The Companion to British History

Charles Arnold-Baker OBE

of the Inner Temple, Barrister-at-law
Formerly Visiting Professor to the City University

SECOND EDITION

London and New York

First published 1996 by Longcross Press Ltd

This edition first published in paperback 2001
by Routledge
11 New Fetter Lane, London EC4P 4EE

Simultaneously published in the USA and Canada
by Routledge
29 West 35th Street, New York, NY 10001

Routledge is an imprint of the Taylor & Francis Group

© 2001 Charles Arnold-Baker

The right of Charles Arnold-Baker to be identified as the Author of this
Work has been asserted by him in accordance with the Copyright, Designs
and Patents Act 1988

Typeset in Garamond by
Wearset, Boldon, Tyne and Wear
Printed and bound in Great Britain by
TJ International Ltd, Padstow, Cornwall

British Library Cataloguing in Publication Data
A catalogue record for this book is available from the British Library

Library of Congress Cataloging in Publication Data
A catalog record for this book has been requested

ISBN 0-415-26016-7 (Hbk)
ISBN 0-415-18583-1 (Pbk)

SCHEME

In thirty years of compilation I have been increasingly conscious of my inadequacies and of the vast size of the subject compared with the small space into which it must be compressed. I conceive that a *Companion* is meant to provide any reader with historical background. In the case of these islands this creates immense difficulties, and it seems to me that the user is entitled to some description of them and some explanation of the way in which I have tried to solve them. I hope, in the first place that having been a soldier, a barrister, a member of a royal commission, a chief executive of a nationwide local government organisation and a Traffic Commissioner, may partially compensate for a historian's other shortcomings.

Period

Logically one might begin with the Anglo-Saxon invasions, but it seemed that these would not be intelligible without reference to the situation, in so far as it is known, before them, so I decided on the date hallowed by tradition, of Caesar's first raid in 55 B.C.

At the modern end, three moments seemed particularly significant, namely the advent of the Wilson government in 1960, accession to the European Community in 1970 and the Single European Act in 1986. The recognisable continuity between our present and our past gave way in 1960 to the mounting tempo of a revolutionary epoch in which 1986 stood out by reason of its effect on our sovereignty. This seemed the moment at which to break off, but amplifications such as Maastricht and the electronic unification of the world exchanges have driven me on sometimes even to 2000.

Geography

It would have been easy but essentially false to concentrate on internal events and produce a Little Englander's book. The truth is far more complicated and intractable. There is no history of England without Scotland, Wales and Ireland, or indeed, apart from the history of our neighbours. But who are the neighbours? The sea, and those who go down to it in ships was the vast if muted fact of English history: the air was the vast if noisy fact of the subsequent World Era, and with the silence and speed of electronics we are entering a newly shrunken globe. The ebb and flow of national energy has made and unmade neighbours not merely in Europe but in all the continents. British history has a habit of expanding and contracting with movements in policy, trade, martial prowess, ambition, inventiveness and self-deprecation. The bowstaves of Agincourt came from Italy and Prussia. Snooker was invented at Ootacamund in the hills of Southern India. Scottish architects built much of St. Petersburg. English speaking nations hold places everywhere, and many independent states owe some of their institutions and attitudes to British example or British occupation of their soil. The only truly international court of justice was the Privy Council.

The choice of material was therefore infinite, and had to be controlled as far as possible by guidelines. I have, to begin with, given the central position to the English who are much more numerous and occupy a much greater area of the British Isles than the other three major nations. Secondly these three have a history of their own of great interest and of intrinsic importance to the whole. Thirdly there is a strong interpenetration between Britain and the European coastal countries, whose relationship with Britain has been strongly influenced by her and their internal politics. Fourthly, the British have ruled other areas, so that their history, at least when under such rule, is an offshoot of the main stem. Fifthly there has been commercial, economic, technical, political and cultural communication and intermigration with many other countries and places. This has varied from time to time but has often been, in some ways or many, significant for the British nations. The Swiss have given us Calvinism, the Poor Law and the Red Cross; portcullises, sugar and cotton were first imported from the Frankish Levant; some legal surnames from Portugal; bananas and steel bands from the Caribbean; soft wheat in bulk from North America. I have treated the five classes as a hierarchy, each accorded less space, relatively, than the one before; but while trying to confine material in each to that which might be relevant in some way to British history, I have attempted, as justice requires, to set it forth not from the British but from the local point of view.

Subjects

The spirit and workings of a society are not to be found exclusively in its politics or its economics, technology or convictions, but in the totality and interaction of its activities, and these include many remarkable and at first sight unremarkable things. Religion and the urge to perform public service have always played an important part; so have the arts and music. The pride of the English gentry in civilian pursuits and sports has made the British army officer the least political in the world. Games, beer and gambling have to find a place. But the spirit changes constantly: in a country where an allegation of cruelty will provoke embittered defence in divorce proceedings, one would hardly suspect the enormous gloating crowds two centuries ago at bull-baitings and executions. In a single generation pride of empire has given way to apology for imperialism. Many things which bulk large in one era matter little in another, and the converse is also true. We may perceive, with a hindsight which contemporaries necessarily lacked, significance in things which they found negligible. The conflict between space and information can be resolved only by conscious determinations.

Omissions

I have made, with regret, two classes of omissions. With a few exceptions such as Gibbon I have left out all historians who are not historical sources unless, like Sir Winston Churchill, they were mentionable for other reasons. I have also, as far as I can, omitted the technical terms of historiography. The output of the historical faculties is now too vast for such a book as this. Secondly, despite their historical and social importance in this aggressive group of nations, I have omitted the histories of the hundreds of individual regiments which have fought for them. I have also without regret omitted definitions of words and concepts unless they happen to be arcane.

Diagrams

The diagrams are intended to clarify only difficult or less known points.

Attitudes

Though I have tried to give room for all points of view, I have my own. I see no reason to belittle the achievements of the British nations. They have borne more responsibility for the conduct of human affairs than any nation since the Romans. There have naturally been terrible, disastrous, foolish or ill-natured episodes but those who have not been involved in vast operations are, despite all the bluster and propaganda, in a weaker position to criticise than those who have.

Similarly, in a work which necessarily depends much on secondary sources I have tended, in a conflict where other things are equal, to prefer the account (allowing for self-interest) of the person who has experience of the issues to that of the outside observer. A human being is made up of intellect, muscle and bone, a system of metabolism, alimentary and sexual tastes, prejudices, passions, physical weaknesses and inherited peculiarities. It is a mistake to assume that world or village events are settled wholly by ratiocination or sense. The decisive event may be a bad night, a quarrel with the cook or, of course, the ruthless pursuit of power or logic. The man of engaged experience is likely to present these problems more realistically than a spectator.

In the ordinary sense history is about people, and it is a deplorable duty to record the follies and massacres as well as the wisdom and achievement; but there is much reason to remember and detest the murderous extremists such as Lenin and Hitler, who avoided emulating Genghis Khan's pillars of skulls only for reasons of expediency. An important test of the essential decency of a society is the number of its people which it kills. By this rule of thumb the United Kingdom emerges with much credit. Moderation, with its exasperating delays, compromises and hypocrisies, does not lead to the slaughterhouse because, within often self-destructively wide boundaries it recognises the value of people and the possibility that their opinions may be right. Even the lucrative and nasty slave trade was abolished by the British, who profited from it more than anyone else, against the opposition of Latin and African powers. Similarly the criminal extremism of religious fanatics engendered the compromise Anglican church. Eighteenth century predatory corruption was defeated before it got out of hand and the movement against the death penalty gathered strength in Britain, while Russian communists and German Nazis perfected industrialised killing.

One may be entitled to private judgments, but in recounting history, however much one may be inclined to moralise, people and events ought to be publicly judged by the standards of their time and place, not by those of another country or another age. It is misleading to apply Lilliputian intolerance to Brobdingnagian customs, and anachronistic to appraise events of one era by ideologies which were fashionable long before or unknown until much later. The double burden on the historian is heavy. He must say what he believes happened but tell the story as far as he can through the eyes of a contemporary. I cannot believe that I have succeeded in this, but certainly I have tried, and when I have deviated out of time or circumstance I have tried to make the fact of the deviation obvious.

It is, of course, true that people and nations generally fall below the level of their ideals, but the underlying assumptions of national outlook and language differ more than is sometimes supposed. Oppression of minorities may, for example, be a necessary consequence of the institutions in one country and an abuse of those in another. Both minorities may suffer equally, but in the one case the oppressor may be ashamed; in the other not. In the former the minority has hope and probably a future. In general the murkier side of British history has been the result of – often highly reprehensible – neglect and sins of omission rather than (save at times in Ireland and China) deliberate viciousness.

All observers of public events have been troubled by the apparent need to choose between free will and determinism, and those who accept a moral content in the make-up of human action necessarily assume an element of choice. Common observation shows that there is something in both points of view. We all live within frameworks to whose original shape we contributed nothing, but which we can, later on, join in altering; and it is a curious fact that the most perfervid of devotees of determinism, the followers of Mohammed, Calvin and Marx, have thrown up the most energetic activists, who have revolutionised societies and conquered continents, as if their particular brand of inevitability was impossible without their intervention. The existence of such experiential contradictions suggests that the full rigour of any moralistic or deterministic doctrine is simply wrong: that the stark choice is illusory and that life is, after all, much more complicated than the purely intellectual have tried to make it.

Calamities

Alongside the insoluble questions of human choice, there have been calamities which men have not controlled and which, strange to say, figure only a little or not at all in the general histories. Epidemics have swept away people and social institutions many times or have provoked the creation of organisations like the Victorian local government system. AIDS has changed the private behaviour of millions. More people died of the Spanish influenza of 1919–20 than were killed in the First World War, and pollution may yet destroy us all. Frosts, too, have decided the fate of nations like Denmark. Tempests have altered coasts, drowned ports and spread conflagrations. The great Lisbon earthquake was felt throughout the Mediterranean and altered the assumptions about the meaning of life.

In a work of this kind it seems to be necessary to allow for all this: to include material, for example, because instinct proposes a relevance which the intellect, or at least my intellect, does not grasp. The user can smile at an entry if I put it in. He cannot give himself that pleasure if I leave it out.

Arrangement and Space Saving

I have made use of one particular space-saving device with a compensation, namely the inclusion where possible of particular cases under generalised headings. This makes them a little harder to find, but gives them, in return, a natural setting which would otherwise have to be repeated. Thus apart from major international figures like Bolivar and some like French monarchs who had direct and important contact with British affairs, I have not given foreign personalities special treatment but have, with the aid of cross-references, left the user to find them under the countries where they were prominent. Many British figures will be found under headings concerned with their families, and similarly many places will be found in areas where they are situated or classified.

Cross-References

The text has not been overloaded with asterisks or typographical devices to indicate cross-references, for I have preferred to rely on the user's intelligence. References outwards from an entry occur only where the subject is not mentioned by name or where it seems to be unexpected, but because of the method of presentation of particulars incorporated in generalised headings, the inward references are comparatively numerous.

Names and Titles

Names have presented special problems. People have only too often changed theirs. I have myself. Cardinal Pacelli emerges from the conclave as Pius XII; Mr Bronstein from the Russian revolution as Comrade Trotsky. It requires some mental agility to grasp that Henry of Bolingbroke, the Earl of Derby, the Duke of Hereford, the Duke of Lancaster and Henry IV were one and the same, or that Lord North was a courtesy Lord and spent his political career in the House of Commons.

I have tried to solve these difficulties in the following way. A person, not a foreigner, will usually be traceable through the name or title by which he is usually known: thus, *Disraeli* not Beaconsfield, but *Marlborough* not Churchill, but the other names or titles with the dates of assumption appear in the heading. Places are sometimes even more difficult because given different names in different epochs or simultaneously by different nations. It is unhelpful to call the Peace of Aix-la-Chapelle the Peace of Aachen, but Ratisbon is sometimes Regensburg and the French call the Battle of Waterloo after *Mont St. Jean,* where much of it was fought, while the Germans use *Belle Alliance* after the farm near Bonaparte's headquarters.

Assistance

It is always a pleasure to acknowledge help. Notably I have received it from my son Henry von Blumenthal who inspired my occasionally flagging spirits and, despite the commitments of a busy life, undertook a variety of arduous jobs, and from other members of my family; from Ann Rowen MBE who typed the original million and a half words; Professor John Pick who supplied material on the stage and music hall; Mrs Charlotte Cubitt for supplying material on Friedrich von Hayek; Dillwyn Miles, Herald Bard of the Welsh National Eisteddford, on the Welsh tongue, Oliver Turnbull, an old friend on almost everything, and Christopher Pounsett Esq on printing. Apart from reference works in six languages, I have over the years consulted mostly English, French and German histories, biographies, economic, medical and geographical works and books on literature and art. They are far too numerous to acknowledge here, but perhaps I may come nearer by thanking the libraries of the universities of Vienna and Zürich; of All Souls, Magdalen and Nuffield Colleges at Oxford; of the London School of Economics, the Wellcome Institute, the City of Westminster and the Honourable Society of the Inner Temple. Errors of fact, synthesis, selection or interpretation are, of course, entirely mine.

The Present Edition

The book was originally published at the end of 1996. I would like to acknowledge again the many dozens of encouraging letters, mostly from strangers, which I have received, and which are a real solace for the difficulties of getting the book into existence. I have, as far as I can, followed their helpful advice in preparing this edition.

Charles Arnold-Daker
Inner Temple, August 2000

A

AACHEN or AIX-LA-CHAPELLE (Germany). K. Pepin (who came from Heristhal not far away) had a palace here in 765. Charlemagne made it his main capital, and Holy Roman Emperors were crowned there from 813 to 1531 when it began to decline. It was the scene of several diplomatic meetings, especially the Congress which settled the European conflicts of 1739-41 at the Preliminaries (30 Apr.) and Peace (18 Oct. 1741) of Aix-la-Chapelle, and the Congress of 1818. Given to Prussia in 1815, in World War II it was almost destroyed by allied bombing.

AALAND Is (Finn: AAHVENMAA) (Baltic). This strategic archipelago at the junction of the Gulfs of Finland and Bothnia, was Swedish until the P. of Frederickshamn (1809) when, with Finland, it passed to Russia. At British insistence it was neutralised under the P. of Paris after the Crimean War (1856). Finland, independent since Dec. 1917 took over the administration in July 1919. In 1921, under a League of Nations initiative, it was demilitarised again, and its people declared a protected minority, under a convention between Britain, France, Italy and all the Baltic states except the U.S.S.R. and its govt. became semi-autonomous.

AARON OF LINCOLN (?-c. 1185). A leading Jewish financier, often made loans to the Crown on the security of local taxes. His advances to private persons led to the requisition of interests in 25 counties, in many of which he maintained agents, while his ecclesiastical loans helped to build abbeys and Lincoln cathedral. At his death his property was seized by Henry II. The outstanding credits amounted to about £15,000 – equal to about three quarters of the royal annual income, and a special department, the *Scaccarium Aaronis* (Lat: Aaron's Exchequer) was set up to liquidate his estate. The debtors numbered over 400 and his customers had included the King of Scots and the Abp. of Canterbury.

ABADAN (Iran). This island in the Shatt-el-Arab passed from Turkey to Iran in 1847 under the T. of Erzerum. The Anglo-Persian Oil Co. established its base under an agreement with the Sheikh of Mohammerah. In 1951 Iran nationalised its oilfields and expelled foreign technicians; as a result the huge refineries came to a standstill. This continued till 1954 when they were reopened by an international consortium including British Petroleum which now owned the interests of the former Anglo-Persian co. The war with Iraq halted its use between 1977 and 1988.

ABATTIS (Fr: Felled) Trees felled side by side with the tops or branches towards the enemy as a military obstacle equivalent to the modern barbed wire.

ABBÉ (Fr. = abbot). Commonly any French clergyman below the rank of bishop, and sometimes even a layman (such as Brantôme) who owned an advowson.

ABBO of FLEURY, St. (?945-1004). French Benedictine, wrote on mathematics, astronomy and papal authority and, at the invitation of Oswald of Worcester, spent the years 985-7 at Ramsey Abbey, which he reformed. He also wrote a *Life of St. Edmund* dedicated to St. Dunstan. In 988 he became Abbot of Fleury. He died in a scuffle at La Réole.

ABBOT, ABBESS, PRIOR. Among the Benedictines and some Canons Regular, the heads of larger monasteries were called Abbots, and their deputies and other important subordinates, Priors. The head of a smaller house was the Prior, but at Winchester, the bishop was the Abbot of the Cathedral and the Lord Prior was the real head of the abbey.

Abbots were theoretically elected by the inmates, usually from their own number but the wealth and secular importance of many abbeys often led temporal rulers to usurp the right of appointment. Abbeys were often exempt from episcopal control and abbots increasingly adopted the episcopal insignia. The first English instance of a papal grant of an episcopal mitre to an abbot was that of Alexander II to St Augustine's, Canterbury in 1063. England eventually had 28 mitred abbots, who with the Lord Prior of Winchester, were peers, though they seldom attended parliament. It being the sacred duty of the monks to obey the Abbot, his authority within his House was absolute, though revolts sometimes occurred (*see* ABELARD). As their wealth increased, many abbots became as splendid as lay nobles, with separate establishments within their house.

The manner of election and the position of Abbesses were similar to those of abbots, but as women they could not perform the spiritual duties of the priesthood, and so were always under episcopal jurisdiction.

In 1513 attendance of mitred superiors in parliament was declared not to be necessary. In 1534 elections to abbacies were made subject to royal licence. All the great abbeys were suppressed between 1536 and 1540.

ABBOT, Abp. George (1562-1633). Calvinist Master of University Coll. Oxford from 1597, though in conflict with High Churchmen led by Laud, gained royal favour in 1606 by an uncompromising defence of monarchy, and in 1608 persuaded the Scots of the lawfulness of episcopacy and arranged a union of the two churches. Bp. of Lichfield, and translated to London in 1609, in 1611 he became Abp. of Canterbury. By his influence the Anglican church was represented at the Synod of Dort in 1618, and many puritans got livings. His Calvinist orthodoxy yet tolerant approach helped to reconcile many advanced Protestants with an episcopal organisation of the church. The rise of determined Laudians led to a loss of influence and suspension in 1627.

ABBOT. Three brothers were distinguished generals in India. **(1) Augustus (1804-67)** artillery commander in the first Afghan War, was considered the ablest gunner of his time. **(2) Sir Frederick (1805-92)** engineer, served in the Burma and first Afghan War and having fought at Sobraon (Feb 1846) bridged the Sutlej with an efficiency which astonished his own forces as well as the enemy, and secured the early fall of Lahore. **(3)** The adventurous **Sir James (1807-96)**, fought in the Afghan War and was sent to Khiva in Dec. 1839 to give diplomatic support to the Amir against Russian pressure. At the Amir's entreaty he crossed Asiatic and European Russia (being waylaid by Kazaks *en route*) and negotiated a settlement at St. Petersburg with the Russian govt. direct. In 1845 he became Commissioner in Hazara. Isolated in the outbreak of the 2nd Sikh war (1848) he raised a private army and held out against much superior forces. He continued to rule Hazara until 1853, and had raised it from a desert to prosperity. The people adored him; Abbottabad is named after him; he spent his whole fortune on them, and left with only a month's pay.

ABBOTT, Sir John Joseph Caldwell (1821-93) secured Argenteuil in the Canadian Parliament in 1857, but only after an election petition. Sol. Gen: East in the liberal Sandfield govt. of 1862, he joined the Conservatives in 1865 on the federation issue. He advised Sir Hugh Allan on the Canadian Pacific Rly venture, and in 1872 they both became directors. The Company disbursed large sums to support the Conservatives in the election of 1873, and this came to public knowledge in 1874; the govt. had to resign, and in the ensuing election it was defeated. Abbot was unseated on petition. In 1878 he was defeated but similarly unseated his opponent. In 1880 it was Abbott's turn. In 1881 he received an overwhelming vote and was undisturbed until 1887, when he was called to the Senate for Quebec, and

1

entered the Macdonald cabinet without a portfolio. He was Macdonald's leading senatorial spokesman until June 1891, and then, on Macdonald's death reluctantly became Prime Minister until ill health forced him to resign six months later.

ABBOTT. *See* TENTERDEN.

***ABBREVIATIO PLACITORUM* (Lat. = Summary of Pleas)** is an abstract of pleas and business during the period 1189 to 1327 in the *Curia Regis*, the Council, Parliament, and the courts, made by Arthur Agarde (1540-1615) and others under Elizabeth I, James I and Charles I. Printed by the Record Commissioners in 1811 it is a source for the workings of the Curia Regis and the early common law.

ABD **(Arab = servant or slave).** A common part of Arab names eg. Abdullah = *Servant of God.*

ABDICATION (LEGAL). Some Anglo-Saxon kings (eg. Ine of Wessex) abandoned their thrones by entering religion, but since then a sovereign has not been able to abdicate without the consent of parliament. In the case of Edward II (1327) a parliament declared him deposed. A delegation then visited him and he agreed to abdicate provided that his son succeeded him. The delegation then renounced homage and allegiance on behalf of the whole kingdom. Richard II (1399) made an extorted resignation to an assembly of Estates. It was represented as voluntary but as a result of criticism a schedule of 33 notorious crimes was presented and it was resolved to deprive him on their account. A commission conveyed the resolution to him. In both cases Acts of Indemnity were subsequently passed to protect the creators of the new regime. At the first forcible abdication of Henry VI (1460) the first parliament of his successor Edward IV declared that the three kings since Richard II were Kings successively in deed and not of right and confirmed their grants; this case was therefore treated as the supersession of a usurping line. James II (1688) fled but never gave up his claims; a convention parliament then declared that as his acts were inconsistent with the nature of the kingship he had abdicated the government and the throne being thereby vacant William and Mary were invited to occupy it. They having accepted, called a new parliament which by Act declared the convention to be a parliament.

The first voluntary abdication was that of Edward VIII (1936); the King executed an instrument of abdication in the presence of his brothers. Parliament was asked to legislate accordingly, and a commission for giving the Royal Assent was issued. His Majesty's Declaration of Abdication Act, 1936, was then passed and came into effect on Royal Assent. The declaration is a schedule to the Act.

ABEL, Sir Frederick Augustus (1827-1902) was Chemist to the War Office from 1854 to 1858 and the first director of the Imperial Institute from 1887. He was an expert on explosives, and with Sir James Dewar invented Cordite and a safe way of making gun cotton.

ABELARD, Peter (1079-1142). This theologian and philosopher was born near Nantes, and after teaching at Corbeil and Melun he came in 1108 to the school of Notre Dame in Paris. Here he had his famous affair with Helöise, daughter of Fulbert, a canon of Notre Dame; the enraged father eventually had him castrated. He then became a monk at St. Denis.

He introduced the western church to the systematic study of Aristotle, and taught that reason is a necessary foundation of faith. He thus came into collision with previously habitual dogmatism, and with the newer mysticism of Bernard of Clairvaux by whom he was assailed. His position against such powerful enemies was not strengthened by his conceit or by his escapade. In 1121 he was accused of heresy and imprisoned by a Council at Soissons. On release he retired to a hermitage at Nogent-sur-Seine, where pupils sought him out in such numbers that he organised a school called Le Paraclet.

He was then sent as Abbot to St. Gildas de Rhys in Brittany, but after ten years he quarrelled with the monks who drove him out. He was allowed formally to resign his abbacy, so that he could revise his works, but he was again condemned by a council at Sens, and died at Cluny on his way to argue his appeal at Rome.

ABEOKUTA. *See* NIGERIA.

ABERCORN, Es. and Ds. of. *See* HAMILTON.

ABERCROMBIE, John (1726-1806), employed as a gardener at Kew, wrote *Every Man His Own Gardener.* It was said to have been submitted to Goldsmith for stylistic correction and returned unaltered. Published in 1767, it had a wide influence.

ABERCROMBIE, John (1780-1844) was a famous teacher of pathological anatomy at Edinburgh.

ABERCROMBIE, Sir Leslie Patrick (1879-1957), Prof. of Town and Country Planning at London University, wrote a well known book *Town and Country Planning* (1933), and prepared plans for Greater London, eight other cities and the West Midlands. He was chairman of the Council for the Preservation of Rural England from 1950.

ABERCROMBY, whig landowners in Clackmannan. **(1) Sir Ralph (1734-1801),** whose mother was a Dundas, was commissioned in 1756, fought at Minden and became ADC to Sir Wm. Pitt. After a further regimental career he was elected by the Dundas influence to Parliament after a bitter contest which included a duel. His habit of considering things on their merits made him an awkward (but always well liked) whig. He eventually resigned, and in 1793 commanded a brigade in the disastrous Flemish campaign. He was the only general who emerged with credit, and he and his subordinate Wellesley (later Wellington) extricated the survivors. In Nov. 1795 he was sent with John Moore, another famous subordinate, to reduce the French W. Indies. He took St. Lucia and Demarara, relieved St. Vincent and reorganised the defences of Grenada. In 1796, with Picton, a third famous subordinate, he took Trinidad. His successes enabled him (from his Flemish experience) to introduce a new and more intelligent discipline (and from his Caribbean experience) better measures (such as mountain stations, sanatoria and more comfortable uniforms) for the troop's health. After a failure at Porto Rico he came home for reasons of health and took command (Dec. 1797) of the unruly forces in Ireland, then threatened with revolt and French invasion. The Irish govt. obstructed his improvements and he resigned, but Henry Dundas promptly found him a divisional command in the Dutch expedition of 1799. In co-operation with the Navy, the Dutch fleet was taken over at Den Helder in Aug. In Sept. he defeated a counter-attack, but was superseded by the D. of York who, though with Russian support, bungled two attempts on Bergen-op-Zoom and then, by the Alkmar Convention, handed over all the prisoners in return for an unmolested evacuation. The disgusted Abercromby refused a peerage.

He was now immensely popular. In June 1800 he reached Minorca as commander of the troops in the Mediterranean, and with V-Adm. Keith made an attempt on Cadiz (Oct.). This was frustrated: Keith reasonably refused to make a prolonged stay on a lee shore, and the equipment necessary in amphibious warfare was not available. They withdrew without loss and were redirected against the French army which Bonaparte had abandoned in Egypt. He spent a month surveying the fortifications of Malta, and recommended that it should replace Minorca as the British Mediterranean HQ. There followed a six weeks delay at Marmaris (Asia Minor) awaiting non-existent Turkish reinforcements and training his men in landing operations. Then he struck at Egypt. He put ashore 14,000 infantry, 1,000 cavalry and his artillery in one day against opposition at Aboukir (Mar. 1801), marched on Alexandria, defeated the French under Menou, but was killed.

As tactician, trainer and disciplinarian, he fathered the spirit of the 19th cent. army, and besides those already mentioned, inspired or advanced John Hope, Robt. Anstruther, James Kempt, Thos. Graham, Rowland Hill and Edward Paget. His brother **(2) Sir Robert (1740-1827)**, after a regimental career mostly in America, went to India in 1788, was mainly instrumental in defeating Tippoo Sahib in 1792, and succeeded Cornwallis as C-in-C in 1793. He successfully concluded the Rohilla wars and suppressed without severity an understandable mutiny among the HEIC's officers. He retired in 1797.

Of the sons of **(1)** above **(3) Sir John (1772-1817)** was his father's military sec. in all his early campaigns, his father's extreme short sight making him dependent on his staff for knowledge of the battle. In 1809 he became C in C at Bombay. During an expedition against Mauritius he was taken and retaken at sea, but went on to conquer the island. In 1812 he was temporary gov. of Madras, but retired in 1813. His brother **(4) James (1776-1858) 1st Ld. DUNFERMLINE** (1839) was an M.P. from 1807 to 1830 and then for Edinburgh in the first reformed parliament. He entered the cabinet in 1834, but after the 1835 election was elected Speaker against Manners Sutton in a highly charged contest, by ten votes. He presided with strength and impartiality in an excitable house until he retired in 1839.

ABERDARE (1) Henry Austin Bruce (1815-95) 1st Ld. (1873), became liberal M.P. for Merthyr Tydfil in 1852. In 1862 he was U/Sec. of State at the Home Office under Palmerston and in 1864 Vice-Pres. of the Council on Education. He was also a Charity and a Church Estates Commissioner. Defeated at Merthyr in 1868, he won Renfrew in Jan. 1869 and entered Gladstone's cabinet as Home Sec. His 1871 Licensing Bill aroused hot opposition from publicans and the liquor trade, and had to be withdrawn. In 1872 a weaker Act was passed, but the event drove the brewers into alliance with the Tories who thereby gained support in the business interests, many of which had been liberal. In 1873, in a cabinet reshuffle, went to the Lords. His political career ended with the fall of the govt. in 1874.

He now devoted himself to voluntary causes. He was chairman of the Committee on Welsh Education in 1880. In 1882 he became chairman of the Nat. Africa Co. which in 1886 bought out rival French interests, received a charter as the Royal Niger Co., and laid the foundations of Nigeria. In 1893 he was Chairman of the Royal Commission on the Aged Poor, and he was elected first Chancellor of the University of Wales. His grandson **(2) Morys (1918-) 3rd Ld.** became Min. of State at the Dept. of Health in 1970 and was subsequently Chairman of Committees of the House of Lords.

ABERDEEN, -SHIRE (Scotland). The modern town, mostly between the mouths of the Dee and the Don, consisted of Aberdeen, inhabited in 8th cent., and chartered in 1179, and Old Aberdeen, properly Aberdon, made a burgh of barony in 1498. As ports and crossing places the twin settlements early had a local importance: the bishopric originated in the 12th cent. and an early castle rebuilt and garrisoned by Edward I was destroyed in 1308 by Robert the Bruce, who bridged the Don in 1310. Most of the military events of Wallace's rebellion took place in the surrounding countryside. By this time the Saxon, Scandinavian and English stock in the towns was spreading into the county, driving the Celts into the hills and building many castles. Border warfare was endemic until the defeat of the Highlanders at Harlaw in 1411. Thereafter there was comparative peace, and by 1494 the town was the seat of an university.

Save in the areas of the Don and the Ythan, the soil is not fertile, but it is suitable for cattle, while the town and other ports, particularly Peterhead and Frazerburgh

sustained a growing fishing industry. There was also granite quarrying, and in due course an export trade in these products encouraged shipbuilding, and the importation of wool and linen for weaving and reexport. North Sea oil wells developed hugely. In the late 1970s they brought many immigrants, investment, building and new industries.

ABERDEEN'S GOVT. (Dec. 1852-Feb. 1855). (13 in Cabinet under the E. of Aberdeen with E. Granville Lord Pres; Gladstone Ch. of the Exch; Vist Palmerston Home Sec; Lord J. Russell Foreign Sec; Sydney Herbert Sec. of War). *See* DERBY'S FIRST GOVT.

(1) This ill co-ordinated coalition had to deal with the drift into the Crimean War, and the European confusion to be accelerated by Napoleon III as self-proclaimed Emperor (Dec. 1852), and by Cavour's recent accession to the premiership of Piedmont. Gladstone reversed Disraeli's fiscal policies. Leaving the interests affected by free trade to fend for themselves, he abolished or reduced duties on partly and wholly manufactured goods and food, extended the legacy duty and prepared to abolish the income tax in stages by 1859, when the Long Annuities were due to end. Such policies presupposed peace, and continued the long-standing neglect of the armed forces, yet Britain was at war in Burma at the opening of 1853, and Russian threats to Turkey were answered by an Anglo-French naval concentration off the Dardanelles in June. The almost watertight bulkhead between foreign policy and home politics is further illustrated by an obsessive, but ineffectual, interest in constitutional and franchise questions. **(2)** Hence the sufferings of the neglected and mismanaged army in the Crimea were hardly surprising, but it was the enhanced power of journalism aided by the electric telegraph, and Florence Nightingale's flare for publicity, which brought down Aberdeen in a general upsurge of angry public opinion. The immediate cause of his fall was Russell's resignation in protest against a cabinet decision to refuse a committee of inquiry.

ABERDEEN AND TEMAIR. *See* GORDON.

ABERGAVENNY (Gwent) (Lat: *GOBANNIUM*) had a Roman legionary fortress, and after the Norman invasion a castle and Benedictine priory. The place was frequently involved in border warfare; Owain Glyndwr burned it in 1404. Strongly pro-Stuart in the 17th Cent., it was sacked by Fairfax and the parliamentarians in 1646, and lost its charter for Jacobitism in 1689. It is primarily an agricultural market.

ABERGAVENNY, Lds. *See* NEVILLE.

ABERFAN (Glam). In 1967 a coal tip collapsed and buried a school full of children. Over 2M was subscribed to a relief fund and the National Coal Board was widely criticised. The offending tips were not cleared away until 1969.

ABERSHAW, Louis Jeremiah or Jerry (?1773-95) a highwayman, terrorised travellers between London and Kingston between 1791 and 1795 but killed a constable at Southwark, and was caught and hanged. His fame was prolonged by his good looks and the panache with which he faced the scaffold.

ABEYANCE. Certain, mostly older, peerages descended, in accordance with the common law rules on the descent of property, to heirs general; if no male heir could be found the rights devolved equally to sisters and their heirs as coparceners, regardless of seniority. A peerage (unlike property) being indivisible, it could not be enjoyed until all the lines of heirs had been reduced to one by intermarriage or extinction. In the interval the peerage was said to be in abeyance. Abeyances have lasted for centuries: e.g. Lords Grey of Codnor 1496 to 1989.

ABERHART, William (1878-1943) was premier of Alberta from 1935 to 1943 with a Social Credit majority, whose policy he was unable to carry out.

ABHORRERS, were supporters of Charles II and his

brother James against the anti-prerogative views of Shaftesbury and his associates. During the Exclusion crisis they promoted addresses expressing abhorrence of their petitions for the summoning of parliament (1679). The name was soon superseded by 'Tories'.

ABIGAIL (*see* 1 SAM. ch 25 vv 24-8) A waiting woman or lady's maid, with special reference to Abigail Hill (Mrs Masham) who, from such a position, ousted Sarah, D. of Marlborough, from Q. Anne's favour.

ABINGDON. *See* BERKSHIRE.

ABINGDON, E. of. *See* BERTIE, WILLOUGHBY.

ABINGER, Ld. *See* SCARLETT.

ABJURATION, OATH OF. (**1**) An oath to leave the realm as a condition of release from sanctuary, abolished with sanctuary in 1624. (*See* BENEFIT OF CLERGY). (**2**) A similar oath imposed upon certain Popish recusants. (**3**) An oath to abjure the claims of the Stuart Pretender, the temporal power of the Pope, and the doctrines that faith need not be kept with heretics and that heretics might be put to death. This oath, first proposed as a condition of public office in 1690, was made compulsory only in 1701. The requirement was renewed in 1714 and again in 1766. From 1778 R. Catholics who took it were relieved of most of their civil disabilities. All oaths of abjuration were abolished in 1871.

ABNAKIS or TARRATEENS, a federation of Algonquian tribes (the Penobscot, Passamaquoddy and Malecite) who ranged from Maine to the St. Lawrence. Allied with the French in the wars of 1689 to 1697, they did much damage in northern New England. Their word 'wigwam' has passed into English.

ABOLITIONISM. *See* SLAVERY.

ABORIGINES' PROTECTION SOCIETY was founded in 1833.

ABORTION. *See* BIRTH CONTROL.

ABOYNE, Es. and Vist. *See* GORDON.

ABRACH, CLAN. *See* CLANS, SCOTTISH

ABRAHAM, The Rt. Hon William (Welsh poetic title MABON) (1842-1922) P.C. (1911) became a miners' agent in S. Wales in 1870. In 1875 he negotiated the sliding scale wage agreement, which related wages to prices and profits, and was miners' chairman of the Joint Sliding Scale Assn until it was abolished in 1903. In 1885 he became a radical liberal M.P. for the Rhondda, and in 1898 first Pres. of the S. Wales Miners' Federation. He went with the Labour Party in 1906 when it became a separate organisation, but was never a strong socialist. The Federation was affiliated in 1909. He tried but failed to prevent the first general miners' strike in 1912. Part of his influence came from his interest in the Eisteddfodau, at which he was a well-known conductor and singer.

ABRAHAM MEN were sturdy beggars common in Shakespeare's time, who simulated lunacy and falsely claimed the immunities of released Bedlamites.

ABRAHAM, PLAINS or HEIGHTS of, above Quebec was the place where the British under Wolfe decisively defeated the French under Montcalm in 1759. Both generals were killed.

ABRIDGMENTS OF THE LAWS were digests or summaries of the Common Law which, with time, became increasingly encyclopedic. Their main interest is as pointers to much earlier law otherwise not directly known. (**1**) **Statham's** contain cases, mostly from the Year Books (YB) down to 1461. It was the first printed English law book. (**2**) **Fitzherbert's** digested some cases from Bracton and from the YBs down to 1506. (**3**) **Brooke's,** published in 1568 is founded on Fitzherbert. (**4**) **Rolle's** continued the process down to 1668. (**5**) **Viner's**, in 24 vols began publication in 1741 and ended with a 6-vol.supplement in 1801. (**6**) **Comyn's** (1762-1822), **Bacon's** (1736-1832) and **Cruise's** (1804-35) were smaller but still very large works.

ABSALOM AND ACHITOPHEL. *See* DRYDEN, JOHN.

ABSENTEES, in social history, were landlords who derived rent from estates but did not live on, or take any direct interest in them, especially Irish landowners who often preferred the civilisation, business advantages and political influence of London to the local discomforts and barbarism. Estate management thus fell into the often oppressive hands of agents employed to screw out money to pay their masters' debts. As agriculture was primitive and life disorderly, even moderate rents soon reached the bottom of the Irish tenant's pocket; the money was too seldom ploughed back into the land, though some model villages and many fine country houses were built and gave employment. English govts disliked absenteeism because the class which had the strongest interest in maintaining the ascendancy was not there to do it. Hence legislation, royal orders and proclamations from the time of Richard II sought, ineffectually, to drive the absentees back to their lands. The Union of 1800 was really a total abandonment of this idea, since the abolition of the Dublin Parliament deprived Irish landowners of yet another motive for staying.

ABSENTEES, ACT of 1537, (Ir), transferred to the crown Irish properties of all English monasteries, and of the D. of Norfolk, Lord Berkeley, the E. of Shrewsbury, and the heirs to the E. of Ormonde.

ABSOLUTISM, a word originating among political thinkers in the 1820s, described the condition of a monarchy which meant to rule without restraint from other institutions in the state. Such a monarchy required an armed co-ercive apparatus and the ability to finance it. An absolutist monarch would seek financial independence of parliaments by, for example, developing crown estates or trading monopolies or by raising existing taxes. He would govern through generally unaristocratic officials dependent on himself, and tended to suppress or penetrate any independent source of power or influence such as the Church, the territorial nobles, parliamentary bodies and legal institutions. It was, with varying intensity, the commonest system in 17th-18th cent. Europe, but was always mitigated by administrative inefficiency and inadequate resources.

ABU (**Arab = father**). On the birth of a first son an Arab commonly changed his name so as to indicate his paternal interest, e.g. Abu Auni, father of Auni.

ABU DHABI. *See* TRUCIAL SHEIKHDOMS.

ABUNA. The patriarch of the Ethiopian Coptic Church, appointed until 1959, by the Coptic patriarch of Alexandria, when the church became antocephalons. The office was abolished by the Marxist govt. in 1975.

ABYSSINIA or ETHIOPIA. (**1**) In 1820 the Egyptians invaded Eritrea, leased Massawa and fortified Kassala. At this time an ancient and once powerful imperial dynasty, descended traditionally from Solomon and the Queen of Sheba, reigned barbarically over the Amhara at Gondar, but the Empire had effectively broken up into sub-states of which Amhara, Gojjam, Tigré and Shoa were the largest. Massawa was in the hands of the Turks.

In 1850 a certain KASSA, a general and official at Gondar began a campaign which culminated in his own coronation in 1855 as Emperor (under the title of THEODORE II), the defeat of Tigré and the temporary subjugation of Shoa. Insufficient resources, defects of character and the disadvantages of usurpership created weaknesses. He lost ground and in 1864 quarrelled with the British and imprisoned British residents and consuls. The ensuing period of diplomatic acrimony was also marked by increasing discontent among the greater provincial rulers. When Sir Robt. Napier invaded the country in 1868 with a British force, Theodore was deserted by many of his feudatories and committed suicide at Magdala. In the course of a long civil war another Kassa (of Tigré) was crowned Emperor as JOHN IV in 1872. He defeated the Egyptians at Gura in 1875 and enforced the submission of the Shoans under their Solomonid King MENELIK in 1879.

(2) The Suez Canal had converted the Red Sea into an international highway. Italy had acquired a foothold at Assab in 1869. In 1885 she occupied Massawa and troops and colonists began to penetrate inland. This was brought to a halt by the Ethiopian army, and negotiations were opened in 1887. At this point Menelik of Shoa acquired arms from the Italians and conquered Harar, while a Mahdist army invaded the west, and in Mar.1889 killed John IV at the B. of Metemma. The Italians seized Keren and Asmara, and in May signed a Treaty at Uccialli with Menelik, promising mutual friendship. Menelik was crowned Emperor in Nov. as Menelik II, and thus the Solomonid dynasty was restored: in Jan.1891 the Italians annexed Eritrea.

(3) The scramble for Africa was in full swing and in 1895 Italy, in abuse of the T. of Uccialli, proclaimed a protectorate over Ethiopia. Menelik mobilised and overwhelmed the invading Italians at the B. of Adowa (Feb.1896). Italy recognised Ethiopian independence by a treaty signed in Oct at Menelik's new capital of Addis Ababa. (Amh = Newtown).

(4) Secure on his Red Sea flank, Menelik now enlarged his Empire by conquering Gambala and Kaffa. Treaties with Italy, Britain and France signed between 1894 and 1908 established its present Southern, Western and Northern frontiers. In 1909 he had a stroke, and rivalry between a regency for his grandson LIJ YASSU and Tafari of Harar weakened the government.

(5) In 1913 Lij Yassu succeeded Menelik II, and in World War I embraced Islam and strongly favoured Turkey and Germany. This brought him into collision with the church and its head, the Abuna (see previous entry). In 1916 the Abuna anathematised Lij and he was overthrown by TAFARI and the Shoans at the B. of Sagale (Oct.1916). Menelik's daughter ZAUDITU became Queen of Kings with Tafari as her regent and heir.

This Tafari, famous as HAILE SELASSIE gradually introduced a modernised administration and replaced feudal rulers by provincial governors, as opportunity offered. European officers trained the bodyguard. The slave trade was put down and in 1923 Ethiopia joined the League of Nations. The church ceased to be subject to Alexandria, and British, French, and American capital was brought in. In 1928 Haile Selassie was appointed King and Vicegerent, and in 1930 ascended the throne as King of Kings.

(6) Italy, since 1922 under a Fascist govt., became aggressive in its efforts to keep up with the new Nazi govt. of Germany. In 1935 a border incident at Walwal was provoked or used as a pretext to invade Ethiopia. Addis Ababa was taken by May 1936 and Haile Selassie escaped to Europe. The ineffectiveness of the League of Nations, which imposed but could not enforce sanctions against Italy, led to an attempted compromise. The British and French proposed a ceasefire in return for far-reaching special Italian rights in Ethiopia. The British public would have none of it; this incident brought Anthony Eden, then U/Sec. of State for Foreign Affairs, into prominence, and his resignation prevented the plan from coming to fruition. Resistance under some local chiefs continued, but an attempt in 1937 on the new Italian viceroy's life led to murderous oppression. Nevertheless much Italian capital came to the country and considerable public works especially roads were constructed. The country was reconquered by the British and the Emperor restored in 1941 and he continued the process of modernisation and made Addis Ababa the seat of the Organisation of African Unity. From 1970 a Russian trained soldier, Haile Mariam MENGISTU organised a sort of creeping revolution. The Emperor was taken into custody in 1974 and eventually died, and a Marxist revolutionary group called the DERGH took over at Addis Ababa. Its corrupt and violent regime met provincial resistance and famine, but Russian subsidies and arms

kept it in power at the centre until 1988, since when its area of influence steadily contracted. In May 1991 Mengistu fled to Zimbabwe.

ACADEMY, ROYAL was founded in 1768 by George III at the request of Sir Joshua Reynolds and others as a central stronghold for the visible arts. It consisted originally of 30 academicians. Associates were introduced in 1769, and the schools shortly afterwards. It was at Somerset House until 1837, on the present site of the National Gallery until 1868 and then settled at Burlington House Piccadilly. Since 1918 academicians and associates over 75 years old have had senior, non-active, status, creating vacancies among the 30. *See also* LANDSCAPE PAINTING.

ACADIE or ACADIA (NOVA SCOTIA). *See* CANADA-6, 10.

ACAPULCO GALLEON. Acapulco, a landlocked deep water harbour on the Mexican Pacific coast, was the eastern terminal of the Spanish trade route from the Philippines and E. Indies, and the destination in the 16th to 18th cents. of their annual treasure galleon whose cargo was sent overland to Nombre de Dios for final shipment *(see* FLOTA) to Spain. Privateers frequently tried to intercept this ship and some, including Drake, Cavendish, Woodes Rogers, and Anson, succeeded.

A.C.A.S. (ADVISORY CONCILIATION AND ARBITRATION SERVICE) set up by the Employment Protection Act of 1975 to bring together opposing sides in industrial disputes, even though they might not be on speaking terms..

ACCA, St. (?-740) Benedictine biblical scholar and disciple of St. Wilfrid who, on his deathbed nominated him Abbot of Hexham, of which also he became Bp. In 732 he left or was 'expelled' and became Bp. of Whithorn.

ACCELERATION of a peerage was, strictly, the calling up to the House of Lords by writ of an heir, in the barony of his father. Such a writ, which did not create a new peerage, could be issued only where the father had more than one. More loosely, the term also meant the conferment, during the lifetime of a peer, of a peerage upon his heir (e.g. in a case where the father had only one). Such a peerage would be limited so as to conform with that which the heir expected to inherit. Of the 12 peers summoned to carry out the Tory peace policy in 1712, three were accelerations. In 1951 the heir to the E. of Ancaster was called up as Lord Willoughby d'Eresby, to perform the functions of the Lord Great Chamberlainship which his father had resigned.

ACCESSION. *See* SUCCESSION.

ACCESSION TO THE EUROPEAN UNION (E.U.), is the process whereby a non-member state joins the E.U. The application is first considered by the Council of the E.U. which obtains the opinion of the Commission, and must then decide unanimously whether or not to admit the applicant state. There follow negotiations to define in detail the terms of the accession. These culminate in a Treaty and Act of Accession containing the agreed terms. This treaty has to be ratified by the applicant state under its own constitutional processes. The Treaty of 1972 admitted Britain, Denmark, Ireland and Norway, but Norway was prevented by a referendum from ratifying. The European Communities Act 1972 made the pre-accession treaties part of English law, enabled post-accession treaties to be incorporated by Order-in-Council subject to affirmative parliamentary resolutions, and provided for the precedence of community over the domestic law in the U.K. The Treaty of 1979 admitted Greece; that of 1985 Spain and Portugal; that of 1995, Austria, Finland and Sweden.

ACCOLADE. The touch, with a sword, on the shoulder to confer Knighthood.

ACCOUNTANCY. Until the 14th cent. accounts were kept on a simple receipts and payments basis with no calculation of profit and loss. Double entry accounting arose from the banking and commercial operations of the Italians soon after 1300. The first English treatise (believed no longer to be extant) was Hugh Oldcastle's of 1543. The first known British full-time Public Accountant was George Watson, who practised at Edinburgh after the Restoration, and by 1800 there were 24 in London. The 19th cent. banking commercial and industrial boom created the first wave of demand for independent accountants not necessarily practising for any particular interest. The Scottish Institute of Chartered Accounts was set up in 1854. The English Institute in 1880; the Society of Incorporated Accountants in 1885; and the Assn. of Certified and Corporate Accountants in 1904. The second wave of demand arose from the enormous burdens of taxation and tax administration imposed upon businesses during two world wars and especially after the second. By 1993 professional accountants exceeded 140,000.

ACCOUNT DUTY. See DEATH DUTIES.

ACCRA. See GHANA.

ACHESON, Sir Archibald (1776-1849) 2nd E. of GOSFORD (Ir) (1807) and 1st (U.K.) Ld. WORLINGHAM (1835) became an Irish M.P. in 1798 and sat for Armagh in the United Parliament from 1801 to 1807; from 1811 he was an Irish representative peer and known for his conciliatory views on Irish affairs. He held minor office in the Whig govt. of 1834, and in July 1835 was appointed Gov. of Lower Canada and Gov.-in-Chief of British N. America with a commission to investigate grievances. His inclinations were conciliatory, and his instructions from ministers even more so: they were modelled on a liberal Home Ruler's view of Ireland. He was to accept Louis Papineau's demands that the assembly should control crown lands and dispose of the local revenues, and that the legislative council was to be elective. These instructions were repudiated by the King. In Oct. 1835 the legislature refused to recognise the commission or vote supplies; riots followed. Gosford's new instructions did not help, and there were similar scenes in Sept.1836. The U.K. govt. sent new instructions which set no limit to the commission's inquiries. Gosford was promptly suspected of going back on his word. Supply was again refused. The commission then issued its report which was hostile to the agitators on all points, and thereupon the Westminster parliament resolved to appropriate the Lower Canadian revenues to the payment of arrears. Papineau organised a rebellion but the local Irish joined with the English urban constitutionalists against it. At its next meeting the legislature again refused supply and protested against the report and the Westminster resolution. Gosford dissolved it. The province then drifted towards anarchy while Gosford issued proclamations. In Sept. 1837, at the verge of civil war, he resigned and left public life.

ACHESON, Dean Gooderham (1893-71) A corporation and international lawyer was U/Sec. at the U.S. Treasury for six months in 1933 under Pres. Roosevelt, but returned to private practice. He was Asst. Sec. of State from 1941 to 1945, and then U/S. of State until July 1947. As such he played an important part first in formulating the Marshall plan and then as Pres. Truman's Sec. of State from Jan.1949 in administering it, and in the creation of the N. Atlantic Treaty Org. Heavily attacked by the Republicans because of the Chinese Nationalist collapse and the Korean stalemate, he resigned in 1953, but remained an active influence in the Kennedy and Johnson administrations.

ACID RAIN damaging particularly to German and Scandinavian forests in the 1970's was attributed to sulphorous and nitric emissions from western British power stations and the prevailing westerly winds. A German outcry ended in the issue of an E.U. directive in 1988 on reducing such emissions.

ACLAND. The family originated in Yorkshire but early became established in Devon which its members represented intermittently in Parliament. **(1) Sir John**

(?-1613) was M.P. for Devon in 1606-7 and conferred many benefactions on the City of Exeter and Exeter College, Oxford. **(2) John Dyke (?-1778)** was M.P. for Callington (Cornwall) in 1774 and served under Burgoyne in America with his better known wife **(3) Lady Harriet (1750-1815)** who shared his adventures. **(4) Sir Thomas Dyke (1787-1871)** was Tory M.P. for Devon from 1812 to 1818. He favoured Catholic emancipation, which annoyed the Tories, but gave him back his Devon seat with Whig support in 1820. On the other hand he voted against the Reform Bill and so was out of Parliament from 1831 to 1857. Thereafter he held North Devon as a Peelite Tory until 1857. His son **(5) Sir Thomas Dyke (1809-98)** was a fellow of All Souls (Oxford), M.P. for W. Somerset from 1837 to 1841 and from 1885 to 1886, and N. Devon from 1865 to 1885. He was mainly responsible for establishing the Oxford Local Examinations. His brother **(6) Sir Henry Wentworth (1815-1900)** was a Prof. of medicine from 1851 to 1894 and Pres. of the General Medical Council from 1874 to 1887. He early saw the need to improve professional standards in medicine and reorganized Oxford medical teaching so as to include general instruction in sciences.

ACONTIUS, Jacobus (ACONZIO, Jacopo) (?1500-?66) Tyrolese engineer, jurist and theologian, migrated from Switzerland to England in about 1559. A theological controversialist and author of *Strategmata Satanae* (Lat.= The Ruses of Satan), he drained Plumstead Marshes between 1562 and 1566, and repaired the fortifications of Berwick. Perhaps more importantly he was the first to propose (in his own interest) to an English govt. (in 1559) the Italian idea that an inventor should be awarded a monopoly patent for his invention.

À'COURT, William. See HEYTESBURY.

ACRE. See HIDE.

ACRE or ST JEAN D'ACRE (Palestine) was captured from the Egyptians in 1105 by Baldwin of Jerusalem with the help of the Genoese, who acquired trading and other privileges there. It was the chief port of the Crusader Kingdom (Outremer) until captured with Jerusalem by Saladin in 1187. The Third Crusade, led by K. Richard I, Philip of France and Leopold of Austria retook it in 1191. Its treatment caused furious disputes between those potentates, and these formed a step in the events leading to Richard's imprisonment. Acre then became the capital of Outremer until stormed by el-Ashraf in 1291. The strategic devastation of Palestine effected at that time led to its permanent decline.

In 1799 it was a small border fortress. Bonaparte's fleet having been destroyed by Nelson, he marched up the Syrian coast to conquer the Ottoman Empire by land. He was stopped at Acre in May by a force of Turks supported by a British squadron under Sir Sydney Smith, and after a fruitless siege retired. See MEDITERRANEAN WAR-2.

ACROPOLIS OF ATHENS. Its temples were more or less intact until 1687 when the Turks used the Parthenon as a powder magazine, and a stray shot during the Venetian siege blew it up. The scattered statuary began to be used locally as building material. The E of Elgin, British Ambassador to the Sublime Porte from 1799 to 1803, obtained permission to collect the remains. He embarked them, but the ship was wrecked and they had to be rescued a second time; eventually they reached England and were sold to the Crown. Now known as the Elgin Marbles, they were placed in the British Museum in 1816, and owe their good condition to this fact. At intervals Greek govts. agitate, for political reasons, for their return.

ACT OF GRACE 1717. See JACOBITES-13.

ACTON (1) Sir John Francis Edward (1736-1811) 6th Bart. entered Tuscan naval service but was employed from 1779 in the Neapolitan govt, which then ruled half of Italy. From 1781 he was effectively prime minister to K. Ferdinand IV, a tyrant upon whom he exercised a moderating influence. His willingness to allow Nelson to use the naval facilities in Naples and Sicily was a decisive element in the victorious B. of the Nile and the maintenance of British naval supremacy during the French wars thereafter. His grandson **(2) Sir John Emerich Edward Daiberg (1834-1902) 1st Ld. ACTON** (1869) was whig M.P. for Carlow from 1859 to 1865. He shared with his friend Gladstone a taste for theology and as a R. Catholic took part in the controversies surrounding the doctrine of Papal infallibility. He was a Lord-in-Waiting in Gladstone's fourth govt. from 1892 to 1895 when he became Regius Prof. of Mod. History at Cambridge. Cosmopolitan and reputedly perspicacious, he planned the Cambridge Mod. History but wrote little. He is credited with the saying 'power tends to corrupt and absolute power corrupts absolutely' (1887) but in 1770 Chatham said 'Unlimited power is apt to corrupt the minds of those who possess it'.

ACTON BURNELL, STATUTE OF (1283) was issued by Edward I and his council from Acton Burnell, near Shrewsbury. The preamble states that foreign merchants will not do business in the country unless they have a ready means of securing payment. Creditor and debtor were to appear before the mayors of London, York, or Bristol, and have the debt recorded. If it was not repaid the mayor was to sell the debtor's goods with the assistance through the royal chancery of the sheriffs of any shires where the debtor had assets. If these did not suffice the debtor was to go to prison. The Statute proved inadequate and was followed by the **Statute of Merchants** in 1285. Under this, further towns were appointed as registries, debtors were consigned to prison immediately the debt was in default, and their lands were given to the creditor until the profits from them repaid the debt. The procedure was modelled on that of the Exchequer of the Jews for regulating Jewish loans.

ACTRESSES. The first actress recorded as having played on the English stage was Margaret Hughes (?-1719), P. Rupert's mistress, who played Desdemona in *Othello* at the Clare Market theatre, London, in Dec. 1660. Charles II licensed theatres to put on plays in which women's parts were played by women instead of boys, in 1662. Male impersonators became rare, save in Pantomime, by about 1710.

ACTS OF PARLIAMENT. *See* BILLS; STATUTES.

ACTUARIAL SCIENCE. Edmund Halley (1656-1742), the astronomer, by his *Breslau Table of Mortality,* and Abraham de Moire (1667-1754), French mathematician who came to London in 1688, by his *Doctrine of Chances* (1711 and 1718) and his *Annuities upon Lives* (1725) provided the groundwork for the practical study of life contingencies, which made possible the successful functioning of the great life insurance institutions.

ADAIR, Sir Robert (1763-1855) a friend of Charles James Fox, visited Germany, Austria and Russia to study the local effects of the French Revolution in the years immediately after it occurred. He was thus an unusually well informed M.P. on continental matters, about which little hard information was at the time available. He was sent on confidential missions concerned with Bonaparte's ambitions to Vienna in 1806 and to Constantinople in 1807 *(see* DUCKWORTH). In the years 1831 to 1835 he was in the Low Countries where a civil war between the Dutch and the Belgians was largely prevented by his exertions.

ADAM, St. (?-1222), Cistercian and Abbot of Melrose was a royal nominee to the bishopric of Caithness, a Norse earldom where he tried to enforce canon law, and progressively to raise the church offerings. This eventually caused a riot in which he was killed.

ADAMANT. A pre-17th cent. term for a lodestone.

ADAM MARSH or DE MARISCO, (?-1259) Somerset Franciscan, nephew of a Bp. of Durham, and a friend of Grosseteste, whom he accompanied to the council of Lyons (1245). He was offered a chair at Paris, but preferred Oxford, where from 1247 he was regent of the Franciscans. Well known and trusted for his intellect and sense, he was much sought by, *inter alios,* Henry III, Simon de Montfort, and Boniface of Savoy, and his learning gained him the admiration of Roger Bacon.

ADAM, Robert (1728-92) with his brothers **William (II),** **John** and **James,** were architect sons of **William (I)** a leading Edinburgh architect. Their style originated with Robert's study in 1754 of the Palace of Diocletian at Split (Yugoslavia). Amongst their many buildings were Portland Place, the Adelphi, Osterley, Fitzroy Square (London), and Sion House.

ADAM, related to the architects **(1) William (1751-1839)** became M.P. in 1774 and from 1779 supported Ld. North and Fox. After 1783 he was chiefly distinguished as a legal M.P. From 1816 he presided in the Scottish jury court. Of his three sons **(2) John (1779-1825)** was political and private sec. to the Marquess Hastings in India, and acting gov-gen. of India for seven months in 1823. As such he suppressed the local English press. **(3) Sir Frederick (1781-1853)** was one of the few competent brigadiers under Wellesley on the Spanish East Coast and was badly wounded in 1813 at Ordall. His brigade enfiladed the French Old Guard at Waterloo, and so ensured its defeat. He was Ld. High Commissioner to the Ionian Isles from 1824 to 1831. **(4) William Patrick (1823-81)** was private sec. to Ld. Elphinstone, gov. of Bombay from 1853 to 1858 and Liberal M.P. for Clackmannan from 1859. He was chief Liberal Whip from 1865 until 1880 and then briefly gov. of Madras.

ADAM OF ORLTON (?-1345) consecrated Bp. of Hereford against Edward II's wishes in 1317, was employed on diplomatic missions to France between 1318 and 1320. He maintained English connections and joined the baronial rising of 1321, and after the defeat at Boroughbridge in 1322 he was charged with treason, refused to plead, and though personally protected by the archbishops, forfeited his property. On the Queen's landing in 1326 he became her chief adviser, and played a leading part in procuring the King's abdication. Under the new regime he was briefly Lord Treasurer, and then employed on diplomatic missions to the Pope and the French court. In 1333 he became Bp. of Winchester by provision and in 1341 he acted as a secret hostile adviser to the King against Abp. Stratford, who successfully accused him of it in Parliament. Shortly afterwards blindness forced his withdrawal from public life.

ADAM OF USK (?1352-1430) wrote a Latin chronicle of English history from 1377 to 1404. He witnessed the Parliament of 1390, was with Abp. Arundel during the campaign of 1399, and was a commissioner for deposing Richard II.

ADAMNAN, St. (?624-704) became Abbot of Iona in 679, and later learned the Roman rite at Monkwearmouth. Unable to introduce it at Iona he furthered it in Ireland. In 697 he presided at the Synod of Birr which adopted the so-called Canon of Adamnan prohibiting the taking of women and children as slaves in war. He wrote a life of St. Columba, and a derivative account of the Holy places.

ADAMS. This famous American family was descended from **(1) Henry (fl. 1630)** who migrated from England to Massachusetts in 1636. **(2) Samuel (1722-1803)** entered politics in 1746, and by 1763 was a member of the Caucus Club which controlled the Boston Town's meeting and had become a telling publicist. A member of the popular faction opposed to oligarchs such as the Hutchinsons, he was, by 1764, drafting instructions for the town's representatives and agitating against the Revenue Acts (1764) and the Stamp Act (1765). After the latter's repeal, he led the agitation against the Townshend Acts, which led to the so-called Boston Massacre (1770), and the Tea Party of 1773. He signed the Declaration of Independence in 1777. His lawyer cousin **(3) John**

(1735-1826) defended the British soldiers court-martialled for the 'massacre', yet represented Massachusetts at the Continental Congresses, and helped to write the Declaration of Independence. In 1778 he was involved in negotiations for the alliance with France; in 1780 he obtained Dutch recognition; he signed the P. of Paris of 1783 and became the first U.S minister to the Court of St. James in 1785. Meantime the Constitution of the U.S.A. had been adopted and between 1788 and 1796 Adams was Vice-President. In 1796 he succeeded Washington as President. As such he had to cope with revolutionary France, with which he narrowly avoided war. His son **(4) John Quincy (1767-1848)** served as minister at The Hague from 1794 to 1797, at Berlin from 1797 to 1801, at St. Petersburg from 1809 to 1814, and in London from 1815 to 1817 when he became Pres. Monroe's Sec. of State. He secured Florida and the 42nd parallel frontier by the Transcontinental Treaty with Spain in Feb.1821, and obtained the recognition of the S. American states (other than Peru) in the same year. He was also the real author of the Monroe Doctrine, which then depended upon the British Fleet, and he negotiated the Oregon Treaties with Britain and Russia. In 1824 he became President by which time most of his international work was done. Defeated for the presidency in 1828, he was elected to Congress in 1830 and remained there till his death. In a sour atmosphere of political manoeuvre and opposition accusations of abuse of patronage, he became associated with the anti-slavery movement and a powerful opponent of the southern doctrine of States' rights. From 1831 to 1845 he delayed efforts to annex Texas. His son **(5) Charles Francis (1807-86)** was minister to London from 1861 to 1868 and had major responsibility for keeping Britain out of the American civil war.

ADAMS, Sarah Flower (1805-48), wrote hymns, especially *Nearer, my God, to Thee.*

ADAMS, William (?-1620), sailed in a small squadron of Dutch traders to the E. Indies in 1598. His ship ended up the sole survivor, with a sick crew, on the Japanese coast. The Shogun Ieyasu, appreciating his knowledge of ships and pilotage, took him into his service and gave him a gentleman's estate near Yokosuka, where he married. In 1612 he made contact with the English trading station at Bantam, when he was visited by a ship of the HEIC. He obtained trading concessions for the Co. and thereafter made many voyages on its behalf from Japan. He survived the accession of the xenophobic Shogun Hidetada, who drove the English merchants out in 1623. His experiences provide a rare insight into contemporary Japanese society, and have formed the basis of a well known novel and film.

ADAMSON (before 1576 CONSTEIN or CONSTANT), Patrick (1537-92). As Abp. of St. Andrew's from 1576 he was (though trained as a Calvinist) repeatedly accused by the General Assembly of offences against the Church, and in 1579 took refuge in St. Andrew's castle where he fell ill. In 1583 he gained the King's favour and became his ambassador to Q. Elizabeth. On his return he proceeded in parliament against the presbyterians, who retaliated in the General Assembly by excommunicating him, but the sentence was quashed as illegal. In 1587 he was again accused, and in 1588, as the Presbyterians grew stronger, he lost the King's support. He then tried to reach an agreement with the Presbyterians, and a forged *Recantation* of episcopacy, allegedly by him, became current in 1590. Thereafter his influence disappeared.

ADAMSON, William (1863-1936), a Scottish miner, union official, and Labour M.P. for W. Fife (1910-31) was after the 1918 general election, in which the Labour leaders lost their seats, leader of the largest opposition party in the Commons. Later, he was Secretary for Scotland in Ramsay MacDonald's two Labour administrations.

ADDEDOMARUS. *See* BRITAIN, PRE-ROMAN-4.

ADDINGTON, Henry (1757-1844) 1st Vist. SIDMOUTH (1805) was a childhood friend of the younger Pitt. This influenced him to enter politics as M.P. for Devizes in 1784. He seldom spoke in debate but studied the procedure of the House, and for this reason Pitt obtained for him the Speakership in 1780. As Speaker he was much concerned with Warren Hasting's impeachment. In other ways he was less than impartial: in 1800 he made a powerful committee speech against Pitt's Irish policy, and when the King declared against R. Catholic relief, Addington undertook to try and bring Pitt round to the King's point of view. When he failed, the King offered him the government with Pitt's support; but Pitt's more powerful associates would not support Addington who had by now resigned the Speakership. In 1801 he formed a government of mediocrities to carry on Pitt's policy without R. Catholic relief. His first major task was to conclude negotiations, already begun, for the popular P. of Amiens (Mar. 1802). The government now undertook a large scale demobilisation and Pitt, believing this to be dangerous, withdrew his support. In May 1803 the war was renewed in disadvantageous circumstances at sea, and with unpopularity at home. Though commanding majorities in both Houses Addington could not face Pitt and his talented supporters. In April 1804 he resigned, but in Jan. 1805 entered the cabinet under the title of Vist. Sidmouth, as Lord President. The reconciliation with Pitt did not last, for Sidmouth voted for the impeachment of Pitt's friend Lord Melville, and resigned in July. He was a member of the brief 'All the Talents' administration after Pitt's death, and then was out of office until 1812, when he was Spencer Percival's Lord President. When Percival was assassinated, he became Home. Sec. under Lord Liverpool. As such he was responsible for most of the repressive measures against social and political unrest in the years after Waterloo. He resigned office in 1821, and from the Cabinet in 1824.

ADDISON, Dr Christopher (1869-1951) 1st Ld. (1937), Vist. ADDISON of STALLINGBOROUGH (1945). Prof. of Anatomy and later Labour politician, he was Min. of Munitions (1916-7), of Reconstruction (1917-9) Pres. of the Local Govt. Bd, which became the Min. of Health in 1918 (1919-21). He then joined the Labour Party and was Min. of Agriculture (1930-1), Commonwealth Sec. (1945-7) and Ld. Privy Seal (1947-51). As Min. of Reconstruction he shared Lloyd George's wish to get back to 1914 standards after World War I, not appreciating the intervening social changes, but he produced results. As Min. of Health he continued reconstruction through local authority house building to be let at controlled subsidised rents. His willingness to accept high building costs got the houses built (but never enough to meet the demand) but it raised prices and attracted criticism, for which Lloyd-George dismissed him, with characteristic disloyalty, in 1921. As Min. of Agriculture his Agricultural Marketing Act 1931 enabled producers to regulate prices through specialist boards.

ADDISON, Joseph (1672-1719) became a fellow of Magdalen, Oxford in 1693 and having obtained an annuity in 1699 through Charles Montague (later E. of Halifax) went to France, met Boileau, and travelled the continent until 1703. Well-known among Whig politicians, he secured a series of lucrative posts, and in 1709 became sec. to Lord Wharton, the Lord-Lieut. of Ireland, and M.P. for Malmesbury. It was at this time that he began to contribute to Steele's *Tatler,* (which ended in 1711), and to publish Whig pamphlets. He also contributed much of the *Spectator* in 1711 and 1712. The Tory victory put him out of office, but at Q. Anne's death he became Sec. to the Lords Justices and retrieved his Irish post. In 1715 he also became a commissioner of trade. In 1716 he married the Countess of Warwick, but escaped periodically from Holland House to a nearby coffee house. He retired in 1718.

ADDLED PARLIAMENT (1614). In this parliament the Commons refused to consider James I's request for supplies and debated a bill against impositions. The Lords led by Bp. Neile of Lincoln opposed the Commons who debated Neile's speech. The King objected to their conduct; they replied with complaints against royal favourites and pensioners, and Parliament was then dissolved. See JAMES I and VI-12.

ADELA OF BLOIS (?1062-1137) This clever and strong minded daughter of William the Conqueror and Matilda of Flanders was a scholar in Latin and Greek and a poet. She married Stephen, Count of Meaux and Brie, in 1080. He succeeded to Blois and Chartres in 1090. She ruled her husband's territories with great ability from 1095 to 1099 while he was on crusade, and was on terms of close friendship with the canonist Ivo of Chartres. She also acted as regent for her son Count Theobald from 1101 to 1109. During this period she and Ivo drafted the Investiture Compromise. When Theobald came of age she took the veil at Marcigny on the Loire, but her interest in politics continued, and in 1118 she negotiated an alliance between Theobald and K. Henry I against Louis of France. She was a generous patron of monasteries and churches.

ADELAIDE, Queen (1792-1849) of William IV was supposed, without much evidence, to have been a reactionary influence on the King, particularly during the Reform Bill controversies, when she was very unpopular. She regained public affection after her husband died, and Adelaide (S. Australia) was named after her.

ADELAIDE (fd. 1836). See AUSTRALIA-8 et seq.

ADELARD OF BATH (early 12th cent.) became one of the most influential scholars of his time. He studied at Tours, taught at Laon and then travelled in Greece and Asia Minor, Sicily, S. Italy, and Spain. He translated into Latin about a dozen mathematical, scientific and astronomical works from Arabic, and Euclid's *Elements* from Greek, defended Democritus' theory of atoms and developed a theory of liberal arts. By these achievements he effected an early introduction of Hellenic learning to the west. He also wrote a treatise on falconry.

ADEUZA OF LOUVAIN (?-1151) Henry I's second queen.

ADELPHI (Gr = *Adelphoi* = brothers) an area between the Strand and the Thames in London, roughly conterminous with the old site of Durham House, was so called because it was developed after 1768 by the brothers Robert, James and William Adam. Until about 1930 it was a fashionable residential area.

ADEN and YEMEN (Arabia). Aden was occupied by the British for a while in 1798 and ceded to the HEIC by the Sultan of Lahej in 1839. The Kuria Muria Is. were added in 1854 and Perim in 1857. The Turks having occupied the nearby Yemen, British troops helped the Sultan to repel them in 1873. It became a valuable coaling station, especially for the route to India. Sheikh Othman was added in 1882, and Socotra in 1886. As a result of fresh Turkish encroachments, the tribes accepted protection from 1882 onwards, and in 1914 a demarcation agreement with the Turks settled the present Yemeni frontier. The Turks occupied most of the tribal areas during World War I, but their collapse established the independence of the Imam of the Yemen, and restored the authority of the tribal chiefs. Yemeni troops, however, often invaded the protectorate with tribal connivance and had to be forcibly expelled. Under a treaty of 1934 both sides agreed to accept the demarcation of 1914. Aden became a Crown Colony in 1937 and its wharves, docks and airfield were an important part of the British Middle East position in World War II. In 1953 an oil refinery was built to replace the declining demand for coal.

The colony became partly self-governing in 1962 before being incorporated with the former Aden Protected Territories in a Federation of South Arabia in 1963 and this in its turn ended in independence (1967) and the liquidation of the British base a year later. Thereupon Russian advisers infiltrated the area, and the ruling National Liberation Front, after internal controversies, began a series of nationalisations leading to the establishment of a new People's Democratic Republic of the Yemen, which, in 1972, fought a short indecisive war with the neighbouring Yemen Arab Republic. The rising prosperity of the Arab Republic contrasted sharply with the declining economy and disorder of the People's Republic so that in the widespread political upheavals of 1989, the two Yemens were amalgamated by popular demand as a (theoretically) western style democracy. Civil War broke out again in 1994.

AD EXTIRPANDA (Lat.= For the extirpation [of heresy]) (1252) bull of Innocent IV excommunicating any ruler who failed to carry out the injunctions of the church.

ADLER (1) Nathan Marcus (1803-90) was chief rabbi in Hanover from 1830 to 1844, when he became chief rabbi of Britain. Here he persuaded the various Jewish congregations to unite. He was the effective founder of English Jewry. His son **(2) Hermann (1839-1911)** succeeded to his position and consolidated his work.

ADMINISTRATIVE LAW (Fr: *DROIT ADMINISTRATIF*) (1) A special system of law regulating the relationship between the organs of the state and between them and the individual. Incorporating an organised hierarchy of specialised courts, it is a feature of French jurisprudence and its derivatives. **(2)** In Britain the ancient, growing mass of such law has not been systematised. Legislation had created many separate codes and provisions, each often administered by different, or a different hierarchy of, tribunals, each constituted in the light of the political circumstances prevailing at the time of enactment. Attempts have been made, with some success, to absorb these varying institutions into the main body of the Common Law by the application of such principles as the Rule of Law, the Rules of Natural Justice, and the prerogative powers, since 1981 applied by way of judicial review, to protect personal freedom and enforce confinement within the ambit of the purposes of given legislation.

ADMINIUS. See BRITAIN BEFORE ROMAN CONQUEST-3.

ADMIRAL,-TY (Arab: *Amir al Bahr* = Sea Lord) The first English admiral, Sir Wm Leybourne, was appointed in 1297 in connection with Edward I's reorganisation of the south coast defences and the Cinque Ports. The High Court of Admiralty (q.v.) was first established in 1360 on the I. of Oléron, the legal jurisdiction and the functions of a naval commander having already parted company, and the lower ranks of vice- and rear-admiral had appeared. Admirals of England were appointed without interruption after 1391, and from 1540 were known as Lords High Admiral. They not only administered the fleet but sometimes commanded at sea e.g. Lord Howard of Effingham against the Armada in 1588. This was inconvenient for administration which was necessarily shore based, and became increasingly complicated and technical, and needed experts. A Navy Board to control the civil side functioned from 1546. In 1628, after Buckingham's murder, the Admiralty was placed in commission, and with a very short interval in 1816 this became the rule after 1709.

The Board of Admiralty then consisted of the First Lord of the Admiralty and a Civil Lord (who were politicians changing with the govt.) and a number of Sea Lords who were naval officers. The First Sea Lord was responsible for fleet movements and naval policy: the Second dealt with personnel: the Third with *matériel,* and later a Fourth and Fifth were appointed.

In the middle of the 17th cent. the fleet was divided into (in order of seniority) Red, White and Blue squadrons distinguished by the still familiar red, white and blue ensigns, with four admirals of each rank in each, except that the Red had no Admirals, the Senior Admiral who would have held such a rank being admiral of the fleet. Since promotion was by seniority, congestion in the flag list was acute, and to bring forward promising junior officers it became customary to place some more elderly but newly promoted rear-admirals of the Blue on a half pay or Yellow list, and not employ them at sea. To celebrate the victory at Trafalgar the Prince Regent 'restored' or rather instituted the rank of Admiral of the Red, thereby expediting promotions throughout the whole of the flag list.

In 1863 the coloured squadrons were abolished, and their ensigns became available for their present uses. Flag officers thenceforth were promoted by selection.

In 1964 the Admiralty became a branch of the Dept. of Defence, the First Lord was replaced by a Minister for the Navy, and the title of Lord High Admiral was assumed by the sovereign. *See* PEPYS, NAVY BOARD.

ADMIRALTY, COURTS OF. When the Admiral was at sea his Court was held for him on land by a deputy. From about 1340 deputies and courts sat for the north, south and west of England. In 1360 a High Court of Admiralty was established at Oléron (Biscay) so as to be accessible to seamen using the major trade route to Bordeaux. It was by this route that the law of Amalfi (near Naples) known as the *Tabula Amalfitana*, originating in the 11th cent and recognised throughout the Mediterranean, came to be received into English law. The original purpose was to try pirates and deal with prize, but civil jurisdiction, extending to all mercantile and shipping cases, soon developed, and the courts were encroaching upon the business of other courts and had to be restrained by Acts of 1389, 1391 and 1401. In the 15th cent. they were dealing with commercial cases again but the Common Law courts managed to restrain them once more. They declined, but revived during the 18th cent. through the vast numbers of prizes taken, especially in the French wars. Many ports had local courts of Admiralty or Vice-Admiralty which, save in the Cinque Ports, were suppressed in 1835. Such courts were also set up for the colonies as and when required. That at Malta became notorious for expense, delay and corruption. Lord Cochrane once unrolled one of its bills of costs the length of the House of Commons.

The High Court was amalgamated with the High Court of Justice in 1875, but the law and practice remains.

ADMIRALTY Is. annexed to Germany in 1885, were occupied by the Australians in 1914, and became part of Papua-New Guinea in 1975.

ADMONITION TO PARLIAMENT (1572), a manifesto against episcopacy and the admission of papists to communion, was perhaps composed by the presbyterian minister John Field who, with his colleague Thomas Wilcox, was imprisoned after attempting to present it to Parliament. It offended those bishops who sympathised with the moderate critics, and alienated even advanced protestants who sought self-reform by the church and unity in the face of the papal bull *(Regnans in Excelsis)* of deposition against Elizabeth I (1570), growing alienation from Spain, and the St Bartholomew massacre of French Huguenots (Aug 1572). The bishop's rejoinder provoked Thomas Cartwright's vigorous *Second Admonition*. In June 1573 both *Admonitions* were suppressed.

ADOLPHUS FREDERICK, Prince (1774-1850) D. of CAMBRIDGE (1801) was 7th son of George III. After service in the Hanoverian and British armies he became a field marshal in 1813, and was viceroy of Hanover from 1816 to 1837.

ADOPTION OF LAW. This is a presumption that the legislature does not, save expressly, intend to derogate from rules of international law, which may therefore be adopted by a court in suitable cases. Many rules of commercial and maritime law have arisen in this way.

ADOPTIVE ACTS contain powers which a local authority cannot exercise unless it acquires them by an adoption process usually including special public notices and majorities. The process avoids the expense and the parliamentary congestion of promoting private bills.

ADRIAN OF CANTERBURY, St. (?-710), African Abbot of Nerida, refused the see of Canterbury in 665, proposed St. Theodore of Tarsus and by request went to Canterbury with Theodore, who made him Abbot of St. Augustine's. Here he founded and for nearly 40 years directed a school where, besides the usual subjects, Roman Law and Greek were taught. Students came from as far as Ireland, and included many future abbots and bishops. He seems to have been an amiable head master, for the miracles ascribed to him include several in aid of boys in trouble with their teachers.

ADRIAN OF CASTELLO (?1460-1521) became papal nuncio in Scotland in 1488, and in 1489 collector of Peter's Pence in England, where he held several benefices. In 1492 he was English ambassador in Rome and in 1502 Bp. of Hereford and in 1504 of Bath and Wells (both in absence). He was away from Rome between 1503 and 1511 and then became involved in a conspiracy to murder Leo X, for which he was deprived in 1518.

ADRIAN IV (Nicholas Breakspear) Pope (r. 1115-9?) though English, spent little of his life in England. He studied in France, eventually entering the Augustinian monastery of St. Rufus, near Avignon, where he rose to be abbot. Appointed Cardinal-bishop of Albano by Pope Eugenius III (1145-53), he was sent on a mission to reorganize the churches of Scandinavia. On his return he was elected pope. In 1155 he crowned the German King, Frederick Barbarossa, Emperor, but a subsequent attempt to claim the empire as a papal fief failed. His relations with Frederick continued to be poor, and at the time of his death Adrian was preparing to put himself at the head of the emperor's Italian enemies.

ADRIATIC (or GULF OF VENICE) (1) From Roman times conditions in this 500-mile long sea strongly affected the rich central European trade and the western trade as far as England, and the associated exchange movements, by way of Venice, and from the 15th cent. the trade to east central Europe via Trieste. The Levantine trade came through the 45-mile wide Straits of Otranto; the Balkan trade along the Via Egnatia to Dyrrhachium (Durazzo or Durres) and Valona (Avlona). The prevailing wind in the south is southerly; in the north, northerly in winter. The currents go north up the Balkan coast and south along the Italian. Shipping naturally concentrated near Corfu on the Balkan side of the Straits; this was a Venetian possession from 1386 to 1797 and, with Venice herself, the strategic basis of Venetian influence over the European oriental trade, and impressively fortified.

(2) The climate forced the important winter shipping to hug the Dalmatian coast, and it needed oared propulsion, but this coast was infested by piratical Narentines, Turks and Uskoks from Segna. To trade in convoy created price fluctuations; to trade individually was risky. Hence the Venetians occupied Dalmatia which, save for Ragusa (Dubrovnik) was their incompletely controlled province from 1420 to 1797. The Uskoks habitually sold their loot in Habsburg Trieste; the Narentines, theirs, at Ragusa, the Turks in Valona and Durazzo. The chances of being captured or wrecked were about equal in these waters.

(3) The highly saline Adriatic formed, together with Venetian Cyprus after 1470, the basis of a salt industry essential to the Balkans. The Venetian salt monopoly ensured that Balkan exports would reach Europe through Venice.

(4) RAGUSA (from which *argosy* is derived) remained independent under Papal protection, yet from the mid-15th cent. also as a Turkish vassal state. The dual status gave this tiny Italo-Slav Republic a disproportionate importance, for its argosies passed unharmed in the conflicts between Christendom and Islam, and between 1550 and 1650 superseded the Genoese in the Levant-Atlantic traffic. Timber exhaustion, however, brought a decisive decline in Adriatic shipbuilding, and after 1640 the trade fell mainly to the British and Dutch.

(5) The 17th cent. Venetian decline affected all the Adriatic, but Bonaparte (as much Italian as Corsican) understood its value as a corridor to the East. His annexation of Venice in 1797 was aimed at Corfu and Dalmatia as well as Venice herself. The Austrians, however, seized Dalmatia (with Ragusa), but Bonaparte took it from them under the P. of Pressburg in 1805. The French here gave the British considerable trouble. Corfu was their nearest base to Egypt, and after they had capitulated in Egypt, they, using Venetian-built ships, interrupted a major route between Britain and her Austrian ally. The Royal Navy had to wage a long Adriatic campaign *(see* HOSTE). Hence the Vienna Congress assigned Venice and Dalmatia to Austria but the British insisted, in order to prevent domination by a single power, that the Ionian Is. become independent under British protection. This Republic of the Seven Islands lasted until 1861, when they were passed to Greece on the British calculation that the newly uniting Italy would balance Austrian predominance.

(6) The Prusso-Italian War with Austria of 1866 gave Venice and its provinces to Italy, but the Italian part of the war had been inglorious, the powerful Italian fleet being defeated off Lissa (Vis). To compensate for Venice, the Austrians developed docks and shipping at Trieste and connected it with Vienna by the Semmering railway. Venice, deprived of its hinterland, consequently declined. This was a major reason why the Italians plotted to desert the Central Powers in World War I. Moreover the Austro-Hungarian naval threat to the Mediterranean caused the Allies to offer a high price for that desertion. The secret T. of London (1915) represented a 'Venetian' arrangement. In return for Istria and most of Dalmatia, the Austro-Hungarian navy was bottled up by a 67-mile barrage at Otranto. The barrage was a large diversion of British naval resources.

(7) The Italians had to be rescued by their allies on land, yet had the advantage by sea, but the accretion of a Yugoslav state around the Serbian monarchy ensured powerful Slav resistance to the T. of London. The compromise T. of Rapallo (Nov.1920) gave the port of Zara (Zadar) and some off-shore islands to Italy and the rest of Dalmatia to Yugoslavia. Istria remained Italian, and Trieste, in turn deprived of its hinterland, declined, but with little advantage to Italy.

(8) In an age of air power, the strategic control of the Adriatic no longer rested with the master of Corfu, and so in 1938 the Italians seized Albania. In the Italian debacle in World War II, however, Albania was lost; in 1948 Yugoslavia took the Dalmatian enclaves, Flume (Rijeka) and Istria save Trieste; and Dalmatia, hitherto linked laterally only by sea was united by a coastal road completed in 1960. *See also* VENICE; ALBANIA; IONIAN IS; YUGOSLAVIA.

ADULLAMITES (*see* 1 SAM. ch 22 vv 1-2) A pejorative name originally used by Pres. Lincoln in 1864 but reused by Bright to describe those Liberals, led by Robert Lowe, who in 1866 abandoned their party rather than support Russell's proposed parliamentary reforms, and forced the govt. to resign.

ADVENTURERS of 1641 (Ir.) were a private parliamentarian Co. which undertook to reconquer Ireland at its own expense after the massacre of 1641, in return for allotments of a 1000 acres at 4s per acre in Ulster, 6s in Connaught, 8s in Munster, and 12s in Leinster. The purpose was to finance the reconquest by the proceeds while isolating the King from the resources of Ireland

recently organised by Strafford. Their private army was assembled at Bristol in 1642, but the Civil War broke out and it was diverted to and defeated at Edgehill.

ADVERTISEMENTS, BOOK OF (Mar. 1566) was issued by Abp. Parker at the Queen's insistence. It laid down the ceremonials to be used in the Anglican Church. It resulted in the suspension of some clergy whose scruples on certain points such as the use of the surplice, had been tolerated hitherto.

ADVERTISING, COMMERCIAL arose in the 18th cent. when the new mass-producers needed to widen their accustomed markets. **(1)** Black and white lettered bills were used by hired bill-stickers to adorn any flat surface such as a house wall. Fly posting, i.e. surreptitious bill-sticking, was common. The many ex-soldiers and sailors thrown onto the labour market after the French wars reduced the cost and, after 1815, crowded the streets with peripatetic placards carried on poles by fantastically dressed men advertising anything from a mummified Egyptian crocodile or an election candidate, to a malt whiskey. They sometimes came in processions with, even, a band, and developed into Charles Dickens' sandwich men with placards front and back, or into horse-drawn floats which obstructed streets and had to be prohibited in 1853. **(2)** Meanwhile advertising in newspapers transformed their finances and raised their circulations by creating a business nexus besides one of mere curiosity, with potential readers, who might buy them for the advertising alone. **(3)** Press advertising expanded from the 1890's as the Board Schools delivered new semi-literate mass readerships. The front page of *The Times* was wholly dedicated to small advertisments until the 1930s. Wall advertising, once owners saw that there was money in it, was expanded by W.H. Smith with his monopoly of station walls in certain railways. Hoardings then appeared in rivalry on land visible from trains and, when motor cars became common, in places visible from roads. These eventually attracted control as part of planning legislation after 1948. The peripatetic placards were mostly crowded out, but sandwich men are still sometimes seen. **(4)** The American method of financing broadcasting by advertising did not appear in Britain until 1954 because of the B.B.C.'s licence financed monopoly. At its controversial introduction a compromise was reached; the B.B.C. continued as before but could not sell advertising while alternative channels permitted advertising-financed franchised companies to encroach on its monopoly. These, to ensure revenue, competed for the semi-educated mass audiences created by the new educational system after 1946, and seemed by 1994 to represent a political threat to the cultural *raison d'être* of the B.B.C.'s licence revenue. Then in 1994, just as the B.B.C., feeling threatened by satellite channels, went over to populism, one commercial radio channel secured an audience for classical music far larger than anyone expected. *See* BROADCASTING; BROADSHEETS.

AD VITAM AUT CULPAM (Lat = to life or fault, i.e. until death or dishonour). The Scottish description of the tenure of an appointment during good behaviour.

ADVOCATES, FACULTY OF (Sc). Advocates existed in the Scottish courts as early as 1410 but were organised into a professional faculty headed by a Dean in 1532 originally with a membership of ten, which however, steadily increased. Its LIBRARY was founded in 1682 and became the biggest library in Scotland. In 1925 the non-legal part of its 750,000 books was transferred to the new National Library of Scotland.

ADVOCATE, LORD. The chief Scots law officer. The office was created by James III in 1480. He was *ex officio* a member of the Scots parliament and gradually acquired most of the Scots administrative powers of govt., particularly between 1735 and 1885 when there was no Sec. of State, and he was in reality a viceroy. The creation of the Secretaryship brought a wholesale transfer of his powers to the new Scottish Office, and the Lord Advocate reverted to being a law officer.

ADVOWRY was a personal commendation of individuals in a marcher or palatine lordship to obtain the right to be protected by the lord's court, which otherwise protected only feudal tenants.

ADVOWSON and TITHE. (1) A clergyman must be *instituted* by the ecclesiastical superior or Ordinary (usually the bishop) to the spiritualities of a benefice, and *inducted* by his authority to the temporalities. Advowson (Lat: *advocatio*) is the right to propose a candidate for these processes. Advowsons are called *collative* if in the hands of the Ordinary, and *presentative* if owned by anyone else.

(2) Said to be of pagan origin, many probably originated in bargains between bishops and lords of manors whereby the latter received the advowson in return for building the church. *(See,* however, para. 7 below). Since the Constitutions of Clarendon (1164) they have been governed by the common law on property; they could be bought and sold, and an Ordinary could be compelled by an action of *Quare Impedit* (Lat: 'Why does he hinder') to accept a presentation unless the candidate was heretical or notoriously immoral.

(3) Papal attempts to override advowsons by *Provision* (i.e. by direct appointment) were therefore considered a threat alike to ecclesiastical independence, and lay property. They provoked four Statutes of Provisors. (a) That of 1351 laid down that patrons should present to their benefices not the pope; (b) That of 1353 imposed the penalties of *praemunire* upon suing abroad or impeaching an English judgment abroad in a matter of advowson. (c) This was confirmed by the Statute of 1365. (d) That of 1389 forfeited benefices accepted contrary to the previous acts, and forbade enforcement of provisions by ecclesiastical process. Provisions, however continued sporadically, particularly where manors had come into the hands of bishops and monasteries, who found difficulty in resisting the Vicar of Christ. The crown seldom intervened as long as the papacy tolerated royal nominations of bishops.

(4) At the Reformation numerous advowsons returned, with former monastic estates, into lay ownership and provided perquisites for younger members of local landowning families. Incumbents, once inducted, were practically irremovable and so the lower clergy were remarkable for independence, variety of opinion and even eccentricity. As a result of Tudor and Stuart religious controversies, the rights of R. Catholic patrons after 1605 were exercised for them by Oxford and Cambridge Universities. Sales of most advowsons have been void since 1898.

(5) **TITHE,** a primitive income tax for the sustenance of the church, was enjoined by a synodal resolution in 786, and began to be legally enforceable in 900. It consisted of 10% of (a) fruits of the ground (**praedial**); (b) the profits of labour (**personal**) and (c) profits partly of one and partly of the other (**mixed**). A further important distinction was between (d) **great** tithes levied on the crops and (e) **small** tithes levied on living things such as beasts, chickens and eggs. Personal tithes lapsed early, and the extensive common lands were not tithable. Hence squatters and cottars usually escaped tithe altogether.

(6) An incumbent entitled to all the tithes was called the RECTOR. Many mediaeval monasteries, however, provided for the religious needs of their adjacent parishes. To defray the expenses they APPROPRIATED the tithe, but subsequently endowed a parson called the VICAR to do the work. The Vicar usually received part of the glebe and the small tithe (which was difficult to collect), leaving the great tithe to the appropriator. If a layman or corporation occupied a position like that of the monastery he or it was said to IMPROPRIATE the tithe,

and was (and is) called the LAY RECTOR. Roughly speaking the great tithe usually amounted to three times the value of the small. Since the appropriator or impropriator nearly always had the advowson to the vicarage, the combined right could be very valuable. This connection between advowson and the great tithe was an important motive behind the treatment of advowsons as property.

(7) Legislation against appropriations was passed in 1404, but it was still lawful to supplement a monastic endowment by appropriation if the work was not neglected. At the Reformation appropriations passed to impropriators, but in the case of those made since 1404, the impropriator had to nominate a PERPETUAL CURATE for the vacant cure. He was licensed by the Ordinary and could be dismissed only on revocation of the license, and he received the small tithe.

(8) By the beginning of the 18th cent. tithes were paid in money or were – rarely – redeemed for a composition. The payments were related to the national value of the harvest. The system, however, was being thrown out of gear by inclosures which cut across ancient holdings and commons. Hence it became usual to reapportion liability by means of TITHE AWARDS (imposed by commissioners) or PAROCHIAL AGREE-MENTS made locally under official supervision. In some cases where the inclosure was made by private act, the lands were charged, in lieu of tithe, with a CORN RENT which was related to an average price over seven years of corn fixed by Quarter Sessions. Thus from about 1700 to 1880 four different systems were operating in varying proportions throughout the country, but the relationship to the average price of corn was usual.

(9) In many parts, moreover, it was difficult to collect because nonconformist conviction and radical opinion encouraged resistance. In 1918 accordingly the tithe was converted into a tithe rent charge and stabilised for seven years regardless of corn prices. From 1925, agitation still continuing, a proportion of the rent charges was to be paid into a sinking fund to redeem all liabilities by 2010. In 1936 tithe owners were given govt. stock bearing interest equivalent to their tithe rent charges which were abolished, and the lands were charged with annuities in favour of the treasury which would redeem the stock by 1996. This finally broke the nexus between advowson and finance. These annuities were redeemable voluntarily, and in the case of small sums compulsorily. By 1989 they had disappeared.

AED. *See* SCOTS OR ALBAN KINGS, EARLY.

AELFGAR, Earl (?-?1062). *See* MERCIA, EARLDOM OF.

AELFGIFU of NORTHAMPTON (fl. 1015-40) unreliably reputed the mistress of St. Olaf, was the able daughter of Aelfhelm E. of Northumbria, born on one of his Northamptonshire estates. Canute took her as a 'hand-fasted wife' soon after 1015. The Church did not recognise the relationship. Consequently Canute was free to marry Ethelred the Unready's widow Emma in 1017, but he treated Aelfgifu as of equal importance and in 1030, after St. Olaf's death at the hands of the Tronds at the B. of Sticklestead, Canute appointed her regent of Norway for their son Swein and co-ruler of Denmark with Emma's son Harthacnut. Canute's policy, which she sought to carry out, was to reduce Norway to order and also to make it profitable by imposing regular public service obligations and Danish taxes. **Aelfgifu's Time** is the Norwegian name for the years 1030-5, regarded as a time of misery (probably due to crop failures) and oppression mainly due to policies which were not hers. In 1035 she and Swein were driven from Norway by St. Olaf's son Magnus and she was acting as K Harthacnut's adviser if not regent in Denmark when Canute died. In the confusion she returned to England, and she and E. Leofric proposed a regency for her son Harold who in due course ascended the throne, because Harthacnut was at war with Magnus and could not be spared from Denmark. She was probably the real ruler until Harold died (1040), but Harthacnut had disliked Harold and perhaps knew her only too well. She retired.

AELFHEAH. *See* ALPHEGE, ST.

AELFRIC (?-1005) after being Bp. of Ramsbury, was Abp. of Canterbury from 995.

AELFRIC (?950-1016) son of Aelthere, earldorman of the E. Mercians, succeeded his father in 983. He was banished in 986, but restored in about 990. Strongly pro-Danish, he refused to fight against them in 1003.

AELFRIC (fl. 1000), pupil of St Aethelwold, was sent in about 987 to take charge of teaching at Cerne Abbas (Dorset) an abbey newly founded by the Thane Aethelmar. In 1005 he became Abbot of Eynsham (Oxon), another of Aethelmar's foundations. He was a prolific writer of English works intended to make Christianity more accessible to the people. His *Catholic Homilies* contain 80 Sunday and Feast Day sermons, while his *Saints' Lives* were designed primarily for monastic festivals. He also wrote a Latin–English grammar and translated parts of the Old Testament into English.

AELFTHRYTH or ELFRIDA (?945-1000). *See* AETHILSTANS' SUCCESSORS-4-6.

AELFTHRYTH or ELTRUDE (?-929) a daughter of K. Alfred, married Baldwin II of Flanders, and was an ancestress of William the Conqueror's wife Matilda.

AELFWINE (?-1047) was chaplain to K. Canute and reputedly the lover of his widow Emma. He became Bp. of Winchester in 1032.

AELLE or AELLA (?-after 491) was one of several Anglo-Saxon chieftains who invaded Britain in about 477. As tradition calls him the first of the *Bretwaldas* it has been suggested that he formulated a strategic plan of simultaneous invasions by way of Essex and Sussex. He certainly commanded the latter himself, his object being presumably the Wealden iron mines. With Cissa and two other sons he stormed the Roman port and fortress of Anderida (Pevensey) in 491, and became the first King of Sussex.

AELLE (?560-88) and **AELLE (?-876).** *See* NORTHUMBRIA.

AENEAS SILVIUS PICCOLOMINI (1405-64) Pope PIUS II (1458), humanist writer and diplomat became prominent at the Diet of Frankfurt of 1442 as a conciliar diplomat, and at subsequent imperial diets and conferences, where he generally appeared as a conciliator between the Pope, the Princes, and the Emperor. By 1456 he was both a cardinal and a prince. In 1460, as Pope, he condemned the doctrine of the supremacy of the church councils. He hoped to end the mutual enmity of Christian princes by uniting them in a Crusade against the Turks who, having captured Constantinople in 1453, were advancing upon Vienna. In 1464 he took the cross himself as an example, but died on the way to Venice. *See* RENAISSANCE-7.

AERENTHAL, Aloys Count LEXA v. (1854-1912) was an Austrian professional diplomat from 1877 to 1906 mostly in Russia. In Oct. 1906 he was appointed Austro-Hungarian foreign minister because it was thought that his knowledge of Russian personalities would ease the path of Habsburg expansion in the Balkans. In Sept. 1908 he met Izvolski, the Russian foreign minister at Berchtold's house at Buchlau, to discuss Austrian annexation of Bosnia-Herzegovina then under Austrian occupation. He said that Izvolski agreed. In Oct. the annexation was proclaimed. Izvolski denied Aerenthal's version and as Aerenthal had omitted to obtain Turkish agreement, he found Russia and all the Balkan powers for once united and against Austria. The annexation also offended Austria's ally Italy, which entertained Balkan ambitions, and the differences with Italy became deeper still when, just before his death, he refused to support the Italian attack on Turkey in 1912.

AERIAL NAVIGATION ACT, 1911. *See* AVIATION RULES-1.

AEROPLANE. *See* AVIATION.

AESCINGS or OISCINGS. The dynastic name of the Kentish kings, after Aesc or Oisc (r. 488-512) *s.* of Hengist.

AESCWINE. *See* WEST SAXONS, EARLY-9.

AESTHETICISM was a reaction, rather than a movement, against the materialism and ugliness of the mid-19th cent. It was represented in different ways by the morally based attitudes of Ruskin and Morris, the literary enterprise of Swinburne and Pater, the French influenced painter Whistler, and Oscar Wilde's conversational brilliance. It attracted a good deal of well-natured satire in *Punch* and at the hands of W.S. Gilbert in *Patience* where Bunthorne

> Walks down Piccadilly
> With a poppy or a lily
> In his mediaeval hand.

AETHELBALD (?-757). *See* MERCIA-5.

AETHELBALD (?-860) King (855). *See* ENGLISH MONARCHY, EARLY-2, 3.

AETHELBERT or ETHELBERT, I and II. *See* KENT, KINGDOM-2, 3.

AETHELBERT, St. (?-794) East Anglian King. *See* EAST ANGLIA.

AETHELBERT (?-866) K. of the West Saxons (860) succeeded his brother Aethilwulf. In 865 some Danes, probably on reconnaissance, wintered in Thanet. He died just as Hingwar's Danish army of conquest arrived. *See* ASHDOWN, B. OF.

AETHELFLEDA or ETHELFLEDA (?-920) *d.* of K. Alfred and Lady of the Mercians. *See* EDWARD THE ELDER.

AETHELING (A.S.) originally meant a member of a noble family (cf Ger: *adel*), but was later often restricted to the blood royal or even to the royal heir apparent. The word continued in use into the 12th cent.

AETHELSTAN. *See* EAST ANGLIA.

AETHELWINE. *See* EAST ANGLIA.

AETHELWOLD, St. (?908-84), a friend of St. Dunstan, was trained at Glastonbury. From 954 he was engaged in restoring the monastery at Abingdon. In 963 he became Bp. of Winchester, and with K. Edgar's support expelled the seculars from the minsters there and at Chertsey and Milton Abbas, and restored true monasticism according to the Benedictine rule from Fleury. He followed the same course at Peterborough in 966, Ely in 970 and Ramsey in 972. The Council of Winchester held in 970 to standardise monastic practices gave him the task of compiling a common rule; and his *Regularis Concordia* was mostly a recension of continental practices. Of long lasting effect on monasticism it also influenced the character of the episcopate, because the method of election he laid down was bound to create a predominantly monastic episcopate. He also wrote a treatise on the circle.

A[E]THILSTAN, King of the English (r. 925-39) (1) a florid but effective propagandist, began by marrying his sister Eadgitha to Otto I (soon Emperor), and another sister to Sigtrygg Gale, the Ostman ruler of York, who was baptised and so alienated from his heathen brethren at Dublin. He died in 926. Athelstan drove his sons Guthfrith and Olaf Kuaran into Scotland, and by agreement (the T. of Emmet or Eamont) with the K. of Scots, the N. Welsh princes and the Northumbrians ratified his kingship in Northumbria, with the administration in the hands of the Bernician alderman Edred, a descendent of Ida the Flamebearer.

(2) The Irish Ostmen had not accepted the loss of York. They could not by themselves recover it, but looked among their own kind in Scandinavia and among the Viking pirate fleets for recruits and allies. Aethilstan sought by diplomacy to prevent them getting either. His sister Eadgifu had already married the Emperor Charles the Simple. Their son, Louis, was educated at Aethilstan's court. Another sister, Ethelreda, married the powerful Hugh the Great, Count of Paris, ancestor of the French kings, but most importantly a neighbour of the Vikings settled in Normandy. His German brother-in-law Otto, was equally a neighbour of heathen Denmark, with Norwegians who had been driven from Norway by Harald Fairhair. In about 927 Aethilstan made an agreement at York whereby he became foster-father to Harald's son Hakon. Harald abdicated in 929 and died in 932. It then seemed as if Norway might fall into hands of the heathen and Danish supported corsair, Eirik Bloodaxe. Thereupon Aethilstan despatched the well indoctrinated Hakon home where, with the help of the great Jarl Sigurd of Lade, he was established as king.

(3) These manoeuvres and his reputation (see below) prevented the Ostmen from securing continental allies. They could not wholly stop the flow of private recruits into the great build-up of the armament at Dublin, nor interrupt relations between the Dublin kings, the Scots, the Picts or the Ostmen of Cumbria. In 937 K. Eric the Red sailed at last. His great fleet landed in the Solway and joined up with Constantine K. of Scots, the Picts and the Cumbrians. Aethilstan met the allies at an unidentified place called Brunanburh in an all-day battle, and though Olaf and Constantine escaped, their forces (including five kings and seven jarls) were annihilated. This resounding victory, celebrated in a famous poem, confirmed the stability of England as an entity, and precipitated the Ostmen into decline. Two years later, however, Aethilstan was dead.

(4) Aethilstan created a tremendous reputation for himself in Europe. This was probably generated by him, backed by his deeds and communicated through his sisters and the church. He made many monastic endowments and was an avid collector of holy relics. His family and court life were happy, and two foreign kings were sent to him for education.

A[E]THILSTAN'S SUCCESSORS. The new English monarchy had depended on the continuous inspiration of strong kings. In the five reigns between the death of Aethilstan (939) and the accession of Ethelred the Unready 39 years later, either royal strength or continuity (or both) were lacking and English vigour was partly dissipated through discord. (1) EDMUND I (r. 939-46) was faced with confusion. Oaths of allegiance to Aethilstan had lapsed at his death. Olaf the Red, the Ostman king of Dublin had been driven out by his brother after the disaster of Brunanburh (937). Like Siggtryg Gale before him he came to York. The Danes of Northumbria and the Five Boroughs took him as their King. Edward instantly overran the Five Boroughs. In 940 Olaf and the Northumbrian Danes marched S.W. and stormed Tamworth, but were chased north by Edward's superior forces. At Leicester Edmund and Olaf exchanged oaths and Olaf and his brother Ragnvald were baptised. Olaf, however, died within the year. Edmund occupied Northumbria, drove out Ragnvald and handed over Cumbria to Malcolm K. of Scots as part of an arrangement for the defence of the west coast against Ireland. Within a few weeks this vigorous King was, for reasons unknown, assassinated. His half-brother (2) EDRED (r. 946-55) took up his policy. The northern arrangement were confirmed; the oaths resworn but then Eirik Bloodaxe (see AETHILSTAN-2) appeared. The Northumbrian Danes renounced their oaths in his favour and elected him K. of York. Edred marched north and they hastily deposed him (947). He went to Denmark. Edred returned south, whereupon they elected his rival Olaf Kuaran (see AETHILSTAN-1). Edred calculated that they would destroy each other and held off. In 949 Eirik returned and Olaf Kuaran fled together with Abp. Wulfstan of York, whom Edred arrested. In 952 Olaf returned by way of Cumbria. In a tremendous battle on the Stainmoor, Olaf's people were defeated but Eirik was killed. Edred then took over Northumbria, returned its administration to Bernician aldermen and moved Wulfstan to the more easily supervised See of Sherborne. Within a year the King was dead. He left two boys (3)

EDWI[G] (r. 955-9) who was twelve, and (4) EDGAR (r. 955-75) aged eleven. They at first reigned jointly under the tutelage of the great Archbishop, St. Dunstan. It was natural for an archbishop to undertake, like Aethilstan, diplomacy abroad and conciliation at home. The factionalism which must be assumed to have underlain Edmund I's assassination now emerged as a kind of party strife among subjects seeking to influence a govt. headed by a churchman who could (sometimes very effectively) persuade but not command. Moreover, times were changing. The sons of the dead Eirik had a claim to Norway in which the Danish King Harald Bluetooth, who was at odds with the Anglophil K. Hakon (see AETHILSTAN-2) supported them. In 961, when there was an epidemic in England, they killed Hakon at the B. of Stord. Known after their mother, the Sons of Gunnhild, representing Danish aggression, began to attract the fissiparous ambitions of the Northumbrian Danes just as Dunstan was trying to persuade all the nations of England and his king into unification. At the same time, there were signs of anti-clericalism or demands that the weak Edgar should be liberated from the Archbishop's tutelage. These ideas represented the ambitions of territorial rulers and aldermen to be free of the royal grasp as wielded by St Dunstan. The pressure grew with time, yet it was not until the King was in his 30th year that the saint liberated him with a characteristically ingenious gesture. He staged at Bath the magnificent sacramental coronation which strengthened the King by raising him above the level of mere politicians. Immediately afterwards Edgar went to Chester where seven kings rowed him on the R. Dee. Such symbolism impressed contemporaries, but Edgar did not enjoy the supremacy long. He died suddenly two years later after an unwarlike reign. He had married twice. His second wife was Aelfthryth d. of alderman Ordgar of Devon and widow of alderman Aethelwold of E. Anglia. By his first he had a son (5) EDWARD surnamed THE MARTYR (r. 975-8) a man of volcanic temper on the verge of manhood who seemed likely to continue the strong policies of Dunstan. A year later all Europe was changed by a catastrophic famine in which not only the crops but the fisheries failed. It disturbed settled habits while people fought for scraps. Factions grew naturally, and in particular around Edward, and Aelfthryth's son Ethelred, a child of ten. While on an informal visit to his stepmother and Ethelred at Corfe, Ethelred's retainers treacherously murdered the King, and buried the body without honour at Wareham (for his body and popular canonisation see ETHELRED THE UNREADY). The earliest known accusation against Aelfthryth dates from a century later, but it is not easy to see who, save himself and her friends, might benefit from the elevation of a child too young to rule, or in a superstitious age, from the disrespect shown to the corpse.

AETHILWULF (?-858) King (828 and 839). See ENGLISH MONARCHY, EARLY-1

AFFIDAVITS. See OATHS.

AFFLUENT SOCIETY. A phrase, from J.K.Galbraith's book of the same name, denoting the western material prosperity evidenced by widespread ownership of expensive machines.

AFFRAY. See RIOT.

AFGHANISTAN. (1) Babur, the Mogul, made Kabul his capital in 1504, but when he conquered India after 1525, Afghanistan became only a province, until overrun (not for the first time) by Nadir Shah of Persia in 1741. At Nadir's assassination in 1747, Ahmad Shah, his guard-commander, made himself King of the Afghans, and ruled from Kandahar with the support of the Durrani tribe. The two greatest clans of this tribe were the Sadozai and the Mohammedzai, and much of the later internal history revolves round their leaders. Ahmad was a Sadozai.

(2) Persia and India were in disorder, and Ahmad could increase his power at the expense of both. He established the present northern and western frontiers of Afghanistan; in 1756 he took Delhi, and in Jan. 1761 resoundingly defended his conquest against the Marathas at the B. of Panipat nearby. By now his dominions also included Kashmir, and his overlordship was recognised in Baluchistan, Sind and Khorassan.

(3) The Maratha war weakened both sides in the face of two other rising powers, namely the Sikhs and the British. In 1762 Abmad restored a Mogul at Delhi, and in 1767 ceded the central Punjab to the Sikhs. His successor (1773) Timur Shah lost the suzerainty of the outlying areas; when he died in 1793 civil wars between his many sons plunged the country into a generation of anarchy, and the advancing Sikhs destroyed the internal prestige of the Sadozais. Eventually in 1826 DOST MOHAMMED, a Mohammedzai, captured Kabul and began to build up an orderly, if restricted, dominion around it.

(4) Meanwhile the British had become alarmed at Napoleonic and Russian threats to India. Three of Timur's sons had intermittently occupied the throne, and with one of these, Shah Shuja, the British had made a defensive treaty in 1809. He lost his throne immediately, but long survived as a nuisance to Dost Mohammed. It was while the latter was distracted by one of his forays in 1834, that the Sikhs seized Peshawar.

(5) Russian expansion was now causing concern; and the Persians, at their instigation, were besieging Herat. In 1837 Lord Auckland sought Dost Mohammed's help against the Persians; but the Dost instead wanted British help in recovering Peshawar. This was refused, whereupon in 1839 he received a Russian envoy at Kabul. The British retorted with a Sikh alliance and a military expedition to replace the Dost by Shah Shuja.

(6) The FIRST AFGHAN WAR (1839-42) was a fiasco of Crimean dimensions. The British forces crossed the Sind desert, losing their transport camels, and reached Kandahar half starved. After storming Ghazni they occupied Kabul in Aug. 1839. The Dost fled to Bokhara; Shah Shuja was duly installed. Leaving garrisons at Kabul, Jellalabad and Kandahar, the main body withdrew. It was only then realised that the Dost was locally respected, whereas Shah Shuja carried no credit at all. The garrisons were isolated amongst a rebellious population. The political officers such as Macnaghten failed to read the signs. Gen. Elphinstone at Kabul was caught in an untenable position when, in Nov. 1841 the city rose. Shah Shuja's authority vanished. In Jan. 1842 the Afghans agreed to let the British go in peace. They accordingly set out, but were attacked in the snow-bound passes. Only one survivor, Dr Brydon, an army surgeon, reached Jellalabad. Lord Ellenborough, the new gov-gen., next organised a face saving expedition under Gen. Pollock which, after three victories, reached Kabul in Sept. Here Pollock was joined by Gen. Nott, the defender of Kandahar, and after blowing up the bazaar the combined army withdrew to India. Shah Shuja, left in the lurch, was murdered and Dost Mohammed returned.

(7) The war had convinced him that for the time being he could not recover Peshawar; but his experiences at Bokhara had made him suspicious of the Russians. For the next few years he used his considerable talents to reassert the rule of Kabul over the northern provinces, and establish a *modus vivendi* with the British. This ended in 1855 with a treaty advantageous to both sides: for during the Indian mutiny the Dost remained neutral, but with his Indian frontier safe he was free to deal with the Persians. In 1863, just before his death, Herat was recovered.

(8) The reign (1863-1879) of Sher Ali, his third son, was marked by growing tension between Britain and Russia, and subversion by the latter who supported Sher Ali's nephew Abdurrahman. This nephew fled to Russia

after a military defeat in 1869. In 1873 Sher Ali requested British assistance which Lord Northbrooke the Gov-Gen. was eager to give; but Northbrooke's hands were tied by the home government and nothing was done. Meanwhile the Russian southeastward movement was gathering speed. Their attack on Turkey in 1877 was accompanied by intense diplomatic activity in the East. Lord Lytton, the first viceroy, planned a British mission to Kabul to counteract a Russian one already there, but Sher Ali refused to receive it and in Nov. 1878 the British (who were deriving much comfort from the Congress of Berlin) declared war.

(9) In the SECOND AFGHAN WAR (1878-80) Three armies now invaded Afghanistan and Sher Ali fled. The new king, Yakub Khan, signed the T. of Gandamak in May 1879, but the British resident, Sir Louis Cavagnari, was murdered in Sept. Kabul was reoccupied and Yakub Khan was deported. ABDURRAHMAN now reappeared with Russian funds and support, and was recognised as King by the British. The war, consequently, turned into a civil war: for Yakub's brother Ayub Khan raised the Sadozais against the British and Abdurrahman. In July 1880 he advanced from Herat, defeated a small British force at Maiwand, and invested Kandahar. This brought down Gen. Roberts, whose march of 313 miles from Kabul to Kandahar in 22 days is a justly celebrated feat of arms. In Sept. Ayub was routed.

(10) There are remarkable similarities between the reigns (1880-1901) of Abdurrahman and Dost Mohammed. British recognition, accompanied by a subsidy, involved the surrender of control over foreign policy. This freed the King to reorganise his chaotic inheritance; a small but properly paid army broke the power of the tribes, and subdued insubordinate provincial chiefs. The civil administration was reformed; communications were improved and irrigation introduced. In 1893 the frontier with India known as the Durand line was fixed by agreement with Sir Mortimer Durand.

(11) Abdurrahman's son Habibulla (r. 1901-19) took further steps to modernise the country; he introduced the first newspaper, built roads and schools and began a tentative industrialisation. He kept Afghanistan out of World War I, but claimed his total independence at the end of it. Before this claim could be made good he was assassinated, and succeeded by his third son Amanullah (r. 1919-1929) who reasserted the claim. After inconclusive fighting, known as the THIRD AFGHAN WAR, Afghan independence was recognised at the T. of Rawalpindi (8 Aug. 1919). Amanullah now set about an overhasty modernisation inspired by the Atatürk reforms in Turkey. He alienated powerful religious elements in Afghan society. In 1929 civil war broke out; in the confusion a brigand called Habibullah seized Kabul. Amanullah went into exile, and his brother Mohammed Nadir (r. 1929-33) returned from France and was elected King. Habibullah and his men were hunted down. A Constitution with a bicameral legislature was proclaimed in 1930, and the King now continued his brother's policy but with parliamentary support. The irreconcilables, unable to organise an insurrection, murdered him in 1933.

(12) His son Zahir succeeded him at the age of 19. He continued the internal policy of his predecessors; and maintained neutrality in World War II. In 1947 Pakistan became independent and there was a series of disputes about the Pathan territories on either side of the Durand line. These were settled in 1963. Meantime the govt. borrowed heavily from the U.S.A. and Russia for development, and built a road network which unified the communications but made the country more easily penetrable by mechanised armies.

In 1973 the monarchy was overthrown by a left wing *coup,* which was followed by a series of further coups. In 1979, when a less murderous regime than some of the others had been replaced by something more moderate, Russian troops entered the country but could not hold the rural areas against local tribal or Islamic guerrillas of varying allegiances, mostly armed by the U.S.A. through Pakistan. Two million Afghans fled to Pakistan. In 1988-9 Russian troops were gradually withdrawn, and an arms supply on the American pattern substituted.

AFRICA, EAST. *See entries for the countries in the area.*

AFRICA, EQUATORIAL (EX-FRENCH) embraced in 1972 the Central African (Ubangi-Shari), Congolese, Gaboon and Chad Republics. The French explorer Lyon reached Chad in 1820; du Chaillu travelled in the Gaboon between 1858 and 1865; Savorgnan de Brazza established French influence on the Congo between 1874 and 1882, de Crampel on the Ubangi in 1891, and Gentil advanced from the Congo to L. Chad in 1900, to meet Lamy and overthrow the Kingdom of Rabab. In step with similar moves in French West Africa, the whole area was organised as a govt.gen. or administrative federation in 1910, to counter the German advance in Africa and incidentally to set limits to the expansion of British interests in Nigeria. The European rivalries culminated in the Tangier crisis of 1911, in which the British opposed the Germans. Until 1958 the capital was at Brazzaville, when the constituent provinces became independent republics of the French Community.

AFRICA, WEST (1) The Portuguese took Ceuta in 1415, colonised Madeira in 1420, reached C. Blanco and Arguin I. in 1443 and C. Verde in 1446. They built a fort at Arguin in 1448 and exchanged cloth, corn, horses and metalwork for civet, pepper, gum, gold, salt and slaves. By 1460 they had penetrated Sierra Leone, by 1475 Fernan do Po, São Tomé and Annobon. After the Portuguese-Castillian war of 1475 to 1479, Castile received the Canaries but the Portuguese trading monopoly was strengthened by forts and settlements in the C. Verde Is. and along the coast. The Gambia, as the most easily navigable access to the continent, was particularly lucrative, and the discovery of the Ashanti gold production led to the construction of the fortress-factory of São Jorge de Mina (El Mina) in 1482. This became the residence of a gov-gen with a garrison. Contacts were made with Benin in 1483, São Tomé became a captaincy in 1485 and Fernan do Po was settled in 1493. Disease and competition from oriental pepper depressed the Benin settlements after 1506, but São Tome, with its slaves and sugar, prospered because its situation in the south easterly wind belt ensured quick passages homeward.

(2) The discovery of the route to India in 1497 confined the lucrative West African trade to gold, slaves and (to a lesser extent) spices. In the 16th cent. the monopoly was infringed by English, French, Dutch, Danish, Swedish and Brandenburgers. In 1580 Portugal fell to Spain and the Portuguese establishments were attacked by the Dutch, since 1572 in rebellion against Spain. By 1642 they had taken them all, and had created sugar plantations in Brazil which they supplied with slaves from W.Africa. Portugal recovered its independence in 1640 and by 1654 had driven the Dutch from Brazil and recovered São Tomé.

(3) Meantime the English and the French had also established American slave-worked plantations. The Royal African Co. was chartered in 1618; English forts were established at Cormantine on the Gold Coast in 1631, and on The Gambia in 1664. The French founded St. Louis at the mouth of the Senegal in 1659 and took Arguin and Goree from the Dutch in 1677. By the time of the T. of Utrecht (1713) the French and English were supreme in the area. The treaty gave the British the right, restricted to 4800 a year, to import slaves into Spanish America but the slave trade grew continually through the **Gold Coast,** the main suppliers being the Ashanti confederacy, which conquered the Denkera in about

1710, Akim in 1732 and the Fanti at the turn of the cent. In 1750 the Royal African Co. was dissolved in favour of an Association which any Africa merchant could join, the British govt. contributing to the maintenance of the forts.

(4) In 1764 a British attempt to set up a Senegambian colony failed, and for some time colonisation was considered to be unprofitable and avoided. By 1785 the trade in slaves had grown to vast dimensions. 74,000 were taken, 38,000 by the British, 20,000 in French ships. The public conscience was stirring. The Danes forbade the slave trade in 1804, the British in 1807, the U.S.A. in 1808, the Swedes in 1813 and the Dutch in 1814. The British maintained an anti-slavery patrol for over half a century, and one consequence of British naval activity was the growth of SIERRA LEONE which, founded in 1787, was later developed as a colony for rescued slaves; another was the annexation of Lagos for its useful position in anti-slavery operations, and the beginning of British development in NIGERIA. Sierra Leone attracted American interest and the American Colonisation Society acquired Monrovia and began settling freed men who spread outwards along the coast. In 1847 Monrovia declared itself a sovereign state called LIBERIA which was recognised by the British in 1848, but not by the U.S.A. until 1862.

(5) An important reason for British official interest in suppressing the slave trade was that the endemic warfare associated with it made exploration and commercial development impossible. The course of the Niger was unknown until Mungo Park mapped part of it in 1795. A Frenchman, Mollien, found the sources of The Gambia, Senegal and Rio Grande in 1818, and Major Laing reached, and was killed at Timbuktu in 1825. Denham, Clapperton, Oudney and the Landers, starting from Tripoli, crossed the Sahara in 1822 and in the next eight years provided reliable accounts of the area from L. Chad to the Oil Rivers. Between 1849 and 1854 Richardson, Barth and Overweg performed a similar service for the Western Sudan. (For British territories in the area *see* their proper names. For French activities *see* next entry.)

AFRICA, WEST (EX-FRENCH) embraced in 1972 Mauritania; Senegal with Soudan, Guinée (French Guinea), the Ivory Coast, the Upper Volta, Niger and Dahomey; and Togoland. The French explorer Mollien reached the source of the Senegal in 1818, and between 1854 and 1865 the Senegal colony was established by the vigorous Gen. Faidherbe. The others grew from coastal trading factories inland until the discovery of the Senegal-Niger route in 1888 made it possible to administer the whole under a single policy. This unification, involving the military overthrow of many local rulers, was carried through between 1887 and 1892. Timbuktu was occupied in 1894. Dahomey was annexed in 1899. It provoked a rival movement from British colonists on The Gambia and in Sierra Leone, but especially from the Gold Coast whose area was extended 400 miles northwards across the Volta in 1898, and from Nigeria which took in the lower 500 miles of the R. Niger, and the basin of the R. Benue, and had reached L. Chad by 1906. One effect of the *entente cordiale* was to limit British enterprise beyond these points, for by 1900 Lamy's advance to the Chad had connected the French Western and Equatorial Africas, and in 1910, in response to German imperialism, the western area was organised into a govt-gen or administrative federation. Ex-German Togoland was annexed to it as a mandated territory in 1919. The capital was at Dakar whose resistance to the Royal Navy was an embarrassing episode in World War II, if only because it blocked the route to Chad, which supported Gen. de Gaulle.

Between 1946 and 1958 the area was a federation of territories with local autonomy. In 1958 the federation was abolished. French Guinea became an independent state. Senegal and the Soudan were federated as Mali and it, together with the remaining territories became members of the French Community but this proved a transitional stage in which all the countries took a practical independence but only Senegal and the Ivory Coast maintained a close relationship with France. Upper Volta changed its name to Burkina Faso (1984). Saharan desiccation had a profound effect upon the inland economies and generally these countries became increasingly dependent upon the International Monetary Fund when French finance dried up.

AFRICAN ASSOCIATION. *See* R. GEOGRAPHICAL SOCIETY.

AFRIDIS of the Indian (now Pakistan) N.W. Frontier, were first encountered by Gen. Pollock's expedition of 1842 in the First Afghan War. There were campaigns against them in 1878 and 1879, but they remained a disturbing element in the frontier population till the end of the British *raj*.

AGADIR CRISIS or PANTHER SPRING (July-Aug. 1911) was a late episode in the scramble for Africa. In Apr. 1911 civil war threatened Morocco, and the French, with the proclaimed purpose of protecting European interests, sent troops to Fez under the Algéçiras (1906) and Franco-German Moroccan agreements (1909). The Germans affected to think that the French meant to absorb Morocco and sent the gunboat *Panther* followed by the much more powerful *Berlin* to the Moroccan Atlantic port of Agadir. Their implicit threat was to support the Sultan against the pro-European and Franco-Spanish supported Glaui. The Admiralty was alarmed at the prospect of a German base in Atlantic Morocco, and Sir Edw. Grey, the Foreign Sec. told the Germans that arrangements made without Britain would not be recognised. They made no reply but demanded huge compensations from the French. This had been their purpose in the first place. To raise the pressure, they started negotiations with local tribes. Accordingly, with the agreement of Asquith, the Prime Minister, and Grey, Lloyd George in a speech at the Mansion House (21 July) threatened war. This brought the Germans to their senses. They retreated, and the disputes were settled by treaties in Oct. 1911 in which the French ceded parts of the Congo to Germany.

AGA KHAN I (1800-81), originally gov. of the Persian province of Kerman, with the title Aga Khan granted in 1818 by the Shah, was also Imam of the Shiite Ismailis. He revolted against Mohammed Shah in 1838 and fled to India, where he helped the British with the Ismailis in the First Afghan War (1839-42) and in the conquest of Sind (1842-1843). He eventually settled in Bombay with a pension. His grandson **AGA KHAN III (1877-1957)** succeeded to the Imamate in 1885, and rapidly became one of India's leading Muslim statesmen. His representations to the Viceroy in 1906 led to the creation in 1909 of the separate Muslim electorates under the Morley-Minto reforms, and he was president of the All India Muslim League in its early years. He was thus one of the true founders of Pakistan. At the outbreak of World War I he rallied the Ismailis to the British in answer to Turkish claims to Muslim leadership, but he always advocated leniency to the Turks at the peace conferences. At the Indian Round Table constitutional conferences of 1930 to 1932 he was chairman of the Indian as well as the Muslim delegation and as such a principal author of the Government of India Act, 1935. He represented India at the League of Nations in 1937, and also became a well known owner and breeder of race horses. His vast fortune, including properties in many European countries passed to **KARIM AGA KHAN IV (1936-).**

AGAPEMONE **(Gr = abode of love)** The adherents of Henry James Prince, and their Abode at Spaxton (Somerset), founded in 1849. They shared everything; their sexual communism soon created local trouble and they dispersed, but revived for a few years in 1890.

AGENAIS, AGEN. *See* AQUITAINE-9 *et seq.*

AGE OF CONSENT AND MAJORITY (1) The minimum age

for marriage and sexual consent, adopted from Roman Law by the Canon Law, was 14 for boys and 12 for girls. From 1885 sexual consent outside marriage was required at 16. From 1929 a marriage under 16 was void save in N. Ireland.

(2) Majority originally was the age at which a person could exercise the calling to which he was born: thus a merchant came of age when he could count money and measure cloth; the ploughboy when he could plough a straight furrow (both about 15); and by 1215 the gentleman when he could fight in plate armour (about 21). Hence tenants by knight service came of age at 21, socagers at 15. In 1660 military tenures were turned into socage, but all fathers were empowered to appoint guardians of their children up to the age of 21, and later, the courts by analogy treated 21 as the age of majority when necessary. This hard and fast rule, strengthened by occasional legislation obtained until 1968 when the age of majority but not of qualification for office was reduced to 18.

AGILBERT (?-690) Frankish scholar trained in Ireland, was Bp. of Dorchester-on-Thames between 650 and 660, when the new See of Winchester was divided from it. He left in dudgeon, but later ordained St. Wilfrid and appeared with him as the senior Romanist prelate at the Synod of Whitby (664). He made Wilfrid his spokesman because of his own linguistic imperfections. He then went home, consecrated Wilfrid at Compiègne and, as Bp. of Paris, entertained Theodore and Adrian instructively on their way to Canterbury.

AGINCOURT, CAMPAIGN and B. of (25 Oct. 1415). Henry V landed near Harfleur on 14th Aug. and invested it. His small professional force suffered from dysentery, but the large French armies at Rouen, Harfleur and Caudebec sent no help to the town, which surrendered on 22 Sept. Henry paroled its leaders to meet him at Calais by 11 Nov. On 8 Oct. he set out with 5000 archers and 900 men-at-arms. Two large French armies shadowed him and prevented his crossing the Somme near its mouth on 13th. He now marched six days up river, found an obstructed but unguarded ford at Béthancourt and was across the river on 20th. He marched for Calais, the French moving parallel to but slightly ahead of him. Neither army knew exactly where the other was until Henry crossed the Ternoise on 24th and saw the enemy ahead. The French, with between 40,000 and 50,000 men, were determined to crush him. The route to Calais lay through a gap about a mile wide between two woods. The English were at the southern end of it; the French occupied the rest. The two armies slept the night facing each other. In the morning the English ran to the defile and set up oblique blocks of men-at-arms with the archers disposed so as to shoot across their front. The French had a mounted vanguard of 5,000-10,000; a main battle behind it of about 30,000 and a rear-guard of about 10,000. English morale was high because of the supine French conduct at Harfleur. The French commanders were ill-disciplined. Their attacks were badly co-ordinated and out of control. In half an hour their first two divisions were immobilised by overcrowding and muddy ground, and defenceless against the storm of arrows and then against their athletic opponents. The French lost about 6,000 men including the Ds. of Alençon, Bar, and Brabant, the Constable d'Albret and the Count of Nevers. The D. of Orleans was captured. The English lost no more than 300. Henry V reached Calais shortly afterwards.

AGIO The difference in value between currency of the same denomination but of different metal or material.

AGISTER. *See* FOREST-5.

AGNEW, Sir James Wilson (1815-1901) assistant surgeon at Hobart from 1845, founded the Tasmanian Royal Society in 1876, became a minister in 1877 and prime minister of Tasmania from 1886 to 1887.

AGNOSTIC, a word coined by T. H. Huxley in 1869, meaning one who does not know if God exists.

AGRA (India) This architecturally famous city was the capital of Sikandar Lodi (1504-1517) and especially of Shah Jahan (1627-1666). The fort walls were built in about 1570, the Taj Mahal between 1630 and 1652, and the Pearl Mosque between 1646 and 1653.

AGREEMENTS OF THE PEOPLE (A) *Oct. 1647.* Leveller document demanding **(i)** parliamentary representation based on constituencies of equal population; **(ii)** the dissolution of the Long Parliament on 30 Sept. 1648; **(iii)** biennial parliaments; **(iv)** the recognition that sovereignty lies in the people whose elected representative may in their name do anything except regulate religion and worship, conscript troops, call in question acts done in reference to the late public differences, make discriminatory laws or laws evidently destructive to the safety and well being of the people.

(B) *15 Jan. 1649.* This was presented by the Council of the Army to the House of Commons. It proposed **(i)** the dissolution of the Long Parliament on 30 Apr. 1649; **(ii)** A Representative of 400 elected in constituencies of roughly equal population; **(iii)** biennial elections from which royalists were to be excluded for seven years; **(iv)** that the Representative should elect a Council of State for managing of public affairs; **(v)** that representers should not hold public offices; **(vi)** that the Representative may not conscript troops, call in question anything said or done in relation to the late wars or public differences or invalidate securities and grants, make discriminatory laws, give judgment where no law has been already provided save in cases of abuse of public trust, or take away common right, liberty, safety or property; **(vii)** Freedom of worship save for papists and prelatists. The influence of these two documents has been exaggerated. Very little has become law.

AGRÉMENT (Fr. = approval). The formal approval of the head of a diplomatic mission by the government to which he is to be accredited, before his appointment. In 1983 British agrément was refused to an Israeli ambassador.

AGRICOLA, Gnaeus JULIUS (A.D. 40-93). See BRITAIN, ROMAN-12.

AGRICOLA, Sextus CALPURNIUS. See BRITAIN. ROMAN-15.

AGRICULTURAL IMPLEMENTS. The **light plough** *(caruca)* incapable of turning the soil and drawn by oxen or harness-banded horses was used until 10th cent., when the heavier **wheeled plough** *(aratrum)* appeared and, drawn more effectively through a horse collar could turn a furrow. The **rotherham plough,** came in probably from Holland in about 1730: the **mole plough** for drainage in 1780. Jethro Tull introduced the horse-drawn **hoe** and **seed drill** at the turn of 18th-19th cent. The mechanical **reaper** was first used in 1831 but first exhibited at the Great Exhibition of 1851, when an animal powered **combine harvester** appeared. Steam ploughing was first attempted in 1830, but only generally adopted after 1865: stationary internal combustion engines were first used for this purpose in about 1890, but tractors were soon introduced and had become common by 1910. Pest spraying by aircraft became common by 1955 and aircraft sowing was begun in 1974.

AGRICULTURAL SOCIETIES to promote advances in agricultural techniques emerged in parallel with the early movements towards industrial revolution, beginning with the Scottish Society of Improvers (1723), the Dublin Society (1731) the Society of Arts (1754) and the notable Bath Agricultural Society (1777). These all organised agricultural shows, which in some cases continue.

AHMEDABAD (India), old capital of Gujarat, was taken by the Moguls in 1572. The Emperor Aurungzib was viceroy between 1645 and 1647, and its prosperity continued with his favour until he died in 1707. A century of decline was only arrested by British annexation in 1818, and the establishment of the cotton industry in 1859 brought about the rapid expansion which has since made it one of the biggest cities in India. There were destructive communal riots in 1919.

AIDAN, King. (fl. 603). See DALRIADA-3.

AIDAN, King of Scots (?-606) was defeated by the Northumbrians at the B. of Degsastan in 603.

AIDAN, St. (?-651), a monk of Iona became, at the request of the newly acceded K. Oswald of Northumbria, Bp. of Lindisfarne in 635, and spread the practices of the Celtic church far and wide in the north of England. He trained St. Chad, and was a great friend of Oswald and his successor Oswi.

AIDE-MÉMOIRE **(Fr. = memorandum).** A diplomatic document delivered to a foreign minister, summarising the points which an ambassador is to make orally.

AIDS, FEUDAL The feudal tenant was expected to come to the aid of his Lord in any special crisis or emergency. At first, such occasions were undefined. Chapter 12 of Magna Carta, however, laid down that no royal aid was to be levied unless by the common consent of the Kingdom save for ransoming the King's person, for making his eldest son a knight and for once marrying his daughter, and Chapter 15 forbade the King to grant the right to take an aid from his free men save for these three causes.

AIDS (= ACQUIRED IMMUNE DEFICIENCY SYNDROME) is the condition created by the H.I.V. (= Human immuno-deficiency virus) when it contaminates the blood through body fluids containing H.I.V. The transmission may occur through sexual or anal intercourse, blood transfusion, the use of contaminated intravenous needles or breastfeeding. It is not transmitted by casual contact or airborne means, and probably not *via* saliva or tears. The incubation period is 5-8 years. It was first conclusively identified in 1981, i.e. from persons infected between 1973 and 1976. It is believed to have originated in C. Africa.

AILRED of RIEVAULX, St. (1110-67), born in Tynedale, spent part of his youth at the court of David I of Scots, but in 1134 entered the Cistercian monastery at Rievaulx's colony at Revesby and in 1147 became abbot of Rievaulx itself. He wrote a genealogy of the English Kings, a *Life* of Edward the Confessor, a tract on the Battle of the Standard (1138) and the *De Institutione Inclusarum* (Lat = The Institute of Closed Houses), a guide to asceticism. His friend Walter Daniel wrote his *Life.*

AIEL **(Norman-Fr = grandfather).** A possessory Assize. See ASSIZES.

AIGUILLETTES. Ornamental cords round one shoulder, worn, in British practice, only by ADC's.

AILLT. See WELSH LAW-1-9.

AINSWORTH, William Harrison (1805-82) wrote 39 novels mostly historical, of which *The Tower of London* (1840) and *Old St. Paul's* (1841) are the best known.

AIRCRAFT CARRIER In Feb. 1913 the first air attack (by bombs) upon warships was made by a Greek pilot against a Turkish squadron in the Dardanelles. In the same year a seaplane carrier, the converted cruiser *Hermes,* joined the Royal Navy and in Aug. 1915 a Turkish transport in the Dardanelles was destroyed by a seaplane-carried torpedo. H.M.S. *Argus* with an unobstructed flight deck joined the Royal Navy in 1918: the first designed specially for the purpose were the Japanese *Hosho* (Dec. 1922) and the British (new) *Hermes* (May 1923). In 1939 Britain, the U.S.A. and Japan possessed the only substantial carrier forces. (*See* NAVY, ROYAL-8.)

In World War II the British conducted the earliest carrier operations in the Mediterranean convoys, in the victorious air attack on Taranto in Nov. 1940, the B. of Matapan in Mar. 1941 and the sinking of the *Bismarck* in May. The destructive Japanese attack on Pearl Harbor in Dec. 1941 was carrier-based, and the American victories of the Coral Sea and Midway (May and June 1942) were engagements between rival carrier forces. Many carriers of smaller tonnage were used as convoy escorts in the battle of the Atlantic (q.v.).

AIRCRAFT PRODUCTION, MINISTRY of. *See* SUPPLY, MINISTRY.

AIR FORCES Though some work had already been done on lighter than air craft, the first British air force was the air battalion of the Royal Engineers, created in 1911. In 1912 the Royal Flying Corps (R.F.C.) was established with a military and a naval wing. It was originally interested mostly in airships. The naval wing became known as the Royal Naval Air Service (R.N.A.S.), and by 1913 the R.F.C. and R.N.A.S. were practically distinct. Both were by then equipped with biplanes, and their main function, reconnaissance, led in World War I to combats with enemy planes on similar missions. Experiments with torpedoes and bombs created a more offensive attitude, and resulted in the formation of the Independent Air Force under Ld. Trenchard for long distance bombing in 1917. This in its turn led in 1918 to the amalgamation of R.F.C. and R.N.A.S. into the Royal Air Force (R.A.F.) under a single Air Council with Lord Rothermere as the first Sec. of State, and Trenchard as chief of staff. Special R.A.F. ranks and uniforms were substituted for the old naval and military ranks. The growth of these forces in World War I had been remarkable: in 1914 R.F.C. and R.N.A.S. together numbered 1,850 of all ranks. In 1918 the R.A.F. reached a total of 292,000.

By 1937, however, the Admiralty had reasserted itself and established an independent naval air force called the Fleet Air Arm. At this time the air forces were being reequipped with monoplanes, and by 1938 the R.A.F. organisation with which World War II was conducted was complete. In the U.K. it was divided into eight functional commands (Fighter, Bomber, Coastal, Army Co-operation, Balloon, Flying Training, Technical Training and Maintenance) to which a ninth (Transport) was later added. The overseas commands, on the other hand, were mixed administrative commands, and it was from these that the Tactical Air Forces, concerned with military battle co-operation, were developed.

In 1963 all the services were placed under a single Ministry of Defence. The number of commands in the U.K. was reduced to two (Strike and Support), plus a strong command in Germany and several minor ones elsewhere.

AIRD, Sir John (1833-1911) a contractor whose first public task was to remove the 1851 Exhibition buildings, erected by his father, to the Crystal Palace site at Sydenham. He built many railways and docks, but especially dams at Aswan and Assiut (Egypt) between 1989 and 1902. He was Tory M.P. for N. Paddington from 1887 to 1905 and first mayor of Paddington in 1900.

AIRE, R. *See* TRANSPORT AND COMMUNICATIONS.

AIRLIE. *See* OGILVY.

AIREY (1) Sir George (1761-1833) held a variety of offices in Minorca, Ireland, Sicily and the Ionian Isles and became a Lieut-Gen. in 1821. Of his two military sons **(2) Richard (1803-81) 1st Ld. AIREY (1876)** was military sec. to Lord Hardinge in 1852, and Q.M. in the Crimea 1854-5 where his mismanagement was a main factor in the disasters of that campaign. In 1855 he was made Quarter-master General and was in a position to pronounce (favourably) upon his own conduct in the Crimea. He was gov. of Gibraltar from 1865 to 1870.

AIR POLLUTION. Efforts to prevent the use of coal in London began as early as 1273, and James I issued a proclamation against it. By the 20th cent. temperature inversion over London combined with the smoke from thousands of open-grate coal fires was occasionally creating total blackout, unknown numbers of casualties from respiratory disease and an estimatedly huge deteriorative burden on the economy. Coal shortage improved matters during World War II but there was a press outcry against smog after a bad (but not as bad as pre-war) day in 1952. The Corporation of London promoted a local Clean Air Act against black smoke, and this proving successful, a general Act was passed in 1956. This did not deal with other kinds of pollution, notably oxides of nitrogen, volatile organic compounds, carbon monoxide or lead in petrol. By the 1970's these were giving serious concern on a world scale because of their climatic and respiratory effects. Lead free petrol was successfully encouraged in the 1980's by preferential taxation, but the volume of the other pollutants, emitted in large part by motor vehicles, continued to rise and was still rising in 1994.

AIRSHIP. *See* AVIATION.

AISLABIE. *See* GEORGE 1-9.

AITKEN. *See* BEAVERBROOK.

AIX-LA-CHAPELLE TREATIES (This town is now usually called AACHEN) (1) The **T. of 1668** ended the War of Devolution. The French received the right to garrison 11 towns in the Spanish Netherlands. **(2)** The **T. of 1748** ended the War of the Austrian Succession and related colonial wars. Cape Breton was returned by Britain to France in exchange for Madras. The Dutch received back the barrier towns. Austria gave up Parma and Piacenza to a Spanish prince, and Silesia to Prussia. Modena and Genoa were restored to their independence by the French. Britain received the Asiento *(see* SLAVE TRADE), and all the powers guaranteed the Protestant succession in Britain, and the Pragmatic Sanction in favour of the House of Hapsburg-Lorraine. **(3)** The **T. of 1818** between Russia, Austria, Prussia and France ended the military occupation of France and created the Holy Alliance.

AJMER MERWARA. *See* RAJPUTS.

AKBAR HYDARI, Sir (1869-1941) after a distinguished career as an Indian govt. financial administrator, became a reforming Dewan of Hyderabad in 1937.

AKEMAN STREET was a Roman road from Verulamium (St. Albans) to Corinium (Cirencester).

AKERS-DOUGLAS, Aretas (1851-1926) 1st Vist. CHILSTON (1911), became Tory M.P. for E. Kent in 1880, and a whip in 1883. He was chief whip and patronage sec. in the Salisbury govts of 1885 to 1892 and became the lynchpin of the composite alliance which formed it. From 1892 to 1895 he was in opposition as chief whip, but when Salisbury returned in 1895 he was made First Commissioner of Works and was largely responsible for the difficult postponed coronation of Edward VII, and the unfortunate memorial to Q. Victoria in the Mall. In 1902 he became Home Sec., a post which he filled quietly but efficiently until he retired in 1905 on the resignation of the Balfour Govt.

AKKERMAN (Turk), CETATEA ALBA (Roum.) or BELGOROD DNIESTROVSKI (Russ) The Akkerman Convention of 1826 was an annex to the Russo-Turkish P. of Bucharest (1812). It provided for the autonomy of Serbia and gave the Russians the right to intervene in Moldavia and Wallachia. Its repudiation by the Turks led to the Russo-Turkish War of 1828, the T. of Adrianople of 1829, and the beginning of Roumanian independence.

ALABAMA (U.S.A.) formed part of the Carolinas chartered in 1663, but the French built Fort Louis on the Mobile in 1702 and stayed until the whole area was definitively ceded to Britain under the P. of Paris of 1763. It was not ceded to the U.S.A. under the P. of Paris of 1783. In the next thirty years Alabama was an ungoverned no man's land, but it became part of the U.S.A. after the T. of Ghent ended the Anglo-U.S. War of 1812. The area was organised as a cotton growing slave territory in 1817, was admitted to the Union as a State in 1819, and joined the Confederacy in the American Civil War of 1861 to 1865.

ALABAMA, THE was a Confederate steam sloop built at Birkenhead (Lancs) during the American civil war. Because of Lancashire's dependence on cotton, local sympathy was with the southern states. When diplomatic moves were made to detain her, she was forewarned and escaped unharmed. She was completed at sea, and armed in the Azores. At large from 24 Aug. 1862 until 19 June 1864, she took 65 Federal vessels, sank a gunboat and immensely increased the cost of Federal freight and insurance. She was sunk off Cherbourg by the U.S.S. *Kearsarge*. Her career sparked off an anti-British outcry in the U.S.A. and diplomatic relations were strained for several years. The Russell govt. refused to pay compensation for the damage or to submit to arbitration. The liberal Gladstone in his first administration agreed to arbitration at Geneva, where an award was made against Britain (Dec. 1871) for £3,229,000 and accepted by Gladstone in Sept 1872.

ALANBROOKE. *See* BROOKE.

ALASKA (U.S.A.) or (until 1867) RUSSIAN AMERICA From 1725 Vitus Bering explored the waters off the N.E. Asian coast for the Russians, and his discovery of the Aleutian Is (1741) eventually attracted trappers. The first Alaskan settlement was at Kodiak (1784) and the first capital was established at Sitka (1806) by a Russo-American Co. under Russian protection, but the Russian trading monopolies were ended in the same year under an Anglo-Russian treaty which fixed the boundaries. The area so defined was bought from Russia by the U.S.A. in 1867. It was admitted to the Union as a 49th state in 1959, and besides fur, soon developed a large natural oil and gas industry and a substantial increase of population. In 1988 a major tanker disaster did grave damage to the marine ecology.

ALBA. *See* ALVA.

ALBAN, St. a pagan of Verulamium (later St Alban's) is reputedly the first British martyr. He was executed either under Septimius Severus (c. A.D. 211) or during Diocletian's persecutions (c. 305) for sheltering a Christian priest. A church was soon built on the site of his execution, and Bede thought that worship there had been continuous until his own day. It has been continuous there ever since, the church being represented by the present Abbey.

ALBAN, ALBANY, ALBION, ALBU 'Albion', the oldest known name for the island of Britain, appears in the *Massiliote Penplus* (7th cent. B.C.). It was called 'Albu' as late as the 10th cent. AD. by the Irish. In the 4th cent. B.C. there was a Celtic immigration from Europe, and Pytheas called the inhabitants 'Pretani' ('Britons'). 'Albion' then apparently meant the country still held by the non-British. The Romans called Roman Britain 'Britannia', and the part north of the Antonine frontier 'Alba'. When Kenneth MacAlpin, K. of Scots, gained the Pictish throne in 843 the combined kingdom, north of the same frontier, was naturally called 'Alba'. Lothian was probably added in about 971, by cession from K. Edgar of England and the British Kingdom of Strathclyde in 1034 by a dynastic arrangement. Alba was then part of the Scots Kingdom, and in 1398 Robert, Earl of Fife, brother of King Robert III, was created Duke of it under the name of 'Albany'.

ALBANIA (Tosk SHQIPERIA) From this largely Moslem part of the Ottoman Empire many high Turkish dignatories originated including the 17th cent. Kiuprili (Köprölü) Grand Viziers, and Mehemet Ali, the founder of modern Egypt. Albanian soldiers in Ottoman and Venetian service were often used to hold down the Greeks; hence an hereditary feud.

When rebellion, fomented by the Serbs and Montenegrins broke out in the Turkish Balkans in 1876, Gorchakov the Russian foreign minister, expecting an Ottoman debacle, proposed Albanian independence, but was frustrated by Turkish victories. The subsequent consolidation of the new Italy made the province – so close to the heel of Italy – an object of Italian ambition; in the 1887 renewal of the Triple Alliance, Austria was prepared to concede a measure of Italian influence if the *status quo* in the Balkans was upset. Italy hoped for

more, and also had ambitions against the Tyrol. This had no immediate result but meanwhile the Serbs also laid claims. The victory of Balkan nationalisms at the end of the Balkan Wars of 1912 led Austria to insist on Albanian independence to frustrate the Serbs and maintain her own prestige. As many Albanians lived in the historic Kosovo district of Serbia, there were frontier troubles leading to an inevitable Serb invasion in 1913. The Austrians quickly stopped it, but it left a legacy of hatred between Serbs and Albanians, who then offered the new throne to Prince William of Wied. He arrived in Mar. 1914, but left when World War I broke out.

In 1915, to bring Italy into the war, the allies offered her the protectorate. In 1917 the Austrians made a similar offer to buy her out, but between June and Sept., she occupied the country, which was in chaos. The Italians were not popular; in 1919 a rebellion broke out. In 1920 the notables set up an independent government at Tirana. This transformed itself, in 1925, into a paper republic with effective power in the hands of a number of rival clan chieftains. One of these, AHMED ZOGU, overthrew the constitution in 1928 and proclaimed himself King.

Weak and isolated, Albania was soon under Italian pressure again, and in Apr. 1939 they attacked. The King fled, and his crown was accepted by King Victor Emmanuel III of Italy as a separate inheritance. Accordingly when the Germans overran the Balkans in 1941, they permitted the Albanian Kingdom to annex Kosovo, with the later consequence that Tito's Yugoslav rising was directed as much against the Albanians as their German and Italian protectors.

The Axis collapse, the Russian advance into the Northern Balkans, and the victory of Tito's communists isolated the Albanians again. A tribal govt. of revolutionary appearance was set up to salvage something from the wreck; it received some Russian economic help, but the Russians pressed for support against Yugoslavia in their quarrel with Tito's regime. The risks did not appeal to the leadership which, after 1961 adopted, through increasing contacts with Maoist China, a distrustful policy towards Russia, and, indeed everyone else. By the '80's the govt. was pretending that the country was under military threat from the West. Anti-communist agitations began in 1989 and developed into sporadic riots and mass migrations to Italy in the next two years. *See also* CORFU INCIDENTS-2; KOSOVO.

ALBANY. *See* JAMES III *and* V OF SCOTS.

ALBANY. *See* FIFE, ROBERT OF.

ALBANY PLAN OF UNION OF 1754 War with France being imminent, the Board of Trade proposed to the American colonies that they should federate for greater security. A congress of delegates from the Assemblies of the seven northernmost met at Albany (N.Y.) to consider a plan of union prepared by Benjamin Franklin, and to negotiate a better understanding with the Iroquois. The plan envisaged ratification by the British Crown in Parliament. The congress approved the plan, but the colonial assemblies would not ratify it. The meeting, however, set a precedent for later congresses, and the plan itself for the later Articles of Confederation, and the United States Constitution.

ALBEMARLE, Ds. of. *See* MONCK.

ALBEMARLE, Es. of. *See* KEPPEL.

ALBERONI, Giulio (1664-1752) negotiated in 1714 the marriage of Elizabeth Farnese to Philip V of Spain on behalf of his employer the Duke of Parma, and through her influence immediately became prime minister of Spain. His influence was originally gastronomic. He improved Spanish trade and armed forces, and revived the Spanish claims to Naples abandoned to Habsburg influence, and to Sicily, allotted to Savoy under the T. of Utrecht, and he also championed the rights of Don Carlos, son of Elizabeth, to the reversions of Tuscany and

Parma. This posed a threat of Spanish Bourbon domination in Italy, objectionable alike to the Habsburgs, their British ally, the Dutch, and also to the French Regent Orleans whose claims as heir presumptive to the ailing child K. Louis XV might be set aside in favour of overpowerful Spanish Bourbons. This would have overthrown the policies for which the War of the Spanish Succession was fought.

The Stanhope govt. in 1718 negotiated a compromise: Austria was to have Sicily and give up Sardinia to Savoy, and Don Carlos was to have his reversions. This was embodied in a treaty of Quadruple Alliance (Britain, Austria, France and Holland) which was to enforce it upon Spain if necessary by arms. Alberoni, however, had already despatched a large fleet to attack Sicily, but Stanhope having sent Adm. Byng to the Mediterranean by way of precaution, the Spanish force was destroyed off Cape Passaro (11 Aug. 1718) before war was declared. A French army with English naval help then invaded Catalonia, and in April 1719 a Spanish equipped Jacobite force landed in Scotland but was defeated at Glenshiel. Philip and Elizabeth then dismissed Alberoni (who retired) and acceded to the purposes of the Quadruple Alliance.

ALBERT, Francis Charles Augustus Emmanuel of Saxe-Coburg-Gotha PRINCE-CONSORT (1819-61) This prince's parents were divorced in 1826 and the influences in his upbringing were his grandmother's and his uncle Leopold, who in 1832 became King of the Belgians. They encouraged his learned and inquiring disposition. Moreover Leopold had taken over functions of quasi-parenthood towards the Princess Victoria after the death of her father the D. of Kent. He, Stockmar his adviser, and the other Coburgs planned to marry Victoria and Albert. She became Queen in 1837. The engagement was announced in 1839 and was very popular. The marriage took place in 1840. Peelite opposition had, however, created parliamentary wrangles about his annuity. This he overcame by tact and intelligence. Three months later, when the Queen was known to be pregnant, he was designated regent by Act almost without dissent. In 1841 he greatly helped the transition from Melbourne (whom the Queen liked) to the priggish Peel, yet it was Peel who encouraged him to take the cultural leadership, in the first instance through his connection with the rebuilding of the Houses of Parliament. In 1842 he reorganised the royal household, and persuaded the D. of Wellington to abolish duelling in the army.

By 1845 he was probably the best politically informed person in the kingdom; he became, in effect, the Queen's private secretary and the chief channel of political and diplomatic approaches to the Throne; his even judgment ensured that his more impulsive wife would not embroil the Crown in partisan situations at home or abroad. There is little evidence that he sought power, rather than influence, but he also had a constructive streak. He thought that the disorders of the 1840's were due partly to poverty, and that the general wellbeing could be improved by industrial development. He was therefore entirely consistent in encouraging the Society for Improving the Condition of the Working Classes and in launching the greatest and most influential of his projects, the Exhibition of 1851. This famous seminal event opened the eyes of the world to technical advances, particularly the industrial leadership of Britain and it also greatly strengthened her diplomatic position.

The incessant routine work of his life from then onwards was effectual but retiring in character. His last service to the country was, however, typical. In 1861, during the American Civil War, he persuaded Lord John Russell, then Foreign Sec. not to react aggressively to the Federal arrest of two Confederate envoys on board the British steamer *Trent*. This prevented a major diplomatic crisis. He died of typhoid.

ALBERT THE GREAT, St. (1206-80) teacher and defender of St. Thomas Aquinas, was prominent at the Council of Lyons (1274) and in Paris. Of very wide interests, he is entitled the Universal Doctor.

ALBERTA (Canada) originally signified a territory constituted in 1882 in the south of the province of Alberta and less than half its size. The present province was constituted in 1905.

ALBIGENSIANS (CATHARISTS or BOGOMILS) (1) were a religious sect (named after the city of Albi) which appeared in Languedoc and Catalonia (as well as Bulgaria) in the 11th cent. They held the Manichaean view that creation was divided into good and bad: the good being spirit, the bad matter. Man had a spirit imprisoned in a material body; procreation therefore led to evil results and suicide was desirable. The sect was divided into 'perfects' who lived austere and vegetarian lives, and who eventually starved themselves to death, and 'believers' who lived more normally but accepted the consolamentum' or entry into perfection when approaching death. Procreation was avoided, if not by continence, then by sodomy. They rejected most of the Bible as pure allegory, and they were fanatically opposed to the church which they held to be an instrument of evil because, *inter alia*, it took the allegories literally.

(2) The sect spread rapidly, especially because of the contrast between the austerity and spirituality of the perfects, and the laxity and materialism of the clergy. Its doctrines were condemned by church Councils at Rheims (1148) and Verona (1184), but continued to spread. Peaceful efforts to convert them mounted; from 1203 St. Dominic worked there for many years and in 1206 a papal legate, Peter of Castelnau was sent to Toulouse. In 1208 Peter was murdered by a believer.

(3) Subversive of the church, the doctrines were obviously equally subversive of lay society. The two suddenly found themselves in alliance; the representative of lay society in this case was the ambitious French K. Philip Augustus (r. 1180-1223) whose policy was to destroy the great feudatories. One of the greatest was the Count of Toulouse in whose domiions the sect was prevalent. Their conquest, too, would outflank the Aquitainian possessions of the English kings. The Albigensian Crusade of 1208, under Simon de Montfort IV was as much a French political operation as a papal crusade. The motives of its opponents were equally mixed. The Count's ally, K. Peter of Aragon, was a believer; as a King he preferred a Toulousaine buffer state on his northern frontier to the uncomfortable proximity of the French monarchy. The seven year war (in which the troubadour civilisation went up in flames) began in 1208. The crusaders sacked Béziers in 1209, and Peter was decisively defeated at Muret in 1213. The Dominican order was established in 1215; when Montfort died in 1219 the formal military operations were over; but guerrilla war continued until the T. of Meaux (1229) which brought the Languedoc under the French crown. After 1233 the extirpation of the sect was the first major operation of the Inquisition.

ALBINI or AUBENEY, PINCERNA (= Butler) Four men called **William. (I) (fl. 1100)** of **BUCKENHAM** married Maud, *d.* of Roger Bigod. Their son **(II) (?-1176) E. of ARUNDEL (?-1139)** by marriage with Adeliza widow of Henry I, was a faithful adherent of K. Stephen, but favoured the settlement contained in the T. of Wallingford (1153) for which he stood guarantor. Henry II trusted him, and used him in diplomatic missions: to Louis VII and the Pope in connection with the quarrel with Becket (1164), and to Henry of Saxony on the marriage of Henry II's daughter to him (1168). In the revolt of 1173 he joined the King in the French campaign in Aug. and the defeat of Leicester at Bury St. Edmunds (17 Oct. 1173). His grandson **(III) (?-1221)** was a member of K. John's court, but went over to Louis of

France when John abandoned Winchester in June 1216. After the B. of Lincoln (July 1217) he abandoned the French connection and served briefly as a justice in Eyre. He died on crusade. His grandson **(IV) (?-1236)** served as a justice in Eyre in 1199 and under John, but supported the anti-royal party on the Charter. He became one of its 25 guarantors but withdrew to Belvoir. In Nov. 1215 he was captured by John at Rochester, but in 1216 redeemed his lands for a large fine. He joined the royalists for Henry III, had a command at the B. of Lincoln, and later served again as a justice in Eyre.

ALBINI (BRITO) William of (?-1156) of Belvoir, fought at Tinchebray (1106) and was in favour with Henry I who employed him as a justice in Eyre. He supported Matilda in the civil wars and consequently lost and then regained his lands.

ALBINUS, Decimus CLODIUS. See BRITAIN, ROMAN-16.

ALBURGA, St. (?-810) half sister of K. Egbert, converted his foundation of canons at Wilton into the well known nunnery.

ALBUQUERQUE, Afonso de (1453-1515) see PORTUGUESE INDIES.

ALCHEMY The importation of alchemical ideas from the Arabs into the West began with Robert of Chester's translation (1144) of *The Story of Khalid and Morienos*. Arabs were interested in medical uses of transmuted materials, and so were Europeans, such as Albert the Great, who had read Avicenna. He was sceptical of the transmutations which he had seen. Others hoped to gain fortunes by transmuting base metals into gold; and yet others cheated. Thus some alchemists pursued genuinely scientific courses (e.g. in developing distillation) while the reputation of alchemists generally sank. There was a papal bull (1307), and an Act of Parliament (1404) against multiplying gold. Meanwhile such thinkers as Roger Bacon and Arnold of Villanova, in pressing the medicinal uses, stumbled towards the idea of the Elixir of Life. This, of course, proved as tempting as the transmutation of metals, with similar results. Charlatans abounded by the Renaissance but some serious alchemists, such as Paracelsus (1493-1541), pursued respectable and fruitful studies. This had the interesting result of displacing the overwhelming authority of Galen in curative medicine. In 1618 the Royal College of Physicians began to accept into their *Pharmacopoeia* useful remedies propounded both by alchemists and Galenists. Sir Isaac Newton, who was an alchemist, almost accidentally destroyed the basis of alchemy in his *Principia*. What was left did not survive Lavoisier's and Priestley's destruction of the phlogiston theory between 1770 and 1790.

ALCUIN or EALWHINE (c. 735-804) studied at the cathedral school at York under Bede's pupil Abp.Egbert, and Egbert's kinsman Aethelberht, a great teacher who created one of the best libraries in W. Europe. In 767, when Aethelberht became Abp, Alcuin took charge of the school, but in 782, during a journey to Rome, met Charlemagne at Parma and was persuaded to become head of his palace school, where he was joined by many of his English pupils. He returned to England for the legatine council of 786 and was in Northumbria from 790 to 793. Charlemagne gave him the abbeys of Terrières and St. Lupus at Troyes, and in 796 the powerful abbey of St. Martin at Tours, which he turned into a centre of learning. One of the foremost intellectuals, liturgists and theologians of his day, he left about 300 letters which are a major source for the English history of the time. He also wrote annals and philosophical works; used dialogue as a teaching method and established the study of Boethius, Augustine and the grammarians. He retired from secular employment in 801. The Carolingian cultural revival, particularly the Carolingian Schools, may be ascribed to him.

ALDEBURGH FESTIVAL, actually held at Snape, was founded in 1948 by Benjamin Britten and Peter Pears.

ALDERMAN or (A.S.) EALDORMAN The Anglo-Saxon ealdorman was one of a small number of men of, under the King, the highest rank, often controlling shires or even larger areas on the King's behalf. They were slowly superseded by Earls (the title is Scandinavian) while the word survived in an urban context to denote the holder of a senior civic office. The two main usages then became **(1)** the chief officer of a guild; **(2)** a senior member of a town council. In London the division of the City into wards under aldermen originated before 1066. Each ward had, and has a wardmote of all the electors, presided over by the alderman, who holds office for life. Elsewhere aldermen became increasingly common in the middle ages, probably under the influence of London. Under the Municipal Corporations Act 1834, the triennially elected councillors of a borough themselves appointed aldermen for six years, who numbered a third of the number of the councillors. Such aldermen were abolished in 1974. In the City of London the aldermen still held office for life in 1996.

ALDERNEY (Fr: AURIGNY) (Channel Is.) like the other islands a part of Normandy which remained in English hands. It was occupied by the French from 1338 to 1340 and granted to the Chamberlain family in 1559, then to the Devereux from 1584 till the Civil War, and from 1661 to 1682 to the Carterets who sold it to Sir Edmund Andros. Through him it descended to the Le Mesuriers. The govt. was placed under Guernsey in 1825. The island supported a hardy but rich-yielding breed of milch kine which constituted its only (but valuable) export. The British fortified it and garrisoned it until 1930 to control the Blanchart Race. The people and cattle were evacuated in 1940 when France fell, and the Germans refortified it until they left, without a shot fired, in 1945, and the people and cattle returned.

ALDERSHOT (Surrey) first became the site of the great military establishments in 1855, in connection with the Crimean War.

ALDHELM (c. 640-709) perhaps a relative of Ine, K. of Wessex (688-725), he spent his youth in the monastery at Malmesbury. Subsequently he studied at Canterbury under Abp. Theodore and Abbot Hadrian. He became Abbot of Malmesbury c. 675 and the first Bp. of Sherborne in 705. One of the more learned men of his day, he wrote a very ornate kind of Latin but was also well known as a composer of English poems, none of which survive. As people were no more willing to listen to preaching than they are now, Aldhelm stood on a bridge where many passed, and sang songs. When a crowd gathered, thinking him a minstrel, he would gradually bring in sacred subjects.

ALDRED (d. 1069) monk of Winchester, Abbot of Tavistock under Canute, he became Bp. of Worcester in 1046. In 1050 he attended an Easter synod at Rome on Edward the Confessor's business and in 1054 led an embassy to Germany to negotiate the return of Edward the Exile, a possible successor to the throne. In 1058 he visited Jerusalem. At this time he controlled the dioceses of Hereford and Wiltshire besides Worcester, and in 1060 became Abp. of York. Although he wished to hold Worcester and York in plurality, Pope Nicholas II forbade him to do so. He crowned both Harold and William in 1066. He had no great reputation for piety but seems to have been an efficient church administrator. His career illustrates the extent to which some churchmen became involved in secular politics.

ALDFRITH (r. 685-704). See NORTHUMBRIA-6.

ALDWYCH. See FLEET (London).

ALE and BEER. Ale was brewed in England from earliest times, but the absence of cane or beet sugar caused it to be, generally, very weak in alcoholic strength unless made with a very large quantity of malt. Strong ale was therefore strong in the taste and brewed for special occasions. Small ale was not only weak but kept badly.

In the middle ages there were therefore practical reasons, as well as the temptation, to drink it in huge quantities now unimaginable. Hops began to be used in brewing in the 15th cent. and this improved the keeping quality, but beer (i.e. ale brewed with the addition of hops) only became common in the 17th cent. when the Kentish hop gardens began to flourish. Beer was first taxed in 1660, and the system of taxation, based upon specific gravity before brewing, was introduced in 1880. The beer duty in 1910 raised about £12.5M. In 1952 it raised almost 20 times as much. In 1992 total alcohol duties raised £5,400M.

ALENÇON (France) The Dukes of Alençon were descended from Charles of Valois who was killed at Crécy in 1346. His grandson fell at Agincourt (1415). The family ended in 1525, and thereafter the Duchy became a perquisite of a royal prince.

ALEUTIANS (or CATHERINE) Is. (*See* ALASKA) Exploited in the 18th cent. and partly mapped by Capt. Cook in 1778, Russian permanent settlement began in 1791. The islands were sold to the U.S.A. with Alaska in 1867. Dutch Harbour was an important U.S. base in World War II and the islands were much used as a surveillance station against Russian ambitions.

ALEXANDER of HALES (where he trained) **(c. 1170-1245)** became a well known teacher in Paris and eventually a Franciscan. With others he wrote an Exposition of the Rule of St Francis. His other works included glosses on the so called Sentences (Opinions) of Peter Lombard and a series of *Questions*.

ALEXANDER I (?1077-1124) K. of Scots (1107), fifth son of K. Malcolm Canmore (r. 1058-93) and Margaret, *d.* of Edward the Exile, an English atheling. After Malcolm's death the throne was taken by his brother Donald, and Alexander fled to England. On the accession of his next brother Edgar (1097), however, he received the earldom of Gowrie. As King he was forced to implement the terms of his brother Edgar's will under which Lothian south of Lammermuir, with Teviotdale and Strathclyde went to his younger brother David. He was closely connected with Henry I of England, marrying his bastard daughter Sybilla, and in 1114 sending a contingent in support of one of Henry's campaigns. Meanwhile he founded the Augustinian priory at Scone, and helped Turgot, Bp. of St. Andrews to effect reforms in the Scottish church whose independence from Canterbury he asserted.

ALEXANDER II (1198-1249) K. of Scots (1214) *s.* of William the Lion, succeeded his father while the English barons were in revolt against K. John. Consequently in Oct. 1215 the Northumbrian barons did homage to Alexander, and in Sept. 1216 he himself did homage for the English northern counties to K. Louis of France, who had invaded England. This drew down a papal interdict against Scotland which was lifted in 1217 after Louis' defeat had forced him to accept Henry III as King. He married Henry III's sister Joan in 1221 and remained in peace with England until 1238. During this period he was active in establishing royal authority in outlying areas such as Caithness, Moray and the West and he tried unsuccessfully to buy Man and the Hebrides from Norway. After Joan's death, relations with England cooled; the English claimed suzerainty; he claimed the English northern counties. His claim was compromised by the grant of English estates and these were confirmed by the T. of Newcastle in 1244. He died on campaign in Argyll.

ALEXANDER III (1241-86) K. of Scots (1249). During his minority English interference was fended off with papal help, and at his marriage in 1251 to Margaret *d.* of Henry III of England, he refused homage. In 1255 Henry's nominees secured the regency, but church intervention nullified their influence. In 1262 he took over the govt. and conducted a successful war with Norway, which included a great victory at Largs and ended in the cession

of Man. (T. of Perth 1266) Thereafter there were 20 years of peace and prosperity. His daughter Margaret married Eric II of Norway in 1282, and their child, Margaret, became the well known 'Maid of Norway'. Alexander's first queen had already died in 1275 and so had all their children. When Alexander was killed in a riding accident in 1286, there was only the Maid of Norway left.

ALEXANDER II, Pope (r. 1061-1073) was elected with the support of Hildebrand, while the Emperor Henry IV had Honorius II elected as anti-pope. The schism was effectively if not technically ended by the Synod of Mantua in 1064. As a reformer he took strong centralising measures such as requiring archbishops to come to Rome in person for their pallium, and it was he who supported William I's invasion of England. *See* STEGAN.

ALEXANDER III, Pope (r. 1159-1181) as Orlando Bandinelli, exercised much influence during the reign of his predecessor the English Adrian IV. When he was himself elected, the Emperor Frederick Barbarossa set up an anti-pope, Victor IV. The 17-year schism which resulted, forced Alexander to live mostly in France, and it created great difficulties for him in his dealings with England, for this was the period of the dispute between Henry II and Becket whose unreliable temperament was an embarrassment to papal diplomacy. The archbishop's murder, however, enabled the Pope to take a stronger line with Henry II and established the privileges of the English church and its dependence for some time on the papacy. This in turn strengthened Alexander against the Emperor, and the schism ended in 1177 with the Emperor's submission at Venice. Alexander's victory was gained partly through his support of the north Italian communes against imperial encroachments, and the Lombard city of Alessandria was named after him. In 1179 he held the Third Lateran Council which established the important constitutional principle that the election of the pope was vested exclusively in a two-thirds majority of the cardinals.

ALEXANDER VI, Pope (1431-1503). *See* BORGIA-2; RENAISSANCE-7 *et seq.*

ALEXANDER VII (1599-1667) (Pope 1655) as Fabio Chigi was nuncio at Cologne in 1639 and took part in the negotiations for the P. of Westphalia. In 1652 he became a cardinal and Sec. of State. As Pope he was much under pressure from Louis XIV who, as a reprisal for a supposed diplomatic slight, occupied Avignon in 1663 and threatened the Papal States. Alexander had to sign the T. of Pisa in 1664, and thereafter Papal policy became French orientated.

ALEXANDER VIII, Pope (r. 1689-91) secured the return of Avignon, seized by Louis XIV in 1663. He condemned the Jansenists outright in 1690 but condemned the Gallican propositions of 1682, yet remained on good terms with the King.

ALEXANDER I, Czar of Russia (r. 1801-25) a 'left wing' autocrat succeeded on the murder of his father Paul I. He began by investigating schemes for liberalisation, and found good reasons for not proceeding with them. Meantime in Apr. 1801 he reversed his father's policy of hostility to Britain and entered into alliances against Bonaparte. The first ended with the Austro-Russian disaster at Austerlitz (Dec. 1805). The second with Prussia, ended with the Prussian defeats at Jena and Auerstedt and the Russian defeat at Eylau (1806). Alexander continued the war, but was beaten at Friedland (June 1807). At the T. of Tilsit (June 1807) Alexander and Bonaparte agreed to co-operate in an aggressive world policy to which the latter contributed nothing. Mutual suspicion led to a conference and treaty at Erfurt (Oct. 1809), and as a result Alexander seized Finland from Sweden in 1809. By this time Bonaparte's economic war with England was damaging Russian trade, and internal resistance to co-operation with the French was becoming dangerous. The T. of Vienna (Oct. 1809) had increased the size of the Polish Duchy of Warsaw against Alexander's wishes; in 1810 marriage negotiations failed and Bonaparte announced his engagement to the Austrian archduchess Marie Louise and seized Oldenburg, with whose ducal family Alexander was related. By 1812 he and Bonaparte had drifted into the war which culminated in the latter's fatal Moscow campaign and eventually his overthrow.

From 1815 to about 1818 Alexander favoured keeping European peace by adherence to a sort of moral order, but the revolutionary movements of the period drove him increasingly to the right. In 1820 at Troppau he accepted Metternich's idea of intervention to maintain public order. In 1821, however, the Greek revolt broke out and as protector of orthodox Christians the Czar suffered yet another change of heart. He died mysteriously at Taganrog on his way towards the Turkish frontier.

ALEXANDER II, Czar of Russia (r. 1855-81) inherited and ended the Crimean War. He liberated the serfs in 1861, modernised the administration and in 1870 repudiated the Black Sea clauses of the Crimean Treaty. In 1875 he became involved in the Bosnian crisis which led to the Turkish War of 1877 and the treaties of San Stefano and Berlin of 1878. He was assassinated on the day that he had approved further liberal political reforms.

ALEXANDER III, Czar of Russia (r. 1881-94) cancelled his father's latest political reforms and ruled as an autocrat. There was persistent Russification of the non-Russian provinces, persecution of the Jews, and expansion in Asia. Merv was occupied in 1884. From 1888 his foreign policy moved from alignment with Germany to friendship with France. French capital began to develop the industries. The Transiberian Rly was commenced in 1891, and in Dec. 1893 an alliance with France was signed at St. Petersburg.

ALEXANDER, MacALEXANDER or McALISTER Scots family descended from John of the Isles and Margaret *d.* of Robert II through their son Alister or Alexander. By 1505 they were settled at Menstry (Clackmannan). **(1) Alexander (?-1580)** was tutor to the E. of Argyll. His son **(2) Sir William (1567-1640) Vist. (1630) and E. (1633) of STIRLING** was taught by Thomas, brother of George Buchanan, and travelled France, Spain and Italy as companion to the 7th E. of Argyll who introduced him to court. James VI made him tutor to Prince Henry and went with the court to England, where, until the prince's death he was mainly notable as a literary figure. In 1614, however, he became a Master of Requests and was engaged for many years in the thankless task of restraining Scottish place hunters. In 1621 James gave him the Charter of **NOVA SCOTIA** which was confirmed by Charles I in 1625, and proceeded to raise money for colonisation by selling Scots baronetcies with Nova Scotia land grants at £150 apiece. The venture created many disputes, but meanwhile in 1626 he became Sec. of State for Scotland, and that country's effective administrator until the Bishops' Wars. *(See* CHARLES I, NOVA SCOTIA*)*. A kinsman **(3) John (?-1743)** was a well known puritan minister in Ulster and Gloucestershire, and another **(4) William (1726-83)** who claimed to be the 6th E. of Stirling, was an American general in the rebellion.

ALEXANDER (?-1148) Bp. of LINCOLN (1123) nephew of Roger, Bp. of Salisbury, and cousin of Nigel Bp. of Ely was appointed A-deacon of Salisbury by his uncle in 1121 and preferred to Lincoln by his uncle's influence. In 1125 he visited Rome with the two Abps. and John Bp. of Glasgow in connection with the York-Canterbury dispute. In 1127 he was at the Council of Westminster which denounced married clergy. At this period he used the revenues of his huge diocese to maintain a somewhat scandalous magnificence, and to build castles at Sleaford, Newark and Banbury. In 1137, however, he founded the Cistercian house at Haveholme (soon transferred to Louth), and in 1138 another at Thame. In 1139 K.

Stephen seized him and forced him to surrender his castles, but the anarchy did not interrupt his building projects for long: in 1140 he established the Augustinian canons at Dorchester-on-Thames, and shortly after re-roofed St. Mary's at Stow (Lindsey) with the earliest of English stone vaults. In 1141 he threw in his lot with Matilda, but his diocesan administration yielded large funds with which he again visited Rome in 1145. On his return he rebuilt Lincoln Cathedral. *See* AARON OF LINCOLN.

ALEXANDER, Harold Rupert Leofric George (1891-1969) 1st Vist. (1946) and E. ALEXANDER of TUNIS (1952) K.G. (1946) O.M. (1959) (1) was brought up in C. Tyrone. He developed great abilities as a sportsman and as a sculptor and painter, but was commissioned into the Irish Guards in 1911. His ambition to retire and become an artist was diverted as a subaltern into a military channel by World War I, where he was continually in action, wounded twice, much decorated and emerged as an acting brigadier-gen. In 1919 he went to Poland under Stephen Tallents on the Allied Relief Commission, and then to Latvia where Tallents put him in charge of a brigade of German Balts with which, besides learning German and Russian, he drove the Red Army out. He returned home in 1920, and in 1922 commanded his regiment in the occupation of Istanbul. There followed routine events in the life of a rising soldier, but in 1934 he was given the Nowshera brigade on the Indian N.W. Frontier, with Auchinleck next door at Peshawar. His style of popular leadership in two very successful campaigns included learning Urdu and always being in the front line. By 1937 he was the youngest major-gen. in the army; in 1938 he was given the 1st Division at Aldershot, and took it to France in 1939.

(2) The retreat to Dunkirk made his name. He threw back the Germans for two days along the R. Scheldt. The C-in-C (Lord Gort) then put him in command of I Corps with orders to save all that could be saved, and his final stand on the perimeters in fact saved 20,000 British and 98,000 French troops. In 1940 he was again promoted and succeeded Auchinleck at Southern Command, which became at once a defence mechanism against expected invasion, and a widespread organisation of Battle Training schools.

(3) In Feb. 1942 he was abruptly sent to Burma to try and extricate the desperately placed army there. The Japanese had nearly surrounded Rangoon which he was ordered, if possible, to hold. He did so till the last possible moment, and then took the army back under appalling conditions across the Indian frontier. Not least among his achievements at this time was that he managed to stay friends with the impossible Chiang Kai-shek and the Anglophobe American Gen. Stilwell.

(4) This dependability in adversity brought further promotion. He was nominated to the 1st Army for Eisenhower's projected N. African invasion, and then switched to the Middle East where he took over as C-in-C in Aug. 1942, with Gott as his army commander. Gott was killed and immediately replaced by Montgomery, whom he knew from Southern Command. This famous combination bore fruit in the successful defensive victory at Alam Halfa (Aug. 1942), the offensive victory at Alamein (Oct-Nov. 1942) and the westward pursuit towards the combined British, French and American force which landed in Algeria in Nov. It was soon obvious that fighting co-ordination was necessary, and at the Casablanca Conference (Jan. 1943) he was appointed Eisenhower's deputy in charge of all troops actually fighting the Italo-Germans. By May the enemy were at their last gasp. An ingeniously contrived blow at their positions near Tunis forced, without much loss, the surrender of 250,000 troops.

(5) The next objective was Sicily, which fell in 38 days to a new combination of air landing and modern amphibious techniques. It amounted to a rehearsal for

Normandy, but because he was deceived as to Montgomery's progress, many of the enemy escaped across the Straits of Messina.

(6) The Normandy plans now dominated Allied war policy. He was given two not wholly compatible instructions: to make troops (seven divisions) and other resources (especially landing craft) available for Normandy, while eliminating Italy from the war and containing as many German troops as possible. He obeyed the first and was nevertheless brilliantly successful in the second. With only three divisions, he landed at Salerno (Sept. 1943) just as the Italians surrendered. Shortly afterwards (Jan. 1944) the promising landing at Anzio, bungled in its development by the American local commander, caused the Germans to divert troops from Russia and Normandy. The capture of Rome reinforced these effects. In the final Italian battle (Apr. 1945) a million enemy troops surrendered to a smaller allied force composed of eleven nations. By that time Alexander was C-in-C Mediterranean and a Field-Marshal.

(7) After the war, Alexander, instead of becoming C.I.G.S. as expected, was invited to become Gov.-Gen. of Canada, a post which he held with success and popularity from 1946 to 1952. He then became Churchill's Min. of Defence but retired in the autumn of 1954. Decorations and honours varying from the Constableship of the Tower to the Presidency of the M.C.C. were showered upon him, but he never lost his aptitude for sport and art. He died suddenly.

ALEXANDER, Helen (1654-1729) covenanting heroine, helped fugitives, prisoners and persecuted presbyterians openly and secretly, and at the end of her life dictated her extraordinary experiences to her last husband in the so-called *Short Account*, first published in 1856.

ALEXANDER (1) James (1730-1802) 1st. 14. CALEDON (Ir) (1790) 1st. Vist. (Ir) (1797), 1st E. (Ir) (1800) an Indian nabob, returned to Ireland, purchased estates and was M.P. for Londonderry from 1775 to 1790. An ardent Tory and supporter of Union. His son **(2) Alexander, 2nd E.** was Tory M.P. for Newtownards in the last Irish parl. and became an Irish rep. peer in 1804. He was the first British gov. of the Cape of Good Hope (1806-11). For a son of the 4th Earl **(3) Harold Rupert Leofric (1891-1969)** *see separate entry.*

ALEXANDER, William (1767-1816) made drawings of China and Chinese life (1792-8), Egyptian antiquities (1805) and other places. Prof. of Drawing at the Military College, he became the first Keeper of Prints and Drawings at the British Museum from 1808.

ALEXANDRA, Caroline Mary Charlotte Louise Julia (1844-1925) eldest *d.* of Christian IX of Denmark, married Edward P. of Wales in 1863. The P. Consort had promoted the marriage before his death. Her beauty and artistic talents, and his sociability made them the leaders of society during Q. Victoria's long widowed seclusion. Except for a personal sympathy with her Danish, Greek and Russian relatives, she took no active interest in politics, save at the time of the Prussian seizure of Schleswig-Holstein. Her persistent and practical concern for the poor and the suffering was widely known and respected. Her limp, from a riding accident, was sometimes imitated as a compliment, and she was immensely popular though congenitally deaf and always late. In 1913 she instituted Alexandra (Rose) Day for the support of hospitals.

ALEXANDRA PARK and PALACE (Haringay, N. London). The park and race course were opened in 1863, the palace, a north London equivalent of the Crystal Palace in 1873, was burned down and rebuilt in 1875. It was not always easy to find an economic use for it, and it was at various times an internment camp, govt. offices and B.B.C. television studios. It was mostly burned down again in 1980 but restored as an exhibition and conference centre by 1988.

ALEXANDRETTA. *See* HATAY.

ALEXANDRIA (Egypt) remained a major entrepôt in the oriental spice trade with Europe even after the Arab conquest, and was prosperous during the Crusades. In 13th cent. all the major European trading cities had factories or agencies there. Its decay began with its sack by Peter I of Cyprus in 1365, and with the silting up of the Rosetta canal due to shortage of labour. Under Ottoman rule after 1522 its decline was rapid and was arrested only with Bonaparte's invasion of 1798, the eventual rise of Mehemet Ali and British commercial interest. It was the Mediterranean terminal for the overland route to the Red Sea before the Suez Canal was opened. In 1882 the British fleet bombarded the defences in connection with Arabi's revolt. It served as a poorly organised supply base in World War I, especially for the Dardanelles campaign, and was the essential base for the Royal Navy and for military supplies during World War II. The large Greek population, derived from antiquity, was mostly driven out after World War II.

ALEXEYEV, Mikhail Vasilyevich (1857-1918) was Russian chief of staff in World War I. He directed the Galician offensives and the retreat from Warsaw, and was effective C-in-C under Kerensky.

ALFGAR (?-?1062) Earl, son of Leofric of Mercia and Godiva. *See* EDWARD THE CONFESSOR-9 et seq.

ALFRED THE GREAT (849-99) K. of WESSEX (871) youngest *s.* of K. Aethelwulf and his first wife Osburh, was born at Wantage (Berks). She taught him to read. At the age of four he went to Rome, where Pope Leo IV conferred consular insignia upon him, and again in 855 with his father, by way of the Frankish court. These travels contributed to his broad outlook and later interest in learning. He grew up to be a man of slight build, with a mysterious recurrent illness (epilepsy?). His extra-ordinary energy must have been a matter of character rather than physique. Aethelwulf was succeeded in turn by Alfred's three brothers, Aethelbald, Aethelberht and Aethelred I, under whom Wessex was invaded by Viking armies. Alfred and Aethelred won the important victory at Ashdown (870) (q.v.) but fighting continued, and Alfred succeeded to the throne in the middle of a military crisis. This ended with a victory at Wilton (871), after which the enemy made peace with the West Saxons and moved into Mercia. In 875, however, they returned to sack Wareham (Dorset), moving from there to Exeter and thence back to Mercia. In Jan. 878, however, they caught Alfred unawares. Some people fled overseas, and others submitted. Alfred took refuge in Athelney, an island in the Somerset marshes, and it is here that the possibly mythical story of the burnt cakes belongs. He must, however, have devised some method of summoning large forces at short notice, for a few months later he raised enough troops to defeat the enemy at Edington (Wilts), and compel their King Guthrum to make peace and accept baptism at Wedmore. Wessex then had peace until 884, when Alfred repulsed a raid on Kent, and again until 892, when an army which had been defeated on the continent again landed in Kent. This force received malcontents from Scandinavian settlements in Northumbria and E. Anglia, and it was 896 before it was finally defeated. The kingdoms of Northumbria, East Anglia, and Mercia having been destroyed by the Vikings, Wessex alone survived, mainly through the quality of Alfred's leadership and his administrative skill, by which he laid the foundations of the English state. He codified the laws (with a modest preface). He devised a defensive system based on fortresses (*burhs*) which served as temporary refuges for the people, but which were also planned as places of habitation and trade capable of supporting garrisons totalling about 27,000 men. He may have organised a fleet.

He was also concerned with the education and spiritual welfare of his people, as he believed that only proper religious observance would secure God's help against the enemy. This involved a revival of learning, for which he recruited scholars (see ALFRED'S SCHOLARS) and himself gave a lead by translating into English Boethius' *Consolation of Philosophy,* Augustine's *Soliloquies,* and Pope Gregory the Great's *Pastoral Care,* a manual for bishops. Other translations included a version of Bede's *Ecclesiastical History of the English People,* and one of Orosius' history of the ancient world. The oldest surviving version of the *Anglo-Saxon Chronicle* dates from his time.

ALFRED, LAWS OF (c. 890). A code selectively incorporating provisions from the Laws of Ethelbert, Wihtraed, Ine, and the Mercian legislation of Offa. It is much concerned with rates of compensation for private wrongs in a disorderly period.

ALFRED'S SCHOLARS were the learned group which the King assembled to preserve or revive English learning and education. The principal ones were the Mercians Plegmund (later Abp. of Canterbury), Werferth, Bp. of Worcester, Werwulth, and Athelstan; and the Flemings Grimbald and John.

ALFRED the ATHELING (?-1036) younger son of Ethelred the Unready and Emma of Normandy, fled with his parents to Normandy when K. Sweyn Forkbeard conquered England in 1013. After K. Canute died (1035) Alfred landed at Dover in 1036 to visit Emma. Godwin, the leader of Hardicanute's faction seized and blinded him so brutally at Guildford that he died at Ely Abbey.

ALFRED Ernest Albert (1844-1900) D. of EDINBURGH (1866) and D. of SAXE-COBURG and GOTHA. Second son of Q. Victoria was elected King of Greece in 1862, but declined the dangerous honour on political grounds. In the course of a conventional naval career he was C-in-C Mediterranean from 1886 to 1889 and at Devonport from 1890 to 1893. His elder brother, the Prince of Wales, having relinquished all rights in Saxe-Coburg and Gotha in 1863, Alfred succeeded his uncle as reigning duke in 1893.

ALGEÇIRAS (Spain) CONFERENCE (Jan. 1906) arose indirectly from the Anglo-French *Entente* which had germinated into an arbitration treaty (Oct. 1903) and a treaty (Apr. 1904) on the Newfoundland fisheries, W. African boundaries, Siam, Madagascar and the New Hebrides, but especially the concession of a free hand to Britain in the Nile Valley in return for a French free hand in Morocco. The Admiralty wished to safeguard the Straits, so there were secret clauses providing for coastal demilitarisation and conceding a north coastal strip to Spanish protection if the Moroccan Sultanate broke up. There was a corresponding Franco-Spanish secret agreement. The French sent a mission to the Sultan with proposals for reform.

The Germans knew about the secret clauses and originally welcomed the treaties. They had no interests worth the name in Morocco, but by Mar. 1905 France's ally Russia was losing battles by land and sea to Japan, and the Germans thought that France in her thus weakened situation might be blackmailed into concessions elsewhere. In Mar. 1905 the Kaiser, William II visited Tangier, and in a series of speeches asserted the Sultan's absolute freedom, the equal rights of all the powers under his sovereignty, and that Germany had growing interests which, as the Kaiser's visit showed, she would defend. The Germans demanded an international conference for Jan. 1906 and agreed its scope with the French. At this point the British renewed their alliance with Japan (Aug. 1905) and a few days later this enabled the Japanese to accept less stringent terms, when the Russo-Japanese conflict was ended at the P. of Portsmouth. The German hope, apart from the concessions, was to split the *Entente.* The conference accordingly met at Algeçiras opposite Gibraltar. Twelve govts. were represented. Only Austro-Hungary supported

the Germans. Britain, U.S.A., Russia and Spain supported a somewhat strengthened France. Italy was neutral. Morocco was to be kept in order by a Franco-Spanish *gendarmerie* under a Swiss Inspector-Gen. Germany got nothing.

ALGIERS and ALGERIA (*see also*** BARBARY) (1)** In 1830 the French, to re-establish their Mediterranean power lost to the British, seized Algiers and expelled the Dey and the Ottoman officials. The Bourbons then fell, and the Orleanist govt. tried to limit the commitment. French action having deprived the interior of even a semblance of government, order had to be restored by conquest, but the Western tribes, led by Abd-el-Kader (1808-1883) put up a stiff resistance until driven into Morocco and defeated on the Isly in 1844. He surrendered in 1847, and the Second Republic declared Algeria French territory in 1848.

(2) Since 1840 colonisation had been encouraged by government land grants. There was consequently a permanent dispute between the military who wanted security, favoured indirect rule, and disapproved of land grants as likely to cause trouble, and the colonists, who wanted civilian rule amenable to their interests. The republic favoured the latter; Algeria was divided into three *departements* each represented in the French Parliament. The militaristic second Empire took the contrary view and tried to protect native landownership, but in 1867 a customs union with France was set up, and from 1865 Algerians could become French citizens by acceding to French law. This rule, maintained until independence, was a source of endless friction. The colonists did not want natives to increase their political influence by acquiring citizenship: the natives did not want citizenship at the expense of polygamy and communal property rights under Islamic law, while the metropolitan French could not understand why the inestimable boon was being rejected. Successive French govts. pursued a policy of assimilation based upon unrealistic assumptions.

(3) The period from 1871 to 1911 was one of sporadic military operations beginning with a Kabyle (Berber) revolt (1871-3), continuing with the pacification of the Moroccan border (1903-10), and ending with the conquest of the south (1899-1911). Colonisation, especially by vine cultivators from the phyloxera-ruined south of France, continued at the expense of the inhabitants; by 1939 there were a million colonists of whom one third were French.

(4) The French defeats in World War II gave the natives their opportunity. In Feb. 1943 Ferhat Abbas published his manifesto on political rights and against exploitation, and founded the *Union Démocratique du Manifeste Algérien* favouring autonomy in association with France. The French moved too slowly and a Statute of 1947 created an assembly with no more powers than a rather limited administrative body. The colonists continued to dominate the scene against a background of increasing violence. In 1954 rebellion broke out, and in 1956 Ferhat Abbas joined the more extremist rebel leaders now ensconced safely in Cairo. In May 1958 the colonists, fearing betrayal by the home govt, seized local power. There were now two mutually hostile rebel movements, and in Sept. Ferhat Abbas set up his own provisional govt. This gathered increasing local and international support, while the colonists' govt. declined. In Feb. 1961 Gen. de Gaulle invited Habib Bourguiba, the Tunisian President to mediate. Simultaneous referenda in France and Algeria gave strong majorities for independence, and in 1962 a cease fire was arranged (Mar.) and an independent govt. under Ben Bella installed (Sept.). This joined the United Nations in Oct. In 1965 Ben Bella was ousted by a coup which brought Houari Boumedienne to power. His govt. and that of his supporters was shaken only in 1990 by local elections in which Islamic extremists gained many seats.

ALGOA BAY (S. Africa) now Port Elizabeth.

ALGONQUIN or ALGONKIN. These Red Indian tribes were a linguistic, not an organised, group which spread across N. America from coast to coast. The most important were the Abnaki, Delaware, Mahican (not to be confused with the Mohawks), Massachusett, Narragansett, Pequod, and Wampanoag between the Alleghenies and the Atlantic; the Cree, Ojibwa, Ottawa and Shawnee inhabited the Middle West. These two groups were bitter enemies of the Iroquois and usually supported the French. Their principal plains tribes were the Blackfoot and Cheyenne. All the Algonquin tribes had defined hunting and fishing areas, but sometimes moved when game was scarce. They regarded agriculture as secondary, but they taught the Europeans how to raise *inter alia* tobacco, tomatoes, pumpkins, and maple sugar.

ALHAMBRA. Celebrated or notorious music hall in Leicester Square, London, opened in 1854, rebuilt after a fire in 1882 and demolished in 1936. Its revues were immensely popular. Its promenade was a resort of high class whores, and 'being thrown out of the Alhambra' was a young man-about-town's entry to society.

ALIEN PRIORIES were daughter houses of monasteries in Normandy or elsewhere abroad. Gifts of English land to foreign houses were fairly frequent between 1066 and about 1180, but John's loss of Normandy (1207) created serious problems of jurisdiction and feudal service, especially in periods of war with France, when Kings were apt to requisition their lands and pocket the revenues, leaving the monks with a bare living allowance. This happened during hostilities beginning in 1295, 1324, 1337 and 1369. Some of the larger priories solved the problem by purchasing letters of denization. After 1369 smaller cells were mostly farmed out to the highest bidder; by an Act of 1414 these properties were taken into the King's hand, and many were in the end transferred to educational or charitable foundations.

ALIENS. *See* ALLEGIANCE.

ALIENS ACT. *See* IMMIGRATION ACTS.

ALIVARDI. *See* BENGAL-5.

ALLAHABAD or PRAYAG (India) always an important place of pilgrimage, was ceded by the Nawab of Oudh to the British in 1801. It was the home of the Nehru family.

ALLAN, WILLIAM (1813-74) Scots trade unionist was Gen. Sec. of the Amalgamated Society of Engineers from 1851 to 1874.

ALLECTUS (?250-296) a minister of Carausius the usurping Roman emperor in Britain, assassinated him in 293 and himself assumed the purple. He was killed in battle. *See* BRITAIN, ROMAN.

ALLEGIANCE (1) The obligation of a subject to support or to do nothing contrary to the interests of his Lord or Sovereign. It was created most often by birth within the Lord's territory; also by denization or naturalisation. In addition, an alien temporarily within the Lord's jurisdiction owed temporary allegiance. The subject could not shake it off without his Lord's consent. The Lord could not forfeit it save by refusing formally to protect the subject.

(2) A different and concurrent allegiance arose as between a vassal and his Lord. Frequently a man might be a vassal of more than one Lord and his obligations might conflict. Hence it became usual in France and then in England for one Lord to be recognised as the Liege Lord, and for oaths sworn to any other to make an exception in his favour. From Henry I's time allegiance to the Crown was always reserved. This merged the two forms of allegiance. *See* FEUDALISM; NATIONALITY; TREASON.

ALLEN v FLOOD **1898 AC 1.** Some ironworkers insisted, by threatening a strike, that their employer should dismiss the shipwrights whom he also employed. The shipwrights sued the ironworkers. The Lords held that the ironworkers' action was not unlawful. The case is the foundation of the law on the closed shop.

ALLEN, Ethan. *See* VERMONT.

ALLEN, Sir Hugh Percy (1869-1946) originally a cathedral organist, in 1901 moved to New College, Oxford, and in 1918 became Prof. of Music, and Dir. of the R. College of Music. His abilities and enthusiasm as an organiser and popularizer were important factors in the 20th cent. English musical renaissance. In 1944 he secured the creation of a musical faculty at Oxford.

ALLEN, John (1476-1534) Card. Wolsey's commissary from 1522, acted in the 1524 suppression of minor monasteries and received preferments from Wolsey. In 1528 he became Abp. of Dublin and Chanc. of Ireland with instructions to enforce Wolsey's legatine authority, which was being resisted by the Primate. Consequently Allen was involved in Wolsey's fall in 1529. He had to compound his *praemunire*, and the chancellorship was transferred to the primate. He was murdered at Clontarf in 1534 by Lord Thomas Fitzgerald's rebels.

ALLEN, William (1532-94) Card. (1587) taught at Oxford until 1561 when he went to Louvain. In 1562 he returned, but finally quitted England in 1565. He believed that the English were really R. Catholic at heart, only awaiting a well trained body of missionaries to bring them back to the fold. Accordingly he founded the English colleges at Douai (1568), and Rome (1575), and the Douai press, which issued the so-called *Douai Bible* under his guidance. His support of the Armada discredited him with many English R. Catholics. He was made a cardinal in anticipation of the need to reorganise the English Church when the Spanish invasion succeeded, and when it failed he moved to Spain and founded another English College at Valladolid in 1589.

ALLENBY, Edmund Henry Hynman (1861-1936) 1st Vist. ALLENBY of MEGIDDO (1919) was a distinguished regimental commander in the Boer War, and inspector-gen: of cavalry from 1910 to 1914; he commanded the cavalry during the 1914 retreat from Mons, the V Corps at the second battle of Ypres in 1915 and the Third Army from 1915 to June 1917 when he became C-in-C in Egypt. Beginning in Oct. with the victory at Gaza he took Jerusalem in Dec. After a pause caused by the withdrawal of troops to France, he attacked again in Sept. 1918, at Megiddo, and after destroying the Turkish forces in Palestine took Damascus on 1 Oct. and forced the Turks to surrender on 30 Oct. In 1919 he became High Commissioner in Egypt; an advocate of local autonomy, he secured the recognition of Egyptian sovereignty in 1922. He retired in 1925, following differences with the Foreign Sec., Austen Chamberlain.

ALLEYN, Edward (1566-1626) was an actor who founded Dulwich College in 1613 and managed it until his death.

ALLOTMENTS were originally lands *allotted* to any person or for any purpose under an inclosure award (*see* INCLOSURES). The word was soon restricted to land so allotted for a public or charitable purpose, the commonest being quarries and sandpits for road making (highway allotments), land from which the poor could gather fuel (fuel allotments), and land leased in small plots at a low rent for their sustenance. By the beginning of the 19th cent. the last usage was the usual one, and there was much Victorian legislation about them. This was consolidated in 1906, and amended at intervals down to 1952. The principle of the legislation was that local authorities should provide them at low rents and with certainty of tenure.

ALLOWANCE. *See* COLONIAL LAWS. VALIDITY-7.

ALL THE TALENTS was the derisive nickname of a coalition govt. based on the whigs, when Pitt the younger died. (Jan. 1806-Mar. 1807). Its leading members were Lord Grenville (Prime Minister), Charles James Fox (Foreign Sec.) and Vist. Sidmouth (Privy Seal) who was a friend of the King. Its opponents, having mostly grown up in power, had much more talent. The ministry began by negotiating unsuccessfully with Bonaparte. They abolished Pitt's recruiting system in favour of short service, but administered it incompetently. In July 1806 Fox's death deprived them of the one personality who could make them a team. They now became a disparate coalition. The general election of Oct. 1806 increased their potential whig support in the House at the expense of Sidmouth's group. This forced Sidmouth (see ADDINGTON), for self-protection, to insist on his own views and rely on royal backing. They could not press Fox's political principles: parliamentary reform might split the nation in time of war. The abolition of sinecures would destroy the basis of their shaky parliamentary influence. They managed, however, to abolish the slave trade (*see* WEST AFRICA) but when they tried to extend the right of R. Catholics to commissions in the army, the King and Sidmouth resolutely opposed them. The King demanded an undertaking that the matter should not be pressed and, unable to carry on without Sidmouth, they resigned.

ALL FOR IRELAND LEAGUE formed by William O'Brien in Aug. 1913 was an organisation for securing Home Rule of a united Ireland by constitutional means. It suggested the Buckingham Palace conference of July 1914.

ALLTUD. See WELSH LAW-1 & 10.

ALLURE The walk behind the parapet of a castle or town wall.

ALMACK, William (?-1781) a valet to the D. of Hamilton, by 1763 had opened a Whig club, now Brooks's in Pall Mall. In 1765 he opened his assembly rooms in King St. The latter remained a fashionable meeting place until 1863.

ALMAINE = Germany.

ALMIRANTA **(Sp.)** The ship wearing the flag of the 2-in-C of a Spanish fleet. *See* CAPITANA.

ALMOHADS (Arab: MUWAHHIDEEN = Unifiers of Religion) Spanish and North African dynasty during the 12th and 13th cents.

ALMORAVIDES (Arab: MURABITEEN = Dedicated) Spanish and North African dynasty in the 11th and 12th cents. The word sometimes reappears as *Marabout,* more recently signifying a religious leader.

ALMOND, St. John (?1577-1612) an itinerant R. Catholic missionary in England from 1602 to 1609. He was arrested but escaped and continued his work until rearrested in 1612. After unavailing efforts to convert him, he was executed.

ALMONER (1) An official who co-ordinated charitable activities, particularly the royal High Almoner who is generally a bishop. **(2)** A social worker attached to a hospital and called prolixly since 1964 a 'medical social worker'.

ALMSHOUSES as shelter for the poor or old were established in the middle ages and some (e.g. St. Cross at Winchester and Richard Whittington's in London) survive but there was a great increase in formations after the dissolution of the monasteries (1536-40) put such people onto the streets, and such establishments represented common acts of charity into the 19th cent.

ALNWICK (N'land) This small town with its castle, first garrisoned in about 1150, was the principal English military H.Q. on the Eastern Border marches, and from 1309 the seat of the Percy family, which was still there in 2000.

ALPACA An Andean cameloid mammal whose peculiarly lustrous and fine wool was introduced into Britain from Peru in 1836; specialised mills to process it were set up by Sir Titus Salt. The result was an influential Anglo-Peruvian economic nexus.

ALPHEGE or AELFHEAII, St. (954-1012) monk of Deerhurst and then Abbot of Bath, became Bp. of Winchester in 984 on Dunstan's recommendation. He preached to the Vikings whenever he could, and in 994 converted the Norwegian K. Olaf Trygvasson when wintering with his army in Hampshire. This caused division among the Vikings and Olaf agreed to make peace. In 1006 Alphege was elected Abp. of Canterbury and received his pallium at Rome. On his return he held a reforming council at Enham (?1009). In 1011 a Danish host under Thorkill stormed Canterbury and captured him. Probably by Alphege's wish, the negotiations for his ransom were protracted while he preached in the Danish camp and made converts. Heathens battered him to death at a drunken orgy near Greenwich in Apr. 1012 when he refused to pay or could not raise the ransom. Miracles soon occurred at his tomb at St Paul's and in 1023 Canute had his body translated with ceremony to Canterbury.

ALPHONSE of POITOU. *See* LOUIS IX.

ALPORT, Cuthbert James McCall (1912-) 14. (1961) was director of the conservative political centre from 1945 to 1950 when he became M.P. for Colchester. From 1957 to 1961 he was at the Commonwealth Relations Office as parliamentary U/Sec. of State and then as Min. of State and from 1961 to 1963 he was High Commissioner to the Fed. of Rhodesia and Nyassaland. He also represented the British govt. in the Salisbury negotiations with Rhodesia in 1967.

ALRIC. *See* KENT. KINGDOM-5.

ALSACE part of the Holy Roman Empire, was penetrated by French influence in the Thirty Years War (1618-48) and ceded, except for Strasbourg, to France at the P. of Westphalia in 1648. Strasbourg remained independent and anti-French during Turenne's Alsatian campaigns, but French rights in Alsace were confirmed by the P. of Nymeguen (1678) and Strasbourg's independence was crushed in 1681. The Edict of Nantes remained in force, and Alsace was outside the French customs frontier until 1789. Full union with France, involving abolition of feudalism, created friction with German princes who had estates there, and was one of the causes of the first French revolutionary war. After the Franco-Prussian War of 1870, it became German *Reichsland* until 1918 when France retook it. It was again annexed by Germany in 1940, and retaken by France in 1944.

ALSATIA (London) The Whitefriars precinct. It was a sanctuary until 1697. The word was used, by extension, for sanctuaries and refuges for persons of doubtful character in general.

ALTEN, Sir Charles, Count von (1764-1840) of a protestant Hanoverian family, served in the Hanoverian army until its dissolution in 1803, when he joined the British army. He raised a German Legion, held various commands on the Continent and in the Peninsula, fought with distinction at Waterloo and then returned in 1818 to Hanover to recreate its army, in which he became a Field-Marshal. He was also Hanoverian Minister of War and Foreign Affairs.

ALTERNAT. Device for avoiding sometimes interminable delays over precedence in signing treaties. A copy was laid before each signatory, who signed and passed it to his left, for further signature and so on.

ALTHORP. *See* SPENCER.

ALTHORP (N'hants) (pron: ALTHROP) a regency mansion imposed by Henry Holland in 1790 upon a core, part medieval, part Tudor, part Carolean. The seat of the Spencer family since 1508. The pictures formed one of the greatest family collections in the world, but some were sold off in the 1980's.

ALTIMARLICH (Wick) B. of (1680) between the Campbells and the Sinclairs, was the last private pitched battle.

ALTRANSTAEDT, P. of (1706). *See* BALTIC-38.

ALTRINCHAM (Ches) originally chartered in 1290, began to develop commercially only with the coming of the Bridgewater Canal in the 1760's, when spinning and market gardening were its chief occupations. These were supplemented by engineering from 1905.

ALUM a sulphate extracted from a rock or shale was essential for dying and making cloth and paper. In the middle ages it came from Asia Minor and Syria, mostly through Genoese shippers. After 1462, new mines found at Tolfa in the Papal States contrived, with war and piracy in the Aegean, to supersede the ancient source. These monopolies in their time financed a trade between the Mediterranean and the English and Flemish cloth making areas, which might otherwise have disappeared. Tolfa remained productive into the 20th cent.

ALUMINIUM was first isolated in 1825; introduced to the public at the Paris Exhibition of 1855, its modern production by electrolysis began in 1886.

ALVA or ALBA, Ferdinand ALVAREZ DE TOLEDO, D. of (1507-82) after military success in Africa, France Germany and Italy, was made Spanish captain-gen. in the Netherlands in 1567 for the purpose of suppressing local privileges and protestantism. Militarily successful, he failed as a governor because he combined ignorance of local conditions and inadequate resources with an impatient cruelty and ruthlessness, which turned the people of all outlooks against him. Unable to suppress the 'sea beggars' or overcome the resistance of Holland and Zeeland, he resigned in 1573. Reports of his treatment of the Dutch formed an influential element in the development of anti-Spanish opinion in England. In 1580 he directed the military occupation of Portugal with equal cruelty.

ALWAR (India). A Rajput state founded in the latter half of the 18th cent., it survived because its ruler supported the British in the Mahratta War of 1803. Always subject to varying degrees of misrule, its affairs became a scandal in 1937 when its govt. had to be taken over by the paramount power.

AMALFI. See ADMIRALTY, COURT OF.

AMALGAMATED PRESS. See HARMSWORTH.

AMAZON. See BRAZIL.

AMBASSADOR, MINISTER, CHARGÉ D'AFFAIRES Ambassadors were representatives of major rulers sent to treat with others of equal power or rank. Ministers went to or from lesser rulers. Ordinary heads of such missions were accredited only for a particular purpose or occasion: extraordinary envoys resided permanently in the capital where they were accredited. Permanent accreditation was mutual and invariably (save between Switzerland and France) by envoys of equal rank on each side. When permanent missions became normal, caretakers had to be appointed during vacancies. These, the chargés d'affaires were accredited not to the ruler but to his foreign minister. The system was codified in the T. of Vienna (1815) but embassies were still confined in 1914 to Austro-Hungary, France, Germany, Britain, Italy, Japan, Russia, Spain, Turkey and the U.S.A., to which by 1939 Belgium, China, Poland and Portugal had been added. After World War II nearly all states exchanged ambassadors, and ministers then became their deputies or heads of department. In the 1950's the U.S. embassy in London had eleven of them. See DIPLOMATIC IMMUNITY.

AMBER. See JAIPUR.

AMBIDEXTER A juryman who took bribes from both sides.

AMBLESIDE (Cumbria) A small village in the calmly beautiful hills about L. Windermere where at one time or another the poet Wordsworth, Thomas Arnold, and Harriet Martineau lived.

AMBOINA. See EAST INDIA COMPANY-2; INDONESIA-2.

AMBROSE, St. (?339-97) the son of a Praetorian prefect of Gaul, was Gov. of Aemilia (at Milan) in 374 when the Christian laity insisted on his becoming bishop as well. He knew the western rulers of his time personally and was an energetic missionary and defender of the Church's and private rights against tyranny. He converted St. Augustine of Hippo in 386. His influence was unrivalled in his day and his fame has lasted ever since. See TE DEUM.

AMBROSIUS AURELIANUS. See ARTHUR, KING; BRITAIN. ROMANO-BRITISH-4.

A.M.D.G. or Ad majorem Dei gloriam (Lat = To the greater glory of God). Found on ecclesiastical monuments, and the title pages of Jesuit publications.

AMERCEMENT. When someone had committed a crime less than felony, which might include a simple failure in a legal proceeding (or 'false claim'), he was considered to be in the King's mercy and, there being no corrective prison system, he might theoretically suffer such physical penalty, short of death as a court might see fit to inflict, from exile, mutilation, whipping or branding at one end of the scale to ducking or ridicule in the stocks at the other. He could buy himself out of mercy, and in practice there was a tariff which was related to his means and the severity which he might otherwise expect. The Crown, always short of money, was usually glad to accept such payments. A felon could not be amerced because all his property was forfeit and therefore he would have nothing from which to pay. See FINE.

AMERICA, 'DISCOVERY' Of. Leif Ericsson or his kinsman Thorfirm Karlsefni established a settlement at L'Anse aux Meadows (Newfoundland) in about A.D.1000, and called it Vinland. Columbus, first sighted the Bahamas in 1492, the Cabots reached Newfoundland in 1497, and Vasco da Gama Brazil in 1498. Amerigo Vespucci accompanied Vasco on some of his voyages; in 1501 he thought that the New World was a separate continent, and in consequence it was named after him by the German geographer Martin Waldseemüller in 1507. In 1513 Balboa reached the Pacific across the Isthmus of Panama but thought that it was an extension of the Indian Ocean, but in 1521 Magellan penetrated the Straits named after him in Tierra del Fuego. He was killed in the Philippines but the circumnavigation of the globe by his flagship established its proper size and consequently the approximate position of America upon it. In 1535 the Viceroyalty of New Spain was established at Mexico and in the next ten years Spaniards explored the southern areas of the present U.S.A., invaded Peru and extended their conquests the length of the west coast.

AMERICAN REBELLION, REVOLUTION or WAR OF INDEPENDENCE (1775-83) (A). *CAUSES* **(1)** The social divergences from the solid stratified society of a well settled England to the mobile, individualistic habits of an almost empty continent, and the contrast between them. **(2)** The repudiation, civil or religious, of the homeland implicit in migration. **(3)** The political need of the colonial oligarchies to distract or divert the energies of their discontented poor. **(4)** Safety from the French after their defeat in the Seven Years War.

(B). *REASONS FOR SUCCESS* **(5)** Unscrupulous and plausible propaganda. **(6)** An inadequate British war effort, and the difficulty of co-ordinating it across an ocean. **(7)** European, especially French, intervention. **(8)** Collapse of British political morale.

(C). *PRELIMINARIES* **(9)** The Grenville govt. especially Shelburne, proposed to divert the pressure of migration from the 13 colonies after 1763 northwards (Nova Scotia) and southwards (Florida). A frontier was drawn to the west and the territory beyond was to be accessible from Canada, thereby conciliating the conquered Canadian French. There were to be superintendents of Indian affairs backed by troops and forts at a cost of £370,000. The main object was temporarily to keep colonists and Indians apart. It was to be financed by the so called Sugar Act and the Stamp Act (1765). The former was practically unarguable: it reduced the sugar duty by half, and earmarked the proceeds for American use. What was novel about it was that it was enforced. The Stamp Act, a tax on legal transactions and newspapers was expected to raise £60,000. It was entirely new and it touched those, such as lawyers, tavern keepers, and journalists who could make the most noise. The objectors, being acquisitive and self confident, saw no reason to close the west, or to pay for defence now that Britain had got rid of the French.

(10) The colonial legislatures were mostly oligarchical. In the winter of 1764 a resolution moved, by Patrick Henry in a rump session of the Virginia Assembly challenged the supremacy of Parliament (not the Crown), but once this lead had been given, the others joined in to distract the populace, currently discontented because of the post-war slump. The Stamp Act congress (Oct. 1765) admitted the supremacy of the Crown and the right of parliament to legislate on imperial matters, but not to tax the colonies internally for revenue. The Rockingham govt. agreed and passed the Declaratory Act, affirming the right to legislate imperially, and repealed the Stamp Act (Mar. 1766). Moreover the duty on French molasses was reduced to benefit Rhode I. rum distillers, who used virtually nothing else.

(11) These measures emboldened the agitators, while removing the grievances so necessary to their political safety. They had to find others. The Declaratory Act was now denounced as the thin end of the wedge. Boston and New York refused even trivial supplies. The latter seized on traditional fears of standing armies to refuse obligations under the Quartering Act (1767). In 1767 America cost the British taxpayer £428,000: in May Charles Townshend introduced the duties (named after him), on lead, glass, paper, painters' colours, and tea exported from Britain to America. These were expected to bring in only £40,000, but met the constitutional point that they did not infringe the rule against raising revenue in the colonies; the rest of the deficit was to be cleared by reducing the frontier garrisons. But since the leading colonists wanted to have their protection without paying for it, the constitutional point hardly mattered to them, save as a battle cry. Samuel Adams drafted a circular from the Massachusetts Assembly calling for resistance on grounds of natural law. John Dickinson of Pennsylvania (the draftsman of the anti-Stamp Act congress) excited opinion through his *Farmers' Letters*. Lord Hillsborough told colonial governors to ignore the Massachusetts Circular. The Massachusetts Assembly was, however, suspended and this magnified the Circular out of all importance.

(12) Smuggling had always been a major activity, and the source of many fortunes. On this were now super-imposed boycotts of English goods *(Non-importation Agreements)*, which added to the unemployment and disorder in the major ports. By this time English opinion, which had on the whole favoured the Americans showed signs of boredom and impatience with the confusion which was damaging the market. English commerce began to look elsewhere while Lord North, who came to power in 1770, repealed all the Townshend duties except the tea tax (worth about £12,000 a year). By then the non-importation campaign was flagging. This phase, however, coincided with the culmination of a Bostonian campaign since 1763 against the behaviour of British troops, whose drunkenness (on Rhode I. rum) and seductive habits were supposed to be corrupting the New England puritans. Terrorist organisations had been suborning or bullying the people into open resistance or hostility since 1766. In Boston a soldier could not go out alone. In Mar. 1770, while the Townshend duties were repealed, a Boston mob attacked troops on guard at the customs house; after a long and patient day the troops fired and killed five. The revolutionary pamphleteers promptly called it the **BOSTON MASSACRE.**

(13) The slump was passing, and there was a general feeling that the Boston extremists had gone too far. Most of the grievances on taxation and western migration had been remedied or exposed. People wanted business as usual. New York abandoned the non-importation agreement, and the trade boycotts collapsed. Until 1773 agitation was kept barely alive artificially by such outrages as the looting of the *Gaspée*. Then came Lord North's reform of the HEIC which, amongst other things

reduced the tax on tea, and permitted the Co. to sell it direct to America. This halved the price, and the rich New York and Philadelphia smuggler barons were faced with ruin. A new boycott was out of the question: once the stuff was landed people would drink it. Therefore their henchmen, disguised as red Indians, boarded the ship and threw it into the harbour. The **BOSTON TEA PARTY** (16 Dec. 1773) was essentially a private operation for the benefit of racketeers. It was British over-reaction which made it a public event. North was seriously concerned at Boston lawlessness generally. He thought that, as in 1770, the other colonies would disown Massachusetts where, therefore, a sharp lesson would be enough; parliamentary opinion already disgusted with the antics of American agents in London, readily supported the closure of the Port of Boston until compensation had been paid. North altered the colony's constitution by making the members of the upper house gubernatorial nominees and, since local juries never convicted in seditious or revenue cases he authorised the governor to transfer trials to England if necessary. Not surprisingly the so called **COERCIVE ACTS** caused uproar. The other colonies supported Massachusetts in defence of their own constitutions, and the remands to England were represented as deportations of innocent men. The situation was aggravated by the Quebec Act, 1774 (*see* CANADA-10), which aroused racial and religious as well as economic and political animosities. George Washington, Patrick Henry, and the Philadelphia land speculators lost large sums in the wreck of the Vandalia land company as a result.

(14) In Nov. 1772 the radical Samuel Adams had set up the Boston Committee of Correspondence to promote rebellion, and by Feb. 1773 there was a network of committees in Massachusetts. In Mar. the Virginia Assembly set up a committee for Intercolonial correspondence, and the idea caught on elsewhere. Hence the extremists had no difficulty in summoning a protest assembly known as the **FIRST CONTINENTAL CONGRESS** to Philadelphia where it met in Sept. and Oct. 1774. The method of summons and the objects of this assembly ensured that it would be an extremist body. The **SUFFOLK RESOLVES,** a series of resolutions by delegates from Boston and other towns of Suffolk (Mass) denounced the Coercive Acts, and demanded a total cessation of British trade, the withholding of taxes, backed if necessary by forcible resistance. The Congress endorsed them, but made exceptions for southern crops. Massachusetts armed its militia and started accumulating munitions. This was the breaking point.

(D). THE WAR (15) Gen. Gage at Boston decided to destroy the colonial magazine at Concord (Mass). This was done, but his troops were attacked at **Lexington** and got back with some loss (Apr. 1775). The affair was magnified into a victorious battle, and the colonists began to arm. British reinforcements under Howe, Burgoyne and Clinton arrived, and in May the **SECOND CONTINENTAL CONGRESS** met at Philadelphia, voted the creation of the **CONTINENTAL ARMY** and appointed Washington as its C-in-C. Howe next dispersed a rebel effort to isolate him in Charlestown by driving them off **Bunker Hill** (17 June 1775); this hard fought action showed that the colonial militia could stand up creditably and fight regulars. Shortly afterwards fighting of a similar character broke out in Virginia.

(16) Both sides were disorientated. Lord North, a champion of financial economy, had pruned the navy and delayed raising troops. The Admiralty already feared French intervention, and wanted to keep the hulk of the fleet in home waters. Adm. Graves, off the endless American coast, had only 27 ships against the swarms of elusive privateers. Meanwhile the rebels, such were the passions aroused by the Quebec Act, staged an autumn invasion of Canada. The French Canadians remained neutral but English troops under Carleton sent it tumbling back in the spring of 1776. Part of the uncertainty arose because neither the rebels nor Lord North were sure whether the rebellion was really a rebellion; but on the rebel side opinion favouring a complete break was hardening with the hard facts of war. The individualistic colonial was difficult to lead: it was rare for more than 15% of the rebel troops to be actually available to fight at any given moment. What was needed was a positive cause and an ally. The flag of independence might supply both; Silas Deane was dispatched to get French help in Feb. 1776. The rising of the Carolina loyalists and their defeat at Morris Creek Bridge (27 Feb. 1776) lent point to Tom Paine's *Common Sense*, which advocated independence and was selling in large numbers. Moreover, Howe with his small force abandoned Boston in Mar. and retired to Halifax (Nova Scotia) to await the arrival of more reinforcements under his greater brother the Admiral, who had power to treat. It was too late: the extremists did not want to treat: the **DECLARATION OF INDEPENDENCE** (4 July 1776) was a consequence of Howe's power to do so.

(**17**) The British promptly counter attacked. They took Long I. in Aug, New York and Rhode I. in Sept, and destroyed the rebel L. Champlain flotilla, while the Indians devastated frontier areas but lost severely to the Virginians. When Gen. Howe went into winter quarters, rebel morale was low but many loyalists had been alienated by the use of Indians. When, however, the Congress moved to Baltimore, Philadelphia showed signs of loyalty. Washington's solution was a surprise attack on Trenton on Boxing Day. Three battalions of Hessians surrendered, and rebels began to return to the fight. By this time Benjamin Franklin was negotiating with the French govt. and the British realised that the war would not peter out on its own. All the same Howe needed at least 20,000 more men but the govt. would give him only 2,500, while it fitted out battleships to meet the potential Franco-Spanish threat, and small vessels to deal with privateers from French and Spanish ports.

(**18**) Victory before foreign intervention was now urgent. Lord George Germain and Burgoyne planned to achieve this by cutting New England off from the rest by a southward movement (under Burgoyne) from Canada *via* Ticonderoga down the Hudson to Albany, and a northward movement (under Howe) from New York up the Hudson to meet it. The snag was that during the long march from Montreal to Albany, the rebel revival after Trenton would continue: Washington's reinforced army indeed overran New Jersey. To wait for Burgoyne at New York might involve Howe in losing the south. He tried to draw Washington into a battle but failed, and then with Germain's agreement, decided to attack Philadelphia. Burgoyne reached Ticonderoga on 5 July and with this knowledge Howe left New York by sea. He was delayed by storms, reached Chesapeake Bay on 25 Aug, and defeated the rebels at Brandywine on 11 Sept. Meanwhile Burgoyne was short of food. He lost a force at Bennington, and his subordinate, St. Leger, who had come about-face via the Mohawk, was checked by Schuyler at Ft. Stanwix. With no news from Howe Burgoyne had either to abandon the enterprise or go on. He went on while Howe took Philadelphia (25 Sept.). Four days later began the series of actions which resulted in Gates blocking Burgoyne into **Saratoga**. Howe defeated Washington at Germantown on 4 Oct., but on 17 Oct. 1777 the starving Burgoyne surrendered with about 7,000 men.

(**19**) The great plan, eagerly watched by British and French alike had failed, but the failure became decisive when Washington, after the defeat at Germantown, managed throughout the winter to maintain a front at **Valley Forge.** This allowed time for France to recognise the U.S.A. and sign a treaty of friendship (Mar. 1778).

North wanted to resign; the Rockingham whigs to grant independence, and win the Americans away from the French. This was the occasion of Chatham's famous oration (7 Apr. 1778) in favour of conciliation but against liquidating the empire which he had won, and of his fatal collapse. European interference had been expected. Bourbon foreign policy sought to redress the verdict of the Seven Years War, and gain prestige to back its sagging financial credit. French assistance started to reach the rebels in May; France and Spain entered the war in June. Negotiations between the govt. and the rebels had failed by Oct., when and perhaps because a French fleet, superior in numbers to Lord Howe's, had arrived under d'Estaing. The Spaniards, by now, were besieging Gibraltar, and the Royal Navy, too slowly redeveloped, was having to fight in four theatres (Channel Blockade, Gibraltar, West Indies, American Coast) besides track down privateers and supply the army across 3,000 miles of ocean. On the whole they were successful: the British were not crippled, whereas inflation and internal disputes nearly crippled the rebels.

(**20**) 1779 was a year of stalemate in the north and of fleeting success in the south; in 1780 rebel troops mutinied and Benedict Arnold rejoined the British. The generals concentrated on the Carolinas, where Cornwallis defeated Gates at Camden (S. Carolina) in Aug., and Greene at Guildford Court House in Mar. 1781. The British, however, controlled only the ground on which they stood and eventually retreated to Savannah, which was held with a small force until the end of the war.

(**21**) There now followed a concentration against Virginia, organised by Clinton, using Arnold and Cornwallis from Carolina. The local militia, reinforced by Lafayette, could not hold them, and in the summer 1781 Cornwallis established a base camp at **Yorktown** between the York and James rivers. The British were thus divided when Washington decided to attack them in detail. He feinted at New York, and then pinned Cornwallis against the coast. The British fleet under Sir Samuel Hood appeared in Aug., but a superior French fleet under de Grasse came on its heels. Hood, after a cannonade, retired to New York to get troops from Clinton. Cornwallis held out until 19 Oct., and then surrendered. Hood returned with the troops on 24th.

(**22**) The surrender of this second force, due to temporary loss of maritime control, did not destroy the British military effort in the colonies, where there was a further deadlock. Its true effect was in London; a Commons motion for a speedy peace was defeated in Feb. 1782 by only one vote. The truth was that if the rebels were recognised as an independent state, they would have to solve their own problems, whereas if they were put down, Britain would have to solve them herself. The British were traders not imperialists and the idea of dominating large land masses had never particularly appealed to them. Moreover they were tired of war. In these circumstances Rodney and Hood brought de Grasse to action at the Saints (W. Indies) on 12 Apr. 1782, and won a great victory which ended the French threat in the Atlantic. It failed to revive political morale. North had already fallen in Mar.

(**E**). ***THE PEACE*** (23) The collapse of British morale was a response to dangers of which Yorktown was a symbol. During the latter part of the war Britain had been threatened not only by France and Spain (joined in 1780 by Holland) but by the Armed Neutrality of the Baltic states which might, by depriving her of naval stores, have crippled the Royal Navy. The danger from Europe thus seemed far greater than any possible gain by victory in America. The new govt. of Rockingham, Fox, and Shelburne was committed to a quick settlement in America and a redeployment of forces to compel a favourable peace in Europe. For such a policy the victory off the Saints was, of course, very helpful.

(24) The negotiations with France and the Americans were both conducted in Paris, Fox as foreign secretary being responsible for Europe, Shelburne as colonial secretary for America. Shelburne held that the Americans should be treated generously, and encouraged to develop the interior of the continent, so that with their goodwill a vast new market might be opened up for British trade; and they might be induced to desert their French ally. By the T. of Paris (30 Nov. 1783) these results were in substance achieved, if actually realised some years later.

AMERICAN TAXATION, ON. A speech made by Edm. Burke in 1774 in favour of repealing the American Tea Duty. The argument is based on precedent as well as expediency.

AMERINDIANS A generic term for the tribal peoples of Mongoloid stock in America, particularly the nomadic ones. They apparently numbered about 1.25M in North America at the end of the 15th cent. Their languages differ phonetically and morphologically, some being agglutinative, some analytic, some inflective and some polysynthetic. Their cultures have depended, to a major extent, on their respective staple foods. Thus the Plains Indians such as the Sioux hunted bison; the Californian Athabaskans gathered acorns; the Salish of the N.W. coast were fisheaters; the Iroquois of the East cultivated vegetables. The diversity of speech and culture has made it very difficult to discern a unifying principle in their history. In the 1980s about 140,000 lived in Canada.

AMERY, Leopold Charles Maurice Stennett (1873-1955) *Times* reporter and historian of the Boer War, was on the War Council staff at Versailles in 1917 and 1918, and then, as Baldwin's Sec. of State for the Dominions and Colonies, twice presided at Imperial Conferences. At the famous debate in the Commons on 5-6 May 1940 when Chamberlain was overthrown after the Norwegian disasters, it was Amery who made the leading attack, quoting Cromwell's words with shattering effect: "You have sat too long here for any good you have been doing. Depart, I say, and let us have done with you. In the name of God, go!" He lost his parliamentary seat in 1945.

AMESBURY (Wilts) was an important Saxon royal manor. The Witan met there in 932; a nunnery was founded in 980; it became very rich and was eventually attached to the Angevin convent of Fontevrault.

AMESBURY, Ld. *See* DUNDAS.

AMHARA. *See* ABYSSINIA.

AMHERST (1) Jeffrey (1717-97) 1st Ld. (1776) was recommended as a boy by the D. of Dorset to Gen. Ligonier who passed him on to the D. of Cumberland. By 1756 he had fought in five battles with distinction, and come to the notice of Pitt who in 1758 promoted him maj-gen. and sent him to America with Wolfe under him and 14,000 men. He took Louisbourg in July and Fort Duquesne in Nov. In 1759 he was in charge of one of the three converging advances on Montreal, taking Ticonderoga in July and Crown Point in Aug. He reached Montreal in Sept. 1760, and was at once appointed Gov-Gen. of British North America. He then had to cope with Pontiac's resistance which was beyond his capabilities. He returned to Britain in 1763 and was made (absentee) gov. of Virginia. He quarrelled with the King in 1768, but his popularity was too great for George III, who received him back into favour. From 1772 to 1782 and from 1783 to 1787 he was acting C-in-C and the govt's main military adviser at home in the American rebellion. His nephew **(2) William Pitt (1773-1857) 2nd Ld. AMHERST, 1st E. AMHERST of ARRACAN (1826)** was sent as ambassador to China in 1816 to protest at alleged exactions by mandarins, but refused to make the abject prostrations required in the Imperial presence and was expelled. In 1823 he succeeded the Marquess Hastings as gov-gen. of India. He arrived in Aug. and found a Burmese war on his hands (*see* BURMA). This was followed by a war of succession in Bhurtpur, in which the rajah recognised by the British had to be restored after a palace revolution. Amherst's hesitations prolonged the disturbance, but the state was eventually pacified in 1826. In 1827 he established Simla as the British summer capital, but soon afterwards he retired through ill-health.

AMICABLE GRANT (1525) In 1523, for the support of Henry VIII's warlike policy against France and Scotland, Wolsey demanded the then huge sum of £800,000 in the form of 4s in the pound of all lands and goods. The Commons refused to be browbeaten, even by the Cardinal in person, and granted a subsidy intended to produce £150,000 over four years. Actually it yielded £136,000 in two, but it was not enough to exploit the French defeat at Pavia. Wolsey accordingly, with the support of the council and the judges, issued commissions for the collection of a nominally voluntary 'amicable' grant of one sixth of the goods of the laity, and one third of those of the clergy. This was a benevolence under another name. As it was not imposed upon lands, it was hoped that the gentry would not oppose it, and the higher assessment of the clergy was intended as a sop to the laity. Opposition, however, was bitter, widespread, and remarkably united on what was perceived to be an issue of principle. It was also stimulated by unemployment and a shortage of coin. The City refused to pay, and there were threatening gatherings. Henry stopped Wolsey's repressive measures, and abandoned the grant. This ended the ambitious continental policy, and the loss of face weakened the King's confidence in Wolsey. It also turned Henry towards a technique of governing through rather than in spite of the notables and their parliamentary machine.

AMIATINUS, CODEX. An 8th cent. MS written at Monkwearmouth and Jarrow under Abbot Ceolfrith, containing the earliest surviving Latin text of the Bible. It is at the Laurenziana at Florence.

AMIENS, B. of (Aug. 1918) called by Ludendorff the Black Day of the German army. During their spring offensive the Germans came close to this railway junction whose fall would have isolated the more southerly British armies from their ports at Calais and Boulogne. Hence an Allied counter-attack was inevitable. Haig was in command and most of the infantry was Australian and Canadian but the main punch of the operation came from 450 British tanks, which created a German moral collapse. Their retreat began and never stopped till the Armistice.

AMIENS, MISE (Fr = Decision) OF (23 Jan. 1264). In Dec. 1263 Henry III and the rebellious barons led by Simon de Montfort submitted their dispute to Louis IX of France for arbitration. Henry's case was that the barons' demands, if conceded, too severely restricted the royal power to govern; the barons' that the restrictions were needed to prevent recurrent and recent abuse. By his *mise,* issued at Amiens, Louis rejected the baronial case and, save for a demand for monetary compensation accepted Henry's. Despite Louis' reputation for justice, the barons had expected a political compromise and would not accept the *mise.* War followed. *See* BARONS' WAR.

AMIENS, P. of (25 Mar. 1802) and PRELIMINARIES OF LONDON (1st Oct. 1801) Austria had concluded the P. of Lunéville with France in Feb. 1801. By the preliminaries, Britain agreed to return to their former owners Elba, Malta, Minorca, Tobago, Santa Lucia, Martinique, Dutch Guiana, the Cape of Good Hope, and the French and Dutch Indian factories. She was to keep Ceylon and Trinidad. France was to evacuate Naples and the Papal territories, guarantee the integrity of Portugal and the independence of the Ionian Is. Malta was to be placed under the guarantee of a third power; Egypt returned to Turkey. The preliminaries were regarded as the definitive treaty; the T. of Amiens substantially reproduced them save for Malta which was to be handed over personally to a Grand Master of St. John, with a

Neapolitan garrison, and guaranteed by Britain, France Spain, Austria, Russia and Prussia. These conditions were never fulfilled and the Is. remained in British hands.

AMIN, Idi (1925-) joined the King's African Rifles in 1946 and had risen to Colonel by 1964 when the British left, and he was given command of the Ugandan army. In 1966 he participated in Pres. Milton Obote's repression of Buganda. In 1971 he overthrew Obote himself and set up an oppressive and corrupt regime under which most of the Asians were expelled and migrated to Britain. Disliked by every other country save Russia, Libya and the Palestinian Liberation Organisation, he was overthrown late in 1978 by Tanzanian troops and returning exiles. In Dec. 1980 in free but not excessively scrupulous elections Milton Obote was restored.

AMOBR **(Welsh).** A marriage fine payable to a Lord *cf. Merchet. See also* WELSH LAW.

AMOUNDERNESS *see* LANCASHIRE; PRESTON.

AMOY, HSIA-MEN or SSU-MING (China) the port of the tea-growing portions of Fukien, attracted British and Dutch traders in the 18th Cent. It was one of the five original treaty ports with a western international settlement created by the T. of Nanking in 1842. British treaty rights were abandoned in 1942.

AMRITSAR (Punjab) 'MASSACRE'. Under the influence of Ghandi, violent opposition to British rule began after World War I. In Apr. 1919 communal and political riots did severe damage in Amritsar and threatened worse. On 13th a large hostile crowd defied a ban on meetings. British troops were sent to disperse the crowd, and fired. Many were killed, as much in the struggle to get through the only exit as in the firing. Gen. Dyer (1864-1927) did not know that there was no other way out. He firmly asserted that, casualties notwithstanding, his action had prevented anarchy in the Punjab. The affair, locally serious, was blown up into the dimensions of a massacre by the press of all countries, and did immense damage to the reputation of British Indian rule.

ANABAPTISTS (after 17th cent. BAPTISTS) administered baptism only to adults. The term is used of some large continental groups, predominantly pacifist and communist in inclination, which first appeared in S. and W. Germany in the 1520's and spread to Switzerland, Moravia and Holland. In 1533 a group established a Kingdom of God at Münster under a dictatorship, and practised polygamy. Their state was cruelly suppressed in 1535; their violence, communism and matrimonial habits brought odium on their name. There were a few Anabaptist refugees in England in the 1530's. The proliferation of sects in the 1640s revived them, and they attracted a following in the parliamentarian army, accepted the State, and took the more respectable name of **BAPTISTS**. The old term remained a pejorative well into 19th cent.

ANAESTHETICS. Observations on the pain-killing effects of nitrous oxide were published by Humphry Davy in 1800, and on ether by Michael Faraday in 1818. General anaesthesia was publicly introduced to clinical practice by Wm. Morton, a dentist at Boston (Mass) in 1846. Anaesthesia in child-birth was used in 1847, but clerical and medical opposition was overcome only when Q. Victoria allowed John Snow to deliver her eighth child under anaesthesia in 1853. Snow was the first full time anaesthetist, and he designed much of the original apparatus. In 1884 Carl Koller's observations on the effects of cocaine in the eye led to the introduction of local anaesthetics.

ANANIAS (1) a deacon in Ben Jonson's *The Alchemist*. The name became a popular word for puritan. **(2)** (Acts V) A term of Victorian abuse signifying one who pretends to be more charitable than he really is.

ANARAWD ap GRUFFUDD. *See* DEHEUBARTH-14.

ANARAWD ap Rhodri. *See* GWYNEDD-13 *et seq*.

ANARCHISM is the political doctrine that government is an evil and that if it is necessary there should be as little of it as possible. It has a long history, but its first modern exponent was William Godwin (1756-1836) who published *An Inquiry Concerning Political Justice* in 1793. He advocated a society of small autonomous communities whose members held their property in common. The word 'anarchist' meantime was used as a term of abuse by the moderate Girondins during the French Revolution against their more extremist opponents. The word 'anarchism' was first used in the 1840s by Proud'hon, who applied it to his ideas on controlling the abuse of property. In the 1870s an alliance of labour groups left the Marxist International and in 1881 attempted to organise an Anarchist International. Bakunin, an opponent of Marx, was a leading figure in this ineffectual development. The doctrine always had a strong appeal: so that the Moscow anarchists had to be violently overthrown by the Communists in Apr. 1918, and the Barcelona anarchists were treated with equal ruthlessness by their communist allies in 1939, during the closing stages of the Spanish Civil War.

ANCASTER, Ds. and Es. of. See BERTIE; HEATHCOTE-DRUMMOND-WILLOUGHBY.

ANCHOR Anchors (other than mere weights) were introduced only with the use of iron; they were highly unreliable and a cause of shipwrecks until the introduction of curved arms in 1813. The patent or stockless anchor was invented in 1821; the Admiralty pattern anchor came into general use in the Royal Navy in 1852.

ANCIENT CUSTOM, *ANTIQUA COSTUMA*. See GREAT OR OLD CUSTOM.

ANCIENT (i.e. former royal) DEMESNE of the Crown which had been granted away. 13th cent. lawyers thought that villeins in them should not be prejudiced by the mere grant, and accordingly they were permitted to sue for remedies in the King's court by the *Little Writ of Right Close*.

'ANCIENT' FRONTIERS OF FRANCE in early 19th cent. diplomatic parlance meant not the ancient frontiers but those of 1792, which included Alsace, Lorraine and followed roughly the modern frontier with Belgium. *See* 'NATURAL' FRONTIERS OF FRANCE.

ANCREN RIWLE An early 13th cent. compendium of advice for women trying to be anchoresses. The unknown author recommends hard work, avoidance of gossip, and a limitation on the number of pets.

ANCRUM, E. of. See KER OF FERNIEHURST-3.

ANDAMAN Is. (Bay of Bengal) were used by the Govt. of India as a penal settlement for long term prisoners and exiles from 1857 until 1942 and occupied by the Japanese from 1942 until 1945. In 1956 they became a union territory of India.

ANDELYS, LES (France). This pair of villages at the confluence of the Seine and the Gambon was strategically important in the defence of Normandy against the French. In 1119 Henry I defeated Louis the Fat at the important B. of Bremule nearby, and in 1197 Richard I erected the great fortress of Chateau Gaillard there. Its capture after an eight month siege by Philip Augustus heralded the French conquest of Normandy.

ANDERIDA. *See* PEVENSEY.

ANDERS' ARMY. After Hitler's invasion of Russia in 1941, Polish prisoners of war captured by the Russians in 1939 were released to fight the Germans. Most of them were anti-Russian, and did not wish to fight on the Eastern Front, so after strained negotiations between London and Moscow this new army, under Gen. W. Anders, left Russia to fight alongside the British. It played an important part in the Italian campaign, among others.

ANDERSON, Elizabeth *née* GARRETT (1836-1917) constantly frustrated in her efforts to practice medicine, eventually obtained a licence from the Society of Apothecaries in 1865, on the basis of which she opened a women's and children's dispensary in the Euston Rd, London, in 1866. This developed into a women's hospital staffed by medical women, especially after she got a doctorate of medicine at Paris in 1870. She helped to form, and until 1903 also worked at, the London School of Medicine for Women. Her determination helped to open all professions to women.

ANDERSON, John (1882-1958) 1st E. WAVERLEY (1952) was educated at Edinburgh and Leipzig, and as a civil servant rose to be Sec. to the Mm. of Shipping (1917-9), and was knighted. He then became civil service head successively of depts. of Local Govt. and Health, Inland Revenue, the Irish Office and the Home Office. After a spell as Gov. of Bengal he was elected as a National M.P. for the Scottish Univs, took office as Ld. Privy Seal at once and in 1939 became Home Sec. and Min. of Home Security. In this capacity he was responsible for the domestic preparations for war, air attack, and invasion. The standard-issue family air raid shelter was popularly known as the 'Anderson'. In Oct. 1940 Herbert Morrison succeeded him as Home Sec, and he became Ld. President and then (1943-5) Chanc. of the Exch. He remained responsible for most domestic matters during the war, and was eventually nominated to the King by Churchill as head of govt. should both Churchill and Eden be killed.

ANDERSON v GORRIE (1895) 1 QB 668. The Court of Appeal dismissed an action against three judges of the Supreme Court of Trinidad for damages for acts done maliciously and without jurisdiction in judicial proceedings, as prejudicial to judicial independence.

ANDOVER (Hants). This ancient royal estate and prescriptive borough, of which Enham formed a part, was a Saxon centre of government and a meeting place for church councils. Alphege held a reforming council there, and it was the meeting place of Ethelred the Unready and Olaf Tryggvasson in 994. It had a sheep fair and associated woollen and parchment industries, as well as an iron market.

ANDOVER WORKHOUSE SCANDAL (1845-6). The local Board of Guardians starved the inmates who became ill with rotten food. The outcry caused an overhaul of Poor Law administration.

ANDRASSY (1) Count Gyula (1823-90) a reforming Magyar nationalist and Kossuth's envoy to the Sublime Porte during the Hungarian revolt of 1848, went into exile after the Capitulation of Vilagos. Amnestied in 1857, he acted as mediator between Deák and the Austrians and eventually, on Deák's suggestion, became Hungarian prime minister in 1867. He feared the growing minorities in the Hapsburg dominions and the danger which they might constitute with Russian support. He therefore believed that the internal *status quo* should be maintained, and that it *could* be maintained only through mutual support between Austrians and Magyars each dominant in their own half. He therefore opposed anything which might upset Austrian hegemony in the non-Hungarian territories, including federalism, and alliances against Prussia; and insisted against Beust on neutrality in the Franco-Prussian war. In Nov. 1871 he became joint Foreign Minister. The Balkan crisis put him in a dilemma because it was dangerous to allow any further increase in Russian influence in the Balkans, but equally dangerous to increase the internal Slav minorities by further annexations. The military occupation of Bosnia and Herzegovina in 1878 under the T. of Berlin was thus intended to check the Russians while avoiding the worst consequences of annexation. It was unpopular in all quarters and failed in its object. Meantime Andrassy negotiated an alliance with Germany which remained the basis of Habsburg foreign policy until the disaster of 1918. The treaty was signed in Oct. 1879 and he then resigned. His son **(2) Count Gyula (1860-1929)** entered the Hungarian Parliament in 1885; he was a

constitutionalist and minister of the interior from 1906 to 1910. In Oct. 1918 he was appointed joint foreign minister to save the integrity of the Empire, a purpose frustrated by Pres. Wilson's intransigence, and by internal revolution.

ANDRASSY NOTE 1875. *See* DISRAELI'S SECOND GOVT-3.

ANDRÉ, John (1751-80) adjutant-gen. to the British forces in the American rebellion, was hanged by Washington for his part in Benedict Arnold's conspiracy.

ANDREW, St. His cult came to Scotland in the 8th cent. St. Andrew's became the chief see in the 10th, and the legend that a 'St. Regulus' or 'Rule' had brought his remains there gave it, under royal patronage, increasing importance. By the end of 12th cent. St. Andrew had superseded St. Columba as patron of Scotland, and his cross had been adopted as the national symbol.

ANDREWES, Lancelot (1555-1626) attracted attention as a preacher at St. Paul's in the late 1580's when he was a royal chaplain and Master of Pembroke Hall, Cambridge. Having declined two bishoprics, he became Dean of Westminster in 1601. Averse to Calvinism and highly regarded by James I, he took a leading part in the Hampton Court Conference (1604) and was one of the translators of the Authorised Version. He defended the Oath of Allegiance imposed after the Gunpowder Plot (1605) in several years of polemical exchanges with Card. Bellarmine, and became successively Bp. of Chichester in 1605, and of Ely in 1609, when he was also sworn of the Council. In 1613 he was one of the commission which tried the Essex nullity suit, and in 1617 he went to Scotland with James I to help, unsuccessfully, to persuade the Scots to accept episcopacy. Promoted Bp. of Winchester in 1619 he sat on the commission which investigated allegations of manslaughter against Abp. Abbot in 1621. He was considered a prodigy of learning, and mastered fifteen languages.

ANDROS, Sir Edmund (1637-1714). *See* CHANNEL IS; GUERNSEY; NEW YORK; NEW ENGLAND-2; VIRGINIA.

ANDROS I. is part of the Bahamas.

ANDRUSSOVO, T. of (1667). *See* BALTIC-34.

ANEIRIN (late 6th cent.), author of the *Gododdin* (Votadini), a poem describing a military expedition by the Britons of Lothian against the Angles of the present Yorkshire. The expedition, in which Aneirin took part, was routed at Catterick (Yorks). The poem exists only in a 13th cent. MS, and it is uncertain how much of it is Aneirin's work, but it seems to portray the outlook of a Celtic military aristocracy.

ANGARY is the right of a belligerent to purchase compulsorily any neutral war equipment or transport in its territory. Its exercise on two Turkish battleships built in Britain by public subscription in 1914 helped to turn Turkish opinion against Britain in World War I.

ANGELL, Norman (1874-1967), journalist, economist, and tireless opponent of war, published his *The Great Illusion* in 1910 as a broadside against the warfare mentality, was Labour M.P. for N.Bradford (1929-31), and received the Nobel Peace Prize in 1933.

ANGERS. *See* ANJOU.

ANGEVINS, ENGLISH (PLANTAGENETS). The English Angevins are reckoned to be the three Kings, namely Henry II (r. 1154-89), Richard I (r. 1189-99) and John (r. 1199-1216) who possessed Anjou by descent from Geoffrey of Anjou and Matilda (*see* STEPHEN, MATILDA). The term Plantagenet comes from *planta genesta* or broom, which was an Angevin badge or favour, but it was used as a family name during the period 1216-1399 after Anjou had been lost, when the family still enjoyed the English crown in the reigns of Henry III, Edward I, II and III, and Richard II. *See also* ANJOU AND FOREIGN ANGEVINS and genealogy in Appendix.

ANGINA. *See* SCARLET FEVER.

ANGLES. A Germanic tribe, which, in the 5th cent. inhabited part of Schleswig, where there is still a district called Angeln. Most of them migrated to England. According to Bede, the East and Middle Angles, the Mercians and the Northumbrians (or their royal houses) were descended from them, and they gave their name to England. *See* MAP

ANGLESEY, Marquesses of, *see* PAGET. **Earls of (first creation)** *see* VILLIERS; **(second creation)** *see* ANNESLEY. *See also* BAILEY-11.

ANGLICANISM (1) The doctrine and practices of those in communion with the see of Canterbury, were formulated with royal encouragement and intervention under Elizabeth I, and Charles I and II, principally by Lancelot Andrewes, Win. Laud, Thomas Ken, Sir Thomas Browne and Richard Hooker. **(2)** Led by Laud in the late 1620s and 1630s it provoked a bitter Puritan reaction, but Laudian loyalty to the old order after Charles I's death, and the mental association created between Puritanism and social disorder, produced the victory of Anglicanism at the Restoration. **(3)** The Anglican Church was a reformed branch of the universal church, its clergy deriving their authority by apostolic succession like those of the earlier churches. Accordingly it repudiated both the systems of church government based on Calvinist models, and the doctrinal and temporal authority of the Papacy. Seeking inspiration in scripture and in the traditions of the earliest Christian centuries, it held that notwithstanding probable predestination for some, free will was possible and freedom from the consequences of original sin might be achieved with divine aid, and could lead to salvation. Since scripture held all things necessary to salvation but was itself sometimes apparently contradictory or inconclusive, it followed that reason had to supplement revelation, and that ecclesiastical development was not only desirable but inevitable. It also followed that it was proper to tolerate wide differences of outlook within the church, and that the method of appointment to benefices should encourage diversity of opinion. This justified advowson and govt. ecclesiastical patronage. **(4)** In later times there have been four main trends of Anglican opinion: (a) *Low Churchmen* were in sympathy with the individualistic attitudes of non-conformity, relegated episcopacy, priesthood and sacraments to a low place, frowned on ceremonial and emphasised the importance of preaching. Their name was coined in the 18th cent. as a contrast with the High Churchmen, but at that time it referred to (b) *Latitudinarians* or *Broad Churchmen* who disliked positive theological definition, and interpreted the Book of Common Prayer in a liberal sense. These nowadays are usually called *Modernists* (c) *The High Churchmen* not only emphasised episcopal authority but, as upholders of the Divine Right of Kings, were strongly allied with the House of Stuart. Many (including an archbishop and six bishops) seceded as 'non-jurors' at the accession of the Calvinist William III, and the rest, excluded from preferment as suspected Jacobites, lapsed into obscurity and left the field open to Low Churchmen until the mid-19th cent. when the *Tractarians* (later the *Oxford Movement)* reasserted the High Church position and gained increasing acceptance. (d) The psychological affinity of High Churchmen with Rome, especially in ceremonial, led in the 19th cent. to the rise of *Anglo-Catholicism* which sought as far as possible to assimilate Anglican practices, if not doctrines, with those of the pre-Reformation Roman church. **(5)** In the lay and political world disturbed by 20th cent. disasters, there was a marked swing towards a materialism which relegated Church affairs to a second or even lower place. This was encapsulated in legislation which created a tricameral Church Assembly (later General Synod) able to legislate by Measure, subject to the reservation of theological issues to the Bishops and a supervisory parliamentary mechanism. This went further than the legislature imagined. Parliament, over the years, washed its hands of

Church issues in increasingly cold water, while there grew up within Anglicanism a belief, evidenced by the substitution of non-statutory liturgies for the Book of Common Prayer, that the Church could and should do as it pleased through its legislative institutions. This was latently opposed to the ecumenism promoted since the 1940s by the Papacy and espoused by Anglo-Catholics. A joint Commission had reported in the 1980s that dogmatic differences between the Anglican and Roman communions were now trivial. The ordination of women, a recent issue arising out of lay anti-discrimination movements, destroyed this understanding; the Papacy claimed only infallible knowledge of the unalterable dogmata on faith and morals, but the Anglican Church apparently claimed a much higher ability to alter them by a majority vote. The nature of priesthood was a crucial issue, since women, dogmatically speaking had always been held incapable of consecrating the sacraments, and their admission to the only order which could do so, necessarily jeopardised the authority of that order and the validity of the sacraments. The Papacy's view of its own powers did not permit it to do this; the Anglican church did it by Measure in 1993. From this moment, as an organisation it, perhaps unknowingly, ceased to acknowledge the immutability of principles and set aside the reservation of theological issues to bishops. *See also VERITATIS SPLENDOR*

ANGLING. This ancient popular English pastime was first analysed by Dame Juliana Berners, a nun, in the *Book of St Albans* published by Wynkyn de Worde in 1486. Izaak Walton's *Compleat Angler* appeared in 1653 and had passed through five editions by 1676. Four centuries later, the Anglers' Association claimed to have over a million members.

ANGLO-AMERICAN WAR 1812-5 (1) During the Napoleonic wars the British sought to regulate all seaborne trade to French controlled areas and to man an adequate fleet to do so. For the first they stopped ships *en route* to French ports or carrying French goods and neutrals engaged in any trade normally closed to their country in peacetime. For the second they boarded all ships to impress British seamen and refused to recognise U.S. men's passports without proof of residence in the U.S.A. before 1783.

(2) U.S. Anglophobia and Francophilia had both been modified by French revolutionary atrocities and by Pitt's determination to maintain the Anglo-American trading partnership, but the problems became important after 1805 because both Britain and France intensified their economic hostilities. U.S. blockade running, very damaging to Britain, then became extremely lucrative. Moreover the succession to the Presidency of Jefferson to Adams brought temperamentally anti-British republicans to power and they had scored a propaganda success by purchasing Louisiana from Bonaparte.

(3) Republican policy was, with ostensible even-handedness, to force both sides to lift their restrictions on neutral traders. This disadvantaged the British because Bonaparte would continue to control British trade landings but the British would be unable to control trade at sea. Naturally (1810) he offered to lift his ineffective maritime restrictions. Meanwhile, as expected, the Americans merrily carried falsely manifested contraband to France. Pres. Madison (Feb. 1811) demanded that the British should follow Bonaparte: the British, that Bonaparte should first begin to dismantle his Continental System (July 1812). By this time he was on the way to Moscow to extend it.

(4) In fact, while Bonaparte's system was collapsing, the Americans were embracing a new continental imperialism. In 1811, in order to open the lands beyond the Mississippi, William Henry Harrison (Indiana) had pre-emptively attacked the Shawnee confederacy under their distinguished chief Tecumseh. British and Spanish influence seemed to stand between the States and continental exploitation. A movement to expel European powers from the Americas developed under Henry Clay (Kentucky), Speaker of the House and Peter Porter (S. Carolina), chairman of its Foreign Affairs Committee, which recommended destroying the British control of the Caribbean trade and northern fisheries and conquering Canada. The British, who had a war on their hands already, did not want another but the temperature of U.S. opinion was rising. Pres. Madison embargoed all U.S. ships, which promptly armed themselves for privateering (Apr. 1812). In July he sent a belligerent message to Congress which voted war. A U.S. squadron opened hostilities before the actual declaration.

(5) The war was fought on three fronts. (a) Very small forces attacked Canada and suffered seven defeats. Tecumseh and the British naturally co-operated and the Americans took and abandoned York (Toronto). British efforts to invade U.S. territory failed because the Americans secured naval control of the Great Lakes. During these indecisive confusions Tecumseh was killed in a skirmish on the Thames. (b) U.S. frigates and privateers harassed the Atlantic fisheries and the Canadian southward trade, but the Royal Navy, more importantly engaged in European waters, spared few ships for the theatre yet held its own, with some individual defeats, against the powerful U.S. frigates operating close to their own bases. It could do little against the mainland even though Adm. Cockburn and Gen. Ross daringly burned Washington D.C. and proclaimed a blockade. The sufferers were the New Englanders who had opposed the war and in 1814 were talking of secession. (c) U.S. privateers sufficiently inconvenienced the Caribbean sugar and tobacco traffic for the British to mount combined operations against their bases in the G. of Mexico.

(6) By the autumn of 1814 both sides (who were never out of diplomatic contact) saw that the war could achieve little but trade a great deal and, besides, Britain and her allies were bringing the French war to a victorious conclusion and could soon redeploy against the U.S.A. The continental imperialists were accordingly sidetracked and negotiations opened just as British expeditions sailed against the Gulf ports. Peace was made on 24 Dec. 1814 at Ghent but the news was unknown when Pakenham unsuccessfully attacked New Orleans (Jan. 1815) and Cockburn and Lambert took Mobile (Feb.).

(7) The peace transferred some islands in Passamaquoddy Bay to Britain but otherwise returned the parties to the *status quo* before the war in a world where Bonaparte's fall had solved the maritime but not the American continental issues.

ANGLO-CATHOLICISM. *See* ANGLICANISM-4.

ANGLO-FRENCH UNION PROPOSAL (June 1940) as a result of the collapse of French armies and obvious impending surrender to the Germans, the British govt through Churchill, proposed an indissoluble union of the two countries with a single govt. and common citizenship. It was rejected out of hand by the French prime minister, Paul Reynaud, under the influence of his pro-German mistress. His resignation cleared the way for the defeatist Marshal Pétain to form a govt. ready to sue for an armistice.

ANGLO-GERMAN NAVAL AGREEMENT (1935) theoretically allowed Germany to build warships exceeding the size permitted under the P. of Versailles (1919) up to a tonnage amounting for capital ships to 35% and for submarines to 45% of the British. In practice it took so long to design and build the capital ships that only two battle cruisers were ready for World War II and the vast *Bismarck* and *Tirpitz* not until 1940.

ANGLO-INDIANS (1) those Englishmen who made a lifelong career for themselves in India in the 19th and 20th cents. They seldom married Indians and were never half-castes. (2) The term was later confusingly used for persons of mixed English and Indian ancestry who nowadays have a distinct culture.

ANGLO IRISH TREATY (1921). *See* IRELAND-1-14.

ANGLO-JAPANESE ALLIANCE (1902). *See* JAPAN-4 & 5.

ANGLO-NORMAN or ANGLO-FRENCH was a western type of French imported into Britain which varied with the origin of the speaker and became increasingly insular. The first important Anglo-Norman literary work was the 12th cent. *Voyage of St. Brendan* and there were didactic and moralising works, *Bruts*, and practical treatises often based on Latin originals. The best text of the *Song of Roland* is in Anglo-Norman. By the 14th cent. it was merging into English, but John Gower's (?1330-1408) Anglo-Norman was still very French. It continued in use in an increasingly barbarous form in legal proceedings until 1708. Certain legal technical terms, e.g. 'cestui que vie' remain.

ANGLO-NORMANS were (1) those leaders who followed William I and who had estates on both sides of the Channel. These descended with varying fortunes and permutations in their families until the French conquest of Normandy in 1207, when most of them were forced to choose between English and French allegiance. Some, however, had already gone, or then went, to Wales, Scotland or Ireland; (2) those leaders who followed Strongbow to Ireland in 1166 or who reinforced the conquest there later on, and who mostly had estates in the Pale, Munster and later in parts of Ulster. Some of their descendents, such as Chris de Burgh the pop singer, were still great magnates six centuries later, though wars in the intervals had moved them from one estate to another many times.

ANGLO-PORTUGUESE COMMERCIAL T. (1654). *See* PORTUGAL AFTER 1640. The occasion of this treaty was the piratical use of Lisbon by the Palatine Princes in 1649, and the resulting damage to Anglo-Portuguese trade. Six articles provided for Portuguese reparations for damage to Blake's fleet and English mercantile interests. Nine others, of permanent effect, gave each party the right to trade with the colonies of the other; permitted English warships to use Portuguese ports for repairs; limited Portuguese customs duties on English goods to a maximum of 23% and exempted English merchants from Portuguese legal process save through a specially appointed Judge-Conservator of the English. *See* METHUEN T.

ANGLO-PORTUGUESE CONGO T. (Feb. 1884). Britain recognised Portuguese sovereignty north of Ambriz, especially at the mouth of the Congo in return for free navigation on the Congo R., and also on the Zambesi. The treaty was abandoned.

ANGLO-PORTUGUESE MARRIAGE T. (1661). *See* PORTUGAL AFTER 1640. Charles II was to marry the Infanta Catherine of Braganza, elder sister of Afonso VI, who was to bring a dowry of 2M cruzados, Bombay and Tangier. Britain was to have free trade in India, and in Brazil at Bahia, Pernambuco and Rio de Janeiro. Ceylon, if recovered from the Dutch, was to be partitioned. In return Britain was to defend Portugal with her fleet against Spain, and, by a secret article, the Portuguese colonies against all comers: Britain was not to make a peace with Spain which restricted her ability to fulfil her obligations under the Treaty.

ANGLO-RUSSIAN CONVENTION (Aug. 1907) was a set of agreed forbearances on points of friction. (1) The two powers agreed not to intervene or send missions to Tibet nor to negotiate with her save through the Chinese as suzerain. (2) Russia would have political relations with Afghanistan only through Britain which would make no changes in the status of that country or take any action there threatening Russia. (3) The two powers recognised three zones in Persia under the Shah's sovereignty; a

Russian N.W. zone comprising the best territory and the most important towns except for Ispahan; a slightly smaller British zone along the Afghan and Indian frontiers and thirdly a neutral zone larger than either in between which was mostly desert or on the Gulf coast. The Russians had built roads and railways towards Persia and their interest was economic, whereas the British interest was strategic. As Russia was already in alliance with France which had an *entente* with Britain, the various agreements between the three powers grew naturally into a Triple *Entente*. The Persian arrangements did not always work smoothly especially after the development of the Persian oil wells in the neutral zone, which were accessible to the British by sea and an object of Russian ambition. The other agreements were observed in spirit at least, till World War II.

ANGLO-SAXONS. The collective name usually applied to the permanently settled Germanic inhabitants of Britain before the Norman Conquest, to distinguish them **(1)** from their British and Celtic predecessors in Britain, **(2)** from the 'Old Saxons' who remained in Europe and **(3)** from the Vikings and Danes of later migrations. *See* ANGLES, ENGLISH. **(4)** English speakers generally.

ANGLO-SAXON CHRONICLE. K. Alfred had the *Anglo-Saxon Chronicle* prepared (890-2) and sent copies to major monasteries for continuation. Seven exist, six in Old English and one partly in Old English and partly in Latin. The oldest, **(A1)** known as the PARKER or WINCHESTER Chronicle begins at A.D. 1, was written at Winchester in a single hand up to 891 and by various scribes until 1001. It was then transferred to Canterbury where Kentish interpolations were made and it was continued until 1070. Its record of events after 973 is scanty. A2, mostly burned in 1731, was an 11th cent. copy of A1. Its contents are known from a printed version of 1643. **B** is written in a single hand and ends at 977. **C** is in various 11th cent. hands and ends at 1066. B and C are thought to be based on a West Saxon Chronicle from Abingdon, possibly kept at Sherborne and distributed. **D** is written in various 11th cent. hands, probably at Worcester, and ends in 1079. **E**, written at Peterborough, ends in 1154 but D and E, where they overlap, probably have a common source (now lost) in the North of England. **F** is in Old English and Latin, and was written at Canterbury. All the versions are customarily called 'The Anglo-Saxon Chronicle' but each contains material peculiar to itself.

ANGLO-SOVIET PACT (1942). The British and Russian govts. were unable to agree in 1941 because the latter wished to keep the proceeds of the Thieves Compact, while demanding premature British landings on the European Channel coast. Accordingly they agreed to pursue the war against Germany (which they could not avoid doing) and resist post-war German aggressions (which would be improbable).

ANGOLA was first reached by the Portuguese in 1482. They founded Loanda in 1575, and by 1617, when they founded Benguela, they had established their sovereignty over the coast. The Dutch attacked in 1640 but were driven out in 1648.

Until 1830 its main wealth lay in the export of slaves to Brazil, and only after this was stopped did exploration, pacification and development exploit the interior resources. Progress, however, was slow because of a continued trade in so-called indentured labour. The Benguela railway was begun in 1902: the inland tribes conquered only by 1915 and forced labour formally abolished only in 1953. A Marxist inspired 'anti-colonial' rebellion began in Feb. 1961 but made little progress until supported by Russian financed Cuban troops. The rebels then took over the towns, while the legitimate parties (now stigmatised as rebels) maintained a successful resistance in the countryside supported by South Africa. The conflict continued till the Gorbachev regime in the U.S.S.R. abandoned adventurist African policies in 1986.

ANGOULÊME and its territory **ANGOUMOIS (Fr.)** in the middle ages was a vassal county of Aquitaine, and mostly shared its fortunes, but in 1373 it was permanently occupied and subsequently annexed by the French.

ANGUS, Es. of. *See* UMFREVILLE; DOUGLAS (RED)

ANHALT (Germany). This otherwise unremarkable and often subdivided Saxon duchy produced three important figures: **(1)** CHRISTIAN I of Anhalt-Bernburg, Chancellor to Frederick V, Elector Palatine and son-in-law of James I *(see* THIRTY YEARS WAR). **(2)** LEOPOLD I of Anhalt-Dessau (1676-1747) (The Old Dessauer) who as a general in Prussian service organised (and often commanded) the armies which won Frederick the Great's victories, and **(3)** his cousin and occasional opponent Sophia of Anhalt-Zerbst, later Czarina of Russia, and better known as CATHERINE the Great (1729-1796).

ANILINE was first obtained from indigo by O. Unverdorben in 1826 and from coal tar by Runge in 1834. The vast German chemical industry originated from these discoveries.

ANJOU (France) and FOREIGN ANGEVINS. Anjou was an organised county in the late 9th cent. when its Count, Robert the Strong (the founder of its **First House)** defeated the Normans. It became one of the most important of the major French fiefs, and its ruthless Count FULK III Nera (the Black) (r. 987-1040) and his four successors widely extended it. FULK V (r. 1109-31) married twice. By his first wife, a Countess of Maine, he had GEOFFREY V, Plantagenet (r. 1131-51); he married Matilda of England and was the father of King HENRY II and of another Geoffrey who ceded his rights in Anjou and Maine to Henry II. Secondly Fulk V married Melisende of Jerusalem, and reigned as King at Jerusalem from 1131 to 1143. Thus England and Jerusalem had related dynasties in the time of the crusading K. RICHARD I.

The inclusion of Anjou in a greater Anglo-Norman empire made local delegation essential, and in 1175 K. Henry II appointed a seneschal whose office became hereditary in the family of William des Roches. Hence when the French K. Philip Augustus seized the county in 1205, he was able to deal with a permanent local administration which maintained the practical independence of the county.

The **Second Angevin House** arose from the enfeoffment by St. Louis of his brother CHARLES I of Anjou (r. 1246-85) whose European ambitions kept him absent, and led through a variety of marriages to the establishment of Angevin ruling houses in Poland, Hungary, Sicily, Taranto and Achaia. His career being ruined by the Sicilian Vespers in 1282, his granddaughter married CHARLES of Valois (r. 1290-1325) and the county passed by inheritance to the French crown at the accession of King Philip VI in 1328.

The **Third Angevin House** arose when King John II enfeoffed his second son LOUIS I in 1360. He was adopted by his relative Joan of Sicily, and in 1383 became King of Sicily. The county and the Sicilian claims of its counts passed finally to King Louis XI of France at the death of CHARLES V of Anjou in 1481. *See* ANGEVINS, ENGLISH

ANJOU, D. of. *See* ELIZABETH I-20 *et seq.*

ANIMALS, CRUELTY TO. Baiting of tethered animals, particularly bulls and bears, cockfighting organised in rounds called 'mains' often in specially built cockpits, and fights between dogs bred for the purpose, were common till the end of the 18th cent. when opinion, encouraged by Methodism, gained ground against such barbarities. The R. Society for the Prevention of Cruelty to Animals was founded in 1824, a similar Scottish society in 1839. Sporadic legislation followed, and was consolidated in the Protection of Animals Act 1911. This was supplemented in 1934 and 1954 by which time the Societies' main activity was directed at the keeping of animals in conditions amounting to cruelty and at cruel methods of slaughter, but the older rules against fighting were still not invariably obeyed and organised cockfights and dog fights were still being uncovered in 1991. An agitation against cruel conditions of animal exports forced a change in the law in 1995.

ANIMAL EPIDEMICS could be catastrophic especially in pre-industrial societies, where they affected a major source not only of food, but of fertilizers and agricultural power.

A pandemic of **cattle plague,** probably imported by the Huns, began in 376, and became endemic in the west. There were unidentified outbreaks in Britain in 466, in Scotland in 502, in Britain and Ireland in 547, and the years 568-82 saw immense animal mortalities everywhere from Italy to Ireland. In 591 a cattle disease, perhaps **anthrax,** almost wiped out the French and Flemish breeding stock and deer. From 689 to 701 **'murrain'** devastated Ireland and, particularly in 694, England. There were further visitations in 770-8. In 791 Charlemagne, at war with the Huns, lost most of his horses by disease. His campaigns also spread **rinderpest** which came to Britain in 809 or 810. Murrain attacked English cattle in 869, and there was anthrax in Britain and Europe in 878 and intermittently till 908. Rinderpest ravaged Europe from 940 to 942, and **dysenteric** epidemics Britain in 986-7 and 995. England suffered in 1054 and in 1085-7, in 1092-4, 1103 and 1110. In 1111-2 an anthrax-like disease carried off men, animals and birds. Calamitous epidemics among cattle and pigs in 1131-4 destroyed ploughing teams, so much that land went out of cultivation. European and English outbreaks of Rinderpest in 1222-3 and 1238 have been ascribed to the Mongol incursions. In 1252 and 1254 a spectacular English visitation of anthrax destroyed animals of all kinds, and birds. In 1274 a merino sheep from Spain brought **ovine smallpox** to Northumberland; this continued until 1312. In the Murrain of 1333, cattle and sheep losses varied from 50% at Maldon to 34% at Basing. Between 1348 and 1410 Norfolk records indicate endemic diseases which killed cattle, sheep, poultry and bees in large numbers. They were lumped together as the **common murrain.** Irish records mention cattle mortalities in 1423, 1443, and 1445-50. In 1479-80 there was a dangerous epidemic in England. Thereafter, though continental outbreaks were frequent, they seem to have attained only a reduced scale in Britain until 1661-3, when diseases attacked all farm animals, particularly sheep. A similar outbreak with a different emphasis littered the countryside with dead cattle. 1693 was an epidemic year for **liver fluke** among sheep, 1714 a year for rinderpest imported from Holland, and in 1735 there was a countrywide outbreak of **sheep rot** which cluttered up the roads with carcases. This disease recurred in 1738. In 1745 there began a severe 12-year outbreak of rinderpest, also of Dutch origin. This had important social and economic effects. Cattle farming became so difficult that much pasture was ploughed up and, assisted by exceptional harvests, the price of grain fell and exports of grain rose sharply. In 1746 there was legislation to suppress the disease with compensation, but it took time to enforce and in 1747 the difficulties were compounded by a further visitation of sheep rot. Rinderpest eventually died down in 1758, but sheep rot returned in 1766 and both recurred in 1769. Ruthless slaughtering ended the rinderpest in 1770 and again in 1781. In the years 1789 to 1794, 1798, 1808 to 1810, 1816 to 1818 and 1823 there were serious recurrences of sheep rot, and in 1828 there began a four year epidemic which destroyed 2M sheep in the winter of 1830-1 alone.

Foot-and-mouth appeared for the first time in 1839 and continued among sheep and pigs as well as cattle till 1841, when it had become endemic. In 1847 **sheep pox** was imported from Germany. In 1857 there was a foot-and-mouth disaster, and sheep rot reappeared on a dangerous scale in 1860. In 1865-6 rinderpest from Russia killed 250,000 cattle in the London area, but a determined campaign stamped it out altogether by 1871. Its place was taken in those years by foot-and-mouth, and in 1872 by a growing incidence of **pleuro-pneumonia** among cattle and in 1878 by **swine fever.** These, with foot-and-mouth accompanied the appalling sheep rot visitation of 1879-81 which killed 6,000,000 sheep. The Black Year (1879) provoked the appointment of the Richmond Commission.

In 1886 the first measures were taken against anthrax and in 1890 an act against pleuro-pneumonia rapidly reduced its incidence. The recent successes and the foot-and-mouth epidemic of 1892 brought the Contagious Diseases of Animals Act, which created permanent powers of compulsory slaughter with compensation, and of movement prohibition. Pleuro-pneumonia was eliminated by 1900 and most epidemic diseases were well controlled until the system was neglected during World War I. As a result there were virulent outbreaks of foot-and-mouth in 1922-5. In 1926, moreover, **fowl pest** made a first and damaging visitation to Britain and thereafter lurked in endemic form, while foot-and-mouth reappeared in Scotland and porcine anthrax in England in 1952. In 1953-5 **myxomatosis** from France wiped out all but a few rabbits, and so greatly increased arable productivity and the stability of coastal dunes. By 1986 the rabbit population was re-establishing itself but meantime **scrapey**, a disease of sheep, had infected cattle where it became known as **mad cow disease.** This also affected humans by 1994. It led to a French-inspired E.U. embargo on British beef in 1998.

ANNALES CAMBRIAE **(Lat = Annals of Wales).** These year by year entries begin in the 5th cent. and, until the 8th cent., are mostly derived from Irish and Cumbrian sources. Thereafter until 13th cent. they were probably compiled at St. Davids.

ANNALS OF ULSTER, compiled in several different monasteries, begin in the 5th cent. but are contemporary with the events which they record only after the 6th. They end in the 10th cent.

ANNAM. See INDOCHINA.

ANNANDALE. See BRUCE-2 *et seq.*

ANNANDALE, MARQUESSES of. See JOHNSTONE.

ANNAPOLIS ROYAL (Nova Scotia) was fd as **Port Royal** in 1605. It was ceded to France in 1632 and became an important French stronghold and an objective of British military planning until captured in 1710. Ceded to Britain in 1713 was the capital of Nova Scotia until 1750.

ANNATES (or FIRST FRUITS) were the first year's revenue of a benefice which a new appointee paid to his superior, or in the case of a bishop or archbishop, to the Papacy. Papal annates became general in 13th cent. through direct papal nominations to livings. In England payment to Rome was restricted by the **Act of Annates (1532)** to 5% of net revenue and the act also permitted consecration by the metropolitan and another bishop if the Pope refused consecrations as a result of the Act. The main inconvenience of Annates as a method of Papal taxation was that an applicant for a benefice had to borrow in order to obtain the benefice. Annates under the Act of 1532 were transferred to the Crown in 1534 (*see* HENRY VIII-11) and to Queen Anne's Bounty in 1704.

ANNE (1665-1714) Queen (1702) was the second *d.* of James D. of York (later James II) and Anne Hyde, who died in 1671. **(1)** James married Mary of Modena in 1673, and in their R. Catholic circle Anne was brought up, at Charles II's command, as an Anglican by Lady Frances Villiers. Her health was always poor. In 1678 and 1679 she was in the Low Countries with her father and in 1680 and 1681 in Scotland. An attempt to marry her to George of Hanover (later George I) was rejected by the Hanoverian court and permanently prejudiced her against the Hanoverians. She married George, brother of Christian V of Denmark in July 1683, and in her new separate establishment (*see* COCKPIT) her childhood friend Sarah Jennings (then Lady Churchill) was a lady of the bedchamber. They addressed each other as Mrs Morley (Anne) and Mrs Freeman (Sarah). By now Anne was estranged from her stepmother, and the religious and political tides were moving against her father; hence her protestant friends ensured that she kept on good terms with her elder sister Mary, the Princess of Orange. When Mary of Modena had a son, she gave some credence to the warming pan myth and escaped from James to William of Orange. The Declaration of Right settled the succession upon her after William and Mary, and their children, if any. In July 1689 she gave birth to William, D. of Gloucester, the only one of her 15 offspring to survive infancy.

(2) From 1690 Anne became increasingly estranged from William and Mary. They distrusted the Churchills. She had a romantic feeling in favour of succession through her father's descendents; her High Anglicanism was out of favour with the Calvinist King; and probably Mary was jealous of her happy married life. The King granted away James' private estate to which she had the best claim, and a related motion in the Commons to increase her civil list, which was really a symptom of William's unpopularity, was taken by him and the queen as evidence of a plot. Early in 1692 matters came to an open breach when the king dismissed Marlborough from all his employments, and Anne promptly retired to Sion House with her Mrs Freeman. There was a partial reconciliation with Mary in Aug. 1693.

(3) In 1694 Mary died childless, and Anne suddenly became important. William reinstated Marlborough at court, and from Mar. 1695 she gave support to William's policies and govt. Nevertheless he kept her in the background and never, for example, conferred a regency upon her during any of his absences. This was understandable from William's point of view, but in July 1700 the young D. of Gloucester died, and a further settlement became urgent. In 1701 she consented to the Act of Settlement which established the Hanoverian succession. Three months later her father died, and Louis XIV provocatively recognised his son as James III. Six months later still William III died and she ascended the throne.

(4) The principal first decisions of the reign were the appointment of commissioners to treat for the union with Scotland, the granting of £700,000 a year to the Queen and £100,000 to her husband, the appointment of Marlborough as Captain-Gen., of Godolphin as Lord Treasurer, of their friends and supporters to other offices and of Sarah as Mistress of the Robes. Always devout, Anne took church patronage into her own hands. Most important of all, war was declared on France (4 May). *See* SPANISH SUCCESSION, WAR OF.

(5) Party politics were still in their infancy, though the distinction between the aristocratic, religiously tolerant or free thinking Whigs and the Tory Anglican squires was (with gradations and eccentricities) recognised. Marlborough and Godolphin were ready to co-operate with those who would help efficiently to prosecute the war. On the whole the Whigs offered the best support, but the parliament of 1702 contained a great many groupings, based mainly on personal relationships. The notion of a single party govt. was still unborn. Tories still held high office and made an Occasional Conformity Bill the price of support. In so doing they appealed to the Queen's Anglicanism: Marlborough and Godolphin, who opposed the bill on practical grounds had to vote for it in order not to upset

her. Nevertheless the bill was thrown out both in 1703 and in 1704.

(6) The risk of Tory mischief-making, and the demands of the Whig Lords (*see* JUNTO) for profit and place created mounting pressure upon Anne to replace Tories by Whigs. The general election of 1705 produced a whig parliament, but it was here that a hidden fissure in English governmental stability revealed itself. Anne was ready to support Marlborough's war policy for the defence of true religion and her crown, but his Tory opponents were more Anglican than his whig supporters who steadily replaced them. Sunderland, Marlborough's son-in-law, became Sec. of State in 1706; in 1708 Wharton became Lord-Lieut of Ireland, and Somers Lord President; the election of 1708 produced a strong whig majority; in 1709 Orford took the Admiralty. Anne's dislike of these changes had been restrained by the victorious course of the war, but no significant victory marked 1707. There was growing estrangement between her and Marlborough's masterful duchess, now turned shrewish. Moreover Marlborough and Godolphin interfered with Anne's cherished powers of ecclesiastical appointment. In these circumstances the soothing appearance at court of the Duchess' Tory cousin Abigail Hill (Mrs Masham), a relative of the Tory speaker Robert Harley, began to undermine the whig position. The victory at the bloody B. of Malplaquet was pyrrhic. The Tories argued loudly for a new war policy to be waged by sea instead of by land, and Harley gathered much varied support and the services of able pamphleteers.

(7) Defeats and the great famine of 1709 had beaten Louis XIV almost to his knees, and he opened peace negotiations. The British unreasonably insisted that Louis should help the Allies to turn his own grandson out of Spain, for the Bourbon victory at Almanza (1707) had made it difficult to do it themselves. Naturally Louis rejected this insult and appealed to the pride in French public opinion. The English longing for peace was very strong, and the whigs could now be blamed for irresponsibly frustrating it. Into this war-weariness burst the extraordinary episode of Dr Sacheverell, a worthless parson who in 1709 preached an inflammatory sermon in London, naming most of the ministers and especially Godolphin as enemies of religion. This coincided with Anne's opinion of them, which Abigail naturally inflamed. The ministers over-reacted and had him impeached, thereby exaggerating his importance and turning him into a popular symbol. There were riots, pamphlets and arson of dissenter's chapels. The Lords convicted him only by 69 to 52, and passed a derisory sentence. In the general jubilation the govt's simultaneous alienation from the people and the throne was plain for all to see. Harley, through Abigail, could safely advise Anne to break up the administration. She dismissed Sunderland in June and Godolphin in Aug. The general elections in Nov. returned a Tory majority. The govt. was now led by Harley, created E. of Oxford, and by Bolingbroke. Somers stayed on in office. Marlborough, as the ablest available general, was necessary as the principal bargaining weapon, for the Tories were unavoidably committed to peace. Their so-called alternative war policy was found to be no alternative at all. In the Low Countries Marlborough had scored the few successes of 1710. By Jan. 1711 Britain's Habsburg ally in Spain was in full retreat. Hence, when the French made secret approaches intended to split the Grand Alliance, the govt. responded by sending Matthew Prior to Paris, for covert negotiations.

(8) The terms were that Britain should abandon her allies in return for trade, and naval and colonial advantages, later mostly embodied in the peace treaties (*see* UTRECHT, P. of 1713). This involved abandoning the Habsburg claimant to Spain. The allies were not, of course, told this, but merely informed that there was to be a general peace congress. To this the Emperor and the

Dutch suspiciously agreed but in Apr. 1711 the Emperor Joseph I died suddenly, and Charles, who was his successor, became Emperor in Oct. There was now need for haste, lest the French come to a separate settlement with him, but the allies did their best to influence parliament, and secured a vote in the Lords against any peace which left any Spanish possession in Bourbon hands. The govt. then retaliated by getting Anne to dismiss Marlborough (31 Dec. 1711) on charges of peculation, which were false but would take time to rebut.

(9) The Congress opened at Utrecht in Jan. 1712. There was no truce, but the instructions to the new British C-in-C, the D. of Ormonde, not to venture a battle or even a siege, were communicated to the French. The allies soon sensed their betrayal, but as the British retired towards Dunkirk the military pressure upon the allies grew. Anne announced Britain's terms of peace (i.e. those already agreed) in June, and on 12 July there was an Anglo-French armistice which Ormonde invited the allies to join. Despite the odds, the allies decided to fight on, but without the support of British troops and money, their case was hopeless. With successive victories, however, the French raised their terms against the allies until in Feb. 1713 the govt. began to fear the destruction of the European balance and threatened to resume the war. As a result the French hastened to a settlement with Britain in Apr., just as the Emperor, goaded by unreasonable French demands in Italy, resolved to fight it out. The Austrian (Rastatt) and German (Baden) peace treaties had to wait another year. In England, Anne helped to drive the necessary legislation through the Lords by creating or accelerating 12 peerages.

(10) The wars and the Civil War had consolidated British opinion against the extreme courses represented not only by puritanism and the Jacobites, but even the Anglican extremism of the Tory govt. manifested in the Occasional Conformity Act of 1711, and the Schism Act of 1714. Anne hated depriving her own family of any right to the throne, and was hostile to the Hanoverians; and the politicians were obsessed with the issue of the succession when Anne fell ill at Christmas 1713. The Whigs were united in favour of Hanover; Oxford and Bolingbroke quarrelled. The identity of those in office at the moment of the Queen's death seemed vital. The Whigs, with some show of right, accused Bolingbroke and Oxford of planning a *coup d'état*. Surrounded by quarrels and intrigues, Anne on her death-bed gave the Treasurership to the neutral D. of Shrewsbury. Bolingbroke fled, ultimately to Jacobite employment.

ANNE, reigning Duchess of BRITTANY (1478-1514). *See* BRITITANY-5,6.

ANNE BOLEYN. *See* BOLEYN HENRY VIII.

ANNE NEVILLE (1456-85) *d.* of Warwick the Kingmaker and Anne Beauchamp, was betrothed at Angers in 1470 to Edward, Prince of Wales, to be married if Warwick's attempt to restore Edward's father Henry VI should succeed. She was one of the wealthiest heiresses of her time. Warwick and Edward were both killed, and in 1474 she married Richard of Gloucester, later Richard III, whom she survived only a year.

ANNE OF BOHEMIA (1366-1394) *d.* of the Emperor Charles II was betrothed to Richard II in 1379, but married him only in 1382. It was originally an unpopular match and her Bohemian retinue was thought to be expensive, but he adored her and she was respected for her piety. She tried unsuccessfully to save the lives of Richard's advisers condemned in the Merciless Parliament of 1388. Though Wyclif's writings came to Bohemia at this time, there is no known evidence that she patronised Lollardy.

ANNE OF CLEVES (1515-1557). Her father was John, Duke of Cleves (q.v.), the most powerful of the West German protestant princes, and so considered by Thomas

Cromwell to be a suitable wife for Henry VIII after Queen Jane Seymour died in 1537. The match was arranged in 1539, and though Henry found her repellent, the marriage took place in 1540. On the failure of Cromwell's policy and his fall, the marriage was annulled by parliament, and she was pensioned off, on the condition that she remained in England.

ANNE OF DENMARK (1574-1619) married James VI and I in 1590 at Opsloe (Oslo) in Norway. After James became King of England she was notable as a patroness of literature (especially of Jonson and Dekker) and of architecture.

ANNESLEY (1) Sir Francis (1585-1660) 1st Ld. MOUNTNORRIS (1628) 1st Vist. VALENTIA (1642) took a leading part in the plantation of Ulster in 1608 and was S. of State for Ireland in 1618. Court faction got him the posts of vice-treas. and receiver-gen. in 1625 in spite of his opposition to Lord Deputy Falkland. He helped to secure Falkland's recall in 1629 and became treas.-at-war in 1632. In 1633 he quarrelled with Lord Deputy Wentworth (Strafford) and was condemned to death for peculation, but only imprisoned. The Commons declared this sentence unjust in 1641, and he later served as S. of State at Dublin under Henry Cromwell. His son (2) **Arthur (1614-86) 1st E. of ANGLESEY (1661)** had been a parliamentary diplomatic agent in Ireland in 1645 and 1647, and M.P. for Dublin in 1658. In 1660 Charles II commissioned him to treat with former parliamentarians for their support when he was also Pres. of the Council of State and he used his position and his seat in the Convention Parliament to promote a Restoration on terms which would reconcile most parties. He was V.-Treas. for Ireland from 1660 to 1667 and Privy Seal from 1672 to 1682. Among their descendants (3) the scandalous **Richard (1694-1761) 6th E., 5th Ld. ALTHAM** and the holder of four other titles had his nephew (4) **James (1715-60)** the rightful Lord Altham, sent to America as a slave, and was subsequently sued, but staved off disaster because James could not afford to press the proceedings. When Richard died, his mistresses claimed his titles for their children and one (5) **Juliana (?-?)** succeeded in relation to the Mountnorris and Valentia peerages.

ANNEXATION, ACT OF (Scot. 1587). *See* JAMES VI-8.

ANNONA. *See* BRITAIN, ROMAN-6.

ANNUAL REGISTER. *See* BURKE.

ANNULMENT. *See* DIVORCE; HENRY VIII.

ANNUNCIATION, CHURCH OF THE. *See* PALESTINE; CRUSADER PILGRIMAGE CHURCHES.

ANNUS MIRABILIS **(Lat = Wonderful Year), 1759.** *See* SEVEN YEARS WAR-7.

ANONIMALLE CHRONICLE, written in French at St Mary's Abbey, York, is a source for the years 1333-81, based on much lost contemporary literature. About half of it is devoted to the years 1376-81, particularly the Good Parliament and the Peasants' Revolt of 1381. The writer is sometimes called *The Anonymous of York.*

ANSCHLUSS (Ger = combination), was the name given to Hitler's invasion and subjugation of Austria in Mar. 1938.

ANSELM, St. and Abp. (1033-1109) born and educated at Aosta, entered the monastery of Bec in 1060, succeeded Lanfranc as prior in 1063 and was abbot from 1078. From Bec he early visited Canterbury where he was admitted a member of Christchurch. His reputation for piety and learning was such that the Conqueror called for him to his death-bed and when Abp. Lanfranc died in 1089 Anselm was universally considered to be his obvious successor. William Rufus, however, kept the see of Canterbury vacant and seized the revenues until 1093, when he thought that he was dying and hurriedly appointed Anselm. The latter resisted appointment strongly, but eventually agreed on condition that all Canterbury estates be restored, that the King should trust his advice in all spiritual matters, and that the reforming Pope Urban II should be recognised in preference to the imperialist anti-Pope Clement III. Discussion on the last and most important was postponed, but had soon to be raised again because Anselm needed a *pallium* to enable him to consecrate other bishops and it could be obtained only from a Pope in person. His request for leave to get the *pallium* precipitated a crisis. At the Council of Rockingham in Feb. 1095, most of the bishops supported the King while the barons supported Anselm.

The decision was postponed and William now tried at Rome to trade recognition of Urban II for the deposition of Anselm. A papal legate, Walter of Albano, accompanied the mission back to England. He conceded the royal rights to exclude papal letters and legates from England and so obtained recognition of Urban II. Then he flatly refused to depose Anselm and left a *pallium* for him. There could be no real reconciliation especially as Anselm habitually denounced the sexual morality of the King and his court. In 1097 William accused him of stinting the feudal levy in Wales, and of other secular malpractices. Anselm several times asked leave to discuss his problems with the Pope and eventually went without. The see was promptly forfeited. In Rome he was received with high honour and in 1099 he was present at the Easter Council which passed decrees against lay investiture, simony and clerical marriage. At Henry I's accession in 1100 he returned to England; he refused a demand (based on custom) for homage on the restitution of his temporalities as being contrary to the decrees. On a personal level he and Henry were on good terms and he raised no objection when Henry proposed to negotiate a modification of the decrees in favour of the English custom. The Pope remained obdurate and in 1103 Anselm even accompanied the King's mission to Rome himself. This too was fruitless; he remained abroad, but in 1105 the Pope excommunicated the King's chief adviser, Robert of Meulan and the Bishops whom the King had invested, and Anselm threatened to excommunicate the King himself. The result was a compromise, probably drafted by Ivo of Chartres and Adela of Blois, ratified in London in 1107. The King gave up spiritual investiture and conceded free elections; Anselm agreed that a bishop should not be refused consecration because he had already done homage for his temporalities. The balance of advantage was with the Crown since elections were always conducted in the royal court. This settlement lasted for centuries. Anselm's theological writings, mostly composed at Bec, have given him a special and enduring reputation, but the most important, *Cur Deus Homo?* (Lat = Why is God Human?) on the Atonement, was written in exile.

ANSON, George (1672-1762) 1st Ld. (1747) circumnavigated the world between 1740 and 1744, capturing the Manila Galleon, which he sold at Canton, on the way. His losses by scurvy inspired Lind's researches into the use of citrus fruits. As C-in-C of the Channel Fleet he defeated the French off C. Finisterre in 1746 and thenceforth as a sea lord he reorganised the navy. He instituted officers' uniforms, classified ships into six ratings, revised the Articles of War, established the naval hospital at Haslar and appointed Lind to it in 1753, and created the corps of Marines in 1755. In the Seven Years War (1756-63) he instituted the Brest blockade, which was the key to British maritime strategy until 1815. *See* WARS OF 1739 TO 1748-2; BLOCKADE.

ANSON BYE-LAW. After the Education Act, 1902, was passed, Sir Win. Anson, Parly. Sec. to the Board of Education, permitted parents to withdraw their children from primary school religious education. The principle was universally applied by the Education Act, 1936, and continued by the Act of 1944.

ANSTIS, John, father (1669-1745) and son (1708-54). The father was Garter King of Arms from 1718, the son jointly with him from 1727. They left collections of heraldic and genealogical material. Chesterfield

apostrophised the younger thus: "You foolish man, you don't know your own foolish business."

ANTARCTICA, originally thought to be a vast southern continent, was gradually whittled down in public imagination after Drake rounded the Horn in 1578; but its true extent only became clearer after Cook's discoveries in 1769-1772. His report of a lucrative fur market at Canton brought British sealers to South Georgia in 1778, and wholesale slaughter, and though the South Shetlands were annexed to Britain in 1819, the fur seal was almost extinct by 1822. This was also the period when the mainland coast was extensively charted by the Russian Fabian v. BELLINGSHAUSEN and by sealers of the English firm of Enderby Bros., who were now concentrating on oil from the elephant seal. There followed an American sealing and exploration expedition in 1830; a French one (1831-8) under Dumont d'Urville; a further U.S. one (1838-9) under Wilkes, and a British one (1839-43) under Sir James CLARK ROSS (1800-62). For the next 30 years the area was left to sealers mostly from New Zealand who operated from Kerguelen and Crozet in the Indian Ocean; overkill soon brought a change to whaling, but by 1890 mineral oils were driving whale oil out of the market. The invention of the harpoon gun and the appearance of the Norwegians led by C. A. Larsen redressed the balance. Meanwhile there was renewed scientific interest. Robert Falcon SCOTT (1868-1912) led an expedition in 1901 to 1904; (Sir) Ernest SHACKLETON (1874-1922) another in 1908, and Scott his second, on which he died, in 1910-11. Shackleton made a second expedition in 1914 and a third in 1922. The British Graham Land expedition (1934-7) made valuable discoveries.

Argentinian claims at Deception I. led to the creation of a British Station there in 1944. In 1947 Argentina set up a station at Gamma; Chile, one at Greenwich I., U.S.A., another at the B. of Whales; Australia, another at Macquaries and Heard Is. In 1950 the French came to Adelie Coast. The **Antarctic T.** of Dec. 1959 provided that Antarctica should be used for peaceful purposes only and that new activity shall not be made the basis of a claim.

ANTHRACITE. This type of Welsh coal was much in demand by navies before the advent of oil, because it burned at great heat and virtually without smoke, thus reducing the distance at which a ship might be detected by an enemy, and increasing the intervals between refuellings. Ability to cut off supplies was a major element in British naval supremacy before 1908.

ANTHRAX, SPLENIC FEVER, or WOOLSORTER'S DISEASE attacks humans and animals, and its spores may contaminate the soil for long periods. Herbivorous animals may thus pick it up and communicate it to each other and to humans. Capable of developing pandemics, especially in S. Europe, it was not identified separately from other "plagues" until 19th cent. The Black Death, long thought to have been bubonic was probably anthrax or coincided with an outbreak of it. Louis Pasteur discovered the appropriate anti-bacterial vaccine in 1881.

ANTI-COMINTERN PACT. (*See* AXIS). This was an extension of the Berlin-Rome Axis agreement of Oct. 1936 to Japan (25 Nov. 1936), to Hungary (24 Feb. 1939) and to Spain (7 Apr. 1939).

The Russo-German Agreement or alliance of 23 Aug. 1939 concluded at Moscow between Ribbentrop and Molotov provided that neither party would join any group of powers directly or indirectly aimed at the other party. Japan immediately denounced the Anti-Comintern Pact.

ANTICIPATION, COMMISSION OF. A Tudor and early Stuart device for appointing collectors of a tax before it fell due.

ANTI-CORN LAW LEAGUE. (*See* BRIGHT, JOHN and COBDEN, RICHARD). The free traders, mostly manufacturers, were originally focused in the so-called **Manchester School** which developed into the Manchester Anti-Corn Law Association and the various Cobden Clubs in other towns. These were all founded during and in response to the depression which began in the autumn of 1836; in 1839 they coalesced into the Anti-Corn Law League. The Irish potato rot of 1845 panicked many Tories into supporting the League, including eventually Peel. The Corn Laws were repealed in June 1846 together with most of the other customs duties on food and many manufactured goods. The repeal made no difference to the price of corn until the mass importation of American soft wheat (which ruined the British countryside) in the 1860s. *See also* CORN LAWS and PEEL'S SECOND ADMINSTRATION.

ANTIGUA (W. Indies) was settled by the British in 1632, and held for its useful anchorages at English Harbour and St. John. Together with Barbuda and Redonda it formed a presidency of the Leeward Is. In Nov. 1940 sites for military and naval establishments were leased to the U.S.A. In 1956 responsible govt. was introduced and in 1960 75% of the U.S. base area was released.

ANTILLES. *See under names of individual islands.*

ANTINOMIANISM is hostility to the rule of law ascribed to certain extreme Christian sects as arising from grace through faith, mostly by their opponents. The sects concerned were all, save the Anabaptists of Münster, small.

ANTISEPTICS and ASEPSSIS. Carbolic acid was introduced by Lister in surgery in 1867.

ANTI-STAMP CONGRESS 1765. *See* AMERICAN REBELLION-10.

ANTLER, or ABBOT'S BROMLEY HORN DANCE, probably represents a pre-Roman or even pre-Celtic fertility ceremony. It is danced on the Monday after 4 Sept. at Abbot's Bromley, by six men. Three hold up red, and three white antlers on their shoulders so as to stand above their heads. They previously visit the local farmers.

ANTONELLI, Card. Giacomo (1806-76) Pius IX's Sec. of State and reactionary adviser. Virtual civil ruler of Rome from 1850 to 1870, he opposed the convening of the Vatican Council.

ANTONINE WALL. Shortly after A.D. 138, the Emperor Antoninus Pius appointed Lollius Urbicus gov. of Britain, with instructions to reoccupy southern Scotland. This Lollius did, building the Antonine Wall as a new frontier across the Forth-Clyde isthmus. At 37 miles, the new fortification was only half the length of Hadrian's Wall. It was built of turf on a stone footing with a fort roughly every two miles. The probable intention was to save troops, but it could be outflanked from islands to the west, and only a few years later there was a revolt by the Brigantes in its rear. It was burned and abandoned. Hadrian's Wall was put into commission again and the territory north of it was evacuated. In the second half of the 2nd cent. the Antonine Wall was briefly reoccupied, but thereafter Hadrian's Wall remained the northern frontier until the Romans withdrew from Britain.

ANTONIO, Dom. *See* ELIZABETH 1-20.

ANTONY HOUSE (Corn.) classical house built for the Carew family between 1711 and 1721.

ANTRIM. *See* MACDONNELL' CLANS-B.

ANTWERP (Belgium) is on the R. Scheldt at the junction of the major sea and mediaeval river routes of W. Europe. It had a 13th cent. cloth industry but had to dispute the advantages of its position with nearby rivals, notably Bruges, Ghent, Amsterdam and England. Thus its rising prosperity was abruptly checked in 1347 when Bruges secured its annexation by Flanders; but from 1406 onwards overmonopolisation, the silting of the Bruges waterways and Burgundian commercial liberalism diverted the trade back to Antwerp. The English Staple was established there; in 1485 the daily commercial exchange was opened, and in 1531 the financial exchange. With the help of the Spanish and American trade the city was now the most important commercial centre in Europe. Its industries included cloth, sugar refining, soap, glassware and especially printing. Its wealth was a foundation of the Flemish art movement.

The decline began with the Dutch Wars of Independence. It suffered a Spanish sack (*The Spanish Fury*) in 1576, a prolonged siege in 1585, and lost its overseas trade when the P. of Westphalia (1648) closed the Scheldt. Thenceforth the control of the Scheldt was a major element in English policy, successfully enforced. Antwerp stayed poor, and when Belgium became independent in 1832 the mouths were, at English insistence, placed in Dutch hands. Nevertheless the port expanded, encouraged later in the century by the Belgo-Congolese connection, and it became a major strategic determinant in World War II after its fall to the Allies in 1945. Hence the Germans held an enclave in the city for two months and then bombarded the area more heavily with V. 1s and V. 2s than any other place, but doing little damage. The port's major revival had, however, to await the rise of the Common Market in the 1960s, which abolished Dutch obstruction in the Scheldt estuary. *See also* STAPLE B-1 & 3.

ANZAC = Australia and New Zealand Army Corps, formed for the Galipoli campaign, landed there in April 1915. Its achievements became widely known and the initials passed into the language as a word.

ANZIO, B. of. *See* ALEXANDER-6.

APOLOGY OF THE COMMONS (1604) was a statement on English constitutional customs provoked by friction between James I and Parliament notably over wardships, purveyance and the control of elections. It declared that freedom of election, of speech and from arrest were parliamentary privileges necessary for the general liberties, and that the Crown could not alter the laws on religion without parliamentary consent. It was not formally presented to the King who, however, certainly read it.

APOSTASY. *See* HERESY.

APOSTOLICAE CURAE (1896) By this encyclical Leo XIII condemned Anglican orders on grounds of form and intention. The Abps. of Canterbury and York issued an effective reply in an encyclical letter of 1897.

APOSTOLIC KING. The King of Hungary.

APOSTOLIC SEE. The Papacy.

APOSTOLIC CHAMBER, headed by the Papal Camerarius or Camerlengo, was originally the papal secular administration, and it carried on the routine govt. of the Papacy during interregna. It also acquired a large extra-territorial revenue (*See* LIBER CENSUUM) and was mostly responsible on the one hand for borrowing, and for selling offices and indulgences and, on the other, for financing building, artistic patronage and the vast papal collections. By 1640 the interest on its debts exceeded its income, and thereafter its mounting indebtedness led to the wholesale neglect and administrative corruption which ultimately caused the collapse of the Papal dominions. With their annexation by Italy, the Chamber ceased to matter save during *interregna*.

APOSTOLIC SUCCESSION. The doctrine that bishops derive their essence and authority through consecration by other bishops, themselves so consecrated in unbroken succession from the Twelve Apostles who received the Holy Spirit on the first Christian Pentecost, immediately after the Crucifixion. Unlike the bishops of other protestant churches, **Anglican** bishops trace their succession without a break from the Apostles through Thomas Cranmer who, though married, was regularly consecrated Abp. of Canterbury with papal approval and by bishops in the succession, in Mar. 1533.

APOTHECARIES, were originally grocers who specialised in imperishables such as spices, drugs, and jam. In France they were sometimes monks. Their earliest professional connection with pharmacy probably arose through Arab contacts in Sicily; the Emperor Frederick II's constitution of Melfi (1231) separated their functions from those of physicians. They figure separately in the Paris *Livre des métiers* (1268) and in 1366 Mandeville mentions them along with 'merchants'. It was not until 1617 that the London Apothecaries Company was separated from the Grocers'.

APPANAGE is the provision made for the children of kings, often by the grant of jurisdictions and their profits. Those for younger children tended to become alienated from the main body of crown possessions by inheritance. Such centrifugal appanages (in particular the Duchy of Burgundy given by John of France to his son Philip the Bold in 1363) were an important feature of French mediaeval history and Burgundy itself very nearly developed into a sovereign independent state. In the case of heirs to thrones there was no such danger, for they merged into the crown at succession. In England the Lancaster estates, a rare example of the former, eventually returned to the Crown, but in so powerfully organised a shape that they have remained a separate organisation ever since. The Duchy of Cornwall is the permanent statutory appanage of the monarch's eldest son.

APPARITORS or SUMMONERS were ecclesiastical court bailiffs and messengers. In the middle ages they had an evil reputation for corruption and blackmail.

APPEAL OF FELONY. *See* COMBAT. TRIAL BY.

APPEASEMENT originally meant the settlement of international issues by conceding reasonable demands. Concession to unreasonable demands such as Hitler's in 1939 increased his appetite. When this was realised the word acquired a pejorative use which has remained. *See* MUNICH.

APPELLANTS. After Card. William Allen's death in 1594 George Blackwell, a strong pro-Jesuit was put in charge of the R Catholic mission in England as arch-priest. The Jesuits favoured the violent overthrow of the Elizabethan govt; the seculars were politically loyal, and thought the Jesuits mistaken. Led by William Bishop they vainly *appealed* to Rome against Blackwell's appointment: the appeal was renewed in 1601, and again in 1602 with the support of the French ambassador, when Blackwell was made to sever his Jesuit connections, and to accept appellants on his council. In 1603 Bishop formally repudiated the use of political means for the conversion of England, and in 1608 Blackwell himself took the oath of allegiance.

APPELLANT, LORDS (1388) were Thomas of Woodstock, D. of Gloucester, Richard II's uncle; Richard FitzAlan, E. of Arundel; Thomas Beauchamp, E. of Warwick; Thomas Mowbray, E. of Nottingham and Henry Bolingbroke, E. of Derby, son of John of Gaunt.

The 'Wonderful' Parliament of 1386, led by Gloucester and Arundel, had forced Richard II to dismiss some of his courtier friends from high office, impeached or arrested others, and had appointed a continual council or commission to supervise state business and the royal household. The King freed his friends, and went on a long progress, mainly to recruit troops and supporters. He also consulted the judges on the legality of the impeachments and the commission. They condemned both in a formal but confidential document witnessed, *inter alia*, by two archbishops and three bishops. The document was betrayed to Gloucester and his friends, who to prevent its use as a manifesto, gathered their forces. In Dec. 1387 they scattered the King's friends at Radcot Bridge, and forced him to call a parliament (later known as the Merciless Parliament) to Westminster in Feb. 1388. Here the five lords formally accused or *appealed* the King's five principal friends of treason in accroaching the royal power, as well as by acts of tyranny and rapine. The King's friends included Aubrey de Vere, D. of Ireland, Michael de la Pole, E. of Suffolk, Sir Robert Tresilian, C. J. of the King's Bench, Alexander Neville, Abp. of York,

and Sir Nicholas Brembre, a former Lord Mayor. Brembre and Tresilian received a tumultuary execution. The other three principals escaped. Many others were condemned and put to death. The Lords Appellant temporarily took over the govt. This lasted until 1389 when Richard declared himself of age (he was 22) and established a normal govt. with the help of his uncle, John of Gaunt.

APPIN MURDER. After the Jacobite rebellion of 1745 many tenants of forfeited Jacobite estates paid a rent to the govt. and another, which was remitted through one Allan Breck Stewart, to their exiled chief in France. The govt. factor, Cohn Campbell of Glenure, evicted some of these tenants and was murdered. Allan Breck was suspected but disappeared. Glenure's sub-factor, James Stewart of the Glens was also suspected and arrested. The Campbells were the hereditary enemies of the Stewarts. There was no evidence against James, who was tried by a court headed by the Chief of Clan Campbell, the Duke of Argyll, as hereditary Lord Justice General. Argyll packed the jury with eleven Campbells, and James was hanged (1752). The event long embittered highland clan relationships, and was the subject of R. L. Stevenson's novel *Kidnapped*.

APPLEBY (Westmorland), on the ancient route from the Vale of York to Carlisle, had a British fort, and later, as protection from Border raids, a Norman castle. The town was always small, but the important market as well as the strategic position led to early incorporation as a borough.

APPLEGARTH, Robert (1834-1925), errand boy, cabinet maker, founder and from 1863 to 1871 sec. to the Amalgamated Society of Carpenters and Joiners, helped to establish the executive co-operation of trade unions with H.Q.'s in London. He became a war correspondent in the Franco-Prussian War, and ultimately the owner of an engineering firm.

APPRENTICES. Since the earliest times of the town guilds the method of entry to industry had been regulated by the guilds themselves. Apprenticeship to a master was essential, but the conditions even within the same industry varied with time and place. In general, however, a master could take on very few apprentices, sometimes only one at a time, in addition to his own sons. He was responsible for board, lodging, equipment, clothing, training, and behaviour. The period of apprenticeship was theoretically seven years and the conditions were often detailed in an indenture, though, since the boy could sue only through a distant next friend, they were often ignored. Where many apprentices gathered together, as in London, their agility in riots and civil commotions had a salutary effect on masters, similar to the activities of a trade union, but provincial apprentices were more likely to be oppressed.

The growth of demand for manufacturers under the Tudors often led apprentices and others to set up on their own without training or before their indentures had expired. This put goods on the market which, because inferior in quality, were cheaper, and undercut the guild masters. The Statute of Artificers 1562 forbade such trading without apprenticeship, but it was soon ignored: in particular manufacturers set up in places where no guilds existed, and the demands of the market were so strong that guild masters broke the rules, and because they controlled the enforcing machinery did so with impunity. By 1814 when the Statute was repealed, it had long been a dead letter.

Apprenticeship was for centuries almost the only form of education available to boys who were not intended for the professions. Hence the pressure to take up indentures diminished with the rise of state education. In 1920 only 13 of boys under 21 were apprentices, and in 1926 even in the industries where apprenticeship was supposed to be the rule, only 20% of employers had apprentices in training; most of these were in metal industries, woodworking, building, printing, and the retail trade.

APPROPRIATION is a constitutional principle that **(1)** supplies granted by Parliament can be expended only on particular objects specified by itself; **(2)** property acquired by a local authority for one purpose cannot arbitrarily be used for another, especially if acquired compulsorily. Since 1974 the powers of local authorities to reappropriate property from one purpose to another, have been much widened.

APPROPRIATION. *See* ADVOWSON AND TITHE-6.

APPROVED SCHOOLS. The population explosion and industrial mortality of the Industrial Revolution resulted in many children being deserted or uncared for. Some ended up in prison where their condition shocked social reformers, who started industrial training schools. Under the Reformatory and Industrial Schools Acts 1854 and 1857, the Home Secretary was empowered to make grants for the maintenance of children in these schools and to inspect them. The system developed under voluntary managers. After 1968 they were called **Community Homes** or **Residential Establishments,** or in N. Ireland, **Training Schools.**

APPROVED SOCIETY (1936-56) was a Friendly Society registered for the purpose of distributing national health insurance benefits.

APPROVEMENT. *See* INCLOSURE.

APPROXIMATION OF LAWS of the member states relating to trade is one of the objects of the E.U. treaties. It is achieved by means of *regulations* which are made by the Council of the E.U. and *directives* also so made. Regulations alter the law of a country directly. Directives require a country to make the necessary alteration itself.

APRÉS MOI LE DÉLUGE **(Fr = after me, the Flood)** Louis XV seems to have said this, perhaps quoting from elsewhere, to Mme de Pompadour, who used it, in the plural, herself. Metternich also used it. It means, either, as in Louis XV's case, that the speaker cannot control the present so as to prevent future disaster, or, as in Metternich's case, that the speaker's disappearance will unleash forces which future generations cannot contain. Metternich was a notoriously conceited man.

APROBATION DES LOIX, confirmed by an Order-in-Council in 1581, sets out the points at which the laws of Guernsey differ from those in the Grand Coustumier de Normandie, and therefore of Jersey. It is the main source of Guernsey law.

APSLEY HOUSE. *See* BATHURST.

AQABA, GULF OF. Aqaba, an Egyptian pilgrim port, was recognised by the Turks as Egyptian in 1841, but it was reoccupied by them in 1892. Captured by T. E. Lawrence in 1917 it then became part of the Hejaz. In 1925 it was occupied by the British, who feared Wahabi control of the Hejaz; they ceded it to the Jordanian Kingdom and improved the communications with Amman. Meantime the state of Israel came into existence, and the closure of the Suez canal to Israeli shipping resulted in the development of a port at the neighbouring village of Eilat after 1949. This was connected with Haifa by an oil pipeline and with Beersheba by a road. The Egyptians blockaded the Gulf in May 1967. This was a main cause of the six day war a month later.

AQUAE SULIS. *See* BATH.

AQUINAS, Thomas, St. (?1225-74), son of a count of Aquino, was related to the Hohenstaufen and Valois families. Against family opposition he became a Dominican in 1244, and from 1245 to 1256 was a pupil of St. Albert the Great at Paris and Cologne. From 1259 to 1269 he taught in Italy mainly at Anagni, Orvieto, Rome, and Viterbo; from 1269 to 1272 he was in Paris and in 1272 he set up the Dominican school at Naples. Here he wrote the extant parts of his incomplete *Summa Theologica*. He died on the way to the Council of Lyons. The *Summa* is now the basis of R. Catholic doctrine, but

his views were condemned by the 13th cent. Franciscans and by Abp. Peckham in 1284. Nevertheless he was canonised in 1323, and pronounced a Doctor of the Church in 1567. Study of his works (Thomism) became obligatory for R. Catholic theological students in 1879.

AQUITAINE or GUYENNE (S. France) (1) Roman *Aquitania* extended from the Loire to the Pyrenees. After successive Visigothic and Frankish conquests and Merovingian confusion, the province became a military governorship or duchy, and passed through four different families, ending with that of Duke WILLIAM III (r. 951-63). His dynasty was celebrated for luxury and literary patronage, especially under the troubadour Duke WILLIAM IX (r. 1086-1127) at Poitiers. It ended in 1137 with WILLIAM X, whose famous daughter ELEANOR first married Louis VII of France, divorced him, and in 1152 married Henry II of England. For the next three cents. the Duchy, comprising 40% of France was to play an important, sometimes predominating role in English politics, culture, shipping and trade.

(2) In 1137 Aquitaine was a congeries of fiefs over which the Duke had little real authority. Eleanor's husbands tried to change all that. Her court at Poitiers was organised on French lines with a local administration on the Norman pattern under six seneschals functioning as sheriffs. This strengthened the local ruler (HENRY II until about 1170) though disorder remained common.

(3) The Duchy had a claim to the suzerainty of Toulouse, which Henry II tried to enforce in 1159, but was defeated by the French. In 1167 a similar situation developed in the Auvergne. In 1169 Henry made RICHARD COEUR-DE-LION titular Duke. In practice this put the duchy into the hands of Eleanor, now estranged from her husband but on good terms with Richard, whom she caused to be enthroned in 1172. In 1173 Toulouse submitted to Aquitainian suzerainty as a result of Henry's encircling diplomacy of Castilian and Savoyard marriage treaties.

(4) The Savoyard treaty of 1173 required the castles of Loudun, Chinon and Mirebeau (in Maine, close to the Aquitainian border) to be given to the Savoyards for Prince John. They belonged to Henry, the young King, as Count of Maine, who was affronted; his brother Richard, the strategist, thought the transaction a danger. Eleanor supported them, and Louis VII financed their discontent. In the ensuing revolt, Eleanor was captured, but the revolt ended only in Sept. 1174 at the P. of Montlouis, in which real power was conceded to Richard. He acquired his military skill in the next nine years putting down rebellious, mostly southern nobles.

(5) In 1180 the treacherous and capable Philip Augustus succeeded Louis VII. Public opinion was against Philip attacking the lands of an absent crusader, but did not prevent him from intriguing with the feudatories; but Richard, after his return from Germany in 1194 kept the disorderly duchy intact till he died. King John's quarrel with Philip, however, led to the legal forfeiture of his French fiefs in 1202. Philip purported to confer Aquitaine upon Aymeri de Thouars, but diverted his strength to the conquest of John's northern fiefs. Thus in Aquitaine he acquired only Touraine and Berry, because John's Poitevin vassals, preferring a distant English to a nearby French ruler, resisted his advance. On the other hand they were a broken reed during John's southern diversion in the disastrous Bouvines campaign. This ended with the Truce of Chinon (1214) which, by successive prolongations, continued for 45 years with three short interruptions.

(6) During the first (1224-1227) Louis VIII occupied Poitou and La Rochelle and gave them to his child brother Alphonse; and when Louis died in 1226, his widow Blanche of Castille overawed the Lusignan Hugh of la Marche and his wife Isabella of Angouleme (Henry III's mother), and secured their obedience by the Ts. of

Vendôme (Mar. 1227). In 1229 by a Convention at Paris, Raymond of Toulouse, in defiance of Aquitainian suzerainty, accepted a French heir if he should die childless.

(7) In the second period of warfare (1229-1231) HENRY III in alliance with the Bretons made an abortive expedition to Nantes which, however, made some impression on his mother, for the third period (1242-1243) arose out of her intrigues. There was to be a confederation against French penetration reinforced by marriages between the Houses of Castille, Provence and Toulouse. Alphonse, now of age, was invested as Count of Poitou in July 1241. Isabella and Hugh refused the homage required by the T. of Vendôme, and widespread hostilities and disorders encouraged another abortive expedition (B. of Saintes). The French forced the count of Toulouse to return to the Convention of Paris (P. of Lorris, Jan. 1243), Henry went home to England, Hugh of la Marche submitted and Isabella became a nun at Fontevrault. For a time the English had nothing north of the Gironde except Oléron and Ré, and in 1249, for good measure, Raymond VII of Toulouse died childless, so that Alphonse succeeded him there. (See WINE TRADE).

Simon de Montfort had become Lieutenant in 1248. A relative of the King and a Gascon, he was too energetic and tactless, and he had a private quarrel with Gaston of Béarn, the most important of the vassals. By 1251 the Duchy was in civil war, and in 1252 there were stormy proceedings before the King's court at Westminster. Simon resigned, but Gaston appealed for support to the new K. Alfonso of Castille, who had claims on Gascony. In the end Henry III imposed peace himself at Bordeaux in 1254, united the Duchy with the Crown, and conferred the govt. upon the LORD EDWARD (later EDWARD I); Alfonso renounced his claims in return for a marriage between Edward and his sister Eleanor, which left Henry freer to pursue his Mediterranean preoccupations (see SICILY). These could not go forward without a treaty with the French.

(8) Accordingly in 1259 the state of war was ended by the T. of Paris. The peace created a new financial, diplomatic and legal situation. Feudal law permitted appeals from the Ducal courts to the King's *parlement* at Paris: therefore Edward, who was fully in charge by 1266, maintained a permanent delegation in Paris, and tried to render appeals unnecessary by a just and efficient administration. Moreover, the customs at Bordeaux yielded a large income which disorder would jeopardise. Gascon money and ships were important in the Evesham campaign (1265) and in 1269 they were the mainstay of Edward's crusade. In Aug. 1271 Alphonse and his wife Jeanne died, and parts of the T. of Paris became the subject of prolonged litigation.

(9) By 1289 Edward I was free to issue the Ordinances of Condom and Condat, which crystallised the administration. It was headed by a salaried seneschal, and beside him was the Constable, who, unusually, was the financial controller. **Gascony** was divided into three areas, Bayonne, Dax and St Sever beyond the Landes, the latter with a sub-seneschal. **Saintonge** and the **Three Dioceses** also had sub-seneschals. These were subordinate to the seneschal but financially accountable to the Constable. The sub-seneschal of **Agen** had his own receiver who rendered the accounts. The Constable was also responsible for fortifications. The seneschal appointed provosts in towns, castellans, and country bailiffs, and also local *defensores* to maintain the ducal interests in matters which might lead to an appeal to Paris. Gascony proper had four courts (Bordeaux, Bazas, Dax and St Sever); Agen two; and in the Three Dioceses of Limoges, Perigueux and Cahors; an English judge attended the French assizes at **Périgord.**

(10) To exploit the territory, over 140 bastides (new towns) were built, and from 1286 a privilege duty of

5s.6d a tun on wine was substituted for the usual variable rates. This was gradually extended to merchants outside the Duchy, and canalised the trade through the Aquitainian ports, whose best customer was Bristol. Prosperity and growth were thus associated in local opinion with the English connection. Piracy, however, was universal, and a battle between the Cinque Portsmen and the Bretons at St Mahé (May 1293) was used as a pretext by Philip IV (The Fair) for bogus legal proceedings covering a mobilisation. In Jan. 1294 he summoned Edward to appear before his *Parlement*, and in May Gascony, declared forfeit for contumacy, was invaded. English authority was confined to Blaye, Bourg and Bayonne until the Anglo-Scots truce (Jan. 1302) and Philip's defeat at Courtrai (July) freed Edward for action. In Dec. Bordeaux expelled its French garrison. In May 1303 Gascony was restored under another T. of Paris. By 1307 its revenues exceeded those of the English Crown.

(11) French encroachments continued, but as Philip IV was at war in Flanders they stopped short of invasion. In 1311 there was a futile conference called the Process of Périgucux. In retaliation EDWARD II deferred homage to Louis X (r. 1314-16) and did homage to Philip V (r. 1316-1322) only in 1320. In 1323, however, Charles IV's attempt to build a *bastide* in the Agenais at St. Sarlat near St. Sardos was resisted by the seneschal, at a time when Edward was procrastinating about homage. The French were attacked, their King cited those responsible and, when they were not given up, forfeited the duchy. The E. of Kent capitulated at La Réole in Sept. 1324. In Sept. 1325 Q. Isabella arranged a peace, in which PRINCE EDWARD (later EDWARD III) was enfeoffed with the duchy less the Agenais, in return for a relief of £60,000. This was the beginning of the revolution against Edward II, but it ushered in seven years of fruitless negotiation (The Process of Agen) arising from the continued French occupation of the Agenais and the Bazadais. Edward III, with a Scots war on his hands, could not force the French to keep their bargain and Philip VI was helping to keep the Scots war going. By 1336 hostilities were inevitable. The first act of the Hundred Years War was a reconfiscation in May 1337, but the duchy was prepared and its people supported Edward III. In Oct. he claimed the French crown; in 1340 he assumed the title and destroyed the French fleet at Sluys.

(12) The concentration of the war in the north drew off most of the French, and Sir Walter Manny and Henry, E. of Derby drove the rest out of Gascony in 1345. The B. of Crécy (1346) and the fall of Calais (1347) ensured that French efforts to retrieve the position would fail. The war stagnated until the BLACK PRINCE became Lieutenant in 1355. He used the duchy as a plundering base, raiding eastwards to Narbonne in the autumn and northwards towards the Loire in Sept. 1356. On his way back with his loot the French, under their King John, attacked him and were destroyed at Poitiers (19 Sept. 1356). The King was sent a prisoner to England, and a truce ripened into the T. of Brétigny (or Calais) under which Edward III was to hold in full sovereignty an Aquitaine enlarged to nearly its ancient extent.

(13) The legal transfer of sovereignty never took place, but Edward behaved as if it had; in 1362 he conferred the Duchy on the Black Prince who held his court at Bordeaux. His expensive magnificence and favouritism soon made him unpopular. Moreover, he went to war in Castille, where Henry of Trastamara with a French army under Du Guesclin, had driven Pedro the Cruel from the throne. The French object was to get control of the Castilian navy. The Black Prince intervened to prevent it, and in April 1367 after a great victory at Nájera restored Pedro, but set his prisoners free. The war required redoubled taxation, and the Lords of Armagnac and Albret entered appeals to King Charles V who asserted his right to try them in Dec. 1368. In Mar. 1369,

as a result of the Prince's ill-considered clemency, Henry of Trastamara overthrew Pedro and secured the Castilian fleet. In June Edward III resumed the French royal title and in Nov. Aquitaine was forfeited yet again.

(14) The French waged a land war of attrition, and the Castilians won a naval victory at La Rochelle in 1372. When the two-year Truce of Bruges was concluded in 1375, the English controlled only a broad strip between Bordeaux and Bayonne. Warfare reopened desultorily in 1378, but in 1394 a 28 year truce was made between RICHARD II and Charles VI. The French made capital out of the political confusion following Richard II's deposition in 1399. They sent armed help to Owen Glendower in 1405, and tampered with the greater Gascon vassals such as the Albrets, Armagnacs and La Hire. Their armed companies roamed the countryside. The towns, led by Bordeaux, made shift to defend themselves and in 1406 a Bordelais fleet defeated the French. The truce was a dead letter, but no help came from England until 1409, and it was only in 1412 that an organised force under Clarence arrived *via* the north.

(15) During HENRY V's reign the fighting was mainly in N. France, and Aquitaine was in a condition of relative peace. French fortunes reached their nadir at the T. of Troyes (1420), but Charles VII's principal support against the Burgundians, and thus the English, came from Aquitainian provinces which had at one time been English. The decisive Joan of Arc episode brought victory in the north, and when the Burgundians deserted the English (1435), Charles recovered Paris.

(16) While English politics paralysed the govt., during the Truce of Tours (1444-8), Charles reorganised his army, and in 1449 resumed the war. The French overran Normandy first and then the Duchy. Bordeaux fell in 1451. A liberating force under Talbot, arrived in Oct. 1453 and the population expelled the French, but on 17th July 1453, Talbot was decisively beaten at Castillon. The final surrender of Bordeaux ended English rule in Aquitaine. Constantinople had already fallen to the Turks on 29th May. Within nineteen months, the Wars of the Roses were to begin. Economic connections, especially a wine trade, continued to modern times.

ARABELLA STUART (1575-1615). See SEYMOUR.

ARAB HORSES, whose purest breeds are still found in the Nejd, were first imported into Britain in the early 18th cent. The **Darley Arabian** was brought from Aleppo in 1704. They form part of the ancestry of most English thoroughbreds.

ARABIA see CALIPHS AND CRUSADES. **(1)** By 900 Arabia was not ruled by the Caliphate. The Holy Cities of Mecca and Medina in the Hejaz were controlled by Aliid sherifs usually under Egyptian suzerainty; Aden flourished on the Indo-Egyptian trade; the central highlands were ruled by Zaidi Shiites, and Oman's interests were mainly in Persia. This fragmentation continued until the Turks conquered the Hejaz in 1517 and the Yemen in 1536. In the East, the Portuguese took control of the Gulf, until Anglo-Persian joint action expelled them (*see* HORMUZ) in 1622. In the 1630s the Zaidis drove the Turks from the Yemen, and in 1650 the local sheikhs expelled the Portuguese from Oman. **(2)** The next hundred years witnessed a new puritanism, notably that of the Wahhabi Saudi Amirs of Dariya, who by 1750 had laid the foundations of a new central Arabian state. By 1806 they had penetrated to the borders of Egypt and Iraq. A counter-attack was mounted in 1812 by Mehemet Ali, Pasha of Egypt, with British support. Medina and Mecca were reoccupied, and in 1818 his son Ibrahim took Dariya. The Saudis moved to Riyadh, and when the Egyptians withdrew in 1840 (and the English were occupying Aden) retook the North West. In 1871 the Turks from Iraq overran Hasa, and in 1885 the Rashidi Emirs of Hail captured Riyadh. The latter, however, quarrelled with each other and with the powerful sheikh

of Kuwait, and in 1902 the Wahhabi Abdul Aziz IBN SAUD was able to regain Riyadh. In 1908 the Sherifs of Mecca, who were influential among the tribes, profited from the confused political situation during the Young Turk revolution and acquired a certain local autonomy. By 1914 they had clashed with Ibn Saud. **(3)** In World War I the British encouraged anti-Turkish elements, particularly the Sherif, the Sheikh of Kuwait, and Ibn Saud; the Sherif HUSAIN, with T. E. Lawrence's advice, proclaimed an Arab revolt, but the mutual suspicions of the Arab potentates, shortage of British material support, and the obstinacy of the Turkish garrison at Medina, halted progress until the end of 1916. By this time an Arab force had been formed with which FAISAL, the Sherif's son, and Lawrence took Aqaba in July 1917. The northern tribes now joined the revolt and with their help the British army drove the Turks back to Turkey. **(4)** Husain meanwhile had quarrelled on doctrinal and political grounds with Ibn Saud, and intrigued with the Rashidis of Hail when British mediation failed. Ibn Saud retaliated in 1921 by capturing Hail. In 1924 he took Mecca and Medina, and forced Husain to abdicate. **(5)** International difficulties centering on the Palestinian Arabs and the Jews, were complicated by overlapping promises made to the Arabs in World War I and pledges for a homeland for the Jews after World War II. **(6)** The economic and political structure of Arabia has been revolutionised by the development of oil resources around the periphery and inland through the establishment of pipelines and oil terminals, since the first discovery of Arabian oil in Bahrain in 1932. *See also* IRAQ; TRANSJORDAN; BALFOUR DECLARATION.

ARABIC NUMERALS or POSITONAL NOTATION with nine digits and a zero, originated in India in the 2nd cent. The system reached Baghdad in the 8th cent, and Spain in the 10th. Gerbert of Aurillac (?945-1003, Pope Sylvester II 999), astronomer and mathematician, used it. It began to be employed commercially at Pisa in 13th cent. and the symbols, which, except for 1 and 9 differed markedly from those used by the Arabs, reached their recognisably modern form in 14th cent. Florence, whence they spread rapidly along trade routes, through the activities of Florentine bankers. The system superseded Roman numerals as a general medium of calculation in 16th cent.

ARABI PASHA. See EGYPT-11-13.

ARAB LEAGUE consisting of Egypt, Iraq, Jordan, Lebanon, Saudi Arabia, Syria and the Yemen was created in Mar. 1945, and in 1947 a central bureau for co-ordinating the N. African independence movements was set up at Cairo. Libya joined the League in Mar. 1953, the Sudan in Jan. 1956, Tunisia and Morocco in Oct. 1958. In July 1961 Iraq resigned because Kuwait had joined, and in Aug. 1961 Algeria joined.

The geographical separation, differing interests and rival ideologies of the member states seldom allowed them to act in unison and many of them actively intrigued against the govts. of others. Thus while Egypt and Saudi Arabia ostensibly placed their forces under a unified command against Israel in June 1954, they still found it necessary to sign a military alliance together with Syria in Oct. 1955. Iraq, with Turkey, Britain, Pakistan and Iran formed the Baghdad Pact of Feb. 1955. In Jan. 1956 Lebanon and Syria signed an alliance. In 1957 Egypt, Saudi Arabia and Syria agreed to subsidise the Jordan. In Feb. 1958 Egypt and Syria agreed to form themselves into a United Arab Republic. In July 1958 as a result of a left wing coup in Iraq, Jordan and Lebanon asked for British, U.S. and Turkish assistance, and in Dec. Egypt and Iraq quarrelled over Syria where the Iraqis were encouraging those Egyptians opposing the rise of a ruling marxist party. In Apr. 1959 the Sudan called a meeting of the League to try and compose these differences, but Iraq, Jordan and Tunisia refused and Libya failed to attend. The other states agreed to condemn Iraqi policy, but did little to enforce their views and in Sept. 1961 Syria withdrew from union with Egypt. Meanwhile in Mar. 1958 Egypt had concluded a similar union with the Yemen which excited Saudi suspicions. This came to an end in Dec. 1961, but in Sept. 1962 a military rebellion in the Yemen led to a civil war in which Egypt supported the republican rebels while Saudi Arabia supported the Govt. In Apr. 1963 Egypt, Syria and Iraq agreed to form a new tripartite state, but in July Egypt withdrew because of the left wing sympathies of the Syrian govt. The League continued to be weakened by dissent over Palestinian issues. After the 1979 agreement between Israel and Egypt, the latter's membership was suspended, and the League's H.Q. moved from Egypt to Tunis.

ARAGON became internationally important when in 1137 RAMIRO II married his daughter to Raymond Berengar of Barcelona. The resulting union created a powerful military, commercial and seafaring state which acquired Roussillon in 1172. PETER II beat the Almohads at Las Navas de Tolosa (1212) but in 1213 he was killed at the B. of Muret by the crusaders against the Albigensians led by Simon de Montfort (IV). JAMES the Conqueror (r. 1213-76) abandoned his French possessions (save Montpellier) and adopted a Mediterranean policy. He took the Balearic Is in 1229; Valencia in 1238. His son PETER (later III) married Manfred's daughter and inherited Manfred's claims to Sicily against the usurping Charles of Anjou. In 1282 the Sicilian Vespers ended the Angevin ambitions in the Mediterranean, and Sicily passed to Peter, whose fleet and commerce dominated the Western Sea. By 1325 the Aragonese were established at Athens. In 1352 their fleet broke the Genoese commercial power in the Levant at a battle off Constantinople.

At K. MARTIN's death in 1410 the succession failed, and the four Cortes of the Kingdom settled the crown upon FERDINAND I (r. 1412-16) a cadet of the House of Castile. His son ALPHONSO V (The Magnanimous; r. 1416-58) overthrew the Neapolitan Angevins and added Naples to his dominions in 1442. He was the richest of the renaissance patrons. When he died, the Two Sicilies passed to an illegitimate son, whose family held it against the French till 1504. His legitimate grandson FERDINAND II (r. 1479-1516) made a runaway marriage with the spirited Isabella of Castile and commenced the slow merger of the Spanish sovereignties legally effected in 1716.

ARAKAN. See BURMA-4 et seq.

ARBALEST. Strictly, a crossbow with a steel bow.

ARBROATH or ABERBROTHOCK (Angus) The rich coastal abbey was founded in 1175 by William the Lion, and dedicated to St Thomas à Becket. Its mitred abbots were invariably conspicuous public personages until the Reformation, and the buildings were used as an occasional royal residence and parliamentary meeting place. Little now remains. See BASS ROCK.

ARBROATH, DECLARATION OF (Aug. 1320). At English instance Pope John XXII cited four Scottish bishops, and published a further excommunication of Robert the Bruce for continuing the Scots war of independence. The Scots barons replied by a letter or declaration drafted by Bernard of Linton, Abbot of Arbroath, Bruce's Chancellor. This asserted Bruce's right to the crown by virtue of his descent, his recognition and consecration, and his services to the Scots nation. It set forth the claims of the Scots to independence, and declared that they fought "Not for glory or riches but only for liberty which no true man would yield save with his life". Despite this famous phrase, the excommunication was not lifted nor Bruce's title recognised until Oct. 1328, after peace had been made with England.

ARBUTHNOT, John (1667-1735) Scottish physician to P. George of Denmark and Q. Anne, became a close friend of Swift's, and thence knew most of the literary folk of his time, they being glad to know him because of his wit. He composed *A History of John Bull* (1712) and other witty political pamphlets. See also SCRIBLERUS CLUB.

ARCADIA, a Peloponnesian district, thought to have been a Greek Eden or country of rustic happiness, after which renaissance poets sighed, notably Jacopo SANNAZZARO (1458-1530), Sir Philip SIDNEY (1554-86) and John MILTON (1608-74), besides a generation or more of painters. *Et in Arcadia ego,* (Lat. = I too am found in Arcadia) refers to death; but has sometimes been altered to *Et ego in Arcadia* (Lat. = I too was in Arcadia) referring to lost happiness.

ARCH, Joseph (1826-1919) besides being a Methodist preacher, worked from 1835 to 1872 as a hedger and ditcher. In 1872 he organised a local farmhands' strike and so began his public career by launching the National Agricultural Labourers Union, with the help of wealthy well-wishers. In 1873, with 100,000 members, he obtained significant wage increases. The agricultural depression caused by rising imports of soft wheat led to unsuccessful strikes and lock-outs, and by 1880 membership had sunk to 80,000. He entered Parliament for N.W. Norfolk as a Gladstonian liberal in 1885, lost the seat in 1886 and secured it again from 1892 to 1902. He remained uncertain of the relative advantages of industrial and political action as a means of improving the life of the agricultural labourer, and the union, which had depended too much on his efficient personality, suffered from his political preoccupations. He retired in 1900.

ARCHANGELSK and MURMANSK (White Sea). The only oceanic ports of European Russia, were seized by Ivan III in 1505. Their importance for over 400 years varied inversely with Russian power in the Baltic. The first recorded English visitors were Willoughby and Chancellor in 1553. The harbour and commercial intendancy at Archangel were developed rapidly after 1670, and in 1693 Peter the Great got English and Dutch seamen to teach him seamanship there. The ports were used for supplying Russia in World War I. At the Russian revolution the British occupied them to protect the depots from the Germans but they soon became bases against the revolutionaries. They were evacuated in Oct. 1919 and in the next years the area was closed and Archangel's beautiful buildings were mostly destroyed. In World War II they were the only point of entry for large scale supplies from the West, and the embattled Murmansk convoys became a major (but unappreciated) part of the British war effort. German attempts to cut the Murmansk railway involved Finland in 1942. The Russians treated British servicemen at Murmansk badly despite British protests.

ARCHBOLD, John Frederick (1785-1870) in 1824 published the treatise on the Criminal Law which in successive editions has held the field as the principal source on the subject. Archbold edited only the first two editions himself. In *Archbold* v. *Sweet* he successfully sued the publishers for libel because they had published a new edition full of mistakes without a statement that he had not edited it.

ARCHDEACONS. Clerics with responsibility for material administration in the whole or part of a diocese. They became common after the Norman conquest, at first as officials in the bishops' household, but soon with territorial jurisdictions. Mediaeval archdeacons were so notorious for corruption as to provoke the question *Num archidiaconus salvari potest? (Lat. =* Can an archdeacon be saved?).

ARCHDUKE (Ger *ERZHERZOG* = Commander-in-Chief). The title from 1453 of the ruler of Austria; then the title of any ruling prince of the House of Hapsburg and after 1806 of any Hapsburg prince.

ARCHER, Thomas (1668-1743), pupil of Sir John

Vanbrugh, was one of the few English baroque architects. He built Heythrop House (Oxon), part of Chatsworth, St Philip's, Birmingham and St. John's Westminster.

ARCHERY was not esteemed in Britain before 1066, but the Normans employed it with success at Hastings. The crusaders encountered Turkish troops armed with the *composite bow* made of horn on the inner side, sinew on the outer with wood in between. This had an extreme range of 800 yards and could be used from the saddle because it was short. The European bow remained a weak instrument (except in the form of the steel *crossbow*) until the Welsh introduced the *longbow*, made of yew, probably in the 12th cent. A six-foot longbow had an extreme range of about 400 yards, but because of its size, it could be used in warfare only on foot. The longbowman usually rode to battle and dismounted to fight. He could discharge 12 arrows a minute against the crossbowman's two, but was more affected by wind; and as rain softened bowstrings he was at risk in wet weather. The need for agility meant that he was unarmoured and needed protection; but, favourably placed, he could do great moral and physical damage to even armoured cavalry.

By the 14th cent. the English had made longbow shooting a national sport, but their military archers were highly paid specialists. The supplies of native yew soon ran out and had to be imported from Prussia (*see* HANSE-4) and Italy.

The dangers of leaving longbowmen unprotected were demonstrated at Bannockburn (1314). The first important victory won by a combination of them with dismounted men-at-arms was against the Scots at Halidon Hill (July 1333). This defensive victory set the tactical pattern for later triumphs against the French at Crécy (1346), Poitiers (1356), and Agincourt (1415). An Act of 1512 required compulsory longbow practice, and archers fought decisively in the offensive victories of Flodden and the Battle of the Spurs at Guinegate, both in 1513. The Act of 1512 was confirmed in 1515, and in 1537 Henry VIII chartered the Company of St. George or Honourable Artillery Company and expressly required it to practice archery. It abandoned the bow in favour of firearms in 1590, but kept archery butts until as late as the 18th cent.

ARCHES, COURT OF, the consistory court of the Abp. of Canterbury, which met formerly in the London church of St Mary le Bow. It was early combined with his Court of Peculiars, and the judge, the Dean of Arches, held both jurisdictions. It heard appeals from diocesan consistory courts, and appeals from it lay only to the Pope until 1534 when they were transferred to the Crown in Chancery. The system of appeals was modified by the Ecclesiastical Jurisdiction Measure, 1965.

ARCHITECTURE (BRITISH)

A. GENERAL (1) *Geology* Architecture is dominated by the materials to hand. Hence before the development of overland transport there were well marked local styles. The most noticeable depended on **(a) Freestone** (such as Bath stone) stretching from Somerset to Lincolnshire. This was workable and the many churches and manor houses were therefor often highly decorated. **(b) Hard Stone** (such as granite) admitted of little ornamentation and produced a severe style in Cornwall and the north. **(c) Flint** in E. Anglia and on the south coast produced variegated wall patterns. **(d) Oak** particularly on the Welsh border and the north-west was the foundation of a half timbered domestic style, as well as of some monumental roof building. **(e) Clay** transformed into **bricks** was much used in river valleys such as the Thames. **(f) Caen Stone** and some **Purbeck Marble** was used in places where it could easily be brought by sea (e.g. Canterbury).

(2) *Climate* A climate which tended to be dull, wet and windy created a natural bias towards enlarged windows (after the introduction of glass), steep roofs, and sheltered or porched outer doors.

B. SUMMARY (3) The following is a conventional terminology which, despite its disadvantages, has passed into the language. It must, however, be understood that the styles associated with particular periods in fact overlapped sometimes for many years. For two examples see paragraph 9 (below).

Norman	1055-1189
Early English	1189-1307
Decorated	1307-77
Perpendicular	1377-1485
Tudor	1485-1558
Elizabethan and Jacobean	1558-1620
Renaissance or Stuart	1620-1714
Georgian	1714-1810
Regency	1810-37

C. SALIENT FEATURES (4) *ROMANESQUE* styles were based upon round headed arches, thick walls and simple vaulting. The few existing **Anglo-Saxon** buildings (e.g. the churches at Earls Barton and Bradford on Avon) are modest, with small doors and narrow windows, sometimes triangular headed, for the Anglo-Saxons built mostly, if sometimes impressively, in wood and only Greenstead Church (Essex) with its nave of tree trunks, has survived. **Norman** architecture introduced by Edward the Confessor was more ambitious, and scores of examples remain (St. Bartholomew the Great, London, Tewkesbury Abbey, Ely Cathedral, the keeps of castles such as Rochester and the Tower of London, the Norman House at Christchurch, Hants). The arches and windows were larger, there were massive piers and solid buttresses, and, especially, the meeting places or cross vaults (hitherto dovetailed) were replaced by ribs which supported stone panels.

(5) *GOTHIC* styles are distinguished by the exploitation of the pointed arch. This simple form probably originated because if diagonal ribs are semi-circular at a vault crossing, the span and height of the arches can be kept uniform only by starting them steeply, and this naturally produces a point. Pointed arches also carried the thrust diagonally downwards towards the ground and could therefore be propped by flying buttresses, of which decorative use could be made.

(6) *EARLY ENGLISH* had plain, tall, lancet windows, often in threes or fives, sometimes with intermediate ribs in the vaulting and clustered columns, with detached sub-columns or pilasters, or using Purbeck marble. West fronts of major churches were often elaborate e.g. the remarkable cases of Lincoln and Salisbury Cathedrals, besides Stokesay Castle and parts of Charney Basset manor.

(7) The *DECORATED* style developed from the Early English by the addition of tracery, and the enlargement of windows (replacing groups of lancets) designed to show off the rapidly developing glaziers art. Buildings rose higher, and in the case of churches began to be elaborately buttressed. A limit to the number of intermediate ribs in vaulting was reached, and the designer's ingenuity thus taxed created the branching or Lierne vault, and the stellar vault. Hence ceilings became a major decorative feature. The main of many examples are the naves of Exeter and Lichfield Cathedrals, parts of Kenilworth and Ludlow Castles, and Penshurst Place.

(8) *PERPENDICULAR.* This soaring and peculiarly English style might be called an upward development of the decorated. The finest example is the nave of Winchester Cathedral, but elaboration of design produced buildings such as Kings College Chapel (Cambridge) which approach the continental Flamboyant. Westminster Hall with its immense timbered roof belongs to this period. A further development was the fan vault first used in stone in the cloisters of Gloucester Cathedral (c. 1375) and in wood at Winchester College Chapel (1395).

(9) *TUDOR* is a development of late Gothic, influenced by the new Renaissance styles spreading from Italy, often adapted to official and domestic rather than ecclesiastical purposes, and sometimes using materials such as brick and timber. Among notable examples are the gatehouse of St. James' Palace, Henry VII's Chapel at Westminster, the remarkable late fan vaulted staircase at Christchurch, Oxford (1630) and St. Mary's, Warwick, which was built as late as 1694.

(10) In the *ELIZABETHAN* and *JACOBEAN* periods renaissance classical ideas penetrated a Gothic habit of mind. The Reformation virtually ended church building; the demands of public order ended castle building; and a new class of rich men wanted opportunities for conspicuous spending. Renaissance decoration increasingly obscured the Gothic framework beneath, until public taste was ready for a complete change. This confused time included such buildings as Longleat, Wilts. (1567-80), Montacute, Somerset (1580-1601), Holland House, Kensington (1607 destroyed in World War II), the Middle Temple Hall (1562-72), Hatfield (1607-11) and the Orders Façade of Wadham College, Oxford (1610).

(11) *RENAISSANCE* or *STUART* architecture derives from the studies of Palladio (1508-80) and other Italian architects made by Inigo JONES (1573-1652) who imported their ideas, known as PALLADIANISM, into England just as public taste was ready for them. He was succeeded by Sir Christopher WREN (1632-1723) who knew Bernini, Mansart and other French architects at Louis XIVs court. Moreover Dutch influence came with cavaliers returned from exile with Charles II. Gothic ideas were consciously abandoned. The new style harked back to the orders of classical Greece and the Byzantine dome combined with the usual need to let in the light, and eventually with the pillared porticoes of imperial Rome. Inigo Jones' Whitehall Banqueting House (1619-21), the Queens House at Greenwich (1618-35) and St. Pauls Covent Garden (1631-8) are refined examples; Wren's Fountain Court at Hampton Court (1690) and St. Paul's Cathedral (1675-1710) are more grandiose. The style proved capable of infinite adaptation, and beautiful examples ranging from chapels and summer houses to colleges and palaces exist in thousands. (*See* BAROQUE)

(12) *GEORGIAN* is an extension of Stuart architecture mainly devoted to domestic buildings, but associated with a complementary style in furnishing, furniture, dress, silver and ceramics, and with the neo-Palladianism (c. 1715-60) of such architects as BURLINGTON, and later with the neo-Classicism (c. 1760-1800) of others such as the brothers ADAM. The period produced many big buildings like Kedleston (Derbys) (1761-5), Syon (Isleworth) (1761), the London Mansion House (1739-57) as well as many of greater modesty, which were nevertheless remarkable, such as Boodles Club (London) (1775) and many town and country houses.

(13) Under the *REGENCY* Georgian taste was affected by the new styles of Bonaparte's Europe, the idiosyncrasies of the Prince Regent, the Greek revival, and the wider distribution of sound fortunes created by the French wars and the new industrial techniques. In architecture it might be called the age of mass produced elegance, typified by the great terraces of classical inspiration in London and Bath, where numbers of families could share surroundings of considerable outward magnificence.

D. REVIVALISM (14) If there was an element of revivalism in Georgian and Regency classical arts, improvements in transport, which gave access to every kind of material, abetted other revivalisms conducted in every conceivable substance. Horace WALPOLE's Strawberry Hill (1753-78) is an essay in stucco Gothic; William BUTTERFIELD's Keble College, Oxford (1870) is brick Gothic in four colours; G. E. STREET's Law Courts (1874-82), a variegated Gothic complex, was the first building to contain air conditioning. Sir Thomas DEANE's Oxford Museum (1855-60), a multi-coloured mosaic of external styles, included a mediaeval kitchen for chemical experiments, and cast iron arches. The most successful building of the **Victorian** era was Sir Charles BARRY's Houses of Parliament (1840-60), a design of great skill and adaptation.

(15) Victorian Gothic has distracted attention from the contemporaneous classical revivalism which seemed at the time to be a mere continuation of the Regency. H. L. ELMES built St. George's Hall, Liverpool (1839) on the model of the tepidarium in the baths of Caracalla. Sir Win. TITE built the Royal Exchange. Sir Gilbert SCOTT, influenced by Palmerston, the public offices in Whitehall. As a fashion, however, the revived **Neo-Classicism** proved the more durable and became the inspiration for most substantial buildings until the outbreak of World War II.

E. SYSTEM BUILDING (16) Mass production of components began to invade the market as a result of continental experiments (going back to 1900) and the redevelopment required after the destruction during World War II. For the first time high building, other than for religious purposes, became common. The new architecture was marked by the features of industrialism, especially repetition, poor quality of detail, and great size. It nevertheless branched out into three discernible movements: the **Vertical,** inspired by American city development, the **Horizontal** intended to exploit soft sites and good landscapes, and a **Free Style** which gave opportunity for great, if sometimes peculiar originality.

ARCOS (All Russian Co-operative Society) was the Russian govt. trading organisation in London. The Baldwin govt. thought that it was a centre of subversion, particularly towards India, and in May 1927 raided it, but found no evidence. The govt. nevertheless broke off relations with the U.S.S.R., thus incidentally giving Stalin an opportunity to take over the aggressive tenets of Trotsky as against those of his more moderate critics, who advocated a more conciliatory foreign policy.

ARCOT (S. India), was the seat of a Nawab who held the Carnatic under the Nizam of Hyderabad. In 1743 the Nawab DOST ALI was killed by the Marathas, who abducted his son-in-law CHANDA SHAHIB. The Nizam accordingly replaced Dost Ali's family with ANWARRUDIN, an old family servant of his. The War of the Austrian Succession brought hostilities between the English at Madras and the French of Pondicherry, both in the Carnatic. Each appealed to Anwaruddin (who was supposed to be impartial) for protection. He would not protect the French against the English fleet since he had no fleet of his own, and in 1746 when the French under Dupleix, besieged Madras, the English appealed to him. His forces arrived too late and were defeated by the small French garrison of Madras. From this circumstance Dupleix deduced the idea of using small highly trained European forces in combination with intrigue at princely courts. When the war ended he agreed to place Chanda Shahib on the Throne of Arcot. Anwarrudin was accordingly defeated and killed at the B. of Ambur (Aug. 1749) by Dupleix' ally, MUZAFFER JANG who had proclaimed himself Nizam, and conferred the Carnatic upon Chanda Shahib. The latter with Dupleix now attacked Trichinopoly where MUHAMMAD ALI, Anwarrudin's son, had taken refuge. To compel the relief of Trichinopoly, Clive with about 500 men surprised Arcot and held it against a powerful army in a victorious 56 day defence (23 Sept.-14 Nov. 1751). Chanda Shahib's army dissolved: he was killed and in 1754 the discouraged French home govt. recalled Dupleix. Muhammad Ali now became Nawab entirely as a dependent of the British. The Nawabs of Arcot soon became the target for unscrupulous Madrasi and English speculators, and their debts were one of the great financial scandals of the late 18th cent. Arcot was annexed in 1801.

ARCTIC CONVOYS. See ATLANTIC, B. OF.

ARCTIC EXPLORATION (1) grew out of a 16th cent. desire to reach the Pacific by routes not under Spanish control. Sir Hugh Willoughby began by attempting a **north-east passage** on behalf of the London Merchant Adventurers in 1553. He reached the Kola Peninsula and died of privation. His colleague Richard Chancellor turned south *via* the (later) Archangel and secured trading concessions from the Czar. Borrough reached Novaya Zemlya, and Pett the Kara Sea in 1556. Twenty years later Martin Frobisher tried the opposite **north-west passage.** He landed in Greenland, reached the Baffin Is. and made further voyages enticed by the hope of gold in 1577 and 1578. John Davis made three voyages (1585-7). He followed many miles of the Greenland coast and penetrated the unknown Baffin Bay through the Davis Strait. By now there was some understanding of the differences in the respective problems of the two passages. **(2)** Pursuing the N.E. Passage, the Dutchman Barents discovered Spitzbergen in 1596. In 1607 Henry Hudson's visit to and reports on Spitzbergen initiated the local whale fisheries. The Russians began systematic explorations of the Siberian coast between 1725 and 1742 with the Dane Vitus Behring in charge. He reached the Pacific through the straits named after him, charted Kamchatka, and landed in America. The Swedish Baron Nordenskjöld made the first through passage (Norway to Alaska) only in 1878-9. **(3)** Pursuing the N.W. Passage, Henry Hudson visited Hudson Bay in 1601, and Thomas Button explored it extensively in 1612 and 1615. In 1616 William Baffin discovered Baffin Bay and the Smith, Jones and Lancaster Sounds. Hence Thomas James and Luke Foxe followed with some confidence, and though they failed to find a western exit, their discoveries inspired the foundation of the **Hudson Bay Co** (1670) with its vast fur trade. Then exploitation replaced exploration until the whalers William Scoresby (father and son) surveyed the Greenland coast between 1806 and 1822, and attracted the attention of John Barrow, the Sec. to the Admiralty. In 1818 a series of naval expeditions began with that commanded by Capt. John Ross. William Parry also attempted to locate the passage between 1819 and 1825, but despite this and many other efforts, the N.W. Passage was first made between 1903 and 1906 by the Norwegian Roald Amundsen. **(4) Polar Exploration** attracted interest comparatively late. Parry had attempted a sledge expedition in 1827. James Clark Ross had found the **magnetic pole** during his uncle John Ross's expedition of 1828 to 1833. Many expeditions, all unsuccessful and many disastrous, followed, but in 1895 the Norwegian Nansen proved that the Arctic was an ice-mass not a land-mass, by the drifting of his ship. In 1900 the Duke of Abruzzi reached 8634 N. In 1909 Peary reached the Pole. In May 1926 Byrd and Amundsen independently flew over it, and in 1958 a U.S. atomic submarine went under it.

ARDEL. A Welsh procedure in which one accused of a crime could stop the proceedings by producing someone to vouch for him. Abolished in 1535.

ARDENNES. A steep, heavily wooded and wild territory in S.E. Belgium and adjacent French districts, assumed to be impassable to armies. The French and Belgian general staffs incorporated the assumption in their defensive plans against the Germans, while in World War I the Germans preferred to circumvent the area to the north. In World War II however, they sprang a strategic surprise through it in the 1940 campaign, and attacked through it again at Christmas 1944.

ARDRES, P. of (June 1546), ended Henry VIII's war with France. He recovered his pensions, and was to hold

Boulogne till 1554 if K. Francis I paid 2M crowns to redeem the pension arrears.

ARDRES, Truce of (Nov. 1396). See CHARLES VI of FRANCE-4.

ARD-RI (HIGH KING), was the title of the Chief King of Ireland. From the 5th cent. the Ard-ri was chosen alternately from the two houses descended from Niall of the Nine Hostages (*see* O'NEILL). The Ard-ri had prestige and certain quasi-priestly and judicial functions, which he exercised from the sacred hill of Tara, but the office carried little revenue or following, and the power of the Ard-ri depended on the personal power of the man himself. Nevertheless the office symbolised, if in shadowy fashion, the unity of Erin. Its usefulness for this purpose was rudely shattered by Brian Boroimh who deposed the Ard-ri Malachy and usurped the office. When he died at Clontarf in 1014 Malachy returned, but the spell was broken and from Malachy's death in 1022 until the Norman invasion in 1167, Ard-ris were appointed by violent rather than legal processes and none was universally recognised. These Ard-ris were known as Kings with Opposition, and symbolised anarchy rather than unity. This represented a psychological factor of some importance in the Irish defeat by the Normans. At the time of the Norman invasion, which began in 1167, the Ard-ri was Rory O'Conor. By 1177 he was a fugitive in Connaught and he died in 1198 in the monastery of Cong.

AREOPAGITICA. See MILTON, JOHN.

ARGENTINA see BOLIVAR. **(1)** Paraguay repudiated the authority of the vast Spanish viceroyalty of La Plata in 1811, and overambitious attempts from 1816 to establish a unitary republic centred on Buenos Aires were reduced to a treaty between Buenos Aires, Entre Rios, Santa Fé and Corrientes and, in Dec. 1824, the calling of a constituent assembly. Within weeks, Bolivia became independent, and the Brazilians invaded the separatist Banda Oriental (now Uruguay). Refugees demanded and the Assembly agreed to the incorporation of Uruguay in Argentina; the resulting war with Brazil forced the Assembly to set up a federal executive. RIVADAVIA was its first president, but the other states contracted out, leaving Buenos Aires to carry the war on alone. She did this successfully, but in 1828 the British, with their ubiquitous navy forced a compromise whereby Uruguay became independent. Rivadavia resigned. An index of British interest in the area may be found in their importation of bloodstock for their horse races.

(2) In Dec. 1829 Juan Manuel ROSAS was elected gov. of Buenos Aires, and obtained dictatorial powers. He acted as informal leader of the provincial dictators, and was thus able to conduct an essentially Bonapartist foreign policy on behalf of a so-called **Argentine Confederation.** This involved intervention in Uruguay, a border war with the Bolivian-Peruvian Confederation in 1837 and in 1838 commercial disputes with France leading to a French blockade of the R. Plate until 1840. In 1843 Uribe, the fugitive *blanco* (conservative) Uruguayan president was, with Rosas' military support, returned to Uruguay. Montevideo held out against him for eight years under Rosas' personal enemy Paez, assisted by the British and French fleets which, in 1845, broke Rosas' Paraná river boom. The British withdrew in 1847, the French in 1848, and in 1850 the latter formally abandoned hostilities on condition that Rosas withdrew his contingent from the siege. This precipitated his fall, for in May 1851 URQUIZA, gov. of Entre Rios, in alliance with Corrientes, Brazil, Paraguay and the *Colorados* raised the siege. Rosas was routed in Feb. 1852 and fled to England.

(3) Urquiza now called a further constituent assembly to Santa Fé. This enacted a federal constitution, to which Buenos Aires would not accede. Thus from 1853 to 1859 there were two rival govts. After a civil war in 1859 Urquiza incorporated Buenos Aires in the confederation after defeating Gen. MITRE, but after a further war in 1861 Mitre, victorious at the B. of Pávon, became national president.

(4) Between 1864 and 1870 Mitre commanded the joint forces of Argentina, Brazil, and Uruguay in a devastating war with Francisco Solano Lopez, the savage dictator of Paraguay, who was killed. Argentina then made some minor annexations on the Paraná and the Pilcomayo.

(5) Mitre's successors, SARMIENTO (1868) and AVELLANEDA (1874) opened a modernising era. Sarmiento suppressed the provincial dictatorships, and established an educational system. Avellaneda encouraged European immigration which raised the white majority by large numbers uninterested in provincialism. Many of these were English, Scots and even Welsh speaking Welsh. There were immense and interrelated expansions (mostly with British capital) of the railways and the export of cereals. ROCA'S ruthless campaigns in 1879 ended the Indian menace. Patagonia was opened up. Under Roca, Pres. from 1880, the rate of immigration and development rose spectacularly, for the advent of the steamship, refrigeration, the silo and barbed wire vastly increased meat production, packing and export (with British banking) from British organised ranches. Argentina had become an international trading state.

(6) Riches brought corruption and political instability. Opposition came from a new phenomenon, the Civic Union, which raised a revolt in 1890, and this in turn led to the financial collapse of 1891 and the first bankruptcy of Baring Bros., the London bankers. Seven further years of confusion led to Roca's second administration whose comparative success was due mainly to disputes with Chile over Tierra del Fuego and the mineral rich Atacama. War was eventually avoided by the arbitration of King Edward VII, but this freed the parties to resume their hostilities. By 1910 the radical Hipolito IRIGOYEN was the dominant influence in politics. In 1916 he swept the polls on personal charisma and the support of the urban bourgeoisie. He kept Argentina out of World War I despite German provocations, and got ALVEAR, his running-mate elected to the presidency in 1922.

(7) Under Alvear the radicals split into the *personalists* who supported Irigoyen, and the *anti-personalists* who were searching for a doctrine. Irigoyen was returned with weakened support in 1928, but was caught by the worldwide slump of 1929 which lowered the price of Argentinian exports. Blamed for the consequent distresses, he was overthrown by a military junta led by Gen. URIBURU, and at the elections of 1931, the conservative Gen. Agustin JUSTO came to power. His govt., based on a coalition of the forces, industrialists and the church interfered with elections but could not, even then, do without the anti-personalist radicals. It attacked the economic troubles by entering into friendly relations with Brazil and the U.S.A., and in 1933 obtained, under the Roca-Runciman agreement, a privileged position in Britain for Argentine meat. It also modernised the bigger cities with British financed and managed electricity, gas and telephone systems.

(8) The election of 1937 was apparently won by a coalition of radicals, liberals and progressives with a compromise radical, Dr ORTIZ, in the presidency, but his health failed and his powers passed to the much less liberal Vice-Pres. CASTILLO. The Lower House refused to co-operate with him, paralysed the internal administration and tried to force him out of neutrality in World War II. Foreign policy became a party issue, in which Castillo was supported by the anti-Americans. In Dec. 1941 he refused to break with the Axis and proclaimed a state of siege, but in June 1942 he was overthrown by the military headed by Gen. RAMIREZ, who was succeeded in Feb. 1944 by Gen. FARRELL. Diplomatic relations with

Germany had been severed in Jan. War was declared in Mar. 1945.

(9) The United Nations, however, had acquired an embarrassing ally, for the new govt, based upon an ambitious and unscrupulous urbanised working class, had fascist characteristics. These provided the environment for the rise of the facile and politically agile Col. Juan PERON and his spectacular wife Evita, then sec. for Labour. The generals quarrelled in Oct. 1945. The Perons took power in Feb. 1946 and kept it for nine years by chauvinism, demagoguery, violence, and control of the economy through Russian type centralised trade unions. His appeal to Latin nationalism stretched beyond the Argentine and survived him. Evita died in 1953; in Sept. 1955 a mutiny under Gen. LONARDI drove Peron into exile. In Nov. Lonardi was succeeded by Gen. ARAMBURU. The Peronistas and the generals had done severe damage to the economy. The 1958 civilian govt. of Arturo FRONDIZI faced an impossible situation, with Peronistas winning elections. The army replaced Frondizi with GUIDO in 1962, but he, unable to stem the Peronistas, was attacked by the navy. Eventually a militarily supervised election achieved a return to constitutionalism in 1963.

(10) The military, however, were soon back in the key posts, with unhappy results. Their unpopularity permitted Peron once more to return to power (1973), and when he died he was succeeded by his second wife, who could hold on only until 1976, when a further coup under Gen. VIDELA brought in a succession of further generals, whose early years were blackened by vigilante terrorism and the disappearance of thousands of citizens. The regime's unpopularity and its economic failures led in 1982 to the Bonapartist attack on the Falkland Is.

(11) Legally, Argentina had no proper claim to these islands. Their allegiance to Britain was a carefully cultivated grievance. Initial apparent success was popular, but prompt defeat led to a collapse, and the resignation of Pres. GALTIERI. The conflict was in any case unnatural for the two countries had long had close links. The British community in Argentina remained large even after Peron had nationalised British-owned enterprises, and was composed of families who liked the Argentine and had made major contributions to the economy and history of the country – not to mention its sports.

ARGLWYDD. See WELSH LAW-1.

ARGONNE. (France), an area north of Paris, was in 1918 the first in which American troops were employed in large numbers in World War I.

ARGOSY. A corruption of Ragusa (now Dubrovnik). See ADRIATIC-4.

ARGOSTOLI (Cephalonia, Ionian Is.). A regular British fleet anchorage down to 1939.

ARGYLL (Gael; EARRAGHAIDHEALL – Gaelic Coast) was gradually settled by independently minded Scots from Ireland between 2nd and 9th cents. when it fell first under the intermittent sway of the rulers (whether Pictish or other) of central Scotland, and then of the Ostmen until their defeat at the B. of Largs (1263). It was then equally intermittently influenced or ruled by the Macdonald Lords of the Isles until their suppression between 1495 and 1506. During all this period Argyll was merely a collective geographical name for a number of tribal, Gaelic-speaking lands, of which (from north to south) Kintyre, Knapdale, Lorne, Morvern, Ardnamurchan and Garmoran with their adjacent islands in the Minch, were the most important. The collapse of the Lordship of the Isles led to civil wars between three branches of the Macdonalds and ultimately to the supremacy of the Campbells, the Gordons and the Mackenzies. The Campbells were soon (1457) headed by an Earl of Argyll and they acquired Lorne and Cawdor, together with sweeping powers as King's Commissioners and eventually the hereditary post of Lord Justice General in the area, whereby, until the abolition of heritable jurisdictions in 1746, they excluded the royal criminal jurisdiction. This Campbell supremacy was due, as much as anything else to the fact that they were mostly presbyterian and adhered to the dominant covenanting side in Scots politics, whereas the Gordons were R. Catholics and shared in the defeats of the 17th and 18th cents. The population of this sparse area has never been large (about 60,000 after World War II) and the principal activities have been cattle and sheep farming. *See also* DALRAIDA; GLENCOE.

ARGYLL, Earls, Marquess, Dukes. *See previous entry,* CAMPBELL; CLANS, SCOTTISH-6,7.

ARIANISM was a divisive Christian doctrine, propounded by **ARIUS** of Alexandria (?250-336), that the Son was subordinate to the Father. It was derived from certain utterances of Jesus in the days before the Crucifixion. In 325 St. Athanasius single handedly persuaded Constantine's Council of Nicaea to condemn the doctrine, but the Eastern Emperor Constantius embraced it while his Western colleage Constans opposed it. This deepened the growing political division of the empire. After Constans died, Constantius tried but failed to enforce Arianism in the West, and it continued to receive imperial patronage (save under Julian) down to the death of Valens in 378. The Emperor Theodosius, after the Council of Constantinople (381) expelled its champions, but it then spread among the Germanic tribes. They invaded the Western Empire, reimported it and tended to persecute their orthodox subjects from whom they remained separate in opinion as well as other things. In 496 Clovis and the Franks changed over to orthodoxy, and so established a working partnership with the Papacy and the non-Frankish population, which led to the gradual disappearance of Arianism.

ARKWRIGHT (1) Sir Richard (1732-92) originally a barber at Bolton, invented a spinning mill in 1769, adapted it to calico in 1773, and combined the whole process of yarn manufacture into one machine in 1775. In 1784 he assisted in the erection of the great New Lanark mills, but in 1785 his patents were cancelled. In 1790 he introduced steampower into his mill at Nottingham. **(2)** His son **Richard (1755-1843)** inherited the business and made a fortune.

ARLES (Fr). *See* BURGUNDY.

ARLES (Sc) A present offered in return for an oath to serve in a mine. If accepted, the man was bound for life. Parents sometimes, probably illegally, allowed their children to be arled, even at birth. The practice was common until the end of the 18th cent. *See* SERVITUDE.

ARLES, COUNCIL OF (314). *See* BRITAIN. ROMAN-22.

ARLINGTON. *See* BENNET.

ARMADAS (Sp = armed forces) (1) 1582-8 (in Spanish irony **La Invencible**). An expedition against England had been in preparation since 1582. The Spanish policy in France and England of religious and political subversion was checked by the execution of Mary Q. of Scots in Feb. 1587. By then the Armada was mostly assembled at Lisbon under the Marquis of SANTA CRUZ. At the end of Mar. he was ordered to sail before the summer, while simultaneously DRAKE sailed from England for Cadiz, which he raided (*The Singeing of the King of Spain's Beard*) at the end of April. Then during May and June he was on the Portuguese coast destroying naval supplies, especially barrel staves essential for naval supplies and water.

The Spanish plan was to sail to Ostend, embark the D. of Parma's army there, and land it in England. This required an acquiescent France (*see* HUGUENOTS). Drake's operations delayed the departure till 1588, by which time Santa Cruz had died and had been replaced by the D. of MEDINA SIDONIA. Brave but without maritime experience, he was expected to discipline the temperamental Spanish admirals by virtue of rank and character. His 130 ships included squadrons of ten large war galleons each from Portugal and Castile, four each of armed merchant galleons from Biscay, Guipuzcoa, Andalusia and the Levant, and four Neapolitan galleasses. The galleons were high decked and armed with short-range heavy guns. The galleasses had oars as well as sails. The remaining 70-odd were light craft or freighters. The English fleet was commanded by the Lord High Admiral, Lord HOWARD OF EFFINGHAM, with Drake as 2-in-C. The fighting force consisted of about the same number of galleons, but with better sailing qualities because they were on average somewhat larger, but longer and narrower in beam. They were low decked and armed with culverins of longer range and lesser calibre than the heavy Spanish. The many other ships were all light craft.

The Armada eventually sailed on 28 May, 1588, but contrary winds delayed progress, and food and water storage (both depending on good barrels) were found to be defective. It therefore headed for Corunna, but was scattered by a hurricane. It eventually sailed for England on 21 July and was reported off the Scillies on 29th. This report came to the Lord Admiral and Drake at bowls on Plymouth Hoe.

There were seven engagements in the Narrow Seas. The first five, at the Lizard (29 July), The Dodman (30 July), Portland (2 Aug.), Isle of Wight (3 and 4 Aug.) were inconclusive; the English kept out of range of the heavy Spanish guns, but their own longer but lighter metal could do little damage. By 6th Aug. the Armada was anchored off Calais, having lost only three important ships, and both fleets were running out of ammunition. If it could be driven past Ostend out into the North Sea, the prevailing Westerlies and the English fleet could prevent contact with the Spanish Army.

On the night of 7 Aug. the Armada was attacked by fire ships. Believing that these might be loaded with gunpowder, it broke up in confusion and was swept through the straits towards the shoals of Gravelines where a final and furious battle took place. A sudden change of wind saved it from the shoals and drove it into the North Sea. Its only hope of survival was now to sail for Spain north about Scotland. On 13 Aug. the English gave up pursuit. About 60 ships were wrecked off Norway, Scotland and Ireland. 68 got back to Spain at the end of September.

(2) *Oct. 1596.* An invasion fleet of 100 sail left Ferrol for England but was shattered by a gale. **(3)** *Oct. 1597.* A further fleet of 136 sail with 9000 troops was also dispersed by a gale. **(4)** *1599.* About 160 ships were prepared for concentration at Lisbon but dispersed to deal with Dutch operations against the *Flota* and the Azores. **(5)** *Sept. 1601-Jan. 1602.* 38 ships landed 5000 men at Kinsale (Ireland). This fleet, the only one to reach its destination, was partly dispersed by storms. The troops were cut off and surrendered in Jan. 1602.

ARMAGH (Ulster) is a fertile agricultural county whose 17th cent. English colonists planted orchards. Later small farmers supplemented their living by linen weaving. It is named after the town of Armagh, a bishopric traditionally founded by St Patrick in 444 and converted into an archbishopric for Ulster at the Synod of Raith Bressail (1111). The names of the archbishops are mostly known, and they became in due course Primates of the Irish church. The Reformation put the ancient cathedral into Anglican hands, and 18th cent. archbishops greatly improved and embellished the town. In the 19th cent. the R. Catholics set up a rival see and cathedral.

ARMAGNACS. *See* CHARLES VI and VII of FRANCE passim.

ARMED NEUTRALITY (1) First (1686-97). Sweden joined the League of Augsburg (July 1686), but it was in the general Baltic interest to sell metals, grain, and ship's stores to both sides. Hence Sweden and Denmark co-operated profitably in the first Armed Neutrality and convoyed Baltic commerce to belligerent ports. Anglo-Dutch maritime superiority over France might have forced the Scandinavians to fight: in practice they preferred not to risk an embargo on the Baltic trade, with which the French could not interfere. Most of this trade favoured Britain and Holland, and Sweden stayed out of the war.

(2) Second (1780-3) The American rebellion was creating a boom in Baltic exports, and for Danish carriers. By Mar. 1777 the Russian territorial claims at the neck of Jutland were liquidated: Oldenburg became a Holstein-Gottorp duchy, but Russian trade was carried more freely through the Sound. Within a year the Franco-American military and commercial treaties (Feb. 1778) had brought France into the American war, and British naval policy, involving the control of neutral trade, was creating unease among the Baltic powers. When Spain entered the war in June 1779 the area of the obnoxious British controls was extended to most of the Mediterranean and S. America. This also affected the Dutch, whose ships carried most of the Baltic naval stores. In Mar. 1780 the Czarina with Sweden, Prussia, Austria, and Denmark proclaimed the Second Armed Neutrality, and were promptly joined by Holland whom the British consequently blockaded in November. Portugal joined the combination in 1782 and the Two Sicilies in 1783. Despite all Britain's troubles and distractions, Baltic naval powers were too weak for this kind of struggle, and the British were prepared to be tactful. They offered a market for most of the products which might have been sold to their enemies, blockaded Holland, and winked at the activities of Danish merchantmen who, for a while, were the only safe carriers, even in the Mediterranean. The war was decided elsewhere and by other means.

(3) Third or Northern Confederacy (1800-1) The French revolutionary wars had been in progress since Apr. 1792 and when Britain became involved in Feb. 1793, her blockading power and economic strength diverted most of the Baltic external trade to British ports. The enormously expanded Royal Navy absorbed every product which the Baltic countries could produce, including the growing production of Russian hemp. This continued throughout the war of the First Coalition, and during the Second Coalition of 1799 until Russia, now under Paul I (1796-1801), left it. Bonaparte's victory at Marengo (June 1800) and his ability to play on European war weariness brought about a reaction in which Baltic dislike of the British monopoly, backed by a naval expedition (Aug. 1800) to Copenhagen played its part. The Confederacy, of Russia, Prussia, Denmark and Sweden, was formed in Dec. 1800 to force peace upon the British. The diversion of Baltic supplies from the British navy to the French, which this envisaged, was deemed a mortal threat to Britain which seized the Swedish and Danish West Indies and despatched a fleet under Parker and Nelson to break up the confederacy. After a battle off Copenhagen the Danes were forced to an armistice in Apr. 1801, whereupon the Prussians occupied Hanover: but the mainspring of the confederacy, the Czar Paul, had already been murdered in Mar. (a fact unknown in the west for some time) at the instigation of Russian exporters, who feared bankruptcy from his policies. The new Czar, Alexander I (1801-25), made haste to be reconciled with Britain. *See* AMERICAN REBELLION-23; BALTIC-34; SECOND COALITION, WAR OF (1799-1801)-4.

ARMENIA and ARMENIAN MASSACRES. The Armenians of their ancient Caucasian and Black Sea kingdoms were early converts to Christianity, and in the 5th cent. evolved their own script, biblical translations and literature. Their territories were fought over by Persians, Romans, Arabs, Byzantines and Turks, and after the Byzantine disaster at Manzikert (1071) many of them migrated southwards and founded the kingdom of **Lesser Armenia** in the safer mountains of Cilicia. This survived until the Mamelukes captured Sis in 1375. In 1514 the Ottoman Sultan Selim settled many of them under Kurdish emirs around L. Van where they proliferated. Some rose to be local chiefs. The Ps. of Gulestan (1813) and Turkmanchai (1828) transferred Karabakh, Erevan and Nakhichevan to Russia: the Moslem populations left and were replaced by Armenians from Persia and Turkey. In each Russo-Turkish war Armenians fled to Russia even though by the *Khatt-i-Humayun* of 1856 they were recognised as a *Millet* of the Ottoman Empire. In 1878 Russia acquired the old Armenian city of Kars, and by the Berlin T. Turkey undertook to improve their condition and protect them from the Circassians and Kurds. This raised unfulfilled hopes. Armenian discontent led to the formation of a nationalist party. In 1894 Armenians raided a bank, and massacres followed at Ersindjan and elsewhere, and in 1896 in Constantinople. A British, French and Russian joint protest resulted in an Ottoman *iradé* on Armenia but no practical results, but Moslem neighbours were formed into irregular cavalry units known after the Sultan as *Hamidiyeh*. These attacked Armenians in 1904 at Mush and during the Young Turk revolution of 1908 at Van and in 1909 at Adana. Some 50,000 perished. In 1914 a new regime for the Armenian provinces (with neutral inspectors) was forced on the Turkish govt by the powers, especially Russia, but World War I broke out.

This type of foreign interference neither endeared the Armenians to the Turks nor inclined the Turkish govt. to the allied side in the War. Consequently when they joined Germany they deported or massacred the Armenians in the militarily sensitive areas by the Russian frontier. This developed into a genocidal policy. By 1916 600,000 had been murdered and the rest dispersed.

When Russia collapsed, there was an attempt to create an Armenian state under American trusteeship, but in Mar. 1921 Turkey and the U.S.S.R. agreed to give each other a free hand with the Armenians in their own territory. The allies did not intervene. There was another massacre at Smyrna in 1922. Apart from creating an Armenian diaspora, these massacres caused great indignation in Britain and kept anti-Turkish sentiment alive. Armenian independence was yet again suppressed. Karabakh was incorporated into Russian Azerbaijan as an enclave, which, in 1988 began a long civil war. *See* AZERBAIJAN.

ARMINIANISM, the doctrine of Jacob **Hermandzoon** or Jacobus **Arminius** (1560-1609) represented a reaction against Calvinist determinism prevalent in the Netherlands. Its most precise statement is found in the **Remonstrance** of 1610 drawn up at Gouda after his death. It repudiated predestination, and the doctrines that Christ died only for the elect, and that the saints cannot fall from grace. More positively, it asserts that Christ died for all men, and that Divine omnipotence is compatible with human free will. The **Remonstrants** allied to Oldenbarneveldt and the Dutch republicans (who favoured peace) opposed the Calvinists allied to Prince Maurice of Orange and more aggressive politicians. Thus the controversy had a bearing on European politics. The condemnation of Arminianism at the Synod of Dort (1619), to which James I sent observers, was a victory for Dutch extremists in church and state. Abp. Laud and his supporters were sometimes called Arminians by their opponents, but were not markedly influenced by Arminianism.

ARMISTICE, TRUCE, TRUCE OF GOD. (1) An **armistice** is an agreement between opposed belligerents temporarily to cease fighting while still remaining at enmity (e.g. by maintaining blockades) in every other respect. **(2)** A **Truce** is a temporary cessation of enmity in which the contestants behave more or less peacefully but without prejudice to the issues for which the war was being fought or the right to take up arms again. A truce may last a long time e.g. 20 years. **(3)** A **Truce Of God** was a close season for fighting imposed by the Church. The Council of Elne (1027) forbade warfare between Saturday night and Monday morning, and later, in Advent and Lent. **(4) The Armistice** of 11 Nov. 1918 marked the end of World War I. The German forces were in dissolution. The German High Command, in so far as it could, surrendered, and the Allies put an end to hostilities while continuing the blockade. The armistice was periodically renewed until the signature of the T. of Versailles. **(5)** The Franco-German Armistice of 1940. That of 1918 had been signed in a railway carriage at Compiègne. The Germans used the same coach.

ARMORICA. Lat = Brittany.

ARMOUR. (Other than tilting or ceremonial armour). Plate armour disappeared with the Romans, and Frankish, Viking and Saxon soldiers wore mail shirts of riveted rings or scales, with an iron helmet. Shields were circular or oblong. Only the Normans used the kite-shape. To hack or batter through such protection, swords, axes and maces became larger and heavier, and so mail became heavier still. To reduce the wearer's discomfort a padded linen *gambeson* was worn underneath and the heat of the sun on crusade led to the adoption of the light *surcoat,* often heraldically ornamented, overall. Mail was vulnerable to penetration by pointed weapons particularly arrows and crossbow bolts, and the wearer could not avoid contusions and broken bones if struck sufficiently violently. Moreover, a knight's horse was at the mercy of English bowmen. Hence during the 14th cent. plate armour began to appear, first at sensitive places, and so did horse armour. By 1400 complete plate armour was being forged so ingeniously that its weight was mostly self supporting, and the shield was abandoned by cavalry altogether. Armourers were highly skilled; their industries congregated in particular places of which the most important were Milan and Venice (Italy), Augsburg, Nürnberg, and Landshut (Germany), Innsbruck (Tyrol), Toledo (Spain) and Damascus (Syria).

Comfortable armour, especially for infantrymen, was extremely expensive and troops preferred to wear less of it than endure a badly fitting suit. Hence infantry began to discard armour before it was seriously threatened by firearms. Cavalry were still wearing very full armour in the Civil War; musketeers, who needed to move very freely had none, but pikemen still wore a great deal of it. The invention of the bayonet (q.v.) outmoded the pike and the pikeman's armour together, and the increasing efficiency of firearms led to the abandonment of cavalry armour in the 18th cent. though French cuirassiers fought at Waterloo.

ARMS, ASSISE OF (1181) required all freemen to provide themselves with arms and practice their use. The object was to provide a local defence militia more efficient than the *fyrd*. A similar measure (The Assize of Le Mans) was adopted for Henry II's continental dominions, and it was copied by the French King and the Counts of Flanders.

ARMSTRONG. There were several personalities of this common Border surname. **(1) John** (?-1528) **(2) William** or **Kinmont Willie** (?1602-?58) and **(3) William** or **Christi's Will** (fl. 1596) were notorious mosstroopers; **(4) Archibald** (?-1672) an Eskdale sheepstealer became jester to **James VI** and **I**, made a fortune and went with Charles to Spain. In 1637 he insulted Abp. Laud and was dismissed. **(5) William** (**1778-1857**) was mayor of Newcastle. His son **(6) Sir William George** (**1810-1900**), **1st Ld. ARMSTRONG of CRAGSIDE** invented the hydraulic pressure accumulator (1850), submarine mines (1854), the breach-loading rifled gun (1858), and the wirewound gun barrel (1880). He established the Elswick warship yard in 1882, and took over Whitworth's gun factory in 1897.

ARMSTRONG, Sir George Carlyon Hughes (1836-1907)

Bart. (1892) editor of the strongly conservative *Globe* from 1871, bought it in 1875, and made it an influential supporter of Disraeli. He had a flair for scoops and *inter alia* published the then secret Salisbury-Shuvaloff treaty in May 1878. He acquired a large interest in the equally Tory *People* in 1882, and retired in 1889.

ARMY (For early customary forces *see* ARMS, ASSISE OF; FEUDALISM; FYRD; LAND TENURE). This note is concerned primarily with paid troops but because forces have mostly been raised *ad hoc* and by the means to hand at the given moment, there was a tendency for several systems to overlap each other in time. Unpaid troops are undisciplined and given to pillage friend and enemy alike with destructive political consequences.

Pre-Gunpowder

(1) Paid armies began to be raised under Henry II. The personnel were of four main types; viz, knights, usually of gentle birth serving as officers, mounted, armoured and providing their own horses; professional mounted men-at-arms, mostly recruited in Wales; skilled specialists such as the Genoese crossbowmen, and the Saracens brought back by crusaders; and dangerous and unruly mercenaries assembled from all over Europe but variously called Brabançons, Navarrese, or Routiers.

(2) Chain mail was expensive, hot and heavy. The armoured man needed a horse: the infantry stood no chance against mailed horsemen unless, like the Scots, they could in mass formation hold them out of arms-reach with **pikes,** which might be 16 feet long. A combination of crossbowmen and cavalry could be dangerous to massed pikemen, but the crossbow had a low rate of fire. **(3)** The **longbow** (*see* ARCHERY) mostly in the hands also of Welsh professionals, came into general use in the early 14th cent., by which time other English infantry was beginning to be armed with the bill, a kind of combined short pike and axe very effective against pikemen pure and simple. **(4) Artillery** in the sense of appliances for projecting missiles to a greater distance or of greater weight than a man could manage, was used before the coming of gunpowder in siege warfare (*see* CASTLES). **(5)** Armies were generally small and contemporary accounts invariably exaggerate their size. The total numbers engaged at Hastings (1066) did not exceed 17,000, at Bannockburn (1314) 27,000. The B. of Towton (1461), said to have been the biggest ever fought in Britain, involved about 50,000.

Gunpowder

(6) English troops had **Guns** at Crécy (1346) for the first time, but gunpowder made little difference to warfare for another 90 years. The ingredients of primitive gunpowder tended to separate in transit and had to be mixed just before use. Hand guns were too heavy, inaccurate and self destructive; cannon were too clumsy and immobile for general use. Thus gunpowder weapons were confined to occasions where they could be used with deliberation. **(7)** The process of improvement, however, continued. Corned powder, which was more powerful and could be transported and used without delay was invented in about 1430. Increased pressures inside barrels instigated improvements in gun metal refining and gun casting. By about 1440 the Turks and the French had reliable cannon. The French, in particular, developed guns which, by previous comparison, were easily moved and with these they enforced the capitulation of many Aquitainian strongholds in the closing stages of the Hundred Years War.

(8) So far these developments had hardly influenced the behaviour or organisation of field armies; but the invention in Spain of the **Arquebus** or hackbut in mid 15th cent. did. This was the first true hand gun; it resembled a large musket, ignited by a matchlock and was generally supported on a forked rest. It weighed up to 30lb, was very slow to load (by the muzzle), and rain invariably put out the match. Its extreme effective range was 200 yards. It was superseded, as the Toledo refiners improved their skills, by the Spanish **Musket** in about 1580. This was lighter and though still fired from a rest, used corned powder and could penetrate armour. **(9)** The armoured knight began to disappear as a result, while infantry had to be armed part with muskets, part with pikes to protect the musketeers while loading. An elaborate drill and standardised organisation was necessary and training became a skill. As muskets became yet lighter the forked rest disappeared, and the introduction of, first, the wheel lock and, then, the flint lock made for greater reliability and protection against bad weather. The proportion of pikemen to musketeers in a unit declined as the rate of fire rose. In the Swedish army under Gustavus Adolfus infantry was trained to fight in a chequerboard formation with musketeers discharging volleys by thirds or quarters down the avenues between solid blocks of pikemen. Swedish-trained officers fought in the Civil War. **(10)** The role of cavalry in the new era was long in doubt. Shock tactics became unfashionable, horsemen being often armed with heavy horse pistols with which they ineffectively peppered the enemy. Hence they were used mainly for reconnaissance and pursuit. Artillery, on the other hand, advanced rapidly. Gustavus introduced a light **Field Gun** manned by soldiers not contractors, and firing a two pound shot.

(11) The next great change was the invention of the **Bayonet,** perhaps at Bayonne in about 1640. The plug bayonet prevented the musket from being fired but the ring bayonet (about 1690) enabled the weapon to serve the purpose of both pike and musket. Pikemen disappeared from the battlefield and the muzzle loading smooth-bore flintlock with bayonet attachment, remained the standard infantry weapon until the Crimean War. The Prussians improved the rate of fire in the 1730's by introducing the iron ram rod. Frederick the Great and his generals Seydlitz and Ziethen greatly improved the use of the mounted arms: limbered horse artillery with mounted gunners could move as fast as cavalry. Seydlitz reintroduced cavalry shock tactics, while Ziethen developed the light cavalry.

(12) Since the control of the army was a main issue in the Civil War, from the Restoration onwards parliament only allowed peacetime military establishments on sufferance, and Army Acts, limited to a year's duration, were passed annually. Hence wartime establishments were invariably run down very quickly as soon as peace was concluded, and large numbers of old soldiers would be suddenly thrown on the labour market or the parish rates. The Royal Artillery, however, became permanent in 1716, the Royal Engineers in 1717 but as there was no staff the regular disbandments after wars resulted in experience being lost and the British army being behindhand with up to date technical ideas. The army, it was said, was always preparing for the last war.

(13) In fact, however pedestrian many English commanders were, the British infantry of the line was the best in the world because the true use of musket and bayonet had been more fully grasped than elsewhere. Musketeers had the best chance of destroying their enemy if they adopted a formation in which they could all fire. The English three rank line firing rolling volleys was superior to the infantry column attacking it. The English square firing by platoons was safe from cavalry.

(14) In the later middle ages the crown raised troops by issuing a commission of **Array** to a local magnate and, in effect, contracting with him for a unit, for which he was paid a fixed amount per head for equipment and wages. This practice developed into the **Regimental System** after the Restoration. In theory regiments were numbered and disbanded in reverse order of number, although sometimes there were political departures from this rule. In practice also particular regiments tended to be recruited from particular areas perhaps related to the

sphere of influence of the original magnate who raised them. Most of the low numbered regiments had a long continuous existence and a noticeable social and corporate identity, recognised by the public. This regimental spirit contributed much to the toughness and endurance of British troops.

(15) The **rifle** was invented early but was not usable as a military weapon until the American phase of the Seven Years War. Rifle units trained as self reliant skirmishing troops began to supplement the line infantry in the 1770's and had a distinguished record in the Peninsular War. It was, however, exceedingly difficult to load a rifle from the muzzle with ball or prevent fouling. In the 1830s, however the Minié rifle using a hollow conical bullet which was easily slid down the rifling and then expanded by the exploding gases, suddenly gave the infantryman an accurate range of 700 yards and swept the cavalry off the battlefield. In 1848 the Prussian needlegun, a breachloader, made it possible for the infantryman, for the first time, to fight lying down. By 1875 all European infantry used breachloaders and by 1900, with the coming of brass cartridges, bolt action repeaters. 25 trained invisible men (such as Boers) could now fire 500 shots at a target half a mile away in one minute. The, at the time obvious, tactical solution was a commensurate improvement in artillery with the introduction of breach loading rifled guns.

(16) Armies grew and each weapon consumed progressively more ammunition. The need for supply services increased in geometrical progression. Armies might live off a well stocked country if their govts were willing to sacrifice the inhabitants' good will. Bonaparte's military plundering was a major factor in his defeat, but in a poor or burned out country such as Russia or Spain it was impossible by requisitions to live at all. Thus supporting services, for one reason or the other, had to convey not merely munitions of war but supply food, medical care, pay and so forth. In the Peninsular War Wellington developed a makeshift but effective system, which withered with the peace. The Crimean War revealed the depth of its inadequacy as well as incompetence and corruption. Luckily the Crimean War came before the greatest logistics explosion, so that military reforms were carried out with such problems in mind. **(17)** The mind, however, had to be created in the form of a **General Staff.** The Staff College was established in 1858. The war had shown how vulnerable a small long service army might be, and in 1859 a volunteer movement was launched which quickly raised a reserve of 180,000 men. By 1870 the lessons of the Austro-Prussian War of 1866 had been digested, and six years service with the colours plus six in reserve replaced enlistment for life. This, of course, rapidly created a fully trained professional reserve alongside the volunteers. In 1871 the curious system of taking commissions and promotion by purchase was abolished. In 1873 a beginning, enforced by Indian exigencies, was made with the linking of battalions, and by 1881 the regiments had all been localised. (*See* REGIMENT). At the beginning of the South African War (1899) the army, considered as a machine, was adequate; the tactics imposed by its commanders were not. There was just time to reform these before World War I.

Mechanization

(18) The professional army reached its apotheosis in the first months of World War I but the strategic deadlock in the winter of 1914-5 brought new problems. **Machine Guns** had been invented as long ago as 1862 and all armies made moderate use of them up to 1914. The recumbent infantry by now protected themselves against shell fire from the vastly increased artillery, by digging in. Machine guns began to sweep the approaches to the trenches, and barbed wire forced attacking infantry to stand up and be shot. Again the military brains demanded more artillery, and battles became massed artillery duels lasting weeks. Tactics had become industrialised and the shape of the army changed accordingly. By now only a minority of the troops actually struck at the enemy. The rest brought up supplies part of which they consumed themselves. The total effort was tactically and economically counter-productive, for the bombardments broke up the drainage and in the winters converted the wire strewn battlefields into impassable quagmires, while entire industries had to be converted from more useful pursuits. **(19)** The murderous inconclusive duels of 1914 to 1916 led a British committee of naval inspiration to propose a solution to the barbed wire and machine gun domination. This was the armoured land battleship or **Tank** based upon the agricultural tractor. Teething troubles and initial mistakes in tactical handling gave it only a limited influence on the outcome of the War, but radically altered the nature of later wars, and meanwhile aircraft had replaced light cavalry for reconnaissance while the bomber formed a new type of artillery. The professional forces which emerged after 1919 were therefore more diverse than in previous eras, though the framework of 1881 still remained, for this framework, by adding new battalions as required, to existing regiments had been found capable of unlimited expansion during the volunteer period up to 1916 and in the conscription period of 1916 to 1918.

(20) In the return to a small professional army, (about 180,000) the possibility of a revival of conscription was never quite forgotten and when Nazi Germany's aggressive intentions became obvious in 1937 the National Service Act, though lackadaisically operated by a hopeful govt., created the necessary administrative arrangements and made the first registrations in 1938*. World War II was fought almost wholly with conscripted forces. *See also* ARMOUR, ARTILLERY

ARMY ACTS. *See* MUTINY ACT.

ARMY BUREAU OF CURRENT AFFAIRS (A.B.C.A.) was organised to inform British service people about the purposes of World War II by lectures and pamphlets, some on social problems. Despite claims that it delivered the service vote to Labour in 1945, its impact on exhausted personnel even during training was small, and during fighting nil.

ARMY COUNCIL was created on the analogy of the Board of Admiralty when the office of Commander-in-Chief was abolished in 1904. *See* ARNOLD-FORSTER.

ARMY MEDICAL CORPS, ROYAL (R.A.M.C.). Before 1854 field units recruited their own medical staff as best they could, and in the H.Q. of the military C-in-C there was a surgeon-gen. who was mainly a medical staff officer. His authority depended wholly on the interest which his C-in-C took in the work, and his effectiveness on the provision made by the Medical Dept. of the War Office for hospitals and equipment. Since medicine was in its infancy, the needs were seldom foreseen or adequately anticipated. The Crimean War scandals resulted in the formation of a Medical Staff Corps. and in 1857 this became the all male Army Hospital Corps. soon officered from the War Office. After various changes of name the corps. and the War Office Medical Department were amalgamated to form the R.A.M.C. in 1898.

ARMY PLOTS (1641). *See* CHARLES 1-16; STRAFFORD.

ARMY SERVICE CORPS, ROYAL (R.A.S.C.) (*See* WAGONERS). The Land Transport Corps, was formed in the Crimean War, merged with the Military Train in 1856 and became the A.S.C. in 1870. In 1880 the ordnance stores

branch was hived off, and a new A.S.C. was formed in 1889. It has been responsible for getting supplies to the troops ever since.

ARNE, Thomas Augustine (1710-78), prolific composer and also band leader at Drury Lane and Covent Garden, is now best remembered for his music to Mallet's *Alfred,* which includes *Rule Britannia* (1740). Dr Burney was one of his pupils.

ARNHEM (Holland) B. of (Sept 1944). The British Airborne Div. under Gen. Browning, was dropped to seize the Rhine bridges in preparation for a rapid thrust, advocated by Gen. Montgomery, into the Ruhr and towards Berlin. A German formation in transit was accidentally present, and the boggy terrain and narrow roads south of the river (of which the generals were advised), enabled the Germans to prevent a link-up between the Division and allied ground forces to the south. The gallant surviving paratroopers were forced to surrender. *See* WORLD WAR II-15.

ARNISTON. *See* DUNDAS.

ARNOLD, Benedict (1741-1801), the American National Traitor, was a Connecticut bookseller who volunteered with the rebels, helped Ethan Allen to take Ticonderoga in 1775, and after winning a victory at Ridgefield (Conn) in 1777 was promoted Maj-Gen. He played a leading part under Gates in the Saratoga Campaign when he was wounded, and in June 1778 took command at Philadelphia, recently evacuated by the British. Here he was accused of peculation by the Pennsylvanian civil authorities, eventually court marshalled and in 1780 partially acquitted. Resentment or a change of heart caused him to offer to surrender West Point to Sir Henry Clinton, the nearest British commander, for £20,000. The correspondence was intercepted, and Arnold fled. He briefly but savagely helped the British to raid Virginia and Connecticut, and went to England in 1781 where he died.

ARNOLD (1) Dr Thomas (1795-1842) was educated at Winchester and Oxford, ordained in 1818 and from 1828 until his death was headmaster of Rugby; he revolutionised the public schools by broadening the curriculum to include, in addition to classics, mathematics, modern languages and history, and by diverting the energies of the boys into team games and evangelical Christianity. An influential supporter of R. Catholic emancipation, he wrote powerfully in its favour. He became regius prof. of history at Oxford in 1841. Three of his sons achieved distinction: **(2) Matthew (1822-88)** was private sec. to the Marquess of Lansdowne from 1847 to 1851 when he became an inspector of schools. He is, however, remembered as a distinguished critic and poet. **(3) Prof. Thomas (1823-1900)** was an inspector of schools in Tasmania from 1850 to 1856, and was a prof. of English Literature in Dublin from 1856 to 1862 and from 1882 to 1900. **(4) William Delafield (1828-59)** was director of public instruction in the Punjab from 1856.

ARNOLD-FORSTER, Hugh Oakeley (1855-1909), grandson of Thos. Arnold, nephew of Matthew Arnold, was adopted by W. E. Forster the liberal statesman. He became his private sec. when the latter became Chief Sec. for Ireland in 1880. His first work, *The Truth About the Land League* (1881) went far to discredit Irish nationalism in England. In 1884 he became sec. of the Imperial Federation League, and a powerful advocate of naval development and colonial preference. He sat as liberal-unionist M.P. for Belfast from 1892 to 1906, and in 1900 became sec. of the Admiralty. The First Lord (Selborne) being in the Lords, Arnold-Forster spoke in the Admiralty in the Commons and had, for a junior minister, an exceptional opportunity for shaping the policy being developed by Adm. Fisher. In 1903 he became S. of State for War and began to reform the War Office on the model of the Board of Admiralty. This was interrupted when the govt. fell in 1905 but bore fruit later

---

*The author believes that he was (accidentally) the first person to register. He was an undergraduate at Oxford where the registration began a week earlier than elsewhere. His surname begins with A and he was at the head of the queue when the office opened on the first day.

on. Thereafter he was slowly pressed into retirement by poor health.

A.R.P. (Air Raid Precautions) were protective arrangements sponsored by the govt. to protect civilians before and during World War II. They included the appointment of air raid wardens, public and private bomb shelters, a black-out of lights in houses, shops and street lighting, air-raid sirens, an extensive voluntary system of fire-watching against incendiaries, and the provision of the whole population with gas-masks. The Royal Observer Corps, a voluntary unpaid body, watched for and plotted approaching raiders. The whole represented a considerable but valuable burden on the war economy. *See* CIVIL DEFENCE.

ARQUEBUS. (*See* ARMY-8.) Edward IV brought some 300 Flemish arquebusiers to Ravenspur in 1471. At the B. of Stoke (1487) the weapon is said to have killed 2000 men.

ARRAN, HAMILTON Es. of *see* HAMILTON; JAMES III AND V OF SCOTS.

ARRAN, Sir Thomas Boyd, E. of *see* JAMES III OF SCOTS.

ARRAS, Bs. of (Apr. 1917) (1) Part of Nivelle's dual offensive, the British advance was small and involved 142,000 casualties, but the Canadians took Vimy Ridge. The R. Flying Corps' large scale reconnaissances lost heavily from aerial fighter ambushes out of the clouds. *See also* WORLD WAR I–11.

(2) (May 1940) During the retreat to Dunkirk, a British armoured brigade in a fairly small engagement inflicted such losses that the Germans are said to have been deterred from attacks later on.

ARRAS, TREATIES OF (1) 1191 *see* ARTOIS; PHILIP AUGUSTUS; **(2) 1414** between Charles VI and John the Fearless; **(3) 1435** between Charles VIII of France and Philip of Burgundy whereby the latter abandoned the English alliance in the Hundred Years War in return for Macon, Auxerre, and parts of Picardy **(4) 1482.** *See* ARTOIS.

ARRAY, COMMISSIONS OF. From the 13th cent. English kings sought to increase the troops raised by contract by reviving the ancient universal duty of military service. Arrayers were commissioned to go into the shires to choose, clothe, equip and pay each a certain number of men. After 1343 such conscripts could buy exemption for cash, although this was not often done. The men thus raised were usually archers and other infantry, and sometimes specialist craftsmen. *See* ARMY.

ARREARS ACT 1881 (Ir) provided that if a tenant were unable to pay his arrears of rent but actually paid the rent for 1880-1881, the Treasury would pay 50% of the arrears due, and the rest would be cancelled.

ARRESTABLE OFFENCE. *See* FELONY.

ARRÊT DE PRINCE. *See* EMBARGO.

ARROMANCHES (Normandy) was the site of the extraordinary floating harbour (code named MULBERRY) which was towed across the Channel as part of the invasion equipment on 6 June 1944. Construction began four days later. It was interrupted on 18th by a prolonged storm but was functioning fully by the first week of July, delivering 15,000 tons a day.

ARROW WAR. *See* PALMERSON'S FIRST ADMINISTRATION-8.

ARTEVELDE, Jacob (?1287-1345) and Philip (1340-82). *See* FLANDERS-11-16.

ARTHUR, King (6th cent.). Traditionally one Uther Pendragon had two sons, a 5th cent. ruler called **Ambrosius Aurelianus** or **Emrys**, and **Arthur**, but it is possible that these three, or two of them in varying combinations, have been confused. Aneirin's poem *Gododdin* (c. 600) mentions a famous warrior called Arthur. It is certain that the British had a powerful and skilful general at this time. Gildas, perhaps imitating Nennius, says that Arthur fought 12 battles (possibly against the South Saxons) culminating in the great victory at Mount Badon (q.v.) in 516.

The much later chivalric romance may possibly represent a tradition that he was a cavalry leader; this would explain the dissemination of local traditions about him from Cornwall to Cumberland. He is said to have died after the B. of Camlan (537) in a war with other Britons. For Camlan, Camelford (Cornwall) where there is a place called Slaughter Field, has been suggested.

The legend of him and his Knights of the Round Table was very popular, and the 12th cent. Geoffrey of Monmouth was only the first of its written embroiderers. Sir Thomas Mallory's *Morte d'Arthur* was a translation from the French. He wrote it in 1469-70 and Caxton printed it in 1485.

ARTHUR, Sir GEORGE, Bart (1784-1854) originally a soldier, was lieut-gov of Honduras from 1814 to 1822 and his despatches on slavery attracted the attention of Wm. Wilberforce. He became Lieut-gov. of Van Diemen's Land (Tasmania) from 1823 to 1837 and of Upper Canada from 1837 to 1841. In 1842 he was gov. of Bombay and in 1846 provisional Gov-Gen., but retired through ill health.

ARTHUR, Prince (1486-1502), elder brother of Henry VII, married Katherine of Aragon in Nov. 1501 at St Pauls, London, but died before his father Henry VII. The marriage may not have been consummated. If not consummated, there was no impediment to Katherine marrying Henry. If consummated, it could be held to nullify Henry's marriage to her, when he found it convenient to get rid of her.

ARTHUR of BRITTANY (1187-1203) as a son of Geoffrey, third son of Henry II, and Constance of Brittany, had a claim to Brittany and a better claim to England than K. John, who was Henry II's fourth son. A child in 1199, when Richard I died, he became a puppet in Anglo-French politics. John seized the English throne; King Philip II of France secured Arthur's custody, and invested him with Richard's French fiefs as well as Brittany. During the ensuing intermittent hostilities John's mother, Eleanor of Aquitaine, was besieged by Arthur and his allies at Mirebeau in 1202; but John relieved the castle, captured Arthur, and in 1203 murdered him. This deed shocked the Anglo-Norman nobility. Philip was able to use it to justify forfeiting and conquering Normandy, and John was never trusted again.

ARTICLES, LORDS OF THE (Sc) were a committee of 41 of the Scots parliament which between 1461 and 1689 (save in the years 1640 to 1661) dominated its affairs. The unicameral parliament having assembled and verified the credentials of its members, the four orders adjourned to separate rooms. The prelates then nominated eight nobles, the nobles eight prelates, prelates and nobles jointly eight lairds and eight representatives of towns. The session was resumed, and the crown nominated eight of its officers and appointed the Lord Chancellor to preside.

The parliament and the crown referred its business by Articles (i.e. agenda items) to the Lords, who sat daily and dealt with them while the other members of the parliament waited, intrigued, roistered or wenched. After about a week, the Lords had finished, the parliament would resume, and the resulting drafts would be laid before it, passed, generally on a single vote, and given the Royal Assent by touch of sceptre. The amount of legislation thus passed could be large. In 1633 between 18th June, when parliament assembled and 28th, when it dispersed, 168 Acts were passed by this procedure.

In the constitution of this peculiarly Scottish body, the 10 or 12 prelates, who were crown nominees, played a vital part since they were like-minded. They could exclude radicals from among the 40 or 50 nobles, but the nobles had little choice of prelates. Similarly their joint choice of lairds and the lowly townsmen would reduce radical membership to a minimum. The crown nominees were all officers who could be dismissed at will. Thus the crown's hold on the Lords of the Articles and therefore on parliament, was very strong and likely to remain as long as the episcopal church was unchallenged.

The method of legislation implied in the existence of

the Articles much more resembled the bargaining at a private council meeting than a public session of a legislature on a bill. Public debate in full parliament occurred before the Lords had been nominated, and very seldom after they had reported.

The presbyterian attack on prelacy was as much political as dogmatic. It was an ultimately successful campaign to take over the legislative process.

ARTICLES OF CONFEDERATION adopted by the American Continental Congress in Nov. 1777. ratified by 12 states by 1779, and by Maryland in 1782, were a multilateral treaty for the common management of foreign and Indian policy, coinage and posts, and for the settlement of inter-state disputes. In the so-called congress each state had one vote, and amendments had to be unanimous. There was no federal executive or judiciary; the states retained all rights not ceded, including taxation and regulation of trade, and often evaded their obligations. By 1786 the defects of the Articles had generated the discussions which led in 1789 to their supersession by the constitution.

ARTICLES OF WAR were royal prerogative regulations governing military discipline and conduct in time of war. They did not apply in peacetime when such matters were regulated, if at all by contract. The first statutory legal framework for the Army was the Mutiny Act 1789 which did not supersede the prerogative. The Mutiny Act of 1803, however, did and discipline has since been governed by successive Army Acts.

ARTICULI CLERI* (Lat: Articles of the Clergy) (1316)** or ***DE DIVERSIS LIBERTATIBUS CLERO CONCESSIS (Lat: Various Liberties Granted to the Clergy). The 16 chapters of this enactment arose from clerical complaints opportunistically brought forward at the Lincoln Parliament in the aftermath of Bannockburn, in Jan. 1316. They were enacted in Nov. They limited the royal power to prevent the levy of certain tithes and also impositions upon religious houses and certain church lands, and, consistently, the power to intervene in ecclesiastical sentences of excommunication commonly used to enforce tithes. They also extended the effect of sanctuary, and purported to abolish royal interference in ecclesiastical elections.

***ARTICULI SUPER CARTAS* (Lat: Articles supplementary to the Charters) (1300)**, confirmed the charters yet again, and then legislated against the tendency of certain royal officials to overstep their jurisdictions. Thus purveyors were forbidden to take more than was necessary, or for any needs but the King's, the marshal was forbidden to hold civil pleas, the Common Pleas were not to be held in the Exchequer, Common Law writs were not to issue under any of the petty seals, escheators were not to commit waste, bailiwicks were not to be let at excessive rents, and sheriffs should be elected. There were other, mainly procedural provisions, but also the important enactment that precious metals should be hall marked.

ARTIFICERS, STAT. OF (1563) ineffectually empowered J.P.'s to fix wages and, more effectually, to regulate apprenticeship. Repealed in 1814.

ARTIFICIAL INSEMINATION, HUMAN. Insemination from a donor (A.I.D.) is rejected as immoral by the R. Catholic church. In *Russell* (1924) AC 687 the Lords held that the essence of adultery was fertilisation *ab extra*. In *MacLennan* 1958 SC 105, the Court of Session held that its essence was bodily copulation only. Hence A.I.D. is adultery with consequent illegitimacy in England, but not in Scotland.

ARTILLERY (MILITARY) first appeared in action in the West at the S. of Cividale (1321). The English first used it at the B. of Crécy (1346), and Henry V took a battery to the S. of Harfleur (1415). The French artillery of the brothers Bureau was reducing English strongholds at the end of the Hundred Years War, and their newly devised field pieces combined with heavy cavalry enabled Francis I to defeat the hitherto invincible Swiss pikemen at Marignano (1515). For the next century, however, war was dominated by fortifications, and battles were uncommon; guns consequently remained heavy and were usually served by civilian contractors. The Swedish K. Gustavus Adolphus was the first to create a true field artillery firing light (2 and 4lb) shot, capable of rapid movement, and used in numbers. This required a specifically military organisation. It demonstrated its success at the B. of Lützen (1632). The French were the first major power to follow suit; in 1671 and 1676 Louvois organised fusilier and gunner regiments, and both sides made extensive use of field as well as heavy artillery in Louis XIV's wars. (*See* ARTILLERY, ROYAL) The French artillery was only fully organised in 1732. French standards introduced by Gribeauval long prevailed. 4, 8 and 12-pounders and large mortars were considered to be field artillery. 16- and 24-pounders and small mortars were siege or fortress artillery. Standardisation improved both training and ammunition supply. Guns could fire between 2 and 5 times a minute and could range accurately up to about 600 yards. Gribeauval also introduced cartridges, caissons and ammunition wagons, and the tangent-sight; his tactical and technical innovations were the foundation of Bonaparte's practice and dominated artillery theory everywhere until about 1825.

The application of rifling to guns in 1858 immensely increased their range, power and accuracy. The rifled explosive shell no longer needed to be spherical which increased its weight and aerodynamic quality, but since muzzle loading of rifled guns was very slow, breach loaders had to be developed. In the 1870 war the Prussians had them, but the French had not. The result was a considerable French effort afterwards. They invented smokeless powder in 1884 and the celebrated quickfiring 75 in 1897. Details of these improvements reached the British by way of the *entente cordiale* in 1910, but the French thought that their new weapons had made heavy artillery out of date. Consequently they were insufficiently equipped for the siege warfare of World War I and it was left to the British to develop the heavy but comparatively mobile 9.2in howitzer.

After the war the British, impressed by the need for mobility and versatility, developed the 25-pounder (a gun-howitzer) and the high velocity anti-tank gun. As World War II tanks grew heavier, anti-tank guns grew from the 2-pounder to the 6-pounder and the 17-pounder, and parallel developments occurred in all other major armies. The limiting factor was weight and viability of the recoil mechanism, and this in its turn led to the development of the recoilless (back blast) gun, the anti-tank bomb projector and the rocket. By the 1980s rocket propulsion was encroaching into the field of ballistics.

ARTILLERY, ROYAL (R.A.). Two companies were raised in 1716 and increased to four in 1727. They depended, however, on civilian waggoners until 1793 when the Royal Horse Artillery (R.H.A.), which always kept its own transport and horses, was formed. In 1794 a Drivers' Corps was formed for the R.A. and (after various changes of name) was amalgamated with the R.A. in 1822. When the Board of Ordnance (q.v.) was abolished in 1855 as a result of the Crimean War, the control of the R.A. passed to the War Office. In 1861 the three Indian artillery corps were amalgamated with it.

ARTISANS AND LABOURERS DWELLINGS ACT 1875 required the City of London, the Metropolitan Board of Works and the Urban Sanitary Authorities to take heed of representations by medical officers of health that an area was unhealthy, and empowered them to clear and rebuild such an area in accordance with schemes which had to be confirmed by a Sec. of State or the Local Govt. Board. The initial expense was to be defrayed by the rates, but ultimately recovered from rents.

ARTOIS (Fr) with **Arras** its capital. (*For early history see* FLANDERS). when Count Robert II was killed at B. of Courtrai in 1302, Artois was adjudged to his daughter Mahaut (Matilda), who by marrying Otto IV brought it to the House of Burgundy, and so at the death of Charles the Bold in 1477 to the Habsburgs. The time between 1302 and 1477 was the period of Arras mediaeval banking and textile prosperity (arras = wall hanging), which was interrupted in the 14th cent. by struggles between guildmasters and artisans, and after the Third T. of Arras (1435) between Charles VII of France and Philip the Good of Burgundy, by the Anglo-Burgundian War. In 1477, Charles the Bold having been killed at Nancy, Arras was stormed and almost destroyed by Louis XI who acquired the sovereignty in 1482 at the fourth T. of Arras and resettled it from other parts of France. In 1492 it was sacked by the Spaniards and retroceded to the Habsburgs in 1492 at the T. of Senlis.

On the partition of Charles V's empire, Artois passed in 1555 to Spain which held it until 1640. During the Thirty Years War it was conquered by France, and ceded by Spain in part at the T. of the Pyrenees in 1659, and in part by the T. of Nimwegen in 1678.

ARTS, ROYAL SOCIETY OF, was founded in 1754.

ARTS COUNCIL OF GREAT BRITAIN (1946) was developed from a wartime Council for the Encouragement of Music and the Arts (C.E.M.A.) in order to exclude political influence from govt. funding of the arts. This was to be done through the *arm's length principle* namely by making it the recipient of annual global sums and leaving it to distribute the money in detail. Its chairmen and 19 members, even though (or because) they could call on advice from specialised panels and committees (often of practitioners) had difficulty in allocating the money so as to encourage the deserving or promising without subsidising the mediocre. Its mistakes between 1946 and 1990 were gleefully reported by its enemies, but there is no means of knowing whether its activities injured or enriched British culture.

ARUNDEL, Es. of. *See* ALBINI; FITZALAN; HOWARD.

ARUNDEL MARBLES from the I. of Paros represent part of a chronicle of Athenian history brought to England in 1627 for Thomas Howard, E. of Arundel. Another part was found in 1897.

ARUNDEL (Sussex), a village dominated by the huge castle, the seat of the D. of Norfolk. The castle was founded in 12th cent, but largely rebuilt in a mediaeval style in 19th. There is also a R. Catholic cathedral for the diocese of Arundel and Brighton.

ARUNDEL, Thomas (1353-1414) Abp. of Canterbury. Third *s.* of Richard Fitzalan, E. of Arundel and Warenne, by his second wife, Eleanor, *d.* of Henry Plantagenet, E. of Lancaster, rose rapidly as an ecclesiastic with influential connections. Archdeacon of Taunton in 1373 he was made Bp. of Ely in 1374. In 1386 he became Lord Chancellor, in 1388 Abp. of York, and in 1396 Abp. of Canterbury, whereupon he resigned the chancellorship. All the while he was much concerned with secular politics, in which his brother Richard E. of Arundel played a leading role. After Richard II's arrest of Gloucester, Warwick, and Arundel in 1397, Thomas was impeached by the Commons and banished. He returned to England with Henry of Lancaster in 1399, was restored to his see, and he crowned Henry on 13 October. In subsequent years he was involved in suppressing Lollardy. He became Chancellor again in 1407, and yet again in 1414.

ARUNDELL is the name of three inter-related Cornish families respectively of Lanherne, Trerice and Tolverne. **(1) Sir John (?-1379)** commanded a naval expedition against Brittany, and defeated a French fleet off Cornwall in 1379, but having raped and drowned a number of nuns was justly drowned in a subsequent storm. **(2) John (?-1477)** was a domestic chaplain to Henry VI and became Bp. of Chichester in 1458. **(3) John (?-1504)** became Dean of Exeter in 1483, Bp. of Lichfield in 1496 and of Exeter in 1502. **(4) Humphrey (1513-50)** sided with and led a Cornish anti-inclosure rebellion in 1549, and was hanged. **(5) Sir John (1495-1561)** known as *Jack of Tilbury* was Vice-Admiral of the West under Henry VII and Henry VIII. **(6) Thomas (1560-1639) 1st Ld. ARUNDELL of WARDOUR (1605)** a soldier, fought the Turks in Hungary, was a favourite of Queen Elizabeth's and was killed in the civil war. His wife **(7) Lady Blanche (1583-1649)** with 25 men defended Wardour Castle for eight days against a parliamentary force of 1300 in May 1643. **(8) Sir John (1576-1656)** known as 'Jack for the King' was governor of Pendennis, commanding the Fal, and sustained a famous five month siege. **(9) Henry (1606-92) 3rd Ld. ARUNDEL of WARDOUR** a R. Catholic was one of the negotiators of the secret treaty of Dover in 1669. Accused in 1678 by Titus Oates of complicity in the non-existent Popish plot, he was impeached along with Belasyse and Stafford. Delays caused by technical disagreements between the Houses gave time for the truth to come out, and saved his life. In 1685 he was freed. James II made him Lord Privy Seal in 1687, but at the King's abdication he retired. **ARYAN** (Sanskrit: noble) formerly referred to the Indo-European group of languages, or those who spoke the Indo-Persian subgroup of it. The 19th cent. Comte de Gobineau and his disciple Stewart Chamberlain propagated a theory of an Aryan race, said to have been responsible for all human progress and morally superior to the Semites, and persons of other colour. In Nazi Germany the term was used to distinguish those whom the regime regarded as racially pure or at least unobjectionable, from others such as Jews, Gypsies and Negroes who were to be exterminated. These racial doctrines contained insurmountable problems of definition and were incapable of lucid development; and 'Aryan' declined into a political term meaning, if anything, those of not too unEuropean appearance or ancestry who were prepared to support Hitler.

ARYA SAMAJ. This monotheistic Hindu sect, founded in 1875 by the Swami Dayannand Saraswati (1824-83) denies the efficacy of the priesthood, is opposed to the caste system and bases its views upon the Vedas. Vigorously reformist, it is comparable in spirit with evangelical Christianity, but intolerant of Christianity and Islam. It furthers female education and inter-caste marriage, and has built shelters for orphans and widows. From its first propagation it has been a factor in the advance of Indian nationalism.

ASAPH, St. (?-?596) St. Kentigern, driven by persecution from Strathclyde to Wales, founded a monastery at Llanelwy. When he returned to Strathclyde in about 570 Asaph succeeded him there, and possibly became the first Bp. of Llanelwy, which was later called after him.

ASCENSION I. (S. Atlantic) discovered in 1501 by the Portuguese João de Nova, was occupied by the British in 1815 as a supplementary patrol station, while Bonaparte was at St. Helena. It remained under Admiralty control until 1922 when it became a dependency of St. Helena. It became a cable centre and B.B.C. relay station, and in 1942 a U.S. airfield was built; this has since been used as an R.A.F. staging post. During the Falklands War (1982) the island was an important staging post for naval and military supplies as well as aircraft.

ASCHAM, Roger (1515-68) a versatile Tudor scholar, wrote a well known treatise on archery (*Toxophilus*), invented a long used method of teaching Latin, and wrote and taught extensively on education (he opposed corporal punishment). Though remembered for these things now, probably was most important as tutor to Princess (later Queen) Elizabeth from 1548 until 1559.

ASCOT. *See* HORSE RACING.

ASDIC. *See* COMMERCE PROTECTION, NAVAL-2.

ASHANTI (Ghana) was a slave-trading West African tribal confederacy with its capital at Kumasi. The British outlawed the slave trade in 1807, and their vigorous action to suppress it eventually deprived the Ashanti of a major source of revenue. The first collision with the Gold Coast British occurred in 1820. The First Ashanti War lasted from 1821 to 1831 when the confederacy acknowledged British suzerainty over the Fanti. In 1872 it attacked the Fanti again and was defeated by Wolseley in the Second War of 1873-4. Intrigues at Kumasi created a probability of further disorder and the Third War of 1896, was a bloodless expedition ending in the banishment of the King, Prempeh, and the establishment of a protectorate. The Fourth War of 1900, however, was an intervention to rescue the Ashanti from their own rebellious subjects and led in Sept. 1901 to annexation to the Gold Coast Colony. *See* AFRICA, WEST.

ASHBURTON. *See* DUNNING; BARING.

ASHBURTON or ASHBURTON-WEBSTER TREATY (1842) fixed the Canada-Maine frontier, by a compromise in which Canada got only about 5000 of the 12,000sq. miles in dispute. The larger portion lay potentially but not actually across the direct route from Quebec to Halifax, and Peel and Ashburton thought it a fair bargain for U.S. help against the Slave Trade, for which the southern states provided the main market.

ASHEY v WHITE. *See* AYLESBURY ELECTION CASES.

ASHDOWN, CAMPAIGN and B. of (8 Jan. 871) In 866 Hingwar of Dublin a son of Ragnar Lothbrok, with Kings Hubba, Halfdan and Baskegg (Bacsaeg) led a Danish army against England. They wintered in Kent, crossed to E. Anglia in 867, and made a treaty with K. Edmund from whom they obtained horses. They then moved to York, and in Mar. 868 destroyed the Northumbrian forces at the B of York Gate. A treaty was forced on K. Buhred of Mercia, but meantime Edmund of E. Anglia, probably realising that the Danes intended permanent conquest, declared against them. He was captured at Thetford, and martyred at Medehamstead, later called Bury St. Edmunds.

Hingwar now went north, where with K. Olaf the White of Dublin he subdued Strathclyde, and eventually died in Dublin. Halfdan and Baskegg remained with the main army, and in Dec. 870 entrenched themselves at Reading. The West Saxon army under K. Ethelred I and his younger brother K. Alfred now came up, unsuccessfully assaulted the fortifications (4 Jan. 871) and retreated along the Ridgeway. The two forces made further contact on 8 Jan. at Ashdown, the Saxons being at the foot of a hill.

Both armies were divided into an advance force of picked men, centrally placed in wedge (boars head) formation, supported by a main body in line, but the Danish boar's head was commanded by their kings and the main body by their earls, whereas the Saxons' was to be commanded by Ethelred, the supporting force perhaps of better quality than the Danish, by Alfred. The Danes came down the hill before Ethelred had finished his prayers: Alfred took over the boar's head, charged uphill, and the two advance forces met with a crash round a stunted thorn. Ethelred then took command of the supporting force, charged past the stunted thorn and drove the Danish earls off the field. K. Baskegg and five earls were killed. Halfdan fought his way back to Reading with heavy losses.

This famous battle represented the first major check to the Danish invasion; it raised Saxon morale and was the first clear indication that the effective leaders against the Danes would be the West Saxon royal house.

ASHLEY, Ld. *See* COOPER.

ASHMOLE, Elias (1617-92), originally a solicitor, became a member of the royal garrison at Oxford during the Civil War and then entered Brasenose College where he studied natural philosophy. At the Restoration the Oxford Court connection proved useful, for Charles II made him Windsor Herald. He was also called to the bar and became a Fellow of the Royal Society. He collected curiosities and also acquired the complete botanical collection of the Tradescants of Lambeth. In 1677 he presented his collections to Oxford Univ. and they became the nucleus of the Ashmolean Museum founded in 1683.

ASHTON or ASSHETON. Lancashire families all distantly or closely related. **(1) Thomas (fl. 1346)** captured the Scots royal standard at Neville's Cross (1346). His son **(2) Sir John (?-1428)** was M.P. for Lancs. in 1413, and in 1416 became seneschal of Bayeux after its capture, and held other Norman offices. Twice married, he had many children of whom **(3) Sir Thomas (fl. 1446)** was an alchemist and had eleven children while **(4) Sir Ralph (fl. 1460-83)** acquired Middleton by marriage. His descendants remained there for 400 years. He was one of Richard III's commanders, V-Constable of England and Lieut. of the Tower. He was assassinated. A kinsman of (1), **(5) Sir Robert (?-1385)** was an M.P. in 1324, in 1359 Capt. of Guines, and in 1362 Lord Treasurer. In 1368 he was custodian of Sangatte (Calais), in 1369 Adm. of the Narrow Seas and in 1373 Lord Treasurer again. From 1380 he was constable of Dover.

ASKARI. An African soldier trained and commanded by Europeans, especially British, German or Italian.

ASKE, Robert (?-1537). *See* PILGRIMAGE OF GRACE.

A.S.L.I.B. (Assn. of Special Libraries and Information Bureaux) was founded in 1924 and merged with the British Soc. for International Bibliography in 1946.

ASKWITH, George Ranken (1861-1942), Ld. ASKWITH (1919), barrister and distinguished govt. negotiator generally in labour disputes and then in the railway branch of the Bd. of Trade, particularly in the years around 1911. He left valuable memoirs called *Industrial Problems and Disputes* (1920). His methods and ideas descended through a variety of conciliation bodies including A.C.A.S.

ASPASIA was the beautiful, cultivated, and witty mistress of the ancient Athenian statesman Pericles. The name is sometimes used for women of similar character in high political society.

AS[S]IENTO **(Sp = contract).** An arrangement permitted by the Spanish Crown whereby the subjects of a foreign country might trade slaves to Spanish America in breach of its own monopoly. *See* GEORGE 1-13; SLAVE TRADE.

ASQUITH, Herbert Henry (1852-1928) 1st E. of OXFORD AND ASQUITH (1925) and ASQUITH'S FIRST and SECOND GOVTS (Apr. 1908-May 1915; May 1915-Dec. 1916) (For the composition of these two cabinets, *see* next two entries) **(A) (1)** The son of a Lancashire woolspinner, Asquith had a brilliant school and Oxford career culminating in a fellowship of Balliol in 1874. He was called to the bar, but made no mark until his gifts were noticed by Sir Henry James (later Lord James of Hereford) in 1883. He became a Gladstonian liberal M.P. for E. Fife in 1886, and spoke effectively against Balfour's coercion of Ireland. He made his name, however, both as barrister and as politician, as junior to Sir Chas. Russell on behalf of Parnell before the Parnell Commission, and became a Q.C. in 1890 just before his first wife died. The Parnell divorce (Nov. 1890) damaged the electoral prospects of the Liberals who were returned in 1892 with a Home Rule pledge and only a majority of 40 to ensure it. Gladstone decided to choose young men for his Cabinet, and Asquith, without previous ministerial experience, became Home Secretary. In this he was a rare success, handling difficult problems such as the Irish dynamiters and the Featherstone riots coolly, administering his Office efficiently and getting the Factory Act, 1895, through the Commons. He married the famous

Margot Tennant (*see* **B**) during this period and when the liberals lost the election of 1895 he went out of office with greatly enhanced credit. In the ensuing internal squabbles he refused to take advantage of Lord Rosebery's resignation from the leadership in 1896 or Sir Wm. Harcourt's in 1898, but supported Sir Henry Campbell Bannerman's claims. Meantime he had broken the conventions by returning, though a Privy Councillor, to the bar.

(**2**) The Boer War created another fissure within the party, and a quarrel with Campbell Bannerman; they agreed in their condemnation of Chamberlain and Milner's policy, but Asquith thought that the war was inevitable while his chief thought it unjust. In these circumstances the party suffered severely in the Khaki Election of Oct. 1900, and the ensuing recriminations almost led to a rupture in Feb. 1902. The war, however, ended in May, and the liberals were able to unite against conservative home policy especially on education and protection.

In 1905 the conservatives resigned. Rosebery (supported by Sir Edw. Grey, Haldane and Campbell Bannerman) disagreed publicly on the Irish question. Grey and Haldane tried to force Campbell Bannerman to leave the leadership of the Commons to Asquith while he became prime minister as a peer. Asquith would have none of it: he induced Grey to accept the Foreign Office and Haldane the War Office, himself becoming Chanc. of the Exch. In 1906 the liberals had a landslide victory at the polls. So began one of the decisive govts. in English history. (*see also* CHURCHILL, WINSTON S.)

(**3**) Campbell Bannerman's declining health made Asquith the leading intelligence at the point – home policy – where liberal policies were most controversial. His three budgets (1906, 1907 and 1908) marked the change from 19th to 20th cent. Britain. Export taxes and taxes on food (such as tea and sugar) were reduced; the tax distinction was made between earned and unearned income; grants to Local Authorities were fatefully substituted for earmarked taxes; and old age pensions were introduced for the first time. When Campbell Bannerman resigned in Apr. 1908 Asquith succeeded without controversy. David Lloyd George succeeded him at the Exchequer.

(**4**) The govt's. duty to safeguard the country against Germany had led to Haldane's military reforms and the launching of the *Dreadnought,* but the latter, by making all other battleships out of date, had put Germany and Britain nearly level in the naval armaments race. Liberal legislation was being increasingly blocked by a Tory and landowning House of Lords. Money was needed for armaments. Asquith and Lloyd George proposed to raise it by a land tax. In Nov. 1909 the Lords threw out the budget in defiance of a 250 years custom that they would not interfere with finance. Asquith immediately obtained a dissolution and in the election of Jan. 1910 secured a majority which, despite Irish doubts, forced the budget through.

(**5**) This affair determined the party to proceed with a project for constitutional reform which it had entertained since 1907. A bill was brought in to reduce the House of Lords absolute veto on public legislation to a suspensory veto effective only for three sessions and two years. It would certainly not pass the Lords without a wholesale creation of peers, and Edward VII refused to create the necessary number until after a second general election in which the constitution was the sole issue. Before parliament could be dissolved the King died (May 1910)

And for the next few months Asquith tried unsuccessfully to negotiate a settlement. Accordingly in Nov. 1910 he obtained a secret undertaking from George V, and in Dec. the elections gave him a majority of 126. The Parliament Bill was now introduced and resisted by the Lords with wrecking amendments. In July 1911, on consideration of their amendments, it became necessary to reveal the King's promise. Resistance collapsed, though with a bad grace.

(**6**) The object, much publicised, of the Parliament Bill was to clear the way for further liberal legislation, of which Irish Home Rule was the most important. Faction made itself evident against the Home Rule bill introduced in Apr. 1912. The Ulster Protestants led by Sir Edw. Carson, arguing that the Parliament Act had taken away their constitutional safety, began to arm in order to assert their right to remain part of the U.K. Prosecution was impossible because the juries would not have convicted. Worst of all, some army officers at the Curragh, on being tactlessly asked if they would obey instructions to coerce Ulster, replied in Mar. 1914 thay they would rather resign. The so-called Curragh mutiny damaged British international prestige and, incidentally, forced Asquith to take over the War Office. Negotiations on the Irish question were still in progress in July when World War I broke out and the whole issue was put in cold storage.

(**7**) Asquith appointed Lord Kitchener to the War Office. Churchill had the Royal Navy at its stations. The British Expeditionary Force reached France without a hitch. The fruits of govt. preparedness in peacetime were being reaped. But weaknesses in war direction shortly became noticeable. The strategic westerners led by Kitchener, thought in terms of a war of attrition in the Flanders trenches; the more imaginative such as Lloyd George and Winston Churchill believed in manoeuvre. The Dardanelles expedition was the product of the latter school. It failed partly through local incompetence, partly because Asquith's govt. gave it inadequate support when it got into difficulties. A similar lack of drive seemed apparent in the question of ammunition supply, vital now that the western front was converting war into an industrial rather than a tactical activity. In May 1915 Asquith met public criticism by re-forming the govt. with trade union and Labour support.

(**8**) This purely political solution to a military situation was unlikely to succeed. The newcomers had much to learn and little to contribute. The great volunteer armies were bleeding to death at the B. of the Somme. The practical but politically unpalatable necessity for conscription became evident at the time of the Irish Easter rebellion of 1916. The far Right joined with Lloyd George's Left and the Beaverbrook Press to frustrate Asquith's policy of immediate Home Rule, while demanding a radical change in the direction of the war. In Dec. 1916 he resigned in favour of Lloyd George and went into opposition. At the 1918 election he even lost his seat, but was returned in 1920 and in 1921 saw his policy of Dominion Status for Ireland adopted by his unwilling opponents. The ex-wartime coalition now collapsed, and the 1922 elections created a three party parliament in which Asquith had the choice of putting conservatives or labour into power with his support. Since liberals and conservatives came mainly from the same social background, a conservative-liberal coalition might have split the nation. With characteristic good sense Asquith supported labour. This statesmanlike decision unexpectedly ruined his party. Co-operation with labour was in fact impossible, and in Oct. 1924 there was another dissolution. The Zinoviev Letter affair stampeded the electors into the Tory Camp. Asquith again lost his seat, and the King offered him a peerage. He accepted it but remained leader of his party. In Oct. 1926 he resigned as a result of Lloyd George's handling of party funds.

(**B**) **Margot (Emma Alice Margaret)** née **TENNANT (1864-1945)** described by Benjamin Jowett as 'the best educated ill educated woman that I have ever met' started a *crèche* in Wapping in 1885 and began factory visiting in Whitechapel in 1886. Through her wealthy father combined with her own intellectual and athletic gifts (she was a famous rider to hounds) she knew everybody of interest or intellectual distinction in England. In May 1894 she married H. H. Asquith. Her forceful and eccentrically candid personality probably did him little damage while her human understanding was an asset.

Herbert Henry's son **(3) Cyril (1890-1954) Ld. ASQUITH of BISHOPSTONE (1951)** became a Lord of Appeal in Ordinary. *See also* BONHAM-CARTER

ASQUITH'S FIRST (LIBERAL) CABINET (Apr. 1908-May 1915) 20 in Cabinet. Lord Chancellor: Lord Loreburn. Ch of the Exch: D. Lloyd George. Home Sec: Herbert Gladstone. Foreign Sec: Sir Edw. Grey. Sec. for War: R. B. (1911 Vist) Haldane. Chief Sec. for Ireland: Augustine Birrell. First Lord of the Admiralty: R McKenna. Pres. of the Bd. of Trade: Winston S. Churchill. In June 1909 Gladstone went to S. Africa as Gove-Gen. Churchill succeeded him at the Home Office and Sydney Buxton succeeded Churchill at the Bd. of Trade. In Oct. 1911 Churchill and McKenna changed places. In June 1912 Haldane became Lord Chanc. In Mar. 1914 Asquith took on the War Office as well as the prime ministership. In Aug. 1914 Earl Kitchener succeeded him at the War Office. *See* CAMPBELL BANNERMAN'S and ASQUITH'S ADMINISTERATION.

ASQUITH'S SECOND (COALITION) CABINET (May 1915-Dec. 1916) 22 in Cabinet. Lord Chancellor: Lord Buckmaster (l). Lord Privy Seal: Earl Curzon (c). Ch. of the Exch: R. McKenna (l). Home Sec: Sir John Simon (l), Foreign Sec: Sir Edw. Grey. Colonial Sec: A. Bonar Law (c). Sec. for War: Earl Kitchener (u). Sec. for India: A. Chamberlain (c). Ch. of the Duchy of Lancaster: Winston S. Churchill (l). Min. of Munitions: D. Lloyd George (l). Att-Gen: Sir Edw. Carson (Protestant Irish). In Jan. 1915 Sir J. Simon succeeded by Sir Herbert Samuel. In July 1916 Kitchener was drowned. Lloyd George succeeded him and Edw. Montague became Min. of Munitions. Birrell was succeeded by H. Duke. (l) = Liberal. (c) = Conservative. (u) = uncommitted.

ASSACH A type of Welsh compurgation in which the accused could clear himself by the oath of three hundred men. Abolished in 1413.

ASSADA. *See* EAST INDIA COMPANY-3.

ASSAM. Tea and teak exporting area in the foothills of the E. Himalayas. *See* BENGAL, BURMA.

ASSART and WASTE. Waste was the cutting down of shrubs and trees so that the stumps and roots still encumbered the ground and reduced the value of the land by more than the value of the things taken. A landlord or a minor coming of age was entitled to impeach waste. i.e. force the tenant or outgoing guardian to account for it. Assart was a total clearance, including grubbing up, whereby the land could be converted to a different purpose such as arable or garden. An assart was land so cleared. Assarts of common land were objectionable to manor tenants who lost pasturage thereby. In forests they required a royal, usually annual licence; they were forfeited to the Crown if made without one but were often regranted for a fine. This practice was the legal basis for Charles I's infuriating attempts to raise revenue by enforcing forest laws against ancient long forgotten assarts.

ASSASSINS. *See* CALIPHATE-10.

ASSENT, ROYAL. *See* BILL.

ASSENT AND DISASSENT, STAT. OF 1430 (Ir) forbade the collection of any local subsidy without the assent of the parliament or Great Council. These subsidies were commonly granted at the demand of the Lieutenant, or Deputy or Lord of the Franchise, by the County Court, for the better government or defence of the county. They were often abused or spent elsewhere, or for a private purpose such as the ransom of someone kidnapped in a feud. Moreover a county which had lately paid a heavy local subsidy might resist central taxation, which

therefore had to be light. Local subsidies thus anticipated national revenue and weakened the govt. Because of the parliamentary procedural complications and delays introduced after 1495 by Poynings Law, the council assumed the power of assent and disassent.

ASSER (?-?909) Bp. of SHERBORNE (?900), a Welshman ordained at St. David's, was asked in 885 by K. Alfred to study with him. He agreed provided that he could return to Wales for six months each year. He wrote a *Life* of the King in 893 which, if not a forgery, is less a systematic account than a human description by a not very clever but enthusiastic bystander at court, and, save what can be inferred from this, little is known of him. He must have spent all his later years in England for he was given the abbacies of Amesbury and Congresbury, and the bishopric of Sherborne was large.

ASSIGNATS. To meet the financial crisis which had provoked the revolution, the French constituent assembly, in Dec. 1789 issued 400M livres of 5% bonds (*assignats*) secured on the crown and church lands and to be redeemed by their sale. They were not popular and the lands remained unsold. The management crises of the *assignats* coincided with political disturbances. In Aug. 1790 as a result of further govt. cash shortages, interest ceased to be paid and a further 1200M livres were issued as currency. Necker resigned and a damaging inflation followed. War in Aug. 1792 brought further increases while the monarchy was suspended and there were massacres in the prisons. By July 1795 there were risings in Brittany and the *assignat* was worth only 3% of face value; by Oct., when the Convention was dissolved 0.15%. In Mar. 1796, with the war in Italy being financed by loot, an attempt was made to replace the *assignats* by *mandats territoriaux* ('land warrants') which were the same thing under a different name. Public confidence in republican paper having disappeared, on 4 Feb. 1797 paper money was abandoned.

The eight year experiment ruined the older financial and banking classes, who had habitually lent money to the govt, and brought into existence the class of hectic and corrupt *Directoire* speculators among whom Bonaparte was able to rise to power.

ASSIGNATION, HOUSES OF, were rooms where persons of substance with a reputation to lose might meet for discreet mutual enjoyment. Usually accessible from two different streets through a dressmaker's (ladies) and a barber's or tobacconist's (gentlemen), they were a source of income for both. They succumbed in World War I to competition from hotels, one of which is said to have considered erecting a tablet *to the women who fell in the war*.

ASSIGNMENT was a mediaeval charge upon a crown fund in favour of a crown creditor. This could be made by **(1) Mandate,** i.e. an order to the Treasurer to pay the creditor. This was payable at sight. **(2) Assigned Tally.** This was handed over by the Issue of the Exchequer but charged against a particular source of revenue, e.g. the customs at Boston. The latter method could be abused, for a tally holder had in theory been paid, and he or his heirs might be called upon to account for money which it had never been possible to collect from some distant source. Tallies could be assigned and holders, therefore, sometimes sold them to finance houses at a discount.

ASSINIBOIA. *See* CANADA-19.

ASSINIBOIN, a northern plains branch of the Sioux, migrated from the Missouri to Saskatchewan shortly after 1800.

ASSISE OF BREAD AND ALE (1) was the fixed price based upon the price of grain; or **(2)** the inspection for quality and quantity.

ASSIZES (Norman-Fr: *sessions, sittings, hence business done at a sitting***) (1)** The King and his council might, before parliaments existed, make enactments, then known as **assizes;** for example the

Assizes of Clarendon (1166) and Northampton (1176) regulated the criminal proceedings by jury; the Assize of Arms (1181) established a system for providing military equipment, and the Assize of Forests codified Forest Law. Eventually the word was commonly applied to legislation dealing with the procedure for settling five kinds of disputes viz.: (a) **The Three Possessory or Petty Assizes** enabled certain cases arising out of possession (as opposed to ownership) of property to be tried by a jury of twelve. That of *Novel Disseisin* (1166) dealt with wrongful dispossessions of freeholds. It was repealed in 1833. That of *Morte d'Ancestor* concerned wrongful possession of land claimed by a plaintiff deriving title from a dead forbear. The procedure could not be used if the land had been devised by will; when all land became devisable under Acts of 1541 and 1661 this assize became inoperable. The Assize of *Darrein Presentment* (Fr: last presentation) was its ecclesiastical equivalent, the plaintiff claiming the right to present to a vacant living. (b). The *Grand Assize* made at the Council of Windsor (1179) allowed a defendant to a writ of right, instead of waging battle, to claim that the better right to a freehold should be decided by the verdict of 16 knights of the county, 12 of whom had to be agreed. If a plaintiff wished to insist on battle, he had to give good reasons. It was abolished in 1833. (c) The Assize *Utrum* (Lat: whether) enabled a jury of 12 to settle whether land was held in frankalmoign (and so subject to the ecclesiastical courts) or by a lay tenure, together with any incidental questions. This took many disputes away from the obsolescent and rapacious church courts and handed the collateral property issues over to the relatively reliable civil courts. Alienations of ecclesiastical property were absolutely forbidden by an act of 1571, and thereafter this assize fell into disuse.

(2) **Commissions of Assize** were issued for the trial of cases under the five assizes, in counties named in them. The limited civil competence thus conferred required legal expertise, and so at least one commissioner was generally, and in due course always a judge. Other commissions, of *Oyer and Terminer* (Fr: To hear and determine) and of **Gaol Delivery**, conferring criminal jurisdiction, were also issued, and it was obviously convenient to issue these to the same persons as the commissioners of assize. Finally the Statute of Westminster 1285 enacted that a case commenced in the Kings Bench or Common Pleas should be tried there on a fixed date unless before (Lat: *Nisi Prius*) that day, the justices of assize came into the county, when they would be tried locally. By arranging regular circuits of judges, local trials by courts with the same authority as the central courts could always be arranged. These sessions, held three times a year at county towns, for such trials came to be known as **Assizes** and were held with great ceremony until 1970 when they were replaced by local permanent Crown Courts; but the practice of sending High Court judges to sit in them for difficult cases continued.

ASSOCIATION. *See* JAMES VI-8.

ASSOCIATION, THE (1695) (*see* WILLIAM III-10) was a bond sworn by protestants throughout England to hunt down and kill any persons who assassinated William III or who might profit from his death.

ASSN. FOR DISCOUNTENANCING VICE (Ir.) was an educational body started in 1791 by private subscription, but supported partly by govt. grants. By 1819 it had 119 schools with about 9,000 children, protestant and R. Catholic in about equal proportions. *See* NATIONAL EDUCATION SCHEME.

ASSUMPTION OF THE VIRGIN MARY, is the ancient belief that she 'having completed her earthly life, was in body and soul assumed into heavenly glory'. The feast ceased to be celebrated in England in 1547, but repeated demands since 1870 for definition in the R. Catholic church led to the issue of the bull *Munificentissimus Deus* (1950) by Pius XII. The doctrine, never universal, is rejected by all Protestant churches; the bull has thus increased the difficulties of Christian reunion.

ASTLEY, Sir Jacob (1579-1652) 1st Ld. ASTLEY (1644) first served in the Netherlands, and was Newcastle's sergeant-major-gen. in 1639 against the Scots. He joined the King's Army as maj-gen. in 1642, but was defeated and captured in 1646.

ASTOR, Nancy (1879-1964) U.S. born conservative married to Vist. Astor was, as M.P. for Plymouth Sutton from 1919, the first and until 1921 the only woman in the House of Commons. A forthright champion of women and families and prohibition, she originally favoured concessions to Germany to correct the injustices of the P. of Versailles but was soon disillusioned by Nazism. During World War II she served as Mayor of the much bombed city of Plymouth.

ASYLUM, DIPLOMATIC. It used to be thought that an embassy was part of the territory of the country which is represented, and that therefore a fugitive who took refuge in an embassy could not be pursued into it by the authorities of the host country, and could be surrendered, if at all, by formal extradition processes which would depend upon the existence of an extradition treaty between the host's and the ambassador's country. Rights of asylum based on these principles were successfully claimed in Greece in 1862 and in Spain in 1875. The modern (post World War II) view, however, is that a diplomatic mission (but not its property) is immune merely in the interests of comity and convenience, and may at its discretion confer the same immunity upon a person who enters its premises. Hence common criminals may be surrendered, or political refugees protected. Thus Card. Mindszenty took refuge in the U.S. embassy in Budapest and lived there for many years.

ATACAMA. *See* BOLIVIA-2 *et seq.*

ATHELING (A.S. = noble) used in poetry to denote good and honourable men – such as heroic figures, the prophets, and the saints. It came, however, to mean specifically princes of the royal house, and was borne by them apparently as a kind of title. Edgar the Atheling, who might have succeeded to the throne on Edward the Confessor's death in 1066, was the last male representative of the West Saxon royal house.

ATHELNEY (A.S. = Royal Island) An island in the Somerset marshes. *See* ALFRED THE GREAT.

ATHENAEUM CLUB (London) was founded in 1824 for the association of individuals known for their scientific or literary attainments, artists of eminence in any class of the fine arts and noblemen and gentlemen distinguished as liberal patrons of science, literature or the arts. In practice there has always been a strong social element, but election to the Athenaeum under Rule 2 is guided by the above quoted criterion and is considered an honour.

ATHLONE (Westmeath, S. Ireland) is strategically placed at a crossing of the Shannon, and has, since the Anglo-Norman conquest been a much demanded military objective, with a castle founded in 1204. This castle held out for K. James II from 1688 to 1691, when it was taken by the Dutch Gen. Ginkel (q.v.) for William III. He took the title E. of Athlone. In later years, though it remained small, Athlone became a road, rail and canal centre, with a textile industry.

ATHLONE COMMISSION. *See* TRANSPLANTATION.

ATHOLL or ATHFOTLA. *See* PICTS

ATHOLL, Ds. of. *See* MAN, I. OF-10 & 11.

ATHOLL, Marquesses of. *See* MURRAY.

ATKINSON, Sir Harry (1831-92) migrated to New Zealand in 1855, fought in the Waitara War of 1860, and became Min. of Defence in 1864. He initiated the policy of self reliance in defence affairs, but the govt. fell in 1865 and he was out of office (and mostly out of

Parliament) until 1873. He then became the champion of the Conservatives, and was in office as Treasurer or Prime Minister or both from 1875 to 1877, 1879 to 1884 and 1887 to 1891. During these periods he substituted a property for a land tax, created a system of protectionist tariffs, abolished the provinces, reduced public expenditure and the pay of ministers, reduced the size of the House of Representatives and ended the outright sale of Crown lands. On the fall of his last Ministry in Jan. 1891, he became speaker of the Legislative Council but died suddenly.

ATKINSON, John (1844-1932) Ld. ATKINSON was solgen. for Ireland from 1889 to 1892 and both att. gen. and M.P. (Londonderry) from 1895 to 1905 when he became a Lord of Appeal (until 1928).

ATKYNS. Family curiously associated with the Court of Exchequer. **(1) Sir Edward (1567-1669)** who defended Prynne before the Star Chamber, was appointed a Baron of the Exchequer by Charles I in Oct. 1640, but the patent did not take effect, and the Commons appointed him in 1645. In 1648 the Lords moved him to the Common Pleas. After the Restoration Charles II moved him back to the Exchequer, and he was on the bench at the trial of the regicides. Of his two sons **(2) Sir Robert (1621-1709)** entered Cromwell's Parliament as M.P. for Evesham, and remained in the Restoration Parliaments. In 1672 he became a judge of the Common Pleas, but was forced by govt. pressure to retire in 1679. He was in much demand as a legal adviser, particularly in political trials such as the Russell impeachment and the Williams trial. After the revolution he became Chief Baron of the Exchequer (in succession to his younger brother) and from 1689 to 1693 (the Great Seal being in Commission) he was also Speaker of the House of Lords. His brother **(3) Sir Edward (1630-98)** became a baron of the Exchequer in 1679, and when Montagu was dismissed for refusing to support the dispensing power in 1686, James II appointed him Chief Baron in Montagu's place. In 1689 he refused allegiance to William III and was superseded by his brother.

ATLANTIC, B. of THE. A misnomer for the biggest, naval war in history. It continued throughout the whole of World War II. German and Italian U-boats sank 2828 merchant ships. 782 German and 85 Italian U-boats were destroyed. **(1)** It comprised six main features: the transport (a) to Britain from Venezuela, the USA and Canada of food and fuel without which Britain would have been starved into surrender; (b) to Britain of troops and arms without which no attack on the enemy from the west could have been mounted; (c) to Russia of war supplies to sustain the Russian war with Germany; (d) from Britain of troops and materials to (i) Malta via Gibraltar; (ii) Egypt round Africa; (iii) India via the Cape. **(2)** This immense and varied traffic was carried in thousands of merchant ships varying from converted liners to tramps and tankers, only some of which could be armed. Mostly, these could be fully loaded in one direction only. They were under constant U-boat and aircraft attack at sea and in British waters. Allowing for the sinkings, it took about two ships to deliver one cargo. Vast industrial efforts were required on both sides of the Atlantic simply to maintain the necessary numbers. **(3)** The war was one of constant attrition in innumerable furious small encounters interrupted by six major events viz: the loss of H.M.S. *Hood* and the sinking of the *Bismarck* (May 1941); the destruction of convoy P.Q. 17 to Murmansk (June-July 1942); the complicated convoy operations which preceded the Allied landings in French N. Africa (Nov. 1942); the successful defence of P.Q. 19 (Dec. 1942); the sinking of the battlecruiser *Scharnhorst* off the North Cape (Dec. 1943); and the sinking of the huge *Tirpitz* (Nov. 1944). **(4)** To illustrate the sheer size of this war, the convoys to Arctic Russia alone landed 24,400 vehicles,

3276 tanks, 2665 aircraft and 693,000 tons of other war materials at Murmansk in 1941-2 and lost about 40% as much again.

(5) The Atlantic War reached its watershed with the Italian surrender (Sept. 1943), after which the shipping and escorts thus saved could be used in, and particularly to sustain, the invasion of W. Europe. In that operation the naval role, after bombarding German coast defences, was confined to marshalling the huge cross-Channel invasion fleet and subsequent traffic, and protecting it from molestation. This turned out to be surprisingly easy because naval superiority had been established to such effect that German naval efforts to interfere in the Channel were trivial. *See* NAVY, ROYAL-11 & 12; COMMERCE PROTECTION C.

ATLANTIC CABLE was first completed in Aug. 1858, but the insulation was unreliable. A successful cable was laid in 1866.

ATLANTIC CHARTER (14 Aug. 1941) was an eight-point declaration of war aims issued by U.S. Pres. Roosevelt and the British Prime Minister Winston Churchill after meetings on board warships in the Atlantic. The points were:- **(1)** That the two countries sought no aggrandizement; **(2)** that all peoples had a right to self determination and **(3)** self government; **(4)** all nations should have equal access to trade and raw materials and **(5)** should establish improved labour standards and social security; **(6)** the establishment of the means to perpetual peace and the abandonment of the use of force in international dealings; **(7)** freedom from fear; **(8)** freedom from want. The Charter's immediate purpose was to reassure neutrals, to outflank American isolationists, and to involve Pres. Roosevelt in the British war effort. It was incorporated in the Declaration of the United Nations of 1 Jan. 1942.

ATLANTIC FLEET, based on Gibraltar, was organised by Fisher in 1905 as part of the naval redeployment, so that the usual Mediterranean strength could be easily available nearer home, in case of trouble with the Germans.

ATLANTIS. A German merchant cruiser which, between Mar. 1940 and Nov. 1941 sank 145,000 tons of allied shipping before being sunk by H.M.S. *Devonshire* off Ascension I.

ATOMIC speculative theory is very ancient, but the originator of the modern practical school was Gassendi, who published an account of it in 1649 as an appendix to his edition of Epicurus, and he was also the first to use the term 'molecule'. His account was developed by Boyle and Newton, whose views were studied and experimentally developed by John Dalton (1766-1844) and, amongst others, Rutherford and Niels Bohr (1885-1962). The various studies led along two separate paths starting from the concept of **Chain Reaction,** first accurately suggested by Enrico Fermi and Niels Bohr at a seminar in Washington in Jan. 1939. One, by allowing a rapid development of the reaction, led to military use as a **Bomb,** the other, concerned with methods of moderating the reaction so as to produce controlled quantities of heat, led to the peaceful provision of electricity. The first **controlled reaction** was achieved at Chicago in 1942 and the first Atomic Bomb was fired at Alamogordo (New Mexico) in July 1945. Though in nuclear terms comparatively small, the violence of this explosion astonished all beholders. Its success led immediately to the atomic bombing of **Hiroshima** and **Nagasaki** (Aug.) and to the abrupt surrender of the Japanese.

In May 1951 the Americans fired the first **Fusion** or **Thermonuclear** bomb. Their example was followed by the Russians in Aug. 1953 and the British in May 1957. World opinion was alarmed at the effects, and negotiations to limit such tests were set on foot. There was a voluntary moratorium which broke down because of the Cuban missiles crisis, and then the Macmillan govt.

negotiated the **Partial Test Ban Treaty (1963)** under which Britain, Russia and the U.S.A. undertook not to test nuclear weapons in the air, under water or in space. Meanwhile more enterprise was diverted towards peaceful uses. The Russians had opened a nuclear power plant in 1954, the British the first large scale **Nuclear Reactor** electric power plant at Calder Hall in May 1956. By 1970 Britain had 27 such stations.

A series of accidents or mishaps in various countries and the fearful disaster to a power plant at Chernobyl in 1986 in the Ukraine (which affected the sheep pastures in Cumbria), created rising public suspicion of even the peaceful uses of atomic energy.

ATREBATES were a Gallic tribe, part of which had migrated to the middle Thames. At the time of the Roman conquest they were apparently under Caractacus, and his defeat in the years A.D. 43-50 entailed their subjection. They do not seem to have acted independently. Their later capital Calleva (Silehester) near Reading, was laid out in about A.D. 80. It acquired a 4th cent. church and survived until the 5th cent. when it was abandoned. No later buildings having covered the site, it has long attracted the attention of more and less skilled excavators. *See* BRITAIN, PRE-ROMAN-3.

ATTACHÉ **(Fr = one who is attached)**. A specialist, most often from an armed service, who is attached to a diplomatic mission as adviser or observer, though not himself a diplomat.

ATTACHMENT, COURT OF. A minor criminal court for a forest.

ATTAINDER and PAINS AND PENALTIES, ACTS OF, were methods of condemning a person by Act of Parliament instead of trial at law. A Bill of Attainder envisaged death, forfeiture of goods, and extinction of the titles of the victim. A Bill of Pains and Penalties was less drastic. Originally Acts of Attainder were passed against persons who fled from a charge of felony, because a conviction had the same consequences. They were used against Yorkist prisoners by a Lancastrian parliament in 1459. In 1461 a Yorkist parliament retaliated. The early Tudors used such Acts against powerful persons but until 1534 it was uncertain whether they were valid if the accused had not been heard in his defence. Thomas Cromwell then consulted the judges in the case of Sir Thomas More, and they reluctantly advised that they were. Henry VIII's embarrassment at the attainder of Q. Katherine Howard in 1541 led to the inclusion of a provision that royal assent to bills might be given by commission; this Act was tactfully renamed The Royal Assent by Commission Act, 1541, by the Statute Law Revision Act, 1948.

In practice most defendants were given a hearing. From the accession of Q. Elizabeth I until 1640, attainders were very rare: the most conspicuous being that of Lord Paget in 1586 and of the Gunpowder Plotters in 1605. Strafford's attainder arose out of the failure of his impeachment, and set a pattern leading naturally to similar acts against the regicides in 1660, Monmouth in 1685 and Sir John Fenwick in 1696. By this time the rise of constitutional parties had rendered the procedure obsolete as an instrument of party warfare, and thenceforth such bills were preferred in connection with rebellions. Thus the Es. of Mar and of Kellie were attainted and other rebels imprisoned in 1715 and another E. of Kellie was attainted in 1746 and other rebels transported in 1747. The last Attainder was passed in 1798 against Lord Edw. Fitzgerald after the Irish rebellion. The whole procedure was discredited by the brilliant defence in the abortive bill of pains and penalties against Q. Caroline in 1820, after which it fell into disuse.

ATTEMPTS. *See* MARCHES, ANGLO-SCOTS-5.

ATTERBURY, Francis (1662-1732) an Oxford divine, became a court chaplain in 1691, and preacher at the Rolls in 1709. He championed the rights of the clergy, led the High Church Lower House of Convocation in their clashes with the Latitudinarian bishops, and is said to have written Sacheverell's speech before the Lords on his impeachment in 1710. He was the effective clerical leader of the Tory clergy. From 1713 he was Bp. of Rochester and Dean of Westminster (the two offices being commonly held together), but in 1720, after the South Sea Bubble he was accused of involvement in a Jacobite plot, condemned in parliament by a bill of pains and penalties, and in 1723 went into exile. *See* GEORGE I-10.

ATTILA (Ger: ETZEL) (?-453) in 434 became joint king with his brother Bleda (whom he murdered in 445) of the Huns. Centred on Hungary, the Huns had the Byzantine Empire paying tribute by 447 and then Attila turned his attention to Gaul. The threat absorbed the energies and attention of the Romano-Gallic authorities who were thus unable to pay much attention to Britain. He invaded Gaul in 451. The Roman general Aetius and Theodoric, K. of the Visigoths, combined to defeat him at Maurica in central France. This saved the far west, but in 452 Attila invaded Italy. He lost heavily through plague and returned to Pannonia, where he died during his wedding night with a girl called Ildico. *See* ANIMAL EPIDEMICS.

ATTLEE, Clement Richard (1883-1967) 1st E. ATTLEE (1955) O.M. (1951) K.G. (1956) (1) was converted to Fabian socialism by his experiences in the East End of London, by the works of Morris and Ruskin, and through employment as sec. of Toynbee Hall from 1910 to 1914. He served in the army in World War I, being twice wounded, and in 1919 he entered politics by getting himself co-opted into the mayoralty of Stepney. He was elected to parliament for Limehouse in 1922 and kept the seat until 1950.

(2) He served as U/Sec. of State for War in the minority Labour govt. of 1924, and as a member of the Indian (or Simon) Commission from 1927 to 1930, Chanc. of the Duchy of Lancaster from 1930 to 1931 and acted as a reforming postmaster-gen. in 1931.

(3) He refused on principle to support Ramsay MacDonald's move to the National Govt. in 1931 but survived the election of that year. As the Labour Party had only 52 seats in the Commons, he had a rare early opportunity to show his mettle, and as deputy leader under George Lansbury he worked harmoniously with Cripps. In 1935 he succeeded Lansbury as leader and was therefore leader of the opposition at the outbreak of World War II (Sept. 1939). It was Neville Chamberlain's war failures which gave him his opportunity, for the Labour Party, guided by him, refused to serve in a coalition under Chamberlain but agreed to serve under 'anyone else'. The 'anyone else' proved to be Churchill who took him on as Lord Privy Seal and Leader of the Commons. His wartime career was singularly suited to his talents. His capacity for sticking to the point made him an ideal colleague in a desperate situation; and he was content to serve where he was most needed in the national interest. Thus, he was Dominions Secretary from 1942 to 1943, and then Lord Pres. and Deputy Prime Minister till 1945. *See* WORLD WAR II; CHURCHILL'S FIRST GOVT.

(4) However much he differed from Churchill and the Tories on internal politics, he put such opinions into cold storage for the duration of the war. On the other hand, he was in general agreement with his war colleagues on policy towards foreign states. He was as hostile to Stalin as all responsible British politicians and understood the need to maintain a certain independence from the U.S.A.

(5) His self control was valuable to the country, and to his party when politics broke out again after the war, and he caught more votes in 1945 than a more flamboyant statesman might have done, because the electorate wanted to preserve the social advances made in the war, but without revolutionary controversy. *See* ATTLEE'S FIRST *and* SECOND GOVT.

(6) As a prime minister he was distinguished for his

mastery of facts, ability to delegate and a capacity to conciliate, supported upon a wide and high experience of difficult office, and an unblemished and well understood integrity. It was a Tory M.P. who, after the years of socialist legislation which he put through, was able publicly to call him one of the greatest living Englishmen.

(7) After his second resignation, he remained leader of the Labour Party until 1955. His speeches were statesmanlike in opposition, especially in his bipartisan approach to foreign policy but the divisions within the Labour Party had hardened, and Attlee, without the authority of a premier, found it even more difficult to reconcile his temperamental followers: for example, he opposed but could not wholly stop Trade Union hounding of Aneurin Bevan and the left wing. He became increasingly withdrawn as if any intervention from any direction might make things worse.

(8) The May 1955 election produced a comfortable Tory majority and it was evident that Attlee would soon retire. Morrison, Bevan and Gaitskell each bid, in their own way, for the succession in the autumn. Attlee, however, held on till the impetus behind Morrison and Bevan had exhausted itself. He announced his retirement at a routine meeting of the parliamentary Labour Party in Dec. 1955, and the leadership went to Gaitskell.

ATTLEE'S FIRST GOVT. (1945-50) 20 in Cabinet. C. R. Attlee Prime Minister and Min. of Defence; Herbert Morrison Lord Pres. and Leader of the Commons; Ernest Bevin Foreign Sec; Hugh Dalton Ch. of the Exch; Sir Stafford Cripps Pres. of the Bd. of Trade; J. Chuter Ede Home Sec; Lord Pethick Lawrence Sec. of State for India; Emmanuel Shinwell Min. of Fuel and Power; Ellen Wilkinson Min. of Education; Aneurin Bevan Min. of Health.

(1) By the end of World War II the social and governmental system had through wartime exigencies developed along real but unavowed socialist lines. Consequently when Attlee and the Labour Party campaigned for nationalisation and social reform they were defending a situation which existed already and which the Tories were proposing to dismantle. The electorate, having put a huge effort into the war which created the situation, naturally gave Labour a landslide victory. This astonished everyone including Stalin and even Attlee who, however, did not become Prime Minister without a challenge by Morrison for the leadership. Attlee's first duty was to replace Churchill at the Potsdam Conference. Fortunately in May 1945 he had accompanied Eden to the foundation conference of the U.N.O. in San Francisco, and on his way back had met Truman and found him a kindred spirit.

(2) The leading cabinet figures formed an exceptionally able but difficult group. Attlee preferred to delegate major areas of policy to ministers whom he trusted, particularly Bevin and Cripps, and so free himself for the major political problems and the business of co-ordination. He preferred to work through the circulation of paper even at the highest level, and liked to concentrate on one thing at a time.

(3) Domestically the first eighteen months represented the rising tide. The Opposition seemed stunned and the govt., having taken over parliamentary time, put legislation through in a flood. By the end of 1946 acts had been passed to nationalise the Bank of England, the coal industry, Cable and Wireless, civil aviation. There had also been legislation, minor measures apart, on National Insurance, New Towns, Trades Disputes and Catering Wages, and an Act to establish a National Health Service. The legislation was passed during a period when there was none of the unemployment which had been feared. Industry was turning smoothly over to peacetime production, but there was little public expectation that there would be close

practical limitations on what could be done. Attlee himself was not over-optimistic for he had been shaken by the abrupt ending of Lend-Lease in Aug. 1945, but he saw that there was no realistic alternative to the difficult conditions placed upon the subsequent American loan, particularly the requirement that Sterling should become fully convertible within a year.

(4) In foreign affairs Stalin was clearly determined to dominate Europe by force or subversion, but it was the uncertainties of American policy, always fundamentally Anglophobe, which most disturbed the govt. Truman's undoubted goodwill was cancelled out by the loan negotiations and the passing of the MacMahon Act by Congress, and the American reaction to Russia was often naive. Moreover there was a divergence over Palestine, for Bevin and Attlee's policy was thought by the Americans to be pro-Arab.

(5) The great change came when Gen. Marshall became U.S. Sec. of State in Jan. 1947. The Truman doctrine, proclaimed in March, secured aid for Greece and Turkey and relieved Britain of the responsibility for them. In 1948 the Marshall Plan was launched and in 1949 the North Atlantic Treaty Organisation (N.A.T.O.) was set up. These ensured the economic recovery and military security of Western Europe. They were as much due to Attlee's and Bevin's persuasiveness as to Stalin's imperialism, but the determination to free India (and forego control of her resources) lent urgency to the govt's diplomacy. This operation had become more complicated than expected. Attlee, who was an expert on India, was convinced by the failure of the Cabinet Mission to India in 1946 that the Muslim League could and would set up an independent Pakistan. Vist. Wavell, viceroy since 1943, was accordingly dismissed and replaced by Attlee's personal choice, the semi-royal Lord Louis Mountbatten, with instructions to negotiate independence within a time limit. He arrived in India in Mar. 1947 and acted with great speed but at a vast price in confusion and human life. *See* AUCHINLECK, Sir Claude

(6) Meanwhile the U.S.A. had been causing concern by withholding atomic information. Attlee had flown to Washington in Nov. 1945 and had had cordial discussions with Pres. Truman who, however, could not, in the face of congressional stonewalling, make even his small promises good. After the passage of the MacMahon Act Attlee had no hesitation in deciding that Britain must make her own atomic bomb, to keep a freer hand with the Americans. The decision and the details were kept from all save a few members of the Cabinet, and large sums were concealed in the parliamentary estimates.

(7) Early in 1947 the govt. ran into trouble. Fuel supplies broke down owing to industrial mismanagement and unrest during a particularly cold winter, and two million people were out of work. Then the Cabinet was shaken by a dispute over the nationalisation of Iron and Steel, and by an economic crisis. Morrison, responsible for the co-ordination of economic policies, was unenthusiastic about the nationalisation and negotiated a compromise with the leaders of the industry. Bevin, Cripps and Dalton raised a storm in the party. This coincided with an exchange crisis which came to a head in July when sterling became freely convertible. The cabinet hesitated for five weeks to go back on its undertaking to the U.S.A. and then suspended convertibility. Attlee was blamed, and Cripps now tried to organise a cabinet *coup* in which Bevin should replace Attlee and Attlee should take the Exchequer. Bevin would have nothing to do with it, but Cripps persisted. He had an interview with Attlee on 9 Sept. It ended with Cripps accepting a new post as Min. of Economic Affairs, but then Dalton had to resign after an indiscretion to a journalist just before his budget speech. He was succeeded by Cripps who thus came to dominate economic policy. His aim was to reconcile two

irreconcilables: to bring the balance of payments into equilibrium and solve the dollar shortage while maintaining the benefits which the govt. believed that it had secured for the working class. Rations, however, had to be reduced to a level lower than their lowest in wartime; housing was cut and the building of roads and hospitals brought virtually to a halt.

(8) The creation of the Organisation for European Co-operation and Development (O.E.C.D.) together with the Marshall Plan implemented in 1948, saved the situation, but the Russian blockade of Berlin had to be met by the, not wholly successful, Anglo-American airlift which in its turn lent urgency to the creation of N.A.T.O. (1949). There was, naturally, a growing movement for unification in Western Europe but the govt. was sceptical and Attlee correctly thought that Britain, at the heart of a Commonwealth, tended to look outwards from Europe.

(9) At the end of 1949 there were signs of exhaustion. Many members of the govt. had seen continuous office for ten years. Most had been ill and had run out of ideas. Inevitably there were the conventional quarrels between the Marxist and the Fabian wings of the Labour Party. A general election was overdue. It took place in Feb. 1950.

ATTLEE'S SECOND GOVT. (Feb. 1950-Oct. 1951) 18 in Cabinet. Principal members were unchanged from the First Administration save Sir Stafford Cripps, Ch. of the Exch; Hugh Dalton Min. of Town and Country Planning; George Tomlinson Min. of Education; Harold Wilson Pres. of the Bd. of Trade; Hames Griffiths Sec. of State for the Colonies and Patrick Gordon-Walker Sec. of State for Commonwealth Relations. The India Office had been abolished.

The govt. had high but unrealistic hopes in the general election of Feb. 1950. British recovery compared well with that of other European countries and the promises of 1945 had been for the most part kept, but at the price of devaluation (in the previous autumn) and hardships which were not expected in time of peace. The result was that the Labour majority in the Commons fell to ten. Attlee remained in office, but achieved little through external distractions and internal quarrels. The Korean War broke out in June 1950 and brought rearmament, inflation and a decline in the balance of payments. Cripps and Bevin had to resign after long periods of ill health. Morrison, who took Bevin's place at the Foreign Office, was a failure there, and Attlee had to intervene directly, especially when the Mussadeq govt. of Persia expropriated the Anglo-Iranian Oil Co. Hugh Gaitskell succeeded Cripps at the Exchequer. This promotion enraged Bevan who was ambitious, commanded much left-wing support, had virtually created the National Health Service and was opposed temperamentally and doctrinally to Gaitskell. The preparation of the budget in Apr. 1951 precipitated the crisis. Gaitskell meant to impose (small) charges for some services which Bevan had previously provided free. Attlee was in hospital, and Morrison, as his deputy, made little effort to reconcile them. When Attlee returned, Bevan, Harold Wilson and John Freeman had already resigned and were soon leading a powerful attack on the policies of their previous colleagues. An alliance which deceived no one was patched up for the general election (Oct.). The Labour vote was the highest hitherto achieved by any party, but the Tories were nevertheless returned to power.

ATTORNEY-GENERAL, SOLICITOR-GENERAL Attorneys practised in Common Law courts, solicitors eventually in Chancery. The crown originally appointed attorneys for particular matters, but from 1399 a standing attorney was appointed for all crown purposes and this was the Attorney-General (A.G.). Since the office was important, and only barristers and serjeants had a right of audience in the courts, it soon came to be held exclusively by barristers, and as royal power grew the A.G.'s and their subordinates the Solicitors General (S.G.), increased in importance.

Such men as Bacon and Coke were A.G.'s, and both advised the House of Lords in that capacity; but the connection with the crown made the Commons suspicious, and it was not until after 1660 that it became normal for the A.G. to be an M.P. With the amalgamation of the Courts of Common Law and Chancery in 1875, the specialisation between the A.G. and the S.G. (also a barrister) – as with attorneys – and solicitors ceased.

These two Law Officers of the Crown are members of the govt. and act as its advisers on legal matters.

ATTORNEY-GEN. v DE KEYSER'S ROYAL HOTEL LTD. (1920). The War Office requisitioned a property under statutory powers requiring lawful compensation, and then proposed to pay, under the prerogative, *ex gratia*. The House of Lords, continuing the reasoning founded on St. John's argument in *The Case of Shipmoney* held that where the subject matter of a prerogative is wholly covered by a statute, the statute prevails because it would be ... meaningless for the Legislature to impose restrictions and limitations upon and to attach conditions ... if the Crown were free at its pleasure to disregard all these provisions, and by virtue of the *prerogative* do the very thing which the *statute* empowers it to do.

ATTWOOD, Thomas (1783-1856) a banker, was High Bailiff of Birmingham in 1811. A powerful and informed opponent of govt. interference in trade, he secured in 1813 the withdrawal of the Orders in Council (restricting trade as part of a war policy, with Europe and the U.S.A.). In 1816 he opposed the reduction of paper currency during a shortage of specie. In 1830 his Birmingham Political Union supported the Reform Bill and in 1832 he became M.P. for the newly enfranchised Birmingham. He supported O'Connell's Irish policy in 1833 and six years later presented the Chartist Petition to the Commons.

AUBIGNY. See JAMES VI-7 *et seq.*

AUBREY, John (1626-97) F.R.S. (1663), antiquarian, collaborated with Anthony Wood on the *Antiquities of Oxford,* and investigated Avebury and Stonehenge, but is best known for his *Brief Lives,* a number of sketches mostly of contemporaries. He left a huge archive to the Bodleian Library.

***A.U.C. or Ab Urbe Condita* (Lat = Since the foundation of the City)** i.e., after 753 B.C.

AUCHINLECK, Sir Claude John Eyre (1884-1981) (1) came of a military family and was commissioned in 1904 into the 62nd Punjabis. In World War I he fought on the Suez Canal and commanded his battalion in the attempted relief of Kut-al-Amara. These events set the tone of his outlook. He and his Indian soldiers developed a lifelong mutual empathy. After routine events he took command in 1933 of the Peshawar brigade on the Indian N.W. Frontier and, like H.R.L.G. Alexander next door, earned a major-generalship. He was appointed D.C.G.S. in India and as a member of the Chatfield Cttee on the modernisation of the Indian Army in 1938-9 he secured the progressive promotion of Indian officers.

(2) Early in 1940 he took over IV Corps in England for transfer to France but with his experience of mountain warfare was hurriedly diverted to Norway which had just been surprised by the Germans. Inadequately equipped and supplied in the face of disaster, and overshadowed by the German onset in the west on 10th May, he nevertheless retook Narvik and was promptly ordered to abandon it. In July, after his return to England, he became G.O.C. Southern Command. In November, as a full general, he became C-in-C in India where his functions resembled those of a war minister rather than a commander. It was his promptness in sending troops to Basra which saved the situation in Iraq. In June 1941 however he and the overdriven Wavell

(C-in-C Middle East) were ordered to change places. He was now under govt. pressure to deliver a victory in the Middle East quickly at a time when, as he found, the equipment with which Wavell had had to fight was too meagre and the reinforcements not acclimatised or adequately trained; but eventually he was ready and in Nov. 1941 he launched into a victorious offensive which relieved Tobruk, took Benghazi and 20,000 prisoners. Rommel, his opponent, was, however, unexpectedly reinforced and drove him back nearly to Tobruk. The result was that Malta could be heavily bombed from African as well as Italian airfields, and again he was under pressure to attack and eventually ordered to do so before 1 June 1942. Rommel however attacked him four days earlier. Auchinleck had misinterpreted his intelligence reports and was the victim of a tactical surprise at Gazala. As a result Tobruk fell, and Auchinleck retreated to El Alamein where Rommel's forces were in July brought to an abrupt halt. Auchinleck was, however, insultingly superseded in August, and consequently worked in India, but for a while refused high appointments. In June 1943 Wavell became Viceroy of India and Auchinleck for the second time became C-in-C there. His previous experience, and high Indian repute fitted him well as a creator of armies, bases and war industries and as a supplier to the Americans and Chinese, with whom, like Alexander, he managed to be on friendly terms. It was primarily on his remarkable achievements in these fields that his warmaking reputation rests and for which he was promoted Field Marshal in 1946.

(3) Partition was now afoot. He hoped systematically and quietly to reconstitute the Pakistani and Indian armies using British officers as honest brokers, so that order could be kept during the partition process. This needed time, and again he was denied it. The cabinet decision, advised, against Auchinleck's deepest convictions, and announced by Mountbatten the Viceroy, to precipitate the two countries into independence in Aug. 1947 instead of 1948 made the task impossible, for the Indian Army, deeply divided by race and religion and partly suborned by politicians, began to disintegrate of itself, and was, as he had foreseen, powerless to prevent the vast massacres which ensued. Nevertheless he tried to salvage something from the wreck by staying on as C-in-C of both armies, but his relations with Mountbatten were, in view of what had occurred, understandably strained. In Sept. 1947 Mountbatten called for and obtained his resignation. He left his beloved India in a mood of despair and, considering the British actions of the time dishonourable, refused a peerage. He left England in 1968 for Marrakesh where he died.

AUCHINLECK. See BOSWELL.

AUCKLAND. See DURHAM-5.

AUCKLAND (N.Z.) was founded in 1840 by Capt. Wm. Hobson the first gov. of N.Z. and was the capital until 1865. Its two fine natural harbours created excellent facilities for overseas trade, and prosperity led to the rise of a great variety of industries. By the 1970's the population was 500,000. The surrounding province contains coal, oil, precious and industrial metals and the remarkable thermal-spring areas around L. Taupo.

AUCKLAND, Lds. and E. of. See EDEN.

AUDLEY FAMILIES (A) (1) Henry (?-1246) was constable to Hugh de Lacy, Earl of Ulster; at his fall in 1214 he joined Ranulf of Chester under whom he served from 1216 to 1221 as deputy sheriff of Salop and Staffs; by acquiring great estates in these counties he became a Lord Marcher. His son **(2) Sir James (?-1272)** was prominent at the court of Richard of Cornwall, King of the Romans, and in 1258 became a royalist nominee to the Council of Fifteen appointed under the Provisions of Oxford. He and his brother-in-law Peter de Montfort were then appointed to negotiate with the Welsh prince Llewellyn, but when in 1263 he resisted Llewellyn's breach of the truce, his castles were seized by rebellious barons. Nevertheless he maintained a force of importance, and fought with the royalists at Lewes and Evesham. In 1270 he became Justiciar of Ireland.

(B) or **AUDELEY, James of (1316?-69)** was a prominent commander under the Black Prince in the French campaigns of 1346, 1350 and 1356, and the Breton campaign 1360. He was governor of Aquitaine for the Black Prince during the 1362 campaign in Spain and died as Great Seneschal of Poitou.

(C) Thomas (1488-1544) 1st Ld. AUDLEY of WALDEN (1538) was a barrister, Town Clerk of Colchester in 1516 and J.P. for Essex in 1521. It was as steward to the Duke of Suffolk that he originally attracted royal notice, and in 1523 he became an M.P. By 1525 he was a member of Princess Mary's Welsh Council; in 1527 he was a groom of the chamber and then entered Card. Wolsey's household. When Wolsey fell in 1529, More succeeded Wolsey as Lord Chancellor and Audley succeeded More as Chancellor of the Duchy. He also became Speaker of the Commons, and as such one of the King's principal managers of the attack on the clergy, and the Queen's divorce. More resigned the Great Seal in May 1532, and Audley was appointed Keeper in the hope that he might be able to remain speaker at the same time, but even the subservient Commons insisted on electing Wingfield, and Audley, in Jan. 1533, became Lord Chancellor and the leading parliamentary manager of the King's and Thomas Cromwell's policy. He pronounced the Queen's divorce (1533), procured the Act of Succession (1534), and the attainder of Anne Boleyn's accomplices (1536). He procured also the passing of the Act of Six Articles, and the attainder of Thomas Cromwell (1539), and in Dec. 1541 he presided over the cases involving Queen Katherine Howard. He resigned in 1543. See also TOUCHET.

(D) Hugh (?-1662) a money-lender, amassed an enormous fortune while holding a post in the court of wards. His activities were a factor in discrediting the court.

AUGEREAU, Pierre Francois Charles (1757-1816) Duc de CASTIGLIONE was a French divisional general by 1795. He carried out the *coup d'etat* of Fructidor (Sept. 1797). Bonaparte made him a marshal and duke in 1808 and he was one of the many unsuccessful French commanders in Spain. He supported the Bourbons at the Restoration, but would not sit on Ney's court martial. Brave rather than clever, his name is proverbially associated with loot.

AUGHRIM, B. of (July 1691). (Co. Galway) William III's Dutch Gen. Ginkel defeated with great slaughter the Franco-Irish army of James II under the French Gen. de St. Ruth, a year after the B. of the Boyne. St. Ruth was killed and by Oct. all Ireland had submitted.

AUGMENTATION (1) A mark of honour added to a coat of arms. **(2)** In Scottish law an addition to a minister's stipend.

AUGMENTATIONS, COURT OF, (1) set up in 1536 to deal with the property of dissolved monasteries was both a court and a finance department, modelled on the Duchy of Lancaster. The Act of 1536 enjoined the dissolution of 372 monasteries worth less than £200 a year. The suppression of pilgrimages in 1537 and 1538 yielded much plate and jewellery from shrines. The great monasteries were all terrorised into surrender, and the Order of St. John expropriated by statute, by the summer of 1540. The royal income was increased by about £40,000 a year, and about £700,000 worth of property was sold. Only about 2% of the land was granted away free. The balance was used to found new bishoprics at Bristol, Chester, Gloucester, Oxford, Peterborough and Westminster; to pension off unemployable religious; and to pay the debts of the suppressed houses. Some of the money stuck to the fingers of the Court's officials. **(2)**

The Court was amalgamated with the Court of General Surveyors in 1546 and dissolved in 1554 when nothing more remained to be done.

AUGSBURG, CONFESSION OF (1530) was drafted by Melanchthon, approved by Martin Luther, and presented to the Emperor Charles V at Augsburg in June 1530. It is a summary of the Lutheran doctrine which, with minor changes, has remained in use ever since. Charles referred it to the R. Catholic theologians Eck, Faber and Cochlaeus who replied in the *Confutatio Pontificia*. Melanchthon's answer, the *Apology for the Confession*, was rejected.

AUGSBURG, INTERIM (1548) and P. of (1555). (1) The Truce of Nuremburg forced upon the Emperor Charles V in 1532 by the needs of a Turkish war, broke down in 1541, when the protestant Philip of Hesse abandoned the League of Schmalkalden for the Emperor's R. Catholic League of Nuremburg. War was resumed. Philip returned to the Protestant fold, but in 1547 Charles V captured him and his ally John Frederick of Saxony at the B. of Mühlberg, and in 1548 dictated the *Interim* which gave toleration, pending the decisions of the Council of Trent, to Lutheran doctrines wherever they were already established, subject to the reintroduction of Roman ceremonial. Rejected by the best informed or the most extreme on both sides, rendered unenforceable by French military intervention against Spain, and overturned by the revolt of the protestant princes in 1552, it was implicitly ignored in the Passau negotiations in 1552, when the princes demanded a peace regardless of religion, and the Emperor conceded a religious division of Germany to last only until the next imperial Diet.

(2) This Diet was held at Augsburg in 1555, and the *Peace* was technically a Recess or final enactment of the Diet. Two faiths only were legalised, the R. Catholic and the Lutheran, but in each territory only one was to be recognised, the choice being with the ruler (Lat: *cujus regio, ejus religio*). An inhabitant who adhered to a faith not of his ruler's choice was free to sell his property and move to a territory where his faith was recognised. Both religions could, however, be permitted in Imperial Free Cities; and Knights and communities who had long practised protestantism in ecclesiastical principalities should, under the so-called *Declaratio Ferdinandea*, continue to do so.

(3) An important feature of the Peace was the *Ecclesiastical Reservation*. Ecclesiastical lands taken by Lutherans before the Peace of Passau (2 Aug. 1552) from prelates who were not immediate vassals of the Empire were to remain in their possession, but any ecclesiastical prince who became a Lutheran was henceforth to lose his office. As neither party agreed to these arrangements, the Emperor included them in the Recess on his own authority, and they were mostly, but not entirely respected.

(4) The Peace prevented major conflicts within the Empire for half a century, and its principles remained an important diplomatic doctrine until the French Revolution, especially so far as Britain was concerned in relation to Hanover and its neighbouring ecclesiastical states.

AUGSBURG, WAR OF THE LEAGUE OF (1688-97) (1) This war, one of the most important in British history and misnamed by French historians, began with Louis XIV's invasion of Germany (Sept. 1688), William III's expedition to England and Louis' declaration of war on the Dutch (Nov. 1688), and, for the purpose of moving against them across Belgium, on Spain (Apr. 1689). Louis also intended to expand into S. Germany. To cover the gap between his Belgian and his South German armies the French devastated the Palatinate as far as Heidelberg and Mainz (Spring 1689). The more active operations, however, occurred in Scotland and Ireland. While James II, with French support, overran Ireland (Mar. 1689) except (London)Derry and Enniskillen, the Scottish

Highlanders rallied to him. An inconclusive naval battle in Bantry Bay (May 1689) failed to isolate him from France, but William III was able to suppress the Highlanders (B. of Killiecrankie, July 1689), relieve Londonderry by Aug., and build up an army in Ulster.

(2) By attracting Savoy into the war (1690), William hoped to divert part of the French forces from their seemingly inevitable conquest of Belgium, while he dealt with the Irish problem. In fact the Savoyard intervention was balanced by a renewed Turkish attack on Austria from whom they took Belgrade, and meanwhile French arms were victorious over the unsupported Savoyards at Staffarda (Aug. 1690), the Anglo-Dutch on land at Fleurus (July 1690) and by sea at Beachy Head (July). The latter battle caused recriminations between William III's two states, but fortunately William himself beat James II next day at the Boyne, the news of which reached the European mainland some time later. These events settled the pattern of the war for nearly two years. In 1691 French expansion continued on the mainland fronts with the fall of Mons and Nice, the conquest of Piedmont, and the bombardment of Barcelona, but the Austrians won a great victory on the Hungarian plains (B. of Szlankamen, Aug. 1691), and William III's generals defeated the Irish Jacobites (B. of Aughrim, T. of Limerick July 1691).

(3) Adm. Russell's victorious six day operations from Barfleur to La Hogue against Tourville (May 1692) wrought changes in the character of the war which the combatants took some time to digest. The French abandoned fleet operations and increased their military effort. They overran Württemberg, captured the important fortress of Namur (1692); their threat to Brussels forced William III into an offensive defeat at Steenkirk (Aug. 1692), and they repelled a Savoyard invasion with loss. At sea, however, the Tripoli corsairs (nominally under Turkish suzerainty) profited by French naval weakness to declare a *Jehad* against France. The French, meanwhile, had gone over to joint-stock privateering based on their Atlantic and Channel ports. This irritating and lucrative activity brought an ineffectual reprisal in a failed amphibious attack on Dunkirk. Again a pattern extended itself into a second year: French troops took Heidelberg (May 1693), involved the allies in another offensive defeat at Landen (July 1693), beat the Savoyards at La Marsaglia (Oct.), and a French force in Catalonia occupied Rosas. Moreover, their privateers, operating at squadron strength brought off a spectacular *coup* by capturing the Anglo-Dutch Smyrna convoy off the straits, while another English amphibious operation failed at St. Malo.

(4) The ensuing commercial uproar in London and Amsterdam brought about, as if incidentally, a radical change in British naval philosophy. Though there was another expensive amphibious failure before Brest (The Camaret Bay Affair, June 1694), a fleet was sent to the Mediterranean initially to protect the Levant trade. It relieved Britain's ally Savoy and prevented a French capture of Barcelona. With no British base available to sustain this effort, the fleet wintered unwillingly at Cadiz and, for lack of funds and facilities had to be withdrawn in the summer of 1695. This weakened the will of Savoy, which was tempted out of the war by the French offer of Casale, but the French troops thus released arrived too late to prevent William III's recapture of Namur (Sept. 1695) and were then wasted in mounting an abortive operation against England which was to begin when William III had been murdered at Turnham Green (Feb. 1696). *See* ASSOCIATION, THE

(5) Two considerations now persuaded Louis to offer peace. Firstly the Austro-Turkish war took a decisively unfavourable turn for France when the Russians joined in and took Azov (July 1696). The harassed Turkish armies facing Austria were pressed back into Hungary and a westward release of Austrian energy was soon to be expected. Secondly it was becoming clear that the Habsburg K. Charles II of Spain would soon die childless, and in any negotiations for the disposal of his inheritance, Louis preferred to be at peace. The war was accordingly terminated by the Ts. of Ryswick (Sept-Oct. 1697) while P. Eugene won his decisive victory over the Turks at Zenta (Sept.) *See also* CARLOWITZ, P. OF.

AUGUSTAN AGE. A literary period, elevated in tone, centring on the reign of the Emperor Augustus, and by analogy the similar periods of classical inspiration in French under Louis XIV and in English at the turn of the 17th-18th cents. It was notable for Pope (1688-1744), Addison (1672-1719) and sometimes Dryden (1631-1700).

AUGUSTINE, St. (?-604 or 605), prior of Gregory the Great's monastery of St. Andrew in Rome, he was chosen by the Pope in 596 to head a mission to convert the English. He and some 40 companions landed in Kent in 597 and soon baptised K. Ethelberht who had a Frankish Christian princess for wife, and was overlord of the kingdoms S. of the Humber. In 601 a second mission arrived and Augustine went to Arles where he was consecrated Archbishop. He restored a church on the site of the present Christ Church, Canterbury, and established his see there. He also consecrated Mellitus Bp. of the East Saxons with his see at London, and Justus Bp. of the Kentish Men at Rochester. He tried but failed to reach agreement with the leaders of the surviving Celtic church. At the time of his death, only the South-East had been converted. *See* MISSIONARIES IN BRITAIN AND IRELAND.

AUGUSTINE of HIPPO, St. (354-430) originator of much Christian dogma especially, in response to Manichaeism that of the omnipotence of God; in response to the Donatists, that of the unity and holiness of the church, the validity of the sacraments, and the foundation of civil coercive authority upon justice; and, in response to the Pelagians, the doctrines of the Fall, Original Sin and Grace. Of his many (mostly polemical) writings, the *Confessions* date from about 399 and the *City of God* between 413 and 426.

AUGUSTINIANS (SCOTLAND). K. David I (r. 1124-53) used this order, whose rule permitted members to go out and serve neighbouring churches, to supersede the Culdees, especially at St. Andrews, Scone and St. Serfs at Lochleven; he recruited from English priories, mostly Merton; he also founded houses at Holyrood, Jedburgh, Cambuskenneth, and, in a Premonstratensian form, at Whithorn. In the 13th cent. Augustinians replaced Culdees at Monymusk and Abernethy. They were relatively more important in Scotland than elsewhere because of their numbers in proportion to the population, and because they substituted communal and regulated, for eremitical and irregular Christian communities.

AUGUSTUS II or FREDERICK AUGUSTUS "The Strong" (1670-1733). (1) Elector of Saxony from 1694 was a major N.E. European figure whose ambitions periodically threatened to embroil himself and his neighbours in the War of the Spanish Succession. At John Sobieski's death in 1696 he stood for the elective Polish throne. To further the candidature he entered the R. Catholic church, which caused bitter offence in Saxony and led his Hohenzollern wife to leave him. In Sept. 1697 he was elected, and in 1699 he brought the Turkish war to a successful end at the P. of Carlowitz. Alarmed at the growing power of Charles XII of Sweden, he made an alliance with Russia and Denmark for the conquest of Livonia for his own family. The Poles refused to support him, and his Saxon army was defeated by Charles XII at Klissow in July 1702. Deposed at Charles' bidding by the Polish nobles, he retreated to Saxony which was occupied and pillaged by Swedish troops. At the T. of Altranstaedt in Sept. 1706 Augustus' surrender was abject: he had to congratulate his supplanter, Stanislas Leszczynski, on his election to the Polish throne and to hand over Patkul the Livonian

patriot and Russian ambassador as a prisoner to the Swedes (who broke him on the wheel). This forced an irreconcilable breach with Russia.

(2) When Charles XII met defeat at Poltava in July 1709, Augustus denounced the treaty, and with Peter the Great's support recovered the Polish crown in Oct. The opposition in the Polish Sejm (Diet) feared him both as an absolutist and as a Russian dependent. He hoped to base his absolutism exclusively on his Saxon resources. By 1715 the opposition had formed the armed Confederation of Tarnogrod to resist his policies. Government ceased: the Russians intervened, and the price of their mediation at the Pacification or 'General Confederation' was the reduction of the Polish army to ineffective proportions. The chaotic Polish constitution was thus re-established with nothing to protect it, and Augustus' later intrigues to strengthen his position were futile.

(3) Very rich and a ready spender, Augustus developed Saxon industries and was largely responsible for the beauty of Dresden before it was bombed in World War II. He built the celebrated *Zwinger* and founded the Meissen china works. His somewhat demure sobriquet alludes to his capacity for fathering children, of whom he had about 360.

AUGUSTUS FREDERICK (1773-1843) D. of SUSSEX (1801), 6th son of George III, went to Göttingen univ. and in 1793 married Lady Augusta Murray in a C. of E. ceremony in Papal Rome. The ceremony being void, it was repeated in London, but George III's consent not having been obtained under the Royal Marriages Act, the marriage was declared void again. The children were called d'Este after a joint ancestor. He had intellectual interests and amassed a huge library. As a Liberal, supported abolition of the slave trade, R. Catholic emancipation and parliamentary reform. He was also Pres. of the R. Soc. of Arts from 1816, and of the Royal Soc. from 1830 to 1839.

AULD ALLIANCE see EDWARD I-15; EDWARD III-12 and Scottish reigns passim.

AULD LANG SYNE, an old song of parting, was first written down by Robert Burns in 1791, but he knew a different tune for it. The present tune may come from *Sir Alexander Don's Strathspey,* current at the time.

AULIC COUNCIL (Ger. REICHSHOFRAT = Imperial Court Council) was set up by the Emperor Maximilian I in 1497 as his supreme executive and judicial body, both for the empire and for his own hereditary lands. It soon acted only for the Empire and consequently its organisation and membership were the subject of provisions in the P. of Westphalia (1648). Since most imperial initiatives were carried on through the hereditary resources, its executive functions dwindled, and it had, in the Imperial Chamber, a judicial rival. Nevertheless it was an important body until about 1712. It had about 20 members and, after a short itinerant period, always sat at Vienna. It disappeared with the Empire in 1806.

AULUS PLAUTIUS. *See* BRITAIN, ROMAN-1 & 2.

AUROCHS. The ancient wild ox which became extinct in the 16th cent.

AUSCHWITZ (or OSWIECIM). *See* CONCENTRATION CAMPS.

AUSGLEIGH **(Ger = settlement or accommodation).** *See* AUSTRO-HUNGARY-1 & 2.

AUSPICIOUS INCIDENT. *See* OTTOMAN EMPIRE-14.

AUSTEN, Jane (1775-1817) was exceptionally well educated by her clergyman father and lived placidly at Bath, Southampton, Chawton (Hants) and finally in a house next to Winchester College, where she had a nephew. She began *Pride and Prejudice* in 1796 and *Sense and Sensibility* and the satirical *Northanger Abbey* in 1797, but the second was published first in 1811, the first in 1813 and the third only after her death. She began *Mansfield Park* in 1811 and published it in 1814, *Emma* in 1815 and 1816, and *Persuasion* , written in 1815 was also published after her death. She was a calm humorous observer of family and neighbourly relationships much appreciated by contemporaries and by the ablest 19th cent. critics such as Coleridge, Southey, Macaulay and Sir Walter Scott, and conjures up, without apparent, but with much real effort, the atmosphere of small household life.

AUSTERITY (1945-51). A policy of the Attlee govts. designed to pay for peacetime socialism by reducing imports, raising exports, raising taxes and rationing even more strictly than during World War II.

AUSTIN (i.e. AUGUSTINIAN) FRIARS were a mendicant order formed by Pope Alexander IV in 1256 originally from some groups of Italian hermits. They followed an adaptation of the Rule of St Augustine of Hippo and were organised on the pattern of the Dominicans. They soon took to urban ministry, and consequently the E. of Hereford built a house for them (whose site still bears the name) in the City of London shortly after their foundation. They had other houses, notably one at Clare, but they never proliferated in England as they did elsewhere. Martin Luther was an Augustiian.

AUSTIN, Herbert (1866-1941) 1st Ld. AUSTIN (1936) went to Australia in 1884 where he received his training in machinery and steel processing. Returned to Birmingham in 1893 he designed the first *Wolseley* car – a three wheeler – in 1895, and founded the Austin Motor Co. in 1905. While Conservative M.P. for Kings Norton between 1918 and 1924 he conceived the idea of popular motoring, which bore fruit as the Austin Twelve of 1921 and the Austin Seven of 1922.

AUSTIN, John (1790-1859). Prof. of Jurisprudence at London Univ. from 1826-32 published his influential treatise on the *Province of Jurisprudence* in 1832. His wife **Sarah (1793-1867)** translated the major works of the German historian Leopold von Ranke. They were both much influenced by the company of their neighbours in Queen Square, London, James Mill and Jeremy Bentham, She also wrote, *inter alia, Germany from 1760 to 1814.*

AUSTRALIA (1) In the 17th cent. Dutch explorers discovered the northern part of the Australian coast from the G. of Carpentaria to Arnhem Land, the western coast at various points and the western end of the south coast. Abel Tasman touched **TASMANIA** (which he called **VAN DIEMEN'S LAND**) in 1642-3. On his return to Fiji he had circumnavigated the continent and proved it to be a vast island. It was still thought that another continent extended to the South Pole, the so-called *Terra Australis Incognita* (Unknown Southern Land).

(2) James Cook's voyages (1769-71; 1772-5; 1776-81) destroyed the myth of the southern continent, but in Aug. 1770 he took possession of **NEW SOUTH WALES (N.S.W.)** on behalf of the Crown. The American rebellion having deprived Britain of some sites for penal colonies, Lord Sydney had criminals transported to N.S.W. on the advice of the botanist Sir Joseph Banks who had sailed with, and for whom Cook had named **BOTANY BAY.** The name became a nickname for convict settlements, though no convicts were ever sent to that particular place.

(3) Colonisation of N.S.W. began in Jan. 1788 with the first penal settlement under Gov. PHILLIP. In 1790 a second fleet brought a special corps called the N.S.W. Corps, and in 1792 its commandant GROSE became Lieut.-Gov. Until 1809 the Corps dominated the colony (*see* BLIGH) through a rum monopoly.

(4) While Bligh was detained, N.S.W. was under a military govt. and the officers engrossed the land and reduced the convict and 'emancipist' labour to virtual slavery: this was not the intention of the home govt; so MACQUARIE was allowed to bring his own regiment and the corps was recalled. He made it easier for convicts to be emancipated, and for emancipists to become farmers. Quite logically he spent much on public works, encouraged exploration, survey and agricultural research, founded a bank and minted a currency to replace rum.

Vested interests protested vigorously and by 1817 false rumours of convict insurrection attributed to Macquarie's laxity were circulating in London. In Mar. 1819 Castlereagh obtained a select committee on the prison system (which, of course, included transportation), a commissioner (J.T. BIGGE) to make local inquiries having already been appointed in Jan. The result was that Macquarie was replaced by Sir. Thos. BRISBANE and, on Bigge's report, an Act of 1823 established councils in N.S.W. and Van Diemen's Land to advise the governors on legislation and local taxes. In 1825 Brisbane was followed by Sir Ralph DARLING who favoured a land owning upper class and made large land grants to applicants with capital, in order to encourage speedy development. Shortage of labour temporarily frustrated his declared object, while leaving large tracts of empty land in the hands of a small group. In Jan. 1831 Goderich decided that henceforth land should only be sold, and Darling, who was unpopular with the majority because of the old policy, now lost face with the rest because of the new.

(5) He was replaced by the more liberal Sir Richard BOURKE, and the home govt. began, not wholly successfully, to encourage assisted migration. Development played into the hands of the more successful emancipists and wealthier native born; they began to agitate for a local legislature with a limited property franchise which would, of course, protect their own interest. Geo. GIPPS became governor in 1838. Transportation ceased in 1840, and in 1842 British legislation created a council consisting of 12 crown nominees and 24 members elected on the desired property franchise; this had no control over the Civil List, land sales or land sale revenue, but its powers were otherwise comprehensive. Rising local self consciousness complicated Gipp's position, for he had also to face an agricultural depression. People (mostly townsmen) in middle income groups demanded local control of land policy; the rich graziers and the poorer squatters (mostly country people) wanted to restore transportation. An attempt to restore it in 1849 was successfully resisted at Melbourne, Sydney and eventually Brisbane.

(6) From the 1820's the demand for grazing had caused outward expansion from the narrow bounds of N.S.W., and fear of possible French competition led to annexation of land in Victoria, the most fertile area on the continent. In 1829 Capt. Freemantle proclaimed British sovereignty over the west coast as a preliminary to the establishment of the Swan River settlement. Curiously, Australia as a single territory was never formally annexed to the Crown.

(7) The westward passage in 1813 over the Blue Mountains had led to the exploration of the inland country. The chief difficulty for those seeking grazing was the rivers, which tended to dry out in the hot season. Capt. Charles Sturt in 1828-30 made two heroic journeys in which he found the courses of the N.S.W. rivers. In 1827 Allan Cunningham had travelled north, discovering good land in the Liverpool Plains and Darling Downs, and had then moved east to the sea at Brisbane.

(8) The new colony founded in 1836 at Adelaide became a base for the exploration of central Australia. It had been inferred that a large central sea or lake fed the Queensland rivers. In 1840 E. J. Eyre discovered Ls. Torrens and Eyre, which were mostly mud and salt water. In 1844 Sturt confirmed Eyre's findings while Eyre himself travelled westward along the equally waterless shore of the Great Australian Bight.

(9) The final stage in establishing the outline of Australian geography comprised the trans-continental expeditions. The German, Ludwig Leichardt, made three journeys (1842-8) from Queensland to Port Essington, east of modern Darwin, dying on the last. In 1858 A. C. Gregory crossed on the other diagonal from Brisbane to

Adelaide. J. M. Stuart, Sturts' lieutenant, reached the north coast from Adelaide at the third attempt in 1862. Melbourne, the rival city to Adelaide promoted another northward crossing by Burke and Wills on a parallel route to the east, but they mismanaged the expedition and died (1861) on the return journey from the G. of Carpentaria. John McKinlay later found their remains and succeeded in reaching the gulf. In 1874 Sir John Forrest pushed across the centre of the continent from the west coast.

(10) By mid-19th cent. the practice of local responsibility in the settled areas made people realise that autonomy depended upon ability to pay for it. In the 1850's this was attainable, and the Australian Colonies Government Act separated **VICTORIA** from N.S.W., gave each and Van Diemen's Land (from 1855 **TASMANIA**) colonial parliaments and created the colony of **SOUTH AUSTRALIA** with a council. These bodies all eventually developed into bicameral legislatures.

(11) In 1851 the former Californian prospector E. H. Hargreaves found gold near Bathurst and within a year £1m worth was produced in Victoria. The ensuing gold rush trebled the population, which was 265,000 by 1860. As mining required a licence whose cost naturally weighed most upon the unsuccessful digger there was trouble in the mining camps and demands for reform. At Balaarat there was a fight with the troops at Eureka Stockade (q.v.) in Dec. 1854. Gold production reached its peak by 1856 after which it fell continually, and diggers began to drift towards agriculture. Here they were met with the results of the old land policies: most of the useful land was held under licence by squatters or graziers, who were interested less in selling than in acquiring better titles. Resolutions in the N.S.W. Assembly to inquire into the issues were defeated until 1859 (when **QUEENSLAND** was separated from N.S.W.), but in the '60s bills were passed both in N.S.W. and Victoria permitting farmers to select land from squatters runs, but giving squatters certain limited pre-emptive rights. Between 1861 and 1866 17,000 family farms were established in N.S.W., and between 1864 and 1878 1,300,000 acres were brought under cultivation in Victoria which in 1866 turned protectionist.

(12) Meantime, however, the absorption of the unemployed went too slowly and the local economies remained depressed. There was a strong demand in the tradition of Macquarie for public works, led, after 1873 by Sir Hercules ROBINSON, gov. of N.S.W. Victoria, and N.S.W. had borrowed over £200M by 1892, of which £64M was spent on railways. The conversion of these vast capital sums into personal income at a time of worldwide depression created a boom, and then a speculative inflation. The overseas markets hardly expanded at all, the London loan supply dried up in 1884 and land development had reached a temporary limit by 1888. The trade unions which had developed from mining inspiration in an atmosphere of expansion had suddenly to face employers no longer able to go on raising wages. Between 1888 and 1895 there was a series of great strikes, but Australian overseas credit had collapsed, and there was nothing from which to satisfy workers' demands.

(13) Financial crisis had engulfed all parts of society: it created a general demand for federation, and a particular demand in organised labour for political rather than industrial action. Federative negotiations had long been in progress and informal machinery existed for approximating local legislation, but the main obstacles to federation were the Victorian State tariff of 1866, and the desire of conservatives (who were strong in the upper houses of state legislatures) to reserve as much power as possible to the states. The pressure for compromise was, however, strong enough for the imperial parliament to enact the Commonwealth of Australia Act, 1900, and the

federation of six colonies (including **WESTERN AUSTRALIA**) came into existence on 1 Jan. 1901. The capital was initially at Sydney with the Commonwealth parliament at Melbourne, but in 1908 it was decided to build a new capital at Canberra.

(14) Though the decision to found Canberra took many years to realise, it marked the point at which Australians became in all but name an independent nation, linked with the UK by sentimental and to some extent economic, but not political links. The country's affairs became important to Britain only when they touched her foreign policy. World War I broke out during a Commonwealth general election, but participation was not in issue. Some 350,000 Australians served overseas as volunteers, first in Egypt and then, with New Zealand troops, at the Dardanelles in 1915. This campaign became a national legend. Thereafter they were employed in numbers on the Western Front. In 1916 the Labour prime minister, W. M. Hughes, became convinced that conscription was essential but was twice defeated in referenda.

(15) In 1918 a country party designed to secure protection for the farmers hastened the collapse of Labour, and a National Country Party coalition, returned in 1923 maintained high tariffs, gave agricultural export bounties and borrowed heavily overseas. By 1927 the rising cost of living provoked strikes, and the govt. was resoundingly defeated. In the circumstances of the world slump of 1929 the United Australia Party set up a coalition very like the National Govt. in Britain in 1931 but it took until 1934 for a very slow recovery to become manifest. This was the year of the Statute of Westminster, which made no more than a formal difference.

(16) In World War II the earliest war efforts of the R. G. MENZIES govt. were directed to the Middle East and large forces were engaged there until the end of 1941. In Oct. 1941, a Labour govt. was formed under John CURTIN and in Dec. the Japanese attacked. By Mar. 1942 most of the Australian troops in the Pacific had been lost and those in the Middle East had to be brought back. The Curtin govt. introduced conscription and labour direction after the Americans had turned the tide, and the govt. (newly returned in Aug. 1943) transferred large numbers from the forces to industry and so laid the foundations of a modern industrial state. Meantime Australian forces were heavily engaged in New Guinea on the very doorstep of the Commonwealth.

(17) Two further factors intervened after the war to develop the trend towards a self-conscious independence. The war had caused a consciousness of territorial emptiness and a need to fill the spaces in self defence. Immigration was encouraged on an enormous scale, and no longer only from Britain and the Old Commonwealth. On average half the immigrants in the years since 1951 have come from elsewhere. This has altered the character of the population. Moreover the new migrants have mostly been accommodated in towns, not as heretofore on the land. The second factor was Britain's accession to the Common Market and particularly the creation of the single market in 1986. This loosened economic ties. The Keeting Labour govt. orchestrated republicanism and Anglophobia by way of distraction, during the election campaign of 1996, from its poor administration, and was overwhelmingly defeated.

AUSTRASIA. See FRANKISH EMPIRE.

AUSTRIA (AS EXPRESSION) before 1919 might mean (a) the two small duchies of Upper and Lower Austria; (b) these with Styria, Carinthia, the Tyrol, the Vorarlberg and, after 1806, Salzburg, a mainly German area roughly conterminous with the modern Austrian republic; (c) the periodically changing assemblage of lands (including the above) owing allegiance after 1556 to the Ferdinandine Habsburgs until the death of the Emperor CHARLES VI (r. 1711-40) and then through the Archduchess and Queen

MARIA THERESA (Empress from 1745 in right of her husband (r. 1740-80), to the House of Habsburg-Lorraine.

AUSTRIA comprising only the area of the present Upper and Lower Austria with Vienna, became a duchy in 1156. In 1192 the Babenberg Duke Leopold II, the captor of Richard I, acquired Styria, which was held with Austria until Frederick the Warlike was killed fighting the Hungarians in 1246. The duchies, with (after 1269) Carinthia and Carniola were then disputed between Bela IV of Hungary and Ottakar II of Bohemia, who had a grant by writ from RICHARD OF CORNWALL as King of the Romans. After Rudolf of Habsburg was elected King in 1273, Ottakar's claims were challenged and he was eventually killed at the B. of Dürnkrut (Aug. 1278). By 1282 Austria, Styria and Carniola were firmly in Habsburg possession.

AUSTRIA (*see previous entry*). **(1)** Under FERDINAND I (r. 1556-64) Germans formed a 65% majority of the population, the rest being mostly Czechs; but the balance shifted continually as non-German areas were acquired and German provinces lost. Progress against the Turks between 1526 and 1718 brought in southern Slavs, Hungarians, Roumanians and Ukrainians. The War of the Spanish Succession added Lombard Italians, and the Flemings and Walloons of Belgium. From 1742, when Silesia was lost to Prussia, the Germans suffered a reduction of about 20%. The First Polish Partition (1772-5) added many Poles, and in Galicia, more Ukrainians. The later partitions increased both these elements, and the rape of Venice (1797) added Italians in the Veneto and Istria besides Croats and Serbs in Dalmatia. The Germanic element, with the dynasty at its head, had become by 1815, a minority of 30% in a conglomerate.

(2) The Holy Roman Emperor had to be a R. Catholic, and four of the Electors were always of that persuasion. The prestige of the office was important and the Habsburgs secured it continuously (save in 1742-5) but paid for it by provoking important minorities. In Bohemia the Hussite tradition, and in Hungary urban Calvinism helped to set their people apart. Police action or persecution had Bohemia in turmoil in the Thirty Years War (1618-48), and Hungary during the War of Spanish Succession (1702-14).

(3) Religion was vital because, willy-nilly, the Habsburgs were the last crusaders, in the front line of European land defence against the huge dynamism of Ottoman Islam. The Turks took the great frontier fortress of Raab (Györ), 70 miles from Vienna in 1594. In 1683 they besieged Vienna itself and raided as far west as Salzburg and Friuli.

(4) With eleven major languages, divergent histories and varying laws, especially of succession, the Habsburg states resembled a huddle of mutually strange political animals round an overworked shepherd in a hurricane. The Habsburg shepherd, however, was acquisitive. His motto AEIOU (*Austriae est imperare orbi universo* Lat = It is for Austria to command the whole world) expressed his outlook, tenaciously pursued through dynastic alliances summarised by Mathias Corvinus as *Tu felix Austria nubes* (Lat = You, lucky Austria, marry). Westward ambition matched the eastward defensive. To re-establish the imperial German authority diminished by the Reformation was an enduring objective even after the P. of Westphalia (1648) proved it impracticable, and Habsburg as much as French diplomacy was concerned (and more profitably) with the succession to the vast inheritance of their Spanish cousin. Austria did not conquer Germany but remained the greatest influence there after 1648. She became predominant in Italy after 1714.

(5) French ambitions set the westward limits, and in wars with both Habsburg families, French rulers habitually sought the alliance of the Turk. Richelieu's intervention in the Thirty Years War prevented the

conquest of Germany. Conversely the Turkish defeats before Vienna (1683), and at Szlankamen (1691) and Zenta (1697) partly freed Austria, with her British and other allies, to prevent a French conquest of the same area.

(6) Louis XIV's aggressions were, by the accident of neighbourhood, indiscriminate. Britain and Holland easily secured the Habsburg alliance, for Habsburg lands were as much threatened as Dutch independence and English religion and trade, but fear rather than common interests held the allies together. If they prevented France from seizing the Spanish empire, France remained, after 1714, with her Spanish family ally, magnificently, if torpidly, dangerous. The Ts. of Utrecht, Rastatt and Baden (1713-4), however, heralded a Turkish attack on Venice preliminary to an attack on Hungary. P. Eugene's two tremendous pre-emptive victories at Petrovaradin (Aug. 1716) and Belgrade (Aug. 1717) forced the Porte to cede (at the P. of Passarovitz in July 1718) wide Danubian provinces, the base at Belgrade and, most importantly, freedom of trade, travel and taxation to Habsburg subjects as far as Persia. The Utrecht settlement had demonstrated the limitations, as allies, of the English who had deserted the cause for trade. The need to develop the war-damaged economies of Hungary and Belgium brought forth in 1719 the Vienna Oriental Co. and in 1720 the Ostend or Austrian East India Co. An outcry in London forced the latter into liquidation in 1727. *See next entry.*

AUSTRIA, POST-PRAGMATIC (1740-1867) (*see previous entry*) **(1)** By 1721 the Hofburg had long been exercised at the likelihood of a female succession. CHARLES VI's court was full of women, including his strongminded Hanoverian Empress, two dowagers, and the Archduchess daughters of both his predecessors besides himself. His elder daughter was MARIA THERESA (properly Theresia). If things were left as they stood, the personally connected Habsburg confederacy would fly apart. Some of the countries were under Salic Law; in others the local estates were entitled to choose or confirm a new line of succession; elsewhere foreign rulers might claim or trump up dormant remainders. Dismemberment would destroy Vienna as an east European nerve centre and command post, and expose Germany if not Europe to French or Turkish conquest. To preserve the inheritance undivided became the pre-occupation of Charles VI as a responsible statesman, of the City and Court of Vienna as vested interests, and of states such as Britain and Hanover which depended on the balance of power. The **Pragmatic Sanction** set forth Charles' intentions. The operations which made it part of European and Hapsburg public law were legally intricate, politically risky, diplomatically sophisticated, and prolonged over nearly twenty years. They were, with two exceptions, remarkably successful.

(2) The first exception was Hungary, which was content to let the Archduchess Maria Theresa be its King (*sic*), but jealously kept its own institutions with its capital at Pressburg and later at Buda. The second, arose from a pardonable miscalculation on Prussia. The splenetic but inconsiderable and loyal Frederick William I, had habitually and publicly humiliated his heir. The Turkish offensive of 1736 to 1739 kept the Austrian armies in the east and ended with the loss of Belgrade (P. of Belgrade Sept. 1739). Six months later that heir, Frederick the Great, ascended his father's throne. Four months later still (Oct. 1740), by the death of Charles VI, the Pragmatic became effective. No one expected much from the despised Frederick. When, therefore, with a full treasury and his father's army he sprang at the Archduchess' uncovered throat (Dec. 1740), he achieved a military and diplomatic surprise. A single battle (Mollwitz Apr. 1741) put him in possession of Silesia, the rich basin of the Oder. Maria Theresa had powerful economic and political reasons for trying to get it back, but meanwhile all Europe rethought, in the light of this Prussian apparition, the principles of European diplomacy. The P. of Berlin (July 1742) ended the First, the P. of Dresden (Dec. 1745) the Second Silesian War, with a cession which she regarded as temporary. In each war the French had intervened against her, and English support had been ineffectual.

(3) Holland had become second rate. The British were weak on land; the Hanoverian possessions of their Elector-King exposed them to French or Prussian blackmail; their traders competed with Austrians in Turkey; they were distracted by colonial rivalries and wars with France and Spain. In 1749 Maria Theresa made her secret conference review her foreign policy. As long ago as Jan. 1715 Louis XIV had canvassed an alliance. In a remarkable submission, Count KAUNITZ proposed it now. The idea sank in. He went to Paris as ambassador in 1750, returned in 1753 with the ground well prepared, and became chief minister. By that time too, the administration, army and finances had been overhauled. The empress did not intend to provoke war; she simply envisaged that the recovery of Silesia should remain possible.

(4) Russian policy, much affected by court disturbances, had oscillated between westward and southward aggression. The latter, in its early stages, benefitted Austria whenever it distracted the Turks. The former, if confined to the Baltic provinces was harmless, but the Russians, no less than the Swedes, meddled habitually in Saxo-Poland, towards which, after the seizure of Silesia, Prussia had realisable ambitions. The Austro-Russian alliance of June 1746 was designed to hold Frederick to the P. of Dresden, and anticipate his probable designs on Poland or Saxony. The P. of Aix-la-Chapelle (1748) gave the Habsburgs less than nothing, since it recognised the already recognised Pragmatic, and the cession of Silesia inconsistent with such recognition. Nobody believed that it would last, and in Sept. 1751 the British, by way of reinsurance for Hanover, acceded to the Austro-Russian alliance. This exhausted the advantages of the British connection.

(5) Anglo-French colonial wars raging since 1751 in India and 1754 in Canada, precipitated the European conflict, (see SEVEN YEARS' WAR) which was preceded by Kaunitz's *Renversement des Alliances* (Fr. = Reversal of Alliances) of Jan. and May 1756. This expressed the effect of a long drift; a French alliance remained the primary feature of Hapsburg foreign policy until the French Revolution. The Empress, through Kaunitz, supplemented it, in the face of the Prussian assault, with a league which included the Empire, Russia, Poland and Sweden. The probable result was not attained. Frederick the Great, at his last gasp, was saved by the Czarina Elizabeth II's unexpected death (1762) and the accession of a pro-Prussian successor. The P. of Hubertusburg (Feb. 1763) still left Silesia in his hands: more serious, however, was the death of Augustus III of Saxo-Poland and the election in Poland of the Czarina Catherine's lover, Stanislas Poniatowski, as a result of a Russo-Polish deal. It was now improbable that Prussia could ever be made to disgorge Silesia or to desist from eastward expansion.

(6) In 1765 the Empress' husband, Francis II, died. (*See* LORRAINE.) Their son JOSEPH II was elected Emperor and became co-ruler with his mother. The Czarina Catherine was, too, interested by her Russian lovers in southern policies. The tremendous Russo-Turkish War of 1768 to 1774 gave the Habsburgs time for further reforms. Personal factors influenced their nature. Francis II, despite his infidelities, had been the backbone of the Empress' life, besides possessing a flair for finance. She was now less sure of herself. Joseph was modern, fiery, tactless and autocratic: Kaunitz cynical, clever and confident. Both, like Frederick the Great, were men of

the new enlightenment without respect for established usages. The First Polish Partition was decisive: the Empress opposed it as immoral, contrary to international comity and her understanding of Habsburg interests, yet bowed to the judgement of her son and ministers. Thenceforth she was the rulers highest and often decisive adviser, but not herself the daily arbitress of events. She died in 1780.

(7) The period from 1772 to Joseph II's death in 1790 anticipated the French Revolution in many ways; he initiated popular education, took over church lands and created a state church, and substituted a centralised govt. with local agencies for the older local establishments and immunities. Making German, now spoken by a minority, the official language touched a concealed nerve of latent nationalism, already irritated by the attack on local privileges. In Hungary it had to be abandoned. It caused unrest in Belgium, depressed by a new and rigorous economic policy, under which the govt. (save in the Tyrol) restricted imports especially of food, metals and textiles, and substituted home products and their export. To prevent Belgian rebellion it needed more than an efficient police. The Anglo-Dutch economic stranglehold had to be broken. In 1782 the Dutch were induced to withdraw the Barrier Treaty garrisons. The next stage was to reopen the Scheldt. This awakened not only British but French opposition. To maintain this direction Joseph had to turn from France to Russia for a guarantee against Prussia and to pay the Czarina by abetting her designs on Turkey. Austrian troop movements distracted the Turks when the Russians advanced on the Black Sea in 1782.

(8) Russia was obviously unreliable, and in 1784 Joseph tried to gain room for manoeuvre. He induced the Wittelsbachs to exchange adjacent and rich Bavaria for rich but troublesome Belgium. Frederick the Great stopped this by forming a League for the Defence of German Liberties, and showed that the Prussian King was more influential in Germany than the German Emperor. Thus Joseph was friendless in 1787. The Russians now invoked his obligation to fight if the Turks counter-attacked. After pyrrhic Austrian victories in an expensive and unpopular war, the Russians acquired interests in the Balkans and Turkey. This threatened Austrian trade more immediately than British competition, and the British interests too.

(9) The French revolutionary impact was first felt in Belgium (Oct. 1789) which rose as the Austrians were occupying Belgrade. Joseph II died and LEOPOLD II (r. 1790-2), advised by SPIELMAN and COBENZL instead of Kaunitz, liquidated the Turkish war and gravitated towards Prussia. He died during the diplomatic preparations for the struggle with revolutionary France and FRANCIS II (r. 1792-1835) succeeded him. In fact Prussia and Russia were negotiating another Polish partition behind Austria's back. At Vienna the principal casualties were Spielmann and Cobenzl, who gave way to THUGUT, a protégé of Kaunitz. The Polish obsessions and mutual hatred of Prussia and Austria inhibited co-operation throughout the French wars of the next twenty years. *See* FRENCH REVOLUTIONARY WARS.

(10) The treaties of Lunéville (Feb. 1801) and Amiens (Jan. 1802) destroyed Austrian influence in Italy and Germany, and brought back Cobenzl. The Holy Roman Imperial Constitution, mainly through Prussian opportunism, was becoming unworkable, while France and Russia might at any moment dispose of Germany as they pleased, and the imperial title with it. In May 1803 the British went to war again and in Aug. 1804 Francis II took, by way of addition, the title of Emperor of Austria. The older title was abdicated in Aug. 1806 by which time military disaster and the P. of Pressburg (Dec. 1806) had cut Austria off from the Adriatic and transferred the Tyrol to Bavaria. Count Philip STADION superseded Cobenzl.

(11) Pressburg and Nelson's victory at Trafalgar (Oct.

1805) were the watershed. French expansion into Germany and Poland gave Austria a breathing space. It also convinced the imperial family advised by Stadion that they must fight Bonaparte for their lives. The political but unmilitary ARCHDUKE JOHN directed legal and administrative reforms, launched (Mar. 1808) a propaganda campaign in all German speaking countries, and persuaded his imperial brother (June 1808) to institute a popular militia. This began the German national movement for which the Prussians later claimed the credit. The Spanish risings and British Iberian intervention (Aug. 1808) created a sensation. A similar rising was planned for the Tyrol. In Feb. 1809 Austria again went to war. In May outside Vienna Bonaparte was beaten off by the military but unpolitical ARCHDUKE CHARLES at Aspern, but won the second round when John failed to reinforce Charles at Wagram. Charles sought an armistice, which in effect sacrificed the Tyrolese. The P. of Vienna ensued. The French hunted down the faithful Tyrolese leader, Andreas Hofer, and shot him at Mantua in Feb. 1810. Austria now had a valuable martyr.

(12) Court factionalism and the Tyrolese disgrace decided Francis II to repudiate his brothers and Stadion. The new, fatefully appointed minister was Count (later Prince) Klemens Lothar METTERNICH (1773-1859), a Rhinelander married to Kaunitz' grand-daughter. Lately ambassador in Paris, his despatches had encouraged Stadion to advise war in Feb. 1809. His appointment represented a change of man rather than policies. Peace and accumulation of resources for the next struggle was the aim, but with whom the next struggle was to be, was not certain. Metterich knew Bonaparte and esteemed his abilities. The Archduchess Marie Louise was to be the means whereby the heir of Kaunitz induced the self-made Emperor of the French to believe in a new *Renversement des Alliances*, with Russia, now active in the Balkans, as the odd man out. The marriage in Feb. 1810 offended the Czar with whom Bonaparte had also been seeking a marriage alliance. In Feb. 1811 the Russians captured Belgrade, but as the Franco-Russian rift deepened, Austria's position improved against both powers. By Jan. 1813 the court was ready to abandon Francis II's brother-in-law even if Metternich was not. The fresh army was mobilised in Bohemia. Despite frantic French diplomacy, Austria entered the war in Aug. with by far the strongest allied contingent; Prince Charles SCHWARZENBERG became allied C-in-C and beat Bonaparte decisively at Leipzig in Oct.

(13) The confederative nature of the Austrian state explains the European objectives of Francis II (who was no cipher) and Metternich, at the interrupted Congress of Vienna (1814-5). It was as essential to maintain it, as it had been at the time of the Pragmatic Sanction. Central European order depended on the dynasty and was now threatened by new movements based on mobile, modern, popularist and secular ideas implanted by French invaders, and potentially hostile to dynasties. Austria needed political outworks to delay infiltration. These were to consist of leagues of dynasts maintaining stiff state structures which would give time for a Christian revival. It was natural to think in terms of confederations. The Austro-Bohemian territories could be involved in a German confederation, where Habsburg rank and prestige would secure the presidency. The Italian lands might similarly join in an Italian confederation under a Holy Father who would surely listen to his Eldest Son. In the north and south there were great problems. The Polish and R. Catholic question nearly brought a rupture with Orthodox Russia, and there were difficulties in launching a Christian revival while discouraging Christian incursions into Moslem Turkey, and encouraging a more political Papacy.

(14) In fact Austrian diplomacy won illusory gains. A weak German Confederation was, indeed, set up, but the Pope would have nothing to do with its Italian counterpart. The Czar was to be King of a separate Poland wholly at his mercy, but irritable from the independent Polish city republic of Cracow on the Austrian frontier. No guarantees against Russian activity in the Balkans could be obtained (June 1815). The Holy Alliance (Aug.), in one aspect an early form of ecumenism, and much derided in England, was a natural second best. If local institutions could not be set up to re-educate the peoples, a concert of dynasts must do it instead.

(15) It was too late. The religious revival was confined to the Habsburg dominions. Elsewhere, apart from Prussia, the states of Germany and Italy could not, or would not, suppress their agitators. As early as 1817 liberal students demonstrated at the tercentenary festival of Luthers XCV theses, at the Wartburg. While allies agreed at AIX-LA-CHAPELLE to end the occupation of France (Sept.-Nov. 1818), police began to trace disturbing Jacobin conspiracies. The murder in Mar. 1819 of the right-wing playwright August von Kotzebue by a student, convinced them that they were serious. At CARLSBAD in Sept. 1819 the German diet voted Decrees against liberals and in favour of censorship and control of universities, but the liberal epidemic knew no frontiers. In 1820 there were insurrections in Spain (Jan.), Naples (July), Portugal (Aug.) and Piedmont. The Final Act of the diet at Vienna (May 1820) authorised larger German states (i.e. Prussia and Austria) to 'help' the govts. of smaller ones to enforce the Carlsbad Decrees. The Czar met Francis at the TROPPAU Congress (Oct-Dec. 1820) to consider what should be done elsewhere, and their LAIBACH (Ljubljana) Congress (Jan-May 1821) authorised Austrian intervention in Naples and Piedmont. There had been revolts against the Turks in Serbia since 1819. In Apr. 1821 the Greeks rose.

(16) The resort to arms of 1821 thus marked the failure of the system. So too did Metternich's appointment as head of the govt. besides its foreign minister; the tired emperor began to leave more and more to him. This meant more police. Not surprisingly, when the Congress of VERONA met (Oct Dec. 1822) to consider Turkish and Iberian issues, the England of Canning vetoed remedial action. This raised the spectre of Turkish partitions, if ever Russia should escape the logic of Metternich's reactionary solidarity and personal magnetism. In 1825 Nicholas I succeeded Alexander I at St. Petersburg. Balkan rivalry now destroyed the *entente* which the Holy Alliance had become. The Anglo-Russian St. Petersburg Protocol (Apr. 1826) on Greek affairs was an early step, leading quickly to the T. of London (July 1827) and the destruction of the Turko-Egyptian fleet at Navarino (Oct.). The Russians wound up a Persian war and invaded Turkey (Apr. 1828). They were in Varna by Oct. and extorted at the T. of Adrianople (Sept. 1829) the independence (i.e. protectorate) of Moldavia and Wallachia. They could now interfere with the Austrian oriental trade. In July 1833 they forced the Turks to close the straits to all but Russian warships.

(17) The rebellious years 1830-1 had forced Austria into the increasingly hated role of European policeman, against the trend of British and French opinion and stirring Prussian ambition. Russia was the blackmailer, but had suppressed a Polish rising. The three treaties of MÜNCHENGRÄTZ (Sept-Oct. 1833) helped to restore the position. Russia, in effect, acceded to the Vienna Final Act, and approved Austrian action against rebels all over Italy. From Palermo to Lübeck liberalism was being held down by forces backed, or supplied by Austria guaranteed by Russia. In 1834, after rioting at Frankfort, the German diet supplemented the inefficient repressive system with a committee of political investigation. In May 1835 the much loved Emperor Francis I died, and

Metternich secured in the ARCHDUKE LUDWIG a pliable regent for his dim-witted successor FERDINAND I (r. 1835-48). Opposition, particularly among the industrialised Bohemian nobility (e.g. the Schwarzenbergs) was growing, for the Minister's rule had become a show of dexterity in the interests of a *status quo* rendered decreasingly sustainable by the prosperity, rising educational standards and cross migrations of an industrial revolution. Political impotence was no longer tolerable in an era of new money and confidence. The long expected upheaval of 1848 was heralded by tremors in Spain (1843), Holstein (1844), Roumania (1845), Portugal and Poland (1846-7).

(18) The popular insurrections of 1848-9, mainly in the Austrian sphere of influence, began in Sicily in Jan. 1848, incidentally overthrew the French July Monarchy in Feb., and broke out in mid-Mar. almost simultaneously in Austria, Italy and in Vienna, whence Metterich fled to England (Mar. 15). Mobs seized control in Berlin three days later, and on Mar. 23rd the opportunist Savoyards invaded Lombardy. In Apr. Prussian troops suppressed the Berlin outbreaks and helped to put down revolts in Russian Poland, while the hitherto liberal Pope, Pius IX, repudiated the Italian movements. Ferdinand and the regency, by leaving Vienna for Innsbruck, had freed their hands. The first tide began to turn in May when loyal troops put down riots at Cracow and beat the Savoyards at Curtatone. In June they suppressed riots in Prague and the strong ARCHDUKE JOHN replaced the weak Ludwig as regent. In Aug. after a triumph at Custozza (July) they drove the Savoyards to an armistice at Vigevano, and the govt. returned to Vienna. In Sept. the Neapolitans recovered Sicily.

The insurrections, whether nationalist, liberal or merely outbursts against unpopular figures, or motivated by half successful ambitions, represented no movement, and exhibited a fatal lack of co-ordination. It was not until mid-Sept. that the Hungarians, after long argument, elected Lajos KOSSUTH as dictator, but they did not move, while in Oct. the govt. suffered and suppressed another rising in Vienna. In Nov. a revolution drove the Pope from Rome to Gaeta, but in Dec. Louis Napoleon Bonaparte became President of France with R. Catholic help, and was preparing to restore him. Thus even though the neighbouring Habsburg D. of Tuscany was hounded from Florence (Feb. 1849), Mazzini's Roman Republic, proclaimed two days later, was doomed in advance.

(19) The ARCHDUCHESS SOPHIE, Ferdinand's sister-in-law, had held the court together throughout these upheavals, and inspired it with aggressive courage. Men of strength and ability gathered round her. Jellacic, the Ban of Croatia, held Agram (Zagreb), Radetzky beat the Savoyards, Prince Windischgraetz had bombarded Prague and then Vienna into submission. Now he set off against Hungary, offering his brilliant brother-in-law Prince Felix SCHWARZENBERG as head of the govt. Schwarzenberg would not serve without a new emperor. Sophie persuaded Ferdinand to abdicate, and her own husband to renounce his rights (Dec. 1848). The Austrian (but not the Hungarian) crown thus passed to FRANZ JOSEF (r. 1848-1916), her son, who, being only 18 was uncompromised by past contentions. It was for Schwarzenberg, a very modern man, to re-establish his empire. He assembled a powerful ministry which included the liberal Stadion, Alexander Bach the administrator, and Bruck, the shipping magnate. He called for (Apr. 1849) Russian aid under the Münchengraetz treaties. By Aug. the Hungarians had capitulated to the Czar at Vilagos, and their country was soon being fairly and incorruptibly administered by hated Austrians, but first some hangings created martyrs. Three years later Schwarzenberg was dead, but he had laid the foundations of an autocracy.

(20) After Schwarzenberg Franz Josef was long his own prime minister and until 1859 Austria seemed triumphant. She had, short of annexations, procured solid advantages from the Crimean War (1854-6): others had fought her battle against Russian interferences in Turkey; the Danube was open to international (mainly Austrian) navigation, and the Black Sea was neutralised. These were won, however, at the price of upsetting both sides. Savoy, not Austria, had helped the allies, and Franz Josef's ultimatum had eventually forced peace upon the Czar, his brother autocrat. So long as other options were open this diplomatic isolation was just tolerable, but in the years 1859 to 1866 they were violently closed. In 1859 Savoy and Cavour, with French help, took the north Italian provinces (Preliminaries of Villa Franca and T. of Zurich, July and Nov. 1859) in 1860, with British applause the rest of Italy, save Rome. Six years later at Prussian hands, this expulsion from Italy was completed by the loss of Venice and matched by expulsion from Germany. The disaster at Königgraetz (July 1866) brought not only this but the political extinction of Hanover, and Prussian control of the Elbe route from Bohemia to the North Sea. (Ts. of Nikolsburg and Prague). Trieste was now the only outlet, and the Balkans the only area accessible to expansion.

(21) As ever the internal constitution and external policy were bound up together. With face-saving politeness Ferenc DEÁK, the Hungarian, demanded *Ausgleich*. In effect Austria was expelled from Hungary (June 1867), the link between the two becoming largely personal. It is hard to see how this much criticised arrangement could have been avoided, but it created structural and political contradictions which were probably irreconcilable. Austria became Austro-Hungary (q.v.).

AUSTRIA (REPUBLICAN) (A) (1) On 21 Oct. 1918 the Austrian members of the *Reichsrat* (the diet of the non-Hungarian Habsburg possessions) resolved themselves into a National assembly for **Deutschoesterreich** (German Austria). The Emperor abdicated on 11 Nov. On 12th the Assembly proclaimed the republic and its adherence *(Anschluss)* to Germany, and on 22nd it defined its territory so as to include those old imperial provinces with a German majority.

(2) The new dispensation was menaced from three main directions: gathering communist subversion with a base in Hungary, provincial separatism and Yugoslav claims supported by Serbian troops. In May 1919 Vorarlberg applied to join Switzerland and the Tyrol declared for secession. In Apr. and June there were communist insurrections in Vienna. The Assembly was forced to adopt a federalist constitution, but the break-up of the Hapsburg army had left the govt. without troops, and the parties had raised their own to fight the communists. The *Anschluss* had to be abandoned because sporadic famine made normalisation urgent, and the Allies refused a peace treaty permitting it. The P. of St. GERMAIN (10 Sept. 1919) thus imposed independence upon a country which was not sure if it wanted it. On the other hand, the southern para-military bodies drove back the Serbs; German speaking Hungary, except Ödenburg (Sopron) joined the republic, while the Swiss rejected the Vorarlberg application. The Germans of Bohemia and Moravia had, however, to be abandoned, and Italy filched the South Tyrol. These events and poverty attended the birth of the republic, and dominated its internal and international position.

(3) From 1919 to 1921 the towns lived mostly on Anglo-American relief, and in 1922 came the great inflation. The treaty had imposed reparations which manifestly could not be paid. In Oct. 1922 the Chancellor, Ignaz Seipel, negotiated the GENEVA PROTOCOLS by which, in return for a large international loan, Austria put her finances under League of Nations inspection and undertook to remain independent until after 1940. The protocols brought prosperity, symbolised by important, if journalistically exaggerated housing and welfare schemes in Vienna.

(4) Unfortunately the armed partisans became increasingly influential within their political parties, and politics more violent and unparliamentary. In July 1927 there was fighting in Vienna between the Social Democrat *Schützbund* (Defence Union) and the Christian Democrat *Heimwehr* (Home Defence Force), which had contacts with the Italian Fascists. The economic crisis of 1931 brought bankruptcies and unemployment. It also brought the rise of Hitler (born in Austria), but a swing of Austrian opinion towards the left. The *Heimwehr* was now threatened simultaneously by Nazis and Communists.

(5) The Christian Democrat Engelbert Dollfuss had a majority of one in parliament, but procedural deadlocks made govt. impossible. In Mar. 1933 he suspended Parliament and turned to Italy. In Aug. at the RICCIONE MEETING Mussolini promised support if the *Heimwehr* were given a predominant place in the state, and allowed to destroy the Social Democrats. This ruined the Marxists, but converted Austria into an authoritarian Italian protectorate. In July 1935 Dollfuss was murdered in an attempted Nazi insurrection, but the Italian guarantee held good, and Hitler repudiated his Austrian creatures.

(6) It was the Abyssinian crisis which destroyed Austria. Italy found herself at odds with all the western world save Germany, with whom she concluded the Axis Agreement of 1936. She could no longer afford to oppose German ambitions, while the League of Nations was discredited by the outcome of the Abyssinian war. Austria was thus isolated. Its destruction, mostly by internal subversion, took 18 months. On 12 Mar. 1938 German troops invaded; *Anschluss* was proclaimed on 13th and confirmed by plebiscite on 10 Apr. Austria, as part of the German *Reich* was now known as **OSTMARK** (Eastern March).

(B) (1) At the Moscow meeting of Oct. 1943 the Allies agreed to restore Austrian independence, and this was confirmed at Teheran. The Russians therefore set up a coalition govt. under Karl Renner, the pre-Dollfuss Speaker of the Assembly, after they took Vienna in Apr. 1945. This govt. was recognised by the other allies in July. The country and Vienna were each divided into four zones of military occupation, which the Russians were determined to prolong because their military communications ran across other states to the east and gave them a pretext for occupying and revolutionising them; they were also engaged in far-reaching industrial looting for the benefit of their own economy. Western diplomacy was much concerned with getting them to leave and preventing the revolutions, and the Austrians themselves confined capital investment to the western zones, so that much of their industry migrated from the Vienna region.

(2) The constitution of 1920 was restored, but Russian behaviour proved so unpopular that the communists were unable to get any support. The country subject to Allied control had govts. of a socialist complexion like the British Labour Party. In 1947 the British declared the state of war at an end, and western troops thenceforth remained mainly to protect the Austrians from the Russians. The deadlock continued until communist regimes had been firmly imposed on the countries of Eastern Europe. At the Berlin Conference of Jan. 1954 evacuation of Austria was raised and in Jan. 1955 conceded. The AUSTRIAN STATE TREATY of 15 Apr. 1955 followed. All troops were withdrawn by 25 Oct. and on 5 Nov. Parliament made a constitutional declaration of perpetual neutrality. The creation and increasing strength of the European Community threatened to put Austria at a permanent economic disadvantage so long as the

declaration had to be maintained, but the collapse of the Russian Marxist system in the late 1980s led to movements in 1991 to join the Community.

AUSTRO-HUNGARY or the **DUAL MONARCHY** (*see earlier entries*) was a vital element in the European balance of power, and in the defence of the Levant against Russian penetration through the Straits. Both were fundamental British interests, and the internal condition of the Dual Monarchy was therefore constantly reported to the British Foreign Office. (1) It was based on the *Ausgleich* of June 1867, conceded by the Emperor Franz Josef to Ferenc Deák and the Hungarians. It consisted of two bodies of territories, namely the geographically solid Kingdom of *Hungary* with its capital and parliament at Budapest, and the sprawling discontinuous imperial territories called the *Lands Represented in the Reichsrat* (L.R.R.) or sometimes *Cisleithenia,* with their capital and parliament at Vienna. In Hungary the old institutions were so manipulated that a Magyar minority unsteadily dominated a disunited and discontented majority of southern Slavs, Slovaks and Roumanians. In the L.R.R. a German speaking minority and aristocracy governed, and managed or owned the industry and agriculture, but was not homogeneous: the Galician landlords of a Ukrainian peasantry were Poles; the Bohemian industrialists, powerful at court, were mostly Czechs. The L.R.R. thus consisted of Ukrainians, Ruthenes, Poles, Czechs and Austrians, at first acceptably ruled by a cosmopolitan body, whose true nationality was Habsburg. The only significant sea ports were Trieste (L.R.R.) and Fiume (Hungarian), but the Danube and its river ports (Linz, Vienna, Pressburg, Komarom, Budapest, Novi Sad, Semlin) handled more foreign as well as local traffic.

(2) As the L.R.R. and Hungary would have been helpless alone, the threat of international predation kept them uneasily together, with a customs union, a common army command (but dissimilar military organisation), and a common foreign policy. The ministries concerned were drawn from both sides and were called *The Common Government*. They were responsible to the crowns and to parliamentary delegations which met separately at Vienna and Budapest. Vienna, however, remained the habitual residence of the Emperor and King, and the centre of civilisation, higher education, and amusement.

(3) The Balkans and Turkey remained theoretically open, but internal and external factors inhibited expansion. Externally Russia had marked down Turkey for her prey, but nationalist cross currents, especially in Greece and Roumania marred the simplicity of her design, and the Straits attracted the apprehensive interest of Britain and France. Moreover the Turkish Empire was still capable of surprising military performances. The 'sick man's' bursts of energy always gave time for suspicious rivals to quarrel downstairs.

(4) Hungary was better located to exploit the Balkans than the more advanced L.R.R., but the annexation of more Slavs threatened to reduce the Magyars to a dangerously small minority in their own country. Similarly the Magyars opposed local autonomy for the nations of the L.R.R. because they would have to follow suit. Worse still, once the Balkans were firmly in the Russian sphere, the Dual Monarchy's precarious great power status, even its existence, would be at risk. Thus from 1867 to 1914 there was a kind of Magyar induced paralysis:- advance or retreat, the opposing dangers balanced each other.

(5) There was, too, a related but separate source of worry. The Danube was vulnerable. An East-West (vertical) Balkan partition would put Russia in control at the mouth. It was ceasing to be respectable to uphold Ottoman integrity. To encourage strong national successor states was, again, dangerous to Hungary.

(6) The *Ausgleich* was enacted in defeat and isolation after the military disaster at Königgraetz. The P. of Prague

with Prussia (Aug. 1866) was barely signed when Franz Josef appointed the liberal Saxon prime minister, Baron BEUST, as his minister. Beust hated, and was hated by, the Prussians, who had just driven him from Dresden. As a foreigner he could be objective about the Dual Monarchy's internal broils. There was to be a new departure. Liberal reforms, at least in the L.R.R., were during the next four years to attract the respect of western powers: rational diplomacy their support and investment. Beust approached the French, the British and the south German states. Bismarck anticipated him by overthrowing the opportunistic Bonapartist Empire of Napoleon III (1870) and forming the German Empire (1871). Beust, who had been trying to secure local autonomy for the Czechs was intrigued out of his post by ANDRASSY, the brilliant Hungarian who ran the joint foreign policy in the interests of Hungary. Despite the slump of 1873, Andrassy was lucky, and by 1874 Austro-Hungary was on friendly terms with Germany and Russia in the vague understandings of the *Dreikaiserbund* (Ger. = League of Three Emperors), and even with Italy.

(7) In July 1875 Franz Josef visited Dalmatia in a pro-Slav mood and unintentionally touched off a revolt in Turkish Herzegovina. This spread quickly. Fear of vertical partition or of new Balkan nationalisms soon caused him and Andrassy to withdraw. International consular mediation was proposed, but the Turks refused it. Then reforms were proposed which trenched so far on Turkish sovereignty that the British rejected them. The Turks now took vigorous action (May 1876). The Bulgarian massacres and Gladstone's famous denunciations paralysed British support for Turkey (*see* BERLIN MEMORANDUM; REICHSTADT MEETING) and while the Powers talked, the Serbs and Montenegrins intervened. The Turks routed them.

(8) Slav feeling forced Russia to come to the rescue. In Jan. 1877 Franz Josef and Andrassy agreed to remain neutral in return for military occupation in Bosnia and Herzegovina, if Russia respected the independence of Roumania, Bulgaria, Serbia and Montenegro. This was unrealistic. The Russians had to cross Roumania and Bulgaria to defeat the Turks, which they did, but they imposed the P. of San Stefano (Mar. 1878) and alarmed all Europe, particularly Britain. At the Berlin Congress, the San Stefano *diktat* was set aside (*see* BULGARIA) and Austrian troops were let into Bosnia and Herzegovina. The Dual Monarchy was isolated as after the Crimean War. The result was dependence on Germany expressed in the Dual Alliance of Oct. 1879. Bismarckian diplomacy delayed the counter-formation of a Russo-French understanding, but only for a time.

(9) The chauvinistic factionalism of the Austro-German liberals had resulted in a long Czech boycott of the *Reichsrat*, and now they objected to the Bosnian occupation. They were in fact gunning for Andrassy. Franz Josef appointed as prime minister Count TAAFFE, a childhood friend and an Irish peer. The character of the L.R.R. had changed far-reachingly since 1848. The abolition of feudalism had created a prosperous R. Catholic peasantry, rising agricultural production and, especially in northern Bohemia, an industrial revolution. Taaffe combined clerical influence, the Hapsburg aristocracy and the Slavs in a coalition represented as 'government above party'. The Czechs returned to parliament. Urban liberal ardour was damped by good cheap food and drink and, besides, Taaffe had charm. It was the heyday of Viennese gaiety. Andrassy had gone, succeeded briefly by Haymerle, and then by the Moravian Count KALNOCKY.

(10) The prosperous peace was seemingly reinforced when Italy joined the Dual alliance with Germany in 1882, but once Russia had recovered, the old bugbear of vertical partition reappeared. Austrian predominance in the western Balkans tempted the Russians to adventures

in the east. In 1886 they kidnapped the Bulgarian Prince and put in a general to advise the govt. Austro-Hungary's objections were not supported by her allies. Italy wanted a share in the western Balkans. Bismarck feared a French attack if Germany were involved in a Russo-Habsburg war. In fact Russian bungled brutality upset the Bulgars, and Bismarck's secret Reinsurance Treaty calmed Russian nerves.

(11) In a conglomerate linked by a dynasty, dynastic affairs loomed large. The Archduke Maximilian had been shot by a Mexican firing squad in 1867. Franz Josef's Empress, the beautiful Elizabeth of Bavaria had long lived in a withdrawn semi-melancholia from which fox hunting in Ireland and the English midlands gave some relief. In Jan. 1889 the Crown Prince Rudolf killed Marie Vetsera and committed suicide at Meyerling. A few months later his brother the Archduke Johann Salvator, renounced his rights and became a ship's captain called Orth. The Emperor and the new heir, his nephew the Archduke FRANZ FERDINAND, disliked each other and disagreed on almost everything, especially policy. Then in 1898 the Empress was murdered at Lausanne, and within eighteen months Franz Ferdinand contracted a morganatic marriage. A feeling of fatalism, almost of doom, sapped confidence in the dynasty's unifying function.

(12) Owing to Taaffe's administrative reforms, Vienna had become a cosmopolitan city. The Language Ordinance of 1880 had made Czech an official language, and since most Czechs knew German, but few Germans spoke Czech, the whole L.R.R. was open to Czech ambition, while Germans were excluded from the best jobs in Bohemia, its richest part. The 1890 elections showed how little, for all his skill and goodwill, Taaffe and imperial patronage had reconciled the nationalities. The inward-looking inexperienced Czechs ousted their more tolerant elders. Christian Socialists and social democrats replaced the bourgeois German liberal factions with a more strident factionalism of their own. Cheap Czech labour was driving Germans from Bohemia; Slovenes were having educational brawls with Germans in Styria. The *Reichsrat* became unworkable. Franz Josef canvassed a combined programme of universal suffrage and social reforms such as shorter working hours and national insurance. The Suffrage Bill was howled down (Oct. 1893) and Taaffe resigned. The Germans walked out of the *Reichsrat* in the course of a dispute about languages in schools. A new prime minister, Count Casimir BADENI, bid for Czech support by a strengthened Language Ordinance. The Germans broke up the *Reichsrat* and rioted. Franz Josef dropped Badeni for administrative rule by decree. While the *Reichsrat* talked, Karl Lueger, the mayor, turned Vienna into a civic model and Ernst von KOERBER, the prime minister, created public services, bridled the police, and made Vienna the railway centre of E. Europe.

(13) Russia, suffering similar stresses, desired repose. In 1897 she and Austro-Hungary came to a sensible and popular agreement. They would take no Balkan territory for themselves, save that the Dual Monarchy might annex Bosnia, Herzegovina and Novibazar if necessary. They would prevent others from doing so, would jointly oppose Balkan domination by any Balkan nation, and consult amicably together. This worked well, offsetting Italian irredentism, holding the ring during the Macedonian troubles of 1903 and the nationalist (Karageorgevich) *coup* in Serbia, and it even helped to balance the factors in the Moroccan crisis of 1905-6. The world pattern had, however, changed. Russia, defeated by Japan and gripped by riots and disaffection, had quarrelled with Germany whose colonial ambitions and naval programme were disquieting Britain. The coincidental entry of Izvolski and AEHRENTHAL to the foreign offices at St. Petersburg and Vienna in 1906 occurred when the powers were already set upon a

diplomatic polarisation, of which the launch of the revolutionary British oil-fired battleship *Dreadnought* was a physical symptom.

(14) Austro-Hungary was the natural market for Serbian pigs, plums and maize (Serbia's only exports). Budapest objected to the competition, Vienna wanted to force the Serbs to buy Bohemian instead of French armaments. Tariffs and quotas (which raised food prices in Vienna) had for some time been imposed to meet both demands. The Serbs held out. They sold their goods elsewhere, but especially aimed for an alternative east-west railway outlet to the Adriatic (uniting them with their Montenegrin cousins) across Bosnia and Herzegovina, now occupied by Austro-Hungarian troops but still Turkish. To the Serbs the issue was more emotional than economic. Aehrenthal did not understand this. He wanted a north-south railway through Novibazar to Salonika; it would alleviate the evils of vertical partition, and so facilitate understandings with Russia. The Serbs should have their Austro-Hungarian market. In 1907 the tariffs and quotas were abolished. Early in 1908 he announced in flamboyant language the railway project. Serb fury was boundless. That they might ultimately benefit from a Salonika railway was nothing to them: the issue was political. The Russian pan-Slav press took it up. Izvolski had openly to denounce a project which he secretly supported. In Sept. 1908 he met Aehrenthal privately at the latter's house at Buchlow near Carlsbad, and three weeks later Franz Josef suddenly annexed Bosnia and Herzegovina but not Novibazar. The Salonika railway was thus abandoned, and Izvolski said that he had been tricked. The pan-Slav press and the insatiable Serbs lashed themselves to further fury. Their Adriatic railway would have to pass through Novibazar as much as the Salonika route. They now wanted Bosnia and Herzegovina.

(15) In these controversies Germany, isolated through the *Entente*, had to support the Dual Monarchy, her only friend; and for reasons of a wholly different character, Russia felt bound to support Serbia. If the major causes of World War I lay elsewhere, there was much tinder lying about in the Balkans, made more inflammable still by the Balkan Wars (q.v.). These, by 1913, made Serbia with her irredentist mission towards Bosnia, into the major indigenous power. It was not the immediate intention of the Serbian govt. to provoke a war with Austro-Hungary in 1914, but the secret nationalist body (The Black Hand) to which many of its members belonged, meant to create trouble in Bosnia. That body organised the murder of the Archduke Franz Ferdinand at Sarajevo in June 1914. The war was not prevented because the Austrians imputed the murder to the Serbian govt, which dared not hunt the criminals down.

AUSTRIAN SUCCESSION, WAR OF. *See* WARS OF 1739-48.

AUTHORS' [PLAYWRIGHTS AND COMPOSERS'] SOCIETY OF, was founded by a group of writers headed by Sir Walter Besant in 1883. The first presidents were successively Tennyson, Meredith, Hardy and Bane. Its quarterly journal *The Author* was first published in 1885. By 1990, under the secretaryship of Mark Le Fanu, most Englishmen who had ever published anything belonged to it, and it was achieving a sound negotiating position particularly with publishers and the media.

AUTHORISED VERSION. *See* BIBLE; HAMPTON COURT CONFERENCE 1604.

AUTO-DA-FÉ (Port) *AUTO DE FÉ* **(Spanish)** (Act of the Faith) was a formal judicial sentence of the Inquisition. Such sentences were usually promulgated publicly, and occasionally cases would be accumulated so that promulgations could take place together. Minor judgements were enforced on the spot, but as the Inquisition had no power of capital punishment, in the case of a condemned heretic the *auto* ended with the latter's transmission to the civil authority, by whom, in

grave cases he was burned or strangled. These public ceremonies and subsequent burnings became confused especially among protestants who called them autos da fé indiscriminately.

AUTOMOBILE ASSOCIATION (A.A.) was founded in 1905 in part to warn motorists of police speed traps. Advised that explicit warnings amounted to a criminal conspiracy, its motor-cycle patrols after World War I were instructed to salute members whose cars carried the A.A. badge, while the members were urged to stop if not saluted and ask why. After World War II it developed into a more conventional service society.

AUVERGNE (Fr) a large mountainous territory centred on Clermont adjacent to Aquitaine. In the 11th cent. it was under the Counts of Poitou who governed it through *Vicomtes* (sheriffs). These promoted themselves to the rank of Count and were intermittently under the not very effectual suzerainty of English Kings in the latter half of the 12th cent. As a result of disputes between their descendants and French royal interventions, the area was divided into four viz.:-

(a) The largest was the **Episcopal County of Clermont,** from which (b) the small **County of Auvergne** was separated by K. Philip Augustus in 1230; (c) **The Dauphine of Auvergne** or **of Clermont** which did not include Clermont; and (d) **The Terre (Land) of Auvergne** which belonged to the Dampierre family but passed to Alphonse of Poitou, and through him to the French Crown in 1271. The territories provided resources for their lords but the divisions prevented the rise of an Auvergnat political power. There was, however, a vigorous local culture and religious life. The First Crusade was preached at the Council of Clermont (1095), there were famous monasteries (e.g. Issoire) and a considerable trade through Lyons with Italy. Aubusson in due course became the centre of a carpet industry. The area fell piecemeal to the French Crown as the English progressively lost those parts of Aquitaine nearby.

AVA. *See* BURMA-2,8.

AVALON. *See* BALTIMORE.

AVANT GARDE **(Fr. = vanguard).** Figurative expression for advanced practitioners in thought or art.

AVEBURY (Wilts.) and its neighbourhood is the site of a complex of early bronze age (c. 1800 B.C.) ritual constructions. These included the main circle of standing stones with huge banks and ditches, now enclosing most of the modern village, the Beckhampton Long Stones, a mile to the S.W.; Silbury Hill, a very high mound, a mile to the S.; and the Sanctuary Circles on Overton Hill 1½ miles to the S.E.

AVERROISM. Averroes (Ibn Rushd 1126-98) was a Cordovan philosopher and physician. Through his commentaries Aristotle became widely known in Europe, and his theories, particularly his view of the unity of the intellect – a kind of mediaeval collective subconscious – caused acute theological controversy especially at Paris, where Albertus Magnus wrote a refutation in 1256, and St. Thomas Aquinas began his *Summa Contra Gentiles* in 1257. Both had, however, to build on Aristotelianism. Averroism was anathematised in 1270.

AVERY, John (?1665-97) or **LONG BEN,** pirate king of his time, operated from Madagascar and once took the Mocha fleet with the Great Mogul's daughter. He retired to Bideford, Devon, but had difficulty in realising his loot and died in penury.

AVESTA. The sacred writings, in a language akin to Sanskrit but in Pali script, of the Parsees. The oldest (Gathas) were probably composed by Zoroaster himself. They represent the oldest literary form of dualism, later professed by the Albigensians, Bogomils and Cathars.

AVIATION. Between Nov. 1783, when the Mongolfier brothers made the first manned flight by hot air balloon over Paris, until the 1860's, aviation was, through lack of propulsion, only a curiosity, but balloons were found to have a practical military use, in the American civil war for observation, and in 1871 for sending messages and politicians out of the besieged city of Paris. The first fundamental change came in 1884 with Renard and Krebs' propelled airship, which was hard to steer for lack of rigidity. This defect was partly cured in Count Zeppelin's first girder framed airship of 1900, but his craft were navigationally at the mercy of winds, so he increased engine power, which necessitated increased size to carry the required fuel.

Meanwhile the brothers Wilbur and Orville Wright were addressing the wind problem from a different direction by using aerodynamics. They inaugurated the second fundamental change when they made the first heavier-than-air flight in the U.S.A. in Dec. 1903. From a British point of view, however, Blériot's crossing of the Channel by aircraft in July 1909 was, and was seen to be, epoch making. Military requirements from 1912 and through World War I led to immense developments in design, quality, quantity, manufacturing techniques and pilotage skills together with basic facilities such as airfields, hangars and beacons. These had been developed by 1919 when Alcock and Brown crossed the Atlantic. Two months later a regular air service was commenced between London and Paris and by 1925 there was a European network of air routes, and most major cities were building airfields or converting military ones.

The probability of war after the rise of Hitler in Germany in 1933 stimulated aviation in a manner similar to World War I, in the design and production of small fighter aircraft and particularly of large aircraft for bombing and transport. The experience and confidence gained from this in World War II (including jet propulsion, first tried successfully in May 1941) was put to world-wide commercial use after it, so that by the 1990's aviation was superseding other forms of long distance transport, and the London airports, for example at Heathrow and Gatwick, had together become the biggest port in the Kingdom, and were handling incoming and outgoing flights at a rate of one a minute. This generated problems of air traffic control, which was much influenced by human factors, so that they could not be solved by enlarging or improving existing airports. New ones had to be built (for example at Luton and Stansted, by way of supplementation) and traffic had to be diverted to other cities such as Manchester. Here a major difficulty was the shortage of suitable sites, for many had already been built up before the era of aviation. Hence a tendency to develop airfields in the country and connect them with city centres by specially provided transport including special bus fleets, railway spurs and helicopters. The result was that flights might be fast and short, but much time might be lost between airports and ground destinations. By 1993 London-Paris flying time might be as little as 50 minutes but a further 4 hours were needed for formalities and travel to the city centres. The rate of development proliferated such problems leaving ground installations chronically short of facilities so that efforts to keep up gave major airports the aspect of building lots.

AVIATION, MINISTRY OF. *See* SUPPLY, MINISTRY.

AVIATION RULES. (1) The first international conference on air law met in 1889 in Paris. The first British Aerial Navigation Act was passed in 1911. The first regular international air service (Paris-Brussels) started in Mar. 1919 and in Oct. the Paris Convention created rules for flights over and between states, the registration of aircraft and their manning and equipment. 38 states (mostly European and Latin American) acceded to it, but the U.S.A. and many S. American states signed the Havana Convention of 1928 instead. 16 acceded to this. They were both superseded by the Chicago Convention of 1944. **(2)** In 1929 an international convention on carriage

by air was signed at Warsaw, and at The Hague in 1955 and Guadalajara in 1961. In 1966 the U.S.A., dissatisfied by the low limits of carrier's liability set by these conventions, denounced them but by the Montreal Agreement agreed to return to the system, as carriers touching U.S. airfields accepted a higher limit and waived certain defences available under these conventions. **(3)** An anti-Hijacking Convention was signed at The Hague in 1970 and an anti-sabotage convention at Montreal in 1971.

AVICENNA (Abu Ali al Husain ibn Sina 980-1037), Arab philosopher and physician, was born near Bukhara and spent a quarrelsome life among the princely courts of Iran. He wrote on many subjects including philosophy, geology, astronomy and music, but his most lasting influence was on medicine, where his encyclopaedic work *The Canon* was for five centuries the leading authority. He also wrote a commentary on Aristotle, and this and *The Canon* were widely known in Europe.

AVIGNON (Fr) was the papal capital from 1309 to 1377 and the residence of anti-popes from 1377 to 1408, and with the surrounding Comtat Venaissin, papal property from 1348. Of the Avignon Popes (q.v.), Clement VI (r. 1342-52) greatly enlarged the Palace and the fortifications. The city became a major European financial and diplomatic centre during this period, and one of the biggest cities in Europe. Later it became a moral embarrassment to the papacy because, as an asylum, it attracted brigands, criminals, whores and predatory mercenaries, so that the estate of the Vicar of Christ turned into a roaringly profligate tourist centre; while, as an enclave in French territory, it was a means through which French govts. exerted pressure by blockade or occupation on him. The cardinals lived, and there was a standing French garrison at Villeneuve just across the bridge, and Louis XIV occupied the Comtat in 1663 and 1688-9. It was annexed by France in 1791 during the Revolution.

AVIGNON POPES. Six French Popes beginning with Bertrand de Got who was elected as **Clement V** (r. 1305-14). He continued to live in France under French political influence. In 1306 he suspended the operation of the bull *Unam Sanctam* in France and in 1307, at the instigation of K. Philip IV began the proceedings against the Templars. He moved to Avignon in 1309 partly to set a little distance from the King. When he died French influence kept the Holy See vacant until the cardinals elected Jacques Duèse, as **John XXII** (r. 1316-34). The double imperial election of 1314 presented an opportunity for him to improve the Papal position in Italy, and in 1317 with French support he claimed the imperial rights there. This brought him into collision with the Bavarian Emperor Ludwig IV who, however, took his rival Frederick of Austria prisoner at the B. of Mühldorf in Sept. 1322. This thrust the Pope still further into the arms of France, whose influence also procured his recognition of Robert the Bruce as King of Scots in 1323. In 1324 John XXII excommunicated Ludwig IV, who in 1327 made a progress in Italy to a secular coronation in Rome in 1328 and then declared John XXII deposed and procured the election of Peter of Corbara as the anti-pope **Nicholas V** (r. 1328-30). In 1334, when John XXII died, Jacques Fournier was elected at Avignon as **Benedict XII** (r. 1334-42). He was succeeded by Peter Roger, as **Clement VI** (r. 1342-52). It was he who purchased the sovereignty of Avignon in 1348. He was followed by Stephen Aubert as **Innocent VI** (r. 1352-62) who realised that the Franco-Papal partnership was bringing discredit on the Vicar of Christ: the English statute of *Praemunire*, for example, was passed in 1353. His first efforts were directed to reform of the Curia and the re-establishment of authority in the Papal states. In 1362 William Grimoard succeeded him as **Urban V** (r. 1362-70); his attempts to reserve the right to appoint abbots and bishops gained him international suspicion. It led in 1365 to a further statute of *Praemunire,* and in 1366 to the refusal of the English tribute. By now papal independence was becoming a pressing issue, and in 1367 Urban went to Rome, but was forced in 1370 to return to Avignon. It was Peter de Beaufort as **Gregory XI** (r. 1370-78) who took the final plunge in 1377 and entered, by way of reinsurance, into a Concordat with England, since 1369 again at war with France. 111 of the 134 Cardinals created during this period were French. *For later events see* SCHISM, GREAT.

AVIS, HOUSE OF. The rise of this Anglo-Portuguese family was due to the political crisis precipitated by the death in 1363 of Fernando, the last of the Portuguese Burgundian Kings. Portuguese independence was threatened by the pro-Castilian dowager Queen regent, Leonor Teles, and her lover the Count of Ourem. There was a popular uprising in Lisbon led by Nun Alvares Pereira and supported by **(1)** Dom **João,** Master of the Order of Avis, a bastard half-brother of the late King. Ourem was murdered, Leonor driven out and João proclaimed King. The Castilians were decisively fought off with the help of English archers at Aljubarrota (Aug. 1385). In May 1386 João concluded the T. of Windsor with England, and immediately afterwards John of Gaunt claimed the crown of Castile and landed at Corunna. His daughter Philippa married K. João at Oporto (Feb. 1387). The Castilian war was abandoned within eight months but the treaties and marriage formularised a growing English influence which was to be lasting. João reigned until 1433. His eight half-English children included **(2) Duarte (r. 1433-8)** and the celebrated Prince **(3) Henry the Navigator (r. 1439-60).** Duarte was succeeded by his infant son **(4) Afonso V (r. 1438-81),** with the dowager Q. Leonor as regent until 1446, and then by Dom Pedro, the second son of João and Philippa. After 1476 Portugal was effectively governed by Afonso's son **(5) João II (1481-95)** who was followed by his cousin and brother-in-law **(6) Manuel I (The Fortunate) (r. 1495-1521)** who left numerous progeny. The eldest succeeded as **(7) João III (r. 1521-57),** but his son died before him, leaving a posthumous child **(8) Sebastian (r. 1557-78)** and the regency was taken first by his grandmother, Q. Catherine (a sister of the Emperor Charles V) and in 1560 by **(9) Henry (1578-80)** her brother-in-law, who was a Cardinal. The regency ended when Sebastian came of age in 1568, but he was killed, together with most of the nobility, at the B. of Alcazar Kebir in Morocco, and Card. Henry succeeded him. At his death the main royal line became extinct. Philip II of Spain claimed the crown in right of Q. Catherine, his aunt, and occupied the country. This interrupted its commercial relations with England. *See* BRAGANZA.

AVON or **AFON.** This name standing by itself or in combination with other syllables (Upavon, Aveton, Avening, Aunemouth) is derived from Old British Abona meaning 'river'.

AVON, BRISTOL. *See* TRANSPORT AND COMMUNICATIONS.

AVON, COUNTY OF, centred on Bristol and Bath with nearby parts of Somerset and Gloucestershire was created by the Local Government Act 1972, and came into existence in 1974. The location of the Gloucestershire boundary provoked the only petition (by the local parish councils) to the House of Lords in the 20th cent. It was successful. The county was dissolved in 1996.

AVON, E. of. *See* EDEN, ANTHONY.

AVON, WILTSHIRE. *See* TRANSPORT AND COMMUNICATIONS.

AVONMORE, Vists. *See* YELVERTON.

AVRANCHES (Normandy). Lanfrane taught law at Avranches before becoming Abp. of Canterbury. In the Hundred Years War the town and district was in English hands from 1380 to 1404; French from 1404 to 1418; English from 1418 to 1438 and finally French after 1438. It was badly damaged in 1944 during the B. of Normandy.

AVRANCHES, CORCORDAT or PACIFICATION OF (May 1172) was the formal reconciliation between Henry II and the Church after Becket's murder. He had to maintain 200 knights on Crusade and take the Cross himself unless excused; to restore the possessions of Canterbury; compensate those who had suffered by supporting Becket; allow appeals to Rome; and renounce rules detrimental to the Church introduced in his time. He was, in fact, excused the Crusade in return for founding three monasteries, and the last condition (an indirect reference to the Constitutions of Clarendon) was a dead letter.

AXE. *See* EXE.

AXHOLME, I. of (Lincs). In 1627 this island in the Lindsey marshes was crown property. Charles I contracted with the Dutch engineer Cornelius Vermuyden to drain the marshes and Dutchmen, despite heated local opposition, settled in the area. The project disturbed local livelihoods and made the King locally unpopular, but it also changed the character and dialect of the population. Disputes persisted, and in 1650 Levellers such as John Lilburne and John Wildman sought to exploit the commoners' demand for a share in the reclaimed lands.

AXIS, THE or ROME-BERLIN AXIS. The 1936 political understanding and later military agreement between Hitler and Mussolini. The term gained general currency from a speech by Mussolini at Palermo in Aug. 1937.

AXMINSTER. *See* CARPETS.

AYCLIFFE. *See* NEW TOWNS.

AYLESBURY (Bucks.) was the centre of a Saxon hundred, and by 13th cent. it had a fair and had become the assize town. It was chartered in 1554 and a parliamentary borough until 1885. It was a municipal corporation, and from 1888 the seat of the county council.

AYLESBURY ELECTION CASES *(Ashley v White* **and the** *Aylesbury Men).* Certain whigs had not been allowed to vote at the Aylesbury election of 1702. The Commons claimed exclusive jurisdiction in election disputes. The courts and the Lords held that the Commons could decide who had been elected, not who was entitled to vote. The dispute was ended by prorogation, with the courts enjoying the advantage of the *status quo.*

AYLESFORD, E. of. *See* FINCH; FINCH-HATTON.

AYLMER OF VALENCE (?-1324) E. of PEMBROKE **(1296),** 3rd *s.* of William of Valence, half brother to Henry III, accompanied his cousin Edward I to Flanders in 1297 and on his Scottish campaign in 1298. He subsequently received Scottish lands and was made a guardian of Scotland after Bruce's revolt of 1306, when he defeated Bruce at Methven. After Edward I's death, he shared the general discontent at the behaviour of Edward II and his friend Piers Gaveston, and took part in the election of the Ordainers in 1310. In 1312 Gaveston was removed from his protective custody by the E. of Warwick and hanged. Aylmer's anger at this dishonourable violence and slight to his rank, led him to give greater support to the King, and to oppose Thomas of Lancaster, also involved in the murder. After a political reconciliation, Aylmer took part in Edward II's disastrous Bannockburn expedition to Scotland (1314). He also continued to support Edward, and shared in the condemnation and execution of Thomas of Lancaster in 1322. He died while on an embassy to Charles IV of France.

AYR-SHIRE (Scot). The town on the R. Ayr was the main Scottish western harbour with a market and a bridge. It was chartered as a burgh in 1202 and became the court and garrison town for the sheriff, who was usually a member of the Loudoun family. Though small, it became a social centre and spa for the Lowland gentry, while the sheriffdom hardened into the shire. When the Clyde ports developed for the traffic of central Scotland, they attracted business from Ayr, but the advent of the railway to Glasgow enabled the burgh to compensate with a new engineering and textile industry which enjoyed a modest prosperity until World War II. The burgh and shire were divided in four as part of the new Strathclyde region in the local govt. reorganisation of 1975.

AYSCOUGH, Samuel (1745-1804) cataloguer at the British Museum, indexed the *Annual Register* from 1758 to 1780, the *Gentleman's Magazine* from 1731 to 1786 and made the first Shakespeare concordance.

AZEGLIO, Massimo Marchese d' (1798-1866), an established painter, married Manzoni's daughter, became a successful novelist, and was attracted into politics in 1843 by his cousin Cesare Balbo. He visited Romagna, and in 1846, in a pamphlet on papal misgovernment called for a public conspiracy against the Italian regimes. This attracted great interest in Britain and originated the pro-liberation British public opinion which later made Garibaldi's expeditions possible. He had hopes of Pius IX and K. Charles Albert of Savoy, but these were dashed in the defeats of the Austrian War of 1848. Recriminations between republicans and monarchists followed. d'Azeglio was offered, and refused, the ministry of war, but in May 1849 he obeyed an express royal order and formed a govt. Despite Austrian pressure he maintained the liberal constitution and even modernised the relationship between church and state, but in Nov. 1852 was forced to resign in favour of a Cavour-Rattazzi coalition, Thereafter he was employed by Cavour in a variety of confidential missions in the interests of Italian unity, and as Royal Commissioner in Romagna in 1859, fomented the enthusiasm which brought about the annexation to Savoy.

AZERBAIJAN (Iran and Russia). This large Moslem area on the Caspian was under Persian suzerainty or rule down to 1723 and from 1735. Russian southward aggression eventually secured Baku under the T. of Gulistan (1813), and reached the present frontier by the T. of Turkmanchai (1828). When revolution broke out in 1917, the Russian Azerbaijanis, with Turkish help, set up an independent state and in May 1918 drove the communists from Baku (with its oil wells). A British force under Maj-Gen. Dunsterville (Kipling's 'Stalky') replaced the Turks in Nov. and controlled the republic until it left in Aug. 1919, In Jan. 1920 the state was recognised *de facto* by the Allies, but was overthrown by the Russians in Apr. A large Armenian Christian enclave, **Nagorno-Karabakh,** was incorporated in it when in 1936 it became a Union republic of the U.S.S.R.

In World War II Persian Azerbaijan was occupied by the Russians who, in Nov. 1945, engineered a communist revolt. An Azerbaijani republic was set up at Tabriz, and a Kurdish one at Mahabed. Western diplomatic support enabled the Persians to re-establish their authority in Dec. 1946 after the Russian troops left. In 1988 Armenian demands for the return of Nagorno-Karabakh brought local fighting along the boundary between Russian Azerbaijan and Armenia, and massacres of Armenians at Bako. These troubles, possibly fomented by Persian Islamic fundamentalists, lasted intermittently for nearly two years and embarrassed the Gorbachov govt. of the U.S.S.R. which was wrestling with other major problems.

AZORES (Atl) though known in the 14th cent. were first colonised by the Portuguese in 1445. They raised sugar for export to Europe and became rich on cattle and vegetables for the shipping which plied to Brazil and the E. Indies. When the Spaniards annexed Portugal (1580) the Azores held out for Dom Antonio, the Portuguese claimant, who had obtained French help, but the Spaniards under Santa Cruz defeated the French fleet at Terceira (July 1582) and overran the islands in 1583. Now Spanish, they were attacked by the English in 1591 (the occasion of the famous fight of the *Revenge)* and again in 1597. After Portuguese liberation (1640) they became even more important as stageing points for British trade until the opening of the Suez Canal (1863) diverted it, and for British naval strategy, and they were often used (under the T. of Windsor of 1336) as anchorages by British fleets. The British occupied them for this purpose in World War II.

AZOV and SEA OF AZOV (Ukraine). Azov, a Turkish fortified port at the mouth of the R. Don, controlled one of the main Ukrainian trade routes to the Black Sea. Peter the Great captured it in 1696 and the Czarina Anne annexed it in 1739. The exit to blue water from the Sea of Azov being controlled by the Crimean Turkish fortress of Kertch, the annexation made a Russian attack on the Crimea inevitable. These operations ultimately cleared the way for the development of Ukrainian agriculture and mining, and for the important grain and coal exports to the west and to Britain, which were carried mostly in British ships.

B

BABINGTON'S CONSPIRACY. John Ballard (?-1586) a R. Catholic priest educated at Rheims, was sent to England in 1581. In 1584 he went to Rome and conceived the idea of assassinating Elizabeth I. In 1585 he returned to England and persuaded Anthony Babington (1561-86) a secret R. Catholic to organise his plot. Babington had become personally devoted to Mary Q. of Scots while serving as a page to her custodian, the E. of Shrewsbury, and had met her supporters in Paris. Ballard's part was to secure the support of the leading English R. Catholics, most of whom he visited. In May 1586 he went to Paris and obtained the interest of Mendoza, the Spanish ambassador and an introduction to Mary. She told him to negotiate, through Mendoza, for the assistance of the Spanish King and the Pope. During these travels he got to know Gilbert Gifford, a R. Catholic but also a secret agent of Walsingham. The latter also intercepted Babington's letters to Mary. Ballard was suddenly arrested on 4 Aug. 1586. Under torture he incriminated Babington. After trial they were executed on 20 Sept. The event precipitated Mary's trial.

BABU or BABOO. This Hindi equivalent of 'Mr', denoted the status which an English speaking Bengali clerk might assume by reason of his contacts with the British administration. Hence one whose book knowledge gave him influence.

BABYLON. (1) The crusader term for Old Cairo. **(2)** A puritan polemical term for Rome, hence the Whore of Babylon for the R. Catholic Church. See Rev XVII.

BABYLONISH CAPTIVITY. The residence or detention of the Popes at Avignon where they were under rigorous French pressure in an exceptionally profligate city.

BACH, Johann Christian (1735-82) 11th *s.* of Johann Sebastian, gained a reputation as an operatic composer at Milan, and from 1762 spent the rest of his life in London. His Hanover Square concerts made him famous and popular. He became the Queen's music master and was the first composer to prefer the pianoforte to other keyboard instruments.

BACHELOR. A man of some slight status or attainment but not of much; hence a young knight without a following or a student who has taken only his first degree.

BACHELOR TAX (1695) was first enacted to help finance the war with France. The income tax of 1798 also discriminated against bachelors.

BACHELOR'S WALK (Dublin) AFFAIR (July 1914). Gun running, particularly at Larne (24 Apr.) and Howth (26 July) ensured an arms supply for protestants and Ulstermen. After the Howth gun-running the police tried to seize the arms with military aid. The Ulster Volunteers, however, got most of their arms safely away. On marching back through Dublin, the troops were stoned by crowds who, probably wrongly, suspected collusion, and at Bachelor's Walk the troops turned and fired killing or injuring 41 civilians. The outbreak of World War I distracted English attention from the incident, but the Irish nationalists continually represented the affair in a light which suited their purposes.

BACKING A WARRANT. A warrant issued in one county required endorsement by a J.P. before it could be executed in another. The consequent delays often enabled wanted persons or their property to disappear.

BACKWELL, Edward (?-1683) Lombard Street goldsmith and successful banker, who issued banknotes and financed Oliver Cromwell, Charles II and the HEIC. Charles II employed him in the sale of Dunkirk and other confidential dealings with Louis XIV.

BACKWOODSMEN. A derisive term for those peers, especially landowners, who never attended the House of Lords until their interests were threatened by Lloyd George's budget of 1909. For the budget debate several

asked the police the way to their own chamber, and one is said to have been found occupying a seat in the House of Commons.

BACON, produced by dry-salting winter-killed pork, is very ancient, but since most of the lean was already eaten, it was mainly fat, which kept for months. The modern type of composite bacon came in with refrigeration.

BACON, John, father and son (1740-99 and 1777-1859) sculptors, executed many monuments. Those to William Pitt at Guildhall and Westminster Abbey, and that to Dr Johnson in St Paul's are by the father. Many others at St Paul's are by the son.

BACON'S REBELLION (1676). Sir William Berkeley, Gov. of Virginia, worked harder to enforce the Navigation Acts upon the colonists than to protect them against the Indians. Nathaniel Bacon (1647-76), a planter affected by the Acts, took the law into his own hands in dealing with the Indians, while his friends were demanding political and economic reforms. A newly elected House of Burgesses was backed by his armed force. Berkeley fled and gathered troops. Bacon then burned Jamestown, but before matters came to a trial of strength, he suddenly died. Charles II deemed Berkeley's subsequent reprisals excessive and recalled him.

BACON, Roger (c. 1210-92), *doctor mirabilis,* was a follower of Robt. Grosseteste at Oxford and then, from c. 1237 to 1247, studied and taught at Paris. He became a Franciscan and returned to Oxford where he wrote his *Opus Majus* (Lat = Greater Work) (1266-8). In Paris he had lectured on Aristotle's *Physics* and *Metaphysics* but not as an Aristotelian, though he had emphasised Aristotle's interest in induction, experiment and mathematics as a means of understanding universals and nature. Like Grosseteste he also studied optics and language: he knew Greek, Hebrew and Arabic. This was all part of his belief in the unity of wisdom or knowledge; different branches of it might be used to interpret each other, with experiment replacing or supplementing deduction from established premises. His work on optics, especially on the working of the eye, remained important until 17th cent. and he took up other technical problems such as flying machines; yet he was also a speculative philosopher in spiritual secrets beyond the limitations imposed in contemporary Parisian philosophy and attainable only in an abyss comparable, perhaps, with the speculations of modern astronomers. Such mental explorations earned him a vast intellectual reputation in the academic and intellectual world, besides two spells of imprisonment at the hands of his order.

BACON (1) Sir Nicholas (1509-79) held minor govt. posts from 1537 and kept his place under Mary I despite his known protestantism. He was Treasurer of Grays Inn in 1552 and a friend and brother-in-law of Sir Wm. Cecil, later Lord Burghley. At Elizabeth's accession he became Lord Keeper and, with a short interval in 1564, remained one of her most trusted men and later one of the most determined opponents of Mary Q. of Scots. For his elder son **(2) Anthony (1558-1601)** *see* ELIZABETH 1-28 et seq. His famous younger son **(3) Sir Francis (1561-1626) 1st Ld. VERULAM and Vist. St. ALBANS (1618),** was called to the bar in 1582 and sat as an M.P. for five different constituencies respectively in 1584, 1586, 1589, 1593 and 1597. He was against religious tests of political reliability and advocated milder treatment for both puritans and R. Catholics. In 1593 he became a confidential adviser to Essex, but in 1594 opposed the triple subsidy for the Spanish war and permanently lost the Queen's favour. He failed to dissuade Essex from his rasher ventures and after Essex's Irish failure and unauthorised return to court Bacon acted as a "friendly accuser" at his examination before the Privy Council (which Essex did not resent);

but, on Essex's abortive insurrection in Feb. 1601, Bacon appeared for the prosecution at Essex's trial and conviction for treason. Such ingratitude in an age of patronage damaged his credit and his reputation followed him into the next reign. He became Sol-Gen. only in 1607 and remained without real influence until after Salisbury's death in 1612. In 1613 he became Att-Gen. when K. James was under Somerset's influence. He accordingly lent his intellectual gifts to the support of the King's despotic view of the prerogative. In *Peacham's Case* he examined Coke when the King ordered the judges to be consulted separately, and in *The Case of Commendams* he instructed the King's Bench not to proceed until they had spoken with the King. Coke, the Chief Justice, refused to countenance this interference and in Nov. 1616 was dismissed. With the support of Buckingham the new favourite, Bacon became Lord Keeper in Mar. 1617 and Lord Chancellor the following Jan. During this time he was very active in the prosecution of Sir Walter Raleigh (1618).

In 1620 (when he published the *Novum Organum*) he became sensitive to the current agitation against monopolies; and, though he had advised the King that the patents were lawful he tried unsuccessfully to persuade the King to recall them. In the parliament of Jan. 1621 he was attacked for his legal advice to the King and then accused of wholesale corruption in the administration of Chancery suits. To the latter accusation he had no defence and sent in a general confession; this put an end to his political career, though he later contended that he had never allowed bribes to sway his judgement.

Bacon's fame depends not on his rather disreputable political career, but on the products of his versatile and inquiring mind. His celebrated Essays were published as early as 1597; his views on scientific training (*The Advancement of Learning*) appeared in 1605; and his philosophical championship of scientific method is contained in the *Novum Organum* which was famous or notorious in its own time. He also produced scientific treatises; a *History of Henry VII;* a collection of jokes; several theological and ecclesiastical tracts; and the *Reading on the Statute of Uses,* which long remained the standard work on the law of property.

He died of bronchitis contracted while stuffing a chicken with snow in order to discover whether a low temperature would preserve meat. *See next entry.*

BACONIANISM, the philosophy pioneered by Francis Bacon mainly in his immense *Novum Organum Scientarum* (Lat = New System of Knowledge), *De Sapientia Veterum* (Lat = The Wisdom of the Ancients), and *De Augmentis* (Lat = Extensions of Meaning) arose out of the impression which inventions made upon Bacon at the period when the renaissance and the collapse of scholasticism had long disturbed established intellectual habits. The observation, recording and description of phenomena would replace the persuasive logic of humanism; it would be increased in value by sharing and publication as well as precision. Its purpose is always practical and designed to improve the human condition and though its method is objective its purpose is related to morality and politics. Accordingly it is the business of the state to support and finance it.

BACONTHORPE, John (?-1348), *doctor resolutus,* a Carmelite who studied at Oxford and Paris, was provincial of his order from c. 1327 to 1333. He taught at Cambridge and possibly at Oxford. As a theologian he composed learned and independent *Commentaries* on Peter Lombard's *Sentences* and was an exponent of the doctrine of the Immaculate Conception. He also wrote on Canon Law.

BACTON (Norfolk). In 1967 the first North Sea gas pipeline crossed the coast at this place.

BADAJOZ (Sp). This fortress on the Portuguese frontier at the latitude of Lisbon was held against the French on their invasion of the Peninsula in 1807, but was betrayed to them in Mar. 1811 by José Imaz, its governor, and strongly garrisoned under Col. Philipon. Its recovery being essential for the reconquest of Spain, two unsuccessful attempts were made in 1811 and in Mar. 1812 Wellington invested it. This siege was fought out with the greatest determination on both sides. It was reported on 4 Apr. that a relieving army under Marshal Soult was five marches away; the place was therefore stormed with a loss of 4000 men on the night of 6th. The fury of the fighting caused the attacking troops to run berserk and the town was sacked.

BADEN, STATES AND RUUNG (ZÄHRINGEN) FAMILY. This principality of scattered lands along the east bank of the Rhine from Basel to Philipsburg, played a brief and equivocal part of importance in the War of the Spanish Succession. In 1535 it had been divided into two: the mutually hostile northern **Baden-Durlach** (later Protestant) and the southern **Baden-Baden.** The result was political ineffectiveness and devastation in the French wars. Ludwig (Louis) of Baden-Baden (r. 1677-1707) spent most of his reign with distinction as an imperial general in Hungary and then, less happily, in association with Marlborough and Eugene against the French. His interests as a general and as ruler of a small state adjacent to France did not coincide and his methods wrecked some of Marlborough's more imaginative plans. Nevertheless his Stollhofen fortifications gave Baden-Baden considerable strategic importance and kept the French out of central Germany until Marshal Villars surprised them in May 1707, just after Ludwig's death. He nearly completed Rastatt while his colleague, Carl Wilhelm of Baden-Durlach (r. 1707-38) built Karlsruhe. In 1771 the two territories were united under Carl Friedrich of Baden-Durlach who reigned until 1811. Imperial weakness and French revolutionary aggression forced him to come to terms with successive French govts. This paid handsomely: in return for unimportant lands west of the Rhine lost in 1796, Baden between 1803 and 1806 was enlarged nearly five-fold with lands of extinguished minor German states, and now extended from Constance to Heidelberg. In 1848-9 local revolutionary violence was suppressed by Prussian troops. After the Austrian defeat in 1866 Friedrich I took a leading part in the movement for the new German Empire of 1871. He was succeeded in 1907 by Friedrich II the last reigning Grand-Duke whose son, Prince Max, was the last imperial Chancellor of Germany. *See* GORDONSTOUN.

BADENOCH, Alexander (c. 1343-1405) Ld. of BADENOCH (1371) E. of BUCHAN (1382), ("The Wolf of Badenoch") was a son of K. Robert II by his mistress Elizabeth Mure. He became King's Lieut. North of the Forth in 1372. In 1380 he quarrelled with the local Churchmen, the Bp. of Moray denying his jurisdiction. The quarrel was decided against him. In 1382 he became Earl by marriage to the Countess of Buchan, but deserted her and lived in open adultery; consequently the Bps. of Moray and Ross denounced him in 1389. He retaliated in 1390 by sacking Forres and Elgin (whose cathedral is still in ruins). His excommunication and subsequent submission to the Church so discredited him that he took no further important part in public life.

BADEN-POWELL, Robert Stephenson Smyth (1857-1941) 1st Ld. (1929) was educated at Charterhouse, where he became interested in the outdoor life. He joined the army in 1876 and served in India and S. Africa. By 1895 he was commanding native levies in Ashanti, and in the Matabele campaign of 1896-7 he was C. of S. It was at this time that he first wore the flat-brimmed sun hat associated with him. During his celebrated defence of Mafeking against the Boers in 1899-1900, he thought of using boys as responsible auxiliaries and messengers, as a method of character training. This led eventually to the foundation of the Boy Scout movement and, later, with the help of his sister Agnes, of the Girl Guides. His book *Scouting for Boys* was published in 1908 and was a best seller.

BADGE MEN were beggars who wore a badge to indicate the parish or other authority, such as a foundation, which licensed them to beg.

BADMINTON. The game was originally played in the 1870s by the British army in India where it was called POONA. Some officers on leave played it at Badminton (Avon) in 1873 and the name stuck.

BADMINTON (Avon), classical mansion built in the 1670s and altered by the Kents in about 1740, for the D. of Beaufort.

BADOGLIO, Marshal Pietro, D. of ADDIS ABABA (1871-1956). Sub-chief of Staff under Armando Diaz, he signed the Armistice for Italy in Nov. 1918. He was Chief of the General Staff until 1921, Gov. of Libya from 1928 to 1933, and finished the conquest of Abyssinia in 1935-6. Chief of Staff again in June 1940, he resigned in Dec. when defeated by the Greeks. He, with Count Grandi and the D. of Aquarone, helped K. Victor Emmanuel III to depose Benito Mussolini on 25 July 1943. He became prime minister and negotiated Italy's surrender to the Allies on 8 Sept. The Fascist party having been formally dissolved, he declared war on Germany on 13 Oct. In June 1944 he was succeeded as prime minister by Bonomi and retired.

BADON, MOUNT or MONS BADONICUS, B. or SIEGE OF (c. 495). The site of these events is conjectured to be either Solsbury Hill near Batheaston or Liddington above Badbury near Swindon. A series of British victories over invading Anglo-Saxons culminated at this place and forced the Anglo-Saxons out of the area between the Thames and Northamptonshire for half a century. It is possible that some of the S.W.-facing "Devils Dykes", defensive Saxon works, were built to contain the British successes.

BADUCING. *See* BENEDICT BISCOP.

***BAEDEKER* RAIDS** were air raids in response to the destruction of Lübeck by the R.A.F. during World War II on certain provincial towns such as Exeter and Canterbury, so named because these places might have been described as 'worth a visit' in *Baedeker's Tourist Guides.*

BAFFIN, William (?-1622). *See* ARCTIC EXPLORATION *for his main career.* He was killed on an expedition against the Portuguese in the Persian Gulf.

***BAGA DE SECRETIS* (Lat = File for secret matters).** A collection of official documents relating to state trials between 1477 and 1813. It includes documents on Anne Boleyn, Sir Walter Raleigh, the Regicides and the Jacobite rebels.

BAGANDA, BUGANDA. *See* UGANDA.

BAGEHOT, Walter (1826-77), banker, shipowner, author and journalist. Educated at University College London. Joint Editor of the *National Review* with R. H. Hutton from 1855 and editor of the *Economist* from 1860 until his death. Of his many writings the most permanently influential was the *English Constitution* (1867), which long remained the model statement of progressive conservative constitutional thought not only in the setting of the Victorian social climate.

BAGHDAD PACT (Feb. 1955), concluded at the instigation of Britain and the U.S.A. between Turkey and Iraq, was joined by Britain (Apr.), Pakistan (Sept.) and Iran (Oct.). The purpose was to contain Russian aggression in the Middle East by co-ordinating measures for defence and security. There was no integration of forces on the N.A.T.O. model and in accordance with Art. 51 of the U.N. Charter, member states undertook not to interfere in each others' internal affairs. The hope that other, particularly Arab, countries might join the Pact was frustrated by, among other things, Egyptian opposition. Efforts to bring Jordan into the Pact led to riots in Amman

and a loss of British influence. Iraq left the Pact in 1959 after the overthrow of her monarchy and, Baghdad being the capital of Iraq, the name was tactfully changed to CENTRAL TREATY ORGANISATION (C.E.N.T.O.).

BAGHDAD RAILWAY, or 'Berlin to Baghdad railway', originated as part of a German 19th cent. policy of penetrating the Middle East with Turkish help. The Anatolian Rly Co was formed in 1889 and the line from Haidar Pasha (opposite Constantinople) to Konia was completed in 1896. A further section was begun in 1903, but progress was erratic until World War I gave the project an urgent strategic role. Under German military direction the line by 1918 was continuous from Haidar via Eskishehr and Afium Karahissar to Adana and thence to Aleppo and Nisibis. This proved of vital importance in the Turkish-Greek conflict of 1922. The line was completed as far as Baghdad in 1940. *See* CHANAK INCIDENT.

BAGIMOND'S ROLL. In 1274 Bajamundus of Vitia ("Bagimond") was sent by Gregory X to Scotland to collect the tithe for the relief of the Holy Land. His register or Roll remained the basis of Scottish ecclesiastical taxation until the Reformation.

BAGNIO. A prison for slaves notably in a north African port.

BAGOT, Sir Charles (1781-1843) negotiated the Rush-Bagot Treaty with the U.S.A. neutralising the Great Lakes (1817) and, as ambassador at St Petersburg, the treaty defining the frontier between Canada and Russian America (later called Alaska) (1825). He was Gov. Gen. of Canada from 1842.

BAGPIPES (1) Three types were developed in the British Is. viz: (a) the Scottish (9 notes in A major with a natural G, the C and F between the sharp and the natural, and two drones) (b) the Northumbrian (15 notes in G with four drones) and (c) the Irish (12 notes in regular A major with one drone). **(2)** The dates of their introduction and the historical relationship between the three types are uncertain but pipes are mentioned in 5th cent. Ireland. There were English court pipers between 1307 and 1603. War pipes are said to have been used by an Irish contingent at the B. of Crécy (1346) and Galileo's father mentioned them in 1581. They spread to Scotland only in 15th cent. when English (*Inglis*) became court pipers at Edinburgh. By mid-16th cent. they were dying out south of Northumbria, but 80 pipers played at Charles II's coronation at Scone in 1651. **(3)** The Scottish popularity of bagpipes was probably due to the schools of piping, of which that of the Macrimmons of Skye (1500-1795) was the most famous. The connection between the Bagpipes and Scots national feeling may be traced to their use after 1642 by Scottish troops, when English troops had adopted a more European style of martial music. Both Scots and Irish pipes played their part at the B. of the Boyne in 1690. **(4)** When British regulars began to occupy permanent garrisons in India after the Mutiny, the bagpipes of Scottish regiments caught the imagination of some local populations, who had similar instruments of their own. Several Indian regiments adopted the Scottish pipes and at Indian independence (1947) the departing British governor of Bombay was sent off with *Will ye no' come back again* by an Indian pipe band.

BAGSHOT HEATH was in the 18th cent. a desolate area, notorious for robbers, stretching along the Surrey-Berkshire boundary.

BAHADUR SHAH. *See* MOGULS.

BAHAMAS. (1) Christopher Columbus first 'discovered' America by a landfall in the Bahamas, probably Watling I. (1221 Oct. 1492). He took formal possession but apart from kidnapping inhabitants to work in the plantations of Hispaniola, the Spaniards showed no interest in these islands. There was an inoperative English grant in 1629 and a French one in 1633. The real history began in 1647. A religious dispute in Bermuda caused a group of

'Pilgrim Fathers' led by Wm. Sayle to migrate to Eleuthera. In 1656 this settlement virtually died out, but further Bermudans colonised New Providence. Sayle, who had returned to Bermuda was appointed Gov. of S. Carolina in 1663 when Charles II granted that colony to 8 Lords Proprietors; through them he interested the D. of Albemarle (Monck) and others who were granted the islands in 1670. They in turn confirmed one John Wentworth, who had been elected by the inhabitants as their Gov. in 1671. (2) The Lords Proprietors having no force with which to back their authority and piracy being much the most lucrative local industry, the islands were internally ungovernable and internationally a nuisance. Consequently they fell victim at intervals to French and Spanish punitive expeditions and English commercial interests pressed the Crown for reform. In 1717 the lords Proprietors surrendered their powers of government and leased the islands to Capt. Woodes Rogers who arrived as the first royal Gov. in 1718 with a sufficient force to establish order. By 1725 he had put down lawlessness and established a prosperous trading colony. The new conditions created a demand for local self-government and in 1729 Rogers, with royal authority, called a general assembly. Until the American revolution the Bahamas were comparatively peaceful, but in 1776 Nassau was taken and then evacuated by the American rebels. In 1782 it was taken by the Spaniards and then retaken after peace had been signed at Versailles but before the news had reached the area. (3) A new era of immigration, mainly of American loyalists, set in and the population, both free and slave, rose quickly. The result was a slavery controversy between the U.K., represented by the governors and the colonists represented by the Assembly. Home opinion was hardening against slavery while the colonists were determined to defend their property. At emancipation in 1834 nearly 8000 slaves were released and the British taxpayer paid roughly £13 a head in compensation. (4) Though piracy had long vanished, wrecking flourished for a century longer, and smuggling, especially during the U.S. periods of civil war and prohibition, has provided the population with a fine livelihood. With such external preoccupations, internal broils have been few, the most important being that which led to the disestablishment of the Anglican Church.

The D. of Windsor (formerly Edward VIII) was Gov. of the Bahamas during World War II.

BAHAWALPUR (West Pakistan) became independent of the Afghans at the end of the 18th cent. It entered into treaty relations with the British in 1838 and joined Pakistan on 7 Oct. 1947.

BAHREIN (Persian Gulf) was occupied by the Portuguese from 1507 to 1602 and by Arab subjects of Iran from 1602 to 1783. It was then seized by the mainland Ateiba tribe, one of whose leading families has ruled it ever since. The British have protected it against claims by the Omanis, the Wahhabis, the Turks and the Iranians since the mid-19th cent. but the oil discoveries there of 1932 gave British local policy a sharp edge, and by 1935 it was the main British naval station. By 1947 1.5M tons of oil was being refined there annually, mostly from crude oil pumped from Saudi Arabia, and the govt. built a free port for the old but now modernised entrepot trade. It was the main Anglo-American base in the war against Iraq in 1990-1

BAIKIE, William Balfour (1824-64) was surgeon and naturalist to the *Pleiad* expedition up the R. Niger in 1854. He took charge when the captain died and brought the ship 250 miles further up river than had been achieved before. In 1857 he led a second expedition but the *Pleiad* was wrecked. The crew went home over-land but he stayed and single-handedly set up an administration which became the nucleus of Nigeria.

BAIL, in criminal process, is the release of a prisoner awaiting trial into the custody of a private person who usually gives security in the form of a bond to pay a sum, varying with the circumstances and importance of the charge, if he fails to surrender the prisoner to the court on the agreed date. The forfeiture of the sum is called **estreat.** Excessive bail was forbidden by the Bill of Rights 1689. The discretion of the courts to grant or refuse bail was limited in 1971 by the enactment of a presumption that a prisoner is entitled to bail unless there are strong reasons why it should have been refused. There was then a rapid increase in the number of people who jumped their bail.

BAILIFF, BAILIWICK. (cf. Fr: *bailli*). To manage their manors, lords had foremen, called *reeves* and *bailiffs* or *stewards*. The functions of the first two were not at first always distinguishable but in time the reeve declined into a foreman, while the bailiff was responsible for collecting rents, keeping the accounts, and also for disciplining the work-force and for prosecuting cases in the lords court. He became the Lord's general manager. The area under his charge, which might include more than one manor, was his bailiwick. Later the term 'bailiwick' meant also a territory in which the sheriff's functions were exercised by a privately appointed bailiff under a Crown grant. Such exemptions from shrieval authority were at one time common (e.g. in the Hundred of Bengeo in Hertfordshire, or the seven hundreds of West Suffolk) but were mostly merged in the surrounding counties by the Liberties Act 1850 and the Cinque Ports Act 1855.

BAILLI **(Fr.)** *BAILO* **(Ital.)** **BAILLIFF (C.I.)** A person to whom, in the middle ages, a ruler's powers had been committed. The Venetian Bailo at Constantinople ruled a quarter of the Latin Empire and was the head of the Venetian community in the city under the Turks. *Baillis* governed Outremer during royal absences or female regencies. The *Bailliffs* of Jersey and Guernsey were and are similarly high officers under the lieut-gov.

BAILLIE, Robert (1599-1662) a distinguished Scottish theologian, was a member of the Glasgow Assembly of 1638. From 1640 to 1642 he was the practical representative of the Covenanters in London and in 1643 he represented the Kirk at the Westminster Assembly. He was a Commissioner who went to Holland to invite Charles II to Scotland. At the Restoration he refused a bishopric but became Principal of Glasgow Univ.

BAILEY. A walled enclosure forming part of a castle and outside the keep or citadel, if any. *See* APPENDIX.

BAIN, Alexander. *See* MIND.

BAIRD, John Logie (1888-1946). *See* TELEVISION.

BAJI RAO I AND II. *See* MARATHAS-B2 & 8.

BAKER, Geoffrey Le (fl. 1341-56). His *Chronicon,* begun after 1341, covers the years 1303-56 and was perhaps written for the Oxfordshire knight Sir Thomas de la More, or the Bohun family. He drew on other writers such as Adam Murimouth and on eyewitness evidence, notably for Edward II's deposition and the exploits of English knights abroad. He alone mentions that the English dug pits to impede the French cavalry at the B. of Crécy (1346).

BAKER, Sir Herbert R.A. (1862-1946), architect, early attracted the friendship and patronage of Cecil Rhodes, for whom he restored Groote Schuur, now the residence of the S. African Prime Minister. He had many commissions in S. Africa, including the Union Buildings at Pretoria. In 1912 he became joint architect with Sir Edwin Lutyens for New Delhi. Their personality clashes are reflected in the layout of that city. In England he built, *inter alia,* Church House, Westminster, the War Cloister at Winchester College, and Rhodes House at Oxford. His style was infused with a spirit of Anglican monarchism very suitable to the moderate imperialism of his greater employers.

BAKER, Sir Samuel White (1821-93) supervised the

construction of the Dobruja (Roumania) Rly in 1856 and in 1861 started up the Nile. He reached Khartoum at the end of 1862 and met Speke and Grant at Gondokoro in Feb. 1863. With their advice he discovered L. Albert in March 1864 and, after further exploration, returned to Khartoum in May 1865. After four years in England he returned to Egypt in attendance upon the P. of Wales, and at the Khedive's request was given command of an anti-slavery expedition in Equatoria. In consequence he became the Khedive's gov-gen of the Sudan until 1873 when he retired in favour of Col. Charles Gordon.

BAKER'S DOZEN, i.e. 13, dates from the time when a baker might be put in the pillory or heavily fined for short weight.

BAKEWELL (Derbys) was an ancient lead mining centre and from 8th cent. an important Mercian royal settlement. There was also chert limestone working, which continued into the 20th cent. It had a modest 17th cent. prosperity which is evidenced by its almshouse (1602) and Grammar School (1637). *See also* EDWARD THE ELDER

BAKU (Russian Azerbaijan). From 1509 to 1723 this oil producing city was under Iranian suzerainty. It then became the capital of a local Khanate under Russian protection until its incorporation into the Russian empire in 1806. During the Russian Revolutionary civil wars it was briefly occupied by British troops under Maj gen Dunsterville (Kipling's 'Stalky') in 1919. It was a powerful magnet for the abortive German offensives in S. Ukraine in World War II and the risk of losing its oil resources was a motive for Muscovite opposition to local separatism in the Gorbachev era.

BALACLAVA, B. (25 Oct. 1854). This indecisive Crimean battle was the scene of three famous feats of arms: namely the repulse of the Russian cavalry by the *Thin Red Line* of the 93rd Highlanders; the *charge of the Heavy Brigade* in which Major-Gen the Hon. James Scarlett in an uphill attack dispersed the Russian cavalry force many times the size of his own; and the suicidal *charge of the Light Brigade* under the Earl of Cardigan when over 500 out of 700 men were lost in strict obedience to a mistaken order.

The battle was provoked by a Russian attempt with superior forces to cut off the British before Sevastopol from their base at the port of Balaclava about ten miles to the south-east. The determination of the British troops in this confused affair held off the Russians and saved the port.

BALAJI VISWANATH. *See* MARATHAS-B11.

BALANCE OF PAYMENTS is the term for the difference between a nation's payments to all other countries and those countries' payments to it. Its main components are on the one hand payments for goods and raw materials, interest on borrowings, the cost of movement by foreign transport, foreign loans and investment, foreign aid, the local net cost of British garrisons and missions abroad and payments by British tourists. Against these are set receipts represented by charges for exports, interest and repayment of foreign loans, foreign investments, the profits of the carrying trade, the profits from the London money and insurance markets, payments arising from foreign establishments in the Kingdom and from foreign tourists there.

The receipts and payments basis of the concept makes no distinction between capital and income transactions. Variation in foreign exchange rates alter the basis of calculation daily, and many transactions (e.g. in the illegal traffic in drugs, arms and stolen works of art) are unreported or untraceable. The unreliability of the balance of payments as a guide to action has been illustrated as follows:

In 1963 Britain was a creditor country on international account for about £1400M. In this and the next three years the balances were:

Recorded items		Balance believed unaccounted for
1963	111	-73
1964	-399	41
1965	-91	67
1966	15	-10

leaving an apparent adverse balance over the four years of £289M. Yet in fact Britain was a creditor country on international account for almost the same (£1400M) in 1966 as in 1963.

BALANCE OF POWER is a method of attempting to keep international peace in the absence of a supranational authority capable of enforcing it impartially. The basic, and generally accurate, assumption is that a state will go to war if, but only if, it is likely to win and remain in a position to reap the profits. Accordingly statesmen at any given moment will consider what country is nearing that critical point and take protective action against its presumed designs. Such action may take different forms such as subversion, or rearmament, but the commonest is the formation of *ad hoc* alliances by countries with a special interest in the existing peace. As states wax and wain in power and yesterday's ally may have grown into today's danger, these alliances are at intervals superseded by other groupings.

This international technique, lasting over centuries, has a number of practical consequences. *Firstly* it places a premium at once on diplomacy and upon timely and accurate information. The European doctrines of the equilibrium were first elaborated in the 16th cent. which also saw the rise of professional diplomats and espionage. *Secondly* it tends towards the destruction of weaker states: partly because great powers may not wish to risk a conflagration over a small matter, and partly because if one secures an advantage, another in the name of the balance of power will demand compensation, and both advantage and compensation will be gained at the expense of the weak. This process is nakedly visible in the 18th cent. Partitions of Poland and in the 19th cent. attrition of the Ottoman Empire. *Thirdly* the so-called balance is seldom stable for long because technical and commercial change (not to mention birth rates) are altering the relative power of states all the time and the personalities of rulers may introduce an element of the unforeseeable. The probable policy of Charles XII of Sweden after Altranstaedt (1706) was a matter of European-wide speculation; and few imagined that the proximate cause of World War II would be an alliance (1939) between Stalin and Hitler. *Fourthly* the doctrine presupposes that war will sometimes be necessary to redress the balance: the wars against Louis XIV and Napoleon I were fought on this ideological basis.

Never wholly effective as a peacekeeping system, the doctrine has broken down. The Great Powers have few areas left in which to trade compensations, and the nature of war is now so terrible at ideological and technical levels, that the idea of a "just" war is difficult to support. Accordingly the 20th cent. has seen a revival of supranational peacekeeping agencies, such as the League of Nations, whose appeal was more spiritual than practical, and the United Nations Organisation whose success (in 1999) was still uncertain.

BALBOA Vasco Nuñez de (?1475-1517) discovered the Pacific at the Isthmus of Darien in Sept. 1513.

BALDWIN (?-1098). Abbot of Bury St. Edmunds from 1065. A Frenchman and Edward the Confessor's doctor, he rebuilt the Abbey.

BALDWIN, Abp. of CANTERBURY (?-1190) described by Pope Urban III as "fervent monk, zealous abbot, lukewarm bishop, careless archbishop" became archdeacon to Bartholomew Bp. of Exeter immediately after ordination but soon resigned and went to Ford Abbey. In

1180 he became Bp. of Worcester. In 1184 he was involved in a disputed election to the archbishopric of Canterbury. The monks of Christchurch chose the abbot of Battle, but the bishops chose Baldwin. The monks then bid for Roman support by substituting Card. Theobald, Bp. of Ostia, for the Abbot. Henry II arranged a compromise whereby the monks elected Baldwin on the undertaking that the bishops' claim to elect the archbishop was abandoned.

No sooner was he consecrated than Baldwin quarrelled with the monks. Christchurch had long been richer than the archbishopric, which was politically and administratively inconvenient. Moreover Baldwin as a Cistercian disliked the monks' luxurious habits. They, in their turn, stood on their privileges and ignored his authority. He seized part of their revenues and founded a rival college of secular priests. They appealed not only to the Pope, but to foreign as well as English sovereigns. The dispute attracted widespread European interest and was not settled until Richard I enforced a compromise in 1189.

In 1188 Baldwin took the cross and made a recruiting progress through Wales and, having crowned Richard I in 1189, he set out for the Holy Land in March 1190, where he arrived in Sept. On reaching Acre on 12 Oct. he had to take charge of the ecclesiastical affairs of the Kingdom because the Patriarch was ill. He therefore accompanied the army, but his own health failed him and on 19 Nov. he died.

BALDWIN, Stanley (1867-1947) 1st E. BALDWIN of BEWDLEY (1937), son of a Worcestershire Ironmaster, was a cousin of Rudyard Kipling and of Burne Jones. He entered politics only in 1908 as a Tory M.P. for his father's constituency of Bewdley, which he held until 1937. He became Parl. Private Sec. to Bonar Law (an acquaintance of his father) on the formation of the War Cabinet in 1916, and was joint financial secretary to the Treasury from 1917 until 1921. In 1919 he published an anonymous letter in *The Times* urging the wealthy to tax themselves voluntarily to reduce the war debt and himself secretly bought £150,000 of War Loan for cancellation. His identity in these transactions remained unknown for many years.

In 1921 he became Pres. of the B. of Trade in Lloyd George's coalition. He found the atmosphere and political attitudes of the govt. uncongenial and he personally detested Lloyd George. In 1922 he felt that peace had been needlessly risked over the Chanak affair. The Conservative leaders – Austen Chamberlain, Balfour and Birkenhead – were planning to fight the next general election under Lloyd George. It was Baldwin's speech at the famous Carlton Club meeting of 19 Oct. 1922 which, as much as anything else, persuaded the Tories to go it alone and overthrow Lloyd George. Baldwin accordingly became Ch. of the Exchequer when Bonar Law took office after the general election.

The first task of the new govt. was to make a settlement of the American War debt and Baldwin and Montague Norman (Gov. of the Bank of England) obtained terms from Andrew Mellon which were rather less favourable than Bonar Law had hoped. They were reluctantly approved just as Bonar Law fell seriously ill; Baldwin then became Leader of the House and in May 1923, when Bonar Law resigned, George V, who had been expected to send for Curzon, chose Baldwin instead. This constitutionally important decision of the King's also had a profound influence on the character of the Conservative Party.

His first administration lasted only eight months. The minority Labour govt. followed and in Nov. 1924 he began his second (until 1929) during which he gained much credit by his firm but fair-minded and expeditious handling of the nine day general strike of 1926. In the slump which followed, he joined Ramsay Macdonald's

national' coalition govt. in 1931 and became prime minister again in 1935. An astute and seemingly indolent politician who liked to keep things calm, he dealt with the Abdication crisis of 1936 and the first moves in the international advance of Nazi Germany. His failure to re-arm has been variously attributed to inability to credit the reported horrors being perpetrated in Germany, a political wish not to antagonise the electorate by raising taxes, and simple inability to decide quickly. In none of these was he unique, but the ultimate effects were nearly catastrophic.

In 1937 he resigned in favour of the far less able Neville Chamberlain.

BALDWIN'S FIRST GOVT. (May 1923-Jan. 1924). *See* LAW'S CONSERVATIVE and BALDWIN'S FIRST GOVT OCT. 1922-MAY 1923.

BALDWIN'S SECOND CONSERVATIVE GOVT. (Nov. 1924-June 1929). 21 in cabinet. Under Stanley Baldwin the main figures were Vist. Cave, Lord Chanc; The M. Curzon, Lord Pres; the M. of Salisbury, Lord Privy Seal; Winston Churchill, Chanc. of the Exch; Sir Wm Joynson-Hicks, Home Sec; Austen Chamberlain, Foreign Sec; L. S. Amery, Colonial Sec; Neville Chamberlain, Min. of Health; The E. of Balfour succeeded Curzon in June 1925. Vist. Hailsham succeeded Cave in Mar. 1928.

(1) In June 1924 Baldwin had abandoned protection, thereby catching much of the Liberal vote and had created an anti-socialist atmosphere which swayed the floating but not the Labour voters. Labour increased its seats in the Commons to 151. The Liberals went down to ruin with only 40. The Conservatives took 419.

(2) Baldwin aimed at tranquillity, uncontroversial politics, routine, an inward-looking 'business as usual' without social or foreign adventures. He had put the great political specialists into offices with which they were unfamiliar. There was a loosened grasp on external affairs. Austen Chamberlain continued the Macdonald policy of harmless guarantees in the curious Locarno Pact of 1925 (q.v.) by which Britain effectively bowed out of European affairs. Its equivalent in the Empire was Balfour's definition of the Commonwealth, adopted at the Imperial Conference of 1926 (q.v.) in response to mistaken Canadian importunities. World War I had destroyed the German menace: revolution the Russian govt. and parties could agree to reduce armaments and their expense, Conservatives because they were unnecessary, Labour because they were ideologically suspect.

(3) In this spirit Churchill returned the country to a gold standard in international but not internal dealings, and left the printing of money to the Bank of England. Similarly Baldwin refused to countenance a bill to abolish the trade union political levy (Mar. 1925). Welfare measures such as unemployment relief and old age pensions were extended, educational expenditure doubled. Local authorities, under the Wheatley legislation of the previous govt, were building 100,000 houses a year. Income tax came down to 20%. Real wages rose, poverty declined.

(4) There was one enormous and misunderstood problem. In 1921 unemployment had exceeded two million in the worst slump hitherto known. By 1925 total industrial production had risen well above pre-war levels, but unemployment had not fallen commensurately because the old exporting industries, notably textiles and coal, were not selling their products. Oil and cheap Ruhr and Polish coal engrossed the European markets. Bombay cotton mills were underselling the British, and not only in India. It was believed that unemployment could be overcome only by reducing export prices, and the employers, especially the coal owners, thought that this could be done only by reducing wages and increasing working hours. Baldwin said that 'All workers have got to take reductions in wages to help put industry on its feet'. Amongst workers he included himself and was identifying with them more than with the employers. He thought the coal owners 'stupid and discourteous'. There was no such reasonable spirit among coal owners and miners' leaders. The result was the nine-day general strike (3-12 May 1926) (q.v.), the miners' strike, which lasted until Nov. and the Trades Disputes Act 1927.

(5) Despite these convulsions the economy continued to expand, mainly for the home market and by 1928, with some redeployment, the workless were down to a million, but there were questionable developments elsewhere. Churchill's fiscal policies increased Treasury power at home. Budgets were balanced by pooling hitherto assigned revenues, and the local councils' independence was undermined by derating their main sources of income (agriculture and industry), and their sense of responsibility eroded by substituting govt. grants. Nobody noticed the effects of these powerful but insidious changes until long after.

(6) Meanwhile the five-year parliamentary term was drawing towards its automatic close and parliament was dissolved in May 1929.

BALDWIN of REDVERS, (?-1155), E. of DEVON was one of the most powerful supporters of the Empress Matilda against K. Stephen. In 1136 he was driven overseas and fled to the court of the Empress's father-in-law at Anjou. He returned with troops in 1139 and successfully held Corfe castle against Stephen. The operation was, however, in other respects a failure and Baldwin, though disposing of large resources, did not act as one of Matilda's war leaders thereafter.

BALEARIC ISLANDS. *See* MINORCA.

BALEWA, Sir Abubakar Tafawa (1912-66) entered Nigerian politics in 1946 and soon attained ministerial office. Well known as a moderate, he became premier in 1957, and was chairman of the Commonwealth conference held at Lagos in Jan. 1966, mainly to discuss Rhodesia. A week later he was killed in an anti-federalist riot.

BALFOUR, Arthur James (1848-1930) 1st E. of BALFOUR (1922), was interested originally in science and philosophy, and wrote several books, of which *Foundations of Belief* (1895) is the best remembered. His uncle Robert ("Bob") Cecil, 3rd M. of Salisbury, induced him to enter politics, and he became M.P. for Hertford near the Cecil mansion of Hatfield in 1874, as a supporter of Disraeli's last govt. In the then aristocratic atmosphere of politics he enjoyed great social prestige through his Cecil connections and liberality, besides his brilliance of mind and graceful manner. As a supporter of Lord Randolph Churchill and as "Bob's" nephew he became a considerable Tory figure, and in 1885 he achieved office as Pres. of the Local Govt. Board. Thereafter his promotion was rapid, giving rise to the comment 'Bob's your uncle'. Sec. of State for Scotland and in the Cabinet in 1886, he accepted the unpleasant office of Chief Sec. for Ireland with a mandate to impose resolute govt. He was subjected to much abuse ('bloody Balfour') but introduced substantial administrative and social improvements, and his cool head and ingenious irony won him considerable acclaim. When W. H. Smith died in 1891, Balfour became leader of the House of Commons and First Lord of the Treasury as well. He thus shared with his uncle the leading positions in the state. Defeated at the general election of 1892 he returned in 1895 as head of the Commons coalition and continued with his Irish policy of resolution and reform. This unfortunately was interrupted by the South African War.

At the Khaki election of 1900 his party's majority was doubled and inevitably when his uncle resigned the premiership in 1902, Balfour succeeded him. The moment was a difficult one for the Tories. The Imperial Conference wanted colonial preference, which meant inroads into the long-held principle of Free Trade, and the taxation of food. The govt. had to deal with the aftermath of the Boer War and with the complications arising from the Russo-Japanese war. There were also extensive educational reforms culminating in the Education Act of 1902 which was largely his work. The Tories were divided and unpopular. Balfour therefore resigned, and in the election of 1906 the Tory Party was overwhelmed. Balfour even lost his seat, but was found a safe one a few weeks later. There followed the great constitutional crisis of 1909 to 1910 in which he acted as chief negotiator in the Lords reform discussions. Determined to keep his party united he advised his die-hards to give way. They refused and pressed their opposition to the Parliament Bill to a division. In Aug. 1911 therefore he resigned the leadership of his party.

During the Irish controversies which followed Balfour tried to exercise a moderating influence but when World War I broke out he began, though an ex-minister in opposition, to attend meetings of the Inner Cabinet and in May 1915 he became First Lord of the Admiralty. After Asquith's overthrow at the end of 1916 he became Lloyd George's foreign sec. and shared with him the British responsibility for the Versailles Settlement, the Washington Conference and the ending of the Japanese alliance. In Oct. 1922 he advocated a general cancellation of war debts and secured the financial rehabilitation of Austria through the League of Nations; he also joined Churchill in the firm stand against the Turks at Chanak.

Between 1925 and 1929, as a peer, he was Baldwin's Lord President and in 1926 it fell to him to produce the definition of Commonwealth relationships which preceded the Statute of Westminster, 1931.

BALFOUR GOVT. (July 1902-Dec. 1915). 21 in Cabinet. Leading figures under A. J. Balfour: E. of Halsbury, Lord Chanc; M. of Lansdowne, Foreign Sec; Joseph Chamberlain, Colonial Sec; George Wyndham, Chief Sec. for Ireland; E. of Selborne, First Lord of the Admiralty; G. W. Balfour, Pres. of the Bd. of Trade; Austen Chamberlain, Postmaster-Gen. In Sept. 1903 Alfred Lyttleton replaced Joseph Chamberlain but Austen Chamberlain was promoted to Chanc. of the Exch. The M. of Salisbury became Lord Privy Seal. In Mar. 1905 Walter Long replaced Geo. Wyndham. The M. of Salisbury replaced G. W. Balfour, and the E. of Cawdor the E. of Selborne.

(1) This govt. superficially resembling its predecessor (see DERBY GOVT, THIRD) brought new energy to the solution of its inherited problems, with important and durable results. The German menace, powerful in the long term had not yet developed so as to exert direct effects upon British internal affairs. Shielded by the Fleet and supported by a profitable colonialism, the govt achieved measures of comfortable domesticity.

(2) The first such measure, passed by Christmas 1902, was the great Education Act 1902 which guided the development of state education until after World War II. The second was the successful Irish Land Purchase Act 1903. The third the Licensing Act of 1903 and the fourth the Unemployed Workmen Act of 1905. (q.q.v.)

(3) Internal affairs were, however, increasingly if obliquely influenced by overseas events. In 1901 two cases in the courts (The *Taff Vale* case and *Quinn v Leathem)* had correctly under the existing law, exposed trade union funds to actions by employers for damages arising out of strikes. They had provoked widespread and angry demands for changes. The Labour Representation Committee (L.R.C.) was formed under the inspiration of the able and respected Keir Hardy. The govt. shelved the issue by appointing a royal commission. L.R.C. support promptly rose from 356,000 to 861,000. In 1902 it won its first parliamentary seat at a bye-election for Clitheroe. At the same time the govt. was having to deal with the financial and political *sequelae* of the Boer War, for which Britain had mostly paid. The colonies represented at the 1902 Colonial Conference had, as a result of their warlike successes, shown a marked disinclination to help with imperial defence and some other centrifugal general attitudes, but means had to be found to reconstruct the mined Boer economies. The Treasury was financing reseeding and stock. It was now proposed locally to import cheap Chinese indentured labour to work the undermanned mines. This would cost the Treasury nothing since the mine owners expected to make a profit. The govt. approved the scheme without adequate thought and tens of thousands of Chinese men were brought in from S. China and enclosed without women in guarded compounds near the mines. Profitable the scheme undoubtedly was, but wholesale and flagrant sexual perversion and deprivation of simple liberties shocked the religious conscience and outraged libertarian traditions. Moreover it raised a new spectre: the possibility that govts. might import cheap labour to combat trade union efforts to raise wages. The controversy was a godsend to the (liberal) opposition. The L.R.C. also won bye-elections at Woolwich and Barnard Castle in quick succession, the latter for the first time with an absolute majority. The Labour Party was on its way.

(4) The Boer War had made Britain widely unpopular. Diplomatic (or proud) isolation was now understood to be expensive and dangerous. There were only four potential friends worth cultivating: the German dominated Triple Alliance with Austro-Hungary and Italy, the Dual Alliance of France and Russia, the U.S.A. and Japan, then a rising but isolated second rank power. The first three seemed to promise no comfort: the Triple Alliance because German aggressive naval and commercial policies were obviously directed against Britain, the Dual Alliance because of potential conflicts with Russia in Central Asia and China and with France in Indo-China and N. Africa, and all three because of their long-standing if differently constituted Anglophobia.

(5) This sentiment was not shared with the Japanese, who were diplomatically isolated off-shore islanders with an ancient monarchy, a respected aristocracy and afraid of the Russian advance. The Derby govt's Japanese alliance (Jan. 1902) benefitted the Japanese by interposing a British naval shield between Japan and Russia's friends, but it failed to deter the Russians. Accordingly the Balfour govt. made approaches to France, while taking precautions against the Germans. A naval base was built at Rosyth on the Firth of Forth and preparations began to change the worldwide deployment of the fleet to a concentration nearer home. In May 1903 Edward VII changed the atmosphere of the French discussions. He single-handedly won over a hostile Paris in four days (May 1903). Henceforth Anglo-French bargaining could go forward in relative good will.

(6) The govt. now faced in concert with France, the German-provoked first Moroccan crisis (see ALGECIRAS CONFERENCE) and took momentous naval steps, jointly planned by the E. of Cawdor and Sir John Fisher (First Sea Lord). The Navy was relocated into three fleets based on Malta, Gibraltar and Britain, and the revolutionary battleship *Dreadnought* was laid down. These represented an open recognition that Germany was the real enemy and, because the relocations passed large Mediterranean responsibilities to the French navy, converted the *Entente* into an alliance against her.

(7) There now emerged a concurrent issue of great international and domestic significance, namely the expediency of substituting protectionism in any form for the long established free trading system by which Britain as the unique industrial country had bought foreign raw materials at highly profitable rates. This era of industrial monopoly had now passed with competition from the U.S.A., Germany and France. The colonies had complained that industrial imports were hindering the development of their own industries. There was a complicated controversy. Many of their imports were British, and in their new mood they might question the advantages of the imperial system and wish to enact general tariffs of their own. On the other hand Britain might abandon free trade, tax foreign imports and raise the domestic cost of living with all its unpredictable political consequences; or thirdly, it might be feasible to strengthen imperial bonds with a new vision of Empire underpinned by a system of imperial preference, which might raise the cost of living a little but appeal to the still significant colonial loyalties. Joseph Chamberlain had already aired the arguments as Colonial Sec. since 1895, and had made himself the apostle of imperial unity, but the colonies in his charge were understandably sceptical of his doctrines as long as the British public showed no disposition to respond to them. This represented a flaw in the structure of the govt. He was succeeded (Sept. 1903) by Alfred Lyttleton and preached accordingly. His powerful charisma soon attracted mass audiences and a following within the Cabinet. The flaw developed into a fissure and then into an unbridgeable gulf. His Tariff Reform League captured the N. Union of Conservative Associations. A cabinet reconstruction in Mar. 1905 failed to solve the difficulties. In Dec. Balfour resigned.

BALFOUR OF BURLEIGH, Alexander Hugh Bruce (1849-1921) 6th Ld. (1869) was the son of Robert Bruce, M.P. for Clackmannan. The fifth Lord was a Jacobite attainted in 1716, but the peerage was restored in 1869. He was chairman of commissions on educational endowments (1882-9); the Metropolitan water supply (1893-4); rating (1896); food supply in war time (1903) and on trade with Canada and the W. Indies (1909). In politics he was a Lord in Waiting in 1888-9, and from 1895 to 1903 he was in the third Salisbury Cabinet as Sec. of State for Scotland. He did much to improve Scots local govt, particularly in the field of health, and thenceforth until his death he was the most prominent figure in Scottish public life. He resigned on the issue of tariff reform in 1903 and joined the Unionist free trade group. In 1916 and 1917 he was chairman of the committee on commercial and industrial policy after the War.

BALFOUR DECLARATION (Nov. 1917) was a letter to the Jewish Board of Deputies signed by A. J. Balfour, then Foreign Sec., on behalf of the govt. It read as follows "H.M. Government view with favour the establishment in Palestine of a national home for the Jewish People, and will use their best endeavours to facilitate the achievement of that object, it being clearly understood that nothing shall be done which may prejudice the civil and religious rights of existing non-Jewish communities in Palestine, or the rights and political status enjoyed by Jews in any other country". *See* ISRAEL; PALESTINE; ZIONISM.

BALFOUR of PITTENDREICH, Sir James (?-1584) was implicated in Card. Beaton's murder and spent three years in the French galleys, but escaped in 1550. Mary Q. of Scots made him a Lord of Session in 1563 and in 1567 gov. of Edinburgh Castle. He turned against her and, after she was dethroned, became Lord President. It then became known that he had helped to draw up the band for Darnley's murder, and fled to France. He later returned. His *Prackticks of Scots Law* was a much used handbook. *See* CASKET LETTERS

BAL[L]IOL, Bernard the Younger (?-1215) probably the son of Bernard the Elder, captured William the Lion at Ainwick in 1174. He was the great grandfather of John Baliol, K. of Scots.

BAL[L]IOL, Edward (?-1364) K. of SCOTS (1332 intermittently to 1356) eldest *s.* of John (II) Baliol, K. of Scots and Isabelle, *d.* of John Warenne, E. of Surrey, succeeded to and lived on his father's French fiefs until 1324 when Edward II began to use him in his Scottish intrigues. When K. Robert the Bruce died, Baliol put himself at the head of the "disinherited", namely the Scots barons driven from Scotland by K. Robert for their

English proclivities. With English finance, 400 men-at-arms and 3000 foot he landed in Fife on 6 Aug. 1332. The regent, the E. of Mar, was surprised and routed at Dupplin Moor on 12th, Perth was seized, and Baliol was crowned at Scone on 24 Sept. In Nov. at Roxburgh he did homage to Edward III and prepared to marry his daughter Joanna who was already affianced to David II (Bruce), but within three weeks he was beaten by Archibald Douglas at Annan, and retreated into England. Here he gathered a large army which defeated Douglas in July 1333 at Halidon Hill and took Berwick. In Feb. 1334 he held a parliament at Edinburgh which agreed the cession of Berwick to England and in June the whole of Lothian was surrendered to the English crown and shired on the English pattern, with English castles and garrisons. The area was not recovered by the Scots kings for a century.

A Scottish reaction now set in. The E. of Moray was publicly recognised as regent for David II and he and Sir Andrew Murray surprised Baliol's troops in the Forest of Culblean and drove him over the border early in 1335. This gave Edward III no alternative but to intervene on behalf of his vassal. Until 1339 Baliol and Edward's generals conducted operations mainly from English territory against the recalcitrant Scots who held their own for David II; then Baliol preferred the peace of his English properties.

In 1341 David returned to Scotland. Five years later he boldly invaded England, but was defeated and captured at Neville's Cross (Oct. 1346). Baliol reappeared, established himself with English troops at Caerlaverock on the Solway and raided as far as Glasgow. He was contained by Robert the Steward the acting regent for David II. He had become virtually a crowned freebooter.

By this time Edward III had had enough of him and preferred to release David. Baliol was pressurised into surrendering his Scottish royal rights to him in return for a pension of £2000 a year. The value of this surrender to the English was that it kept an English claim alive and threatening David II even if he was the recognised K. of Scots.

Baliol died at Wheatley near Doncaster.

BALIOL, Henry (?-1246) was Chamberlain of Scotland from 1219 to 1231 He had many English estates and accompanied Henry III to the Gascon war in 1241.

BALIOL, John (I) (?-1269) was one of the richest magnates of his time, possessing many estates (including Barnard Castle) in England and half the lands of Galloway in Scotland. He was one of the Scottish regents for Alexander III until 1255 when his lands were forfeited for treason at the instance of Henry III. He came to terms with Henry, whom he supported in the Barons War, and though he was captured at the battle of Lewes he, with the northern baronage, continued to oppose Simon de Montfort. He and his wife, Devorguila, endowed Baliol College, Oxford.

BAL[L]IOL, John (II) (c. 1240-1313) K. of SCOTS (1292-6) was the third son of John Baliol (I). By the successive deaths of his brothers (1271 and 1278) and mother (1290) he built up a vast inheritance in Normandy, England and Scotland, as well as a claim to the Scottish throne, disputed at the death of the Maid of Norway. At the suggestion of Frazer, Bp. of St. Andrews the dispute was submitted to K. Edward I of England, who accepted jurisdiction on the basis of a feudal paramountcy of the English crown over Scotland. At a general assembly of the English and Scots nobility and commons at Norham on 10 May, 1291, the Scots were required to admit this paramountcy which they did on 2-4 June. Certain castles were then handed over to Edward and the various claimants swore fealty to him. A court of 24 English and 40 Scots was appointed to try the issues and this sat at Berwick from 2 Aug, 1291 until 17 Nov 1292, when John Baliol was declared King. On 30th he was crowned at

Scone and on 26 Dec. he did homage for Scotland at Newcastle.

A consequence of the admission of feudal superiority was that John's subjects began to appeal from Edinburgh to Westminster, the first such case being that of *Roger Bartholomew* of Berwick. John's protests were ignored; he was moreover vulnerable to English pressure because most of his wealth was in England and Normandy. Consequently when summoned to appear at Westminster at the suit of the E. of Fife, he first refused and when condemned, yielded, attended a parliament (May 1294) and upset the Scots. The major issue under discussion was a French war which Baliol opposed, but he was bullied into making a three year aid for the war, and surrendered Berwick, Roxburgh and Jedburgh as security. This naturally excited the further indignation of his Scottish subjects.

When he returned to Scotland he found them in no mood to join in the French war: a summons to send troops was ignored and a parliament at Scone in 1295 insisted on the dismissal of all the English at his court, the forfeiture of all fiefs held by Englishmen and the appointment of a committee of Scots lords and bishops to advise him. By these he was compelled to make an alliance with the French, and when in 1296 Edward I invaded France, a Scottish army ravaged Cumberland. Edward promptly turned about, stormed Berwick on 30 March 1296 and by July had overrun Scotland and received the submission of most of its leaders. Baliol surrendered the Kingdom at Montrose on 10 July and was taken to England and imprisoned. Released in 1299 he eventually settled in obscurity on his Norman estates and took no further part in public affairs, though the insurrection of William Wallace was raised in his name.

BALKAN *ENTENTES*. (1) In Oct. 1930 the foreign ministers of Greece, Roumania, Turkey and Yugoslavia met in the so-called First Balkan Conference. Their proclaimed object was to assist collaboration between all the Balkan states, with a view to ultimate union. Inertia, dissimilarity of outlook and language, mutual jealousies and Italian diplomacy prevented further development until the temperature of the European situation worsened with the rise of Hitler. In 1934 the four powers accordingly signed the Pact of the Balkan *Entente*, which provided for mutual consultation in diplomacy and support in defending the Balkan frontiers. It was ineffective because the combined strength of the four states was less than that of the increasingly aggressive Nazi Germans, or in the case of Roumania, of Hungary backed by them, or of the U.S.S.R. **(2)** A further attempt by Greece, Turkey and Yugoslavia to form a new *Entente* in 1954 broke down for similar reasons.

BALKAN WARS 1912-3 contributed material causes to World War I, created the explosive atmosphere in which it was ignited and deeply influenced its course.

(1) The leaders of Serbia, Bulgaria, Greece and Montenegro, backed by Russia, conspired to deprive Turkey of her European dominions by aggression. While Turkey was distracted by the Italian attack on her in Sept. 1911, military negotiations began between Bulgaria and Serbia, and were concluded on 13 Mar. 1912. Bulgaria and Greece reached a similar agreement on 29 May; war was decided upon in Sept. and Montenegro was drawn in and made treaties with Bulgaria and Serbia in Oct. This network of agreements constituted the BALKAN LEAGUE.

(2) *The First War.* In accordance with their agreement with Bulgaria, the Montenegrins attacked on 8 Oct, and by 18th war had become general. The Bulgars invaded Thrace and defeated the Turks at Kirk Kilisse (22-3 Oct.) and Lüle Burgas (29-31st). The Serbs won a great victory at Kumanovo (23 Oct.). On 8 Nov. the Greeks took Salonika, but on 18th, when the Serbs entered Monastir the Bulgars were heavily defeated before the Lines of Chataldja above Constantinople. On 28 Nov. the leading men of Albania met at Avlona and declared their country's independence. An armistice was concluded on 3 Dec. but on 23 Jan. 1913 the Young Turks led by Enver Pasha seized power to prevent the surrender of the isolated city of Adrianople, the second city of the Ottoman Empire. The League then denounced the armistice and, after a prolonged siege, Adrianople capitulated to the Bulgars on 26 Mar.

(3) The great powers now stepped in to limit the conflict and to settle it in their own interests. After embittered negotiations, preliminaries were initialled at London on 30 May 1913. The great powers reserved to themselves the settlement of the Turkish European frontier (temporarily only 6 miles from Constantinople), the status and extent of Albania and the disposal of the Aegean islands. The division of the remaining Turkish mainland provinces was left to the victorious powers themselves.

(4) *The Second War*. The London Preliminaries pleased no one and settled nothing. On 1 June the Greeks and Serbs made an alliance to divide Macedonia on lines which differed from those previously agreed by the Serbs with Bulgaria. The Roumanians now entered the scene with demands for Silistria and the S. Dobruja (both part of Bulgaria), while the Greeks approached the Turks for support against the Bulgars, who demanded Salonika. Hitherto Russia had inclined towards the Bulgars, and Austro-Hungary had favoured them as a counterweight to Serbia, but Bulgarian demands became so pressing and unreasonable that neither power was willing to do more than mediate. This was misunderstood by the Bulgars who, on 29 June, launched a surprise attack on their Serb and Greek allies, expecting a walkover. Restrained neither by Russia nor by Austro-Hungary, the Roumanians then invaded Bulgaria (11 July), taking the Bulgarian army in the rear and the Turks denounced the second armistice and recovered Adrianople on 22nd. Bulgaria sued for peace, which was signed at Bucharest on 10 Aug. 1913.

(5) *The T. of Bucharest*. Save that Montenegro was later absorbed by Yugoslavia, and Bulgaria retained a Mediterranean littoral at Dedeagath (now Alexandoupolis, surrendered to Greece after World War I), the T. of Bucharest established the south Balkan frontiers on the lines where, with only minor variations, they have since remained, and Bulgaria obtained most of the Aegean islands save the Dodecanese, already taken by Italy. Further north, however, the situation was different. The partition between Serbia and Montenegro of the Sanjak of Novipazar deprived Austro-Hungary of her rights under the T. of Berlin of 1878 in the Sanjak, interposed a solid barrier to her southward expansion, and foreshadowed the Serb imperialism which ultimately took the form of a South or Yugo Slav state. Moreover Austrian diplomatic support for Albania angered the Serbs and so inclined the Bulgars towards Austria, and this in turn inclined Roumania in the contrary sense. Finally it brought to power the nationalist and pro-German Young Turks whose alignment of Turkey with the Central powers in World War I had catastrophic results for Turkey and Russia.

BALL, John (?-1381) a radical priest, began his career in York but moved to Colchester where, in 1366, the public was forbidden to listen to him. In 1376 he was excommunicated. His social opinions were egalitarian and in the circumstances revolutionary, and his theology seems to have been derived from Lollardy. He was immensely popular. At the outbreak of Wat Tyler's rebellion in June 1381, the rebels liberated him from the Archbishop's prison at Maidstone and he became one of their leaders. On the march to London he preached a celebrated sermon at Blackheath on the popular text:

When Adam dalf and Eve span,
Who was then a gentleman?

He was present at Wat Tyler's murder at Smithfield, whence he fled to Coventry, but was caught and hanged on 15 July.

BALLADS. The ballad of *Sir Aldingar* relates a story found in William of Malmesbury (1140). *Sir Patrick Spens* concerns an event which probably happened in 1281, and *Chevy Chase* and *Otterburn* both tell of the B. of Otterburn in 1388. Actually there are only five ballad texts (*Riddles Wisely Expounded, Robin Hood and the Monk, Robin Hood and the Potter, St. Stephen and Herod* and *Robyn and Gandelyn*) which can with certainty be dated before 1500 and they are not earlier than 1420; but Robin Hood is mentioned as being a hero of song in *Piers Plowman*, and *Judas*, though not a ballad, is a 13th cent. poem in ballad form. The general conclusion seems to be that minstrels were composing these narrative songs from the 13th cent. onwards and that they were spread originally by word of mouth and casually embroidered and developed.

The number of pre-19th cent. ballads is very large. There are more than 50 about Robin Hood. The composition of new ballads almost died out in the 19th cent. and early 20th, but the principle or form seems to have acquired a new life in the 1960s through the influence of the W. Indian calypso and the widespread use of the electric guitar.

BALL[A]ARAT (Victoria, Australia). Gold was found in 1851 and a gold rush followed. The govt. prohibited exploitation of Crown lands and imposed an annual licence fee for a mining right. By 1854 digging began to fail and the diggers demanded abolition of both prohibition and fee. Being voteless, they stockaded themselves at the **Eureka** goldfields. Troops stormed the stockade killing 30 diggers in Dec. 1854. This precipitated the Victorian constitutional reforms of 1855. Digging ended in 1911.

BALLARD, John (?-1586). *See* BABINGTON'S CONSPIRACY.

BALLET (1) of the modern kind originated in Italian court entertainments, where dancers appeared as part of the floor show at state banquets. Leonardo da Vinci designed settings for some of the festivals of the Milanese court, and one in particular at Tortona in 1489 is usually held to have been the first ballet performance. Catherine dei Medici introduced these entertainments into France, and the first ballet of which there is a detailed account was the *Ballet Comique de la Reine* by Baldassarino de Belgiojoso for the marriage of the D. of Joyeuse and Margarite of Lorraine in Oct. 1581.

(2) In England masques were introduced from Italy under Henry VIII and these developed into a form of aristocratic entertainment similar to the French court ballet, which was a courtiers' pastime not a professional performance. Louis XIV was himself a performer until he was thirty.

By 1660 there was a shortage of dancers and a patent inability of courtiers to satisfy the growing technical demands of dancing masters. Louis XIV therefore founded the Academie Royale de la Danse in 1661, another for music in 1669 and a school for professional dancers in 1672. These shortly after were united into a single Academy better known as the Paris Opera. The first prima ballerina was Mlle Lafontaine in 1681.

(3) In England Marie Salle appeared with the mime John Rich in the 1720s and in 1734 she created in London the revolutionary ballet *Pygmalion* in which the formal French costumes were discarded and there was a deliberate attempt to unify music, décor and dancing. Thirty years later Noverre converted her methods into a theory which was not acceptable in Paris, so that much of his work was done in other European centres including London. It was not until 1770 that Gaetan Vestris was able to arrange a performance of Noverre's *Medée et Jason* at the Paris Opera and to discard the masque still worn by male dancers.

(4) The advent of romanticism was as much due to British influences (such as Scott and Byron) as to any other and as it happens just after 1800 women began to dance on the points of their toes. The most sensational and the earliest performer in this new style and technique was the celebrated Marie Taglioni who made her debut in Vienna in 1822; and took the lead in the first performance of her father's ballet *La Sylphide* in March 1832. This inaugurated the modern style of (so-called) classical ballet and dress; and it was followed in 1841 by Carlotta Grisi who took the title role in *Giselle* which Gautier had written specially for her while Taglioni was in Russia.

(5) There had been a Russian court ballet since the time of Catherine the Great, but Taglioni was there from 1831 to 1842, and then for over sixty years (1847-1910) St. Petersburg ballet was dominated by a remarkable Frenchman Marius Petipa who was responsible for the introduction and much of the choreography of *Sleeping Beauty, Swan Lake* and the *Nutcracker*. These in their turn became known in the west through Serge Diaghilev who in 1909 brought to Paris a troupe of dancers on holiday from the Maryinski theatre. With Diaghilev came Anna Pavlova who exercised a profound influence in England, where she danced regularly from 1908 to 1930. She chose and trained a number of English dancers and also fired the imagination of Edris Stannus, better known as Ninette de Valois, who opened a ballet school in 1926, and became director of the Vic-Wells ballet in 1931. In 1957 this was renamed the Royal Ballet. The principal ballerina was for many years the English dancer, Margot Fonteyn, in due course partnered by the Russian, Rudolf Nureyev, who had sought asylum in the west. Especially since World War II ballet has become immensely popular.

BALLOT. The word comes from the Italian, especially Venetian practice of using small balls for secret voting (cf. 'blackball'). In Britain voting at elections was open until the Ballot Act received the Royal Assent on 18 July 1872. This immediately affected Irish politics. Influenced or intimidated by land owners, Irish voters had mostly voted for one or other of the English parliamentary parties. Parnell now saw an opportunity to form an Irish party for which Irishmen could vote without interference. The long term effects were more important. It virtually abolished the hitherto substantial influence of non-voters in public affairs, and strengthened the case for extending the franchise.

BALLPLATZ (more fully BALLHAUSPLATZ) (Vienna). The location of the Austrian Foreign Office from the mid-18th cent. onwards.

BALLYMENA (Co. Antrim) became, with the introduction of linen manufacture in 1733, a textile centre of importance to the Irish economy and for agricultural industries in adjacent areas, because linen, unlike wool, was not subjected to British import duties.

BALMERINO (1) James Elphinstone (1553-1612) 1st Ld. (1604) became a judge and secretary to James VI, and went with him to London. He was attainted of treason in 1609, as a result of some correspondence between him and the Pope in 1599 (i.e. before James went to England), but released. **(2) John (?-1649) 2nd Ld.**, was implicated in the Scottish opposition to Charles I and in 1634 was sentenced to death but released. He was close to Argyll and was one of the Scots commissioners in London in 1644. **(3) Arthur (1688-1746) 6th Ld.** went into exile as a Jacobite and returned to Scotland in 1733. He joined Charles Edward in 1745, marched to Derby, fought at Falkirk, was taken at Culloden and executed in Aug. 1746.

BALMORAL (Scotland) was bought by the Prince Consort in 1847 and first used by the royal family in Sept. 1848, by which time a journey of such distance from London could readily be made by train. The present castle was built between 1853 and 1856 and the Prince bequeathed it to Q. Victoria at his death. He was responsible for the use of tartan in the decoration and furnishings, and also for the invention of the Balmoral Tartan itself.

BALTIC EXCHANGE for arranging cargoes for ships and aircraft, originated as coffee-house meetings in London between merchants and ships' captains in the 17th cent. After 1744 they met at a coffee house called *The Baltic*. Moved to St. Mary Axe in 1903.

BALTIC (1) This shallow sea with its gulfs and estuaries is a vast area of convergence for trading outlets and navigable rivers of the European and Scandinavian land masses north of a line from Frankfort to Moscow, and has long been a trunk route to the Atlantic world, especially Britain. Comparatively placid but foggy, obstruction by ice (for a few weeks in the central areas and up to five months in the north) creates an annual traffic cycle. The skerries and creeks of Sweden and Finland were the nursery of Vikings; the mouths of the great European trading rivers had advantageous sites for armed merchant and pirate communities viz: R. ELBE, Lübeck; R. ODER, Stettin, Greifswald, Stralsund; R. VISTULA, Danzig; R. DVINA, Riga; R. NARVA, Narva; R. NEVA-VOLKHOV, Viborg. There are also historically strategic islands; SEELAND, the cradle of Denmark, with Copenhagen and Elsinore, dominates the western exit by the Sound; RÜGEN and WOLLIN, the mouth of the Oder; ÖSEL, the G. of Riga; the ÅLAND Is., the junction of the Gs. of Bothnia and Finland; GOTLAND, with Visby, the central area; STOCKHOLM, the sea entry to the lakes where the Swedish monarchy began.

Importance to Britain **(2)** Always important, but especially from the 14th cent to the mid 19th, the Baltic was commercially and navally vital to Britain, and its politics correspondingly interesting. In exchange for wool, cloth, and latterly coal, the Baltic countries exported silver needed to maintain the value of Sterling, and provided masts, spars, cordage, hemp, tar and later copper without which English sailing ships could not have moved or remained afloat. Its importance naturally grew with the development of English sail-driven shipping. In addition there was Prussian yew for the bowstaves of the feared English archers, amber, furs, beer, pickled fish, Russian wax and later still vast amounts of Swedish iron. More spectacular policies nearer home have diverted attention from this rich but quiet activity, without which those policies might not have been supported at all. This can be recognised from relationships with the Hanse, diplomatic activity such as that under Henry IV and the powerful expeditions sent there. *See* BALTIC EXPEDITIONS, BRITISH; HANSE.

Formation of the Riparian States. **(3)** At the end of the Viking era (c. 1100) the DANISH, SWEDISH and NORWEGIAN Kings had power nuclei respectively on Seeland, near L. Mälar and at Bergen; the sparse populations paid deference to their rank, but their power scarcely extended beyond bowshot from royal estates. The plains and forests from Finland to the Vistula were tribal wandering grounds backed by the vaguely defined and governed areas of Poland and Lithuania, and by the crumbling Varangian states of Kievan Russia. Here and there, especially along the water route from the G. of Finland to Constantinople, Russia suffered under Scandinavian trading and slaving colonies. It was also beginning to feel the disruptive effects of Asiatic incursions.

(4) German power had reached the southern littoral in the 10th. cent and POMERANIA acknowledged German overlordship in the 11th. The Wendish duchies of MECKLENBURG, OLDENBURG and HOLSTEIN, and the Danish duchy of SLESVIG, clustered about the neck of Jutland, and the Scandinavian pirate guild at Jomsborg, still functioned, but only HAMBURG, a Christian missionary centre, had so far developed as a German town. Seaborne trade was neither controlled, nor protected from piracy.

(5) The most advanced Baltic state was Denmark under Canute's nephew Sweyn II (r. 1050-74). Seeland was then at the centre of the Danish realm, which included the present areas of SCANIA (Skåne), BLEKINGE and HALLAND. The Danes flourished by taxing, robbing or enslaving passing traders, and Sweyn perceived and his Five Sons (1074-1134) reaped the advantages of an alliance with the church, which helped the monarchy to convert sporadic (private) piracy into respectable (crown) protection. They were helped, too, by the death of Harald Hardråda of Norway at the B. of Stamford Bridge (1066) and his successors' preoccupation during the next forty years with the Hebrides, Man, Ireland and Wales. By 1103 the Danish church had become a missionary province with its own archbishopric at Lund in Scania.

(6) The Swedish Vikings had operated the trade *via* Russia to the Byzantine and Islamic orient. This passed through Åbo (Turku) and along the Finnish coast to the Neva. Finland was soon part of the Swedish world. Of the seven Swedish bishoprics founded by 1120 from Lund, one was at Åbo. The cessation of Viking activity created opportunities too, for the sailor-peasants of Gotland, who carried on business with Novgorod and the south coast.

Trade 1120-1227 (7) The consolidation of Denmark regularised the flow of trade through the Sound at a price paid in tolls until the mid-12th cent. when during civil wars (Norway 1130-61, Denmark 1134-58, Norway 1184-1202, Sweden 1156-1202) it became precarious again. The power spheres of the monarchies were beginning to press upon each other especially along the Kattegat where the greater and obstinate landowners had estates in more than one country and long amounted to a fourth power in tripartite Scandinavia. The Swedish eastern trade, too, was becoming precarious and now required an annual armada called the *Ledung*.

(8) The background was the rise of German mercantile enterprise and of Danish political competition with it *(see* HANSE-1). The Danes acquired Schleswig-Holstein as far as the Elbe in 1214, beat the *Ledung* in 1220, and laid the trade of Gotland under contribution. In the temporary eclipse of the Hanse, the Norwegians tried for the Anglo-Baltic carrying trade. Danish supremacy, however, was short. Attempts to stop the overland trade between Lübeck and Hamburg provoked the Wendish Hanse, whose militia overthrew the Danish feudal host at Bornhöved in 1227, the year after the Teutonic Knights arrived in E. Prussia.

East-West Conflict 1241-90 (9) There were now fundamental reorientations. The Hanse never had a central govt: from 1241 Denmark, through dynastic disputes, was without one. The traders of the two competed in disorderly fashion everywhere, but for a new type of trade. The Mongol onrush was blocking the trans-Russian routes at the moment when Swedish silver, copper and iron, from mines developed with Lübecker capital, were coming onto the market. Swedish furs even for a while superseded Russian. A main element in Baltic history was to be the division of the profits of a vast carrying trade. The "easterners" (with the northerners and the Hanse) wanted a free passage westwards, the "westerners" (Denmark, Schleswig and Holstein) to levy tolls. The western interest was to unite Denmark and Schleswig-Holstein and barricade the routes. Short of conquest, the easterners wanted to keep them apart and in competition. Until 1290 an uneasy Baltic peace was maintained by Swedish diplomacy, Hanseatic patrols, and the Teutonic Knights' subjugation of Prussia, while faction and civil wars kept Denmark weak.

The Teutonic Knights 1290-1340 (10) From 1290 until 1323 there was a dangerous breakdown of international maritime order, due mainly to dynastic quarrels in Sweden, and the demise of the Ascanian rulers of Brandenburg, but the Teutonic Knights, having exterminated the Prussians, colonised Livonia and Courland, and stabilised the local semi-nomads as serfs. The clearances created a timber and then a grain trade. The Knights became rich and dominated the Polish outlets. They could levy tolls at a time when further internal confusion (1326-40) prevented the Danes from doing so.

Danish Advance and Retreat 1332-70 (11) In 1332 K. Magnus of Sweden took over the protection and then the govt. of Scania. This gave him and his Hanseatic allies a dominant position which gravely injured the economy of Denmark. A Danish *coup d'état*, however, ended in the election of the ruthless K. Valdemar Atterdag, who built up his own power, and by selling Estonia to the Knights (1346) made them rivals of Sweden in the Russian trade (see also LANCASTER FIRST FAMILY-4). By 1359 Sweden was itself involved in dynastic troubles. In 1360-1 Valdemar struck. The lost provinces were recovered; Gotland was seized; the Hanse was defeated in the Sound (1362), and a Danish sponsored claimant ruled in Stockholm (1365). But Valdemar's excessive shipping levies provoked a reaction. The League of Cologne included the North Sea as well as the Baltic ports and the Teutonic Knights. It warred the Danes down, and in 1370 (P. of Stralsund) they had to hand over the Sound fortresses for 15 years and concede to the Hanse the right to veto the next election to the Danish throne.

Margaret and the Union of Calmar 1375-1401 (12) The wars left a trail of maritime disorder with which, after Valdemar's death (1375) his remarkable daughter Margaret had to cope. She was consort to the Swedish King of Norway, but persuaded the Hanse to use their veto to give the Danish throne to her son Olaf. She thus became his regent in Denmark and when Olaf succeeded in Norway (1380) Norwegian regent too. In 1387 one side in a Swedish civil war offered the crown to Olaf and so she became their regent as well. The need was great, for the *Vitalienbrüder* (= victuallers) a piratical confederacy based on Stockholm, Gotland and Mecklenburg, were strangling trade by constricting the food supply. They even sacked Bergen. In 1391 Margaret persuaded the magnates of the three kingdoms to crown her great-nephew Eric as King of all three, with herself as regent. English merchants were prepared to speculate. The Prussia Merchants were incorporated in the same year. By 1401 this UNION OF CALMAR had cleared the seas, in co-operation with the Knights.

English and Dutch Traders 1401-41 (13) This assisted English commerce. K. Eric married Philippa of England. The Company of Baltic Merchants was incorporated in 1408 (*see* CHARTERED COMPANIES) and in 1409 the future Henry V made a commercial treaty with the Knights. He was already too late. A Polish war opened with the Knights' decisive defeat at Tannenberg (July 1410). When Margaret died in 1412 disputes broke out in the Union. By 1435 (P. of Vordingborg) Denmark ceased to control Schleswig and (P. of Brest) the Knights ceased to control the Polish estuaries. Torn by its jealousies the Union began to break up. Baltic carriers lost heavily by interruptions in timber supplies and shortage of seamen. Dutch carriers began to take their place despite bitter Hanseatic opposition, which forced a treaty upon them at Copenhagen in 1441.

Slav Advances 1441-1515 (14) In practice the Dutch could not be stopped. The Hanse was threatened in the east by the Muscovites, who were interfering with Novgorod's valuable trade on the Northern Dvina, and in the south by the Poles, to whom the Knights were steadily losing ground. From 1448, when the Danes and Swedes elected different kings, there were wars or civil wars in all the Scandinavian countries. In the absence of secure bases and orderly hinterlands, the Baltic carriers gave way to the better secured Dutch. Moreover by 1466 the Knights had had to move their capital to Königsberg and submit E. Prussia as a fief to the Polish crown. Further north Great Novgorod fell to the Russians who, like the Poles, now began to control their own sea exports. They expelled the Hanse in 1496 and annexed Pskov in 1510. In 1515 Estonia, Livonia and Courland reverted to a revived Order of the Sword.

End of Union of Calmar 1481-1523 **(15)** Meanwhile the Danish-Schleswig-Holstein combination with its Dutch friends, was putting pressure on the Hanse in the west. K. John (Hans) (r. 1481-1513) confined agricultural exports to town staples. In 1520 Christian II (r. 1513-23) felt ready to re-establish the Union of Calmar. He took Stockholm and put most of the leading Sture family to death. This "Stockholm Massacre" was counter-productive. Gustavus VASA, a principal supporter of the Stures, rallied the nation, drove out the Danes with Hanseatic help, and in 1523, by taking the Swedish crown, formally ended the Union.

The Reformation 1523-44 **(16)** This affair focused attention on a new dimension in Northern affairs. Some of the Stures had died as condemned protestants. Christian's uncle Frederick I (r. 1523-33) D. of Schleswig-Holstein, who supplanted Christian, was a Lutheran. Between 1523 and 1536 the Reformation swept the Baltic like a political hurricane. In 1525 the High Master of the Teutonic Order, Albert of Hohenzollern, turned protestant with his brethren and they converted E. Prussia to their own hereditary use. The monarchies, bankrupted by centuries of conflict, were desperate for money. They had always been jealous of the acquisitive church. In Denmark, Sweden and Finland, it owned about a third of the cultivable land, With true protestant fervour the new Swedish monarchy's popular supporters put church property in Sweden and Finland at the disposal of the Crown (June 1527). In Denmark Frederick began seizing church property in 1530, but in 1531 Christian II tried, with the help of Charles V, his imperial brother-in-law, to recover the Crown *via* Norway. Frederick captured him by a trick in 1532, but died in 1533. There followed a devastating religious, social and commercial war with foreign interventions known, after the Catholic Christian of Oldenburg (the main intervener) as the COUNT'S WAR. The bigger cities and the greater nobles supported the Count. The new King, Christian III (r. 1534- 59) and the Rantzau family, perforce protestant, got Swedish aid.

(17) The protestant victory (1536) brought a long chain of consequences. For the next two centuries Norway was ruled from Copenhagen. The Dutch ousted the Hanse in the Atlantic coastal carrying trade, and the Hanseatic *Kontors* at Bergen and in England declined. A war (1542-4) with Charles V ended in Holstein being separated from Schleswig (T. of Speyer 1544). The Danish-Dutch partnership seemed to grip the Baltic.

Rival Routes and the End of the Sword 1544-63 **(18)** Two developments upset the balance. Firstly, overland communications from France to Poland (and beyond) improved; this by-passed the Dutch and created a new foreign interest in Polish and German affairs. Secondly, in 1561 the lands of the Sword were partitioned. At the entreaty of the Reval merchants, Estonia went to Sweden. Poland took Livonia and the Grand Master Ketteler became D. of Courland under the Polish Crown. Osel was sold to Denmark. Then came dynastic complications. Gustavus Vasa was succeeded by the brilliant but erratic Eric XIV (1560-8) in Sweden, but had left Finland to an ambitious younger son John. Eric, by parliamentary action, sought to reduce John's power: John, by marrying a Polish princess (Catherine Jagiellonica) (1562) to increase it. John lent money to Sigismund Augustus of Poland on the security of the Livonian castles. Eric and Sigismund both intended to

step into the political void left by the demise of the Sword. Eric seized John and his wife at Åbo (Aug. 1563) and took over the Livonian castles.

The Northern Seven Years War (1563-70) **(19)** There was now a land war between Sweden and Poland for the Baltic Provinces and a commercial and naval war with Poland's allies, Denmark and Lübeck, concentrated about the G. of Finland, Ösel, Gotland and the Sound. The Swedes developed a navy. The Danish Frederick II took Älvsborg and marched into Sweden, The Swedes occupied Jämtland and Häjedalen in Norway. The allies' professionally commanded, but unpaid mercenaries pillaged everywhere. On the other hand Sweden, without generals of much ability, had a disciplined and patriotic native army. Agriculture, industry and seaborne commerce fell off. There were local famines. Lübeck's financial power was crippled. In the background was the growing Russian power and threat to Poland, constituting a favourable diversion for Sweden. At the centre was the unbalanced Swedish King who quarrelled with his nobles at the height of the war. The Danes devastated southern Sweden: the unprotected southern nobles overthrew the King and replaced him with John III (r. 1568-92) of Finland.

The Union of Lublin and the Russian Troubles (1569-1613) **(20)** The Danes had been driven back. John III was brother-in-law to the K. of Poland, who had just united (1569) the two parts of his dominions at LUBLIN. The Scandinavians were tired of the war. Imperial mediation secured the P. of STETTIN (1570). There was to be a mutual restitution of territories between Sweden and Denmark, but in the event, the Baltic provinces remained Swedish, despite a Russian invasion repulsed before Reval in 1571. In 1572, at the death of K. Sigismund II, the Polish throne fell vacant and Russian attention was now, when not distracted by Turkish problems, transferred to Poland.

(21) After a prolonged crisis, during which the Polish crown became elective, and a French prince reigned briefly, Stephen Bathory (r. 1575-86) became King. Poland had a defender; Sweden, in Pontus de la Gardie, found a general. The Polono-Swedish combination was effective. In 1581 the Swedes took Narva. The P. of JAM ZAPOLSKI (1582) recognised their sovereignty in Estonia and cut off Russia from the Baltic again. From 1584, when Ivan the Terrible died, until 1613, Russia, plunged into her TIME OF TROUBLES, was helpless.

Danish and Polish Decline 1587-1613 **(22)** Poland now began its decline into an ungovernable confederation. The Swedes stepped into the coastal vacuum. They aspired to control the trade outlets and took over the anti-Danish policies of the old Easterners and the moribund Baltic Hanse. Moreover the English defeat of the Armada (1588) saved Holland and her energetic shipmasters. With timber and minerals, a rising industry, Dutch transport and a hardy and aggressive population Sweden seemed ready to take on the world. In 1587 the half-Polish Sigismund of Sweden was elected K. of Poland against Maximilian of Austria. An ensuing civil war was ended at the P. of BEUTHEN. Subsequently Swedish statesmen treated Sigismund's presence in Warsaw as some guarantee of Polish neutrality, and this had profound effects on Swedish internal history too.

(23) In 1588 the child Christian IV (r. 1588-1648) began his brilliant and disastrous reign in Denmark. In 1592 Sigismund succeeded in Sweden. His new subjects distrusted his religion, and their leaders, especially Charles, D. of Södermanland, hoped to keep him in Poland. A long political crisis and civil war culminated in Sigismund's defeat at the B. of Stangebro. In 1599 he was dethroned in Sweden. In 1600 Charles executed Sigismund's supporters, and in 1604 was proclaimed King as Charles IX (r. 1604-11). Since Sigismund would not yield, Poland and Sweden were at war which, after battles around Riga in 1605, subsided, until Sigismund's death in 1632, into mutually hostile forays in Russia.

(24) Through the Sound tolls and commercial entrepots in Ösel, Visby, and Scania, Denmark had since the T. of Stettin (1570) acquired riches, still evidenced by the architectural splendours of Copenhagen. But after 1604 Sweden had a stable government, a ruthless King and a change of policy. There had long been Norwegian boundary disputes and there were commercial and navigational disputes all over the Baltic. Charles IX founded GOTHENBURG on the Kattegat, to evade the Sound tolls and, additionally, gave it exclusive trading rights in the far north, but in 1611 he was dying. Consequently Christian launched the disastrous preventive *War of Calmar*, where most of it was fought. He encountered the military genius of Charles IX's seventeen year old son GUSTAVUS ADOLFUS (r. 1611-32). James I of England, Christian's brother-in-law, mediated and by the P. of KNAEROED (1613), the Swedes gave up their northern border claims, bought back the lost fortress of Älvsborg near Gothenburg, but acquired freedom from the Sound tolls. Christian understood the change which this represented, and in the next years fortified his Swedish frontier and developed Copenhagen.

Swedish Imperialism 1613-21 (25) An aggressive policy demanded an effective force. Gustavus Adolfus created the first modern army with its various arms and services, its pay and promotion structure, depots and training, all based on a patriotic reservoir of potential recruits.

(26) The first victim was the Czar Michael Romanov (r. 1613-45) who lost all access to the western seas (P. of STOLBOVA 1617); the second, preoccupied by a Turkish as well as a Swedish war, was Sigismund of Poland, who was swept finally out of Livonia (1621). With a toll-free Sound, Sweden was mistress of the Russian trade.

The Thirty Years War 1618-54 (27) Meanwhile spectacular events were unrolling in the west. The Thirty Years War broke out in 1618, when Brandenburg acquired E. Prussia. Wallenstein's northward drive represented the appearance of an aggressive imperial Germany threatening English and Dutch Baltic interests and the Danish hold on the western exits. By the T. of THE HAGUE (Dec. 1625) the first two undertook to subsidise Danish intervention in the war, but in Aug. 1626 Christian was beaten at Lutter; the imperialists occupied Holstein and Jutland for over a year and in 1628 Wallenstein took Mecklenburg for himself.

(28) Wallenstein's plans broke down. In Aug. 1628, Stralsund, fed by Sweden, drove him off. The P. of LÜBECK (May 1629) ended Danish intervention and prestige, but it dawned on Europe that Sweden too had a fleet. Gustavus thrust a truce (of ALTMARK Sept. 1629) upon the Poles (who left him in control of the Prussian ports), negotiated a French subsidy and landed in Pomerania (July 1630). His army was a sensation. To Sweden, the famous campaign which took Gustavus far into Europe and ended with his victorious death at Lützen (Nov. 1632) was a costly irrelevance. Moreover the throne passed to a girl, CHRISTINA (r. 1632-54), unfitted by temperament to rule, while the real govt. under Axel OXENSTIERNA (?-1654) was isolated somewhere in Germany; but the terror of Swedish arms and Oxenstierna's skill brought success out of danger, despite military setbacks in Silesia (1633) and at Nördlingen (Sept. 1634). The 26 year truce of STUHMSDORF (Sept. 1635) sacrificed the Prussian ports but ended the Polish entanglement. In 1640 Frederick William (r. 1640-88) (The Great Elector), succeeded in Brandenburg, and in July 1641 made a truce with Sweden which simplified the North German situation; finally a victory at the Breitenfeld (Nov. 1642) ensured the safety of the Swedish army.

(29) Since 1613 Swedish shipping had been free of the Sound tolls. The Danes confined the privilege to ships sailing from Sweden; the Swedes insisted that it applied to all ships (including English and Dutch) cleared from ports under their control. The Swedish contention would have freed most of the Baltic trade and favoured the Dutch. The impoverished Danish govt. could not afford it. The Swedes attacked, as the negotiators were assembling to settle the Thirty Years War, and imposed the T. of BRÖMSEBRO (Aug. 1645) on Christian IV. They took Ösel and Gotland, two Norwegian provinces, the Kattegat province of Halland, and enforced their own toll policy. Further victories against the imperialists gave them, at the P. of Westphalia (1648) West Pomerania, Bremen and Verden, that is to say the power to close the Oder, the Elbe and the Weser. Frederick III (r. 1648-70) succeeded to a shaken Danish throne.

The Swedish Empire 1654-75 (30) The Swedish Baltic empire depended upon too many uncertainties. It needed a friendly and united Poland, a powerless and divided Russia, continued divisions in north Germany and, in the absence of a large native merchant marine, compliant foreign carriers. Swedish manpower could not suffice to ensure stability if something went wrong and the successors of Q. Christina, who abdicated, and Oxenstierna, who died in 1654, seem to have been overconfident.

(31) Christina's Palatine (Zweibrücken) cousin succeeded her as Charles X (r. 1654-60). Relations were already strained with the Dutch, who found Sweden's little finger thicker than Denmark's loins. Their carrying monopoly was also deemed a threat to the growing trade in metals and ship's stores with Cromwellian England, and in the short Anglo-Dutch War of 1652-3 Britain and Sweden were aligned against Holland and Denmark. Cossack revolts began the disintegration of Poland, by drawing Russian intervention and creating Polish feudal unrest. In 1655 the militarist Charles X, with his unemployed army, decided to intervene for the recovery of the Prussian ports. The campaign, superficially brilliant left him isolated in a hostile countryside. Denmark declared war in the spring of 1657. The Poles, by ceding the suzerainty of E. Prussia (T. of WEHLAU Sept. 1657) bought over the Great Elector, who promptly changed sides. Charles X now had a stroke of luck. Marching from Poland, into Jutland in the hard winter of 1657-8 he crossed to the Danish islands on the ice. The T. of ROSKILDE (Mar. 1658) was abject: Scania, Bleckinge and Halland passed for ever to Sweden; the Norwegian provinces of Bohuslän and Trondheim temporarily; the Sound was to be closed to foreign shipping and Copenhagen ruined.

(32) The weather and preoccupations with the decline of the Commonwealth had prevented English and Dutch intervention, but the T. of Roskilde was intolerable and the Dutch mobilised. Frederick III was persuaded to repudiate it, and was besieged in his capital. A Dutch fleet fought its way in (Oct. 1658). The Great Elector overran Pomerania. The coming Restoration in Britain put Charles X's only available ally out of action. Moreover when he died suddenly at Gothenburg, the crown passed to a child, Charles XI (r. 1660-97).

(33) Pacification was in the air. By the T. of The Hague (May 1659) the French, English and Dutch had agreed to impose peace in the Baltic. After their P. of the Pyrenees (Nov. 1659) with Spain, the sated French, entrenched in Belgium, were free to act. Of the northern peace treaties, OLIVA (May 1660) and COPENHAGEN (June) reopened the Sound, returned Trondheim to Denmark, forced the Great Elector to return Pomerania, but confirmed his sovereignty over Prussia and its ports; and KARDIS (June 1661) established peace between Sweden and Russia.

(34) Military frustration brought political unrest.

Frederick III established a popular autocracy in Denmark. In Sweden there was an aristocratic regency of doubtful legitimacy and wisdom. Poland, defeated by the Turks, had to cede Smolensk and Kiev to the Russian intervener (T. of ANDRUSSOVO Jan 1667). The Swedish regency supported Britain and Holland against France in 1667-8, but English and Dutch traders were diverting Russian commerce round the North Cape. Meantime Denmark acquired OLDENBURG and Frederick III and Christian V (r. 1670-99) were preparing their revenge. The new star in the firmament, however, was Brandenburg-Prussia, whose patient Great Elector was the true heir, at once, of Wallenstein and the Teutonic Knights. His immediate and obvious objective was Swedish Pomerania. Thus Britain, Holland, Denmark and Prussia had interests and made treaties inimical to Sweden, whose Russian frontier was distantly threatened. Not surprisingly the regency, like Gustavus Adolfus, approached France (Apr. 1672). The result was unfortunate, for Sweden became involved in Louis XIV's aggressions and in 1674 invaded Brandenburg to support them. Slackness had weakened the Swedes. The Great Elector routed them at Fehrbellin (June 1675); the Danes, assisted by a peasant uprising, invaded Scania, and the garrisons in the Baltic Provinces had to be reduced to meet them. The young Charles XI, who had come of age in 1672, took charge and defeated the Danes at Lund (16/6) and Landskrona (16/7), but the Great Elector overran Swedish Pomerania, Rügen and Courland. In 1678-9 the Treaties of Nijmegen brought a moratorium in Louis XIV's wars and his diplomacy was free to rescue his ally. The P. of St. GERMAIN (June 1679) restored all the Brandenburg conquests to Sweden; the P. of FONTAINEBLEAU (Sept. 1679) all the Danish.

The Swedish Disaster 1679-1709 (35) Charles XI used his triumph to institute a revolution. The immense crown debts were to be paid by wholesale reductions (resumptions of crown grants). The old aristocracy was driven from office and ruined, and Acts of the Estates of 1680 and 1682 empowered the King to act and legislate on his own. These measures undermined credit and patriotic initiative; a new kind of administration required a royal bureaucracy. Meanwhile the new revenues revived the forces and financed a naval base at Karlskrona in formerly Danish Blekinge. But the house was built on political sands. Reductions, tolerable and precedented in Sweden, were subversive of society in the Baltic Provinces. Their nobles protested; their leader Johann Reinhold PATKUL was condemned to death. He escaped, and began his tragic career of intrigue on behalf of his alienated peers at foreign courts. With Russia under the weak regency of the Czarina Sophia (r. 1682-9) and Poland embroiled in Turkish wars (1683-99) this did not seem important, but actually the Turkish repulse from Vienna (Sept. 1683) had already altered the balance of Baltic power. Meanwhile there were profits to be made from the War of the League of Augsburg. *See* ARMED NEUTRALITY-1 AND NEXT ENTRY-1

(36) Great changes were impending. The Great Elector died and was succeeded by Frederick III (r. 1688-1713). Peter the Great (r. 1689-1725) ascended the Muscovite throne and by 1696 had reached the Ukrainian coast at Azov. In 1697, while Sweden mediated at the T. of Ryswick, AUGUSTUS the Strong of Saxony was elected King of Poland, and CHARLES XII (r. 1697-1718) succeeded his father at the age of 15 in Sweden. In the next year Peter destroyed the Strieltzy, his anti-westernising praetorian guard, but as the P. of Carlovitz (June 1688) left the Turks free to deal with him, he looked to the north, where Frederick IV (r. 1699-1730) had just come to the Danish throne. The P. of Ryswick had ended the need for the Danish-Swedish Armed Neutrality: the old enmity was resumed: the Danes still wanted their three lost provinces and Charles XII,

grandchild of a Holstein-Gottorp, supported Holstein to restrain them.

(37) Patkul's Baltic disaffection seemed to promise easy victory to a coalition whose members, however, had incompatible aims. Peter wanted a port on the G. of Finland, and Estonia if he could get it; Augustus to conquer Livonia and Courland with his Saxon troops; Frederick of Brandenburg wanted Stettin and Pomerania, and an end to Polish suzerainty in Prussia. The Danes aimed both at Holstein and the Three Provinces. Moreover the accomplices failed to co-ordinate their movements, and Denmark miscalculated the need of the Atlantic Powers to keep the peace while the Spanish succession was being settled. No one anticipated the mad military genius of Sweden's teenage King.

(38) Charles XII forced the Danes out of the war in the first fortnight. When Augustus advanced on Riga, Peter was not ready. Brandenburg, next within Charles XII's reach, cooled off. Moreover the Elector Frederick saw an opportunity to extract international recognition of his total independence. By Sept. Augustus had run out of supplies and retreated; by Nov. Frederick was King in Prussia, and Charles, free to concentrate against Russia, had defeated Peter at Narva. In June 1701 he turned the Saxons out of the Baltic provinces and invaded Poland; he took Warsaw in May 1702, defeated Augustus at Kliszow and captured Cracow in July. His garrisons could not prevent Peter from founding St. PETERSBURG in Swedish Ingria in May 1703. Peter grasped the G. of Finland while Charles played Polish politics. His victories had strengthened the anti-Saxon nobles. In July 1704 (while Marlborough was marching to Blenheim) they elected Stanislas Leszczinski King: Peter meanwhile took Narva and Tartu (Dorpat) and fortified Kronstadt. He could now devote more resources to helping his Saxon ally, who still had powerful Polish support. Charles became bogged down in a civil guerrilla. By 1706 he had decided on a direct blow at Saxony itself. The Russians and Saxons were beaten at Fraustadt in Feb. and Saxony, methodically laid waste, was beaten to her knees. At the P. of ALTRANSTAEDT (Sept. 1706) Augustus was forced to renounce the Polish crown and surrender Patkul who, as Peter the Great's ambassador he should have protected, thereby creating a personal hatred between Peter and Augustus, and Charles broke Patkul on the wheel in Poland to discourage Baltic disloyalty. Neither manoeuvre availed him.

(39) To attack Peter on his own ground, Charles now sought the alliance of Mazeppa, the Hetman of the Cossacks and having taken Vilna (1707) entered the Ukraine (1708). Peter's propaganda was successful. The Cossacks needed a protector against the Turks. For this role Poland, in dissolution, was no longer suitable and Charles' little Swedish army commanded only the ground where it stood. The Cossacks deserted Mazeppa. In July 1709 Charles' army was forced to surrender by superior numbers at POLTAVA; and Charles took refuge in Turkey. As a logical consequence Augustus dethroned K. Stanislas at Warsaw, but retook the Polish crown as a Russian puppet.

Turkish Sideshow 1709-18 (40) The main Swedish army had gone; the lawful ruler was now at Bender on the R. Diester, arguing with the grandees of the Sublime Porte. There was no effective regency at home. In 1710 apart from Riga, the Baltic Provinces were lost. Finland, the best Swedish recruiting ground, could not be properly defended; the Russians spread steadily across the south. Only in Scania there was some comfort: the governor, Magnus Stenbock, routed a Danish invasion. A total Baltic revolution was prevented only by Charles' Turkish intrigues and the maritime powers. A W. European famine followed the great frost of 1709; in 1710 Britain and Holland guaranteed the neutrality of the Swedish German possessions in return for the blockaded grain trade of the Baltic provinces. In 1711 Turkish armies invaded Russia. Peter, surrounded on the Pruth, had to retrocede Azov. The Turks demanded nothing for Charles, but they had distracted the Czar from the north.

(41) This Swedish diplomatic success was threatened by the prospect of peace in W. Europe. The Utrecht negotiations might release many vultures onto the Swedish imperial corpse. Charles resolved to go home. Stenbock's army set out from Stralsund to meet him, but was shepherded by Russo-Saxon opposition into the Holstein fortress of Thöding, where, in 1713, he was starved out. His King, meanwhile, was taken into custody by the Turks whom, however, he quickly persuaded of the threat of an Europe pacified by the Ts. of Utrecht, Rastatt and Baden (Apr. 1713 to Sept. 1714). Set at liberty, Charles rode from Pitesti in Roumania to Stralsund in sixteen days (Oct-Nov. 1714). His suspicions were correct. In May 1715 Sweden faced a coalition of Denmark, Hanover, Prussia and Saxo-Poland; by Dec. the Prussians were in Stralsund, his last German possession. He made another legendary escape, this time by boat, gathered an army at home and counter-attacked against Danish Norway; but some Swedes, at least, had had enough of these heroics. A bullet, not fired from enemy lines, killed Charles XII at Fredrickshald (Dec. 1718).

The Rise of Russia 1716-43 (42) One symbol of the new age was the Russian occupation of Mecklenburg in 1716 (see next paragraph). Charles XII's successor was his sister Ulrica Eleonora with her husband Frederick of Hesse (K. 1720-51). They decided to cut Sweden's losses and leave others to deal with Russia. The others soon appeared. Austria, Polono-Saxony, Britain and Hanover signed an alliance at VIENNA against Russia and Prussia (Jan. 1719). In Nov. Sweden ceded Verden and Bremen (i.e. control of the Weser and the Elbe) to Hanover for 1M thalers and the protection of the British fleet. With the Royal Navy in the Baltic, Prussia could safely allow herself to be bought off. A *coup d'état* ended the Swedish autocracy and put Frederick I on the throne as a crowned chairman. The T. of STOCKHOLM (Feb. 1720) returned Pomerania and Stettin to Prussia. In the P. of Fredericksburg with Denmark, Sweden renounced her Holstein alliance and her freedom from the Sound tolls. The Russian forward position, essentially a military attempt to circumvent the same tolls, collapsed but the P. of NYSTAD (Sept. 1721) gave Peter E. Karelia (the route to the White Sea), Ingria (the route to St. Petersburg) and the Baltic provinces. Power had shifted from the Scandinavian to the Continental shore. Peter could even afford to put Sweden in his debt for the tolls, by exporting tax free grain to her.

(43) Peter, who had reconnoitred Europe in person, had taken over the interests of the easterners. He naturally meddled in Jutland. The marriage of his half niece Catherine to the D. of Mecklenburg had already given him military rights in that Duchy. Another marriage was equally sinister. The D. of Holstein-Gottorp was the husband of an elder sister of Ulrica of Sweden, whose accession therefore infringed his wife's rights. Ulrica's govt. thus had good reason to injure him even more. By happily abandoning the Holstein alliance in the P. of Frederiksborg, they enabled the Danes to seize and annex ducal Schleswig. Peter's niece Anne was, however married to the Holstein heir presumptive: whereby both the Duchy and the political opposition inside Sweden acquired a powerful and dangerous patron, able at any moment to tax Swedish bread. In comparison with this, the marriage of Catherine's sister, another Anne, to the last D. of Courland would, but for the accidents of Russian politics, have been a minor matter.

(44) Peter had killed his son in 1718 and died without nominating a successor in Feb. 1725. A court faction successively elevated his ignorant Livonian widow Catherine I (r. 1725-7) and Peter II (r. 1727-30). The

Moscow boyars then invited Anne of Courland (r. 1730-40) to the throne as another crowned chairman. She accepted and then by a military *coup* re-established the autocracy and moved the capital to St. Petersburg. Famines, culminating in the disaster of 1735, accompanied these events and stopped Russia from exerting the westward pressure which might have been expected from Peter's arrangements. Moreover in 1733 Augustus (II) of Saxony, the Russian protected K. of Poland since Poltava, died. Austria and Russia supported his son Augustus III for the elective throne: France, Stanislas Leszcynski. In the WAR OF THE POLISH SUCCESSION Russian troops chased Stanislas into Danzig; Austria was trounced by the French in Italy; the British seized the opportunity to make a commercial treaty with Russia (1734); Danzig fell (June 1734) and by the P. of VIENNA (Oct. 1735) the powers recognised Augustus II (r. 1735-63) as King of Poland, which steadily declined into a Russian protectorate. (*See also* LORRAINE; SICILY; TUSCANY; PARMA.)

(45) In Sweden half a generation of peace had bred a war party. Just after the Empress Anne had settled the Polish business for her husband, the last Ketteler D. of Courland, died (1737). She forced her lover, Count Ernest Biron, upon the nobles and undertook another Austro-Russian enterprise, this time against Turkey. It failed, and by the T. of BELGRADE (Sept. 1739) both powers had to make substantial cessions. This rocked her regime. A Swedish backed palace intrigue was soon afoot. It centred on her sister Elizabeth. Anne died. The throne passed to a baby with Anne's niece, yet another Anne as regent. While Prussia and Austria were distracted by their first Silesian conflict, and in the hope of a favourable coup, the Swedes launched their troops into the Baltic provinces. Elizabeth indeed seized the throne, but without their help (1741) and disposed of Biron. More competent than her sister, she adopted Peter of Holstein-Gottorp, while her generals routed the enemy and advanced to the G. of Bothola. The price of peace was the election of Adolf Frederick, another Holstein-Gottorp, as Crown Prince of Sweden and, for the safety of St. Petersburg, Southern Karelia (P. of ABO 1743). Swedish prestige never recovered.

Baltic Peace 1743-56 (46) Adolf Frederick never meant to be the Czarina's tool and his strong minded wife, Louisa Ulrica, was Frederick the Great's sister. The immense but empty Russian realm had outgrown its strength. During the confusion engendered by the Wars of the Austrian Succession, reconstruction kept the Baltic at peace. An Austro-Russian alliance against Prussia was countered by a Prusso-Swedish alliance of May 1747. The first might have upset Frederick's P. of DRESDEN with Austria (Dec. 1745); the second might have redressed the balance. The two emerged as preliminaries to the P. of AIX-LA-CHAPELLE (Oct. 1748).

As crown prince, Adolf Frederick had supported the ruling anti-Russian party (the so-called "Hats") because he thought that they would increase the royal powers when he came to the throne. In 1751 he succeeded, but they broke their promises. He and Q. Louisa began to build a court party and in 1756 attempted an unsuccessful *coup*. These events placed the Hats even more firmly in power: they also paralysed Swedish foreign policy.

The Seven Years War 1756-63 (47) The great Anglo-French colonial war had already broken out, and Austria was preparing to reconquer Silesia. The RENVERSEMENT DES ALLIANCES was the natural expression of the probabilities. An Anglo-Prussian alliance (WESTMINSTER Jan. 1756) for the protection of Silesia and Hanover was countered by an aggressive Austro-French alliance at VERSAILLES (May).

(48) Frederick anticipated the stroke by invading Austria's ally Saxony on the way to Bohemia where, however, he was defeated at Kolin (June 1757).

Opportunism brought Russian troops into Poland ostensibly to fight the battles of her Elector-King, and the Swedes joined them. The Russians overran E. Prussia (B. of Gross Jägersdorf Aug. 1757), the Swedes moved on Stettin, the French conquered George II's Hanover (B. of Hastenbeck July 1757; Convention of KLOSTER ZEVEN, Sept.) and advanced against Frederick's Saxon flank, and the Austrians were advancing into Silesia. Frederick's tactical genius, however, saved his dynasty. He routed the French at Rossbach (Nov. 1757), and the Austrians at Leuthen (Dec. 1757), and then repelled the slower Russians at the pyrrhic B. of Zorndorf (Aug. 1758). By now he was receiving large British subsidies: the British naval threat was keeping the Swedes at home and the Anglo-Hanoverian army had taken up arms again. He now, however, suffered four defeats (Oct. 1758-June 1760), but the British victories at Minden (Aug. 1759) and Quiberon Bay (Nov.) staved off for a year a collapse which sheer weight of hostile power would have made inevitable. Despite two victories late in 1760 the Austrians overran most of Silesia and the Russians Pomerania.

(49) Frederick, who could only hope for a miracle, was saved by one. The Czarina Elizabeth died in Jan. 1762. The unstable but wildly pro-Prussian Peter III halted his armies. British subsidies dried up in Apr. By June Prussia had signed peace with Sweden and Russia had changed sides. The oscillation was too violent for the Russian court, where the Czarina Catherine (r. 1762-96) had Peter murdered and began her remarkable reign (July); but it dispersed the Austrians and enabled Frederick to concentrate. He beat them at Bürckersdorf and by Nov. had negotiated a truce. The P. of HUBERTUSBURG (Feb. 1763) virtually re-enacted the P. of Dresden.

(For the first Polish partition *see* POLISH PARTITIONS; for the second Armed Neutrality *see* ARMED NEUTRALITY.)

British Trade Supremacy 1763-1806 (50) The P. of Versailles of 1783, by freeing the U.S.A. from British economic control, opened up a new potential market for Baltic products, and U.S. commercial treaties with Sweden and Prussia soon followed. But industrial Britain was the mart of the age, and British ships, always familiar in the Baltic, now, along with the Danes, replaced the Dutch. Denmark became prosperous and could abolish her urban staples – so oppressive upon Norway, and develop an extensive trade via the Danish settlements and factories in Africa and India. Danish commercial prosperity was matched by Swedish primary exports. (See also next entry-3,4.)

(For the Second and Third Polish Partitions *see* POLISH PARTITIONS. For the Third Armed Neutrality *see* ARMED NEUTRALTY-3.)

Anglo-French Economic War 1806-15 (51) The Czar's realism in dissolving the Armed Neutrality was justified. By May 1803 the peace movement represented by the Ts. of Lunéville (Feb. 1801) and Amiens (Mar. 1802) had broken down. France and Britain were again at war; a war whose economic features had been recognised by the British before the French. The British policy was to deny France all seaborne supplies of war or potentially warlike materials, while exporting to Europe, including France, anything which Europeans would buy, especially for specie. The victory at Trafalgar (Oct. 1805) destroyed Napoleon's hope of breaking the blockade. The BERLIN DECREES (Nov. 1806) closed ports under French control to British trade. The greatest gap in this, so-called CONTINENTAL SYSTEM, was the Baltic. Here British trade poured in torrents openly to Scandinavia and Russia, and covertly to the disaffected ports and creeks of Bonaparte's subjects. Russian refusal to join the system brought on a war ending at the T. of TILSIT (July 1807) with a Franco-Russian alliance, Russian accession to the system and the dismemberment of Prussia. The British cheerfully retaliated with a vast and profitable smuggling industry based on off-shore islands. Bonaparte planned a counterstroke designed also against Anglo-Swedish trade. He would seize the Danish fleet and close the Sound, while his new Russian ally invaded Finland, and he himself occupied Swedish Pomerania.

(52) The Czar indeed invaded Finland in Aug. 1807, but in Sept. the British bombarded Copenhagen and seized the Danish fleet for themselves. Bonaparte's troops occupied Pomerania and in Oct. the Danes, perforce (*see next entry-5*), were allied with him. It was to no avail. Local disaffection helped the Czar in Finland; the Estates elected him their Grand Duke. French troops, meanwhile, could not reach Sweden in the face of the British fleet under Saumarez, who operated in the Baltic for three years. The Czar, whose new title was conceded by Sweden at the P. of FREDERICKSHAMN (Sept. 1809), was glad that they could not. An opportunity to convert Sweden peacefully to the Continental System now seemed to appear. Gustavus IV (r. 1792-1809) was dethroned in a military *coup* in Mar. 1809 in favour of his childless uncle Charles XIII (r. 1809-18); and a prince of Holstein was elected crown prince. He died immediately and the govt. ostensibly joined the Continental System and sought Bonaparte's advice. One of the envoys privately approached Marshal Bernadotte. The marshal was well known in northern Europe. Bonaparte disliked him but, believing that as a Frenchman he would be pro-French, raised no objection to his candidature. Elected Crown Prince in Aug. 1810, he became effective head of the govt. His policy was wholly Swedish. He abandoned the claims to Finland which, he believed, would only create trouble with Russia. He aimed, instead, at Norway, long partially isolated from Denmark by the British blockade, and he refused to prosecute the normal hostilities and trade embargos against Britain. The British and Swedes never exchanged a single shot, while Bonaparte made menacing annexations as far as the Holstein frontier. See *next entry-6 and* FRENCH COASTAL ANNEXATIONS.

Norway and Denmark Separated 1813-45 (53) On their own during the wars, the Norwegians had drifted away from Danish habits and the Danish economy. In 1812 Bernadotte joined the allies in return for the promise of Norway. After the B. of Leipzig (Oct. 1813) the Swedes invaded Denmark, and forced the Danes to exchange Norway for Swedish Pomerania (T. of Kiel, Jan. 1814). The Norwegians ignored the treaty and proclaimed a constitution at EIDSVOLD (Apr. 1814). Swedish troops appeared, but sense prevailed and the CONVENTION OF MOSS (Aug. 1814) arranged for local autonomy under the Swedish crown. Finally the Congress of Vienna allotted Swedish Pomerania to Prussia and compensated Denmark with Lauenburg. Bernadotte succeeded in Sweden and Norway as Charles (XIV) John (r. 1818-44). He was well liked in both countries.

(54) Her merchant marine destroyed and her Norwegian agricultural market gone, Denmark lurched through private and public bankruptcies until the repeal of the British Corn Laws (1846) gave her an outlet and a modest prosperity. Sweden could still export metals, but the steel industry succumbed to British competition, and was replaced by timber. The revolutions of 1848 left Scandinavia largely unscathed because it had been moving towards constitutionalism for some time. The Danish autocracy (more nominal than real) was formally ended.

The Rise of Germany 1848-95 (55) Popular participation in govt. however, reawakened the dormant Schleswig-Holstein question. The German language and German separatism had been making headway in the duchies since 1830. Holstein (but not Schleswig) was part of the German confederation; different laws of succession obtained in Denmark and the Duchies, giving the greatest of the landowners the D. of Augustenburg, real claims;

the urban liberal separatists had close connections with the German liberals; the pro-Danish parties had affinities with the Danish conservative nationalists who, having secured power at Copenhagen, sought to incorporate Schleswig in Denmark (Mar. 1848). Simultaneous revolutions in Holstein and Berlin established a German govt. with Prussian support. After sporadic fighting Britain, France, Russia and Sweden compelled the Prussians to retire, and guaranteed the autonomy of the duchies under the Danish crown by the CONVENTION OF LONDON (Aug. 1850).

(56) The Crimean War (1854-6) had some repercussions in the Baltic (see BALTIC EXPEDITIONS-7) and Sweden joined the anti-Russian alliance in Nov. 1855; this probably helped to hasten a settlement. In the general confusion the Americans refused to pay the Danish Sound tolls, other nations and the Copenhagen merchants supported them, and in Mar. 1857 they were abolished in return for international compensation. The effect was to divert trade away from Holstein and Hamburg to Copenhagen, and gradually increase German discontent. This in turn brought a Danish reaction, against which the separatists appealed to German public opinion, now manipulated by Bismarck. The role of the Schleswig-Holstein war of 1864 in hastening the expulsion of Habsburg influence in Germany has often been noted, but the seizure of the duchies and Lauenburg was not less important for the control which it gave to Prussia over the Baltic trade exits other than the Sound. After the proclamation of the Empire in 1871, the Germans were soon planning to exploit the advantage. The modern KIEL CANAL was surveyed and built between 1887 and 1895. Some of the trade which had benefitted Copenhagen since 1857 was now attracted back through Hamburg and, moreover, the German navy, built in support of a trans-oceanic colonial policy could, by means of the canal, also dominate the Baltic.

Anglo-German Rivalry 1895-1917 (57) Denmark had become an economic dependency of Britain. Norway had suffered from Swedish economic domination and a low standard of living, which sent many Norwegians to North America. The advantages of a British association were becoming apparent to Norwegians just as the growth of German industrial and naval power were attracting or compelling Sweden, In the pre-Dreadnought era, Sweden could build a navy which, in combination with Russia, might keep Germany at bay but in 1905 the Japanese destroyed the Russian seapower. Hence Norway preferred independence with British trade and protection, to German influence through the Swedish economy. In Sept. 1905 she became, with little fuss an independent constitutional state under a Danish prince suitably entitled King Haakon VII.

(58) The enormous new demands of the German engineering and shipbuilding industry were added to the older demands of the British. Debased by defeat and racked with internal confusion, Russia could not protect Scandinavia against Germany. Sweden's prosperity as a primary exporter concealed her political impotence. Meanwhile new prospectors were opening up the mineral riches of the far north. The new Narvik railway created a route which avoided both the Baltic ice and the German navy. Moreover in 1906 the British launched H.M.S. *Dreadnought* which was ready for sea in 1907. This was nowhere more important than in the Baltic. The great German battle fleet was out of date overnight, and with it the superiority over Russia, for the Russians could start building *Dreadnoughts* as soon as the Germans. Moreover *Dreadnoughts* were too big for the Kiel Canal, which the Germans worked from 1908 energetically to widen. In fact Russian warship building fell behind the German, just as the German fell behind the British, but the widened canal, reopened in June 1914, converted the Baltic into a German lake, across which Swedish metals

and timber flowed despite British submarines (see next entry-8), under German naval protection and behind Swedish minefields into the German armaments industries throughout World War I. Much of the Danish agricultural production went the same way. Norway, menaced in her neutrality by the unrestricted U-boat campaigns from 1915 onwards, maintained her economic independence, but the immense and ancient Russian trade ended for a generation.

Effects of Russian Revolution and German Defeat 1917 onwards (59) When the two great powers of the south and eastern coasts collapsed in defeat and revolution, the dependent economies suffered disaster as well. Moreover the coastal minorities of the Russian empire seized the opportunity to set up as independent states. The Germans had assisted this process by trying to establish the Teutonic Knightly families as the ruling elements of the Baltic provinces, and by intervening against the revolutionaries in Finland. The British, having impounded the German navy, took good care to sink as much of the Russian fleet, now in rebel hands, as they could. (See next entry-9.) With Russia at war with herself, this type of allied support heartened the local nationalists, and so from 1921 to 1939 Baltic geography had superficial resemblances to the mediaeval situation. Poland was an inland economy connected to the open sea through the free state and port of Danzig. East Prussia was separated, like a Polish duchy, from the main body of Germany. Russia had her window to the Baltic only through St Petersburg renamed Leningrad. Otherwise the Russian interior was cut off by the territory of the Three Baltic Provinces, slightly rearranged into three republics named, after their majority languages, ESTONIA, LATVIA and LITHUANIA.

The often brutal expulsion of the Germanic country landowners and town merchants began the modern German westward retreat. It also deprived these three republics of most of their educated population and it cut them off from the west, just as their linguistic exclusiveness cut them off from the east. They lived, by the grace of Russian revolutionary weakness, in a kind of daydream until 1938. Finally, FINLAND was at last established as an independent state. There were, however, two major differences. The Baltic was now not so much a channel between East and West as a cul-de-sac of the West; and during the post-war depression, even the north-south traffic languished.

Nazi Aggression 1933-44 (60) That daydream began to fade when Hitler came to power in Germany in 1933 (see POLISH PARTITIONS, FOURTH). The three republics handed over bases to the Russians in Oct. 1939, Poland having been partitioned by Sept. Only Finland challenged fate and was well rewarded. For three months from Nov. 1939 she fought Russian armies to a standstill and, by the sacrifice of Viborg (Vipuri) maintained her independence (Mar. 1940).

(61) In Apr. 1940 the Germans seized Denmark and attacked Norway. The venture cost them much of their surface fleet but, besides giving them access to the Arctic Atlantic, it cut Sweden, apart from daring air and motor-boat contacts, off from the outside world and incorporated her metals and timber into the German war economy. The Baltic again became a German lake and this made it easy for Hitler to turn on his Russian ally (June 1941). His armies reached the environs of Leningrad (Sept.). The German grip was not broken until late in 1944.

Russian Resurgence 1944-89 (62) In the post-war settlement, based upon the Western Yalta miscalculations, the Russians were easily the greatest gainers. Finland maintained a certain independence subject to a Russian military enclave at Hangö and a commercial agreement which for a decade harnessed the Finnish economy to Leningrad. The three Baltic republics were suppressed and the Russians began deportations which, by 1962, had reduced the indigenous populations to minorities in their own countries. By creating a Poland under a Communist tyranny like their own and, at Winston Churchill's suggestion, shifting it bodily west of any area previously understood by the name, the Russians obtained the advantages of a Polish Partition and, they hoped, a permanent dependency anxious for protection against the Germans, many millions of whom had been brutally driven out to make way for Poles. The ancient German eastward drift was violently reversed in eighteen months. Russia now dominated the Baltic.

At the same time Russia had to rebuild her, in any case primitive war-battered economy, and this could not be done solely by looting the conquered territories. Overseas trade had to be revived to supply the basic essentials of a society with industrial ambitions, because these could be had only in the West. The historic role of the Baltic as a passage between east and west was revived in the 1960s, together with an increasingly productive and ingenious Russian shipbuilding industry, with its Polish outlier at Danzig (now Gdansk). *See also* ARMED NEUTRALITY; BALTIC EXPEDITIONS – BRITISH; POLISH PARTITIONS.

(63) The immediate effect of the Gorbachov-Yeltsin era in Russia was economic collapse throughout much of the former Soviet Union, a consequent slackening of trade and the somewhat shaky re-emergence of the three Baltic republics as independent states. Leningrad became St. Petersburg again. *See* CRUSADES, BALTIC.

BALTIC EXPEDITIONS, BRITISH. The immense importance of the Baltic in British history was mainly indirect until the end of the 17th cent. because the govt's naval resources did not, before the reign of William III, run to direct interventions. The chief British expeditions to the Baltic were:

(1) In **1700** William III expected a French attack which would have endangered the Baltic naval supplies and crippled British and Dutch commercial and naval shipping. An Anglo-Dutch expedition to impose mediation in a war just launched against Sweden by a shaky alliance of Denmark, Brandenburg, Polono-Saxony and Russia, reached the Kattegat but the Swedish K. Charles XII put Denmark out of the war before it could arrive. The expedition, however, saved Danish independence (P. of TRAVENDAL Aug. 1700) but did not stop the war.

(2) Charles XII having been killed (Dec. **1718),** Sweden seemed likely to be at the mercy of Russia and Prussia with Danish support. To protect British commercial and maritime interests, Britain offered a million thalers and the protection of the Royal Navy to Sweden in return for the cession of Bremen and Verden (i.e. the control of the R. Weser) to Hanover. The agreement was signed in Nov. 1719 and the British fleet accordingly entered the Baltic and checked Sweden's enemies. *See* BALTIC-42.

(3) In **1800** a naval demonstration before Copenhagen was meant to reassure the Baltic powers against Bonaparte's propaganda after his victory at Marengo (June 1800). It failed and provoked the formation of the Third Armed Neutrality. Accordingly

(4) a fleet under Sir Hyde Parker, with Nelson as 2-in-C, was sent early in **1801** to secure the dissolution of the Armed Neutrality, if necessary by destroying its principal fleet, which was Russian. This fleet was divided between Reval and Kronstadt and immobilised by ice. The first stage was to establish safe communications by requesting the Danes not to molest British ships in the narrows. This was refused, and in April the B. of Copenhagen was the result. The Danes having capitulated, the passage was clear, but Parker's methods were so dilatory that even after his supersession by Nelson, it was not possible to reach Reval before the ice

broke. Technically the operation was thus only a partial success, but unknown to Parker and Nelson the Russian Czar, Paul I, had been murdered ten days before the battle, and Russian policy became slowly less hostile.

(5) 1807. This expedition, an indirect consequence of the Berlin Decrees (1806), is still resented in Denmark but hardly remembered in Britain. It was a much larger operation than the previous one. It consisted of 25 ships of the line and 40 other warships under Adm. James Gambier, and 27,000 troops under Lord Cathcart carried in 377 transports. Cathcart's original objective had been Stralsund and the I. of Rügen, so that the various components of the force arrived before Copenhagen from opposite directions. The object was to seize the Danish fleet, which could not be done against opposition without besieging the city. The city in its turn could not be besieged if the main Danish army in Jutland, reinforced by the French, could cross to Seeland where it stands. Time was essential because most of the Danish ships were laid up in the Arsenal and would need several weeks to be made ready for sea. Hence light squadrons isolated Seeland while the city was invested, bombarded from landward and set on fire. There was much naval skirmishing too. The city surrendered in Sept. It took six weeks to fit out the 15 Danish ships of line and others, and take them to England.

(6) 1808-11. This important operation under Sir James Saumarez captured traders, mostly Danish; turned small islands such as Anholt (Kattegat) into trading depots; protected British traders breaking the Napoleonic decrees against British trade and prevented Bonaparte and the Russians from gaining Sweden. In theory Britain was at war with Sweden, but no shot was ever fired, and eventually Saumarez induced Sweden to change sides.

(7) 1855. In this British naval foray during the Crimean War, most Russian Baltic trade was stopped and, because the fleet occupied the strategic Åland Is., the Swedes felt they could safely join the allies (Nov.). These activities materially hastened the assembly of the Paris Peace Congress (Feb. 1866). *See* PALMERSTON'S FIRST GOVT.

(8) 1914-5. Brave but not very effective submarines ran through the German and Swedish minefields to harass the German timber and metal supplies from Sweden.

(9) 1918-20. After the German Armistice of Nov. 1918, a British force entered the Baltic in support of the Russian anti-communist republicans, and by motor torpedo-boat attacks (Aug. 1919), on the Red fleet at Riga and Kronstadt sank two battleships and a cruiser.

BALTIC STATES. The collective name of the republics of Lithuania, Latvia and Estonia during their independence.

BALTIMORE (1) George, (?1580-1632) 1st Ld. (1625) became private sec. to Sir Robert Cecil in 1605; in 1698 he was a clerk of the council and he was M.P. for Bossiney in Oct. 1609. He was employed on foreign and Irish affairs and became S. of State in Feb. 1619. With Sir Thos. Wentworth he was M.P. for Yorkshire in 1621 and had to put the case for the King's war in the Palatinate. In 1625 he resigned, declared himself a R. Catholic, and took no further part in English affairs.

Since 1621 he had been interested in colonising Newfoundland having established a small colony at Ferryland; he secured in 1623 a charter for the colony under the name of Avalon. This prospered at first, but in 1627 he had to go there himself to set it in order. In the spring of 1628 he went there again with his family for eighteen months, during which he repulsed a French naval attack. By the autumn of 1629 he had concluded that the climate was too rigorous and moved to Virginia, where he met with opposition from the Virginia Company. He therefore returned to England to negotiate a new charter for lands elsewhere, but met similar opposition and delays. He died before the Charter of Maryland was sealed on 20 June 1632, and the colony (named after Charles I's queen) was accordingly founded by his son **(2) Cecilius**; his second son **(3) Leonard (?-1647)** was its first governor. *See* MARYLAND.

BALUCHISTAN is now divided roughly in the proportions of one to two between Iran and Pakistan, having at one time been wholly under Iran and between 1595 and 1638 wholly under the Moghuls. Moslem dominance was established in the 17th cent. The precarious independence of the principal state of Kalat depended upon an easily disturbed balance of power, after Moghul protection had lapsed, and Nadir Shah's defeat of the Afghans resulted in the Khan of Kalat being appointed Iranian gov. in 1739. Ahmad Shah Durrani's refoundation of Afghan power enabled Kalat to exchange Persian for the much less dangerous Afghan overlordship in 1748 until 1839 when British armies traversed the country and stormed Kalat during the First Afghan War. Between 1840 and 1876 all the govts. in the adjacent areas were weak, and the Baluchis were left mainly to themselves, which meant rural anarchy and murderous intrigue at Kalat.

Some order having been restored, the British by a treaty of 1876 recognised the Khan's internal autonomy in return for his co-operation, and occupied the Quetta area so as to end Afghan influence and protect India against invasion from the N.W. The arrangement suited both sides.

The T. of Gandamak (1879) began the process of creating (so-called) BRITISH BALUCHISTAN to protect the military communications of Quetta. The area then acquired was progressively enlarged back to the Indian frontier by extensions and perpetual leases in 1891, 1899 and 1901, while the Khans of Kalat and their feudatories continued to rule in the State. Of these feudatories LAS BELA was virtually independent, and KHARAN and MAKRAN became independent in the 1940s. In 1952-3 the four states joined Pakistan as the Baluchistan States Union and in 1955 they were merged with W. Pakistan.

BAMANGWATO. *See* BECHUANALAND.

BAMBRIDGE, Thomas (fl. 1728-30) bought the wardenship of the Fleet debtors' prison in Aug. 1728 for a large sum. By Mar. 1729 a Commons' committee had reported on appalling cruelties and extortions but in 1729 and in 1730 he was acquitted of murdering prisoners. He was himself later imprisoned in the Fleet. His examination before the Committee was portrayed by Hogarth.

BAMBURGH (N'land). The fortress was founded in 6th cent. by Ida, K. of Bernicia. St. Aidan founded a mission on the nearby isle of Lindisfarne and died there in 651. Bamburgh remained an important seat and stronghold of the Northumbrian kings and later of the Es. of Northumberland. The Normans rebuilt the castle, and it was improved from time to time until 1464, but was gravely damaged by artillery when Henry VI and Q. Margaret were besieged there in 1462. Grace Darling was born there.

BAMPFIELD, Thomas (?-1663) represented Exeter in the Cromwellian parliaments of 1654, 1656 and 1658. In the last he was elected Speaker for the time being, because Sir Lislebone Long, the deputy for the sick Speaker Chute, died. Chute then died, and Bampfield was confirmed in the substantive office until the dissolution of 22 Apr. 1659. He also sat in the Convention Parliament of 1660.

BAMPTON LECTURES. The Rev John Bampton (1698-1751) left a sum to finance theological expositions annually or biennially delivered at St Mary's Church, Oxford, by distinguished divines.

BAN and **BANNS.** The word originally meant a solemn proclamation and therefore, as ban, a public notification that someone or something is proscribed by the govt; and as banns that those named in the proclamation intend to marry.

BANBURY, B. of (556). The Britons were defeated at Banbury probably by Ceawlin coming from Cambridgeshire. The battle marks the resumption of the Anglo-Saxon advance after the check at Mount Badon half a century earlier.

BANBURY PEERAGE CASES (*see* KNOLLYS) were intermittent *causes célèbres* from 1641 to 1813. Elizabeth Howard, wife of the 1st E. of Banbury had two sons, the younger being born at the house of the 4th Lord Vaux, whom she married five weeks after the Earl's death. The House of Lords rejected their legitimacy and right to the peerage, but the King's Bench recognised their legitimacy and right to the property. As the Lords were not acting as a court of appeal from the King's Bench but as a committee of privileges in a peerage claim, the two conflicting judgements stood, and successive Knollys called themselves Earls of Banbury without being able to take their seat. **William (1763-1834),** 8th so-called Earl made the last, unsuccessful, claim to have the Lord's decision reversed in 1813.

BANCROFT, Abp. Richard (1544-1610) became chaplain successively to Sir Christopher Hatton, a favourite of Elizabeth I, and then Abp. Whitgift. His abilities and anti-puritan sentiments gained him membership of the High Commission in 1587, and a sermon against the opponents of episcopacy at St Paul's Cross brought him considerable fame in 1589. In 1597 he became Bp. of London and because of Whitgift's senility he was the real head of Canterbury province. His opposition to Calvinism, his high claims for episcopacy and his ruthless orthodoxy widened the differences within the Church. After a diplomatic visit to Denmark in 1600 he led the prelates' side of the Hampton Court conference in 1604, and he became prolocutor of convocation and then Abp. of Canterbury. Pious, learned and competent, he was well suited to organise the Authorised translation of the Bible, which continued until his death.

BAND (Scots). A bond, especially a political agreement between great noblemen.

BANDA, Dr Hastings Kamuzu (?1906-97), a mission-school educated Malawi peasant, worked in a gold mine and then studied medicine in the USA and Britain, practising it at Liverpool and on the Tyneside, and afterwards in London. From 1954 to 1958 he was at Kumasi (Ghana), after which he returned to Nyasaland and took the leadership of the Malawi Congress Party. During the year's state of emergency, which began in Mar. 1959, he was under detention, but became a Minister in 1961 and Prime Minister in 1963. This office he retained when Nyasaland became independent as Malawi in July 1964. In 1966 he was elected President when his country became a republic.

BANDAR ABBAS (Iran). The Portuguese having seized Hormuz (Milton's 'Ormuz') in 1507, Shah Abbas I built Bandar Abbas nearby in 1623 to replace it, and permitted an English factory. The English then assisted Abbas to destroy Hormuz, and Bandar Abbas became the chief trading city of the Persian Gulf. A century later Nadir Shah began to develop Bushire and when the HEIC's factory at Bandar was destroyed by the French in 1759 the company moved to Bushire.

BANDOENG (Java) CONFERENCE (Apr. 1955) held on the initiative of Indonesia with the support of Burma, Ceylon, Pakistan and India, included 29 Asian and African countries. The occasion was growing disquiet at the possible consequences of tension between the U.S.A. and China, and a desire to increase the world influence of the newly emerged countries of Asia and Africa. The formal agreements effected little but the discussions and especially the declaration against "colonialism and all its manifestations" have had far reaching influence. The delegations accepted the view that Russian expansion, especially in Europe, was a form of colonialism equivalent to that of France in North Africa, but accepted equally the genuineness of Chinese pacific aspirations as expounded at the conference by Chou En Lai. The declaration thus amounted to a qualified welcome to China and a rebuff to Russia.

BAND OF HOPE. A temperance organisation founded at Leeds in 1847 and organised nationally with a London H.Q. in 1855.

BANFF,-SHIRE (Scot) The town was chartered as a royal burgh as early as 1163 by Malcolm IV, but Pictish and mediaeval remains in the surrounding county show that the area had a substantial and active population long before. Because of its position on the Moray Firth Norse pirates made it a landfall and there were frequent conflicts between Norwegians and Scots until the end of the 13th cent., since when its history has been uneventful.

BANFF, Es. of. *See* OGILVIE.

BANGKA (Indonesia) was ceded to the British by the Sultan of Palembang in 1810 and exchanged for the Dutch possession of Cochin in India in 1814.

BANGLADESH formerly E. PAKISTAN is part of Bengal and became an independent republic within the Commonwealth after the Indo-Pakistani War of 1971. Until it seceded it was the more highly populated of the two parts of Pakistan, although prevented from playing its proportionate part in the political affairs of that Moslem state. Much of it is close to sea-level and has always suffered from terrible and decimating floods.

BANGOR (Ulster). St. Comgall founded a monastery here on the south side of Belfast Lough in c. 555 and was its first Abbot. His pupils included important missionaries such as St Columbanus. Comgall died c. 601 and shortly afterwards the monastery was the first Irish house to Romanise itself. It became the largest in Ireland and for a while had a European reputation.

BANGORIAN CONTROVERSY. In 1717 Benjamin Hoadly, Bp. of Bangor, preached before George I and also contended in print (on the basis of the text "My Kingdom is not of this world") that Christ had not left any authority to anyone in this world. It seemed to follow that civil government had no authority over the church (save perhaps in an emergency) and perhaps also that no member of the church, even a bishop, had any authority over any other. This created a widespread and bitter controversy; the lower house of Convocation prepared to launch an attack on the bishop as subverting church and state. To avoid this Convocation was prorogued and not, in fact, recalled for over a century.

BANISTER, John (1630-79), composer and violinist. Charles II liked his playing, sent him to France to study, and made him master of his band when he returned in 1663. He lost the place in 1667 but set up on his own, and in 1672 organised the first public concerts in Europe at his house in Whitefriars, London.

BANK CHARTER ACT 1844. See BANKING-5; BULLION COMMITTEE (1810).

BANKES, Sir John (1589-1644), a distinguished lawyer, became M.P. for Wootton Basset in 1624 and for Morpeth in 1628. He opposed the royal position in the tunnage and poundage debate of 1629, but received preferment, becoming Att-Gen. to P. Charles in 1630 and King's Att-Gen. in 1634. At this time he bought Corfe Castle. In 1637 he led for the Crown in the Star Chamber against Prynne, Williams and others, and against Hampden in the *Case of Shipmoney*. In Jan. 1641 he became Chief Justice of the Common Pleas and also served as temporary speaker of the Lords.

He followed the King to York and then to Oxford, and though he favoured a compromise he was steadfastly on the King's side; he contributed substantial sums to the King's War funds while his redoubtable wife, **Lady MARY,** defended Corfe Castle for three years against the parliamentarians. He was a privy councillor from 1641 and so continued until his death at Oxford. He was widely respected even by his enemies for his ability, moderation and integrity.

BANK FOR INTERNATIONAL SETTLEMENTS (Basel) was created to deal with German reparations payments after World War I and generally to deal with operations between central banks. It started business on 20th May 1930, its capital being guaranteed in equal shares by the central banks of Britain, France, Belgium, Italy and Germany and also two bank consortia of Japan and America. The Japanese connection was severed in 1948 and most of the American shares have passed to European holders. As a result the bank is really a European institution: and it became in 1947 the agent for the internal European balancing operations required under the Marshall Plan and in 1950 for the European Payments Union of the Organisation for European Economic Co-operation.

BANK HOLIDAYS. When the Bank of England and the clearing banks are closed, bills of exchange cannot be presented or cleared. During the 18th cent. the Bank closed on about 40 (red letter saints' and anniversary) days in the year. The commercial inconveniences resulted in these days being gradually reduced so that by 1834 only 4 remained. Lord Avebury's Act of 1871 prevented further reductions by providing that the banks were to close on days specially appointed by Proclamation, and four particular days namely *in England* Easter and Whit-Monday, the first Monday in Aug. and Boxing Day, and *in Scotland* Christmas and New Year, the first Mondays in May and Aug. and Good Friday. In 1968 the first Monday in Sept. was substituted for that in Aug. and New Year's Day became an additional day in England. With occasional variations these practices continue.

BANKING. (1) The simpler banking practices carried on under the Romans by money changers, survived in the East after the fall of the Western Empire, and soon spread westwards again as trade revived. In the 13th cent. most major Italian cities had pawnbrokers, money changers or deposit bankers, and the crusading orders, particularly the Templars, provided public safe deposits.

(2) At the end of the cent. the unprecedented category of merchant bankers appeared in N. and central Italy, as large partnerships. Initially they served only the merchants of their own towns, but as the latter dealt mainly through the N. European fairs, these bankers funded dealings at these fairs. Money lent at one fair would be repaid at another, and so the bankers were the suppliers of credit: but they made their profits from exchange transactions rather than by discounting borrowers' promises. They spread along the western trade routes to Aragon, the Languedoc and the Low Countries, so that by the 14th cent. at Bruges one in thirty is said to have had a bank account and in the 15th 30% of the population of Barcelona had dealings with banks.

(3) Italian merchants and their banking practices were found in England under Henry III and Edward I. Italian bankers ("Lombards") became major lenders to the Crown. The Riccardi of Lucca advanced some £400,000 between 1272 and 1294, and the Florentine Frescobaldi about £150,000 between 1296 and 1310. The Peruzzi and Bardi of Florence were lending to English and French govts. at the end of the 13th cent. and became so unpopular that in 1339 Edward III repudiated his debts to them. Habitual govt. dishonesty has led to many bank failures since that day, notably the Fugger disaster of 1548-52 and the Welser crash of 1614.

(4) Modern banking began with the foundation of the Banco della Piazza di Rialto at Venice in 1587 and the Bank of Amsterdam, modelled upon it, in 1609. Both these institutions lasted until the early 19th cent. In England the older form was carried on by the de la Poles and Sir Thomas Gresham, but the modern English banking system originated with the City Goldsmiths; their deposit receipts were circulating as a type of currency in the 17th cent. and very soon they were issuing bank notes by way of loan. They suffered from the usual round of govt. defalcations, especially under Charles II.

After the revolution the coincidence of public mercantile ambition and royal financial difficulties led to the foundation of the **Bank of England** in 1694. It made a large loan to the govt. in return for its charter. In 1697 it was given a monopoly of joint-stock banking; in 1707 it took over virtually the whole of the circulation of Exchequer Bills and in 1715 it managed for the first time the issue of a govt. loan. By 1755 it was the recognised banker of all the main govt. departments, and by 1770 the London private bankers had ceased to issue their own notes and relied on those of the Bank of England. It had thus become a central bank.

Meantime private banking developed rapidly as the central bank became more dependable after 1750. Such banks could not have more than six partners and varied very greatly in usefulness. Crashes were common; nevertheless, especially in the provinces they were an essential element in the financing of the industrial revolution. For example, Taylor and Lloyd financed much of the prosperity in Birmingham, and eventually developed into Lloyds Bank. These country banks continued to issue their own notes and the country bank note was virtually the only paper money circulating outside London until after 1830.

(5) The wars of 1793 to 1815 led to further developments. The Bank of England was forbidden to honour its notes in gold in 1797, and thereupon increased its note circulation. This and war finance produced an inflation in which foreign exchange rates fell and the price of bar gold rose above the mint price. The result was a govt. inquiry; the leading academic economists Malthus, Ricardo and Thornton convinced the committee that inflation was directly related to the volume of the note circulation. It followed not only that the bank ought to regulate its issues in harmony with the general condition of the economy, but that no one else should be able to interfere with its ability to do so. The Bank Charter Act of 1844 separated the trading and issuing functions of the Bank of England and provided for the gradual erosion of the country bank note issues. *See* BANK NOTES.

An important characteristic of English banking which gave it a lead over continental systems was that the courts treated cheques as negotiable instruments and so made large scale deposit credit possible. This in its turn led to the wholesale discounting of foreign bills; in the mid-19th cent. London became the banking centre of the world. The tidal flow of money and credit increased the importance of the Bank of England as a reserve and central bank. Bank rate manipulations and open market operations became a feature of its methods after 1844, and in 1890 it was the Bank of England which rescued Baring Brothers from failure by raising a guarantee fund.

(6) The effect of these events was to produce closer co-operation between the Bank of England and the private banks. Private joint stock banking had been lawful since 1833 but bank amalgamations became common only after 1890. The clearing bankers committee was established in 1911. By 1914 the system consisted of only 16 major banks to whom the Bank of England could and did give polite hints on policy through the committee. When it was nationalised in 1946 these became formal directions and the Bank began to supervise the banking system. It was not wholly successful as the fraudulent affairs of the Bank of Credit and Commerce International (1990) and Barings (1995) showed.

BANK NOTES. The exclusive privilege of issuing bank notes in England and Wales, other than by banking partnerships of six persons or less, was restricted to the Bank of England in 1800, but the Country Bankers Act of 1826 permitted private banks to do so outside a radius of 65 miles from London. The Bank of England alone was allowed to compound annually for stamp duty on bank notes by the Bank Charter Act of 1844, which also forbade any banks formed after the Act to issue notes. The last private English note-issuing bank, Fox Fowler and Co., of Wellington (Som) was taken over by Lloyds Bank Ltd in 1921. The liability of the Bank of England to make payments in lieu of Stamp Duty was abolished in 1929. The Currency and Bank Notes Act, 1954, required the Bank to make a fiduciary issue of £1575M, but gave the Treasury power to vary the amount by Treasury Minute, which must be laid before Parliament.

Certain Scottish banks were still issuing notes up to a total of £20.8M in 1994.

BANK RATE was the rate of interest at which the Bank of England lent money. It effectively controlled general interest rates, the level of credit and investment and the strength of sterling in relation to other currencies. It was, and, under other names, is the first recourse of govts seeking to influence the economy. It was renamed **MINIMUM LENDING RATE** after 1972, and later still **BANK BASE RATE.** The differences are technical rather than real.

BANKRUPTCY is a process whereby the state takes possession of a debtor's property and shares it out between the creditors in accordance with rules of priority and equity between them; it generally involves a change in the status of the debtor who while bankrupt cannot hold public office or be a company director, or do business without disclosing his bankruptcy. There has never been a Common Law on bankruptcy, and the need for rules was first discerned in the two great Tudor periods of land and trade speculation, by which time it had become the ineffectual practice to imprison most kinds of debtors, with the result that the dishonest concealed their assets, purchased a comfortable prison life and waited for creditors to compromise, while honest debtors could not work to repay their debts. Hence the most threatening creditors were paid first, regardless of equity. 16th and early 17th Privy Councils sometimes imposed settlements and there was legislation in 1542, 1571, 1604 and 1623 with many later amendments. In 1825, during a depression, an Act, though subsequently repealed, laid down the main lines of present legislation which, after many intervening statutes and amendments, are to be found in the Insolvency Act 1989. A false imputation of bankruptcy was held libellous in 1842.

Always open to abuse, the system worked adequately as long as there was a moral consensus, but was considerably abused after World War II when it was inadequately policed. Less scrupulous business people accumulated debts while transferring assets at heavily discounted prices to other persons or companies under their control. Theoretically the rules made it possible to reopen such fraudulent transactions. In practice the expense and difficulty left many defrauded creditors with only small proportions of their entitlements.

BANKS, Sir Joseph (1743-1820) Bt. (1781) wealthy botanist, visited Newfoundland; helped to finance Cook's expedition and accompanied him round the world (1768-71). Botany Bay (N.S.W.) was named from the variety of plants which he found there; visited Iceland in 1772; Pres. of the Royal Society (1778-1820) and P.C. from 1797.

BANKS, Thomas (1735-1805), sculptor and pupil of Peter Scheemakers, executed works at St. Petersburg and in Westminster Abbey and St. Paul's. He was a friend of Home Tooke and, on that account, suspected of treason.

BANKSIDE (Southwark, London) was a pleasure area facing the City across the Thames and early occupied by fairs, taverns, brothels and bull and bear baiting rings. Theatres (The *Globe, Rose, Swan* and *Hope)* were erected under Elizabeth I. It began to decline as an entertainments' centre at the turn of the 17th-18th cents. In the 19th railways were built across it in various directions with large stations (London Bridge and Waterloo), and after World War II a power station was built opposite St. Paul's cathedral though hotly opposed by the Chapter. This opened in 1952 and was extended until 1970. The Royal Water Colour Society transferred its gallery to Bankside in the same year, and the Shakespeare *Globe* Trust started to build a renewed *Globe* theatre in 1980. In 1999 the power station was converted for the Tate Gallery.

BANNERET, KNIGHT, rode with his arms on a small square banner, while his inferior, the Knight Bachelor, used a triangular penant. The Banneret was paid twice as much as the bachelor and commanded several bachelors' followings or a large squadron of his own. He was perhaps, comparable with the modern major.

BANNOCKBURN, B. of (24 June 1314). Robert Bruce had driven the English out of all Scotland save Stirling Castle whose surrender if not relieved, was promised for the 24 June. Edward II assembled a large army for the reconquest, and his first objective was the relief of the castle. The battle was therefore fought a mile or two to the south of it.

The English force consisted of armoured cavalry, archers and infantry. The Scots, who were fewer, consisted mostly of pikemen and a body of light horse. On 23 June the English van under Robert de Clifford appeared and, because time for the relief was short, crossed the marshy Bannockburn rivulet and pressed towards the castle. Bruce had anticipated this and had encumbered the ground with pits to trip horses and posted a flanking force under Moray to drive them back. His plan succeeded, and the English were also worsted in two other skirmishes arising out of attempted reconnaisances of the main Scottish position. At nightfall therefore, both sides encamped: the Scots on higher ground just over a mile north of the stream, the English astride it with most of their troops on the south side.

Next morning the English were faced with the choice of losing Stirling Castle or fighting then and there. Time being on Bruce's side, he did not move and they were forced to cross the river and deploy on ground too restricted for their full force. When the confusion and crowding of the deployment was at its height Bruce launched three of his four forces ("battles") of pikemen down hill to attack. Desperate fighting ensued. The pikemen were galled by the English archers who, however, were dispersed by a charge of Bruce's cavalry. The English front line held on but the space behind was crammed with supporting troops who could neither move forward to reinforce the front nor move aside to allow it to retreat nor make space for a cavalry charge. The English armoured cavalry was thus effectively immobilised all day. When English disorganisation and exhaustion seemed complete Bruce led in his fourth battle and broke their front. The collapse which followed was materially assisted by a charge of spectators and camp followers who had been watching from a neighbouring bill. Many of the English were unable to get back across the marshy stream and were either caught and killed, or drowned. Edward II escaped but most of his army was lost. Scottish casualties were light and Stirling Castle surrendered at once. This battle ended English mediaeval attempts to conquer Scotland.

BANTRY BAY (Ireland). This sheltered deep anchorage, an important point of entry to Ireland, was the focus of much naval activity: **(1)** On 11 May 1689, the squadron covering the landing of a French force to assist the Irish Jacobites was unsuccessfully attacked by the English Admiral Herbert. **(2)** In Dec. 1796 a French expeditionary force against Ireland reached Bantry Bay in disorder and was compelled by storms to return to France. **(3)** It was used as a British Atlantic patrol base in World War I.

BANTU. This word is used in three distinct senses. **(1)** The speakers (regardless of culture) of any one of 400 or so Bantu languages which prevail almost everywhere in Southern Africa south of the 5th parallel north. **(2)** A short form of 'Interlacustrine Bantu' meaning the tribes inhabiting the areas around and between the great African lakes. These are not all Bantu speaking, but had a certain common culture, and strong monarchies. **(3)** Particularly in S. Africa, any coloured person who is not of European, Asian or Hottentot descent, regardless of language or culture.

BAPTISTS (1) hold that membership of the Church can only be conscious and voluntary; baptism is the symbol at once of agreement with its doctrines by the individual, and of acceptance of him by the Church. Accordingly only baptism of a responsible adult can be valid.

(2) Modern Baptist Churches derive their origin from English separatists under the influence of continental ANABAPTISM. In 1609 John Smyth, a separatist exile in Amsterdam, founded a gathered Church whose members underwent adult baptism. Led by Thomas Helwys, a group from Smyth's Church returned to London and founded the first Baptist Church in England in 1612. Helwys, who was soon arrested and died in prison, put forward one of the earliest arguments for total liberty of conscience in his *A Short Declaration of the Mystery of Iniquity.*

(3) The movement spread, but in 1633 it split between the 'General Baptists' who believed in free will and therefore in the general mission of the Church, and the 'Particular Baptists' who held in the Calvinist manner that only the particular elect could attain salvation, and that therefore there was no purpose in freely preaching the gospel. The two groups did not reunite until 1891. In spite of its divisions, the Baptist movement emerged from the Interregnum and the intermittent persecution of the post-Restoration period, as one of the three major Nonconformist denominations alongside the Congregationalists and Presbyterians.

(4) The influence of these earnest people had been out of proportion to their numbers or social position. John Bunyan, the author of *Pilgrim's Progress*, is often described as a Baptist although much of his work was conducted amongst Independents and he stood for local associations of Baptists and Paedobaptists. The now universal Anglican custom of hymn singing was a Baptist invention. Catherine Sutton's collection of hymns was published in 1663; Benjamin Keach introduced them to the London congregations in the following years and the habit later inspired Isaac Watts and the Wesley brothers.

(5) Like other Nonconformist Churches the Baptists lost a number of individuals and congregations to rationalism and Unitarianism in the course of the 18th cent., but enjoyed a renaissance with the Christian revival of the late 18th and early 19th cents. Their evangelical influence became world-wide. Led by William Carey (1761-1834) a group of Northamptonshire pastors founded the Baptist Missionary Group in 1792, and as a result Joseph Hughes (1769-1833) of London formed the British and Foreign Bible Society in 1804. This was of immense importance in the development of linguistics as well as colonial history.

(6) In the 19th cent. Baptism spread to most countries so that in 1905 the Baptist World Alliance was formed with headquarters in Washington.

BARALONG AFFAIR. On 19 Aug. 1915, the German submarine U.27 was about to destroy the British steamer *Nicosian*, when the Q-ship *Baralong* attacked and sank the U.27, part of whose crew escaped to the *Nicosian*. The *Baralong*'s boarding party killed these men, apparently to prevent them destroying the *Nicosian*'s cargo of mules. The American muleteers made accusations of inhumanity to the American press, and the British govt. offered to submit to an international tribunal provided that British accusations of German inhumanity in three other cases were also investigated. The Germans refused. The episode was a significant event in the Anglo-German competition for the support of American opinion in World War I.

BARBADO[E]S (W. Indies) was visited by the Portuguese before 1518, and by 1536 it had apparently been depopulated. It was first claimed for England by Capt. John Powell in 1605 and colonised some twenty years later after James I had given a charter to Sir Wm. Courten. He sent settlers under Henry Powell (brother of John) who founded Bridgetown in 1628. Meanwhile the charter lapsed and Charles I in 1627 granted a new one to Lord Carlisle. Accordingly Barbados was held for the King by Lord Willoughby of Parham in the Civil War until captured in 1652.

The Instrument of Surrender ended *de facto* proprietary rule, and set up a governor, council and assembly with control of taxation vested in the legislature. At the Restoration, the proprietors claimed their rights under the patent of Charles I, and these were compromised for a 4½% duty on exports which lasted until 1838. Subject to this the constitutional system of the colony remained unchanged until 1954 when a form of ministerial responsibility was inaugurated by convention.

The history of Barbados has mostly been peaceful. There was some disorder at the liberation of the slaves in 1834 and an attempt to federate the island with others led to rioting in 1876. The colony did not escape the difficulties which overtook the Caribbean territories in the world depression of the 1930s and in common with other islands there was rioting in 1937.

BARBAROSSA (Ital = red beard) **(1)** The sobriquet of the Emperor Frederic I of Hohenstaufen, who was elected in 1152 and drowned in Asia Minor in 1190 on the Third Crusade. **(2)** Also of the Barbary pirate admiral Khair-ed-Din who became Turkish beglerbeg of Algiers in 1518 and captured Tunis in 1534. In 1536 he became C-in-C of the Turkish fleet, and died at Constantinople in 1546. **(3)** The code name of the German operational plan for the invasion of Russia which was put into effect on 22 June 1941.

BARBARY (1) is called after the Berbers of Morocco and Algeria, where most of them are now called Kabyles. The much larger coastal area known as the Barbary States extended from the Egyptian frontier to the Atlantic and comprised (from East to West) the territories (beyliks) of Tripoli, including Benghazi, Tunis, Tlemçen and Algiers together with the Kingdom of Morocco, whose corsairs mostly sailed from Salee opposite Rabat.

(2) The Barbary corsairs operated roughly from 1490 until 1840 and constituted an important economic and social burden on European commerce and settlement. They raided all the Christian populations along the Mediterranean and penetrated as far as the English Channel. Open coastal villages were often moved inland as a result, and there were many English charities for the redemption of their captives. A number of factors made all this possible. The spread of Turkish power along the African coast, at the end of the 15th cent., coincided with the flight of the Moors from Spain and these Moors provided many of the first crews. The doctrine of the Holy War or *Jehad* provided a moral backing alike for the Moorish desire for revenge, and the Turkish desire to exploit it. In the 16th cent. the corsairs formed an important element in Turkish naval strength. *See also* MORISCO etc.

(3) By 1595 profitability, especially at Venetian expense, had made religion a thin pretext. The Anglo-Spanish peace of 1603 deprived English seamen of their favourite prey. Hence many, even whole ship's crews, joined the corsairs.

(4) Europe was distracted by the wars which followed the Reformation, so that the naval powers only

intermittently had resources available to deal with the problem, and as the power of the Ottoman Sultanate declined, the Beys became increasingly unruly until, in the late 18th cent, Turkish suzerainty amounted to little more than a right of appointment – usually exercised in favour of the most likely claimant – on the spot.

(5) Blake operated against the corsairs in 1655 and there were uncoordinated French, Dutch, English and Venetian expeditions throughout the 18th cent. Nevertheless by 1750 the beys conducted foreign affairs much as they pleased, and levied protection money (called "tribute") on traders and trading states. The grumbling tolerance of this situation gave rise to some curious diplomatic arrangements. To give the protection of his flag to his corsairs against international action for piracy, a bey would regularly declare war against any Christian states capable of being milked; this did not disturb the rights of certain European powers, who by treaty were entitled to ransom their captured subjects and who maintained permanent consular missions at the local court to do so, war or no war. By the end of the century even the Americans were paying the tribute, but in 1801 (their navy being disengaged) they attacked Tripoli and in 1812 Algiers. In 1816 and again in 1824 a British fleet bombarded Algiers, but the corsairs were finally put down in the 1830s when the French occupied Algeria. *See* SHIPS, SAILING.

BARB[ARY] HORSES, whose purest breeds are found in Morocco, were introduced early into Spain and the Netherlands, but the earliest pure bred introduction into Britain was probably a gift by Ferdinand of Aragon to Henry VIII. These horses formed a large element in the ancestry of the later English thoroughbred. The Godolphin Arabian may have been a Barb.

BARBER-SURGEONS. A decree of the Council of Tours (1163) articulated the ecclesiastical view that the shedding of blood was incompatible with holy office, and so minor surgery came to be practised by laymen, particularly barbers. Professional surgeons emerged later. The London Barbers had a guild from 1308, the surgeons from 1368, but the barbers continued to practice surgery. The two guilds came to an agreement on surgical practice in 1493, but kept their separate identities until 1540, when the Company of Barber-Surgeons was formed by Act of Parliament.

BARBICAN. An outwork to a mediaeval fortified gate. By the late 12th cent. it was the practice to build them as a safeguard against surprise and bombardment. This continued with increasing elaboration e.g. the gatehouses of such castles as Bristol (c. 1220), Lincoln (1224-5) and Shrewsbury (1233-4). Later barbicans were virtually independent sub-castles.

BARBICAN (London), takes its name from the gates to London Wall which is just to its south. Devastated in World War II, the rebuilding of the area was long obstructed by communist provoked strikes. Between 1960 and 1982, however, offices, theatres and over 2000 flats were built, two of the blocks of flats being 43 storeys high

BAREBONES or BARBON. (1) Praise-God (?1596-1680) was an earnest London leatherseller whose activities as a preacher and anti-royalist attracted attention: he was summoned by Cromwell to sit in the Nominated Parliament (q.v.) which met in July 1653. Though he seems to have taken no part in the proceedings this body was later known as Barebones' Parliament. After the restoration he made no secret of his opinions, and was twice briefly in custody. See COMMONWEALTH. **(2) Nicolas (?-1698)** was probably the son of Praise-God. He was a considerable speculative builder, but is remembered as the originator of fire insurance after the Great Fire of London in 1666.

BARBOUR, John (c. 1320-95), Archdeacon of Aberdeen by 1357, later studied at Oxford and Paris and was then employed by K. Robert II in his court and Exchequer. He wrote *The Bruce* (c. 1375) a metrical history of Robert I in the Lothian English dialect and modelled on French metrical narratives. He also wrote the *Buik (Book) of Alexander* (c. 1368). Several other poems have been uncertainly attributed to him.

BARBUDA. *See* ANTIGUA.

BARCELONA, SIEGES OF. In the 17th and 18th cents. Barcelona was the largest and richest city in Spain, but its Catalan population was restive and separatist. In 1705 the allies against Louis XIV resolved to oust the Bourbon Philip I and put the Austrian Archduke Charles (Charles III) upon the Spanish throne. An expedition was fitted out at Lisbon under the E. of Peterborough and Prince George of Hessen-Darmstadt who as governor had made a popular defence of Barcelona in 1697 against the French. It was resolved, after discussions, to enter Spain through Barcelona which was attacked by sea and land in Aug. 1705 and captured in Oct. A French counter offensive followed: in Apr. 1706 the city was invested by Tessé and a French fleet. A desperate resistance was organised by Charles III who held out just long enough to be relieved by the English fleet under Adm. Leake. Tessé withdrew with heavy losses in men and material to France.

BARCLAY'S BANK originated with the banking activities of the goldsmith John Freame, who took his brother-in-law James Barclay into partnership in 1736. Some of the Barclays were quakers and had connections with other quaker businesses. The modern bank arose through fusion in 1896 with a total of 19 other banks, many of quaker affiliation. The most important were Bouveries', and Ransom's (London), Gurney's (Norwich) and Backhouse's (Darlington), all old-established. During World War I it acquired the United Counties, the London and Provincial, the South-Western and many other smaller banks. The present name dates from 1925. *See also* BANKING-4.

BARDI. *See* BANKING-3.

BARDS were Celtic poets, singers and minstrels who commonly resided in princely and noble households. The bard's principal function was to praise God and his patron, whose genealogy he was expected to know. This connection with genealogy was, in a largely oral culture, politically important. The chief Bard of a Welsh principality was called the PENCERDD. He attained the office by competition and was highly honoured. When the principalities were destroyed (1536), the bards organised circuits for visiting the houses of the gentry of princely descent, and their genealogical skills helped to preserve the memory of old families. The bardic assemblies (Eisteddfodau) now assumed importance as a means of regulating and training bards, especially those at Caerwys in 1523 and 1568, but the system broke down in the 17th cent. civil war. It was artificially revived for literary purposes in 1822. *See* DRUIDS; EISTEDDFOD; LYON; KING OF ARMS.

BARFLEUR and LA HOGUE, Bs. of (29 May 1692). After the Jacobite collapse in Ireland, Irish troops were concentrated around Le Havre in Apr. 1692 for a direct attempt on England. The French Mediterranean and Brest squadrons were to unite under Tourville and convoy the troops across. The Mediterranean squadron was stopped by bad weather but after some delay Tourville was ordered to sail without it. In the interval the English and Dutch fleet had had time to unite, so that when Tourville's squadron met them off Cape Barfleur they had 90 ships against his 44. He managed after nightfall to extricate his ships, but some had sustained serious damage especially to their rigging.

Tourville now retreated southwards as fast as the crippled state of his fleet would allow, with the allied pursuit not far behind all day. Twenty of his ships came successfully through the Race of Alderney and got into St Malo. Fifteen were unable to make the passage and took refuge in the open roadsteads of Cherbourg and La Hogue where Rooke's English squadron attacked and burned them.

This battle set the seal on the English revolution of 1688; damaged French prestige by demonstrating that Louis XIV had not the power to restore a R. Catholic to the English throne; and ensured the subordination of Ireland to Britain for two centuries.

BARHAM, Adm. Charles Middleton (1726-1813), 1st Ld. (1805), first came to public notice in 1761 for his services to trade protection in the West Indies. After routine commands he was Comptroller of the Navy (1778-90). He also became M.P. for Rochester (1784) and Rear Admiral in 1787. In 1794-5 he was one of the Lords of the Admiralty and was promoted Admiral in 1795. On the resignation of Lord Melville, Middleton, though nearly eighty, became First Lord on 1 May, 1805. He was thus in charge of the Admiralty during the Trafalgar campaign. This was fortunate: he was a practical sailor in all types of ships, besides having long experience of Admiralty staff work and policy; and he knew the sailing conditions in all the waters from Corsica to the West Indies where the rival fleets operated. The dispositions which he was able to order calmly and at short notice, were precisely those most certain to frustrate Bonaparte's intentions. He left office on the change of govt. in Jan. 1806 and retired.

BARING. Well-known English family descended from **Johan** Baring of Hamburg, who started a cloth business near Exeter in 1717. His sons **Francis** and **John** founded the London firm of Baring Brothers in 1770. The most distinguished members of the family were **(1) Sir Francis (1740-1810)** a director of the HEIC and M.P. from 1784 to 1806, who was a strong supporter of Pitt and is said to have died the richest merchant in Europe; **(2) Alexander, 1st Ld. ASHBURTON (1774-1848),** who developed the firm's S. American interests and was an M.P. from 1806 to 1835; **(3) Sir Francis, 1st Ld. NORTHBROOK (1796-1866),** joint secretary of the Treasury, Ch. of the Exch. and First Lord of the Admiralty; **(4) Edward Charles, 1st Ld. REVELSTOKE (1828-97),** who was head of the firm when the S. American crash happened in 1890 *(see* ARGENTINA-6); **(5) Maurice (1874-1945)** journalist, diplomat, critic, poet and wit; **(6) Evelyn, 1st E. CROMER (1841-1917),** virtual ruler of Egypt from 1883 to 1907; **(7) Rowland, 2nd E. (1877-1953),** Lord Chamberlain from 1922 to 1939; **(8) George (1918-), 3rd E.,** Gov. of the Bank of England from 1961 to 1966.

BARKER FAMILIES. (1) (a) Sir Christopher Barker (?-1549) was Garter King of Arms from 1536 to 1549. His great-nephew **(b) Christopher (?1529-99)** was Queen's Printer and was succeeded in that function by his son **(c) Robert (?-1645). (2) (a) John (1771-1849)** was British pro-Consul and Consul at Aleppo from 1799 until 1825, and Consul-Gen at Alexandria from 1825 until 1829. He not only introduced vaccination into the Middle East but also by means of his botanical garden near Antioch introduced many oriental plants and trees to England and western plants and trees to Syria where he improved the quality and variety of the fruit and also culture of cotton and silk. His son **(b) William Burkhardt (?1810-56)** was a distinguished orientalist who began the study of Turkish in Britain. **(3) (a) Samuel (1686-1759)** his son **(b) Thomas (1722-1809)** and their relative **(c) William Higgs (1744-1815)** were all Hebraists.

BARKING (Essex) had a wealthy double monastery founded by Erkenwald, Bp. of London, in c. 666. It was destroyed by the Danes in about 870 and refounded by K. Edgar in 970. The large city church of Allhallows, Barking by the Tower was in 1385 appropriated to the monastery, of which nothing now remains.

BARLOW, Sir George (1762-1846), the Indian revenue expert carried through the Bengal Land Settlement under

Shore and Cornwallis; he became Chief Secretary in 1796, a member of the Council in 1801 and provisional Gov. Gen. in 1802. On Cornwallis' death in 1805, Barlow temporarily succeeded him: but was superseded in 1807 by Lord Minto. He was compensated with the governorship of Madras, where he antagonised the army, and by his lack of tact and his ill manners caused a mutiny among the Company's officers. This was firmly suppressed. He retired in 1821.

BARMOTE COURTS are ancient courts regulating leadmining and related rights in the High Peak (Derbys.) and at Wirksworth.

BARNACLES. About a dozen species of these creatures, all of pre-human origin, have long been important because they foul the underwater parts of marine installations particularly wooden ships on long voyages (e.g. to India). Speed might be reduced by as much as 50-70 miles a day. This constituted an important burden on commercial economics. In the late 18th cent. barnacles were countered by copper sheathing ships' bottoms. This was expensive but reduced the rate of fouling, protected the wooden structure and added as much as 30% to a ship's useful life. Metal is not by itself immune to such fouling but can be protected by special paints.

BARNARD CASTLE. See DURHAM-6.

BARNARDISTON, Sir Samuel (1620-1707), a Levant merchant and Dep-Gov. of the HEIC from 1668 to 1670, became involved in a quarrel between the Houses of Parliament. The Company had seized a ship of one Skinner as infringing its monopoly. The Lords awarded damages against Barnardiston; the Commons voted the award illegal. The Lords put him in custody for contriving a libel of their House. The Commons voted these proceedings illegal too.

In 1672 with this record Barnardiston stood for parliament in Suffolk but, though he received a majority of votes, the Sheriff (Soames) sent up a double return because he was in doubt about the qualifications of some of the voters. The Commons pronounced in favour of Barnardiston, who then brought an action in the King's Bench against Soames for malice, and obtained damages. On a writ of error, the Exchequer Chamber and later the Lords reversed the judgement, but these proceedings established the exclusive right of the Commons to pronounce on elections.

He sat thenceforth in all the parliaments until 1701 and steadily supported the Whigs. In 1681 he was foreman of the grand jury which threw out the bill against Shaftesbury. In 1684 he was tried for seditious libel before Jeffries and heavily fined. In 1690, however, he was a prominent member of the Committee which for the first time made an effective audit of the public accounts.

BARNARDO, Dr Thomas John (1845-1905) of Spanish and German extraction, was converted during a protestant revival in Dublin in 1862, and thereafter spent much of his spare time evangelising. In 1866 he entered the London Hospital (Stepney) as a missionary medical student. In the cholera epidemic of 1866-7 he became obsessed with the condition of destitute children and abandoned his missionary calling in order to devote himself to them. In July 1867 at Stepney Causeway he founded the East End Juvenile Mission from which 'Dr Barnardo's Homes' developed. In 1887 his financial management was attacked. He was exonerated, but handed over the properties to trustees.

BARNARDS INN. See INNS OF COURT AND CHANCERY.

BARNATO, Barnett Isaacs (1852-97) was educated at Spitalfields. In 1873 he went to S. Africa as a conjurer. He assumed the name of Barnato there and became a Kimberley diamond trader. By 1880 he was able to establish his London diamond firm of Barnato Bros. In 1881 he floated his mining co. at Kimberley and in 1888 he joined up with Cecil Rhodes' De Beers Co. He also sat in the Cape Assembly for Kimberley in 1888 and 1894. In 1895 he seems to have been the chief market-rigger in the boom in Kafir (S. African gold mining) shares. By a series of misjudgements he was left with more stock on his hands than he could support and jumped off a ship on the way to Cape Town.

BARN ELMS (Barnes, Nr. London) was a fashionable country walk and a well-known duelling place in the 17th and 18th cents.

BARNES, Thomas. See WALTER, JOHN-2.

BARNET, CAMPAIGN AND B. OF (1471). Warwick ("The Kingmaker"), now middle aged, invaded England in 1470 and drove Edward IV to take refuge with Charles the Bold, D. of Burgundy. The latter financed a return expedition which crossed from Walcheren to Ravenspur (Yorks) in Mar. 1471. Edward marched on London and the rival armies met at Barnet (Herts) in a fog on 14 Apr. Warwick's troops attacked each other by accident and this gave rise to cries of 'treason'. Part of his army was defeated elsewhere in the fog. Co-ordination was lost and Warwick's own wing was overwhelmed. He was killed while looking for a horse.

BARNETT, Samuel Augustus (1844-1913) and his wife **Henrietta (1851-1936).** He was vicar of St. Jude's Whitechapel from 1872 to 1894 and together they started the Children's Country Holiday Fund (1878), formed the Whitechapel Art Gallery (1901) and Toynbee Hall, of which he was the first Warden, and (from 1910 to 1914) Clement Attlee secretary.

BARODA (CITY now VADODARA) and STATE was an important Maratha principality founded in about 1721 by Pilaji Gaekwar (properly GAEKWAD). It consisted of scattered territories in Gujarat and Kathiawar. By 1800 its ruler was at war with his overlord the Peishwa, and in 1802 the British guaranteed his independence. Thereafter its history was unimportant save for the deposition of the Gaekwad Mathar Rao for gross misgovernment in 1875. It acceded to India in Aug. 1947, achieved responsible govt. in Sept. 1948, and was merged with Bombay in May 1949.

BAROMETER. The first measurement of atmospheric pressure by means of a barometer was made in 1643 by Torricelli, a pupil of Galileo. See METROROLOGY.

BARON originally seems to have meant "man" in relation to or in comparison with others, e.g. in law-French "baron et feme", man and wife. In particular it was used of one who held of a feudal superior by an honourable service such as knight service or serjeanty. In this sense the term was interchangeable with "homo", man. Thus a feudal superior became entitled to homage, the oath to be his man, from each of his barons; the barons or free tenants of a manor were collectively known as the homage, and the manor court held by a lord for his free tenants was called (in England) the Court Baron. By the early 13th cent. the word usually meant one of the King's barons and from the early 14th cent. only the greatest of these, whose standing entitled them to be summoned personally to parliament; this latter usage resulted in barons becoming the lowest grade of the peerage. Meanwhile the older and slightly wider connotation of King's Barons survived in a variety of local ways: thus the highest officials and the judges of the Court of Exchequer were until 1875 called Barons of the Exchequer and were headed by a Chief Baron. The Cinque Ports still elect barons who carry the canopy at the sovereign's coronation; and the freemen of certain anciently important towns such as London and York, which were considered to hold directly of the Crown, were called barons.

In Scotland a baron court or court baron was a court of justice held by a lord or proprietor for his barony; where the court was held for a burgh of barony he usually appointed a bailie to preside who was then known as a baron-bailie.

A few academic writers use the term 'Honorial Baron' to denote a leading military tenant of one of the Crown's principal tenants-in-chief. Such people were often called 'barons' and were socially indistinguishable from their lords. They qualified for their status mostly by birth and social position as long as they had some real military substance such as an ability to put at least five knights into the field. *See* FEUDAL SERVICES.

BARONET. James I, to raise funds for the English colonisation of Ulster, invented baronetcies (which were hereditary) and sold them for £1095 apiece. The first baronet (1611) was Sir Nicholas Bacon. Baronetcies of Ireland, for similar purposes were created in 1619; and baronetcies of Nova Scotia to aid Scottish colonisation were created in 1624. As there were not enough Scots candidates, English and Irishmen became eligible in 1633. In 1638 new Scottish creations ceased to carry land grants in Nova Scotia, and at the Union of 1707 separate creations for England and Scotland ceased, and the dignity became purely honorific. This development was unpopular. Gentlemen felt obliged to purchase baronetcies in order to maintain their family precedence in the county where hitherto it might have been taken for granted. This was a matter of some importance in a hierarchical society.

BARONS WAR. (1) This civil war lasted from May 1263 to May 1267, though according to Edward I's interpretation of the Dictum of Kenilworth, it began legally on 4 Apr. 1264, and ended on 16 Sept. 1265. **(2)** Pope Alexander IV released Henry III from his oath to the Provisions of Oxford (1258) by a bull published in England in 1261. In the ensuing two years the King gradually freed himself from their effects: but as he did so, opposition grew. At the same time certain younger barons, mostly Lords Marcher had formed an alliance against the Lord Edward (the future Edward I) who had important interests in Wales. Led by Roger Clifford they invited Simon de Montfort, E. of Leicester, over from France to help them. He met them at Oxford in May 1263 and decided to exploit both their power and the popular discontents. An ultimatum was made to the King and rejected. The barons then made widespread attacks on the King's supporters in the countryside. These events created anti-baronial feeling, but the barons secured the Welsh border and the Severn Valley. Earl Simon marched to Reading and thence to the Cinque Ports, whilst the Londoners attacked the Queen. In July the King capitulated and the barons took over the govt.

(3) Both sides now asked K. Louis IX to mediate, but he accepted as if it were a submission to arbitration. He heard the arguments on both sides, and in Jan. 1264, in an award known as the *Mise of Amiens* pronounced for the King on all points. Earl Simon was temporarily incapacitated at Kenilworth by a riding accident; the Mise astonished and confused the Barons, and the Lord Edward struck quickly from Wales, drove the Barons across the Severn and met the King at Oxford in 1264. The Barons rallied at Northampton: here on 6 Apr., the Lord Edward captured some of the more prominent leaders. Earl Simon avoided Northampton, and while the royalists were plundering in the midlands, reached London. He and his powerful ally Gilbert of Clare then laid siege to Rochester Castle. The King, who could not afford to be cut off from his kinsmen or lands in France, came south in force. The two armies met at Lewes on 14 May, and the King and Edward were captured after a half-day battle. In Aug. a peace was signed at Canterbury which provided for the readoption of the most significant of the Provisions, and the Lord Edward became a hostage for their implementation. At Louis IX's suggestion the Pope had in the previous Nov. appointed a legate, Card Gui of Sabina, to deal with English affairs. Gui was now at Boulogne demanding admittance to England. The barons temporised and in Aug. he summoned them to admit him, or to justify their refusal. He also demanded the renunciation of the Provisions, which they naturally refused. On 21 Oct. he excommunicated and interdicted the upholders of the Provisions. He was then recalled to assume the tiara as Clement IV. This ensured that the Papacy was still against Earl Simon.

(4) The Earl was in difficulties: besides the opposition of the Church, his vigorous govt. had alienated some barons, and the promotion of his friends and sons had caused jealousy among others. The Marchers and Gilbert of Clare changed sides. A conspiracy was formed. In May 1265 the Lord Edward made an arranged escape, from the custody of Gilbert's brother Thomas, to Ludlow where he, both Clares and the Marchers raised an army. Earl Simon delayed in order to make a deal with Llywelyn ap Gruffydd, the Welsh prince whom the Marchers were meant to control: this did not improve Simon's reputation and as the prince temporised it gave him no new troops. Meantime in July the royalists had, by seizing the Severn crossings, nearly penned him into South Wales, but he made a forced march past Hereford, forded the river at Kempsey on 2 Aug. and arrived at Evesham. Meantime the Lord Edward was at Worcester, and Simon de Montfort the Younger, marching slowly from the south to join his father, had reached Kenilworth Priory. There on 1 Aug. Edward surprised him and captured most of his barons and knights. On 4th he attacked the father, now without hope of reinforcement, at Evesham. The Earl and his principal supporters fell fighting.

(5) On 16 Sept, all acts done in the King's name since the B. of Lewes having been annulled, a general peace was proclaimed, but the next day an ordinance was made confiscating the lands of Earl Simon's supporters. Some of these were still safely in arms at Kenilworth, Southwark, the Cinque Ports, the Isles of Ely and Axholme and Chesterfield. The ordinance drove many who had laid down their arms to take them up again. The so-called 'disinherited' prolonged the war.

(6) On the royalist side wiser counsels soon prevailed. Clement IV's new legate, the distinguished and well informed Card. Ottobuono Fieschi, arrived in Nov. Those bishops who had supported Earl Simon were suspended. The Lord Edward negotiated compromises at Axholme, Sandwich and Winchelsea. In May 1266 the army and Legate moved to Kenilworth, where the settlement known as the *Dictum of Kenilworth* was worked out with his help and proclaimed on 31 Oct. 1266. Kenilworth then surrendered. *See* STATUTE OF MARLBOROUGH.

BARONY. *See also* BARON. **(1)** In England a barony was the territory within which a baron or other Lord had acquired or usurped powers usually exercised by the crown. Such territories were rare save in the Marches, and they were seldom compact. **(2)** In Scotland a barony was any large freehold estate regardless of the proprietor's rank, carrying with it civil, and till 1747, criminal jurisdiction. **(3)** In Ireland a barony was a subdivision of a county equivalent to an hundred or wapentake, and originally representing the territory of a local chief at the time when he submitted to the English. Such territories previously belonged not to him but to his clan or sept, and in Irish eyes such submissions were suspect.

BAROQUE. A post renaissance artistic, especially architectural, style originating in Italy at the end of the 16th cent. It is characterised by the use of exuberant decoration and colour upon a fundamentally classical base, but in such a way that the decoration itself forms a coherent design embracing the whole composition. The usually accepted origins are Carlo Maderna's (1556-1629) façade of Santa Susanna at Rome, and the nave of St. Peter's (1607). The ideas then spread quickly; in particular they were taken up in the Low Countries by Peter Paul Rubens and his friends. One, Francart, built the Béguinage church at Malines, and this prepared the way for Hesius' church of St. Michael at Louvain.

The close contacts between Britain and the Low Countries brought the style across the water, but for only a limited time and in a somewhat sober version. Inigo Jones (1573-1652) knew all about it, but his banqueting hall at Whitehall (1638) shows how much he kept it to himself. Sir Christopher Wren (1632-1723) was equally restrained even at his grandest (St. Paul's Cathedral 1675 onwards; Greenwich Hospital 1698). Sir John Vanbrugh (1664-1726), as one might expect from his writings, was less inhibited, and in Blenheim Palace (1705), Castle Howard and elsewhere he showed himself the only notable English exponent of baroque in the continental manner. His pupil Thomas Archer (1668-1743) was the last.

BAROTSE-LAND (Zambia) A tribal federation which apparently reached the Zambesi in the 17th cent. They were dominated by one of their number, the Aluyi, till 1838 when the Kololo, Basuto migrants driven northwards by unrest in Zululand replaced them. In 1864 the Aluyi, now called Malozi, defeated the Kilolo and re-established themselves. Missionaries began to work in the area in 1884, and in 1890 and 1900 treaties were signed with the British S. Africa Co, which obtained mining rights. The Malozi received tribute from the rest, and most of the work on the land was done by a class of serfs, who were not, however, slaves. Labour shortage and the demands of the Co. resulted in pressure to liberate the serfs, and so make them available for work away from home. This was done in 1906. In 1924 the country was placed under the Colonial Office, and in due course became part of an independent Zambia.

BARR, Archibald (1855-1931), a Scottish inventor and prof. of engineering, invented, with Stroud, the naval range-finder and other instruments for gun-control which revolutionised early 20th cent. naval policy.

BARRACOON. A Portuguese and later a Dutch slave compound or depot in W. Africa. cf BAGNIO.

BARRIER ACT 1697 of the General Assembly of the Church of Scotland was designed to hinder speedy changes in church law by requiring that Acts involving such changes should be approved both by the presbyteries and the Assembly. *See* SCOTLAND, KIRK OR CHURCH OF.

BARRIER TREATIES between Great Britain and the Netherlands were signed on 29 Oct. 1709, 29 Jan. 1713 (incorporated in the T. of Rastatt) and 15 Nov. 1715. The principle behind them was that, in return for Dutch support of the protestant succession in Britain, the British would procure an adequate military barrier to protect the Netherlands against France. This barrier was to consist of the citadel of Ghent and a number of Belgian fortified towns.

BARRINGTON. (1) John Shute (1678-1734) 1st Vist. (Ir 1720) was called to the bar in 1700. By 1705 he had come to the notice of Lord Somers, then Sec. of State, as the writer of some able papers and pamphlets on religious toleration. Somers employed him to win Presbyterian support for Anglo-Scottish union and rewarded his success with a commissionship of customs. In 1709 he inherited the estates of a relative called Barrington and changed his name. In 1715 he was M.P. for Berwick-on-Tweed, and much respected as a man of moderation and sense. He was again elected for Berwick in 1722. He was, however, expelled from the House for his connection with the Harburg Lottery scandal, and though he found many defenders he just failed of re-election and left public life. Of his ten children four are noticed below. **(2) William Wildman, 2nd Vist. (1717-93)** entered Parliament in 1740 for his father's old constituency of Berwick. He was a Lord of the Admiralty from 1746 to 1754, M.P. for Plymouth and Secretary-at-War in 1755. In 1761 he was Ch. of the Exchequer, but

preferred to become treasurer of the navy in 1762. In 1765 he again became Secretary-at-War at the King's express wish and he held this post until 1778. **(3) Dames (1727-1800)** was second justice at Chester and in his day a well known scientist. His writings induced the Admiralty to send the Phipps and Lutwidge expedition to the Arctic. He was a friend of Gilbert White. **(4) Adm. Samuel (1729-1800)** after routine commands under Hawke and Rodney went as C-in-C to the West Indies in 1778. When war broke out he attacked the French island of St. Lucia, and with a very weak squadron managed to bluff d'Estaing's much superior Toulon fleet away until the island fell. He was reluctantly superseded by Adm. Byron, and in 1779 took an able part in the battles off Grenada and Basseterre. He refused the command of the Channel fleet several times because of the jobbery prevailing in it, but in 1782 accepted a post as 2-in-C to Lord Howe. He thus took part in the fighting for the relief of Gibraltar (Oct. 1782). **(5) Shute (1734-1826)** became Chaplain in Ordinary to George III in 1760 through the influence of his brother the second Viscount. In 1769 he became Bp. of Llandaff, and was translated in 1782 to Salisbury, and in 1792 to Durham. He was notable for his charity and toleration, but inflexibly opposed to the granting of political rights to R. Catholics. A punning friend called him 'The Licensed Poacher' because on formal occasions he sometimes had to begin with the words "I, by Divine Permission, Shute..."

BARRINGTON alias WALDRON, George (?1755-?+) a remarkable pickpocket, moved in Society. He relieved Prince Orloff of a diamond snuff box, and after other exploits was transported. He published a description of his voyage to Botany Bay, and the following lines have been uncertainly attributed to him:

True patriots we, for be it understood
We left our country for our country's good.

BARRISTERS-AT-LAW. (1) Dissatisfied with standards of advocacy and judicial administration, Edward I (1272-1307) encouraged or instituted the Inns of Court (Lincoln's and Gray's Inns and the Inner and Middle Temples) as training schools in the Common Law. Apprentices-at-Law (i.e. trainees) first appear in a Year Book of 1356. They were the forerunners of barristers, first so-called in the 15th cent. The term refers to the mock trials called *moots*. A trainee who made a *gaffe* was made to dance on the spot. Those who reached proficiency were *called* to sit on the raised outer or utter benches outside the bar, at which apprentices put their cases and where dancing was not possible, and were called Utter Barristers. By Q. Elizabeth I's time barristers had ousted attorneys from the Inns of Court precincts, and senior barristers called (from their position in the moots) Benchers, acted as the Inns' governors and set up the preliminary training schools called Inns of Chancery. From the Utter Barristers were chosen the Serjeants-at-Law who, on appointment by the Crown, left their Inn and joined one of the two serjeant's Inns. Serjeants had a monopoly in the Court of Common Pleas, and they alone could be judges.

(2) James I introduced the degree of King's (or Queen's) Counsel; the holders in due course developed into leading advocates in courts other than the Common Pleas. K.C.'s could become judges by becoming serjeants for one day beforehand. Alternative educational opportunities at Oxford and Cambridge caused the Inns of Chancery to decline.

(3) When the courts were amalgamated into a single Supreme Court, the serjeants' monopoly in the Common Pleas lapsed; judges no longer needed to have been serjeants and no new ones were appointed. The surviving Inns of Chancery disappeared. The serjeants sold their Inns in 1877; Lord Lindley, the last English serjeant died in 1921. An important consequence was that barristers who became judges had nowhere to go and stayed in their own Inn whose governing body they came increasingly to dominate. Hence in 1883 barristers who had hitherto needed no unified organisation of their own formed a Bar committee, which was succeeded in 1894 by the General Council of the Bar. In 1966 the four Inns delegated most of their educational and disciplinary functions to a Senate of the Inns (see INNS OF COURT). This arrangement proved unsatisfactory and in 1985 the General Council in effect took back its main representative functions.

(4) The tendency of the judges to monopolise the government of the Inns became, with the large increase in their number, increasingly marked after World War II. From 1989, however, this was checked by self-denial. Meanwhile the number of barristers was increasing (from about 1500 in 1948 to over 7000 in 1995) and so were the numbers of solicitors (about 60,000 by 1992) and the latter began to agitate to be entitled to invade the barristers' monopoly in the higher courts. Though no fully coherent reasons for this were ever advanced, by 1992 they had virtually succeeded.

BARROSA, B. of (Feb. 1811) arose from an Anglo-Spanish operation under Lapeña to relieve Cadiz which was being besieged by the French under Victor. The allied force was ferried from Cadiz to Tarifa and then marched back to take the French in the rear. The road to Cadiz ran along a peninsular whose landward end was blocked by a forest with the Barrosa ridge behind it. The Spanish troops cleared the French out of the forest and the combined force then marched for Cadiz. 7000 French troops now began to occupy the ridge but when information of this reached Sir Thomas Graham, the commander of the British component, he decided to storm the ridge with the 4000 men readily available before the French could properly establish themselves. This was done and the way to Cadiz was cleared.

BARROW, Isaac (1630-77). Originally a theologian, became Prof. of Greek at Cambridge in 1660, then Gresham Prof. of Geometry in London (1662) and Lucasian Prof. of Mathematics at Cambridge in 1663; eventually he became Master of Trinity in 1673. He wrote *inter alia* on optics, geometry, and papal supremacy, and was acknowledged as a great inspiration by his famous pupil, Isaac Newton, for whom he resigned the Lucasian chair in 1669.

BARROW IN FURNESS (Cumbria). Furness Abbey and Piel Castle lie nearby, and there were veins of a very pure iron ore. The Abbey had Irish connections, but the place remained a tiny village well into the 19th cent, despite its large trade in the ore. In 1841 the first ironworks was built and the railway came in 1846. Large scale steel making by the Bessemer process began in 1859 and shipbuilding in 1873. The local ore being virtually exhausted by 1950, the industries were thenceforth supported on ore and scrap brought from elsewhere.

BARROWS. It is arguable that if the houses of the dead were modelled on the habitations of the living, the natural cave was the pattern for the megalithic passage grave, which was often covered with a mound and when so covered was the earliest form of barrow. The earliest examined in Britain date from c. 3400 B.C.

Megalithic barrows date from the period 2500-1800 B.C. They were designed for mass burial and are either *round* or *long*. The round barrows occur in Brittany, Jersey, Ireland and Orkney, but not in England. Megalithic long barrows on the other hand are very common, and consist of three types. Nearly all have a passage covered with earth; the earliest types have an entrance at the east end, and burial chambers branching off on either side; then the east entrance became a dummy while the real concealed entry was made elsewhere; and finally side chambers degenerated into cists or niches.

There were also long barrows constructed as if they concealed a passage but which in reality had burial chambers let into them along their sides. The builders of these long barrows were people of a Mediterranean race who migrated from France and the Peninsula to Ireland and Western Britain. When the 'Beaker Folk' arrived, they built round barrows of which 18,000 are known, and these are therefore later than the long barrows. These are of various types, but mostly have a shallow, possibly ritual, ditch round them and a pit containing cremated remains. Sometimes the ditch encloses more than one mound and mounds vary from the large or "bell" type to the flat or "disc" variety. It is believed that the disc barrows were made after the bell barrows and that they date from 1400 to 1200 B.C. when cremation came in.

Later it became common to make interments in urn fields or even to insert urns into existing barrows, but in the period 500 to 300 B.C. there was a type of iron age barrow which was round and small. These are usually found in groups close together.

The Romans sometimes buried in barrows which are steep and conical in shape. There is usually a brick chamber and the cremated remains are found in a green glass jar.

The early Saxons built barrows, some of which consisted of very large mounds of earth, containing cremated remains. With them the custom of barrow building died out.

BARRY. A family to whose talents in the sphere of building London owes much of its character. **(1) Sir Charles (1795-1860),** was an architect and built, amongst others, the Travellers and the Reform Clubs in Pall Mall, London; the Athenaeum at Manchester; and he reconstructed the Treasury at Whitehall. By far his most famous work was, however, the Houses of Parliament on which he was engaged with Augustus Pugin from 1840 until his death; **(2) Edward Middleton (1830-80),** his elder son was also an architect. He completed his father's work on parliament, designed Covent Garden Opera House and the Charing Cross Hotel, and was prof. of architecture at the Royal Academy from 1873. **(3) Sir John Wolfe-Barry (1836-1918)** was Sir Charles' younger son and an engineer. He helped Sir John Hawkshaw to build the railway bridges at Charing Cross and Cannon Street; he built extensions to the Underground, bridges at St. Pauls and Kew and many dock extensions and improvements on the Thames, at Grimsby and at Cardiff. His famous work, however, was Tower Bridge completed in 1894.

BART, Jean (1650-1702). French corsair trained under the Dutch, joined the French navy in about 1669 and made money, rank, and fame as a commerce raider, mostly from St. Malo, during the War of the League of Augsburg.

BARTHOLOMEW COTTON'S CHRONICLE was probably copied as far as 1290 from a composite Norwich chronicle which is an independent source for local events from 1264 to 1279, and from 1279 to 1284 mainly a copy of the St Edmunds Chronicle. For the years 1288 to 1298 (when Cotton died) it is again original. He was a monk at Norwich and had access to local archives. The *Continuation* is a source for the years 1290 to 1307, especially for the political conflicts in 1297. The writer shows some interest in the mercantile community, the parliamentary Commons and the baronial case against Edward I.

BARTHOLOMEW FAIRS were held on or during the week of 24 Aug. (St. Bartholomew's Day) in most large towns, but the greatest were at Smithfield (London) and at Oxford. They were always occasions of celebration, but the Smithfield fair was the main cloth exchange for England until the 15th cent, though there were also extensive dealings in cattle, leather and pewter. Its sideshows were notoriously profligate. After various 19th cent. efforts at reform, the shows were moved in 1840 to Islington, and the Fair suppressed in 1855.

BARTHOLOMEW'S DAY, St. (24 Aug. 1662). The day when about 2000 English clergy resigned rather than assent, as required by the Act of Uniformity, to everything contained in the Book of Common Prayer.

BARTHOLOMEW'S DAY, St., MASSACRE (24-27 Aug. 1572). See HUGUENOTS-7.

BARTHOLOMEW'S HOSPITAL, St. (London) was founded in 1123 by Rahere (?-1144), a prebendary of St. Paul's, who obtained a charter in 1133 and was its first master from 1137. Govt. proposals to close it were made and were still being resisted in 2000.

BARTOLIST, after the Italian jurist Bartolo (1313-57), was a person skilled in the Civil Law.

BARTOLOZZI, Francesco (1727-1815), Italian engraver, came to England in 1764, was employed in George III's library and was a founder member of the Royal Academy. He died in Lisbon.

BARTON (1) A West country term for demesne land or for a manor house. **(2)** More generally a home farm.

BARTON, Elizabeth (The Maid of Kent) (c. 1506-34). During an illness in 1525 she had prophetic trances. After recovery a small rural chapel became a popular shrine for her, but she lived at and travelled from St Sepulchre's convent at Canterbury. She became the focus of a group of priests and Observantine friars interested in resisting Reform, which was by now entangled with Henry VIII's "divorce". Her later visions and prophecies were hostile to the divorce; they transmitted them to the public and she once denounced the King to his face in Anne Boleyn's presence. In 1532 the Reforming Cranmer succeeded the conservative Abp. Warham. She was examined before him and admitted the falsity of her visions. She was executed by attainder and seven Observantine houses were suppressed as centres of disaffection. See MONASTERIES, DISSOLUTION OF – 4.

BARTON, Sir Edmund (1849-1920) was elected by the Univ. of Sydney to the N.S.W. legislature in 1879; was Speaker of the House of Assembly from 1883 to 1887 and Att-Gen in 1889. He founded the Sydney Federation League in 1893 which led to the Hobart conference of premiers on federation in 1895 and succeeded Sir Henry Parkes as leader of the Federation Movement in 1896. He led the delegation which negotiated the Commonwealth constitution in 1900. In 1901 he became the first Prime Minister of the Commonwealth of Australia, but retired from politics in 1903 to become a judge.

BAR, TRIAL AT. A criminal trial by jury in the presence of a full bench of judges, used only in cases of great moment or difficulty, such as (1904) the trial of Col. Arthur Lynch for treason, (1905) the Petition of Right on claims against the Transvaal govt. The last case was the trial of Sir Roger Casement for treason (1916). The creation of the Court of Criminal Appeal made such trials obsolete.

BARUCH, Bernard Mannes, (1870-1965) began his public career in 1916 as chairman of the Allied Purchasing Commission in the United States, and subsequently of the powerful War Industries Board. After World War I he was the American member of the Reparations Commission and the Supreme Economic Council, and as such became well known in Britain. He was much trusted by Pres. F. D. Roosevelt, and it was he who as early as 1937 made recommendations to the Senate Military Affairs Committee about wartime industrial mobilisation. Roosevelt employed him at intervals on highly confidential missions particularly to his old friend Churchill, and in 1943 he became special adviser to James Byrnes, the American war mobilisation director. During 1946 and 1947 he was a member of the United Nations Atomic Energy Commission, He gave large sums to research and charity and retired in 1947. See next entry.

BARUCH PLAN. In 1946 Dean Acheson and David Lilienthal proposed an international atomic energy authority with exclusive control of fissionable materials, and the production and custody of atomic weapons. Bernard Baruch as a member of the U.N. Atomic Energy Commission adopted this idea and added a proposal that there should be international inspection of atomic developments, and a suspension of the veto power in the Security Council on atomic matters. The proposal foundered on the opposition of the U.S.S.R. which argued that it contravened a fundamental principle of the United Nations Charter.

BASEBALL evolved from the English childrens' soft ball game now called 'rounders'. The word is found in doggerel verses of 1744, Lady Hervey's letters (1748) and *Northanger Abbey* by Jane Austen (1798). The journal of George Ewing refers to soldiers playing at Valley Forge in 1778. The first games in their modern hard-ball form were instituted by Abner Doubleday (later a general) for military cadets at Cooperstown N.Y. in 1839. The first code of standard rules for this game was drafted in 1845.

BASEL, COUNCIL OF (1431-49) was assembled in defiance of Pope Martin V and existed throughout the reign of Eugenius IV (r. 1431-47). Its assumptions of power amounted to a schism. In 1435 it purported to abolish annates and first fruits. In 1436-7 it made a compact with the Hussites and in 1439 it declared conciliar authority a dogma, and summoned Eugenius. He meanwhile held his own councils at Ferrara and Florence, and negotiated union with the Greek church (1439). As he refused the summons, the Basel Council declared him deposed. He excommunicated them, whereupon they elected the lay Amadeus VIII, D. of Savoy, Pope (Felix V). Eugenius ignored this and busied himself with Italian politics and dogma. The bulls *Exultate Deo* (1439) and *Cantate Domino* (1441) reflected the latter, his re-entry into Rome (1443) which he had been forced to leave in 1434, the former. The council by now was running out of steam and Eugenius, having secured his base, reached Concordats with German princes, and his successor Nicholas V (r. 1447-55) with the Emperor. In 1449 Felix V resigned and the attenuated council, by now at Lausanne dissolved.

BASHI BAZOUK. These irregular Turkish mounted troops were armed but not paid by the govt; they were consequently inclined to pillage civilians and became notorious in the Balkans during the 19th cent. The term also refers sometimes to a kind of mounted Ottoman provincial gendarmerie.

BASIC ENGLISH. The Orthological Institute was founded in 1927 and Basic English, developed between 1926 and 1930 by the British linguist, Charles Kay Ogden, was the first outcome of its researches. It consisted of some 600 nouns, 150 adjectives, 18 verbs and about 100 miscellaneous operative words such as 'not', making about 850 in all. By 1939 there was an international organisation which was disrupted by World War II. Sir Winston Churchill publicly supported the principle of Basic English as an international language in Sept. 1943, and the Basic English Foundation was established with the aid of a British govt. grant in 1947.

BASILDON. See NEW TOWNS.

***BASILIKON DORON* (Gr. = Royal Gift)** by James VI and I was a book on the art of govt. written for the benefit of his son Henry in 1597.

BASILISK (16th Cent.) A large brass gun.

BASING. London City Aldermanic family after which Basinghall St. and Bassishaw ward are named. They were mostly wool, and later cloth, traders and flourished from early 12th to mid-14th cent. The most remarkable was **Adam,** mayor in 1251-2, who was primarily a Household merchant.

BASING "HOUSE" (Hants) belonging to the R. Catholic M. of Winchester, comprised two rich adjacent mansions astride the London-Wiltshire road near Basingstoke. He turned them into a single royal fortress in the Civil War and partially controlled the London wool trade. He was besieged from July to Oct. 1644 when he beat off a major assault with slaughter. After the royalist disaster at Naseby (June 1645) Hampshire and Wiltshire royalists took refuge there and Cromwell besieged and stormed it (8-15 Oct. 1645). Many, including women, were massacred. The sale of the loot brought in dealers from London and lasted for days.

BASINGSTOKE CANAL. *See* TRANSPORT AND COMMUNICATIONS.

BASKEGG or BACSECG. *See* ASHDOWN, CAMPAIGN AND B. OF.

BASKERVILLE, John (1706-75), of Birmingham, described as the finest printer of modern times developed his eponymous type between 1750 and 1757 when he printed his *Virgil.* In 1758 he issued a famous edition of Milton, and as printer to Cambridge University from 1763 he produced a magisterial edition of the Bible. Beaumarchais bought his plant at his death.

BASKET. (1) Foundling hospitals left baskets out of doors to receive abandoned babies: hence *basket* for *bastard.* **(2)** Prisons similarly left baskets for people to leave food for poor prisoners.

BASRA (Iraq), port on the Shatt-el-Arab about 70 miles from the Persian Gulf, was founded as a base for Arab operations against Iran, and has mostly been oriented to that purpose. The Turks took it in 1534, and one of the governors made himself independent in the 17th cent. and opened the port to Portuguese, Dutch and English shipping. It was disputed between Turkey and Iran during the 18th cent. but finally fell to the Turks in 1779. The modern port was developed with British capital under British occupation during World War I and so it became the main port of the new state of Iraq. It remained a target of Iranian ambition and was much damaged in the 1980s war between Iraq and Iran.

BASS ROCK (Firth of Forth). St. Baldred had a hermitage here in early 8th cent and in the middle ages it was the property of the Lauders from whom it was bought by the govt. in 1671. A castle prison was then erected there; this was seized by Jacobites at the revolution, and held against William III until Apr. 1694; it was the last place to submit to him.

BASQUE ROADS (Fr), B. of (11-12 Apr. 1809) 14 French battleships were at anchor behind a boom in this anchorage near Rochefort. Lord Gambier watched them, and Lord Cochrane attacked them with explosion- and fire-ships at night. This attack itself did no damage but the French panicked and cut their cables, and 12 ran aground. Next morning Cochrane tried to destroy these helpless vessels, using his own frigate and other vessels of light draft, but Gambier delayed sending reinforcements and eight French ships got away. Cochrane, an M.P., opposed a vote of thanks to Gambier in the Commons, on the ground that Gambier had neglected to make the victory complete. Gambier demanded a court martial. A packed court honourably acquitted him and Cochrane was forced to retire.

BASSEIN (India) 28 miles N. of Bombay was ceded to the Portuguese in 1534 and was a wealthy trading centre until taken by the Marathas in 1739. The British annexed it in 1818 but the proximity of Bombay prevented anything more than a modest prosperity thereafter.

BASTIDES were small towns fortified on a square pattern by the English in Aquitaine, mostly between 1150 and 1320 as part of a policy of military and economic development, especially under Edward I. They mostly had charter privileges designed to attract settlers and to create a local vested interest in English rather than French overlordship. Their liberties were reduced and sometimes suppressed by the French crown.

BASTILLE. Originally a tower, the word also meant the castle prison in Paris (cf 'Tower of London'), to which people might be committed by arbitrary royal order. It was demolished in a popular riot on 14 July 1789, when it actually held only seven prisoners. The event became part of the revolutionary myth and July 14 the French national day. The word was used in Britain to denote a prison, and in 19th cent. social polemics, a workhouse.

BASTWICK, Dr John (1593-1654), vituperative controversialist, published his *Flagellum Pontificis* (Lat = The Priest's Whip) in favour of presbyterianism in 1633, and was fined and imprisoned by the High Commission. In prison he wrote and in 1636 published Πραξεις Των Επισκοπων (Gr. = On the Habits of Bishops), an attack on the High Commission. A year later he published his *Letanie of Dr John Bastwick,* denouncing bishops as enemies of God. For this he was prosecuted in the Star Chamber at the same time as Prynne (for his *Histrio-Mastix)* and Henry Burton. Sentenced to lose his ears in the pillory, a fine of £5000 and life imprisonment, he was released in 1640 by Parliament and returned to London in triumph. As a captain of Leicester trained bands, he was captured by the royalists in 1642, but soon released. In 1648 he reused his style in two violent tracts against Lilburne and the Independents.

BASUTOLAND (now LESOTHO). (1) In the 18th cent. several Zulu and Sesuto speaking tribes settled along the Caledon river. In the early 19th cent. their area was persistently ravaged by the Zulu Chaka and the tribes were broken up and mostly perished. The remnants were gathered together by Moshesh who retreated into the Basutoland mountains, and here Chaka was held off.

(2) Meantime Europeans, especially Boers, had been encroaching from the South and in 1833 Moshesh invited missionaries to his country to advise him. The first came from the Paris Evangelical Society and he and they co-operated loyally for many years. Boer penetration, however, continued and their Orange River colony began to expand at Basuto expense. Moshesh therefore obtained British protection in 1843. In 1848 British sovereignty was also proclaimed over the Orange River country, but abandoned six years later. Thus after 1854 Moshesh had to defend his country against the Boers, Bantu and unruly English. War was almost continuous until 1868 when Britain stepped in again to stop advances across the Caledon. Moshesh died in 1870 and Basutoland was reluctantly annexed to Cape Colony in 1871, by a govt. anxious to limit its commitments.

(3) Direct rule was not a success, and culminated in a revolt, known as the "Gun War" (1880), caused by attempts to disarm the people. This insurrection ended in 1883; the chiefs asserted their loyalty to the British Crown but asked for the withdrawal of direct rule. This was arranged in 1884. The chiefs were encouraged to rule the country in accordance with their own customs, and the descendants of Moshesh were successively recognised as Paramount. Lerotholi, a grandson, established a genuine predominance by 1898. He died in 1905.

In 1909, on the establishment of the Union of South Africa, the Basutos petitioned to remain independent, and assurances were given; these were reaffirmed in 1935 and again in 1956. The country was constituted an independent kingdom under the Lesotho Independence Act, 1966, as from 4 Oct. 1966, the Paramount Chief being recognised as King.

BATAVIA (Java) now JAKARTA.

BATAVIAN REPUBUC. *See* NETHERLANDS.

BATE'S CASE (1606). The Levant Co. had under its charter been levying an extra duty of 5s. 6d. per cwt upon currants imported by non-members of the company. It paid £4000 a year to the Crown for its privileges and was therefore indirectly a tax farmer. The outcry against monopolies forced the Company to surrender its charter, and James I thereupon collected the extra duty to compensate for the loss of the £4000. Bate, a Levant merchant, refused to pay, on the ground that this was a new tax requiring parliamentary sanction. He was sued in the Court of Exchequer in Nov. 1606 and condemned. The court held that this type of impositions could be made under the King's 'absolute' prerogative to conduct foreign policy, which implied a power to lay taxes on foreign goods.

BATES, Sir Percy Elly, Bt. (1879-1946) became deputy chairman of the Cunard Steamship Company in 1922 and chairman in 1930. In 1931 he initiated the policy of constructing the two immense liners *Queen Mary* and *Queen Elizabeth,* and in 1935 negotiated the Cunard-White Star amalgamation. The existence of these two ships influenced the strategy of World War II because they could carry a whole division at a voyage.

BATH (Somerset) (Latin AQUAE SULIS; Anglo-Saxon AKEMANCEASTER) was a Roman town, developed particularly under Agricola (78-84). The Latin name refers to Sul a local Celtic goddess. There was a Roman bathing establishment of which much remains. The town declined during the later Roman period and the Saxon invasions. It was sacked in 577 and temporarily abandoned. After a while the population returned, and an Abbey was founded in 944 by monks from St. Omer. By 973 this had reached sufficient splendour to be used for K. Edgar's coronation, and while it was being rebuilt by John de Villula of Tours (Bp. of Wells, 1088-1122) the Normans transferred the bishopric of Wells to it. The Norman church was replaced between 1499 and 1616 by a perpendicular structure. (But *see* BATH AND WELLS, SEE OF.)

Until the end of the 17th cent. Bath was primarily a local market town with, as Chaucer's *Wife of Bath* testifies, a hand weaving industry, which depended on the Cotswold and Mendip sheep runs. To this, after the accession of Q. Anne, was added a revived interest as a spa. Anne visited it herself in 1702, and it became normal for the London gentry to stay there for extended periods; the Assembly Rooms were built and social life organised in them by Beau Nash. Dr. Oliver (after whom the biscuit is named) organised the hospital. The Woods, father and son, with Ralph Allen rebuilt the town in stone in its present classical style. It became a meeting point for the wealthy and influential, especially at times when Parliament was not in session, and since the wealthy were also the patrons of literature it became essential for budding authors to go there too; hence the many literary references to Bath especially in the works of Sheridan, Smollett and Jane Austen.

The city was damaged by bombing in World War II and suffered much from neglect and municipal incompetence thereafter, but it was still in 1969 one of the most beautiful towns in Britain.

BATH. (1) *for* **MARQUESSES OF,** *see* THYNNE. **(2)** *for* EARLS OF, *see* GRENVILLE for the first creation and PULTENEY for the second.

BATH, ORDER OF THE, so called because the Knights were supposed to take a bath before their installation, was founded in 1399 but died out and was not revived until 1725. It consisted only of Knights (K.B.) until 1815, when it was organised into civil and military divisions each of three grades, the Knights of that time being given the highest.

BATH AND WELLS, SEE OF. An indirect outcome of K. Alfred's victories was the reinforcement of the church in the West of England by the partition of the see of Sherborne by his son Edward the Elder in 909 and the creation of the see of Wells out of it. Glastonbury Abbey provided most of the bishops until 1088 when the see was moved to Bath Abbey. The title 'Bath and Wells' was sanctioned by Pope Honorius III in 1219 and in 1245 Innocent IV ordered elections to be held alternately in Bath and Wells by the two chapters, the bishop being enthroned at the place of election. This continued until the dissolution of Bath Abbey in 1540, when Wells once more became the sole cathedral.

BATHILD, or BALDHILD, St. (?-680), Anglo-Saxon slave in the house of the Frankish mayor of the palace, attracted K. Clovis II whom she married in 649. From 657

to 662 she was regent for her eldest son and besides founding monasteries, campaigned against the slave trade. After a palace revolution, she was secluded in her nunnery at Chelles (q.v.).

BATHING and SWIMMING. These practices were restricted in the middle ages by superstitions about water and especially sea bathing. Sea bathing as a fashion was started by a Dr. Russell of Lewes who, in the 1750s, persuaded his patients that it was good for them, especially at Brighton where he believed the sea to be exceptionally saline. The vogue spread, and by 1787 when the P. of Wales began to build the Pavilion, it was common. George III helped by bathing (from a bathing machine to the sound of a brass band) at Weymouth in the 1780s. The railways brought many holiday makers to the seaside from about 1840, but until about 1870 men habitually bathed naked while devout ladies protested against Sunday bathing (naked or otherwise). Women seldom bathed (save at night) until bathing suits were invented in the 1850s, and by the 1880s they had imposed their habit on the men. Brighton had byelaws against 'indecent' bathing in 1896, when swimming was included in the first modern Olympics. Women's swimming was included in 1912.

BATHURST FAMILY. Many members of this prolific and long lived family have achieved public distinction. Of two brothers of the first generation **(1) Sir Benjamin (?-1704)** was gov. of the HEIC and treasurer to Q. Anne. **(2) Ralph (1620-1704)** was dean of Wells and later Pres. of Trinity Coll. Oxford. During the Commonwealth he was a member of the group of Oxford scientific men which was a germ of the Royal Society.

In the next generation **(3) Allen (1684-1775) 1st E. BATHURST (1772)** was M.P. for Cirencester from 1705 to 1712 when he was one of the twelve Tories ennobled to force the ratification of the P. of Utrecht through the Lords. He was a strong critic of Walpole, and briefly obtained minor office after Walpole's fall. He was a friend of Pope, Swift and Congreve. His nephew **(4) Henry (II),** one of 36 children, became Bp. of Norwich in 1805. Allen's son **(5) Henry (I) (1714-94) 2nd E.** was M.P. for the family seat at Cirencester from 1735 to 1754 and a supporter of the Pelhams. He also gained preferment by supporting Frederick P. of Wales and so became solicitor and then att-gen. In 1754 he became (as was usual) a Justice of the Common Pleas. After a tranquil period on the Bench he was a commissioner of the Great Seal in 1770 and then, to general surprise in view of his modest legal talents, he became Lord Chancellor until 1778 and so presided over the trial, *inter alia,* of the Duchess of Kingston. In 1779 until 1782 he was Lord President under North.

(6) Henry (III) (1762-1834) 3rd E. was M.P. for Cirencester from 1793 to 1794. He was a personal friend of Pitt and held various minor but lucrative offices from 1783 to 1802 and from 1804 to 1807. From 1807 to 1809 he was Pres. of the Board of Trade under the D. of Portland, and in 1809 he was for a few months Foreign Sec. Under Lord Liverpool he was Sec. for War and Colonies, and ended under the D. of Wellington as Lord Pres. Henry (II) had a son **(7) Benjamin (1784-1809)** who was a diplomat first at Leghorn and then at Vienna. While taking despatches from Berlin home via Hamburg he inexplicably vanished.

BATTA. See INDIAN MUTINY-2,3.

BATTENBERG or MOUNTBATTEN, P. Louis Alexander of (1854-1921) M. of MILFORD HAVEN (1917), eldest *s.* of P. Alexander of Hesse, was naturalised and joined the Royal Navy in 1868. In 1902 he became Dir. of Naval Intelligence and by 1908 C-in-C Atlantic Fleet. After a period as 2nd Sea Lord, he became First Sea Lord and in July 1914, with war threatening, decided with Churchill to keep the Reserve Fleet in commission at the end of the summer exercises. Despite this timely and peaceful mobilisation against the Germans he was forced to resign in 1914 by a press campaign which harped unscrupulously on his German background. He married a grand-daughter of Q. Victoria and was the father of the future E. Mountbatten of Burma.

BATTLE. A substantial force or a main division of a mediaeval army, usually commanded by a nobleman.

BATTLE (Sussex). The parish 6 miles N.W. of Hastings where the *Battle* of Hastings was fought. In fulfilment of a vow, William the Conqueror founded an abbey there, with its high altar on the spot where K. Harold's standard had fallen. Work was begun by monks from Marmoutier, and William took a close interest in the construction. In 1076 the Abbot received benediction there. In 1087 the church was ready for dedication and William, near death, urged his son to arrange the matter speedily, but William Rufus did not see Abp. Anselm consecrate it until 1094. The church was built on a French plan, probably with an apse surrounded by an ambulatory and radiating chapels. Much of it was destroyed in the Reformation but the façade facing the village remains and the terrace facing the opposite direction gives an excellent view of the battlefield from the English point of view.

BATTLE ABBEY ROLL, purporting to list the families who came over with the Conqueror, was probably compiled in the 14th cent. The roll itself does not now exist but there are 16th cent. versions, all said to be imperfect, in Leland, Holinshed and Duchesne.

BATTLE HONOURS commemorate special episodes in the history of a regiment, most commonly by placing names of battles or campaigns on regimental colours (if any), but other devices are used such as the back-badge of the Gloucestershire Regiment, a change of name (e.g. the Grenadier Guards for defeating the French Grenadiers at Waterloo), the extra drum horse of the 3rd Hussars to carry drums taken at Dettingen, or the oak leaf given to the Cheshire Regiment by George II at the same battle.

BATTLESHIP. *See* WARSHIP TYPES.

BATTLE, TRIAL BY. *See* COMBAT, TRIAL BY.

BAVARIA (Ger: BAYERN) and its RULING HOUSE. (1) Because of its size, location and affiliations, the Duchy of Bavaria was, from about 1550, exerting a leverage upon those major powers, namely France, Austria and later Prussia with which Britain maintained friendships or rivalries. Though R. Catholic, natural competition with their Hapsburg neighbours made its Wittelsbach rulers rely during the Reformation on Protestant allies and French subsidies, the first of which was paid in 1532; but when the Palatinate (also a Wittelsbach state) turned Protestant in 1546, Bavaria changed sides and remained mostly in the Habsburg camp for nearly a century. Bavarian power tipped the scales in favour of the Habsburgs at the start of the Thirty Years War and the Duke was made an Elector. After changing sides twice the Dukes not only kept their electoral bonnet, but emerged at the P. of Westphalia with most of the Palatinate which had belonged to James I's son-in-law.

(2) A period of reconstruction followed, but from 1700 to 1803 the country was prey to the ambitions of its misguided rulers. The Elector Max Emmmanuel, who was also gov. of the Spanish Netherlands and hoping, with French help, for much more, sided with France in the War of the Spanish Succession. This constituted a lethal strategic danger to Vienna and provoked Marlborough's Blenheim (q.v.) campaign (1704). The Elector was driven out of his country. His son, Charles Albert, tried to exploit the death of the Emperor Charles VI by having himself elected Emperor and claiming Bohemia. During the War of the Austrian Succession he was driven from his country too. His early death and the P. of Füssen signed by his successor ended the war, but Maximilian III, the signatory, died without heirs and Bavaria passed to Charles Theodore, of the Palatine Wittelsbachs, whose children were illegitimate. He negotiated with the Austrian Emperor Joseph II to cede a third of Bavaria to Austria if his children could keep the rest. The heir presumptive, Charles of Zweibrücken, supported by Frederick the Great, protested and a War of the Bavarian Succession ended in 1779 at the P. of Teschen, which secured the succession to Charles but transferred the Innviertel to Austria.

(3) At the start of the French Revolutionary Wars, the Palatinate was lost in 1792 and Moreau briefly overran Bavaria in 1795. In 1799 Maximilian of Zweibrücken succeeded Charles; an Austro-Bavarian army was defeated at Hohenlinden in Dec. 1800, and the country had to submit to the P. of Lunéville (Feb. 1801). Maximilian's new minister Montgelas now proposed a change of policy. With French help, compensation and more might be exacted at the expense of other states. In Aug. 1801, a French alliance was made at Paris, and in 1803, in compensation for the lost Palatine lands, Bavaria received 16 ecclesiastical states and 17 imperial cities. Appetite whetted, the Wittelsbachs gave important help to the French in the Ulm and Austerlitz campaigns against Britain's successive allies, and at the P. of Pressburg (Dec. 1806) received further dividends in the shape of Tirolese lands extending over the Alps almost to Verona. They were, however, unable to digest the Tirolese who, led by Adreas Hofer, remained obstinately pro-Austrian, and in two successive rebellions in 1809 chased the Bavarians out. The south Tirol was abandoned to France by the Austrians under the T. of Schönbrunn in Oct. 1808 and Bavaria, which had supported the French in the Wagram campaign, made further gains 'in compensation' for the loss of the Tirol.

(4) Bavarian support for France continued until the real military effects of Bonaparte's 1812 debacle in Russia had become evident, but in Oct. 1813, a few days before the B. of Leipzig, the King (as he had been since 1806) staged a timely desertion. For this he was in 1816 rewarded with parts of the Palatinate and the important city of Würzburg, to console him for the loss of the Schönbrunn compensations.

Bavaria was now, after Austria and Prussia, the third largest German state, and for the next half century her object was to maintain independence against the other two. As Prussian power grew, Bavaria leaned increasingly on Austria; as Austrian power waned Bavaria tried to create a third force of secondary German states as a reinsurance.

(5) In 1818 Bavaria had become a parliamentary state in which, for the most part, internal administration was in the hands of ministers, while foreign policy was conducted by the crown with ministerial help. The personal foibles of the Wittelsbachs continued to attract attention, but in a new form. Ludwig I (1825-48) was an extravagant patron of the arts (particularly abroad) with, in Lola Montez, an expensive Irish mistress who dabbled in political patronage. The Bavarian conservatives were strongly clerical; the radicals equally strongly parliamentarian. Much as they hated each other, they hated Lola Montez and the King's extravagance more. When the 1848 revolutions broke out they joined to drive him from his throne.

(6) His successor, Maximilian II (r. 1848-64) continued the policy of arts patronage, but concentrated expenditure in Munich where vast works gave employment. The reactionary von der Pfordten govt. had to be dismissed in 1859 after prolonged parliamentary struggles: Schrenk-Notzing's, which followed, adopted a cautious but practical policy of administrative and judicial reform, but this was impeded by Maximilian's death in 1864, and by the Prussian defeat in 1866 of Austria, Bavaria and her 'third force', the so-called Alliance of Four Kings. Of the four kingdoms, Hanover was extinguished and Saxony lost half her territory. A French hint at 'compensation' in the Palatinate enabled Prussia to

pose as the true maintainer of *The Watch on the Rhine* and in the uproar Bavaria, though a defeated power, changed front, supported Prussia and joined in the attack on France in 1870.

(7) In 1866 the new King Ludwig II was an unstable 20-year-old aesthete; his habits were as expensive as his grandfather's, with an additional passion for the new grand opera of Richard Wagner, who lived in Munich from 1865 to 1871. Bismarck offered an enormous bribe in the form of the looted funds (The Welfenfonds) of the Hanoverian royal family. The result, in Dec. 1870, with ministerial agreement, was a letter (drafted by Bismarck) from the King inviting the King of Prussia to become German Emperor, and an agreement whereby Bavaria kept a separate military and communications system and even a separate diplomatic service and status. These curious arrangements remained till the imperial collapse in 1918.

(8) The *Welfenfonds* were used to beautify Munich and Bayreuth and financed five fantastic country residences for Ludwig II who was becoming increasingly eccentric. In 1886 he was falsely declared insane; his ambitious uncle Luitpold became Regent for Ludwig's actually insane brother Otto, and three days later Ludwig drowned himself in L. Starnberg. Luitpold continued as Regent until his death in Dec. 1912, when he was succeeded in the regency by his son. Though Otto did not die until 1916, the new Regent was made King as Ludwig III in 1913. The dynasty was deposed on 8 Nov. 1918 just before the Berlin revolution.

BAWBEE. A coin worth sixpence Scots (halfpenny English) first struck in 1542 and named after the mint master at that time, the Laird of Sillebawby.

BAWDY COURTS was the popular name for episcopal courts which were still dealing with a variety of sins, especially sexual, at the beginning of the 17th cent. They excited some of the opposition to episcopacy at the bottom of the Root and Branch Petition, and Sir Henry Vane (the younger) tried to have their powers transferred to mixed courts of lay and clerical commissioners.

BAXTER, Richard (1615-91), presbyterian divine ordained in 1638, became a headmaster at Dudley. Moving to Bridgnorth (Salop) he refused the "et cetera oath" and his studies in this connection led him to reject episcopacy, as it then was. In 1641 he became curate at Kidderminster and famous as a preacher and social worker there. Though no republican, he supported Parliament in the Civil War, yet opposed the political and religious Independents. He preached much to the troops, mainly at Coventry. After the war he worked at Kidderminster until 1660, strongly advocating political moderation, which in that immoderate age earned him many enemies. In particular he repudiated the Solemn League and Covenant, opposed the Engagement, and sought to unite ministers of good will in the 'Association'. He also denounced the Regicides and argued against the deposition of Charles II. When he left for London, he was already in close contact with the party of the Restoration, and by his vigorous preaching to the City and the Commons played a prominent part in it. He became one of Charles II chaplains but of course refused a bishopric. He took a prominent part in the Savoy House Conference (1661).

When the Act of Uniformity was passed (May 1662), he left the Church of England and for a while retired, but as soon as the Conventicle Act expired he began to preach again and attracted, like a modern television personality, immense audiences. This made him obnoxious to the increasingly powerful High Churchmen and R. Catholics; he was harried from meeting house to meeting house and, during 1685 and 1686 imprisoned. On his release he entered into the protestant coalition which overthrew James II.

His immense influence arose from his skill in the use of words (he was a prolific and popular writer as well as a preacher), his saintly life, intellectual reasonableness, and inflexible determination. Moreover he was a person whom everybody liked.

BAYEUX TAPESTRY is not a tapestry but a long narrative embroidery in wool on linen, belonging to the town of Bayeux (Normandy). Probably commissioned by Bp. Odo of Bayeux (?-1097) William the Conqueror's half-brother, traditionally for his new cathedral at Bayeux, it was more probably made to decorate the great hall of one of his castles. It shows, in such details as the spelling of place names, that it was made by English craftswomen, who were then famous.

It pictures the events justifying and leading up to William's invasion of England and his victory (of which Odo was an eye witness) at Hastings, and as it concentrates on such matters as feudal loyalty and treachery it seems to be comparable with the mediaeval *chansons de geste.* The Tapestry is, however, unique as a secular narrative in the form of an 11th cent. strip cartoon.

BAYONNE (S. Fr) at the junction, four miles inland, of the Rs. Adour and Nive, has long been the principal French Biscay port S. of Bordeaux and the capital of the French Basques. In the 10th-11th cents. it maintained a precarious quasi-autonomy, supported on its carrying trade, the importation of iron and the export of timber, and a long-lasting armaments industry. (*See* BAYONET.) It passed, with the rest of Aquitaine, to the English kings, as Dukes, in 1199 and reverted to the French crown only in 1451. It was the scene of the controversial meeting between Catherine de' Medici and the D. of Alba in 1565 (*see* HUGUENOTS). several times refortified, notably by Vauban in the 17th cent., it fell to Wellington in 1813.

BAYONNE DECREE. *See* PENINSULAR WAR-2.

BAYONET was probably invented at Bayonne early in the 17th cent. It brought about, in its successive forms, a revolution in military organisation and tactics. The plug bayonet enabled the same man to act *either* as pikeman or as musketeer. In 1688 the French began to arm their troops with the socket bayonet, which enabled the same man to act as both at once. The older mixed units of pike and musket disappeared between 1660 and 1680. The socket bayonet was universally adopted by 1700.

Efficient bayonets were the foundation of the British system of platoon firing, so effective against the French in the Napoleonic Wars, because of the safety which they afforded in line when part of a force was reloading. The adoption of machine guns and machine pistols towards the end of World War I rendered them tactically obsolete.

BAZALGETTE, Sir Joseph William (1819-91). A great but neglected Victorian, became chief engineer of the Metropolitan Commission of Sewers in 1852 and of the Metropolitan Board of Works which superseded it in 1855. He designed and built the vast London sewerage system (1859-65), the Victoria and Albert Embankments (1860-70), the Chelsea Embankment (1871-4), Northumberland Avenue, and Putney and Battersea Bridges. Save for the last, all these tremendous works, despite the 100-fold increase in the weight of traffic, were in use in 2000.

BAZAS, BAZADAIS. *See* AQUITAINE-11.

BAZOOKA. Infantry anti-tank rocket weapon first used by American troops at the North African landings in Nov. 1942.

B B C. *See* BROADCASTING.

B C P = Book of Common Prayer.

BEACHY HEAD, B. of (10 July 1690). In the struggle for Ireland after James II's flight, neither side tried to interrupt the other side's communications: French reinforcements regularly reached James through Cork, and English came in through Belfast and Carrickfergus. In June 1690 William III reached Ireland, while simultaneously the French main fleet under Tourville came up the English Channel in search of the combined English and Dutch. This led to a crisis: in the absence of the King and army and with an insecure political situation it was deemed necessary to order the English Adm. Herbert to fight. In ignorance of William's victory on the Boyne (1 July), Herbert, with 58 ships, attacked Tourville's 75.

In very light winds, the allies bore down slowly in line abreast upon the almost stationary French. The allied van (right) and rear (left) came to close range, but the centre maintained a distance. This enabled Tourville to send some of his disengaged centre to double the allied van which was soon crushed. At this moment the wind dropped altogether. The allies, better informed of the local tides, anchored but the French were carried out of action. The allies were, however, so badly damaged that when the tide changed in the evening, it was resolved to destroy their 16 damaged ships and escape. Herbert, accordingly, made all sail with the rest eastwards, was half-heartedly pursued by the Downs, and reached safety in the Thames.

The battle, which might, if Tourville had exploited it properly, have decided the Irish war, served only to prolong it for a year.

BEACONSFIELD. *See* DISRAELI.

BEAKER FOLK. *See* BRONZE AGE.

BEALE, Dorothea (1831-1906) principal of Cheltenham Ladies' College from 1858 until her death was one of the most influential advocates of women's higher education and suffrage. Her evidence in 1865 to the Endowed Schools Commission was a turning point in the education of English girls, and her subsequent successes were caused mainly by her willingness and ability to put her views into practice. Thus while carrying on her Cheltenham principalship with distinction, she found time in 1885 to create a training college for women secondary school teachers (St. Hilda's, Cheltenham), and in 1893 St. Hilda's Hall, Oxford, to give trainee teachers the advantage of a period at Oxford. This developed into the well-known women's college.

BEAR AND BULL BAITING. The worrying of a tethered animal by dogs. This was a popular, often tumultuous spectacle which, especially in Tudor times, took place at fairs and at the Southwark Bear Gardens, which acquired a proverbially uproarious reputation. In 1591 the Privy Council closed the Southwark theatres on Thursdays to give the baitings a competition-free day. The practice was suppressed in 1835.

BEAR AND RAGGED STAFF. The badge of the Es. of Warwick, is the origin of the name of many public houses called 'The Bear'.

BEARDSLEY, Aubrey Vincent (1872-98), tubercular artist, achieved a scandalous success by his illustrations to the *Morte d'Arthur* (1893), *Salome* (1894), contributions to the *Yellow Book,* and through his open representation of a hitherto socially suppressed eroticism. His drawings were of great simplicity and power, and influenced firstly by the pre-Raphaelites and then by the Japanese Ukiyo-e content in *Art Nouveau*. His style and the critical uproar which surrounded it permanently changed the direction of West European art.

BÉARN (France) was a French Pyrenean frontier area. Under the Catalan House of Monçada it maintained a precarious independence against the English and French Kings especially during the reign of Gaston VII (1229-90). After his death it passed to the Counts of Foix, through them to Navarre and finally to France at the accession of Henry IV.

BEARSTED, Sir Marcus Samuel (1853-1927) 1st Vist. (1921) formed the Shell Transport and Trading Company in 1897. He was Lord Mayor of London in 1902-3, when he was concerned mainly with shipping oil between Russia and the Far East. In 1907 he negotiated the amalgamation of the British and Dutch oil interests in Borneo and during World War I managed the business so that despite Dutch neutrality most of the oil came into British rather than enemy hands. He was made a peer in 1921.

BEATING BOUNDS. Boundaries were important because of the existence of local and lucrative jurisdictions, and because, later, rating and poor law were administered upon the geographical basis of parishes only. In the absence of good maps or surveyors, the recollection of boundaries was ensured by making periodical perambulations round them, in which, for obvious reasons, children always took part. Memorable ceremonies were staged, which might be agreeable, such as a feast or almsgiving at important points, or disagreeable such as the thrashing of a child at each boundary mark.

BEATLES. A group of four singers who pioneered a vigorous and loud type of popular music which attracted huge popularity in the 1960s and became known as the *Liverpool Sound*. Their style was unsuccessfully imitated by less talented groups all over the English speaking world. They separated in 1970.

BEATON or BETHIUNE (1) Abp. James (c. 1470-1539) and his nephew **(2) Card. David (1494-1546)** were Abps. of St. Andrews (James 1522-39, David 1539-46). Each was a determined, even cruel, upholder of R. Catholicism in Scotland, and each rose to be among the most distinguished men of his day. James was made Abbot of Dunfermline in 1504 and held the rich Abbacies at Kilwinning and Arbroath at the same time. He became Lord Treasurer in 1505, Abp. of Glasgow in 1509, Chancellor in 1513 and, on becoming Abp. of St. Andrews and Primate in 1522 he resigned Arbroath to David, who by Papal dispensation did not even take orders till 1525.

During the minority of James V, Albany the regent spent much of his time in France, leaving the govt. in the hands of a commission of regency in which James was the richest and most influential personality. Meanwhile David was a permanent Scots representative at the French court; he was appointed Lord Privy Seal in 1528 and after being consecrated Bp. of Mirepoix (France) became a cardinal in 1537. On his uncle's death he succeeded to the primacy.

As elsewhere, there was an intimate relationship between political activity and religious persuasion; the traditional Scots policy of estrangement from England and alliance with France was mainly supported by the R. Catholics, and the Beatons, by training and position were its natural champions; they used their diplomatic and personal skills as well as the power of their church against their protestant and political opponents. David negotiated the marriage of James V first with Magdalen of France and then with Mary of Guise and, under his uncle's primacy and his own, several distinguished protestant divines, including Patrick Hamilton (1528), were burned.

Self protection and the progress of the reformation in England naturally inclined the protestant, mainly Calvinist, party to bring about a revolution in Scottish policy by encouraging friendship with England. At the unexpected death of James V in 1542 the estates set aside a commission of regency naming the cardinal co-regent with the earls of Argyle, Arran and Huntly, and appointed Arran, a protestant, as sole governor. The cardinal was arrested. Treaties of marriage and alliance were then negotiated with England but meanwhile Beaton had secured appointment as papal legate *a latere* and Seaton, his custodian, returned him to his fortress at St. Andrews. With this rare combination of military and spiritual power he raised a great force, took control of the Queen and in Sept. 1543 compelled Arran to change sides and repudiate the English treaties. The English declared war but their operations in 1544 were ineffectual.

Card. Beaton was now the most powerful person in Scotland and he determined to settle accounts finally with the protestants. Early in 1546 their most popular preacher, George Wishart, was condemned before a provincial assembly at Glasgow and burned in March. This was the preliminary to a move designed to eliminate the power of the rising protestant nobility, particularly in Fife where the Leslies were influential. Before the Cardinal could carry his designs any further, John and Norman Leslie and their feudatory Kirkcaldy of Grange murdered him in his bedroom at St. Andrews on 29 May 1546.

This murder eliminated the most powerful and able of the R. Catholic leaders at the height of his success, and is commonly regarded as a turning point in Scottish history. His nephew **(3) James (1517-1603)** was the last R. Catholic bishop of Glasgow.

BEATTY, Adm. of the Fleet **Sir David (1871-1936) 1st E. BEATTY (1919)** saw aggressive service on the Nile and during the Boxer Rising in China, and in 1910 became the youngest flag officer for a century. He was Winston Churchill's naval secretary in 1912, and took command of the Battle Cruiser Squadron in 1913. During World War I he was responsible for the partial victories at Heligoland Bight (Aug. 1914) and the Dogger Bank (Jan. 1915); but his handling of the battle cruisers at Jutland (31st May, 1916) and his influence on their training have been the subject of controversy ever since. When Jellicoe became First Sea Lord in Dec. 1916, Beatty succeeded him as C-in-C of the Grand Fleet, and accepted the surrender of the German High Seas Fleet in Nov. 1918. From 1919 until 1927 he was First Sea Lord; as such he opposed without conspicuous success, the reduction of the navy, but established a Fleet Air Arm separate from the R.A.F. and took the first steps to establish a fortified base at Singapore.

BEATTY v GILLBANKS **(1882).** The Queen's Bench Division held that a public assembly which is in its nature lawful, does not become unlawful because others who disagree with its objects, threaten and execute violence upon its members.

BEAUCHAMP (Pron: Beecham). **(1) William (?-?1212)** was Lord of Elmley and hereditary castellan of Worcester. His son **(2) Walter (?-1236)** commenced the family's association with Wales by marrying a daughter of the marcher Roger Mortimer in 1212. He was also sheriff of Worcestershire in 1216. Having declared for Louis of France, he was excommunicated and the marchers seized his land. This was doubtless a friendly seizure for he was instantly reconciled and restored. He witnessed the Great Charters of 1216 and 1225 and was a justice in eyre in 1227-8. By reason of the marriage of his otherwise undistinguished son **(3) William** to the heiress of the Es. of Warwick, his grandson **(4) William (?-1298)** became **E. of WARWICK.** He was an active commander in Wales and the father of **(5) Guy (?-1315) 2nd E.,** who received Scottish grants from Edward I in 1298 for his conduct at the B. of Falkirk and was employed in military and political capacities in Scotland down to Edward I's death. He was well acquainted with Edward II's proclivities and passion for Gaveston. He adhered to the party representing the policy of the late King, helped to procure Gaveston's banishment in May 1308, and alone opposed his recall in 1309. By Oct. 1309 he had the support of Thomas of Lancaster, who took over the leadership of the opposition, together with the Es. of Arundel, Lincoln and Oxford. They refused the royal summons to York but came in arms to the Westminster meeting (Mar. 1310) where he was appointed one of the Ordainers. He was sufficiently involved in administering reforms to excuse himself from service on a Scottish campaign in the summer.

He helped to seize Gaveston on his return in Jan. 1312 but refused to take part in his murder in June. A peace was finally forced on the King in 1313 and Guy again refused to take part in a Scottish campaign which culminated in the disaster at Bannockburn. This left him much respected and in a key position but a year later he suddenly died. His son **(6) Thomas (1315-1401) 3rd E.** married Margaret Ferrers of Groby. He followed Guy in opposition to the King. In the 1379 Parliament he was appointed, by common consent, governor to the young Richard II. In 1385 he joined with the Es. of Derby and Gloucester in the embryonic opposition to Richard and in 1387, with Gloucester and Arundel, he appealed the King's advisers of treason, defeated a royal force at Radcot Bridge and, with others, summoned the 'Merciless Parliament' of 1388 which exiled, imprisoned or executed the King's chief supporters.

The King gradually gathered a new following, and in 1397 Gloucester (his uncle), Arundel and Warwick were arrested and themselves, with some justification, charged with treason. Warwick pleaded guilty and threw himself on the King's mercy. His honours and estates were forfeited and he was banished to the Isle of Man where he was harshly treated by the governor William le Scrope. He was liberated when Henry IV took the throne in 1397. He was a disagreeable character and attempted to deny his confession of guilt in 1397, but was silenced by Henry and he also urged Henry to put Richard to death.

His cousin's grandson **(7) John Ld. BEAUCHAMP and KIDDERMINSTER (?-1388)** was steward of Richard II's household. Impeached by the Lords Appellant, he was executed. The *s.* of **(6), (8) Richard (1382-1439) 4th E.** was notable, even in that age, for his courage and chivalry and, though a godson of Richard II, was an important supporter of Henry IV, for whom he defeated Owen Glyndwr and fought at Shrewsbury in 1403. He was absent from 1408-10 on a magnificently conducted pilgrimage to Jerusalem during which he was received in honour by many European potentates. Through his military association with Prince Henry who, as Henry V, made him deputy of Calais (1414) he became a negotiator with Burgundy and France. Meanwhile he was also involved in Henry's anti-Lollard policy and led an English mission to the Council of Constance. He returned in time for the Agincourt campaign, but was sent from Harfleur via England to Calais where, in 1416, he received the Emperor Sigismund and the D. of Burgundy.

He was now employed in military capacities, dividing the Norman command with Clarence, and being responsible for the capture of Caen, Domfront and eventually Rouen (Jan. 1419) and then in 1420 Aumle and Melun. He had also arranged the preliminaries of the T. of Troyes and the marriage of Henry V and Katharine of France, but was still on campaign when Henry died in 1422.

Henry bequeathed the care and education of the baby Henry VI to him and he carried out his duties assiduously until the King's coronation in 1429. Thereafter he resumed the role of diplomat and soldier, arranging a Scottish truce in 1430, capturing the French general Pothon de Xantrailles at Beauvais in 1431 and protecting Calais from the Burgundians in 1435. He became Lieut. of Normandy and France in 1437 and died at Rouen.

BEAUCHAMP. (Pron: Beecham). Of these distant kinsfolk of the Es. of Warwick **(1) Sir Walter (?-?)** was a lawyer and speaker of the Commons in Mar. 1416. Of his sons **(2) William (?-?)** became **Ld. St. AMAND** in right of his wife (1449) and **(3) Richard (?1430-81)** became Bp. of Hereford in 1448, and was translated to Salisbury in 1450. In 1475 he was appointed Chancellor of the Order of the Garter, being in constant attendance on the King. He became additionally dean of Windsor in 1478, and procured the incorporation of the chapter.

BEAUCHAMP. *See* LYGON.

BEAUCLERK. Surname given by Charles II to his son by Nell Gwynn **(1) Charles (1670-1726) D. of St. ALBANS (1684).** He had a distinguished military career in the imperial army against the Turks in 1688 and with William III in the Landen Campaign of 1693. Among his descendants were **(2) Amelius (1771-1846),** a successful and eccentric admiral; **(3) Aubrey (1710-41)** a naval captain killed at Cartagena; and **(4) Topham (1738-80)** the friend, after 1757, of Dr. Johnson, who married **Lady Diana Spencer,** the divorced wife of Vist. Bolingbroke, a scandalous society figure. She was also an artist.

BEAUFORT, Sir Francis (1774-1857). See METEOROLOGY.

BEAUFORT FAMILY named after John of Gaunt's castle in Champagne where his three children by Katharine Swynford, his mistress and from 1396 third wife, were born. They were legitimated by Parliament in 1397. As the D. of Lancaster's children they were half-brothers to K. Henry IV, uncles to Henry V and great-uncles to Henry VI, and played commensurately important roles in Lancastrian politics, but by an Act of 1407 they were barred from the throne. See GENEALOGY.

The most distinguished of those in the table were **(1)** Gaunt's third son **Thomas (?-1427) D. of EXETER for life** (1416) Adm. of the North in 1403, who in 1405 took a leading part suppressing the northern revolt. He was Lord Chancellor from 1410 to 1412 and from 1416 he was appointed Lieut. of Normandy where he had campaigned since Agincourt (1415). He spent the years 1418 and 1419 fighting again in Normandy and in 1420 negotiated the T. of Troyes. In 1421 he and Clarence were defeated at Baugh, and in 1422 he was one of Henry V's executors. Though a member of the Council under Gloucester, he seems thereafter to have exerted little individual influence, unlike his elder brother **(2) Henry (?-1447) Card.** and Bp. of Winchester, who was the cleverest of the family, and outlived his brothers, most of their children and two Lancastrian kings. He studied law at Aachen; became Chancellor of Oxford Univ. in 1397; and Bp. of Lincoln by Papal provision in 1398. He was Lord Chancellor in 1403, but resigned in 1404 on succeeding William of Wykeham in the rich see of Winchester. He had a strong business sense and amassed huge sums. To this Winchester owes the completion both of its immense Cathedral and the Hospital of St. Cross; but at the time other consequences seemed more important, for he became the leading financier of the Lancastrian house and without his very large loans its policies could not have been carried on.

He had known the prince, the future Henry V, from childhood and became his principal adviser at a time when Henry IV was advised mainly by Abp. Arundel, much of the time Lord Chancellor. The King and Arundel preferred peace by repression and consolidation after the King's usurpation and the subsequent rebellions: the younger elements about the prince and the Beauforts favoured a more energetic policy abroad against the French erosion of English possessions in Gascony, and extending the great trade through the English fortress market at Calais.

Arundel's resignation as Chancellor in 1409 and the King's worsening health gave the bishop great influence which increased at Henry V's accession in 1413. While Henry was prosecuting his successful wars with Beaufort finance, the bishop was engaged in high diplomacy. In 1417 he attended the Council of Constance: it had been English policy to insist on a church reform before the ending of the Great Schism by the election of a single Pope. In return for the Emperor Sigismund's support against France this policy was now reversed and a new universal Pope (Martin V) was elected with English support. Martin in 1418 offered Beaufort a cardinal's hat and a legatine commission. Henry V forbade him to accept either.

At Henry V's death in 1422 a council, in which the bishop was a leading figure, took over effective government from Humphrey, D. of Gloucester the protector named by the late King. Consequently when the Duke was abroad Beaufort virtually administered the kingdom and, when the Duke was in London he found the bishop unwilling to defer to him. He was also Lord Chancellor from 1224 to 1226, when he at last became a cardinal, and legate for preaching a crusade against the Hussites. Meantime the French war had broken out again, and the crusaders enrolled in 1429 were diverted to defend the English possessions now under attack by Joan of Arc. The English military collapse and the coronation of Charles VI made peace desirable: Cardinal Beaufort accordingly led an English delegation in the abortive congress of Arras in 1435. He made a further effort for peace in 1440, and inspired the matrimonial treaty and marriage of King Henry VI with Margaret of Anjou in 1445.

(3) John (II) (1403-44) became first **D. of SOMERSET** and capt-gen of Aquitaine and Normandy in 1443. **(4) Edmund (?-1455) 2nd D.** began promisingly as a soldier in 1431. He retook Harfleur in 1440 and relieved Calais in 1442. From 1443 as lieutenant of France his operations were a failure. In 1447 he and others arrested the D. of Gloucester at St. Edmundsbury. Gloucester died a few days later and was widely (but wrongly) thought to have been murdered. The D. of York now became heir presumptive to the crown unless the Act of 1407 barring the Beauforts were repealed. The French war was going from bad to worse. In 1452 he claimed the succession in arms. In 1453 the French possessions except Calais were finally lost, but the King went mad and Q. Margaret gave birth to a son. These events shut York out of the succession but gave him a moral and legal title to the protectorship. Somerset was imprisoned. In 1454 the King recovered: York ceased to be protector and Somerset was released. The rival parties with their retainers met at St. Albans in 1455. In the street battle which ensued Somerset was killed.

(5) Henry (1436-64) 3rd D. after defeating the Yorkists at Wakefield in 1460, made his submission to Edward IV (York) after the B. of Towton in 1461, and was taken into favour, but in 1463 he went over to the Lancastrians again and was captured and executed at Hexham in 1464. As he died attainted his brother **(6) Edmund (II) (?1438-71)** though styled the fourth Duke, never inherited his dignities. He was taken at the B. of Tewkesbury in 1471 and executed. **(7) Lady Margaret (1443-1509).** In 1455 Henry VI married her to his half-brother EDMUND TUDOR, E. of Richmond, who died within a year. Their posthumous child was HENRY (later Henry VII). When the Wars of the Roses broke out she retired with Henry to Pembroke, and married Henry Stafford, s. of the Lancastrian D. of Buckingham. Consequently she was an honourable captive after the Yorkist triumph in 1461. The effect of Henry IV's victory at Tewkesbury in 1470 was, however, to make her son Henry the principal Lancastrian claimant to the crown; he therefore fled to Brittany, but remained in touch with his mother. She then took as a third husband Lord Stanley, later E. of Derby. She conspired against Richard III, and in particular negotiated the important marriage between her son and Elizabeth of York. As a result of the abortive rising of 1484 Richard deprived her of her property, but could not proceed to extremes because he dared not offend her powerful husband. It was the Stanleys who gained the B. of Bosworth for Henry.

Lady Margaret was now the richest subject in the country. Influenced by John Fisher, she retired from politics and began to create the educational foundations for which her name has ever since been celebrated. These included professorships of Divinity at both universities, Christ's and St. John's Colleges at Cambridge, and a school at Wimborne Minster (Dorset).

BEAUHARNAIS. *See* BONAPARTE-11 to 13.

BEAULIEU ABBEY (Hants) (pron: Bewly) was a Cistercian house generously supported and endowed by K. John and Henry III, save during the interdict of 1208-13 when, however, its Abbot, Hugh, acted as intermediary between John and the Pope. The monks took joyful possession of their church in 1227. The other buildings were completed only in 1246, when Beaulieu was already establishing daughter houses. Isabel of Gloucester, wife of Richard, E. of Cornwall, was buried before the high altar in 1239, and the Earl's subsequent foundation of Hailes Abbey (Glos) was begun with 20 monks and 30 lay brothers from Beaulieu. By the 1270s Beaulieu was the richest Cistercian house in the Canterbury province.

Many of the buildings survived its dissolution (1538). The refectory (c. 1230) is now Beaulieu parish church. The present Palace House is the former 14th cent. gate house, drastically restored in 1872.

BEAULIEU. *See* MONTAGUE.

BEAUMARIS (Anglesey). The local Welsh royal manor of Llanfaes was the ferry terminal between Anglesey and Snowdonia. Llywelyn the Great founded a Franciscan friary there in 1237. Anglesey was shired in 1284. Edward I's decision to build a castle was probably concerned with the control of the corn supply from the isle to mainland Wales. Building was not begun, however, until 1295, shortly after the Welsh revolt. The town of Llanfaes was destroyed, and a new fortified borough was built beside the castle and chartered in 1296. Castle building continued until the 1330s by which time the exterior was more or less complete, but not the interior. It remains in this condition. *See* EDWARDIAN CASTLES IN WALES.

BEAUMONT, DE, MEDIAEVAL FAMILY. Its fortunes were founded by **(1) Roger (?-c. 1095)** who was given the Norman fief of Beaumont and married the daughter and heiress of Waleran, Count of Meulan. His eldest son **(2) Robert (c. 1046-1118) Count of MEULAN** and perhaps **E. of LEICESTER** was the first to break into the English palisade at the B. of Hastings (1066) and was well rewarded with estates in Warwickshire. He and his brother **(3) Henry (c. 1048-1119)** of Newburgh or Neubourg near Beaumont, **E. of WARWICK,** were supporters of William Rufus who gave them their earldoms. Henry was a friend of Prince Henry and the brothers were among those who chose the Prince as King in 1100, and were among the few magnates who were faithful to him in the rebellion of the next year. Robert fought for Henry I at the B. of Tinchebrai (1106). He rebuilt St. Mary's Abbey at Leicester; Henry and his son Roger endowed and made collegiate St. Mary's church at Warwick. Robert was reputed a cold and crafty statesman.

His estates were divided between his twin elder sons **(4) Waleran (1104-66)** and **(5) Robert (1104-68).** Waleran took the Norman fiefs of Beaumont-le-Roger and Meulan, Robert the English lands. They began as Stephen's chief advisers, Waleran perhaps being made E. of Worcester by him but, because of the King's exasperating superficiality, each by 1152 was supporting Matilda. Robert had quickly gained Henry II's confidence and, at or just after his accession, was made Steward of England and Normandy and in 1155 Justiciar. Effectively he was Henry's English viceroy from 1158 to 1163, from 1165 to 1166 and from Oct. 1166 until his death. He headed the list of signatories to the Constitutions of Clarendon of 1164. His only son **(6) Robert (?-1190) E. of LEICESTER** and Steward of England and Normandy, broke with the family tradition by joining a rebellion, when the young Henry, son of Henry II, revolted in 1173. The King forfeited Robert's English lands and destroyed his town and castle of Leicester, but after the rebellion had been crushed returned his lands at the Council of Northampton (1177). He was restored to court favour and carried a sword of state at Richard I's coronation. He

went on pilgrimage to Jerusalem and died on the way back.

His second son and heir **(7) Robert (?-1204) E. of LEICESTER** fought with K. Richard on Crusade and, on his return, became a partisan of K. John and acted as Steward at his coronation in 1199. Childless, and with one brother in holy orders and the other a leper, his title and inheritance passed through sisters to their husbands' families of de Montfort and de Quincey.

BEAUMONT, Louis de (?-1333) was related to Edward II and his wife Isabel of France. In 1316 there was a disputed election to the bishopric of Durham. The monks, despite threats from Louis, elected someone else. With Isabel's help and a series of simoniacal transactions the bishopric was given to Louis by Pope John XXII. He held it until his death.

BEAUMONT or DE BEAUMONT. LATER FAMILY. This talented if erratic family included: **(1) John (?-?1555)** who was a double reader of the Inner Temple in 1537 and Master of the Rolls in 1550. In the latter capacity he made corrupt bargains with litigants and appropriated some £20,000 of royal revenue. For these and other offences he was heavily fined and compelled to resign. **(2) Sir John (1583-1627)** 1st baronet was in his day a celebrated poet; his brother **(3) Francis (1584-1616)** was a poet and friend of Ben Jonson, but is best known for his collaboration as a playwright with John Fletcher, which began in 1605 and ended only with his death; **(4) Sir George (1753-1828),** 7th baronet was a painter and patron of the arts. He knew Dr. Johnson, was an intimate friend of Sir Joshua Reynolds, helped Wordsworth, and habitually entertained Sir Humphry Davy, Byron and Sir Walter Scott. He was a discriminating collector of pictures and sculpture, and it was he and his friends who successfully persuaded govts. to create the National Gallery, of which the Beaumont Collection formed an important part.

BEAVERBROOK, William Maxwell Aitken (1879-1964) 1st Ld. (1917) was born in Canada and by 1909 had made a fortune in banking, transport and power mergers. He then migrated to England; in 1910 he became conservative M.P. for Ashton-under-Lyne, and in 1911 Bonar Law's parliamentary private secretary. When war broke out in 1914 the Canadian govt. asked him to act as its eye-witness in France, where he remained for some time: his reports had a considerable influence on war policy in both Britain and Canada. Lloyd-George came to power in 1917 and Aitken was given his peerage and became from 1918 to 1919, the newly created Minister of Information. He now began to interest himself in newspapers: he took charge of the *Daily Express* in 1920, established the *Sunday Express,* and bought the *Evening Standard.* He had strong views on, particularly imperial, policy which he sought to impose upon the Tory party by the supposed ability of his papers to win elections for them. The electorate trusted the Beaverbrook press less than its owner expected; Labour won the election of 1929. Beaverbrook now launched his Empire Free Trade policy, which represented one facet of his increasingly outmoded view that Britain should "live of her own". He was hostile to the League of Nations: thought that Britain should never be involved in another war: opposed intervention against the Italians in Ethiopia, and favoured Franco in Spain; and he was one of the principal apologists of the Munich agreement on Czechoslovakia.

Nobody however doubted his patriotism, and when the Chamberlain govt. fell in May 1940 Churchill made him Minister of Aircraft Production. In this capacity he lent a sense of urgency to developments which had already been planned, but though production doubled during his year of office, it seems likely that this would have happened anyway. In Aug. he became a member of the War Cabinet. He was Minister of State in 1941, returned briefly to production as Minister of Supply, and finally was Lord Privy Seal from 1943 to 1945. After the war he continued to press his peculiar world outlook upon the public through his papers with a marked lack of success. The Tories suffered a landslide defeat in the General Election of 1945 and his vigorous campaign against joining the Common Market failed and indeed possibly encouraged opinion to support it. In the end he admitted that his policy was in ruins.

BEC. This Norman abbey, founded in 1034, became a famous school and training place in the 11th and 12th cents. It attracted scholars and pupils from all over Europe, especially under Prior Lanfranc, before he became Abp. of Canterbury in 1070. His most distinguished pupil was Anselm, successively Prior and Abbot and an inspired teacher and scholastic, who also became Abp. of Canterbury in 1093. Anselm's pupils included William of Corbeil, Abp. of Canterbury from 1123 to 1136, Alexander, Bp. of Lincoln, and Nigel, Bp. of Ely. William of Corbeil's successor at Canterbury, Theobald, was also trained there.

BECHUANALAND, BOTSWANA. In 1813 a request by the Batlhaping tribe to the London Missionary Society brought about the earliest significant contacts between Europeans and the tribes of this area. A mission was established at Kuruman, first under Campbell and then under Robert Moffatt. The country was badly disordered by crowds of refugees from Chaka's Zulu armies, and in 1823 Moffatt saved the Batlhaping only by enlisting Griqua mercenaries. When the Matabele under Mzilikazi broke away from the Zulus in 1826, they settled in the Transvaal and raided Bechuanaland regularly until driven north by the Boers in 1837.

By now the Great Trek was in full swing, and inevitably led to clashes between land hungry Boers and the tribes who were supported, for differing reasons, by Livingstone and the British missionaries, and the British traders. In 1852 the Boers raided Dimawe and Livingstone's mission was sacked. The discovery of gold in 1867 near the Tati river made things worse. The area was claimed by both Bamangwato and Matabele, and in 1868 Pres. Pretorius tried to annex it to the Transvaal as well. The British stopped him but refused the Bamangwato request to occupy the country themselves. Boer encroachment and inter-tribal warfare continued until 1881 when the British sought to impose a solution by defining the Transvaal boundaries (*The Pretoria Convention*). The immediate practical result was that so-called European volunteers crossed the new frontiers as "supporters" of local chieftains and set up the two small republics of Stellaland and Goshen. Paul Kruger, now Pres. of the Transvaal, then tried to secure a revision of the Pretoria Convention to take in these republics. Under the London Convention of 1884 he obtained some frontier revisions.

Opinion against further Boer encroachments was hardening. The missionaries led by John Mackenzie campaigned vehemently for native rights; Cecil Rhodes favoured British control in the interests of trade and colonisation, and Foreign Office opinion was alarmed by German advances in South West Africa nearby. A protectorate was proclaimed and deputy commissioners (first Mackenzie, then Rhodes) were sent without arms or funds to establish order. Naturally they failed. The Goshen freebooters attacked Mafeking, seized native lands and tried to establish another local republic. Kruger tried to annex the lands along his frontier. In reply a strong force under Sir Charles Warren entered Bechuanaland in Sept. 1885; the southern part was made a Crown Colony, the rest by proclamations of 1885 and 1892 became a British protectorate. In 1895 the crown colony was annexed to Cape Colony and so passed eventually to the Union.

Meanwhile Rhodes was maturing plans to colonise (Southern) Rhodesia, using the protectorate as a base. A struggle now began between the tribes and missionaries on the one hand, and the trading interests on the other. A tribal delegation consisting of Khama, Bathoen and Sebele visited London in 1895, and obtained an assurance from Joseph Chamberlain that the territory would not be administered by Rhodes' British South Africa Company, but would remain under crown protection. This position was maintained by successive British govts, notably in a declaration of 1935, against mounting South African pressure.

Between 1948 and 1956 there were tribal difficulties centring on the personality of Seretse Khama, the Chief of the Bamangwato, who had married an English wife and who had ambitions for his tribe. He was exiled and the British govt. meanwhile moved towards the establishment of a broadly based legislature. Seretse was allowed to return in 1956 after renouncing his chieftainship, and the new constitution was promulgated in 1960 and worked smoothly. On 30 Sept. 1966 the protectorate became an independent republic.

BECKET, Thomas [à], or Thomas of London, or St. Thomas of Canterbury (1118-70) (1) was the son of Gilbert Becket, a Rouen merchant settled in London and his Norman wife. He received a business training and, after studying in Paris, became a notary in the service of Abp. Theobald, whom he accompanied to Rome in 1143. He then went to Bologna and Auxerre to study canon law, in which he became very proficient, and was Theobald's legal adviser at the Council of Rheims in 1148.

(2) Becket was ambitious, exhibitionist, competent and could immerse himself completely in whatever he was doing. He had, for example, mastered such noble diversions as hunting and hawking and so became popular with the rising court generations. By 1154 when K. Stephen died his abilities were much in demand. As a business man he was appointed archdeacon of Canterbury and took deacon's orders; and Theobald and Bp. Henry of Winchester pressed his appointment to the chancellorship because, as a friend of both King and Archbishop, he might reconcile the interests of church and state. As chancellor he threw himself into K. Henry's affairs which he conducted with his usual ability to the King's great satisfaction, but not to that of the church. In 1159, for example, he was blamed for the heavy taxes imposed on the church for the Toulouse campaign.

(3) Since 1135 the power of the church in lay affairs had considerably increased, due to the weakness of the crown under Stephen and the rise of canonists encouraged by Theobald. Church courts (which were mostly corrupt) claimed (*see* BENEFIT OF CLERGY) not only exclusive jurisdiction over criminous clerics, but by extensions of the doctrine of breach of faith started to compete with the royal courts in matters of debt and lay fees. When Theobald died in 1161, the King thought that he saw an opportunity to control these abuses by making his friend the chancellor archbishop. Becket rejected the suggestion, but was overpersuaded by the Papal legate and the King. In June 1162 he was ordained a priest and consecrated archbishop by Henry of Winchester.

(4) The King had miscalculated. Becket resigned the chancellorship, and as a priest, devoted himself exclusively to the church, whose liberties he asserted with tactless vigour. He opposed the King in everything; defended church leniency towards a series of gross crimes committed by clerics, and, contrary to established law, excommunicated a tenant-in-chief without royal permission. In less than a year King and archbishop were open enemies.

(5) At the council at Westminster in Oct. 1163 the King demanded that criminous clerks should be punishable by the civil authority after degradation by the church court. The bishops led by Becket refused; and when the King required them to swear to abide by the ancient customs of the realm, all but one qualified their oath with the phrase 'saving our order'. Later, however, most of the bishops had second thoughts, and Becket, feeling isolated, appealed for papal support.

(6) It happened that there was a schism. Pope Alexander III dared not offend the King of England lest he transfer his support to the imperially sponsored antipope. As a compromise he urged Becket to accept the customs without qualification and this in Dec. 1163 Becket did.

(7) At this point Henry II overplayed his hand. In Jan. 1164 at a council at Clarendon he proceeded to codify the customs and demanded the bishops' adherence to this code, since famous as the CONSTITUTIONS OF CLARENDON. The bishops unanimously refused, until Becket suddenly gave way and agreed, as he put it "to perjure himself". The reduction of the vague customs to defined rules had, however, to be sent to Alexander III for ratification; but as most of them were against Canon Law he condemned all but six. Thereupon Becket withdrew his consent and did penance for his "perjury".

(8) The King now took steps to ruin Becket. At a council at Northampton in 1165 he was suddenly called upon to account for all public money which had passed through his hands during his eight years chancellorship. After a week's altercation Becket fled to the Abbey of Pontigny in France. Here he remained for nearly six years conducting a polemical correspondence with all the parties involved and attracting international partisanship. He excommunicated his English opponents, and even threatened the King, but the sentences were revoked by the Pope. The French King made several efforts at reconciliation which all broke down.

(9) In 1170 Henry II wanted to secure the succession by the coronation of his son Henry, to whom fealty had been sworn by the barons when Becket was chancellor. Coronation was the exclusive prerogative of the archbishop of Canterbury, but as he was in exile the King prevailed upon Roger Abp. of York to crown the young Henry without papal licence in the presence of six other bishops in June 1170. This offended the Pope and the French King as well as Becket. Nevertheless in July Becket and Henry II met and were nominally reconciled. Actually Becket had secured the Pope's authority to proceed against the offending bishops, whom he suspended or excommunicated in Nov. In Dec. he returned to Canterbury and found the civil authorities and especially the young Henry understandably hostile, while the suspended bishops hastened to Normandy to complain to the King. In his Christmas sermon Becket denounced his enemies and excommunicated them. Four days later four of the King's knights murdered him in his Cathedral, as a result of words spoken by the King in a rage.

(10) The shock to Christian opinion was tremendous; Becket was shortly canonised and Henry had to bargain with the Pope for readmission to the good graces of the church. *For details see* AVRANCHES, CONCORDAT OR PACIFICATION OF.

BECK'S CASE (1904). Adolf Beck was identified by several women as a fraudulent person called Smith and convicted. In prison he discovered that Smith was a Jew and was by his own lack of circumcision, able to demonstrate his innocence. The case helped to bring about the creation of the Court of Criminal Appeal.

BECKFORD (1) William (1709-70), Lord Mayor of London in 1762-3 and 1769-70 was a wealthy absentee sugar planter who combined city business with rural life. He became M.P. for Shaftesbury in 1747, and for the City from 1754 to 1770. Strongly radical, he supported the elder Pitt until the latter's retirement. From 1761 he was the first effective critic of the system of parliamentary representation, and after he quarrelled with the govt. over the terms of the P. of Paris (1763) he gave sustained support to John Wilkes, especially during the 1769

agitation to abolish rotten boroughs, and he supplied the ideas and brains of the radical movement. His even wealthier son **(2) William (1759-1844)** also an M.P., wrote (in French) his repellent oriental novel *Vathek* (c. 1781). It emerged in an English translation in 1786. He also built a vast mansion, Fonthill, designed by John Wyatt, and resembling a mediaeval abbey. Here he lived a secluded life. The gigantic tower eventually collapsed.

BEDE or BAEDA, the Ven (c. 672-735) entered the monastery at Wearmouth (Northumbria) at seven, and apart from visits to the sister house at Jarrow is known to have made only two journeys away in his life. His Abbot, Benedict Biscop, educated him and gave him the use of the fine libraries which he had assembled in the two monasteries. He learned Latin thoroughly and Greek fairly well.

Apart from two commentaries on the *Acts of the Apostles* (c. 710-20) he wrote a famous *Ecclesiastical History of the English People,* completed in 731, in Latin. Its carefully assimilated sources included writings and conversations, and was designed to present a picture of the way in which the English Church had achieved its order and unity. In particular he portrayed the history of each diocese and its ascertainable succession of bishops, and argued for Papal authority and the Roman rite. Paganism still lurked in the country and so he was much inspired by the Romans whom he regarded as a chosen people. Hence he was influenced by writers such as Orosius. The *Ecclesiastical History* also presented moral examples of good men to be imitated and hurtful actions to be avoided.

Abp. Egbert, the founder of the school at York, was one of his pupils and he in turn trained Alcuin.

BEDESMAN, -WOMAN (cf Ger: beten = to pray) One who receives alms, usually a small pension, on condition that he prays for his benefactor. In Scotland bedesmen were also licensed beggars. *See also* CHANTRY.

BEDFORD. The Saxons under Cuthwulf defeated the Britons at Bedcanford (said to be Bedford) in 571. It was sacked in 1010 by the Danes who subsequently settled it. In 1561 a native, William Harpur, then Lord Mayor of London, endowed a grammar school, and his charity (along with streets named after him in London and Bedford) still survives. The town was a stronghold of sectarianism in the 17th cent. and John Bunyan preached and was imprisoned there.

BEDFORD, DUKES AND EARLS OF. *See* LANCASTER. RUSSELL AND TUDOR.

BEDFORD LEVEL. *See* FENS.

BEDINGFIELD, Sir Henry (1511-83) was M.P. for Suffolk in 1553 and was one of the first to rise for Q. Mary on the death of Edward VI. In consequence he was made Privy Councillor. In 1554 he was given custody of the Pr. Elizabeth and conducted her from the Tower to Woodstock. He is said to have treated her harshly yet, by his care, to have saved her from assassination. He sat in the parliaments of 1553, 1554 and 1557 for Norfolk, but not after the accession of Elizabeth, although she seems to have borne him no ill will.

BEDLAM (Corruption of BETHLEHEM) A Royal Hospital was founded in 1247 as a lunatic asylum in Bishopsgate, London. Henry VIII handed it over to the City Corporation in 1547. It became famous, but abuses crept in and eventually it was notorious for brutalities to its inmates, who were exhibited as a public amusement. It was moved to Moorfields in 1675; to St. George's in 1815 and finally to Shirley near Croydon.

BEDOUIN. Nomad pastoral tribes originating in the Hejaz and Nejd. They spread to N. Arabia, Syria, Iraq and later to the Sudan and Saharas as far west as Tunisia. Originally Arab speaking and of Arab stock, their habits and language were adopted by certain African peoples. In the Syrian and Iraqi fertile crescent they tended first to become marginal cultivators, then from generation to generation part-time agriculturists and eventually full time farmers before losing their tribal identities and merging in the indigenous populations. Elsewhere or in their nomadic state they were constantly at feud and treated strangers as victims unless recognised as worthy of safe conduct or actually provided with one from their sheikh. They habitually plundered unarmed caravans, so that the Ottoman govt. paid a regular toll to the tribes around Medina and Mecca to protect the pilgrimages. They formed an organised military recruiting ground for the British, whom with T. E. Lawrence they assisted in disrupting the Ottoman Empire in World War I.

BEECHING, James (1788-1858) in 1851 invented the self-righting lifeboat.

BEECHING, Richard (1913-85) Ld. BEECHING (1965) a physicist with varied experience in industry, including ICI, was appointed in 1961 as chairman of the British Railways Board with instructions to inquire into the means by which the railway system could be reduced. His report was published early in 1963 and implementation was begun at once, because he had been assured of the govt's acceptance. His wholesale closure of branch lines and stations deprived most rural areas of their public transport. Later he was commissioned to investigate the management of the legal system. His report proposed, and the Courts Act 1971 imposed, civil service control of the system. This vastly increased its expense, prolonged the delays and began the erosion of judicial independence.

BEEFEATER. *See* YEOMAN OF THE GUARD.

BEEFSTEAK CLUBS were theatrical dining clubs composed of wits, actors and politicians. The actor Richard Estcourt founded the first in 1709. John Rich, the manager of the Covent Garden Theatre founded the *Sublime Society of Steaks* in 1735; its members included Garrick, Hogarth, John Wilkes, John Kemble, the E. of Peterborough and the P. of Wales and it was for long a kind of radical discussion group. It moved to the Lyceum theatre in 1808, and was dissolved in 1867. Thomas Sheridan, the actor father of Richard, founded another at the Theatre Royal, Dublin, of which Peg Woffington was pres. The fare was limited to steaks.

BEER. *See* ALE AND BEER.

BEET. *See* SUGAR.

BEETON, Isabella Mary (1836-65). *See* COOKERY.

BEGGA, St. *See* MISSIONS TO EUROPE.

BEHAVIOURISM. This word, originating in 1913, represents a method of psychological study based upon the objective observation of behaviour. The objectivity implies that the information to be studied must be limited to that which can be measured. In this sense, it is related to Hobbes' rather vague idea that a man is a superior kind of machine.

BEIRA (Mozambique) owes its existence to the building of the rly from Salisbury (Rhodesia) under the Anglo Portuguese Agreement of 1891. It was administered by the Mozambique Co. until 1941.

BEIT, Alfred (1853-1906), a German, learned the diamond trade in Amsterdam and went to Kimberley in 1875; in 1879 he met Cecil Rhodes and became his lifelong collaborator. In 1880 he became a partner in Jules Porges and Co., one of the largest contemporary mining concerns, and in 1888 he and Rhodes formed the de Beers Consolidated Mines Co. which practically ruled both Rhodesias until 1923. His business acumen was essential to Rhodes throughout his career, and Beit was involved in all his friend's vicissitudes including the Jameson Raid. He became a British subject in 1898.

BEK. This distinguished Lincolnshire family descended from Walter Bek, Lord of Eresby included **(1) Anthony (I) (c. 1240-1310)** who had been knighted and made a King's clerk while still at Oxford. He was a friend of the Lord Edward with whom he went on crusade in 1270; and in 1274 Edward made him his Chancellor. He also

served as a diplomat in the 1280s and 1290s. In 1283 he had been elected Bp. of Durham on Edward's nomination, and under him the palatinate's autonomy reached its peak. He delighted in splendour which he and the bishopric could easily afford. Unfortunately his assertion of visitatorial rights over the cathedral priory brought on a major conflict with the Prior, accompanied by local hatreds and much diplomacy at Rome, where Bek was only partially successful against the Prior. As a result he fell from royal favour and lost the Liberty of Durham. He recovered both at the accession of his personal friend Edward II. Other members of the family included **(2) Thomas (I), Bp. of St. David's (1280-93), (3) Anthony (II), Bp. of Norwich (1337-43)** and his brother **(4) Thomas (II), Bp. of Lincoln (1342-7).**

BEKYNTON or BECKINGTON, Thomas (c. 1390-1465) entered the service of D. Humphrey of Gloucester in 1420 whereby he secured many lucrative church preferments between 1422 and 1438. During much of this time he was in secular employments, first with the Duke and then as a diplomat.

In 1432 he was sent on a peace mission to France; in 1437 he began to act as one of the King's secretaries; in 1439 he was in the negotiations with the French at Calais, and in 1442 he was sent to negotiate a marriage treaty with them. All these missions failed because of the justified belief of the French that they were winning the war.

His international standing got him a papal nomination to the see of Salisbury, but he had to exchange it for Bath and Wells, to which he was consecrated in Oct. 1443. His chief monuments are his magnificent buildings at Wells, and his many bequests to places (such as Winchester, Eton and Lincoln College, Oxford) with which he was connected.

BELASYSE. This influential Durham and Yorkshire family included: **(1) Anthony (?-1552),** a master in Chancery, a notable pluralist who also secured large grants of former monastery property. This founded the family fortune. He left his wealth to a nephew **(2) William** whose grandson **(3) Thomas 1st Ld. FAUCONBERG (1645)** was the father of **(4) Henry (d. before 1652)** who was concerned in the attempted arrest of the Five Members. Henry's younger brother **(5) John (1614-89) 1st Ld. BELASYSE (1645)** was M.P. for Thirsk in the Short and Long Parliaments, but took the King's side. He had a very active career as a soldier. He went into exile after the war, returning in 1650 to be a key figure in the royalist plans of the 1650s. In late 1653 on Charles II's instructions he helped found the *Sealed Knot,* a group of six designed to co-ordinate royalist activity in England. As the only R. Catholic member he was expected to maintain links with the northern recusants. As relative or neighbour of disgruntled northern Parliamentarian officers such as Fairfax and Lambert, he was frequently urged, and sometimes agreed, to sound them out. In 1654 his personal quarrel with Sir Richard Willys compounded the damage done to the Sealed Knot by its inability to control the wilder royalist adventurers. For the rest of the decade he urged caution and stood aloof from rebellion although this did not save him from spells of imprisonment. After Cromwell's death he was involved in tentative negotiations with Presbyterians, abortive plans to win over members of the Cromwellian circle (including Richard himself) via Fauconberg (*see* 6 *below*), and the early approaches to Monck. His willingness to join the 'Trust' in early 1660 helped to strengthen royalist co-ordination. The nature of the Restoration vindicated his earlier caution, but Clarendon's enmity arising from differences of approach in the 1650s ensured that he held only routine appointments until made Gov. of Tangier in 1664. As a R. Catholic he refused the oath of conformity and resigned in 1666. He was imprisoned without trial from 1678 until 1683 as a result of Titus Oates's fabrications, but under James II was First Lord Commissioner of the Treasury. The son of **(4)**, **(6) Thomas (1627-1700) Vist. (1652) and 1st E. FAUCONBERG (1689)** supported Parliament in the Civil War and married Cromwell's third daughter Mary in 1657. His links with his uncle Lord Belasyse and his royalist circle, and with conservative Cromwellians, made him a natural go-between should the chance arise. Such hopes and suspicions grew with some justification after Richard Cromwell's fall. After the Restoration he became a member of Charles II's privy council. He was one of the lords who invited William III to England.

BELFAST (Ulster) began as a castle built in about 1177 by John de Courcy to command a local ford. This survived until it was replaced in 1611 by Sir Arthur Chichester's castle. He obtained a charter for the adjacent settlement in 1613 and this gave Belfast representation in Parliament; the town, alone in Ulster, successfully resisted the Irish insurrection of 1641. By 1685 (when the Edict of Nantes was revoked) the beginnings of industry (brick making and ships' stores) had appeared and the town was becoming the chief port of Ulster. To this the Huguenots added improved methods of linen making. The first water-driven cotton mills were erected in 1784 and the first steam-powered mills in 1811, by which time the first shipyard (1789) had already been opened by William Ritchie. The Harbour Commission was established in 1847. Queens College was founded in 1849, a medical school was added in 1866 and the whole was converted into an University in 1909. The City became the capital of Northern Ireland in 1920 and was severely bombed in World War II. *See* ULSTER.

BELFRY or (Fr) *BEFROI* was a mediaeval siege tower, commonly on wheels or rollers, designed to overtop the walls of a besieged place. It usually had a projecting penthouse roof just above ground level to protect those who were filling up the moat or undermining the wall, and a boarding drop-bridge from the top storey, and the whole was covered with hides as a protection against fire.

BELGAE were a group of tribes inhabiting the area between the Seine, the Maine and the Rhine (later called *Gallia Belgica)*. Early in the 1st cent. B.C. members of this group began to invade and settle Britain, and as a result of Caesar's invasion of Gaul, more followed. He regarded the British coastal tribes as recent Belgic arrivals.

It is uncertain which tribes or kingdoms in pre-Roman Britain were Belgic and which merely under Belgic influence. The Atrebates, west of the Weald, were undoubtedly Belgic; the powerful Catuvellauni probably were. The peoples inhabiting modern Kent, and the Durotriges and the Dobunni were probably only under Belgic influence. Significantly, Caesar considered the Kent Britons to be the most civilised of the British inhabitants.

BELGIAN CONGO. *See* ZAIRE.

BELGIUM (*see also* NETHERLANDS; BRABANT; LUXEMBOURG). **(1)** The separate history of the area now called Belgium begins with the Spanish victory at Gembloux over the Dutch in June 1578. This ensured that it should be R. Catholic as against protestant Holland, centred on Brussels and Antwerp rather than on Amsterdam, and commercially, temperamentally and politically distinct. The presence of many fortresses made Belgium internationally important because they obstructed French northward aggression after 1620. Britain, Holland and other European states therefore had an interest in keeping this fortified 'Barrier' out of French hands. Under Bonaparte the Low Countries were really part of his empire. At the Congress of Vienna in 1815 it was British policy to man the Barrier by strengthening the Dutch; so the latter received Indonesia back, a loan of £2M to bring the fortifications up to standard, and a 'Benelux' state was created under the name of the Kingdom of the United Netherlands. The union was not a success. In Aug. of the revolutionary year 1830 risings in Brussels and elsewhere drove out the Dutch. Part of British policy thus collapsed, but the July revolution and dynastic change in Paris prevented France from taking advantage of it. In Nov. a national congress declared for Belgian independence, and the Dutch mobilised.

(2) In the previous Feb. Britain, Russia and France had agreed at London on Greek independence, and the crown of Greece was accepted by Leopold of Saxe-Coburg-Gotha. Finding the task impossible, he abdicated in May; the Belgian crown was now offered to him. The country thus acquired, as its head, one of the ablest and best connected diplomats of the period. Meantime the London Conference, fearing a renewal of European revolution or war, had by Nov. 1831 in principle decided on Belgian independence, and at Leopold's request, the French in Nov. 1832 turned back a Dutch invasion by occupying Antwerp. It took seven more years of diplomatic haggling on the details before independence was contractually guaranteed by the European powers in the T. of London (19 Apr. 1839).

(3) The Belgian state was thus born in revulsion against the Dutch, and preserved by the action of foreign powers. Both facts are cardinal. The first made French for a time the official language; this gave an advantage to the French-speaking Walloon minority, and sowed seeds of dangerous internal controversy. The second gave Belgium 75 years of security, and put at a moral or propagandist disadvantage any power which violated her territory. This was to be important in 1914.

(4) When Leopold I, who was Q. Victoria's uncle, died in 1865, Belgium was becoming rich through coalmining, industry and the international dealings favoured by free trade. The bourgeoisie were numerous and well to do. Their position was an object of ambition for the less fortunate. This state of affairs soon created a politically conscious but as yet unenfranchised class.

(5) In 1880 as a result of Stanley's Congo revelations, an International Africa Association was formed under the presidency of Leopold II (*see* CONGO), to suppress slavery and exploit the rubber and ivory of the vast and wealthy Congo basin. In 1885 this became, as the so-called Congo Free State, virtually the King's private estate, but the advantages also benefitted the Belgian economy as a whole. By 1890 affluence and discontent combined to create a labour party, and in 1892 a series of strikes forced the govt. to widen the franchise. The upward trend in the standard of living also brought to the surface Flemish intellectual discontent. The first achievement of the new Flemish revival was the establishment of the Flemish Academy in Ghent in 1886; and the extended franchise of 1892 accelerated the process, because it enfranchised more Flemings than Walloons. Henceforth the movement towards linguistic equality was continuous.

(6) As the 19th cent. drew to a close, the possibility of war oppressed responsible politicians. Leopold II urged conscription, but everyone feared the cost and inconvenience. In 1900 the King was forced to hand over the Congolese interests to parliament in a will for which he received £2M, but then the malpractices of Congolese (mostly Belgian) concessionaires came to light, and there was an organised outcry to anticipate the will by annexation. Thus conscription and annexation (which, the politicians hoped, would foot the bill) came about together in 1908. Leopold II was succeeded by Albert I in 1909.

(7) Within five years Belgium was, save for Ypres, overrun by the Germans. The new army, in Aug. 1914, contributed materially to the decisive German check on the Maine in Sept. but the country suffered four years of occupation, and the fighting round Ypres ruined the westerly frontier areas for a generation. The deeds of the conscripts in war made universal male suffrage inevitable in 1919, and it was hoped that German reparations would pay for reconstruction.

(8) German defalcations, and the economic disaster of 1929 to 1931 brought political unrest and dissension. Moreover, in 1934 the war-hero K. Albert was killed in a climbing accident, and was succeeded by the young Leopold III. The contemporary European movement against parliamentary democracy appeared in Belgium in the form of the Rexist Party, and the language controversy reappeared, in a political form, as Flemish separatism. The old Catholic and Socialist parties, both in reality alliances, were divided among themselves and had lost their appeal. To crown all in 1934, the end of free trade (upon which much of Belgian prosperity depended) put 25% of the labour force out of work. The result was a coalition for economic rehabilitation under Paul Van Zeeland, Vice-Gov. of the Bank of Belgium, who became Prime Minister in 1935. The Rexists won 26 seats in the elections of 1936, but the truth about Nazism caused them to lose all but four in 1939.

(9) Meantime Hitler's territorial appetite was growing, and the powers who had guaranteed Belgian independence seemed too weak or too pacifist to be reliable. Appeasement was in the air; the special Belgian contribution to it was to denounce the guarantees in Apr. 1937, to strengthen the forces and the fortresses, and to declare strict neutrality when war came in Sept. 1939. These gestures were futile: in 1940 all the Low Countries were invaded on 10 May: the Dutch army surrendered on 28th. The cabinet and govt. moved to London whence it governed the Congo in the King's name.

(10) German war policy began as old fashioned colonialism in the Marxist sense. The Belgian franc was devalued, and huge quantities of goods were exported to Germany. But in June came the invasion of Russia, and with it a more direct control of the economy, featuring rationing, the imposition of war contracts on Belgian firms, and labour direction. This engendered obstruction particularly in the civil services which the Belgian Nazi organisations could not overcome. The feeling that Britain could not be attacked encouraged resistance movements. In 1944 these made major contributions to the German defeat; after the June rly strike the Germans never got the railways working properly again, and in Sept. a resistance organisation prevented the Germans blowing up the port of Antwerp.

(11) The liberation brought a scramble for power and office which tended to be personal in scope and methods, and it created problems for the allied armies which needed tranquillity behind their lines. The many resistance movements claimed rewards in place and pension; the émigrés and escapees who had fought in a more orthodox fashion had similar claims; there were many in public positions who had stuck to their posts by govt. order, and many in business who had made fortunes on the black markets or at the expense of the Germans. Lastly there were the traitors. In the struggle for power, tribunals were overwhelmed with accusations, mostly of personal or political origin. Thousands were detained for many months pending trial. On the other hand the resistance organisations were disarmed, often with goodwill, and the black market fortunes were mopped up by a currency reform. The Pierlot govt. thus achieved a pacification at the expense of those who held office during the German occupation.

(12) Leopold III had been deported by the Germans and his brother P. Charles, Count of Flanders, was elected Regent in Sept. 1944 by parliament. In Feb. 1945 Achille Van Acker, a trade unionist, became Prime Minister of a coalition and in May the Americans liberated the King in Austria. This created a splendid opportunity for divisive tactics by the communists, who campaigned against the King ostensibly for his conduct as a wartime prisoner. They were joined by most of the socialists and

some liberals, and in July the govt. introduced a bill to prolong the regency. The Catholics ("Social Christians") promptly left the coalition. There was a general election in Feb. 1946 in which the Catholics and Socialists gained most of the seats, and from Aug. 1946 until Mar. 1947 the Prime Minister was Camille Huysmans, the socialist.

(13) He was succeeded by Paul-Henri Spaak and another predominantly socialist coalition which lasted until May 1949; this was a very important short administration for on July 3, 1947, the Benelux treaty was ratified; In Mar. 1948 the Brussels treaty was signed and on 4 Apr. 1949 Belgium signed the North Atlantic Treaty.

(14) From this time Belgian affairs, though journalistically exciting because of the linguistic and royal controversies (settled in July 1951 by Leopold's abdication in favour of his son Baudouin), were overshadowed partly by Congolese problems, but mainly by integration with other Benelux countries and Europe, and the establishment in Brussels of the European Commission and its vastly influential cosmopolitan bureaucracy.

BELGRAVIA (London) is a residential area financed by the Grosvenor family, named after one of their Leicestershire properties. They employed Thomas Cubitt to do the work. It represents one of the largest town engineering projects in history. Cubitt removed the clay topsoil of the waterlogged site both for drainage and for brickmaking and replaced it with earth excavated from St. Katharine's Docks. The operations lasted from 1825 to 1870.

BELIZE or BRITISH HONDURAS (C. America) became known to Europeans as a source of Campeachy or Log wood in about 1638. The wood is of great value as a source of a mordant black dye. British interest crystallised with the capture of Jamaica (1655) which formed a staging post for settlers. The wood gave Britain a preponderance in the contemporary dye trade, and the settlers soon came into conflict with the local Yucatan Indians and with the Spaniards who attacked regularly till 1668 and again in 1717 and 1754. Meanwhile the settlers managed their own affairs under the occasional protection of the Royal Navy. In 1786 another Spanish invasion was driven back. British claims in the Mosquito Coast were exchanged for Belize and a dormant constitutional charter, issued in 1765 was put into effect. Nevertheless a last Spanish attack had to be defeated at the B. of St. George's Bay in Sept. 1789. In 1840 an executive council was set up; in 1853 a legislature under a Lieut-Gov. under Jamaica and in 1884 British Honduras became a separate Crown Colony and so remained until 1960, its economy being underpinned by the demand for dye for black stockings. Belize, the capital, has a poor harbour obstructed by sand bars and is devastated about once in a generation (as in 1931 and 1961) by hurricanes. The name is said to derive from a Spanish corruption of 'Wallace'.

BELL, Alexander Graham (1847-1922) migrated with his father to N. America and in 1873 became prof. of vocal physiology at Boston univ. His experiments in speech measurements led to his invention and patenting of the telephone in 1876, but its possibilities remained unrecognised until it was inspected by the Brazilian Emperor Pedro II at an exhibition at New Orleans in 1885.

BELL, Charles Frederick Moberley (1847-1911) was *Times* correspondent on Egyptian matters from 1865 until 1890 and founded the *Egyptian Gazette* in 1880. In 1890 he became the manager of the *Times* and in 1901 started the *Literary Supplement*. He published the 9th Edition of the *Encyclopaedia Britannica* in 1898 and established the Times Book Club in 1905.

BELL, Gertrude Margaret Lowthian (1868-1926) was the first woman to obtain first class honours in history at Oxford. She was a friend of Sir Frank and Lady Lascelles, and stayed with them, especially in Teheran, where she learned Persian. In 1897 she published a translation of the *Diwan* of Hafiz. In 1899 she went to Jerusalem to learn Arabic. From visits to Petra and Baalbek she acquired a taste for desert travel and Syrian archaeology, but she returned to Europe and spent much of 1901-4 climbing in the Alps. She returned to the Levant, travelling in 1905 from Jerusalem to Konia in Asia Minor; and in 1909 from Aleppo down the Euphrates to Kerbela, and thence *via* Baghdad and Mosul into Asia Minor again. Already known as a writer on archaeology now, in publishing *Amurath to Amurath* gave a political account of the Young Turks whom she had met on this long journey. In 1913 she started from Damascus for Arabia but was turned back at Hail, and ended up in Apr. 1914 at Baghdad. At the outbreak of World War I she returned to Europe and reorganised the London HQ of the Red Cross with alarming energy and success, but her Eastern journeys had given her a knowledge of Arabian personalities and politics possessed by no one else, and so when wartime Arab movements against Turkish rule began to take shape, she was recruited by the Arab Intelligence Bureau in Cairo, which she reached in Nov. 1915. She was almost immediately attached to the expeditionary force from India which conquered Mesopotamia. By Mar. 1917 she was in Baghdad acting as oriental secretary to the chief political officer (later civil commissioner) Sir Percy Cox, and his successor Sir Arnold Wilson. In this capacity she prepared a masterly *Review of the Civil Administration of Mesopotamia* which was published as a White Paper in 1921.

She favoured early political independence for the Arabs, and was trusted by most of their leaders. She was a known opponent of direct British rule on Indian lines, and when her views were adopted and Feisal was elected to the throne of Iraq, she became for a while the most influential person in Baghdad, acting as adviser simultaneously to the high commissioner (Sir Percy Cox again) and the Arab ministers. She was still oriental secretary at Baghdad at her death.

BELL, Henry (1767-1830) as builder of the *Comet* steamship in 1812 was the originator of practical steam navigation in Europe. The *Comet* plied between Glasgow and Greenock until 1820 when she was wrecked. *See* SHIPS, POWER DRIVEN.

BELL or INCHCAPE ROCK (Scot) a navigational hazard nearly opposite the mouth of the R. Tay. Southey wrote a ballad about the efforts of the abbey of Arbroath to warn mariners by means of a bell. In 1799 seventy ships were wrecked on it during the great gale. As a result Robert Stevenson designed a lighthouse 120 ft high which Rennie completed in 1811.

BELLAMY'S VEAL PIES. There are two versions of the younger Pitt's last words. Viz "Oh my country, how I leave my country!" or "I think I could eat one of Bellamy's veal pies".

BELLE ISLE. *See* PARIS. P. OF (10 Feb. 1763); SEVEN YEARS WAR-10 TO 13.

BELLÊME or TALVAS, Robert (?-1114) E. of SHREWSBURY (1098), was the eldest son of Roger, Lord of Montgomery, and Mabel, heiress of the hated house of Talvas. He initially inherited great estates on the borders of Normandy and Maine. He was arguably one of the nastiest characters in English history. He supported the Norman baronial revolt in 1077 against the Conqueror and that of Odo and the English baronage against Rufus in 1088. Driven back to Normandy after the fall of Rochester, he was soon in rebellion against D. Robert, and subsequently he engaged in violent and irresponsible local forays. These were purely freebooting excursions carried out with skill and with a cruelty so appalling that his name was still a byword in Normandy in the 19th cent. In 1098 he succeeded to his brother's Earldom of Shrewsbury together with Arundel and Chichester, and began to fortify Bridgnorth and other fortresses, and in

1101 he succeeded to the county of Ponthieu. He thus became a menace to all security and order. Summoned before the King's Court in 1102 on 45 grave charges, he refused to come. After many sieges beginning with Arundel and ending with Shrewsbury, K. Henry deprived him of his English fiefs and deported him to Normandy. His Norman fiefs promptly rebelled but he put them down with his habitual cruelty. He then led a further rebellion himself but fled from the field at the B. of Tinchebrai (28 Sept. 1106). Nevertheless he supported William Clito against Henry and at a later date Fulk of Anjou. In 1112 he sought the intervention of Louis VI of France, and the latter tactlessly sent him as ambassador to K. Henry who seized him. He died in prison at Wareham.

BELLEROPHON, H.M.S. After his second abdication Bonaparte went to Rochefort intending to escape to America. The *Bellerophon* (Capt. Frederick Maitland) in Basque Roads frustrated this ambition and between 9 and 15 July 1815 Bonaparte attempted to negotiate for an unmolested passage or a passage in a British ship. Maitland, however, stuck to his instructions to accept only an unconditional surrender. Bonaparte on 13th signed a letter to the Prince Regent claiming the protection of English law. On 14th Maitland saw this letter and undertook to receive him and convey him to England, but as before refused (but not in writing) to give any undertaking about his treatment. On 15th Bonaparte surrendered. Later he fraudulently exploited the absence of a written document to allege that asylum had been granted, and that he had been tricked. This became an important element in the St. Helena propagandist myth which later intermittently soured Anglo-French relations.

BELLE SAUVAGE. This inn on Ludgate Hill was called Savages' Inn or The Bell on the Hoop in 1453. It was well known for dramatic performances and bull baiting in 16th and 17th cents, and as a starting point for coaches in 18th. The name may have been a revival by mental association with Pocahontas. *See* ROLFE SMITH, JOHN.

BELLOC, (Joseph) Hilaire (Pierre) (1870-1953) French born, English educated poet, essayist and historian was naturalised a British subject in 1902 and was a Liberal M.P. from 1906 to 1910. His vast literary output included 16 novels, 8 works of general and military history, 13 biographies varying from Danton to Milton, travel books, a considerable body of essays on serious and less serious matters, and some enduring absurdities such as the *Bad Child's Book of Beasts*. His passion for things English and command of style made him a formidable because unselfconscious upholder of morale in both World Wars.

BELL THE CAT *see* JAMES III OF SCOTS-2.

BELMEIS or BELESMAINS ('Fair Hands'). The name of three distinguished churchmen. **(1) Richard Rufus (?-1127),** a prominent royal minister managed Robert of Bellême's forfeited earldom of Shropshire from c. 1103 till at least 1123. He was nominated Bp. of London in 1108, and devoted much of his ecclesiastical revenue to the rebuilding of St. Paul's cathedral and founding St. Osyth's priory in Essex. **(2) Richard (?-1162),** his nephew was a youthful prebendary of St. Paul's, and also became Bp. of London in 1152. **(3) John (?-c. 1203),** a native of Canterbury brought up in Abp. Theobald's household, was a close friend of Becket. Henry II got him out of England by having him made Bp. of Poitiers. From 1176 he became a leading persecutor of Albigensians in the Toulouse area, and in 1181 was elected Abp. of Narbonne, but was translated to the more important see of Lyons. He retired from Lyons in 1193 to St. Bernard's abbey of Clairvaux.

BELORUSSIA or WHITE RUSSIA, was a constituent republic of the U.S.S.R. and, though it had no discernible international independence, it was forced upon the international community (on the false analogy of the British dominions) as an original member of the United

Nations Organisation. It became more really independent, with its capital at Minsk, as a member of the Commonwealth of Independent States, constituted in succession to the defunct U.S.S.R. in 1991.

BELPER, Edward Strutt (1801-80) 1st Ld. (1856) as a young man was a friend of Bentham and John Stuart Mill, and from 1830 to 1847 was liberal M.P. for Derby. Unseated on an election petition, he sat for Arundel in 1851, and for Nottingham from 1852 to 1856. He was Chanc. of the Duchy of Lancaster in the Aberdeen coalition govt. from 1852 to 1854. He was considered an authority on free trade, law reform and education, and in later life was much sought by the ablest intelligences of his time, including Macauley, Romilly and Grote.

BELSEN was one of the 600 Nazi concentration camps. Though by no means the largest or worst of these murder factories, conditions there so appalled the British troops who captured it in 1944 that parliamentary witnesses were flown out specially, lest the facts were disbelieved. The name has become a byword.

BELTAIN FIRES AND CAKES. On 1 May all fires were extinguished and a new one, lit by friction, started on a hilltop. A cake was divided between those present, and anyone who received a piece identified as unlucky might be the victim of a mock sacrifice (Scotland) or might have to leap over the bonfire (Wales). This echo of human sacrifice persisted with local differences in Scotland until the end of the 18th cent.; in Wales to the 19th, in the I. of Man until the 1840s and at Stapleford Hill (Notts) even later.

BELTON (Lincs.) a classical mansion built, perhaps, by Wren in 1685 for the Brownlow family.

BELVOIR (Pron. **Beaver**) (**Leics.**) seat of the Rutland family since Tudor times. The present mansion, on a conspicuous eminence, is an astounding Strawberry Hill Gothic confection built by James Wyatt in 1816.

BENARES, BANARAS, VARANASI or KASHI (India), the Hindu holy city in the Mogul province of Oudh, was ceded by Safar Jang, the Nawab of Oudh, to the HEIC in 1775. One Balwant Singh, a local landowner was already practically independent of the Nawab, and helped the British at the B. of Buxar (1764); his son Chet Singh was exiled by Warren Hastings, but his grandson was reinstated; an exchange of land left the family in possession of their properties, while the British administered Benares. By this time the head of the family was known as a rajah, and during the Indian Mutiny he ruled his lands like a prince, and supported the British. His successor Prabhu Narayan Singh was recognised as maharajah as late as 1910, when his lands were turned into a native state in deference to his high character and to Hindu opinion. The state was enlarged by the addition of Ramnagar in 1918, but was merged in Uttar Pradesh at independence.

BENBOW, Adm. John (1653-1702), was Master of the Fleet at the B. of La Hogue (1692) and commanded against French privateers in the next two years. In 1698 he was concerned in trade protection in the West Indies. In Aug. 1702 his flagship was left unsupported, by the insubordination of other ships' captains, in a fight with four French ships off Santa Marta; though his leg was shot off he continued on deck on a chair, but died three months later. His exploits made him a popular hero.

BENCH. This word was used in the sense of a seat of honour. Hence the Common Bench was the early name for the Court of Common Pleas which always sat at Westminster, as opposed to the Court of Kings Bench which, in theory, travelled with the King. Other common uses were the Bench of Bishops meaning originally the seats reserved for them in the House of Lords and so the episcopate; the Bench of aldermen; and the Bench or governing body of an Inn of Court.

BENCOOLEN (S.W. Sumatra) H.E.I.C. trading station from

1685. It ceased to be viable after 1815 and was ceded to the Netherlands in 1825.

BEN CRUACHAN (Argyll) This otherwise unremarkable mountain contains the largest hydro-electric pumped storage scheme in Europe. It was opened in 1965.

BENEDICT BISCOP or BADUCING (c. 628-89). A well born thegn of K. Oswy of Northumbria, made five journeys to Rome and became an important influence in the life or aesthetics of the English church. After his second journey he became a monk at Lérins, and he returned from the third in the company of Theodore of Tarsus. During his travels he acquired relics, chalices, pictures and a celebrated library. He brought back glaziers and masons from Gaul, and a singing master returned with him from Rome. When Theodore became Abp. of Canterbury in 669, Benedict became Abbot of St. Peter and St. Paul there. In 674 he went north and founded the monastery at Monkwearmouth, and in 681 the sister house at Jarrow where Bede spent his life.

BENEDICTINES. Some years before 529 St Benedict founded a series of monastic communities near Nero's ruined palace at Subiaco. Forced to move in 529, he established the monastery at Monte Cassino, which has been the headquarters of the order during much of the time since. He died in about 547. The Lombards sacked Cassino in about 580 and the community moved temporarily to the Lateran in Rome. In this way Pope Gregory the Great got to know their rule. He observed it himself and used it to train many of his most distinguished pupils, including St. Augustine and the members of his mission to England in 596. In Britain the rule spread vigorously. English monks not only converted most of Britain, but laid Christian foundations in Holland, Scandinavia and central Germany. St. Margaret founded the first Scottish house at Dunfermline as late as 1190.

The Lateran Decree (1215) committed the govt. of the order to triennial provincial synods of abbots. These were held regularly in England from the first at Oxford in 1218. There was a papal reorganisation in 1336. At the Dissolutions of Henry VIII there were nearly 300 English houses, of which Westminster Abbey was the most famous. *See* CASSINO.

BENEFICIUM **(Lat 'favour').** A grant of land, or income such as a money fief or prise made for services. On the continent this often meant a lay fief, but in mediaeval England connoted a reward, a (spiritual) benefit conferred by a religious house, and especially a benefice or paid office in the church. The commonest such ecclesiastical benefices were parochial incumbencies.

BENEFIT OF CLERGY, SANCTUARY AND ABJURATION.
(1) Originating in the holiness of the church or its servants, these two mitigations of the older rigorous criminal law had distinct histories.

(2) *Benefit of Clergy.* In the 12th cent. the church contended that all clerks, including clergy in minor orders, should be tried only by their own courts. This was resisted by lay rulers especially in relation to clerks accused of secular crimes; the controversy reached a climax in the dispute between Henry II and Becket. The 3rd clause of the Constitutions of Clarendon (1164) set out arrangements which, according to Henry, represented existing English law: a clerk must first be accused before a temporal court and then only if he pleads his clergy, is he handed over to the ecclesiastical court. At his trial before the latter a royal officer must be present, and if found guilty he is degraded by the ecclesiastical court and then being now a layman, arrested by the officer and handed over to the royal court for punishment. Becket, following accepted canon law, resisted accusation before a lay tribunal, and the presence of a royal officer at the ecclesiastical court, and contended that the proceedings after the finding of guilt were wrong because they involved two punishments for one offence. This latter contention was not at the time supported by the Papacy, but the outcry after Becket's murder in 1170 forced the Crown to give way to it, with the natural consequence that royal officers ceased to attend ecclesiastical courts. But for practical reasons the initial accusation and plea of clergy continued to be made in the royal court. Since the church courts continued to use compurgation in criminal cases, criminous clerks usually got away scot free, and the proceedings were widely regarded as a farce. Accordingly pressure was exerted by the Crown; royal courts would hold an inquest to discover a clerk's innocence or guilt, communicate their opinion to his bishop, and impound his property pending trial. Forest offences were excluded from the benefit even in Henry II's time: by 1260 misdemeanours had also been excluded, but under the statute *pro clero* in 1350 the privilege had been extended to secular as well as religious clerks. These included such persons as bellringers and sextons.

(3) The stage was now set for a revolution in the whole concept. A conviction for felony involved not only capital punishment of the accused but the ruin of his family through the forfeiture of all his property. The courts with merciful intention began to interpret *pro clero* so as to include all who could read, and eventually to anyone who read the first verse of the 51st Psalm. This, the so-called "neck verse" was therefore learnt by heart by all professional criminals. The fiction of handing over to the bishop for compurgation was abolished in 1576; and the royal courts were empowered to award a year's imprisonment not in orders who pleaded his clergy was branded. By 1660 therefore a male felon could, subject to statutory exceptions, escape punishment for a felony once, but the brand made it impossible to claim the privilege again. In 1692 an Act enabled women, who could never be ordained, to plead clergy like men. Statutory exceptions began, however, to grow into a tangle of complicated and technical rules as more and more acts creating new felonies were passed, and interpreted in favour of accused persons by the courts. The whole system and principle was abolished as late as 1827.

(4) *Sanctuary and Abjuration.* Criminals could escape justice by taking refuge on consecrated soil, but if they were allowed to remain indefinitely, such sanctuaries would become dens of thieves. Therefore a criminal must choose between accepting the benefit and burden of the law and surrendering to its officers, or giving up both and leaving the country, in which case he swore before the coroner to go by the most direct route to a port assigned to him and to embark within a fixed time. Once embarked he was treated as legally dead. If he broke his oath he could be killed.

(5) Sanctuary is of pre-Christian origin. Abjuration was probably connected with the Anglo-Saxon custom of outlawry. There were certain mostly obvious cases where the rules did not apply: sanctuary could not be claimed by clergy, or by persons already condemned, or caught with stolen goods or who had committed offences in churches. By 1250 a person who refused either to surrender or abjure could, after forty days, be starved. In 1379 courts were empowered to seize the goods of debtors evading process, but in 1529 the banishment consequent on abjuration was replaced by relegation for life to a permanent sanctuary, and in 1540 the number of sanctuaries was reduced, their boundaries carefully defined and arrangements enacted for the discipline of sanctuary-men. This did not work well; in 1603 the common law was restored, whereupon the sanctuaries became a haven for the fraudulent. In consequence sanctuaries were abolished in 1623.

(6) A number of technically miscalled sanctuaries (such as the Rolls and the Savoy) continued, however, to exist mainly in London. These were in fact enclaves

which had their own "police privileges". Criminals could not be pursued into them by peace officers from outside, who had to rely upon the non-existent or corrupt peace authorities of the enclave. By the time these could be got to move, the bird had usually flown. Much eroded by rebuilding and the pressure of public opinion they were assimilated with their surrounding areas in 1839.

BENELUX. Under the T. of London (5 Sept. 1944) Belgium, the Netherlands and Luxemburg agreed to form a customs union which came into full force in Mar. 1948. In 1958 they joined the Common Market.

BENEŠ, Eduard (1884-1948). This Czech statesman was one of the earliest collaborators of Thomas Masaryk. Except when Prime Minister (1921-22) he was in effective charge of Czechoslovakia's foreign policy from 1919 until his election as President in Dec. 1935. He resigned on 5 Oct. 1938, after the Munich Agreement, and went to Chicago. During World War II he was head of the Czech govt. in exile in London and returned to Prague in May 1945. He formed a coalition and was re-elected President, but in Feb. 1948 he was compelled by the Russians to set up a fully communist govt. He resigned in June and died a few weeks later.

BENEVENTO. *See* TALLEYRAND.

BENEVOLENCE was theoretically a voluntary gift by a wealthy person to the King, but in practice it was paid under pressure. Benevolences seem to have grown out of the forced loans raised under Edward II and Richard II, but the word itself was not used until about 1473 when the intention to repay was discarded. They were declared illegal by an act of Richard III in 1484 but in 1485 he circumvented the act by a technical promise to repay. Benevolences were common under Henry VII and VIII (who could bully their nobility) but were not instituted under the later Tudors (who could not). In 1614-15 James I revived the practice despite sporadic opposition, and in 1622 Vist. Saye and Sele was imprisoned for protesting against the last of them.

BENGAL (India) (1) The Portuguese established the first European settlement at Hooghli in 1579. The Moguls under Akbar were at the height of their power and Bengal, Bihar and Orissa together formed their richest viceroyalty; it was ruled from Dacca by a Nawab responsible to the Emperor at Delhi, together with a revenue minister or Diwan appointed by the Emperor himself. In the ensuing 180 years, dynastic civil wars, the instability and religious intolerance of the Emperor Aurangzib (1659-1707) and the rise of the Marathas, Persians and Afghans, corrupted the Mogul system and destroyed most of the direct power (but not the influence) of the imperial throne. By 1720 the Nawabs had become semi-independent; their relations with other powers and provinces had characteristics resembling foreign policy; and the internal politics of the viceroyalty had become more important than the politics of the Great Mogul. The changing balance between Delhi and Dacca formed the background of European activities.

(2) The Portuguese offended the Imperial Prince, Shah Jehan, by refusing to support him against his father Jehangir, with the result that after coming to the throne he destroyed their trading post ('Factory') at Hooghli in 1632. A year later the HEIC stepped into their shoes and by 1640 had, besides Hooghli, factories as far afield as Dacca and Patna (six in all). These, through a Bay Council, were subordinate to the Company's Agent and Council at Madras. There were also Dutch, and later Danish, factories along the river Hooghli, and in 1673 the French founded their principal and lucrative Bengal settlement at Chandernagore.

(3) Official corruption and arbitrary levies made unprivileged trade unprofitable. The company decided in 1686 to fortify the post at Chuttanuttee (later Calcutta), but they were driven out by the Nawab. In 1690, however, they secured peace and a licence to fortify from

the Emperor Aurungzib; Job Charnock, their Agent, accordingly founded Fort William at Calcutta and in 1696 Aurungzib granted the *zamindari* there and so took the town effectively out of the Nawab's jurisdiction. Starting from nothing, this privileged enclave grew very quickly: fifty years later it had 400,000 inhabitants.

(4) In 1704 the Diwan in Bengal, Murshid Kuli Khan, quarrelled with the Nawab, and moved to Muksabad which he renamed Murshidabad after himself. His virtually independent administration imposed such onerous levies on the English that a company embassy went to Delhi to ask for redress. In 1717 they obtained a *firman* ('phirmaund') or charter of privileges whose meaning was disputed for many years; but though Nawabs habitually construed it in their own interests, the *firman* and *zamindari* gave the English a long start over their rivals.

(5) Murshid became Nawab in 1713 and reigned until 1725. He was succeeded by his son-in-law, Shuja Khan, whose administration was peaceful and efficient. He had a favourite, Alivardi, Gov. of Patna who, by influence at the Mogul court, secured a patent as Nawab of that place in 1736. In 1739 (when Delhi was sacked by the Persians) Shuja Khan died, and in 1740 after a short civil war, Alivardi seized the viceroyalty. Within a year Bengal was attacked by the Marathas, and after a long and bloody war Alivardi ceded Orissa to them in 1751. Thereafter until his death in 1756 there was peace.

(6) During Alivardi's reign causes of friction between the Nawab and the English had multiplied. They had become rich and abused their privileges. The *firman* permitted them to protect and judge their own Indian servants, and to trade custom-free. They began to sell passes to the Nawab's subjects, which prejudiced his revenue, and they levied all sorts of imposts in the *Zamindari*, thus subjecting to customs the very people with whom they traded custom free. The Nawab predictably made levies and took other action which the English called infringements of the *firman*. Nevertheless a *modus vivendi* was precariously maintained until 1756 when Alivardi was succeeded by his grand-nephew Mirza Mohammed, an unstable eighteen-year old, usually known by his title Suraj-ud-Daula.

(7) His attack on Calcutta coincided roughly with the outbreak of the Seven Years War and Clive, who was sent to the rescue from Madras, was able to drive out the French and overthrow Suraj-ud-Daula in the campaign which culminated on 23 June, 1757, at Plassey. This event fatally weakened the shaky finances of the French East India Co, and the English made enormous quick profits. In 1757 Clive received the perpetual revenues of the XXIV Pargannas, an area larger than Cornwall. In 1760 the Company received, revenue free, territories four times as large, around Midnapore, Burdwan and Chittagong. In 1765 Clive accepted for the Company the office of Diwan for the whole viceroyalty, in exchange for a fixed rent payable to Delhi.

(8) This change was revolutionary. The Nawabs now had to look to the Company for money, because it collected the taxes; and as revenue collection and property jurisdiction went together (*see* INDIAN LAND SETTLEMENT) its officials were soon involved in the daily administration. By 1770 the Governor and Council at Calcutta were the real govt. and the Nawab's court at Murshidabad a puppet show.

(9) Bengal was now, in everything but name, part of the British Empire; it was much the richest possession of the Company, and its affairs had national and international implications. They attracted the attention of Parliament, and much of the late 18th cent. legislation on India was really framed to meet the situation in Bengal (*see* EAST INDIA COMPANY, HON.). Calcutta became the Company's Indian capital, and the seat of the Governor-Gen. who from 1773 to 1785 was Warren Hastings.

(10) His reign was a period of administrative difficulty and experiment, as well as political and military danger. Hastings saw that the Company was changing from a primarily commercial undertaking exploiting an investment, into a governmental body, whose commerce had to take second place after the welfare of the population. The change was not always welcomed by the Company's local servants; the Gov-Gen. had only a casting vote on his own council, whose members habitually overruled him, thwarted his policies, and eventually had him impeached. It took him and his successor, Cornwallis (1786-93) twenty years to establish proper habits of administrative integrity.

(11) By 1786 the administrative system of Bengal was established, and it became the rough pattern for other parts of India. Officials were properly paid and so harder to corrupt; each district had its district officer; the judicial system had been rationalised; the tax assessments had been placed on a permanent footing and, unfortunately, the *Zamindars* had been given the status of property owners. This bred injustices to the peasants (ryots) who, as the population rose, had to be given more and more protection against their new and ingenious landlords. Bengal Tenancy Acts were passed for this purpose in 1859, 1885, 1928, 1938 and 1941.

(12) In 1826 Assam was added to the immediate responsibilities of the Gov-Gen., who soon found that he had too much to do. Therefore in 1854 he became responsible solely for India as a whole, and Bengal, Bihar, Orissa and Assam were given Lieut-Governors. In 1874 Assam was hived off under a Chief Commissioner, but in 1905, against Hindu protests (*see* YUGANTAR) the area was reshuffled into a western province comprising W. Bengal, Bihar and Orissa, and an eastern one comprising E. Bengal and Assam. This did not last, and in 1912 Bengal was united under a governor, Bihar and Orissa were united under a lieut-governor and Assam had its separate chief commissioner again.

(13) The united Bengal received a new constitution under the Montague Chelmsford Reforms of 1921. In 1937 Bengal was constituted an autonomous province under the Government of India Act, 1935.

(14) When India and Pakistan became independent in 1947 Bengal with its large Moslem population was divided between them, the eastern part becoming the new province of East Pakistan with its capital at Dacca. *See* BANGLADESH.

BENGAL FAMINE (1943) By building railways in the 19th cent. the British had averted famines in India but in 1943 the Japanese blockade of the Burmese and Siamese rice supply, together with shipping difficulties, meant that there was no rice to send by rail, and led to hoarding. In the resulting famine a million people died. The central govt. did not intervene until the arrival of Wavell as viceroy. As a condition of an armistice at the end of war, the Siamese were required to deliver 1.5M tons of rice.

BENGHAZI, seaport and capital of Cyrenaica, changed hands five times during World War II and was finally taken by the British in Nov. 1942. *See* BARBARY.

BENIN (Nigeria) This city, nation, state and religious centre for much of W. Africa was already highly organised when first visited by the Portuguese Joao Afonso d' Aveiro in about 1485. Portuguese traders and missionaries were active there till the mid-17th cent. by which time they had been gradually ousted by the Dutch. Trade was mostly in palm oil, pepper, ivory and especially slaves. By about 1700 the area was in decline because of endemic civil war. Later the economy was further unhinged by the progressive suppression of the slave trade in which the British were active.

Though Thos. Wyndham visited the coast as early as 1553 British influence was unimportant till the establishment of the coastal protectorate in 1885.

Attempts to wean the *Oba* (King) from the practice of human sacrifice failed and culminated in the murder of an unarmed mission in Jan. 1897. A punitive expedition under Sir Harry Rawson then stormed the city and the Oba was deported to Calabar where he died in 1914. The area is now part of Nigeria.

BENN, Anthony Neil Wedgwood (1925-) 2nd Vist. STANSGATE (1960-3) was elected as a left wing Labour M.P. in 1950 and soon made a strong, if not invariably favourable impression by his wit and intellectual elegance. He introduced a bill to permit himself to renounce his right and obligation to assume his father's peerage (and continue in the Commons). This was defeated on the ground that a general rule was needed, not merely one for the benefit of Mr Benn, but the manoeuvre drew attention to the problem. In 1960, accordingly, he went to the Lords on his father's death, but in 1962 the Tory govt. introduced the Peerage Bill, which was passed in 1963. In July 1963 he was able to disclaim his Viscountcy in time for the 1964 general election which returned a Labour govt. under Harold Wilson. He served as Postmaster-Gen., and then from 1966 to 1970 as Min. of Technology. In the next Labour govt (1974-9) he was Sec. of State for Industry and Min. of Posts and Telecommunications under Wilson and then for Energy from 1975 to 1979 under Callaghan. He had always been at variance with the Fabian and consensus based leadership of his party but was too valuable and charming a colleague to be driven out. He sought to convince his public in *Arguments for Socialism* (1979) that the Keynesian state was dead and should be replaced by high public investment and expenditure, and extensive public ownership combined with self management at the shop floor. The resources for such a programme were to be found in an economically low-profile foreign policy involving withdrawal from Ulster, N.A.T.O. and the E.E.C. This seemed to be both too clever and to ignore the contemporary revolutionary ambitions of the U.S.S.R.

BENNETT (Enoch) Arnold (1867-1931) novelist whose "Five Towns" Burslem, Hanley, Longton, Stoke-on-Trent and Tunstall form the background of many novels, published between 1902 and 1925 portraying, in minutely detailed drabness, the life of the Potteries and other run down areas. He was also a distinguished journalist and theatre critic.

BENNET (1) Sir John (?-1627) became Abp. of York's Vicar-Gen. in spirituals in 1590, M.P. for Ripon in 1597 and a member of the Council of the North in 1599. He was M.P. again in 1601 (York) and 1603 (Ripon) when he became judge of the Canterbury Prerogative Court, and M.P. for Oxford Univ. in 1614 and 1620. He was then appointed to the High Commission, but was involved in Bacon's fall, being himself impeached for auctioning the administration of intestate estates. The impeachment was adjourned *sine die,* but in July 1624 he was fined £20,000 in the Star Chamber. He paid without difficulty. He was three times married and in 1624 had 10 children and 40 grandchildren living. Two of his sons were also wealthy lawyers. One of the grandchildren **(2) Henry (1618-85) Ld. (1663) E. of ARLINGTON (1672)** was wounded in the Civil War. In 1654 he became sec. to P. James in exile, and in 1658 he was Charles' successful representative to Spain. In 1661 he became Keeper of the Privy Purse and, with Sir Chas. Berkeley, manager of the King's mistresses. With Lady Castlemaine's help he became Sec. of State and, with Buckingham and Bristol, he led the opposition to Clarendon. From 1664 he was chiefly responsible for foreign affairs by reason of his experience and linguistic talents, and he had married Isabella, a daughter of Louis of Nassau. He was, however, a R. Catholic and had become a member of the celebrated Cabal. As such he was responsible for hoodwinking his protestant colleagues over the secret T.

of Dover in 1670, and in advising the issue in 1672, and the withdrawal in 1673 of the Declaration of Indulgence. Afraid of the political and practical probabilities arising from the policy of Clifford and James, D. of York, he betrayed the T. of Dover to Shaftesbury, supported the passage of the Test Act which ruined Clifford, and advised Charles to dismiss James. In Jan. 1674 the Commons, not surprisingly, debated his impeachment and though the articles were thrown out, his public repute was destroyed. In Sept. he resigned as Sec. of State and became Lord Chamberlain and, in Dec. 1674, he went to Holland to negotiate with William of Orange for a general peace and for his marriage to James' daughter Mary. The mission failed. Shortly after, as a result of a quarrel with Danby, he retired. His daughter **(3) Isabella (?-1723)**, married Henry 1st D. of Grafton, a bastard of Charles II by the Duchess of Cleveland.

BENNETT, Richard Bedford (1870-1947) 1st Vist. BENNETT (1941), New Brunswick lawyer, migrated westward in 1897. He served successively in the legislature of the NW Territory and Alberta, and entered the Canadian House of Commons in 1911 as a Conservative for Calgary after Laurier's fall in the general election which brought Sir Robt. Borden to power. In 1916 he was appointed director-gen. of National Service: this involved organising a war effort – especially in military manpower – which would give Canada a standing in world opinion independent of Britain. When negotiations for a coalition to carry conscription broke down, the govt. fought a khaki election and enacted conscription on its own. This enhanced Canada's international standing and she signed the peace treaties as an independent power; but it damaged Canadian Conservatism by alienating the French of Quebec. Borden was followed by Meighen in the conservative leadership, but political and economic unrest led to electoral defeat in 1921, and for the next seven years Bennett was in opposition. In 1927, however, he became leader of his party, and having won the general election of 1930 became Prime Minister.

This was the second period of post war depression. Bennett was both a Canadian and a Commonwealth nationalist, holding that his country's interests were best served as a loyal but equal partner of the British Commonwealth. The Statute of Westminster, 1931, and the Ottawa trade agreements were really his monuments. The first represented the establishment of legal equality; the second the replacement of legal ties by mutual economic interests. But the internal political situation remained precarious and in 1935 Bennett's govt. was swept away by a liberal-French coalition under Mackenzie King. He was never in power again. He died in England. *See* CANADA-28.

BENNETT, Sir William Sterndale (1816-75), violinist, pianist, organist, composer and musical organiser, was a close friend of Mendelssohn. He inspired the foundation of the Bach Society in 1849, was conductor of the London Philharmonic from 1855, Prof. of Music at Cambridge from 1856 and Principal of the Royal Academy of Music from 1866. Though the distractions caused by his other work probably explain the decline of his early promise as a composer, the survival of a widespread Victorian musical taste probably owes more to him than to anyone else.

BENOIT or BENEDICT of STE MAURE, a troubadour patronised by Henry II. Among his works are a verse history of the Dukes of Normandy.

BENSON. This Yorkshire family included **(1) George (1699-1762)** a very learned presbyterian divine. **(2) Robert (1676-1731) 1st Ld. BINGLEY (1713)** who, as an M.P. from 1702, was a supporter of Harley and Ch. of the Exch. in 1711. **(3) Edward White (1829-96)** had a brilliant academic career at Trinity College, Cambridge. He was ordained in 1853 and in 1859 married Mary

Sedgwick and was offered by the Prince Consort the mastership of the newly founded Wellington College. Under his guidance it became not merely a charity school for sons of officers, but a famous public school. In 1874 he left Wellington and became Chanc. of Lincoln Cathedral, and in 1877 Disraeli offered him the newly created see of Truro. He organised it, ensured that a cathedral would be built and at the same time played a part in church affairs at large. In 1882 he succeeded Tait as Abp. of Canterbury. The R. Commission on Education was set up in 1886 on his initiative; in the same year he established an advisory House of Laity for the Canterbury province, and this became the precedent for the tricameral convocation. His judgement in the *Case of Dr King* (1889), the saintly bishop of Lincoln who was tried for ritual offences, was a model of legal and historical erudition. He was a powerful opponent of disestablishment, and created the Anglican bishopric in Jerusalem. He also made friends with the Russian orthodox church. Of his three sons **(4) Arthur Christopher (1862-1925)** was an influential master at Eton between 1885 and 1903 but resigned and became a fellow of Magdalene College, Cambridge. In 1907 he published (with Vist. Esher) a three volume selection of Q. Victoria's letters, over a hundred other volumes including works on Rossetti, Fitzgerald, Pater and Ruskin, and voluminous diaries. He wrote the words of *Land of Hope and Glory* for Elgar's previously composed music. In 1915 he became Master of Magdalene. He died in office. **(5) Edward Frederic (1867-1940),** a prolific and sentimental novelist, had a power of recall which made his works of family reminiscence valuable as social history. He also wrote popular horror stories. **(6) Robert Hugh (1871-1914),** Monsignor was ordained in 1895 but was received into the Roman church in 1903. He became well-known as a preacher and, with the family literary gifts, a writer of Catholic apologetics and a novelist.

BENTHAM, Jeremy (1748-1832), the Utilitarian philosopher produced an immense literary output, but the dates of composition and of publication of his works were often separated by many years. Educated at Oxford and Lincoln' s Inn, he conceived a moral and intellectual contempt for Sir William Blackstone whose law lectures he heard at Oxford in 1763. In 1776 he published his anonymous *Fragment on Government,* a masterly critique of Blackstone's commentaries. This caused a sensation and Lord Shelburne sought him out and befriended him. He was introduced to most of the leading progressive statesmen of his day and left memoirs of such figures as Camden and Pitt. His influence, based on his incisive intelligence, was thus much increased by personal acquaintanceship with those who could put his ideas into effect, and many of his works were written at Shelburne's house. In 1789 he published his most important book, the *Introduction to Princlples of Morals and Legislation* which contains the clearest statement of his utilitarianism; utility is "that property in any object whereby it tends to produce benefit, advantage, pleasure, good or happiness, or to prevent the happening of mischief, pain, evil or unhappiness to the party whose interests is considered". The two sovereign motives of mankind are gain and pleasure, and it is the function of the moralist and the legislator to advance them. Having defined the sources of pleasure and pain he proposes yardsticks by which pleasures and pains can be evaluated: they can be related to their intensity, duration, certainty, propinquity, likelihood of repetition or reaction, their extent and the number of people likely to be affected. Pleasures and pains are then classified, and this classification can be used for measuring the propriety of laws.

It was consistent with this outlook that Bentham invented words (like *minimise)* when he needed them, and that his visit in 1785 to Russia (where his brother, Sir Samuel, was an engineer) led him to investigate the uses of penal employment; he in fact spent much time and energy in perfecting his "pan-opticon", a prison where all inmates could be supervised from a single central point.

In 1792 he inherited a fortune and thenceforth lived an independent existence writing and studying seven or eight hours a day. Already famous, he was made an honorary citizen of France by the French National Assembly at the instance of Brissot, another of his friends. He took up an extraordinary variety of public causes: in 1795, for example, he published an attack on Law Taxes, and proposed a form of death duty. In 1798 he turned his attention to the Poor Law and to a project for raising govt. loans by the issue of annuity notes. In 1807 he was engaged on the reform of Scottish legal procedure; in 1808 on the death rate in Mexico; in 1809 he completed but did not publish a critique of the law of libel; in 1817 he finished an examination of the Pauline doctrines and their influence in the Church of England, and in 1818 he exposed the hypocrisy of taking oaths. He was also gradually completing a legal codification and a programme of parliamentary and electoral reform. His readiness to do the research and drafting himself was an important source of his influence. By this time he was also conducting an enormous world wide correspondence with, amongst others, Bolivar, the Czar Alexander, Quincy Adams, Daniel O'Connell and Mehemet Ali.

Most of his works were edited during his lifetime by Dumont, a Genevan Swiss, and by J. S. Mill.

BENTINCK FAMILY. This family, already distinguished in the Netherlands, entered British history when **(1) Hans Willem (1649-1709) 1st E. of PORTLAND (1689)** visited England in 1670 with William of Orange. He and William were very intimate: in 1675 Bentinck personally nursed him through the small-pox; in 1677 he came to England to negotiate his friend's marriage to Pr. Mary, and ten years later he achieved the understanding with Frederick III of Brandenburg (heir presumptive to the Orange possessions) by which William's English expedition was covered against French military counter-moves. After William's coronation he accompanied the King on his Irish campaign; he was mostly employed in diplomacy, and partic ularly in 1697 when he negotiated the preliminaries of the P. of Ryswick with Marshal Boufflers. By this time he had irritated William III by his jealousy of Albemarle, another Dutchman, and though the King remained personally friendly, Portland was sent to Paris as ambassador to negotiate the problems of the Spanish Succession. This period ended with the abortive First Partition T. of 1699, when Portland resigned. In 1700 the Second Partition T. was signed and in 1701 the Commons voted to impeach him for his part in the proceedings, but the impeachment was dismissed. After William's death his career was unimportant. **(2) William Henry Cavendish (1738-1809) 3rd D. of PORTLAND (1762)** as Marquess of Titchfield was M.P. for Weobly in 1761. He was a whig, a friend of Rockingham, and from 1765 to 1766 was Lord Chamberlain in the latter's first govt. He was then in very active opposition, partly because the govt. arbitrarily ignored his title to the Inglewod estates in Cumberland: and his and the D. of Grafton's animosity became so notorious that Portland was even suspected of being "Junius". He remained in opposition throughout Lord North's period of office, but when Rockingham returned briefly to power in 1782 he was Lord Lieut. of Ireland, while his brother-in-law Lord John Cavendish was Ch. of the Exch. In an age of wit his reputation has suffered because he lacked it; all the same he was an influential and useful politician, and could preside over the many rival intelligences who would not concede primacy to each other. Thus in 1793 as First Lord of the Treasury he was nominal head of the Fox-North coalition; during the difficult and riotous second period of Pitt's first govt. he was Home Sec. from 1794 to 1801; under Addington he became Lord President in July 1801, and he remained in the govt. when Pitt returned from 1804 until the latter died in 1806. For a short while out of office during the period of "All the Talents", he was First Lord of the Treasury with Perceval, Canning and Castlereagh from 1807 to 1809, when Perceval succeeded him. His son **(3) Ld. William (Cavendish) (1774-1839)** served in Suvarov's H.Q. in Italy in 1799 and with the Austrians in 1801. From 1803 to 1807 he was gov. of Madras, but being held responsible for the Velore mutiny was recalled. He commanded a brigade under Moore in the Corunna campaign (1808-8) and in 1811 was appointed to command the British forces in Sicily. The mainland possessions of the Neapolitan Kingdom were in French hands, and K. Ferdinand's court was at Palermo under British protection and subsidy. The King, who was in contact with the French, was involved in constitutional quarrels with the Sicilian baronage over taxation, and Bentinck was urged by many Sicilians to intervene, if only to safeguard the British military position. He threatened to withdraw the troops and the subsidy, and so compelled the King to form a liberal govt. and a parliament on the English model. He proceeded in 1812 to establish wholesale reforms in taxation, justice, property and status: these were later known as the 'laws of the Good Lord Bentinck', who in 1813 resumed his military career first in Spain and then at Genoa.

After a long interval without significant public employment, he went to India in 1827 as Gov-Gen. of Bengal. He reduced the cost of the services, recovered fraudulently alienated revenue, began the tax settlement of the northwest, and reformed the judicial system. In 1833 he became the first titular Gov-Gen. of India. He suppressed widow-burning (Suttee) and the Thugs, and intervened in grossly maladministered native states such as Coorg and Mysore. His knowledge of the Russians also led him to renew the alliance with Ranjit Singh, and to make a commercial agreement with the Amirs of Sind. Though personally not liked by the English in general, he formed a friendship with Macaulay whose promotion he assured. In 1835 he left India and in 1836 became liberal M.P. for Glasgow.

BENTLEY, Edmund Clerihew (1875-1956) journalist and novelist invented the four line rhymed epigram of extremely irregular scansion named *clerihew* after him:

> Henry the Eighth
> Had a thucthethion of mateth
> He thought that the monkth
> Were a lathy lot of thkunkth.

BENTLEY, Richard (1662-1742) immensely learned and quarrelsome scholar, made his first mark with a dissertation on John Malalas in 1691. He was Boyle Lecturer in 1692, Keeper of the Royal Library from 1694 and DD (Cantab) in 1696. He now began a prolonged quarrel with the Hon. C. Boyle which was connected with the *Epistles of Phalaris*. He proved them spurious. In 1700 he became Master of Trinity (Cambridge). He quarrelled with the fellows and was deprived by the Visitor. In 1717 he got himself elected Regius Prof. of Devinity (*sic*). His scholarly output, especially on classical texts, was enormous and his influence lasting.

BENTLEY, John Francis (1839-1902), a R. Catholic church architect, designed and mostly built Westminster Cathedral. His only instruction from the client was that it should not resemble Westminster Abbey.

BEORHTRIC (?-802) K. of the West Saxons succeeded Cynewulf in 785 and married Eadburh *d.* of K. Offa of Mercia. The two Kings appear to have shared a dislike for Egbert, Beorhtric's next of kin, who was driven overseas. Eadburh, however, hated her husband and eventually poisoned him. Egbert then ascended the throne of the West Saxons.

BEORN (?-1049) was a nephew of Gytha, wife of E. Godwin and brother of Sweyn Estrithson, K. of Denmark. When Edward the Confessor married Godwin's daughter Eadgyth (Edith) in 1045, Beorn received the earldom of the Middle Angles. In 1046 on the banishment of Godwin's son Sweyn, Beorn took his Mercian fiefs. Sweyn murdered him at Bosham three years later.

BEORNWULF (?-826) K. of the Mercians deposed Ceolwulf in 823. He spent the next two years consolidating his position, especially by settling the disputes of his predecessor with the church. In 825 war broke out with Egbert of Wessex who defeated him with slaughter at Ellandun. As a result the East Anglians came over to Egbert. Beornwulf then undertook a punitive foray against them but was killed.

BEOWULF. An Old English epic composed of several different episodes, which survives as a M.S. of c. 1000. In its 10th cent. West Saxon English can be discerned a 7th or 8th cent. Anglian original containing orally preserved verses recounting some events which actually took place in the early 6th cent., in western Sweden and Jutland. The poem has a Christian setting but deals vividly with the deeds of a hero, Beowulf, of pagan times.

BERAR (India) A province of Hyderabad permanently leased to the British in 1853. The heir to the throne of Hyderabad used the title Prince of Berar.

BERBER. *See* SOMALIA *and* BARBARY.

BERBICE (Guyana) was settled by the Dutch in 1627 and separated from Surinam in 1732. The British seized it along with Demerara and Essequibo in 1796, and again in 1803 when the Dutch were allied to Bonaparte. English colonisation ensured that the three places were not returned to Holland in 1815. They were united to form British Guiana in 1831. It was long the source of the well known brown sugar called Demerara sugar.

BERCHTESGADEN (Bavaria), a German salient amid magnificent scenery on the Austrian border, contained the private retreats of Adolf Hitler and some other Nazi grandees. He first rented *Haus Wachenfeld* in 1925 and after his rise to power converted it into the *Berghof* by which name it is better known. It was at the *Berghof* that Neville Chamberlain had his first interview with Hitler on 15 Sept. 1938.

BERCHTOLD von und zu UNGARSCHITZ, Leopold Count (1863-1942), became Austro-Hungarian ambassador to St. Petersburg in Dec. 1906. He took a leading part in the Bosnian negotiations of 1908 when Aerenthal and Izvolski met at Buchlow, his country house in Moravia. In Feb. 1912 he unwillingly succeeded Aerenthal as foreign minister, for temperamentally he was a diplomat rather than a policy maker.

His method of securing Balkan advantages by negotiation failed against not only Russian opposition and Serb intransigence, but for lack of support from Austria's German and Italian allies. Moreover, the triumphs of the Balkan states over the Turks in the Balkan wars had made them ambitious and Serbia, in particular, was trying to subvert the imperial territories towards the Adriatic. By 1914 he recognised that a peaceful policy had failed and when Serbs murdered the Archduke Franz Ferdinand at Sarajevo on 28 June 1914, he advised a final settlement with Serbia (war).

At the outbreak of the war, his efforts to induce Italy to intervene on Austria's side in accordance with its treaty obligations, broke down in the face of exorbitant territorial demands. In Jan. 1915 he resigned the Foreign Ministry and held only court posts until the fall of the dynasty. Thereafter he took no part in public affairs.

BERE ALSTON (S. Devon). This small place on the Cornish border had lead and silver mines from the end of the 13th cent. and a fair from 1295. It was a parliamentary borough, mostly under Treasury control, from 1584 to 1832.

BERENGARIA (?-c. 1230) Q. of Richard I, *d* of Sancho VI of Navarre and Blanche of Castille, was one of the wittiest and most beautiful women of her age. In 1191 she voyaged after K. Richard to marry him, and was wrecked on the coast of Cyprus. Richard attacked and conquered Cyprus and married her at Limassol in May 1191, but saw very little of her. After his death she lived mostly at Le Mans, but K. John seized most of her property and she was, for a queen, very poor until after his death.

BERENGARIA. Former German 52,000-ton liner *Imperator* taken in reparations after World War I and operated by the Cunard Co on transatlantic services until 1936.

BERESFORD (1) John (1738-1805) second *s.* of Marcus E. of Tyrone and Lady de la Poer, sat for Waterford in the Irish Parliament from 1760 to 1800 and became an Irish Privy Councillor in 1768. In 1770 he was made a commissioner of Revenue and Chief Commissioner in 1780. In these permanent positions he wielded great influence over Lords Lieutenant who were temporary. He was Pitt's main adviser on Irish affairs, and he and Grattan were bitterly opposed particularly on questions of trade. When Lord Fitzwilliam came to Ireland in 1795 to embark on a new policy of conciliation, Beresford was dismissed, but recalled when the policy failed. He now became one of the chief advocates of union, and from 1800 represented Waterford in the united parliament. He remained, however, in Ireland until 1802 to settle the fiscal problems arising out of the new arrangements. **(2) William Carr (1768-1854) Vist. BERESFORD (1814)**, a soldier, was with Hood and Nelson in 1794 at the capture of the three Corsican fortresses. In 1799 he went to India and thence, in June 1801, to Egypt where he led a celebrated march across the desert from Qosseir. He next assisted in Baird's seizure of Cape Town (Jan. 1806) and in Popham's unsuccessful attack on Buenos Aires. He was captured but escaped to England in 1807. He was then given military command of an expedition to Madeira, which he took in Dec. 1807. Here he learned Portuguese; he was then sent to Wellesley's force in Portugal and afterwards took part in Moore's tragic retreat to Corunna. In Feb. 1809 he was seconded to the Portuguese army which he spent the next two years in training. He became a Portuguese count and field-marshal.

In the spring of 1811 he took command of Hill's corps, and on 16 May he and Hardinge won the hard fought B. of Albuera against Soult. He was in most of Wellington' s later Peninsular battles, and was given his peerage at the Duke's special request.

After the B. of Toulouse (Apr. 1814) he returned to Portugal and in 1817 put down a mutiny at Rio de Janeiro. He finally left Portuguese service in 1819, and from 1822 was a supporter of Wellington in the House of Lords. **(3) Charles William de la Poer (1846-1919) Ld. (1916)** an able and ambitious sailor, quickly gained promotion. He was Tory M.P. for Waterford from 1874 to 1880, and was also a society figure and a friend of the P. of Wales. From 1882 to 1885 he served in the Mediterranean, taking part in the bombardment of Alexandria (1882). He was re-elected for E. Marylebone in 1885, secured no political office but became Fourth Sea Lord. In this administrative office he proved a difficult colleague, for he occasionally attacked the Admiralty in Parliament. He resigned in 1888 but continued in the ordinary course of promotion and by 1906 had been appointed C-in-C in the Mediterranean. From this post he openly opposed the Sir John Fisher's far reaching naval reforms, and in 1909 was ordered to haul down his flag. He at once challenged Fisher by a document which he sent to the Prime Minister. In the resulting inquiry Fisher's policies were upheld, but he was returned to the Commons for Portsmouth in 1910 and continued to hold the seat until made a peer in 1916.

BERG. *See* JÜLICH.

BERGSON, Henri (1859-1941), part French, part English philosopher. In examining the non-mathematical sciences, he argued that time has an aspect of real duration in the indivisible continuity of change, of which everyone is conscious. He also thought that the mind, in acting on matter, introduced an element of unpredictability, freedom or spontaneity into events. The past does not cease to exist, and memories are not simply stored records of it, but the brain acts as a censor, admitting at any given time only that part of consciousness of the past relevant to the practical activity of the moment.

Evolution is not due wholly to the preservation of chance or naturally selected variations, but is affected by *l'élan vital* (Fr = Life enhancing momentum), a psychological factor common to all organisms, pre-disposing them to transmit advantageous variations. In the world as a whole, organic life strives continually upwards against the obstruction of inert matter.

Though Bergson's working life was spent mostly in France, he was Pres. of the London Soc. for Psychical Research in 1913.

BERIBERI is caused primarily by the dietary deficiency of vitamin B1, particularly where the staple food is polished rice. The wholesale polishing of rice by steam processes began in the 19th cent. in India and Malaya, where the disease caused widespread debilitation. Its cause was not suspected before 1895, nor established until 1911.

BERING SEA DISPUTE (1881-93). In 1881 U.S.A., in order to control seal hunting off Alaska, claimed that the Bering Sea was an internal sea, as it had been before it acquired Alaska from Russia. Britain rejected the claim. In 1886 USA began seizing sealing vessels, mostly Canadian. By 1891 the British had forced an agreement for the joint patrolling of the area and for an arbitration. The arbitrators sat in Paris in 1893, found against the U.S.A. and awarded damages. The dispute showed that differences between Britain and the U.S.A. could at last be settled amicably.

BERING STRAITS. At the request of Peter the Great, the Danish navigator Vitus Janassen Bering (1681-1741) commanded a trans-Siberian expedition to determine if Asia and America were separate continents. The journey lasted from 1725 to 1728 but the results were uncertain and he did not see Alaska. His second expedition in 1741 reached Alaska and this opened the area to Russian trappers and fishermen. He died during the journey, at Bering I. His reports were largely ignored by the Russian bureaucracy, but his cartography was confirmed by Capt. James Cook in 1778.

BERKELEY FAMILY of Berkeley Castle (Glos) trace their ancestry to **(1) Eadnoth the Staller (fl. 1067)**, an Englishman who swore allegiance to William I and was given a military command. His grandson **(2) Robert Fitz Harding (fl. 1153)**, a Bristol merchant supported the Angevins and was rewarded with land in the royal manor of Berkeley (c. 1153) and later with the whole manor. The family generally avoided politics in 13th cent. but improved its estates. In 14th cent, however, it continued to increase its lands but became politically active. **(3) Thomas (II) (?-1321)** holder of the barony 1281-1321, apparently fought in 28 skirmishes or battles, some of them against the men of Bristol, and was taken at Bannockburn (1314). His son **(4) Maurice (III) (?-1326)** joined the Barons against Edward II, was captured and died in prison at Wallingford. Maurice's son **(5) Thomas (III) (?-1361)** who married a daughter of Roger Mortimer, supported him and Isabella and so got back his lands, but with lasting infamy, for he was a commissioner for deposing Edward II and it was to Berkeley Castle that the latter was taken in Apr. 1327 and brutally murdered in Sept.

(6) Thomas (?-1417) 4th Ld. BERKELEY gained some 24 manors by marrying the heiress of Warn, Lord of

Lisle. Their only child **(7) Elizabeth (?-?)** married Richard Beauchamp, E. of Warwick and when Thomas died she gained the Lisle lands, but the barony of Berkeley passed to her cousin **(8) James (?-1463)**. This split of title and lands caused a violent family feud lasting nearly two centuries and culminated in a battle at Nibley Green in 1470. It was settled only in 1609.

(9) Sir William (1639-66) as a rear-admiral, was accused of cowardice in the battle of 3rd June 1665, but was promoted and was killed in gallant circumstances in the Four Days B. (June 1666). **(10) Sir William (?-1677)** was gov. of Virginia from 1641, with a short parliamentary interruption till 1676 when he was recalled for incompetence in connection with Bacon's rebellion. **(11) John (?-1678) 1st Ld. BERKELEY of STRATTON (1658)** went on an embassy to Sweden in 1636; he was M.P. for Heytesbury in 1640 and was expelled in 1641 from the House on charges of subverting the army in the King's interest. He served the King with distinction in the Civil War. In 1643 he took Exeter but in Mar. 1644 he and Hopton were defeated at Alresford. In Apr. 1645 he nearly captured Taunton, but was himself forced to surrender at Exeter in the following Jan. He then made abortive attempts to negotiate between the King and Parliament, but when arraigned by parliament retired to Paris where he held minor appointments at the fugitive court. Between 1652 and 1656 he served under Turenne at whose request he was given his peerage. He became Pres. of Connaught in 1661, a privy councillor in 1663 and spent the years 1670 and 1671 as Lord Lieut. in Ireland where he showed favour to R. Catholics. From Dec. 1675 until May 1677 he was one of the English plenipotentiaries at Nijmegen. His son **(12) John, 3rd Ld. (1663-97)** was one of the admirals involved in the disastrous repulse at Camaret Bay in June 1694.

(13) George (1628-98) 1st E. of BERKELEY was M.P. for Gloucestershire in 1654 and 1656 and one of the commissioners for inviting Charles II to return in 1660. In 1661 he was a member of the Council for Plantations; in 1663 a founder of the Royal African Co, and in 1668 he was a member of the new Board of Trade. He became gov. of the Levant Co in 1680, and was a member of the provisional govt. which took over after the flight of James II. **(14) James (1680-1736) 3rd E.** was Rooke's flag-capt. at the B. of Malaga (Aug. 1704), a Lord of the Admiralty from 1717 to 1727 and C-in-C in the Channel in 1719. **(15) George (1685-1753) Bp. of CLOYNE** was the celebrated philosopher and scientist. **(16) George Charles Grantly (1800-51)** was M.P. for W. Gloucestershire from 1832. On his initiative, women were admitted to the gallery of the House of Commons in 1836. His brother **(17) Francis Henry (1794-1870)** was M.P. for Bristol from 1870. He brought forward motions or bills in favour of the ballot in every session from 1848 till his death. The Ballot Act 1872 was largely the result of this activity. His brother **(18) Craven (1805-55)** was a liberal M.P. for Cheltenham from 1832. **(19) Randal Thomas (1865- 1942), 8th E.** and F.R.S., was a distinguished scientist in the field of crystallography.

BERKSHIRE (Eng.) seems to have been a no-man's land until as late as A.D. 779 when Offa annexed it to Mercia. It was taken over by Wessex in about 845 and K. Alfred was born at Wantage in 848. The wealthy abbey of Abingdon claimed to have been founded in 675 by Cissa. Until the Reformation the crown and the church each owned about a quarter of the land; after the crown, Abingdon being much the biggest landowner. The lay holdings were all small. At the Reformation the ecclesiastical estates were quickly dispersed, so that the county has never been dominated by exceptionally big lay landowners.

In the middle ages Wallingford was the principal town, but the trade was diverted in 1416 by a low bridge at Abingdon which was the county town until the railways created a junction at Reading and passed Wallingford and Abingdon by.

BERLAIMONT, PALAIS. The glass and steel building in Brussels which houses the Commission of the European Community; or the commission itself.

BERLIN (Germany). (1) The adjacent towns of Berlin and Kölln became the Hohenzollern capital in the late 15th cent. but were separately administered until 1709. The university was founded in 1809 to compensate for the loss of Halle to Bonaparte's new kingdom of Westphalia. The city's prosperity kept pace with the 19th cent. expansion of Prussia and the unification of Germany: in 1816 the population was under 200,000. In 1871 826,000, in 1905 it was over 2M and by 1939 it was nearly 4.5M.

(2) The population was always mixed, Dutch refugees and engineers arrived in the 17th cent., Huguenots in the 18th, and Scandinavian, Polish and Jewish elements thereafter. The local dialect reflects some of the migrations, which gave the population a different character from the rest of Prussia. The Berliners were on the whole more sceptical of Nazism than other Germans.

(3) The city (especially the centre) was badly smashed up by allied bombing and Russian artillery during World War II, and when it fell to the Russians in May 1945, the population had fallen to about 3M crowded into a ring of suburbs. In addition the Russians pillaged the city, other than their own sector, for industrial equipment.

(4) The city was divided into four sectors, each under a major allied power and a four-power military administration (The Kommandatura) was set up. This soon became unworkable. The Russian policy was to encourage the Communists by providing industrial employment in their sector (having made it temporarily impossible in the others). The electors were not deceived, and in the 1946 elections the policy met total defeat. Thereupon the Russians separated their sector from the rest, and in June 1948 tried to blockade the others: this was met by smuggling, by an eleven-month long allied airlift of essentials, and by counter-measures against East German communications passing through the Western Sectors. The East German regime replied by building loopways through their own territory, and these were completed in 1952.

(5) The separation between the western and the Russian sectors deepened with time. After the blockade, West Berlin undertook a reconstruction programme which, in twenty years, transformed it into a modern western city. East Berlin, being geared to the Russian economy, got off to a much later start. The political differences widened. In West Berlin the communist vote vanished: in the East no other party was allowed. Refugees flooded into the West from the East at rates varying from 15,000 to 30,000 a month and anti-communist riots in both halves brought Russian military intervention in 1953. The refugee drain on eastern manpower and prestige eventually caused the communist regime in Aug. 1961 to wall the Western city in as part of the larger Russian Iron Curtain and thereafter the flood of refugees fell to a trickle.

(6) The wall was destroyed in 1989 in the general movement against communism in Eastern Europe, and in Oct. 1990 the two parts of the city were reunited and proclaimed the German capital again. See IRON CURTAIN.

BERLIN CONGRESS AND T. (July 1878) The bases of the treaty and collateral agreements had already been agreed beforehand, though partly leaked by a Foreign Office clerk. The Congress, organised by Bismarck, therefore had little to do save settle details and the actual document was signed at Lansdowne House in London, but it made Germany a party to settlements in areas where she had not hitherto been directly involved. The main provisions were **(1)** The Greater Bulgaria of the T.

of San Stefano was divided into an autonomous principality north of the Balkan range, a semi-autonomous Turkish province of Eastern Rumelia under a Christian governor south of it, and Macedonia and the Aegean littoral which remained fully Turkish. (2) Austro-Hungary was to administer Bosnia and Herzegovina and garrison the Sanjak of Novi Bazar. (3) Russia retook Bessarabia and acquired the Turkish fortress and port of Batum. (4) The Turks undertook to Britain to improve the treatment of their Christians. (5) Britain took an effective right to send her fleet into the Black Sea at will, and occupied Cyprus as a base.

BERLIN DECREE (21 Nov. 1806), by Bonaparte against British commerce on the pretext of the British Orders in Council of 16 May 1806, falsely alleged that the right of blockade applied only to fortified ports, and plausibly that the Royal Navy could not maintain the blockade proclaimed by the Orders. It then declared a blockade of the British Isles, denied access to French controlled ports to any vessels coming from Britain or her colonies and declared neutral property of British origin liable to confiscation. The decree was a dead letter until after Bonaparte returned to Paris after the T. of Tilsit (July 1807) (see THIRD COALITION, WAR OF, SECOND PHASE) because of evasions and a relaxed interpretation by the Minister of Marine. By Sept. 1807 enforcement regulations had been made and Bonaparte, in overruling his incredulous minister, announced that it was intended that French armed vessels should seize any neutral carrying goods of British origin. *See also* BALTIC; BALTIC EXPEDITIONS; CONTINENTAL SYSTEM; MILAN DECREE.

BERLIN MEMORANDUM (June 1876) was a joint proposal by Russian, Austria and Germany that they, with Britain, France and Italy, should intervene in the Bosnian-Bulgarian revolt against the Turks by forcing reforms upon the latter. The Sultan Abd-el-Aziz abdicated and in the ensuing confusion Serbia and Montenegro attacked the Turks (early July). *See* REICHSTADT MEETING; DISRAELI'S GOVT.

BERLIN PACT (Sept. 1940) between Germany, Italy and Japan crystallised attitudes which had long been in gestation. The three powers agreed (1) to respect the German and Italian New Order in Europe and the Japanese concept of a Great East Asia euphemistically named the Co-prosperity Sphere; (2) to assist one another by all means if attacked by a power not at that time involved in the European or Sino-Japanese war. The latter was designed to keep the U.S.A. out of the wars. Its immediate effect was that the British reopened the Burma road so that munitions could be supplied to the nationalist Chinese. The closure of this road thus became an object of Japanese policy and a major reason for their later invasion of Burma.

BERLINE. A light, fast four-wheeled travelling carriage with a separate hooded seat at the back designed about 1670 for the Elector of Brandenburg in whose capital, Berlin, it was first used.

BERMONDSEY (orig: Beormund's Eye). An example of urban evolution. (1) St Peter's monastery was built in the 8th cent. on this islet in the marshes south of the Thames nearly opposite the Tower of London. It was replaced under William II by the Cluniac priory of St Saviour with monks from La Charité. Mainly by land reclamation, it became very rich. The subordination to Cluny ended in 1399 when it was elevated to an abbacy. It was a lodging for notables on the way to Canterbury or France, and home to Qs Margaret of Valois and Elizabeth Woodville. At dissolution in 1537 it passed to Sir Thomas Pope.

(2) The population of the area grew steadily, and after the Plague and Fire of London (1666-7) it was settled by the well-to-do. This gave it a garden suburb character which, from 1820 gave way to docks, the railway and rural and Irish immigration for employment in new, especially food processing and leather, industries.

The attendant slums and epidemics were not fully overcome until the period between WW I and WW II.

BERMUDAS or SOMERS Is. (Atlantic) and Co. The Is were known in 1515 but were colonised as a result of the wreck there in 1609 of Sir George Somers' ship *Sea Venture* on its way to Virginia. His narrative was used by Shakespeare for *The Tempest*. The castaways reached Virginia in 1610. In 1612 the islands were granted to the Virginia Co. which sold them to the London Somers Isles Co, and this Co began systematic settlement. In 1684 the Co surrendered its rights to the Crown, which used the island as a naval base for over two and a half centuries. In 1941 the U.S.A. was granted naval and air bases on a 99-year lease, and in 1952 the British naval dockyard was closed as such and began to be developed as a free port. The islands have had a representative Assembly since 1620. *See* CHARTERED COMPANIES.

BERNADOTTE, Jean Baptiste (1763-1844) Marshal (1804), Regent (1810) and King (1818) of SWEDEN, and (1815) and (1818) of NORWAY served under Bonaparte in Italy in 1797, and was then ambassador to Vienna where his ostentatious republicanism made him obnoxious. He was briefly minister of war after the *coup d'état* of Prairial, and after Brumaire he offered his services to Bonaparte and married Desirée Clary, the latter's former fiancée. He was governor until 1805 of Hanover and from 1807 to 1809 of the Hanseatic ports (see BALTIC) though still much employed on campaigns. He was a popular governor and made European and Baltic contacts, but Bonaparte dismissed him from his military employments after the Austrian campaign of 1809.

The Swedish King Charles XIII, being insane and without heirs, the Swedish estates now offered to elect him Crown Prince; he accepted with enthusiasm, while Bonaparte agreed because he, not very sensibly, believed that he would gain an ally. Bernadotte thus became regent of Sweden as **Carl Johann.** Entirely devoted to the interests of his new country, he formed alliances with Britain and Russia and helped to defeat Bonaparte at Leipzig in 1813. His reward at the Vienna settlement was the transfer of Norway from Denmark (which had remained in alliance with the French) to Sweden, but the Norwegians established a constitution of their own with Carl Johann as regent under a separate crown. In 1818 he succeeded Charles XIII. He ruled conservatively in Sweden and encouraged Norwegian aspirations and culture.

BERNARD OF CLAIRVAUX, St. (1090-1153) Burgundian nobleman, entered the monastery of Citeaux in 1113 and was commissioned in 1115 by the abbot St. Stephen Harding to establish a new house. This was Clairvaux which, under his direction, became the most influential ecclesiastical centre in Europe. Bernard's power rested upon a strong, if conservative, intellect and an overwhelming but obviously saintly character, with a determination to hold people to their sense of responsibility. In 1127 he drafted the rules of the Knights Templar and secured their acceptance at the Synod of Troyes (1128) of which he was secretary. At the disputed papal election of 1130 his support secured the tiara for Honorius II against Anacletus, and Honorius conferred privileges upon his order which incidentally increased Bernard's influence. In 1140 he persuaded the council of Sens to condemn Abelard. In 1145 a former pupil of his became pope as Eugenius III.

In 1144 the crusader city of Edessa, whose immunity was supposed to have been guaranteed by Christ, had fallen to the Seijuks and Bernard used his prestige and influence to exploit the resulting sensation and launch the Second Crusade (1147-9). Its failure embittered his last years.

BERNHARDI, Gen. Friedrich von (1849-1930). This German general's unimportant career would have been forgotten had he not, after his retirement in 1909, become a writer on military and political subjects. Like Treitschke he held that war was inevitable, and that Germany's right of self-preservation justified any measures to win it. In 1912 he published his main work *Germany and the Next War*. The English translation caused a sensation because of the importance attached by contemporaries to German generals; and it helped to harden British opinion against German aggressiveness.

BERNICIA, centred on Bamburgh, and **DEIRA,** centred on the Yorkshire Wolds, were Celtic named areas settled in the late 5th cent. by Angles under related royal houses. They expanded in different directions: Bernicia into the country from the Tees northwards and Lothian, which was thinly populated by reason of the earlier south-westward emigration of the British Votadini: Deira westwards to comprise most of Yorkshire. The earliest historical King of Bernicia was IDA the Flamebearer (r. 547-59): in Deira the earliest was AELLE (r. c. 550-600). AETHELFRITH of Bernicia (r. 593-616) inflicted a great defeat on the migrating Votadini at Catterick and in 603 another on the Scots of Dalriada at Degsastan (unidentified). Soon afterwards he secured control of Deira, thus establishing a combined Northumbrian state from the Humber to the Forth. The Deiran fumily continued, however, to exist and at Aethelfrith's death the Deiran EDWIN (r. 616-32) the first Christian King, seized Northumbria while the Bernician family took refuge with the Picts and Scots. This perhaps led Edwin to fortify Edinburgh, named after him. At Edwin's death OSWALD (r. 633-44) later canonised, returned with the Bernician family, bringing many Scots, and especially Celtic trained monks with them. This had complicated doctrinal and cultural consequences for the area later. *See* NORTHUMBRIA.

BERNSTORFF. This remarkable Mecklenburg family included **(1) Andreas Gottlieb von, (1640-1726),** a minister in Hanover to George I; **(2) Count Johann Hartwig,** Chief Minister of Denmark from 1751 to 1770; **(3) Count Andreas Peter,** Danish foreign minister from 1773 to 1780 and Chief Minister from 1784 to 1797, who was the architect of the first Armed Neutrality; **(4) Count Albrecht,** Prussian Minister and German Ambassador in London from 1854 to 1861 and 1862 to 1873; and **(5) Count Johann Heinrich,** German Ambassador to Washington from 1908 to 1917 and to the Sublime Porte from 1917 to 1918.

BERRY. This Merthyr Tydfil family included three brothers of great financial ability. **(1) Henry Seymour (1877-1928) 1st Ld. BUCKLAND (1926)** was associated with the great mining enterprises of his friend D. A. Thomas (Lord Rhondda), and eventually became chairman of steel companies including Guest Keen & Nettlefolds. **(2) William Ewert (1879-1954) 1st Ld. CAMROSE of LONGCROSS (1929)** founded the Advertising World in 1901 and he with his brother **(3) Sir (James) Gomer (1883-1968) 1st Ld. KEMSLEY (1938) 1st Vist. (1945)** acquired control, *inter alia*, of the *Sunday Times* and the *Financial Times* and in 1927 the Amalgamated Press. In 1928 they, with Sir Edward Iliffe, also acquired the *Daily Telegraph*.

BERRY. *See* AQUITAINE-5.

BERTHA. *See* KENT, KINGDOM-2.

BERTHA, BIG. (After Bertha Krupp, the owner of Krupps, the German armaments firm). This nickname was mistakenly given to two howitzers made at the Skoda works in Austro-Hungary for German use against the Liége forts. Specially designed to smash them quickly, they opened the way to the rapid German occupation of Belgium in 1914.

BERTHIER, Louis Alexandre, Prince of NEUCHATEL and WAGRAM (1753-1815), first became Bonaparte's Chief of Staff for the Italian campaign of 1796. He organised the Italian Republic in 1798, took part in the *coup d'état* of Brumaire and was briefly minister of war.

Thereafter he was Bonaparte's actual chief of staff (whatever his title) in all his major campaigns until the fall of the Empire in 1814. Disillusioned, he made his peace with Louis XVIII, and on Bonaparte's return left France for Germany, where he died unexpectedly. It has been argued that his absence was a major contributing factor to Bonaparte's defeat at Waterloo.

BERTIE, Francis Leveson (1844-1919) 1st Vist. BERTIE of THAME (1915) was Asst. Sec. of State for foreign affairs from 1894 to 1903, ambassador to Rome from 1903 to 1904 and then became a rapidly and deeply respected ambassador to Paris from 1905 (nine months after the conclusion of the *Entente Cordiale*) until 1918. He was a champion of Anglo-French co-operation in the Tangier crisis (Mar. 1905), the Algeçiras conference (1906), the Agadir crisis (1911) and throughout World War I.

BERTIE. (1) Richard (1517-82), a servant of the E. of Southampton, went during Q. Mary's reign to Germany and Poland. In or about 1552 he married **(2) Catharine (1520-80)** *d.* of the 8th Lord Willoughby de Eresby, widow of Charles D. of Brandon, who had been executed in 1545. Their son **(3) Peregrine (1555-1601) 9th Ld. WILLOUGHBY DE ERESBY (1580)** was born at Cleves (Germany) and absorbed some of his father's cosmopolitanism. Elizabeth I employed him to negotiate a Danish treaty, mostly for trade, in 1582 and another for Danish intervention in favour of the Huguenots in 1585. He then campaigned in the Low Countries, succeeded Leicester in command there in 1587 and defended Bergen (1588). He commanded the Dieppe Expedition of 1589-90. Disillusioned, he went abroad, until in 1598 Essex obtained for him the Governorship of Berwick with the Wardenship of the E. March. He died in office. His son **(4) Robert (1582-1642) 1st E. of LINDSEY (1626)** commanded the fleet against La Rochelle (1628) and was Lord High Admiral in 1636. He had settled in Lincolnshire, and during most of James I's reign his great work had been the reclamation of 30,000 acres of fen. He raised local troops for the King at the beginning of the Civil War, and was killed at Edgehill. His son **(5) Montague (?1606-66) 2nd E.** was a judge at the trial of the regicides.

BERTRAND, Henri Gratien, Count (1773-1844) was one of Bonaparte's few personal friends. They met in Egypt in 1798 and he became A.D.C. after the B. of Austerlitz (1806). He directed the building of bridges for the B. of Wagram (1809) and organised the retreat of the Grand Army after the disaster at Leipzig (1813). In the same year he became Grand Marshal of the Court. He accompanied Bonaparte to Elba, held a command at Waterloo and stayed at St. Helena until his master's death. He brought Bonaparte's remains from St. Helena in 1840. His sometimes misrepresented devotion to Bonaparte has obscured his very real talents as an executive and as the channel for the dissemination of the 'Napoleonic Legend'.

BERWICK (N'land) –SHIRE (Scot.) The area had British and Roman settlements and was subsequently colonised by Northumbrian Angles. It was much fought over but from 1018 it was considered part of Scotland. Of its three parts, Lammermuir was mostly occupied by Lindsays, Lauderdale by Maitlands and the Merse ('march') by Homes. The town with its castle controlled the mouth of the R. Tweed and consequently the trade of Lauderdale as well. It was bounded on the south by the Bp. of Durham's franchise of Islandshire. The agriculture was based mostly on oats and barley, with much cattle and sheep encouraged by monasteries at Coldingham, Dryburgh and Coldstream, and by the feudalised clan centres at Fast and Hume. There were also important coastal fisheries.

The town grew up round the castle and was chartered by David I (r. 1124-53) some years before his accession. He established or revived a market and set up a mint. It became one of the Four Boroughs and in 1296 it was one of the six which ratified the French Alliance. It then had about 1500 inhabitants. At that time its strategic and economic importance was very great and Edward I occupied it. He equipped it as his Scots administrative capital, with an exchequer and laid it out on the most modern principles of town planning. In 1318 (as a distant consequence of the B. of Bannockburn) the Scots retook it, and it was granted its own govt. and tax settlement at a perpetual fee ferme of £333-6-8. This lasted only until 1333, when the English took it back, and annexed it to their East March. Apart from short Scots incursions, including an occupation from 1378 to 1379, the burning of the town in 1383, and an occupation of the castle in 1384, the town and castle stayed in English hands until 1461. At the turn of the 14th-15th cents, they suffered not only from border unrest but from the politics of the Percy family, whose rebellion led in 1405 to a royal occupation. Between 1174 and 1406 the town is said to have changed hands between Scots and English 13 times. It was also a regular meeting place for representatives of the Wardens of the Marches on both sides, for diplomatic encounters and even occasionally for parliaments. It finally fell into English hands in 1482 and was maintained as a powerful and expensive garrisoned fortress, financed not only by its local taxes but by the wool customs of Newcastle and Hull. The defences were reorganised by Henry VII in 1489, by Henry VIII in 1522-6 and extensively rebuilt under Elizabeth from 1560 onwards. It had been a county on its own since 1551. See ACONTIUS.

The Union of English and Scots crowns ended the international function of Berwick and it soon declined into a minor coastal port. It survived as a borough until 1974.

BERWICK, James FitzJames (1670-1743) 1st D. of (1687) (1) a son of K. James II by Arabella Churchill, was thus a nephew of the first D. of Marlborough, as well as a cousin of King Louis XIV. Educated mainly in France, in 1686 he served under the D. of Lorraine at the capture of Buda from the Turks. He returned to England in 1687, and at the Revolution of 1688 took his father's side, and fought at the Boyne. After James left Ireland for France in July 1690 he commanded the cavalry at the successful defence of Limerick and, when Tyrconnel the Viceroy went to France in Sept. Berwick was for a few months C-in-C; recalled by his father in Jan. 1691, he served under Marshal Luxembourg at Steenkerk (1692) and Landen (1693) where he was taken prisoner. By this time he was a French Lieut-gen and committed to a professional military career.

(2) In 1696 Berwick secretly visited England to concert a Jacobite plot and during the short peace after the T. of Ryswick he was sent on a diplomatic mission to the Pope.

(3) On the further outbreak of war he returned to the army; served with success under Boufflers in the Low Countries, and was naturalised a French subject. From now on his ascent was rapid. In reply to allied operations in Spain he was sent there as the head of a military mission. In 1705 he was appointed to succeed Villars in suppressing the Camisard revolt in the Cevennes, and later that year he commanded frontier operations against Savoy and captured Nice. In Feb. 1706 he was promoted Marshal of France and sent to Spain again. Here matters had come to a crisis because the English and Portuguese, in furtherance of the claims of Charles, the Hapsburg candidate for the Spanish throne, were threatening invasion. Berwick, like Wellington, experienced all the difficulties of co-operation with Spanish generals, and by midsummer Charles was proclaimed in Madrid. Berwick then began to experience, similarly, the advantages of Spanish popular support. On 25 Apr. 1707 he defeated Galway's Anglo-Portuguese army at Almanza and so put an effective end to the Hapsburg claims in Spain.

(4) Returning to France he commanded defensive

undertakings in Alsace and came to Vendôme's rescue after Oudenarde (1708). These and similar defensive operations in Savoy continued until the P. of Utrecht in 1712. This left a Bourbon King on the Spanish throne, and Berwick was employed until the end of 1714 in reducing Catalonia (which had supported Charles III) to obedience. When he returned to France, Anne had been succeeded by the Hanoverian George I. The Jacobite revolt of 1715 followed: but he refused the Old Pretender's request to go to Scotland and take charge, because he was now a Marshal of France and a French subject.

(5) Thereafter he lived as an ordinary nobleman in and out of court in France until the War of the Polish Succession, when he was killed at Philipsburg.

BESAÏEL. See ASSIZE.

BESANT, Annie (1847-1933) *née* WOOD, married and left a clergyman; joined the Secular Society in 1873; and the Fabians in 1874. In 1888 she organised the matchmaker's strike and formed their union. She then became interested in Theosophy and from 1895 tried to reconcile it with Hinduism, founding a Hindu College in 1899 besides other Hindu institutions. In this way she became involved with the Indian, preponderantly Hindu, National Congress. She launched the Indian Home Rule League in 1916 and was even Pres. of the Congress in 1918. By this time Congress was launched on its campaigns; she protested against the violence and, as an Englishwoman, lost her influence. She remained actively concerned with Theosophy until she died.

BESSEMER STEEL PROCESS, involving the blowing of air through molten iron, was invented by Sir Henry Bessemer (1813-98) in 1856 and was widely adopted after 1864. Sydney Gilchrist adapted the process to phosphoric iron in 1878 by lining the converter with dolomite. These inventions first made the mass production of steel possible.

BESSBOROUGH. See PONSONBY.

BESSIERES, Jean Baptiste, D. of ISTRIA (1768-1813), first made Bonaparte's acquaintance in Italy in 1796 and was rapidly promoted for his skill as a commander of cavalry. He became a marshal in 1804, and was given his first independent command in Spain where he won a spectacular victory over the Spaniards at Medina del Rio Secco in 1808. He was recalled for the Essling and Wagram Campaigns, but in 1810 he successfully defended Walcheren against the British. In 1811 he returned to Spain as Masséna's 2-in-C and took part in the B. of Fuentes d'Onoro. He was killed on reconnaissance in Russia.

BESS OF HARDWICK (1518-1608). This formidable lady, d. and coheiress of John Hardwick married **(1) Robt. Barlow of Barlow; (2) Sir Wm. Cavendish; (3) Sir Wm. St. Loe** and **(4) Geo. Talbot, 6th E. of SHREWSBURY.** She inherited the property of all four; immensely rich, she built Chatsworth and Hardwick Hall, and in 1569 had custody of Mary Q. of Scots at Tutbury. She married her daughter Elizabeth Cavendish to Mary's brother-in-law Lord Chas. Stuart and was briefly imprisoned for it. See TALBOT.

BESTIALITY. See BUGGERY.

BETHALL, Richard (1800-73) 1st Ld. WESTBURY (1861) was a Liberal M.P. from 1851, sol-gen. in 1852, and att-gen. in 1856. He secured the Probate Act, 1857, and the first Statute Law Revision Act, 1861, when he became Lord Chancellor, but resigned in 1865 when the Commons passed a censure motion against him for inattention to his duties. A distinguished lawyer, he sat in the Lords and the Privy Council thereafter to hear appeals.

BETHEL (Gen. c. 28 v. 19 = *House of God*) became the generic term for Methodist places of worship. They commonly used Old Testament names for them, of which *Bethel* was the commonest.

BETHMANN-HOLLWEG, Theobald von (1856-1921) became German Chancellor in 1909 in succession to Prince Bülow. He was a weak liberal attempting through parliamentary compromise to achieve progress in a country where only military virtues were respected; hence he achieved successes only where the prestige of the military was not involved. For this reason his negotiations for naval reductions with Britain failed because of the opposition of Adm. von Tirpitz and the Kaiser, but he carried reforms in taxation and in the administration of Alsace-Lorraine and, in co-operation with Sir Edw. Grey prevented the Balkan wars of 1912 from expanding into a direct conflict between Austro-Hungary and Russia.

In Nov. 1913, however, the ZABERN INCIDENT occurred. The Alsatian population of Zabern (Saverne) was placed illegally under martial law by a local colonel because somebody had objected to the truculence of one of his subalterns. Bethmann-Hollweg tried to play the affair down with the worst results: the conservatives demanded apologies for imagined insults to military honour: the liberals demanded courts martial. Both sides joined in carrying a vote of censure in the *Reichstag*.

Though his authority was fatally damaged, Bethmann-Hollweg clung to office; and when the war fever of 1914 precipitated the Sarajevo crisis, he found that, with the Kaiser's connivance, others had taken real charge of policy and that he, as head of the govt., had no effective function except as a 'front man'. This accounted for his notorious but bitter comment that the Belgian guarantee was 'a scrap of paper'. In Jan. 1917 he had so far abdicated any concern with war policy that he refused to advise for or against unrestricted submarine warfare. Not surprisingly by the summer he had forfeited the support of the *Reichstag* which debated a peace resolution. The military, led by Ludendorff and Hindenburg, intervened to influence the debate but the resolution was passed on 19th July. The Kaiser was faced with the alternatives of a military *coup* or getting rid of Bethmann-Hollweg who, at long last, retired.

BETHOC (fl. 1018) *d.* of Malcolm II of Scots. *See* SCOTS AND ALBAN KINGS, EARLY-15.

BETTAGHS (Irish) were Irish serfs.

BETTERMENT is the increase in the value of property resulting not from direct improvement but by the actions of neighbours or public authorities, e.g. an agglomeration of buildings in a town, with the betterment arising from the presence of the buildings near each other. The provision of water, sewerage and electricity will have similar effects.

BETTING AND GAMING. (1) Games were legal at common law, but govts felt that they interfered with military training; the Unlawful Games Act, 1541, is entitled "The Bill for Maintaining Artillery and Debarring Unlawful Games", and made common gaming houses and virtually all games illegal as a waste of time. This affected the legality of sums wagered upon the outcome of a game, and in general the courts habitually refused to enforce betting agreements.

Betting and gaming, however, are a national passion, and both have been carried on merrily in defiance of the law ever since 1541, so that enormous sums and, in the 18th cent. great estates, changed hands on the turn of a card. It was therefore sought to ameliorate what could not be controlled, and Acts of 1710, 1728, 1738, 1739 and 1744, dealt with details such as securities, illegal lotteries, fashionable but particularly pernicious games (such as 'roly-poly otherwise roulet'), and gaming houses.

(2) By 1845 the absurdity of the law was recognised and the connection with military skill abandoned. The Gaming Act, 1845, legalised games of skill; rationalised the rules against common gaming houses and cheating, and declared betting and gaming contracts unenforceable. There followed a spectacular growth in betting establishments which were not caught by the Act, and draconian legislation was passed against them in 1853 and 1854. In 1874 it was necessary to forbid advertising of betting facilities by, amongst other means, telegrams and placards. The total effect of the Victorian legislation was to drive the industry into the streets, where it throve vigorously. Accordingly street betting was made a criminal offence in 1906: this effected little, because everyone was in the conspiracy and street betting was simply conducted by 'runners', that is by people who were fleeter of foot than the police.

(3) By 1928 a change of attitude was discernible: the Racecourse Betting Act created the Totalizator and so gave the horseracing industry a cut of the profits of bookmaking; and the Betting and Lotteries Act of 1934 was passed to take the fashion for dog racing into account. By this time football pools had started and in 1947 their profits were sufficient to attract the attention of the Treasury. A first Pool Betting Duty was enacted in 1947.

(4) By 1960 the absurdities of a law, which was internally inconsistent and habitually flouted, were no less obvious than the somewhat different absurdities of 1845. Accordingly the Betting and Gaming Act of 1963, while retaining the legal unenforceability of bets, legalised the setting up of private casinos. These blossomed everywhere, and brought with them some of the social evils which the earlier law had been designed to suppress. By 1968 there were demands for detailed control. A national lottery was instituted in 1994.

BEUNO, St. (?6th cent.) a Herefordshire monk who worked influentially in Clwyd, Gwynedd and Anglesey, which contain villages and many churches named after him.

BEUST, Count Friedrich Ferdinand von (1809-86) began his remarkable career as a Saxon diplomat. He became Saxon minister for foreign affairs, education and religious worship in 1849. He was the strong man of the govt. and responsible for suppressing the local revolutionary disorders of that year. In 1853 he became Prime Minister. He was the leading champion of the small German states against Prussia and so supported Austria against Prussia both in 1851 and 1866. He had thus achieved the undying hatred both of German liberals and of Bismarck. After the defeat of Austria and Saxony in 1866 Bismarck refused to treat with him, and he resigned. He immediately received the remarkable offer of the foreign ministry of Austro-Hungary, which he accepted.

In this new capacity he led the negotiations for the *Augsleich,* and subsequently as Austro-Hungarian minister-president secured the establishment of a parliament. In foreign policy he remained resolutely anti-Prussian and worked for an understanding with France. In 1868 he became Chancellor. His policy came to nought with the collapse of France in the war of 1870, and in 1871 he was dismissed, but appointed ambassador in London where he served until his transfer to Paris in 1878. He retired in 1882. *See* AUSTRO-HUNGARY-6.

BEVAN, Aneurin (1897-1960), courageous miner and son of a Welsh miner, held his first trade union post at 19. He had experienced unemployment and inadequate sickness benefits, and in the 1926 conflict with the mine owners organised relief, besides making fighting speeches. He became a Monmouthshire County Councillor in 1928 and Labour M.P. for Ebbw Vale from 1929 (until his death). In 1934 he married **Jennie Lee**, and from 1942 to 1945 he was editor of *Tribune*. He was a bitter and sometimes wrong-headed critic of wartime policies and methods, even though his party was part of the govt. conducting it. He was also strongly anti-American. When Labour won the 1945 general election he became Min. of Health, and presided over the creation of the National Health Service advocated by Lord Beveridge. His vituperative speech in 1948, characterising the Tories as 'vermin' is said to have cost his party 1M votes. In 1951 he became Min. of Labour, but resigned in April in protest at the introduction of prescription charges and increased military expenditure in Gaitskell's budget. As the Labour Party lost the general election in the following autumn, Bevan never held office again.

He spent the next years of his life at loggerheads with his own party on the question of arms; he believed that it was the purpose of Russian policy to drive Britain into rearmament, and so divert resources to unproductive ends which would result in the economy 'rotting underneath'. In 1955 Gaitskell defeated him for the leadership of the Labour Party by 157 votes to 70, but in 1956 he was elected party treasurer. Realising that a split party could not win general elections, he managed in 1957 to compose his differences with Gaitskell, and became his shadow foreign secretary. He died before this change could be tested.

BEVERIDGE, William Henry (1879-1963) 1st Ld. BEVERIDGE of TUGGALL began his varied life as a law fellow (1902-9) at University Coll. Oxford, and from 1903 to 1905 was also sub-warden of Toynbee Hall and (1905-8) a member of the Central Unemployed Body for London. From 1906 to 1908 he was also a leader writer for the *Morning Post*. In 1909 (till 1912) he was Director of Labour Exchanges under Winston Churchill at the Bd. of Trade. During World War I he became Permanent Sec. to the Min. of Food but in 1919 he accepted the directorship of the London School of Economics and held it till 1937. In 1934 he reverted to his interest in welfare by accepting the chairmanship of the Unemployment Insurance Statutory Committee (until 1944) and in 1941 and 1942 he was, at Churchill's instance, chairman of the Inter-departmental Committee on Social Insurance and Allied Services. The results of the experience gained in these committees appeared in 1942 as his celebrated ***BEVERIDGE REPORT*** properly called *Social Insurance and Allied Services* (Cmd. 6404 of 1942). It proposed a social insurance scheme intended to cover every citizen against 'interruption or destruction of earning power, and for special expenditure arising at birth, marriage and death'. This was to be based upon six principles viz: (a) a flat rate of subsistence benefit; (b) a flat rate of contribution; (c) adequacy of benefit; (d) unification of administrative responsibilities; (e) comprehensiveness; and (f) classification. The document made a tremendous public impression, and with varying changes was the foundation of the social security legislation passed between 1948 and 1960 much of which, though eroded, was still in place in 2000.

BEVERLEY MINSTER (Yorks.). St. John of Beverley was Abp. of York from 705 to c. 718. He founded the church and school at Beverley and consecrated it to St. John the Evangelist. In 866 it was destroyed by the Danes, and later refounded and endowed by K. Athelstan; he dedicated it to its original founder who had by then been canonised. It was a seat of learning and culture throughout the middle ages, as the beauty of the church testifies. The foundation was dissolved in 1547.

BEVIN, Ernest (1881-1951), illegitimate son of a village midwife, experienced much hardship in his early years. He was a strong Methodist who at one time contemplated entering the ministry, but gradually turned to politics. By 1910 he was chairman of the Carmens' branch of the Dockers' Union and by 1920 he was the dockers' foremost spokesman. In 1922 he negotiated the amalgamation of 45 unions into a single Transport and General Workers Union and became its gen. sec. He was also a prime mover in building up the *Daily Herald*. His union supported the General Strike of 1926, though he personally thought that it was unintelligently planned.

He had no very high opinion of Parliament, preferring to influence events by participation, for example, in the World War I dock labour and transport committees, and between the wars in the Macmillan Commission on the banking system. Nevertheless he was drawn into the political system by World War II, for Churchill made him Min. of Labour and National Service in 1940 and consequently Bevin had to find a seat in the Commons. He represented Wandsworth Central until 1950 and then East Woolwich.

He was a key figure in the conduct of the war; he had to mobilise the manpower so that it was properly employed in the right proportions, yet without offending the main bodies of political and industrial opinion. In this he succeeded: in particular by creating a parity of esteem between armed and industrial service by conscripting both. ***BEVIN BOYS*** were young men who at call up for military service in World War II chose work in the coal mines. The scheme, an example of his common sense, provided a useful alternative for conscientious objectors and others, while alleviating the labour shortages in the mines.

When the Labour Party won the 1945 general election, Bevin became Attlee's foreign sec. He soon made himself internationally celebrated by his forthright attachment to liberalism in international dealings, and his resistance to Russian aggression. He championed liberty of travel, and simplified British passport procedures. When the Russians obstructed a final peace settlement he became one of the leaders in the alternative policy which took shape in Mar. 1948 in the T. of Brussels, and in Apr. 1949 in the North Atlantic T. He originated the idea which eventually became known as Marshall Aid, and presided over Britain's withdrawal from Palestine and her subsequent *de facto* recognition of the State of Israel.

BEZA, Theodore (1519-1605) joined Calvin at Geneva in 1548, and became professor of Greek at Lausanne. He defended Calvin for burning Servetus in 1554. Rector, from 1559, of the Geneva Academy, he was the true political successor to Calvin himself on his death in 1564. His tract *De jure magistratuum* (Lat: The Basis of Civil Authority) appeared in 1574 shortly after the St. Bartholomew's massacre; in it he defended the right of revolt against bad govt. and so provided the intellectual justification for the special claims of the Huguenots in France. He corresponded with statesmen and learned men all over Europe, and presented the *Codex Bezae* to Cambridge University.

BEZANT. Byzantine gold coin in widespread use until 15th cent: hence, in heraldry, a round yellow disc.

BHARATPUR. *See* RAJPUTS.

BHONSLA (Nagpur). *See* MARATHAS-8 *et seq.*

BHOPAL (India) was an important principality founded by the Afghan, Dost Mohammed Khan, in 1723. Its rulers were consistently friendly to the British, whose protection was unsuccessfully requested in 1809, but granted in 1817 under a treaty made in connection with the Pindari war. The rulers (who from 1844 to 1926 were women) respected their treaty obligations during the Mutiny and in both world wars. The state was merged in Madhya Pradesh in 1956.

BHUTAN (Himalayas). When the British first penetrated Bengal, Bhutan extended southwards into the foothills and eastward nearly to Darjeeling. Like a number of Asian states, it had a dual govt. vested in the spiritual Shabtung Rimpoche and the temporal Deb Raja. The former was believed to be a reincarnation and each Shabtung Rimpoche had to be discovered after his predecessor's death. The Deb Raja was in practice the nominee of the governor of one or other of the two halves (Paro and Tongsa) of the state.

Contacts with the British began in 1772 when Warren Hastings came to the aid of Cooch Behar, whose Rajah had been captured by the Bhutanese. A treaty followed in 1774, but efforts to open up the country commercially failed. In 1826 the British occupied Assam and took the Assamese districts of Bhutan in return for a derisory rent, but the Bhutanese habitually raided across the borders (mainly for slaves and plunder), and by 1863 military reprisals had to be taken because the Deb Raja could not or would not keep order. The state was subjugated and reduced to its modern proportions by a treaty of Nov. 1865, the British govt. however, undertaking to pay an annual subsidy of 50,000 rupees.

The Deb Raja now died; there was a long ensuing civil war between Paro and Tongsa ending in 1865 with the victory of Tongsa. The Shabtung Rimpoche died at this time and no reincarnation was found. His functions were 'temporarily' vested in a Deb Raja, while the temporal govt. was carried on by the victorious governor. In 1907 the latter was elected Maharajah and all the functions of govt. were concentrated in him. This enabled him to negotiate a revision of the treaty of 1865; British and Bhutanese mutual goodwill was increased by a Chinese claim to suzerainty, and in 1910 Britain agreed not to interfere in Bhutan's internal affairs and Bhutan agreed to be guided by Britain in her external relations. The subsidy was doubled, and the Chinese Court was informed that Bhutan was an independent state. In 1942 the subsidy was raised to Rs 200,000; in 1949 to Rs 500,000 by the Indian govt, and in 1951 a small district in the foothills was retroceded.

BIAFRA. *See* NIGERIA.

BIARRITZ (S. France) This Biscay fishing village became a fashionable watering place through the patronage of Napoleon III's Empress Eugenie, who liked it because of its proximity to her native Spain. It soon attracted many English (who built villas there) and other visitors, including Q. Victoria in widowhood, and Edward VII.

BIBBY LINE, a shipping firm between Britain, Burma and Ceylon, was founded by John Bibby in 1807 and has been operated by Bibby Brothers, Liverpool bankers, ever since.

BIBLE. (1) The great variety of versions and translations of both Testaments circulating in the early church led Pope Damasus to encourage St. Jerome (c. 345-419) to make a fresh Latin version of the whole Bible. This, known as the VULGATE, gradually superseded all others throughout the west and was pronounced authoritative for the R. Catholic Church by the Council of Trent in 1546.

(2) There is no complete Anglo-Saxon version of either Testament, only some free renderings and word-by-word translations of portions. There are also metrical translations of certain books, particularly Genesis and Exodus, in Middle English, and the 14th cent. Lollards made anonymous versions of some books in various dialects. There is a tradition that John Wycliffe translated the whole Bible; no translation can certainly be ascribed to him, but two contemporary versions by Nicholas of Herford and John Purvey remain from the period 1380-1408. The Council of Oxford forbade new translations or the use of translations made 'in the times of John Wycliffe or since', but Lollard manuscripts continued to be made.

(3) The Vulgate was first printed in 1456, the Hebrew text in 1488, Erasmus' Greek text in 1516 and the Complutensian Polyglot (in Hebrew, Greek and Latin) in 1522. These opened the way for detailed study. William TYNDALE projected his New Testament translation in 1523, but failed to get ecclesiastical patronage and fled to Germany in 1524; here he met and became an admirer of Martin LUTHER. Luther's German New Testament had already appeared in 1522 and was soon to have a profound effect on German style. Tyndale's New Testament, after vicissitudes, was published at Worms in 1526, and copies soon reached England. He continued to make translations and print them in the Netherlands until he was burned as a heretic near Brussels in 1536. By this time there were many versions current, and Canterbury Convocation having petitioned Henry VIII in 1534 for a complete translation, Miles Coverdale published a Bible dedicated to Henry in 1535. He used Tyndale wherever

he could, and translated elsewhere from Luther's and Zwingli's German. The poetic quality of his Psalms led to their retention into modern times in the Book of Common Prayer.

(4) In 1537 a revised Bible known as MATTHEWS BIBLE appeared and was the first bearing royal authorisation. It was printed in Antwerp and its editor was John Rogers. In 1539 Coverdale's version, somewhat revised, reappeared in a very large format and became known as the GREAT BIBLE. Its use was enforced in churches by Thomas Cromwell and Abp. Cranmer until Mary I's accession, when the Vulgate was made required reading instead. The policy was reversed at the accession of Elizabeth I. During Mary's reign Whittingham prepared the so-called GENEVA or Breeches Bible (because in it Adam and Eve are said to have taken fig leaves to make themselves breeches), based upon Tyndale and the Great Bible, but influenced by Calvin and Beza. This was very popular after the accession of Elizabeth I, and it was the first to be divided into verses. Abp. Parker produced a revision of this version in 1566. This was known as the 'Bishops Bible', but because the editors worked without co-ordination, its quality varies from book to book. While this protestant activity was going on, the English College in France was producing a translation of the Vulgate. The New Testament was published from Rheims in 1582, the Old from Douai in 1609; the whole is known as the Douai Bible.

(5) The multiplicity again available by 1600 was such that the Hampton Court Conference proposed a new version to James I. He commissioned 54 divines to do the work which was based upon the Bishops Bible, though the best resources of contemporary scholarship were exploited as well. They organised themselves into friendly partnerships. The result in 1611 was the AUTHORISED or King James Version which exhibited a remarkable unity of style and was instantly successful. It superseded all other English translations in a generation, and had a profound influence on English thought and outlook.

(6) The REVISED VERSION was produced between 1881 and 1885. Its pedestrian accuracy opened the gates to many later private versions, some unworthy.

BIBLE CHRISTIANS. *See* METHODISM; O'BRYAN.

BICKERTON, Adm. Sir Richard, 2nd Bart (1759-1832) as rear-adm. commanded the blockade of Cadiz in May to Oct. 1800, and that of Egypt until the evacuation of the French army in 1801. He was C-in-C in the Mediterranean during the short peace of Amiens and 2-in-C to Nelson in the blockade of Toulon in 1804 and 1805. In May 1805 when Nelson set off for the West Indies (*see* TRAFALGAR) Bickerton was recalled to the Admiralty where he remained until he retired in 1812.

BICYCLE. The *Hobby Horse* or *Velocipede* came into use in Paris in 1816; it consisted of two wheels and a cross bar upon which the rider sat while propelling himself by his feet on the ground. The first true bicycle was built by MacMillan of Dumfries in 1839; the first driven by cranks by Lallement in Paris in 1865. The latter was known as a *boneshaker*. The invention of rubber tyres made greater speeds tolerable and led to enlargement of the driving wheel (the front) in the period 1872-85 while the back wheel grew smaller; this type of 'ordinary' bicycle was commonly called the *Penny Farthing*. Finally Lawson introduced the geared up chain transmission to the rear wheel in 1876 and so inaugurated the low, and so-called 'safety' bicycle upon which all modern types are based.

BIDLE, John (1616-62), virtual originator of English Unitarianism, published his *Twelve Arguments* against the divinity of the Holy Ghost in 1647, and was imprisoned for it. In 1648, he published his *Confession of Faith Touching the Holy Trinity Etc* in which he cited the Fathers of the church in support of his *Twelve Arguments*. He was banished to the Scilly Is. from 1655 to 1658. In

1661 he was sentenced to a heavy fine which he could not pay, so he stayed in prison and died there.

BIENVILLE. *See* LE MOYNE.

BIG BEN. The great bell in the clock tower of the Houses of Parliament was named after the impressive Sir Benjamin Hall, who was chief commissioner of works from 1855 to 1858 when it was cast.

BIG FIVE. (1) at the Versaille negotiations in 1919 were President Wilson (U.S.A.), Lloyd George (Britain), Clemenceau (France), Orlando (Italy) and Prince Saionji (Japan). **(2)** During World War II the phrase meant U.S.A. or Roosevelt, Britain or Churchill, U.S.S.R. or Stalin, (Nationalist) China or Chiang Kai-Shek, and France or de Gaulle: these countries secured permanent seats and a veto in the Security Council of the United Nations. The **Big Four** were the first four in either above paragraph. The **Big Three** the first three.

BIGGE, John Thomas (1780-1843). *See* AUSTRALIA-4.

BIGHAM, John Charles (1840-1929) 1st Vist. MERSEY (1916) lawyer and from 1895 to 1897 a liberal M.P., became a judge in 1897 and a leading member in 1902 of the important Commission which, as a result of the P. of Vereeniging, reviewed the S. African court-martial sentences. He was Pres. of the Probate, Divorce and Admiralty Division of the High Court from 1909 to 1910. In 1912 he held the inquiry into the sinking of the *Titanic.*

BIGNOR (Sussex) has the remains of a large 2nd to 4th cent. Roman villa with exceptionally fine mosaics still in good condition after their discovery in 1811.

BIGOD. (perhaps from Norman expletive 'bi Got'), a Norman knightly family which rose to power and eminence mainly in the eastern counties between 1070 and 1306. Its main members were **(1) Roger (I) (?-1107)**, a major landowner in Norfolk and Suffolk and Lord of Framlingham. He was steward to William II and Henry I. His second son **(2) Hugh (?-1177) E. of NORFOLK (1140)** swore before the Abp. of Canterbury that Henry I on his deathbed had disinherited Matilda. He remained a fairly regular supporter of K. Stephen until the last year of the reign when he held Ipswich for Henry of Anjou. Henry confirmed his earldom and stewardship at his accession in 1154, but imposed a full submission by a show of force in 1157. In 1173, however, Hugh joined Pr. Henry's revolt against his father but had to submit and had his castles dismantled. He died on pilgrimage to the Holy Land, a tactful form of exile. His son **(3) Roger (II) (?-1221)** came to prominence first at the accession of Richard I when he was reconfirmed and sent to arrange details of the crusade with the French court. He supported the royal interests after K. Richard left for Palestine and in due course became custodian of P. John's castle at Hereford. In 1193 he negotiated in Germany for K. Richard's release and in 1194 took office as Justiciar, and so remained in the early years of K. John. In 1213 he quarrelled with John who briefly imprisoned him, and in 1215 he was a leader of the magnates in the Magna Carta negotiations and became one of the 25 trustees for its enforcement. At Henry III's accession he rallied to the Crown, and spent the rest of his active life as a court administrator. His grandson **(4) Roger (III), 4th E. of NORFOLK** and Earl Marshal was a justice in Eyre for Essex and Herts. In 1244 he was one of the twelve representatives of the estates deputed to secure reforms of the alleged royal extravagance. He also led an embassy to the Council of Lyons to protest against papal taxation. In 1246 he became Earl Marshal in right of his mother who was a daughter of the E. of Pembroke, and in 1253 he was one of those responsible for extracting the promises of reform which preceded the abortive Gascony campaign. He was one of the baronial leaders in the Provisions of Oxford but suspecting, with others, the ambitions of the Montfort's he went over to the King. This allegiance was short lived for when the French King

who was supposed to be impartial set aside the Provisions of Oxford, Bigod rejoined Simon de Montfort and held Oxford for him. After Edward I's accession in 1272 he retired into obscurity and died without issue. His brother **(5) Hugh (III) (?-1266)** was Chief Justiciar from 1258 to 1260. His son **(6) Roger (IV) (1245-1306) 5th E.** and Earl Marshal figured with Humphrey Bohun (q.v.) as one of the baronial leaders against Edward I in the political and fiscal controversies before the *Confirmatio Cartarum* (1297). He is the subject of the anecdote about his alleged duty to go overseas: "By God, Sir Earl", said the King, "you will either go or hang", to which Bigod replied "By God, Sir King, I will neither go nor hang". Bohun died in the following year and this affected Bigod deeply. After the final reconfirmation of the charters at the Lincoln parliament (1301) he was financially embarrassed and in return for royal funds surrendered his marshalcy and entailed the earldom which, accordingly, became extinct at his death.

BIHAR (India) through invasions and migrations acquired large Afghan settlements and was conquered in 1529 by Babur as a precaution against Afghan power in the West. Akbar added it to Bengal in 1576. It remained under the Nawabs of Bengal, through whom it passed to the British (*see* BENGAL). They maintained the administrative connection with Bengal until 1912 when it was combined with Orissa as a new province. The two parts were reseparated in 1937. Hence Bihar became an original state of the Indian Union at independence.

BIKANER (India). Rai Singh the first rajah was one of Akbar's generals. After the collapse of Moghul power there was intermittent war between Bikaner and Jodhpur; this was ended by British intervention in 1818. In the five years after 1830 civil war and banditry were rife, and the territory was policed from 1835 to 1842 by a British force at the maharajah's expense. Maharajah Ratan Singh assisted the British against the Sikhs, and his son Sardar Singh remained loyal during the Indian Mutiny. There was a feudal (Thakur) insurrection in 1883 arising from attempts to raise the dues ("scutage") payable in lieu of military service. This led to the permanent establishment of a British political agent at Bikaner. The principality was incorporated in Rajasthan in Mar. 1949.

BIKINI (Marshall Is, Pacific). The scene of United States atomic bomb tests in July 1946. The revealing garment of the same name is popularly supposed to have been worn by the younger female inhabitants.

BILBO (apparently from Bilbao in Spain). **(1)** was a particularly sharp and elastic sword which could be bent in a circle; **(2)** as BILBOES, was an iron bar with sliding shackles for confining a prisoner especially on shipboard.

BILL. (Med.) An infantry staff weapon, mainly for wielding rather than pushing. The head had a sharp hooked blade on one side, a spike on the other and a sharp tip.

BILL, PARLIAMENTARY, is a draft of a law which has not yet received the assent of parliament and the Crown. There are eight main types. **(1)** A *public bill* is introduced into either house by a member of that house. **(2)** A *government bill* is introduced into either house by or on behalf of the govt. **(3)** A *private members bill* is a public bill introduced by a member of either house on his own initiative, and not as part of govt. policy. The distinction between **(2)** and **(3)** did not exist before the emergence of ministerial responsibility to parliament. **(4)** A *private bill* affects the interests of a person as such, and is introduced into either house by means of a petition from someone who is not a member of that house. **(5)** A *local bill* is a private bill having purely local effects. In the 16th and 17th cents. many members regarded the passage of such bills for the benefit of their constituents as their primary task. **(6)** A *personal bill* is a private bill concerned with the affairs of a private person, for example formerly, for divorce or naturalisation, or the settlement of a large family estate. **(7)** A *hybrid bill* is partly public and partly private in its effects, and in particular affects the interests of a person as such and not as a member of a class. This part has to be dealt with as a private bill (see below). **(8)** A *money bill* must be introduced into the House of Commons, and must be founded upon a resolution of the whole House. Since the Parliament Act 1911, after passing the Commons it may be certified by the Speaker to be a Money Bill, and the Lords cannot then delay it for more than a month.

Outline of Modern Procedure. Disregarding, temporarily, exceptions and frills, the procedure is as follows:-

(a) The bill is *brought in and read a first time*. This constitutes mere notice of intention; often the bill has not even been drafted, and only the short and long titles will be public. The eventual text must not go beyond the scope of the long title, otherwise the effect of the notice would be misleading. *but see* **(h)** below.

(b) *Publication.*

(c) Second Reading. An order is moved that *the bill be read a second time*. On this motion only the main principles of the bill are discussed. If the motion is defeated the bill falls to the ground.

(d) Committee Stage. In the 17th cent., and in modern times in the case of very short and urgent bills (e.g. Edward VII's abdication) the House might proceed direct to the Third Reading, but the normal course is to *send the bill to a committee* for detailed examination. Here it is debated clause by clause and detailed amendments are made. An amendment which would destroy the main purpose of the bill is not allowed. The committee may, and until 1939 usually did consist of the whole House, but this, though still usual in the Lords, is now rare in the Commons, where the committee will consist of between 25 and 40 members.

(e) Report. The bill is next *reported* with or without amendment to the whole House, whose members then have an opportunity to make amendments themselves.

(f) Third Reading. The bill, as finally amended, is debated as a whole on the motion that it *be read a third time*. Fourth readings occurred in the 18th cent.

(g) Passage. The bill is finally *passed*: that is to say, to the other House or to the Crown for agreement as necessary. A motion to pass a bill is nowadays seldom debated because everything will already have been said.

(h) NOTE. Since 1999 govt. bills have mostly been published extraparliamentarily before first reading. The foreshortening of draftman's time and possible second drafts before introduction may lead to opposed First Readings.

Procedure in Special Cases. (i) A bill passed by one House and rejected by another cannot be revived in the same session, but a public bill passed by the Commons and rejected by the Lords may, under the Parliament Acts 1911 and 1949, be presented to the Crown for its Assent over the heads of the Lords a year later, if passed in exactly the same form by the Commons in the next following session; this procedure, not possible before 1911, has been used only five times.

(ii) A bill passed by one house and amended by the other is returned to the first house. If it agrees to the amendments the bill is presented for the Royal Assent. If it disagrees then either the bill fails, or the Parliament Act procedure may be used.

(iii) A money bill, that is a bill involving a levy upon the subject, must originate in the Commons; it must be moved on behalf of the Crown, and cannot proceed to its Committee Stage until the relevant authority has been given by a resolution of the whole house. It does not, since 1911, require the agreement of the Lords, who cannot delay it for more than a month, but who can and usually do debate it. The rights of the Lords depend on whether or not the bill has been certified by the Speaker as a money bill, and sometimes the certificate is deliberately withheld, so as to enable parts to be considered and if necessary amended in detail in the Lords.

(iv) After second reading, opposed private bills are referred to a very small select committee which hears evidence from the promoter and opponents, in the manner of a trial. If it is unopposed, it will be considered by an unopposed bill committee where it may be vigorously attacked by civil servants. Proceedings on most other stages of private bills are usually short.

Effects of Bills. A bill has no effect until it has received the Royal Assent, and no action or defence in legal proceedings can be founded upon one pending in either house. A Financial Resolution of the House of Commons does, however, give temporary authority for the collection of an existing tax, until the passing of the Finance Act founded upon such resolution.

BILLIARDS. The first British description appeared in 1674, but pictures of a similar game go back to 1635. Before this the meaning of the word is uncertain and may have referred to games differing as widely as shuffle-board and croquet. It was fashionable in the 18th cent. when a broad headed cue was used. The first book on it appeared in 1807. The india rubber cushion was introduced in 1835 and slate beds in 1836. *See* SNOOKER.

BILLINGSGATE (London). Market tolls were collected there under K. Ethelred (979-1016). It specialised in fish in the 16th cent. and was closed in 1975. The name has been used as a synonym for a peculiarly elaborate or foul-mouthed form of abuse for at least four centuries.

BILLINGTON-GREIG, Theresa (1877-1964) was twice imprisoned as a leading suffragette but came to doubt their tactics and broke with them in 1911.

BILL OF RIGHTS 1688 begins by reciting that on 13 Feb. 1688 the Houses "assembled at Westminster lawfully fully and freely representing all the estates of the people...", tendered to William of Orange and Mary a declaration setting out 12 heads of accusation against James II, that he had abdicated, that the Houses had met in response to letters from William and Mary, and that they "for the vindicating and asserting their ancient rights liberties" declared 13 propositions, the first 12 of which relate to the 12 heads of accusation. These 13 propositions are that:- **(1)** the suspending power without parliamentary consent is illegal, **(2)** the dispensing power "as assumed and exercised of late" is illegal, **(3)** the court of High Commission and all other courts of like nature are illegal, **(4)** levying money for the use of the crown without grant of parliament is illegal, **(5)** The subjects are entitled to petition the crown, **(6)** "the raising and keeping a standing army within the kingdom in time of peace, unless it be with consent of parliament is illegal", **(7)** protestant subjects may bear arms, **(8)** parliamentary elections should be free, **(9)** freedom of speech and debates and proceedings in parliament should not be questioned in any court or place outside parliament, **(10)** excessive bail should not be required; nor excessive fines imposed; nor cruel and unusual punishments inflicted, **(11)** jurors should be empanelled and returned and in treason trials they should be freeholders, **(12)** grants and promises of fines and forfeitures of particular persons before conviction are illegal and void, **(13)** parliaments should be held frequently.

The bill then continues that, encouraged by William and Mary's response they tendered the crown to them, that they accepted it, that thereupon the new King and Queen intimated that the Houses should continue to sit as a parliament. Thereupon it was enacted that the propositions in the declaration are the law of the land, that William and Mary be King and Queen but that the royal functions are to be exercised by William only in their joint names. The bill then proceeds to limit the succession to William's heirs, papists excluded. Finally it saved all charters, grants and pardons issued before 23 Oct. 1689, and invalidated all future dispensations unless allowed by statute or specially allowed by acts passed in the present parliament. No such acts were passed, probably because a general act of indemnity for William's supporters made them unnecessary.

BILLS. *See* MARCHES. ANGLO-SCOTS-5,6.

BILLS OF EXCHANGE. *See* BANKING-5.

BILLS OF MORTALITY. In 1592 the Worshipful Company of Parish Clerks began to publish weekly returns of deaths for the 109 parishes in and about the City of London. This area, which did not remain constant, became known as "within the bills of mortality".

BILLS OF SALE transfer the ownership of chattels without transferring possession, but they have most often been used as chattel-mortgages. To prevent frauds on creditors, the Bills of Sale Act, 1854, made an unregistered bill void against a judgment creditor. An Act of 1882 had the different purpose of protecting the unsophisticated against 'sharks'; it laid down the exact form of the bill and required attestation by a solicitor and registration in the High Court. The procedural inconvenience virtually put an end to them.

BILNEY, Thomas (c. 1495-1531), a Cambridge theologian, attacked pilgrimages and images, recanted in 1527 but resumed his preaching and was burned as a heretic.

BIMETALLISM, i.e. the use of both gold and silver coins as legal tender, was an intermittent feature of 19th cent. economics. It was based on a ratio of 31 silver to 2 gold. Before 1848 it was primarily a French institution and the ratio was maintained by regulating the output of the mints. From 1848 to 1860 the Californian and Australian gold rushes vastly increased the gold production and spread bimetallism to other European countries and the U.S.A. This, and the perpetual tendency of India to absorb gold for decoration maintained the ratio. After 1870 silver production rose steeply while gold production fell, and in 1873 the Germans went over to a gold standard and sold vast amounts of silver. This upset the bimetallic currencies and the silver based Indian rupee. Monetary conferences at Paris in 1878 and 1881 and at Brussels in 1892 failed to overcome German obduracy and the issue affected U.S. elections in 1896 and 1900. By 1914 a gold standard was normal save in China, and to some extent in India. The issue became outdated with the rise of managed or mismanaged paper currencies. *See* GOLD STANDARD

BINDHACHAL (Uttar Pradesh, India). A place of pilgrimage for Hindus to the shrine of Vindyeshwari, but better known as the place where Thugs worshipped at a temple of Kali.

BINGHAM or BYNGHAM. A Dorset family of some fame and notoriety. **(1) Sir Richard (1528-99)** fought at Lepanto, in Cyprus, and with the Dutch in the Low Countries; from 1579 to 1583 he was in Ireland where he suppressed the Desmond rebellion, and drove out the Spanish Smerwick expedition. In 1584 he became Pres. of Connaught which at first he administered with fairness and leniency but, feeling betrayed by successive insurrections in Galway, Clare and Mayo in 1586 he inaugurated a reign of terror and confiscation which has not been forgotten, and which was disapproved by the Lord Deputy, Sir John Perrot. He spent much of the next ten years in dispute with Perrot who complained formally to the Queen in 1592 of his cruelty and insubordination. In 1596 he came to London without leave, allegedly to secure justice; he was for a while imprisoned, but in 1598, on the outbreak of the O'Neill rebellion, he was reinstated. **(2) John (?-1605)** was granted the Burke estate of Castlebar which eventually descended to **(3) Sir John (?-1749)** a gov. of Mayo who deserted James II at the B. of Aughrim in 1691. He married a niece of the E. of Lucan whose title became

extinct. The title was revived in **(4) Charles (1735-99),** second son of Sir John who was made **E. of LUCAN** in 1795. His grandson **(5) George Charles (1800-88) 3rd E. (1839),** a soldier and M.P. from 1828 to 1830, was a maj-gen. by 1851 and put in command of the Cavalry Division in the Crimean War (1854-5). As such he was unjustly blamed for the manner of the charge of the Light Brigade, commanded by his subordinate and brother-in-law the E. of Cardigan (Oct. 1854). He was recalled, refused a court martial and so was forced to vindicate himself in the House of Lords. His social importance, however, far exceeded the publicity of these spectacular events, for he led the policy of 'improving' his great Irish estates at Castlebar (Co. Mayo) by demolishing the villages, driving out the tenants and turning the land over to sheep, thus adding to the enduring hatred felt by the rural Irish for the English Ascendancy. His descendent **(6) Richard John (1934-?) 7th E. (1964)** vanished in Nov. 1974 after allegations against him of murder.

BIOLOGY, EARLY. European biological inquiry virtually ceased with the death of Galen in about A.D. 200, and did not revive until Arabic translations of the works of the Greek scientists such as Aristotle became known in Latin between 11th and 13th cents. Michael Scot translated Aristotle in South Italy in the 1230s. The first major advances were, however, made by the Renaissance artists notably Botticelli (1444-1510), Leonardo da Vinci (1452-1519), Dürer (1471-1528) and Michelangelo (1475-1564) who examined what they saw, instead of theorising from accepted texts. The first biological text-books were botanical works produced by Otto Brunfels in Germany in 1542. Pierre Belon of le Mans made detailed drawings of animal physiology in the middle of the 16th cent. and by the end of it Fabricius was teaching anatomy at Padua. One of his pupils was William Harvey (1578-1657) who in 1616 first expounded his discovery of blood circulation, and published his treatise on it in 1628. The compound microscope, originally designed by Galileo in 1610, was used by Marcello Malpighi (1628-94) to corroborate Harvey's findings by detecting capillary circulation; Leeuwenhoek (1632-1723) used it to discover and investigate bacteria as early as 1683, and the discovery of the cellular structure of animals and plants followed in the 18th cent. This cleared the way, after a number of false starts, for the emergence of the 'progressive' school of biologists, and Darwin's *Origin of Species* appeared in 1859.

BIRD, Francis (1667-1731) sculptor and pupil of Grinling Gibbons and Caius Gabriel Cibber, to whose business he succeeded. He worked for Wren on St. Paul's Cathedral, especially on the scene depicting St. Paul's conversion, and executed a famous statue of Dr Busby, headmaster of Westminster, for Westminster Abbey.

BIRDCAGE WALK and COCKPIT STAIRS (St. James' Park, London). The walk was named after birdcages set up there under James I. Cockpit Stairs, connects the Walk with Storey's Gate. *See* COCKPIT.

BIRDS, PROTECTION OF. The first British legislation (1869) protected Sea Birds and in 1872 was extended to some other species. A close season for wildfowling was first imposed in 1876 and bird sanctuaries were authorised by an Act of 1896. The law was consolidated and extended by the Protection of Birds Act 1956, and again in 1967.

BIRDWOOD, Field-Marshal Sir William Riddell (1865-1951), 1st Ld. of ANZAC and TOTNES served in India and then in the South African War. He was Kitchener's assistant military sec. in India from 1902 to 1904, and then military sec. until 1909. Kitchener gave him the command of the Australia and New Zealand Army Corps (ANZAC) with which he landed at Galipoli in Apr. 1915. He also carried out the skilful withdrawal from the Dardanelles. In 1918 he commanded the Australasian troops on the Western Front. He was C-in-C in India from 1925 to 1930, and Master of Peterhouse, Cambridge, from 1931 to 1938.

BIRINUS (?-650) probably a German, came to Britain as a missionary at the instance of Pope Honorius I, and worked among the West Saxons. In c. 635 he baptised their K. Cynegils. He built a number of churches including that at Dorchester-on-Thames where he also founded a see. He seems to have failed to convert Cynegils' family, yet his diocese had to be divided within seventy years of its foundation.

BIRKBECK, Dr George (1776-1841), became prof. of natural philosophy at Anderson's College, Glasgow, in 1799 and noticing the difficulty which the intelligent poor had in acquiring scientific knowledge, began in 1800 to give inexpensive lectures for artisans. These were immensely successful, and in 1823 developed into the first Mechanics' Institution, though in 1804 he had migrated to London, where he practised as a physician. The *Gentlemans Magazine* suggested in 1824 that London should follow Glasgow. Birkbeck immediately took action, found the money and became Pres. of the London Mechanics' Institution later called the Birkbeck Institution and finally Birkbeck College. These examples were followed all over the country. Meanwhile he joined in the agitation for a London University and in 1827 became one of its founders. He was also prominent in securing the repeal of the Newspaper Duty in 1836.

BIRKENHEAD. *See* LIVERPOOL.

BIRKENHEAD, first Earl of. *See* SMITH. F.E.

BIRKETT, Norman (1883-1962) 1st Ld. BIRKETT of ULVERSTON (1958). A very successful barrister who was a liberal M.P. in 1923-4 and 1929-31. He was Chairman of the Committee on Defence Reg. 18B which dealt with cases of persons who had been detained on security grounds during World War II. In 1959 he settled a grave printing dispute and two days before his death he persuaded the House of Lords to throw out Manchester Corporation's scheme for turning Ullswater into a reservoir.

BIRLAYMEN or BOORLAWMEN. Members of a jury of 4 to 14 in, mostly lowland, Scottish courts of barony who with the laird or his bailiff settled agricultural problems (cf English court baron).

BIRMINGHAM (Eng.) was unimportant until the 16th cent. when the iron masters began operations. It supplied Parliament with weapons in the Civil War, but by 1700 the population was not above 12,000. It had no corporation or guilds, and being over five miles from any place where the "Clarendon Code" applied, was unhampered by religious discrimination. Enterprising people could therefore settle easily and in the 18th cent. amongst others Matthew Boulton, James Watt, Erasmus Darwin, Joseph Priestley, Herschell, Smeaton and Josiah Wedgwood came there. It was the building of the canal complex, of which it was the centre, combined with the operations of Taylor's and Lloyds Bank, and Boulton and Watt's partnership which launched the town into its modern importance. It had no parliamentary representation until 1832 nor a local authority until 1838. It made history by the modernism of its civic administration under the leadership of Joseph Chamberlain, who was first elected to the Council in 1869. Its boundaries were extended in 1911, 1928 and again in 1966, and it was heavily damaged by air raids in World War II. *See* TRANSPORT AND COMMUNICATIONS.

BIRMINGHAM POLITICAL UNION was founded by Thomas Attwood to agitate for the Reform Bills and slowly declined after its main purpose was achieved in 1832.

BIRMINGHAM POST. Radical journal founded in 1857 by John Feeney and Sir John Jaffray. After the split in the Liberal Party over Home Rule, it became Unionist but was later associated with the views and propaganda of Joseph

Chamberlain. It drifted steadily to the right and by the 1970s was generally conservative in its views.

BIRON. This branch of the French Gontaut family had five marshals among its members. **Charles Armand (1663-1756)** was captured at Oudenarde in 1708 and **Armand Louis (1747-93)** known until 1788 as the Duc de Lauzun, played a prominent role in the American War of Independence; supported, as a deputy, the French Revolution; commanded revolutionary forces, but was guillotined during the Terror.

BIRR, SYNOD OF or ADAMNAN'S SYNOD (696). The meeting at which Adamnan converted Irish churchmen, other than those under obedience to Iona, to the decisions of the Synod of Whitby (664).

BIRELL, Augustine (1850-1933), liberal M.P. for West Fife (1889-1900) and for Bristol (North) (1906-18) was Pres. of the Board of Education from 1905 to 1907. His 1906 Education Bill, designed to remedy grievances which nonconformists were alleged to suffer, was thrown out of the House of Lords through a combination of bishops and conservative peers. This was an early warning of Lords' opposition to Liberal legislation which ultimately led to the crisis of 1910. Birrell became Chief Sec. for Ireland in 1909 and held the post until 1916. More interested in administration than in policy making, he got on well with Redmond and the Irish moderates, but he and they were taken by surprise by the Easter Rising of 1916 and he resigned. *See* CURRAGH INCIDENT.

BIRTH CONTROL. Thomas Robert Malthus (1766-1834) a clergyman and economist advocated limiting the population before it outran the food supply. His book, the *Essay on Population,* created a sensation in 1798, but he did not advocate artificial interference with fertilisation. Francis Place, who had 15 children, published a pamphlet urging contraception in 1822, but offered no ideas on method. The American, Robert Dale Owen, son of Robert Owen the reformer, published a more practical work in 1831 called *Moral Physiology* and in 1832 in Boston (Mass) Francis Knowlton, a doctor, published the *Fruits of Philosophy* for which he was imprisoned. In 1876 Annie Besant and Charles Bradlaugh republished the *Fruits of Philosophy* in England and were prosecuted but acquitted in 1877. This prosecution gave enormous publicity to the subject and led to the foundation of the Malthusian League, the establishment in 1921 of the first birth control clinic in London, and later still the widespread distribution through the League of the works of Marie Stopes. The Nat. Birth Control Assn was formed from 8 distinct groups in 1931 and changed its name to the Family Planning Assn in 1939. The contraceptive pill for oral consumption was developed after World War II; it came into general use in 1961-2, and superseded the condom, but the onset of AIDS reinstated the condom as a protection against disease rather than impregnation. *See* STOPES, MARY.

BIRTH RATE. *See* POPULATION AND VITAL STATISTICS.

BISCOE, John (1794-1843), commissioned in 1830 by Samuel Enderby & Sons to seek new sealing and whaling grounds, circumnavigated Antarctica in 1831, and claimed Graham Land for Britain.

BISCUIT, SHIPS was made of flour with a minimum of water, kneaded into thick flat cakes, slowly baked hard and enclosed in barrels. The process preserved the flour, but before the days of metal containers it was often infested with weevils. It remained the basic essential of ship's food for long voyages from 16th cent. till about 1921. *See* NAVIGATION.

BISHOP, William Avery (1894-1956) V.C. (1917) was a Canadian fighter pilot who is credited with having shot down 72 enemy aircraft in World War I. In 1918 he joined the Canadian general staff and rose steadily to the rank of Air Marshal by 1938. From 1940 to 1944 he directed recruiting for the R. Canadian Air Force.

BISHOPS are distinguished from other priests mainly by

their power to confer holy orders and to administer Confirmation. They are consecrated by three other bishops, one of whom is usually the metropolitan of the province. A bishop must be of mature age (usually thirty) and must be "chosen" or "elected". In most places the electors were originally the cathedral chapter, but in the R. Catholic church their powers have mostly long since been superseded by the Pope, and in the Church of England the Chapter cannot elect without a royal licence called a *congé d'élire* and must elect the person mentioned in royal Letters Recommendatory. The Anglican bishops are thus, in fact, appointed by the Prime Minister who, however, since 1979 has always formally consulted an advisory commission of the Church. Previously some kind of informal consultation was in any case normal.

In 1995 the Abps. of Canterbury and York and the Bps. of London, Durham and Winchester had permanent seats in the House of Lords together with 21 other diocesan bishops in order of seniority of appointment.

BISHOPRICS. See ADVOWSON AND TITHE-3; PLURALISM.

BISHOPS' BOOK (1536). See TEN ARTICLES.

BISHOPS CASTLE (Salop), called after the castle built there by the Bishops of Hereford, was a place of some importance in the strategy of the Marches but otherwise inconsiderable. It sent two M.P.'s to parliament from earliest times until 1832. The castle had by then fallen into ruin. The population never exceeded 1300 but it remained a borough until 1974.

BISHOPS' WARS 1639 AND 1640. See CHARLES I-12.

BISLEY (Surrey). The rifle competitions were transferred from Wimbledon to Bisley in 1890.

BISMARCK. A powerful German battleship which with the cruiser *Prinz Eugen* broke into the Atlantic from Norway in May 1941. On 24th she was attacked by H.M.S. *Prince of Wales* and by H.M.S. *Hood* which blew up. On 27th the *Bismarck* was sunk by the Home Fleet, but the *Prinz Eugen* escaped to Brest. See COMMERCE PROTECTION. NAVAL C-6 & 9.

BISMARCK or NEW BRITAIN ARCHIPELAGO. The Germans occupied it in 1885. They surrendered to the Australians in 1914, and Australia administered it under a League of Nations mandate after 1920. The local Germans were all deported. Parts of it, particularly Rabaul, were occupied by the Japanese in World War II, since when it has been an Australian trust territory. See NEW GUINEA.

BISMARCK-SCHÖNHAUSEN, Otto von (1815-98) Prince (1871). (1) In 1847, when first elected to the united Prussian diet, he married Johanna v. Puttkamer and so came into the circle of protestant conservative nobles who advised Frederick William IV. At first he favoured the Austrian policy of repression after the 1848 insurrections. In May 1851, however, he became Prussian representative to the federal diet at Frankfurt where he soon concluded that Austrian influence must be extruded from Germany. This view related to a Prussian ambition (dating from Frederick the Great's time) to control the German ports and the fluvial communications across Europe to them. As these were mostly in the hands of independent states (particularly Hanover and Denmark) guaranteed by Austria, the expulsion of Austria from Germany was a precondition of such control. The King and his foreign minister, Manteuffel, thought that Prussia should wait until Austria got into difficulties with Russia or France: Bismarck, who had no use for social conservatism, thought that Prussia should make trouble in order to snatch at a great future. At the same time he thought that the Balkans were none of Prussia's business. Hence Austria could be compensated for expulsion from Germany by gains in the Balkans.

(2) In 1858 Frederick William IV went mad and his brother William became regent. Prussian policy became more liberal, and the reactionary Bismarck was despatched in 1859 from Frankfurt to St. Petersburg as ambassador. In 1861 the regent became King as William I, and there followed a dispute about the military estimates between the King advised by Albrecht v. Roon, his War Minister, and Parliament. The liberal majority wanted to reduce the length of service in the army: Roon the size of the militia (*Landwehr*). The controversy reached to the roots of the Prussian state because the militia was a territorial and popular organisation, whereas the army was authoritarian and efficient. To encourage the militia was to encourage Prussian liberalism: to enlarge the army was to provide the instrument for an energetic foreign policy. The liberals increased their majority in the general election and Roon urged the King to make Bismarck Minister-President. The King sent for him, but though he wanted the larger army, he was alarmed at Bismarck's ideas which might, of course, involve the overthrow of many of the King's princely relatives. Bismarck was, therefore, sent as ambassador to Paris. Within six months he was recalled to become (22 Sept. 1862) Minister-President. In internal politics he depended on the King, but he was also necessary to the King so long as there was a liberal, that is hostile, majority in parliament. Bismarck's habitual refusal to co-operate with the liberals was aimed as much at his master as at them. In fact, however, he was interested in other things.

(3) He believed in the principle of practical and therefore limited achievement. This was what he meant by *realpolitik*. The limited achievement which he sought was a Germanic unit small enough to be dominated by Prussia, but big enough to be, as a leading European state, worth dominating. From this point of view his career falls into three distinct but overlapping phases:- **(i)** The defeat of the Habsburgs and the Partition of the German speaking world (1862-6); **(ii)** The absorption of non-Austrian Germany and the defeat of the French (1866-71). **(iii)** Peace and digestion (1871-90). See PRUSSIA-17 to 18.

(4) At the P. of Frankfort (May 1871) the French were required to pay an indemnity and cede most of Alsace-Lorraine. This cession was required on military advice and exacerbated Franco-German relations until as late as 1945, and Bismarck later regretted it. For the next eight years he, now Imperial Chancellor, co-operated with the national liberals in the *Reichstag* (Imperial Parliament) to transform Germany into a modern state with a single civil code, currency and central bank. This was not in fact liberalism but paternalistic utilitarianism, but Bismarck shared with the liberals a distrust of the R. Catholics. The central issue was education. The R. Catholics claimed to train and license teachers; Bismarck demanded that the state should train and license priests. The *Kulturkampf* (Battle of Cultures) in 1876 reached an intensity where priests defied the law and were imprisoned, and episcopal sees were left vacant. This so far identified Bismarck with liberalism that his conservative and protestant friends began to have doubts about him. His position was further complicated by his diplomacy to prevent a French war of revenge. As this could only come about if imperial Austria or Czarist Russia supported France, he encouraged French republicanism, and constituted in 1873 the so-called *Dreikaiserbund* (League of Three Emperors) as a method of settling disputes between them.

(5) The League could not succeed because any major dispute was likely to be vital. This happened in the Balkans where, as Russian intervention against Turkey in 1877 grew more dangerous, an Austro-Russian war became probable. Germany's position depended on a balance between these two and Britain. In 1878 he presided over the Berlin Congress and mediated successfully between the powers. The Congress also demonstrated that Germany could not live without allies. France was hostile, Britain distant, Russia unstable. In

Oct. 1879 an alliance was signed with Austro-Hungary against bitter opposition from K. William.

(6) The years 1878 and 1879 also marked a decisive change in German internal politics. Bismarck's attack on the R. Catholics was intended to distract the electors. By 1877 the revenue was insufficient for the military budget. Bismarck feared direct taxation, which would make the govt. dependent upon the *Reichstag,* and demanded that indirect taxes should be voted for an indefinite period. The liberals demanded constitutional guarantees and a parliamentary ministry as their price. In June 1878 someone tried to assassinate the King. The *Reichstag* was dissolved; Bismarck launched an anti-socialist campaign which put the liberals in a dilemma, for they had either to renounce their progressive principles or risk accusations of complicity with assassins. They were swept away and Bismarck, who had bought the estates about Varzin from the v. Blumenthals, made a deal with the junker landowners (most of whom were army officers) and the industrialists to protect their respective interests by tariffs which paid for the army. This alliance of industrialists, junkers and the army became a standing feature of German political life.

(7) But Bismarck was a man without a party. The liberals had gone; the other parties could always combine to defeat him in the *Reichstag*. To maintain his position he had to unite or distract the nation periodically by scares and foreign crises. In 1884 he generated a series of disputes with Britain, and in the course of one year acquired the Cameroons, South West and East Africa and part of New Guinea. In 1886 the unification of Bulgaria was used as a further distraction and resulted, after a general election, in the passing of a seven years Army Appropriation.

(8) By now Bismarck was getting old, and in 1888 K. William I died. Frederick III was a known liberal and Bismarck as a counter-weight had encouraged his son, the new Crown Prince, to be insubordinate. Frederick III died three months later and William II ascended the throne. Bismarck's tactics now rebounded on himself. The Emperor was young and romantic. He understood modern Germany better than his elderly Chancellor. He thought that the rising social democrats would be less dangerous if courteously conciliated. The laws of 1878 against them were due to expire in 1890. The *Reichstag* would not renew them. In the general election of 1890 those who agreed with Bismarck were roundly defeated. He proposed a *coup d'état* to the Emperor who in return dismissed him. He spent the rest of his active retirement at Varzin blackening William II's character.

BISON. These large plains buffaloes used to migrate in herds sometimes a million strong, in a regular cycle in the American mid-west between the Gulf of Mexico and Central Canada. They provided the plains Red Indians with food but trampled down any cultivations over which they happened to pass. Arable settlement in bison country was impossible until vast numbers had been slaughtered by trappers who sold the fur and skins for export. This led to fighting with the Indians. Their destruction, mainly in the 1860s, was an important phase in the history of the N. American continent.

BIZERTA (locally **BEN-ZERT,** formerly **HIPPO ZARYTUS) (Tunisia).** Its excellent but decayed harbour was redeveloped after 1881 by the French who turned it into a fortified naval station. The Germans seized it in World War II and used it as a supply base, whose importance increased as their troops retreated towards it before the Anglo-American armies, who took it in May 1943.

BJÖRKÖ, T. of (24 July 1905) between the Kaiser William II and the Czar Nicholas II at an island in the Baltic, was a defensive alliance against attack by any European power, though mutual aid was to be given only in Europe. The Russians had just been defeated by the Japanese and feared that the Japanese might renew the

war with British help, but they already had a French alliance and needed French finance. As the T. was really inconsistent with the French alliance, and peace was made with American mediation on 5 Sept., the Russians had to choose between France and Germany. They chose France and the treaty never came into effect.

BLACK ACT (1723) was passed for three years against large armed gangs in Waltham (Epping) Forest who because they blackened their faces, were called the Waltham Blacks. As protection racketeers, they terrorised the area and its environs from about 1720, and the Act had to be extended several times.

BLACK ACTS (Sc.). (1) Stuart statutes printed in black letter type (1535-94). **(2)** Acts of 1584 to suppress presbyterianism and restore episcopacy. They declared the King's supremacy, handed the functions of the Kirk presbyteries and Assembly to the bishops and made it treason to attack episcopacy. Repealed in 1592.

BLACK AGNES. The swarthy Countess of Dunbar, who successfully defended Dunbar Castle against the English in 1338.

BLACK AND TANS. The nickname of a body of militarised police volunteers, theoretically recruits to the Royal Irish Constabulary, raised in 1920 and used by the British Govt. to fight the I.R.A. (Irish Republican Army). The name is also used to include a distinct and much more brutal body called the Auxiliary Division ('Auxis').

BLACK BALL LINE was formed by James Bains at Liverpool in 1852 to convey immigrants to Australia during the Gold Rush. Very prosperous at first, it declined towards 1858 with the decline in migration, revived as it rose and collapsed in 1866 with the collapse of its bankers.

BLACK BOOK (Scots). A 14th cent. transcript of Scots council proceedings.

BLACK BOOK OF THE ADMIRALTY (temp. Henry VI) is a compilation of rules for the conduct of the fleet, and the law on prize and collisions. It contains a copy of the Laws of Oléron, upon which shipping law is based, and an exposition of the Civil Law procedure of the Admiralty Court. The illuminated M.S. is in the Public Record Office.

BLACK BOOK OF CHIRK (c. 1200). The oldest MS of the Venedotian code of Welsh Laws.

BLACK BOOK OF THE EXCHEQUER (13th cent.) contains memoranda on appointments to various Exchequer posts in the mid-13th cent. and under Henry VI and Edward IV. The different LITTLE BLACK BOOK OF the EXCHEQUER (also 13th cent.) contains an account of Henry II's household and the *Dialogus de Scaccario* (both also found in the Red Book of the Exchequer) and some treaties, papal bulls and charters.

BLACK BOOK OF THE TOWER or *CODEX VETUS* (Lat = old roll) was a collection of extracts from the Parliament Rolls of Edward I and II, first printed in 1661.

BLACKBURN, Helen (1842-1903). *See* SUFFRAGETTES.

BLACKBURN (Lancs) is at the Pennine entrance to the Ribble valley. Woollens produced from Pennine sheep gave it a moderate but reliable prosperity, evidenced by the 12th cent. Norman style rebuilding of its 6th cent. church and by the Elizabethan Grammar school. The wet climate encouraged cotton processing which was already established when James Hargreaves (locally born) invented the Spinning Jenny (*see* INDUSTRIAL REVOLUTION) in 1764. Rioting spinners drove him out, but cotton had replaced woollens by 1790 and inspired related activities such as weaving, carpets and building the appropriate machines, all much developed by Sir Robert Peel, the statesman's grandfather. The population rose. The village became a municipality in 1851 and a county borough in 1888. By 1913 it was the world's leading cotton weaving centre, and accumulating capital for diversified engineering. With this secondary industrial substructure, the mid-20th cent. decline in cotton affected Blackburn less than some other Lancashire towns. It now produced, besides machinery, electrical goods, chemicals and paints, paper and footwear, and it maintained its population.

BLACK CAP. A black cloth folded into a flat square and worn over the wig by a judge when passing sentence of death or swearing in the Lord Mayor of London.

BLACK "CODES" were collections of enactments dealing with slaves in the American slave owning colonies. Though they varied in detail, their common principle was that slaves were chattels, not persons, and that the law must protect their owners. The status of a child depended on that of the mother. Slaves could not own property, make a contract, strike a free person even if attacked, or give evidence against a free man. They might not assemble in groups, or be absent from home without their owner's permission. They could not have firearms and might not be taught to read or write. The codes were severely, but seldom capitally, enforced by the courts.

BLACK DEATH. *See* PLAGUE.

BLACK DINNER. *See* JAMES II OF SCOTS-2.

BLACKETT, Prof. *See* COMMERCE PROTECTION, NAVAL C-8.

BLACKFEET. *Similar to* WHITEFEET.

BLACKFOOT INDIANS or SIKSIKA, a large fierce tribe of Algonquian stock in Montana and Saskatchewan, who wore black moccasins. A smallpox epidemic destroyed 60% of them and their power in the years after 1780.

BLACK FRIARS. *See* DOMINICANS.

BLACKFRIARS BRIDGE (London). The first was in use from 1770 to 1860; the second, in use from 1869, was widened and doubled for trains in 1907-9.

BLACK FRIDAYS (1) The day, 11 May, 1866 when Overend and Gurney's Bank of London failed. **(2)** The day, 24 Sept. 1869, when Jay Gould's and James Fisk's corner in the gold market brought about a crisis on the New York stock exchange. **(3)** In left wing parlance the day, 15 Apr. 1921, when the railway and transport workers' union refused to support the miners in an imminent strike and effectively ended their triple alliance.

BLACK GALL. Danish Vikings in Ireland.

BLACKHEATH (London) was occasionally used for very large assemblies such as the rally of Wat Tyler's supporters in 1381; Henry V's triumphal return from Agincourt in 1415; the assembly of Jack Cade's followers in 1450; and of Lord Audley's in 1497. The army met Charles II there at his restoration.

It is said that K. James I introduced golf to England by playing it on Blackheath in 1608. In recent times it has become better known for a rugby football club named after it.

BLACK HOLE (OF CALCUTTA). Originally a black hole was the prisoners' cell in a military guardhouse. On 19 June 1756 Suraj-ud-Dowlah, the Nawab of Bengal, confined 146 Europeans in the very cramped Black Hole at Calcutta and most of them died of heat-stroke during the night. One prisoner, Holwell, survived to write a harrowing but substantially true account. Indians have challenged this as an atrocity story, but it is difficult to exonerate those responsible, for they must have known what the consequence of such a mass confinement in such heat would have been. *See* PLASSEY.

BLACK JACK. (1) The black pirate flag, seldom, if ever, garnished with a skull and crossbones. **(2)** A name for bubonic plague.

BLACK, Joseph (1728-99) in a thesis, *De Humore Acido a Cibis Orto et Magnesia Alba* (Lat = Acidity rising from food and chalk) submitted at Edinburgh in 1754, proposed a chemical method based upon the exact use of the balance, observed that chalk lost 60% of its weight when burned for lime, and concluded that this was due to the escape of a gas which he called 'fixed air' (later identified as carbon dioxide). He also by experiment established the existence and nature of latent and specific heat. He was a friend of James Hutton and James Watt.

BLACK KNIGHT OF LORNE. *See* JAMES II OF SCOTS-1.

BLACK LIST. This old phrase, dating from 17th cent., signifies a list kept by someone of people of whom he disapproves, particularly a govt. list of wartime neutrals or neutral firms known to trade with the enemy, or a union list of employers who employ non-union labour or of goods produced by employers involved in a trade dispute or a list kept by employers of workers active in Trade unionism.

BLACKMAIL. *See* MARCHES. ANGLO-SCOTS-10.

BLACK MARKET. A market in goods which are officially restricted and under official price control but where buyers and sellers defy the law to deal in greater quantities, for which they are prepared to accept higher prices. The expression is said to come from the Italian Fascist blackshirts who controlled scarce goods after 1923.

BLACK MICHAEL. *See* HICKS BEACH.

BLACKMORE, Richard Dodderidge (1825-1990), market gardener and novelist, wrote *inter alia, Lorna Doone* (1869) about the primitive people of Exmoor a generation earlier.

BLACKMORE, Sir Richard (1653-1729), physician to William III and Q. Anne, wrote didactic epics ridiculed by Pope but praised by Addison and Dr Johnson.

BLACK PRINCE or EDWARD of WOODSTOCK (1330-76), D. of CORNWALL (1337) by Act of Parliament, P. of WALES (1343), eldest son of Edward III, accompanied his father on his first invasion of France and early showed the promise of his life long military career, being knighted at La Hogue in 1345. In 1346 he commanded the van at the B. of Crécy and carried his part of the field on his own resources; he was also active in the taking of Calais. In 1350 he was in the sea-battle off Winchelsea with the Spaniards. On the renewal of hostilities with France in 1355 he invaded Aquitaine from Bordeaux; this was part of a co-ordinated plan for reducing the French with simultaneous attacks in Normandy and Brittany, but the Prince's short autumn campaign degenerated into a profitable expedition. In July 1356 he set out again, intending to join his father in Normandy; he plundered and burned as far as Bourges, by which time the French K. John had assembled an army to prevent his crossing the Loire. The Prince, therefore, retreated towards Bordeaux by way of Poitiers, but was there cut off and brought to battle. Using the tactics of Crécy, he was completely victorious (19 Sept. 1356) and reached Bordeaux with the French King and many nobles as captives. This enabled him to impose a two year truce while he went home. In 1459 he returned to France and in 1360 was nominally the chief negotiator of the T. of Brétigny.

The second phase of his career now began. He married his beautiful cousin Joan of Woodstock in 1361. In 1362 he was granted the Principality of Aquitaine and Gascony, and went to live at Bordeaux. She bore him two sons in France, one of whom was Richard II. He was one of the richest of continental rulers and deeply involved in French and Spanish affairs. The high cost of his govt. made him internally unpopular and his power constituted a strong motive for the greater families to intrigue with the French court. In wars for Normandy and Brittany in 1364 the great Gascon family of Albret sent troops to the French side. His attempt to suppress the free companies (mostly English raised) created further difficulties, for they promptly took service with the French commander du Guesclin in Castile and helped to dethrone his father's ally Pedro the Cruel in favour of Henry of Trastamara. The French purpose was to secure the Castilian navy. This required military action, and the prince led a combined invasion of Castile which ended in the defeat of Henry of Trastamara at the hard fought B. of Najera (Apr. 1367). The prince had financed Pedro with a loan secured by a mortgage on the province of Biscay: Pedro now refused to pay or surrender the province. To pursue his claim the prince bullied the Estates of Aquitaine into granting a five year hearth tax but the Albrets, Armagnacs and other magnates refused to levy it, and appealed to the French King. At this point Henry of Trastamara returned and defeated Pedro at Montiel in Mar. 1369 and in May Charles V, deeming the moment militarily favourable, denounced the peace of Bretigny, invaded Aquitaine and took Limoges. In 1370 the prince counter-attacked, stormed Limoges and massacred its people, but the situation continued to develop favourably for the French.

Meantime Edward III had become a sick man; in 1371 the prince had to return to England to help the King deal with Welsh insurrections, and agrarian and parliamentary unrest. In 1372 he resigned Aquitaine, which was mostly lost by 1375. In England he figured as a respected but not very powerful personage, until his death during the Good Parliament.

BLACK PROPAGANDA is disseminated in enemy territory and so presented that it seems to originate in that territory, whose residents may be induced to believe that it comes from a secret but reliable dissident source. In World War II the British did this with some success. While the BBC purveyed mostly the truth, the British black propagandists, purporting to be speaking through transmitters in Germany or enemy-held territory (such as *Soldatensender Calais*, actually at Dover) broadcast reports which were mainly fictional, seemed reliable, and were devised to alter the attitudes and morale of the audience. Much of this was done by Sefton Delmer and other journalists from the *Express* group of newspapers.

BLACK ROD, GENTLEMAN USHER OF THE. This court official, who is the chief royal usher, and usher to the Order of the Garter, has been on permanent loan to the House of Lords since the 14th cent. and acts as its chief servant, administrative officer and messenger. He performs in certain parliamentary ceremonies, of which the best known is the summoning of the House of Commons to the royal presence. On this occasion the door of the Commons is slammed in his face.

BLACKSTONE, Sir William (1723-80), fellow of All Souls, Oxford from 1744, called to the bar in 1746, first Vinerian Professor of English Law from 1758 and Principal of New Inn Hall. His academic success brought success in London, where simultaneously he practised at the bar and from 1761 to 1770 sat in the House of Commons. His celebrated four volume *Commentaries* (1765-9) enjoyed a vast success and still form the basis of much teaching in the Common Law states of the U.S.A. In 1770 he became a judge of the Common Pleas, where he served (with a short interval on the King's Bench) until his death.

Though his lectures and writings were trenchantly criticised by Bentham, their influence was profound, mainly because they contained a systematic description of the Common Law as it stood in his day after a long period of self-generated development, but before the tempo of social change provoked wholesale interference by statute.

BLACK THURSDAY, 6 Feb. 1857 when an enormous bushfire devastated most of Victoria, Australia.

BLACKWALL FRIGATES were fast 800-ton merchantmen built by Smarts of Blackwall for the India trade between 1837, the HEIC having lost its monopoly in 1833, and 1869 when clippers entered the market. They did the run from Bombay to London in 85 days. They were also built in Sunderland and on the Tyne.

BLACKWELL (1) Elizabeth (1821-1910), British but educated in the U.S.A., secured a U.S. medical degree and later became a Prof. of gynaecology at the London School of Medicine for Women. Her sister **(2) Emily (1826-1910)** also graduated in the U.S.A., was the first major woman surgeon and founded the New York Infirmary.

BLADEN, Thomas (1698-1780) was gov. of Maryland

from 1742 to 1747 and thereafter became an M.P. The boundaries of the state are mainly due to his treaties with the Iroquois, and his negotiations with Pennsylvania.

BLADENSBURG, B. of (24 Aug. 1814). *See* ANGLO-AMERICAN WAR OF 1812.

BLADON parish church is near Blenheim Palace. The graves of Sir Winston Churchill and his father, Lord Randolph Churchill, are in the churchyard.

BLAIR, Anthony Charles Lynn (1953-) PC (1994) educated at Durham Choir School, Fettes and St John's Coll: Oxford, was called to the bar in 1976. He married Cherie Booth (later QC) in 1980. He entered Labour politics in 1982, became MP for Sedgefield in 1983 and joined the Shadow Cabinet in 1988 as front bench spokesman (Energy) in 1988-9, (Employment) 1989-90, (Home affairs) from 1992 to 1994 when he was elected Leader. *See next entry.*

BLAIR GOVT. (1997-) (Labour): Twenty-two in Cabinet under Anthony Blair with John Prescott, Deputy PM and Sec. of State for the Environment, Transport and the Regions; Gordon Brown, Ch. of the Exch; Lord Irvine of Lairg, Lord Ch; Robin Cook, Foreign Sec; David Blunkett, S. of S. for Education and Employment; Jack Straw, Home Sec; Margaret Beckett, Trade and Industry; Donald Dewar, S. of S. for Scotland (d. 2000); Dr Margaret (Mo) Mowlem, for N. Ireland. 97 Junior ministers

(1) In a House of 659, the 165 Tories were overwhelmed by 481 Labour with (encouraged by participation in a minor cabinet committee) 46 Liberal Democrats. The new Labour MPs, who included over 100 women, mostly had experience of local but not national or international issues. Hence the govt. could use its huge majority to dominate parliament, and the knowledge and experience of its senior nucleus to dominate its supporters. The decline in the prestige of the House of Commons was reflected in the emptiness of its benches as seen on television.

(2) An emollient Queen's Speech was quickly followed by actions which were hardly understood by the Labour majority nor adequately criticised by the opposition. The Bank of England's powers of economic control were reduced: its supervisory functions over investment and banking being transferred to govt. boards in return for supervised routine powers to fix interest rates. The twenty-two major bills for a session lasting from May 1997 to the Autumn of 1998 were ill drafted due to congestion, and inadequately discussed. These included measures against supposed bad teachers and failing schools, and against assisted places at public schools. Pensions were to be reviewed. There was to be a huge house building programme with enormous protective measures for the environment. Hence the budget of July 1997 attacked untaxed resources including pensions, allowances, mortgages and medical insurance instead of instituting staff economies, and substituted large loans for student grants. Pressure through the lately combined Dept. of Education and Employment was directed towards the economical construction of a caste society based on job-orientated instruction.

(3) Meanwhile constitutional changes were planned. 47 life peers (only 5 Tory) were created in Aug, the govt. having already a few days before proposed a Scottish parliament (involving a reduction of 12 Westminster MPs in 2004) and a Welsh Assembly. In Sept. the Scots electorate supported the Scots proposal by 74.3%, but the Welsh (with a turn-out of 50.3%) voted by only a 0.6% majority in favour of the Welsh one.

(4) A semi-American moralistic but feeble thread was woven into foreign policy with the aid or to the pleasure of the U.S. Pres. Clinton who visited Britain in connection with Ulster in May. The vast international drug rackets were to be combatted by an attenuated MI6. Overseas Development Funds were to be allocated upon quasi-charitable rather than commercial considerations; human

rights were to be everywhere upheld; the Persian Gulf problems were to be settled and the Foreign Secretary tactlessly suggested British arbitration in the 50 year old Kashmir dispute.

(5) European policy was less straightforward. The E.U. was told that N.A.T.O. must remain the core of security. Since the disappearance of a Russian threat, this was sensible both militarily and politically, because it hindered the growth of E.U. forces. Britain was accordingly ready to concede the settlement of an E.U. (toothless) foreign policy by qualified vote in the Council of Ministers instead of unanimity, save on immigration, frontier control and in emergencies. These policies, seemingly meant to safeguard British interests were really compensations for persistent govt. asseverations of intention to surrender Sterling to the Euro.

(6) The Good Friday Agreement for Ulster and the Queen's Speech in Nov. 1998 amplified the govt.'s constitutional proposals by announcing bills on Welsh and Scots Devolution and the exclusion of hereditary peers from the Upper House. The devolution bills were passed without much fuss in July 1999 (Wales) and Nov. (Scotland) save that there was a difficulty where Scots MPs might vote on English issues but not English on Scots. The govt. sought to deal with this by reviving the dormant Commons regional affairs committee. On the other hand the Irish proposals ran into storms which continued into the year 2000. (*See also* HOUSE OF LORDS BILL, GOVERNMENT OF WALES ACT, SCOTLAND ACT.)

BLAKE, George, a relatively effective Russian spy working in Britain, apparently betrayed at least one British agent in E. Europe. He was convicted in 1961 but escaped and went abroad.

BLAKE, Robert (1599-1657) (1) was educated at Oxford and took on his father's business as a merchant at Bridgwater, where he probably acquired his knowledge of ships. He served in the Short Parliament and was elected to the Long Parliament in 1645. He earned praise for his resolute conduct against the royalists when Col. Fiennes surrendered Bristol to them in July 1643. His triumphant defence of Lyme against P. Maurice with ten times his numbers, then gained him promotion. In July 1644 he seized Taunton and held it till the war ended in 1645. He continued there as a successful civil administrator in circumstances of misery and famine.

(2) Early in 1649, with Deane and Popham, he took joint command of the fleet against Princes Rupert and Maurice, whom he blockaded in Kinsale. He was blown off station in an Oct. gale, and the princes escaped to Lisbon where the Portuguese, against remonstrances, gave them shelter. By seizing Portuguese cargoes and then their Brazil fleet, Blake forced the Portuguese to expel them. He then caught and destroyed some of their ships in the neutral Spanish port of Cartagena. The rest escaped to Toulon, to which Blake applied the methods which had been successful at Lisbon, with like results. The princes then set sail for the W. Indies.

(3) Meanwhile Blake was recalled. In June he seized the Scillies and in Aug. Jersey. From Dec. 1651 to Mar. 1652 he was a member of the Council of State, but when war with Holland became imminent he was appointed General-at-Sea and on 19 May he and Bourne held their own against Tromp's much larger fleet off the Downs. On 22 Sept. 1652, Blake missed an incoming Dutch India Fleet under de Ruyter, who joined up with de Witt off Dunkirk. Blake followed them, and a fleet action developed on 28th off the Gabbard and Kentish Knock (Thames Estuary). Severely but not fatally damaged, the Dutch retreated next day.

(4) The English now over confidently dispersed much of their fleet, but the Dutch made great sacrifices to improve their own. Hence, on 29 Nov. Tromp, with 80 ships, caught Blake off the Goodwins with 29. Tromp was actually covering the passage of some large merchant fleets, but Blake stood his ground, relying on his pilots' superior local knowledge. The Dutch, carried to leeward by currents, could not at first attack: after various manoeuvrings a partial action was fought off Dungeness in which both sides suffered equally, but Blake retreated to the Downs while the Dutch trade safely passed Boulogne.

(5) It was now the turn of the English, and during the winter nearly 80 ships were assembled at Portsmouth. On 18 Feb. 1653 Tromp's fleet was sighted off Portland with over 200 merchantmen in convoy. The three English squadrons were widely separated: Penn's being to the South and Monck's to the leeward. Blake could, accordingly, be attacked in force. A desperate battle ensued; Blake was wounded but, as Penn and Monck began, towards evening, to come up, the Dutch drew off, passed the convoy up Channel and fell in behind it. In the ensuing two-day eastward chase Tromp lost nine warships and over 30 merchantmen, but got the rest away.

(6) Blake's wound put him ashore for the rest of the war, but in July 1654 he showed the flag in the European parts of the Mediterranean and in Apr. 1655 he destroyed a corsair squadron in Tunis. This enabled him to secure a treaty with the Bey of Algiers in May. In June, however, war broke out with Spain, so he blockaded Cadiz until Oct. when he came home. In the following spring, he and Montague resumed the blockade, thus enabling Sir Richard Stayner to capture the Plate Fleet in Sept. Montague and Stayner then went home and Blake, for the first time in British naval history, maintained the blockade throughout the winter. As a result he got wind of a Spanish American fleet, whose 16 ships he destroyed with small loss at Santa Cruz (Tenerife) on 20 Apr. 1657. He was now a sick man and died aboard his flagship as she entered Plymouth Sound.

(7) One of the greatest Englishmen, his reputation has suffered because he served the wrong govt, but his example was the foundation upon which the later successes of the Royal Navy were built.

BLAKE, William (1757-1827), poet, engraver, artist opened his first print-seller's shop in 1784, published *Songs of Innocence* in 1789, made the acquaintance of Godwin, Tom Paine, Fuseli and other radicals in 1791, and published *Songs of Experience* in 1794. His other works belong more to the history of literature and art, but the romantic pity of his outlook on the social and religious scene had a powerful influence on the reformers of his day and helped to soften up the opposition to them.

BLAKENEY, William Blakeney (1672-1761). *See* MINORCA.

BLAMEY, F-M Sir Thomas Albert (1884-1951) began his career as a teacher but joined the Australian army in 1906. He saw service at Galipoli and in France and then became Australian Defence Representative in Britain from 1919 to 1923. From 1925 to 1939 he was police commissioner in Victoria. Recalled to the army, he commanded an Australian corps in Palestine in World War II. and became Dep. C-in-C Middle East under Wavell in 1941. From 1942 onwards he was C-in-C Allied Land Forces in the SW Pacific under the American Gen. MacArthur.

BLAMIRE, William (1790-1862). Cumberland farmer and, from 1831, Whig M.P., carried the Tithe Commutation Act. 1836. instigated the Ordnance Survey of 1842 necessary for the administration of the Act: and inspired the Copyhold Enfranchisement Act, 1841. *See* CIVIL SERVICE.

BLANCHE OF CASTILE (1188-1252) was the daughter of Alfonso VIII of Castile and Eleanor, *d.* of Henry II of England. She married Louis (later Louis VIII) of France in 1200, and organised his base at Calais during his invasion of England in 1216. At his death in 1226 she became Regent of France until Louis IX came of age in 1232, and again in 1248 when be was on Crusade. During these regencies it was largely her personal determination which kept the Kingdom together in the face of feudal rebellion and English aggression.

BLANDFORD FORUM (Dorset), an ancient settlement with many Roman remains. It was virtually destroyed overnight in 1731 in a fire during a gale.

BLANKETEERS. In Mar. 1817 a body of working men met at St. Peter's Fields, Manchester. and having provided themselves with blankets marched to London to press their grievances upon the govt.

BLASPHEMY was a canon law offence in the middle ages, and as it and heresy were easily confused, blasphemers were occasionally burned, the last in 1612. This process and punishment were abolished in 1677. Meantime the Court of High Commission having been abolished, the King's Bench assumed the jurisdiction. It held in 1676 that denial of the truth of Christianity was punishable, but since then convictions have been obtained only if there was an element of contumely or ribaldry, and the number of cases was always minute. In 1883, in *Bradlaugh's Case* it doubted if Christianity had ever been part of the law.

In virtual desuetude since 1922. the subject was revived by the publication of Salman Rushdie's *Satanic Verses* and the Iranian Ayatollah Homeini's sudden fatwa encouraging Shia Moslems to murder him. This act of war led to moslem demands that the offence should cover Islam, and to counter demands that it should be abolished. In 1995 the controversy was still unresolved.

BLAST FURNACES. See DARBY, ABRAHAM; CORT.

BLATCHFORD, Robert (1851-1943), journalist on the *Sunday Chronicle* from 1885 to 1891, turned socialist, was dismissed, and with three others founded the *Clarion,* an enthusiastic socialist journal for the thinking artisan. His articles were reprinted as *Merrie England.* He remained influential until about 1900.

BLATHWAYT, William (c. 1648-1717), trained and preferred by his uncle, Thomas Porey, the D. of York's treasurer, he became Sec. to Sir Wm. Temple, ambassador at The Hague in 1668, moved to the Plantation Office in 1675, became Sec. at War by purchase in 1683 and in 1686 Clerk to the Privy Council. A purely formal witness at the trial of the Seven Bishops, he retained office until 1704 and was also a commissioner of trade from 1696 to 1706.

BLEDDYN ap CYNFYN (?-1075) was a half-brother of the Prince Gruffudd ap Llywelyn; he with his brother Rhiwallon succeeded to Gruffudd's lands at his death in 1063, but as a vassal of Edward the Confessor. In continuation of Gruffudd's policy he supported the Mercians against the crown; he allied himself with Edric in 1067 and with Edwin and Morcar in 1068. In 1070 he had to fight the sons of Gruffudd, whom he killed at the B. of Merchain. He then had to deal with Norman penetration into North Wales to the Clwyd, and in 1073 he was nearly captured by Robert of Rhuddlan in an ambush. He was assassinated at the instigation of Rhys ab Owain, K. of Deheubarth. He was much praised for his virtues, and was one of the few princes who amended the Laws of Hywel Dda. He was the ancestor of the later princes of Powys.

BLEGYWRYD (fl. 945) Welsh lawyer and principal draftsman of the Laws of Hywel Dda. The so-called *Book of Blegywryd* contains the Demetian version of the Laws as current in Deheubarth. See WELSH LAW.

BLENCH. See FEU.

BLENHEIM (BLINDHEIM or HOCHSTÄDT) B. and CAMPAIGN of (1702-4). In the coalition against Louis XIV the main strategic concentrations were in the Low Countries under Marlborough, and in Austria whose security was threatened not only by the French in northern Italy. but, at her back, by a Hungarian revolt. By 1702 the Elector of Bavaria Max Emmanuel, who was also gov. of the Spanish Netherlands (Belgium), had built up an army with French subsidies. and in Sept. he suddenly

seized Ulm and declared for Louis XIV. He thus interposed a hostile belt across the direct route between Austria and her allies in the Low Countries, and gave the French a springboard for an offensive in south Germany. This was particularly menacing because most of the local Austrian troops were hired from German principalities which were likely to be threatened.

In 1704 a French force under Marsin had already joined the Elector. Louis XIV now proposed to send reinforcements under Tallard and take Nuremberg and Nördlingen. This involved reducing the French armies in the Low Countries and putting them on the defensive. Austria was then to be overwhelmed through a combined attack by Vendôme and the Grand Prior from Italy, and by Tallard, Marsin and the Elector in S. Germany. The victorious French and Bavarians would then return to the Low Countries and deal with the British and Dutch.

Marlborough's planned reply was to fight a battle in S. Germany, to destroy the Franco-Bavarians and eliminate Bavaria. As troops had to be left in the Low Countries to face the still formidable French, only part of his command could be used. Therefore it was necessary to effect an unimpeded concentration with coalition forces coming from other fronts.

On 19 May 1704 Tallard passed reinforcements to Marsin in Bavaria and on the same day Marlborough began his march to the Danube. This celebrated operation was distinguished by three features: by efficient finance and logistics the march was never impeded by shortages. Secondly, for half the distance the troops followed the Rhine and so threatened successively the French on the Moselle and in Alsace. Thirdly, though the troops had to march upstream at a foot's pace, they could return downstream to the Low Countries in a matter of hours by barge. Hence the French were immobilised from Strasburg to the Channel by doubt, until 11 June, when Marlborough crossed the Neckar and plunged eastwards towards Ulm.

Meantime P. Eugene came from Vienna and took command of most of the imperial forces in S. Germany. In the last days of June his and Marlborough's armies joined at Ulm. They were now superior to Marsin and the Elector, but to make their superiority effective they had to secure a reliable crossing-point over the Danube and to change their line of communications from the north-westerly alignment vulnerable to the French in Alsace, to a north-easterly alignment based on Nuremberg, which was now safe. The combined force therefore moved rapidly eastwards to the old Danubian fortress of Donauwörth, and on 21 July stormed the Schellenberg which dominates it, before it could be reinforced. Both sides suffered, but the way was now open for the next stage, namely the taking of such systematic reprisals against Bavaria either to compel the Elector to make peace and fatally compromise Marsin's army, or to force the combined Franco-Bavarians to risk a battle. Louis XIV, anticipating this, sent a further army under Tallard himself to join the others. After brushes with Eugene in the Black Forest, he reached Ulm on 29 July and met them about 20 miles south of Donauwörth on 5 Aug. By this time the allies were besieging Ingolstadt further to the east along the Danube and Marlborough lay, as if to cover the siege, between Tallard and the fortress. Tallard therefore crossed to the north side of the river to seize the Schellenberg and encamped for the night. The whole of Eugene's and Marlborough's armies then concentrated on the north bank in front of Donauwörth and on 13 Aug. advanced to the attack.

The Battle. Though not expecting to be attacked, the Franco-Bavarians took up a strong position facing east between the Danube on their right and a thickly wooded range of hills on their left. Their four mile front was covered by a small river, the Nebel, and its marshes and was strengthened by three villages on their own side of the Nebel namely Blenheim near the Danube; Oberglau on their left centre, and Lutzingen slightly behind their extreme left in the wooded foothills. Tallard commanded the right hand half of the combined army and his infantry reserve was behind Blenheim: Marsin and the Elector commanded the left including Oberglau. The weakness of their position was that the ground resembled a funnel with the Nebel at the widest point, and the line of retreat depended mainly upon a road through Blenheim. The French thus tended to magnify, with disastrous consequences, the importance of that riverside village.

Marlborough and Eugene had 56,000 troops against their opponents' 60,000. Marlborough commanded the left two-thirds from the Danube to Oberglau and Eugene the right in the hills. The approach march had to be made close to the river, so it took Eugene two and a half hours to reach his positions on the right after the first British troops under Cutts had crossed the Nebel in the centre at 10am. Cutt's troops were drawn up, unusually, with infantry in front, then cavalry and then a last line of infantry. They suffered heavily from French artillery. At 12.30 Eugene attacked Marsin and the Elector, while simultaneously Cutts and Holstein-Beck violently assailed Blenheim and Oberglau. All three attacks were pressed with determination and daring, and though in a local sense they failed, nevertheless Marsin and the Elector's wing was bent back over a mile to Lutzingen; the forces at Oberglau were immobilised and prevented from intervening elsewhere and, most important of all, Clérambault, the French commander in Blenheim, drew all the local reserves including Tallard's infantry, into the defence of the village.

Thus by 3pm (when the attacks on the two villages were suspended), Tallard's central front had been denuded, but Marlborough's main force had been able to cross the causeways between Blenheim and Oberglau with only minor molestation; his infantry could rely on the combination of bayonet and firepower against Tallard's cavalry, which was almost all he had left, while their own cavalry crossed behind. By 14.30 Marlborough had a superiority of fresh troops at a decisive point and a general advance was ordered all along the line. Tallard's forces broke, and the large numbers in Blenheim were surrounded and captured; but Marsin and the Elector by prompt disengagement made good their escape in the dusk because the victorious army was too exhausted to pursue.

The Consequences. The three Franco-Bavarian armies lost three quarters of their effectives and Tallard was captured. The remnants fled to Strasburg; the Elector abandoned Bavaria which ceased to count. The reputation of the French as the foremost of military powers was broken, and the morale and determination of their opponents raised so that the war could be continued. This in its turn guaranteed the Habsburgs a further two centuries of survival, and to the British the certainty of the Protestant and Hanoverian succession.

BLESSINGTON, Margarite Countess of (1789-1849) *d*. of Edmund Power, a small landowner, was brought up in Ireland, early showing great precocity; and at fourteen was married to an insanely irascible Capt. Farmer, whom she refused to accompany to the Curragh. Her beauty became famous in Dublin and in 1807 Lawrence painted her portrait. She then went to London, and, Farmer having fallen out of a window in the King's Bench Prison, she married the rich E. of Blessington in 1818. Her beauty and talent and his money soon made them the centre of London social life, until in 1822 they began a European tour in company with the celebrated Count Alfred d'Orsay. In 1823 they made friends with Byron in Genoa, and in 1827 her husband's only legitimate daughter Harriet Gardiner married d'Orsay at Naples. The Earl died suddenly in Paris in 1829, but she stayed through the 1830 revolution, and only in 1831 resumed

her leadership of London society at a house in Seymour Place but, having nothing but a jointure, took to authorship to maintain her standard of life. She wrote or edited many books including novels, *belles lettres* and straight reporting and she was one of the first salaried correspondents of the *Daily News*.

In 1836, d'Orsay joined her and they lived happily together until his death. Their income and earnings became insufficient to support their mode of life and between 1845 and 1858 her jointure (charged on Irish estates) disappeared because of the potato rot. They fled from their creditors in Apr. 1849 to Paris where she died two months later.

BLETCHINGLY (Surrey). This picturesque small village was owned by the de Clares, then the Staffords and in due course by Anne of Cleves. It returned two members to Parliament from earliest times to the reforms of 1832.

BLETCHLEY PARK. *See* ENIGMA.

BLICKLING (Norfolk), HALL and HOMILIES. This village had a large 14th cent. manor where Anne Boleyn lived as a child. Sir Henry Hobart pulled it down and he and his son employed Robert Lyminge, the architect of Hatfield, to build the well known Jacobean mansion which, however, was internally converted and extended between 1765 and 1770. The BLICKLING HOMILIES were, and are, kept there. They consist of 19 sermons dating from 960, in a post-Alfredian prose style.

BLIGH, Vice-Adm. William (1754-1817), whose irascibility and courage have left their mark in history and folklore, sailed with Cook on his second circumnavigation in 1772 to 1774 and discovered the bread-fruit at Otaheite. After various routine (but strenuous) appointments as navigator and cartographer, he was sent in 1787 to Otaheite in command of the *Bounty* to collect bread-fruit for acclimatisation in the West Indies. He sailed from Otaheite for the West Indies but the crew being demoralised by luxury and Tahitian women, and Bligh being hot-tempered, a mutiny led by Fletcher Christian followed, and on 28 Apr. 1789, Bligh and eighteen others were set adrift in an open boat. The mutineers settled in Pitcairn I. where their descendents still live.

Bligh navigated his boat over 3000 miles to Timor, obtained a schooner and reached England in Apr. 1790. In 1794 he made further geographical discoveries in the Society Is. In 1797 he fought at Camperdown and with great courage put down a mutiny at the Nore. He was personally thanked by Nelson for his services at Copenhagen in command of the *Glatton* on 21 May 1801, and was elected a Fellow of the Royal Society on the same day.

In 1805 he was appointed governor of N.S.W. where he made enemies by harsh treatment of subordinates, and by honourable efforts to reduce drunkenness and the import of spirits. There was yet another mutiny in 1808, and Bligh was deposed and imprisoned until 1810 by the military commander who was later cashiered. Bligh returned to England and was promoted rear-admiral and in 1814 to vice admiral, though his active life had ended in 1811.

BLIGHTY (from Hindi 'belati' = a distant country). World War I soldier's expression for home.

BLIMP, COLONEL A furious corpulent moustachioed figure who began his outbursts with the words "Gad, Sir", used by the cartoonist David Low to personify last ditch conservatism.

BLIND JACK OF KNARESBOROUGH, or John METCALF (1717-1810) was blinded by smallpox at the age of six but made himself a good horseman and swimmer. He recruited for the royal forces during the Rebellion of '45 and took part in the Bs. of Falkirk and Culloden. He then operated a stage coach between Knaresborough and York and crowned his remarkable career by building 200 miles of turnpike.

BLITHFIELD HALL *(Staffs)* a Georgian house with some Tudor remnants and 19th cent. pastiche, was the seat of the Bagot family, who settled there in the 14th cent.

***BLITZKRIEG* (Ger = Lightning War).** The principle of deep disruptive penetration by units moving so fast that they can afford to do without flank protection, may be traced to Gen. Leonhard von Blumenthal as C. of Staff to the Crown Prince's army in the Prussian advance into Bohemia in 1866, but the term *Blitzkrieg* originated with the World War II German general Guderian to describe such an attack on a large scale by a combination of armoured and motorised ground forces and close support aircraft. Most of the German army, even in World War II, depended on horse-drawn transport, but it was conceived that a *blitzkrieg* by specialised forces penetrating regardless of flanks and communications, far into enemy territory would create such confusion, terror and paralysis of will that a military collapse would ensue before counter measures, especially against weak German communications, could be taken. *Blitzkriegs* were tried with complete success against Poland (1939), the Low Countries and France (1940) and Yugoslavia and Greece (1941) but by 1941 the technique was beginning to be understood, and later applications in Russia, N. Africa and the Ardennes encountered a law of diminishing returns.

BLITZ, THE. A British civilian term (derived from *Blitzkrieg)* for the German air raids in 1940-1, particularly the 90-odd night attacks on London.

BLOCKADE (AS WAR POLICY) (In this entry, the blockaded power is called the 'enemy'.) **(1)** The earliest blockades attempted in modern times arose in the Seven Years War. Originally a blockade was designed to prevent entry and exit from an enemy port. Its object was six-fold: **(a)** to prevent blockaded warships from leaving port; **(b)** to deprive enemy warships at large of a base; **(c)** consequently to open the high seas to the military and mercantile shipping of the blockading power and **(d)** to deny them to enemy shipping; **(e)** to weaken the enemy by depriving him of things useful to his war effort, and **(f)** to give the traders of a blockading power a monopoly, as against the enemy, of accessible markets. A strong naval power therefore had every temptation to impose a blockade if it could, and the enemy the strongest grounds for breaking it. Neutrals, however, introduced complications peculiar to naval strategy: the high seas are common to all nations, belligerent or neutral; a blockade raises prices in an enemy country, and the more effective it is the higher those prices will be. The blockaded area becomes an increasingly tempting market for neutral traders.

Blockades were likely to be penetrated in two principal ways: directly by blockade runners using ships or, nowadays, aircraft, and indirectly by re-exports through neutral countries. The Confederate blockade runners carried on a roaring trade with the neutral (British) Bahamas during the American Civil War, and the British (that is to say enemy) flew ball bearings from Sweden during World War II. Indirect penetration became more important as overland communications improved: in World War II the Germans obtained huge supplies from the Russians until they attacked them.

(2) Blockades, therefore, give rise to conflicts between belligerents and neutrals. Neutral govts intervene on behalf of their traders who, in the eyes of their national law, are reaping a legitimate profit from a seller's market. Blockading powers, on the contrary, treat neutrals who are supplying their enemy with warlike goods as abettors of their enemy and liable to warlike action. A belligerent cannot be expected to allow neutrals to frustrate its war policy.

(3) In the naval aspects of a blockade a curious international jurisprudence arose from this tension. A blockading power sets up Prize Courts to deal with intercepted ships and property: those found to be contraband are condemned to seizure, the others released. Clearly it is unreasonable – and so may provoke neutral reprisals – that property should be condemned for breach of a blockade whose existence or nature is unknown to traders. Accordingly a blockade, to be lawful, must be openly notified. Secondly trading neutrals have urged with only varying success that traders cannot, without compulsion, be expected to obey a law not their own, and that they ought not to be molested save where the absolute needs of belligerency require; therefore a notified blockade, to be lawful, must also be effective, for otherwise 'paper blockades' can and do cause a kind of officially sponsored piracy. Thirdly there has been a continually widening area of dispute about the definition of contraband. Weapons were always seized, but as war involved more of the people and resources of belligerents, the definition widened. As early as Jan. 1798 the French Directory decreed the seizure not only of all British goods but, regardless of flag, of the ships and cargoes in any ship found to contain such goods.

(4) The technique of blockade developed with the advance of modern economics. Originally ships lay off a port and stopped vessels coming from or going into it. Then a blockading power would invite or require neutrals to call at its ports for clearance. Then, finally, neutral ships were invited to obtain clearance at their port of departure from the consul of the blockading power. These technical advances gave contraband trade through adjacent neutral states an increased importance. Means were sought, especially in World War II, to close this broad avenue by restricting the trade of such countries to quotas based upon their previous peace-time trade. This, of course, created further diplomatic conflicts resolved more or less in favour of the enemy in proportion to the power of the neutral concerned, and it also spread belligerent economic espionage and counter espionage in neutral countries.

(5) Meantime an enemy would seek to retaliate. Some enemy armed ships could always penetrate the cordon and prey upon the blockading power's shipping. This type of warfare was waged extensively in the Wars of 1793 to 1815 by the French and became known as *guerre de course.* Its nuisance value was high, but it reduced the British trade by only 2½%. The introduction of submarines, however, made a significant, almost a decisive change. In World War I the Germans proclaimed a counter blockade, and when anti-submarine techniques made it dangerous for submarines to challenge shipping on the surface, they notified and carried out their intention to sink all ships in the blockade area without warning. In World War II they adopted the same tactics supplemented by aircraft and powerful surface warships. The damage in both wars nearly decided the issue.

(6) Counter blockade and *guerre de course* involve violence on the high seas, and provoked counter measures by neutrals. Of these since 1790 the most important has been the U.S.A. which for this reason was at war with France from 1798 to 1800, and which counted it as an important reason or pretext for entering World War I against Germany in Apr. 1917.

The following are the principal historic blockades:

Blockading Power	Enemy	Date
Britain	France	1756–63
Britain	American rebels	1775–81
Britain	France	1793–1802 1803-14
U.S. Federals	Confederates	1861–65

Britain and Allies	Germany Austro –Hungary Bulgaria Turkey	}	World War 1914–18
Britain and Allies	Germany Italy Japan	}	World War II 1935—45

BLOCKADE, SAILING. NAVAL FEATURES (1) The object, in the 18th-19th cent. French wars was to prevent the enemy in their scattered ports from combining into a fleet strong enough to clear the British home waters. Blockade kept the Royal Navy at sea in a state of constant practice and efficiency. It kept the enemy in port without opportunities for training in gunnery or seamanship. Insofar as it interrupted coastwise movement, it starved the enemy fleets of timber and other essential supplies. Any British ship was consequently a match for any French ship of similar class, even though the French were usually better designed. Both sides knew this. Blockade was thus a source of positive strength to Britain, not merely an inhibitor of enemy action.

(2) The technique of the blockade depended upon the fact that large square rigged warships could not beat out of port against a wind blowing from any point in the seaward 90 degrees (or more for some difficult ports). Since this was also the moment when it was dangerous for a blockading squadron to be off the coast, it would withdraw to safety, knowing that its enemy was bottled up. When the wind changed the blockaders would resume station. In the Channel the fleet used Torbay and Plymouth for shelter and revictualling; the Mediterranean was less easy, for Gibraltar and Malta were far from Toulon and meat had to be bought in Africa. Nelson, however, found an imperfect but better placed anchorage at Maddalena in northern Sardinia.

(3) Tactically, one or two frigates watched the enemy port and were connected by a seaward chain of ships at signalling intervals to the main squadron below the enemy's horizon. Daylight flag signalling was well developed; complicated messages could be repeated across 40 miles of sea in half an hour. Night signalling was primitive, and in fog communication beyond speaking distance stopped. Such conditions gave the enemy the chance to escape, but created navigational and seamanship difficulties for them too, so that their under-trained squadrons could seldom profit.

BLOEMFONTEIN. See ORANGE FREE STATE.

BLOEMFONTEIN CONFERENCE (May-June 1899). See SALISBURY'S THIRD GOVT-12.

BLOEMFONTEIN CONVENTION (Feb. 1854) between Sir George Clerk for the British govt. and the representatives, mostly Dutch, of the Orange River Sovereignty. By it the British abandoned the sovereignty and left the white inhabitants to manage their own affairs on terms similar to those of the Sand River Convention, save that the British maintained a treaty with the native Adam Kok.

BLOIS, COUNTS OF. Between 1066 and 1453 when English Kings had extensive French possessions, the counts of Blois were important in Anglo-French relations because of the family connection between Blois on one side of the Ile de France and Champagne on the other. Both territories were united in 1165 under Count THIBAUD IV, considered the most powerful Frenchman of his time. At his death (1152) Champagne passed to his eldest son Henry, and Blois to the second son Thibaud V (1152-91) who as a rule sided with the French King against the Plantagenets; but his successor Louis I made an alliance with K. Richard II to safeguard himself against Capetian claims, while he went on the fourth Crusade. He became D. of Nicaea but was killed at Adrianople in 1205. Thereafter the county was weakened by debt and

division and declined rapidly. In 1391 it passed to the Dukes of Orleans by sale, and in 1498 to the French crown by the accession of its owner Louis XII.

BLOMFIELD, Robert (1766-1823) agricultural labourer and apprentice shoemaker, came to London where he used to read the speeches of Burke and Fox to his fellow workmen. He thus painfully acquired an education and, expanding his reading, ultimately wrote the *Farmer's Boy* (1800). Having little access to paper or pen, his compositions were first evolved in his head, being gradually committed to paper as opportunity served. *The Farmer's Boy* was set (not by him) to an excellent and rousing tune, and became vastly popular. He also wrote rural works under the patronage of the D. of Grafton who got him a paid sinecure and made him an allowance. He died, however, a bankrupt.

BLONDEL, a troubadour, was, according to a pleasant 13th cent. legend, a friend of K. Richard I, who was himself a poet. When the King was imprisoned in 1192 at Dürrenstein by the D. of Austria, Blondel set out to find him. Learning that Dürrenstein apparently housed a special prisoner, Blondel sang under the window a song which only he and Richard knew, and heard a voice complete the verse. The discovery is said to have simplified the negotiations for the King's release. This Blondel may – or may not – be the same as the celebrated trouvère BLONDEL DE NESLE.

BLOOD, CIRCULATION OF. See HARVEY. WILLIAM.

BLOOD, 'Colonel' Thomas (?1618-80). An adventurer of outstanding boldness, Blood obtained property in Ireland under the Commonwealth. After the Restoration he lost his land, and plotted to kidnap the Lord Lieutenant, the D. of Ormond, in Mar. 1663. The plot was betrayed and most of his associates were hanged, but he escaped, reached Holland and served under de Royter. In 1665 he returned and after dealings with the Fifth Monarchy Men, joined the Covenanters' revolt in 1666. After further adventures in Ireland, he reappeared in the limelight by rescuing his friend Capt. Mason, who was being taken for trial, and in 1670 he actually kidnapped Ormond, intending to hang him at Tyburn, but was overtaken by the military escort. He remained free, and six months later made his famous, and almost successful, bid to steal the crown jewels from the Tower of London. This time he was taken, but he insisted that he would confess personally to the King. Charles II, impressed by his story, pardoned him and restored his Irish estates. The story has provoked the suspicion that he had contacts at court before his arrest.

BLOODY ASSIZES (1688). After the defeat of Monmouth's rebellion at the B. of Sedgemoor, Lord Chief Justice Jeffreys held assizes in the affected areas, mostly in Somerset. Nearly 400 were executed and 1200 sold as slaves for the Trinidad and Barbados plantations. The name arose because execution for treason involved (for men) castration and quartering while alive and covered the scaffolds with blood. Women were burned. A colony of whites, known as red-legs, in Trinidad, are said to be the descendants of those sold at this time.

BLOODY FLUX. See DYSENTERY.

BLOODY HAND (1) One with blood on his hands, who under Forest Law was presumed to have illegally killed a deer. **(2)** The badge of Ulster; and, consequently, **(3)** that of English baronets who were originally supposed to be an hereditary colonial aristocracy. The mythological origin of (2) and also a similar detail in the arms of Antwerp is that a certain lord granted it to that of two brothers swimming for it "whose hand should first touch the land". The slower swimmer cut his hand off and threw it.

BLOODY SUNDAYS (1) 13 Nov. 1887. Radicals had used Trafalgar Square for meetings since 1884. Sir Chas. Warren, the Commissioner of Metropolitan Police, wanted to reduce this practice and in 1887 prohibited some meetings. To defy him the Social Democratic Federation called a meeting designed also to attract the Irish by demanding the release of William O'Brien, M.P., then in custody (*see* SALISBURY'S SECOND GOVT-6). Organised bodies marched on the square from all sides led by John Burns and R. Cunningham Graham. The police were overwhelmed. The Guards were called out and cleared the Square. Many police and demonstrators were injured. Two demonstrators died. The socialists, having got their martyrs, kept the memory of this, the biggest riot between 1850 and 1900, green. **(2)** 22 Jan. 1905. The Czar's troops fired on a peaceful procession at St. Petersburg. This strengthened Russophobe opinion outside Russia and helped to precipitate the 1905 insurrections. **(3)** 30 Jan. 1972. In Londonderry British troops fired on a prohibited R. Catholic demonstration against internment. 13 demonstrators were killed.

BLOOMERS, a type of Turkish trousers, were introduced by Amelia Bloomer (1818-94) of New York in the 1860s. They enabled women to ride bicycles with becoming modesty and so contributed to female emancipation.

BLOOMSBURY SET or GROUP. Certain influential writers and artists met between 1907 and 1930 at the Bloomsbury houses of Clive and Vanessa Bell (formerly Stephen) and Adrian and Virginia Stephen (later Virginia Woolf). The group was much influenced by G. E. Moore and Bertrand Russell, and included the art critic Roger Fry, the economist Lord Keynes, the Fabian Leonard Woolf (husband of Virginia), Desmond McCarthy and Arthur Waley the sinologist, and Lytton Strachey. Aldous Huxley and T. S. Eliot were well known among them. They had a close-gathered but free social life little trammelled by contemporary moral conventions.

BLORE, Edward (1787-1879) originally an artist and engraver, became an architect, and made his name with Sir Walter Scott's neo-Gothic house at Abbotsford (1816). He became Architect to William IV and Q. Victoria, and finished Nash's original Buckingham Palace, and his work is also to be seen at Hampton Court, Windsor Castle, the Pitt Press at Cambridge, Merton College Chapel, and the North Wing of the Clarendon Press at Oxford. He also designed, but never saw, Government House at Sydney (Australia).

BLOUNT FAMILY (1) Sir Thomas (?-1400) was a supporter of Richard II and refused to recognise Henry IV's title to the throne. With John and Thomas Holland, Es of Huntingdon and Kent, he plotted Richard's restoration. The E. of Rutland betrayed the plot and Sir Thomas was caught and cruelly executed. **(2) Sir Walter (?-1403)** was a professional soldier with the Black Prince in Spain (1367) and with John of Gaunt in Castile (1386). He was M.P. for N. Derbyshire in 1399 and was killed at the B. of Shrewsbury. His son **(3) Sir John** was gov. of Calais in 1413. **(4) Walter (II) (?-1474) 1st Ld. MOUNTJOY,** probably the son of Sir John, fought for the Yorkists at Towton in 1461, became gov. of Calais and in 1465 Lord Treasurer. His sons **(5) Sir James (?-1493)** and **(6) John (?-1485) 3rd Ld.** were successively captains of Hammes (near Calais). **(7) William (?-1534) 4th Ld.** studied in Paris under Erasmus whom he brought to England in 1498. He was a close friend of Henry VIII as prince and King, becoming Lieutenant of the Calais Marches in 1509, and bailiff of Tournai in 1514. He was engaged during the years 1520 on the complicated diplomacy of the Field of the Cloth of Gold and the subsequent meetings with the Emperor Charles V. His principal claim to fame lies in his friendship and patronage of scholars including, besides Erasmus, Leland, Whytforde and Richard Sampton. The French connection and the patronage of learning was maintained by his son, **(8) Charles (I) (?-1545) 5th Ld. (9) Charles (II) (1563-1606) 8th Ld. and 1st E. of DEVONSHIRE,** a grandson of the 5th Lord, was M.P. for Beer Alston in 1584 and 1586. From 1586 to 1593 he served as a soldier in the

Netherlands, against the Armada and then in Brittany. In 1593 he served a further session in the Commons and in 1597 was 2-in-C of the troops in Essex's expedition against the Azores. He is said to have been implicated in Essex's conspiracy, but in 1601 was in fact made Lord Deputy of Ireland in his place and led the repulse of the Spanish at Kinsale and the suppression of Tyrone's revolt. He was a pacifier and disapproved (unavailingly) of religious persecution until James I's accession (1603), when he was promoted Lord Lieutenant. He then returned to England and held lesser administrative posts. In 1605 he married Essex's sister Penelope, the divorced wife of Lord Rich. She had some years before been his mistress and had had by him a son **(10) Mountjoy (1597?-1666) 1st (Irish) Ld. MOUNTJOY and E. of NEWPORT.** He served as a soldier in the Low Countries in 1622 and was rear-admiral in the La Rochelle expedition of 1628. Though he supported the opposition to Charles I in the Long Parliament he would not rebel against his sovereign, but being of an independent disposition he quarrelled with Newcastle, his military superior, during the civil war and was from 1642 to 1644 in custody. He fought for the King at Newbury in 1644 and was captured by the parliamentarians at Dartmouth in 1646. They released him on bail, but in 1655 he was committed to the Tower on a probably justified suspicion of treasonable conspiracy against the Commonwealth. At the Restoration he was given a pension by Charles II. **(11) Sir Christopher (?1565-1601)** was a cousin of (9) above. He was closely identified with Essex's interests and was in fact his stepfather. He was camp master in Essex's Cadiz expedition in 1596 and in the Azores in 1597. In 1599 he was marshal of Essex's army in Ireland and, being involved in Essex's conspiracy, was executed.

BLÜCHER, F-M Gebhard Leberecht von, PRINCE OF WAHLSTADT (1742-1819). This famous commander began in the Swedish army, from which the Prussians captured him in 1760. He threw in his lot with them, but resigned on being passed over for promotion (for excessive public wenching and drinking) in 1773. In 1787 he returned, and as a result of a series of distinguished cavalry actions between 1789 and 1794 he was given the *pour le mérite* (a rare Prussian decoration for bravery in command). By 1801 he was a lieut-general. He was the only Prussian leader to emerge with credit from the disastrous B. of Auerstedt (14 Oct. 1806) where he commanded the cavalry; he extricated some of them from the capitulation at Prenzlau and carried on the war until forced to surrender for lack of supplies. He thus became the military hero upon whom Prussian national sentiment was focused.

When the War of Liberation began in 1813, Blücher was given a corps command and fought at Lützen and Bautzen. He then became Prussian C-in-C in Silesia with Gneisenau as his chief of staff; he beat Macdonald on the Katzbach, and his victory over Marmont at Möckern (16 Oct. 1813) made Bonaparte's defeat at Leipzig (in which he also took part) inevitable. He pursued the Emperor with great energy into France, refusing to be put off by checks in the five Bs of Brierme, La Rothière, Champaubert, Vauxchamps and Montmirail. On 9-10 Mar. 1814, however, he finished the business by a great victory at Laon.

During Bonaparte's 'Hundred Days', Blücher commanded the Prussian army of the Lower Rhine, and collaborated with Wellington in the Waterloo campaign. He retired shortly afterwards.

He was a man of extremes. Speed of action was matched by a sang-froid amounting to personal indifference. He greeted Wellington amid the welter of Waterloo with an observation about a laxative. His patriotism was romantic and tactless, and he was narrowly dissuaded from sacking Paris in 1815.

BLUE BOOK. An official report of, or to parliament or the privy council setting forth actual or supposed information, as opposed to a white paper which sets out a govt's intentions.

BLUE COAT. This was formerly the dress of servants and so thought appropriate for beadles, almspeople and charity children; hence it became the uniform of the scholars of charity schools all over England. Many of these still survive, the most famous being Christ's Hospital, London.

BLUE FUNNELL LINE formed as the **OCEAN STEAM SHIP CO.** by Alfred Holt in 1865 to trade to China and received great encouragement by the opening of the Suez Canal in 1869. The opening of the Panama Canal in 1915 enabled it to operate world wide despite World War I, but in World War II it lost nearly half its ships and was unable to combat foreign competitors and airlines which had stepped into the breach. It went into liquidation in 1988.

BLUE GOWN (1) In England, the dress given to a whore in a house of correction. **(2)** In Scotland, the garb of royal bedesmen, to the number of years of the King's age, privileged to beg anywhere in Scotland.

BLUE LAWS were draconian laws on personal behaviour and Sabbath keeping in force in early Connecticut and New Haven.

BLUE NOSE. A Nova Scotian.

BLUE STOCKING. This term for a learned or pedantic lady originated in certain mid-18th cent salons held by Mesdames Montague, Ord and Vesey, where literary discussions and diversions replaced the usual cards, and dress was informal, which meant that the *men* wore blue stockings.

BLUES (MUSIC) originated among the negroes of the Southern states of U.S.A. At a mayoral election in Memphis the band engaged in the interest of Mr Crump was so popular that he was elected. Hence the music became known as "Mr Crump" or "Memphis Blues". Gershwin's *Rhapsody in Blue* was first heard in 1922 and finally established world-wide interest in Blues.

BLUM, Léon (1872-1950). This French statesman first became a deputy in 1919, and spent the next five years reconstructing the Socialist Party. In 1924 he supported Hériot's radical coalition, though he refused to serve in it. In the election of 1932 the Socialists obtained over 100 seats and Blum (who was a Jew) negotiated for a popular front against Fascism. The 1936 elections during the economic depression were won by his Popular Front, and Blum became prime minister. His govt. introduced a number of socialist reforms, which made it unpopular with the right, while pursuing a policy of "non intervention" or neutralism in Spain and other foreign concerns, for which it was attacked from the left. It became impossible to pass necessary financial legislation, or to get the co-operation of industrialists or trade unions. In June 1937 he resigned, but served in the succeeding Chautemps govt. as Vice Premier. In Mar. 1938 he came back as Prime Minister, but later refused office under Daladier. He was arrested by the Vichy govt. in 1940 and put on trial in Feb. 1942, but his defence so embarrassed the prosecution that the trial was abandoned; he was kept in administrative imprisonment. After the liberation he was head of the brief caretaker govt. of Dec. 1946, but thereafter retired.

BLUNDELL'S SCHOOL (Tiverton, Devon) was founded by Peter Blundell in 1604. Blackmore, a pupil there, mentions it in *Lorna Doone.*

BLUNDERBUSS. A bell-mouthed scatter gun, commonly loaded with nails and stones, used by guards of stage coaches as a protection against highwaymen.

BLUNT, (Sir) Anthony (1907-83), Surveyor of the King's and Queen's Pictures (1945-72) and Director of the Courtauld Institute (1947-72) was a Russian double agent who helped Burgess and Maclean to escape to Russia and was himself caught in 1972 through information from the F.B.I.

BLUNT, Wilfrid Scawen (1840-1922) R. Catholic poet and diplomat, left diplomacy in 1869 and married the Arabic scholar Lady Anne Noel, who was famous among the Bedouin. They travelled the Middle East and India, and published the prophetic *Future of Islam* in 1882. He was opposed to British imperialism and was briefly imprisoned in 1888 for taking part in an Irish riot.

BOADICEA or BOUDICCA (?-61). The Iceni tribe (Norfolk area) were initially friendly to the Romans and their King Prasutagus became a Roman client. He made the Emperor co-heir at his death, with Boadicea and his daughters, presumably for their protection. Roman discipline broke down. Plunderers despoiled the tribesmen, flogged the King's widow and raped the two daughters. In A.D. 60 Boadicea led the Iceni and their neighbours the Trinovantes (Essex area) into a ferocious rebellion. *See* BRITAIN, ROMAN-9.

BOARD OF CONTROL. *See* EAST INDIA COMPANY. HON-9.

BOARD OF TRADE. *See* TRADE AND PLANTATIONS.

BOARD OF TRUSTEES (Sc.) officially COMMISSIONERS AND TRUSTEES FOR IMPROVING FISHERYS (*sic*) AND MANUFACTURES IN SCOTLAND (1727) was originally set up under an Act of 1726 to regulate standards of linen manufacture, but in response to petitions on the Scots economy, its scope was widened as its name indicates. It was given various accumulated funds, the surplus of the malt duties, and in 1751 an annuity. In co-operation with the Forfeited Estates Commissioners, especially after 1752, it devoted its resources to linen and fisheries (43% each) and coarse woollens (14%) mainly by encouraging invention and importing foreign experts and instructors. In the linen industry the trustees exerted a powerful leverage. Output rose from 4M yards in 1740 to 13M in 1772. English competition in the manufacture of coarse woollens and Dutch in the fisheries (until the French Wars of 1793-1815) caused the Board to concentrate on linen still further: production was 22M in 1797 and 31M in 1822.

BOARD SCHOOLS. *See* EDUCATION ACTS.

BOAT RACE, OXFORD AND CAMBRIDGE. First held in 1829 and held annually since 1856. As it is still in theory casual, the losing side sends a formal challenge in the next year.

BOBBY Slang term for police after Sir Robert Peel who established the force. They were also called "Peelers".

BOCAGE (Fr.) A countryside much enclosed by hedges with trees, and having many small woods and copses. Western Normandy, eastern Brittany, and Vendée are mostly *bocage* which was the terrain of the various Vendée revolts, and of the fighting in Normandy in World War II.

BOCCACCIO, Giovanni. *See* RENAISSANCE-2.

BOCHE (Fr) A World War I pejorative for a German.

BOCLAND, FOLCLAND, LAENLAND. Bocland in Anglo-Saxon law was land granted by means of a charter (or 'book'). The 'book' was of ecclesiastical origin, and contained a pious preamble and a minatory conclusion. Grants by book were made mostly to the church but otherwise to kings, or great men. In any case they needed royal permission, for the land was freed from all except the most basic common burdens. The rights and duties of the grantee were defined in the 'book', in contrast with the rights and burdens in 'folcland' which were defined by the custom of the local community (or folk).

Laenland was a loan of land for up to three lives. The grantee sometimes owed service or rent. More often he took the land as repayment of a lump sum. It was thus usually a lending transaction, and commonly the borrower was the superior in status. The church was the commonest lender. The transaction was usually made by 'book'.

BODIAM (Sussex). At this unremarkable inland village 14 miles from Hastings, Sir Richard Dalyngrydge built

Bodiam castle in 1386. Still picturesque in its water-lily covered moat, it remains externally complete because it had no military history whatever.

BODICHON, Barbara (1827-91) *d*. of Benjamin Leigh-Smith, a Progressive M.P. who gave her the same educational and financial opportunities as a man. She campaigned for employment opportunities for women and the book *Women and Work* (1857) was a landmark. In 1866 she was a founder of the Women's Suffrage Committee and, with Emily Davies, of Girton Coll., Cambridge she was a landscape artist and the pattern of George Eliot's *Romola*.

BODIN, Jean (1530-96) French philosopher and economist who in his *Six Livres de la République* (1576) (Fr = Six Books on the State) propounded the first modern systematic exposition of political science. He visited England in 1581 as secretary to the Duc d'Alençon, when the latter was seeking Q. Elizabeth I's hand.

BODLE. A copper coin worth 2d. Scots.

BODLEY. Exeter family. Three brothers became well known. **(1) Sir Josias (?1550-1618),** a military engineer, went to Ireland in 1598 and was trenchmaster at the sieges of Kinsale (1601) and Waterford (1603). From 1604 to 1607 he was employed on fortifications, but his important work was his Survey of Ulster in 1609 for the great Ulster Plantations. **(2) Lawrence (?-1615),** a Canon of Exeter, persuaded his Chapter to give many early manuscripts, including the Leofric Missal, to Oxford University, of which he was a doctor. **(3) Sir Thomas (1545-1613)** was educated at Wesel, Frankfort, and Geneva as well as at Oxford, and travelled Europe acquiring linguistic and political knowledge between 1576 and 1580. He then became a gentleman usher to Q. Elizabeth, and was M.P. for Plymouth in 1584. In 1585 he was sent on a mission to Frederick II of Denmark and German protestant princes to organise support for Henry of Navarre and the Huguenots. In 1586 he was M.P. for St. Germans and he married in 1587. In 1588 he returned to diplomacy, undertaking a highly confidential mission in May to Henry III of France, when the latter left Paris to escape the Duke of Guise. On his return he was appointed resident ambassador to the United Provinces, a post which he held until 1596. A remarkable feature of his position was that he was entitled to sit and vote in the Dutch Council of State. The work was difficult and wearisome, and though Bodley was twice canvassed for Sec. of State he left public life on his return from Holland and never re-entered it.

His work for Oxford University Library named after him in Feb. 1598 engaged his attention continuously until 1611. He appealed, successfully, to his wide acquaintanceship to give or subscribe for books; and he persuaded the Stationers' Company to give a copy of every book which they published. This is the origin of the rights of the modern copyright libraries. He also began the permanent endowment of the library and drew up its original statutes.

BODOTRIA. The Roman name for the R. Forth.

BOECE, BOETHIUS or BOYIS, Hector (c. 1465-1536), a Scot, was a friend of Peter Syrus, John Gasser and Erasmus whom he met in Paris as a young man. He, with others, brought the new learning to Scotland when he returned in about 1498. He made friends with William Elphinstone, Bp. of Aberdeen, who in 1494 had secured a papal bull for the creation of a university there; and it was mainly Boece's abilities which enabled the bishop to put the bull into effect. Boece is thus remembered as the real founder. He wrote in Latin *The Lives of the Bishops of Mortlach and Aberdeen* printed in 1522, and a famous *History of Scotland* (to 1460) published in Latin in 1527, in Scots in 1531, and in English in 1577.

BOER WAR (12 Oct. 1899-31 May 1902). *See* SOUTH AFRICAN WAR.

BOGNOR REGIS (Sussex). The title *Regis* (Lat = 'of the King') commemorates George V's convalescence there in 1929. Some authorities hold that the King's last words were "How is the Empire?" Others who were trying to persuade him to go to Bognor again for his health report "Bugger Bognor".

BOGOMILS. *See* ALBIGENSIANS.

BOHEMIA. (1) There was an especially intellectual, mediaeval connection between England and Bohemia, which perhaps explains why the most popular English carol concerns K. Wenceslas (St. Vaclav), a Bohemian king murdered in 929. In 1212, by the Golden Bull of the Emperor Frederick II, Bohemia became independent of the Holy Roman Empire but with a king entitled to vote in the imperial elections. The incumbent Premyslid dynasty ended in 1305, and in 1310 the diet offered the crown to John of Luxemburg, who married a Premyslid princess but spent his life as a soldier in French service and was killed by the English at Crécy in 1346. Meanwhile the country was governed by a Czech noble, Henry of Lipa.

(2) John's son, as Charles IV, became Emperor in 1355. He re-established the royal authority, beautified Prague and in 1348 founded its university. He also took cautious steps to meet the growing demand for church reform. This coincided with the rise of Lollardy in England; Wycliff's *de civile dominio* (Lat = Civil government) appeared in 1376. Charles died in 1378 and Wycliffs *de officio regis* (Lat = a King's duty) was published in 1379. Lollard works and doctrines were brought to Bohemia by Jerome of Prague. They spread rapidly and were studied by John Hus, who became Dean of Philosophy at Prague in 1401. Charles' successor Wenceslas IV was involved in simultaneous conflicts with the nobles and between the religious reformers led by Hus, and the Church hierarchy. In 1414 Hus accepted safe conduct from Wenceslas' brother Sigismund, King of the Romans, to attend the Council of Constance. His trust in his King's brother was misplaced. He was seized as a heretic and burned. Most Bohemians being Hussites, a revolt followed immediately. The Hussites carried the King with them and the war became a national uprising against foreign interference. Wenceslas, however, died in 1419. The anti-Hussite Sigismund claimed the throne and the war became a civil war as well. His papalist and German crusaders invaded Bohemia from all sides. In 1421-2 Hussite generals defeated two such invasions. In 1427 they routed the English Card. Beaufort (B. of Tachov) and in 1431 they put to flight the greatest invasion of all. These events ensured an enduring English interest in Bohemian affairs. By 1436 the Hussites (despite bloody internal disputes) had, in the Compactata of Prague, obtained the substance of their demands: expropriation of church property, communion in both kinds and an independent church under an elected archbishop. The analogy with Henry VIII's church settlement is clear. The Compactata remained law until 1620.

(3) The confirmation of the Compactata was the price which Sigismund paid for recognition as King. He died in 1437 and his son-in-law Albrecht of Austria was elected in his stead. He died in 1439 leaving a pregnant widow. The country had slipped into elective monarchy. The Diet recognised the infant Ladislas Postumus in 1443 but practical govt. was paralysed in a deadlock between the Hussites led by George of Podiebrad and the R. Catholics led by Rosenberg and Menhart of Hradec. In 1448 George cut the Gordian knot by seizing Prague and the Emperor confirmed his act by appointing him governor. Hence when Ladislas was released from tutelage and crowned in 1453 Hussites held all the key posts and he had to rule by their advice. Himself a fervent R. Catholic, his presence helped to secure the loyalty of the outlying provinces of Moravia, Silesia and the two Lusatias, but in

1457 he died suddenly and George was elected in his place. He was less successful with the four provinces, notably Silesia. His international security depended upon the willingness of the Hungarian K. Matthias Corvinus (Matyas Hunyadi) to hold the Austrians and Poles in check. Negotiations with the Pope broke down. A R. Catholic party was formed among the nobility and in alliance with the city of Breslau (Wroclaw). George declared his loyalty to Hussite doctrines in 1462. In 1463 Pope Paul II excommunicated him and encouraged Matthias to change sides. In 1469 the R. Catholic nobles of Bohemia and Moravia proclaimed him King. There followed another ideological civil war with outside interventions.

(4) George Podiebrad died in 1470, and the Hussite diet elected Vladislav, a R. Catholic son of Casimir IV of Poland. The civil war ended eight years later by an agreement that Vladislav was to have Bohemia and the reversion of the four provinces while Matthias was to have the four provinces for life. By this time, however, the Turks were threatening Hungary, and when Matthias died in 1490 Vladislav was elected as Ulaszlo II to its throne. Bohemia was thus uneasily reunited with its provinces but without a real king, for Ulaszlo II was now too busy in Hungary. His infant son Louis was crowned, but led by Leo of Rozmital, a relative of the English royal family, the nobles took over effective power. By 1526 (when Louis died after the Turkish victory at Mohacs) they had imposed virtual serfdom upon the peasants and so created a social cleavage beneath the religious unity.

(5) At Louis' death, the Austrian Archduke Ferdinand asserted a claim by hereditary right. A Bohemian diet rejected his claim but was prepared to elect him King. The four provinces on the other hand conceded the hereditary claim, and Ferdinand, thus strengthened, was able to encroach steadily upon Bohemian liberties. In 1546 he demanded Bohemian help in his war with the Lutherans. The diet refused but the Protestant defeat at Mühlberg in 1547 rendered them helpless. Their leaders were hanged, and the diet compromised on the hereditary principle by recognising four successive heirs to the throne in the father's lifetime. At the same time a vigorous Jesuit campaign split the Hussites and over-persuaded many of them to return to R. Catholicism. National feeling remained strong but religious unity had disappeared. Nevertheless the religious guarantees were respected up to the Emperor Rudolf's Letter of Majesty of 1609.

(6) The Emperor Matthias, who followed Rudolf in 1611, moved the Habsburg court from Prague to Vienna, which caused commercial discontent and political suspicion. His successor, recognised in 1617 was the astute and strongly R. Catholic Archduke Ferdinand of Styria, who well before Matthias' death, had started to return former church lands to the Roman church. The political explosion which he provoked had vast European repercussions. In Mar. 1618 the protestants of Prague rose and threw Ferdinand's leading regents out of the window of the Hradcin. See THIRTY YEARS WAR-2.

BOHUN (pron: BOON). This powerful Anglo-Norman family from Bohon in Normandy amassed many honours and estates. **(1) Humphrey (I) (?-1113)** came to England at the Conquest and gained the lordship of Tatesford (Norfolk). His grandson **(2) Humphrey (III) (c. 1110-87)** married Margaret, *d.* of Miles of Gloucester; E. of Hereford. He supported Matilda in the civil wars under Stephen, and held Trowbridge for her. He was a loyal supporter of Henry II and one of the draftsmen of the Constitutions of Clarendon (1164). In 1173 he campaigned against the Scots when William the Lion tried to assist the rebellious P. Henry, and in Oct. defeated Henry's general, Robert of Beaumont at Fornham in Suffolk. In 1174 he witnessed William the Lion's submission at Falaise. His son **(3) Humphrey (IV) (?-**

1182) inherited the earldom of Hereford and the office of Constable of England from his mother. He married the semi-royal Margaret of Huntingdon, a granddaughter of David I of Scots and widow of Conan, E. of Brittany and Richmond. Because he predeceased his father his son **(4) Henry (1176-1220)** was E. of HEREFORD and Constable only from 1187. He married Maud of Essex. He supported the baronial opposition to K. John and was one of the twenty-five trustees for the due performance of Magna Carta. Nevertheless at John's death he adhered to the party of Louis of France and was captured at the B. of Lincoln (May 1217). He died on a tactful pilgrimage to the Holy Land. His son **(5) Humphrey (V) (?-1274) E. of HEREFORD and ESSEX,** and Constable, supported Richard of Cornwall against Henry III and was Sheriff of Kent from 1239 to 1242. He deserted the King's French expedition in 1242, and in 1244 was fighting Welsh risings, one of which is said to have been provoked by his greed. He went on Crusade in 1248, but on his return in 1252 he joined Simon de Montfort and three years later he had another quarrel with the King in France, and in 1254 was again fighting the Welsh. By 1258 he was openly in opposition, on the baronial side over the Provisions of Oxford, and then a member of the Council of Fifteen, while acting also as a Justice in Eyre in the Welsh Marches. When civil war was renewed, however, he came over to the King, while his son **(6) Humphrey (VI) (?-1265)** stayed with Montfort. The father was taken prisoner at the B. of Lewes, but steadfastly supported the King, and was partly responsible after the royal victory at Evesham (Aug. 1265) for the *Dictum of Kenilworth*. The son died immediately after the battle. **(7) Humphrey (VII) (?-1298)** succeeded to the family honours only at his grandfather's death in 1274. He and his friend Roger Bigod, E. of Norfolk, played an important part in resisting Edward I's reforms and in securing the *Confirmatio Cartarum* (1297); and in 1298 they obtained a reconfirmation as the price of their military service against the Scots. After the B. of Falkirk (July 1298) he came home to die. His son **(8) Humphrey (VIII) (1276-1322)** married Elizabeth, *d.* of K. Edward I, in 1302 and entailed his honours as part of the marriage contract. In 1308 he and Gloucester campaigned against the Scots; in 1309 he took part in the baronial protest against papal exactions and in 1310, though, or perhaps because he was intimately connected with the court, he became one of the twenty-one Lords Ordainers responsible for banishing Gaveston (Jan. 1312). On Gaveston's recall Bohun and Lancaster took up arms and put him to death and, in Oct. 1313, extracted a pardon from the King. There followed the disastrous Bannockburn campaign in which he was captured and then exchanged for Robert the Bruce's wife.

This setback for the nobility led to the encroachment of the Despensers upon the King's favour. Bohun and others secured the removal of the elder Despenser at a parliament at York (Sept. 1314) but in the subsequent period of disorderly peace, Bohun was much engaged in forays against the Welsh and the Despenser power in Glamorgan. There was a brief closing of the ranks when Bruce invaded Northumberland in 1318, but Lancaster's refusal to take part in the counter-attack forced a truce in the next year.

There now followed a baronial revolt which Bohun and Mortimer led against the King and the Despensers. Bohun appeared in arms at the Parliament of 1321, and the Despensers were sentenced to exile. The King then made a surprise mobilisation and at the B. of Boroughbridge (Mar. 1322) Bohun was killed. The honours descended successively to his sons **(9) John (?-1335)** and **(10) Humphrey (IX) (?-1361).** The fifth son **(11) William (1310-60) E. of NORTHAMPTON (1337)** was a distinguished soldier as well as a friend and cousin of Edward III, whom he helped against Mortimer in 1330.

In 1337 William was sent to France to make the King's claim to the French crown, and later to Scotland to treat with David Bruce. He took part in Edward's expedition to Flanders (July 1338) and in the naval victory of Sloys (June 1340). In 1342, as military commander in Brittany he beat the French at Morlaix. During the French truce of 1342-5 he campaigned in Scotland, but returned to France in 1345 and fought at Crécy (Aug. 1346). In the period 1349 to 1351 he negotiated first a French and then a Scots truce. The rest of his career consisted of routine military appointments. By Elizabeth, widow of Edmund Mortimer, he had a son **(12) Humphrey (X) (?-1372)** who united in his own person the three Bohun earldoms and the Constableship. On his death these became extinct, but his daughter **(13) Elizabeth (?-1410)** married Henry Bolingbroke, for whom the Hereford title was revived as a Dukedom in 1397, and she brought much of the vast Bohun inheritance into the Bolingbroke family.

BOLDON BOOK. This survey of the Bp. of Durham's demesne manors between Tees and Tweed was made for Bp. Hugh du Puiset. The name derives from one of the first entries, for Boldon, and the area to which it relates is not covered in Domesday. The original is lost but four copies survive.

BOLEYN or BULLEN. (1) A distinguished or notorious Tudor family, originally London merchants. They invested profits in land, and by the 15th cent. were established as Norfolk gentry and were marrying Butlers and Howards. Sir Geoffrey bought Blickling from Sir John Fastolf ('Falstaff'). His grandson **(1) Sir Thomas (1477-1539) Vist. ROCHFORD (1525) E. of WILTSHIRE and ORMONDE (1529)** was a partisan of Henry VII and a personal friend of Henry VIII, with whom he used to joust. He had also made money in the Flanders trade, and at his friend's accession he became Keeper of the lucrative exchange at Calais and of the foreign exchange in England. From 1511 to 1513 he and Poynings were engaged in diplomacy in the Low Countries, and helped to negotiate the Holy League of 1513 against France which led to the short war of 1514. In 1519 he agreed with K. Francis I on the arrangements for the Field of the Cloth of Gold (June 1520). He was accidentally unable to be there, but was present at the interview with Charles V at Gravelines in the next month. Thereafter he was much employed in negotiations with the Emperor at Oudenarde, and on the T. of Windsor of June 1522. By this time his daughter Mary and his second daughter, the famous and tragic Anne, had attracted the King's attention, and this doubtless accelerated his promotion. He was Treas. of the Household in 1522; in 1523 he received lucrative Forest appointments, but was captured and ransomed by Breton pirates while on mission to Spain.

As early as 1527 the King had taken the first steps to obtain annulment of his marriage to Q. Katherine, and by 1529 Anne had become his mistress. In 1530 her father became Lord Privy Seal and was sent to treat about the annulment with Charles V, who was Katherine's nephew, and with the Pope who was in Charles' power at Bologna. This embarrassing mission was not a success. On his return he lived the life of a minor court nobleman. His *d.* **(2) Anne (1507-36).** Her elder sister Mary had already been Henry VIII's mistress when she first came to close quarters with the King at the age of fifteen in 1522. They fascinated rather than loved each other, and she resisted his advances for some years, possibly until 1529, that is, two years after he began proceedings against Q. Katherine. He was not, however. the only man in her life and there was much court gossip. The King's infatuation nevertheless helped to strengthen his theological opinions and political resolution. In 1531 Henry was separated from his wife, and at Easter 1533 it was announced that he had married Anne, who was pregnant, in the previous Jan. Abp. Cranmer then pronounced

sentences annulling the previous marriage, and Anne was crowned Queen at Whitsun. She gave birth to the future Q. Elizabeth I in Sept.

Everything began to go wrong. Like the Queen whom she had supplanted, she had only a daughter. She was said to be a witch, having six fingers on one hand. She was less complaisant as a wife than as a mistress, and made jealous scenes which, of course, encouraged the infidelities at which they were aimed. She had never been popular, like Katherine, and the gossip about her was doubly malicious. In 1534 and in Jan. 1536 she had miscarriages caused, probably, by the King's syphilis. Katherine had died in the same Jan. and the King thought, or professed to think, that God was punishing him for his behaviour with his wives by depriving **him** of heirs by either. In May Anne, her brother Vist. Rochford and four court officials were arrested on charges of incest or adultery and after trial, executed. **(3) Mary (1507-36)** *see* HUNSDON. **(4) George (?-1536)** Vist. HUNSDON was Anne's elder brother and employed, not unlike his father, in a variety of minor diplomatic missions. His probable bastard **(5) George (?-1603)** was Dean of Lichfield. **(6) Q. Elizabeth I** (q.v.).

BOLINGBROKE. *See* GEORGE I; ST. JOHN; WARWICK.

BOLIVAR Y PAIACIOS, Simon (1783-1830) was born in Caracas (Venezuela) of aristocratic and rebellious ancestry. From 1810 until his death his activities provide a conspectus of S. American Spanish politics which makes it unnecessary to treat of the Spanish American republics before 1830.

(1) The abdications of Charles IV and Ferdinand VII of Spain at Bayonne in favour of Bonaparte, and the simultaneous popular insurrection against the French (May 1808) shook the political society of Spanish America. The possibility that Spain might be conquered encouraged local separatism, and during 1809 many Spanish governors were superseded by self appointed juntas. The Spanish defeat at Ocaña led, in Jan. 1810, to the substitution of a regency for the Junta Central at Cadiz. In Apr. Bolivar's friends and relations engineered a royalist *coup* at Caracas against the pro-French Capt. Gen. and Bolivar went to London to secure arms and British support.

(2) On his return he, with Francisco Miranda, led a republican movement which brought about a declaration of VENEZUELAN independence on 7 July 1811. As the British were in alliance with such Spanish authorities as existed, against the French, they could not openly support colonial revolts against Spain, but the City of London favoured local independence which would break up the Spanish trading monopoly.

(3) Resistance to the Caracas revolutionaries was supported by much of the poorer local population which had long relied on the Crown for protection against the planters. The result was a confused and destructive civil war, in which Bolivar rose to eminence mainly through Napoleonic ambition, lack of scruple and breadth of vision.

(4) The first Spanish counter attack in July 1812 destroyed the new Venezuelan state. Bolivar and Miranda fled to La Guaira, but Bolivar purchased his own safety by betraying Miranda, who died four years later in prison at Cadiz. He himself escaped to Curaçao; then, by way of the secessionist port of Cartagena, he launched a new campaign up the Magdalena river in Dec. He soon found that he had to create some slogan to attract an indifferent population, and to find a resource from which to pay his troops. He discovered both in racialism, and proclaimed "War to the Death" against Spaniards as such in June. By Aug. 1813 he had retaken Caracas; in Jan. 1814 he proclaimed himself dictator of Venezuela, and in Feb. hundreds of Spaniards (whose property had already been seized) were murdered in the prisons.

(5) A second Spanish counter attack succeeded at La

Puerta (June 1814) and Caracas had to be abandoned. The dictator's lieutenant, Urdaneta, moved or drove most of the population westwards towards New Granada (now Colombia), while Bolivar sailed from Carupano round to Cartagena which was still in secession, and launched an attack against New Granada from the north. In Dec. the capital, Sante Fé (now Bogota) was taken and a Union of NEW GRANADA proclaimed. The new govt. commissioned Bolivar to attack the pro-Spanish port of Santa Marta, which was about to be reinforced. He used the troops to attack independent Cartagena instead. While the inhabitants beat him off, the new Spanish army under Morillo arrived at Santa Marta. In May 1815, accordingly, Bolivar fled to British Jamaica, moving to Haiti in Dec., while Morillo organised the third Spanish counter-attack, took Cartagena and in Mar. captured Bogota.

(6) In July 1816 ARGENTINA, under the name of the United Provinces of LA PLATA declared its independence while Bolivar was, with Haitian finance, seizing the I. of Margarita off Guayana (Jan. 1817) and extending his operations into Guayana itself. Simultaneously the Argentine gov. of Mendoza, San Martin, crossed the Andes into CHILE, defeated the Spaniards at Chacabuco (Feb.) and took Santiago. Chile broke into civil war. Bolivar, though defeated by Morillo (Mar. 1818) at el Semen, managed to hold onto Margarita and in Apr. to set himself up at Angostura, where he assembled a congress and received British volunteers. In the same month San Martin decisively beat the (mostly Chilean) royalists at Maypo. It was now only a matter of time before he attacked Peru and reached the frontiers of New Granada.

(7) Liberation by anyone else gave Bolivar no pleasure. He made a special effort (May-June 1819), marched from the Orinoco into New Granada, defeated the Spaniards in a small but decisive skirmish at Boyaca, and occupied Bogota for the second time. Much of the country was cleared of Spaniards, and the Angostura congress then proclaimed the Republic of COLOMBIA consisting of Venezuela, Colombia, together with Quito (now Ecuador) yet to be conquered. Bolivar was to be President.

(8) In these enormous areas troops were thin on the ground and small forces could produce great effects. The Spaniards were still dangerous in the north; the southward expedition towards Quito failed; Cochrane, the British admiral in Chilean pay, assembled a small navy and started to clear the Peruvian ports. The new Colombian republic was without money or organisation, and on the verge of collapse. In Jan. 1820, however, the Riego *pronunciamiento* took place in Spain and the new Spanish govt. sought to negotiate. Throughout 1820 there were local and eventually general armistices, which Bolivar and San Martin used to strengthen their positions at opposite ends of the continent. Bolivar at least never meant peace, and in Jan. 1821 he seized Maracaibo on the Caribbean, while a riot at the port of Guayaquil (Ecuador) gave it to his supporter Sucre. In May the war was resumed in full. A composite force of *llaneros* (cowboys) and British volunteers under Paez took Caracas for the third time, defeated the Spaniards, finally so far as Venezuela was concerned, at Carabobo (24 June 1821) and drove them to the coast. Again, almost contemporaneously, San Martin landed at Callao, and on 12 July entered Lima, the capital of Spanish South America. The Repubic of Colombia was now recognised by the U.S.A.

(9) Though the royalist war was to continue until 1826, the emphasis now shifts from the liquidation of Spanish authority to attempts to create a unitary or at least a federal state out of the ex-colonies. As Bolivar wanted to rule them all himself, a pre-emptive southward offensive was set on foot (Autumn 1821) which met

desperate resistance in the border territories of Pasto, whose people, despite massacre, rose three times against the armies of liberation. Eventually Sucre advanced on Quito, defeated the Spaniards at Pichincha (May 1822) and occupied the city. Thus when Bolivar and San Martin met at Guayaquil in July, Bolivar was in possession of (modern) Ecuador. Shortly afterwards San Martin resigned in Peru, and Bolivar turned aside to pacify or devastate Pasto.

(10) In Feb. 1823 the Spaniards beat the Peruvian San Martinistas at Torata, and there followed a *coup d'état* at Lima in Bolivar's interest. In Sept. he took over the govt. on the pretext of saving the country. The real problem was whether the Spanish armies were likely to be reinforced. In Nov. the Spaniards in Venezuela capitulated. In Dec. the U.S.A. proclaimed the Monroe Doctrine, which the British alone could – and would – enforce. The Peruvian royalists thenceforth had to rely on their own resources. In Feb. 1824 they achieved their last success by taking Callao, but they were weakened by desertions, and Bolivar defeated them in Aug. at Junin. On 9 Dec. the viceroy surrendered after a token engagement at Ayacucho. British recognition of the republic of Colombia followed immediately. A few royalist commanders continued the fight for another year, but Bolivar was now free to establish a constitution for Upper Peru, which in due course called itself BOLIVIA.

(11) Bolivar had lived a hard life and had always over-indulged his exceptional sexual appetite. By 1826 his energies, but not his ambitions, were declining. Moreover he had for so long used words as weapons that the purity of his motives was everywhere questioned by those with much experience of him. Thus when in July 1826 he secured almost dictatorial powers in Peru, Paez the *llanero* raised an insurrection in Venezuela; this in turn gave Bolivar the opportunity to obtain dictatorial powers in New Granada. As he made little headway against Paez, they were reconciled in Jan. 1827, upon the basis that Paez should be effective ruler of Venezuela. A revolt immediately occurred in Peru, and this had spread to Bogotá by June. The Republic of Colombia proclaimed at Angostura was now neither Colombian nor a republic, and Bolivar was having to rely increasingly upon his troops against growing unpopularity.

(12) In Apr. 1828, therefore, a constitutional convention met at Ocaña (in the Magdalena Valley) just as a further rebellion broke out in Bolivia. Sucre, Bolivar's local gov. left La Paz, and the Peruvians supported the Bolivians. There was now no chance of a united states of Spanish America unless New Granada would support a war against Peru, and no chance of the latter if the "liberals" of Ocaña got their way. Bolivar staged a *pronunciamiento* at Bogotá in June, and in Aug. began operations against Peru. In reply the Liberals, among whom were many soldiers, conspired to get rid of him, and in Sept. local mutinies coincided with an attempt on his life which was foiled mainly by Manuela Saenz, his mistress. The principal mutineer was Obando who had himself deserted the Spaniards.

(13) Preoccupied with Granadine affairs, Bolivar left Sucre to fight the Peruvians; he defeated them at Tarqui and they surrendered in Feb. 1829. Bolivar went south and in June a Bolivarist coup happened at Lima; but before he could take advantage of it, he had to return to New Granada to deal with further mutinies and conspiracies. By the autumn he had destroyed some of his own following, and Paez, in Jan. 1830 led the final secession of Venezuela from Colombia. By Apr. it was obvious that Bolivar himself was the main obstacle to peace, and he first delegated his functions and then resigned in May. He had resigned so often before that nobody believed him and politics continued regardless. In June Obando murdered Sucre, his ablest lieutenant, but two months later Bolivar staged a revolution at

Bogotá. He was, however, a dying man and four months later he collapsed.

(14) His life and character profoundly changed the ways of half a continent and uprooted the Spaniards from Guayana to Ecuador. His wars ruined immense tracts of prosperous country. His personal abilities did not suffice for his ambitions, and his dream of a new empire gave place to a series of unstable and impoverished republics.

BOLIVIA (formerly UPPER PERU) (1) Its separate existence dates from 1825 when Bolivar's army under Sucre overthrew the Spaniards at the B. of Tumusla (2 Apr. 1825). A constitutional congress proclaimed independence under the new name and a constitution which Bolivar drafted was ratified at Chuquisaca in 1826. Sucre became the first president. In 1828 he was ousted by the Peruvian Gamarra. By a series of coups Santa Cruz established an union in 1836, but this was unacceptable to Chile, and after three years of war Chilean troops restored Gamarra in Peru and Santa Cruz went into exile. Gamarra promptly invaded Bolivia, but was killed in 1841.

(2) From then till 1879 Bolivia was a land of violence and maladministration. The many regimes can be classified into three: the responsible despotisms (1841-61), the irresponsible tyrants (1864-79) and the ephemeral praetorians who killed each other in the intervals, but by 1879 Bolivia was involved in the international fertilizer problem. Between the Bolivian port of Antofagasta (just north of the Chilean frontier) and the highlands lies the Atacama desert. In Atacama and the adjacent Peruvian province of Tarapaca large guano and nitrate deposits had been discovered in the 1840s. American, British, Brazilian and Chilean financial interests began to prospect and invest, for the discovereries were of world-wide agricultural importance. Chile was stable and powerful: Bolivia and Peru in confusion. Naturally foreign investors based their operations in Chile. The frontiers between the three states had been only approximately settled in this hitherto unimportant desert. Now Chileans and foreigners flocked through Antofagasta into the mining camps and supported Chilean claims. Peru and Bolivia in 1873 made a secret military alliance to halt the Chileans and in 1879 the Daza govt. demanded that they should pay a tax on exported nitrates or have their stocks seized. In the ensuing Nitrate War the Chileans defeated Bolivia first and then Peru, and a truce was imposed in 1881. Peace negotiations were not concluded till 1904. Bolivia lost her coastline, but Chile, in return, gave free access through north Chilean ports and built a railway from Antofagasta to La Paz. During this period Bolivia had to cede the rubber bearing Tierra do Acre to Brazil.

(3) The collapse in the Nitrate War led to the establishment of a series of competent govts. based upon true political parties, and, save for a *coup* in 1898, internal politics were tranquil until 1930. This was a period when tin mining for the international market developed and brought wealth, but this in its turn provoked interest in a direct outlet to the Atlantic along the Paraguay river. The vital area was the Chaco, a large jungle in which, as in Atacama, frontiers had been vague for a century. Oil had been found in the adjacent Bolivian areas. Paraguayans and Bolivians alike hoped that there was oil in the Chaco. They fought an exhausting and bloody war from 1932 to 1935. The peace, signed in 1938, gave Bolivia neither the Chaco nor the outlet.

(4) The war had created a strong Bolivian nationalism demanding a new dispensation. World War II raised the profits on Bolivian exports. The period 1938-52 was therefore one of unrest and rising standards of living. This culminated in the revolution of 1952 and the establishment of Estenssoro's reforming govt. It nationalised the mines, reduced the army and distributed land among the peasants. Unfortunately it had also to

contend with falling export prices, which made the revolution less attractive to its intended beneficiaries, and from 1964 Bolivia was under military govts. In the early 1980s these included an increasing civilian proportion.

BOLL. An old Scots measure also used in N. England and the I. of Man. It was the equivalent of 6 bushels for grain and peas, 8 for potatoes, and 140 lb flour. A boll of land was about an acre. The Linlithgow or standard Scots boll contained, for oats, barley and potatoes, 6 bushels, for meal 140 lb.

BOLSHEVIK. In 1898 nine Marxists met at Minsk and formed a Russian Social-Democratic Labour Party from the scattered groups which they represented. In July 1903 at a second congress in Brussels there were strong differences about the nature of the party. Lenin and his faction held that it should be a militant exclusively activist elite; Martov that it should embrace all who subscribed to its principles and funds. The congress moved to London in Aug. and on one particular day a vote was taken and carried (with a majority of one) by Lenin's side. His faction immediately called themselves Bolsheviks (i.e. the majority) as against the others whom they stigmatised as the minority **(Mensheviks).** This difference in organisation concealed fundamental differences on policy, since Lenin advocated revolution by any means, whereas Martov was prepared to try constitutional methods. The party was represented as a unit in the Russian Duma, but at the Prague congress on 1912 Lenin succeeded in expelling his opponents. The party was then re-christened the Russian Social-Democratic Labour Party (of Bolsheviks); in 1918 it changed its name to the Russian Communist Party (of Bolsheviks) and in 1925 to the All-Union Communist Party (of Bolsheviks).

BOLTON (Lancs), an old textile town with a school dating from 1524, owes it present industries to the fact that Sir Richard Arkwright, the inventor of the spinning frame (1768) and Samuel Crompton who invented the spinning mule (1779) both lived there, and that there was plenty of water power. *See* MANCHESTER.

BOLTON ABBEY (Yorks). Robert de Meschines and his wife founded an Augustinian house here in 1121, and it moved to the banks of the R. Wharfe in 1151. Part of the nave was used as the parish church after 1170. The Abbey was dissolved in 1540 and the materials mostly used for building.

BOLTON, Dukes of. *See* PAULET.

BOLTON, Sir Francis John (1831-87), army officer, invented a system of visual day signals and oxy-calcium light for night signals. His Army and Navy Signal Handbook was used in the Abyssinian campaign of 1867.

BOLTON, Sir Richard (?1570-1684) published the Statutes of Ireland in 1621, was Chief Baron of the Irish Exchequer from 1625 and Irish Lord Chancellor in 1639. He was one of Strafford's advisers in the creation of strong Irish govt. and proclaimed the peace with the Irish rebels in 1646. The parliamentary victory and death of Charles I drove him from office.

BOMBA, **(short for bombardatore = the bombarder).** The nickname of Ferdinand II (1830-59) of the Two Sicilies, derived from his bombardment of Messina during the Sicilian uprising of 1848.

BOMB KETCH. A strongly framed ship with a pair of heavy mortars instead of the foremast, designed to bombard towns and fortified harbours, especially on the Barbary coast, otherwise inaccessible to conventional attack. *See* SHIPS, SAILING-8.

BOMBAY (India) CITY and PRESIDENCY. (1) The HEICs first Indian settlement was established at Surat in 1612, and Surat and Portuguese Goa were intermittently at war till 1632 when their governors agreed to keep the peace. This was ratified in 1642, and in 1654 the Portuguese conceded free trade as well. The islands of Bombay, ceded by Bahadur Shah of Gujarat to the Portuguese in 1534, passed to the British Crown (*see* CHARLES 11-20) in

1661. They were occupied in 1665 and leased to the Co. in 1668. In 1672 Gerald Aungier, the Co's president at Surat, moved his H.Q. there; though unhealthy, it was comparatively safe from attack. He enforced religious toleration and so brought in the Parsee merchants of Gujarat. Their capital was invested, *inter alia,* in shipbuilding and, aided by the decline of the neighbouring Portuguese colonies, Bombay became one of the world's principal trading ports. Clive and Watson destroyed the Maratha pirate base at Vijayadurg in 1756.

(2) During the first century, Bombay policy continued to be chiefly concerned with the Marathas, and its prosperity depended upon peace in their areas. By the 1760s the Maratha govt. was breaking up and from 1773 there was a dispute for the office of Peishwa. Under North's Regulating Act Bombay had just become subordinate to Bengal, but in 1776 the Bombay Council intervened independently in the dispute. This gained them the important ex-Portuguese island of Salsette nearby, but involved them in a war in which the Bombay army was forced by the Marathas, with French help, to surrender at Wargaon (1779). Bengal, in the person of Warren Hastings, had to come to the rescue; a force under Goddard marched across India from Bengal to Surat. The Marathas were divided diplomatically and defeated in detail, and eventually made peace at Salbai (17 May 1782). By 1804 the adjacent Maratha rulers had all accepted protection, and in 1818 the lands of Poona and Satara (the territories of the Peishwa and his nominal overlord) were annexed.

(3) Bombay now became the principal centre for British dealings with the Rajputs .and the rulers of the lower Indus. Sind was annexed in 1843.

(4) The reduction of the Marathas turned the Presidency after 1819 into a huge peaceful hinterland for the city which was the principal focus of European trade with half the sub-continent. From 1838 there was a 45-day scheduled service to England, via Suez and Alexandria. When the Suez Canal was opened in 1869 it was reduced to 30. Between 1853 and 1864 Bombay became the central terminal for a railway network, and during the American civil war (1861-5) there was a tremendous local cotton boom. This led to the building of the great Parsee-financed cotton mills in the 1880s. The Parsee Tata family was also responsible for the city's hydroelectric schemes completed in 1915; these formed the basis for a very wide industrial diversification.

(5) In 1937 Sind became a separate province and Aden was transferred to the Colonial Office.

(6) The Presidency did not long survive independence even as a State of the Union. In 1956 it gained eight Marathi speaking districts from Madhya Pradesh and ceded four Kanarese to Mysore. In May 1960 this altered area was partitioned between the new states of Gujarat to the north, and Maharashtra to the south.

BONAPARTE or (before 1796) BUONAPARTE. This prolific Italian family originated near Milan and moved to Corsica, then a Genoese possession, where **Carlo Maria (1746-85)** married **Letizia Ramolino (1750-1836),** later entitled **MADAME MÈRE,** in 1764. Corsica was ceded to France in 1769. Of their 13 children eight survived. This article is concerned with those of their biological descendants and connections who were public figures. It illustrates the Italian family outlook as well as the prerogative still naturally accorded to ruling families.

(1) Joseph (1768-1844) ("Tio Pepe"), K. of NAPLES (1806), K. of SPAIN (1806-13) married Julie CLARY whose sister DESIRÉE was firstly engaged to Napoleon (below) and then married **(2) Charles Jean Bernadotte (1763-1818)** Marshal of France, Crown Prince of Sweden (1810) and K. of SWEDEN and NORWAY. Their descendents still occupy the Swedish throne. **(3) Napoleon I (1769-1821)** changed the surname to its French version and married (a) **Josephine Tascher de la Pagerie,** widow of Vicomte

ALEXANDRE de BEAUHARNAIS with whom she adopted (i) **Eugene de Beauharnais (1781-1824)** Napoleon's viceroy of Italy (1805-14) later D. of LEUCHTENBERG, and (ii) **Hortense (1783-1837)** for whom see (6) below. Napoleon divorced Josephine in 1809 and married (b) the Archduchess **Marie Louise (1791-1847)** (later Duchess of PARMA) by whom he had (iii) **Francois Charles Joseph (1811-32)** K. of ROME (1811) called NAPOLEON II by Bonapartists (after 1816 D. of REICHSTADT). Napoleon did not marry (c) **Marie** Countess WALEWSKA by whom he had a bastard (iv) **Count Alexander Walewski (1810-68)** whose adventurous life included being French ambassador in London and Foreign Min. (1855-60) of the French Second Empire. For Napoleon I see also separate article. **(4) Lucien (1775-1840)** whose clear headedness as Pres. of the Council of Five Hundred saved Napoleon during the *coup d'état* of Brumaire (Nov. 1799) but who otherwise refused to have much to do with him. He was captured by the Royal Navy on his way to America and remained in Britain till 1814. By his second wife **Alexandrine de Bleschamp** he had 9 children of whom (a) **Charles Lucien (1803-57)** P. of CANINO married **Zenaide,** *d.* of K. Joseph (above). (b) **Pierre (1815-81)** who murdered the journalist Victor Noir in Jan. 1870. Charles Lucien's 10 children included **Lucien (1828-95),** a Cardinal. **(5) Eliza (1777-1820)** Princess of PIOMBINO (1805) and LUCCA (1806) and Grand Duchess of TUSCANY (1809) where her rule was competent and popular. Later Countess of COMPIGNANO. **(6) Louis (1778-1846)** K. of HOLLAND (1806-10) married the well loved and respected Hortense (see 3-a-ii above). Her third (legitimate) son was (a) **Charles Louis (1808-73)** Pres. of the French Republic (1848-52) and as **Napoleon III,** Emperor (1852-70) (*see separate article*) who by his wife **Eugenie Guzman de Montijo** had a son **Napoleon Eugene (1856-79),** the PRINCE IMPERIAL, killed in the Zulu War. Hortense by her widely seductive lover **Charles Joseph Comte de Flahaut (1785-1870)** had another son (b) **Charles Auguste** Duc de MORNY (1811-65), a vastly influential financier as well as the Emperor's half-brother under the Second Empire. **(7)** The fiery **Pauline (1780-1825)** Princess BORGHESE sold her Paris mansion to Wellington for use as an embassy, which it remains. She perhaps inspired and probably financed Napoleon's escape from Elba. **(8) Caroline** married **Joachim Murat,** Marshal of France and K. of NAPLES (1808-15), later Countess of LIPONA. **(9) Jerome (1784-1860)** K. of WESTPHALIA (1807-13) and Pres. of the Senate under the Second Empire, whose grandson of his first marriage to **Elizabeth Patterson** of Baltimore (a) **Charles Joseph (1851-1921)** was Pres. Theodore Roosevelt's Sec. of the Navy in 1905 and later U.S. Att-Gen., and whose descendents by **Catherine of Württemberg** married into the royal houses of Italy and Belgium

BONAPARTE, (Charles) Louis Napoleon (1808-73) Pres. of the French Republic (1848-52), Emperor of the French as NAPOLEON III (1852-70), *s.* of Louis Bonaparte, K. of Holland and Q. Hortense (de Beauharnais), brother and step-daughter of Napoleon I. **(1)** He entertained high ambitions from his youth. He flirted with Carbonarist conspiracies in Italy, imbibed St. Simon's economics and wrote embroidery of the 'Napoleonic Legend'. He made two ill-organised attempts to gain power at the ages of 28 and 32. Detained in the fortress of Ham, he escaped in disguise to London in 1846. This was a time of bad harvests corruption, scandals, recession and diplomatic defeat by Britain over the Spanish marriages. Thus the existence of an adventurous Bonaparte was significant when the boring bourgeois monarchy was falling into disrepute. In Feb. 1848 K. Louis Philippe was driven from the throne. *See* SECOND REPUBLIC-FRANCE.

(2) With the left defeated in June, the right was

attracted by a Bonapartist. Louis Napoleon stood for the July bye-elections and was returned in four *departements*. His slow delivery and lack of wit did not impress the assembled politicians. There was no Bonapartist party, and it was too early for the strong royalist factions to put up a presidential candidate. Insofar as he had organised backing for the presidency he secured it by promises to them and the R. Catholics, which he never meant to honour. They, for their part, thought him conveniently naive and cheerfully publicised him. In the upshot he outmanoeuvred them and astonished the world and himself by getting 70% of the total vote.

(3) France now had a head of state who knew almost nothing of the country. In the first parliamentary elections under the new constitution (May 1849) the electors voted 3 to 2 in favour of the right, but royalists took 5 out of every 7 seats. These results provoked another unsuccessful Parisian insurrection. He felt himself dependent on, even a prisoner of, the R. Catholic right. Since Europe was still preoccupied with its own insurrections, he had no need for a vigorous foreign policy, but as a Bonaparte he would not seem authentic without one. The contradiction was apparent in his first compromise steps in Italy. In 1849 his troops, to please his R. Catholics, saved the Pope's mismanaged temporal states by turning Garibaldi and Mazzini out of Rome, but simultaneously he interposed his mediation to shield from Austria, the major Catholic power, the Savoyards who were hostile to the Pope.

(4) A President was ineligible for consecutive re-election and the royalists meant to get rid of him when his term expired in 1852. They pursued a policy of retrenchment to reduce the (Bonapartist) army, disfranchised 40% of the electors, and at the legitimist court in Austria, and the Orleanist in England, plotted a *coup d'état*. With republicanism discredited and people tired of violence, the Bonapartists promised continuity. His presidency resembled an election campaign. He visited the provinces, inspected regiments and cultivated financiers. His party's demands could not be met without constitutional amendments which were persistently refused. In Dec. 1851, by an operation considerably less bloody than Cavaignac's (1848), he imposed his own rule, and got the extensions approved by a plebiscite under universal suffrage by an 11 to 1 majority. A new, mainly cosmetic constitution was followed by a plebiscite which called him to the imperial throne (Nov. 1852).

(5) Napoleon III's new régime had fundamental but as yet invisible weaknesses. Its support was emotional rather than organised. It was an autocracy, but the autocrat was a sick and lecherous man, who had to depend on a camarilla of friends, such as Persigny, various relatives including the bastards Morny and Walewski, and a new, beautiful, tempestuous Spanish wife. Eugenie was ambitious but had neither the tact of an empress-consort, nor the brains for politics and besides, in the era of the *grandes horizontales* she was unfashionably chaste.

(6) Such a dispensation would survive in good weather, and an economic upswing gave it six years of apparent success. The great banks and department stores opened, steel production was multiplied by 4, railway mileage by 6, and France went into transoceanic shipping. The govt. rebuilt most of Paris. Good rural roads stabilised urban food prices. The Emperor, mindful of his uncle's fall, determined to avoid conflicts with Britain where, unlike him, he had lived. One later result was the Cobden commercial treaty (1860), a more immediate one was co-operation with Britain in the Crimean War. This ended with a prestige success. The peace congress in Paris (Feb.-Apr. 1856) was the summit of his fortunes, and if the adventure had cost 100,000 men it strengthened French interests in the Levant and Egypt. The French Suez Canal surveys were beginning.

(7) Every good Bonaparte would strive to re-establish the "natural" frontiers of France denied by the treaties of 1815. No heir to the French revolution could ignore the idea of nationality. As a former Carbonarist Napoleon favoured Italian aspirations. He could rely on British opinion which was infuriated by the savage misgovernment at Naples and romantically enthusiastic about gallant little Piedmont. He was also spurred on by the Orsini plot (Jan. 1858) and induced by Cavour and the charms of the Countess of Castiglione (in the secret Pact or deal of Plombières) (July 1858) to attack Austria in return for Savoy and Nice. Another 100,000 men were sacrificed in the short victorious campaign (May-July 1859) of Magenta and Solferino, while Cavour fomented revolution elsewhere in the peninsula. From opposite points of view, Prussia and Napoleon III saw suddenly that things had gone far enough. The Prussians mobilised to support the shaken Habsburg monarchy: Napoleon stopped to avoid further damage to the Papacy and French R. Catholic opinion, and was also horrified by the casualties and their sufferings. The P. of Villafranca (July 1859) gave Lombardy to Piedmont, but all Italy execrated it as a betrayal. The revolutionaries redoubled their efforts and, apart from the Roman campagna, united Italy. The Savoyard-Papal B. of Castelfidardo (Oct. 1860) encapsulated the contradictions of French policy: Mohammedan mercenaries (The Papal Zouaves) in French pay fought for the Vicar of Christ against the Italians, while French troops garrisoned Rome.

(8) The war had shaken the imperial position. The Italian public, remembering Gladstone, transferred its affections to the British, who apart from volunteers had done nothing, and the disturbance of the Franco-Austrian balance in S. Germany created a vacuum which Napoleon dared not fill. To appease his domestic critics the constitution was liberalised (Nov. 1860-Dec. 1861). France now had a dual system in which parliamentary institutions exercised a growing autonomy, while the throne conducted foreign policy as if it were a private estate. The decadence of Bonapartism was not, however, without its successes. The public was entertained by victories in Algeria, a punitive expedition in aid of Levantine Christians, the bombardment of Foochow, the imposition of commercial capitulations on China, aggression in Indo-China. None of these adventures touched vital foreign interests or investments: that of Mexico, launched (Oct. 1861) while the U.S.A. was incapacitated by its civil war, did. As a result of political credulity and inadequate military appreciations, the expedition was too weak, had to be reinforced and ended up as a debilitating struggle, whose six year duration gave time for the Federal victory in the U.S.A. and the revival of the Monroe doctrine. The enterprise was a roundabout contrivance to help appease the Italian appetite for Rome, by establishing in the New World an Austrian throne to compensate for the cession of Venice to Italy, and it collapsed just as Prussia was ousting Austria from Germany (1866). The Italians received Venice at Prussian, not French, hands, the Mexicans shot their French intruded and deserted Austrian emperor (June 1867) and the cup was filled when French troops had, on behalf of the Pope, once more to fight Garibaldi, now a revered world hero. Napoleon then chose this moment to demand 18th cent. style compensations for the Prussian annexations in N. Germany. He proposed Landau, Mainz, part or all of Belgium and the Orange duchy of Luxemburg. Bismarck mocked and published these claims which embroiled France with the remaining German rulers, the Dutch, the Belgians, and the always subliminally anti-Bonapartist British.

(9) The Emperor, now diplomatically isolated and humiliated, was, though he did not realise it, militarily weak. The army, despite the experience of six wars, was

intellectually backward, unbalanced in organisation and weaponry, and overstretched. The empress' triumphal opening of the Suez Canal (1869) did not prevent liberals defeating nearly half the govt. candidates in a general election. A further measure of appeasement followed. In Sept. 1869 he conceded a theoretical ministerial responsibility to Parliament. A govt. under Emile Ollivier took office in Jan. 1870 and drafted a new and more democratic constitution, which the electors ratified by 5 to 1 (May 1870). Meanwhile Napoleon's privately conducted diplomacy continued.

(10) Bismarck had been ambassador in Paris and knew his man. A Sigmaringen candidature for Spain was withdrawn in the face of French opposition, but when Napoleon sought assurances against a renewal, Bismarck exaggerated the Prussian King's courteous refusal into a gross insult. Without waiting for confirmation, the sick Emperor half decided and was half bullied by his wife into a war to re-establish the dynastic prestige. Enormous majorities in the Chambers supported war. Bismarck and his King united all Germany against this French bellicosity. The French declared war on 19 July 1870. The Germans mobilised by railway and struck on 3 Aug. One month later one French army was besieged in Metz, the other, with the Emperor, had surrendered at Sedan. The Assembly voted the end of the Empire on 4 Sept. After six months honourable custody near Cassel, Napoleon joined Eugenie at Chislehurst.

BONAPARTE, Napoleon I (Personal) (1769-1821). General 1793; **FIRST CONSUL OF FRANCE 1799-1804;** Pres. of the Italian Republic 1802-4; Mediator of the Swiss Confederation 1803-14; **EMPEROR OF THE FRENCH 1804-14**; K. of Italy 1805-14; Protector of the Rhenish Confederation 1806-14. Sovereign of Elba 1814-5. **EMPEROR OF THE FRENCH again 1815. (1)** Was born at Ajaccio (Corsica) and trained as an artillerist. His direction of the batteries against the British fleet at Toulon (1793) earned him his first military laurels. He was an organising genius, a pitiless iron-willed egoist with a comprehensive intellect and memory, an unscrupulous and not always wise propagandist who habitually appropriated other people's credit, and an unrivalled manipulator of lesser men's best and worst feelings. Save when he lost his temper he was incapable of a spontaneous act. With a broad, handsome face and grey, penetrating cold eyes, he was short, strongly built and, after 1806, inclined, though of temperate habits, to corpulence. He could assume a public charm. Talleyrand thought him a very great man, but ill bred. He twice deserted an army under his command. See FRENCH WARS OF 1793-1815.

(2) He was unusually lucky. He was associated at Toulon with Robespierre's brother Augustin, whose praises won him promotion. He was disobediently in Paris in 1795 sharing a mistress, Josephine de Beauharnais, with the Director Barras, on whose behalf he cleared the streets with grape-shot when the sections rose (Oct. 1795). In Mar. 1796 he married Josephine and was sent to Italy where his whirlwind victories and plunder gave him a semi-independent position; from this he was able to settle preliminaries with the Austrians at Leoben (Apr. 1797) and the P. of Campo Formio (Oct.) without regard for the govt.

(3) He succeeded in drawing advantage even from his Egyptian disaster, deserting to France (Oct. 1799) just as the nation feared invasion and further Jacobin terrorism, and when his failure was still unknown. The politicians persuaded him to direct another *coup d'état* (Brumaire) (Nov. 1799) for them. He took the power for himself. He went on to the 12 victories of his second Italian campaign. This culminated at Marengo (June 1800), won mainly by Desaix, who was killed. These, with the peace treaties of Lunéville and Amiens and the Concordat of 1801 established his dictatorship and

enabled him to move from consulate to empire. (*See* TALLEYRAND.)

(4) Despite wars, it was in the period 1801 to 1811 that Bonaparte made his greatest impact. He reorganised the central and local administration and the state finances, and founded the *Banque de France*. His tree lined road and canal network served the comfort of the armies as well as the economy. He formed the present judicial system and gave it the so-called *Code Napoleon* (already mostly drafted by Cambacérès before the Revolution). He established an aesthetic style for the reign and an educational organisation. He created a new nobility. He also imposed a narrow censorship, an official press, and an all-pervasive police and delation system, of which the modern *concierge* is a survival. His system did little and was intended to do little for women.

(5) In the conduct of foreign affairs he was unable to grasp the nature or conditions of sea warfare or, understandably, the unprecedented character of the English economy. His propaganda concealed his many defeats. Apart from Acre and Waterloo, Eylau (Feb. 1807) is forgotten because of Friedland (June 1807); Essling (May 1809) because of Wagram (July 1809). The enormous wastage of these middle campaigns was already beginning to tell in 1806 when he called up the conscription of 1807, and his overdrafts upon his country's human resources continued upon a rising scale for the unparalleled series of Spanish and Russian disasters (1809-13), and for the catastrophes at Dresden and Leipzig (1813). His habitual application of violence to the solution of international problems ruined the French economy and destroyed the morale and much of the manhood of a generation.

(6) As he grew older in association with inferiors and yes-men and with declining health, his self criticism and grasp on facts diminished, and he became impatient of good advice. Moreover his preoccupation with aggrandisement, by whatever means which came to hand, meant in the end that nobody could place any faith in his word.

(7) He never ceased to fight even when relegated in 1815 to St. Helena, where he created the so-called NAPOLEONIC LEGEND, a mixture of half truths, lies, special pleading, spurious appeals to justice and sentiment, which was all the more telling for being related to real achievements. *See* LOWE, HUDSON.

BONAPARTISM. (1) The view that France should have an imperial monarchy vested in the Bonaparte family. **(2)** A political policy, attributed by H. A. L. Fisher especially to the Bonaparte emperors, in which an energetic foreign policy distracts the public from authoritarian methods at home.

BONDED WAREHOUSES. The use of Indian and Persian silks being at the time illegal in the U.K., bonded warehouses were permitted for purposes of re-export in 1700. From 1709 pepper and from 1742 rum could be stored in both bond for importation and for re-export. These experiments were in due course extended to tea, rice and tobacco, with further extensions in 1803. The system reduced the need for working capital otherwise tied up in customs deposits, kept markets steady by enabling importers to release goods to them regularly, and increased the flexibility of trade at no cost to the exchequer.

BONDFIELD, Margaret Grace (1873-1953) came from a poor, nonconformist, but radical home. At 13 she became a shop assistant in Brighton. She moved to London, where she was revolted at the conditions under which shop assistants in the capital had to live and work. Learning of the N. Union of Shop Assistants, she joined it and became Asst. Sec. in 1898, and in 1921 Sec. of the N. Fed. of Women Workers. In 1923 she was elected as the first woman chairman of the Trades Union Congress and M.P. for Northampton. As parliamentary sec. of the

Ministry of Labour in the Labour Govt. of 1924 she was British delegate on the International Labour Office and at the Geneva International Labour conference of that year. From 1926 to 1931 she was M.P. for Wallsend, and was Minister of Labour from 1929 to 1931 in the second Labour Govt. She was the first woman to enter the British Cabinet.

BOND STREET (London). The southern ("Old") section of this famous shopping street was built in 1686 by Sir Thomas Bond, a member of Q. Henrietta Maria's household. The northern ("New") section was built in 1721. It was famous for whores between 1900 and 1950.

BONEDDIG. See WELSH LAW-1 & 5.

BONHAM-CARTER, Helen Violet (1887-1969) Lady ASQUITH OF YARNBURY but better known as Lady VIOLET BONHAM CARTER was the *d.* of H. H. Asquith. One of the wittiest speakers of her generation, she campaigned over many years on social and political issues from a liberal point of view.

BONHAM'S CASE (1610) 8 Co. Rep. 113b. Dr Bonham, a Cambridge doctor of physic, practised in London; he was forbidden to do so by the Royal College of Physicians. He persisted. They fined him twice and then imprisoned him. He brought an action for false imprisonment. The College pleaded its charters and acts. The case is one of the authorities **(1)** for the doctrine of *ultra vires*, since they could punish for bad practice but not simply for practice; **(2)** for the doctrine of natural justice, for they prosecuted, tried, sentenced and received the fines. The case is also remarkable for the judges opinion that the Common Law could "control Acts of Parliament and sometimes adjudge them to be utterly void: for when an Act of Parliament is against the common right and reason or repugnant or impossible to be performed, the common law will control it and adjudge such Act to be void". Cases of 1335 (*Tregor's Case*) 1449 and 1574 (*Strowd's Case*) were cited in which this had been done. Coke's part in this judgement shows that the causes of parliamentary govt. and the supremacy of the Common Law were not identical until after the revolution.

BONIFACE, St. (675-754) "the Apostle of Germany". *See* MISSIONS TO EUROPE-3.

BONIFACE OF SAVOY, Abp. of CANTERBURY (c. 1215-70) was the uncle of Eleanor of Provence, Queen to Henry III, who nominated him to Canterbury in 1241. He first visited England in 1244 and, finding the see in debt, set about raising money by stretching his metropolitical prerogatives of visitation. Between 1245 and 1249 he was abroad. On his return his visitations and fines created opposition and riot in London, so he went abroad again from 1250 to 1252. In 1253 he supported the barons against Henry III and for a while administered his province with the advice of Grosseteste, but his worldly inclinations were too strong and in 1255 he went to Turin at the head of an armed force to rescue his brother, who had been imprisoned in an uprising. Returning in 1256 he led the bishops in resisting royal and papal exactions and after the Provisions of Oxford in 1258, he was one of the council of fifteen entrusted with their execution. By 1262 he was abroad again, this time in France, and in 1264 he argued the King's case at Amiens before K. Louis. Thereafter he was of little account: he offered to accompany the Lord Edward on a crusade in 1269, but went as far as Savoy where he died.

BONN (Germany) was the residence of the Abp-Electors of Cologne, who founded the university there in 1786. Beethoven was born there. It passed to Prussia in 1815 and existed as a distinguished if placid university town until 1945, when the West German govt. made it their temporary capital because it was the only sizeable town in Germany which was undamaged. The politicians and their institutions overshadowed the university until 1991 when Berlin was redeclared the capital of the re-united

Germany, and the federal institutions began a long, slow migration eastwards.

BONNAUGHT or BONNACHT (Irish) was an Irish mercenary, or the military service due to an Irish clan chief.

BONNER or BONER, Edmund (?1500-69), a hated and presumably sadistic bishop, began as a chaplain to Card. Wolsey. After Wolsey's fall Cromwell and Henry VIII employed him from 1532 to 1534 in diplomacy touching the papal attitude to the King's second marriage. In 1534 he was on mission to Denmark and N. Germany, and in 1538 to the Emperor and to the French court where his manners angered K. Francis I. In the same year he was elected Bp. of Hereford but translated to London in 1539 and appointed to the Commission to enforce the Six Articles. He was execrated for the severity of his sentences and was pictured personally birching some of his victims. In 1542 and 1543 he was ambassador to the Emperor, and then until 1547 continued on the Commission and in administering his see.

At the accession of Edward VI he rejected Privy Council control of the church during the royal minority and after some controversy was imprisoned by the Star Chamber at the instance of Hooper, Latimer and Cranmer. Here he remained until Mary I's accession in 1553 when he repossessed his bishopric. He then set about restoring Roman practices with some vigour, but does not seem to have taken much part in inquisitorial persecutions until directly ordered to do so by royal admonition. Thereafter he was responsible for many sentences on heretics and he degraded Cranmer at Oxford in Feb. 1556.

At Elizabeth I's accession he retained his see and seat in parliament but, like all the bishops except one, was deprived for refusing the Oath of Supremacy in May 1559. He spent the rest of his life in prison. The Queen, it seems, disliked him.

BONNET LAIRDS were small farmers or peasants S. E. and W. of Glasgow and in Galloway, who worked their land themselves with a few servants.

BONNY, Anne (fl. 1720). *See* READ, MARY.

BOOKLAND. *See* BOCLAND.

BOOK OF COMMON PRAYER (B.C.P.). *See* PRAYER BOOK.

BOOK OF DISCIPLINE (Sc. 1560) *see* BUCHANAN, GEORGE; CALVINISM; MARY Q OF SCOTS-7.

BOOK OF FEES. *See* TESTA DE NEVILL.

BOOK OF KELLS. A splendid illuminated Gospel, possibly written at Iona c. 800, in a combined Celtic and Northumbrian style never surpassed.

BOOK OF RATES. *See* TARIFF.

BOOK OF SPORTS issued by James I in 1618 and again by Charles I in 1633, encouraged certain harmless diversions but was seized upon by puritans as another pretext for attacking the Anglican church.

BOOK OF ST. ALBANS was published in 1486 by a press at St. Albans soon after Caxton had started printing at Westminster; it contains treatises, probably by different authors, on the gentlemanly subjects of hawking, hunting and heraldry, the whole attributed to the possibly well connected Juliana Berners, prioress of Sopwell (Herts).

BOOKS. After the collapse of the Western Roman Empire the production of books was for six centuries almost entirely in the hands of monks; for example, Cassiodorus after his retirement in 540 founded a monastery with a *scriptorium* at Vivarium. Books were not dictated but copied by sight and hand, and production was slow.

The rise of the universities created a new demand for secular books, and by the 13th cent the stationers who supplied them were mostly controlled and regulated by universities. Booksellers began to appear in the next century. In 1357 writers of text hand were exempted from London jury service, and in 1403 the Stationers Company petitioned for their own ordinances.

Though printing by MOVEABLE TYPE was known in

China many centuries earlier, the European invention is usually ascribed to Johan Gutenberg of Mainz who was experimenting as early as 1439. Printed books first came on the market in the 1450s, the earliest dated book being Fust and Schoeffer's *Mainz Psalter* of 1457; Caxton was operating at Westminster in the '70s and his *Dictes and Sayenges of the Phylosophers* came out in 1477.

The modern form and layout of books was established by 1520, and the early printing press was so advanced that it remained practically unaltered until Stanhope produced his iron press in 1800. The statutes were first printed in 1503, and in 1557 the Stationers Company received its charter and set up its copyright register.

16th cent. printers were really publishers; printing created a new legal situation, where no law existed to protect authors and printers from piracy. Registration at Stationers Hall was effective as a form of protection, but it discriminated against printers who were far from London. Moreover those who had the ability or time to read were still a minority (if a large one) of the population. Only professional people owned books in any numbers.

In the 17th cent. this situation began to change; literacy and interest in reading spread widely; moreover it was a time when such giants as Shakespeare, Newton and Cervantes were being published. The number of new issues and editions is estimated to have been 1,250,000. In the 18th cent. it rose to 2,000,000. In the 19th to 8,000,000. By the beginning of the 20th cent. the demand was so great that there were not enough printers to cope with it, and this, combined with restrictive practices, created a steep rise in wages in the printing industry. This led to a search for new or improved techniques. The photo-offset process was invented in 1904 and high speed presses began to appear in the 1960s. *See* CHAINED BOOKS.

BOOKSELLERS ASSN. Was formed in 1895.

BOOKSELLER'S ROW. *See* HOLYWELL ST.

BOON WORK is an obligation by a tenant to perform unpaid, but commonly specified work, for his lord, particularly an obligation to plough or dig or hoe a given area of land, in the early middle ages three acres.

BOONE, DANIEL (1734-1820) explored Kentucky in 1769 for Judge Richard Henderson, and negotiated a large purchase of land from the Cherokees there. His incompetence in paper work prevented him from validating his titles and he became the proverbial adventurer trapper of the frontier. He penetrated Missouri, then Spanish territory, and after the Louisiana Purchase made expeditions into Kansas. He was already a legend when he died.

BOOT, Jesse (1850-1931) 1st Ld. TRENT (1929). The son of a Nottinghamshire herbalist, he opened his first Chemist's shop there in 1877. The business expanded nationally and internationally, and by 1892 Boots Cash Chemists Ltd were manufacturers as well as retailers of drugs, dealt in many other commodities and ran subscription libraries. He gave much of his money for the benefit of his home town and founded the University of Nottingham.

BOOTH, The Rt. Hon. Charles, F.R.S. (1840-1916) was a partner in Alfred Booth and Co. the shipowners. His interest in social questions impelled him to write his influential *Life and Labour of the People of London* between 1891 and 1903. Intimate with many leading figures in industry, administration and politics, his ideas formed the basis of the Old Age Pensions Act of 1908.

BOOTH or BOTHE, Laurence (?-1480). *See* DURHAM-9.

BOOTH, "General" William (1829-1912), Mrs Catherine (1829-90) and William Bramwell (1856-1929). The elder William was apprenticed to a Nottingham pawnbroker. Moved by his experience of alcoholism and poverty he felt the call in 1844. He moved to London,

became in 1852 a Methodist preacher and in 1855 married Catherine Mumford, who had been excommunicated by the Methodists as a reforming extremist. In 1861 he broke with Methodism and he and his wife preached together at Gateshead until they started their Christian Revival Association at Whitechapel in 1865, and gave it the title of Salvation Army in 1878. They published many tracts of which *In Darkest England and the Way Out* (1890) was the best known. He was a gospeller and moralist without much education, or theology, or organising ability, but he compelled attention by the strength of his personal sanctity. It was left to his son, William Bramwell, chief of staff of the Salvation Army from 1880 to 1917, to create an efficient and international organisation. It was the latter who was associated with W. T. Stead in the campaign against prostitution which culminated in the Criminal Law Amendment Act of 1885. He was general of the Salvation Army from his father's death until his own.

BOOTHBY, Robert John Graham (1900-86) Ld. (1958) Tory M.P. from 1924 to 1958 and a strongly placed back bencher as a nationally known broadcaster and television personality, was also for many years the lover of Harold Macmillan's wife.

BOOTHIA. *See* ROSS, SIR JAMES: ROSS, SIR JOHN.

BOOTH'S RISING (Aug. 1659) was a premature royalist and presbyterian revolt led by Sir Geo. Booth and suppressed by Lambert.

BOOTS being difficult to make and expensive, were worn so much by the nobility and gentry that in the 16th cent. they were a mark of rank. The dissemination of prosperity led persons of lesser distinction to use them and early in Charles I's reign some gentry unsuccessfully petitioned the Crown to forbid this new fashion.

BOOTS or BUITS (Sc). An instrument of torture consisting of a wooden boot for the victim's leg and wedges which were driven in to tighten the pressure until he either confessed or fainted. Not used after about 1707.

BORDAR (from Med: Lat *Borda* = a hut) in most counties was a non-free tenant with between one and five acres for which he rendered labour services, and who otherwise earned a living by day labour where he could find it.

BORDEAUX (France) was a possession of the English Kings in right of the Duchy of Aquitaine from 1154 to 1453. The wine trade was important to the development of Bristol and Southampton in the middle ages. *See* AQUITAINE.

BORDEN, Sir Robert. *See* CANADA-25.

BORDER. (1) This word used alone means the frontier between England and Scotland. It now runs from just north of Berwick, along the Tweed and the watershed of the Cheviots and then along the R. Sark to the head of the Solway Firth. The latter is an obvious natural obstacle, and the Romans began the western end of Hadrian's Wall here, even though the Brigantes had spread or at least hunted to the north of it. The Wall's eastern end, however, was not on the Tweed but at Wallsend on the Tyne, and the modern location of the Border was not established till the reign of Richard I. Berwick town remained in dispute till Tudor times.

(2) The WELSH BORDER fluctuated more than the Scots. In the north the Statute of Wales (1282) attached the county of Flint to the Palatinate of Chester, but Welsh law was nonetheless mostly observed west of Offa's Dyke, both in the six counties created by the Statute, and in the Lordships Marcher. The boundaries of Lordships varied with the fortunes of war. The jurisdiction of the Council of the Marches set up by Henry VII included the English Border counties as well as Wales. An Act of 1536, sometimes called the Act of Union, set up the remaining Welsh counties, but detached Flint from Chester. An Act of 1543 attached Monmouth to England. These two Acts virtually obliterated the border by giving English and

Welsh the same law and rights. Local Government Acts of 1958 and 1972 have, however, treated Monmouthshire, under the name of Gwent, as part of Wales and have tended to increase administrative differences again. *See* MARCHES; WALES, GOVT. OF, ACT 1998

BORDER COMMISSION. *See* CUMBERLAND-13; **COUNCILS,** *see* CUMBERLAND-12.

BORDERER. One living on the edge of a common.

BORDER MEETING. *See* MARCHES, ANGLO-SCOTS-5 to 6.

BORDER WARRANT (Sc) was a warrant issued to arrest the person or goods of a resident in England to compel him to appear in a Scottish court.

BORGIA (Ital) or BORJA (Sp). This powerful Aragonese family included the Dukes of Infantado and became internationally famous when **(1) Alonso (?-1458)** Bp. of Valencia accompanied Alfonso of Aragon to Naples and was in 1444 made a cardinal. In 1455 as CALIXTUS III he succeeded Pope Nicholas V. Some of his relations moved to Rome where their name became Italianised. He made his uterine nephew **(2) Rodrigo (?-1503)** Abp. of Valencia and Sixtus IV made him a Cardinal. In 1492 he was corruptly elected Pope as ALEXANDER VI, and was called upon to preside over great events. On 4 May 1493, by the bull *Inter cetera divina* (Lat: among a variety of divine matters) he made the original division of the New World between Spain and Portugal (*see* TORDESILLAS. T. OF). In 1495 when Charles VIII had overrun Italy, he formed the Holy League whose forces fought the French at the decisive B. of Fornovo in July. In the same year he made Card. Ximenes Abp. of Toledo, and began the policy against Savonarola which ended with the latter's execution in May 1498. In this same year Machiavelli became Sec. of State at Florence; Vasco da Gama reached India; Columbus found Guiana, and Cabot Labrador; and Erasmus came to Oxford. In the period from 1500 (a year of Jubilee) until his death, the events occurred which put the Kingdoms of Naples and Sicily into Spanish control; and extended the Papal States into Romagna. He was a famous sybarite and patron of the arts. By his mistress Vannozza dei Cattani he had five children who were officially his nephews and nieces (hence the word 'nepotism'). Of these **(3) Cesare (1476-1507)** was an archbishop and cardinal at nineteen, but in 1499 was allowed to renounce his orders and married Charlotte of Navarre. As a soldier he conquered Romagna for his father. The seductive **(4) Lucrezia (1480-1519)** married Giovanni Sforza and (much later) a D. of Ferrara. Death carried off so many of those near this famous lady that she has been accused or credited with a catalogue of crimes on evidence which would not satisfy a court. **(5) St. Francis Borgia (Francesco) (1510-72)** was a cousin of Alexander VI and became the third General of the Jesuits. He was canonised in 1671.

BORING. *See* DRILLING MACHINERY.

BORNEO. *See* INDONESIA; SAMUEL.

BORNHOLM. *See* BURGUNDY.

BORNU (Nigeria) was ruled by native chiefs until 1893, when Rabah Zobeir collected the remnants of the Sudanese army defeated at Omdurman, marched across Africa to Lake Chad and conquered it. Under the Berlin agreement of 1894 Bornu was partitioned between Britain, France and Germany and in 1900 Rabah was killed by the French at the B. of Kusseri. The native line was re-established over the British and French territories in 1902, the German part remaining under a separate emir of the same family. In 1917 the German part was annexed for administration to the British part, and in 1937 the emirate was reunited.

BOROUGH (A.S: BURH) meant originally a settlement which was safe or walled against (mainly Danish) marauders, and then a town organised for defence, the common ownership of property or the conduct of a market. Most were founded by Anglo-Saxon kings on royal property, and Athelstan, to encourage trade, gave

each a mint. Houses were often annexed to particular manors, whose lords thus had access to the market and the burghal privileges as well as a refuge in trouble. The residents were free men.

(1) *English boroughs* appear in Domesday, but they were not corporations. Their courts (if any) began as Hundred Courts, but they developed or preserved special customs which became increasingly distinctive when privileges were granted by seigneurial or royal CHARTER. The charters, originally individual, began in the 12th cent to confer privileges by reference to other charters (e.g. Oxford received the London customs in 1155) and town clerks began to compile customals as guides to practice. The early boroughs were very small. Domesday Oxford had only 243 taxable houses, the remaining 478 being ruinous. London, easily the biggest, had 126 parish churches and was already connected with Westminster by a continuous suburb, but as late as 1796 open country began half a mile north of the Thames. The ancient borough of Montgomery was still a village of 1000 people in 1969. Boroughs with royal charters were part of the royal demesne and their people were liable to pay the tallage. Other boroughs came to be treated similarly. The amounts were negotiated and by the end of the 13th cent. this negotiation was done through representatives. This probably inspired borough representation in parliament. The right to such representation was conferred by royal charters, which usually laid down the constitution of the borough, and the manner of electing its M.P.s and sheriffs. Though permanent if carefully observed, they could be forfeited for acts committed in breach of their terms, and many were forfeited or surrendered in 1682, 1683 and 1684 and replaced by others drawn more stringently in favour of Charles II's govt. The Reform Act, 1832, abolished franchise by charter and the Municipal Corporations Act, 1835, replaced most of the old ones by a standard type of charter under which councils consisted as to three quarters of councillors elected for three years by the ratepayers, and as to one quarter of aldermen elected for six years by the councillors, the whole council electing the mayor. The 178 boroughs chartered under the Act began to acquire statutory administrative powers mainly concerned with public health, and so became administrative units fundamentally different from their original character. When the Local Govt. Act, 1888, created county councils, 61 boroughs became COUNTY BOROUGHS and were thus administratively autonomous from the surrounding counties; by 1964 these had increased to 84; in 1865 three were absorbed into Greater London. Meantime the non-county boroughs also increased in number so that by 1958 there were 318. As from 1974, the Local Govt. Act 1972 created districts in which the boroughs were amalgamated with adjacent urban and rural districts. The new combined districts could, and mostly did, apply for borough charters whose effect was purely ceremonial.

(2) *Irish boroughs* mostly developed in the manner of the English boroughs, allowing for the fact that they were often colonies of English settlers in an alien landscape. Many of their early charters were modelled on the custom of Breteuil in Normandy. *See* LOCAL ADMINISTRATION.

BOROUGH, THE. *See* SOUTHWARK.

BOROUGHBRIDGE, B. of (16 Mar. 1322). Retreating from Edward II's forces, Earls Thomas of Lancaster and Humphrey (de Bohun) of Hereford moved north from the Lancastrian stronghold at Pontefract. At Boroughbridge (Yorks) on the S. bank of the R. Ure they were intercepted by experienced border levies under Sir Andrew Harclay. He arranged his troops as pikemen on foot supported by archers. These tactics, resembling those of Bruce at Bannockburn (1314) and Edward III at Halidon Hill (1333) succeeded and, after the death of the E. of Hereford, Harclay gained a mass surrender including that of Thomas of Lancaster and the other rebel leaders. Pontefract capitulated and Lancaster was executed there on 23rd.

BOROUGH ENGLISH. A tenure in some English boroughs under which the whole inheritance passed to the youngest son or, occasionally, failing sons, to the youngest daughter.

BOROUGH HOLDER. See BURGAGE.

BOROUGH MONGER. One who traded in parliamentary rotten boroughs. A term of late 18th and early 19th cent. polemics.

BOROUGH, BURROW or BORROWS, Stephen (1525-84) and his brother **William (1536-99)** went with Chancellor on the first English northabout voyage to Russia in the *Edward Bonaventure* in 1553 and made other voyages there in succeeding years. In 1558 Stephen went to Spain and in 1560 to Russia again. In 1563 he became chief pilot in the Medway. In 1570 William was fighting pirates in the G. of Finland and in 1587 he commanded the *Lion* under Drake at Cadiz, but questioned the wisdom of the attack on Lagos and was nearly cashiered. He commanded the *Bonavolta* against the Armada. These brothers represented a new and growing generation of English professional seamen.

BORROW, George (1803-81), traveller, especially as a Bible colporteur in Spain from 1835 to 1840, was a gifted linguist. His *Bible in Spain* (1842) is an idiosyncratic and protestant view of Spain; *Lavengro* (1857) and *Romany Rye* (1857) opened the public eye to gipsy life. His *Wild Wales* (1864) dealt with commonly unnoticed detail. The books are much concerned with the open air life and such sports as boxing, and stood outside the literary conventions of the time. For this reason they attracted and still attract a following. He wrote several other works and helped to compile the *Newgate Calendar*. An early unselfconscious but full-blooded sociologist, he kept open house to dukes and tramps at Oulton Broad.

BORSHOLDER. See FRANK PLEDGE.

BORSTAL INSTITUTIONS were custodial schools, the first being set up at Borstal (Kent) in 1908, to supplement the reformatory schools functioning since 1854. See RUGGLES-BRISE.

BOSA (?-705). See MISSIONARIES IN BRITAIN AND IRELAND-11 to 13.

BOSCAWEN (Non: Pescorn) Edward (1711-61), a distinguished but neglected Cornish seaman, was a grandson of Arabella, sister of the great D. of Marlborough. After routine positions he served as a volunteer with Adm. Vernon in the successful attack on Porto Bello in 1739, and stormed the Boca Chica Battery at Cartagena in Mar. 1741. In 1747 he was with Anson at the victory of C. Finisterre, and being promoted rear-adm. was appointed C-in-C by sea and land in the East Indies. Here he waged war against the French under great difficulties until learning in 1750 of the peace signed in 1748. In 1755 he commanded squadrons in American waters and in 1757 was 2-in-C to Hawke and then C-in-C off the American coast. Returning after the fall of Louisburg, he took command in Feb. 1759 of the Mediterranean Fleet and in Aug. destroyed the French Toulon squadron, which was on its way to Brest, in a series of actions near Gilbraltar and Lagos. During the rest of his life he commanded the British fleet which, after Hawke's famous victory, was based on Quiberon Bay.

BOSCOBEL (Salop). The place where Charles II was hidden by members of the Penderel family for two days after the B. of Worcester (3 Sept. 1651), part of the time in an oak.

BOSE, Sir Jagadir Chandra (1858-1937). See BOTANY.

BOSE, Subhas Chandra (1897-?1945) was an ardent Indian nationalist and a somewhat inconvenient supporter of Gandhi. He joined the Swaraj (Independence) movement in 1920, was Pres. of the All India Trades Union National Congress from 1929 to 1931 and in 1939 became Pres. of the Indian National Congress. He went into hiding when Japan entered World War II, escaped to Japan and tried to form an Indian nationalist army from captured prisoners to fight alongside the Japanese, who do not seem to have put much faith in him. He was killed in an air crash.

BOSNIA AND HERZEGOVINA (Balkans). The broils in these two Balkan provinces long affected British diplomacy **(1)** The Turks had originally appointed 48 hereditary Kapudans, whom in 1580 they divided between eight Sanjaks under a Pasha at Sarajevo. By 1739 the area north of the Sava with Hercegnovi and parts of Bosnia proper were in Austrian hands. These mainly Croat areas were R. Catholic and used the Latin script. The mainly Serb areas were Othodox and used Cyrillic.

(2) The Greek revolt of 1821 and the later Greek wars inspired Bosnian revolts mainly against Sultan Mahmoud II's reforms, which threatened to increase Turkish efficiency. They were put down and in 1837 the office of Kapudan was abolished. Yet other revolts followed, and till 1850 the area was virtually independent, until reconquered by the Croat Omer Pasha. His centralising policies naturally provoked an outbreak which simmered on from 1862 to 1875 because the new methods encroached on the fortunes of the former Kapudans, but did little for the population. In 1875 a general insurrection coincided with or was inspired by another in Bulgaria and a *coup d'état* at Constantinople.

(3) This was the time of the Bulgarian Massacres and European intervention. In Jan 1876 the powers proposed a limited form of autonomy. Egged on by Serbia-based Slav nationalists, the Bosnians rejected it. In June Serbia and Montenegro, stiffened with Russian volunteers, attacked the Turks and the insurgents proclaimed their solidarity with them. This combination was, however very thoroughly defeated by the Turks before the end of Oct.

(4) Austria and Russia, the two immediately interested powers, had hoped that the disintegrating Turkish Balkan power would be replaced by a series of weak, but self-generated, national states whom they could dominate but need not administer. The Turkish victories compelled a revision of their ideas. At Budapest in Mar. 1877 they agreed a partition: Austria was to occupy Bosnia and Herzegovina under Turkish suzerainty and stand aside while Russia attacked Turkey. See ROUMANIA.

(5) The Bosnian nationalists now found themselves fighting the Austrians instead of the Turks, but by Oct. 1878 they had been overcome. The area remained legally and economically Ottoman, but from 1880 to 1908 it was administered by the Austrian Finance Ministry, particularly from 1881 to 1903 by Benjamin Kallay whose administration was efficient and just. He encouraged Bosnian local sentiment and culture as a counter-weight to Serbian ambitions, and this policy was inherited by Burian, his successor; by 1907 there was an Assembly which was being allowed to formulate reforms for autonomy *within* the Turkish Empire. Slav feeling, however, was the mainspring of the idea.

(6) The Young Turks now overthrew the Constantinople govt. and demanded that Bosnia be represented in their proposed new Pan-Turkish parliament. For Austria this created a situation which could be solved only by cutting the Gordian knot, and on Aehrenthal's advice the territory was annexed to both the Austro-Hungarian crowns, with Russian agreement. This solved nothing. Neither Austria nor Hungary would allow the other to upset the internal balance of the Empire by acquiring Bosnia which, therefore, had to be governed as part of neither. Hence the Bosnians had no say in foreign policy, yet foreign attachments of a pan-Slav, or Serbian kind, were their ruling passion. Moreover, the new local diets were elected on a communal basis and had no control over the executive, and the executive was itself divided between a military governor (Potiorek) who took his orders from the General Staff, and a civil governor (Bilinski), responsible to the Min. of Finance.

(7) The confusion made it easy for violent nationalist groups to form, abetted and armed by the Serbs across the border. The people were stirred by the Serbian victories in the Balkan Wars of 1912, and Bosnian nationalist groups agitated amongst the younger Slavs in all the great cities of the Empire.

(8) Hungarian brutality in nearby Croatia exacerbated the situation and so did the bullying Potiorek, who acted increasingly without consulting Bilinski. He dissolved Serb societies and prorogued the Diet. The decision to bring the Archduke Franz Ferdinand to Sarajevo was made behind Bilinski's back. It was a Bosnian Serb, one Princip, who murdered the Archduke at the second attempt on 28th June 1914, and so precipitated the First World War. Princip is commemorated as a Serbian national hero. After the war the area became part of Yugoslavia.

(9) The dissolution of Yugoslavia in 1990-2 resulted in a Serb provoked civil war which (1994-5) European and United Nations peacekeepers seemed unable to stop.

BOSPHORUS. See STRAITS.

BOSS from Dutch 'baas' = master: South Africa and New York having been Dutch colonies in their time.

BOSTON (Lincs.). St. Botolph founded a monastery here in 654 and the name Boston is said to be a corruption of 'Botolphs Town'. The monastery was sacked by the Danes in 870, but revived after the Norman Conquest and became the most important English port trading with the Hanse and northern Europe. The great 14th cent. tower (The Stump) was built partly as a navigational landmark and lighthouse. By the 16th cent. the river was silting up and the trade was declining. In 1545 the town received a charter. In 1764, however, an effort was made to deepen the river, and the Grand Sluice was built, and in 1882 a dock and new cut were constructed for ships up to 2000 tons. Trade, however, continued to decline in the face of large tonnage Imports of grain and meat to the bigger ports. This trend was reversed only after World War II when the demand for lorry-borne fresh vegetables in Birmingham created considerable traffic with Holland.

The Pilgrim Fathers made their first (unsuccessful) attempt to leave England from Boston in 1607.

BOSTON (Mass) was mapped by Capt. John Smith in 1614 and visited from the Plymouth Plantation in 1621. The Massachusetts Bay Co's colony was inaugurated at Salem in 1628 and the govt. of the Co was transferred from London to Massachusetts in 1630 when John Winthrop and his followers settled at Boston, which then received its name. It became the capital of Massachusetts in 1632. By 1640 the population had reached 10,000, and by 1750, 15,000. (For the significance of the Boston "Massacre" (Mar 1770) and the Boston Tea Party (Dec. 1773) *see separate entries and* AMERICAN REVOLUTION AND WAR OF INDEPENDENCE). An important political factor of the 1770s was that the city was governed by a Town's meeting where all the voters discussed public affairs. As Boston contained most of the Massachusetts citizenry, the Town's Meeting had a locally predominant position as late as 1822.

BOSTON 'MASSACRE' (Mar. 1770). *See* AMERICAN REBELLION-13.

BOSTON TEA-PARTY (Dec. 1773). *See* AMERICAN REBELLION-14.

BOSWELL. This talented Scottish family included (1) Alexander 14. AUCHINLECK (1706-82), who became a Lord of Session in 1754. His son (2) James, the elder (1740-95) was a biographer and friend of Dr Johnson. (3) Claude Irvine, Ld. BALMUTO (1742-1824) was a nephew of Alexander and became a Lord of Session in

1799. (4) Sir Alexander (1775-1822), the elder son of the biographer, was a poet and antiquary.

BOSWORTH FIELD, B. of (22 Aug. 1485). Henry Tudor landed from France at Milford Haven with a weak force on 7 Aug. 1485, knowing that the Stanleys (one of whom was married to his mother) and the Welsh would support him. He marched across Wales unopposed, gathering support, including that of Sir John Savage, a Stanley relative who was one of Richard III's commanders. Richard, at Nottingham, thought that Henry would be crushed by his lieutenants in Wales, and did not know of the unopposed march until Henry appeared at Shrewsbury on 15 Aug. He sent for reinforcements from the south and himself moved south to Leicester: Henry came on through Stafford (where he interviewed Sir William Stanley) and Lichfield, and at Atherstone had another interview with the Stanleys. Their problem was that Lord Strange, Lord Stanley's son, was a hostage with Richard.

The main armies now faced each other east and west about three miles apart to the south of Market Bosworth. The Stanley force was to the south opposite the gap between them. At this stage they could not risk Strange's life by joining Henry, but would not join Richard when he threatened to have Strange killed. Thus the next day's battle was a three sided affair.

On 22nd Richard occupied some high ground towards Henry's army and Northumberland, another of his unreliable commanders, posted himself at the southern edge of it, to watch the Stanleys. Richard's vanguard, under Norfolk, held the western edge against an attack by Henry's advanced troops under Talbot, and drove them back, but Norfolk was killed. Henry's main force now came up and Richard decided to make a decisive stroke against him. This could be done only by advancing across the front of the Stanleys; everything therefore depended on Northumberland. In reply to a message Northumberland refused to move. Richard decided to take the risk and charged. When he was irretrievably committed, the Stanleys attacked him in the flank and Richard and most of his supporters were killed.

BOTANIC GARDENS. The Chelsea Physic Garden, London, was established by the Society of Apothecaries in 1673 and enlarged by Sir Hans Sloane in 1722. The Royal Botanic Gardens were established at Kew in 1757 by Princess Augusta of Saxe-Gotha. She engaged William Aiton, who was trained at Chelsea, to lay it out.

BOTANY. *See* HALES, STEPHEN. John Gerard (1545-1612) was superintendent of Burghley's gardens and published his well known *Herbal* in 1597. Thomas Johnson (?-1644) issued a plant catalogue in 1629 and an edited version of the *Herbal* in 1633. The Sherard brothers, William (1659-1728) and James (1666-1738) endowed a professorship at Oxford and William, while the Turkey Co's Consul at Smyrna (1702-16) made botanical journeys in Anatolia, besides others in Switzerland and Italy. In 1721 Sir Hans Sloane founded the Chelsea Botanic Garden, which attracted and inspired the celebrated Swedish botanists LINNAEUS and Peder Kalm, and indirectly popularised the Chelsea Flower Show. Meanwhile John Ray had published his *Historia*, which led to Linnaeus' *Species Plantarum* (Lat = Kinds of Plants) of 1753, which set the science on the way which it has ever since followed. In modern times Sir JAGADIR CHANDRA BOSE (1858-1937), the Bengali botanist, became a world authority on plant life, partly through his ingenuity in creating instruments for detecting movement in plant tissue, and founded the Botanical Research Institute in Calcutta, named after him. His studies were fundamental to the manipulation and scientific application of plants in agriculture.

BOTANY BAY (N.S.W.) was the place where Capt. Cook first set foot in Australia on 29 Apr. 1770. A penal settlement was established nearby in 1788, but later moved to Sydney.

BOTHA, General Louis (1862-1919). (1) This respected Boer personality began his public career in 1884 as commissioner to delimit farms allotted in Zulu territory to Lukas Meyer's Volunteers. He was subsequently field cornet and native commissioner at Vryheid, and led the local burgher force during the Jameson raid (1895). In 1897 he was elected to the first Transvaal *Volksraad,* and supported Joubert in conciliating the Uitlanders; but when the South African War broke out in 1899 he raised the Vryheid commando and soon became one of the ablest Boer generals. He defeated Buller at Colenso, Spion Kop and Vaalkrantz, and when Joubert died in Mar. 1900 took over the chief command. He reorganised the Boer forces, but too late to stave off defeat at Doornkop (May 1900) and Diamond Hill (June 1900); nevertheless, he carried on guerrilla warfare for nearly two years and secured fair terms at the P. of Vereeniging in May 1902. Shortly afterwards he visited England and was warmly received.

(2) When he returned he, with other prominent Boers, created a nationalist organisation called 'Het Volk' which was launched in 1905. In 1906, when the Transvaal received responsible govt., he was Prime Minister and, true to his principles, he favoured reconciliation between Boers and British and co-operation between the four provinces. He and Smuts were the principal architects of the Union (1909) and on 10 May, 1910, he became its first Prime Minister.

(3) His first difficulty was with Hertzog and de Wet, the Dutch extremists of his own party, who were stirring up hatred of the British population. Botha dismissed Hertzog and converted his own party. The next problem was that of the Indian indentured labourers who claimed citizen rights on the expiry of their indentures. Their leader was the later to be famous Mohandas Karamchand GANDHI. This dispute was compromised through the efforts of Jan Smuts. While it was being negotiated, a white general strike broke out on the Rand in July 1913 when only British troops were available. Clashes between the troops and a Johannesberg mob endangered Botha's policy of reconciliation. In Dec. a railway strike followed, but this time Botha was ready: a citizen force was mobilised: the strike leaders were deported and the strike collapsed, not without criticism of the deportations which had to be legalised by an Act of Indemnity.

(4) The instability of the Union was now powerfully illustrated at the opening of World War I. Botha and the British agreed that the British garrison troops should be replaced by South African units, and that the Union should conquer German South-West Africa. Before anything could be done he was faced with a military revolt led by, of all people, Solomon Maritz, the officer commanding on the German frontier, with de Wet and Christian Frederick Beyers, the commandant-gen. of the burgher forces. The rebels object was neutrality and the Germans had tampered with some of them. Botha was distressed but not frightened. He was determined to enter the war, and negotiations therefore broke down. He then characteristically called out commandos from Dutch areas only in order to avoid racial trouble, and being much abler than the rebel commanders, broke them in Oct. and Nov. 1914. The whole revolt was over by Feb. 1915 and a combined force of both nations invaded the German territory, which surrendered in July.

(5) Botha continued in office throughout the war and in 1919 attended the Versailles Peace Conference where, as one who 'also came from a conquered nation', he made a moving appeal for lenient terms; but he was dying, and though personally esteemed, his views carried less weight than was their due.

BOTHMER. *See* GEORGE I-2.

BOTHWELL. *See* HEPBURN.

BOTHWELL BRIG, B. of (July 1697). In this skirmish, Monmouth defeated an amateur force of oppressed Lanarkshire covenanters, who had risen as a result of the govt's over-reaction to the murder of Abp. Sharp near St. Andrews in May. *See* MACKENZIE-SEAFORTH-3.

BOTSWANA. *See* BECHUANALAND.

BOTTLES. *See* WINE TRADE-5.

BOTTOM in the 18th cent. meant solidity of character: reliability, substance or staying power. A desirable characteristic in politics. Hence the "Broad-bottomed Administration" and caricatures of the "Bottomless Pitt".

BOTTOMLEY, Horatio William (1860-1933). This bizarre trickster, after an adventurous early life, started a printing business and in 1884 launched the *Hackney Hansard,* and other similar papers; in 1890 he promoted the Hansard Publishing Union with a capital of £500,000, and in two years went bankrupt. At the ensuing trial for fraud he defended himself and was in 1893 acquitted. He continued his career as a promoter of nearly 50 companies involving £20M in capital, and made £3M out of it himself. Between 1900 and 1905 sixty-seven writs and bankruptcy petitions were filed against him; at the same time he was spending immense sums in high living. He was also involved in journalism where he had real ability, and so in newspaper management where he had none. He bought the *Sun* in 1898 and founded *John Bull* in 1906, when he entered parliament for South Hackney.

But he was in difficulties. The shareholders of one of his trusts petitioned for liquidation. Most of the books were missing; in 1909 he was acquitted of fraud, but lost in a civil action for £50,000. In 1911 he himself presented a petition in bankruptcy and applied for the Chiltern Hundreds, but many of his assets were found to be in his wife's name. Public indignation was diverted by war in 1914, and he then achieved a national reputation by patriotic speeches and articles for which he was handsomely paid. In 1915 his old confidence had returned and he was promoting companies again. He received subscriptions of nearly £900,000 and in 1918 paid off his old creditors; his bankruptcy was discharged and he returned to Parliament as an independent.

This sparked off further investigations. His affairs were too complicated; there were widespread demands for repayment; an associate published defamatory allegations; Bottomley prosecuted and failed. A receiver was appointed to investigate his affairs: in May 1922 he was convicted on 23 counts of fraudulent conversion and in Aug. expelled from the Commons.

BO-TREE (Sansk: *Bodhidruma* = Tree of intelligence) *ficus religiosa* or peepul tree is a fluttering spiky-leafed Moracea important in two Indian religions sharing common origins. **(1)** HINDUISM in which Vishnu, the second in the Hindu trinity beside Brahma and Siva, takes a major part. Vishnu was supposedly born under a Bo-tree. This probably explains the tree's significance in the second religion. **(2)** BUDDHISM. Gautama, the Buddha, was an historical figure, Pr. Siddhartha (c. 620-c. 540) of Kapilavastu in Oudh. At about the age of 30 he escaped from his wife and other restraints to a long period of reflection sitting under such a tree, whose location is now unknown. It survived for 1200 years and cuttings from it were taken to Ceylon, whence further cuttings were taken to Burma, Thailand and other centres of veneration.

BOUCHAIN (France) Siege of (8th Aug.-12th Sept. 1711). This was the last military operation undertaken by the D. of Marlborough. Having pierced the so-called *Ne Plus Ultra* lines at Arleux he moved east and invested Bouchain. The French army under Villars was in superior numbers and manocuvred for the relief of the fortress so that Marlborough's army had not only to attack the garrison but to fight Villar's force as well. Bouchain, nevertheless, was captured in five weeks.

BOUFFLERS, Louis François (1644-1711) D. of (1694). After service under Turenne, Boufflers was wounded at

169

the siege of Mons in 1691. He became a marshal of France in 1693. He defended Namur in 1695 and Lille in 1708 and, though compelled to surrender on both occasions, won high esteem. He and Villars were in joint command in 1709 at the defeat of Malplaquet, and he extricated the French troops with great skill after Villars was wounded. He retired, worn out, immediately after.

BOUGAINVILLE, Louis Antoine de (1729-1811), French South Pacific explorer, made many notable voyages of which that of 1767-9 to Tahiti, Samoa, the New Hebrides and the Solomon Is was the most important. His Voyage Round the World (1772) helped to popularise the contemporary admiration for the noble savage.

BOULEVARD. This word, connected with the English 'bulwark', originally indicated a town wall. When town walls began to be pulled down in the 18th cent. the word was transferred to the wide streets laid out on their sites. Their width and linear plan permitted effective use of artillery against urban disorder, and this is said to have been an important motive for the plan of modern Paris.

BOULOGNE (France) belonged to the Counts of Ponthieu from 965 to 1234, to the Ds. of Brabant until 1419, to Burgundy until 1477 when Louis XI of France seized it. Despite its shortage of natural facilities, it has always had an importance from its closeness to the English coast. The English besieged it and took it in 1544, but the French retook it and kept it. From 1803 to 1805 it was the scene of Bonaparte's preparations for the invasion of Britain, and of much indecisive small-boat fighting in which Nelson figured. In World War I it was a major British supply port and under British military administration. In World War II the Germans used it as a submarine base. *See* FLANDERS-2 & 8.

From the mid 19th cent. it was a port for the increasingly regular cross-Channel steamers to Folkestone. After World War II the ferry services through Folkestone increased considerably because of the wartime damage to Dover, which was not fully repaired until the 1970s. It became the French end of the Channel Tunnel in the 1990s.

BOULOGNE (Lat = BONOVIA). English Honour entitled in 1219 to the service of 108-122 knights and some parts of them; it comprised a varying number of manors in Essex, Cambridgeshire, Hertfordshire, Suffolk and Huntingdon with outliers in Oxfordshire and Somerset.

BOULTON, Matthew (1728-1809), a Birmingham engineer, began in his father's business as a silver stamper, but showed an inspired inventiveness first in his father's work and then in methods, such as by inlay, in dealing with other metals. In 1775 he went into partnership with James Watt, and Boulton & Watt became famous as pioneers of machine tools. In 1797 their minting machines produced the entire new British copper coinage. He also invented an impulse pumping system.

BOUNDARY COMMISSIONS are of three types. **(1) INTERNATIONAL.** The only case in the U.K. was the 1924 Commission to settle the Ulster-Eire frontier. It consisted of members from both sides under a neutral chairman and its function was, like other such commissions, to act as an arbitrator between agreed limits. In contrast, the next two types do not arbitrate but propose boundaries at intervals of 10-15 years in accordance with criteria imposed by statute but in the light of local representations. **(2) PARLIAMENTARY.** These review House of Commons constituencies in order to achieve, where possible, equality of electorates within respectively England, Scotland, Wales and N. Ireland. The criteria for the four areas differ so that England is slightly under-represented, the others over-represeneed. Actually, equality is seldom attained and the predominant statistical criterion tends to result in local ties being ignored (*see* GERRYMANDER). **(3) LOCAL GOVT.** Separate commissions exist for the four countries to keep local govt. areas under review with a view to effective and convenient administration in the light of demographic changes. This principal also ignores local ties and modern districts have mostly become aggregations based on resources.

Boundaries proposed by (2) are subject to parliamentary confirmation: those by (3) by the responsible minister (in 1996 the Sec. of State for the Environment). In practice both sorts of commissions take longer than their statutorily allotted periods and, the purpose being different, their proposals seldom coincide.

BOUNTY, H.M.S. *See* BLIGH.

BOUNTY. (1) Was the sum paid at naval recruiting offices in wartime from about 1700 onwards. It was in two parts. The Royal bounty was 30s for an able seaman and 25s for an ordinary seaman, to which the borough might add £2. By 1795 these figures had risen to £4 and, in London, to as much as £40. "Bounty hunters" under this system took the money, deserted, changed their name and applied at another office. Bounties were abolished in 1857. **(2)** An old expression for a govt. grant to encourage a particular activity. **(3)** *See* TARIFF.

BOURASSA, Henri (1868-1952). Canadian and especially Quebec nationalist, who opposed Canadian involvement in the Boer War, and conscription in World War I.

BOURBON. (1) The first association of this great Lordship with French royalty began in 1272 when Beatrice of Bourbon married Robert, the sixth *s.* of Louis IX. Their descendants were Ds. of Bourbon until the death in 1505 of Pierre who had married Anne, *d.* of Louis XI. Their only child Suzanne married a relative, Charles of Montpensier. At his death the fief passed to Antoine, who was descended from an ancestor of Charles of Montpensier and the Condé and Conti families. Antoine married Jeanne d'Albret, heiress of the Kingdom of Navarre, and on her father's death in 1554 Antoine became K. of Navarre in right of his wife. Their son, Henri, was thus heir both to Navarre and to Bourbon. He also had a distant claim to the French crown by descent from Louis IX. Through deaths and civil wars, this claim was made good in 1589 when he ascended the throne as Henri IV.

(2) *The French Bourbon Kings* were Henri IV 1589-1610 (assassinated), Louis XIII 1610-43; Louis XIV 1643-1715; Louis XV 1715-74; Louis XVI 1774-93 (guillotined). "Louis XVII" the child of Louis XVI disappeared during the Revolution and was never traced; Louis XVIII 1814-24; Charles X 1824-30 (abdicated) and finally Louis Philippe 1830-48 (abdicated) who was descended from Louis XIV's brother, Philippe, D. of Orleans.

(3) *The Spanish Bourbons.* In 1700 Louis XIV accepted the Spanish Crown for Philippe D. of Anjou, the Dauphin's second son (*see* SPANISH SUCCESSION. WAR OF). He became Philip V 1700-46; He was followed by Ferdinand VI 1746-59; Charles III 1759-88; Charles IV 1788-1808 (deposed by Bonaparte); Ferdinand VII 1814-33; Isabella II 1833-70 (abdicated); Alphonso XII 1875-85; and Alphonso XIII 1885-1931 (abdicated). *See* CARLISM. ESP.-4,5.

(4) *The Neapolitan Bourbons.* The alliance between Spain, France and Savoy against Austria under the T. of Escorial (1733) brought a Spanish army under the future Charles III of Spain. He quickly overran the Kingdom, and was recognised in 1738 as K. of Naples and Sicily, but these monarchies were to remain distinct from Spain. Hence, when Charles succeeded in Spain in 1759, he resigned them to his son who became Ferdinand IV of Naples and III of Sicily, and changed his title to Ferdinand I of the Two Sicilies. He reigned, with Bonapartist and Muratist interruptions, until 1825, and was followed by Francis I 1825-30; Ferdinand II (*Bomba*) 1830-59, and Francis II 1859-60 (abdicated).

BOURCHIER or BOURGCHIER. The founder of the family eminence was **(1) Robert (?-1349) 1st Ld. BOURCHIER** who, though a layman, was Lord Chancellor in 1340-1, but was chiefly distinguished as a soldier in the French wars. His grandson **(2) William (?-1420)** was brilliantly wed to Anne (c. 1382-1438) *d.* and heiress of Thomas of Woodstock and widow of Edmund Mortimer, E. of Stafford. He served the King in France, fighting at Agincourt (1415) and was later Capt. of Dieppe and E. of Eu. Three of his sons became peers **(3) Henry (?-?), E. of ESSEX** was thrice Treasurer. **(4) William (?-?)** was **Ld. FITZWARIN** by marriage and **(5) John (?-?)** became **Ld. BERNERS (?-?)**. A further son of (2), **(6) Thomas (c. 1410-86) Bp of Worcester (1435-43), of Ely (1443-54), Abp. of Canterbury (1454)** had not gone far at Oxford when he gained a clutch of prebends, and, before he became Chanc. of the University (1434-7), Henry VI had recommended him for the see of Worcester, to which, despite papal protests against his youth, he was elected. He rose steadily by brains and tact and was briefly Lord Chanc. in 1455-6. Politically, he was a modest mediator between York and Lancaster, and in 1467 Edward IV got him a cardinalate but he had to wait till 1473 for his hat. Parts of his manor at Knole (Kent) survive. **(7) John 2nd Ld. BERNERS (1467-1533)**, grandson of the first Lord, served with distinction as a soldier in France and Scotland and was an accomplished courtier. He devoted much of his leisure to literary pursuits especially in translations from French and Spanish, of which Froissart's *Chronicles* (1523-5) is the best known for its distinctly English style.

BOURKE, Sir Richard (1777-1855). *See* AUSTRALIA-5.

BOURNE, Hugh (1772-1852), a Staffordshire carpenter and popular Methodist preacher, repeatedly defied resolutions of the Wesleyan Methodist Conference and was expelled in 1808. His congregations supported him and in 1812 he established the new denomination of Primitive Methodism, which differs from the Wesleyan by an even greater simplicity of habits. His later travels spread interest to Ireland, Canada and the U.S.A.

BOURNEMOUTH (Dorset). Always, after the coming of the railway, a holiday resort, the population rose from 695 in 1851 to 37,000 in 1890 when it was incorporated, and to 144,000 in 1972, by boundary extensions as well as natural increase. In 1974 it was transferred to Dorset.

BOURNVILLE. *See* CADBURY, GEORGE.

BOURSE **(Fr = purse). (1)** 500 Turkish piastres. **(2)** A stock exchange, especially in Paris or Brussels.

BOUVERIE. *See* PLEYDELL-BOUVERIE.

BOUVINES, B. of (27 July 1214). In pursuit of his political ambitions Philip Augustus of France supported the Hohenstaufen claims in Germany, and attacked his more independent vassals at home. This resulted in a coalition between the Emperor Otto IV, some French vassals, including Raynald of Boulogne, Ferdinand, Count of Flanders and K. John of England, who wanted to recover Normandy and other lost Angevin possessions. The continental allies, with an English contingent, would assemble in Flanders in the spring of 1214 and advance upon the Isle of France from the north, while John landed at La Rochelle, raised Anjou and Aquitaine, and marched up from the south-west. The advance from Flanders did not take place, and Philip Augustus had plenty of time to assemble and dispose his forces. In the upshot he advanced against Flanders, while John was defeated at La Roche-aux-Moines in Poitou early in July. Meantime Philip Augustus manoeuvred the other confederates out of their entrenched camp at Valenciennes. After some further marching and counter marching the armies met south of Lille, and after desperate fighting the confederates were overthrown. The emperor fled, and Raynald and Ferdinand were captured. This event had great repercussions. Otto could no longer resist the claims of his rival Frederick II; Philip Augustus had no further trouble with his northern feudatories; and John was so weakened and impoverished that he could not oppose the baronial demands which culminated in Magna Carta.

BOW. *See* ARCHERY.

BOW CHURCH (London), so-called from the arches (bows) of its crypt, was well known because of its position on the London market street of Cheapside, to which traders resorted from all parts. The Abp. of Canterbury's chief court (the Court of Arches) sat there, and still did i.e. in 1976 for the confirmation of episcopal elections. Birth within the sound of its bells, or those of the rival church at Stratford-after-Bow, is said to be the qualification of a Cockney. The original church, except the crypt, was destroyed in the Great Fire, rebuilt by Wren, largely destroyed in World War II and restored.

BOWDLER, Thomas (1754-1825) published his *Family Shakespeare* in 1818, and later, an edition of Gibbon's *Decline and Fall of the Roman Empire*. He wrote in the former that 'those words and expressions are omitted which cannot with propriety be read aloud in a family', and published the latter 'with the careful omissions of all passages of an irreligious or immoral tendency'. Commonly but erroneously considered typical of the Victorian era (which he never saw), his name has passed into the language amid ridicule.

BOWER, Walter (1385-1449). Abbot of Inchholm, from 1418, had to fortify this island monastery against English raiders, but meanwhile spent the dangerous summer seasons on the mainland, *inter alia* raising James I's ransom (1423-4). He was also custodian of the secluded Countess of Ross (1430-2) and in Oct. 1432 successfully opposed the English peace terms on the ground that the Scots could not make peace without French consent. Between 1440 and 1447 he amplified and continued the *Scotichronicon* version of Fordun's *Chronica Gentis Scotorum* (Lat = Chronicle of the Scottish Nation). The passages on the period 1418 to 1447, when it ends, are well informed.

BOWLER HAT, BILLYCOCK, BROWN DERBY or GOODGODSTER (Fr = *Chapeau Melon*). This singular headgear, regarded by foreigners as the mark of the true Briton, originated when William Coke, known as Billy Coke, E. of Leicester, to reduce the effects of hunting accidents, asked the brothers Bowler, hatters of Bermondsey, to design a hard hat. In 1837 he wore a brown one at the Derby where it was greeted with universal surprise. The French novelist, Proust, at a loss for a name, described it horticulturally.

BOWLING, NINE PINS, TEN PINS or SKITTLES is said to have originated in Germany as a religious ritual converted into a monastic game. In England it was amongst the games forbidden in 1365 in favour of archery. Later attempts to suppress it were entirely ineffectual, and in 1530 Henry VIII set a bad example by adding a bowling alley to Whitehall Palace.

BOWLS, already in vogue in 13th cent., became the object of hostile legislation in 14th and 15th because bowlers' use of village greens interfered with archery. When firearms superseded the bow, legislative hostility continued because of the games' association with taverns, but, with the 16th cent introduction of the bias, its popularity grew, as witness Drake's famous match at Plymouth Hoe in 1588; James I and his sons played and so did many notabilities after the Restoration. After 1688 it again declined into a tavern pastime, from which it was rescued by Scottish and Australian interest at the end of the 19th cent. Modern organised bowls on sophisticated greens originated with the formation of the Scottish Bowling Assn. in 1892. Similar bodies had covered the rest of the U.K. by 1904.

BOWRING, Sir John (1792-1872), linguist, friend and executor of Jeremy Bentham and M.P. from 1835 to 1837 and from 1841 to 1849. He became consul at Canton (1849-53), and Gov. of Hong Kong in 1854. His high-handedness mainly caused the unjustifiable *Arrow* war. Later he negotiated a useful commercial treaty with Siam.

BOW STREET, -RUNNERS near Covent Garden (London).

The early 18th cent. brothels, disorderly drinking booths and petty crime of the immediate area made some sort of magisterial authority desirable, and from 1735 Sir Thomas Vail, an acting J.P., found it convenient to live in Bow Street and hold courts in his house. His successor, the novelist Henry Fielding, established the Bow Street Runners, who were process servers and a primitive police and detective force. Fielding and his brother persuaded Parliament to enact the Gin Tax which had a powerfully calming local effect. The Runners continued to operate until superseded by the new police in the 1830s.

BOXER 'RISING'. *See* CHINA-33 to 35.

BOXING. 17th cent. London Prize fighters fought barefisted and with no holds barred. The first recognised Champion of England (in this style) was James Figg who held the title from 1719 until, probably, 1734. Jack Broughton was champion from about 1736 to 1750. His standing enabled him to establish the first rules, and also in 1747 the first boxing school, in the Haymarket. This attracted the gentry, and the sport began to be respectable. He also invented a rudimentary boxing glove. He lost his position in 1750 to a foul by one Jack Stack under whom boxing reverted to a form of brawl. This lasted until about 1780 when Tom Johnson became champion, re-established Broughton's rules and was in his turn defeated by Ben Brain in 1791.

Ben Brain was shortly afterwards defeated by Daniel Mendoza, celebrated as the first scientific boxer. In 1795 Mendoza was defeated by the even more famous Gentleman Jackson (who grabbed his hair). It was Jackson who taught the English upper classes to box. Broughton's rules were in due course revised, and adopted in 1839 under the name of the London Prize Ring Rules. These introduced the 24 foot roped ring, and prohibited kicking, gouging, butting and biting.

In 1860 there was a notorious or famous fight at Farnborough between the American John Heenan and the English Tom Sayers, which went on for 37 rounds when the crowd invaded the ring. It then continued for five more before being declared a draw. This and other disorderly events impelled John Chambers of the Amateur Athletic Club to devise new rules: gloves were to be worn and wrestling forbidden. The match was divided into standard rounds and the count of ten introduced. These rules appeared in 1867 and the 8th Marquess of QUEENSBURY lent his name to them in order to win back the support of the gentry who had begun to drift away. The Queensbury Rules gradually gained gound, though many famous boxers continued under the old rules or even under both new and old until the end of the century. By this time magistrates were beginning to frown on prize fighting both in Britain and in the U.S.A., and in the last decade of the 19th cent. it became extinct. In the 1970s even boxing under the Rules was criticised for its possible tendency to result in brain-damage.

BOYCOTT. In Sept. 1880 Capt. Charles Boycott, Lord Erne's estate agent in Co. Mayo, Ireland, refused to reduce rents and at Parnell's instigation was the first to be ignored and isolated by the local population which had been organised by the Land League. The harvest had to be gathered by imported labour under guard, and Boycott had eventually to leave the district.

BOYD, distinguished and notoriously anti-English family of western Scotland. **William (1704-46) 12th Ld. BOYD, 4th E. of KILMARNOCK (1717),** a dissipated lord who succeeded to an encumbered estate, joined the Jacobite rebellion of 1745 to better himself by a change of dynasty. Captured at Culloden (1746) he was condemned for treason, and was the last peer to be publicly beheaded for it.

BOYD-ORR, John Boyd-Orr, 1st Ld. (1880-1971). Nobel prizewinner in 1949 he published his book *Food, Health and Income* in 1936 and this became the foundation of the very efficient British food rationing system which did so much to assist the victory in World War II. He was director of F.A.O. from 1945 to 1948.

BOYER, Abel (1667-1729). Huguenot who settled in London in 1689. He published an Annual Register (of events) from 1703 to 1713, a monthly periodical called *The Political State of Great Britain* from 1711, Anglo-French dictionaries, and *Histories of William III* (1702) and *Queen Anne* (1722).

BOYLE. This famous and versatile mainly Irish family originated at Ledbury (Herefords), but some members of the mediaeval family moved to Faversham in Kent. **(1) John (1563-1620)** was Bp. of Cork. His younger brother **(2) Richard (1566-1643) 1st Ld. YOUGHAL (1616) and 1st E. of CORK (1620)** the ('Great Earl'), began as clerk to Sir Richard Manwood, then Chief Baron of the Exchequer. There being no future with him, Boyle went in 1588 to Ireland with introductions to all the best people, and obtained an escheatorship. He was prosecuted on several charges involving dishonesty, but the Munster rebellion of 1592 supervened and Essex offered him employment. Later he was examined before the Star Chamber on the charges but successfully countercharged his accuser, Sir Henry Wallop, and obtained his dismissal from the treasurership of Ireland. He then became clerk of the council of Munster under the presidency of Sir Geo. Carew who enabled him to buy out Sir Walter Raleigh's immense southern Munster estates for a mere £1000. This founded the family fortunes and gave Boyle himself immense power as well as riches in Munster, for he developed the land and industries as well as built castles. By 1612 he was an Irish privy councillor: and by 1633 when Strafford became Lord Deputy, he was the greatest man in Ireland.

The two clashed on public and personal issues. Strafford intended to establish an efficient royal govt. The existence of powerful feudatories like Cork was contrary to this design. The King's poverty led to inquiries into the titles to private estates: Cork's titles were not always good. Strafford was domineering and tactless, Cork patient and devious. The Irish, both native and colonial, recognised Cork as their best protector. There was never an open quarrel, but Strafford found himself decreasingly able to carry out his policy in the face of local indifference; and all the while suspicion of his military intentions against England grew. Eventually Strafford was recalled and impeached, and Cork gave evidence against him with apparent reluctance. In 1641 on his return the Irish rebellion broke out, but Cork was ready for it, raised his tenantry, and put down the Munster rebels at the B. of Liscarrol (3 Sept. 1642).

Of his fifteen children seven married noblemen, four were ennobled in his lifetime, and one was the famous scientist. His eldest having died at Liscarrol, he was succeeded by his second son (*see* **(6)** *below*). Of his cousins **(3) Michael (1580-1645)** was Bp. of Waterford; **(4) Richard (?-1645)** was Bp. of Tuam and his son **(5) Michael the younger (?1609-1702)** was Abp. of Armagh. **(6) Richard (1612-97) 1st E. of BURLINGTON and 2nd E. of CORK** was a strong supporter of Charles I in the Civil War, but lived relatively unmolested in Ireland under the Protectorate. He was Lord Treasurer of Ireland from 1660 to 1695 and built Burlington House, London, where he lived and made his reputation. He managed to combine these activities with the Lord Lieutenancy of Yorkshire. His brother **(7) Roger (1621-79) 1st Ld. BROGHILL and 1st E. of ORRERY (1660)** was much trusted for his personal character by both King and Parliament. Though sympathetic to royalists, he fought the Irish rebels in the 1640s. Charles I's execution caused him to leave public life but he eventually decided to offer his services to Charles II. His intentions became known to Cromwell who, recognising his Irish experience, persuaded him to accept a commission in the army then setting out to conquer Ireland. Accordingly he was involved in Cromwell's and Ireton's reconquest, though not in the memorable atrocities. He also sat in Cromwell's 1654 parliament for Cork, and in 1656 not only for Cork but for Edinburgh where he was for a year a popular Lord President of the Council. In 1657 he became one of Cromwell's peers, and a prime mover of the idea of making Cromwell King. After Oliver's death he tried to establish Richard Cromwell in the Protectorship, but when it became clear that the Commonwealth was ending he went to Ireland and secured it for the King. He spent most of the rest of his active career as President of Munster, resigning in 1668. He was also a poet and playwright. **(8) Robert (1627-91)** the scientist, though said to have been averse from linguistic studies, mastered French, Italian, Greek, Hebrew, Syriac and Chaldee. He knew Wren and employed Robert Hooke. After various adventures he settled in Oxford in 1654 and set up his laboratory. He invented the air pump in 1659; published the proof of 'Boyles Law' in 1662 and was a leading founder of the Royal Society. It elected him president in 1680, but he refused office. Among his achievements was the formulation of an atomic theory which has formed the basis of physics ever since. **(9) Richard (1695-1753) 3rd E. of BURLINGTON and 4th E. of CORK,** held a variety of local posts and in 1715 was Lord Treasurer of Ireland. He is, however, famous as an architect, as a patron of arts and as the reconstructor of Burlington House. He furthered the career of Bp. Berkeley, the poet Gay, the architect Kent, the sculptor Inigo Jones and the composer Handel. **(10) Henry (?-1725) Ld. CARLETON (1714),** a grandson of the first E. of Burlington was M.P. for Tamworth from 1689 to 1690, for Cambridge University from 1692 to 1705 and for Westminster from 1705 to 1710. He was Lord Treasurer of Ireland from 1704 to 1710 and from 1708 to 1710 Sec. of State in England in succession to Harley. From 1721 to 1725 he was Lord President under Walpole. He left Carlton (*sic*) House to the Prince of Wales. **(11) Henry (1682-1764) 1st E. of SHANNON (1756),** a grandson of the first E. of Orrery was an Irish politician and a member of the Irish House of Commons from 1715 until 1756. In 1729 he organised a successful resistance to Walpole's attempt to gain a 21 year grant of taxes, and in 1733 he became Speaker as well. The grandson of **(7), (12) Charles (1676-1731) 1st Ld. BOYLE (1713) 4th E. of ORRERY (1703)** was an English M.P. from 1701 to 1705, then a general, and then helped to negotiate the P. of Utrecht. He was a Lord of the Bedchamber to George I and a patron of Graham the astronomer, who named his astronomical invention an 'Orrery' after him. His son **(13) John (1707-62) 5th E. of CORK (1753) and 5th E. of ORRERY** was mainly a literary patron. A descendent **(14) William Henry (1873-1967) 12th E. (1934)** a naval captain in World War I co-operated with T. E. Lawrence in his Hejaz campaign; in 1933 he became C-in-C Home Fleet and in 1937 C-in-C Portsmouth. He became Admiral of the Fleet in 1938. In 1939 he was given command of the countermanded Finnish expedition and so, as it were, inherited the naval aspect of the Norwegian campaign, suffering the disadvantages of the character of Gen. Mackesy, its military commander. The govt. solved the impasse by putting him in supreme command. The Narvik victories resulted, but by then the German strategic threat to France forced the abandonment of the campaign.

BOYNE, B. of the (1 July 1690). The Franco-Jacobite forces of James II had failed to conquer Ulster, which became a point of entry for the troops of William III. French troops under Lauzun reached Dublin in Apr, but these were exchanged for Irish regiments. In June William's infantry and artillery arrived at Belfast and Carrickfergus, and he advanced southwards. James and Lauzun barred his way behind the tidal R. Boyne near

Drogheda, but neglected to link up with the Drogheda garrison on their right, or to occupy effectively a ford and bridge beyond their left, or to fortify their front. William planned to launch a frontal attack across the river when the tide had fallen, and simultaneously to force the bridge and ford and so outflank the Jacobite left. Nothing happened as planned. The flanking force set out too late to come into action, but the frontal assault was a greater success than expected, for some raw Irish Jacobite troops in the centre fled. When James realised that a threat was developing on his left he beat an orderly retreat towards Dublin which was abandoned a few days later. The casualties on both sides were slight. Nine days later, however, the Anglo-Dutch fleet was defeated off Beachy Head.

Appreciating the professional quality of William's troops, James went to France to raise reinforcements or possibly take advantage of the temporary French naval superiority to make a direct attempt on England; but the French preferred to sustain the war in Ireland, which continued for another year until the Jacobite disaster at the decisive B. of Aughrim. The B. of the Boyne thus has a greater symbolic than real importance, especially for Northern Irish Protestants who still invoke its memory.

BOY PATRIOTS. *See* GEORGE II-7.

BOY SCOUTS. *See* BADEN-POWELL.

BOYS, John (1749-1824) agricultural writer, developed the Southdown breed of sheep.

BOYS' BRIGADE was founded in Oct. 1883 by William Alexander Smith (1854-1914) as an Anglican welfare organisation for boys. Not dissimilar in technique from the Boy Scouts, it antedated them by a quarter of a century.

BOYS CLUBS and NAT. ASSN. of. The Boys Club movement was launched to alleviate the post-World War I depression for children of the urban poor and unemployed, especially in the East End of London, by encouraging self-reliance. The idea spread rapidly assisted by funds and practical help from many public schools, and the Assn. was formed in 1925. By 1972 there were about 2000 such clubs. *See* GEORGE VI.

BRABANT. The modern Dutch and Belgian Brabants with Antwerp, were disputed from 1106 to 1159 between the Houses of Louvain and Limburg when the Louvains prevailed. Henry I of Louvain changed the name of the area, now a Duchy, to Brabant in 1190. John 1(1261-94) bought Limburg in 1283 and defeated and killed John of Luxemburg at Woeringen in 1298. John II (1294-1312) and John III (1312-55) conceded the fiscal and judicial liberties which culminated in the 'great charter' celebrated as *La Joyeuse Entrée* (Jan. 1356).

Brabant had become the leading mercantile and manufacturing area in Europe and factionalism between burgher and guild interests was endemic. This now broke into dynastic struggles which were really class wars between the husbands of John III's daughters, namely Wenceslas of Luxemburg who had married Johanna and was supported by the guilds, and Louis II of Flanders who had married Margaret and upheld the burghers. By 1383 Johanna's party had secured a precarious hegemony, and her husband was dead. The disposal of her interests was of enormous European importance, not least to England which, having taken Calais nearby in 1346, had established her wealthy trading staple there. In the upshot, she bequeathed her interests to Margaret's daughter, Margaret of Flanders, who had married Philip the Bold of Burgundy, and accordingly through the passage of Brabant in 1406 to their second son Anthony, to the main Burgundian family in 1430, English trade and politics became entangled with Burgundian affairs. By the marriage between Mary of Burgundy and the Archduke Maximilian, and the T. of Arras, Brabant eventually passed to the Habsburgs in 1482, and so to Spain.

During the Dutch wars of independence, Brabant was

conquered by Maurice and Frederick Henry of Orange, and ceded to the United Provinces by Spain at the P. of Westphalia (1648). As it was administered for the benefit of the other provinces this part then became known as the **Lands of the Generality**. South Brabant was ceded to Austria under the P. of Utrecht (1713). The two parts remain respectively part of Holland and Belgium.

BRABAZON, Lord. *See* MOORE-BRABAZON.

BRACKEN, Brendan (1901-58) 1st Vist. (1952). A wild youth, he was shipped off to Australia to work on a sheep farm in 1916. A legacy enabled him to return to Britain where, though 19, he was accepted as a pupil at Sedbergh. In the early 1920s he met Winston Churchill with whom he was associated until his death. In 1924 he became a publisher, and also showed a flair for journalism and ran the *Financial News*. In 1929 with Churchill's help he became M.P. for N. Paddington. In 1939 he was Churchill's P.P.S. first at the Admiralty and then from 1940 at 10 Downing Street. His knowledge of journalism led to his appointment as Min. of Information in 1941, and this office he held until 1945 when he was briefly First Lord of the Admiralty in Churchill's caretaker govt. He then lost N. Paddington but was returned for Bournemouth. In 1951 he declined office but accepted a viscountcy. His health was deteriorating. He never took his seat in the Lords and he died of cancer in 1958.

His somewhat brash and fiery personality led to unfounded speculation that his constant presence with Churchill could be explained only if he were Churchill's illegitimate son. Clementine Churchill mistrusted his influence over her husband. He left his fortune to Churchill College, Cambridge.

BRACKNELL. *See* NEW TOWNS.

BRACTON or BRATTON, Henry (?-1268), a west countryman employed as a Justice in Eyre and of the King's Bench in the 1240s and 1250s. he settled down as Archdeacon of Barnstaple, and from 1264 as Chancellor of Exeter cathedral. His *De Legibus et Consuetudinibus Angliae* (Lat = The Laws and Customs of England) is a detailed account of almost the whole of English law in his time. It relies on decided cases and references to Roman law, but may have been of composite authorship first written in the 1220s and 1230s, and then revived by him in the 1250s. Many 13th and 14th cent. copies were made and there is a Norman French version called BRITTON. Historically minded lawyers used the Latin text increasingly in the late 15th cent, and in the 16th it was printed. This gave it a new lease of life, mainly as a source of political ammunition in the Tudor and Stuart controversies.

BRADDOCK, Maj-Gen Edward (1695-1755) was C-in-C in North America in 1755, and led the disastrous expedition against Fort Duquesne in which much of his force was lost and himself mortally wounded under the irregular tactics of the French-led woodsman.

BRADFORD (Yorks) was a trading centre from early times, receiving a market charter in 1251, and a fair in 1294. In 1311 there was already a fulling mill, and by Henry VIII's reign the cloth trade was well established. Woollens declined in the 17th and 18th cents, but in 1798 the first steam powered worsted mill was erected; alpaca processing was begun by Salt in 1836 and mohair in 1840. Silk manufacture was introduced shortly afterwards, and the wool exchange was built in 1867 to accommodate the dealings of the great already existing international wool market. The manufacture of and dealings in woollens and raw wool continued on a large scale till World War II when interruption of imports and bombing brought an abrupt decline from which the industry did not recover. The diversification which followed was accompanied in the 1970s by a considerable immigration, especially of Indians.

BRADFORD-ON-AVON (Wilts). Cenwalh of Wessex fought a battle here in 652 and there was a royal manor as well as a monastery over which St. Aldhelm ruled until 705. The Danes sacked the monastery in 1003; shortly after, the manor was granted to the Nunnery of Shaftesbury which held it until the Reformation. In the middle ages the place was very rich as a centre of the wool trade and a manufactory of broadcloth, and Flemish merchants settled there under Edward III. After the Reformation there was a long slow decline despite the eventual introduction of weaving machinery; the last cloth mill closed in 1809.

BRADLAUGH, Charles (1833-91), free thinker and politician, entered political journalism in 1853, published articles and pamphlets under the pseudonym of 'Iconoclast' and spoke at open air meetings. In 1858 he launched his platform campaign based mainly on religious free thought and republicanism, and soon acquired an extremist following. In 1860 he founded the weekly *National Reformer;* in 1866 he joined the parliamentary reform league and at a riotous meeting in Hyde Park persuaded it to defy the police. He wrote the first draft of the Fenian proclamation of 1867.

He stood unsuccessfully for Northampton in 1868 (when he abandoned the pseudonym) and 1874, but was elected at his third attempt in 1880. It then took him six years actually to take his seat in the House, for he refused to swear the oath of allegiance on the Bible and the authorities (at one time or another a select committee, the House as a whole and the courts) would not accept an affirmation (*see next entry*). His opponents' motives were more political than legalistic, but after seven exclusions or expulsions and re-elections, the issue was settled in his favour after the elections of Nov. 1885 by the new Speaker.

He was simultaneously involved in other battles. He was prosecuted in 1868 for refusing to give security that no blasphemy or sedition would appear in the *National Reformer,* and made the govt's case appear so ridiculous that the requirement was withdrawn. This was a notable step in freeing the press. At the same period he obtained a change in the law of evidence enabling the courts to hear evidence from free-thinkers. His advanced views made it impossible after 1870 to get a regular job, and he lived on the willing support of his friends and by writing, and in 1874 he began his eleven year long collaboration with Annie Besant in the *National Reformer*. In 1878 they were unsuccessfully prosecuted as publishers of a pamphlet on birth control. In 1885 they parted company because she would not support his objections to socialism, and during the four and a half years of his unchallenged membership of the Commons he was a liberal, but markedly active in supporting private members bills, and in Indian matters. In 1889 he attended the Indian National Congress at Bombay. He also became very popular with the Commons who just before his death unanimously expunged his expulsions from its journals.

BRADLAUGH v GOSSETT (1884) *(See previous entry).* The House of Commons resolved not to allow Charles Bradlaugh to take the oath as an M.P. and directed that he be excluded until he engaged not to attempt to take the oath in disregard of the resolution. He attempted to enter and Gossett, the Serjeant-at-Arms, ejected him. Bradlaugh sued Gossett for an injunction to restrain him from carrying out the Order of the House. In giving judgement for the defendant, the Queen's Bench Division held that some rights are to be exercised out of Parliament and will be protected by the courts, while others must be exercised, if at all, within the walls of the House, and are dependent upon the resolutions of the House. In such matters it must be assumed that the House is acting within its own view of the law, and the court cannot inquire into it. This amounted to a declaration that the House is in sole control of its proceedings.

BRADLEY, James (1693-1762), Savilian prof. of astronomy at Oxford from 1721, and Astronomer Royal from 1742, had calculated the propagation of light from the sun to earth and developed the theory of the aberration of light by 1729. He published his discovery of the nutation of the earth's axis to the Royal Society in 1747, and his calculations helped Lord Macclesfield to harmonise the English and Gregorian calendars. By now well known to politicians, he persuaded the govt. in 1752 to provide funds to make important improvements at Greenwich Observatory.

BRADMAN, Sir Donald George (1908-), a sensational cricketer who dominated the game from 1929 to 1948. He began by scoring 452 runs (not out) against Queensland and 334 against the M.C.C. and finished with 29 centuries.

BRADSHAW, John (1602-59), a prominent and also a fanatically republican barrister, presided over the court which tried Charles I. He had to overrule the legal objections to the court's legality, but obstructed the King's conduct of his own case. Later, he attacked Cromwell's dissolution of the Rump, opposed the Protectorate and was compelled to retire. He was buried at Westminster Abbey but dug up again and gibetted at the Restoration.

BRADWARDINE, Thomas (?-1349), *Doctor Profundus,* established between 1320 and 1335 a reputation as a theologian, philosopher and mathematician. His distinguished *De causa Dei contra Pelagium et de virtute causarum ad suos Mertonenses* (Lat = God's case against Pelagius and the power of causality, delivered to his friends at Merton) was completed in 1344. He countered the nominalist views of Ockham and others by logical and mathematical arguments based on the Augustinian theology of grace. He held human actions to be devoid of all merit and man as incapable of overcoming the least temptation without the grace of God.

By 1335 he had joined the household of Richard de Bury, and shortly afterwards he became a King's chaplain and probably confessor to the royal household. He died of the Black Death within a week of his consecration as Abp. of Canterbury.

BRAEMAR with CRATHIE constitute a parish larger than some older Scots counties. Braemar was the scene of the E. of Mar's Jacobite meeting (Aug. 1715) which decided to support the Old Pretender and raised his standard. The castle, built by a previous Earl in 1628 was garrisoned after the rebellion of 1745 and given artillery fortifications. The well-known annual Braemar Gathering for Highland music and sports was started in 1832 by a Wrights' Friendly Society and acquired impetus when Balmoral (in the parish) was bought by Q. Victoria.

BRAG. A bluffing card game (the predecessor of poker) fashionable in the 18th cent.

BRAGANZA. *See* AVIS. Portuguese royal house, descended from Afonso, D. of Braganza (?-1451), an illegitimate son of K. João I. Duke João I claimed the throne at the death of the childless K. Henry II in 1580, but was driven out by the Spaniards. He died in 1583 and his claims passed to Duke Antonio whom the English supported. When Portugal regained its independence in 1640 Duke João II, grandson of Duke João I, became king as João IV. His pious and likeable daughter Catherine married Charles II.

On the French invasion in 1807 João VI moved, with British help, to Brazil whence he returned in 1821 leaving his son Pedro behind as regent. Pedro proclaimed himself Emperor of an independent Brazil as Pedro I in 1822. In 1826 he also became K. of Portugal, but resigned that throne to his young daughter Maria, with his brother Miguel as regent. Miguel predictably proclaimed himself King, but could not hold the position, and was driven into exile in 1833 in favour of Maria. Meanwhile Pedro I abdicated the throne of Brazil in 1831 in favour of the infant Pedro II, who reigned under the regency of a series of non-royal politicians until declared of age by parliament in 1840. In Portugal Maria was followed in 1833 by Louis, who reigned until 1889, when the Emperor Pedro II of Brazil abdicated in favour of a republic. Louis was succeeded on the Portuguese throne by Carlos who was assassinated in 1908, and then by Manoel II who abdicated in Oct. 1910.

BRAHE, Tycho (1546-1601) the Danish astronomer installed his first observatory at Herritzvad in 1571 and discovered the new star of Cassiopeia on 11th Nov. 1572. In his *De Nova Stella* (Lat = The New Star) published in 1573, he proved that Cassiopeia was beyond the moon. Between 1576 and 1598 he built Uranienborg and Stellaborg (the forerunners of all modern observatories) on the island of Hven, and compiled his star catalogue. At the accession of Christian IV in 1596, he moved to the protection of the Emperor Rudolf II at Prague in 1599. He was joined shortly before his death by Keppler.

BRAHMANISM. *See* HINDUISM.

BRAHMAPUTRA RIVER or TSANGPO or JAMUNA (Tibet and India). The Bengal section of this immense river flowed south-eastwards through Mymensingh (Nasirabad) down to Bairab Bazar and so through the Meghna, until the early years of the 19th cent. when there was a catastrophic change of course southwards to join the Ganges 90 miles to the west. The identity of the Brahmaputra with the Tsangpo was first established for British authorities in 1884-6, but the actual connection between the two was not fully surveyed until 1924.

BRAHMIN. *See* CASTE.

BRAHMO SAMAJ. Hindu reformist sect founded or inspired in Bengal by Ram Mohan Roy in about 1828, but properly organised by Devandranath Tagore (1817-1905) on a monotheistic basis in 1842. It regarded the Vedas as divinely inspired, but for tactical reasons opposed the abolition of caste. It spread to most north Indian provinces and Madras, but after 1857 it began to split between the purely religious followers of Tagore, and social reformers who followed Keshab Chandra Sen (1838-84). Sen's movement again split in 1878 when, despite its condemnation of immature marriage, Sen married his infant daughter to the Maharajah of Kutch Behar. The younger members then formed the anti-Christian (i.e. nationalist) **SADHARAN SAMAJ.** *See also* TAGORE, RABINDRANATH.

BRAINWASHING. A coercive technique of conversion used by Chinese communists between 1921 and 1958. It attracted attention in the west between 1949 and 1953 as a result of the confessions and apparent conversions to communism of western prisoners in the Korean and Vietnamese wars. It appears to leave the convert (whether or not reconverted) with an abiding sense of submission to his mentor.

BRAITHWAITE, John (1797-1870), an inventive mechanical engineer, ventilated the House of Lords by forced draught, designed the donkey engine, built the first workable fire engine, with Ericsson built the locomotive Novelty which achieved 60 mph in 1829, and fitted a canal boat with a propeller.

BRAKE, BRACK (Scot.) Ground *broken* for cultivation.

BRAMAH, Joseph (1748-1814), a versatile inventor interested in fluids, responsible amongst other things for the public house beer engine, a hydraulic press, and the first screw propellers for ships. His work drew attention to the need for standardised parts.

BRAMHAM PARK (Yorks). Q. Anne mansion built by 1st Ld. Bingley between 1698 and 1710.

BRAMWELL, George William Wilshere (1808-92) 1st Ld. (1881) usually known as Baron Bramwell. This exceptionally gifted lawyer drafted (with James Willes) the important Common Law Procedure Act, 1852, and was mainly responsible for the Companies Act 1862. He became a judge as a Baron of the Exchequer in 1856 and was a member of the Judicature Commission of 1867 whose labours resulted in the reorganisation of the courts by the Judicature Act 1873. He refused a seat on the Privy Council in 1871.

BRAN THE BLESSED (BENDIGEIDFRAN) son of LLYR. A towering British king devoted to poetry and music who was converted into a saint by the Church. His head was buried on the site of the White Tower in the Tower of London, but exhumed by K. Arthur.

BRANDENBURG or MARK (i.e. March of) BRANDENBURG or briefly THE MARK. Recent Brandenburg arose after the collapse of the older Margraviate of Brandenburg which had become an electorate under the Golden Bull of 1356. In 1411 the Roman K. Sigismund appointed Frederick VI of Hohenzollern (r. 1411-40), Burggraf of Nuremberg, as his local hereditary gov. and in 1415 conferred on him the dormant electorate. He is known as the Elector Frederick I. He was succeeded by the 'Iron Elector' Frederick II (r. 1440-70). Between them they reassembled its scattered, illegally alienated and largely ungoverned lands including Berlin (then unimportant) and Cölln on the Spree opposite it. Albert Achilles (r. 1470-86) established an efficient financial administration, and by the *Dispositio Achillea* of 1473 laid down the indivisibility of the dynastic lands and the rules of succession. His nephew Joachim I (r. 1499-1535) established an uniform legal code and a university at Frankfort on the Oder. He also in 1529 obtained the reaffirmation and imperial confirmation of a Pact of Mutual Succession made with the princes (Piasts) of Pomerania in 1388. This treaty (of Grimnitz), because it involved the possession of the great port of Stettin, had important results later on. So had the activities of the Teutonic Order which was converted to Lutheranism. Its lands were partitioned. In 1525 the High Master, Albrecht of Hohenzollern, appropriated East Prussia and set himself up as the hereditary Duke under the Polish Crown, and the rule of the Order in the Duchy was liquidated.

Joachim I, however, remained a determined enemy of the Reformation. Not so his successor Joachim II (r. 1535-71) who carried through a church reform and monastic secularisation on the Saxon model, nor Johann Georg (r. 1571-98) who annexed several adjacent bishoprics.

Thus far the electoral power had, in a territorial sense, expanded gradually. It was now to become not only much enlarged but far flung. In 1614 Johann Sigismund acquired the detached western territory of Cleves, and in 1618 he inherited the equally detached Duchy of Prussia from the last descendent of Duke Albrecht. These events and the reversionary claim to Stettin involved the Hohenzollerns in European politics from Russia to Holland. Johann Sigismund died in 1619 at the opening of the Thirty Years War; George William (r. 1619-40) his pacific son was unable to protect his territory from the warring armies. By 1640, at the accession of Frederick William, called the GREAT ELECTOR, the inheritance had been devastated by famine, pestilence and the Swedes, and had to be rebuilt from its foundations. The Great Elector concluded that a state with such widespread political involvements must be militarily strong or go under. This was the principle of his refoundation which created the Prussian state. *See* PRUSSIA.

BRANDING. A man was entitled to benefit of clergy only once. If he had enjoyed it he was branded on the thumb as a simple and indelible record of the fact.

BRANDON, Charles (?-1545) 1st Vist. LISLE (1513) and D. of SUFFOLK (1514) (both of the second creation). This unscrupulous upstart was the son of William Brandon, Henry VII's standard bearer killed at Bosworth. Brought up at court, he became a personal friend of P. Henry (Henry VIII) who began to promote him as soon as he became King. By 1512 he had accumulated many lucrative minor offices and also the wardship of Elizabeth Grey, Viscountess Lisle, with whom, though already

married, he contracted a marriage in 1513. Later she repudiated the marriage. In the same year he was marshal of the army in the operations against Thérouanne and Tournai, and shortly after was sent to negotiate support for a further campaign with Margaret of Savoy, regent of the Netherlands. It seems that he (now D. of Suffolk) made amorous advances to her. In Oct. 1514 he went to Paris as ambassador, technically to the coronation of Mary, Henry VIII's sister, as Queen to Louis XII, but actually to arrange a meeting between the two kings. Louis, however, died in Jan. and Suffolk was immediately returned on a further mission to his successor Francis I. This time, if not before, he made successful advances to the newly widowed queen, whom he secretly married. This marriage was not only polygamous: it scandalised the caste-conscious older nobility, and it had to be regularised by a papal bull. His position and probably his life were saved by Card. Wolsey. Suffolk, however, maintained his place by always agreeing with the King. When Wolsey failed to secure the Aragon divorce, Suffolk turned against Wolsey. He was Lord High Steward at the coronation of Anne Boleyn, and helped to suppress the Yorkshire and Lincolnshire rebellion of 1536. In 1541 he was one of the commissioners who tried the 'accomplices' of the unlucky Q. Katherine Howard. In 1544 he commanded the attack on Boulogne. He died in his bed.

BRANDON, Gregory (?-?) and his son **Richard (?-1649)**, common hangmen of London. Richard beheaded Strafford, Laud and Charles I.

BRANDY. *See* SPIRITS.

BRANKS (mostly Scots). An iron headpiece with a bar projecting into the mouth used as a gag for scolds.

BRANT, Joseph. *See* IROQUOIS.

BRASENOSE. *See* OXFORD UNIVERSITY.

BRAOSE. A Norman family which succeeded in the gap left by the fall of the house of Montgomery in the Welsh March and was later, like others, enmeshed in the affairs of Munster. **(1) Philip (fl. late 12th cent.)** was Lord of Brecon and commanded some of Henry II's troops against Wexford, as a result of which he was granted as much of the Waterford country as he could conquer in 1177. He failed to make the conquest and his nephew **(2) William (?-1211)** bought the rights, such as they were, in 1201. K. John also granted him further rights of conquest in Wales and he took Abergavenny, Brecon, Builth and Radnor, but provoked by that monarch's rapacity, rebelled and fled to the French court. John seized his wife and a young son and starved them to death at Windsor. Of his other sons **(3) Giles** was Bp. of Hereford and **(4) Reginald (fl. 1214)** recovered his father's lands in 1214, married Gwladys *d.* of the Welsh P. Llywellin and became one of the most powerful Marcher lords until his death.

BRASIL, BRAZIL or HY BRAZIL, a legendary Atlantean island still marked on some charts as late as 1853.

BRASSES used as church monuments are in fact made of latten. The earliest (1231) surviving is at Verden (Germany). The earliest (1277) in England is at Stoke d'Abernon (Surrey). Brasses were made regularly until about 1610 and then very intermittently until 1773. A few modern revivals exist.

BRASSEY (1) Thomas (1805-70), famous for his incorruptibility, was contractor for many large railways including the Great Northern from London to Yorkshire (1847-51), the Canadian Grand Trunk (1852-9) and others in the Crimea, Australia, Argentina and India. His son **(2) Thomas (1836-1918) 1st E. of BRASSEY (1886)** became liberal M.P. for Hastings in 1868, and served in political offices in the Admiralty from 1880 to 1885. In 1886 he founded *Brassey's Naval Annual,* an international naval reference work. He was gov. of Victoria from 1895 to 1900. His wife **(3) Anna (1839-87)** was a well known traveller, especially by sea.

BRATTICE, BRETTASCHE or _HOURD_. A wooden gallery built out from the top of a castle wall to command its base. Later replaced by a stone equivalent called MACHICOLATION.

BRAWLING is fighting in a church or churchyard. It became common during the mid-16th cent. when rival sects were apt

> To prove their doctrine orthodox
> By apostolic blows and knocks.
> (Samuel Butler: _Hudibras_)

It was made an offence in 1551.

BRAY, VICAR OF. A ballad of unknown authorship tells how the Vicar of this Thameside village kept his ecclesiastical living between the reigns of Charles II and George I. Despite the words of the ballad, it is believed that the story of the vicar's fickleness of faith is about Simon Alleyn, vicar from 1540 to 1588. In any case,

> This is the law I will maintain
> Until my dying day, sir,
> That whatsoever King may reign
> I will be the Vicar of Bray, Sir!

BRAY, Sir Reynold (?-1503) served in Lady Margaret Beaufort's household and so came to the notice of and got employment with Henry, D. of Richmond, for whom he recruited troops in Wales. Henry as King made him Chanc. of the important Duchy of Lancaster and from 1492 he generally concerned in financial administration of royal private property. He was also a distinguished architect. He designed, built, left his insignia in and was buried at St. George's Chapel, Windsor and is credited with the very similar Henry VII Chapel at Westminster, most of St. Mary's at Oxford and the tower of St. Mary's Taunton.

BRAZIL. (1) In 1500, acting on Vasco da Gama's sailing directions, Pedro Alvares Cabral, on his way to India, bore too far west and on 22 Apr. sighted Brazil. As it was within the demarcation of Tordesillas he claimed it for Portugal, which however took little further till 1533. Then João III divided it into fifteen hereditary captaincies and distributed them for colonisation. Only two, São Paolo in the south and Pemambuco in the north, flourished. Meanwhile French corsairs helped themselves to the valuable red brazil wood, and government scarcely existed. In 1549 João changed the system and appointed a governor; he made Bahia the capital, introduced a rudimentary crown administration, and protected the important places. This at last encouraged substantial colonisation.

(2) The new measures were timely, for in 1555 the French under Villegagnon seized the Rio de Janeiro. Part of the impetus behind this came from protestant support, which was withdrawn when Villegagnon broke his promise of religious toleration; and he was forced to surrender to the Portuguese, who then founded the city as a protection against future incursions.

(3) With Portugal under Spain between 1580 and 1640 Brazil became a natural target for Spain's enemies, particularly the Dutch. They briefly occupied Bahia in 1624, and in 1630 a great expedition seized Pernambuco, and set up a colonial administration under a prince of the House of Orange. His policies, however, proved too enlightened for his financial backers in Amsterdam; in 1644 he resigned. His successors being both less competent and more oppressive, unrest among the Portuguese settlers led to a revolt under João Fernandez Vieira, who expelled the Dutch in 1654.

(4) Brazilian subsequent history has four major features. In the first two centuries the main wealth was in sugar, especially around Pernambuco. It was exported to Europe, and was a great source of revenue to the Portuguese kings. This needed much capital, machinery and especially slaves (imported from Angola), and so there was endemic border warfare and sustained penetrations of the interior. In the south these took the form of expeditions called bandeiras which sometimes lasted for years and resembled Great Treks. Brazil, thus, secondly, expanded westwards far beyond the Tordesillas line. Thirdly, the discovery of gold in 1693 brought on a gold rush which resulted in further large imports of African slaves and the transfer of the capital to Rio de Janeiro in 1763. The fourth, a modern bandeira stage into the Amazon basin, occurred late in the 20th cent.

(5) Colonial reforms were begun in mid-18th cent. by the Marquis of Pombal; these included permitting migration from the Azores and Madeira, and recognition of equality between Indians and Portuguese. As in Spanish America, such enlightenment by a metropolitan govt. was not locally popular, and there were minor uprisings including one in 1789. In 1808, however, the situation was transformed; the French attacked Portugal; the royal family crossed the Atlantic, and Rio de Janeiro became the capital of Portugal. The tables were now turned; the Portuguese commercial monopoly had to be abolished, whereupon English commercial interests stepped in. By 1845 Brazil and the home country were on an equal footing, and when a Portuguese cortes tried in 1822 to put the clock back Brazil declared her independence, with Pedro, the Regent, as Emperor. _See_ COCHRANE-5

(6) The spectacular period of the empire lasted until 1889. Despite foreign wars, the population almost trebled, the gross national product increased tenfold, the public revenues 14-fold, and as a net creditor country, there was no foreign debt, but the political issue which overthrew the monarchy was slavery. Brazil had agreed to abolish the slave trade in 1831 but suppression was not effective until 1853 and brought the great slave plantation families into opposition to the crown. Emancipation in the U.S.A. increased the pressure on the govt. In 1871 the children of slaves were declared free; but the pressure for immediate emancipation of the rest simply increased. With intervening stages all slaves were freed in 1888. A conspiracy between the army and the 'best people' followed, and Pedro II was driven into exile in 1889.

(7) The honesty and order which had marked the last fifty years of the empire were now replaced by maladministration and confusion. Social conditions changed but little, for slave labour was replaced by immigrants from the Mediterranean; but the administration was corrupt, and the army had become a political force.

(8) Thus in forty years three govt. candidates for the presidency were declared elected contrary to the probable justice of the case. In 1930 after the last of these, Getulio Vargas led a successful military rebellion, seized power and established a centralised and authoritarian administration, known as the _Estado Novo_. He curtailed the rights of the states, introduced a censorship, bid for mass support by social legislation and, like other similar rulers, pursued a vigorous foreign policy. By Aug. 1942 Brazilian troops were fighting in Italy against the Axis, but with the end of the war see-saw politics began. Vargas was overthrown by the army, the Estado Novo was superseded by a more democratic dispensation, Vargas returned and tried to secure his position by inflationary wages and labour legislation, but in 1954 the army forced him to resign again and he committed suicide.

(9) After a further 18 months of political manoeuvring Kubitschek became Pres. with Goulart, Vargas' former Minister of Labour, as his vice-Pres. They inaugurated an era sometimes described as 'nationalism and public works', during which the new city of Brasilia was begun.

The capital was transferred there from Rio de Janeiro in 1960. The enormous investment was mostly sustained by foreign borrowing, and by 1989 Brazil had the highest *per capita* foreign debt in the world.

(10) Meanwhile social pressures, mainly upon the land, combined with the need for economic development to deal with the country's debts led to vast technologically supported migrations into the Amazon basin, accompanied by massacres and clearances for cattle farming. The brutality and possible ecological consequences of these operations were provoking worldwide protests in the 1990s.

BREAD. *See* YEAST.

BREAD AND ALE, ASSISE OF. Henry II attempted to establish a fixed relationship between the price and weight of a loaf by reference to the price of grain, and by inspection for quality. This was elaborated under Henry III in the assises of bread, wine and ale (probably 1256), and later legislation extended the principle to other foodstuffs such as fish. The system worked tolerably until the Black Death destabilised the cost of living and labour.

BREADALBANE, John Campbell (1635-1716) 1st E. of (1681). *See* CAMPBELL OF GLENORCHY-2

BREAKSPEARE, Nicholas (HADRIAN IV). *See* MISSIONS TO EUROPE-5.

BRÉAUTE, Fawkes de (?-1226), an unpleasant Norman mercenary and intimate of K. John, began a disreputable career as Sheriff of Glamorgan. In the civil war of 1215 he commanded a force to watch London. With this he took Bedford, and apparently in reward, was given the hand of Margaret, a wealthy heiress and connection by marriage of the Es. of Albemarle and Devon, together with several midland castles including Windsor and Northampton. He used their garrisons to despoil the I. of Ely.

At John's death Fawkes, presumably to ingratiate himself with the regency for Henry III, supported the new King against the French, and his troops fought in the victorious B. of Lincoln (1217). This brought him six shrievalties, and the ownership or control of his wife's and the E. of Devon's lands, but the regency demanded the surrender of the royal castles. He then gave covert support to Albemarle's insurrection, and when it failed took the Cross (it being unlawful to interfere with a crusader's property) but did not go. He assisted Hubert de Burgh in putting down the London insurrection of 1222, but sympathised with the Welsh rising of 1223, and was implicated in a baronial conspiracy to seize the Tower. This was connected with an attempt to secure the dismissal of Hubert who replied by calling the Council of Northampton the same year, at which Fawkes was at last compelled to surrender the castles. In 1224 judgment was given against him for 16 novel disseisins, and his brother William kidnapped one of the judges. Thereupon Fawkes was outlawed; he lost all his lands and was banished.

BRECON or ABERHONDU and BRECKNOCK or BRYCHEINIOGG. There had been a Roman fort close to Brecon, but otherwise little is known of this sparsely occupied country until Bernard of Newmarch killed Bleddwn ap Marenearch, the local chief, in 1091, built the castle in 1092 and later the Benedictine priory. A small town with guilds grew up and was chartered by the Bohuns. The area became a marcher lordship and the scene of continuous war and disorder. Llywelyn was killed in a foray near Builth. The wars lasted as late as the Act of Union of 1536 and the formation of the shire, and perhaps accounts for the deserted aspect of some of the landscape. Peace enabled a wool and leather industry to flourish in the towns in the 17th and 18th cents., and iron was worked until the opening of the S. Wales coalfields caused a workers' migrations southwards. The population has remained small. In 1951 it was under 50,000 and Brecon, the only borough, had 6500.

BREDA (Netherlands). Charles II lived in Breda during the later part of his exile and his manifesto before his restoration was issued from, and became known as the Declaration of Breda. The treaty which ended the second Anglo-Dutch war in 1667 was signed here.

BREECHES were worn in the 18th cent. mainly by the wealthy and the titled, but began to be superseded by trousers early in the reign of George III. They were so much a mark of class distinction in France that the revolutionaries called their supporters the breechless *(sans culottes)*.

BREECHES BIBLE otherwise the **GENEVA BIBLE (1560)** *see* BIBLE-4.

BREHON LAWS (Brehon = judge). These ancient Irish laws seem to have been written down and perhaps consolidated in about 438, but the only existing records are 8th to 13th cent. partial transcripts with commentaries and glossaries. The language is often archaic and obscure, but where they can be understood, they throw much light on ancient Celtic law and life. They deal with the training and work of judges, the nature of clans and their property, personal status, crime, contracts and the law of distress.

The Norman and English invaders brought their own law. This differed in most respects from the Brehon, especially in that Anglo-Norman land law was founded on feudal relationships based on ties of blood, whereas Brehon law presupposed the collective vesting of land in whole tribes, many of whose members were volunteers. The two systems, mutually incompatible as they were, existed side by side, but it was the policy of the invaders to impose their own at the expense of the other. Hence they frowned upon Anglo-Normans who went native, because intermarriage or concubinage between Norman and Irish too often resulted in feudal property coming under Brehon rules. Edward Bruce's invasion of 1318 accelerated this defeudalisation, but it was halted in 1366 by Clarence's statutes of Kilkenny: these imposed savage penalties on Anglo-Normans who 'went Irish' or intermarried with the Irish. The weakness of English rule resulted, however, in feudalism being confined to the Pale and a few other small areas for a century. When English power increased again the hold of Brehon law was loosened by the so-called surrenders and regrants (q.v.). In the 1390s, the 1530s and later, defeated Irish chieftains were allowed to make their peace on condition that they surrendered their lands; these were then regranted to them by the crown. Under Brehon law the chief could do no such thing because the land was owned collectively by the tribe: therefore a chief who made a surrender and accepted a regrant was necessarily repudiating the ways of his ancestors. This, combined with the successive Tudor colonisations ('plantations') steadily reduced the effective sway of Brehon law, which was ultimately abolished as law by an Irish Act of 1613.

BRENDAN, St. (or BRANDON, BRANDAN or BRENAIND) (c. 486-575) founder and Abbot of Clonfert (Galway). He seems to have travelled to the Scottish Is. and up the Clyde, and possibly to Wales. Such travels were not uncommon amongst Irish ecclesiastics, but his gave rise to the *Navigation of St Brendan,* in which he appears as the legendary hero of a sea voyage by a band of monks, in which a possible visit to America may be discerned.

BRENIN (Welsh = King). *See* WELSH LAW-1.

BRENNER PASS (Alps). Though this pass had a Roman road it was not a major trade route until the 14th cent. when it became important to the enormous Venetian spice trade; but there was no carriage road until 1772. The railway was completed in 1867. The Italian frontier was fixed at this pass in 1919.

BRENTFORD, Vist. *See* JOYNSON-HICKS.

BRENTON, Sir Jahleel (1770-1844), American loyalist, migrated to Britain, joined the Royal Navy, fought at Cape St. Vincent (1797) and was Saumarez's flag capt. at the B. of Algeçiras. He was a prisoner from 1803 until exchanged in 1806 and in 1810 single-handedly defeated a Franco-Neapolitan force off Ischia consisting of two ships, a cutter, a brig and seven gunboats, taking the brig. R-Adm. in 1830, he was Commissioner at the Cape from 1840.

BREST (France). The importance of this magnificent natural harbour in western Brittany was recognised very early. It was in English hands from 1342 to 1397. Richelieu began to develop it as a naval base in 1631, and Vauban fortified it in the 1660s, after which it became the principal French naval station on the Atlantic.

BREST-LITOVSK (BRESC) Ts. of (Dec. 1917-Mar. 1918) were negotiated during World War I between Germany (represented by von Kühlmann) and Austro-Hungary (Count Czernin) on the one side, and on the other the Russians (Joffe and Trotsky) and the Ukrainians (Sevryuk and Holubowiez). The situation was confused. The Russians were in the throes of military defeat by the Germans and of civil war. Lenin's Bolsheviks had gained much support by alone promising the war-weary population peace at any price. The Ukrainians demanded independence from Russia, and hostilities between them and the Russians broke out during the negotiations. Austro-Hungary was starving; Germany also needed food, but above all needed to bring her troops back for a decisive blow on the Western Front before American reinforcements turned the military scale against her.

Hence, the Russians wished to drag out the discussions; the Germans were determined to impose a quick settlement, while the Austrians were prepared to make concessions for Ukrainian grain; and the Ukrainians wanted a separate peace. On 9 Feb. 1918 the Ukrainian treaty was signed against Russian opposition, and Trotsky refused to negotiate further. On 18th the Germans resumed military operations, invaded Estonia and threatened Petrograd. On 24th the Russians agreed to negotiate again and the Russian treaty was signed on 3 Mar. Poland and the Baltic states were to be detached from Russia which was also to cede Kars, Ardahan and Batum to Turkey. There were also trade and indemnity provisions. The Ukrainian treaty was never effective for lack of a properly constituted Ukrainian national authority able to carry it out. The Russian treaty was annulled at the general armistice in Nov. 1918, but many of the ideas behind it survived and found their way into the final peace settlements.

BRÉTIGNY or CALAIS, T. of (1360) Edward II had captured the French K. John II at the B. of Poitiers (1356). This put him in a strong negotiating position when peace talks began at Brétigny near Chartres in May 1360. A truce was quickly agreed until Michaelmas 1361, and the principal negotiators, the Black Prince and the Dauphin, took back a draft treaty for ratification by the two Kings. This was to be a definitive peace under which Edward III renounced the French Crown and suzerainty over Brittany and Flanders in return for full sovereignty over all Aquitaine and of Montreuil, Ponthieu, Guines, Marck and Calais in the north. The three last constituted the Pale of Calais. John II was to be ransomed for 3M gold crowns, 600,000 cash down with hostages for six annual instalments of the rest. At Calais in Oct. 1360 the terms were amended by means of the so-called CLAUSULA *CEST ASSAVOIR* ("it is to be understood") so that the mutual renunciations of sovereignty were to be conditional upon the mutual transfer of ceded or conquered lands before Nov. 1361. These included the return of Normandy to France. The transfers could not physically be made in time. The formal renunciations never took place. Edward accepted 400,000 crowns and the hostages for John's release. The rest amounted to a tacit execution of the treaty. Edward dropped the title of King of France and ruled his French territories as alods without any protest from John, and the balance of the ransom was not paid.

In later times each side used the informal and partial execution of the treaty as an argument against its permanence, thus reviving when convenient the English claim to the French crown, and the French claim to the overlordship of the territories mentioned in it.

BRETT (1) William Baliol (1815-99) 1st Ld. ESHER (1885) 1st Vist. (1897) was Tory M.P. for Helston from 1866 to 1868 and sol-gen. in 1868 when he became a judge and in 1883 Master of the Rolls. His son **(2) Reginald Baliol (1852-1930) 2nd Vist.** was private sec. to the M. of Hartington from 1878 to 1885 and Liberal M.P. for Penryn from 1880 to 1885. He became a personal friend and courtier of Q. Victoria and organised her Diamond Jubilee in 1897. In 1902 he became a member of the R. Commission on the Conduct of the Boer War, and consequently in 1903 chairman of the War Office Reconstruction Committee which led to the creation of the Army Council and the General Staff. He joined the Committee on Imperial Defence in 1904, and gave powerful expert support to Haldane's military reforms at court and with ministers. In World War I he was engaged as a confidential liaison official with the French.

BRETTON WOODS AGREEMENT (July 1944) was the result of a United Nations monetary and financial conference which took place in the town of that name in New Hampshire, U.S.A. It was agreed to set up the International Monetary Fund, and the International Bank for Reconstruction and Development.

BRETTES AND SCOTS, LAWS OF, were Celtic codifications in use among the Britons (Bretts) of Cumbria and Strathclyde, and the Highland Scots. Their surviving fragments are concerned with *cro* (roughly *wergild*) computed in cows and based upon the status of the person killed or injured. They went out of use in England as a result of legislation by Edward I, and through desuetude in the 14th cent. in Scotland.

BRETWALDA ('Ruler of Britain'). A title used in the *Anglo-Saxon Chronicle* to distinguish K. Egbert and seven other kings of Anglo-Saxon states who had dominated their contemporaries. These seven were Aelle (Sussex) (c. 477); Ceawlin (Wessex) (560-91); Ethelbert (Kent) (560-616); Redwald (East Anglia) (616-27); the Northumbrians Edwin (616-32); Oswald (635-41) and Oswy (654-70). The *Chronicle* took the list (though not the title) from Bede. K. Ethelbald of Mercia (d. 757), for at least the last twenty years of his reign, claimed to be Bretwalda.

BREVET. A document promoting a military officer in rank without conferring more pay. The practice began in the British army after the Restoration, was common during and after the Peninsular War, and is not extinct.

BREVIA PLACITATA (Lat = Pleaded writs) is an anonymous collection in Law French of writs followed by their corresponding counts or pleadings. It dates originally from about 1260 and was used much as a precedent book by 13th cent. lawyers who added to it as the occasion arose.

BREVIARY. The number of different psalm and service books needed to ensure the proper observance of all festivals was inconveniently large, and as early as the 8th cent, Alcuin attempted to provide an abridgement (i.e. breviary) for general use. The reform of the liturgy of the Roman curia by Gregory VII (1073-85) produced the first authoritative "Roman" breviary though the earliest complete manuscript dates from 1099. It was adopted and spread throughout Europe by the Franciscans, but it did not supersede local breviaries until Pius V made it obligatory in 1568 in every diocese which could not show two centuries unchallenged use of its own. An adaptation of the Roman Breviary for private use was made by Card. Quiñones in 1535 and suppressed in 1558. This version was much used by the compilers of the English Prayer Book of 1549.

BREWSTER SESSIONS. The justices' meeting held annually in the first fortnight of Feb. to deal with liquor licences.

BRIAN BORU, BOROIMH, BORUMA or MacKENNEDY ('of the Tribute') (926-1014) youngest of three sons of Cennetig (or Kennedy) whose family claimed the alternate succession to the chiefship of Cashel, helped his brother Mathgamain in a series of campaigns against the Vikings, who were sometimes allied with some native Irish. In 967 they defeated the Limerick Vikings, and Mathgamain made himself K. of Munster but was murdered by a conspiracy of Munster chiefs. Brian then became head of the family or sept called the Dal Cais. He gradually overcame his brother's enemies and by 978 was chief of Cashel and thus K. of Munster.

Brian now led the Dal Cais against other provinces, and in 984 was acknowledged as K. of Leinster. In 988 he joined with the other Irish over-king, Mael Sechnaill II, in gaining a major victory over the Vikings, and shortly afterwards they divided the overlordship between them, but in 1002 they quarrelled and Brian led the Munstermen against the men of Connaught under Mael Sechnaill and established himself as sole effective overlord or High King of Ireland. The sub-kings and the Vikings recognised his position by giving hostages and visiting him at his palace at Kincora on the Shannon.

As High King, Brian's direct authority in the domestic affairs of the sub-Kingdoms, other than his own, was very limited, and his position as High King was uncertain because it was novel. It is doubtful if he would have consolidated it before he perished after his great victory over the Vikings and Irish rebels at Clontarf (1014), for he was already a very old man.

BRIAND, Aristide (1862-1932) a liberal socialist French statesman first became prime minister in July 1909 and held the office on ten subsequent occasions. His most important political acts included the introduction of three year military service in 1913 in reply to the Germans; the supersession in 1916 of General Joffre for General Nivelle; the negotiation of the Locarno Pact in 1925 and the Kellogg Pact of 1928. He was the most influential supporter of the League of Nations, and the principle of collective security.

BRICE'S DAY MASSACRE, St. (13 Nov. 1002). See ETHELRED II-6.

BRICG BOT (A.S. = Bridge duty). The landholder's obligation to maintain a bridge.

BRIDEWELL (= St Bridget's or St Bride's well) is in the City of London. Card. Wolsey built a palace there, which passed to the crown at his fall. This was given to the City in 1553 as a training institution for homeless apprentices who at that time were sturdy and often violent. The cells, meant for the more unruly, were soon used to confine other sorts of prisoner, especially vagrants and prostitutes, and so the place was long used simultaneously as a charitable teaching foundation and prison; hence the word "bridewell" came to mean a house of correction. The prison was closed in 1860 and the building demolished and replaced in 1863. The charity remains and the funds are used mainly to support K. Edward's School, Witley.

BRIDGE. Of the three varieties of this game, Bridge Whist superseded Whist between 1893, when it was introduced in New York (London 1894), Auction Bridge was introduced in London possibly from India in 1903, and adopted by the Portland Club in 1907. Contract Bridge developed simultaneously with Auction but did not become popular until Harry S. Vanderbilt devised his scoring system in 1927. By 1931 it had virtually supplanted Auction everywhere, and the players were numbered in tens of millions. The boom reached its peak in 1934.

BRIDGE OF SIGHS. From this enclosed but noticeable bridge, connecting the inquisitorial rooms in the Venetian ducal palace and the prison, the prisoners on their way could briefly glimpse busy waters and a public bridge below. The bridge, whose aspect was well known to European travellers, thus became a romantic symbol of hope and hopelessness.

BRIDGEMAN, Charles (?-1738) was gardener to George I and George II. He began the English naturalistic style of layout and designed Kensington Gardens, the Serpentine, and probably also the gardens at Richmond. He was the forerunner of Capability Brown and the Kents.

BRIDGEMAN (1) John (1577-1652) a chaplain to James I, was Bp. of Chester from 1619. As a strong opponent of nonconformity he was driven into retirement during the Commonwealth. His son **(2) Orlando (c. 1606-74)** became Chief Justice of Chester in 1638. He was M.P. for Wigan in the Long Parliament and sat in the Oxford Parliament in 1644. In 1660 he was made Chief Baron of the Exchequer and presided over the trial of the regicides. He immediately became Chief Justice of the Common Pleas. He was Lord Keeper from 1667 to 1672. As a lawyer he developed conveyancing techniques, particularly the 'strict settlement' by which English landed families could keep their estates in the family by a succession of bargains in each generation between life tenants and their successors, involving the breaking and re-creation of entails. The object was to prevent wastrels from eroding the family fortune (see BETTING), but it made it difficult to raise new capital for improvements.

BRIDGET, St. (1303-73) worked in Sweden from 1344 to 1350 and in Rome from 1350 until her death. She founded the Brigittine Order in 1370 and was the mother of St. Catherine of Sweden. She is not to be confused with the St. Bridget or Bride of early church dedications, who was probably a Celtic deity.

BRIDGETOWN. See BARBADOS.

BRIDGWATER Ds. and Es. of. See EGERTON; CANALS; TRANSPORT AND COMMUNICATIONS-4.

BRIDLEWAY. See HIGHWAY-1.

BRIDLINGTON AGREEMENT between the trade unions that they would not attempt to poach each other's membership.

BRIDPORT (Dorset). The earliest Charter of this town dates from 1253; from 1295 until 1868 it returned two members to Parliament and then until 1885 one. It was incorporated in 1619. Its main importance through many centuries lay in its rope-walks, some of which survived until 1950 and supplied the Royal Navy with most of its cordage from the 16th cent. onwards. See HEMP.

BRIDPORT. See HOOD.

BRIEF, originally meaning simply a letter, came to mean a letter from an authority, and so, often, a 'writ'. More specialised meanings include a papal letter of advice or remonstrance, or concerning discipline; a royal letter patent licensing a national church collection for a charitable object, and the collected papers and instructions used by a barrister or advocate to conduct a case in court.

BRIGANTES. This large British tribe occupied most of northern England except Humberside. At the coming of the Romans it was much divided by factions led by members of the royal family, some of whom intrigued with outside powers. In A.D. 50 the Queen, Cartimandua, made a treaty with the Romans, and in 51 handed over Caractacus to them, perhaps in accordance with the treaty. In 57 she quarrelled with her co-ruler and husband, Venutius, and seized his relatives, whereupon he fled over the frontier, raised a force and returned. The Romans intervened to restore order and confirmed Cartimandua in her position, but during the Roman civil wars of 68-9, Venutius drove her away. At the end of the civil war, the established Emperor Vespasian's new governor, Petillius Cerealis, methodically reduced the Brigantes (71-4), occupied York with the Ninth Legion and built the road from York to Carlisle. The subjugation was rounded off by Agricola's campaigns and fortifications in the Lowlands of Scotland between 79 and

84, and the construction of Hadrian's and the Antonine Walls. These deprived the tribe of its northern allies.

In c. 154-5, however, the Romans suffered disasters at the Walls in a widespread Brigantine revolt. This had to be suppressed with continental reinforcements in a campaign which seems to have put an end to the tribe as an entity.

BRIGGS, Henry (1561-1630), first Prof. of Geometry at Gresham College (1596 to 1620), persuaded Napier to use 10 as the logarithmic base. His immense set of logarithmic tables were the foundation of all subsequent such tables.

BRIGHAM and SALISBURY Ts. (1289-90) arose from negotiations between Edward I, Eric of Norway and the Scottish regency about the future of Eric's daughter Margaret (The Maid of Norway) who was also Edward's grandniece and who had succeeded to the Scottish throne at the age of three in 1286. Edward's suzerainty over Scotland was assumed, but by the Salisbury Agreement (Nov. 1289) Eric agreed to send the child to Scotland by Nov. 1290 free of marriage contracts, that she should not marry without Edward's consent, that Scots might be substituted for Norwegians in her household, and that Edward's mediation should be sought in issues and disputes touching the welfare of Scotland. Meanwhile Edward had obtained a papal dispensation for a marriage between his son Edward and Margaret (Nov. 1289), and in Mar. 1290 the Scottish magnates confirmed the Salisbury agreement at Brigham (near Berwick). The already advanced marriage negotiations were concluded at Brigham in Aug. 1290. The young Edward was to become K. of Scots, but Scotland was to remain separate under its own laws and customs. Margaret, however, died in Sept. The result was the turmoil in Scotland which Edward sought to resolve by the Great Cause (1291-2).

BRIGHT, John (1811-89), son of a Rochdale miller, first became prominent between 1834 and 1841 by his speeches against religious intolerance, church rates and capital punishment. His opposition to the Corn Laws brought him, from 1835, the lasting friendship of Cobden, and in 1840 he became treasurer of the Rochdale Anti-Corn Law League. In 1842 he and Cobden extended the campaign to the whole country and in 1843 he was elected M.P. for Durham. His indignation at the policies of the landed interest led him into some anomalous situations: in 1845 he defeated a proposal to reduce child factory-labour from 12 hours a day to 10 on the ground that shorter hours would raise costs, reduce demand and so raise unemployment. He also opposed the Maynooth grant. In the autumn of 1845 came the potato and other crop disasters, and the consequent Irish famine led to the repeal of the Corn Laws in 1846. The League was then dissolved. Meantime Bright became M.P. for Manchester and turned his attention to Ireland's difficulties after the famine. He favoured fundamental changes such as the partition of land amongst the cultivators, the sale of encumbered estates, and the disestablishment of the Irish church. His family interests also led him to an inquiry into the cotton trade, and he uncovered much evidence of maladministration in the HEIC as a result. This led him to advocate in 1853 the transfer of the govt. of India to the Crown. Events proved him right sooner than even he expected.

After 1853 he steadily opposed the drift towards war with Russia and the war itself and supported the peace negotiations. This made him unpopular, and in the election of Mar. 1857 he lost his seat: in 1858, however, he returned as M.P. for Birmingham just in time to make highly informed contributions to the debate on the Government of India Bill. In the next year he made probably the most important proposal of his career, namely the creation of common commercial interests as the basis of a treaty with France, so as to minimise mutual distrust and military expenditure. In 1860 he

and Cobden negotiated such a treaty and piloted the necessary fiscal legislation with difficulty through the Commons. Part of the bill (a repeal of the paper excise) was rejected by the Lords, and Bright then found himself in the thick of a constitutional crisis, which the Commons preferred to settle by a declaratory resolution.

The drift of the U.S.A. into civil war found Bright (though a cotton miller) on the side of the North at a time when most parliamentary opinion favoured the Confederates. In 1863 by a public campaign (and the unobtrusive support of the Prince Consort) he frustrated a motion in the Commons to recognise the Confederacy. His belief in liberty and popular govt. never waned, and in 1866-7 he was engaged in the furious franchise controversies of that time. In 1868 he became Gladstone's Pres. of the Board of Trade. In 1870, however, his health broke down and he resigned; and though still much engaged in politics, his influence was much attenuated. He held only minor office in the liberal govts. of his later years.

BRIGHTON (earlier BRYGHNESTON, BRIGHTHEMP-STON and BRIGHTHELMSTONE) was a minor fishing village until Richard Russell published his book on the medical uses of sea water, and settled there in 1754. His theories about sea bathing became fashionable when the P. of Wales (later George IV) first went there in 1783. The Prince patronised the place until 1827 and during this period, amongst other things, he spent many hundreds of thousands on the Pavilion. This attracted the nobility and gentry to Brighton, which developed an extensive, not invariably proper, hotel trade and became exceedingly prosperous even before the railway connected it to London in 1841. Q. Victoria sold the Pavilion to the Corporation in 1850. The original Chain Pier was built in 1823 and destroyed in a storm in 1896. The University of Sussex was established in 1964. Especially after World War II the town acquired a conference industry, one by-product of which was a spectacular I.R.A. attempt to blow up Mrs Thatcher, the then Prime Minister.

BRIGHT YOUNG THINGS, a fashion rather than a group among the wealthier generation which came of age just after World War I. They took refuge from the horrors of the war in a determined, sometimes alcoholic and often promiscuous, frivolity distantly related to the extra-vagances of surrealism. They figure a great deal in con-temporary humorous magazines and are portrayed in Evelyn Waugh's *Vile Bodies* (1930), by which time they were virtually extinct.

BRIGID or BRIDE, St. *See* MISSIONARIES IN BRITAIN AND IRELAND-3.

BRIG O'DEE. *See* JAMES VI-10.

BRILL, BRIEL or BRIELLE, a port on the estuary of the New Maas in Holland, was captured by the Sea Beggars in 1572, and held against the Spanish authorities. This was the beginning of the overt and eventually successful revolt of the Dutch mainland against Spain. *See* ELIZABETH I-14, 28.

BRINDABAN (Oudh, India). Sacred and popular place where the Hindu god Krishna dallied with the milkmaids.

BRINDLEY, James (1716-72) was the great engineer of the canal era. His first work was the coal canal from Worsley to Manchester in 1759, and he later built 370 miles of canals including the D. of Bridgwater's Manchester and Liverpool system, and the Grand Trunk Canal. *See* TRANSPORT AND COMMUNICATIONS.

BRINSLEY, John (?1570-1650) master of Ashby-de-la-Zouche school, published *Ludus Literarius* (Lat = The Letters Game), a treatise on the Grammar school curriculum in 1612, and was ejected on religious grounds from the mastership in 1620.

BRISBANE (Queensland) was discovered and settled as a penal colony in 1824 for the purpose of keeping the worst convicts away from Sydney. It was named after Sir Thomas Brisbane (q.v.). Free settlers were discouraged, but explorers and squatters were opening up the grazing country inland of the mountains. When transportation to N.S.W. was abolished in 1840 it became a civil parish and the land became available for purchase. As numbers grew, the settlers began to resent being governed from Sydney (600 miles away) and their demands for separation were granted.

BRISBANE (1) Sir Charles (?1769-1829), adventurous naval officer captured Curacao in 1807, and was gov. of St. Vincent from 1808. His brother **(2) Sir James (1774-1826)** helped to capture the Ionian Is. and establish the Republic of the Seven Isles (1808-10), and as C-in-C East Indies, concluded the First Burma War in 1825.

BRISBANE, Sir Thomas Makdougall (1773-1860) as gov. of N.S.W. from 1821 reformed the penal settlements and encouraged free immigration against heavy local opposition. He was also a distinguished and hard-working astronomer, who catalogued thousands of stars and established observatories at Brisbane, Largs and Makerstoun.

BRISTOL. This commercial port was important enough in the reign of Ethelred the Unready (978-1016) to have a mint, and it was part of a royal manor in Domesday. Its first charter (1155) was the model for other charters, notably in Ireland, whose original invasion was partly financed by Bristol merchants. The first mayor was elected in 1216. By the 13th cent. the growing trade made it necessary to enlarge the walls and docks, and in the 14th cent. there was a cloth industry based upon the Cotswold sheep runs, exporting to Ireland and the Spanish Peninsula with a return trade in wine from Bordeaux. The town became a separate county by charter in 1373. The extensive maritime activity led naturally to the transatlantic voyages of the Cabots, Pring, and James in the 16th cent. and to the incorporation of the Society of Merchant Venturers in 1552. It led equally naturally to the 17th cent. exploitation of slave and sugar trades, and to Caribbean piracy. Commercial rivalry with London created a small royalist majority in the early Civil War, and P. Rupert stormed the city in July 1643. It then became a major royalist economic and financial centre until the decline of the royalist fortunes after the B. of Naseby. In Sept. 1645 Fairfax retook if from Rupert.

The enormous fortunes made in the 18th cent. in slaves, sugar and piracy helped to found the great glass and pottery works, the new textile and leather industries and the tobacco and sugar businesses. At the same time Wesleyan and Quaker influences became strong and led to the sustained national agitations against the slave trade, which was suppressed in 1807. At the end of the 18th cent. Bristol began simultaneously to be used as a spa (which led to the building of Clifton) and to lose its primacy as a western port. Liverpool and the rising northern industries engrossed much of the shipping interest while the West Indian trade languished. With the rise of the railways the industrialisation of the south and the building of the motorways this trend was reversed in the 20th cent. with the development of Avonmouth, and its port. The university was chartered in 1909.

BRISTOL, Frederick Augustus Hervey, 4th E. of BRISTOL and Bp. of DERRY (1730-1803), a very rich man, known in his time as the Bishop of Bristol for short, inherited the title and the fortune in 1779. He travelled Europe in such style that large hotels in many capitals were and are named after him.

BRISTOL. *See* DIGBY; HERVEY.

BRISTOL RIOTS. *See* REFORM BILLS (1831-2)-4.

BRISTOL, T. of. *See* ELIZABETH I-15.

BRITAIN, B. of (10 July-15 Sept. 1940). The French surrender on 22 June, 1940, left Britain alone against the Germans (with their Russian supporter) and the Italians. The German Air-force *(Luftwaffe)* now devoted its strength to its attacks on Britain. These mass air operations are known as the Battle of Britain, but in fact there were two battles of which the second was in three phases with an epilogue known as the "Blitz". The Germans were under the supreme authority of Reichsmarschall Goering: on the British side the battle was fought by Fighter Command under Air Marshal Sir Hugh Dowding and No. 11 Group under Air Vice Marshal Park.

The *first battle* lasted from 10 July to 13 Aug. The *Luftwaffe* attacked merchant convoys in the Channel. The Germans lost 300 planes against 150 British, but the convoys were stopped. On 16 July Hitler ordered preparations to invade Britain, and on 13 Aug. the *second battle* began. The German object was to pave the way for the subjugation of Britain. This involved two not wholly consistent policies: firstly to destroy R.A.F. superiority in British skies, prevent harassment of a German seaborne invasion, and attack British naval and ground units; secondly to destroy British national morale and compel surrender by bombardment. The *Luftwaffe* was unequal to either task, but tried both.

In the first phase (13-18 Aug.) the *Luftwaffe* tried to provoke an air battle by attacking south east England in daylight with combined fleets of fighters and bombers. Dowding concentrated on the bombers and destroyed 236 aircraft for a loss of 95. The second and most dangerous phase now opened: the *Luftwaffe* concentrated on the single task of destroying the Kent fighter bases. This nearly succeeded: between 30 Aug. and 6 Sept. the Germans lost 225: the British losses had mounted to 185 and the fighter pilots were becoming exhausted. By now autumn was approaching and with it the end of invasion weather. Moreover on 25 Aug. the British began bombing German towns by night, including Berlin. Hitler wanted to reassure his public and to bring about a collapse in British morale before invasion became impossible. Thus on 7 Sept. at the moment when the *Luftwaffe* was nearest to victory, it was diverted to bombing London by day. This, the third phase, was a welcome relief. The main daylight effort was made on 15 Sept. The Germans lost 56 planes, the British 26. On 17 Sept. Hitler postponed the invasion until further notice. On 12 Oct. it was cancelled for the winter.

The final figures of aircraft losses were: Germans 1733, R.A.F. 915. These were much less than the respective pilots had reported from the heat of the battle.

The Blitz. A fourth phase, the night bombing of British cities, began contemporaneously with the third phase. This was known as the Blitz. London was bombed every night from 7 Sept. to 2 Nov. (long after the invasion had been postponed). Thereafter attacks were made on ports such as Liverpool, Newcastle and Plymouth, and industrial centres such as Manchester and Coventry. The last major raid took place at Birmingham on 14 May, 1941. Altogether 30,000 people were killed and 3,500,000 houses damaged or destroyed.

BRITANNIA FLAVIA. *See* BRITAIN, ROMAN-20; **INFERIOR.** *See* BRITAIN, ROMAN-16; **MAXIMA.** *See* BRITAIN, ROMAN-20; **PRIMA.** *See* BRITAIN, ROMAN-20; **SECUNDA.** *See* BRITAIN, ROMAN-20; **SUPERIOR.** *See* BRITAIN, ROMAN-16; **VALENTIA.** *See* BRITAIN, ROMAN-24.

BRITAIN BEFORE THE ROMAN CONQUEST (*see* CAESAR'S INVASIONS) **(1)** Spanish tin superseded British in the Roman market after Caesar's conquest of Brittany and, because it was nearer to Italy, held its own. The two important routes for general trade between the British Is. and the continent ran (i) from Ushant mostly by sea past or across Cornwall, and up the Irish Sea to Man, Ireland, Lancashire and Strathclyde; and (ii) from the Pas de Calais across the Straits, mostly by land to Kent and the midlands. The latter was liable to be disturbed by the politics of East and South Britain: the former only by the Atlantic weather. In 50 B.C. Caesar's ally Commius abandoned him and moved to Britain. He set up a Belgic kingdom in Sussex, and also dominated the Atrebates of Surrey and Hampshire. Roman civil wars prevented counter-action, and he was peacefully succeeded in 25 B.C. by his son Tincommius whose capital was at Silchester *(Calleva)*. There was much trade with the empire and some absorption of Roman culture in the South East, but meanwhile Catuvellaunian ambitions (cut short by Caesar) revived. Their King, Tasciovanus, took advantage of Roman frontier troubles (20-16 B.C.) to attack the Trinovantes, but Augustus warned him off. There was also a Roman political arrangement with Tincommius, who was under Catuvellaunian pressure; a Roman technical mission went there. Hence Tasciovanus turned his energy towards the midlands, already relatively well populated and cleared. He had subjected most of Northamptonshire by the time (about A.D. 5) his son Cymbeline succeeded him, with his capital at *Verulamium* (St. Albans). **(2)** The political movements which now follow represent the activities of small bodies of Belgic heroes or aristocrats and their retainers. Eppillus drove out Tincommius, who fled to Rome. He also superseded Dubnovellaunus, a chieftain in Kent who crossed the Thames and overthrew Addedomarus, the Trinovantian ruler. The latter so far had held his own against the Catuvellauni (A.D. 1-7). The Romans did not try to restore Tincommius, but recognised Eppillus upon whom they conferred the title of King *(Rex)*. The reason was that the confusion among the Trinovantes had drawn in Cymbeline who overran them (A.D. 9); a civil war might lead to the Sussex and Hampshire Belgae sharing their fate. Another palace revolution, however, brought Eppillus' brother Verica to power, and thereafter Eppillus' influence was confined to Kent. Cymbeline tried to take similar advantage of this situation, but Verica fended him off. A.D. 9 was the year when Varus' legions were lost in the Teutoburger Wald, and Cymbeline's aggressions were related to Roman inability to intervene. By this time he had established his capital at Colchester *(Camulodunum)*.

(3) The early period of Cymbeline and Verica was prosperous. Britain, through the two states, exported cattle and hides, corn, slaves and hounds, iron, gold, silver and pearls, and imported wine, glass and jewellery in return. The balance was so much to the Roman advantage ("beads for the natives") that they made alliances with both to keep the peace. Unfortunately relations could not remain static. Cymbeline was expanding into Kent and along the Upper Thames, while a brother, or half brother Epaticcus, was encroaching on the Atrebates. He took Silchester in A.D. 25. By A.D. 42 Verica's territory was reduced to a coastal strip around Chichester. A rebel son of Cymbeline, Adminius, invited Caligula to intervene in A.D. 40 but the troops mutinied. In 43 Verica went to Rome to invoke his alliance, and Claudius agreed. Cymbeline had just died, and his ambitious sons Caratacus and Togodumnus overran his territory besides that of the Dobunni. They demanded his extradition and instigated anti-Roman disturbances (perhaps coastal raids) when it was refused.

(4) Claudius' motives for invasion were probably (a) the need to re-establish prestige after Caligula's fiasco; (b) personal pride; (c) to reduce the dangerously strong military establishment in Gaul; (d) to tap British minerals and manpower; (e) to suppress political disaffection in Gaul associated with Druidism arising out of Roman hostility to human sacrifice as practised by the Druids. *See* BRITAIN, ROMAN.

BRITAIN, ROMAN. *See previous entry.* **A.** *Conquest –* *First Period* **(1)** The Claudian expedition of A.D. 43 under Aulus Plautius consisted of four legions (II Augusta, IX Hispana, XIV Gemina and XX Valeria) with auxiliary cavalry. It landed at Rutupiae (Ricliborough), crossed Kent, forced the Thames and stormed the Catuvellaunian capital at Camulodunum (Colchester). The chief, Togodumnus, was killed, his able brother Caratacus fled to Wales.

(2) The XX Legion garrisoned Colchester. The others fanned out building the following roads as their axes of advance. II (Great West Road). Commanded by Vespasian (later Emperor) this legion probably restored Verica and his Kingdom *(see para. 7 below)*. It proceeded steadily, storming hill forts in Wilts, Hampshire and Dorset (including Maiden Castle) and eventually reached Isca (Exeter). XIV (Watling Street) reached Ratae (Leicester). XI (Great North Road) reached Lindum (Lincoln). It was imperial policy to occupy only the fertile lowlands; and the Fosse Way, a *limes* (q.v.) was built from Exeter via Bath and Leicester to Lincoln and Brough-on-Humber. Plautius had completed it when he was succeeded by Publius Ostorius Scapula in A.D. 47.

(3) Caratacus raised the Silures and Ordovices with others, and attacked the *limes*. Scapula disarmed the tribes in his province, and counter-attacked. The original policy was abandoned. The XIVth legion extended Watling Street to Viroconium (Wroxeter) where it built a fortress. Colchester and Verulamium (St. Albans) became *coloniae* (municipalities of old soldiers) and the XXth advanced to Glevum (Gloucester). These moves, completed by A.D. 51, proved inadequate to enforce peace in the midlands. The XIVth with other elements reached the Dee. Thereupon Cartimandua, Q. of the Brigantes, sought Roman protection against a party hostile to her in her state. Scapula now led a punitive expedition against the Ordovices in Snowdonia; Caratacus fled to Brigantia and was betrayed by Cartimandua (A.D. 52). *See* CAER CARADOG.

(4) Cartimandua's Brigantian enemies were led by Venutius, her husband, who took the opportunity of a change of governor to attempt a palace revolution. Thus Aulus Didius Gallus (A.D. 52-7) and Quintus Veranius (A.D. 57-8) had to deal with a civil war just outside the province in which the aggressive Silures and the Britons of Anglesey supported Venutius. A philo-Roman victory was ensured only in A.D. 58 by Caius Suetonius Paullinus, the next gov., who attacked the Silures and destroyed the headquarters of Druidism in Anglesey.

B. *The Administration.* **(5)** The governor, styled *Legatus Augusti pro Praetore* (Delegate of the Emperor with praetorian powers) had his H.Q. at Colchester. He had two major officials who, however, were responsible direct to the emperor: these were the *Legatus Juridicus* (judicial delegate) and the *Procurator Augusti* (Representative of the Emperor). The former settled disputes involving Roman citizens or matters in which Roman laws specifically applied, but not disputes between natives under their own laws. The *Procurator* was responsible for raising taxes, remittances to Rome and accounting for taxes spent locally. His office was in London. The *Procurator* and the *Legatus* to some extent kept a watch on each other.

(6) The principal taxes were the *Annona*, paid in grain to supply the army; and two taxes paid in money, namely the *tributum soli* (land tax) based upon a survey carried out periodically by a high ranking senatorial *Legatus ad census accipiendos* (delegate to hold a census) specially appointed for each; and the *tributum capitis* (head tax) on property other than land. In addition the govt. disposed of public slaves and the revenues from large imperial estates.

(7) Within the province friendly tribes were ruled by their existing princes, but their authority did not automatically pass to their heirs under tribal custom. Verica's Kingdom *(Regnum)* was, however, unique in the empire in that Verica and Cogidubnus, his successor, bore the title *Rex et Legatus Augusti* (King and Delegate of the Emperor). The arrangement lasted until Cogidubnus' death in about A.D. 73. Its people became known as the *Regneses* (People of the Kingdom). The tribes were, as far as possible, organised into *Civitates* (states) each with a capital. Most capitals had a double name, of which the second part was the tribal name in the genitive plural (e.g. *Isca Dumnoniorum* = Isca of the Devonians = Exeter). The subunit of the *civitas* was the *pagus* (clan), mostly a village or two, and below this was the *vicus* (hamlet), perhaps only a country house with its labourers. The population, especially in the midlands and Wiltshire, was considerable, exceeding the mediaeval population. Roman *coloniae* were progressively intruded, land being expropriated and shared among ex-soldiers by way of pension. The tribal capitals were encouraged to Romanise themselves with fora, baths and so forth.

(8) The legions and the *Alae* (cavalry squadrons) were recruited elsewhere in the empire, the legions being quartered in fortified depots whence they garrisoned outposts, often for long periods. In addition there was the *Classis Britannica* (The British Fleet) based on Boulogne. These warlike formations tended, with time, to recruit locally, shed retired soldiers to become colonists and so to alter their own character and that of the population.

C. Confusion. (9) In the absence of most of the troops, there was an insurrection of the Iceni led by Boadicea (Boudicca) provoked by the behaviour of the procurator's representatives; they were joined by the Trinovantes who were discontented perhaps by land requisitions for the new *coloniae*. Colchester was burned; the IXth legion under Quintus Petillius Cerealis was ambushed and mostly destroyed. The commander of the IInd refused to move. Paullinus reached London with XIVth while Boadicea burned St. Albans. London had to be abandoned and was burned, but the tribes were defeated and Boadicea slain in a battle on Watling Street, probably near Towcester. Some 70,000 people had perished in the sack of the three towns. Paullinus was unbendingly severe in his treatment of the defeated.

(10) The Rome govt, however, had other ideas. Tyranny had provoked the rebellion, and extreme severity was only tyranny prolonged. The procurator was superseded and Paullinus was followed by Publius Petronius Turpilianus (62-3) and then by Marcus Trebellius Maximus (63-8). The attempt to subdue Wales was suspended and a more liberal regime sought to rebuild the economy. The time available, however, turned out to be short. Reinforcements were needed in Gaul whither the XIV had to be sent, and so the IInd Augusta was moved to Gloucester (A.D. 67). The XIVth returned, but civil war broke out in 68 (The Year of the Four Emperors) and the XIVth went abroad again and never returned. Thereupon Venutius overthrew Cartimandua, the Brigantes became permanently hostile and the peacekeeping arrangements which depended upon a permanent alliance with the Brigantes broke down. Vetius Bolanus (A.D. 68-71) could do no more than hold his own.

D. Conquest – Second Period. (11) In A.D. 71 Cerealis returned as gov. with a new legion (II Adjutrix) and a reversion to the forward policy. The IXth was advanced to Eboracum (York) in Brigantian territory where it could also protect the philo-Roman trading Parisi. IInd Adjutrix replaced it at Lincoln. Between A.D. 74 and 78 his successor, Sextus Julius Frontinus, campaigned extensively in Wales. These endless and expensive forays in hostile, largely mountainous country revealed the Roman dilemma. To retain the province profitably involved a limited military commitment which sooner or later tempted the adjacent tribes into aggression. To extend the area of military action to prevent such aggression not only reduced profitability but sucked into potential conflict further tribes in the background. No more troops being available, successive governors made do with varying forms of the same compromise, namely to maintain a military area north of the civil province.

(12) The policy was systematically followed by Gnaeus Julius Agricola (A.D. 78-84) who had served

under Paulinus and Cerealis. He began by a violent campaign in north Wales and Anglesey (*see* DRUIDS) to clear his flank and open up the lead and silver mines. There followed parallel northward movements by XXth from Chester (where it was replaced by the II Adjutrix) and IXth from York. In 81 he built a *limes* across the Forth-Clyde isthmus, which was narrow as well as a linguistic and tribal boundary between Caledonians and Britons. The Votadini (*see* GWYNEDD) were under pressure from the Selgovae whom Agricola overthrew. They became permanently philo-Roman. A campaign in A.D. 82 against the Novantae might have pacified the Lowlands if the Caledonian confederacy outside the new *limes* had not been aggressively restive. While the fleet reconnoitred the west coast Agricola campaigned in the eastern lowlands in 83 and eventually reached the area of Inverness; this led in A.D. 84 to a victorious battle at *Mons Graupius* (Fife), which crippled the highland tribes for fifty years.

E. Weakness. (13) These events did not please the govt. They were expensive and there was trouble in Dacia. Sallustius Lucullus (84-9) probably superseded Agricola. In 85 the Dacian war broke out and the British garrison could not be kept up to strength. The XXth accordingly was withdrawn to Chester (87) and IInd Adjutrix was moved south. Lucullus, however, was involved in a military conspiracy and executed in A.D. 89 by Domitian, and in A.D. 91 IInd Adjutrix was moved to the Danube. These events are probaby connected with the establishment of coloniae at *Lindum* (Lincoln) in c. 90 and at *Glevum* (Gloucester) c. 96 under Publius Metilius Nepos (95-7) who was succeeded by Titus Acilius Quietus (97-100) and then Lucius Neratius Marcellus (100-1). Troops were progressively moved to other parts of the empire, and in 105 and 106 (Brigantian?) rebellions caused the abandonment of the Scottish lowlands. There was war in Britain under Marcus Atilius Bradua (115-8) and again under Pomperius Falco (118-22). It seemed that Britain would either have to be reinforced or abandoned. In 121 the Emperor Hadrian arrived with the VIth Victrix to decide what should be done.

F. The Walls. (14) HADRIAN'S WALL was originally built hastily and partly of turf in order to deal with an urgent crisis. It was constructed from Tyne to Solway by VIth Victrix under Falco and the next gov. Aulus Platorius Nepos (122-5). The scheme was workable only if the rear was safe, but in the governorship of Marcus Appius Bradua (128-31) there was a Brigantian rebellion, the IXth Legion disappeared and VIth had to move to York. It seems likely that the wall, by interfering with long established traffic, provoked disturbances which seem to have been endemic under Sextus Julius Severus (131-5) and Publius Mummius Sisenna (135-8). Accordingly Quintus Lollius Urbicus (138-42) reverted to Agricola's policy, probably in response to an attack by the Selgovae and Novantae on the pro-Roman Votadini. First the Brigantes were violently assailed, and then the XXth Legion with reinforcements from Wales and the Pennines moved to the Forth-Clyde isthmus. They built the ANTONINE WALL, opened Hadrian's Wall and pacified the lowlands enough to enable the Votadini in the time of Gnaeus Papirius Aelianus (144-?) to abandon their hill forts.

(15) The previous pattern now reasserted itself. The troops were inadequate to maintain order in the rear. There were revolts, not only in Brigantia but in the Province, where Verulamium was burned. The Scots lowlands were evacuated again (154-5), and the names of the governors are unknown until Lucius Verus (155-8) arrived with reinforcements and reoccupied Hadrian's Wall. His successor (Longus or Longinus 158-61) briefly occupied the Antonine Wall but Marcus Statius Priscus Licinius Italicus (161-3) withdrew, and Sextus Calpurnius Agricola (163-?) replaced the turf parts of Hadrian's Wall with stone, and abandoned the Antonine frontier for the last time. This, however, failed to secure lasting order (*see also* BLACK DEATH OR PLAGUE). In 169 there was a rebellion in Wales and in 178 the tribes crossed the Wall and a gov. called Caerellius was killed in battle. In 180 Lucius Ulpius Marcellus arrived, and after successful punitive expeditions, negotiated the formation of the Lowland tribal confederacy of the Maeatae, to resist the Caledonians. This seems to have made for stability along Hadrian's Wall.

G. *Political Mutinies and Reorganisation* (16) In about 183 Priscus, Marcellus' successor, raised a mutiny which developed into a short rebellion. It was put down by two new legions which arrived in advance of the new gov. Publius Helvius Pertinax (185-7). In 192, however, the Emperor Commodus was assassinated. Decimus Clodius Albinus (gov. since 191) had been faced with Saxon seaborne raids and had had most of the towns turf walled. In 196 he proclaimed himself Emperor and took the legions to the continent where, in Feb. 197, he was defeated and killed by Severus. There were wholesale confiscations in the provinces (Spain, Gaul and Britain) which had supported Albinus, and these for some while disrupted the overseas trade, especially in Spanish wine. Moreover Caledonians and Maeatae raided the north while the Brigantes took to rural brigandage. Severus' representatives, Virius Lupus the gov. and Sextus Varius Marcellus the procurator were, however, able to lay the foundation of a new type of regime. The old province was reconstituted as *Britannia Superior* with a Consular governor: the north became the province of *Britannia Inferior* with a Praetorian governor. Coastal forts were built by the Consular Gaius Valerius Pudens (202-5) and the Praetorian L. Alfenus Senecio (205-6).

(17) In essence this represented civilian administration within an armoured shell; the new arrangements were consolidated by the arrival in 208 of the Emperor himself. His son Geta was put in charge of Brit. Sup. and was probably responsible for the martyrdom of St. Alban. The programme of fortification was pressed ahead, the Caledonians were attacked by sea (209) and a rebellion of the Maeatae put down (210). Severus died at York in 211. Caracalla completed the operations but provoked a brief military mutiny when he murdered Geta (212).

H. *Tranquillity.* (18) The new arrangements ushered in a frontier tranquillity which was to last until 296. It was a period of prosperity and social advance encouraged by Roman technology and education, and the example of the *coloniae*. In addition the capital towns of the tribal *civitates* acquired a strongly Roman character and in Brit. Sup. a farming economy based on large country houses ("villas") was widespread. The mines were exploited by Roman corporations or under military supervision, and a considerable industry worked for the occupying army and under its control. The general success of this administration may be gauged from the remarkable colonia at York, established in 237, and the pacification of the Brigantes by 244. The imperial civil wars which began in mid-century left the island unaffected, even though politically it formed part of Postumus' *Imperium Galliarum* (Empire of the Gauls) from 259 to 274.

(19) Three serious trends now developed. Rival emperors debased the coinage. This upset trade and formed the basis of an imperial inflation. Secondly, the Edict of the Emperor Caracalla, which enfranchised almost all free men, brought everyone under Roman law but exposed citizens equally to purely economic pressures, and, thirdly there were agrarian disturbances leading, from 245 to further urban fortification. After 268, Saxon piratical forays from Frisia affected the east coast as far as the Wash and also the Channel. The navies of the period were unable to keep up continuous patrols, but to improve matters a base for the *Classis Britannica*

was fortified at Richborough and another at Burgh Castle (Norfolk).

I. *Carausius, Further Reorganisation and Prosperity* (20) Aurelian reunited the empire in 274 and re-established confidence by a thorough reform of the coinage (274-84). The creation of defences against seaborne attack now went steadily ahead. Marcus Aurelius Mausaeus Carausius, praefect of the *Classis Britannica,* had a composite and wide ranging command against external, mostly seaborne incursions in the north-west of the empire. He apparently won a great victory in 285 in defence of Britain, but complicity with Saxon pirates was made a pretext for ordering his execution in 286. He was evidently plotting rebellion, for he subverted the XXXth legion in Holland, as well as the Classis and moved to Britain where the garrison received him enthusiastically as emperor. He defeated Diocletian in the Channel in 288 and there followed five years of military quiescence (due to the govt's other preoccupations) during which Carausius persistently sought recognition and Diocletian determinedly refused it. He brought the British coinage up to the reformed imperial standard, and had a mint too at Rotomagus (Rouen).

By 293 Diocletian had imposed the framework of his tetrarchic reforms, and was ready to mount his offensive to fit Carausius' territory into them. The Caesar Constantius won over the XXXth and took Boulogne. At this point Allectus, Carausius' finance minister, murdered him and assumed his throne. He had no hold on the British public; and when Constantius landed in 296 he was received as a saviour from the rapacity of Allectus' Frankish troops.

(21) Diocletian's empire-wide reforms effected a local intensification of the policy of Severus. From about 300 there were four civil provinces (*Britannia Maxima* based on London, *Prima* based on Caerleon, and *Secunda* and *Flavia* based on York and Lincoln). Each was governed by a *Praeses* under a *Vicarius* or Deputy (residing in London) to the Prefect of the Gauls. The army, however, was a separate command under the *Dux Britanniarum* (General of the British Provinces) and coast defence was another under the *Comes Litoris Saxonici* (Count of the Saxon shore), who disposed of a fleet, forts and signal stations on the east and Channel coasts and even in Wales and Lancashire. Irish piracy was beginning too. All the same the new dispensation provided security in which the economy flourished: the Romans introduced certain fruit and nut trees, many types of root, vetch, flax, rye and oats, geese and pheasants; they improved the cattle, and bee-keeping was widespread. They also made extensive use of corn drying. The expanding towns provided a market for such foodstuffs, but there was a considerable export trade as well, in which woollen cloths figured.

(22) The new dispensation was organised in detail while Constantius with his son Constantine was in Britain in 305. He campaigned against the Picts (or Caledonians), reached the far north of Scotland and took effective steps also against the Scots (then in Ireland). He died at York in mid-306 and the army there proclaimed Constantine emperor. This proved premature and his title was recognised only in 307. It seems that an Allemanic chieftain, Crocus, was concerned in this and that there was some small settlements of Saxons on the east coast at this time. In 313 Christianity was recognised by the Edict of Milan and in the next year each British province was represented by a bishop at the Council of Arles. The tranquillity on the frontiers lasted a generation and allowed the new religion to spread mainly, if not wholly, in the towns.

J. *Decline* (23) In 342, however, there began the long slow collapse first of Roman rule and then of Romano-British civilisation. A dangerous Pictish invasion required a personal visit by the Emperor Constans in 343.

The garrison could not be reinforced and he made political arrangements: the Votadini received local autonomy and undertook the defence of their sector, thus releasing troops for other uses. In 350, however, a usurper of British origin, Magnentius, made a bid for the imperial throne and took all the garrison to the continent. He was defeated in 351 by Constantius II at the B. of Mursa where high casualties on both sides permanently reduced the manpower of the already inadequate military establishments. Moreover Constantius took reprisals against anyone associated with Magnentius. In its weakened state Britain was now unable to control mounting barbarian pressure, even though the economic prosperity continued. A grain surplus, for example, was specially imported by Julian to the Rhineland in 359. In 360 there were both Pictish and Scots raids; in 365 a concerted attack by Picts, Scots, Saxons and Allacotti; in 367 these tribes co-ordinated with a Frankish attack on Gaul. Since most of these movements were waterborne, static, especially linear, defences broke down. The Count of the Saxon Shore was killed and the Dux apparently captured; the situation, out of hand for two years, was saved mainly because the attackers' purpose was plunder not conquest.

(24) The crisis caught the emperor distracted by a major war. Two distinguished commanders were sent to Britain and superseded, before Count Theodosius the Elder, arrived in 369. His far-reaching measures might have been effective. A fifth province *(Britannia Valentia)* was based on Carlisle. The wall was rebuilt and garrisoned with locally raised farmer militias. The fortresses at York, Chester and Caerleon and many other forts and signal stations were built or rebuilt. All the important towns were refortified with bastion towers and wide ditches. Fleet bases were established in the Humber, Tees and Tyne, and at Holyhead, as well as a shipyard on the Severn; and some troops were brought from the continent to raise the strength of the small field army. Most important of all, the Romanised tribes of the Lowlands, the Votadini and the Damnonii, whose wealth depended on inclusion in the Roman economic area, were themselves victims and could be treated as allies. They became independent but with Roman honours, took responsibility for their own sectors and thus lent depth to the defences of the north. Such arrangements were workable because, despite the local destruction, which caused the collapse of some rurally situated industries, the prosperity continued for another generation; militarily they depended upon a mobile strategic reserve.

(25) Magnus Maximus, who was probably Dux, and a popular figure in Britain, planned to become Emperor. To secure his rear he campaigned against the Picts in 382 and put the Novantae on the same political basis as the Votadini. He then took the field army, including the XXth from Chester, to Gaul. The resulting civil war drained Britain of troops and lasted until his defeat and death in 388. Meantime Scots, and Pictish seaborne raids recommenced, especially in the Irish Sea. The departure of the XXth (which never returned) unhinged the north western defences. The northern Welsh tribes had to be converted into allies.

K. *Roman Withdrawal* (26) Gaul was under heavy attacks which spread to Italy. Such troops as there were were needed to defend Italy, the heartland of the Western Empire. The Wall was abandoned in 405, the year when Nial of the Nine Hostages raided Cornwall. The last Roman troops left in 407, to be involved in the civil wars. By 410 the Roman administration had mostly gone or been expelled, and the imperial govt. authorised the Britons to defend themselves. This was really a repetition for Britain as a whole of the precedents already set for outlying tribes.

BRITAIN, ROMANO-BRITISH. (1) After the Roman evacuation, a central authority of some kind was maintained, and passed into the charge of Cornovian princes of unknown name who used the title *VORTIGERN* (sublime leader, dictator). Pictish raids caused widespread devastation and disrupted civilian communications, so that regular trade and exchange collapsed and many cultivations were abandoned. Save in a few restricted localities coinage went out of use.

(2) The Vortigern, unable to raise sufficient force to deal with the Picts, had to moderate between rival opinions: to try to revert to Roman rule (showing signs of revival under Aëtius) or to seek help from the growing numbers of armed Teutonic tribesmen (Angles, Jutes, Saxons and Frisians) who appeared on the coasts. The Pelagian controversy was raging and Pelagianism, by making headway in Britain, was isolating her from the Roman Church. The Vortigern preferred Teutonic military settlements (c. 425) and the Jutish ones are traditionally associated with two chiefs denominated Hengest and Horsa. The bishops, on the other hand, sent calls for help against the Pelagians. The continental church with, it may be assumed, the encouragement of the lay authorities, responded by sending over (429-30) the remarkable St. Germanus (St. Germain) of Auxerre, a strong minded general. He organised resistance not only to Pelagianism but to an Irish based Scots invasion in N. Wales for which he efficiently trained British levies (The ALLELUIA Victory). If the Vortigern cleared the way for Cunedda's migration of the Votadini from Lothian to Gwynedd at that time, it suggests some political co-operation between him and Germanus, for the Votadini were settled there to protect the area from pirates.

(3) There was a plague in 433, which had serious local effects but did not reduce the rate at which Teutonic migrants came into their settlements. These by now were not confined to the East coast, but were to be found at fluvial sites inland. In 442 a Jutish revolt broke out in Kent, and the other Teutonic settlements mostly joined in. The speed of their success suggests an initial surprise, or even collusion. In 446, the Britons, or at any rate those who still favoured the Roman connection, petitioned Aëtius for help. In this document, known as the *Groans of the Britons,* they say that they are being driven into the sea. St. Germanus made a second visit. If he rallied them, the success was relatively short-lived; by 460 western Britons were migrating en masse to Armorica, soon to be called Brittany.

(4) By 470 the Anglo-Saxon offensive had blocked off the east coast from direct continental, other than Teutonic, contacts, and communication from the Roman world ran from Spain and Southern Gaul via Brittany, across or round Cornwall and thence up the Irish Sea to Man, which became the centre of a Celtic sea province. The inhabitants on both shores had much in common and there was intermigration. The Saxons had by then advanced too far, and the Britons, led by Ambrosius Aurelianus, possibly a cavalry leader, began to resist more strongly. Under his successor Arthur, they won a great victory at the B. or S. of Mount Badon (near Bath or Swindon) in 490, and drove the Anglo-Saxons back as far as London and the borders of Norfolk. Many re-migrated by way of Cuxhaven to Germany.

(5) There followed a sixty year period of peaceful coexistence interrupted by a serious epidemic in 530. In 550 the Saxon advance was resumed.

(6) British leadership did not survive in England beyond the 7th cent. but Britons in varying, often large numbers did. The inherent probability that comparatively few invaders would prefer to enslave rather than exterminate a large conquered population, though not portrayed in written sources, is confirmed by a miscellany of other evidence including place names, estate and parish boundaries, excavations, similarities of parts of Kentish and Welsh Law (*see* GAVELKIND) and statistical

analyses of the height, features and colouring of 19th cent. army recruits.

BRITANNIA. The original model for the figure of Britannia was Frances Theresa Stuart. She was probably not a mistress of Charles II, but later became Duchess of Richmond. The figure appeared on British copper coinage from 1672 to 1970, and subsequently on 50-pence pieces.

BRITISH AND FOREIGN BIBLE SOCIETY was founded in 1804 initially to provide Bibles in Welsh. *See also* BAPTISTS.

BRITISH ASSOCIATION FOR THE ADVANCEMENT OF SCIENCE was founded by Sir David Brewster and others in 1831.

BRITISH CENTRAL AFRICA PROTECTORATE. *See* NYASALAND.

BRITISH COLUMBIA. Capt. James Cook in 1774 repaired his vessels in Nootka Sound and traced the general outline of the coast. He also obtained sea-otter pelts which he sold at great profit at Macao on the way home. This led to a boom and to disputes with Spain. Consequently Capt. George Vancouver was sent to map the coast north of San Francisco in 1792 to 1794, and during this period Alexander Mackenzie reached it overland. By 1821 the coast was occupied by trappers and traders of the North West Co. which in that year amalgamated with the Hudson Bay Co. When the international frontier was extended to the Pacific in 1846 the Company moved its headquarters from Vancouver in the state of Washington to Victoria, and three years later Vancouver I. was made a crown colony. The mainland Canadian territory, however, continued to be run for the benefit of the fur trade as hitherto until the 1858 gold rush made a more official form of govt. desirable. The mainland was then proclaimed a Crown colony, and in 1866 amalgamated with Vancouver I. as British Columbia. In 1871 it became part of Canada, but on condition that the transcontinental railway should be built quickly. The result was that the Canadian Pacific Rly was completed in 1885 and the new city of Vancouver founded in 1886.

In the 20th cent. the greatest interest has attached to the development of the enormous hydroelectric resources, and to the discovery of oil and natural gas which began production in significant quantities in 1956.

The province is politically interesting because it elected the first Social Credit govt. in the world in 1952. This was prevented by federal law from carrying out the most remarkable feature of its programme, namely the introduction of an automatically taxed currency. *See also* NOOTKA SOUND.

BRITISH COMMONWEALTH. In 1925 Mackenzie King, the leader of the Canadian liberals, won a general election by alleging (wrongly) that Lord Byng of Vimy, the Governor General, had acted under pressure from Britain in refusing him a dissolution and granting one to his rival. At the Imperial Conference of 1926 he used these allegations as a pretext for demanding that the practical independence of the larger colonies should be translated into reality. He was supported by other colonies who wished to avoid indirect commitment through Britain to the Locarno T. Balfour accordingly drafted the statement which defined the new relationship of Britain and the major colonies as "autonomous communities within the British Empire, equal in status, in no way subordinate one to another in any aspect of their domestic or internal affairs, though united by a common allegiance to the Crown and freely associated as members of the *British Commonwealth* of Nations". In accordance with this formula, governors-general began to be appointed on the advice of the local not the British govt; a Dominions Office was set up, and in June 1930 a separate Secretary of State was appointed. In 1931 parliament passed the Statute of Westminster under which independence under the Crown ("Dominion Status") was conferred upon Canada, Australia, New Zealand, South Africa and Newfoundland.

Since that time there have been many changes in the status of the various territories. Many have remained Kingdoms or Dominions of the Crown (now styled Realms), others have become republics within the Commonwealth, yet others have left the Commonwealth altogether but some have returned and some have been absorbed into other or larger units. Amongst the countries remaining in the Commonwealth some have abolished and others retained judicial appeals to the Privy Council. These changes are indicated in the Table.

D = Dominion, Kingdom or Realm under the British Crown
RC = Republic within the Commonwealth
O = Outside the Commonwealth
K = Kingdom within the Commonwealth but not under the British Crown
PCA = Privy Council Appeals abolished
Former protectorates are in *italics*.

Aden etc	RO	1967
Antigua & Barbuda	D	1981
Australia	D	1931
	PCA	1975-1986
Bahamas	D	1973
Bangladesh	RC	1972
Barbados	D	1966
Botswana	RC	1966
Brunei	K	1984
Burma (Myanmar)	RO	1947
Canada	D	1931
	PCA	1949
Ceylon (Sri Lanka)	D	1948
	PCA	1971
	RC	1972
Cyprus	RC	1961
Dominica	RC	1978
Gambia	D	1965
	RC	1970
Ghana	D	1957
	RC	1960
	PCA	1961
Grenada	D	1974
Guyana	D	1966
	RC	1970
India	D	1947
	RC	1950
Irish Free State		1922
	RO	1949
Jamaica	D	1962
Kenya	D	1963
	RC	1964
		1965
Kiribati	RC	1979
Lesotho	K	1966
Malawi	D	1964
	PCA	1965
	RC	1966
Malaya	K	1957
Sarawak, N. Borneo and Singapore		
added		1963
	PCA	1983
Malaysia, *see* Malaya		
Maldives	RO	1965
	RC	1982
Malta GC	D	1964
	RC	1974
Mauritius	D	1968
	RC	1992
Namibia	RC	1990
Nauru	RC	1966
Newfoundland	D	1931
Governed by a British Commission		
United with Canada		1949

New Zealand	D	1931
Nigeria	D	1960
	PCA	1963
	RC	1963
Pakistan	D	1947
	RC	1956
	RO	1972
	RC	1989
Papua-New Guinea	D	1975
St Kitts & Nevis	D	1983
Saint Lucia	D	1979
St Vincent & the Grenadines	D	1979
Seychelles	RC	1976
Sierra Leone	D	1961
	RC	1971
Singapore	RC	1965
Solomon Is	D	1978
South Africa	D	1931
	PCA	1950
	RO	1961
	RC	1994
Swaziland	K	1968
Tanganyika formerly		
mandated	D	1961
	RC	1962
became with Zanzibar		
Tanzania	RC	1964
	PCA	1964
Tonga	K	1970
Trinidad & Tobago	D	1962
	RC	1976
Tuvalu	RC	1978
Uganda	D	1962
	RC	1963
	PCA	1963
	2nd RC	1976
Vanuatu	RC	1981
Western Samoa	RC	1970
Zambia	D	1964
Zanzibar	K	1963
see Tanganyika		
Zimbabwe	RC	1980

BRITISH COMMONWEALTH GAMES. The idea was first mooted by the Rev. Astley Cooper in 1891 and a small meeting was held in London in 1911; the first full scale meeting of the established quadrennial series was held at Hamilton (Ontario) in 1931.

BRITISH COUNCIL was founded in 1934 to encourage the understanding of English language and culture in foreign countrIes. It has branches in the U.K. as well as foreign capitals.

BRITISH COUNCIL OF CHURCHES was formed in 1942 under the presidency of William Temple, Abp. of Canterbury. Membership consists of most protestant churches in the British Is. and some interdenominational groups such as the Y.M.C.A. R. Catholic observers have attended since the late 1960s.

BRITISH EAST AFRICA. Formerly a collective term for Uganda, Kenya, Tanganyika and Zanzibar. From 1948 to 1961 it possessed a High Commission consisting of the governors of the first three, responsible for providing common services such as posts, and a high court. When Tanganyika became independent on 9 Dec. 1962, the High Commission was replaced by a Common Services organisation, but the revolutions in Zanzibar and Uganda effectively destroyed what vestiges of unity remained.

BRITISH EAST AFRICA CO. accepted a strip ten miles deep along the Tanganyika coast from the Sultan of Zanzibar in 1887 and was formally incorporated in 1888. Unable to raise capital from the British Govt. to develop this acquisition, the company started operations in Uganda instead. This proving unprofitable too, the company surrendered its charter, and the coastal strip was sold to the British Govt. for £250,000 in 1895.

BRITISH EMPIRE GAMES. See BRITISH COMMONWEALTH GAMES.

BRITISH EXPEDITIONARY FORCES (B.E.F.). See WORLD WARS I AND II.

BRITISH GUIANA. See GUYANA.

BRITISH HONDURAS. See BELIZE.

BRITISH INDIAN OCEAN TERRITORIES, formerly OIL Is. (because they provided coconut lamp-oil) are eleven small islands separately administered from 1965 after the independence of Mauritius and the Seychelles. The I. of Diego Garcia was later let to the U.S.A. as a base, some 2000 islanders being evicted to accommodate it.

BRITISH KAFFRARIA. See XHOSA.

BRITISH LEGION. Until 1921 there were four ex-servicemen's organisations, viz: The Comrades of the Great War, the Nat. Assn. of Discharged Sailors and Soldiers, the Nat. Fedn. of Discharged and Demobilised Sailors and Soldiers, and the Officers' Assn. After agreement in 1920 they united as the British Legion at a general meeting of ex-servicemen in 1921. It received a royal charter in 1925.

BRITISH LEYLAND arose from a merger, fostered by the Industrial Reorganisation Corp. in 1968, of the British Motor Corp. (B.M.C.) and Leyland Motors (L.M.). L.M. specialised in heavy vehicles; B.M.C. was itself a merged group of passenger car firms, of which Austin-Morris was the biggest. British Leyland's industrial relations were abysmally bad and it needed govt. help in later years. It eventually became a new type of state corporation. From about 1978 its industrial relations improved and it entered into co-operative arrangements with Japanese car-building firms.

BRITISH LINEN CO. and BANK originated at an uncertain date in the EDINBURGH LINEN COPARTNERY, which advanced money upon the security of expected finished linen to enable weavers to buy their raw materials. The industry expanded quickly, and demand for this short term credit outran the Copartnery's resources. Lord Milton, its leading spirit, procured the formation of the Co. in 1746. Despite its name it was Scottish. It was buying Russian flax and establishing warehouses at Glasgow, Leith and London in 1747, when it launched its banking operations by issuing notes in payment for goods. It gradually withdrew from manufacturing and by 1790 it was wholly a bank, which it remains.

BRITISH MEDICAL ASSN. (B.MA.) was founded as the PROVINCIAL MEDICAL AND SURGICAL ASSN. (P.M.S.A.) in 1832, and transformed as a result of discussions in 1854-5 into the existing Assn. in 1856. Some of the moral impetus came from events in the Crimean War, which led to a parliamentary enquiry, the passage of the Medical Act, 1858, and the creation of the related but distinct GENERAL MEDICAL COUNCIL (G.M.C.) (q.v.). The BRITISH MEDICAL JOURNAL was founded by the P.M.S.A. in 1840, and was taken over by the B.M.A.

BRITISH MUSEUM (London). The collection and house of Robert Cotton, an Elizabethan antiquary, were given to the nation by his grandson under a private Act of 1700; this vested them in a body of official and family trustees. When Hans Sloane made his bequest to the nation, a further act, the British Museums Act, 1753, was passed to fuse the management of the two gifts, and to provide for the purchase of the Harley manuscripts by funds raised by a lottery. This was the first of eighteen acts passed between 1753 and 1962 concerned with the Museum. George II presented the royal library in 1757, and with it he made over the right of compulsory copyright. The new museum was opened at Montagu House in 1759; the Kings Library (to house George III's collection) was added in 1827.

Montagu House was demolished in 1845 to make way for the monumental front completed in 1852, and the great domed reading room was opened in 1857. The museum was financed mainly by gifts and the invested proceeds of the original lottery, plus occasional govt. grants. In the 1960s it derived large amounts from its interest in the copyrights left by George Bernard Shaw, especially "My Fair Lady", the musical version of the play "Pygmalion".

The British Museum Act of 1963, attacked by Lord Radcliffe as a breach of faith, repealed all the previous legislation, created a new body of trustees who are publicly appointed, and separated the Natural History Museum from it.

BRITISH NORTH AMERICA ACTS (B.N.A.A.) contained the Canadian Constitution. The Act of 1867 united Canada, Nova Scotia, and New Brunswick into a single Dominion under the name of Canada and divided it into *four* provinces, namely Quebec, Ontario, Nova Scotia and New Brunswick. It created the Dominion and Provincial Constitutions, allotted certain powers to the latter and reserved the rest to the Dominion. It also provided for the admission of other colonies.

Since the Canada thus created was still subject to the United Kingdom, the Act contained no provision for constitutional amendment, which had to be effected from time to time by the Westminster Parliament in successive B.N.A.A.s. Such acts were passed in 1871, 1886, 1907, 1915 and 1930. When Canada became independent under the Statute of Westminster, 1931, this situation was not altered in form, but the British Parliament thenceforth enacted constitutional amendments in further B.N.A.A.s of 1940, 1946, 1949 (twice), whenever so requested by the Canadian legislature. By the 1949 No. 2 Act, however, the Canadian parliament was empowered to amend the constitution in so far as such amendment did not affect the exclusive rights of the provinces. The practical effect was that British legislation was passed thereafter automatically at the request of a conference of the Dominion and provincial premiers, which thus became in fact, if not in theory, the constitutional amending body, and further acts were passed by this method in 1951, 1960 and 1964.

In 1982 a new Dominion constitution was enacted in the Canada Act. This terminated the previous arrangements and provided that future amendments could be made by the Canadian parliament. The change was criticised by many Canadians on the ground that it eroded the constitutional safeguards of minorities.

BRITISH SOMALILAND. See SOMALIA.

BRITISH SOUTH AFRICA CO. was formed by Cecil Rhodes and Alfred Beit, and chartered in Oct. 1889. The immediate purpose was to exploit the MATABELE territories (now Rhodesia and Zambia) north of the Transvaal and west of Mozambique, and in the long run to establish a continuous belt of British territory all the way to Egypt, linked by a British railway. The British Govt. was unwilling to annex or protect these areas but, under its Moffatt T. (Feb. 1888) with Lo Bengula, the Matabele King, the latter would make no foreign treaty without British consent. The pressure of new settlers, and previous experience with the Boers in Bechuanaland, gave Rhodes good reason to fear that the Moffatt T. would not prevent the Germans (on the West) and the Portuguese (on the East) from getting in first. In Oct. 1888 therefore his agent, C. D. Rudd, bought for him all the mining rights in Lo Bengula's country for £100 a month, some rifles and a steamer. The 'Rudd' Concession was the foundation upon which Rhodes raised £1,000,000 initial capital; and his company was accordingly empowered for 25 years to exploit concessions and administer a territory (whose northern and western boundaries were left undefined), subject to the control of the Colonial Office.

Once the operations began in earnest the govt. found that it could not avoid protecting them: in 1891 the territory was declared a protectorate, and in 1894 on the basis of agreements with the BAROTSE, the company took over the administration of further territories to the north. In 1895 these two parts became known as SOUTHERN and NORTHERN RHODESIA. In 1915 the charter was renewed for a further ten years, but the administrative rights were surrendered to the British Govt. in Southern Rhodesia on 1 Sept. 1923, and in the North on 1 Apr. 1924. Compensation of £3,750,000 was paid. In 1933 the Southern Rhodesian Govt. bought the mining rights for £2,000,000. The company paid its first dividend in May 1924, and became a purely trading venture ever since, with extensive properties also in Malawi and Botswana. Until 1964 its copper royalties amounted to about £1.75M a year. Threatened with expropriation by the new Zambian govt. its mineral rights were surrendered for £4M. It ceased to operate independently in 1965.

BRITISH SURVIVAL. See BRITAIN, ROMANO-BRITISH-6.

BRITISH WEST AFRICA. A collective term for the former British colonies, trust territories and protectorates of the Cameroons, Gambia, the Gold Coast (now Ghana), Nigeria and Sierra Leone. It never had much political or administrative significance, but a West African Currency Board functioned from 1912 to 1956.

BRITAIN, BRITON, GREAT BRITAIN. It is uncertain whether the name Britain is of W. Germanic or Old Celtic origin. The Romans called the island *Britannia,* and the term Briton is today used, save in journalism, to indicate the inhabitants from the time of the Romans until their defeat by the Teutonic invaders in the 5th and 6th cents.

In the middle ages the term Britain was used only as a historical term. It came back into practical uses under Henry VIII and Edward VI, in connection with efforts to unite England and Scotland and as a result of investigations into the island's past unity. It has been ingeniously but not very plausibly suggested that the name Great Britain originated in the punning title of a book – John Major's *Historia Majoris Britanniae* (Lat = history of Great Britain or Major's History of Britain).

In 1604 James I and VI was proclaimed 'King of Great Britain' probably because this collective name sounded more impressive than the component parts added together.

BRITON, THE. A weekly published in 1762 by Smollett for Lord Bute. It provoked the publication of Wilke's *North Briton.*

BRITTANY, ARMORICA, BRITANNIA MINOR, Fr: BRETAGNE. (1) When the Roman empire broke up, Brittany became a haven for refugees from the Anglo-Saxon invasions of Britain. (*See* BRITAIN, ROMANO-BRITISH). By the mid-6th cent. much of the peninsula had been thus occupied and Armorica had become Brittany.

(2) Carolingian suzerainty was nominal, and a local dynasty, the House of Cornouailles, maintained links with England: for example Edward the Elder was received into fraternity by the canons of Dol, and when the Vikings devastated Brittany in 919, there was a return migration to England. K. Athelstan was godfather to Alan of the Twisted Beard, grandson of Alan the Great, the last ruler of all Brittany, and protected him. In 936, with Athelstan's help, he led many of his people back and established himself in the counties of Vannes and Nantes. Conan I (r. 987-92) imposed order mainly by establishing powerful fiefs, with whose lords adjacent rulers later habitually intrigued.

(3) On the basis of the invasion of 919, the Ds. of Normandy claimed the overlordship, and the Bayeux tapestry shows Harold Godwinsson assisting D. William on an expedition against Conan, D. of Brittany. William's Anglo-Saxon opponents got much help from Bretons in the years just after the Conquest: William consequently besieged Dol, but was warned off by K. Philip of France. Other Bretons, however, came to England with William in 1066, and Domesday Book shows Count Alan, a cadet of the ducal house, as one of the greatest holders of English land, including the earldom of Richmond (Yorks). Partly because of this connection, the 12th cent. Ds. of Brittany had close ties with and could be pressurised by the English royal family. Constance, *d.* of Conan IV (r. 1156-70), the last of his dynasty, was married to Henry II's son Geoffrey who thereby gained the duchy; but he rebelled against his father and then died prematurely (1186) and his posthumous son Arthur was murdered by K. John (1203). Meantime the Breton lords competed for Constance's hand and for 20 years did what they liked until the marriage of her *d.* Aliz to a relative of the French royal house, Peter of Dreux, whose descendents ruled in peace and a fair prosperity until the death of John III in 1341. The Dreux period was distinguished by a growing imbalance between the areas of the more prosperous French-speaking (ARGOET) inland agricultural population and the less advanced coastal, mainly sea-going ARMOR. This continued the fissiparous tendencies in the duchy and deprived it of the political strength which unified direction might have imparted.

(4) At John III's death, a war of succession broke out between his younger half-brother John, Count of Montfort, supported by the Armor, and his niece's husband, Charles of Blois, supported by the Argoet. Edward III gave Montfort the earldom of Richmond and promised military aid in return for his acceptance of Edward's title to the French Crown. Philip IV of France, of course, supported Charles of Blois militarily and his troops captured Montfort. This did not stop the war, for Monifort's wife Joan fought on. The conflict was frequently savage, but made famous by the deeds of such soldiers as Duguesclin, Sir Walter Manny and Sir Thomas Dagworth. The English mercenaries, however, left in 1361 under the T. of Brétigny, but the war continued until the death of Charles of Blois at the B. of Auray (1364) assured the succession to Montfort's son. By the P. of Guérand (1365) the separatist John of Montfort was recognised as Duke but did homage to the French King. He died in 1399. His widow Joan, while regent, was married to Henry IV. If, which is uncertain, Henry had hoped thereby to secure a safe channel for English shipping, the move failed. Armor piracy was too ingrained to be lightly rooted out.

(5) French preoccupation with the English and Burgundians ensured that for over a century Brittany was unmolested. The last Duke, François II (r. 1458-88) being without a son, sought to ensure autonomy by foreign alliances. His young daughter Anne was married by proxy to the Emperor Ferdinand in 1470, but under French pressure she repudiated the marriage as unconsummated, and then married in turn Charles VIII (1491) and Louis XII (1498) and her daughter Claude married François I. Under the marriage treaties Brittany was to remain autonomous. Its sovereignty merged with that of France only in 1519 at the accession of Henri II, the son of Claude and François I. The local autonomy, however, survived until the French Revolution. (*See also* ELIZABETH I.)

(6) The Franco-Breton union put Anglo-Breton trade under French control and enabled French govts. to develop the naval arsenal at Brest, which represented a threat to British maritime interests in the 18th and 19th cents. from the French, and from the Germans in World War II. On the other hand it led to a decline in Armor piracy and the tranquillisation (in co-operation with Henry VII's navy) of the Narrow Seas, though violent fisheries disputes continued into the 20th cent.

BRITION. *See* BRACTON.

BRITTON, John (1771-1857) published an immense series of drawings of English and Irish architectural antiquities between 1805 and 1835. These formed one of the "quarries" of information for the Gothic revival.

BRITTON, Thomas (?1654-1714), small-coal merchant, chemist, bibliophile and musician, started weekly concerts in a room over his warehouse at Clerkenwell in 1678. All the ablest musicians and cognoscenti of the day attended or played, and the concerts became a social institution and landmark in the development of English musical practice.

BROAD ARROW. This simple symbol was originally the badge of the Sydney family; Vist. Sydney was master-gen. of the Ordnance from 1693 to 1697 and the mark has been used to distinguish govt. property since his time.

BROAD BOTTOM MINISTRY was the coalition formed in 1744, at the fall of Carteret, between the Pelham administration and the opposition led by Chesterfield. Pitt joined it in a junior post in 1746, and it lasted with small changes till Henry Pelham died in 1754.

BROADCASTING. (1) Wireless telegraphy by Morse Code dates from 1896 and was used in the Russo-Japanese war of 1904-5. Thermionic valves made speech transmission possible during World War I, and in Feb. 1920 the Marconi Co. started broadcasts embroidered with entertainment. In June 1920 they excited great interest by broadcasting the soprano Nellie Melba, but in the autumn the Post Office forbade further transmissions as interfering with communications. In Feb. 1922, however, "2MT" was allowed to broadcast for one hour a week from Chelmsford. Later in 1922 "2LO" at Marconi House, London, was licenced, and in the autumn all concerned were induced by the Post Office to surrender their interests to a monopolistic BRITISH BROADCASTING CO. which began operations in Nov. J. C. W. REITH became the managing director and P. P. ECKERSLEY the chief engineer. These two became world renowned.

(2) By Dec. 1924 there were 8 main stations and 11 relay transmitters able to reach 70% of the population by a signal receivable on a CRYSTAL set (mostly in towns), with many of the rest able to receive a service on VALVE receivers. The ninth main station opened in Belfast in 1924, while the Daventry long wave transmitter (1925) made full rural coverage at last possible. Simultaneous broadcasting was hampered by defects in the Post Office telephone network, but by 1932 this was overcome by putting it through special underground cables. The screened grid valve, introduced in 1927, eliminated mutual interference by valve receivers.

(3) Meanwhile the multiplication of continental stations was creating new interferences and the GENEVA CONFERENCE (1925) worked out a system of international waveband allocation. One practical consequence was that the British system of stations had to be abandoned in favour of five twin-wave transmitters, sending two programmes. This drove the crystal receiver out because only in the hands of an expert could it separate the two programmes.

(4) Though George V broadcast from the Wembley Exhibition in 1924, the newspapers successfully opposed outside broadcasting until 1927, when the B.B.C. became a non-profit making corporation. The B.B.C. also began empire broadcasting at this period through the discovery that low wavelengths could be made to reach distant targets by reflection from the ionosphere. Both developments, but particularly the problems created by time zones in long distance transmissions, brought a need for recording equipment, and from 1930 this was somewhat rudimentarily met by the Blattnerphone. BROADCASTING HOUSE (London) was opened in 1932.

(5) Though the CATHODE RAY TUBE was invented as early as 1897, no practical TELEVISION (T.V.) system was developed until Baird's experiments of 1925 to 1929. By 1932 the B.B.C. had opened a T.V. studio and was collaborating on development. Electrical and Musical Industries Ltd (EMI.), however, were developing with not

only 240 lines but interlaced scanning and the iconoscope camera. As a result of Baird's complaints to the P.M.G. a committee was set up which in Jan. 1935 recommended that the B.B.C. should experiment with both systems. Baird's 30 line system was abandoned shortly after, but thereupon E.M.I. changed to 405 lines and set up their studios at ALEXANDRA PALACE. The Baird E.M.I. 240 line experiments were discontinued in Feb. 1937. Few (very expensive) T.V. receivers were sold before World War II.

(6) Portable radio and recording equipment for outside broadcasts were well developed by 1938, so that radio reporting was feasible by the beginning of the war. At this time there were 9,000,000 licensed receivers. It became necessary to guard against the use of transmitters as directional beacons by enemy aircraft. This was done by broadcasting from several transmitters on the same frequency and shutting off one when enemy aircraft came too close to it.

(7) In June 1946 the suspended T.V. service reopened and the 1947 royal wedding gave it great impetus. By 1948 there were 50,000 receivers picking up the Alexandra Palace programme. By Aug. 1952 four high power B.B.C. transmitters could reach 80% of the population, by 1956 95%. The supply of receivers ran behind the demand.

(8) The Television Act, 1954, ended the B.B.C. monopoly. In Sept. 1955 the INDEPENDENT TELEVISION (later BROADCASTING) AUTHORITY's (I.T.A.) London transmitter started up, with programmes financed by advertising, and by 1956 this medium could reach about 50% of households.

Though T.V. achieved a predominating position it did not supersede radio for which a daytime (especially morning and car-born) demand remained, as well as a growing evening demand for concerts and a multi-lingual World Service. This was encouraged by the introduction of FREQUENCY MODULATION at very high frequencies and the introduction of TRANSISTOR receivers.

(9) Since 1953 European T.V. had generally accepted a 625-line standard and a new European frequency agreement was made at Stockholm in 1961. One reason why Britain entered this was that the new standard was more suitable than 405 line for COLOUR television. The first result was the establishment of the B.B.C.'s second (B.B.C.2) network in 1964. Colour T.V. was begun on this network in July 1967. The B.B.C., however, did not neglect radio. There were four programmes and LOCAL RADIO stations began to be opened. By Nov. 1973 there were two in London just as the B.B.C.'s radio monopoly was ended. A second independent television channel started to operate in 1982.

BROAD CHURCH. *See* ANGLICANISM.

BROADMOOR (Berks) criminal lunatic asylum was opened in 1863.

BROAD PIECE (1) A gold coin of Charles I, which appreciated from £1 to £1 3s. 9d. (2) Sometimes, the Spanish piece of eight.

BROADS, NORFOLK AND SUFFOLK. These shallow lakes represent the flooded sites of immense diggings, from which Norwich and other local towns were supplied with peat for fuel, and flints for building and for a flint-knapping industry which was still not quite extinct in the 1980s. The digging continued until the end of the 13th cent. (when flooding became serious) and was abandoned in the 14th. Thereafter the Broads became valuable as highways and fisheries, and in the 19th cent. a holiday trade began. In the first 50 years of the 20th cent. they were badly neglected, so that nearly half of them became unnavigable.

BROADSHEETS, BROADSIDES AND STREET BALLADS. Broadsheets were popular or vulgar poems, long printed in black letter on one side of a single sheet, and often illustrated with a primitive woodcut. The earliest in existence is Skelton's celebration of the victory of Flodden printed by Richard Fawkes in London in 1513. By 1540 they were a common form of propaganda, and watched with suspicion by the authorities. Protestant broadsheets were suppressed (as far as possible) and R. Catholic ones allowed under Mary I; under Elizabeth the situation was reversed. The broadsheets dealt with every imaginable subject, from grave political and religious issues to the latest robbery. They partly anticipated the popular press. By the 17th cent. more sophisticated poets were writing proper ballads, and soon after literary figures like Marvell and Cooper were also in the business. Though all these poems were intended to be – and were often – sung, this development resulted in a division between the older popular broadsheet and the newer longer and better written variety, which reached fewer people and merged eventually into the main stream of literature.

In the mid-18th cent. black letter type went out of fashion, but the production of broadsheets continued unabated until the 1850s when it began to fall off. The end was hastened by the rise of the press and the music halls. Most of the broadsheets after 1880 were reprints of music hall songs.

BROADSWORD was a heavy broad bladed weapon designed for cutting not thrusting used by highland Scots who usually held a small round shield in the other hand. It required considerable strength of wrist and shoulder.

BROCHS are free-standing drystone circular towers rising sometimes to a height of 40ft with walls at the base about 15ft thick surrounding a space about 30ft in diameter. After about 6ft the wall becomes double with a space from 2ft to 4ft wide between the inner and the outer shell. There was only one entrance. The circular interior was probably thatched. Of 600 known brochs, most are in N.W. Scotland and the Western Isles, usually near good land in river valleys and along the coasts. Many were occupied throughout the Roman Iron Age. The earliest probably date from the 2nd cent. B.C.

BROCKWAY, Fenner (1888-1990) Ld. BROCKWAY (1964), strongly Marxist professional supporter of anti-western and pro-Bolshevik front-movements, was imprisoned as a conscientious objector in World War I; organised a 'No More War' faction (1923-8); supported Indian independence and became a Labour M.P. (1929-31) and became gen-sec. of the I.L.P. (1933-9) by which time he had, by reaction against Stalinism, embraced the essentially militarist doctrines of Leon Trotsky and become a founding organiser of the Fourth International. After Trotsky's murder he reverted to more orthodox communism and was Pres. (from 1970) of a British Peace in Vietnam faction and co-chairman (from 1979) of the so-called World Disarmament Campaign.

BRODIE, William (?-1788) a town councillor and Deacon of the Edinburgh Wrights and Masons, was also the head of a local gang of burglars one of whom sensationally turned King's evidence in 1788. Deacon Brodie fled, but was traced to Amsterdam, brought back and hanged.

BRODRICK. Anglo-Irish family which received many thousands of forfeited acres between 1653 and 1670 around Cork. These were erected into the single manor of Midleton, and gave the family an influence in Munster almost equal to that of the Boyles. **(1) Alan (?1660-1728) 1st Ld. MIDLETON (1715), Vist. (1717)** lawyer and Orangeman, was attainted by the Patriotic Parliament and naturally rose quickly after the Jacobite defeat. He became an Irish M.P. in 1692, Irish sol-gen. in 1695 and Speaker in 1703. He was strongly opposed to the Tests and lost the solicitor-generalship when the House refused to pass some bills. Pembroke's appointment as Lord-Lieut heralded a change, and in 1707 he was made Att-Gen. and sent to London to persuade the govt. to repeal the Tests. He failed, but nevertheless became C.J. of the Irish Queen's Bench in 1710. He was, however, dismissed by the Tory govt. in 1711. In 1713 he became an M.P. and Speaker again, and having secured the protestant succession, became Irish Lord Chancellor in 1714. At the same time he became an English M.P., supporting Walpole against the Peerage Bill, but subsequently quarrelling with him. He became involved in the Wood's Halfpence affair because, as Irish Lord Chancellor, he avoided sealing the patent. The govt. got the Irish Lords to pass a censure upon him for his absence: the Commons promptly praised him for his attention to duty. He continued to oppose the patent but favoured prosecuting Swift for his *Drapier's Letters*. A descendent **(2) (William) St. John (1856-1942) 9th Vist. (1907) and 1st E. of MIDLETON (1920)** was a Tory M.P. from 1880 until 1906. He was financial sec. to the War Office from 1886 to 1892, and when in opposition discovered the shortage of army ammunition which led to Rosebery's fall in 1895. In that year he became U-Sec. of State for War, and in 1898 for Foreign Affairs. He took over the War Office in 1900 at the height of the Boer War, and in 1902 inspired the creation of the cabinet committee later known as the Imperial Defence Committee. A military hat (for which he was not responsible) was also named after him.

Feeling responsible for the inefficiency of the army during the Boer War, he secured a transfer to the India Office where, from 1903 to 1905 he was Sec. of State. He was instantly plunged into acute, and to him distressing, controversy with his old friend Curzon, the Viceroy, whose forward Indian foreign policy, particularly in Tibet and Afghanistan, was at variance with that of the cabinet. He attributed Curzon's independence and arrogance to his personal anxieties and physical pain, and was thus disinclined to publicise the details of the disagreement. Accordingly when Curzon was forced to resign in 1905 Broderick was the target of much ill informed vituperation, and lost his seat in the election of 1906.

In 1907, however, he succeeded to his father's peerage, which was based upon the estates near Cork; he reverted to an earlier interest in Irish affairs, on which he had always been notably well informed. In 1917 he tried, but failed, to induce the north and south to settle their differences through the Irish Convention, on the basis of Irish autonomy within the Empire. After the convention broke down he refused Lloyd George's offer of the Lord Lieutenancy because it would have involved the simultaneous pursuit of the two incompatibles, namely autonomy and conscription. This increased his credit with the Irish, and in July 1921 it was at de Valera's invitation that he persuaded the Govt. to accept the truce. He disapproved of the eventual settlement and thereafter left public life for good.

BROGHILL, Lord. *See* BOYLE.

BROKE, Capt. Sir Philip Bowes Vere, Bart. (1776-1841) commanded the frigate H.M.S. *Shannon* which was blockading Boston. On 1 June 1813 Capt. Lawrence, in command of the more powerful but not well manned U.S. frigate *Chesapeake*, over-confidently put out from Boston. There had been a long line of American successes in single ship actions, and the population turned out in crowds to watch. Broke captured the *Chesapeake* in 15 minutes. The action became famous, and Broke's improvements in gunnery practice were vindicated, and later adopted by the Royal Navy.

BROKEN HILL PROPRIETARY (B.H.P.) (Australia). In 1883 a boundary rider found traces of silver-lead at Broken Hill (N.S.W.) and with five others subscribed 600 to start a mine. It proved very rich. The BHP Co. was formed in 1885. In 1889 it leased iron deposits at Spencer Gulf for smelting, and in 1911 it opened what was to be the biggest steel plant in the British Empire on the Newcastle coalfields (N.S.W.) with another at Port Kemble which, by 1965, overshadowed it. BHP had by then become a nationwide vertical and horizontal monopoly producing its own raw materials, processing, transporting and exporting them and controlling most of the workshops which used them including, from 1937, an aircraft industry. It penetrated most corners of the Australian economy.

BRONTË. *See* NELSON.

BRONTË, Charlotte (1816-55), Emily (1818-48) and Anne (1820-49) *ds.* of Patrick Brontë, an Irish Anglican parson and his Cornish wife Maria, lived mostly at Haworth, an isolated parsonage beside the Yorkshire moors, together with their drunken brother Branwell, but had periods as governesses, notably Charlotte and Emily in Brussels in 1844-6 when Charlotte had some kind of temperamental crisis. In 1845 she discovered Emily's poems which, because of the masculinity of the literary world, were published (unsuccessfully) under the pseudonyms of CURRER, ELLIS and ACTON BELL. Among their works, Currer's *Jane Eyre* was a success in Oct. 1847, Ellis' *Wuthering Heights* and Acton's *Agnes Grey* in Dec. 1848, by which time they had revealed their sex and become a sensation. Charlotte's *Shirley* appeared in 1849, *Villette* in 1853. Their stylistic power and imaginative range refuted the contemporary notion, largely entertained by publishers, that women could not write and advanced the social emergence of Victorian women.

BRONZE AGE. The use of bronze (a mixture of copper hardened with a small amount of tin) began in central Europe in about 1800 B.C. and spread in the time of the Mycenaean civilisation, encouraged by trade with the tin mines of Cornwall and Wexford (Ireland) and the copper mines of Wicklow, Waterford, Cork and Kerry. The trade routes ran through southern France and Brittany and through N.W. Germany and the Baltic, with Wessex at the crossroads.

The first 'Beaker' people came from Brittany and settled in Wiltshire (1700-1600 B.C.). They began the building of Stonehenge. In the middle Bronze Age (c. 1400-800 B.C.) gold ornaments were made as well as weapons and tools of bronze. The reconstruction of Stonehenge and hundreds of round barrows testify to the power and organisation of this civilisation.

Iron technology began to spread after the downfall of the Hittites, and bronze versions of iron swords were imported into Britain from c. 700 B.C. British iron working began about 50 years later, with the introduction from the continent of the horse.

BROOKE, Alan Francis (1883-1963) 1st Vist. ALANBROOKE of BROOKBOROUGH, F-M and C.I.G.S. (1941-6) spoke French before he spoke English, and passed into Sandhurst via tutors and a crammer. He was an artillery officer in World War I, and in World War II commanded II Corps, which did much damage to the Germans in the retreat to Dunkirk. As CIGS and chairman of the Chiefs of Staff Committee he could stand up to Churchill yet would examine any possibly viable idea. He was very influential and practical and he was a powerful advocate of the African and Italian landings before those in Normandy. The Americans, and of course the Russians, wrongly believed that his motives were political. He contributed more than any other soldier to the success of the western allied land operations. He was a great expert on birds.

BROOKE, Sir James. *See* SARAWAK.

BROOKE, Ld. *See* GREVILLE.

BROOKE, Rupert Chawner (1887-1915), conspicuous and much liked undergraduate at Cambridge, perceived the aggressive features of German society while in Berlin and published his Poems in 1911. He became a fellow of Kings in 1912 and travelled in the English speaking world. Joined up in 1914 and died at Scyros. His *1914 and Other Poems* were published posthumously. His prophetic intelligence and ability to encapsulate English attitudes won him wide acclaim.

BROOK'S (Pall Mall, London) a gambling, political club, founded by Almack in about 1750 and especially associated with Chas. James Fox, and Sheridan.

BROTHELS. Turkish baths (otherwise *bagnios,* hothouses or stews) were introduced during the Crusades. These were used freely by both sexes; from the time of Henry II they were generally confined to Southwark, and turned gradually into brothels. Their conduct was regulated by an Ordinance of 1161, and there were 18 of them. In 1351 the City Corporation required prostitutes to wear particular clothes. In 1380 all the *bagnios* were owned by William Walworth (*see* RICHARD II). Henry VII closed them in 1506, but reopened twelve in 1507. Henry VIII closed them all in 1546. The result was that prostitution and hothouses spread elsewhere, especially Covent Garden. The Restoration *bagnios* did not have resident girls but kept lists and sent for them on request. They were quiet, luxuriously appointed places. The best known, all at Covent Garden (near the clubs), were Molly King's, Mother Douglas or Cole's, Mrs Gould's and Mrs Stanhope's. Brothels on French lines with resident girls, known as *Seraglios,* were introduced by a Mrs Goadhy in 1750 in Berwick St, Soho. Charlotte Hayes followed suit in King's Place, Pall Mall, and Mrs Mitchell, Mrs Prendergast and the negress Miss Harriet, settled there too. Of the later brothel keepers, the most distinguished was Mary Wilson (fl. 1815-30), who had successive establishments in Old Bond St, St. Pancras and St. John's Wood. She wrote several books on the subject, and translated Aretino.

By 1840 Leicester Square was the main centre. The subject is inherently open to exaggeration: one contemporary improbably estimated the number of brothels in London at 1500 and another at 5000. The former also mentions long rooms of taverns where 200 (*sic*) prostitutes assembled at one time. Brothels had, however, spread to certain ports and garrison towns. From 1864 prostitutes had under the Contagious Diseases Acts 1864-9 to be medically examined in 11 such towns; from 1869 in 18. In 1885 brothels were prohibited, and in 1886 Mrs Josephine Butler's campaign ended medical examination. The combination drove prostitutes onto the streets, mainly in Soho, Whitechapel and Paddington. There were recognised areas in most other large cities. The prosperity of the independent prostitute varied considerably, but probably reached its peak in World War II when there were large numbers of American troops with money to spend.

In 1958 a newspaper inspired campaign to "clean up our streets" led to inflated reports of the number of street women, and the passage of the Street Offences Act, 1959. This forbade soliciting in public and encouraged the telephone summoned call girl reminiscent of the Restoration. It also, later, failed to suppress street soliciting, and by the 1990s protection rackets related to public prostitution were growing up in many larger towns.

BROTHER'S CLUB was founded in opposition to the Kit-Kat Club, by St. John in 1711, and was frequented by Tory ministers and their propagandists such as Arbuthnot, John Freind, Prior and Swift. It advised on literary patronage.

BROUAGE (S. Brittany). The salt pans, exploited from earliest times, were the chief source of salt in the west from 14th to 17th cents (*see* HANSE) and, because of the high French salt excise, a hotbed of smugglers.

BROUGHAM, Henry Peter (1778-1868) 1st Ld. BROUGHAM and VAUX (1831) was called to the Scottish bar in 1800 and in 1802 helped to found the *Edinburgh Review.* He came to London in 1803. In 1806 he was secretary of the Rosslyn-St. Vincent mission to Lisbon, and in 1808 he was called to the English bar. He was already well known from his support of liberal causes such as the anti-slavery movement. In 1810 he became M.P. for Camelford, and in 1815 accepted Winchelsea from Lord Darlington. He soon became one of the most effective opposition speakers. He opposed repression and restriction, and spoke against the Six Acts, but he was really a whig and despite Benthamite leanings, openly disliked radicals. In 1818 he secured the appointment of the committee on education, and its investigations into charitable foundations such as Eton, Winchester and the universities, revealed many scandals. He was a friend and adviser of the Princess of Wales, and when in 1820 she became Queen he became her att-gen. She and her husband had long been estranged and she was at Geneva; Lord Liverpool's govt., through Brougham, offered her 50,000 a year if she stayed abroad, but Brougham did not pass the offer on. In June she arrived in England, and from Aug. to Oct. his brilliant advocacy before the House of Lords defeated her divorce bill. This gave him immense prestige and popularity.

From 1822, when Canning became Foreign Sec. Brougham was a powerful backbencher who acted in general support of a liberal policy; he attacked the Holy Alliance, inveighed against French interference in Spain and Austrian tyranny in Italy, favoured R. Catholic emancipation and in 1828 brought forward fruitful proposals for law reform. In 1830 he was elected for Yorkshire, and prepared a parliamentary reform bill of his own. When Grey formed his whig govt. of 1831, he threatened to proceed with his bill if he was not offered a seat in the cabinet, and accordingly became Lord Chancellor. This gave him an opportunity to carry out some of his law reforms; he accelerated Chancery procedure; and instituted the Central Criminal Court. At the same time he engaged zestfully in the struggles around the great Reform Bill. His natural flamboyance on one of these occasions seems to have overreached itself: ending a speech in an attitude of prayer, he was helped to his feet by friends who thought that he was drunk.

His personal vanities, boastfulness, and intriguing habits were meanwhile undoing his reputation. He was suspected of a hand in the indiscretions which forced Grey to resign in 1834; and annoyed the King by undignified behaviour in Scotland; his manipulation of the *Edinburgh Review* became widely known, and at the time of Melbourne's resignation in Nov. 1834, he betrayed to *The Times* a confidential interview between Melbourne and the King. Not surprisingly, when Melbourne returned in 1835, he refused to have Brougham with him. Accordingly, Brougham became the effective leader of the opposition peers (though theoretically a govt. supporter) and when the Melbourne Ministry fell, though he then went officially into opposition, he gave much support to Peel. Thereafter he gradually faded out of public life; but he contributed to the unfortunate defeat of the Westmorland life peerage claim in 1856.

BROUGHTON CASTLE (Oxon) was built in 1306 and passed in 1451 to the Lords Saye and Sele. It was transformed into a Tudor mansion between 1554 and 1599.

BROWN, Douglas Clifton (1879-1958) Vist. RUFFSIDE (1951). Unionist M.P. for Hexham from 1918 to 1923 and from 1924 to 1951, became dep. chairman of Ways and Means in Nov. 1938, a privy councillor in 1941, and chairman in Jan. 1943. Within two months Mr Speaker Fitzroy died and he succeeded him in an eight years old House well disciplined by his predecessor and untroubled by home politics. In 1945, however, with the great Labour victory, the climate changed abruptly, for the opposition, especially, was unwilling to accept rulings tamely. His patience and good temper now replaced Fitzroy's authoritarianism, and was so successful and popular (despite occasional difficulties) that he was re-elected unanimously after the election of 1950. The very small govt. majority inevitably created much procedural wrangling foreign to his temperament, and he retired in 1951.

BROWN, George Alfred (1914-85) Ld. GEORGE-BROWN of JEVINGTON (1970) was Labour M.P. for Belper, and after junior posts became Min. of Works (1951) and in the first Wilson govt. took over the Dept. of Economic Affairs, designed to formulate a national economic plan. He was Foreign Sec. from 1966 to 1968 but then resigned because the govt. had virtually abandoned his ideas on economic planning. He belonged to his party's right wing, was its deputy leader from 1960 to 1970 but failed to gain the leadership against Wilson. After 1970 his enthusiasm waned and he finally supported the new Social Democrats. Convivial and charming, his ebullient outspokenness often entertained the public if not everyone. Nikita Khrushchev, who walked out of a London dinner after getting into an argument with him, called his conversation 'scandalous and completely unacceptable', a compliment which delighted George Brown.

BROWN, Sir George (1790-1865). See CRIMEAN WAR.

BROWN, Sir John (1816-96) the owner of the vast Atlas steelworks at Sheffield, invented the conical steel spring railway buffer (which greatly improved the performance of trains) in 1848, and the method of armourplating warships (then just begun) with rolled steel plate.

BROWN, Sir John (1880-1958), territorial soldier, became chairman of the British Legion in 1930 and in 1937 was drawn into the War Office as Deputy Dir-Gen. of the Territorial Army by Leslie Hore-Belisha who was then reforming the army. Immensely successful and popular, his activities helped to lay the foundations of the World War II army. He retired in 1941.

BROWN (1) Lancelot ("Capability") (1715-83) Northumbrian born, he began as kitchen gardener to Lord Cobham at Stowe at the time (1740) when William Kent was landscaping the grounds. He soon developed Kent's ideas. His comparatively naturalistic gardening style superseded the French geometrical patterns hitherto in vogue. He designed or remodelled the gardens at, amongst others, Kew, Blenheim, Chatsworth and Nuneham Courtenay. His designs sometimes included Gothic 'ruins', in imitation of landscape paintings by Claude. He was also a successful architect whose houses were better known for their comfort and practicality than their aesthetic appeal. He made a fortune, was widely respected and in 1770 was High Sheriff of Huntingdonshire. His son **(2)** also **Lancelot** was for twelve years between 1780 and 1794 an M.P.

BROWN (1) Peter (1784-1863), a Canadian journalist, founded the *British Chronicle* in New York in 1838 and then moved to Toronto and renamed it *The Banner* in 1843. It was an organ of Scots Free Church opinion. His son **(2) George (1818-80)** founded the Toronto *Globe* in 1845 to support the reform party but broke with them, and from 1851 to 1861 and from 1863 to 1867 was an extreme radical M.P. in the Canadian Assembly. He was one of the earliest to advocate a federation of British North America. He tried but failed to form a govt. in 1858 and was briefly president of the council in 1864. In 1873 he became a Senator. He was assassinated by one of his own dismissed employees.

BROWN, Adm. William (1777-1857) was pressed into the Royal Navy in 1796. He eventually became a merchant captain and settled at Buenos Aires, where in 1814 the republican govt. offered him the naval command. He twice defeated Spanish squadrons and made a fortune privateering. In the Argentine-Brazilian wars of 1826 and 1827 he also won successes but was eventually caught with inferior numbers and forced to surrender. He commanded operations against Uruguay between 1842 and 1845.

BROWN, William John (1894-1960) joined the civil service as a boy clerk in 1910, and in 1912 caused a sensation by giving evidence on behalf of other boy clerks to the royal commision on the civil service, which accepted his views. In 1919 he resigned to become gen. sec. of the new Civil Service Clerical Association, which involved him in running battles with conservative politicians; having failed in 1922, 1923, and 1924 to gain a parliamentary seat for Labour he was elected for W. Wolverhampton in 1929. He soon disagreed with his own party on unemployment policies, in Mar. 1931 he refused the whip, and in the elections of Oct. 1931 and 1935 he was defeated as an independent. In 1942, however, he succeeded at Rugby against national but with local Labour support. With his markedly independent outlook, he was opposed both by Labour and Conservative parties in 1945 but held the seat. He had resigned the secretaryship of his union in 1942 to become its parliamentary representative and from then until 1950 he was one of the few independent M.P.s. A strong upholder of personal liberty, he concentrated his generally trenchant criticisms upon left wing politicians, communists, and the govt. in power. In 1951, however, he lost his seat on a split vote and never got back. He remained until his death influential, partly through journalism (as "Diogenes" in *Time and Tide*) and as a radio and television personality.

BROWNE (1) Sir Anthony (?-1548) was a half brother of William Fitzwilliam, E. of Southampton. He was one of Henry VIII's esquires; ambassador to France in 1528 and 1533 and master of the horse in 1539. He also served as a justice in eyre in 1545 and was named guardian of P. Edward and P. Elizabeth. He acquired Battle and was already wealthy when he inherited Cowdray from his half brother. His son **(2) Sir Anthony (1526-92) 1st Vist. MONTAGUE (1554)** a R. Catholic by conviction and briefly imprisoned for recusancy in 1551, was entirely loyal to the political settlement with which his fortune was bound up. He was also master of the horse, and was sent on embassy to the Pope in 1554. He served before St. Quentin in 1557, and Elizabeth I employed him as ambassador to Spain in 1561. He was also member of the commission which tried Mary Q. of Scots in 1587.

BROWN[E], George (?-1556) Abp. of DUBLIN (1535), originally English provincial of the Austin Friars, was the prime executant and champion of the Irish Reformation. By opposing the claim of the bishops to be a separate estate in the Irish parliament he frustrated their opposition to reformist legislation, and introduced the bills for securing Irish first fruits to the Crown and for dissolving the monasteries. He is described by Irish religious opponents as ignorant, greedy, profligate, gluttonous, drunken and corrupt, but he successfully defended himself to the govt., and his Anglicanisation of the institutional church endured for three centuries. His substitution of an English for a Latin prayer book made little difference to the Irish who understood neither.

BROWN, Field-Marshal George, Count (1698-1792). This Irish soldier of fortune found his way to the Russian army in 1730. Taken prisoner and enslaved by the Turks in 1737, he was redeemed and then served in Finland against the Swedes in 1743. In the Seven Years War he was a material contributor to two of the few defeats – Kollin in 1757 and Zorndorf in 1758 – inflicted on Frederick the Great. He ended up as Gov. of Livonia.

BROWNE, Hablot Knight ("Phiz") (1815-82), illustrator and especially the creator of the visual image of many of Dickens characters.

BROWNE, Sir Richard (?-1669) a presbyterian officer of London trained bands, disarmed the Kent royalists in 1642, and suppressed a rising there in 1643. As a major-gen. he reduced the royalist vicinity of Oxford in 1644 and took the surrender of the city in 1646. He was a commissioner for receiving Charles I from the Scots in 1647. Elected M.P. for Wycombe in 1645 he acted with the so-called Presbyterian party of Holles, who wished to restore the King on reasonable terms. Hence he supported the disbandment of the Army, opposed its interventions in politics and was considered a candidate for the command of the alternative force based on the London trained bands. He was therefore purged from the House by Col. Pride (Dec. 1648) and imprisoned until 1653. He was prevented from taking his seat in 1656 in common with other opponents of Cromwell, but became M.P. for London in 1659 in Richard Cromwell's parliament. He was now committed to the recall of Charles II who knighted him in 1660 when he was Lord Mayor. In 1661 he suppressed Venner's rising.

BROWNE, Robert (?1550-1633). See CONGREGATIONALISM.

BROWNE, Sir Thomas (1605-82) was educated at Winchester and Oxford, and studied medicine at Monpellier, Padua and Leyden (Doctor 1633). He lived near Halifax until 1637 when he moved to Norwich, and also became a Doctor of Medicine of Oxford. He was now famous as a physician but meanwhile he had, as early as 1635, written for private circulation his well-known *Religio Medici* (Lat = A doctor's religion). It was pirated from a bad copy, so he published an authorised version in 1643. It attracted instant attention, for at a time of religious and political passion it set forth with ingenuity and attractiveness, a reasonable man's view of the fundamental questions then agitating opinion. He was an Anglican who took his Bible as his primary guide and, where it was silent, the Church; but he felt free to use his intelligence where both were silent or in conflict. As, however, it is necessary to use intelligence to study the texts, reasoned criticism is apt to reveal anomalies and lacunae which must be explained or reconciled by further reading. Thus private judgement, at least of able people, is not so unimportant as might at first appear.

Browne's sympathies were royalist, and royalists admired his book, but this did not reduce the respect in which he was held in parliamentary E. Anglia. He wrote much else, including his learned *Hydrotaphia* (Urn Burial) and the *Garden of Cyrus*, a fantastical disquisition of the history of horticulture. Charles II knighted him in 1671 on a state visit to Norwich. He left large collections of documents, plants, birds eggs and curiosities.

BROWNISTS. See CONGREGATIONALISM.

BRUCE. A family of Norman barons and Scottish Kings, originating at Brix or Bruis near Cherbourg, and possibly related to the Ds. of Normandy. **(1) Robert (I) (?-c. 1094)** and other Bruces came over with the Conqueror, and he was given 43 manors in North Yorkshire. His son **(2) Robert (II) (c. 1078-1141)** obtained in addition the Honour of Annandale from David I of Scots, with whom he had been friendly at the Court of Henry I, but fought against him at the B. of the Standard (1138). Of his sons the elder **(3) Adam** took English lands, while the younger **(4) Robert (III) (?-1189)** had saved the Scottish Honour for himself by joining the Scots at the battle. He was conveniently captured by his own father. He was a powerful magnate in S. W. Scotland and founded the fortunes of the Scottish Bruces, but kept up English connections, especially by way of the family foundation of Guisborough Priory. His son **(5) Robert (IV) (?-1190)** married Isabel, *d.* of K. William the Lion, but father and son died within months of each other, and Annandale passed to the second son **(6) William (?-1215)** and at his death to **(7) Robert (V) (?-1245)**. He married Isabel, the second *d.* of David, E. of Huntingdon, the younger brother of William the Lion. These royal connections founded the family's claim to the Scots Crown, and the great Lordship of Annandale made Robert V one of the most powerful men in Scotland until his death. Their son **(8) Robert (VI) (1210-95)** called *The Competitor,* succeeded to his father's Scottish lands in 1245 and to his mother's share of the Huntingdon properties in 1251. He also married a daughter of Gilbert of Clare, E. of Gloucester. He was thus a personage of consequence in both Kingdoms. In 1238 the childless K. Alexander II recognised his claim to the throne; but Alexander III's birth in 1241 voided the recognition, and on the latter's succession as a minor in 1255 Robert, with John Baliol the elder, became one of the fifteen regents. With interest in both countries, he naturally favoured a policy of friendship with England and negotiated the King's marriage to Margaret, *d.* of Henry III, who appointed him sheriff of Cumberland. He had served at intervals as a justice of the English Kings Bench, and supported Henry III in the Barons War. As a result he became Chief Justice in 1268, but forfeited English judicial office on the accession of Edward I. He then returned to Scotland. In Feb. 1283-4 Robert was present at the meeting of the Scottish estates at Scone which recognised the rights of Margaret, the Maid of Norway, but when Alexander III died in 1286, an indecisive civil war broke out between the nobles of South and West Scotland headed by the Bruces (i.e. Robert VI and his son) **(9) Robert (VII) (1253-1304) E. of CARRICK** (in right of his wife) and the Comyns and Galwegions headed by John Baliol. This ended in the compromise of Brigham in 1290 whereby the crowns of England and Scotland were to be united by the marriage of Margaret and Prince (later King) Edward. Margaret, however, died in Oct. whereupon thirteen claimants for the Scottish throne came forward. Of these three were taken seriously, namely John Baliol the Younger, Robert (VI) Bruce and John Hastings.

John Hastings claimed that Scotland was divisible between the descendants of the three granddaughters of David I as parceners. The Baliol claim rested on primogeniture among the granddaughters. The Bruces' claim was based on Robert (VI) being closer in generation to David I than the others. The matter was referred to K. Edward I in May 1291: he appointed a court of 24 English and 40 Scots which awarded the crown to Baliol in Nov. 1292. Robert the Competitor then resigned his claims to the E. of Carrick who avoided attending Baliol's first Parliament, and in 1293 married his daughter to Eirick, K. of Norway. When the Competitor died in 1295 Carrick became the castellan of Carlisle for Edward I; he sided with the English when Baliol tried in 1296 to assert his independence, and it was with English help that he recovered his Annandale lands from the Comyns to whom Baliol had awarded them in consequence. Thereafter he lived in England. His son **(10) Robert the Bruce (1274-1329)** was the famous K. of Scots who reigned as **Robert II** (q.v.) from 1306 to 1329. Of his children **(11) Marjory** married Robert the Steward (Stuart) of Scotland. They were the ancestors of the royal house of Stuart. **(12) K. David II (1324-71).**

BRUCE. See ABERDARE AILESBURY; KINCARDINE.

BRUEYS D'AIGUILLIERS, François Paul (1753-98). French naval officer, discharged for royalism in 1793 but reinstated in 1795, was rapidly promoted because of the shortage of naval talent. He commanded the fleet in Bonaparte's Egyptian expedition of 1798, seized Malta, landed the troops at Alexandria and lost his fleet and his life to Nelson at the B. of the Nile (Aug. 1798).

BRUGES. See FLANDERS-2 *et seq.*; HANSE *passim*; STAPLE B-2,3,7.

BRUMAIRE, COUP D'ÉTAT OF. The 18th Brumaire of the year VIII (9 Nov. 1799) was the day on which Napoleon Bonaparte, acting on the advice of Siéyès, moved to overthrow the French Directory. He lost his nerve and the day was saved by his quick witted younger brother Lucien, who was President of the Chamber. This enabled Bonaparte to establish the Consulate. See SECOND COALITION, WAR OF, 1799-1801.

BRUMMAGEM, a corruption or literal spelling of the pronunciation of BROMWICHHAM, an early form of Birmingham. The word was used for an article, especially a cheap-jack article made there.

BRUMMEL, George Bryan "Beau" (1778-1840). His grandfather, William, let apartments in Bury St, London to, *inter alia*, Charles Jenkinson, later first E. of Liverpool. Through this acquaintanceship Beau's father, also William, acquired lucrative appointments and was for many years private sec. to Lord North. In 1790 he sent his son to Eton and left him about £30,000 at his death in 1795.

At Eton Beau got to know the P. of Wales. This, together with his remarkable social gifts and fastidious taste, made his house the hub of London society, and himself the arbiter of fashion and manners. This might have lasted even after he quarrelled with the Prince in 1814, but in May 1816 he fled from his gambling debts to Calais and never returned. His many friends often visited him there and supplied him with money in quantities which, however, were quite insufficient for his habits. He was briefly imprisoned for debt in 1835. In 1837 he began to show signs of mental derangement and he died at an asylum in Caen.

BRUNANBURH, B. of (937). See AI[E]THILSTAN-3.

BRUNEI. See BORNEO; INDONESIA.

BRUNEL, Isambard Kingdom (1806-59), polymath and civil engineer, began his independent career by designing the Clifton Suspension Bridge at Bristol, followed by the harbour and docks there, and at Monkwearmouth, Brentford and Milford Haven. In 1833 he became engineer to the Great Western Rly and, railways being then in their infancy, carried into effect his later controversial broad gauge layout with its appurtenances including the great Albert Bridge at Saltash. He was also responsible for railways in Italy, Australia and Bengal.

In 1836 he turned to shipbuilding. His aim was to build ships capable of carrying enough coal for their outward transatlantic run. His *Great Western* was the first steamship designed for such a scheduled service. His experiments and observations convinced him of the practicality of screw propellers in the Royal Navy (1845). The *Great Britain* was the first large screw-propelled ship. Between 1853 and 1859 he built the *Great Eastern* which had propellers, paddles and sails, and in which he introduced the hitherto unknown double skin construction. This ship, huge in terms of contemporary construction, was a failure as a transatlantic liner.

Amongst his other achievements were improvements in heavy guns, a hospital in Turkey and experiments in the use of carbonic acid gas for propulsion. He was also an enthusiastic promoter of the Great Exhibition of 1851 and a member of the committee responsible for the Crystal Palace.

BRUNELLESCHI. See RENAISSANCE-4.

BRUNO, Giordano (1548-1600), a lapsed Dominican, after quarrelling with the Geneva Calvinists, enjoyed Henri III's protection at Paris in 1581, and then lectured on mathematical and cosmological subjects at Oxford. Received with hostility, he moved to London where he joined the intellectual friends of Robert Dudley, and wrote a number of works which seem to anticipate modern quantum mathematics. After adventures in France and Germany he went to Venice, and in 1593 was seized by the Inquisition and ultimately burned at Rome.

BRUNO, St. of COLOGNE (?1030-1101) founded the Carthusian Order in 1084.

BRUNSWICK (Ger = BRAUNSCHWEIG). This much partitioned duchy was briefly united in the 16th cent. and then divided in 1569 between the families of Dannenberg (later Brunswick-Wolfenbüttel) and Lüneburg-Celle, who later became Dukes, Electors and eventually Kings of Hanover and Great Britain. Bonaparte annexed Brunswick Wolfenbüttel to the Kingdom of Westphalia, but it reverted to its Duke in 1814. He was killed at the B. of Quatre Bras in 1815, and the Duchy was ruled by the British Prince Regent as regent for the next duke, who came of age in 1830 and abdicated. His brother, William, then reigned until 1884. Social and military connections between Britain and Brunswick were close until 1830 and

traces of them such as Brunswick Square in London and the uniforms of the Rifle Brigade (copied from the Brunswick Hussars) remain. Duke William was unmarried. The connection between the Hanoverian and the British Crowns ceased in 1837 at the accession of Q. Victoria by reason of Hanoverian Salic Law. By Prussian annexation of 1866, K. George of Hanover (also D. of Cumberland) lost his throne. In 1879 he claimed the succession to Brunswick as next of kin. Prussia objected because he had never renounced his Hanoverian claim. At Duke William's death, ex-K. George's son, Ernest, D. of Cumberland, claimed the throne, but the Council of Regency appointed a Prussian Regent and then a Mecklenburger. In due course his son P. Ernest Augustus of Cumberland renounced his family's claim to Hanover, was recognised as Duke and married Kaiser William II's only daughter.

BRUNSWICKIAN CLUBS were bodies of Ulster Orange extremists formed in 1827-8 to resist R. Catholic relief.

BRUSSELS (Belgium), at the crossing of the R. Senne and the road from Cologne to Bruges, was no more than the centre of a 13th cent. textile industry, but its wealth created a burgher class which, as early as 1229, secured municipal and commercial privileges from the Ds. of Brabant. English competition destroyed the woollen trade in the 14th cent. and the clothiers and weavers migrated, some to England, some to Italy, but the town's prosperity based on lighter textiles and foreign exchange continued to grow. The fortifications were much enlarged between 1357 and 1379. A generation later the Dukes moved their capital from Louvain to Brussels which, when Brabant was joined to other Burgundian possessions in 1430, became the capital of the Low Countries. The decline of the Hanseatic Kontor at Bruges caused much financial business to migrate to Brussels, and when Charles V became Emperor it was the effective financial and political capital of Europe. It was also the H.Q. of the imperial postal system and the seat of a brilliant court over which three remarkable women presided as governors: the emperor's aunt Margaret of Austria (r. 1507-15 and 1518-30), then his sister Mary of Hungary (r. 1531-56) and finally his illegitimate daughter Margaret of Parma (r. 1559-67).

Tolerance in matters of opinion was traditional with the local patriciat ("lignages") and the Dukes. Brussels was a centre of heretical opinions in the 14th cent. The bégards preached there contemporaneously with the English Lollards, and Tyndale and other translators of the Bible resorted there under Mary I. This safety ended with K. Philip II's change of policy in 1567 when the D. of Alva was appointed to suppress heresy and disorder by force. Margaret of Parma resigned to avoid participation in the new approach which, beginning with the execution of Egmont and Hoorne (June 1568) had provoked the Dutch into full rebellion by 1572. With the Emperor now in Vienna, and the Low Countries divided by war, the city's practical importance would, in any event, have declined but thereafter civil commotion and the wars waged in Belgium (including a destructive bombardment in 1695) eroded its prosperity still further. Its decline was arrested only after 1706 when Marlborough drove out the French, in occupation since 1701, and established great military depots there. The revival continued on a modest scale after the P. of Utrecht (1713) had transferred Belgium to Austria (*see* BELGIUM; BRABANT). It was Wellington's military base in 1815 and became the Belgian capital in 1831, deriving until 1914 much prosperity from its connection with the Congo. Its post World War II prosperity began with the establishment in 1957 of the H.Q. of the E.E.C. (later E.U.) there, but was fully launched by the World Fair of 1958. *See also* EUROPEAN COMMUNITIES.

BRUSSELS CONFERENCE (1920). See REPARATIONS.

BRUSSELS TREATY (17 Mar. 1948) created the West

European Union, a defensive alliance between Britain, France, Belgium, Holland and Luxemburg. It provided for defence committees of ministers, and a combined general staff in Paris. F-M Vist. Montgomery was the first C-of-Staff with Gen. de Lattre de Tassigny as his deputy. These institutions were absorbed into the North Atlantic Pact signed at Washington in Apr. 1949, which developed into the North Atlantic Treaty Organisation (N.A.T.O.) in 1950-1.

BRUSSELS, T. of, or ACCESSION T. (1972) admitted Denmark, Ireland, Norway and the United Kingdom into full membership of the European Economic Community. Norway did not ratify the treaty and so only the other three were actually admitted. *See* ROME, T. of.

BRUT, *BRUT Y TYWYSOGION* (Welsh = Brut or Chronicle of the Princes). In the early Anglo-Saxon period, British chroniclers began to claim Trojan ancestry for the British Kings, starting their history with the splendid K. Brutus. A complete saga of Brutus and his successors was first given to the world in the 12th cent. *Historia Regum Britanniae* (Lat = History of the Kings of Britain) by the Welshman Geoffrey of Monmouth, who claimed to have read of Brutus in a very ancient book in the British tongue, brought from Brittany and given him by Walter, Archdeacon of Oxford. Nothing else is known of this book.

Brutus, he said, came from Troy, conquered the local giants and built London (called Trinovantium or New Troy). From his eldest son sprang the line of the Kings including Bradud, builder of Bath, and his son Lear; Gorbaduc and in the time of Julius Caesar, Cassibelaunus (or Cymbeline) and his brother Lud (who gave his name to London). King Coel (Old King Cole) of Colchester was succeeded by his son-in-law Constantius (father of Constantine), and in the time of the Saxons there was Vortigern, the Roman Aurelius Ambrosius and his nephew Arthur who were successively victorious over the invaders. The story ends with the defeated British taking refuge in Brittany whence they will eventually return to claim their own.

The tale was an instant success, and as the British History or Brut it became the standard opening of mediaeval histories of England, whilst in mediaeval Wales it was to start the *Chronicle of the Princes*. It was widely believed even in Tudor and Stuart times when historical inquiry was often synonymous with discussion of its authenticity.

BRYCE. (1) James the elder (1767-1857), a Glasgow minister, moved in 1805 to Killaig near Londonderry and founded the Associate Presbytery of Ireland. His third son **(2) James the younger (1806-77)** was a distinguished mathematician and geologist. His son **(3) James (1838-1922) Vist. BRYCE (1913)** F.R.S., O.M. was a lawyer statesman and historian. His *Holy Roman Empire* (1864) won international acclaim, and in 1866 he made a well-received report to the Schools Inquiry (or Taunton Commission) on schools in the W. Midlands and Wales. From 1868 to 1874 he lectured on law at Manchester, where he was very active in developing the university, and from 1870 to 1893 he was Regius Prof. of Civil Law at Oxford and made many visits to Russia and the Caucasus, making himself an expert on Near Eastern affairs. He was a liberal M.P. from 1880 to 1906. He also made three extended visits to the U.S.A. and wrote a well-known book, *The American Commonwealth*, on its institutions. The family connection with Ireland gave him an insight into Irish affairs. He voted for the Coercion Bill in 1881 but against the Crimes Bill of 1882, and in 1885 he concluded that Irish problems could be solved only by Home Rule. In 1892, when Gladstone reorganised his last govt., Bryce entered the Cabinet as Chanc. of the Duchy, and was in the Cabinet Committee which prepared the Irish Home Rule Bill. When Gladstone retired in 1894 he became Pres. of the Board of Trade under Rosebery, and

he also acted as Chairman of the Royal Commission on Education of 1894-5. The principles of the Bryce Commission's report were the foundation of the English educational system for the next 80 years.

Shortly afterwards he visited South Africa. As he concluded that war with the Boers was avoidable, he was not electorally popular during the Boer War. His views were shared by Campbell Bannerman, but when the reunited liberal party won the election of 1905 it was necessary to reconcile the liberal imperialists to Campbell Bannerman's leadership; Bryce was offered the Chief Secretaryship for Ireland and accepted it as reluctantly as every other holder of that office. His administration was not a success, for the liberal victory had raised Irish expectations which Bryce now seemed unable to satisfy. In Dec. 1906 he resigned, and became Ambassador to Washington. Here he was both popular and respected, and brought off a number of valuable diplomatic operations including the arbitration convention on American-Canadian disputes. When he returned in 1914 he became a member of The Hague Tribunal.

At the start of World War I Bryce was invited to investigate German atrocities against Belgian civilians. His experience of this led him to conclude that after the German defeat permanent international machinery for the prevention of war had to be set up; in 1917 he submitted (after much correspondence with American statesmen) a memorandum to the British govt. in which he proposed the structure of a League of Nations much as it later emerged. He believed that American participation was necessary, but was disappointed.

In 1918 he was chairman of the abortive joint conference on House of Lords reform, and in 1921 he addressed the Lords in support of the Irish treaty.

BRYDGES (1) Sir John (?1490-1556) 1st Ld. CHANDOS of SUDELEY (1554), a companion of Henry VIII, was Lieut. of the Tower from 1553 to 1554 and helped to put down Wyatt's insurrection in 1554. For this Mary I ennobled him. He had to supervise the burning of Bp. Hooper at Gloucester in 1555. **(2) Grey (1579-1621) 5th Ld. (1602),** called 'The King of the Cotswolds' was imprisoned for supposed complicity in Essex's rebellion in 1601 but became a favourite of James I. He was immensely rich and given to lavish entertainment and display. **(3) James (1673-1744) 9th Ld. (1714) 1st E. of CAERNARVON (1714), 1st D. of CHANDOS (1719)** was M.P. for Hereford from 1698 to 1714 and paymaster of the forces abroad from 1707 to 1712. He was a patron of Handel, who wrote the Chandos Anthems for him and stayed in his house. He built a great mansion at Canons, Edgware, and started another in Cavendish Square, London.

BRYDON, John McKean (1840-1901) architect of many neo-classical buildings, including the large govt. offices facing Parliament Square, London.

BRYTHONIC LANGUAGE GROUP. *See* CELTS.

BUBBLE ACT (1720). *See* COMPANIES.

BUBONIC PLAGUE. *See* PLAGUE.

BUCCANEERS were named after a process of preserving meat for use at sea, called boucanning. They flourished in the Caribbean in the 17th cent. because of the Spanish trading monopoly, and congregated particularly at the French island of Tortuga (La Tortue), whose governors issued letters of marque without asking too many questions, and later at Port Royal, Jamaica, after its capture by the British in 1655. Their activities were often highly organised in a democratic, if commercial, way and were carried on in the twilight zone between rank piracy and legitimate privateering made feasible by wars, the slowness of official communications and the temptations of smuggling encouraged by the Spanish monopoly.

Some had distinguished careers on both sides of the law: for example Henry Morgan stormed Porto Bello in 1668 and after he had taken Panama in 1670 absconded with most of the loot; yet in 1671 he was knighted and subsequently became deputy governor of Jamaica with a commission to suppress buccaneering. Other buccaneers were William Dampier; Morgan's pupils John Coxon and Bartholomew Sharp, and John Cook. The last important buccaneering operation was the unsuccessful attack on Panama in 1684. In 1689 the great wars against Louis XIV broke out and buccaneering was technically ended by all the buccaneers becoming lawful privateers. Many of them and much of their wealth vanished in twenty minutes in the great Port Royal (Jamaica) earthquake of 1692.

After the P. of Utrecht (1713) there was some sporadic buccaneering, which was universally outlawed.

BUCER, Martin (1491-1551), an early associate of Luther, was one of the first priests among the reformers to marry. Henry VIII consulted him on his divorce, and after moving to Strasburg he led the reformers there. He and Luther had doctrinal disagreements as Bucer moved closer to Zwingli and became a leader of reformed churches in Switzerland, but they never became enemies. Much of Bucer's continental life was spent trying to reconcile the various protestant sects. He refused to support the Interim of Augsburg and when it was enforced against Strasburg he moved to England, where he acted as Abp. Cranmer's adviser and contributed to the 'reformed' rather than the Lutheran tone of English protestantism. He was Regius Prof. of Divinity at Cambridge from 1549 and died there.

BUCHAN, John (1875-1940) 1st Ld. TWEEDSMUIR (1935), one the most articulate men of his generation, was called to the bar and had already published three books by 1901 when he became Lord Milner's private secretary in South Africa. In 1903 he became a director of Nelson's, the publishers, and continued to write. *Prester John* appeared in 1910; *The 39 Steps* in 1915 and *Greenmantle* in 1916. They made him famous. He was also, in World War I, on the H.Q. staff of the British Army in France, and in 1917 he became Director of Information at the War Office. In 1927 he became an M.P. for the Scottish universities, and was Lord High Commissioner to the Scottish Church Assembly in 1933-4. Throughout this period his books came out regularly and increased his fame. They included, besides the novels, biographies of Julius Caesar, Montrose, Sir Walter Scot and Oliver Cromwell. In 1935 he was appointed Gov-Gen. of Canada, an office which he held with dignity and success until his death.

BUCHAN, EARLS OF. *See* COMYN *for the first creation;* STEWART *for the second.*

BUCHANAN, George (1506-82). A learned and much travelled Scot, began his influential contacts with politics when tutor in Paris of Gilbert, E. of Cassilis. He returned to Scotland in 1536 where he was tutor to an illegitimate son of K. James V. Arrested as a heretic during Card. Beaton's persecution in 1539, he escaped to England and then to Paris, and was invited to Bordeaux by Govea, the Portuguese principal of the College of Guienne. Montaigne was one of his pupils, and the elder Scaliger one of his friends. From 1547 he helped Govea to organise the new Portuguese University at Coimbra, but was secluded by the inquisition for suspected heresy on Govea's death.

Released in 1552 he went first to England and then to France where, as tutor to the children of the Marshal de Brissac, he acquired military experience. By 1562 he was back in Scotland, teaching classics to Q. Mary, and taking part in the govt. of the reformed church as a lay member of the General Assembly in 1563 and of the commission which revised the *Book of Discipline*. He was moderator of the Assembly in 1567. This was the year of Darnley's murder (10 Feb.) and Bothwell's marriage to the Queen (15 May): Buchanan joined her opponents and acted as secretary of the Scottish deputation at the conference convened by Q. Elizabeth at York to inquire into Mary's position. He was thus implicated in the production of the "Casket Letters", an important element in the negotiations, but it is not thought that he himself forged them.

Mary having fled to England, the council appointed Buchanan in 1570 to be tutor to James VI (then four years old), a duty he performed actively until 1579. Though a man of personal moderation and charm, he did not make upon his pupil the impression which he intended but he corresponded with the learned all over Europe, ranging from Tycho Brahe and Roger Ascham to Theodore Beza, and in 1579 he composed (as a parting gift) the most influential of his writings, the *De Jure Regni* (Lat = The Law of a Kingdom), an exposition of limited monarchy and the right of resistance to tyrants. This became a standard work and provided intellectual inspiration for the English parliamentary opposition to his pupil James VI and I and to Charles I. *See* TRUE LAW OF FREE MONARCHIES.

BUCHAREST, T. of (10 Aug. 1913). *See* BALKAN WARS OF 1912.

BUCHAREST, T. of (7 May 1918). Roumania capitulated to the Central Powers in World War I. It was nullified by the defeat of those powers in Nov.

BUCHLAU. *See* AUSTRO-HUNGARY-13 *et seq.*

BUCK. Vigorous, well dressed young men, often of a somewhat ruthless character, were known as bucks throughout the 18th cent. but the term has been specially applied to men-about-town during the Regency.

BUCKHURST, Ld. *See* ELIZABETH I-12,13.

BUCKINGHAM, Ds. of. *See* STAFFORD for first creation; VILLIERS for second creation; and SHEFFIELD.

BUCKINGHAM, E. of. *See* THOMAS OF WOODSTOCK.

BUCKINGHAM AND CHANDOS, Ds. of. *See* GRENVILLE.

BUCKINGHAM AND NORMANBY. *See* SHEFFIELD-5.

BUCKINGHAM PALACE formerly HOUSE (London) was originally built for John Sheffield, D. of Buckingham and Normanby. George III bought it in 1761 for his queen, and it was known as the Queen's House until the 1820s. Nash rebuilt it for George IV, but Q. Victoria was the first sovereign to live there. The entrance was through the Marble Arch, but this was moved to the Hyde Park end of Oxford Street in 1851. After her death the large memorial to her was erected in its place, and the facade of the palace was refaced by Sir Aston Webb to match it. Nash's work fortunately survives on the garden fronts. It was bombed during World War II and the destroyed chapel was rebuilt as an art gallery to exhibit to the public selections from the vast royal art collections. The State Rooms were opened to the public in 1993.

BUCKLE, George Earle (1854-1935), Wykehamist, Fellow of All Souls and, from 1884 to 1912, Editor of *The Times*. Hostile to Irish Home Rule, he published the series on *Parnellism and Crime* which led to the setting up of the Parnell Commission with its accidentally disastrous financial effects on *The Times*. After 1912 he collaborated with W.F. Monypenny in the classic *Life of Beaconsfield*.

BUCKLE, Henry Thomas (1821-62), son of a shipowner, travelled the continent and learned its main languages between 1830 and 1843. He then bought and condensed many hundreds of books, and between 1853 and 1861 wrote a famous but uncompleted *History of Civilisation* based on environmentalist theories.

BUCKMASTER, Stanley Owen (1861-1934) 1st Vist. (1915) entered politics as a liberal M.P. for Cambridge from 1906 to 1910 and for Keighley from 1911 to 1915. He became Sol-Gen. in 1913, and Director of the Press Bureau in 1914. From 1915 to 1916 he was Lord Chancellor, and thereafter served only as a judicial peer.

BUDDHISM (1) began traditionally in the 6th cent. B.C when Gautama opened his career as a teacher at Benares (India) with a sermon known as "Turning the Wheel of Doctrine", in which he expounded the *Four Noble Truths* namely the nature of pain, its cause in craving, its cessation by detachment from craving, and the Path which leads to the cessation of pain. This path is called *The Eightfold Path* and involves self control and avoidance of the extremes of indulgence and self-mortification. Since life never stops but is represented by a succession of states, the proper pursuit of the Path leads upward through successive lives towards ultimate assumption or *Nirvana,* an eternal condition free of impurity, transcending birth and death. A few renounce nirvana in order to remain in the world to help others. These are called ARHATS. Gautama organised his followers into a regular community monastic in kind called *The Sangha*. The rules were simple, forbidding extremes, enjoining morality and requiring certain duties such as periodical preaching. Entry to the Sangha involved a period of novitiate and then a ceremony whose essential feature was the utterance of a triple request for help called the *Threefold Refuge,* the *Three Jewels* or the *Three Treasures*. These refuges are the Buddha, his Doctrine and the Sangha. The Sangha was to be supported by free will gifts from the laity.

(2) Like other religions, Buddhism developed rival sects. Beginning in the 5th cent. B.C., the older or more conservative teachers (the so-called School of Elders or THERAVADA) carried Buddhism to southern India and Ceylon, where their Pali scriptures are preserved. Thence they spread along trade routes to Burma, Thailand, Indonesia and so eventually to China and Japan. A very similar school known as SARVASTIVADA wrote its scriptures in Sanskrit and spread to Gandhara, Kashmir and also eventually to Tibet and China.

(3) In contrast with the strict doctrines and practices of these, there grew up a more liberal body called the School of the Great Assembly or *Mahasanghika* and eventually, about the year A.D. 1, the so-called *MAHAYANA* or Great Vehicle (of Salvation). Its adherents called the Theravadists *HINAYANA* or Little Vehicle in derision. The primary differences between the two outlooks may be shortly summarised as follows: The Theravadists hold that Gautama and his doctrines are the foundation, and that a Buddha is one who successfully follows the Eightfold Path. The Mahayanists believe Gautama to be one of an endless succession of Buddhas and that therefore the individual can seek strength from them as well as Gautama.

(4) Buddhism began to decline in north India after A.D. 500, where the psychological affinity between the dominant Mahayanists and surrounding Hinduism made it hard to maintain its distinctive characteristics. By 1200 it had virtually disappeared in the North West but survived elsewhere diluted with Hindu and magical practices called *TANTRISM*. In this form it was practised in Tibet until the reforms of Tsongkapa (1356-1418) led to the establishment of the *GELUKPA* ("Virtuous Way") sect, of which the Dalai Lamas have all been head.

BUDGET (1) in politics is an account of the state finances and proposals for the future presented by the Chanc. of the Exch. to the Committee of the whole House of Commons. As the accounts are made up to the 31 Mar. and the tax year ends on the 5 Apr. and with it the legal validity of existing taxes, the *annual* budget was presented soon after the latter date. It is usually preceded by White Papers surveying the economy, national income and expenditure and the balance of payments.

(2) The budget statement is made at about 2.30pm and falls into two logical parts. The first is an account of the govt's financial out-turn in the past year, and this is invariably prolonged until after the Stock Exchange closes at 3.30 so that the markets are not violently disturbed by the second part which contains the proposals for changes in existing taxes or the creation of new ones (or both) and the changes in the applications of public funds. These are all kept very secret until the instant of disclosure. The immediate debate is therefore apt, despite

the preceding white papers, to be scrappy because nobody outside the cabinet will have had time to consider the budget's effects. This debate ends, usually the same night, with a series of resolutions under the Provisional Collection of Taxes Act. These enable existing taxes to be levied, if necessary at the new rates, for four months until the full Finance Bill legalising them has been passed. New taxes have, however, to await special enactment, sometimes in a separate bill.

(3) Interim or provisional budgets, usually in the autumn, were presented in times of actual or supposed crisis. In 1994 the full budget was transferred to Nov.

(4) Wartime budgets contain only token figures, to avoid disclosure to an enemy.

BUDGET PROTEST LEAGUE. A Tory organisation specially created to fight Lloyd George's 1909 budget.

BUGANDA (Uganda) was the largest (and Bantu speaking) kingdom of Uganda. The capital, Mengo, was the seat of the Kabaka (King) and Lukiko (legislature). The Kabaka appointed saza (roughly county) and gombolola (district) chiefs. The state levied a systematised tribute and was defended by a conscript army based on a census, and the law was enforced by a judiciary. The economy was based on agriculture, especially the banana. The Kabakas had already been converted to Methodism when, in 1890, the reigning one made a Treaty with the British E. Africa Co, which undertook to recognise him as long as he accepted its advice. The country was on a rising curve of prosperity especially after Uganda became a British Protectorate in 1893. It reached its peak in 1914 when an appalling epidemic, the decisive event in Bugandan history, of sleeping sickness killed over 2M of the 3M people. This shook society and Bugandan leadership of the Ugandan states. By 1950 the British were proposing to form an E. African Federation, in which Buganda would have only a minor role. The Kabaka, Mutesa II, protested and demanded independence by a fixed date. The govt. as inheritor of the Treaty of 1890 considered this a breach of it and exiled Mutesa in 1953. His people stood by him and forced a compromise whereby he should return and eventually become Pres. of Uganda, which he did in 1962.

BUGGERY committed with mankind or beast was an ecclesiastical offence until 1533 when it was made a felony until 1535. It was revived and made perpetual in 1540, but in 1548 the felon was not to suffer in lands, goods or by corruption of blood. Under Mary I all felonies created since 1509 were repealed (1553). In 1562 parliament, lamenting that "sithence ... divers evil disposed persons have been the more bold to commit the said most horrible and detestable vice..." revived and perpetuated the Act of 1533 in its original form. The law, re-enacted in 1861, remains in force save as between adult consenting men.

BUGGY. *See* CARRIAGES.

BUILDING BYE-LAWS AND REGULATIONS. Local authorities began to control the materials and manner of building under the Public Health Act 1875, by making bye-laws. Then to achieve greater uniformity the Local Govt. Board issued model bye-laws which, in theory, they were free to reject. In practice it was easier to accept them because it took time to get bye-laws other than the model, approved. Eventually the Sec. of State for the Environment took power under the Public Health Act 1961 to issue uniform and universal regulations himself. In 1972 the Queen's Bench Div. held that a local authority which had inspected a building for these purposes was liable for negligence if the inspection was improperly carried out and damage resulted. In 1991 the House of Lords confined this rule to the first owner of the building.

BUILDING SOCIETIES. First established in Birmingham in 1775, they originally consisted of a fixed number of subscribers who formed a society for housing themselves and dissolved it when all the members had been housed. These 'terminating' societies began to be replaced towards 1800 by societies which borrowed money from outside. Money could be accumulated and people housed more quickly and there was no need to dissolve. Such societies were called 'Permanent'.

Building Societies first became certifiable under the Friendly Societies Act, 1829, and special legislation was passed in 1836. Compulsory safeguards and tax exemptions led to rapid development. By 1850 there were over 2000 societies, and in 1870 a royal commission was appointed which led to further legislation in 1874 assimilating building society law as nearly as possible to company law. The capital assets of the societies grew from £51,000,000 in 1890 to £4,000,000,000 in 1965. Legislation in the 1980s enabled them to undertake banking activities and as a result many of them became public companies.

BUKEREL. London City aldermanic family after which Bucklersbury ward is named. They flourished mainly as spice and hide merchants, and as court financiers from the conquest to the mid-13th cent. **Andrew (?-1237)** was mayor from 1231.

BUKHARA or BOKHARA (Usbek S.S.R.) attained its highest prosperity in the 16th cent. but by the 19th the weakness of its amirs was attracting British and Russian attention. Two British envoys – Stoddart and Conolly – were put to death there in 1842. In 1866 the amir was defeated by the Russians and Bukhara became a Russian vassal state in 1868. In 1920 a revolution broke out, but in 1922 the Turk Enver Pasha, with the help of the fugitive amir organised a pan-Turanian counter revolution. The resulting war with the Russians ended with Enver's death in Aug. 1922.

BULAWAYO. See RHODESIA.

BULGARIA. (1) Nationalism began in 1820s when Bulgar was first printed. A Bulgarian school was opened in 1835. Hitherto the educated spoke Greek or Turkish, and Bulgars were represented at Constantinople by the Orthodox Patriarch as head of the Millet-i Rum (see MILLET SYSTEM). when the nationalists sought to revive the language and secure a separate church, Bulgaria began to figure in British diplomacy because, against Russian southward penetration it was thought that the stability of the Ottoman Empire was an important safeguard which Bulgarian separatism might disrupt. The separate Church was secured in Feb. 1870 by Ottoman *firman*. This encouraged local nationalisms still further; the Bosnians rose in 1875, the Bulgars in sympathy in May 1876. They were put down with atrocities made notorious by a famous diatribe of Gladstone's (see also AUSTRO-HUNGARY-7). Hence the Turks irretrievably lost credit and the dismemberment of their empire became respectable.

(2) This defeat for Foreign Office policy was underlined when Russian armies, now advancing across Bulgaria, were joined by local volunteers. The Russians, to secure Bulgarian allegiance, imposed upon the Turks a treaty (San Stephano, 3 Mar. 1878) which created a "Greater Bulgaria". This included everything which any Bulgar had ever claimed. It provoked other powers into intervention, and at Berlin in July they substituted something more reasonable, and so made the Bulgars permanently Russophil. Bulgaria between the Danube and the Rhodope Mts became a principality under nominal Turkish suzerainty: the southern part (Eastern Rumelia) was turned into a province with a special regime and a Christian governor. This could not last. The Assembly (*Sobranie*) of the principality called P. Alexander of Battenberg to the throne. Related to the Russian imperial family, he pursued a pro-Russian policy with Russian trained officials and a conservative minority, and suspended the constitution. The liberals, led by Tsankov, espoused an irredentist nationalism hostile alike to Russia and Turkey. In Eastern Rumelia the govt.

upheld the Berlin arrangement with pro-Russian conservative help: therefore the local liberals demanded union with the principality. As tension rose, Alexander recalled the Sobranie. A liberal govt. was installed and in 1885 the E. Rumelian liberals seized the governor with the connivance of Alexander, who became governor himself. A brief Serbian attempt to frustrate the inevitable was defeated at Slivnitza, and the new situation was confirmed in the Convention of TOP-KHANE (5 Apr. 1886). Not for the last time, the natural course of events was interrupted by a Russian conspiracy. In Aug. 1886 the prince was seized and transported to Russia. A counter revolution by Stambulov, the President of the Sobranie, and Col. Mutkurov ejected the conspirators, but the Russians refused to return the prince. They attempted to rig the election of their candidate to the vacant throne, but the Bulgars got Ferdinand of Saxe-Coburg-Gotha to accept it. Ferdinand's difficulties would have overwhelmed a less supple man. Western recognition was postponed by the diplomacy of the Russians, who intrigued against him through the church and twice tried to kidnap him. Hence Stambulov had to govern despotically and bid for Turkish friendship. By 1894 Turkish control of school and church foundations had passed to the Bulgars.

(3) These were substantial successes but did not make Ferdinand safe. He wanted Russian recognition, but Stambulov believed that it could be secured only by subservience to Russian interests. He was succeeded in 1894 by the conservative Stoilov who proclaimed an amnesty, but was promptly assassinated by Stambulov's partisans. Nevertheless the prince persisted: Turkish strength was ebbing: Austria was taking her place as the alternative support for Bulgarian independence. Ferdinand, to please Austria, had in 1893 married a R. Catholic, and Stambulov had obtained the Sobranie's consent to a Roman education for the offspring. In 1896, however, Ferdinand caused Boris, his heir apparent, to be baptised into the Orthodox faith with the Czar Nicholas II as sponsor, and so publicly repudiated an Austrian alliance. Russian support was now forthcoming. Ferdinand obtained the legal confirmation from the Porte of his position in both parts of Bulgaria and was recognised on all hands. A secret military convention with Russia followed in 1902.

(4) All Bulgarian rulers had to live with irredentism. As many Bulgars lived under Roumania, Serbia and Turkey as in Bulgaria itself, and nationalism was a part of the contemporary ideology. No statesman opposed to it could hope to stay in office or even live. The so-called MACEDONIAN PROBLEM was really the Bulgar Problem. It engendered a permanent hostility towards the smaller neighbour states. The liberalism of the nationalists inclined them against autocratic Russia, and Austrian fear of Serb nationalism created an affinity between Austrians and Bulgars. The baptism of Boris was thus an example of that wily diplomatic agility necessary to small expansionist states; the prince acquired the European sobriquet of 'Foxy Ferdy' and in 1908 seized the occasion of the Austrian annexation of Bosnia to get rid of Turkish paramountcy. The two parts were made into a unitary Kingdom with himself as Czar. The Russians could hardly complain, and with their support the new country was internationally recognised in Apr. 1909.

(5) The internal nationalist grievance having been liquidated, the public could not be distracted from external irredentism. Alone, the Turks might have bowed out gracefully, but Serbia, Montenegro and Greece were waiting greedily in the wings. The Turks tried to play one off against the other, but the Balkan states conspired against them and in the First Balkan War (see BALKAN WARS) drove Turkey from her European territories (May 1913). They then quarrelled over the spoils; Bulgaria attacked her late allies but was defeated by the intervention of Roumania. Under the T. of Bucharest (10 Aug. 1913) Bulgaria lost the rich Dobruja, but gained Mediterranean ports at Dedeagatch (later Alexandropolis) and Lagos. Most of Bulgarian Macedonia went to Greece and Serbia. On the outbreak of World War I there was thus a govt. predisposition in favour of the Central Powers: the Germans persuaded the Turks to make concessions on the Macedonian issue, the allies failed to persuade Greece and Serbia. Accordingly Bulgaria joined the Central Powers in Oct. 1915 and, being on the losing side, had to cede her newly gained Mediterranean littoral to Greece at the T. of NEUILLY and the conference of San Remo (Apr. 1920).

(6) From 1918 until 1935 Bulgarian politics were dominated by a struggle (often murderous) between the liberal-agrarian opinion seeking rapprochment with the Balkan neighbours and reform at home, and extremists varying from the communists to armed irredentist organisations such as I.M.R.O. (International Macedonian Revolutionary Organisation). Disorder, the '30s depression and the example of Mussolini's Italy created the inevitable demand for strong govt. and ended with rival coups which brought K. Boris actively into politics as a stabiliser. In 1938 a parliament with a small tolerated opposition was called and non-aggression pacts were signed with the Balkan Pact countries. This new diplomatic dispensation under Germany's shadow enabled Bulgaria to re-arm, and German military missions appeared at Sofia. There must, in view of later events, have been military collusion even at this early stage. In any case after the great German victories of 1939 and 1940 there was a pause and the Filov govt. on 1 May, 1941 signed the Axis pact. In Apr. the Germans entered the country and used it as a base for operations against Yugoslavia and Greece. Bulgaria's reward was Macedonia, the Greek littoral and the Southern Dobruja, but she did not enter the war actively until Dec. 1941 when Germany declared war on the U.S.A.

(7) In Aug. 1943 K. Boris died mysteriously, and a regency was appointed for his infant son. The country was now for the second time involved with Germany in defeat, and in June 1944 Bagrianov, a friend of the late King formed a govt. to extricate the country. When Roumania surrendered to the Russians the govt. disarmed all the German troops, but as no armistice terms were offered by the Russians Bagrianov resigned and made way in Sept. 1944 for an all party govt. under Muraviev. This declared war on Germany on 8 Sept. Next day the Russians declared war on Bulgaria, invaded the country and installed a communist govt. There followed a reign of terror during which Georgi Dimitrov, the pre-war Communist leader, arrived from Russia to take over. By Sept. 1947 democratic institutions had been destroyed and the country was, and remained, a Russian satellite until the Russian collapse of 1989.

BULK PURCHASE of materials from abroad on long-term contracts was part of the Attlee govt's policy. In a rising market it obtained favourable prices as exemplified in the Canadian wheat agreement; but it brought its own nemesis: so great was the gain at the time that sellers became reluctant to renew agreements which fell due. Then, after the Korean War, prices fell and bulk purchases became a liability. The policy had, however, already been abandoned.

BULL, IRISH (cf Icelandic 'bull' = nonsense, or the vulgar 'balls'). A self inconsistent statement to which, according to the English, the Irish are prone; e.g. a witness before the Parnell Commission is reported to have said that it was 'better to be cowardly for an hour or two than dead for the rest of one's life'. Sir John Mahaffey, an Irishman, in a learned article, observed, however, that 'an Irish bull is always pregnant'.

BULL, Dr John (c. 1563-1628) was a singing man at the Chapel Royal, prof. of music at Gresham College from 1597 to 1617, organist of Antwerp cathedral until his death. His many works included secular and religious works for voices and for the organ, virginals and stringed instruments. He probably did not compose or transcribe the national anthem but he was a leading inspiration to the English composition of his time.

BULL, PAPAL. *See* PAPAL CHANCERY.

BULLER, Gen. Sir Redvers (1839-1908) V.C. (1879). He was Wolseley's chief of intelligence in 1882 at Tel-el-Kebir, and chief of staff in the relief of Khartoum in 1884. In Dec. 1899 he commanded the British force in Natal and was defeated by the Boers at Colenso. His role in the Boer War was thereafter subordinate to Lord Roberts. Not a distinguished general, he was very popular with the troops.

BULLION COMMITTEE (1810) As a result of the French wars, the Bank of England obtained parliamentary powers in 1797 to restrict the redemption of its notes by coin. The note issue and prices then rose, sterling fell on the foreign exchanges and gold stood above its mint price. A parliamentary select committee inquired into this new situation and in 1810 it recommended that the note issue should be reduced by 1813 so that gold could come down to mint prices, and cash payments be resumed. The Bank contended that the rise in prices was not due to excessive note circulation, and Parliament threw the recommendations out. The controversy had important effects later for it led to the adoption of the principle, first embodied in the Bank Charter Act 1844, that the govt. should be entitled to limit the Bank's right to issue notes.

BULLIONISM. The pre-mercantile theory that a country's wealth is determined by the amount of gold and silver it possesses. An outlook rather than a theory, it had a powerful influence on Spanish and Portuguese colonialism.

BULLOCK REPORTS by govt. committees under Alan, later Lord, Bullock. **(1) 1975** proposed progressive, largely unsuccessful, methods of teaching English in schools **(2) 1977** on the introduction of industrial democracy, fell with the 1979 electoral defeat of the Labour Party.

BÜLOW, Count Bernhard von (1849-1929) Prince (1905) son of Bismarck's State-sec. for foreign affairs, became minister in Bucharest in 1888, ambassador to Rome in 1893 and state-secretary in 1897. He succeeded Hohenlohe as Chancellor at the end of 1900. He wanted to be an exponent of German Bonapartism. For this it was necessary to build a fleet and develop an overseas investment, but there was always the risk that once German expansionism was recognised, other powers would combine to crush Germany before she became too strong. Bülow therefore believed it to be his function to ease Germany past the danger points by diplomatic means until she had a clear lead. He spoke of his activities as "greasy" and was called "the eel" by Kiderlen. During his Chancellorship the Germans pressed on with their projects for the Berlin to Baghdad Rly; they interfered in Morocco and supported the Austro-Hungarian annexation of Bosnia-Herzegovina. Meantime the German navy was being built up at a rate and by means not wholly under his control. By 1908 the outcry in England against the German building programme was creating the kind of situation, exacerbated by imperial indiscretions, which he was trying to avoid. In June 1909 he resigned and retired to his estates. He reappeared briefly in 1915 on a mission to Rome to try to persuade the Italians to stay neutral by offering them parts of Austro-Hungary. As the Austrians would not co-operate, the mission failed.

BULWER and BULWER-LYTTON. This versatile family included **(1) William Henry Lytton Earle Bulwer (1801-72) 1st Ld. DARLING AND BULWER (1871)** who acted in Greece for the Greek revolutionary committee in 1824 and reported diplomatically on the Belgian revolution of 1830, and became in 1849, ambassador at

Washington where he concluded the Clayton-Bulwer T. He was commissioner to the Danubian principalities in 1856 and ambassador at Constantinople from 1856 to 1865. He then returned to the Commons from 1868 to 1871. **(2) Edward George Earle Lytton Bulwer-Lytton (1803-73) 1st Ld. LYTTON (1866)** as **'Edward Lytton'** was a famous novelist. He was an M.P. from 1852 until 1866, and from 1858 to 1859 Colonial Sec. under Lord Derby; as such he was responsible for organising the new colonies of British Columbia and Queensland. He was much traduced by his wife **(3) Rosina Bulwer-Lytton neé Wheeler (1802-82)** also a novelist, who wrote pasquinades against him and made him the villain of her novel *Cheveley*. Their son **(4) Edward Robert Bulwer, 2nd Ld. and 1st E. of LYTTON (1831-91)** was both a poet (under the name of **Owen Meredith**) and a diplomat. He held routine appointments until 1873 when, as Minister in Lisbon, he succeeded to his father's peerage. In 1875 he declined the Governorship of Madras, but in 1876 to his surprise, Disraeli pressed upon him the *durbar* at which the Queen was proclaimed Empress. He was then faced with a famine in the south which he overcame by drastic administrative changes, and anticipated future trouble by systems of railways and irrigation and a policy of revenue accumulation known as the 'famine insurance'. Meantime fear of Russian encroachments on Afghanistan led to a war in which two successive Amirs were overthrown, and a British Resident established at Kabul. Lytton's bold decision to support the new Amir Abdurrahman proved one of the most far sighted in central Asian history, and secured friendship with the Afghans for half a century. Two other Indian achievements stand to Lytton's credit; he overhauled the system of indirect taxation and abolished internal customs; and he reserved one sixth of all places in the Indian civil service to Indians. He resigned the viceroyalty in 1880 and withdrew for seven years into private life, to become, however, ambassador in Paris in 1887 until his death. As such he was immensely popular. **(5) General Sir Edward Earle Bulwer (1829-1910)** as adj-gen for auxiliary forces from 1873 to 1879 did much of the staff work of Cardwell's military reforms. **(6) Victor Alexander George Robert, 2nd E. (1876-1947)** began his public career in 1901 as private sec. to George Wyndham, the Chief Secretary for Ireland. Though his affiliations were tory he was liberal in outlook, being, for example, an outspoken supporter of free trade and of women's suffrage. Consequently he did not achieve public office until World War I; he was at the Admiralty first as civil lord and then as parliamentary sec. in 1916 and 1917. In 1918 he was British Commissioner for propaganda in France; in 1919 civil lord again, and in 1920 parliamentary USec. of State for India. This restarted the family connection with India; in 1922 he became Gov. of Bengal and later acted as Viceroy in Lord Reading's absence. Despite violence and rioting he was liked by the Indians who, after he returned to England in 1927, asked him to lead their delegations to the League of Nations. It was this international activity which now engrossed him. He helped to found the League of Nations Union, and was Chairman of the Mission which investigated Japanese Manchurian aggression against China, and issued the celebrated Lytton Report upon it in 1932. This, which condemned Japan, was widely acclaimed and as widely ignored. The failure of the League govts to enforce his recommendations was the first long step towards the collapse of that organisation. After this he avoided public office and devoted himself to voluntary public causes such as the National Theatre, Sports and Boys Clubs.

BUNDI. *See* RAJPUTS-4.

BUNKER HILL, B. of (17 June 1775). This battle for a key point near Boston (Mass) was fought not on Bunker Hill but on Breeds Hill, a low mound nearby. The British under Gen. Howe carried the hill after a bitter struggle and with heavy losses. Their victory was not followed up. The battle was therefore tactically and strategically indecisive, but it showed that Americans, with courage, could stand up to British regulars, and revealed defects in American discipline and organisation which Washington could later point out and remedy.

BUNYAN, John (1628-88) served in the parliamentary army at Newport Pagnell in 1644 to 1646. His conversion took some eight years, beginning with the death of a comrade in arms who had taken his place on the duty roster, and ending with an overheard conversation between some poor women in Bedford, whose Independent church he joined in 1653. In 1656 he was chosen deacon and began to preach; but the local presbyterians indicted him for illegal preaching in 1658. At the Restoration he was again indicted and intermittently imprisoned until 1672, but released under Charles II's Declaration of Indulgence. His long imprisonment had been much mitigated by privileges. In 1675 he was again briefly imprisoned, and it was then that he wrote *Pilgrim's Progress,* published in 1678. Thereafter he preached and wrote as he pleased. His many works were first published in a collected edition in 1736.

BURBAGE, (1) James (1530-97) and his son **(2) Richard (1657-1619).** *See* DRAMA-4.

BURCHARD (?-754). W. Saxon assistant to St. Boniface in Germany, and energetic first Bp. of Wüzburg; as leader of a diplomatic mission to Rome in 749 he secured decisions favourable to the Carolingian succession.

BURDETT and BURDETT-COUTTS. (1) Sir Francis (1770-1844) married Sophia, a daughter of Thomas Coutts the banker, on his return in 1793 from Paris, where he had witnessed the early years of the French Revolution. He had thus acquired an unfashionable radicalism combined with financial independence. In 1796 he became M.P. for Boroughbridge, and a thorn in the flesh of the authorities. He attacked encroachments on public liberties, such as the successive suspensions of the *Habeas Corpus* Acts; he opposed the war with France as a futile exercise in repression; he expounded the effects upon the poor of rising war taxation; he exposed scandals in the prisons and he became a friend of Horne Tooke and voted against his expulsion from the Commons.

In 1802 he stood for Westminster as a parliamentary reformer, but prolonged litigation on the result determined him in 1806 not to stand again; so he subscribed heavily to the funds of Paull, another parliamentary reformer, instead. A misunderstanding and duel with Paull followed: the committee urged Burdett to stand after all, and after a tumultuous contest he came out top of the poll. This Westminster Election of 1807 represented a major step towards reform, because the Westminster (potwalloper) electorate was both large and strategically placed. Burdett continued to sit for Westminster for thirty years.

He continued to campaign against abuses. He was against military flogging; he moved for inquiries into parliamentary corruption and placemen; he was recognised as one of the ablest constitutional lawyers of his time, and corresponded extensively with Bentham on law reform. There were two spectacular incidents: in 1809 he flouted the rule against reporting the proceedings of Parliament, defied attempts to arrest him and was committed to the Tower only after a four day siege, when troops had been brought in to control his enraged London supporters. In 1820 his observations on the govt's conduct in the 'Peterloo' affair brought a fine of £2,000 and three months imprisonment at Leicester assizes.

But his major interests were R. Catholic emancipation

and parliamentary reform. The former was effectively set in motion by his resolution, accepted by the Commons in May 1828; and he was one of the consistent supporters of the Reform Bill of 1832. His youngest daughter **(2) Angela Georgina (1814-1906), Baroness BURDETT-COUTTS (1871)** in about 1830 attracted the attention of the Duchess of St. Albans, who was Thomas Coutts' widow (and therefore her step-grandmother). She left her immense fortune to Angela who in 1837 became the richest heiress in England, and added Coutts to her name. She entertained and knew everybody who mattered at court and in politics in France as well as Britain. She managed her property herself, and played an important part in the conduct of Coutts Bank. Her greatest interest, however, was in philanthropy. It is possible only to give a few examples. She endowed four colonial bishoprics and the Westminster Technical Institute. She was the main founder of the N. Soc. for the Prevention of Cruelty to Children, and was for a long time Pres. of the R. Soc. for the Prevention of Cruelty to Animals, and she tried to lower the cost of food in London by creating a new market in the East End.

BUREAU, Jean and Gaspard. These brothers created the superior French artillery which battered down the English strongholds in the latter part of the Hundred Years' War. Gaspard designed and cast the guns; Jean supplied the ammunition, for example at the sieges of Montereau (1438) and Meaux (1439). They collaborated at Pontoise in 1441, Dax in 1442, at Cherbourg in 1451 and in the Bs. of Formigny and Castillon. Their designs and methods were the foundation of most land artillery until the time of Gustavus Adolphus in the Thirty Years War.

BURFORD (Oxon). An ancient and still beautiful village with many mediaeval houses, where K. Ethelbald of Mercia was defeated by Cuthred of Wessex in 752. It had a corporation well before 1250. In 1306 it was required against protests to send a member to Parliament, and petitioned successfully not to have to do it again. The corporation was dissolved in 1861, but in 1894 it acquired a parish council which after World War II restored the Tolzey or guildhouse and converted it into a museum.

BURGAGE. A tenure by which land in a city or town was held of the Crown direct. In England a definite rent was always payable and the land could be bequeathed; in Scotland there was an obligation, more nominal than real, to provide watch and ward. English burgage tenements usually carried a parliamentary vote, and where the number of other voters had declined or even, as at Old Sarum, disappeared, the burgagers (sometimes called borough holders) could dispose of a parliamentary seat to the highest bidder or could sell the electoral rights altogether by selling their tenement. Burgage was thus the foundation of the Rotten Borough (q.v.).

BURGERS, Thomas Francois (1834-81), Pres. of the Transvaal from 1872 to 1877.

BURGESS, Guy (1913-63) and MACLEAN, Donald (1911-63) converted to communism as undergraduates at Cambridge and were employed in the Foreign Office until they fell under suspicion and fled together to Russia in May 1951. They had been controlled by H.A. "Kim" Philby, a journalist, who had also reached a high position in MI6. (q.v.)

BURGHAL HIDAGE is a record made under Edward the Elder (899-925) of the arrangements for maintaining the defensive system in Wessex, Sussex and Surrey, probably designed by his father Alfred in c. 890. Every town and village was within 20 miles of a fortress, which was to be repaired and garrisoned by the men of the surrounding area. In wartime every perch of wall needed four men, each of whom was supported by one hide of land in a 20 mile radius. *See* BURH; BURH BOT.

BURGHERS. *See* SCOTLAND, (PRESBYTERIAN) CHURCH.

BURGH, DE; DE BORGO; BURKE or BOURKE. This distinguished and prolific Norman-Irish family of uncertain provenance included **(1) Hubert (?-1243) E. of KENT (1227).** He was K. John's ambassador to Portugal in 1200 and his Chamberlain from 1201. He had the custody of Arthur of Brittany at Falaise in 1202 but refused to kill him. In 1203 he headed an unsuccessful peace mission to K. Philip II of France, but the situation in Normandy was militarily hopeless, and on his return Hubert was sent south. In 1204 he held Chinon and in 1205 had to fight his way out and was gravely wounded. In 1214 he returned to become Seneschal of Poitou. Always willing to uphold lawful Crown authority, he would have no part in the tyrannical and arbitrary acts of the King. After Magna Carta (1215) he became Justiciar and one of the Conservators of its provisions. John died in 1216 leaving Henry III a child. The country was in disorder and partly occupied by the French. While William the Marshal became Regent, Hubert defended Dover Castle against them in 1216 and after the rout of Lincoln destroyed their fleet off Sandwich in the next year. His rise became rapid. In 1215 he had married Avice, K. John's divorced wife and widow of the Justiciar Geoffrey FitzPeter. She and the regent died in 1217 and Hubert, together with Stephen Langton and the legate Pandulf, took over the govt. In 1221 he married Margaret, the sister of Alexander II of Scotland, and became the greatest magnate in England.

All men of goodwill agreed that it was essential to good govt. to secure the royal castles, most of which had been given foreign mercenary garrisons by K. John. The comparative quiet of the external situation provided an opportunity. The castles were demanded, Hubert surrendering his own, and placed under episcopal 'trustees'. Only Fawkes de Bréauté resisted, but by 1223 the resumption was complete.

To associate him with this important act the King had been accorded a limited majority. When, however, in 1227 he was declared of full age, Hubert's fortunes declined. He was now only a party leader against whose moral authority the King chafed. His growing wealth in the west combined with military failures in Wales created opposition and weakness. On the advice of Peter des Roches, Bp. of Winchester, the King dismissed and imprisoned him at Devizes (1232) whence he was rescued and placed in safety by Richard the Marshal. Thereafter he lived in retirement. He was deeply respected. Matthew Paris tells of a blacksmith who refused to manacle him in 1232 with the words 'Is not that Hubert most faithful and courageous who has so often snatched England from spoiling by foreigners and restored it to itself Who served the Lord King John in Gascony, Normandy and elsewhere with such fidelity that our enemies themselves praised it? Who preserved Dover for us, the key to England against the King of France and his skilled forces for a long time and secured our safety by overthrowing our enemies on the sea?'. His brother **(2) William (?-1206),** known in Connaught as 'the Conqueror', came with Prince John to Ireland in 1185. He was the ancestor of the de Burghs or Burkes Es. of Ulster and of the Burkes of Connaught and Munster. He married a daughter of Donnell O'Brien, Chief of Thomond, and after Donnell's death in 1193 maintained an alliance with his sons. In about 1195 he received a speculative grant of Connaught or of lands there from John, and in 1200 he was Gov. of Limerick. A feud in the royal house of Connaught then gave him his opportunity: one of the contestants, Cathal Carragh, invoked his aid against the reigning K. Cathal Crovderg, whom William attacked. In the ensuing civil war William acquired great possessions in the province, but Cathal Crovderg was supported by the de Courcys and eventually by the Crown. Thereupon William changed sides, but in 1203 on a rumour that he was dead, the Connaught Irish rose and attacked his troops, and when he retaliated upon Cathal Crovderg he was deprived of his Connaught lands by K. John. His son

(3) **Richard (I) (?-1243)** was restored to his father's lands only in 1222. He was continually at war with the Irish, particularly Aedh O'Conor, and conquered most of Connaught. Aedh died and Richard became Justicier of Ireland in 1228. The fall of Hubert de Burgh in England involved Richard who was superseded in 1232 by Peter of Rivaux and forced to surrender his conquests, but nevertheless he attacked the Irish lands of Richard the Marshal. In 1234 he was partly restored to favour, but Connaught had to be conquered all over again in 1235, and from 1237 onwards he spent his time organising its govt. Of his sons (4) **Richard (II) (?-1248)** succeeded to some of his lands in Connaught while (5) **Walter (?-1271) E. of ULSTER,** married Egidia, d. of Hugh de Lacy, E. of Ulster, who died in 1243. Richard had lands in Munster and, during the Barons war was created E. of Ulster by the Lord Edward in exchange for them. Not only was Ulster in a disturbed state but the Geraldines espoused the baronial side and attacked him. Nevertheless he held his own and established strong govt. in the province. His son (6) **Richard (III) (?1259-1326) (the Red Earl)** being minor, Ulster suffered a civil war between William FitzWarin, the King's Seneschal, and the Mandevilles. Richard came of age in 1280 and sided with the Mandevilles, and FitzWarin was eventually expelled. Richard was considered the head of the de Burghs, and ruled both Ulster and Connaught. With his Irish family background he was able to lead or dominate the Irish in his territories as well as the English. By 1296 the northern half of the country was at peace, and the English Kings referred to him more than to their own Justiciars.

Ireland now became involved in the Anglo-Scots war. The Red Earl was summoned to military service in Scotland, but his sister Egidia married James the Steward of Scotland who had submitted to Edward I. Summoned again in 1301 he did not go, and in 1302 his daughter Elizabeth married Robert the Bruce. When Bruce murdered the Red Comyn and raised the Scottish revolt in 1306 he took refuge in the islands on the Ulster coast. After Edward I died in 1307 the Scottish war began to go against the English and Richard took the opportunity to strengthen his position at home by further marriages between his children and the Clares and Geraldines. The period between 1306 and 1315 was the summit of his career.

Robert the Bruce's victory at Bannockburn in 1314 altered the position. The Scots went over to the offensive and, commanded by K. Robert's brother Edward, landed in Ulster in May 1315; they defeated Richard at Connor in Sept, and the feudatories of Meath at Kells in Nov. They induced the Connaught Irish to rebel, and that province fell into anarchy. The English had to turn aside to reconquer it, and an English army under Richard's kinsman Sir William de Burgh slaughtered the Connaughtmen at the B. of Athenry in Aug. 1316. Shortly afterwards Robert Bruce arrived to reinforce his brother and the two marched far south pillaging as they went. There was no force to resist them, but two crop failures had created a famine from which the Scots as well as the Irish suffered. They retreated to Ulster. Robert went home and Edward was killed in Oct. 1318, at the B. of Faughart, in which Richard took no part. The Scots in Ulster and the confusion in Connaught had destroyed his power. He spent the rest of his life trying, against odds, to rebuild it. He was succeeded by his grandson (7) **William (1312-33) 3rd E.** who obtained legal possession of his lands in 1328; but the old authority could not be re-established. In particular the subfeudatories of Ulster and the reconquerors of Connaught had acquired a grip on their territories which they were unwilling to relinquish. In June 1333 E. William was murdered by Robert de Mandeville, one of his own vassals, leaving only a daughter, Elizabeth, who eventually married Lionel of Clarence. This ended the de Burgh earldom of Ulster, but in Connaught two sons of Sir William de Burgh, the victor of Athenry, adopted the Gaelic custom of male succession and seized, with Irish help, such lands as they could. They and their descendants held them in the manner of Irish chiefs for two centuries without any English legal title. Of these two (8) **Edmund (?-?)** was the ancestor of the Burkes or Lower MacWilliams of Mayo and (9) **Ulick (?-?)** of the Burkes or Upper MacWilliams of Clanrickard in Galway.

BURGHERSH, Lord. *See* FANE.

BURGHLEY (N'hants), immense Elizabethan mansion built for the Cecil family. It later passed to the M. of Exeter.

BURGHLEY, Lord. *See* CECIL-3; ELIZABETH I-23.

BURG[H]RED. *See* MERCIA.

BURGHS (Scots). (1) were incorporations for purposes of trade. Some, such as Dunfermline or Stirling, were natural communities, but most were deliberately planned beside the new castle centre of a sheriffdom (e.g. at Banff, Berwick, Edinburgh, Elgin, Forres and Inverness the main street ran direct to the castle). This association of market and castle was convenient. The surplus of royal estates could be sold and the profits easily paid to the sheriff. The assemblage of traders would supply the castle's needs and create a market for the whole sheriffdom too, and the burgh would be protected. By 1150 there were at least 15 ROYAL burghs but leave was occasionally given to barons and the church to erect burghs of BARONY of their own. Thus Glasgow and St. Andrews (whose three main streets converge on the cathedral) were episcopal burghs, Arbroath, Canongate and Kirkintilloch baronial. The burgh-founding policy was designed to stimulate the economy.

(2) Besides Scots, the new burghs were inhabited by foreign traders, English, Danes, Normans and especially Flemings. Since trade deals in movables easily looted, the burghs were all fortified sooner or later. Burgh building was encouraged by privileges. The new settler had a period, usually a year and a day (see KIRSET) during which he had to build a well secured tenement. He then became entitled to the property (burgage) subject to a crown rent, usually of 5d. for every 20 feet of frontage, and to a share in the town lands. Such a new burgess was a free man on an 'island' in a feudal 'sea'. He could divide his burgage; could go where he pleased; marry or give in marriage without leave or payment. His heir paid no relief. The wardship of his children was governed by burgh not feudal law, and he had his disputes settled quickly (within three tides) according to the international custom of merchants by the burgh court, composed mostly of people like himself. In return he had to keep order and defend and maintain the walls (watch and ward), and in addition to the rent, he paid the petty custom or toll on market sales, the Great Custom which resembled the English Great Custom, and an occasional *auxilium* (Lat = aid) to meet special royal needs e.g. in war. The issues of justice also belonged to the lord. The Tolbooth was the office at which the sheriff or other royal official controlled proceedings. Central oversight was exercised by the royal Chamberlain, who was supposed, on ayre, to see that the court did justice, to hear appeals and to gather the revenue paid in.

(3) As population and sense of community grew, the burghs began to elect their own officers. By the 13th cent. this was done at Michaelmas by an annual Head Court consisting of all the burgesses. The *provost* or *alderman* was the head of the burgh and often exercised the functions of the King's Officer. The *bailies* presided in the burgh court, the *liners* defined the burgage holdings, and other officials supervised the quantity of goods. In the 14th cent. it was found convenient to grant Charters of perpetual FEU FERME, the first being issued by Robert I (the Bruce) to Aberdeen (1319) and Berwick (1320). These charters usually fixed the ferme at a higher figure

than the previous total, but inflation quickly gave the advantage to the burghs. They were never, however, exempted from the Great Custom. On the other hand they were usually granted a trading monopoly within the adjacent sheriffdom.

(4) Since the law of the burghs was different from and occasionally in conflict with the law of the rest, a kind of burgh parliament developed in the late 13th cent. This was called the COURT OF THE FOUR BURGHS, originally Berwick, Edinburgh, Roxburgh and Stirling, but owing to English occupation Lanark and Linlithgow replaced Berwick and Roxburgh in 1369 and others were added later. The King's Chamberlain presided, and it heard disputes between burghs, appeals from burgh courts and from the Chamberlain's ayre, and generally declared the law of the burghs. By 1455 it included representatives from all the burghs south of the Spey.

(5) Meanwhile the exigences of foreign affairs required large sums which the burghs had to help to find. In 1296 six leading ones (Aberdeen, Berwick, Edinburgh, Perth, Roxburgh and Stirling) ratified the French alliance with their common seals. In 1326 Robert I in a parliament at Cambuskenneth forewent his rights of purveyance in return for a grant of 10% of the annual revenues of the earls, barons, freeholders and the burgesses of his burghs. In 1328 the burghs were expected to ratify the English peace treaty, because they would have to find part of the £20,000 payable under it. In 1357 they were summoned to parliament to consider the problem of David II's ransom, and in this year they were denominated one of the three estates. After 1367, though in theory summoned only for financial reasons, they were always summoned, because there was always financial business. By 1405 the pretence of special reasons was dropped, but their interest in finance remained. Thus the legal functions of the Court of the Four Burghs long continued, and when it withered away in the 15th cent. it was replaced by the Convention of Royal Burghs, which was a pressure group, rather than a constitutional organ, directing the parliamentary activity of its representatives.

(6) General Councils sometimes made decisions involving taxation (e.g. peace and war). Between 1366 and about 1450 some burghs were represented at them but the practice was then dropped. Agitation against this anomaly resulted in a concession (1504) that they should be warned and consulted if taxes were in issue. In 1563 they gained the right to be summoned on such occasions, and four years later to take part in the discussion of weighty matters – in practice everything. Hence the Great Council became in effect a convention of estates.

(7) The main effect of creating burghs was to concentrate and regulate trade, and the royal burghs had an initial advantage over the others because their parliamentary position enabled them to secure monopolistic legislation. The many creations of baronial burghs broke into their position, especially as the Crown began to promote. Glasgow and St. Andrews became royal burghs in 1611 and 1620 respectively. Five other such promotions occurred in the first half of the 17th cent., but nearly 100 burghs of barony were created between 1660 and 1707. In 1693 the royal burghs, to stem the urge for promotion offered free trade to those baronial burghs willing to relieve them of 10% of their land tax. This arrangement did not work well, but was in any case superseded at the parliamentary union of 1707, which left the royal burghs with only 15 members in the United Parliament.

(8) The principal burgh officials (see para 3 above) anciently carried on the day to day business which might be judicial and military as well as administrative but they were now appointed by close corporations. Big towns also had Deans of Guild, whose courts settled traders disputes and even questions of land use. From 1833 the

66 royal and 13 parliamentary burghs had Town Councils elected by £10 householders, but the £10 householders of royal burghs or burghs of barony could in addition adopt a 'police system' ('police' here means 'improvement') and choose 'commissioners of police' to administer lighting and watching, and public health functions such as water and sewerage. Councillors could be police commissioners and one fifth of the commissioners had to be appointed by the council. The result in many instances was a dual administration. From 1847 councils could become police commissioners and from 1850 burghs of barony could adopt the police system. In 1892 the Burgh Police Act ended dual administration by requiring the election of Town Councils or Police Commissioners but not both, and in 1900 the term 'commissioners of police' was abolished and all burghs used the historic terms provost, bailies and town councillors.

(9) In 1929 the law was consolidated into a single Scottish Local Govt. Act. but the whole system was swept away and geographically reformed in 1975. These reforms involved the abolition of the burghs as such.

BURGOS (Spain). The most ancient capital of Castile. In 1812 Wellington took it with difficulty in the later stages of the Peninsular War. It was the seat of Gen. Franco's rebel govt. during the Spanish Civil War until his victory in 1940.

BURGOYNE, Gen. John (1722-92) (Gentleman Johnnie) was at school with Lord Strange, heir to the E. of Derby, and eloped with his sister in 1743. With a small sum which the angry E. gave her he bought a captaincy, but resigned in 1746 and went to France to evade his debts. In 1756 at the outbreak of war he returned, was reconciled with the earl and through him obtained military posts leading in 1758 to a lieutenant-colonelcy in the Guards, and his first active service at St. Malo. In 1759 he persuaded the War Office to let him raise the first English regiment of light horse (the Queen's Light Dragoons); in 1761 he was elected M.P. for Midhurst, and in 1762 he went to Portugal as a brigadier-gen. and assisted the Portuguese against a Spanish invasion, with some success.

In 1768 he moved his parliamentary seat to the Derby borough of Preston; he was an effective speaker on foreign and strategic matters and was popular in social and literary circles (his last play *The Heiress* is still sometimes shown). He was a favourite at court, and by 1772, in addition to several military sinecures, he had become a major-gen. He was in America under Gage from Sept. 1774 until Nov. 1775, when he returned in disgust at the inactivity of many British commanders. In June 1776 he went as 2-in-C to Sir Guy Carleton in Canada, but left for England after the (in his view criminal) failure to take Ticonderoga. He then proposed a pincer movement against the rebels through New York colony. 12,000 men were to come down from Canada through Ticonderoga and Albany, to meet another force under Clinton detached by Sir Wm. Howe from the south. He was sent as C-in-C to Canada to lead the northern forces. The plan failed. He had been given only half the necessary troops and Clinton hardly moved. On 17 Oct. 1777 he had to surrender at Saratoga.

Made the scapegoat for the disaster, he threw in his lot with the political opposition to the crown, and Fox and Sheridan argued that his defeat was caused by the incapacity of the govt. Hence, when the Whigs came to power (June 1782) he was briefly C-in-C in Ireland. He also played a leading part in exposing Indian corruption, and led in the impeachment of Warren Hastings.

BURGUNDY. The name refers to many different territories and govts. (1) An original seat in the Baltic island of Bornholm or Borgundarholm. (2) After migration, an area (c. 435) on the R. Main centred on Worms and then Imperial Savoy, from which the area spread into Franche Comté and was annexed by the Merovingian Franks in

534. (3) On the division of the Merovingian Kingdom, a Burgundian Kingdom stretched from Arles to Chartres, but between 879 and 888 it was divided into three: Lower, Jurane including Franche Comté, and Carolingian Burgundy. The first two were united in 933, and after 1032 its Crown was attached to the Imperial dignity as the Kingdom of Arles. (4) This connection became largely honorific with the passage of time, for the various provinces were taken piecemeal by France; thus Provence passed to Charles of Anjou in 1246; Lyon was annexed in 1312; Dauphiné was purchased in 1343; FRANCHE COMTÉ became part of the lands of the Valois dukes of Burgundy; and by 1481, when Provence came into the hands of the French King, there was nothing left except Savoy and French Switzerland. (5) Meantime the territory kept by the Carolingians was attacked by the Normans in the last years of the 9th cent, and Richard the Justiciar, Count of Autun, was given the local command against them. He was the effective founder of the DUCHY of Burgundy which always formed part of France. His son Raoul (or Rudolf) was K. of France from 923 to 936. After a variety of wars and intrigues, the Duchy was conferred by the Capetian K. Robert the Pious upon his own second son Henry in 1031, and it remained in his family until the line failed in 1361. It then escheated, and was granted in 1363 by K. John to his fourth son Philip of Valois ('the Bold'). (6) Under the four Valois Dukes a new middle European state known as Burgundy very nearly came into existence. Philip married Margaret of Flanders, and so in 1383 acquired Flanders as well as the Franche Comté and Artois. Hainault and Brabant were acquired by Philip the Good in 1428 to 1430, and Luxembourg in 1443. (7) With the defeat and death of Charles the Bold at Nancy in 1477, Valois Burgundy collapsed. The Duchy was seized by France; Charles' daughter Mary married the Archduke Maximilian of Austria; but by the T. of Arras of 1482 Franche Comté was to go to France on the marriage of Margaret, their daughter, to the Dauphin. The marriage did not take place, and so all the Valois lands except the Duchy passed to the Habsburgs. Franche Comté eventually became part of France in 1684. (8) The long history of local autonomy resulted in the province of Burgundy having a privileged position under the French Crown. From 1631 to 1789 its governors were the semi-royal Princes of Condo; the taxes, which were lower than elsewhere, were voted by the local estates, which sat triennially under the presidency of the Bp. of Autun. Talleyrand got his early political experience as Bishop. The provincial administration was practically separate: it did much to develop the roads and canals, and so provided the substructure for the development of the wine growing industry. The province of Burgundy disappeared officially in the French Revolution.

BURGUNDIAN SUCCESSION, WAR OF (1477-82). *See* LOUIS XI OF FRANCE.

BURH (A.S. = fort). Fortified towns designed by Alfred, Edward the Elder and his sister Ethelflaed as refuges against Viking forays, and garrison towns to hold down conquered territory. They had markets and mints had to be located in them for security. Almost all of them had the same street plan. *See* BURGHAL HIDAGE.

***BURH BOT* (A.S. = fort duty).** The obligation to maintain and, when necessary, garrison a local fort. *See* BURGHAL HIDAGE.

BURIAL ACTS 1852-1906. A series of prolix and complicated acts intended to govern the management of closed churchyards after they had filled up, new burial grounds and cremation. They represented an early example of adoptive legislation. They were all repealed and replaced at the instigation of the present writer by the Local Government Act 1972, which empowered ministers to make orders on the subject matter instead.

BURKE, Edmund (1729-97) originally became known through his writings on political philosophy. In 1759 he founded the *Annual Register,* and took service under William Gerard Hamilton, who in 1761 became sec. to the E. of Halifax in Ireland. In 1765 Burke became sec. to Lord Rockingham, then First Lord of the Treasury, and in Jan. 1766 he became M.P. for Wendover. Almost at once he became involved in the American controversies as an outspoken defender of the colonists. He favoured receiving the petition from the American congress, the repeal of the Stamp Acts, and freedom of navigation. In 1774 he stood for Bristol, and in a famous election address urged that an M.P.'s duty lay to the whole country, and that therefore he could not be bound by the opinions of his electors. His intellectual abilities were vast, and his oratorical style was compelling to the point of fascination, but overuse lessened its impact and Rockingham's fall reduced his influence within the govt. Until 1782 he was out of office; in days when the party whips were weak and Parliament sometimes voted on merits, his achievement was still considerable, particularly in creating a climate of opinion favourable to administrative reform. This culminated in 1782 and 1783 in Crewe's Act disenfranchising revenue officers. Clerk's Act disqualifying state contractors from the House of Commons, and Burke's own Acts regularising the accounts of the Paymaster Gen. and regulating the Civil List, which at that time included ministers' emoluments.

In practice, however, his interests were extra-territorial, in America, Ireland and India. He was a prime mover in granting legislative autonomy to the Irish Parliament in 1782. As a member of the Fox-North coalition he was in the Select Committee on the HEIC and in 1783 prepared the draft of Fox's East India Bill. As he had criticised North and particularly his 1773 Regulating Act, this did not improve his reputation. He was attacked as an Irish adventurer. People remembered that he had said that principles should be subordinate to govt. All the same his interest in the relief of oppression was genuine. He supported Wilberforce against slavery. He thought that Warren Hastings was an oppressor of the Bengal population and worked from 1785 to 1794 on his celebrated impeachment. He retired from parliament just before the acquittal was announced.

He viewed the French Revolution of 1789 differently from Fox. The latter hailed the fall of the Bastille with enthusiasm. Burke, in his *Reflections on the Revolution in France* (1790) more correctly prophesied bloodshed and tyranny. Though in the short term, Burke was not a successful politician, his influence was powerful and lasting, because he turned into a commonplace the idea that taxpayers were entitled to a return on their money and to know what that return was, and that therefore govt. should not be a mystery in the hands of initiates. He and his younger contemporary Bentham owed much to each other. *See* AMERICAN TAXATION.

BURKE, William and HARE, William murdered at least 15 unknown wayfarers and sold the corpses to an Edinburgh school of anatomy. They were caught in 1829. Hare turned King's evidence and Burke was hanged.

BURLINGTON. *See* BOYLE.

BURMA, locally **MYANMAR. (1)** originally consisted of five nations or states (Burmese, Shans, Karens, Talaings and Pegu) with divergent histories. The country became known in the west through Marco Polo in 14th cent. and some other Italians between 1415 and 1504. The first systematic contact, however, arose by way of the Portuguese settlement (1510) at Malacca. In 1519 the T. of Martaban with the K. of Pegu allowed them to establish trading factories, but throughout the 16th cent. the states were at war with each other and with the Siamese.

(2) By the early 17th cent. British and Dutch traders had established themselves at Portuguese expense in Burma and Indonesia. Rivalry between British and French

in India and the East led to further fighting in Burma where both nations supplied arms to the contending states. The British had a depot at Negrais and a factory at Bassein: both English and French had factories at Syriam in Talaing territory where most of the business was done, and both were under the control of ill-informed governors in India. Locally neither had a settled policy which could rise above the level of opportunism. In the end, however, the English obtained the favour of the adventurous "Huntsman-Captain" who, as Alaungprah (Alomprah), had risen to the throne of Ava, while the French supported the Talaings. His capture of Syriam (July 1756, a month after the B. of Plassey) and of Pegu in 1757, gave the English in Burma a decisive advantage over the French, but a commercial treaty came to nothing because English traders sold arms to Talaing rebels, and so their settlement at Negrais was razed.

(3) Alaungprah died in Siam in 1760, and his successors inherited his confident and aggressive outlook. They successfully attacked Manipur in 1764: in 1765 they invaded Siam and sacked its capital Ayodhia, after a two year siege. The vast loot went to adorn the great Shwedagon pagoda at Rangoon, and Tenasserim was annexed. The Siamese royal house perished and their throne was eventually taken by Phaya Tak, who became a Siamese Alaungprah.

(4) Ayodhia fell just in time for the army to be able to repel four Chinese invasions (1765-9) from Yunnan. This war arose from commercial disputes which were compromised in 1770. In the next years Phaya Tak slowly freed Siam from the Burmese, but the latter turned westward into Manipur, raided the neighbouring state of Kachar (1782-4) and collided with the British in Bengal. Arakanese fugitives used British territory for raids on Burma. The Burmese would neither expel nor control them nor allow a Burmese right of pursuit, and from 1811 to 1815 an Arakanese chief even maintained a kind of bandit monarchy on British soil.

(5) Ambition and self-protection alike inclined the Burmese to intrigue with Indian, especially Maratha, princes. From 1807 their missions, ostensibly with religious or learned objects, visited sacred places such as Benares and Buddh Gaya, and political centres as far off as the Maratha capital at Poona. The British did not realise until 1813 that the purpose of these missions was to acquire Assam and Bengal as far as the R. Brahmaputra. Burmese designs on Bengal, however, were frustrated by the overthrow of the Peishwa of Poona in 1817. They were more successful in Assam, a native state which the Burmese general Maha Bandoola conquered and annexed in 1821.

First Burma War (6) The British were now alarmed. Early in 1824 their troops fought the Burmese in Kachar and near Chittagong. They were determined to protect Kachar, and after an ultimatum they drove them from Assam and Manipur (early 1825). Meanwhile an amphibious force surprised Rangoon (May 1824) and started up the Irrawaddy. Once recovered, the Burmese put up a stiff resistance, but despite losses from illness and bad administration the British made headway. Maha Bandoola, recalled from Arakan, assaulted their positions around Rangoon, but was driven off. The expedition then began to make its way north to Danubyu, which was heavily stockaded and had to be besieged. In Apr. 1825, however, Bandoola was killed. His death broke the back of the resistance. Alternate armistices and advances eventually brought the British to Yandabo near the capital, where peace was signed (Feb. 1826). Assam, Arakan and Tenasserim were ceded. Pegu was to be occupied till half the war indemnity had been paid, and the King undertook not to interfere in Manipur or Kachar.

Second Burma War (7) Pegu was soon evacuated, to the distress of the Talaings who suffered for their friendliness to the British; and the Burmese viceroys practised indiscriminate extortion on foreigners as well. British protests seeming ineffectual, Pegu was invaded and annexed (1852-3).

(8) Under the T. of Yandabo reciprocal embassies were to be maintained at Ava and Calcutta. The arrangement did not work because the Burmese preferred to entertain no relations with the west. In 1852, however, the new King, Mindon Min (Meungdaung Meng) tried to change the policy. Diplomatic missions were exchanged; efforts were made to modernise the country and Burmese ministers toured Europe. Unfortunately the King died in 1878, and the murderous lady Supayalat, wife of Thibaw, one of Mindon Min's 48 sons, engineered a palace revolution and massacred his brothers.

Third Burma War (9) Some British traders had long been agitating for control: the massacre gave them a handle. The Govt. was unwilling to move for fear of Burmese discontent in the British provinces; but its hand was forced. The French were advancing through Tongking. Supayalat and Thibaw began to negotiate with French concession hunters and banks. An English loan was soon spent; a further loan was requested from a Rangoon company and when refused the company was fined the same amount. Intervention became unavoidable; in the Third War of Nov. 1885, Thibaw and Supayalat ("Soup-plate" to the British troops) were deposed, and the Kingdom annexed to India, of which administratively it formed a part until 1937. The Shan states became feudatories of the British Crown. (*See also* CHURCHILL, LORD RANDOLPH.)

(10) Economically British rule was highly beneficial. Between 1824 and 1941 exports from Rangoon rose from 10,000 tons to 4 million. The Irrawaddy delta became the greatest rice exporter in the world; oil was exploited after 1900, wolfram, tin, silver and lead after 1912. On the other hand dacoity (violent crime) rose quickly after 1905. In 1931 it assumed the proportions of an insurrection in which the nations of the country fought each other in the jungle. This problem was not solved even in 1992.

In 1937 Burma received a constitution which gave it internal autonomy, and a ministry responsible to a popularly elected lower house. Govts. consisted of fluid coalitions, and had short lives. Ba Maw's govt. lasted until Feb. 1939, Pu's until Sept. 1940, Saw's until Jan. 1942.

(11) Meantime in 1942 Aung San and the THIRTY FRIENDS went to Japan, and received military training; in Jan. 1942 the prime minister, Saw, was interned for contacting the Japanese in Portugal, and shortly afterwards the Japanese invaded the country and brought the Thirty Friends back. They and their 4,000 followers were not a success, and Aung San had to reform and discipline them, while British-led guerrillas continued to fight their friends the Japanese. In Aug. 1943 the Japanese accepted Ba Maw (who, ironically, had been interned by Saw for contacting the Japanese) as President; he then proclaimed Burma's independence, and declared war on the British. In 1944, however, Aung San made approaches to the British and changed sides in Mar. 1945.

(12) The British undertook to confer independence as soon as possible, but meanwhile to try to restore order and the economy. Huge numbers of weapons were in circulation and these, when not used in mere dacoity, formed part of the equipment of bandit armies masquerading as political parties. The politicians' (especially Aung San's) bids for their support destroyed all hope of disarmament, but Aung San called into being an alliance of them called the Anti-Fascist Peoples Freedom League which secured most of the cabinet seats in Sept. 1946. In Jan 1947 he headed a delegation which reached agreement with the Attlee govt, and in Apr. the League won a landslide victory in the elections. Thereupon, in July, Saw, who had been

allowed to re-enter public life, had Aung San and six colleagues assassinated. Aung San's friend Nu succeeded him and Saw was arrested and in due course executed. Nu signed an Anglo-Burmese treaty in Oct. and proclaimed the Independent Union of Burma on 4th Jan. 1948. The treaty expired in 1954 and was not renewed.

(13) In 1962 a military revolutionary govt. under Gen. Ne Win seized power and adopted a Socialist constitution in 1973, but the Burmese faction which he headed was constantly at war with the Shans and Karens, which all sides financed by exporting opium and heroin through Siam. The country became virtually inaccessible, for the Burmese areas were under a military dictatorial oligarchy which cut off access to the Shans and Karens and prevented movement abroad. Foreign economic and moral pressure induced the govt. to hold elections in 1988, but to its surprise the opposition led by the Oxford educated Suu Aung San won a landslide victory, whereupon it annulled the elections and interned her until 1995.

BURNE-JONES, Sir Edward Coley (1833-98), a friend of William Morris, Dante Gabriel Rosetti and other pre-Raphaelites, painted a long series of romantically other-worldly paintings, which caused sensations between 1877 and 1881. The inspiration was not pre-Raphaelite and he has been occasionally stigmatised as an escapist.

BURNELL, Robert (?-1292) before 1260 was a clerk to the Lord Edward, by whom he was soon employed in negotiations. By 1270 he was archdeacon of York and about to accompany the prince on a crusade, when the archbishopric of Canterbury fell vacant by the death of Boniface of Savoy. Edward forcefully pressed Burnell's candidacy upon the Canterbury monks without success; he then appointed him together with Roger Mortimer and the Abp. of York to act on his behalf in his absence, and so in Nov. 1272 these three became regents of the Kingdom when the crown passed to Edward. In Sept. 1274, after Edward's return, Burnell was appointed Chancellor and in Jan. 1275 he became Bp. of Bath and Wells. At this point his ecclesiastical career was arrested by papal dislike of his personal failings. His wealth, represented by 82 manors, was inordinate. His nepotism in church appointments was regarded as excessive, and the provision which he made for his daughters was only slightly less scandalous than the fact that he had daughters at all. Edward's further attempts to obtain for him Canterbury in 1278 and Winchester in 1280 accordingly failed.

Burnell's career is distinguished chiefly in the fields of civil administration and diplomacy. The Statute of Westminster I (1275) was mainly his work. Between 1275 and 1277 and again in 1282-3 he was engaged with the difficult problems of Llywellyn and North Wales, and he helped to draft the Statute of Rhuddlan (1284). In the previous year a parliament had been held at his house at Acton Burnell, and in 1285 he presided over the passage of the Statutes of Westminster II and Winchester. His interest, as Chancellor, in judicial administration was practical and active. He fixed the seat of the hitherto itinerant chancery permanently in London, and in 1289 (after a long absence with the King in Aquitaine) he headed the inquiry which led to the great judicial purge of 1290. It was probably through his influence and expertise that Edward I compelled the lawyers to establish the educational system which grew into the Inns of Court and Chancery. Scottish affairs occupied the last months of his life, but he died just before the end of the Baliol-Bruce arbitration.

BURNET. Persons bearing this lowland Scots surname included **(1) Abp. Alexander (1614-84)** who began his career as chaplain to the E. of Traquair and after fleeing to England to avoid taking the Covenant, took Anglican orders. He was ejected from his living in Kent in 1650 for loyalty to the King, whom he joined for a while abroad,

but he seems to have been in Kent in 1657. His brother was the King's physician. After the Restoration he became chaplain to the gov. of Dunkirk, Lord Rutherford, a distant relative. By 1663 he thus had sufficient interest to obtain the see of Aberdeen. and in Apr. 1664 he became Abp. of Glasgow and a privy councillor shortly afterwards. A persecuting Laudian, his policy is said to have been a cause of the Pentland insurrection of 1666; it brought him eventually into collision with Lauderdale, who initiated a policy of conciliation in 1667 and who, under the Scottish Act of Supremacy of 1669, compelled Burnet to resign in Dec. 1669. By 1674, however, Lauderdale's policy had changed. Burnet was restored and five years later, after the murder of Abp. Sharp, became Primate. **(2) (a) Robert,** a Lord of Session, of Edinburgh, had two sons **(b) Sir Thomas (?1632-1715),** a celebrated physician, and **(c) Bishop Gilbert (1643-1715),** scholar, scientist, broad churchman, politician and historian, who began his extraordinary career by taking his M.A. degree at Marischal College, Aberdeen in 1657 at the age of fourteen. In 1661 his learning earned the offer of a living at Saltoun (which he refused) and in 1663 he came to Oxford and London where he made the acquaintance, amongst others, of Boyle and Sir Robert Moray. Moray introduced him to Lauderdale and Abp. Sharp, and he impressed both of them (though but twenty-one) with his forceful liberalism. In 1665 he was a founding fellow of the R. Society; and also accepted Saltoun where, in the ensuing five years, he acquired public respect by his generosity and attention to pastoral duties. At Saltoun he was soon recognised as the prophet or brains of the parties of moderation, and with Abp. Leighton and Lauderdale he worked unceasingly for an understanding between the covenanters and episcopalians. From 1669 to 1673 he held office at Glasgow, but in fact became one of Lauderdale's most trusted advisers in London, until the change to a persecuting policy in 1672. Despite the altered climate at court Burnet stood his ground and was frank with Lauderdale and the King; this did not lessen their respect for him; it was in 1675 that he left the arena of Scottish politics for England, and became chaplain at the Rolls. Here he contributed materially to Lauderdale's impeachment, through his confidential knowledge of the latter's political designs. Consistently with this he refused to be stampeded in the "Popish Plot", and defended its earliest R. Catholic victims. By 1680 he was intimate enough with Charles II to remonstrate with him about his private life, and he apparently converted one of the King's mistresses. As with William Penn, Charles knew a good man when he saw one, and it was widely known that Burnet's integrity gave him influence at court. Stafford in 1680 and Russell in 1683, though of opposed persuasions, asked him to intercede for their lives.

Burnet's preference for conciliation kept him away from the vengeful supporters of the D. of York after the Exclusion crisis, and he maintained contacts with leading Whigs. This led to eventual trouble with the Duke and later King, whose influence rose as Charles II's will to rule declined. By 1684 Burnet was forbidden the Court and at James' accession in 1685 he went abroad and was in due course, invited to stay with William of Orange. He became one of William's principal advisers; he was mainly responsible for the moderation of William's manifestos in 1688; it was on his advice that James II was allowed to escape, and that indulgence was shown papists afterwards. Early in 1689 this influential personality for the first time acquired high public office as Bp. of Salisbury.

As at Saltoun, he contrived to combine public service of national importance with a model of pastoral activity. He proposed (with William's connivance) the Hanoverian succession in 1701, and thereafter maintained a vigorous correspondence with the electress Sophia. Since 1698 he had been a member of the commission for exercising the royal powers in ecclesiastical matters and in 1704 after eight years of negotiation he secured the establishment of Queen Anne's Bounty. He opposed the separate peace with France in 1713.

His *History of His Own Time* (first published in 1723) represents an account by an active participant in the affairs described, and though honestly composed, is sometimes partisan. Of Gilbert's three wives the first, **(d) Margaret (?1630-85)** was a well known "character" in her day and the third **(e) Elizabeth (1661-1709)** a well-known religious writer. Gilbert's son **(f) Sir Thomas (1694-1753)** by Mary, his second wife, became in 1741 a justice of the Common Pleas.

BURNEY (1) Charles (1726-1814) often called simply Dr Burney, pupil of Thomas Arne, was organist at King's Lynn (1751-60) and at Chelsea Hospital from 1783: he travelled widely in Europe and published accounts of his journeys in 1771 and 1773. He was a composer, and also wrote musical biographies and, between 1776 and 1789 a *History of Music*. He was a well loved social figure in his day. His son **(2) Charles (1757-1817)** was distinguished classical scholar whose sister **(3) Frances d'Arblay** known as **Fanny Burney (1752-1840)**, author of *Evelina*, was a diarist and successful novelist who belonged in youth to the literary circle of Dr. Johnson and Burke.

BURNHAM BEECHES (Bucks). The remains of an ancient forest, acquired for its beauty by the City of London in 1879.

BURNHAM, Edward Levy-Lawson (1833-1916) (1) 1st Ld. (1903) began as dramatic critic on his father's *Sunday Times*. In 1855 his father, Joseph, acquired the *Daily Telegraph and Courier* and reorganised it with half its title. With Cobden, Bright and the rest of the press they agitated against the newspaper duty, whose abolition in 1861 much improved the prosperity of the press and the Levy-Lawson papers. In 1885 Edward took control of them and opposed the Liberal Irish Home Rule policy, and they became leaders of the conservative press. His son **(2) Harry Lawson Webster (1862-1933) 2nd Ld., 1st Vist. (1919)** was a Liberal M.P. from 1885 to 1892, twice a member of the London County Council (1889-92 and 1897-1904) and then M.P. for Mile End from 1905 to 1906. He found his party uncongenial under Lloyd George and was elected at Mile End and sat till 1916 as a Unionist. He then became interested in labour relations. He presided at the Geneva International Labour Conference in 1921, 1922 and 1926 and a committee under his chairmanship set up the precedent-setting Burnham Award for teachers' salaries. He sold the *Daily Telegraph* in 1927.

BURNS, John Elliot (1858-1943), trade unionist, cricketer and politician, established the Battersea Labour League as his political base in 1889 when he led the Dock Strike, and became a member (until 1907) of the London County Council. He became an M.P. in 1892 and gradually changed from socialist to liberal opinions. Liberal (but rather reactionary) Pres. of the Local Govt. Board from 1905 to 1914, he prevented the Poor Law reforms proposed by the Hamilton Commission of 1909. Owing to his growing unpopularity he was transferred to the Board of Trade in 1914, but resigned against entering World War I and left politics.

BURNS, Robert (1759-96) the Scottish poet first began to write in 1775; he composed some of his best work (such as 'To a Mouse' and 'Holy Willie's Prayer') in 1785 and 1786, when he discovered that his 'Twa Herds' (a satire on two Calvinists) was circulating widely in manuscript. This encouraged him to get his poems published, in order to raise money to take a job as a plantation overseer in Jamaica. The poems were favourably reviewed, and he went to Edinburgh instead of Jamaica. A second edition was published in 1787. By this time he

had made himself well-known as much by his drinking, wenching and social exuberance as by his poems. He wrote 'Auld Lang Syne' and 'Tam o' Shanter' in 1789 and 'Scots wha hae' in 1792. He fell asleep in a ditch after a carouse and contracted a fever of which he died. His poems range from extreme tenderness to savage satire, and from public patriotism to private bawdiness. This reflected the kind of man he was: he made a living at one time or another as a smuggler, a surveyor, a farmer and an exciseman; he was said to be irresistible to women, and could undoubtedly drink any man under the table. In none of this was there any concealment: he combined full bloodedness with moral courage, and so represented to the Scots the ideal personality which they would have liked to have themselves. This was expressed in the vernacular poetry which made them proud of their dialect as well. This all happened at a time when many people remembered the suppression after the Jacobite rebellion of 1745, and the consequent depopulation of the Highlands. Burns made the Scots feel that after all they were not a conquered people. His birthday, called *Burn's Nicht* (25 Jan.) is the opportunity for a Scots national carouse.

BURROUGH or BOROUGH, Stephen (1525-84) was master of the only ship of the first English expedition to reach Russia in 1553. He made further voyages around the North Cape in 1556 and, in charge of trading squadrons in 1560 and 1561. Thereafter he was the chief pilot on the Medway. *See* MUSCOVY CO.

BURNT CANDLEMAS **(1356)** was a devastating English foray from Roxburgh to Edinburgh in retaliation for a Scottish attack on Berwick.

BURSLEM. *See* STOKE-ON-TRENT.

BURT, Cyril Lodowick (1883-1971), educational psychologist of London Univ. *See* ELEVEN PLUS EXAMINATION.

BURT, Thomas (1837-1922) began as a coal hewer, became sec. of the Northumberland Miners Assn. in 1865, Liberal M.P. for Morpeth in 1874 and held minor office under Gladstone. He was interested in mass organisations such as Trade Unions and Co-Operatives as a power base, rather than separate representation of a Labour Party in parliament, thus starting a train of thought which has lasted throughout the 20th cent.

BURTON. *See* PAGET AND BAILEY-6.

BURTON, Decimus (1800-81), partly trained as an architect by his builder father, was befriended by John Nash and developed a much applauded classical style, which strongly influenced 19th cent. British townscapes either because he designed the buildings (e.g. the Athenaeum, Charing Cross Hospital and four mansions in Regents Park, all in London; estates at Liverpool, Fleetwood, Folkestone, Glasgow and Tunbridge Wells, and Adelaide Crescent at Brighton) or because others followed his example. His energy was enormous and the number of his designs probably uncountable.

BURTON, Henry (1578-1648), a friend of Prynne (q.v.).

BURTON, Sir Richard Francis (1821-90) was brought up in Italy, France and Oxford, and commissioned into the Indian army in 1842. He had an astonishing aptitude for languages and for 'getting inside people's skins'. He is said to have mastered 35 Indian languages before learning others in other parts of the world, and as an assistant on the Sind Survey, passed as a native. He published a book on Sind in 1849. He then made an unscathed pilgrimage to Mecca and Medina (forbidden to Unbelievers) and his book on it made him famous. After a visit to Harrar, a disappearance into the desert and a spell in the Crimea, he accompanied Speke to the equatorial African lakes. In 1860 he made a study of the American Mormons. He married Isabel Arundell in 1861 and she was with him on all his later journeys. He also became Consul successively at Fernando Po, Santos (Brazil), Damascus and finally Trieste. He also wrote five works on his explorations, and found time to make a famous, if odd, translation of the *Arabian Nights* (from the Arabic), another of Camoens *Lusiads* (Portuguese) and the poems of Catullus (Latin). Lesser men suspected him of nameless vices.

BURY. *See* MANCHESTER.

BURY, Richard (?1287-1345) spent ten years at Oxford, left without a doctorate and joined the household of Edward II. In the years before 1330 he helped to build up support for Edward, and organised the coup which re-established the royal power. In 1333 he was rewarded with the rich, strategic bishopric of Durham. He was a notable encourager of learning, and the greatest book collector of his age. Perhaps with the assistance of Robert Holcot he wrote *Philobiblon* (Gr = Booklover), as a sort of handbook to his library at Durham College Oxford. *See also* DURHAM.

BURY ST. EDMUNDS (Suffolk) was called **BEODRICSWORTH** until the remains of K. Edmund the Martyr were moved there in the 10th cent. In 1020 the Benedictine abbey was given a charter of endowment and liberties by Canute, to serve Edmund's shrine, and in 1044 Edward the Confessor gave the abbot the right to appoint the bailiff of the surrounding eight and a half hundreds (nearly half of Suffolk). By 1100 the abbey had its own mint, markets and fairs, and by 1200 the Abbot was one of the most powerful lords in the Kingdom. It was at the Abbey in Nov. 1214 that the nobles agreed to impose Magna Carta on K. John. The separate administration of western Suffolk by the abbots hardened into a permanent institution, so that when the abbey was dissolved under Henry VIII, the eight and a half hundreds received a separate commission of the peace, and eventually became the administrative county of West Suffolk under the Local Govt. Act 1888. It was amalgamated with East Suffolk in 1974.

BUSBY, Dr Richard (1606-96) Headmaster of Westminster from 1638, a highly disturbed period, was distinguished for his loyalty to the Crown, classical learning, determination and violence. He taught and flogged Dryden, Locke, Atterbury and the Hoopers but his powerful personality protected the school (at the very threshold of Parliament) against political, especially Roundhead, interference and preserved it into the new age. Effectively he was the school's second, if often criticised, founder. It seems likely that the sombre tone of Locke's *Thoughts on Education* was inspired by his experiences under Dr Busby. His violence was not directed exclusively at his pupils. He once flogged a parliamentary messenger.

BUSHELL'S CASE (1670) 1 St. Tr 869. A trial judge fined a jury 40 marks each for bringing in a patently perverse verdict. Bushell, the foreman, refused to pay. The judge committed him to prison. He took out a writ of habeas corpus. Vaughan C. J. set him free. The case decided that a jury is free to reach a verdict independently of the court's opinion.

BUSHIDO (Jap = The Way of the Soldier), was the moral code of the Japanese leaders, supposed to inculcate simplicity, honesty, courage, justice and determination. It sometimes degenerated into arrogance and brutality. *See* SHINTO.

BUSHIRE (Iran), BUSHEHR or ABUSHEHR. An important Iranian port on the Persian Gulf. An HEIC factory was established there in 1763 but, mainly because of the climate, the British moved to Basra in 1769. It remained, however, the most important naval base after 1778 because though shallow and hot it could provide necessary supplies.

BUSHMEN or KHOISAN (Southern Africa) had until recently a palaeolithic culture, and because of the resemblance of their cave paintings (not made since 1850) with Aurignacian stone-age cave paintings in Spain, it has been proposed that they brought the earliest extant culture to S. Africa through migrations from the north,

ahead of other peoples of more powerful physique. Their languages are monosyllabic, using clicks as additional consonants, and they live mainly by hunting, each group of families reserving to itself a hunting district. They have long been found in numbers in the mountains of the Cape Prov., the Kalahari and in Damaraland.

BUSHRANGERS were Australian bandits, often escaped prisoners, who terrorised country districts, particularly in Tasmania. In reply to martial law proclaimed in 1815, they banded together in often large gangs to fight the police. Special legislation was passed against them in 1830. The most notorious and almost the last was Ned Kelly who, with three others, wore armour and held up villages in Victoria. In 1880 the four were besieged in a hotel at Glenrowan. The other three were shot and Kelly was taken and hanged.

BUSKERS AND STREET ENTERTAINMENTS. The 18th cent. expansion put money in limited amounts into more pockets than hitherto. If theatres, concerts, operas and assembly rooms admitted only the well-off, the less well-off spared pennies or less for more modest entertainments. Since time out of mind individuals had preferred to beg as singers or musicians than merely to beg (*see* ALDHELM). Boys played hurdy-gurdies. These resembled lutes with a handle to a resinated wheel turned by the right hand while the tunes were played with the left. Men, mostly Italians, merely turned the handle of portable barrel-organs and later in the 19th cent. both were mostly superseded by the pedal operated pianola or the hand-turned street piano. There was also the one man band who either made his tune on pan-pipes and carried a drum, bells, tambourine and other contrivances operated as accompaniment by feet, elbows, head as well as hands, or who played an instrument such as a violin accompanied by pedal-played instruments mounted on a wagon. There were also street bands of professionals between engagements. Besides these musical diversions there were portable Punch and Judy shows which were glove-operated from below, Fantocini marionettes string-operated from above, prints exhibited for sale in upturned umbrellas and travelling shows such as peepshows ("a penny a look"), and George Wombwell's (1778-1850) three menageries. These and sellers of bread, muffins, milk, flowers, fruit, hot food, household goods like brooms, and petty craftsmen such as chairmenders and knife-grinders, all drew attention by recognisable cries or bells. The street uproar even provoked legislation in 1839 and 1864. Most of these were driven out by industrial competition, but milk-floats and muffin-men survived until 1935, a knife-grinder was seen in 1992, buskers still entertain theatre queues and Underground passengers and *Punch and Judy* is still to be seen at seasides.

BUSS. A two or three masted herring fishing boat of 50 to 80 tons, used especially by the Dutch who maintained as many as 1,000 of them in the northern North Sea in the 18th cent.

BUSS, Frances Mary (1827-94) pioneer of womens' education, founded N. London Collegiate School for Girls in 1853.

BUSSACO, B. of (26 Sept. 1810). Masséna, directing the third French invasion of Portugal, crossed the frontier at Almeida and marched towards the coast. Wellington's intention was to draw him down to the lines of Torres Vedras protecting Lisbon, the while inflicting casualties and embarrassing his communications. Bussaco is about 20 miles from the coast half way between Viseu and Coimbra; the British occupied a strong position on a ridge and after repulsing the French with heavy losses (including five generals) in a fog, made an unmolested retreat. This defensive victory greatly heightened the morale of the British troops and of the Portuguese guerrillas *(ordenanza)* who shortly afterwards captured the French base details at Coimbra.

BUSTAMANTE. *See* JAMAICA.

BUTCHER, or SWEET WILLIAM. Terms applied, according to the point of view, to William D. of Cumberland, second s. of George, who suppressed the rebellion of 1745.

BUTE (Scot). A county comprising some islands in the Firth of Clyde, taken from the Norwegians by K. Alexander of Scots in about 1263.

BUTE, John Stuart 3rd E. of (1713-92), a kinsman of the 3rd D. of Argyll, married Mary, the wealthy daughter of Lady Mary Wortley Montague. In 1737 he was elected a representative peer for Scotland, but took little part in debate. His interests were then scientific and literary (he gave Dr Johnson a pension and encouraged George III to lay out Kew) and he had a passion for amateur theatricals, then an important court diversion. In 1747 he became intimate with Frederick, P. of Wales ('Poor Fred') Said to have had the shapeliest legs in London, he became even more intimate with the Princess, and dominated their court; particularly after Frederick's death in 1751 he helped to bring up P. George (later George III). He became the Prince's Groom of the Stole and his main political adviser after he came of age in 1756 during the Seven Years' War. As Frederick and George were successively at loggerheads with George II, their household – Leicester House – was a natural centre for the opponents of the govt. Argyll died in 1761, and his heir being non-political, Bute followed him as leader of the Scots representative peers, and especially as manager of the Scots M.P.s. Thus Bute became an influential open as well as backstairs advocate of peace, against Pitt. Moreover George II was more Hanoverian or continental in his outlook than either of the princes, who identified themselves with Pitt's subsidy for Hanover's neighbour and ally, Frederick of Prussia, while Leicester House was ready to abandon him. A change of reign was, therefore, certain to make great changes of policy.

In 1760 it happened. Bute became a leading member of the govt and in Mar. 1761 S. of State. Shortly after, peace negotiations were begun. These hung fire because, though Britain had all the military and naval advantages, the French were secretly persuading Britain's nominal Spanish ally to change sides. Pitt was apprised of this, and of the resulting treaty signed in Aug. He advised instant war with Spain before the Plate treasure fleet could reach Cadiz, but being overruled by Bute and the cabinet resigned in Oct. The Plate fleet having arrived, the Spaniards declared war in Jan. 1762 but suffered the capture of Manila and Havana as a result of Pitt's previously well laid plans. Meanwhile Bute, by May, had as First Lord of the Treasury succeeded Newcastle as head of the govt. He appointed Fox to manage the Commons. Prussia, largely occupied by Austrian and Russian troops, now had a somersault of fortune and policy. In Jan. 1762 the Czarina Elizabeth died. Her successor, Peter III of Holstein, changed sides and agreed to help Frederick against Austria, in exchange for a free hand in controlling Denmark. This would not only prolong the war, but threatened the main Baltic supply of British naval stores. The Prussian subsidy was switched to Portugal in case of a Spanish invasion; the Prussian treaty was allowed to lapse; and peace negotiations were reopened. These resulted in the Preliminaries of Fontainebleau initialled in Nov. 1762 and approved by parliament on 2 Feb. 1763. Contrary to rumour Bute did not obtain the approval by wholesale bribery, and Prussian interests were secured by a separate convention, negotiated immediately afterwards. The Peace was signed at Paris on 10 Feb.

The country wanted peace and retrenchment, but it proved difficult to taper off the war expense. To avoid still further borrowing, a cider tax was proposed and driven through against virulent opposition, which destroyed Bute's nerve. In Apr. 1763 he resigned public office in the hope of continuing as the King's private adviser. This was resented by his successor Grenville, who almost prevented all contact until he himself resigned in July 1765. Bute's last act of importance was to advise the King to send for Chatham in July 1766.

BUTLER. Of the sons of Hervey Walter of Amounderness, two were brought up in the household of Ranulf Glanville, Justiciar to Henry II. One, Hubert (q.v.) became Abp. of Canterbury, while his elder brother **(1) Theobald Fitz Walter (?-1206)** came to Ireland with P. John in 1185. John made him a large speculative grant of Ormonde (Munster) and created him chief Butler of Ireland with the immensely valuable prisage on wines belonging to the office. By 1199 he had reduced Ormonde to obedience. He was followed in Ormonde by **(2) Theobald (11) (?-1230); (3) (III) (?-1248); (4) (IV) (?-1285) and (5) (V) (?-1299); (6) Edmund (?-1321)** s. of Theobald (IV) was Justiciar of Ireland in 1315 and 1316 during the invasion of Edward and Robert Bruce. Unable to repel it he was superseded by Roger Mortimer. His son **(7) James (?-1338) 1st E. of ORMONDE (1328)** so created at the instance of Mortimer, had married Eleanor Bohun, a grand-daughter of Edward I in 1327. Consequently his son **(8) James, 2nd E. (1331-82)** was known as the noble earl. He was well liked at the court of Edward III who educated him; he served in higher posts in Ireland under Clarence, being associated with him in the passing of the Statutes of Kilkenny (Nov. 1366) and was a lord justice of Ireland from 1376 to 1378; nevertheless under him Upper Ormonde was lost to the O'Kennedy's. **(9) James, 3rd E. (?-1405)** however consolidated a semi-independent lordship in Tipperary and Kilkenny by acquiring the Despenser lands in 1391. He was the most powerful English lord in Ireland, and Richard II's chief adviser in the pacifications of 1395. **(10) James, 4th E. (?-1452)** "The White Earl" was Lord Deputy of Ireland in 1407. He then served with Thomas of Lancaster and later with Henry V in the French wars. In 1420 he returned to Ireland, where he was regarded as a dependable standby and, in the intervals of other dispensations was head of the administration as Justiciar, Deputy or Lieutenant in 1420, 1424, 1426, and from 1443 to 1446. As the period was one of turmoil and slow English retreat, this increased the relative importance of the Butler family among the Anglo-Irish. Of his three childless sons **(11) James, 5th E. (1420-61) and 1st E. of WILTSHIRE (1449)** was Lord Deputy from 1450 to 1451 and Lord Lieutenant from 1453 to 1455. By this time he was much involved in Lancastrian politics. He became Lord Treasurer of England in 1455 and fought at St. Albans (1455), Wakefield (1460), Mortimers Cross (1461) and being captured at the B. of Towton in Mar. 1461 was beheaded and attainted. His brother **(12) John, 6th E. (?-1478)** was attainted with him, but crossed to Ireland and raised his Kilkenny followers. He was, however defeated by Thomas, E. of Desmond, at Carrick-on-Suir in 1462, and he and his brother **(13) Thomas (?-1515)** 7th E., left Ireland permanently. John and Thomas however, were pardoned in the 1470s When Thomas died the Earldom of Ormonde, thus revived, was disputed between his grandson Sir Thomas Boleyn (*see* BOLEYN) and **(14) Sir Piers (?-1539) 1st E. of OSSORY (1528)** who was very active militarily in Ireland and was Lord Deputy from 1521 to 1524, and then Lord Treasurer In 1527 he surrendered his claim to the Earldom of Ormonde to Sir Thomas Boleyn, and received that of Ossory instead. Since 1477 the great Geraldine family of Kildare had dominated and mostly ruled Ireland against the interests of the Crown. Their supremacy was now to be overthrown by an alliance of the Butlers and the Boleyns. Complaints against Kildare's rule led to his recall and arrest in 1534. His son, Lord Offaly, raised a rebellion. This was suppressed in 1535 by Sir Piers who was handsomely rewarded with more lands. Sir Piers and Sir Thomas Boleyn both died in 1539, and the earldom of Ormonde and Ossory were accordingly united in the person of **(15) James (?-1546)** whose son **(16) Thomas 10th E. (1532-1614)** was the famous Black Earl. Brought up in England, he came to Ireland for the first time in 1554, and was Lord Treasurer in 1559. The years from 1560 to 1583 were largely spent in a war in Munster with the E. of Desmond. This was partly a family feud but partly a war of policy in which Desmond represented the native Irish, and Ormonde was trusted by Q. Elizabeth who, however, tried to enforce a peace. Desmond was killed in 1583, and Ormonde became military commander in Munster shortly afterwards. He helped to round up the Armada survivors in 1588, and 1597 as lieut-gen. supported Essex's unsuccessful attempts to suppress the O'Neill rebellion in Ulster. He and Essex made mutual accusations of incompetence and disloyalty, but in view of Essex's behaviour, the Queen believed Ormonde. His grandson **(17) Walter (1569-1633) 11th E.** was involved in a dispute as result of which he was imprisoned for 8 years and deprived of his palatinate of Tipperary. His grandson **(18) James, 12th E. (1610-88) and 1st D. (1684)** married Elizabeth, the heiress of the Desmonds, in 1629 and so ended the feud. He first visited Ireland in 1633, and soon became a prominent, if independently spirited, royalist. Wentworth (later E. of Strafford) became Lord Deputy in the same year, and came to trust him. Indeed Strafford commissioned him to raise the Irish troops in 1640, when he himself left for England. In 1641 Ormonde became the King's Lieut-Gen. of the forces in Ireland. The situation was a triangular one with Ormonde, the royalist, heading the army; the Lords Justices, pro-parliamentarian, heading the civil govt. and Irish rebels ready to fight all corners. To keep the troops busy, the Lords Justices naturally impeded Ormonde's operations, while Ormonde's purpose was to pacify the country and send the troops to help the King. He defeated Preston at the B. of Ross in Mar. 1643, and was later instructed to conclude a peace with the rebels. The armistice was signed in Sept. and the best troops were then despatched to England where in Jan. 1644 they were involved in the rout at Nantwich. By this time Ormonde had been appointed Lord Lieutenant, and his principal preoccupation was to prevent the Scots army in Ulster from returning to Scotland which had declared for Parliament. They, however, attacked the Irish R. Catholics and so broke the truce. With insufficient forces Ormonde was now in an impossible situation, unable to restrain the Scots without rebel help, or the Irish without parliamentary help. In the upshot he negotiated a general pacification and left the country. His conduct was later approved by the King.

In 1648 he visited Paris to advise the Queen and Prince on Irish affairs, and at the King's execution in 1649 proclaimed Charles II in Ireland, took Drogheda and invested Dublin, but the rising was put down with great atrocities by Cromwell and Ireton, and Ormonde had to go overseas. He remained at Charles II's fugitive court as one of his principal advisers and most active agents until the Restoration, when he resumed his palatinate of Tipperary and most of his other Irish estates; in Nov. 1661 he went to Ireland as Lord Lieutenant. He ruled this difficult country in the aftermath of civil war until 1668, and again from 1677 to 1685. His grandson **(19) James, 2nd D. (1665-1745)** like his grandfather, was a strong protestant and a relative of Marlborough's colleague, the Dutch Veldt-Marskal Overkirk. He assisted in the over-throw of James II and fought for William at the Boyne in 1689, at Steenkerk in 1692 and at Landen in 1693. He also commanded the troops in Rooke's expedition against Cadiz in 1702. He was Lord Lieutenant of Ireland from 1703 to 1706 and again from 1710 to 1712. He now lent

himself to transactions which have discredited him with posterity. In Dec. 1711 Marlborough was dismissed at the instance of the Tories as a preliminary to ending the War of the Spanish Succession, and Ormonde was offered the Captain Generalcy in his place. In Apr. 1712 he took command in Flanders and within a fortnight the secret "restraining orders" arrived enjoining him to take no part in a siege or battle without further orders. Since this put his colleague P. Eugene of Savoy at a decisive numerical disadvantage against the French, he was being expected to act as the instrument of British treachery to her allies. He carried out his orders until peace came.

Almost immediately after George I's accession he was deprived of his many offices and his impeachment being voted in 1715 he fled to France. His estates were then forfeited by attainder. He died in France.

BUTLER, Joseph (1692-1752) son of a presbyterian linen draper, was converted to Anglicanism while studying for the presbyterian ministry, and took his Oxford degree in 1718. His abilities had become known, and he was immediately appointed Preacher at the Rolls and given the living of Houghton-le-Skerne (Durham) and in 1725 the 100-square-mile parish of Stanhope. Fifteen of his sermons were published in 1726 when he resigned the Rolls in favour of pastoral work at Stanhope, but he kept his contacts and in 1733 was made Lord Chancellor's chaplain and in 1736 Clerk of the Closet to Q. Caroline. As she powerfully influenced church appointments, so did he but she died in 1737. He then became Bp. of Bristol (1738), Dean of St. Pauls in 1740 and, as Clerk of the Closet to George II from 1746, he was in an even stronger position of influence, which he exercised disinterestedly. He refused Canterbury in 1747 but accepted Durham, which he knew, in 1750. As Bp. of Bristol he had asked John Wesley not to preach in his diocese and this may have originated the improbable rumour that he died a R. Catholic.

BUTLER, Josephine (Elizabeth) (1828-1906) *d.* of John Grey of Dilston (1785-1868), an assistant of Clarkson in the anti-slavery campaign, was originally involved in the movement for women's higher education but, having settled in Liverpool in 1866, was so appalled by the state of working girls and prostitutes that she espoused their cause at a time when the mere mention of such subjects by a woman in educated society brought obloquy and ostracism. She organised, and from 1869 to 1886 managed, the Ladies Nat. Assn. for Repeal of the Contagious Diseases Act. She also campaigned vigorously and successfully on the continent against the white slave traffic. *See* STEAD, WILLIAM.

BUTLER, Pierce (1652-1740) 3rd Vist. GALMOY, "E. of NEWCASTLE", one of the distinguished Irish R. Catholics who maintained their loyalty to James II. He was Lord Lieut. of Kilkenny and as a colonel of horse took part in the Jacobite siege of Londonderry (1689), the B. of the Boyne (1690) and the decisive B. of Aughrim (1691). He commanded Irish cavalry in the French service during the War of the League of Augsburg and was attainted and lost his estates just as it ended (1697). He continued in French service throughout the remaining wars of Louis XIV.

BUTLER, Richard Austen (1902-82) Ld. BUTLER of SAFFRON WALDEN (1965) ("RAB") as a Tory politician and Min. of Education (1941-5) instituted, through his Education Act 1944, the most far-reaching social reform of the 20th cent. by creating a framework within which everybody had access to education at secondary, further and university levels. This required widespread building and recruitment, the enlargement of existing universities, the establishment of new ones and polytechnics, and the erosion of older hierarchical attitudes. His career thereafter, though brilliant, was an anti-climax. He was Chanc. of the Exchequer (1951-5), Leader of the House of Commons under Eden till 1957, Home Sec. under

Macmillan until 1962, and deputy prime-minister until Macmillan resigned in Oct. 1962. He finally served as Foreign Sec. under Sir Alec Douglas-Home till 1964 and retired to the Mastership of Trinity, Cambridge. At each Tory prime minister's resignation after 1955 he was expected to be the successor but never was.

BUTLER, Samuel. There were three too-easily confused men so-called. **(1) The satirist (1612-80)** was a page to the Countess of Kent and clerk to a variety of J.P.s; he travelled abroad and then became Steward of Ludlow where he wrote *Hudibras,* his witty and popular satire against the Puritans, for Hudibras'

> ... religion it was fit
> to match his learning with his wit
> Twas presbyterian true blue
> For he was of that errant crew
> Whom all men grant
> To be the true church militant

(2) The classical scholar (1774-1839) published a 4-volume edition of Aeschylus (1809-16) during his successful headmastership of Shrewsbury, whose reputation he remade. **(3) The polymath (1835-1902)** farmed sheep in N.Z. from 1859. On his return he wrote the Utopian but prophetic *Erehwon* (1872) and the *Way of All Flesh* (1873-85). This novel was published only in 1903 and had a formidable effect on moral attitudes. He also wrote against Darwinism; was a successful painter, and published travel books and critical works on Homer. His *Erehwon Revisited* came out in 1902; his well-known *Notebook* in 1912. George Bernard Shaw thought him one of Britain's great men and his insights as 'future-piercing'.

'BUTSKELLISM', portmanteau of (R.A.) BUTLER (Tory) and (William) GAITSKELL (Labour) used in the 1950s and 1960s to denote a broadly similar outlook in policy which as Chanc. of the Exch. they both pursued in the economic and social situation of the time.

BUTT, Isaac (1813-79). Irish barrister, entered politics in 1836, as a convinced eloquent but reasonable Home Ruler opposed to Fenian violence. His constitutionalism failed to make the necessary impact in parliament and in 1877 his party replaced him by Parnell.

BUTTERFIELD, William (1814-1900) neo-Gothic architect mainly of religious buildings who refurnished Winchester College chapel with "smart yellow pews" and built buildings such as Keble College (Oxford), best seen in moonlight.

BUTTON'S COFFEE HOUSE (Russell St., Covent Garden, London) was a literary and gambling rendezvous in the 17th and 18th cents. Most of the habitués at Will's Coffee House also frequented Button's. Button had been an old servant of Addison's, and at meetings in his coffee house he assumed Dryden's function as arbiter of taste.

BUXAR, B. of (23 Oct. 1764). Shuja-ud-Dowlah, the Moghul vizier and Nawab of Oudh, and Mir Kasim, Nawab of Bengal, assembled some 50,000 men to reconquer Bengal, which had fallen to the HEIC after the B. of Plassey. The offensive was met by a British force of 7000 under Major (later Sir Hector) Munro, on the south bank of the Ganges at Buxar near Shahabad in Bihar. After a violent conflict the Indians retreated with a loss of 2000 men, but their force was much reduced by desertions as well. This defeated Mir Kasim's claim to Bengal. It also raised the Co's prestige and heavily depressed that of the Moghul govt. In practice the victory made the Co. a govt. as well as a trading concern, though it did its best to conceal the fact.

BUXTON, Sydney Charles (1853-1934) Vist. (1914) E. (1920) became a Liberal M.P. in 1883. There were two memorable events in his Westminster career: in 1909 (as Postmaster General from 1905 to 1910) he opened the Post Office telegraph system and (as Pres. of the Board of Trade from 1910 to 1914) he successfully moved the Fair Wages resolution in the Commons, and may therefore be regarded as a founder of modern socio-economic policy. As gov-gen. of S. Africa he had to cope with the treasonable activities of some Boer nationalists.

BUXTON, Sir Thomas Fowell (1789-1845) was one of the group of early 19th cent. idealists. He married Harriet Gurney, Elizabeth Fry's sister, and was M.P. for Weymouth from 1818 until 1837 when he lost that corrupt borough through opposition to corruption. Meanwhile he had taken up, with his relatives by marriage, the related causes of prison reform and slave emancipation. In 1824 he succeeded Wilberforce as leader of the anti-slavery movement. He continued, on the whole successfully, to disturb the Victorian conscience till his death.

BUYS, Paulus (1531-94) Catholic leader of the Dutch revolt against Spain, came in 1575 to London with van Marnix and Maelson to offer the protectorate of Holland to Q. Elizabeth. He was an organiser of the Union of Utrecht in 1577, and supported the House of Orange as a likely source of efficient govt. Consistently with this he favoured an English rather than a French alliance in the Spanish War, and concluded the T. of Westminster of 1585 which led to Leicester's operations in Holland. Unfortunately he quarrelled over the financial management of the campaign with the overbearing Leicester, who had him arrested on a trumped up charge of peculation.

BUYS, Willem (1661-1749) was Pensionary of Amsterdam from 1693 to 1725 and a leading colleague of Heinsius. He conducted the negotiations with England in 1705 and 1706. In general he was a leader of the Dutch peace party and took part in the abortive Gertruydenburg negotiations of 1710. In 1711, however, he and his party had observed the disadvantages of a peace made by Britain, and he was sent unsuccessfully to dissuade the new Tory administration from that course. He was a principal Dutch negotiator for the P. of Utrecht (1713).

BUZONES appear in Bracton as the leading men of a county, with whom the judge in the county court confers: perhaps the forerunners of the later knights of the shire.

BYE PLOT or WATSON'S PLOT (1603) was a plot of R. Catholics and Puritans together, to kidnap James I and extort religious toleration from him. It was thought, if it ever existed, to have been connected with the Main Plot.

BYERLEY TURK, THE, was one of the stallions, imported in 1690, from which most English racehorses are now descended.

BYLAND ABBEY (Nr Easingwold, Yorks), a large Cistercian house founded at an uncertain date at Old Byland, and moved 7 miles to Byland in 1177, was a successful agricultural undertaking until the Reformation when it was dissolved and demolished, mostly for its building materials. Its reclamations and husbandry left a lasting mark on the Easingwold countryside.

BYNG. This service family included **(1) Adm. George (1663-1733) 1st Vist. TORRINGTON (1721)** who repulsed the Old Pretender's fleet in 1708 and destroyed the Spanish fleet at Cape Passaro in Aug. 1718. For his son **(2) John (1704-57)** *see* MINORCA. **(3) Sir John (1772-1860) 1st E. of STRAFFORD (2nd creation) (1835)** was C-in-C in Ireland from 1828 to 1831, M.P. for Poole from 1831 to 1835. In 1855 he became a field-marshal. His grandson **(4) Julian Hedworth George (1862-1935) 1st Ld. BYNG of VIMY (1919) 1st Vist. (1928)** raised the S. African Light Horse in the Boer War. He commanded the 3rd Cavalry Division at the first B. of Ypres in 1914 and then the Cavalry Corps. He evacuated IX Corps from Suvla (Galipoli) in 1915. In 1916 and 1917 he was a popular commander of the Canadian Corps, and in Apr. 1917 took Vimy Ridge. He prepared the unsuccessful B. of Cambrai as Commander of the 3rd Army, but offered powerful resistance to the German offensive in Mar. 1918. He was Gov-Gen. of Canada from 1921 to 1926. In this office he was personally liked, but was involved in a constitutional crisis in 1926 when he refused a dissolution to W.L. Mackenzie King. From 1928 to 1931 he was commissioner of the Metropolitan Police which he reorganised. He became a field marshal in 1932.

BYRD, William (?1542-1623) was educated to music under Thomas Tallis, and became organist at Lincoln in 1563. He composed with great distinction for almost every instrumental and vocal medium available in his time. Some of his works seem to have been written in the interests of the oppressed R. Catholics, but appreciation of his remarkable talent has had to wait until modern times.

BYRHTFERTH (?-1015) mathematician and astronomer of Ramsey Abbey and writer of a manual for parish priests on the *Compotus* in English and Latin.

BYRHTNOTH (?-991). *See* MALDON, B. OF.

BYRON, George Gordon, 6th Ld. (1788-1824), the poet, was much criticised in Britain for his unorthodoxy, irregular life and oriental literary background. Having travelled in Greece and the Levant, he took his seat in the House of Lords in 1812 just as the first two cantos of his *Childe Harold* were causing a sensation. In 1813 he married a convenient heiress, whom he left a year later. Thereafter he divided his time between Venice, Ravenna, Pisa and Genoa, and wrote the greater part of his poetry. Though he and English society were at loggerheads, his poetry served as a powerful introduction of romanticism, and it was in a romantic (and not very practical) spirit that many Englishmen supported the Greeks in their revolt against Turkey. This movement attracted Byron too. He went to Greece and died of fever at Missolonghi. The death of an English Milord and famous poet in such circumstances created an immense sensation, especially on the continent, and contributed powerfully to that anti-Turkish orientation of European opinion which led to the B. of Navarino (1827) and to the foundation of the Greek state. His death made him one of the founders of modern Greece. As a result of the difference between his English and continental reputations, and the divergences between English and continental romanticism, he has always been more widely known abroad than in his home country.

BYZANTINE or EASTERN ROMAN EMPIRE (1) was that part of the Roman Empire whose capital was established at Byzantium (Constantinople) by the Emperor Constantine in 330. The term "Eastern Roman" refers to the period before 565 when Latin was still the official language. By the end of the 5th cent. Roman authority west of Trieste and Cyrenaica was mostly a legal abstraction, but JUSTINIAN (r. 526-65) reimposed practical sovereignty over most of Italy, North Africa and Southern Spain in a series of campaigns conducted by his generals Belisarius and Narses. Architects and town planners such as Anthemius developed a pronounced civil and military architectural style, and the great lawyer Tribonian codified the Law. The powerful influence of these achievements spread westwards by cultural and commercial osmosis not through direct power, for between 602, when major Persian wars broke out, and 678 when the Arab four-year siege of Constantinople collapsed before a combination of military skill, desperation and the invention of Greek fire, the Empire was locked in a series of terrible oriental conflicts.

(2) The work of re-establishing the empire had been complicated by Slavonic invasions across the Danube, and by further religious controversy (The Iconoclastic heresy) which estranged Byzantine Christendom from the Roman variety. Nevertheless, the Heracleids and their successors the Isaurians, who were Iconoclasts (717-802) organised a state stretching from Palermo to the Caucasus, which was compact enough to be governable, but large enough to be a great power. Within this area Byzantine civilisation, by now wholly Greek speaking, flourished, and its military power grew. By 969 the

Amorian and Macedonian dynasties had extended Byzantine power to the Euphrates; the Arabs had been driven from the Aegean and Cyprus, and Antioch had been retaken. With the rise of the powerful Fatimid pseudo-Caliphate in Egypt, equilibrium was reached in the south-east, and during the long reign of Basil II Bulgaroctonos (r. 976-1025) (Bulgar slayer) it seemed that the problems caused by Slavonic immigration into the Balkans might be settled as well, and that a period of security might result.

(3) There was, however, a dangerous break of continuity. During the 40 years after Basil II, the throne was occupied by eleven rulers who were really party leaders, and the military and civil organisation suffered from corruption and deceit. As a result the Lombards increased their influence in north Italy at Byzantine expense; the Slavs, especially in Croatia and Serbia, began to organise principalities under native rulers within the confines of the Empire; and the Normans by 1071 had overthrown Byzantine authority in southern Italy and were preparing to attack Sicily. This western indiscipline was, as usual, worsened by war in the East. The Seljuk Turks had secured control of the Baghdad Caliphate, and the general pressure of their westward migration was building up. In these circumstances the military landholding families secured control at Constantinople and the Cappadocian general Romanus Diogenes took the throne in 1068. His attempt to drive back the Turks was defeated at the B. of Manzikert in 1071; and within ten years most of Asia Minor was lost to a Seljuk sultanate established at Konia (Iconium), and a series of Danishmend principalities set up in the north-east.

(4) Manzikert was the central disaster of the Byzantine history and so recognised at the time. Romanus was deposed and blinded by his political opponents, but the need for a strong military monarchy was pressing. The devastation of Asia Minor destroyed the soldier-peasant. The great landowners represented the best remaining military resource. In 1081 the able Alexius Comnenus, a great landowner, became emperor and founded a dynasty which ruled for just over a century.

(5) Under the Comneni the character of the Empire was transformed. The native organisation became more feudal, and the new military and naval necessity to hire mercenaries and acquire allies forced the emperors to grant mercantile concessions to western states such as Venice; thus began the impoverishment of the trading classes. At the same time the Crusades erupted into Levantine politics.

(6) It was only in theory that the arrival of western armies to re-establish the eastern frontier of Christendom was welcome to Byzantine statesmen. The Western Roman and Orthodox Eastern worlds had long been politically and doctrinally estranged. The crusading armies consisted of ill disciplined partly armoured mobs of barbarians led, however, by potentates whose rank could not be ignored. They marched the length of the Empire. They were suspicious of the inhabitants; and there were constant robberies and clashes with the imperial police. They refused to take advice, and then blamed Byzantine authorities when things went wrong. When they reached Syria, instead of restoring it, as they promised, to the Roman Empire, they set up weak and incompetently governed crusader states on their own. And finally they irresponsibly stirred up conflict in the Levant for which in the end the local Christians paid.

(7) In spite of all, Alexius Comnenus defeated the Italian Normans in 1107. His son John checked the Hungarians, defeated the Danishmends and in 1136 re-established Byzantine rule in the Taurus mountains and then the emperor Manuel, by military and diplomatic means, secured his western frontier and, briefly, a Byzantine ascendancy over Norman Antioch. In 1176, however, at Myriocephalon he suffered a second

Manzikert at the hands of the Seljuks, and nine years later the dynasty ended in a series of political riots at Constantinople.

(8) Its successors, the distantly related Angeli, did not last long, for in 1204 Constantinople was stormed by the so-called Fourth Crusade. This terrible event had a variety of close and distant causes. Venetian commercial imperialism was reinforced by the crusaders sense of adventure and greed. The Crusades had increased the mutual dislike of Easterner and Westerner. The religious fanaticism of the unsophisticated tended to treat oriental heretics as worse than the enemies of the faith. Alone the Papacy, to its credit, condemned the venture.

(9) The Empire was divided. A Latin Emperor reigned at Constantinople but hardly ruled over a number of Latin vassal states which stood in a western feudal relationship to his crown. These occupied, roughly, the territory of modern Greece. The best harbours and trading stations fell to Venice. Byzantine authority, however, survived in three areas: a Comnenian govt. at Trebizond, an Angelid despotat in Epirus and at Nicaea a true imperial court under Theodore I. Lascaris, the brother-in-law of the last Angelid Emperor. He and his successor, John Vatatzes, drove the Latins from Asia Minor, established bases in Europe and undermined the power of the Angeli in Epirus. In 1258 Michael VIII Paleologus succeeded the last of the Lascarids. In 1261 he retook Constantinople and so founded the dynasty with which the empire was to end.

(10) Though much diminished it was still an important state. The Seljuk Sultanate of Rum (Konia) had broken up into petty shifting principalities; in the West the ambitions of Charles of Anjou, who had succeeded to Norman pretensions, had been abruptly checked in 1282 by the Sicilian Vespers, in which Byzantine diplomacy had a hand. Nevertheless the position could not be held. Turkish pirates stopped unarmed long distance trading. The imperial family was disunited, and the antagonists in the civil wars did not scruple to call in foreign, even Turkish, aid. When the Ottoman Turkish principality was established under Osman at Brusa only 100 miles from Constantinople in 1326, the imperial princes were too preoccupied to intervene effectively; in any case the empire was at war with the Serbs.

(11) European disunity now favoured the Ottoman Turks. In 1353 they crossed the Dardanelles, the Genoese making fortunes ferrying them over. In 1361 they took Adrianople and made it their capital. The Serbs were defeated at Kossovo in 1389; a western crusade at Nicopolis in 1396. In 1400 the Emperor Manuel II ineffectively toured Europe to secure help for his country, which was now assailed on all sides and shrinking daily. The imminent disaster did not, however, occur. In 1402 a great Mongol army appeared in Asia Minor under Timur (Tamberlaine). The Turks were overwhelmed at Ankara and their Sultan, Bayazid (Bajazeth) was captured. The Mongols, however, retired and the pressure soon rose again. The capital was intermittently invested; the few outlying territories frequently attacked. Diplomacy and offers of ecclesiastical union with the west produced nothing effective. In 1444 the Sultan Murad II (Amurath) defeated the Hungarians at Varna.

(12) The city was by now practically all that remained. On 29 May, 1453, after nearly two months of siege, the Sultan Mohammed II (The Conqueror) stormed it.

BYZANTIUM. *See* CONSTANTINOPLE.

C

CAB (from Fr: *cabriolet*) (1) originally a one-horse bright yellow two wheeled chaise for two passengers with a hood and apron. Cabs began to ply from a rank in Great Portland St. (London) in 1819, at 75% of the Hackney fare. Two-horse four-wheel broughams and Clarences supplemented them from 1836. They were called **growlers** because of the sound of their wooden shod brakes. **(2)** The **hansom cab** could carry two passengers. It was driven from a dickey with the reins over the roof, and the passengers were weather-proof, and could speak to the driver through a hatch above their heads. It was patented in 1834 and became progressively lighter and faster. From 1886 to 1896 there were about 4000 growlers and 7000 hansoms. The last hansom plied in 1951. **(3)** The hackney was a horse bred from a cross between a racehorse and a carthorse, especially suitable for use with carriages, and kept at livery stables for hire. Hence a hackney cab was one available for hire. **(4)** A **taxi** was originally any cab fitted with a taximeter to measure the fare by time or distance or, since the advent of the motor vehicle, a combination of both. Taxis began to drive horse drawn cabs and hackneys out of business after 1897.

CABAL, originally meaning a group of intriguers, was applied perhaps pejoratively, under Charles II to a small body of privy councillors forming an embryonic cabinet; and particularly to the five ministers Clifford, Arlington, Buckingham, Ashley and Lauderdale. *See* CHARLES II-11-16.

CABINET (1) (Fr: Ruler's private room) is a meeting of those of the sovereign's advisers whom the prime minister chooses to consult on policy. All are privy councillors (and therefore sworn to secrecy) but the cabinet is not a committee of the Privy Council but, in theory, an informal meeting of some of its members. Charles II in exile had experienced and temperamentally preferred the French method of settling policy by private discussion with ministers in his cabinet, to debate in the Privy Council. Despite parliamentary hostility the practice continued under William III. An attempt to revert to Privy Council procedure was incorporated in the Act of Settlement, 1701, but repealed in 1706 before it ever came into effect. The most important practical development began in 1717; owing to language difficulties and antipathy between himself and the P. of Wales, the German King George I ceased to be present regularly, and by the end of the reign he had ceased to come at all, thereby much reducing the influence of the monarchy.

(2) Theoretically the monarch could appoint whatever ministers he liked. In real life he tended to appoint those whose views and temperament coincided, and who could command support of groups in parliament who, at least, were not hopelessly at variance. Hence the chief man in the cabinet was he who could obtain, by management and policy, the adherence of enough parliamentary groups to get working support. In this power of management, this chief minister was not alone, for the monarch, as fountain of honour, the source of patronage and the dispenser of places and pensions, had a powerful parliamentary influence of his own, supported by the contemporary glamour of royalty and, from 1714 to 1830, the independent resources of Hanover. Royal influence could form and shepherd a cabinet often without the use of the legal powers of appointment and dismissal. All the same, after 1689 two factors predominated; the Crown revenues were insufficient to carry on the govt. and the Bill of Rights, 1689, had declared a standing army to be illegal; hence the Crown had annually to seek parliamentary authority for continuance of the army and for pushing foreign policy to extremes, and it had to resort frequently to the Commons for money.

(3) Robert Harley, Sec. of State in 1704, was the first to be appointed because of his backing in the Commons, but the term **prime minister** was not used until after Sir Robert Walpole came to power in 1721, and then mainly as a term of abuse. Since the cabinet had to manage the Commons, it could hardly do so unless its members were agreed and those who attended were naturally those most concerned with Commons' business. Money being the root of the matter, the prime minister was usually and now always is First Lord of the Treasury. The Secretaries of State and dignitaries such as the Lord Chancellor, Lord Privy Seal, First Lord of the Admiralty and the Lord President were almost always members. Other ministers might or might not be.

(4) By 1760 the detailed and much of the policy control of govt. had passed from the monarch to the cabinet and cabinet ministers. George III set out to change this, not by altering or overthrowing the constitution or practices of the previous century but by breaking away from the influence of the parliamentary groups which had been managed with such elegance by Walpole and the Pelhams in the two previous reigns. Into the vacuum stepped the more modern political party. When in 1784 he and Pitt defeated Fox and North, the Tory Party was established in power permanently until 1830. Pitt would not be controlled by the monarch and appealed to public opinion to reinforce the prime minister's control of his cabinet. By 1846 it had become on the whole politically homogeneous, and collectively responsible to crown and parliament and, further, through George III's illness, the loss of Hanover, and Victoria's youth and sex, much of the royal patronage and influence had passed to the prime minister.

(5) Constitutionally the sovereign invites somebody to form a govt. The list of ministers is agreed with the sovereign, but the prime minister nominates those whom he will call to the cabinet. In 1874 there were 12 of these; by 1914 it had risen to 19, by 1938 to 22. The extreme informality of the whole arrangement was witnessed by the fact that the prime minister received no *official* mention until accorded precedence above the Abp. of York in 1902, and the cabinet first appeared as such in a statute in 1937. *See* CABINET OFFICE.

(6) World War I enforced changes. As a body it was unwieldy, and in 1916 Lloyd George formed a **war cabinet** of only five members (later, with the addition of Smuts, called the **Imperial War Cabinet**) and instituted a **cabinet office** under Sir Maurice Hankey. In World War II there was a War Cabinet of nine members under Winston Churchill.

(7) In general the cabinet settles only major issues of policy and seldom, if ever, votes or debates at length. Controversial matters are referred to committees to thrash out compromises. Consequential details are similarly referred to lesser committees.

CABINET MISSION TO INDIA sent in 1946 by the Attlee govt. consisted of Lord Pethick-Lawrence, Sir Stafford Cripps and A. V. Alexander. It tried but failed to reconcile the Indian National Congress with the Muslim League and then made its own proposals for progress towards independence under an interim govt. These fell through because mutual distrust prevented agreement on the communal composition of the interim govt.

CABINET OFFICE. Until the middle of World War I, Cabinet business was conducted without regular papers or even minutes; the Prime Minister simply reported its conclusions to the Sovereign. In 1917 Lloyd George appointed a permanent secretary, Maurice Hankey, who with his office prepared papers, minuted the conclusions and circulated them to members and the sovereign. This office steadily gained importance and staff, so that by the

1960s it was a significant co-ordinating instrument, accounting for the development of 10 Downing St into the large bureaucracy which it had become. By the 1990s it formed the base for a number of senior advisers to the Prime Minister and such bodies as the Central Statistical Office and the Central Policy Review Staff. The constitutional position of these advisory bodies is uncertain but in 1989 a Chanc. of the Exch. (Nigel Lawson) resigned apparently on the ground that the Prime Minister was publicly taking economic advice from these bodies which conflicted with his own.

CABINET, IMPERIAL WAR. See LLOYD GEORGE'S WAR CABINET.

CABINET, WAR. See CHAMBERLAIN'S ADMINISTRATION. CHURCHILL'S WARTIME ADMINISTRATION.

CABLE. See also TELEGRAPHY. The earliest permanently successful telegraphic cables were operated overland in England in 1839; under water between England and France in 1851; across the Atlantic in 1866, and across the Pacific in 1902.

CABLE ST., London (Nov. 1936). The British Union of Fascists had been conducting a provocative campaign with often violent meetings (e.g. at Oxford) on the Nazi model. It was to culminate in a grand uniformed march to intimidate this Jewish area. The Jews forcibly halted it and strong police action was needed to stop the fighting. The event demonstrated Nazi realities and the govt. secured legislation which, amongst other things, forbade political uniforms.

CABOT (1) John or Giovanni (1450-98), a Genoese naturalised in Venice but trading at Bristol, was granted a patent in 1496 and sailed in search of the North West Passage in May 1497. He reached Newfoundland or possibly C. Breton Island in the belief that he had reached Asia, and discovered the Grand Banks Cod Fisheries. In 1498 he set out with five ships to reach Japan and the Moluccas by following the American coast southwards. They may have reached the Chesapeake, but his ship was probably wrecked off Newfoundland, and the others returned. His son **(2) Sebastian (1474-1557)** was educated at Venice and accompanied his father in 1497. He was cartographer to Henry VIII in 1512, and to Ferdinand of Aragon from 1512 to 1516 and, after a period in England, pilot-major to the Emperor Charles V from 1519 to 1526, when he investigated the problem of compass variation. From 1526 to 1530 he commanded an unsuccessful expedition to the Plate, and as a result was banished to Oran. Re-employed as pilot-major from 1533 until 1544, he then published a map of the world. He left Spain for England, where in 1548 he was pensioned. Charles V demanded his return in 1550. In 1551 he arbitrated between London merchants and the Hanse, and proposed the formation of a London Co. of Merchant Venturers. He had always been interested in the possibilities of a North-East passage, and in 1553 (when his return was again demanded) and in 1556 he planned and supervised the expeditions to Russia.

"CAB RANK RULE" provides that where briefs fall within a barrister's fee-range and specialisation, he must accept them in the order in which they are offered regardless of merit, otherwise difficult, unusual, weak, inadequate or unpopular litigants might never gain a hearing.

CACHET, LETTRES DE **(Fr: Letters under the signet)** were orders issued by French Kings to perform administrative acts of many different sorts, but one particular kind, the order to detain a person in the Paris Bastille without legal process, which could be obtained by private individuals with influence at court, led to unjust detentions, sometimes lasting for years, arising out of private quarrels. This practice was never common, and mostly used to deal with lunatics, but it was regarded with propagandist abhorrence at home and abroad as a symbol of the tyrannical character of French govt.

CADAFAEL (fl. 640). See GWYNEDD-5.

CADBURY, George (1839-1922), a Quaker, took over the family cocoa and chocolate business at Birmingham with his brother Richard in 1861, and moved it to Bournville in 1879. He began to lay out the Bournville housing estate with its gardens and amenities in 1895 as a self-supporting classless venture, and sold or let the houses without reserving any for his own employees. His brother died in 1899 and he became Chairman of the Co. He then transferred his interest in the estate to a Village Trust. The estate became the model for most late English public and private suburban development. As a religious man Cadbury furthered Quaker evangelism and was one of the founders of the National Free Church Council. As a Liberal he became principal shareholder of the London *Daily News* (afterwards the *News Chronicle*) in 1901 and his family bought the *Star* in 1909.

CADE, 12th cent. family of cloth merchants and money lenders from St. Omer, with connections and partners all over Europe and much business, and a house, in London. **William (?-1166),** his brother **Ernulf** and his son **Eustace (?-?)** were the main figures in this banking house which lent large sums to the Crown and Crown officials between 1155 and Becket's fall in 1164.

CADE, John ('Jack') (?-1450) and **CADE'S REBELLION.** The surname is common around Ashford (Kent) but an Irishman of this name employed by the Dacres in Sussex, was wanted for murder and fled to France in 1449. Ashford was the heart of the Kentish rising of 1450. Large numbers under a Cade's leadership gathered at Blackheath early in June, at first receiving assistance from some prominent Londoners and countenance from Yorkists and others hostile to the D. of Suffolk. Some of this support was soon alienated. On 6 July Cade agreed with certain royal councillors to disband his following, and about 2000 from Kent, Sussex, Surrey and Essex were pardoned. He then went to besiege Queenborough Castle (Sheppey) but was mortally wounded there on 12 July. Cade had not co-ordinated the many discontented people in the Home Counties, but the sequels show that grievances were strongly felt, for there were lesser risings in the next four years in Kent, Wiltshire and London. These were put down more ruthlessly.

CADELL ap GRUFFUDD. See DEHEUBARTH-15.

CADELL ap RHODRI (fl. 930). See DEHEUBARTH; GWYNEDD-14.

CADET FORCE for teenagers, was inaugurated in 1858 and rapidly extended during the patriotic (mainly anti-French) volunteer movement of 1859. Public schools formed cadet units which, from 1908, were called Officers' Training Corps and subsidised by the War Office. The subsidy was interrupted between 1930 and 1937. It accelerated the training of officers in World War II.

CADI, KADI or QAZI. A civil judge under Islamic law.

CADIZ (Sp) (Lat: GADES), a prosperous port from Roman times, on the sea route from the Mediterranean to Portugal, Biscay, the British Is. and the Baltic, owed its advantages to its well protected anchorage against Atlantic weather. It became immensely important after the establishment of the Spanish American colonies, especially after the port of Seville began to silt up. Hence it was the target of English attacks by Drake in 1587, Essex in 1596. It repulsed another with loss in 1625. One reason for holding Gibraltar after 1707 was the comparative ease with which Cadiz could be blockaded from there. During the Peninsular War it was the seat of the Spanish resistance govt. against Bonaparte. *See also* ELIZABETH I-22,26.

CADOG, St. or CATWG the WISE (fl. c. 450), a Celtic missionary and teacher of royal origin, who founded the monastery at Llancarfan (Glam), trained many Welsh clergy and probably preached in Cornwall and Brittany. This was the period of grave disturbance in the life of Celtic Britain and he seems to have been remembered as a kind of hero. He is reputed to have visited Rome and Jerusalem.

CADOGAN (1) William (1601-61) served under Strafford in Ireland where, by 1641, he was a Capt. of Horse. In 1649 as a major of horse under Cromwell he put down the Irish in the Dublin neighbourhood and became gov. of Trim. His grandson **(2) William (1672-1726) 1st Ld. CADOGAN of READING (1716)** and **1st E. CADOGAN (1718),** Marlborough's coadjutor and friend, served under William III in Ireland and Flanders, where Marlborough noticed his brilliance as a military administrator. In 1701 he was at Hamburg organising the movement of Danish and other troops to Holland, and in 1702 Marlborough made him his chief of staff ("Quartermaster-Gen"). His career was inseparable from his chiefs until he was badly wounded at the siege of Mons in Sept. 1709. He then became Lieut. of the Tower (until 1715) and British diplomatic agent at The Hague. He shared Marlborough's growing political unpopularity and was removed from The Hague by an intrigue at the end of 1710. He returned to Marlborough and served with the army until it retired to Dunkirk in 1712. He then went into exile in Holland with Marlborough for whom he acted as principal intermediary between the whigs and the German princes interested in the Hanoverian succession. He returned to England before Q. Anne's death, and played a quiet but important part in ensuring the succession of George I. Reinstated in his honours, he went as ambassador to The Hague, where he negotiated the Barrier T. of 1715. When the Jacobite rebellion broke out he embarked Dutch troops direct to Scotland, reinforced and then superseded the D. of Argyll, and rapidly brought the revolt to an end. He then returned to The Hague and in Sept. 1716 signed a defensive alliance with France and Holland. A Jacobite attempt to impeach him for peculation failed in 1717. In 1720 at Vienna he negotiated the accession of Spain to the alliance of 1716, and in 1722 at Marlborough's death, he became C-in-C, and took charge of the military security required by the contemporary Jacobite plots. He was thereafter one of the Lords Justices appointed to act during the King's many absences in Hanover. His later years were somewhat clouded by litigation with the Duchess of Marlborough. His brother **(3) Charles (1691-1776) 2nd Ld.,** served under Marlborough and married a daughter of Sir Hans Sloane, whereby Chelsea became the property of the Cadogans. His son **(4) Charles Sloane (1728-1807) 1st Vist. CHELSEA and E. CADOGAN** of the second creation (1800) was M.P. for Cambridge from 1749 to 1776 and Master of the Mint from 1769 to 1784. His son **(5) George (1783-1864) 1st Ld. OAKLEY (1831) and 3rd E.** was a distinguished Admiral. His grandson **(6) George Henry (1840-1915) 5th E.,** was M.P. for Bath from 1873, USec. for War (1875 to 1878), for the Colonies (1878-80), Lord Privy Seal (1886-92) and Lord Lieut. of Ireland from 1895 to 1902. Of his children **(7) Sir Edward Cecil George (1880-1962)** was M.P. for Reading (1922-3) for Finchley (1924-35) and for Bolton (1940-5). His brother **(8) The Rt. Hon. Sir Alexander, O.M. (1884-1968),** after a normal diplomatic career, became Per. USec. of State for Foreign Affairs in 1938, and was British representative to the Security Council of UNO. from 1946 to 1950.

CADRE **(Fr: frame).** Originally the nucleus of officers and N.C.O.s which could, with the addition of recruits, build up and train a military unit. Among oriental, especially Chinese, influenced communist parties it signifies the body of trained executives and propagandists who are to lead and indoctrinate populations towards a particular party policy.

CADWALADR ap CADWALLON (r. 633-64). *See* GWYNEDD-5.

CADWALLON ap CADFAN. *See* GWYNEDD-4.

CADWALLON LAWHIR (fl. c. A.D. 500). *See* GWYNEDD-2.

CADZAND (Zeeland) B. of (1337). Sir Walter Manny and the E. of Derby defeated the Flemings here.

CAEDMON, St. and Poet (?-680). This ox-herd entered Whitby abbey as an elderly man after 658. Possibly of British origin and certainly unlettered, he had a natural or, according to Bede, a miraculous power of English verse composition. He is said to have composed many poems, virtually none of which survive.

CAEDWALLA. *See* WEST SAXONS, EARLY.

CAEN (Normandy) was made the capital of Lower Normandy by William the Conqueror, who built a great castle there and founded the Abbaye-aux-Hommes where he was buried, and the Abbaye-aux-Dames where his wife Matilda was buried. It was lost to the English with the rest of Normandy in 1204. Recaptured in 1346 by Edward III, it was held only intermittently until 1417 when it became the centre of the English financial administration of Normandy. Henry VI founded a university there in 1432. It finally passed to France in 1450. It had international connections long before and since, because its immense quarries could easily ship building stone to any place accessible by water. Several English cathedrals (e.g. Winchester) were built of Caen stone. Later it was strongly protestant and many of its people fled to England and the Low Countries when the Edict of Nantes was revoked in 1685. It was badly damaged in the Normandy battle of 1944.

CAEN, *CONSUETUDINES ET JUSTICIE* **OF (Lat: Customs and Rules)** (July 1091), sometimes called the T. of CAEN, was an agreed statement of ducal, and by implication feudal tenants' rights in Normandy, drawn up jointly for K. William Rufus and his brother Robert, D. of Normandy after a formal inquiry. It was needed because the Duchy had been in chaos and William wished to restore to order the counties of Aumale and Eu, and the lordships of Conches and Gournai with Fécamp Abbey, which Robert had made over to him earlier in the year without partitioning the Duchy. These places were therefore held by the King as fiefs of the Duke.

CAER CARADOG and LLANYMYNECH (Salop). Caractacus reputedly made his last stand against the Romans at one of these places. Tradition favours the first; archaeology the second.

CAERLAVEROCK Castle on the Scots shore of the Solway was the stronghold of the Maxwells of Nithsdale. A contemporary poem in French celebrates Edward I's capture of it, but it was retaken and demolished in 1313. Another castle was built on a nearby site in c. 1335, but later in the cent. the foundations of the original castle were reused for a further building. The partly reconstructed ruins of the latter still stand. See BALLIOL, EDWARD.

CAERLEON (Lat. ISCA SILURUM) (Gwent) on the R. Usk, was a major Legionary fortress of nearly 50 acres surrounded by embankments, and first garrisoned by the IInd Augusta in c. A.D. 74. It was rebuilt in stone in about 100-120, and the garrison was then reduced. The place was neglected until the period 213-22 when a full garrison was restored. Regular military occupation ceased in about 380 by which time troops were needed more for coast defence and very little for police-work. Thereafter it ceased to matter.

CAERNARVON (Lat: SEGONTIUM) -SHIRE. See GWYNEDD. The area was occupied by the Ordovices when the Romans came. The latter conquered it between A.D. 71 and 78 and built outlying forts from Chester to Canovium (Caerhin) and Segontium. These were abandoned between 380 and 390, by which time Christianity had possibly arrived; it was well established in the 6th cent. The area was divided into the three cantreds of Arllechwedd, Arfon and Llyn which were subdivided into commotes. After the Edwardian conquest (1283) the three cantreds, with the commotes of Eifionydd and Creuddyn, were combined to form the county (Stat. of Rhuddlan 1284), while Caernarvon, Conway and Criccieth received charters. Edward I and his successors built the castle-palace at Caernarvon (1283-c. 1330) on a lavish scale with Roman eagles in the decoration, but never quite completed it. A powerful castle was also built at Conway. Pwllheli and Nevin were chartered in 1355. Despite Owain Glyndwr's revolt (1400-15) which did great damage, the Edwardian system remained until the Acts of Union of 1536 and 1542 established quarter sessions and approximated the shire govt. to the English pattern. By this time there were many landed proprietors who, in 18th cent, began to develop the granite and slate quarries. These exported their products through the developing ports to the expanding industrial towns, whose workers needed slate for cheap houses, while their employers used granite for more monumental purposes. The rly from Chester to Bangor, built in 1848, brought holiday makers and converted the small ports into resorts. The shire ceased to be a county in 1974 when it was incorporated into the much larger modern county of Gwynedd.

CAERPHILLY (Glam), the centre of the Commote of Senghenydd, was nominally subject to the Lords of Glamorgan, but the inhabitants remained bellicose until Gilbert of Clare built a castle to restrain them in 1260. Llywellyn ap Gruffydd destroyed it in 1270, and thereupon a vast fortress in an artificial lake was built. The ruins of its unusual design with a fortified dam and keepless ward are still remarkable. It remained inviolate until Owain Glyndwr stormed it in 1403. Thereafter it declined into a prison. The market which grew up round the castle traded chiefly in the well-known local cheeses, and in the mid-18th cent. the town became a stronghold of Calvinistic Methodism. After 1830 the main activity was mining.

CAERWENT (Gwent) (Lat: VENTA SILURUM) was a small exclusively Roman town established in S. Wales while the nearby Caerleon (Isca Silurum) was being built.

CAESAR (1) Adelmare (?-1569) an Italian originally called Cesare Adelmare was physician to Qs. Mary and Elizabeth I. His son **(2) Sir Julius (1558-1636)** was a judge in Admiralty in 1584. He was an M.P. four times between 1589 and 1601, Chanc. of the Exch. in 1606, M.P. twice more between 1607 and 1614, Master of the Rolls from 1614, and M.P. yet again in 1620. His son **(3) Sir Charles (1590-1642)** was M.P. in 1614, a master in chancery from 1615 and a judge of the court of audience from 1626. Exceedingly rich, he bought the Mastership of the rolls from Charles I for £15,000 in 1639 but died of smallpox.

CAESAR'S INVASIONS OF BRITAIN. (1) The pre-Roman Britons had extensive tribal (especially Belgic) and trading (especially in Cornish tin) connections with Gaul and the Roman world. Apart from natural sympathy, British tribes were likely to be pro-Gallic because the tin trade was mostly in the hands of the Veneti of Brittany. The Romans exterminated the latter in 56 B.C. and disrupted the trade. Britain also became a political refuge for Gauls, and Julius Caesar needed fresh victories to keep his name before the Roman electors and to justify his continuing Gallic command.

(2) He decided to invade Britain, probably in 57 B.C. but Gallic disturbances delayed him until Aug. 55 when a reconnaissance in force with two legions landed near Walmer and Deal, but withdrew after six weeks. He returned in July 54 with five legions and 2000 horses but was delayed by a Channel storm which gave the British time to combine. He advanced from Deal and Sandwich to the ford at the present Canterbury. There were battles at Bigbury and Harbledown with the Catuvellaunian commander Cassivelaunus, and the advance was resumed via Rochester and London. The Catuvellauni were a Belgic aristocracy, and at this point some of their subject tribes, notably the Trinovantes under Mandubracius, came over. The Catuvellaunian capital, an immense fortified circuit at Wheathampstead, was then stormed and treaties were imposed freeing six tribes (Trinovantes,

Cenimagni, Segontiaci, Ancalites, Bibraci, Cassi) from the overlordship of the Catuvellauni and placing them and the latter in tributary alliances with Rome. Caesar evacuated Britain in Sept. The treaties were scarcely honoured, if at all. *See* BRITAIN BEFORE THE ROMAN CONQUEST.

CAETH. *See* WELSH LAW-1,11.

CAGLIOSTRO, "Count Alexander" alias Giovanni Balsamo (1743-95) a widely travelled rogue and forger who set his sights high, was of solid appearance and made fortunes all over Europe as a supposed physician, salesman of elixirs and necromancer. He was implicated in the Diamond Necklace scandal at the French court in 1785, and after a spell in the Bastille came to England, ran up debts and was committed to the Fleet. He obtained his release, went abroad and died in a papal prison.

CAGOTS. Ancient untouchable and underprivileged clans of Aquitaine and Brittany, some perhaps descended from 6th cent. lepers; they acted as cattlemen and slaughterers.

CAHORS, CAHORSINS. This ancient, once great, city lay on the main mediaeval route from Toulouse to Paris. It was the capital of Quercy (a fief of Toulouse) and of a large now vanished wine industry supplying Bordeaux, and it was in English hands throughout much of the middle ages, being occupied by the French only in 1428. In the 13th and 14th cents. it was a centre for Italian bankers and exchange dealers, who became known as Cahorsins and whose operations extended as far as England and Denmark.

CAICOS Is. (W. Indies) were occupied by the British in 1764. In combination with the Turks Is. they became a Crown Colony in 1962.

CAILLAUX, Joseph Marie Auguste (1863-1944), French radical-socialist was Finance Minister under Waldeck Rousseau (1899-1902 and 1906-09) when he estranged the Right by introducing income tax. He became prime minister in 1911 and negotiated the Agadir bargain (part of the Congo to Germany, protectorate over Morocco for France) behind his foreign minister's back. Criticism drove him from office, but in Dec. 1913 he was finance minister again and this time got the income tax bill passed. An unsavoury press campaign against him and his wife resulted in Madame Caillaux shooting the editor of *Figaro*. She was acquitted but he had to resign and was denied office in World War I. He thought that the war should be ended quickly and his alleged friendship with German agents led to the removal of his parliamentary immunity, accusations of defeatism, imprisonment from 1917 until impeachment and condemnation by the Senate in 1920. Amnestied in 1924, he was Finance Minister under Painlevé (Apr. to Oct. 1925), Briand (June 1926) and Bouisson (June 1935). His pacifism led him to support Daladier's efforts to negotiate with Hitler in 1938 and 1939, but after the fall of France (1940) he retired to the country and refused to co-operate with the Vichy govt.

CAIRD, James (1816-93), in *High Farming: the Best Substitute for Protection* (1849) and *English Agriculture* (1851) contended that the Corn Laws having been repealed in 1846, machinery, improved drainage (both already developed), chemical fertilisers and better education would maintain farm prosperity, which was not actually threatened until the mid-1860s. In 1874, when N. American soft wheat and improved transport had already created the agricultural slump he published *The Landed Interest and the Supply of Food* in which he blamed the trouble on *laissez-faire,* bad management and insecure tenancies.

CAIRNCROSS, Sir Alexander Kirkland (1911-), lecturer at Cambridge from 1935 to 1939, became Dir. of Programmes at the Min. of Aircraft Production in 1945 and then held a series of high economic advisory posts e.g. at Berlin (1945-6), B. of Trade (1946-9), O.E.E.C. (1949-50), H.M. Govt. (1961-4) as well as academic posts, culminating in 1969 in the mastership of St. Peters Coll., Oxford. He was a widely respected writer on economics, particularly in relation to state intervention in economic situations.

CAIRNS, Hugh McCalmont (1819-85) 1st Ld. CAIRNS (1867) 1st E. (1878) became M.P. for Belfast in 1852 and was a leading parliamentarian by 1858 when he became Sol-Gen under Lord Derby. In 1866 he was Att-Gen and then became a Lord Justice in Chancery. He was Lord Chancellor in 1868, leader of the Tory opposition in the Lords from 1869 to 1874, and Lord Chancellor again from 1874 to 1880. An exceptionally able but utterly humourless lawyer and evangelical churchman, his main activity was opposition to Irish disestablishment.

CAIRO (Egypt). The Byzantine town of BABYLON was captured in 641 by the Arabs under 'Amr who built FUSTAT on the site of his own camp. In the 9th cent. the Tulunids built AL KATAI to the north. In 970 the Fatimids founded the mosque and University of AL AZHAR while their general Johar al Rumi founded AL KAHIRA (The Triumphant) hence "Cairo". Saladin built the Citadel in about 1195, but the architectural peak was reached between 1250 and 1517 under the Mamelukes who made it, with Damascus, joint capital of their domains. It fell to the Turks in 1517 and remained a provincial town until Mehemet Ali massacred the last of the Mamelukes in 1811. It then became effectively a capital again. It was British occupied from 1882 to 1946.

CAIRO CONFERENCES (1) 22-26 Nov. 1943. Pres. Roosevelt (U.S.A.), Churchill (U.K.) and Gen. Chiang Kai-shek (China) met to declare a joint far Eastern policy. This was formulated in the Cairo Declaration as unconditional surrender from Japan, the independence of Korea, and the restoration to China of Manchuria and the Pescadores Is. **(2)** 4-6 Dec. 1943. Roosevelt and Churchill met Pres. Inönü (Turkey) and tried but failed to persuade the Turks to join the war. It was also agreed to appoint the American Gen. Eisenhower to command the proposed Normandy invasion.

CAITHNESS (Scot) was an area of Pictish settlement early invaded from Scandinavia; until 1231 the earldom was held by the Norse earls of Orkney. After prolonged confusion James II conferred it in 1455 on William, the third Sinclair E. of Orkney, and the Sinclairs held it in growing splendour until 1677 when George, sixth Sinclair earl, transferred his rights to Sir John Campbell of Glenorchy, later E. of Breadalbane, in payment of his predecessor's debts. The Sinclair tribesmen led by George Sinclair of Keiss refused to recognise the transfer until Glenorchy defeated them in 1680 at Altimarlich, the last Scots clan battle. See also SINCLAIR.

CAITHNESS, Es. of. *See* SINCLAIR.

CAJETAN, Thomas de Vio (1469-1534) Card. (1517) became General of the Dominicans in 1508; urged self reformation on the Lateran Council of 1512; as a Cardinal he entered into discussions with Luther in 1518; played an important part in the imperial election of Charles V in 1519 and of Pope Hadrian VI in 1522. His connection with Charles V made him an influential opponent of Henry VIII's divorce in 1530.

CALABAR (Nigeria) exported many slaves in the 18th cent. until the trade was suppressed in 1807. It then made itself rich on the export of palm oil. See NIGERIA.

CALAIS (Fr) (1) fell to Edward III in Aug. 1347 after his victory at Crécy (1346). He spared the population at the intercession of Q. Philippa, but deported it to make room for English colonists. **(2)** The place was annexed, and tin, lead and cloth staples were established in 1348. English sovereignty was recognised at the P. of Brétigny (1360) and the initially most important wool staple came in 1363. The French war and the economic policy of Burgundy caused the staples to be moved to Middleburg from 1384 to 1388, but the truces of 1389 and 1394 brought them back permanently. **(3)** Calais and its March

or Pale soon became the most important single English possession. It consisted of the fiefs of HAMMES, HERVELINGHEN, MARCK, OYE, SANGATTE and WISSANT with the county of GUINES, and marched with Flanders to the East and Artois to the South. The customs revenue from the staples amounted at times to a third of the English govt's revenue. As an enclave without natural defences, its territory had to be fortified and garrisoned, but its traders made a huge turnover in N. France and the Burgundian lands. The harbour was the main base for policing the Channel against Breton and Flemish pirates and, when necessary, for blackmailing the Hanse. The garrison or *Lieutenancy,* whose expense was charged on the local customs, was the largest permanent English professional force. The governorship or *Captaincy* was a highly prized public office. Northumberland was Capt. in 1389; Sir Thos. Swynford in 1400; York in 1454; Warwick from 1458. The famous Dick Whittington was simultaneously Lord Mayor of London and *Mayor of the Staple* in 1407, and many M.P.'s were Staplers, e.g. seven in the parliament of 1422. Its prosperity was further attested by many 15th cent. diplomatic congresses. **(4)** After the Franco-Burgundian accord at Arras in 1435, the Burgundians attacked it and thereafter the cost of the military and naval establishments was always high, though defrayed from local revenue. This gave the Capt. a position of quasi-independence if he chose, and from 1455 when York became Capt, until 1471, when Warwick was killed at Barnet, Calais was the indispensable refuge of the Yorkist grandees. The Wars of the Roses could probably not have been fought without it. **(5)** Interrupted occasionally by political disturbances, the wool trade prospered progressively less because of the rise of the cloth trade conducted by the Merchant Adventurers. They were encouraged to evade the staple, and made immense fortunes trading direct to continental markets or through the Hanse *Kontor* at Bruges. By 1536, when the population was 12,000, the number of wool merchants had sunk in 20 years from 5450 to 150. The retention of Calais now became a matter of expensive prestige rather than economics, and the development of armaments made it hard to hold by purely military means. The fortifications decayed. As long as the Franco-Burgundian frontier was near the town, France and Burgundy, while coveting it, preferred it in English hands rather than in each others. The enormous increase in the power of centralised France by the end of the 15th cent. overset the balance. When the Burgundian and Spanish lands came into the hands of a single Habsburg, a French war was inevitable. Mary I's marriage with Philip of Spain involved England, yet the garrison had been reduced and border fortifications even dismantled. The French D. of Guise took Calais in 1558 by a *coup de main,* and so, by ending 211 years of English rule, gained for himself immense prestige in the confused politics of contemporary France. *See* STAPLE B-6 *et seq.*

CALAIS, P. of (1360). *See* BRÉTIGNY.

CALAS, Jean, Affair. This Huguenot of Toulouse was corruptly convicted and barbarously executed in 1762 on a false charge of murdering his son to prevent his conversion to R. Catholicism. The case aroused European indignation when, at the widow's instance, Voltaire took it up. His best selling pamphlet *Sur la Tolérance,* virtually destroyed the moral authority of the French Church and shook the stability of the regime too closely identified with it, besides securing a posthumous reversal of the judgement.

CALCULUS. *See* STONE.

CALCUTTA (India) or **FORT WILLIAM IN BENGAL,** founded by Job Charnock in 1690 as an HEIC factory at Sutanati, was fortified in 1696 and acquired its name from the zamindari of KALIKATA purchased in 1698. It became the seat of a Presidency in 1700 and the fort was completed in 1716. In 1717 the Co. acquired the right to free trade in Bengal, and this vastly increased its prosperity. By 1735 the population was 100,000. As a result of the B. of Plassey (1757) and the transfer of the revenue offices to it (1772) Calcutta became the effective capital of Bengal, rather than the Nawab's seat at Murshidabad. The Regulating Act of 1773 made the Gov. of Bengal Gov-Gen, and Calcutta became the British Indian capital, and so remained until 1912 when the capital was moved back to Delhi. The Madrassa was founded by Hastings in 1781; the Medical College by Bentinck in 1835 and the University by Lord Canning in 1857. Administered mainly by local justices, the city was incorporated only in 1876. Its powers were gradually increased until 1899 when Lord Curzon radically reduced them. Thereupon the Indian members resigned – an early example of "non-co-operation". Responsible local govt. was restored in 1923, by which time the population had reached 1.25M, and the port had a virtual monopoly of the jute trade and much of India's coal. By 1990 the population was thought to have reached 6M. *See* CHOLERA.

CALDECOTE, Sir Thomas Walker Hobart Inskip (1876-1947), 1st Vist. (1939) became Conservative M.P. for Bristol in 1918. He was a law officer in all Tory administrations from 1922 to 1936; he opposed Prayer Book revision in 1927 and 1928 and piloted the Govt. of India Act in 1935. In 1936 he became Min. for Co-ordination of Defence, in 1939 Sec. of State for the Dominions, and then Lord Chancellor, but from 1940 to 1947 he was Lord Ch. Justice.

CALDER, Sir Robert (1745-1818) commanded the squadron placed to intercept Villeneuve on his way back from the W. Indies during the Trafalgar campaign, but failed to press him in an action in July 1805 off C. Finisterre. He took two ships. His greed for prizemoney was notorious, but Nelson sent him home to his court martial in a first-rate to show his confidence.

CALDER HALL (Cumbria) nuclear power station was opened in 1956 to produce military plutonium with electricity as a by-product.

CALDER, R. *See* TRANSPORT AND COMMUNICATIONS.

CALEDON. *See* ALEXANDER.

CALEDONIA was the Roman name for **(1)** Scotland north of the Forth-Clyde isthmus; **(2)** a forest possibly in Perthshire; and **(3)** the area occupied by the Caledones of Glenmore.

The Romans under Agricola occupied the southern parts in about A.D. 82 and built a legionary fortress at Inchtuthill on the Tay (Perths.) with auxiliary fortresses blocking the highland passes at Callander, Dalginross, Fendoch, Cardean and Stracathro. Marching camps have been found as far north as the Pass of Grange (Banffs.). Inchtuthill and all the sites north of the Earn were abandoned in A.D. 88, and not approached until c. 142 when the Antonine Wall was built at the isthmus, and the road to the Tay reoccupied. Intermittent warfare led to the abandonment of the area N. of the Cheviots in about 185. Large Roman punitive expeditions were mounted c. 210 and 306 but the area was otherwise left alone.

CALEDONIAN CANAL. *See* TRANSPORT AND COMMUNICATIONS.

CALEDONIAN MARKET (London), originally for cattle, was built to succeed the old Islington cattle market and was associated in 1885 with and slowly superseded by a more general market. This was partly closed in 1929 and finally in 1939.

CALGACUS. *See* MAEAETAE.

CALGARY (Alberta) was founded as a fort by the North-West Mounted Police in 1875. The Canadian Pacific Rly reached it in 1883, and it was incorporated in 1884. Large scale irrigation was begun. Gas was discovered in the neighbourhood in 1914 and oil not far off in 1947. The festival and rodeo called the Calgary Stampede originated as a farmers' fair soon after the arrival of the railway, and by 1923 had become an annual event.

CALICO JACK. *See* READ, MARY.

CALICUT (Malabar, India), CALICO. The Portuguese reached Calicut in 1488, and after intermittent hostilities stormed it in 1501. They established a factory there in 1513. After Goa it became the greatest 16th cent. emporium for Indo-European trade, specialising in printed and painted cotton cloths named after it. The French seized the factory at the end of the century and an English one was established in 1616. The Dutch negotiated a pepper monopoly in 1661 with the local ruler (The Zamorin). In the latter part of the 18th cent. calico began to be woven in England and France. This was much encouraged in England because Hyder Ali captured the town in 1766. The British returned in 1782, but in 1789 it was almost entirely destroyed by Tipoo Sahib. From this disaster and European competition it never recovered.

CALIFORNIA (U.S.A.) was first settled in 1769 and accumulated a mixture of British traders, Russian fishermen and Spanish missionaries. It was under Spanish control until 1821 and then formed part of Mexico. In July 1846 American settlers raised a rebellion. The Mexicans having been defeated in the resulting war, the area was ceded to the U.S.A. under the T. of Guadalupe Hidalgo (Feb. 1848). Nine days before the treaty was signed, gold was found at Sutter's Mill, and the consequent gold rush raised the population to a point at which a regularly constituted state could be established. This was admitted to the Union in 1850.

CALIPHATE (Arab: Khalifa = Successor) (1) The stability of this intermittently powerful institution was directly and indirectly important to Europe because of its ability to rally Islam in aggressive courses, to police a huge economic area and to transmit significant, especially Greek elements of civilisation to the West. Immense hoards of Iraqi silver coins have been found on the Baltic island of Gotland, Aristotelianism came to mediaeval Europe through the Caliphate of Cordova (Spain), and the Caliph's influence, even in decline, had to be taken into account by the rulers of the British and French empires.

(2) The prophet **MUHAMMAD** ruled Arabia from the twin capitals of Mecca and Medina. He died in 632, and the new ruler, his foremost disciple ABU BEKR, took the modest title of 'Successor'. He ruled until 634 and he with OMAR (r. 634-44), OTHMAN (r. 644-56) and ALI (r. 656-61) are known as the 'immediate' or 'orthodox' Caliphs.

(3) The development of Islam and the Caliphate down to the present day was profoundly influenced by a feud among the Koreish, the Prophet's tribe, dating from some 40 years before his birth, between the descendants (BENI) of Hashim, his great-grandfather, and those of Umaiya, Hashim's nephew. The Prophet had no sons, but a daughter FATIMA. Othman was an **Umaiyid**. He was murdered and Ali, his successor, was a Hashimid, married to Fatima, by whom he had two sons, HASAN and HOSSEIN. By this time the Arabs had conquered Persia, Syria and Egypt. Ali's authority was rejected by the Umaiyid MOAWIYA, gov. of Syria and Egypt, who became Caliph after Ali was assassinated in 661 at Kufa in Iraq.

(4) Moawiya (r. 661-80) was originally recognised by all Islam. The **UMAIYID** Caliphate which he founded ruled from Damascus. When he died, the Iraqis invited Hasan and Hossein to lead them, but they and their households were massacred by the local Umaiyid governor. This outrage upon the Prophet's near descendents delivered a blow to Umaiyid moral prestige and Islamic unity from which neither recovered. In the course of a twelve year civil war the two parties, which later crystallised into sects emerged: these are the **SHIITES** who supported the descendants of Ali and Fatima, the ALIIDS, and the **SUNNIS** who originally supported the Umaiyids. Politically the Shiites were inlanders, the Sunnis of Mediterranean outlook. In the short run the Shiites were driven underground and developed a doctrine of a mystical or hidden Caliph (called the IMAM) with spiritual attributes transmitted from father to son, as distinguished from the purely secular rule represented by the Immediate and Umaiyid Caliphs. One day an Imam would appear as a MEHDI or champion, and inaugurate an era of peace.

With the Umaiyid victory in 692, the Arab advance was resumed across N. Africa and Spain. In 732 it was checked only in France by Charles Martel at the B. of Tours. Meantime the Arab empire engrossed the Eastern trade and cut it off from Western Europe.

(5) The political resources of the Umaiyids were now overstretched, and vice and weakness at Damascus were undermining the administration. A new Hashimid candidature appeared in the shape of the descendants of Mohammed's uncle Abbas, with support from the Shiite areas. In 750 these **ABBASIDS** overthrew the Umaiyids at the B. of the Zab, and then massacred nearly all of them. The first Abbasid Caliph is known as AS-SAFFAH, the Shedder of Blood.

(6) The Abbasid's capital was Baghdad, and they rewarded their Persian supporters at the expense of the Arabs, who now ceased to be the ruling aristocracy. Not being descendants of Ali, they attracted Shiite hostility and Sunni support. Their rise began a process of polarisation between Mediterranean and Asiatic Islam. An Umaiyid survivor, ABDUL RAHMAN, reached Spain in 755 and founded at Cordova the rival Caliphate of **ANDALUS**. An Aliid revolt at Mecca was suppressed in 762, but IDRIS IBN ABDULLA escaped and founded the first Shiite Kingdom in Morocco. The oriental Caliphate at Baghdad continued in mounting splendour until it reached its summit under the famous HAROUN-AL-RASHID (786-809) the contemporary of Charlemagne. He nevertheless permitted one IBRAHIM IBN AL AGHLAH to establish an hereditary appendage which, under the name of Ifriqiya, included most of Algeria, Tunis, Tripoli and eventually Sicily and Sardinia. The African frontier of Abbasid power was now at Alamein, while in the East the Caliph MAMOUN (r. 813-33) had established another semi-independent, and soon really independent, state in Khorassan.

(7) The Baghdad Caliphate, the centre of a great economic complex, had come to rely increasingly on foreign, mostly Turkish, troops. In 861 the Turkish generals murdered the Caliph MUTAWAKIL and set up a series of maltreated puppets. Their govt. was centred on Samarra until 892, when it moved back to Baghdad. Their action discredited the political Caliphate and broke up oriental Islam. Attempts by later Caliphs to re-establish control failed in the face, especially of Shiite Carmathian, that is Arab Puritan, revolt. The provinces now paid only lip service to the throne. In 945 Baghdad was seized by the Persian **BUWAIHIDS**, also Shiites, who dominated the Sunni Abbasids for a century. Under such influence the Baghdad Caliphs withdrew from politics and devoted themselves to spiritual matters.

(8) The chaotic period between the death of Mutawakil and the Buwaiyid *coup d'état* saw the rise of the **ISMAILIS**. This Shiite sect, to whom the Carmathians originally adhered, flourished in the Yemen and favoured the claims of the descendants of Ismail, fifth in descent from Ali and Fatima. and ancestor of the Aga Khan. Their missionaries were active among the Algerian Berbers: there was a successful revolt against the local Sunni Aghlabid dynasty. In 910 an Ismaili (or as it called itself **FATIMID**) Caliphate was established at Kairouan in Tunisia and in 969 Egypt was conquered and a new capital built at Cairo. Confusion at Baghdad and order at Cairo diverted the eastern trade to Egypt, and since the Fatimids hated the Abbasids more than the Christians, this trade continued into Europe. Egypt became, about the year 1000, as splendid as Iraq had been in 800. and so

remained well into the 12th cent. The Caliph AZIZ, however, died in 996 leaving a child of eleven called HAKIM, who later suffered from religious delusions and vanished in 1021 in unexplained circumstances. A sect, the **DRUZES,** looking to him as a saviour, took root in Syria where it remains, but the reign of Hakim set a precedent also for the rule of powerful ministers who carried on the real govt. Fatimid primacy was recognised throughout Arabia, most of Syria and Africa, but their direct power was soon confined to Egypt and Palestine.

(9) The Buwaihid masters of Iraq had never been cohesive or statesmanlike. The 10th cent. Byzantine Empire enjoyed a revival largely at their expense, while the lands east of the Persian Salt Desert were divided between unstable local rulers at Bokhara and Ghazna. More important, however, was the rise of the Seljuq Turks in central Asia. They burst into Persia and in 1038 overthrew the Ghazhevid army near Nisapur. In 1055 they entered Baghdad at the Caliph's request and replaced the Buwaihids. In 1071 they defeated the Emperor Romanus Diogenes at the decisive B. of Manzikert (Malazkirt) and soon overran central Asia Minor. Henceforth the Abbasid Caliphs were respected primarily as religious figures in a Turkish political world. In 1077 the Seljuqs also came into collision, in Syria and Palestine, with their Fatimid rivals, and almost incidentally provoked the long reaction of the Crusades.

(10) Throughout these disturbed years Fatimid or Ismaili propagandists had been busy in Abbasid lands, and in 1090 one HASAN IBN SOBBAH seized the north Persian castle of Alamut. He set up the much feared Shiite ascetic order of the **ASSASSINS** who in due course spread to Syria, and whose grand master was known in the west as the Old Man of the Mountain. Fear of political murder gave this sect a power throughout the middle east out of all proportion to its numbers, until the coming of the Mongols.

(11) The establishment of the Crusading states in the Levant worked further changes in Egypt. The Fatimid Caliphs employed numerous slave troops (MAMELUKES). These encroached increasingly upon the civilian govt. By 1150 Egypt was in confusion and invaded both by Seljuqs and Crusaders. In 1172 the mameluke Saladin put an end to the Fatimid Caliphate in the name of the Abbasids of Baghdad. and Egypt became a mameluke state. In 1258 the Mongols destroyed the Assassin strongholds in Persia, sacked Baghdad and ended the true Abbasid Caliphate. In 1260, however, they were repulsed from Egypt at the B. of Ainjalud, and in 1263 Rukn-al-Din Baibars, Sultan of Egypt, discovered an Abbasid living in Syria and installed him at Cairo as a kind of hereditary religious official with the title of Caliph and the function of validating the rights of each successive Sultan. This shadow Caliphate descended in the same family upon mameluke nomination until the Ottoman conquest of Egypt, and in or about 1521 its last holder (another Mutawakil) surrendered his rights to Suleiman the Magnificent.

(12) The title of Caliph was thenceforth born by the Turkish Sultans. In 1922, on the proclamation of the Turkish republic the Sultan continued as Caliph only. In 1924 the Caliphate was abolished as well.

CALIXTUS III, Pope. See BORGIA.

CALIXTUS III (anti-pope 1168-78) was set up by Frederick Barbarossa in opposition to Paschal III's successor Alexander III, whom he drove out of Rome. His existence was a diplomatic complication for Alexander throughout the Becket controversy in England.

CALLAGHAN, James, Rt. Hon. (1912-) Ld. CALLAGHAN of CARDIFF (1988) became a Labour M.P. in 1945. was Parl. Sec. to the Min. of Transport in 1947, and to the Admiralty in 1950-1. He was Ch. of the Exchequer from 1964 to 1967, Home Sec. from 1967 to 1970 and Foreign Sec. from 1974 until he succeeded Sir Harold Wilson as Prime Minister in 1976. Defeated on a parliamentary vote in 1979 he resigned, lost the subsequent general election and was, owing to the continuity of the Thatcher administrations thereafter, pressed slowly into retirement.

CALLAGHAN GOVT. (Apr. 1976-May 1979). James Callaghan succeeded to Harold Wilson's Labour govt with Anthony Crosland (until 1977) and then David Owen as Foreign Sec. and Peter Shore at the Dept. of the Environment. Barbara Castle resigned and was replaced at the Dept. of Health by David Ennals. Michael Foot became Lord Pres. In Sept. Roy Jenkins became an E.C. Commissioner and was replaced at the Home Office by Merlyn Rees. William Rodgers entered the Cabinet as Min. of Transport and Roy Hattersley replaced Shirley Williams at Prices and Consumer Protection. The govt had to have a working arrangement with the Liberals because of its small majority.

(1) There was an economic upturn in 1977, thanks mainly to North Sea oil; there was also a large international loan and cuts in govt expenditure. In 1978 inflation fell below 10%. possibly assisted by the influence of the Price Commission. In place of Wilson's 'social contract', the govt issued guidelines on wage settlements. These were sometimes observed but at the end of 1978 the govt., to match economic growth issued a guideline of 5% increases which the unions would not accept. Members of the weaker unions had already suffered from previous wage restraints, and the stronger unions believed that they could get more. Strikes made the winter of 1978-9 a winter of discontent among the public which concluded that the Labour Party's special relationship with the unions made the govt at least indirectly responsible for the trouble.

(2) Rising living standards were now accompanied by rising imports. Domestic industries suffered from foreign competition. Production began to fall even though the direct effect was masked by new oil production. Nationalisation Acts in 1977 had sought to reorganise the aviation and shipbuilding industries. Unemployment rose and restraining schemes were mere palliatives.

(3) The govt. valued its reputation for compassion and raised pensions and supplementary benefits. Another Race Relations Act (1976) had made it an offence to create racial discord or in most cases to discriminate between races. A new Police Complaints Board was set up. The Health Services Act had been directed against the use of public facilities by private doctors and patients; directed at assuaging understandable jealousy, it did little for the Health Service.

(4) In Ulster there was the usual hope and hopelessness. In Rhodesia guerrilla movements presaged unpredictable upheavals but the govt interfered as little as possible. Meanwhile in Uganda Idi Amin created embarrassments, which could not be shrugged off, and bursts of Asian refugees arrived in Britain. All these issues were handled calmly on the assumption that Ian Smith in Rhodesia and Amin would depart one day, but meanwhile those present until then suffered.

(5) Mar. 1979, following the winter strikes, the govt. was defeated by one vote in the Commons and easily lost the inevitable general election.

CALLEVA ATREBATIUM (SILCHESTER). *See* ATREBATES.

CALMAR or KALMAR, UNION OF. *See* BALTIC-12 *et seq.*

CALONNE, Charles Alexandre de (1734-1802) became the French Controller-General of Finance in 1783. He had inherited a vast debt from court extravagance and wars, especially in support of the American colonists. He reinstituted the sinking fund, reformed the gold coinage, supported the Anglo-French commercial treaty of 1786, and tried to revive credit by extensive public works especially at Le Havre and Cherbourg. Unable without reforms to deal with an annual deficit of 100M livres he proposed *inter alia* a land tax payable by all orders, and the abolition of internal customs. These were submitted to an assembly of notables in Feb. 1787. They rejected

them, he was dismissed and the crown was forced to call the States-General which brought on the Revolution. He left France, and from 1790 to 1792 he was the chief effective adviser to the *emigrés*.

CALNE (Wilts), a Saxon royal burgh, was the scene of a synod in 978 at which a floor collapsed and precipitated all the participants into a cellar except St. Dunstan. There was also a council in 997. It returned two M.P.'s from 1295 to 1832. In the 14th cent. it received an influx of Flemish weavers and it long remained, as its older houses attest, a prosperous wool centre.

CALTROP a small set of iron spikes for wounding horses' hooves arranged so that one always points upwards. They were sowed in numbers by mediaeval armies as a defence against cavalry (cf ABATTIS).

CALUMET (Norman Fr = tobacco pipe). The long Amerindian communal pipe. To present it to someone represented an offer of amity: to refuse it, a declaration of enmity.

CALVERT. *See* BALTIMORE.

CALVIN[US] (Lat = form of CHAUVIN) Jean (1509-64) decided not to enter the Church but read law at Orléans where he also studied with his relative the scriptural translator Pierre Olivetan and then at Bourges with the Greek scholar Melchior Wolmar. From 1529 to 1532 he was in Paris, speaking at large against the Church. Forewarned of impending arrest he fled *via* Nérac, the residence of the radical Queen of Navarre, to Basel where, in 1535-6 he published his long-meditated *Institute* (see CALVINISM). In 1536, while passing through Geneva, he was persuaded to help impose a strict and godly dictatorship. In 1539 a liberal opposition whom he called the Libertines, drove him out, but he returned in 1541 and devoted himself to tyrannising Geneva and propagating his doctrines, particularly in France, Holland and Poland through his printing presses, while his disciple John Knox converted Scotland and others preached, less successfully, in England. He also lured his doctrinal opponents Castellio and Servetus with safe conducts to Geneva and burned them. He is said to have been personally charming.

CALVINISM is the theological system of John Calvin as set forth mainly in his *Institutes,* published originally in 1535 and revised in 1539. It is very elaborately worked out, but its central feature is the doctrine of absolute predestination. God is omnipotent, therefore he knows everything including the future. Therefore he must have willed both grace and sin, and also their respective consequences, the salvation or damnation of particular creatures. Since the Fall (willed by God) man is no longer free: all human activity is sinful but good works by Christians are excused through the merits of Christ, and those who have divine justification have a perfect assurance of salvation. The true church consists, therefore, of the elect of God: persons who are necessarily superior to other beings. It is therefore reasonable that the church should rule over the state – and that John Calvin should tyrannise Geneva.

Though the *Institutes* are the foundation they are too long for ordinary reading. A more widely influential summary is contained in the *Second Helvetic Confession* drafted by Bullinger in 1562 (before Calvin died) but issued only in 1566 in response to a request by the Palatine Elector Frederick III. This was accepted in all the Swiss Protestant Churches: by the French Huguenots, the Scottish reformers led by John Knox, and by many of the English puritans. Under Edward VI it was nearly imposed on the English church and the XXXIX Articles contain much material derived from it. The doctrine also spread along the Rhineland, and by 1622 Calvinism was the state religion in the Netherlands. It strongly influenced the course of the Thirty Years War, since Bohemia, a Hussite country, was claimed by a R. Catholic Habsburg and by the Calvinist Elector Frederick V. In

Britain it provided much of the moral and intellectual backbone of the opponents of the crown until the decapitation of Charles I in 1649, and it was during this early period that it spread to N. America. Puritan excesses discredited its more extreme forms in England under the Commonwealth.

One of its most remarkable features was the energy of many of its champions. Far from lapsing into a passive acquiescence of the foreordained, the early Calvinists were endowed with an invincible conviction of their own rightness and a determination to impose themselves upon the world. Their numbers were never large, yet their religious influence was world wide and their politics affected every country in Europe.

CALVINISTIC METHODIST. *See* METHODISM.

CALVIN'S or COLVILLE'S CASE (1604). *See* POSTNATI.

CALYPSO. A type of W. Indian rhythmical shanty for which words were made up impromptu. It became well known in Britain in the years just before 1935, and famous because of the many calypsos composed about the abdication and activities of K. Edward VIII.

> As he saw Wally in de street
> He couldn't control dat body-beat.
> Love, Love alone
> Made King Edward lose de t'rone.

CAMBERLEY (Surrey), became the seat of the new Military Staff College in 1858.

CAMBODIA. *See* INDOCHINA.

CAMBON (1) Paul (1843-1924) French diplomat. As Resident at Tunis from 1882 he negotiated the terms of the protectorate. In 1886 he became ambassador to Madrid and in 1890 to the Sublime Porte. Here he failed to negotiate a British withdrawal from Egypt then under nominal Turkish suzerainty. In 1898 he began his 22-year tenure of the French embassy in London. It was a difficult moment because of Anglo-French tension arising out of the Fashoda incident in the Sudan. He achieved great distinction in reducing Anglo-French colonial rivalry, and particularly in the establishment of the *Entente Cordiale* in 1904. He further encouraged friendly relations between Britain and Russia and effectively associated Russia with the *entente* in 1907. His brother **(2) Jules (1845-1935)** became gov. gen. of Algeria in 1891 where he established the main lines of French colonial policy. As ambassador at Washington from 1897 he negotiated the Spanish-American peace treaty, and in 1902 became ambassador at Madrid. His great skill earned him the embassy at Berlin which he held from 1907 to the outbreak of World War I, and his discernment there was an important factor in the formation of Anglo-French policy. From 1915 to 1919 he was Sec-Gen. of the Min. of Foreign Affairs.

CAMBRAI, B. of (Nov.-Dec. 1917) was conceived as a large scale but limited raid by 381 British tanks and 8 divisions on the Hindenburg line, which was surprised and penetrated. Haig, the British C-in-C decided to exploit the attack but there were no reserves. Further advances petered out and an equally surprise German counter attack drove the British back.

CAMBRAI, LEAGUE OF (1508-9). *See* JAMES IV OF SCOTS.

CAMBRAI, P. of, or LADIES PEACE (Aug. 1529) negotiated by Louise of Savoy for Francis I of France and Margaret of Austria for the Emperor Charles V, broke up the coalition between France, England and Venice against the Emperor by establishing a separate peace between France and the Empire. Charles surrendered his claims to his grandmother's Burgundian lands and Francis his claims in Italy and his feudal rights in Artois and Flanders, and Francis married the Emperor's daughter, Eleanor.

CAMBRIA derived from Welsh *Cymry* and related to CUMBRIA was the Latin term for both Wales and Strathclyde.

CAMBRIDGE, (1) Adolphus Frederick (1774-1850), 1st D. of (1801) 7th son of George III, was a soldier who served in the continental campaign of 1794-5. He became a Field Marshal in 1813 and was viceroy of Hanover from 1815 to 1837. His son **(2) George William (1819-1904) 2nd D.** was the last (and reactionary) C-in-C of the British Army, a post which he held from 1856 until forced to resign in 1895. His sister **(3)** was the mother of Mary of Teck, Queen to George V.

CAMBRIDGE'S CONSPIRACY (July 1415). Richard, E. of Cambridge, Lords Gray of Heton and Scrope of Masham conspired to murder Henry V, who was at Southampton organising the French (Agincourt) campaign. Their object was to place Edmund, E. of March, on the throne with the support of the K. of Scots, the Percys and Owen Glendower. This represented a revival of the Tripartite Indenture of Henry IV's reign, and it was probably related to the French negotiations in which the French plenipotentiaries had just denied Henry V's title to the English throne. Edmund, however, revealed the plot on 1 Aug., the day fixed for the assassination. The main conspirators were seized, tried and executed. The expedition sailed on 11th.

CAMBRIDGESHIRE, CAMBRIDGE AND ITS UNIVERSITY (A.S. GRENTBRYCGE). The area including HUNTINGDONSHIRE and ISLE OF ELY was occupied by the Romans. They drained parts of it which later went back to marsh. The earliest Saxon settlements were made in 5th cent. and later it was included in the Danelaw. By this time it was divided between North and South Gyrwas representing Huntingdonshire and Cambridgeshire respectively, while the Fens stretched to within a few miles of Cambridge and were developing into the Isle of Ely. When Edward the Elder conquered the Danes he included the area in East Anglia, but it was later overrun by the Danes again, and in 1010 Cambridge, which had become a Saxon military centre, put up a desperate resistance to them. In 1086 the shire system was established, the three areas having, however, a single sheriff, and in 1109 most of it was separated from the diocese of Lincoln under a bishop at Ely, who also held the Isle of Ely as a franchise.

In the middle ages the area produced much wool, hops and leather as well as fish, baskets and saffron. The Stourbridge Fair held at Barnwell was said to be the largest in Christendom, and dealt in all these commodities. It declined after 17th cent. and was last held in 1934. The Reach Fair dealt mainly in horses, an activity which has survived in the racing stables at Newmarket.

CAMBRIDGE UNIVERSITY began by a migration from Oxford after a Town-and-Gown riot in 1209, and when scholars were driven from Paris in 1229 Henry III offered quarters at Cambridge to some of them. The town received a corporation at about this period. The townspeople were no more friendly than those at Oxford, and in 1231 it was necessary to require that no scholar should remain who was not being supervised by a master. Peterhouse, the first college, was founded in 1284 partly to help solve the recurrent disciplinary problems. In 1318 the university was recognised as a *studium generale* by Papal Bull, and by 1388 there were eight colleges, but it did not approach the repute of Oxford until Lollardy began to influence the latter and frighten the govt at the end of the cent. Thus King's College was founded in 1441 with three more before 1500, and Lady Margaret Beaufort's foundations came in the early years of the 16th cent.

Erasmus was Lady Margaret's Professor from 1511, and by 1535, when Thomas Cromwell became chancellor, the university was a hotbed of protestantism, and attracting royal patronage which was, of course, withdrawn under Mary I. Elizabeth I gave it statutes in 1570 which vested the govt. of the university in the heads of colleges. Meantime "left wing" religious opinions grew at Cambridge. Since the Reformation bishops of Ely have customarily been Cambridge graduates and so have many of the clergy in the surrounding area. Their opinions strongly influenced the area, taking the form of puritanism in the 17th cent, so that it was the principal recruiting ground for the Parliamentary New Model Army in the Civil War. Cromwell himself came from Huntingdonshire. The area thus played at this point a decisive part in English history.

When the troubles were stilled, intellectual modernism at the university continued. The Lucasian professorship of Mathematics was founded in 1663; Isaac Newton, Professor from 1669 to 1699, created the famous mathematical school. The only honours degrees available were in mathematics until 1824. The classical tripos instituted in 1824 did not lead to a degree until 1850. By this time the university as an institution was far behind the times. Under an Act of 1856 new statutes were framed. One result was the foundation of the Cavendish Laboratory of experimental physics in 1871. In 1877 a financial reorganisation was attempted but failed because of the agricultural depression which reduced the income from college endowments. Meantime local govt. reorganisation had overtaken the area, and Cambridgeshire, Huntingdonshire, Peterborough and the Isle of Ely became separate administrative counties in 1888. In 1897 the university launched an unsuccessful public appeal for funds and in 1914 applied to the govt. for money. This was renewed in 1919 and led to the appointment of a royal commission and new statutes in 1923.

In 1965 a further local govt. reorganisation amalgamated Peterborough with Huntingdonshire, and Cambridgeshire with the Isle, and made some locally drastic boundary changes.

CAMBRIDGE, STAT. of, 1388. Of the 14 clauses, II forbade obtaining office by suit or bribery. III to IX represented an attempt to regulate the labour market by fixing wages, forbidding migration without a royal recommendation, punishing beggars, depriving labourers of weapons (but requiring them to practice archery instead of playing games), extending the Stat. of Labourers to boroughs and cities and inquiring into cases of foreign imprisonment. X provided for the appointment of six J.P.s per county.

CAMBUSKENNETH (Stirling). This wealthy Augustinian abbey was founded by David I in 1147 and it had a special relationship with the crown until the reformation. Several Scots parliaments were held there including that of 1314, which outlawed those Scots who fought for Edward II at Bannockburn nearby, and that of 1326 which included commissioners for the burghs. Its abbots were always influential, sometimes by virtue of their office, sometimes because a powerful office holder was given the abbacy as payment for services.

CAMDEN, William (1551-1623) second master of Westminster School and Headmaster from 1593 to 1597, first published (in Latin) his well-known and learned *Britannia* in 1586. He revised it, edition by edition, until the 6th in 1607. The first English version came out in 1610. Meanwhile in 1597 he became Clarenceux King of Arms. He endowed the Camden professorship of ancient history at Oxford.

CAMDEN. *See* PRATT.

CAMELOT, the seat of K. Arthur, is believed by rival schools to be Caerleon, Winchester, the large Cadbury Camp near Queen Camel (Som) and Tintagel castle near Camelford (Cornwall). The two latter seem more probable.

CAMERON, CLAN. *See* CLANS, SCOTTISH.

CAMERON, Sir Ewen (1629-1719), CAMERON of LOCHIEL (c. 1647) was gigantic, ferocious and respected. He joined the royalists with his clan after the death of Charles I and fought in the Glencairn rising for Charles II in 1653. Gen. Monck never succeeded in overcoming the clan, and in 1658 he and Lochiel came to terms. The Protector Oliver having died, the Commonwealth was in decline, and Monck, with Lochiel in company, hastened its fall by his march from Coldstream to London. Lochiel remained an important pro-Stuart influence. He was knighted in 1681; joined the Scottish resistance to Dutch William and played an important part in the victorious ambuscade of William's troops in the Pass of Killiecrankie (July 1689). He is reputed (not improbably) to have killed an enemy by tearing out his neck muscles with his teeth.

CAMERON AND HUNT REPORTS (Sept.-Oct. 1969) by commissions concerned with the disturbances in Ulster in 1967-8, described discrimination against R. Catholics, particularly in housing, criticised the R. Ulster Constabulary (R.U.C.) and the para-military B. Specials. As a result the latter were disbanded and the R.U.C. placed under an English Chief Constable.

CAMERONIANS were followers of Richard Cameron (killed 1680) who adhered rigidly to the Scottish Covenants despite the political and religious changes which occurred after 1649. They refused to take part in the affairs of an uncovenanted nation, and until 1863 still disciplined their members for voting in elections. Some of them formed a regiment used by William III's govt. to patrol the Scottish Highlands. This eventually became the Scottish Rifles (Cameronians), which should not be confused with the Cameron Highlanders.

CAMEROONS. In 1832 John Beecroft starting trading at Bimbia. The missionary Alfred Saker settled there in 1845. In 1849, when Spain was about to occupy Fernando Po, Beecroft was appointed consul, and in 1850 a British Court of Equity was established to deal with disputes between chiefs and Europeans. A treaty for the abolition of slavery and human sacrifice followed in 1852. Saker also founded many coastal European settlements. Between 1868 and 1874 the Woermann and other Hamburg companies began to trade there, and demanded a German consul. The Germans anticipated the British at most points and by 1884 they were installed. The Dualas objected and were bombarded by German warships. In 1885 the Germans appointed a governor and in 1886 and 1887 German rights were recognised by international agreement. The eastern frontiers were defined in 1893 and 1894, and there were further annexations from French Africa in 1911 as a result of the Moroccan agreement. In 1916 an Anglo-French force drove the Germans into Spanish internment and a temporary partition giving Britain the richest 10% of the area, was crystallised in the London Declaration of 1919. Both areas came under League of Nations mandates in 1922, the British part being integrated with Nigeria. The French part supported the Free French movement in World War II, and Douala was for some time Gen. de Gaulle's H.Q. The resulting local feeling led eventually to the grant of independence to the French Cameroons in Jan. 1960. Thereupon the British put the issue of reunification to a plebiscite, and in Oct. 1961 the south joined the ex French Cameroons while the north stayed with Nigeria.

CAMISARDS (Fr = shirt wearers) Louis XIV persecuted the protestants of the Cevennes and Bas Languedoc, partly by quartering dragoons upon their houses. As a result of these *dragonnades* during the War of the Spanish Succession, the protestants rose in revolt (July 1702). They wore white shirts for mutual recognition during night attacks. In Gédéon and Pierre Laporte they had able guerrilla commanders; the local population supported them and they maintained arsenals and levied taxes. By 1703 the govt. (most of whose troops were elsewhere) was unable to suppress them, and Marshal Villars had to be called in. The main operations against them ended in Apr. 1705, but guerrilla war continued until Oct. 1710. The episode diverted significant military resources from other fronts.

CAMPAIGN FOR NUCLEAR DISARMAMENT (C.N.D.) was organised in the late 1950s after a public relations exercise in which public places were plastered with an unexplained (but later well known) symbol. Expectations having been aroused, the movement was explicitly launched against the adoption by the British govt. of atomic weapons as a safeguard against the enormous Russian military manpower. Many leading members were to the far left in politics: many of its supporters, idealists with an instinctive and reasonable horror of atomic destructive capacity. There was much talk of Hiroshima and Nagasaki, and its most successful publicity gambit was an annual march to the Atomic Research Establishment at Aldermaston (Berks). Much of the press characterised it with fair accuracy as a left-wing movement. Its variations in intensity and support tended to coincide with western reactions to Communist Russian provocations, and it never campaigned against Russian atomic weapons. Not surprisingly, it faded out when in 1989 communism ceased to be fashionable. It did, however, serve the useful purpose of calling attention to a dangerous problem.

CAMPBELL, CLAN and FAMILIES. From the middle ages to the 15th cent. this federation of clans dominated the Scots west coast, against opposition, from the Clyde to C. Wrath; members of it sometimes dominated the whole of Scotland. *See* CLANS. SCOTTISH.

CAMPBELL OF LOCHOW (ARGYLL) (A) (1) is the leading sept of the prolific Clan Campbell. Its Chiefs, also entitled **MACALLUM MOR** are the chiefs of that clan, holders since 1455 of the Lordship of Lorne and since 1457 of the Earldom (or higher) of **ARGYLL.** and between 1529 and 1746 hereditary Lords Justice-Gen. of Argyll. The clan has since remote times been at feud with the Macdonalds.

The Campbell country with its Atlantic-facing sea-lochs and islands was held together by waterborne communications, symbolised by the lymphad (a kind of ship) in Campbell heraldry, but the sparse overland communications into the rest of Scotland were confined to defensible passes at Tyndrum and Rannoch into Perthshire and Inverlochy at the entrance of the Great Glen. The territory was to some extent intermixed with Macdonald country and the feud arose, folk resentments and particular memories apart, from land hunger and fisheries disputes. The tendencies of these chiefs to acquire properties E. and S. of the passes arose when they became intimately involved with national affairs.

B (1) Colin (?-1493) 2nd Ld. CAMPBELL (1453) 1st E. was Lord Chanc. in 1483 and one of the conspirators against James III in 1487-8. His *s.* **(2) Archibald (?-1513) 2nd E.** was Lord Chanc. in 1494 and from 1499 a joint governor of the Lordship of the Isles, where he savagely put down a revolt in 1504 and extended his jurisdiction to the Argyllshire islands in 1506. He fell at Flodden (see JAMES IV OF SCOTS). His son **(3) Colin (?-1530) 3rd E.** successfully contested a Macdonald resurgence in the Isles over the years 1513-7, established himself as the ruler of the W. Highlands and, having become one of the regents in 1525, lent his powerful support to James V against Angus. His *s.* **(4) Archibald (?-1558) 4th E.** on succession had to put down a rebellion in the Argyllshire islands and was imprisoned on the thin pretext that his oppression had caused the rising. He and the Gordons opposed the Regent, the E. of Arran, from whose custody they took the child Q. Mary, and having successfully defended the Clyde against Lennox, he got the forfeited Lennox estates around Glasgow. Calvinism was spreading and while he led opposition to the English and commanded a wing at the B. of Pinkie (1547) he also moved over to the new religion, entertained and protected John Knox and in 1557 signed the Engagement. By his death his great western territorial power was

supplemented by popular Calvinistic support in the Lowlands. His *s.* **(5) Archibald (1530-73) 5th E.** had signed the Engagement too, but assisted the Queen Regent (Mary of Guise) to suppress protestant rioters in Perth. This did not prevent him signing the new Engagement in 1559 or in assisting at the sack of St. Andrews cathedral and becoming a leading Lord of the Congregation in their march against the Queen Regent. He took Perth and Edinburgh and brought in his clansmen to attack the French at Leith. He pursued his own interests as a 'half-king' by offering assistance to the English in Ireland (which would strengthen his grip in Kintyre and Bute) in return for help and their artillery on the Forth (which would strengthen his Lowland following). He also became the official destroyer of Popish monuments. Hence he stood at the head of a primarily reformed country when he received Mary Q. of Scots at Leith in 1561 and entertained her on his lands in 1563. She, however, would not, on religious and political grounds, put herself into his hands; there was an obvious risk that this over-mighty subject might supersede the Stewart dynasty with his own; but given the power of other parties in the state, he and she had to intrigue and make changing alliances to make their own kind of headway. Her Darnley marriage was against Argyll's interests but Elizabeth I would not support him against his lawful, and her fellow, Queen and cousin, so he and Mary established a kind of truce which ripened into co-operation when she fell out with Darnley. He knew of the plot to kill him and unwisely supported the Bothwell marriage, whereupon his Calvinist following, incited by John Knox's fiery sex-hating mysogyny, changed sides. He could not, or in view of her fascination, would not turn back. He tried to have her released from Lochleven (close to Campbell country); was attacked in the Kirk Assembly ostensibly for his adulteries (which came close to the bone) and consequently could not support her adequately at the B. of Langside (1568). Her flight to England was a major event in Campbell history for, without a royal balancing factor in the east, his direct power was confined to the west. He recognised this by joining the govt. so as to compete for the control of the child King James VI, and was briefly Lord Chanc. before he died. His half-brother **(6) Colin (?-1584) 6th E.** succeeded to his outlook, practically manifested in opposition, with the Atholls, to the Regent Morton. In the long run this led to Morton's overthrow and execution, and to further contests for the control of James in and after the Ruthven Raid (1582). During the youth of his son **(7) Archibald (1566-1638) 7th E.** the family was in eclipse and at the age of 18 he was defeated by the R. Catholic Gordons in Glenlivet (1584). Imprisoned at Edinburgh, he secured his liberty by an understanding with them. He and they joined in driving out the MacGregors (1608) and he became a R. Catholic. With his back thus covered to the north, he took up the 5th Earl's south-westerly ambitions and subdued the Macdonalds of Kintyre (1615) but he borrowed heavily and, having made over the estates to his son, fled from his creditors to Flanders in 1619. Taking Spanish service he was, because of brief hostilities, attainted but in 1621 restored. He died in London. His squinting son **(8) Archibald (1586-1660) 8th E. and M. of ARGYLL** was effective head of the clan from 1619. he became a Scots Privy Councillor in 1626 and a Lord of Session. Charles I sought his advice after the renewal of the Covenant in 1638 but while in London he discovered that the King had authorised the Irish Macdonnell, the E. of Antrim, to take over Kintyre. Convinced of royal bad faith, he accepted the General Assembly's abolition of episcopacy and raised his clan. He could thus negotiate or impose the P. of Berwick between Charles and the Scots in 1639 and this led naturally to a quarrel with the royalist M. of Montrose. He led the Estates in continuing to sit in defiance of the King's order, pillaged the properties of royalist nobles and thereafter he successfully obstructed royal efforts to raise Scottish support until he went with the army to England in Jan. 1644. His absence was a proximate cause of the subsequent disturbances, for in Apr. Huntly and the Gordons rose in the north, Montrose crossed the western Border and there was an Irish foray in the west. He went back as military commander, but Montrose beat him in a series of small battles and vengefully ravaged Argyll. It was only after Montrose's capture that Argyll recovered his influence at Edinburgh and became the head of the ruling Scots committee. In Oct. 1646 he invited Cromwell to the capital.

He led most other Scots in the revulsion against Charles I's execution and in Feb. 1649 proclaimed Charles II and himself crowned him at Scone in Jan. 1651, but failed to overcome Charles' innate dislike of self-righteous Calvinism and Scotsmen, or his distrust of himself. His practical help was feeble and the Scottish army relied more on the Lord of Hosts than on dry powder. Argyll was chased into Inverary and submitted to the Commonwealth (Aug. 1652). After further intrigues he became an M.P. in the Commonwealth parliament of 1658. This involved formally repudiating allegiance to any monarchy but in 1660 he came to welcome Charles II. He was arrested, tried at Edinburgh and executed. His son **(9) Archibald (?-1685) 9th E.** commanded Charles II's bodyguard, fought at Dunbar and raised most of his clan for the King but quarrelled with the Highland royalists and parted from them. Not pardoned by Cromwell, he remained in arms but, by the King's direction, made his peace in Mar. 1655. The King was nursing his Highland strength and Archibald was naturally suspected of fomenting a new royalist conspiracy and imprisoned from 1657 to 1660. He joined Charles II at the Restoration and was well received but subsequently incriminated by Middleton and Lauderdale, sentenced to death (Aug. 1661) but respited in June 1663 released and restored to his honours. He was now employed in a series of police operations: against Covenanters in Kintyre (1665); for quieting the Highlands (1667); against the Macleans of Mull (1674-8) and for disarming Highland Papists (1679); and in 1680 his Highlanders were quartered on covenanting districts (*see* HIGHLAND HOST). He protested at the severity of most of these measures but, his advice being ignored, he incurred the unpopularity of executing them. In 1681 he hotly opposed the Scottish Test Act but fell victim of a charge of treason in Dec., was sentenced to death but in 1682 escaped to Holland. He now took desperate courses, being involved with the Rye House plotters in 1683 (*see* CHARLES II-27) and in 1685 becoming Monmouth's leader in Scotland. He proclaimed Monmouth at Cambelltown in May but his clansmen refused to come out and he was taken and summarily executed under his existing sentence. His son **(10) Archibald (?-1703) 10th E. and 1st D. of ARGYLL (1701)** was maintained from his father's estates after the forfeiture of 1681. In 1685 he offered to resist his father's incursion and turned, probably tactically, R. Catholic but joined William of Orange in Holland and went with him to England. In Mar. 1689 he took his seat as E. of Argyll in the Scottish Estates and was commissioned to offer the Crown of Scotland to William III and Mary II. In May he became a Scots privy councillor and in June was formally restored to his honours. Thereafter his knowledge was used to pacify the country (*but see* GLENCOE, MASSACRE OF 1692). His son **(11) John (1678-1743) 2nd D., E. (1705) and D. of GREENWICH (1719)** served as an officer in Flanders in 1702 and became a useful mover in the negotiations for the Anglo-Scots parliamentary union of 1707 (his English earldom being part of the mechanism). He served again with distinction in Flanders between 1706 and 1709, was politically hostile to Marlborough and in 1711 was moved as C-in-C to Spain and in 1712 to

Scotland. He strongly opposed the malt duty of 1713 which weighed per head more heavily on the Scots than the English. Meanwhile he crushed Mar's part of the 1715 Jacobite rising but was dismissed in 1716 for continued opposition to the malt duty. In 1719 he reached an understanding with the govt., was re-employed and abandoned his opposition to the duty, but by 1738 he was again in open opposition to Walpole who had him dismissed in 1740. He held office briefly in 1742. The son of (10), **(12) Archibald (1682-1761) E. of ISLAY (1705), 3rd D.** was educated at Eton, read law in Holland, served under Marlborough and became Lord Treasurer of Scotland in 1705 for the financial negotiations for parliamentary union. Elected as a Scots representative peer in 1707, he became Lord Justice-Gen. in 1710. In 1715 he raised his clan for George I and fought at Sheriffmuir. After 1725 he was Walpole's chief adviser on Scotland. It was by his advice that the govt. started to raise Scots regiments in the wake of the Jacobite rebellion of 1745. He rebuilt Inverary.

(C) The Heritable Jurisdictions Act 1746 destroyed the power of pro-Hanoverian as well as Jacobite chiefs over their clansmen and transferred the functions of the local Lord Justice-Generalship to the Scots Lord Justice-Gen. in Edinburgh, but it left their rights as landowners untouched and the clansmen continued to some extent to render them deference. Hence the local prestige of the Ds. of Argyll declined only very slowly and they remained prominent figures. Thus **(13) John Douglas Sutherland (1845-1914) 9th D. (1900)** called until 1900 the **M. of LORNE** was a liberal M.P. (for Argyll of course) in 1868; married Princess Louise in 1871 and was gov-gen. of Canada from 1878 to 1883.

CAMPBELL OF GLENORCHY. There were lairds in Glenorchy from 14th cent. and **(1) Sir John (?-1686)** 10th Laird, became wealthy and married Mary Graham, *d.* of the E. of Monteith. His son **(2) John (c. 1635-1717) 1st E. of BREADALBANE (1681)** supported the Glencairn rising of 1654 in favour of Charles II and won the respect of Gen. Monck who suppressed it. Later he advised Monck to declare for a free parliament, thereby precipitating the Restoration. He sat for Argyll in the first Restoration parliament, where his abilities were widely recognised and secured him much influence in the Highlands. Meanwhile he had lent large sums to George, 6th **E. of Caithness,** and in 1672 undertook to meet his debts in return for his earldom and other titles, estates and jurisdictions. From 1677 (when the earl died) until 1681 he was thus E. of CAITHNESS, but the transaction was disputed by George Sinclair of Keiss, whom he defeated in a pitched battle at Altimarlich (June 1680). Meanwhile the Scots privy council decided that he had obtained the Caithness estates and titles by fraud, and returned them to Sinclair of Keiss, but John Campbell was strong enough to secure a compensation in the form of the Earldom of Breadalbane. Notorious for greed and cunning he nevertheless had a stronger hold on Highland loyalty than his kinsman, Argyll, who had been too much involved in the national politics of Edinburgh. Hence in 1689 William III's govt. regarded him as the key figure in Highland politics and left the pacification to him. He pocketed most of the £20,000 given him for the purpose, and in 1692 was involved in the Glencoe Massacre (q.v.). Nevertheless his tact and circumspection kept the Highlands quiet and himself safe from prosecution. Like other chieftains, he dallied with Jacobite emissaries but gave such lukewarm support to the Old Pretender in 1715 that the govt. felt no need to proceed against him. His grandson **(3) John (1696-1782) 3rd E. (1752)** was Min. in Denmark from 1718. He became M.P. for Saltash in 1727, ambassador in Russia in 1731 and M.P. again for Saltash in 1734, for Oxford in 1741 when Walpole made him a lord of the admiralty. He became a Scots representative peer in 1752. His son **(4) John**

(1762-1834) 1st M. of BREADALBANE (1831) was a whig of no particular talent who received besides the marquessate an U.K. peerage to improve the govt's position in the Lords. His son **(5) John (1796-1862) 2nd M.** as Lord Glenorchy, was a whig M.P. for Okehampton from 1820 to 1826 and after the Reform Act for Perth from 1832 to 1834.

CAMPBELL (LOUDOUN) (1) John (1598-1663) Ld. LOUDOUN (1620) 1st E. (Sc) (1641) acquired the barony by marriage and sat in the Scots parliament of 1622. Strongly anti-episcopalian, he was a leader in organising the Covenant (1637-8) and in the armed rising of 1639 to enforce it. He was a disgruntled Scottish commissioner to Charles I who imprisoned him in 1640 for communicating with the French, but he was soon released and promptly joined the Scottish army. In 1641 he became Scots Lord Chancellor, and frequently represented the Estates in dealings with the King between 1642 and 1647. He became progressively disillusioned with the different brands of extremism in both countries, and so favoured Charles II's claims but with covenanting safeguards. Hence he fought at Dunbar, joined the Highland rising of 1653 and was excepted from Cromwell's Act of Grace in 1654. He ceased to be Lord Chancellor at the Restoration. His grandson **(2) Hugh (?-1731) 3rd E.** was joint Sec. of State for Scotland in 1704, a champion of the Union and a frequent Lord High Commissioner to the Church Assembly.

CAMPBELL, Sir Colin (1792-1863) Ld. CLYDE and F-M (1858), the son of a Glasgow carpenter, joined the army, fought in the Peninsular War with conspicuous courage and went, in 1842, to China as a Lieut-Col, and then to India where he won wide respect and a knighthood for his conduct in the Second Sikh War. He commanded the Highland Brigade and then the First Division in the Crimea, but came into confrontation with the incompetent high command, and returned, much traduced, to England. Fortunately Palmerston recognised his abilities and high character and when the Indian Mutiny broke out (1857) he procured his appointment as C-in-C in India. He started from London within 24 hours of the appointment. The speed and skill with which he led the troops and co-ordinated a group of able subordinates brought about the relief of the besieged garrisons (his name gave prominence to the bagpipe tune *The Campbells are coming, Hurrah*) and the rapid suppression of the mutiny. Military disarmament and pacification occupied him until 1860 when he retired.

CAMPBELL, Gordon (1886-1953) V.C. (1917). To counter the German unrestricted submarine campaign in World War I, he devised and trained the Q-ships. These were warships under various careful and innocent disguises of a kind which submarines would be tempted to challenge on the surface, and which could, by unmasking, surprise the submarine before it could dive. They destroyed only a few submarines, but lowered the aggressive morale and so the destructive capacity of German submariners.

CAMPBELL, John (1779-1861) Ld. CAMPBELL of ST. ANDREWS (1841), a distinguished reforming lawyer, was a whig and liberal sol-gen (1823-4), att-gen (1834-41) and then briefly Lord Chancellor of Ireland in 1841. In 1850 he became C.J. of the Queen's Bench; in 1859 he returned to politics as Lord Chancellor, but retired for ill health after a few months. He combined these activities with biographical composition, of which *The Lives of Lord Chancellors* (1845-7) and the *Lives of Lyndhurst and Brougham* (1860) earned him about equal indignation and acclaim and have been unjustly allowed to obscure his legal reforms.

CAMPBELL, John Frands (1822-85) though Sec. of the Commissioners for Northern Lights, published a great collection of Highland songs, legends and Gaelic texts.

CAMPBELL, Sir Malcolm (1884-1949) and his son **Donald (1921-67)** were world leaders in the development of fast motor cars and speed-boats. The father reached a land speed of 203 mph in 1927, and 305 mph in 1935; The son, 401 mph in 1964. The father achieved a water speed of 129 mph in 1937, and 142 mph in 1939; the son 276 mph in 1964 and was killed at over 297 mph.

CAMPBELL, Mrs Patrick (1865-1940), actress, born TANNER, of an English father and an Italian mother, married Patrick Campbell, who was killed in the Boer War, but kept his name professionally when she married George Cornwallis-West. From 1893, when she triumphed as Paula in *The Second Mrs Tanqueray,* to 1914 as Eliza Doolittle in *Pygmalion,* she dominated the London stage by her passionate acting and beautiful diction. In private life she was extremely witty and entertaining. After World War I she went into film acting, which may have paid better but suited her histrionic talents less well.

CAMPBELL, Thomas (1777-1844) poet of patriotism and heroic deeds, wrote *Ye Mariners of England* and *Hohenlinden,* a battle which he happened to witness.

CAMPBELL-BANNERMAN, Sir Henry (1836-1908) became a Liberal M.P. (Glasgow) in 1868. He held minor office from 1871 to 1874 and 1880 to 1884. As Chief Sec. for Ireland for 1884 to 1885 he supported Home Rule. He was Gladstone's Sec. of State for War in 1886 and again from 1892 to 1895, and advocated service innovations such as short service, an army reserve, and linked battalions which were consistently obstructed by the D. of Cambridge, the C-in-C. An inquiry into military and naval administration between 1888 and 1890 led to the Duke's resignation and the abolition of his office in 1895, but Campbell-Bannerman provoked the "cordite vote" which brought down the Liberal govt. in the same year. Nevertheless when Harcourt resigned in 1898, Asquith made it easy for him to become the Liberal leader. He refused to denounce the Boer War but attacked the way in which the Boer civil population was treated. The problems of party unity which this compromise created dissolved after the war was over and was replaced by a new unity in defence of free trade against Chamberlain's tariff campaign in 1903. This enabled him to adopt a gradual approach towards Irish Home Rule which the party as a whole, but not Lord Rosebery, accepted. When Balfour resigned he insisted on forming a minority govt. with a programme of internal reforms (*see next entry*) but defeats in the Lords led Campbell-Bannerman to lay the foundation for the threat to the Lord's powers which were to culminate in the Parliament Act, 1911. Meanwhile he was dying and in 1908 resigned in Asquith's favour.

CAMPBELL-BANNERMAN and ASQUITH'S GOVT. (Dec. 1905-Apr. 1908). ASQUITH'S GOVTS. (Apr. 1908-Dec. 1916). (1) In 1905 the Conservatives resigned. Rosebery (supported by Sir Edw. Grey) Haldane and Campbell-Bannerman disagreed publicly on the Irish question. Grey and Haldane tried to force Campbell-Bannerman to leave the leadership of the Commons to Asquith, while he became prime minister as a peer. Asquith would have none of it: he induced Grey to accept the Foreign Office and Haldane the War Office, himself becoming Chanc. of the Exch. In 1906 the liberals had a landslide victory at the polls. So began one of the decisive govts. in British history. There were important social measures, notably the Trades Disputes, Merchant Shipping, and Smallholdings Acts of 1906 and the Evicted Tenants Act, 1907, free school meals for poor children and medical inspection in elementary schools. In 1907 women were qualified to serve on urban local authorities, but bills on plural voting and education were heavily amended or thrown out by the Lords.

(2) In overseas affairs, the Transvaal and O.F.S. were given responsible govt. in 1907 (*see* CHURCHILL) and there were unsuccessful efforts to end the arms race at the abortive Hague Conference, yet service costs were cut, but by way of re-insurance, a general staff and expeditionary force were created, military conversations were held with France and Belgium and a convention initialled with Russia.

(3) Campbell-Bannerman's declining health made Asquith the leading intelligence at the point – home policy – where liberal policies were most controversial. His three budgets (1906, 1907 and 1908) marked the change from 19th to 20th cent. Britain. Export taxes and taxes on food (such as tea and sugar) were reduced; the tax distinction was made between "earned" and "unearned" income; grants to Local Authorities were fatefully substituted for earmarked taxes; and old age pensions were introduced for the first time. When Campbell-Bannerman resigned in Apr. 1908, Asquith succeeded without controversy. David Lloyd-George followed him at the Exchequer, and Churchill followed Lloyd-George at the Board of Trade. The govt's duty to safeguard the country against Germany had led to Haldane's military reforms and the launching of the *Dreadnought*, but the latter, by making all other battleships out of date, had put Germany and Britain nearly level in the naval armaments race. Liberal legislation was being increasingly blocked by a Tory and landowning House of Lords. Money was needed for armaments. Asquith and Lloyd-George proposed a land tax. In Nov. 1909 the Lords threw out the budget in defiance of 250 year old custom. Asquith immediately obtained a dissolution, and in the election of Jan. 1910 a majority which, despite Irish doubts, forced the budget through (*see* PARLIAMENT BILL CRISIS 1910-11). The Parliament Act 1911 settled a constitutional distraction provoked by two important realities. Pensions and other such benefits had to be financed and so had battleships.

(4) During the crisis the govt. had reason to apprehend German aggressive intentions. In Jan. 1911 Haldane had induced Asquith to have the problems of mobilisation investigated. The result was the important *War Book*. In July the Germans provoked the Agadir crisis. The War Office wanted to be able to send six divisions to France as soon as war broke out, but apparently the Admiralty could not guarantee their arrival. Haldane and the First Lord, McKenna, each supported their professional adviser. Asquith made McKenna change places with the Home Sec., Churchill (Oct. 1911), and Churchill proceeded to reorganise the Admiralty.

(5) Tempers rose in the hot summer (97 degrees in Aug.) of 1911. In *Osborne v. Amalgamated Society of Railway Servants* (Jan. 1911) it had been held that a trade union could not lawfully finance its parliamentary representation by a compulsory levy. 16 of 40 Labour M.P.s lost their salaries in the middle of a wave of nationwide strikes and lockouts, mainly in coal, engineering, cotton, the railways and the docks. Often trivially provoked, the strikes were sometimes directed as much at the trade union's H.Q. as at the employers. One of them included a three day riot at Tonypandy in the Rhondda (*see* CHURCHILL). This trail of labour unrest left miners' minimum wages legislation behind, but it was not the only sort of unrest. Home Rule was, to Ulster protestants, a prospect of domination by their hereditary enemies in a parliament at Dublin. They came out in armed opposition, led by Sir Edw. Carson, actually a Dubliner. His Ulster Volunteers began to arm and drill in Jan. 1912, in anticipation of the expected Home Rule Bill. This was introduced in Apr. By Nov. Bonar Law and most Conservatives were supporting them. Thus the Tories of the Parliament Bill crisis, were now apparently supporting prospective rebellion. Then there were the suffragettes. From June 1909 until early in 1913 hunger strikes and widespread arson, bombings, window smashings, picture slashings and false fire alarms harassed the services. By 1913, however, suffragette rage was becoming discredited, and their moderates were gaining a hearing.

(6) The domestic violence had an European analogue. The German provoked Agadir crisis (1911) was followed by an Italian attack on Turkish Tripoli (1912). This in its turn brought other jackals to the feast. The Balkan wars (q.v.) were, however, really front actions for the great powers. If Russia went to war with Austro-Hungary, France and Germany would be drawn in. Any major war would disrupt Britain's seaborne trade, and the govt. would have to exclude the powerful German fleet from the Channel and so go to war as well. Hence Sir Edw. Grey did his utmost to restore peace by setting up a conference of ambassadors in London. He was much assisted by the German ambassador, Prince Lichnowsky, and his minister, Baron v. Kühlmann. They were not, however, assisted by their govt. In Jan. 1913 the latter had concluded that war between the Dual Alliance and the Central Powers was inevitable and that therefore they must fight at a time and on ground of their choosing. To be able to carry out the Schlieffen Plan, they increased the annual conscript intake, raised a capital levy for military purposes and timed the completion of the widened Kiel Canal (which otherwise could not pass Dreadnoughts between the North Sea and the Baltic) for Aug. 1914 when the new conscripts would be fully trained.

(7) The 1910 election had been fought on the Parliament Bill, an issue which obscured the sub-divisions of power. Asquith's ministers were all Liberals, because their party had 272 M.P.s out of the 392 who had supported the bill. The others were 80 Irish and 40 Labour. Bonar Law's conservatives also began with 272 seats, but by Aug. 1914 had gained a net 16 in bye-elections. The dependence of the Liberals upon the other two parties came to the fore. They could not help pursuing Irish Home Rule and Welsh Disestablishment. The Parliament Act had now made both measures possible. Both bills passed the Commons three times. Britain entered World War I on 4 Aug. The two bills were presented for the Royal Assent over the heads of the Lords just afterwards, but instantly suspended 'for the duration' by further Acts. The Anglo-Irish Union of 1801 thenceforth subsisted only provisionally. In the final stages Asquith had repudiated coercion of the Ulstermen. The unity of Ireland thus became provisional too. The Irish M.P.s, if they had something to fear from the conservatives, now had nothing to gain from the Liberals.

(8) With the belligerents bogged down in the west behind barbed wire and machine guns, two rival war philosophies developed. The westerners wanted to bash a way through, the others wanted to go round. Kitchener, the alarming Sec. of State for War, to whom all deferred as to an oracle, could not make up his mind or give anything but confused guidance, so others pressed their own ideas. Churchill, an outflanker, developed the Dardanelles campaign, whose second naval phase, through local incompetence, failed in Mar. 1915. Then the westerners tried their hand. In three battles (10 Mar.-25 May) the western front remained unpierced. The C-in-C, Sir John French, blamed the failures on shortage of shells. Then, due to lack of drive among the commanders, the military phase at the Dardanelles was bogged down on the western pattern (Apr.)

(9) Lord Northcliffe, who owned the *Daily Mail* and *The Times*, now heard about the shell shortage, essentially a responsibility of the Govt. He planned a campaign to overthrow it on that ground at the time when solutions for the practical problems were already being sought. To expand the factories, the skilled labour long entrenched in the engineering industries had to be diluted. The unions accepted this provided that it was carried out voluntarily, temporarily and under their direction, that profits would be restricted and that industry should be directed through local joint committees of employers and trade unionists. Lloyd

George, as the govt's. labour conciliator, accepted this in mid-Mar. (during the first of the three battles) at a meeting of the Treasury. He called this Treasury Agreement 'the Great Charter for Labour', and it began to be thought that he alone could create a popular war effort. His next move was to obtain a cabinet committee on munitions (Apr.) On 13 May the opposition (contrary to their leader's wishes) put down a motion on the shell shortage. On 15th, Fisher, Churchill's First Sea Lord, suddenly resigned (*see* CHURCHILL). The opportunity to attack Churchill was too good to be missed by Tories, westerners and tariff reformers alike. On 17 May Bonar Law and Lloyd George agreed for different reasons that a coalition was needed: Bonar Law to prevent his backbenchers from getting out of hand, Lloyd George to strengthen his populist position. Asquith accepted the coalition principle for yet other reasons: to expose the conservatives to the coming Northcliffe storm and to the odium for getting rid of Kitchener, in whom, though a national idol, he had lost confidence. Churchill was sacrificed to Tory hatred. It was only now that the Northcliffe campaign was properly unleashed.

(10) ASQUITH'S SECOND ADMINISTRATION was a coalition in that all parties perforce supported it, but the non-liberals had little more than a toe-hold in the Cabinet. Northcliffe's campaign did not, as he intended, overthrow the Liberals. It benefited Lloyd George for whom a special Ministry of Munitions was created, and put him in intimate contact with workers and business men throughout the 18 months of Asquith's covertly disunited coalition, where the prime minister acted more as a referee than a leader. Moreover the Ministry of Munitions was a success. The armaments came forward in a flood encouraged by new welfare improvements such as works canteens, and by the recruitment of nearly 2M women. It began a social revolution. War pressures, however, were splitting the govt. In Sept. 1915 McKenna raised income tax to 17½% and lowered the exemption limit. He imposed a new tax on war profits (Excess Profits Duty) at 50% (80% in 1917) and a 33⅓% import duty on so-called luxury goods such as motor cars and watches. These all struck at the Free Enterprise and Free Trade roots of liberalism. So, in another fashion, did inflationary finance. So even more did the agitation for conscription to replace the voluntary system. In Jan. 1916 the Military Service Act imposed compulsion on unmarried men between 18 and 41, save those who conscientiously objected. It produced less than half the voluntary rate of recruitment. There was another agitation – to include married men. Lloyd George threatened to resign if this was not carried: Grey and McKenna if it was. Asquith, fearing his govt. might fly apart, presented a compromise to a second session of the Commons. It pleased no-one, but then on Easter Sunday 1916 there was an insurrection in Dublin, and on the Wednesday came news of Gen. Townshend's surrender to the Turks at Kut-el-Amara (Iraq). Asquith could now satisfy popular demand without worrying too much about liberal principles. But realising that it was not his policy, to some he seemed more interested in manipulation than principle. Doubts whether such a man could win the war became widespread. Two other events shook the govt. yet further. On 5 June Kitchener (still a popular idol) was drowned. The generals wanted to replace him by the E. of Derby, a puppet. Bonar Law and Lloyd George wanted Lloyd George and forced him upon Asquith (July 1916).

(11) Simultaneously the dreadful B. of the Somme began. By Nov. it had destroyed Kitchener's volunteers. Asquith's credit ran out. Carson organised a Unionist revolt. It became known that between 49 and 80 Liberals would support Lloyd George, who then proposed to Asquith a War Council of three with himself in the chair. Asquith naturally replied that it must be subordinate to the Cabinet and that he must be in the chair himself.

Bonar Law told his Unionist colleagues that he supported Lloyd George. They to his surprise determined to resign, not in support of Lloyd George, but to force a quick decision. Asquith accepted Lloyd George's proposal. Before it could be announced his liberal colleagues heard of these manoeuvres for the first time and were furious with him. Asquith withdrew his acceptance. Lloyd George resigned. So did Asquith, thereby ending the govt. (5 Dec. 1916) and defied Bonar Law or Lloyd George to form one. The King sent for Bonar Law, who would do it only if Asquith joined. Asquith refused. Bonar Law then advised the King to send for Lloyd George. Apart from Asquith's leading Liberal friends, Lloyd George was supported by all other shades of political opinion, though Lord Robert Cecil, Austen Chamberlain and Curzon stipulated that neither Northcliffe nor Churchill be given office. On 7 Dec. 1916 Lloyd George kissed hands as Prime Minister.

CAMPBELL v HALL (1774). Lord Mansfield C.J. of the King's Bench, held that the crown could govern a conquered territory (in this case Grenada) by prerogative, but that by conferring a representative legislature without reservations on the territory, it had irrevocably divested itself of this prerogative (cf The CASE OF SHIPMONEY).

CAMPEGGIO or CAMPEIUS, Lorenzo (1472-1539) papal nuncio at the Imperial Court from 1513 to 1517, Card. in 1517, in 1518 was sent to England by Leo X to preach a Turkish crusade. He was on good terms with Henry VIII, and so later became Protector of England in the Roman curia. In 1523 he was made Abp. of Bologna. and in 1524 Bp. of Salisbury. In 1528 he came to England about Henry's divorce, instructed ostensibly to find facts in consort with Wolsey, but privately assured by Clement VII (who was in the Emperor's power) that the matter would be called to Rome before he could pass final judgement. This charade annoyed Henry, and Campeggio left England for good in 1529, for the imperial coronation. He was deprived of Salisbury by Act in 1532.

CAMPERDOWN, B. of (11 Oct. 1797). The French Gen. Hoche and the Irishman Wolfe Tone, persuaded the French Directory to attack Ireland in the summer of 1797 where an insurrection was plotted. 15,000 troops were assembled at the Texel (Holland) to be convoyed by the Dutch fleet. A special and prolonged combination of wind and tide was necessary to get the whole armada out of the Texel at once, and this failed to materialise for three months. Eventually the battle fleet sailed and was attacked by a better armed British squadron under Adm. Duncan. After a desperate fight more than half the Dutch fleet was captured. Hence when the rebellion duly broke out in Mar. 1798, the French could give it only minor support. *See* IRELAND, D-5.

CAMPION, St. Edmund (1540-81), a fellow of St. John's College Oxford, joined Wm. Allen at Douai in 1571, became a Jesuit in 1573, was ordained in 1578 and in 1580 returned to England together with Robert Parsons and the first Jesuit mission. He was an effective preacher and reached large audiences. As a result the authorities soon became aware of him. He was arrested and late in 1581 he was executed for conspiracy. He was canonised in 1970.

CAMPION, Gilbert Francis Montriou (1882-1958), Ld. CAMPION (1950), became a clerk in the House of Commons in 1906 and by 1914 had become an expert on comparative parliamentary procedure. In 1919 he was Sec. of the Lowther Conference on Devolution and in 1937 became Clerk of the House of Commons. His radical proposals for procedural reform in 1945 were only partly accepted, but in the meantime he had recast Erskine *May*. After his retirement in 1948 his advice was much sought by legislatures elsewhere, and he became the first Clerk of the European Consultative Assembly.

CAMPO FORMIO, "TREATY" of (17 Oct. 1797). Bonaparte, then French C-in-C in Italy, barely consulting the wishes of his govt. imposed a political settlement on northern Italy by agreement with Austria, and created the conditions in which British maritime and commercial interests could be threatened. **(1)** The new French-created Cisalpine Republic received the Austrian duchies of Milan and Modena, and parts of the Padane territory of the Venetian Republic. Austria accepted Venice and the Venetian territories in Istria and Dalmatia, the Venetian govt. having been bullied into liquidating itself. **(2)** The threat to Britain consisted in the cession of Belgium by Austria to France, and in the French annexation of the strategically important Venetian Ionian Is. **(3)** In addition to the Venetian bribe, the Austrians were led to understand that France would support territorial adjustments in their favour in Germany.

CAMP, ROMAN. A standard square (2017 × 2017 Roman feet) was surrounded by a ditch whose earth was thrown up inwards to form a rampart. The interior was unequally divided by a 100 ft roadway or *via principalis* crossed midway by another or *via decumana*. These both had gates at each end. The *praetorium* or H.Q. was at the crossing. This design whether temporary as marching camps or permanent as legionary depots, was used for some six hundred years. Many examples still remain all over Europe, some (e.g. Porchester) with stone walls; and their presence influenced the layout of cities (e.g. Chester). They were capable, at a pinch, of holding a legion plus legionary cavalry but such congestion was seldom required.

CAMULODUNUM. See BRITAIN; ROMAN-1; COLCHESTER; TRINOVANTES.

CANADA (1) was apparently sighted by Bjarni Heijolfson in about 986; Leif Ericsson attempted a settlement from Greenland in about 1000. He called it **Vinland.** The Cabots made their first significant landfall from Bristol in 1497. They also discovered the Newfoundland cod fisheries which were exploited by the English, French, Portuguese and Spaniards from 1500 onwards.

A. NEW FRANCE (2) The coast was explored in the 1520s, and in 1534 by Jacques CARTIER (1491-1557) who entered the St. Lawrence and staked a vaguely defined claim for France under the name of New France. He reached Montreal and unsuccessfully founded a colony near Quebec, but these explorations were more important in opening up the fur trade. In 1600 Henri IV granted a monopoly of it to Pierre Chauvin on condition that he would settle 50 colonists a year. The trade was well established as far as the Great Lakes by the time Samuel de CHAMPLAIN (?1565-1635) arrived to manage the fur monopolies in 1603. He helped to found the first French Canadian colony at Port Royal (now Annapolis Royal) in 1604, and in 1608 he took the crucial step of settling and fortifying the St. Lawrence narrows at Quebec itself. His explorations stretched south to L. Champlain and westward as far as L. Huron.

(3) The too slow development of Quebec led Card. Richelieu to establish the COMPANY OF 100 ASSO-CIATES in 1627. In return for a grant of New France, and a 15-year fur trade monopoly from 1629, the Co. was to bring in 400 settlers a year. Unfortunately the Co's first fleet and Quebec were captured by the English in 1629 and though Quebec was restored in 1632 (T. of St. Germain) the Co. never fully recovered.

(4) Cartier and Champlain had made friends with the Hurons and Algonquins, who had driven the Iroquois southwards. Iroquois raids on trading parties developed into a war. By 1650 they had destroyed the Huron confederacy and the Francophil tribes had migrated beyond L. Michigan. French explorers and missionaries accompanying them reached Wisconsin but the base colony was left in extreme danger. A desperate appeal was made to the crown. The colony was converted into a province with a governor (in 1659) intendant, bishop and garrison. In 1663 the charter was also cancelled. The

Iroquois were defeated and forced to make peace in 1666, and thereafter colonisation proceeded in earnest. Over 3000 settlers (more than the residents) including marriageable girls, arrived between 1663 and 1670. Westward exploration was now pressed still further; Louis JOLLIET (1645-1700) established that the Mississippi flowed into the G. of Mexico, and in 1671 Simon d'Aumont, sieur de St. LUSSON (?-1673) claimed the interior of the continent for France at Sault St. Marie.

(5) In 1672 Louis de Buade, Comte de FRONTENAC (1622-98) became gov. There was a clash between the Crown policy of encouraging settlement, which involved arduous forest clearances, and the get-rich-quick who could live an entertaining life and make fortunes by exchanging furs for imported brandy. Frontenac encouraged the fur traders (called *coureurs de bois* = wood rangers), to join westward expeditions under such leaders as René, sieur de LA SALLE (1643-87) who reached the G. of Mexico in 1682. The short-term profits were vast, but brandy demoralised the friendly Indians and scandalised the church. Moreover, the trade excited the cupidity of the warlike Iroquois. The Jesuits told the home govt. that Frontenac's activities were immoral, disobedient and tending to Indian wars. In 1682 he was recalled. The brandy trade was reduced, but the Iroquois were fought (only with partial success) until 1686.

(6) New France was now faced with the English who had conquered the New Netherland (New York) from the Dutch in 1664; and had founded the Hudson Bay Co. in 1670. The former began to encroach on the fisheries of **Acadie** (Nova Scotia); the latter to divert the furs. The French captured the Hudson Bay posts in 1686 and 1687. The Iroquois, now allied with the English, attacked Montreal and with the outbreak of a European War, an English force under Sir William PHIPS (1651-95) occupied Acadie in 1690. Frontenac was brought back. He held Quebec and ravaged the Iroquois country, while his subordinate Pierre le Moyne sieur D'IBERVILLE (1661-1706) recovered Acadie and conquered Newfoundland. At the P. of Ryswick (1697) New France kept Hudson's Bay but returned Newfoundland. In 1700 the Iroquois made peace.

(7) The European peace was, however, only temporary and the resumed wars of Louis XIV soon spread. In 1710 the British occupied Acadie, and at the P. of Utrecht they kept it but not Cape Breton, recovered Hudson's Bay, and limited the French rights in the fisheries. For a generation this did not hinder the expansion of New France; westward exploration was resumed, and in 1738 Pierre GAULTIER DE VARENNES and others had pushed up the Red River to the Missouri, and made a fortune by 1744 in fur trading on the Saskatchewan. The population rose at an average rate of 800 a year. Farming, lumber and ship-building developed, and the law was altered so as to force landowners to let land for clearance. There were riverside villages from Quebec to Montreal, both by now substantial towns, and a great protective fortress on Cape Breton I. at LOUISBURG.

(8) During the war of the Austrian Succession Louisburg was captured in 1745 by New England forces, but returned in 1748 at the P. of Aix-la-Chapelle. This peace was not wholly effective in N. America. The fanwise movement of the French conflicted with the interests of the Hudson Bay Co. to the north and hemmed in the New England colonies in the Middle West. In 1749 the French claimed the OHIO Valley, and in 1754 built Fort DUQUESNE (now Pittsburg). The Virginian George Washington, sent to expel them, was driven back and in 1755 Gen. Edw. BRADDOCK was defeated and killed there too, just as other British forces were occupying Acadie and expelling settlers who refused British allegiance.

(9) These colonial wars formed part of the causes of

the world wide Seven Years' War (1756-63), during which French Canada, after an initial stand, was conquered by the British. Louisburg fell in 1758. Wolfe took QUEBEC and destroyed the main French army in 1759, he and his opponent, Montcalm, both being killed. The T. of Paris, 1763, left France with nothing but St. Pierre, Miquelon and some Newfoundland fisheries, together with New Orleans and her claims to territories known as LOUISIANA, west of the Mississippi.

B. BRITISH COLONIES. (10) The New Englanders preferred Acadie, now renamed **Nova Scotia** which, since 1758, had had a gov. and an Assembly on ordinary colonial principles, and in 1769 **Prince Edward Island** was also constituted a separate colony with most of the land allotted to about 100, mostly Scots, proprietors. These very slowly brought in settlers. **Quebec,** however, remained French in character and speech and accordingly the Quebec Act, 1774, while bringing in English criminal law, preserved French civil law, protected the R. Catholic Church, admitted R. Catholics to public office, and placed the govt. in the hands of a gov.-in-council.

(11) The Act included in Quebec the former French territories north and east of the Ohio and Mississippi, thus frustrating the ambitions or greed of the New Englanders, and creating friction between them and the mother country. The great American Rebellion was fought partly over New England colonial claims in these areas, which were ceded to the U.S.A. when it was recognised at the T. of Paris in 1783. It was followed by the arrival of some 40,000 UNITED EMPIRE LOYALISTS from the U.S.A. and the creation of **New Brunswick** out of part of Nova Scotia in 1784, and (by the Canada Act, 1791) of **Upper Canada** (the future ONTARIO) and **Lower Canada** (the present province of Quebec) with legislatures of their own.

(12) Within a year Britain was plunged into the French revolutionary wars which lasted virtually without interruption until 1815. Completely protected by the Royal Navy, British North America boomed because the interference with the Baltic trade created an enormous English market for Canadian timber. The only interruption occurred in 1812 when Britain's blockade, having frustrated American efforts to profit from the war, caused the Americans to enter it on Bonaparte's side. An American invasion of Canada was repelled by the Canadians themselves.

(13) Peace brought depression in Britain and a fall in the timber market. Malaise succeeded comfort in Canada and created new political problems. Executive officers from the governors and the councils downwards were mostly irremovable, with predictable incomes, and were often English, and they represented an obsolescent attitude to colonial administration. The elected houses of the legislatures, on the other hand, were dominated by local populations whose living had become precarious and who, in Lower Canada (Quebec) had no English background. The exhaustion of the shallow soil of the Montreal area caused a collapse of wheat farming, which raised the cost of living against the poor, and put many French Canadians out of work. It was thought, perhaps naively, that these problems would be solved by bringing the scapegoat executive and the population into greater mutual sympathy. The extremists led by Louis Joseph PAPINEAU (1786-1871) in Lower Canada and William Lyon MACKENZIE (1795-1861) in Upper Canada, favoured popular election of governors and officials on the American model. The moderate reformers led by William Warren (1775-1844) and his son Robert (1804-73) in Nova Scotia championed the English principle of executive responsibility to the legislature. Papineau's friends really wanted independence. The Lower Canadian legislature withheld supply: the executive impounded revenues. The legislature replied with the extremist NINETY-TWO RESOLUTIONS of 1834 which frightened the moderates. The British govt. sent out a commission of investigation under Lord Gosford, who was also to act as gov. of Lower Canada. The commission's findings differed from Papineau's known views, but Gosford's policy of 'conciliation without concession' irritated the British moderates almost as much as the French extremists. Gosford, who was fundamentally liberal in outlook, resigned because he could not break the deadlock. The Papineau rebellion (Papineau actually fled to the U.S.A. on the first night) followed and was quickly put down.

C. THE DURHAM REFORMS. (14) The British govt. now despatched the E. of Durham as gov. gen. and royal commissioner. The insurrection having discredited extremism, Durham's celebrated Report (1839) offered solutions for the two major problems. The local problem of French Canadian separateness was to be overcome by the creation of a unitary province of Canada in which the French and English were to mingle. The constitutional issue, which affected every other British overseas possession, was to be settled by locally responsible govt. in local matters. The two provinces were combined in 1840. The instructions to Lord Elgin, gov-gen. from 1846, marked the introduction of the new local responsibility. When in 1849 he refused to veto the Rebellion Losses Bill, local autonomy was firmly established in Canada and had become a British commitment in every other possession.

(15) Since 1821, when the Montreal North-West Fur Co. and the Hudson Bay Co. had united, the official connection between Canada and the Northwest had become tenuous, The monopolist Co. traded in and, so far as necessary, ruled the northern half of America from the Atlantic to the Pacific. In the 1840s, however, American traders from St. Paul (Minnesota) reached the border, and settlers, especially those on the Red River, began to defy the monopoly by trading with them. Moreover, American settlement was increasing these difficulties further west where in 1846 the Oregon had to be partitioned along the 49th parallel. Then came the British Columbia gold rush and the British Gov. of Vancouver I. had to maintain British sovereignty and order on the mainland. The result was the creation of the colony of **British Columbia** in 1858.

(16) Local autonomy had deprived Canadian Tories of outside support. Moreover, the repeal of the British Corn Laws in 1846 had abolished the preferential tariff for Canadian wheat in favour of no tariff at all for anyone. This gave farmers a justified sense of grievance, for the market naturally expanded. In fact it bore more heavily upon nascent Canadian industries, because it lowered the true cost of British manufactured exports in the 1850s. There was some wild talk of joining the U.S.A. but economic solutions found more favour. These were to bring in raw materials quickly and cheaply by reciprocal trade agreements and the development of the railways. The latter also facilitated the great commodities boom of the Crimean War (1854-7).

(17) The early years of the union were uncontroversial and marked by much structural and technical legislation in the field of property, govt., church relations and legal codification. The Canada Act, however, had never fully united the two provinces: and it had laid down equality of representation for the two parts. As the Papineau rebellion receded in the memory, and economic and governmental changes created new party attitudes, differences became more marked and the latent antagonism of French and English emerged in a habit of mutual veto. The idea of substituting a federation for the decreasingly workable legislative union was propounded in 1858 by Alexander Galt and advocated to the British govt. by the gov-gen., Sir Edmund Head. Three sets of conditions all favoured federation. The Atlantic colonies were in high prosperity through their fisheries, shipping and lumber but further development could hardly be expected in the absence of an enlarged hinterland. At the same time the Hudson Bay Co. monopoly was due for revision in 1859. Its continuance was unlikely, and there were strong influences favouring the annexation of the North-West to Canada West (Ontario). This sudden prospective increase in the English population unsettled the French. They wanted a partition of the Province of Canada so that they could have a place of their own. In Sept. 1864 the Atlantic colonies considered federation at the CHARLOTTETOWN CONFERENCE. The Canadian provincial govt. asked to join in and the conference reopened at QUEBEC in 1865.

(18) The result was the BRITISH NORTH AMERICA ACT, 1867, by which the British Parliament divided the Province of Canada into Quebec and Ontario, and at their own request as from 1 July 1867, united them with Nova Scotia and New Brunswick into a federation called the **Dominion of Canada.**

D. THE DOMINION. (19) In 1869 it was necessary to make adjustments in favour of Nova Scotia and immediately afterwards there was trouble in the middle west. The transfer of the Hudson Bay Co's territories and jurisdiction had been negotiated without consulting the local officials or the settlers. The latter, part French, part Scots and mostly part Indian, numbered 12,000 and formed an independent-spirited community along the Red River called ASSINIBOIA. Road building and survey parties alarmed them and they feared an invasion by Anglican Ontario farmers. Their leader was Louis RIEL (1844-85), who proclaimed a provisional govt. and negotiated terms. The resulting **Manitoba** Act, 1870, carved a new province with its capital at Winnipeg out of the territory and added it to the Dominion. Riel, however, was driven into exile by a charge of murder.

(20) The Act of 1870 had brought the Dominion to the frontiers of British Columbia where a movement for union was springing up. Negotiations began at once. The main condition agreed was that a railway to the Pacific Coast should be commenced within two years. The colony entered the federation in 1871, and in 1873 **Prince Edward I.** also entered. In 1880 Britain transferred the ARCTIC islands to Canada by Order in Council.

(21) The railway undertaking to British Columbia ran into difficulties. The T. of Washington (1871) and the boundary settlement with the U.S.A. had created trouble for the Conservative govt. of John Alexander MACDONALD (1815-91) in the 1872 general election. The govt. negotiated finance for the railway as part of their platform, won the election, but had to resign after revelations of corruption (*see* PACIFIC SCANDAL). The Liberals who followed were caught by the business recession of 1873 and could not raise the capital. Attempts to negotiate a postponement brought charges of bad faith from British Columbia. Construction and the unification of the country therefore proceeded, but slowly.

(22) The conservatives now came forward with a new policy. Unification was to be achieved by protectionism against the U.S.A. With the cry of 'Canada First' they won the election of 1878 and imposed protective tariffs. Rising prosperity also made it easier to raise capital. The CANADIAN PACIFIC CO. was floated and given 25,000,000 acres of western land as well as $25M. This, the true heir of the Hudson Bay Co., completed the railway to the Pacific in 1885, but not without one important interruption. Louis Riel reappeared as the champion of the Indians and half breeds along the Saskatchewan. They were alarmed at the destruction of the bison and perhaps disappointed that the railway had not taken the Saskatchewan route. He repeated his Assiniboia tactics of 1870, set up a provisional govt. and tried to negotiate. This time the attempt was crushed by force and Riel was hanged for treason.

(23) The conservatives maintained their position in the general elections of 1887 and 1891, but meantime Riel's execution had offended French sentiment in Quebec, where the govt. had passed an Act to compensate the Jesuits for losses arising from their suppression in 1773. The Pope was asked how the money should be distributed. Protestants objected to papal intervention and carried their campaign into Manitoba where in 1870 French ceased to be an official language and hitherto denominational schools were made undenominational. The French and R. Catholics contested this in the courts, which held that Manitoba was entitled to legislate as it had, but that the Dominion legislature was bound to pass remedial legislation. The govt. failed to carry the necessary bill in time and in the 1896 general election it was overthrown by the Liberals led by (Sir) Wilfrid LAURIER (1841-1919) who, however, depended heavily on the fundamentally reactionary Quebec voters.

(24) The Liberals were committed to free trade, but Canadian industries had grown up under a tariff shelter and would have collapsed in the face of unrestricted U.S. competition. 1897 was the year of Q. Victoria's Diamond Jubilee, and Laurier was able by a brilliant compromise to steal the conservatives' patriotic clothes. He instituted IMPERIAL PREFERENCE. The year was brilliant in other ways. The colonisation of the U.S.A. middle west was ending, and migrants were beginning to look to Canada for land. At this moment gold was found in the Yukon. The last great land and GOLD RUSH (1897-8) into Manitoba and the North-west followed. Wheat farming spread across the prairies. Two more transcontinental railways (The Grand Trunk and the National Trans-continental) were built and in 1905 the provinces of **Alberta** and **Saskatchewan** were created to form with the other seven the permanent political framework of the dominion. The rapid development of these areas led also to the beginnings of the base metal mining and wood pulp industries, and the exploitation of hydro-electricity. One consequence of the Rush was a too close acquaintance with Americans, and a dispute with the U.S.A. about the Alaska frontier. This was settled by arbitration in 1903 on a basis which seemed to Canadians too favourable to the U.S.A. It was seen that Britain could not always exert herself fully on behalf of Canada: but more strongly, that American greed must be resisted by Canada acting on her own. The Liberals, still phil-osophically committed to free trade, began in 1911 to negotiate a reciprocity treaty with the U.S.A. which could have made wide markets available to the prairie farmers. This alarmed industrialists, bankers and railwaymen. Laurier misjudged the situation. In the general election of 1911 the Liberals and free trade were swept away in a wave of patriotic and anti-American sentiment.

(25) The Conservative Govt. under (Sir) Robert BORDEN (1854-1937) had not long to continue the economic *status quo*. The German invasion of Belgium and France in 1914 united Canadians in supporting Britain in World War I. A Canadian volunteer force, amounting in the end to four divisions, went to Europe. Vast quantities of food and timber were shipped across, or sunk in, the Atlantic. War profits encouraged rapid industrialisation. The demand for raw materials created inflation and the West Front casualties pointed the contrast between the soldiers in the mud and the profits at home. Conscription became an issue. In 1917 Borden asked Laurier to form a coalition to carry it. Laurier refused because of opposition in Quebec. This split the Liberals, some of whom helped Borden to carry it without Laurier. A 'Union' govt. was formed and in the ensuing general election the English and French were aligned against each other. Much of the process of national unification was undone.

(26) On the other hand, participation in the War

created international recognition. Borden was a member of the Imperial War Cabinet from 1917: Canada was separately represented at the Versailles peace conferences, and entered the League of Nations in her own right.

(27) The end of the war knocked the bottom out of the primary products market, but continued protection kept manufacture prices high. Hence earnings sank but prices stayed level. This hit the farmers and other rural dwellers. Moreover, industrial unrest culminated in the six-week Winnipeg strike (1919), the arrest of the strikers' leaders, and a general movement towards left wing trade unionism. Borden retired in July 1920 and was succeeded by the much less competent Arthur MEIGHEN (1874-1960). On the other hand Sir Wilfrid Laurier was succeeded in the leadership of the Liberals by the astute and fiery William Lyon MACKENZIE KING (1874-1950) who was acceptable to the Quebecois. But farming interests were now emerging as a third force called the Progressive Party. In the elections of 1921 the Liberals carried every seat in the Quebec legislature, but only half in the Dominion House of Commons, while the Progressives carried many seats in other provincial legislatures and held a balancing federal position. The result was a liberal progressive coalition under King until 1926 and a stronger liberal govt. after the general election of that year. Canadian initiative at the Imperial Conference of 1926, however, instigated the Commonwealth Declaration, and eventually the Statute of Westminster of 1931.

(28) Up to 1929 progress had been steady, but the 1929 depression resulted in a conservative victory at the 1930 elections. The govt. of Richard Bedford BENNETT (1870-1947), however, made little progress and in 1935 was swept from office. The long depression had also brought some other parties into the public eye. The Social Credit Party captured Alberta and tried to impose local monetary panaceas. The Union Nationale, a French nationalist party, took control of Quebec in 1936.

(29) The depression continued until, once again, Canada was lifted out of it by a war. She entered World War II in Sept. 1939 and large Canadian forces crossed the Atlantic. There was the usual industrial and timber boom but the most important single Canadian contribution to the western effort was probably the facilities provided for the training of air pilots.

(30) After the war Canada emerged as a self conscious industrial power strengthened in the 1950s by the discovery or development of iron in Labrador, and oil, natural gas and radium, and in 1948 Mackenzie King retired in favour of Louis Stephen ST. LAURENT (1882-1973). The most tangible work of his govt. was the building of the St. Lawrence Seaway but in 1957 the liberals lost the general election and it was left to the conservatives to complete it in 1959. It did not prove as successful as had been hoped. Conservative rule lasted until 1963 when the Liberals under Lester PEARSON (1897-1972) came in as a minority govt., a position which they were unable to improve at the elections of 1965. In 1967 Pearson resigned in favour of the Quebecois Pierre Elliott TRUDEAU (1919-) who managed to win a clear majority in 1968 and dominated Canadian politics until 1984.

(31) Trudeau's leadership coincided with a resurgence of French Canadian separatism. Its terrorist exponents were soon suppressed but a nationalist provincial govt. in Quebec passed legislation enforcing inter alia, the primacy of the French language in the province. The autocratically minded Trudeau, though no separatist, was necessarily pre-occupied with eastern, particularly Quebec-related issues. This brought him into collision with provincial govts. which, in the west wanted more attention and in the east less interference. His tenure was interrupted from May 1979 to Feb. 1980. On his return he showed his anti-separatism by campaigning

successfully in the 1980 Quebec referendum on 'sovereignty-association'. He followed up with the campaign for the largely cosmetic Canada Act 1982, but detailed implementation had to be negotiated at Meech Lake in 1987 by Brian Mulroney's Progressive Conservatives and by June 1990 Newfoundland and Manitoba had refused to ratify. In the interval, however, after a bitterly fought general election in 1988 the govt. signed (in 1989) the important free trade agreement with the U.S.A. which was a counterpart of Britain's accession to the E.E.C. *For constitutional devolution see* BRITISH NORTH AMERICA ACTS.

CANADIAN PACIFIC RAILWAY. *See* CANADA-22.

CANALETTO or Giovanni Antonio CANAL (1697-1768), Venetian painter, got many English contacts through Joseph Smith, British consul at Venice, and stayed in England from 1746 to about 1755. He painted many celebrated scenes for English collectors, such as the D. of Bedford at Woburn, and is sometimes regarded as a forerunner of the 19th cent. landscape painters. The demand for his painting declined after a while as his studio adopted increasingly obvious mass production techniques, but they represent an interesting record of London, Venice and Warsaw in his time.

CANALS, CANAL ERA. *See* TRANSPORT AND COMMUNICATIONS.

CANALS (OVERSEAS). The most important in modern times were the Canal du Midi between the Mediterranean and the B. of Biscay opened in 1681; the Kiel Canal 1895, enlarged by 1914; the Panama Canal 1915; the Suez Canal 1869, closed 1967 to 1975, and the St. Lawrence Seaway 1959. *See also* KIEL.

CANARY Is. (Atlantic), partly occupied by the Portuguese, were ceded to Castile in 1479 under the T. of Alc çovas. Castilian control was not complete until 1496. Thereafter the islands became a staging point for the Americas and the E. Indies. Homeward bound ships habitually loaded spare space with Canary Wine which was thus plentiful and cheap in England during the century, until over-cultivation exhausted the soil. The position and uses of the islands made them the object of occasional Moorish and English attacks. In 1936 Franco's Nationalist insurrection began in the Canaries.

CANBERRA (Australia) (Aboriginal = meeting place) was originally a squatters' settlement. Following the Washington precedent of a separate capital for a federal state, the site was adopted for a Commonwealth capital and planned by the winner of an international competition, the American Walter Burley Griffin. Construction began in 1913. The Commonwealth parliament was transferred there from Melbourne in 1927.

CANDIA otherwise **HERACLION,** the chief port of Crete. The name, especially under the Venetians (1207-1669), was synonymous with Crete.

CANDIDA CASA. *See* WHITHORN.

CANDLEMAS or the **PURIFICATION OF THE VIRGIN MARY (2 Feb.)** is the day when candles were consecrated for use throughout the coming year, and in Scotland it is the first of the quarter-days for the making of periodical payments.

CANICE or KENNETH, ST. *See* MISSIONARIES IN BRITAIN AND IRELAND-3.

CANNAE, B. of (216 B.C.). The encirclement and virtual obliteration of a large Roman army by a smaller Carthaginian force became the doctrinal inspiration of Prussian military thinkers, particularly the elder Moltke and Schlieffen, after the formation of the General Staff.

CANNES CONFERENCE (Jan. 1922). *See* REPARATIONS.

CANNIBAL. *See* CARIBBEAN.

CANNING FAMILY included three men of the highest distinction in 110 years namely **(1) George (1770-1827)** a prime minister and leading politician; **(2) Charles John (1812-62) E. CANNING**, gov. gen. of India and his cousin **(3) Stratford (1786-1880) 1st Vist. STRATFORD DE REDCLIFFE** the diplomat. *For all three see below.*

CANNING, Charles John (1812-62) Vist. CANNING (1837) 1st E. CANNING (1859), s. of George (below) became M.P. for Warwick in 1836. He was a Peelite Tory, and was USec. for Foreign Affairs under Peel from 1841 to 1846, and P-M-G under Aberdeen and Palmerstone from 1853 to 1855 when he succeeded Dalhousie as Gov-Gen of India. He arrived at Calcutta in Feb. 1856 and the Indian Mutiny, mainly the result of Dalhousie's policies and methods, exploded a year later. Much criticised for inadequate measures when the danger was known and for vacillation and excessive clemency, he in fact created a fair balance between the military need to establish order and the political need to maintain confidence. The former he left to the very able generals and administrators who understood the business: the latter he reserved to himself and refused (against military advice) to abandon the frontiers already established. In this he was triumphantly right and the territorial framework of British India survived the Mutiny. The HEIC however, which had nominally appointed him, did not; but in 1858 he was continued in office as the first viceroy. The labours of Hercules now descended upon him. He had to restore the shattered finances, reorganise the army, reform the administration and judiciary, establish the rudiments of education and reorientate govt. attitudes to the Princes. In these tasks he was largely successful.

CANNING, George (1770-1827) was brought up by a whig banker uncle. He became an M.P. in 1794, and a Pittite by reaction from French revolutionary excesses. He was Pitt's Foreign USec. of State from 1796 to 1799, a member of the India Board until 1800, when he made a rich marriage, and then Paymaster-Gen. until 1801 when he went into opposition to Addington. A man of intellectual speed and wit, he lived on his nerves and was derisive of Addington. From May 1804 to Feb. 1806 he was treasurer of the Navy. He refused to serve under Grenville, but in 1807 became Foreign Sec. under Portland and had the main responsibility for seizing the Danish fleet (1807) and for initiating intervention in Spain. Meanwhile Castlereagh, as Sec. at War, was responsible for troop dispositions: he restricted reinforcements to Moore in Spain and then diverted resources to the Flushing expedition (1808). As the M. Wellesley had accepted the Spanish Embassy on condition that he would have an army at his back, the disarray in political policy was strongly criticised by others besides Canning. Finally, in 1809 Castlereagh's friends got the Cabinet to approve the Convention of Cintra at a meeting from which Canning happened to be absent. This amounted to a public repudiation of the Peninsular policy. Canning (the senior) threatened to resign if Castlereagh were not dismissed, but Portland would not take the necessary steps and eventually Canning resigned (Sept. 1809). Even then Castlereagh only discovered by accident the nature of the issue on which Canning had resigned; the result was a duel. Canning, out of office, supported those Tories who championed a vigorous Peninsular policy, but when Perceval was assassinated (1812) he refused the foreign office because Castlereagh was to be leader of the Commons. He disbanded his parliamentary following and in 1814 was briefly ambassador at Lisbon. He returned via France in 1816, and was given the important office of Pres. of the Board of Control (of the HEIC). He practised his talent for administration and acquired a considerable understanding of Indian affairs and oriental trade. In 1820 came the unfortunate affair of Q. Caroline. Canning, a friend of the Queen, did not wish to be involved with the Ministry's bill and offered to resign. George IV would not accept the resignation so Canning went abroad. He returned after the Bill had been abandoned and resigned. She died (Aug. 1821) and Liverpool then tried to get him back, but the King, incensed by the actions of his political friends, would not have it. It was therefore

natural to send him to India as Gov-Gen. (1822). Before he could leave England, however, Castlereagh committed suicide and Liverpool and Wellington together argued the King into giving him the Foreign Office. Castlereagh's foreign policy had become bogged down in its own inconsistencies and disregard for English opinion. Canning, who disliked the contemporary agitation for parliamentary reform, advocated, and secured useful practical legislation to demonstrate that parliament would not always defend abuses. In a similar spirit he refused to be associated with French interference in Spain (1823-4) or Austrian intervention in Naples (1822-4) or Spanish in Portugal (1825-7) because these favoured oppressive regimes. Little could be done directly to help the more progressive elements in the countries concerned, but their insurgent colonies were another matter and the independence of Rio de la Plata, Mexico, Colombia and Brazil was recognised at this period. This action was motivated by the vast increase in British investment and trade with S. America since the breakdown of the Iberian monopolies. but it served the old principle of excluding French influence from S. America while securing popular support.

The potential French threat to the Americas represented by the French army in Spain caused Canning to propose a joint Anglo-American declaration of policy (Aug. 1823). The Royal Navy held the key, for it could protect the new countries against all comers. The Americans, however, chose to enunciate the Monroe doctrine, and in doing so acted alone in order to reassert their independence and republicanism. Since they had not the power to enforce it, the doctrine was 75 years ahead of its time. Simultaneously with the Latin European and American problems, Canning was faced with the complex issues of the Greek revolt. The romantic English public clothed these brigands and pirates with the aspect of Demosthenes, while Byron postured in a toga at Missolonghi. The govt. was under pressure to support the rebels unconditionally. This might be done by joining with Russia in partitioning the Ottoman Empire but, apart from French and Austrian opposition to such an outcome, it was important to maintain Ottoman integrity against Russian southward pressure. By 1825 the Turco-Egyptian forces under Ibrahim had the Greeks by the throat, and England was hearing only of Turkish atrocities. The St. Petersburg protocol signed by Wellington in Apr. 1826 proposed Anglo-Russian mediation and a Greek Peloponnesian tributary state, with the threat that the western powers would withdraw their embassies and unilaterally recognise an effective Greek state if the Porte refused the mediation. An important motive for this démarche again was trade: the struggle was disorganising Levantine shipping, for the Turks were concentrating on the Pelopennese, leaving the Greek island pirates free. The protocol failed because Austria and Prussia would not adhere to it, and because no Greek authority emerged which could be recognised as a state. Accordingly by the T. of London (27 July 1827) between Britain, France and Russia, the objects of the protocol were reaffirmed, but under a secret article the powers were to impose an armistice if the Porte refused to agree to one. Canning, however, was publicly against coercing the Turks, for he foresaw that coercion meant partition. Both sides paid lip service to the armistice, which they covertly evaded when they could.

CANNING GOVT (Apr.-Aug. 1827). In Apr. Liverpool had a stroke and Canning had succeeded him. Wellington and Peel resigned while four whigs entered a 12-strong cabinet. This govt. represented a stage in the break up of the Tories and the rise of the Liberals but it was not put to the test because in Aug. George Canning died suddenly.

CANNING, Stratford (1786-1880) 1st Vist. STRATFORD DE REDCLIFFE (1852) cousin of Charles (above) was appointed a writer in the Foreign Office by his other cousin George in 1807; and in 1808 he was First Sec. to Adair's embassy to the Sublime Porte. When Adair left in 1810 he took over the mission as Min. Plenipotentiary. His extraordinary career may be summarised as follows: 1810-12 First Mission to the Porte. 1812-19 Swiss Mission. 1820-24 Mission to Washington. 1824-5 Mission to St. Petersburg. 1825-9 Second Mission to the Porte. 1830-2 Third Mission to the Porte. 1832-41 Membership of Parliament. 1842-58 Fourth Mission to the Porte.

In the first mission to the Porte he was left without instructions and had to develop a policy of his own. The situation was relatively simple. Britain's two major interests were the protection of her Levantine shipping and the defeat of Bonaparte. The Ottoman govt. was weak. Privateers preyed on British trade and sold their prizes in Turkish ports. In a particular case (at Nauplia) he cheerfully called on the British local naval commander who sank a privateer under the Turkish fort. This brought the traffic to an abrupt halt. To defeat Bonaparte he persuaded the Porte to accept British rather than French influence and negotiated a Russo-Turkish peace on good terms for Turkey. This released Russian troops for the War and secured Turkish goodwill; it was obtained through his intelligence service, which got evidence that the French were simultaneously planning an attack on Russia in concert with Turkey and Austria, and an attack on Turkey in concert with Austria. The P. of Bucharest was the result (28 May 1812).

In the mission to Switzerland he was secretary of the Viennese negotiations which established the new Swiss federation and neutrality, induced the Swiss to accept the results, and at their request planned their military system.

The mission to Washington produced little in specific effects but led to a lowering of the diplomatic temperature, raised by British impressment on the High Seas, and suppression of the slave trade.

The mission to St. Petersburg and the Second and Third Missions to the Porte were dominated by the issue of Greek Independence: the Russians wanted international mediation, but George Canning opposed coercion, without which mediation would have been ineffectual. Turkey under the reforming Mahmoud II was stronger than before and disinclined to brook rebellion as contemplated in the St. Petersburg protocol (Apr. 1826). Stratford Canning had almost persuaded the Turks to concede a tributary state confined to the Peloponnese in order to maintain, in peace, their growing strength, but the B. of Navarino (Oct. 1827) precipitated a conflict which ended with the establishment of an independent Greek state south of Arta and Volos. This conflict was damaging to British interests, for it arrested the Turkish revival which in his view was important for the protection of the Levant.

During the Parliamentary period he was respected for his knowledge of Levantine affairs but was otherwise an undistinguished backbencher.

During his Fourth Mission to the Porte he was for 16 years the most influential single man in the Ottoman Empire through his knowledge of Turkish habits, speech and personalities and his friendly personal relationship with the young Sultan Abd-el-Mejid. His view was that if Turkey could be made respectable by internal reform and development, she could attract enough western support to become a real obstacle to Russian southward ambitions. Turkey was at peace from 1841 to 1853 and the moment seemed propitious. Thus much of the Great Elchi's (Turk = ambassador) diplomatic efforts were concerned with Turkish internal affairs such as the establishment of equality between religions, the guarantee of personal liberty and property and other such western notions foreign to the whole basis of Ottoman society. Such a policy was bound to break down for lack of proper instruments and because it

tended towards a revolutionary situation which it was precisely his task to prevent.

By 1853 he was effectively in control of such international policy as centred in Istanbul, and it was largely his skill which marshalled western opinion just before the Crimean War.

CANNON. *See* ARTILLERY.

CANON LAW. (1) A canon is a rule laid down by the church for its members and enforced primarily by ecclesiastical sanctions, sometimes supported by the civil authority. Collections made at synods or by councils began to appear in the 4th cent. In 550 Dionysius Exiguus brought out a seminal Latin translation of the recorded Greek canons. The canon law applied in England as throughout the Western Church, but local supplementary canons were made by local authorities too, the mass of general church law and custom being kept relatively uniform and up-to-date by appeals and references to Rome. The academic systematisation came through the study of Roman civil law in Italy, especially at Bologna, in the early 12th cent. Ivo of Chartres compiled his **Panormia** in imitation of the Pandects of Justinian, and then in about 1140 Gratian produced his systematic **Concordia Discordantium Canonum** (Lat = Reconciliation of Canons) or **Decretum** (Lat = The Decree). It was almost immediately adopted as a textbook at Bologna and rapidly gained authority in ecclesiastical courts. In 1230 Gregory IX commissioned Raymond of Peñaforte to make a further digest of post-Decretum papal decretals, known as the **Five Books of Decretals** (1234); further collections followed: the **Sext** or Sixth Book (1298), the **Clementines** (by Clement V in 1317), the **Extravagantes** of John XXII containing 20 of his bulls (1500) and the **Extravagantes Communes** containing decretals of various Popes (also 1500). These books collectively form the **Corpus Juris Canonici** (Lat = Body of Canon Law).

(2) Ecclesiastical courts were staffed by trained canonists, but few parish clergy were familiar with their jurisprudence; hence summaries for their use were made by provincial and diocesan bodies. Some of these synodal constitutions contained customs applicable only in a particular area, but came to be well known in the Church as a whole. In 1430 William Lyndwood assembled them in the **Provinciale**, the constitutions promulgated in the Province of Canterbury by the archbishops from Stephen Langton to Henry Chichele. He provided each constitution with a commentary, referring each clause to its source in the law books.

(3) In 1532 the Church was forced to request a royal commission to sift through its canons to bring them into conformity with God's laws and those of the realm, and Statutes and a royal injunction ended papal jurisdiction over England, the power to promulgate provincial constitutions without royal licence, and the study of canon law at the universities. The Act of Submission 1534 laid down that existing canon law had force only by royal authority and provided for the royal commission. This completed its collection of canons by 1535, but it never received royal approval. Thus the Church and its courts continued to use the existing canon law, subject to various statutes, and purged of 'popery'. Canon law, through church courts, touched laymen at many points, notably heresy, matrimony, the law of wills and intestate estates, and the rules on penance. The Reformation put an end to questions of penance in protestant countries, and the jurisdiction in heresy (*see* BLASPHEMY). The English Probate and matrimonial jurisdiction continued in the hands of church courts until 1857.

CANONISATION in the R. Catholic Church is the declaration (which can be made only by the Pope) that a person has entered into eternal glory, and can therefore properly be the object of a cult. The process was introduced to control irregularly instituted popular cults, the first attested canonisation taking place in 993.

CANON (1) of SCRIPTURE. The Biblical books, i.e. the Old Testament and New Testament but not the Aprocrypha, accepted by the Christian churches as genuine or inspired. It was laid down by St. Damasus at the Council of Rome in 382. **(2) LITERARY.** The disputed body of English literary works regarded as essential reading by university literary faculties. **(3)** *See* CANONS.

CANONS (1) Regular or Augustinian lived under a semi-monastic rule. **(2) 'Secular'** were the staff of a cathedral entitled to share in the endowments and bound to a common life, though permitted before 11th cent. to own private property. Of the seculars, the Canons **Residentiary** are now the permanent salaried staff; the **Non-Residentiaries** are unsalaried and the **Minor** Canons are chosen for their voices, but have no say in the management.

CANOSSA (Italy) was the place where the excommunicated Emperor Henry IV surrendered to Pope Gregory VII after waiting three days in the snow. The word is occasionally used for any abject submission. *See* GREGORY VII.

CANTATE DOMINO (Lat = Sing unto the Lord) **(1441)**, bull of Eugenius IV ascribing to the Church a monopoly of the means of Grace.

CANTELUPE. This family of Welsh border magnates included **(1) William (?-1239) 1st Ld. CANTELUPE,** who was K. John's sheriff of Warwick, Leicestershire, Worcestershire and Hereford and in 1203 Justiciar. He supported Henry III against the French in 1216. Of his sons **(2) William (?-1281) 2nd Ld.,** was Henry III's steward and ambassador to the papal court at Lyons in 1245 and **(3) Walter (?-1266)** was a royal clerk by 1215 and by 1227 was acting as the King's proctor at the Roman Curia. He was elected to the see of Worcester (1236) when still in minor orders but proved to be a fine reforming bishop who vigorously visited and administered his diocese. His resistance to papal taxation got him into trouble with the King so that at the Oxford Parliament (1258) he was elected on the barons' side as one of the 24 governors of the realm. In the civil war he sided with his friend Simon de Montfort and was present at the Bs. of Lewes (1264) and Evesham (1265). Respected as a peacemaker, arbitrator and bishop, the royalist chronicler Thomas Wykes wrote that but for his support for Montfort he would have deserved canonisation. **(4) St. Thomas (c. 1218-82).** His uncle Walter had him educated at Oxford, Paris and Orleans; he became an eminent scholar and in 1261 Chanc. of Oxford Univ. He supported the barons against Henry III and became Chanc. of England in 1265, after their victory at Lewes (1264). He lost office in 1266 after Simon de Montfort's defeat and returned to his studies at Paris and then Oxford, where he became Chanc. (1273) for a second term. As bishop of the poor see of Hereford from 1275 he lived in ascetic rigour. In maintaining the rights of the see against Abp. Peckham he appealed to Rome and died on his way there. His heart and other relics were brought back to Hereford and though pronounced excommunicate by Peckham, a cult sprang up at his tomb and in 1320 he was canonised. The offerings of the many pilgrims to his shrine financed much building at his cathedral.

CANTERBURY (Kent) (Lat = DUROVERNUM CANTIACORUM) was a pre-Roman settlement of the Belgic Cantiaci on a ford above the tidal confluence of the R. Stour with the ancient Wantsum, which connected the English Channel with the Thames Estuary. Hence it was a port and market for the continent and, in due course, the natural crossing point for the Roman roads from the Channel to London. The Romans had fortified it by A.D. 200 and again in 270. Its prosperity continued until they left (c. 411) and seems to have been little reduced when the Jutes attacked Kent, for it became the seat of their kingdom of Kent in mid-6th cent. and from 597 the centre from which St. Augustine (who had found a Roman building in use as a church) began the R. Catholic conversion of Britain. To this it owes the fact that it became the English primatial see. Augustine founded two great, and sometimes controversial, other institutions, namely the monastic Cathedral of Christchurch whose often turbulent (later Benedictine) monks claimed the right to elect the archbishop and frequently exercised it against royal and other opposition, and the Benedictine Abbey of Sts. Peter and Paul, later rededicated in his own name, which outshone it in splendour and whose monks throughout the middle ages provided teachers and preachers and were at constant feud with Christchurch.

Despite Viking raids, including the sack of 1011, Canterbury was not only the primary southern English centre of civilisation and religion, but at intervals the principal economic one as well. It had one of the earliest recorded guilds in England and enjoyed extensive rights of self govt. The Archbishops operated a mint for centuries. Its trade survived devastating fires in 1161 and 1198, but its secular decline began as the central institutions of govt. tended to concentrate in London. The archbishopric was such an institution and soon the primates acquired a London establishment (at Lambeth), seldom visited the city and left their diocesan duties to coadjutors. Meanwhile the Wantsum was silting up and diverting seaborne trade round the North Foreland direct to London. This economic decline was abruptly arrested in 1170 by the murder in Christchurch of Abp. Becket, who rapidly became a popular saint of European repute. The monks of Christchurch made much of their heaven-sent opportunity (they publicly flogged Henry II for it in 1174 and took credit for the victory of the Standard next day) and soon Canterbury was rivalling Compostella as a pilgrimage centre. Christchurch now overtook St. Augustines. The city was a tourist resort with many inns and in an unpoliced era highly disorderly. By the mid 14th cent. it had, however, acquired a charter and in the Wars of the Roses it successfully freed itself from the jurisdiction of the Sheriff of Kent by becoming a county itself (1461). A tourist economy is always precarious and liable to depression at the slightest rumour of human or natural calamity. In 1529, however, the monasteries were suppressed and with it the cult of St. Thomas. This was fundamental and the town languished. Its decline was only partially arrested by the arrival of protestant refugees, first from Flanders and then from France, from the latter half of the 16th cent. These were mostly weavers, but many of them preferred to be nearer the Cotswold and Norfolk sheep raising districts, and only a small improvement resulted. The city drowsed in a golden haze of old pre-eminence and present precedence, and when County Councils were introduced (1888) it did not even become the centre of county administration. It suffered severely from an air raid in 1942 and acquired a university in 1965. In 1974 it was merged into the surrounding district, which acquired the inappropriate title of city. *See also next notice;* COINAGE; PILGRIMS WAY.

CANTERBURY, SEE OF. St. Augustine landed in Kent in 597 with instructions to organise two ecclesiastical provinces based upon London and York. As the Kentish King's Christian Q. Bertha had come from France, she had a bishop called Liudhard at Canterbury already. Augustine's dioceses were set up at Canterbury for the Men of Kent and for the Kentish Men at Rochester a few years later. The two between them were conterminous with the Kentish kingdom. The delay in reaching London caused Canterbury to remain the southern metropolitical see. Later there was a long struggle for precedence between Canterbury and York which ended in 1353 when the Abp. of York was recognised as Primate of England but he of Canterbury, Primate of All England.

CANTERBURY (N.Z.), plains whose principal towns are Christchurch and its port of Lyttleton. English settlement began in 1843 and it soon became famous for wool and mutton.

CANTERBURY, Vists. *See* MANNERS-SUTTON.

CANTON (S. China). The HEIC established a factory here in 1685 and began regular sailings to this important port in 1699. The French followed suit in 1725. The Chinese authorities confined western trade to Canton and traders (including, after 1761, the Dutch) to a special area and in 1757 forbade all dealings save through a local merchant guild called the Hong. This arrangement lasted until 1842 when, after the Opium War (1839-42) by the T. of Nanking, the Hong monopoly was replaced by five privileged Treaty Ports and the British acquired Hong Kong whose development into one of the greatest emporia in the Far East led to rival development at the Cantonese deepwater port at Whampoa. This disseminated a Cantonese version of Chinese culture all over the world. The return trade brought western ideas into China, so that Canton became the centre from which the agitation against the Manchu dynasty began, and from which the Kuomintang later set out to overthrow the northern war lords.

CANTREF **(Welsh = 100 trefs).** The pre-Norman administration of Wales differed (like the language) as between N. Wales (Gwynedd) and the South, and varied with the nature of the country. An *erw* (= "Welsh acre") was a necessarily varying area which an 8-ox team could plough in a day, and was divided into, usually, 8 *cyfars* (= shares) of about an English acre, representing the share of a family which had contributed to the ploughing. In some places, however, cyfars were only half an acre and there were 16 to the erw. This was called the *Erw of Hywel Dda,* but even within the same Lordship an erw might contain as few as 4 or as many as 24 cyfars.

A *rhandir* was generally 312 erws, and these were grouped into free *trefs* (= vill) of 4 rhandirs, or unfree trefs of 3, one in either case being left fallow each year.

In South Wales trefs were the basic units of assessment; but in Gwynedd 13 tribal and 7 settled trefs respectively constituted a *maenol,* which was the basic unit. In South Wales, however, there were *maenors* (or *Swydds*) consisting of a group of 13 free or 7 unfree trefs, and 4 maenors made up a *commote* which supported a royal residence. A northern commote consisted of 4 settled and 8 tribal maenols, and two such commotes made up a *cantref* and supported the residence. Hence in the north military and judicial administration was more likely to be based on the cantref, in the south on the commote, and these units tended, respectively, to be the geographical basis of Anglo-Norman lordships.

CANUTE AND HIS SONS. (1) CANUTE, CNUT or KNUT (?991-1035) K. of Denmark 1014, of half and then the whole of England 1016, of Norway 1026 (*see* ETHELRED THE UNREADY: EDMUND IRONSIDE) was the *s.* of K. Swein Forkbeard of Denmark. As a result of the mutual succession T. of Olney, he succeeded Edmund Ironside. He began sensibly by killing Edric Streona and bigamously marrying Emma, K. Ethelred's widow. The English had to suffer the biggest Danegeld yet, to pay off Canute's army, but 40 shiploads of professionals ("Thingmen") remained to be supported on the *heregeld.* This expensive force was the principal instrument of public order, and the country preferred to support it instead of returning to the previous chaos. The King established a comparatively efficient central administration, under churchmen led by Abp. Wulfstan II of York; the clerks trained in it tended to become bishops later on. This had a unifying effect on the church too. In local administration he was less successful. The supervision of the disorganised counties was committed, in the form of great earldoms, to his main supporters, who expected rewards and became great territorial magnates within their earldoms. Moreover, most of the earls were Danes; only the English family of Leofwine, earldorman of the Hwiccas survived from Ethelred's reign but Godwin, a relative of Edric Streona, began his remarkable career as one of Canute's thingmen. In due course he was to marry the King's sister. The initial problem was to unite English and Danes into a single nation which, under Danish rule, meant winning over the English. With politic impartiality, Canute raised a memorial church at Assendun to all who had died there, outlawing not only an English eorlderman. Aethilweard. but the great Thorkel, who was sent to Denmark. His greatest gesture of conciliation, however, was his translation of the relics of St. Alphege to Canterbury. Thereafter Englishmen thought of him as their King and even fought for him in his Scandinavian wars. In 1025 he defeated the Norwegians and Swedes on the Holy River (Helge-aa). In 1027 he made a pilgrimage, as the mightiest King in Europe, to Rome and witnessed the coronation of the Emperor Conrad II. On his return Malcolm II of Scotland submitted to him, while his forces overran Norway and in Aug. 1030 he killed St. Olaf at the B. of Sticklestead. The last years of his reign were peaceful. Then the great empire fell to pieces. One son. Sweyn, took Norway. There was controversy in England about the other two **(2) HARALD HEREFOOT (?-1040)** and **(3) HARDICANUTE (Harthaknut) (?-1042).** The Wessex magnates, led by E. Godwin, wanted Emma's son, Hardicanute: but he was in Denmark where he had been brought up. The northerners wanted Harald who was present and had been educated in England, and whose mother, the able Aelfgifu (Algiva) of Northampton, though not royal, was English. In the end they compromised by electing both, with Q. Emma to represent Hardicanute until he should come. Aelfgifu dominated Harald. This essentially Scandinavian arrangement was upset in 1036 as a result of Godwin's atrocious mutilation of the atheling ALFRED, the son of Ethelred and Emma. There was a revulsion against Godwin and his party and Harald and Aelfgifu had Hardicanute deposed on the pretext of his absence (he was detained by a revolution in Norway). Emma fled to Bruges with most of Canute's treasure. Hardicanute eventually reached Bruges, where he and his mother bickered over a projected invasion of England. Meantime Harald's reign was not fortunate. In 1039 Gruffydd ap Llywellyn of Gwynedd made a devastating raid and there was war on the Scots border and between rival northern earls. When Harald died in 1040 Hardicanute and Emma (and so Godwin) were accepted with relief, but not for long. The King came with a far more expensive body of Thingmen than ever Canute had needed, and they had to be paid by unprecedented gafols. He was childless, possibly epileptic and dominated by Emma who kept the purse strings. Moreover, harvests were bad and cattle disease rampant. Superstition and policy pointed to an alternative. The only surviving representative, since the death of the Atheling Alfred, of the old Saxon royal house, was EDWARD (surnamed The Confessor), a child of Ethelred and Emma. He was consecrated as joint-king just before Hardicanute died.

CANUTE, LAWS OF, promulgated at Winchester between 1016 and 1035 dealt with ecclesiastical and secular matters. A third part on forest law is a Norman forgery of about 1185.

CANVAS (Lat = *cannabis* = hemp) or SAILCLOTH, essential to a sea trading nation before the age of steam, was made of Dorset or Russian hemp until difficulties with the Baltic trade and the 18th cent. introduction of the power-loom led to supplementation with Irish flax, Indian jute and American cotton.

CANYNGES. This great trading family flourished at Bristol in the late 14th and 15th cents. Under Richard II **John** and **William** the elder produced and exported cloth.

William the younger (?-1474) seems to have begun as a merchant but became a shipowner. His fleet was manned by nearly 800 men and he controlled about a quarter of Bristol's shipping, making enough money to rebuild the large and beautiful church of St. Mary Redcliffe.

CAPE BRETON I. *See* WARS OF 1739-48-11; PARIS. P. OF (FEB. 1763); SEVEN YEARS WAR. CANADA-7.

CAPE COAST CASTLE was first settled as CABO CORSO by the Portuguese in 1610. The Swedes secured it and built the castle in 1652. In 1659 it was taken by the Dutch who in 1664 lost it to the British. It was the capital of the British Gold Coast Colony until 1876 when it gave way to Accra.

CAPE COLOUREDS (C. of Good Hope) are a substantial mixed body of descendants from usually illicit interbreeding of Europeans, Hottentots, Bushmen and slaves imported by the Dutch from Indonesia, Ceylon, India and Madagascar. Self conscious as differing from both negroes and Europeans, they have tended to be mutually supporting and amounted in 1890 to about 2500 of the population of the Cape and in 1910 40%. After a long and unscrupulous campaign by the nationalist govt. between 1951 and 1956, they were deprived of their vote on the common roll and allowed limited parliamentary representation by whites only.

CAPE OF GOOD HOPE, TOWN, COLONY and PROVINCE. Jan van Riebeek first settled the Cape for the Dutch East India Co. in 1652 and by 1781 close farming settlements had been established within a pastoral ring many miles inland. The Town had about 15,000 people and it throve, too, as a staging point on the route to India. For this reason the French occupied it from 1781 to 1784 during the American Rebellion and, after French revolutionary pressure was imposed on Holland, the British took over from 1794 to 1802, and from 1806 onwards. The British abolished the monopolies and the slave trade, introduced wool farming and the mohair goat; they permitted unlimited immigration and built ports at Durban and Port Elizabeth. As their numbers increased they clashed with the slave holding Dutch farmers, whose way of life, narrow religion and independent-mindedness made for later trouble. From 1836 the latter began the GREAT TREK into the interior where British administration might be unable to reach them. It involved clashes with the tribes who were moving in the opposite direction. The British built roads over the mountains and in due course caught up with the trekkers if only to establish some kind of frontier order. The trekkers, well aware of the superiority of their firearms over tribal weapons, moved on. In this piecemeal way the coastal enclaves acquired a vast, largely abandoned, hinterland which was very slowly being filled in by heterogeneous, though predominantly British, secondary settlers. On the missionary trail to Bechuanaland some Dutch pastoralists discovered diamonds in 1867, at the Orange River crossing. The nature of the discovery was not at first understood, but further discoveries north of the river brought a rush of mostly British immigrants. The inchoate Dutch republic of the Orange Free State laid claims to the area (called Griqualand West) and the British replied in 1871 by annexing it. In 1873 they started to extend the Cape Town-Wellington railway towards Kimberley, and built other railways inland from Port Elizabeth and East London. These ventures were a response to immigration: but immigration in turn responded to them. By 1884 the railway had reached Kimberley and the European population of the Cape and its province, predominantly British, was causing apprehension among the Dutch. In 1885 the British proclaimed a protectorate up to Lat 22°S, but in 1886 the discovery of inland gold brought a further rush and in 1895 caused the incorporation of all the land up to the Botswana frontier. A further consequence of these movements and of the South African War was a certain degree of industrialisation, and the development of the docks at Cape Town, but local administration in the area was fragmented until 1913. The Colony became a Province of the Union of South Africa in 1910. At that time about 25% of the population was European: about 30% tribal and 40% Cape Coloured. *See* SOUTH AFRICA; TREK; SOUTH AFRICAN WAR.

CAPE HORN (S. America) was probably sighted by Drake in 1578, but actually recorded in 1616 by the Dutchman, Schouten, who called it after Hoorn, his birthplace.

CAPEL. Of this royalist family **(1) Arthur (?1610-49) 1st Ld. CAPEL of HADHAM (1641)** was M.P. for Herts. in 1640 and again in 1647. Parliament confiscated his estates in 1643 when he was the King's Lieut.-Gen. in Shropshire, Cheshire and N. Wales. He was one of the King's commissioners at Uxbridge in 1645, escorted the Queen to Paris in 1646 and, having obtained leave to settle in Herts. again, helped the King to escape from Hampton Court in Nov. 1647. He joined in the second Civil war but having surrendered at Colchester was condemned and executed in 1649. His son **(2) Arthur (1631-83) 1st E. of ESSEX of the seventh creation (1661),** as Lord Lieut. of Herts. did much for royalism in the county, but opposed Charles II's R. Catholic and absolutist tendencies. In 1672 he became Lord Lieut. of Ireland, but was recalled in 1677 for opposing crown grants to the King's friends. He was an opponent of Danby, took Titus Oates' side in the 'Popish Plot', supported the Exclusion Bill in 1680. opposed the holding of the Oxford parliament in 1681 and became involved with Monmouth in 1682. As a result he was put in the Tower where he committed suicide. His brother **(3) Sir Henry (?-1696) 1st Ld. CAPEL of TEWKESBURY (1692)** supported the Exclusion Bill in 1680 and was a commissioner of the Treasury in 1689. A Lord Justice in Ireland in 1693, he was promoted to Lord Deputy in 1695 and as such obtained the repeal of James II's Irish legislation.

CAPEL COURT. A lane outside the old London Stock Exchange where, during booms, dealers chaffered in the open air after hours or because the Exchange was overcrowded.

CAPETIANS or ROBERTINES, EARLY. The recurrent themes in the progressive imposition of this dynasty upon the populations of Gaul were (a) the central position of the Ile de France; (b) undisputed successions from father to son and (c) mostly long reigns from 987 to 1314; (d) ambition; (e) the mystique of royalty. Moreover (f) a King can, with some show of legality, claim the allegiance of his vassals' sub-tenants. Three other factors were also important: (g) the high, and not always unattractive, abilities of some of these rulers; (h) the pervasive influence of the Crusades in which the Franks took a leading part; (i) the improvement in 12th cent. communications.

Early Developments **(1) Robert the Strong (?-866)** of Anjou, Warden of the Neustrian frontiers became D. (i.e. military governor) of Paris in about 853. His son **(2) Eudes (?-898)** repulsed the Vikings from the town in 885. He represented the effective defence against them. There being a Carolingian minority, the notables conferred the crown on Eudes in 888. The Norman wars, however, prevented him making his power good: in 893 the legitimate Carolingian, Charles III (the Simple) was invested at Laon. He did not, for the time being, take the royal title, but Eudes' brother and successor **(3) Robert (?-923)** recognised him. This Robert was **D. of FRANCE,** count in addition of Anjou, Blois and Tours, and the strongest man in Gaul. He and Charles got rid of their western troubles in the T. of St. Clair-sur-Epte (911) (*see* NORMANDY). They then turned eastwards and invaded Lorraine. Robert was the leader in these campaigns and the reality of power seemed to be slipping into his grasp. Charles dismissed him. Robert accordingly had himself crowned at Rheims (June 922) but was killed in the ensuing war. His claims were taken over by his son-in-law **(4) Raoul or Ralph of Burgundy (?-936),** who deposed Charles and reigned as King, and then Robert's son **(5) Hugh the Great (?-956).** He helped the Carolingian Louis IV (*d'Outremer*) to the throne, and both married sisters of the German King Otto I who in 951 took the Lombard crown as well. Their uneasy partnership ended in 954 with Louis' accidental death. While Otto was distracted by Slav and Magyar invasions, Hugh established Louis' son Lothaire on the Gallic throne in return for the dukedoms of Burgundy and Aquitaine. Until he died he was the greatest potentate of the west.

His son **(6)** the famous **Hugh Capet (?-996)** (he wore a *capet* or bonnet as lay abbot of St. Martin at Tours) and Lothaire were both wards of Otto, who in 962 was crowned emperor at Rome. Lothaire coveted Lorraine, now fallen back into Germanic control, and in 978 made a surprise attempt on Otto and his Byzantine empress Theophano. Otto overran much of Gaul, proclaimed Lothaire's brother Charles of Lorraine King, but was repulsed from Paris by Hugh. In 986 Lothaire eventually died; his son Louis died in 987.

Establishment of the Monarchy. The great men now assembled, first at Compiègne and then at Senlis where they rejected Charles of Lorraine and offered the crown to Hugh. He was sworn at Noyon (July 987). His domain, much smaller than his father's, was confined to two disconnected areas about Paris and Orleans. In the struggle with Charles, Hugh tried to win over Arnulf, Charles' nephew, by giving him the vacant see of Rheims. The bribe failed and Hugh deposed him in favour of Gerbert of Aurillac, confessor to Otto III. This embroiled Hugh with the Papacy and raised the issue (later called Gallicanism) of the King's powers over the Gallic church. Gerbert, strong in his connections, went to Rome where the Pope (John XV) was the nominee of the Crescentii, local petty nobles. While negotiations proceeded Hugh captured Charles, who died in 992. In 995, however, John XV pronounced for Arnulf and then, in 996, he and Hugh both died. The new Pope, Gregory V, was a nephew of Otto III and a friend of Gerbert. An accommodation was delayed by the matrimonial confusions of **(7) Robert the Pious (r. 996-1031).** On accession he had repudiated his wife (daughter of an Italian King and widow of the Count of Flanders) and, against Gerbert's advice, had married Bertha of Chartres, a cousin within the prohibited degrees. He was excommunicated, but the Crescentii staged a revolution at Rome. Gregory V abdicated. Otto III came in force; the anti-Pope John XVI was expelled, and Gerbert accepted the tiara as Sylvester II (999). Relations between the Papacy and K. Robert now improved. In the end he married Constance of Arles. This connection helped him to conquer Burgundy, which he gave as an appanage to his younger son **(8) Robert the Old (?-1076).** His descendants reigned as Dukes of Burgundy until 1361, and formed a distinct, German-supported, nucleus of power eastward of Paris. The Germans defeated K. Robert in 1006.

The Rise of Norman Influence. In the reign of **(9) Henry I (r. 1031-60)** Normandy was experiencing population pressure; after 1035 when its Duke, Robert the Devil, died, the Duchy was in confusion and in 1047 Henry aided the young D. William to put down his rebels at the B. of Val-s-Dunes. This had unforeseeable consequences. Enterprising landless Normans under Robert Guiscard invaded Saracen and Byzantine Italy in 1054, and founded the later Norman Kingdom of Sicily. In 1066 D. William was to repeat the exploit nearer home. Henry himself married the Varangian Anna of Kiev. His attempts to impose his will on Normandy foundered at the Bs. of Mortemer (1054) and Varaville (1058). Of his children the younger **(10) Hugh (?-1102)**

founded the House of Vermandois; **(11) Philip I (r. 1060-1108)** drew important advantages from the First Crusade (1096-9). The crusade was first preached by Urban II, a Gallic Pope, at Clermont, and appealed strongly to the Gallic imagination. It drew off much manpower and many leading vassals (including Hugh of Vermandois) whose territories thus became more amenable to Capetian influence. Philip, like other Kings, stayed behind; he more than doubled and consolidated the royal domain.

Dissemination of Royal Influence. The century preceding the reign of **(12) Louis VI (the Stout) (r. 1108-37)** had seen notable developments in trade, communications and, by the readoption of three-fold rotation, of agriculture. This economic quickening was fostered mainly by the Cistercians and protected by the feudal castles, and it had encouraged self conscious towns. The castles, with their exactions, were now a nuisance; the King offered privileges and status to the towns, thereby weakening the local lords and, near the royal domain, campaigned against the castles. This clearance of the central communications helped to diffuse a new culture. The Abbot SUGER, friend to the King and his son Louis VII, first popularised the Gothic style at his new abbey of St. Denis. The fashion soon spread. The royal prestige was felt throughout Gaul. In 1124, in the war with England and the Emperor Henry V, the King could summon troops from all parts. When D. William X of Aquitaine died in 1137 the King married his son Louis (later Louis VII) to the Duke's famous heiress Eleanor. Of his other sons **(13) Robert the Great (?-1188)** founded the Capetian houses of Brittany and Dreux and **(14) Peter (?-1183)** was the ancestor of the Courtenays. *For later personalities of this dynasty see* LOUIS IX; CHARLES OF ANJOU; PHILIP III; PHILIP IV, and CAPETIANS, LAST.

CAPETIANS, LAST. Philip (IV) the FAIR was succeeded first by his eldest son **Louis X (r. 1314-6)** and then by his second son **Philip V (r. 1316-22),** who set aside a daughter and a posthumous son of Louis X. The daughter, Jeanne, however, inherited Navarre (acquired by Philip the Fair), which thus for a while became separated from the French crown again. Philip V was followed by his brother **Charles IV (r. 1322-8),** while his daughters retained their mother's rights in Franche Comté The short reign of Charles IV contained one incident, the War of St. Sardos (1322-4), of major importance. As a result of a border fracas in Gascony and delays in Edward II's homage for it, Charles sequestrated the duchy of Aquitaine. Subsequently the Pope (John XXII) persuaded Edward to send his queen ISABEL (1292-1358), who was Charles' sister, to negotiate and suggested that the P. Edward should do homage on behalf of his father. The advice was followed and the dispute settled, but Isabel refused to return and, without French help, set up the conspiracy which brought about Edward II's downfall. *See* SALIC LAW.

CAPE TIMES (1876). Oldest S. African daily paper.

CAPE TO CAIRO RAILWAY was an unrealised ambition of Cecil Rhodes.

CAPE VERDE Is. were sighted in 1460, and in 1462 colonised by Portuguese who were given a monopoly of the Guinea slave trade. In 1495 the islands became part of the Portuguese royal estate, and the wealth of Riberra Grande attracted the attention of Drake, who sacked it in 1585 and again in 1592. In 1712 the French also sacked it with such ferocity that the islands were partly abandoned. The good harbours formed useful refuges on the India route, but water shortage always prevented them becoming a major staging point.

CAPGRAVE, John (1393-1464) Augustinian at Lynn (Norfolk) from c. 1410 and later prior there, wrote Latin religious writings, and historical works and saints lives in English. He was Humphrey D. of Gloucester's confessor and also wrote for Henry VI. He dedicated his *Chronicle* of *England* (1461), the first history of England in English, to Edward IV.

CAPIAS (Lat = seize). There were two writs **(1)** *Capias ad respondendum* ('Seize him so that he must answer') was used to bring a recalcitrant defendant before a court. In 1347 it was held that where this writ could be used **(2)** *Capias ad satisfaciendum* ('Seize him to satisfy') would also lie. This was the foundation of the law on imprisonment for debt.

CAPITANA (Sp.). The flagship of a Spanish fleet. *See* ALMIRANTA.

CAPITAL BURGESSES were persons who, under some old municipal charters, had a special position, like that of a councillor or alderman, or special voting rights. The *capitouls* were similar magistrates in some southern French towns under English Kings. They survived only at Toulouse.

CAPITAL-ISM: INTEREST: PROFIT. The following summary of the definitions in this controversial subject may be helpful.

Fixed Capital is that part of capital (such as land or machines) which does not change its form: *Circulating Capital* is that part (such as money, saleable goods or stocks of raw materials) which may do so in the course of production. The *Classical School* (Adam Smith, David Ricardo and John Stuart Mill) thought that capital originated in accumulations from excess of production over consumption, but were faced with the difficulty of fitting land into this definition. The *Marginalist* or *Austrian School* (Eügen Böhm-Bawerk, Stanley Jevons, Irving Fisher, Léon Walras) defined capital by reference to its length of existence, called the *Production Period*, or its rate of amortisation. Both types of theory regarded interest or profit as an inducement to accumulate and apply capital. From the point of view of the consumer his willingness to accept an enhanced price was a form of *abstinence* so that the benefit of that application might continue. The *Marxists* thought that there was no benefit: capital was merely an extract from the accumulated labour of the past and interest and profit were derived from the power of the capitalist into whose hands that extract had come. Their view was essentially political. *Keynes* held that the rate of interest, whose variability had baffled all theoretical economists, depended upon the population's total demand (*liquidity preference*) for money. If new money is not created to meet a rising demand, interest rates will rise: if it is not destroyed in the face of falling demand interest rates will fall. This places a premium on govt. intervention in market economics.

CAPITAL GAINS TAX (1965) is in principle levied on the difference between the cost of purchasing, and the larger sum realised by selling, a capital asset. It is charged at a specified rate on the total amount of a person's chargeable assets in a given year of assessment after deducting allowable losses and a free allowance, originally £1,000, but raised to £3,000 in 1980. Since 1982 the allowance has been related to the retail prices index.

CAPITAL LEVY, apart from death duties, was imposed under the name of SPECIAL CONTRIBUTION only once in recent times by a Labour govt. in 1948.

CAPITAL PUNISHMENT in practice was not common in the Middle Ages except for treason and piracy, because the Church disapproved. In the late 15th cent. the increase of population was not accompanied by improvements in law enforcement and this led to greater reliance on capital punishment, in public and sometimes with barbarous accompaniments, as a deterrent. Thus treason, both high and petty, was punished in the case of a man with hanging, drawing and quartering, in the case of a woman with burning. A pirate was slowly drowned. Other felonious offences were visited with hanging, and their number was steadily increased as population pressure and social confusion brought one offence after

another to the fore. By 1790 the number of capital felonies had reached 200, though the practical effects were much mitigated by perverse acquittals, Benefit of Clergy and the refusal of monarchs to sign execution warrants in minor cases. As a result of the ceaseless campaigning of Samuel Romilly and Jeremy Bentham, the number of capital offences was reduced to 15 by 1834 and all the cruel accompaniments had gone; the institution of an efficient police force soon demonstrated the purposelessless of most of the remaining 15 and by 1861 they had been reduced to four, namely treason, piracy, arson in naval dockyards and murder. Public executions were abolished in 1868. The death penalty for murder was abolished in 1965; for arson in naval dockyards in 1968. *See* SILVERMAN, SYDNEY.

CAPITAL TRANSFER TAX (1974-94) was in principle levied on a cumulative basis on gifts and transfers during life and at death, subject to exempt amounts. It was not levied on transfers between spouses. It replaced Estate Duty.

CAPITULARY was originally a collection of civil laws, especially of the Merovingian and Carolingian Kings.

CAPITULATIONS (1) were privileges, mostly economic in character granted by oriental states to the subjects of major western countries during the period 1569 to 1932. The oriental states concerned were Japan (16 cent.-1900), China (1840-1932), the Indo-Chinese States and Siam (17th cent.-1932), Persia (19th cent.-1928), Egypt (1697-1932) and the Ottoman Empire (1569-1923). In form the grants were freely made: in fact they were originally offered as bargaining counters and later extracted under pressure.

(2) The most important capitulations concerned the Ottoman Empire, which in 1569, the date of the first of them, extended from Hungary to Algeria; the word, without qualification is generally understood to refer to these. They included the recognition of communities of foreign merchants, whose disputes were to be settled by their own consuls under their own law; security and freedom of travel, transport and sale of goods; and freedom of navigation in Ottoman waters. Privileges of this kind were not new, for they had been conceded to the Genoese and Venetians by Byzantine and Seljuk rulers, and had been continued in some form or other to the Venetians after the fall of Constantinople in 1453. It was an impending war with Venice which induced Selim II to offer the capitulations of 1569 to France; and the war was ended in 1573 by a dangerous Franco-Spanish understanding, which eventually led to the English capitulations of 1580. English naval successes and commercial penetration of the Mediterranean resulted in large reductions in Ottoman export duties to England, as well as most favoured nation treatment (1601), and European traders began to use English ships. In 1604, however, the French obtained special capitulations for monks and pilgrims at Jerusalem (a distant *casus belli* of the Crimean War) and in 1673 they secured the position which England had lost in the 17th cent. political confusion.

(3) The Ottoman defeat at Vienna (1683) led to a Habsburg counter-offensive, and the Porte began offering capitulations in return for political assistance. Hence also the Franco-Habsburg peace of 1697 (T. of Ryswick) led to special British ones including the monopoly of trade between Istanbul and Egypt, where a British Consulate was for the first time set up. By the Ts. of Carlowitz (1699) and Passarowitz (1718) Habsburg subjects were admitted to extensive capitulations including freedom of navigation on the Danube, and in 1739 France, by the offer of virtually unhindered economic access to the Ottoman dominions, was induced to help Turkey to secure the T. of Belgrade. Russia secured important capitulations under the T. of Kuchuk Kainardji (1774).

(4) By 1800 capitulations were unpopular because

they were grossly abused, especially by consuls who sold patents of protection in large numbers to Ottoman subjects. The govt. attempted to redress the balance by excluding internal trade from them and establishing export monopolies. This was frustrated by British pressure and reversed in the Convention of Balta Liman (1838). The precedent was followed by the other major powers, so that the Empire became a vast western market in which local businesses could not accumulate capital and over which the Ottoman govt. had only minimal control. In 1856 the govt. demanded the abolition of the capitulations as part of the settlement of the Crimean War, but was forced to renew them in 1862. There were now two opposed currents: Ottoman reformers sought to eliminate the abuses, while Europeans sought to extend the general scope to the public administration. By 1890, so far as the subjects of Britain, France, Russia and Austro-Hungary were concerned, the Sultan was no longer sovereign in his own dominions. Extreme Turkish xenophobia was the natural result; it helped to precipitate the Young Turks' revolution of 1908 and allied procrastination on the issue in 1914 caused Turkey to join the Central Powers in World War I, and abolish them. They were theoretically restored by the inoperative T. of Sèvres (1920) but their end was admitted by the T. of Lausanne (1923). *See* CHINESE TREATY PORTS.

CAP OF LIBERTY or PHRYGIAN BONNET. On manumission a Roman slave was capped to hide his shaven head. The red Phrygian bonnet was the head dress of Marseilles galley slaves, and when the Swiss galley slave survivors of the Nancy mutiny (1791) were freed, they continued to wear it as a political emblem.

CAPRI (Med). This small island within sight of Naples was captured by the British in 1806 and used as a minor base against Bonaparte Italy until 1808 when the French stormed it. It was returned to the Kingdom of the Two Sicilies in 1813.

CAPRIVI, Leo (1831-99) Count (1891), a soldier, was head of the German admiralty from 1883 and favoured the defensive torpedo arm against supporting a forward colonial policy with a large fleet. He resigned in 1888, but in 1890 succeeded Bismarck as Chancellor. As he expected a war on two fronts he concentrated on defensive armaments and the Austrian alliance. He traded Zanzibar to the British for Heligoland to reduce British hostility and safeguard the Bight ports, and in 1891 renewed the Triple Alliance with Austria-Hungary and Italy. He also tried to reduce the international temperature by commercial treaties. These lowered the corn import duties (provoking opposition from landowning *Junkers*), but reduced the price of German manufactured exports. A loyal monarchist, he believed in crown govt. above and so in spite of, parties in the legislatures. This could function only with the Emperor's favour but his policy needed liberal support which alienated the Emperor's court. His Prussian school reform upset the liberals because it favoured the churches, and the increase in defence forces required by external policy had to be bought by a reduction in the length of compulsory service. This finally alienated the Court. He was dismissed in 1894.

CAPTAIN. Until Tudor times a captain was an officer usually with martial duties in charge of a unit which was not necessarily military. A captain might raise a company of troops or, as at Calais, might be both military and civil governor of an important colony. The title clung to the unit but, as in the army, companies (the original units) came to be combined into larger formations and captains ceased to be contractors raising their own companies. Higher titles were created for their commanding officers and this tended to depress the captains. Nevertheless they continued to be company commanders until 1941. A naval ship's captain was originally its fighting commander, while the Master was responsible for sailing the ship. Until late in the 17th cent. military officers moved freely between land and sea. As the fighting importance of specific seafaring talents became recognised, the functions of captain and master merged. The ship, however, had to remain the basic unit of command in the Royal Navy, but as ships varied very widely in size it was necessary to distinguish between commanders of different sized ships, notably by inserting ranks below that of Captain, particularly Commander.

CAPUCHINS. *See* FRANCISCANS.

CARACCIOLO, Prince Francesco (1732-99) English trained Neapolitan admiral. When the French took Naples in 1798 he escorted the Neapolitan court to Sicily and then returned and became a convert to liberalism. On the recovery of the city in 1799 he was captured and condemned to death by a Neapolitan court martial sitting in Nelson's flagship. The Q. of Naples was his enemy; her friend, Lady Hamilton, Nelson's mistress, prevailed on Nelson to have the sentence carried out within hours. The affair caused a widespread scandal.

CARADOG ap GRUFFUDD ap RHYDDERCH. *See* DEHEUBARTH-10, 11.

CARADON, Ld. *See* FOOT.

CARATACUS. *See* BRITAIN BEFORE THE ROMAN CONQUEST-5; ROMAN BRITAIN-2,3; CATUVELLAUNI.

CARAUSIUS, Marcus Aurelius Mausaeus (?245-93). *See* BRITAIN. ROMAN-20.

CARAVEL. *See* SHIPS. SAILING.

CARBERRY. *See* VAUGHAN.

CARBINES, CARBINIERS, CARABINIERS. A carbine was the light version, suitable for cavalry, of any current standard infantry firearm. Dragoons armed with muskets were originally mounted infantry. In 1692 the 6th Dragoons were made into Carabineers to make them more like cavalry, and were henceforth known as *The Carabineers.*

CARBONARI (Ital = Charcoal Burners). Originally there were republican-minded fraternities of charcoal burners in the Black Forest and the Jura in the 18th cent. Their ideas and masonic type customs spread through French and Swiss officers of anti-monarchist (i.e. anti-Bonapartist) leanings in Italy to Murat's Neapolitcan army. The Italian Carbonari were mostly nobles and officials. After 1815 they transferred their animosity to the Neapolitan Bourbons and they were active in the Naples rebellion of 1820, which began with a military mutiny. Garibaldi was a *carbonaro*: Napoleon III as a young man, oddly enough, probably was. The movement was again active in the disturbances of 1831 after which it petered out. It had, nevertheless, provided Italian liberals with mutual contacts which remained useful throughout the *risorgimento*.

CARBON DIOXIDE was first identified by Bergman in 1774. An important component of motor vehicle emissions, it became a major factor in global warming when the number of these vehicles multiplied between 1950 and 1995.

CARDIFF (Welsh CAERDYDD) was first occupied as a Roman auxiliary fort (c. A.D. 75) and heavily fortified in the 3rd and 4th cents. Depopulated in Saxon times, the Norman reoccupation represented a new start (c. 1090) under Robert fitz Hamo. E. of Gloucester. He raised the motte and bailey castle on the site of the fort and made it the capital of the Norman lordship which superseded the old Kingdom of Morgannwg. His son-in-law, Robert E. of Gloucester (?-1147), a bastard of Henry I, probably built the stone keep. The parish church already existed in 1100, and William of Clare, E. of Gloucester (1147-83) established a borough outside the walls. The city's wealth was founded on trade, leather-working and wool. In Owain Glyndwr's revolt, parts of it were burned down, and it did not fully recover until the 16th cent. In the meantime the seigneury passed through the Clare, Despenser, Beauchamp and Neville families to Richard III and Henry VII, who gave it to Jasper Tudor. It was then acquired by the Lewises of Van through whom it descended *via* the 2nd Ld. Windsor's *d.* Charlotte to the 4th E. of Bute in 1766. His descendants, the Es. and Ms. of Bute, built the docks for the Welsh coal trade and the Victorian Gothic castle. Between 1955 and 1970 the govt. of Wales was progressively established there.

CARDIGAN (ABERTEIFI) and CARDIGANSHIRE (CEREDIGION). The minerals (especially the metals) attracted the interest of the early Irish, and the hilltop earthworks were probably thrown up against them. The Romans showed a similar interest and the area was later still raided by the Ostmen. The town is, as its Welsh name shows, at the mouth of the R. Teifi. St. David traditionally preached from Llandewibrefi, and in the 8th cent. St. Padam from Llanbadarn fawr. This religious focus of early Wales perhaps encouraged literary activity too. After the fall of the Welsh kingdom of Deheubarth in 1093, Ceredigion became a battleground but in 1100 the area was apparently granted to Gilbert fitz Richard of Clare, and there was a Norman castle and bridge at the town, but in 1135 the Welsh won a great victory at Crug Mawr-Banc y Warren, and Norman authority collapsed. By 1171 Rhys ap Gruffydd (The Lord Rhys) was in possession of the town. He rebuilt the castle in stone and was safe enough to hold the first national Eisteddfod there in 1176, and in or before 1184 he founded the great Cistercian abbey of Strata Florida further north. Llywelyn took over the area in 1231 but when he died in 1240 the town passed permanently into English control. Though it was at the far west of the new shire, in 1284 Edward I made it the capital of his shire of Cardigan, by the Statute of Rhuddlan. It received a charter and the shire was divided into six hundreds, but the assizes were fixed at Carmarthen. The arrangements worked badly, probably because of the combined weakness and self-will of the marchers, and the incessant feuding between the English valley settlers and the hillmen. In the 15th cent. Owain Glyndwr took over the govt. without difficulty. By the Act of Union (1526) the fully shired area was enlarged to include the marches of Tregaron and Cardigan, and was given its own assizes. It also began to send members to parliament, and from 1554 Cardigan and Aberystwyth did so too. In the 18th cent. Ceredigion was the most important area of Welsh Methodism. The bad roads forced trade to go mostly by sea to Bristol, to which minerals (especially lead) were shipped. This trade grew steadily in volume and value until 1870 when problems of transport and obsolescent machinery made it vulnerable to foreign competition. By 1890 most mining had ceased and there was extensive emigration which continued into the 1970s. *See* DEHEUBARTH.

CARDIGAN, James Thomas Brudenell (1797-1868) 9th E. of (1837) as Lord Brudenell was a Tory M.P. from 1818 to 1837. He had entered the army in 1824 and by 1832 had purchased the command of the 15th Hussars. His spoilt and unreasonable nature brought him into conflict with his officers, one of whom (Capt. Wathen) he court martialled. The court acquitted Wathen and censured Cardigan. He resigned. His father, a friend of William IV, got him the command of the 11th Hussars, with whose officers he quarrelled equally. The result was a duel with a Capt. Tuckett, Cardigan's arrest and trial by the House of Lords, who acquitted him on a technical point. He retained command and was promoted to - maj-gen. in the ordinary course of affairs in 1847. He commanded the Light Brigade with utter incompetence in Bulgaria and the Crimea, but as a result of mistaken orders became the hero of the Charge of the Light Brigade (*see* BALACLAVA). He was inspector of cavalry from 1855 to 1860.

CARDINALS. Rome and its neighbourhood had 50 parishes, 7 (later 14) districts for poor relief and 6 local ('suburbicarian') bishoprics. The parish priests were called *cardinal priests* and the district deacons *cardinal deacons.* They gradually formed the so-called SACRED COLLEGE which helped to manage the Holy See, and to this the 6 bishops were added as cardinals in the 8th cent. when the papacy had become so busy that the help of neighbouring bishops was needed. The local duties of these spiritual grandees soon became nominal. Assembled in CONSISTORY, the cardinals act as the Pope's chief councillors; since the middle ages they have ranked as royalty with the title 'Eminence' (= Highness). They are nominated by the Pope. Since 1179 the cardinals have had the exclusive right to elect the Pope; since 1271 this has always been done in a temporary state of seclusion, called CONCLAVE, designed to prevent outside influence. The emperor Charles V, however, gave lists of undesirable papal candidates to friendly cardinals, and Philip II of Spain had his own lists published. Louis XIV and so Austria and Spain claimed a formal right to veto (or "exclude") one candidate; this *exclusiva* was exercised through a cardinal who had to act before an election was complete. In 1586 the maximum number was fixed at 70 and a two-thirds majority was required. The *exclusiva* was abolished in 1904. In 1930 the required majority was increased by one. In 1966 the limitation to 70 was abandoned, but in 1970 the power of election was restricted to cardinals under 75 years of age.

CARDINGTON (nr Bedford) has two gigantic hangars, built in World War I and preserved as industrial archaeology, for the construction, originally, of the huge R Class hydrogen lifted airships, and then abandoned after the R 101 disaster. They are now used for the more modest but safer helium lifted types.

CARDONNEL, Adam (de) (?-1719), son of a Huguenot and clerk at the War Office, was the D. of Marlborough's military sec. from 1692. M.P. for Southampton from 1701, he fell with the Duke in 1710. Marlborough's inability to secure for him the post of Secretary-at-War indicated the Duke's decline and Cardonnel's expulsion from the Commons on allegations of army peculation in Feb. 1712 formed an important element in the general campaign against Marlborough's position. He was in fact a faithful public servant.

CARDS, PLAYING, probably brought from Asia to N. Africa and Europe in mid 14th cent. were common through stencilled reproduction by 1400, and in England common enough by 1463 for makers to petition for protection against the now printed imports. The Tarot pack had 78 cards: 22 'greater arcana' consisting of picture cards used in a form of divination and 56 'lesser arcana' divided into four suits of 14. The modem 52 card pack of 4 13-card suits is derived from the latter. Cards were taxed from 1615 onwards; the tax (2s 6d per pack) reached its peak in 1789 which was the summit of the gambling mania. It remained at this level until 1828, when it slowly declined. The tax paid was shown in the design of the ace of Spades. The modern cards were developed through the printer Thomas de la Rue's lithography method, which made mass production in colour possible.

CARDWELL, Edward (1813-86) 1st Vist. CARDWELL (1874) entered parliament as a Peelite Tory in 1842. He was Sec. to the Treasury from 1845 to 1846 and Aberdeen's Pres. of the Bd. of Trade from 1852 to 1855, and was responsible for the Merchant Shipping Act 1854. He served under Palmerston as Chief Sec. for Ireland from 1859 to 1861 and as Colonial Sec. from 1864 to 1866. Under Gladstone he was Sec. for War and undertook the reorganisation of the Army against much opposition. He abolished transportation, introduced short service commissions and replaced the permanent colonial garrisons with a system of linked battalions in territorially based county regiments; and by the use of a Royal Warrant abolished the long established system of purchase of commissions. His career was that of a practical administrator rather than a political animal.

CAREW. (1) Sir John (?-1362) was escheator and for a year (1349) justiciar in Ireland. A substantial Munster landowner and expert on Irish affairs, he advised on Clarence's expedition in 1362. His grandson **(2) Thomas (?-1431) Ld. CAREW,** was a military figure in the wars of Henry V and Capt. of Harfleur in 1419. His grandson **(3) Sir Edmund (1464-1513)** was a military supporter of Henry VII. Of his grandsons **(4) Sir Peter (1514-75),** after a life of truancy and military adventure abroad, returned to England in 1530 where Henry VIII, impressed by his knowledge of soldierly techniques and French, employed him about the court and in the army. In 1547 he was Sheriff of Devon and then retired to his wife's Lincolnshire estates. In 1549 he severely repressed local risings against the new prayer book, but in 1553 helped to proclaim Mary. Nevertheless he joined the conspiracy to prevent her marriage to K. Philip and had to go abroad, but was kidnapped in Antwerp in 1556 and put in the Tower. He came back into favour when Elizabeth came to the throne. In 1572 he obtained leave to pursue his family's claims in Munster and spent the rest of his life fighting for them. His cousin **(5) George (1555-1629) 1st Ld. CAREW (1605) and E. of TOTNES (1625)** entered his service in Ireland in 1574, volunteered for Sir Henry Sydney's Irish army in 1575, became lieut-gov. of Carlow in 1576 and defeated Rory Oge O'More in 1577. After a voyage with Sir Humphrey Gilbert in 1578 and further Irish service, he murdered several Irishmen suspected of killing his brother. This brought him notoriety and the disapproval of the govt. but he won over the Cecils and the Queen and became one of her gentlemen-pensioners in 1582. Sir John Perrott, the Irish Lord Lieut. knighted him in 1586 and from 1588 to 1592 he was Irish Master of the Ordnance. He then became English Lieut-Gen. of the Ordnance and took part in the expeditions to Cadiz in 1595 and the Azores in 1597. In 1599 he became Treasurer-at-War, but in Jan. 1600 succeeded Sir Henry Wallop as Pres. of Munster and was Lord Justice between Essex's departure and Mountjoy's arrival. His ruthless military and administrative activity soon reduced Munster and smoothed Mountjoy's way, and he and Mountjoy left Ireland together in 1603. James I liked him. He received appointments in the Queen's household, and was M.P. in the parliament of 1604. He was Master of the Ordnance from 1608 to 1617, gov. of Guernsey from 1609 to 1610, a councillor for Virginia from 1609 and privy councillor from 1616. In 1621 he, with Buckingham and Middlesex, received the gunpowder monopoly and in 1624 he was a member of the committee which considered the advisability of going to war over the Palatinate (*see* THIRTY YEARS' WAR); as such he attracted some of the obloquy arising out of Mansfeld's expedition early in the next reign. Of antiquarian tastes, he left many papers on Ireland and was a friend of Camden, Cotton and Bodley, as was a kinsman **(6) Richard (1555-1620),** a poet and distinguished antiquary who was M.P. for Saltash in 1584 and for Michell in 1597. His brother **(7) George (?-1612)** was secretary successively to Sir Chris. Hatton, Lord Chancellor, and to Sir Thomas Egerton and Sir John Puckeridge, Lords Keepers. In 1598 and 1599 he was on a diplomatic mission to the Baltic states. He was also M.P. for various Cornish boroughs from 1584 to 1601. From 1605 to 1609 he was ambassador in France. He was a large landowner in Cornwall. His nephew **(8) Sir Alexander (1609-44),** M.P. with Sir Bevil Grenville for Cornwall in the Long Parliament, quarrelled with Sir Bevil by voting for Strafford's attainder. He was given command by parliament of the island fortress of St. Nicholas at Plymouth Harbour but tried to surrender it to the King, for which he was court-martialled and executed. His half brother **(9) John (?-1660)** met the converse fate. Also an M.P. in the Long Parliament, he sat at the "trial" of Charles I and signed his death warrant. He

was a member of Cromwell's third (1651) and fourth (1652) Councils of State; as a Fifth Monarchy Man he opposed Cromwell's rise to quasi royal power and was imprisoned in 1655 and again in 1658. At the Restoration he was excluded from the Indemnity Act, tried and executed for treason.

CAREY, George Leonard (1935-) BD., M.Th., Bp. of Bath and Wells 1987-91. Abp. of Canterbury 1991. *See* ANGLICANISM – 5.

CAREY. (1) Henry (?1524-96) 1st Ld. HUNSDON (1559), *s.* of Q. Anne Boleyn's sister, was from 1547 to 1555 M.P. for Bucks. where he received lands from the Protector Somerset. He was ennobled by his cousin Q. Elizabeth to whom he had always been faithful; he received many more properties, became a Privy Councillor and was an important figure at court. In 1564 he was ambassador to France and from 1568 gov. (not always resident) of Berwick. He was responsible for defeating the northern rebels in 1569-70 and afterwards received large Yorkshire estates. He was said to have favoured the Queen's marriage to the D. of Anjou. In 1583 he became Lord Chamberlain, and in 1586 was one of the court which tried Mary Q. of Scots. In 1587 he was sent to Edinburgh to stabilise relations with the Scottish court and his success was followed by the award of the warden-generalship of the Marches, which was a largely diplomatic post. In 1588 he commanded the infantry assembled at Tilbury during the Armada crisis. Of his sons **(2) George (1547-1603)** was envoy to Scotland in 1582, gov. of the I. of Wight from 1582 to 1589 when he returned to Scotland briefly; and succeeded his father as Lord Chamberlain in 1597. His brother **(3) Robert (?1560-1639) 1st Ld. LEPPINGTON (1622) and 1st E. of MONMOLITH (1626)** was M.P. for Morpeth from 1586 to 1593. He was employed on diplomatic business in Scotland in 1588 and 1593 after which he held positions in the administration of the Scottish border. He was commissioned to bring the news of Q. Elizabeth's death to James VI and then entered the service of the P. of Wales, whose Chamberlain he was from 1617. He went with the Prince to Spain in 1623. His brother **(4) John (?-1617) 3rd Ld. HUNSDON** was deputy warden of the Eastern Marches and Marshal of Berwick and proclaimed James VI and I in 1603.

CAREY, Henry (c. 1687-1743) London poet and playwright between 1715 and 1739, who wrote *Sally in our Alley.*

CARFAX or CARFUKES (Lat: *Quadrifurcus* = four forked), any major cross-road particularly in a town such as Exeter, London or Oxford where the name survives.

CARIB-BEAN. The Caribs were a warlike nation of the W. Indies believed by the 16th cent. Spaniards to be man eating. The word 'cannibal' is a form of their name, and the Caribbean Sea is called after the islands where they lived. They were all exterminated by the end of the 17th cent. The Caribbean Federation represented an attempt by the British govt. to combine the various small island colonies into a stronger unit. It was established in 1957 with Ld. Hailes as gov. gen. but Jamaica voted to leave it in 1961 and Trinidad in 1962. Thus deprived of its main resources, the federation was dissolved in Apr. 1962.

CARISBROOKE (I. of Wight) had a 3rd cent. Roman fort. William FitzOsbern built a castle just after the Norman Conquest and the Redvers family improved it. In 1293 it was sold to the crown. 16th cent. artillery fortifications were added against Spanish dangers, and it became the residence of the governors of the I. of Wight. Charles I was in custody from Nov. 1647 to Sept. 1648.

CARLETON, Sir Dudley (1573-1632) 1st Ld. CARLETON (1626), Vist. DORCHESTER (1628) was M.P. for St. Mawes from 1604 to 1611. Suspected of being a Gunpowder plotter, he nevertheless was ambassador to Venice from 1610 to 1615, to The Hague from 1616 to 1625 and to Paris in 1626, when he returned to The

Hague. He was Sec. of State from 1628. His voluminous papers survive.

CARLEY (Ir.) or CARLINE (Sc.) (Gael = Old Woman). The last sheaf cut at harvest, regarded as a potent symbol of good or ill luck, and the object of many ceremonies as late as 1890.

CARLILE, Richard (1790-1843), freethinking radical tinsmith, published or republished subversive literature including the works of Tom Paine and was often imprisoned. His publications were never successfully suppressed.

CARLILE, Wilson (1847-1942) usually called 'Prebendary Carlile'. *See* CHURCH ARMY.

CARLINGFORD. *See* TAAFFE.

CARLISLE (Cumbria) (Lat: *Luguvallium*; Welsh: *Caer Luel*) was reached c. A.D. 70 by the Romans who began with a marching camp, but turned it into a substantial town for retired soldiers with a cattle market and a fortified camp called Petriana at Stanwix. They held it until 383. K. Egfrith bestowed it on St. Cuthbert for his see of Lindisfarne in 685, and the saint saw the Roman walls and a fountain, but the Danes completely destroyed the town in the 9th cent. Edmund I ceded it to Scotland with Cumberland c. 945 as part of common arrangements against the Ostmen, and it remained Scots until 1092 when William II built the walls and castle. It became a bishopric in 1163. The Scots held it again from 1136 to 1157 when it finally passed to the English and was granted a charter. Thereafter it was the main English base for the defence of the western March. Burnt in 1292 and 1460 and several times besieged, it maintained a turbulent and disorderly existence until 1561 when the Elizabethan govt. enforced order. This was much assisted by the union of the crowns in 1603. The cathedral was badly damaged by Scottish troops in the civil war. It was granted a comprehensive municipal charter in 1634 which governed its affairs until 1834. Carlisle was a centre for Irish labour during World War I and when the workers had nothing else to do, the public houses were disorderly. Hence a state liquor enterprise was set up in 1916 which was returned to private enterprise only in 1971. *See also* CUMBERLAND; CIVIL WAR-12,14.

CARLISLE, Es. of. *See* HAY HOWARD.

CARLISM (Spain). *See* SPAIN (HABSBURG) **(1)** Originally a Spanish King's daughters might succeed to the throne in default of sons. The first Bourbon King, Philip V (1700-46) superseded this by the Salic Law practised by his House. Don CARLOS, the younger brother of the later Ferdinand VII, was born in 1788. In 1789, on the petition of the Cortes, K. Charles IV agreed to revert to the older custom, but the necessary decree (known as the Pragmatic Sanction) was not promulgated. Ferdinand VII (r. 1815-33) had three childless marriages, but in 1829 he took as a fourth wife the ambitious and seductive Bourbon, Maria Cristina of the Two Sicilies. She was soon pregnant and in May 1830 at her importunity Ferdinand promulgated the dormant Pragmatic. In Oct. Cristina gave birth to the first of her two legitimate daughters, ISABEL. Her rights of succession thus depended on the Pragmatic, but Carlos contended that as it had been agreed after his birth it could not deprive him of his vested rights under Salic Law, and that its promulgation after 41 years by a different King was ineffectual without the consent of a new Cortes. Ferdinand died in Sept. 1833 and Cristina proclaimed the three-year-old child Queen as Isabel II with herself as Regent.

(2) Carlos, supported by Basque, Catalan and Valencian separatists, raised an ill-organised revolt and then escaped by sea to England. Palmerston refused support so Carlos, thinly disguised, returned to N. Spain overland. The revolt now had a second wind. Represented as reactionary, it was Catholic, rural and anti-Castilian. Its only partial later suppression was the main reason why, in the period 1834-1941, Spain remained a poor and second class state unable to recover its rebellious empire which was consequently exploited by British capital. It was also contemporaneous with a similar disturbance in Portugal. France had just been forced to concede Belgian independence and Palmerston feared, correctly, that she might want compensation in Spain: but as she professed liberalism and feared the Holy Alliance, she needed British support. Palmerston persuaded her to accept a Quadruple Alliance (Britain, France and the *de facto* Portuguese and Spanish govts.) to maintain 'liberal' regimes in the Peninsula. The British fleet intervened decisively in Portugal and the French allowed 4000 Foreign legionaries to enlist under the Queen Regent, while Palmerston encouraged and the D. of Wellington obstructed the recruitment of a British volunteer Legion under Col. Geo. de Lacy Evans M.P. to do the same. 10,000 men were rapidly recruited and landed at San Sebastian in July 1835. Mostly untrained and many unfit, their effective numbers were reduced to 5000 by disease in the following winter. Both govts. professed to be neutral. The civil war was accompanied by massacres on both sides and though Britain was distracted by the fall of Peel's govt. in Apr. 1835, Chartism in 1836, Q. Victoria's accession in 1837 and outbreaks in Canada and Afghanistan, British diplomats negotiated several local conventions (mostly honoured) between rival commanders which saved the lives of thousands of prisoners. The French legionaries were withdrawn in 1836 by which time the Carlists seemed to be winning. The British govt. therefore authorised limited naval intervention, which the local admiral (Lord John Hay) interpreted enthusiastically, and his marines were soon fighting far inland beside the Legion which, however, dissolved in June 1837. The marines occupied Passajes, a port near San Sebastian, until the Carlist military collapse of 1840. Carlism, however, survived as an old-fashioned but strong local sentiment centring on Carlos' descendants.

(3) Isabel II grew up dignified, politically incompetent and tactlessly promiscuous. Public opinion eventually turned against her and a *coup d'état* by Gen. Serrano (her first lover) and Gen. Prim drove her into exile in 1868. The Carlists were not organised and there was an interregnum in which a Cortes declared Spain a constitutional monarchy but excluded all Bourbons from the throne. Serrano having been assassinated, Prim searched for a new sovereign. Of the possible candidates, Bismarck's manipulation of French objections to Leopold of Hohenzollern precipitated the Franco-Prussian War, but in 1870 the Cortes elected Amadeus of Savoy by 191 votes with 119 dissentients. He was rudely received even in Madrid and the Carlists were, of course, against him. His unhappy reign ended in an abrupt abdication (Feb. 1873) and the republicans stampeded the Cortes into proclaiming a Republic. The Carlists naturally became anti-republican.

(4) They had by now acquired a young and likeable leader in Carlos, the original Carlos' grandson, who united the old Carlist ideals with the championship of monarchy as a principle. The start of his rising (The Second Carlist War 1873-6) resembled his grandfather's, but it came to an unexpected end. The republican govt. was weak and despised and distracted by a Cuban rebellion. Adroitly guided by the legitimists Canovas de Castillo and Primo de Rivera, Isabel II's handsome son Don Alfonso, an officer cadet at Sandhurst, issued a manifesto from Sandhurst in Dec. 1874. He appealed to liberal sentiment against the republicans yet undercut the Carlists by claiming the throne and asserting his Spanishness and Catholicism. The republican-governed areas received him with rapture and in a month he was King as Alfonso XII. Many anti-republican Carlists came over. By Mar. 1876 Carlos had been driven out.

(5) The Carlists survived, ultimately as a force for

anti-republicanism but especially for local autonomy in the Civil War of 1936-40; and Gen. Franco, whom they mostly supported, sought to reconcile them to his unitary state. In this he was lucky, for the direct Carlist Bourbons had already died out in 1931, while their indirect representative had disqualified himself by marrying Irene, the future Queen of Holland. Franco's nominated successor, Don JUAN CARLOS, grandson of the abdicated Alfonso XIII, thus merged the rival Salic and Pragmatic claims in the Crown when he became King in 1975.

CARLOWITZ, P. of (Jan. 1699) ended the Eastern part of the War of the League of Augsburg. The defeated Turks ceded Hungary, Transylvania, Croatia and Slavonia to the Habsburgs, Podolia and their Ukrainian provinces to Poland and the Peloponnese and some Aegean islands to Venice. It also guaranteed freedom of worship to R. Catholics within the Turkish empire and so provided a standing excuse for Habsburg interventions in the future. It also formed the precedent for a similar Russian imposed provision in favour of orthodox Christians a century later. The treaty marked the beginning of the long Turkish decline.

CARLSBAD CONFERENCE (6-31 Aug. 1819) of major German states was summoned by Mettenich. Prussia, Bavaria, Saxony, Hanover (then under an English King) and six other states were also represented. The occasion was the recent revolutionary outrages, including the murder of Kotzebue: the purpose to take measures against liberalism. Metternich announced the agenda as (a) matters of urgency and (b) the fundamental constitution of the German confederation. On the *matters of urgency* it was unanimously decided to recommend to the Diet the introduction of a uniform press censorship, the supervision of universities and schools, the suppression of the *Burschenschaften* (Ger = Young mens' associations) and the establishment of a permanent inquisitorial commission. These measures are the notorious DECREES. On the issue of fundamental constitutions Metternich met defeat. He wanted to abolish those representative legislatures already established in some German states, as incompatible with the Confederate Constitution, which permitted only 'assemblies of estates'. Effective resistance was led by Württemberg, and the issue was abandoned.

CARLTON CLUB, launched in 1831 and relaunched in 1832, was the effective H.Q. of the Tory, and later the Conservative, Party until the formation of the Conservative Central Office in 1870. The directing organ was its political committee; the executive work was done by F.R. Bonham, a follower of Peel until the Corn Law crisis of 1846, and thereafter by the Conservative Chief Whip. From 1852 to 1870 the constituency agency work was done by Disraeli's solicitor, Philip Rose. The club's limited membership led to the foundation of the Junior Carlton Club in 1864. It was the scene of the well-known CARLTON CLUB MEETING in 1921 at which the Conservatives ended the coalition with Lloyd George and his career in office. *See* CHANAK INCIDENT.

CARLTON HOUSE, built on the site now occupied by the D. of York's column in London, was owned by the bachelor L. Carleton, who at his death in 1725 left it to Frederick, P. of Wales. He lived there from 1732. In 1783 it became the residence of the P. of Wales and future P. Regent, George IV. The name was used in both cases to describe the clique or party of the heir to the throne. It was demolished in 1827, the portico being reused for the National Gallery.

CARLYLE, Thomas (1795-1881) after various unsuccessful literary ventures in Scotland moved to London in 1831. He published *The French Revolution* in 1837 which created a sensation: and became known also as a lecturer. His other publications included *Chartism* (1839); *Heroes and Hero Worship* (1841); *Oliver Cromwell* (1845); *Frederick the Great* (1858-65). He despised weakness and

exhibited a stridently expressed passion for strong men and strong govt.

CARMARTHEN (CAERFYRDDIN Lat: MARIDUNUM)-SHIRE. In the 1st cent. the area was mostly occupied by the Demetae (commemorated in Dyfed) and the town, originally Roman, became their centre of communications and for the operation of gold mines in the hills. The town was abandoned in 5th cent. and the area suffered much from Irish and Ostmen raids until protected under Rhodri the Great. The Welsh rulers were centred on Dynevor. Norman penetration began (c. 1080) from the sea, with coastal castles at Kidwelly, Llanstephan and Laugharne, from which they spread inland, but Carmarthen and its castle were destroyed by Llywellyn the Great in 1214 and had to be rebuilt in stone under Henry III. The castle then became the local centre, and by 1227 the town could be chartered. In 1284 the Statute of Rhuddlan made about two-thirds of the area into a county, with Carmarthen as the assize town for Carmarthen and Cardigan. It was a useful port, and in 1353 it became the staple for a large wool trade. The remaining marcher lordships were added to the County by the Act of Union in 1536, when both town and county began to send members to Parliament. The town was converted into a county by itself in 1604, and the presence of coal in the east made it possible to operate an iron smelting works there from 1747. This was the beginning of steadily developing industrialisation, especially at Llanelly and Ammanford, which absorbed migrants from Cardiganshire towards the end of the 19th cent. The county was amalgamated into Dyfed in 1974. *See* DEHEUBARTH.

CARMARTHEN, M. of *See* OSBORNE.

CARMELITE ORDER (WHITE FRIARS), founded in Palestine in about 1154 by St. Berthold, originally practised extreme asceticism. With the collapse of the Crusades it migrated to Europe, where it was reorganised by the Englishman St. Simon Stock (c. 1165-1265). An order of sisters was founded in the Low Countries in 1452 and spread rapidly. Discipline was seriously relaxed in the 15th and 16th cents. and this led to the reform of the sisterhood by St. Theresa of Avila between 1562 and 1582, and of the Friars by her disciple St. John of the Cross between 1570 and 1591. Consequently in 1579-80 the order was divided into a 'Calced' (sandalled) branch following the more relaxed rule, and the 'discalced' or reformed branch. The order has produced a number of important Christian mystics.

CARNARVON, two Es. of the Herbert family. **(1) Henry Howard (1831-90) 4th E. (1849)** was Tory Colonial USec. in 1858 and Sec. of State in 1866. He piloted the British North America Act through the Lords in 1867 and in 1878 resigned over Disraeli's Eastern policy. His interview as Lord Lieut. of Ireland (1885) with Parnell when he offered a Home Rule compromise led to his second resignation. His son **(2) George Edward (1866-1923) 5th E.,** financed Egyptian archaeology from 1908 and with Howard Carter made the famous discovery of Tutenkhamun's tomb in 1922.

CARNATIC. *See* GEORGE II-15; ARCOT.

CARNEGIE, Andrew (1835-1919), a Scot, began in the Pennsylvania Railroad, and during the American civil war reorganised the Union Telegraph System. From 1868 onwards he developed the Pittsburgh steel industry and amassed a huge fortune. In 1889 he published a widely read article called *The Gospel of Wealth*. He argued that the rich should use their wealth for the public advantage. In 1901 he sold his interests to the U.S. Steel Corporation, retired to Scotland and began to put his principles into practice. He created several institutes and foundations in the U.S.A. and in Britain the philanthropic Carnegie United Kingdom Trust and a great many public libraries.

CARNOT (1) Lazare Nicolas Marguerite (1753-1823) was elected to the French National Assembly in 1791, became a member of the Committee of Public Safety and as such reorganised and disciplined the revolutionary armies. He later became known as the Organiser of Victory. He retired in 1801 because he objected to Bonaparte's ambition, but later supported him in his final efforts to stem the allied invasion of 1814. The Bourbons exiled him and thereafter he worked mostly as a scientist. His son **(2) Nicolas Sadi (1796-1832)** founded the modern science of thermodynamics. A grandson **(3) Marie François Sadi (1837-94)**, an engineer, organised the resistance to the Germans in Normandy in 1870 and was elected a deputy in 1871. In 1885 he became Min. of Finance and in 1887 President. He was assassinated by an Italian anarchist.

CAROLAN, Turlough (1670-1738), blind, much honoured Irish itinerant harper.

CAROLINA, NORTH AND SOUTH. (1) Giovanni da Verazzano apparently visited Carolina in 1524, and Sir Walter Raleigh tried three times in 1584 and 1587 to colonise Roanoke I. His last settlement under John White existed until 1589, when it vanished without explanation. Charles I gave the patent to Sir Robert Heath to colonise a large area south of Virginia, but apart from naming it Carolina after the King, Sir Robert effected little because of the English Civil War; it was left to Virginians in the 1650s to begin settlement spontaneously along (the later named) Albemarle Sound. In 1663 Charles II superseded Sir Robert Heath's patent by a new one to eight persons called collectively the Carolina Proprietors. The most important of the eight (all well known in English public life) were the Barbadian planter, Sir John Colleton, then Chanc. of the Exch. and Sir Anthony Ashley Cooper, later E. of Shaftesbury; the others were Clarendon, George Monck, D. of Albemarle, Lords Craven and Berkeley, Sir George Carteret and Sir Wm. Berkeley. In 1665 they drew up the *Concessions and Agreements* which defined the rights of resident landowners so as to attract capital and settlers, and in 1669 they commissioned Locke to draw up a constitution which, being too elaborate, never operated. They had already appointed a separate governor for the basically Virginian Albemarle Sound Colony in the north, and in 1680 they colonised Charleston (named after Charles II) in the South, with Barbadians and English and French protestants.

(2) This early distinction between the two parts was recognised in 1691 when Albemarle Province was renamed North Carolina and was expanded inland quickly by thousands of German and Swiss settlers. By 1710 there was Indian opposition. A destructive war with the Tuscaroras lasted from 1711 to 1713 but they were defeated and migrated north to join the Iroquois. Meantime South Carolina had suffered from sporadic French and piratical attacks in the War of the Spanish Succession, and in 1715 had to face and defeat an equally destructive invasion by the Yamassees from Florida.

(3) As the Proprietors had made no profit, their interest had languished, and the colonies had fended for themselves in these troubles. Proprietorial rights were now resented and in 1719 the South Carolina assembly usurped them: the charter was locally superseded and the crown henceforth appointed the governors. In 1729 a parallel development in the North resulted in the crown buying out the Proprietors and so N. Carolina became a Crown Colony as well. Crown influence in these self reliant areas was slight, but the association with Britain brought economic benefits through the trade in rice, hides and indigo.

(4) Wealthy coastal Carolinans showed an independent mindedness and contributed to revolutionary ideas; these Carolinans first defied the Stamp Act of 1765, and in the Second Continental Congress of 1776 the North Carolinans were the first to vote for independence. The Carolina frontiersmen, however, were disaffected towards the coastal ruling

classes and in the war Charleston was occupied by the British from 1780 to 1782.

(5) Both states were among the original 13 to form the U.S.A., but both disliked interference and early showed secessionist tendencies, particularly South Carolina which, led by John Calhoun, became the foremost champion of States Rights. In 1860 South Carolina was the first to secede from the Union, and the Civil War began in Apr. 1861 with the bombardment of Fort Sumter in Charleston harbour.

CAROLINE Is. (Pacific) vaguely occupied by the Spaniards in the 19th cent. were sold by them to Germany in 1898, Seized by the Japanese in 1914, they were under a Japanese mandate from 1922. The Japanese built extensive warlike installations which were captured by the Americans in World War II; the islands became American U.N. Trust territories in July 1947.

CAROLINE of ANSBACH (1683-1737) married the Electoral P. of Hanover in 1705 and when the Elector became King of Great Britain in 1714 she and her husband moved to London where her wit, political intelligence and association with Walpole preserved relations between the King and his son (who hated each other) until the latter ascended the throne as George II in 1727. She then became (until she died) a major political figure in partnership with Walpole, through her ability to manage her husband. She had strong literary and intellectual tastes and knew most of the philosophers and literati of her time.

CAROLINE of BRUNSWICK (1768-1821) a hoyden who married George IV as P. of Wales in 1795. They separated in 1796. She was accused of adultery but cleared by an inquiry in 1805. In 1811 George, as Prince Regent, excluded her from court; she went abroad in 1814 and thereafter developed an adulterous relationship with her Italian servant Bartholomew Bergami. Her husband was a controversial political figure, so when she came to England, after his accession, "to claim her rights as queen", she was loudly applauded by the opposition. He then sought a divorce by parliamentary bill (then the only means available) but the evidence was demolished in hearings before the House of Lords and the bill had to be abandoned. Since the facts about her were publicly unknown she was a popular heroine, whom the King further injured by having her excluded from the coronation. She died a few days later.

CAROLINE MATILDA (1751-75) youngest child of Frederick, P. of Wales, married the perverted K. Christian VII of Denmark in 1766. Count Holck had secured an ascendancy by pandering to his sexual tastes. The queen, left alone, fell in love with a new and intelligent court physician, John Frederick STRUENSEE, who had political ambitions. By 1770 Struensee was the court favourite by reason of his skill as a physician to the King and as a lover of the Queen. She behaved with such indiscretion that the King necessarily knew of the relationship. In July 1771 Struensee became chief minister and effective ruler but an aristocratic conspiracy was being hatched in collusion with the Queen Mother, Juliana Maria. In Jan. 1772 Struensee and Caroline Matilda were separately seized, she being sent to Elsinore. He confessed under torture to sexual relations with her, she admitted them when shown the confession. The Queen Mother browbeat the King into signing Struensee's death warrant and Caroline was tried and divorced. The British govt. intervened to save her from seclusion, and she died at Celle in Hanover.

CAROLINGIANS or CARLOVINGIANS. This Frankish dynasty started with **(1) Pepin of Landen (?-640)** and his son **(2) Grimoald (?-656)** successively mayors of the palace (Chamberlain and chief minister) to the Merovingian Kings of Austrasia. Grimoald's nephew **(3) Pepin of Herstal (?640-717)** was also mayor from 680. He accumulated great wealth and defeated the Neustrians at the B. of Tertry in 687 and so became the ruler of all Frankish territories. The mayoralties of Neustria and Burgundy were given to dependents. When he died there was a civil war between his widow, Plectrude, regent for two child grandsons supported by the Neustrians, and a famous bastard **(4) Charles Martel (?-741)** who established his rule by 725, just in time to turn back the Berber invasions in his great victories at Poitiers (or Tours) and Narbonne in 732. At his death the mayoralty was divided between his sons **(5) Carloman (?-754)** and **(6) Pepin the Short (?-768)**. The latter soon ousted his brother, and by 747 held all the mayoralties. In 751, with papal blessing, he deposed Childeric III, the last Merovingian, and was anointed King himself, and in 753 he overthrew the Lombards. At his death the kingdom stretched from the Danish frontier to Rome and the Pyrenees, and from Brittany to the Elbe. His sons **(7) Carloman (?-771)** and **(8) Charles** known as **Charlemagne (?-814)** divided the territory but quarrelled and Carloman, like his uncle and namesake, was defeated and deposed. Charlemagne's principal problem was to conquer the Saxons (*see* EPIDEMICS, ANIMAL) and to build up an administration which would hold his dominions together. The only existing framework was the church, which was on his side. In 800 the imperial idea was revived when Leo III crowned him Emperor, but the clerical order was too weak to stand up to the violence and corruption of the military, while too much depended on the emperor's personal ability to control the latter. As long as Charlemagne lived there was some hope, despite family scandals, but as distances grew in the growing empire, the influence of a peripatetic court diminished and his successors were not of his calibre. Since 781 his son **(9) Louis the Pious (?-840)** had been K. of Aquitaine. He succeeded to the imperial throne and married twice. The children of Ermingard, the first wife, quarrelled over the inheritance long before his death. Of these **(10) Pepin I (?-838)** and his son **(11) Pepin II (?-865)** were Kings of Aquitaine from 817 to 865. Another **(12) Louis the German (?-876)** was K. of Germany from 833. When he died the eldest son **(13) Lothair I (?-855)** became titular emperor and the son of Louis' second wife, Judith, **(14) Charles the Bald (?-877)** became K. of France. A civil war had supervened and ended in the T. o Verdun (843). The empire was divided so that Louis retained the Germanic territories, Charles the Frankish (subject to the local claims of the Pepins), while Lothair received a passagelike area extending from Rome over Switzerland and along the valley of the Rhine to its mouth. It was Charles the Bald's court which K. Aethelwulf and the future Alfred the Great visited in 855 and his descendants and Burgundian collaterals reigned (with one interruption) in France until displaced by the Capetians in 986. At Lothair's death his territory was divided. His eldest son **(15) Louis II (?-875)** became emperor and took the south. The second son **(16) Lothair II (?-869)** took the northern part, now named 'Lorraine' (Lotharingia) after him. When the emperor Louis II died, Charles the Bald became emperor until 877. The empire was briefly reunited by Louis the German's son **(17) Charles the Fat (?-888)** who was emperor from 881.

CAROLINGIAN SCHOOLS. *See* ALCUIN.

CARPENTER, Edward (1844-1929), moral reformer and originally a clergyman, renounced his orders in 1874, became a university extension lecturer and absorbed the aesthetic socialism of Ruskin and Morris. He adopted the form of open air communalism advocated by the Americans Emerson, Thoreau and Whitman. Consistently with this he championed sexual, including homosexual, freedom, women's rights, nudism and vegetarianism.

CARPENTER, John (1370-1441). Town clerk of London from 1417 to 1438 left an educational endowment from which the City of London School was founded. *See also* WHITE BOOK.

CARPENTER, Mary (1807-77) started ragged and other schools in the poorest part of Bristol and also in India. She became very knowledgeable about destitute children and her book *Juvenile Delinquents* inspired the Juvenile Offenders Act, 1854.

CARPET BITERS. Those whose rages border on insanity. The class includes Henry I and Adolf Hitler.

CARPETS are of oriental origin and began to be used in England extensively in Tudor times. They were being made at Axminster and Wilton in the late 17th cent. and the weavers in both places were chartered in 1701. Ingrain carpets were being made at Kidderminster by 1736, and in 1740 French weavers were settled at Wilton where they introduced Brussels carpeting. This soon developed into so-called Brussels or cut pile carpet. In 1745 the manufacture of Brussels and Wilton commenced at Kidderminster which soon became the chief carpet making centre in the country. By 1835 the Axminster weavers had gone out of business; the Wilton weavers lasted only a few years longer.

CARR or KER, Robert. *See* SOMERSET.

CARRACKS. *See* SHIPS, SAILING.

CARRIAGES, CARTS and COACHES. (1) Horsed or cattle-drawn carts for moving produce locally have always been used, and big ones were used on the continent, but larger long distance vehicles were rare until 16th cent. because of bad roads. A rough Tudor system for repairing roads resulted in the building of the first known English coaches by Walter Rippon for the E. of Bedford in 1555 and for Elizabeth I in 1564. These, though unsprung, soon developed into fare earners which (after a fashion) carried passengers outside as well as in. In the late 17th cent. constant jolts were exchanged for occasional coach-sickness by slinging the body above the chassis on straps, as in the existing coach of the Lord Mayor of London built in 1751. The first stage (i.e. with planned stops) coaches ran between London and Coventry in 1659. Mail coaches first replaced post-boys between London and Bristol in 1784. In 1789 John Warde, the fox-hunting man, introduced springs and soon fast and then lighter coaches plied the London-Brighton run in 11 hours. Aided by macadamisation, a network of stage services rapidly covered the country and flourished until the coming of the railways in the 1830s.

(2) Coaches apart, the main types of carriage were (a) *Two-wheelers* (i) One, horse, two person, open and driven from the seat: **gigs, chaises** and **cabriolets;** (ii) similar but with a dickey for one or two grooms: **curricles;** (iii) similar but covered and driven by a coachman from the dickey: **hansoms;** (b) *Four-wheelers* (i) one or two-horse, two person, open and driven from the seat: **buggies** and **phaetons;** (ii) two-horse two to four person, open and driven from a front box: **barouches** and **victorias;** (iii) similar but two-person and covered: **broughams;** (iv) two or four-horse, four person, closed with dickey and grooms, driven from a front box: **landaus.** All the open types had adjustable canopies. A special doubled overcoat was developed for coachmen and grooms who worked in the open. Victorias, barouches and landaus were and are ceremonial vehicles, when open.

(3) Horses being expensive to maintain, private carriages were confined to the well-to-do, but in 1824 300 were passing Hyde Park Corner daily. Broughams, introduced in 1829, were common in towns and still seen in London as late as 1930. Heavily horsed **drays** delivered coal until 1939. Gigs, usual in the country, are probably not extinct. See also CAB.

CARRIAGEWAY. *See* HIGHWAY.

CARRICK. *See* BRUCE.

CARRINGTON. *See* PRIMROSE; SMITH.

CARRON (Stirling); CARRON COMPANY, CARRONADE. The Carron ironworks were opened in 1760. In 1776

Gen. Robert Melville invented a short cannon with a large bore and a small firing chamber intended to smash rather than penetrate fortifications and ships' hulls. These were called *carronades* and were widely used by the British in the Napoleonic wars. *See* ARTILLERY; FIREARMS.

CARSON, Edward Henry (1854-1935) Ld. CARSON (1921) (1) Irish barrister (1877), became sol-gen. for Ireland and M.P. for Dublin University in 1892, was called to the English Bar in 1893, became a Q.C. in 1894 and established a brilliant reputation in 1895 by his handling of the defence in *Oscar Wilde* v *The Marquess of Queensbury*. He refused office but in 1900 became English Sol-Gen. in the Unionist govt. which continued until 1905.

(2) The maintenance of the Anglo-Irish union was the political passion of his life and in Jan. 1910 he became leader of the Irish Unionists in the Commons; he refused to be considered for the leadership of the Tory party in 1911 because unionism was more important to him. In the debates over the Parliament Bill he used his eloquence to demonstrate that if the bill were enacted, Home Rule could follow automatically. Consistently with this view the Ulster Unionists began to arm and offered him their leadership, which he accepted. By Apr. 1912 the Ulster Volunteer Force (U.V.F.) had grown to many thousands and Carson was able to say that Ulster could not be ruled from Dublin save as a conquered province. As a result a liberal backbencher moved an amendment to the govt's Home Rule Bill excluding four of the Ulster counties. Carson advised acceptance, but meanwhile organised the signature of the *Ulster Covenant* (Sept. 1912) and then moved to exclude the whole of Ulster. This was defeated and the bill was then thrown out by the Lords. It now became clear that the govt. intended to use the Parliament Act to get the bill through and the arming of the U.V.F. was stepped up. The importation of arms was prohibited in Dec. 1913, the U.V.F. took to gun running, the navy was despatched to Arran to deal with it and in Mar. 1914 the "Curragh Mutiny" brought home to all concerned the real possibility of a civil war. The govt. offered a county option limited to six years; a conference at Buckingham Palace broke down in July, but at this point World War I broke out and the controversy was put into cold storage by the passage and suspension of the Home Rule Act, and a promise of amending legislation before the suspension could end.

(3) Carson disliked this, but thought that the war was more important, and persuaded the U.V.F. to enlist *en masse*. He became Att-Gen. in Asquith's govt. (May 1915) but was soon disenchanted with the muddled prosecution of the war. Moreover, when the Easter Rebellion of 1916 occurred, the govt. proposed to negotiate to bring the Act into force immediately, subject to the exclusion of six Ulster counties. Carson undertook to persuade the Ulstermen to agree on the basis that the exclusion would be permanent. The Irish nationalists agreed on the basis that it would be temporary. The negotiations broke down. In July 1916 Lloyd George gave an assurance that the six counties would never be forced into home rule, but Carson doubted the govt's willingness or ability to stick by the pledge and resigned in Oct. This precipitated Asquith's fall, and Carson then became First Lord of the Admiralty in Lloyd George's new govt. until July 1917, when he joined the War Cabinet.

(4) He had taken office on the understanding that Ulster would not be put under Home Rule. In Mar. 1917 T.P. O'Connor raised the issue, and with Carson's agreement a convention of representative Irishmen under Sir Horace Plunket discussed the issue for many months. Lloyd George said that he would introduce legislation if substantial agreement was reached. None was, but Lloyd George determined in Jan. 1918 to introduce legislation based on the majority (southern Irish) report. Carson promptly resigned. At the election in Dec. 1918 Lloyd George and Bonar Law both undertook not to put the Home Rule Act into effect until Ireland was sufficiently settled, and the govt. announced its intention to amend it. The Act could be brought into force at any time simply by a legal termination of the war, but there was no amending bill. The situation of Ulster was thus highly precarious, and when the govt's amending bill was introduced in Feb. 1920 Carson had to support it because there was no hope of repealing the Act. In Feb. 1921 he resigned the leadership of the Ulster Unionists and in May became a Lord of Appeal. A savage and powerful advocate and orator, Ulster owed its existence to his passionate sincerity and organising ability. *See* IRELAND F; NORTHERN.

***CARTAE BARONUM* (Lat = Baronial writings)** (1166) were tenants-in-chiefs' returns of the number and names of their enfeoffed knights. Relatively few knights' fees had apparently been created since 1135. Most of these tenants alleged, in effect, that they had already enfeoffed more knights than they needed to perform their military obligations. Henry II accordingly made little progress in raising the obligations correspondingly.

***CARTAE NATIVORUM* (Lat = Charters of peasants or villeins)** was a 14th cent. register of deeds of Peterborough Abbey lands. Most concerned small areas (1 rood to 2 acres) and most of the parties were peasants or even villeins. It illustrates an active small scale land market which must have been operating for some time. Unlike a manorial court roll, grants are recorded for a rent and the transactions are drafted as for free land.

CARTAGENA (Venezuela), the largest and richest port of the Spanish Main, was founded in 1533. It had the largest slave market in America and as a starting point for the *Galeones* annually accumulated huge stocks of silver and merchandise. Though powerfully guarded it was sacked by pirates in 1544 and by Drake in 1586.

***CARTA MERCATORIA* (1303)** exempted West European, German, Lombard and Tuscan merchants from municipal dues for paving, bridges and walls and granted freedom to deal wholesale, to export and to lodge where they pleased. They were entitled to summary justice 'according to the law merchant' from municipal officials who became punishable for misdoing. If the mayor and sheriffs of London did not hold their court daily, another judge was appointed to supplement their jurisdiction. In all but capital cases half the jury was to consist of foreign merchants, and future municipal charters were not to infringe the rights thus conferred. In return they were liable to pay the New, Little or Petty Custom (q.v.). The financial effect of the charter, when the Petty Custom was not in suspense, was to transfer taxable resources from the municipal corporations to the Crown. The value to the Crown rose only slowly as and when cloth exports outstripped imports. In Tudor times the low rate tended to favour foreign traders in unfinished fabrics.

***CARTE BLANCHE* (Fr = blank paper).** Originally an unconditional surrender, because the surrendering commander sent a signed blank sheet to his opponent, leaving the latter to fill in his terms.

CARTEL (1) is an association of businesses for the purpose of raising, through monopolistic practices, the profits of each. The word was first used by a German liberal deputy in 1879. A *domestic* cartel is confined to a single country. A *horizontal* cartel is an association, at a given level, of businesses which would otherwise be in competition. A *vertical* cartel is an association of businesses at different levels which ties each to the one above, e.g. of a wholesaler with retailers of the same goods. One special form is the *Interessengemeinschaft* (Ger = Community of interests) which involves pooling profits. Another is the *group*, in which a major or *holding co.* controls a series of *subsidiaries* by owning a majority of its shares. These are sometimes acquired by means of a take-over bid in which private shareholders are persuaded to sell to the holding company at a price well above the current market value. This process is encouraged by the common undervaluation of assets. See MONOPOLIES LEGISLATION. **(2)** A ship flying a flag of truce. **(3)** An arrangement to exchange prisoners during a war.

CARTERET. Jersey family. **(1) Sir Philip de (1584-1643)** seigneur of St. Ouen and Sark was lieut-gov. of Jersey from 1626. He showed kindness to Wm. Prynne, who was confined there, and when accused by the islanders in 1642 was excused from appearing before the Lords on Prynne's intervention. His nephew **(2) Sir George (?1616-80),** a naval officer, served in Rainborough's second expedition against Sallee, and when the civil war broke out established himself at St. Malo, whence he supplied the royalists in the west and the Channel Is. He developed Jersey as a supply and privateering base. His royalism and skill were rewarded by a knighthood and by the grant of New Jersey. He repulsed a commonwealth attack in 1650, but was forced to surrender in Dec. 1651. He then entered the French navy but was imprisoned in 1657 and thereafter went to Venice. At the Restoration he became V-Chamberlain of the Household and a privy councillor, and in 1661 an M.P. He was also Treasurer of the Navy and during the Great Plague kept the fleet at sea largely on his personal credit. As a result of defeat by the Dutch he was obliged to exchange his post for the dep. treasurership of Ireland in June 1667, but a parliamentary inquiry revealed much laxity in the financial administration of the navy and he was suspended from the Commons. All the same, in 1673 he became a commissioner of the Admiralty as well as a member of the Board of Trade and the Tangier Committee. Not surprisingly he became very rich, though Pepys, who found him difficult, thought him honest. Charles II intended to elevate him to the peerage just before he died, but in the event the peerage had to be conferred upon his grandson **(3) George (1667-95) 1st Ld. CARTERET of HAWNES (1681).** His son **(4) John (1690-1763) 1st E. GRANVILLE (1744)** entered the Lords in 1711 as a supporter of the Hanoverians. He became a gentleman of the Bedchamber to George I in 1714 and Bailiff of Jersey in 1715. In addition his mother, who was co-heiress of the wealthy third E. of Bath was created Countess Granville with remainder to him. In 1717 he became a supporter of Sutherland and in 1719 he secured the first opportunity for his negotiating talents as ambassador to Sweden. The Baltic being vital to English shipping, he mediated in the local war being waged by Sweden against Denmark and Russia, obtained freedom of navigation for British trade and persuaded the powers to sign the P. of Stockholm in Mar. 1720. In 1721 he became Sec. of State (southern dept.) under Walpole, against whom he began to intrigue. He was the only minister who spoke German to a King who spoke no English. He apparently furnished the opposition with the facts leading to the scandal of Wood's Halfpence, which created uproar in Ireland. Walpole retaliated by having him made Lord Lieut. of Ireland in 1724. He became intimate with Swift, to whose advice he often listened, and his Irish administration was locally popular. Dismissed in 1730, he joined Pulteney in opposition. In Feb. 1741 he moved a sensational but unsuccessful prayer for Walpole's dismissal. When the govt. however fell in Jan. 1742, Carteret became Sec. of State (north) under Wilmington. Noted for his fondness for the bottle, a brief ascendancy over the Hanoverian King was labelled the "Drunken Administration". His pro-Austrian policy against Prussia was unpopular because it was thought to be carried on in the interest of Hanover without consulting his colleagues. Henry Pelham became Prime Minister in July 1743 and in Dec. Carteret was savagely attacked by Pitt. Shortly after succeeding to his mother's Granville title in 1744 he resigned. In 1746 he made an unsuccessful attempt to form a govt. but in 1751

he became Lord President, an office which he continued to hold regardless of the govt. in power until his death. As a personal friend of the King, he exercised through this political anomaly much of the function of the modern constitutional monarch. See WARS OF (1739-48)-5-9.

CARTHUSIAN ORDER (WHITE MONKS). A monastic society was formed by St. Bruno in 1084 at La Grande Chartreuse (whence its name) in the French Alps, to seek union with God through contemplation, silent solitary spiritual exercises and celebration of the liturgy. Bruno never intended to form an order and wrote no rule, but as other communities wished to adopt the Carthusian way of life the prior, Guiges du Chatel, set down the customs of La Grande Chartreuse for them in 1127. Several Carthusian houses (*Charterhouses*) were set up in England, notably the first at Whitham by St. Hugh of Lincoln in 1175-6, and the important one at Clerkenwell, London, by Edward III's general, Sir Walter Manny, in 1349.

CARTIER, Jacques. See CANADA-2.

CARTIMANDUA. See BRIGANTES; BRITAIN, ROMAN-3,4.

CARTOGRAPHY. Before 1300 maps were mainly illustrations of preconceived ideas. In about 1270 pilots' books of sailing directions called PORTOLANS began to have charts derived from observation. These related to the Mediterranean, the Black Sea and parts of the European Atlantic and were drawn by Italians. In 14th cent. cartographical skill moved to Barcelona and a Catalan map of 1375, made for the K. of France, shows the results of exploration. Mauro's Venetian map of 1459 represents the world as a wheel, but contains much accurate information on Africa and Asia. Ptolemy's *Geography* was printed in Latin in 1475 and Martin Behaim, a German employed by P. Henry of Portugal, made a terrestrial globe in 1492. At this time the earth was believed to be much smaller than it is, and this led to attempts to reach China by sailing westwards. The discoveries created great interest in map making. The Casa da India at Lisbon and the Casa de la Contratacion at Seville (as responsible pilotage authorities) naturally led the way. Their *plane charts* were drawn by compass bearing and dead reckoning; they distorted East-West distances in high latitudes and made no allowances for magnetic variations which were extreme in the Americas. Triangulation was being discussed in the 1530s and it circumvented some of these difficulties. The Flemish geographer, Gerardus MERCATOR's (1512-94) projection of 1569 solved the first of the problems: but attempts to deal with the magnetism were made earlier and, in the nature of the case, had to be pursued longer. By 1575 interest in navigation had transferred the foremost of the cartographic centres to Antwerp (then under the Spanish Crown) and the first printed seaman's atlas was Waghenaer's *Spieghel der Zeevaerdt* (Mirror of Navigation) of 1584. Dutch inspiration soon reached England where Molyneux's globe was made in 1592. For a while technical progress was slow until the Paris Observatory was opened in 1671. Thenceforth the world survey, with improved instruments, proceeded. The British Ordnance Survey was set up in 1791; the Hydrographic Office in 1795. During World War I aerial photography came into use and increased the speed and accuracy of surveys. By the end of World War II the R.A.F. had mapped virtually the whole of enemy occupied Europe in great detail.

CARTWRIGHT (1) John (1740-1820) was a man of principle. He was a successful junior officer in the Royal Navy but retired in 1777 because he was against American taxation and did not wish to sail with the fleet against the rebels. He became an ardent political reformer who published tracts and held meetings on every public subject, especially manhood suffrage, slavery, freeing Greece and the Spanish autocracy. His brother **(2) Edmund (1743-1823),** a clergyman and fellow of Magdalen College, Oxford, while visiting weaving shops at Matlock thought of a weaving mill and patented his power-loom in 1785-7. In 1787 he built a power-loom works at Doncaster, but went bankrupt because of local, sometimes violent, opposition. He was eventually rewarded by parliament.

CARTWRIGHT, Thomas (1535-1603) was a presbyterian intellectual who systematised puritan doctrines. His controversies with Abp. Whitgift and his attack on the Elizabethan Anglican settlement provoked Hooker to write his great *Laws of Ecclesiastical Polity*. Whitgift deprived him in 1570 and thereafter he travelled the continent, with intervals in the Fleet prison.

CARUCATE, CARUCAGE. *See* HIDE.

CARVEL. *See* SHIPS, SAILING.

CARVER, John (?1575-1621) was an English Congregationalist who went to Leyden in 1608 where he became a deacon of Robinson's church. In Sept. 1620 he sailed in the *Mayflower* with the Pilgrim Fathers whose expedition he had encouraged. They made him gov. of the Plymouth Colony in Dec. In Mar. 1621 he made a treaty with the Indians. He was re-elected gov. next day, but died in Apr.

CARVETII. Small British tribe around Carlisle.

CARY (1) Sir Henry (?-1633) 1st (Scots) Vist. FALKLAND (1620) fought on the continent, was a gentleman of the bedchamber to James I from 1608 and became Comptroller of the Household and a Privy Councillor in 1617. He was Lord Deputy of Ireland from 1622 and, after trying to intensify action against R. Catholic priests, was active though not very skilful in Charles I's negotiations with the Irish on the so-called Graces: in return for £120,000 the Irish Catholics were to be permitted to practice at the bar, to hold certain minor offices, and land titles for 60 years back were to be validated. The whole settlement was to be confirmed by an Irish Act. They paid the money but puritan influence prevented the passing of the Act, so that land titles remained doubtful. Falkland, who had difficulty in working with Ld. Loftus, the Irish Lord Chancellor was recalled in 1629. His wife **(2) Elizabeth (1585-1639)** was a R. Catholic and a literary defender of her faith. They separated in 1625. Their son **(3) Lucius (?1610-43)** was brought up mainly by his mother. He was M.P. for Newport (I. of Wight) in the Short and Long Parliaments where he was of a strongly 'liberal' disposition. He denounced Laud's ecclesiastical policy and supported Strafford's attainder, but would have nothing to do with the proposed abolition of episcopacy. With Hyde he helped to form, in the autumn of 1641, a party against Pym and his allies. He became Charles I's Sec. of State and went with him to York. He tried to negotiate a settlement with parliament in Sept. 1642 but his efforts foundered on parliamentary intransigence and royal unreliability. Despairing of civil peace he threw away his life at the first B. of Newbury.

CASABLANCA, Louis de (1755-98) Corsican commodore commanding the French flagship *Orient* at the B. of the Nile. His son "stood on the burning deck" and perished with him when the ship blew up. They are celebrated in verse by Mrs Hemans and André Chenier.

CASABLANCA CONFERENCE (Jan. 1943) between the U.S. Pres. Rooseveldt and Winston Churchill, was held to deal with political problems arising from the allied landings in N. Africa of the previous Nov., especially the claims of Gen. de Gaulle to represent the French. *See also* ALEXANDER, H.R.L.G.

CASEMENT, Sir Roger David (1864-1916) served on the Niger from 1883 and in 1895 became Consul-gen. at Lourenço Marques, Loanda and in 1898 at Boma (Congo). His sensational report, published in 1904, on the cruel European trading practices on the Congo led, in 1908, to the transfer of the Congo from the Belgian crown to the Belgian State and reforms in its govt. From 1906 to 1911 he held consular posts in Brazil and in 1911 published a similar report on trading along the Putumayo R., for which he was knighted.

In 1913 he retired to Ireland where, as an extreme nationalist, he took part in forming the Irish National Volunteers. After World War I broke out he went via the U.S.A. to Berlin. Here he tried, and failed, to recruit an Irish brigade from prisoners of war. He also found that the Germans could not risk an expedition to Ireland and so, on hearing of the plans for an Irish rising, he tried to prevent it. A shipload of arms was, however, sent and a submarine landed Casement (who said that he meant to stop the rising) on the Kerry coast in Apr. 1916. He and the arms were captured and after a trial for treason he was hanged.

CASE OF THE ARMIE truly stated **(Oct. 1647)** issued by new regimental agitators, demanded that as soldiers the troops should have arrears of pay and indemnification, but as free commons they had rights and liberties. A law paramount should provide for biennial parliaments freely elected by all citizens over 21 and the Commons alone should be able to make or repeal laws. Social grievances were to be mended and in particular customs duty on foreign imports should replace excises on English products, especially beer, cloth and stuffs. The agitators were seeking to minimise the divergence of interest between the military and the civilians who paid for them, and direct criticism from both at the parliamentary majority. They also attacked the high command for diluting the army's demands and trying to damp down radicalism. At the PUTNEY DEBATES, the agitators surprised the officers by bringing in the more moderate AGREEMENT OF THE PEOPLE, but many of Cromwell and Ireton's arguments were directed against the Case. *See* CHARLES I-27.

CASEY, Richard Gardiner (1890-76) Ld. BERWICK (1960) became an Australian M.P. in 1931 and held several lesser ministerial posts until he became Min. for Supply and Development in 1939. In 1940 he left politics to become Australian minister at Washington, where he impressed everyone with his ability to such an extent that Churchill invited him to become a member of the British War Cabinet as Min. of State in the Middle East. He held this position from 1942 to 1943 and then became gov. of Bengal from 1944 to 1946. He then rejoined Australian politics as Pres. of the Liberal Party and in 1951 became Min. of External Affairs. He resigned on becoming a life peer, but in 1965 returned yet again to Australia, this time as Gov-Gen. He was made a KG in 1969

CASHEL (a rocky outcrop in C. Tipperary, Ireland) and its **SYNODS.** It was the seat by the 7th cent. of the Kings of Munster, and from 1111 was the second Archbishopric of Ireland. A cathedral was built on the rock in the early 12th cent. and in the 13th cent. a more ambitious Gothic building replaced it. Remains of each survive. The Synod of 1101, when the King gave Cashel to the Irish Church, promulgated major reforms which went far towards freeing the Church from secular controls. The Synod of 1171-2, after Henry II's invasion, completed the approximation of Celtic with Western church practices both liturgically and administratively, especially in an organised system of tithes.

CASKET LETTERS were eight letters and some sonnets allegedly written by Mary Q. of Scots to Bothwell in French. Letter II, if genuine, implicated Mary in the murder of Darnley. Bothwell is supposed to have kept them in a silver casket and given them to Sir James Balfour of Pittendreich who, after the defeat at Carberry Hill (June 1567) caused them to be taken by the protestant lords, after he or William Maitland had abstracted a bond to murder Darnley. Translated into Scots and English they were used to discredit Mary and prevent her return from England. The E. of Morton had them until his execution in 1581 when they passed to the E. of Gowrie, who refused to part with them to Q.

Elizabeth. At his execution in 1584 they disappeared. To this not very probable story is opposed a story equally full of difficulties, that the crucial letter II is a protestant forgery. *See* DOUGLAS (MORTON)-3

CASSANDRA. A Trojan prophetess who always foresaw the true future and was never believed. The name was, oddly enough, used as the pseudonym for a column in the *Daily Mirror* between the World Wars.

CASSEL, Sir Ernest (1852-1921) *s.* of a Cologne banker, worked his way up from a Liverpool corn chandlers office until he became one of the richest financiers. *Inter alia* he financed the Aswan dam in Egypt (1898) and the London central tube line (1900) and negotiated state loans for foreign countries including Mexico and China. He was also an important philanthropist. He retired in 1910.

CASSILLIS. *See* KENNEDY.

CASSINO, MONTE. *See* BENEDICTINES. In World War II it was turned into a stronghold by the Germans and almost destroyed in the Allied advance from Salerno (1943).

CASSITERIDES. The source of tin in the ancient world. Described as islands, they may have been Cornwall or some islands off C. Finisterre.

CASSIVELAUNUS or CASWALLON. *See* CATUVELLAUNI.

CASTE is a functional division of society sanctioned by custom, law or religion and social pressure. Entry to a caste is strictly limited, often simply by birth: exit is possible only by expulsion for breach of a social taboo or ceremonial pollution. A member of a caste is, and feels, set aside for the social purpose of the caste. In this rigid form caste has not been a feature of European society, and though social distinctions have always been accepted, there has been a degree of social mobility, particularly in England. Hereditary caste, however, was a fundamental characteristic of the Hindu population of India before and during the British involvement. The castes were minutely specialised and extremely numerous: there were even castes of robbers. This extremity of subdivision made Indian society uniquely static. It was possible, especially among the lower castes, to change status only by a change of religion, by flight or during civil turmoil. The Europeans (French, Portuguese, English, Dutch and Danish) fitted fairly well into this situation; they were treated by local custom as a caste of their own. As a generalisation castes were divided into four main groups. Theoretically *Brahmins,* the highest, were priests and teachers; the *Kshatriya,* the next, were warriors; the *Vaisya* were the merchants and skilled artisans; the *Sudra* were the manual labourers. *Outcasts* were those originally of any caste who for some reason such as ceremonial pollution had lost, but might regain, their caste. At the bottom of the scale were the *Untouchables.* Very common in the south, they probably represented the remnants of an ancient Dravidian aboriginal stock; the Sudras possibly a later invasion; the Brahmins and Kshatriya a still later imposed and subsisting aristocracy. The system was not, however, tidy. The princes, for example, were mostly Kshatriya, but some were Brahmins. In some areas physical contact between an Untouchable and anyone else would pollute the latter. In others it would pollute only a Brabmin. In the south a Brahmin could be polluted by the mere sight of one. In yet others anyone might be polluted by contact with someone of any caste inferior to his own. A journey across the ocean, and the consumption of beef, were both widely held to involve pollution of the gravest kind. The practical effects of pollution were serious. A person had a position in a village and rights in the communal property by virtue of his function, which depended on his caste. Loss of caste made him not only ritually unclean and socially unapproachable, but had much the same effect as expulsion from a trade union in a closed shop. Ritual cleansing to regain his status might take time, involve elaborate and nasty ceremonies and cost

large sums in fees to the priesthood. Though the caste structure was hierarchical and gave privilege, power and in practice wealth to the three highest castes, Hindu thought and law also contemplated correlative obligations. In theory, at least, criminals were to be punished with increasing severity the higher their caste, and renunciation of worldly advantage was, and is, widely respected.

CASTELNAUDARY (Fr). A strategic town in the gap between Toulouse and Carcassonne, often besieged by the English or the French in the middle ages.

CASTIGLIONE, Baldassare (1478-1529), an Italian statesman, wrote his conversation piece *Il Cortegiano* (It = The Courtier) in 1514 and published it in 1528. The scene is the court of Urbino under the presidency of the Duchess, and sets forth every qualification of the perfect courtier. Sir Thomas Hoby (1530-66) translated it into English. A *chef d'oeuvre* of classical Tuscan, it is regarded as a companion piece to *The Prince* (1519) by Castiglione's contemporary, Niccolo Machiavelli. The book influenced Tudor writers, e.g. Sidney, Spenser, Surrey and Wyatt, and the social habits of ruling families, their friends and the ambitious all over Europe. Castiglione visited the court of Henry VII in 1506.

CASTILE and LEON (Spain). Castile was united under one crown with Leon from 1037 to 1065 and again from 1072 to 1157. In 1188, however, Alfonso VIII forced the King of Leon to do homage. By this time Castilian territory marched with Aragon and reached the Tagus, but the Leonese did not accept the Castilians' superiority and refused to join with them in the Almohad Wars. In 1230, however, Ferdinand III succeeded to both thrones and the two countries, with their capital at Burgos, were never separated again. By now their political hegemony in Spain was a recognised fact. In the years 1383 to 1385 John I of Castile failed to conquer Portugal in right of his wife. He was defeated by an Anglo-Portuguese force (*see* AVIS) at Aljubarrota (1385) and the Anglo-Portuguese T. of Windsor (1386) was followed by a joint counter-attack which equally failed. Castile naturally allied herself with the French (*see* AQUITAINE) and it was a Franco-Castilian intrigue which in 1412 placed the Castilian Ferdinand of Trastamara on the vacant Aragonese throne. *See* SPAIN 1406-1516.

CASTLE, Barbara (1910-) Lady CASTLE of BLACKBURN (1979), *Daily Mirror* journalist and left wing local councillor, was Labour M.P. for Blackburn from 1945 to 1979 and a strong supporter of Aneurin Bevan and Jenny Lee. She was Harold Wilson's Min. for Overseas Development in 1964-5, and Sec. of State for Transport from 1965 to 1968. Though her efforts at transport co-ordination mostly failed, she was memorable as the introducer of breathalisations. She then became Sec. of State for Employment (to which Productivity had been tacked to indicate a departure) but her policy to reduce industrial unrest (set out in her White Paper *In Place of Strife*) by compulsory delays and strike ballots was frustrated by a combination of the T.U.C. and the Labour left wing. In the second Wilson govt., as Sec. of State for Health, she secured the doctrinaire abolition of pay-beds in hospitals. Callaghan offered her no office. She opposed the manner of European integration as settled by the various treaties and was a Euro-M.P. from 1979 to 1989 in order, not very effectually, to influence events. Widely regarded as of prime-ministerial timber, she was exposed to political dangers by accepting her offices under Wilson.

CASTLE GUARD, a common obligation of knight service, was more regular and often more burdensome than service in the field, because from 1066 until well into the 14th cent. castles needed garrisons. Richmond Castle (Yorks) needed bi-monthly shifts of 30 knights. It was sometimes performed at a considerable distance. The 40 knights of Bury St. Edmunds did three months a year each at Norwich; some Northamptonshire knights had duties at Dover and those near Abingdon had to hold Windsor. The weight of these impositions early led to commutations for money, which were fixed under Henry II at 6d or 8d per day per knight. Such sums were still being paid long after the strategic purpose of the castle had vanished; even sometimes as late as the 18th cent.

CASTLEMAN. A free, but socially low, tenant in the north who was obliged to serve in the garrison of a local castle, especially in Durham. *See* DRENG; DURHAM-5.

CASTLES. *See* MILITARY ARCHITECTURE. MEDIAEVAL-2 *et seq.*

CASTLE ASHBY (N'hants) built in 1574 was refaced by Inigo Jones in 1635. The seat of the M. of Northampton.

CASTLE CHAMBER, Court of the. The Irish equivalent of the Star Chamber.

CASTLEHAVEN, Es. of. *See* TOUCHET.

CASTLE HOWARD (Yorks). Palladian palace built by Vanbrugh and Hawksmoor between 1699 and 1726 for the Howard Es. of Carlisle.

CASTLE or CORNWALL SCANDALS (Ir) 1884. William O'Brien in the *United Irishman* exposed a coterie of sodomites, some of whom were govt. officials. He successfully defended a libel action and those concerned were prosecuted. His purpose was to vilify the Lord Lieut.

CASTLEMAINE, Barbara, Countess of. *See* VILLIERS and PALMER.

CASTLEREAGH. *See* STEWART.

CASUS BELLI **(Lat = occasion for war).** Self defence has always been a *casus belli*. Ultimata were habitually drafted to throw the blame on the other side. Apart from self defence, the Charter of the U.N. now restricts *casus belli* to wars authorised by the Security Council.

CAT. *See* COLLIER; WHITTINGTON.

CATALOGUS SANCTORUM HIBERNIAE **(Lat = List of the Holy Ones of Ireland) (9th or 10th cent.)** classified the old Irish churchmen into three orders of diminishing sanctity, viz:- The First, consisting of northerners instructed by St. Patrick; the Second, mostly Munster presbyters, instructed by the Welsh saints David, Gildas and Docus; and the Third, consisting of hermits and anchorites Bishops were rare The author seems to have meant to exalt the northern church, at the expense of the earlier southern churches.

CATALONIA. In 1137 the Catalan Count Raymond Berenger IV married Petronilla of Aragon, and thenceforth Catalonia and Aragon were under one ruler, but remained distinct. Catalan commercial and mercenary interests under a Catalan dynasty dominated the Mediterranean and the union, until the dynasty died out in 1410. It was succeeded by the inland Aragonese family of Trastamara. Dissatisfaction developed into rebellion in 1462, which was suppressed by John II in 1472. His son Ferdinand, married Isabella of Castile, and in the resulting Hispanic federation Catalonia was relegated to a still less significant position. Crown policy reserved the exploitation of the New World to the Castilians, while Spanish naval effort failed to protect Catalan trade against Turkish and Barbary fleets. The decline of Catalan prosperity was aggravated by attempts to restore the collapsing finances of the crown, now involved in the Thirty Years' War. Philip IV and Olivares sought in 1626 to impose a centralisation which infringed the charters (fueros) of the two provinces. Both *cortes* blocked the proposals until 1635, when war broke out with France. Rising taxes and Castilian billeting brought a revolt in June 1640. French armies supported the rebels, and Catalonia was mostly under French occupation until 1659, and again between 1689 and 1697, during the War of the Grand Alliance. In the War of the Spanish Succession the Catalans in defence of their *fueros* supported the Habsburg claimant Charles against the French from 1705 onwards and so lost all their political rights when, as a result of Britain's abandonment of her allies at the T. of

Utrecht, the Bourbon Philip I became K. of Spain. This was the origin both of political Carlism and later Catalan nationalism, which remained impotent but latent until 1930. At this time a left wing Catalan coalition, the *Esquerra Republicana,* arose under Francesco Macia, won the municipal elections of Apr. 1931 and proclaimed a republic. In Sept. 1932 a statute of autonomy was agreed with the provisional republic at Madrid. In consequence the Catalans formed the principal support of the Republicans in the Civil War of 1936 to 1939 and suffered the worst repression under the nationalist regime.

'CAT-AND-MOUSE ACT' (1913) was passed against determinedly hunger-striking suffragettes. It enabled them to be released and re-arrested instead of force-fed.

CATCH. A humorous or witty form of distinctively English musical round. Catch clubs were common gentlemen's assemblies especially between 1660 and 1750; the catches sung were not, invariably, proper. *See* MUSICAL CLUBS; GLEE.

CATCHLAND (Norfolk). Land common to more than one parish. The parson who first seized the tithes could have them for the year.

CATECHISMS are elementary prescribed manuals of Christian doctrine, often in question and answer form. The word was first used in the 16th cent. but the council of Lambeth issued one in 1281; Gerson wrote his *A.B.C. des Simples Gens* at the beginning of the 15th cent. and Colet another in about 1510. Protestantism with its emphasis on teaching released a flood of them. Thereafter the most important were:- Martin Luther's *Kleiner Katechismus* (1529); *The Shorter Catechism* (1547) (Anglican); St. Peter Canisius *Summa Doctrinae Christianae* (1554) (R. Catholic); the *Heidelberger Katechismus* (1563) (Calvinist); the revised *Shorter Catechism* (1604) (Anglican); and the *Penny Catechism* (1898) (R. Catholic). The so-called *Roman* Catechism (1566) is a manual for priests.

CATERANS. Highland irregular swordsmen or bandits, and the Lowland term for them or other marauders.

CATESBY, Robert (1573-1605) a wealthy R. Catholic fanatic was wounded in the Essex revolt of 1601 and heavily fined. In 1602 he was intriguing with Spain and in 1603 he was briefly imprisoned as part of the precautions to anticipate Q. Elizabeth's death. Placing no faith in James I's promises of partial toleration, he decided in May 1603 to blow up the King and Parliament, but postponed action. The proclamation against priests of Jan. 1604 decided him to go forward and he took his cousin Thos. Winter, his friends, Thos. Percy and John Wright, and Guy Fawkes, a professional soldier, who was to be the technician, into his confidence. The plot was 18 months in preparation. Catesby widened the circle of conspirators and among these was Thos. Tresham. The latter's note to Ld. Monteagle led to the discovery of the plot. Catesby was killed resisting arrest in Staffordshire.

CATHARI. *See* ALBIGENSIANS.

CATHAY. China.

CATHCART. (1) Charles (1721-76) 9th Ld. (Sc) CATHCART, a soldier and protégé of the D. of Cumberland, was minister at St. Petersburg from 1768-71 and thereafter C-in-C in Scotland. His son **(2) Sir William Schaw (1755-1843) 10th Ld., 1st Vist. (1807), 1st E. (1814) CATHCART** served against the rebels in America, became a Scots representative peer in 1788, served at Quiberon in 1793, ingloriously in Hanover from 1794 to 1795 and as C-in-C in Ireland from 1803 to 1805, when he was briefly and unluckily again in Hanover. In 1807 he bombarded Copenhagen. He was military commissioner with the Russians from 1813 to 1814 and ambassador to St. Petersburg from 1814 to 1821. His son **(3) Sir George (1794-1854)** as C-in-C in S. Africa (1852-4) won important victories over the Basutos and Kaffirs, and commanded the 4th Division in the Crimea, where he vainly urged a speedy attack on Sevastopol, and was killed at Inkerman.

CATHEDRAL is a church which contains a bishop's throne (Cathedra). It or its predecessor was the original church of the see, served by the bishop and his household, but as parish churches were built and bishops acquired private chapels, its management was committed to a separate corporate foundation called the **Chapter.** In mediaeval England the cathedrals of Chichester, Exeter, Hereford, Lichfield, Lincoln, Salisbury, Wells and York had secular chapters (now called Old Foundations) while Canterbury, Durham, Ely, Norwich, Rochester, Winchester and Worcester were Benedictine and Carlisle was Augustinian.

After the Norman reforms the secular chapters were headed by a Dean; and there was a Precentor responsible for music and ceremony, a Treasurer and a Chancellor responsible for preaching and the Cathedral school. The bishops generally appointed the members of such chapters other than the Dean, and in theory it elected the bishop, though papal and royal encroachment steadily reduced the election to a mere ceremony. Most chapters were free of episcopal jurisdiction.

At the Dissolution (1539-40) the monastic chapters were superseded by so-called New Foundations in which the Dean, as successor to the monastic head was, and is, a more powerful figure than the Dean of an Old Foundation. In addition, part of the funds of the monasteries was applied to convert the collegiate churches at Bristol, Chester, Gloucester, Peterborough and Westminster into cathedrals with New Foundations, while a bishopric was endowed at Oxford, where the episcopal throne was established at Christchurch. The bishopric of Westminster was suppressed in 1550, but the Abbey remained collegiate.

The number was not increased until 1836 when the creation of new modern dioceses and further New Foundations began with Ripon. In the modern foundation the head of the Chapter is called the Provost.

CATHELINEAU, Jacques (1759-93), linen draper and saintly leader of the Vendee peasant revolt against the French revolutionaries, was killed while storming Nantes. His death took the heart out of the movement.

CATHERINE or CATHARINE. See also KATHERINE or KATHARINE.

CATHERINE OF ARAGON (1485-1536) d. of Ferdinand of Aragon and Isabella of Castile (The Catholic Kings) and aunt of the Emperor Charles V, was married at sixteen to Arthur, P. of Wales, in 1501 but he died in 1502 and she was betrothed, under Papal dispensation, to his next brother Henry, who was twelve. She was kept in England until he became King as Henry VIII in 1509 when the marriage was celebrated. They were happy at first despite his bullying temperament and promiscuity and had five children, of whom only the future Mary I survived infancy. When, however, the Boleyns came to court, he first took Mary Boleyn to bed and then fell for her younger sister, Anne, who managed him with greater skill. By 1526 he had decided to doubt the validity of his marriage and separated physically from Catherine, ostensibly until its validity should be confirmed. Actually he began annulment proceedings and Card. Campeggio arrived as legate to hear the case but with instruction to avoid pronouncing sentence, if necessary by adjournment to Rome. This suited Catherine, for the Pope was virtually a prisoner of her nephew (*for later events see* HENRY VIII-12-16; WOLSEY, THOMAS; REFORMATION). She was exiled to various country houses and died at Peterborough.

CATHERINE OF BRAGANZA (1638-1705) d. of the late K. João IV and Q. Luisa de Gusmão, regent of Portugal, married Charles II in 1662 (*for the political and commercial considerations see* CHARLES II-8). They had a lifelong affection rather than passion (which the King reserved for his mistresses) for each other and after initial religious suspicions she was respected for modesty and charity. She had no political influence, but he protected her whenever anyone suggested that she had. She left England in 1693 and died in Portugal.

CATHERINE HOWARD (?-1542), niece of Thomas, 3rd D. of Norfolk, met Henry VIII in 1539. His growing affection for her at the expense of Q. Anne of Cleves assisted Norfolk and his conservative faction against Thomas Cromwell. Anne's marriage to Henry was annulled on 12 July 1540. He married Catherine on 28th. In Nov. 1541 Abp. Cranmer, himself threatened by the religious hostility of the Howards, provided evidence of her pre-marital unchastity with Henry Mannock and Francis Dereham and of her adultery (abetted by her cousin Lady Rochford) with Thomas Culpepper. Dereham and Culpepper were hanged in Dec. A bill of attainder was brought in Jan. 1542 against her and Lady Rochford, by then insane, and passed on 11 Feb., the Royal Assent being given (to spare the King's embarrassment) for the first time by commission. The two were executed on 13th. The speech which she made before putting her head on the block was both touching and elegant. Norfolk's condemnation of his niece failed to preserve the influence of his faction.

CATHERINE DEI MEDICI (1519-89) Q. consort of Henry II of France (r. 1547-59) was of little political account during his reign as against his mistress, Diane de Poitiers. After Francis II died in 1560, however, she became regent for Charles IX and appointed L'Hôpital as Chancellor. She sought to maintain the increasingly precarious position of the throne by balancing the noble and religious factions against each other. As a result she was distrusted by all. The regency ended formally in 1563, but she dominated the court until 1572, when the massacre of St. Bartholomew temporarily gave the supremacy to the Guises and ended hopes of compromise for a generation. Henry III succeeded Charles IX in 1574 and the rise of the Bourbon interest slowly thrust her into the political background. *See* HUGUENOTS-2-13 *and also* COOKERY.

CATHERINE PARR (1512-48), the intelligent and attractive d. of Sir Thos. Parr of Kendal, had been twice widowed by 1542 and was preparing to marry Q. Jane Seymour's brother, Sir Thomas, when she met Henry VIII. She married Henry in July 1543. Her moderate protestantism probably strengthened the influence of Cranmer and Hertford at the end of the reign and she survived attempts, notably in 1546, to intrigue Henry into moving against her and Cranmer as heretics. She lent stability, sensible kindness and association with humanist scholars to the lives of Henry's three children. Immediately after Henry's death she married Sir Thomas, now Lord Howard of Sudeley, who had become the custodian of the Princess Elizabeth. She died in childbirth.

CATHERINE THE GREAT. *See* RUSSIA, PETEINE~8, 9; ANHALT.

CATHERINE OF VALOIS. *See* TUDOR-7.

CATHOLIC ASSOCIATION, founded by Daniel O'Connell in May 1823, began as a body of Irish R. Catholic gentry subscribing £1 a year to redress those particular and practical grievances which could not await emancipation. It was a failure, and in Feb. 1824 he converted it into a mass organisation based on a subscription (the *Catholic Rent*) of 1d a month. It was an immediate success; by 1825 he found himself at the head of a popular movement with substantial funds. This, and his extraordinary character, enabled him to secure R. Catholic emancipation in 1829, when the Association was dissolved. To forestall O'Connell's practice of founding new associations, the Lord Lieut. was given special powers to suppress any potentially subversive society.

CATHOLIC ASSN. OF IRELAND (1902) was formed to give preferential treatment in all branches of activity to R. Catholics, and therefore to boycott protestants. The protestants formed a counter organisation, the SOCIETY FOR THE PROTECTION OF PROTESTANT INTERESTS. The Catholic Assn. was condemned by Abp. Walsh and the Ulster R. Catholics in Jan. 1904 and collapsed.

CATHOLIC COMMITTEE, IRISH (1759-95) was a constitutionalist committee organised mostly by trading and business interests to secure R. Catholic emancipation.

CATHOLIC DEFENDERS. *See* HEARTS OF STEEL.

CATHOLIC HERALD **(1887),** weekly, was founded by Charles Diamond.

CATHOLIC KINGS, THE. A papal title bestowed in 1494 upon Ferdinand of Aragon and his queen, Isabella of Castile (*see* SPAIN 1406-1516 3-7) and used by Spanish sovereigns ever since.

CATHOLIC LEAGUE. *See* HUGUENOTS-13.

CATHOLIC RELIEF ACTS. ("Roman Catholic Emancipation Acts"). (1) By an Irish Act of 1778 R. Catholics were allowed to own land upon taking an oath of allegiance; priests ceased to be liable to proceedings on common information, and it ceased to be an offence to keep a R. Catholic School. The Gordon riots followed. **(2)** By an English Act of 1791 those who took the Oath of Allegiance were freed from the effects of the Statutes of Recusancy, and excused from the Oath of Supremacy. R. Catholic schools and worship were tolerated and the legal and military professions were opened. **(3)** In 1793 R. Catholics in Ireland were admitted to the Irish franchise, universities and professions. **(4)** By the English Act of 1829 most disabilities were abolished except those relating to public religious celebrations and the validity of R. Catholic marriages. **(5)** The Act of 1926 abolished all other restrictions except that the Sovereign, the Regent, the Lord Chancellor and Lord Keeper may not be R. Catholic; that R. Catholics may not exercise advowsons; and that R. Catholic priests may not sit in the House of Commons.

CAT HOUSE. An open sided wheeled shed used to provide cover for besiegers trying to break through a wall with rams or picks.

CATNACH, James (1792-1841) of Seven Dials, London, published many chapbooks, broadsides and ballads concerning past sensational events, mainly robberies, trials and executions. He bought old woodblocks and circulated, as a result, 16th and 17th cent. illustrations which might otherwise have been lost.

CATO'S LETTERS **(1720-22)** by the whigs JOHN TRENCHARD (1662-1723) and THOMAS GORDON (?1691-1750), long series of political articles in the London press, dealt with the constitution, problems of govt. and the dangers of majority rule. They were widely read and often reprinted, especially in the American colonies where, more than any other written opinions, they influenced political activists in favour of a limiting constitution.

CATO, Marcus Porcius (232-147 B.C.) Roman statesman celebrated for his unbending morals, hostility to Carthage and simplicity of life. A type of the republican virtue admired (at a safe distance) by 18th and 19th cent. political writers and historical propagandists.

CATO ST. CONSPIRACY was a wild plot to murder Castlereagh and his cabinet while dining at Ld. Harrowby's in Feb. 1820, and then to set fire to London, seize the Bank and the Mansion House and overthrow what was left of the govt. One conspirator, a butcher, came with two bags for the heads of the ministers. Its leader, Arthur Thistlewood, and four others were hanged. Five others were transported. The discovery caused a sensation because of the disturbed state of the country.

CATTLE. (1) BEEF. *Shorthorns or Durhams* from Teesdale began to be improved through selective breeding by the brothers Colling in the 1780s and the *Shorthorn Herdbook* first appeared in 1822. *Herefords* were already being exported in 1817 (*Hereford Herdbook* 1846). *Aberdeen Angus* breeding began in the early 19th cent. (*Polled Herdbook* 1862). This encouraged the breeding of *Galloways. Devons* were originally used draft animals, but were improved for beef in the 19th cent. (*Devon Herdbook* 1851). *Red Polls* arose in 1846 through the merger of the

Norfolk beef cattle with the *Suffolk* milch kine. **(2) DAIRY.** *Jerseys* and *Guernseys* were legally protected in their respective islands in 1789 and the first English Jersey herd was founded in 1811. *Ayrshires* originated by selective breeding in Scotland in the 1790s. *Frisians,* very common for centuries in Europe, were never much favoured in Britain because their very large milk output was of low quality.

CATTLE ACTS 1663 and 1667 restricted the importation of cattle from Scotland and Ireland into England. The Scots restrictions lapsed at the parliamentary union of 1707; the Irish continued until 1759 and seem to have encouraged the salting of beef for shipping.

CATUVELLAUNI. A powerful Belgic tribe which migrated to Britain in about 120 B.C. Its capital was at Wheathampstead (Herts) at the time of Caesar's invasions (55-4 B.C.) when its King was CASSIVELAUNUS; he was followed by TASCIOVANUS, who in or about A.D. 5 was succeeded by CUNOBELINUS ('CYMBELINE'). He moved the capital to Camulodunum (Colchester) and expanded his power into the S. Midlands and along the Thames Valley. In about A.D. 40 he drove Verica, chief of the Atrebates, into exile. Verica appealed to the Emperor Claudius, and a Roman army under Aulus Plautius landed in Kent in A.D. 43. Cymbeline's sons TOGODUMNUS and CARA(C)TACUS were defeated on the Medway and Claudius himself took Camulodunum. Togodumnus was killed, Caratacus fled to (modern) Wales. The Romans then subdued or took into clienthood the former subject tribes, but their area was continually raided by Ordovices and Dobunni, led by Caratacus, until he was treacherously surrendered by Cartimandua, Q. of the Brigantes, with whom he had taken refuge. Colchester, the principal Roman town in Britain at the time was sacked in Boadicea's (Boudicca's) Icenian rebellion (A.D. 60) probably with Catuvellaunian help, and Roman reprisals ended the tribe as a recognisable entity.

CAUCHON, Pierre (?-1443), execrated Bp. of Beauvais, responsible for the trial and condemnation of Joan of Arc. There is no doubt that there was a mistrial, later reversed by Calixtus III, but the extent to which Cauchon contrived it is less certain.

CAUCUS is a private meeting or group of politicians to concert action, particularly in a constituency. The word, of American origin, spread from the American colonies to Britain in the 1760s.

CAULAINCOURT, Armand Augustin Louis de (1773-1827) Duc de VICENCE (1808) became Bonaparte's A.D.C. in 1802, engineered the kidnapping of the Duc d'Enghien in Mar. 1804 and immediately became Grand Equerry. From Nov. 1807 to Feb. he was ambassador in Russia, where he seems to have tried to keep the peace; on his recall and during the Moscow campaign he was abused as pro-Russian, but he accompanied the Emperor when he abandoned the army and fled to Paris. In June 1813 he negotiated the Silesian armistice, and after the B. of Leipzig replaced Maret as Foreign Minister. Bonaparte used his peaceful intentions as a front, but when his defence crumbled, Caulaincourt negotiated the agreement with the Emperor Alexander which gave Bonaparte imperial status and Elba. During Bonaparte's 100 days he again acted as foreign minister, but Alexander saved him from Bourbon vengeance.

CAUTIONARY TOWNS (1598-1616). *See* JAMES I AND VI-4,14.

CAVALIER. (1) A military partisan of Charles I. The term was originally derogatory. The stereotype of the flamboyantly dressed, long haired Cavalier, contrasting with the sober, short haired Roundhead, is a myth. On both sides personal inclination determined appearance. **(2)** A high fortification or tower built astride of the wall or other works.

CAVALIER or PENSION PARLIAMENT. *See* CHARLES II-4; RESTORATION-8.

CAVAL[L]IER, Jean (1681-1740) adventurous Languedoc

CAVAL[L]IER, Jean (1681-1740)

peasant and baker at Geneva, lead the Camisard revolt in the Cevennes from 1702 to 1704 when he was induced to surrender, commissioned by Louis XIV, but later escaped from Versailles to Switzerland and, after serving with the Piedmontese, raised a Dutch regiment for the English service in Spain. He was wounded at the B. of Almanza (1707) and in 1708 pensioned by the British govt. After a residence in Ireland he became gov. of Jersey.

CAVALRY (*see also* ARMY) **(1)** Ponies were often used to carry mediaeval English and Scots specialists, mainly archers and their equipment, to battle, but mounted fighters were relatively few because of the cost and difficulty of raising powerful chargers. These were needed by heavily protected knights (i.e. officers) as mobile vantage points from which to set an example and direct the fighting. Moreover the English and Scots developed infantry tactics for dealing with organised bodies of horse and routed them at Stirling Bridge, Halidon Hill, Crécy, Poitiers, Agincourt and elsewhere. A British infantry tradition grew up and was maintained in this branch of tactics into the age of firearms, until horses ceased to be used in battle after 1900.

(2) There was a social distinction between foot- and horsemen because the latter originally supplied their own horses and those of their following. They had to be richer and (if officers) were in practice of higher standing and (if troopers) reflected their leaders' status. This social tradition survived long after horses were officially supplied. Knightly valour was their pronounced feature and led, for example, on the same day at Balaclava (1854) to the disaster of Cardigan's Light Brigade and the great victory of Scarlett's Heavy Brigade. Combined with equine excitement, this valour was the probable reason why British cavalry, as at Waterloo, often got out of hand. Once precipitated into a charge there was no stopping them. Relying much on the weight of their mounts to administer battle-shock, the main units of this type were guards and dragoons.

(3) Like pitched battles, onslaughts by cavalry were rare and short. Its main, mostly unsung, work consisted of (a) military and topographical reconnaissance (intelligence). Countrysides being unmapped until the 20th cent., cavalry officers became proficient at sketching landscapes; (b) screening main forces from enemy observation (tactical counter-intelligence); (c) outpost work (security) and (d) message riding (communications). For these vital functions lightly accoutred men with fast, rather than strong, horses were needed and raised as Light Cavalry or Hussars. Lancers, equipped to overreach infantry bayonets, were somewhere between light and heavy cavalry.

(4) Outside battle, horses continued to be used until motorisation came between the World Wars. In this the British Army was ahead of the others. There being more fodder than oil in Europe the German Army, apart from its armoured crust (about 15%) remained horse-drawn and, as the state of the roads attested, fearfully vulnerable to allied air attack on its communications.

CAVAN. *See* LAMBART.

CAVANAGH or CASWALLON. *See* KAVANAGH.

CAVE, Edward. *See* GENTLEMAN'S MAGAZINE.

CAVE, George (1856-1928), Vist. CAVE (1918) was unionist M.P. for Kingston from 1906, became Sol-Gen. in 1915 and in 1916 Home Sec. The wartime Home Office was responsible for compulsory military service, the control of aliens and the administration of censorship, in that war an important branch of intelligence. In Jan. 1919 he went to the House of Lords as a Lord of Appeal. He was Lord Chancellor in 1922, and from 1924 to 1928. He was a respected lawyer rather than a politician and is chiefly remembered in North America as the adjudicator of the boundary between Canada and Newfoundland.

CAVEAT EMPTOR **(Lat: buyer beware)** A distinctive doctrine originating in *Chandelor* v. *Lupus* (1603) Cro.Jac

4, of the English law of sale. A seller was not liable to a purchaser for a defect in a chattel, other than food, unless he expressly warranted that it was free from that defect. The widespread implications were codified in the Sale of Goods Act 1893, since modified by the Unfair Contracts Terms Act 1977.

CAVELL, Edith (1865-1915) became matron of the Berkendael Institute at Brussels in 1907. This became a military hospital in 1914 and when the Germans overran Belgium she helped allied soldiers to escape. She was arrested by the Germans in Aug. 1915 and court-martialled and shot in Oct. The shooting of a woman and nurse at this time caused a sensation and was much used by allied propagandists.

CAVENDISH (Devonshire). (1) Sir John (?-1381), a leading common lawyer, became C.J. of the King's Bench in 1372. One of his judgements is well known: a lady, to defeat a grant made jointly by her husband and herself, alleged her own minority, and finding difficulty in proving it, offered to abide by Cavendish's opinion. He replied "No man in England can be certain whether someone is of full age or under age, for there are women of 30 who seem to be 18". He became Chanc. of Cambridge University in 1380 and was murdered at Bury St. Edmunds in June 1381 during the Peasant's Revolt. His descendent **(2) George (1500-?61)** was an intimate servant of Card. Wolsey from 1526 and wrote a life of him which circulated in garbled form until an edition by Grove in 1761. He introduced his brother **(3) Sir William (?1505-57)** to Court in 1530. A Commissioner for dissolving monasteries and in 1541 auditor of the Court of Augmentations, he acquired former monastic lands. From 1546 he was treasurer of the Royal Chamber and sworn of the P.C. He acquired still more land under Edward VI yet managed to keep his offices under Mary I. His third wife was the formidable and wealthy **(4) Bess of Hardwick (?-1608)** who remarried, her last husband being George Talbot, 6th E. of Shrewsbury. As a result the Talbot and Cavendish children were brought up together and intermarried or were political allies. By her, Sir William had **(5) Henry (?-1616),** M.P. for Derbyshire in 1572. He became a personal friend but not an adherent of Mary Q. of Scots who was confined in Talbot and Cavendish houses. His brother **(6) William (?-1626) 1st Ld. CAVENDISH (1605)** and **1st E. of DEVONSHIRE (1618)** was M.P. for Derbyshire in 1588. Bess gave him most of her fortune and he also inherited Henry's. He owned Hardwicke, Oldcotes and Chatsworth and patronised Thomas Hobbes. He also largely financed the colonisation of the Barbados. For his brother **(7) Charles (I)** *see* CAVENDISH (NEWCASTLE). His sister **(8) Frances (?-?)** married Sir Henry Pierpoint and was the ancestress of the Ds. of Kingston. Her sister **(9) Elizabeth (?-?)** married Charles Stuart, E. of Lennox. The grandson of **(6)**, **(10) William (1617-84) 3rd E. (1628),** a prominent civil war royalist fined by Parliament, was an original fellow of the Royal Society (1663). His brother **(11) Charles (II) (1620-43)** was a successful royalist commander in Notts. and Lincolnshire until killed attempting to relieve Cromwell's siege of Gainsborough. The mother of **(10)** and **(11)**, **(12) Christiana (?-1675)** was a courageous and ingenious royalist who took charge of Charles II's property after the B. of Worcester, entertained royalists at Roehampton throughout the Protectorate and was the channel through which Monck communicated his intentions to Charles II in 1660. The son of **(10)**, **(13) William (1640-1707) 4th E. and 1st D. (1694)** became M.P. for Derby in 1661. He was a notoriously hot tempered duellist. By 1675 he was in opposition to the court and one of Shaftesbury's supporters in the "Popish Plot" affair. He was a member of Charles II's Privy Council of Thirty in 1679 but resigned in 1680. He consistently promoted exclusionist legislation but refused, after Shaftesbury's flight, to resort to extremism and was received into favour. Though he moved to debate James II's first speech from the Throne, he would have nothing to do with Monmouth or his rising and he had a brawl in 1685 in the King's presence with Col. Colepeper (who called him an exclusionist), was fined £30,000 in the King's Bench although he pleaded privilege of Parliament, but escaped to Chatsworth where he imprisoned the pursuing sheriff's posse. The Lords compelled the King's Bench to retract in 1689. He spent the next years building Chatsworth with Talman, Verrio and Thornhill and plotting James II's overthrow. He signed the invitation to William III of June 1688. He led the local forces and protected the Princess Anne with his militia. In the subsequent convention parliament he argued for conferring the crown on William and thereafter he was one of comparatively few Englishmen whom William trusted, being the only lay peer always appointed a Lord Justice to act during the King's many absences. He opposed efforts to vacate William's Irish land grants in 1699 and was a strong supporter of Anne's succession, and the French war. He was also a leading figure in the successful Anglo-Scots union negotiations of 1706. He left many bastards. His grandson **(14) William (1720-64) Ld. CAVENDISH (1751) 4th D. (1755)** was M.P. for Derbyshire from 1741. Through his marriage in 1748 with **(15) Charlotte, Lady CLIFFORD,** heiress of the E. of Cork, he acquired huge Irish properties and increased political importance and in 1751 he was called to the Lords by writ. In Mar. 1755 he became a popular Lord Lieut. of Ireland. At the outbreak of the Seven Years' War public opinion demanded Pitt as prime minister in place of Devonshire's relative, the D. of Newcastle, but the whigs successfully obstructed his appointment. Accordingly Devonshire was recalled to be a compromise prime minister with Pitt as Sec. of State for War (16 Nov. 1756). He was not a success and his leader of the House of Commons, Robinson, was inept. Pitt made an alliance with Newcastle and from 1757 until 1762 Devonshire was Lord Chamberlain instead. His brother **(16) Ld. Frederick (1729-1803)** succeeded him in 1751 as M.P. for Derbyshire and was M.P. for Derby from 1754 to 1780. He was a regular soldier as well (ending as Field-Marshal in 1796) and owned Twickenham. His brother **(17) Ld. John (1732-96)** was M.P. for Weymouth from 1753 to 1761 and then for Knaresborough as a Whig. Rockingham made him a whip in 1765. From 1768 to 1782 he was M.P. for York and served as Ch. of the Exch. under Rockingham from Mar. to July 1782. He refused office under Shelburne and in Feb. 1783 carried the motion which forced Shelburne to resign. In Apr. his niece's husband, the D. of Portland, became Prime Minister and Cavendish became Ch. of the Exch. again, only to be ousted in Dec. when Pitt resumed office. In 1790 he lost his seat but was elected for Derbyshire in 1796. Not a prominent public figure, he was influential by his birth, assiduity and ability as a forceful advocate. A cousin **(18) Henry (1731-1810)** began his scientific investigations in about 1760 and sent his first chemical paper to the Royal Society in 1766. He published papers on electricity in 1776. His discovery of the composition of water dates from 1777 but was published only in 1783. His paper on terrestrial density was published in 1798. He was a brilliant, absent minded recluse. **(19) Georgiana (Spencer) (1757-1806)**, wife of the 5th Duke, famous for her beauty and charm, the queen of London intellectual society and a friend of Selwyn, Sheridan and Fox, had strong political convictions and during a canvass for Fox at the Westminster Election of 1784 visited the stews and traded kisses for votes. Her son **(20) William Spencer (1790-1858) 6th D. (1811)** was Lord Chamberlain in 1827 and 1828 and from 1830 to 1834. He employed (Sir) Joseph Paxton as his estate manager and his immense conservatories at Chatsworth were the model for the Crystal Palace. His cousin **(21) William (1808-91) 2nd E. of BURLINGTON (1834)** succeeded him as the 7th D. He was M.P. for Cambridge Univ. from 1829 to 1831, lost his seat for supporting the Reform Bill, but was returned for Malton instead and then for N. Derbyshire. From 1834 he concentrated wholly on science and business. He financed the Barrow-in-Furness iron mining and steel industry, and docks, railways in southern Ireland and the development of Eastbourne and Buxton as resorts. He was chairman of the R. Commn. on the Advancement of Science, endowed the Cavendish Laboratory at Cambridge and was a founder of the Royal Agricultural Society. He was also an important breeder of shorthorn cattle. His son **(22) Spencer Compton (1833-1908) M. of HARTINGTON (1858)** and **8th D.** was liberal M.P. for N. Lancs. from 1857. A forceful and logical speaker, he carried the resolution of no-confidence against the Derby govt. in June 1859 and after holding minor office became Sec. of State for War in the Russell govt. of 1866. He supported Irish church disestablishment and lost his seat in 1868, but was returned for the Radnor boroughs instead. He was Postmaster-Gen. in Gladstone's govt. in 1869 and steered the Ballot Act through the Commons in 1870. He then became Chief Sec. for Ireland and had to pass the "Coercion Act". When Gladstone resigned in 1875 he became leader of the Liberals. As a whig he opposed (in the face of Russian pretensions) a forward policy in Afghanistan, but supported Ottoman rule in the Balkans. In 1880 he was M.P. for N. Lancs. and having refused the premiership became Sec. of State for India under Gladstone (1880-2). He was thus responsible for the withdrawal from Afghanistan and as Sec. of State for War from 1882 to 1885 was involved in the Sudan events ending with Gordon's death at Khartoum. By this time he was out of sympathy with the more radical Liberals; he acted as moderator in the franchise and redistribution controversy of 1884 and refused to support the Gladstonian Home Rule policy in 1885. Elected for Rossendale, he refused office under Gladstone in 1886 and founded the new Liberal Unionist Party with which, in combination with Salisbury, he overthrew Gladstone. He again refused the premiership and supported Salisbury independently, meanwhile acting as chairman of a R. Commn on naval and military administration (1888-90) and on industrial relations (1891). After his succession to the dukedom he moved the rejection of Gladstone's Home Rule Bill in the Lords and was Lord President from 1895 to 1903 under Salisbury and Balfour, but resigned against Balfour's fiscal views. His brother **(23) Ld. Frederick Charles (1836-82),** Liberal M.P. for the W. Riding from 1865, held minor offices close to Gladstone. Appointed Chief Sec. to the Lord Lieut. of Ireland in 1882 he was murdered in Phoenix Park, Dublin. His nephew **(24) Victor Christian (1868-1938), 9th D.** became M.P. for W. Derbyshire in 1891 and was financial Sec. to the Treasury from 1903 to 1905. He was Gov.-Gen. of Canada from 1916 to 1921 and Colonial Sec. from 1922 to 1925. In the latter office he was responsible for the Wembley Exhibition, whose finances he personally guaranteed. He retired an invalid in 1925.

CAVENDISH (Newcastle). (*See* CAVENDISH-DEVONSHIRE). **(1) Charles (?-1617)** settled at Welbeck (Notts.) and married Catherine, the heiress of the wealthy Ld. Ogle. His son **(2) William (1592-1676) 1st Vist. MANSFIELD (1620), 1st E. of NEWCASTLE (1628), 1st. M. (1643), 1st D. (1665)** was very rich and spent heavily to get court preferment. In 1638, through Strafford's influence, he became governor to the P. of Wales (later Charles II) and taught him his realism and horsemanship. When the Bishop's Wars broke out Newcastle lent the King £10,000 and raised a troop. In 1641, however, he retired from the court, perhaps because his name was associated with the so-called Army Plot. When the civil war was about to begin he tried to seize Hull for the King; he later joined him at York and was C-in-C in the four northern counties. He occupied Newcastle and raised troops through his Ogle connections. He was the most effective royalist commander in the north until the disaster at Marston Moor (2 July 1644) and then went to Paris by way of Hamburg and in 1647 to Holland. In 1650 he joined Charles II's privy council, but played only a modest part because of the influence of Hyde, with whom he disagreed, especially in that he advocated winning Scottish support at any price. From the Restoration he was heavily occupied restoring his ruined estates and paying debts, many contracted in the King's interest. He wrote many plays, patronised Dryden and Shadwell and published two works on Horsemanship, on which he was the acknowledged European authority. His son **(3) Henry (1630-91), 2nd D.** was, as Vist. Mansfield, M.P. for Northumberland from 1661 to 1676. He was a powerful local figure in the north where he held many offices, but refused to swear allegiance to William and Mary in 1689 and retired. The many family honours became extinct at his death.

CAVENDISH LABORATORY (Cambridge) was founded by the 7th D. of Devonshire, the head of the Cavendish family, in memory of the scientist Henry Cavendish (1731-1810) (*see* CAVENDISH-DEVONSHIRE-17). Between 1918 and 1939 it was a centre for, among other things, the nuclear research pursued by Cockcroft, Rutherford, Chadwick and Walton.

CAVOUR, Cainhilo Benso, Conte di (1810-61), a Piedmontese French speaking nobleman with a Calvinist mother, and one of the most important statesmen of the 19th cent. was dismissed for liberalism from the court of K. Charles Albert of Savoy and from 1831 managed the family estates where, like Coke of Norfolk, he introduced foreign techniques and new strains of crops and animals. He also tried English drainage methods, popularised artificial manure, founded the Turin Agricultural Society, developed agricultural banks, planned railways and wrote on the English poor law. In 1847 the King granted press freedom and Cavour founded the newspaper *Il Risorgimento* which gave its name to an era. Cavour disliked republicanism and believed that constitutional monarchy would provide the vehicle in which an aristocratic democracy would bring liberation to the oppressed. He persuaded Charles Albert to save the monarchy by granting a parliamentary constitution early in 1848, just as the Milanese rose against the Austrians. He then persuaded the King to go to war; in order to forestall the Milanese republicans. The campaign was a failure; meantime Cavour, after hesitations, stood in the new parliamentary elections. The King went to war again in Mar. 1849 but, disastrously beaten at Novara, abdicated at once in favour of Victor Emmanuel II. In June 1850 Cavour was elected, by Oct. he was a minister under d'Azeglio and by Nov. 1852 prime minister. His object was "the aggrandisement of Piedmont" and he seized every opportunity to make Savoy appear the champion of Italians generally, and simultaneously raised the world esteem of his little country by acting upon an international stage. For this reason he joined with France and England in the Crimean War, though Savoy had no quarrel with Russia at all, and so was recognised as the leader of Italy by the powers at the peace conference. The next stage was to provoke a war with Austria, in which in 1859 he succeeded by trading Savoy and Nice for French help; French victories were pyrrhic and France concluded an armistice at Villafranca behind his back. Though Savoy received most of Lombardy, Cavour resigned (July 1859). In Jan. 1860 he was back, and in the T. of Turin (Mar. 1860) got the French to withdraw their opposition to Austrian expulsion from Italy; with the aid of suitably managed plebiscites, Savoy and Nice were now definitely ceded to France and Parma, Tuscany,

Modena and the Romagna were incorporated in the Piedmontese constitutional monarchy. These intrigues, involving the loss of Italian territory to a foreign state, led to a break with Garibaldi, a Niçois who decided to adventure against Bourbon Naples and Sicily alone. Garibaldi's famous Thousand were assembled at Genoa, Cavour taking care not to know about it until it had sailed. He then made sure that they were supplied. With Garibaldi's saintly leadership and the hysterical support of the populations, Bourbon authority collapsed in Sicily and Naples and Cavour induced his parliament in Mar. 1861 to annex them and the Papal states (other than Rome) too. He died shortly after, having made Italy.

CAWDOR. *See* REBECCA RIOTS.

CAWNPORE, now KANPUR (India). *See* INDIAN MUTINY.

CAXTON, William (c. 1422-c. 92), a businessman in the Low Countries, was Governor of the English merchants at Binges from 1462 and much involved in Anglo-Burgundian commercial transactions. By 1468 he had also begun literary translation, encouraged by Edward IV's sister Margaret, Duchess of Burgundy. After 1471 he learned the art of printing, probably at Cologne and possibly from Johann Veldener. Later at Bruges he persuaded Colard Mansion to set in type the first book printed in English, the *Recuyell of the Historyes of Troye*. By 1476 he had moved to Westminster and, doubtless with royal contacts, had set up the first English press. He printed the *Canterbury Tales* in 1476. He was well known at the courts of Edward IV, Richard III and Henry VII. He published over 70 different works before he died.

CAYMAN Is. or TORTUGAS (Sp = turtles) or DRY TORTUGAS. Columbus saw them swarming with turtles in 1503. The turtles, sometimes drysalted, and the coconuts being both very nutritious, became a regular source of food for English, French and Dutch ships and troops after the British took Jamaica in 1655. Consequently Jamaicans colonised them, and until Jamaican independence the islands were a Jamaican dependency. Thereafter they were placed under the London govt.

CEADWALLA. *See* KENT. KINGDOM-4.

CEAWLIN. *See* KENT. KINGDOM-2,3.

CEAWLIN (r. 560-93). K. of the West Saxons. By his important victory with Cuthwine over the Britons in 577, the West Saxons gained the valley of the lower Severn and split the Britons into two groups, north and south-west of the Bristol Channel. He was considered the overlord of the English south of the Humber perhaps until 584 when he fought an uncertain battle with the British. His achievement of 577 was not undone but he was driven from his Kingdom in 592 and perished in 593. Historically an important ruler, the reasons for his fall are uncertain but possibly reflect a family feud.

CECIL or CECYLL FAMILY, courtiers, perhaps of Welsh origin, who rose with Henry VII. At any rate **(1) David (?-1541)** was one of the yeomen of the chamber in 1507, but by then had properties at Stamford. Henry VIII liked him and he held offices and acquired property in Northamptonshire. His son **(2) Richard (?-1552)** was a royal page at the Field of the Cloth of Gold. He left substantial, mostly ex-monastic, estates in Rutland and N'hants. His famous son **(3) William (1520-98) 1st Ld. BURGHLEY (1571)** married twice. His first wife was Mary (?-1544), sister of the Greek scholar John Cheke. His second wife was Mildred (?-1589) whose father, Sir Anthony Cooke, was tutor to Edward VI. She, with her sister Ann (who married Sir Nicholas Bacon) and Lady Jane Grey were said to have been the most learned ladies of their time. It was a very influential protestant contact. William, who was trained as a lawyer, became Protector Somerset's master of requests and then secretary. In Nov. 1547 he was M.P. for Stamford. When Somerset fell William was briefly imprisoned, but by now his extraordinary ability and objectivity were recognised and

Protector Northumberland made him Sec. of State in 1550. In 1552 he added his father's considerable wealth to his own. This was important for he resigned rather than support Northumberland's attempt to set up Lady Jane Grey, but was not Romanist enough to please Mary I. Hence he developed Wimbledon and Burleigh and accepted diplomatic tasks, in 1554 to bring Card. Pole to England and in 1555 with Pole to mediate between France and the Emperor. He was an M.P. again in the autumn and it was apparently his opposition which defeated a bill to confiscate the properties of protestants who had fled abroad. This oblique demonstration of his lack of sympathy with the persecutions was supplemented with contacts with the Pr. Elizabeth, whose confidence he won and who probably guided her conduct at this period by his advice. On the day Mary died Elizabeth, at Hatfield, appointed him her Sec. of State, concluding the formalities three days later with a well known speech: "This judgement I have of you, that you will not be corrupted with any manner of gifts, and that you will be faithful to the State". He was also prodigiously and methodically industrious; able, like her to speak French, Italian and Latin with facility; a patron of architects, musicians and gardeners and a student of genealogy and heraldry. Above all he and Elizabeth knew each other's minds and she understood that his value far exceeded that of other glamorous persons who attracted her more. In a political sense the period 1558 to 1598 was a joint reign, though it sometimes seemed to the outside world that others, notably Leicester (Northumberland's son) might disrupt the unity. This became decreasingly likely with time. William, too, had independently useful sources of influence. He had been a Sec. of State. His brother-in-law, Bacon, was Lord Chancellor. His father-in-law, Sir Anthony Cooke, chaired the Commons Committee which drafted the 1559 Act of Supremacy. In 1561 he began, as Master, to reform the Court of Wards, which increased its revenues and yet reduced its unpopularity. In the same year he set up an investigation into the causes of popular disorders and discontents and an intelligence system for foreign affairs. Through him the Queen could learn all that was necessary for her to carry on her role as a great popular leader.

The fugitive arrival (May 1568) of Mary Q. of Scots in England marked a major change. It was now necessary to provide for hostile and potentially successful movements against the Queen inside the country. The fact that William already had a foreign intelligence organisation facilitated this, for most movements hoped to, or actually did, make foreign contacts. In his outlook on such matters he was entirely modern. If he could open diplomatic mail without detection he did. At the same time it was obvious that treasonable activities would lose sustenance if foreign powers could be cajoled into neutrality. Huguenots were sustained against Spanish supported Guises, Dutch rebels against their lawful Spanish sovereign and English piratical raiders against the authorities of the Spanish Main, yet for nineteen years without provoking Spain into open war. Mary Q. of Scots had her uses. As long as she was alive K. Philip II could hope that local R. Catholic action might supplant Elizabeth with her and avoid all the expense of an expedition. Though he had already given up that hope and prepared the expedition when Mary was executed, the diplomatic achievement is remarkable. His son by Mildred Cooke **(4) Sir Robert (?1563-1612) 1st Ld. CECIL (1604), 1st Vist. CRANBORNE (1604), 1st E. of SALISBURY (1605)**, a delicate hunchback, was M.P. for Westminster in 1584 and in 1588 belonged to Derby's mission to Spain. In 1589 he was M.P. for Hertfordshire and by 1590 he was much employed by his father in state business. This unofficial but useful arrangement was confirmed when the Queen knighted him at Theobalds (May 1591) and called him to the Privy Council (Aug.).

He was now a kind of secretary to the joint rulers. In 1596 he became S. of State jointly with his father. It was in this capacity that he went, with Lord Brooke, Sir Walter Raleigh and others, on the extraordinary mission to Paris in 1598 to try and prevent a Franco-Spanish alliance. Four months later his father died and Sir Robert was faced with a situation which, in some ways, resembled his father's under Mary I; a successor was waiting in the wings and potentially hostile aspirants to power, in the shape of Essex and his interest, occupied public attention. The difference was that the Queen supported him against Essex and the last crisis of the reign was played out two years before it ended. Sir Robert had time to correspond with James VI of Scots and arrange for a smooth succession. James confirmed him in office and ennobled him. He was Lord Treasurer from 1608. Until he died the routine management of the English was, despite court rapacity and James' lack of dignity, in his hands. In this he represented an Elizabethan influence projected into a new era, where revolutionary thought was confronted by a weaker crown authority. In 1607 James gave him Hatfield in exchange for his beautiful house at Theobald's, and the mansion and gardens which he laid out have remained the seat of the Salisbury family ever since. It cost him a fortune, and the inheritance in his successors of debts combined with only ordinary talents thrust the family into the background of affairs. His elder half-brother by Mary Cheke **(5) Thomas (1542-1623) 2nd Ld. BURGHLEY, 1st E. of EXETER (1605)** was president of the Council of the North from 1599 to 1603. His son **(6) Sir Edward (1572-1638) 1st Vist. WIMBLEDON (1625)** was a professional soldier and sailor trained in Germany and a protégé of Buckingham, who made him the effective general of the 1625 Cadiz expedition. Its failure was largely his fault but he remained the acknowledged English military expert until his death. **(7) James (?-1683) 3rd E.** was an exclusionist imprisoned in the Tower from 1677 to 1679. **(8) James (?-1693) 4th E.** perhaps by reaction was imprisoned briefly as a R. Catholic and in 1692 as a suspected Jacobite, but until the mid-19th cent. the family nursed its estates. It also became allied with the City family of Gascoigne. **(9) for Robert (1946-) Vist. Cranborne** see HOUSE OF LORDS BILL 1998; GASCOIGNE-CECIL.

CEDED PROVINCES (India). The collective name of the territories ceded to the HEIC by the Nawab of Oudh in 1801 viz: Allahabad, Bareily, Cawnpore, Etawah, Gorakhpore and Moreadabad together with Farrukhabad, ceded by its ruler in 1802.

CELESTIAL EMPIRE. China.

CELESTINE III (?1106-98) Pope (1191), an Orsini, defended Abelard at Sens (1140) and as a cardinal from 1144 advocated conciliation with Frederick Barbarossa and between Becket and Henry II. His preference for compromises had become a weakness for a pope in old age, just as the second crusade was on its way. In particular he crowned Henry VI emperor but failed to enforce the European peace needed during a Crusade. Thus Henry pursued his conquests in S. Italy and Sicily (1191-4), encouraged the imprisonment of Richard I (1192-4) and consequently French intrigues and aggression in S. France.

CELIBACY OF CLERGY. In the East priests and deacons may be married before ordination but not after; bishops must be celibate. In the West celibacy was enjoined in 386, but Pope Leo 1(440-61) forbade higher clergy to put away their wives on ordination and required them to live as brother and sister. Later ordination was refused to married men until they and their wives had exchanged vows of continence and the wives then entered a convent or were enrolled as deaconesses or widows. This remained the rule until 1917 when ordination of married men was forbidden altogether. Clerical concubinage was common in 10th and 15th cents. Celibacy of clergy was abolished in the Anglican Church in 1549.

CELLE (Ger.). *See* GEORGE I; CAROLINE MATILDA.

CELTS, CELTIC LANGUAGE, GAELS, GALATIANS, GAUCIANS, GAULS, SCOTS, WELSH. Roman and Greek writers used the word *Celt* of several interrelated tribes inhabiting Transalpine Europe and the Peninsula (Galicia). They or their aristocracy were tall, strong and blonde. They invaded Italy in 400 B.C. and settled the Po Valley, thereafter called Cisalpine Gaul. They sacked Delphi in 279 B.C. and colonised northern Asia Minor (Galatia) in 276. Early in the 1st cent. B.C., Teutonic pressure drove many across the Rhine; there was extensive migration to Britain, which by Caesar's time was a Celtic speaking country with, in some parts, local branches of Celtic tribes.

Ireland seems to have had several Celtic colonisations; some early movements being related to Rhenish Celtic cultures, others to British and explicable as flights from the Roman Conquest, while the old Irish languages had some affinities with Galician.

Celtic languages were spoken throughout Europe between c. 500 B.C. and A.D. 500 In the Atlantic West they developed into two broad types, viz: GOIDELIC or Q-Celtic which broke up into OLD IRISH, MANX and the GAELIC of the Scots, and BRYTHONIC (a form of P-Celtic) which developed into WELSH, CORNISH and BRETON. Brythonic had many Latin loanwords but the geographical distribution was the result of the Anglo-Saxon invasions which also imported Saxon loanwords. The difference between northern and southern Welsh may be due to the arrival of the Votadini in N. Wales from Lothian. *See* CLANS, SCOTTISH; GWYNEDD.

CELTIC CHURCH. The collapse of the British church during the Anglo-Saxon invasions was only partial, for Augustine found British church leaders when he arrived in the 6th cent. but Christianity in Wales and Cornwall changed its institutional character. In the early 6th cent. St. Illtud, possibly a Briton of Brittany, set up a monastery in Wales; among his pupils were St. Samson and St. David, the one a wanderer, the other an extreme ascetic. Such men set a pattern for the Celtic Christianity which had also reached Ireland. It came to be identified with certain practices, notably the observance of Easter on the 14th of the moon after the spring equinox, tonsure from ear to ear and domination by monasteries governed by abbots. Its bishops exercised their sacramental functions under abbatical direction and there was no diocesan organisation. Celtic monks followed an ascetic regime of prayer, fasting and public and private confession. They originated the penitential code later adopted by the rest of the Church. Worship followed the conventional Roman pattern with certain variations such as the omission of compline. The liturgy itself was not Roman but probably Gallican. The Celtic church was never totally severed from the Continent to which it looked for intellectual material and books. Education was esoteric rather than practical and in the 6th and 7th cents. it kept Latinity alive the Irish having, since St. Patrick's time, substituted Latin for the vernacular in their usage. Men such as Columbanus were reputed the leading Latin scholars in Europe. If there was no formal schism between the Celtic and the Roman churches, outlook and practice made them drift apart until the Celts thought of themselves as different and stubbornly defended their practices against criticism by Roman trained missionaries and such Roman adherents as St. Wilfred at the Synod of Whitby (664). By the end of the 8th cent., however, Roman practices and organisation had permeated the English church, but some of the Celtic aesthetic sense continued to flourish and Celtic monks taught their beautiful half-uncial penmanship to the Anglo-Saxons.

CELTIC FRINGE. Scotland, Wales and (between 1800 and 1920) Ireland.

CELY FAMILY and PAPERS. This London based Stapler family, was engaged in the wool trade and had business interests in Calais and Bruges, besides London and the Cotswolds. As a result of a partnership dispute in 1489, about 450 of their letters and business papers from the previous 15 years survive. These are the only so far uncovered substantial collection of a mediaeval English merchant family's papers.

C.E.M.A. (Council for the Encouragement of Music and the Arts). *See* ARTS COUNCIL.

CENEDL (Welsh = kindred). A clan or tribe. cf Irish CINEL or KINEL. *See* WELSH LAW-5,8

CENHEDLOEDD. *See* WELSH LAW-5.

CENOTAPH (Gr = empty tomb) Whitehall, London. Originally a wooden structure erected for the peace procession in July 1919, it was superseded in 1920 by the stone memorial to "Our Glorious Dead", designed in a single night by Sir Edwin Luytens and used as the focus of the annual state commemoration on or near 11 Nov. (Armistice Day).

CENSORSHIP is the compulsory submission of material intended for publication to authoritarian control before publication. **A. In Peace Time (1) Press Licensing.** Proclamations against heretical and seditious books were issued in 1529 and importations were in theory regulated in 1533. From 1538 books had to be licensed by the Privy Council or its representatives. In 1547 and 1549 there were orders against popish books. Mary I permitted nothing else and in 1557 chartered the STATIONERS CO. and confined the right to print to its members or special patentees. In 1559 Elizabeth I's **Injunctions** required all books to be licensed by her or by six privy councillors or by certain bishops. So many books had to be read for licensing that this system never worked. In 1586 the Star Chamber ordered that presses should be confined to London, Oxford and Cambridge and that no new presses were to be set up until depreciation had reduced the number to those considered sufficient for the needs of the realm by the Abp. of Canterbury and the Bp. of London. In 1588 Abp. Whitgift appointed 12 licensors of printed books to combat puritan pamphleteering (*see* MARPRELATE TRACTS). The system served to impede the rise of an effective journalism, but in 1622 certain stationers were licensed to publish fly-sheets or CORANTOS about the Thirty Years' War. The publication of corantos was prohibited by the Star Chamber in 1632, which also issued an ordinance against offending printers in 1637; but in 1638 Nathanial Butler and Nicholas Bourne received a monopoly of news from abroad. These were replaced by NEWS BOOKS or DIURNALS, but the Long Parliament and the Commonwealth continued and strengthened the royal system of censorship and this was extended in 1662 until 1664, and then to 1679, and after an intermission was reimposed from 168S to 1694, when the licensing system was finally abandoned.

(2) Criminal Libel, Sedition, Search. Between 1679 and 1685, and after 1694, the authorities relied upon the common law as then understood. Two MESSENGERS OF THE PRESS were appointed to track down authors and publishers of obnoxious material, which was placed before the Treasury Solicitor. On his advice Secs. of State issued warrants to arrest or search, which might be followed by prosecutions or bindings over to keep the peace. The usual punishments were fines, pillory or prison. Defoe was pilloried in 1/03 for his pamphlets on church matters; but John Matthews was executed for treason in 1719 for asserting that the Old Pretender was James III. Even when prosecutions failed, the warrants were a means of ruining printers: the Freeholder's Journal and the *True Briton* were ruined by such harrassments in 1723 and 1724. Secs. of State took to issuing GENERAL WARRANTS for the seizure of unspecified papers or for the arrest of unspecified persons. John Wilkes ended general warrants for papers by successfully suing the responsible U/Sec. of State in 1763 in connection with No. 45 of the *North Briton* (*Wilkes* v *Wood*). General warrants against persons were held illegal in 1765. Prosecutions nevertheless continued on a diminishing scale. Paine fled the country in 1792 rather than face prosecution for his *Rights of Man,* and in 1810 Cobbett was sentenced to a fine and imprisonment for denouncing military flogging. By mid-19th cent, however, censorship prosecutions were virtually obsolete, save under special legislation in the two World Wars.

(3) Parliamentary Proceedings. After Charles I's attack on parliamentary privilege, both Houses became shy of publishing their proceedings and it became a breach of privilege to do so. The *Vote* contained (and contains) no more than the barest summary of decisions. From 1720, however, some unofficial reports began to circulate, notably Boyer's *Political State of Great Britain* (1702), the *Historical Register* (1716), the *Gentleman's Magazine* and the *London Magazine* (1732). The Commons passed threatening resolutions in 1738, but the reports continued, often under transparent disguises. In 1771 the Commons unsuccessfully took action against certain printers and their City supporters, again including John Wilkes. Since then the Houses have tacitly let the matter drop.

(4) Stamp Duty. In 1712 a stamp duty of ½d on half sheet periodicals and 1d on every whole sheet was imposed, to drive the many smaller papers out of existence. In 1725 the rate was consolidated at ½d per half sheet. The intended effect was only temporary, but the duty was not abolished until 1855.

(5) Drama. Originally players belonged to guilds or were under royal or noble patronage. Control of stage performances, which probably began in 1549, was aimed at strolling players: it started with licensing of plays and in 1554 applied the law on vagabonds to them. Elizabeth's Injunctions of 1559 forbade plays treating of religion or the govt. and required interludes to be licensed by the mayor, lord lieutenant or two J.P.s. The court on the whole favoured drama, the corporation of London was hostile to it: hence in 1574 the E. of Leicester's men were patented to play in all towns, whereupon the Act of Common Council required all plays to be licensed by the corporation, which proceeded to refuse licenses wholesale. As a result the first permanent theatre was built in Finsbury outside the City boundary. At the same time the licensing of plays throughout England was transferred to the Master of the Revels, while particular companies under James I and Charles I were exempted from his jurisdiction by patent. Between 1642 and 1660 plays were forbidden, though sometimes performed. At the Restoration there was, of course, a revival. D'Avenant and Killigrew were granted monopolies in London and Westminster, but this led to a dispute with Sir Henry Herbert, Charles I's Master of the Revels, who was still alive and asserted his right to licence plays. When he died Killigrew succeeded to his post and admitted every kind of political and religious reference as well as indecency. In William and Mary's time there was a reaction and in 1697 the master was forbidden to licence plays contrary to religion and good manners. By 1714 his functions had virtually passed to the Lord Chamberlain, his superior, and this was made statutory by the Licensing Act, 1737, passed in consequence of several satirical plays hostile to Walpole. The Lords Chamberlain in fact appointed **examiners of plays** to do the work and these were often men of literary distinction themselves. A Commons' Select Committee of 1832 resulted in the licensing of theatres as well as plays by an Act of 1843. There was another Select Committee in 1909. The whole institution was persistently and often wrongheadedly attacked until, in 1969, it was abolished. This led to fears that playwrights and actors might be prosecuted for works performed on stage, and one such prosecution was launched but failed on a technicality.

(6) The **filtering or adaptation of material** by editors and programme controllers, especially if it suits a commercial interest or proprietorial opinion, is an important little noticed form of censorship even if it is exercised for a private rather than an official purpose. It seemed in 2000 to be on the increase.

B. Wartime censorship is carried out through confidential notices to editors and programme controllers issued by defence departments. These are called "D NOTICES".

CENSUS. *See* POPULADON; LIBER CENSUUM.

CENTRAL AFRICAN FEDERATION of Northern and Southern Rhodesia with Nyasaland, lasted from Sept. 1953 until Dec. 1963. Created by Act of Parliament, it ultimately collapsed before the centrifugal force of African nationalistic particularism.

CENTRAL AFRICAN REPUBLIC. *See* EQUATORIAL (EX-FRENCH) AFRICA.

CENTRAL CRIMINAL COURT ("OLD BAILEY") erected in 1834 and maintained by the Corporation of London, is the principal criminal court for (roughly) the Greater London area. The Recorder of London and the Common Serjeant are the permanent judges and High Court Justices also sit there in rotation.

CENTRAL ELECTRICITY (1) The Authority set up in 1954 was a board appointed by the Min. of Power to co-ordinate the nationalised electricity industry and operate 274 power stations selling power to the twelve electricity boards. The arrangements were cumbersome and **(2) The Generating Board** superseded the Authority in 1957. By 1965 power stations had been reduced to 233, nearly 9000 miles of high votage transmission lines built, supply more than doubled and atomic plants were being designed.

CENTRAL INDIA AND BERAR. *See* MARATHAS. 'Central India' was originally a British term for Malwa, after it came into their hands in 1818, but the Saugor Nerbada territories were administered under Agra; Gwalior, Indore and other Central India states were protected. In 1853 Nagpur lapsed to the HEIC and Berar was assigned by Hyderabad nominally to defray the expenses of the Hyderabad Contingent. In 1854 Bundelkhand and Baghelkand were added to Malwa. There was violent fighting up and down the area during the Indian Mutiny (*see* JHANSI) and in 1861 with the addition of the Saugor Nerbada territories it was organised as Central India subdivided into the Residencies of Gwalior and Indore and Agencies for major states or groups of lesser ones.. In 1902 Berar was placed on permanent lease. In 1907 two agencies were amalgamated. In 1921 Gwalior was removed from Central India and in 1931 two further agencies were amalgamated.

CENTRALISM, DEMOCRATIC. The technical communist term for the doctrine that once the party policy has been settled, all party members must conform to it whether they agree with it or not. Those who do not conform are DEVIATIONISTS.

CENTRAL POWERS. A common term for Germany and Austro-Hungary in alliance and sometimes for the coalition which they formed with Bulgaria and Turkey to fight the allies in World War I.

CENTWINE (r. 676-85). *See* WEST SAXONS, EARLY-10.

CENWALH (r. 643-72). *See* WEST SAXONS, EARLY-8.

CENWULF. *See* MERCIA.

CEOLFRITH, St. (?-716) was prior, under Benedict Biscop, of Wearmouth from 674. In 678 he visited Rome and in 682 became abbot of Jarrow. In 684 he went to Rome again and from 689 added Wearmouth to Jarrow. He greatly extended the abbey scriptoria and persuaded the Irish in 704 and the Picts in 710 to accept the Roman Easter. He died on the way to Rome.

CEOLNOTH (?-870) became Abp. of Canterbury in 833 and reconciled Egbert and Ethelwulf, Kings of the W. Saxons. He bought off the Danes in 864. *See* KENT-6.

CEOL(RIC) (r. 591-7). *See* WEST SAXONS, EARLY-5.

CEOLWULF, St. (?-764). Bede dedicated his *Historia Ecclesiastica* to him as K. of Northumbria from 729. He was dethroned and restored in 731, but abdicated in 737.

CEORL (A.S.). A freeman lower than a thegn but higher than a serf.

CERDIC (r. 519-34). *See* WEST SAXONS, EARLY-1.

CEREALS. (1) *Barley, Millet* and *Wheat* have been known in Europe since earliest times. Soft wheat for breadmaking was normal in Britain in the middle ages. Hard wheat and millet were grown in S. Europe. Barley was grown from the Mediterranean to Scandinavia and was used for porridge and ale and fed to animals. **(2)** *Oats, Rye* and *Spelt* entered Europe as weeds and separate cultivation began only in the middle ages. Oats and rye can grow in cold climates. Oats were used for porridge and beer; rye for bread; both for fattening stock. **(3)** *Buckwheat,* brought by the Mongols in 15th cent. had reached Brittany under the name *Sarasin* by 1500. **(4)** *Rice* was cultivated in Sicily in the 13th cent. and had reached Lombardy by 1475. **(5)** *Sorghum* was grown in Italy in small quantities in the 9th cent. and was later widely adopted. **(6)** *Maize* was brought to Mediterranean areas from Mexico in 16th cent. *See* CORN LAWS.

CERNE GIANT. *See* HILL FIGURES.

CERTIORARI. *See* PREROGATIVE WRITS.

"CESSION, WAY OF." The French scheme for ending the Great Schism (q.v.) by getting both Popes to resign. *See also* CHARLES VI OF FRANCE-1,4,10.

CETSHWAYO or CETEWAYO. *See* ZULUS-4.

CEYLON, SRI LANKA or SERENDIB (1) From about 13th cent. internal confusion made it impossible to prevent Tamil settlement in the north. By 1500 there was a Tamil ruler at Jaffna, while the Sinhalese had rival capitals at Kotte near Colombo and at Kandy.

(2) Ceylon, long a resort of merchants from China, Malaya and the Levant, had become a staging and transhipment area on the commercial routes which ran from the Orient *via* the Persian Gulf or the Red Sea eventually to Europe. Much of the entrepot trade was in the hands of the Moslems ('Moors') from Arabia and Gujerat settled at Colombo. Portuguese exploration, designed to bypass such middlemen, reached Colombo in 1505. Their naval bases at Goa and Diu in India and Hormuz at the entrance to the Gulf diverted some of the trade round the Cape and helped them to acquire gradual control of the westward trade through Ceylon. A mere permission to trade in cinnamon in 1505 developed into a factory and fort in 1518 and then into governors and armies. By 1543 Kotte was protected and Jaffna tributary. In 1546 came the first war with Kandy and in 1597 Philip of Spain, now K. of Portugal, annexed the Portuguese territories in the island. Portuguese rule brought Christianity to part of the population as well as the Portuguese language and surnames.

(3) Spanish interference, however, attracted Dutch hostility and in 1602 the first Dutch fleet reached Batticaloa and offered to help the K. of Kandy. Dutch-Kandyan co-operation was never more than nominal because the Dutch simply wanted to step into Portuguese shoes. In 1639 they took Trincomalee and the Portuguese were wholly ousted when Jaffna fell in 1658. Their former territories were now ruled by the Dutch East India Co. (which introduced Roman-Dutch law) but in 1739 the Sinhalese dynasty at Kandy died out and was succeeded by Tamils.

(4) British influence began in 1761 (during the Seven Years' War) through contacts with Kandy; Trincomalee was briefly occupied and lost in 1782, but in 1795 when Dutch independence was threatened by France, the stadholder ordered the local council to admit British troops, which they refused to do. Thereupon the British landed by force at Trincomalee and conquered the Dutch areas in a year. It was administered from Madras by the HEIC until 1798 when it became a Crown Colony and

was confirmed to Britain in 1802 at the P. of Amiens. An attempt on Kandy inspired by a Sinhalese conspiracy was beaten back in 1803.

(5) In 1814 the Sinhalese chiefs of Kandy rebelled against their Tamil King and asked the British gov., Sir Robt. Brownrigg, for support. The King was deposed and in 1815 the territory was annexed, but the chiefs' prerogatives were guaranteed. In 1818 a further chiefs' rebellion created an opportunity to abolish their privileges.

(6) Under the Constitution of 1833 the Kandyan territories were amalgamated with the maritime provinces, though Kandyan Sinhalese remained under Kandyan personal law. An Executive Council of five and a Legislative Council of ten officials was also set up. Two unofficial nominated members were added in 1837. This began a process whereby the unofficial proportions were intermittently but significantly increased, especially in 1910, and eventually election substituted for nomination in 1923.

(7) The principal export had been coffee, but between 1880 and 1890 disease destroyed the plantations. This led to the substitution with English capital of quinine and then of tea which became and remained the chief export. Rubber was also cultivated from about 1895 and coconuts, long a peasant crop, began to be planted as well. These profound economic changes created a need for the constitutional developments.

(8) In 1915 the mishandling of a communal riot led to the creation of a National Congress on the Indian model, mostly among the English educated Sinhalese. Dissatisfaction with arrangements of 1923 led in 1927 to the appointment of the DONOUGHMORE COMMISSION. It recommended a constitution in which Defence, Law and Finance were to be in the hands of three non-voting officers of State, who with 50 territorially elected members and 8 nominees to represent minorities, constituted the legislature. (The State Council.) This was enacted in 1931 just as the first independent Dominions were being created by the Statute of Westminster.

(9) The Japanese advance in World War II created a demand for Dominion status. In 1943 the British govt. declared its intention to introduce responsible govt. and asked ministers to draft a new constitution. This was examined and endorsed by the SOULBURY COMMISSION in 1945; a cabinet system was introduced by negotiation with D. S. SENANAYAKE, the leader of the State Council and a White Paper promised dominion status. This was formally requested in June 1946. Agreements on defence and external affairs were signed on Nov. and the CEYLON INDEPENDENCE ACT, 1947, came into force with Senanayake as Prime Minister on 4 Feb. 1948.

(10) He held office until he died in 1952. He was succeeded by his son, DUDLEY, who in 1953 gave way to Sir John KOTELAWALA. Their United National Party was defeated in 1956 by a republican coalition.

(11) Since the republic, successive govts, despite their ability to impose most of their expenses on the tea-drinking world by an export tax, have failed to maintain stability and have been much harassed, despite the recognition of Tamil as an official language, by a young guerrilla movement called the TAMIL TIGERS which, despite or perhaps because of cruel repression, established a hold in the north with the help of the far more numerous Tamils in southern India. Indo-Ceylonese diplomatic relations have ever since been dominated by the difficulties created by this connection.

CHACO WAR (1932-5). *See* BOLIVIA; PARAGUAY.

CHAD. *See* EQUATORIAL (EX-FRENCH) AFRICA.

CHAD or CEADDA, St. (?-672) was made Bp. of Northumbria when Wilfrid, already nominated to this see was in France seeking consecration. When Wilfrid returned in 669, Chad was deposed, but he was so respected for his humility, devotion and competence that he was instantly reconsecrated as the first Bp. of the Mercians. It took him less than three years to set up the see at Lichfield, with a full diocesan organisation. He died leaving a great reputation. An 8th cent. copy of the Gospels, once said to have belonged to him, is preserved in Lichfield Cathedral.

CHADWICK, Sir Edwin (1800-90). In 1829 his article on *Preventive Police* gained him the friendship of Jeremy Bentham. In 1833 he became chief Poor Law Commissioner and also a member of the R. Commission on the Condition of Factory Children. When the Poor Law Commissioners were reconstituted in 1834, he became their first sec. (until 1846). He was also a member of the sanitary commissions of 1839 and 1844 and of the Board of Health from 1848 to 1854. A man of powerful and practical intellect and character, he laid the foundations of the later system of Local Govt. In 1871 he proffered a scheme for the drainage of Cawnpore, which was adopted by the local authorities.

CHAINED BOOKS. Books being rare and valuable, chaining them represented a compromise between the desire to make their contents available and suspicion of the readership's morality. The practice was common in the 15th and 16th cents. The Great Bible, Foxe's *Book of Martyrs* and the *Paraphrases* of Erasmus were chained in most parish churches. All Saint's Church, Hereford, has a chained library instituted as late as 1715 but it was probably the last.

CHAIN REACTION. *See* ATOMIC THEORY.

CHAIRMAN, LORD. Apart from an occasion in 1971, the House of Lords has always conducted its committee stages in committee of the Whole House. The Lord Chancellor, a cabinet minister appointed by the Crown, presides in state from the Woolsack over the House but without the powers of the Speaker of the Commons; the Lord Chairman, elected by the House itself, presides less formally over the Committee from the Table. He also manages the proceedings on private bills. Without the public acclaim of Speaker or Lord Chancellor but with the backing of the House's authority, Lords Chairman such as the 3rd Lord Merthyr have achieved a high degree of respect within the whole parliamentary system.

CHAKA or SHAKA. *See* ZULUS.

CHALKING THE DOOR (Sc.). 40 days' notice of eviction by marking a door in the presence of witnesses.

***CHALLENGER EXPEDITION* (1872-6)** was undertaken jointly by the Royal Society and the Admiralty as a result of the Lightning and Porcupine expeditions of 1868-70. The wooden steam corvette *Challenger* was commanded by Capt. (later Sir) George Nares; Prof. (later Sir) Charles Wyville Thompson led the scientists. They determined the areas of oceanic temperature, mapped the main outlines of the oceanic basins and traced their currents, surveyed considerable mileages of coast and made extensive biological investigations. The sheer bulk of the discoveries, which included reports on zoology, botany, physics, chemistry and deep sea deposits, published in 50 vols between 1890 and 1895 has seldom, if ever, been surpassed in the history of exploration.

CHALMERS, Thomas (1780-1847), theologian, writer and welfare reformer. *See* FREE CHURCH OF SCOTLAND.

CHAMBER, CITY. *See* CHAMBERLAIN-4.

CHAMBERLAIN. This title has five distinct uses. **(1)** The office of *Lord Great Chamberlain* became hereditary in 1133 in the family of the de Veres, Es. of Oxford. In 1779 it passed to the co-heiresses of Lord Willoughby d'Eresby and so became vested in three families who take it in turns, reign by reign. The Es. of Ancaster take two reigns, the M. of Cholmondeley and Ld. Carrington one each. Apart from ceremonial functions at the Coronation, the Lord Great Chamberlain was until 1960 active head of the administration of the Houses of Parliament, which sits

technically in the royal Palace of Westminster. Since that time most of his functions there have been carried out by two committees. **(2)** The *Lord Chamberlain of the Household* is appointed by the sovereign and is the director of the royal household. Until 1968 he was responsible for the censorship of plays (*see* CENSORSHIP-5). Between 1714 and 1830 the office was political. **(3)** When there is a King, his Queen usually has a Lord Chamberlain of her own; his functions are almost wholly ceremonial. **(4)** In the City of London the Chamberlain, as head of the City Chamber, is by indenture the treasurer and financial officer of the Corporation, but he is elected by the Livery and not the Corporation. A similar situation existed formerly at York. **(5)** In Scottish local authorities the Treasurer was an elected member of the Council, the Chamberlain the chief professional financial officer.

CHAMBERLAIN (1) Joseph (1836-1914) probably the most influential British politician in the 19th cent. never to have been prime minister, and a 'social imperialist'. The son of a London footware manufacturer, he went to Birmingham in 1854 to represent his father's interests in his uncle's screw-manufacturing business (Nettlefolds), and here his interest in moral improvement and elementary education eventually led him into local politics. In 1868 he reorganised the Birmingham Liberals and helped to found the National Education League. He became a borough councillor in 1869 and mayor in 1873. During his mayoralty he initiated many municipal improvements and, in 1876, became, as a result, one of the borough's M.P.s together with John Bright. In 1877 he became Pres. of the Nat. Liberal Federation and set about reorganising the constituency parties and preparing for the victory of 1880. In that year he became Pres. of the Board of Trade with the aid of Sir. Chas. Dilke, the two of them representing the radical wing of the party in the govt. He took a strong interest in Irish affairs and the negotiations with Parnell (*see* KILMAINHAM T.) and pressed for an Irish Govt. Bill to devolve responsibility for all but justice and police. This was defeated in cabinet. Consistently with this he favoured local self-administration under British protection in other parts of the world. He pressed for this in Egypt and the Sudan, where Gen. Gordon had to be rescued in Khartoum, and advocated, by means of protectorates, resistance to German influence in the Cameroons, Samoa, New Guinea and E. Africa. Frustrated by Gladstone's Irish Home Rule policy he turned, in the new context of the widened franchise of 1882, to policies of a more collectivist type at home (Jan.-Apr. 1885). "What ransom to wider social needs was property prepared to pay for its privileges?", he asked. Goschen and Gladstone both recoiled from his so-called UNAUTHORISED PROGRAMME of reforms and he, for his part, moved into the orbit of the Unionists in order to frustrate Gladstonian Irish Home Rule. In 1887 and 1888 he served Salisbury's govt. as plenipotentiary in the Canadian-U.S. fisheries dispute and he was Salisbury's Colonial Sec. from 1895 to 1903. Here his interests lay in capital investment and the promotion of Anglo-Colonial trade and other bonds. The London and Liverpool School of Hygiene and Tropical Medicine owe their origin to his interest; the W. African territories were rationalised. He wanted to extend self-govt. in all the territories heavily populated by white settlers but feared the likelihood of conflict in S. Africa with the pro-German govt. of Paul Kruger's Transvaal. This preoccupied him from 1895 until the Boer War broke out in 1899, yet the war itself did not prevent him piloting the Australia Bill through parliament in 1900. He also had some energy to spare for domestic issues in the years before the S. African conflict. In particular he set up a committee to investigate the feasibility of old age pensions (1896) and piloted the long-sought Workmen's Compensation Act, 1897. Returning to Britain from a reconciliatory trip to S. Africa (1902-3) he resigned from Balfour's cabinet to pursue his dream of an Imperial Preference which might lead to political union, and agitated for his schemes through the TARIFF REFORM LEAGUE (1903-31). The election of 1906 failed to secure protection and imperial preference, or maintain an effective Conservative and Liberal-Unionist coalition, but shortly after it he had a stroke and retired. His *s.* by his first wife, Harriet Kendrick **(2) (Joseph) Austen (1863-1937)** was educated at Cambridge, Paris and Berlin. He became M.P. for East Worcs. as a Liberal Unionist and instantly became a junior whip in 1892. In 1900 he became Financial Sec. to the Treasury (then a minor office) and in 1903 Ch. of the Exch., when his father and the freetraders left Balfour's cabinet. Balfour fell in Dec. 1905 and Austen, in opposition, took up his father's Tariff Reform ideas and in 1910 voted with the Diehards against the Parliament Bill. He stayed out of office until Asquith formed his wartime coalition in 1915 and offered him the India Office where he stayed until Asquith resigned in 1917, but in 1919 he became Ch. of the Exch. once more. On Bonar Law's retirement he became leader of the Tories in the Commons, but his reluctance to end the post-war coalition made him unpopular with his party and he was ousted from the leadership by Stanley Baldwin at the notorious CARLTON CLUB MEETING on the evening of 19 Oct. 1922 (*see* 1922 COMMITTEE). After the brief Labour interlude, he returned as Baldwin's Foreign Sec. in Nov. 1924. He negotiated the Locarno Ts. and supported German admission to the League of Nations. When Chinese hostility to the foreign treaty concessions developed, he accepted the need to protect Shanghai with troops but abandoned the concession at Hankow in central China. It is uncertain whether he was the originator or the first victim of the so-called Foreign Office Mentality, but many in his party were again discontented with him and he was moved to the Admiralty in 1931, but resigned soon after to advance his half-brother's career at the Exchequer (1931-4) yet it is perhaps an irony that he spent much effort on the back benches warning of the need to rearm. His half-brother by Joseph's second wife, Florence Kendrick, **(3) Neville (1869-1940)** was educated as a metallurgist and engineer, but became an accountant and at 21 took charge of his father's estate in the Bahamas. His father and half-brother had already advanced to high office before he returned to Birmingham in 1897 to go into business. He was interested in the local municipal and charitable life but was first elected to the City council after his father's death. Like the latter he took a radical line in pressing slum-clearance and rebuilding schemes through the council and he helped to establish a municipal bank in 1916. Lloyd George, on this account, made him Director of National Service but in 1916-7 his political advance was not assured and these two wholly contrasting personalities soon quarrelled. He resigned and returned to Birmingham and in 1918 became a Tory M.P. He gradually developed an opposition to the persisting Lloyd George coalition, in which his half-brother was serving as Ch. of the Exch. Now in 1922 he accepted the Postmaster-Generalship under Bonar Law and within a year was promoted, *via* the Min. of Health to the Exchequer himself. This remarkable rise was checked by the advent of Ramsay Macdonald's first Labour govt. and when Baldwin returned to office, Neville refused the Exchequer because of his party's continued adherence to unfettered Free Trade. Winston Churchill, therefore, took his place and he went back to the Min. of Health (1924-9) which had much of local govt. in its remit. He led for the govt. in the derating legislation of 1925, which strongly influenced housing, and the Local Government Act 1929 which abolished the Poor Law guardians. He was again out of office from 1929 to 1931 but acted as a successful Chairman of the Conservative Party Central Office which engineered the landslide victory of 1931. As a result he went back to the Min. of Health in Macdonald's first 'National Govt' and then (in Nov.) became Ch. of the Exch. yet again. Now, in the background of the Slump, his father's idea of a general tariff (at 10%) and Imperial preference began to be realised with the aid of the Imperial Economic Conference at Ottawa in 1932, but like many Tories of his time he relied wishfully on disarmament conferences to avoid spending on the forces. In 1935 he was budgeting for defence only £1500M over 5 years. Under trade protection, his domestic social goals as well as national safety might well have been approached by higher spending on arms. With Baldwin's resignation (May 1937) he became prime minister and led an unprepared country into war. After the German occupation of Norway (May 1940) and despite his majority in the Commons, he bowed before public indignation and resigned in favour of Churchill. He continued as Lord President of the Council until he died later in the year.

CHAMBERLAIN GOVT. (May 1937-May 1940) was a continuation of Baldwin's National govt., but with Neville Chamberlain's promotion from the Exch. to which Sir John Simon moved from the Home Office. Sir Samuel Hoare took his place. Anthony Eden remained at the Foreign Office. The vital service ministers were Duff Cooper (from 1938 Lord Stanhope), Admiralty; Lord Swinton (later Sir Kingsley Wood), Air; and Hore-Belisha, War; Sir Thos. Inskip (from 1939 Lord Chatfield), Defence Co-ordination. Vist. Halifax was Lord Pres. but succeeded Eden on the latter's resignation in 1938.

(1) Hitler's aggressions (*see* WORLD WAR II-1-4) overshadowed the domestic scene and the govt. moved towards intervention in the economy with a Coal Mines Act (1938) to nationalise the coal seams but not the mining companies. Another nationalisation created British Overseas Airways. Meanwhile Hore-Belisha built barracks and made the army more comfortable.

(2) In the German crisis Chamberlain took the management out of Eden's hands (*see* APPEASEMENT) and eventually caused Eden to resign. The cabinet was temperamentally divided between those who did not want a conflict and those who thought it inevitable. Moreover, Chamberlain's natural anti-Bolshevism helped to lure him to the well-meant but tragic Munich agreement (q.v.). Meanwhile rearmament went qualitatively forward in the development of radar and good fighter aircraft, and conscription was introduced, but naval expansion lagged because of the time needed to build ships. By Aug. 1939, however, the govt. felt itself in a position no longer to tolerate Hitler's demands.

(3) On the eve of war, the Min. of Transport, Leslie Burgin, became Min. of (War) Supply. On the outbreak all the members of the cabinet offered their resignations and a War Cabinet was formed composed of Chamberlain, Hoare, Simon, Halifax, Hore-Belisha, Kingsley Wood, Churchill, Chatfield with Lord Hankey as Min. without Portfolio.

(4) Although Chamberlain's uncomprehending conduct of the war ended with an enforced resignation, his govt. can be credited with the foundation of a fair rationing system combined with subsidies for basic foodstuffs, which between them ensured that the wartime British were well nourished. In addition it instituted the sterling area, a world-wide system of sea-traffic control as part of the British blockade and an excess profits tax against war profiteering. The British Expeditionary Force was successfully transported to France.

(5) As a result of the disastrous Norwegian campaign, a Labour vote of censure was supported by a significant and influential body of conservatives and the govt. fell on the day when the Germans invaded the Low Countries in order to outflank the Maginot Line. In an atmosphere of mounting gravity, Chamberlain, who enjoyed power and phone-tapped his political opponents, proposed a coalition but Labour refused to support one led by him. He was forced to advise the King to send for Churchill.

CHAMBERLAYNE (1) Edward (1616-1703); (2) John (?-1723) both learned, published *Angliae Notitiae or the Present State of England*, a handbook modelled on *L'Estat Nouveau de la France* (Paris 1661) with statistics and names of public officers. The first edition appeared in 1669. A certain John Miege plagiarised the work from 1691 in *The New State of England*, the last, 22nd, appeared in 1723 and booksellers published 14 further ones, the last in 1755.

CHAMBERLEN. A family of male-midwives of Huguenot origin which settled in England in 1559. **Peter (1560-1631)** invented the modern obstetric forceps. It enabled the family to deliver more women with greater safety than anyone else and they kept it a close secret. They practised with great credit at court until the death of **Hugh (c. 1700)** His widow then hid the forceps, which came to light only in 1813.

CHAMBERS OF COMMERCE AND TRADE. The first Chamber of Commerce so-called, was established at Marseilles in 1599 to settle merchant law and customs of the port, to appoint consuls in the Levant and to deal by way of diplomacy or reprisal with the Barbary States. In 1700 such Chambers were created at other French ports. These French Chambers were really local trade authorities. The first English chamber for the protection and promotion of common interests was formed in 1768 in Jersey where it was natural to use a French name for an institution which was essentially different, being voluntary not official. In the United Kingdom Chambers of Commerce were primarily organisations of manufacturers and wholesalers. The earliest were at Glasgow and Belfast (1783), Edinburgh, Leeds and Manchester (1785); they then spread widely. The Birmingham Chamber was founded in 1813. The ASSOCIATION OF BRITISH CHAMBERS OF COMMERCE was founded in 1860, the powerful London Chamber in 1881. Meantime there also grew up a parallel and sometimes rival system of CHAMBERS OF TRADE for retailers. Some small town chambers of trade were called chambers of commerce. These were smaller but very numerous. The NATIONAL CHAMBER OF TRADE, founded in 1897, had 800 affiliates.

CHAMBER OF SHIPPING founded in 1878 to defend the interests of British shipping, by then beginning to feel the effects of not always scrupulous competition. In alliance with business generally it sought to remove barriers encourage equal safety standards and expand world trade. In 1921 it promoted the International Shipping Conference, later the International Chamber of Shipping.

CHAMBERS, Sir William (1726-96) went to China as a supercargo in 1742 to 1744, subsequently became an architect, settled in London in 1755 and was employed at Kew where he laid out the landscape and built the pagoda. He also wrote a *Treatise of Civil Architecture* (1759). A pioneer of English *Chinoiserie*, he nevertheless designed Somerset House (London) in 1775. He was lampooned for his Chinoiserie but his classification of Greek and Roman architectural styles, based on careful measurement and observation, has influenced architectural thought ever since. He also designed the royal coronation coach.

CHAMILLART, Michel (1652-1721) became Louis XIV's Intendant of Finance in 1690, *Controleur-General des Finances* in 1699 and Sec. of State for War in 1701. An honest but limited man, he nevertheless made possible the fielding of large armies during most of the disastrous wars of the Spanish Succession. The financial business was transferred to Desmarets in Feb. 1708 and Chamillart resigned the rest of his posts in 1709.

CHAMPAGNE (France) and its FAIRS. In 966 the counties of Troyes and Meaux were united and became the nucleus of the later feudal state of Champagne, under the House of Vermandois, which intermarried with the House of Blois. Hence, when the Vermandois died out in 1023, Champagne passed to Blois (*see* ADELA, NORMAN RULERS 1087-1154). There was a partition between 1089 and 1125 followed by a reunion. Count HENRY I (1152-81) married Mary, *d* of Louis VII of France. His son HENRY II (v. 1181-97) a leading crusader, married Isabel of Jerusalem in 1192. His nephew THEOBALD IV (v. 1201-53) a celebrated troubadour, succeeded his uncle Sancho VII as K. of Navarre in 1234 and thereafter until the death of HENRY III, Champagne and Navarre were held by the same family. Henry III's *d.* JOAN married Philip the Fair of France in 1284. He became King in 1285. In 1305 she died leaving Champagne to her son LOUIS, who unified it (but not Navarre) with the French Crown when he became Louis X in 1314. The county derived its political importance from its threatening position on either side of Paris and the development of the great mediaeval CHAMPAGNE FAIRS. Six were held every year: one each at Lagny and Bar, two each at Provins and Troyes. They lasted seven weeks each, the second to the fifth being devoted to trading. Goods from all over Europe were sold and the fairs developed into a primitive banking institution, especially for clearances. They began to decline at the beginning of the 14th cent. because of the rise of the Hanse and of Paris, and the diversion of trade over the Alps and along the Rhine.

CHAMPERTY. *See* MAINTENANCE.

CHAMPION, KING'S or QUEEN'S. By a judgement of the Lord High Steward in 1377 the holder of this already old ceremonial office is the Lord of the manor of Scrivelsby (Lincs.), held by the Dymoke family until the reign of George VI. The Champion's function, of challenging anyone who disputes the sovereign's right, is performed only at coronation banquets, which have not been held since 1728. As the lordship is now owned by a gravel company, it is uncertain what would happen if they were revived.

CHAMPLAIN, Samuel de. *See* CANADA-2.

CHANAK INCIDENT (1921). By the T. of Sèvres (1920) the allies imposed a theoretical peace upon Turkey, whereby there was to be a neutralised area on the Asiatic side of the Dardanelles; most of Thrace and the Aegean coast of Asia Minor was given to Greece and the rest divided into British, French and Italian spheres of influence. This, of course, provoked a strong nationalist reaction led by Mustafa Kemal (later Atatürk). A provisional capital was set up at Ankara, out of reach of allied troops and naval guns; the Turkish army was reassembled and turned on the Greeks, who were decisively beaten at the B. of the Sakaria (Aug. 1921). It now advanced towards Chanak on the Dardanelles and on Smyrna. Evidently a new treaty must be made with Turkey or Kemal be opposed by force. The French and the Italians (now anti-British) repudiated their guarantee, leaving the British as the only protectors of the neutral zone. The Dominions were lukewarm. Lloyd George, who was pro-Greek, ordered the local commander Gen. Harington, to resist, but he thought that he would be overwhelmed and sensibly negotiated an armistice at MUDANIA. English opinion would not have supported a new war. This left the Turks with a free hand at Smyrna. Those of the Greek population who had not fled were massacred when the town was taken. Lloyd George was hotly criticised at home for his pro-Greek stance and for having exposed Britain to this humiliation. Led by Bonar Law, the Conservatives, at their CARLTON CLUB MEETING, used the opportunity or pretext to abandon their coalition with the Liberals, and Lloyd George fell from power. It was left to Curzon, as Foreign Sec., to clear up the international imbroglio at the Lausanne Conference and T. (1922-3). This settled the main outline of the Turkish State on the lines of Kemal's demands and ended the allied occupation of Constantinople but, at

British insistence, neutralised the Straits by demilitarisation and the creation of an international permanent commission.

CHANCELLOR OF THE EXCHEQUER (*see also* TREASURY). In Norman times the Lord Chancellor attended the sessions of the Exchequer with his clerk. By the reign of Henry III the clerk, by now known as the Chancellor of the Exchequer, was deputising for him. When the Exchequer for which, with the Treasury, the Lord Treasurer was responsible, passed to the Treasury Commission as a whole the Chancellor of the Exchequer became a member of the Commission. Before long it was accepted that he could act for the Treasury Board. Thus his rise dates from his membership of the Treasury Commissions of James I and Charles I and was subsequently unaffected by the decline of the mediaeval Exchequer. The new style Treasury Commission set up by Charles II in 1667 increased his importance still further. The Lord Chancellor and the Secretaries of State, who overshadowed him on the earlier Commissions, were no longer members and when, from the 1750s, the First Lord became preoccupied with the wider functions of First Minister, the Chancellor developed into the working head of the Treasury. The change was slow. As late as the early 19th cent. the office did not always carry Cabinet rank. The first modern holder, charged with the efficiency and economy of the whole machine of govt. and concerned through finance with most lines of govt. policy, was Gladstone, whose periods of office (1852-5, 1859-66, 1873-4 and 1880-2) totalled 13 years. Gladstone commissioned the Northcote-Trevelyan Report on civil service reform during his first tenure; during his second he set up a unified govt. administration and a unified system of expenditure control to match it. In 1866 his Exchequer and Audit Departments Act gave this control statutory force. The Northcote-Trevelyan reforms of 1870 (instituted by Sir Robert Lowe) created a civil service which could operate it.

CHANCELLOR, Richard (?-1556), after sailing the Levant, commanded a ship and was pilot-general in Sir Hugh Willoughby's North-East Passage expedition in 1553. He lost touch with the rest of the fleet but reached Archangel. He then continued overland to Moscow where he impressed the Czar Ivan the Terrible and obtained trading privileges for the English. He returned in 1554. In 1555 he visited the Czar's court again but was wrecked on the way back. The negotiations of 1554 opened the way for the formation of the Muscovy Co.

CHANCELLORS' ROLLS were duplicates of the Pipe Roll kept as a check upon it. The series, with some gaps, runs from 1163 to 1831.

CHANCERY, CHANCELLOR, LORD HIGH. (Lat = *Cancella* = screen, hence a screened off place, or office, cf Ger = *Kanzel*). (1) The chancellor was the earliest of the King's official secretaries. He managed the written business of govt. and affixed the King's seal, later the Great Seal, to official documents. The Chancery was originally in the Household, and since it moved with the King, the screens were doubtless portable. In a primitive administration the Chancery (a) *received* communications relating to policy which would be brought before the King or his council and petitions or requests for justice or mercy which would be settled somehow; (b) *issued* the King's commands and decisions. Thus on the policy side the Chancery provided the secretariat for the council; on the executive side it issued writs and other orders embodying decisions; and on the more personal side it dealt with injustices. These functions arose under the pressures of necessity and were not departmentalised, or even closely thought out. The paper simply passed through the Chancery.

(2) The Chancellor had to be a man of exceptional capacity and high education, such as could be found or rewarded only in the high ranks of the church. Before 1238 he was generally a well-beneficed churchman holding office for (on average) four years. Thereafter he was paid a fixed sum out of which he maintained his clerks and by 1320 the Great Seal fees were being paid to the Exchequer. If the Chancellor was not, at least, a bishop he very soon became one. His prestige was a compound of association with the crown and the royal council, high ecclesiastical rank, sheer ability, power to grant or influence favours and regular presence at the seat of the govt. Originally decisions promulgated through the chancery were made by the King, or the Council or by councillors brought in to advise. As the volume of business grew, its scope was extended, specialisation set in and routines developed.

(3) The first extensions arose from the injustices for which the common law envisaged no remedy. The chancellor probably settled minor PETITIONS himself from the earliest times. By mid 13th cent. petitions needing some kind of litigious treatment were habitually referred by the King or the Council to him, and he was driven more and more into dealing with them judicially. Simultaneously the problem of making law courts sit and dispense justice had been solved by the invention of ORIGINAL WRITS, which came to be issued by the Chancery as a matter of course, rather than discretion.

(4) The association with the Council, the business of issuing writs and the function of dealing with petitions and improving the law brought about a natural connection with Parliament when it began to develop. The Chancery issued the WRITS OF SUMMONS: the Chancellor was already the King's mouthpiece to the people. He naturally became his mouthpiece in parliament and so, by a short step, the permanent presiding officer of the House of Lords. Significantly he did not need to be, for this purpose, a member of the House, for the magnates who composed it managed their own procedure. In 1995 this was still true.

(5) The issue of a new original writ was tantamount to legislation. The Common Law courts tended to resist them by nonsuiting plaintiffs or rejecting their claims as unknown to the law, and the barons disliked them. The Provisions of Oxford (1258) required that no new original writ should issue without the authority of the King or Council. The Stat. of Westminster II (1285) permitted new ones if they were in *consimili casu* (closely analogous to settled precedent) but required other cases to be referred to the next parliament. Thenceforth the list of such writs could effectively be extended by parliament alone. The Chancellor's power directly to develop the Common Law thereafter flowed through other channels: mainly the drafting of legislation and the development of the **Court of Chancery,** but an important contributing factor was the size and work of the Chancery. It was inconvenient to keep it as a department of a peripatetic royal household. Though commonly settled at Westminster, it was still following the King occasionally after 1300. When it became stationary, its public image as a tribunal naturally became more prominent. By 1340 it was being treated as a major court alongside the others, but its decisions were regarded as acts of council, and common law judges as well as councillors were often summoned to take part in the discussions (cf Star Chamber). It was not until 1474 that the Chancellor began to issue decrees by his own authority and this practice arose because in the Wars of the Roses, the magnates of the Council were in mortal conflict, the jurisdiction of the courts was in parts unenforceable and the Chancellor had to act alone or not act at all. Very soon it became a habit.

(6) The separation into an independent institution was now accelerated by three other factors. Many cases had always fallen outside the common law and had, therefore, to be settled by the Chancellor and Council. The most important concerned alien traders and the commonly overlapping subject of maritime disputes, and ecclesiastical law; since 1360 an Admiralty court had been functioning and so had the important ecclesiastical Court of Arches, of still older foundation. The council increasingly diverted cases to these courts. Secondly there were areas or times when disorder prevented the proper functioning of ordinary courts and the council had to take stern measures of a quasi-criminal character to get the law obeyed. These were taken through the process of the PRIVY SEAL, which was cheaper, more expeditious, more secret but in the long run less secure than the Great Seal procedure of the Chancery. The Lord Privy Seal presided in the Council acting in this criminal capacity. Hence property titles requiring security were left to the Chancery: short term issues related to order remained with the Council and its new offshoot, the STAR CHAMBER. Then, thirdly, the Chancery had to create a jurisprudence capable on its own of supplementing the Common Law, especially in the matter of remedies, for the Chancery could compel performance of a specific act upon pain of imprisonment, where the common law courts could award only monetary compensation (*damages*).

(7) This supplementary jurisdiction developed into the important branch of law called **Equity.** It was still an era when the idea of changing the law by statute was being only reluctantly propounded and therefore a jurisprudence capable of adapting it to new cases was welcome. Under the Chancellorship of Sir Thomas More (1529-32) nearly 500 suits were commenced. Under James I the *annual* average was over 1450. Chancellors, being politicians with other calls on their time, were overwhelmed with judicial work which accumulated delays; eventually, too, they had to be lawyers. After Card. Wolsey (1515-29), More and Audley (1529-44) were lawyers. Wriothesley (1544-7) was a politician. Rich (1547-51) was a lawyer. Godrich, Gardiner and Heath (1552-8) were not lawyers. Thereafter the only non-lawyers were Sir Chris. Hatton (1587-91), Bishop Williams (1621-5) and the E. of Shaftesbury (1672-3), who was, however, well acquainted with Chancery business.

(8) Congestion attracted staff. There had always been Chancery officials called **masters,** *collaterales* or *socii* (associates) or *praeceptores*. Their number was fixed at twelve and they assisted the Chancellor in hearing cases and often examined witnesses or investigated other evidence. They lived collegiately and their head, who also supervised the chancery records, was the **Master of the Rolls.** By 1623 he was the recognised Lord Chancellor's deputy and even, sometimes, called the Vice-Chancellor. He controlled a body of clerks, of whom the chief were the **Six Clerks** (with the Sixty Clerks under them), who drafted all the major documents. These clerks originally acted for litigants, but the press of business eventually made this impossible and by 1605 litigants were beginning to employ professionals who knew whom to solicit, i.e. **solicitors.**

(9) The other expedient for relieving congestion was the conciliar COURT OF REQUESTS which was set up in 1493 and functioned until 1642.

(10) Chancery officials were paid by fees; hence they resisted efforts to increase their number and reduce their incomes. Too few for the growing work, they employed under-paid deputies, who did the work badly or took bribes for expedition. The offices were habitually bought: the price of a mastership in 1621 was £150. In 1703 a Six Clerkship passed for £5000. Everyone who understood the system had a vested interest in maintaining it, while suits might be expensively protracted for years: a tithe suit commenced in 1644 for £4 ended in 1666 having cost £200.

(11) The jealousy of common lawyers (who had mostly supported parliament) and the manifest abuses in the Chancery made attack inevitable. The Nominated Parliament (1653) resolved to reform it, but the bill fell

when the Parliament was dissolved. Cromwell enacted this bill as an Ordinance in 1654. It was largely unworkable and the lawyer commissioners of the Great Seal resigned, leaving the court in the hands of two army officers. The Ordinance lapsed in 1657 and was not replaced. There were then scenes of confusion when the old officials returned to claim their places. The old system, with its abuses, was restored at the Restoration and though there were widespread complaints and even reform bills (1690, 1691, 1692), select committees (1729-33) and a royal commission (1740) nothing was done. Meanwhile the disappearance of the Star Chamber and the Court of Requests had increased the congestion, the abuses and the profits. The price of a mastership was £1000 in 1689 and £6000 by 1702. The reason was that interest on funds in court was paid to them. When the South Sea Bubble burst, a deficit of over £1M was found in four masters' accounts. They were deprived of the control of funds in court and their offices then became unsaleable.

(12) The court was reformed after 1813, when a Vice-Chancellor was appointed. In 1831 the Bankruptcy jurisdiction was passed to a new Bankruptcy Court. After 1833 Masters were appointed by the Crown. In 1842 two more Vice-Chancellors were appointed and the Six Clerks abolished and in 1851 a Court of Appeal in Chancery was set up. The Court was amalgamated into the High Court in 1873. The administrative and parliamentary functions continue.

CHANCERY WARRANTS (*see* WALTON ORDINANCES) were warrants under the Privy Seal authorising and limiting the use of the Great Seal while the King (in the case of the originator, Edward III) was overseas from 1338.

CHANDERNAGORE (Bengal) was a site, granted to the French East India Co. in 1673, where they built a factory in 1690-2. Captured by Clive and Watson in 1756, it was restored to the French as a demilitarised trading centre in 1763. It was merged in India in 1950.

CHANDOS. *See* BRYDGES.

CHANDOS CLAUSE was an amendment moved by the M. Chandos to the second Reform Bill and accepted by the govt. It extended the county franchise to £50 tenants at will who, under open voting, could be controlled by their landlords.

CHANDOS, Sir John (?-1370) K.G. (1349) fought at Crécy (1346), saved the Black Prince's life at Poitiers (1356), became Edward III's Lieutenant in France in 1360 and Constable of Guienne in 1362. He won the victory at Auray (Brittany) in 1364 and fought at Navarete (Spain) in 1367. In 1368 he resigned but was persuaded to return and became Seneschal of Poitou in 1369. He died of wounds at the B. of Mortemer.

CHANGKUFENG (Korea) (1938) and NOMANHAN (Outer Mongolia) (1939) "INCIDENTS" were considerable Russo-Japanese pitched battles provoked by Japanese attempts to secure debatable border lands, and in which the Japanese were defeated. They led in Apr. 1941 to a Russo-Japanese non-aggression pact because both powers looked forward, for different reasons, to a Japanese attack on the U.S.A. Actually the Germans surprised Russia ten weeks later. The Russians broke the pact once the Allies had defeated Japan.

CHANNEL FLEET, based on Portsmouth and Plymouth, existed so long as France was the main maritime danger. The Admiralty used the Anglo-French Entente of 1904 to move ships to the Atlantic and North Sea from the Mediterranean and by Feb. 1909 the Channel Fleet was deemed unnecessary and it was incorporated with the Home Fleet.

CHANNEL Is. (Fr = *Isles Normandes*) (*see also* ALDERNEY; GUERNSEY; HERM; JERSEY; MINQUIERS; SARK). The islands were taken over from Bretons by Normans in the 10th cent. and when Normandy fell to France this remnant of the Duchy remained under the English Kings. The local law continued to be based on the Coûtumier of Rouen and the two bailiwicks of Jersey and Guernsey developed slightly divergent institutions besides an entrepôt trade between England, Normandy and Gascony which could be policed only from their own harbours. It was thus convenient for the Crown to leave them with their institutional and fiscal autonomy. At the Reformation they were transferred from the diocese of Coutances to Winchester, but Jersey was effectively Calvinist until 1823 and Guernsey until 1662. In the Civil War Jersey was royalist, Guernsey parliamentarian save for Castle Cornet. Jersey and the castle fell to the parliament together in 1651. Wartime privateering and peacetime smuggling were the main sources of prosperity between 1670 and 1815 and the latter is still not unknown, though it now supplements greenhouse cultivation.

CHANNEL TUNNEL. In 1876 an Anglo-French protocol followed by legislation in each country permitted the formation of a Channel Tunnel company which by 1882 had dug 2000 yds. of tunnel at each end near Dover and at Sangatte (Fr.). Operations were then suspended on military grounds. The idea was taken up and dropped in 1914 and in 1930 a Committee reported that it was desirable to proceed. After World War II further surveys were languidly undertaken, but the French and British govts. announced in 1964 that they intended to go ahead. Several years of further surveys preceded actual construction, which was hotly opposed by ferry operators, environmentalists and local pressure groups all the way to London. Construction was completed in 1994. The controversy about the rail and road links was not stilled in 1996.

CHANTREY BEQUEST. Sir Francis Legatt Chantrey **(1781-1841),** a Sheffield grocer's boy, was apprenticed to a woodcarver and from 1802 practised as a portrait sculptor and painter. By 1804 he was exhibiting at the Royal Academy and in 1822 he made a bust of George IV. Knighted in 1835, he bequeathed his property to the Royal Academy.

CHANTRIES were benefices for chanting masses for the soul of a deceased and often comprised a chapel inside a church. The chantry priest could not interfere in the functions or share the revenues of the incumbent and therefore he had no pastoral work. As a result many chantry priests acted as schoolmasters and chantry schools were an important feature of English 14th and 15th cent. education. In 1545 an Act of Henry VIII ineffectually vested Chantry revenues in the King for life, but in 1547 under a new Act nearly 2400 chantries were suppressed. The funds were to be applied to charity and for pensions to chantry priests, but were widely embezzled. Some of the suppressed chantries developed into the "Edwardian" grammar schools.

CHAPELS ROYAL belong to existing and former court establishments. There were ten in 1970. They are subject not to a diocesan bishop but to the Dean of the Chapels Royal, who is usually a bishop. Royal chaplains are often influential figures at court and the Chapels have a long and important musical tradition.

CHAPLIN, Sir Charles Spencer (CHARLIE CHAPLIN) (1889-1977) spent his childhood in Kennington (London). He started in music hall at the age of ten and got his first important part (as Billy in a play about Sherlock Holmes) at the age of 16. He first appeared with Fred Karno in the U.S.A. in 1910 and made his first film in 1913. His famous appearance from which he never deviated was first devised for his second film *Kid Auto Races at Venice* in 1914. In 1919 he helped to found United Artists. He had strong opinions about the plight of the weak and oppressed and some of his films got him into trouble with right-wing opinion. He nevertheless became very rich. At one time he was notorious for his passing affairs, but was much assisted by his wife, Oona.

CHAPMEN were itinerant door-to-door traders who bought and sold things likely to be wanted by householders and local craftsmen such as, in earlier times, iron and salt and later buttons, lace, sewing thread or chap books. They virtually died out in the 19th cent. Those who use the word as a surname and are armigerous commonly have arms, though unconscious of any relationship, with the same basic characteristic which is found not only in Britain viz:- *per chevron, a crescent counter-changed*.

CHAPTER. *See* CATHEDRALS.

CHAPUYS, Eustace (?-1556) was imperial ambassador to Henry VIII during most of the years 1529 to 1545 and the mouthpiece of the Emperor Charles V in his support of his aunt Katharine of Aragon. His partisanship affected the quality of his many surviving despatches.

CHARCOAL was used in iron smelting from very early times and the Sussex Weald was the great centre of English charcoal-burning ancillary to the large local early and mediaeval iron industry. Later, charcoal was in demand for gunpowder and from the 16th cent. also for drying hops. Charcoal burners were called 'colliers' which, in various forms, became a surname. The industry declined as supplies of wood ran down in the 17th cent. and in the 18th, coal and then coke began to supersede charcoal in smelting and heating, while gunpowder was replaced in the 19th by other explosives.

CHARING CROSS (London) was erected to mark the last halting place of the body of Eleanor of Castile, Edward I's queen, before her burial at Westminster. It was originally on the site of Charles I's statue in Whitehall. The cross now in the forecourt of the railway station is a copy.

CHARITY. A. Nature. Legal charity is a branch of public administration rooted in private benevolence. A private gift of identified property for a clearly charitable object is valid even though it infringes the Rule against Perpetuities (*see* LAND TENURE). The object of the gift must be public, i.e. directed to the benefit of the community or part of it, and not contrary to the policy of the law. In addition such a gift must still fall within one of five categories. Four of these have been deduced (*see* PEMSEL'S CASE 1893) from the preamble to the statute 43 Eliz I c.4. which gives examples rather than a definition. The guiding principle (not always consistently applied) may be described in non-technical terms as help to people who are weak in body, spirit or attainments or who are in a weak situation. The first four categories are thus **(1)** relief of poverty; **(2)** education; **(3)** the advancement of religion; **(4)** miscellaneous unclassifiable objects including provision of bridges, life belts and public water, relieving the parish rates and redeeming captives from slavery. The fifth class, recognised by statute in 1958, is the provision of recreational facilities for the public or so as to improve the condition of life of people in need of them.

B. Administration. A charity is not to fail for lack of somebody to run it; therefore the att-gen. could, in the last resort, apply to the Lord Chancellor to appoint trustees. Conversely a charity being perpetual, its objects might become obsolete in the course of time so that the trustees have an accumulating fund which cannot or should not be spent. The provision of bridges, for example, is now a function of local and central govt. Accordingly the trustees could ask the Lord Chancellor to make schemes changing the management or objects of the charity. Such *schemes* had theoretically to be made *Cy près,* i.e. as close in intention as possible to that of the original founder. This has not always been done.

Older trusts sometimes laid down who should nominate trustees or make schemes, but the Lord Chancellor's powers passed via the Chancery Court to the High Court. In 1853 the Charity Commissioners were created to exercise the courts' powers in non-contentious and administrative matters so that in practice 99% of the central work was not done by the court at all. Under the Charities Act, 1960, trustees were required to register their trusts. Failure to register did not invalidate the trust. Registration, on the other hand, conferred powerful benefits. Charities being for the public benefit have never been taxed and have had rating privileges varying from time to time. The principal advantage of registration was that entry on the register was conclusive of charitable status and therefore of entitlement to fiscal privileges.

C. Importance. The total value of charitable funds at any given moment is unknown but very large. They include the major religious and educational endowments and many thousands of benevolent and other funds. Of 107 people who left over £500,000 to charity in 1993-4 many left over £1M, and two left £98M between them.

CHARLECOTE (Warks.). Tudor mansion built in 1551 for the Lucy family which occupied the site from 1189 to 1946.

CHARLEMAGNE. *See* CAROLINGIANS.

CHARLES I (1600-49) D. of ALBANY (1600), D. of YORK (1605), P. of WALES (1616). (1) In 1616 there were abortive negotiations for a marriage with Pr. Christine of France and from 1617 to 1618 with the Infanta Maria of Spain. The latter were revived in 1622 and the prince and BUCKINGHAM went to Madrid in 1623, but political and religious obstacles prevented a match. (*See* JAMES I.)

(2) On their return they became the effective rulers of the Kingdoms in James' dotage and rode the crest of a popular clamour for a Spanish War in the interests of protestantism, Charles' Palatine sister ELIZABETH and the plunder of the Spanish trade. A French marriage and alliance was sought; alliances with Holland and Denmark made (June 1624); an army under Mansfeld was assembled. (*See* THIRTY YEARS' WAR-1-11.) Charles became King in Mar. 1625 and married **Henrietta Maria** of France in May, but the French refused to intervene in favour of the Palatinate and borrowed ships against their own Huguenot rebels. Mansfeld's army melted through disease. The Dutch were to blockade Spanish Flanders and supply a 20% contingent for an English naval attack on Spain under Buckingham. This expedition, crippled by shortage of money, dishonest victuallers and incompetent pressed crews, sailed in Oct. for Cadiz and returned baffled and diseased. Since parliament would not vote funds to prosecute the war properly, it degenerated during the next four years into ill conducted private forays against the Spanish coast, while Dunkirk privateers made havoc of English trade.

(3) The use of English ships against the Huguenots was inconsistent with the protestant policy and a scandal in England: so when the defeated Huguenot, Soubise, arrived as a refugee the govt. could not act against him as Richelieu wanted. Public opinion wanted the opposite. In Feb. 1626, however, Richelieu, through English mediation, came to terms with the Huguenots and in Mar. (T. of Monzon) to a partial settlement with Spain. Alliance with France had become obviously impossible: war much more likely, especially as the Huguenots now expected English protection. The Spanish war provided the occasion. The English seized French ships trading with Spanish territory: the French embargoed English ships. Anti-papist feeling forced Charles to expel his queen's R. Catholic attendants when the protestant armies were severely defeated in Germany. The wreck of the Cadiz expedition was now reinforced for a campaign against France. The Huguenots rose and in Aug. 1627 Richelieu besieged them in La Rochelle. The adjacent Ile de Ré beat back a first relieving expedition under Buckingham and a second under his brother-in-law Denbigh: Buckingham, waiting to take command of a third, was murdered at Portsmouth in Aug. 1628 by John Felton, a victim of the Cadiz disaster.

(4) The resources for these ventures had been raised by doubtfully legal means which encountered skilfully engineered unpopularity. Charles had continued to collect tonnage and poundage after the parliamentary grant of 1625 ran out and imposed forced loans amounting to five subsidies as well. The ragged troops and sailors had been billeted upon villages as they made their destructive way to the ports; martial law had been used to enforce coat-and-conduct money and other military exactions. The issues were raised in the *Five Knights Case,* and in June 1628 by the PETITION OF RIGHT. Buckingham's murder was greeted with an enthusiasm which offended the King. He felt entrapped and bearing the discredit for a failure, for which lack of parliamentary support was really to blame; but in Oct. 1628 La Rochelle surrendered and the *casus beii* disappeared.

(5) Charles now resolved to rule without a parliament and after the Commons had voted the THREE RESOLUTIONS he dissolved it (Mar. 1629). The economies of peace became essential to his political policy. The P. of Susa (14 Apr. 1629) settled the French conflicts, but a Spanish peace was more difficult to obtain and eventually more humiliating. The T. of Madrid (5 Nov. 1630) virtually restored the Anglo-Spanish position of 1604, but Charles had to abandon his allies and his Palatine sister to secure it. Thenceforth he had no foreign policy.

(6) Having eliminated his biggest single expense, the King next sought to dispose of his debts, of just over £1M. Creditors were charmed, cajoled or bullied into accepting partial satisfaction by grants of crown land or a pension, or by patronage expedients such as the proceeds of a jurisdiction, a monopoly or a sinecure. Then the new Lord Treasurer, Richard Ld. WESTON (c. 1628) reduced the expenses of the court and, by ignoring the debts, very nearly balanced the books at about £600,000 for seven years running. This, however, was done by means which successively alienated important interests. The treatment of the debts undermined the King's credit and the attempted court economies divided the court. But it was the systematic development of unparliamentary revenues which engendered increasing opposition. The continued collection of tonnage and poundage from passively resisting merchants invaded trade and parliamentary privilege. Compounding for infringements of old Acts against inclosures, struck at major landowners who sometimes even had to rebuild demolished villages. Distraint of knighthood irritated the middle-sized estate owners. The strict enforcement of forest laws affected thousands who happened to live in long forgotten forests such as nearly all Essex. New fees in the Court of Wards served as an onerous inheritance duty especially upon those who hoped to dispose of their property by will. Tax farming exacerbated the public mood, for the farmers, like monopolists, were friends or favourites at court and took between 25% and 30% of the proceeds.

(7) Above all, these exactions, lawful or not, were a constitutional hypocrisy: the legal justification of any one of them was not a true statement of the purposes to which the money was to be put. Thus the extension in 1635 of ship money levies from coastal counties, which had always been liable, to the whole Kingdom, became the symbolic grievance. The King was judicially advised that he might impose levies for the defence of the realm against danger, of which he was the sole judge. There were no dangers against which warships had to be financed by ship money, yet Charles persisted in levying it. Since the budget was already balanced, ship money might give the King a permanent surplus: he might be able to pay a standing army, never call parliament again and impose an autocracy. Moreover the tax was regressive, weighing it was said (with some exaggeration) intolerably on the poor.

(8) The opposition to autocracy ran deeper than economics or law. The most efficiently autocratic of Charles' advisers was Sir Thomas Wentworth (Vist. from

1628), E. of STRAFFORD (from 1640). He struck up an alliance and friendship with the Arminian William LAUD, who became Abp. of Canterbury in 1633. The strong and numerous puritan sects feared a King who believed in his Divine Right, with Strafford at his table, Laud at his altar, an army at his back and a French R. Catholic in his bed.

(9) A motley coalition thus began to form, but since there was no parliament in which to proclaim its ideas or make its deals, it was resolved to use the law courts. John HAMPDEN, a rich Buckinghamshire squire, refused to pay 1's worth of ship money and in 1637 contested its legality. The proceedings excited immense interest for it was necessary to argue the extreme cases: on the crown's behalf, for the prerogative, on the defendant's side for parliamentary control of taxation. The success of this opposition exercise in public relations may be gauged by the ship money defalcations. These were in 1634, 1%; in 1635, 2½%; in 1636, 3½%; in 1637, when Hampden's case began, 9%; in 1638, when judgement was given against him, 20½%.

(10) Two Scottish events, given Charles' character, began his fatal decline. Under the Scottish Act of Revocation (1625) the crown resumed all Scots church and crown lands alienated since 1542. By confiscations, forfeitures and alienations in good faith most Scots landowning families were affected to their fury. The Scots nobility whose leaders formed the backbone of the Scots Privy Council were permanently antagonised. To make matters worse, the judicial Lords of Session were called progressively less often to the Council, which was manned by persons of only mediocre local standing and knowledge. Hence the King was no longer properly in touch with the drift of Scottish events. Thus the second seminal occurrence was his Scots coronation at Edinburgh in June 1633. He had no idea how much its high episcopal ceremonial offended the strongly presbyterian population. Deviations from a proper Anglican mode could, he thought and as Laud advised, be corrected by new canons (May 1635) and a new service book (1637). The attempt to use it at St. Giles' Edinburgh led to a riot, an alliance between the nobles and the Kirk and wholesale defiance of the King's authority by a population united against "Popery" and traditionally hostile to England. By Feb. 1638 the leadership had drawn up the Scots NATIONAL COVENANT and between 27th Feb. and 9th Mar. almost every adult male in Scotland signed it. It prevented an accommodation with the King, for he refused to abandon his theoretical outlook or even, despite advice, the Service Book.

(11) The only possibility seemed to be temporary (i.e. insincere) concession. A General Assembly of the Kirk was summoned to Glasgow for Nov. 1638: the Estates for May 1639. The Assembly was elected (to the impotent royal displeasure) on a presbyterian model and promptly demanded that bishops should be held responsible to it. To the King this was intolerable. His Commissioner, Hamilton, refused it. The Assembly persisted. Hamilton dissolved it. The Assembly defied him and continued to sit (Dec. 1638). It had now become a revolutionary body. It proceeded to re-establish presbyterianism and deprive non-presbyterian ministers of their livings; the new canons and the FIVE ARTICLES OF PERTH went the same way. Whatever the law might be (and the Assembly's Acts were questionable) they had the support of the nation. From Charles' point of view the Kingdom was in rebellion. Both sides armed.

(12) While the Scots fielded an army under Swedish trained officers, Charles could not afford a professional army at all. He had to rely upon the northern train-bands and the followings of disaffected lords. The FIRST BISHOPS' WAR consisted of a skirmish at Turriff (24 May 1639) followed by the T. of Berwick (18 June). The Scots agreed to disband, Charles that ecclesiastical affairs

should be determined by the Assembly and civil matters by the Estates. The Assembly promptly abolished episcopacy and the Service Book, while the Estates enacted that the Lords of the Articles should consist of members chosen by their respective estates. Control of the Scots parliament consequently passed from the crown to a committee of presbyterian nobles and burgesses.

(13) The English Privy Council's Scottish Committee (Committee of Eight) advised that an English Parliament should be summoned, and that meanwhile a loan (eventually amounting to £230,000) should be raised to form an army; the SHORT PARLIAMENT, however (13 Apr. 5 May 1640), refused to vote any supplies and efforts to raise ship money and City loans failed. Strafford had suggested using the Irish army, but the southern train bands were mobilised instead. Thereupon the Scots returned. In the SECOND BISHOPS' WAR the train bands proved useless and by Aug. the Scots had overrun the north-east nearly to York. Charles was against calling another parliament: the opposition launched the Petition of the Peers in favour of one. Charles attempted something less by calling the last Magnum Concilium to York. This body dominated by the opposition peers urged the calling of a parliament and to ensure that its views would prevail, negotiated the T. of Ripon, whereby the Scots should continue to occupy Northumberland and Durham and be paid £850 a day. The King's purse could not stand this for long. Writs for a new parliament were issued in Oct.

(14) The famous LONG PARLIAMENT met on 3rd Nov. 1640 in an atmosphere of panic. Pym intended to impeach the King's ministers; Strafford to arraign him and his friends for treasonable dealings with the Scots. The charge was inherently probable but no evidence, *stricto sensu*, survives. Each side learned of the other's intention, but Pym got in his blow first. The Articles of Impeachment were passed and hastily carried to the Lords who ordered Strafford's arrest. After this excitement came an anti-climax: the Commons could not make their case, for it depended upon a paltry attempt to twist Strafford's advice in the Committee of Eight into advice to use the Irish army against England. The Lords, who mostly disliked Strafford, were increasingly incredulous. By Mar. 1641 it was obvious that the tiger might be let out but there had been discussions between courtiers and some malcontent soldiers and rumours of these were blown up into an ARMY PLOT; and besides, Charles had refused to disband the Irish army. The radical Sir Arthur Heselrigge played upon fear of Strafford's revenge. Judicial processes were abandoned for political ones. A bill of attainder was introduced, and on 21 Apr. passed by a majority of 204 to 59 to the Lords. Mobs were mobilised by sinister versions of the Army plot, by talk about the Irish army. To this tension the King contributed by attempting unsuccessfully to regarrison the Tower. The overawed Lords passed the bill. Charles had undertaken to protect the earl, and the earl had absolved him from his promise. Charles was no coward, but there was more than his own life at stake. With screaming mobs pressing the palace, where the queen and his children were, he gave way. The earl went to the block with a clear conscience, in the presence of the largest crowd ever assembled on Tower Hill.

(15) The opposition pressed home the attack. The unnerved King assented on the same day as the attainder to Acts which provided for triennial parliaments and made the present parliament indissoluble save with its own consent. As in Scotland the demolition of the royal power structure now proceeded, but in a manner appropriate to a different society. Parliament concentrated on fiscal law and the government machine. In granting a tonnage and poundage, the previous exactions and impositions were declared illegal; so were writs of ship money. No taxes were henceforth to be levied

without parliamentary consent. The Star Chamber, the Councils for Wales and the Marches and for the North, as the punitive instruments of royal secular policy, and the Court of High Commission, their spiritual counterpart, were swept away. New men seized the key positions: puritans, presbyterians and other sectaries could emerge into the public forum and multiply their claims. They immediately collided with the more settled elements, broke the unity of the opposition and caused a rupture between the Houses. The immediate, but only one of the enduring reasons for this strife was religion and its organisation.

(16) The King did not mean to accept the abridgement of his prerogative and his opponents, knowing this, had yet one more reason to distrust him. To divide them was now his major purpose. As Lords and Commons quarrelled over episcopacy in the ROOT AND BRANCH bill and over doctrine in the PROTESTATIONS, Charles, to the anger of the English Commons, decided to go to Scotland. When the Commons, on the analogy of the Covenant, wanted to make signature of the Protestation compulsory, the Lords threw the bill out. The Commons then decided to proceed alone. The Lords, to preserve unity, drew attention to the dangers of Charles' visit to Scotland and moved that commissioners accompany him. The Lord Keeper refused to seal their commission and the two houses thereupon commissioned them by joint Ordinance. This was unconstitutional but usurpation was to follow. In Sept. 1641 the Commons voted a declaration on the Protestation making changes in the service and an end to Sunday amusements and requiring compliance to be certified to itself. The King's physical absence seemed to permit the break-up of the ancient constitution.

(17) Charles' visit to Scotland was a partial success. By assent to the legislation establishing presbyterianism, he gave it a legal as well as moral status alarming to English moderates; but his efforts to win over covenanting nobles collapsed because of the *Incident*, an affair like the Army Plot of doubtful authenticity, involving an alleged plan to kidnap the E. of Argyll. In England, however, the religious extremists had provoked a moderate reaction, which tended to abate respect for the parliament; nevertheless a major obstacle to an alliance between the King and the public continued to be a fear of Popery, deliberately fuelled by abuse of Charles' French queen. All the same, his political position seemed to be improving when the rebellion known as the IRISH MASSACRE erupted (Oct. 1641).

(18) The migratory connection between Ulster and Scotland made this rebellion important in all three Kingdoms; Laudian bishops had driven Ulster presbyterian ministers from their parishes back to Scotland, where they had a loud voice in the revolution. During the Bishops' Wars Wentworth had imposed the Black Oath on all substantial persons except R. Catholics and had severely punished those who refused it: he had also attempted to deport unlanded Ulster Scots to Scotland. Simultaneously he alienated the Irish and the landowners of Connaught by manipulating the crown inquests ostensibly to extend the plantation system but actually to raise revenue. In Roscommon the landowners lost a quarter of their lands, in Galway a half. Star Chamber proceedings were launched against the Corporation of London for failures at Coleraine, which ended in forfeiture and a fine of £70,000. The analogy with the abuse of Forest proceedings in England was obvious. The difference was that the basic population was R. Catholic, secretive and Gaelic speaking. Moreover, when Strafford's Irish army was disbanded and paid off at less than half its entitlement in May 1641, the mostly R. Catholic soldiers joined the discontented underground. Strafford's policy had infuriated large sections in all parts of Irish society and could be pursued only by Strafford

himself. When he had gone there was aimlessness at Dublin Castle and those, whether Irish, English, Anglo-Norman, Protestant or R. Catholic, whom he had terrorised, began to pluck up courage. Nevertheless, the outbreak, when it occurred, reminded all good protestants of St. Bartholomew's Night. Many thousands were murdered or died of privation. Some of the Irish claimed (like the Covenanters) to be acting in the King's name. The English and Scots opposition found it convenient to believe that he was privy to their designs.

(19) Since July the opposition had been attempting to recover ground lost through extremist extravagance. A Commons Committee under Pym and Vane was at work framing a remonstrance. It began as a list of grievances and continued with the remedies so far enacted. The addition of aspirations created trouble, for they involved ecclesiastical reform, an attack on the bishops and established forms of worship, and behind them on the large body of episcopalian opinion which apprehended with the King, that the transformation of the church would weaken, change or perhaps destroy the throne. The Irish rebellion precipitated the division: it was necessary to raise an army to put it down. Pym thought with some reason, that an army commanded by the King's officers would be used against the parliament. He carried through the Commons an instruction to the commissioners with Charles in Scotland that the King must appoint officers whom parliament could trust and that if he refused, parliament would make its own arrangements: in other words raise an army itself. It was now the turn of the episcopalians, who thought, with equally good reason, that this army would be used against themselves. With the Bishops' Wars just past they went over to the King. One result was that the committee on the Remonstrance added propagandist clauses designed to attract the support of the moderates and blaming bishops and popish lords in the Upper House for frustrating the work of reform. Thus the GRAND REMONSTRANCE ceased to be a parliamentary and became a purely Commons document, recording at once the royal misgovernment and the disarray of the opposition. The debate on it was of unprecedented heat and length (8-22 Nov. 1641) but the crisis came not with the Remonstrance's passage, but on the question whether it should be printed. Widespread dissemination would involve something new: an appeal by the Commons to the ordinary citizenry, against the King, over the heads of the Lords and ignoring established aristocratic components in the constitution. The proposal to make this decisive shift in political habits all but caused a fight in the House. On 1 Dec. the Grand Remonstrance was presented to the King, who had returned from Scotland on 25 Nov. On 2nd he observed that he was ready to grant "what else can be justly desired ... in point of liberties, or in maintenance of the true religion that is here established". Moderate opinion and the Lords, he knew, were with him. The Commons then claimed that as they represented the public they could approach the Crown with bills to which the Lords had not consented. They followed this up on 15 Dec. by passing the motion to print and by introducing a bill to create a Parliamentary Lord General in whom, in effect, the royal military powers would be vested. On 21 Dec. the City wardmotes mostly elected puritans to the common council. The effect of publishing the Remonstrance seemed to be visible. The army bill might be forced through by the same means as Strafford's attainder.

(20) It was becoming dangerous for the King to wait, in the hope that the quarrel between the Houses would paralyse the opposition; Pym and his allies were taking practical steps to control the realities of power. The provocations offered by the Commons besides were creating an extremist clamour in his court. His determination to act was sensible; some of the action

taken was not. There was fear in the air. He put the swashbuckling Thomas Lunsford into the Lieutenancy of the Tower in place of the puritan Sir William Balfour and increased the fears. He declared against reform of the church, but the mob stopped the bishops coming into the House of Lords. When Pym refused to restrain the mob the bishops protested that anything done in their absence was illegal. At this point Charles made a crucial mistake; by countenancing their protest he seemed to undercut the authority of the Upper House; the Lords, his best allies, were furious. Meanwhile Pym was encouraging rumours that the Commons might impeach the Queen for conspiring against public liberty and instigating the Irish Massacre. Charles decided to get in first. On 3 Jan. he had articles of impeachment against Pym, Hampden, Holles, Hesilrige, Strode (THE FIVE MEMBERS) and Lord Mandeville presented to the Lords for treason in attempting to subvert the fundamental laws, deprive the crown of its rightful powers and alienate the affections of the people, and in inviting a foreign army to invade England. There was no precedent for a royal impeachment; the alienated Lords voted a committee to inquire into the precedents and refused to arrest the accused. Charles then sent the serjeant at arms to the Commons to arrest the five, but the Commons repelled the serjeant and said that they would consider the matter. The Queen, who was, or who was thought to be, in real danger, now intervened and drove Charles next day (4 Jan.) to attempt the arrest himself. This was exactly what Pym wanted. The House, which had been sitting at Guildhall, moved back to Westminster. With escape boats carefully arranged, the Five Members waited for the King to commit himself. He entered the House of Commons but found that "the birds are flown". They had gone to the City; the Common Council appointed Philip Skippon to command the trainbands for its and their defence. They were not only safe, but triumphant. Six days later Charles left Whitehall for the last time as a free man. Next day the five returned amid jubilation to a reunited parliament. The rejoicings were premature. (*See* CIVIL WAR 1642-6.)

(21) The King lost the subsequent civil war, but it was not the parliament which won. Confusion continued in Ireland; Charles surrendered to the presbyterian Scots; and in England the means of waging the war against him had changed its character. A substantial minority of the parliament had been royalist: it had been expelled and was now fugitive. Other members had died or been expelled for disagreement with the dominant faction of the moment. The Lords were a powerful handful. In the Commons a presbyterian majority lead a shrunken assembly, which no longer represented anything but itself. The representation of the broader mass of opinion had passed to the army, whose religious independency was anathema to presbyterians and would in due course break the Solemn League and Covenant with the Scots. Superficially the King's surrender to the Scots was an ingenious political manoeuvre, holding out some hope that he might rescue something from his disaster. They took him to Newcastle.

(22) In fact the Scots would concede nothing unless Charles signed the Covenant which, for conscience sake he could not do; and the parliamentarian PROPOSITIONS OF NEWCASTLE, with their insistence on presbyterianism were equally offensive to him. His only hope was to spin out time, but meanwhile the Scots, the parliament and the Independents negotiated round about him. The Covenanters' position was growing weaker for their troops were unpaid and hungry and Montrose's victories had demonstrated the disunity of Scotland. To hand the King over to the parliament meant the collapse of covenanting policy in London: to receive him in Scotland might mean the overthrow of the covenanting govt. in Edinburgh. They tried desperately and tactlessly to convert him, while they negotiated for their unpaid arrears with the parliament. They still controlled London's coal supply. Eventually a monetary agreement was initialled. The Commons ordered the sale of episcopal lands to raise the first instalment. The Scots now had to choose: go with the King, or leave him behind. On 16 Dec. the Scottish estates voted that they could not receive Charles. On 23rd, the financial agreement for the Scots evacuation was concluded. On 24th he tried, unsuccessfully, to escape. The first half of the English payment arrived and the English Commissioners appeared at Newcastle on 2 Jan. 1647. The Scots marched out on 30 Jan. and Charles was taken into ceremonial custody at Holmby House in Northamptonshire. The allegation that the Scots sold him was untrue, yet not convincingly deniable.

(23) Immediately the Commons quarrelled with the army. It was obviously desirable to reduce the cost of the forces in England and raise troops for Ireland. The reduced English establishment was published first: that for Ireland followed. It was to be recruited from the New Model. Simultaneously it was voted that no member of parliament and no one refusing to sign the covenant (i.e. Cromwell and his supporters) should hold a commission. Further, in a recent case, the court had held that the soldiers were liable for damage to life and property in the late war. When parliamentarians arrived at the army H.Q. at Saffron Walden to enlist volunteers for Ireland, they were met with demands for information on pay, for arrears already owing (18 weeks for the infantry, 43 for the cavalry) and for indemnification against past acts. The parliament men offered six weeks pay on discharge. The soldiers added to their demands freedom from future impressment, widows' and orphans' pensions and compensation for war losses. From cloud cuckoo land the parliament denounced all petitioners and threatened prosecution. Only about 20% of the men needed for Ireland had volunteered. The regiments now elected representatives called agents or agitators, who met in council and began to assume the aspect of a rival govt. The parliament thereupon ordered each regiment to a separate place where the soldiers were to choose between Irish service and discharge. The regiments did nothing of the sort. They all marched to Newmarket, where they agreed the SOLEMN ENGAGEMENT while Cromwell sent Cornet George Joyce (?-1670) and 500 horse to secure the King; he was brought to Newmarket too.

(24) The army immediately issued its political demands in the DECLARATION OF THE ARMY and then impeached eleven presbyterian leaders in the Commons. The eleven left when the army threatened to move on London and the generals began to negotiate with the King on the basis of the HEADS OF THE PROPOSALS elaborated by the Council of the Army. Charles rejected these with such bitterness and determination that even his followers began to think that he had secured support elsewhere. The military were disillusioned, but meanwhile riots in London brought the reinstatement of the eleven, whereupon the Speakers of both Houses and about 60 Independents fled to the protection of the army. The army moved. London was occupied; Charles was brought to Hampton Court and the Independents were restored to their places (24 Aug. 1647). They immediately made Fairfax Constable of the Tower. They were heartened, too, by the news that a parliamentary force under Col. Michael Jones (to whom Ormonde had handed over Dublin) had defeated the Irish confederates at Dangan Hill (8 Aug.). All the same, the presbyterian majority continued obstinate and had to be overawed by a military presence. The army was quartered mainly at Putney between Hampton Court and Westminster.

(25) Political discussions dragged on and by Oct. the soldiers had grown impatient with the delays in

implementing the Solemn Engagement. Most regiments replaced their existing agitators and they, and the Levellers in the army, issued respectively two draft manifestoes: THE CASE OF THE ARMIE and the AGREEMENT OF THE PEOPLE. These were debated in the Council of the Army at Putney for a fortnight in the presence of the generals. The debates loosened military discipline but threw up a demand for Charles' life. Alarmed by the threat to discipline, Cromwell carried a resolution to return representative officers and agitators to their regiments. The Council was replaced by a general council of officers, and there were sporadic mutinies, which continued until May 1649.

(26) The King was indeed finding other support. He had never ceased to deal with the Scots. On 16 Nov. 1647 he escaped to the I. of Wight but, to his surprise, the governor of Carisbrooke took him into custody. Nevertheless while he was there the ENGAGEMENT with the Scots was made (26 Dec. 1647). The parliament did not know its terms, but soon realised that an agreement had been reached. At Cromwell's insistence they passed Votes of No Addresses to the King, dissolved the Committee of Both Kingdoms and conferred its powers upon its English members, who were thenceforth known as the DERBY HOUSE COMMITTEE. They were just in time. The army was unpopular about London; revolts broke out in Kent, Essex and South Wales; half the navy deserted to Charles' commander Batten. A Scots invasion was obviously imminent. This SECOND CIVIL WAR was, from the royalist angle, ill co-ordinated. In Scotland the Engagers led by Hamilton, mostly nobility and their dependants, were denounced by the Kirk for aiding an uncovenanted King. The result was a slow mobilisation and they could not use Leven's experienced army. Cromwell put down South Wales: Fairfax, Kent; and Cromwell was well on his way north by the time Hamilton with his raw force crossed the western Border in July. He cut them off from home and destroyed them at Preston (17 Aug.). The Essex royalists surrendered at Colchester at the end of the month.

(27) The parliament chose this time to repeal the Vote of No Addresses and negotiated with Charles direct at Newport (I. of Wight). During Sept. and Oct., while Fairfax was hanging royalists, and army feeling against the King was growing, the presbyterians were trying to do a deal with him. The Second Civil War made military men feel that the King was faithless and a man of blood. The Newport treaty made the parliamentary presbyterians seem little better. The military seized the King again and took him to Hurst Castle (1 Dec.) and then to Windsor (23 Dec.). Col. Pride occupied the House of Commons under orders to suppress it, but independent members persuaded him to limit his action to a PURGE (6 Jan. 1649). The Independent remnant, numbering about 60, passed an Ordinance erecting a court to try the King. See CHARLES I, TRIAL AND EXECUTION.

CHARLES I, TRIAL AND EXECUTION OF (20-23 Jan. 1649). The Ordinance for the trial, passed by the 60 members of the purged House of Commons on 6 Jan. 1649, erected a court of 135 named commissioners under John Bradshaw. The trial was held in Westminster Hall.

Less than half those named were willing to act. The charge was that Charles, being entrusted with a limited power to govern according to law, had violated that trust to erect an unlimited and tyrannical power. The King refused to plead to any charge until the court could produce a lawful commission by virtue of which he could be tried; he could not acknowledge an usurped authority, for the liberties of the people were bound up with his own. He maintained this position for three days while the London mob showed signs of getting out of hand. There were fears of rescue. On the fourth day formal evidence of his participation in the civil war was heard and he was condemned to death. Even then there was difficulty and

the soldiers had to bully the Independents into signing the death warrant. Eventually 59 members of the court did so. These are known as the Regicides and were exempted from pardon at the Restoration.

Charles was beheaded outside the Whitehall Banquetting House on 30 Jan. 1649; a very large force of troops held back the crowd from which a loud groan escaped when the axe fell. The immediate appearance of the anonymous *Eikon Basilike* capitalised upon public sympathy and converted him into a retrospective martyr. The Anglican Church canonised him as a martyr in 1661 and offices are said for him in some churches each 30 Jan.

CHARLES II (1630-85) P. of WALES (1638) (*see also* SCOTLAND 1660-89) was with his father in the Civil War until Mar. 1645. He then moved to Bristol and thence westwards by way of Barnstaple and Falmouth. In Mar. 1646 he went to the Scillies, in Apr. to Jersey and in July to Paris where he remained until July 1648. The Fronde having broken out in France, he prepared a squadron at Helvoetsluys and raided the Thames.

(2) **KING** on 30 Jan. 1649 by the execution of his father (*see* COMMONWEALTH-1 *et seq*), he was proclaimed at Edinburgh on 5 Feb. and at Dublin. He then went to Paris, briefly to Jersey and in Jan. 1650 to Breda, where he received the Scots Commissioners in Mar. Having been forced to undertake to sign the Covenant, though he believed "presbytery not a religion for a gentleman", he landed in the Cromarty Firth and reached Falkland in June. Here, though under the control of Argyll and the Presbyterians, he made secret contacts with the R. Catholics. In Sept. Cromwell defeated the presbyterian army at Dunbar and Charles tried, but failed, to escape to the R. Catholic Gordons.

Presbyterian extremists now presented a Remonstrance against him, but this was condemned by a Resolution of the Estates. The RESOLUTIONERS, to carry on the war, joined with the royalists, who were strong in S.W. Scotland. They repealed the Act of Classes of 1649 and Charles was crowned at Scone in Jan. 1651. Meanwhile Cromwell overran the southern Lowlands and reached Perth. While his army was at Stirling, the King marched for England by way of the south western recruiting ground, hoping to raise support when he crossed the border. But the Scots were so unpopular that none appeared and he was defeated at WORCESTER in Sept. After an adventurous escape (*see* LANE, JANE) he lived in poverty in Paris until June 1654. He then went *via* Cologne and Middleburg to Bruges, where he set up a small and notoriously dissolute court. His departure from France had been hastened by peace negotiations between the Protectorate and France, preliminary to a British attack upon Spain. In Apr. 1656 he therefore agreed to retrocede Jamaica, lately taken by the Protectorate in return for Spanish armed assistance. From Feb. 1658 he was mostly in Brussels and during the year following Oliver Cromwell's death (Sept. 1658) observed the confusion in Britain from Brittany whilst fomenting a royalist conspiracy. When this failed (B. of Nantwich, 19 Aug. 1659) he travelled to Fuentarabia (Spain) to persuade Mazarin and the Spanish negotiators to finance him, but the P. of the Pyrenees (Nov. 1659) destroyed his Spanish Jamaican agreement. He returned to Brussels in Dec., later moving to Breda.

(4) (*See* RESTORATION.) At Brussels he began to receive English and Scots emissaries from the presbyterians and Monck. Apart from the benefits of a tolerant Spanish hospitality, he returned to England without obligations to any foreign powers. Landing at Dover in May 1660 and the Restoration settlement having been enacted, the Convention parliament was dissolved (Dec. 1661).

(5) The disappearance of the anti-royalist laws, and an anti-puritan revulsion combined to bring in a parliament (The CAVALIER or PENSION PARLIAMENT) of

middle-aged royalist gentry and veterans, prepared to honour the King but not yet be governed by him. They favoured checks, balances, dispersal and dilution of power to prevent too much government. In this the Lords Lieut., whom the King perforce nominated from their like had a key role. In local administration the county justices became supreme. The Lord Lieut., as *Custos Rotulorum* stood at their head and recruited their numbers by nominations to the crown. The Lord Lieut. and his friend, the annually appointed High Sheriff, organised the election of county M.P.s which, under open voting, they could powerfully influence. These country M.P.s, though a minority in the House, remained, as ever, its leading element. Lords Lieut. always sat with the visiting judges at Assizes which, for a further half-century, were still to have some of the character of an Eyre. They were in addition the ear and mouth of the govt. A revived aversion to standing armies made a local militia the only available military force, and the Lords Lieut. commanded it. The office holders were unpaid part-timers. The county organisation was broken down into fragments, many of them some days distance from the centre. Local magistrates had to rely upon a local following, or influence, to enforce their will, for there were no regular soldiers or police. Only if centre and periphery agreed could a policy be made and enforced. Extremism was apparently ruled out.

(6) Yet a paradoxical form of extremist moderation emerged at once. Charles and Hyde (E. of Clarendon) were at odds on religion: The minister was royalist because he was Anglican. His sceptical master had a soft spot for R. Catholics, whose sympathy had perhaps saved his life. Both were political creatures but Charles was tolerant by policy and inclination, Clarendon by policy only. On 4 Nov. 1660 Charles had declared in favour of an ecclesiastical compromise, devised to please the Presbyterians by James Ussher Abp. of Armagh, by which a synod was to be associated with each bishop. A bill had been introduced and bishops and presbyters met at the Savoy, but the result was a double fiasco. Court cavaliers frustrated the bill, while Richard Baxter and his presbyters bungled the conference.

(7) After 20 years bitter experience the Cavalier parliament was determined to drive their puritan erstwhile oppressors from public life, while making use of the still lively public fear of Popery and the Spanish Inquisition. Meanwhile Charles' English coronation was joyfully celebrated (Apr. 1661). The CORPORATION BILL took shape, was introduced in the autumn and passed in Dec. Protestant nonconformity, strongest in the towns, was now driven out of town govt. which ensured that none but Anglicans could be elected to parliament. It was the urban counterpart to rural control through Lords Lieut. This was the first measure of the misnamed *Clarendon Code,* which was a succession of opportunist enactments spread over some four years, for which Clarendon was not primarily responsible.

(8) Money and foreign policy now preoccupied the govt. Charles had no doubt about the importance of overseas trade and its concomitant, a strong navy. The P. of the Pyrenees (1659) justified the retention of Spanish Jamaica, while a Portuguese marriage (with **Catherine of Braganza**) brought a dowry of £880,000 together with TANGIER and eventually BOMBAY (23 June 1661). Weakening Spain by protecting Portugal was popular; Louis XIV, who had assumed personal control of his govt. in Mar. naturally favoured it too, after 24 years of war with Spain. The new alliance also restrained the Dutch from disrupting the Portuguese empire. The Anglo-Portuguese relationship was thus mutually advantageous: Britain obtained commercial rights and took over two possessions which Portugal could not maintain. In Aug. Charles and Louis forced a peace treaty with the Portuguese upon the Dutch, who evacuated northern

Brazil but kept Ceylon. While parliament was preoccupied with the Uniformity Bill (passed 19 May) 1662, the eyes of the court were fixed on trade. A new Guinea Co. was incorporated to compete with the Dutch round the Cape, and great engineering works were put in hand in Tangier harbour. Tangier, however, might be expensive to defend against Moorish hostility. Louis wanted Dunkirk (which Cromwell had reclaimed) as a point of command against the Low Countries. Charles sold it to him for £400,000 (27 Oct. 1662).

(9) The ACT OF UNIFORMITY complemented the Corporation Act by defining the means whereby the Corporation Act would be operated against non-Anglicans, for the Prayer Book was a schedule to the Act, its content being settled by Convocation, who incorporated concessions offered to the presbyterians at the Savoy. It was not debated by parliament. By its Calvinistic formularies the church hoped to comprehend some of the less rigid presbyterians, but only partly succeeded. About 1000 puritan clergy and six bishops (The NON-JURORS) refused to swear to it and in 1662 were driven from their cures. Charles thought that politically motivated Anglican intolerance was inconvenient and divisive and was prepared to dispense with the Act of Uniformity in particular cases. Meanwhile he continued to strengthen his aggressive commercial policy. He incorporated the ROYAL AFRICAN CO. with his brother, **James D. of York** as gov., excluded Irish shipping from the colonial trade and an Anglo-Portuguese army defeated a Spanish invasion of Portugal at Ameixial (8 June 1663), but his FIRST DECLARATION OF INDULGENCE (Dec.) proposing legislation in favour of the religious dispensing power caused a *furore* which Clarendon was unfitted by conviction to put down. The Lords threw the bill out.

(10) Clarendon, increasingly didactic, began to bore Charles. His daughter Anne's affair with the R. Catholic James, and their marriage in 1660 (both of which excited his furious indignation) had gained him some protestant court enemies but no friends. His present parliamentary failure shook his position at the Palace; he was also widely (if unjustly) believed to have profited from the sale of Dunkirk. He tactlessly opposed the African expeditions instigated by James, which provoked the SECOND DUTCH WAR, but defended the even more provocative annexation of New York (Aug. 1664). A war was in full swing whatever he said, yet he stayed in office to administer it. Clarendon was suspected of clinging to power for private gain, while his ostentatious rectitude gave increasing offence. Moreover, Sir Henry Bennet (later E. of Arlington) Sec. of State since 1662 (who favoured the Dutch war) hated him and traduced him through Charles' mistresses. It was the business of Clarendon, as Lord Chancellor, to maintain a working relationship between Crown and Parliament (because Charles direct support in the Commons was weak) but he was manifestly failing to do so. Plague (1665), fire (1666) and naval disaster (1667) combined to create an atmosphere of quarrelsome political depression in which a scape-goat was sought. The P. of BREDA (31 July 1667) ended the war. A month later Clarendon was dismissed. Threatened with impeachment, he went to France.

(11) If the E. of Arlington was now the most influential politician, the young D. of Buckingham, witty, dissolute and rich, amused Charles more. Moreover there were the King's mistresses, especially the Duke's distant and promiscuous kinswoman, Barbara Villiers, Countess of Castlemaine (Duchess of Cleveland from 1670) who dabbled in foreign politics (*see also* GWYNN, ELEANOR; KEROUALLE. LOUISE DE; WALTER, LUCY). The recriminations which had ended the war centred on court accusations of parliamentary parsimony and parliamentary counter-accusations of court profligacy and malversation. A Commons committee of accounts (the first of its kind)

drove the charges home. It was necessary to broaden the basis of the govt. Sir Thomas Clifford, a crypto-Catholic M.P. for Totnes and a friend of Arlington's, was brought in as Treasurer of the Household. Anthony Ashley Cooper (since 1661 Ld. Ashley and under-Treasurer), a presbyterian enemy of Clarendon, was called in along with Lauderdale, the effective ruler of Scotland. From their initials these five were known as the CABAL.

(12) When the Cabal entered office, the WAR of DEVOLUTION (1667-8) was revealing to all Europe the designs of Louis XIV upon its 'liberties'. His minister, Colbert, had fostered agricultural and industrial production. A vigorous policy of tariffs, bonded warehouses and export subsidies, navigation laws, harbour dues on foreign shipping and the development of overseas trading and shipbuilding, had both raised France to a high level of prosperity and alarmed the Dutch, whose best market France had been. Strategically placed and populous, with a centralised administration and an efficient diplomatic service (all in the hands of a young and vigorous autocrat) she stood before the choice of continental domination or overseas enterprise for which Colbert was preparing. Louis reversed Colbert's policy. Charles II of Spain (r. 1665-1700), a sickly simpleton, was unlikely to have an heir. Under the P. of the Pyrenees, Louis had secured a Spanish wife and dowry. She had renounced all her Spanish rights, but the dowry was not paid. Suspicions that Louis might try to pick up the vast Spanish inheritance in Europe and America now acquired substance when Louis speciously claimed the isolated Spanish possessions along his northern and eastern borders in right of his wife and began to negotiate for the total waiver of her renunciation. His troops occupied the Spanish Netherlands without Spanish resistance; the Dutch flew to arms; English opinion sympathised with the Dutch. The latter could obviously not defeat France single handed on land. It looked as if, contrary to an old principle of English policy, the coast from Hamburg to Bayonne might fall under the control of a single power. In Jan. 1668 Charles and Arlington concluded an alliance at The Hague with the Dutch. In Feb. French troops occupied Franche Comté and Louis came to an understanding with the Emperor under whose suzerainty the occupied territories lay. These developments at least induced Spain to liquidate one distraction, by recognising Portuguese independence (13 Feb. 1668). The Dutch republicans would sacrifice much (especially if it belonged to Spain) to avoid a war in which the House of Orange would be bound to lead, and they neared an understanding with France; they also attracted Sweden into the Alliance of The Hague and so induced Louis to confine himself temporarily to moderate courses. By the P. of AIX LA CHAPELLE (2 May 1668) he gave up Franche Comté, but kept 12 Flemish fortified towns. Of these he developed and fortified Lille, regardless of expense.

(13) Traditional Anglo-Dutch enmities were not so easily buried. Dutch traders still swarmed upon the seas, to the discontent of English commercial and shipping interests. The French danger was, in a daily sense, less obvious. Charles, a Francophile, also hated the Dutch. Bye-elections were slowly changing the complexion of the faithful Commons. Elderly Cavaliers were being replaced by old Roundheads or their sons. This changing Commons was inclined to trust the King and Arlington with money even less than the King and Clarendon. Louis now mounted his diplomatic offensive to isolate the Dutch by buying their potential allies. Charles was in the market, but drove a hard bargain in a worldly sense (see DUTCH WARS, 17TH CENT-15). It was at the moral level that he got himself into difficulties. Temperamentally sceptical, yet troubled by older religious survivals, he was bargaining with a persecuting R. Catholic. In the T. of DOVER (1 June 1670) he undertook to join in a war

against the Dutch but he also engaged to receive a subsidy, declare his own conversion to the old faith at some future date and then accept a French force into England if this caused a major disturbance. The combination of money and religion was inflammable. It had to be negotiated in deep secrecy through Charles' sister Henrietta (Minette). The war treaty was public; at home only Arlington and Clifford knew the rest. This guilty secret gave Louis a powerful hold over Charles.

(14) The perennial money troubles which lay behind the treaty were exacerbated by Clifford's incompetence at the Treasury. Neither additional parliamentary grants in 1669 to 1672, nor Louis' money after the T. of Dover sufficed to cover Charles' deficits. By Jan. 1672, a year's revenue had been anticipated and £1M was owed to bankers. The fleet could not otherwise have been equipped. The govt. defaulted on its interest to the bankers (THE STOP OF THE EXCHEQUER), causing a panic and bankruptcies in the City. When payment was resumed a year later, interest had to be paid on delayed interest. Charles began to sell fee farm rents; it was a bad start for a war.

(15) (See DUTCH WARS, 17TH CENT.) Charles never announced his promised conversion, but as war came (Mar. 1672) he issued his SECOND DECLARATION OF INDULGENCE suspending by his prerogative the penal acts against R. Catholics and Dissenters alike. This reasonable move towards national unity entirely failed. Both the Declaration and the war came suddenly with parliament prorogued and the Exchequer stopped. There was something about the French alliance which ministers could not, or would not, explain; Popery was suspected in high places: Arlington, Clifford, James and his duchess were presumed to be papists. Their faith was associated in the public mind with autocracy, and autocracy with Louis XIV. The amalgamation of the Guinea and Royal African Cos. and their slave monopoly was another blow at protestant Holland which enriched papistical shareholders. The Church was endangered on both flanks; the constitution seemed under a formless shadow.

(16) When parliament met (Feb. 1673) the govt. was desperate. The Commons were willing enough to vote war subsidies to despoil the Dutch, but only on conditions which dissolved the Cabal. Charles had to withdraw the Declaration on the most humiliating terms: worse still, he had to assent to a TEST ACT which drove Arlington, Clifford and James from office. Though unpopular, his court influence as heir presumptive remained, now that he was no longer at sea. The Test was focused against the protestant survivors of the Cabal, particularly Shaftesbury. The Dutch broke the blockade in Aug. Shaftesbury (Lord Chancellor since Nov. 1672), a leading champion of the war, was dismissed in Nov. 1673. On 19 Feb., by the T. of WESTMINSTER, Britain abandoned the war.

(17) Shaftesbury had voted for the Test. By marrying Mary of Modena and refusing the Test, James set Anglicans and Dissenters against himself. Shaftesbury now tried to lead these forces against the King, but Charles, it seemed, had taken much of the wind out of their sails; his new minister, Sir Thos. Osborne (soon E. of DANBY) was financially competent and following the T. of Westminster, seaborne trade was driven, for lack of Dutch carriers, into British ships. The revenue was buoyant; Danby got on well with the City and managed the Commons with places and bribes. For advice on foreign affairs he relied on Sir William Temple, a pro-Dutch former ambassador to The Hague. It was intimated to Louis that money was needed to keep Britain from joining his enemies. In 1675 it was agreed that if parliament voted supply on condition that Britain went to war, Charles was to dissolve and receive £100,000. Parliament merely demanded the recall of English auxiliaries in the French army but Charles prorogued

from Nov. 1675 to Feb. 1677 and Louis paid. During this recess the two Kings, by personal letters, agreed to make no alliance without the other's consent.

(18) Shaftesbury and the opposition now wanted a general election. When parliament met again they argued that by force of an old statute the parliament had been illegal since 1662. The angered peers sent Shaftesbury to the Tower. Meanwhile Danby got a vote of £600,000 for the fleet because of continuing French successes, but demanded an offensive alliance with the Dutch as a condition of the money being made available. By another secret arrangement, Louis paid £166,000 for a prorogation until May 1678. Danby needed, however, to make a convincingly Francophobe gesture, but Charles wanted an end to European war. One avenue to exploit might be the intermittent talk of marrying Mary, d. of James, to WILLIAM OF ORANGE, a heroic and successful protestant champion against the French. Such a match, when the heir presumptive was a R. Catholic, would also be a reinsurance for the House of Stuart. Under the marriage treaty, Charles was to mediate between the Netherlands and France. The momentous wedding took place in Nov. 1677: the mediation was ineffectual. Louis now stopped his payments and in Jan. 1678 Laurence Hyde signed a defensive alliance with the Dutch, Charles recalling parliament for 7 Feb. He also released Shaftesbury from the Tower and asked for war subsidies in a belligerent speech. 30,000 men and 90 ships were to be raised and some troops landed at Ostend.

(19) As the Dutch had not ratified the alliance and the Commons were slow to entrust the King with the money or the men, he proceeded to ask Louis for some £500,000 a year for three years in return for his mediation between Holland and Spain (25 Mar. 1678). Louis found it cheaper to bribe the opposition and blocked Charles' attempts to raise funds and troops by playing on the old fear that a standing army might be used at home. They also attacked ministers, especially Lauderdale. When, however, Charles adjourned parliament, Louis hurriedly offered the £500,000. At the resumption (23 May) Charles announced that peace was imminent and got £200,000 to pay off his forces, subject to an embargo on French imports. There was a hitch in the peace parleys and the army was kept on foot. On 15 July parliament was prorogued again, and on 26 July Temple made a Dutch alliance. Unfortunately by 10 Aug. the Dutch republicans had taken control and signed the P. of NYMWEGEN with Louis. The isolated Spaniards now had to give way and by the second P. of Nymwegen (17 Sept.) Louis added four more Flemish fortresses and the Franche Comté to his gains.

(20) It was a feature of the years 1668-78 that England and France both profited overseas from Dutch pre-occupations at home. When Charles handed over Bombay to the HEIC in 1668, the French also set up their first Indian factory-house. P. Rupert formed the HUDSON BAY CO. in 1670. The govt. of the English W. Indies was organised in 1671. In 1672 the French occupied Pondicherry and other Coromandel coast sites and, while the English Guinea and African Cos. were being amalgamated, formed their own Senegal Co. In 1673 they also settled at Chandernagore in Bengal. When the P. of Westminster of 1674 conceded British sovereignty in New York and New Jersey, the French consolidated their colony in Guiana and under the P. of Nymwegen (1678) took African Goree. The base lines of a century of global struggle were being traced.

(21) There now supervened the extraordinary and fictitious "POPISH PLOT". Mary of Modena's secretary, Edw. Coleman, seemed to be implicated in a plot to establish a papist autocracy under Charles' brother James. Titus Oates, the informer, had made a deposition to Sir Edmund Berry Godfrey who sent him to the Privy Council: they heard him on 6 Oct. 1678. Godfrey was

found dead on 22nd. In the hysterical atmosphere, Shaftesbury saw his opportunity. He demanded James' removal from the Council. A bill, amended by the Lords to make an exception for James, was now passed to exclude all R. Catholics from parliament. Its passage was accompanied by a reign of terror, as R. Catholics were hurried through treason trials with perjured witnesses supported, if not suborned, by Shaftesbury, who now turned his attention to the army. The Court wanted to maintain this force against the rising political storm; the opposition to deprive Charles of its use; Louis XIV to get rid of a military threat. In Dec. the disbandment money was voted, but it was resolved to by-pass the royal Treasury and disburse it through the City Chamber.

(22) Louis now decided to overthrow the pro-Dutch Danby. He had already incurred a general unpopularity for, like Charles, he doubted the authenticity of the Plot. A party to keeping the troops on foot, he had yet annoyed Charles by advising the concessions extorted by Shaftesbury. He had been involved in Charles' secret financial dealings with Louis and these were known to Ralph Montague, a former ambassador in Paris. With great skill and dramatic presentation these dealings were revealed to the Commons. Their fury was boundless and a long list of Articles of Impeachment was voted. The probable reaction of the Lords was only too plain. With the case of Strafford before his eyes, Charles dissolved the longest parliament in English history (3 Feb. 1679) and advised James to leave the country (28th). Whatever the electoral future, no other action was possible.

(23) Continued trials, rumours and lies kept the nation in a state of excitement. A majority of the electors (influenced by the bad eggs and dead cats of the rest) voted against Popery and the K. of France. Charles' interest among the new Commons fell from 150 to 30. They promptly revived Danby's impeachment and when it was delayed, sent up a Bill of Attainder. Charles fought with skill and tenacity to save Danby in the Tower and the rights of his brother in Brussels; in the process he had to let men convicted on perjured evidence die, despite their evident innocence. He also, on Temple's advice, reconstructed the govt. A new, reduced Privy Council of thirty was set up, half of ministers, half of representatives of the various orders of peers and commoners. Shaftesbury was made Lord President. The arrangement did not work. Though now in office, Shaftesbury behaved as leader of an opposition, his friends introducing a bill to exclude James from the throne. Naturally the King worked with Sunderland, Laurence Hyde and others favourable to his own views. The council fell apart and the bill passed the Commons overwhelmingly. Against the advice of a majority of the council, Charles dissolved parliament again, thereby also stopping Danby's attainder. He now dismissed Shaftesbury and ended the council of thirty.

(24) In the second general election of 1679 James future was a more conspicuous issue than Danby's past. Charles was ill and had, but in secrecy, to allow his heir presumptive back, first to Windsor and then to Edinburgh. In the sharpened atmosphere, the electors returned another exclusionist house. Shaftesbury, however, now made a strategic error. If James were set aside, his daughters would naturally succeed him. Both were protestants and one was married to William of Orange. Instead Shaftesbury backed the claims of the unsuitable D. of MONMOUTH, Charles' bastard by Lucy Walter. Rumours were put about that Charles had married her and efforts were made to bully him into admitting it. Charles loved Monmouth dearly but had every reason for doing no such thing. He would neither tamper with the laws of succession, nor set up a rival claimant, nor insult his Portuguese in-laws. He sent Monmouth abroad when James went to Edinburgh. Shaftesbury persisted; his bill passed the Commons (May 1680), whereupon Charles

prorogued parliament. By now Shaftesbury had set up a national organisation, and Monmouth, who had defiantly returned, toured the West Country making speeches. The heated debate generated the term WHIG (for the exclusionists) and TORY (for supporters of hereditary monarchy). Meanwhile Charles wooed the more reasonable elements, the public was sickening of the disembowelments at Tyburn, the courts were suspicious of the inconsistencies in the evidence. Charles appealed to a sense of natural order. The bishops would support him; entailed landowners feared a precedent which might threaten their legitimate offspring. The world was no longer to be "turned upside down" and Shaftesbury's position under Cromwell was remembered. A reaction was coming.

(25) When parliament met (1 Nov. 1680) a new Exclusion Bill passed the Commons as before, but in the E. of Halifax the Tories had found a leader. He was assisted by the difficulty in finding an alternative to James. The bishops voted solidly with him and the Lords threw out the Exclusion Bill by 63 to 30. Shaftesbury's weapon of terrorism, the 'Popish Plot', was now hopelessly blunted and the crowd all but rescued Vist. Stafford (one of the last victims) from the scaffold. For the third time parliament was dissolved (20 Jan. 1681).

(26) Before the next parliament met on 29 Mar. Charles laid a careful plan. Laurence Hyde examined the finances for him and reported that with care, no foreign adventures and a small foreign subvention, the King could live of his own. He could, therefore, offer a compromise and reinsure himself with Louis. This was done by an oral agreement between Hyde and Louis' ambassador, Barillon. For safety parliament was to be summoned to Oxford, away from Shaftesbury's gangs; whig grandees and M.P.s came with armed retinues. On 29 Mar 1681 parliament, as strongly whig as ever, met in the Convocation House at Oxford. The King's guards were with him; other troops on the approach roads. A Tory M.P. explained the King's proposed compromise: a Popish sovereign could reign but not rule. Parliament should thus assemble without writ at his accession. His children should be educated as protestants, his prerogative exercised by a Protector who should be none other than the P. of Orange. The Commons would not listen. On Sat. 5 Apr. they rejected the compromise and resolved to bring in the Exclusion Bill. The King had to fall back on his contingency arrangements. On Mon. 7 Charles, in one sedan chair, the regalia in another, came to the Lords. The Commons being suddenly summoned, they found him robed and crowned on the throne. The words of dissolution were pronounced. The surprise was complete. Violent resistance was not attempted: the horror of civil war was still upon men. The members scattered. On 8th, the first instalment of French money was paid. In the next three years Charles received some £400,000.

(27) The circumstances of Charles' last parliamentary dissolution converted Britain into a passive spectator of Louis XIV's European aggressions and left Charles free to press his counter-attack on the Whigs. The foolish Monmouth gave him splendid opportunities with his bravoes and inflammatory talk. In July Charles had Shaftesbury indicted for fomenting rebellion, but a City grand jury threw out the bill. One Stephen College, however, was convicted at Oxford on much the same evidence. Shaftesbury fled to Holland where he died (Jan. 1683). Whigs were indeed discussing armed revolution, but independently of them came the abortive RYE HOUSE PLOT (June) to murder the King. Here was real evidence of whig intentions comparing favourably with the murderous fancies of the Popish Plot. Some prominent Whigs were implicated, fled, committed suicide or died on the block. Revulsion swept the country. Charles, on the crest of success, turned his attention to the boroughs which, since the Second Declaration of Indulgence (1672) had been the main base of Whig parliamentary influence. Crown lawyers, by *Quo Warranto,* forfeited the charters of Evesham, Norwich and London for various technical breaches of their provisions. The new charters given in substitution remodelled their franchises to Tory advantage; thereupon 63 other boroughs made their surrenders and obtained similar regrants (1684). These arrangements were not tested in Charles' lifetime. Fears that dissent bred rebellion revived anew. Ministers and lecturers were rounded up and punished under the "Clarendon Code".

(28) Though Charles had secured control of the institutional machinery, there were larger forces with which he could not settle. One was a widespread economic depression which began in 1682 and deepened as the Turks approached Vienna; while Louis disturbed Europe and expelled the Huguenots, his other policies were driving the Orange party in Holland to desperation and dividing the interest of the House of Stuart. Parsimony and corruption had lately reduced the navy to impotence. Charles saw danger approaching and took measures in 1684 to restore the fleet. These plans matured only after his death a few months later.

(29) An astute politician and promiscuous as a man, Charles II was courageously wedded to the principles of legitimate monarchy. He was clever and valued intellect and invention, and as many of his acts showed, he respected goodness and integrity and tried in his generation to help at least some of the poor or ill.

CHARLES IV of FRANCE (r. 1322-8). *See* CAPETIANS, LAST.

CHARLES V (1500-59) Holy Roman Emperor (1519). (*See* SPAIN 1406-1516.) **(1)** inherited (a) Castile with America; (b) Aragon with Naples, Sicily, Sardinia and the Balearic Is.; (c) the Burgundian territories, primarily Flanders and Franche Comté; (d) the Habsburg possessions, primarily Austria and the Tyrol. Of these (a) and (b) had lately been associated by the marriage of their sovereigns and Flanders was already closely tied economically to Castile through wool, salt and the movement of pilgrims. Austria had commercial connections with Franche Comté, but was threatened increasingly on the East by the Turks.

(2) He became effective ruler of these lands in 1516 and was elected Emperor while in Spain in 1519. Though Flemish by birth and upbringing, he spent six periods aggregating 16 years in Spain as a ruler and became much Hispanicised. This was not surprising, for as Flemish taxpayers were increasingly burdened with the cost of his overstretched activities, Castilian resources tempted him forward and were called into account at a time of progressive European, but especially Spanish, inflation. During most of his reign he was fighting on more than one, and sometimes as many as four, fronts while his Castilian subjects uninterruptedly expanded his American empire. Hence he was preoccupied with financial transfers between his varying policy theatres; his funds were seldom in the right places at the right times and he had to rely increasingly on deficit financing through Genoese and German bankers until his debts ruined him and them.

(3) The year of his imperial election typified his problems. Hernan Cortes invaded Mexico, Luther extended the scope of his controversy with the Papacy and there was revolt in Valencia. The latter was followed by the Castilian xenophobic uprising of the Comuneros which lasted until 1521. His Spanish authority was not properly established until 1522, by which time he was at war with the French in Italy; the rationalisation of Castilian and American govt. (1524) had to proceed under the shadow of German religious divisions. His defeat and capture of Francis I at Pavia (Feb. 1525) gave little rest. To help finance his foreign policies, foreigners (i.e. his bankers) were permitted to trade in the Caribbean, which created bad feeling in Castile, and still his army was unpaid and in 1527 sacked Rome. All the same, he made an ambitious marriage with his splendid and able cousin Isabel of Portugal, who made a perfect empress and regent until her premature death in 1539 and ultimately brought Portugal to their son Philip. Meanwhile the Castilian church was moving Heaven and his council to stop fresh enslavements in America, which created ill feeling there. By the time that the decree against enslavement was issued (1530) there were menacing developments in the opposite direction. In 1526 the Hungarian kingdom had collapsed before the Turkish armies which, in 1529, besieged Vienna. Simultaneously the Barbarossas, Turkish protected corsairs, seized Algiers.

(4) The essential pattern, with permutations, was repeated in the next decade. While the religious and political quarrels surrounding Henry VIII's marriage with Catherine of Aragon (Charles' aunt) were reaching their climax, Pizarro overthrew the Peruvian Incas (1531) and sent back much gold, but by 1534 the decree against enslavement had to be revoked in the face of threats of colonial mutiny. But in that same year the army was organised into its final and best known form, with its *tercios* (brigades) of combined pikes and arquebuses. This came only just in time, for the Barbarossas took Tunis and their corsairs harried the coasts of Italy and Spain and interrupted the Aragonese trade routes between. In 1535 Tunis was briefly retaken. Despite the useful acquisition by imperial escheat of Milan as a staging point between the Mediterranean and Germany, the defence of both the Austrian land frontier and the Mediterranean sea frontier was becoming burdensome. Moreover in 1538 the Castilian Cortes compelled Charles to exclude foreigners from America but insisted on maintaining aristocratic tax exemption. Charles replied in 1539 by re-enforcing the *Tasa del trigo* (*see* SPAIN 1406-1516-6).

(5) American trade and bullion imports grew steadily, while the church fastened its influence upon Spanish outlooks. The late 1530s were the period when the Inquisition (never established in America) came into its own and when the friars campaigned successfully against American enslavements. At the same time the French wars were petering out (T. of Toledo 1539) which seemed to permit a great crusading effort against Algiers. This ended disastrously in 1541, but the govt. pressed on with the *Nuevas Leyes* (= New Laws) of America which forbade enslavements on any pretext (1542). It was all of a piece with this, that the *Consulado* or merchant chamber was set up at Seville to supplement the *Casa de la Contratacion* (*see* SPAIN 1406-1516-5) in the management of the Atlantic trade, and in 1545 virtue seemed to have been rewarded by the discovery, in the area of modern Bolivia, of the fabulous silver mines of Potosi. The beginnings of new wealth enabled the Emperor at least to catch up with inflation and win, at Mühlberg, military victory over German protestant princes.

(6) Then came appalling disaster: between 1545 and 1548 America was swept by the first of its two great plagues, which were by 1600 to cut the population by 80%. The event confused production, commerce, exchanges and social life. While the govt. fought to protect its Indian subjects against forced labour in the mines (1549) there was a crisis in the Castilian cloth trade which had repercussions in Flanders, and while Turkish naval pressure continued to rise, bankers' confidence began to fall. Silver imports on crown account in 1546 to 1550 were more than double those of 1540 to 1545. In 1551-5 they more than redoubled, yet the service of accumulated loans left nothing over and mortgaged the ordinary taxes of Castile. In 1552 the greater German princes, led by Maurice of Saxony, fearful of growing imperial power, changed sides and attacked Charles who could not pay his army. Charles' flight from Innsbruck to

Villach represented the victory of German rebellion and heresy. The context of the marriage between his son Philip and his cousin Mary I of England was defeat and the despair of the Castilian and Flemish taxpayers. The exhausted emperor made the best of things. He reorganised the Italian administration; his brother Ferdinand took over the Austrian lands; in 1556 he abdicated in Spain and the Netherlands in favour of Philip and lived out the remaining 18 months of his imperial reign at the Spanish monastery of Yuste. *See* SPAIN (HABSBURG).

CHARLES V of France (Lieutenant of the Realm 1356-64, K. 1364-80) (for events before his accession *see* JOHN II). His disordered inheritance was impoverished by disaster and diminished by his father's improvidence, but he had managed to strengthen its administration, initially to collect his father's ransom. The new machinery institutionalised the pre-existing *gabelle*, the new *maltot* and the hearth tax (*fouage*) lately established by the Estates. For the first time the crown had an income which was substantial and regular. It was now possible to recruit a standing army. In this Charles was fortunate in discovering, in Bertrand du GUESCLIN, a general of genius. In 1364 he defeated Charles of Navarre at Cocherel and re-established royal control of the Seine. A Breton campaign was a failure but du Guesclin set about recruiting free companies into so-called Great Companies for a contest in Spain. They were to be hired to Henry of Trastamara, a bastard claimant to the Castilian throne, occupied by England's ally Peter the Cruel. The object, apart from turning this important southern neighbour of English Aquitaine from an enemy into a friend, was to secure the use of the Castilian navy and interrupt Aquitainian trade. And, win or lose, the troublesome companies would have been marched off French soil. Militarily the operation failed. The Black Prince, as D. of Aquitaine, defeated du Guesclin at Najera in Apr. 1367, but having won the war lost the peace. K. Peter did not, as promised, pay his army which had to be supported from additional Aquitainian taxes, and two of the greater feudatories, Armagnac and Albret, repelled the tax collectors, appealed to London and then to Paris. Charles took high legal advice and in 1368 concluded (correctly but with too much logic) that he could lawfully entertain the appeals. Meantime two diplomatic events strengthened the French position. Louis of Mâle, Count of Flanders, had requested an English husband for his daughter Margaret, but Charles persuaded the Pope to refuse the necessary dispensation. Consequently in 1369 she married Philip of Burgundy whereby, for a while, French influence ousted English in that important area. During the same period the Black Prince had understandably scrupled to hand over prisoners taken at Najera to K. Peter. Set at liberty they made no mistake. Peter was murdered (Mar. 1369) with Charles' privity; moreover Charles had publicly accepted the Armagnac and Albret appeals. This, of course, destroyed the tacit basis of the T. of Calais and Edward reassumed his title as K. of France. Charles declared Aquitaine forfeit. The new French army was soon making headway near Paris (Sept. 1370), in Maine (Dec.) and in the south, while the Black Prince's callous sack of Limoges (Sept.) alienated potential supporters. An English naval success against the Flemings off Bourgneuf in 1371 was amply avenged in June 1372 by a Franco-Castilian victory off La Rochelle. In Aug. the French army took Poitiers, in Sept. Angoulme and La Rochelle. By this time the emissaries of Robert II (r. 1371-90), the first Stewart, had concluded at Vincennes the formalities of the AULD ALLIANCE already operative in practice. In 1373 John of Gaunt marched from Calais to Bordeaux, but du Guesclin refused to be tempted into battle; and an effort was made to neutralise Castile by inciting Portugal and Aragon to attack her. These manoeuvres failed: Castile and Aragon made peace in

1374 while Albret and Armagnac attrition of Aquitaine continued. By June 1375, however, Charles had run out of funds. The TRUCE OF BRUGES (June 1375) left the English in control only of Calais and a broad stretch of coast from Bordeaux to Bayonne. In an atmosphere of popular unrest and of depression at the Black Prince's death (June 1376) Edward III died (June 1377). The French raided the English coast; the Welsh rose and the Scots seized Berwick (1378). Despite all pressure, however, the abandoned Gascons held out; a Breton rising expelled the French partisans, the English retook Berwick (1379) and in June 1380 they defeated a Franco-Castilian fleet off Ireland. It was at this point that Charles V died, irresponsibly abolishing as an act of death-bed repentence the maltot and fouage upon which his successes had been founded.

CHARLES VI of France (1368-1422, K. 1380), child of Charles V, **(1)** like his kinsman Richard II, was mentally unstable. He succeeded in a period of Anglo-French truce but factions and uncles with large appanages (*see* JOHN II) disputed and fought at court. In the Great Schism, which began in 1378, France, Spain, Sicily and Scotland supported Clement VII at Avignon; England, Austria, Bohemia, Hungary and most of the Italian states recognised Urban VI at Rome. A single Papacy was a unifier and pacifier: two in rivalry encouraged world conflict and court factionalism. Events proceeded despite the effectively paralytic French govt. In a Venetian war the Genoese disaster at Chioggia (1381) dislocated the finances of international trade in the S. of France. There was Flemish urban unrest and the English Peasants' Revolt, and while the French urban *Maillotins* were rising in 1382, the Flemish francophile nobility routed the pro-English city of Ghent at Roosbeke (Nov.). In Portugal John, Grand Master of Avis, became regent in 1383 and appealed for English help against France's ally Castile, yet in Feb. 1384 the Anglo-Scots war was resumed. Then the Burgundian **Philip the Bold** succeeded in Flanders, Artois and Franche Comté, creating a loose but wealthy assemblage of unFrench lands and effectively reversed the verdict of Roosbeke. Thus when the truce ended in May 1385, the French court had for several years been helpless witnesses to the decline of their friends. The trend continued. In Aug. an Anglo-Portuguese force inflicted the 'Portuguese Bannockburn' on the Castilians at Aljubarrota.

(2) For the time being the interests of Charles VI and his Burgundian uncle ran parallel. By Philip's good offices, Charles married **Isabel of Bavaria** (?-1435) in July 1385 and a great fleet was built at Flemish ports to threaten Calais or (with Scots help) England. It never sailed, but John of Gaunt, now campaigning in Castile, failed to end Castilian raids on England and English shipping and, under the additional naval threat, returned home. In 1388 the great Marcher defeat at Otterburn induced the new English govt. of Thomas of Woodstock to make the, regularly extended, TRUCE OF BOULOGNE (1389).

(3) Internal politics disposed the two kings to repose; external claims, the two crowns to war. Richard and Charles, when lucid, were both intent on personal rule. The truce of Boulogne had become feasible because Charles had dismissed his uncles to their appanages and recalled his father's ministers (called derisively by the uncles *Marmousets* = stokers). They ran the govt. while Charles and his brother LOUIS (1372-1407), D. of Touraine and (from 1392) of ORLEANS, egged on by Q. Isabel, enjoyed a riotous life. Her sexual demands speeded Charles' decline. In 1392 he was seized with a homicidal mania. The uncles, with Isabel, formed a regency and imprisoned the *Marmousets*. In 1393, after signs of recovery, a distressing incident at a court function (*le Bal des Ardents* = The Dance of the Burning Men) finally upset the balance of his reason. Isabel said

that he had lucid moments and sexual intercourse with her. As she was widely believed to have it with others, this became important when her eldest son CHARLES (later VII) was born.

(4) In negotiations during the truce Richard II would not give up the French title or Calais and the regency would not forego the Scots alliance but, in Nov. 1396, the two govts. signed a further 28-year truce at ARDRES, sealed by the marriage of Richard to Charles' *d.* **Isabel (1389-1409).** Richard was Francophil and loved his new Queen. The French court undertook to aid him against his own lieges: he to aid them in their Italian schemes (*see* para 5) and in settling the Schism by the abdication of both Popes (the so-called *Way of Cession*). The Regency did not understand how suspicious English nobles were of a French alliance, how the Way of Cession offended the English Urbanist clergy or how financial demands for a foreign adventure would raise opposition in the Commons. The truce itself was kept, but the regents became disenchanted with Richard's inability to honour his side of the bargain. When John of Gaunt died in 1399, Richard confiscated the Lancastrian lands; the heir, Henry of Lancaster, was welcomed in France and permitted to organise the expedition by which he usurped the English throne as Henry IV.

(5) In 1391, LOUIS II of Anjou and Provence became K. of Naples. The co-regent **Orléans,** now married to **Valentina Visconti (1366-1408),** also entertained Italian ambitions based on his wife's county of Asti. The regency forced French suzerainty on nearby Genoa in 1396. Thus far Burgundy supported Orléans. It was now proposed to create a N. Italian Orléanist state which was to include the Papal Marches. This dismemberment of the Papal states was clearly inconsistent with the Way of Cession. The Regents quarrelled, the Burgundian drifting towards the Roman pontiff, Orléans to the Avignonese. Moreover Orléans moved against his uncle's policy of Burgundian territorial continuity by acquiring part of Luxemburg in 1402. In 1404 Philip of Burgundy was succeeded by his son **John the Fearless (r. 1404-19)** and Orléans became sole Regent.

(6) They saw an opportunity in Glyndyr's Welsh revolt: patched up their quarrel, intervened (1405-6) jointly, while Burgundy moved against Calais and Orléans against Gascony. This complex of moves failed and each blamed the other. The old quarrel was inflamed by personal dislike and Burgundy's jealousy of Orléans' influence over the intermittently mad King. In Nov. 1407 he had Orléans assassinated in Paris (then strongly pro-Burgundian). The new young D. of Orleans, **Charles (?-1465)** shortly married a daughter of the experienced Bertrand of Armagnac, whose family had caused the Anglo-French breach of 1369. The anti-Burgundian and ultimately anti-English Orléanist faction became known as **Armagnacs.** The fearless John, having suppressed Flemish communal stirrings in Sept. 1408, raised the Paris mob and with the compliance of Q. Isabel, drove the royal dukes from the court. By agreements at Gien and Poitiers (1410) they, with the Armagnacs, formed a party, to which most of the nobility and the west and south adhered. Both sides sought English help. Burgundy realistically offered Gravelines, Dunkirk, Dixmude and Sluys and aid in conquering Normandy. In 1411 a joint force marched on Paris and cleared the Armagnac troops out of the suburbs. Armagnac emissaries now appeared and offered the lost provinces of Aquitaine. There had been a change of political personalities in the English Council, which concluded the T. of Bourges (1412) with the Armagnacs on those terms. *See* HENRY IV-11,12.

(7) John the Fearless, with typical opportunism, had already announced that his King had commissioned him to drive the English from Bordeaux. When the news of the T. of Bourges arrived he took the *oriflamme* and marched off to drive the traitor dukes out of the South.

The armies faced each other, but on Charles VI's (lucid or wild) orders the Armagnacs renounced their agreement with England. Burgundy renounced his. There were reconciliations (T. of Auxerre July 1412) all unknown to the English, who landed a powerful force in Normandy under the D. of Clarence. He marched *via* Anjou to Blois, declined to accept the Armagnac change and then entered the Duchy of Orleans. The French dukes hurriedly bought him off at Christmas 1412.

(8) There were now further changes in the two govts. In Mar. 1413 Henry V succeeded in England. As prince he had supported the Burgundians, but as King he entertained approaches from both sides, perhaps to raise his price with each. But the two sides were themselves in no hurry for, at the Estates General of 1413, each was bidding for the mastery of the whole. The assembly debated reforms in an atmosphere of growing disorder. The Paris extremists (or *Cabochiens*) pressed for wholesale changes to be supervised by the D. of Burgundy. Their atrocities embarrassed him and brought a reaction in Paris. The moderates came to terms with Armagnac (T. of Pontoise, 1413), admitted him to the city and massacred the Cabochiens and their allies. The Armagnacs could now claim to be a French govt. Burgundy resembled a foreign state. In the summer of 1414 diplomatic duplicity reached new levels. Henry negotiated marriage alliances simultaneously with France and Burgundy. Burgundy agreed joint military action with England while undertaking to the French to forego English alliances. In the end it seemed that Henry was prepared to trade his claim to the French crown for sovereignty over western France from Calais to the Pyrenees, with the unpaid balance of John II's ransom. The French rejected the contention that any claim to the Crown existed but remade the offer contained in the T. of Bourges (1412). With only slight variations the parties remained in these positions. Henry therefore had his war.

(9) His troops landed in Normandy in Aug. 1415 and Harfleur fell in Sept; in Oct. at AGINCOURT the Armagnac army was destroyed and the D. of Orléans captured. Bertrand of Armagnac, however, survived to the south and Burgundy to the north-east now hoped to step into the shoes of the Armagnac party as guardian of the Kingdom. Both were hostile to Henry, whose forces did not suffice for the offensive action on two fronts necessary to conquer Normandy. The Anglo-French war petered out into a truce.

(10) The Council of Constance had met in 1414 to resolve the Great Schism and reform the Church. The Emperor Sigismund III wished to enforce the Way of Cession. Pope John XXIII was deposed in May 1415; Gregory XII resigned in July. The main obstacles to progress were Benedict XIII at Avignon and the Anglo-French war. Sigismund travelled first to S. France to persuade the Aragonese to withdraw obedience from Benedict; then to Paris where he found Bernard of Armagnac determined to retake Harfleur (which he rightly considered vital to the security of Paris) and, despite the truce, blockading it. Thence he came to England where he was magnificently received (May 1416). In June the French occupied the I. of Wight and blockaded Portsmouth, but decided in June to negotiate all the same. In such circumstances no peace was possible and in Aug. Sigismund signed an alliance with Henry (T. of Canterbury). The same day the D. of Bedford defeated the Genoese blockading squadron in the Seine and relieved Harfleur. The French now agreed to negotiate with Henry and Sigismund at Calais, and Burgundy was invited; these negotiations broke down but a truce was agreed until Feb. 1417. Burgundy was not a party and his troops harried the Armagnacs, while Henry prepared further operations.

(11) In Aug. 1417 a great English army landed. Burgundy was steadily isolating Paris; by Feb. 1418

Henry had taken Caen and Falaise, but the Burgundians were in possession of Rouen and both Vexins. Not wishing to frighten them into the arms of the Armagnacs, the English continued in the west. By May 1418 they held Orbec and Pontaudemer.

(12) It was time for another Burgundian somersault. They had entered Paris, massacred their opponents and killed Bertrand of Armagnac. The Dauphin CHARLES (later VII) escaped, but in July D. John, with Isabel, entered the capital and announced that they would fight for Rouen if it were attacked. Since the Armagnacs controlled most of the routes to the city, no action against the English was possible without their support. The local commanders made ineffectual agreements which the Dauphin refused to ratify. By July 1418 Henry had taken all the castles of W. Normandy: in Jan. 1419 Rouen capitulated to him. The Dauphin and the Burgundian (with Isabel and Charles VI) now decided to negotiate separately with Henry, but both sets of negotiations broke down because the Dauphin and D. John had agreed at Pontoise to bury the hatchet (July 1419); they agreed to meet at Montereau in Sept. to co-ordinate operations. At this meeting the Armagnacs murdered John.

(13) The murder of Montereau opened a gulf of hatred between Armagnacs and Burgundians and substituted for the slippery John the Fearless, **Philip the Good (1407-67)** who could be trusted to hate reliably for some time. Henry seized the diplomatic opportunity: in the convention of Arras (Christmas 1419) he and Philip were allied on the basis that Henry would marry Catherine of France and one of his brothers a sister of Philip, that he would help Philip to track down the murderers (i.e. the Dauphinists) and that he would secure from Charles VI lands for Philip by way of amends. The allies then proceeded to reduce Armagnac strongholds all over N.W. France (in the course of which they occasionally came to blows) and marched by way of Rheims to Troyes where Charles VI and Isabel were. Here the tripartite T. of TROYES (q.v.) was sealed in May 1420.

(14) In June Henry married Catherine and captured Montereau. In Nov. Meaux fell and in Dec. the two Kings and Burgundy entered Paris. The Estates General made obedience to the treaty a legal obligation, the murderers of Montereau were condemned in absence and the Dauphin pronounced ineligible for the throne. Isabel's part in these transactions at Troyes and Paris inferentially cast doubt upon his legitimacy.

(15) But the Dauphin was not without forces. Henry went to England leaving Clarence in charge; Clarence invaded Anjou and was defeated and killed in Mar. 1421 at Baugé. The English occupying forces were too small to stand on the defensive. Henry hastened back, drove the Dauphin into Touraine and set about reducing the Dauphinist strongholds in N. France. At Meaux his troops suffered much from dysentery, which he too contracted. He died at Bois de Vincennes in Aug. 1422 leaving his English crown and French inheritance to Henry VI, a child of eight months. Charles VI died in Oct.

CHARLES VII of France (uncrowned King 1422, crowned 1429-61) (*for previous life see* CHARLES VI). (1) His legitimacy was originally doubted even by himself. His supporters, who continued to be called *Dauphinists* were weak and suffered from a certain aimlessness of method. The strong English war direction hitherto centralised in Henry V now gave way to conflicts of interest; for France he had appointed Burgundy as regent or failing him John, D. of Bedford: for England, he could only propose Humphrey, D. of Gloucester ("Duke Humphrey"), who had acted as Guardian of England in his absences on campaign; but there were English precedents for other arrangements. A power struggle within the baronage distracted English attention from French affairs, while Burgundy pursued an increasingly divergent course. The war, for some years, was fought by the weakened but capable Bedford. In July and Aug. 1424 he brought off spectacular victories at Cravant and Verneuil over combined French and Scots forces in which most of the Scots and the majority of the French commanders perished.

(2) In 1422 Gloucester had married Jacqueline, heiress of Hainault who was already, perhaps illegally, married to the refugee John of Brabant. In June 1423 Bedford was betrothed to Anne, Burgundy's sister. Gloucester's action had offended Burgundy who was occupying Hainault: he now proposed to conquer Hainault for his wife. The embarrassed Bedford tried to stop his foolishness, but in Oct. 1424 Gloucester led an expedition there which failed and returned in Nov. Hence England and Burgundy were enemies in the Low Countries but theoretical allies in France.

(3) By Dec. 1425, with the occupation of Maine and Anjou and a victory over the Bretons at St. James de Beuvron, the tide of English conquest had reached its height. Bedford now had to go to London on political business and was away until Mar. 1427, leaving Lord John Talbot in command. On the Dauphinist side an able new commander, Dunois, had arisen while most of the Burgundians had been withdrawn to Flanders because of the quarrel with Gloucester. Minor operations dominated the scene until July 1428 when the E. of Salisbury reached Paris with a substantial re-enforcement and attacked Orléans. By Oct. the strongly defended city was isolated, but Salisbury had died of wounds and Suffolk, his much less energetic successor decided to rely upon a winter blockade. JOAN OF ARC (q.v.) now appeared. After victories in the vicinity she marched to Rheims and crowned her King Charles VII. A Burgundian embassy was present (18 July 1429). The foundations of the English political position were breaking up. Henry VI was brought over to France to advertise the legality of the English position and Joan, now a prisoner, was tried and burned for heresy and sorcery to discredit the moral foundation of the French successes. Subsequently Henry was crowned at Paris (Dec. 1431). These events impressed no one. The essential coronation oath of the French Kings could be sworn only by an adult in the true line of succession. Charles VII's legitimacy had been miraculously certified and he had sworn as an adult. Henry VI was but ten years old. Moreover his guardians were quarrelling.

(4) Since 1429 Martin V had reigned as the only Pope and there was greater strength in the conciliatory functions of the Holy See. Philip the Good's approaches at Troyes began to ripen. There was a proposal for a diplomatic conference at Auxerre in Apr. 1430; Burgundy, Charles VII and Bedford were to attend: The D. of Savoy was to be host and the Holy See to act as mediator. Martin V and his successor, Eugenius IV, commissioned Card. Albergati for the purpose. The conference never met but Albergati did hold four separate peace discussions: with the French and Burgundians at Semur (Aug. 1432) and with the English, French and Burgundians at Auxerre (Oct.), between Corbeil and Melun (Mar. 1433) and at Corbeil (July). During this period the English military position deteriorated. Hence the discussions broke down on preliminaries, because the English would not release their noblest prisoners (Orléans, Bourbon and the Count of Eu) and the French would not concede a truce. All the same, thorough-going hostilities had been diluted with diplomacy. Moreover in 1433 the Constable of Richemont (a relative of the D. of Brittany) had replaced and put to death the factious and unintelligent La Trémoille, who for too long had been Charles VII's principal confidant.

(5) French royal policy now settled into a more logical pattern. There could be no discussion about the French crown: large concessions might be made to secure Burgundy's adherence and Orléans must take part in any negotiations. In 1434 the Burgundians found that Suffolk hoped for a peace and they wanted to include Savoy and Brittany: moreover the Holy See had inferentially recognised Charles as King and the removal from his court of the murderers of Montereau had extinguished one source of Franco-Burgundian contention. In a climate of mounting royalist prestige a tidal set towards peace was bound to advantage Charles VII, for the English could be represented as intruders prolonging the agonies of war and sporadic French operations during *pourparlers* as the lawful recovery of stolen property. The English position depended upon the contract made at Troyes: the French upon divine condemnation of the contract through a convenient miracle.

(6) René of Bar, D. of Lorraine since 1431, was territorially a thorn in the flesh of Philip the Good, by whom he had been captured. By his influence Philip met the D. of Bourbon and the Constable of Richemont at Nevers. There were three agreements. One settled disputes between Burgundy and Bourbon; the second provided for an international peace congress at Arras; the third that if no peace emerged at Arras Philip would strive for union and, if he abandoned the English alliance, he should have the Somme towns which had come to him as the dowry of his first wife MICHELLE of France.

(7) Accordingly delegations from the interested states met at ARRAS (15 Aug.-6 Sept. 1435). The English offered a 20-year truce or until Henry VI came of age, so that the principal issues could then be settled. The French pitched their demands unacceptably high. There was to be a definitive peace then and there: the English were to recognise Charles' title to the French crown and surrender all their holdings or claims in France. Lands ceded to them were then to be held as fiefs of the French crown. The English, of course, left. Philip was now held to the Nevers agreement. Albergati was ready to absolve him from oaths sworn to the T. of Troyes. The Somme towns were handed over but the French gave up the right to tax Artois in return for a right to repurchase the towns for 400,000 crowns. No homage was to be due from Philip during his and Charles VII's lifetime and none of his vassals should be liable for service under the crown. In return there was a Franco-Burgundian defensive alliance. 1435 (the year of the Ps. of Vordingborg and Brest) marked the point at which the downturn of English fortunes in France became irreversible. Bedford died a week before it was sealed. Soon the French were in Dieppe; In Apr. 1436 the Constable of Richemont entered Paris in triumph.

(8) By now the English Council had a new Lieutenant of France in the person of Richard of York but were again contemplating peace. Negotiations broke down in 1437 but the murder of James I of Scots led in July 1438 to a northern truce. Hence Richard was replaced by Warwick, a soldier, to combat a determined French attack in Aquitaine. New negotiations were started on the basis of ransoming the captured D. of Orléans, who would then act as mediator in further negotiations. These hopes were forlorn: since 1436 a French taxation system based upon the *gabelle,* a tax on non noble property (*taille*) and another on sales (*aide*) had been made permanent in order to recreate the professional army. In 1439 the new army was constituted. Charles VII meant to use it. Other administrative reforms, however, delayed him. To form a body of competent administrators it was necessary to recruit both those who had been loyal before 1435 and the more reliable Burgundian officials. Moreover administrative service was beginning to attract ennoblement. The territorial feudatories and military nobles began to feel shut out from the important decisions. The result was the PRAGUERIE (1440), a revolt led by the Dauphin. Charles VII bought them off quickly by a measure which set the social tone of France for three and a half centuries. Though a professional army had just been created, the *noblesse de l'épée* (nobles of the sword) in consideration of their feudal obligation of military service were relieved of all obligation to pay taxes.

(9) Orléans' mission was brought to nothing by further royal successes. In Sept. 1441 the army took Pontoise. Orléans, Alençon and Burgundy now suggested in the spirit of the *Praguerie* that Count John of Armagnac be detached from the King by a marriage between Henry VI and one of his daughters. But except for Burgundly, the days of private wars and peaces were over. Charles VII was advancing on Bordeaux. In Oct. 1442 an English mission could not reach Armagnac and Charles overran La Réole and the Landes. Thereupon the English govt. tried a new tack. A French princess was to be sought for Henry VI in return for a long truce pending final settlement. The claim to the French throne was, if necessary, to be abandoned. With this in view the E. of Suffolk led a mission to Tours and in May 1444 concluded a truce until Apr. 1446. Orléans, Charles of Anjou and René of Bar, K. of Sicily, were present besides Charles VII. A marriage with Margaret, *d.* of René of Sicily, was soon arranged and in June Suffolk returned to London amid rejoicing. As Charles VII and René were preoccupied with further military reforms and a local war around Metz from Nov. until Mar. 1445, the bride could not reach England until Apr. The French ambassadors reached London in July.

(10) The return of Maine to René had been discussed at Tours and his ambassadors expected it. Q. Margaret urged Henry VI to make the cession and Charles VII let it be known that it was the best avenue to peace. In Dec. 1445 Henry promised to hand over by May 1446 and so the truce was extended to Apr. 1447. But Henry found it difficult to comply: the garrison demanded pay and compensation and the courts haggled. A personal meeting of Kings was proposed, but by now Charles thought that further war was the only solution. On the basis of a promise that Maine really would be ceded by 1 Nov. 1447 the truce was extended to Jan. 1448. Thereupon the local commander, Osbern Mundeford, refused to hand over without Dorset's authority, which Dorset would not give. The French blockaded Le Mans which fell in Mar. The truce was again extended but within a fortnight other English local commanders had seized St. James de Beuvron and sacked Fougres and the French retaliated by taking Pont de l'Arche, Conches and Gerberoy. There were, moreover, disorders in England. It might seem that the English govt. was not in full control of its territory. Charles VII decided to take control himself; the truce was in practice at an end. By Oct. 1449 his armies had occupied Rouen. In Apr. 1450 the last effective English force in Normandy went down at the B. of Formigny.

(11) In England faction and Cade's rebellion paralysed the govt. Dunois, with Castilian naval assistance, besieged Bordeaux and took it in June 1451. Leading Bordelais went to England and pleaded for rescue. In Oct. 1452 a small force under John Talbot, E. of Shrewsbury, landed and the major Gascon towns expelled the French. In the spring of 1453 three French armies moved against Bordeaux and in July Talbot was defeated and killed at the B. of Castillon.

(12) To the English who still had the rich area and powerful fortresses of the Calais Pale, as well as partisans and contacts in Normandy and Aquitaine, this was not final. Charles VII was determined to make it so. In the *Grande Ordonnance of Montil-lez-Tours* (1454) he established *parlements* at Toulouse, Grenoble and Bordeaux and *Cours des Aides* (Tax Commissions) at Montpellier and Rouen. While the French Q. Margaret

became a leading figure in the Wars of the Roses, Charles seized the lands of John of Armagnac in 1455. Alençon was imprisoned for treason in 1458; the impatient Dauphin, having risen in league with Savoy, fled to the protection of Burgundy and there remained until he came to the throne as Louis XI.

CHARLES VIII of France (r. 1483-98) was fourteen at his accession. His father, Louis XI, had conferred the effective regency upon the very competent **Anne of Beaujeu,** Charles' elder sister, but this cut across the ambitions of her brother-in-law, **Louis, D. of Orléans.** He secured the convocation of the radical Estates General of Tours in 1484. France was thus in a state of crisis while Richard III was expecting a Tudor rebellion.

Henry Tudor had escaped to Brittany and his supporters were gathering in France. Richard leaned towards the Burgundian connection, but Maximilian, K. of the Romans, was quarrelling with the Flemish estates (*see* LOUIS XI) and was temporarily a broken reed. The best Richard could do was to obtain a Scottish truce (Sept. 1484) and he offered Francis II of Brittany the revenues of the honour of Richmond (long associated with Brittany) in return for Henry Tudor's arrest. The plot failed by hours and Henry was given refuge and financial support by the regency (Oct-Nov. 1484). By this time the Estates General, mollified by the disgrace of some of Louis XI's ministers and a reduction in the *taille*, had dispersed without helping Orléans. Anne of Beaujeu could pursue a harder line. The situation at court was complicated by a personal feud: Orléans had long wanted to divorce Anne's sister JEANNE (Plain Jane) and marry Anne. Anne was in love with Orléans but refused to be compromised. He took mistresses and embittered both women. There were quarrels and conspiracies while Henry Tudor prepared his expedition with French money. In July he set sail from the Seine and by Nov. 1485 he was King; but meanwhile Anne had twice ordered Orléans' arrest and on the second occasion he had fled to Brittany. The Albrets and the Count of Foix sympathised. Another League of the Public Weal seemed to have arisen, complicated by Breton particularism. The aged D. Francis II of Brittany had two daughters, Anne and Isabel. Rival anti-French factions sought to bolster up Breton independence by contracting these to suitable outsiders. In 1484 Anne had been more or less promised to Orléans, who was already married. In Mar. 1486 the Breton estates arranged to marry her to the Emperor Maximilian and Isabel to his son, Philip. Then the duke promised Anne to Alain of Albret. Breton independence was moreover an important English interest and Henry VII, a newly established dynast, could not abandon it, however much he wanted peace. The French regency suspected a threat to the integrity of France or a conspiracy to overturn or dominate its govt. In 1487 the army attacked: it made slow but steady progress. Maximilian, still in dispute with the Flemings, was of little use and from Feb. to May 1488 virtually a prisoner in Bruges. English efforts at compromise failed both at Paris and at Rennes. An unofficial expedition under the English Queen's uncle, Lord Scales, compromised Henry's diplomacy and in any case was destroyed in a general disaster at St. Aubin du Cormier (28 July 1488). Orléans was imprisoned and by the T. of Sable (20 Aug.) Francis II acknowledged his vassalage and promised not to marry Anne without French consent. He also undertook to dismiss all foreign troops and to hand over four towns in pledge. On 9 Sept., however, he died and the fiercely Breton Marshal des Rieux became guardian of the two daughters. The French regency promptly claimed the wardship and disputed Anne's title to the Duchy. Obviously France was now seeking annexation. The Bretons tore up the treaty, fighting was renewed and the marshal with the duchess applied for English help. In Dec. Henry VII sent missions to Brittany, to Maximilian and Philip, to Portugal and to Ferdinand and Isabella of Spain, who wanted to recover Roussillon and Cerdagne. In Jan. 1489 parliament voted a war tax and mobilisation began. Naturally a peace embassy went to France but by 10 Feb. (T. of Redon) he had agreed to procure 6,000 troops for the duchess' service provided that she paid them, made no alliance or marriage without his consent and undertook to help him recover his lost French dominions. On 14 Feb. he re-established with Maximilian the Anglo-Burgundian alliance of 1478 and on 27 Mar. at Medina del Campo a Spanish treaty of marriage and political alliance was initialled whereby neither side was to make peace with France unless France surrendered Normandy and Aquitaine to England, or Roussillon and Cerdagne to Aragon. The English war tax was never fully collected and provoked a northern rebellion in Apr. The Spanish sovereigns had ratified the T. of Medina del Campo at once and by Apr. Henry's 6,000 had arrived in Brittany. Meanwhile Flemish faction fights developed into a French supported rebellion against Maximilian, whose few troops were besieged in Dixmude. They appealed to the Capt. of Calais, Lord Daubeny, who obtained reinforcements. Quarrels between des Rieux and his duchess stultified the Breton operations, but Daubeny brought off a brilliant victory at Dixmude (13 June 1489).

The diplomatic scene now shifted to Frankfort, where the Imperial Diet met on 6 July, and made Maximilian sign a peace with France on 22nd. The Duchess adhered to this treaty which effectively combined the P. of Arras of 1482 and the T. of Sable. The Breton collapse was temporary: English troops were in Concarneau and Morlaix and despite all the French regency's diplomatic efforts, Henry VII retained his aggressive posture and angled for further foreign agreements. There were commercial treaties with Denmark (Aug. 1489 and Jan. 1490) and Florence (Apr. 1490) and with the Sforza D. of Milan against France (4 Oct.). By Christmas the T. of Frankfort had been apparently set aside by an Anglo-Imperial alliance and the proxy marriage of the Duchess to Maximilian.

The reality was otherwise. Maximilian was too involved in a Hungarian war. The Spanish sovereigns, mobilising against Granada, withdrew most of their troops from Brittany. The marriage angered Albret who (Apr. 1491) surrendered Nantes to the French. They spread over the duchy and besieged the Duchess Anne in Rennes. Charles VIII (now of age) had already provided himself with necessary papal dispensations. Her treasury exhausted, her troops mutinous and her confessor corrupt, Anne at last was really married on 6 Dec. to the K. of France under a T. (at Langeais) which bound her to marry his successor if he died without an heir. That successor would be Orléans who, if only for appearances, was set at liberty.

But the transaction had world-wide ramifications. The papacy was alarmed at the continued Ottoman advance (the Turks had briefly occupied Otranto in 1480 and raided Rome in 1481). The crusading idea, cynically regarded by politicians, still attracted some support. There was to be a European effort against the Paynim for which peace in the west was an essential preliminary. Charles VIII was attracted by the offer of the leadership of a crusade for which a base in Southern Italy was needed.

At a less elevated level he was the heir to the Angevin claims to Naples, held since 1435 by an Aragonese dynasty, whose present representative was the bastard Ferrante, a brutal and unpopular usurper. Moreover the emperor's second wife was Bianca Sforza, sister of Lodovico, regent of Milan, and he was on bad terms with Ferrante. Lodovico encouraged Charles to listen to the appeals of Ferrante's subjects, calculating that a French incursion would also help to protect Milan against his imperial brother-in-law. A policy of western

peace came into effect. Henry VII, who had arrived at Calais in force, was bought off at the T. of Étaples (3 Nov. 1492) by instalment reimbursements of the "Picquigny Pension" (see EDWARD iv-14) and his Breton expenses and these continued to be paid until 1511. The Breton marriage had destroyed the basis of French rights in Artois and Franche Comté under the P. of Arras (1482): by the T. of Senlis (23 Jan. 1493) they were returned to Maximilian. Finally, under the T. of Barcelona (19 Jan. 1493) Roussillon and Cerdagne were returned to Aragon. Though Sicily was the granary of Spain the Spanish Sovereigns were not, temporarily, on good terms with their Neapolitan relatives; and if the Borgia Pope wanted to welcome the French in Italy his enemy Card. della Rovere was urging Charles VIII to depose him and put an end to the dynastic ambitions of his son Caesar. In Sept. 1494 Charles leapt into Italy and took its rulers by surprise. In Nov. he occupied Florence, in Dec. Rome, in Feb. 1495 Naples. There was European alarm. The Pope, the Spanish, Maximilian, Venice and Milan signed a League of Venice (30 Mar. 1495) and Charles had to fight his way out. By a lucky victory at Fornovo (6 July 1495) he made good his escape, but Ferdinand's diplomatic reaction had distant and historic effects. In Aug. 1496 he sent his daughter Joanna (the Mad) to marry Philip of Burgundy. In Oct. he agreed to marry Henry VII's son Arthur and the celebrated Katharine of Aragon. Henry, though formally adhering to the League, did not intend to embarrass France, with whom he made a commerical treaty in May 1497. Nevertheless the marriage treaty was ratified in July and in Sept. Spanish mediation procured the Anglo-Scots P. of Ayton. Within months Charles VIII was killed in a tennis court accident and Orleans was King as Louis XII.

CHARLES EDWARD LOUIS ("BONNY PRINCE CHARLIE") (1720-88), the Young Pretender. See JACOBITES AND THEIR PRETENDERS 1 *and* 17 *to* 22.

CHARLES of ANJOU (1226-85). *See* ST. LOUIS IX; PHILIP III.

CHARLES MARTEL. *See* CAROLINGIANS-4.

CHARLESTON. *See* CAROLINA.

CHARLOTTE, Princess (1796-1817) only daughter of George (later IV) married Leopold of Saxe-Coburg, who later became Leopold I of the Belgians and one of Q. Victoria's most influential correspondents.

CHARLOTTE AUGUSTA MATILDA, Princess (1766-1828) eldest *d* of George III, married in May 1797 the P. of Würtemberg, who became reigning D. in Dec. 1797 and a French client King in 1806. He died in 1816.

CHARLOTTE SOPHIA of Mecklenburg-Strelitz (1744-1818) married George III in 1761 and managed his household during his insanity in 1788 and from 1810 to 1818. She was of a practical and sympathetic disposition, but powerless politically. She tried to use her social position to ameliorate the condition of the poor. She invented apple charlotte, which was both cheap and tasty, for them.

CHARLOTTETOWN CONFERENCE. *See* CANADA-17.

CHARLTON OR CHERLETON (1) John of (?-1353) 1st Ld. CHARLTON of POWYS (1313), a Shropshire landowner, became chamberlain to Edward II in 1307, secured the Powys estates by marriage in 1309 and raised Welsh troops for the King in 1310. From 1313 until 1330 he was almost continuously at feud with Welsh neighbours. In 1321 he supported Lancaster's revolt, but was pardoned in 1322. He joined Mortimer's rising in 1326. In 1337-8 he was briefly in Ireland as Lord Lieutenant. His brother **(2) Thomas (?-1344)** was Edward II's Privy Seal, but became Bp. of Hereford in 1327 when, like his brother, he deserted the King. From 1328 to 1330 he was Lord Treasurer. In 1337 he accompanied his brother to Ireland where he became Lord Chancellor and from 1338 to 1340 Lord Lieutenant. A kinsman **(3) Lewis (?-1369)** became Bp. of Hereford in 1361. **(4) Edward (1370-1421) 5th Ld. (1401)**

obtained Caerleon and Usk by marrying the widowed Countess of March in 1398, supported Henry IV in 1399 and was involved in border wars and local truces with the Welsh from 1402 to 1409. He captured Sir John Oldcastle in 1417. A later relative **(5) Sir Job (1614-97)** was M.P. for Ludlow from 1659 to 1679 and speaker in 1673. A justice of the Common Pleas from 1680, he was dismissed by James II for opposition to the dispensing power.

CHARNOCK, Job (?-1693) was the HEIC's agent at Kasimbazar from 1658 to 1664 and at Hooghli in addition until 1686. Highly successful, the hostility of local rulers forced him to withdraw to an island in the Ganges delta, whence he was recalled in 1688 to Madras. In 1690 he returned and obtained a grant from Aurungzib of a site at Sutanati, where he founded the settlement which developed into Calcutta.

CHAROST, HOTEL DE (Paris). The palace of Pauline Bonaparte from whom the D. of Wellington bought it in 1815, since when it has served as the British Embassy.

CHARTER. (1) ENGLAND. A document issued by the crown or its delegate to create, expressly or by implication, a legal person distinct from the individuals composing it, such as a borough or company, with a name and common seal, and conferring rights, duties or privileges upon it. Such a charter, if granted under the prerogative, would be forfeited by the procedure of *Supersedeas* if its terms were abused or exceeded, or by *Quo Warranto* if those purporting to exercise the rights were not entitled (e.g. by defective election) to do so. A charter issued under parliamentary authority, on the other hand, could not be forfeited because forfeiture would amount to the repeal or dispensation of a statute by the crown alone. Hence acts committed *ultra vires* (e.g. excesses, abuses and usurpations) can be corrected only by equity proceedings such as mandamus and injunction and, in govt., by audit.

(2) In older practice the word referred to a solenm document or agreement, to which the crown was sometimes a party, setting forth certain important matters such as the ownership of lands or the law, for example, as stated in the Magna Carta. Sometimes, too, it was the equivalent of a conveyance.

(3) In SCOTLAND the foregoing uses were also normal, but charters were much more often used to convey lands than in England.

CHARTER ACTS (India) 1793, 1813, 1833, 1853. *See* EAST INDIA COMPANY.

CHARTERED COMPANIES. (1) The London Weavers Co's first charter dates from Henry I, but craft-based guilds seldom had charters before the 15th cent; being essentially similar to the fraternities such as parish guilds which mostly owed their constitution to authority deputed to them by their city. After a royal inquiry into the guilds in 1349, the London trade fraternities began to seek royal charters which, in England, were of two main types.

(2) The earlier or *Regulated* Company was an association, usually superseding a staple and formed or encouraged by the Crown; its members traded with their own funds in accordance with the Co's regulations. By the mid-15th cent. the leading London craft guilds had received charters which developed the guild principle for distant trading and were designed to ensure that a given trade was conducted in accordance with state policy. They often granted rights of search, necessary to preserve their monopolies outside London. This monopoly aspect mostly broke down because of the trouble involved in enforcing these rights at a distance. The lesser and poorer Cos. tended to lag behind. Half were still unincorporate in 1531.

(3) The later or *Joint Stock Co.* had a common capital contributed by members and traders for their profit. The practice originated in 14th cent. Italy, especially at Genoa, whose bank, by 1453, administered nearly all the Genoese foreign possessions including Corsica (cf the HEIC). Many such companies originated in business partnerships and the main utility of a charter was to give corporate personality to what was otherwise often a large and unwieldy association of individuals.

(4) The development from the earlier to the later type was neither simple nor quick; for example in the original East India Co. investors subscribed only for a voyage at a time and there was no permanent joint stock until 1657. In some companies the dividend was paid in commodities which the members then sold, or the commodities were bought at a valuation by the members who retailed them. Moreover some monopolistic companies reverted from joint-stock to regulation, as a result of public criticism, because regulation facilitated participation. The main justification of the great monopolistic chartered companies was that they had to perform governmental functions or maintain military establishments abroad and when govts. entered this field they declined or vanished. The following list of major chartered companies gives the date of foundation and whether they were regulated (R) or joint stock (JS). Those marked C were colonising companies.

Prussia Merchants R 1391
Merchant Adventurers R 1407,
   rechartered in 1505 and 1564
Baltic Merchants R 1408
Havre Company R 1409
Merchants of Andalusia R 1505 and 1529
Russia Company JS 1566 R 1669
Society of Mines Royal JS 1568
Society of Mineral and Battery Works JS 1568
Levant Company JS 1581. R 1605
Eastland Company R 1579 (a development of
   the Baltic Merchants)
East India Company, Honourable R 1600 JS 1657
Virginia Companies JS 1606
The France Company R 1611
C Newfoundland Company R 1611
C Bermuda or Somers Is. Company JS 1612
Kings Merchants of the New Trade R 1616
C New England Company JS 1620
C Hudsons Bay Company JS 1670
Royal African Company JS 1672
Bank of England JS 1694
South Sea Company JS 1711

CHARTERHOUSES (Fr = "Chartreuse" = Carthusian monastery) were established in various places in England of which the principal, in London, was founded by Sir Walter de Manny in 1371. Dissolved in 1535 it eventually passed into the hands of Thomas Sutton (c. 1532-1611) of Knaith, who in 1610 endowed an almshouse and school. It was the subject of the *Case of Suttons Hospital,* an important precedent in the law of charities and trusts. The school became famous especially for literary teaching and its pupils included Crashaw, Lovelace, Addison, Steele and Thackeray, as well as Roger Williams who founded Rhode I., Blackstone the lawyer and John Wesley. The school was moved to Godalming (Surrey) in 1872. The almspeople remain.

CHARTER SCHOOLS (Ir). An Incorporated Society was set up in 1700 to provide protestant schools in every diocese for the education of R. Catholic children. It was financed until 1800 by parliamentary grants.

CHARTERS OF LIBERTIES: HENRY I, STEPHEN, and the 'UNKNOWN'. An Anglo-Saxon King took a coronation oath whose earliest form is set out in the pontifical of Abp. Egbert of York (mid-8th cent.) and later in the influential coronation order composed by Abp. Dunstan for K. Edgar in 973. He promised to keep the laws and the customs of his predecessors (or in the earliest form to forbid injustice), to protect God's church and people and to do justice with mercy. By the 12th cent., when the King's sacral nature was again being promoted, his coronation was the obvious time when he might be forced or persuaded into other promises. Henry I, Stephen and Henry II each came to the throne after an uncertainty or dispute over the succession and each conceded a coronation charter which guaranteed what the church and the baronage expected of him. These engendered the notion that the King was somehow under the law. Henry I's charter was issued with attention to its publicity value and it gained importance with time, for copies were made for each county and it served as a model for later charters including Magna Carta. After Ranulf Flambard's escape from the Tower (Feb. 1101), Henry had writs sent to every county to reaffirm it. Stephen owed his crown mainly to the Church. His coronation came within three weeks of Henry I's death and his charter was a hurried statement of intentions, filled out in Apr. 1136 by a more explicit and far-reaching document. The Church was to be free from lay interference: its elections were to be canonical; during vacancies, sees were to be in the custody of the clergy or honourable men, and the clergy should be able to leave their effects by will. These opportunist clauses were only partly honoured. Henry II succeeded to the throne from a position of greater strength and his charter, very generally couched, was little more than a confirmation of the laws and customs of Henry I. John succeeded in England and Normandy without dispute and made only the customary oath to maintain the laws of Edward the Confessor. His mercurial incompetence, however, brought him into collision with a powerful Pope, Innocent III, an aggressive French King, Philip Augustus, and a hostile English baronage, sometimes in combination. He lost Normandy to Philip in 1204 and exposed England to a papal interdict from 1208 to 1214, whilst northern and eastern barons exploited a growing resentment at his arbitrary rule and extortions. When he was reconciled with Abp. Stephen Langton in 1213 he merely had to renew his coronation oath, but when the barons made their alliance with Philip Augustus, they formally renounced their homage to John (Apr. 1215) and occupied London. This forced him to negotiate and a draft, the so-called 'Unknown Charter' (found in Paris) was the result. It recites Henry I's coronation charter and of its 12 clauses eleven reappear in Magna Carta. The twelfth, which restricts the obligation of foreign service to Normandy and Brittany, does not. On 9 May John accepted the baronial demand of trial by due process of law. Some of his councillors, including William Marshal and Hubert de Burgh, encouraged him to negotiate but Stephen Langton probably had in mind a settlement for the benefit of all classes. The first fruit was the so-called *Articles of the Barons* which John sealed on 15 June 1215 in a Thameside meadow 'between Staines and Runnymede'. Greater importance, however, would have been given to the *Inspeximus,* which was sealed by Langton and the bishops and the papal legate, as specially provided in the last clause. Other copies were distributed to every county. *See* MAGNA CARTA.

CHARTISM (1832-50) was an amorphous movement arising from the pressure of high food prices and industrial competition upon the practitioners of older established crafts. Its leaders were mostly independent artisans such as cabinet makers and tailors; the following, mostly workers in declining industries such as linen and handloom weaving, but there were great local variations. The doctrines dated back to John Cartwright's (1740-1824) *Take Your Choice* (1771) and the London Corresponding Society (1792), but the Poor Law of 1834 with its indifference to dignity and pride of independence, provoked the action. This took the old fashioned shape of a demand for parliamentary reform,

embodied in the PEOPLES' CHARTER; a draft bill designed to secure (a) annual parliaments; (b) universal manhood suffrage; (c) equal electoral districts; (d) no property qualification for M.P.s; (e) secret ballot; (f) payment of M.P.s. It represented a protest against the Reform Act, 1832, but on the occasions in 1839, 1842 and 1848 when it was taken, accompanied by huge demonstrations, to Westminster, it was accompanied by a petition expatiating on social, economic and political ills.

The leading personalities were William Lovett (1800-77), sec. of the British Assoc. for Promoting Co-operative Knowledge, Francis Place (1771-1854), the radical tailor friend of Sir Francis Burdett, and John Arthur Roebuck (1801-79), barrister and M.P. for Bath from 1832 to 1837 and from 1841 to 1847, together with five radical M.P.s, but the central organisation was weak and the membership lost interest after 1842, with the return of prosperity. At this time Feargus O'Connor (1794-1855) a temperamental politician, who had made his journal, the *Northern Star* the main organ of Chartism, took over the leadership, but his style was unsuited to the new circumstances. Though there was a brief revival in 1848, induced by European events, Chartism ceased to matter after 1850. Some of its adherents, however, remained as a new movement led by Ernest Jones (1819-69), an extremist who, with a small following, gained control of the National Charter Assoc. in 1850. This new Chartism, related to European revolutionary movements, was both violent and ineffective. *See* PEEL'S SECOND GOVT.-1,2.

CHARTRES (Fr.). The intellectual and religious effort which went into the architecture, sculpture, wood carving and glass of its cathedral, made its erection and adornment one of the most influential events of mediaeval Western Europe. It was built on the site of a previous Cathedral burned in 1194. One window (*Notre Dame de la Belle Verrière*) is of 12th cent. glass. The building was carried out in three distinctly marked stages (a) the early part of the main building and sculpture of a forceful early style was completed by about 1240; (b) the rest of the main building and the Old Belfry with much further sculpture of a later style was finished and glazed by about 1290; (c) the New Belfry was completed in about 1510.

CHASE was an unenclosed area held by prescription or royal grant for hunting game (*see* PARK). It was not subject to forest law.

CHASE-ABOUT RAID (Aug. 1565). *See* MARY Q. OF SCOTS-11.

CHÂTEAU. A French country house. A castle is a *Château fort.*

CHÂTEAU GAILLARD. *See* ANDELYS; PHILIP (II) AUGUSTUS; RICHARD I.

CHÂTEAUBRIAND, Francois René, Vicomte de (1768-1848), went to America in 1791 and lived among the Iroquois. In 1792 he returned, joined the royalists and after accidents and illness found his way to England, where in 1797 he published his *Essaie sur les Revolutions.* This alienated his *émigré* friends with its rejection of Christianity. In 1800 he returned to France at the invitation of his fashionable publisher friend Fontanes and in 1802 issued his celebrated *Genie du christianisme,* which attracted the more pious royalists. He was also prominent in the salon of Pauline de Beaumont, who became his mistress. In 1803 he became sec. to Bonaparte's uncle, Card. Fesch, and then chargé d'affaires in the Valais, but resigned on the murder of the Duc d'Enghien. Until 1811 he travelled in the Middle East, N. Africa and Spain and at the Restoration he became a member of the House of Peers. In 1822 he was ambassador in London; after a short time at the Congress of Verona he was foreign minister in 1823.

CHÂTEAU-RENAULT, Francois de Rousselet, M. de (1637-1716) commanded the troop convoy to support James II in Ireland in 1688, and a squadron under Tourville at Beachy Head in 1690. He succeeded

Tourville as V.-Adm. of France in 1701 and in 1702 escorted the *Flota*. Secretly instructed to bring it to a French port, he got it into Vigo, where Sir George Rooke's Anglo-Dutch fleet took or destroyed every ship in the harbour. Originally a soldier, he was not again employed at sea, but next year became a marshal of France.

CHATELHERAULT, D. of (?-1575). *See* HAMILTON (ARRAN)-7.

CHATFIELD, Alfred Ernie Montacute (1873-1967) 1st Ld. (1937) was Beatty's flag-captain in World War I and his fourth Sea Lord in 1919. In 1929 he was C-in-C Atlantic, from 1930 to 1932 C-in-C Mediterranean and from 1933 to 1938 First Sea Lord. As such he was responsible for the effective arming of the Royal Navy for World War II and for its training especially in night actions. In 1939 he held the shortlived office of Min. for the Co-ordination of Defence. A gunnery expert, he was one of the ablest naval officers of his generation and as a trainer laid the foundations of the Royal Navy's successes in World War II, especially in the Mediterranean.

CHATHAM, Es. of. *See* PITT.

CHATHAM (Kent). The naval dockyard was founded in 1588 and transferred to a better site in 1662. It remained one of the principal naval bases until 1967 and was closed in 1989.

CHATHAM CHEST. A charitable fund raised by Sir F. Drake and Sir J. Hawkins in 1581 for sick and wounded seamen. Naval court martial fines were paid into it until 1688 and Charles II endowed it with land. After 1688 it was maintained, like the N. Health Service before its time, by deductions from seamen's pay. In 1802 it was moved to and incorporated with Greenwich Hospital. The deductions ceased in 1829.

CHATHAM HOUSE (ROYAL INSTITUTE OF INTERNATIONAL AFFAIRS) originated at the peace conference of 1919. It was begun as an Anglo-American venture, but the Council of Foreign Relations at New York split off and developed separately. All the major Commonwealth countries developed similar institutes in close relationship with it.

CHATHAM Is. (Pacific), 360 miles E. of New Zealand, were found by a Lieut. William Broughton in 1791 when they had about 1000 inhabitants, whom he called Morioris. Maoris from New Zealand invaded and conquered the islands in 1831 and all but exterminated the Moriorios. The islands remain a dependency of New Zealand.

CHÂTILLON, CONFERENCES OF (5 Feb.-19 Mar. 1814) between allied diplomats and Caulaincourt, representing Bonaparte, were carried on while operations were in progress. The allies had won the B. of La Rothière on 1 Feb., and proposed the French "ancient" frontiers. Between 9 Feb. and 1 Mar., when the French won victories, Bonaparte demanded the "natural" frontiers. As the allies began to advance in the North and Wellington was approaching Bordeaux (1-11 Mar.), Caulaincourt progressively abandoned claims "beyond the frontiers". When the allied victory was certain these offers were rejected.

CHATSWORTH (Derbys.) became the main residence of the Cavendish family when the present house was erected on the site of a previous mansion between 1687 and 1706 by William, 1st D. of Devonshire. It was extended in 1820.

CHATTAN, CLAN. *See* CLANS, SCOTTISH.

CHATTELS, CHATTELS REAL. *See* REALTY.

CHAUCER, (1) Geoffrey (c. 1344-1400) son of a prosperous London vintner, began as a page to Elizabeth de Burgh, wife of Lionel, D. of Clarence, at the centre of court society. He was captured during the Brittany expedition of 1359, but Edward III ransomed him and later sent him on diplomatic or trade missions to France, Genoa and Florence, where he met Boccaccio and possibly Petrarch. On his return from Italy he became comptroller of the lucrative London customs, and so became familiar with the world of business and could afford to marry Philippa de Roe(l)t (c. 1366), sister of Katherine Swynford, John of Gaunt's mistress and wife. Between 1359 and 1372 he wrote the French influenced *Boke of the Duchess*, and some parts of a translation of Lorris' *Roman de la Rose,* and between 1372 and 1386 the Italian influenced *Hous of Fame*, the *Parlement of Foules, Troylus and Cryseyde* and the *Legend of Good Women*. He was M.P. for Kent in 1386 when he was deprived of his customs posts. He drafted some of the famous *Canterbury Tales* at about this time and made the Canterbury pilgrimage in 1388. The twenty-three surviving verse *Tales* evoke with much wit, ribaldry and occasional indecency the life and tastes of the people at all levels from knights to cooks and are cast in the form of a party on pilgrimage telling each other stories to wile away the time between Canterbury and London. His son **(2) Thomas (c. 1367-1434)** married an heiress, Matilda Burghersh, and doubtless benefitted from having John of Gaunt as his uncle. Save between 1418 and 1422 he held the valuable office of Chief Butler; from 1399 to 1434 and from 1400 onwards he was regularly an M.P. for Oxfordshire, where he had several estates. He was Speaker in 1407, 1410 and 1414. In 1415 he was with Henry V in France and was at the B. of Agincourt. He was Speaker again in 1421 and a member of the Council from 1424.

CHAUMONT, T. of (Mar. 1814) was largely the work of Castlereagh. Austria, Britain, Prussia and Russia undertook to keep 150,000 men each in the field against Bonaparte. Britain paid her partners a total of £5M; and the parties agreed not to negotiate separately. The treaty, defensive in the case of a settlement, was to be offensive in the absence of one, and of indefinite duration. There were to be periodical meetings to deal with common problems. *See* LIVERPOOL GOVT., WARTIME PHASE; FOURTH COALITION, WAR OF.

CHAUTH was a forced contribution of 25% of the revenue assessment levied by an Indian military commander upon a territory which he had overrun but not annexed. In practice it was a kind of 'Danegeld' paid by Hindu and Moslem rulers to the Marathas.

CHAUVINISM. Nicholas Chauvin was a veteran soldier absurdly conspicuous for his blind devotion to Bonaparte. Hence the word properly means an unheeding nationalism and contempt for foreigners. Since 1970 it had been used occasionally by feminists as a term of vague abuse.

CHEAP (O.E. céap = commercial dealing) forms part of many local names and signifies the presence of an ancient market e.g. Cheap St. in Sherborne. Early mediaeval London grew up around two markets. **Eastcheap,** near London Bridge, was the centre for waterborne goods, especially fish, whilst the spinal Westcheap or **CHEAPSIDE** partly followed a Roman road and was the main craft centre. At its western end was the corn market and close by was the site of the folkmoot. It remained the main shopping street into Tudor times. It was rebuilt and partly resited after the Great Fire of 1666.

CHEDDAR (Som.) was a royal manor with large halls where the witan is known to have met in 941, 956 and 968. While riding near the celebrated gorge, the Saxon K. Edred had an uncertain telepathic experience related to St. Dunstan, who was 20 miles off, which, he was convinced, saved his life. The manor continued a royal residence until K. John's time and he erected fresh buildings there. In 1215, however, it passed to Wells Cathedral. The market and stock fair doubtless served to publicise the well-known cheese made since the 15th cent. and mass produced, not only in Cheddar, in the 20th.

CHEKE, Sir John (1514-57), a protestant professor of Greek at Cambridge from 1540 to 1551 and tutor to the future Edward VI from 1544, was M.P. for Bletchingly in 1547 and Provost of King's College, Cambridge from 1548. In 1553 he supported Lady Jane Grey and was imprisoned under Mary I until 1554 when he went abroad, teaching Greek for a living until he was arrested near Brussels in 1556, by order of Philip II, now Mary's husband. He was sent to the Tower where under threat of torture and already in ill health, he recanted his protestantism and obtained his release.

CHELLES NUNNERY, nr Paris (Fr), was founded (c. 660) by Bathild, Anglo-Saxon Queen to Clovis II. It was influential in England, for St. Hilda of Whitby possibly and her sister certainly went there. As St. Mildred and St. Milburga of Wenlock were educated there, it must have been well known to their mother St. Ermenburga, who founded Minster in Thanet. Wenlock was founded by K. Merewalh of Mercia, Milburga's father, who placed it under St. Botolph's direction. Botolph made Liobsynde, also from Chelles, its first abbess.

CHELMSFORD (Essex) (Lat = *Caesaromagus*). The bridge over the Chelmer, built in 12th cent., diverted the main London-East Anglia road into the town, which by 1227 had become the seat of the shrievalty and assizes for Essex.

CHELMSFORD. *See* THESIGER.

CHELSEA (A.S. = *chalk wharf*) was a royal manor, the house being occasionally used by Henry VIII, and Sir Thomas More lived there too. The Society of Apothecaries instituted the Physic Garden for botanical and medical research in 1673. The porcelain works operated from about 1745 until 1784 and Henry VIII's manor was pulled down in 1760. By this period Chelsea was a residential village whose beauty and seclusion attracted 19th cent. artists and writers such as Turner Whistler, Carlyle and Wilde. In a comparative sense, the atmosphere continued into the 20th cent. because though building continued, the underground avoided the area. By the 1960s the Kings Road was synonymous with youthful fashion and art.

CHELSEA ROYAL HOSPITAL was founded by Charles II, on the inspiration of Nell Gwynne, as a home for 'worthy old soldiers broken in the wars' and opened in 1694. Sir Christopher Wren was the architect. The Board under the Presidency of the Paymaster Gen. was responsible for military pensions until 1955. The 558 uniformed pensioners remain and are a well known feature of London life.

CHELTENHAM (Glos.) became a spa after the discovery of mineral springs in 1716 and in the 19th cent. it became an educational centre based on the Grammar School (originally a chantry school). Cheltenham College was founded in 1841; the Ladies College in 1853 and Dean Close in 1886. *See* BEALE, TOBACCO.

CHEMICAL WARFARE is not easy to define, since sulphur fumes, the Byzantine Greek fire, all explosives, napalm and the defoliants are products of warlike chemistry. The phrase, however, most often refers to substances generically but inaccurately called gases. Of these only Chlorine and sulphuretted hydrogen, the least effective, are true gases. C.S. or tear-gas and the volatile offspring of phosgene are vapours whilst the most practically dangerous is mustard gas, which is a treacly liquid. Attempts have been made to abolish or limit the use of 'gas' by international convention, notably The Hague Declaration of 1899 to which Britain adhered in 1907. The German use of chlorine in 1915 brought them world-wide obloquy which assisted the Allied cause in World War I. At the Washington Conference of 1922 the powers agreed to prohibit the use of gases. The Germans used them in their extermination camps but were deterred by British threats in World War II from using them in their Russian campaigns.

CHEMINAGE. A toll for passage through a forest.

CHEMISTRY (*see* ALCHEMY). Joseph BLACK (1728-99) of Edinburgh made the fundamental discovery that air could take part in combustion in 1756. Oxygen was discovered in 1772 and between 1770 and 1790 Antoine Lawrent LAVOISIER defined combustion. This led naturally to the analysis of chemical compounds and elements; by 1808 John DALTON (1766-1844) had propounded the idea of atomic weight and in 1811 Avogadro that of molecular weight. Developments from these fundamental ideas made possible the opening of the study of ORGANIC CHEMISTRY by Kekulé in 1858 and of PHYSICAL CHEMISTRY in 1875.

CHEPSTOW (Mon.) at an important crossing of the R. Wye was fortified in British, Roman and Saxon times and the castle was founded by the Normans in about 1080. The protection thus given encouraged a town, later fortified, and a port and the establishment of **Tintern Abbey** four miles up the river. Chepstow was chartered in 1524 and the port, mainly for agricultural products, throve until about 1850 when growing modern ships became too large for it.

CHEQUE is an order by the signatory to somebody (nowadays always a bank) who has his money, to pay it to a third person. The latter had to endorse it when presenting it for payment and could then cash it at the bank or endorse it to yet another party and so on. Endorsement made endorsers liable upon the cheque in succession (if more than one), if the bank failed to pay. By 1950 multiple endorsements had virtually died out. A receipt for money was not valid unless it had been **stamped** with a 2d stamp and all cheques were so stamped before use. The Cheques Act, 1957, enacted that an unendorsed but paid cheque was evidence of receipt of the money, whereupon separate stamped receipts fell out of use. Receipt and cheque stamps were accordingly abolished in 1960.

CHEQUERS (Bucks.) an Elizabethan house built by Wm. Hawtrey in 1565 but with Neo-Gothic alterations, was acquired in 1909 by Lord Lee of Fareham and made over with an endowment in 1917 as an official country residence for the Prime Minister. The first to use the house was Lloyd George in 1921.

CHERASCO, B. of (15 May 1796). The French defeat of the Austrians at the Bridge of Lodi (10 May 1796) isolated the Sardinians who were compelled by Bonaparte to make peace, cede Savoy and Nice and renounce their Austrian alliance.

CHERBOURG (Fr.) is an ancient starting point for cross channel trade. William I gave it a hospital and a church. Its strategic importance greatly increased under Philip Augustus and in mediaeval wars, and especially in 1295, it was often attacked and pillaged by the English who held it continuously from 1418 to 1450. Vauban began to develop the fortified harbour in 1687 and the works were continued under Louis XVI, Bonaparte, Louis Philippe and Napoleon III whenever there was a war scare.

CHEROKEES, an Iroquoian tribe, occupied throughout the 18th cent. an area between the Ohio river and Alabama, and were consistently allied to the British against other tribes, the French and finally the American rebels.

CHERTSEY (Surrey) had a Benedictine Abbey founded in 666 and refounded in 964 after a Danish raid. The fertility of the district and the fairs and markets established in 1129 and 1282 soon made it immensely prosperous and it became one of the largest monasteries in the world. It was totally destroyed at the Dissolution.

CHERWELL, Ld. *See* LINDEMANN.

CHESHIRE, CHESTER. (Lat = DEVA; A.S. = LEGACEASTER) (1) The Roman legionary city was built in about AD. 71 as a base against N. Wales and the N. West, first for the IInd Legion and after A.D. 90 for the XXth, which was stationed there during two reconstructions until 383. It was then moved to Gaul by Magnus Maximus and the town began to decay. It was sacked probably in 615 by Aethelfrith of Northumbria, who defeated the Welsh there. The houses collapsed into elongated piles of rubble which formed the foundations for the Rows, the elevated arcades long a prominent feature of the city. The area remained isolated until c. 830 when it was overrun and annexed by the Mercians. In about 907 Aethelflaed, the Lady of the Mercians, refortified the city against the Danes. By 1000 it was an important port and market with its own mint. It held out against William I until 1070.

(2) In 1070 he established the city and county as a Palatinate. It included most of Lancashire up to the Ribble and as much of N. Wales as could be reached. Its purpose was the same as that of the Roman legionary fortress and its first E. was William's relative HUGH of AVRANCHES (?1047-1101), but the earldom's wealth depended mostly on vast estates outside Cheshire in richer and more settled areas. Hugh founded the great abbey.

(3) He was succeeded by his son RICHARD (?-1 120) and then by his nephew RANULF le MESCHIN (The Nasty) (?-1129) who, apart from large estates at Bayeux, had also acquired the honour of Carlisle. Hence his son RANULF de GERNONS (?-1153) was an important and virtually independent potentate more powerful than K. Stephen, his liege lord, whom he fought at Lincoln in 1141. His son HUGH of CYFEILIOG (?-1181) was also immensely powerful. He supported and survived the rebellion of 1173 against Henry II. Two reasons for the impunity of the Chester earls were that they guarded the frontier against the powerful Welsh principality of Gwynedd, and Chester was now important to the communications with Anglo-Norman Ireland.

(4) Hugh's son RANULF of BLUNDEVILLE (?-1132) was the most spectacular of his line. He married Constance of Brittany and Richmond and for his loyalty to K. John and Henry III was custodian of Leicester and Lancaster and was made E. of Lincoln. His position was in fact a threat to the stability of the Govt. and in 1218 the regency, with papal support, persuaded him to take the Cross. He died on crusade in 1237 leaving his vast estates to be divided among parceners. The County thus came to his nephew JOHN the SCOT (?-1237) **E. of HUNTINGDON.** This was the period of Henry III's Provençal marriage (1236) and in the ensuing financial and political crisis the earldom was one of the prizes and was escheated in 1241. In 1254 Henry conferred it upon the Lord Edward and it formed the base from which he, as prince and King, conquered N. Wales. This was completed by 1284 but the separate palatine organisation was retained and the county and city enjoyed great prosperity throughout the 13th and 14th cents. through the Irish trade and its important salt workings. The Earldom after 1301 was conferred only on heirs to the throne. In the middle of the 14th cent, however, the silting of the Dee brought a decline at Chester and under Henry VIII the palatine status of the county was virtually abrogated except for the judicial organisations. In 1541, however, Chester became a bishopric and in 1543 the County for the first time sent members to parliament. In the 16th cent. a trade to Spain and Portugal developed, but attempts to improve the Dee were overtaken by the 18th cent. rise of Liverpool.

CHESTERFIELD (Derbys.) given charter privileges in 1204 (John) and 1233 (Henry III) was incorporated in 1598. It was the place at which Devonshire and others met in 1688 to plan the overthrow of James II. The curious, twisted and bent spire of its hilltop parish church is, of course, ascribed to the Devil.

CHESTERFIELD. *See* STANHOPE.

CHESTER-LE-STREET. *See* DURHAM-1.

CHETWODE, Field Marshal Sir Philip Walhouse Bt. (1869-1950) 1st Ld. CHETWODE (1945) commanded 5th Cav. Brigade (1914-5) and the 2nd Cav. Div. (1915-6) on the Western Front, then the Desert Column in Egypt (1916-7) and XX Corps against Jerusalem. From 1920 to

1922 he was Dep. C.I.G.S; from 1923 to 1927 C-in-C Aldershot; he then went to India as C.G.S. (1928-30) and became C-in-C (1930-5) at a difficult time, when Indian nationalists were demanding Indianisation of the army command. The proportion of Indian officers was much increased with an Indian 'Sandhurst' at Dehra Dun. An Indian Air Force was established and the Indian Marine became the Indian Navy. It was largely through his qualities of imaginative leadership that the Indian forces were developed smoothly until the disruptions after World War II.

CHEVAGE. A payment by a villein to live outside his lordship.

CHEVAUCHÉE **(Med. Fr. = a ride).** A massed cavalry raid intended, unscathed, to ravage a district and bring back loot.

CHEVIOTS. These border hills between England and Scotland were long the fastness of cattle raiders. They attacked the lowland farms, which were in consequence often fortified as PELE CASTLES. The sheep of the area produced a special wool suitable for a kind of serge called Cheviot Cloth. *See* MARCHES, ANGLO SCOTS.

CHEVREUSE, Marie de Rohan-Montbazon, Duchesse de (1600-79) was Superintendant of the Household to Anne of Austria, Queen to Louis XIII, in 1625 when she became the E. of Holland's mistress during his embassy to Paris in connection with the betrothal of Henrietta Maria to Charles I. She then tried to promote a liaison between Henrietta and Buckingham and committed other indiscretions. She later became an important politician at the French Court and suffered a series of exiles – one in England from 1639 to 1641.

CHEVY CHASE. *See* OTTERBURN.

CHIANG KAI-SHEK (1887-1975) Japanese-trained soldier, in 1918 joined Sun Yat-Sen, the Chinese nationalist (KUOMINTANG) leader against the local warlords who had arisen after the overthrow of the Manchus and of Yuan Shih-Kai. Success was impossible without a separate army and in 1923 Chiang studied communist military methods in Russia. He returned to found the Whampoa military academy on Russian lines near Canton. In 1925 he became C-in-C and launched his campaign, based on the Whampoa force, against the warlords. This carried him to Pekin by 1928, when he established the national capital at Nanking. Unfortunately he had suppressed rather than overthrown the warlords, and the Communists had set up their own separate organisation, especially in country areas. In 1931 the Japanese took over the govt. of Manchuria, but Chiang decided that the communist threat was the worse of the two and concentrated against them. The Japanese invasion of 1937 was thus militarily a success in which Chiang was driven westwards and the communists repeated their Yugoslavian pattern of fighting the govt. and its foreign enemy impartially. Moreover the Japanese occupation of Burma cut him off from his western allies. He was exhausted when the allies defeated Japan and the communists were able to throw their full resources against him. Between 1946 and 1949 his govt. was driven from the mainland to Formosa (Taiwan) where it remained as the nominal Chinese govt. until expelled from the United Nations in 1971.

CHICAGO (U.S.A.) was used as a portage in 1673 by Jolliet and Marquette and in the early 18th cent. it was an occasional military camp, Indian village and council place and trading post. It had a U.S. garrison from 1803 to 1812, but there was no permanent settlement until the defeat of Black Hawk in 1832. A mail route to Ottawa was opened in 1834. Its position at the hub of the expanding U.S.A. has tended to draw interest away from the north shores of the Great Lakes, so that expansion at Chicago was matched by relatively slow growth at Toronto.

CHICAGO AIR CONVENTION 1944. *See* AVIATION RULES-1.

CHICAGO TRIBUNE is an influential conservative Republican newspaper founded in 1847. From 1914 it was controlled by Robert McCormick and did much to lead and create U.S. economic and political isolationism.

CHICHELE[Y] Henry (c. 1362-1443) Bp. of St. DAVIDS (1408) Abp. of CANTERBURY (1414). William of Wykeham maintained him at Winchester College and financed his law studies at Oxford. As a Doctor of Laws he was engaged in ecclesiastical diplomacy concerned with the Great Schism, especially in missions to the Roman Curia in 1404 and 1406-8 and to the Council of Pisa in 1409. From 1410 he was a member of the Council and as a diplomat went to the French court in the same year, to Arras in 1411 and negotiated with the French and the Burgundians again in 1413. As Abp. he helped in the complicated Calais negotiations with the Emperor Sigismund in 1416. He was with Henry V in France in 1418-9 and he helped to secure the capitulation of Rouen. With Henry he joined in resisting papal control of the English church and, in particular, in preventing the grant of a legatine commission to Henry's uncle, Henry Beaufort (1418). After Henry's death in 1422 he was involved in disputes over the regency between Gloucester, Bedford and the Council, and with Beaufort and the Papacy over provisions. In 1427 he was suspended from his metropolitan and legatine powers by Martin V and forced, with other bishops, to try for the repeal of the Statute of Provisors. They failed, but the whole episode damaged his reputation and increased the influence of Beaufort. He remained, however, an important political figure but concentrated on church and educational work. Thus he raised the endowment of Canterbury cathedral; established the Chichele Chest for poor scholars at Oxford and founded All Souls College there in 1438.

CHICHERIN, Georgi Vasilievich (1872-1936) left Russia in 1904 and spent 12 years in Menshevik conspiratorial activities in Berlin, Paris and eventually London, where he organised philanthropic work for Russian refugees in order to maintain revolutionary contacts. When Russia started to negotiate with the Central Powers he was interned and in Jan. 1918 exchanged for Sir George Buchanan. He took part in the Brest-Litovsk negotiations in Mar. 1918. In May he succeeded Trotsky as Commisar for Foreign Affairs of the R.S.F.S.R. and in 1922 went as Commisar for the U.S.S.R. to the Genoa peace conference, during which he negotiated the T. of Rapallo with Germany. He continued to conduct Russian foreign policy until the end of 1928 when illness forced him to retire.

CHICHESTER (Ssx) (Lat = NOVIOMAGUS REGNENSIUM = Noviomagus of the Men of the Kingdom; A-S. = CISSECEASTRE) was the capital of "The Kingdom" of Cogidubnus, recognised by the invading Romans. Fishbourne, in the outskirts, had a Roman villa, the long occupied centre of a prosperous estate. Aelle's son Cissa occupied it (c. A.D. 500) without destroying it and it remained important under the South and West Saxon Kings, with a mint as early as Athelstan's time (r. 925-39). Sea inroads forced the bishops to move here from Selsey and the first cathedral was dedicated in 1107. Stephen granted the city rights of guild merchant and borough. The citizens acquired the farm of the city and possibly the right to elect the mayor, in the 1220s, and secured them permanently in 1316. The mediaeval town flourished as a market, especially for cattle but, lacking direct access to the sea, its seaborne commerce was always precarious. It was represented in parliament by two M.P.s from 1295 to 1867 and by one until 1886. Four of its five fairs were abolished in 1889 and its life stagnated until the late 20th cent. when its arts festival began to attract attention.

CHICHESTER. See PELHAM.

CHICHESTER, Arthur (1563-1625) Ld. CHICHESTER (1613) lived in Ireland after assaulting a royal purveyor, but after his pardon served against the Armada and in all the major overseas expeditions. In 1597 he was knighted and in 1598 a Col. at Drogheda. As gov. of Carrickfergus from 1599 to 1603 he gained great experience in dealing with Irish rebels and an understanding of Irish problems and from 1604 he was an able and determined, as well as long lasting, Lord Deputy. He favoured religious toleration and the translation of the B.C.P. into Irish and encouraged the surrender of clan lands and their regrant in fee to the chieftains. The English govt. policy was inconsistent with these views. Apart from a determination to persecute, James I meant to colonise Ulster with Scots and this involved wholesale evictions. He carried out the policy of repression without much conviction from 1605 to 1607, but the plantation of Ulster with considerable efficiency between 1608 and 1614. He is the founder of modern Ulster. On refusing to resume repression in 1614 he was recalled, but made Lord Treasurer of Ireland. James employed him on a mission to the Elector Frederick V in 1622.

CHICHESTER, E. of. See LEIGH.

CHILD, Sir Francis (1642-1713), a freeman of the Goldsmith's Co. from 1664, married into the Wheeler family, London goldsmiths, inherited their fortune and banking business and with it founded Child's Bank.

CHILD, (1) Sir John (?-1690) was dep-gov. of Bombay from 1679 to 1681 and Pres. of Surat from 1682 to 1690. He was the first person to take charge of all the HEIC's undertakings in India. His brother **(2) Sir Josiah (1630-99)** advocated political power as well as commercial monopoly for the HEIC, of which he became a director in 1677. From 1682 he was its leading spirit and virtual dictator and his attitude set, psychologically, the Company's course for the next century.

CHILDREN, CHILD LABOUR, INFANTS, MAJORITY etc. (1) Originally an infant (Lat = one who cannot speak for himself) came of age when he could pass the test for entry into his station in life: thus a ploughman's son when he could plough a straight furrow (at about 15); a knight's son when he could fight in armour (about 21). The latter eventually became universal. Until then the father was entitled to his services and could chastise him, but originally was not bound at law to maintain him unless lack of maintenance amounted to an offence, even though he had the custody of a boy until majority and of a girl until majority or earlier marriage. The age of consent was 14 for a boy and 12 for a girl.

(2) The absence of efficient birth control, the inefficiency or absence of a system of matrimonial registration and the lack of an enforceable obligation of maintenance, created a huge problem of destitute children, many of them bastards or assumed bastards; hence the ease with which charlatans assembled the Children's Crusade (1212) and the social advantage of being a royal or nobleman's bastard. Monasteries and foundling institutions alleviated the condition of many abandoned children.

(3) The Dissolution of the Monasteries destroyed the welfare system and left children to the parish. The clergy as guardians of morality were supposed to frown on fornication and adultery, and the spread of parish registers, especially after 1603, facilitated the ascription of parentage. Public or at least parish opinion could put pressure on irresponsible parents. After the Poor Law was enacted (1600) this moral pressure became a pleasure, for if the child was not maintained by its parents, the ratepayers did. A major vice in the system was that either way there was an inducement to put children out to work in order to save the parents' pocket or the ratepayers', and this undercut the wages paid to adults. The custom of compulsory apprenticeship (men until 24, girls until 21 or marriage) was incorporated in the Act of 1600. It was, however, the Poor Law Act of 1662 (the so-called Settlement Act) which obliged paren ts to maintain their bastards.

(4) The system thus established worked after a fashion until the population explosion which accompanied the industrial revolution; it then quickly became monstrously, if unexpectedly, cruel. Destitute children congregated in larger towns and were apprenticed as soon as possible by Guardians of the Poor who were under heavy pressure from their burdened ratepayers. Often the distant places and conditions into which they were apprenticed were unknown to or quietly ignored by the Guardians. It amounted to an internal slave trade or a parental slavery much mentioned in literature. Many children simply died of overwork, undernourishment or tuberculosis at factory looms in the north, or in inhuman employments such as chimney sweeping.

(5) The public conscience was disturbed when particular facets of this complicated problem were brought to its notice, so that improvements were made piecemeal, for example, in factory conditions, or by the activities of welfare minded educationalists such as Robert Raikes and the E. of Shaftesbury. Ill-treatment and neglect of apprentices and servants and the exposure of infants became offences in 1861; parental neglect in the matter of necessaries in 1868. It was only with the foundation of the National Society for the Prevention of Cruelty to Children (1884) that the problem began to be considered as a whole. Legislation against cruelty in the home began in 1889; regulating baby farming (1897); casual occupations (1903); fosterage (1908) and restricting or prohibiting imprisonment of offenders under 14 and creating Borstals for their reformation. The Education Acts 1918 and 1921 restricted employment during school age. By 1933, when the law was consolidated, most of the abuses were under control; after 1948 the Education Act thrust all children safely into schools between the ages of 5 and 15 and fed them there until Margaret Thatcher as Sec. of State began the erosion of school meals.

(6) Paradoxically there was a public tendency to degrade the family and belittle natural affection. Taxation discriminated against marriage and drove mothers as well as fathers out to increase production, leaving some children unsupervised outside school times and sometimes in bad company. Juvenile crime rose. Simultaneously the media whipped up fears of parental sexual abuse. Sexual allegations always lead to exaggeration. At least one Council recruited social workers on the assumption that 10% of all children were subjected to it. There were early morning raids on homes and officious child seizures, later raised in parliament and subjected to public inquiries, but in the 1990s there was a marked increase in the children in care.

CHILE (see BOLIVAR) (1) The natural poverty of Chile caused the secondment of mostly second rate officials from Spain; and economic activity was controlled by the Viceroy of Peru at Lima. When Bonaparte invaded Spain in 1808, Chile was a backward country whose local opinion was directed against Peru rather than Spain. Thus the cabildo abierto of Santiago, established as a govt. in Sept. 1810, relaxed trading restrictions and began the abolition of slavery in defiance of the viceroyalty, but without formal assertion of independence. Division on this issue contributed to defeat by the Hispano-Peruvians at Rancagua in Oct. 1814 and the reassertion of viceregal control. The principal extremists led by Bernardo O'HIGGINS (1778-1842) fled to Argentina, raised troops and marched with San Martin's army over the Andes to defeat the govt. at Chacabuco and Maipo (1818). Chile became independent with O'Higgins as President-Dictator.

(2) His most important concern was to create a small navy to protect the unique seaborne communications and effect physical unification (see COCHRANE-5), but domestic controversies over church and land culminated in civil wars which in 1830 brought to real power Diego PORTALES PALAZUELOS, who established an economically progressive, yet otherwise obscurantist, dictatorship. Trade, communications, agriculture and mining prospered and the govt. attracted scientists and intellectuals from all over the world. In 1836 he attacked Bolivia and Peru. He was assassinated by mutineers, but the war was carried to victory in 1839. Two years later the govt. was taken over by Manuel BULNES PRIETO, who pushed Chilean claims to Patagonia and Tierra del Fuego, brought in German settlers into Araucania and so opened nearly a century of controversy with Argentina.

(3) Meanwhile Chilean copper production and prosperity attracted international, especially British, investment. The national debt was redeemed and tax surpluses went in establishing a university and higher schools and academies. The responsible minister, Manuel MONTT, who became Pres. in 1851, followed, however, the policy of Portales in economic development and educational backwardness, but conditions had changed. Industrialists and their employees were creating the prosperity and demanding a voice.

(4) Unable to agree on a successor, the politicians accepted a series of compromise liberal candidates who initiated social reforms, but the world depression of the 1870s was aggravated in Chile by local famines. The copper market fell and the govt. sought to meet its deficits by inflation which naturally distressed the poor.

(5) An imperialist seizure of the Peruvian nitrate areas (of vast importance to world agriculture) seemed an easy way out. A victorious Nitrate War against Peru and Bolivia ended in 1883 under the presidency of Domingo SANTA MARIA GONZALES. It not only brought the great nitrate area into Chile but gave her the temporary, artificially prolonged to 48 year, occupation of the Peruvian provinces of Tacna and Arica. The world demand for copper and nitrates, however, led to overdependence upon mineral exports, a neglect of industry and the urbanisation of Santiago, while the govt. of Jose Manuel BALMACEDA (r. 1881-91) did nothing to remedy inflation. By 1890 he was in armed conflict with the Congress.

(6) A new dispensation was marked by foreign disputes, notably with Argentina on the Atacama and Andes frontiers. These were settled by British arbitration in 1899 and 1904. On the other hand, Chile did not enter World War I, but took the profits from the resulting boom in copper and nitrates on which she was already too dependent. The blockaded Germans developed the extraction of nitrate fertiliser from air and while industrial workers, excluded from politics, went on strike, the bottom fell out of the minerals market in 1918 and the nitrate market never fully recovered. In 1920 the Liberal Alliance, a sort of Labour Party under Arturo ALESSANDRI PALMA, won the presidential election but with insufficient support in Congress. In Sept. 1924 he was overthrown by a military junta which enacted his programme but was itself removed by another junta under Carlos IBANEZ DEL CAMPO. On their invitation Alessandri returned on condition that a presidential constitution on the American model were enacted. Ibañez, however, remained on friendly terms with the landowners and encouraged foreign investment. In 1929 the govt. also settled the long-running Peruvian dispute by retroceding Tacna.

(7) Next came the worldwide depression. The copper and nitrates could not be sold. There was widespread unemployment. Foreign exchange dried up and Chile defaulted on her external debt. Efforts to meet deficits by raising taxes aggravated the troubles. A widely supported students' revolt drove Ibañez into Argentiian exile (July 1931) and 18 months of civil disorder ended with the return of Alessandri in Dec. 1932 with individualist and

right wing support which crystallised into the Radical Party, composed of landowners and industrialists conmitted to democracy, social reform and economic diversification. Its leaders also secured control of the Popular Front parties. In 1934 they turned against Alessandri and in 1938 won the presidency for Pedro AGUIRRE CERDA. His policy resembled Roosevelt's New Deal, but by the time he died (1941) the Popular Front had broken up because the Communists supported Germany in World War II. His successor, Juan Antonio RIOS, got the support of the Christian Socialists instead. The war created the usual export prosperity but he gave greater priority to industrialisation than to social questions.

(8) At Rios' death in 1946 his successor Gabriel GONZALES VIDELA had to court the left wing to achieve power because the export boom was ending, but in 1948 he outlawed the Communist Party. His main objective was industrialisation which, he believed, needed friendly relations with the U.S.A. He failed because post-war foreign capital was too short to finance his policy and the resulting inflation oppressed the poorest. Hence in 1952 Carlos Ibañez, having learned from Peronista methods in Argentina, returned and was elected president on the slogan "Bigger Loaves". He wholly failed to come up to expectations and in 1958 he was succeeded by Jorge ALESSANDRI, son of Arturo, who narrowly defeated Salvador ALLENDE of the Marxist Popular Front. Videla's spiritual successor, Alessandri, succeeded where Videla had failed in getting foreign capital, but the austerities needed to meet the interest fell too readily on the workers. Strikes aggravated the food shortages and inflation. Between 1960 and 1964 the exchange rate fell by 80%. The right wing parties could find no credible successor and the contest of 1964 was between Allende, who had moved further to the left, and Eduardo FREI, a Christian Democrat. Frei was elected and the right-wing conservatives and liberals were so weakened that they merged as the National Party. Frei now pursued social and land reforms to take the wind out of Marxist sails but too slowly, and inflation continued to match the increase in the gross national product. A self-conscious democracy became increasingly aware of the disparities of wealth. This was the background of Allende's victory in 1970 on a minority vote. It was soon evident that he was heading for a Marxist revolution. A reaction gathered way, ending in Sept. 1973 in a military coup during which he perished.

(9) The military govt. under Gen. Augusto PINOCHET Ugarte was originally believed to be a transitional stage in a return to a free enterprise parliamentary normality but by 1977 it had proscribed Communists, Socialists and Radicals and suspended all the other parties. International copper prices fell, which created poverty and discontent. The govt. instituted a murderous police dictatorship and many fled the country including 40,000 to Britain. U.S., Church and military pressure however forced the constitutional election in 1989 of Pres. AYLWIN who, however, had to keep Pinochet as C-in-C.

CHILTERN HUNDREDS. An M.P. cannot resign, but since 1707 has vacated his seat on accepting an office of profit under the Crown, unless that office is statutorily exempted. The purely nominal offices of Steward of the Three Chiltern Hundreds (Desborough, Burnham and Stoke), of the Manor of Northstead and, until 1920, the Escheatorship of Munster, were first used for this parliamentary purpose in 1750, being technically offices of profit. The appointment is made by the Chanc. of the Exchequer and the holder may be re-elected. The practical value of the arrangement is that as the assent of the crown is, in effect, required, an M.P. cannot commit himself irrevocably to any other body by handing over an undated letter of resignation, as communist deputies had to do in France.

CHIMNEY SWEEPS were small boys employed or driven to climb into chimneys and smoke traps to clean them. They often suffered from burns, semi-asphyxiation or a soot-caused condition called Chimney Sweep's Cancer. In 1805 George Smart invented his sweeping appliance, a stiff radiating rattan brush on a long jointed cane capable of being indefinitely lengthened with new sections. This made the use of these wretched children unnecessary, but nevertheless repeated Acts of Parliament (1840, 1864, 1875 and 1894) were needed to stop the practice.

CHINA. (1) The great distances between China and the West have until about 1880 obscured the economic influence of this vast power, because intercourse has been in the hands of successions of middlemen, whereby immediacy of conscious impact has been lost. The political influence has also been screened off by intervening powers which would, however, have played deeper roles in western history had they not had to look over their shoulders at the Chinese behind them.

(2) Mediaeval Sino-European trade passed either (a) by the SILK ROAD from Sian on the Yellow R. to Alma Ata, then north of the Caspian, to Tana (Azov) or the Crimea, and thence by sea to Constantinople, or (b) by fleets of junks from southern ports via the Malacca Straits to CEYLON, where goods were transhipped for the Persian Gulf or Egypt in Arab dhows. Part of the Gulf trade reached Genoa via Levantine ports such as Alexandretta. Goods for Egypt were unloaded at Tor, brought overland to Alexandria and bought mostly by Venetians. The northern route was originally the main channel for the Chinese silk monopoly, but in the early 6th cent. the Byzantines began raising silkworms. Merchants then tended to exchange silk in Asia for other commodities such as furs, ivory and slaves, which fetched high prices at Constantinople. There was never enough silk and in Europe it remained expensive and often a privilege of very high rank. On the southern route the Chinese exported some silk and spices (e.g. ginger) and exchanged south Chinese products for others (e.g. pepper) all of which were sold in Ceylon. Arms and bullion were the main return cargoes. There was a net outflow of gold and silver to the east.

(3) The goods passed through many hands. People hardly ever made even half the journey. Despite their commercial relations, Europeans and Chinese remained for centuries absurdly ignorant of each other.

(4) The two routes, drawing on different parts of China, were not in competition. Their usefulness depended in the north on govts. able to maintain order in Asia and in the south on the control of Egypt and the Red Sea at one end and the policing of the pirate infested Annamese and Indonesian waters at the other. Strong Chinese govts. tended to intervene in Central Asia and Indo-China.

(5) China, that is the area where written Chinese came into use, became strongly identifiable in the period of the TANG dynasty (618-907) which was also the great time of Islamic conquest in the Middle East and Africa and of the Viking raids in the West, but between 907 and 960 (the time of the FIVE DYNASTIES) China was in confusion. What western traffic there had been before 626 was only sporadically resumed after reunification under the Kai-feng based NORTHERN SUNG (960-1126). Kai-feng, however, was stormed by Ju-chen armies from the Mongolian north in 1126, but a prince escaped to re-establish the dynasty much further south at Hangchow (or Kinsai) in 1136; hence the next dynastic period is called the SOUTHERN SUNG. Their territory was marked off from the Juchen kingdom of CHIN by the R.Huai.

(6) The great Jenghiz Khan seized the headship of the Mongol tribes in 1206. By 1223 he had overrun Siberia and much of Russia and by 1234 his successor had absorbed China. The pacification of Asia soon inspired the Venetian Polos to explore the northern

route, while in 1250 the Mongol assault on the Southern Sung began. By 1271 Kublai Khan had taken the Chinese throne under the dynastic title of YÜAN, with a newly founded capital at Khanbaluc (Pekin or Beijing). The Polos returned home by the southern route.

Confuciansim (7) A major element in the Chinese political atmosphere was the pervasive unity of the ancient Confucian doctrine and customs, which penetrated to every level. Society was to be established by a hierarchy of obligations: respect and obedience were due by women to men, by the junior generation to the senior, by the family to its ancestors. But society had also to be administered and it would be prosperous and happy only if it was managed by virtuous men. The discovery and promotion of virtue was a vital function of the state, and in a theoretically static society ancient learning was an important component of virtue. The headship of the state was institutionalised in the Throne by a sort of corporate analogy with the headship of the family. The Throne discovered and promoted virtue by *inter alia* an examination system based upon the classics. Open to most it was the high road to honours. The ideal was a comfortably static population ruled through a benign, essentially pacifist, scholar bureaucracy.

(8) Since all authority came from above this system was unsuitable for determining the occupancy of the Throne. The imperial rights of a dynasty were conferred by Heaven through a revocable mandate. The practical ability of the Throne to enforce its will, in other words a dynastic founder's successful rebellion and the ability of his successors to maintain their position, was regarded as evidence of the issue or withdrawal of the divine mandate. There was, accordingly, nothing illogical in the Throne being occupied by foreigners, since Heaven can confer its mandate on whom it pleases. On the other hand there was room in the world for only one Throne, for the heavenly mandate was obviously indivisible. Co-equal national sovereignties were inconceivable. All prostrated themselves before the Throne.

(9) In this vast, rich and populous country there were naturally wide gaps between Confucian principles and human failings. Northern domination and the two Sung tragedies brought a specifically Chinese consciousness into being, and as the Mongol realm declined a Chinese claimed the mandate of Heaven. The MING dynasty (1368-1644) was established at Nanking in the Yangtze Valley. Politically stable, artistically decadent, intellectually enterprising, the Ming emperors extended their prosperous sway to a vast area. China was ringed with terrified tributary states: Korea, Manchuria, the Mongolias, Sinkiang, Tibet, Nepal, Sikkim, Bhutan, Burma, Siam and the Indo-Chinese monarchies all owned the supremacy of the Celestial Throne and helped to insulate Chinese ideas from the outside. In the south they pacified the sea route to Ceylon, encouraged or driven by immense Chinese naval expeditions, some of which in the early 15th cent. reached even East Africa and the Persian Gulf.

(10) The Ming empire attained its economic plateau just as the Ottoman Turks took control, at Constantinople, of the terminals of the northern route. They soon threatened the southern route too. By 1500 the Portuguese, too, had their regularly functioning third route round the Cape; by 1520 Egypt and the Levant were in Turkish hands, but the Portuguese were failing to divert all the traffic through their own establishments and felt compelled to seize local bases, or trade direct in their own ships. The seizure of bases in China and her tributaries was too hazardous (though it succeeded in Indonesia) but their merchantmen had already reached Canton (then Kuang Chou) in 1514. From 1542, however, the Ming regime was weakened and the Silk Road disorganised by Mongol Oyrat wars, and in 1557 the Portuguese were, *faute de mieux*, permitted a fortified

factory at Macao. Spaniards reached Canton in 1575 and brought Jesuits in 1583, but the Iberians failed to monopolise the seaborne trade, which continued to pass through Egypt as well as by the Cape until the 1590s.

(11) English and Dutch aggression and conflict on the one hand, border wars and the Muscovite encroachment on the Tartar states on the other coincided with, and partly caused a weakening in, the internal vigilance of the Ming dispensation, the corruption of officialdom, disorder and military failure. This encouraged R. Catholic activity in the south and the unification of the Manchu clans which had by 1616 become a military power based on Mukden and Jehol. Their forces crossed the Great Wall soon after. The disorganised Ming armies were no match for them, while behind their backs the Dutch attacked Macao, seized Formosa and traded in the southern provinces; in 1637 the English too bombarded Canton and compelled the locals to trade. By 1644 the Ming govt. was in dissolution and the Mandate of Heaven was transferred to Abahai, with the reign title Shun Chi. His Manchu or CHING dynasty exhibited a temperamental affinity with the Mongol Yüan, and reigned from Pekin; but it failed to establish order in the South until 1678.

(12) The new dynasty practised a type of racialism: Manchu is not related to Chinese and administration was bilingual; thus, far more high posts were given to Manchus than their numbers warranted. Intermarriage with Chinese was, in theory, forbidden and the two races were distinguished by enforced differences of dress and hairstyle. The govt. depended for its military security on the Bannermen, divisions of troops enrolled on a hereditary basis and mostly Manchu.

(13) In spite of this emphasis on privilege, relief at the cessation of disorder strengthened the govt. which also profited from long reigns. There were only five in 177 years (Shun Chi, 1644-61; Kang Hsi 1661-1722; Yung Cheng 1723-35; Chien Lung 1735-95; Chia Ching 1795-1821). Moreover the Kang Hsi and Chien Lung emperors were exceptionally able and ruled their vast territories through Chinese institutions in which Manchus played an, on the whole, inoffensive part.

(14) The pacification of the south was urgent but could not be achieved without peace in the north. In 1689 Kang Hsi settled the Manchurian-Siberian frontier at the T. of NERCHINSK with Russia which, by this time, could absorb all the trade of the northern route; it thus ceased to supply western Europe. The Red Sea and Persian Gulf routes also declined in the face of European technical superiority, but the total westward traffic rose through the natural expansion of the European marts and the demand for tea. The increase in the numbers and tonnage of ships added silk, cotton, lacquer, furniture and pottery. Europe was learning something of China through the south, but at a time when the Manchu govt. was trying to cope with tribal and tributary rebellions and the subversive ideas which confused the southern scene. The ideas were ascribed in part to missionaries. Restriction of western influence became a policy. The latest of several Rites Controversies ended in the proscription of Christianity in 1720. It was not wholly effective. A further treaty (of KIAKHTA 1727) settled the Russo-Mongolian frontier. In 1757 Chien Lung restricted the Portuguese to Macao and the British to 13 houses on the waterfront at Canton. Both nations were required to trade through members of a corporation called the Hong. In regard to other Europeans, the British and Portuguese did the emperor's work for him. Their partial monopoly made fortunes for East India merchants, but it flourised in an atmosphere of suspicion, which was the political root of the monopoly itself.

(15) 18th cent. China was prosperous and, mainly by internal colonisation, aggressively enterprising. Between 1683 and 1794 the population rose from 150M to 313M.

Thenceforth resources grew more slowly than the population, which by 1850 had reached 450M. In the 1780s, when the boom was about to end, East India merchants began to export opium from Bengal to China: the European price of tea came down with a run, but the immorality of the new trade horrified the better officialdom and created a shortage of silver in the southern provinces. The govt. resolved to suppress it. Their measures upset the tea exporters as well as the opium profiteers, and the British too. The result was Lord Macartney's abortive embassy to Pekin in 1793. It failed because Macartney refused to prostrate himself before the Throne. Official doctrine could not tolerate such behaviour: but some officials caught the idea that some – admittedly barbarous – nations of the Western Ocean had no such elevated notions about the Dragon Throne as they had themselves.

(16) In the Chia Ching era (1795-1821) the opium trade, driven underground, flourished mightily with British and Dutch backing. It was an immense source of corruption and exacerbated official difficulties as the economy took a downward turn. There were natural calamities. Some southerners had never forgotten the Mings and remembered that their rulers were as much foreigners as the British. For eight years (1796-1804) the White Lotus rebellion convulsed the S.W. The Manchu banners had become decadent. Local militias had to be raised. The cost was formidable; the dislocation and destruction widespread and those local forces encouraged the independent pretensions of provincial governors. The Tao Kuang emperor succeeded (1821) to a shaky inheritance: but the golden lustre of the great reigns invested the Throne with a prestige which held the empire together and he himself took steps to bring order into the finances by enforcing economy at court. The decline was arrested, but not reversed.

(17) These were the conditions in which the epoch-making OPIUM WAR (1839-42) took place. A special anti-opium commissioner, Lin Tse-hu, was appointed at Canton. 70% of the British China trade was in opium, much of it illicitly brought in via the Hong. The HEIC backed by the home govt. stood up for its profits. Modern weapons and discipline overmatched the obsolete and confused local forces, but the govt. at least profited by the diversion of southern xenophobia from itself to the British. The war ended in the first of the *unequal treaties* at NANKING (1842). The Hong and the restrictions on trading were abolished and Hong Kong ceded to Britain (*see* CHINESE TREATY PORTS). This easy victory excited the cupidity of other powers. To avoid international complications the British negotiated the T. of THE BOGUE (1843). In return for extra-territorial status for British subjects, the two sides agreed the MOST FAVOURED NATION CLAUSE:- the British in the confidence that they could outstrip any other country which benefitted, the Chinese in the belief that western countries might not demand concessions which they would have to share with their rivals. Both calculations were only partially justified; similar treaties with the U.S.A. (Wanghia) and France (Whampoa) were signed in 1844. Western trading in the 1830s had brought in protestant missionaries alongside the never inactive R. Catholics. The Chinese reaction to them was to have important effects. Hung Hsiu-chuan, a Hakka peasant who had met a protestant convert in 1836, had crypto-Christian visions about the redemption of the world from Confucianism, and gathered converts. In 1851, the commencement of the Hsien-Feng reign, Hung proclaimed himself the Third member of the Trinity, as Heavenly King of the Kingdom of Great Peace (Taiping) at Yung-an in the Kwangsi mountains. His nationalist armies advanced northwards. In 1853 they took Nanking and set up a govt. on the usual Chinese imperial pattern. Thus a movement to overthrow the Throne developed

into an attempt to supersede the Manchus upon it. It happened to be accompanied by a spectacular natural calamity. The Yellow R. broke eastwards through the Hopeh sandhills and shifted its mouth from the Yellow Sea to the G. of Pechihli. The rebels, meanwhile, did not practice the virtues they preached and their corrupt violence destroyed the economy and reduced their own following. The southern maritime provinces were held against them and in 1853-4 they failed against Pekin. This was the turning point. By 1856 imperial armies were constricting their areas of control from north and south amid fearful carnage.

(19) The Hsien-Feng emperor had 28 Manchu wives and concubines chosen in 1852. Of these the gentle Niuhuru became the Empress; the concubine Yi (known by the first of her many later tides as TZU-HSI) was her friend. In 1855 Tzu-hsi bore her lord his only son. This birth gave her a pre-eminence which her abilities and strength of character enabled her to exploit. It began her rise to power.

(20) Tzu-hsi's emergence was hardly auspicious. True the Taipings were under increasing pressure in the Yangtze valley, but the long Nien-fei revolt (1856-68) broke out in the north, mainly in Shantung and Chihli. While the Pekin govt. wrestled with it, the southern Viceroy, Yeh Ming-ch'en faced demands for the renewal of the British, French and American treaties. He was firm to a point of rudeness and in Oct. 1856 he seized the *Arrow* (which flew, but was not entitled to, the Union Jack) for smuggling and piracy. The British seized the Canton forts and bombarded Yeh's *Yamen*. The Cantonese burnt the foreign factories and warehouses. As a French missionary had been executed in Kwangsi the French joined in gleefully. An Anglo-French alliance followed, but Palmerston was defeated in the Commons and had to spend the spring of 1857 electioneering and vilifying Yeh. When the election was won Lord Elgin was sent as a plenipotentiary to bring the Chinese to reason by force. He had, at Singapore, to release his troops to deal with the Indian mutiny; his attempts at persuasion failed; reinforcements, the French, Yeh's obstinacy and mercantile fury brought action. In Dec. Canton was stormed, Yeh captured and the city put under a puppet administration supervised by British, French and Americans.

(21) Taiping, superficially a Christian protestantism, had impressed the British and Sir George Bonham, gov. of Hong Kong had visited them at Nanking. Bearing in mind the political centralism of Confucian doctrine, this made foreigners rebels in the eyes of Pekin. The govt. refused to treat. Elgin and the French envoy, Le Gros, with American and Russian 'observers' proceeded north with a powerful force and in May 1858 stormed the Taku forts at the mouth of the Peiho, 100 miles from Pekin. In the ensuing negotiations the main issues were the European demands that resident ambassadors should be established at Pekin and entitled to audience without prostration, and that the interior of China, especially the Yang-tse (much of it still under Taiping control) should be open to trade. The two sides were at cross purposes: the mercantile concessions were the more important in European eyes, the diplomatic ones in Chinese. That the latter might initiate a social revolution was unintelligible to the British. They threatened to march on Pekin and the Chinese negotiators gave way. By the T. of TIENTSIN (26 June 1858) the two points were conceded; the opium trade was legalised, additional ports opened. Moreover the envoys accepted the toleration of Christianity because they feared British intervention on the side of the Taipings, once trade on the Yangtse started in earnest.

(22) The court was staggered and in subsequent negotiations on tariffs at Shanghai, Elgin was persuaded to accept modifications. The ambassadors would return in a year to exchange ratifications; they would be received with great ceremony then, and thereafter they would reside in a treaty port. Elgin was beginning to understand that a collapse of central authority would vitiate his commercial purpose. The govt. began to raise trained armies, which in the ensuing year drove the Taipings back to the vicinity of Nanking. Unfortunately the new British and French ministers, Frederick Bruce and de Boubulon, arrived to exchange ratifications. The Chinese sent distinguished commissioners to meet them at Shanghai: they refused to see them and sailed, with 18 warships, for the Peiho. Not surprisingly the Taku forts fired on them. Bruce ordered an assault and four of his ships were sunk (June 1859). After nine months of parliamentary debate a firm line was decided. Bruce issued an ultimatum demanding apologies and indemnities and declaring that the Shanghai modifications were void. In Aug. 1860 Elgin and le Gros joined him and a combined force again stormed the Taku forts. It was symptomatic of European confusion about Chinese problems that simultaneously French and British troops were helping to repulse a Taiping attack on Shanghai.

(23) In new negotiations the govt., faced with an unfamiliar situation, vacillated between the fears of the impressionable and hedonistic emperor and the belligerence of Tzu-Hsi. Fighting broke out again and the Chinese took prisoners; the allies seized the vital bridge at Palichao and in Sept. the court fled to Jehol leaving Prince Kung, the emperor's half brother, in charge at Pekin. The French began to loot the Yuan Ming Yuan, the vast and beautiful imperial summer pleasances 20 miles outside Pekin. The British joined in. The allies now demanded that the South Gate of Pekin be surrendered in pledge and Prince Kung, fearing further damage, complied and released his prisoners. A date for the ratification of the unamended T. of Tientsin was fixed; an immense war indemnity was paid; but Elgin was not quite satisfied. He resolved, as "a solemn act of retribution" and perhaps to cover the traces of the looting, to destroy the Yuan Ming Yuan. Upwards of 200 buildings were sacked and with their gardens and woods burned (Oct. 1860).

(24) The first repercussion was a Russian diplomatic *coup*. P. Kung, persuaded of English and French ill faith, ceded the Amur and Ussuri lands and the important harbour of Haishenwei, renamed Vladivostok (T. of PEKIN, 14 Nov. 1860) in return for Russian military support: there was no need, for the allies indeed left. Next the long ailing emperor died, overwhelmed with shame (Aug. 1861). There was a sharp struggle for the regency on behalf of Tzu-Hsi's child. When the court returned to Pekin, she and Niuhuru emerged as regents with P. Kung as chief minister. The new govt. had general support and sophisticatedly pursued policies of co-operation with the west. Nevertheless, the most lasting effect was to confirm the latent Chinese xenophobia.

(25) Things now went better. The Europeans had evacuated Canton (Oct. 1861). A new determination was symbolised by a change of reign title from Chi-hsiang to Tung Chih (= Restoration of Order). The first priority was to put down the rebellions. The C-in-C, Tseng Kuo-fan, and his lieutenants, Tso Tung-t'ang and the famous Li Hung-chang were scholar-soldiers of a new type with no inhibitions about using western methods. Locally raised troops were trained on European models, one such force being led from 1863 by Charles Gordon (of Khartoum fame). By May 1865 the Taiping leaders were hunted down. It had cost 20M lives and the devastation of provinces.

(26) These successes and four years experience emancipated Tzu-Hsi from P. Kung. The govt. centred in the Palace, had always been penetrated from all directions by the thousands of household eunuchs. Tzu-Hsi, who genuinely liked them, ensured their personal loyalty to herself by tolerating their increasing corruption.

With their aid she degraded the Prince and then restored him to a position shared with others. The senior co-empress, Niuhuru, was too ill-educated and silly to matter. Tzu-Hsi was without a rival.

(27) The generals now redeployed their forces. In 1868 they stamped out the Nien-fei and then dealt with national minority rebellions among the Miao in Yunnan, and the Moslems in Shensi and Kansu. These later revolts cost as much in lives and devastation as the Taiping. By 1873 there was an exhausted peace. Despite enlightened measures of rehabilitation, including wholesale tax remissions, Sino-Manchu ruthlessness had left a permanent scar. The young Tung Chih emperor officially (if with motherly advice) assumed his powers and Li Hung-chang rose to supremacy at Tseng Kuo-fan's death. Unfortunately, the emperor had inherited his father's dissipated character. In 1875 he died.

(28) Tzu-Hsi staged a comeback. The household and her overwhelming personality secured an unprecedented and ill-omened change in the succession: there was to be another child emperor for whom, of course, Tzu-Hsi was to take up a second regency. The reign title was Kuang-hsu. The arrangement shocked many sections of opinion. Since the notorious T'ang empress Wu, the Chinese had been hostile to gynocracy. The Manchus held by the Kang Hsi Emperor's legislation against eunuch influence. Moreover, the Empress-Regent's greed was not a pattern for virtuous govt. The displeasure of Heaven was soon manifest. In 1877 there was drought and famine on a vast scale. In 1877 and 1878 moreover the bonds of unity were weakening. The provincial forces formed a power base for local governors. Central direction became erratic: it was no longer easy to protect the tributary states, which began to come to terms with foreign colonialism. Moreover each accession had seen the opening of new treaty ports. The increasing penetration by foreign merchants and consuls revealed the weakness. Between 1871 and 1877 the Japanese engrossed the Ryu Kyu island chain. The Russians penetrated Ili and then sold it back in 1881. Then a Japanese squadron appeared off Korea and in 1882 the U.S.A. signed a separate treaty with the Koreans. By 1883 the English and French, long before the *Entente Cordiale,* had a working understanding in the Far East. The French demanded the protectorate of Nam Viet (as Annam) and bombarded Foochow (Aug. 1884). After fighting in Tongking and Formosa, the cession was made (1885). In 1886 the British conquered Upper Burma. Japanese-inspired reforms in Korea had led to bitter dispute in 1883. Korea was close to Pekin. Burma and Annam were far away. On Li Hung Chang's advice the distant territories were relinquished while his troops occupied Seoul. A treaty of 1885 with Japan virtually neutralised the area.

(29) Li Hung Chang respected westerners and saw the advantages of European technology. As viceroy in Northern China he floated companies, financed railways, developed mines, harbours and telegraphs and built arsenals. He became fabulously rich like his empress, with whom he shared the profits. He had foreseen the Japanese danger and began to provide a modern navy based on Wei-hai-wei, and he fortified Port Arthur. The north began to outstrip the war ravaged south. This caused perturbation in Meiji Japan, whose statesmen were indeed planning mainland expansion nearby.

(30) The race against time now took an ironical turn. In 1889 Tzu-Hsi could no longer resist the pressure for the Kuanghsu emperor to assume his functions. Her household influence, however, remained and as he conducted affairs from the palace he was morally and to some extent physically her prisoner. She once had two of his wives beaten. Her power rested on an obsolescent oriental palace organisation supported upon the power of westernising scholar soldiers. The emperor, however, was interested not only in the technology of the west but in

its liberal ideas, but he could not enforce them without destroying his own Throne or himself, for the tide of xenophobia was mounting. The most favoured nation clauses extended extra-territorial status to almost all foreigners and to the lengthening totals of their families and servants; and the Chinese were at an obvious disadvantage in the extra-territorial courts. As more treaty ports opened they and their privileges irritated more people; so did the activities of the missionaries, who openly derided long held ideas of propriety and religion and built their extra-territorial churches where they pleased, regardless of susceptibilities. It needed little to cause a civil explosion.

(31) In 1893 the Japanese resolved to attack before Li Hung Chang's armed power could develop further. The objective and the pretext were alike in Korea, where they landed troops. The decisive naval battle was fought in July 1894, before war was declared, in the mouth of the R. Yalu. The Japanese were victorious and followed up with destructive torpedo attacks on Wei-hai-wei. Reinforced with impunity, their troops drove Li Hung Chang's Huai army to the Manchurian frontier. The threat to Pekin was too clear. In Apr. 1895 Li signed a humiliating peace at SHIMONOSEKI. Formosa, the Pescadores and Port Arthur were ceded to Japan. The great viceroy, his domestic power in ruins, was dismissed.

(32) The European powers scrambled for 'compensations'. Germany, France and Russia forced Japan to give back Port Arthur (May 1895); Russia helped herself to the Chinese Eastern Rly (q.v.) across Manchuria (1896) and Germany took Kiao-Chow (Nov. 1897). While the govt., its only effective forces destroyed, wrestled with disorder, the Yellow R. began a destructive series of annual floods. In Mar. 1898 the Russians occupied Port Arthur, whereupon the British hurriedly took Wei-hai-wei opposite, and Kowloon by Hong Kong for good measure. Not to be outdone the French claimed a sphere of economic interest in the provinces adjacent to Indo-China and seized Kwang chou-wan.

(33) There now supervened two reactions of opposite character: one popular, the other official. In the south bands of young men practising a type of boxing analogous to Zen Buddhism started a movement against missionaries and foreign traders. It spread like wildfire, fed by the resentments and humiliation of the people, and its leaders meant to restore the authority of the Throne. The so-called Boxer Rebellion was not a rebellion at all, but a popular war on foreigners. While this typhoon was rising in the south, the reformers in Pekin persuaded the emperor to institute a thorough-going westernisation. During the Hundred Days of Reform in 1898 a stream of decrees remodelled the govt., enjoined the creation of schools, reformed the taxes, the forces and anything else which seemed appropriate; but the reformers were too few; the imperial will was backed by inadequate resource, and the Emperor feared, with justification, that Tzu-Hsi would frustrate his purpose. He relied on Yuan Shih-Kai, the trainer of the Huai army, to neutralise her. Yuan betrayed him. The empress had properly gauged public opinion. The people wanted reactionary revenge, not barbarian innovations. The emperor was secluded in an island wing of the palace and, like Niuhuru, became a cypher (Sept. 1898). The Boxers approached and the Empress smiled upon them. In May 1900 they burst in, looting foreign goods and besieging the European diplomatic quarter. The siege lasted for 10 weeks until an international force (which included Prussian Horse Marines) was landed in the Peiho and relieved them. The Empress fled with the captive Emperor to Jehol, while the international army sacked Pekin (Aug.).

(34) The court could not stay at Jehol because the Russians were threatening. While they occupied Manchuria (Oct. 1900) the court made a long westward journey through the countryside and for the first time since childhood Tzu-Hsi witnessed grinding rural poverty. Peace at all costs and modernisation were the only hope. The former was achieved by another humiliating T. of PEKIN (7 Sept. 1901). The treaty, however, involved repudiating the Boxers and so destroying the one remaining support of the dynasty. The mandate of Heaven would soon be exhausted.

(35) While the indomitable tyrant remained internally formidable, the Japanese and the Russians fought each other for Korea in a war which took place entirely on Manchurian soil and in Chinese waters (1904-5). The educated classes were turning away from the Confucian society. Newspapers published in Tokyo, Hong Kong and Shanghai nourished republicanism. In 1908 the emperor and empress died within 24 hours of one another and the new emperor was yet another child. The Throne itself was seen as an incapable anachronism. A republic was proclaimed in 1912. By then the Japanese were firmly in possession of Korea and encroaching steadily in Manchuria.

(36) The republic began badly, balanced between Sun Yat-sen's republicans and the soldiers of Yuan Shih-kai, who at one stage attempted a restoration with himself as emperor. By 1917 a Manchu-dominated govt in the north was at war with the southern republicans and by 1924 some provincial grandees had made themselves virtually independent as war lords. The confusion of self appointed jurisdictions compelled the western powers, especially the British, to maintain their interests by means of shallow-draft river gunboats. These penetrated far inland and, because they represented an element of security, were not always unwelcome.

(37) While the northerners disintegrated, the republicans of the south organised the KUO MIN TANG party under Chiang Kai-shek, who was Moscow trained. Moscow made great efforts to help through its local commissar, Michael Borodin, particularly through the training and indoctrination of military officers at the Whampoa Academy. From 1926 the power of the Kuomintang spread steadily northwards, but its success naturally engendered internal disputes about the uses of victory. Many of its guiding spirits might be communist inspired: most of its supporters had a more traditional outlook. Chiang Kai-shek and his wife, a daughter of Sun Yat-sen, broke with the communists in 1931. A six year civil war ensued.

(38) The Japanese decided to invade China in 1937 and soon made themselves hated by their cruelty and ineptitude. Chiang Kai-shek rightly saw in them a powerful anti-communist force and though he was never in alliance with them, he pressed the war against the communists with great energy. They were driven into the fastnesses of Yenan. Bearing in mind his training, Chiang may well have got his priorities right. The communists, however, saved themselves by an appeal to nationalism against the Japanese: "Chinese do not kill Chinese" was the slogan which gradually won over popular support. Moreover the nationalist Chinese commanders, even after they secured American help in World War II, were not noticeably competent. When the Japanese defeat cleared the field in 1945, nationalist credit was lower than communist. A further civil war, in which MAO TZE-TUNG, his wife, Chiang Ching and Chou-En-lai emerged as the leading communist figures, ended in 1949 with the defeat of the Kuomintang. Chiang Kai-shek set up a fugitive govt. in Formosa (retroceded by Japan) and certain off-shore islands, where in 1996 the Kuomintang still ruled. The western concessions and enclaves, except Hong Kong and Macao, were all surrendered by 1950.

(39) The communist victory did not bring the longed for tranquillity. There was a period (1949-52) of Reconstruction, designed to establish necessary material

sufficiency after the ravages of the long wars. Then came the move to Socialism (1953-7), involving wholesale expropriations and liquidations. With the economy in state hands there followed the industrial Great Leap Forward accompanied by the establishment of the Rural Communes (1957-61). The disturbances and general poverty caused by these vast operations brought a need for Readjustment (1961-5) or relaxation before a new period of strenuous innovation known as the Cultural Revolution (1965-8). These phases in the development of Communist China reflected the controversies of rival groups in the leadership, rather than any coherent policy line. The Cultural Revolution, despite its name, was an extremely violent affair and the ideological hooligans on whom Mao Tze-tung and Chiang Ching relied had, in due course, to be sent home for a further period of Reconstruction (1968-71). For the next 20 years the oscillation between common sense pursuit of economic improvement and Marxist forays against ideological deviants, such as the massacre of students in Tienanmen Square at Beijing in 1989, continued a feature of Chinese affairs, complicated by the collapse of the similar, if not always friendly, regime in Russia. The effect was a kind of reverse image of the impact of co-equal sovereignties upon the underlying principles of the old Imperial Throne. The Pekin govt., having imported Marxism from Russia, was now defending a foreign importation which its originators no longer wanted. Hence, the decision in 1992 to create a hydro-electric complex involving a 400-mile lake on the Yangtze and the displacement of millions of villagers had an air, in so vast a country, of "internal Bonapartism". *See also* HONG KONG; CHINESE TREATY PORTS.

CHINA INCIDENT. A Japanese euphemism for the Kwantung Army's war with China from 1932 onwards.

CHINA TRADE. *See* EAST INDIA COMPANY-2,10.

CHINA(WARE), is a type of porcelain made from a combination of china clay, china stone and bone ash. It was first introduced into Britain in about 1806 by Spode at Stoke-on-Trent and Barr at Worcester.

CHINDITS are the fiercely stylised guardian lions of S.E. Asian sculpture. In World War II they were adopted as the insignia of, and gave their name to, Gen. Wingate's forces, which operated behind and among the Japanese in the Burmese and Malayan jungles.

CHINESE LABOUR QUESTION. In 1891 the Transvaal gold-mine owners told the Boer govt. that low grade ore might be profitable if the native hut tax were raised and the natives forced into the mines for low wages. When Kruger's govt. rejected the argument, the owners threatened to close the mines, whereupon the govt. took power to confiscate and work closed mines. After the Boer defeat, Milner doubled the hut tax (1903) and set up an inquiry into the adequacy of mine labour. This reported that 129,000 more hands were needed than were locally available. Hence, early in 1904, the Transvaal legislative council passed an ordinance for the importation of Chinese indentured labourers, but the Cape legislature in May forbade them in the Cape Colony. Milner supported the Transvaal, for he thought the idea a sensible form of post-war reconstruction. The Balfour govt. sanctioned the Transvaal ordinance. The first contingent arrived in June and there were 60,000 by 1906. This was politically inept. There was uproar in Britain on moral grounds and because it interfered with a potential field of immigration and might create a precedent for undermining unions elsewhere. It also affronted the nonconformists and the philanthropists, for the coolies, when not engaged in hard work underground, were enclosed in compounds without their women. They were not, in theory, slaves, being paid 15 times as much as they got at home, but the incident, inflated by extremist politics, damaged the govt.'s reputation. At the general election the Chinese became a major issue and contributed to the Conservative defeat in Jan. The Liberals granted a constitution to the Transvaal in 1907 and the Boer party, having secured a majority in the new Assembly, started repatriation which was completed in 1910. *See* SOUTH AFRICA-2.

CHINESE EASTERN or CHANGCHUN RLY, connecting the Siberian rly system with Vladivostok across Manchuria, was built with French and Russian capital between 1898 and 1903 and its construction was a factor in provoking the Japanese attack on the Russians in 1904. The Russians sold it to the Japanese controlled Manchurian govt. in 1935 and it was converted to western (4'8½") gauge by 1936. In 1945 the trunk line and that of the S. Manchurian rly were placed under Sino-Russian joint administration, but in 1952 the whole system reverted to China.

CHINESE TREATY PORTS. The Portuguese were conceded a settlement at Macao in 1557. The arrangement was acceptable to the Chinese because it facilitated their control of movement and customs. On a similar principle the HEIC was confined to trading at Canton and through a merchant guild there called the Hong. By the Ts. of Nanking (1842) after the OPIUM WAR, Amoy, Canton, Foochow, Ningpo and Shanghai were opened to British trade and residence, and Hong Kong was leased to Britain. By the T. of The Bogue (1843) British subjects acquired extra-territorial rights. In 1844 similar privileges were conceded to France (T. of Whampoa) and the U.S.A. (T. of Wanghia). The four Ts. of Tientsin (1858) with Britain, France, U.S.A. and Russia, were enforced by the Pekin Convention (1860) and resulted in the opening of further ports (Chin-Kiang, Chingwangtung, Hankow, Kiu-Kiang, Kinchow, Nanking, Newchwang, Swatow, Wenchow). The Chefoo Convention (1876), ratified in 1885, opened Ichang, Pakhoi and Wuhu to Britain. In 1898 Britain took Wei-hai-wei, France Kwang-chow Wan, Germany Kiao-Chow and Russia Port Arthur. There were also many minor treaty ports. Japan took Port Arthur from Russia in 1905; Britain took Kiao Chow from Germany in 1914 and returned it to China in 1919 and Wei-hai-wei in 1930. The whole system began to collapse with the advent of nationalist sentiment on both sides in the Chinese civil wars and was abrogated after World War II. *See* GUNBOATS.

CHINOISERIE, a primarily decorative habit derived from Chinese porcelain, lacquer and paintings in the later 18th cent. It affected the design of many smaller objects including furniture (e.g. Chinese Chippendale) and even of whole rooms, e.g. the Chinese Room at Schönbrunn. Some *chinoiserie*, of a very elaborate kind, is present in Nash's Pavilion at Brighton (1815-21) and it survived in gentlemen's fancy waistcoats down to 1939. *See* CHAMBERS.

CHINON, TRUCE OF (Sept. 1214) between K. John and Philip Augustus of France arose through John's repulse at La-Roche-aux-Moines (2 July 1214) and the French destruction of the army of English, Germans and Flemings at the B. of Bouvines (27 July). It was to last until Easter 1220. It was often renewed, so that until it was superseded by the P. of Paris (1259) there were hostilities (of a very desultory kind) only from 1224 to 1227, from Aug. 1229 to July 1231 and from June 1242 to Apr. 1243. Throughout these 45 years the issues left open by the truce were the refusal of Henry III to recognise the French King as D. of Normandy or any French prince as Count of Poitou and by the French Kings to recognise Henry as D. of Aquitaine.

CHINOOK. A group of tribes inhabiting the American and Canadian Pacific coast. They traded extensively with the British and Americans, largely in salmon. **Chinook Jargon** was a combination of Indian, English and French used locally as a *lingua franca*.

CHINSURA (Bengal) was a Dutch East India Co. factory from 1653. Clive took it in 1759 and retroceded it as a demilitarised trading post in 1763. It was exchanged for some British property in Sumatra in 1825.

CHIPPENDALE (1) Thomas (1718-79) a famous Yorkshire cabinet maker, was in partnership with James Rannie in London from about 1748 until 1766 and with Thomas Haig from 1771. His fame rests more on his *Gentleman and Cabinet Makers Director* (published in 1754) than on his work. The book set the tone for a comparatively refined style and distinctive method of furniture making, which was copied widely but depended much on the use of rosewood, which eventually ran out. His son **(2) Thomas (1749-1822)** carried on the business until 1821.

CHIRK (Denbigh), the seat of the Myddleton family, had a powerful 11th cent. castle rebuilt in the 14th. It was restored as a residence in the 17th cent.

CHIROGRAPHS. *See* INDENTURES; FEET OF FINES; PAPAL CHANCERY.

CHISHOLM (1) William (?-1564) as Bp. of Dunblane from 1527 to 1564 gave the episcopal property to his illegitimate children. His real or presumed nephew, the able **(2) William (?-1593)** was his coadjutor from 1561 and succeeded him as Bp. of Dunblane in 1564. From 1565 to 1567 he was Mary Q. of Scots representative in Scotland in connection with the Darnley marriage, but fled to France in about 1569 and became Bp. of Vaison in 1570. He was deposed from Dunblane in 1573 and after leaving Vaison in 1584 became a Carthusian and eventually prior at Rome. His nephew **(3) William (?-1629)** succeeded his uncle at Vaison in 1584 and after an abortive intrigue in favour of the Scots R. Catholics became Rector (i.e. governor) of the Venaissin.

CHISWICK (Middx). The remarkable Palladian villa designed by the E. of Burlington with interiors by William Kent, was built between 1725 and 1727.

CHITRAL. Only the 180-mile long but narrow and disorderly Afghan valley of the R. Panja cushioned off the Emirate of Bokhara and the Pamir plateau (both to be annexed by Russia) from the weak N.W. Indian border states of Swat and Kashmir, save that these were for the most part in turn separated from the Panja by the Chitral (or Mastuj) R. valley, forming only a slightly wider territory with a fortified capital at Chitral near its southern end. Control of Chitral was thus essential in view of Afghan weakness to save Swat and Kashmir from pressure and penetration from the north. In 1889 and again in 1891 its Mehtar agreed, with some persuasion, to accept a British subsidy and advice on foreign relations and defence. In 1895 the state became a British protectorate and so remained until the end of the British *raj.*

CHITTAGONG. *See* BENGAL-7; BURMA-6.

CHIVALRY, i.e. that which pertains to knights, came to mean a self denying courage and generosity combined with courtesy, as well as martial skill. Brains, and self restraint, were not necessarily included. The subject has attracted a huge, but commonly tragic, literature in which, too often, knights perish by the hand or influence of those more cunning than themselves.

CHIVALRY, COURT OF, was initiated by Edward III under the Lord High Constable and Earl Marshal to exercise summary jurisdiction over knights and in military matters. Under the Earl Marshal alone it dealt with heraldic questions and precedence. The criminal jurisdiction lapsed because the Constable ceased to be appointed. The heraldic jurisdiction was exercised with decreasing regularity until 1737, but was suddenly recalled into existence in 1954 to try a dispute between the Manchester Corporation and the Manchester Palace of Varieties. The Lord Chief Justice sitting as the Earl Marshal's Surrogate, held that its jurisdiction had not lapsed.

CHLORINE was first prepared in 1774 by Carl Wilhelm Scheele and identified as an element in 1810 by Sir Humphrey Davy. *See* CHEMICAL WARFARE.

CHOCOLATE, a drink of Mexican origin, was a Spanish secret until it somehow spread to France in 1620. A French chocolate house was opened in Bishopsgate, London, in 1657. Such houses spread rapidly, rivalling the coffee houses as meeting places. White's Club (St. James') was originally a chocolate house. The cocoa trees began to be transplanted to the coastal states of the Gulf of Guinea in the 18th cent. where they became an important constituent of the local economy. Eating chocolate, which required cocoa butter to be pressed out, was not introduced until about 1820. With the addition of subsidised W. Indian sugar it made the fortune of a group of midland Quaker families centring on the Frys. African swollen shoot disease reduced supplies and encouraged dilution after World War II.

CHOIRS. Gregory the Great established the Schola Cantorum (Lat = Singers' School) at Rome in the 6th cent. and the Gregorian Chant and the choir school were brought to England by Benedict Biscop and St. Wilfrid a century later. Monastic and cathedral choirs were about the only music schools in the English middle ages, the knowledge being transmitted orally until musical notation was invented in the 11th cent. In the 15th cent. harmony began to supplement plain chant and lay singers to augment the choirs, which had by then become numerous and, according to a Bohemian diarist, distinguished by their sweetness. Church music became increasingly elaborate until by the 18th cent. it had reached a peak of complication and professionalism symbolised by the isolation of many choirs in galleries at the west end of churches. In 19th cent. movements towards greater public participation in ritual brought them back to the chancel to lead congregations and created a demand for simpler music and this in its turn encouraged the rise of specialised choirs interested in concerts, where oratorios were a major feature.

CHOISEUL. This French military and diplomatic family produced two notable statesmen **(1) Etienne Francois (1719-85) Comte de STAINVILLE** and **(1757) Duc de CHOISEUL.** As ambassador at Rome from 1754 to 1757 he settled the *Unigenitus* dispute; briefly ambassador at Vienna, he became Foreign Secretary in 1758 and strengthened the Austro-French alliance by the T. of Vienna. In 1761 he negotiated the FAMILY COMPACT and passed the foreign ministry over to his cousin **(2) César Gabriel (1712-85) Duc de PRASLIN,** himself taking on the ministries of war and marine and maintaining overall supervision of policy, including the peace negotiations of 1763. This arrangement between the cousins continued until 1766 when they exchanged the ministries of foreign affairs and marine. Between them they introduced military and naval reforms, fortified Brest, encouraged Pacific exploration and secured the annexation of Lorraine (1766) and Corsica (1768). In internal affairs they protected the *parlements,* suppressed the Jesuits and encouraged the Encyclopedists. Strongly patrician, their irreligious outlook eventually gave offence at court and in 1770 they were both dismissed.

CHOLERA, "ASIATIC", a disease transmitted mainly by faecally contaminated drinking water. The following represents the main events in its recent history. Endemic in Java, there were major destructive outbreaks in 1629 and 1689. It moved to Pondicherry and the Coromandel Coast in 1769 and in 1781, when it spread to China. The great epidemic of 1817-23, starting in Bihar, reached Turkey and Russia. The Bengal epidemic of 1826 spread steadily westwards and by 1831 had reached Poland, Egypt and finally Britain, where it caused 32,000 deaths. After a preliminary outbreak among the Indians and Afghans in 1840, a great wave of it rolled across Europe between 1846 and 1849. This caused 50,000 deaths in England and then passed over to Northern and Central

America in 1849-50. The scourge returned to England in 1853-4. By now it was endemic in the filthier areas of many European towns and its vibrio was described by Filippo Pacini in 1854 during an outbreak in Florence. His work was republished in 1866 without much effect on medical opinion, but the likelihood of transmission through infected water was beginning to be understood in England. Hence improvements in water supply, effected under local acts and Public Health legislation between 1848 and 1874, reduced the English mortality at the 1865 visitation to 14,378 of which 5,600 were in London. The last major English outbreak was in certain ports in 1873. The movement of the disease seemed to be associated with the **Haj.** This, and the great Bengal epidemic of 1875 hastened Disraeli's important **Public Health Act** of 1875 which codified and imposed generally some geographically piecemeal measures, set up port health authorities and local boards and established regular means of financing them. Meanwhile a further terrible Indian outbreak in 1879 reached Europe in 1883 and inspired Robert Koch in 1884 to re-identify the vibrio and to prove its means of transmission and its source in the water tanks of the Ganges delta. The invention of a vaccine did not, however, prevent a million deaths in Russia in 1892 or deaths on a similar scale in China, the Philippines and Russia in 1902. Thereafter it was thought that the main danger had been overcome. In 1947 a serious outbreak in Egypt belied these expectations as did the much more dangerous Far Eastern one of 1961-6. In 1970 a middle eastern epidemic reached Russia and Czechoslovakia. *See* EPIDEMICS, HUMAN.

CHOLMONDELEY (Pron: Chumley). Cheshire family. **(1) Sir Hugh (1513-96)** a soldier, served against the Scots in 1542 and after important local appointments became acting V-Pres. of the Marches. His son **(2) Robert (?1584-1659) 1st Vist. (Ir) CHOLMONDEY of KELLS (1628) 1st Ld. (Eng.)** 1645, E. of LEINSTER (1646) raised royalist troops in Cheshire and was fined by parliament. A descendant **(3) George (?-1733), Ld. NEWBOROUGH (1724)** was a professional soldier who raised troops for William of Orange at the revolution and subsequently fought in his wars.

CHOPS OF THE CHANNEL. The Atlantic entrance to the English Channel, formerly sometimes called The Slieve.

CHOUANS **(Fr = Screech owls)** were rebels led by Jean Cottereau or Chouan in Normandy and Brittany against the French revolutionary govts. The movement arose from a combination of dislike for the govt's irreligious policies and its interference with their dealings in contraband salt, but open revolt was provoked by the conscription of Feb. 1793 and, together with the Vendée revolt, rapidly developed into a major threat to the French state. The joint forces were defeated at Savenay, but in 1795 they raised 15,000 men for the émigré attempt on Quiberon. Thereafter the movement degenerated into a guerrilla which petered out only in 1801, with the concordat between Bonaparte and the Papacy.

CHOU EN-LAI (1898-1971) worked among Chinese in Europe from 1920 to 1924 and then joined both the Chinese Communist Party and the Kuomintang, serving in 1926 as political commissar of Chiang Kai-shek's 1st Army. From 1927 to 1930 he was sec. of the unsuccessful Communist Revolutionary Cttee. and in 1931 joined Mao Tse-tung in Kiangsi. He reconciled Mao to the Communist Central Cttee. and eventually established him as its leader. Driven from Kiangsi by Kuomintang troops, he and Mao in 1934 and 1935 led the Long March to Yenan where he, in effect, became the foreign and propaganda minister of the rebel regime. During and after World War II Chou was mainly in Nanking, Wuhan and Chungking as principal negotiator with Chiang Kai-shek and the Americans. When the Kuomintang was driven from the mainland in 1949 he became premier and foreign minister of the communist govt. He passed the foreign

office to Chen Yi in 1958. As premier he was an important figure in international affairs and seemed to present a reasonable face to other foreign powers.

CHOULTRY COURT. The HEIC court at Madras which settled disputes between Indians. *See* EAST INDIA CO. COURTS.

CHRISTCHURCH (Dorset) (A.S. = THUINAM) was an important port in Iron Age times and until the 10th cent. It was granted to the Redvers family at the Conquest and the great Augustinian priory, whose name it now bears, was established in 12th cent. It was transferred from Hampshire to Dorset in 1974 and in 1993 was the scene of a bye-election in which a liberal democrat converted a Tory majority of 23,000 into a liberal democrat majority of 16,000.

CHRISTCHURCH CATHEDRAL. *See* CANTERBURY; PILGRIM'S WAY.

CHRISTCHURCH (Oxford) was founded as CARDINAL COLLEGE by Wolsey in 1525, suppressed at his fall, refounded as KING HENRY VIII's COLLEGE and in 1546 established as a combined college and Cathedral chapter when the seat of the bishopric of Oxford (created in 1542) was established there. Cambridge scholars imported by Wolsey are said to have introduced Lutheran ideas to Oxford.

CHRISTCHURCH (N.Z.) was founded by J. R. Godley and the Canterbury Assn. as a model Church of England establishment in 1850. It was the last and the most successful of Edw. Gibbon Wakefield's projects.

CHRISTIAN BROTHERS. A R. Catholic educational body founded in 1802 at Waterford (Ir.) by Edmond Ignatius Rice. It spread to many other Irish places and subsequently to Britain, Australia, N. America and India.

CHRISTIAN SCIENCE is a doctrine principally concerned with healing and based upon the idea that matter is an illusion, expounded in *Science and Health* by Mary Baker (1821-1910) who published it in 1875 and in 1879 married the businesslike Mr Eddy, who organised the sect. The first church was opened in Boston (Mass.) in 1879 and the Metaphysical College in 1881.

CHRISTIAN SOCIALISM was an Anglican movement founded by John Ludlow, Charles Kingsley and Thomas Hughes in reaction against High Anglican indifference to social questions, but opposed mainly to the fashionable Utilitarian and *laissez-faire* doctrines of Bentham and Mill. It aimed to reform people and society by the application of Christian principles in social relationships. A manifesto to the workman of England was issued just after the Chartist failure in 1848 and there was a periodical called *Politics for the People* which quickly failed because those who could read disagreed with its views and those for whom it was intended could not read. All the same the group attracted sympathy and employed its energies in practical relief work. This included the opening of craft workshops and evening classes and by 1854 the Working Men's College in Gt. Ormond St. London. A further periodical, *Tracts on Christian Socialism* failed too.

As a movement it died out under church hostility, workers' indifference and the distractions of the Crimean War (1856), but its ideas continued to influence events, in particular in the field of trade unionism, the co-operatives and education and in colouring the views of the early English socialists with a Fabianism rather than revolution.

CHRISTIANSBORG (Ghana), a Danish settlement was ceded to Britain in 1850.

CHRISTINA OF MARKYATE (c. 1097-c. 1161) came of a wealthy Anglo-Saxon family in Huntingdon. In 1112, at St. Alban's abbey, she made a private vow of chastity, which she preserved against the seductions of Bp. Ranulf Flambard and of her parents who wished to marry her off. After 1123 she lived mostly at Markyate (Hunts.) where she attracted so many disciples that a nunnery became established. She maintained links with St. Albans and with its Abbot, Geoffrey (?-1147).

CHRISTMAS (25 Dec.) was the first of the midwinter Twelve Days of Christmas when farm work was at a halt and country people had time for fun, but the main celebration and present giving was, as it still is in Spain, the last or Twelfth Night (6 Jan.) which was the Feast of the Three Kings bringing gifts (*see also* YULE). The Reformers frowned on the Kings and fun moved back to Christmas day, which in turn attracted Puritan hostility. The Protectorate declared it a solemn fast. It revived with a confused enthusiasm at the Restoration but declined slowly in the rationalist 18th cent. Q. Victoria. with the Pr. Consort's new German Christmas trees, reanimated it for her and everybody else's children. Carols, never extinct, were revived through the many choirs. Charles Dickens published his *Christmas Carol* in 1843. Cards appeared in the 1850s. Commercialisation set in during the 1930s, was interrupted by World War II, but expanded back until shop displays and street illuminations were starting in November.

CHRIST'S HOSPITAL (BLUE COAT SCHOOLS) was founded for boys and girls in Newgate, London, in 1553. The girls school moved to Hertford in 1790, the boys to Horsham in 1902.

CHRONOMETER. With the growth of English world trade, shipwrecks were too often caused out of sight of land by the inability of seamen to establish their longitude (the difference between the time at a fixed point such as Greenwich and the actual time at the location of the ship). In 1714 the Admiralty offered large prizes for a practical method of achieving this, accurate to half a degree (30 seconds), and they appointed Commissioners of Longitude to test the applications. The prize was won only in 1761 by John Harrison whose chronometer, after 6 weeks at sea between London and Jamaica, was found to be only $1\frac{1}{4}$ seconds out. This revolutionised not only long distance navigation of ships but the hydrography upon which they depended.

CHUDLEIGH, Elizabeth. *See* KINGSTON'S CASES; FREE MASONRY.

CHUNGKING (Szechwan, China) was the wartime capital of China from 1938 to 1945.

CHURCH, Sir Richard (1784-1873) fought at Maida in 1806 and as commandant at Capri from 1806 to 1808 carried out much secret work on the mainland. In 1809 as Gen. Oswald's Chief of Staff in the Ionian expedition, he made contact with Kolokotronis and other Greek exiles and formed two Greek regiments in English pay with the object of training a Greek military cadre. These were disbanded in 1814. Church pleaded the Greek cause unsuccessfully in London and Vienna and then took service with the Neapolitan govt. until 1827 when he sailed from Greece to become C-in-C of the Greek insurgent army. He resigned publicly before the Greek National Assembly in 1829 in protest against Capo d'Istria's govt. but his propaganda in England at least won guarantees for the area which he had liberated. In 1832 he settled in Greece, became a Greek citizen and member of the Council of State and Inspector-Gen. of the army.

CHURCH ARMY was founded by the Rev. Wilson Carlile (1847-1942) as a result of working in the London slums, the Church Army developing from the Westminster Mission which he set up in 1882. He was Rector of St. Mary-at-Hill (London) and a prebendary of St. Pauls from 1891 to 1926 and this enabled him to conduct and extend the work of his army conveniently. By 1926 it had spread extensively overseas, especially in the U.S.A.

CHURCH ASSEMBLY (NATIONAL ASSEMBLY OF THE CHURCH OF ENGLAND) was created by an Act of 1919. It consisted of three Houses: Bishops, Clergy and Laity. Those of Bishops and Clergy consisted of the combined membership respectively of the two houses of the convocations of Canterbury and York. The House of Laity was elected quinquennially by representative electors of

Diocesan Conferences. Theological pronouncements were reserved to the convocations, but on other subjects the Assembly legislated by means of Measures. These, when passed, were sent to the Ecclesiastical Committee of Parliament (created by the Act) which submitted them to Parliament with or without comment. A Measure confirmed by Parliament had the force of law. Parliament could reject a Measure but not amend it. It was superseded by the **GENERAL SYNOD** which appears to be entitled to make changes in faith and doctrine by majority vote, a power never claimed even by the most ultramontane of the Popes. *See* ANGLICANISM.

CHURCH BUILDING SOCIETY was founded in 1818. Parliamentary grants for church building were made in 1818 (£1M) and 1824 (£500,000) and by 1833 £4.5M had been raised in addition from other sources.

CHURCH COMMISSIONERS (1) In 1704 Q. Anne formed a fund called **Queen Anne's Bounty** ("Q.A.B.") to receive the annates and tenths payable to the crown since 1534. It augmented the livings of the poorer clergy. From 1777 it made loans and from 1803 disbursements for the repair of parsonages. Between 1809 and 1820 it received over £1M in parliamentary grants and it regularly accepted private benefactions. From 1925 it collected and distributed the tithe rent charges and it received govt. stock in compensation when the rent charge was extinguished in 1936. Meantime **(2)** in 1836 the **Ecclesiastical Commissioners** (E.C.) were created by statute to hold church property and prepare schemes to alter and redistribute ecclesiastical revenues. They consisted of all the episcopacy, three deans, five cabinet ministers, two judges and some laymen but **(3)** the real work was done by three **Church Estates Commissioners** (one appointed by the Abp. of Canterbury, two by the Crown) who *inter alia* were joint treasurers to the E.C. **(4)** In 1948 Q.A.B. and E.C. were fused into a new body called the Church Commissioners who, in addition, can reorganise parishes and fix fees. This is an even larger body but as before most of the work is done by the Church Estates Commissioners. Its recent investment policy does not seem to have been invariably sound. *see* BURNET-2C

CHURCHILL. (1) Sir John **(?-1685)** became Att-gen. to the D. of York (later James II) in 1674 and in 1675 was imprisoned by the Commons for appearing in the Lords in a Chancery appeal against an M.P. In 1685 he became master of the rolls. His kinsman **(2)** Sir Winston **(?1620-88)** married Elizabeth Drake, a niece of George Villiers, D. of Buckingham, and in 1661 became M.P. for Plymouth; he had court appointments and sat continuously in the Commons until his death. Of his eleven children, four reached high honour or notoriety **(3)** Arabella **(1648-1730)** became lady in waiting to Anne Hyde, Duchess of York, and so the Duke's mistress. Of their children **(a)** Henrietta **(1670-1730)** was the ancestress of the Es. Waldegrave and **(b)** James **(1671-1734)** was the Marshal D. of Berwick. **(c)** Henry **(1673-1702)** was created E. of Albemarle by his father after 1688. Arabella's famous brother **(4)** John **(1650-1722)** was the 1st D. of Marlborough. His brother **(5)** George **(1654-1710)** fought in both the Dutch Wars of Charles II, held minor naval posts and like John abandoned James II for William in 1688. He became M.P. for St. Albans in 1700 and principal adviser to P. George of Denmark, Q. Anne's husband when, in 1702, he became L. High Admiral. Until the prince died he was thus chiefly responsible for naval administration. He was often attacked as a means of harrying P. George and Marlborough. His brother **(6)** Charles **(1656-1714)** began in the household of P. George, entered the army in 1688 and in 1693 captured his nephew, the D. of Berwick, at the B. of Landen. M.P. in 1701, by 1702 he was a lieut.-gen. and at the B. of Blenheim (1704) he commanded the English Centre. From 1706 he commanded the British troops in Belgium in his brother's absence, but suffered a stroke which ended his career in 1708. By the marriage of the daughter of **(4)**, **(7) Anne (?-1716)** to Charles Spencer, 3rd E. of Sunderland, the dukedom of Marlborough descended after her sister **(8) Henrietta's (?-1733)** death to Charles, 5th E. of Sunderland. See CHURCHILL, SIR WINSTON; SPENCER; and SPENCER-CHURCHILL.

CHURCHILL, Charles (1731-64) ferocious satirist and supporter of John Wilkes, published the *Rosciad* in 1761.

CHURCHILL, Lord Randolph (1849-95) (1) became M.P. for his family seat of Woodstock in 1874 as a supporter of Disraeli, but until 1878 was mostly in Dublin (where his father the 7th D. of Marlborough was Lord Lieut.) helping to organise charities and, with his remarkable capacity for absorbing facts, becoming very well informed on the Irish.

(2) He made a spectacular return to Westminster with a vituperative attack on the 'old gang', i.e. the subordinate members of his own front bench. He was re-elected in 1880 when the heavily defeated Tories went into opposition. Salisbury was then little known, Disraeli (now E. of Beaconsfield) ill and Sir Stafford Northcote too conciliatory. Lord Randolph, with Sir Henry Drummond Wolff, John Gorst and sometimes A. J. Balfour, seized their very first opportunity at the swearing in of the agnostic Charles Bradlaugh, to raise a public outcry against Northcote's compromise over the oath. They were soon nicknamed the Fourth Party and they attacked Liberal policies in the name of a new Tory radicalism unfamiliar to many conservatives, combined with parliamentary obstruction which eroded the govt's legislative programme. Especially while arguing for the fullest administrative conciliation and a settlement of the fundamental Irish land question, they refused to countenance any form of Home Rule and denounced Gladstone's association with the Parnellites. He had a talent for the vivid phrase and invective ("The constitutional function of an opposition is to oppose…"; and for restoring Egyptian rule in the Sudan Mr Gladstone was "the Moloch of Midlothian"). All this kept him usefully in the public eye so that he could refashion the Tory party through caucuses, the Primrose League and advocacy of Tory democracy which, though never completely expounded, was encapsulated in the phrase 'trust the people' and handed on to his famous son. By 1884 he had captured the party organisation.

(3) Woodstock was to be disfranchised and he agreed to stand at Birmingham against John Bright. Meanwhile he went to India. In the Nov. 1885 election he stood both in Birmingham and Paddington. Bright defeated him by 773 in a turn-out of 9000, but Paddington returned him next day, consequently on Gladstone's resignation the new govt. could not resist his claim to office. He became Sec. of State for India. In his six months as such he financed the neglected defences, negotiated an Afghan agreement with Russia, conquered Upper Burma and organised the Indian Midland Rly.

(4) In Jan. 1886 the govt. was defeated on Home Rule and Gladstone returned with a new Home Rule Bill. 1886 was spent fighting it. He called Gladstone 'an old man in a hurry' and was returned again at Paddington with an increased majority in July. His party was now in a strong position and Salisbury made him Chanc. of the Exch. and Leader of the Commons. It was the summit of his career.

(5) Character defects brought him down. His publicly displayed Tory radicalism offended senior cabinet colleagues who understandably felt insulted by his contemptuous abrasiveness. There were furious cabinet disputes which came to a head over service estimates. Salisbury and others wanted to raise them: he, on social grounds, did not. He resigned in a fury. Salisbury accepted his resignation before he could retract (Dec.

1886). He never held office again, but entered an accelerating syphilitic decline which rendered him incoherent by 1894.

CHURCHILL, Sir Winston Leonard Spencer (1874-1965) O.M. (1946) K.G. (1953) Hon. American Citizen (1963) Royal Academician Extraordinary (1948) Fellow of Churchill College, Cambridge. **(1)** In his only novel, *Savrola* (1900) the hero inspires the British nations to put up a victorious defence of freedom against the mass invasion by a tyrannical continental coalition. By that prophetic moment the author had been commissioned into the 4th Hussars (1895), visited (and reported for the *Daily Graphic*) the Cuban rebellion against Spain (1895), fought on the Indian N.W. frontier (1897) about which he published the *Story of the Malakand Field Force* (1898), fought under Kitchener with the 21st Lancers against the Dervishes at Omdurman and Khartoum, taking part in the last proper charge of the British cavalry and published *The River War* about it (1899); and had been ambushed by the Boers in a S. African armoured train. Imprisoned at Pretoria, he had leapt into fame through a lavatory window, reached Durban, joined the S. African Light Horse and reported the war to the *Morning Post* by despatches which he turned into two more books.

(2) He was now ready to enter politics, which he did in his usual electrifying manner. He was returned for Oldham (Oct. 1900) as a Unionist in the khaki election but excited conservative suspicion in his Commons maiden speech by saying that if he were a Boer he hoped he would be fighting in the field. It was Joseph Chamberlain's proposals for tariff reform which brought Churchill to formulate his own free trade convictions and to realise that the Tory party was not for him. By Dec. 1903 the Oldham Conservatives had disowned him. In May 1904 he crossed the floor of the House amid execration and took his seat with the Liberals.

(3) His objective reportage, which incidentally served his ambition with money and publicity, had extended into historical research. In Jan. 1906 he issued his election address as a Liberal candidate for N.W. Manchester. Next day he published the two volumes of his remarkable biography of his father *Lord Randolph Churchill*. He was, of course, elected and, refusing the Financial Secretaryship of the Treasury, characteristically chose to become parl. USec. for the Colonies. His chief, Ld. Elgin, the former Viceroy of India, being in the Lords, Churchill thus became the govt. spokesman for this vast interest in the Commons. This was not obviously the decisive step in his political career, but in Jan. 1906 he persuaded Elgin to establish a fully responsible govt. in the Transvaal and so made Jan Christian Smuts a friend for life and earned the even deeper hatred of the Tories. He had also to cope with the artificially envenomed issue of Chinese labour on the Rand. In the summer of 1907 he arranged to write for the *Strand Magazine* to finance a tour of E. Africa. In the inevitable *My African Journey* (1908) he visualised harnessing the Nile for industrial development and then turned, quite naturally, to social reform and the minimum wage at home. In Apr. 1908, when Asquith succeeded Campbell-Bannerman as Liberal Prime Minister, Lloyd George replaced Asquith at the Exchequer and Churchill was asked to replace Lloyd George at the Bd. of Trade. In the ensuing bye-election then required Churchill, amid Tory jeers, was narrowly defeated but in Aug. he announced his engagement and in Sept. was married to Clementine Hozier and elected at Dundee. This commenced his socially decisive alliance with Lloyd George, but whereas Churchill's main preoccupation was the alleviation of distress, his partner meant to redesign the state. Churchill began with the neglected subject of sweated labour. His Trade Boards Act 1909 empowered him to set up regulatory boards for oppressively conducted industries and at the same time he brought in the later famous William Henry (later Lord) Beveridge to set up labour exchanges (now job centres) and inserted a wholly new unemployment insurance into the National Insurance Act 1911.

(4) By now, however, the German militaristic threat was casting its shadow. The problem was how to finance all these social reforms and pay for the new expensive *Dreadnought* type battleships needed for defence. Lloyd George inevitably in his "people's budget" proposed to tax the rich, especially the landed interest. The Lords threatened to abandon their 250-year-old convention against interference with budgets. In the famous Parliament Act controversy (1910-11) Churchill supported Lloyd George with a convert's enthusiasm and yet again added to the Tory hatred of, this time, a renegade ducal grandson. He was rewarded (1910) with the Home Office.

(5) He promptly went to work. Books and entertainments were introduced into prisons. The sentences of all child prisoners were reviewed. The Mines Act 1911 improved the pits, the Shops Act hours in the retail trades. From 1911 to 1939 he was Pres. of the Early Closing Assn. Much of any Home Secretary's time is taken up with law and order, but two episodes raised doubt, especially among radicals, about the genuineness of his typically aristocratic radicalism. In Nov. 1910 rioting miners at Tonypandy (S. Wales) were dispersed by metropolitan policemen using rolled up mackintoshes instead of truncheons, but troops arrived when the riot was over and Churchill was long falsely branded with having used them. The other episode in Jan. 1911 was the Sydney Street Siege in which he was photographed apparently directing troops to ambush a gang.

(6) Nevertheless with a Home Secretary's responsibility for national security he began to take an interest in defence. He read the papers of the Committee of Imperial Defence (C Imp D). He was the Kaiser's guest at the German army manoeuvres. The Agadir Crisis (July-Aug. 1911) led him to contemplate what might happen if that army had to be fought. He pointed out to Asquith that the Admiralty had no emergency plans, nor a General Staff on the model of the War Office. During a golfing holiday Asquith suddenly asked him to change places with McKenna at the Admiralty and Churchill found himself First Lord (Oct. 1911). He appointed David (later Lord) Beatty, the youngest flag officer in the Navy as his naval sec. and set about creating a staff. His capacity for concentrating on the matter in hand was immensely beneficial to the obsoletely organised Navy, even if Lloyd George was soon complaining that he would "only talk of boilers". He got Cabinet and C Imp D backing and by Aug. 1912 had reorganised the Admiralty Board into three divisions, Operations, Intelligence and Mobilisation, all under a Chief of Staff. In the first instance the new staff could be advisory only: there were no trained staff officers, and a staff course had to be instituted at Portsmouth and even then sea service, gunnery and navigation remained the usual avenues of promotion. World War I was already in progress before the roles of the First Sea Lord (who had to be relieved of much administration) and Chief of Staff became fused, but meanwhile beforehand active co-ordination with the War Office via the C Imp D became feasible so that an Expeditionary Force might be despatched across the Channel.

(7) In the material field, one far reaching decision on Fisher's advice was to build the fast, oil-fired 15"-gun battleships of the Q. *Elizabeth* class. This was unpopular with M.P.s from mining areas. It foreshadowed the eventual abandonment of the close worldwide network of coaling stations, but meanwhile made it necessary to acquire distant oil fields and the Anglo-Persian Oil Co. Pointing in the same direction the Royal Navy was already experimenting with aircraft which Churchill enthusiastically encouraged. He often flew himself and

took lessons as a pilot. War later revealed a variety of inadequacies: in anti-submarine protection, in ammunition hoists to gun turrets, in the quality and design of shells. Churchill had already strained his relationship with the Cabinet and nearly everyone else to get improvements, but praise came from two unexpected quarters: the German naval attaché, reporting to Grand Admiral v. Tirpitz, ascribed major energetic impulses and aspiration in the Navy to him; and Kitchener, with whom he was never on friendly terms, said (May 1915) "There is one thing at least they can never take away from you. When the war began, you had the Fleet ready". He had indeed. He had ordered a trial mobilisation (July 1914) as less expensive than fleet manoeuvres and in view of the Austrian ultimatum to Serbia, P. Louis of Battenberg (the First Sea Lord) cancelled the dispersal. When war came Churchill simply sent the fleets to battle stations.

(8) His next acts have been questioned. At the request of the Cabinet he went to Antwerp and personally superintended its defence against the wheeling swing of the German invasion. He gained a week and possibly saved the French Channel ports, but part of the new Naval Division was lost and Churchill, who enjoyed the whole affair, was accused of frivolously neglecting his real duties. He now made the mistake which led in part to his first political downfall. Public prejudice had forced P. Louis to resign and Churchill, against advice (the King's especially) called in Fisher. An arrangement involving such domineering characters who habitually worked by incompatible daily routines, could not work.

(9) There had been some setbacks and after a defeat at Coronel (2 Nov. 1914) victory at the Falkland Is. (Dec.); Churchill soon saw clearly, as others did not, that the alternatives were to break through the Western slough of mud, barbed wire and machine guns by new methods, or to outflank it. He pursued both by establishing (Feb. 1915) the Admiralty Land Ship Committee which ultimately inspired the tank (*see* TENNYSON-DEYNCOURT) and by investigating the possibility, first, of attacks on the N. German coasts and then, on the opposite wing, the opening of the passage to Constantinople to relieve the staggering Russians who, in Jan. 1915, had appealed for a demonstration to lessen the pressure upon the Caucasian front. Fisher was willing to use obsolete battleships but Kitchener would not divert troops to the Mediterranean. Churchill consulted Admiral Sir. S. H. Carden, C-in-C Eastern Mediterranean, who thought that the Dardanelles could not be rushed but "might be forced by extended operations". This was enough, especially as Fisher suggested that the Q. *Elizabeth* should conduct her gunnery trials by bombarding the forts. Churchill got enthusiastic Cabinet approval and, if the operation appeared successful, Kitchener promised the 29th Division to supplement the ANZACs and Churchill added the Naval Division. Meanwhile delays compounded each other. *See* DARDANELLES CAMPAIGN.

(10) It was now that politics blew up in Churchill's face. Fisher had for some while been in a highly nervous state. He and Churchill had agreed a draft list of ships for the Dardanelles. To this Churchill added two submarines. Fisher resigned. Three other Sea Lords threatened to resign with Fisher. Sir Arthur Wilson dissuaded them but Asquith, attacked by *The Times* over the shell shortage in France was trying to form a coalition. The conservatives demanded as a condition that Haldane should leave the War Office and Churchill the Admiralty. Asquith accepted this and an astounded Churchill left the Admiralty a week after Fisher. He became Chanc. of the Duchy of Lancaster with, still, a seat on the War Council which, however, was downgraded to a Dardanelles Committee and then had little to do and was soon replaced by a smaller committee in which Churchill was not included. He resigned from "a post of well-paid inactivity" and in Nov.

1915 joined his yeomanry regiment, the Oxfordshire Hussars, as a major in France. After a brief attachment to a reluctant 2nd Bn. Grenadier Guards to learn trench warfare, he was posted as commanding officer to the 6th Bn. R Scots Fusiliers with Sir Archibald Sinclair as his 2-in-C. He was a fearless and well-liked commanding officer.

(11) When the 6th and 7th Bns. had to be merged in May 1916 Churchill, urged by Beaverbrook, returned to his parliamentary work but Lloyd George formed his govt. in Dec. 1916 without him. All the same, through Beaverbrook and Sir George Riddell, he sought to attract Churchill, and at a meeting behind the Speaker's chair in May 1917 Lloyd George assured him of his determination to have Churchill at his side. He became effectively the Prime Minister's colleague, but it was not until July that Lloyd George felt strong enough to overcome, with Bonar Law's help, organised Tory prejudice. Churchill then resumed office (though outside the War Cabinet) as Min. of Munitions.

(12) He instantly set up a Munitions Council of businessmen already working in that sprawling ministry and a War Priorities Committee under J. C. Smuts. Stoppages, because of Churchill's imaginative approach, were seldom long or serious. He kept in close touch with his French and American counterparts and was at pains as the War Cabinet's "shop man" to deliver the goods. He even wore down Haig's suspicions. Lloyd George gladly availed himself in private of his buoyant resourcefulness, as well as his eyewitness reports of visits to Clemenceau Foch and a tank attack near Amiens.

(13) Attracted by an implied offer of post-war Cabinet rank he fought and was returned at Dundee in the general election of Dec. 1918 as a coalition liberal. Lloyd George asked him to take over the War Office and Air Ministry to deal with demobilisation. With Haig's agreement he instituted a scheme based on age, length of service and wounds "to let 3 men out of 4 go and pay the fourth double to finish the job". Over 2.5M were released, leaving one million whilst the peace was being negotiated. Lloyd George wanted to end British aid to the anti-Bolsheviks in Russia as soon as possible but Churchill, with some Tory support, favoured the opposite view. War weariness however, sapped the crusading will and Allied interventions ebbed away leaving Churchill stranded.

(14) He was soon off on another tack. Impressed by the economical interventions of the R.A.F. in Somaliland, he supported Sir Hugh (later Vist.) Trenchard's struggle for an independent Air Force as an imperial fire-brigade in the new controlled territories particularly of the Levant. Lloyd George enthusiastically welcomed the idea of putting the Colonial Office in charge of them with the R.A.F. to keep order and sent Churchill to the Colonial Office. He organised a Middle East dept. and called a conference at Cairo to deal with the future of the area. The Emir Feisal was to be placed on the throne of Iraq, the Emir Abdullab on that of the Transjordan. The troops in Iraq should be recalled and security entrusted to the R.A.F. and there was to be an adjustment in the immediate Jewish-Arab disputes in Palestine. These dispositions lasted longer than anybody expected.

(15) Then in Sept. 1922 came the Chanak Affair. Churchill had been trying to dissuade the pro-Greek and increasingly rude Lloyd George from over-enthusiastic courses, but joined him in a solemn warning to Mustafa Kemal (later Atatürk). Churchill's request as Colonial Sec. for Dominion support and their refusals became public. The CARLTON CLUB MEETING ensued (Oct. 1922) and Lloyd George resigned. At the Nov. election Churchill lost Dundee.

(16) Politically isolated, as ever he wrote. In Feb. 1923 *The Times* began to serialise the *World Crisis*. Balfour called it 'a brilliant autobiography disguised as a

history of the universe'. Churchill fought his last election as a liberal and free-trader at Leicester West where F. W. (later Lord) Pethwick-Lawrence took the seat for Labour. When Asquith let Labour take minority office in Jan 1924 Churchill stood as an independent anti-Socialist for the Abbey Div. of Westminster. He was beaten by 43 votes in Mar. Sir Archibald Salvidge, his father's old Liverpool friend, found him a way back into the Tory party. Free Trade, the issue on which he had left it, no longer mattered so much in a period of national industrial rivalry, and a form of imperial preference seemed acceptable. He was elected at Epping (Sept. 1924) as a Constitutionalist with a majority of 10,000. When Neville Chamberlain chose the Min. of Health, the Prime Minister (Baldwin) invited Churchill to become Chanc. of the Exch.

(17) In his first budget he returned reluctantly to the gold standard but his other measures made small impact on the country's position in the new international economy. On the other hand he resumed his old interest in pensions and his suspicion of defence expenditure. He made the Ten Year Rule (q.v.) reapplicable from successive annual starting points. With a change in the balance between direct and indirect taxation, income tax was reduced to 20% and he was hand in glove with Chamberlain when (1929) he transferred the Poor Law powers from the old Unions to the counties and boroughs while Churchill absorbed the saving by derating industry and abolishing the tea duty.

(18) Politically isolated again by the 1929 slump, he served his political purpose yet again by writing, this time the magisterial biography (1933-8) of his famous ancestor John, D. of Marlborough, meanwhile fighting the govt's India Bill clause by clause: but his isolation made it harder to secure an audience for his well informed vaticinations about the growing threat from Germany. In Dec. 1936 K. Edward VIII's abdication restored Baldwin's reduced popularity while Churchill was shouted down in the Commons. He had, however, gathered an extra-parliamentary following which challenged govt. foreign policy, but Neville Chamberlain, now Prime Minister, would not listen.

(19) When the euphoria after the Munich Agreement (1938) had subsided, Churchill's consistency gathered appreciation, but it was not until the German attack on Poland (1 Sept. 1939) that he was offered a place in the govt. "Winston's back" the Admiralty signalled the Fleet. There were some successes: the *Graf Spee* scuttled in the R. Plate; the rescue of the prisoners from the *Altmark* in Norwegian waters, but the disastrous Norwegian campaign brought, in Apr. 1940, the celebrated debate which overthrew Chamberlain. Two days later the Germans invaded the Low Countries and France and the Labour Party demanded a coalition. It refused to serve under Chamberlain and Churchill became Prime Minister.

(20) He also became Min. of Defence with a cabinet defence committee which he dominated, consisting of service ministers, chiefs of staff and some others. Given his vast experience and fighting flair and his dynamism 'the deadly problem of civilians-versus-generals in wartime was solved'. In home affairs he was mainly concerned with morale, rationing, and the balance between civilian and service needs, especially in allocating shipping. He left manpower problems to the huge figure of Ernest Bevin, who backed him to the hilt. The result was few stoppages and only two back bench revolts.

(21) To avoid misunderstanding everything was submitted in writing. He began daily with a sec. on one side of his bed feeding him with papers and a shorthand writer on the other taking down the answers or recording the inspirations. Routine or regular issues apart, he had an independent means of evaluation in Prof. Lindemann's special statistical office and, in due

course, a rising flood of decrypted enemy wireless traffic. He thus set up a war direction which was so coherent and well informed that it mattered little if sometimes his brain was hyperactive and his wish to exploit openings too furious. Yet, his greatest and earliest virtue was compassion. He lived well, drank prodigiously without effect but despite his cigar-smoking image he seldom smoked. He always took his siesta.

(22) He had also to inspire the British people. They, of course, rose to his offer of nothing but "blood, toil, tears and sweat", but it was beyond anyone to inspire the French and few dreamed how bad their case was. He made five dangerous and abortive visits and an offer of union and then decided to send no more metropolitan fighter aircraft to France. His aim, if France collapsed, was to reduce the gain to the enemy and the loss to Britain and show the Americans that Britain would not give up, for he was sure of victory, if not 'until, in God's good time, the New World with all its power and might, steps forth to the rescue'.

(23) Thus his first success against American isolationism was to open a sustained correspondence with Pres. Roosevelt five days after he came to power. The first letter contained a very frank list of British needs; and American deliveries began a month later. Lend-lease kept them going until the end of the war. In view of the long historic nexus between France and the U.S.A. he now faced a grave dilemma. He dared not let the enemy take the French fleet, yet direct action against it might offend American opinion. He personally supervised the plans against French warships outside France and Adm. Sir James Somervell destroyed three battleships which refused his ultimatum at Oran. This more than anything else demonstrated to the world that the nation meant to fight it out. Within days he had made Sir Alan Brooke C-in-C Home Forces and, convinced that a German invasion could not succeed without air supremacy, he set Beaverbrook's frenetic energy to the acceleration of aircraft production. He gave priority to technical measures such as Dr R. V. Jones bending of German air navigational radar beams and sent Sir Henry Tizzard to Washington with power to pass to the Americans every technical secret the British possessed. He initiated the impulse to form the commandos and airborne troops. By Aug. he had got from the Pres. fifty obsolete destroyers in exchange for long leases for U.S. bases in the W. Indies, Bermuda and Newfoundland, thus entangling U.S. and British interests.

(24) By Sept. 1940 (see BRITAIN, B. OF) he knew that the invasion threat must recede and he instantly despatched tanks, no longer needed at home, through the Mediterranean to Egypt and strengthened Adm. Sir A. B. Cunningham's fleet there. Three months later Gen. Sir Archibald Wavell launched his brilliant 'right and left' offensives in the Western Desert and Ethiopia which annihilated the Italian Cyrenaican army and destroyed an empire; the German threat to Greece, however, prevented the conquest of Tripoli.

(25) Meanwhile the Blitz (from Sept. 1940) had been withstood under Churchill's and the King's personal example. This again reminded the Americans that Britain deserved support and, too, Sir John Anderson having succeeded (Sept.) the dying Chamberlain as Lord Pres. Chamberlain's death (Nov.) simplified the political situation. Churchill succeeded him as leader of the Conservative party, which assured his parliamentary majority. By this time the Embassy in Washington had become an offshoot of the War Cabinet. The sudden death of Ld. Lothian, the ambassador, led to other ministerial changes. Ld. Halifax succeeded him and Anthony Eden replaced Halifax at the Foreign Office while David Margesson, the Conservative Whip, succeeded Eden at the War Office. Almost immediately (Jan. 1941) Harry Hopkins, personal envoy of Pres.

Roosevelt arrived. Churchill's conversion of him forged a further link with Roosevelt.

(26) This was not too soon. Eden with the C.I.G.S. (now Sir John Dill) had had to post off to Cairo, Athens and Ankara to try to fence the Germans out of the Balkans, but Yugoslavia capitulated and Allied forces, controversially but unavoidably sent to Greece, had to withdraw, some to Crete, the rest to N. Africa. Yet the morally essential operation paid off. It gained time. Roosevelt appreciated it and it cost the Germans their only airborne division. In May 1941 Churchill easily secured the confidence of the House. He felt a need, however, to forestall German designs on Iraq furthered by a local insurrection. At his request Sir Claude Auchinleck, C-in-C India, rapidly sent troops to Basra, while Wavell invaded pro-Vichy Syria. The latter operation probably contributed to the failure of the 'Battleaxe' offensive in the Western Desert which had already been scheduled for this time. Impressed by Auchinleck's celerity and unimpressed by the far greater burdens on Wavell, Churchill made them change places and, for good measure, sent Oliver Lyttleton as Min. of State to assist Auchinleck at Cairo.

(27) Russia was clearly Hitler's next target and Churchill warned Stalin, who took no notice. When the attack began (22 June 1941) Churchill put his anti-Bolshevism into cold storage. "If Hitler invaded Hell, I would at least make a favourable reference to the Devil in the House." Britain and Russia agreed to make no separate peace with Germany (July). Hurricane fighters were despatched to Murmansk to protect northern shipping, while another supply route was opened through Iran. In Sept. 1941 an Anglo-American supply conference reallocated some British supplies to Russia. The threat in the Atlantic over which they came had long been a serious anxiety. Churchill had the Western Approaches command moved from Plymouth to Liverpool and persuaded Canada and the U.S.A. to extend their operational radii. This only stemmed the rate of sinkings by U-boats and long range aircraft. In May Churchill put the ministries of Transport and Shipping under Fred. Leathers of the P & O Co. and sent him to the Lords as a peer. Soon afterwards the monstrous German battleship Bismarck had broken out into the Atlantic and after destroying H.M.S. Hood was herself sunk.

(28) Fortunes in the Atlantic war were thus swaying back and forth when Churchill (in the new battleship Prince of Wales) met Roosevelt at Placentia Bay (Newfoundland) in Aug. Here they made two decisions of vast, if differing, range. The Atlantic Charter set out the ideals for which the war was being fought, even though the U.S.A. was still technically neutral, and the U.S. Navy undertook to convoy supplies as far as Iceland. The Germans could not now attack these supplies without involving the U.S.A. in the war as a belligerent.

(29) This curious arrangement lasted only four months, for on 7 Dec. 1941 the Japanese surprised Pearl Harbor and the European War became world-wide. Hitler's declaration against the U.S.A. followed instantly and strengthened Anglo-American resolve to defeat Germany first. Churchill and a staff crossed the Atlantic in the Duke of York (sistership of the Prince of Wales) and presented three strategic papers proposing American intervention in N. Africa to relieve the Mediterranean, American troops in N. Ireland to relieve the army and the bombing of Germany from the U.K. to assist Russia. On 26 Dec. Churchill addressed both Houses of Congress but on his return to the White House had a small heart attack. This did not interrupt business. It was decided to set up a united S.W. Pacific command under Wavell and a Combined Chiefs of Staff Committee in Washington with Dill as the senior British representative on it. The post-Pearl Harbor news continued, however, to worsen.

Japanese aircraft sank the *Prince of Wales* and the *Repulse*. The Germans took Benghazi, the Japanese Singapore. The Dutch Adm. Doorman's forlorn command was destroyed piecemeal. The German battle cruisers *Scharnhorst* and *Gneisenau* with the heavy cruiser *Prinz Eugen* passed, not undamaged, through the Channel into the North Sea.

(30) Churchill now reconstructed his govt. Sir R. Stafford Cripps had returned from the Moscow embassy and as the foremost pro-Russian became Lord Privy Seal and Leader of the Commons. By way of balance Attlee became Dep-Prime Minister and took over the vital Dominions Office. Beaverbrook went to the U.S.A. and Oliver Lyttleton succeeded him at the Min. of Production. Sir James Grigg replaced Margesson at the War Office and was found a seat in the Commons.

(31) Britain, instead of being the only and whole hearted enemy of Germany, was now allied to two vast powers who were prepared to profit by Britain's injuries as well as to fight Germany and Japan. In Apr. 1942 Churchill wanted to visit Roosevelt because the Pres. and his representative in Delhi, Col. Louis Johnson, were meddling intrusively in Indian affairs. The War Cabinet had several members with Indian experience but it disagreed on this monstrous distraction from the enemy. It was eventually decided to send Cripps, a friend of Jawaharlal Nehru and Gandhi, to discuss Dominion status after the war. Churchill was glad to see him go and the mission petered out harmlessly. Moreover, American Pacific successes had made the problem less urgent.

(32) Then Stalin began through his Foreign Min. Molotov to press disruptively for recognition of the Russian frontiers of 1941 and for a "second" front in Europe. The first could not be conceded without betraying Poland. The second subtly degraded the existing second front in Africa. Churchill stuck to his joint Anglo-American assault on French N. Africa. He also agreed on the manufacture of the atom bomb in the U.S.A. not in Britain. Next came the fall of Tobruk with the loss of 25,000 prisoners, but Roosevelt instantly ordered 300 tanks and 100 self-propelled guns to Egypt. When Churchill returned to London he defeated a Commons motion of censure by 475 votes to 25. On 25 July the Americans agreed with the British Chiefs of Staff that Europe could not be invaded in 1942 and settled finally for French N. Africa. Churchill accordingly appointed Sir Harold Alexander C-in-C Middle East, but the latter's choice for command of the 8th Army, Lieut-Gen. Gott, was killed and Lieut-Gen. B. L. (later Vist.) Montgomery replaced him.

(33) Churchill now (Aug. 1942) flew to Moscow to announce the substitution of the attack on French N. Africa for the cross-channel invasion of Europe and to explain the advantages of attacking the soft underbelly of the Axis. This meeting went well. The first, eastern stage of the N. African offensive began at Alamein (23 Oct.). The Americans surprised Algeria and Morocco (8 Nov.) but with the African victory on its way Churchill took the precaution of saying in a speech at the Mansion House that he had "not become the King's First Minister to preside over the liquidation of the British Empire". In Jan. 1943 he and Roosevelt conferred again, this time at Casablanca (Mor.). Brooke persuaded Churchill and Gen. Marshall that a cross-Channel operation even in 1943 was impossible because of Pacific calls on shipping and got the Americans to accept an attack on Sicily. Churchill and Roosevelt tried to settle N. Africa by reconciling Gens. de Gaulle and Giraud, and Roosevelt proposed and the British accepted the principle of unconditional surrender. The conference cheerfully dispersed after putting Alexander in charge (under Eisenhower) of all fighting in N. Africa. The countervailing effect was that Stalin had to be told of the further delay in the cross-Channel offensive (Overlord) and also of the diversion of Murmansk

shipping for the attack on Sicily. Anglo-Russian friction reached a new temperature when the German discoveries at Katyn confirmed the long suspected Russian massacres of Polish officers. Churchill now sought to convince the Americans that the underbelly strategy against the Italian mainland was right, but Eisenhower delayed commitment until he knew the outcome of the Sicilian attack, not due until July. Hence Churchill's message to Stalin was angrily received.

(34) Meanwhile landing craft sufficed for *Overlord* or the Mediterranean but not both. Churchill really wanted to relieve pressure on the Russians and the Italian operation did so, therefore despite American suspicions he wanted to keep the landing craft as long as possible in the Mediterranean and after the fall of Sicily the Combined Chiefs of Staff came round to a landing at Salerno, Fascist Italy collapsed (July 1943) and a new meeting became necessary, this time at Quebec (mid Aug.) Here the British and Americans disagreed, for the latter wished to give priority to opening the Burma Road and establishing airfields to bomb Japan. Churchill met them by agreeing to an offensive in Burma under the Supreme Commander in S. E. Asia, Lord Louis Mountbatten.

(35) The Italian events had indeed reduced the pressure on Russia and despite the usual insults Stalin agreed to meet Roosevelt and Churchill at Teheran. The westerners conferred on the way at Cairo where, to Churchill's irritation, Chiang Kai-shek joined them and the Americans refused to keep the landing craft in the Mediterranean. Churchill's plans for a full attack on Rhodes and for large supplies to Yugoslavia had to be restricted. Two Supreme Commanders were agreed: for *Overlord*, Eisenhower; for the Mediterranean Sir Henry Maitland Wilson.

(36) In Dec. 1943 Churchill fell ill at Tunis, but while recovering at Marrakesh the German Battle-cruiser *Scharnhorst* was sunk off the North Cape and the Americans after all agreed to use landing craft to threaten Rome, in order to end the bloody stalemate further south. The principle of the landing at Anzio, an outpost of Rome (Jan. 1944), was excellent: the American execution incompetent. Alexander, deprived of troops transferred to *Overlord*, was consequently unable to take Rome until June.

(37) Home from Marrakesh in Jan. 1944 Churchill turned his full attention (with the aid of a special committee) to the *Overlord* preparations, especially *Mulberry* and *Pluto* (q.v.), the plans for parachute drops, naval bombardment and for the use of allied bombing under Sir Arthur Tedder, to isolate the invasion areas from early reinforcement.

(38) The King and Churchill agreed with equal reluctance that neither should go to sea on D-day and Churchill, with Smuts and Bevin, went to the vicinity of Eisenhower's H.Q. at Portsmouth, where Gen. de Gaulle made last minute and exasperating difficulties. This, however, was overshadowed by the appalling weather. The great British-led invasion eventually began on 6 June and the British *Mulberry* harbour was installed with hardship at Arromanches. The other, because of storms, was never fully completed and the Americans maintained their rates of landing only by great feats of improvisation. Hence the initial brunt of the immense battle was borne by the British and Canadians and Churchill's influence was powerful. After Eisenhower took command of the more balanced forces on 1 Sept. it diminished. Churchill could not dissuade him from reinforcing at the expense of the Mediterranean and in the dispute about later developments the Supreme Commander objected to Churchill's intervention.

(39) Churchill had more influence and enough to do elsewhere. In the Mediterranean most of the forces and the command were British. The Russian betrayal of the

Warsaw Poles (1 Aug.-2 Oct. 1944) made their intentions clear. Their henchmen were preparing a *coup* for the German retreat from Greece. With American agreement British airborne forces reached Greece in the nick of time (24 Sept.) while Churchill and Roosevelt were together.

(**40**) At this meeting there was controversy about the Pacific. The Americans, especially Adm. King, wanted it to themselves. Churchill insisted on a substantial British contribution and Mountbatten was ordered to reconquer Burma. Meanwhile the western impetus had diminished and the Arnhem defeat had not helped. Churchill therefore decided to go to Moscow. Roosevelt, who still trusted Stalin, would not go and it was left to Churchill to extract an agreement about Greece and Poland. It was a paper agreement only, for each side had power where its troops were and Stalin had no intention of showing mercy to the Poles. Had the agreement taken American views into account it might have been even worse.

(**41**) On his return Churchill got American recognition of de Gaulle's govt. in France, and on Armistice Day 1944 made a triumphal entry into Paris.

(**42**) The Greek situation was now exacerbated by the time it took to get control of Athens and by a press leakage of Churchill's instructions to Gen. Scobie, the British commander, not "to hesitate to act as if you were in a conquered city where a local rebellion is in progress", but he obtained Roosevelt's agreement to the appointment of Abp. Damaskinos as regent, pending elections, and the return of the Greek King.

(**43**) By now a tired Churchill was influencing the Americans decreasingly, the Russians not at all and through his intermittent absences losing his grip on an equally tired cabinet. Attlee, in a letter (Jan. 1945), upbraided him with lack of cabinet method and with paying too much attention to Beaverbrook and Bracken. This was part of the dissolving background of the Big Three meeting at Yalta (Crimea) in Feb. Roosevelt (who unknown to everyone else was slowly dying), agreed to staff talks on the way at Malta G.C., but refused long discussions with Churchill lest they seem to be ganging up on Stalin. Such appeasement, designed to get Russia into the Japanese war, did not help the Poles and required too many concessions to Stalin. Naturally he and his camarilla were cordial. But there was worse to come. Eisenhower had already told Stalin direct how he planned to advance across Germany and had thus put it out of his own power to forestall the Russians in Berlin, as Churchill wanted. With Roosevelt's support he made them a present of Prague as well. The fundamental American Anglophobia was working to the top.

(**44**) At this point (12 Apr. 1945) Roosevelt died. Churchill felt this deeply but did not yet realise that his great colleague had been succeeded by another equally great. In May he expressed his concern to Pres. Truman at the proposed early American withdrawal from Europe. The response was Truman's swift and strong reaction against the Yugoslavs at Trieste.

(**45**) Victory in Europe was followed by a widespread lassitude. To all save Churchill Japan was far away. His proposal to maintain the coalition until victory over Japan (assumed to be 18 months hence) was rejected by the Labour Party. He resigned and the King asked him to form a caretaker govt. pending elections. Churchill's campaign was high-sounding, Attlee's modest. They met by arrangement at the Potsdam Conference where the Americans told them of the successful atom-bomb tests in New Mexico. There was no argument about using it against Japan. A few days later (26 July 1945) Labour won the general election easily. The electorate knew Churchill as a hero, but disliked his friends. He at once advised the King to send for Attlee.

(**46**) Once again he wrote, this time his *Second World War*. A world rather than a party leader, he preached European unity in the Cold War at Fulton (Missouri)

(Mar. 1946) and at Zurich (Sept.) and, against State Dept. scepticism, the holding of summit meetings for British, American and Russian statesmen. All this kept him in the public eye while the Attlee govt. ran out of steam, so that in 1951 he returned (albeit with a narrow majority) to office. He did not at first realise that he was himself running out of a different sort of steam. He had a second minor stroke in June 1953; he failed at Bermuda (Dec.) to get Eisenhower, now President, to call a summit meeting. There was a minor cabinet reshuffle. It was obvious that he could not lead the Tories in the next general election. On 5 Apr. 1955 he resigned in favour of Eden. The Queen offered him a Dukedom but he preferred to stay in the Commons. Increasingly infirm, M.P.s took turns to wheel him in and out of the House yet, when Eden's health broke down during the Suez crisis, he was consulted by the Queen about a successor. He recommended Harold Macmillan.

(**47**) He visited the Commons for the last time on 27 July 1964 and died six months later. His state funeral was attended by a public display of passion which almost equalled that accorded 13 years before to his wartime constitutional master, K. George VI.

CHURCHILL'S CONSERVATIVE CARETAKER GOVT. (May-July 1945) (*see previous entry*). It was formed to govern until the general election set for July and to carry on the war against Japan. Churchill, Eden and Anderson retained their former posts and there were some new recruits, notably Sir John Grigg (War), Harold Macmillan (Air), Brendan Bracken (Admiralty) and R. A. Butler (Labour). At the election the conservatives and their allies held 214 seats against 393 for Labour and resigned.

CHURCH MISSIONARY SOCIETY was founded in 1799 by a group of evangelical clergy as the Society for Missions in Africa and the East. The present name was adopted in 1812 because it wished to extend the area of its work to parts not mentioned in the original title.

CHURCH RATE was leviable by the vestries, in theory to maintain the parish church: though it was often spent on other things. In the early 19th cent. nonconformists began to complain that they ought not to pay for churches which they did not use, or for festivities, such as church ales, which it sometimes financed. Abolition was proposed in 1834 and 1837, it being argued that better management of church estates and higher pew rents could replace the money. It was defeated on both occasions by the bishops; their attitude was coloured by fear of a whig-dissenter coalition, which might reform both Parliament and the church. Meantime local disputes and refusals to pay increased, especially in Cornwall, Wales and the northern counties. In 1868 Gladstone's govt. made it voluntary.

CHURCHSCOT. A payment in kind to the parson on St. Martin's day.

CHURCH TEMPORALITIES ACT, 1833 (Ir.). Until 1833 18 Irish prelates receiving between £4,000 and £15,000 a year, managed a church of 500,000 souls. English bishops receiving between £2,000 and £15,000 managed a church of 6,000,000. Out of 1385 Irish benefices 424 had less than 100 souls. The Irish church had 600,000 acres of land besides tithes. The matter had become scandalous. The Act suppressed 10 bishoprics, created ecclesiastical commissioners, abolished the Vestry Cess and substituted a small annual tax on benefices in lieu of First Fruits. It also made the first provision enabling Irish tenants (in this case of bishoprics) to buy the land with govt. help.

CHURCH UNION or ENGLISH CHURCH UNION was founded in 1859 for the defence of Anglicanism against Erastianism, rationalism, puritanism and all attempts to alter its marriage laws or divert its endowments.

CHURCHWARDENS. Under canon 89 of 1604, the incumbent and parishioners were to appoint one each at the Easter vestry if they could not agree on both. They were to manage parish property and finance and present offenders against ecclesiastical law. The latter obligation soon facilitated efforts by some advanced protestant incumbents to introduce an equivalent of the Calvinist discipline through lay elders, but this did not outlast the 17th cent. With the advance of Methodism they ceased altogether to make presentations in the 19th cent. and most of their other functions were taken over by the parochial church councils in 1921.

CHURCHYARDS are often older than their church and were sometimes pagan holy places or places for secular gatherings such as markets, assemblies and trials. It was thus natural to preach and perform Christian services and then to consecrate them and later build a church on them. Every Christian, and then every parishioner, was entitled to burial in his parish churchyard save an unpardoned felon or an excommunicate. As the population grew in the 18th cent. graves were reused, surface levels rose, retaining walls began to collapse; many churchyards became unsightly, insanitary or scandalous and the law of mortmain hindered the acquisition of new land. Accordingly Burial Acts 1853 to 1906 (q.v.) authorised closures by Order of Council, the creation of Burial Boards to provide public burial facilities and the maintenance of closed churchyards at the expense of the rates. These functions passed in due course to local authorities.

CHUTE, Chaloner (?-1659) was a much employed conservative counsel: in 1641 he appeared for the bishops and in the 1640s he defended Att-Gen. Herbert, Laud, the eleven M.P.s impeached by the army, and Hamilton. Elected M.P. for Middlesex in 1656 he was promptly excluded. In 1659 he was re-elected and made Speaker. His illnesses forced the House to elect two successive temporary Speakers, the latter of whom, Thomas BAMPFIELD was confirmed in the Chair when Chute died.

CIANO, Galeazzo (1903-44) Conte di CORTELAZZO took part in the 'March on Rome' in 1922, married Edda, Mussolini's daughter in 1930, became Italian minister of propaganda in 1934 and after commanding a bomber squadron in the Abyssinian war became foreign minister in 1936. He advocated the aggressive policy in the Spanish Civil War, the invasion of Albania, the Axis pact and Italian intervention on the German side in World War II. After the defeats of 1942 he favoured a separate peace and Mussolini relegated him to the post of ambassador to the Vatican in Feb. 1943. In July he voted against Mussolini at the meeting of the Fascist Grand Council which engineered the dictator's fall. Captured by fascist partisans in Oct. 1943, he was judicially murdered in Jan. 1944.

CIARAN or KIERAN, St. See MISSIONARIES IN BRITAIN AND IRELAND-3.

CIBBER[T] (1) Caius Gabriel (1630-1700) Slesvig sculptor, settled in England where he decorated St. Pauls Cathedral and other buildings. His son **(2) Colley (1671-1757)** comic actor, playwright and from 1711 manager of Drury Lane theatre, was appointed, to the fury of the literati, poet laureate in 1730 and was the absurd hero of Pope's *Dunciad* in 1747. Dr Johnson greeted the appointment thus:

> 'Augustus still survives in Maro's strain;
> And Spenser's verse prolongs Eliza's reign;
> Great George's acts let tuneful Cibber sing;
> For Nature formed the Poet for the King'

(For Q. Caroline's view, *see* SAVAGE, RICHARD). He was not a successful writer or a good poet; his sense of humour appears in his autobiography *The Apology for the Life of Colley Cibber, Comedian,* and the chaphook *Colley Cibber's Jests* and also, perhaps, when he induced by the gift of a particularly ugly statue, the Fellows of Winchester College, to accept his son **(3) Theophilus (1703-58),** also a successful actor and pamphleteer.

CIDER, home made, was taxed at 1s.3d per hogshead from 1661 to 1706; at 5d in 1707-10; at 4s. from 1710 to 1767. Imported cider was taxed basically at 10s from 1661 to 1678; at £4 from 1679 to 1708 but there were additional levies against foreign importers. An attempt to tax cider additionally in 1763 under Bute helped to precipitate his fall. From 1767 home made paid 6s; foreign £3 a tun. These levies were habitually surrendered in return for the civil list, until they were abolished in 1901. Thus cider was untaxed until World War II.

CIGARS, CIGARETTES. Cuban natives taught the Spaniards to smoke tobacco, but cigars were introduced into the English-speaking world only in 1762 when Gen. Putnam came, after the capture of Havana, from Cuba to the American colonies. Cheroots became common in India after the First Burma War (1824-6). Cigarettes, originally rolled by the smoker, were a Spanish 19th cent. invention: their mass production in packets began in the 1870s (*see* Bizet's *Carmen* Act I-1875). Cigarette smoking developed into a major scourge and source of govt. revenue after World War I.

CILTERNSAETAN were a Mercian folk who settled north of the Chilterns in 6th cent.

CINEMA. The phenomenon called the persistence of vision was long known, but first exploited through various gadgets such as the ZOETROPE of 1834. George Eastman's invention of celluloid film strip for Kodak cameras opened the way in 1889; the first projector was used in 1890; the first cinematic showings to paying audiences took place at the Grand Café des Capucines in Paris in Dec. 1895 and at the Empire in London in Feb. 1896. Dramatic films appeared in 1901 and specialised cinemas began to be built in 1908. By 1909 the art was so widespread that the U.S. National Board of Censorship was instituted at New York. American film making stepped into the gap caused by the collapse of the European industry during World War I. *Birth of a Nation* was made in 1915, *Intolerance* in 1916. A powerful sales drive made it supreme and European govts. replied with quota restrictions in the 1920s. Anti-Americanism also boosted over-praised Russian propagandist films such as Eisenstein's *Battleship Potemkin.*

Hollywood then turned to mass entertainment and the 1930s produced the musical, the Disney cartoon and the horror and gangster film, while the French specialised in social satire. World War II fertilised both the British documentary and the oriental film industries, which by the 1950s were occupying a large previously under-exploited market. The cost of production in the old film countries was now pricing their films out and a new, economical style was developing in Europe and especially Scandinavia, often related explicitly to sado-masochism. The public appetite for large scale picturesque films had now to be satisfied through internationally financed and marketed epics. *Waterloo* (1970) employed actors of all nationalities and 20,000 Russian troops. The advent of television and particularly colour television brought a decline in the size of cinema audiences in Britain.

CINQUE PORTS (Norman Fr = Five Ports) is a confederacy in Kent and Sussex of the **five** ports of Hastings, Romney, Hythe, Dover and Sandwich to which the **Two Ancient Towns** of Winchilsea and Rye and some 30 other places (called Limbs) were added at intervals. It began before the Conquest for trade protection and piracy in the Narrow Seas. Its habits were long those of a semi-independent state, which made treaties and waged wars. It blockaded Great Yarmouth a number of times to get control of the Fair. Essex ports were similarly treated. Ships from the West Country and the French Basque ports were regularly attacked. Treaty relations subsisted with the Norman and Spanish ports. The objects were to secure carrying monopolies primarily in outward bound wool and Wielden iron and in inward wines, salt and spices. The seven headports were free of English taxes and made their own laws as long as they provided the Crown with 57 ships for 57 days a year at their own expense. The Confederacy reached the summit of its prosperity in the 13th cent. and played an influential role in the Barons' Wars. By a charter of 1278 Edward I, who was familiar with the Biscay trade, sought to control and channel these energies. Their obligation to provide shipping was widened and he and his successors habitually used it outside the Narrow Seas as far as Bristol and S. Wales. A **Warden** was installed at Dover Castle with wartime powers and an Admiralty court. The 30 Limbs were associated by agreements with individual headports whereby they contributed to the finances in return for privileges in the relevant port. The accounts were expressed in Purses of a standard sum to which each headport and limb contributed a fixed proportion. The representative assembly was called the Court of Brodhull (where it met) and disputes were settled, between ports, at Guestling and between others at Shepway. The courts of Brodhull and Guestling coalesced into a quasi-parliamentary assembly called the *Court of Brotherhood and Guestling* which still exists.

The Confederation's decline began in 14th cent. through changes in the coastline. Erosions damaged lands. Silting clogged havens or even cut Rye and Winchilsea off from the Channel. The portsmen could not compete with the steady enlargement of commercial ships because their harbours became too shallow to admit them. They still contributed five ships against the Armada (1588) but their function as a shipping, even a fishing, organisation had virtually endled by the mid 17th cent. Instead they acquired a vigorous prosperity through smuggled French brandy and tobacco off-loaded at sea from West Indiamen. The contraband was hidden in caves and cellars, especially at Rye. The result was a large increase in customs men, many of whom were smugglers too. This had a curious political effect for until 1688 at least eight of their 16 M.P.s were in practice nominated by the Lord Warden. This now became unnecessary, for the customs men, instantly dismissable by the Treasury, could be depended upon to vote as they were told. The Reform Act 1832 reduced the M.P.s to three and perceptibly reduced the customs element in the electorate. The Lord Warden, meanwhile, had become a largely ceremonial (if paid) figure with an official residence at Walmer Castle. The D. of Wellington held the office for many years as a reward, but took the duties seriously. The Admiralty court continued to function until 1914. George VI by a symbolic inspiration nominated Winston Churchill to the office in 1941 at the height of World War II and it has since been held by statesmen of high distinction. The Confederacy was expressly preserved by the Local Govt. Act 1972.

CINTRA, CONVENTION, 22 and 31 Aug. 1808. *See* PENINSULAR WAR (1807-14)-4.

CIPHER. *See* CRYPTOGRAPHY.

CIRCAR or SARKAR (Persian = business head) in India it meant (1) 'authority' and hence the state or the HEIC; (2) a high official; (3) an administrative division of a Moghul province. The **Northern Circars** (of Madras) stretched along the east coast from Guntur south of the Kistna almost to Juggernaut near the Mahanadi. They were granted as *jagirs* to the French general de Bossy to maintain his troops protecting Hyderabad. The British drove him out in 1759 and their possession was confirmed by the Moghul Shah Alam in 1765. The Hyderabad claims were finally commuted in 1823.

CIRCINN. *See* PICTS.

CIRCUITS, JUDICIAL (*see* ASSIZES) were seven groups of county towns which judges, acting as Commissioners of Assize, Oyer and Terminer and Gaol Delivery, visited three times a year to deal with accumulated business. The practice began in the 12th cent. Each circuit had a Bar

Mess which functioned as a kind of Inn of Court for the circuit. When the assizes were abolished in 1971 the number of circuits was reduced to six, centring on branches of the High Court at Birmingham, Leeds, Manchester, London, Cardiff and Bristol.

CIRCULATING LIBRARIES (1730-c. 1948) were proposed by SAMUEL FANCOURT (1678-1768), a dissenting minister who established one in London in 1730. *See* RICHARDSON, SAMUEL. Public libraries made them redundant two centuries later.

CIRCULATION OF THE BLOOD. *See* HARVEY.

CIRENCESTER (Glos.) (often pron: Sissester or Sisseter) (Lat: CORINIUM) was the chief town of the Dobunni tribe. Under the Romans it was centrally placed at the crossing of the Fosse Way, Akeman Street and the road from Silchester (Calleva) through Gloucester (Glevum) to S. Wales and the legionary fortress at Caerleon (Isca). The traffic must have been considerable for the town was, after A.D. 90, the second largest in Roman Britain. The West Saxons took it in 577 but in 628 it passed under the Mercians. In 1117 a college of prebendaries was turned into an Augustinian Abbey, to which Henry II leased the manor; in 1215 and 1253 it received fair charters and in 1403 a guild merchant which, however, was abolished by Henry V (r. 1413-22). Its wool fairs had been the largest in England but with the supersession of the wool trade for cloth the town's wealth and population declined in the 15th cent. The abbey was destroyed at the Dissolution. All the same its surrounding agriculture and important cattle market maintained a certain continuing prosperity evidenced by the beauty of its church and many later houses and the growing local interest in fox-hunting and other equestrian sports. The Royal Agricultural College was also established there.

CIRCUMSPECTE AGATIS (Lat = Be careful) If an ecclesiastical court held a marriage null (thereby bastardising the children), or a will void (thereby destroying the bequests) the consequences would be serious for those with expectations depending respectively on legitimate descent or the will. To prevent this indirect effect on property and feudal obligations, people began to sue out royal *writs of prohibition* to forbid an ecclesiastical court from proceeding with a given case. This might be reasonable where property issues might arise and the Crown was interested in the feudal obligations, but might be an abuse if used against the settlement of purely church matters or in disputes solely between clerics. Hence the Crown was unwilling to forego the Prohibitions: the Church unwilling to submit to them. Edward I forced the issue by issuing ordinances to enforce Prohibitions generally and in Jan. 1286 commissions to inquire into infringements by the Bp. of Norwich and officials who were distinguished canon lawyers. The result was a compromise in which the validity of the writs was assumed but judges and sheriffs were enjoined to "Be careful in the matter touching the Lord Bishop and his clergy, not punishing those things which are exclusively spiritual" namely (1) Penances, whether corporal or pecuniary, imposed by prelates for mortal sin; (2) punishment for ecclesiastical dilapidations; (3) Tithes and oblations; (4) Disputes between incumbents for amounts of less than a quarter of the value of a benefice; (5) mortuary dues; (6) ecclesiastical pensions; (7) assaults on clergy; (8) Actions for defamation not involving damages. "In all such cases the spiritual judge may proceed notwithstanding the King's prohibition". It quickly developed into a rule of the general law.

CISALPINE REPUBLIC was set up by Bonaparte and recognised by Austria in the T. of Campo Formio (Oct. 1797). It consisted of Lombardy, the Cispadane and the western half of Venetia. The capital was Milan. Novara was added in 1800. Its constitution was modelled on the French Directory. In 1800 Bonaparte took over the govt.

against strong local opposition and used it as a nucleus of his new Italian Republic. *See* FRANCO-AUSTRIAN WAR 1795-6; SECOND COALITION WAR 1799-1801-3.

CISTERCIANS (WHITE MONKS) (1) a branch of the Benedictines, was founded at Cîteaux (Burgundy) by St. Robert of Molesme in 1098 and rose to favour through its association with St. Bernard of Clairvaux. Its constitution, the CHARTER OF LOVE, was drawn up by the English Abbot, St. Stephen Harding in 1119. Each house managed its own affairs in accordance with ordinances laid down by an annual General Chapter at Citeaux, at which each house was represented. This became the model for the govt. of all other monastic orders after 1215. **(2)** The most important English houses were established at Waverley in 1128 and Rievaulx in 1131. **(3)** The Cistercian Rule enjoined simplicity, manual labour and seclusion. Houses were to be founded only in remote places. As a result they had a profound influence as agricultural pioneers and innovators and established the agricultural landscape of wide areas especially in the north of England.

(4) In Scotland K. David I (r. 1124-53) founded or helped to endow houses at Dundrennan, Holmecultram (Cumbria), Kinloss, Melrose and Newbattle. These were colonised from Rievaulx (Yorks). Melrose and Dundrennan subsequently established houses at Balmerino, Coupar-Angus, Culross, Deer, Glenluce and Sweetheart. They were all in fertile areas and the monks, being good farmers, helped to spread up-to-date agricultural practices, besides bringing new land under cultivation. As their farms spread they acquired increasing numbers of lay brothers to do the work so that by the 14th cent. the monks formed a minority in their own communities and tended to become idle or corrupt and the abbots or priors rich. These headships attracted the cupidity of monarchs, who forced their own, often unworthy or even lay, nominees upon the house. In 1532 James V thus forced one of his baby bastards on Melrose.

CITIZEN, ARMY (Ir) was formed in Jan. 1914 as an armed branch of Philip Larkin's labour movement, itself centred on the Irish Transport Workers Union. The occasion was the collapse of the Board of Trade inquiry into the 1913 strike. Land was taken outside Dublin and an English soldier, Capt. White, drilled the members without govt. interference. It was amalgamated with the Irish Volunteers in Nov. 1915.

CITRINE, Sir Walter (1887-1983) 1st Ld. CITRINE as Gen-Sec. of the Trades Union Congress (T.U.C.) from 1926 to 1946, secured trade union predominance in the Labour Party, a fact which became obvious in 1931 when his opposition to the second Macdonald Govt's proposed expenditure reductions helped to bring it down. He and Ernest Bevin hit Macdonald expelled from the Labour Party and thenceforth they could dominate Party policy through a Joint Council, because the Trade Unions provided most of the money for the party funds. He and Bevin were both strong men but utterly opposed to Communist, Fascist and Nazi violence and they (Bevin in the Cabinet, Citrine as his "agent") swung the T.U.C. behind the Churchill war policy. They also established a basically socialist system through production boards to further the war effort. This simplified post-war nationalisations. As chairman of the Central Electricity Authority he from 1947 to 1957 developed the practical workings of a newly nationalised industry.

CITY, CITIZEN (Lat = CIVITAS). In English usage a city was a cathedral town, usually established as a borough. Since the middle ages the Crown has asserted an exclusive right to confer city status. Ely, though a city, was not a borough and the borough of Ripon was made a city in a local gas act. A citizen was a member of the city corporation and, formerly, abbreviated as 'Cit' the word meant a tradesman. The American use of 'citizen' to denote nationality spread to the British Commonwealth

as a result of the independence of an increasing number of its parts. Citizenship then denoted the local nationality (e.g. Canadian) of a British subject.

CITY AND GUILDS INSTITUTE (London) was founded in 1878 and chartered in 1900 for technical education mainly for craftsmen and operatives. By 1980 its activities had covered a very wide spectrum and its examinees numbered many tens of thousands.

CIVIL DEFENCE planned at the Home Office in 1937-8 was that part of the war potential concerned with maintaining morale, transport, housing, water, sewerage, gas, electricity and supplies necessary to enable civilians to take part in the war effort of World War II, despite enemy aerial and naval attack. Much of the work was done by part-time volunteers. *See* ARP.

CIVIL DISOBEDIENCE. The term originated in the title of a powerful essay (1849) by the American Henry David Thoreau (1817-62). He justified action to ignore rules laid down by a state when either those rules seem contrary to some higher morality or when the existence of the state seems to infringe some basic right of humanity. "There will never be a really free and enlightened State until the State comes to recognise the individual as a higher and independent power from which all its own power and authority are derived." Abolitionist behaviour in the U.S.A. before the ending of slavery is an example of the former; Gandhi's campaigns against the salt monopoly in British India of the latter. Civil disobedience is difficult to justify in a true democracy, since it is necessarily practiced by a minority impatient of democratic institutions.

CIVILIAN. An expert in Roman **CIVIL LAW** as opposed to a Canon lawyer or an English Common lawyer. The lawyers at Doctors Commons were civilians and had a monopoly in ecclesiastical and admiralty courts which were influenced by Roman law. They also practised in arbitrations involving foreign law and in some cases before the Star Chamber and the Court of Requests. They were all doctors of law at Oxford or Cambridge. **Civil Law** is the group of legal ideas and systems ultimately derived from Roman Law, but heavily overlaid by Germanic, ecclesiastical, feudal and local practices. Derived from the *Corpus Juris* (527- 65) of the Emperor Justinian, it was received into the Holy Roman Empire partly because it was considered to be imperial law, and it spread in Europe mainly because its students were the only trained lawyers. It became the basis of Scots law, though partly penetrated by the Common Law. In England it was taught academically at Oxford and Cambridge but underlay only the law on wills and marriage (by way of canon law) and on maritime matters (by way of the Bordeaux trade). In Europe codifications were completed by Denmark (1687), Sweden (1734), Prussia (1794), France (*see* CAMBACERES) (1804) and Austria (1811). The French codes were imported into areas which Bonaparte conquered and were later adopted with modifications in the Netherlands (1838), Italy and Roumania (1865), Portugal (1867), Spain (1888), Germany (1900) and Switzerland (1912). These codifications were respectively imported into colonies at one time or another by most of these countries. The Swiss version was adopted in Brazil (1916) and Turkey (1926). Uncodified civil law, much influenced by Common Law, obtains in Quebec, S. Africa and Rhodesia, Ceylon and Mauritius.

CIVIL LIST (1) originally comprised the civil expenses of govt. i.e. those other than debt service and armed forces. These were defrayed by Crown hereditary revenues viz: from Crown estates and, after 1661, from an excise of 1d per gallon of beer, cider and perry, created to compensate for the abolition of the feudal incidents. In 1689, however, the Commons had to add £600,000. In 1697 the first Civil List Act granted £700,000, any surplus to be at the disposal of parliament. The latter condition was abolished in 1700. Under Anne this sum was inadequate and parliament paid off debts of £1,200,000. Under George I: £1,300,000. Under George II £800,000 (subject to certain royal annuities) was guaranteed by parliament, the King to surrender the hereditary revenues but to keep any surplus. George III's political use of these funds created substantial debts: parliament paid off £513,000 in 1769 and £618,000 in 1777 when the Civil List was raised to £900,000. The result was an attack on the whole system and the Civil List Act of 1782 abolished secret pensions payable during pleasure and many sinecures, imposed restraints on the use of Secret Service funds, introduced an accounting system and divided the Civil List into classes.

(2) Meanwhile, in the early years of George II, parliament had been voting sums (beginning with £200,000) for 'miscellaneous services'. These developed into a civil govt. provision outside the Civil List. Civil List indebtedness continued sporadically: nearly £3,400,000 was paid off between 1782 and 1820 though the List was raised to £1,083,000 in 1816. By this time the miscellaneous services vote had reached £2,000,000 and the idea of transferring charges for ordinary civil govt. to this head from the Civil List had firmly taken root. Hence George IV received £845,000; all such charges were removed under William IV, who received £510,000; and the liability for pensions was removed under Victoria, who received £385,000 with the right to grant pensions for public services from public funds on ministerial advice. These so-called Civil List pensions were limited to £1200 a year, raised in 1937 to £2,500 and in 1952 to £5,000.

(3) Edward VII and George V received £470,000, but in 1916 George V gave £100,000 towards the cost of World War I and further gifts between 1931 and 1935 because of the depression. Edward VIII was to have received £410,000 (less £40,000 and the Cornwall revenues until marriage) and George VI the same without such deductions. In 1948 George VI transferred £100,000 saved in World War II to the consolidated fund. From her accession Elizabeth II received £475,000, but by 1970 the Civil List was heavily in debt through inflation and in 1972 was increased to £980,000. Besides the Civil List the monarch receives the revenues of the Duchy of Lancaster. The heir apparent, if male, as D. of Cornwall possesses the Cornwall Duchy revenues, which otherwise go to the crown as well. In recent times his provision has been restricted until the age of 21. Since all taxes are paid to the monarch, the monarchs could hardly tax themselves. In fact between 1842 and 1910 they paid a voluntary contribution to the exchequer equivalent to the income tax on their investments. It was then discontinued in return for the Civil List bearing the cost of foreign state visits. In 1992 a press circulation war led to a search for sensationalism and the American owned Murdoch press ran a prolonged anti-monarchy campaign in which taxation of the monarch was a major feature. The result was a review of the Civil List and of arrangements for taxing the monarch's private income. The constitutional implications have not so far been worked out.

CIVIL REGISTRATION ACT 1836, instituted central registration of births, marriages and deaths. *See* DIVORCE AND NULLITY-2

CIVIL RIGHTS ASSN. (N. Ireland) was a kind of Irish nationalist popular front which organised marches in 1968 to provoke protestant retaliation. Naturally the R. Ulster Constabulary became involved. Riots provoked the so-called Freedom March from a Catholic area of Belfast to the protestant stronghold of Londonderry (Jan. 1969) and led the O'Neill govt. to propose reforms notably in local govt., but a Unionist revolt forced O'Neill to resign.

CIVIL SERVICE (1) The term originated (c. 1785) in the HEIC to distinguish between the civil and the military side of its organisation. The Tomlin Commission (1929-

31) defined a civil servant broadly as 'a servant of the Crown (not being a holder of a political or judicial office) who is employed in a civil capacity and whose remuneration is wholly paid out of monies provided by Parliament'. This excludes staff of Crown Agents, Church Commissioners, Trinity House and local authorities because not paid by parliament, and also industrial workers, and reduces the term to non-industrial grades concerned with administrative rather than productive work in central depts.

(2) The earliest govt. depts. were the Chancery (11th cent.), the Treasury (12th cent.) and the related Royal Mint and Customs (13th cent.). After a long interval came the Privy Council Office (1496) and after another the Post Office (1657), the reorganised Ordnance (1683), the Admiralty and Navy Boards (1690), the Inland Revenue (1694) and the War Office (1704). Most of these existed in an embryonic form already. After a shorter interval came the Board of Woods and Forests (1760), the Home and Foreign Offices (1782), the Board of Control (concerned with the HEIC) (1784), the Stationery Office and the reorganised Board of Trade (1786). The Irish and Colonial Offices followed in 1801. After a fourth interval came the Poor Law Board (1834), the reorganised Paymaster-Gen's Office (1836) and some minor agencies.

(3) These were recruited by recommendation or patronage and though burdened with sinecures intermittently corrupt and reviled retrospectively as such, they sustained business with small staffs and, especially between 1683 and the mid-19th cent., during a brilliant period of British history.

(4) Utilitarianism and the Pitts eliminated many sinecures between 1756 and 1806. Methodism introduced a new seriousness. The French Revolution had disseminated the principle of *la carrière ouverte aux Talens*. The result was the Northcote-Trevelyan Report (1853-4). Sir Charles Edward Trevelyan was an assistant sec. at the Treasury who had already worked in India; Sir Stafford Northcote had been Gladstone's sec. and later entered politics.

(5) The authors' purpose was to eliminate patronage. They proposed two classes of civil servants, the mechanical and the intellectual, to be recruited by competitive examination respectively between the ages of 17-21 and 19-25. Promotion was then to proceed on merit rather than seniority. The proposals were cautiously received. A Civil Service Commission was set up in 1855 and created a pass examination system; appointment still rested with departmental heads, but their choice was now confined to successful examinees. In 1860 a select committee recommended multiple candidacies for pooled vacancies. An Order-in-council of 1870 required competition save in rare authorised cases. This was the true beginning of the modern service. In 1874-5 the Playfair Committee proposed a division into four classes. A committee of 1919-20 classified these into a very small highest administrative and secondary executive grades and two clerical grades. This pattern has broadly speaking remained, but wars and welfare induced a great expansion and new, especially scientific, discoveries and made it necessary to recruit specialists. The following figures illustrate the trends.

	1939	1965
Administrative	2100	3500
Executive	19300	77800
Clerical & Typists	129000	228000
Specialists	11000	79000
Others e.g. porters	207000	304000
Total	387400	697600

(7) The advent of the Thatcher and Major govts. ostensibly dedicated to reducing state administration has

not greatly reduced totals, but has led to transfers to differently named accounts.

(8) The extent of (a) the power and (b) the influence of the Civil Service is disputed. (a) Ministries observably have continuities which survive changes of political ministers and they have reserve policies where no policy of party origin is in force. It is well known that some depts (e.g. the Home Office and the Dept. of Education) are less tractible than others. These represent real but not decisive types of power for they habitually turn a winning party manifesto into legislative and executive shape once the result of a general election is known. (b) Influence is much harder to assess. The civil servants are more permanent and usually better informed than their newest political master who is very likely to exchange outlooks with them, unless personality clashes (e.g. between Richard Crossman and his Permanent Sec. at the Min. of Housing and Local Govt., Dame Evelyn Sharp) drive them apart. There is an exchange of colour varying between different depts. and the depth of pigmentation will depend upon experience of previous govts. as well as length of time in office.

CIVIL WAR 1642-6. (*See* CHARLES I-1 to 21.) The King left London (Jan. 1642) with only 40 men. Edward HYDE now began to guide his wiser policies, but he had by him George, Lord Digby, who was less sensible. The Opposition armed but doubted whether Charles could raise a force; its demands therefore became extravagant. To these, on Hyde's advice, Charles took up a position of reasoned legality. Many of the demands were obviously unlawful and they, by now, hardly represented the nation. They rather than he seemed to be acting arbitrarily and moderate men began to look to him. Moreover, the parliament men were divided: Anglicans against Presbyterians and both against the new champions of toleration. There was danger to the church, but these divisions made it seem that the defence of the church might succeed. Charles remained in the Home Counties for some weeks and only reached York in Mar. but he was beginning to have a following. He summoned Hull (Apr.) where the depot for the Bishops' Wars was but the governor, Sir John Hotham, refused to hand over the magazines. Despite this peaceful clash the parliament still did not believe that the King could fight. Charles, meanwhile, appealed with mediocre success to the Yorkshire gentry and in July tried again at Hull, but with the same result.

(2) In the propagandist war on the whole the King and Hyde were the more successful. On 1 June the opposition sent him their extremist Nineteen Propositions which Charles rejected resoundingly. In Aug. he moved to **Nottingham** with 800 horse and 300 foot and set up his recruiting standard. Ominously, it was blown down in a storm; useful support came in only slowly. His cause still seemed forlorn when on 6 Sept. the parliament declared that it would impose the cost of its war preparations upon the estates of malignants, delinquents and other disaffected persons and that it would not demobilise until Charles had abandoned to its justice all those whom it voted to be delinquents. This was govt. by attainder. It convinced all royalists, at last, that they had to fight.

(3) The **First Civil War** was the highest common factor of struggles waged in three Kingdoms, each of which had its own civil war. The national issues in each differed sharply and the factions in one Kingdom would seek to get the better of their opponents by alliances of convenience with factions in others. Underneath was a mass of folk who were less involved than the leading champions hoped. Thus party intrigue, diplomacy and propaganda were as much part of the warlike techniques as and more continuous than the fighting. Moreover there were local issues, temperaments and feuds within each of the Kingdoms themselves and these created, from time to time, theoretically illogical alignments. Put crudely, the King and the English royalists confronted the parliament over predominantly secular questions, but because the parliamentarian alliance threatened the Anglican church, churchmen supported the King. In Scotland Presbyterians and the settled lowlands confronted (with an important exception) the tribal and sometimes R. Catholic highlands and their social controversy was expressed in predominantly religious terms. The exception was the Campbell confederacy of the west coast whose Chief, the E. of Argyll, was the leading covenanting statesman of his day. The ancient feud between the Campbells and Macdonalds (or Macdonells) involved the isles of the western sea and Ulster, where both had important colonies. The Irish rebels were initially native, tribal or nomadic and R. Catholic. They wanted to recover their lands lost in successive plantations of English and Scots and to re-establish the glory of their church oppressed by Anglicans and Presbyterians, but many Irish were not rebels and some colonists were. Many Irish lived as tenants on plantations and depended upon colonists for jobs. The Macdonells of Ulster under their chief, the E. of Antrim, joined the rebels: in Munster the O'Briens, under Ld. Inchiquin, and in Galway the Norman-Irish Ld. Clanricarde, supported the English.

(4) The Irish rebels had covert help from France and Spain who both allowed Irish soldiers to return to their native land. In particular two generals in Spanish service, Thomas Preston and Owen Roe O'Neill, Chief of the O'Neills, arrived and formidably improved their effectiveness. The King could not help the settlers and the E. of Ormonde, his faithful Norman-Irish Lieutenant, had to make do as best he could with an openly parliamentarian council and a small army. He relieved blockaded Drogheda in Mar. 1642 and defeated the Kilkenny rebels under Mountgarret at Kilrush in Apr. Courted by Parliament and King, he was congratulated by both.

(5) By the end of Sept. 1642 the English armies had assembled. The King's was raised and paid privately: the opposition's was partly financed from public funds. The navy declared for parliament but there were many royalist privateers. The Thirty Years' War then raging prevented direct foreign military intervention but the navy could, without wholly closing the seas, prevent Charles from getting much other assistance, for which his Queen was busily negotiating in Holland. He had to win early or be worn down. An inadequate victory over the E. of Essex at Edgehill (23 Oct. 1642) gave him Banbury and Oxford, but his advance upon London was turned back by the massed London train bands at Turnham Green (13 Nov. 1642).

(6) Yorkshire was divided between a royalist gentry and the parliamentarian clothiers of the West Riding, with Hotham still holding Hull. In Dec. 1642 Norfolk, Suffolk, Essex, Cambridgeshire and Hertfordshire formed the parliamentarian **Eastern Association** and in Jan. 1643 the royalists tried to conquer the West Riding but were expelled from Leeds. A second effort ended in their losing Wakefield and being besieged in York. In May Huntingdonshire joined the Eastern Association, but in June the E. of Newcastle relieved York and at last overran the West Riding after defeating the Fairfaxes on Adwalton Moor (30 June 1643). By this time Sir Ralph Hopton had beaten the Somerset parliamentarians at Stratton (16 May 1643) and conquered all the West except Barnstaple, Exeter and Plymouth. Returning towards Bath he suffered severely in an engagement with Sir William Waller at Lansdowne (4 July) but was reinforced from Oxford by P. Maurice and defeated Wailer completely on Roundway Down above Devizes (13 July 1643). He then joined P. Rupert before Bristol, which was taken (26 July 1643).

(7) Charles had reached his peak but had failed to touch the main enemy resources in London and the East.

In Sept., indeed, Lincolnshire joined the Association. Charles' solution might have been a concentric offensive, but the powerful garrisons of the parliamentary ports threatened the homes and morale of the unpaid and ill disciplined troops. Hopton's army besieged Plymouth and would not come east. The M. of Newcastle, after taking Lincoln and Gainsborough (where he was roughly handled by the Association's rising cavalry commander, Oliver Cromwell) retreated to attack Hull. Hopton wasted the summer. Newcastle was eventually foiled altogether.

(8) The King now resorted to a second best. The parliamentarian city of **Gloucester** commanded the Severn Valley, interrupted the communications between Bristol and his forces in Shropshire and Worcestershire, and also those between his Welsh and Midland supporters. Its territory and trade would be valuable. Its fall would complete his interior lines against the north and east. Moreover its governor, the young Col. Massey, seemed ready to surrender the place. In Aug. therefore the royal army moved on the city which held out stoutly. The E. of Essex mounted a rescue operation from London and forced the King to raise the siege (5 Sept.) but the King cut him off from London and short rations forced him to fight. The first **B. of Newbury** (20 Sept.) was bitter and prolonged and at the end the royalists still blocked the way, but short of ammunition, they let Essex pass the next day. With hindsight Sept. 1643 can be seen to be the watershed of the war. It was not obvious at the time.

(9) Each side was trying to break the seeming deadlock by seeking help from without. The King tried Ireland, parliament, Scotland. The Anglo-Irish had joined the Irish rebellion, which had spread to all the provinces. In May 1642 the R. Catholic clergy met at Kilkenny and, on the analogy of the Scottish Covenant, drew up an oath of confederation for the re-establishment of their church. A council of representatives from each province was set up and in Oct. it convened a general assembly pledged to uphold the R. Catholic faith and the King's authority. They appointed Generals for each province and proposed to finance their undertaking at the expense of protestants, neutrals and the Irish Church. Charles had instructed Ormonde to negotiate with the confederation and on 15 Sept. 1643 Ormonde signed a year's truce called the **Cessation**, pending a settlement. The confederates would not support Charles militarily but gave him £30,000. The practical advantage to the royal cause was that troops engaged against the Irish rebels could be released for use in England. The great disadvantage was that the Cessation confirmed the Scots worst suspicions about latent Popery at Charles' court. Despite a royalist rising at Kings Lynn (Aug-Sept. 1643) and Rupert's seizure of the strategic point of Newport Pagnell, the negotiations between the parliament and the Scots had almost broken down; the parliament wanted a military and political alliance which allowed for religious independency, but the Scots were determined to impose the uniformity of their all inclusive Covenant. The godly propagandists trumpeted forth that the troops from Ireland were 'idolatrous butchers' of protestantism. Both sides felt equally threatened and flew into each others arms. The resulting **Solemn League and Covenant** (25 Sept. 1643) papered over the doctrinal fissure but secured a Scottish army which, under the E. of Leven, was better found in all respects than Charles' Irish. Meanwhile the E. of Manchester defeated the Newport Pagnell royalists at Winceby (Oct. 1643) and Sir John Meldrum relieved Puritan Hull.

(10) Pym had died in Nov. The parliament now took an important constitutional step. In setting up the **Committee of Both Kingdoms** it united the Scots and English war effort against the King. The new committee instantly had to face a period of crisis.

(11) The hopes raised when Leven's Scots crossed the Border in Jan. 1644 were not initially fulfilled. Leven was held up besieging Newcastle: his troops suffered from snowbound communications and royalist cavalry under Sir Marmaduke Langdale, who also dispersed the elder Fairfax's new levies at Pomfret. Sir John Meldrum was resisted at the royalist stronghold at Newark. By Mar. in a London long deprived of coal, it seemed that the Yorkshire royalists would not be ground between the Scots and the northern parliamentarian millstones after all and meanwhile fear of the King's Irish reinforcements grew. Scots and English leaders were bitterly at feud over religion and finance. The Committee's fears were justified. P. Rupert at Chester (the port for Ireland) gathered a force and marched so rapidly upon Newark that Meldrum was surrounded and forced to surrender (24 Mar. 1644). Consequently the parliamentarians had to give up Lincoln, Gainsborough and Sleaford but a royalist offensive was developing against Sir John Waller's Hampshire army lying just south of the Winchester-London road. The Committee thought that London was directly threatened from the north by Rupert; it ordered Waller to give up his cavalry to the E. of Essex, whose army was to defend these northern approaches. This would deprive Waller of his offensive potential and perhaps his defensive capacity too. There was a real risk of total defeat in detail. Waller saved the situation by deciding to attack the superior royalist forces before the cavalry left. The B. of Alresford (29 Mar. 1644) was a major parliamentary victory.

(12) The improving weather at Newcastle now released Leven. On the same day as Newark he pushed the royalists across the R. Wear. The M. of Newcastle withdrew worriedly towards Durham. On 11 Apr. his strategic situation collapsed. The royalists under Sir John Bellasis, who were to hold the Fairfaxes at Hull, were unexpectedly routed at Selby. The Marquess abandoned everything to save York, which he reached on 16th. Leven and the Fairfaxes promptly blockaded him. During the six weeks while the troops of the Eastern Association (under Manchester and Cromwell) took Lincoln and marched to the siege, and while Rupert gathered troops for its relief, there had been an ill co-ordinated royalist rising among the Gordons in Scotland. This had been suppressed by Argyll but it ended with the establishment of the M. of Montrose on the border at Carlisle. More was to be heard of him. Simultaneously the King, against Rupert's advice, concentrated the southern troops by abandoning Reading and Abingdon: Waller was now able to surround Oxford on three sides and threatened the exit to the west. Charles had to get out in a hurry towards Worcester.

(13) All these troubles would be set to rights by the defeat of the three parliamentary armies about York. On 16 May Rupert marched from Shrewsbury; picking up Byron's force from Chester he took Stockport and on 28 stormed Bolton. Goring's cavalry joined him and he took Liverpool, but failed to capture the supplies there. Consequently he had to send to the King for powder and wait until it arrived. During this delay there was trouble in the west. P. Maurice, who had ill-advisedly besieged Lyme for nearly two months, was driven off by Essex, who took Weymouth and moved on Exeter. The Queen was ill at Exeter. The King called for Rupert's decisive stroke; Rupert set out and shortly afterwards the King succeeded in inflicting a sharp reverse on Waller at Cropredy Bridge (29 June). Rupert reached Knaresborough on 30th and brilliantly relieved York next day. The decisive stroke planned for 3 July was anticipated by the parliamentarians and turned into a disaster on Marston Moor on 2nd. Newcastle and many of his officers went overseas. York surrendered.

(14) Rupert, with Langdale and Goring and reinforced from Montrose, made good his retreat into Lincolnshire. Apart from garrisons at Pontefract,

Scarborough and Newcastle, the north east was lost. Lancashire soon followed, yet at this moment the royal cause began to revive. Irish Macdonells under Alaster M'Coll Keitach or Alexander Macdonald landed at Ardnamurchan and advanced unresisted to Badenoch. This drew part of Leven's Scottish army northwards. In the west Essex had failed to capture the Queen, had pressed on into Cornwall and was trapped at Lostwithiel against the Fowey estuary by the King's army coming up behind. The cavalry cut its way out and Essex escaped by sea (31 Aug.). The rest had to surrender their equipment and guns (1 Sept.). By this time Montrose with two companions had crossed Scotland from Carlisle. He found Alaster McColl about to fight a battle with the Stuarts and Robertsons at Blair Atholl. He reconciled them and with the combined force (about 2000) marched on Perth. His own Grahams joined him on the way. After defeating Ld. Elcho's covenanters at Tibbermore, he entered the city in triumph and then with Ogilvie and Gordon reinforcements marched for Aberdeen. The covenanting Scottish Estates sent for the troops on the border. On 13 Sept. Montrose defeated the Aberdonians and sacked his city. In the far south the King marched eastwards driving his disorganised enemies before him. By 20 Oct. he had overrun Hampshire and relieved his important garrisons at Basing and Donnington Castle. The only anti-royalist success was the storm of Newcastle which surrendered to the Scots on 22nd.

(15) Montrose abandoned Aberdeen and led the E. of Argyll's powerful army on a wild goose chase all over the Highlands. In the south the parliamentary leaders quarrelled over politics but decided that, to stop the rot, it was necessary to attack. Manchester, Essex, Waller and Cromwell accordingly forced a long but indecisive engagement at Newbury (27 Oct. 1644). Charles and Rupert united their forces immediately afterwards and the battered contestants lurched apart. Both sides were feeling the need to reorganise: with Scotland preoccupied the King and his enemies concentrated on their local concerns.

(16) The King's reorganisation depended too much upon Rupert (now C-in-C) who had his enemies and who could not be everywhere at once. Money was short, the troops had to live on the country and discipline was consequently weak save where the Prince was personally present. The opposition's problem was different. Their troops were paid, but by their counties and though better disciplined they, with their higher commanders, felt local allegiances which hindered combination. The leaders tended to negotiate rather than plan together. Cromwell advocated a unified army under central management. Recognised as the ablest of the officers he was feared as the leader of Independents, who were strong in the army of the Eastern Association. The reorganisation was seen as a threat to the presbyterian majority in parliament, whom Essex supported. Moreover Cromwell and Manchester, who were temperamentally incompatible, had quarrelled on ends and timing: Cromwell wanted to win the war be the consequences what they may for the King: Manchester did not recognise even the possibility of his overthrow. The presbyterians were in a cleft stick: the King would destroy them if they lost the war: the war could be won only by an army which for other reasons might destroy them too. Yet more parliamentarians welcomed victory than feared it. The pressure for reorganisation grew, but it could not happen without the removal of some of the higher officers. In these circumstances on 9 Dec. 1644 Zouche Tate and Cromwell moved the ingenious **Self Denying Ordinance,** probably devised by Harry Vane. It provided that no member of the Lords or Commons should hold any military or naval command. Ostensibly, it would purge the army of politics: actually it gave members of the Commons who could resign their seats a choice denied

to peers, who could not. Essex and Manchester would leave the army: Cromwell would remain.

(17) The political drama at Westminster unfolded to military accompaniments in the Highlands. The snow halted operations in mid-Oct. when Montrose got his force into Blair Atholl. During the hard Nov. he was joined by men from all the western seaboard, but especially Macdonalds. In the mild Dec. they grew restive and Montrose led them, with the MacNabs, in a surprise attack on their hereditary Campbell enemies. The E. of Argyll escaped and his castle at Inveraray held out, but his country was devastated and too many of his people put to the sword. The Self Denying Ordinance passed the Commons on 19 Dec. The Lords rejected it on 13 Jan. They demanded an inquiry into some allegations made by Manchester against Cromwell, his subordinate. The Commons pointed out that accusations against M.P.s involved privilege: an issue which might not arise if the Ordinance had been passed. The Ordinance was necessary to military discipline.

(18) The King now decided to negotiate. The contact might help further to disrupt his enemies while he prepared for the next campaign. The Scottish war was going still better than he knew: his Irish concerns worse; the Cessation, extended at intervals between Ormonde and the Confederates, was not fully effective. Covenanters and MacDonells were fighting in Ulster: Inchiquin and the O'Briens declared for the parliament in Munster. In any case Confederate opinion was hardening against a final agreement without total restoration of the Irish Roman Church. Thus Charles had the moral odium of the Cessation without the military benefits. Accordingly he commissioned the E. of Glamorgan to negotiate with the confederates behind Ormonde's back. Before Glamorgan left, royal and parliamentary commissioners met at Uxbridge for negotiations in which neither side believed: the Commons were now dominant in London and their extremists were determined to enforce their demands; but news of Montrose's great victory at Inverlochy (2 Feb. 1645) over the Campbells arrived in the middle of the proceedings. The meeting dispersed on 22 Feb. If victories in Scotland had stiffened the King, the passage of the Ordinance for the New Model Army had strengthened the Independents. The losers were the moderates on both sides and the presbyterians in both countries.

(19) Immediately, Charles' fortunes took a turn for the worse. The royalists abandoned Weymouth as the parliamentarians surprised Shrewsbury. Then Cromwell took Devizes and pressed on into Dorset. The King's country was coming to pieces at the seams while his enemies **New Modelled** their army. The county contributions became payable to parliament and the new force, of 21,000 men, was to receive equal pay from parliament, the commanders being forbidden to attract men from each other's units or to permit looting. Sir Thomas Fairfax, soldierly and acceptable son of a parliamentarian Lord, was to be C-in-C. Cromwell was to command the cavalry. Philip Skippon was major-general (Chief of Staff). The self denying ordinance was passed on 3 Apr. after Essex and Manchester had resigned. Their troops to a man re-enlisted under the new conditions.

(20) Rupert and the more sensible courtiers saw that Charles still had enough to save something by a negotiated peace but not enough to win, but the King still hoped for too much from Ireland (where Glamorgan was negotiating on the basis of a secret treaty while Ormonde was attempting an open one) and was buoyed up by Montrose's further exploits. On 4 Apr. he had raided Dundee.

(21) The King was adamant and Rupert advised a northern campaign which could lend help to Montrose. Cromwell, however, struck from London northwards of Oxford on 23 Apr. while Fairfax marched towards Dorset.

The King's forces were now to concentrate for the northern campaign but his commanders were a quarrelsome lot; Rupert detached Goring to the West to get rid of him; and to hold Fairfax he himself marched for the north. The Committee of Both Kingdoms ordered Fairfax to leave the West and make for the threatened Midlands; the parliamentary siege of Chester was abandoned. Thereupon Rupert and the King stormed Leicester, having first recalled Goring. Goring, however, disputed his orders: he wanted a south western not a northern campaign. Fairfax and Cromwell's forces were united on 2 June. On 14 June 1645 they together fought the King without Goring's cavalry at **Naseby.** If Rupert's advice had been followed the battle would not have been fought. The King lost his infantry, guns and secret correspondence and fled with the remnant of his cavalry to Wales. On his way he heard of Montrose's success at the B. of Auldearn (9 May). Fairfax and Cromwell now turned south-west and trounced Goring at Langport (10 July) but further cheerful news came in from Montrose who had beaten the covenanters at Alford and had, on 16 Aug., won a great victory at Kilsyth. The Scots govt. fled. Glasgow and Edinburgh fell. Charles decided to go north with his cavalry after all, but changed his mind at Doncaster and, looping clockwise via Huntingdon (which he sacked), drove away Leven's remaining Scottish troops from before Hereford. Brilliance and euphoria illuminated the morale of his court while the real soldiers fought it out at Bristol. Fairfax and Cromwell formed the siege on 21 Aug. On 10 Sept. the faithful Rupert surrendered the city. The furious King arrested him. It was not treachery or incompetence which lost Bristol, but the resolution of the anti-royalists, however much they hated each other, to stick together. So much a horrified perusal of the King's correspondence had taught them.

(22) Rupert's disgrace (he was soon released) was the work of the foolish and egocentric Digby, who had put it about that he had betrayed the King for money. Deprived of his best general by the fall of Bristol, Charles moved from south Wales with the rest of his cavalry to Chester, which was besieged on three sides. Here, on Rowton Heath, his effort to break up the siege was defeated with slaughter (24 Sept. 1645). Chester, too, was now unsafe. The King moved to Newark while his southern strongholds, Devizes, Winchester (5 Oct.) and Basing House (15 Oct.) fell to Cromwell. By now the parliament knew, but the King did not, that Montrose had met disaster at Philiphaugh on 15 Sept. Digby urged Charles to send his cavalry north to Montrose, partly because Rupert and Maurice were approaching with their friends to demand an inquiry into the defence of Bristol. Two disasters swiftly followed. Digby took the Northern Horse north and lost them at Sherborne-in-Elmet, while the Newark garrison mutinied in favour of Rupert. Suddenly the King had no field army. With the enemy closing in he escaped to his garrison at Oxford (3-5 Nov.).

(23) The King's only hopes now lay in foreign intervention, division among the enemy and Ireland. The continental realists moving towards a settlement of the Thirty Years' War either could not act or saw no reason to help a helpless or faithless King. Moreover the R. Catholic powers were influenced by the Vatican which now intervened disastrously and decisively in Ireland. Innocent X's nuncio to the Confederates, Giovanni Batista **Rinuccini,** arrived in Oct. 1645. He knew nothing of Irish or English affairs, but soon persuaded many Confederates to insist on nothing less than the re-establishment of the Roman church and a R. Catholic Lord Lieut. He did not know that Charles had a religious conscience too; he disregarded the power of the New Model; unlike the Norman Irish lords, he did not understand that a compromise might enable the Irish and the King to stand together and hold their position.

Rinuccini's intransigence destroyed the King's Irish hopes, split the Confederates and in the end exposed all Ireland to the intolerant savagery of triumphant republican sectaries. The parliament had already ordained that Irish prisoners should be hanged.

(24) The parliamentarians were methodically reducing royalist garrisons while parties of the King's troops moved at large in the open country and royalist officers tried to recruit in Wales. Nothing could come from Ireland, but the perennial quarrel between presbyterians and Independents suggested a slight chance of an accommodation with the Scots. In Jan. 1646 a captured copy of Glamorgan's treaty with the Confederates reached London. Apparently the King was conceding the very things which his conscience forbade him to concede. This double dealing divided his friends and once again united his enemies. In a kind of despair, Ormonde and Digby (who had reached Ireland from Yorkshire) arrested Glamorgan. The King publicly repudiated him, but the damage was done. Then Chester surrendered (3 Feb.) and the King's last considerable force, under Lord Astley, was routed at Stow-on-the-Wold (21 Mar. 1646).

(25) The English parliamentarians had, since Feb. been behaving as if the war was won. They ignored the Scots and drew up peace terms to suit themselves. Since the independents dominated them through their army this was scarcely surprising, for the Scots were still intent on a presbyterian establishment for both countries. (*See* SOLEMN LEAGUE AND COVENANT.) on 2 Apr. the French ambassador, Montreuil, left Oxford for the Scots H.Q. at Newark to negotiate an accommodation between them and Charles. On 11th the Scots commissioners publicly denounced the English terms. The Scots at Newark offered no concessions to Charles and on 21st he approached the Independents through Ireton. Cromwell publicly rejected the King's appeal to the Commons on 25th. On 27th the King vanished. He made a circuitous ride via Harrow and Downham Market and appeared, much to their astonishment, at the Scots H.Q. at Southwell on 5 May. On 8th they took him to Newcastle against the angry protests of the English parliament. On 19th they made him order Montrose to disband, but on 5 June Owen Roe O'Neill's confederates routed the Scots general Munroe at Benburb in Ulster and reminded both Scots and parliament of the unfinished Irish confusion. *See* CHARLES I-21 TO 34.

CIVIL WAR, SECOND 1648. *See* CHARLES I-28.

CIVITAS. **(Lat = state).** *See* BRITAIN, ROMAN-7.

CLACKMANNAN (Scot). A very small agricultural county long disputed between Scots and Picts until Kenneth MacAlpin's local victory over the Picts at Tullybody in 844. It remained an arena for clan disputes until 1648 and was later extensively undermined from without for coal. Its M.P., as the only elector before the Reform Bill of 1832, habitually elected himself but enthusiastically supported the Bill.

CLAIM OF RIGHT (Apr. 1689) passed by the Scottish Estates, asserted that James VII and II had been deposed and set out the reasons, and the terms on which the crown was to be offered to William of Orange. The Scots equivalent of the English Bill of Rights.

CLAIRVAUX. *See* BERNARD, ST.

CLANCARTY. *See* MACCARTHY.

CLAN-NA-GAEL A Fenian secret society, with H.Q. in Chicago, formed in 1883; its agents were responsible for several murders and explosions in the 1880s.

CLANS or SEPTS, IRISH. (As Irish clan records and traditions have suffered even more than the Scots, for a vista of the development of clan history generally, *see* CLANS, SCOTTISH.) Because of the immunity of Ireland from attack in the first eight cents. of the Christian era and the sea-dominated nature of the first such attacks by the Ostmen (whose settlements hardly ventured beyond the ports) some Gaelic clans, though they continually fought each other, became associated with particular areas (e.g. the Macmorroughs in Wicklow) much earlier than their Scottish counterparts; though some (e.g. Maclachlan and Mac Torcaill) originated with or thought that they remembered a Norwegian ancestor. The Normans began to break them up by imposing their continental style feudalism in much of Leinster and Munster. Meanwhile the descendents of Conn of the Hundred Battles, mostly MacDonalds, reached Argyll and the Inner Hebrides. They began to colonise the Ulster coast within sight and soon founded the Irish Macdonnells of the Isles, of the Glens and of Antrim (*see next entry*-6). The Normans themselves originated clans too: notably several in Munster (q.v.), but their English successors tried with varying success to impose an English form of society and a sort of *apartheid* in the ten obedient shires (*see* KILKENNEY, STATUTES OF). They tried to combine this with a policy of *surrender and regrant* designed to convert clan chiefs into landowners and their followers into tenants. Where this was actually achieved, it strengthened the clan loyalty of the tenants, while the landless clansmen became household or armed retainers or gallowglasses. The policy did nothing for order, while creating obstacles to English colonisation. It was superseded by *plantation*, begun experimentally under Mary I (1553-8) in Offaly and Leix and, fired by sectarian fanaticism, eventually developed to monstrous proportions especially under Cromwell. The people of Leinster and Munster were driven into Connaught and Clare and though many returned they had lost their organisation and returned as individuals not as clansmen, while in Ulster the leaders of the R. Catholic tribes were replaced mostly by Scots protestant landlords who employed the local Irish as labourers. Thus the Irish clans had ceased to matter as clans by the Restoration.

CLANS, SCOTTISH, AND CLAN TARTANS. (Clann: Gael = kindred) (1) The basis of the Scots clan is an extended family with its descendents, branches and accretions, in earlier times living in a group. The chief descendent of the head of the original family was, and is if known, the chief of the clan. The clansmen owed him deference, loyalty and military service and accepted his jurisdiction in disputes. He was bound in return to give protection and support (often of a violent kind) in disputes with outsiders and help in distress. With his personal retainers he often forced his will or policy on his clansmen by burning their crofts.

(2) The clans are not uniform in origin, organisation or tradition, but it is convenient to divide them into Highlanders (those tribes which still occupied Highland territories in the 16th cent.) and Lowlanders. Of the 97 major clans about 50 are of Celtic tribal origin, 10 are Norse and a few have accepted progenitors who were Norman, Saxon, French and Breton. The remainder are emancipated off-shoots of other clans, or aggregations of families, or tribes which have absorbed broken tribes, while some originate in land grants followed by settlement by personal adherents of the original grantee. Many clans have sub-clans or septs, and there are families which became associated and eventually merged with a clan or sept of a different name.

(3) The early Highlander history is mostly undocumented but rich in oral tradition. It seems that there were a number of distinct migrations of Q-Celtic or Goidelic speakers from the west into the predominantly P-Celtic or Brythonic speaking Pictish Caledonians. These Scottish migrants were in six groups, the last five of which remembered or sang of distinct ancestries, and they arrived behind each other, pushing their predecessors away from their west coast landing areas. The earlier arrivals were thus ground between the still resistant Picts in front and their Scottish relatives in the rear; they suffered severe casualties, broke up or became

seriously disorganised and sometimes merged with the Pictish or Brythonic population to become Lowland Clans. Meanwhile the later arrivals had time to grow until involved in struggles with still later arrivals.

(4) If the foregoing view is correct then the oldest migrations were those of the Caithness Clans (particularly the Mackays of Strathnaver and the Clans Abrach and Kinloch) and the descendants of Fearchar Fada MacFaradaig later found on the east coast. The Caithness clans accepted a mutual kinship but had no tradition of common ancestry. The descendents of Fearchar were the Mormaers of Moray, from whom came the family confederacy of Clan Chattan, the MacDuff Earls of Fife, the Mackintosh, the Clan Vurich or Macphersons, the Macnaughtons, together perhaps with the Camerons and Macleans.

(5) The next migrations were those of the descendants of Cormac mac Oirbertaig and of Krycul. The latter became the MacNicols of Assynt and the Macraes. The descendants of Cormac became Earls of Ross who commanded a widespread allegiance. This included five tribes of Grants, the Mackenzies (MacKenneths) and Matthiesons of Lochaish, Geraldine Clans which transferred their allegiance to the Earls of Seaforth in 1476. It also included the Siol Alpine, an assemblage of loosely allied kindreds, including Macgregors, Grants of Strathspey, Mackinnons, Macquarries or McGuires, MacNabs, MacDuffies and Macaulays. This group, particularly the Siol Alpine, suffered tragically from the pressure of the next migrations and virtually ceased to exist as an entity. (*See next para.*)

(6) The third major wave consisted of the descendents of Conn of the Hundred Battles and of Feargus Leith Dearg. Conn's main clan was the Macdonalds who, as Lords of the Isles, nearly founded an independent state in the northwest and eventually broke up into the six major septs of Clanranald, Sleat, Kintyre, Keppoch, Glencoc and Glengarry and a residually broken yet named body descended from the Macdonalds of the Isles and their retainers. They subjected about half the families of the Siol Alpine and were associated with Robertsons, Macfarlanes and, with other loose kindred, the Siol Gillevray, composed of Macneills, Maclauchlans and Macewans.

(7) While the Macdonalds were destroying or scattering the more northerly clans of Cormac mac Oirbertaig, the descendents of Feargus, particularly the Campbells, were settling further south in the Macgregor country. It was the Campbells who drove the Macaulays into the Lowlands and converted the Macgregors into landless robbers. The other branch of Feargus, the Macleods, settled in Harris, Lewis and Skye, and in due course collided with the Macdonalds. Since Campbells sided with the crown in the 15th cent. struggles which ended the Macdonald Lordship of the Isles, the Macdonalds were permanently at feud with both the Macleods and the Camphells. Moreover their defeat left them open to attack from the east. The Camerons, particularly, of Lochaber acquired much of the Clanranald lands; the Macleans settled in Ardgour, as well as Dewart, Lochbuie and the I. of Coil.

(8) By about 1580 the clans each occupied fairly well defined localities: most being in the Highlands or Islands. These areas continued to vary in extent with time and with the effects of clan warfare, disease and food supply. Nevertheless, by the 17th cent. the clan was considered to be a group of families associated with a place. In each such place the weavers tended to produce from local materials and dyes a distinctive but standardised local TARTAN pattern called a sett, likely to be worn by most of the inhabitants. It was not originally a uniform but a convenience. Clans also tended to have plant badges, which probably originated as charms, and they mostly had distinctive war cries and, later on, peculiar pipe melodies.

(9) The clan chiefs were, accordingly, not powerful in money, which was scarce, nor in acreage which, though sometimes vast, was very poor. Their power depended on their following and its size.

(10) The decisive event in modern clan history is the Rebellion of 1745. The defeat of the Highlanders and the harrying of their territories reduced their numbers. Legislation designed to weaken clan loyalties abolished the jurisdiction of the chiefs and until 1782 forbade the wearing of highland dress or other clan distinctions. One result was that the old art of making the vegetable dyes was lost. Another that the *sett* adopted by the chiefs family came to be regarded as the clan tartan, after tartan could be legally worn again.

(11) Nearly 800 families are part of the clan system, but do not bear the name of the clan to which they belong. In view of the importance of these loyalties and associations, especially in pre-1745 history, the following lists show the connections. The names of the clans appear, each with a number, in the first list. The names of the families in the second list each have a number in parentheses indicating association with the numbered clan in the first list.

Clan and *Chief*

1a	Agnew of Lochnaw	31	Erskine
1	Armstrong		*E. of Mar and Kellie*
2	Baird	32	Farquharson
3	Barclay		*Farquharson of*
4	Brodie		*Ivercauld*
	Brodie of Brodie	33	Ferguson, Fergusson
5	Bruce, Brus		*Ferguson of Kilkerran*
	E. of Elgin	34	Forbes
6	Buchanan		*L. Forbes*
	Buchanan of that ilk	35	Fraser, Frazer
7	Cameron		*L. Fraser*
	Cameron, L. of Lochiel	36	Gordon
8	Campbell of Lochow		*M. of Huntly*
	D. of Argyll	37	Graham of Monteith
9	Campbell of		*Graham of Gartmore*
	Breadalbane	38	Graham of Montrose
	E. of Breadalbane		*D. of Montrose*
10	Campbell of Cawdor	39	Grant
	E. of Cawdor		*L. Strathspey*
11	Campbell of Craignish	40	Grant of Glenmoriston
12	Campbell of Inverawe	41	Gunn
13	Campbell of Loudoun	42	Hamilton
	E. of Loudoun		*D. of Hamilton*
14	Campbell of Melfort	43	Hay
15	Campbell of Strachur		*E. of Erroll*
16	Carnegie	44	Home
16a	Chattan, Clan		*E. of Home*
17	Chisholm, Chisholme	45	Innes
	Chisholm of Chisholm		*Innes of that ilk*
18	Cockburn	46	Johnston, Johnstone
19	Colquhoun		*Johnston of that ilk and*
	Colquhoun of Luss		*Annandale*
20	Cranston	47	Kennedy
21	Crawford		*M. of Ailsa*
	Crawford of	48	Kerr
	Auchinames		*M. of Lothian*
22	Cumming	49	Lamond, Lamont
	L. of Alfyre		*Lamont of that ilk*
23	Cunningham	50	Lauder
	Cunningham of	51	Leslie
	Kilmaurs		*E. of Rothes*
24	Dalzell	52	Lindsay
25	Davidson		*E. of Crawford*
	Davidson of that ilk	53	Macalistair
	or Tulloch		*Macalistair of the Loup*
26	Douglas	54	MacAlpin, MacAlpine
	Douglas of Douglas	55	MacArthur
27	Drummond		*MacArthur of*
	E. of Perth		*Tirracladdich*
28	Dunbar	56	Macaulay
29	Dundas		*Macaulay of Ardincaple*
	Dundas of Dundas	57	MacBain
30	Elliot		*MacBean of that ilk*
	Elliot of Stobs	57a	MacBeth

57b	MacCallum		*Mackinnon of*
	D. of Argyll as		*Mackinnon*
	MacCallum More	88	Macmillan
58	MacDonald		*Macmillan of*
	L. MacDonald		*Macmillan*
59	MacDonald	89	Macnab
	MacDonald of		*Macnab of Macnab*
	Clanranald	90	MacNauchton
59a	MacDonald of Kintyre		*MacNaughton of*
60	MacDonald		*Dunderawe*
	MacDonald of Sleat	91	MacNeil
61	MacDonald		*MacNeil of Barra*
	MacDonald of	92	McNeil of Gigha
	Arnamurchan		*McNeil of Gigha*
62	MacDonell	93	MacNicol
	MacDonell of		*Nicolson of Scorrybreac*
	Glengarry	94	Macpherson
63	MacDonell		*Macpherson of Cluny*
	MacDonell of Keppoch	95	Macquarrie
64	Macdonell of Antrim		*Macquarrie of Ulva*
	E of Antrim	96	Macqueen
65	Macdonald of		*Macqueen of*
	Glencoe		*Corribrough*
66	MacDougall	97	Macrae
	MacDougall of	98	MacTavish
	MacDougall and		*MacTavish of*
	Dunollie		*MacTavish*
67	MacDuff	99	Malcolm
	Duff of Braco		*Malcolm of Poltulloch*
68	MacEwan or	99a	Matheson
	MacEwen	100	Maxwell
69	MacFarlan		*L. Hermes*
	MacFarlane of that ilk	101	Menzies
70	Macfie or Macfee		*Menzies of that ilk*
	MacDuffie of Colonsay	101a	Montgomerie
71	MacGillivray	102	Morison, Morrison
	MacGillivray of		*Morrison of Barras and*
	Dunmaglass		*Duneystein*
72	MacGregor	103	Munro or Munroe
	MacGregor of		*Munro of Foulis*
	MacGregor	104	Murray
73	Macinnes		*E. of Tullbardine, D. of*
74	Macintyre		*Atholl*
	Macintyre of Glen Noe	105	Ogilvie
75	Mackay		*E. of Airlie*
	Mackay of	106	Ramsay
	Strathnaver, L. Reay		*E. of Dalhousie*
76	Mackintosh	107	Robertson
	Mackintosh of		*Robertson of Struan*
	Mackintosh	108	Rollo
77	MacLachlan	109	Rose
	MacLachlan of		*Rose of Kilravock*
	MacLachlan	110	Ross
78	Maclaine		*Ross of that ilk*
	Maclaine of Lochbuie	111	Ruthven
79	MacLaren	112	Scott
	MacLaren of		*D. of Buccleuch*
	MacLaren	113	Seton
80	Maclean	114	Sinclair
	Maclean of Duart		*E. of Caithness*
80a	Maclean of Coll	115	Skene
81	Maclennan		*Skene of Skene*
	Logan of Drumderfit	116	Stewart
82	MacLeod of Harris		*Stewart of Appin*
	MacLeod of that ilk of	117	Stewart of Atholl
	Harris		*E. of Atholl*
83	MacLeod of Lewis	118	Stewart of Galloway
	MacLeod of Lewis		*E. of Galloway*
84	Macleod of Raasay	118a	Stewart of Garth
85	MacKenzie	119	Stuart of Bute
	MacKenzie of Kintail	120	Stuart, Royal
86	Mackinlay	121	Sutherland
	Mackinlay of		*Sutherland of that ilk*
	Kynachan	122	Urquhart
87	Mackinnon		*Urquhart of that ilk*

Abbot 89. Abbotson 89. Abernethy 51. Adam 36. Adamson 76. Adie 36. Airlie 105. Alexander 53, 62. Allan 59, 69. Allanson 59, 69. Allardice 37. Alpin 54. Anderson 110. Andrew 110. Angus 73. Arthur 15. Ayson 76.

MacNachdan 90. MacNachton 90. MacNaghten 90. MacNair 69, 90. MacNamell 66. MacNaughtan 90. MacNaughton 90. MacNayer 90. MacNeal 91, 92. MacNee 72. MacNellage 91. MacNeiledge 91. McNeil 92. MacNelly 91. MacNeur 69. MacNichol 8. MacNider 69. MacNie 72. MacNiel 91, 92. MacNish 72. MacNiter 69. MacNiven 22, 76, 90. MacNuir 90.

MacOmie 76. MacOmish 41. MacOnie 7. MacOran 14. MacOShannaig 59a. Macoul, Macowl 66. Macourlie 7. MacOwen 8.

MacPatrick 49, 79. MacPeter 72. MacPhail 7, 75, 76. MacPhater 79. MacPhedron 56. Macphee or Macphie 70. MacPheidiran 56. MacPhilip 63. MacPhorich 49. MacPhun 99a.

Macquaire 95. Macquey 75. Macquhirr 95. Macquire 95. MacQuistan 58. MacQuisten 58. Macquoid 75.

Macra 97. Macrach 97. Macraild 82. MacRaith 58, 97. MacRankin 80a. MacRath 97. Macritchie 76. MacRob 41, 69. MacRobb 69. Macrobbie, MacRobie 107. MacRobert 107. MacRorie, MacRory 58. MacRuer 58. MacRune, MacRury 58.

Macshannachan 58. MacSimes 35. MacSimon 35. MacSorley 7, 49, 58. MacSporran 58. MacSuain 96. MacSwan 96. MacSween, MacSwen 96. MacSwyde 96. MacSymon 35.

MacTaggart 110. MacTary 45. MacTause 8. MacTear 74, 110. MacThomas 8, 76. MacTier, MacTire 110.

MacUlric 7. MacUre 8.

Macvail 7, 76. MacVanish 85. MacVarish 59. MacVeugh, McVey 80. MacVean 57. MacVicar 90. MacVinish 85. MacVurie 59. MacVurrich 59, 94.

MacWalrick 7. MacWalter 69. MacWattie 6. MacWhannell 58. MacWhirr 95. MacWhirter 6. MacWilliam 41, 69.

Magrath 97. Mathie 99a. Mayor 45. May 58. Means 101. Meikleham 49. Mein of Meine 101. Mengues, Mennie 101 Menteith 37, 120. Meynefs 101. Michie 34. Middleton 45. Mill, Milne 36, 45, 105. Miller 69. Minn, Minus 103. Mitchell 45. Monach 69. Monro or Monroe 103. Monteith 37, 120 . Monzie 101. Moray 104. More 51. Morgan 75. Mowat 121. Munn 119. Murchie 6, 58, 85. Murchison 6, 58, 85. Murdoch 58, 94. Murdoson 58, 94.

Napier 69. Neal 91. Neil or Neill 91. Neilson 75. Neish 72. Nelson 41. Nicholl 83. Nicholson 83. Nicol or Nicoll 83. Nicolson 83. Nish 72. Niven 22, 76, 90. Noble 76. Norman 52.

O'Drain 58. Oliphant 121. O'May 58. O'Shaig 58. O'Shannachan 58. O'Shannaig 58.

Parlane 69. Paterson 79. Patrick 49. Paul 7, 75, 76. Peter 72. Philipson 63. Pitullich 58. Polson 75. Purcell 58.

Rae 97. Rankin 80a. Rattray 104. Reid 107. Reidfuird 45. Reoch 32, 58. Revic 58. Riach 32, 58. Risk 6. Ritchie 76. Robb 69. Robison, Robson 41. Ronald 63. Ronaldson 63. Rorison 58. Roy 107. Ruskin 6. Russell 22.

Sanderson 62. Sandison 41. Shannon 58. Shaw 76. Sim, Sime, Simon 35. Simpson 35. Small 104. Smith 16a. Sorley 7, 49, 58. Spalding 104. Spence, Spens 67. Spitall or Spittel 6. Sporran 58. Stalker 69. Stark 107. Steuart, Stuart 120. Swan 96. Swanson 41. Syme 35. Symon 35.

Taggart 110. Tarrill 76. Tawesson 8. Tawse 32. Taylor 7. Thain 45. Thomas 8, 76. Thomason 8, 69, 76. Thompson 8. Thoms 76. Thomson 8. Todd 36. Tolmie 84. Tonnochy 107. Tosh 76. Toshach 76. Toward, Towart 49. Train 58. Turner 49. Tweedie 35. Tyre 74.

Ure 8.

Vass 103, 110.

Wallace, Wallis. Warnebald 23. Wass 103, 110. Watson 6. Watt 6. Weaver 69. Weir 69, 90. Wemyss 67. Whannell 58. Wharrie 95. White or Whyte 49, 72. Williamson 41, 75. Wilson 41. Wright 74.

Yuill, Yuille 6. Yule 6.

CLAPHAM SECT was an influential group of serious minded evangelicals which started to gather round the Rev. John Venn (1759-1813), rector of Clapham in about 1790. It included William Wilberforce, Henry Thornton (1760-1815), gov. of the Bank of England; Granville Sharp (1735-1813) the philanthropist; John Shore, first L. Teignmouth (1751-1834) gov-gen. of India from 1793 to 1798; Charles Simeon (1759-1836) vicar of Holy Trinity, Cambridge; Zachary Macaulay and Hannah More (1745-1833) the playwright and, after 1788, evangelical propagandist. They inspired and founded the Church Missionary Society in 1797 and the British and Foreign Bible Society in 1804; they inveighed effectively against the slave trade and then against slavery itself and they encouraged and Hannah More founded free schools for the poor. They never advocated revolutionary methods of reform but relied with remarkable success upon the conversion of those interested in abuses.

CLARA EUGENIA, Infanta. *See* ELIZABETH I-32,33.

CLARE FAMILY was descended from a bastard of Richard the Fearless, D. of Normandy, but the English family's fortunes began with **(1) Richard Fitz Gilbert (?-c. 1090)** who came over with William I and was granted the lordship and castle of Clare (Suff.) As William's joint Justiciar, he suppressed the revolt of 1075 when William was in Normandy. He was succeeded by his son **(2) Richard (?-?)** who was the first of the family to adopt Clare as a surname. His son **(3) Gilbert (?-1114)** conquered extensive lands in Wales. Of his children the eldest **(4) Richard (?-1136)** was the ancestor of the Es. of Hertford and Gloucester while a younger son **(5) Gilbert (?-1148) E. of PEMBROKE and STRIGIL** established himself in Wales and was the father of the celebrated **(6) Richard (Strongbow) (c. 1130-76)** who had apparently lost most of his estates by 1168 when, probably, he met Dermot MacMurrough, lately driven from his kingdom of Leinster. Richard promised his assistance in return for the hand of Dermot's eldest daughter and the succession to Leinster. In 1170 Strongbow landed in Ireland with about 200 knights and 1000 foot, captured Waterford for Dermot and duly married Aoife (Eva), his daughter. Within weeks he took Dublin and then (May 1171) Dermot died. Strongbow, as Dermot's heir, was now confronted by all Dermot's enemies in Ireland and the hostility of Henry II who had already ordered all his subjects to return home. Moreover Roderick O'Connor of Connaught besieged him in Dublin. He was seeking terms from Roderick when a sudden sally drove the besiegers away. He then returned to England where Henry II accepted his renewed fealty and granted him most of Leinster other than Dublin, in fee. He then served with the King in Normandy during 1173 and 1174 and was rewarded with Wexford, Waterford and Dublin. His interests were inherited by his daughter **(7) Isabel (?-?)** who later married William Marshal whereby the earldom descended in the Marshal family, but he gained only a part of her father's estates because his Irish fief had been broken up. The son of **(4), (8) Gilbert (?-c. 1152) 1st E. of HERTFORD** (by a doubtful grant from K. Stephen) and his first descendents were S. Wales magnates of no great distinction, but his son **(9) Roger (?-?)** married Amice, daughter of William fitz Robert, E. of Gloucester, and so brought that earldom into the Clare family. **(10) Gilbert (1243-95)** "The Red", **E. of CLARE, HERTFORD and GLOUCESTER** was, after Simon de Montfort, the second leader of the Baronial party against Henry III. The negotiations before the B. of Lewes were conducted in his and Simon's name and they were denounced together as traitors; it was to Gilbert that the King surrendered his sword when he lost the battle. Within weeks the two earls had quarrelled over the treatment of royalist barons who had taken refuge in the Marches, and subsequently Gilbert too went over to them. Early in June 1265, after the Ld. Edward had escaped, he joined and fought for him at Kenilworth and Evesham, but sought to prevent the forfeiture of the estates of the vanquished. His vast lands passed at his death to his son **(11) Gilbert (?-1314)** who seems to have been as moderate in partisanship as his father. He took no side over the banishment of Gaveston, presumably because Gaveston had married his sister Margaret. He died fighting at Bannockburn. The estates were then divided between his sisters as parceners. The most celebrated of these was **(12) Elizabeth (?-1360)** commonly called ELIZABETH DE BURGH after her first husband John de Burgh. She outlived him and two others and devoted the wealth from her lordship of Clare to pious causes, especially the foundation of Clare College, Cambridge.

CLARE. *See* HOLLES.

CLARE ELECTION. *See* WELLINGTON GOVT.

CLARENCE. *See* GEORGE PLANTAGENET (1449-78); LIONEL OF ANTWERP (1338-68); THOMAS OF LANCASTER (1389-1421); WILLIAM IV.

CLARENCE HOUSE, built by John Nash for William IV as D. of Clarence, is part of the St. James's Palace complex and was a residence of Q. Elizabeth the Q. Mother after 1952.

CLARENCIEUX. *See* HERALDS.

CLARENDON (Wilts.), about 3 miles from Old Sarum, was a royal property in the centre of the Forest of Clarendon. In 1164 Henry II converted it from a hunting lodge into a palace to accommodate the Council which drew up the *Constitutions*. Henry III spent much on its refurbishment with paintings of the Exploits of Alexander the Great, the History of Antioch and the Combat between Richard I and Saladin. Excavations have revealed tile pavements and fine sculpture. 13th cent. Clarendon equalled the palaces at Guildford and Woodstock in beauty and importance.

CLARENDON, ASSIZE OF (1166), issued by Henry II instituted a system of investigation into serious crimes committed since 1154. Twelve men of each hundred and four of each township had to report on oath those suspected of being robbers, murderers, thieves or harbourers of such. Gaols were to be erected to house those caught. It also contained instructions for Justices in Eyre, who began a tour of the country immediately afterwards. The assize was revised and reissued from **NORTHAMPTON** in 1176 (when forgers and arsonists were added). It was repeated in the Assize issued by Hubert Walter in 1195 which also imposed sanctions against failing to follow the Hue and Cry, and required all above the age of 15 to swear to keep the peace before Knights especially assigned for the purpose. William the Lion's **POLICE ASSIZES** of 1175 and 1197 followed the pattern of the English assizes of 1166 and 1195.

CLARENDON. *See* HYDE: VILLIERS.

"CLARENDON CODE" (1661-5), despite its name, was opposed by Charles II and Edw. Hyde, 1st E. of CLARENDON, who was Lord Chancellor when its five acts were passed. **(1) The Corporation Act 1661** which required all holders of municipal office (a) to renounce the Solemn League and Covenant, a test which excluded most presbyterians; (b) to take the oath of non-resistance, which excluded Republicans and (c) to take the Anglican sacraments which excluded R. Catholics and some nonconformists. As many municipal corporations elected M.P.s and the rest could influence such elections, this weighted the scales in borough elections heavily in favour of the royalists: it was repealed in 1828. **(2) The Act of Uniformity (1662)** required all clergy to make a declaration of assent and consent to everything contained in the Elizabethan Book of Common Prayer as amended by the convocations and required all teachers in schools and universities to conform to the Liturgy contained in it. About 2,000 mostly presbyterian clergy (out of 10,000 in all) refused the declaration and were ejected (*see* BARTHOLOMEW'S DAY, ST.). **(3) The Conventicle Act, 1664,** made meetings of more than five persons (in addition to a household) for worship illegal unless conducted in accordance with the Book of Common Prayer. It was aimed at the ejected ministers, many of whose congregations followed them. A further **(4) Act of 1670**

mitigated the penalties but simplified the powers of repression. Never very effective, both were repealed by the **Toleration Act, 1689. (5) The Five Mile Act, 1665,** forbade any minister of religion to come within five miles of any city or town corporate or any place where he had preached or held a living, unless he took the oath of non resistance and declared that he would not attempt any alteration in the govt. of church or state. This deprived dissenting congregations of their ministers and, because they were mostly in towns, made it hard for dissenters to get religious ministrations acceptable to them. The group of villages on the site of modern Birmingham happened to be more than five miles from any of the places mentioned in the Act, and so became the focus of midland nonconformity. This in its turn hindered the erection of Birmingham into a borough. Clarendon and Charles II, with his brother James, wished, for different reasons, for greater toleration: James in particular to allow the spread of R. Catholicism (*see* DECLARATION OF INDULGENCE). The "Code" reflected the country gentry's reasonable belief than an Anglican political settlement would protect them against a puritan dictatorship, which they had experienced, and the Caesaro-Papalism which they saw developing across the Channel.

CLARENDON COMMISSION (1861) reported on the state of nine greater public schools. These were in process of reforming themselves and the commission's proposals (affecting only Eton, Winchester, Charterhouse, Harrow, Westminster, Rugby and Shrewsbury) were mostly overtaken by events.

CLARENDON, CONSTITUTIONS OF (1164) were drawn up after research and discussion in the *curia regis* but show evidence of compromise. They are described as a "record of the customs, liberties and dignities of the Kings predecessors" particularly of his grandfather K. Henry which ought to be kept and observed in the Kingdom "for the avoidance of disputes between lay and ecclesiastical authorities and as being made in the King's presence" and that of a lengthy list of lay and clerical magnates. The 16 clauses may be considered in four groups: **(1)** *to prevent excessive church interference in royal policy* (Cl.4) ecclesiastics were not to leave the realm without royal licence and might be required to give security for good behaviour abroad; (Cl.7) The King's Tenants in Chief and principal household officers were not to be excommunicated or their lands interdicted before the King had an opportunity to refer the issue to the appropriate royal or ecclesiastical court and (Cl.10) a similar provision permitting interdict but not excommunication related to tenants of royal estates, castles and towns; (Cl.8) appeals to Rome were not to proceed without royal assent. **(2)** *to protect the royal revenue and influence* (Cl.11) ecclesiastical tenants in chief were to hold their baronies subject to the same conditions as other baronies; and (Cl.2) the royal assent was required to the permanent alienation of churches held of the King. (Cl.12) The King was entitled to the revenues of vacant sees, abbacies and priories and elections to these were to be held in the royal chapel by persons summoned for the purpose. Those elected had to give fealty and do homage saving their order, before consecration. (Cl.14) Goods forfeit to the King were not to be detained by ecclesiastical bodies. **(3)** *to maintain royal jurisdiction in matters of property,* (Cl.1) disputes about advowsons and presentations and (Cl.9) whether (*utrum*) property is held by a lay tenure or in frankalmoign and (Cl.15) pleas of debt, even involving issues of conscience, were reserved to the royal courts. **(4)** *to maintain public order* (Cl.13) the King was to restore ecclesiastical rights usurped by nobles, and the church was to join in restoring usurped royal rights generally; (Cl.13) accused clerics were to appear before a royal justice and then be tried in the ecclesiastical court, if necessary in the presence of a royal officer, and conviction there was not to protect the criminous cleric against civil punishment; on the other hand (Cl.5) excommunicates were disqualified as sureties and compurgators but (Cl.6) laymen were to be accused only by reputable named persons in the presence of the bishop, though not so as to deprive the archdeacon of his rights, and if people dared not bring an individual to justice, the sheriff might empanel 12 men of the vicinity to declare the truth in the bishop's presence; and finally (Cl. 16) villeins' sons were not to be ordained without their lord's consent. Abp. Becket had, of course, habitually infringed the provisions in group (1). Cl.14 (group 2), Cl.15 (group 3) and Cl.6 (group 4) represented efforts to suppress growing extensions of church jurisdiction or its abuse, while Cls. 3 and 16 (group 4) were concerned with the abuse of ecclesiastical privileges. Becket objected histrionically to Cl.3, against the weight of contemporary canonist opinion. Alexander III felt bound to support him in condemning it (Decretal *At si clerici*) but Innocent III, the most ultramontane of Popes, reversed Alexander's condemnation (*Novimus*). In practice only the limitation on appeals to Rome was destroyed by the Becket crisis.

CLARENDON PRESS (Oxford). *See* OXFORD UNIVERSITY PRESS.

CLARET. *See* WINE TRADE.

CLARKE, George Sydenham (1848-1933) 1st Ld. SYDENHAM (1913) passed first into and first out of Woolwich and entered the Royal Engineers. His talents were soon recognised. In 1885 he reported prophetically against the armoured cupola forts at Bucharest, preferring the Turkish earthworks. He was sec. of the Navy and Army Administration Commission (1888-90) and favoured inter-service co-operation. From 1901 to 1903 he was Gov. of Victoria and then was a member of the War Office Reconstitution Committee in 1904, and in 1907 he became Gov. of Bombay. As a Liberal the non co-operation of self-styled Indian liberals such as Tilak disappointed him and when they preached violence he used the heavy hand and was duly criticised for it; meanwhile he affected great material improvements such as paving and sewering Bombay and laying the foundations for the Sukkur barrage. In the end Indians came to respect and consult him. He retired in 1913, but acted as chairman of the Royal Commission on Venereal Diseases. He was disappointed that the govt. would not employ him in World War I. After the war in speeches and writings he expressed his pessimistic view of the future of the British Empire and of western civilisation.

"CLARKE, John". *See* CROMWELL-2.

CLARKSON, Thomas (1760-1846) began his lifelong and powerful campaign against slavery with a prize essay in 1786. He urged abolition upon the French during the Revolution and upon the Czar in 1818.

CLASS. Overworked term of collective differentiation connoting either **(1)** the hierarchical differences, of mediaeval origin, between nobles, gentry, commons and serfs or **(2)** an English, mostly tacit, social classification related to education at a public school as opposed to any other, and sometimes marked by a difference of speech or accent, or **(3)** the Marxist division by economic function in a prerevolutionary society into workers, capitalists and a middle or distributing group, or **(4)** the grouping created in a socialist society by fission between a privileged party bureaucracy or New Class and the rest or **(5)** the N. American tacit differentiation based on the size of a person's bank balance and the use which he makes of the money.

CLASSES, ACT OF 1649 (Scots) excluded from Scots public office and military command Hamilton's party (The ENGAGERS) and other royalists. It made Charles II dependent upon Argyll and the sterner presbyterians who, trusting too much in the Lord of Hosts and excluding good potential soldiers, contributed to their own defeat at Dunbar. Its repeal in Jan. 1651 cleared the

way for Charles II's coronation at Scone and the broader based, if unsuccessful, Worcester campaign.

CLASSICAL ASSN. was founded in 1903 to arrest the decline of classical studies.

CLASSIS BRITANNICA. *See* BRITAIN, ROMAN-7,20.

CLAUSE FOUR of the 1918 Labour Party constitution committed the party to nationalisation of large industries. By the 1950s some, including Gaitskell, thought that this commitment was too rigid and also damaging to the party's electoral prospects. Proposals to drop it aroused strong opposition, decisive at the time. After Gaitskell's death the controversy continued to have disruptive effects into the 1990s.

CLAUSENTUM. *See* SOUTHAMPTON.

CLAUSEWITZ, Karl von (1780-1831) as a student at the Berlin young officers' school got to know and was respected by Scharnhorst. He saw low-ranking service in the Napoleonic Wars and became a maj-gen. and director of military schools only in 1818. He never saw active service after 1815. He wrote two distinguished campaign studies and especially a *Life and Character of Scharnhorst* which he published in 1832 simultaneously with his famous monograph *On War*. The latter, a unified theory of tactics in relation to strategy and strategy in relation to politics and economics, though a separate book, was drawn from his interpretation of Scharnhorst's career in the context of the Prussian defeat and revival. Since the Prussian victory over Austro-Hungary in 1866 no staff college has been without it.

CLAVEL, John (1603-42), a well connected highwayman, was condemned in 1627 and then pardoned. He left a metrical autobiography (*A Recantation of an Ill-led Life*) describing the rules and organisation of highway bandits, warning inn-keepers and travellers of their ways and appearance.

CLAYMORE (Gael = Great Sword). A two-handed sword used by Scots highlanders. Not to be confused with the single-handed Broadsword.

CLAYPOOLE (1) Elizabeth (1629-58) 2nd *d.* of Oliver Cromwell, married in 1646 **(2) John (?-1688)** who raised a parliamentary troop in 1651 and became Oliver's Master of the Horse. He was an M.P. in 1654 and a peer in 1657. In the parliament of 1656 his attack on the rule of the major-generals was seen as a signal from his father-in-law. She is said to have developed an unpleasant arrogance on her father's elevation, yet to have exercised a moderating influence in favour of dissidents including presbyterians and royalists.

CLAYTON, Sir Robert (1629-1707), self-made City of London financier and alderman from 1670 to 1689, he was an associate of Shaftesbury, a strong exclusionist and on the City delegation which met William of Orange in 1688. He was a City member of the Convention parliament of 1689 besides later parliaments, a Commissioner of Customs and a Director of the Bank of England. He had already founded the R. Mathematical School in 1673 to train boys as navigators. Very rich by 1690, as Pres. of St. Thomas' Hospital and Christ's Hospital (a school) he contributed to their reconstruction.

CLAYTON-BULWER T. (1850). Britain and the U.S.A. agreed jointly to guarantee the neutrality of an isthmian canal (probably to be built in Nicaragua) and neither to seek control of the isthmus, erect fortifications nor acquire new C. American colonies. The canal was not built and the treaty was made obsolete by U.S. C. American imperialism manifested in the Spanish American War of 1898 and the intrigues in Colombia leading to the Panama revolution. *See* HAY-PAUNCEFOTE T. (1901).

"CLEANSE THE CAUSEWAY". *See* JAMES V OF SCOTS-1.

CLEARANCES, HIGHLAND (Scot). The dispossession of Highland crofters, which began for the purpose of getting rid of Jacobites after the B. of Culloden, and continued in order to breed sheep. Many migrated to Canada.

CLEARING HOUSE, LONDON BANKERS was first established in 1770.

CLEMENCEAU, Georges (1841-1929) ('The Tiger') was a French radical statesman and prime minister in the difficult years 1917-8 when French military morale had to be upheld by a ruthless determination. He was not popular, but respected as a strong man. He presided vengefully over the Paris Peace Conference in 1919 and left office in 1920. His wartime relationship with Lloyd George, another ruthless politician, was excellent, but being the kind of patriot which he was, took a more grasping line on German reparations and, because of the old French pro-Polish sentiment, a more aggressive line on Bolshevism; this included the unfortunate loan of Gen. Weygand to the Poles, who fortunately ignored his advice.

CLEMENT V Pope (r. 1305-14). VI Pope (r. 1342-52). *See* AVIGNON POPES.

CLEMENT VII Pope (r. 1523-34), was a son of Giuliano de' Medici. This worldly and intelligent man was intent on defending papal political and territorial interests. He first sided with the French against Charles V and so in 1527 provoked the occupation and sack of Rome; and then, being in the power of Charles V, he prevaricated over Henry VIII's divorce of Catharine of Aragon in 1529. As a Medici he patronised the leading artists including Michelangelo, Raphael and Benvenuto Cellini. Preoccupied with politics and culture, he failed in his primary pastoral function of reforming the church; thus protestantism rapidly gained ground in Europe and papal authority was virtually ended in England.

CLERGY DISCIPLINE ACT 1892. The clergy are expected not to commit crimes or engage in extra-marital sex and on proof of such acts in an ordinary court, are liable to deprivation. They can also be prosecuted under the Act by a parishioner before the consistory court for an immoral act and conviction empowers the bishop to suspend or deprive them.

CLERICAL SUBSCRIPTION. The rule that a parson must declare his acceptance of the XXXIX Articles by subscribing his signature as a condition of ordination into the Church of England and of preferment. Instituted by canon in 1604 in a rigorous form, the declaration was modified by an Act of 1865.

CLERICIS LAICOS (1296), a very short bull of Pope Boniface VIII forbade lay taxation of the clergy without papal authorisation and automatically excommunicated all concerned in unauthorised taxation. It had been received but not promulgated in England when Edward I demanded a clerical subsidy. The clergy refused but Edward, regardless, ordered its collection. The clergy were thus put in a dilemma: excommunication if they paid, seizure of their lands if they resisted. Abp. Winchelsea threatened to excommunicate Edward, who stood his ground, and finally gained the subsidy on the pretext of necessity and because lay protests throughout Europe had caused the Pope to issue the face saving bull *ETSI DE STATU* (July 1297) bringing within the authorisations envisaged by *Clericis laicos* states of emergency, which were to be defined by the ruler.

CLERKENWELL (London) was so-called after the Clerk's Well beside St. Mary's nunnery. This was the scene of mediaeval miracle plays performed by the parish clerks. The priory of St. John of Jerusalem was nearby, both priory and nunnery having been founded in the 12th cent.

CLERKS OR CLERICS. In the middle ages bishops, priests, deacons and, after 1207, subdeacons were clerks in Holy or Major Orders; porters, lectors, cantors, exorcists and acolytes were clerks in Minor Orders. They were all entitled to ecclesiastical privileges, but the latter were not bound to celibacy. There were many public officials of varying eminence each known as a Clerk. The principal ones were:

Administrative and Household: Of the King's House: a financial official of the household: **Of the Acts:** secretary of the Admiralty: **Of the Cheque:** responsible for yeomen at court: **Of the Pells:** an exchequer official who entered receipts and payments: **Of the Pipe:** an exchequer official who kept the Pipe Roll and passed the Sheriff's accounts: **Of the Signet:** effectively the Private Secretary of the principal Sec. of State: **Of the Crown:** *inter alia*, the Lord Chancellor's secretary and custodian of parliamentary writs.

Parliamentary: Of the House of Commons: the secretary of that body: **Of the Parliaments:** the secretary to the House of Lords: **Register, Lord:** a hereditary official who acted as clerk of the Scots Parliament and presided over the election of Scottish Representative peers.

Judicial: Of the Peace: the administrative officer of Quarter Sessions: **Of Arraigns:** the Court Officer in charge of criminal indictments.

CLERMONT, COUNCIL OF (1095). *See* CRUSADES-3.

CLEVELAND, Duchess of. *See* VILLIERS.

CLEVELAND, Stephen Grover (1837-1908) Tariff reforming Pres. of the U.S.A. 1885-9 and 1893-7 (Democrat).

CLEVELAND MESSAGE (17 Dec. 1895). *See* JAMESON RAID-2.

CLEVES (Ger.) This county passed to the Counts of La Marck in 1368, was made a duchy in 1417 and combined in 1521 with the duchies of Jülich and Berg. These faced each other across the Rhine near the Dutch frontier with only a narrow corridor of the ecclesiastical Electorate of Cologne in between, and comprised important parts of the modern Ruhr. As early converts the dukes represented the best placed and greatest Lutheran power in W. Germany. They were the focus of intense manoeuvring among major powers when it became apparent that the last Duke would die (as he did in 1609) without heirs. In 1614, by the Compromise of Xanten, Cleves alone passed to Brandenburg but the other duchies remained objects of controversial diplomacy, especially between Brandenburg-Prussia and Austria, for over a century. *See* ANNE OF CLEVES; BRANDENBURG; JÜLICH.

CLIFFORD. Of this rich family of R. Catholic landowners in Devon. **Thomas (1630-73) 1st Ld. CLIFFORD of CHUDLEIGH (1672)** was M.P. for Totnes from 1660, fought in several naval actions and then, partly by Arlington's interest, was Comptroller of the Household from 1666 to 1668, a commissioner of the Treasury from 1667 to 1672 and Treasurer of the Household from 1668. He was one of a group of so-called 'young men' who opposed and steadily undermined Clarendon. In 1669 he became a member of the 'Cabal'. As Charles II's financial adviser he was mainly responsible for the secret T. of Dover (1670) and from Nov. 1672 to June 1673 he was Lord Treasurer. He championed the King's Declaration of Indulgence and was forced to resign under the Test Act as a declared R. Catholic. He apparently committed suicide.

CLIFFORD (1) Walter (?-1190) Ld. CLIFFORD, a border magnate, was sporadically at war with the Welsh from about 1157 to 1164. His *d.* the celebrated **(2)** Fair **Rosamond (?-1176)** was Henry II's mistress. She lived with him at Woodstock but was not, as was supposed, poisoned by Q. Eleanor. The family continued to prosper and **(3) Robert (1273-1314) 5th Ld. and 1st Ld. WESTMORELAND** acquired lands in Westmorland and from 1297 was Forest Justice north of the Trent, gov. of Carlisle and warden of the Western March. He captured Caerlaverock from the Scots in 1300, acquired some of Bruce's English estates in 1306 and became Castellan of Skipton in 1310. Though a friend of Edward II, he joined the opposition in 1311 but made his peace and, after failing to relieve Stirling, was killed at Bannockburn. **(4) Roger (1333-89) 9th Ld. and 5th Ld. WESTMORELAND (1352),** a soldier, fought in Flanders (1345-50), Gascony (1355 and 1359-66) and Ireland (1361 and 1368). From 1370 he was also a warlike warden of the Western Marches and from 1377 gov. of Carlisle. He died on campaign in Brittany. His son **(5) Thomas (?-1391) 10th and 6th Ld.**, an adherent of Richard II, succeeded his father as warden and gov. but was driven into exile and killed in Germany. **(6) Thomas (1414-55) 12th and 8th Ld. (1422)**, another soldier, campaigned with Bedford in France in 1435, relieved Calais in 1452 and 1454 and was among the Lancastrians killed at the B. of St. Albans. His son **(7)** Butcher **John (?1435-61) 13th and 9th Ld.**, raised a force to avenge his father in 1458; reached an agreement with the Yorkists and was attainted with them in 1459. In 1460 the attainder was reversed to win him back to the Lancastrians with whom he sided at the B. of Wakefield (1460). He fell at Ferrybridge under a Yorkist attainder. His son **(8) Henry (?1455-1523)** was brought up as a shepherd and only restored as **14th and 10th Ld.** in 1485 on a further reversal of the attainder. He pacified Yorkshire in 1486 and became in addition first **Ld. VESCI** and commanded a detachment at Flodden in 1513. His son **(9) Henry or Harry (1493-1542), 15th, 11th and 2nd Ld.** and first **E. of CUMBERLAND (1525)**, a page of Henry VIII, commanded against the Scots in 1522 and was warden of the Western March from 1523 to 1534. He supported Henry's divorce in 1529, took Skipton from the Pilgrimage of Grace in 1536 and was given vast church estates. His son **(10) Henry (?-1570), 2nd E.**, lived on his estates after 1547 and was an ineffectual partisan of Mary Q. of Scots in 1569. His son **(11) George (1558-1605), 3rd E.**, wasted the estates as a gambler and court favourite and spent much of his life after 1585 as an unsuccessful privateer. He had been a ward of Francis, 2nd E. of Bedford, whose daughter **(12) Margaret (1560-1616)** he married. They separated and their daughter **(13) Anne (1590-1676)** during a quarrelsome marriage with Richard Sackville, 3rd E. of Dorset, was much involved in litigation with her parents' creditors. She claimed the Lordship of Clifford in 1628 and in 1630 married, equally unhappily, Philip Herbert, E. of Montgomery and Pembroke, a prominent parliamentarian. She got possession of the Clifford properties in 1643 which thus passed to the Herbert family.

CLINK was a prison in Southwark destroyed in the Gordon riots of 1780.

CLINTON, Edward Fiennes de (1512-85) 9th Ld. CLINTON (1517) 1st E. of LINCOLN (1572) married in 1534 Elizabeth Blount, widow of Lord Talboys and mother of Henry VIII's bastard, Henry Fitzroy, D. of Richmond. He served afloat under L. Lisle (later D. of Northumberland) in the Scottish and Boulogne expeditions of 1544 and in the Channel in 1545. In 1547 he commanded the fleet which co-operated with Somerset's invasion of Scotland and, as the last Gov. of Boulogne (1547-50), his unsupported but effective defence earned him the post of Lord High Admiral and other minor or lucrative offices including the Tower and the Lord Lieutenancy of Lincolnshire. Expected to support the Dudleys, he in fact made peace with Mary I and in 1554 helped to suppress the Wyatt rebellion. He commanded a contingent at St. Quentin in 1557. Mary had deprived him of the Admiralty, but now reinstated him to command the fleet in the Channel. He retained the office at Q. Elizabeth's accession. He commanded the army, with Warwick, against the Northern Rebellion (1569) and mobilised the fleet in connection with the papal excommunication of the queen in 1570. He retired to comfortable courtiership after attending the marriage of Marguerite of France with Henry of Navarre in 1572.

CLINTON, William Jefferson (1946-) was an Oxford Rhodes Scholar, and thereafter a practising and academic lawyer. He entered US politics as a Democrat and, despite his almost childish appearance, from 1979 to 1981 and from 1983 to 1992 he was Gov. of Arkansas. In 1993 he was elected Pres. of the U.S.A.. A shrewd political tactician with a sub-imperialist foreign policy, attacks on his moral character (related to corruption in Arkansas and sexual adventures at the White House) failed to damage his position or party.

CLIPPER, originally any very fast sailing ship, was first an American Baltimore schooner used to run the British blockade in 1812 and later in the slave trade. They had long low hulls, deeper astern than forward, with a sharp-raked stem and overhanging counter. The first square-rigged clipper was built in 1832 but the first true clipper was the *Rainbow* of New York (1845). The gold rushes in California (1949) and Australia (1850) with the opening of the English China trade in between, created a tremendous demand for fast passages which the Americans monopolised until the 1857 slump and the American Civil War (1861-5). British clippers then overtook them, particularly on the valuable tea trade. As London tea prices rose steadily towards each autumn, the first China tea-clipper home got the best price for its cargo. Accordingly they raced from Foochow to London (16,000 miles). The voyage took about 180 days, the rivals generally docking within hours of each other. The opening of the Suez Canal (1869) undermined the system, though the most famous race between the *Thermopylae* and the *Cutty Sark* took place in 1872. Thereafter the clippers carried wool from Australia, the *Cutty Sark* until 1895, and then, save as training ships, went out of service.

CLIVE (1) Robert (1725-74) 1st Ld. CLIVE (Ir. 1762) set out for India in 1743 but, being blown to Brazil, was detained there for nine months and learned a little Portuguese. When he reached Madras in 1744 he was in debt and his single introduction had left. After two years of poorly paid boredom, war broke out with France in 1746. He escaped from surrendered Madras, volunteered and became notorious for quarrelsomeness and courage at Boscawen's siege of Pondicherry in 1748. After the P. of Aix-la-Chapelle he returned to his clerkship with the HEIC but immediately volunteered for a military expedition to restore the rajah of Tanjore. His reckless courage at Devicotab changed the direction of his career, for the commander of the expedition, Stringer Lawrence, found him a quasi-military post as commissary and thereafter, as one of the few Europeans, he was constantly in charge of troops. In 1748 there were disputed successions in the *Suba* of the Deccan and its vassal the Carnatic. The French supported Mirzaffa Jung, the grandson of the late Subadhar, against Nazir Jung, his son; and Chanda Sahib, the son-in-law of the late Nawab of the Carnatic, against his son, Anwar-ud-Din. The British took the opposite side. The two pretenders joined forces and, strengthened by the French, beat their rivals at Ambur (Aug. 1749). Anwar-ud-Din was killed, but his second son took refuge in Trichinopoly. Mutineers killed Nazir Jung and then his rival Mirzaffa Jung. The French were already strong in Hyderabad and if Trichinopoly, now besieged by Chanda Sahib, fell, the chances of British survival would be slight. Clive was sent with 500 men and three guns to reinforce it, but proposed an attack on Arcot, the capital of the Carnatic instead. The enemy fled because he marched through a furious thunderstorm (Aug. 1751), but returned heavily reinforced with troops diverted from Trichinopoly and besieged him for seven weeks. Their failure was decisive in S. Indian history, for it reduced French prestige and enabled the British to regain their strength for the subsequent wars around Madras. With prestige and promotion, he was now profiting and trading on his own account in partnership with the future Company historian Robt. Orme. In 1753 he returned, rich, to England, was much fêted for his exploits and entered politics on Henry Fox's advice, but his election to parliament was overturned, so he went back to India as Lieut-Gov. of

Fort St. David in Dec. 1755. In June 1756 Calcutta fell to Suraj-ud-Dowlah. The 'Black Hole' incident followed. Clive was promptly put in charge of the counter-measures and sailed with 900 British and 1500 Indian troops from Madras in Oct. He took Hooghli, the French settlement at Chandernagore, and while Eyre Coote retook Calcutta, he won the extraordinary complex of intrigue, chicanery and fighting known as the B. of PLASSEY (June 1757). The HEIC in consequence made him Gov. of its Bengal possessions while Mir Jafir, the Nawab, gave him £250,000 and, as a Jagir, the £30,000 a year paid by the HEIC for Bengal. Shortly afterwards he fought and beat the Dutch. In 1760 he again went home, becoming M.P. for Shrewsbury and sponsoring his father and his associate, John Walsh, into Parliament. He also had a powerful holding in the HEIC, but contentious company politics and a feud with the leading civilian director, Lawrence Sullivan, soured the rest of his life. His enemies in the Co. challenged and confiscated his jaghirs and until 1774 HEIC politics revolved around Clive's attempts to secure his fortune. In 1763 his political influence and friendship with George Grenville secured the Indian clauses of the P. of Paris, especially those concerning the exclusion of French forces from Bengal and the N. Circars. During this period Bengal had deteriorated under his corrupt and uninspiring successors. Extortion and incompetence had disorganised trade, there had been a terrible massacre of Europeans at Patna, and a war with Oudh and Mir Jafir's successor, Mir Kassim, was going badly. Clive was asked to return and accepted on condition that the existing Chairman of the HEIC, Sullivan, should be replaced. His 22 month second governorship (1765-6) was almost as important as his first. Civil servants were to be paid properly and forbidden to trade privately or accept presents. The HEIC took over the defence of Bengal and the Nawab's army was disbanded. He restored discipline in the HEIC's army. He secured a *firman* conferring the Dewani of Bengal on the HEIC and out of the revenue he paid the Nawab a fixed amount for his expenses and the cost of justice. This Dewani vastly enlarged the HEIC's income and political importance, but exacerbated corruption at home and in India and misgovernment in Bengal, for which, despite Clive's reforms, he was unfortunately blamed. On his return, in poor health, he was naturally the target of much abuse and accusation, to which he eventually replied in a well known speech in the Commons. A parliamentary inquiry, completed in May 1773, found that he had received large sums, but had done great and meritorious service to the state. He died, perhaps by his own hand, a year later. His son **(2) Edward (1754-1839)** 2nd Lord, and **1st Ld. CLIVE (Eng. 1794) 1st E. of POWIS** of the second creation (1804), was gov. of Madras from 1798 to 1803 and as such provided the financial and administrative backing for Wellesley's (later Wellington's) campaigns against Mysore, the Pindaris and the Marathas, and he carried out the annexation of the Carnatic. A dependable but not brilliant man, he retained unusual physical vigour until very late in life.

CLIVEDEN SET. *See* ASTOR.

CLOCKS. The scientist Pope Sylvester II built a weight-driven example in A.D. 996 and water clocks called 'horologes' existed at St. Pauls and at Westminster at the end of the 13th cent. Weight-driven apparatus for striking the hours (Ger: *Glocke* = bell) spread from Italy and reached England in about 1386 when a patent was granted to three clockmakers from Delft. The first pendulum apparatus was completed by Huygens in 1656: the dead-beat escapement by Geo. Graham in 1715. The three-legged gravity escapement was introduced by E. B. Denison into Big Ben in 1859. Electric clocks, though devised as early as 1894, came into use only in the years 1918 to 1922. The proliferation of timekeepers of all kinds had enormous social and industrial effects, e.g. fast transport could be scheduled, employment hours standardised and payments regulated, a generally more strenuous (if not necessarily beneficial) way of life and such expedients as daylight saving, introduced. The most advanced examples are now atomic clocks used as master timekeepers. *See* CHRONOMETER.

CLONTARF. *See* PEEL'S SECOND GOVT.-4.

CLOSED SHOP. The restriction of employment under a given employer or in a particular department (or "shop") of a business to members of a particular trade union. Originally a tactic designed to protect workers against wage variations and strike breakers, closed shops were found mostly in industry under agreements forced on employers by threat of, or actual, strikes, or by the semi-strikes known as 'go slow' or 'work to rule'. The agreements often provided that no new worker should be employed in a shop without the consent of the shop. A price was commonly extracted for such consent, such as a direct increase in wages or an indirect increase through a reduction in official working hours and consequent payment of overtime pay (at a higher rate) for necessary work outside them. This in its turn encouraged slow or inefficient working, for the less done in official hours, the more overtime was needed to make up shortfalls. Closed shops thus led to a slow attrition of industry and of the workers' general prosperity. The Thatcher govt. (1979-91) made it illegal for a closed shop to be imposed in any given business without the consent (given through an independently conducted secret ballot) of 85% of those employed in it. This made it legally impossible for a trade union to coerce an employer or the employees by means of direct or secondary strikes. See also HARRIS TWEED. CLOSED SHOP.

CLOSE ROLLS were records of closed (or folded) letters under the Great Seal directed to particular persons for particular purposes and not considered suitable for public inspection. They included certain writs to sheriffs, but private persons often had their own deeds and conveyances enrolled on the back of the Close Rolls for safety. Over 20,000 survive from 1204 onwards.

CLOSURE. *House of Commons* **(1)** In 1880 and 1881 Irish M.P.s prolonged discussion to compel action on their country's grievances and to resist the Irish Coercion Bill. Business became so congested that the Annual Army Act might have expired and no Finance Bill passed. No agreement short of abject concessions seemed possible with the Irish and thereupon the Gladstone govt. adopted the expedient of limiting debate by resolution (Nov. 1882). Such limitations on debate take two forms. (a) **The Guillotine** is a simple motion during a debate that the "Question be put". If carried the debate on that question ends and the question is voted on. Such a resolution is not debatable, but cannot be moved without a quorum. (b) **The Kangaroo** is a timetable resolution moved in advance and laying down the moments when particular stages in a given piece of business must end. Its effect is to limit the number of speakers and inferentially to confine debate to the more important personalities; in a committee or report stage it forces the opposition to press only those amendments which it deems most important. Thus politically minor matters which may be technically or socially important tend either to be missed or to be settled by negotiation between interested parties outside Parliament. Timetable motions are debateable and often passionately debated. It is the nature of closure motions that, save for guillotines on private members business, in practice only the govt. will move them and that they will not be carried without a whip. They have consequently strengthened the disciplinary features of party govt. At the same time the limitations on debate have been slightly mitigated by the Speaker's complementary power to select amendments at the Report stage, so that discussion in a timetabled committee will not invariably cause a particular amendment to be stifled.

(2) The precedent of 1882 was adopted by later Liberal and then Labour govts. to put extensive programmes of controversial legislation through the parliamentary machine, to the detriment of minorities; these had to rely increasingly for protection on the House of Lords and the likelihood of reversal at a later date. After World War II this was wearing thin. The steel industry, for example, was nationalised, partly denationalised and then renationalised.

House of Lords **(3)** A peer cannot be expelled from the House, but there is an ancient form of Closure motion which brings to an end a contumacious peer's activities on a particular issue. This is a motion that he 'be no longer heard'. In addition there is a type of curtailment of debate which has the same effect as a closure. When the date of a prorogation is known, debate in the Lords has to be ended so that bills can be passed and presented for the Royal Assent. Failure to end the debate automatically kills the outstanding bills and would in controversial cases provoke a political crisis. Some hundreds of amendments to the Local Govt. Bill were passed in 20 minutes before the prorogation of parliament in 1972.

CLOTA. The Roman name for the R. Clyde.

CLOTHING (*see* TEXTILES). **(1)** clothes were required for protection or vanity or modesty. It is supposed that furs and skins, products of a hunting economy, enabled temperate zone dwellers to penetrate colder climates, while textiles later permitted movement into hotter areas and were the product of a more settled agricultural life. In either case fabrication techniques were always related to the individual user and maker (unless, like the Scottish plaid, the design was very simple) being confined, apart from minor accessories, to the use of punches and hooks, for drawing thongs through skins, knives and scissors, and for textiles, bone, and in the Middle Ages, iron needles. Hand work remained the only method of fabrication until the early 19th cent. During this long period styles were seldom, if ever, dominated by cut, because cloth was never sufficiently uniform in weight or tension. Uniformity was based upon habit and general design, diversity upon ornament. The popinjay appearance of earlier fashionable clothing distracted attention from its poor fit. Moreover washing was either only partially effectual or destructive. A Roman toga, a woollen garment always washed white, usually with fuller's earth, lasted about a year. Soap, though known to the Romans, came into widespread use only in the late 18th cent.

(2) The mass production of textiles after 1770 rapidly outran the capacity of tailors, dressmakers and their assistants to make clothes. Sewing constituted the obvious bottleneck and in 1830 the Parisian Barthelemy Thimonnier began making uniforms with a bank of single thread sewing machines which were naturally destroyed by a mob. Elias Howe, an American, ran into similar trouble in the U.S.A. with his hand-operated lockstitch machine and sold his patents in England. Isaac Singer's famous pedal driven machine came into use in the U.S.A. in 1851. This transferred the bottleneck to cutting. The band knife was introduced to England in 1860, but could not be fully exploited until spreading machines, introduced at Bradford, could be trusted, after 1895, to lay the cloth accurately. At the turn of the century mechanical solutions were also found to the problems of pressing and buttons.

(3) This sequence of events kept garment mass production in English and American proprietorship well into the mid-20th cent., but being always labour intensive, it tended to be the resort of refugee labour, sometimes sweated. In addition the reputation of English bespoke tailors was pre-eminent until World War I; until 1914 German naval officer's uniforms were all made in Savile Row. Parisian model dressmaking, on the other hand, had a similar position until about 1960.

CLOTH MAKING. *See* TEXTILES.

CLOTH OF GOLD, FIELD OF (1520) was a conference between Henry VIII and Francis I of France, arranged by Card. Wolsey. It was marked by expensive splendour designed to celebrate the friendship of the two kings, but concealed simultaneous and ultimately successful negotiations for an alliance with Francis' enemy, the Emperor Charles V. *See* VALOIS-29; WOLSEY, CARD. THOMAS.

CLOTWORTHY. *See* SKEFFINGTON.

CLOUD OF UNKNOWING (c. 1380). This mystical work was composed by an unknown, theologically able, priest in the E. midlands who also composed works such as *The Book of Privy Counselling,* besides three translations from the Latin. The *Cloud* is inspired by the 6th cent. treatises of Dionysius the Areopagite and their mediaeval commentators. The writing is quizzical, even humorous, but asserts principles of division between the spiritual and the material and might have appealed to the Albigensians.

CLOUGH (1) Richard (?-1570) was Sir Thomas Gresham's factor at Antwerp from 1552 and suggested the idea of the London Royal Exchange to him. He became immensely rich. Among his probable relatives **(2) Arthur Hugh (1819-61),** the poet, was a fellow of Oriel Coll. Oxford from 1841 and then Principal of University Hall, London from 1849 to 1852 while his sister **(3) Anne Jemima (1820-92),** a leading champion of women's education was, from 1871, head of the women's hall which she transformed into Newnham Coll. Cambridge.

CLOVESHO, SYNODS OF. In 672 representatives of the church and of the Kings south of the Humber agreed that a synod should be held annually at this place (so far unidentified). It is unlikely that this rule was kept, but at least seven were held between 742 and 825. That of 747 enacted strict adherence to the Roman rite. That of 803 appears to have abolished the archbishopric of Lichfield (created in 782) and transferred the Mercian sees to Canterbury.

CLOVIS (?466-511). *See* FRANKS-1.

CLUB or BAT PARLIAMENT (1426) held at Northampton. To prevent violence between Gloucester and Beaufort factions the regent, the D. of Bedford, forbade participants to carry arms, so they brought clubs (bats) instead.

CLUBMEN in the Civil War were groups of cudgel armed farmers, mostly in the west, who tried forcibly to keep the armies off their land.

CLUBS. There was a dining club called **Le Court de Bone Campagnie** under Henry IV, and Sir Walter Raleigh founded the **Friday Club,** which dined at the Mermaid Tavern. Ben Jonson apparently founded the **Apollo Club** in 1616 at the Devil Tavern. These were all literary and near Temple Bar. When coffee houses started in the 1650s landlords tended to allot club rooms free and the word "club" came into use. The political clubs began at this time, viz. James Harrington's **Rota or Coffee Club** (Republican) in 1659; the **Sealed Knot** (Royalist) in 1660; the **Royal Navy Club** in 1674 and Patersons **Wednesday Club,** at whose meetings the idea for founding the Bank of England evolved. **Whites Club** began as a purely social club in 1693. The **October Club** was a Tory anti-Harleian club founded in 1710. The **Cocoa Tree** of the same year was Jacobite until 1746. **Whites** became Tory in 1784. Its rival was **Brooks's,** a social club founded in 1764 which became Whig in 1782. **Boodles** founded in 1763 as the **Scavoire Vivre** was a gourmet's club after it got its modem name in 1774. The various services clubs began as a result of the Napoleonic and later Wars: the **Guards** in 1813: the **United Service** in 1815, the **Junior United Services** in 1827 and the **Army and Navy** in 1837. The outstanding 19th cent. political clubs were the **Carlton** (Conservative), founded in 1831, and the

Reform in 1834. The **Athenaeum** was founded in 1823 and moved to its Pall Mall building in 1830.

CLUNY. (1) The influence of this monastery in Burgundy, founded in 910 by William, D. of Aquitaine, began to spread only under its second Abbot St. Odo (r. 927-42). The object was to re-establish the strict Benedictine Rule, to cultivate a personal spiritual life, to ensure the splendour of public worship and to develop economic independence of monasteries. A centralised organisation began to appear under Abbot Odilo (r. 994-1048); Paschal II and Innocent II were Cluniac trained and many Cluniacs being of noble birth, the order had great influence with lay rulers.

(2) The first English house was founded at Lewes (1077) and by mid-12th cent. there were 36 houses in England. They were never under the effective control of the mother house. William I, Henry I and Stephen made important benefactions and Henry I even completed the nave of the mother house itself.

(3) The principal Scottish houses were founded at Paisley and Crossraguel under Malcolm IV (r. 1153-65).

CLYDESIDE, a Glasgow shipbuilding district noted in the 20th cent. for the strong leftward inclination of its population. During World War I the shop stewards' movement developed there and it was a stronghold, inspired by James Maxton, of the Independent Labour Party. The decline of the industry after World War II broke up the old community and its collective attitude.

CLYNES, John Robert (1869-1949), the son of an evicted Irish labourer who migrated to Lancashire, got his interest in politics from reading newspapers to three blind men to supplement his earnings in a cotton mill. He became Lancashire Sec. of the Nat. Union of Gas Workers and General Labourers (later General and Municipal Workers) in 1896. He represented his union on the 1900 Labour Representation Committee and became M.P. for N.E. Manchester in 1906 as a member of the first parliamentary Labour Party. In 1909 he joined his party executive and became Pres. of his union in 1912. In 1918 he became Food Controller and a Privy Councillor and in 1921 Chairman of the Parliamentary Labour Party. Ramsay MacDonald defeated him for the leadership in 1922. In 1926 he opposed the principle of a general strike, but supported the miners when they turned out. He served under MacDonald as Dep. Leader of the Commons in 1924 and as Home Sec. from 1929 to 1931 when he refused the party leadership and also lost his seat. He returned to the Commons in 1935 content to be regarded as an Elder Statesman of the Labour movement.

COAL. (1) was burned by the ancient inhabitants of Glamorgan; by Roman garrisons on Hadrian's Wall; and occasionally by Saxon monasteries in the north. Northern monks used it in their forges in the 11th cent. and Newcastle 'sea coal' was being brought to London by sailing barge in 13th cent. Inefficient combustion created highly unpopular pollution and there were proclamations against the domestic use of coal from Edward I to James I. In practice lack of good chimneys and the coming of wholesale brickmaking in the early 16th cent. restricted the market, while the authorities, especially the Crown and the corporations at Newcastle and London, levied duties, which gave them an interest in encouraging the trade.

(2) Coal was originally picked up on the seashore, as in Durham and Northumberland, or dug from hillside outcrops. Then it was followed into the hill until the difficulty of removing the spoil above, or the danger of not doing so, forced miners to use shafts, slopes or drifts as appropriate. By the 18th cent. English mines had been worked so far or deep that there were serious difficulties in bringing coal from face to shaft (done hitherto by human or animal power) and lifting it to the surface (hitherto by ladders or in hand-or-horse-winched baskets). Moreover, water was apt to restrict mining

depths and the woods near the mines had been devastated for pip props.

(3) The enormous 18th cent. acceleration of demand imposed solutions. Newcomen's steam (coal fired) pump was introduced at Northampton in 1711. Watt's rotary engine began winding coal at Walker (Durham) in 1784. Stephenson's steam engine first pulled coal tubs to shaft bottoms in 1812. These opened enormous possibilities. The ancient northern and S. Wales mines grew and mining began or was extended from Fife to Lanarkshire, in the central and western midlands, in Lancashire, Flint and Denbigh, and in Somerset and Kent. An immense seaborne trade – outward coal, inward pit props – developed; the variations of type of coal produced variations in the design of steam driven machinery and railway engines; and certain royalty owners (e.g. the Bishopric of Durham) became exceedingly rich.

(4) The world demand soon outran the expanding British supply and other countries developed mining themselves. Of these the most important were the U.S.A. and Germany, but even as late as 1869 Britain was producing 118M tons out of a world supply of 230M. The British peak, at 302M, was reached in the years 1910 to 1914 when the world average had risen to 1358M and Britain was exporting 10-20% of her output.

(5) Initially coal was in demand for heat and then for steam power or for coke for smelting. From about 1850 it came into use as the raw material for increasing chemical and light oil industries of astonishing and still multiplying variety. These include paint, soap, perfumes, ammonia, dyestuffs, explosives, disinfectants and insecticides.

(6) The industry began to decline through labour shortages, mismanagement and exhaustion after World War II and in 1992 a govt. proposal on grounds of unprofitability to close most of the residue provoked a furious political reaction. In 1996 a mine at Hirwaun in S. Wales, bought by its own work force, was working at a profit. *See* MINES ACT.

COALBROOKDALE. *See* DARBY.

COALITION, WARS OF THE FIRST and SECOND. *See* FRENCH REVOLUTION AND CONSEQUENT WARS.

COARB. In the Celtic churches abbots were often hereditary and concerned mainly with an abbey's temporal affairs. Where an abbot was unfit (e.g. through nonage or lack of consecration) for spiritual functions, these were performed by a specially elected co-arb. Six Scottish clans claim descent from abbots.

COASTGUARD. In 1661 the responsibility for coast defence was transferred from the maritime counties to the militia, but smuggling was supposed to be prevented by a Waterguard employed by the Revenue. These "revenue men" were underpaid and often hand in glove with the smugglers. Moreover, in certain boroughs, notably 20 in Cornwall, they comprised most of the electorate; hence about 30 parliamentary seats were in the gift of the Exchequer. To lend some backbone to the revenue collecting system, two mobile independent bodies were organised. These were the Riding Officers on land and the Revenue Cutters at sea. The three bodies were amalgamated in 1822 for practical reasons and because borough corruption scandals were not regarded with the old equanimity. This Preventative Service was renamed the Revenue Coastguard in 1829, transferred to the Admiralty in 1831 and to the Board of Trade in 1925.

COASTING TRADE of the British Is. has always been more important than its invisibility to landsmen has made it seem. It has carried mainly coal, oil, wood, building materials, scrap iron, grain and potatoes. London, in particular, has depended almost wholly for supplies of these things as they became available, between 1660 and 1960. Averaged over the century before 1960 coasters have carried about 20% of the ton-mileage of all goods moved in the Kingdom. The proportion was higher before the time of good roads and the railways. Until

1854 the trade was confined to British vessels and, though then opened to foreign competition, British vessels still carried nearly 85% of the trade a century later.

COBALT, long used in compounds to impart a blue colour to paints, glass, glazes and ceramics, was first separately identified c. 1735 and confirmed in 1742 by a Jewish chemist, George Brandt. Big deposits were found in New Caledonia (1874), Ontario (1905) and Katanga (1920). Before 1914 it was used mostly in dyes, since then mostly in hard alloys, but experiments have been made with an atomic bomb.

COBB & CO. A Wells Fargo type of coaching Co. founded by three Americans in Australia in 1854. It provided a legendarily reliable transport service between Melbourne and Bendigo and later acquired a virtual monopoly in Victoria, N.S.W. and Queensland. It declined in the face of the railways and the last run took place in 1924.

COBBETT, William (1762-1835), a gallant, versatile and skilful self-publicist, served in the ranks from 1783 to 1791 in Nova Scotia and after an honourable discharge wrote in support of increased soldiers' pay and tried to expose some army scandals. He soon had to leave England, first to France and then in 1793 to Philadelphia where a pro-British pamphlet of his attracted anti-Jacobin attention in Britain. He remained in the U.S.A. writing pamphlets and running a bookshop until 1799 and in 1802 founded the *Political Register*. He lived at Botley (Hants) from 1805, pursued agricultural experiments and wrote strongly in favour of better agricultural labouring conditions. He also took the popular side in politics and in 1809 his support helped to end the traffic in military commissions run by Anne Clarke, the D. of York's mistress. An article against military flogging provoked a prosecution; he was fined £1000 and imprisoned for two years (1810). This temporarily ruined him, but in 1816 he reduced the price of the *Register* and so acquired a huge popular circulation. In 1817, however, on the suspension of *Habeas Corpus*, he went to the U.S.A. until 1819, when he returned to run a seed farm in Kensington and loudly to support Q. Caroline. It was in 1821 that he began the well-known series of political journeys recorded in his *Rural Rides* (1830). In 1831 his pugnacious journalism was at the service of parliamentary reform and a prosecution for sedition failed. He was M.P. for Oldham from 1832.

COBBOLD, Cameron Fromanteel (1904-87) 1st Ld. COBBOLD (1960) entered the Bank of England as adviser in 1933 and rose through it to be gov. from 1949 to 1961. In 1962 he was chairman of the Malaysia Commission and from 1963 to 1971 Lord Chamberlain.

COBDEN, Richard (1804-65), enterprising son of a poor farmer, set up with friends in calico printing near Clitheroe (Lancs) in 1831 and made money. He lived at Manchester and became one of its first aldermen and also wrote reformist pamphlets. In 1838 he, with other Manchester merchants, formed the Anti-Corn Law League; this was also the effective origin of the Manchester School of economists. In 1841 he became M.P. for Stockport. He and Bright now organised a powerful movement in and out of Parliament against the Corn Duties, whose repeal they secured in June 1846, but his labours distracted him from his business which was ruined and rescued only by a public subscription. His outlook on world trade made him critical of the currently fashionable aggressive policies and he attacked the govt. over the Crimean War, the *Arrow* affair at Canton and the Indian mutiny. This went against popular feeling and in the general election of 1857 he lost his seat. He went abroad, but in 1859 was offered and refused the Presidency of the Board of Trade by Palmerston. He returned to parliament. In 1860, as a private citizen, he began to negotiate a celebrated commercial treaty with France, on the basis of mutual tariff reductions. This strikingly improved Anglo-French relations and the international terms of trade. Thereafter he strongly opposed interventionist foreign policies, particularly in the American Civil War and the Danish-German war of 1864.

COBENZL, Ludwig Count (1755-1809), as Austrian ambassador to Russia from 1779 to 1797, negotiated the two later partitions of Poland. In 1797 he agreed the P. of Campo Formio with Bonaparte and ceded the left bank of the Rhine to France. After a further two years in Russia he signed the P. of Lunéville in 1801 when he became Vice-Chancellor. He represented Austria at Rastadt in 1803 as Foreign Minister. Further French aggression, notably in Italy, led to the formation of the Third Coalition with Russia and Britain, which ended in the defeat at Austerlitz. He was dismissed a few weeks later.

COBHAM or BROOKE. Kentish family. **(1) Thomas (?-1327)** was elected Abp. of Canterbury by the cathedral monks while absent in Paris but, faced with a rival supported by Edward II and the Avignon Papacy, settled in 1317 for the bishopric of Worcester. **(2) John 3rd Ld. COBHAM (?-1408)** was frequently employed as a negotiator with the French from 1374 and was one of Richard II's councillors at his accession. He continued his work in govt. and diplomacy but in 1388 he was one of the King's commissioners for trying those accused by the Lords Appelant, and in 1397 was impeached for his conduct on that occasion. This was one of the grounds for the deposition of Richard II. He was recalled in 1399 when already very old. His granddaughter **(3) Joan's** five husbands included the Lollard Sir JOHN OLDCASTLE (q.v.). A relative **(4) Eleanor (?-?1446)** became the mistress of Humphrey D. of Gloucester in about 1429. She was condemned for sorcery in 1441 as part of the political moves against him and died in prison. **(5) Sir Henry (1538-?1605),** was a diplomat much employed by Elizabeth I, mainly on missions to the Netherlands (1570), Spain (1570, 1574) and as resident at Paris (1579-83). He was M.P. for Kent in 1586 and 1589.

COBHAM. *See* OLDCASTLE; TEMPLE.

COBLENZ MANIFESTO. *See* FRENCH REVOLUTIONARY WAR. APR. 1792-FEB 1793-2.

COBURG. *See* ALFRED ERNEST; SAXE-COBURG.

COCHIN (India). This large Hindu state early established trading relations with the Portuguese who dominated it politically until the Dutch drove them out in 1662. In 1765 it became tributary to Mysore as a result of the rise of Hyder Ali and so passed under British protection with the death of his son Tippoo Sahib at Seringapatam in 1799.

COCHRANE. (1) Sir William Blair of Blair (?-1686) married ELIZABETH COCHRANE of Cochrane and assumed her name. **1st Ld. COCHRANE of DUNDONALD (1647) 1st E. of DUNDONALD (1669).** He amassed huge estates in Renfrew and Ayr and was a royalist M.P. in the Scots parliament of 1644. In 1648 he was in Ireland collecting the Scots troops and in 1653 he had acquired and set up a splendid household at Paisley. He compounded for 'delinquency' (i.e. loyalty) in 1655. At the Restoration he became a Scots privy councillor and commissioner of the treasury. His son **(2) Sir John (?-1695)** was implicated in the Rye House Plot (1683) but escaped to Holland. Attainted in absence under James II, he took part in Argyll's rising of 1685, was captured but escaped execution by his father purchasing a royal pardon. **(3) Archibald (1749-1831) 9th E. (?)** was an inventor and scientist who ruined the family fortunes in the pursuit of successful experiments ahead of his time, particularly in the manufacturing of soda, coal tar and fertilisers. His brother **(4) Sir Alexander Thomas (1758-1832)** was a successful seaman, being 2-in-C at the B. of San Domingo (6 Feb. 1806), gov. of the captured I. of Guadeloupe from 1810 to 1814 and C-in-C off N. America from 1814 to 1815. The son of **(3), (5)**

Thomas (1775-1860) 10th E. (1831) combined in the highest degree the qualities of his father and uncle, with a sometimes disastrous outspokenness. As commander of the 4 pdr brig. *Speedy,* the frigates *Pallas* from 1805 to 1806 and *Imperieuse* from 1806 to 1809 his exploits in the Mediterranean became legendary. He had, however, a genius for making enemies as well as friends. He had secured election to parliament at Honiton in Oct. 1810 and with Sir Francis Burdett for Westminster in Feb. 1807. He promptly moved a resolution in the Commons against naval abuses. It failed for bad timing and made more enemies. He then returned to the Mediterranean but came back for reasons of health in 1809 and moved against the abuses of the Maltese Vice-Admiralty Court. He also proposed an ingenious attack on the French fleet in the Basque Roads which failed of its proper effect because his C-in-C (Lord Gambier) refused to support it properly. Thereupon he opposed a parliamentary vote of thanks to Gambier but would not prefer court martial charges against him. This ruined his British naval career. He was next accidentally and innocently involved in a Stock Exchange scandal for which he was expelled from the Commons, fined £1000 and sent to prison for a year, but the Westminster electors enthusiastically re-elected him. He refused for a while to pay the fine but eventually did so because continued imprisonment was affecting his health (July 1816). His debts were paid by popular subscription. In 1817 he accepted an invitation to take command of the Chilean fleet in the rebellion against Spain. He defeated the Spaniards and by Nov. 1821 (when he resigned) he had driven them from the coast. In Mar. 1823 he took command of the Brazilian Imperial navy with equal success against the Portuguese and resigned while in England in Nov. 1825. He was then invited to take command of the insurgent Greek navy, an ineffectual body of quasi-pirates who could not be induced to do anything before the B. of Navarino (1827) settled the naval problem without them. In 1832 William IV annulled his convictions and he became a rear-adm. Dundonald now devoted himself to the development of screw steamers for naval purposes and designed the steam frigate *Janus* himself. He was C-in-C West Indies from 1848 to 1851. In the Crimean War he volunteered, with the aid of a secret weapon, to destroy Kronstadt but was dissuaded from pressing his proposal.

COCKADES. Under Charles I the royal cockade was red. Charles II changed to white. William III, of course, used an orange one, and so white became a Stuart and ultimately a Jacobite emblem. Hence the Hanoverians used black, and black cockades have been used by men-servants of royalty and other grandees ever since.

COCKATOO I. (Sydney, Austr.). Convict prison from 1839.

COCKBURN, Henry Thomas (1779-1854) Ld. (1837), a well-known Scots lawyer and from 1837 a Lord of Session, was the principal instigator of the foundation of Edinburgh Academy.

COCKBURN, William (1669-1739) invented a secret remedy for scurvy which was, for its day, very successful and with which he supplied the Royal Navy for 40 years.

COCKBURN (pron. *Coburn*). This well connected and widespread lowland Scots family originated in one of Robert the Bruce's supporters who fell at Bannockburn. **(1) Sir William (?-1513)** obtained lands at Langton in Berwickshire, married Anna Home, and was killed at Flodden. **(2) Adam (1656-1735) Ld. ORMISTON (1692)** represented Haddington in the Convention of Estates of 1678, in the Scots parliament of 1681 and in the Convention and parliament of 1689 which appointed him a commissioner for the abortive Union. He was the first to introduce enclosure and long leases into Scots agricultural practice. In 1692 he became Lord Justice Clerk and in 1695 a Scots Privy Councillor and member of the inquiry into the Glencoe massacre. He was consequently violently assailed in Argyll. In 1699 he

became Treasurer-Depute but in 1705 reverted to Lord Justice Clerk and became a Lord of Session. In 1710 he was superseded in the clerkship, but received a life grant of it in 1714 from George I for political services. He was a strong whig and presbyterian and an active suppressor of Jacobites after 1715. **(3) Sir George (1763-1847)** distinguished himself in the defence of Gibraltar (1782-4) and secured the patronage of the E. of Harrington, then Col. of the 65th Foot to which Cockburn had been posted in 1785. As a result he was sent to study foreign military methods, especially the Prussian, Austrian, French and Spanish between 1785 and 1789. He became a maj-gen. in 1803 and in 1810 was in command in Sicily, where he witnessed and took some credit for Campbell's defeat of Cavaignac's attempted invasion. He returned the same year to England where he became an eccentric whig local politician. **(4) Sir James (1771-1852) 7th Bart.** was a maj-gen., Sec. of State in 1806 and gov. of Bermuda in 1811. His brother **(5) Sir George (1772-1853) 8th Bart.** became a Lieut. in Hood's flagship off Toulon in 1793 and quickly got the command of the frigate *Meleager,* first under Hotham and then under Nelson. In 1796 he took command of the *Minerve,* a large captured French frigate flying Nelson's broad pennant. With her he had many daring adventures and took many prizes until 1802. From 1803 to 1805 he commanded the frigate *Phaeton* and then held more conventional commands in the W. Indies, being employed in 1811 to mediate (unsuccessfully) between Spain and her insurgent American colonies. In 1812 he was rear-adm. in charge of a squadron off the Chesapeake against the Americans. In 1813 he, with Maj-Gen. Ross, was joint commander and main inspirer of the expedition which, after the victory at Bladensburg (24 Aug. 1813), took Washington and burnt it. In 1815 he convoyed Bonaparte to St. Helena and remained there as gov. until 1816. His nephew **(6) Sir Alexander (1802-80)** a famous linguist and lawyer, built up a practice in election cases and in 1834 became a member of the Commission which bore fruit in the Municipal Corporations Act, 1835. He acquired thereafter notoriety as a barrister and in 1847 became a liberal reformist M.P. for Southampton. In 1850 he made a celebrated defence against Gladstone of Palmerston's action in the Don Pacifico case and within hours was denouncing Austrian reprisals in Hungary. In July 1850 he was sol-gen; in Jan. 1851 att-gen. and again from Dec. 1852 to Nov. 1856. He simultaneously maintained a vast and lucrative private practice at the bar, but when Sir John Jervis died he accepted the Chief Justiceship of the Common Pleas and was Chief Justice of the Queen's Bench from 1859, presiding with panache in most of the *causes célèbres* of the day. He also represented the British side in the *Alabama* arbitration at Geneva in 1872. In 1875, by operation of the Judicature Acts, he became the first Lord Chief Justice of England.

COCKCROFT, Sir John Douglas (1897-1967), under Rutherford who had foreseen the possibility in 1919, split atoms for the first time in Apr. 1932. From 1941 to 1944 he was in charge of air defence research; from 1946 director of the Atomic Energy Establishment at Harwell. In 1960 he became Master of Churchill Coll. Cambridge on the nomination of Churchill himself.

COCKFIGHTING was introduced very early into England and Henry VIII set up a palace cockpit at Whitehall. It apparently reached Scotland only in 1681. Most towns had cockpits by 1800 and the most famous main (match) was for 5000 gns. at Lincoln in 1830. Strongly condemned at all times by religious opinion, cockfighting went into a slow decline thereafter, hastened by anti-cruelty legislation. Though prohibited in England in 1849, in 1993 it was still not wholly extinct.

COCK LANE GHOST, was an imposture perpetrated in a house off Giltspur St. London in 1762. It attracted the interest of thousands before its exposure.

COCKNEY (M.E. coken-ey = cocks egg, i.e. a misshapen egg) meant a sport or milksop such as was to be found in a town, as against the hardy countryman, and so a Londoner, particularly one born within the sound of Bow Bells. Two churches, however, claim the honour of thus casting their campanological mantle: St. Mary le Bow, Cheapside, in the City and St. Mary-atte-Bow in the East End outside the City. Cockney is, or was, also a London East End dialect with Danish features, notable also for the curious habit of rhyming slang, i.e. of using expressions which rhymed conventionally with the idea intended to be meant, e.g. "Duke of Kent" for "rent", or "apples and pears" for "stairs". This might then be shortened into a code e.g. "Duke" means "rent" and "you comin' up the apples?" was an invitation. The habit was common until 1945 when the dispersal and dilution of the East End population through war and rehousing ended it. By reason of artificial revivals it was, however, sometimes heard in the 1990s.

COCKPIT, THE. The house in Whitehall on the site of the present Treasury Chambers which became the home in 1683 of the Princess Anne on her marriage to P. George of Denmark. Also the group of political associates including Marlborough, Sarah his wife, Godolphin, Russell and sometimes Shrewsbury, who met each other and the princess there. It was pulled down in 1816 after many years of disuse.

COCKPIT OF EUROPE. Belgium.

COCOA TREE, a coffee house which between 1727 and about 1750 was a meeting place of Tory parliamentarians.

COCOS or KEELING Is. (Indian Ocean) were first settled by Alexander Hare with his Malay harem and slaves (1826-31). In 1827 John Clunies Ross settled there and he and his descendents planted coconuts. Taken under British protection in 1857 and placed under Ceylon in 1878, the islands were granted in 1886 to Geo. Clunies-Ross in perpetuity. In 1903 they became part of the Straits Settlements and in Nov. 1914 the German cruiser *Emden* was destroyed at North Keeling. In 1945 an airstrip was built at West Keeling and in 1955 the islands were transferred to Australia, subject to the rights of the Clunies-Ross family. In 1972 John Clunies-Ross relinquished his authority.

COD FISHERIES. In the European Atlantic these extend from Biscay, northwards to Iceland and thence to Novaya Zemlya; in the American Atlantic from C. Hatteras to Greenland. In the Pacific a slightly different species is fished northwards of a line from Oregon to Japan, as far as the Bering Straits.

CODRINGTON (1) Christopher (1668-1710), fellow of All Souls from 1690, was a successful soldier in Flanders (1694-5); then succeeded his father as gov. of the Leeward Is. from 1697 to 1703. He endowed the vast Codrington Library at All Souls and Codrington's College, Barbados. A kinsman **(2) Sir Edward (1770-1851)** became naval C-in-C in the Mediterranean in 1826 and commanded the combined fleet which destroyed the Turkish-Egyptian squadron at Navarino (20 Oct. 1827). His second son **(3) Sir William (1804-84)** was a maj-gen. at the Alma and Inkerman and became C-in-C at Sebastopol after its fall in 1855. His brother **(4) Sir Henry John (1808-77)** was a rear-adm. in the Crimean War and slowly rose to be an Admiral of the Fleet. He was a well known theoretical tactician with few opportunities for action.

COD WARS. *See* ICELAND.

COERCION ACT 1880. *See* IRELAND.F.-9.

COERCIVE ACTS 1774. *See* AMERICAN REBELLION-13.

COFFEE first came to West European notice from its use, by the late 16th cent. in the Levant. Coffee houses appeared in Italy and elsewhere in the early 17th cent. The first English one opened in Cornhill, London, in 1652. Coffee houses soon entertained political and literary gatherings. The price fell and consumption rose

as cultivation of the plant spread from Arabia to Ceylon in 1658, Indonesia in 1696, Hispaniola in 1715, Guiana in 1718, Brazil in 1727 and Jamaica in 1730. *See* CEYLON; CHOCOLATE.

COGGESHALL (Essex). The people were reputed to be short on logic. When a mad dog bit a wheelbarrow, they are said to have chained up the wheelbarrow to prevent the epidemic spreading.

COGIDUBNUS or COGIDUMNUS was recognised under the Emperor Claudius as King of an area which included at least part of the former territory of the Atrebates. This Regnum (realm) was probably centred on the Chichester area and it is supposed that the uniquely magnificent villa of A.D. 80 at Fishbourne (near Chichester) was built for him in his old age. Tacitus, writing in about A.D. 97, says that he 'survived, ever most loyal to the Romans to within our own memory'. Accordingly he cannot have taken part in Boadicea's revolt.

COGNAC, LEAGUE or T. (1526) between Francis I, Venice, Milan and the Papacy against the Habsburgs, ushered in the French aggressive policy in Italy which ended only with Italian unification in 1860.

COGS. *See* SHIPS, SAILING.

COIF was a white, close fitting, cap worn by lawyers as a mark of their profession. By Tudor times it was reserved to serjeants at law, who were sometimes spoken of as 'coifs'. cf 'silk' for Q.C., in reference to the Q.C.s silk gown.

COIFI. 7th cent. pagan priest at the Northumbrian court who desecrated his shrine because, according to Bede, his gods had failed to bring him prosperity.

COIGN or COYNYE was the ancient customary right of an Irish chief to quarter his armed retainers upon private persons or to exact an impost ostensibly to maintain them. Since this amounted to a right of private taxation not controlled by English law, it was strongly disapproved by English govts. *See* ELIZABETH 1-17.

COINAGE. (1) Military confusion closed the Gallic mints in mid-4th cent. In Britain this diminished the money supply, which ended completely when the Roman legions left c. 395. Coins (probably copper) continued in use in certain Romanised places such as Caerwent and the Kentish coast. Foreign trade revived in the 6th cent., for Merovingian gold coins have been found in the south.

(2) English minting began under the stimulus of commerce between Kent and Gaul and the marriage of Ethelbert of Kent with Clovis' d. Bertha in c. 595. The earliest coin, the gold 20-23 grain THRYMSA, was copied from the Merovingian ⅓ solidus (*Tremissis*), itself copied from a tremissis of Constantine used in the W. and E. Roman empires until 8th cent. The earliest mints were at Canterbury and London and, perhaps, at Winchester.

(3) Contemporaneously with the Thrymsa, 20-grain silver coins now known as SCEAT (treasure) were being minted and rated at 1/20 of a "shilling". These were also imitations; the thrymsa ceased to be minted by about 640 and Sceats represented a debasement or inflation and were themselves gradually debased by addition of copper alloy or reduction in weight to as little (at London) as 14 gr. by 750. Under Offa of Mercia (757-96) the southern coinage was reformed, but sceats continued to circulate in Northumbria and, until the Danish Conquest of that Kingdom in 867, were struck by the royal and archiepiscopal mints at York. By c. 785 new sceats were mostly copper. There was also a small copper STYCA (mite), perhaps the tiny Roman or post-Roman coin found occasionally in hoards.

(4) Offa and Jaenbert, Abp. of Canterbury, introduced the silver PENNY at 16-20 gr. in about 775. This was a revaluation. In about 791 Offa and Abp. Aethelheard further revalued to 22½ gr. or 240 to the "Tower" pound, to correspond with the Carolingian reforms. They struck millions of these pence. These were based upon 240 to the Gallic, later Troy, pound and involved the demonetisation of gold. Pennies were normally marked with the moneyer's name until the mid-13th cent. The Canterbury mint was three-handed (royal Mercian, royal Kentish and archiepiscopal) all under Mercian control. There was another mint at Thetford and, after 830, pennies were struck at London. Until 1344 they were the only coins struck in England. Other denominations mentioned in the texts were moneys of account as follows: POUND = 240 pence; MARK (Scots. MERK) = 160; SHILLING = originally 20, then 12; a GOLD MARK = 1440 appears in Domesday.

(5) The Mercian collapse (825) brought the Canterbury mint under W. Saxon control and coins were struck in London from 827 and intermittently at Winchester. After 870 Viking rulers issued coinages from previously established mints (e.g. London, Thetford, York) which they took over and from Lincoln. Alfred's succession (871), however, brought a wide development; new mints opened at Bath, Exeter, Gloucester and Oxford, and the English advance brought further multiplication. There were mints in 26 towns under Athelstan (925-39) who, by the earliest surviving English coinage law, sought to standardise their production. At the same time Hywell Dda was issuing pennies in Wales. Under Edgar the number of mints rose to 40, all supplied with centrally produced dies. The need to pay Danegelds under Ethelred the Unready (979-1016) created an unprecedented demand for coin: 84 mint towns are known and older mints were enlarged. Six gelds absorbed 155,000 lb of silver (about 3.9M silver pence). By the Norman conquest, which made little change in the nature of the coinage, the number of mint towns had, however, fallen to 70.

(6) Under the developed Saxon and Norman system, a mint was permitted only in a fortified town. It was always associated with an independent exchange under a warden. Bullion was acquired through the exchange, struck by the moneyer and issued through the exchange. The moneyer was a person of substance who lived rent free and was responsible to the King. He was liable to savage punishment for forgery. The warden had a vested interest in maintaining the propriety of his moneyer's coinage, since his stake in the prosperity of the exchange would otherwise suffer. The King's share in the profits was secured because the moneyer had to buy his dies from the King's graver (in Norman times a post hereditary in the descendants of Otto the Goldsmith) and pay the King's dues (20s) at the time of purchase. To ensure a regular royal income from this source the detailed design of the penny was changed frequently: for example in the combined reigns of William I and II (1066-1100) there were 13 types; under Henry I (1100-35) 15 and there were regular recoinages. In Henry's time there was serious debasement which extreme remedies such as castration of moneyers failed to remedy, and twelve mints closed but one opened in Wales. At Carlisle the moneyer was the head of the wealthy lessors of the Cumberland silver mines and he struck both for Henry and for the Scots.

(7) An important detail was the existence of franchise mints belonging to the Abps. of Canterbury and York, the Bps. of Durham, Lincoln and Rochester and the Abbot of St. Edmundsbury; the last coin issued in the name of the Abp. of Canterbury appeared in 914, but all these dignitaries continued to take the profits down to the 16th cent. The mints were an important part of their temporalities. The civil war of Stephen's reign (1135-54) led not only to rival coinages in his and Matilda's name, but to private coinages such as Henry of Anjou's issue of 1149 (called *Duke's money*), Eustace fitzJohn's coinage from York and Robert of Stuteville's pennies.

(8) The monetary confusion lasted until 1158, when Henry II made an important reform, consisting of a sole currency of uniform design necessitating a new method of controlling moneyers and collecting royal profits. These poorly designed TEALBY pennies (so-called from a find at Tealby in 1807) were issued until 1180. They were then replaced by the SHORT CROSS pennies, which were issued in four reigns but always bore the name *Henricus*. These coins were easily clipped so that the currency became fraudulently debased. In 1247 the old coinage was replaced by pennies whose LONG CROSS extended to the rim and which were declared illegal if the ends of the cross were not visible. The coins of Henry III continued to be issued until 1279 and the cross was deeply indented to allow division for small change.

(9) In 1279 all royal mints were placed under a single newly created MASTER OF THE MINT, as part of a comprehensive recoinage, and moneyers' names, save at Bury St. Edmunds, disappeared. The silver FARTHING and HALFPENNY were introduced to make division unnecessary and the Long Cross pence were replaced. A new 4d coin, the GROAT, was also introduced. There was a great new issue in 1300 and by this time, apart from the ecclesiastical franchise mints, production was stabilised at 7 mints.

(10) After 1307 output was low and there was movement of English coinage abroad; consequently in 1335 silver halfpennies and farthings were ordered and declared legal tender save for tax payments. The franchise mints had been operating at a low rate for some years, but since they could only strike pennies this brought them to a halt. By 1343 there was a currency crisis and in Jan. 1344 the gold FLORIN (made by two goldsmiths from *Florence*) was issued at a value of 72 pence together with $\frac{1}{2}$ and $\frac{1}{4}$ forms. In Aug. these were supplanted by the gold "ship" NOBLE (80 pence). The weights of these coins and of the silver penny progressively altered until a gold-silver ratio of 12:1 was reached in 1351, when the GROAT (4 pence) and HALF GROAT (2 pence) were introduced. A mint was opened at Calais in 1363 but struck only gold after 1365.

(11) For various reasons including undervaluation, the currency drain continued. Import and export duties and prohibitions on the export of coin impeded trade without halting it. The supply of bullion gave out and the amount coined fell to negligible amounts. The Calais mint was suspended in 1411, by which time foreign base metal coins (e.g. Venetian GALLEY HALFPENCE, Flemish SUSKINS and DOITS) were widely used for small change. Radical measures to alleviate the difficulties were taken in 1412. The ratio of gold to silver was fixed at 100:9 and new nobles of 108 gr. and pennies of 15 gr. were put into circulation at the same value as their heavy predecessors. This was successful and attracted enough bullion to enable most mints to resume production. The mints at York reopened in 1423, at Calais in 1424. Gold, however, soon ran out: by 1433 very little was minted anywhere. Silver followed suit: by 1448 coinage was generally at a low ebb and so remained until 1464.

(12) In 1465 the gold coinage was reformed by the issue of the 120 gr. RYAL or ROSE NOBLE valued at 120 pence (with halves and quarters in proportion) and the 80 gr. ANGEL valued at 80 pence (with halves in proportion), and at the same time the penny was reduced from 15 gr. to 12 gr. English mints could now compete with foreign, and large amounts of bullion were coined; ryals, however, ceased, save for special issues, to be struck after 1470.

(13) The modernity of the Tudor dynasty is evidenced by coinage developments which began in 1489 with the issue of the 240 gr. gold SOVEREIGN and the substitution of real portraits for the mediaeval conventional royal faces. An Act of 1504 forbade the currency of clipped coins and in about 1505 or 6 the King's graver struck some experimental silver portrait TESTOONS (Fr. *téte* = head) at a value of 12 pence, as well as many portrait groats. The health of the English

currency was guaranteed under Henry VII and remained for a while under Henry VIII until he had spent his father's accumulations: but danger signs were apparent from 1510 onwards, when not only foreign small change but gold as well as illegal clipped coins began to circulate and there was the usual flight abroad. In 1526 Henry began to debase coinage. A new 22 Ct. CROWN OF THE ROSE (54 pence) was equated with the French *ecu:* standard gold was used for the Sovereign (now 270 pence) and other existing denominations, and a new GEORGE NOBLE (80 pence) was issued. The silver weight of the penny was reduced from 12 gr. to 10⅔ gr. and the Troy (or French) pound of 5760 gr. was substituted for the Tower pound of 5400. This coinage, for which Card. Wolsey was responsible, lasted until 1542 when further debasements began with gold 23ct, and silver at 10 oz. In 1544 silver was reduced to 9 oz. This was the year in which the testoon was put into circulation, the weight of the penny came down to 10 gr. and gold was revalued on the basis of 96 pence to the Angel. In 1545 gold sovereigns were struck at 22 Ct., 192 gr. and a value of 240 pence and silver to 6 oz. and in 1546 at the same weight and value sovereigns were debased to 20 Ct. and silver to 4 oz.

(14) The damage to the economy was a matter of urgent concern to later statesmen. In 1548 the govt. began striking 8 oz. silver for SHILLINGS (12 pence), the renamed testoons, and efforts were made to raise the fineness of the other denominations. In 1551 debased silver coins were reduced in value by half; standard gold was used for a sovereign which, consequently, rose in value to 360 pence and 11oz. SILVER CROWNS, HALF CROWNS, SHILLINGS and SIXPENCES were issued. Unfortunately the needs of the Treasury compelled the mint to continue with debased issues at the same time, Henry VIII's testoons often being used as a source of bullion. Monetary confusion was further compounded because many issues of Edward VI were made in the name of Henry VIII. All the same there was progress which Mary I continued by issuing gold coins only of standard gold.

(15) Elizabeth I initiated a determined attack on base currency. The worst testoons were counter marked for ½ and ¼ pence respectively in 1559 and demonetised in 1561. The new currency was of standard gold and 11oz. silver with 22ct. gold for 240, 120, 60 and 30 pence pieces. In 1560 silver was raised to 11oz. 2dwt., shillings were suspended and coins valued at 6, 3, ½ and ¼ pence added to the series. Despite rumours of devaluation current in 1562 it was possible in 1572 to strike a new silver coinage of standard metal, but in 1601 there were very slight reductions in the weight both of gold and silver coins. James I continued this but because gold was leaving the country, he added a lighter gold UNITE of 240 pence, a THISTLE CROWN of 48 pence, the 60 pence crown being named the BRITISH CROWN. In 1605 he also struck a ROSE RYAL of standard gold valued at 360 pence. In 1611 the value of gold coins was raised by 10% and those more than 2 gr. in 120 pence short of weight demonetised. These measures failed to prevent the leakage of gold. Meanwhile there was a chronic shortage of small change, leading in 1613 to a decision to issue copper TOKEN FARTHINGS, saleable at 1056 for 240 pence. The patent for this was issued to Lord Harington, whose widow sold it to the D. of Lennox in 1615. The tokens were not tender and they were not popular. In 1616 Lennox established a permanent London exchange for them. The patent passed to Lennox's widow, the Duchess of Richmond, in 1624 and to Ld. Maltravers in 1634. There were many reasons for their unpopularity; in particular local traders, guilds and city corporations issued tokens themselves and it was easier for local users to obtain redemption of these. Moreover they were easily forged.

(16) An effort to introduce the French mill and screw presses in 1578 had come to grief on conservative craftsmans' opposition. Charles I's able French engraver Nicholas Briot succeeded with the King's active support. The quality of the coinage henceforth was greatly enhanced. Briot persuaded Charles not to debase the coinage, despite his financial difficulties. During the civil war the Tower mint was in parliamentary control, but continued to issue coins in the King's name, which was needed to maintain credit. The King had mints at York, Aberystwyth, Shrewsbury, Oxford, Bristol, Exeter, Weymouth and Combe Martin. Both sides collected and coined vast quantities of private plate, so that very little pre-civil war plate now survives. In addition SIEGE PIECES were struck or cut from plate in the besieged royal fortresses of Carlisle, Colchester, Newark, Scarborough and, finally, Pontefract. The King's image and titles disappeared from new coinage after his death and was succeeded by a Commonwealth coinage showing two shields so drawn as to be known as the BREECHES COINAGE "a fit stamp" according to Ld. Lucas "for the coin of the Rump". It was instantly demonetised at the Restoration.

(17) The great change in the nature of the coinage from a govt. warranted measure of precious metal to a currency of notional denomination began in the reign of Charles II. The shortage of small change, leading to an enormous proliferation of private tokens after 1648 led the way, by accustoming the public to the use of nominal currency. In 1672 copper halfpence and farthings were ready and the proclamation which put them into circulation forbade the use of tokens. The operation was a great success: the price of copper being much below the face value, the mint netted large profits for a generation, but others wanted a share and a brisk forgery trade grew up. Forgery of silver and gold was a felony: of copper only a misdemeanour.

(18) Meanwhile silver continued to be undervalued, being coined after 1688 at 62 pence per oz. but fetching 63½ pence abroad. In the ensuing years there was a stampede to the continent leaving only clipped, light or defaced silver in Britain and by 1694 the guinea had risen to 360 pence. A general recoinage was undertaken in 1695 and by 1698 the guinea had fallen 258 pence. All the same the export of silver was not stopped and in 1717 Sir Isaac Newton was commissioned to investigate. He reported that the HEIC alone was exporting £2M a year and on his recommendation the GUINEA was fixed at 252 pence (21 shillings).

(19) The developing situation had other features. The shortage of means of exchange brought a proliferation of bills and, after 1694, the issue of banknotes by the Bank of England. The premium of silver drove the silver penny out of circulation in about 1731. The acquisition of large amounts of bullion was a public event of such interest that coins were marked to record it: hence special coinages were marked for the bullion brought in by the Royal African Co. (1675), captured at Vigo (1702-3) brought in by the South Sea Co. (1723), the HEIC (1729 and 1739) and captured off Peru by Anson (1744).

(20) In 1754 forgery led the govt. to suspend copper issues, so that for 40 years there was virtually no silver or official copper in circulation. The public supplied its own remedies. Copper blanks were made, often at Birmingham, sold to counterfeiters who stamped them and then sold to wholesalers at 50%, who resold to traders at 66%. Trade tokens flourished, especially after 1784, and were issued by corporations and businesses of every kind. Many towns had clearing houses for them. Rare small issues apart, gold alone was minted.

(21) In 1797 the 2oz. copper "CARTWHEEL" 2 pence piece was issued with the 1oz. penny and in 1799 ½ oz. halfpenny. These were inconveniently clumsy for common use, but further demands were met by issues of

pence, halfpence and farthings in 1806 and 1807, farthings in 1820 and pence and halfpence in 1825. A few of these pieces were still circulating in country districts as late as 1940. In 1797, too, Spanish dollars, valued at 57 pence, were hall-marked as currency: in 1804 the Bank of England issued silver dollar tokens and in 1811 banknotes became legal tender. From this it was a short step to establishing the GOLD STANDARD of 1816 based on the celebrated George and Dragon sovereign, with silver and copper subsidiary currency without intrinsic value. This was possible because, for the first time, the price of silver had fallen below the mint price.

(22) In response to an agitation for decimal currency the silver FLORIN was issued in 1849. In 1920 the silver content was reduced to 50%; in 1931 the gold standard was abandoned and in World War II the silver content of the "silver" coinage was wholly abandoned because the photographic industry's use of silver compounds had raised the price of silver far above the content of the silver coinage.

(23) Decimal coinage was introduced in 1971 and the shilling disappeared. A new coinage of thick yellow-metal pound coins and ugly multiangular pence denominations was introduced, occasionally varied by special commemorative issues. By now the coin collectors were beginning to influence certain kinds of circulation: in particular, as they were prepared in continental markets to pay more than the face value of some commemorative issues, these seldom circulated in numbers for long. No doubt the whole English system will be swept away altogether when all European currencies are superseded by the ECU, renamed EURO in 1995.

COKE, Sir Edward (1552-1634) (sometimes called Ld. COKE or COOKE) called to the bar in 1578, made a brilliant common law practice which brought him to the notice of the Cecils. By their support in 1585 he became Recorder of Coventry, in 1586 of Norwich. In 1589 he was M.P. for Aldborough; in 1592 Recorder of London and Sol-Gen; in 1593 Speaker. He now became heavily engaged in the Star Chamber, then a very popular court, and was acquiring a reputation for ferocious advocacy. In 1594 there was a dispute (see ELIZABETH 1-28) about the Attorney-Generalship, between Essex, whose candidate was Francis Bacon, and Sir Robt. Cecil, who wanted Coke. In allowing his name to go forward Coke took a decisive step, by siding with institutional conservatism and alienating the more ardent spirits in public life. He got the job (then very lucrative) and in 1598 nailed his colours to the mast by marrying (against competition by Bacon supported by Essex) the wealthy Lady Elizabeth, who was Burghley's grand-daughter and Sir Wm. Hatton's widow. In 1600, when he led with all his well-known savagery, the prosecution of Essex and Southampton, he began to publish his *Law Reports* which established in writing, in a short time, the foundations of the Common Law. He was, logically enough, an important pillar of the Stuart succession in 1603; James I mistook his uncompromising prosecutions of Raleigh (1603) and the Gunpowder Plotters (1605) for political allegiance to royal policies and rewarded him in 1606 with the Chief Justiceship of the Common Pleas. James thought of himself as a lawyer and believed that he recognised a kindred spirit, but Coke refused to support the prerogative imposition of customs duties, yet in 1607 decided *Calvin's Case* in the sense which the King favoured. He had come to the politically far-reaching conclusion that the Common Law, of which he was the most distinguished expositor, was a governing framework of rules which settled the relative rights, responsibilities and duties of all persons and estates; and that, therefore, the courts which administered it were pre-eminent institutions and should be independent of all others. Judges were paid by fees and this doctrine had financial advantages for the C. J. of the Common Pleas. The feud,

dating from Essex's time, with Bacon (now Lord Keeper) was rationalised in a determination to limit the jurisdiction of the Chancery Court. The King's autocratic and episcopalian leanings supported each other; they had to be curbed too. The result was a series of judicial conflicts. Coke granted writs of prohibition against ecclesiastical courts and the Court of High Commission when even trivial property was involved, and took similar action against the Chancery. He decided against the royal claim to make law by proclamation (1610). Since the Common Pleas and Chancery jurisdictions were related mainly to property, Bacon (whose income was threatened), persuaded James to promote Coke to the King's Bench, but this simply transferred the controversies to different battle grounds. Coke refused to convict a liar in the prerogative court of Requests, of perjury on the ground that the court was not a court. He rejected a royal effort at co-ordination by opposing James' practice (hallowed by tradition) of consulting the judges on points of law and in the *Case of Commendams* rejected the writ *de non procedendo rege inconsulto* (Lat = Not to proceed without consulting the King) (1615). Suspended from his functions in 1616, he was ordered to expunge cases unfavourable to the prerogative from his *Reports,* the 11th part of which had just been republished; continuing obstinate, he was dismissed.

Coke was an improbable hero. The disagreeable courage which made him obnoxious to James and Bacon made him equally dislikeable to others. He shamefully maltreated his wife (whom he tried to shut up in 1617) and was an associate rather than a friend of the growing opposition group centred on Hampden and Pym. Both sides, however, needed his brains. He was restored to the privy council in 1617 and employed on several commissions, but as M.P. for Liskeard from 1620 to 1622 he furiously and successfully attacked monopolies and the Spanish match, advocated a Spanish war and championed parliamentary privileges. He was also a prime mover in the impeachment which ended the career of his old enemy Bacon (1621). The incensed King briefly committed him to the Tower in 1622. More important he had joined the opponents of the real rulers, Charles, P. of Wales and his friend Buckingham. Coke was M.P. for Coventry in 1624 and for Buckingham in 1625 and 1626, when he opposed the royal demand for money. The court ingeniously prevented his re-election in 1626 by picking him for sheriff, but he was returned in 1628 and spoke powerfully against Buckingham's policies and the consequent taxations and detentions which, in his authoritative view, were illegal. When parliament was dissolved he published the first part of his famous *Institutes of the Laws of England* (generally known as "Coke on Lyttleton") and his papers were promptly seized. His retirement was thenceforth occupied with writing under difficulty the remaining parts. Part 2 was published in 1642, Part 3 and the unfinished Part 4 in 1644. The unfinished Parts 12 and 13 of his *Reports* were published between 1656 and 1659.

COKE, Thomas William ("Billy" or Coke of Norfolk) (1752-1842) 1st E. of LEICESTER (2nd creation) (1837) succeeded to the family estates at Holkham (Norfolk) in 1776 and, save in 1784-90 and 1806-7, he was a zealous Whig M.P. for Norfolk until 1832. He was a popularising, almost revolutionary, farmer from 1778, particularly in breeding Southdown sheep, South Devon cattle and Suffolk pigs, and in substituting (under continuous crop rotation developed from the Townshends) wheat for rye. His scientific management multiplied the income from his farms ten-fold in his lifetime. This was administratively achieved by taking unimproved (often unenclosed) land into his own management as leases fell in, improving it and then granting new leases imposing new contractual obligations. His methods created the pattern for temperate farming all over the world. He was also a famous social and racing figure. *See also* BOWLER HAT.

COLBERT, Jean Baptiste (1619-83) M. de SEIGNELAY, began as Mazarin's agent and became Louis XIV's *Intendant des Finances* in 1661. He brought system into the Kingdom's chaotic finances by suppressing abuses and standardising the *taille* (excise) levied on non-noble tenants in the central *pays d'election*. He encouraged colonisation and the formation in 1664 of the French East India and West India Cos. and instituted a high protective tariff for French manufactures: this provoked retaliation, especially by the Dutch, and so created much internal discontent. From 1668 he was also sec. of the navy. He instituted the maritime conscription: built or rebuilt the bases at Toulon and Rochefort and fortified Calais, Dunkirk, Brest and Le Havre. He engaged the ablest naval architects, and French warships were long the best designed in the world. From 1669 Colbert was also responsible for the royal household and in this capacity founded the French system of art patronage. His interest in economics was far-reaching. He improved agriculture and horse and sheep breeding, introduced labour legislation, protected forests and encouraged ship building. Unfortunately Louis XIV's wars swept away the profits, but his civilising influence survived.

COLCHESTER (Lat: CAMULODUNUM) (Essex). When K. Cunobelinus (Shakespeare's Cymbeline) of the Catuvellauni conquered the pro-Roman Trinovantes (A.D. 5-10) he made his capital here in their territory. Claudius regarded its capture as a major step in the Roman conquest and made it the provincial capital; but the town was taken (partly from within) and destroyed by Q. Boadicea in A.D. 60. A fresh *colonia* was set up after its recapture, but though the town's population eventually reached 20,000 it never regained the pre-eminence which it had lost to London as a result of the disaster. Scandinavian raids led to the building of a tower in 11th cent. and the place was fortified in the 12th. It flourished in the middle ages as an agricultural market and port and in the 14th cent. through cloth making. In that century the population rose from about 2000 to over 4000. Under Elizabeth I and James I Flemish weavers settled there. In the 19th cent. the depot of the Essex regiment was established there and the town was crowned with a gigantic and conspicuous water tower.

COLDBATH FIELDS (Clerkenwell, London). The baths, for curing nervous and rheumatic disorders, were established in 1697. There was a prison from 1794 to 1877. The area has since been built up.

COLDINGHAM (Berwicks). K. Oswald of Northumbria founded a double priory here under his sister Ebba in 640. It became a rich and influential Scots monastery, but later fell under the protection and control of the Humes who, from time to time, took much of its revenue. James IV disputed control with them and though he obtained a papal bull of suppression it could not be enforced and the house survived until the Reformation.

COLDSTREAM (Berwick) was the place where Gen. Monck crossed the border into England to restore the King in 1660 with the troops which were later exempted from the general demobilisation and became the Coldstream Guards.

COLD TROD. *See* MARCHES, ANGLO-SCOTS-5.

COLD WAR was the name of the armed tension provoked by Communist Russia against the non-communist bloc from the end of World War II and throughout the 1950s. It included such episodes as the murder of Jan Masaryk, the Berlin Blockade and airlift and the persistent obstruction of the work of the U.N.O. by Russian vetos.

COLE, Sir Galbraith Lowry (1772-1842), soldier, volunteered for the attacks on the French W. Indies in 1794 and after service at the War Office, in Egypt and at Malta, was 2-in-C at the B. of Maida (1806). From 1809 he commanded the 4th division under Wellington in the

Peninsula with great skill. He saved the B. of Albuera (1811) and took part in most of Wellington's later peninsular victories. In 1812 he became M.P. for Fermanagh (until 1823). He was a well liked gov. of Mauritius from 1823 to 1828 and of the Cape from 1823 to 1833.

COLE, George Douglas Howard (1888-1959) was a prolific writer on labour and industrial relations and taught these subjects at Oxford. As a frequent contributor to the *New Statesman and Nation* he strongly influenced the socialist thought of his day. With his wife he wrote thrillers.

COLENSO, John William (1814-83) became Bp. of Natal in 1853. He would not insist on the divorce of polygamous converts; in 1861 he publicly rejected the doctrine of eternal punishment, the sacramental system and the traditional authorship and accuracy of the Pentateuch. In 1863 his Metropolitan, Bp. Grey of Cape Town, declared him deposed. This created a long maintained sensation. On appeal in 1865 the Privy Council upheld Colenso, because his appointment antedated Grey's. In 1866 Grey excommunicated him but Colenso, in later litigation, maintained his position. He also published a Zulu grammar. In 1869 Grey, nonetheless, consecrated W. K. Macrorie as Bp. The Natal schism lasted until 1911.

COLERIDGE, Samuel Taylor (1772-1834) friend of Charles Lamb and Robert Southey, with whom he planned a communistic community on the Susqehanna. He published his first poems in 1796 when he began to take opium, under the influence of which he wrote *Kubla Khan* in 1797. From 1798 until 1811 the Wedgwoods financed him so that he could devote himself to literature. He translated Schiller's *Wallenstein* in 1800 and generally stimulated English interest in German literature and thought. In 1807 he met his fellow addict, Thomas de Quincey, and in 1808 he abandoned his family and battened first on Wordsworth and then on any friends who would harbour him.

COLERIDGE-TAYLOR, Samuel (1875-1912) son of a W. African negro and an English mother, was a pupil of Stanford. He composed *Hiawatha* (1898-1900) and was the first European champion of African negro music.

COLET (1) Sir Henry (?-1505) was Lord Mayor of London in 1486 and 1495. His well known son **(2) John (1466-1519)** through influential relatives got several wealthy livings and preferments before he was even qualified for ordination. He then studied civil and canon law at various continental universities, as well as philosophy, in which he developed a preference for Origen and Jerome over the scholastics. He also began to learn Greek. Ordained in 1498, he delivered lectures at Oxford on the *Epistles to the Romans and to the Corinthians* and by abandoning the scholastic word-by-word method of commentary attracted large audiences including Erasmus, whom he converted away from the schoolmen; Grocyn, Linacre and Thomas More were among his intimates. In 1505 he became Dean of St. Pauls and this brought him into constant contact with increasingly influential leaders of renaissance opinion. He also inherited his father's huge fortune and in 1509 used part of it to found St. Pauls school; here he laid down educational methods which were liberal for their day. Meantime he preached at St. Pauls. In 1512 a convocation to extirpate Lollardy was summoned but in the opening sermon Colet attacked the ignorance and materialism of the clergy. This brought attempted reprisals. He was prosecuted for heresy before Abp. Warham who, however, dismissed the charges as frivolous. In 1513 he preached against Henry VIII's aggressive foreign policy: the King summoned him to a discussion in which both made concessions and parted with mutual admiration. In 1515 he preached at Wolsey's elevation to the cardinalate. Thereafter his ill health narrowed the circle of his activities.

COLIBERTI (Lat = persons freed together) according to *Domesday Book* represented a considerable element in Wessex and W. Mercia. Their nature and exact status is unknown, but the word suggests group manumissions of slaves, who would be more likely to have been of British than of Anglo-Saxon stock.

COLLATION. *See* ADVOWSON.

COLLECTOR (India) was, owing to the importance of the Mogul land revenue settlement, not merely the tax collector but the administrative head and chief judicial officer of the district. The reason was that liability to pay tax was the test of entitlement to land and the collector in assessing the one was settling the other and had to enforce both.

COLLEGE OF JUSTICE (Sc) is the collective name of those concerned in the administration of justice in the Edinburgh Court of Session. The Lords of Council and Session are its Senators, advocates, writers to the Signet, clerks of session and the bills and of the Exchequer, the directors of the Chancery, the Auditor and some others but not solicitors unless Writers to the Signet, are members. *See* SESSION. COURT OF.

COLLETTS INN. *See* KINGS INNS.

COLLEY or COWLEY, later WESLEY or WELLESLEY, were a Gloucestershire family settled in Ireland in the 16th cent. where they received large estates in Co. Wexford. **(1) Richard (?1690-1758) 1st Ld. MORNINGTON (Ir. 1746)** also succeeded to those of his cousin Garrett Wesley and assumed this name. His son **(2) Garrett (1735-81) 2nd Ld., 1st Vist. WELLESLEY and 1st E. of MORNINGTON (1760)** was a versatile musician who married Anne Hill, *d.* of the 1st Vist. Dungannon. She was a cold and not very intelligent woman. Their remarkable progeny included the first D. of Wellington, the first M. Wellesley; the first Ld. Maryborough and the first Ld. Cowley.

COLLIE, BORDER, SCOTS, WELSH. These sheep-dogs were used very early in Scotland and then spread to the Border and later to Wales, differentiating as to breed as they went. They began as shepherds' companions and guard-dogs in turbulent times, but were soon found to be potent labour savers and, as part of dog-and-stick farming, unconscious agents of much rural unemployment.

COLLIER. In the 16th and 17th cents. coal was carried (mostly for household purposes) 300-400 tons at a time, along the coast, notably between the Tyne and London. A particularly strong deep-waisted type of collier of 600-ton capacity built on a Norwegian model known all over the northern seas was called a CAT. It continued in use until mid 19th cent. and was the type of ship favoured by Capt. Cook (who had been in the coal trade) in his explorations. When steamships appeared they needed coaling stations and this, with the new steampowered industry, led to the development of a, soon very common, steam collier carrying about 6000 tons. Such ships, a majority English built, carried on a world-wide coal trade until industry and shipping took to oil. Nevertheless there remained a large demand for coal, for purposes other than power supply, and the 6000-tonners were superseded after World War II by far fewer 25,000-tonners.

COLLINGWOOD, Cuthbert (1750-1810) 1st Ld. (1805) went to sea at 11 and reached the Captains' List in 1780. He was a friend of Nelson under whom he served in the W. Indies in 1780 and from 1783 to 1786. He fought under Howe at the Glorious First of June (1794) and under Jervis at Cape St. Vincent (Feb. 1797) and, though humourless and taciturn, his courage and ability in both battles won him the respect of the whole fleet. As a V-Admiral from 1803 he was constantly at sea. He commanded the starboard column of Nelson's fleet at Trafalgar and took successful command of the fleet at his friend's death. It was not his fault that most of the prizes were lost in the ensuing tempest. He stayed in command and maintained British supremacy in the straits and off Cadiz from his H.Q. in Gibraltar until he died, worn out, at sea.

COLLINS, Michael (1890-1922) from 1906 to 1916 lived in London where he was an active Irish republican. He took part in the Easter Rebellion (1916) and after a short imprisonment became the organiser of the Irish Volunteers and Sinn Fein. He became Irish Min. of Home Affairs on the declaration of independence in 1919 and was director of organisation for the volunteers. When all Irish revolutionary organisations were declared illegal he operated underground, raising loans. In 1921 he led the delegation which negotiated the Irish T. and in Jan. 1922 became chairman and finance Min. of the provisional govt. but had to deal with organised opposition to a treaty which broke out in civil war in June. Although not known at the time, he ordered the murder of F.M. Sir Henry Wilson. He took command of the Free State Army and put down opposition in Dublin but was murdered himself.

COLMAN, St. (?-676) an Irish monk of Iona succeeded St. Finan as Bp. of Lindisfarne in 661.

COLNEY HATCH (Pron "coney") (Middx). A lunatic asylum opened in 1851. It became proverbial.

COLOGNE (Ger.) became an archbishopric in the 9th cent. but the city slowly freed itself from archiepiscopal control by 1288. It was a centre for banking, wine and cloth and had important trading connections with England. The town of Cologne was ruled by the *Richerzeche* (Millionaires Boozer) until 1396 when the 22 guilds took over. It was recognised as a free imperial city in 1475. In 1801 Cologne was occupied by the French and in 1802 the Archbishop-elector died and was not replaced. The area passed to Prussia in 1815. *See* HANSE; FLANDERS-6.

COLOGNE, LEAGUE OF. *See* BALTIC-20; HANSE-6.

COLOMBIA or NEW GRANADA (*see* BOLIVAR) was formed at the death of Bolivar in 1830 by the secession from GRAN COLOMBIA of Venezuela and Ecuador. It was hardly governed at all until 1858 when the so-called GRANADINE CONFEDERATION was set up. This collapsed in 1863 and the present constitution, name and organisation was not established until 1886. An alliance of conservatives and practically minded liberals held power until 1899 when the liberal challenge led to a civil war. This wrecked the economy, but ended with a govt. victory in 1902. Meanwhile the Americans and French were intriguing in Panamá. The Colombian govt. had granted a concession to the French Panamá Canal Co. as far back as 1878, but corruption in Paris and malaria stopped the work, much of which had been done by 1898. The U.S.A. decided, after turning the Spaniards out of Cuba, to build a canal either in Nicaragua or at Panamá, but triangular negotiations broke down. The French and Americans then instigated a local insurrection, the U.S.A. prevented the Colombian govt. from putting it down and in 1903 recognised Panamá as an independent state. The conservatives survived even this and retained their hold on the govt. until the depression of 1930. In 1930 the liberals were returned to power under Enrique Olaya HERRERA (pres. 1930-4). They seized all public offices, declared a moratorium on debts and used their political advantage to pursue the habitual local feuds. The conservatives prepared for civil war which was, however, averted in 1932 when all parties were distracted by a two year border war with Peru. Meanwhile the liberals sought to modernise the state by introducing state education, a public health system and a redistribution of land. These policies were pursued by Herrera's liberal successors Alfonso LOPEZ Pumarejo (pres. 1934-8 and 1942-5) and Eduardo SANTOS Montejo (pres. 1938-42). The rise in export earnings caused by World War II facilitated these policies. The slump at its end split the liberals whose right wing believed that, for the time at least, the reforms could go no further, for the feuding had broken into local violence and the real condition of the country resembled the fragmentation of the 1850s. After political confusion in 1946 a moderate conservative Mariano OSPINA Perez (pres. 1946-50) was elected (against two rival liberal candidates) but with a liberal legislature. His supporters began to take over public office and in Apr. 1948 Jorge Gaitan, the left wing liberal candidate, was murdered. Furious riots broke out in all the major cities; the govt. proclaimed a state of siege and used the special powers conferred by it to eliminate its opponents. The extreme conservative Laureano GOMEZ (pres. 1950-3) was, in effect, a dictator and when Gen. Gustavo ROJAS Pinilla (1953-7) overthrew him in the name of liberty the dictatorship continued. The liberals and conservatives, however, recognised that autocracy at the centre and civil war between local political bosses was no substitute for a govt. Alberto LLERAS Camargo, a liberal, negotiated an agreement called the NATIONAL FRONT whereby the parties shared the spoils of office equally and the presidency by rotation, and there was to be a return to constitutional govt. Elected pres. on this basis (1958-62) Lleras was able to abolish the state of siege in many areas and the legislature functioned again, but civil disorder continued sporadically under him and his two successors. The National Front arrangement was in any case due to expire in 1974. In fact the Front was being already challenged by the right wing Peronista-style ANAPO movement. Meanwhile poverty led to the cultivation and processing of heroin and political fragmentation was extended in the form of organised and immensely profitable drug rackets, particularly by exports through Panamá, especially from MEDELLIN, whose CARTEL was recognised in the 1980s as a threat to international order.

COLOMBO. See CEYLON.

COLOMBO PLAN. In 1950 Australia, Britain, Ceylon, Canada, India, New Zealand and Pakistan agreed to discuss S.E. Asian development planning and economic problems annually and to establish a permanent body concerned with technical assistance. Finance for projects was arranged bilaterally or with the International Bank for Reconstruction and Development. Originally a purely Commonwealth organisation, it was joined by the U.S.A., Cambodia and Laos in 1951; Burma and Nepal in 1952; Indonesia in 1953; the Philippines, Japan and Thailand in 1954; Malaysia in 1957; South Korea and Bhutan in 1962; Singapore in 1965 and Iran in 1966.

COLONIA. See BRITAIN. ROMAN-7.

COLONIAL CONFERENCES. FIRST (1887). Prompted by the Imperial Federation League in the knowledge that all the premiers of the self-governing colonies would be attending Q. Victoria's golden jubilee (June), Ld. Salisbury assembled his conference in Apr. to encourage imperial co-operation for self-defence against the new overseas ambitions of European powers. The calling of the conference was more important than its achievements, which were insignificant. It was not suggested that similar conferences should be repeated regularly, but all later colonial and imperial conferences descend from it. **SECOND (Ottawa 1894),** was originally a meeting to discuss Pacific cables, at which Britain was represented only by the 7th E. of Jersey, a former gov. of N.S.W. It discussed imperial preference at Canadian instigation, but reached no important conclusion on it. **THIRD (June-July 1897)** was held during Q. Victoria's Diamond Jubilee celebrations. **(1)** Joseph Chamberlain (Colonial Sec.) presided and the premiers of Canada, Newfoundland, the six Australian colonies, New Zealand, Cape Colony and Natal attended. **(2)** The idea of uniting the Empire was in everybody's mind, but the discussions centred round three facets, politics, defence and trade. Chamberlain hoped for a political council of representative plenipotentiaries, which might grow into a

federal council. The premiers (except Seddon of New Zealand and Braddon of Tasmania) treasured their parochial independence and feared that Britain would dominate the policy of such a body, adherence to which would restrict their freedom of dissent. They agreed, however, that conferences should meet at intervals but fixed no dates. A similar parochialism dominated defence: the Admiralty wanted a single world navy, the War Office interchangeability of military formations. The Australians wanted a squadron in their waters, the Cape offered (but later withdrew) the cost of a battleship. **(3)** Local protectionism had created too many local vested interests to permit of a customs union, but the premiers agreed on imperial preference and the denunciation of treaties (with Germany and Belgium) inconsistent with it. **FOURTH (July-Aug. 1902)** at the coronation of Edward VII, Joseph Chamberlain presided and Australia, Canada, Cape Colony, Natal, Newfoundland and New Zealand were represented. Chamberlain hoped that imperial co-operation in the recent S. African war might encourage the formation of a council of empire and an imperial defence policy. In fact it had increased the colonial sense of separate nationality; the British per capita contribution to defence was many times that of the others, yet despite their protectionism, Canada offered nothing and the rest made only trifling additions to their naval contribution. The conference resolved, however, **(1)** to meet every three years; **(2)** that imperial free trade was impracticable, but imperial preference desirable and **(3)** that Britain and those colonies which had not practised imperial preference should do so. **FIFTH (1907).** This was the conference at which the parties disagreed over imperial preference and the Canadians resisted a proposal to set up a permanent or standing commission or Imperial Council. Future conferences were, however, to be held every four years and the term 'Dominions' was to be used for self governing units of the Empire. See IMPERIAL CONFERENCES.

COLONIAL (later COMMONWEALTH) DEVELOPMENT CORPORATION was originally established in 1948.

COLONIAL LAND EMIGRATION BOARD (1840-76), set up to support colonial settlement mostly in Australia and New Zealand. From 1842 it was financed through the Waste Lands Act, 1842, which fixed a minimum price for land and took half. Its operations naturally declined as the colonies became more self conscious.

COLONIAL LAWS AND THEIR VALIDITY. (1) The word 'Colony' was used initially only of those places deliberately called colonies. Other British overseas communities were called Islands (e.g. Man), Plantations (Ulster), Factories (Bombay), Dominions (New England), Settlements (Malacca) or Fortresses (Gibraltar). After 1889 whatever local term was used, the word 'colony' meant any British possession except the U.K., the Channel Is., Man and India, but it never included a protectorate even if it was indistinguishable from a colony in other ways, nor Cyprus which was handed over by the Porte subject to contingent restoration.

(2) In 1722 the Privy Council on appeal from a foreign plantation came to the following conclusions or resolutions which distinguished between **Settled (1)** and **Conquered or Ceded (2 and 3)** colonies viz: "1st, That if there be a new and uninhabited country found out by English subjects, as the law is the birthright of every subject, so, wherever they go, they carry their laws with them, and therefore such new found country is to be governed by the laws of England; though, after such country is inhabited by the English, acts of parliament made in England, without naming the foreign plantations, will not bind them; but that secondly, Where the King of England conquers a country, it is a different consideration for there the conqueror, by saving the lives of the people conquered, gains a right and property in such people; in consequence of which he may impose upon them what laws he pleased. But, thirdly, Until such laws given by the conquering prince, the laws and customs of the conquered country shall hold place; unless where these are contrary to our religion, or enact any thing that is *malum in se* (Lat = bad in itself) or are silent; for in all such cases the laws of the conquering country shall prevail."

In practice treaties of cession provided for the retention of older developed systems of law in ceded colonies. Hence the basic law by which Quebec is governed is the *Coutumier of Paris* as at 1769, Mauritius the *Code Napoléon*, Ceylon, British Guiana and S. Africa various forms of Roman Dutch Law and Trinidad Roman-Spanish law. These were subsequently varied by the Crown in Council, or in due course by local legislatures irrevocably granted by the crown.

(3) Initially colonial policy, being external to the U.K., was a matter for the royal prerogative, which in this respect was not limited by parliamentary law. Therefore the Crown could and did legislate in a colony and alter its laws. (4) The Crown's prerogative was exercised by the governor, but under the control of the Colonial Office. (5) Local organs of a legislative character were progressively created. There were ten types of these. (The examples are as at 1953.) (a) a mere executive council of officials whose advice the governor took but could reject (St. Helena) (b) a legislature with an official majority and an unofficial nominated minority; (Hong Kong) (c) a legislature with an unofficial majority of nominated members; (Malaya) (d) a legislature with an official majority and an unofficial elected minority (Fiji). In 1907 classes (a) to (d) above comprised 17 colonies in all. (e) a legislature containing an elected majority (Falkland Is.) (f) a legislature with an unofficial majority but with elected members of the legislature in the executive council (Gibraltar); (g) a representative legislature without control of the executive (Mauritius). In 1907 classes (e) to (g) included the Canadian provinces and seven other colonies; (h) a representative legislature which controlled the executive by convention (Barbados); (i) semi-responsible government (Jamaica); (j) self-governing places (Malta G.C.).

(6) In addition there were the Channel Is. and the I. of Man. These were important because they provided the constitutional precedents for the treatment of colonial law.

(7) As colonial law was theoretically subject to the prerogative, appeals from local courts lay to the Crown, not to the English courts, and were invariably referred to the Privy Council. A judicial committee of the Council grew up and was eventually constituted (1833) by statute. In practice it consisted of judges and latterly included judges from overseas territories. It is perhaps significant that colonial policy was originally managed through another privy council committee, that for Trade and Plantations, which eventually developed into the Board of Trade.

(8) Once a colony had a legislature of any sort it became necessary to settle its and the governor's respective spheres of competence, bearing in mind that he represented not only the Crown but the Home govt. and its policy. As Crown representative he could assent to or refuse assent to legislation or he might refer bills to London for ALLOWANCE OR DISALLOWANCE. This was known as RESERVATION and to maintain some consistency the Colonial Office would issue governors with INSTRUMENTS OF INSTRUCTIONS setting out what types of bills might respectively be assented to, refused or reserved. These instruments were public documents and as time went on and the telegraph bound the empire over more closely together, their drafting became increasingly specific. This created a growing number of difficulties: in particular (a) where there was an elected

legislature it was argued that the governor was constitutionally bound to assent if assent was permitted in his Instructions; (b) an assent might be attacked as void at home if it contravened the instructions.

(9) Moreover there were doubts about the relationship between colonial laws and United Kingdom statutes which were invading larger spheres of activity than hitherto. There was no legal doubt that parliament could legislate for the colonies, though certain of its legislation had provoked the American rebellion. The problem was the extent to which colonial legislatures could legislate in the same field and whether a governor was bound to refuse assent to or at least reserve such legislation if it was REPUGNANT to a U.K. statute. Moreover there were doubts about the occasions when such a statute applied: were express words or necessary intendment required or were all statutes applicable unless shown not to be?

(10) These issues were brought to a head by a constitutional crisis in S. Australia in 1864 and were resolved by the brief Colonial Laws Validity Act, 1865. This applied British Acts of Parliament to colonies only when they contained express words or were applicable by necessary intendment. Even in this limited class of statutes, local legislation was to be void for repugnancy only to the extent of the inconsistency, and was not to be void because assent had been given contrary to instruction. Colonial legislatures were empowered to establish courts of law and those with an elected majority could, within the rules laid down by their constitutions, make constitutional laws. The Act also expressly validated the disputed S. Australian legislation.

(11) The practical autonomy of colonies grew, especially in foreign affairs. In 1871 the Prime Minister of Canada was made a plenipotentiary to negotiate the T. of Washington and by 1879 the U.K. habitually requested adherence on behalf of individual colonies so that they could be consulted. In 1899 self governing colonies were permitted to withdraw from such treaties and from 1905 they could adhere to such treaties even though the U.K. had not.

(12) These developments in practice reduced the governor's discretion to refuse assent or reserve bills and made disallowance increasingly difficult and rare. This led to attempts in various constitutional enactments to define the occasions when these powers might be, or must be, used: for example, certain types of Canadian provincial legislation had to be reserved and could, since the Statute of Westminster 1931, be disallowed on the advice of the Canadian govt.

COLONIAL OFFICE was set up in 1854. *See* DOMINIONS OFFICE.

COLORADO. *See* NEW MEXICO.

COLOURS, MILITARY. A military unit might be raised privately and the colonel then provided his own rallying flag. For reasons of identification in battle, its colours reflected the colours of the uniform which he provided. Such *regimental* flags only accidentally indicated the nationality of the unit; hence from Q. Anne's time infantry units were given a second, or *sovereign*'s colour based upon the union jack, save in the Foot Guards where the practice was reversed. The troops which had no colours were: rifles and light infantry because their tactics made them unusable; Engineers, who never fought as a unit; Artillery, who treated their guns as colours and the Royal Marines because of their fragmentation among ships. Household Cavalry and dragoon guards carried a single standard: other cavalry a guidon. These arrangements subsist, even though the cavalry are now armoured. Apart from the basic design, colours are embroidered with the regimental badges and with the battle honours represented by the names of victorious engagements in which the unit has distinguished itself. Some are entitled to more than there is room for.

Colours, when worn out, are laid up in churches and a new set is consecrated bearing the honours omitted from the previous set.

COLQUHOUN (pron *Ca-hoon*) **Patrick (1745-1820)** spent six years in Virginia, returned to Glasgow in 1766 and set up as a merchant and local politician. He founded the Glasgow Chamber of Commerce in 1783, moved to London in 1789 and became a metropolitan magistrate in 1792. Alarmed by the incidence of crime, he wrote *Treatises* on *Police of the Metropolis* (1795) and on *Indigence* (1806) which paved the way for later police and social improvements and on the *Wealth, Power and Resources of the British Empire* (1814) which is a quarry of economic information.

COLUMBA or COLUMCILLE, St. (c. 521-97). Of royal Irish ancestry, he trained as a monk and founded monasteries at Derry (546), Durrow and probably Kells. In 563 he took twelve companions to Iona, off the W. Scots I. of Mull, and from the monastery which he founded there they conducted fearless and successful missions throughout much of Scotland. He converted the King of the northern Picts, and Irish settlers in Scotland followed his spiritual leadership. His biographer St. Adamnan and the Venerable Bede both admired him. He died in the year when St. Augustine landed in Kent, by which time he had so established the Iona monastery that it maintained a supremacy over the northern church for a century. This was so far recognised that at the Synod of Whitby (663) St. Wilfrid put the choice between the Roman and the Celtic Easter as a choice between Sts. Peter and Colomba.

COLUMBAN, St. (c. 543-615) a Leinsterman, spent at least 20 years in the Irish monastery of Bangor before taking twelve companions to Gaul in 590. He resolutely adhered to the customs of the Celtic Church, and his monastery at Luxeuil (in the Vosges) came under heavy criticism from the Frankish church. He was banished in 610 ostensibly for denouncing royal immorality and founded a fresh monastery at Bobbio (in the Apennines). His rule, which was severe, never became popular, was not observed in Britain and was, anyhow, largely superseded by that of St. Benedict. He was a fine Latinist, like others of his Irish contemporaries, and Luxeuil and Bobbio contributed significantly to the survival of Latin civilisation.

COLUMBIA UNIVERSITY (New York) was chartered as King's College in 1754 and closed at the rebellion in 1776. It reopened under the name of Columbia in 1784.

COLUMBUS (Sp. COLON), Christopher (1451-1506), a Genoese, married in 1478 the daughter of a Portuguese seaman trained by P. Henry the Navigator. With his brother Bartholomew, a cartographer, he formulated the (not new) theory that 'the Indies', i.e. the Far East, could be reached westwards instead of by the long haul round Africa. Underestimating the distance, they persuaded Ferdinand and Isabella of Spain to finance a voyage. The expedition, consisting of 90 men in three small caravels (*Santa Maria, Niña* and *Pinta*) left Palos on 3 Aug. 1492 and sighted a Bahamian island on 12 Oct. He explored the coast of Cuba and part of Hispaniola and, the *Santa Maria* having been wrecked, brought the sensational news back to Palos in the other two ships on 15 Mar. 1493. His 'Letter' describing these events was published in Apr. and volunteers flocked to him. In Sept. he set sail again with 1200 men in 17 ships and, after exploring the Leeward and Virgin Is. and Puerto Rico, reached Hispaniola and, in Jan. 1494, began building a settlement at Isabella. The crew, unsuitable for such a task, mutinied in his absence and, returning to Spain, accused Columbus of fraud. Accordingly he had difficulty in organising his third expedition, which did not set sail until 1498. He reached Trinidad and the mouths of the Orinoco, but meantime a royal commissioner had been investigating the Isabella colony and the two Columbus' were arrested. Returned to Spain, they were released but had forfeited

royal favour. Other navigators such as Magellan and Vespucci were now in the field. Columbus' fourth and last venture, a private affair, took place in the years 1502 to 1504. He reached Honduras and Darien (Panama) but returned ill and incapacitated. Until he died he believed that his discoveries were somewhere near China. *See* RENAISSANCE-8; SPAIN 1406-1516-5.

COLVILLE (1) James (?-?1540) sat in the Scots Parliament in 1525, 1531, 1535 and 1536. In 1532 and 1535 he was a Lord of the Articles. In 1532 he became one of the first Lords of Session and a commissioner for the English peace at Newcastle. In 1538 he took the part of the Douglases and was summoned for treason. **(A)** His illegitimate son Robert was the ancestor of **(2) Robert (?-1662) 1st Ld. COLVILLE of OCHILTREE (1650),** a strong royalist ennobled by Charles II during the Scottish campaign. **(B)** A legitimate son **(3) Alexander (?1530-97)** supported the opponents of Mary Q. of Scots and was appointed a Lord of Session by Morton in about 1575. He also acted as arbitrator in the Gordon-Forbes feud in 1578 and was a Lord of the Articles and a commissioner for defining the jurisdiction of the church. He retired in 1587. His nephew **(4) James (1551-1629) 1st Ld. COLVILLE of CULROSS (1604)** was a protestant soldier under Henry IV of France, but occasionally came to Scotland where, in 1571, he held Stirling for James VI against Lennox; in 1582 he was involved in the Ruthven Raid for which he was pardoned in 1583. In 1589 he apparently acquired the barony of Culross and was thereafter employed on diplomatic missions to France and in 1594 to England. (See also CALVIN'S or COLVILLE'S CASE.) A descendent **(5) Alexander (1717-70) 7th Ld. (1741)** became an Admiral, reduced Louisburg in 1758, relieved Quebec in 1760 and conquered Newfoundland. Another descendent **(6) Charles (1818-1903) 10th Ld. (1849) and 1st. Vist. (1902)** was a court official and Scottish representative peer from 1852 to 1885 and from 1880 to 1895 as chairman of the Great Northern Rly Co. was one of the earlier peers to turn to big business. He died rich. A further descendent **(7) John Mark (1933-) 4th Vist. (1945)** was Minister of State at the Home Office in 1973-4 and subsequently Chairman of the Parole Board.

COMBAT, TRIAL BY, WAGER OF BATTLE or APPEAL OF FELONY. This Norman, but not Anglo-Saxon, method of trial was, in theory, an appeal to God. It was originally applicable in most cases, including international negotiations, where a duellist sometimes accompanied negotiators to settle incidental points. In a criminal case accuser and defendant commonly fought in person and the defendant, if defeated, was hanged instantly. Clergy, infants, women and persons over sixty could decline battle or appoint champions and so give themselves advantages over ordinary litigants. In civil cases the latter might eventually appoint professional champions (of whom there were many) too and the appeal to God degenerated into a judicial brawl. Armed with horn pick-axes, the parties laid about each other until one was beaten into surrender. Innocent III withdrew church approval at the Lateran Council of 1215 and, though the method continued in sporadic use in England in real actions on the Grand Assize and in appeals of murder, it was rare after 1300 because other methods of trial were fairer. One case (which ended in a fiasco) was a nine days wonder in 1571. Charles I stopped another in 1638. In 1818 (*Ashford* v *Thornton* 1 B & Ald 451) the court was forced to hold that the method still existed but battle was avoided. It was hurriedly abolished in 1819.

COMBERMERE. *See* COTTON.

COMBINATION ACTS 1799 AND 1800 imposed, on summary conviction (i.e. by J.P.s), three months imprisonment or two months hard labour on anyone who conspired with or solicited another to alter wages or working hours. Previous legislation in 1795 was concerned with wartime dangers. These acts had a reactionary social purpose. Though in form directed against masters as well as workpeople, they were in practice applied only to working men. They were repealed in 1824 through the agitation of Francis Place and Joseph Hume.

COMBINED (18th cent. 'CONJUNCT') OPERATIONS (1) are those involving the co-operation of fighting men trained for different elements. Migrations apart, they have been an unavoidable part of wars involving sea-girt Britain. The details of Caesar's two attacks are only slightly known, those of other, pre-14th cent. operations not at all, but Edward III's victory at Sluys (1340) may have been an early case. Of a few, among many examples, failures included the 1588 Armada, Tollemache's landing at Camaret Bay (Brest 1694) and the Anglo-Austrians' at Toulon (1707): successes included the capture of Quebec by Wolfe and Saunders (1759), Abercromby's carefully rehearsed victory in Aboukir Bay (Egypt 1801), Cochrane and Ross's burning of Washington (1814), the Anglo-French landings at Calamita Bay (Crimea 1854) and the bungled, if gallant, landings at Gallipoli (1915).

(2) These were necessarily confined to land-sea frontiers but despite their long history and common features, no doctrine on their conduct was developed save by Abercromby who was killed within days of his success. Such operations require (a) detailed information, (b) careful staff-work before the men and resources are chosen and assembled, (c) convenient assemblage, (d) time for all the foregoing, (e) during which surprise is safeguarded by efficient security or distraction, (f) temperamental affinity and shared knowledge between service commanders, (g) correlative rehearsal at subordinate levels, (h) a sense of urgency at the time of impact. Much must be unpredictable but all that is humanly foreseeable must at least be considered. Of the eight above examples at Sluys, only Aboukir Bay met all those criteria. The Armada met none and could never have succeeded 'save by a miracle', Camaret Bay failed on (e), Toulon on (f), (g) and (h). The success at Washington was opportunistic, that at Calamita Bay unplanned. The pyrrhic attacks at Gallipoli succeeded tactically on the basis of (f), (g) and (h) but failed later for inadequate political will.

(3) With World War II, a third element was involved, namely the air, which was, unlike the others, in overall rather than linear contact with the other two. The planned, if navally disastrous, German attack on Norway (Apr-June 1940) and the improvised Anglo-French militarily disastrous reaction, opened eyes in London. Thus, while the improvised German attack on Crete was locally successful but entailed the loss of the irreplaceable airborne force, in the Churchill govt's aggressive spirit, a **Combined Operations Staff** was created for the first time in world history and developed doctrines and techniques for operations of all types and sizes from the tiny (but significant) Bruneval and the strategically important St. Nazaire raids (Feb. and Mar. 1942) to the partial but useful failure at Dieppe (Aug. 1942). A tested corpus of understanding was thus available to the Americans when faced with Japanese planned operations and their own improvised reactions.

(4) From the time (c. May 1942) when the Japanese onslaught was contained, the proper planning and execution of combined operations were seen to be an initiating condition of victory, and large Anglo-U.S. intellectual and material resources (such as air co-operation techniques, enterprising staffs and directors such as Ld. Louis Mountbatten and landing craft) were devoted to it. In the west these produced the spectacular landings in French N. Africa (Nov. 1942), Sicily (July 1943) and Salerno (Sept. 1943), the failure for want of urgency at Anzio (Jan. 1944), the huge invasion of Normandy (June 1944) and the landings in Provence (Aug. 1944). In the East there were the bitter U.S. island operations, but after the British Arakan (Apr-May 1945) and Australian Celebes (July 1945) attacks, further efforts were rendered unnecessary by the Japanese surrender to atomic power.

COMETS. The trajectories and periodicity of many comets have been calculated, beginning with Halley's comet, which with a period of orbit of 76.09 years appeared *inter alia* in A.D. 1066,1759,1910 and 1988.

COMGALL, St. *See* MISSIONS TO EUROPE.

COMINFORM (Communist Information Bureau), the organisation for disseminating revolutionary communism, was set up at Belgrade to replace the Comintern (Communist International) in Oct. 1947, by agreement between the communist parties of the USSR, Eastern Europe, France and Italy. The Yugoslavs were expelled in June 1948 and it moved to Moscow. Its functions were transferred to the International Department of the USSR Communist Party's Central Committee in April 1956.

COMINTERN ('Communist International') or THIRD INTERNATIONAL was founded at Moscow in 1919 as the directing organisation for world revolution. After 1924, when the Russian civil wars had ended and the Russian communists constituted the most powerful force in the Comintern, its independence gradually disappeared and from 1929 it was run on Stalin's behalf by Molotov, Manuilsky and the Finn Kuusinen and had, in fact, become an instrument of the Russian Foreign Office. It held no congress after 1935. After Russia was attacked by Germany in 1941, the Russians urgently needed the help of powers which the Comintern was pledged to overthrow, and its existence became embarrassing. In 1943 it was accordingly dissolved: but this by itself made no difference to Russian influence in other communist parties.

COMITADJI. A Macedonian anti-Turkish guerrilla or bandit.

COMITY. A system of international mutual forbearance and helpfulness based upon convenience, whereby states of similar outlook will enforce under their own laws private rights acquired under the law of another state. It is sometimes stated to be the principle underlying private international law.

COMMANDANT (1) An Irish major; **(2)** An officer commanding troops in a garrison area; **(3)** The commander of any French ship, no matter how small.

COMMANDER-IN-CHIEF (C-in-C) (1) the title, which superseded that of CAPTAIN-GENERAL, of the highest commander of the British Army in the 18th cent. Until 1855 he was virtually independent of the War Office and even thereafter, the holder being the very conservative royal D. of Cambridge, not very amenable to its influence. He was succeeded at his death by E. Roberts, who resigned in 1904 in favour of an Army Council, and the office was abolished. **(2)** The title of the commander of a major, exclusively British, war force in a theatre of operations. The naval usage dates back to 1760, the military to World War I. **(3)** Where a large force is a combination of several modes or several nations, the World War II title was SUPREME COMMANDER.

COMMANDERY or PRECEPTORY. A territorial sub-unit, sometimes very extensive, of a military order. The Knights Templar had four in the Middle East and eight (of which England was one) in Europe. The Hospitallers later called them *Languages*. The administrator was called the *preceptor*.

COMMANDO was originally the administrative and tactical unit of the Boer army. It consisted of all males between 16 and 60 in a given electoral area. In World War II the word meant a British unit trained in the skilled technique of raiding, especially from the sea.

COMMAND PAPERS are papers presented by the govt. to the Houses of Parliament. They include reports of the work of govt. depts, Royal Commissions and Departmental Committees and materials relevant to policy discussions. Originally printed as appendices to the *Commons Journal,* they have since 1833 been issued in five consecutive series viz: Nos. 1-4222, *1833-69,* C.l-C.9550 *1870-99,* Cd.1-Cd.9239 *1900-18;* Cmd.1-9889 *1919-56;* Cmnd. 1 *et seq 1956 onwards.*

COMMENDA. A type of mediaeval short term partnership common throughout Europe, in which a *commendator,* who stayed at home, lent money to a commendatarius, who used it to finance and manage a venture in return for his expenses and 25% of the profits.

COMMENDAMS. A (1) A person (the *Commendatarius*) was said to hold an ecclesiastical benefice *in commendam* if the revenues had been granted to him during a vacancy. It was considered an abuse if he were a layman and the practice came to be (very) slowly restricted to pluralities with another benefice of higher status. Originally the papacy issued Letters Recommendatory to the patron who disregarded them only on peril of excommunication. The *commendatarius* took the stipend and if he did not carry out the duties he appointed a curate or vicar at a pittance to do so. The purpose was to ensure that the holder of the higher office was properly paid; the circumstance which gave rise to it was the extreme unevenness of church endowments. The practice was often abused and was a matter of recurrent complaint against the Papacy, many of whose later and highly pluralist *commendatarii* never set foot in England. After the Reformation the crown adopted the papal practice, but restricted it almost wholly to benefices in its own gift. By the 18th cent. the practice had become a system. Eight of the poorest bishoprics were always held with particular benefices viz:-

Bristol with a residentiary prebend of St. Pauls and the Rectory of Bow.
Chester with the rectory of Stanhope.
Gloucester with a prebend of Durham.
Oxford with the Deanery of St. Pauls.
Peterborough with the Vicarage of Twickenham.
Rochester with the Deanery of Westminster.
St. Davids with the Rectory of St. Anne's Soho and the Vicarage of Greenwich.
Llandaff with a canonry of Windsor.

*These were new bishoprics set up by Henry VIII. The practice died out with the centralisation of endowments under the ecclesiastical commissioners. **(2)** Separately from this the custody of an ecclesiastical benefice might be temporarily given to a layman or clergyman during a vacancy. The *commendatarius* received the revenues. The practice was grossly and continually abused, some benefices being held almost permanently in commendam. Abolished in 1836.

COMMENDATION was the personal submission, perhaps in troubled times, of a free man to the protection of one greater than himself for his service. Permanent settlement and repetition by successive generations of the same family might sometimes harden into a feudal relationship. It was essentially pre-feudal.

COMMERCE PROTECTION, NAVAL. In her major wars Britain, with or without allies, mostly commanded the sea while her opponents resorted to commerce destruction. **(A)** During the **Wars of 1793-1815 (1)** this was effected mainly by privateers. There were 87 substantial ones based on the French Channel ports in 1800, besides fishing and rowing craft; the fewer Biscay privateers had to be larger, some reaching frigate tonnage; the Martiniquais and Guadaloupois used schooners and brigs against the long distance traffic and row boats against inter-island shipping. In the Indian Ocean Robert Surcouf and others, against the large scattered East Indiamen, operated ships of substantial tonnage from I. Bourbon

and Mauritius and, after 1795, from Sumatra and Java. At least 829 French commerce raiders were captured between 1793 and 1800.

(2) The damage was inflicted mostly on isolated British vessels, 490-520 a year being taken between 1793 and 1815. This represented about 2½% of the volume of British overseas trade: trading vessels other than East Indiamen then averaged about 120 tons.

(3) As merchant seamen were essential for naval crews, the loss of commercial shipping particularly affected the Royal Navy as well as the war economy in general. The CONVOY ACTS of 1798 and 1803 compelled ships to take convoy and pay for it. The resulting fall in insurance rates easily compensated ship owners for the outlay. Convoys were gathered at the entrance of the Baltic, the Chops of the Channel, Gibraltar, Malta, Kingston (Jamaica) and Bombay. They were very large: 200-300 ships were usual. In 1810 600 were delayed by headwinds in the Little Belt: even 1000 were known. Convoys, however, created their own problems. They took time to collect and sailed at the pace of the slowest. Voyages were more expensive; perishable cargoes were at greater risk. They created gluts on arrival between periods of relative dearth and caused acute price fluctuations to the advantage of local speculators and warehousemen. Under sail there was, in any case, a tendency for ships to part company from convoys in bad weather, and enterprising owners were tempted to "go it alone" in order to be first in the market.

(4) These vessels, isolated by misfortune, bad management or opportunism, had nevertheless to be protected and patrols, consisting of frigates and sloops of war (said to be on cruise) were established at areas where the commercial routes converged. These were casually reinforced by the many warships passing between Britain and their stations with despatches, or going in for or returning from repairs and, of course, by British privateers. Between 15% and 20% of captures by the enemy were recaptured, entitling their rescuers to salvage. The ships in the cruise areas were responsible for taking most of the enemy commerce raiders.

(B) In WORLD WAR I **(1)** there was no privateering and the technical circumstances had altered. Mines closed the Baltic to the British, the Straits of Dover partly to the Germans and the Mediterranean to the Austrians; power driven ships, though dependent on fuelling points, were less liable to part company with convoys and radio simplified the control of patrols and convoys generally. The German surface attack on commerce had to come north about Scotland, where it risked engagement by the powerful 10th Cruiser Squadron, or it had to radiate from colonial bases at Tsingtao, Rabaul and the E. and W. African colonies. These bases had all fallen by the Spring of 1915.

(2) Accordingly the Germans resorted to the newly invented submarine (U-boat). This could not capture a ship when it was itself submerged and was vulnerable when surfaced. Consequently, though U-boats in safe situations did attack on the surface with the gun, countermeasures kept them increasingly under water, whence they could use only torpedoes, usually without warning. This was a sanguinary and bitter form of warfare in which prisoners were seldom taken.

(3) At the start of the war there were only 34 U-boats, of which in practice only 8 could keep the sea at one time. Their attack on commerce began immediately and sinkings averaged (world figures) 60,000 tons a month in the first six months. Seven were lost. In Feb. 1915 a change in the German naval high command brought an intensification; U-boats appeared even in the Irish Sea and during the next 12 months monthly sinkings were about 90,000 tons. By this time, despite evasive routes, zig zagging, intensified patrolling, the arming of merchantmen and the activities of Q-ships, the effectiveness and number of U-boats at sea rose; in the fourth half year monthly averages were 140,000 tons; in the fifth (to Jan. 1917) nearly 300,000. By now the Germans were putting 8 new U-boats a month into service and losing less than three. With a peak in Apr. 1917 of 881,000 tons, sinkings averaged no less than 642,000 tons in the sixth half year, eight times the rate of replacement. Moreover zig zagging and roundabout routes sensibly diminished the usefulness of the remaining shipping: steamers covered as much as 2,500 miles on the 1,300 mile run from Gibraltar to London.

(4) Dependence upon patrols was losing the war. Lloyd George personally forced a change to convoys upon a reluctant Admiralty: for coal to France in Mar. 1917, to Scandinavia in Apr. Success, facilitated by the development of the hydrophone, was immediate. In Apr. the U.S.A. entered the war but gave no naval help in the Atlantic until Aug. where, consequently, convoys could not be organised until Sept. In Oct. they became the rule in the Mediterranean. Average sinkings now fell in the seventh half year to 365,000 tons and continued to decline even though at the opening of 1918 there were 134 U-boats (about 35 at sea) and replacements were still exceeding losses. The Admiralty's organisation of shipping combined with drastic import restriction made it possible to carry to France in British ships more than half of the U.S. army.

(C) In WORLD WAR II convoys were instituted at once; the heterogeneous but fast units of the home based German surface fleet had, however, to be watched and at the start there was such a shortage of escorts that merchant shipping could be convoyed only during the two or three most dangerous inward or outward days. There had to be a rendezvous and dispersal zone measuring 200 × 500 miles for merchantmen and warships just west of Rockall, extending from the lat 61°N to 55°N whence the shipping lane ran via the North Channel to the Clyde and Liverpool. To this zone all transatlantic shipping came, either singly or in fleets. The Mediterranean and African or Far Eastern ships used Cardiff and Avonmouth. They were partially protected from Gibraltar and there was some helpful, but incomplete, cover by Coastal Command of the R.A.F. In the greater part of the oceans ships sailed unescorted and frequently unorganised. The ports were continually bombed. The war in defence of commerce may perhaps be considered in nine phases.

(1) The German U-boats at the start were few and used defective torpedoes. The battlefleet engaged much of the Royal Navy's attention, while surface raiders, such as the pocket battleship *Graf Spee,* threatened the unguarded oceans and then drew off some of its strength. This enabled German destroyers to mine the sea areas off Newcastle, the Humber, Cromer and the Thames. Their magnetic mines sank 76 ships.

(2) The Norwegian campaign (Apr. 1940) crippled the German surface fleet, but the invasion threat after the German capture of the Channel and Atlantic ports, substituted a new distraction for the Royal Navy. The German torpedo defects were overcome and the French had betrayed the Asdic, which could not detect surfaced U-boats. A German aerial and U-boat offensive, begun in June, was soon sinking 500,000 tons a month. The British believed that they could not build enough escort warships to avoid defeat before their mass production reached the sea in the following Apr; they tided over the gap by 50 old U.S. destroyers in exchange for bases in Newfoundland, Barbados and the W. Indies. In fact overstrain slackened the Germans' offensive even though they were using French ports.

(3) Against the reinforced escorts the Germans now adopted pack tactics, already rehearsed before the war. A U-boat which sighted a convoy would signal its position to the German Admiralty (Seekriegsleitung: SKL) and

shadow it. Other U-boats would be ordered up and a combined, usually surface, attack delivered preferably on the first night. The packs were assisted by a cipher breaking service. This began in Sept. 1940. Convoy HX72 (from Halifax, Nova Scotia) lost 12 ships out of 53. In Oct. they sank 21 out of 34 ships in convoy SC7 (from Sydney). German losses rose too, but British losses did not decline because the German airforce joined in. It was taking about two British ships to deliver one cargo.

(4) The British defence, however, induced SKL to switch operations further out into the Atlantic where, however, the strain on crews was very great. The rate of sinkings could be maintained only by the refurbished surface fleet. Between Jan. and Mar. 1941 capital ships and merchant cruisers entered the N. and S. Atlantic, the Indian Ocean and the South Seas, sinking 843,000 tons. The policy of heavy ship intervention ended with the destruction of the *Bismarck* in May 1941, but sporadic merchant cruiser activity continued as late as the Spring of 1943.

(5) Since Mar. 1941 the U.S.A. had convoyed her own ships to mid-Atlantic. From July, when U.S. troops occupied Iceland, their supply convoys covered other flags and destinations and from 1st Sept. the U.S. navy started to patrol the Denmark Strait. Since the Germans had turned on their Russian ally in June, the latter had been clamouring for western supplies. From Sept. the P.Q. convoys were run along the edge of the pack ice from Iceland to Murmansk. SKL ordered U-boats not to get involved with U.S. sponsored sailings, but accidental clashes were unavoidable and that same Sept. an incident (U.S.S. *Greer* and U.652) gave the U.S.A. its pretext, in the name of anti-piracy, for declaring *de facto* war (11 Sept. 1941) and escorting HX and SC convoys to mid ocean. By this the British had some of the advantages of a U.S. alliance: the Germans the disadvantages of her neutrality. It was not until Pearl Harbor (7 Dec. 1941) that Hitler felt able to declare war (11 Dec.). The U-boats first attacked the P.Q. convoys in Jan. 1942.

(6) The apparent threat to the P.Q. convoys was increased when the battlecruisers *Scharnhorst* and *Gneisenau* broke north through the Channel (Feb.), but in practice the assault was sustained by U-boats and aircraft, with the great battleship *Tirpitz* stationed in the background at Trondheim (Norway). Unknown to the Admiralty, SKL suspended capital ship operations in Feb. because of an oil shortage; but there were destroyer forays; and at the end of May PQ16 was attacked by aircraft. The important PQ17, however, was ordered to disperse when the *Tirpitz* moved north and U-boats and aircraft sank 24 of its 37 unprotected ships (June).

(7) The U.S. war took SKL by surprise. Out of 165 operational U-boats, only 22 were in the N. Atlantic, none of them on the U.S. coast. In Jan. and Feb. 1942 the unorganised U.S. shipping could be attacked by only 5 U-boats, but the damage was, nonetheless, serious. When counter-measures began to bite, the attack, supported by submarine tankers, was switched to the Caribbean. Between Jan. and June 1942 these long range U-boat operations sank 460 ships. Only single ships sailed for Murmansk during the long Arctic summer days, partly because the allies were assembling shipping for the N. African landings, but in July 1942 the now augmented U-boat force was moved back to the N. Atlantic. Packs of 20-25 attacked the convoys, but the defence was stronger too. Aircraft from Newfoundland and Britain progressively narrowed the uncovered central Atlantic zone and the escorts were better equipped and trained. In Dec. the Russian convoys, beginning with JW51, were resumed. JW51A reached Murmansk without incident. A surface attack on JW51B was repulsed.

(8) The success of the N. African landings and of JW51 led to the fall of Grand-Adm. Raeder, who made

way for the U-boat expert, Adm. Dönitz, at SKL. Hitler was narrowly dissuaded from scrapping his big ships, but the main effort was to be made through U-boats. They had, however, already been anticipated. The turning point was the period Feb-Apr. 1943. The Allies sailed in large convoys with powerful escorts, as recommended by Prof. Blackett; carrier-borne aircraft closed the air cover gap and ship-borne High Frequency Direction Finding (*Huff-duff*) instantly detected the position of transmitting U-boats. In May 41 U-boats were sunk and convoys were comparatively safe; on 24th SKL recalled the rest for re-equipment but the Allied lead was far too great to be overtaken. The end was near.

(9) The British determined to use the 1943 summer suspension of the Russian convoys to put the *Tirpitz* out of action. This was done by midget submarines in Sept. at Altenfjord. This coincided with the watershed of the Atlantic War when the Italians surrendered for, a few U-boats apart, the command of the Mediterranean was no longer disputed, the southern fronts no longer had to be supplied round Africa and the shipping and escorts thus saved could be used in and to sustain the invasions of W. Europe. Moreover, in Dec. a German surface attempt on convoy JW55 brought on the B. of the North Cape when the *Scharnhorst* was sunk. The *Tirpitz*, partly repaired, was damaged again in Mar. 1944 and sunk by bombing in Nov.

COMMERCIAL PROPOSITIONS (1784) (Ir) were in the form of a bill in the Irish House of Commons, a draft commercial treaty between Britain and Ireland. The tariffs of both countries were to be equalised, but Ireland was to control the linen duties of both countries and foreign linen was to continue to be excluded from Britain. In return, if the yield of the Irish duties were to exceed £650,000 the surplus should go to the expenses of the navy. Grattan proposed that a naval contribution should be made only when revenue exceeded naval expenditure, i.e. never. Pitt, who genuinely wanted to prevent mutual economic injuries, brought even this before the British parliament, which threw it out. *See* GENERAL CHAMBER OF MANUFACTURERS.

COMMINATION. The precautionary cursing, enjoined for each Ash Wednesday in the B.C.P., of impenitent committers of nine types of covert, no longer confessed, evil deeds such as contract killing, incest and moving landmarks, inherently hard to detect. As, presumably, Anglicans no longer do these things, comminations have been omitted from the modern orders of service.

COMMISSAR, PEOPLE'S. A minister in the U.S.S.R. before World War II.

COMMISSARY means, in particular, **(1)** a, usually local, representative of a bishop, perhaps in a detached part of his diocese or **(2)** in Scotland, because jurisdiction over wills had originally been ecclesiastical and so delegated to a Commissary, the term was used for the Commissary Courts which dealt with the confirmation of executorships. They were combined with the Sheriff Courts in 1874. Or **(3)** a civilian official responsible for supplying an army, hence *commissariat*.

COMMISSION is a document issued by a sovereign authority empowering a person to perform acts required in furtherance of the authority's functions or policy. Thus commissions are or were issued by the Crown to military officers and judges; to groups of persons (e.g. formerly the Admiralty and the Treasury) to perform the functions of some great officer of state; and, since the end of the 18th cent., to inquire into particular issues, e.g. the govt. of India (1932), the future of common lands (1955) or corruption in local govt. (1974). The commissioning authority cannot confer a power which it does not itself possess. Prerogative commissions set out the limitations of the authority conferred; parliamentary commissions are limited by the terms of the Act which authorises them. The distinction is often blurred, for if a prerogative commission (e.g. the Treasury) exists for a long time, parliamentary powers may be added to it.

COMMITTEE OF BOTH KINGDOMS (*see* CIVIL WAR-9 *et seq*) was formed by the parliament as a means for putting the joint direction of the war, envisaged by the Solemn League and Covenant, into practical effect. Hitherto the war had been prosecuted politically by the English Committee of Safety and Council of War, which latter included soldiers not in either House of Parliament. The Scots acted as independent allies. With some difficulty Harry Vane and St. John, with Cromwell (and Ireton) in support secured the new committee, which combined the functions of both bodies and included the Scot's commissioners in London. It sat in some state at Derby House and, as a supranational authority, tended to reduce the prestige of the Westminster parliament. Its leaders, on the English side, were Vane, St. John and Cromwell, on the Scottish, John, Ld. Maitland.

COMMITTEE OF IMPERIAL DEFENCE, set up in 1860, was a body of civil and service experts who considered the relative priorities in the naval and military estimates. In 1903-4 Balfour strengthened it by making the prime minister its ex-officio chairman. During World War I it included service ministers, the professional service heads and the heads of the service intelligence depts. After the war interest shifted from estimates to imperial defence for which the U.K. took major responsibility and the ministers concerned with overseas affairs were added. In 1936 a Minister for Co-Ordination of Defence was created and became V-Chairman. The committee met roughly bimonthly, most of the work being done by sub committees, of which that of the Chiefs of Staff was the most important. This sub committee, with the Prime Minister, became the strategic direction of the war under Churchill. The Committee was replaced by the Defence Committee in 1947.

COMMITTEE STAGE. When a bill in either House of Parliament has passed its second reading and (in the Commons) has, if necessary, been supported by a money or financial resolution, it is considered line by line by a committee of the whole house or a standing committee, each clause in the bill being separately put after amendments to it have been considered. The procedure, similar to that of the parent house, requires considerable intellectual agility on the part of the Chairman, especially on a controversial bill to which many, sometimes hundreds, of mutually inconsistent amendments may be proposed. In practice where a private member's amendment on a matter of importance is acceptable to the sponsor (usually the govt.) the sponsor will ask the private member to withdraw in return for an undertaking (always honoured) to introduce a similar amendment himself. This gives time for details and drafting to be considered by the experts. When the stage is finished the bill, as considered, is reported to the House.

COMMITTEE OF THE WHOLE HOUSE. Each House of Parliament may resolve itself into committee under the chairmanship, in the Commons, of the Chairman of Committees (never the Speaker) and in the Lords, of the Lord Chairman (never the Lord Chancellor). Such a committee may take the Committee Stage of any public bill and in the Lords almost invariably does so. In the Commons it deals with financial and money resolutions, financial legislation and bills of major constitutional importance. These committees originated at a time when the Speaker was a crown favourite who might influence debate excessively in the royal interest. *See* STANDING COMMITTEE; COMMITTEE STAGE.

COMMIUS. *See* BRITAIN. PRE-ROMAN-3.

COMMON AGRICULTURAL POLICY (C.A.P.). An E.E.C. or E.U. policy, politically difficult to dismantle, for keeping farmers in business by buying up and storing surplus products in order to keep prices *up* to a pre-determined level. It was the converse of the much better English policy, developed in World War II, of keeping prices *down* to a pre-determined level by subsidies. *See* MARKETING, AGRICULTURAL.

COMMON CARRIERS held themselves out to carry goods for reward. At common law they must accept them at a reasonable charge. The inadequacy of the rules for mass transport, such as railways, led to statutory control of railway charges from 1845 onwards. Charges had to be published after 1873. The Board of Trade settled classifications after 1888.

COMMON COUNCIL. A body which emerged in most boroughs either through the general commonalty setting it up because a mass meeting was too unwieldy, or through the mayor associating prominent citizens with himself as advisers. The constitution was locally determined and varied very widely, but the mayor (by whatever title known) presided and in the most important boroughs there were two grades of membership, viz Alderman and Councillors (respectively, by whatever title known). In seven cases there were three grades. Save in London and York they all sat together and, save in London, they lost ground to the corporate magistrates, who were mostly aldermanic, in the period 1689 to 1725 and were mostly moribund, save in London, when abolished by the Municipal Corporations Act, 1834.

COMMON GOOD was the property of a Scots burgh held for the general advantage of its community. Alienable properties are those which were, or could, be exploited as investments. Inalienable properties were those (e.g. churches or greens) dedicated to a particular purpose.

COMMON INFORMERS (*see also* MONOPOLIES). In the absence of police forces, penal statutes from the 15th cent. onwards offered a share in any penalty imposed, to any informer who set the statute in motion, and the Star Chamber sometimes promised informers a share of the fines which it imposed in certain types of case. The system was liable to abuse. Forgotten acts might be revived to gratify personal spite; threats to sue were an easy means of blackmail and an undesirable class of informers grew up. All the same new statutes were constantly passed inviting the informers' attention. The crown then sought to restrict the evils by empowering particular persons to act as an informer, restraining others from doing so, allowing such effective monopolists to compound with offenders and even (e.g. a Mr Dyer in the leather trade in 1593) to dispense with observance of a statute. Such patents were often granted in association with patents of monopoly and were abolished by the Statute of Monopolies 1624. The Common Informer revived, and survived in decreasing numbers as public enforcement agencies were multiplied, into the 20th cent. *See* SUNDAY OBSERVANCE.

COMMON LAW. (1) That part of the law of England common to all the country and anciently declared by the judges of the Courts of Kings Bench, Common Pleas and Exchequer, in the course of deciding cases brought before them and so developed from precedent to precedent. It consists partly of principles deduced from cases, but incorporated a considerable jurisprudence derived from early statutes such as the Grand and Possessory Assizes and Magna Carta. When a statute had been sufficiently long in force for its effects to be fully worked out, it came to be regarded as part of the Common Law and this included legislation as late as the Statute of Uses (1535) and the Statute of Frauds (1677). **(2)** It was distinguished from custom which was local and which it upholds if certain and reasonable. Custom was administered by local courts. **(3)** It was primarily concerned with ascertaining strict rights and wrongs and was distinguished from *Equity*, a system of jurisprudence later developed by the Chancery to achieve by supplementation of the Common Law, a nearer approximation to justice. **(4)** It was distinguished from

Canon Law administered by ecclesiastical courts and from *Probate* Law originally administered by them and from *Admiralty* Law derived from international models administered by the Court of Admiralty. These systems were derived directly or indirectly from Roman law.

COMMON LAW STATES, are those parts of the world in which, as a result of British imperial expansion and subsequent secondary colonisation, the English Common Law became the foundation of the local legal system. These areas thus exclude Scotland, the Channel Is., Malta, Cyprus, Aden, S. Africa, Mauritius, Malaysia, Ceylon and Quebec, but include other British and ex-British areas as well as most of the U.S.A. Even in the excluded areas particular Common Law doctrines and court procedures are often found, while legislation and local habits have led to wide practical divergences between the included ones. These similarities are of more than academic importance for decisions in the courts of common law states have a mutually persuasive influence. The Common Law in member countries of the European Union (Britain and Ireland) is being eroded by E.U. legislation, especially since the T. of Maastricht.

COMMON MARKET. *See* EUROPEAN UNION.

COMMON OR OPEN FIELDS. *See* INCLOSURE, LAND TENURE (ENGLAND)-3.

COMMON ORDER, BOOK OF. *See* KNOX, JOHN.

COMMON PETITIONS in mediaeval parliaments were those which were addressed to or considered to affect the common or general interest, as opposed to private petitions concerning a special interest or limited case. Cf the modern distinction between public and private bills. *See* BILL.

COMMON PLEAS, COURT OF (*see* CURIA REGIS-5) tried cases between subjects. **(1)** It was the first non-itinerant part of the royal court and it was required to "be held in some certain place" by Magna Carta cl 17. It was not a distinct court until Henry III came of age in 1224. His own court then began to travel, leaving the Common Pleas to be settled at Westminster. Within a year or two these were being entered on separate rolls, the *De banco* (Lat = "from the Bench") rolls, as opposed to the *Coram Rege* (Lat = "In the King's Prescence") rolls. By 1237 the distinction was sufficiently understood to be pleaded in bar of the Curia's jurisdiction and in 1272, with the appointment of Gilbert of Preston as its first Chief Justice, the separation was complete. It was not required to stay at Westminster, only to stay in some certain place, presumably for a reasonable period, and there were public complaints under Edward III about its movements when it was at York (1337). All the same it was there again in 1392, at St. Albans in 1544 and at Hertford in 1581.

(2) The judges were originally clerics, but late in the 13th cent. professional lawyers began to replace them. After 1316 every Chief Justice except one was a Serjeant-at-Law and the serjeants had exclusive right of audience there. This lasted until 1847. The procedure was primarily by Compurgation.

(3) The Court had a monopoly by way of real actions and the older personal actions (account, covenant, debt and detinue) of disputes between subjects unless, which was rare, a charter otherwise provided. It was extremely busy in the middle ages, but its procedure became increasingly expensive and cluttered with technicalities, so that the Courts of King's Bench and Exchequer were able, through legal fictions, to attract business away to their own cheaper, more certain and more expeditious, methods. Thus varieties of actions for trespass, involving an allegation of breach of the King's peace, could be used to settle an issue of title to land: an allegation of diminished ability to pay a crown debt, to settle an account. The court also supervised the old local courts, either by writ of *Pone* (Lat = place), to transfer a case to itself, or by various writs of *False Judgment* to correct their mistakes. This initially brought it business and hastened their decline, but again the King's Bench invented better remedies by *Writ of Error*. Thus by the mid 16th cent. the court, though great in dignity, was stagnant. It so continued until the amalgamation of the courts into the High Court in 1875 and it ceased to be a separate division of the High Court in 1880.

COMMON PRAYER, BOOK OF (B.C.P.) (*see also* BREVIARY). Abp. Cranmer and others wanted to simplify, shorten and translate the mediaeval Latin services. His draft was considered by a conference of scholars in 1548 and this became the *First Prayer Book of Edward VI* enforced by the Act of Uniformity of 1549. Criticism by the more advanced reformers led to a revision known as the *Second Prayer Book of Edward VI* of 1552. At Mary I's accession in 1553 the old services were restored by the Act of Repeal. After her death the *Elizabethan Book* of *Common Prayer* was issued under the Act of Uniformity of 1559. This was nearly the same as the Second Book of Edward VI. Strongly attacked in the Millenary Petition of 1604, James I caused it to be revised after the Hampton Court Conference. From 1645 to 1661 it was superseded by the Puritan 'Directory of Public Worship' but after the Restoration a further conference at the Savoy failed to agree; consequently it was slightly revised by Convocation and enacted in the Act of Uniformity of 1662. This version has remained in use ever since, though attempts to introduce a new prayer book were defeated in Parliament in 1927 and 1928. Despite its lack of authority the new book was much used. The use of alternative services approved by the General Synod was authorised experimentally in 1965 and permanently in 1974. Despite their uninspired diction they are slowly ousting the proper Book.

COMMON RECOVERY. See JOHN DOE AND RICHARD ROE.

COMMON RIGHTS. See INCLOSURE LAND TENURE (ENGLAND)-3.

COMMONS, HOUSE OF (to 1604) (1) The examples which furnished the *idea* were, perhaps, the growing bicameralism of the Common Council of London and the composite assemblies habitual in Sicily and the Papal states, of which Edward I probably knew. The *practical need* arose from the reluctance of magnates to tax their tenants for the benefit of the King and the difficulty of taxing substantial and angry towns, respectively, without their consent. The original *political impulse* seems to have been Simon de Montfort's desire to strengthen himself against his opponents. His parliament of 1265 included knights from some shires and 2 representatives from a number of boroughs.

(2) At Easter 1275 burgesses from many market towns were summoned in connection with the new duty on wool, but though they apparently assented to other measures, this was not regarded as a precedent. Whether and what sort of meetings should be called was determined by expediency. If finance was the main reason for calling in the knights and burgesses, it was not the only one. In eleven parliaments after Easter 1275, knights but no burgesses appeared at four, while in three where both classes appeared, there was no financial business. In questions other than taxation, the function of the commons was to assent to proposals made by their betters, but no doubt the proposals would have been affected by private, unrecorded, discussions. The govt. measures could not always be embodied in petitions and if they required legislation they appeared in drafts corresponding to the later bills.

(3) The so-called "model" parliament of 1295 was not a very stable model. Besides 37 shires, 100 towns were represented, but of the larger some (e.g. Deal) were never summoned again before 1485 and only 25 (e.g. Portsmouth) were always represented along with 24 (e.g. Lostwithiel) not summoned in 1295. Some of the rest (e.g. Torrington) were represented occasionally but so were others (e.g. Ilchester) not summoned in 1295. Wales

and the palatinates of Chester, Durham, Redesdale and Hexham were not represented. The number of knights of the shire remained roughly constant at 70-80. From 1297 they and burgesses were always present but, save for London, Norwich, York and Bristol, the boroughs were villages; on average 70 were represented between 1307 and 1327, rising to 85 by 1399.

(4) Little is known of the elections. Attendance at parliament was an unsought and sometimes alarming burden, consuming travelling time and involving, as at Gloucester, discomfort. Sheriffs, who returned the members, had to find able men who could treat on behalf of their people and who, therefore, had to have the confidence of those who mattered locally. Consequently they settled procedures so as to bring the most locally respected forward. The 70-80 "knights" (who soon ceased to be necessarily knights) by reason of their education, personal standing or place in local administration, were for centuries more influential than the rest, save for the great businessmen, mostly of London.

(5) Though parliament might meet at any place in the Kingdom, accommodation (mostly in large monasteries) limited the choice. If the Commons had no regular meeting place they probably used the same kind of room (if possible) wherever they were summoned. At Westminster, the increasingly frequent venue, this was originally the not very convenient monks' Chapter House and, after 1400, their refectory. It is uncertain if they met separately from the first but they did so from 1344; they had royal officials as advisers and they sometimes invited sympathetic magnates to sit with them. Moreover, between 1373 and 1384, business was often considered by joint meetings of delegations from lords and commons, besides these bodies separately. By 1399, however, this was considered unusual, but such consultations were held in 1404 and 1406 with magnates whom the Commons seem to have named themselves.

(6) The negotiation of taxes took the form of the drafting of indentures between the Commons and the King, with the assent of his lords. The advantage of the indenture was that its exact words could be enforced without further evidence or interpretation.

(7) Petitions to the crown and council in parliament were an important feature of business. Originally the Commons did not themselves present them, but any petition presented with their public knowledge or in their presence necessarily gained cogency thereby. Such petitions formed a specially important class. After a while the Commons began petitioning on their own (e.g. against the price of fish in 1357). Since the crown could turn petitions into law by consulting the magnates and assenting to them they were an ancestor of legislation. As early as 1348 the Commons had demanded that answered petitions should not be altered.

(8) It is a short intellectual step from petitioning for the redress of a wrong to demanding the punishment of a wrong doer. Impeachments, however, marked a new stage: for to formulate one required a procedure; to present it, a spokesman. Until 1376 the Commons communicated with the King through *ad hoc* spokesmen or deputations. The first permanent spokesman or Speaker (Sir Peter de la Mare) was elected in the Good Parliament (1376), the scene of the first impeachment. This represented an accumulation of habit and procedure crystallised by the exigency of the moment. It was natural, and probably required by the Crown, that the Speaker should be the presiding officer and his habitual control of proceedings, to which he early brought a judicial manner, developed and refined the proceedings themselves. In 1384 the commons were, for the first time, formally instructed to elect a Speaker and to present him on the second (or between 1413 and 1427 a later) day. Speakers were not imposed, but the crown paid them and the Commons sought a man of standing and sophistication, which meant someone with court or administrative, besides parliamentary, experience. The wealthy Thomas Chaucer (son of the poet), five times Speaker, was the King's chief Butler and in 1453 only 5 counties were represented by men with no court connections. Moreover, many burgess representatives were no longer borough residents but gentry, officials, or leading retainers of great nobles and of increasingly independent mind (*see* FORTY SHILLING FREEHOLDERS).

(9) The parliamentary politics of Richard II had quickened interest, especially in the potential leverage of finance. In 1401 the Commons tried to secure redress of grievances before granting supply and thereafter there were irregular efforts to have the council nominated in parliament, so that expenditure might be monitored. The old distinction between ordinary expenditure, which the crown should meet from its own resources, and extraordinary (e.g. warlike) expenditure, which might be defrayed by subsidy, was very real and the Commons favoured restoring the ordinary resources by resumptions and control of alienations. They also sometimes tried to appropriate subsidies for particular uses (e.g. to pay 590 archers in 1474).

(10) The destination of parliamentary petitions reflected the Commons' growing prestige. In 14th cent. few were addressed to them, even in conjunction with the King and Council. Under Henry IV, however, about 15% of common and 10% of private petitions were so addressed and under Henry VI the figures were about 40% and 30%. Petitions were an avenue for legislation. A petition agreed by the Lords and the royal answer to it represented a decision (*statutum*) which was then reduced to law French by the clerks and the two chief justices and enrolled. In 1414 the Commons had demanded (not wholly successfully) that petitions should be answered as they stood and that the editing process should not alter their sense. This was very close to process by bill, which the Lords were using (complete with three readings) by 1454. (*See* BILL, PARLIAMENTARY.)

(11) The first statute of Edward IV (1461) was made "at the Commons special request" but thereafter the Crown asserted a legislative initiative which it kept for nearly 150 years. In practice this meant more bills, which were drafted in the Council and brought into either house, as convenient, by trusted members. This hardly affected the growing independence of the Commons. In 1471 they demanded that money bills should originate with them. In 1476 they delayed payment to the King. In 1512 (*Strode's Case*) they asserted the latest of a line of claims against interference in their proceedings. In 1523 Sir Thos. More, Speaker, included freedom of speech in the customary Speaker's claim and in the same session the Commons flatly refused to be interrogated by Card. Wolsey.

(12) The Union with Wales (1523) increased the membership but commerce, a rising proportion of the economy, was increasing the relative influence and the number (now 110) of the boroughs represented. The first burgess Speaker, Humphrey Wingfield, was elected in 1533. The Kings needed public support for their doubtful title, their help against overweaning magnates and popular acclaim for the economic and social revolution associated with the attack on the church. In 1543 (*Ferrer's Case*) the Commons themselves enforced their freedom from arrest at the instance of any inferior court and received in support from Henry VIII the most splendid of royal declarations on Crown and Parliament. In the course of the long alliance between Crown and commons, the latter acquired also regular experience of statecraft and of the way to control the general line of policy. They refused, for example, in 1558 to finance Q. Mary I's deviation into a French war.

(13) Under the thrifty Elizabeth I the Commons

exerted little power through the purse since in peacetime the queen could live of her own and they were willing to support her wars; but conflicts demonstrated the limitations upon the freedoms so far won. They might say what they pleased on subjects within their competence, but the Queen enforced very clear views on what those subjects were. They did not include her prerogative, especially touching religion, the succession, foreign policy and trade. She exerted her influence in public pronouncements and through privy councillors in the House and the Speaker. In 1571 she barred Walter Strickland from the House for introducing a bill to reform the liturgy. In 1572 she impounded two bills with the same object. In 1575 the House itself sent Peter Wentworth to the Tower for a vehement attack on her policy and the subservience of the House to it. In 1580 she made the Commons apologise for resolving on a public fast without first consulting her. In 1587 she confiscated a draft bill to reform the church and when Peter Wentworth, in consequence, presented a number of questions on the liberties of the House, he and Anthony Cope, the sponsor of the bill and his supporters, were committed to the Tower. In 1591 Peter Wentworth was again imprisoned, this time for publishing a pamphlet on the succession and in 1593 he proposed a conference with the Lords to prepare a petition to the queen on the subject and was hailed off to prison again with his supporters. In the same session the queen forbade the Speaker to read a puritan bill against the powers of ecclesiastical courts.

(14) That seven such major incidents in 15 years did not overly disturb contemporaries is shown by the outcome of the celebrated monopolies incident of 1601. There had already been embittered debates on the incidence of the war subsidy and the numerous monopolies amounted to a form of private taxation. There was excitement, confusion and popular muttering. The House could not agree whether to launch a petition, bring in a bill or send for and cancel the monopoly patents itself. The second course would have been an infringement of her trade prerogatives: the third a usurpation. Before any conclusion was reached she intervened 'to take present order for reformation' herself and in a famous and spirited oration won all hearts.

(15) In fact the Queen's action had hardly saved the prerogative and it encouraged the Commons, as men in possession, when they faced her less able, less dignified and foreign, successor (1604). James I provoked them at once by trying to have elections reviewed in the Chancery. They forced him to concede such control to the House. Then they attacked purveyance as illegal and wardship as scandalously abused. Prompted by the Lords they offered a grant in return for abolishing most of the feudal incidents. He hectored them. They rejoined with an *Apology* which foreshadowed a determination to discuss prerogative questions. The confrontations of the reign were related to the decline in the numbers of privy councillors in the House, so that members looked for leadership amongst themselves and if the King sought to exclude them from high policy they retaliated in kind. A new device for excluding royal influence was the Committee of the Whole House over which the Speaker, still a link with the crown, could not preside.

(16) The issue whether the Commons should consider any matter of national or govt. concern, how (if at all) govt. policies should be financed and how the armed force for imposing those policies should be controlled was fought out in litigation, civil war and revolution over the ensuing century. *See entries on succeeding reigns,* CIVIL WAR; COMMONWEALTH PROTECTORATE; RESTORATION; ASQUITH'S ADMINISTRATION.

COMMONWEALTH AND PROTECTORATE. (1) The Commonwealth of 1649 was founded upon a Common's resolution of 4 Jan. 1649 that they as representing the people, in whom all original power lay, could make laws without the King's or the Lords' concurrence. This usurpation was necessary, *inter alia*, as a foundation for the trial of the King. A proclamation against proclaiming a new King was issued on the day (30 Jan.) when he was beheaded, but the Scots proclaimed Charles II on 5 Feb. The House passed Acts for abolishing the monarchy on 17 Mar. and the House of Lords on 19th. Thus the 59 strong remnant of the Commons (derisively and for all time called the RUMP) made itself the formal sovereign and the Speaker the highest dignitary, to whom all formal communications were addressed.

(2) Meanwhile the threat from Scotland remained only potential because of the political confusion there; nearer home there were military mutinies of Leveller inspiration, which Cromwell managed to put down in Apr. 1649. The generals then resolved to tackle Ireland. The Irish confederates and the royalists had come to an agreement in Jan. 1649 and Charles II had continued Ormonde's commission as Lord Lieut; Ormonde gathered forces for the recovery of Dublin, hoping to forestall the republican expedition, but he was defeated by Michael Jones at Baggot Rath just before Cromwell landed with a powerful army on 15 Aug. Cromwell moved instantly. Drogheda in the north was stormed and its garrison, after refusing to surrender, massacred on 11 Sept; Wexford to the south suffered the same fate on 11 Oct. This military terrorism destroyed the largest formed bodies of Irish royalists and frightened other places into surrender, but it was never forgotten in Ireland and remained a symbol of hate for generations. By the winter the Irish east coast other than Waterford was in English hands. Ireton, Ludlow and Fleetwood were left to complete the conquest.

(3) The Scots composed most of their disputes and sent commissioners to Charles II at Breda (Holland). They arrived in Jan. 1650. There followed a long wrangle, for they insisted that he should sign the Covenant as a precondition of their military allegiance, and he could not afford to alienate his Irish or Scots R. Catholic supporters, or the downtrodden Anglicans by doing so. But the Irish disasters made the issue less important, though the delay enabled Cromwell to return with much of his army in the spring. Eventually Charles set sail and signed the Covenant at sea, whereby news of it would not leak out for some time and it could be said that he was acting under duress. He arrived in Scotland in June. By now the great royalist M. of Montrose had been defeated and hanged; Argyll and the Covenanters could consequently treat their King with Old Testament arrogance. They required public humiliations of him, but worse still, they purged the army of unsanctified veterans, while Cromwell marched steadily north with his force of Independents.

(4) Cromwell tried persuasion, but the proud presbyterians trusted in the God of Battles. Their general, David Leslie, skilfully manoeuvred Cromwell into a difficult position at Dunbar but came down from his hills to be able to interfere with Cromwell's embarkation. The result was another Marston Moor. The righteous army was destroyed (3 Sept. 1650). One result, after furious argument (*see* REMONSTRANCE (SCOT) 1650) was that the Scots politicians were politer to their King. Edinburgh Castle surrendered to Cromwell on 19 Dec. On 1 Jan. 1651 Charles was crowned, with all due ceremony, to the sound of 80 pipers at Scone. He got away to his reorganised army about Stirling before Cromwell reached Perth and marched for England with Cromwell in pursuit. He was totally defeated at Worcester (3 Sept. 1651).

(5) The Commonwealth govt., while much concerned with overseas trade, tried hard to keep the peace with mostly hostile foreign powers, while it established itself at home. The French, however, banned cloth imports from regicide England; this provoked counter-measures against

French wines and silks, whereupon French privateers were let loose on English shipping. William II of Orange was Charles II's brother-in-law and the Dutch, who possessed much of the Atlantic carrying trade, were hostile too. One cause of dispute with them was eliminated by the settlement of N. American colonial frontiers in the autumn of 1650 and William II died in Nov. Thus, while Charles II was marching south towards Worcester a mission led by Oliver St. John went to Amsterdam to negotiate with the temporarily supreme oligarchical rivals of the House of Orange. The English wanted a close political union; the Dutch a treaty on the lines of the *Magnus Intercursus* of 1496 and the mob abused St. John. Then he proposed terms against the reception of each side's rebels which might involve the confiscation of property of the widowed Mary of Orange. The Dutch angrily put forward a treaty of commerce on equal terms and mutual military aid, provided that the other party paid. St. John went home. The B. of Worcester then made Dutch friendship less important and the Commons passed the Navigation Act (9 Oct. 1651), possibly as a negotiating weapon. The Dutch remained unperturbed. They knew that in the existing state of English shipping the Act was unenforceable. A few days later Charles II escaped to France but immediately afterwards Limerick surrendered (27 Oct.).

(6) The parliament had been building warships since 1647 and the programme was accelerated. The policy of the Navigation Act and the unofficial war with the French pointed to the same conclusion: the navy began to search Dutch ships for French goods. This move towards foreign aggression had, however, to be balanced by conciliation at home. The royalist landowners were having to compound for their 'delinquency' at between 33% and 10% of the value of their estates (at 20 years purchase) and some of the major ones had their entire estates sequestrated. Much land was thrown simultaneously on the market, prices fell. Speculators came in, to the discontent of tenants and besides, many parliamentary officers were rewarded with royal or episcopal or confiscated property. The result was distress, confusion, abrupt changes in old customs and habits and agricultural disorganisation. Accordingly in Feb. 1652 an Ordinance of General Pardon and Oblivion was passed. This contained so many exceptions that it was received derisively as a fraud, especially as a confiscation act against some 600 estates was passed at the end of the year. Then sequestrated estates began to be sold to pay for the navy, as friction with the Dutch grew. In May 1652, however, Galway, the Irish rebel stronghold, surrendered but by now the States-Gen. had ordered its admirals to protect their merchantmen. Large rival fleets cruised and anchored close to each other: on one of these occasions a fight broke out in the Downs over salutes; freed from the Irish troubles the Commonwealth declared war (30 June 1652).

(7) During the two years of the furiously contested First Dutch War public expenditure, which might have declined by a reduction in the army, rose to highest levels (£2.5M per annum) but the Commons, who were expected by Cromwell and the soldiers to pursue a policy of 'healing and settling', behaved as if there were no war in progress. The army was now interested in reform, religion and a general election. Reform disappeared in a welter of committees and debates. The presbyterian Commons wanted to abolish the Anglican church, recusancy fines and tithes, so that ministers of religion could not have been paid, but did nothing to simplify the lot of Independents or meet the social onslaught of Levellers, diggers and Fifth Monarchy Men. A self regarding policy of inertia was, if anything, an encouragement to many subversive elements (from Royalist to Leveller) which, during a major war, threatened the stability of the state. Hence a replacement of the legislature in a general election became the essential and the foremost of the Army's demands. It was the one thing which the Rump of the Commons would not concede. Great exertions elicited a decision to dissolve on 3 Nov. 1654; but as members' corruption and complacency caused increasing unrest, the generals tried to advance the date. The Rump then prepared a bill to perpetuate themselves and be the sole judge of other candidates elected. Cromwell and other officers summoned a meeting and urged them to drop the bill. They went back and started to rush it through. The news reached Cromwell, who took a few files of musketeers of his own regiment with him to the House and, after listening to the debate, cleared it. The Council of State was dismissed too (20 Apr. 1653).

(8) As the object of the *coup d'état* was to get new legislators, the army set up the NOMINATED or BAREBONE'S PARLIAMENT whose membership, nominated at the suggestion of the congregational churches in each county, might have been expected to agree conveniently with the army's views. This cheerfully ineffectual body of 140 godly debaters abolished the corrupt and inefficient Court of Chancery but provided no solution for the problems which were left over as a result. It established civil marriage to the indignation of most decent citizens. It abolished church patronage and debated disestablishment without regard to the practicalities. At this point Maj-Gen. John Lambert and some other officers drew up an amateur constitution; early in the morning of 12 Dec. 1653 they induced their many parliamentary supporters to surrender their functions into Cromwell's hands. This apparently surprised Cromwell and brought the Commonwealth formally to an end.

THE PROTECTORATE (1653-59). (9) The officers urged Cromwell to adopt their constitution and this document, the INSTRUMENT OF GOVERNMENT, became the fundamental law by adoption on 16 Dec. 1653. There was, however, an important interval of nine months before the first parliament assembled. The new govt. made good use of the time. The Dutch had lost their C-in-C (Marten van Tromp) and most of their fighting fleet at the B. of the Texel (9 Aug. 1653). By Feb. blockade and the winter cold were forcing them to their knees. The war was nearly over. It had transferred the naval preponderance to Britain. International negotiations now marched side by side with the settlement or spoliation of Ireland. The P. of Westminster (5 Apr. 1654) ended the war: a treaty with Holland and Denmark's enemy Sweden followed six days later. Then the Irish began to be transplanted to Connaught and Clare and new settlers started to arrive; on 10 July the Portuguese were forced by the seizure of their annual Brazil fleet to make peace, expel P. Rupert's fleet and concede to the English the right to trade with their colonies.

(10) Peace and Irish loot failed to secure an entirely complaisant parliament, which was summoned for 3 Sept. 1654. The new electoral qualifications had brought many English republicans and moderate presbyterians to Westminster. Instead of responding to the Protector's appeal for conciliation and stability, they remembered the old House of Commons and fell to discussing the Instrument of Government. Since this contained no means whereby it might be amended, they set about trying to amend it themselves. On 11th Sept. the Protector sent for them and told them that each must sign a pledge to uphold a govt. consisting of one person and a parliament before he could re-enter the House. Thirty refused and were excluded. Apart from this he told the members that parliament must not perpetuate itself, that there must be liberty of conscience and that neither the Protector nor parliament must have absolute control of the forces. The Danish peace followed on 14th. The purge, however, failed to secure harmony. Parliament

amended the Instrument so that members of the Council of State had to be confirmed in office by a new parliament within 40 days of its first sitting; and it wished to exclude those guilty of certain blasphemies and heresies of which it was to be the judge. Then it proposed that the joint military control of the forces should last only during Cromwell's life and it refused to provide funds for 27,000 of the 57,000 men under arms. Since the Instrument itself comtemplated only 30,000 and the country was at peace they had some justification, but the military disagreed. Cromwell and the Army were determined to impose on the country what they believed was for the country's good. On 22 Jan. 1655 the Protector dissolved parliament.

(11) The Council of State had concluded from the Mediterranean aspect of the First Dutch war that distant naval operations required distant bases; but the object of naval war was to extend seaborne trade and the trade to the Spanish Main was particularly prized. The govt. wanted to relieve the Huguenots, and France, having been at war with Spain for 20 years, tried in 1654 to barter military help to Spain for free trade. This the Spaniards would not have. Consequently the govt. veered to the opposite policy and sent an amphibious expedition under Robert Venables and Sir William Penn against the Spanish W. Indies. It sailed in Dec. 1654, just before parliament was dissolved.

(12) Cromwell had said that he dissolved parliament because of the bickering and discontent which it had caused. In Mar. 1655 there was trouble of another kind in a rising of Wiltshire royalists under Col. Penruddock. It was easily suppressed, but shortly afterwards the Venables and Penn expedition was repulsed at San Domingo and began to move on Jamaica. A Spanish war was bound to be declared sooner or later. Thus the govt. was tempted to impose rigorous order at home. The policy of 'healing and settling' was abandoned. Penruddock's supporters were transported to Barbados and other royalists put under restrictions and severities, notably the Decimation Tax of 10% on rents. The landings (May) in Jamaica were unopposed, but the Spaniards held the interior in a prolonged guerrilla war. The slide towards aggression continued. It was determined to attack the Tunisian pirates. Thorough-going military rule was imposed. The country was divided into eleven districts each under a maj-gen. who, besides supervising the militia and repressing royalists, acted as tax collector, police commissioner and guardian of morals. Assemblies for racing, cockfighting, bear baiting and other amusements were dispersed as ungodly and convenient for conspiracies. Laws against drunkenness, swearing and blasphemy were enforced. Theatres, gaming houses and brothels were closed: so were hundreds of alehouses. At the end of 1655 Blake's expedition to Tunis was a complete success but meanwhile military righteousness thundered on under its own momentum. The Long Parliament had ordained (ineffectually) that Christmas should be kept as a fast. Other festivals joined the dismal list and Anglican services became illegal (24 Nov. 1655). A commercial treaty which ended the undeclared French war (24 Oct.) enriched the shipping interests but did nothing to increase the popularity of the govt.

(13) After the accommodation with France a Spanish war took on the air of inevitability (Feb. 1656), especially as Spanish corsairs from Dunkirk had been attacking British shipping for some time. Their efforts were now redoubled. In Apr. 1656 Charles II signed a treaty with the Spaniards for military aid against the Protectorate in return for the surrender of all British rights in the W. Indies, but at about the same time Blake took a squadron into Spanish waters and intercepted the *Flota*. By a formal *rapprochement* with France against Spain, Britain was to receive Dunkirk and Mardyk in exchange for naval assistance (5 Sept. 1656). During Aug. a new parliament was elected, but at the instigation of the military, the Council of State purged it of about 100 members, mostly from the old strongholds of opposition to the King. The purged parliament met on 17 Sept. It happily voted funds for the war. Dunkirk was blockaded at great expense and not very effectually and a force was assembled to assist the French in besieging it. The Spanish army in Flanders was dwindling through lack of money; for this the British fleet was largely responsible, for Blake and the Council of State maintained the blockade of the Spanish coast and the Mexican silver fleet dared not sail until late in 1657.

(14) The unpopularity of the military grew. Parliament refused to continue the 10% tax on royalists for the support of the militia and the rule of the major generals. Their administration began to fade away at the end of 1656. There was a widespread desire to have done with experiments and return to old familiar ways. The result was the first HUMBLE PETITION AND ADVICE (31 Mar. 1657) offered to the Protector as the British troops began to land near Dunkirk. Parliament wanted him to assume the crown. There was a furious quarrel between him and the republican army at the height of the war in Flanders. As Anglo-French forces closed on Durkirk, Blake destroyed another treasure fleet at Santa Cruz (20 Apr.)

(15) Between Mar. and the end of June 1657 the constitution was converted into a bicameral one with an Upper House of 42 peers, including 7 relatives of Cromwell, and 17 regimental commanders and with the Protector as an uncrowned King. The naval blockade crippled Spanish finances: the Spanish invasion of Portugal melted away and their defence of Flanders slowly dissolved. The French took Mardyk (3 Oct.) while parliament was in recess and the new Lords were being chosen. Parliament met at the turn of the year. It proved no more tractable. An alliance of fanatics, fifth-monarch men and disaffected officers planned to carry a snap vote for the restoration of the republic and the recall of the Long Parliament. For the second time in his life Cromwell hurried to Westminster and, as Protector, dissolved parliament (4 Feb. 1658).

(16) The Protectorate now faced a situation similar to that of Charles I before the calling of the Long Parliament. There was war, albeit victorious, but inadequate revenue with which to finance it and no constitutional authority to raise additional taxes. There was further cause for concern in the Swedish conquest of Denmark (see BALTIC-42), which threatened to put the navy at the mercy of the Swedish govt. The Council of State had started, in a small way, to import spars from N. America in 1653 but the Dunkirk war was going slowly and the danger seemed acute. Moreover ships were being kept at sea for lack of money to pay them off and unpaid troops lived at free quarters, intensifying the political hatred of the military govt. But the Spaniards were desperate too and organised a last offensive. They were beaten at the B. of the Dunes. Dunkirk (25 June 1658) and Gravelines (24 Aug.) fell. The fleet could be released to succour the Danes. At this point, however, Oliver Cromwell fell ill and died (3 Sept. 1658).

(17) Richard Cromwell, inexperienced, amiable and weak, succeeded his father by nomination. He failed, as George Monck advised, to reduce the army and dispense with politically ambitious officers such as Fleetwood, Disbrowe and their supporters (collectively known as the Wallingford House Party). They wanted to separate the office of C-in-C from the Protectorship and secure the immunity of soldiers from dismissal save by court martial: thereby converting the army into a state within a state. Their demand was too strident as well as premature. A new parliament was elected: most members were moderate presbyterians known as the New Courtiers

ready to support the Protector, together with a few cavaliers and a small but able body of republicans (The Commonwealth's Men) led by Hesilrige, Scot and Vane. The opposition failed to prevent the new Commons from recognising the Protector's succession or the existing membership of the Lords. The Lower House, as a whole, was hostile to the army. Many of the new lords were high army officers who had become territorial grandees out of touch with their units. Some, such as John Lambert, had further enriched themselves by purchasing soldiers pay rights at a discount. No money was being raised to pay the troops arrears, but the fleet was winning victories in the Kattegat (Nov.). A deep fissure was developing between the armchair generals and the real (and financially cheated) fighting men in the south.

(18) The Commonwealth's men now sought to unite all the disaffected by bringing forward the same petition which had led Oliver to dissolve his last parliament. It demanded a restoration of a single chamber govt. unrestrained by the protectorship; provision for extreme sectarians such as Fifth-monarchy men and Unitarians and military immunity from dismissal save by court martial. They sought and sometimes got sympathy from moderates by attacking the conduct of Oliver's major generals. The Commons even voted to impeach one of them (William Butler) and began receiving royalist petitions against arbitrary acts. By this time the Protector's prestige with the military had fallen to nothing. The army was in fact a state within a state; but the tone of the Commons remained hostile to it and the presbyterian majority would do nothing for sectaries who, of course, formed a majority of the troops. The field officers now petitioned that arrears of pay be satisfied, republican principles reasserted and liberty of worship restored, and they tried to persuade the Army Council to impose as a new test for office an oath deposing to the belief that Charles I's execution was lawful and just. To this parliament replied with resolutions that no officer should hold his commission unless he undertook not to disturb the parliament and that the Army Council should not meet without the consent of the Protector and both Houses. Richard communicated these resolutions to the Council, which refused to disperse and demanded the dissolution of parliament. Fleetwood was ordered to attend the Protector at Whitehall to explain. Instead he summoned the troops to St. James's. The Protector issued a counter summons to Whitehall. The troops followed Fleetwood. On 22 Apr. 1659 he forced Richard to dissolve parliament.

(19) The southern army now controlled as much of the machinery of govt. in London as seemed to suit it, but other forces, especially Monck's Scottish garrison, were differently inclined and other govt. agencies, especially those such as the Privy Council and the Admiralty, concerned with foreign policy, functioned almost independently. On 7 May the Rump of the Long Parliament was recalled by the troops, who demanded of it a commonwealth without protector or peers, an act of oblivion for all public acts done during the Protectorate, liberty of conscience for all Christians except Papists and Prelatists, the exclusion of royalists from office, a speedy general election and the office of C-in-C for Fleetwood. They also wanted the new legislature to consist of popular representatives and a co-ordinate but vaguely defined select senate, with administration under a council of state. On 21 May the govt. agreed at The Hague with Holland and France who imposed peace in the Baltic. Four days later Richard, with a touch of realism, abdicated.

THE RESTORED COMMONWEALTH. (20) The Rump, led by Hesilrige, Vane and Ludlow, was now under the impression that it was supreme, whereas the military intended that it should be merely a conductor through which the army's political policy should be imposed. It treated their demands with scant attention. Nothing was done to establish a senate. Fleetwood indeed became C-in-C, but the power to nominate officers was vested in a parliamentary commission. Cromwellian officers were dismissed, while those whom Cromwell had dismissed were reinstated. The latter were mostly political extremists opposed to the Rump. The Bill of Oblivion caused great resentment and nothing was done for the sectaries. The higher officers incurred the suspicion of their rank and file by not insisting on their demands.

(21) At this point there were sporadic rebellions of royalists and presbyterians both of whom, for different reasons, wanted to destroy the army. Moreover the fleet returned from the Baltic under Adm. Montague, who had had discussions with an envoy of Charles II. The uprising was put down and the admiral superseded by John Lawson, an ardent republican. Lambert's force at Derby now petitioned that the army's demands should no longer be ignored and that public offices should be purged of 'malignants'. Parliament replied by ordering Fleetwood to admonish the officers responsible. He assembled the southern officers and they presented a further petition in support of the Derby petitioners and again demanded military immunity from dismissal, save by court martial (5 Oct.). The Rump had in June received assurances of fidelity from Monck and felt strong enough to resist. A bill was introduced to make void all acts of the protectorate not confirmed by the Rump and then Lambert and Disbrowe were dismissed. For the second time the Rump was expelled by the army (13 Oct.) but it was only Lambert's and Fleetwood's army.

(22) George Monck had indeed proclaimed the superiority of the civil over the military power. He first purged his army of some 140 disaffected officers and then took great care to gain the confidence of the rest. His propaganda consolidated his own force and disintegrated the southern army. He said that the army could not in law or decency expel the parliament for which it had fought and which it had restored, that it was wrong to precipitate the country into civil war in the private interests of the southern military grandees and that as there was no authority for raising taxes, the troops would not only lose their arrears but infuriate the population by living at free quarters. Fleetwood and his supporters wasted time discussing paper constitutions while their men robbed households and levied so-called taxes on city businessmen. Members of the deposed govt. sent Monck a commission as C-in-C and persuaded the gov. of Portsmouth to declare for a free parliament. Troops sent to besiege the port changed sides and thereupon the fleet in the Downs did so too. The Irish army followed suit. With the disintegration of his political position at hand, Fleetwood recalled the Rump (26 Dec.).

(23) The Rump behaved with unrealistic perversity. It dismissed officers wholesale, expelled even more of its own members (including Vane), denied admission to excluded members and returned to the old principle of recruitment rather than election. Monck's army concentrated at Coldstream and marched on London. Lambert's army melted away while the population petitioned Monck to establish a full and free parliament. He reached London on 3 Feb. 1660 and told parliament that excluded members must be readmitted and a date for dissolution fixed. The Rump ordered him instead to dissolve the City Corporation, arrest eleven leading citizens and demolish the City gates for refusing to pay taxes to the 'representative' parliament, which he did but the citizens preferred pillage to taxation by the Rump. The latter ordered him to continue. At this Monck's patience ran out and he peremptorily required that vacancies in the House be filled at once. The City fêted him. Monck only had to withdraw guards from the House to enable the excluded members to return, but before he did so he extracted a promise from them to settle the

command and pay the arrears of the army, to issue writs for a new parliament to meet on 20 Apr. 1660 and to dissolve as soon as possible. They kept their promise and the Long Parliament and Restored Commonwealth came to their end on 16 Mar. 1660. *See* RESTORATION.

COMMONWEALTH. *See* BRITISH COMMONWEALTH.

COMMONWEALTH CONFERENCES. *See* IMPERIAL CONFERENCES.

COMMONWEALTH DAY. EMPIRE DAY was inaugurated in 1902 on the Sovereign's official birthday (the second Saturday in June). The name was changed in 1956.

COMMONWEALTH INSTITUTE was founded in 1962.

COMMONWEALTH('S) MEN (1) *1530-40s* were a self-named circle of humanists gathered particularly around Thos. Cromwell and the Protector Somerset, who advocated economic and social reforms and mostly linked their views to protestantism. **(2)** were doctrinal republicans who supported the republican form of the Commonwealth established in 1649, overthrown by Cromwell in 1653 and briefly re-established before the Restoration (*see* COMMONWEALTH-16). **(3)** *Late 17th and early 18th cent.* were a diffuse body of writers and thinkers who favoured a return to classical republican virtues, though for practical reasons they did not advocate the overthrow of the monarchy. They favoured the old "country" opposition to standing armies, large financial interests and bureaucracy.

COMMONWEALTH RELATIONS OFFICE. *See* DOMINIONS OFFICE.

COMMONWEALTH SECRETARIAT was established in 1965 at Marlborough House, London. It services Commonwealth conferences and organs of co-operation.

COMMONWEALTH PARTY was founded by Sir Richard Acland, a former Liberal, during World War II. It appealed to egalitarian sentiment and hence more to potential labour and liberal voters than to Conservative. One of its proposals was that all incomes should be subjected to an absolute upper limit. Not a party to the wartime electoral truce, it offered voting opportunities to those discontented with the coalition and actually won three bye-elections. It disappeared when party warfare was resumed in 1945.

COMMONWEALTH SETTLEMENT. The Empire Settlement Act, 1922, empowered the govt. to agree schemes with any public authority in any of the colonies (now Dominions) in co-operation to finance migration from the U.K. to the colonies. The powers were extended in 1937 and 1967.

COMMORTH CALAN MAI (Welsh) was a tribute of cattle payable every other May by the Welsh community to a marcher lord.

COMMOTE. *See* CANTREF.

COMMUNAL AWARD (India) (4 Aug. 1932). With the connivance of the Viceroy (Ld. Minto) a Moslem deputation requested the British govt. in 1906 to provide in the new projected Indian constitution for separate Moslem representation, and the Govt. of India Act, 1909, created special Moslem landholders' constituencies on the ground that in a property qualified electorate the Moslems would be otherwise under-represented because of their relative poverty. The precedent once set, demands for separate representation spread to other minority groups. In further constitutional discussions in 1932, Ramsay Macdonald, then prime minister, adopted the principle for Sikhs, Parsees, Jains, Christians, certain tribal people and the depressed Hindu castes as a preliminary to the Second London Round Table Conference. Gandhi threatened to fast to death and the Award was altered by the POONA PACT (24 Sept. 1932) which kept the depressed castes in the Hindu communal representation, but gave them special representation as well. These conclusions were enacted in 1935.

COMMUNE. A popular self-generated town govt. There were two major types with many variations. **(1)** A revolt against feudalism as in Switzerland. **(2)** A revolt of small workers on raw materials against the entrepreneurs who imported or otherwise controlled them (*see* HANSE). In Britain feudalism was neither as oppressive nor as comprehensive as in parts of Europe and overlords and the Crown forestalled agitation by timely grants of town charters. Similarly the entrepreneurial monopolies could always be evaded by setting up in business outside the town boundaries. Hence the *communard* incidents in British municipal history never led to demands for independence. In any case most mediaeval towns were, by modern standards, villages with a basically rural way of life and many communal agitations were really rural phenomena.

COMMUNICATIONS. *See* TRANSPORT AND COMMUNICATIONS.

COMMUNIST PARTY OF GREAT BRITAIN. (1) William Gallacher, a communist, was arrested for his activities in Glasgow in 1918 and others took part in such affairs as the *Jolly George* or talked of planting the red flag on Buckingham Palace. The party as such was founded in 1920.

(2) In the 1922 election two communists, with Labour support, won parliamentary seats and one lasted, with a break, until 1929, but in 1924 the Labour Party, which had (with hindsight, wisely) refused Communist Party affiliation, additionally barred communists as members and Labour candidates. Communists, therefore, concentrated on trade union militancy.

(3) The party seemed to gain support in the late 1930s when it focused on Fascism and claimed to lead a struggle against it, using the Spanish civil war as a mirror; but in the first months of World War II it opposed the war against Stalin's ally Hitler. As its newspaper, *The Daily Worker*, was suppressed for a while at this time few people noticed. On the other hand it obtained some reflected glory from the Red Army's victories in 1943-5. Its support increased and in 1945 it won two parliamentary seats. It was, however, soon discredited because of its obvious subservience to Russia with her revolutionary imperialism and campaigns of world-wide subversion, and later with the internal difficulties over de-Stalinisation, the forcible suppression of Hungarian, Czech and Polish movements for local autonomy by Russian troops and the brutal maintenance of the Berlin Wall. Communist M.P.s disappeared from the Commons in 1951. The party continued as an industrial nuisance, especially on London building sites into the 1970s.

(4) The party was Bolshevist, i.e. in accordance with Lenin's doctrine, the term 'party' meant not a body of persons of like opinion, but a restricted group of political activists more akin to a religious order. In this sense the number of party members probably never reached five figures. Its active support sometimes reached 20,000 with a body of electoral voters who mostly thought that it stood for a pure form of socialism.

COMMUTATION ACT, 1784, cut the Tea Tax from 112% to 25% and altered the incidence of the window tax against large houses. This represented Pitt's calculated shift from general indirect to selective direct taxation.

COMMUTATION OF LABOUR SERVICES, customarily owed to a Lord, developed at rates varying with the money supply in a primarily barter economy, and with the labour supply and the relative power of the lord. Great lords such as the King or the Church could demand or refuse commutation more easily than ordinary landowners. In the 12th cent. it spread fairly quickly, but in the 13th cent. manorial lords were sometimes able even to reimpose service. The pace increased in the first half of the 14th cent. but the labour market was disturbed and confused by the huge mortality of the Black Death and later epidemics (*see* PLAGUE). The more scarce labour was, the more lords wanted service in kind, while labour wanted commutation and advocated a fixed standard rate. This was a major issue in the Peasants' Revolt. The revolt was put down but the movement continued because a labourer whose offer of commutation was refused simply ran away. By the end of the 15th cent. most services had been commuted and tenants paid contractual rent for their land and lords used the money to hire labour.

COMPANIES, COMMERCIAL. (For regulated and joint stock cos. *see* CHARTERED COMPANIES.) From joint stock cos. it was a short step to pooling money which the Co. then adventured for a variety of purposes such as manufacture. The Bank of England (1694) and the South Sea Co. (1711) were finance houses. The difference between a corporate body liable for its debts only to the extent of its resources and an unincorporate body whose members were all equally liable for all its debts was not fully understood by the public and many unincorporate bodies behaved as corporations and, especially at the time of the South Sea Bubble (1711-20), attracted funds by illegitimate methods and later incompetently or fraudulently ruined their subscribers. The Bubble Act 1720 confined the right to have transferable stock to corporate bodies, but made the incorporation process difficult and expensive. The rise of the modern **Limited** Co. began only with the repeal of the Bubble Act in 1825 but opportunities for fraud were still enormous and so company registration was introduced in 1844. The Act was amended in 1848, 1849, 1855, 1856 and 1857. Eventually the whole statutory structure was recast and the use of the expression "Limited" (Ltd) was introduced in the Companies Act 1862, whose principles have, with further amendments, been followed ever since.

COMPASS, MARINERS'. *See* NAVIGATION.

COMPIÈGNE (Fr.) was an important French royal and imperial residence from earliest times and so the scene of great events, including the capture of Joan of Arc (1429) and the Treaties of 1624 and 1635 (*see* THIRTY YEARS' WAR). It was the German H.Q. in the 1870 war and it was the place where the Germans signed the Armistice of 11 Nov. 1918 and where the French signed their surrender to Hitler on 22 June 1940. The same railway carriage was used on both the latter occasions.

COMPOSITION (Ir.). *See* PERROT-1.

COMPOTUS (perhaps a mistake for Lat: *Compostus* = well arranged or Late Lat: *Computus* = a computation). The understanding of the perplexing Church Calendar. Books on it were written by Bede and Byrhtferth of Ramsey.

COMPOUNDING FOR RATES. Before 1867 a landlord could pay a lump annual sum for rates upon all his properties. He recouped himself by commensurately raising his rents. The public advantages were that the Guardians received large sums early and avoided borrowing, and for this they allowed a discount. Disraeli's Reform Bill of 1867 enfranchised all who paid their rates direct to the Guardians. A liberal M.P., Geo. Hodgkinson, proposed an amendment to abolish compounding, thereby indirectly conferring the parliamentary vote on all ratepayers. Disraeli accepted this, though it increased the electorate by some 400,000 more than he originally intended. It made little other practical difference because landlords then paid their tenants' rates as agents and were allowed a discount for collecting them.

COMPREHENSIVE SCHOOLS are state schools to which children of high and low ability are sent instead of being separated by the system of the Education Act 1944, which provided grammar schools for the promising, with more numerous secondary modern schools for the others. Even under the 1944 Act some areas with strong Labour parties instituted the comprehensive system, and in 1959 the Labour Party, with its interest in social engineering, adopted comprehensivation as a policy. Subsequently Labour govts. encouraged or pressed local education authorities into ending the dual system. The benefits claimed for the comprehensive were that it was less socially divisive and that very large schools could offer more subjects. The first claim remained unreal because it was political rather than educational and there were in any case educational arguments for an alternative system. The second claim was only partly made good because it fell victim to reduced educational expenditure. *See* ELEVEN PLUS EXAMINATON.

COMPTER or COUNTER. A debtor's prison attached to the mayor's or sheriff's court in a borough. The City of London had two, closed in 1854 and 1917.

COMPTON. Originally a Warwickshire family. **(1) Sir William (?1482-1528)** page to Henry VIII as D. of York, became his Groom of the Stole and holder of many other, mostly sinecure, offices. He commanded the rearguard in the French war of 1513 and, save for service in the Flodden campaign, was permanently in attendance on the King. By marriage to Werburga Brereton, widow of Sir Francis Cheyney, and through his offices which included from 1513 to 1516 the Chancellorship of Ireland, and from 1516 the life shrievalty of Worcestershire, he amassed estates in 18 counties. This fortune founded the power of the Compton family, for his grandson, otherwise undistinguished, was ennobled as the 1st Lord Compton and his son was **(2) William (?-1630) 1st E. of NORTHAMPTON (?-?).** His son **(3) Spencer (1601-43), 2nd E.,** became Master of the Robes to Charles I as P. of Wales in 1622 and accompanied him to Spain. In 1626 he was summoned to the Lords as Lord Compton. He was strongly royalist, yet favoured the calling of a parliament at the beginning of the second Bishops' War, but when forced to choose sided with the King and raised troops for him. After the B. of Edgehill he, with his three sons, commanded in the Banbury area until he was killed at Hopton Heath (Mar. 1643). His third son **(4) Sir William (1625-63)** as a lieut-col. held Banbury against constant parliamentary attack until May 1646 and Colchester in 1648. Much respected for his exemplary character by both sides, he was involved in royalist plans for a restoration throughout the Commonwealth, and was in custody in 1655 and 1659. At the Restoration he became M.P. for Cambridge and Master of the Ordnance. His brother **(5) Henry (1632-1713)** served as a private soldier in the Civil War and in Flanders and was commissioned in 1661 into the Horseguards but disliked the life and in 1662 was ordained. In 1666 he became rector of Cottenham, in 1667 Master of St. Cross (Winchester) and in 1669 a canon of Christchurch. By 1673 he was preaching, not well, at court and in 1674 he became Bp. of Oxford and in 1675 Dean of the Chapel Royal. Hence in Dec. 1675 he was translated to the See of London. He was a great personal friend of Danby's and strongly protestant. This earned him the dislike of James, D. of York, and the responsibility for the religious education of James' daughters Mary and Anne, who both liked him. He was a strong personal influence at court and was able in 1677 to force the dismissal of Edw. Coleman, the Duchess' R. Catholic secretary (*see* POPISH PLOT). He spent much effort, as diocesan, not only campaigning against R. Catholics but in reconciling other dissenters, especially French protestant refugees. Naturally he became the object of royal animosity with the change of reign in 1685. In Nov. 1685 he declared in the House of Lords that the King's dispensations of the Test Act endangered the constitution. Early in 1686 he refused to suspend Dr Sharp for attacking popery and thereupon a Court of High Commission suspended him from his functions (Aug.). Popular support favoured him and he had the large income of the *see* and could live, an active and dangerous figure, at Fulham Palace, from which he unofficially ruled his clergy. He was one of the instigators of the Seven Bishops refusal to read the Declaration of Indulgence (May 1688) and in June Danby got him to join the powerful secret committee which organised James' overthrow. At the Revolution he conveyed Anne out of London, met the E. of Devonshire's escort for her at Nottingham, and took command of it. In Dec. he waited on William of Orange, in Jan. 1689 voted in the Lords for him and, since Abp. Sancroft would not do so, crowned William and Mary in Apr. Sancroft was suspended and as the most influential of the commissioners appointed to administer the archbishopric, Compton was now virtually head of the church; he was also a commissioner for Trade. He worked vigorously for protestant comprehension at home and the anti-French alliance abroad. Nevertheless when Sancroft died (1691) and again in 1694 he was passed over for the primacy. This embittered him and alienated him from the Whigs who mainly supported the war. When Anne came to the throne (1702) he was again a personally influential figure, yet basically out of sympathy with the war policy. Consequently he supported the Occasional Conformity Bill (1705) and Dr Sacheverell in 1710. His Tory propaganda, however, provoked powerful retaliation. Apart from his political activities, Compton built many churches (including St. James' Piccadilly) and hospitals, and organised Queen Anne's Bounty. His main interest, however, was botany and the gardens at Fulham were an important experimental ground. His nephew **(6) Spencer (?1673-1743) Ld. WILMINGTON (1728) E. (1730)** became a Tory M.P. for Eye in 1698 but turned whig and became in 1705 chairman of the committee of privileges and in 1707 Treasurer to the Queen's husband, P. George of Denmark. In 1709 he was one of the managers of Sacheverell's impeachment. He failed of election in 1710 but was returned again in 1713 and held the speakership throughout the reign of George I (1714-27). From 1722 he was also Paymaster-Gen. In the new reign he was induced not to supplant Walpole in the headship of the govt. and in 1730 he gave up the paymastership for the Lord Presidency and the Privy Seal. He refused to vote for Walpole in the crisis of 1742 and became First Lord of the Treasury but not effective head in the Newcastle administration. A collateral relative **(7) Spencer Joshua (1790-1851) 2nd M. of NORTHAMPTON (1828)** followed Spencer Percival as M.P. for Northampton from 1812 to 1820 and was a practical Tory. He favoured direct against indirect taxation, supported the anti-slavery movement and criminal law reform. He lived in Italy from 1820 to 1828 and thereafter was notable for promoting scientific and literary movements, especially the Geological Society, the British Association, the Royal Society (of which he was Pres. from 1838 to 1849) and the Archaeological Society. His son **(8) Alwyne Frederick (1825-1906)** was Bp. of Ely from 1886 to 1905.

COMPTON CENSUS (1676) was a religious census instigated by Danby and conducted by **(5)** in the previous entry. The bishops made the returns from figures compiled by their parishes. The figures seemed to show that 21 out of 22 people were Anglicans – which is probable only if all who took communion in the Anglican manner genuinely adhered to the Church of England.

COMPTON WYNYATES (Warwicks) formerly moated great mansion begun in 15th cent. and completed in about 1520. The seat of the M. of Northampton.

COMPULSORY ACQUISITION (1) The Crown has always taken property for defence purposes, but otherwise land was first taken compulsorily for inclosures (q.v.). It was assumed that compensation would be made. In the case of inclosures this was commonly done in kind by the allotment of other land for the extinguished rights; expropriators and expropriated being mostly the same people redistributing their property. **(2)** Apart from *assart* private parliamentary Acts were mostly necessary. These contained four elements (i) authorisation, (ii) selection of land, (iii) acquisition and (iv) compensation. The clauses in these Acts developed a pattern which was institutionalised into standard inclosure clauses by an Act of 1801. Another Act of 1848 abolished the need to proceed by Private Act by creating a standardised method, and the Lands Clauses Act of the same year introduced for other Compulsory Acquisitions, standard clauses similar to the Inclosure clauses of 1801. This Act applied to public undertakings of which railways and harbours were then the most common, but they came to be applied to expropriations by public bodies (democratically elected by 1895) for their own purposes (e.g. roads). From 1909 these could apply for ministerial orders subject to parliamentary confirmation or challenge instead of promoting standardised Acts. Since 1965 the cases needing parliamentary intervention have been steadily reduced. **(3)** Especially under Labour govts., which readily confirmed Compulsory Acquisitions and never sold land or permitted local authorities to do so, by 1980 the total amount of lands acquired (by compulsion or agreement) by public bodies and the govt. exceeded the area of six average counties. The Thatcher govt. meant to restore some of this to the open market (*cf* the Dissolution of the Monasteries) by forcing local councils to sell unneeded land, but reduced the potential enthusiasm for the policy by centrally controlling the proceeds. It also retained compulsory purchase powers for itself and these were used to promote huge road building programmes, often on relatively cheap amenity land. Public discontent in the 1990s led to riots e.g. at Twyford Down (Winchester), in N. London and near Bath.

COMPURGATION or WAGER OF LAW was a method of trial adopted by the Church from the tribes which overran the Roman Empire. It early became part of the Common law. A defendant, to clear himself of a civil claim, was required to deny it in a set form of words and to support the denial by the oaths (originally in the same form) of a certain number of other persons called compurgators. If he or they stumbled in the words or he could not procure enough compurgators he lost and the compurgators would be liable for perjury. In 1215 the papacy laid down that compurgators need only swear that they believed the defendant; this destroyed much of the procedure's efficiency because they could seldom be prosecuted for perjury. Their number was originally uncertain and in the judge's discretion, 3 or 6 being usual in a manorial court; but in 1342 it was settled at 12. The method could never be used where the Crown was a party, which excluded it from criminal proceedings and the Court of Exchequer. Primarily used in actions of Debt, Detinue and Account (all in the Common Pleas) it fell slowly into disuse as these actions were superseded by proceedings in the King's Bench, or Chancery. Ecclesiastical courts, however, continued to use it in matters of penance and since accused clerks could usually obtain skilful clerical compurgators, the rule that those pleading benefit of clergy should be handed over to the ecclesiastical court for purgation became farcical and was abolished in 1576. In civil proceedings the method was last used in *King* v *Williams* (1824) and it was abolished in 1833.

COMPUTER. The earliest analogue computer was Lord Kelvin's tide predictor of 1872. The Electronic Numerical Integrator and Calculator was demonstrated in 1946; the stored programme computer in 1949. Commercial versions of the latter came into use in 1953.

COMYN or CUMIN, powerful Anglo-Scots family with Highland connections, which acquired wide lands in Galloway, Wigtown, Nithsdale and Tyneside. The traditional founder of the family's fortunes was **(1) William Cumin (?-?)** a clerk to Henry I's chancellor Godfrey, Bp. of Durham, in 1133, who became chancellor to K. David of Scots. His nephew **(2) Richard (?-?)** established the family in the Badenoch highlands (Inverness) but married into a Border family through whom the Comyns later claimed descent from the 11th cent. Scots K. Donald Bane. His descendent **(3) William (?-1233)** became **E. of BUCHAN** in right of his wife. Of

his sons **(4) John** (?-1274), justiciary in Galloway, was an influential magnate at the Scots court from 1249 to 1255. He was also involved in English politics under Henry III, being against the King in 1258, for him in 1263, against him in 1264 and finally rewarded by him in 1265, while **(5) Alexander (?-1289) 2nd E. of BUCHAN (1233)** justiciary of Scotland from 1253 and a leading member of the Scots court from 1257, became Chief of the Comyns in 1258. He tried to build up a semi-independent lordship in Galloway and Wigtown, from which he ravaged the Western Is. in 1264. In 1266 he acquired the sheriffdom of Wigtown and became Constable of Scotland in 1270. He supported the arrangements relating to the Maid of Norway and became one of the Guardians of the Realm in 1286. His kinsman **(6) Walter Comyn of Badenoch (?-1258) E. of MENTEITH (1230)** built many castles in Galloway and was a leading figure at the Scots court from 1249 to 1255. Alexander and Walter were responsible for seizing the King in a *coup d'état* at Kinross. These Comyns resented Henry III's interference in Scottish affairs (partly on behalf of his daughter Margaret, Q. to Alexander III) but an understanding was reached and relations between them, and their descendants and the English crown were generally friendly for the next 30 years (*see* 4 above). The son of **(4)**, **(7) John the Black (?-1300)** "The Claimant", Ld. of Badenoch from 1258, also supported the Maid of Norway's title and became one of the Guardians in 1286. In 1291 he laid claim to the throne himself, but getting little support he became a partisan of John Balliol, whose sister he had married. This son **(8) John**, called the RED COMYN **(?-1306)** thus became the Balliol claimant when John Balliol renounced his rights. He was captured at Dunbar in 1296 but released. He fought at Falkirk (1298) and was elected joint Guardian in 1299. He attempted to get rid of the English administration in 1303 but failed and submitted in 1304. Supporters of Robert the Bruce murdered him in Dumfries church. One of them came out of the church and said 'I doubt I've killed the Red Comyn' to which Bruce replied 'I'll mak' sicker' (= sure) and went back in. The son of **(8)**, **(9) John (?-?1313) 3rd E. of BUCHAN,** a friend of Edward I, initially shared Balliol's fortunes and was sent to Scotland to hinder Wallace's revolt, raised in Balliol's name (1297), but in 1303 he sought French intervention and forfeited his English properties. These, however, were soon restored and in 1305 he acknowledged Edward I's suzerainty. After the Red Comyn's murder he was at blood feud with the Bruces, yet Isabelle, his wife, supported Robert the Bruce who was crowned with her circlet at Scone. His fortunes quickly declined and his estates were seized in 1313.

COMYN, John (?-1212) as a young man was a diplomat in the service of Henry II with the Emperor, the Curia, Castile and Navarre, but from 1169 to 1179 he was a justice in Eyre and, though not in Holy Orders, a canon of St. Pauls, Archdeacon of Bath and custodian of two vacant bishoprics. In 1181 Laurence O'Toole, Abp. of Dublin, died. At Evesham Henry browbeat the Dublin clergy into electing Comyn. He went to Rome for his pallium and in 1183 was ordained and consecrated there by Lucius II himself. He reached Ireland in 1184 where he headed the reception of P. John as Lord of Ireland. In 1185 he was at Henry's Christmas court at Guildford and nominated to receive Card. Octavian who was sent to crown John as King of Ireland. Abp. Baldwin, however, persuaded the Cardinal to leave without doing so. Thenceforth Comyn was a mediator between the royal sons and their father yet, like everyone else, he quarrelled with John. His essentially diplomatic outlook kept him travelling in England. He administered his province mostly through supervised delegates and made important donations to the Dublin church. He died a very old man.

CONACRE (Ir.) was a licence to take a crop off land. There were two varieties **(1)** where the owner permitted the land to be tilled and **(2)** where, before doing so, he prepared and manured the land at his own expense. The crop planted by the conacre holder could not be removed until he had paid for it.

CONALL. *See* DALRIADA.

CONCENTRATION CAMPS (1) represented a military technique aimed at impounding and controlling civil populations likely to help guerrillas. They were used for this purpose by the British in the S. African war and had no penal purpose; but maladministration created discomfort, ill health and a rising mortality much criticised by the British public.

(2) The Nazi govt. of Germany instituted an entirely different type of political camp to eliminate and murder its opponents. These were called 'concentration camps' (or 'K.Z.') in order to divert suspicion from their activities. Six of these (Buchenwald, Dachau, Flossenburg, Mauthausen, Ravensbück and Sachsenhausen) were set up in 1938 for Jews. The beginning (1939-40) of World War II created an immense demand for labour and the system was extended on the Russian model to provide slave labour camps, to which foreign labourers were deported. There were several hundred camps of which nine were very large, housing many thousands at a time. Two of these (Auschwitz and Lublin) were in Poland, inmates being overcrowded, starved and worked to death. In the concentration, as opposed to the labour camps, conditions were barbarous. Prisoners were used for medical experiments or tortured. In either case the vast number of dead were cremated. The final development was the Extermination Camp, a death factory, whose purpose was to wipe out unwanted populations. At the principal one, Auschwitz, between 1 and 3 million people perished.

(3) From 1923 the Russian govt. set up so-called corrective labour camps to which enemies or alleged enemies of the regime were sent, especially during the farm collectivisation campaign between 1928 and 1932. By this time the convenience of a large slave labour reserve resulted in a change of policy; camps were set up to work difficult industries such as arctic gold mining, fisheries and lumber, and offences against the state became a pretext for providing the labour. The camp population was maintained also by importing people from foreign areas or minorities dominated by Russia, especially during World War II. The system continued until Stalin's death when it began to be reduced and humanised. It was finally (it is believed) ended under Gorbachov.

CONCERT OF EUROPE. A vague expression for Europe as settled at the P. of Vienna (1815) and the understandings between great powers to maintain the settlement.

CONCILIATION HALL (Dublin) was the H.Q. of the Repeal Movement.

CONCLAVE. *See* CARDINALS.

CONCORDAT **(Lat.)** originally any treaty, is now the technical term for an agreement between church and state and especially an agreement to which the Holy See is a party.

CONCRETE. A cement mixed with varying proportions of other solids. The Romans varied the weight by mixing it with stones low in a building or with lighter materials such as clinker higher up (e.g. in the Colosseum). Its composition seems to have been forgotten in Europe with the collapse of the Empire, because it has to be kept moving before use. This could then be done only by slaves or cattle which ceased to be adequately available with the rise of Christianity and the barbarian invasions. This oblivion radically conditioned the construction of large works and buildings until after its rediscovery in Britain in 1824.

CONCUBINAGE. HEIC officials and officers and plantation owners in the Americas often kept concubines (the latter being slaves) but in Britain such relationships were unrecognised until the 1960s when an unofficial, but socially understood, concubinage developed, often between employers and secretaries or between young people. It has been so far officially recognised by the abolition of the disadvantages of illegitimacy and the payment of allowances to single parent families.

CONDAT, ORDINANCES OF (1289). *See* AQUITAINE-9.

CONDÉ and ENGHIEN, branch of the Bourbon family. **(1) Louis I (1530-69) P. of CONDÉ**, brother of K. Anthoine of Navarre, was implicated in the conspiracy of Amboise (1560) and with Coligny led the Huguenots in the first two Wars of Religion. In the second he was killed at the B. of Jarnac (1569). His son **(2) Henri I (1552-88)** succeeded him in the Huguenot party, setting himself as a leader of the extremists. This was something of an embarrassment to his cousin, Henry of Navarre, the future Henri IV. He was killed at the B. of Coutras. **(3) Henri II (1588-1646)** was brought up as a R. Catholic and after Henri IV's death in 1610 raised a series of rebellions against the regency, which succeeded in 1616 in apprehending and imprisoning him until 1619. Thereafter he consistently supported the govt. and even Mazarin. His notorious or famous but insufferable son **(4) Louis II (1621-86) Duc d'Enghien** until 1646, was later called LE GRAND CONDÉ. He obtained Mazarin's favour and the command of an army at the age of 21. He instantly (in 1643) won the decisive victory over the Spaniards at Rocroi. In 1644 he and Turenne seized Phillipsburg and in 1645 won the B. of Nördlingen. In 1646 he campaigned in Spain and in 1648 in Flanders won the B. of Lens over the Spaniards against heavy odds. On his return his rank involved him in the Fronde and in 1650 Mazarin had him detained for a year. Turenne raised a revolt on his behalf and in 1651, when the govt. had to give way and dismiss Mazarin, he was released and raised troops himself. In the civil war of 1652 after Mazarin's return (in which Turenne changed sides) he was defeated. He then entered the Spanish service, where he won great credit at Arras (1654), Valenciennes (1656) and Cambrai (1657). He returned to France in 1659 after the P. of the Pyrenees. In 1674 he defeated William of Orange at Seneffe. In 1675 he replaced the dead Turenne in Alsace from which he drove the Austrians. Thereafter he retired. His great-grandson **(5) Louis Henri, Duc de BOURBON-CONDÉ**, was Louis XV's chief minister from 1723 to 1726. His great-grandson **(6) Louis Antoine Duc d'ENGHIEN (1772-1804)** was kidnapped and murdered on Bonaparte's orders for supposed complicity in Georges Cadoudal's conspiracy.

CONDOM, ORDINANCES OF (1289). *See* AQUITAINE-9.

CONEY-CATCHER. A catcher of rabbits, i.e. simpletons: a Tudor confidence trickster.

CONFEDERATES, IRISH. *See* CIVIL WAR-9 *et seq*; COMMONWEALTH-2 *et seq.*

CONFEDERATE STATES OF AMERICA viz Virginia, Georgia, N. and S. Carolina. Alabama, Tennessee, Louisiana, Arkansas, Mississippi, Florida and Texas, seceded from the U.S.A., set up a confederacy (Feb. 1861) with a constitution similar to the U.S.A.'s under the presidency of Jefferson Davies, a flag showing stars but with vertical bars instead of horizontal stripes and a capital at Richmond, Virginia. The Confederacy was never recognised by any other state. Its member states were forced to rejoin the U.S.A. after their defeat in the Civil War (1865) and the Confederate debt was repudiated.

CONFEDERATION. *See* ARTICLES OE CONFEDERATION.

CONFEDERATION OF BRITISH INDUSTRY (C.B.I.) was formed in 1965 by the amalgamation of the Federation of British Industries, British Employers Confederation and the National Association of British Manufacturers.

Although it offered various practical services to its approximately 13,000 member-companies, it attracted most attention as a pressure group, with its president (elected for a two-year term) regularly placing its views before ministers.

CONFESSION OF FAITH. See MARY Q. OF SCOTS-7. John Knox and five others drafted the First Confession of Faith of the Scottish Church, it is said, in four days and then had it approved by the Scots Parliament (1560). It was superseded only by the Westminster Confession of 1647. See COVENANT-ERS

CONFEDERATION OF FREE TRADE UNIONS (C.F.T.U.). The World Federation of Trade Unions was set up in 1944 but abused by the Russian trade unions which were making it into an instrument of Communism. The British T.U.C. and the American Congress of Industrial Organisations accordingly left and set up the C.F.T.U. in 1949.

CONFIRMATIO CARTARUM **(Lat = Confirmation of the Charters) (1297)** confirmed Magna Carta and the Forest Charter and required them to be copied and published in all boroughs and read twice a year in cathedrals. Judgements repugnant to them were to be void and bishops were to excommunicate those who broke them. The statute continues by declaring that aids, tasks and prises recently granted do not constitute a precedent, that the new wool custom is released and that the King will not take them in future 'but by the Common Assent of the Realm and for the common profit' saving the ancient aids and prises and previous customs on wool and hides. See EDWARD 1-18.

CONFLICT OF LAWS is a branch of private international law concerned with the solution of legal problems arising out of the presence, in a given case, of a foreign legal element; for example the effect in England of a French contract. It is said to be based upon a doctrine of comity between the judicial institutions of civilised countries, that is, that the courts of a country will uphold the decrees of another if not positively repugnant to their own domestic law. In fact the issue is mainly one of common sense: if a dispute with a foreign element comes before a court that element is as much a fact as any other and has to be taken into account. The relevant doctrines originally grew up in the middle ages around commercial, maritime and matrimonial practices.

CONFUCIANISM. See CHINA-7.

CONGÉ **(Fr = permission).** The expulsion of an ambassador by the govt. to which he is accredited (cf AGRÉMENT).

CONGÉ D'ÉLIRE, the royal licence to a cathedral or monastic chapter to elect a bishop or abbot. This was one of the rights retained by the Crown, along with the right to consent to the election of a prelate and to enjoy the revenues of his lands during a vacancy, in K. John's charter of 1214 granting freedom of elections to the church. The *congé d'élire* was accompanied by Letters Recommendatory which, after the passing of the Statute of Praemunire, laid down whom the body concerned was to elect under pain of a Praemunire. The Statute was repealed in 1967 and there is now no sanction against disobedience of the Letters Recommendatory.

CONGESTED DISTRICTS (Ir.) were rural areas mostly in Connaught, Donegal, Clare and Kerry, where there was a high proportion of peasant holdings so small or poor that they did not support a decent living. Nationalists and churchmen denounced emigration: politicians the prohibition on further subdivision. A Congested Districts Board was set up in 1891 with powers to buy, build upon, improve and resell land so as to increase the productivity or size of holdings and to make grants. The members of the Board were all Irish. They encountered obstruction, terrorism, refusal either to migrate or to accept migrants and the apathy of migrants themselves. The Board imported new strains of stock, built piers, established cottage industries and by 1914 had bought,

rearranged and resold 2.5M acres with 68,000 tenants. It failed to develop any industries.

CONGLETON BEARS. Bear baiting was so popular in this Cheshire town that, just before a Wakes week, money apparently intended to buy a new Bible was appropriated to buy a new town bear.

CONGO (BRAZZAVILLE). See EQUATORIAL (EX-FRENCH) AFRICA.

CONGO FREE STATE. H. M. Stanley's explorations in the Congo basin led Leopold II of the Belgians to set up the *Association Internationale du Congo* in 1876 with Stanley as its chief agent, to exploit the area. With French and U.S. support, Leopold defeated an Anglo-Portuguese attempt to establish Portuguese control of the river mouth in 1884 and, during the Berlin W. Africa conference of 1884-5 by bilateral agreements, secured his personal recognition as sovereign of a Congo Free State. His financial resources were inadequate but after 1891 a strong demand for rubber (for tyres) developed and vast quantities of wild rubber was secured by atrocious methods through the seizure of vacant lands, enforcement of labour service instead of taxes, premiums to officials and grants to concessionaires. The Congo had, in effect, become a private slave state. Growing international scandal and the publication of Roger Casement's report (1904) on the rubber producing areas inspired the Congo Reform Movement and mounting protests in Belgium. Leopold was induced by Anglo-American pressure to hand over his colony, which in 1908 was annexed by Belgium. See BELGIUM.

CONGREGATION, LORDS OF THE (FAITHFUL). The Calvinist party in Scotland, inspired by John Knox, who in 1559 rose under the leadership of Argyll, Morton and Arran against Mary of Guise. To achieve their purpose it was necessary to end the French alliance and rely on English help. An English naval intervention saved them from defeat and by the T. of Edinburgh (Feb. 1560) they secured most of their aims. See MARY Q. OF SCOTS-6 *et seq.*

CONGREGATIONALISM, BROWNISM or INDEPENDENCY, is based upon the priesthood of all believers and on the principle that congregations are bound in equality together and with God by a covenant which places them outside state or church control. Such bodies had appeared in England by 1550; they multiplied under Elizabeth, once she evidently did not mean to dissolve the established church. Their earliest and most influential thinker was Robert Browne (?1550-1633), a relative of William Cecil. He founded congregations at Norwich, was imprisoned and, being released by Cecil, fled to Holland with his congregation. Here in 1582 he issued *The Life and Manner of All True Christians* and a *Treatise of Reformation without Tarrying for Any.* He then quarrelled with his congregation and, after wanderings in Scotland and elsewhere, was reconciled with the church and died as Rector of Abchurch, Northants. His original doctrine, however, gathered adherents now called Brownists, and even martyrs such as John Greenwood, who was hanged in 1593. Some, however, were driven overseas. Influential congregations continued to be formed in Holland, especially Leyden, and soon in America. In Massachusetts, in particular, Independency was the *de facto* state religion, for citizenship depended on membership of the recognised church of a given area, and the doctrine was orthodox Calvinist. The underground groups in England, however, were composed of individual enthusiasts and lacked co-ordination. Particular preachers led many such groups to diverge from one another and sometimes from Calvinist orthodoxy. The English Congregationalists of the 1640s thus included, besides a variety of separatist groups, followers of the New England way, who differed from the Presbyterians on organisation above parish level. Presbyterians stigmatised both as "sectaries" and both types of Congregationalist, who were strong in

Cromwell's army, were allied to prevent the imposition of a Presbyterian system of govt. Pride's Purge effectively ended Presbyterian encroachments and the resultant system of independent parishes with some national intervention to ensure minimum standards reflected the New England practice. The Savoy Declaration of 1658 set forth the views of the ministers who favoured this system, but they moved away from the New England model in their preference for a wider toleration, born of their struggle with the Presbyterians. The modern movement flowed from this. Their history had made them odious to the Restoration govt. and they did not win liberty until the Toleration Act 1689. All the same the sect prospered because of its evangelical fervour and (as compared with Presbyterians) intellectual freedom. Excluded from universities, they set up Dissenting Academies and in the end were responsible for founding London University. Their London Missionary Society, founded in 1795, began operations in Tahiti in 1796 and spread to Asia and Africa in the 19th cent. In 1832 they founded the Congregational Unions as co-ordinating and advisory bodies. In 1966 the Assembly of the Union agreed to form a Congregational *Church* in England and Wales, thus abandoning one of the distinctive features of their outlook. This naturally opened the way in 1972 to union with the Presbyterian Church to form a United Reformed Church. Some continuing congregational churches opposed this and maintained their independence.

CONGRESS POLAND. The truncated Polish Kingdom under Russian domination set up in 1815 under the T. of Vienna and slowly destroyed in the next 15 years.

CONGRESS SYSTEM was to be a means of settling European problems, agreed between Austria, Britain, Prussia and Russia in the T. of Paris (Nov. 1815). Four congresses were held. **(1)** At **Aix-la-Chapelle** (Sept.-Nov. 1818). France was admitted to the system and the allied army occupying her was reduced from 150,000 to 30,000, but Castlereagh would not countenance a Russian proposal of mutual guarantees of the monarchies. **(2)** At **Troppau** (Oct-Dec. 1820) adjourned to **Laibach (Ljubljana)** (Jan-May 1821), the issues proposed were measures against, respectively, German liberalism and Italian and Greek nationalism. Castlereagh and then Canning sent only observers, on the ground that the system was never intended as a union for the superintendance of the internal affairs of other states. **(3)** Britain withdrew from the Congress of **Verona** (Oct-Dec. 1822) in order to be free to oppose military intervention in the Peninsula and Greece.

CONGREVE, William (1670-1729) was a fellow student with Swift at Trinity Coll., Dublin and a friend of Dryden. In 1692 he began writing plays including *Love for Love* (1695) and the *Way of the World* (1700). He derived his income from several minor public offices and was much patronised as a wit. He wrote little after 1710.

CONGREVE, Sir William (1772-1828) an artillery officer, invented rocket artillery and formed largely unsuccessful rocket batteries in 1809. He was an M.P. from 1812 and comptroller of the Royal Laboratory at Woolwich from 1814.

CONNAUGHT, CONNACHT. This sparsely populated province whose boundaries with Meath, Ulster and Leinster have fluctuated a good deal, recognised Kings from two families (the Ui Briuin and Ui Fiachrach) from 5th to 12th cent. Of the last of these Turlough O'Connor (?-1156) and his son Rory (?-1224) were considered to be High Kings of Ireland. Rory's brother, Cathal Crovderg (?-1224), however, could not maintain his position against rising English colonisation. K. John granted lands in Connaught to William de Burgh, who had difficulty in establishing himself and in 1227 Henry III granted the Lordship to William's son Richard. His family held it with Ulster until 1461 when it escheated. It was, however, controlled thereafter by junior branches of the de Burghs,

the Mayo and Clanricarde Burkes. The province was shired in 1576 (Galway, Leitrim, Mayo, Roscommon and Sligo) and subsequently became a dumping ground for Irish driven from their lands in the various Irish plantations. It, with Co. Clare, was long the only part of Ireland where R. Catholics might own land. As a result it remained strongly Gaelic. The capital was Galway, which maintained trading links in the middle ages with Spain, but the province raised only sheep, cattle, oats and potatoes so that the volume of trade was small. The archbishopric was at Tuam. *See* ELIZABETH I-17.

CONNAUGHT AND STRATHEARN, Arthur William Patrick Albert, D. of (1850-1942), third son of Q. Victoria, had a conventional military career beginning in 1866 and ending as a Field Marshal in 1902. He had in 1899 renounced his rights in the duchy of Saxe-Coburg-Gotha and in 1902 he began a new career as an English prince. He was at the Delhi Durbar in 1903; opened the S. African Parliament in 1910; from 1911 to 1916 he was gov-gen. of Canada and in 1921 he opened the legislature in India. His rock-like common sense was unobtrusively useful to the overseas politicians with whom he had to deal.

CONNECTICUT. There were traders from New Amsterdam and the Plymouth Co. on the Connecticut R. from 1614. Settlers from Massachusetts Bay reached Hartford in 1633, where the Dutch built a fort. Further settlements were founded at Saybrook (1635) and New Haven (1638) and in 1639 the people of Windsor, Hartford and Wethersfield agreed upon FUNDAMENTAL ORDERS, under which there was to be an annual assembly and an elected governor (*see also* CONGREGATIONALISM). The British ousted all Dutch authority from the area in 1654. The colonies were entirely agricultural, but because of the fertility of much of the soil expanded quickly under John Winthrop jun (1606-74), who was elected governor annually from 1657 until his death. In 1662 the Fundamental Orders were replaced by a Royal charter, which remained in force until 1816. In 1665 the River and the New Haven settlements were united into a single colony. The Charter conferred rights on residents in a strip as wide as the Colony and of unlimited length and led to constant conflicts with Pennsylvania, which were not resolved until after independence, at which time the population was almost wholly of English origin. The State supported the Union in the Civil War.

CONQUERED PROVINCES (India). The collective name given to Aligarh, Agra and Saharunpoor, conquered by the HEIC from Scindia, and Bundelkhand conquered from the Peishwa.

CONRAD, Joseph (1857-1924) originally TEODOR JOSEF KONRAD KORZENIOWSKI, Polish patriot and seaman, was naturalised British and obtained his ship's masters ticket in 1886. He sailed the Malay archipelago, explored the Congo and visited the Ukraine. He published *Almayer's Folly*, his first novel in 1895, *Lord Jim* in 1900, *Nostromo* in 1904 and other novels and stories down to 1922. Writing wholly in English, he was accepted as a master of prose style in his lifetime.

CONSCIENTIOUS OBJECTOR. One who declines warlike service on the genuinely held conviction that fighting is wrong. When conscription was introduced into Britain in 1916 and again in 1939, special provision was included to exempt those (e.g. Quakers) with real scruples. In particular willingness to undertake dangerous non-combatant work such as in field ambulances was regarded as evidence of a genuine conviction. The arrangement was unique to Britain.

CONSCRIPTION in modern times was started in Prussia by the *Kantonreglement* of 1733. Carnot introduced universal military conscription in France in 1793 and the word itself first appears in the Law of 19 Fructidor of the Year VI (1798), the so-called *Loi de Jourdan*. It remained in force until 1814. The many exemptions in Prussia were abolished in 1813 and 1814, just as the French restored monarchy abolished conscription altogether. In 1818, however, Prussian power made it necessary to restore it in France. The Prussian act of 1814 was amended in 1860 so as to abolish the difference between army and militia (Landwehr) service and in this form the institution was extended to all the states of the North German Confederation and then of the German Empire. The French system was amended so that both countries entered World War I with conscript armies. In Britain, until Jan. 1916 voluntary recruitment had raised about 2,500,000 men, but it was foreseen that the demands of the Western Front would outpace the rate of such recruitment, while many volunteers were skilled men likely to be more useful remaining at their jobs. Conscription was introduced, at first for unmarried men only, in Jan. 1916. The U.S.A. introduced it in 1917 and, like Britain, abandoned it when the war was over. In Apr. 1939 the British govt. took the belated step of introducing it in peacetime; the eight-month period of service was overtaken by World War II and detained conscripts for the duration. In the mid-1940s British conscripts could choose to serve in the coalmines instead and were known as 'Bevin Boys'. From 1941 to 1947 women were also liable for conscription, but as they were often replacing men in jobs out of which the men had been called up, large numbers were kept compulsorily in certain civilian pursuits considered of value to the war effort. These pursuits were called 'reserved occupations' and, unlike in World War I, no stigma attached to them. *See* CONSCIENTIOUS OBJECTOR.

CONSERVA-NCY-TORS were Commissioners or trustees under local Acts for the management of rivers. They could usually build weirs, locks and towpaths, make byelaws and levy tolls. Depending on their Acts, they might own the bed and banks of the river or merely the right of passage. Their jurisdiction did not generally extend to tidal waters. Some 40 rivers including all the main ones were under conservators deriving their authority from over 300 acts. The earliest such acts were passed during the 18th cent. canal mania of which they really formed a part, but often the conservators took over from pre-existing commissioners of sewers. *See* TRANSPORT AND COMMUNICATIONS.

CONSERVATIVE. This word was first used politically in the *Quarterly Review* for Jan. 1830: "...what is called the Tory, but which might with more propriety be called the Conservative Party", but in 1819 a correspondent of the D. of Wellington had written of his *"esprit conservateur"* and conservatives were sometimes called *conservators* until 1832.

CONSERVATIVE CENTRAL OFFICE was constituted in 1870 but the name came into general use in 1871. The first agent was J. E. Gorst, who also became Sec. of the Metropolitan Conservative Alliance. In 1871 he, with Chas. Keith-Falconer, became joint-secs. (until 1875) of the Nat. Union of Conservative and Constitution Associations, whose H.Q. moved into the same office, where it has since remained. The Nat. Union became, in effect, the propaganda dept of the Central Office.

CONSERVATIVE RESEARCH DEPT. was established in 1929 by J. C. C. Davidson. Its first chairman was Ld. Eustace Percy, followed by Neville Chamberlain. Joseph Ball, a former officer of MI5, was director from 1930 to 1939. Ralph Assheton revived it in 1945 under R. A. Butler.

CONSERVATIVE WORKING MEN'S ASSOCIATIONS. *See* NAT. UNION OF CONSERVATIVE AND CONSTITUTION ASSOCIATIONS.

CONSIDERATION is a peculiar characteristic of English contract law. A contract to be legally binding, if not made as a deed, must consist of an agreement whereby each party does or forebears to do something in consideration of a forebearance or act by the other.

CONSISTORY. (1) *See* CARDINALS.

(2) Church of England. A diocesan court of ecclesiastical law, particularly probate and matrimonial cases. These were transferred away from them in 1857, leaving little save faculty jurisdiction over church alterations.

(3) Presbyterian Churches. The minister and elders of a local congregation responsible for supervision and discipline. Known in Scotland as the Kirk Session.

CONSOLIDATED FUND is the account at the Bank of England, in the name of the Exchequer, into which all revenue is paid and from which all issues are made under statutory authority. Usually issues are authorised annually by Act, but certain issues such as judges' salaries and the interest on govt. annuities are permanently authorised and these are said to be "charged on the consolidated fund". It was set up in 1752 to simplify the management of the various govt. stocks and annuities raised in 1731, 1742-5 and 1750 and these became known as Consolidated Annuities or CONSOLS. Similar arrangements were made in Ireland. The Act of Union with Ireland of 1800 left the two funds in being but they were amalgamated by the U.K. (Consolidated Fund) Act, 1876. Under the National Debt Act, 1870, the whole of the interest on the national debt was charged on the fund.

CONSOLIDATION is a process of statutory codification whereby old enactments dealing with a particular subject are repealed and re-enacted so as to bring them conveniently together. A proper consolidation is not intended to alter the law. Consolidation bills are usually introduced in the House of Lords and then referred to a joint committee of both Houses. They are then certified by the Lord Chancellor as consolidation measures and pass their remaining stages in both Houses formally.

CONSOLS. *See* CONSOLIDATED FUND.

CONSORT is a spouse of a sovereign of equal rank. The wife of an English King, though his subject, is equal to him in dignity. The husband of a reigning Queen is not even that. Philip of Spain, as husband of Mary I, was King-Consort. Mary II was Queen-Consort of William III. Victoria's affection for Albert led to the conferment upon him of the anomalous title of Prince Consort, which was purely ornamental.

CONSPIRACY ACT, 1875 legalised an agreement or combination to do any act in contemplation of a trade dispute if that act would not be a crime if committed by one person.

CONSTABLE, LORD HIGH (England). A post-Conquest office of the royal household. At first there was more than one, but later a single Lord High Constable emerged. He had charge (including provisioning) of the military side of the King's household and supervised the officials connected with the royal sports. His subordinate was the Marshal. Both were, by the 13th cent., great officers of state and the Constableship was hereditary in the Bohun family. The political significance of these positions was evident when the Constable and Marshal resisted Edward I in the crisis of 1297. The office was forfeited by the attainder of the D. of Buckingham (descended from the Bohuns) in 1521. Since then it has been conferred only for particular occasions such as coronations. The D. of Wellington acted as Lord High Constable at the coronations of George IV, William IV and Victoria. *See* next entry.

CONSTABLE AND MARSHAL, COURT OF THE; or COURT OF CHIVALRY. (1) All armies need a disciplinary institution and mediaeval armies were commanded by nobles and their relatives. Hence this court also had jurisdiction over contracts relating to deeds of arms such as prisoners and prize, and all things touching war in or out of the realm such as the hiring of troops.

(2) The jurisdiction was founded on a book of articles of martial law drawn up when hostilities began and therefore existed only in time of war; but 'time of war' was an elastic phrase and the quasi-civil jurisdiction tended to enlarge itself. The political crisis under Richard II led to restrictions. From 1304 the court could be statutorily enjoined by writ of privy seal. From 1399 appeals for matters done within the realm had to be tried in the Common Law courts. Thenceforth it had unlimited jurisdiction only abroad; at home it was confined to alien enemies and cases arising from actual or past war. Edward IV conferred an illegal jurisdiction over treasons in 1462 and 1467 which did not last, but the Tudors tried a more subtle extension by using the court when war was merely apprehended.

(3) In 1521 the office of Lord High Constable was forfeited and thereafter High Constables were appointed only occasionally and *ad hoc*. This shook the courts institutional stability.

(4) The court's encroachments were part of the parliamentary grievances against Charles I, but by now a workable definition of war had been found, namely a time when the central courts were closed or the King's writ could not be executed. The Petition of Right condemned it within the realm in time of peace.

(5) During the Civil War the discipline of the new modern armies was handled by their officers, especially on the parliamentary side and after the Restoration Royal codes, modelled on the parliamentary ones, were issued in 1666, 1672 and 1686. The legality of these codes and the courts martial which administered them were doubtful until the Mutiny Act 1689, which inferentially rendered the Court's disciplinary jurisdiction unnecessary.

(6) To limit duelling, a bill to extend the Court's jurisdiction over slanders of noblemen was introduced in 1668 but dropped and this jurisdiction disappeared. The heraldic jurisdiction, however, continued but in 1695 it was held that prohibition lay against it and in 1702 the Queen's Bench, in defiance of the council, held that it was improperly constituted without the Constable. Hence from 1737 it apparently ceased to function, only to be revived in 1954 when the Earl Marshal's Surrogate (who was also the Lord Chief Justice) held that its existence had not been interrupted.

CONSTABLE OF SCOTLAND. A heritable chief office (still vested in the Es. of Errol) of the Scots Royal Household with, until 1746, jurisdiction over transgressions committed within four miles of the King, Parliament or Privy Council.

CONSTABLES, POLICE are the holders of ancient common law offices organised together for efficiency. They are the PETTY CONSTABLES who originally had to serve for a year without pay. These are first mentioned in 1252 and were then appointed by the Sheriffs Tourn or Leet for each township, but came to be appointed by the Quarter or Petty Sessions on the nomination of the parish vestries. They acted as executive agents of the Justices but had various statutory duties imposed upon them. By 1600 they were responsible for keeping the peace and for executing the orders and warrants of the justices. They were customarily sworn in and by 1662 could be appointed in default of nomination. They were regarded as under the control of the HIGH CONSTABLE, originally required by the Statute of Winchester (1285) to be appointed in each hundred to inspect armour. As the functions of High Constables became obsolete, so did their authority decline. The office was unpopular and constables often appointed paid deputies who were the original professional police. Never very satisfactory, they fell into disrepute and the larger disorderly towns secured local acts empowering Improvement Commissioners to set up police forces. The Town Police Clauses Act, 1847, codified such provisions which could be locally adopted. Thus statutory forces of police constables slowly spread and by 1872 it was no longer necessary to appoint parish constables.

CONSTANCE, COUNCIL OF (1414-8). *See* SCHISMS-8-10.

CONSTANCE OF CASTILE. *See* LOUIS VIII.

CONSTANTINE, DONATION OF. *See* FALSE DECRETALS.

CONSTANTINE MacFERGUS (?-820), a Pictish King. His power originally reached to the W. coast, including Dalriada, but was apparently shaken or destroyed by constant raids by Vikings, who sacked Iona in 806. He founded, perhaps as a result, the important monastery at Dunkeld.

CONSTANTINE I, II, III. *See* SCOTS OR ALBAN KINGS, EARLY.

CONSTANTINOPLE, BYZANTIUM, NEW ROME, MICKLEGARTH, TZARIGRAD or ISTAMBOUL. Constantine the Great founded his new capital in 330 at the Greek town of Byzantium. It was enlarged in the 5th cent. and the powerful triple walls (still visible) were built in the 6th cent. Its maritime advantages and defensive strength gave protection and cohesion to the later Roman empire; it repulsed enormous assaults by the Kotrigurs (558), the Avars (626), the Arabs (673-7) and the Varangians (941). The population at this time was about 500,000. As the centre of govt., finance, ecclesiastical affairs, trade and industry for a vast area it was long the greatest emporium of the west. It engrossed the spice and silk trade after the 11th cent. and dealt in Russian and Bulgarian wheat, Russian furs and slaves, dyes from Cyprus, wine from Crete, Italy and Greece, Adriatic and Cypriot salt and Dalmatian timber. Its principal manufactures were textiles (including silk) and all types of jewellery and ornament. There was also a pilgrim and a tourist industry and the immense financial operations of the govt. The economy attracted colonies of traders. The Bulgars had their suburb in the 8th cent, the Varangians in the 9th. The Venetians secured govt. favour in 992. Alexius Commenus freed them from customs, settled them at Galata and placed the Amalfitans under their jurisdiction. In 1111 the Pisans and in 1155 the Genoese received privileges, but only a 40% tariff reduction. These developments, with Arab pressure and the Crusades, made the City increasingly cosmopolitan and turbulent. Foreigners now dominated the economic life and shipping and rioted in the streets. The decline was hastened by the Latin sack of the city in 1204, from which the Venetians profited at the expense of the Genoese and took an autonomous quarter for themselves. When the Romans returned in 1261, the positions were temporarily reversed, but the govt. eventually moved the Venetian enclave to Galata, the Genoese to Pera. It then tried to enmesh other western interests in those of the empire, now threatened by the Turks, and gave concessions to the Catalans in 1290, the Provençals a few years later and the Florentines in 1436. Imperial shrinkage, the diversion of trade routes and three terrible plagues depopulated the city as Ottoman pressure grew. A Turkish attack miscarried in 1422. By 1453 the Emperor could raise only 7,000 men and had to rely for money and ships mostly on the Genoese, because the Venetians had commercial treaties with the Turks. The city, nevertheless, sustained a six weeks' siege before it fell on 29 May 1453 to the Sultan Mahommed (Mehmet) the Conqueror. The Sultan immediately set about restoring its prosperity. Many immense Roman monuments, such as the Hippodrome, were demolished and the materials used for mosques, the great palace of Topkapi and two huge Bazaars. Trade and manufactures were encouraged to return. From 1540 to 1650 the city enjoyed a prosperity similar to that of the 9th cent. and the late Byzantine pattern of life began in some sense to recur, if not for the same reasons. The Ottoman govt. was essentially military. Commercial and professional activities tended to fall into the hands of subject nationalities or foreigners; Ottoman diplomacy leaned heavily, for example, upon the Greeks living around the Orthodox patriarchate in the Phanar. Commercial shipping, after the 16th cent., was mostly Italian and French. Armenians became rich and unpopular as bankers. Moreover, the Janissaries, originally a special corps of converts, declined, once they were allowed to marry, into a rich, violent and corrupt Praetorian caste. This parasitic body was massacred in its barracks in 1826 by Mahmud II and the victory of the modernisers brought important changes. The first Golden Horn bridge was built in 1838. The great European embassies were established soon after; the European railway system arrived in 1871 and a healthy water supply in 1885. The development towards an international metropolis was, however, abruptly ended by World War I. The vast empire of which it was the centre suddenly vanished and the city's vulnerability to western seaborne power caused Kemal Atatürk to move the capital to Ankara. It remained, however, the greatest of Turkish cities. The first bridge over the Bosphorus was completed in 1973.

CONSTANTINOPLE CONFERENCE 1876-7. *See* DISRAELI'S SECOND GOVT.-4.

CONSTANTINOPLE CONVENTION (Oct. 1888). *See* SUEZ CANAL.

CONSTITUTIO DOMUS REGIS **(Lat = The Organisation of the King's House)** written by a senior member of the royal household, perhaps Bp. Nigel of Ely, Treasurer to Henry I, possibly for the instruction of Stephen. It describes the three main divisions: the chapel under the Chancellor, the Hall under the Steward and Master Butler and the Chamber under the Treasurer. The Constable and Marshal ordered the military side and security and employed the outdoor servants. The Chancellor received the highest official salary, namely 5 shillings a day, one best loaf, two ordinary loaves, one wax candle and 40 candle ends.

CONSTITUTION (1) in its paramount or political sense is an aggregation of laws, customs and habits which identify the ruling personalities of a country, regulate their decisive processes and their mutual relationships in those processes; they define the ways in which the ruler's decisions are enforced and the limitations upon such enforcement. In the foregoing sense every country has its constitution, even when the govt. is a tyranny, since the tyrant must take advice from and placate those whose support ensures his survival.

(2) It is, however, usual to appraise the **constitutionalism** of a state by reference to the extent to which the activities of the rulers and the rights and duties of the ruled are regulated by enforceable and durable laws. Thus an arbitrary despotism is said not to be a constitutional govt. but a govt. whose activities can be checked, challenged and supervised by peaceful and permanent machinery is. Under such a regime an act which contravenes these checks is said to be unconstitutional.

(3) Struck by the 18th cent. defeats of their country at the hands of the British, French political philosophers contrasted the disorderly and stagnant tyranny of France with the ebullient constitutional libertarianism of Britain and sought to explain the latter (*inter alia*) in terms of constitutional checks and balances. They evolved a celebrated tripartite analysis: the functions of govt. were divided into the legislative (parliament), the *executive* (Crown) and the *judicial* (courts). It was believed that liberty, personal initiative, enterprise and prosperity were ensured where these three functions were exercised by different people or groups acting in their own right independently of each other and thus able to prevent the excesses of each. This doctrine of the **separation of powers** was not the law or the practice of 18th cent. Britain; the two most important means of execution (taxation and the army) were ultimately controlled by the legislature, the judiciary was appointed by the executive and many persons with executive and judicial functions such as magistrates and naval officers were members of the legislature. All the same the spirit of the doctrine or at

any rate personal restraint which seemed to conform with it was to some extent observed.

(4) The Americans, faced with the need to reconcile the conflicting interests of thirteen countries and to present a common front to the British, started from their colonial charters (of English origin) and the French analysis (inaccurate though it was) of the British constitution. They were used to **written constitutions** (embodied in these charters) and they thought that British colonial authoritarianism was due at least in part to a breakdown traceable to the **unwritten** character of the British model. In any case the terms of a permanent association between the 13 states had to be embodied in a document. This distinction between written and unwritten constitutions necessarily gave prominence to the distinction between the ways in which the checks and balances were maintained: the unwritten depending more upon spirit, customs and habit, the written more on law. Thus under written constitutions the judicial element seemed to be the pivot of the rest. If, however, the concept of "the People" is substituted for "the Crown" then, bearing in mind the circumstances, the American constitution is, even in some detail, a remarkable written copy of the British as it was interpreted by the French.

(5) The most important difference between the British and the American systems was the distinction between the **unitary** and the **federal** constitution. In the unitary, local powers owe their authority (if any) to central institutions: in the federal, the central institutions have only as much authority as the local powers concede to them. The principal guarantee of legalism in a federation is the power of the constituent states. In practice these have to have existed in working order before the federation is set up. Australia became a federation of former colonies with surprisingly divergent outlooks; on the other hand, despite the even greater divergence of its four provinces, S. Africa became a unitary state because the founding statesmen distrusted legalism and there was not sufficient local interest to withstand them.

(6) Written constitutions usually provide for constitutional amendment by means more solemn or elaborate than the formalities required for the passage of ordinary legislation. Where constitutional provisions are thus protected, the constitution is said to be **inflexible:** where they can be changed by ordinary legislation they are **flexible.** In this sense the British constitution is flexible; but these terms are misleading. A constitution is more than its laws, and profound alterations can be made by shifts of custom or habit alone. In Britain the biggest single constitutional amendment in the century after 1832 was the decision to recruit a civil service by examination. The Statute of Westminster 1931 shifted, until 1982, the *practical* ability to amend the Canadian constitution from the British Parliament to a conference of Canadian Federal and Provincial prime ministers. It is said that under a flexible constitution it is possible by timely changes to anticipate political crises before the heat rises to dangerous heights. The evidence for this is weaker than the nature of the proposition would lead one to expect. The American crisis of 1931 was overcome without formal constitutional change at all and so was the British.

(7) A consideration of great practical importance is the extent to which public affairs are carried on within the constitutional framework or behind or outside it. There is, of course, always unofficial bargaining and discussion whose effects are expressed in constitutional forms. The extent to which those forms affect the decision determines whether the constitution is real, nominal or a sham. In the latter category may be found the pre-1988 constitution of the U.S.S.R., where all decisions were taken in the organs of the Communist Party. In Britain the House of Commons exercised virtually no control over the Budget between 1917 and 1990.

CONSTITUTIONAL CONFERENCE (1910). K. Edward VII died just as the Asquith govt. was about to press the Parliament Bill through parliament, if necessary by advising the sovereign to create enough peers to vote it through the Lords. The new King, George V, to avoid this, proposed a round table conference and for nearly six months four liberals and four conservatives discussed proposals for constitutional reform. They failed because the conservatives did not wish Irish Home Rule to be subject to the reformed procedures otherwise almost accepted.

CONSTITUTIONS OF LONDON (1319) was an *inspeximus* issued by Edward II in the York Parliament confirming ancient liberties, together with letters patent containing rules for the govt. of the City, amongst others, that executive officials were to be elected and could be dismissed by the commonalty; that aliens could be admitted to the franchise only by the authority of six members of his craft or of the full Hustings; that tallages were to be controlled by auditors appointed by the commonalty; that aldermen should pay the same taxes as the rest and be annually elected. *See* LONDON CHARTERS, 1327.

CONSTITUENT ASSEMBLY. *See* NATIONAL ASSEMBLY.

CONSTRUCTIVISM is the belief that human institutions will serve human purposes if, perhaps only if, consciously or deliberately designed for those purposes. This widely accepted idea is the basis of such constructions as the U.S. constitution and the British Town and Country Planning Acts. Such a rational approach to social and political difficulties tends to discount the large irrational element in human activity. It also presupposes in the designer more information than can normally be amassed and encourages large bureaucracies, numerous and populous learned bodies and large accumulations of facts.

CONSUBSTANTIATION. A doctrine that, after consecration, the communion elements are changed into the body and blood of Christ in their spiritual substance but not in their physical accidents, as opposed to transubstantiation, which holds that the change takes place in both. The mediaeval Roman church feared that it would undermine the sacramental power of priests, rendering the apostolic succession of bishops redundant and relegating the episcopacy and the Pope to positions of honoured leadership only. Subsequently, the R. Catholic church has tended to an acceptance of consubstantiation theory. The Church of England has also gone much of the way to meet Rome, particularly under the influence of Newman's Tract 90, in which he argued that the language of the XXXIX Articles does not militate against Catholic doctrine on the Eucharist. The Anglican-Roman-Catholic International Commission's Final Report (1981) effectively reduced the differences over Eucharistic doctrine between Rome and Canterbury to a matter of words.

CONSULS were originally commercial magistrates in Mediterranean ports. They usually followed the 15th cent. Catalan custumal called the *Consolat or Consulate of the Sea*. The custom of accrediting consuls to settle disputes between their own nationals in foreign ports was not common until the 19th cent. The British consular service was instituted in 1825. It and others soon developed into a system of quasi-diplomatic assistance to nationals in any commercial centre. *See* CIVIL SERVICE.

CONSUMER PROTECTION. The idea is very ancient, as the assises of bread and ale testify, and many guild regulations had the purpose of protecting the reputation of a craft by protecting customers against abuses. In more modern times industrialised production changed the relationship of producer and consumer by introducing an element of distance between them. Hence acts about

weights and measure were passed (from 1878); in 1934 the courts recognised the tort of negligence, which arose out of an industrialised process; and further legislation dealt with Food and Drugs (from 1955), Trades Descriptions (from 1966) and Fair Trading.

CONSUMPTION. *See* TUBERCULOSIS.

CONTAGIOUS DISEASES ACTS 1864-9. *See* BROTHELS.

CONTEMPT is disobedience or open insult offered to a properly constituted court, including Parliament and its two Houses. Contempt in the face of a court is punishable summarily on the spot. The power to enforce court orders by process for contempt against the person was the foundation of the Lord Chancellor's jurisdiction in Equity.

CONTIGUOUS ZONES. *See* TERRITORIAL WATERS.

CONTINENTAL ARMY. *See* AMERICAN REBELLION-15.

CONTINENTAL CONGRESS, FIRST. *See* AMERICAN REBELLION-14. **SECOND.** *See* AMERICAN REBELLION-15.

CONTINENTAL SYSTEM (1806-13). *See* BALTIC-58-59; BERLIN DECREES (1806); FRENCH REVOLUTIONARY WARS and the phases of the wars therein mentioned; ORDERS-IN-COUNCIL.

CONTRABAND. *See* BLOCKADE.

CONTRACEPTION. *See* BIRTH CONTROL.

CONTRACTING OUT. *See* POLITICAL LEVY.

CONVENTICLE. An unlawful religious body or gathering.

CONVENTION, FRENCH (1792-5) was the revolutionary assembly elected after the collapse of the monarchy. It proclaimed the republic, waged war on Kings, established the committees and the Terror and was the arena in which the Girondins were overthrown by the Jacobins and in which the latter and Robespierre were themselves overthrown with the aid of the army. Thereafter it set up the Directory and dissolved itself. *See* FRENCH REVOLUTIONARY WAR, APR. 1792-FEB. 1793-2.

CONVENTION OF ESTATES (Sc.). This term is sometimes interchangeable with "Parliament" and sometimes means a parliamentary assembly not summoned by a monarch. Since Scottish monarchs were often absent or children there were many such cases.

CONVENTION PARLIAMENTS (Eng.) are bicameral assemblies constituted exactly as parliaments are but, not being summoned by the crown, are not parliaments. There have been two. **(1) 1660.** The Long Parliament dissolved itself in Mar. 1660. A general election without the King's writ was held and the convention met in Apr. It proclaimed Charles II King on 8 May. In June it declared itself a Parliament and thereafter (a) passed an Act of Indemnity and Oblivion pardoning all except 50 named persons; (b) restored royal and church lands but not private lands to their owners and (c) settled £1,200,000 a year upon the King from taxation and the hereditary revenues. It was dissolved in Dec. and the first true Parliament of the reign (1661) confirmed its purported legislation. Since Charles II had legally been King since his father's murder, the legality of this Parliament and so of its competence to confirm the acts of the convention was never in doubt. **(2) 1689-90.** After James II had fled, William of Orange, by the advice of an assembly of notables, called for a general election and the resulting convention met in Jan. 1689, settled the Crown on William and Mary and drew up the Declaration of Rights. They accepted it on 13 Feb. when the convention also declared itself a Parliament. It was dissolved only in Feb. 1690 and its acts were confirmed by the next Parliament. The legality of these proceedings has always been open to attack, for James did not abdicate, the convention parliament could not enact, but did declare, that he had, and if William's title depended upon a vacancy on the throne which was neither created by act of parliament nor by the will of the King himself, then the second "parliament" was not summoned by the crown and could not confirm the acts of the convention.

CONVERTIBILITY (1) The right of a holder of a banknote to be paid out in specie at its face value. Since 1931 Bank of England notes have not, despite their wording, been convertible in this sense. (2) The free ability of a holder of a particular currency to exchange it for the currency of another country.

CONVERSI (Lat = converts) were lay brothers in the Benedictine orders and so by extension in other orders.

CONVOCATIONS OF CANTERBURY AND YORK. Provincial assemblies of the English clergy were first held under Abp. Theodore of Tarsus (668-90) and after 733 York had its separate convocation. These originally consisted of prelates and their advisers, but in 1225 Abp. Stephen Langton summoned proctors for chapters of cathedrals and monasteries and in 1258 archdeacons were convoked with letters of proxy from their clergy. Finally Abp. Peckham in 1283 summoned Bishops, Abbots, Deans, Archdeacons, two proctors for the clergy of each diocese and one for each chapter. In this form the Convocations endured until the Reformation. Originally unicameral, convocations began to sit in two Houses in the 15th cent., the Upper consisting of the Bishops and mitred Abbots under the Abp., the Lower consisting of the rest under an elected *Prolocutor*. The Lower House could initiate synodical action by presenting *gravamina* (heads of complaint) or *reformanda* (draft legislation) through its prolocutor to the Upper House. Convocations claimed and with Papal support after 1295 successfully upheld their exclusive right to tax the clergy and grant supply to the crown. This privilege became less important after the dissolution of the monasteries had deprived the church of much of its wealth and the convocations of many of their most important members. In 1532, by the Submission of the Clergy, convocations surrendered their right to enact new canons without royal licence and this was embodied in an Act of Parliament in 1534; it allowed the King to appoint commissioners to review the canon law. One other consequence was that thenceforth convocations and parliament were always summoned and dissolved together, with the exception of the convocation of 1640. The right of self-taxation was surrendered in 1664, which also began another difficult period of doctrinal and political dispute. After 1688 the High Church (sometimes Jacobite) bishops were slowly replaced by Whigs who were often at loggerheads with their higher High Church clergy. Eventually these quarrels were silenced in 1717 as a result of the Bangorian controversy, when the Crown prorogued the convocations. There was no further discussion of any business until 1852. In that year Canterbury convocation resumed discussion under the influence of the Oxford reformers and the Evangelicals and in 1862 York followed suit.

CONVOYS, CONVOY ACTS 1798 and 1803. *See* COMMERCE PROTECTION, NAVAL. A. B, C.

CONVULSIONS. *See* INFANTILE DIARRHOEA.

CONWAY or CYNWY (Caernarvonshire) had one of the eight castles built by Edward I in N. Wales. With Caernarvon, Harlech and Beaumaris, it was constructed after the fall of Llywelyn, P. of Wales, in 1282 to overawe and control the still restless people of the principality. It stood at the mouth of the river, isolating the entrance to Snowdonia from the north coast and the coast road. The small attached fortified town was the administrative, as well as the military, centre. The castle and town walls were completed in 1287.

CONYNGHAM, Henry (1766-1832) 1st M. CONYNGHAM (1816) and his beautiful wife **Elizabeth (DENISON) (?-1861).** He, as an Irish peer was a vigorous supporter of the Union. His wife was mistress to the P. Regent and they were a powerful influence at court during the latter's reign as George IV.

COOCH-BEHAR (W. Bengal), a Moghul tributary state, sought protection from the British in 1772 against invading Bhutanese and became one of the earliest Treaty states.

COOK Is. (Pac.) were annexed to New Zealand in 1901.

COOK, James (1728-79), as an apprentice to a haberdasher near Whitby, quarrelled with the haberdasher at the age of 12 and boarded a collier, of which he soon became mate. At 27 he joined the Navy and became Master (navigating specialist) in slops. He was present at the fall of Quebec and charted the St. Lawrence and the Newfoundland and Labrador coasts. On the strength of this work the Royal Society invited him to conduct, with Sir Joseph Banks, an expedition to observe the transit of Venus. The *Endeavour* was built on the strong lines of the North Sea colliers under his supervision and with her he reached Tahiti where, in a makeshift observatory of his own devising, he made the necessary observations on 13 Apr. 1769. He now set out for the *Terra Australis Incognita* (Lat = Unknown Southern Land) but encountered New Zealand whose configuration, including its division into two islands, he established during a six month circumnavigation. He then sailed for Australia (then called New Holland), explored the nearest coast, called it New South Wales and claimed it for the Crown. He returned *via* New Guinea and Java to England in June 1771. He was promoted Capt. and with the *Resolution* and *Adventure*, sailed on his second, epoch making voyage, in July 1772 to investigate the *Terra Australis*. He was eventually driven north and wintered in the Society Is. He then followed the Tropic of Capricorn from Easter I. to the New Hebrides and named New Caledonia. He also reached Fiji. In Jan. 1774 he gave up the attempt to find the *Terra* and came home. The peculiar importance of this voyage was that he established experimentally that sauerkraut, and better still, lime juice, were reliable preventatives for scurvy and returned, hitherto uniquely, without having lost a man. This revolutionised long distance seafaring and seaborn trade. He next volunteered to command an expedition to discover the N.W. Passage. This was to be attempted from the Pacific. He sailed in the *Resolution* with the *Discovery* in company in June 1776, passed and renamed the Hawaiian Is. the Sandwich Is. and followed the American coast as far as Cook Inlet in Alaska but was turned back by ice. The expedition returned to Hawaii where he was killed in a fight with tribesmen.

COOK, Thomas (1808-92), originally a religious temperance reformer, organised the first publicly advertised train excursion from Loughborough to Leicester for the South Midland Temperance Assn. in 1841. So successful was it that he made the organisation of excursions into a business, published tourist handbooks, issued the first hotel coupons and, in 1864, moved to London and founded 'Cooks Tours' from which the mass holiday industry sprang.

COOKERY. The mediaeval English cuisine was reputed the best in W. Europe with the Burgundian slightly and the French far behind. Levantine ideas were, however, penetrating the hedonistic papal and Tuscan states, and the Turks, who invented puff-pastry and the escalope, were influencing the Austrians. The great event in the development of European systematic cookery was the introduction in 1533 of Italian cooks to the French court by the Florentine Catherine dei Medici (whose cousin was Pope Clement VII) and her encouragement of them until her death half a century later. English cookery, however, remained static because the excellence of English meat and vegetables offered no challenge to ingenuity whereas the inferiority of French raw materials did. The rise of French fashions by the influence of Louis XIV also helped to spread French ideas so that the part played by good cuisine in household wealth and economy began to be understood and publicised in Britain by such writers as John Nott (*The Cooks Dictionary* 1726), Richard Brindley, a Prof. of Botany (*The Country Housewife and Lady's Director* 1727-32), Hannah Glasse (*Art of Cookery made Plain and Easy*

1747), William Verral, a pub keeper (*The Cooks Paradise* 1759) and Mrs Elizabeth Raffald (*The Experienced English Housekeeper* 1769), who ran the first known English catering school at Manchester. Then industrialisation made Britain rich and leading French cooks such as Soyer were attracted to English great houses, so that the more sophisticated French ideas became well known. By the mid-19th cent. the charming Heidelberg-educated Isabella Beeton (1836-65) had published her modest, but brilliantly presented, *Household Management*. It was and so much remains a best seller that successive recensions have turned it into an encyclopaedia. Such books, while attracting the well-off to continental habits, had little impact on a largely illiterate population and ordinary English cooking, bereft of educated inspiration, became a joke, even a terror to European palates. This, through insularity, spread to and with the Empire. A 400-page guide to Indian housekeeping (1866) devoted three pages to Indian recipes. Such an attitude predominated where the British gathered in large numbers until the 1960s. Two considerations raised the standard. The first was the realisation during World War II that good cooking saved food and made rationing more tolerable. It caused the Army to retrain thousands of its cooks. The second was the enormous tourist trade which gave most of the British public experience of food other than their own and a taste for the more exotic. By 1980 every type of cuisine in the world was available in London and, by way of example, Chinese restaurants, confined in 1930 to Soho and Tiger Bay, were found in thousands throughout the Kingdom.

COOPER, Alexander (?-1660) and his brother **Samuel (1609-72)** were court miniaturists and nephews of the miniaturist John Hoskins, who taught them. Samuel was much acclaimed and some 70 of his miniatures survive, of Commonwealth and Restoration notables including the best-known likeness of Oliver Cromwell. Alexander travelled abroad and later took service under Q. Christina of Sweden.

COOPER, Alfred Duff (1890-1954) 1st Vist. NORWICH of ALDWICK (1952) was educated at Eton and Oxford and married the famous Lady Diana Manners in 1919. He was Unionist M.P. for Oldham from 1924 to 1929 and for St. George's from 1931 to 1944. He was financial sec. at the War Office from 1928 to 1929 and again from 1931 to 1934 and at the Treasury from 1934 to 1935 when he became Sec. of State for War. In 1937 he became First Lord of the Admiralty and resigned against the Munich Agreement in 1938. Sociable, literate and cosmopolitan, he wrote distinguished biographies of Talleyrand and Haig and other works. Churchill took him in as Min. of Information from 1940 to 1941 and then he was Chanc. of the Duchy of Lancaster until 1943. He was a brilliant ambassador to Paris from 1944 to 1947.

COOPER, Anthony Ashley (I) (1621-83) 1st Ld. ASHLEY (1661), 1st E. of SHAFTESBURY (1672), orphaned by the age of ten, inherited wide estates from part of which his guardians cheated him. In spite of this he stayed rich. He made a mark at Oxford and, in 1639 a good marriage connected him with the Coventrys and the Saviles. He was illegally elected M.P. in the Short Parliament. He took little part in the early Civil War, but joined the King as a local supporter in Dorset in 1643 and then went over to the parliament in Jan. 1644, and having been commissioned by them for Dorset instead, led the reduction of the county until Apr. 1646. He then retired into semi-private life until 1652, when the Rump appointed him a member of Hales' law reform commission.

(**2**) His main career began in 1653 when, after the Rump had been expelled, Cromwell appointed him to the Council of State, but in Dec. 1654 he resigned and in 1655 took as a third wife an aunt of the young E. of Sunderland. In 1656 he became an M.P. for Wilts and headed a coalition of presbyterians and republicans

unfriendly to the Protector. He remained, however, on good personal terms with the Cromwells. In the successive dispensations which ended in the Restoration, he maintained a republican and unicameral position until Monck's arrival in London made it untenable. He then started to work with Monck, sat for Wiltshire in the Convention and was one of the 12 Commons delegates sent over to invite Charles II home. He was sworn of the Privy Council in May 1660 and was one of the Commissioners for trying the regicides. He also became Ch. of the Exchequer.

(**3**) He was increasingly noticed as a witty and compelling speaker and by 1663 he was in opposition to Clarendon, but he was also heavily involved in the Carolina, Barbados and Guinea investments. He opposed monopolies and supported measures which increased the royal access to public funds. His purpose was to ingratiate himself with Charles and he assiduously attended, too, the salons of Lady Castlemaine, where Clarendon's overthrow was plotted. Consequently he became a member of the ill-assorted Cabal, in which the King, Clifford and Arlington hoodwinked the others over the Dover Treaties of 1669-70 and then induced them to support the Dutch War. In 1672 he became Lord Chancellor, in which office he intrigued with the Scottish nobles against Lauderdale. Dismissed in 1673, he was offered large inducements to return a few days later, for it was evident that he now knew of the Dover Treaties, but he refused. (*For the rest of his political career see* CHARLES II-11 *to* 27; POPISH PLOT.) His grandson, (**III**) **(1671-1713) 3rd E. (1699)** was influential as a thinker, mainly on the continent: Diderot's *Essai sur le Mérite et la Vertue* is a free translation of his *Inquiry Concerning Virtue*; Leibniz followed many of the ideas in his *Characteristics of Man, Manners, Opinion and Times*. His descendent (**VII**) **(1801-85) 7th E. (1851)** personally austere reformer, became an M.P. in 1826. His first interest was in the condition of lunatics; his second, factory working hours; his third, the condition of women and children in the mines and then of child chimney-sweeps. In 1846 he took up the Ragged School Movement (himself teaching in them for many years every Sunday). In 1848 he helped to launch the Refuge and Reformatory Union (Shaftesbury Homes) and in 1851 persuaded parliament to legislate for the regulation of lodging houses. He was also much concerned in the Peabody Housing Schemes. He had for some while been interested in the practical side of public health, and the army sanitary commission, of which he was chairman virtually saved the Crimean army. He also helped the British and Foreign Bible Society, the City Mission, the Church Missionary Society and the Y.M.C.A. He was immensely respected in all levels of society. Palmerston habitually sought his advice. 40 London burglars asked him (successfully) to meet them. They brought 400 others to the meeting.

COOPER, Richard (1) (?-1764) portrait engraver, mostly worked in Edinburgh. His son (**2**) **(?1760-1814)** also an engraver and painter, well known between 1780 and 1809.

COOPER or COUPER, Thomas (?1517-94), saintly Elizabethan divine and Master of Magdalen College School, Oxford. He published a Latin-English dictionary in 1565 and the Queen's admiration of it brought him promotion to the Deanery of Christchurch (1567). He was Bp. of LINCOLN from 1570 and translated to WINCHESTER in 1584. He was hotly attacked in the Marprelate tracts (1588-9) but seems to have got the best of the argument.

COOPER, Thomas (1805-92) grew up in a strict, but poverty stricken, home but by native intelligence and hard work educated himself. After periods as a shoemaker and schoolmaster he turned to journalism. An ill-tempered man, he quarrelled with Gainsborough Methodists, moved to Stamford, then to Lincoln and in

1840 to the *Leicester Mercury*. In 1841 he became Sec. of the Leicester Chartists and from then until the collapse of the movement was a leading figure among them. In 1843 he was imprisoned for two years for inciting workers to strike until the Charter became law. In 1846, true to form, he broke with the other Chartist leaders and thereafter earned his living writing and lecturing.

COOPER, Thomas Thornville (1839-78), adventurous traveller, made between 1855 and 1870 journeys in the interior of Australia, in Central India, Burma and in many southern provinces of China; he ended as political agent at Bhamo, where he was murdered.

COOPERAGE was the sale of spirits, mostly Dutch gin, to North Sea fishing boats at sea. This lucrative trade caused so many accidents that an international fishery conference at The Hague in 1887 agreed to stop it. In Britain the result was the North Sea Fisheries Act 1888.

CO-OPERATIVES. Robert Owen (1771-1858) advocated co-operative industrial communities and some of his supporters laid the foundations of later workable experiments. The first to associate the co-operative idea with retail supply were the ROCHDALE PIONEERS (1844), whose main principles were open membership, members' control, the limitation of interest on capital and the distribution of surpluses in proportion to the value of purchases. The idea spread, mainly as a painless savings movement centred in Manchester. Trade backing was created in 1863 by the establishment of the Manchester Co-operative Wholesale Society (C.W.S.) which began to operate factories of consumer goods and soon developed an immense turnover. A similar Scottish C.W.S. was set up in 1868. By now the enthusiasts were seeking new fields. The Co-operative Union (1869) was launched as an advisory, propagandist and political body and soon there were Co-operative Insurance, Permanent Building and Press Societies and an International Co-operative Alliance (I.C.A.) (1895) with its office in London. The ideas preceded the establishment of I.C.A. to many European and Commonwealth countries, but took root primarily in rural, especially farming, communities. The claimed membership of the so-called Movement has always been very large (13,000,000 in Britain in 1964; 120,000,000 for I.C.A.; 32,000,000 in the U.S.S.R.) but this covers membership for purposes differing as widely as active and strenuous participation in an Israeli Kibbutz and the merely passive right to receive a dividend calculated on a housewife's grocery purchases. Hence the foundation of the CO-OPERATIVE PARTY (1917) was not attended by any marked increase in political influence and since Co-operative M.P.s invariably took the Labour whip, the Labour Party simply acquired a source of funds. This was recognised, for the Co-operative Union became, along with the Trades Union Congress and the Labour Party, a member of the National Confederation of Labour. From 1948 its candidates stood as 'Co-operative and Labour' and in 1959 their members were limited to 30.

COORG (India) was an ancient Vijayanagar state claimed by Tippoo Sahib. In 1788 Ld. Cornwallis made a treaty with Vira Raja, the claimant, and in 1792 Tippoo ceded his own claims so that Vira Raja was recognised as King. He died in 1809. Vira Raja II, who ascended the throne in 1820, was deposed by Ld. William Bentinck in 1834 for gross misgovernment and the territory was thereafter administered separately by a British Chief Commissioner.

COOTE (1) Richard (1636-1701) 1st E. (Ir.) of BELLAMONT (1689) was M.P. for Droitwich in 1688 and strongly supported William III, who gave him lucrative Irish appointments and in 1695 appointed him gov. of New York to put down pirates. Here he arrested the notorious Capt. Kidd. His descendent **(2) Sir Eyre (1726-83)** went to India as a soldier in 1754 and it was on his advice that Clive fought the B. of Plassey. He was specially promoted and sent to Madras in charge of the troops. The French were attacking Trichinopoly, and

Coote, with a much inferior force, distracted them by seizing Wandewash. In Jan. 1760 he defeated them there against odds of 5 to 1 and in Jan. 1761 he and Adm Stevens took the French capital at Pondicherry. After controversial, but unimportant, activities Coote as a lieut-gen. was appointed C-in-C in Bengal in 1779. By 1780 Hyder Ali of Mysore had overrun much of the Carnatic and Coote was sent to Madras for the second time. After an arduous and dangerous campaign he and Adm. Hughes first held Porto Novo and then defeated Hyder Ali there (1 July 1781) again against odds of 5 to 1 and followed up his victory, after which bad health compelled him to hand over command.

COPE. A mineral duty payable to the crown by Barmote mines.

COPENHAGEN. The name of the D. of Wellington's horse.

COPENHAGEN, B. of (21 May 1801). *See* BALTIC EXPEDITIONS; NELSON.

COPENHAGEN FIELDS (Islington, London). An open space for the largest meetings and demonstrations, until occupied by the Caledonian market in 1885. *See also* TRAFALGAR SQUARE.

COPERNICUS or KOPPERNIK, Nicolas (1473-1543) of Thorn (Torun) in Prussian Poland first developed the hypothesis that the earth and the planets revolve around the sun and that they revolve on their axes. A short popular account was published in 1530; the full exposition *De Revolutionibus Orbium Celestium* (Lat = The Revolution of Celestial Bodies) in 1543. It made an immense impression but the thesis was not formally proved until Kepler (1609) and Galileo (1610) published their findings.

COPLEY, John Singleton (1) (1738-1815) Massachusetts painter and engraver, was already well-known in England when he settled in London in 1776. He made a fortune as an historical painter of such romantic subjects as "Chatham's Last Appearance in the Lords" and "The Repulse of the Spanish Floating Batteries at Gibraltar". His son **(2) (1772-1863) 1st Ld. LYNDHURST (1825)** made his name at the bar by a successful and popular defence of a Luddite at Nottingham in 1812, an intricate patent case in 1816 and the defence of Arthur Thistlewood, the Cato St. conspirator, in 1817. In 1818 he became a Tory M.P. In 1819, as Sol-gen., he conducted the case against Q. Caroline in the House of Lords and in 1824 was Att-gen. In 1825 he became Lord Chancellor under Canning and retained the office under Goderich and Wellington until 1830. He was noted as a dangerous debater and remarkable for the impartiality of his appointments. On the fall of the Tories the whig govt. appointed him Ch. of the Exchequer. In 1834 he briefly Lord Chancellor again under Peel and then led the Tory opposition in the Lords. From 1841 to 1846 he was again Peel's Lord Chancellor. He was by now personally popular and respected in political circles, though much abused as a reactionary by liberal journalists.

COPPER and its alloy **BRONZE** were mostly superseded by iron before the Roman Conquest, but its decorative use continued and it was utilised increasingly where a rust-free metal was needed, e.g. in the fastenings and sheathing of wooden ships, or a light metal, e.g. for casting light cannon. The main European sources before 1800 were Cyprus and Britain and demand rose only slowly. The development of electricity, however, quickly quadrupled the demand and created vast opportunities for the new N. and S. American, Japanese and Australian mines while British production fell to negligible amounts. After 1910 Britain was almost wholly dependent on imports.

COPSIGE (?-1067), a thane of Tostig's, took part in the Stamford Bridge expedition against Harold, submitted to William I at Barking and was murdered by Oswulf (?-1067).

COPYHOLD. *See* LAND TENURE (ENGLAND)-3; CUSTOMARY COURT.

COPYRIGHT. A BRITISH. The Stationers Co. of London was incorporated in 1557 and all printers had to serve an apprenticeship as a member. The right to publish was controlled by royal licences and patents, which were granted to printers as a form of censorship (*see* IMPRIMATUR) and every printed publication was supposed to be entered (registered) at Stationers' Hall. This gave the Co. a virtual control over copyright, but did not give an author or other creative artist any right to protect himself from plagiarism or piracy. This became a scandalous problem. The first attempt to establish such protection in the courts concerned Bunyan's *Pilgrim's Progress* in 1679. When the Licensing Acts expired, publishers procured the Copyright Act, 1709, which created the author's monopoly in his own written works for 14 years from first publication and, if living at the end of that period, a further 14 years. Acts of 1734, 1736 and 1777 protected prints for 28 years, an Act of 1798, sculptures. In 1814 the author's and sculptor's period was extended to the longer of life or 28 years. Dramatic pieces were covered in 1833, musical works in 1842, when an author's period was extended to life plus seven years or 42 years, whichever was the longer. Pictures and photographs were protected from 1861. The Copyright Act, 1911, repealed all the previous legislation and substituted, with minor exceptions, a single code for all subject matter. It abolished the need for entry at Stationers' Hall and copyright henceforth depended on creation of the work, not on formality. The Act of 1956 repealed and re-enacted that of 1911 and covered films, recording and television and sound broadcasts. With certain exceptions, the period became the author's life plus 50 years. The 1911 Act was brought into force at different times in Commonwealth countries, so that entry at Stationers' Hall continued to be required in some of them for many years after 1911. British Copyright was consolidated with amendments in 1988. This act was neither more intelligible nor of greater benefit to authors. Its application to electronics is uncertain.

B. INTERNATIONAL. Pirating in foreign countries, especially the U.S.A., was a serious abuse. Britain passed the first International Copyright Act in 1833 and the first multilateral copyright convention was signed at Bern in 1886. This was revised at Rome in 1928 and at Brussels in 1956. Meanwhile a rather lower-standard convention (The Universal Copyright Convention) was established in 1952 and both sets of treaties were revised together at Paris in 1971. Until 1982 U.S. Copyright was dependent upon publication, but thereafter U.S. law was approximated to the convention of 1952. Communist bloc countries were not party to any of these conventions but started to come in after 1983.

C. E.U. In 1995 as a result of E.U. legislation the period of copyright was extended to the author's life plus 70 years.

COPYRIGHT LIBRARIES. Since 1911 a copy of every book must be deposited with the British Library (formerly the Reading Room of the British Museum) and, on demand, to the National Library of Scotland (formerly the Advocates Library) and also the university libraries of Oxford, Cambridge, Trinity College Dublin and the National Library of Wales. The rights of Trinity College, Dublin, are now unenforceable.

CORAM (Lat = in the presence of). Used to indicate the person or judge before whom a dispute was argued.

CORAM, Thomas (1668-1751). A Dorset venturer and businessman, settled in London where he was so moved by the plight of the poor that, with Hogarth's help, he established the Foundling Hospital beside the large square still called Coram's Fields. His charitable work so impoverished him that in old age he had to subsist on a small annuity subscribed by admirers. Until 1965 no adult was allowed in Coram's Fields unless accompanied by a child.

CORBEIL, William of (?-1136), a Norman pupil of Anselm at Laon, became clerk to William II's influential minister, Ranulf Flambard, Bp. of Durham and in 1104 witnessed the consecration of his cathedral. He then became a canon of St. Augustine's Canterbury and was soon Prior of St. Osyth (Essex). He was by now well-known among the higher echelons of Church and State. In 1123 Henry I bullied the chapter of Christchurch Canterbury into electing him Abp., but the conferment of his *pallium* at Rome was postponed when Abp. Thurstan of York revived the old controversy about the primacy between York and Canterbury. The Papacy was unwilling to settle the issue definitively because, *inter alia,* it involved questions of Anglican jurisdiction in Scotland. He received his *pallium*. A legatine inquiry at Westminster by John of Crema in 1125 was inconclusive, but in 1126 Honorius II by-passed the problem was appointing William Legate in both kingdoms. Like other magnates he swore at Henry I's insistence to Matilda's succession in 1126 (before he or they realised what kind of person she was) but most of his energy was spent in necessary administration. His council at London pursued the papal policy against marriage of the clergy. He rebuilt the cathedral at Rochester and completed that at Canterbury. He constructed the huge castle at Rochester to protect the diocese and the Medway ports. Like many of his lay and ecclesiastical colleagues, he felt absolved from his oath to Matilda by her marriage to Geoffrey of Anjou, and so far consented to Stephen's succession that he crowned him. This was his last important public act.

CORBEIL, T. of (1258). By this treaty K. James of Aragon ceded his lands N. of the Pyrenees and, therefore, E. of the Aquitainian frontier, to Louis IX of France at the time when Anglo-French negotiations (leading to the T. of Paris in 1259) were in progress about rights to Normandy and the northern frontier of Aquitaine. It weakened the English position.

CORBRIDGE (Lat: CORSTOPITUM) (N'land) at the crossing of the R. Tyne by Deer Street into the Scots lowlands just S. of Hadrian's Wall was an important Roman garrison post. It was also the site of two Viking victories over the Northumbrians in about 918.

CORBY. *See* NEW TOWNS.

CORDELIERS were a French revolutionary club formed in May 1790 and led by Marat and Danton. It consisted mainly of shopkeepers, students and artisans. Between May and July 1791 it organised violent anti-royalist demonstrations. After the fall of the monarchy the club's leadership passed to Hébert. Its revolutionary and atheistic programme led to conflict with the govt. and in Mar. 1794, after an unsuccessful insurrection, the club was suppressed.

CORDON SANITAIRE (Fr). The line of guards around a quarantine area or, figuratively, any comparable arrangement designed to contain the spread of dangerous or subversive influences.

CORDOVA (Spain). Capital of Andalusia, celebrated for its leather. The name is the origin of the Fr. Cordonnier (Shoemaker) and the Eng. Cordwainer.

CORFE CASTLE (Dorset). According to an unreliable legend K. Edward the Martyr was murdered here in 978. The Normans began the castle and by the 13th cent. it was a powerful fortress. K. John starved Matilda de Braose and her son to death in the prison. In 1646 Lady Bankes held it for six months against a parliamentary force, which blew up the defences after she surrendered. The place sent two M.P.s to Parliament from 1295 to 1832.

CORFU. *See* IONIAN ISLES.

CORFU AFFAIRS (1) Aug. 1923. An Italo-Greek incident. The Italian fleet bombarded Corfu and the League of Nations acted as mediator. **(2) 1946.** The Albanian govt. mined the international waters of the Corfiote Strait without public notification and in peacetime and two

British destroyers were damaged. The British govt's demand for compensation for the considerable loss of life and material was refused and the British impounded the Albanian gold reserve lodged in the Bank of England. This was not the only piratical action of the Albanians at the period. The dispute was not settled for forty years.

CORFU PACT (1917) was an agreement between the Serbian govt., then in Corfu with the base details of the Serbian army, and the South Slav (Yugoslav) committee based on London. It envisaged a unified Serb-Croat-Slovene Kingdom and was inconsistent with the promises made to Italy in the secret T. of London.

CORITANI, a British tribe occupying the areas of modern Leicester and Lincolnshire conquered by the Romans before A.D. 47.

CORK (Ir), CITY and COUNTY (*see* also DESMOND; MUNSTER). The town with Cobb (pron. Cove) or Queenstown has a magnificent harbour and fisheries and attracted a trade especially with the W. of England, Brittany and Spain. It was a Christian centre in the 6th and 7th cents. The Vikings burned the town in 821 and shortly occupied it and established a trading centre. They remained, with interruptions, in control until the place surrendered to Henry II in 1172. The area, which now included part of Desmond, was prosperously farmed in the valley bottoms and coastal plains and there were important copper mines, producing also some gold and silver in the west. There were many monastic houses especially in the city and at Cloyne and Buttevant. K. John shired the area, in which the Es. of Desmond long possessed a dominating influence, for there was a fairly steady trickle of English and Welsh immigrants throughout the middle ages. After the earls fell, more thought was given to colonisation and at the end of the 16th cent. the Crown allotted extensive lands to planters such as Sir Walter Raleigh, Edmund Spencer and, especially, the Boyle family. Richard Boyle, 1st E. of Cork, settled many English colonists and founded or rebuilt eight towns (including Bandon, Baltimore and Youghal) which became parliamentary boroughs and gave the Boyles strong influence in the county and at Dublin. Since R. Catholic emancipation the town (which acquired Queen's College in 1849) has been a centre of nationalist agitation.

CORK, Es. of. *See* BOYLE-I *et seq.*

CORNAGE was an obligation mostly in the north to provide a horned beast, particularly a milch cow, subsequently commuted to a payment. (*See* also CUMBRIA. CUMBERLAND-8-10, 13.) A popular but erroneous etymology ascribes an obligation to blow a horn on certain ceremonial occasions or to wind a horn when the Scots were seen crossing the border.

CORNBURY. *See* HYDE.

CORNET. The lowest commissioned rank in the cavalry, it was redesignated 2nd Lieutenant in 1871. Field Cornets were subordinate officers in a Boer commando.

CORNICHE. *See* FRANCO-AUSTRIAN WAR 1795-7-4.

CORNISH LANGUAGE. *See* CELTS; CORNWALL.

CORNISH REBELLION (1497). *See* FLAMMOCK.

CORN LAWS 1661-1861 originally called *Acts for the Encouragement of Tillage* **(1)** embodied efforts to keep a balance between an economic agriculture and a well fed population when local, national and world crop prices fluctuated uncontrollably and the only effective (if intermittent) long distance transport was by water. They applied in order of price to (i) wheat (highest); (ii) rye, beans and peas (usually treated together); (iii) barley and its two varieties 'beer' and bigg; (iv) oats (lowest) and (v) flour and biscuit made from these. In this article the price of (ii) and (iii) should be understood as being between those quoted for (i) and (iv). The prices were always quoted for the *quarter* of 64 gallons.

(2) The Act of 1660 prohibited exports until prices had fallen to 40s for wheat and 16s for oats: that of 1663

substituted 48s and 13s 4d. Meanwhile the Act of 1660 imposed a small duty on imports at 42s. for wheat down to 28s. for barley, but in 1670 this was altered to a high duty on wheat at 33s. and a low one when it reached 35s. For oats the figures were 16s. and 18s.

(3) The prohibitions and duties applied to the prices reigning at each port. From 1685 the county justices fixed the price by the oath of two independent witnesses not in the corn trade. The procedure for price fixing became very important when an Act of 1688 added export bounties for corn carried in British ships with three quarter British crews. (*See* NAVIGATION ACTS.) The bounties were 5s. when wheat reached 48s. and 2s. 6d. for barley at 24s. The system of prohibitions, tariffs and bounties set up by the Acts of 1663, 1670 and 1688 remained until 1773, but evasions and corrupt assessments led to the transfer of price fixing to county grand juries in 1732 and then to a method whereby J.P.s returned the averages of 2 to 6 markets in each county to the Treasury which published them quarterly.

(4) In 1773 bounties were altered to 5s. for wheat at 44s. and 2s for oats at 14s. In 1781 prices began to be determined by market inspectors in open Quarter Sessions on the basis of weekly returns from corn factors. To prevent transmarine fraud these arrangements were adequate, but as a result of better roads and new canals corn imported duty free at one port might undercut dutiable corn landed at another. Accordingly in 1789 prices were fixed in relation to twelve regions combining several counties each.

(5) The legislation of the previous 112 years was codified in 1791 with amendments. The bounty prices and rates remained the same (*see para 4 above*). The export prohibition prices were 46s. for wheat and 15s. for oats but import duties distinguished between European corn and Irish and colonial. European wheat was taxed at 24s. when the price was 50s. or under, oats at 6s when the price was 17s. or under. Between 50s. and 54s. for wheat the tax was 2s. 6d. and for oats between 17s. and 18s, 1s. Above these prices the tax was nominal. Irish and colonial corn was taxed at about 80% of these rates. These rules applied until 1804 when, in expectation as a result of the P. of Amiens of a glut of European corn, the prices at which such imported corn was to remain taxable were raised by a little under 20% as was the export prohibition price. These provisions continued in force throughout the rest of the wars. Bonaparte did not interfere with such cross Channel traffic in grain as there was, but wartime dislocations and bad harvests on both sides prevented the Acts' effective operation.

(6) In 1813 (when prices fell because of an excellent harvest) it was feared that the end of the French wars would bring about a price collapse and the wholesale abandonment of marginal farms. A Select Committee of Inquiry concluded that the reasonable prices were 80s. for wheat, 53s. for the rye group, 40s. for barley and 27s. for oats. In 1815 total import prohibitions on European corn were enacted until the prices should reach these figures. Irish and colonial corn were let in at 67s. to 22s. These rules (which were slightly below the effect of the Act of 1804) became the subject of heated controversy during the post war depression. In fact wheat prices seldom reached 64s. and fell to 38s. in 1833. A farmers' outcry drove the govt. back to the pre-1815 system. Export prohibitions (wheat 80s., oats 28s.) were combined with high and low import duties (High: wheat 80s. and under, 12s; oats 28s. and under, 4s; Low: wheat 80s. to 85s., 5s; oats 28s. to 30s., 2s). This raised protection only a little. Prices rose less than the farmers wanted and the govt., attacked by those who had to pay more, lost the support of those who expected to receive more. Accordingly in 1827 it edged over towards the consumers and substituted sliding scales, tapered down to 1s. when wheat stood at 73s. and oats at 31s. Much grain was imported during the bad years 1828 and 1829 and the good harvests of 1830 and 1835 muted controversy.

(7) From the industrial depression of 1836 onwards agitation revived. Manchester founded the first Anti-Corn Law Society; a national Anti-Corn Law League was launched in 1829, a bad year. Enthusiasm grew until halted by good harvests in 1842-4. In 1842 Sir Robt. Peel had, in any case, reduced the duty at the lower end of the scale to prevent foreign speculation. The urban, especially unemployed, poor suffered from high corn prices and their complaints against the Corn Laws were championed by employers hoping for cheaper labour. They were supported, too, by radicals quite differently motivated. To them Anti-Corn Law agitation was a means of levelling, or reducing the standing and pretensions of the (landed) aristocracy. Their economists argued that cheap imported corn would reduce the price of industrial exports and so contribute to the rightful prosperity of the democratic towns. Cobden and Bright, the leaders of the movement, were genuinely and idealistically concerned to benefit the urban masses and had strong non-conformist and evangelical connections.

(8) The defenders of the system included not only Tories but Chartists. They believed that its abolition would ruin all save the most prosperous or specialised farms and that the resulting unemployed would migrate to the towns and depress the labour market; the country, on this argument, would suffer while the towns would not benefit. The Chartists, besides, thought that the Anti-Corn Law League was a distraction from their proper programme of enfranchisement for the unenfranchised.

(9) The decision was made on a political calculation and obscured by a famine. The Tory, Sir Robt. Peel, half convinced that the Anti-Corn Law League was right, concluded by 1845 that either the violence of public feeling would disrupt the Tory Party or that the Corn Laws would constitute an electoral millstone around its neck. Right or wrong they had to go. In 1845, however, there were horrifying crop failures. Potato rot destroyed the staple crop of 80% of Ireland and of some parts of England. It was not feasible to feed Ireland from depleted Enghsh stocks. It was argued that corn had to be let into the country and the Act of 1846 (which came into effect in 1848) lowered the sliding scale for European corn (wheat 48s. to 53s., oats 18s. to 22s.) and subjected colonial corn to a uniform nominal duty of 1s.

(10) These manoeuvres, which in the long run saved the Tory party and instantly ruined Peel, had little effect on the people's bread. Britain was nearly self-supporting in good years (when the corn duty would matter little) and continental and British bad harvests usually coincided; more distant corn growing countries had not yet developed agricultural mass production or suitable transport for it. Thus neither the towns nor the country experienced the effects expected by their respective advocates until 25 years later. Peel's Act was repealed by a Statute Law Revision Act in 1861. *See also* CAIRD, JAMES.

CORNOVIL. British tribe occupying the modern counties of Cheshire, Shropshire, Staffordshire, Clywd and Powys and conquered by the Romans by A.D. 50.

CORN PRODUCTION ACT 1917 guaranteed farmers a good price for their cereals to save importing them in ships which the Germans were sinking. Its repeal in 1927 created rural difficulties akin to a sudden slump.

CORN RENT. *See* ADVOWSON AND TITHE-9.

CORNWALL, KERNOW or DYVNAINT, COUNTY and DUCHY. Pressure from the east, the good harbours and the trade in tin and copper, tended in early times to make Cornwall a starting point for migration. Moreover, southward voyagers from Ireland and Wales preferred to cross Cornwall rather than round Lands End. Christianity, possibly, came in Roman times; there are crosses dating from 6th cent., but St. Piran is said to have been sent by St. Patrick. The pressure in early Anglo-Saxon times led to a colonisation of Brittany (where one district was long called Cornouaille), but the area was not successfully attacked until Egbert compelled some kind of submission between 815 and 823. In 823 the Cornish supported a Danish invasion which was crushed at the B. of Hingston Down and in 928 Athelstan banished Cornishmen beyond the Tamar. Up to this time Cornwall was really a separate country organised and ruled largely by its church. Athelstan, however, conquered it in 936, and in 1018 it was placed under the bishopric of Crediton (later Exeter). By 1066 most of the land was owned by Englishmen, who were then replaced by Normans; Robert of Mortain was the most important of these. His honour of 248 manors became the foundation of the Earldom and, later, Duchy of Cornwall which, since 1337, has been vested in the Sovereign's eldest son. The county's peculiarities and remoteness gave it a difference of outlook from other areas. Cornish (a relative of Welsh) was the common language down to about 1600 and was used in public worship until 1678. The people were strongly Lancastrian and supported both Flammock and Warbeck in 1497 and Arundell in 1549. Corish piracy and smuggling in the 16th cent. were a nursery of famous seamen including Sir Richard Grenville and in the 17th cent. the area was strongly royalist. By this time the habits of the seafarers led to the creation of many customs posts, whose holders, in league with the smugglers, could make a good living. The customs patronage was important in its own right, but also influenced the many parliamentary boroughs where the voters were mostly customs men. From 1295 the county and six boroughs elected two M.P.s each. Between 1547 and 1584 15 more boroughs were similarly enfranchised, so that from 1584 to 1821 there were 44 Cornish representatives in parliament. This gave heirs (particularly Hanoverian heirs) to the Throne an important influence in the unreformed House of Commons. The tin miners were from ancient times subject only to the STANNARY court, save in cases affecting limb, life or land, and paid a small tax. (*See* STANNARIES.) Deep copper mining was begun in 1718 and by 1850 the copper mines of Devon and Cornwall were producing a third of all the copper in Europe. The tax on tin and the stannary jurisdiction were abolished in 1838 and the Council of the Stannaries then became exclusively a body for managing the Duchy estates.

CORNWALL, Ds. of. This dukedom, created by parliamentary charter in 1337 in favour of the monarch's eldest son, has since been held by every male heir apparent, except George III, who was George II's grandson. The administration was much improved after 1970 by Charles P. of Wales.

CORNWALLIS. This Suffolk family settled at Brome near Eye in the 14th cent. and members were sometimes M.P.s for Suffolk. **(1) Sir Thomas (1519-1604)** as sheriff of Norfolk and Suffolk declared for Mary in 1553. He resisted Wyatt's rebellion (1554). He acted as escort to princess Elizabeth but protested against proposals to exclude her from the succession. From 1554 he was the last Treasurer of Calais. A strong but loyal recusant, he was regarded with suspicion by Q. Elizabeth's govt. His son **(2) Sir Charles (?-1629)** was ambassador at Madrid from 1605 to 1609. His nephew **(3) Frederick (?-?) 1st Ld. CORNWALLIS (1661)** fought for Charles I and accompanied Charles II on his travels. A descendent **(4) Frederick (1713-83) Abp. of CANTERBURY (1768)** became a royal chaplain in 1740, a canon of Windsor in 1746 and Bp. of Lichfield in 1766. As Abp. he was personally liked for his generosity but criticised because his wife held routs at Lambeth on Sundays. His kinsman **(5) Charles (?-1762) 1st E. CORNWALLIS (1753)** had improved the family fortunes by marrying a Townshend, who was also a niece of Walpole's. His son **(6) Charles (1738-1805) 2nd E. and 1st M.** (1792) had a conventional but active military career until he inherited the earldom; he then joined the Whig opposition to Bute. He virtually retired from politics in 1768 when he married, having opposed the parliamentary right to tax the American colonies. In 1776, however, he was despatched in command of a division to America under Howe. He then became 2-in-C under Clinton and was much the ablest of the British generals. His capitulation at Yorktown (1781) was never blamed on him and in 1782 he was offered the gov. generalship of India, which he refused because he disliked Pitt. He accepted in 1786. He had to reform the corrupt Bengal administration (which he did by paying proper salaries) and reorganise the army, which had been shaken in the previous wars. These labours were interrupted by the Third Mysore War in 1789. This arose because of weakness and incompetence by the Madras govt. and the ambitions of the Maharajah, Tippoo Sahib. Cornwallis had to leave Calcutta to intervene personally. He secured the help of the Marathas and Hyderabad and advanced in Jan. 1792 towards Tippoo's capital, Seringapatam, which was invested in Feb. Tippoo sued for terms which included the division of half his territory between Hyderabad and the Marathas and a large indemnity (T. of SERINGAPATAM Mar. 1792). Cornwallis immediately returned to Calcutta where he promulgated the Bengal Permanent Revenue Settlement (22 Mar. 1793). He returned home in 1793 and in 1795 became Master-Gen. of Ordnance with a seat in the cabinet, to direct military policy against the French. Meanwhile discontent and confusion reigned in India and Cornwallis was persuaded to go back there, but this proved unnecessary and he was sent as Lord Lieut. and C-in-C to Ireland in 1798 instead. Here he suppressed rebellion and pressed for Union. This meant supporting Castlereagh's traffic in seats and peerages which converted the Irish parliament from opposition to voting its own extinction. He believed that R. Catholic emancipation was vital to Irish peace, actively promoted it and resigned in 1801 when the govt. refused to act. In 1801 he negotiated the P. of Amiens, in which he is sometimes thought to have been outwitted by Joseph Bonaparte and Talleyrand. He then retired but in 1805 was recalled to India where he died. His brother **(7) James (1742-1824) 4th E. (1823)** was a Kentish pluralist and then Bp. of Lichfield from 1781. His brother **(8) William (1744-1819)** was one of the finest seamen of his time. At the B. of St. Kitts (Jan. 1782), in command of the *Canada*, 74, he prevented the French flagship *Ville de Paris*, 120, from breaking the British line by throwing his ship in her path. From 1788 to 1793, as commodore on the Indian coast, he commanded the blockading operations which prevented French assistance and supplies from reaching Tippoo Sahib's French trained army in the Third Mysore War. Because of lack of developed dockyards, high-rated ships could not be maintained in the area and this long naval campaign had to be conducted mostly with frigates and lesser craft. He was automatically promoted to flag rank and came home where he took command of one of the squadrons blockading the French coast. In June 1795, with five ships of the line, he was attacked by 12 French in the Bay of Biscay and after a nine-hour cannonade extricated his squadron virtually without loss. Not surprisingly, he was thanked by both Houses of Parliament, and in 1796 was appointed C-in-C in the W. Indies, but could not proceed and after a court martial and other wrangles, struck his flag. After a brief period of inactivity he was given command, in 1801, of the Channel Fleet. The command was much attenuated in the brief period of peace after the T. of Amiens (Mar. 1802-May 1803) but became the operational strategic centre of defence against the combination of the invasion army and its flotillas at Boulogne and the changing pattern of enemy squadrons moving between their bases (especially Brest)

along the Franco-Spanish Atlantic coasts. His tenacity in the face of appalling storms prevented the enemy fleets from ever making a full combination in support of the Boulogne forces and his nursing of his command made possible the formation of Calder's and Nelson's fleets, which frustrated the purpose of Villeneuve's return from the W. Indies and permitted the overwhelming victory at Trafalgar. He has been undervalued because his brother, the Marquess, attracted more limelight and, also, he was exceptionally modest and refused honours. Moreover, his patient slogging and foresight did not attract attention whereas the famous victories which he facilitated for other men did. He retired in 1806.

CORNWALLIS CODE (India) of 1793 originated in Bengal and divided the HEIC govt. into commercial, judicial and revenue branches. Local, i.e. Hindu or Moslem personal, law was administered but the dependence of land titles upon revenue liability favoured larger landowners. The system spread to most other HEIC territories and remained the basis of administration until 1833.

CORONATION. The English royal rites first emerged with the coronation of K. Edgar at Bath by St. Dunstan in 973. Probably modelled on a Frankish *Ordo* of c. 900, it was widely copied in Europe. It reached an elaborate form in the *Liber Regalis* of Edward II in 1308 and of Richard II in 1377, which included the homage of the peers. It was translated into English for the coronation of James I, when the penitential psalms were omitted and the communion made to conform with the Book of Common Prayer. Abp. Sancroft made major departures for James II, a R. Catholic, but the old order was resumed for William III and Mary II, with the addition of an oath to defend protestantism. Handel's magnificent *Coronation Anthems* were composed for George II and one, namely *Zadok the Priest* has been used ever since. In 1902 the homage of the peers was restricted to one for each order. For the coronation of George VI the oath was adapted to take account of the independence of the Dominions.

CORONEL, B. of (1 Nov. 1914) (Chile). Count Spee's German squadron of armoured and light cruisers was based on Tsingtao (N. China) until Japan entered the war. It then dispersed in part, the light cruisers seeking targets in the Indian Ocean, Spee himself with the armoured cruisers crossing the Pacific to attack British shipping from the south. The British S. American squadron was sent against them but its two armoured ships under Adm. Sir Christopher Cradock were overwhelmed by the famous gunnery of Spee's ships and sunk. *See* FALKLAND IS; WORLD WAR 1-7.

CORONERS or CROWNERS originated as keepers of pleas, i.e. as officials with whom complaints and answers to them were deposited pending trial or consideration by justices in eyre. The office probably originated in the 12th cent. Their special function was to ensure that the King's rights (much entangled with litigation) and property were safeguarded. The freeholders in each county court elected two. The Statute of Westminster (1275) required that they should be knights, but later a knight's qualification (lands worth £20 a year) was enough. This requirement on status arose because coroners were often expected to act as a check on the sheriff, whose duties they had to perform if he were absent. When certain boroughs got the privilege of electing their own sheriffs, they generally elected their own coroners too, and as the importance of the sheriffs declined so did that of the coroners. They were early regarded as responsible for inquiring into events likely to result in a forfeiture to the crown, and for this they had to summon a jury. Such INQUESTS were eventually confined to cases of treasure trove and apparently unnatural death, (and in the City of London, fire), and since the 18th cent. have been concerned with causes rather than fiscal consequences. Since 1926 coroners have had to be barristers, solicitors or doctors.

CORPORAL PUNISHMENT is mostly a euphemism for the

enforcement of discipline by applying canes, whips or birches to the buttocks. It was normal and accepted in schools other than St. Paul's until 1939, but declined after 1945 and was suppressed in state schools in the 1990s. When applied to other parts of the body, as in the pre-20th cent. services, it was called **FLOGGING**. The word **CORPORAL** when used as a military rank is derived from continental words such as *caporal* (Fr.), meaning 'charge hand'.

CORPORATION is a legal entity created by charter and distinct from the persons composing it. Nowadays the right to create corporations is vested, apart from statute, exclusively in the crown or its delegates. Some early charters appear to have been issued by others, but have always been regarded as valid, as in such cases delegation is presumed. A *royal charter* is made to a body of named persons. It incorporates them, gives them a corporate name and seal, lays down the purposes of the incorporation and sets forth the ways in which the corporation is to be managed and its governing body appointed. If it exceeds its objects, or abuses its powers or otherwise acts ultra vires, the charter can be forfeited. A *parliamentary charter* is granted by the appropriate authority named in a statute for the purposes of that statute. A certificate of incorporation to a limited company granted by the registrar of companies is a very common example. A parliamentary charter cannot be forfeited. A person who has reason to complain of the acts of the corporation must use the redress laid down in the statute or, if none, proceed in the courts by *mandamus* or *injunction*.

CORPORATION ACT, 1661. See CHARLES II-7; CLARENDON CODE 1661-5.

CORPORATION TAX, leviable on the income, profits and capital gains of businesses other than partnerships, was introduced in 1966. Like P.A.Y.E. it imposed a considerable hidden charge upon the economy through the accountancy and administration needed to operate it.

CORPORATIONS, MUNICIPAL pre-1834, VARIETY. The incorporated places received their charters at different times, for differing reasons and motives, and under a variety of influences. Hence there was no principle of uniformity in the town constitutions before the Municipal Corporations Act, 1834. The following eight Suffolk cases illustrate the variations possible within a single county. The first date is that of the first charter: the second is that of the governing charter in 1833. The population is that of the 1801 census.

Aldeburgh 1529-1637, pop. 804. There were 12 Capital Burgesses elected for life and 24 Inferior Burgesses. These 36 comprised the Common Council which chose Inferior Burgesses from the Freemen, but the Freemen and the two Bailiffs were appointed by the Capital Burgesses alone, and the latter were alone eligible for office. Only burgesses and freemen could vote for the two M.P.s. The offices were habitually bought: in 1834 the Capital Burgesses were the M. of Hertford, his family, friends or employees; none of the Inferior Burgesses and only 4 out of 33 freemen resided at Aldeburgh (see ORFORD *below*).

Beccles 1540-1605, pop. 2788. The charter was designed to regulate Beccles Fen. There was a Company of XII and a Company of XXIV. The XII filled their vacancies by co-option for life from the XXIV, and they appointed the Portreeve and the three Surveyors of the Fen. The two bodies filled vacancies in the XXIV for life from the freemen.

Bury St. Edmunds ?-1607, pop. 7655. There were 12 capital and 24 council Burgesses who, together as a Common Council, elected the Alderman from the Capital Burgesses. These 36 elected the two M.P.s. They also elected the Capital Burgesses from the council Burgesses and the latter from the inhabitants, but in the 18th cent. they left it to the Alderman to appoint tradespeople as Council Burgesses. The Common Council invariably elected one Fitzroy and one Hervey nominee to parliament, regardless of their, or anyone else's political opinions.

Dunwich 1199-1698, pop. 184. This place, already much eroded, was mostly washed away by the sea in the 18th cent. It had 32 Freemen (about half the adult male population) of whom two patrons nominated 8 each. This reduced the cost of bribing the rest. They elected 12 councilmen, 10 aldermen and 2 bailiffs and also the two M.P.s.

Ipswich 1199-1678, pop. 11277. The Freemen elected the two M.P.s and annually two bailiffs who had to be either Portmen or Chief Constables. The 12 Portmen and the 24 Chief Constables were elected for life by their own body or the major part of them, but by 1810 the Portmen had fallen to 5 and could not elect any more. The place was riven by party strife between the Blues (Tories) and the Yellows (Whigs) and every appointment, even that of Crier, was bitterly and corruptly contested.

Orford c. 1340-1605, pop. 751. There was a mayor, eight Portmen and 12 Capital Burgesses. The mayor and Portmen appointed the Portmen and Capital Burgesses for life from the inhabitants. The Portmen nominated two of their number annually for Mayor and the inhabitants chose one. The Portmen and Capital burgesses elected the two M.P.s. Most of the Portmen were relatives, friends or employees of the M. of Hertford. The Corporation was described as "a political club, formed to legalise the nomination of two members of the House of Commons by a member of the House of Lords". (*See* ALDEBURGH *above*.)

Southwold c. 1540, pop. 1054. The assembled resident payers of scot and lot elected two bailiffs annually and a High Steward for life. These nominated the other offices and managed all the business. This democratic and fairly uncorrupt place was not represented in parliament.

Sudbury ?14th cent.-1664, pop. 3283. There was a mayor, six aldermen and 24 Capital Burgesses. Aldermen were co-opted from the Capital Burgesses. From the resident freemen the whole council selected the Capital Burgesses; these annually elected an alderman to the mayoralty with the assent of 24 freemen, whose acquiescence was ensured because the mayor and aldermen nominated them. Freemen were admitted by birth, purchase or apprenticeship, but the corporation caused riots in 1771 by refusing admissions and was for the same reason successfully sued in 1813. The reason was that from 1702 freemen had successfully asserted their right to vote for the two M.P.s and the bribes brought money into the town. Sudbury, the model for Dickens' Eatenswill, was deprived of its parliamentary seats in 1844 for corruption, gross even for the period, in 1841.

CORPORATIONS OF THE POOR represented efforts to improve the efficiency of the Poor Law by incorporating several parishes and pooling their resources. The first was created in London in 1647 and there were a number of rural, particularly E. Anglian, incorporations by private act until 1750. The system was eventually extended in the form of "Unions" (q.v.).

CORPUS DELICTI **(Lat = the substance of the wrong).** Something whose existence must be proved in order to prove that a crime has been committed in relation to it.

CORRESPONDING SOCIETY was founded in London in Jan. 1792 by John Frost (1750-1842), an attorney and Thomas Hardy (1752-1852) a radical bootmaker, to encourage constitutional discussion. It soon had affiliates in Manchester, Norwich, Sheffield and Stockport. It derived its ideas from Locke and Rousseau and preached manhood suffrage, annual parliaments, a simpler legal system, an end to inclosures and cheaper govt. Membership cost 1d. a week and gathered much popular support. Originally attacked by the French revolutionaries, Frost and others presented addresses to the French Convention (Nov. 1792). Frost was sent to prison for six months for sedition in Feb. 1793 and after a sort of congress with other popular societies at Edinburgh in Dec. other members were transported. In 1794 Hardy, with John Thelwall (1764-1834) and Horne Tooke were charged, but acquitted, of treason. Meanwhile disillusion with French revolutionary excesses set in and in 1798 the Society considered setting up a loyal corps, to resist French invasion. The organisation was suppressed under the Combination Acts in 1799.

CORROBOREE. An Australian aboriginal dance of a festive or warlike type, performed at night.

CORRODY, an annuity in kind comprising food, clothing and usually lodging, granted by a monastery. From the mid 13th cent. corrodies became a serious drain on monastic resources. Some were sold to lay benefactors to provide the corrodian with security in old age and the abbey with cash, but a long-lived corrodian became a prolonged liability. Patrons might demand corrodies for relatives or dependants, and the king frequently required royal abbeys to provide for his elderly servants.

CORRUPT AND ILLEGAL PRACTICES. Bribery of judicial officers was always a misdemeanour. The House of Commons prohibited spending more than £10 at an election by an ineffectual standing order of 1677. The first of many acts against bribery and treating by parliamentary candidates was passed in 1695. Bribery at a local election was held a misdemeanour at Common Law in 1724: of members of corporations in 1723: of privy councillors in 1769. The Public Bodies (Corrupt Practices) Act 1889 introduced a statutory code alongside the Common Law. Other acts extended it in 1906, 1916 and 1967. Representation of the People Acts distinguished between practices which were corrupt in intention and those which were prohibited regardless of intention. In 1974 councillors were required to undertake to observe a mostly trite National Code of Local Govt. Conduct written by civil servants and in 1989 local authorities were required to make paid appointments on merit, though merit was not defined.

'CORRUPT COTERIE', a creation of the sensational press in 1912-4 was supposed to consist of young people who were conspicuously relaxed in the pursuit of sexual and alcoholic satisfaction.

CORRUPTION OF BLOOD. (Legal). An effect of attainder or conviction for treason or felony, namely the extinction of the ability of the convict's posterity to inherit his titles or entailed estates.

CORSICA (Med.) awarded by Papal bull to Pisa in 1090, passed in 1367 to the Genoese republic. Misgoverned for over three centuries, its people developed a violent and independent disposition. In 1734 a revolt led by **Hyacinth Paoli** was suppressed, but his son **Pascal Paoli (1725-1807)** led a more successful revolt in 1755, in which the Genoese were almost driven out. They obtained French assistance in 1764, but being unable to pay their debts to France ceded their rights instead in 1768. Pascal Paoli then led resistance to the French, but being defeated at Portonovo in 1769, cut his way through to an English frigate. He lived in England while French government steadily fastened on the island, made possible the recruitment of Corsican notables (among them the Bonapartes) into the French cultural orbit. In 1789 Paoli was recalled by the French National Assembly, became maire of Bastia and was in 1790 appointed gov. When Louis XVI was murdered he turned against the French, solicited a British protectorate and, with Nelson's help, drove them from the island. It remained substantially independent as a British base throughout Bonaparte's wars, though Paoli, balked of the viceroyalty, died in England in 1795. Corsica was returned to France in 1815. Its strategic importance to Britain was not exclusively geographical. Its forests supplied much of the timber needed by the French navy. *See* FIRST COALITION, WAR OF THE.

CORT, Henry (1740-1800) invented the puddling process for purifying iron in 1782 and lived by royalties on the invention. He was a navy agent at Fareham and in 1789, as a result of the prosecution of his partner's father for embezzlement, his own fortune and patents were seized and manufacturers were able freely to adopt his process. He was granted a pension in 1794.

CORTES were Spanish parliaments. In Castile and Leon they reached their influential summit in the 14th cent; in Catalonia a little earlier, in Aragon and Valencia a little later. They all declined in the 16th cent. In Castile the Crown, with its American income, could afford to exempt nobles from taxation and therefore participation: in the other three direct confrontation wore the Cortes down. In Catalonia and Valencia they were not summoned after 1645, in Castile only irregularly after 1665. Those of Aragon, Valencia and Castile were merged in 1709. The Catalan followed suit in 1724. By this time the sessions were purely formal.

CORUNNA. *See* ELIZABETH I-24, PENINSULAR WAR.

CORVETTE. *See* WARSHIPS, MODERN.

COSTA RICA. Spanish rule ended in 1821 and from 1824 to 1839 Costa Rica was one of five states of the short-lived Central American Federation. Coffee growing, introduced between 1835 and 1842, was the stay of the economy until 1871 when the first concession was made to the U.S. United Fruit Co. The latter introduced bananas and, with U.S. govt. backing and a U.S. pattern constitution, soon dominated the country. Boundary disputes with Nicaragua were settled in 1889 and with Panama in 1944. A unicameral constitution was introduced in 1949 and Costa Rica became the most stable of the Central American republics. From about 1981 left wing guerrillas, in pursuit of so-called grievances, began to cause anxiety.

COTES (1) Francis (?1725-70) portrait painter who taught his brother **(2) Samuel (1734-1818),** portrait painter and miniaturist. They were of Irish extraction but worked in Bath and London.

COTGRAVE, Randle (?-1634) secretary to Ld. Burghley, wrote the earliest English-French dictionary (1611).

COTSWOLD GAMES were athletic contests of ancient origin. They were reorganised in 1604 by a Capt. Robert Dover and held near Chipping Camden until the end of the 18th cent.

COTSWOLD HILLS were the breeding ground of large sheep with long, coarse wool. These were raised from 10th cent. onwards in enormous numbers on great open pastures, and the wool either sold (at times through the Adventurers) or converted into cloth. The area became very rich and the profits were extensively invested in magnificent churches and private houses built of peculiarly beautiful local stone. Many still survive at such places as Broadway, Burford, Chipping Campden, Cirencester, Malmesbury, Moreton-in-the-Marsh, Northleach and Stow-in-the-Wold. There were also weaving industries at Witney and Stroud which still survive. In the 18th cent. inclosure (with drystone walls) brought a change to mixed farming in a changed landscape and the sheep were often moved elsewhere to be crossed with Merino and Rambouillet.

COTTAGE COUNTESS. At 17, Sarah Hoggins (?-1797) married Henry Cecil in 1791. She became Countess of Exeter when he succeeded to the earldom in 1793. The affair caused some excitement because his previous wife had run away with a parson and Sarah was the daughter of a smallholder.

COTTAR was often a village specialist such as a craftsman, cowman, shepherd or goat herd, whose work was not directly concerned with communal cultivation of the soil. He had a very limited share in the village fields, perhaps 5 acres or less, with correspondingly light labour services attached to them. The cottars might also represent a reserve of labour, which could be hired by the lord or the more prosperous villeins, especially when circumstances such as an animal epidemic, temporarily deprived them of their normal work.

COTTILLION (Fr = pettycoat). An energetic square dance of a mildly erotic character, in which the ladies held up their skirts and, in politer society, showed their pettycoats.

COTTON grows naturally only in hot, dry climates, to which mediaeval Europe had only indirect access, save in Asia Minor and Syria. The Moors introduced the manufacture of cotton cloth into Spain and in the 14th cent. fustian began to be made in France. The Portuguese brought cultivation to Brazil in the 16th cent. (two Portuguese Grand Masters of Malta were called Cotoner) and it soon spread to the southern colonies of British America. The result was the foundation of the Lancashire cotton industry in the 17th cent., encouraged by mercantilist policy and, by contrast, the humid climate needed for manipulation. When the spinning, and later the weaving and carding machines, were invented in the 18th cent. the proximity of water as a source of power compounded the advantages of Lancashire, which gained yet again in the steam age by the nearness of the coal fields and the construction of the Bridgwater and other canals (*see* COMMUNICATIONS).

Lancashire consumed and re-exported the greater part of the world's surplus cotton until the 1870s, after which other places set up large industries; the Bombay industry was founded in 1850, the Japanese and U.S. in about 1873. All the same the market and consequently the acreage continued to expand. Hence by 1914 Lancashire's share of the world market was about 20%, but this represented a consumption of 2,100M lb of raw cotton as against 25M in 1790 and about 60% of the world trade in manufactured cotton goods. War and competition rapidly reduced this. By the years 1936 to 1938 British exports had fallen by about 75%, internal consumption of raw cotton by 37% and about 45% of the Lancashire industry was at a standstill. World War II exacerbated the situation and afterwards labour shortages accelerated the decline. The volume of manufactured exports in 1951 was only 50% of 1938: in 1960 it was 24% and still declining. *See* CLOTHING TEXTILES.

COTTON. London merchant family. **(1) Joseph (1745-1825)** commanded East Indiamen and became a director of the HEIC in 1795. He was also deputy master of Trinity House from 1803 to 1823. His son **(2) William (1786-1866)** became a director of the Bank of England in 1821 and an inventor of some ingenuity. He was greatly interested in social questions: in particular he stopped the practice of paying workpeople on Saturdays by orders on a public house, by ensuring that enough small change was minted; he overhauled the administration of the London Hospital; he established church building funds and built 10 London churches himself and he was one of the founders of the National Society.

COTTON and COTTONIAN LIBRARY (1) Sir Robert Bruce Cotton (1571-1631) amassed books and documents which were used by distinguished people of his time. He was a friend of the E. of Somerset and got into trouble for trying to forge exculpatory letters on his behalf in 1616. In the Parliament of 1625 he was M.P. for Thetford and circulated some notes on constitutional precedents which offended the court. His great library eventually passed to his grandson **(2) Sir John (1621-1701)** who decided to give it to the nation but died prematurely. His grandson **(3) John (1679-1731)** procured the passing of a private Act for that purpose in 1702. It was transferred from Cotton House to Essex House in the Strand in 1712 and thence to Ashburnham House in Deans Yard in 1730. Here part of it was damaged in a fire. It came to rest in the British Museum in 1753.

COUNCIL LEARNED IN THE LAW (c. 1498-1509) was a committee of the Council set up by Henry XII to identify those elements of the law which could be used to the royal financial advantage. Reginald Bray was the original leader: later it was consulted by Empson and Dudley.

COUNCIL OF EUROPE was established at Strasbourg in 1949 and its Assembly included representatives of 14 nations. Not to be confused with the European Parliament under the T. of Rome.

COUNCIL OF STATE (1649-60) (1) was Oliver Cromwell's executive. It was appointed annually and consisted for the first two years of 41 members of whom 31 were members of the residual House of Commons. 16 were regicides. In the third year only 21 previous members were elected and 20 new ones appointed. This rule was followed in the next two years. It operated in standing committees, notably those for foreign affairs, Ireland, the Army and the Navy.

(2) Under the Instrument of Government it had 15 members named in the Instrument and, besides being the executive it could, with the Protector, make Laws and Ordinances during the long intervals when the parliament was not to be in session. After the general election for the second parliament, it scrutinised the returns and forcibly excluded about 100 members who had been lawfully elected.

(3) Under the Instrument as amended after the Humble Petition and Advice, it was renamed the PRIVY COUNCIL. The Protector nominated its members with the concurrence of the existing members and subsequent parliamentary approval. When he dispensed with the parliament, it became a kind of collegiate sub-dictatorship dominated by the Protector but, like him, strongly influenced by the military men. With Oliver's death it ceased to matter.

COUNCILS OF ACTION (1) 1920, were trade union organisations set up to combat British govt. intervention in the Russian civil war and invasion of Poland. **(2) 1938,** Lloyd George set up similarly named, but entirely different, bodies to expound his policies and Keynes' style economics against the slump, and support for the League of Nations.

COUNCILS, BOROUGH, COMMUNITY, COUNTY, DISTRICT, PARISH. *See* LOCAL ADMINISTRATION.

COUNT (Lat. *Comes* = companion) (1) was originally a trusted friend or associate of a late Roman ruler, often as a member of his council or as responsible for a particular charge, e.g. *comes stabuli* (constable or stable keeper). Visigothic and Frankish rulers tended to quarter such companions in particular places to act as their local representatives. In this way the *comes* developed into a territorial official during the 6th and 7th cents. His territory was originally called a *pagus* (sept or clan), but later a *comitatus* (band or gang, and then county) but his office was regarded as a function not as a property, even if properties were attached to the office and the office itself passed from one member of a family to another. Anarchy accelerated the movement towards heredity and by the 11th cent. the count was a feudatory of a Duke, save in Flanders and Toulouse where the Count was supreme. **(2)** The word *comes* was used in English Latin documents for Earl, and *comitartus* for shire. An Earl's wife is called a countess. **(3)** The word *Count* was used as the equivalent of the German *Graf* who was commonly much less important than an earl, save for the *Pfalzgraf=* Count Palatine (of the Rhine).

COUNTER-REFORMATION (1492-1648) is a misleading name for a R. Catholic revival which began before the Reformation; and gained at least as many successes among non-Christians as against Protestants. Though not a movement in any co-ordinated sense it had certain recognisable strands. It may be said to have begun with the appointment of Francisco XIMENEZ as confessor to Q. Isabella of Castile in 1492 and his reform of the Castile

Franciscans with her help. The idea of the state correcting the church was not new, but the moral earnestness of the Spanish Catholic Sovereigns, who concluded the last effective crusade by taking Granada in 1492, contrasted sharply with the luxury and cynicism of the Western Church elsewhere. They used state power to protect and encourage the church to reform itself and extend its activities. In North Germany, on the other hand, princely intervention was direct and active; it deprived the church of room for manoeuvre and the political Reformation was the result.

(2) The second feature of the counter-reformation was the foundation of new religious orders. Luther published the XCV Theses in 1517 and made the break with the Papacy final in 1520-1. The Theatine order was constituted in 1524; the Capuchines (*see* FRANCISCANS) in 1529. These early dates suggest that some such movement would have occurred without Luther's external stimulus. Loyola's conversion, similarly, dates from events in Spain in 1521 and, though his Jesuit order – authorised in 1540 – was to become a major force in the struggle with protestantism, one of Loyola's companions, St. Francis Xavier, sailed for India in 1541, visited Japan in 1549 and died in China in 1552.

(3) The new seriousness led Pope Paul III (Alexander Farnese) to undertake a full scale doctrinal and functional reappraisal. It 1545 he convened the **Council of Trent** (Tyrol). It began in Dec., moved to Bologna in 1547 and ended its first series of sessions in 1549. His successor, Julius III, held a series in 1551 and 1552. Pius IV (Giovanni Medici) the third and last in 1562 and 1563. The Council's conclusions dominated Church doctrine and policy for over four centuries. These included the equal validity of Tradition and Scripture as guides to faith, the exclusive right of the Church to interpret Scripture and the restriction of scriptural texts to a revised Vulgate. The doctrine of Justification, merit and the seven sacraments were set forth in a sense opposed to the views of the reformers, and Papal Supremacy over the Church was eventually recognised. The Council also instituted the revision of the Index. With the Church united under a centralised direction, Paul IV, Pius V and Sixtus V reorganised the Curia, disciplined the bishops and, with Spanish help, introduced the Inquisition into most of Italy, except Venice.

(4) The weakening of the Church by the Reformation led to greater use of, and sophistication in, diplomacy. Where the Papacy could no longer command it could persuade, induce or subvert. Papal nuntii replaced the legates; secular political parties began to have Roman inspired programmes. Political rulers, especially the Habsburgs, adopted counter-reformist policies as an adjunct to more worldly ambitions. South Germany was preserved for the faith and Bohemia, reconquered in the 1620s, was reconverted in the next twenty years. By 1650 Poland had been reconverted as well.

(5) By this time French ambitions, opposed to those of the Habsburgs, broke the unity of the counter-reformist states; Richelieu, the French Cardinal Prime Minister, was forced in the course of the Thirty Years' War to support Protestant states against the Habsburg political advance. Thus the European Counter-Reformation is considered to have ended with the settlement of the War at the P. of Westphalia (1648), the last major treaty in which the Papacy negotiated as a principal.

COUNTRY KEEPERS. *See* CUMBERLAND-13.

"COUNTRY PARTY". A conventional term for those, neither especially rural nor originally organised as a party, who welcomed the Restoration because it ended centralised and military dictatorship, puritan gloom and the persecution of the English church. They drifted into loose association when they perceived a trend from a different direction towards similar vices, namely royal absolutism and a Romanist and Jesuitical church and army personified in a suspected R Catholic King, his professedly R. Catholic heir, the D. of York, and evidenced indirectly by policies which seemed to favour the aggressions of Louis XIV against European order and the world economy and his persecution of protestants. Nothing was proved until near the end of Charles II's reign but it was hard to understand how the court policies could be financed unless by the French King. This gut-feeling against absolutism, Romanism and France in association, and in favour of overseas commerce, generated the early whig party.

COUNTRY WALK. (17th and 18th cent.) often a euphemism for a duel, duels being illegal. *See also* BARN ELMS.

COUNTY OR SHIRE. (1) 'County' comes from the Latin comitatus = either a war-band or the following of an earl. 'Shire' meant an official charge or circumscription and was not strictly appropriate to old kingdoms (e.g. Essex, Kent and Sussex) or to border nomanslands (e.g. Cumberland or Northumberland) or tribal areas (e.g. Devon, Cornwall, Norfolk or Suffolk) which were not anciently allotted by superior authority to somebody's responsibility. This still accords with popular, if subconscious, usage.

(2) As will already be obvious, the origins of old counties are widely diverse. Apart from those already mentioned Wiltshire, Hampshire, Dorset and Somerset were internal shires of Wessex. The very large shire of York was based partly on what remained of Northumbria after the formation of the episcopal County Palatine of Durham, which was never a shire. Yorkshire was divided into ridings (= thirds) but had only one sheriff. Five shires were formed round the Mercian fortified boroughs at Bedford, Cambridge, Huntingdon, Northampton and Buckingham. The E. Midland shires of Leicester, Nottingham, Derby and Lincoln were similarly centred on four Danish boroughs after they had surrendered and been garrisoned. Lincolnshire, however, was composed of the Parts of Lindsey, Kesteven and Holland with a single sheriff, but these Parts reflected much older historical entities. Lindsey, in particular, having once been a kingdom and Holland an area with a peculiar marsh economy. In the W. Midlands the shires of Gloucester, Hereford, Worcester, Shropshire and Cheshire were military governorships against the Welsh. Warwickshire was an artificial creation. Lancashire, Westmorland and Cumberland, perhaps for sparcity of population, were not defined until the 12th cent. The two last shared a sheriff.

(3) In Wales, shiring was related to the method and sequence of Anglo-Norman conquest. The North Welsh principality was conquered ultimately as a whole and shired by the Statute of Rhuddlan (1282) into Anglesey, Caernarvon and Merioneth. These three had, however, been mapped out with Flint and embryonic areas further south around Cardigan and Carmarthen by the Statute of Wales in 1264. In other parts of Wales there was a jumble of private and partly shifting marcher lordships, mostly but not all vested in Anglo-Norman families. These areas were all shired under the Act of Union (1536) which created Brecknock, Denbigh, Glamorgan, Merioneth, Montgomery, Pembroke and Radnor, and the definitive boundaries of Cardigan and Carmarthen. Monmouthshire, however, was detached from Wales (and its Great Sessions) and included in the English judicial circuit system.

(4) Irish counties were defined so as to be consistent with the boundaries of the provinces, but fluctuated with the ebb and flow of conquest and resistance. The earliest shires were in Munster, followed by Leinster, then Ulster and finally Connaught.

(5) The old English shires had the most marked military significance, with the shire levies under the control of an ealdorman or earl. After the Conquest, these

forces were mostly put under the sheriff (or shire-reeve) more, save along the borders, for police than defence.

(6) In England, Wales and Ireland the shire had important legal and administrative features. Within its defined boundary the Common Law was in force. Hence the shiring of N. Wales by the Statute of Rhuddlan (1284) and that of the Irish Pale brought in Common Law and ended Welsh or Brehon Law. There was accordingly a shrieval power to enforce it, usually exercised by a sheriff, though sometimes, in a liberty, by a bailiff. Beyond the county boundary the sheriff's power did not reach without the backing of the neighbouring sheriff, if any. In particular the seaward boundary marked the transition from Common Law enforced by a sheriff against people to Admiralty Law enforced by an Admiralty Marshal often against things, e.g. ships. The shrievalty was thus the essential feature of a county; a place (e.g. Poole or Haverfordwest) which was allowed a sheriff of its own became, *ipso facto,* a county.

(7) The Common Law county acquired secondary characteristics derived ultimately from this fact. The dispersal of the sheriff's original power resulted in other bodies or officials being appointed to exercise some of his functions. Thus coroners took office for his area, commissions of the peace were drawn up for it and Quarter Sessions supervised local govt. functions such as roads, bridges and the Poor Law based upon it.

(8) In Scotland a *county* was another word for *sheriffdom* and denoted the area round the castle of a sheriff, who was a judicial officer. Thus the county was an enforcement area for a law which was presumed to apply anyhow. The southern counties owed their geography to prolonged English occupation and an English type of shiring. Fife was probably a kingdom. The Highland counties were tribal confederations. The east coast lowland counties were areas of settlement from the west.

(9) The English and Welsh counties survived, minor boundary changes apart, in their original shape until 1974 when some new ones were carved out of them, notably the "metropolitan" counties, with Avon and Cleveland and there were some amalgamations such as the Parts of Lincolnshire and Westmoreland and Cumberland, while Monmouth was transferred, as Gwent, to Wales, Glamorgan was partitioned into three and the remaining eleven Welsh counties were amalgamated into five. In 1992 a Local Govt. Commission was set up to reduce the three tiers of local councils to two, by eliminating either districts or counties as convenient. The Major Govt. favoured eliminating the counties but this provoked public protest. The names are habitually (and in this work) used to designate geographical areas.

(10) The Scottish counties were mostly degraded to the status of districts in newly created regions in 1973.

COUNTY CORPORATE (*see* COUNTY). 20 Boroughs became at various times counties corporate and so formed no part of the surrounding county, hundred or district. They had their own sheriffs (whom they elected), assizes and quarter sessions held before their recorders. These were the cities of London, Bristol*, Canterbury*, Chester*, Coventry*, Exeter*, Gloucester, Lichfield, Lincoln*, Norwich*, Worcester* and York*, the boroughs of Berwick upon Tweed, Caernarvon, Hull*, Newcastle upon Tyne*, Nottingham* and Southampton* and the Towns of Poole and Haverfordwest. The two last were created to deal with problems of piracy in their enclosed waters, Poole by charter, Haverfordwest by statute. Those marked * became county boroughs under the Local Government Acts 1888-1933. The status was abolished by the Local Government Act, 1972.

COUNTY or SHIRE COURTS (ANCIENT) were assemblies before the Eorlderman, the bishop and the King's Reeve (Sheriff). Their form and meeting place varied somewhat according to the history of the shire concerned; originally they were composed of the more substantial persons such as royal officials and landowners, but by the 12th cent. the Eorldermen had disappeared and the bishops were usually too busy, leaving the sheriff mostly in charge, with county notables who included bailiffs, hundredors and freeholders. The need for such assemblies declined as seigneurial and royal itinerant courts encroached on the judicial work on the one side, parliament gradually engrossed the political work on the other, and the need to keep order created the justices of the peace and reduced the prestige of the sheriff. By the 15th cent. their principal functions were to elect the Knights of the Shire, appoint the grand jury and proclaim outlawries.

COUNTY COURTS (MODERN). In 1750 statutory courts held before the county clerk and a jury were set up in each hundred of Middlesex, with a jurisdiction limited to 40s. These became the model for a general system of courts of jurisdiction limited to £20 created by the County Courts Act, 1846. The country was organised into 59 circuits, with a County Court Judge for each. The jurisdiction has been steadily increased and in 1976 stood at £750 or in some cases more. One important function was to deal (since 1914) with cases under the Rent Acts. In 1988 they were given the routine cases hitherto triable in the High Court up to a value of £50,000.

COUPON ELECTION (1918). The general election of 1918 was called to exploit the victorious end of World War I and incidentally to strengthen the hand of the Lloyd George-Bonar Law coalition in the peace negotiations. Candidates supporting the coalition were sent a joint letter of encouragement by Lloyd George and Bonar Law. This was derisively called the Coupon by those, such as Asquithian Liberals and Labour candidates, who refused it.

COURCI, John de (?-?1219) of legendary valour, conquered Ulidia (i.e. the Down and Antrim area of Ulster) between 1176 and 1180 when he married Alfreca, *d* of Guthfrith, K. of Man. He was the royal representative in Ireland from 1185 to the early years of Richard I, but was in opposition to Richard's nominee Hugh de Lacy. He was at war with the Lacy's for much of the rest of his life. *See* ULSTER

COURLAND (Baltic) was conquered by the Germanic Knights of the Sword in 1237. Russian pressure proved so heavy in the 16th cent. that the grandmaster Kettler followed the Hohenzollern example in Prussia and ceded the territory to Poland as a vassal duchy with himself as duke. The Kettlers reigned until 1737 when the widow of the last of them, who had become the Empress Anne of Russia in 1730, conferred the duchy on her lover Biron. His son abdicated in 1795. The territory was then annexed by Russia but continued to have a substantial German speaking, especially landowning, population which provided officers for the imperial navy. *See* BALTIC; BALTIC REPUBLICS; HANSE.

COURT BARON or sometimes *LIBERA CURIA* (Lat = Free Court) was a civil court held by the Lord of a manor for its free tenants, or homage. It was not always distinct in practice from the Courts Leet (disciplinary) and Customary (for unfree tenants).

COURTENAY, a family from the Gatinais. Louis VII drove Renaud de Courtenay from France and he sought his fortune in England under Henry II. By marriage the family came to inherit the Redvers earldom of Devon Several became bishops. **(1) William (?-1396) Bp. of LONDON (1375-81), Abp. of CANTERBURY (1381).** Two of his brothers fought with distinction against France and were Knights of the Garter. William himself rose quickly becoming a Doctor of Both Laws and Chancellor of Oxford University before becoming a bishop at twenty-eight. In 1376 he first came into prominence through his determined defence of William of Wykeham and though but thirty four, was translated to the politically sensitive see of London. His firmness stopped Wycliffe's ill-steered anti-clericalism. Feeling was running high against clerical wealth and Caesarian bishops but his courage, moderation and saintliness won through. His integrity was respected even by his opponents. At the Good Parliament of 1376 he was one of the committee of magnates appointed to assist the Commons in their deliberations. His acceptance shows that he was himself a critic of the mismanagement of Edward III's govt. At this moment, however, there was an untoward incident. In Jan. 1377 he published, as in duty bound, papal bulls against Florentines in his diocese, for Florentines had lately been designated enemies of the Papacy. The Londoners joyfully plundered the warehouses of Florentine merchants and William was angrily ordered to retract. This represented a victory for John of Gaunt, D. of Lancaster, a protector of Wycliffe and an enemy of Wykeham, then in disgrace. Gaunt's triumph was short-lived. In the next month William and the bishops insisted on suspending Convocation until Wykeham, who had been excluded by Abp. Sudbury in response to court pressure, was allowed to attend the meetings. The next step was to summon Wycliffe to St. Pauls for his contumacy and denunciations of the clergy. Wycliffe came with John of Gaunt, Henry Percy (Marshal of England) and an armed following. Percy invited Wycliffe to sit down and make himself comfortable. This provoked an exchange of insults between William and Percy and the trial ended in uproar. Gaunt, Percy and their men thrust their way out into the streets full of angry Londoners who roared their abuse at the Lancastrian party for insulting their bishop. Next day there was a riot in which William saved Gaunt's palace of the Savoy from destruction. On the accession of Richard II, he became a member of the council of govt., but it was the outbreak of the Peasant's Revolt (1381) which brought him to the fore. Abp. Sudbury was murdered and William was the obvious replacement. He was also briefly Chancellor after the suppression of the Revolt. In the ensuing difficult years it needed his strong leadership to overcome the pressure from the Commons for higher taxation of the clergy. In 1390 he led the prelates in a formal protest against the Statute of Provisors and in 1393 against the Statute of Praemunire. During these years too he had to grapple with, in his view, serious heretical threats to the Church. Heretics, especially Lollards, were burnt. He was also troubled by the young King's extravagance and misgovernment and in 1385 he publicly reproved Richard, who reacted with a violent outburst and a threat to seize the temporalities of his see. Nevertheless, Richard seems to have respected his Archbishop, for when William died in 1396 before the tragic end of the reign, he was buried at Canterbury in the King's presence. **(2) Richard (?-1415) Bp. of NORWICH (1413),** son of Sir Philip of Powderham Castle and grandson of Hugh, 2nd E. of Devon, was brought up by his uncle the Archbishop who left him his best mitre in his will "in case he should become a bishop". He became a Doctor of Both Laws and Chancellor of Oxford University and lived on various ecclesiastical preferments until in 1406 he succeeded to the family property. As Chancellor of Oxford he had made a spirited stand against Abp. Arundel's claim to make a metropolitical visitation of the university to root out heresy. Richard was perfectly orthodox but his efforts on behalf of academic privilege failed. He made, however, a different contribution to the university's future, by completing the library which had been the gift of Bp. Cobham. He was an old friend of Henry of Monmouth, as P. of Wales and on his accession he became Treasurer of the royal household and in 1413 was elected Bp. of Norwich on the King's recommendation, but never visited his diocese because of diplomatic employments. In 1415 he went with the King

to Harfleur where he fell ill and died. **(3) Peter (?-1492) Bp. of EXETER (1478), Bp. of WINCHESTER** (1487) was involved in the unsuccessful West Country revolt against Richard III in 1484. Condemned in parliament to the loss of his temporalities he fled to Brittany where he acted as Henry Tudor's secretary. From Henry's accession in 1485 Peter, as Keeper of the Privy Seal for the first two years of the reign, played an active part in establishing the new regime until his translation to Winchester. **(4) Edward (?-1509) 1st E. of DEVONSHIRE (1485)** received his earldom and large Devonshire estates in return for supporting Henry against Richard III. He also held Exeter against Perkin Warbeck in 1497. Of near royal descent, his son **(5) Sir William (?-1511)** was a cousin of Henry VII and, suspected of plotting for the crown, was attainted but not executed in 1503. He was released from the Tower at Henry VIII's accession (1509) but died before the reversal of the attainder was completed. His son **(6) Henry (?1496-1538) 2nd E. (1511), M. of EXETER (1525)** was an early friend of the King, became a councillor and received wide estates and many offices. He also supported the King in his divorce, acted as his commissioner for dissolving the smaller monasteries in 1535, was a member of the court which tried Anne Boleyn and led the royal forces in suppressing the Pilgrimage of Grace (1536). Becoming an enemy of Thomas Cromwell, he too fell under suspicion as of royal blood and was attainted and executed (1538).

COURTESY TITLES. If a duke, marquess or earl has a second title lower in rank, his eldest son is known by that title, e.g. the D. of Wellington's eldest son would be called the M. Douro. A younger son would be called (say) Lord George Wellesley. In Scotland the heirs to certain peerages are called Masters, e.g. the E. of Stairs' eldest son was the Master of Stair. These titles carry no rights and their holders could always sit (as did Lord North) in the House of Commons. They are not to be confused with Irish peerages whose holders could sit in the British House of Commons if they had no seat in the Lords. Occasionally the rules of inheritance for a second title may differ from those governing the major one, in which case the second title may resume an independent existence in a different line and cease to be a courtesy title. An heir to a renounced peerage could not use the courtesy title of the renouncing peer because it must be renounced too.

COURT LEET, a minor criminal but private court possibly related to a sheriff's tourn in the hundred and hence to the view of frankpledge. Most private franchises in the 13th cent. were of this kind and might be exercised over fewer manors than those comprising a hundred. The Lord of a leet held his tourn twice a year and took the profits which would otherwise have gone to the sheriff. The matters dealt with included withdrawal of services, nuisances, bloodshed and brawling, false measures and non-attendance at a view of frankpledge itself. A manor court leet was said to be *intrinsec* its own manor but *forinsec* other manors where it had jurisdiction. Much of this type of jurisdiction was superseded by the Quarter Sessions in 1368.

COURT OF BURGESS AND FOREIGN (at Pontefract). *See* COURT OF RECORD; BOROUGH.

COURT OF LAW, subject to special exceptions, sits in public to determine issues in accordance with law. Its members must be present throughout a proceeding and none must take part in any decision in which he is personally interested. It has power to take evidence on oath. English courts are classified in three ways. **(1) *Royal and non-royal.*** The non-royal courts were the old county courts, palatine courts and manor courts. All the rest, even though the judges were not appointed by the crown were royal courts because they administered common law. **(2) *Courts of Record and not of Record.*** A Court of Record has power to punish for contempt of itself or other offences; its proceedings (records) are conclusive evidence of what they record and formerly its proceedings could be corrected only by writ of error. Courts not of record do not have these features and were formerly corrected by writ of false judgement. **(3)** *Superior and Inferior.* Inferior courts originated as local courts such as manor, hundred, borough and the ancient county courts. Nothing (as to subject matter or geography) was within their jurisdiction unless it was shown on the face of the proceedings that the particular matter was within it; therefore a judgment involving a question of jurisdiction was not final and a successful plaintiff could not plead the judgement if he executed a defective process. An inferior court was always liable to be corrected by a superior one whose jurisdiction, unless expressly restricted, is without limit and final. The old Courts of the Common Pleas, Exchequer, Kings Bench and Chancery were all royal, superior courts of Record and so is the Supreme Court into which they were amalgamated.

COURT OF PLEAS (at Yeovil). *See* COURT OF RECORD; BOROUGH.

COURT OF RECORD, BOROUGH, was a petty borough civil court which probably grew out of a local court baron. Usually its jurisdiction was confined to matters arising within the borough and sometimes to personal actions only, with a monetary limit on the damages or debt involved, varying from £5 to £20. Theoretically the judges might be all the aldermen or councilmen or capital burgesses, but in practice the Mayor, Recorder and Town Clerk conducted it. Many of these courts had disappeared by 1834 when many were extinguished; the rest, except the Mayor's and City of London Court, disappeared in 1972.

COURT PRESENTATIONS were formal introductions of persons to the sovereign, each by a sponsor who had already been presented or, in the case of a foreigner, the appropriate ambassador. Presentation gave social access to any British ambassador and the right to be presented by him at a foreign court. Ladies were presented at drawing rooms, gentlemen at levees. No levees were held after 1939 or drawing rooms after 1958. The practice was replaced by the Garden Parties at Buckingham Palace and Holyroodhouse.

COUSINS, Frank (1904-86) attracted attention as the leader of the unsuccessful London 'bus strike in 1958. He was Gen. Sec. of the Transport and General Workers' Union and engineered the absorption of a number of other small unions into it. He became Harold Wilson's Min. of Technology in 1964 and was Labour M.P. for Nuneaton from 1965 to 1966. He resigned against the govt's policy of pay restraint but later served on many councils and commissions.

COUTANCES, Walter of (?-1207), a Cornish canonist, as Archdeacon of Oxford was employed in diplomatic business to the Count of Flanders and the King of France in 1177. In 1183 he became Bp. of Lincoln and in 1184 Abp. of Rouen. As such he acted as a diplomatic guardian of Normandy against French encroachments. When Henry II died he secured the immediate recognition of Richard I in Normandy and then in England. In 1190 he went with Richard on crusade as far as Messina. Here he mediated between the King and the local authorities, whose hostility Richard had provoked. Richard, moved by reports of trouble in England, sent him back and he represented the King's interests as Justiciar in the intrigues surrounding Longchamps and P. John. Throughout most of this time his activities ran counter to John's interests. When John became King he found no difficulty in transferring his allegiance to the French King whom he occupied Rouen.

COVENANT-ERS (1) Local covenants of a presbyterian type began to be signed in Scotland after 1555. In 1561 John Knox and colleagues placed a 'national programme

for spiritual reform' before the nobility. An important influence was John Craig (q.v.), who joined Knox at the Edinburgh High Kirk in 1562. When the D. of Lennox returned from France (*see* JAMES VI-7) and a return to Popery was feared, Craig drew up a Calvinist statement of belief (1581). It was signed by James VI and his household and became known as the KING'S CONFESSION. All parish clergy and, after 1584, all graduates had to sign it. There were reaffirmations in 1590 and 1595. **(2)** became the basis of the Scottish NATIONAL COVENANT of 1638 but with additions by Alex. Henderson (?1583-1646) notably an oath (*see* CHARLES I-12) to defend the reformed worship in Scotland against changes not agreed by the Assembly or Parliament.

(3) This Covenant became, in its turn, the basis of the English SOLEMN LEAGUE AND COVENANT of 1643 (*see* CIVIL WAR-9).

(4) Further local covenants were signed in the aftermath of the Cromwellian conquest of Scotland and the enforcement of toleration and, subsequently, during the long disorders which preceded the compromise establishing the Church of Scotland in 1690. The word covenanter thus means either a supporter of the covenant or a Calvinist extremist ready to overthrow the govt. in Edinburgh rather than tolerate episcopalian church govt.

COVENT GARDEN (London). The 'convent' of Westminster Abbey grew and sold vegetables there. In 1552 it passed to the 1st E. of Bedford. Between 1630 and 1633 the 4th E. employed Inigo Jones to lay it out as an arcaded square on the model of Lisbon. The 5th E. and 1st D., who was greatly interested in cultivation, reclaimed much of the Fens and obtained from Charles II in 1671 a Charter which enabled it rapidly to become the main vegetable and flower market for London, and successive Dukes built buildings and enlarged them. Between 1690 and 1800 the place and adjacent streets were also famous for their coffee houses and brothels. In 1732 a theatre was built. In 1858 this was replaced by the Royal Opera House. The Dukes transferred their interest to a family company in 1918, which continued to operate the market until the Charter was revoked in 1961 by a local act which also set up the Covent Garden Market Authority. In 1969 this body began to clear a site at Nine Elms, S. of the Thames, to which the marketing activities were moved by 1978. The old market became a covered area of small shops and a popular promenade.

COVENTRY (Warks.) grew up around a Benedictine monastery founded in 1043 by E. Leofric and his wife Lady Godiva, who became a sort of secular patron saint for the town. It became the co-see of Lichfield in 1102 and Ranulf of Gernons, E. of Chester, granted its first burgess charter in 1153. In 1191 Bp. Hugh Nonant, with Papal support, expelled the cathedral monks but they returned in 1198. It had two M.P.s from 1295 but the earliest extant Charter of incorporation dates from 1345. There were also important market charters in 1348 and 1445. These arose from the local cloth making and dying industry established since the beginning of the 14th cent. which soon made the town large (it was the fourth for size in the kingdom) and rich. The magnificent 14th cent. Cathedral was one result. When cloth-making moved to the Pennines in the 18th cent. mechanical trades such as clock-making replaced it and these were supplemented by bicycles in 1868 and motor cars in 1896. Rayon spinning came in 1904 and electrical equipment in 1907. These important industries were a target for German raids in World War II and in Apr. 1941 the city centre, the cathedral and some 50,000 houses were destroyed in a famous raid. This, in its turn, led to the construction of the controversial modern cathedral between 1954 and 1962.

COVENTRY (1) Sir Thomas (1547-1606) became a judge of the C.P. in 1606. His son **(2) Thomas (1578-1640) 1st**

Ld.. COVENTRY of AYLESBOROUGH (1628) was a recorder of London (1616), sol-gen. (1617), att-gen. (1621) and Lord Keeper from 1625. In 1629 he tried to arrange a compromise between Charles I and the opposition and, this failing, sided with Strafford and the King. His son (3) Henry (1619-86) went into exile with Charles II and later undertook diplomatic missions to Sweden (1664-6), Holland (1667) and Sweden again (1671). He was a hard worked but undistinguished Sec. of State from 1672 to 1679 (*see* CHARLES II-15 *et seq.*). His brother (4) Sir William (?1628-86) was sec. to James, D. of York from 1660 to 1667 and M.P. for Great Yarmouth from 1661 to 1679. James got him a commissionship of the navy in 1662 and he was a friend of Samuel Pepys. He became opposed to the court, attacked Clarendon in 1667 and the Cabal in 1668. As a result he was dismissed from his offices and briefly imprisoned, but remained in parliament until 1679 when he retired. His nephew Halifax put his name to *The Character of a Trimmer*, for Sir William, though he disclaimed the authorship, believed in a moderate middle party against the extreme.

COVENTRY CYCLE. *See* N-TOWN PLAYS.

COVERDALE, Miles (1488-1568). *See* BIBLE-3.

COVERED WAY. In artillery fortifications there was a parapet on the outer edge of the moat. The covered way was immediately behind and sometimes underneath it as well. Its garrison could both defend the parapet and shoot from behind anyone who got into the moat. An assault on the main curtain behind the moat was thus not practicable until the covered way had been mastered.

COWCHERS. Working selections of Duchy of Lancaster charters and records. (1) GREAT assembled by John Leventhorpe, Receiver-Gen. of the Duchy at Kenilworth between 1402 and 1420. (2) LITTLE were mostly rules, orders and forms.

COWLEY (1) Henry Wellesley (1773-1847) 1st Ld. (1828) younger brother of the 1st D. of Wellington, served in India from 1799 to 1800 when he went home to explain the Mysore War and settlement on behalf of his older brother, the M. of Wellesley, the gov-gen. He then returned to govern the ceded territories of Oudh (1801-2). He came back to England, became an M.P. in 1807, Sec. to the Treasury in 1808-9 and then embarked on the distinguished diplomatic career which was to occupy the rest of his life, first as ambassador to the Spanish *Junta* at Cadiz from 1809, then to the restored Spanish court at Madrid until 1822. He was then moved to Vienna until 1831 and finally to Paris from 1841 to 1846. These were all difficult assignments in which his tact and sense were notably suited to the periods of local turbulence and had a calming effect on European events. His son (2) Henry Richard Charles (1804-84) 1st E. (1857) inherited his father's talents and imbibed his training as attaché at Vienna. He became Min. to Switzerland in 1848 and then briefly to the German Confederation in 1851. Thereafter he was ambassador to Paris from 1852 to 1867, i.e. almost the whole duration of the Second Empire. He negotiated the alliance for, and the end of, the Crimean War, the abolition of privateering (1856), the French aspects of the Italian Risorgimento and the French trade treaty of 1860.

COWLEY. *See* COLLEY OR COWLEY; WELLESLEY.

COWPER TEMPLE CLAUSE (s. 14 of the Education Act, 1870) forbade local authorities to support denominational instruction from the rates. It did not affect the payment of govt. grants for this purpose. A. F. Cowper Temple (1811-88) was chairman of the Broad Church Group.

COWRY SHELLS were used as small change in most of India and on the E. African coast. In India they were reckoned at 1280 to the rupee in 1870. They continued in use as late as 1920.

COX, Sir Percy (1864-1937) worked as a diplomat in Oman and S. Persia from 1896. He became political resident for the Persian Gulf in 1909 and so acted as political adviser to the Mesopotamian expeditionary force in World War I. From 1918 to 1920 he was minister at Tehran and from 1920 to 1923 High Commissioner in Iraq where he, Gertrude Bell and K. Feisal were the true founders of the state.

COX, Richard (?1500-81), was discovered to be a Lutheran in the 1520s and forced to leave Christchurch Oxford to become headmaster of Eton. In 1537 he became chaplain to Henry VIII, Cranmer and the Bp. of Lincoln. He assisted in the consolidation of Henry's Reformation and received many preferments, becoming Dean of Christchurch (Oxford) in 1547 and Dean of Westminster in 1549. He had also been Chancellor of Oxford University from 1547 to 1553. He was an intolerant but not an extremist puritan and so, while removing all traces of Romanism from Oxford, he encouraged foreign theologians there. He took a considerable part in drafting Cranmer's Prayer Books of 1549 and 1552. In 1553 Mary I had him imprisoned briefly, but he escaped to Frankfurt, where he bested John Knox in a liturgical controversy and got him expelled. The issue, whether the exiles should continue in Cranmer's practices or move towards Calvin's, foreshadowed controversies later in the century. In 1559 he returned and Elizabeth made him Bp. of Ely. His intolerance of both extremes made him much disliked. In 1575 the Queen forced him to convey Ely Place in London to her friend Sir Christopher Hatton with the following letter:

Proud Prelate!

Remember what you were before I made you what you are, and if you do not immediately comply with my request, I will unfrock you, By God.

CRABBE, George (1754-1832) self taught, mostly absentee, clergyman and rural poet, befriended by Edmund Burke.

CRACOW was made an independent republic in 1815 as a result of the Vienna Congress. It was about 35 miles square. It was seized by Austria in 1846. *See* POLAND.

CRADOCK, R-Adm. Sir Christopher (1862-1914). *See* CORONEL, B. OF.

CRAFTSMAN, THE (1726-36) opposition journal run by Nicolas Amhurst (alias Caleb d'Anvers) with contributions from Bolingbroke and Pulteney. It maintained sustained, but not always scrupulous, criticism of Walpole, particularly his Excise Bill.

CRAGGS (1) James (1657-1721) and his younger son (2) James (1686-1721). The father began as an army clothier and, suspected or accused of peculation, was imprisoned in 1695 by the House of Commons for refusing to open his books to one of their committees. He was an able and trusted adherent of the D. of Marlborough and at Q. Anne's accession and the Duke's accession to power became M.P. for the Treasury Borough of Grampound (until 1713), Sec. of the Bd. of Ordinance (until 1714) and, in combination with the clerkship of the deliveries, was efficiently responsible for routine supplies to the armies. He became very rich. The son was employed by the Duke as a quasi-diplomat and travelled between Berlin, Hanover, The Hague and Brussels on many confidential missions, in the course of which he became friendly with the Elector George Lewis. Soon after the latter became King as George I, the son became a Sec. of State (1715). He was a discerning literary patron and a friend of Alexander Pope who wrote of him privately:

A soul as full of Worth, as void of Pride,
Which nothing seeks to show or needs to hide,
Which nor to Guilt, nor Fear its caution owes
And boasts a Warmth that from no Passion flows.

He and his father were among the promoters of the South Sea Co. When the bubble burst, they were objects of partisan fury. The son died, unexpectedly. Charges were in preparation against the father when he committed suicide.

CRAIG, John (?1512-1600) important and adventurous Scots divine, as a Dominican at St. Andrews was imprisoned for heresy but in 1536, having failed to get a place at Cambridge became, with Card. Pole's help, Master of Novices at Bologna and then Missioner in Chios. On his return to Bologna he became Rector. He came across a copy of Calvin's *Institute* in the library of the Inquisition. This so affected his outlook that he was condemned to be burned at Rome but was respited for the Jubilee of Paul IV. He escaped and, after wanderings, reached Vienna. Here he was befriended by the Archduke Maximilian, who refused to surrender him to the papal inquisition and gave him a safe conduct to England. He preferred his native Scotland and in 1561 offered his services to the presbyterians, preaching, to much public satisfaction, in Latin and becoming Knox's colleague at the Edinburgh High Kirk in 1563. He was now involved in the swirling politics of the time. He was probably privy to Rizzio's murder and, though Edinburgh was in Bothwell's hands, he refused to publish the banns for his marriage to Mary, Q. of Scots and accused him before the Council of adultery, ravishment, collusion and the murder of Darnley. He was, however, regarded as more accommodating than Knox, who had left the city, and he attempted conciliation on the principle that "whatsoever party shall be overthrown, the country shall be brought to ruin". Outspoken, yet a compromiser, he offended politicians of all sides and was sent out of the way to the north "to illuminate it". He returned to Edinburgh in 1579 as a King's chaplain, helped to draft the Second Book of Discipline and the N. Covenant of 1580 and, in 1581, to anticipate a papistical revival led by the D. of Lennox, drafted the Confession known, because the King had to sign it, as the King's Confession (*see* COVENANT- ERS). His last major public acts were to denounce the Black Acts, but he mediated in the dispute between Melville's presbyterian extremists and the court by means of an oath acknowledging the royal supremacy 'as far as the Word of God allows'.

CRAIGAVON, James Craig (1871-1940) 1st Vist. (1927) Ulster Unionist M.P. from 1906, was Carson's 2-in-C against Asquith's Home Rule Bill. He was member of Lloyd George's govt. but resigned with Carson in 1918. In 1921 he became Prime Minister of N. Ireland. During his long premiership he virtually created the Ulster state. The legislation providing social services, housing, drainage and schools were largely his work.

CRAMP RINGS were rings blessed by English sovereigns and given away on Good Friday to cure cramp and epilepsy. The practice ended with Mary I (cf KING'S EVIL).

CRANBROOK. *See* GATHORNE-HARDY.

CRANFIELD, Lionel (1575-1648) E. of MIDDLESEX (1622), an apprentice who married his master's daughter and became a successful London mercer on the £800 dowry, attracted James I's attention during an appearance on behalf of the Mercers Co. before the council in 1604. He was appointed receiver of customs for Dorset and Somerset in 1605 and surveyor-gen. of customs in 1613. After he made Sir George Villiers' (Buckingham) acquaintance they helped each other and he became Master of the Wardrobe in 1618 and chief navy commissioner in 1619. He was a capable administrator and introduced order and economy. He also got, in 1619, the lucrative office of Master of the Court of Wards. In 1620 he was sworn of the Council and he joined in the hue and cry which led to Bacon's fall in 1621, but his very competence made him obnoxious to the Commons, while his elevation to an earldom attracted the jealousy of the nobility. When articles of impeachment were launched by Coke on grounds of peculation in the court of wards in 1624, Buckingham and the P. of Wales abandoned him: he was condemned by the Lords, fined £50,000 and imprisoned but was pardoned at Charles I's accession.

CRANMER, Thomas (1489-1556) was a Cambridge philosopher and theologian. In a chance conversation in Aug. 1529 with Stephen Gardiner, the King's Sec. and Edward Fox, the Almoner, about Henry VIII's matrimonial difficulties with Katharine of Aragon, he suggested consulting the European universities. He was commissioned to write a book and Richard Croke did some research for him in Italian universities. The book, though never printed, made Cranmer famous: it also made him successful in the King's eyes, for Oxford, Cambridge, five French and three North Italian universities pronounced for the King's view. This failed to convince the Pope. In 1530 he accompanied Anne Boleyn's father, now E. of Wiltshire, on an embassy to Charles V (Katharine's uncle) who dominated the Pope. This too failed but the embassy also sought the support of reformist German princes and in 1532 Cramner secretly married Margaret, *d.* of Osiander, the Nuremberg theologian. Abp. Warham died in Aug.; Cranmer's intellectual views commended themselves to Henry, who nominated him in succession. The Pope, who wanted English and French allies to counterbalance the Emperor, raised no objection because of Cranmer's moderation in language. He was consecrated in Mar. 1533. (*See* APOSTOLIC SUCCESSION.) By this time Henry had secretly married the pregnant Anne Boleyn (25 Jan.). The Act in Restraint of Appeals was passed; convocation under Cranmer's presidency decided that Henry's marriage to Katharine was against divine law and he then obtained a royal licence under the Act to try the case. His court sat at Dunstable priory: Katharine refused to appear. On 23 May 1533 he declared her marriage void; on 28th Anne's marriage valid. He was now in no position to resist the Act of Supremacy 1534. Cranmer, though head of the body of clergy had to submit to Thomas Cromwell as the King's Vicar-Gen. The bishops were involved first in the compilation of the *Valor Ecclesiasticus* and then in 1535 and 1536 some 220 monasteries with incomes of less than £200 were suppressed. In Jan. 1536 Anne Boleyn had a miscarriage and in May she was indicted for high treason based upon a series of adulteries. She was executed on 19th and on 21st Cranmer pronounced her marriage void *ab initio* (possibly on the ground either of a precontract with Northumberland or of Henry's sexual relations with her sister) thereby making nonsense of the charges of adultery, but clearing the way for another royal marriage to Jane Seymour, which took place on 30th. Meanwhile Cranmer, supported by several other bishops, was moving towards doctrinal reform, based on the writings of Melancthon. He was, however, hotly opposed in a convocation over which Cromwell or his proctor, William Petre, presided instead of himself. Controversy was silenced in July by the publication of the King's Ten Articles, supplemented in Aug. by the Royal Injunctions. These failed to satisfy the reformers, while alienating the conservatives. The Pilgrimage of Grace (Oct-Dec. 1536) confirmed Henry's view that he had gone far enough, if not too far. The Bishops' Book represented a further retreat from reformist doctrines, despite Cranmer's efforts to continue their study, while Cromwell launched a successful assault of financial origin on images and pilgrimages, especially upon the shrine of St. Thomas of Canterbury. Vast sums in treasure and jewels were taken to enrich a crown which could dictate doctrine as it pleased. Nevertheless Cranmer quietly persisted, in particular by advocating the "Matthews Bible" for use in churches. This was installed during 1539, when Cromwell's dissolution of the greater monasteries was far advanced. Cranmer, however, failed to defeat the Act of Six Articles and had to put away his wife. Q. Jane Seymour had died in 1537 and Cromwell had negotiated the unfortunate political marriage with the protestant and sexually repellent Anne of Cleves. The conservatives, guided by Stephen Gardiner, were gaining

Henry's ear by political arguments and the attractions of Catherine Howard, niece of the strongly Romanist D. of Norfolk. In June 1540 Cromwell was attainted and though Cranmer, almost alone, spoke for him was executed in July. Not surprisingly it was Cranmer who brought to Henry's notice in the autumn of 1541 the adulteries of Q. Catherine Howard, which brought her to the block in Feb. 1542. Henry, who astutely maintained a balance of power at the centre, refused either to dismiss Gardiner and his friends or to countenance their attacks on Cranmer, who successfully defended the Great Bible against Gardiner's detailed criticisms in 1542 and himself from accusations of heresy in the three following years. In these years he began his great work on the Anglican Liturgy, based upon the Sarum Use, and in 1546 he was converted from the doctrine of the Real Presence by Nicholas Ridley. Consequently, as a member of the council appointed at Edward XI's accession, he was in a powerful position after the protestant victory of 1549. He also invited continental divines, notably Peter Martyr and Martin Bucer, to England and supported some simplification of services and the wholesale destruction of statuary and stained glass. All the same, he kept his distance from the political manoeuvring which led to the replacement of Somerset by Northumberland, but meanwhile some reformist bishops replaced Romanists and began to investigate the competence of their parochial clergy, with startling results. By 1552 the reformists were demanding an even simpler liturgy. This, the Prayer Book of 1552, was drafted by Cranmer and approved by the royal chaplains (i.e. Northumberland's ecclesiastical dependants). He was as much in Northumberland's grip as he had been in Henry VIII's. Edward VI would obviously not live long. Neither Northumberland nor the degree of reform reached by the church might survive the accession of the determinedly Romanist Mary. Hence Northumberland induced Edward VI to devise the Crown to the protestant and learned Lady Jane Grey, to whom he hoped to marry his son Guilford. For ecclesiastical reasons and with religious conviction Cranmer, with a hundred others, signed the will. Hence when Mary triumphed in July 1553 Cranmer was attainted and imprisoned. Protestant bishops were superseded by Romanists. Early in 1554 Convocation appointed delegates to dispute with Cranmer, Ridley and Latimer at Oxford. In Apr. all three were pronounced heretics and re-imprisoned. In Nov., however, the old legislation against heresy was revived, when Card. Pole received England back into the Roman Church. Cranmer's case was now investigated by Papal delegates who reported against him. He was canonically degraded and the decision to burn him was taken but he was induced to sign recantations and then told to prepare for death. On 21 Mar. 1556, in the University Church at Oxford, he publicly repudiated his recantations and was hustled off amid confusion to the stake.

CRANNOGS are circular farm houses built on artificial islands in Scottish lochs. They date mostly from 1st cent. B.C. *See* BROCHS.

CRANWELL (Lincs.). The Royal Airforce College was founded in 1920.

CRANWORTH. *See* ROLFE.

CRAPAUD (Fr = Toad). "Johny Crapaud" was a rude phrase for a Frenchman.

CRAVEN (1) Sir William (?1548-1618) of Yorkshire origin, became a rich merchant taylor of London. In 1610-11 he was Lord Mayor and entertained Christian of Anhalt, the Palatine Minister. Most of his huge wealth passed to his elder son **(2) William (1606-97) 1st Ld. CRAVEN (1627) and 1st E. of CRAVEN (1665)**. In 1632 he entered the military service of the Elector Palatine (*see* THIRTY YEARS' WAR) and became a devoted adherent of Elizabeth, the Winter Queen. He returned to England but in 1637 he led and largely financed another expedition, whose defeat resulted in his imprisonment alongside P. Rupert until 1639. In the 1640s he joined the widowed Elizabeth at The Hague where he maintained her court mostly at his own expense. His fortune was similarly at the disposal of the royalists, particularly Charles II, during the Commonwealth. He returned in 1661 and Elizabeth lived in his house until she died in 1662. His brother **(3) John (?-1648) Ld. CRAVEN of RYTON (1642)** founded the Craven Scholarships.

CRAWFORD. *See* LINDSAY.

CRAWLEY. *See* NEW TOWNS.

CRÉCY, B. of (26 Aug. 1346) Edward III had plundered northern Normandy and sacked Caen. The French K. Philip VI moved from Paris to defend Rouen. Edward was diverted by broken bridges over the R. Seine but eventually evaded Philip, quickly repaired the bridge at Poissy and reached Crécy by fording the R. Somme. He then deployed on a height and on the pattern of the B. of Halidon Hill (1333). Philip accepted the advice of his belligerent, but less experienced, knights to attack. His Genoese slow firing crossbowmen opened the attack but they were overwhelmed by the hail of English arrows. They fell back just as the French cavalry advanced and were ridden down in some confusion. During the ensuing hours of hard fighting, the English remained well under control and slew many of the French commanders, including the blind K. of Bohemia and the Counts of Flanders and Blois. Philip escaped to Amiens. Edward forbade pursuit because of his small numbers and, keeping his force together, marched on 30 Aug. for Calais. The victory confirmed Edward III's military reputation and the power of archery based on armoured support. *See plan in Appendix.*

CREDITON (Devon), the birthplace of St. Boniface, became the see for Devon which was separated from that of Sherborne in 909. In 1040 Cornwall was added to the see and in 1049 Bp. Leofric moved it to Exeter for greater safety, where it remains.

CREES were a powerful Algonquian hunting tribe inhabiting Manitoba in the 18th cent.

CREEVEY, Thomas (1768-1838) possibly an illegitimate son of the 1st E. of Sefton, was an M.P. for Thetford from 1802 to 1819 and from 1820 to 1826. A friend of Grey and Charles James Fox, his unrivalled charm made him one of the best known men in London political life. His correspondence *The Creevey Papers,* is consequently a mine of information on the period but mostly of a social character.

CREIGHTON or CRICHTON (1) Robert (1593-1672) prof. of Greek at Cambridge (1625) and a chaplain to Charles I became dean of Wells (which he restored) at the Restoration. Charles II respected his outspokenness against his own morals and made him Bp. of Bath and Wells in 1670. His son **(2) Robert (?1639-1734)** was also prof. of Greek at Cambridge from 1662 to 1674.

CREIGHTON, Mandell (1843-1901) took a leading part in organising the new see of Newcastle in 1881 and published his *History of the Papacy* between 1882 to 1894. In 1884 he became prof. of Ecclesiastical History at Cambridge and from 1886 to 1891 and was the first ed. of the *English Historical Review*. In 1896 he became Bp. of Peterborough and in 1897 Bp. of London. He wrote lives of *Card. Wolsey* (1888) and *Q. Elizabeth* (1896) and was widely respected for his practical sense as well as his learning. As Bp. of London he had to deal through his episcopal authority with the ritualistic controversy and imposed his will without offending those who disagreed with him.

CREMATION. The Queen's surgeon, Sir Henry Thompson, moved by the dreadful condition of British cemeteries, formed the Cremation Society in 1874 but cremation was not adjudged to be lawful until *R. v Price* in 1884. The first Cremation Act empowering Local Authorities to provide crematoria in 1902. By 1992 more bodies were being cremated than buried.

CRENELLATE, CRENELLATION. The characteristically indented top of a battlement, hence the battlement itself or even the building to which it belonged. The grant of a LICENCE TO CRENELLATE, i.e. to fortify a building or erect a fortification has always been within the exclusive prerogative of the Crown, even if the rule was subject to wholesale dispensation, as probably happened under William the Conqueror, or ignored, as under K. Stephen.

CREODA. *See* WEST SAXONS, EARLY.

CREOLE. (Sp. Criollo = native to the locality) means either **(1)** any person regardless of descent born or naturalised in Spanish America, Louisiana, Mauritius or especially the W. Indies, as distinct from mixed race descendants, usually called mulattos, quadroons, octoroons or mestizos; or later **(2)** any such person of mixed European and negro ancestry or **(3)** a liberated, especially Anglican, slave or his descendants now residing in W. Africa.

CRESSWELL, Madam (?-1684) a whore and procuress, much patronised after 1670 by courtiers and politicians, at Clerkenwell in the winter and at Camberwell in the summer. In later life she turned religious.

CRETE (Med.) was prosperous under Venetian rule from 1204 until the Turks attacked it in 1645. By 1648 all the island had been lost except Candia, which was besieged for twenty-one years. In the peace treaty Venice retained only three enclaves, also lost by 1715. There were abortive revolts against the Turks in 1770. In 1821 when revolt broke out in Greece the Sphakiots occupied the open country and drove the Moslems into the towns; but they were reduced in 1824 by Egyptian troops and from 1832 to 1840 Crete was part of the pashalik of Egypt. It retained its Egyptian-appointed Albanian gov. Mustafa until 1852. His benevolent rule was a golden age. After him Ottoman governors became more oppressive and corrupt and from 1856 to 1866 the island was in a turmoil. As a result of the Berlin T. (1878) and a local insurrection, the British acted as mediators for a compromise (the Pact of **Halepa)** under which a constitutional type of govt. was created. This functioned corruptly but peacefully until 1889 when the conservatives, finding themselves in a minority, took to the mountains and the Turks promptly imposed martial law. Negotiations amid civil disorder continued until a full-scale revolt in 1897. Greek troops were landed but the powers expelled them and Crete became autonomous under Turkish suzerainty. The Turkish troops were evacuated and a Greek High Commissioner, P. George of Greece, was appointed. In 1905 his govt. provoked a local reaction led by Eleutherios Venizelos, who proclaimed union with Greece to get rid of him, with important results. An international force occupied the island. In 1906 the prince was succeeded by Alexander Zäimis, who got the international force out in 1909. On the eve of the First Balkan War in Oct. 1912, Venizelos, now prime minister of Greece, admitted Cretan deputies to the Greek Parliament and by the T. of London (1913) Crete was ceded to Greece. In World War II Crete was considered to be an important outwork of the allied position in the Middle East and was violently attacked by the Germans in May and June 1941. Their conquest was a pyrrhic victory involving the loss of their only trained airborne division. *See* WORLD WAR II-7.

CREWE (Ches.) was a hamlet until the railway reached it in 1837 and the Great Central Rly opened its locomotive works there.

CREWE, E. of. Robert Uffley Ashburton CREWE-MILNES (1858-1945) was a rich, respected and cultivated Liberal. He was Lord Lieut. of Ireland (1892-5) and as Sec. of State for India (1910-5) led the Liberals in the Lords during the stormy passage of the Parliament Act 1911. He was Pres. of the Bd. of Education in 1916 and Chairman of the London County Council in 1917. He was briefly Sec. for War in the 1931 National Govt.

CREWE'S ACT 1782, passed by the Rockingham govt. disfranchised and disqualified revenue officers who formed a noticeable element in the electorate of coastal pocket boroughs, especially in Cornwall. Intended to reduce govt. influence in elections it, in practice, effected little. It was repealed in 1874.

CRICCIETH. *See* CAERNARVONSHIRE.

CRICHEL DOWN AFFAIR (1952-4). Crichel Down (Dorset) was requisitioned by the Min. of Ag. in 1937. In 1952 the former owner attempted to exercise his right to buy it back but was constantly obstructed by ministry officials. A parliamentary storm led to a public inquiry, which found no corruption but criticised official partiality. Sir Thos. Dugdale, the minister, was forced to resign.

CRICKET is supposed to have been played at Guildford School in 1550 and by Oliver Cromwell as a boy. The earliest circumstantial reference was at Winchester College in 1650, the first eleven-a-side match apparently took place in 1697 and the first county standard match recorded in detail was Kent *v* All England at Finsbury Artillery Ground in June 1744. Shortly afterwards the Hambledon Club at Broadhalfpenny Down (Hants.) began to dominate the scene. In 1777 this village club beat All England by over an innings and its career, which ended in 1793, permanently influenced the technique and rules. The Marylebone Cricket Club (M.C.C.) was established in 1787 and revised the laws of cricket in 1788. In 1813 Thomas Lord finally established the cricket ground named after him at St. Johns Wood. County cricket began in 1873 and Test Matches started in 1876. The Australian victory at the Oval in 1882 gave rise to the comic announcement that British cricket was to be cremated, from which the term 'Ashes' (The test match prize) springs.

CRIMEAN WAR. (1) Since about 1840 the Czar Nicholas I had sought to control the Ottoman Empire as a whole, rather than seek a partition, by securing the allegiance and becoming the protector of the **Millet-i-Rum** (*see* MILLET), that is, of the entire body of orthodox Christians throughout the Ottoman dominions, representing about 40% of the population. This might have given Russia not only control of the Straits and the Aegean coasts, but could have extended her influence to the Adriatic in one direction and to N. Africa, the Red Sea and the Persian Gulf in the other. This was unacceptable to France (Bonapartist by 1853), who had special interests and growing ambitions in Egypt and N. Africa; to the Austrians, who feared Russian penetration in the Balkans and to the British who saw a weak but still functioning and dependent Ottoman Empire as their best guarantee for the safety of the approaches to India.

(2) The pretext for Russian pressure on the Sublime Porte was a monkish dispute about the custody of certain holy places at Jerusalem. The R. Catholics, supported by Louis Napoleon, obtained judgement from the Ottoman authorities against the Orthodox, who angled for Russian support. The Orthodox Czar demanded the reversal of the judgement and recognition as Protector of the Millet-i-Rum. These demands were made on 19 Apr. 1853. On the advice of Ld. Stratford de Redcliffe, the British ambassador, the Porte offered a compromise on the first and refused the second on 21 May; on 4 June an Anglo-French fleet assembled off the Dardanelles. On 2 July Russian troops began to occupy Moldavia and Wallachia, the semi-autonomous Roumanian principalities under Turkish suzerainty, as hostages for the fulfilment of the Russian demands. A conference at Vienna failed on 20 Sept. The Porte issued a 15-day ultimatum requiring the evacuation of the principalities and declared war on 4 Oct. While Turkish troops put up a spirited resistance in the Bulgarian quadrilateral, the Russian fleet sank a Turkish squadron at **Sinope** on 30 Nov. *See* IRONCLADS.

(3) This epoch making Black Sea victory under (it was pictured) the very noses of the Anglo-French navies, excited political opinion in London and Paris. British troops were sent to Malta and the combined fleets received Ottoman permission to enter the Black Sea in Dec., just as the Russians made a further central Asiatic advance by annexing Khiva. It soon became apparent that it was not enough to confine the fighting to the land. On 12 Mar. 1854 Britain, France and Turkey signed an alliance and jointly demanded Russian withdrawal. This was refused; on 27 and 28 Mar. France and Britain declared war, while in Apr. Austria and Prussia signed a defensive alliance against Russia.

(4) A British force began to reach Constantinople at the end of Apr. and was quartered at the gigantic Selimiye barracks at Scutari (Üsküdar), opposite the city. It consisted of a cavalry division and five infantry divisions of varying strength under Ld. Raglan. The fighting troops were excellent regulars under competent regimental officers. The generals and staff were second rate and untrained. The medical and supply arrangements, where they existed, were appallingly bad and corrupt.

(5) The Ottoman Empire was in the grip of a cholera epidemic, which soon began to kill off the British troops. The probability of a Russian breakthrough in the Quadrilateral also made a move essential. In June the army sailed to Varna on the flank of an expected Russian line of advance, but the Turks were making good their defence and the Russians, who were dying of cholera too, had already decided to abandon the Roumanian principalities when the Austrians demanded that they should. At the end of June, therefore, they retreated and their troops in Roumania were everywhere replaced (with Turkish agreement) by Austrians. The Russians had thus lost the principal means whereby they were seeking to dominate Turkey.

(6) The only remaining issue, therefore, related to Western fears about the Straits. Neither the Porte nor the Western powers wanted a permanent Anglo-French naval presence in the Black Sea; Sinope seemed to point to the destruction of Russian naval power there as the only alternative. That power was based on the Crimean port of Sevastopol. It was resolved to invade the Crimea.

(7) The Anglo-French landed at Calamita Bay north of Sevastopol on 14 Sept. On 20 Sept the seemingly impregnable Russian position on the heights behind the **R. Alma** was stormed by the infantry in three hours. The victory was not, however, followed up and the allies, instead of marching quickly upon the north of the fortress marched round it and began a leisurely investment from the south and east, based upon the inadequate ports of Kamiesh and Balaclava. This gave Todleben, the garrison engineer, time to design and build very effective fortifications where virtually none had existed before and Menshikov, the Russian C-in-C time to form a large army outside the allied lines which prevented the allied investment from ever being complete.

(8) The first effort at relief was an unsuccessful attack from the east on **Balaclava** (q.v.) on 25 Oct. His second a combined attempt from the City and from the north against the British position at **Inkerman** on 5 Nov. This was repelled after desperate fighting in a fog in which allied losses were so great that it was deemed impossible to take the port by storm. More deliberate siege works were therefore undertaken but the winter of 1854-5 was exceptionally severe throughout Europe and the British (but not the French) army was inadequately equipped for the cold, or medically equipped to recover from the effects of disease. Half the British army was lost in that winter. The Austrian posture kept most of the Russian army in Poland and so prevented the Russian Crimean army from being reinforced, but in the spring of 1855

large French and less British reinforcements arrived. On 18 June the works were attacked. The French successfully occupied the **Mamelon,** a large work in advance of the vital Malakoff fortification, the British were murderously defeated at the **Redan.** The fall of the Mamelon, however, enabled the French to approach the Malakoff by trenching, at which they had become very expert; and the allied bombardment was doing fearful damage. The Russian C-in-C (now Gortshakov) therefore attempted a further relief from the north and on 16 Aug. was bloodily repulsed by the French on the **R. Chernaya.** Gortshakov now decided to evacuate the city and a bridge of boats was built to the north side of the inlet. On 8 Sept. in a combined assault the French surprised the Malakoff and the British were again repulsed at the Redan, but the fall of the Malakoff being decisive, the Russians withdrew and made good their escape. On 26 Nov., however, they captured the Turkish Causasian fortress of Kars. Peace preliminaries were signed on 1 Feb. 1856. *See* PARIS, CONGRESS OF 1856.

CRIMES AGAINST HUMANITY and AGAINST PEACE. *See* WAR CRIMES.

CRIMINAL APPEAL, COURT of, was set up in 1907.

CRIMINAL LAW. The subject, in detail, is beyond the scope of this work, but *see* FELONY; MISDEMEANOUR.

CRIMP. One who made a man drunk, got him to sign naval or regimental articles of service and took the recruiting bounty. The practice was not extinct in 1911.

CRINAN CANAL. *See* TRANSPORT AND COMMUNICATIONS.

CRINOLINE, originally a stiffening material of horsehair and linen, and then the large hooped skirts made fashionable by Q. Victoria during her first pregnancy. The latter made women physically unapproachable yet (to some) more seductive. It went out of fashion in about 1868.

CRIPPS (1) Charles Alfred (1852-1941) 1st Ld. PARMOOR (1914) was a conservative M.P. for Stroud from 1895, when he became the P. of Wales' Att.Gen. He was subsequently M.P. for Stretford (1901-6) and High Wycombe (1910-4). He was against the war and moved over to the Labour Party, being Lord Pres. in their govts. of 1924 and 1929 to 1931. He also had ecclesiastical interests and was Vicar-Gen. of York from 1900 to 1914 and of Canterbury from 1902 to 1924, as well as Chairman of the House of Laity from 1920 to 1924. Meanwhile his famous son **(2) Sir (Richard) Stafford (1889-1952)** became a highly efficient dep-super-intendent of the Queensferry explosives factory in 1915, where overwork ruined his health and condemned him to a life of austerity. From 1919 he had a brilliant career at the bar and in 1930 Herbert Morrison persuaded him to join the Labour Party. He became Sol-Gen. and in 1931 M.P for Bristol East, but refused to join Ramsay MacDonald's National Govt. and moved rapidly to the far left of the time. He was a leading member of the Socialist League: he wanted to abolish the House of Lords, expected "opposition from Buckingham Palace" and advocated establishing socialism through the mechanism of orders under a blanket Emergency Powers Act. In 1936 he was a prime mover in an attempt (The United Front) to combine the Labour, Independent Labour and Communist parties. The Labour Party reacted by ruling that members who appeared on platforms with the other two would be automatically expelled, but re-elected Sir Stafford to its own executive in 1937. He then began to advocate a wider, but necessarily looser alliance (The Popular Front) which would have included the Liberals and even some Tories, and whose purpose was to oust the Chamberlain govt. In the autumn of 1938 he announced the programme and, having refused the Labour Party's request to withdraw it, was expelled in Jan. 1939. He was now a lone hand but his extraordinary gifts, his private charm and his capacity for inspiring loyalty kept him many followers. After World War II broke out (Sept. 1939) he went, at Ld. Halifax's instigation, on an important world tour. In India he met and liked most of the leading politicians; in Moscow he formed the naive conclusion that it was not only necessary but possible to prevent the Germans and the Russians from becoming active allies. Churchill, just become prime minister, sent him in June 1940 back as ambassador to Moscow where, in view of the recent partition of Poland, he was belatedly disillusioned. The mission was a total failure, given a spurious aura of success only by the Germans' treachery. He happened to be in London when they invaded Russia (June 1941) and was instantly sworn of the Privy Council and sent back to negotiate the mutual assistance pact of July 1941. In Jan. 1942, when he returned, he came in on the crest of Russian popularity engendered by public relief that Britain at last had an effective European ally. He became leader of the House of Commons, Lord Privy Seal and a member of the cabinet. Within weeks he was sent to India to obtain fuller Indian support for the war, but his discussions with Indian Congress leaders eventually failed, sabotaged, he believed, by Gandhi who took no part in them. The failure reduced his popularity and created disagreements with Churchill, He resigned in Nov. 1942 and was appointed (largely as a result of his technical experience in World War I) Min. of Aircraft Production, in which post he was a great success. Consequently, when the Labour Party won the post-war election, Cripps was readmitted to it and became Pres. of the Board of Trade. While wrestling with the economic problems, he also had to go to India, again as the effective leader of a cabinet mission. This again failed, for though Cripps had done his utmost to involve Gandhi in the discussions, the Congress withdrew its acceptance of Cripps' proposals after the Moslem League had accepted them. He had, however one success: he convinced the rival parties that the British really meant to leave. In Oct. 1947 Cripps, who had achieved a powerful influence in the Home economy, became Min. for Economic Affairs and then (because of Dalton's indiscretion) almost immediately Ch. of the Exchequer. By force of argument and sincerity he established the only successful voluntary wages and profits freeze, which lasted from Feb. 1948 to Sept. 1949, but ended with the dollar crisis and the devaluation of the pound. By now overwork was destroying his vitality and in Oct. 1950 he resigned from sheer exhaustion. His son **(3) Sir John (Stafford) (1912-93)** was Chairman of the Rural District Councils Association from 1967 to 1970 and of the Countryside Commission from 1970.

CRISP, Sir Nicholas (?1599-1666) enterprising financier and royalist, received with five others the monopoly of the Guinea trade in 1632 and the farm of the great and petty customs in 1640. Expelled from the Commons as a monopolist in 1641, he was fined for having levied customs without parliamentary authority. In 1643 he was discovered raising funds in the City and sending them to the King. He got away to Oxford where he used his London connections to foment plots to raise the City against the Parliament. He also raised a regiment. In 1644 he was commissioned to form a naval squadron, but in 1645 when his property was sequestrated, he fled to France. He was a supporter of Monck's Restoration in 1660 and in 1662 he bought the royal debts to the HEIC.

CRISPIN, Gilbert (?-1117) entered the Abbey of Bec (Normandy) as a child oblate and became a pupil of the future Abp. Lanfranc, about whom he recorded a great deal in his *Life of Abbot Herluin* of Bec. In 1080 he joined Christ Church Canterbury, now under Lanfranc's leadership, and in 1085 became Abbot of Westminster. He was one of a small but important group of scholar administrators who became heads of English monasteries through Lanfranc's influence.

CROATIA. *See* HUNGARY; YUGOSLAVIA.

CROCKFORD, John (?1823-65), printer and **COX, Edward William (1809-79)** had offices in the same building and so a loose business association. Cox had founded the LAW TIMES in 1843; Crockford his CLERICAL DIRECTORY in 1858. This absorbed the CLERGY LIST in 1917.

CROCQUET was originally played in a French convent in Ulster, whence it spread to England after 1852 and became quickly popular. *Alice in Wonderland* (1865) shows that its potential readership knew the game.

CROFT, Henry Page (1881-1947) was a conservative M.P. from 1910 to 1940. He published the *Path of Empire* in 1912 and in 1918 made opposition to Lloyd George's sale of honours a part of his election programme. He attacked Lloyd George's negotiations with the Irish and in the mid-1930s was a fervent opponent of concessions to the Indian National Congress.

CROFTS are smallholdings in the Scottish western and northern coastal counties and the islands. They cannot exceed 50 acres (though most are of less than 25) excluding common rights, and the rent could not exceed £50. Since 1886 tenants have been protected against eviction and entitled to various compensations. Since the Crofters Act, 1955, which set up the CROFTERS COMMISSION, they have been entitled to certain grants.

CROMARTY (Scot.). The lands of Cromarty belonged to the Mackenzies, who acquired other estates scattered throughout Ross-shire, particularly at Ullapool and Loch Fannich. These all descended to the 1st E. of Cromarty (1630-1714) who got them annexed to his Sheriffdom of Cromarty in 1685 and 1698. They thus formed a single but scattered shire which was not unified with Ross until 1889.

CROMIER. *See* EGYPT.

CROMMELIN, Samuel-Louis (1652-1727) and his brothers **Alexander, Samuel and William** were rich Picard Huguenot flax growers and spinners who migrated to Amsterdam in 1685 and set up as bankers. In 1698 William III asked Samuel-Louis to report on the Huguenot colony at Lisburn (Ulster) (*see* TEXTILES; IRELAND) and as a result he received a patent and himself lent the govt. £10,000 to carry out necessary works. He improved the excellent Irish spinning wheel, imported 1000 looms from Flanders and Holland, trained Irish apprentices, got in Dutch farmers to teach the locals how to grow flax and imported skilled workmen from Cambrai ("Cambric"). By 1701 Irish linen and cambric were superseding foreign in England and Ireland and new factories were opened at Kilkenny (1705), Rathkeale, Cork and Waterford (1717) and Rathbride (1725).

CROMWELL (1) Oliver (1599-1658). Second son of a declining gentry family, became M.P. for Huntingdon in 1628 and in 1629 spoke in favour of religious freedom of speech for those reformers who rejected the Elizabethan and Laudian settlement. At 39 he experienced a religious mortification, now describing himself as 'the chief of sinners'. As M.P. for Cambridge in 1640 he moved the second reading of Strode's bill for annual parliaments and spoke for the exclusion of bishops from the House of Lords. His practical bent began to show when politics developed towards civil war. He moved the establishment of the military Committee of Safety in 1642, provided money and then took the field, commanding a troop of horse under Essex at Edgehill, where he observed the need for professionalism in training. Recruiting his troop into a regiment, he spent the next 18 months equipping it and developing its tactical abilities in E. Anglia. In 1643 he used it to suppress royalists at Lowestoft and capture Stamford, thus cementing the newly formed EASTERN ASSOCIATION; he was then gov. of the I. of Ely where he recruited and trained more troops. Now recognised as the ablest of the parliamentary officers and his 'Ironsides' being universally respected, he became the E. of Manchester's 2-in-C, worsted a substantial royalist force at Gainsborough and commanded a wing at the B. of Marston Moor, which was won mainly by him and his troops. (*See* CIVIL WAR-12.13.)

His men were specially chosen as Independents temperamentally inclined to political liberty and religious nonconformity, welded together by his personality into a sternly disciplined military force for whose welfare and rights he felt responsible. They suffered the miseries of war, while presbyterians at Westminster tried to impose their own religious tyranny. When Oliver claimed the credit for Marston Moor for his men he entered the highest level of politics. Sensing that control of the army was necessary to defeat both King and presbyterians, he then set about achieving it. His position of strength was confirmed when the Self-Denying Ordinance (q.v.) purged the army of peers. When the army overthrew the King and purged Parliament, religious independence was saved at the cost of autocracy. Cromwell, seeing the inconsistency of his position, laboured to re-establish a constitutional balance, but as each experiment failed the next approximated more closely to the formal monarchy which his army had abolished. His use of Hampton Court Palace and acceptance of lands worth £4000 a year was consistent with this and at least he prevented those reforms conceded before the civil war from developing beyond a point where Restoration might have become impossible. After the final defeat of the Scots royalists at Worcester in Aug. 1651 his membership on the committees to select commissioners for law reform and for the Propagation of the Gospel promised legislative change informed by a new tolerance. His victories over the Scots covenanters had provided evidence of the penalties of intolerance (*see* CIVIL WAR; COMMONWEALTH AND PROTECTORATE-3,4). 'I had rather that Mahometanism were permitted amongst us than that one of God's children should be persecuted.'

The outbreak of the Dutch war and its finance from Royalists' possessions suggested other less liberal trends. The ending of the Long Parliament over his and the Army's objections to a bill to enfranchise those formerly neutral (or deserters), shows the brief limits to the tolerance vaunted in 1651. The Little Parliament which followed confirmed his common feelings for the *junta* which must necessarily impede any democratic and levelling tendencies. Ordinances against duelling, cock-fighting, horse-racing, adultery and swearing commenced a Cromwellian legislative onslaught on current manners (*see* COMMONWEALTH AND PROTECTORATE-12).

The difficulties of his situation were also reflected in his foreign policies. No sooner had the internal wars to establish the Commonwealth been ended (Surrender of Limerick Oct. 1651) than war broke out with the Dutch (*see* DUTCH WAR-1). This was partly in pursuit of the shipping and commercial interests of the City which had backed the parliament in the overthrow of the King. It was also necessary to keep the grossly inflated forces busy. The Dutch War having ended with a treaty favourable to Baltic trade in Apr. 1654, a Spanish war was immediately commenced and a trade treaty concluded with the Portuguese. After the seizure of Jamaica (May 1655) the fleet was sent to bombard Tunis. Then the Flota was destroyed in Santa Cruz (Apr. 1657) while troops went to the help of the French at Dunkirk.

Of his character little good is said. The charitable Richard Baxter (q.v.) said that 'he thought Secrecy a Vertue, and Dissimulation no Vice, and Simulation, that is in plain English a Lie, or Perfidiousness to be a tolerable Faith in Case of Necessity'. Thus 'he kept fair with all, saving his open or unreconcileable enemies'.

His son **(2) Richard (1626-1712)** was M.P. for Hampshire in 1654 and for Cambridge in 1656 and a member of the Committee for Trade and Navigation from 1655. Oliver twice nominated him as his successor (31

Aug. and 2 Sept. 1658) and he succeeded on 3 Sept. A type of the respectable country gentleman, he was temperamentally unfitted for his father's office and abdicated on 25 May 1659. (*See* COMMONWEALTH AND PROTECTORATE-16-18.) In 1660 he retired to Paris where he lived under the name of John Clarke until 1680. Returning to England he lived modestly on his country estate, while his abler brother **(3) Henry (1628-74)** became a parliamentary colonel and drove Inchiquin into Limerick in 1650. M.P. for Ireland in Barebone's parliament of 1653, Henry then returned to Ireland to deal with extremists, becoming Irish maj-gen. (C. of Staff), a member of the Irish Council in 1654 and responsible for carrying the transplantation of the Irish into effect – an operation of great thoroughness. Becoming Lord Deputy in 1657, he attempted to reform the administration and army. When his father died he became gov-gen. of Ireland and it was on his advice that Richard Cromwell called a parliament. Loyally resisting royalist approaches in 1659, he retired to England when it was evident that the regime was collapsing. Although his English properties were forfeited, those in Connaught and Meath were confirmed at the Restoration.

CROMWELL, Ralph (1394-1456) 3rd Ld. CROMWELL, a member, though young, of the council during Henry XI's minority, was a financial official and eventually Lord Treasurer from 1433 to 1443. He owned Tattersall and built the castle and quarrelled, apparently over local issues, with William de la Pole, D. of Suffolk, who in 1449 tried to have him murdered. Accordingly he supported the moves which ended in Suffolk's death in 1450.

CROMWELL, Thomas (?1485-1540) I.d. CROMWELL (1536) E. of ESSEX (1540), son of a dishonest and drunken Putney odd job man, learned soldiering with the French in Italy, banking in Florence and business in Antwerp, where he acquired connections in the cloth trade. On a second visit to Italy he introduced himself to Pope Julius II, it is said, in song. He settled finally in England in 1512, married a wife with money and engaged in money lending, cloth trading and legal practice. He became acquainted with Card. Wolsey and from 1520 became his man of business. He entered parliament in 1523 and made himself potentially dangerous and necessary to Wolsey by drafting a speech against taxation to finance the current war with France. In 1524 he was called to the bar by Gray's Inn. Wolsey's disastrous experiment with the Amicable Grant was followed in 1525 by an inquiry, on which Cromwell served, into the state of lesser monasteries (18 had been suppressed in 1518 for the benefit of Wolsey's colleges). By now he was the Cardinal's influential secretary, fully conversant with all considerations of policy. He was also ready to be useful to Norfolk and his friends and understood something of parliamentary management.

(2) The attack on clerical prestige began, as Wolsey's policy was failing and he in disgrace, by Acts against various abuses of probate, sanctuary and pluralities, in the parliament of 1529. Cromwell, who had some hand in this, must have been in contact with the King but he spoke for Wolsey in the Commons. In Nov. 1529 the Cardinal was charged in the King's Bench and at some time afterwards Cromwell had a long private interview with Henry. What was said is unknown; Wolsey, however, was pardoned in Feb. 1530 but surrendered much of his wealth (including Hampton Court) to the King. In Nov. the attack on him was resumed but he died. The King's attorney then raised a *praemunire* against the entire clergy for having recognised Wolsey's legatine commission (Dec. 1530) and they appeased the King with £118,840. His pardon was ratified in parliament with an indemnity to the laity (Feb. 1531) and an admission of the royal supremacy in ecclesiastical affairs.

(3) Henry's intrigue with Anne Boleyn was by now

far advanced: her father, as the new Lord Privy Seal, was no match for the conservative More as Chancellor and Gardiner as Secretary. Cromwell had become a privy councillor in 1530, though he had had the King's ear for sometime already, and the tactics of a break with Rome by means of a series of Statutes were probably his idea. In Mar. 1532 the Commons presented the *Supplication against the Ordinaries*, an extremist attack on clerical jurisdictions and on the independent right of the convocations to pass canon laws. Cromwell was responsible for the cohesion of this attack, derived from a mass of separate grievances presented in the previous session. The convocations began to prepare reforms but Henry invited them to consider the abolition of their legislative powers. They insisted on their rights but suggested that canons should require a royal licence. Gardiner, who had drafted their reply, was disgraced and in May Henry asserted that the clergy were 'but half our subjects' and had the bishops oath of papal obedience read in parliament. The result was the *Submission of the Clergy* (15 May 1532). Next day More resigned.

(4) Cromwell now secured the lucrative Mastership of the Wards, the lordship of Romney (S. Wales) and the Chancellorship of the Exchequer and began to conduct the King's imperial correspondence. The Act in Restraint of Appeals to Rome, drafted by Cromwell, enabled Cranmer as Archbishop to pronounce finally against Henry's marriage and in 1533 the King acknowledged his marriage with Anne, and Cromwell naturally took over the Secretaryship from Gardiner and in 1534 the Mastership of the Rolls as well. With a foot in every important govt. agency he could influence the advice reaching Henry from departments not his own. The Act of Supremacy 1534 declared the royal supremacy in ecclesiastical affairs and in Jan. 1535 he became the King's Vicar General and Vicegerent in Spirituals. The year was spent in compiling the *Valor Ecclesiasticus:* in the next year this formed the basis of the first monastic visitation. Some 220 smaller monasteries were suppressed, with the acquiescence of parliament and especially of the relieved parliamentary abbots.

(5) Meanwhile in the political crisis surrounding Anne Boleyn's execution (May 1536) convocation, under Cromwell's chairmanship, ratified the retrospective annulment of her marriage (*see* CRANMER, THOMAS) and went on to accept the *Ten Articles* under which he later issued the *Royal Injunctions*. He also became Lord Privy Seal and, as such, the leading member of the Star Chamber and Court of Requests.

(6) The reformist policy which he now pursued, provoked the *Pilgrimage of Grace* (1536) which, in its turn, led to the creation of a new Council of the North. The expenses of suppression were, however, very great and the result was, first, an attack on pilgrimage shrines, which yielded large sums and then on the surviving monasteries. Between 1538 and 1540 they and the establishments of the Order of St. John were suppressed.

(7) In Dec. 1538 the Pope ordered the execution of the papal bull of excommunication against Henry, originally issued in 1535. Henry and Cromwell tried to secure imperial or French allies by marriage offers which were rebuffed. The imperialist duchess of Mantua said that she had only one head; the French that their ladies were not to be inspected like ponies. Hence Cromwell fatally resorted to a second best. By the T. of Westminster (4 Oct. 1538) Henry was to marry Anne, sister of William, D. of Cleves, a reforming but not Lutheran ruler who had just acquired Gelders. The marriage tied in with a new policy of reciprocity in wool dealings with the Low Countries but it proved to be diplomatically unnecessary because France and the Emperor neutralised each other by mutual hostility. Anne then arrived (1 Jan. 1540) and Henry found her repellent, but dutifully married her (6th). He thus harboured resentments against Cromwell

for international and more intimate reasons, which the attractions of Norfolk's niece, Catharine Howard, did nothing to allay. Moreover Cromwell had too many offices and, it seemed, too much money was passing through his hands. A Howard intrigue brought him down. The King was convinced that he was too powerful. On 10 June he was suddenly arrested on allegations of treason at the Council Table. Attainted on 29th he was beheaded a month later. It turned out that corrupt though he was, he was much less wealthy than was generally believed and that some of his fortune was being used to maintain the poor

CROP ROTATION. The mediaeval open fields were commonly and, subject to local variation, arranged in threes, annually changed: viz (i) winter sown cereal (rye or wheat), (ii) a spring cereal (barley or oats) and (iii) fallow or beans. 16th and 17th cent. experiments led, after the Restoration, to a four year rotation viz (1) autumn cereal (usually wheat); (2) roots (turnips or mangolds), potatoes or cabbage; (3) spring cereal; (4) peas or beans and clover. This system improved the land and made it possible to feed more cattle in the winter and fold more sheep. It spread from Norfolk and multiplied the productivity of the flatter, well drained areas many times. It has since been modified for 5 to 8 year rotations. *See* COKE.

CROPS, CROP-EARS or CROP-EARED. One who had lost his ears in the pillory. The phrase was used, by royalists, of Puritans or Roundheads.

CROSLAND, Charles Anthony Raven (1908-77) became a Labour M.P. in 1950, Min. of State for Economic Affairs in 1964; Sec. of State for Education in 1965, Pres. of the B. of Trade in 1867 and Sec. of State for Local Govt. from 1969 to 1970.

CROSS BENCHES. Seats facing the woolsack in the House of Lords. Deemed not to be on either side, they are considered the proper place for non-party peers. The similarly placed seats in the Commons only occasionally have this association.

CROSSBOW. *See* ARCHERY.

CROSSMAN, Richard Howard Stafford (1907-74), a Wykehamist, took a first in Greats at Oxford (1930), became a fellow of New College, but travelled for a year in Germany during Hitler's rise towards power. This awakened his political instincts. He was an ebullient and successful lecturer but had become heavily involved with the Labour Party. From 1940 to 1945, impelled by Hugh Dalton, he organised propaganda. He became M.P. for Coventry in 1945. Able but mistrusted, he was denied office for 19 years, so turned to internal Labour politics and assisted the rise of Aneurin Bevan and later of Harold Wilson. In the Wilson govt. of 1964 he was Min. of Housing and Local Govt. and as such set up the Redcliffe-Maude Commission; in 1966 he became Lord Pres. and leader of the Commons when he originated the system of departmental committees. Between 1968 and 1970 he organised the Dept. of Health and Social Services. He left the govt. in 1970 and became Ed. of the *New Statesman* but was dismissed in 1972. In his published *Diaries* he later made lucrative use, without permission, of much confidential experience and information.

CROUCHBACK, sobriquet of **(1)** Edmund, E. of Lancaster (1245-96), son of Henry III, **(2)** Richard III.

CROUP. *See* DIPHTHERIA.

CROWE (1) Eyre Evans (1799-1868) worked on the *Morning Chronicle* and as Ed. of the *Daily News* from 1849 to 1851. He also wrote historical works. Of his two sons **(2) Eyre (1824-1910)** an artist, was sec. to W. M. Thackeray, the author and **(3) Sir Joseph Archer (1825-96)** had sensational journalistic assignments in the Crimea, the Indian Mutiny and the Franco-Austrian War of 1859 and then progressed from the consul-generalship in Saxony (1860) to that in Westphalia and the Rhineland

(1872) and then to the office of Commercial Attaché in Vienna (1880) and so for the whole of Europe, centred on Paris (1882). He married a German wife and his career contributed notably to the distinction of his son **(4) Sir Eyre Alexander Barby Wichart (1864-1925).** He also married a German wife and entered the Foreign Office in 1885. He was one of the best informed critics of German attitudes and policies of the time. He had a strong influence in the formation of the *Entente* and in 1907, in particular, composed a powerful memorandum on the reasons for it and the aggressive tendencies developing in Germany. In 1912 he became permanent U. Sec. of State at the Foreign Office. In 1914 he advocated supporting France and he was a British plenipotentiary at Versailles in 1919.

CROWLAND or CROYLAND (Lincs.) was a fen island in the 7th cent. when St. Guthlac (?-714) set up a hermitage there. K. Ethelbald built the first abbey in 716. This was destroyed by the Danes in about 860 and rebuilt between 948 and 975. It was already very rich by the Conquest, but its great period extended from 1392 to 1470. The buildings mostly survived until they were bombarded by Oliver Cromwell in 1643.

CROWLEY, Sir Ambrose (1658-1713) had three ironworks near Newcastle on Tyne, several distributive warehouses and was a major naval supplier in the Wars of Louis XIV. He also became a director of the South Sea Co.

CROWN. The English regalia having been sold under the Commonwealth, a new St. Edward's Crown had to be made for the Coronation of Charles II in 1661. The Imperial State Crown used on occasions other than the Coronation was made for Q. Victoria in 1838. The arches of the Scottish Crown date from 1489; the circlet from the reign of James V (151342).

CROWN AGENTS (FOR THE COLONIES). 18th cent. colonial governors sometimes appointed agents for commercial and quasi-diplomatic purposes in England. In 1833 these were consolidated into a single body of JOINT AGENTS-GENERAL FOR CROWN COLONIES. The name was changed in 1863; they ceased to' be under Treasury control in 1880. In 1967 their principals included 80 govts. and 120 overseas public authorities.

CROWN COURT. *See* QUARTER SESSIONS-5.

CROWN ESTATE or LANDS. The various crown demesne lands, managed respectively by the Crown Estate Commissioners (who succeeded the Crown Lands Commissioners in 1956), the Dept of the Environment (which succeeded the Ministry, formerly the Board of Works), the Forestry Commission and other depts. *See* CIVIL LIST.

CROWN (GOLD). *See* COINAGE-15.

CROWN MATRIMONIAL (Scots). The right of the husband of a Scottish Queen regnant to reign as King.

CROWN OFFICE (Eng) managed the CROWN SIDE, i.e. the criminal and the prerogative business of the Court of the King's Bench. Its head was the King's Coroner and Attorney (otherwise the Master of the Crown Office) and its clerks and other officers who, paid by a burdensome system of fees, had a monopoly of Crown practice. In 1843 the staff was reduced, subordinated to the Chief Justice and became salaried, while attorneys were admitted to the Crown Side. It was amalgamated with the Central Office of the Supreme Court in 1879 but some of the procedures which it operated still survive.

CROWN PROCEEDINGS. At Common Law **(1)** the sovereign could not be impleaded in his own court. **(2)** The crown had special legal privileges and immunities, particularly immunity from liability for damages for torts committed by its servants and special methods of enforcing its own claims against subjects, particularly by way of writs of *capias, subpoena* and appraisement. **(3)** The only ways of proceeding against the crown were by Petition of Right which, if granted the royal *fiat*, was tried in court and ended with a judgement (which in theory might be ignored) or by action for a declaration against the Attorney-Gen. or by action against ministers or departments which had been incorporated or declared liable to suit by Statute. **(4)** The Crown Proceedings Act, 1947, abolished all these ancient rules save that the Sovereign still cannot be personally impleaded.

CROWN (SILVER). *See* COINAGE-14.

CROWTHER, Geoffrey (1907-72) Ld. CROWTHER (1968), on the advice of J. M. Keynes, was appointed Banking adviser to the Irish govt. in 1932 and on the same advice a member of the staff of the *Economist,* which he was to edit from 1938 to 1956. His skill and style quintupled the readership. In World War II he was employed in the Min. of Supply (1940-1) and then of Information (1941-2) and eventually as Head of the Joint Production Staff. After he resigned the editorship he went into business as chairman of Economist Newspaper Ltd and the Commercial Union Assurance. He created the Trafalgar House property group and was chairman of Trust Houses when they merged with Forte Holdings. He was also Chairman of the Central Advisory Council for Education (1956-60), which produced the well-known report (*see below*), Chanc. of the Open University and Chairman of the Royal Commission on the Constitution.

CROWTHER REPORT (1959) recommended that the school leaving age should be raised from 15 to 16. *See previous entry.*

CROYDON was a summer residence of the Abps. of Canterbury from 1086 to 1758, and from 1808 to 1896 they had a palace at Addington Place. The historically important aerodrome was opened in 1915, became the London airport in 1926 and was closed in 1959. The borough was transferred from Surrey to London in 1963. The palace became the H.Q. of the English School of Church Music.

CROYDON TREASURE was a hoard of Arabic, Frankish and English 9th cent. coins found in 1862. The depositor was presumably a Viking from Sweden where large amounts of Arabic coinage have been found.

CRUISER (1) Under sail a cruiser was a warship large enough to maintain itself at sea so as to cruise for long periods. Hence all line-of-battle ships and frigates were cruisers. Smaller craft, dependent upon other ships, were not. **(2)** Under steam a cruiser was smaller and faster than a battleship with much lighter guns and little or no armour, but capable of venturing into any seas. The BATTLE CRUISER was a compromise between a Dreadnought type of battleship and a cruiser, but closer to the former. An ARMOURED CRUISER was a similar compromise in the pre-Dreadnought period. Many ships survived from one period into the next and by 1960 the term had become technically almost meaningless.

CRUSADES, BALTIC (1) differed from southern crusades. They were campaigns, ideologically to conquer and convert heathens and schismatics (i.e. Russian orthodox Christians) and mundanely to suppress the lawlessness which interrupted trade and depopulated the coasts; and they seldom had an amateurish constitution, being mostly directed by the Danish and Swedish monarchies and the Teutonic Knights.

(2) Crusades against the Wends at the neck of Jutland and in the Eastern Baltic began simultaneously in 1128. The latter had achieved superficial conquests by 1137: the former went on till 1185 and went deeper. By 1228 when the Teutonic Knights became active the work in the east had to be done again, and it was not till 1283 that operations began in Lithuania, or 1295 when the Orthodox Russians of Novgorod were attacked. The Swedes meanwhile entered S.W. Finland, the Danes Estonia, and the Knights attacked the Prussians. The dispersal of effort led to unreliable results. The attackers were powerfully armed but heavily outnumbered by enemies who knew the lakes and forests better than they. Progress was fitful.

(3) Tactically a base would be set up, from which, when the ground was firm, raids (*reysen* = journeys) were launched into the neighbourhood – two around Christmas and a large one between May and Sept. They never lasted more than two months. Big battles were rare but the human and material damage might, in wearing down tribal resistance, impoverish the conquest. Nevertheless, with secondary colonisation, the crusaders set up four states or jurisdictions namely Finland (Swedish), Estonia (Danish) Prussia and Livonia (Knights).

(4) These movements reached natural limits when Muscovy and Polono–Lithuania began to feel the need for Baltic commercial outlets, unobstructed by coastal powers. From 1400 Muscovy intervened in the Norgorod–Pskov region. The Poles overwhelmingly defeated the Knights at Tannenberg in 1410. By then Baltic crusading was stagnant.

CRUSADES, SOUTHERN. (1) The West Christians ingested the idea of a holy war from the Mohammedan *jihad*, initially in reaction to the Moorish sack of St. James of Compostella in 997. Moslem raiders sacked Narbonne in 1020. K. Sancho the Great of Navarre tried and only partially succeeded in forming a Christian alliance (1014) but he did obtain powerful Cluniac propagandist support. Hence the assassination of K. Ramiro I of Aragon by a Moslem in 1063, on the eve of a campaign against the Moors of Valencia, electrified European opinion and Pope Alexander II promised indulgences for those who joined it. Campaigns with Papal blessing took place in 1064, 1073, 1078 and led to the capture of Toledo in 1085. The Almoravid counter-attack provoked further desperate expeditions in 1087, 1096 and 1101.

(2) These mainly French and Aquitanian crusades were partly inspired by the loss, through Moorish aggression, of the valuable **pilgrim traffic.** The leaders, if not English, were related to Anglo-Norman nobles and though English govts. were not involved, these crusades exercised their magic on opinion and continuously influenced trade, whether across the Languedoc isthmus or through the Straits. English people often joined privately and, as will be seen, five later crusades profoundly influenced English and Norman affairs.

(3) Urban II (Pope 1088-99) was interested in Christian unity and had to deal simultaneously with the split (since 1054) between the Western and the Orthodox churches and a more local schism. By 1095 he had mastered the western schismatics and was on friendly terms with the orthodox churches. He wanted to divert the divisive military energy of the west to constructive uses; Byzantine diplomats addressed his Council of Piacenza (1095) on a middle eastern offensive against the declining Seljuk power. It might free the pilgrim routes to the Holy Places, perhaps the Holy Land itself, but it required western troops because the Eastern Empire was short of soldiers. The concept of a middle eastern holy expedition was thus likely to kill several birds with one stone but the West and the Byzantines were at cross-purposes.

(4) **FIRST (1095-99)** Urban II launched the so-called First Crusade in a stage-managed call to arms at the Council of Clermont in Nov. 1095. Adhémar, Bp. of le Puy, was to command but the movement soon got out of hand. Apart from minor companies it consisted of six migrations viz: (a) popular assemblies, the French under Walter Sans Avoir and a much larger disorderly crowd from many countries under Peter the Hermit, moved from Cologne across Germany and Hungary, through the Balkans via Constantinople, and met disaster in Oct. 1096 at Cibotus (Civetot) on the Marmara, but Peter was rescued by the Byzantines and given quarters in Constantinople. (b) Three German rabbles massacred Jews in German cities and in Prague and became,

effectively, freebooting expeditions. They were stopped by the Hungarians and dispersed. (c) A well organised force of Walloons with some English and Lorrainers under Godfrey of Bouillon, D. of Lorraine, and his brothers Eustace III and Baldwin of Boulogne followed Peter the Hermit's route and, apart from an outbreak at Selymbria, reached Constantinople in an orderly fashion in Dec. 1096. They were just preceded by Hugh of Vermandois who had come via Rome and Durazzo. They found Peter the Hermit and his remnants there, loudly but falsely attributing their defeat to Byzantine treachery. The Emperor Alexius I Commenus wanted these princes to swear allegiance to him before proceeding, for they were disorderly, dangerous and proposing to conquer former Byzantine territory. Godfrey refused. Alexius reduced their food supply. They sacked the suburbs and were forcibly brought to heel (Apr. 1097). (d) A powerful Sicilian Norman army under Bohemond came via Brindisi and Avlona, reaching Constantinople in late Apr. 1097. (e) A mainly southern French force under Raymond IV of Toulouse and Adhémar of le Puy marched along the Dalmatian coastal tracks to Durazzo and arrived at Constantinople at the end of Apr. 1097. (f) A Norman-Flemish force jointly commanded by Robert, D. of Normandy, brother of William Rufus, his brother-in-law Stephen of Blois and his cousin, Robert II of Flanders,. There was only one English noble, Ralph E. of Norfolk, but many English and Scots soldiers and Norman knights. The proceeds of an English Danegeld were lent to Robert of Normandy to finance it and he pledged his Duchy to William Rufus for it. This led ultimately to the English conquest of Normandy. The crusade moved via Rome to Caserta and Calabria. Robert of Flanders reached Constantinople in Apr. 1097; the others in May.

(5) All the princes except Raymond having sworn to Alexius, the combined army (with Byzantine troops) took Nicaea, the Seljuk capital, in June. In July they won a great victory at Dorylaeum. In mid-Oct. they reached the suburbs of Antioch by which time the Byzantines had re-secured the Aegean provinces of Asia Minor. In Mar. 1098 Baldwin of Boulogne had taken Edessa, of which he became Count. Antioch fell in June but fighting in the vicinity, internal quarrels and the death of Adhémar, the statesmanlike legate, delayed them. The crusaders who mistrusted the Byzantines now began to appoint Latin bishops and Bohemond became P. of Antioch.

(6) The remainder set out southwards in Dec. accepting the submission of various Emirs, especially of Tripoli. They crossed the Fatimid Egyptian frontier (just N. of Beirut) in May 1099 and took Jerusalem on 15 July; in a two day massacre nearly all the Moslem and Jewish inhabitants perished. The leaders then offered the crown to Godfrey who preferred the title 'Defender of the Holy Sepulchre' and in Aug. they destroyed a large relieving Egyptian army at Ascalon. Godfrey died in 1100 and, after a short civil war, was succeeded by his brother Baldwin of Edessa, who took the title of King.

(7) The Frankish Kingdom of Jerusalem with its dependent states (Antioch, Edessa and Tripoli) (*see* OUTREMER) and its four major fiefs (Galilee, Toron, Nablus and Oultrejourdain) expanded into the countryside surrounding the conquered strongholds while, in 1101, two forces, a Lombardo-French under Stephen of Blois and Raymond, who had returned, and an Aquitanian-Nivernais were destroyed in the Anatolian Bs. of Mersivan and Heraclea. These ensured the survival of the Seljuks in central Asia Minor and that the new Kingdom would not be nourished immediately with European colonists and would have to depend upon sea communications. Turbulent internal politics and the foolish hostility of most Franks to the Byzantines made it weak and dependent for survival upon Moslem disunity. Nevertheless, western colonists did come, notably Fulk of Anjou, who accepted the Crown and married his

daughter Matilda to Henry's son, the atheling William and endowed her with Maine and prospects of Anjou in order to raise the necessary funds. This ended a Norman border war and was the precedent for the later Angevin marriage after the atheling was drowned, which gave England an Angevin dynasty.

(8) SECOND (1146-8). This Crusade, provoked by the fall of Edessa (whose immunity was believed to have been guaranteed by a letter from Christ himself) was preached at Vezelay by St. Bernard on the prompting of Pope Eugenius III. K. Louis of France was put in charge and K. Conrad of Germany was persuaded to join. While they were mobilising, an English expedition set out by sea under Henry of Glanville. It helped Afonso-Henriques, Count of Portugal, to take the Moorish capital at LISBON in Oct. 1147, but few of its people continued eastwards. Disorderly Germans followed a month later, while disciplined French went overland to Constantinople. Suspicious alike of the Byzantines and each other, they crossed separately into Asia. Then, ignoring Byzantine advice, the Germans were wiped out at the second B. of Dorylaeum (Oct. 1147). The French rescued the survivors, left Conrad to return to Constantinople and pressed on to the port of Attalia with heavy losses (Feb. 1148). The King went on by sea. The rest struggled on by land. K. Conrad reached Acre in a Byzantine ship in Apr. In June the crusader chiefs decided to attack Damascus, the only Moslem state friendly to the Franks. The attack failed, the crusade broke up leaving things in a worse state than before. The Byzantines had to take over the western part of the county of Edessa. The Franks began to understand the need for Byzantine friendship.

(9) In 1153, while palace revolutions distracted Egypt, K. Baldwin III captured the Egyptian fortress of Ascalon but in 1154 Nureddin seized Damascus. He and the Franks now competed for the control of Egypt by supporting rival Egyptian factions. K. Amalric, successor to Baldwin III who died in 1162, and Shirkuh Nureddin's general, fought wars in Egypt in 1164 and 1167 which brought Shirkuh's brilliant nephew Saladin into prominence. In 1169 Shirkuh engineered a *coup d'état*, took over the govt. and died leaving his power to Saladin as minister to a puppet Caliph. A joint Byzantine Frankish naval expedition failed before Damietta, while Nureddin sought to assert his authority over Saladin. In 1174, however, Amalric and Nureddin both died and in the ensuing political confusion Saladin took over most of Nureddin's dominions, while Jerusalem was under a disputed regency for a leprous child King. These events had immense repercussions further north, where Nureddin's influence had kept the Seljuks quiet. An Anatolian war broke out between them and the Byzantines which culminated in the overthrow of the Emperor Manuel Comnenus at the B. of Myriocephalum (Sept. 1176). The Moslems were now united and confident: the Christians suddenly weak. Worse still, the royal authority over the feudatories had almost disappeared. It was, however, possible to patch up a truce, yet the govt's inability to control the gangster Reynald of Chatillon (*see* OUTREMER-6, 8, 10) who persistently raided merchant caravans and the Haj, decided Saladin to substitute his own power. He invaded, and annihilated the Frankish army at the Horns of Hattin (July 1187). Acre surrendered a week later; Jerusalem in Oct. By 1188 two Hospitaller and one Templar castle and the towns of Antioch, Tripoli and Tyre alone remained. *See* OUTREMER-11

(10) THIRD (1189-92). The King had been appealing to the West ever since 1175, but the public had been unwilling to recognise the danger. Conrad of Montferrat, who had taken charge of the crowded refugees at Tyre, sent Josias, its archbishop, to Europe to make clear the extent of the disaster. The first and

decisive aid came from Sicily to Tyre. In Nov. Gregory VIII issued his public summons. Rumour had gone ahead, for Richard of Poitou (the future RICHARD I) took the cross in Sept. In Jan. 1188 Josias persuaded Kings HENRY I and PHILIP AUGUSTUS to make a peace in which Philip of Flanders joined. Henry ordered the raising of the SALADIN TITHE, a 10% tax on lay movable property. Collection proceeded, but in the spring a Poitevin rebellion and a local war involving Richard, the Count of Toulouse, and Philip Augustus delayed matters until Richard succeeded Henry on the throne and he and Philip patched up a peace. He went home, was crowned and raised vast sums to finance the expedition (*see* RICHARD 1-1-3). Richard and Philip then agreed to set out together from Vézelay in Apr. but the death of Isabella of France delayed them until July.

(11) There were three other major expeditions. In Sept. 1189 a large Danish and Flemish fleet had arrived in the Levant and a separate English squadron helped the Portuguese to take SILVES before sailing east. Meantime the Emperor Frederick Barbarossa, with a powerful German army, reached the Byzantine frontier in June. He wintered at Adrianople, crossed into Asia in Mar. 1190 and was drowned near Seleucia in June. The disheartened army reached Antioch. Meanwhile K. Guy, captured at Hattin, had been released by Saladin. Conrad of Montferrat refused to let him into Tyre but he assembled a force and in Aug. 1189 laid siege to Acre. Saladin appeared and besieged Guy, both besieged forces being intermittently supplied by sea. This intricate double siege lasted nearly two years and attracted all the major leaders on both sides.

(12) Philip Augustus and Richard reached Messina, respectively, in Aug. and Sept. 1190. Here Richard quarrelled with the Sicilians about their treatment of his sister, the dowager Q. Joanna, and his troops sacked most of the city. Philip was drawn into the dispute which smouldered until Apr. 1191 when the Kings left for the Levant. Philip went straight to Tyre, picked up Conrad and took him on to Acre. Richard ran into storms and Joanna was stranded on the Cypriot coast where Isaac Comnenus, the usurping local ruler, mistreated her. Richard, aided by Franks from Acre, proceeded to conquer this Christian island. He collected a vast loot and reached Acre in June. The Crown of Jerusalem was disputed between Conrad (who had saved Tyre) and the discredited K. Guy. Philip supported Conrad. Guy's party had helped in the conquest of Cyprus in return for Richard's support. Thus the Franco-Angevin quarrel was extended to the camps before Acre. Moreover Philip of Flanders had just died childless and while K. Philip claimed his inheritance, Richard was determined to prevent him obtaining it Nevertheless Acre surrendered in July. The various contingents quarrelled about the allotment of quarters and Leopold of Austria, as leader of the Germans, demanded equal treatment with the Kings. The famous insult, when Richard's men threw Leopold's standard into the ditch, was to have fateful effects. It was agreed meanwhile that Guy should remain King for life and that Conrad should succeed him. K. Philip now set off home.

(13) Richard had sworn to liberate Jerusalem and in Aug. he marched south along the coast accompanied by his fleet. He retook successively Haifa and Caesarea, defeated Saladin in a pitched battle at Arsuf (Sept. 1191), occupied and fortified Jaffa as a base for his inland advance and demolished Ascalon. But the odds were too great. There was trouble in Cyprus, of which Richard disposed by sale to the Templars; the quarrels between Guy's and Conrad's factions were renewed and reinforcements reached Saladin from Egypt. The advance failed (Jan. 1192). By now the obvious need for peace was strengthened by news of Philip's and P. John's machinations at home. There had been intermittent negotiations with Saladin. In Apr. the Crusader barons settled the crown issue in Richard's presence in favour of Conrad, who was instantly murdered by Assassins. The Kingdom passed to Henry of Champagne while the Templars, who were regretting their purchase, sold Cyprus to Guy. Richard then stormed Daron, the last Egyptian coastal fortress, and defeated Saladin in two battles outside Jaffa. A military stalemate was ended by a peace signed in Sept. 1192. Richard left on his disastrously adventurous journey home in Oct. (*See* RICHARD I-5.)

(14) Saladin died in 1192 and his dominions were partitioned between his quarrelsome sons. Moslem disunion was matched by a relative Frankish unity, for Cyprus and Acre co-operated and at Henry of Champagne's death (1197) K. Amalric of Cyprus took his crown. He died in 1205 but.the peace was maintained.

(15) FOURTH (1201-4) originally assembled at Venice against Jerusalem, was diverted to Zara and Constantinople where, on the analogy of K. Richard I's conquest of Cyprus, it attacked a Christian state, established the Latin Empire over part of the Byzantine territory and ended the E. Roman Empire as a major power.

(16) FIFTH (1217-21) launched by Pope Honorius III, began under K. Andrew of Hungary and Leopold of Austria. Andrew went home by land in 1218 having achieved nothing. A Friesian fleet then arrived and in May the mainly German force attacked Damietta in Egypt. A three year war there ended in defeat.

(17) SIXTH (1228-9) was an expedition by the Emperor Frederick II, then excommunicate. He recovered Jerusalem by a treaty which was execrated alike by Christians and Moslems; the city remained Frankish until 1244 but he left the Kingdom and Cyprus in political disorder.

(18) SEVENTH (1239-40), a French expedition under Tibald of Champagne and Navarre, recovered some castles and RICHARD, D. of CORNWALL who arrived as it left, took advantage of a Moslem civil war to extend the Kingdom into Galilee (1241), but Jerusalem and the more recent gains were all lost in 1244, when a combined Frankish and Damascene army was defeated by the Egyptians under Rukn-al-Din Baibars at La Forbie.

(19) EIGHTH (1244-54) arose from a vow by Louis IX made in 1244. It sailed from Aigues Mortes in Aug. 1248 and reached Cyprus in Sept. Louis spent eight months there taking advice and attempting to make contact with the Mongols whose advanced forces were at Mosul. He sailed for Egypt and captured Damietta in June 1249. After a pyrrhic victory at Mansourah (Feb. 1250) he and his army were captured (Apr.). After he was ransomed he remained at Acre until 1254. In 1260 the Egyptians defeated the Mongols at Ain Jalud and Baibars became Sultan of Egypt.

(20) NINTH (1270) was organised by Louis IX but diverted, on Charles of Anjou's urging, to Tunis where Louis and many of his troops perished of disease. A small Spanish crusade had meanwhile gone to Palestine where it had provoked a local war with Baibars. He captured the remaining inland castles and was about to attack Antioch when news of a further crusade arrived. This was the Crusade of EDWARD of ENGLAND who arrived with a small force at Acre *via* Sicily and Cyprus in May 1271. He found that the Genoese were in control of the Egyptian slave trade and the Venetians supplying Egypt with arms; Cypriot knights were refusing to serve on the mainland and nobody was trying to get the help of the Mongols. His power was inadequate to bring sense into the situation and in May 1272 he negotiated a 10 year truce, after which he was wounded by the poisoned dagger of an Assassin instigated by Baibars. He was ill for some weeks but left for home in Sept.

(21) After the fall of Acre and the destruction of the Frankish states (1291) there were a number of expeditions called crusades. These included an attack from Cyprus on Alexandria in 1365; a Savoyard attack on Galipoli in 1366, a French defeat at Tunis in 1390 and the great international crusade against the Ottoman Turks which met with disaster at the B. of Nicopolis in 1396.

CRWTH. A Welsh lyre, originally plucked but bowed from the 12th cent.

CRYPTOGRAPHY is very old. It was in use in Venice in 1226. Roger Bacon (?1214-94) described several ciphers and is said to have written a book never since deciphered. The first comprehensive work was Trithemius' *Polygraphia* (1500). Charles I was an expert. Down to the end of World War I all methods depended either upon invisible ink or upon manual or machine systems for confusing the message. An accumulation of evidence would betray the characteristics of the system, but on the other hand cipher breaking at high levels required immense, sometimes uneconomic, effort. More recent developments have included shrinkage by microphotography to reduce a message to undetectable minuteness, or by high speed radio transmissions of unheralded messages whose true nature is unsuspected by monitors. In addition codes with a print-out of random combinations of figures created a cipher which in World War II was unbreakable. *See* WAAD-2; WALLIS, JOHN.

CRYSTAL PALACE. *See* GREAT EXHIBITION 1852.

CUBA was discovered by Columbus in 1492. Diego Velazquez began Spanish colonisation in 1511 at Baracoa and by 1515 there were seven municipalities with *cabildos* (council). The local Indians were used as serfs, but a slave trade from Africa began at once and by 1551 the Indian population had declined to a few thousand. Disease, hurricanes and the activities of freebooters, pirates and protestant European states retarded development until about 1700 because the island had little gold and Spanish colonists mostly went elsewhere. Havana, however, acquired a certain prosperity as a supply point for the *flota* and as a market for the cattle ranches and tobacco farms. As everywhere in the Spanish Caribbean smuggling was endemic.

The great change came with the rise of the sugar industry, with which the slave trade was connected. The Havana Co., formed in 1740 to stimulate both, was a failure but after 1763 (the close of the Seven Years' War) a working arrangement with the British brought dramatic results. In the century after 1763 the population, free and slave, increased tenfold and after 1838 mechanisation of the sugar industry destroyed the forests. By 1860 an annual production of 500,000 tons of sugar represented 30% of the world supply. In theory the slave trade had been abolished in 1820 under an Anglo-Spanish agreement. In fact the Cubans insisted on continuing the trade and the Spanish govt. was long powerless to stop it. Nearly 500,000 slaves were imported before it was finally ended in 1865, but this brought rising costs, discontent with Spanish rule and a long abortive insurrection (1868-78) which the richer planters and the slaves understandably refused to support. By this time most of the sugar was being exported to the U.S.A. whose business interests were increasingly dominant.

Slavery was abolished in 1886 and the sugar industry continued to decline. The exiled rebels organised a new rebellion in 1895 which developed into a ruinous civil war, destroying the value of U.S. investments. An explosion in the U.S. battleship *Maine* at Havana was made a pretext for intervention in 1898 and, with American help, the Cubans received their independence at the P. of Paris (10 Dec. 1898), but U.S. troops remained in occupation until 1901.

Political confusion followed and there was a second U.S. occupation from Sept. 1906 until Jan. 1909. Thereafter govt. was a corrupt political game played in a country where 75% of the useful land and 40% of the sugar production was in foreign ownership. In 1953 Fidel Castro, a communist, launched an insurrection against the last and worst of the govts. under Juan Batista and by 1959 had overthrown him and taken over. He established diplomatic relations with Russia which replaced the U.S.A. as Cuba's principal trading partner and became her military protector. By 1962 the Russians were establishing nuclear missile bases, but were forced by U.S. threats of war to withdraw them. Cuban troops took part in the establishment of the Angolan communist govt. in 1975. *See also* PARIS, P. OF 1763; SEVEN YEARS' WAR-12.

CUBITT. The more notable members of this family connected with the building industry were **(1) Thomas (1788-1861)** who began as a carpenter, built parts of Belgravia (London), the E. front of Buckingham Palace and supported the Thames Embankment scheme. He was interested in drainage and sewerage. His brother and partner **(2) William (1791-1863)** was M.P. for Andover from 1846 to 1861 and Lord Mayor of London in 1860. His cousin **(3) Sir William (1785-1861)** was a large scale builder of canals, docks and railways. His son **(4) Joseph (1811-72)** built the Great Northern and the London Chatham and Dover Rly. and Blackfriars Bridge, London.

CUCKOLDS HAVEN or POINT, on the Thames below Rotherhithe, was traditionally named from a miller's wife who favoured K. John. He is supposed to have compensated the miller with as much land as he could see from his house.

CUERDALE HOARD (Lancs) found in 1840 consisted of over 7,000 coins, some 5,000 of which came from Viking controlled areas of England, particularly Yorkshire, and others from Dublin.

CUJUS REGIO EJUS RELIGIO **(Lat = The country's religion is that of its ruler).** A summary of the German religious compromise reached at the P. of Augsburg (1555).

CULDEES, *CELI DE* **(Ir = Companions of God)** were disciplined communities of secular priests in Scotland, Ireland and Brittany, representing an 8th cent. development or critical reaction from monasticism. They were mostly connected through family relationships; their members could own private property; they made their rules themselves; but some usually became hermits. Many communities were established, notably at Iona and St. Andrews. They represented the main priestly resources of the Scottish church. Their practices, like those of Irish monasteries, were out of line with the rest of the Western Church and in the 11th cent. St. Margaret started to introduce reforms, notably by establishing Benedictines at Dunfermline and by securing a reversion to Roman rites. Her sons, particularly David I (1124-53) reorganised the church on Roman principles, particularly the diocesan supremacy of bishops. He introduced Augustinian canons, whose rule was not dissimilar, into culdee houses such as Abernethy and Monymusk and slowly absorbed the culdees into the new system.

CULEN. See SCOTS OR ALBAN KINGS, EARLY.

CULLEN, William (1710-90) re-established the Glasgow medical school in 1744. He was prof. of medicine there but subsequently prof. of chemistry at Edinburgh. He was an inspirer and teacher of the next generation of scientists.

CULVERIN. *See* ARMADA-(1).

CUM ADVERSUS HAERETICAM PRAVITATEM **(Lat = when, against heretical wickedness) (1245)** bull of Innocent IV approving the Emperor Frederick II's incorporation of heresy into the law as a capital offence.

CUMBERLAND, CUMBRIA, CARLISLE (1) Hadrian's Wall divided the area, which thus had no initial unity or name. **Luguvallium (Carlisle; Welsh, Caer Luel)** survived the Roman withdrawal in 383 and was the nucleus of local life. There are widespread traditions of K. Arthur, but St.

Ninian had to undertake a series of missions against heathenism from Withorn (north of the Solway) in about 405. The mountains, poor soil and wet climate made for a sparse but refractory population and a territory easy to occupy only temporarily. Thus the areas of modern Cumberland and Dumfriesshire were of doubtful allegiance, with a few refuges around which rival groups and clans fought.

(2) The Strathclyde Britons, successors to anti-Roman tribes, made determined incursions from the, north and, as they were converts of Withorn, their K. Rederich's victory over Gwenddoleu, son of Ceidio, at Arthuret (Arderyd) in 573 was represented as a Christian triumph; St. Kentigern preached in the area as a result. This was, however, politically shortlived; in the early 7th cent. the Angles of Northumbria penetrated via the Tyne. By 685 their Christian K. Ecgfrith could give Carlisle and its environs to the See of Lindisfarne. He, however, suffered a disaster at Nechtansmere in that year and the Anglian northward penetration was stayed.

(3) Though the area remained part of the see of Lindisfarne and later of Durham, the Angles could not repel renewed British aggression or immigration and the local church remained Celtic in character. The name **Cumbria** (related to Cymri = British) first appears in 9th cent. documents. Meanwhile, as Northumbria was overwhelmed from the east by the Danes, the Cumbrian coast was assailed from the west by Ostmen coming via the Minch or from Dublin and Man. They destroyed Carlisle and began to settle in the political vacuum. The alarmed tribes were leaderless, but by 900 the W. Saxons had turned back the Danes in southern England and were reaching north. In 924 the W. Cumbrian tribes submitted to or sought protection from Edward the Elder; in 926 Athelstan exacted oaths from all Cumbria at Dacre and in 937 defeated the combined Ostmen, Scots and Britons at BRUNANBURH. The effects of this famous battle are uncertain, but in 945 K. Edmund considered that an Anglo-Scots understanding was necessary. Having expelled two Ostmen chiefs he made Cumbria over to the K. of Scots while he consolidated his own hold in Northumbria. The Scots, however, had their own preoccupations, for by the year 100 Cumbria was held, though thinly, by Scandinavians.

(4) The Danegeld provoked a type of dispute which was, in one form or another, to recur. The Cumbrians claimed exemption and K. Ethelred attacked them. In truth their claim represented a local separatism. They sought to embroil the Scots by appealing to their King as overlord. The tactic was ineffectual and, for the next two generations, Cumbria was attached to Northumbria, whose earls represented what little authority was maintainable, mostly about Carlisle. These Saxon earls survived into the Norman period.

(5) The Norman invasion was not immediately effective beyond the Midlands. The probability of an English civil war emboldened the K. of Scots to re-occupy Cumbria in 1068 and to give Dunbar to the fugitive E. Gospatric (II), after Edwin and Morcar's rebellion of 1069. The Conqueror's devastating reaction isolated Cumbria permanently from Northumbria and temporarily from England in general. It remained in Scottish hands until 1092.

(6) Real Norman authority in the north-west did not extend above the Mersey until in 1092 William II re-occupied Cumbria against weak opposition. In about 1106 he conferred it upon Ranulf de Briquessart, known as *le Mesquin* (The Nasty) who set up his H.Q. at Appleby and organised the two defensive border baronies of BURGH BY SANDS and LIDDEL IN ESK. His rule lasted until 1120 when, on the death of a kinsman in the *White Ship* disaster, he took over the earldom of Chester. Henry I took the lordship into his own hands and altered the local dispositions. Appleby was too far south for control of the border or its barons. He built and garrisoned a castle at Carlisle. In 1130 he appointed a Sheriff for **Westmorland** and in 1133 obtained a separate bishopric. The first bishop was Adelulf. The geography of the historic county dates from this time (*See* para. 8.)

(7) One of Stephen's first acts was to buy Scots support against Matilda by ceding Cumbria (1136). K. David enlarged Carlisle castle. His rule was locally acceptable and Cumbrians fought for him at the B. of the Standard (1138) and his defeated army took refuge in Carlisle (*see* DURHAM). In the anarchy, however, Ranulf le Mesquin laid claims which the Scots could barely fend off, but which he was not quite strong enough to enforce. In 1149, however, Henry of Anjou (the future Henry II) bought Ranulfs support by giving him S. Lancashire in return for these claims. Hence when Henry had restored order as King he re-annexed Cumbria (1157), together with Northumbria and gave a charter to Carlisle. The town became the main English base for the defence of the West March. Subsequently he had other distractions but K. Malcolm IV thought it wise to confine his attention to the conquest of Galloway (1160). There was no serious Scots incursion until the rebellion of Henry II's sons in 1174 tempted William the Lion, who was ignominiously captured.

(8) This victory brought a major change. **Cumberland** and Westmorland were shired separately in 1177. A new method of defence was organised to deal with clan feuding and cattle rustling rather than grand strategy; the tenants were required to turn out armed at warning, but were excused service with the royal army save as van and rear guard when crossing the border. By 1212 most of the tenants paid coinage, a pastoral levy in lieu of a horned beast. The system was inadequate in a declared war, as the Scots capture of Carlisle in that year (when John was at loggerheads with the barons) proved.

(9) The bishopric since the death of Adelulf in 1156 had been vacant because of its unattractive poverty, most of the local church revenues having been long vested in the priory at Carlisle, which also took over the episcopal revenue. Hence no bishop could be found until Richard I's friend, the truant Abp. Bernard of Ragusa, was induced to take the see in 1202. By 1212 he was dead and the canons of Carlisle treasonably and contumaciously elected a Scot, the K. of Scots being then excommunicate. Hence the Papacy and the English regency were able in 1218 to act together. The canons were expelled, part of the priory's wealth was transferred to the see and loyal canons were appointed. Thereafter episcopal succession became regular. Like other border bishops, these churchmen were important militarily. The perennial disturbances inhibited monasticism: outside Carlisle the Augustinians had only one large house, at Lanercost; the Benedictine priories at Wetheral and St. Bees were cells of St. Mary's Abbey at York and the Cistercians had houses only at Calder and Holmcultram. The latter, of Scots origin, was not subject to episcopal visitation. The others were Norman foundations. In addition Carlisle had a Dominican and a Franciscan friary and two hospitals and there were Augustinians at Penrith and Carmelites at Appleby.

(10) Papal concern in English affairs after K. John's death brought peacemaking on the Border. Papal arbitrations of 1237 and 1242 settled the location of the frontier save in the **Debateable Land,** and the Customs of the March were codified (*see* MARCHES, ANGLO-SCOTS). Unfortunately, Edward I's effort to conquer Scotland and the successful Scots guerrilla reaction inaugurated a long war as well as brigandage and feuding. The watch had to be strengthened; the tenants were allowed to build many fortifications, the county was divided into five wards (Carlisle, Lyth, Eskdale, Allerdale and Coupland) for local control and the whole was placed under a Warden of the West March (c. 1300). Significantly, the most efficient and

famous warden, Andrew of Hartcla (fl. 1322), who became E. of Carlisle and, with Church assistance, established a truce from 1322 to 1335, was the least popular.

(11) Most Anglo-Scots warfare in the ensuing centuries took place east of the Pennines. On the Cumberland side hostilities were more of a private, almost a sporting, nature and those involved were as much of a nuisance to their own govts. as to each other. Carlisle was permanently turbulent and disorderly. The appearance of artillery, always in royal hands, in 1383 made a difference. By this time Carlisle castle was a disused ruin but in 1388 it was possible to agree that new castles should not be built (i.e. the local people foresaw that they would be battered down). By mid 15th cent. official wars were an excuse for larger border forays, while in times of peace or truce the skirmishes, mainly about fights in the Debateable Land, were being settled under the Laws of the Marches. Thus local support for the Lancastrians in the Wars of the Roses could be significant. The truce of 1463, the war of 1481 to 1484 and the successive truces of 1484, 1488 and 1491 to 1496 and thereafter, made little difference to the condition of the West March, but the Scots disaster at Flodden (1513) did. Scottish govts. were temporarily too weak to control their frontier clans; the English started to garrison the March and there were local demands for a definition of the Debateable Land. This became feasible when, after the Scottish rout on the Solway Moss (1542), the English occupied Dumfriesshire. The boundary settlement (1552) after the Truce of Norham (1549) partitioned the Debateable Land. When Mary Q. of Scots landed on the coast in 1568, though Carlisle had been efficiently policed since 1561, it was still not considered a place of safe custody and she was quickly hustled south. The surviving nuisance value of these lands was, however, much reduced with the overthrow of the Dacres in the Northern Rebellion of 1570.

(12) Border raiding soon started again and developed into a series of private wars, due again mainly to the weakness of the Scots govt. They led in 1596 to the famous rescue of Kinmont Willie (*see* MARCHES, ANGLO-SCOTS) from Carlisle Castle.

(13) The union of the Crowns (1603) ended the military functions of Coinage tenants. The crown argued that local privileges connected with them, such as freedom from other feudal incidents, lapsed. The tenants argued that their privileges were independent of coinage but that their subtenants' rights had lapsed. The threat of a local revolution was eventually averted by long leases to the subtenants.

(14) The tenants' claim, however, amounted to one of special local, virtually palatine status and, since a modernising parliament was less likely to tolerate such peculiarities than the crown, the shire supported the King in the Civil War, even though Carlisle was initially held for the Parliament. Later it sustained a long siege for the King.

(15) The leadership of the shire, especially the Lowther family, favoured the protestant and whig side in the disorderly politics after the Restoration so that consistent support was given to William III in 1689 to the Hanoverians in 1715 and 1745; this involvement in national issues was, however, skin deep. The localism of the population and perhaps official pressure against papists, made military effort totally ineffectual; the assembled county levies refused to stand against rebel forces a tenth of their number in 1715 and 1745.

(16) Agriculture (and its concomitant, tanning) apart, the earliest and most profitable INDUSTRIES were the great sea and salmon fisheries and mining. There were lead and silver mines at Carlisle and also at Alston, where the miners were specially privileged by 1170. The King took one ninth of the metal and a royalty of a fifteenth on the rest, but provided a skilled smelter (*drivere*) at his own expense. The Alston miners habitually harboured bad characters. Almost as early were the iron mines and forges of Coupland and the coastal saltpans between the Esk and Duddan Sands. Copper mines (which had some silver and gold) began to be worked at Keswick early in the 14th cents and coal, to be important later, was unsystematically mined at outcrops shortly afterwards by monks at St. Bees and by the Dacres at Tindal. Scottish incursion soon made the latter, and other mines, unworkable and in 1478 all the metallic mines were leased to Germans and Flemings. These 'Almain' miners worked against mounting unpopularity (there were riots at Keswick in 1566) and with diminishing profit due to exhaustion of the mines until the Civil War, in which their smelting houses were destroyed and they themselves mostly perished.

(17) Large scale COALMINING began in about 1650 in West Cumberland and in East Cumberland in about 1690 when winding and haulage made penetration beyond outcrop distances possible. It also forced entrepreneurs to introduce drainage and calculated ventilation. All the machinery was horse driven, yet the mines were already advancing under the sea. Mining below natural drainage (adit) level was negligible before the introduction of Newcomen's steam pump by Sir James Lowther at Whitehaven in 1715. Airlocks came in 1760. The first winding engine, which accelerated the rate of delivery, was set up there in 1791. Mechanical ventilation, attempted in 1840, was not successfully introduced until 1870. In the 1890s much coal was lost by sea flooding due to mismanagement.

(18) The conversion of coal into coke on the Cumberland coast encouraged iron smelting and helped to keep the older iron mines going, but the French wars from 1790 created an immense demand for armaments and the Scots Carron foundry was soon receiving 20,000 tons of HAEMATITE a year from Crowgarth near Whitehaven. In 1825 great discoveries were made nearby. In 1849 production was 100,000 tons, in 1857 over 320,000 tons. The railway connections made in 1857 brought Whitehaven production up to nearly 470,000 tons in 1860 and the Victorian iron boom of the 1870s raised it to about 1,600,000 tons annually in 1880 to 1884. In 1869 there were only nine furnaces in blast, in 1880 there were 40. In 1864, moreover, operations began at Hodbarrow near Millom. This was the greatest strike in the country: between 1870 and 1900 this single pit was producing over half as much as the rest of Cumberland.

(19) The ore had been sold to British and foreign buyers but the simultaneous growth of British industry and of Spanish iron exports were restricting custom to Britain: after 1882 exports were negligible and by 1900 imports of Spanish ore had risen to 94,000 tons. This prevented a continuous price rise, so that in the period 1891-1900 the average price per ton at 11s. 10d. was below the 1861-70 prices of 13s. 6d. and well below the boom price of 19s. 6d. The effect on local employment was not, however, great for the rearmament programmes before World War I absorbed the output and the war itself caused govt. sponsored war industries to be set up in and around Carlisle. There was a shortage of labour and many unskilled Irish were brought in from depressed Irish counties. A curious consequence of this influx of new untutored spending power was that it was deemed necessary to nationalise the public houses (1916) of the Carlisle district. These remained in state ownership until 1971.

CUMBERLAND, Ds. of (1) *see* P. RUPERT (1619-82). **(2)** *see* GEORGE P. OF DENMARK (1653-1708). There were three controversial Hanoverian Dukes viz **(3) William Augustus John (1721-65),** *s.* of George II was trained for the Navy, served under Sir John Norris, transferred to the army and as a maj-gen. fought at Dettingen (1743)

under his father. In the Jacobite Rebellion of 1745, Wade having taken command of the first army, Cumberland commanded the second and then took over the first, beat the Scots at Culloden and from his H.Q. at Fort Augustus hunted down rebels and burned their crofts. In 1747 he commanded the allied troops against France and was defeated by Marshal de Saxe at Lauffeld. He brought the army back to Maastricht, returned to England and set about encouraging horse racing (of which he was inordinately fond) by building the racecourse at Ascot, In 1757 at the opening of the Seven Years' War he took command of the defences of Hanover, was defeated at Hastenbeck by the Marshal d'Estrées and signed the Convention of Kloster-Zeven which put Hanover out of the war. His father was furious, so he resigned. A *dilettante* soldier, he was variously known as Sweet William and Butcher Cumberland. His nephew **(4) Henry Frederick (1745-90)** had to pay £10,000 damages for adultery with the Countess Grosvenor and secretly married a Mrs Horton in 1770 which caused his equally furious father, George III, to procure the passing of the Royal Marriage Act 1772. His brother **(5) Ernest Augustus (1771-1851)** was wounded at the B. of Tournay (1794), retired to England and, besides acquiring a sinister sexual reputation, became a reactionary politician who opposed R. Catholic emancipation (1808) and the Regency Bill (1810). He was for a while dep. Elector (i.e. governor) of Hanover. In 1832 he opposed the Reform Bill. He also became grandmaster of the Irish Orangemen. Q. Victoria being unable to succeed in Hanover under Salic Law, he became K. of Hanover as William IV's next of kin. He immediately abolished the parliamentary constitution, became a popular autocrat and in 1840 granted a new constitution.

CUMBERNAULD. *See* NEW TOWNS.

CUMBERNAULD, BAND OF (Aug. 1640) was a political agreement signed by Montrose, Seaforth and other Scottish lords to resist the creation of a Scottish dictatorship in the hand of subjects i.e. of Argyll and the Edinburgh presbyterians.

CUM INTER NONNULLOS (Lat = When, amongst some) **(1323)** Bull by John XXII which condemned the Franciscan belief that Christ and his disciples held no possessions.

CUM UNIVERSI (Lat = When, of all) (1192) otherwise *FILIA SPECIALIS (Lat = The special daughter)* Bull of Celestine III making the Scottish church dependent on the Holy See, reserving the right of excommunication in Scotland to the Pope or a legate a latere and confining legatine office, save when sent direct from Rome, to Scotsmen.

CUNARD, Sir Samuel (1787-1865) began as a merchant at Halifax, Nova Scotia, and established the shipping co. then called the British and North American Royal Mail Steam Packet Co. in 1839. It was later known simply as Cunard.

CUNEDDA. *See* BRITAIN, ROMAN-27; GWYNEDD.

CUNLIFFE-LISTER. *See* SWINTON, LORD.

CUNNINGHAM. Group of lowland Scottish families led by the family of **(1) Alexander (?-1488) L. KILMAURS (c. 1450) 1st E. of GLENCAIRN (1488)**, killed at the B. of Sauchieburn. **(2) William (?-1547) 4th E.** represented Scotland in the marriage negotiations between James V and Mary of Guise (1538). He was captured at Solway Moss in 1542 and thereafter followed a course of ineffectual opportunism, first supporting the reformers and acknowledging the suzerainty of the English crown; then after defeat by Arran he betrayed Coldingham to the English (1544) but went over to Mary of Guise. On bad terms with his son **(3) Alexander (?-1574) 5th E.,** whom he handed over as a pledge for the alliance of 1544; Alexander secured his position at his father's death and was gradually won over to Calvinist ideas. Intellectual and determined, he became the principal inspiration of the reforming opposition to Mary of Guise. He invited Knox to Scotland in 1557, successfully delayed the Catholic advance against Perth in 1559, headed the appeal for English help and in 1560 went to England to seek intervention against French interference. This achieved, he became a member of the Scots council and commissioner for the destruction of monuments of idolatry (including monasteries) in the west. Not surprisingly, he and Mary Q. of Scots were mutually hostile and he continued in opposition politics until 1571 when he retired. **(4) William (?1610-64) 9th E**, was a royalist Scots politician, councillor and, in 1646, Lord Justice-General. He commanded Charles II's Scottish forces in 1653 but, having been defeated at Dunkeld in 1654, was imprisoned by Monck until the Restoration. He was Lord Chancellor of Scotland from 1661.

CUNNINGHAM (1) Andrew Brown (1883-1963) Ld. (1945) Vist. (1946) CUNNINGHAM of HINDHOPE early showed his humorous ingenuity, tact and tenacity when, as a midshipman, he slipped into the up-country Naval Brigade in the Boer War. He commanded destroyers in World War I partly under Keyes and in the Baltic in 1919, and became Capt. of H.M.S. *Rodney,* one of the largest warships afloat. He reached flag-rank in 1934, was Dep. Chief of the Naval Staff in Dec. 1938 and then, in June 1939, C-in-C Mediterranean. In 1940 by firmness and tact he induced the French at Alexandria to immobilise their own ships and in July, while escorting a convoy, he crossed an Italian fleet similarly engaged and boldly pursued it to the Calabrian coast, inflicting damage. In Nov. his torpedo bombers put half the Italian battleships out of action at Taranto and the rest retired to Naples. This eased the path of British (E-W) and hindered that of Italian (N-S) convoys and until Jan. 1941 he could dominate the Central Mediterranean. The German airforce now arrived and wrecked his only aircraft carrier (*Illustrious*) and he had to wait until Mar. to take the offensive to cover convoys to Greece. In the B. of C. Matapan (May) he sank three Italian cruisers and two destroyers, but his replacement carrier (*Formidable*) was bombed a few days later. Of the Cretan evacuation he said "it takes the Royal Navy three years to build a ship and three hundred to build a tradition. We must not let the army down" and, though bereft of air cover, he made the promise good. After four months as head of the British component of the Combined Chiefs of Staff in Washington he was appointed, at U.S. insistence, naval commander under Eisenhower. He covered the N. African, Sicilian and Salerno landings and received the surrender of the Italian fleet (Nov. 1942-Sept. 1943). He reverted to C-in-C Mediterranean but in Oct. succeeded the dying Sir Dudley Pound as First Sea Lord. As such he finished the war. He was showered with honours and at his funeral the preacher "thanked God for such a man at such a time". His brother **(2) Sir Alan Gordon (1887-1983)** after a conventional military career became G.O.C. E. Africa in 1940. He conquered Abyssinia in four months (Jan-May 1941). When Auchinleck replaced Wavell as C-in-C Middle East (June 1941) he gave Cunningham the Eighth Army. His attack on Rommel was defeated and Auchinleck replaced him by Sir Neil Ritchie. Between Nov. 1945 and Dec. 1948 he was High Commissioner to Palestine and Transjordan.

CUNNINGHAM, Sir Henry Dacres (1885-1962) (no relation to the above) had a brilliant career as a R. Navy navigator, but reached flag rank only in 1936. At the Admiralty in 1937 he was put in charge of the Fleet Air Arm. He commanded cruisers in the Norway campaign (early 1940) and the naval side of the failed Dakar expedition (late 1940). He was not blamed and returned to become Fourth Sea Lord. In June 1943 he became C-in-C Levant and in Dec. succeeded his namesake as C-in-C Mediterranean. He was responsible for the Anzio and Provence landings and then in May 1946 followed his namesake as First Sea Lord. In 1948 he became chairman of the Iraq Petroleum Co.

CUPAR (Sc.). A place where people were reputedly hanged first and tried afterwards. *See also* JEDBURGH.

CURA PASTORALIS **(Lat = pastoral care)** by Pope Gregory the Great (r. 590-604). *See* ALFRED THE GREAT.

CURIA REGIS **(Lat = The King's Court). (1)** This early mediaeval term meant (i) the place where the King happened to be, with his officials and household; (ii) The King's Court considered as the govt; (iii) A court held by a justice commissioned by the King.

(2) The Anglo-Saxon kings had a group of clerks and a small assembly of notables or great men, the WITAN, composed of men with territorial or ecclesiastical power or influence, high royal officers and friends. The Curia Regis, by contrast, was a somewhat more formalised body used by the Norman Kings and modelled on the Curia Ducis (Lat = Duke's Court) of Normandy. It consisted in principle of feudal tenants-in-chief holding their fiefs as baronies and the King's chief officials, namely the Justiciar, Chancellor, Treasurer, Chamberlain, Constable, Marshall and the Justices. The Chancellor's presence incorporated the clerks in the Curia. There was thus a functional succession but not an institutional continuity from the Witan.

(3) The Curia followed the King about. Its records had to be portable and sparse and those with business at court might have to pursue it across the Channel. On the other hand, an energetic ruler like Henry I or II expedited business and sometimes heard cases and petitions himself.

(4) The Curia's work would now be called administrative, judicial and legislative, but these distinctions were not clear intellectually or differentiated practically in Norman times. Much administration was judicial in character or conducted by way of a hearing in a judicial manner, probably because of the scarcity of literate persons. In real life the Curia took two forms: a smaller body of officials and adherents, who commonly managed the routine business including the receipt of taxes, and a fuller assembly for important occasions or decisions. Like the Witan, the latter met in the King's presence at Christmas, Easter and Whitsun, if he was in England. The influence of either form of curia, however, depended upon the King's character, the nature of the business and the technical issues. It had no formal rights against the King, just as a diocesan synod had no formal rights against the bishop. William I amended the laws of Edward the Confessor by its advice and consent; but it seems to have been used rather as a repository of information for drafting the Constitutions of Clarendon (1164) and it was assembled simply to be informed of the terms of the Saladik Tithe (1188). All the same, and especially if the King was weak, young or absent, it considered and influenced high matters of state such as war and peace, royal marriages and even, in 1177, an international arbitration. It also acted as a court for the Tenants-in-Chief.

(5) Though the larger Curia on one occasion successfully opposed a new tax (1198), there was no technical distinction between the larger and the smaller forms until about the time of Magna Carta (1215). The differentiation was slow and was caused by the concurrence of practical solutions to administrative difficulties and by political necessities. There was firstly the growing need to establish a treasury and an accounting system which, because of its size, had to stay in one place. It was kept at Winchester and some time around 1118 the exchequer was established there, and in due course another was set up for Normandy at Rouen. Each helped the other with staff, and funds were regularly transferred between them. Secondly Henry II's legislation greatly increased the Curia's judicial business, which was no longer confined to the affairs of great men.

Small men could not afford to follow the King. Itinerant royal delegates had occasionally toured the country even under William I and this became a habit by the 12th cent. Moreover by 1178 there were Justices permanently at Westminster to settle disputes between subjects (*see* COMMON PLEAS, COURT OF).

The political necessities pulled the magnates into opposition under John, so that the larger form of the Curia became critical of him and of the regents and the King in the next reign. Magna Carta was in form a royal enactment made in this larger body. In fact the great men were tending to draw aside into a separate, if loosely constituted, group (*see* LORDS. HOUSE OF).

(6) The smaller part of the Curia naturally continued but so did the process of differentiation. Thus tax collection and accountancy were one thing; the settlement of tax disputes another, and by 1234 the Barons of the Exchequer had ceased to be ordinary treasury officials and were acquiring a mixture of administrative and judicial functions. (*See* EXCHEQUER, COURT OF.) A similar process was occurring in the functioning of the judicial side of the itinerant Curia. The last Justiciar vacated office in 1234 and the civil wars of Henry II's reign gave rise to much business concerned with violence, quasi-criminal matters and the abuses of lower, especially franchise, courts. The first Chief Justice of the King's Bench, Robert de Brus, was appointed in 1268 but the King still sometimes presided. (*See* KINGS BENCH, COURT OF.) The direct connection between the Curia and the King's Bench had, however, virtually disappeared by 1400.

(7) By this time a parliament had become the recognised principal legislator and corrector of the King's Bench; the House of Lords, as part of it, was acquiring both an original and an appellate jurisdiction, yet the uncertainties and shortage of skilled manpower were extreme and the Curia, now developing into the later King's Council, still had much work of all kinds. In the early 15th cent. the Chancery became a Court of Equity (*see* CHANCERY, COURT OF) besides a secretariat and a little later the Council began to split yet again into a largely executive body and a kind of high executive court sitting in a particular building, from which it got its name (*see* STAR CHAMBER).

(8) The Council, being a continuing body, had to consist of professional public servants. The magnates who claimed to sit, generally found it impossible to do so for long. Moreover Parliament never had time in which to deal with all the petitions before it and statutes were often in need of amplification or promulgation. Thus the council acted administratively to deal with some problems, legislatively by proclamations and orders to deal with others and judicially to deal with yet others. The Tudors could make extensive use of this body because its powers were undefined and represented the residual functions of the crown. This continued until the Long Parliament abolished the Star Chamber, and later parliaments seized financial control of the state.

(9) The judicial function, however, survived beyond the seas. *See* PRIVY COUNCIL, JUDICIAL COMMITTEE.

CURRAGH, THE (Co. Kildare) was a large common 32 miles S.W. of Dublin used from 1822 as a racecourse and then as a training ground for volunteers. It developed into the British Army's principal Irish cantonment.

CURRAGH "MUTINY" (Mar. 1914). Carson's Ulster Unionists threatened forcibly to resist inclusion in the united Irish Free State to be set up under a liberal Home Rule Bill of 1912. Certain British cavalry officers at the Curragh signed a letter indicating that they would resign rather than coerce them. Maj-Gen. Sir Arthur Paget then got from Seely, the Sec. of State for War, a promise that Ulster-domiciled officers would be allowed temporarily to 'disappear' if their units were ordered to fight Carson. This amounted to connivance at mutiny. Paget made the

concession widely known, whereupon Brig-Gen. Hubert Gough and 57 out of 70 officers of the 3rd Cavalry Brigade announced that they preferred dismissal to obedience to the orders, if given. The govt. weakly allowed Gough and the three regimental commanding officers to go go to Whitehall and negotiate with the War Office because, with a German war imminent, the Expeditionary Force might otherwise be disorganised. Apart from a sensation and continental speculation about the reliability of the British army, the final result was a cabinet reshuffle. The outbreak of World War I shortly captured attention.

CURRENCY, IRISH. Ireland had its own currency until 1827. The Irish pound was variably below par of the English. There was always an extreme shortage of specie and what there was habitually clipped, so that coins were, to the end, always weighed and tokens and tallies were normal. In country areas banknotes and even coin were pawned for less than their value and barter was common but on the decline, because local worthies such as blacksmiths were issuing notes of low denomination for village circulation.

In 1804, owing to war, the Banks of England and Ireland suspended payment in specie. There was a rush to multiply paper and to start new banks to issue it. The number of banks rose from 12 to 70, paper in circulation quadrupled and the Irish £ fell to 80% of the English. In 1820 there were wholesale bank failures and in 1821 English and Irish currency were assimilated by English currency becoming tender in Ireland.

CURSITORS were 24 administrative, as opposed to judicial, officers of the Exchequer, the highest being called Cursitor Barons. Their name survives in the name of a street off Chancery Lane, London.

CURTANA. A broken sword, symbolising mercy, carried at English coronations.

CURZON, George Nathaniel (1859-1925) 1st Ld. CURZON of KEDLESTON (1898) (Ir.) 1st E. (1911) 1st M. (1921) was educated at Eton and at Oxford, where he became a Fellow of All Souls in 1883. He already had the spinal trouble which put him in lifelong pain, necessitating a harness. It imposed a rigidity on his demeanour and, as he never mentioned it, this made him a target for much malice. He was a wit and stylist in English and Latin with a vivid sense of humour and self-mockery. He also had a restless sense of grandeur. He wrote the following for the *Balliol Rhymes* as an undergraduate:

My name is George Nathaniel Curzon
I am a most superior person.
My hair is soft, my face is sleek
I dine at Blenheim twice a week.

(2) He became an M.P. in 1886 and, in that capacity set out on a series of travels (in 1887-8) via N. America to Japan, China, Singapore, Ceylon and India; (in 1888-9) via Russia to the Caucasus and Turkestan; (in 1889-90) to Persia; (in 1892) repeating his first journey as far as China and then to Cochin China and Siam; (in 1894) to C. Asia and Afghanistan. He became a considerable orientalist and a leading authority on Asiatic affairs. He was drawn to the policy conclusions, hard to gainsay, that Britain's welfare depended on her world influence and that her main source of wealth and influence was India, which had, therefore, to be cherished, developed and protected.

(3) Being the sort of man he was, he resolved to do it himself. In 1891 he became U. Sec. for India; from 1895 to 1898 he was Foreign U-Sec. under Salisbury, but resigned against Salisbury's relaxed attitude towards Turkish oppression, and violence in Venezuela. Better informed than anyone else, he publicly denounced French aggressions in Siam and the German occupation of Kiao-Chow as threats to British imperial interests. As this was the time of imperial euphoria during Q.

Victoria's Diamond Jubilee, he caught a public mood and his brilliant appointment at 39 as Viceroy of India was popular and appropriate.

(4) He entered India (Jan. 1899) in pomp and popularity, incessantly travelling in state, settling disputes, studying assessments, coping with educational problems. He reached a *modus vivendi* with the Afghans and established a powerful position in the Persian Gulf. He believed that British and Indian interests were complementary but thought in terms of princely India (a third of the country) rather than the partly destabilised communal and religious tensions of British India, because in viceregal splendour he had, in a sense, become the greatest of the princes himself. Thus the first years of his viceroyalty were a rising curve, reaching a tremendous climax at the great Delhi Durbar of 1903 which, with his eye for symbolism and tradition, powerfully stimulated Indian archaeology and art and at which Delhi, the capital of the Moghuls, resumed its position as the imperial capital.

(5) Thereafter the curve was downward. The removal of the administration from Calcutta to Delhi upset Bengali business interests and, because Bengal contained a noticeable proportion of British educated, politically conscious Hindus, commerce and politics came into alliance. An administratively sound partition of Bengal gave moslems a majority in the new western part. Strident Hindu agitation and communal violence ensued and coincided with troubles nearer home. Some of his English political associates misunderstood or personally disliked him. The trend towards *entente cordiale* conflicted (since Russia was allied with France) with his fundamentally anti-Russian policy and he quarrelled with Kitchener, his C-in-C, who was a skilful and ruthless intriguer. Moreover, by mid 1905, it was obvious that his friends at home were about to be replaced by his opponents. In Aug. the govt. ignored his recommendation on an appointment to his own council. He resigned and returned to England in Nov. In Dec. Campbell-Bannerman's Liberals came to power.

(6) He was now in eclipse. In deference to the wishes of Edward VII he did not then re-enter politics and in July 1906 his wife died. He hid from his frustrations and grief by becoming Chancellor of Oxford University and throwing himself into its affairs. He was elected to the House of Lords as an Irish representative peer. The Royal Geographical Society and the National and Tate Galleries felt his organising talents. He restored Bodiam and Tattershall castles (which he bequeathed to the nation) but meanwhile he could not keep out of national affairs. He supported Lord Roberts' campaign for conscription; attacked the Anglo-Russian convention of 1907 and at first urged the Lords to resist the govt. in the developing constitutional crisis and then sensibly advised them to accept the Parliament Bill.

(7) He and Milner were both friends of the romantic and bilingual best-selling novelist Elinor Glyn, whose red hair and green eyes bewitched the society of Paris, London and St. Petersburg. In 1907 she published *Three Weeks*, a brief affair between an Englishman and a Balkan queen. It was widely reprobated and read, particularly for an incident on a tiger skin. Curzon and Milner promptly each presented her with a tiger skin. Contemporary opinion saw more in this than was probably justified. She was almost certainly not Milner's mistress: despite his spinal problem she probably was Curzon's. He was for years the blazing sun in her romantic firmament.

(8) All this kept him in the limelight. So did his coronation peerages of 1911. The public noticed that they had an underused elder statesman. The politicians were less enthusiastic and it took until nearly the second year of World War I (May 1915) for Asquith to take him into the cabinet as Lord Privy Seal and keep him out of the war committee. This did not stop him pursuing his convictions. Better informed on Russian and Levantine affairs than most, he passionately espoused Churchill's Gallipoli campaign. He publicly demanded conscription and refused a Garter until Asquith had promised to introduce it. As chairman of the Shipping Control Committee he had to fight his colleagues as well as the U-boats on the crying need to reduce imports. As Pres. of the Air Board, designed to reconcile the competing claims of the soldiers and the Admirals, he pressed for a separate Air Ministry. In Dec. 1916, after Asquith's fall, Lloyd George invited him into his war cabinet.

(9) A month later he remarried, and Elinor said that he never told her. His second marriage was as happy as the first.

(10) He was now as busy as he wished to be. With his new wife, his house again became a social centre. He was Lord Pres. and Leader of the Lords and Lloyd George's War Cabinet met 500 times before the Armistice. On the other hand, as a leading Conservative in a govt. pledged to many liberal policies, he was in an anomalous position. He opposed the Balfour Declaration but had to swallow it. He announced the govt's promise of Indian progress towards responsible govt. but hotly opposed the Montagu-Chelmsford reforms. At the Dublin rising at Easter 1916, though a Unionist, he chaired, at Lloyd George's request, the drafting of an Irish bill but Lloyd George threw it out in favour of a Convention which Curzon had to defend in the House. This failed and Curzon had, in announcing the suspension of Irish negotiations, to make another volte face. Such humiliations were bad for his image. His treatment of women's suffrage seemed (but was not) worse, He had been Pres. of the Anti-Suffrage League since 1912. Though the Commons had passed the Suffrage Bill in 1917 by seven to one, the League expected him to lead the opposition to it in the Lords. Consistently with the advice which he gave on the Parliament Bill in Aug. 1910, he thought that the Views of the Commons should prevail and voted for it. He had not resigned his presidency. Naturally his High Tory friends never forgave him.

(11) After the Armistice (Nov. 1918) Balfour (Foreign Sec.) went with Lloyd George to the Paris peace conference, while Curzon took charge of the Foreign Office at home. In Oct. 1919 Balfour resigned against Lloyd George's recklessness and Curzon, thinking that he could do better, accepted the succession. He was mistaken. The Foreign Sec. was not now properly in charge of foreign policy and this became painfully clear over (his very own) Persian issues. The troops were to be withdrawn from Persia for demobilisation. Curzon, before the troops left, sensibly negotiated a treaty putting Britain in charge of Persian finances and the army. The troops then left. The Persians repudiated the treaty and negotiated another (Feb. 1921) in the opposite sense with Lenin. It was left to the helpless Curzon to announce the failure.

(12) This taught him something of the new dynamics of Levantine politics. His friend Milner, who had been in Egypt from Nov. 1919 to Apr. 1920, advised a new Anglo-Egyptian alliance. By Feb. 1920 parliament had approved heads of agreement and Zaghlul Pasha's mission arrived for the final settlement in July. A Commonwealth Conference had, meanwhile, stressed the importance of the Suez Canal. The cabinet was now, against Curzon's advice, less conciliatory; Zaghlul went home without his treaty and the British authorities there deported him. Fortunately more intelligent counsels prevailed. Lord Allenby, the High Commissioner, proposed a unilateral declaration that, subject to the maintenance of the British position in the Canal and the Sudan and with, in return, a promise of British military defence against foreign interferences, the British protectorate be abolished.

(13) Despite Curzon's warnings, Lloyd George had

persisted in delaying peace with the French-supported Turks, who were at war with Greece. The pro-Greek Lloyd George constantly sabotaged Curzon's efforts to lay a foundation for peace by an agreement with France and, by making Curzon's impartiality look like a front, injured his Foreign Sec's international standing. He also forced Edwin Montagu to resign over the Viceroy's manifesto on the Caliphate. The new French prime minister, Poincaré, embarked on a studiedly pro-Turkish policy just as Curzon at last got the cabinet to make the Egyptian Declaration (which was to have profound effects on World War II). The Turks now drove the Greeks out of Asia Minor. Despite this, Lloyd George continued to conduct intrigues with foreign govts. behind Curzon's back. In Oct. one such came to light and Curzon had had enough. When the Chanak Incident and the Carlton Club Meeting crystallised opposition to Lloyd George, Curzon had already refused to support him (Oct. 1922).

(14) He continued as Bonar Law's Foreign Sec. and instantly set out for the Lausanne Conference, where he dominated the proceedings, got the respect of the Turks, outwitted the French and Italians and got what he wanted, namely the Mosul oilfields and the freedom of the Straits. Technically the conference was aborted by the French who, meanwhile, had seized the Ruhr. Further Anglo-French friction followed. The French thought that the Germans could pay their reparations but would not, the British that they would if they could. Curzon's suggestion that an international jury of experts should find out lowered the tension and germinated the Dawes and Young Plans. In truth both sides were wrong. The Germans could not pay and would not have paid if they could.

(15) There now ensued a curious episode. In May 1923 Bonar Law resigned the prime ministership. The King's private sec. (Lord Stamfordham) summoned Curzon urgently from Montacute to London. When he arrived, Stamfordham told him that the King meant to send for Stanley Baldwin. For some hours the disappointment put this passionate man into a state of collapse. Then, magnanimously, he offered Baldwin his support.

(16) He stayed on as Foreign Sec. where his main achievement was to make the Russians honour Lloyd George's trade agreement with Britain. In Aug. 1923 the Anglo-French quarrel over reparations blew up for the first time under Curzon, who published the British case to a great deal of simulated Parisian fury. In Jan. 1924 Baldwin having, against Curzon's advice, fought and lost a general election, the govt. resigned. A year later Curzon was dead.

CURZON LINE was an armistice line proposed by Ld. Curzon in July 1920 between Poland and Russia based upon the line which Polish troops had occupied in Dec. 1919.

***CUSTODES PACIS* (Lat = Keepers of the Peace).** The meaning of this term was variable. They are recorded in 1195 as assistants to sheriffs in the maintenance of order. In 1205, when England was under threat of a French invasion, constables were appointed for each hundred and township and these were sometimes called *custodes pacis*. During the period of baronial unrest, the barons appointed keepers of the peace to counter the influence of the royal sheriffs and later the King appointed his own to help restore order. Their work was connected with the leadership of the local militia and in 1287 the keepers were made inspectors rather than leaders of the militia and were expressly commissioned to enforce the Statute of Winchester (1285). By the mid-14th cent. they were superseded by the more numerous Justices of the Peace.

CUSTOM. A local legal rule proved by evidence of habit. It must be confined within a definite or definable area, be clear and reasonable. Customs are very diverse and include shaking hands on a horse bargain; drinking a mug of ale on a Severn towage contract (being had for a mug); paying on the nail (a metal post outside the Guildhall at Bristol); various Stock exchange bargains. A claim by custom to be able to turn out an unlimited number of animals on a common was held unreasonable because it would exhaust the land.

CUSTOMARY COURT or HALL-MOOT was held for the unfree tenants of a manor in virtue of the Lords seignorial rights. The Manor Steward commonly presided. The matters handled always included the conveyancing of villein tenements, but might include, according to area, applications to marry and delinquencies such as shirking boon work, careless ploughing, and *leyerwite*, a fine for concubinage or other illicit associations. The disciplinary functions were eroded by commutation and contractual tenancies, or superseded by the itinerant assizes. The conveyancing survived as a means of passing and registering dealings and enfranchisements in copyhold land, i.e. land originally of villein tenure depending on possession of a copy of the court roll. From the mid 18th cent. the steward was often the Lord's solicitor and the court held in his office, which might be in London. In this attenuated form these courts survived until 1926 when all copyholds were enfranchised. *See also* COURT LEET.

CUSTOMS (1) were crown revenues enjoyed by virtue of (i) ancient prerogative (*see* GREAT CUSTOM); (ii) acquisition of franchises; (iii) parliamentary grant (*see* SUBSIDY-3); (iv) agreements with English or foreign trading bodies (*see* CARTA MERCATORIA); (v) ancient local custom. The charges might be levied on imports or exports; under Henry I (1100-35) the amount was at discretion.

(2) The primitive origin of the customs was threefold (i) the crown right of prise, caption, emption or purveyance (effectively a tax payable in kind) which was sometimes commuted in favour of a trader or class of traders for a money toll; (ii) the right to restrain or regulate trade, for which fines for grants of exemption were levied; (iii) the supervision of these activities at the Kings ports and the levying of port dues there.

(3) New customs duties were created from time to time and these were usually levied separately, not as additions to an existing tax. The system became increasingly confused and administratively expensive, especially if parts of the revenue were subject to assignment or farmed by Crown creditors. Full information on the rates was not assembled into a single book until Charles II's time, a new book being issued under George I, but new imposts and rates continued to be created and by 1785 the customs were a corrupt chaos.

(4) Pitt's Customs Consolidation Act, 1787, abolished all existing duties and substituted on each article a single duty equivalent to the aggregate of the previous duties on it. The act had to be founded on about 3000 commons financial resolutions. It also simplified customs administration. The savings on manpower and dishonesty were very large. There were further consolidations in 1853, 1876 and 1952.

***CUSTOS ROTULORUM* (Lat = Keeper of the rolls)** was the senior J.P. and later combined the office with that of the Lord Lieut. In either capacity he made recommendations for the Commission of the Peace.

CUTCH (India) a large, flat, hot peninsula was under Rajput rule from 1546 to 1760 when a Muslim Sindhi govt. was set up. It came under British rule from 1815.

CUTHBERT (?-758) after being abbot of Liminge (Kent) became Bp. of Hereford in 736 and Abp. of Canterbury in about 740. He advised Ethelbald of Mercia and the Synod of Clovesho of 742 and himself summoned another there in 747 to regulate the work of monks and priests.

CUTHBERT, St. (c. 634-87) as a young man served a Benician thane, first as a shepherd and then as a warrior. He entered the Celtic abbey of Melrose in 651. In about

664 he became Prior of Lindisfarne. He accepted the rulings (q.v.) of the Synod of Whitby (664), but never rejected the spirit of Celtic Christianity and his preaching, simplicity and empathy with birds and animals belonged to the tradition of St. Aidan. He spent many years as a hermit in the Farne Is. but reluctantly agreed to become Bp. of Lindisfarne in 684. After his death, admiration for his saintliness inspired masterpieces such as the trappings of his burial (pectoral cross, stole and the coffin itself) and the Lindisfarne Gospels. During the Danish invasions the Lindisfarne monks carried his body from place to place, coming eventually to rest in 997 in the church at Durham. It remained uncorrupt for centuries. In the middle ages he was especially revered in the north country and was considered the protector of Durham and its see. An anonymous monk of Lindisfarne and Bede wrote lives of him.

CUTHBURGA, St. (?-725) was sister of K. Ine of Wessex and queen to the learned and religious K. Aldfrith of Northumbria, from whom she separated in about 703. She became a nun at Barking and in about 706 founded the great double monastery at Wimborne.

CUTHRED (?-754). See WEST SAXONS, EARLY-16.

CUTPURSE, Moll alias FRITH, Mary (?1584-1659) a pickpocket, fortune teller and forger, was the subject of Middleton and Dekkers *Roaring Girle,* and did penance at St. Pauls Cross in 1612. Her determination to mend her ways was strengthened by alcohol and of short duration and she apparently widened her activities to highway robbery, on one occasion at the expense of Gen. Fairfax.

CUTTS, John (1661-1707) 1st Ld. CUTTS of GOWRAN (Ir. 1690) served, after a period in Monmouth's entourage at The Hague, as a volunteer against the Turks in Hungary and was Adj-Gen to the D. of Lorraine in 1686. He returned to England with William III in 1688 and was an M.P. from 1693 to 1707. He fought as Col. of William's Guards at the Boyne in 1690. In 1695 he commanded with distinction at the S. of Namur and was a plenipotentiary for the T. of Ryswick in 1697. From 1701 to 1704 he was one of Marlborough's most determined field commanders. In 1705 he became C-in-C in Ireland.

CWICHELM, K. (fl 614-36). See WEST SAXONS, EARLY.

CWMBRAN. See NEW TOWNS.

CYCLOTRON for accelerating electric particles was originally invented in 1931.

CYFAR **(Welsh).** See CANTREF.

CYLCH **(Welsh = circuit).** In Wales (a) the King, his queen and daughter and the Penteulu, respectively, travelled the Kingdom periodically to supervise justice, administration, military affairs and to hunt; (b) each *maer* and *canghellor* travelled his jurisdiction twice a year; (c) the royal huntsmen, grooms, bodyguards and falconer also travelled on circuit. The cost of entertainment and shelter was imposed in the case of (a) upon all at the night's stopping places, in addition to *gwestfa,* save in Arfon, which was privileged against the Penteulu. In cases (b) and (c) the cost fell only upon the unfree. *See* WELSH LAW, SOCIAL

CYMBELINE or CUNOBELINUS (?-43), of the family of Cassivelaunus, founded Camulodunum (Colchester) in about A.D. 10 and, as K. of the Catuvellauni, was overlord of South East Britain. *See* BRITAIN BEFORE THE ROMAN CONQUEST-2 *et seq.*

CYMMRODORION, HONOURABLE SOCIETIES OF. The first was founded in 1751 by London merchants to foster Welsh culture. It was dissolved in 1787 but a **CYMREIGYDDION Society** founded in 1772 took up its work and revived the *Eisteddfodau.* The original society, refounded in 1820, organised further, more literary *Eisteddfodau* from 1821, but declined and had to be refounded yet again in 1873.

CYNAN ap Rhodri. See GWYNEDD-8.

CYNEGILS (r. 611-42). See WEST SAXONS, EARLY-7.

CYNEWULF (?-785). See WEST SAXONS, EARLY-17.

CYNHASEDD **(Welsh)** was a fee paid to a lord for the right to possess land otherwise than by lineal succession.

CYNRIC (r. 534-60). See WEST SAXONS, EARLY-3.

CYPRUS. (1) The Cypriot church was autocephalous and the island formed a peaceful Byzantine province until overrun by the Arabs in 647. A relative or wet nurse of Mohammed was killed in this invasion and this led to the establishment of an important Moslem shrine. The Arabs withdrew in 680 and the island was not fully controlled by Romans or Arabs until 965, when it was reincorporated into the Eastern Empire. In 1185 Isaac Comnenus (a relative of the Emperor) usurped the govt., but in 1191 he was overthrown by RICHARD I of England on crusade; Richard sold Cyprus to the Templars and it passed to Guy of Lusignan, the deposed K. of Jerusalem. (*See also* CRUSADES-12 *et seq.*)

(2) It thus became the principal crusading state after the fall of Acre in 1291. In alliance with Venice and the Knights of Rhodes, Smyrna was taken from the Turks in 1344 and Adalia (Attalia) in 1361. As Constantinople declined, it became the main entrepôt of the Levant trade and all the great Mediterranean trading states established factories or bought trading privileges; its fertility and climatic variety, combined with the export of sugar, silks and especially salt, gave it great prosperity but after K. Peter I's assassination in 1369, the govt. was weak. The Genoese were able in 1373 to take over Famagusta, the main port, and from 1426 tribute had to be paid to Egypt. In 1460 James II, formerly Abp. of Nicosia, seized power and in 1464, with Egyptian help, expelled the Genoese. In 1472 he got rid of Egyptian suzerainty by a treaty with Venice. He married the Venetian patrician Catharine Corner (Cornaro) who was declared a Daughter of the Republic. At his childless death in 1473 the Venetians ruled the island in her name until 1489 when they persuaded her to abdicate and acquired full sovereignty by succession. It remained profitably in their hands until 1570 when it was attacked by the Turks. The newly fortified Nicosia was stormed and Famagusta, equally newly fortified, fell after a year's bombardment from which it never recovered.

(3) This was the heyday of Ottoman civilisation and the just and intelligent rule of Suleiman the Magnificent brought notable benefits. Prosperity continued through incorporation in the Ottoman economic zone; Turkish taxes were initially lower than the Venetian and the Turks abolished serfdom. There was a good deal of conversion and Turkish immigration.

(4) The decay of the Ottoman central administration led, however, to provincial corruption. Cyprus represented a rich plum for ambitious ministers and the governorship was granted for short periods in turn to court magnates to enjoy the pickings. The archbishopric had (as elsewhere) always represented the Orthodox population (*see* MILLET SYSTEM). In an island it served to maintain Greek consciousness. Rebellions, more or less bloodiedly suppressed, against Turkish corruption took place in 1764, 1804 and in 1821 when the gov. hanged all the bishops.

(5) Western pressure for the liberalisation of the Ottoman empire brought a show of local self govt. in 1838 and again in 1856. This was done by nominating local worthies to the governor's *divan* until it was safe to get rid of them.

(6) The British supported the Turks against Russian Mediterranean ambitions. Cyprus seemed a convenient centre where a military presence could lend backbone to the Turks and protect the Suez Canal. As part of the Berlin settlement of 1878, British troops occupied Cyprus under Ottoman sovereignty. As it had no adequate harbours, the British never developed it for their original purpose, but they greatly improved the administration, if little else. At the outbreak of war with Turkey in 1914, they annexed the island and in 1915 offered it to Greece if she would help Serbia, then being slowly destroyed by the Central Powers. Greece refused and the offer was withdrawn. The Turks recognised the annexation by the T. of Lausanne (1924) and in 1925 Cyprus became a Crown colony with a legislative council.

(7) By 1929, the year of the great depression, political opinion had crystallised into three main groups. The Turkish minority preferred the *status quo*, but hoped that the new Turkish republic (which had just won a resounding victory over Greece) would, if necessary, protect them. The Orthodox church, long the only leadership of the Cypriot Greeks, with its large following, wanted as much autonomy for Cyprus as was consistent with the safety of its immense properties, for in Greece church property was vested in the state. Finally, a small but violent faction wanted union (enosis) with Greece. As a result of disturbances in 1931, the legislative council was abolished and thenceforth the island was under governor's rule until the end of World War II.

(8) After the war the enosis agitation in the shape of EOKA (Ethniki Organosis Kypriakou Agonos) acquired the characteristics of a fifth column. Arms and terrorists, infiltrated from Greece under the direction of Col. Georgios Grivas (or Dighenis), were used to stampede or intimidate Cypriot Greek opinion. To keep control, the church had to outbid EOKA. Makarios (1913-77) ordained in 1946 and elected Bp. of Citium in 1948 was the author of the new policy. In 1950 he was elected Archbishop.

(9) The church now placed itself at the head of all but the most extremist opinion and claimed self determination for Cyprus. Mainland Greek nationalists did the same. Attacks on Cypriot Turks led to the formation of Turkish fortified enclaves in Nicosia, Famagusta and the Kyrenia mountains. The Turkish republic took offence. By 1955 the island was on the verge of a civil war in which Greece was covertly and Turkey might be openly, involved. A conference in London in Sept. failed. The British considered that no solution was possible until order had been restored. Military reinforcements were sent and Field Marshal Sir John Harding made governor. EOKA now started murdering British soldiers, which it represented as a patriotic war. As the archbishop could not and would not repudiate EOKA he was deported in Mar. 1956. This was a mistake for it deprived the Greek Cypriots of their accepted leader, leaving only EOKA terrorism; much exaggerated in the foreign press it could not be entirely suppressed, but its perpetrators were no statesmen. EOKA could not manage without Makarios. In Mar. 1957 it offered to suspend activity if the archbishop were released. The bargain was struck; the more stringent security measures were lifted and in Dec. Sir Hugh Foot became gov.

(10) To the Turkish Cypriots, led by Dr. Fazil Kütchük, the course of events was leading towards *enosis*. Kütchük demanded partition (i.e. a rearrangement of the enclaves) instead. In the summer of 1958 EOKA attacked the Turks again and in the autumn Makarios as a compromise, proposed that after a fixed period of self govt., Cyprus should become an independent state.

(11) This solution was accepted by the mainland Turks (who knew that he meant it) and negotiations at Zurich between the Greek and Turkish govts. in Feb. 1959 brought an agreement which the British govt. quickly approved. In the independent Cypriot republic, Greek-Turkish Parliamentary and administrative representation was to be divided on a 70 to 30 basis with a Greek President and a Turkish Vice-President. The British were to have in full sovereignty about 100 sq. miles in the south-east for service bases, whose presence would contribute enormously to the Cypriot economy. The island was neither to be partitioned nor to enter into any political or economic union with any other state: Britain, Turkey and Greece would guarantee its

independence and Turkey and Greece would respect British sovereignty in the bases.

(12) In the general elections all the 15 Turkish seats fell to Dr. Kütchük, and of the 35 Greek Makarios obtained 30 and AKEL (the communists) 5. The republic came into existence in Aug. 1960 and was admitted to the U.N. In Mar. 1961 it was formally retained in the British Commonwealth.

(13) The arrangements were soon in confusion because the Greek mainland nationalists had no intention of abandoning their attack on Cypriot independence. EOKA terrorism, mostly discredited, was succeeded by a covert invasion. Grivas had been promoted to general and the disturbances were kept going by Greek troops in disguise. The British tried to keep order, but in Mar. 1964 a mixed U.N. force arrived to replace them outside the bases. Outbreaks were frequent and dangerous until the advent in Greece of 1968 of the regime of the colonels, who abandoned the policy of the previous govts. In 1972 a U.N. force was still keeping peace. In 1974, however, Makarios was overthrown and fled to Europe and the Turks invaded and occupied the northern part of the island where they set up an independent administration. They, but no other country, recognised this as an independent republic. Makarios then returned as President of the *de facto* southern part. He died in 1977, leaving the island still divided and the British enclaves still in the southern half.

CYRENAICA. *See* LIBYA.

CZAR. *See* ROMAN EMPERORS-I.

CZECHOSLOVAKIA. *See* AUSTRO-HUNGARY. (1) A Czech (as opposed to Slovak) national sentiment began to revive after 1848 mainly among educated Czechs denied public office if unable to speak German. The sentiment was exploited by allied propaganda in World War I; deserters were formed into Czech legions in Russia, France and Italy and in Feb. 1916 the Czechs Thomas Masaryk and Eduard Benes set up a "Czechoslovak" National Council in Paris. Masaryk courted the Slovak organisations in the U.S.A. and in May 1918 negotiated the PITTSBURGH AGREEMENT, which contemplated the union of Czechs and Slovaks in a state. Masaryk's purpose was to provide the industrialised Czech areas with cheap food from Slovakia. It is doubtful if the Slovaks outside the U.S.A. ever heard of these manoeuvres. In Sept. 1918 the Allied powers allowed themselves to be persuaded by Masaryk's propaganda and charm and recognised his council as a provisional govt.

(2) In Oct. proclamations of independence were issued in Prague, but the south Sudeten areas declared their adherence to the new Austrian republic. In Nov. a provisional Czech national assembly elected Masaryk president; the various Czech legions arrived home and were immediately set in motion first against Slovakia (overrun by Feb. 1919) and then against the Sudetens whose govt. was liquidated by Sept. Thereupon Bela Kun's Hungarian socialist govt. drove the Czechs out of Slovakia. Allied intervention, however, settled the form of the new state so as to include not only Bohemia, Moravia, the Sudeten territories and Slovakia, but also Ruthenia, part of the Teschen coal mines and some minor Austrian and Silesian areas.

(3) The constitution of Feb. 1920, based on a French model, emphasised the unity of the state; govt. currency, legal, administrative and land reforms were designed to break with the Austrian and Hungarian pasts of the two halves of the country. In practice this meant centralisation in Prague, Czech dominance in most depts. of state and policy and, consequent unrest first in Slovakia and Ruthenia and then, as Germany and Hungary recovered from the effects of defeat, among the Sudetens and Hungarians. Successive govts. resisted demands for local autonomy and sought outside support in understandings with the other two major successor states of the

Habsburg monarchy, Yugoslavia and Roumania. This LITTLE ENTENTE, strong enough to bully Austria and Hungary, was otherwise ineffectual without French support, upon which the Czech govt. increasingly relied.

(4) The world-wide slump of 1929 created acute tension in the industrialised Sudeten area, as it did in neighbouring Germany, where by 1933 Hitler had taken over. The Sudeten parties naturally looked to the growing aggressive power in the west and the Czechs naturally opposed them. They coalesced into the Sudeten German Party, a Nazi organisation led by Conrad Henlein. When the French came to an understanding with Russia in self defence against the Germans, it was natural for the Czechs to adhere to it in self defence against the Sudetens (May 1935) and France and Czechoslovakia began the construction of frontier fortifications. In Mar. 1939, however, the Germans outflanked these by seizing Austria, which was immediately followed by an intensification of Sudeten agitation. The failure of a British mission of conciliation under Ld Runciman (Sept. 1939) now made it clear that the dissolution of the Czechoslovak state was imminent.

(5) Hitler's demand for annexation of the Sudeten areas would put Czechoslovakia at his mercy; for they contained all the military strategic points, most of the industry and stretched to within a mile of the Skoda Armament Works. Since nobody was willing at that moment to fight the Germans, his demands were conceded by Chamberlain at Munich; the Germans marched in Oct. 1938. Eduard Beneš, the president, fled. Edmund Hacha, a politician acceptable to the Germans, succeeded him and Slovakia and Ruthenia were accorded local autonomy in a loose federal structure, which instantly collapsed; for Hungarian demands on the Slovak frontier areas were agreed by Hitler in the First Vienna Award, while the Poles seized Teschen. In Mar. 1939 the rump of Slovakia was proclaimed an independent state; the Czech area was compelled to accept German protection and Hungary seized Ruthenia. The whole was now part of Hitler's New Order.

(6) Until 1942 these areas, though suffering under German persecution of Jews and intellectuals, remained relatively quiet. A rudimentary resistance arose after the first German defeats in the east in May 1942 and the reprisals following the assassination of the police terrorist Reinhard Heydrich, the German Protector, in June. Meanwhile the Beneš govt. in exile in London called for the expulsion of the Sudeten Germans once victory was won.

(7) The Yalta agreement put the area firmly under the "tutelage" of the Russians. They annexed Ruthenia, under the name of Subcarpathian Russia, in 1946. Beneš, though President, had to accept a pro-communist coalition under Fierlinger, because the Russian army was everywhere. The Sudeten Germans and collaborators were driven out and this facilitated industrial nationalisation. Thereupon Klement Gottwald, a communist, was forced upon the country as prime minister (July 1946) and in Feb. 1948 he engineered a *coup d'état*, destroyed the lawful govt. and had Jan Masaryk (son of Thomas), the foreign minister, thrown from a window. This second Defenestration of Prague made the republic a Russian satellite.

(8) Economic decline, due to mismanagement and Russian rapacity, led to criticism inside the local communist party. This culminated in Jan. 1968 in the replacement of old guard communists by a more liberal type led by Alexander Dubcek (the so-called PRAGUE SPRING). Their purpose was, without calling Russian leadership in question or abandoning one-party govt., to establish a partial market economy and greater freedom of expression. This met with stern disapproval from all the Iron Curtain bloc countries except Roumania, which tried to act as broker in Russo-Czech discussions in July and Aug. 1968. The Russians never intended that these discussions should do more than make time for mobilisation and in Aug. they, with their Hungarian and Bulgar allies, invaded the country, reversed all the new policies and instituted a permanent military occupation. This lasted until the collapse of the Russian communist system in and after 1988.

(9) Comparative liberal revolution in Prague was followed almost at once by something more nationalist in Bratislava, where the Slovaks moved towards independence. In 1992 this was achieved and Czechoslovakia ceased to exist. Economic connections, however remained.

D

d (for Lat. denarius) denoted a penny before decimalisation.

D'ABERNON. *See* VINCENT.

DACCA (India) became the seat of the Moghul military govt. of Bengal in 1608. The HEIC established a Muslin factory there in 1663 but despite the transfer of the govt. to Murshidabad in 1705 the town flourished until the competition of Manchester textiles in the 19th cent. brought a decline. Severely damaged in an earthquake in 1897, it was the capital of East Bengal with Assam from 1905 to 1912 and in 1947 became the capital of E. Pakistan, now Bangladesh.

DACOITS are members of gangs of robbers in India and in Burma where they have been especially prevalent.

DACRE, Lds. *See* FIENNES; BRAND.

DACRE (1) Sir Richard James (1799-1886) commanded the R. Horse Artillery in the Crimea and became a field-marshal in 1886. His brother **(2) Sir Sidney Colpoys (1805-84),** a sailor, captured Castro Morea for the Greeks in 1828; commanded a ship off the Crimea and in 1863 became C-in-C in the Channel.

DAFYDD I ab Owain (r. 1170-1203). *See* GWYNEDD-25.

DAFYDD II ap Llywellyn. *See* GWYNEDD-28.

DAFYDD III ap Gruffydd. *See* GWYNEDD-30.

DAGGER MONEY. A sum formerly given to the judges at the Northumberland assizes on leaving Newcastle so that they could buy daggers with which to defend themselves against convict's relatives and Scottish raiders.

DAGGER SCENE IN THE COMMONS. Edmund Burke, in peroration on the French revolution, threw down a dagger exclaiming "...Such is the weapon which the French Jacobins would plunge into the heart of our beloved King!" Sheridan brought the house down with, "Where's the fork?"

DAHL, Michael (1656-1743) prolific but dull Swedish painter of most of the personalities at the English court from about 1688.

DAHOMEY (W. Africa). Jakin was founded on the coast at Porto Novo, and Dan-Homey inland at Aboncy in 1625. In 1710 Dan-Homey secured a coastal outlet at Ouida or Wydah. Both states traded slaves to the French, English and Portuguese who had been building coastal forts since 1671 and Wydah was the only African slave exporting port against which the Slave Trade Acts were not enforced. Dan-Homey's aggressive policies were interrupted by civil wars until the reign of K. Ghezo (r. 1818-58), who reorganised the army and introduced female regiments. In 1850 he signed a commercial treaty with France which took Jakin and Wydah under protection in 1863. This involved the abandonment of the legal slave trade from Wydah, already depressed by the U.S. civil war. Dan-Homey continued to press upon these protectorates and so between 1890 and 1893 the French overran it. Dahomey became part of the French community in Dec. 1958 and independent in 1960. *See* AFRICA, WEST, EX-FRENCH.

DAIL EIREANN, the Irish legislature, came into existence when 73 Sinn Feiners were returned at the Gen. Election of Nov. 1918 and refused to go to Westminster. They then set themselves up as an Irish parliament.

DAILY CHRONICLE was founded in 1877 as a liberal paper and gave radical support to Lloyd George, but turned against him after the Maurice affair. Shortly before the Armistice in 1918, Lloyd George persuaded his friend Dalziel, a press magnate, to buy it with the help of funds accumulated from the sale of honours. Bought for £1M, it was sold in 1926 for £3M. In 1930 it was amalgamated with the *Daily News* to form the **NEWS CHRONICLE,** which succumbed to competition in 1960.

DAILY COURANT (1702-35) this, the first English daily paper, contained foreign news translated from foreign journals. Based upon a Dutch model, it profited from the improvement in the cross-Channel packet system after 1691. It consisted of a single sheet.

DAILY DISPATCH. *See* DAILY NEWS.

DAILY EXPRESS was a halfpenny popular newspaper launched in imitation of the *Daily Mail* in 1900 by C. Arthur Pearson. It was equally successful. Ld. Beaverbrook acquired control in 1922. Sales reached 2M by 1933 because, uniquely, the *Daily Express* attracted readers from all levels.

DAILY GRAPHIC *See* DAILY SKETCH; THOMAS, WILLIAM LUSON.

DAILY HERALD was founded as a Labour journal in 1911 and was taken over in 1922 by the Labour Party which then passed its interest to the Trade Union Congress. In 1960 control passed to Odham's Press who undertook to maintain the paper's policy. In 1961 Odham's passed it to the *Daily Mirror* group (later called the International Publishing Corporation) and in 1964 it was replaced by the *Sun* which, as part of the Murdoch group, was a popular tabloid which cherished no socialist ideals.

DAILY INDEPENDENT (Ir.). *See* NATIONAL PRESS.

DAILY MAIL was a halfpenny newspaper launched for the popular market by Alfred Harmsworth and Kennedy Jones in 1896. In its first year daily sales averaged 202,000. Ld. Salisbury said that it was written by office boys for office boys, which was not far from the truth, for it appealed to the new business people, many of whom had never got beyond primary school.

DAILY MIRROR was founded by Alfred Harmsworth in 1904 as a woman's newspaper. As such it failed, but he instantly changed it to another daily picture paper, which then appealed more to women than before and made large profits.

DAILY NEWS was founded by Charles Dickens in 1846 and was strongly Liberal. It acquired the *Star* in 1909, the *Westminster Gazette* in 1928 and was amalgamated with the *Daily Chronicle* in 1930 to form the *News Chronicle* (*see above*).

DAILY SKETCH (1909), originally a Manchester penny picture paper absorbed the *Daily Graphic* in 1926. It changed its name to *Daily Graphic* but in 1955 back again and in 1971 was absorbed by the *Daily Mail.*

DAILY TELEGRAPH (AND COURIER) was launched by Arthur Sleigh in June 1855 and transferred to Joseph Levy (who dropped the name Courier) in Sept. It was Liberal until 1878 and then Conservative. The Levy family sold it to the Berrys in 1928 and it absorbed the *Morning Post* in 1937.

DAILY UNIVERSAL REGISTER was started by John Walter in Jan. 1785 and changed its name to *The Times* in 1788.

DAKAR (Senegal). After the French surrender in June 1940 a French squadron including the powerful new battleship *Richelieu* arrived at Dakar to prevent Senegal from going over to the Free French. A joint British and Free French expedition was sent to seize the port but was repulsed in Oct.

DAKOTA, NORTH AND SOUTH. The N.W. part of this area passed to the U.S.A. under the Louisiana Purchase; the S.E. was ceded by Britain when the 49th parallel became the U.S-Canadian frontier in 1818. The area is named after the powerful and handsome Indian tribe whose feathered headdress is erroneously considered to be typical of Indians generally.

DALAI LAMA. *See* TIBET.

DALADIER, Edouard (1884-1970), French radical politician first took office in the Herriot Govt. of 1924 and in June 1933 as premier negotiated the abortive four power pact (France, Britain, Germany and Italy). From June 1936 to Apr. 1938 he was Min. of Defence under Blum and Chautemps and then, as premier again, signed

393

the Munich agreement. His govt. fell as a result of military defeat in Mar. 1940 and he served under Reynaud until June.

DALE, Sir Henry Hallett (1875-1968) Nobel Prizeman (1936) O.M. (1944), medical research scientist, directed the Wellcome Physiological Research Laboratories from 1904 to 1914 and the N. Inst. for Medical Research from 1928 to 1942. He was chairman of the War Cabinet Scientific Advisory Committee from 1942 to 1947, Sec. of the Royal Society from 1925 to 1935 and Pres. from 1940 to 1945. The width of his contributions to scientific advance included such discoveries as the active principle of ergot, the nature of pituitrin and the chemical mediation of nervous impulses, and he negotiated many international agreements to standardise biological preparations.

DALHOUSIE. See RAMSAY.

DALKEITH (Midlothian), the seat of the Ds. of Buccleuch. See SCOTT.

DALMATIA (Adriatic) except Ragusa (Dubrovnik) was a Venetian province from 1420 until 1797 though the extent of Venetian jurisdiction was disputed with the Turks and local free companies called *Uskoki* until 1617. The large trading ships built in the area were known in England as 'argosies', a corruption of Ragusa. Annexed by Austria in 1797, Dalmatia was ceded to France by the P. of Pressburg (1805) but reassigned to Austria in 1815. Under the secret T. of London in 1915 a large part of it was promised to Italy in return for her support in the war. This was much resented by the Slavs and could not be enforced when the Kingdom of Yugoslavia was formed. Eventually at the T. of Rapallo (Nov. 1920) Yugoslavia obtained the whole area save a few islands and the port of Zara (Zadar), kept by Italy. These passed to Yugoslavia in 1945. This mountainous country, interconnected only by sea, was linked together by a coastal road in the years 1950 to 1960.

DALRIADA may be considered as the bridge by which the Scots ("Irish raiders") crossed from Ireland to Caledonia (later Scotland). The Dalriada were a royal sept of N.E. Ireland. In the 2nd cent. some of them crossed to the Caledonian mainland and islands visible across the water. The Irish called themselves Gael and some of their new settled area eventually became known as Argyll (Irish = Eastern Irish). Later they expelled or conquered the local Picts, possibly at the request of the Strathclyde Britons.

(2) By the late 5th cent. FERGUS MOR 'held part of Britain' and, in the time of his son DOMINGART, Dalriada embraced territory on both sides of the sea. There was intermittent war with the Picts and in 559 Brude, s. of Maelchon, the Pictish King, severely defeated K. CONALL. Hence St. Columba, who crossed to Argyll in 563, received Iona from Brude not Conall. Columba converted Brude, patched up a kind of peace and when Conall died in 574, secured the election of K. AIDAN, whom he consecrated.

(3) The position of Dalriada astride the straits created disputes about its relationship with the mainland potentates on both sides. In 575 the Irish High King held an important assembly at Drumceat which dealt, *inter alia,* with the problem of Dalriada. Columba negotiated the settlement. Dalriada was to continue to pay military service to the High King: but naval service only to the ruler of Argyll. This led to practical independence in two generations, for the declining High Kings became unable to exact their due on the one side, while the advance of Dalriada into Argyll abolished Pictish ability to exact it on the other. By the 7th cent. Caledonian Dalriada was the more important part of the Kingdom. Its people were penetrating Strathearn, possibly the Great Glen and were spreading southwards. Eventually they collided with the Northumbrian Angles, who were advancing north from the Humber to Bamburgh and Dunbar and thence west. In 603 the Angles overthrew K. Aidan at Degsastan (site

unknown), then attacked Strathclyde and campaigned northwards across the Forth. This pressure on the Celtic tribal states of the north did not prevent them from fighting each other; K. Donald IV (The Freckled) was killed at Strathcarron by the Strathclyde Britons in 643. The pressure ended only when the Pictish K. BRUDE, son of Bile, defeated the Angles at Nechtansmere (or Dunnichen) near Forfar in 685.

(4) While the Anglo-Saxon colonisation caused war and confusion in southern Britain, Ireland was comparatively tranquil, if externally aggressive. Caledonian Dalriada was being steadily reinforced at a time when the Picts and Strathclyde Britons were fighting the Angles. Moreover, Iona, the centre of northern Christianity, was in Dalriada. War and the unifying influence of Christianity worked in favour of the Dalriadan Kings.

(5) These processes were suddenly interrupted by the Vikings. In 795 they raided Iona. Soon after 802 the Norwegians were settling the Hebrides and Man. In 830 the abbey at Iona was abandoned, the monks moving to Armagh. K. KENNETH MacALPIN (r. 832-60) was reinforced from Ireland in 836, but in 839 the Vikings simultaneously founded Dublin and inflicted a grave defeat on the Picts. It was in these circumstances that Kenneth became King both of the Scots and the Picts. (*See* SCOTS OR ALBAN KINGS, EARLY.) Irish Dalriada remained subject to rulers of his house in the face of increasing difficulties, but by 880 the two parts were effectively separated by Viking naval supremacy. By 950 neither part was a separate entity and the name Dalriada fell into disuse.

DALRYMPLE, Alexander (1737-1808). *See* METEOROLOGY.

DALRYMPLE, Sir James (1619-95) Vist. STAIR (1690) was sec. to the commissioners for treating with Charles II in 1649 and 1650 and a Lord of Session from 1657. It was he who in 1660 advised Monck to declare for a free parliament. In 1670 he became Pres. of the Court of Session, whose procedure and fees he revised in 1672. He was M.P. for Wigtownshire from 1672 to 1674 when he became a Scots privy councillor. On the whole a man of moderate views, he opposed Lauderdale's treatment of the Covenanters in 1677 and tried to reduce the severity of the Test Act, 1681, which drove him away from Scotland to London. Here he published his classic *Institutes of the Law of Scotland.* In 1682, however, suspicious of James D. of York and of Claverhouse, he fled to Holland. Here he became a political associate of William of Orange, with whom he came to England at the Revolution of 1688. As one of the King's principal Scots advisers, he was partly responsible for the Glencoe massacre of 1692. Of his seven children **(2) John (1648-1707) MASTER of STAIR (until 1695) 1st E. of STAIR (1703),** a presbyterian, came into conflict with Claverhouse, a R. Catholic, during his father's absence in Holland and was a prisoner from 1682-3 and 1683-6. By James II and Sunderland's policy of uniting the extremes against the centre, he was made King's Advocate in Feb. 1686 and all charges against him and his father's family were dropped on condition that he operated the dispensing power. As, however, he permitted illegal 'field conventicles' the Advocacy was passed to Sir J. Foulis and he became Lord Justice-Clerk. In 1689 he was elected to the Convention of Estates for Stranraer, moved the forfeiture of James II's crown and was one of the Commissioners who offered it to William III. He then became Lord Advocate and chief govt. spokesman in the Scots parliament. As he had profited under James II, he became the target of a jealous Presbyterian-Jacobite coalition called "The Club". His skill as a tactician and debater preserved his position and in Jan. 1691 he became joint Sec. of State (*See* GLENCOE, MASSACRE OF 1692.) The report of the Commission on the Glencoe affair (June 1695) led to his resignation and after he succeeded to his father's peerage he had to avoid taking his seat in Parliament until 1700. Sworn of the Privy Council at the accession of Q. Anne (1702), he held no office in her reign, but was the govt's chief adviser on Scottish affairs and the principal activist in the private negotiations and public debates leading to the Act of Union. He died during these debates in the Scots parliament, having substantially achieved his purpose. His brother **(3) Sir Hew (1652-1737)** was Pres. of the Court of Session from 1698 to 1737. He achieved a unique reputation for learning, fairness and courtesy. His brother **(4) Thomas** was physician to the continually ill Q. Anne. His brother **(5) Sir David (?-1721)** a Scots M.P., in 1703 was a commissioner for the treaty of union in 1707, represented Haddington in the first Union Parliament from 1708, was Queen's Advocate from 1709 and Auditor to the Scots Exchequer in 1720. The son of **(2)** above **(6) John (1673-1747) 2nd E. (1707)** accidentally shot his elder brother dead at the age of eight. He became A.D.C. to Marlborough in 1703 and greatly distinguished himself at the Bs. of Oudenarde (1708) and Malplaquet (1709). He was then sent on a diplomatic mission to Saxony but returned to the army in 1710. He was recalled by the Tory govt. in 1711 and went to Scotland where he became a leader of the Whigs. At the accession of George I he returned to favour and was appointed Minister to Paris. This was one of the most successful diplomatic missions in British history. He made friends with Orléans before Louis XIV died, and so was on good terms with the next govt. He compelled his predecessor, Matthew Prior, to surrender the correspondence implicating the Jacobites, on the basis of which Bolingbroke was impeached. He got the Old Pretender expelled from Paris and knew all the activities of the Jacobites. He was completely informed about Card. Alberoni's policies and negotiated the Triple and Quadruple alliances which frustrated them. His lavish expenditure as ambassador had, however, undermined his fortune. This he tried to repair by stock jobbing in the schemes of the Scotsman Law, whom he introduced to Card. Dubois, and to Stanhope, the Sec. of State. Law obtained for a while a predominant influence in the French regency and Stanhope began to use him rather than Stair who, after protests, was withdrawn in 1720. He then busied himself with his Scottish estates and with political opposition to Walpole and Argyll, the govt's ruler of Scotland. He was thus out of office until Walpole fell in 1742, whereupon he was given command of the British forces supporting the Pragmatic Sanction in the War of the Austrian Succession. He was outmanoeuvred by the French, but under the personal command of George II, won the victory at Dettingen. The King refusing to accept proposals for exploiting the victory, he resigned with honour. His nephew **(7) John (1720-89) 5th E.,** a Scottish representative peer from 1771 to 1774, opposed the policies which led to the American revolt and, in 1774, presented a petition from Massachusetts. A great grandson of **(5)** above, **(8) David (1726-92) Ld. HAILES (1766)** became in 1766 a Scottish judge unusually distinguished for his humanity. His brother **(9) Alexander (1737-1808)** was Hydrographer to the HEIC from 1779 and in 1795 became the first Hydrographer to the Admiralty. In this position he organised a service which remained unique in the world for nearly two centuries. The son of **(7)** above **(10) John (1749-1821) 6th E.,** fought in the American Revolutionary War, was Min. to Poland from 1782 to 1785 (between the first and second partitions) and from 1785 to 1789 to Prussia. The grandson of **(3)** above **(11) Sir Hew Whitefoord (1750-1830),** a general, touched the nadir of an undistinguished career by signing the so-called Convention of Cintra (1808) whereby the French army under Junot, just defeated by Wellington (then Wellesley), was suffered to escape.

DALTON (Edward) Hugh (John) Neale (1887-1962) Ld. DALTON (1960), son of an eccentric canon of Windsor, was educated at Eton and Cambridge. He imbibed the fashionable Fabian socialism of his time. In 1924 he became a Labour M.P. but had few opportunities to exhibit his political and administrative talents until World War II, when Churchill gave him the important post of Min. of Economic Warfare, which he filled until 1942. He was then promoted to the Presidency of the Bd. of Trade. He became Attlee's Chanc. of the Exch. in 1945 but in 1947 he incautiously let slip a budget confidence to a journalist, when on the way to the Commons to introduce the budget, and honourably resigned. He returned to office in 1948, being Chanc. of the Duchy until 1950, Min. of Town and Country Planning (T&CP) and then of Local Govt. and Planning until 1951. As such he set up much of the system whereby T&CP has been jointly administered between central and local govt. ever since.

DALTON, John (1766-1844) mathematician and scientist, maintained the electrical nature of the *aurora borealis* in 1793, published his confirmation of colour-blindness in 1794, but became known to the European scientific public first by papers on mixed gases and then on the Expansion of Gases by Heat (1801), by which scientific meteorology became possible. He became famous by his discovery of the laws of chemical combination and tabulation of atomic weights (1805).

DALYEL, DALZEL, DALZIEL (pron: "D-L"). Of this Lowland Scots family **(1) Sir Robert (?-1639)** became **1st Ld. DALZELL and 1st E. of CARNWATH** in 1628. His son **(2) Sir Robert (?-1654), 2nd E.,** was accused by the Scots Convention of betraying secrets to the Queen and declared forfeit. He later fought incompetently for the King at Naseby and then served with Ld. Digby north of the Trent. He sacrificed his liberty to save P. Charles at Worcester (1651) and was, for a while, committed to the Tower. A cousin **(3) Thomas (1599-1685)** was a soldier and also captured at Worcester, but escaped from the Tower and in Mar. 1654 assisted the Highland rebellion. He escaped again and served as a Russian general against the Poles, Tartars and Turks but, in 1666, he was returned at Charles II's request and became C-in-C in Scotland. As such he was responsible for the brutal repression of covenanters in the Pentlands rising (1666). He was a Scots M.P. for Linlithgow from 1678 and a Privy Councillor from 1667. His eccentricities and his beard (respected by the Russians) made people think of him as a wizard. He was a great favourite with Charles II, who called him "Tom". Another cousin **(4) Robert (?1687-1737)** took part in the Jacobite rising of 1715 and was attainted but spared. A kinsman **(5) Robert (1662-1758),** a general, became treasurer of the *Sun* Fire office in 1720 and chairman by 1750. At this period this was the only insurance Co. operating outside the London area. **(6) Robert Alexander (1768-1839),** also a general, obtained the restoration of the earldom forfeited through the attainder by means of a private Act in 1826.

DALZIEL (pron: "D-L"). Three of seven brothers **(1) Edward (1817-1905), (2) George (1815-1902)** and **(3) Thomas Bolton (1823-1906)** ran Dalziel Bros., a celebrated firm of engravers, printers and publishers from 1839-1893. *Inter alia* they made the blocks for *Punch,* the *Illustrated London News;* Lear's *Books of Nonsense* and Lewis Carroll's *Alice* books and gave a style to the age. Their nephew **(4) Davison Alexander (1854-1928) 1st Ld. DALZIEL (1927)** founded a newsagency in 1893 and was Conservative M.P. for Brixton in 1910. Another relative **(5) James Henry (1868-1935) 1st Ld. DALZIEL of KIRKCALDY (1921)** was Liberal M.P. for Kirkcaldy from 1892 to 1921; he owned *Reynolds Weekly* and the *Pall Mall Gazette* and, as a supporter of Lloyd George, helped him to buy the *Daily Chronicle.*

DAMARALAND. *See* s.w. AFRICA.

DAMASCENING, DAMASK. In the 10th to 14th cents. Damascus was an important industrial centre, specialising particularly in armaments (mainly cutting weapons) and fine textiles (originally silk). The former is commemorated in the use of the word *damascening*, the technique of the latter was brought to Flanders and applied to linen in the 12th cent. and established in Ireland in the 17th.

DAMASCUS (Syria) (*see* CALIPHATE, *and previous entry*). This ancient city was taken by the Ottoman Turks in 1516 and under them it became the main assembly point for the Mecca caravan. The Ottoman governorship was practically hereditary in the Azm family throughout the 18th cent. In the 19th cent. its prosperity and population developed rapidly through western trade and it was, logically enough, the original terminus of the Hejaz rly. It accordingly became the German and Turkish military H.Q. against Egypt in World War I. *See* SYRIA.

DAMASUS, St. (?303-84) elected Pope after much violence in 366, secured imperial support for the primacy of the Roman See in 378. He established the Papal archives and commissioned St. Jerome, his secretary, to prepare the Vulgate. At the Council of Rome of 382 he laid down the canon of scriptural books. He also did much to encourage the veneration of saints and to suppress the Arian, Donatist and other heresies.

DAME SCHOOLS were common in the 18th and 19th cents. They taught the three Rs and practical arts such as sewing to young village children. The teachers were usually elderly or widowed and paid by subscription.

DAMPIER, William (1652-1715) joined the Buccaneers in 1679, took service with a French pirate in 1681, returned to English piracy in S. America in 1685, sailed for the E. Indies in 1686 and was marooned at Nicobar in 1688. He escaped and became (captive) master gunner of the Bencoolen fort belonging to the Sumatran Kingdom of Achin. In 1691 he escaped on board the *Defense,* reached England and published two accounts of his voyages (1697) and a treatise of winds (1699) which got him employment as a govt. hydrographer. He surveyed the coasts of New Britain but was wrecked at Ascension in 1701 on the way back. After various ill-executed privateering ventures he became pilot of the *Duke* which rescued Alexander Selkirk ("Robinson Crusoe") from Juan Fernandez (1709). The *Duke* returned with some £200,000 in booty in 1711. His share was not paid out until four years after his death.

DANAKILS, a Moslem pastoral people similar to the Somalis, inhabit the area between the Abyssinian mountains and the Red Sea. Their disregard of frontiers caused friction between the Abyssinians and neighbouring European colonies between the World Wars.

DANBY. *See* DANVERS; OSBORNE.

DANCE (1) George (1700-68) was the architect of the London Mansion House. His elder son **(2) Nathaniel (1736-1811),** a portrait painter and founder member of the Royal Academy, inherited a fortune in 1776, gave up painting and became an M.P. His brother **(3) George (1741-1825)** rebuilt Newgate prison; built the front of the Guildhall and was Prof. of architecture at the Royal Academy from 1798 to 1805. The two Georges were successively surveyors of the Corporation of London between 1735 and 1815.

DANEGELD or GAFOL: HEREGELD. Danegeld was an occasional tax of 2s. per hide (though 4s. and 6s. occurred) first levied under Ethelred the Unready (978-1016). It was used from 991 to 1016 to buy off Danish raiding armies, the sums so paid being called *gafols.* It survived its purpose and was last levied as late as 1162. The word *Danegeld* only appeared after the conquest. *Heregeld* was an annual tax instituted in 1013 to pay the Danish crews in Ethelred's service. It was last levied in 1050 (*see* COINAGE-5) and replaced by so-called *dona*

(gifts) taken from the shires, and *auxilia* (aids) from the towns.

DANELAW. Danish settlement began in earnest in the years 876 to 80, in the territory extending roughly from the Tees southwards to Watling Street. It was most dense around the Five Boroughs (Lincoln, Nottingham, Derby, Leicester and Stamford) and probably least in Suffolk. In all this area Danes kept their own law, as distinguished from the West Saxon laws which obtained south of the Thames or the Mercian law between Watling Street and Wales. Doubtless they imposed it also upon some of their tenants. In any case it was well established and the area continued to have Danish legal and social features after the Saxon reconquest (900-24) and well into the 12th cent., particularly a numerous free peasantry, reflected in Domesday Book. A few technical features survived as late as 1926.

DANES. *See* VIKINGS.

DANGERFIELD, Thomas (1650-85) trickster, forger and perjuror, falsely denounced the D. of Monmouth to Charles II in 1679. The King did not believe him. He then invented the Meal Tub Plot, ascribed to the Countess of Powys. With Titus Oates he gave evidence on the supposed Popish Plot of 1680, personated the D. of Monmouth and was finally convicted of his perjuries and hanged.

DANGEROUS TRADES. Lewis Carroll's Mad Hatter was an example of the hatters, who were made eccentric by the use of a dangerous chemical in the course of their trade. Clergy and welfare reformers were long aware that in particular trades the mortality or incidence of illness was unusually high. In 130 trades handling lead compounds such as paint, glazing, plumbing, printing and red and white lead, expectation of life was low. Woolsorters died of anthrax. Miners, masons and users of grindstones suffered from dust-induced respiratory diseases: those handling pitch and tar (e.g. shipbuilders) from ulcers. The nature of the connection between a substance and the related disorder was often long unknown and still unknown when the Factory and Workshops Act 1883 was passed to improve health at places of work. In 1891 the Home Sec. acquired powers to regulate any industry certified to be dangerous to health and, backed by a growing research organisation, some hundreds of trades have been specially regulated ever since.

D'ANNUNZIO, Gabriele (1863-1938), Italian author and poet, began as a journalist whose brilliance and flair for self advertisement kept him constantly before the public. So did his tempestuous affair with the actress Eleonore Duse, which began in 1894. From 1897 to 1900 he served as a parliamentary deputy, all the while pouring out a stream of poetic and other works. In 1910 he moved to Paris, where life was less expensive and, while maintaining his public in Italy, became strongly Francophile. At the outbreak of World War I he threw all his gifts into converting Italy from her German alliance to intervention on the side of France. His influence was an important, possibly decisive, factor in securing the change of front. When Italy went to war in May 1915 he volunteered for service first in amphibious operations and later as an air squadron leader. His public did not fail to hear of his exploits and when the war ended he came forward as a nationalist. It was proposed to hand over Fiume (Rijeka) to Yugoslavia: in the ensuing diplomatic disagreements D'Annunzio seized the town with a band of volunteers and the help of the local Italians in Sept. 1919, proclaimed the *Italian Regency of the Quarnero* and held the area until bombarded out of it by the Italians on Christmas day 1920. He spent the rest of his life in picturesque retirement on L. Garda.

DANTE ALIGHIERI (1265-1321), a Florentine Guelph, sought refuge in philosophy when his *inamorata* ("Beatrice") married Simone de' Bardi in 1290 and in 1295 he became active in politics. Between these dates he composed the *Vita Nuova*. In 1300 he was one of the city Priors who banished the leaders of the Black and the White Guelf factions. Dante sympathised with the Whites. While in Rome on an embassy in Oct. 1301, the Blacks seized power in Florence. Thereafter he wandered, settling eventually at Ravenna. His uncompleted treatise on linguistics *De Vulgari Eloquentia* (Lat = Common Speech) was begun in 1303 and the equally incomplete Convivio (It = Symposium) in 1304. In the *De Monarchia* (Lat = Monarchy) (1309-12) he discussed the components of Christendom, arguing that a universal empire is both necessary to mankind and ordained by God and that imperial power in temporal matters, being derived from God, is independent of the church. His celebrated *Divina Commedia*, begun at an unknown date, was finished in 1320. It represents a visit through Hell and Purgatory guided by Virgil and through an aesthetic Heaven guided by Beatrice and might be called a symbolic fusion of late mediaeval ideas and renaissance attitudes. It has never ceased to influence thought. *See* RENAISSANCE-2.

DANUBE, navigable from Ulm eastwards, has for centuries been impeded by winter ice, summer low levels, shallows at its mouths and rapids at the Iron Gates. The T. of Paris (1856) which ended the Crimean War, set up an eight power international commission at Galatz to improve the mouths. This functioned until 1918 when its membership was reduced. After provisional arrangements the T. of Versailles in July 1921 internationalised the whole river from Ulm to the Black Sea, established the equality of all flags and set up a new commission and a special organisation to improve the Iron Gates. Economic difficulties impeded its working and the Germans dissolved it in 1940. In 1948 the U.S.S.R. with its satellites repudiated the agreement of 1921 and set up a commission of its own consisting exclusively of riparian eastern countries. Austria joined the commission in 1960.

DANUBE PRINCIPALITIES (MOLDAVIA, WALLACHIA). *See* ROUMANIA.

DANVERS. By reason of a duel in which a Wiltshire neighbour was killed, the brothers **(1) Sir Charles (1568-1601)** and **(2) Henry (1573-1644) 1st Ld. (1603) and 1st E. (1626) of DANBY** were outlawed in 1594 and pardoned in 1598. Sir Charles went to Ireland as a colonel with Essex in 1599. He was also a friend of Henry, E. of Southampton. He was executed for complicity in Essex's rebellion. Henry served under Maurice of Nassau. In 1602 he became Sjt-Maj-Gen. in Ireland. His brother's lands had been forfeited in 1601 but James I gave him the succession in 1603. From 1607 (when the earls fled) he was Pres. of Munster until 1615 when he returned to England and sold the office for £3,200. In 1621 he was given the, mainly non-resident, governorship of Guernsey. Another brother **(3) Sir John (1588-1655)** was four times M.P. for Oxford University and then became a parliamentary colonel. He was M.P. for Malmesbury in 1645. He signed the King's death warrant in 1649 and was a member of Cromwell's Council of State until 1653. His daughter ELIZABETH married **(4) Robert Wrighton Villiers or Vist. PURBECK** (1621-74), a bastard of Frances, *d.* of Sir Edw. Coke. He was elected M.P. for Westbury in 1659 but was expelled. In 1660 he also became M.P. for Malmesbury but was imprisoned for his strong republicanism. Eventually he became a Fifth Monarchy Man and died in France.

DANZIG (GDANSK) (Poland) was, by 1260, the leading Baltic exporter, mostly of grain from the Vistula basin, and timber. In 1308 the Teutonic Knights, who wanted to engross the trade, stormed it. Coveted equally by the Poles, it was continually disputed until the Poles secured possession in 1466. United with its hinterland, it now entered a long period of prosperity. Grain exports (mostly westwards) rose from 25,000 tons in 1492 to 150,000 in 1541 and to 200,000 by 1754. The population rose from 30,000 to nearly 80,000 and it was the richest and largest (as well as the most beautiful) city of eastern Europe. As such it excited the greed of the Prussian Kings, who had territory on both sides. The First Polish Partition (1772) cut it off from Poland and destroyed most of its trade. The Second (1793) incorporated it in Prussia and a mild revival followed. From 1807 to 1814 it was a Free City garrisoned by Polish troops from the Duchy of Warsaw, but in 1815 it reverted to Prussia.

(2) In 1919 Danzig, by now a completely German town, was converted into a Free City, to which Polish trade should have free access along the so-called Polish Corridor. The Poles, however, built a rival port at GDYNIA, but there was more than enough trade for both. In 1938 Hitler (the Nazis having obtained a local parliamentary majority) demanded its surrender to the Reich, but this was refused by Poland and made a pretext for mounting German threats. At the opening of World War II it was annexed by Germany.

(3) In World War II Danzig was badly smashed up by bombing and street fighting and suffered the usual industrial looting by the Russian authorities. The empty shell was ceded to Poland under the Yalta agreement and colonised by Poles. Reconstruction soon began and by 1965 it was a prosperous port again. It was the scene of riots in 1970 and 1974 and the seat of the shipbuilders union which gave birth to SOLIDARNOSC under the leadership of Lech Walesa. *See* BALTIC-44,60,62; HANSE-4 *et seq.*

DAPIFER (Lat = Waiter). The official whose *ceremonial* duty was to wait upon a high personage at a banquet. Normally he was a Chief Steward of a King's or nobleman's household or the Chief Bailiff of an Honour.

DARBY, Abraham I (1678-1717) began the method, suggested by a boy, John Thomas, in his employ, of casting iron in sand moulds and set up the Coalbrookdale Ironworks in 1709. His son **II (1711-63)** perfected the method used by his father of smelting iron ore with coke. His son **III (1750-91)** built the first iron bridge. *See* IRONBRIDGE.

D'ARCY or DARCY. A scattered Irish family originating perhaps in **(1) John (?-1347) Ld. DARCY,** a sheriff in the counties of Nottingham, Derby and Yorkshire who became a Lord Justice in Ireland. He fought at Halidon Hill (1333) and in France in 1346 and was an ambassador to Scotland in 1347. **(2) Patrick (1598-1668)** was a member of the Irish H. of Commons in 1640 and a member of the Confederate Supreme Council. **(3) Patrick (1725-79),** in French service, was captured in the Jacobite rebellion of 1745 and then had a conventional military career. **(4) Charles Frederick (1859-1938),** an Ulster Unionist churchman, was Abp. of Armagh from 1920.

DARCY, Robert (1718-78) 4th E. of HOLDERNESS, was envoy to Venice from 1744 to 1746 and at The Hague from 1749 to 1751. He then became S. of State until 1761 when he was replaced by the E. of Bute.

DARCY, Thomas (1467-1537) Ld. (1505), K.G. (1509), a soldier, became Capt. of Berwick in 1498, temporary Constable and Marshal to hold courts-martial on Perkin Warbeck's supporters in 1500 and warden of the E. March in 1505. He volunteered to go on crusade in Spain in 1511, but returned to the Border where he indulged in occasional raiding. He originally supported the "divorce" of Henry VIII and Catherine but in 1532 had scruples on which, in 1534, Chapuys, the imperial ambassador, played. Consequently at the Pilgrimage of Grace (1535), feigning compulsion, he surrendered Pontefract Castle to the rebels but was pardoned after having suppressed Francis Bigod's insurrection in 1537. All the time he was having treasonable correspondence with Robert Aske and when this was found out he was executed.

DARCY v ALLEN (1602). *See* MONOPOLIES.

DARDANELLES OPERATIONS (Mar. 1915-Jan. 1916) (*For the grand strategy see* WORLD WAR I-4,5,6)

(1) The French objected to any men or equipment being diverted from the Western Front. Fisher opposed diversion from his Baltic plan. Kitchener suggested a mere naval demonstration. Churchill at the Admiralty, with his strategic insight, seized upon this and decided to develop it. The local naval C-in-C (Adm. Carden) submitted a plan for forcing the Dardanelles by naval bombardment and mine clearance. To mollify Fisher the force would be drawn from the many obsolete armoured ships still in use and the French agreed to provide a squadron.

(2) Controversies and inertia delayed the concentration and meanwhile the Turks had suffered winter disaster (B. of Sarikamish Jan. 1915). Since the Russians wanted Constantinople for themselves and were no longer in danger from the Turks their enthusiasm cooled. The fleet reached the Straits in Feb. 1915 without their blessing. It bombarded and demolished the Outer Forts; landing parties, virtually without opposition, blew up the guns. It then entered the Straits and engaged the next forts. There was panic at Constantinople for, apart from the fortress artillerymen, the shores were almost ungarrisoned and ammunition was low. By midday half had been shot away. On the other hand four battleships struck mines in a position believed to have been swept. Drifting mines or shore torpedo tubes were suspected. Carden retired, everyone thought, temporarily.

(3) The attack was a sensation. The Greeks offered to come in at once and land troops at Bulair if assured of Bulgarian neutrality. The Russians promptly vetoed this. Meanwhile the govt. had already had second thoughts. In Feb. troops had been sent to the Aegean island port of Mudros. This half pace towards a combined operation became a full pace in Mar. Sir Ian Hamilton was appointed military commander and arrived in time to witness Carden's attack. His troops, which included the ANZAC Division, however, did not and the new naval C-in-C, de Robeck, would not move without them. The military and shipping confusion forced Hamilton to shift his base back to Alexandria. Security was non-existent and the force took six weeks to organise for action. When it landed at Gallipoli (Apr. 1915) the Turks had been reinforced. A brilliant tactical surprise was achieved but marred by incompetent divisional leadership and the promptitude of Mustafa Kemal (later Atatürk) in charge of the Turkish reserve. The allies dug themselves in close to the beaches.

(4) Unable to get on without reinforcement Hamilton, to the indignation of the French, secured five divisions from the govt. By the time these arrived in Aug. the Turkish opposition had increased to 15. All the same Hamilton achieved a second tactical surprise and was again disappointed by the foolishness of his subordinates. Better ones, long demanded, arrived later. August gloom and rain soon set in. The govt. was losing heart but feared the moral and political effects of withdrawal. In the hope that he would advise it, Hamilton's opinion was sought. He thought otherwise and was superseded by Sir Charles Munro, who evacuated the force without losing a man (Dec. 1915-Jan. 1916).

(5) Success was likely on three occasions (Mar., Apr. and Aug. 1915) and would, with the Turkish capital and only munitions industry at Haidar Pash in mercy, have put Turkey out of the war, reopened the Black Sea to allied navies and supplies to Russia, made the Arabian, Syrian and Mesopotamian campaigns unnecessary and kept Bulgaria neutral. These gains would have materially shortened the war. They might have warded off the Russian revolution. Churchill resigned from the Admiralty.

DAR ES SALAAM. *See* ZANZIBAR.

DARFUR (Sudan). The Sultan Abdel Rahman al Rashid (r. 1787-1802), established at the present El Fasher, took advantage of Bonaparte's invasion of Egypt to subdue the local Arab tribes and his policy was followed by

Mohammed al Fadhl (r. 1802-39) who, however, lost Kordofan to Egypt. Husain (r. 1839-73) came into conflict with Arab slave raiders who had seized the Bahr al Ghazal, an important source of slaves and ivory, which the Darfurians had always sold down river to Egyptian middlemen. The Egyptian govt. supported the Arabs and in 1874 his son and successor, Ibrahim, was killed in battle. Darfur now came under the rule of Slatin Pasha, a German in Egyptian service. In 1883, however, he was expelled by the Mahdi and until 1899, after the Khalifa's defeat at Omdurman, the area was under Mahdist rule. The new Anglo-Egyptian govt. recognised Ali Dina, a descendant of Mohammed al Fadhl, as sultan, but in 1915 he rebelled, as a result of Turkish and Abyssinian intrigues and was killed in Nov. 1916. Darfur was thereafter incorporated as a province in the Sudan.

DARIEN (E. Panama) (1) Ojeda founded the first settlement in 1510 and Balboa's march to the Pacific started from there in 1513. After Panama was founded in 1519, the Darien colony was slowly abandoned. **(2)** In 1693 London merchants, frustrated by the HEIC monopoly, promoted an Act in the Scots parliament for the Encouragement of Trade. This declared Scottish merchants free to form companies to trade anywhere in the world not at war with the crown. The purpose was to circumvent the monopolies of the Royal African and HEI Cos. A further Scottish Act of 1695 created the Co. of Scotland Trading to Africa and the Indies, with a perpetual right to trade in Africa and Asia and a 31-year right to trade in America. The London promoters fixed a capital of £600,000 sterling, half to be subscribed in Scotland. The Scottish organiser was Wm. Paterson, a founder of the Bank of England. The sum was larger than ordinary Scots resources could find. In Dec. 1695, when the English half had been subscribed, the HEIC brought hostile political pressure on the English M.P.s to impeach 23 of the English for technical irregularities, HEIC shares having fallen 45% in the course of these actions. The main witness absconded but they frightened the English subscribers out of the Co.

(3) In reply the Scots, between Feb. and Aug. 1696, set out to raise £400,000 sterling and by a national effort all was promised and half paid up. Paterson advised the colonisation of Darien. The Co. was misinformed about the site, the local resources, the climate and the political conditions. Spain was then an ally of Britain against France and the proposal would infringe her sovereignty. Moreover, in July 1698, when the first expedition sailed, the P. of Ryswick had united the powers in an effort to pacify the Caribbean.

(4) When the Spaniards protested William III ordered British governors to refuse help to the Scottish colonists. By Sept. 1699 three expeditions to Darien had been totally lost. The furious Scots turned their rage upon the English (*see, however,* EQUIVALENT).

DARK AGES. An obsolescent name for the period of W. European history between the collapse of Roman culture in the 5th cent. and the rise of the Mediaeval in the 11th.

DARLAN, Adm. Jean Louis Xavier François (1881-1942) was French naval C. of S. from Dec. 1936, C-in-C from Aug. 1939. On the French capitulation in July 1940 he became Pétain's Min. of Marine and in Feb. 1941 he succeeded Flandin as head of the govt. and added to his other posts the ministries of the Interior and Foreign Affairs. His policy was to save French influence from the Germans by keeping them out of French Africa and preventing them from getting possession of the Toulon fleet. The Germans sensed his fundamental hostility and in Apr. 1942 Laval returned with their acquiescence and ousted him from most of his departmental power. He was still a personage to be reckoned with, however, and when the Anglo-Americans invaded N. Africa in Nov. 1942 he became the French Commissioner-Gen. there. He arranged for the scuttling of the Toulon fleet, negotiated a Franco-Allied armistice and then assumed the office of Head of the French State in N. Africa. This provoked a furious reaction from the Gaullists and widespread agitation in the allied left wing press. In Dec., however, he was assassinated by a French royalist.

DARLEY ARAB, THE was a stallion, imported c. 1692, from which most English racehorses are now descended.

DARLING, Charles John (1849-1936) 1st Ld. DARLING (1924), appointed a justice of the Queens Bench Division in 1897, was famous for his mordant wit on the bench. He presided in the *Crippen* (1910) and *Casement* (1916) appeals and retired in 1923.

DARLING, Grace Horsley (1815-42), daughter of the Farne lighthouse keeper, rescued five people from shipwreck in 1838.

DARLING, Sir Ralph (1775-1858). *See* AUSTRALIA-4.

DARLINGTON (Co. Durham), a market town and prescriptive borough, had an ancient dyeing industry and naturally attracted textile and carpet weaving in the early industrial revolution. Its modern growth began with the building of the railway to Stockton (the first steam driven railway) in 1825. Later a substantial engineering industry grew, related to railway and bridge construction. The place was first represented in parliament in 1868.

DARNELS or the FIVE KNIGHTS CASE (1627-8). Charles I tried to enforce the forced loan of 1627 by imprisonment; and Sir Randolph Crew, C. J. of the Kings Bench, had already been dismissed for denying the legality of forced loans. Sir Thomas Darnel and four others who were in custody applied for a writ of *habeas corpus* to bring the question before the Kings Bench. The return showed only that they had been imprisoned 'by special command of the King'. Darnel now refused to go on but the rest argued that they were entitled to bail, while the Att-Gen. argued that they should be kept in custody until the King was ready to bring them to trial. The judges ordered a remand because there was no precedent for bail in such a case without the King being consulted and because in any case the prisoners could sue out another *habeas copus* immediately. This much misunderstood affair led the public to believe that the substantive issue on the legality of forced loans had been decided against the Knights. This belief probably arose because the King's intention to bring them to trial was widely doubted.

DARNLEY. *See* MARY, QUEEN OF SCOTS-10-14; **STEWART.**

DAROGA was a governor or superintendent in India.

DARREIN PRESENTMENT. *See* ASSIZES.

DARTFORD PROGRAMME. *See* SALISBURY'S SECOND GOVT.-2.

DARTMOOR (Devon) originally mostly wooded, was settled early. There are stone avenues and circles as well as many bronze age circles and round harrows and an iron age camp. Grazing and other quasi-common rights are of ancient, probably Celtic, origin and so are the diggings for potters clay near Bovey Tracey just outside the moor. Tin mining was practised since the 12th cent. These activities and the accompanying demand for fuel rapidly cleared the woods and widened the grazing. The moor, though called a Forest, was never afforested but was managed as part of the Duchy of Cornwall and the Stannaries. Offenders against the tin mining regulations were imprisoned at Lydford. The common rights were from ancient times graded among three classes of people: viz: the holders of the ancient tenements have pasture, turbary and housebote; the inhabitants of the adjacent, so-called VENVILLE parishes can claim turbary, housebote and day pasture on payment of a rent to the Duchy; and all other inhabitants of Devon may hold pasturage only. The prison at Princetown was built to house French war prisoners in 1809 and was converted into a high security convict prison in 1855.

DARTMOUTH. *See* LEGGE.

DARTMOUTH (Devon). The college for naval cadets was

established here in H.M.S. *Britannia* in 1863 and moved ashore in 1905. *See also* PIRACY.

DARWIN (1) Erasmus (1731-1802), a physician with wide interests (he corresponded with Rousseau) formed a dispensary and a botanical garden at Lichfield and founded a Philosophical (i.e. Scientific) Society at Derby. He refused to become George III's doctor and wrote poems about plants which are less appreciated than they were. He also evolved an evolutionary theory, later elaborated by Lamarck, which helped to trigger the genius of his grandson **(2) Charles Robert (1809-82)** who had already at 22 achieved such standing that he was invited to be a naturalist on the *Beagle* scientific expedition to S. America in 1831. On this he studied the botany, zoology and geology of the area and acquired a vast body of knowledge which, impeded by illness, he published after his return in 1836 until 1844 when he first wrote down his evolutionary theory based on natural selection. He was encouraged by friends, especially Charles Lyell, whom he had met as Sec. (1838-41) of the Geographical Society, to develop these ideas. In 1858 a naturalist, A. R. Wallace, sent him a manuscript on a theory of the origin of species which was the same as his own. He immediately published it with a letter outlining his own theory and in 1859 published his own definitive theory in his celebrated *Origin of Species,* this decisively redirected not only biological but religious and ethical outlooks. He wrote on a very wide spectrum of subjects varying from *The Formation of Vegetable Mould through the Action of Worms* to his other famous work, *The Descent of Man* (1871) and a biography of his grandfather.

DAS, Chitta Ranjam (1870-1925). Indian nationalist. Joined the Congress Party in 1906 and became president of it in 1921 when he was sentenced for sedition. In 1923 he entered the Bengal legislative council and in 1924 was the first mayor of Calcutta.

DASHWOOD, Sir Francis (1708-81) 15th Ld. DESPENCER (1763 by termination of abeyance), was the riotous friend of Frederick, P. of Wales. He became a member (and eventually president) of the Dilettanti Society in 1736 and became an M.P. in 1741 as an opponent of John Wilkes. In 1755 he founded the notorious Hell Fire Club at Medmenham (Bucks). To this Bute, the E. of Sandwich, Paul Whitehead and Wilkes belonged. He was re-elected an M.P. in 1747, 1754 and in 1761-2, when Bute made him Ch. of the Exchequer. Fortunately the skills required in that office were less than they became later, for his incompetence was legendary. He fell with Bute and in 1763 became Master of the Wardrobe. From 1770 to 1781 he was joint Postmaster-Gen. The duties of this office could mainly be performed by deputy.

DAUBENEY, Giles (?-1508) 1st Ld. DAUBENEY (1486) was a professional soldier under Edward IV. He supported Buckingham's abortive rebellion in 1483 and fled to Henry, E. of Richmond, in Brittany. He acquired high honour when the Earl became Henry VII. He was a privy councillor and master of the mint in 1485. Lieut. of Calais in 1486, he negotiated the fateful marriage treaty between P. Arthur and Katharine of Aragon in 1488. He captured Ostend in 1489, commanded a field force to support the Bretons against the French in 1490 and negotiated the T. of Étaples in 1492. In 1495 he became Lord Chamberlain but in 1497 his military talents were again employed against Perkin Warbeck's second insurrection and a Cornish revolt. In 1500 he was with Henry VII at Calais but thereafter he went into gradual retirement.

DAUPHIN, DAUPHINÉ. Originally the name of the lords of Vienne in southern France, the word Dauphin developed into their title, and their territory came to be named after the title. Humbert III, the last independent Dauphin, ceded the province to the French crown in 1349 on condition that the title should always be borne by the eldest son of the French King.

D'AVENANT, Sir William (1606-68), perhaps Shakespeare's godson; his comedy *The Wits* was first acted in 1633. He became poet laureate in 1638. A determined royalist, he was captured on a mission for Q. Henrietta Maria to Virginia in 1650 and imprisoned, but released by Milton's efforts. In 1656 he produced *The Siege of Rhodes* (the first English opera) and in 1658 *The Cruelty of the Spaniards*. His operas came to an end at Oliver Cromwell's death, but at the Restoration he was able to form a new (The Duke's) company which performed Shakespearean adaptations.

DAVENTRY (Northants) became important in the world of radio when the B.B.C. set up its high powered long-wave station in 1925. Medium-wave transmitters followed in 1927 and short-wave in 1932.

DAVID I (?1080-1153), son of Malcolm Canmore and St. Margaret, **E. of HUNTINGDON (1113), K. of SCOTS (1124)** spent his youth and early manhood at the English court and acquired the earldom of Huntingdon by marrying E. Waltheof's daughter Matilda, widow of Simon of Senlis. Strongly influenced by his upbringing, he encouraged Anglo-Norman social institutions in Scotland and introduced the main features of feudal landownership into the south, with new methods of warfare and the building of motte-and-bailey castles. He obliged his magnates to keep order and to do justice and many important positions in state and church came to be held by men whom he had attracted from England. Hence southern Scotland acquired a French-speaking aristocracy. He was also a champion of a continental type church. For this he needed a strong episcopal organisation under his own control; hence he offered determined resistance to the claims of the archbishops of York to metropolitical authority over Scottish bishops. At his accession, moreover, Scotland had had only three monasteries. He caused the Culdees to be absorbed into rather similarly organised houses of Augustinian canons and built the new Augustinian Abbey of Holy Rood just below his castle at Edinburgh. Its abbot was later to become his chaplain. In the 1130s he came into contact with the Cistercians and founded the notable Abbey at Melrose (1136) and later the abbeys at Dundrennan, Kinloss and Holm Cultram in Cumberland. The widening economy encouraged and was encouraged by this and by the establishment of at least 17 burghs, beginning with Berwick and Roxburgh. These grew up around royal castles, and Berwick and Roxburgh minted the earliest known Scots coinage. As an English earl he had to chose between Stephen and Matilda and invaded northern England in Matilda's interest. The last such foray was defeated by a popular effort led by the Abp. of York at the B. of the STANDARD in 1138. Thereafter he devoted himself to more enlightened tasks.

DAVID II (1324-71) K. of SCOTS (1329), was the only surviving son of King Robert I by his second wife, Elizabeth de Burgh. His father, enfeebled by hardship and age had, however, arranged by the T. of Northampton for the infant David to marry Edward III's young sister Joan of the Tower (1321-62). The marriage took place in July 1328. David was crowned at Scone in 1331 with his cousin Randolph E. of Moray as his regent. Moray, however, died prematurely in 1332 and was succeeded by Donald, E. of Mar, but he was killed the same year when surprised in Edward Baliol's invasion of Fife, at Dupplin Moor. Baliol was then crowned at Scone but other Scots resisted, and K. Edward III, who had turned a blind eye to the original invasion, now gave powerful support culminating in the important defeat of the Scots at Halidon Hill (July 1333). Their resistance still continued but in 1334 David, then aged ten, and his wife were sent to France for safe keeping by Philip VI, so that the Scots could regain the kingdom without

encumbrance. By 1341 it was safe for him to return and in 1342, though he had spent the impressionable years as a Frenchman, and was now but eighteen, he assumed personal rule. In 1346, at the outbreak of the Anglo-French war, he sought to profit from the resulting apparent English military weakness in the North, to invade England. His large ill found army with a savage Galwegian element provoked local resistance, and he was brought to battle by Q. Philippa and the Abp. of York at Neville's Cross and captured. He spent the next eleven years as a well treated prisoner, and this had the effect of anglicising him. Hence Edward III perceived him as a potential ally. Ransom negotiations were opened in 1348 and by 1356 the English were offering a 10-year truce and the return of David for 100,000 crowns. Edward's puppet, Baliol, renounced the Scottish throne.

At his restoration David found himself in great difficulties. The Scots had managed without him for a long time. He was childless, and disliked his much more competent heir presumptive, Robert the Steward. He was deep in debt for the ransom. Then in 1362 his Queen died and shortly afterwards he married Margaret, widow of Sir John Logie. From the baronial point of view, Logie had been an upstart. From Robert the Steward's point of view the possibility that she might bear him a son would endanger his succession In 1364 David suggested to Edward III that the English and Scots crowns should be united at his own death, in return for the cancellation of the balance of the ransom. The Steward's friends had been in armed opposition for some time. Not surprisingly the result was open rebellion. David was forced to divorce Margaret in 1369 and to reign rather than rule till his death.

As might have been expected in such a weak and largely absentee reign, the Scottish barons had developed governing institutions of their own, particularly through the creation of parliamentary committees of Lords Auditors, for judicial business, and the Lords of the Articles for legislation.

DAVID or DEWI, St. (?-?601), an ascetic Bp. of Menevia, must have been very active among the British for the monasteries of Glastonbury, Leominster, Repton, Crowland, Bath and Raglan, besides churches in S. Wales, Cornwall and Brittany, are legendarily ascribed to his foundation. By the 11th cent. he had become a Welsh spiritual hero and in 1120, when he was canonised, Menevia was already called St. Davids. Rhygyfarch, an 11th cent. Bp. of St. Davids wrote his biography, from which most of the legends about him are derived.

DAVIDSON, Randall Thomas (1848-1930), Dean of WINDSOR (1883), Bp. of WINCHESTER (1895), Abp. of CANTERBURY (1903), was a friend of Q. Victoria and Abp. Benson. He was interested in social questions and thought that with some modernisation of detail the Anglican church was aptly constituted to embrace all forms of protestant opinion. Though he dealt firmly with clergy who flouted the norms of public worship, he favoured prayer-book revision, extended the Lambeth Conferences, developed missions and yet opposed Welsh disestablishment. During World War I he opposed the grosser types of anti-German propaganda and air and gas reprisals. Later he strongly supported the League of Nations. He was on friendly terms with nonconformists and the Greek Othodox churches and welcomed the beginnings of Ecumenism at the Malines conference of 1921 to 1926. In 1926 the B.B.C. refused to broadcast his appeal to the govt., the mineowners and the miners to end the General Strike and the *British Gazette* refused to publish it. He resigned in 1928.

DAVIES, Christian (1667-1739) or Christopher Welsh, a woman, enlisted c. 1693, fought at Blenheim (1704); being wounded at Ramillies (1706), her sex was discovered and she was dismissed, but still followed the army. In 1712 she was pensioned. She married three soldiers successively.

DAVIES, Clement (1884-1962) M.P. (1929-62) for Montgomery, succeeded Sir Archibald Sinclair as leader of the Liberal Party in 1945 and in 1951, preferring to maintain the distinctive political liberalism, refused a cabinet post under Churchill. His party sank to only 6 M.P.s. He was succeeded by Jo Grimond in 1956.

DAVIES, Sir John (1569-1626) was M.P. for Corfe in 1601, Sol-Gen. for Ireland in 1602 and Att-Gen. from 1606 to 1619. Conscious of the misery and misgovernment of Ireland, about which he wrote, his solution was protestantism and investment. He secured the banishment of R. Catholic priests and from 1608 was on the committee for the plantation of Ulster. In 1613 he was M.P. for Fermanagh and speaker of the Irish Parliament and in 1614 and again in 1621 he added membership of the English House of Commons to his other posts. As such he supported the legality of Charles I's forced loans.

DAVIES, (Sarah) Emily (1830-1921), helped to found the women's college at Hitchin in 1869, which in 1873 became Girton College, Cambridge with, until 1875, her as Mistress. She remained its hon. sec. until 1904. She was also a pioneer in the movement for women's franchise. Because of her fame as a champion of women's education, she was elected to the first school board for London under the new Education Act.

DAVIS, Jefferson (1808-89) U.S. Senator for Mississippi (1847-51) Sec. for War (1853-7) Senator again (from 1857). When Mississippi seceded in 1861 he left the Senate and became pres. of the Confederate provisional govt. From Feb. 1862 he was **Pres. of the Confederacy** throughout the Civil War. The military side of his administration, despite the irritability of the generals, was remarkably successful and prolonged the war, but his failure to get foreign recognition probably lost it. Captured in 1865 and charged with treason, he was released on bail in 1867 and never brought to trial. In 1881 he published *The Rise and Fall of the Confederate Government*.

DAVIS, Sir John Francis (1795-1890), an HEIC servant at Canton, accompanied Amherst's abortive embassy to Peking in 1816, became pres. of the Canton factory in 1832 and was joint commissioner with Ld. Napier in China in 1834. From 1844 to 1848 he virtually controlled all British political and commercial activities in China, combining the functions of plenipotentiary, superintendant of Trade and Gov. of Hong Kong.

DAVISON, Emily, a suffragette, threw herself in front of the horses at the 1913 Derby, in the presence of the King and was killed.

DAVISON, William (?1541-1608), temperamentally a diplomat, was the English resident at Antwerp from 1577 through whom the States Gen. raised a loan of £50,000 in 1579, when he secured the reversion to the clerkship of the Treasury. The Queen employed him in 1583 in Scotland to prevent a Franco-Scots alliance and in 1585 he was English commander at Flushing with a largely diplomatic function. He had also worked under Walsingham. Consequently Leicester used him in 1586 to explain away to the Queen his unauthorised acceptance of the governorship of the Low Countries. His handling of this impossible mission apparently impressed the Queen, who made him her secretary and a member of the privy council. He was immediately entangled in the problem of Mary Q. of Scots; he was a member of the commission which tried her and had the custody of her signed death warrant. He was persuaded to despatch it before the Queen was ready and Mary was executed accordingly. The furious Queen insisted on a scapegoat and he was in custody in the Tower from 1587 to 1589. Thereafter he lived comfortably upon profits of office.

DAVITT, Michael (1846-1906). *See* LAND LEAGUE.

DAVOÛT, Louis Nicolas (1770-1823) Marshal (1804), D. of Auerstedt (1806), P. of Eckmühl (1808), was the ablest and least appreciated of Bonaparte's commanders. Save in a minor role in Egypt, he never actually fought the British, but as an independent commander he gallantly held Hamburg and excluded British trade throughout 1813-4 and as Min. of War in 1815 he organised, armed and supplied the Grand Army for the Waterloo campaign.

DAVY, Sir Humfry (1778-1829) published his first volume of chemical and philosophical researches in 1799 and became director of the Laboratory of the Royal Institution in 1801. He demonstrated the existence of potassium, sodium and chlorine by the use of a 'galvanic' battery in 1807 and in 1812 made Faraday his assistant. In 1812-3 he developed the miner's safety lamp which from 1815 greatly reduced accidents and raised production.

DAVYS or DAVIS, John (?1550-1605) made three exploratory voyages between 1583 and 1587 to Greenland and Canada, reaching Lat 73° on the W. Greenland coast while searching for the N.W. Passage. He later acted as pilot on East India expeditions and was killed off Singapore by Japanese pirates.

DAWES, Charles Gates (1865-1951) was the first director of the U.S.A. Budget (1921) and in 1923 the Allied Reparations Committee appointed him to devise plans for overcoming German inability or unwillingness to pay reparations. **The Dawes Plan (1924)** provided for the reorganisation of German finances with American investment backing. From 1924 to 1928 he was Vice Pres. of the U.S.A. and from 1929 to 1932 U.S. Ambassador in London, where he represented the U.S.A. on the Naval Conference of 1930. *See* REPARATIONS.

DAWN BWYD **(Welsh)** was an annual levy in varying kind payable by an occupier of unfree land to the lord.

DAWSON, Bertrand Edward (1864-1945) 1st Ld. DAWSON of PENN (1920) 1st Vist. (1936). This physician, as chairman of the Ministry of Health council on medical services in 1919 to 1920, originated the ideas on which the later National Health Service (N.H.S.) was based. He attained increasingly influential positions in the medical world as president of a variety of medical organisations and as George V's physician from 1914 to 1936, and spoke often in the Lords on medical matters. In 1944 he was a member of the British Medical Association's Planning Committee, on whose reports the N.H.S. was largely based.

DAWSON or ROBINSON, (George) Geoffrey or "Robin" (1874-1944) as Robinson served under Milner in S. Africa from 1901 to 1905 and was ed. of the Johannesburg *Star* from 1905 to 1910. He then joined *The Times*, becoming ed. in 1912. In 1917 he changed his name to Dawson. He resigned in 1919 but returned in 1923. He was a friend of Cosmo Gordon Lang, at that time Abp. of York, and of Stanley Baldwin and Neville Chamberlain, respectively Prime Minister and Chancellor of the Exchequer in 1923. Under his second editorship *The Times*, while not always agreeing with conservative policies (or lack of them) helped to create the somewhat smug 'back to normality' attitudes associated with them. Lang became Abp. of Canterbury in 1928. The slump obsessed conservatives with retrenchment, commercial recovery and fear of communism which Russian patronage of the Comintern did nothing to allay. The rise of Nazism was thought to set a military barrier against Russia, which might avoid the need for Britain to rearm. In the abdication crisis of 1936 *The Times* voiced the right-wing prejudices of Baldwin and the Anglican textbook morality of Lang. By this time the aggressive intentions of Hitler were beginning to work in practice. Like many Englishmen, Dawson was prone to self denigration and vulnerable to endlessly repeated German complaints (dating from pre-Hitler times) of the injustices of the T. of Versailles. The policy of appeasement was born of an emotional desire to right supposed wrongs and to gain an ally against

Russia. In this Dawson was no more blind than the govt., even though his independent sources of information did not tally with foreign office doctrine. Disillusion came a month after Munich (Sept. 1939) when German activities were seen to be destroying the Czechoslovak state and threatening Poland. He retired in 1941.

DAY, Francis. See MADRAS.

DAY (1) George (?1501-56) became Bp. of Chichester in 1543, helped to draft the first English prayer book in 1548, but voted against the first Act of Uniformity. Imprisoned in 1551, he was released and restored by Q. Mary. His brother **(2) William (1529-96)** was a reforming provost of Eton and became Bp. of Winchester in 1595.

DAY[E] or DAIE, John (1522-84) leading printer under Elizabeth I, was patronised by Abp. Parker. He held various ecclesiastical monopolies and published Foxe's *Book of Martyrs* (1563) and the first book of English church music (1560).

DAY OF THE MARCH was a conference, usually held at a border, between representatives of marcher lordships to settle disputes.

DAYLIGHT SAVING or SUMMER TIME. William Willett, a Chelsea builder, incurred ridicule when, in 1907, be proposed putting the clocks an hour forward in summer, but the idea was adopted when World War I made it desirable, in 1916. It was made permanent in 1925. During World War II the advance was two hours in 1941-5 and also 1947.

D-DAY. The World War II technical term, used for security, for the day on which it was planned to launch an operation. H-Hour was the actual time during such a day when it was to begin. The term D-Day came to be popularly identified with the launching of the Normandy invasion. Fixed for 5th June 1944, it had to be postponed until the 6th because of appalling weather. Days after D-Day were called D+1, D+2 etc; hours similarly H+1 etc.

DEAKIN, Arthur (1890-1955) became a full time trade union official in 1919 and in 1932 national sec. of the General Workers Group of the Transport and General Workers Union (T.G.W.U.). He became Bevin's assistant in 1935 and in 1940, when Bevin went to the Cabinet, took his place as sec. of the T.G.W.U. He supported the Labour Party's policies on wage restraint after World War II and as an anti-communist broke up the World Fed. of Trade Unions (of which he was the president) in 1951 because of the use to which it was put by the Russian unions. He was a strong supporter within the Labour Party of Attlee against Aneurin Bevan.

DEAL (Kent) was a limb of the Cinque Port of Sandwich and its importance is due to the sheltered Downs anchorage. The population made a good living by victualling and smuggling and the place too was regarded as a military danger point. In 1539 Henry VIII built the nearby artillery castles of Deal, Sandown and Walmer, which became the residence of the Lord Warden of the Cinque Ports. Elizabeth I established a navy yard, which flourished throughout the sailing era and by 1699, when a charter freed it from the jurisdiction of Sandwich, Deal had become an important port for France and Holland. The wars diverted the commerce elsewhere and the navy yard was closed in 1864.

DEAN. See CATHEDRAL.

DEAN, FOREST OF (Glos.). This area, forest probably from Celtic times, contains coal and iron mines, worked by FREE MINERS, being sons of freeminers born in the Hundred of St. Briavels who have mined in the forest for a year and a day and registered. They are exclusively entitled to leases of crown mines and formerly to timber for them, and their rights were administered by their Mine Law Court. The separate commoners' rights were administered by the Verderers court and both courts met at the Speech House (now a hotel) in the Forest. Free miners were often commoners too. Charles I disafforested and sold most of the area to Sir John Winter, but it was reafforested by Act of Parliament in 1667. The Mine Law jurisdiction was transferred to the local County Court, but the Verderers continue to meet.

DEAN OF GUILD, originally the head of the guild brethren in a Scottish burgh, was the local judge in merchant and maritime cases. He also had the oversight of buildings, so that eventually his chief function was to ensure that they were erected according to law and remained safe. From 1834 he was *ex officio* a member of some larger town councils. In Edinburgh his Court, which included councillors and architects, was since the 18th cent., in effect, a planning and public health authority with power to prevent the construction, demolition or alteration of any building. The court was abolished in 1975.

DEANE, Henry (?-1503) became Chancellor of Ireland and Bp. of Bangor in 1494 and Lord Deputy and Justiciar in 1496. As such he attempted to protect the Pale by a wall. He was keeper of the Great Seal from 1500 and in 1501 became Abp. of Canterbury. In 1502 he led the delegation which negotiated the marriage of Princess Margaret to James IV of Scotland.

DEANE, Richard (1610-53) commanded the parliamentary artillery at Naseby in 1645 and the right wing at Preston in 1648. He led the army's hostility to further negotiations with the King, helping to promote the Remonstrance of 1648 and taking part in the King's 'trial' in 1649. He then became briefly a gen. at sea in charge of the south and, after fighting at Worcester as a maj-gen., was C-in-C of the garrison in Scotland, which country he pacified in co-operation with the M. of Argyll. In 1652 he returned to sea where he showed his mettle as a naval administrator. He was with Blake at the B. of Portland in 1653 and was killed at Solebay.

DEANS, RURAL, minor officials with authority, often specifically delegated over a part of an archdeaconry sometimes coinciding with a hundred, wapentake or grouping of them. Originally appointed by the archdeacon, by the 13th cent. they were mostly appointed by the bishop from resident clergy supposed to have local knowledge. They were required to supervise clergy discipline, inquire into church dilapidations and vacancies of benefices and generally carry out episcopal or archidiaconal orders.

DEARNE AND DOVE CANAL. See TRANSPORT AND COMMUNICATIONS.

DEATH DUTIES (1) A *legacy duty* (Scots: *Inventory Duty*) in the form of a stamp tax on receipts for legacies was imposed in 1694. Amended in 1783 and 1789 it was superseded in 1796 by a duty on legacies and residual personal property payable by beneficiaries except wives. The rate of the tax rose as the relationship of the beneficiary to the deceased grew more distant. It was abolished in cases arising after 1949. **(2)** *Succession duty,* first imposed in 1853, resembled legacy duty but applied to land. It too was abolished in cases arising after 1949. **(3)** *Probate duty* in the form of a stamp tax upon grants of probate and letters of administration of personal estate over £600 was imposed in 1801. Since executors could not act without such authority, the tax was payable on and out of the deceased's estate. **(4)** *Account duty,* first imposed in 1881, resembled probate duty in which it closed some loopholes. Both were abolished in 1894. **(5)** *Temporary Estate duty* was imposed in 1889 additionally to probate and account duty and in some cases of succession duty on estates worth more than £10,000, in connection with deaths occurring before June 1896. It was abolished in 1949. **(6)** *Estate duty* was imposed in 1894 upon the value of all property, whether settled or not, which passed on a death. It was replaced by *Capital Transfer Tax* in 1975. **(7)** *Settlement Estate duty* was imposed in 1894 upon most settled estates in connection with deaths arising before June 1914.

DEBASEMENTS. See COINAGE.

DEBATEABLE LAND was a territory between the Esk and

the Sark (Cumb.) claimed before 1603 by both England and Scotland and the scene of much fighting. *See* CUMBERLAND-10 *et seq*; MARCHES, ANGLO-SCOTS-9.

DEBRETT, John (?-1822) published his *Peerage* for the first time in 1802 and his *Baronetage* in 1808.

DEBT. *See* CLARENDON, CONSTITUTIONS OF (1164).

DEBT, PUBLIC. *See* NATIONAL DEBT.

DECCAN STATES (S. India). (1) In 1482 most of the Deccan was divided between the Hindu **Vijayanagar** in the south and the Moslem **Bahamani** Sultanate in the centre. By 1518 the latter had expanded and broken up into five viz: **Golconda, Bijapur, Ahmednagar, Bidar** and **Berar.** They defeated Vijayanagar at Talikota in 1565. Golconda, based upon a suburb of modern Hyderabad, was politically unstable but its diamond mines attracted the wonder and greed of Europeans and other Indian rulers. Ahmednagar annexed Berar in 1574; Bijapur absorbed Bidar in 1619. These states were now progressively subjected to the Moghuls, Golconda falling to Aurungzebe in 1687. Moghul power, especially in the north, was superseded by the Marathas who between 1706 and 1724 isolated the Moghul governor, the Nizam-ul-Mulk Asaf Jah in Hyderabad. He, therefore, set himself up as the independent (in all but name) ruler of a somewhat shrunken but still large Hyderabad State.

(2) Thus at the time when the British and French were rapidly ousting the Portuguese and Dutch in the overseas trade, the Deccan was divided between the four great states of the Maratha Hindu confederacy in the north, the Moslem Nizamate of Hyderabad and a Hindu dynasty in Mysore. In 1761 the latter was overthrown by the Moslem adventurer, Hyder Ali.

(3) The interplay of Moghul, Maratha, Hyderabad, Mysore, British and French enabled nine small western states to stay independent. These were **Jankhandi, Sangli, Savantvadi, Kolhapur** (the largest), **Jath, Aundh, Phaltan** with **Bhor,** and (the most important) **Janjira** which was ruled by the Abyssinian hereditary admirals of Bijapur and later of the Moghuls. *See* GEORGE 11-15; MYSORE.

DE CAUS or CAUX (1) Salomon (?1577-1626) Norman engineer and architect and mathematical tutor to Henry, P. of Wales, was an expert on hydraulics and laid out the gardens for P. Elizabeth of Bohemia ("The Winter Queen") at Heidelberg. His son or nephew **(2) Isaac (fl. 1640-50),** also a mathematician and hydrologist, laid out the famous formal gardens at Wilton.

DECEANGLI. British tribe of northern Wales conquered by the Romans between A.D. 48 and A.D. 77.

DECIMALISATION. The French revolutionaries introduced their metric system to much of Europe and, after 1815 France restarted to influence world trade. There was an attempt to pave the way for a decimal pound sterling in 1849 when florins (one tenth of a pound) were issued but, though widely circulated ever since, public opinion held resolutely to the practical advantage of the 240d pound, divisible by 2, 3 5 and several multiples of them as against 100, which is divisible by no multiple of 3. This consideration did not apply to other units of measurement and the metric system was habitually used by scientists but, nevertheless, the old systems retained their hold on public opinion. The rise of the E.U. brought an apparent (if unproved) need to approximate the British systems with the continental, despite the binary basis of computerisation. The Weights and Measures Act 1963 introduced a transitional stage by legalising both imperial and metric units and defining the mathematical relations between them. Imperial measures ceased to be taught in schools in the 1970s and the decimal pound sterling became the only currency on 15 Feb. 1971. Imperial measures of length, weight and capacity (particularly the pint) were still in habitual use in 1993. They became criminally illegal in 1995, if still widely observed. *See also* COINAGE; WEIGHTS AND MEASURES.

DECIMATION TAX (1655-6) was a 10% tax levied on the rents of royalist landowners to defray the cost of the Protectorate's militia. *See* COMMONWEALTH-1 2-14.

DECLARATION OF THE ARMY (June 1647) issued at Newmarket after the seizure of Charles I, asserted that the army was not a mere mercenary force, but had enlisted to defend fundamental rights and liberties and would continue to do so. Hence it demanded the purging of parliament of delinquent, corrupt or unfairly elected members and that it should name a day for its own dissolution; that the people should be able to choose their representatives at frequent intervals and that after justice had been satisfied by a few grand examples, an Act of Oblivion should be quickly passed. *See* CHARLES I-26.

DECLARATION OF INDEPENDENCE (1) U.S. (4 July 1776) was a manifesto signed by 55 representatives of the 13 American colonies explaining why the Continental Congress had voted for independence (by 12 votes, New York abstaining) two days before. The principal draftsman was Thomas Jefferson. Its resounding phrases about equality were more influential than true and did not mention that many of the signatories owned slaves. In France it was hailed as crystallising the ideas of those increasingly critical of the govt. and social system. Its continuing power is perhaps illustrated by the declaration issued in **(2) RHODESIA (11 Nov. 1965)** which copied much of its wording.

DECLARATIONS OF INDULGENCE. *See* CHARLES II; JAMES II.

DECLARATION OF RIGHTS (Feb. 1689). *See* BILL OF RIGHTS.

DECLARATION OF RIGHTS, IRISH 1782. This was to be a motion by Grattan in the Irish parliament, modelled partly on the U.S. Declaration of Independence but asserting that the people of Ireland are a free people under a distinct Imperial Crown with a parliament of its own and that only this crown and parliament can bind them by legislation. More particularly Grattan demanded **(1)** the repeal of the perpetual part of the Irish Mutiny Act; **(2)** and of Poynings Law; **(3)** the abolition of the claim of the English parliament to legislate for Ireland; **(4)** abolition of appeals to the English House of Lords and of any authority of the King's Bench in Ireland; **(5)** the restoration of the final appeals to the Irish House of Lords. The equality of England and Ireland meant that none of these changes could be changed again without Irish consent. The Crown virtually accepted the principles before the resolution was moved.

DECLARATION OF RIGHTS 1774 (U.S.A.) was adopted by the first Continental Congress and amounted to an ultimatum to Britain to repeal the Coercive Acts.

DECLARATIONS OF PARIS (1856) AND LONDON (1909) concerning maritime hostilities. That of Paris declared that **(1)** privateering is abolished; **(2)** blockades, to be lawful, must be effective; **(3)** a neutral flag covers hostile goods except contraband; and **(4)** neutral goods, except contraband, are not liable to seizure under a hostile flag. That of London, drawn up by the International Naval Conference, modified **(3)** and **(4)**. It was adopted with some changes by Order in Council in 1914, but the German declaration of unrestricted submarine warfare, ostensibly based on a declaration of blockade, contrary to point **(2)** made **(3)** and **(4)** unworkable and they were abandoned.

DECLARATOR (Sc.). A proceeding in a Scottish court, in which a pursuer seeks the declaration of a right but seeks no other remedy against a defender.

DECLARATORY ACT 1719 of the British parliament, affirmed its right to legislate for Ireland.

DECLARATORY ACT, 1766. *See* AMERICAN REBELLION-10, 11.

DECOLONISATION (1) is the process of reducing or ending the dominance of colonial powers in their colonies. The *word* is related to the Leninist use of the term 'colonialism' but originated after World War II. The *process* began with the recognition of the U.S.A. in 1783.

Spain abandoned S. and Central America between 1804 and 1830, the Portuguese Brazil later. Meanwhile French, Russian, Dutch and German (enthusiastic) and British (reluctant) imperialists were still acquiring colonies, yet the British were simultaneously and pragmatically relinquishing their authority, if not always their economic advantage, in some of them, e.g. Australia, Barbados, Canada and New Zealand.

(2) Decolonisation first became an issue of principle in the post-World War I negotiations on the future of the German colonies and the ex-Turkish territories. The victorious powers wanted to share in their exploitation. This led to the concept of the **MANDATE** whereby a territory was committed for administration to a power which was supposed to be responsible to and supervised by the League of Nations. Ruanda and Burundi were mandated to Belgium; other ex-German African territories to Britain (c. 80%) and France (c. 20%); the major German Pacific colonies to Australia; some islands to New Zealand and Japan. In the Levant, Syria was mandated to France; Iraq and Palestine to Britain.

(3) The League's direct influence was actually small, but the idea of responsibility under mandate remained potent because of the currency of the American idea (imposed in parts of Europe) of self-determination, alongside Leninism. World War II strengthened these notions because France suffered total and Britain partial defeats and British resources were depleted by the huge effort to defend civilisation, and no longer sufficed to maintain her authority. The Russians, besides, achieved a major success by getting included in the U.N.O. a decolonisation committee which inherited the Mandates and whose remit did not include Russia.

(4) The post-war British Labour govts. were ideologically committed to imperial liquidation and, with the French, Belgians and Portuguese limping behind, carried out world-wide decolonisations, sometimes amid carnage. By 1985 only Russia and China were colonial powers. It was left to the collapse of institutional communism in 1989 to inaugurate a decolonisation era in E. Germany, Eastern Europe and the republics adjacent to Great Russia.

DECOMMISSIONING. Irish term meaning (as moderates hoped) the surrender and ending of the importation of weapons by extremists, or (as extremists meant) merely a forebearance of their use. It leaves out of account home manufacture, particularly of fertiliser-based explosives.

DECORATED. See ARCHITECTURE, BRITISH-7.

DECREE in England was a judgment of a court whose jurisdiction arose from Roman or canon law, including matters of probate and admiralty. Now used mainly in connection with divorce.

DECRETAL. See PAPAL CHANCERY.

DECURIO (Lat.). A Roman provincial town councillor.

DEDIMUS. (*Lat* = **We have given**). A writ conferring power to administer oaths.

DE DONIS CONDITIONALIBUS **(1285) (Lat = concerning conditional grants)** was the statute which established entails and the Writ of Formedon (corruption of *Forma doni* Lat = according to the tenour of the grant) to protect them by empowering a landowner to make conditional grants of land so as to restrain the rights of the grantee and his heirs to alienate it. This would enable him to make provision for junior branches of his family while ensuring that ownership would eventually return to the main line. The clause, drafted by Ralph Hengham, began "the King has enacted that the will of the donor manifestly expressed in the charter of gift be observed henceforth". Without amendment, this might have destroyed the free market in land. Its full force was later eroded by legal fictions (particular *fines* and *recoveries*) and by judicial interpretation.

DEE, Dr John (1527-1608). His stage effects at Cambridge in 1546 gave him a lifelong reputation as a magician,

though acquitted of sorcery by the Star Chamber in 1556. He proposed the formation of a royal library of manuscripts to Mary I. Elizabeth patronised him as a court scientist: he was widely travelled and had some understanding of geography, astronomy and surveying. In 1578 he consulted German physicians on the Queen's behalf and, from 1595 to 1604, he was warden of Manchester College. He also dabbled in Rosicrucianism, astrology and alchemy.

DEED. A solemn document in formal language originally engrossed on parchment. It had to be sealed in the presence of a witness and brought into effect by delivery, that is, by some act such as handing it over or utterance declaring it operative. An undelivered deed is called an ESCROW. It was commonly signed as well. The need for parchment and a seal was unfortunately abolished in 1990. Statements in a deed cannot be denied by the person who makes them and the deed cannot be revoked, but the obligation undertaken in it can be released by a deed of release in which the original beneficiary undertakes not to enforce his rights. Used primarily in land dealings.

DEEMSTER, a Manx judge.

DEENE PARK (Northants), Tudor mansion, the property since 1514 of the Brudenells.

DEER, BOOK OF. This 9th cent. Scots manuscript contains many 11th and 12th cent. entries on St. Columba's foundation of the monastery of Deer and on grants of lands and rights which throw much light on Celtic social organisation.

DEFAMATION is disparagement of character. It has four legal forms. LIBEL (Lat: *libellus* = a little book), whether civil or criminal, is a disparagement originally in written and, since the *Yousoupoff Case* (1934) in any permanent form such as a film. **(1)** CIVIL LIBEL is a private wrong based upon statements which are false and which bring the victim into hatred, ridicule or contempt. He is entitled to damages unless the defendant can show either that the statement is true or that it was made in good faith in privileged circumstances, i.e. where he owes a duty to someone to make it if it is true, or that it did not in fact disparage him. **(2)** CRIMINAL LIBEL was any published writing, true or false, tending to cause a breach of the peace. The perpetrator was liable to punishment and truth was a defence only if the public interest required that the statement should be published. SLANDER is a disparagement in a spoken or other fugitive form. **(3)** SLANDER ACTIONABLE PER SE is actionable as if it were libel and applies in cases where there is an imputation (a) of loathsome disease (e.g. syphilis) or (b) of incompetence or dishonesty in the way of a person's business, profession or vocation (e.g. adultery in the case of a priest) or, since 1891, (c) unchastity in the case of a woman. **(4)** SLANDER SIMPLICITER. This is now a residual class of cases in which the victim has to prove not only the actionable disparagement but that he suffered injury thereby.

Defamation actions were comparatively unimportant and rare until the rise of mass media made it possible for false statements to inflict enormous damage. Fox's Libel Act 1792 asserted in a statutory form the Common Law rule that it is for the jury to decide whether a statement is defamatory, and transferred from the judge to the jury the duty of assessing the amount of the damages. Hence defamation actions are the only civil ones which must be tried before a jury. Juries have tended to make awards which, to the displeasure of the press, have (roughly) reflected not only their dislike of defamation but the consequent success of the media in increasing their readerships and audiences.

DEFENCE BONDS. See NATIONAL SAVINGS MOVEMENT.

DEFENCE, MINISTRY OF. An ineffectual minister, Sir Thomas Inskip, for the co-ordination of defence was appointed in 1938, but his functions were swallowed up in the Churchillian direction of World War II. In 1947 a minister of defence was appointed with similar purposes and effect but in 1963 the direction of the three services and the Min. of Aviation was unified under a Sec. of State for Defence with a Defence Council, while Navy, Army and Air Force Boards replaced the previous Admiralty, Army and Air Force Councils.

DEFENCE AND OVERSEA POLICY COMMITTEE replaced the Defence Committee in 1963. Under the chairmanship of the Prime Minister it consisted of the Secs. of State concerned with overseas affairs and defence with other ministers as necessary, and with the Chief of the Defence Staff and the service Chiefs of Staff in attendance.

DEFENCE OF THE REALM ACT ("DORA") (Nov. 1914) authorised Orders in Council for the prosecution of the war and the trial by court martial or magistrates of offences against them. It also authorised the Admiralty or Army Council to requisition the output of arms factories and works or the factories and workshops themselves. In May 1915 opening hours for public houses were controlled and the state liquor monopoly in Carlisle established. Closure during the afternoon survived until 1990; the Carlisle monopoly until 1970. The name Dora was popularised by Scrutton J. during a trial and was personified by the popular press as a statutory Mrs Grundy.

DEFENCE REGULATIONS were made by Order-in-Council under the Emergency Powers (Defence) Acts 1939 and 1940 or by Ministers under those Orders-in-Council. They established a legal dictatorship for waging World War II and affected all walks of life. The Acts expired on 24 Feb. 1946 but some of the Regulations were continued or extended by the Supplies and Services Acts 1945 and 1947 and the Emergency Powers Acts 1946, 1947 and 1953.

DEFENDER OF THE FAITH (Lat = *FIDEI DEFENSOR*). A title conferred at his own request on Henry VIII by Pope Leo X in recognition of the book *Assertio Septem Sacramentorum* (Argument for Seven Sacraments) which he wrote with John Fisher against Martin Luther. The title was given parliamentary authority in 1544, after the Reformation, and has been used by English sovereigns ever since.

DEFENDERS (Ir) were R. Catholic secret organisations formed against the protestant Peep-o-Day or Break of Day Boys after about 1772. They became aggressive and also spread to non-protestant areas and sometimes degenerated into gangsters. The best were absorbed into the United Irishmen.

DEFENESTRATION OF PRAGUE (23 May, 1618). *See* THIRTY YEARS' WAR-3.

DEFOE (originally FOE), Daniel alias Andrew MORTON (?1660-1731) fought for Monmouth in 1685 and for William III in 1688. In 1692 he took to popular pro-govt. journalism for which he held until 1699 a job in connection with the glass duty. He advocated and defended the French War especially in the *True-born Englishman* (1701). In 1702 in a pamphlet called *The Shortest Way with Dissenters* he ironically proposed the total suppression of all dissent regardless of consequences. The humourless supporters of the Occasional Conformity Bill put him in the pillory where the populace drank his health. In a subsequent imprisonment he wrote a Pindaric *Hymn to the Pillory* (1703) and started the *Review*. He then became a govt. informer or agent and worked as such in Scotland (which helped him to avoid his creditors) until 1709. In 1710 he changed sides and started working for Harley and the anti-war party; in 1712 he was imprisoned for a series of ironical anti-Jacobite pamphlets and in 1713 the *Review* was suppressed. In 1715 he was convicted of libelling Ld. Annesley, but pardoned through the influence of Ld. Townshend, who had employed him. In 1716 he started the *Mercurius Politicus,* a Whig journal, but thenceforth

withdrew slowly into more literary activities. Among his 250 known works he published *Robinson Crusoe* (1719), *Moll Flanders, A Journal of the Plague Year, Peter the Great* (1722), *Roxana* (1724) and *A Tour Through Great Britain* (1724-7).

DE HAERETICO COMBURENDO (Lat = Concerning a heretic who is to be burnt). The name of a writ. **(1)** An Act of 1392 recited that itinerant preachers were spreading heretical doctrines and ignoring summonses from bishops and required lay authorities to arrest and detain them until justified (acquitted) by the diocesan authority. A further Act of 1400 recites that these measures were inadequate or unfulfilled and that preachers of "a certain new sect" were, additionally, holding conventicles and confederacies, running schools, writing and making books and wickedly instructing and informing people. Accordingly (a) no one, save incumbents in their own parishes, might preach or teach without the diocesan bishop's licence; (b) no one might write or make books or hold conventicles; (c) all books were to be delivered to the diocesan within 40 days upon pain of detention in prison; (d) unlicensed preachers convicted under canon law were to pay a fine to the Crown and if they refused to abjure their doctrines or having abjured, relapsed, were to be handed over to the sheriff for public burning. The writ was the authority for the burning.

(2) In 1534 these were amended to require lay authorities to make initial arrests. In 1547, at the accession of Edward VI, all three Acts were repealed. In 1553, under Mary I, they were revived. In 1558 Elizabeth I had them repealed but in 1678 it was found that the writ itself, though not issuable, had not been abolished and as a sop to the anti-Catholic lobby, an Act remedied the omission.

(3) The Acts of 1382 and 1400 were directed against Lollards, and burnings, notably that of Sir John Oldcastle, took place under Henry IV and Henry V. The terror drove most Lollards into hiding and perhaps accounts for the scarcity of the once numerous Lollard writings. Thereafter the civil authorities had other preoccupations. There were several burnings at the end of Henry VIII's reign and about 300 under Mary I. These discredited the legislation. The three Acts do not specifically mention Lollards, but the repeal of 1547 does.

DE HAVILLAND, Sir Geoffrey (1882-1965) O.M. (1962) designed an aircraft engine and pusher biplane in 1908 and in World War I was chief designer and test pilot for the Aircraft Manufacturing Co. He formed his own company in 1920, mass produced the *Gipsy Moth* and pioneered the British Flying club movement. In World War II he produced the first wooden *Mosquito* and built the first British jet-propelled fighters. After it he designed, and his Co. built, the *Comet* jet airliner. The company was absorbed into Hawker Siddeley in 1962.

DEHEUBARTH (C. Wales) was originally an independent kingdom. When Rhodri the Great died in 877 his son **Cadell** took the southern part of his dominions and in 918 his son **(1) Hywel Dda (the Good)** did homage to K. Alfred for his inheritance, which he actually received in 920. His wife ELEN OF DYVED brought him Dyved (Pembrokeshire). In 928 he submitted to K. Athelstan and in 938 visited Rome. After the death of Idwal Foel in 942, when he took possession of Gwynedd, Hywel was regarded as the Chief of all the Welsh. Like Alfred, he thought that a codification of the law would help to calm the confusion of the times (*see* HYWEL DDA, LAWS OF; WELSH LAW-2). His son **(2) Owain (?-986)** did not preserve the unity of the territories and his son **(3) Maredudd (?-999)** ruled with him for some years. This King, the grandfather of Gruffudd ap Llywelyn, reunited Deheubarth and Gwynedd until his death, when a civil war resulted in the accession of an usurper **(4) Rhydderch ap Iestyn (?-1033).** At his death the heirs of Hywel Dda, the brothers

(5) Maredudd (?-1035) and **(6) Hywel ab Edwin (?-1044)** ruled, at first jointly. The latter had to deal with Viking attacks on his coast and invasions directed by Gruffud ap Llywelyn, who drove him overseas in 1042. He returned in 1044 with Danish allies and was killed on the Towy. There followed another interregnum during which the country was disputed between **(7) Gruffudd ap Llywelyn (?-1063)** (*see* GWYNEDD) and **(8) Gruffudd ap Rhydderch (?-1055)** who, despite Danish intervention, held most of it until he was killed. Gruffudd ap Llywelyn then held Deheubarth entire until he died, when it reverted to the line of Hywel Dda in the person of **(9) Mareddud ab Owain (?-1072)**. He was the first Welsh ruler to feel the Norman impact and, after a brief resistance, he came to terms in 1072 involving an exchange of lands in Gwent for others in England. These English lands passed to his son **(10) Gruffudd** when he was killed by the adventurous Caradog ap Gruffydd ap Rhydderch (?-1081), while the kingdom went to his brother **(11) Rhys (?-1078)**, also killed by the same Caradog. In 1081, however, the latter was killed at the B. of Mynydd Cam by Rhys' cousin **(12) Rhys ap Tewdwr (?-1093)**, who took the Kingdom. When William the Conqueror came to Wales in arms in 1082 he conceded tribute. In 1088 he was driven to Ireland by troops from Powys, but returned with Danish help. In 1091 some of his vassals tried to restore Gruffudd (10) who was killed. Meanwhile William's death had removed control over the Norman border barons, who were tempted by the confusion to encroach on Deheubarth. Rhys was killed in the ensuing border wars. He was the last King, for his child son **Gruffudd ap Rhys (?1090-1137)** had to be taken to asylum in Dublin and, during his minority, Norman rule was fastened on S. Wales. In 1113 he returned to claim Deheubarth but the rising (in 1116) failed. Henry I, however, gave him a manor in Caeo and he lived as an English feudatory until the general rebellion of 1136, during which he died. His sons **(14) Anarawd (?-1143)** and **(15) Cadell (?- 1175)** at first ruled jointly. With Danish and North Welsh help they drove the Clares out of Ceredigion and the Cliffords from Llandovery and in 1155 their half brother **(16) Rhys (1132-97)** as he grew up and campaigned with them, succeeded to most of the old kingdom. With the revival of English power after the end of K. Stephen's civil wars Rhys made a formal submission to Henry II in 1158 but this did not prevent him going to war with Clare and Clifford Marcher lords in 1159. In 1163 Henry II compelled him to give up Ceredigion and the title of King, and he is known to history as **'The Lord Rhys'**. During the revolt of 1164 he re-established himself in Ceredigion and in 1167 took over Cyfeiliog. His path was much eased by the departure of many Normans to conquer Ireland after 1170, for the King came to terms, confirmed his possession of Deheubarth and made him justice and virtual viceroy of S. Wales. Though he adopted Norman manners and lived in the style of a Norman lord, he is credited with holding the first Eisteddfod. He suffered in later life from the unruliness of his sons and under Richard I he was in constant war with Norman neighbours. Of his sons **(17) Gruffud ap Rhys (?-1201)** was killed in a family feud while **(18) Maelgwn (?-1230)** and **(19) Rhys Gryg (?-1234)** fought over the inheritance and intrigued, alternately, with the King and Llywellyn ap Iorwerth to get it. Rhys Gryg's sons **(20) Maredudd (?-1272)** and **(21) Rhys Mechyll (?-?)** behaved in a similar fashion in intriguing with the King and Llywellwyn ap Gruffydd. **(22) Rhys ap Maredudd (?-1291)** succeeded to part of the lands and in 1277 he paid homage as a marcher to Edward I. In 1282 he sided with Edward against Llywellyn ap Gruffydd's revolt and in 1285 married Ada of Hastings. In June 1287 he raised a revolt which was partly against the exactions of royal officials, but partly an extension of a feud with the Giffords. His lands were overrun by royal armies and he was eventually executed at York. *See also* GWYNEDD.

DEI GRATIA (Lat = By the grace of God). A royal style first used, perhaps, by Ine (c. 690) as a declaration against heathenism and widely copied by other Christian monarchs.

DEINIOL or DANIEL, St. (?-?584), first Bp. of Bangor, but of north British origin, founded two monasteries (Bangor Fawr and Bangor Iscoed) which numbered apparently over 2,000 monks until they were overthrown by the Northumbrian K. Ethelfrith at the B. of Chester. His pastoral influence, strong in Gwynedd, was felt further south and he and Dyfrig were friends of St. David, whom he persuaded to go to the anti-Pelagian synod of Brefi (545).

DEIRA. *See* BERNICIA AND DEIRA.

DEISI or DESI (sometimes spelt DACEY) were a southeastern Irish military family or dynasty which migrated under the leadership of Eochaid Allmuir (?-?) to Dyfed c. A.D. 400, probably with the agreement of Magnus Maximus and established a monarchy there which lasted until the death of Maredudd ap Tewdwr in 796.

DEISM is the assumption that there is one and only one God and that the true propositions of theology can be known by rational means alone. Thus God's virtues are necessarily perfect and his activity is embodied in natural laws constituting a general providence which makes miracles impossible. The natural laws require a moral life, which is the perfect, perhaps the only true worship. Most deists have, with rather less rationalism, asserted the immortality of the soul and the likelihood of eternal salvation or retribution and have been willing to attack and, where expedient, suppress religious views inconsistent with deism. It was mainly an 18th cent. intellectual fad.

DE JAGER v ATT-GEN. OF NATAL [1907] A.C. 326. De Jager, an alien living in Natal, helped the Boers when their troops occupied the area. The Privy Council held that by his resistance in British territory he owed allegiance and was thus guilty of treason.

DEKKER, Thomas (?1570-?1641), dramatist and popular pamphleteer, wrote much about the reality of the contemporary London underworld with which, through poverty and imprisonment for debt, he was familiar.

DELAGOA BAY. *See* MOZAMBIQUE.

DE LA MARE, Peter (fl. 1375) was steward to the E. of March when he was elected M.P. for Herefordshire in the Good Parliament of 1376. The Commons chose him as their Spokesman or Speaker, perhaps on account of his social connections and he requested the meeting with representative lords to voice the Commons' accusations against certain councillors, Ld. Latimer the King's Chamberlain, other royal servants and Alice Perrers, the King's mistress. When Latimer demanded to know who his accusers were, De la Mare replied that he and his fellows would maintain their charge in common (as later became the practice in impeachments). John of Gaunt reversed the proceedings of this parliament in 1377 and De la Mare was thrown into Nottingham gaol, but freed on the accession of Richard II later in the year. In his first parliament (1377) De la Mare was again chosen Speaker. He revived the criticism of the govt. and, on his recommendation, the Commons petitioned for a responsible council to conduct the govt. during the King's minority.

DELANE, John Thadeus (1817-79) became editor of *The Times* in 1841 and by 1845 had organised the speedy collection and transmission of information which, together with a ruthless turn of mind, made him one of the more influential men in Britain. Thus in 1849 he forced Palmerston to apologise to the Neapolitan govt. In 1854 and 1855 he published William Howard Russell's despatches on the deficiencies of supply and medical care in the Crimean War and these led eventually to extensive military and hospital reforms. In 1864 the attitude of *The Times* restrained the govt. from intervening against the Austro-Prussian attack on Denmark. He retired in 1877.

DE LA POLE. *See* POLE.

DELAWARE (U.S.A.) (*after de la Warr family see* WEST) was explored by Henry Hudson in 1609 and got its name in 1610. In 1633 the joint Swedish-Dutch New South Company was formed and in 1638 a party of Swedes and Finns under the Dutchman Pieter Minuit established New Sweden with its H.Q. at Christina (now Wilmington). A reorganisation in 1642 brought the colony under the Swedish crown and precipitated hostilities with the New Netherland Dutch who, led by Pieter Stuyvesant, conquered it in 1655. This Swedish interlude brought the log cabin to America. The D. of York's (later James II) conquest of New Netherland brought Delaware under his personal authority and in 1682 he transferred his rights to the Quaker Wm. Penn. Consequently Delaware became, as the Three Lower Counties, part of Pennsylvania, though in 1703 they were accorded a separate assembly under Penn's charter. The connection ended only at the rebellion in 1776 and Delaware was the first of the original 13 states of the Union. In 1787 it prohibited the import of slaves, while still permitting slavery; it supported the Union in the Civil War.

DELCASSÉ, Theophile (1852-1923) was elected to the French chamber as a radical in 1889. As minister for the Colonies from 1894 to 1895 he was responsible for much colonial development, especially in Madagascar. As Foreign Minister from 1898 to 1905 he fostered the *Entente Cordiale*. He was minister for the Navy from 1911 to 1913, Ambassador to St. Petersburg from 1913 to 1914 and again Min. for Foreign Affairs from 1914 to 1915. In all these capacities he was a key figure in the anti-German front.

DELEGATES, COURT OF. A court (of King's delegates) created in 1534 by statute to hear appeals from archbishops' courts when Henry VIII took over the papal jurisdiction. A separate mixed commission, of judges and laymen, was appointed for each case. The court's functions were transferred to the Judicial Committee of the Privy Council in 1833.

DELFT WARE, an earthenware glazed with tin, was first made in Holland in about 1520 in imitation of majolica. Its manufacture was introduced into Norfolk in 1571 whence it spread to Lambeth, Bristol and Liverpool It was only after 1584 that it was made at Delft.

DELHI (India) became the Moslem capital in 1193. Old Delhi remained the centre, but Moslem rulers built at least seven separate settlements in the area beginning with Siri and ending with Humayun's Old Fort built between 1530 and 1540. During all this time it remained the metropolis, apart from three short periods at Agra under the Moguls and it was famous for its wealth. The city was sacked by the Afghans in 1739 and 1757, dominated by the Marathas from 1771 but captured by the British in 1803; it remained, however, the seat of the Mogul emperor, though the British Resident was the effective authority. It was seized by the mutineers in May 1857 and recaptured in Sept. In 1858 the emperor was deposed and Calcutta became the capital; but in 1912 Delhi recovered its status. The British built an eighth settlement, New Delhi, for the purpose; this became, in due course, the capital of the Indian republic.

DELHI PACTS (1) (Mar. 1931). The Indian National Congress launched the Civil Disobedience movement in Apr. 1930 to drive the British govt. into constitutional concessions. The govt. replied by issuing repressive ordinances and taking Congress leaders into custody. Negotiations between Gandhi and the Viceroy (Ld. Irwin) culminated in the Pact whereby the ordinances were withdrawn and the prisoners released in return for which the Congress agreed to take part in the Round Table

conference on constitutional reform scheduled for 1932. *See* COMMUNAL AWARD. **(2) (1950)** The prime ministers of India (Jawaharlal Nehru) and Pakistan (Liaqat Ali Khan) agreed to let refugees return to their homes during the violent and confused period of relations between India and E. Pakistan (now Bangladesh).

DELICATE INVESTIGATION. *See* GEORGE IV-6.

DELINQUENT. A parliamentarian term for a royalist.

DELIUS, Frederick (1862-1934) son of a Bradford wool merchant of German origin, was prevented by his parents from pursuing a musical career and went to Florida as an orange planter. There he learned the piano and the violin and went to Leipzig, where Grieg persuaded him to make a musical career. He settled in France in 1890 and became mainly known in Germany until Sir Thomas Beecham recorded his main works, three of which were played for the first time in England in 1908.

DELLA CRUSCANS were a group of English poets living in Florence led by Robt. Merry (1755-98) and Hannah Cowley (1743-1809). They so-called themselves after the *Accademia della Crusca*, a Florentine body dedicated to purging the Tuscan language of chaff (*crusca*), but are best known for the ridicule which their sentimental utterances attracted.

DELVAUX, Laurent (1695-1778), Flemish sculptor (under high Habsburg patronage) who executed works in bronze and marble in England. He worked with Peter Scheemackers and taught Joseph Wilton.

DEMERARA. *See* GUIANA.

DEMESNE. That part of a manor exploited directly by the lord. *See* FEUDALISM.

DEMETAE. *See* DYFED.

DEMILUNE. *See* APPENDIX ON FORTIFICATIONS.

DEMI-REP[UTABLE]. Defined by Fielding as a woman "whom everybody knows to be what nobody calls her".

DEMOCRACY. This much abused word originally meant rule by the citizen body (*demos*) in certain Greek states, notably Athens. This excluded the large majority of inferior persons such as women, resident immigrants and foreigners, slaves and youths, besides those who lived too far out of town to be able to attend meetings. The expression ceased to be of more than antiquarian interest after the fall of Greece to the Romans and came back into use in the 18th cent. by a way of contrast with (monarchical) absolutism, aristocracy and oligarchy. It now carried with it previously unknown overtones of egalitarianism, as brilliantly enunciated in the American Declaration of Independence by the slave-owning fathers of the American dream and for practical reasons acquired a permanent association with representative elections, usually by secret ballot.

DEN(N). A Kentish pig pasture.

DE NATIVO HABENDO (Lat = concerning the possession of a villein) a royal writ requiring a sheriff to return a fugitive villein to his lord. Trial of the writ determined whether the defendant was a villein and, if so, whether the plaintiff was his lord.

DENBIGH. *See* VILLIERS.

DENBIGH (DINBYCH)-SHIRE. The area was part of Gwynedd until after the Normans came, and the town was a Welsh border fort until Edward I's conquest, when the area was converted into seven Lordships Marcher, four English (Denbigh, Rhos, Rhyfoniog and Ruthin) occupying the Perfeddwlad or Midland between the Clwyd and the Conway and three Welsh (Bromfield, Yale and Chirkland). There were castles at Denbigh (belonging to the de Lacys), Ruthin (Chester) and Chirk (Mortimer). These withstood the onslaught of Owain Glyndwr in 1402 when Denbigh town was sacked, but the area was much fought over in the Wars of the Roses. The Act of Union 1526 united the seven lordships into one county which was strongly royalist in the Civil War. In the 18th cent. Wrexham and Gresford became important for coal mining and steel.

DENBIGH (1) Willing Feilding or Fielding (?-1643) 1st Ld. FIELDING (1620) 1st E. (1622) married Buckingham's sister. Master of the Wardrobe in 1622, he went with Charles and Buckingham to Spain in 1623. He was naval commander in the attempt to relieve La Rochelle in 1628 and in 1631 made a voyage to India. His son **(2) Basil (?1608-75) 2nd E.** was summoned to the Lords by writ in 1628. Ambassador to Venice from 1634 to 1639, on his return he sided with the parliament, acting as regional commander in the W. Midlands. He was victorious at Dudley in 1644, but suspended for insufficient zeal. In 1645 he was one of the Uxbridge negotiators. In 1649 he refused to have any part in the King's "trial", but was nevertheless a Councillor of State from then until 1651. Increasingly disillusioned with Commonwealth policy, he slowly became a royalist. **(3) Rudolph Robert (1859-1939) 9th E.** erected the first British sugar-beet factory at Cantley (Norfolk) in 1912.

DENGUE. An acute disease of hot climates carried by mosquitoes, mainly *Aedes Aegypti,* originally confused with Yellow Fever. The two diseases seem to be mutually exclusive. It was first reported simultaneously in Java, the Coromandel Coast and Egypt in 1779, but had probably been some while endemic in Java. It came to N. America in 1780 and Peru in 1817. There were serious epidemics in India (1824-5), America (1826-8) and in India again (1853-4) and a great pandemic affected the eastern hemisphere from Africa to China between 1870 and 1873. It has remained endemic in the Caribbean and its adjacent mainland e.g. there were 27,000 cases in Puerto Rico in 1963-4 and nearly 17,000 in 1968-9. *See* EPIDEMICS, HUMAN.

DENIZEN, DENIZATION. *See* NATIONALITY-2.

DENMAN (1) Thomas (1779-1854) 1st Ld. DENMAN (1834) became an M.P. in 1818 and, as Sol-Gen. to Q. Caroline, defeated the bill of Pains and Penalties against her at the bar of the Lords. He drafted the Reform Bill of 1832 and later in that year became Lord Chief Justice. In 1835 he was Speaker of the Lords. He gave judgment against Commons privilege in *Stockdale* v *Hansard* and carried legislation to abolish the death penalty in several cases in 1837. From 1843 he was an outspoken opponent of the slave trade and in 1848 he secured the retention of the naval anti-slavery squadron. He left the bench in 1850. His son **(2) George (1819-96)** was an M.P. from 1859 to 1865 and from 1866 to 1872. He was responsible for important amendments to the law of evidence in the so-called Denmans Act, 1869. He became a judge in 1872.

DENMARK. *See* BALTIC; VIKINGS; HANSE.

DENNY, Sir Anthony (1501-49) favourite of Henry VIII, profiteer from the dissolution of the monasteries, was appointed counsellor to P. Edward in 1547, when he also became M.P. for Herts. He helped to suppress Ket's rebellion in 1549.

DEODAND (from Lat = that which should be given to God), was any object which caused the death of a human being. It was forfeit, originally to the Church, but later to the Crown, theoretically for pious uses. The practice was abolished only in 1846.

DEOGAUN, T. of (1803). *See* MARATHAS.

D'EON DE BEAUMONT, Chevalier Charles (1728-1810) reputed hermaphrodite, was a French secret agent and later a diplomat at St. Petersburg between 1755 and 1760. In 1774 he came to London as minister plenipotentiary, but fell foul of the French ambassador who plotted to murder him. The French govt. pensioned him on condition that he lived as a woman, which he did until 1785 when he returned to England and made his living by displays of swordmanship. At his death he was found to be a man.

DEOXYRIBONUCLEIC ACID (D.N.A.). The hi-helical structure of this, which carries genetic guidance in all organisms, was established in 1953.

DEPRESSION (1) AGRICULTURAL (1868-1914); (2) "GREAT" (1873-96). In the *first,* American soft wheat brought by improved transport, and Argentine chilled beef and N.Z. chilled mutton brought in refrigerator ships, easily undercut British production (other than fresh meat) unprotected since 1846. The countryside was ruined, the rural unemployment migrated to the towns and the rural big houses were maintained on industrial investment income capable of supporting only a little employment. The *second* was more a psychological matter. British manufactured exports continued to rise, but foreign manufactures rose faster. World markets expanded, but the British proportion of them fell. As most people of consequence had landed affiliations and saw the social effects of the first, they were inclined to regard the second with the gloom induced by it.

DEPRESSION, THE GREAT or SLUMP (1929-34). *See* MACDONALD'S SECOND LABOUR GOVT.-3,7-8.

DEPTFORD (London), a hamlet until 1513 (when Henry VIII began the naval yard), it soon became one of the most important shipbuilding centres in Europe, for which reason Peter the Great worked there in 1698. It continued to turn out warships of all sizes up to the end of the Napoleonic wars, was closed between 1832 and 1844, then reopened until 1869. By this time the comparative shallowness of the river had made it unsuitable for metal shipbuilding. *See* EAST INDIA CO-1; TRINITY HOUSE.

DEPUTY (1) A continental term for an M.P. **(2)** A Common Councilman entitled to act in minor ways for an alderman of the City of London.

DEPUTY, LORD. Strictly speaking, a deputy appointed by the Lord Lieut. of Ireland to act on his behalf. In practice the *de facto* governor under an absentee Lord Lieut. and usually appointed by the crown.

DE QUINCEY, Thomas (1785-1859) read German and Hebrew and took opium at Oxford from 1803. In 1807 he got to know Coleridge, Wordsworth and Southey, and Charles Lamb in 1808. He subsequently studied German metaphysics and, with Coleridge, tried to popularise German thought. Accordingly he published a *Prolegomena of all Future Systems of Political Economy* in 1819, but is better remembered for *Confessions of an Opium Eater* (1821), a translation of the *Laocoon* (1826) and *On Murder as One of the Fine Arts* (1827). He deliberately cultivated a 17th cent. prose style.

DERBFINE and TANISTRY were basic features of the Irish law of succession. The chief did not own his country, but was entitled to the respect of his tribe and their following in battle and he could requisition food for his army in war. Otherwise he had only a demesne called the MENSAL LANDS, certain customary rights and payment from such of his tribe as were also his tenants. All male descendents of a chief down to the fourth generation had an equal right to the succession, the office being conferred by election, theoretically upon the strongest or best. This group was called the **derbfine.** In practice there were difficulties: there might be disagreement about qualifications, or one party might refuse to recognise an election, or it might be accepted that the best man was too young or would soon be too old. Accordingly it could be decided to elect a young chief and a parallel ruler or guardian called the **tanist** who would hold office until the chief came of age. The Tanist might be the choice of a rival party for the chieftainship. In this way unity was maintained and too frequent elections avoided. Tanists generally retired with good grace and their sons seldom made special claims. The system was unstable and, in comparison with feudalism, led to weak leadership and disunion. On the other hand, the sheer numbers in a derbfine made it much harder to exterminate an Irish royal family than a Norman feudal one. The system lasted down to 1603.

DERBY. *See* STANLEY.

DERBY, EARL OF. *See* HENRY IV.

DERBY HOUSE COMMITTEE. *See* CHARLES 1-28; CIVIL WAR 1642-7.

DERBY SCHEME (1915) was an effort during World War I to avoid conscription. The E. of Derby, who actually favoured conscription, was deputed to set up arrangements whereby men of military age declared their willingness to serve when called, provided that the unmarried were called first. The scheme obtained two and a half million signatures but was abandoned because public opinion and the press demanded one rule for all.

DERBY STAKES. A horse race instituted in 1780 by the E. of Derby and run annually at Epsom, Surrey. It has always attracted huge concourses and there is a celebrated crowd picture by George Stubbs.

DERBY,-SHIRE. The neighbouring Little Chester was the Roman DERVENTIO. The Mercian town of Derby was called NORTHWORTHIGE, but when the Danes made it one of their Five Boroughs after the T. of Wedmore (878) they called it DEORABY. The area was much devastated in the Danish wars. Derby was occupied by Aethelflaed in 918, but later lost and Bakewell became from 924 until 941 the principal English centre. It was finally taken in 942, and the shire was probably organised by Athelstan (r. 925-39). It was closely associated with Nottinghamshire with which it shared many customs, as well as a High Sheriff and assizes, until 1566. The miners (mostly lead) had their own administration under a bailiff who held the BARMOTE Courts to regulate their affairs. The burgesses of Derby had a cloth dyeing monopoly under a Charter of K. John. The area was mainly royalist in the Civil War. The silk industry came to Derby in 1719, porcelain in 1750 and cotton in 1787. The development of heavier industries began at about this time with the opening of the coal fields.

DERBY'S FIRST GOVT. (Feb.-Dec. 1852) (13 in Cabinet under the E. of Derby, with Disraeli as Ch. of the Exch. and Leader of the Commons and the E. of Malmesbury as Foreign Sec.) *See* RUSSELL'S FIRST GOVT.-6. Disraeli offered to give up the leadership of the Commons to Palmerston if he would join this Tory govt. but he would enter no govt. not committed to free trade. This was the very point which had split the Conservatives since 1846. Derby already thought that his party must abandon protection, but as custom dictated that peers did not make speeches at elections, the country did not know this. In the general election of July 1852 they increased their membership at the expense of the free trade Peelites, but were still in a minority. Disraeli said that he accepted free trade, but in view of his treatment of Peel nobody believed him. His budget showed that he meant what he said. He proposed to compensate three interests for the effects of free trade: the land by reducing the malt tax, ship owners by abolishing some of their dues and sugar by permitting refining in bond. The compensation was to be found by taxing earned incomes of £100 and unearned of £50 a year and houses rated at £10. Gladstone united the opposition groups in an attack on this and the govt. resigned.

DERBY'S SECOND GOVT. (Feb. 1858-June 1859) (13 in Cabinet under the E. of Derby, with the M. of Salisbury, Lord Pres; Disraeli, Ch. of the Exch; the E. of Malmesbury, Foreign Sec. and the E. of Ellenborough, Pres. of the Board of Control). *See* PALMERSTON'S FIRST GOVT. This conservative govt. took office without any important difference of political principle from its predecessor, but having inherited a commercial crisis and overseas problems over which it had little control. The Indian Mutiny was being put down and it was determined to end the HEIC and transfer the formal responsibilities to a Sec. of State (Nov. 1858). Chinese negotiations matured into the T. of Tientsin (July) but the French began their incursion into Indo-China (Dec.) and had secured de Lessep's Suez Canal concession. The movement for incorporating Oregon as a state into the U.S.A. provoked

the proclamation of the colony of British Columbia (Dec.). There was a nasty dispute with the Lords about the admission of Lionel de Rothschild (a Jew) as M.P. for the City, which ended in a compromise permitting each House to settle the religious form of the appropriate oaths for itself (July) and, at the same time, the govt. secured the abolition of M.P.s property qualifications. Meanwhile Cavour and Napoleon III had met at Plombières to concert the expulsion of Austrian influence from Italy and the overthrow of its govts. (July) and by Mar. 1859 a major crisis was obviously developing there, accompanied by a secondary one in Schleswig-Holstein. British naval power could exert little influence in such theatres, soon to be dominated by large armies and, anyhow, British opinion, led by Palmerston, romantically favoured Italian unity. Turning their back on Europe, the govt. had let Disraeli persuade it to undertake a little electoral reform, for in the arbitrary state of its franchise, the opposition would in due course do it, if they did not. Their bill, to reduce the county house occupation franchise for £50 to £10 and give more seats to Middlesex, S. Lancashire and the West Riding, was defeated on an amendment (Mar. 1859). In Apr. revolutions broke out in Italy and the Austrians declared war on Piedmont. The French intervened in May. The govt. just had time to create the new colony of Queensland of N.S.W. (May) and call a general election, in which the conservatives gained some, but not enough, seats. It was forced to resign on a vote of no confidence at the reassembly of parliament.

DERBY'S THIRD GOVT. (June 1866-Feb. 1868). (15 in Cabinet under the E. of Derby; Disraeli, Ch. of the Exch; Spencer Walpole, Home Sec; Ld. Stanley, Foreign Sec; Sir Stafford Northcote, Pres. of the Board of Trade; Vist. Cranborne, Sec. for India; Ld. Naas (later E. of Mayo), Ch. Sec. for Ireland).

(1) Russell's second govt. resigned on an opposition amendment to a Reform Bill and Derby took office without a majority. Politicians were thus obsessed with electoral details while Prussia attacked Austria and her German allies and Prussia's Italian ally was beaten at Custozza and Lissa. The decisive defeat of Austria at Königgrätz, however, ended the war in six weeks and Prussia annexed (*inter alia*) Hanover, and Italy Venice.

(2) Parliament met in Feb. 1867 and the govt. introduced its own Reform Bill, but its weakness forced it to make substantial concessions, both in the electoral qualifications and in the redistribution of seats. Cranborne resigned. The Act, passed in Aug., almost doubled the electorate. In the meantime Canadian opinion had been moving towards federation, and Parliament, with insignificant debate, passed the British North America Act (July) to effect it.

(3) Since electoral reform was essentially a House of Commons matter, the proceedings brought Disraeli, as leader of that House, forward as the virtual leader of the govt., for Derby's health was declining. In Feb. 1868 Derby had to resign.

DE ROBECK, Sir John Michael (1862-1928) Bart (1919) was 2-in-C to Adm. Carden at the Dardanelles in 1915, took over command in Mar. and carried out the withdrawal in 1916. He was C-in-C Mediterranean Fleet (1919-22) and of the Atlantic Fleet (1922-4).

DE RUYTER, Michael Adrienszoon (1607-76), Dutch seaman, as a rear-admiral of Zeeland, defeated an attack by Sir George Ayscue on a convoy at the beginning of the First Dutch War (Aug. 1652) and then fought under Adm. de Witt at the Kentish Knock (Sept.), Dungeness (Nov.), Portland (Feb. 1653) and the North Foreland (June). As a result of the latter defeat, he and Marten Tromp persuaded their govts. to rebuild their fleet. After naval campaigns against the Barbary pirates and the Swedes he commanded the Dutch in the Second Dutch War (victoriously against Monck in the Four Days' Battle

(1666), but less successfully on St. James' Day, because Tromp failed him). In 1667 he carried out the famous raid on the Medway in which he destroyed or took home 8 English ships. In the Third Dutch War he held off the combined Anglo-French fleets at Solebay (May 1673) and won a tactical victory over them at the Texel (Aug.). In Aug. 1674 he sailed for the Mediterranean and, after an indecisive encounter with the French off Stromboli (Jan. 1676) beat Duquesne near Messina, but was mortally wounded (Apr.).

DERVISH is a member of a Mohammedan religious confraternity. Each fraternity derives a spiritual descent (*silsila*) from God, through Gabriel to Mohammed and thence to the initiating teacher and his pupil, who is expected to memorise his *silsila*. The organisation superficially resembles Christian monasticism, but the spiritual exercises tend to be hypnotic or ecstatic, sometimes including feats of endurance, dancing, whirling or howling. Many followers of the Sudanese Mahdi were dervishes, but their most permanent centre has been at Konia in Asia Minor.

DERWENT, DERBYSHIRE. See TRANSPORT AND COMMUNICATIONS.

DERWENTWATER. See RADCLIFFE.

DESBOROUGH, DESBOROW or DISBROWE, John (1608-80), an ill-advised opportunist, married Jane, one of Oliver Cromwell's sisters, in 1636. He was a successful parliamentary soldier and M.P. in 1654 and 1656. He opposed the offer of the Crown to Oliver and also Richard Cromwell's succession in 1659, preferring at first Fleetwood and then favouring the dissolution of the parliament. The Rump made him a member of the Council of State, but he was dismissed for his connection with the Army Petition (Oct. 1659). At the Restoration he was initially arrested, then involved in a plot to kill the King and then engaged in republican intrigues in Holland, but in 1666 he returned to England and was briefly imprisoned. He died at Hackney.

DESBOROUGH REPORT. See POLICE-3.

DESCARTES, René. See RENAISSANCE-14.

DESIGNS were first protected by the Copyright of Designs Act, 1875. See PATENTS, ETC. ACT, 1883.

DESMOND, Es. of (*see* FITZGERALD) **(1) Maurice** son of **Thomas (?-1356) 1st E. (1329),** apparently related to the royal family, was left wide lands in Munster and married Catherine, *d.* of Richard de Burgh, E. of Ulster. This only temporarily assuaged the feud between his family and the Burkes, with whom he was at war from 1326 to 1328. In 1329 he received the palatinate of Kerry, but neglected it for his quarrels with Ulster and the Dublin govt., which imprisoned him in 1331-2. In 1339, however, he defeated the Kerry Irish. Meanwhile a new London policy of governing Ireland through English officials rather than settlers caused the earl to lead a protest at Kilkenny (Oct. 1341). This was ignored and he and others refused to attend parliament at Dublin. The Deputy, Ralph of Ufford, treated this as a rebellion, seized and forfeited his lands and imprisoned him. Ufford, however, died in 1346 (the year of Crécy) and his successor gave him a safe conduct to England where he surrendered to the King, served at the siege of Calais (1347) and was restored to his lands upon which he lived quietly until, in 1355, he was briefly Lord Lieut. Of his sons **(2) Maurice (?-1356) 2nd E.** died just after his father and **(3) Gerald (?-1398) 4th E.** was at the same time captured by the Irish. The result was great confusion all over Munster. After his release Gerald obtained Maurice's lands and the custody of an idiot brother, and spent nearly ten years pacifying the province, by a mixture of violence and appeasement, in which his position approximated increasingly to that of a native Irish chief. He was a poet both in Gaelic and in French. In 1367 he succeeded Clarence as Justiciar, but he had on his hands the usual Irish tribal feuds. He was superseded

in 1369 by Sir William of Windsor and then captured by Brien O'Brien, Chief of Thomond, who also sacked Limerick. Windsor rescued him in 1370 but the O'Brien war continued intermittently and from 1377 he had wars with the Munster Burkes and Butlers. The result was an alliance with the O'Briens who fostered his son **(4) James (?-1462).** This James usurped the earldom. His son **(5) Thomas (1426-68) 8th E.** became Clarence's Lord Deputy in 1463 and fought the Butlers at the same time, but he built castles in Offaly to exclude the O'Connors from the Pale and then launched at least partly successful expeditions against the O'Briens. He was superseded in 1467 by John Tiptoft, E. of Worcester, and was attainted with his relative, Kildare, and executed. The reasons for this are uncertain. His fate may have been related to English politics, but the actual charges were treason with the Irish. His daughter-in-law **(6) Katherine (?-1604)** lived to be at least 114. During her lifetime the earldom was disputed but eventually came to **(7) James (?-1558) 14th E.** who was on excellent terms with the O'Briens and acted as the chief English ruler in Munster from about 1540 until his death. His son **(8) Gerald (?-1583) 15th E.,** notoriously picked a quarrel over the prizes at Youghal and Kinsale with the Butler E. of Ormonde, fought him and then refused to submit before the English Council (1562). Q. Elizabeth put him in custody and in 1564 he returned, having accepted peace articles. He instantly involved himself in one of the O'Brien feuds and in 1563 he was at war with Ormonde again. Both earls were summoned to London and bound over but he continued his violence and in 1567 Sir Henry Sidney arrested him again. He remained in custody in England until 1573. When he returned he was rearrested but escaped. He spent the rest of his life waging a private guerrilla in Munster, in which he was eventually killed and the earldom was forfeited. His son **(9) James (?1570-1601)** the TOWER or QUEEN'S E., was born in the Tower of London and remained there, effectively as a prisoner, until 1600 when he was taken out and paraded in Ireland as the Earl in order to split the Tyrone rebellion by attracting (unsuccessfully) the loyalty of the Fitzgerald followers of **(10) James (?-1608)** the SUGAN E., son of a bastard of **(7)** above. He raised a rebellion and assumed the title of Earl of Desmond in 1598 in order to resist the Elizabethan plantation of Munster. He was beaten near Aharlow (Oct. 1600), captured in May 1601 and died in the Tower.

DESPARD, Charlotte (1844-1939) wealthy novelist inclined to extreme opinions. She helped to set up the Women's Freedom League in 1907 and from 1914 took to pacifism, Irish independence and, after 1920, Russian communism.

DESPARD. Of two brothers **(1) John (1745-1829)** fought and was taken prisoner by the rebel Americans at York Town and was military commandant on Cape Breton I. from 1799 to 1807. **(2) Edward Marcus (1751-1803)** as commandant at Rattan, captured the Spanish possessions on the Rio Negro in 1782 and was superintendent of H.M. affairs there from 1784 to 1790. He was suspended by Ld. Grenville on frivolous charges and in 1798 imprisoned when he claimed compensation. He then devised a plot to murder the govt. and was executed for treason.

DESPATCH BOX. A strong leather-covered box in which documents passing between high state personages are locked during transit. The sovereign's boxes are purple in colour; minister's red; other's (e.g. members of royal commissions) black. They are to be found, naturally, on the tables of legislatures and hence *to speak from the despatch* box means to speak on behalf of the govt.

DESPENSER (1) Hugh (I) (?-1265), a friend of Richard, K. of the Romans, was a partisan of the Provisions of Oxford. After experience as a sheriff and royal castellan he joined the baronial opposition and was one of its 12 representatives, elected in the Oxford Parliament (1258) to the council of 24. In 1260 the five baronial electors appointed him Justiciar and Nicholas of Ely Chancellor. He was also nominally in charge of the Tower of London. When the King resumed personal control in 1261, Hugh was deprived of both his functions, but when Simon de Montfort regained power in 1263 he was reappointed Justiciar. He fought at Lewes and was one of the arbitrators appointed to try and make peace after the battle. He also tried unsuccessfully to mediate between Montfort and the E. of Gloucester. Later in 1265 he was killed with Simon de Montfort at the B. of Evesham. His son **(2) Hugh (II) (The Elder) (1262-1326) E. of WINCHESTER (1322)** had served Edward I well in Gascony, Scotland and Flanders. He gave equal loyalty to Edward II and stood by the King's unpopular favourite Piers Gaveston. After Gaveston's murder in 1308 it was Hugh who represented the King in negotiations with the Ordainers. Unlike his bitter opponent, the E. of Lancaster, Hugh supported the King in the disastrous Bannockburn expedition of 1314. Edward II yielded to the severe limitations on his power imposed under the Ordinances; Lancaster now gained ascendancy and Hugh was dismissed from the Council (1315). Hugh and his son Hugh the Younger now became the core of an anti-Lancastrian party. They received extensive territorial grants from the King and the elder Hugh became involved in his son's ambitions in the Welsh March.

Marcher Lords, the so-called middle party and Lancaster saw these as a threat, which they represented as greed and, forming a coalition, had both Hughs banished in 1321. The King, however, managed to recall them a year later and with their help made a resolute effort to defeat his opponents. This bore fruit in the victory at Boroughbridge, Lancaster's execution and the Despensers' reinstatement. In the same year the Despenser dominated York parliament annulled the Ordinances and for the next four years Despenser policies guided the course of govt. They aimed, in particular, at strengthening the royal authority and improving the administration. This was generally beneficial, but increased Despenser power and consequently unpopularity. The elder Hugh acquired many Lancastrian estates including the Marcher Lordship of Denbigh alongside his son's already immense power in S. Wales. Failures in relations with Scotland and France and Q. Isabella's growing alienation from the King provoked a crisis. In 1326 Isabella and her paramour, the powerful Marcher lord, Roger Mortimer, effected a *coup d'état* and the elder Hugh was summarily hanged at Gloucester. His son **(3) Hugh (III) (The Younger) (?-1326)** was a contemporary and friend of Edward II, who gave him the hand of his niece, Eleanor, eldest of the three sisters of Gilbert of Clare. When Gilbert was killed at Bannockburn (1314), the great Clare inheritance was divided among the husbands of the three sisters, Roger Damory, Hugh of Audley and the younger Hugh, who seems to have seen his share as a base from which to widen his interests; these clashed with those of neighbouring magnates. This eventually drew him away from the earlier association with the baronial party towards the King's side. In 1318, apparently with general approval, he was appointed Chamberlain, but henceforth devoted his energies to extending his territories in S. Wales. He had received the Clare Marcher Lordship of Glamorgan, but attempted to expand it by force and guile. By challenging Marcher customs of succession he claimed the Braose lordship of Gower. His various other aggressions provoked a hostile Marcher alliance which included his brothers-in-law, the E. of Hereford and the Mortimers of Chirk and Wigmore. The alliance ravaged the March lands of both Hughs in 1321 and, as a result of charges laid against them in Parliament, they were banished. The younger Hugh briefly supported himself,

possibly with royal connivance, on piracy. He was fully associated with his father in the policies established in the York parliament after the victory at Boroughbridge in 1322 and in the efforts to widen the royal authority through the use of the royal household. The younger Hugh concentrated on the Chamber, which became active as a land management and acquisition department, but his greed was unabated: he exploited his position for personal gain and, in particular, encroached increasingly upon the interests of the dangerous Roger Mortimer of Wigmore, already his enemy and now Q. Isabella's lover. At the *coup d'état* of 1326 he, like his father, was hanged. (*See also* STAPLE.) His grandson **(4) Henry (1341-1406) Bp. of NORWICH (1370)** was in fact a soldier and had served in Italy in the wars of Urban V, who provided him to the see of Norwich. He was energetic and resourceful and personally defeated the peasant rising in Norfolk in 1381. Because of his reputation as a warlike bishop, he was put in charge of the so-called Norwich Crusade in 1383. Urban VI had proclaimed a crusade in Flanders against his rival Clement VII. His bulls were considered at the parliament of Oct. 1382 together with an alternative scheme for an expedition to Castile under John of Gaunt. The Commons favoured Flanders because the French had seized Ypres and Bruges and the English wool staple at nearby Calais was therefore in danger. Gaunt and the Lords would have preferred that the expedition should be in royal or at least lay hands, perhaps in the hope of diverting it to Spain, but the Commons urged that because it involved no expense to the Exchequer, the Bishop's offer should be accepted. It was. Urban had offered plenary indulgences to supporters and gold and jewels poured in, much of it offered by women. Wyclif wrote bitterly against the scheme and its finances. Gravelines and Dunkirk were soon taken. Then the men of Ghent persuaded the Bishop to invest Ypres. Long and disastrous operations ensued. His recruits were an indisciplined rabble intent on loot and many deserted. Early in Aug. 1381 a French army approached under Philip of Burgundy and the siege had to be abandoned. The French offered bribes to English captains to avoid action. Unable to maintain discipline, the Bishop sacked Gravelines and returned with his rabble to England. At the autumn parliament, Michael de la Pole the Chancellor, caused the Bishop to be deprived of his temporalities for two years. Some of his captains were briefly imprisoned.

In the crisis at the end of the reign Henry was one of the few who remained loyal to Richard II. The new king imprisoned him and he did not make his peace until the parliament of 1401. A great grandson of **(3), (5) Thomas (1373-1400) E. of GLOUCESTER (1397)** married Constance, daughter of his guardian Edmund Langley, E. of Cambridge. In 1397 he supported Richard II when he appealed Gloucester, Arundel and Warwick of treason and the Gloucester earldom was transferred to him by way of reward. He went with the King to Ireland in 1399. After the landing of Henry of Lancaster, Thomas was suspected of murdering Humphrey, the late Gloucester's son. He eventually deserted and helped to depose Richard II but was soon involved in a rebellion against Henry IV and was lynched by the hostile citizens of Bristol (1400). His daughter **(6) Isabel (?-?)** married Richard Beauchamp, E. of Worcester. The Despensers succeeded the Clares as patrons of Tewkesbury Abbey, where there are fine chantry and stained glass memorials to them.

DESPOTISM is rule which is arbitrary in application and restricted (usually by assassination) only in an extremity or by foreign intervention.

DESTABILISATION, was the Communist Russian policy in African countries and elsewhere such as Aden and Guiana, of encouraging disorder and civil strife. The purpose was to create REVOLUTIONARY SITUATIONS favourable, under Marxist theory, to the establishment of regimes under local communists ready to impose DICTATORSHIPS OF THE PROLETARIAT. Professional disturbers such as the Congolese Patrice Lumumba were trained in Russia; arms were supplied wholesale to terrorists and insurrectionary groups such as the Kikuyu and (*via* Czechoslovakia) to the I.R.A. in Ulster; finance was provided for the Cuban invasion of Angola; excessively favourable trade terms were arranged with or offered as inducements to govts. such as the Libyan to throw off their western connections; anti-monarchical coups were organised; propaganda varying from the scurrilous to disguised school curricula was focused upon susceptible populations and, to enhance Russian prestige, some spectacular projects such as the Egyptian High Dam were pressed regardless of consequence and expense. The whole was underpinned by the maintenance of a large and otherwise unnecessary navy. The cost in human lives and misery (e.g. in Mozambique, C. Africa and Syria) was incalculable besides imposing a heavy burden on the primitive Russian economy. By 1985 it was plain that the way towards a prosperous tranquillity could be unblocked only by the improbable overthrow of the Russian govt. When this surprisingly happened in 1989-90 the effects were soon manifest in widespread restabilisations (e.g. in S. Africa), the overthrow of externally supported Marxist regimes (e.g. the Ethiopian Derg) or their democratisation (e.g. in Tanzania).

DESTROYER (orig. TORPEDO BOAT DESTROYER) was developed in the 1890s as a fast ship with guns capable of destroying the primitive steam torpedo boats so far introduced. The stability needed for the guns required a larger ship which was then found to be more suitable for the operation of torpedoes than the torpedo boat. The latter were almost wholly superseded by the Russo-Japanese War of 1904-5 in which Japanese destroyers played a spectacular part. Large numbers were built for the Royal Navy and operated in both World Wars.

DESUETUDE. A Scottish but not an English legal rule that a rule or statute can be abrogated if long disregarded in practice. It does not apply to statutes made since 1707.

DETECTIVE STORIES. This thriving element of popular culture started with the genuine *Mémoires* (1829) of Eugene Vidocq, a real life French thief who turned detective. The first fictional detective was Edgar Allan Poe's Auguste Dupin (1845) but the English fashion began with Wilkie Collins Sergeant Cuff in *The Moonstone* (1868) and was launched into popular acclaim by Sherlock Holmes in Conan Doyle's works beginning with *A Study in Scarlet* (1887) and continued in short stories in the *Strand Magazine*. After Holmes' death, resurrection was forced upon the author by an indignant public which conferred upon Holmes a quasi-immortality at his address at 221B Baker Street, London; its owners are still dealing with his correspondence. Very soon the mode was taken up by writers in all parts of the English speaking world and with the advent of radio and television, it crowded into other media, so that no day passed in the 1990s without a broadcast detective story. In non-English speaking countries the native detective literature in the years up to 1995 had been insufficient to satisfy public craving which subsisted mainly on translations from the English.

DETERMINISM. Laplace in 1814 argued that with the aid of Newtonian physics the state of the universe could, at any moment, be described, at any rate by a superhuman intelligence. This universal determinism differs from the predestination of Calvin, St. Augustine and St. Paul, based on the foreknowledge of an Almighty, and from logical determinism which, based upon the proposition that a prediction is either true or false, led to the curious Aristotelian result that historical foreknowledge is impossible because the basic proposition is false. It is only human to reject the full rigour of deterministic doctrines as inconsistent with free will and moral responsibility, yet it is equally human in the interests of intellectual order to attempt analyses and classifications which, if extrapolated, lead to a deterministic result. Hence most historiography has shown uneasy compromises in which the issue (if there is one) is unsettled. The two major deterministic trends may, however, be called the *cyclic* and the *linear*. The main exponents of cyclic theories have been Giambattista Vico (1668-1744), Oswald Spengler (1880-1936) and A. J. Toynbee (1889-1975). Vico in 1725 visualised nations as passing through a religious, then a heroic, and finally a human stage each characterised by decreasing stability and leading to a collapse and to the religious recommencement of the cycle. Spengler in 1919 thought that the intelligible units of historical exposition were cultures, i.e. groups, of people sharing a common conception of their world. He identified nine of them and portrayed two in detail. These, over a period of about 1000 years, passed through four stages: an agricultural and heroic spring; an aristocratic summer; an urban and autocratic autumn and an over-rich tyrannical winter. At this point development ceases but the culture may survive unless it falls victim to external aggression. Toynbee elaborated elements drawn from both views. His unit of discussion was the civilisation, of which he identified 21. A civilisation is formed by the response of a creative minority to a challenge and the majority accepts the minority until the latter ceases to respond. At that moment the creative minority uses its power to dominate rather than lead and establishes the final stultification, a universal state; this breaks up in a Time of Troubles, from which a new challenge will perhaps emerge.

Of the linear theories Auguste Comte (1798-1857) writing in 1830, thought that the accumulation of knowledge necessarily resulted in endless progress which would not be thwarted, while many readers of Darwin after 1859 inferred a similar conclusion from natural selection. Marx, who regarded the theory as a means or tool of action, had a form of determinism thrust upon him by Engels, Kautsky and other Germans. They thought that less advanced modes of production always generate higher modes and that when a society is in conflict with its mode of production it is replaced by a society not in such conflict.

All the cyclic and linear theories have been attacked because they cannot be squared with the known facts.

DETROIT (U.S.A.) was founded in 1701 by Antoine de la Mothe Cadillac as Fort PONTCHARTRAIN du Detroit, a fur trading post. It was taken by the British in 1760, ceded to the U.S.A. at the P. of Paris (1783) but remained under British occupation until 1796.

DEUSDEDIT (d. 664), the first Saxon Abp. of Canterbury, consecrated in 655.

DEVA. (Lat = CHESTER). *See* CHESHIRE.

DE VALERA, Eamon (1882-1973). Anglophobe, if heroic, Irish Spaniard born in New York, was educated in Ireland, joined the Irish Volunteers in 1913 and took part in the Easter Rising (1916) as commandant of its "Dublin Brigade". He was caught, sentenced to death and released in 1917 under the general amnesty. He instantly became Pres. of the Irish Volunteers and of Sinn Fein. Rearrested in May 1918 he escaped from Lincoln prison in Feb. 1919. He then became Pres. of the shadow "Irish Republic", rejected the Anglo-Irish treaty in Dec. 1921, launched the civil war of 1922-3 and, not surprisingly, was again imprisoned from Aug. 1923 to July 1924. From 1927 to 1932 he was leader of the opposition in the Free State parliament. His party, by now called Fianna Fail, then won the elections and he became prime minister. His govt. instituted social and land reforms and enacted a new constitution declaring Ireland (i.e. the whole island) a sovereign R. Catholic republic. It also, by threatening to withhold the Land Annuities (representing compensation for extruded landowners), secured British abandonment of the southern Irish Atlantic naval bases. During the B. of the Atlantic in World War II this created grave difficulties for Britain and few advantages for Ireland. He also insisted on maintaining Irish neutrality and even permitted a Nazi legation in Dublin. There were unverified rumours of U-boats in Irish sea loughs. After the war, with alternate swings of electoral favour, he was in opposition from 1948 to 1951, prime minister again until 1954, in opposition until 1957, prime minister until 1959 when he became Pres. of the Republic.

DEVALUATION, REVALUATION, DEPRECIATION, APPRECIATION. (1) The first two are deliberate changes in a managed currency's exchange rate against foreign currencies; the second two are natural changes of an unmanaged and, therefore, floating currency. Devaluation makes exports temporarily more competitive until other countries retaliate, and imports more expensive and less competitive at home. With depreciation these effects occur more slowly. Under revaluations and appreciations the converse is the case. Devaluation is thus often an emergency interference in natural events during a balance of payments crisis. **(2)** The British returned to the Gold Standard in 1925 and thus fixed the sterling exchange rate in relation to other gold-based currencies at 4.80 dollars to the £1. After its abandonment in 1931 the pound floated between $3.30 and $5. In 1945 $4.03 was chosen as the fixed rate but the 1949 devaluation brought it down to $2.80 and another in 1987 to $2.40. In 1972 sterling was allowed to float.

DEVANAGARI. The alphabet of Sanskrit.

DEVELOPMENT. *See* TOWN AND COUNTRY PLANNING.

DEVELOPMENT AREAS, DISTRICTS. (1) The Distribution of Industry Act, 1945, named four development areas, viz: *North East* (Co. Durham and adjacent areas of Yorkshire and Northumberland); *West Cumberland; South Wales and Monmouthshire* (Glamorgan, much of Carmarthen, Pembroke, the southern part of Brecon and most of Monmouthshire); and the *Scottish Development Area* (Glasgow, Dumbarton, Lanark, Renfrew and parts of Ayr, Dumfriesshire, Stirling, West and Midlothian and the city of Dundee) which were losing population or might experience difficulty in providing jobs. It empowered the Board of Trade to buy or improve land, provide buildings and make favourable loans for new industries and other ministries to give financial support for basic public services.

(2) The Act was replaced by the Local Employment Act, 1960. This substituted Development Districts which were areas where there was, in the Board's opinion, a high rate of actual or expected unemployment. Most of the previous Development Areas became Development Districts. The Act also introduced Industrial Development Certification. A planning authority might not thenceforth give planning permission for a substantial or important industrial building unless the Board had certified that the development would be consistent with a proper distribution of industry. *See* SPECIAL AREAS.

DEVELOPMENT BONDS. *See* NATIONAL SAVINGS MOVEMENT.

DEVELOPMENT PLANS. *See* TOWN AND COUNTRY PLANNING-4.

DEVEREUX (1) Walter (?-1558) 1st Vist. HEREFORD (1550), a soldier, became C.J. of S. Wales in 1525 and became a privy councillor as a support for the new govt. at the overthrow of Somerset in 1550. His grandson **(2) Walter (?1541-76) 2nd Vist. and 1st E. of ESSEX (1572)** helped to suppress the northern revolt of 1572 and in 1573 undertook to conquer Ulster. His efforts to drive out the Scots failed and he allied himself with them against the Irish. After the treacherous murder of Sir Brian MacPhelim in 1574 and a destructive but useless raid on Rathlin he was recalled to explain his conduct. His son **(3) Robert (1566-1601) 2nd E.** was distinguished for bravery at Zutphen in 1586. His brilliant personality and good looks also helped to earn him the Queen's favour,

even if he refused her a kiss at the age of ten and wore his hat in her presence. In 1587 he became Master of the Horse. He had personal quarrels with the Blounts and Sir Walter Raleigh, of whose influence with the Queen he was jealous. In politics he favoured an all-out anti-Spanish policy and the establishment of the Braganzas on the Portuguese throne; he commanded troops in support of Henry of Navarre in France in 1591 to 1592. In 1593 he became a privy councillor and, in 1594, with Portuguese help uncovered the improbable Lopes plot against the Queen's life. In 1596 he commanded a naval expedition which took Cadiz but produced no other noteworthy results, though for reasons now uncertain, he advocated a march through Andalusia. He sailed unsuccessfully against the Azores in 1597. On his return he was given the military and ceremonial office of Earl Marshal for by now the anti-Spanish essentially naval policy was exhausted. In 1598 he quarrelled with Burghley who wanted to end it. He was by now well past his zenith. The Queen supported Cecil after Burghley's death and relegated Essex to the Lord Lieutenancy of Ireland in 1599, but with a sufficient force to re-establish English power there. As it was suspected that he might try to use his Irish base to enhance political power in England, he was ordered to invade and subdue Ulster. Instead he made a truce with Tyrone, the Ulster chieftain, and came to London where he was arrested and charged in June 1600 with unlawfully leaving his govt. Released in Aug. he contrived an ill-regulated plot to depose Cecil; and in Feb. 1601 attempted to raise the City. He was tried and condemned. The Queen delayed but in the end permitted the execution. His son **(4) Robert (1591-1646) 3rd E.** was a Vice Admiral in the Cadiz expedition of 1625; in 1628 he consistently opposed Charles I's policy, voting for the Petition of Right in 1628 and for Strafford's death in 1641. He was C-in-C of the Parliamentary Army from 1642, fought at Edghill, took Reading and relieved Gloucester in 1643. He resigned over Cromwell's Scottish policy in 1645. *See* CIVIL WAR.

DE VESCI (1) Eustace (?1170-1216) crusaded with Richard I. He was a prominent military figure in the Scottish Marches and also an opponent of K. John and a witness to Magna Carta. He was killed besieging Hugh Balliol's Barnard Castle. He married a bastard of William the Lion. His son **(2) William (?-1253),** Lord of Alnwick, Malton and other estates in Northumberland and Yorkshire, died in Gascony when his son **(3) John (?-1289)** was a minor. Henry III gave the wardship to Peter of Savoy and, as a result, the family joined Simon de Montfort's faction for anti-Savoyard reasons. He was wounded and then taken at Evesham and compounded under the Dictum of Kenilworth. He joined a further rising in 1267, but the Lord Edward treated him with such persuasive consideration that he became devoted to him and went on crusade with him. By 1273 he was Castellan of Scarborough and he helped to defeat the Manx in the Scottish expedition of 1275. He served in Wales in 1277, became Edward's confidential adviser and, in 1279 and then in 1280, contracted, with Edward's applause, a Lusignan and then a Beaumont marriage. Edward employed him in 1282 to negotiate the Aragon marriage and in 1285 another with Holland. His brother **(4) William (?1249-97)** succeeded to the family estates in 1289 and in 1290 to his mother's enormous Irish estates, including Kildare, for she was a co-heiress of Walter Marshall, 5th E. of Pembroke. He was immediately appointed Justiciar of Ireland, when he promptly colluded with the Geraldine John fitz Thomas in supporting rivals for the Kingship of Connaught. Charges and countercharges ended in his removal, with honour, from the Justiciarship. He died after all his legitimate sons and so arranged, by surrender and regrant, for his estates to pass, but for life only, to his Irish bastard **(5) William of Kildare (?-1314)** who was killed at Bannockburn.

DEVIATION is to communism what heresy is to Christianity, namely any development of Marxist doctrine which conflicts with the views of a ruling communist party and especially any such doctrine differing from that currently professed by the govt. of the former U.S.S.R. *See* CENTRALISM, DEMOCRATIC.

DE VILLIERS, John Henry (1842-1914) 1st Ld. (1910) South African barrister and member of the Cape House of Assembly from 1867, became Att-Gen. in 1872 and C. J. in 1873. He was a powerful champion of union, being largely responsible for drafting the Pretoria convention (1881). Widely respected for his determination and gifts of conciliation, he was pres. of the national convention of 1908-9 and became first C. J. of the Union in 1910, despite the defeat of the federalist ideas which would have strengthened the Supreme Court.

DEVIL'S DYKE, a massive post-Roman earthwork about 5 metres (16 feet) high stretching across the Icknield Way from Wood Ditton to Reach in Cambridgeshire. Like the Fleam Dyke it faces S.W. and must have been erected by Germanic invaders who had been forced to abandon the Upper Thames after defeat at British hands c. 571. It later formed part of the boundary between E. Anglia and Mercia.

DEVILS PARLIAMENT (Nov. 1459) was so-called by the Yorkists. They had been defeated at Ludford Bridge (Oct. 413 1459) and the parliament was hurriedly summoned to Coventry to pass wholesale attainders of their leaders.

DEVIZES (Wilts). Roger, Bp. of Salisbury, built a palace-castle in about 1132 and the town grew up around it, with a prosperous wool market from 1340 and a cloth industry from 1520 to 1820. The builders of the Kennet and Avon canal contrived a remarkable curved staircase of locks in the late 18th cent. and there is a monument commemorating the dangers of false swearing.

"DEVOLUTION" (1) (1978-9). (1) The upsurge of apparent support for Welsh and Scottish nationalism in the early 1970s tempted the Wilson govt. to try and gain political mileage by appointing the Kilbrandon Commission to investigate. In 1978 it recommended elected legislative assemblies for Scotland and Wales, with fiscal powers subject to a central veto, but Scottish and Welsh seats in the Commons were to be retained. In 1978 an enabling Act was passed with the proviso that, to take effect, at least 40% of the Scots and Welsh total electorates would first have to give an affirmative vote in separate referenda. In Mar. 1979 the referenda were held. Realising that indirect subsidisation by England would disappear, the Welsh electorate supported devolution by only 13% and the Scots by 33%.

(2) 1997-99. The Blair govt. planned to devolve initially unspecified functions to Scotland, Wales, N. Ireland (*see* GOOD FRIDAY AGREEMENT), Greater London and English Regions. (a) The proposal for a Scots parliament was supported by 74.3% of the Scots electorate in Sept 1997. (b) In Wales, on a proposal for a non-legislative Assembly without financial powers the support was 25.9%. Only 50.6% voted. (c) In Greater London a similar proportion of an even smaller proportion favoured a "mayor" with a small council. (d) In the regions the proposals fell even flatter. The govt. accordingly legislated for (a), (b) and (c) and set up vaguely endowed regional assemblies. *See* SCOTLAND ACT 1998; GOVERNMENT OF WALES ACT 1998.

DEVOLUTION, WAR OF (1667-8). One of the precursors to the War of the Spanish Succession. Philip IV of Spain died in 1665. He was succeeded by the sickly and deformed Charles II who was expected to die early and childless. By his will, Philip reserved the eventual succession to the descendents of his daughter, the Infanta Margareta, married to the Emperor Leopold I, in preference to her elder sister, the Infanta Maria Theresia, who on her marriage to Louis XIV had renounced her rights. Maria Theresia's dowry had not been paid.

Arguing that it would have represented compensation for his queen's rights (as the elder) in the Burgundian territories of the Spanish royal house, he asserted that they devolved upon her notwithstanding Philip's will and, seizing the opportunity presented by the current Anglo-Dutch war, invaded and overran most of Belgium (May-Sept. 1667). This engendered a reversal of Anglo-Dutch relations. The victorious Dutch conceded the P. of Breda (July 1668) and looked for other allies. In Feb. French overran Franche-Comté, while the hard pressed Spaniards, prompted by English diplomacy, recognised the legal as well as the actual independence of Portugal. By Apr. 1668, when Sweden joined the Anglo-Dutch alliance, Louis was offering terms to the Spaniards; these ripened into the P. of Aix-la-Chapelle (May 1668) under which Louis returned Franche-Comté in exchange for the cession of the important Flemish strip containing Douai, Lille, Armentieres, Valenciennes and Maubeuge. *See* CHARLES II-10-12; DUTCH WARS, 17TH CENT.-14.

DEVON (from British tribal name DUMNONIA). **(1)** was independent of the Anglo-Saxons in mid 6th cent. when Gildas admonished a local British ruler called Constantine; a hard pressed K. Geraint corresponded with St. Aldhelm about the date of Easter in about 690. By this time the W. Saxons were in E. Devon and had probably taken Exeter. In 710 the rest of Dumnonia was overrun by a joint W. and S. Saxon assault and there was extensive Saxon settlement. The western boundary remained uncertain for over two centuries. In about 932 K. Athelstan, provoked by Cornish risings, expelled the British inhabitants of Exeter and fixed the western frontier at the R. Tamar. Most (but not all) Celtic place names were obliterated, but Saxon colonisation was slow. The persistence of Cornish-Devonian feuds into modern times suggests that it was fairly dense. Devon (with Cornwall) had a separate bishopric (at Crediton) from 909. The fixing of the Tamar boundary did not divide this diocese.

(2) Devon had a balanced economy with ancient, pre-Roman trading connections arising from tin mines, but copper, lead, iron and china clays were also worked. Apart from Dartmoor, it was and is highly fertile and productive of much cattle and grain, and wool which supported related industries such as tanning. It enjoyed the advantages of ten fjord-like accesses to the Channel, besides the double entry into the Atlantic on Bideford Bay. Hence it bred seamen and developed successful fisheries and shipbuilders.

(3) Between the Norman Conquest and 1214 the tin output rose ninefold, mainly after 1198 when the Stannaries were put under a Warden with a special jurisdiction. K. John issued a special charter to the miners in 1201 and in 1204 the county, by paying the large sum of 5000 marks, obtained a total disafforestation, save for Dartmoor and Exmoor.

(4) The late date of the Saxon conquest meant that conquerors and conquered were alike Christian. There were major monastic houses at Hartland, Tavistock, Buckland and Plympton in the west, at Ford and Dunkeswell in the east and at Totnes and Torr in the south. Exeter had its great cathedral after the See was moved from Crediton in 1050. The cathedral, rebuilt in the later middle ages, is probably the finest late Gothic structure in England and well attests the local prosperity of the period. Little survived at Crediton.

(5) Wealth and seamanship were the foundation of a substantial trade to the Peninsula and the Mediterranean which, incidentally, involved Devonians in disputes and piracy not only against foreigners but their English rivals, the Portsmen and the Staplers further east. The Castilian and Portuguese expansion into the Atlantic and the Indian oceans merely created new fields in which to poach. John Davis, Sir Francis Drake, Sir Humphrey Gilbert, Sir Richard Grenville, Sir John Hawkins and Sir

Walter Raleigh were Devonians. They were adventurous mariners who knew where to raise capital. Their enterprise endangered peace and changed the pattern of world trade. *See* PIRACY, BRITISH WATERS, GENERAL. LEGAL.

DEVON, Es. of. *See* COURTENAY.

DEVONPORT (before 1824 PLYMOUTH Dock). *See* PLYMOUTH.

DEVONSHIRE, Ds. of. *See* CAVENDISH.

DEWAN. *See* BENGAL.

D'EWES, Sir Simonds (1602-50), lawyer and antiquary, helped Sir Robt. Cotton to establish Robert Vere's claim to the earldom of Oxford in 1626, when he was knighted. M.P. for Sudhury in 1640 he was purged by Col. Pride in 1648. He compiled the important *Journals of all the Parliaments during the Reign of Queen Elizabeth.*

DEWESBURY (W. Yorks), an ancient place where Paulinus preached to the local heathen in 627. It grew into an important wool market and subsequently developed a cloth industry powered from the neighbouring coal mines.

DE WET, Christian (1854-1922), a member of the O.F.S. *Volksraad* in 1897, fought in the Boer War as a Boer leader and general. After brilliant surprises as Sanna's Post and Reddersburg, he became a formidable guerrilla leader who was never caught. He took part in the peace negotiations in 1902 and in Nov. 1907 became Min. of Agriculture in the Orange River Colony. He helped James Hertzog to form the Nationalist Party in 1912 and staged the rebellion on the outbreak of World War I. This was defeated by a combination of Gen. Botha's ability and the motor car which rendered his guerrilla expertise obsolete. Convicted of treason he was sentenced to six years' imprisonment but released on the condition that he took no futher part in politics.

D'EYNCOURT. *See* TENNYSON-DEYNCOURT.

DHARMASHASTRA. The ancient, and vast, body of Indian jurisprudence still in force subject to statutory changes made by British and, increasingly, by Indian legislation.

DHIMMIS (Arab = protected people) under Islam are conquered People of the Book, i.e. with a scriptured religion (viz Jews, Christians and Parsees). They were allowed to keep their places of worship but might not build new ones. They paid a ground rent for any land which they occupied (*kharaj*) and the men able to bear arms paid *jizya*, a capitation tax, as well. They were also subject to conditions: the *necessary* were enforced by outlawry, the *desirable* less rigorously. The necessary were that they must not revile Islam, attempt to harm, convert or marry a Moslem, assist an enemy or harbour spies: the *desirable*, that they respect their conquerors by wearing distinctive clothing, by not building houses higher than Moslem houses or mounting horses; that they should not draw attention to their religion, or do in public what is forbidden by Islam but permitted by their religion, namely keeping pigs and drinking wine. A *dhimmi* could escape this social, religious and fiscal inferiority by converting to Islam and vast numbers did. They were still a social problem in all Moslem areas where power had passed to the British.

DHOLPUR. *See* RAJPUTS-4.

DIALECTS, ENGLISH. Versions of speech mostly comprehensible to speakers of other versions are numerous and in Britain are said to form six groups brought during the Anglo-Saxon conquest (6th-7th cent.) or formed just after it (8th cent.). These are east midland Anglian which developed into literary, standard or educated English, East Anglian, Southern and Western Saxon, Northern and Lallans or Lowland Scots. Differences of pronunciation (e.g. southern *grāss* against northern *grӑss*), of words (e.g. northern *ginnel;* southern *alley,* or Lallans *teind;* elsewhere *tithe*), of word usage (western *port = market*) and grammar (the London double negative) separated the dialects, and they were themselves influenced by isolation (e.g. in Gwent) or

specialised surroundings (e.g. mines) or by local importations from abroad such as different proportions of Norman-French, or Danish and Welsh intonations. Some developed their own spelling (e.g. Lallans *guid* = good, *quhilk* = which). Some dialects, partly transmuted by history, were re-exported e.g. 17th cent. East Anglian to America and they influenced each other.

(2) Better roads began the pressure towards standardisation of speech and words in a midland Anglian mode because influential provincials on business at the capital had to understand each other and their Westminster contacts. Printing hastened the process and standardised spelling, but the differences remained very great. As late as 1940 troops recruited in London could barely understand N.C.O.s from Cheshire. Cinema and broadcasting, however, accelerated the erosion of differences so that by the mid 1980s the fear that dialects might vanish led the B.B.C. to introduce dialect speakers who, with broad Scots accents, could be heard adjuring still uncomprehending southerners.

(3) Re-exported dialects, having been further mutated in other climates, were re-imported (often from the U.S.A.) through radio and television. There is also an embryonic Euro-English artificially created from literal translations of continental words (e.g. *Sheep Meat* from Ger. *Schafffleisch* = mutton).

DIALOGUS DE SCACCARIO (Lat = Dialogue on the Exchequer), by Richard Fitzneale or Fitznigel, treasurer of England from 1169 to 1198, was a textbook on the law and practice of the exchequer and the royal revenues. It throws much light not only on central govt. but on local matters related to it, such as the King's forest rights.

DIAZ, Armando (1861-1928) D. of the Victory (1921) commanded the Italian attack which in Oct. 1918 ended in the victory of Vittorio Veneto. From 1922 to 1924 he was Mussolini's first Min. of War.

DIAZ, Bartholomew (?1455-1500) found the C. of Good Hope in 1487.

DICETO, Ralph of (?-1201), archdeacon of Middlesex from 1152 and Dean of St. Paul's from 1180, was a historian active in public life and a friend of such eminent men as Gilbert Foliot, Richard fitz Neal, Hubert Walter, William Longchamp and Walter of Coutances. His principal writings were the *Abbreviatio Chronicorum* (Lat – Abbreviation of the Chronicles) and *Ymagines Historiarum* (Lat = Pictures of History) from the Creation to 1148 and from 1148 to 1200, respectively. He understood legal problems and his account of the controversy between Henry II and Thomas Becket is a moderate one.

DICEY, Albert Venn (1835-1922) Vinerian Prof. of Law at Oxford (1882-1909) published his *Law of the Constitution* in 1885 and *Law and Public Opinion in the 19th Century* in 1905. The former remained the standard text-book on the British Constitution for half a century. The latter, under the name of "Collectivism", propounded an analysis of social development closely related to socialism. He was a prominent political controversialist.

DICKENS, Charles John Huffam (1812-70) was a Commons lobby correspondent from 1823 to 1833 after which he began to write his novels and serial stories of social comment. His vogue in England and America, which he visited in 1842, was enormous and has remained ever since.

DICTATOR,-SHIP. A Roman dictator was an officer of state appointed for six months to deal with a particular crisis and into whose hands all the powers of executive govt. were surrendered for that period. The modern term is an abuse of the Latin, connoting a permanent non-royal individual in whom is concentrated all powers of political decision. Under modern conditions dictatorship is unworkable and turns into a composite rule by intriguing camarillas seeking to influence the decision maker.

DICTATORSHIP OF THE PROLETARIAT. The Marxist

technical term for the period between the Revolution and the establishment of the new socialist order, during which all bodies, influences and persons not conducive to the latter are ruthlessly liquidated, in practice by firing squads. All known examples of such dictatorships have developed into personal dictatorships with an ideological varnish.

DICTATUS PAPAE (c. 1075) (Lat = Notes dictated by the Pope). This was a series of propositions, drawn up by Gregory VII, bearing on papal supremacy over general councils and the emperor. They are based upon a collection of canons called LIBER LXXIV TITULORUM (Lat = Book in 74 Titles) which, though apparently very ancient, included much material from the forged PSEUDO-ISIDORE, then believed to be authentic.

DIDIUS GALLUS, Aulus. *See* BRITAIN. ROMAN-4.

DIEFENBAKER, John George (1895-1979). *See* CANADA.

DIEHARDS or MIDDLESEX REGT. (57th FOOT). At the B of Albuera (1811) Col. Inglis, commanding the 57th Foot, adjured his men to 'die hard'. The phrase, connoting irremovable obstinacy, especially of the conservative kind, derives from this phrase.

DIEMEN (or MEEUWISZ), Anthony van (1593-1645), the most successful of the gov-gens. of the Dutch East Indies (1636-45), organised exploration *inter alia* by Tasman, who circumnavigated Australia in 1639 to 1643.

DIEPPE (Fr.) (1) Norman seaport and holiday resort in a cleft in the cliffs on the Channel opposite Newhaven. It was reoccupied by the English from 1420 to 1435 and was later a strongly Huguenot town until the Revocation of the Edict of Nantes (1685), when most of the Huguenots migrated to England. An Anglo-Dutch bombardment in 1694 further depressed it. **(2)** In World War II it saw a famous Allied raid. 7000 troops, of which 5000 were Canadian, took part. It was designed to keep German troops from the Russian front, gain experience for further landings with, as subsidiary purposes, to train the Canadians and destroy a dangerous German radar station. Surprise was lost when the ships ran into some German trawlers and, amid scenes of great gallantry, over half the force and many aircraft were lost. The main purposes, however, were achieved. Dieppe was chosen as an objective despite its tactical unsuitability because any other might have compromised plans for invasion landing places later. *See also* ELIZABETH I-25.

DIESEL, OIL or THERMAL ENGINE (because ignition was by compression-induced heat) was originally patented for locomotives by the Yorkshireman Herbert Akroyd-Stuart (1864-1927) in 1890. The road version was first developed by the German Nikolaus Otto, together with Crossley Bros. in England. Rudolf Diesel's prototype was run (and blew up) in 1893. Priestman's of Hull began to build oil-engined small locomotives and Diesel's developed model was ready in 1894. The locomotives came into use in 1896: mass production of Diesel's types began in 1897.

DIES NON [JURIDICUS]. A day, viz: Sunday and the Feasts of The Purification, Ascension, All Souls and Michaelmas, when the courts did not sit.

DIEU ET MON DROIT (Fr = God and my right), was Richard I's password at the B. of Gisors (1198) when he defeated the French. It has been the motto of English sovereigns since Henry VI.

DIGBY FAMILY of Sherborne, Dorset. **(1) Everard (?-?)** wrote the first English treatise on swimming. A kinsman **(2) Sir Everard (1578-1606)** was one of the Gunpowder plotters. **(3) John (1580-1653) 1st Ld. DIGBY (1618) 1st E. of BRISTOL (1618),** primarily a diplomat, was involved in Spanish marriage negotiations in 1611, 1614 and 1617. In 1621 James I commissioned him to attempt mediation between Frederick V of the Palatinate and the Emperor (*see* THIRTY YEARS' WAR) and in 1622 he returned to Spain on further marriage negotiations and, knowing Spanish customs, offended the P. of Wales and

Buckingham because he rightly thought and said that their frivolity would be offensive. He was in consequence never in favour with the court of Charles I. On the other hand his outlook, in the controversies between the King and the parliament, was that of a contemporary moderate constitutionalist. He advised the King privately and in the *Magnum Concilium* at York to call a parliament and he originally inspired the Petition of Right, but he saw the dangers in the proceedings against Strafford and he and his son (4 below) organised opposition and spoke out against the attainder. He was, in fact, trying to form a middle party and as late as 1644 advised Charles to conciliate the independents. After the surrender of Exeter in 1646 he went to France. He died in Paris. His son **(4) George (1612-77) Ld. DIGBY (1641), 2nd E.,** as M.P. for Dorset from 1640 was on the committee for Strafford's impeachment in 1641 but opposed the attainder because Strafford could not legally be convicted of treason. He and his father tried to moderate opinion, but George became a full royalist, escaped from London *via* Holland, joined the King with troops but gave up his command after quarrelling with P. Rupert. Charles made him Sec. of State in 1643 and he was, for a while, the King's most influential, but not the wisest, adviser. In particular it was on his, and against P. Rupert's advice, that the B. of Naseby was fought, and he lost the King's secret correspondence in the subsequent rout (June 1645). In Nov. he lost the Northern Horse near Newark and his own secret correspondence as well. He then went indefatigably to Ireland, Jersey, the Queen's court near Paris and back to Ireland and, after the Irish disasters, returned to France. Here, after various adventures, he became Charles II's Sec. of State from 1657 until 1659. He tried but failed to impeach Clarendon in 1663. Thereafter he pursued minor literary activities. His handsome polymath cousin **(5) Sir Kenelm (1603-65)** visited the French court in 1620 but escaped the excessive interest of Q. Marie de Medici by going to Florence and, ultimately, joined the P. of Wales and Buckingham in Madrid (1623). He then became a seaman and commanded a small squadron which beat the French and Venetians at Alexandretta in 1629. In 1630 he came home and found favour at court, where Charles liked his scientific interest and Henrietta Maria his Romanism. He gave enough help to the Queen's committee for raising funds from R. Catholics to incur the hostility of the House of Commons in 1641 but was busier writing a work, *Of Bodies*, on human anatomy (1644). He became the Queen's Chancellor in 1644 and the King sent him on a mission to the Pope in 1645, which confused the negotiations in Ireland. He was banished in 1649 and got to know Descartes in France. In 1654 he was allowed to return and was then apparently employed as a Protectors' agent abroad, returning, however, at the Restoration. He was an original member of the Royal Society and discovered the dependence of plants on oxygen. The family interest at Sherborne has continued into modern times.

DIGEST. The compilation and codification of Roman laws and legal opinions made under Justinian in the 6th cent. It formed the basis of later legal systems outside England.

DIGGERS CONFERENCE. The extremist gold miners of Bendigo (Victoria) wanted to supersede the ordinary govt.; the majority wanted representation in the Victorian legislature and abolition of mining licences. In Sept. 1853 the N.S.W. legislature proposed to abolish licence fees, but the Victoria legislature merely reduced them and legalised miners customs. Disappointment at Bendigo led to the formation in Jan. 1854 of the conference which the extremists hoped to form into an alternative govt. The movement failed. Later licence fees, whose uniformity discriminated against less successful miners, were replaced by a duty on gold when exported.

DIGGES (1) Leonard (?-1571), Oxford mathematician and Copernican, wrote primarily geometrical treatises and anticipated the invention of the telescope. His son **(2) Thomas (?-1595)** was an M.P. in 1572 and 1585, mustered the Walcheren expedition of 1586 and helped to equip expeditions of exploration in 1590. He was also a mathematician and published his father's works, besides his own. He introduced the notion of the infinite universe and influenced Tycho Brahe. His son **(3) Sir Dudley (1583-1639)** was interested in the HEIC and also an M.P. in 1621, 1624, 1625, 1626 and 1628. He attacked Buckingham and other ministers and helped to draw up the Petition of Right in 1628. His nuisance value earned him lucrative posts during the period of the King's personal rule and he was a member of the High Commission from 1633 and Master of the Rolls from 1626.

DILETTANTI SOCIETY (1734), of persons who had made the Grand Tour, was founded primarily to help artists to travel abroad. After the original Foundling Hospital exhibitions (1740), the Society, as representing patrons, tried but failed to organise annual exhibitions of living artists who refused to allow the patrons to choose the pictures, but the discussions kept the issue alive and contributed to the movement which founded the Royal Academy in 1768. See GRAY, SIR ROBERT AND SIR JAMES.

DILHORNE, Vist. See MANNINGHAM-BULLER.

DILIGENCE (1) In Scots law, enforcement of a judgment. **(2)** A large four- or six-horsed stage coach.

DILKE. Radical family. **(1) Charles Wentworth (1789-1864)** edited *The Athenaeum* from 1830 to 1846 and was the first English editor in the 19th cent. to obtain foreign contributors. From 1846 he managed the *Daily News*. He wrote a defence of Wilkes and published a critique of the *Letters of Junius*. His son **(2) Sir Charles Wentworth (1810-69) Bart (1862)** probably suggested the Great Exhibition of 1851 and was one of its executive committee. He was M.P. for Wallingford from 1865 to 1868 and died at St. Petersburg. His elder son **(3) Charles Wentworth (1843-1911) 2nd Bart,** was M.P. for Chelsea from 1868 and one of the radical opponents of Forsters' Education Bill in 1870. His republicanism also gained him notoriety. He was an effective speaker and by 1880 was the acknowledged leader of the liberal radicals and a close ally of Joseph Chamberlain. He then became U-Sec. of State at the Foreign Office where his knowledge of foreign affairs made him as influential as Granville, his chief. In 1882 he entered the cabinet as Pres. of the Local Govt. Board and in 1884 he piloted a Redistribution Bill with conspicuous skill. In Aug. 1885 an indiscretion cut short his potentially brilliant future. McDonald Crawford, M.P. for Lanark, cited him as a co-respondent in divorce proceedings. The case failed against Dilke and his wife Emily (q.v.) stood by him, but the public thought him guilty. He was defeated for Chelsea in 1886. Further proceedings by Crawford against his wife confirmed the public's view of his conduct and he retired from Parliamentary activity. In 1892 he was elected for the Forest of Dean which he represented until he died. His wife **(4) Emily (1840-1904)** widow of Mark Pattison, who had married him in 1885, independently a campaigner for women's rights, was Pres. of the Women's Trade Union League from 1902. His brother **(5) Ashton Wentworth (1850-83)** travelled in Russia, was editor of the *Weekly Despatch*, translated Turgenev and was M.P. for Newcastle from 1880.

DILKE CONVENTION (Feb. 1884). Britain recognised wide Portuguese claims at the mouth of the R. Congo. France, Germany and K. Leopold of the Belgians objected that this disposed of their interests without consultation. As Britain at this time depended upon German goodwill in Egypt, Ld. Salisbury withdrew from the convention.

DILL, Sir John Greer (1881-1944) fought with distinction in World War I and then gained a reputation as an able staff officer. He became C-in-C in Palestine and Transjordan in Sept. 1936 and G.O.C. 1st Corps in France in 1940. After Dunkirk he became C.I.G.S. but Churchill

thought him cautious and in 1941 he became British representative on the Chief of Staff's Committee. He died in the U.S.A.

DILLON. This family of Irish exiles included **(1) Sir James (?-?1670),** gov. of Athlone and Connaught, who took part in the Leinster revolt of 1652 and, being denied pardon, took service in Spain. **(2) Arthur (1670-1733)** was a commander of French Jacobite troops from 1690 to 1714. He then became the Pretender's agent in Paris. His son **(3) Arthur Richard (1721-1806)** was Abp. of Toulouse from 1758 and of Narbonne from 1763, but died in London. His nephew **(4) Arthur Richard (1750-94)** was gov. of St. Kitts in 1784. He then became gov. of Tobago and deputy for Martinique in the National Assembly and served as a republican gen. in the Argonne in 1792 when he was replaced by Dumouriez. He was guillotined. His daughter **(5) Fanny** married Bonaparte's Gen. Bertrand and was with Bonaparte at Elba and St. Helena. **(6) Theobald (1745-92)** a lieut-gen. in Dillon's regiment, took part in the fighting at Grenada in 1779, became a brig-gen. in 1791 and was murdered by his own republican troops. **(7) Edouard (1751-1839),** Col. of the Provence regiment, formed a new Dillon regiment in 1791, had become a Napoleonic lieut-gen. by 1814 and was ambassador to Saxony from 1816 to 1818.

DILLON, John (1851-1927) Irish orator and surgeon, joined Parnell in his American campaign for the Land League in 1879 and was elected in absence M.P. for Tipperary. A habitual instigator of rural boycotts, he was twice imprisoned in 1881 but released in 1882 as part of the Kilmainham T. In 1885 he became M.P. for E. Mayo and helped William O'Brien in the formulation of his Plan of Campaign. He was again imprisoned and released in 1888 and in 1890, after a further arrest, escaped with O'Brien to the U.S.A. He was thus absent during Parnell's divorce, but on his return and reimprisonment (1891) went over to the anti-Parnellites and became their chairman in 1896. Though a determined opponent of the Irish landlords he supported in the interest of political unity the more moderate John Redmond from 1900 and broke with O'Brien in 1904. In 1908 he inspired the establishment of the National Univ. of Ireland; in 1914 he represented, with Redmond, the Irish nationalists at the Buckingham Palace conference and in 1916 he tried to secure Home Rule by agreement (July 1916) after the Easter Rising. Shortly afterwards he became chairman of the Irish Party and drifted into extremist courses in alliance with Sinn Fein, whose forcible resistance to Irish conscription he openly supported. In the ensuing fragmentation of nationalist opinion he was for the first time defeated in the General Election of 1918. He then left public life.

'DILLY or DERBY 'DILLY. The nickname of a group of Whigs, the D. of Richmond, Ld. Ripon and Sir James Graham led by Edw. Stanley, who resigned from the govt. in 1834 over the appropriation of Irish church revenues for lay purposes.

DIMES v GRAND JUNCTION CANAL (1852) 3 HLC 759. In this case a decree made by a late Lord Chancellor was set aside by the House of Lords because he had been a shareholder in the canal co. involved. There was no suggestion of bias or corruption. The case established finally that a man must not be a judge in his own case.

DIMBLEBY, Richard (1913-65), journalist, became the B.B.C.'s first news commentator in 1936. He achieved world fame as a leading war correspondent in World War II. He went freelance in 1946.

DINAR (Lat = *denarius*). An oriental coin: in gold, the equivalent of a mohur; in silver, of a rupee. Also the standard currency of Serbia and Yugoslavia.

DINDINGS. See MALAYA.

DINEFWR. See WELSH LAW-2.

DINGANE or DINGAAN. See ZULUS-2.

DINKA. A large nomadic Nilotic negro tribe in the S.

Sudan. Their principal wealth was in cattle and was long supplemented by the sale of their women who are much prized for their beauty. This trade, mainly to Arabia, subsisted into the 1960s and perhaps later.

DIOCESAN ENCLAVES. *See* PECULIARS.

DIPHTHERIA (formerly sometimes CROUP or ULCERA SYRIACA), a frequently fatal disease, especially in children under ten, was often mistaken in the 17th cent. for Scarlet Fever. It is of ancient origin. An outbreak in Flanders in 1337 spread to England where, in 1382, there was another and serious epidemic. Thereafter there were sporadic European visitations, notably in Germany (1492), France (1576) and from 1583 to 1618 in Portugal and Spain. The latter caused a disastrous importation into Peru in 1614 and into North America, where it became endemic after an outburst in 1659. A great English epidemic in 1734 just preceded a series in America (1735-40) and in France (1745-50). George Washington died of it in 1799. The great pandemic of 1856-8 compounded the medical horrors of the Crimean War period, which themselves created interest in medical reforms and research. Hence the major outbreak in the U.S.A. (1870) was followed by the discovery of an immunization method in 1890. *See* EPIDEMICS, HUMAN.

DIPLOCK COURTS (N.I.) Intimidation of jurors and witnesses by political terrorists led the govt. to set up non-jury courts in 1972 to try cases of political violence after an inquiry by the able judge, Ld. Diplock.

DIPLOMATIC originally meant the science of official or original documents and particularly palaeography; and a diplomatist was an expert in such matters. The modern meaning apparently arose from the title of Dumont's *Corps Universel Diplomatique du Droit des Gens* (1726) which used the phrase 'corps diplomatique' in its original sense, but dealt with international relations.

DIPLOMATIC CONGRESS is an assembly of diplomats and statesmen from all or most of the countries in a large area, designed to establish an international order based upon the settlement of multiple differences. The outcome is generally a series of interlocking treaties, or a many sided treaty with interlocking provisions. The strength of such a settlement depends upon the expectation that the major participant powers will not simultaneously wish to upset it and that their power will remain in balance. Such settlements often formally supersede pre-existing treaties which, however, have generally been rendered obsolete by the events (usually wars) which caused the Congress to assemble.

Event	Congress
Thirty Years' War	Westphalia or Münster 1647-8
Franco-Dutch War 1672-8	Nijmegen 1678-9
War of the League of Augsburg 1688-9	Ryswick 1697
War of the Spanish Succession	Utrecht 1712-4
War of the Polish Succession	Vienna 1735-8
Seven Years' War 1756-63	Paris 1763
War of American Independence	Paris 1783
Napoleonic Wars	Vienna 1814-5
Crimean War	Paris 1856
Russo-Turkish War 1877	Berlin 1878
World War I	Paris 1919-21
World War II	San Francisco 1945*

*This congress drew up the Charter of the United Nations but signed no formal peace treaty to end the war.

DIPLOMATIC IMMUNITY has always been accorded for practical reasons by the custom of nations to ambassadors sent to conduct particular negotiations, but the immunity of the resident ambassadors instituted in Tudor times was not generally recognised until about 1650. In Britain their freedom from process was not defined until a Russian ambassador was arrested for debt

and the furious Czar demanded that those responsible be put to death. It was explained that the Queen of Great Britain could not do this and the Diplomatic Privileges Act 1708 having been passed a placatory illuminated copy of the Act was presented to him with the explanation. The immunity covers ambassadors, their missions, families and households, representatives of Commonwealth countries and certain organisations such as E.U. and U.N.O. and consuls. The immunity can be waived but a diplomat is not otherwise amenable to criminal process or to civil process arising from his diplomatic activity, though he may be detained pending expulsion.

DIPLOMATIC SERVICE. *See* CIVIL SERVICE.

DIRECTORY or *DIRECTOIRE*. The French govt. from 27 Oct. 1795 to 9 Nov. 1799 and the period when it existed. There was a Council of 500 and a Council of Ancients. The Executive Directory itself had five members who were elected by the 500 from a list proffered by the Ancients and renewed thereafter annually one by one. The first Directors were Barras, Carnot, La Revelliere-Lepeaux, Letourneur and Rewbell. The period was distinguished by the expeditions to Italy and Egypt under Bonaparte (of whom the Directors almost wholly lost control), financial confusion, peculation and sexual licence, but gave its name to a style, especially in furniture and in dress whose flimsy character led to the introduction of the ladies' knickers ever since named after it. It was violently overthrown by Napoleon and Lucien Bonaparte and Siéyès in the *coup d'état* of Brumaire.

DIRECTORY OF PUBLIC WORSHIP. *See* COMMON PRAYER.

DIRTY TRICKS (ELECTIONEERING), are slanders based on contrived false identity. Commonly one party uses impostors claiming membership of another party in whose name they do discreditable things or make outrageous statements so that their employer can indignantly attack them.

DISALLOWANCE. *See* COLONIAL LAWS, VALIDITY-7.

DISARMAMENT. The First Hague Conference had already piously agreed before World War I that a reduction of excessive armaments might possibly be the ideal aim of govts. but the issue was first placed squarely on the international agenda by the fourth of Pres. Wilson's 14 Points in 1919, and Art. 8 of the P. of Versailles called for disarmament consistent with national safety and the enforcement by common action of international obligations. To implement this the League of Nations set up a series of committees and the non-governmental MIXED COMMISSION which drew up the GENEVA PROTOCOL (1924). This defined aggression, proposed systematic arbitration and the sanctions. Though welcomed by the League Assembly, it was a dead letter because the great powers saw it as a threat to their position and, in particular, the Dominions having rejected any obligation to intervene in any further European war, the British felt bound to be able to take such initiatives as they wished. The commission had, however, also proposed a disarmament conference and for this the League set up a PREPARATORY COMMISSION. Between May 1926 and Dec. 1930 it had reached a tentative consensus on five issues: **(1)** budgetary limitations; **(2)** limitation of the size of armed forces and **(3)** of length of service; **(4)** renunciation of chemical and bacteriological war; and **(5)** the establishment of a permanent Disarmament Commission. The DISARMAMENT CONFERENCE, under the chairmanship of Arthur Henderson (Britain) consequently began in Feb. 1932 and was attended from 59 states. It failed through a threefold disagreement of principle: the French wanted to ensure their own security on the basis of an international police force, the German theirs on the basis of military parity and the British theirs through qualitative disarmament in which they would keep the arms vital to themselves. By Oct. 1933 (when Nazi Germany left the League) the conference was effectively dead. After World War II the U.N. General Assembly passed a resolution favouring disarmament on 14 Dec. 1946. It was not taken seriously by the great powers, mainly because of the aggressive policies of the U.S.S.R. and China, but the collapse of the former in 1989 made some real progress possible at last.

DISCIPLINE (1) A scourge or **(2)** the act of scourging, in either case, for penance, the Higher upon the shoulders, the Lower upon the buttocks.

DISCIPLINE, BOOK OF (1561) was a programme by John Knox and his coadjutors for establishing a Godly Commonwealth with but one church. All Scots were to be members of it; the state was to heed and enforce its interpretation of the moral law, but the church was to be independently entitled to discipline and correct those faults which the civil authority neglects or cannot touch. The latter included drunkeness, excess, fornication, oppression or cheating of the poor or ignorant, wanton words and licentiousness. These rules were to be complemented by a national system of education and relief for the deserving poor and the whole structure was to be financially supported through a re-appropriation of the property and teinds (tithes) of the old church in roughly equal proportions to ministers, education and poor relief.

The book was submitted to a convention of nobility and lairds and penal legislation against various sins followed (adultery 1563; fornication 1567). In 1572 excommunicates were declared incapable of taking oaths and, therefore, unable to hold office or give evidence. From 1609 they could not enjoy lands or rents. There was legislation against drunkenness in 1617. After 1640 political excommunications became common and exacerbated the bitterness of the civil wars. Consequently the civil consequences were abolished in 1690 in order to reduce the power of the restored General Assembly. The criminal consequences were abolished in 1712. *See also* SABBATH BREAKING.

DISCLAIMER OF PEERAGE. Before 1963 the heir to a peerage succeeded willy-nilly and, if an M.P., vacated his seat and, in a political sense, became disqualified from those higher offices customarily held by M.P.s. The Peerage Act, 1963, permitted a peerage to be disclaimed, in the case of an M.P. within one month of succession, in other cases within a year. The disclaimer operated only for the lifetime of the disclaimant and he could return to the House of Lords only as a life peer. Thus the 14th E. of Home disclaimed, became an M.P. and Prime Minister, but subsequently returned to the Lords as Ld. Home of the Hirsel. The issue was first wittily raised in the Commons by Anthony Wedgwood Benn, who succeeded as Vist. Stansgate in 1961 but was later able to disclaim and return to the Commons. The number of disclaimers between 1963 and 1999 was quite small.

DISCOVERIES. *See* EXPLORATIONS.

DISESTABLISHMENT is the expulsion of a denominational organisation from the machinery of the state. The Church of England's position arises from the inter-related history of the two ideas, the sacerdotal aura of the monarchy and the temporal and political aspects of episcopal pastoral functions. The crown makes, in practice, all high church appointments and two archbishops and 24 bishops sit in the House of Lords,

The Anglican church was disestablished in IRELAND by Act of 1869 which came into force in 1871.

For Wales a liberal bill failed in 1895. A Royal Commission was appointed in 1906 and a bill introduced in 1909. It was enacted under the Parliament Act in 1914 to come into force in 1915, but World War I led to postponement and it came into force in 1920. In INDIA the Anglican church was disestablished in 1927.

In SCOTLAND the Established and United Free (Presbyterian) churches were united and became

independent of the state in matters of religion in 1929 but the disestablishment is not complete.

DISINHERITED, THE (ENGLAND). After Simon de Montfort's death at the B. of Evesham (Aug. 1265) an ordinance was made at Winchester (17 Sept.) taking or requiring the surrender of the lands of all his accomplices into the King's hands. In a burst of irresponsible enthusiasm many of these lands were quickly given away to royal favourites and supporters before the Montfort faction had broken up. This prolonged the civil war, for those thus *disinherited* held out at various places, particularly Southwark, the Cinque Ports, the Is. of Axholme and Ely and Kenilworth, and Montfort had had many supporters in most counties. Campaigns brought about surrenders with negotiated terms of all the above except Ely and Kenilworth whose blockade and siege dragged on into the summer of 1266. The Papal legate, Ottobuono Fieschi, then induced a settlement known as the DICTUM OF KENILWORTH (31 Oct. 1266) which laid down the procedure whereby rebels might redeem or regain their lands and the tariff of payments for doing so. Distinctions were drawn between those who fought with Earl Simon by choice and those who had been swept into the movement and who had got out of it as soon as they could, with other categories of complicity between these extremes. As a result Kenilworth surrendered on 14 Dec. but trouble at Southwark and Ely continued until June 1217. The administrative and judicial problems created by the Ordinance and Dictum were not fully solved until the end of the century.

DISINHERITED, THE (SCOTLAND) were those who landed with Edward Balliol at Kinghorn in 1332 to claim the Scots crown from the infant David II. The most prominent among them were Balliols and Comyns, who had been deprived by Robert the Bruce, but they included English archers and other supporters and after their victory at Dupplin Moor (24 Sept.) they were joined by resident Scots such as William Sinclair, Bp. of Dunkeld. Balliol's Edinburgh Parliament of Feb. 1334 restored their lands and some of the English received important grants including Henry de Beaumont (Earldom of Buchan), Richard Talbot (Mar), John of Warenne (Earldom of Strathearn).

DISPENSARIES (sometimes PEOPLES') were created by subscription and benevolence in most 18th and 19th cent. towns to provide free medicines or treatment (or both) for the poor. Subscribers could often nominate patients.

DISPENSATION and SUSPENSION. (1) Dispensation is a power to licence an individual to do something which would otherwise be illegal. The church has always exercised it, mostly on laws considered not to be of natural or divine origin. By the later middle ages it was reserved to the Pope and his delegates. In England this papal power was transferred in a restricted form in 1534 to the Abp. of Canterbury who seldom uses it. The English Kings habitually gave dispensations notwithstanding (Lat = *Non Obstante*) the general law, in the interests of convenience, e.g. to allow a corporation to own land, and this was unquestioned until the 1680s, when the R. Catholic James II granted them wholesale to circumvent the parliamentary policy in favour of protestant holders of office. For examples *see* GODDEN V HALES; MAGDALEN COLLEGE, OXFORD EXPULSIONS.

(2) Suspension was a more far-reaching and controversial claim to arrest or place in suspense the entire effect of an act of parliament. This amounted to more than the cumulative effect of wholesale dispensations, because it could affect relationships not only between crown and subject but between private individuals. The Declarations of Indulgence of 1672 and 1687 both contained attempts to suspend statutes and directly challenged the doctrine of joint sovereignty of the crown and parliament.

(3) The suspending power was declared illegal in the

Declaration of Rights (12 Feb. 1689) and the dispensing power as 'used of late' was also condemned, but the ratification of this instrument by the Bill of Rights in Oct. did not maintain this distinction and both powers were accordingly abolished.

DISPLACED PERSONS. A politicians' and bureaucrats' euphemism for the millions driven from their homes in World War II or by post-war, mostly Marxist, aggressors.

DISRAELI or D'ISRAELI. Italian Jewish family settled as London merchants since 1748. **(1) Isaac (1766-1848)** was a prolific writer and journalist. His son **(2) Benjamin (1804-81) 1st E. of BEACONSFIELD (1876)** began as a social novelist with *Vivian Grey* (1826). He became, after three attempts, an M.P. in 1837, by which time he had written a number of political tracts and six novels including *Contarini Fleming* (1832). He was a man-about-town, but dressed astonishingly, thus ensuring that he would be noticed. He was re-elected in 1837 (William IV having died) and his maiden speech was laughed out. His career was, however, properly launched in 1839 with a famous speech on Chartism, when he described the rights of labour as "as sacred as the rights of property". He married the rich widow of Wyndham Lewis, a political colleague, and bought Hughenden in 1848. In 1841 he was returned as a Peelite M.P. but Peel refused him office. It is uncertain if this rankled, for Disraeli did not publicly differ from Peel until Aug. 1843 when he and his political associates (known as Young England) were roundly denounced by Peel over the Irish Arms Bill. Meanwhile Peel had been drifting away from the protectionism which Disraeli supported on social and political grounds. He became the main, and also the wittiest, spokesman of Peel's Tory critics and his glittering shafts went home, partly because Peel was a lecturing humourless prig. In 1844 Young England broke up over the Maynooth Grant; Disraeli published *Coningsby* and in 1845 *Sybil,* which caused a rare political sensation. The public eye was thus fixed on him when Peel, by repealing the Corn Laws "like the Turkish Admiral who had steered his fleet right into the enemy's port", gave him his opportunity. Peel was overthrown and soon after, when Bentinck died, Disraeli became the leader of the Conservatives in the Commons. The middle part of his career, from now until the Reform Act of 1867, was frustrating. It was the defeat of his budget as Derby's Ch. of the Exchequer in 1852 which overthrew the Derby govt. He then launched *The Press,* a journal devoted to criticising the Aberdeen govt. and inspired it until 1858. In the Derby govt. of 1858-9 he was again Ch. of the Exchequer and led the House in the abortive Reform Bill and the debate on confidence which brought the govt. down. It is said that the vote would have gone to the govt. if he had published Malmesbury's despatches, which vindicated the govt's European policy, but that he refused to do so. The result was six years of discontent in his own party when in opposition. He often occupied the front bench alone. In 1865 Palmerston's mantle fell to E. Russell, with Gladstone leading in the Commons. The govt. introduced a rental franchise bill, while refusing to disclose its proposals for redistribution of seats. Disraeli organised a combination of Tories and Liberals to turn the govt. out. Derby's and Disraeli's alternative Act of 1867 was followed by Derby's resignation on grounds of health and Disraeli became Prime Minister. The new enlarged electorate promptly turned him out. There ensued a long duel between Gladstone and Disraeli over Ireland. Both had much sympathy for the Irish but Disraeli, with his usual wit, criticised Gladstone because he thought that the Irish troubles were settling themselves and that appeasement would only revive them. Not only Ireland gave him openings. There were the Black Sea Conference, the Washington Treaty, not to mention Ewelme Rectory. By 1872 he had, in his own words, reduced the Treasury bench to "a range of extinct volcanoes". In 1873 Gladstone resigned over the Irish Universities question and returned when Disraeli refused office. At the election of Jan. 1874 Disraeli secured his majority. In Aug. 1876, finding the leadership of the Commons too strenuous, he went to the Lords. He resigned after electoral defeat in Mar. 1880. *See* DERBY'S FIRST GOVT; PEEL'S SECOND GOVT-1.

DISRAELI'S FIRST GOVT. (Feb.-Dec. 1868) was similar in composition to Derby's Third govt. which it succeeded, save that G. Ward Hunt took over the Chancellorship of the Exchequer and the E. of Mayo left to become Viceroy of India. The Irish troubles, inherited from the previous govt. and nourished by Irish Americans demobilised from the American civil war, had simmered down but had impressed Gladstone with the dangers of delay in Irish reforms. In Apr. he carried a motion in favour of Irish church disestablishment against the govt. Parliament was dissolved in the autumn and the Liberals won a majority of 112 seats in the general election. Disraeli resigned without meeting parliament.

DISRAELI'S SECOND GOVT. (Feb. 1874-Apr. 1880) (Twelve in cabinet under B. Disraeli, from Aug. 1876 E. of Beaconsfield. Ld. Cairns, Ld. Chanc; Sir Stafford Northcote, Ch. of the Exch; R. A. Cross, Home Sec; E. of Derby, Foreign Sec; E. of Carnarvon, Colonial Sec; M. of Salisbury, Sec. for India). **(1)** succeeded Gladstone's first govt. after its electoral defeat in Jan. 1874. There was a clear conservative majority, but as an unexpected result of the Ballot Act, 1872, 59 Irish Home Rulers led by Isaac Butt. It inherited an Ashanti war, successfully concluded (Mar. 1874) by Gen. Sir Garnet Wolseley, at the T. of Kumasi, in which the Ashanti renounced the coastal forts, promised free trade, an open road to Kumasi and an indemnity and undertook to stop human sacrifices. This auspicious start for a strong cabinet was hardly matched by a weak and divided opposition, for Gladstone retired in favour of the progressive whig Ld. Hartington, who had to reconcile the older whigs and liberals with new radicals such as Sir Chas. Dilke and Joseph Chamberlain.

(2) The govt. had inherited other distant problems. 1873 had seen the beginning of the great European recession, the election of a Bonapartist, Marshal MacMahon, as Pres. of France and Russia's seizure of Khiva and Bokhara, followed by her adoption of universal military service. In Mar. 1874 the French proclaimed a protectorate in Annam. The European scene was, however, tranquil. In Oct. 1874 the Berne Convention established the Universal Postal Union and there had been a Russian-convened conference at Brussels on the laws of war. The govt., remembering French interest in the early history of New Zealand, annexed Fiji. In the circumstances it was possible to reduce income tax and pass some innocuous legislation, two Statute Law Revision Acts and a Factory Act. In 1875, however, the govt. went forward with a notable programme of reforms. The Conspiracy Act altered Gladstone's trade union legislation of 1871 in a sense favourable to the unions. The Food and Drugs Act endured until 1928. The Public Health Act was the foundation not only of sanitary legislation and its administration, but of later law on local govt. Without its prosaic arrangements for water, sewerage and the like, an Artisans Dwellings Act could not have established the beginnings of public housing. By the essential radicalism of these measures the govt. not only outbid the liberals, but established a working relationship with Chamberlain (now Mayor of Birmingham) and other radicals. Other enactments created the New Sinking Fund, an organisation for land registration (The Land Transfer Act) and introduced compensation for tenant's agricultural improvements (Agricultural Holdings Act).

(3) While Disraeli was redeeming the promises of social reform upon which he had been elected, overseas affairs claimed his interest. There were tax riots (June

1875) in the Turkish province of Bosnia, which was coveted alike by Austro-Hungary and Serbia. Fed by Serbian volunteers, these spread rapidly into a rebellion, and the Sultan Abdul Aziz promised paper reforms (Oct.). Meanwhile his bankrupt vassal, the Khedive of Egypt, was seeking a market for his $\frac{7}{18}$th share in the Suez Canal Co. On 9 Nov. Disraeli, at the Guildhall, asserted British interests in Ottoman affairs and on 25 Nov., with a Rothschild loan, bought the Khedive's shares. Then Count Julius Andrassy, the Austrian foreign minister, persuaded Russia and Germany to issue a joint note (30 Dec.) expressing the fear that Bulgaria would rise in the spring and proposing further Turkish reforms. Andrassy's purpose was to forestall the Serbs; Russia's to gain time for military dispositions. Abdul Aziz accepted the proposals in principle but obstructed them in practice, while Turkish pride was aroused. The Bulgars indeed rose in the spring. Moslem rioters then murdered the French and German consuls at Salonika and Abdul Aziz sent Bashi Bazouks to suppress the Bulgars (May), which they did with fearful brutality. Before the Bulgarian massacres were known Andrassy issued the Berlin Memorandum (May) demanding a two month armistice with the rebels pending implementation of the Andrassy Note. This interference between the Padishah and his subjects was felt to be intolerable by the most modern and therefore the most nationalistic elements among the Turks. When it seemed that Abdul Aziz would give way, a reformist cabal deposed him. Reform in this Turkish context meant technical, largely military, improvement.

(4) The reformers were strengthened by the British. Disraeli had, a week earlier, dissociated Britain from the Berlin Memorandum and, for fear of Russia, ordered the fleet to Besika Bay. His fears were justified. In July the Russian-officered Serbs declared war and the Austrian Emperor and the Czar met at Reichstadt to share the loot. By this time the *Daily News* had reported the massacres and British public opinion turned against the Turks who, however, routed the Serbs, made nonsense of the Reichstadt agreements and, in a further political orgy, deposed another Sultan (Murad V). The Prophet's Mantle now passed to the famous or infamous Abdul Hamid II, who had to meet the inevitable Russian war. In the face of Gladstone's invective and British revulsion, Disraeli dared not support him. Salisbury attended a conference of the powers (Dec. 1876 to Jan. 1877) at Constantinople and sought to save the peace by forcing an armistice with Serbia and agreeing a new programme of reforms with the other powers. These Midhat Pasha, the Grand Vizier, refused to accept because he believed (correctly) that Russia was reluctant to fight and (incorrectly) that Britain would support him. The conference broke down and after delays the Russians invaded (Apr. 1877) in overwhelming numbers.

(5) The Turks again surprised everyone by their skill and bravery and produced a reversal of sentiment aided by the accidental participation of some Englishmen in their defence of Plevna. Anti-Russian feeling revived, subconsciously nourished by the recent (Jan. 1877) proclamation of the Indian Empire. Thus when the Turkish defence eventually broke down the govt. was able to send the fleet to Constantinople (Jan. 1878). Russian exhaustion and Disraeli's moderation brought an armistice. In Mar. the belligerents signed the Pan-Slavist P. of San Stefano which, however, was unacceptable to Britain and Austria. The cabinet (with the abstention of Derby) called up the reserves (Mar.) and ordered Indian troops to Malta. Derby resigned and Salisbury took his place. The bluff succeeded. In a Circular Note Salisbury convinced the powers that a European Congress should settle the Balkan problems. In fact a series of bilateral secret agreements narrowed the field of disagreement before the Congress, held at BERLIN (June- July 1878). It set aside the P. of San Stefano, recognised a British

occupation of Cyprus and kept back the Russians from the Mediterranean. Since these fitted Disraeli's world picture of a British Kingdom linked with an Indian Empire *via* a Middle Eastern route well defended against northern threats, he returned in a blaze of triumph speaking of "peace with honour".

(6) It was the watershed of his govt's popularity. Four main factors combined against it. The first was the depression and especially the destruction of British arable farming by the competition of cheap N. AMERICAN WHEAT. Continental powers imposed tariffs to preserve their best countrybred military manpower. The British govt., interested in cheap food for the urban industrial masses who were suffering from economic dislocations, sacrificed the farmers. The whigs now supported the extension of the rural franchise, hitherto demanded by the radicals. In 1876 Joseph Chamberlain entered the Commons after a bye-election in Birmingham and in May 1877 he became the first pres. of a new Nat. Liberal Federation. The opposition was uniting.

(7) The second factor was the supersession, among the Irish Home Rulers, of the constitutionally minded Isaac Butt by a group of militants led by Chas. Stewart Parnell. By mid-1877 their persistent obstinacy had severely lamed the parliamentary machine. In 1878 Butt resigned the leadership to them. The sacrifice of agriculture ruined an English minority interest; in Ireland it ruined the whole nation. The (Irish) tenants could no longer pay rents to their (English) landlords. Agrarian murders began again and developed into a revolt organised by Michael Davitt (1846-1906) and the American John Devoy. In June 1879 Parnell came out in support. In Oct. the Irish National LAND LEAGUE was publicly launched by four Fenians, with Parnell as President. Organised violence in the Irish villages and something very like it in parliament soon created an impression of govt. impotence at home.

(8) The third and fourth factors tarnished the govt's foreign laurels. They both arose on colonial frontiers. In Jan. 1879 the ZULUS wiped out part of a British force at Isandlhwana and compelled the govt. to fight an unwanted war. Simultaneously it became involved in an AFGHAN WAR intended to forestall Russian interference (Jan-May 1879). After the P. of Gandamak (May) a British resident (Sir Louis Cavagnari) was installed at Kabul but in Sept. the Afghans murdered him and the war had to be recommenced. These events strengthened Little Englander sentiment at home and gave opportunities for Gladstone's thunderous energies. His Midlothian Campaign (Nov-Dec. 1879) set a new fashion in political technique. It also united all the Liberal factions and gave them an influence which the govt. did not suspect. Govt. success in two bye-elections emboldened Disraeli to seek a dissolution (Mar. 1880). The ensuing electoral disaster astonished both Disraeli and the Queen. He resigned before parliament met.

DISRUPTION of the Established Church of Scotland (1843). In 1834 the General Assembly, by the so-called Veto Act, gave the presbyteries the right to object on reasonable grounds to a presentation to a benefice. This led to many conflicts at local level and in the courts and culminated in the secession in May 1843 of about a third of the ministers who, led by Thomas Chalmers (1780-1847) formed the Free Church of Scotland. It showed much energy and self-sacrifice and had, within four years, raised £1.5M and built 650 churches. *See* SCOTLAND, PRESBYTERIAN CHURCH OF.

DISSENTERS. *See* NONCONFORMISTS.

DISSENTING ACADEMIES. *See* CONGREGATIONALISM.

DISSENTING DEPUTIES. In 1732 the Presbyterian, Baptist and Independent congregations within 10 miles of London each elected two deputies who in turn appointed a committee to act as parliamentary lobbyists. The organisation continued active until 1914.

DISSOLUTION OF THE MONASTERIES. *See* MONASTERIES.

DISSOLUTION, PROROGATION. When Parliament is dissolved a new parliament can be called only after a General Election has been held. When it is prorogued, the existing Houses can be summoned again. Both processes are in the prerogative of the Crown and both bring a session and the existence of the parliament to an end and therefore "kill" all legislation uncompleted at that moment.

DISTRAINT OF KNIGHTHOOD. A man with property of a certain annual value could be compelled to become a knight. The value was often set as low as £20, but sometimes at £40 or higher. Drives for distraints occurred frequently in the 13th cent. in connection with military crises (e.g. 1241, 1252, 1285 and 1293) and were really a form of taxation, for knights were liable to scutage and fines for exemption were profitable to the Crown. In addition, the govt. needed to maintain the numbers available for grand assize juries and those administrative functions which had to be performed in the shires by knights. (*See* FEUDALISM D.) The practice almost died out in the 15th cent., though Charles I caused great irritation by trying to revive it in the 17th. It was formally abolished in 1661.

DISTRESSES, STATUTES OF (Stat. of Marlborough 1267; Stat. of Westminster I 1275). Distress is the seizure of the goods of a defaulting debtor and, in a mediaeval context, mostly of one whose sole resources were his animals and tools. He might seek redress for an unlawful distress by means of a writ of replevin, but this was not very helpful in practice because if the creditor had the debtor's tools and beasts, work on the debtor's holding would be stopped and delays would usually outrun the season. Hence unlawful distresses were common because the agricultural debtor would pay up rather than starve. Alternatively a distress, lawful or not, might be violently resisted and cause disorders. Consequently the statute of 1267 forbade distresses between neighbours, thus restricting them to disputes between lord and tenant; amounts were to be reasonable; sheep and plough cattle were not to be taken; owners were to be allowed to feed their impounded beasts; no sales were to be held for 15 days; illegal distresses were punishable and distresses upon the highway or the common street were to be levied only by the King's officers. The statute of 1275 forbade distresses to be taken out of the jurisdiction and empowered sheriffs to storm fortified places in which illegally distrained animals were detained. Later in 1275 a royal determination called *Districciones Scaccarii* (Lat = Exchequer Distresses) aligned the King's rights with those of subjects so as to restrict extortion by royal officers in purported exercise of the King's prerogative. The preamble to the Statute of 1267 and the nature of the legislation gives a picture of the prevailing lawlessness, particularly of great men and of official corruption, both of which Edward I was determined to put down.

DISTRIBUTION, CENSUS OF, taken by the Board of Trade, for 1950, 1957 and 1961 covered retail, service and repair trades and wholesalers. The number of establishments fell between 1950 and 1961 and 1966 from 583,000 to 577,000 but turnover and numbers engaged rose respectively from £5,000M to £9,800M and 2.4M to 2.5M. This census was taken over by the Dept. of Trade and Industry which published later editions.

DISTRICT COUNCILS. *See* LOCAL ADMINISTRATION.

DISTRICT NURSING. *See* NURSING.

DIUMA, St. (?-658), Irish monk, was consecrated Bp. of the Mercians and Middle Angles by St. Finan of Lindisfarne. He led a successful mission among them after K. Penda's death (654).

DIVAN or DIWAN, originally a Persian word, meant a bundle of writings and hence (*inter alia*) a book of accounts or minutes, then a govt. office or a court of revenue or justice and so a council of state or a govt. and a place in which such dignatories met or a piece of furniture upon which they sat. *For its Indian variant* DEWAN *see* BENGAL.

DIVINE RIGHT OF KINGS. A post Reformation doctrine that princes (i.e. the govt.) are entitled to all authority and obedience and do not share it with anyone else, e.g. the Pope or Parliament. In the *Homily Against Wilful Rebellion* (1569), rebellion is denounced as a sin, the goodness or badness of Kings being God's reward or punishment to a nation. Where active obedience is morally impossible, the subject must submit willingly to penalties for non-compliance. This doctrine of PASSIVE OBEDIENCE was held by most leading Anglicans under the Stuarts. Luther owed his safety to princes who were faced by peasant insurrections. He preached it too. John Knox and the Huguenots, both objects of official persecution, thought otherwise. It is distinguishable from, but related to, LEGITIMISM, which identifies the King to whom obedience is owed, by reference to an immutable hereditary right of succession. The NON-JURORS who could not accept William III mostly professed passive obedience though their position was really based upon the sanctity of their earlier oath to James II. The Non-Jurors included Wm. Sancroft, Abp. of Canterbury, Thos. Ken, Bp. of Bath and Wells, seven other bishops, about 400 lesser clergy and a few laymen. They were deprived and their successors appointed by Act of Parliament and consequently non-juring clergy regarded these bishops as their true superiors. Though James II issued *congés d'élire* in 1694 to enable an episcopal succession to be maintained, they slowly died out after the Jacobite rebellion of 1745.

DIVISION (1) FRANCHISE. The official name for a constituency. **(2) VOTING.** In a House of parliament the Chair or Woolsack determines the sense of the House on a voice vote, but any member may demand a vote by division, in which case the lobbies are cleared, bells ring, four members are appointed tellers, two for the *ayes* (in the Lords *contents*) and two for the *noes* (*not contents*); four minutes later the members walk through lobbies, ayes or contents by the chair or Throne, noes by the bar. The tellers count and clerks record them, and the tellers jointly report the ·result at the Table, those for the winning side standing on the right. The four minute interval enables members not in the chamber or in the buildings and homes in the 'Division Bell Area' of the adjacent streets to reach the lobbies before counting ceases. The process takes only eight minutes.

DIVISION (Mil.). The smallest military formation comprising a balance of different kinds of troops. Its main battle force is commonly either infantry or tanks or reduced components of both; the supporting services include artillery, engineers, signals, supply and reconnaissance units and medical formations. It is usually commanded by a major-gen. and has between 17,000 and 20,000 men. An airborne division is smaller yet similar in design, but the equipment and training are specialised for carriage by aircraft and, at least in part, for landing by parachute. The Roman Legion of about 6000 men was, in the above sense, a divisional force. It was commanded by a military tribune.

DIVORCE AND NULLITY, ENGLAND (1) Before 1857 matrimonial causes were under ecclesiastical jurisdiction. Declarations of NULLITY (i.e. that the parties had never been married at all) could be granted for want of consent, incapacity, insanity and impotence; and by decrees in JACTITATION a person could be inhibited from asserting that he or she was married to a particular person. Marriage, being a sacrament, was indissoluble by the ecclesiastical courts, hence the development of an elaborate jurisprudence on nullity and jactitation. If, however, a marriage was established, the courts could in theory only try to enforce or release its secondary effects; a spouse who deserted or refused sexual intercourse might be directed to return to matrimonial duty by a decree of RESTITUTION OF CONJUGAL RIGHTS. Adultery, petty treason, cruelty, buggery and disobedience to a Decree of Restitution could be grounds of a decree of SEPARATION otherwise called DIVORCE *A MENSA ET THORO* (Lat = from table and bed). Alongside these rules there had to be consequential rules on the legitimacy of children, upon which the devolution of property depended, but the ecclesiastical courts had no jurisdiction over property; proceedings concerning the status of parties had to be fought through the ecclesiastical courts, but the consequences to the property would then have to be litigated at Common Law or in Chancery. A divorce in the modern sense, then called a DIVORCE *A VINCULO* (Lat = from the bond) could be obtained and the consequential issues settled all at once only by a PRIVATE ACT OF PARLIAMENT, the bill for which could never be introduced until a divorce *a mensa et thoro* had been obtained. The total cost was prodigious and divorce *a vinculo* was available only to the very rich.

(2) There were serious consequences: people who found a marriage insupportable simply deserted and sometimes (forced by the pressure of custom) remarried elsewhere, thus risking prosecution for bigamy, which was a capital felony. Alternatively some never married and their children were bastards: often the lack of 'marriage lines' was unknown especially if they migrated, because the only registers were the local parish registers and the law presumed legitimacy if possible; but the creation of the Central Register Office and the universal introduction of birth, marriage and death certificates in 1837 closed this escape. In 20 years the situation became intolerable and in any case movements for legal reform were afoot.

(3) The MATRIMONIAL CAUSES ACT, 1857, transferred all the ecclesiastical jurisdiction previously described to a civil Court for Matrimonial Causes, which was also empowered to divorce parties *a vinculo,* at the instance of the husband, on grounds of adultery by the wife; and at the instance of the wife (apart from some special cases) on the combined grounds of adultery with cruelty or desertion. The courts had a certain jurisdiction over ancillary matters, but when it became a branch of the High Court it was fully able to exercise all the property jurisdiction at Common Law and in Equity.

(4) The inconvenient restriction of the grounds of divorce to behaviour involving adultery brought the widespread development of fictional or (theoretically penalised) collusive adulteries. The legislators had never dreamed of the extent of the problem of unsatisfactory marriages and by the 1920s there were hotels whose housemaids and room registers were constantly required in court. Chivalry required the husband to be, if possible, the guilty party but the sporting instinct leans against cruelty and it was virtually impossible to hoodwink the court by a collusive desertion, which was easy to detect and liable to lead to proceedings for perjury. Too many limping marriages were thus preserved until 1923, when wife and husband were put on the same footing. Collusive adulteries now became a commonplace and the subject of much public entertainment and scandal. A. P. (later Sir Alan) Herbert campaigned against this with humour and effect. In 1936 he stood for Parliament at Oxford University solely on the issue of the divorce laws. His Matrimonial Causes Act, 1937, permitted divorce for adultery, cruelty, desertion for three years, incurable insanity for at least five years, presumption of death and, by the wife only, for rape, buggery or bestiality but, save exceptionally, permitted no proceedings in the first three years of a marriage. It also extended the grounds of nullity to include wilful refusal to consummate, mental deficiency, venereal disease and pregnancy by someone other than the petitioner.

(5) This Act might have established a norm for a very long time if World War II had not caused many prolonged separations and ill considered marriages. Though cruelty was still abhorred, adultery became common if not normal and desertion all too frequent. Greater freedom of travel complicated the issues more often with foreign law. After the war divorces were being granted at a rate of 40,000 a year, petitions for adultery and desertion being seldom resisted, those for cruelty being usually bitterly contested. The question before practising lawyers was thus not whether a given marriage ought to be dissolved, but the quickest and cheapest way of dissolving it. Public opinion began to be alarmed at the cavalier attitude to matrimony which this seemed to imply and the Matrimonial Causes Act, 1967, abolished all previous grounds of divorce and introduced the concept of IRRETRIEVABLE BREAKDOWN, of which adultery, cruelty, desertion and so forth might be evidence.

DJEZZAR, Ahmed (c. 1735-1804) PASHA, called THE BUTCHER, was a Bosnian slave who rose to be gov. of Damascus and Acre and as such decisively defended Acre with the help of Sir Sidney Smith against Bonaparte in 1799. Bonaparte massacred his 4000 prisoners and retreated to Egypt.

DJIBOUTI. See SOMALIA.

DJILAS, Milovan (1911-95) was a member of the Yugoslav communist party central committee from 1938, of its politburo from 1940 and a cabinet minister in 1945; he advocated independence from Russia and in 1953 became Vice-Pres. of the republic under Tito. His practical experience and highly critical intellect led him to propound the important development of Marxism which led to his dismissal and imprisonment. This was published in 1957 as the *New Class* in which he argued that the revolutionary concentration of the means of production, distribution and exchange inevitably placed great power and ultimately wealth in the hands of the communist political bureaucracy which became a new class, divisive of society. This class had already engrossed power and surplus resources in Russia where it was responsible for the backwardness of the workers.

DOBSON, William (1610-46) was a pupil of Van Dyck, who introduced him to Charles I. He became the King's serjeant-painter in 1641. Sometimes regarded as the characteristic exponent of the 17th cent. English artistic temperament, he was one of the earliest English portrait and subject painters of ability.

DOBUNNI. A tribe centred on Bagendon (Glos.) and spread across modern Gloucestershire, Avon, parts of Somerset, Oxfordshire and the Border counties. It was tributary to the Catuvellauni, and came over to the Romans after the Catuvellaunian defeat in A.D. 43. *See* CIRENCESTER

DOCK STRIKE 1889, a landmark event, demonstrated that Labour, if sensibly organised, could by trade union action achieve a defined objective.

DOCKYARDS, ROYAL, were originally established at Chatham (c. 1520), Deptford (c. 1490), Devonport (1689), Portsmouth (1540) and Woolwich (c. 1520). These were naval yards but as the navy had increasingly to adopt a world role, Woolwich was closed, Deptford became a victualling yard and further dockyards were established at Sheerness (1703), Rosyth (1909) and Haulbowline (1894) in S. W. Ireland. Others were established at Gibraltar (1704), Malta (1800), Halifax (1749), Bermuda (1780), Simonstown (1902), Trincomalee (1796), Singapore (1928) and Hong Kong (1860). The decline of Britain as a world power led to a corresponding reduction after World War II. By 1980 the last overseas dockyard at Gibraltar was facing closure while at home only Portsmouth, Plymouth and the specialised nuclear submarine establishments at Faslane and Rosyth remained.

DOCTORS COMMONS was the equivalent, for Civil

Lawyers, of the Inns of Court for Common Lawyers. Membership was confined to doctors of law at the two universities; they had a monopoly at the bar and on the bench of the ecclesiastical and Admiralty Courts. The association was formed in 1511 by Richard Blodwell, then Dean of Arches. In 1565 it found premises in Knightrider Street (London) and the courts concerned sat in the gallery of St. Benets Church nearby. It was dissolved in 1857.

DOD, Charles Roger Phipps (1793-1855), published his annual *Parliamentary Companion* for the first time in 1832.

DODECANESE (Aegean). These strategic islands off the S.W. corner of Turkey included Rhodes and Leros. They were under Byzantine rule until 1306, when the Knights of St. John (then in Cyprus after the destruction of Outremer) in league with a Genoese pirate, attacked Rhodes and reduced it by 1308. The islands remained the base of their Christian piracy until Dec. 1522 when the Turks drove them out after a six months siege. The islands remained Turkish until the Italian attack on Turkey in 1912. Under Italian govt. Rhodes prospered and, after World War I, Leros was converted into a vast modern fortress intended to influence Turkey and the Near East. Its existence had a marginal effect on the strategy and diplomacy of World War II. In 1945 the islands passed to Greece.

DODINGTON (Avon), classical mansion built for the Codrington family by James Wyatt in about 1780 with a park laid out by Capability Brown.

DOFRAETH **(Welsh) (1)** The equivalent of *firma unius noctis,* the obligation to provide one night's sustenance for the King's household. It was eventually payable only after Christmas. **(2)** A lord's right to quarter his retainers on his unfree Welsh tenants (cf: COIGN). This developed into **(3)** a right to require certain quantities of oats from the tenant.

DOGE **(It).** The title of the head of the Venetian and Genoese Republics.

DOGGER BANK. A large North Sea shoal 60 miles east of Northumberland, particularly sought by English, Scots, Dutch and Scandinavian fisherpeople for its riches, after the migration of the Baltic herring from the coast of Scania in the 14th cent. It supplied most of the ports from Aberdeen to Hastings. An Anglo-Dutch naval battle was fought off the southern end of it in 1781. A Russian fleet fired on English trawlers in Oct. 1904; and there was a considerable Anglo-German naval action in Jan. 1915. *See also* JAMES I AND VI.

DOGGETTS COAT AND BADGE. Thomas Doggett (?-1721) an actor, founded an annual and still continuing rowing competition for Thames watermen in 1716 in honour of the accession of George I. The prize is a scarlet coat and a large silver badge showing the Hanoverian horse.

DOGMA is a technical term meaning the distinctive tenets of a particular philosophy or sect and so a religious truth established by divine revelation and defined by the church, or in the case of the R Catholic church, by the Pope.

DOGS were first valued because their watchful sensitivity enabled human family groups to sleep and create the surplus energy needed to make the long climb into civilisation. They can seldom have been much use for hunting until humans had learned to control them so well that they would return to their master.

DOG WHIPPER. One who kept worshippers' dogs, mostly collies and turnspits, in order during church services. It was still necessary to appoint one at Exeter Cathedral in 1856.

DOIT. A Dutch coin worth half a farthing.

DOLBEN (1) John (1625-86) fought as a major for Charles I, privately maintained the Anglican service throughout the Commonwealth and was dean of Westminster from 1662 to 1683, as well as Bp. of Rochester from 1666.

From 1683 he was Abp. of York. His brother **(2) Sir William (?-1694)** was recorder of London in 1676 and a judge of the King's Bench from 1678 to 1683 and in 1689. John's son **(3) Sir Gilbert** was M.P. for Ripon in 1685 and for Peterborough from 1689 to 1707. He was also a judge of the Irish Common Pleas from 1701. In 1704 he was a leading advocate of Common's jurisdiction in election matters. He represented Yarmouth (I. of W.) in 1710 and 1714. His grandson **(4) William (1726-1814)** was a leading abolitionist and M.P. for Oxford Univ. from 1768 to 1806.

DOLE (1) originally a weekly allowance to the unemployed, dates from 1919. *See* NATIONAL INSURANCE. **(2)** In Scots law, a corrupt or evil intention.

DOLLAR ($). The Holy Roman Mint at Joachimsthal in Habsburg Bohemia began coining silver from a neighbouring mine in 1519. The coins, known as Joachimsthaler (shortened to *thaler* and corrupted to daler, dollar etc.) circulated in N. Germany, including Hanover. In the Habsburg Spanish American empire the Peso or Piece of Eight was known to the English as a Spanish dollar and was coined from Mexican and Peruvian silver. Thus the dollar was a monetary unit much used in the Americas, based on a silver standard. The U.S. dollar developed naturally from this fact, its value being fixed by law in 1792 by alternative reference to silver and gold. The U.S. dollar at 50d sterling was worth slightly less than the Spanish dollar and its value in terms of sterling remained more or less constant until after World War II. The "S" stands for Sterling, the two vertical strokes for the Spanish symbol of the Pillars of Hercules.

DOLLY'S BRAE AFFAIR (July 1849). Orangemen, celebrating the B. of the Boyne, marched through the R. Catholic Dolly's Brae area. In the ensuing riot there were many casualties and most of Dolly's Brae was burned. A commission of investigation blamed the Orangemen and particularly their nearby Grand Master, the third E. of Roden.

DOLMEN. A megalithic structure composed of 2 or 3 upright slabs surmounted by a table-top, the whole representing the burial chamber of a grave mound from which the earth has been eroded by floods or weather.

DOMESDAY BOOK (1086) is the result, unique in Europe, of a royal survey. **(1)** It covered England south of the Tees, the Cumbrian Derwent and the Shap, but included Flint and the small parts of Wales then in Shropshire and Herefordshire. **(2)** William I decided to make it at the Christmas Court at Gloucester in 1085. Commissioners, sent out in groups, collected the information by the sworn evidence of, usually four, good men of each village or borough. This was collated at county courts and sent to Winchester for further redaction. The East Anglian parts arrived late and the result was two volumes: the main volume was finished: the second, East Anglian, was written in an unrevised form. The whole process took about seven months. **(3)** The object was to discover, mostly by reference to men and stock, the value of each holding and the amounts owed in services by the tenant of each. Since many of the obligations depended upon arrangements existing in the time of Edward the Confessor (*tempore regis Edwardi* = TRE) the names of the tenants of that time as well as the existing tenants and their respective obligations usually appear. **(4)** The book contains errors, omissions, inconsistencies and some oddities, but where it is explicit it was regarded for nearly two centuries as conclusive on matters of tenure and in certain other matters (such as ancient demesne) this evidential authority continued to 1922. **(5)** Though the survey was made geographically, it was recompiled not geographically but by feudal holdings and the compilers introduced the term *manor* to signify the unit of feudal lordship. A manor might, as often happened in the Midlands, be co-terminous with a village but it might consist of several scattered farmsteads (e.g. in Devon) or a village might be divided between several manors (e.g. in Cambridgeshire). Many areas (e.g. Kent, the I. of Wight, the Danish boroughs) had special characteristics and there were many peculiar local customs. The survey incidentally provides, through evidence of waste, information on the movements of Norman armies in the course of the conquest and the subsequent rebellions.

DOMESDAY MONACHORUM (Lat = of the Monks) in three parts written respectively c. 1100, 1150 and 1200 at Christ Church, Canterbury, contains **(1)** lists of Kentish churches and dues payable by them; **(2)** a note on Romescot (Peters Pence); **(3)** surveys of the Kentish manors of the sees of Canterbury and Rochester and of Christchurch; **(4)** a list of the knights of the archbishop and **(5)** some miscellaneous documents.

DOMESTIC SERVICE. Little, save that it was common is known of this before Tudor times when, in a developing cash economy, young people found jobs often by the year in larger households able to pay them. Later, mostly women servants were recruited from local families which thus supplemented their income while their men worked as artisans or on the land. Such women were often in the same service for life and regarded as members of the family. If a household could no longer employ her, she might be passed to a relative who could, and who probably knew her already. The agricultural slump of 1868 onwards drove away many of the families from which servants had been recruited, so employing households recruited more haphazardly often through servants' *registry offices* (not to be confused with register offices), a tendency increased by the households being smaller and owned by town-based business people. Numerically domestic employment reached its peak in the early 1880s. World War taxation destroyed its economic base and domestic machinery superseded the previous need for it.

DOMETT, Alfred (1811-87), barrister, poet, politician and friend of Browning who lamented his migration to New Zealand in 1842. Here he became M.P. for Nelson in 1855, was prime minister from 1862 to 1863 and was registrar-gen. of land, an important post in a country in the course of colonisation, from 1865 to 1871 when he returned to England.

DOMICIL(E) is the English legal concept of home: i.e. the place where a person is established in his way of living. At Common Law every person's country of birth was his domicil *of origin;* his domicil *of choice* was the country to which he or his guardian had chosen to move and settle permanently and where he had actually arrived. One domicil of choice could be superseded by another, but where a choice lapsed and was not superseded, the domicil of origin revived. In 1968 Brussels Convention on E.U. Judgments etc, was enacted into the laws of the U.K. in 1982. This altered the British rules. An individual is now domiciled in the U.K. if he resides there and the nature and circumstances of his residence indicate a substantial connection with it. Residence is presumed (unless the contrary appears) if it has lasted for three months. This materially separated the U.K. from other Common Law countries such as the Commonwealth and the U.S.A.

DOMINGART. See DALRIADA.

DOMINICA. See PARIS, P. OF (10 FEB. 1763); SEVEN YEARS' WAR-10.

DOMINICAN or PREACHERS' ORDER. St. Dominic, of the noble Spanish Guzman family, preached in the Languedoc against the Albigensians from 1203 onwards and in 1207 founded a mendicant order at Casseneuil especially for their conversion. It followed the Rule of St. Augustine modified to encourage teaching and study. This received papal approval in 1216. He travelled ceaselessly thereafter in Italy, Spain and France and held the first Chapter General at Bologna in 1220. The Order reached England in 1221 and was welcomed by Abp.

Langton. They established over 50 convents in England and a firm footing in the universities. Robert Kilwardby (Abp. of Canterbury 1273-8) was a Dominican. It also had an elaborate system of schools and colleges. The 14th cent. decline of the mendicant orders is noticed by Chaucer in the person of his dissolute and greedy friar. Dominicans worked extensively in the Inquisition and were habitually used in diplomatic missions. Their system of self-govt. is thought to have provided the model for the English convocations.

DOMINICAN REPUBLIC. See HISPANIOLA.

DOMINION originally meant a territory outside England (such as Ireland) or Great Britain (such as the American colonies) under the sovereignty or suzerainty of the crown. Hence "The Old Dominion" = Virginia. It was given as a title to Canada in 1867 and to New Zealand in 1907. It became a technical term denoting independence from the British parliament under the Statute of Westminster, 1931. See BRITISH COMMONWEALTH.

DOMINIONS OFFICE was hived off from the Colonial Office as a result of the Statute of Westminster, 1931; it was renamed the **COMMONWEALTH RELATIONS OFFICE** in 1950 when some of the Dominions ceased to be monarchies and amalgamated with the Foreign Office in 1969.

DON, R. (1) (Aberdeen) was channelled at Aberdeen in 1750. **(2)** (Yorks.) was a meander until regulated by Vermuyden and his successors in the 17th and 18th cents. **(3)** (Russia) has been a major trade route since earliest times.

DONALD I and II. See SCOTS OR ALBAN KINGS, EARLY-2,6.

DONALD BANE. See SCOTS OR ALBAN KINGS, EARLY-20.

DONALDSON (1) Sir Stuart Alexander (1812-67) made a fortune in Australian wool; he was a member of the council of N.S.W. from 1848 to 1859, first minister in 1856 and finance min. from 1856 to 1857. He returned to England in 1859. His son **(2) St. Clair George Alfred (1863-1935)** was Abp. of Brisbane from 1905 to 1921 and thereafter Bp. of Salisbury.

DONATION OF CONSTANTINE. See FALSE DECRETALS.

DONATION OF PEPIN (?-754). A lost grant to the papacy of Lombard lands belonging to the Eastern Empire, by the Frankish Pepin the Short, to Pope Stephen II. Generally considered the foundation charter of the Papal States.

DONCASTER (Yorks.) (Lat = *DANUM*) had a Roman military post; and the street names suggest a Danish occupation. It was first chartered in 1194 and was a prosperous market and manufacturing town in the middle ages. It was royalist in the Civil War and the growing importance of the coalfield soon made it rich thereafter. The St. Leger race was established in 1776 and with the coming of the railways it acquired an important carriage and locomotive industry. It was a county borough from 1926 to 1974.

DONCASTER. See HAY (CARLISLE).

DONCASTER PETITION (1321). See EDWARD II-8.

DONEGAL (Ireland). See TYRCONNELL.

DONGOLA (Sudan) was inhabited by Nubians and ruled by Egypt from 1820 until the Mahdist conquest in 1885. It was reconquered under Kitchener in 1896 and incorporated in the Anglo-Egyptian Sudan.

DONIEBRISTLE, MURDER. See JAMES VI-II.

DÖNITZ, Grand Adm. Karl (1891-1980) was appointed in charge of German U-boats in 1935 and commanded and developed the techniques of the German submarine campaign in World War II. In Jan. 1943 he succeeded Adm. Raeder as C-in-C and on 1st May, 1945 he briefly succeeded Hitler as Chancellor of the Reich. In 1946 the War Crimes Tribunal sentenced him to ten years imprisonment.

DONNE, John (1572-1631), remembered as a harsh and powerful metaphysical poet, was connected through his mother with the family of Sir Thomas More and, through a long friendship, with Sir Henry Wotton. He read law at Lincoln's Inn, took part in Essex's expedition to Calais in 1596 and became sec. to the Lord Keeper, Sir Thomas Egerton. In 1601 he married Egerton's niece and was imprisoned for it. The subsequent lawsuit (and 12 children) practically ruined him, but in 1610 he began to attract court patronage as a poet. He took orders in 1615 and was Dean of St. Paul's, where he preached his famous sermons, from 1621. He died of consumption but not before he had had his portrait painted clad in a shroud.

DONNYBROOK (now a suburb of Dublin). The FAIR (c. 1210-1855) was a cheerfully riotous August festival.

DONOUGHMORE. *See* HELY HUTCHINSON; CEYLON-8.

DONOUGHMORE COMMISSION. *See* CEYLON-8.

DON PACIFICO AFFAIR. Don Pacifico, a Gibraltarian in Athens in 1847, had his property destroyed in a riot. Denied compensation, after over two years he appealed to the Russell govt., in which Palmerston conducted foreign affairs almost regardless of his colleagues and the Queen. He exuberantly sent the fleet to the Piraeus (Jan. 1850) and threatened bombardment. The Greek govt. paid up. Attacked in the Commons by Gladstone, Bright and Cobden he overwhelmed them in a celebrated demogogic appeal called the *Civis romanus sum* (Lat = I am a Roman citizen) speech. The context of this much criticised affair was the primitive corruption reigning in the many underdeveloped countries with which Britain was trading.

DONUM **(Lat = gift)** was a royal tax levied for perhaps 40 years in the 12th cent. With the decay of the Danegeld, the crown needed casual levies under a different form. The interchangeable *dona* and *auxilia* (aids) existed before 1130 and were still being levied in the 1150s, initially upon towns and shires, but soon only on the King's own lands and the cities and boroughs. They were levied concurrently with a scutage, but these *auxilia* were not feudal aids. The amount might be the subject of bargaining. In the royal demesne manors these euphemisms were superseded by the more forthright *tallage* before the 13th cent. but for a time the terms *dona* and *auxilia* were retained for levies upon the towns.

DOORNKOP. *See* JAMESON RAID.

DORCAS SOCIETY (see Acts ix v 36). A church ladies' assn. which made clothes for the poor.

DORCHESTER (Dorset) (Lat = *DURNOVARIA*). *See* DORSET.

DORCHESTER. *See* CARLETON.

DORCHESTER COMPANY (1624-6). This joint stock Co. of Dorset men planted some 50 farmers and fishermen at Cape Ann (Mass.). The plantation was not a success and after three years the colonists parted, some for Naumkeag (later Salem) and others for home, where their experience inspired the Massachusetts Bay Co. *See* MASSACHUSETTS.

DORCHESTER ON THAMES (Oxon) (Lat = *DOROCINA*) was a walled Roman town at a river crossing. In 634 it became the seat of the Bp. of the West Saxons. It was an important Saxon royal manor. The bishopric was moved to Lincoln in 1092 but an important Augustinian abbey was built there in 1140. It has a sculptured Jesse window.

DORDRECHT or DORT (Holland). The independence of the Netherlands was proclaimed here in 1572 and the **SYNOD** of 1618-9 of protestant theologians supported by the House of Orange condemned Arminianism supported by many republicans. *See also* STAPLE B-1.

DORSET was the area of the Durotriges, who were centred on the immense fortress of MAIDEN CASTLE. It was turned into a Roman tribal canton administered mainly from Ilchester and DORCHESTER (Durnovaria), which superseded Maiden Castle when the Romans seized it from the Belgae in A.D. 43. The West Saxons conquered but did not settle Dorset in the years after 658, but they set up the diocese of Sherborne in 705. By 939, however,

Dorchester was a royal manor with a mint. A planned lowland manorial system had been established by Domesday (1086), when Wareham had long been the shrieval seat because of channel piracy. In the 12th and 13th cents. there was a castle at Dorchester whose materials were used for a Franciscan priory in the 15th. The town returned two M.P.s from 1295 and, though granted bailiffs under Edward II and markets and fairs under Edward III, it was not incorporated until 1610. Meanwhile wool was exported first through Wareham, then through Weymouth and Melcombe and finally through Poole, which became the staple in 1433. These changes were probably caused by the increase in the tonnage of ships. In 1569 Poole became a separate county and the discovery of the Newfoundland fisheries brought great prosperity to all the coast, rope walks being established at Bridport with associated hemp cultivation nearby, and curing developed at Lyme. From the middle ages the inland areas throve on wool, which was supplemented by dairying in the 17th cent. and there was a well organised smuggling industry in French wines and brandy, and in W. Indian tobacco which continued for two centuries because of the difficulty of patrolling the coast ("Brandy for the parson, baccy for the clerk"). These rural parts suffered heavily in the Civil War, where the farmers banded together as Clubmen to keep both sides out, and under the Bloody Assize of 1685; the so-called Tolpuddle Martyrs came from them in 1834. By the 1950s sheep were practically extinct, but dairy farming was booming. The county was enlarged in 1974 by the addition of Poole and Bournemouth. *See* DIGBY.

DORSET, Es. of. *See* SACKVILLE.

DOUAI. *See* ALLEN; FLANDERS.

DOUBLOON (Sp = *Doblon*) was a Spanish gold coin worth *two* pistoles (about £1-14 in the 17th cent.).

DOUGHTY, Charles Montague (1843-1926) oriental and African traveller, published his famous *Travels in Arabia Deserta* in 1888.

DOUGLAS. This powerful family has been traced to Sir William "Longley" (?-?1288) who held manors on both sides of the Scottish border. He had two sons, of whom William "The Hardy" or "the Rash" (?-1298) married Elizabeth Stewart and, after her death, raped and married Eleanor of Lovain, an English ward. This embroiled him with Edward I both as K. of England and as suzerain; but the Scottish regents, one of whom was his first wife's brother, refused to proceed against him; in the opening stages of the Scots War of Independence he was an opponent of Balliol yet gave military help to Sir Wm. Wallace. He surprised Sanquhar Castle by stopping a cart under its portcullis. His English properties were forfeited. Eventually taken, he died in the Tower and Edward I bestowed his Scottish estates on Sir Robt. Clifford. His career, not surprisingly, imported an anti-English tradition to his family. His many descendents included the Es. of Douglas, Angus, Morton, Forfar and Dumbarton, the Ms. and Ds. of Douglas and the Ds. of Hamilton and of Queensberry. *See* below.

DOUGLAS, Ds. and Ms. of. *See* DOUGLAS ("RED")-11 *et seq.*

DOUGLAS ("BLACK") (1) Good Sir James (?1286-1330) *s.* of William "the Hardy" (*see above*) was educated in France. He found the Cliffords in possession of his estates when he returned and, being refused readmission by Edward I, joined Robert the Bruce when he was crowned (1306) at Scone. He shared Robert's wanderings and became a resourceful and ruthless guerrilla leader. He twice destroyed his own castle (*see* DOUGLAS LARDER), massacred an English force at its Palm Sunday devotions and, with his men, took Roxburgh Castle by pretending, in the twilight, to be cows. He commanded the right wing at Bannockburn (1314) and then, as Warden of the Marches, conducted from a stronghold at Lintalee on the Jed a furious and successful war, full of extraordinary incidents which have passed into legend. Under the

Peace of 1328 he received the family's English lands back and Robert I gave him many estates and baronies in the south Lowlands, together with the Emerald Charter. He died crusading in Spain, while carrying Robert's heart to the Holy Land. The epithet "good" referred to his irresistible charm and kindness to friends. His brother **(2) Sir Archibald (?1296-1333)** surprised and routed Edward Balliol at Annan in 1332, became regent for David II in Mar. 1333 but was killed at Halidon Hill (July). (*See* also DOUGLAS (MORTON).) His son **(3) William (?1327-84) 1st E. of DOUGLAS (1358)** and **MAR** (1374) was educated in France and had to drive the English from his estates when he returned in 1348. He received (1354) confirmation of his father's and his uncle's Scottish lands together with those of his kinsman, the Knight of Liddesdale, whom he had killed in 1353. He was in the Newcastle negotiations for the ransom of David II and then went to France where, in 1356, he was nearly captured at the B. of Poitiers. On his return he became Warden of the East March and then joined the opposition to the King based upon widespread suspicion of the King's treatment of the ransom. The nobility preferred a poor King, the border magnates a Scottish King. He remained in rebellion until the parliament of 1363 when the issue was openly debated but otherwise acted as a Warden and border grandee. In 1271 he swore allegiance to Robert II and his powers were reinforced by a patent as Justiciary S. of the Forth, i.e. outside his lands as well as within them. (*See* EMERALD CHARTER.) In 1378 his troops defeated Sir Thos. Musgrave's raid on Melrose but he took the opportunity afforded by the troubles in England to settle a truce in 1380 with John of Gaunt, then his border opposite number. His son **(4) James (?1358-88), 2nd E.,** married Isabel, *d* of Robert II in 1373. He was an active border fighter and. commanded the joint Franco-Scottish operations of 1385. The French, under Jean de Vienne, however, paid him a large sum to be allowed to go home, but this corrupt transaction did not end the war, which culminated in his victory over the Percys at Otterburn (Chevy Chase) where, however, he was killed. Being childless his honours passed, by special entail, to a bastard of Good Sir James **(5) Archibald (?1328-1400)** "The Grim", **3rd E.,** who was a long-term hostage in England as a young man and returned in about 1361. He served as Warden of the Western March in 1364 and 1368 and then, as ambassador to France in 1369 and 1371, renegotiated the French alliance. On his return (1372) he bought the lordship of Galloway where his imposition of a form of feudalism (to which the mainly Celtic Galwegians were unaccustomed) earned him his nickname. He was much involved in border wars, especially in 1389, but sought to have Scotland included in the Anglo-French negotiations of 1389 and 1391. He also took a step towards civilising the Border by codifying its customs. His son **(6) Archibald (?1369-1424)** "The Tyneman" (Sc = the loser), **4th E., 1st D. of TOURAINE (1423)** married Margaret *d.* of Robert III in 1390 and by 1400 had worked himself into a strong position as Warden of the Marches and Keeper of Edinburgh Castle. As such he was an uneasy ally of Albany's ambitions (1402) but was captured at Milfield by Hotspur during a raid and so came to fight for him and was again captured at Shrewsbury (1403). He was not ransomed until 1408. After a period on the Marches he went to France to negotiate a Burgundian treaty (1412) and thereafter waged border war, particularly to recover Roxburgh, until, as a result of the T. of Troyes Henry V sought a pacification (1421). Henry's death, however, put all at large and in 1423 Douglas took a mercenary contingent to France, for which he was paid with an uncertain duchy and other shaky offices. He was defeated and killed at Verneuil (1424). His son **(7) Archibald (?1391-1439) 5th E. and 2nd D.,** fought under the French at Beaugé (1421) and brought James I home from

England in 1423. James never trusted him and he was intermittently under restraint until 1432. Not surprisingly, he was a member of the regency after James I was murdered (1437) and, as Lieut-Gen., was effectively sole regent from 1438. He died suddenly and his son **(8) William (?1423-40) 6th E. and 3rd D.** with his brother David were murdered by the Crichtons and Livingstons at the notorious Black Dinner in Edinburgh Castle. Hence the honours passed briefly to the elderly son of Archibald the Grim **(9) James (?1371-1443)** "the Gross" **7th E. and 4th D.,** who was suspected of being privy to the murders. At the succession of his son **(10) William (?1425-52) 8th E. and 5th D.,** the Douglas dominated the territories south of the Forth, save in the Merse; they were powerful in Edinburgh and attracted public sympathy as well as respect. They had understandings and later *bands* with the Crawfords and the Lords of the Isles, and William, who was much of an age with James II, was on intimate terms with him. James, however, was determined to master overmighty subjects in his chaotic Kingdom and played them off against each other. In 1443, with Douglas help, he removed Sir Wm. Crichton from the chancery. In 1449 (after an interval of border and royal matrimonial negotiation) Douglas helped the King and Crichton to get rid of the Livingstons and acquired some of their property. He was thus the most dangerous man in the Kingdom. In 1450 he went to Rome and stayed at the Burgundian court on the way out and at the English court on the way back. James was busily undermining his influence while he was away and his Burgundian and English contacts and some lawless acts were made pretexts for a parliamentary arraignment on his return. He formally submitted and received a regrant of his lordships. This admission of dependency was a major blow to his prestige, but meanwhile the King, through the Gordons, had been preparing a stroke against the Crawfords. It could not succeed so long as the Crawfords were protected by the Douglas. At Stirling James demanded that the Douglas-Crawford *band* should be broken. William refused and James murdered him. His brother **(11) James (1426-88) 9th E,** who had been on William's Roman journey, withdrew his allegiance from the murderer, but meanwhile the Gordons overwhelmed his allies and he was forced to submit in 1452 (with the loss of Wigtown and Stewarton) and apply himself to his local duties as Warden of the West March. By way of rejoinder he married his brother's widow, the Maid of Galloway, in 1453 and at the same time arranged a border truce. The King anticipated the expected revolt by winning over his relatives, the Red Douglas and his ally John of the Isles. In 1455 William's brothers and relatives were defeated piecemeal, his estates were forfeited and he fled to England where he became involved in, perhaps instigated, the Westminster-Ardtornish agreement for the partition of Scotland with English help. He remained in English service but is said to have given himself up on a border raid, so that an old retainer might earn the price on his head. He died a monk.

DOUGLAS, ("RED") or ANGUS (*See* DOUGLAS ("BLACK")-3) **(1) George (1380-1403) 1st E. of ANGUS (1389),** brother of James, 2nd E. of Douglas, *m.* Mary *d.* of Robert III and was killed at the B. of Homildon Hill. His son **(2) William (?1389-1437) 2nd E.,** an opponent of Albany, though mainly a Forfarshire magnate, was a successful Warden of the Middle March and drifted away from the mainstream of Douglas allegiance. Hence his younger son **(3) George (?1412-62)** was induced to command the force which overthrew the 9th E. of Douglas in 1455; he acquired a share of the lands and defended the border against various attempts by him to return with Percy and Yorkist help. By his death the family primary interests had moved from Forfar to the Marches. His son **(4) Archibald the Great (?1449-1513)** called "Bell-the-Cat", **5th E.,** Warden of the East March from 1481, though courageous and the leading noble of his day, had neither the resources nor the influence of the Black Douglas, but he led the faction which opposed James III and his favourite Mar, and undertook to neutralise ("bell") the latter ("the Cat"), which he did by hanging him at Lauder Bridge. In the policy disputes of which this was a symptom, he generally favoured Albany and joined in his English intrigues, but was exiled with him. An attempt to overthrow James from England met, however, with no public sympathy. He was captured, forcibly tonsured and died a monk at Whithorn. His grandson **(5) Archibald (?1489-1551) 6th E.,** in 1514 married, perhaps forcibly, Margaret Tudor, Q. dowager to James IV, killed at Flodden. With his uncles **(6) Gavin (?1414-1522)** Abp. of St. Andrews and later Bp. of Dunkeld and **(7) Sir Archibald (?1480-?1540)** Lord Treasurer in 1526, he was involved in a running fourteen year struggle with his wife and the Arrans over the control and custody of the infant James V. By 1526 he had outwitted them and killed Lennox but he returned without the King, who was now old enough to rule his own fate. From 1526 Angus governed the Kingdom in James' name until 1528 when the King escaped and with the aid of the Hamilton's and Lennox's, forfeited the Douglas and drove him into exile. He did not return until James' death in 1542 when he naturally contested power with the regent Arran. The result was a compromise. They agreed to fight the English and divide the administration territorially, Angus taking the area S. of the Forth. Hence it fell to him to defend the Border in the Pinkie campaign (1547) and Wharton's incursion (1548). In 1554 he, in effect, retired when the regency passed to Mary of Guise. The career of his grandson **(8) Archibald (1555-88) 8th E.,** is intertwined with that of his uncle and guardian James, 4th E. of Morton (see DOUGLAS (MORTON)) until Morton's execution in 1581 and he remained hostile to crown encroachments. He was involved in an English intrigue, fled to England and returned as a result of the *coup d'état* (The Gowrie Conspiracy) effected by Gowrie and Mar. As a result he was attainted in 1584 after they were overthrown and again fled to England. In 1585 he recrossed the border as part of a widespread conspiracy against the regent, the E. of Arran, seized Stirling Castle and became the dominant party's Lieut. of the Kingdom. His death from tuberculosis was attributed to sorcery. The earldom and estates passed to a distant cousin **(9) William (1533-91) 9th E.,** a minor political figure whose troops helped Mary Q. of Scots to defeat the Gordons at Corrichie (1562) but presided over Bothwell's conviction in 1567. His son **(10) William (1554-1611) 10th E.,** educated in France, was converted to catholicism and formed the northern R. Catholic party by bringing together the Atholl Stewarts and the Gordons. This led to the affair of the Spanish Blanks for which he, Atholl and Huntly were forfeited, but they kept much of their following and seized Aberdeen in 1594. The rapid advance of Calvinism, however, threatened their position and in 1597 they signed a confession of faith, received their lands back and he became Lieut. of the March. He remained suspect and as the union of the Crowns reduced the functions of his lieutenancy, he became increasingly vulnerable. In 1608 the General Assembly excommunicated him. He died in France. His son **(11) William (1589-1660) 11th E. and 1st M. of DOUGLAS (1633),** though brought up a Calvinist, experienced the conflicting loyalties of the period. He obeyed' the summons to help Charles I in 1639 (The Bishop's Wars), yet signed the National Covenant in 1644 but joined Montrose in 1645; he was taken and imprisoned but emerged to become a member of the Committee of Estates which supported Charles II. For this he and his son **(12) Archibald (1609-55) E. of ORMONDE (1651),** who had similar conflicts of loyalty, were heavily fined under the Protector's Act of Grace in 1654. Archibald's

brother **(13) George (?1636-92) E. of DUMBARTON (1675)** helped to put down Argyll's rising against James II in 1685 and ended, with James, at St. Germains. For his brother **(14) William see DOUGLAS (HAMILTON).** The son of (12), **(15) James (?1646-1700) 12th E. of ANGUS (1655), 2nd M. of DOUGLAS (1700)** lost most of the family estates through the peculations of his factor, one William Lawrie. His brother **(16) Archibald (1653-1712) 1st E. of FORFAR (1661),** early perceived the dangers to be apprehended from the views of the D. of York (James II and VII) and was a leading figure in organising the Scottish part of the Revolution. His son **(17) Archibald (1692-1715),** a soldier and Hanoverian supporter, was killed at Sheriffmuir. The son of (15), **(18) Archibald (1694-1761) 3rd M. and D. of DOUGLAS (1703),** like Forfar, raised a regiment against the Pretender and fought at Sheriffmuir. With him the titles became extinct, but the properties passed to the descendents of his sister **(19) Jane (1698-1753).** See DOUGLAS LAWSUIT.

DOUGLAS, Es. of. See DOUGLAS ("BLACK").

DOUGLAS (1) Sir John Sholto (1844-1900) 8th M. of QUEENSBURY (only distantly related to the Es. and Ds.) (1858), patron of prize fighters and boxers, is known mainly for the Queensbury Rules of boxing, which he drew up in 1867 and for his involvement in the series of civil and criminal proceedings provoked by his hated son **(2) 14. Alfred Douglas ("Bosey") (1870-1945)** leading to Oscar Wilde's conviction. Bosey was himself later involved in many legal actions and was convicted of a criminal libel on Winston Churchill in 1923.

DOUGLAS (HAMILTON). (1) William (1635-94) 3rd D. of HAMILTON (1660) was the son of the 1st M. of Douglas (see DOUGLAS ("RED")-11). He married Anne, Duchess of Hamilton, and was created duke on her petition and by way of solace for the heavy fines which his family had suffered under the Protectorate. He was a Scots privy councillor from 1660 and, faithful to the Douglas tradition, was soon leading the local Scots nobility in opposition to Lauderdale's demands for funds for the royal troops. In 1672, with others, he carried his opposition to the point of refusing to pay the new land tax and in 1673 he opposed supply for the Dutch War. In 1676 he was dismissed from the Council and promptly went to London to lay the general grievances of the Scots against Lauderdale's conduct before the King. Lauderdale threatened legal proceedings which hindered him from pressing his case. He benefited from the change of political climate after Lauderdale's death (1680) and became an English privy councillor under James II (1687), yet as William III's commissioner to the Estates in 1689 and 1693. His son **(2) James (1658-1712) E. of ARRAN and 4th D. (1698)** was ambassador at Versailles from 1683 to 1685 and commanded troops for James II in 1688. Intermittently imprisoned, he eventually became Duke when his mother resigned (*see above*). He was also an early but influential Scottish nationalist who sought to maintain the autonomy of Scotland by encouraging economic growth, much hindered by the English Navigation Acts. The Scottish Co. for Trading with Africa and the Indies (Darien Co.) was founded in 1695 as a rival of the HEIC and he promoted its interests in the Scottish parliament of 1700. In 1703 the first negotiations on Union broke down mainly on English unwillingness to concede Hamilton's demand to let the Scots trade lawfully with the colonies, and in the last Scottish parliament (1707) he represented the angry crowds who opposed union, but resolutely prevented violence. In 1708 he was arrested for unproved complicity with the Jacobite attempt of that year but released and elected a Representative Peer. Naturally he gravitated towards the opposition and in 1710 supported Sacheverell and became a Tory privy councillor and in 1712 as Master-gen. of the Ordnance had some responsibility for abandoning the allies in the French War. He was nominated ambassador to Versailles during the Utrecht negotiations but was killed in Hyde Park in a duel over their wives' inheritance, by the Whig duellist Lord Mohun, who also died,

DOUGLAS-HOME, Sir Alexander Frederick (1903-95) known as **Ld. DUNGLASS (1918-51), 14th E. of HOME (1951-63), Ld. HOME of the HIRSEL (1974).** After Eton and Oxford he was a Conservative M.P. from 1931 to 1951 and was Neville Chamberlain's P.P.S. from 1937 to 1940. He was charming and intellectually able. After succeeding to the earldom he was Sec. for Commonwealth Relations (1955-60), then Lord Pres. and Leader of the Lords and Foreign Sec. (1960-3) under Harold Macmillan. He was persuaded to stand against R. A. Butler when Macmillan resigned and, having disclaimed his earldom, was accepted as Tory leader and became prime minister. Owing to an administrative delay, he was actually in the Lords for some days as prime minister. He served until the 1964 general election which he nearly won. From 1970 to 1974 he was again Foreign Sec. and then regained the Lords with a life peerage.

DOUGLAS' LARDER (c. 1309). An incident in the life of Good Sir James Douglas. He stormed his own castle, flung the corpses of the English garrison into the great hall cellar, held a banquet above, fired the building and disappeared.

DOUGLAS LAWSUIT (1762-9). This *cause celebre* arose as follows. Lady Jane Douglas, the maltreated sister of the D. of Douglas (*see* DOUGLAS ("RED")-18), broke her engagement to the E. of Dalkeith in 1720, was then prevented from entering a French convent and in 1746 married a Col. John Stewart, but in secrecy to prevent the duke cutting off her allowance. She had twins in Paris in 1748 and informed the duke who disowned her. One of the twins, the English educated ARCHIBALD JAMES EDWARD (1748-1827) 1st Ld. DOUGLAS (1790) changed his name to Douglas and claimed the Douglas estates after the duke died in 1761. He was resisted by the heir presumptive, the D. of Hamilton, as either illegitimate or an impostor. The sensational proceedings in the Court of Session and the House of Lords ended in victory for the claimant, who settled down to the life of a country landowner in Forfarshire, of which he became Lord Lieut. and an M.P.

DOUGLAS, Margaret (The Fair Maid of Galloway). *See* JAMES II OF SCOTS-2,3.

DOUGLAS, Margaret (1515-78). *See* MARY Q. OF SCOTS.

DOUGLAS (MORTON). This distinct line of Douglas, descended from Sir Andrew (fl. 1259) a son of Sir Archibald (?1296-1333 *see* DOUGLAS ("BLACK")-2) was established with wide lands including Loch Leven, in Fife and on the Border, especially in Liddesdale and Eskdale, by 1340 and at Morton in Nithsdale and Dalkeith in Galloway by 1381. They were much married with legitimate and bastard relatives of Stewart kings. In particular **(1) James (?-1550) 3rd E. of MORTON** married KATHERINE, a bastard of James IV by Margaret Boyd, and had three children of whom **(2) Elizabeth,** married **(3) James Douglas (?-1581) 4th E. (1553)** a descendent of the 5th E. of Angus (*see* DOUGLAS ("RED")-4); he acquired the earldom by the enforced resignation of his father-in-law. In early life he was a farm overseer (for a relative) and then a soldier. His notorious drinking and wenching affected his reputation but not his abilities and he early showed a bias towards protestantism. In 1557 he signed the first reformers' band, but he refused to support them against the Queen regent, Mary of Guise, and consequently became a member of Mary Q. of Scots Council on her arrival and Lord Chancellor in Jan. 1563. He disliked Darnley, but mainly on family grounds favoured his marriage to the Queen. He had always been on good terms with Argyll, Moray and other committed protestants and hoped to maintain a middle position. The queen mistrusted him. In these circumstances the moves

planned by Mary and her advisers against Moray and Argyll, by destroying the protestant leadership would have made his balancing act impossible; he therefore supported the protestants. He nailed his colours to the mast by taking a leading part in Rizzio's murder, fled but returned by the mediation of Bothwell, who proposed Darnley's murder. Though not directly involved in the murder, he signed Mary and Bothwell's betrothal agreement, but when Bothwell carried her off he formed a confidential group of lords to oppose Bothwell's rise and in due course drove him from the Kingdom and put Mary into custody at Loch Leven (1568). It was at this time that he disclosed the existence of the Casket Letters, of which (if they were spurious) he must have been the chief forger. His object (to place Moray in the regency) was only briefly realised for Moray was assassinated and it became necessary to appoint the weaker Lennox. Morton was henceforth the real ruler and after Knox's death (1572) he became regent until overthrown in 1578. He was executed for his part in Darnley's murder. The title passed to the descendents of **(3),** of whom **(5) William (?-1606) 6th or 7th E.** was the owner of Loch Leven and a strong supporter of James, the 4th E. After many trials, he became Lieutenant for the South from 1594. His grandson **(6) William (1582-1650) 7th or 8th E.,** was Scots Lord Treasurer from 1630 to 1635. At the beginning of the Civil War he sold Dalkeith to raise money for the King and received a mortgage on Orkney and Shetland for three years in return.

DOUGLAS (QUEENSBURY). This branch of the Red Douglas received favours from James VI and I and the earldom of Queensberry was created when Charles I visited Scotland in 1633. **(1) William (1637-95) 3rd E. and 1st D. of QUEENSBURY (1684)** a Scots privy councillor, was Lord Justice Gen. from 1680 and also Scots Lord Treasurer from 1682 to 1686. He obstructed James II's ecclesiastical policy but became pres. of the Council in 1688. He was, however, abruptly dismissed at the instance of the newly R. Catholic E. of Perth (who had become James II's S-of-State) on allegations of maladministration. His son **(2) James (1662-1711) 2nd D. and 1st D. of DOVER (1708),** already a privy councillor in 1684, threw in his lot with William III in 1688 and became Lord Treasurer in 1693. William took his advice on Scottish affairs and sent him to Scotland as his Commissioner to the Estates, to frustrate the agitation caused by the failure of the Darien Scheme. He succeeded despite the opposition of Hamilton, his relative. He became Sec. of State for Scotland in 1702 when the first negotiations for legislative union began, but these broke down through English commercial intransigence and the Scots retaliated by admitting French wines (in wartime) and passing the Act anent Peace and War. The extremism of both sides made his position impossible and he resigned but was recalled in 1705 as Lord Privy Seal. In 1706, the new negotiations having proceeded more happily, he presided as Queen's Commissioner over the Estates which accepted the T. of Union. He acted as third Sec. of State from 1709, though Marlborough thought him a nonentity. His son **(3) Charles (1698-1778) 4th E. and 2nd D.,** married Lady Catherine Hyde (1720) and was Lord Justice-Gen. from 1763. His cousin **(4) William (1724-1810) "OLD Q" 4th D., 1st (British) Ld. DOUGLAS of AMESBURY (1786),** a dissolute friend of the P. of Wales, tried to develop horse racing as a science and left over £1M to his legatees. Being without legitimate offspring, his titles were dispersed among various members of the Scott family.

DOUGLAS REBELLION. See JAMES II OF SCOTS *passim*.

DOUGLAS, R. See TRANSPORT AND COMMUNICATIONS.

DOURO (Port) or DUERO (Sp) river along the Portuguese part of which lie the Port vineyards developed by British

18th cent. capital and exporting their products through the British factory house at the river port of Oporto. *See* WELLINGTON.

DOVER (Kent) (Lat = DUBRIS), the nearest haven and gap in the cliffs to France, has always been a cross-Channel port. It was the Roman terminal of Watling Street and they built a fort and lighthouse on the site of the castle. The latter was built or enlarged by successive rulers, while the people acted as navigators, pilots, merchants and pirates. They formed a prescriptive corporation owing (according to Domesday) the service of 20 ships for 15 days to the Crown in lieu of *sac* and *soc*. Harold had fortified the castle and Henry II built the keep in the 1180s. By then it was prosperous from the pilgrim traffic, for which the 13th cent. Hubert de Burgh built the Maison Dieu as a hospice. Henry VIII established a naval Crown victualling office. In the 19th cent. its prosperity was diversified by the fashion of seaside holidays and the exploitation of the nearby Kentish coalfield and it was again refortified. In World War I its large, navigationally difficult, artificial harbour was the main base of the Dover Patrol (qv). In World War II it was somewhat damaged by aerial and long-range artillery bombardment and its heavy guns took part in the action against the *Scharnhorst* and *Gneisenau*. After World War II its under-used harbour was developed for the expanding cross-Channel motor vehicle ferry and hovercraft traffic and in 1993 the Western Docks railway station was closed in response to the opening of the nearby Channel Tunnel. *See* CINQUE PORTS.

DOVER PATROL was established at the beginning of World War I to prevent enemy naval operations against the Channel, to aid the allied seaward flank in France and Belgium, to cover cross-Channel troop movements and to search neutrals. A keystone of allied war policy, it consisted of minefields combined with hundreds of anti-submarine drifters, minesweepers, light craft, monitors, submarines and other ships. It was commanded by Adm. Ballard (1914-5), Adm. Bacon (1915-7) and then by Adm. Keyes. Its most famous operation was the attack on Zeebrugge (Apr. 1918).

DOVER, secret Ts. of (1670). *See* CHARLES 11-13.

DOWDESWELL (1) William (1721-75) was M.P. from 1747 to 1775 and Ch. of the Exch. from 1765 to 1766, but refused office under Chatham and in 1767 carried a motion against the govt. for the reduction of the land tax. His son **(2) William (1761-1828),** an M.P. in 1792, was gov. of the Bahamas from 1797 to 1802, served under Lake at Bhurtpore and was C-in-C India from 1807 to 1810.

DOWDING, Air Chief Marshal Sir Hugh Tremenheere (1882-1970) 1st Ld. (1943) was from 1930 member of the Air Council responsible for research and development of all-metal monoplanes such as the *Hurricane* and *Spitfire,* introduced (inter alia) radar, the fighter control system and the air-cooled Browning machine gun. In 1936 he became C-in-C Fighter Command, his success in the B. of Britain being largely due to his foresight in his previous capacity. A man of great moral courage, he incurred the hostility of the politicians, and though he saved Britain in the earliest major crisis of World War II he was denied the recognition proper to his achievements.

DOWELLING MONEY. A mediaeval parochial levy on each dwelling.

DOWLAND, John (1563-1626), the greatest lutenist of his time, being unappreciated in England, became court lutenist to Christian IV of Denmark. His four volumes of compositions (1597-1613) were, however, a great success in England. He became one of Charles I's lutenists in the last year of his life.

DOWN, Co. DOWNPATRICK. St. Patrick began his mission to Ireland in this area in 432 and the famous monastic school at Bangor was established in the 6th cent. It was conquered by the de Courcis in the 12th cent. and colonised, but not officially planted under James I.

DOWNING (1) Sir George (?1623-84), second graduate at Harvard, was Cromwell's scoutmaster-gen. in Scotland, became M.P. for Edinburgh in 1654 and for Carlisle and Haddington in 1656. He led the movement to offer the Crown to Oliver in 1657 and then became ambassador at The Hague. After the Restoration he procured the arrest of three of the regicides and in 1665 his resolution in the Commons began the practice of appropriation of supply. M.P. for Morpeth from 1669 to 1670 he was again ambassador at The Hague in 1671, but was forced to leave in 1672 because of his quarrelsome temperament. His grandson **(2) Sir George (1684-1749)** the builder of Downing Street, London, was M.P. for Dunwich, Suffolk in 1710, 1713 and 1722 to 1749. He left an endowment in default of heirs to found a Cambridge College which, after much litigation, was founded in 1800.

DOWNING STREET, LONDON. No. 10 is the residence of the prime minister, No. 11 the Ch. of the Exch. The whole complex, which is connected with the Privy Council offices and the Treasury, was rebuilt between 1960 and 1968 at a cost of about £4M. *See* DOWNING.

DOWNS, THE. An anchorage 8 miles long from the North to the South Forelands (Kent) and 4 miles broad between the Kentish coast and the Goodwin Sands. It was safe in all weathers and, therefore, a gathering point for sailing traffic up-Channel and, from the Thames, the East Coast and the North Sea ports outwards to the Atlantic, the Mediterranean and the Far East. In the 18th and 19th cents. ships often congregated there in many hundreds awaiting convoy or revictualling at Deal and were, in wartime, despite the proximity of the English coast and naval patrols, targets for nocturnal privateers. Its importance declined with the advent of steam and the long 19th cent. naval peace.

DOYLE, Sir Arthur Conan (1859-1930) was an Edinburgh physician whose celebrated fictional detective SHERLOCK HOLMES appeared between 1887 and 1896. He was knighted for medical work in the Boer War. *See* DETECTIVE STORIES.

DOYLE (1) John (1797-1868) and his son **(2) Richard (1824-83),** of Irish origin, were caricaturists and humorous artists of a moderate character which superseded the extremism of Gillray and Rowlandson. Richard worked for *Punch* from 1843 to 1850 and designed its longest lasting cover.

DRAFTSMEN, PARLIAMENTARY, are highly qualified salaried lawyers who draft govt. bills, They are so few in number that govt. agreement to allow a private member's bill to be drafted by one is tantamount to support for the bill. When private amendments to govt. bills are accepted it is the normal practice for the minister concerned to undertake to amend at a later state so that the draftsmen can consider the wording. The pursuit of verbal unambiguity by modern draftsmen has produced a legislative jargon frequently unintelligible to those whom it may affect. This was not entirely the draftsmen's fault because they have to work at great speed.

DRAGOMAN (from Arab = interpreter) was originally a Christian diplomatic official at the Sublime Porte, employed because the Ottoman Turks objected to speaking infidel tongues. (*See* PHANARIOTS.) The word later meant any intermediary between Europeans and orientals.

DRAGONNADES. *See* CAMISARDS.

DRAGOONS, originally mounted infantry armed with a short musket (chaced with a dragon) were first raised by the French in 1600. Six English regiments of Dragoon Guards with carbines were raised by James II in 1685 against Monmouth's rebellion; a seventh in 1689 to aid William III against James. Their role was changed to that of heavy cavalry by Frederick the Great's tactics in the Seven Years' War (1756-63). 20th cent. amalgamations and mechanisation reduced the number to four by 1959 and still further by 1993.

DRAKE, Sir Francis (?1540-96) pirate and seaman of genius, was the only survivor of Hawkins' disaster at Nombre de Dios in 1567. He sailed annually against the Spanish Main from 1570 to 1573, burning Porto Bello in 1572 and Vera Cruz in 1573. After a period in Ireland under Essex, he set sail in the *Pelican,* renamed the *Golden Hind* en route, from Plymouth in 1577 on his famous **Circumnavigation.** After executing Thos. Doughty, one of his senior officers, on flimsy charges he passed the Strait of Magellan in 1578 and in 1579, his presence in the Pacific being a complete surprise to the Spaniards, sacked Valparaiso, took the fabulous Acapulco galleon, crossed the Pacific and Indian oceans and in 1580 touched at Sierra Leone. In 1581 he reached England. A part of the plunder went to the Queen who knighted him. In 1582 he was mayor of Plymouth and in 1584 M.P. for Bossiney. In 1585 he obtained letters of marque, destroyed Santiago and Vigo, captured San Domingo and Cartagena and in 1586 returned via Virginia, whose colonists he brought home. In 1587 he "singed the King of Spain's Beard" at Cadiz and cashiered his Vice-Adm. Wm. Burrough at the same time. He played an important and controversial role in the Armada Campaign in 1588 and in 1589 a vigorous part in Norris' expedition against the Spanish coast. In 1590 he established the Plymouth water supply. He died off Porto Bello during an unsuccessful expedition with Sir John Hawkins. *See* ELIZABETH 1-21 *et seq.*

DRAMA (1) Mimicry and impersonation are no doubt spontaneous. To do them for a purpose follows naturally and, in their earliest organised form, served religion or pious fraud. Town guilds (mysteries) early began to exhibit plays or tableaux, commonly mounted on moving floats, at festivals and there were Nativity plays in which many simple people took part. These were all edifying visible sermons. Some were even called Morality Plays.

(2) The Renaissance classical revival made the court and learned professions aware of plays for entertainment, but the gloomy atmosphere of religious and political terrorism during the latter years of Henry VIII and the reigns of Edward VI and Mary I was not encouraging and few plays were written before the accession of Elizabeth I.

(3) The great Queen would not "make windows into men's souls" and the ideas which had been flourishing within were allowed to burst out. Udall's *Ralph Roister Doister,* the earliest known comedy, was written under Mary I but published under Elizabeth. Norton and Sackville's *Gorboduc,* the first tragedy, was performed in the Inner Temple Hall in 1561; the farce *Gammer Gurton's Needle* at Christ's College, Cambridge in 1566. Plays were intended for select audiences which owned the building (designed for other purposes) in which they were performed by doubtless talented amateurs got together for the occasion.

(4) Then came the dramatic revolution. A professional company of actors under the E. of Leicester's patronage was formed in 1574. In 1576 one of its members, James Burbage (?-1597), originally a carpenter, built the first specialised and public playhouse, **The Theatre,** of wood in Shoreditch. With the machinery in place, playwrights came forward to work it and the Queen took an interest. The **Curtain** theatre was built nearby. There were court prose comedians like John Lyly (1554-1606) in the 1580s, the many productions of George Peele (1558-?97), himself an actor, the horrors of Kyd's *Spanish Tragedy* (1586) and the strong concentration and stylistic splendour of Christopher Marlowe (1564-93) who, between 1586 and 1592, wrote *Tamburlane the Great, Dr. Faustus, The Jew of Malta* and *Edward II.* Public interest quickened. Theatres were built in **Southwark** which attracted custom away from Shoreditch. The first of Shakespeare's public plays (*Henry VI, Part I*) was staged at the **Rose** in Southwark in 1592. *Venus and Adonis* made him famous in 1593, but as it happened he was left for a while with little competition by the contemporary deaths of Marlowe (1593) and Kyd (1594). Meanwhile Burbage opened a second theatre at Blackfriars opposite Southwark in 1596 and in 1598 his son **Richard** (1557-1619) moved The Theatre bodily to Southwark as the **Globe.**

(5) With 37 plays between 1592 and 1613, Shakespeare was versatile as well as prolific, but his contemporary reputation is quite uncertain and the public was voracious. There was plenty of room for others. Encouraged by court and royal interest, Ben Jonson, George Chapman, Thomas Dekker, Thomas Heywood, John Webster and Beaumont and Fletcher all wrote famous plays (still performed) varying from light and airy to the unrelievedly horrible.

(6) It is likely (but not demonstrable) that this tremendous momentum would have reached a natural exhaustion; but the religious and political events of the Civil War and Interregnum in fact stopped it. The godliness which the puritans sought to impose, being inefficient, was not total. Dancing, masquing and other frolics continued throughout at the Inns of Court but drama suffered because the puritans thought all actors immoral and suppressed them. In the joyful upsurge of the Restoration the actors returned and were given comedies to play. These were distinguished by wit, ingenuity or indecency, withheld since 1640. The strenuous or murderous politics of the later Stuarts and the wars of Louis XIV now provided enough serious consideration: actors provided the amusement. The Restoration *genre* did not run out until the death of Q. Anne (1714).

(7) There was now, as ever, a reaction, this time into sentimental unreality amid the relative peace and commercialism of the age of Walpole. It distantly resembled a return to the morality plays, with the unsubtle characters as symbols of immaculacy contrasting strongly with the prevailing well-mannered promiscuity and corruption. Sooner or later the public was bound to be bored. Then enormous events changed the landscape. The Wesleys launched Methodism in 1742. Wars broke out and continued with only short intervals until 1815. Revolutions, industrial and political, engulfed established ideas and institutions. Drama reacted suddenly to a more penetrating, though not necessarily serious or tragic, type. Oliver Goldsmith managed, against professional prejudice and opposition but with Dr. Johnson's support, to get *She Stoops to Conquer* staged in 1774 amid a storm of applause. This was immediately followed by Sheridan's *The Rivals* (1775) and *The Critic* (1779) which heralded a new flight of drama besides an interest in Shakespeare which had hitherto been less than close. Nicholas Rowe had written his first serious biography in 1709. To 18th cent. critics his genius was 'natural' (i.e. eccentric) because he wisely ignored the Three Unities of the classical, mostly French doctrinaires. By the turn of the 18th-19th cents. he was being proclaimed with honour, with especial stridency by Coleridge and Carlyle.

(8) It was not wholly fortunate that this new interest was overtaken by the Romantic Revival or reaction after the witty Rococo of Sheridan. To penetrate the carapace of post-war serious religion and serious business with serious Shakespeare, the actors had to shout. They also isolated the poet by declaiming the words as verse. The declamatory style of Victorian acting gave the drama a ceremonial tinge reflecting the new ceremonialism of the Church. The new mass public created by the rising birthrates of industrialism turned to the music halls for relief or ran to seed in melodrama which, now hilarious, was then taken solemnly.

(9) There was, however, a major disaster. New safety

legislation, by requiring facilities which many theatres could not provide, closed over 200 of them at the end of the 1860s. The connection between the stage and popular outlooks was severed. There was a tendency towards academicism in the study of literature in the universities which then catered for a very small minority of the population. Drama thus interested far fewer people than before, namely those who had been brought up to it and could afford the seats in a relatively small number of theatres. The new popularity began to recover (if at all) only with the arrival of the cinema in the 1920s and television in the 1950s and classical drama also gained immeasurably when actors reverted to the practice of speaking the lines as ordinary speech.

DRANG NACH OSTEN (Ger = Eastward pressure). The tendency of German policy to seek economic and political predominance *via* the Balkans, in Turkey and the Levant, or *via* Bohemia and Poland, in the Ukraine.

DRAPIERS LETTERS by Swift. *See* WOOD'S HALFPENCE.

DRAVIDIANS. Original dark-skinned inhabitants of the Deccan (India) who spread to the far south and Ceylon and also Baluchistan. There were over 70M of them in 1920. Their main languages are Tamil, Telugu, Malayalam and, in Baluchistan, Brahui. The Tamils have, since Indian independence, become a strong political force with their own state in the south (Tamil Nadu) and in N. Ceylon where their terrorists, called the Tamil Tigers, began to be active in 1970.

DREADNOUGHT H.M.S., the first all-big-gun, turbine driven, oil-fired battleship, was designed in 1905 and built in secrecy at Portsmouth in 1906. Her advent revolutionised naval armaments, changed the terms of the Anglo-German naval race and postponed the strategic effect of the Kiel Canal to 1914. *See* TENNYSON-DEYNCOURT.

DREAM OF THE ROOD. Ceolfrith, Abbot of Jarrow and Wearmouth, was in Rome when Pope Sergius I discovered a fragment of the True Cross. He returned in 701 and erected a great Celtic cross at Ruthwell (Dumfriess) upon which is inscribed this Old English poem. It describes a mystical experience in which the poet addresses the Cross (Rood) and meditates upon it and the Cross speaks to him of the Crucifixion and Resurrection in the familiar contemporary terms of loyalty between lord and man. The inscription is in runic characters. There is an expanded version in the Vercelli Book.

DRENG was a personally free man holding land by a measured obligation to plough, sow and harrow the demesne and do certain additional services such as keeping the lord's dog or horse, carting or taking messages. There was occasionally an obligation to fight for the King. The tenure of drengage was common in the north, especially in Durham, and survived vestigially into the 16th cent. Drengs were often castlemen.

DRESDEN, the beautiful capital of Saxony was, in a military sense, needlessly and atrociously devastated on 13-14th Feb. 1945 by the western air forces at the insistent demand of the Russians. About 150,000 people, mostly refugees from the Russians, perished. *See* also AUGUSTES THE STRONG; SAXONY.

DRILLING MACHINES. The first rock drill was patented in 1849; the major developments in their use arose from the driving of the Franco-Italian Mont Cenis tunnel in the 1850s and 1860s.

DROITWICH (Worcs.) has brine springs, which from early times were the point of origin of a widespread and important salt trade. It was a Saxon royal manor and was first chartered by K. John in 1215. The place was fully incorporated in 1554. It became a spa after 1830 when a cholera victim fell into a brine vat and recovered. The salt industry was moved to Stoke Prior in 1922.

DROGHEDA (Ir) is on the lowest ancient ford on the Boyne four miles from the Irish Channel. It had Augustinian and Dominican houses, a considerable salmon fishery, shipped quantities of grain to Liverpool and later had a linen industry. It suffered fearfully in the Cromwellian sack and massacre of 1649, from which it never fully recovered.

DROITS OF ADMIRALTY were the right to certain property found at sea or upon the shore. They were **(1)** *great fish;* **(2)** *deodands* viz: objects which had caused a death; **(3)** *wreck;* **(4)** *Flotsam* and **(5)** *Lagan,* i.e. goods found respectively afloat and on the sea bottom after a ship has sunk and **(6)** *Jetsam,* i.e. goods thrown overboard to lighten a ship in danger. They belonged to the crown unless granted to a lord of a manor such as Corfe, or a corporation such as Dunwich or Southwold. They could be valuable and sometimes led to prolonged disputes.

DROLE TELLER, a Cornish strolling minstrel.

DROLIS or DROLL-HUMOURS were performances designed to evade the Commonwealth ordinances of Sept. 1642 against plays. They were mostly extemporised and farcical shows in taverns or at fairs.

DROUGHTS are technically periods of more than a fortnight without rain, but in popular, more accurate estimation, a dry period needs longer to become a drought. There was no harvest in 1177 and on two mediaeval occasions the Thames was crossed on foot. There were severe intermittent droughts in England between 1715 and 1750. The 1854 drought caused epidemics which prepared the public mind for the Crimean medical scandals. There were also severe droughts in 1921, 1933 and 1934, the two latter being accompanied by great heath and forest fires. 1947, 1992 and 1995 were also drought years.

DROVE. *See* HIGHWAY.

DRUIDS were highly trained Celtic priests, learned men bards, sorcerers, diviners and physicians. They are known almost wholly from their Roman and later Christian enemies. They conducted their rites in the alarming depths of sacred oak groves, revered the mistletoe and practised occasional human sacrifice. Their powerful influence among the Celtic tribes was a particular object of misunderstanding and animosity by the Romans who elected rather than trained their priests. The Gaulish tribes all sent their young aspirants for training to Britain where their H.Q. was Mona (Anglesey). This religious traffic between Gaul and Britain was politically disturbing and provided the Romans with an important motive for intervention in Britain. They eventually (in AD. 61) stormed Mona, massacred all the druids they could catch and felled the groves. Thenceforth they survived as a recognisable order only in Ireland where, in due course, they incurred Christian hostility, evidenced in the many stories of encounters between them and Irish saints. The Gaelic clan bards and *sennachies* represent an attenuated descent from the druidical tradition. Merlin, the shadowy benevolent wizard at the court of the Romano-British Arthur, credited with millenial life, was doubtless a druidical survivor.

DRUMCEAT AGREEMENT. *See* DALRIADA-3.

DRUMCLOG, Fight at (June 1679). During the Scots covenanters' rising after the murder of Abp. Sharp, an armed conventicle beat off Graham of Claverhouse with considerable loss.

DRUM HEAD COURT MARTIAL. One held at short notice by regimental officers in the field, using the big drum as a table. The acquittal rate was not high.

DRUMMOND. Stirlingshire family descended from a Hungarian companion of Edgar the Atheling, rose to high prominence through marriages and other relationships, between its women and the Scots royal family. **(1) Margaret** was David II's mistress and, from 1363, his second wife. **(2) Annabella (?1350-1402)** married John Stewart of Kyle, later Robert III in 1367. **(3) John (?-1519) 1st Ld. DRUMMOND (1488),** a friend of James (later James IV), was commissioned to negotiate a marriage between James and Anne de la Pole in 1484; he became one of the King's principal councillors at his accession in 1488. He put down the Lennox rebellion in 1489. His daughter **(4) Margaret (?1472-1501)** was James' much loved mistress and probable wife. She and her two sisters were poisoned together possibly by Lord Fleming. Her father was opposed to the Albany regency at James' death and was imprisoned for a year (1515-6), but subsequently supported the regency against the Anglophil policies and intrigues of the dowager Q. Margaret Tudor. His descendent **(5) William (1585-1649)** was a distinguished poet and scientist who protested against the Solemn League and Covenant and is said to have died on hearing of Charles I's death. **(6) William (?1617-88) 1st Vist. STRATHALLAN (1686)** commanded a royalist brigade at Worcester in 1651, escaped to Russia and became gov. of Smolensk. He returned to Scotland in 1666 and became maj-gen. of the forces there. He represented Perthshire in Scots parliaments between 1669 and 1686 and became lieut-gen. of the forces in 1685. Despite his elevation in 1686 he disapproved of James II policies. **(7) James (1648-1716) 4th E. of PERTH** and titular **Duke (1716)** was a member of Lauderdale's Scots privy council from 1678 but later supported Hamilton. He became Lord Justice-Gen. in 1682 and Lord Chancellor in 1684. He was a partner with Penn in the settlement of New Jersey. Properly suspected of Jacobitism, he was arrested in 1689 and allowed to leave the country in 1693. His brother **(8) John (1649-1714) 1st E. of MELFORT (1686)** was Sec. of State for Scotland from 1684 until the revolution when, with his brother, he adhered to James II. He was suspected of treason to Jacobitism at the end of his life. The son of **(6)**, **(9) James (1675-1720). 5th E.**, was imprisoned as a Jacobite in 1708, commanded Jacobite cavalry in 1715, was attainted and died in Paris. His son **(1) James (1713-47), 6th E.**, commanded the Jacobite left wing at Culloden. His brother **(11) John** (?-1747) titular **4th D. of PERTH**, was mainly responsible for the Jacobite victory at Falkirk in 1745. A grandson of **(6)**, **(12) William (1690-1747) 4th Vist. STRATHALLAN,** fought for the Jacobites in 1715, was amnestied but was killed as a Jacobite commander at Culloden. A descendent of the Perth and Strathallan families **(13) James Eric (1876-1951), 16th E.**, was private sec. to a series of British statesmen including Vist. Grey of Fallodon (1915-6) and A. J. Balfour (1916-8). As a result of his work at the Peace Conference he became the first sec. gen. of the League of Nations in 1919 and held the post until 1933. From 1933 to 1939 he was ambassador in Rome.

DRUMMOND, Edward (1792-1843) was private sec. to Ripon, Canning, Wellington and Peel. He was assassinated in mistake for Peel by a mad Scotsman called Macnaghten. In Macnaghten's trial the court was faced with the need to define madness for purposes of criminal liability and concluded that a person could not be held guilty if he was under delusions involving factual errors such as would prevent him from knowing what he was doing or that what he was actually doing was wrong.

DRUNKEN PARLIAMENT 1661 (Scots.) met in the full flush of the Restoration. So-called by its presbyterian detractors, it repealed the proceedings of the Scots parliaments since 1639 and voted an annual subsidy so large (£40,000) that the govt. managed virtually without parliaments until 1685.

DRURY LANE (London) was named after the Drury family's 15th cent. house, Drury Place. The famous theatre there was built by Thomas Killigrew and opened in 1663. It was burned down in 1672. The second building, designed by Wren, was replaced by a third in 1794. This was burned down in 1809 and Holland's present structure (with its back to the lane) was opened

in 1814. Its auditorium was rebuilt in 1921. In 1939 it became the H.Q. of E.N.S.A. for World War II.

DRUSES. See CALIPHATE-8.

DRYBURGH (Berwicks) a rich Premonstratensian abbey founded by Hugo de Morville in about 1150. English troops burnt it in 1322. Robert the Bruce restored it but the English sacked it again in 1385. It was ruined in 1544-5 but parts have survived sufficiently to house the tombs of Sir Walter Scott and the 1st E. Haig.

DRYDEN (1) John (1631-1700) was clerk to his cousin Sir Gilbert Pickering, Cromwell's Chamberlain, and wrote a death-panegyric (*Heroic Stanzas*) on the Protector. He also celebrated the Restoration (*Panegyric* 1660, *Astrea Redux* 1661) and in 1667 published *Annus Mirabilis*. In 1670 he became Poet Laureate. Technically the most accomplished of the Silver Age poets, his plays and poems mostly had a covert or explicit political purpose; in 1679 he was beaten up by thugs instigated by Rochester. His most famous political satire *Absalom and Achitophel* was published in 1681. It was mainly an attack on Shaftesbury and he followed it up in 1682 with *The Medal* and with *MacFlecknoe*, an attack on Shaftesbury's supporter Shadwell. He also wrote a defence of Anglicanism in *Religio Laici* and was awarded a collectorship of customs by Charles II, whom he praised in two operas in 1685. The accession of the R. Catholic James II coincided with his conversion to R. Catholicism. James employed him as a pamphleteer. When William III expelled James, Dryden lost his laureateship but he remained a well-known literary but not political figure in London until his death. Of his sons **(2) Charles (1666-1704)** was a papal chamberlain, **(3) Sir Erasmus Henry (1669-1710)** was subprior of a convent at Bornheim from 1697 to 1700 and thereafter a R. Catholic missioner in Northants.

DUALA or DOUALA. See CAMEROONS.

DUAL ALLIANCE (Oct. 1879) negotiated by Bismarck, between Germany and Austro-Hungary. Each agreed to support the other if attacked by Russia (*see* TRIPLE ALLIANCE). The term is sometimes confusingly used for the Franco-Russian alliance of 1894.

DUAL MONARCHY. Austro-Hungary between 1867 and 1918.

DUB. See SCOTS OR ALBAN KINGS, EARLY.

DUBLIN, City and County (*see* VIKINGS). St. Patrick is reputed (not unnaturally) to have preached there, but Dublin was probably founded on the S. side of the Liffey by Ostmen who were permanently established by 825 as sailors, traders and pirates. The King of Dublin was usually the leading Ostman chief and even after Brian Boru's victory at Clontarf (in the modern suburbs) in 1014, the town remained largely Scandinavian. It still had a Danish govt. when the Normans took it in 1170. The Danes then crossed the Liffey and settled Oxmanstown ('Ostmen's town') and after Richard Strongbow took it in 1170-1, Henry II chartered it and gave it to Bristol (which had long traded with Ireland) as a colony with Bristol customs. St. Patrick's was begun outside the walls in 1190. It was architecturally and organisationally modelled on Salisbury and eventually rivalled and virtually superseded the existing Augustinian cathedral of Holy Trinity.

Meanwhile the place attracted colonists from other places in England besides Bristol and from Scotland, Man and France. This cosmopolitan expansion created friction with the Irish who attacked and inflicted heavy casualties on the colony in 1209. The Anglo-Normans then started to build the castle, which was completed and became the seat of English govt. with an Exchequer in 1220. It remained the viceregal seat until 1920. Parliaments often met in Dublin and after 1660 invariably did so. The city was valiantly and successfully defended against the Bruces, who besieged it in 1315 and Richard II held magnificent court there in 1394.

The surrounding county formed the major part of the mediaeval Pale, but its southern boundary was not defined until 1606 when Co. Wicklow was shired. The gradual pacification of the tribes created prosperity in the city, whose population rose to 68,000 by 1688. In the 18th cent, especially under the inspiration of the influential ROYAL. DUBLIN SOCIETY (founded in 1750) much of the city was developed with great architectural elegance. By 1798 the population was nearly 170,000. Despite the union of 1800 the city continued to expand steadily and this process continued after independence. In 1970 the population was about 500,000.

DUBNOVELLAUNUS. *See* BRITAIN BEFORE THE ROMAN CONQUEST-2.

DUCAT (*Ducatus* = Duchy). Silver ducats (worth about 3s. 6d.) were first struck by Roger II of Sicily, *Duke* of Apulia in 1140. Gold ducats (worth about 9s.) were first struck by the Venetian *Doge* Giovanni Dandolo in 1284. The word 'ducatus' appeared in the inscription on the latter and the wide extent of Venetian trade popularised the coins and their name.

DUCKING STOOL. An armchair on the end of a pivoted see-saw beam beside a pond. A delinquent was tied into it and immersed amid the plaudits of the villagers. It was used against shrews, scolds, sometimes quarrelling couples and in some districts dishonest tradespeople, especially bakers and brewers. Apparently a post-Reformation invention, the last recorded case was that of a Sarah Leake at Leominster (Salop) in 1817, but fortunately for her the pond was empty.

DUCKWORTH, Sir John Thomas (1748-1817) 1st Bart. (1813), as R-Adm. took possession of the Danish and Swedish W. Indies in 1801 and was C-in-C at Jamaica from 1803 to 1805. In 1806 he defeated a French squadron off San Domingo. In 1807 a squadron under his command penetrated the Dardanelles, anchored off Constantinople and compelled the Sublime Porte to observe neutrality in the French War. He was Gov. of Newfoundland from 1810 until 1813 when he retired.

DUDLEY or SUTTON. North country baronial family. **(1) John (?1401-87)** was Lieut. of Ireland from 1428 to 1430 and employed on various diplomatic missions. The Yorkists captured him at the B. of St. Albans (1455) and he then changed sides. His son **(2) William (?-1483)** was dean of Windsor from 1473 and Bp. of Durham from 1476.

DUDLEY (1) Edmund (?1462-1510) originally a lawyer and adviser to Henry VII, was associated with Empson in his financial expedients and attracted Empson's unpopularity, particularly in the King's use of large fines, for political as well as financial ends. They also almost trebled the income from wards and royal estates. Dudley was Speaker of the Commons in 1504. He was arrested after Henry VIII's accession and in prison wrote *The Tree of the Commonwealth*, an exposure of administrative absolutism. He was executed on trumped up charges of constructive treason. Of his sons **(2) Sir Andrew (?-1559),** admiral of the north in 1547 and Keeper of Westminster Palace in 1553, supported Lady Jane Grey, his nephew's wife, but though condemned was released from prison in 1555. For his brother **(3) John (1502-53) Vist. LISLE (1542), E. of WARWICK (1547), D. of NORTHUMBERLAND (1551)** *see separate entry and* EDWARD VI AND MARY I. Of his six sons **(4) Ambrose (?1528-90) E. of WARWICK (1561),** also a pardoned supporter of Lady Jane Grey, was master of the ordnance from 1560 and was involved in the attempt (1562) to succour the Huguenots of Le Havre, where he was ultimately besieged and captured (1563). He was a member of the council from 1573 and of the court which tried Mary, Q. of Scots in 1586. For his unremarkable brother **(5) Guilford (?-1554),** who married Lady Jane Grey in 1553, *see* EDWARD VI, MARY I. His brother **(6) Robert (?1532-88) E. of LEICESTER (1564)** married

Amy Robsart in 1550, was M.P. for Norfolk and proclaimed Lady Jane Grey Queen at Kings Lynn in 1553 but was pardoned. He, with other Dudleys, took part in the fighting at St. Quentin in 1557 but he had made the acquaintance of the P. Elizabeth and became a privy councillor on her accession. (For the mutual attraction between him and the Queen and the death of Amy *see* ELIZABETH I-7.) Ambitious, but without real ability, he was disliked as an upstart by the nobles and by Cecil. The Queen honoured him with dignities and kept him at bay but he was not above encouraging the conspiracy against Cecil before the Northern Rebellion (1569) or of betraying it when it seemed unlikely to advantage him. In 1573 he secretly married Lady Sheffield and after her death he married in 1578 Lettice Knollys, the newly widowed countess of Essex. His unpopularity is attested by the groundless but persistent rumours that he had poisoned the husbands of both ladies. Meanwhile he had drifted into the anti-Spanish and pro-Dutch lobby and by 1581 was in correspondence with the Prince of Orange. The formation of an Association to defend the Queen's life, which he proposed in 1584, therefore suited him since it helped to popularise feeling hostile to Spain and Romanism and advertised him as the Queen's national champion. Such an organisation was capable of being dangerous and so she put him in charge, which he could hardly refuse, of the expedition to the Netherlands which left in Dec. 1585. He began, in flat disobedience to his instructions, by accepting the governorship of the Netherlands. He allowed widespread corruption among the officers, misdirected the campaign funds and quarrelled with his best commanders while the ill supplied troops died in hundreds of malaria. Subordinate commanders took Axel and Doesburg and stopped the Spaniards at Zutphen without his help. In Nov. 1586 he returned and was involved in the proceedings against Mary Q. of Scots, who was executed in Feb. 1587. In May 1587 he was despatched with reinforcements to secure a truce pending negotiations with Spain. This second expedition was no better than the first: the Dutch would have nothing of peace and an attempt with P. Maurice of Nassau to relieve Sluys failed for lack of co-operation. He was recalled in Nov. when a major Spanish attempt on England was already certain. He was now in poor health and though put in command of the troops at Tilbury in the Armada crisis, died shortly afterwards. His bastard **(7) Robert (1574-1649) D. of NORTHUMBERLAND and E. of WARWICK** by Holy Roman Patent (1620) explored Guiana in 1594, fought at Cadiz in 1596 and after repudiating his wife in 1605 settled with his mistress, Elizabeth Southwell, at Florence and entered the service of the Grand Duke Cosimo II. He drained the marshes behind Leghorn and built the port, and he commanded against the Barbary pirates. In 1645-6 he published his *Arcano del Mare*, which contains the first collection of charts on Mercator's projection, details of all known navigational instruments and shipwrights practices and a plan for a newly organised fighting navy.

DUDLEY, John (?1502-1553) Vist. LISLE (1542) E. of WARWICK (1547), D. of NORTHUMBERLAND (1551) (1) became deputy-gov. of Calais in 1538 and in 1542 warden-gen. of the Scottish Marches as well as High Admiral. In 1543 he was sworn of the council and in 1544 took a leading role in the capture of Boulogne of which he was gov. from 1544 to 1546. **(2)** (*See* SEYMOUR, EDWARD ?1506-52.) **(3)** At Edward VI's accession, Lisle, as another soldier with Hertford, held the greatest influence and when Hertford, as D of Somerset, became Protector, Lisle's importance in the council was emphasised by his promotion to the semi-royal earldom of Warwick. Ambitious and greedy, he had a political sense which Somerset lacked and, while the Protector was distracted by Scottish campaigns, foreign policy difficulties and short finance, Warwick quietly went about creating an interest and a party in the council and administration and ingratiating himself with the King. The first blow at the Protector's power was the execution, by the King's leave, of Thomas, the Protector's brother (Feb. 1549) without trial at the council's instance. **(4)** Warwick's party comprised the laymen who had partly despoiled the church and wanted more; and the doctrinal reformers behind whose arguments that spoliation might be furthered. They had no regard for the economic or social consequences and treated Somerset's sympathy for the victims as a nuisance. Moreover, their interest in property overlooked the claims of trade. The rebellions of 1549 which Warwick and his supporters put down enfeebled the Protector's authority and enhanced theirs'. They were able to depose him (Oct. 1549) with the acquiescence or support of some R. Catholics; but their position could not be maintained if the country was at war. They hastily withdrew from Scotland and surrendered Boulogne (Mar. 1550). Since their policy naturally involved the destruction of the P. Mary's right to the throne, they had to abandon the alliance with Mary's relative, the emperor, and rely upon France, yet France had designs not only on Calais but on the British Is. Scotland under Mary of Guise had a French regent supported by French troops and there were French intrigues in Ireland. Thus while Warwick, now become D. of Northumberland, relied upon the country's ancient enemies, the attack on the church and its property went forward. Reforming bishops were trying to raise the sometimes appallingly poor standards of their clergy while they and the govt. attacked ceremonies and images. Iconoclasm and simple looting of churches were often indistinguishable. Meanwhile Warwick and his friends helped themselves and not only to church lands. Royal property was used to reward past service to the state. In these circumstances the Commons refused to grant more than a minimum of taxation, well knowing where the money would probably go, and the govt., pressed for cash, reduced or abandoned garrisons and became ever more dependent upon French goodwill. In July 1551 the King's betrothal to Mary, Q. of Scots, was renounced and he was instead engaged to Elizabeth of France (T. of Angers); in Oct. (when Warwick became D. of Northumberland) Mary of Guise was received in state on a journey from France to Scotland, Somerset having been rearrested beforehand. In Jan. 1552 he was dead. **(5)** The alliance with R. Catholic France was accompanied by a shift towards the more extreme protestantism. The period after the T. of Angers was occupied with establishing (under penalties) a new prayer book, passed by parliament three months after Somerset's execution; and the Forty-Two Articles were then prepared under royal authority only. By 1553 there were danger signs. The govt. was unpopular and the King in even poorer health. The religious and political dispensation had no hope of survival without a speedy change in the succession. Northumberland decided to try and supersede the Tudors by the Dudleys. To this end the dying King was induced to devise the crown to Jane, granddaughter to Henry VIII's sister Mary and of Henry Grey, D. of Suffolk. Jane was married to Northumberland's son, Lord Guilford Dudley, and other relatives of his were married to other possible claimants to the throne. **(6)** Edward VI died in July 1553. Two days before, his sister Mary left Hunsdon for Howard country. He proclaimed Jane Queen but she (or rather he) was received without enthusiasm. He then set out against Mary: she was gathering adherents at Framlingham while he lost his on his journey to Cambridge. In a fortnight his venture had collapsed; he was arrested and executed.

DUDLEY. American family. **(1) Thomas (1576-1653)** sailed for Massachusetts in 1630; was Gov. Winthrop's deputy and later four times Gov. He was one of the founders of Harvard College. His son **(2) Joseph (1647-1720)** graduated at Harvard and became the colony's agent at the Court of St. James where, contrary to his instructions but much in his own interest, he secured the replacement of the colony's charter with a new one. He became Gov. in 1702 and held the post in growing unpopularity until 1715.

DUDLEY, Dud (1599-1684) foreran Abraham Darby in smelting iron, using coal in a blast furnace.

DUELLING. A gentleman's courage was part of his honour and he had to be prepared to defend it with his life. If it were insulted (e.g. by high words, a slap in the face or the seduction of his wife) he challenged his opponent. This was called *demanding satisfaction* and might at once lead to a fight. Alternatively if the demandant were a powerful nobleman, he might send a gang to murder his opponent in a *killing affray*. Duelling was always an offence and death in a duel, murder, but public opinion tolerated regulated duels, which developed under the late Stuarts, because they were better than killing affrays. The rules were very strict. The challenger nominated one or more seconds. A second now visited the defender to demand the satisfaction. If he refused it he nominated his own second and chose the weapons. The seconds arranged the place (usually secluded) and time (usually early when nobody was about). This was called *arranging a walk in the country*. The principals and seconds met as arranged. The seconds made a last attempt at reconciliation. If this failed the rivals were carefully placed. A second gave a signal by dropping a handkerchief and the duel began. Sometimes, but not often, the seconds fought too. As soon as blood was drawn they stopped the fight and persuaded the principals to declare that honour was satisfied. The usual weapons were swords (often lethal) or pistols (which usually missed). There were habitual bullies who provoked duels for the fun of killing. In 1712 Lord Mohun (a bully) fought the D. of Hamilton in which both died. The younger Pitt and Tierney fought in 1798; Canning and Castlereagh in 1809; the D. of Wellington and the E. of Winchilsea in 1829. In the last, in 1840, the E. of Cardigan wounded a Capt. Tucket and was acquitted on a very technical point by the House of Lords.

DUFF. Ancient northern Scottish family and **Es. of FIFE. James (1729-1809) Ld. DUFF (1790),** M.P. from 1754 to 1790, an enlightened landowner, reorganised much of Banffshire farming methods and greatly improved the strains of Highland and Angus cattle.

DUFFERIN AND AVA. *See* HAMILTON TEMPLE BLACKWOOD.

DUGDALE (1) Sir William (1605-86) published *Monasticon Anglicanum* Vol. I (1655), Vol. 11(1661), Vol. III (1673). *Origines Juridiciales* (1666), the *Baronage of England* between 1675 and 1676 and became Garter King-at-Arms in 1677. His son **(2) Sir John (1628-1700)** continued his father's researches and became Norroy King-at-Arms in 1686.

DUGUAY-TROUIN, René (1673-1736) Baron (1709), a privateer of St. Malo, took many small English and Dutch prizes between 1689 and 1694 when he was captured. He got a young woman to help him escape from Plymouth. In 1695 he took the *Nonesuch* and was commissioned into the French navy. As a piratical commander of small squadrons he raided the Dutch whalers at Spitzbergen in 1703, the Portuguese *flota* in 1706, an English convoy off the Lizard in 1707 and held Rio de Janeiro to ransom in 1711. These profitable ventures confirmed French naval policy makers in the erroneous doctrine that naval war could be waged successfully without dominating the sea.

DUKE (Lat = *dux* = general). The first English duke was the Black Prince, made D. of Cornwall in 1337. The first in Scotland was Robert II's son, made D. of Albany in 1398. Mostly restricted to royalty or descendents of royalty, the British title is still rare; in 1995 there were only 29.

DUKE, Henry Edward (1855-1939) 1st Ld. MERRIVALE

(1925), a journalist, was called to the bar and by 1899 was a Q.C. He was unionist M.P. for Plymouth from 1900 to 1906 and for Exeter from 1910. He was a conciliatory Chief Sec. for Ireland, after Birrell and the Dublin rising, from 1916 to 1918 when he became a Lord Justice of Appeal. From 1919 to 1933 he was Pres. of the Probate, Divorce and Admiralty Div. of the High Court.

DUKERIES (Notts.). This district contained the estates of several dukes, Welbeck (Portland), Clumber (Newcastle), Worksop (Norfolk), Thoresby (Kingston) as well as the residences of other noblemen.

DULEEP SINGH. See SIKHS-4,5.

DULLES (1) John Foster (1888-1959), a lawyer, served with the U.S. Peace Mission in 1919 and was a delegate to the San Francisco Conference in June 1945. He inspired and probably did not foresee the consequences of the main provisions of the Japanese Peace T. of 1953. He was Sec. of State under Pres. Eisenhower from 1953 to 1959 and was mainly responsible for the policy of containing Russian aggression by alliances. His brother **(2) Allen (1893-1969)** was director of the U.S. Central Intelligence Agency (C.I.A.) from 1953 to 1961 when its conduct raised international suspicions that it was the real power in U.S. diplomacy. He was forced to resign after the failure of the Bay of Pigs invasion of Cuba, as much to allay these suspicions as to atone for the failure.

DUMA **(Russ = Assembly).** The Russian pre-revolutionary parliamentary assembly. Its powers and franchises were restricted but it had influence. Four Dumas were elected: First in 1906; second in 1907; third 1907 to 1912; fourth 1912 to 1917.

DUMBARTON, DUMBREATAIN (= British Fort) or ALCLUITH (= Clyde Hill) is said to have had a Roman naval station. The great hill fortress, the centre of Strathclyde, was captured from the Britons by the Picts in 736 and from them by the Ostmen in 870. Later it became the capital of the Es. of Lennox who ceded it to the crown in 1222. It then became a royal burgh, but was disputed between the English and the Scots until the English were finally driven out. In the 1560s it was a R. Catholic centre and only stormed in 1571. James VI later confirmed its privileges including the levy of shipping tolls on the Clyde. These were transferred to Glasgow in 1700. From 1777 until 1847 there was a glass staple and the first steam navigation company was set up there in 1815 by which time shipbuilding was the main industry.

DUMBARTON, E. of. See DOUGLAS ("RED")-13.

DUMBARTON OAKS CONFERENCE (1944) was a meeting of British, U.S., Russian and (Kuomintang) Chinese experts to draft proposals for the world security organisation which eventually took shape as U.N.O. As the Russians would not meet the Chinese, the first sessions (Aug-Sept.) were held without the Chinese and the second (Sept-Oct.) without the Russians. It crystallised two problems, viz: the Veto difficulties and a Russian demand that all the 16 republics of the U.S.S.R. should have separate membership. See UNITED NATIONS ORRGANISATION.

DUM-DUM (W. Bengal). The British cantonment and arsenal was established in 1783 and it was the H.Q. of the Bengal artillery until 1853. The expanding bullet was invented there in 1897.

DUMFRIES-SHIRE (Scot.). This area (or STEWARTRY) was occupied by the SELGOVAE under the Romans, who constructed forts and roads. It was later conquered by Irish Scots and later still occupied by the Saxons. It retained Celtic customs, however, well into the 12th cent. The town was chartered by William the Lion before 1214 but the area was divided; the Bruces, Lds. of Annandale, were supported by the countryside, the burgh favoured the Balliols and Comyns. The burgh's attempts to engross the trade, as well as the local feuds, explain its sufferings not only by Douglas and Bruce raiding, but by constant attacks from across the border. Evidently the border was,

however, an important source of prosperity, for the town voted against union in 1706 and rioted against it in 1707, although it refused to support either Jacobite rising. Clan warfare continued sporadically until the middle of the 18th cent.

DUMNONII. See DEVON.

DU MOURIEZ, Charles Francois du Périer (1739-1823), a French regular officer, became a Jacobin in 1790, though a royalist at heart and, as foreign minister, was responsible for the declaration of war in Mar. 1792. In Sept. he drove back the Prussians at VALMY and in Nov. the Austrians at JEMAPPES. In Mar. 1793 he was defeated at NEERWINDEN and then conspired with the Austrians to effect a royalist *coup d'état*. This failed and he fled first to Austrian protection and then to England. In 1808 he was in Spain advising Spanish guerrillas. He died in England.

DUMPING (1) The sale of goods below the market price or even below the cost of production in order to destroy established businesses which will bankrupt themselves by underbidding. **(2)** The export of goods similarly underpriced in order to destroy by the same means the businesses in the markets of the importing country. **(1)** is a fairly common practice which relies upon the likelihood that the customers do not realise that once the trade rivals have been bankrupted they will have to pay more. **(2)** is sometimes a political rather than an economic tactic, particularly by communist countries, but can be defeated by special customs' duties levied by the govt. of the importing country. These are called anti-dumping duties.

DUM SOLA ET CASTA **(Lat = while single and chaste).** A condition in a marriage settlement or maintenance order that the widow or ex-wife should be paid an income only so long as she remained unmarried or uninvolved.

DÚN (Celt = fort). An element in place names such as Dunbar, Dumbarton and London.

DUNBAR (E. Lothian). The castle was an important barrier to military advances on Edinburgh from the south from 856 when it was probably begun, until it was slighted by Moray in 1568.

DUNBAR, Lds. and Es. of, were descended from the Northumbrian E. Gospatric. The 5th of these earls married Ada, a bastard of William the Lion. Their descendent **(1) Patrick, 8th E.** was thus a lesser Competitor for the Scots throne at the death of Alexander III. Dunbar, controlling the coastal pass from Berwick to Edinburgh, was an important military position reinforcing the Scottish East March. Patrick became the first **E. of THE MARCH.** The family's attitude to Anglo-Scots policies was often equivocal. In particular **(2) Patrick (1285-1369), 2nd E.,** professed English allegiance and sheltered Edward II after Bannockburn (1314) but changed sides to Robert I and David II, one of whose armies he commanded at Dupplin Moor (1332) and he defended Berwick against Edward III. In 1333, after the B. of Halidon Hill, he transferred his support to Edward Balliol. From 1334 he was a loyal Scottish nationalist because of Balliol's cession of the southern shires to England and, with Douglas of Liddesdale and Moray of Bothwell, killed Atholl, Balliol's lieutenant, in Culblean. In 1338 Patrick's wife "Black Agnes", spiritedly held Dunbar against the E. of Salisbury. This Patrick resigned the earldoms to his son **(3) George (?-c. 1420)** whose *d.* **(4) Elizabeth** married the D. of Rothesay, presumptive heir to the throne, but after consummation he repudiated her, married Mary Douglas bigamously, repudiated her too and was murdered at Falkland by the regent Albany and the young E. of Douglas. As a result George of the March defected to England (1400) where he became a favourite of Henry IV. An abortive English invasion followed, but in 1401 George, with the E. of Northumberland and Henry Percy, helped to defeat a Scots counter-invasion at Homildon Hill. Nevertheless he began to acquire the lands of his English neighbours the Percys, and when the latter rebelled in England in 1403, George urged Henry IV to strike quickly and protected his person at the subsequent B. of Shrewsbury. Here Henry Percy was killed and George did well out of the consequent confiscations. The Scots King, however, forfeited Dunbar and Annandale and gave them to the Douglas, who kept Annandale when George was rehabilitated in 1408. In 1434, however, the Scottish parliament confirmed the forfeiture so as to exclude his son.

DUNBAR, William (?1460-1530). Scottish diplomat and poet, accompanied the embassy to negotiate the marriage between James IV and Margaret Tudor. He wrote the *Thrissill and the Rois* as a political allegory on it and many other poems satirical, elegiac and allegorical including the *Lament for the Makars* (= Poets) and *In Honour of the City of London*.

DUNBLANE (W. Perthshire), an ancient bishopric, around which a small town grew up with a wool market and cloth industry. Its mediaeval importance and resources justified the rebuilding of the cathedral in the 13th cent. and it was often used as a political meeting place. With the growth of Glasgow and Edinburgh, its importance declined and the Reformation ended its function as a religious centre.

DUNBOYNE. *See* BUTLER.

DUNCAN I (1034-40). *See* SCOTS AND ALBAN KINGS, EARLY-16.

DUNCAN II (r. 1094). *See* SCOTS AND ALBAN KINGS, EARLY-21.

DUNCAN, Sir Patrick (1870-1943), classical scholar, entered the S. African Inland Revenue Dept. under Milner in 1894, rose rapidly and became Transvaal Colonial Treas. in 1901, Colonial Sec. in 1903 and Lieut-Gov. in 1906. He was one of a small group who drafted the S. African constitution of 1907 as for a unitary state preferring, despite his own leanings, to keep the lawyers out of politics. He hated racialism and held that the black population should share fairly in the benefits of European development. He practised at the bar from 1908 but became a S. African M.P. as well. He was Smuts' Min. of the Interior, Health and Education from 1921 to 1924 and, after Smuts, he was the most prominent opposition figure from 1924 to 1933. He then became Min. of Mines in the Hertzog coalition. This post was vital in the economy and in relation to the welfare of the vast numbers of blacks employed in the industry. In 1937 he became Gov-Gen. This turned out to be a key position because when Hertzog was defeated over S. African neutrality in World War II on 4 Sept. 1939, he was able to refuse a dissolution, called Smuts to form a govt. and so ensured that S. Africa would be committed against the racialist enemy. He probably did not foresee the lengths to which the nationalists would eventually go to manipulate the constitution of 1907 against his principles after he died in office.

DUNCAN, Adam (1731-1804) 1st Vist. DUNCAN of CAMPERDOWN (1797) was C-in-C North Sea from 1795 to 1801. *See* CAMPERDOWN.

DUNCAN, Henry (1774-1846) Minister at Rothwell (Dumfries) from 1798 to 1846, founded the first Savings Bank in the U.K. at Rothwell in 1810. It was probably based on an Austrian model.

DUNCES' or UNLEARNED PARLIAMENT was the Coventry parliament of 1404; allegedly so-called because there were no lawyers in the Commons, it was criticised by grandees because the Commons financial proposals included resumption of crown grants made since 1366, and their enactments involved new taxes on rents and landed income and surrender of the current year's income from crown annuities, profits and sinecures.

DUNDAS of Arniston. Scottish lowland, legal and political family. Those who became Lords of Session successively took the title of **Ld. ARNISTON. (1) Sir James (?-1679)** M.P. for Edinburgh and member of the committee of Estates in 1648, became a Lord of Session in 1662 but, having signed the Covenant, preferred to resign in 1663 rather than repudiate it. His son **(2) Robert (?-1726)** was a Lord of Session from 1689 and M.P. for Midlothian from 1700 to 1809. His son **(3) Robert (1685-1753),** Scottish Sol-Gen. from 1717 to 1720 and Lord Advocate in 1720, was M.P. for Midlothian from 1748 to 1753. His eldest son **(4) Robert (1713-87)** was Scottish Sol-Gen. from 1742 to 1746, Lord Advocate and M.P. for Midlothian from 1754 and Pres. of the Court of Session from 1760. For his brother and brother's descendants, see next entry. His son **(5) Robert (1758-1819)** was Scottish Sol-Gen. from 1784, Lord Advocate from 1789, M.P. for Edinburgh from 1790 to 1796 and Chief Baron of the Scottish Exchequer from 1801. His brother **(6) Francis (?-1824),** a soldier, was acting Gov. of the Cape from 1798 to 1799 and from 1801 to 1803. His brother **(7) William (1762-1845)** was M.P. for various Scottish burghs from 1796 onwards until 1831 and was Sec-at-War from 1804 to 1806 under Pitt.

DUNDAS (Melville). (*See* previous entry-4.) **(1) Henry (1742-1811) 1st Vist. MELVILLE (1802),** Scottish Sol-Gen. from 1766, M.P. for Midlothian from 1774 to 1790 and for Edinburgh from 1790 and Lord Advocate from 1775 to 1783. He moved the recall of Warren Hastings from India in 1782 and became Treasurer of the Navy from 1782 to 1783 and then from 1784 to 1800. In 1786 he championed Hastings' conduct over the Rohilla War and after a period from 1791 to 1793 as Home Sec. he was Pres. of the Board of Control until 1801, at a crucial period of Indian history, particularly in the Deccan. As such he spoke for the HEIC in parliament. From 1794 to 1801 he doubled these posts with that of Sec-at-War and planned and organised the Egyptian campaign of 1801. He had long been a personal friend, besides able colleague, of Pitt, who in 1804 made him First Lord of the Admiralty. In this post he was involved in 1805 in financial malpractice by a subordinate, dismissed and, in 1806, impeached. He was acquitted, as considered to have been only negligent, but the event nevertheless shook the political fortunes of the govt. His son **(2) Robert Saunders (1771-1851) 2nd Vist,** was M.P. for Hastings and then Rye (1794 and from 1796) and then M.P. for Midlothian from 1801. He too was Pres. of the Board of Control in 1807 and 1809 and then until 1812 a successful and popular Chief Sec. for Ireland. He too was First Lord of the Admiralty, from 1812 to 1827. He thus presided over the demobilisation of the immense wartime navy but took a special interest in hydrography and exploration. He acted on Thos. Hurd's (the first Hydrographer's) advice to place all charts on sale and laid the foundation for the publication of the *Light Lists* and *Sailing Directions*. The name of Melville Sound commemorates these interests.

DUNDEE (Scot.) was a Celtic settlement occasionally occupied by Roman troops. There was probably a Pictish and certainly a Scots royal residence there in the 11th cent. and it became a royal burgh c. 1190. It was the leading Scottish town in the 13th cent. and possessed many monasteries and churches, at least 19 of which are known to have been destroyed. The English sacked it in 1291 and 1303. The Scots Council which recognised Robert the Bruce as King was held there in 1309, by which time Edinburgh was coming to the fore. It remained important as a leader of Lowland opinion, so that despite a further sack in 1547, Geo. Wishart's conversion of Dundee (1550-60) was a leading event in the Scottish Reformation. By this time there were the beginnings of an important linen industry based on locally grown flax and this grew steadily, though the town was sacked in 1645, this time by the R. Catholic M. of Montrose. In 1651 it was held against and stormed by Monck and about 20% of the inhabitants perished. It subsequently suffered from the decline which followed the Hanoverian succession and declared for the Pretender in 1745. The recovery dated from the close of the French Wars and the building of an adequate harbour between 1815 and 1830. It became a prosperous port for the middle Scots hinterland and took advantage of the expansion of the jute industry consequent upon the U.S. Civil War. One result of this prosperity was the foundation of a univ. college (connected with St. Andrews) in 1881, but by this time Indian jute was undercutting Scottish and by 1914, as also between the wars, depression had to be alleviated by diversification into such things as electrical goods and mechanical contrivances.

DUNDEE, Vist. *See* GRAHAM OF CLAVERHOUSE.

DUNDONALD. *See* COCHRANE.

DUNEDIN, i.e. Edwin's Fort, was a poetic name for Edinburgh.

DUNEDIN. *See* MURRAY, ANDREW.

DUNEDIN (N.Z.) was founded as a Scots Free Church Settlement in 1848. The Otago gold rush of 1861 brought much prosperity and it was incorporated in 1865.

DUNFERMLINE, ancient capital of Fife and royal town, had a Celtic monastic settlement which was superseded in about 1072 by a Benedictine abbey. A royal residence was also established and the abbey and palace grew and attracted a population. Part of the abbey was reconstructed as a palace in the 14th cent. and it remained a favoured place of the Kings down to the Reformation. Much of the monastery was destroyed in 1560 and in 1624 the whole town was destroyed in a fire. In 1718 a linen and damask industry developed. Later, Rosyth naval dockyard and local coal mines contributed to its growth and because Andrew Carnegie was born there, the Carnegie Trusts have their H.Q. there.

DUNFERMLINE, Ld. *See* ABERCROMBY; SETON.

DUNGANNON CONVENTION (Feb. 1782) of Irish Volunteers voted that Britain should not legislate for Ireland or regulate Irish trade; that the Irish parliament should be entitled to pass Mutiny Bills at any interval it pleased instead of perpetually and that Ireland should have an independent judiciary. The Rockingham-Fox coalition accepted this programme in principle and while postponing consideration of the relationship of the two countries to a future conference, legislated against the particular grievances. *See* GRATITAN'S PARLIAMENT.

DUNK, George Montague (1716-71) E. of HALIFAX, as Pres. of the Board of Trade from 1748 to 1761 achieved much success in extending American colonial commerce and in helping to establish Nova Scotia where Halifax is named after him. He was absentee Lord Lieut. of Ireland from 1761 to 1763, first Lord of the Admiralty in 1762, Lord Privy Seal in 1770 and ended as Sec. of State. He was regarded as one of the great organisers of the empire.

DUNKELD (Perth). Reputedly founded by St. Adamnan c. 700, the abbey at this important Celtic centre was rebuilt by K. Constantine of the Picts for the fugitive Iona monks in 815. In about 850 K. Kenneth MacAlpin translated St. Columba's relics there from Iona, and Dunkeld became the episcopal see of the Kingdom until superseded by St. Andrews in 908. The place remained ecclesiastically important until the Reformation.

DUNKIRK (Fr.) was formerly a Flemish port and therefore in Spanish control after 1556. The French burned it in 1558 and occupied it in 1582-3. In 1639 the Spaniards heavily fortified it after the defeat of their local squadron by the Dutch. It was taken by an Anglo-French force in 1658 and ceded to England. Charles II, however, sold it to France in 1662. It then became the H.Q. of destructive or lucrative privateering mostly at English expense and so under the T. of Utrecht (1713) the harbour and fortifications were dismantled and the town placed under British occupation. It was only redeveloped after the P. of Paris of 1763. *See* CHARLES II-8; WORLD WAR II-3.

DUNKIRK, T. of (1947) between Britain and France, provided for strong mutual assistance against Germany in case of need. A stable door being closed after the departure of the horse?

DUNMOW and its **FLITCH. (Essex).** There is an old comic practice, mentioned by Chaucer and still in use, of awarding a flitch of bacon annually to a married couple which proved that it had not quarrelled in the preceding year and a day. The proceedings were public; any evidence was admissible, and anyone could ask questions but might not necessarily get truthful replies.

DUNNING, John (1731-83) 1st Ld. ASHBURTON (1782) was whig M.P. for Calne and Sol-Gen. from 1768 to 1770. Re-elected in 1774 he carried in 1780 the celebrated resolution that 'the influence of the crown has increased, is increasing and ought to be diminished'. *See* WILKES, JOHN.

DUNOIS and LONGUEVILLE, Jean Comte de (?1403-68), the BASTARD OF ORLEANS, an illegitimate cousin of Charles VII of France, defeated the English at Montargis in 1427, collaborated with Joan of Arc and commanded the campaigns which led to the fall of Chartres (1432). He negotiated with the English at Gravelines in 1439 and on the truce of 1444. In 1449-50 he conquered Normandy and in 1451 Guyenne. The rest of his adventurous life is part of French internal history.

DUNOON (Argyll). Covenanting Campbells hanged 36 allegedly royalist Lamonts here in 1643.

DUNRAVEN. *See* WYNDHAM-QUIN.

DUNS are enclosures with walls thick enough to contain cells and galleries. The layout is variable but the internal space usually amounts to about 3,000 sq. ft. There are many in the far west of Scotland. They are thought to date from the 1st cent. B.C. *See* BROCHS.

DUNS SCOTUS (Lat = The Scot), Johannes (?1264-1308) 'DOCTOR SUBTILIS', Scottish Franciscan philosopher, was educated at Oxford (1290-3), Paris (1293-6) and at Oxford again (1297-1301). He taught at Paris and Oxford and died at Cologne. He originated a R. Catholic school of thought which differed from that of St. Thomas Aquinas particularly on the matter of form; in holding that the natural law depends on God's will rather than His intellect and is therefore mutable; and that the beatific vision proceeds from love of God rather than from intellectual comprehension. He thus drew a sharp distinction between theology and philosophy. The humanists used his name ('dunce') to ridicule the scholastic subtleties of which many Dun's men in the universities were masters.

DUNSTABLE (Beds) was an important wool and grain market which grew up under Augustinian and royal patronage after the time of Henry I. Watling Street runs straight from London to Dunstable: hence the phrases *Dunstable way* and *plain as Dunstable* meaning direct and simple. The railway was later direct and simple too, but faster and as it went by way of Luton, Luton superseded Dunstable.

DUNSTABLE, John (?-1453) an advanced early polyphonic composer whose far-reaching influence upon his contemporaries helped to lay the foundations of the great 16th cent. schools of music. When serious modern study of his works began in the 19th cent. the main collections were found in Bologna, Modena and Trent.

DUNSTAFNAGE near Oban (Argyll) was a coastal fortress and later a castle at the place, important in seaborne strategy during the Viking era, where the Firth of Lorne, the Sound of Mull and Lochs Linnhe and Etive meet, and was the seat of the Kings of Dalriada. When the Scots absorbed Dalriada, they moved the royal coronation stone (Stone of Destiny) from Dunstafnage to Scone. Robert the Bruce stormed the castle in 1308 and committed it to Clan Campbell as much to hold against sea raiders as in the royal interest, but as that type of warfare declined, so did the importance of Dunstafnage. It remained in Campbell hands until 1745 and two Campbell chiefs still have hereditary functions concerned with it.

DUNSTAN, St. (924-88), artist, musician, smith and statesman, was educated by Irish scholars at Glastonbury and befriended by K. Athelstan. Court jealousy led to an accusation of witchcraft (probably of a sort commonly made against smiths) and he was exiled. He was then, with his friend and future colleague Ethelwold, professed by Aelfheah, Bp. of Winchester. It was perhaps soon after this that he was supposed to have pinched the Devil's nose with his smith's tongs. He returned to court under K. Edmund, but being nearly a victim of further intrigues, returned with the king in about 945 to Glastonbury where Edmund installed him as Abbot. Edmund's friendliness is ascribed to a narrow miraculous escape from death in a stag hunt. Dunstan instituted a reorganisation of the abbey. He began a new church and set up a school which was soon famous. For a third time he returned to court, this time as treasurer and principal adviser to K. Edred, who ascribed an escape from injury at the Cheddar Gorge to a telepathic experience involving Dunstan, who was 20 miles away. It was by Dunstan's advice that Abp. Wulfstan of York was relegated to Sherborne after the Danish civil war in Northumbria in 952. To strengthen the govt. in a superstitious age and to raise the King above the magnates at his court, he taught a sacramental view of royalty. This required some moral effort by the King himself. Consequently, when K. Edwy left his coronation feast in 955 to bed a mistress, Dunstan caused a sensation by publicly denouncing him. He seems also to have fallen foul of the King's wife, Aelfgifu, and her mother, for he denounced the marriage on grounds of consanguinity and was again driven from the court. He fled to Ghent where Count Arnulf of Flanders sheltered him and he spent the next years in the well-known reformed monastery there but returned after Edwy's abdication. K. Edgar received him with joy and promptly made him Bp. of Worcester (957) and, additionally, of London two years later. In 960 he became Abp. of Canterbury. By his work as such he became one of the founders of the English nation. During the peace which he counselled he organised, in collaboration with Bps. Ethelwold of Winchester and Oswald of Worcester, the teaching or conversion of the Danish settlers, suppressed secular influence in monasteries and encouraged the Benedictines, reformed church discipline and established a co-operative relationship with the strongly Scandinavian see of York. With St. Oswald now Abp. there, he carried out the great coronation of Edgar at Bath. This famous event, the first of its kind, permanently impose a religious impress on the English monarchy (973). Two years later Edgar died and, after controversy, Dunstan secured the choice of Edward, who was murdered in 978 at his stepmother's instigation. It was at the Synod of Calne in the same year that the floor collapsed, precipitating everyone except Dunstan into the cellar. The extraordinary, if dimly described, personality of this great (but diminutive) Englishman made an enormous contemporary impression, which doubtless accounts for the miraculous aura which clings to him.

DUNSTER CASTLE (Somerset), begun in 1070 by William de Mohun, was extended in the 13th cent. From 1376 it was the seat of the Luttrell family.

DUNSTERVILLE, Lionel Charles (1865-1946) (Kipling's STALKY) had an active and adventurous minor military career in Asia and commanded the British force which occupied Baku (Azerbaijan) from Jan. to Sept. 1918.

DUNWICH (Suffolk) was the seat of the South Folk of the East Angles, founded by St. Felix, a Burgundian sent there by Abp. Honorius of Canterbury. The place suffered from Danish raids and tidal encroachments and the bishopric was absorbed into the Diocese of Norwich in 1094. Dunwich is now under the sea.

DUPLEIX, Joseph Francois, Marquis de (1697-1763) served in India under the French E. India Co. from 1715 and from 1742 to 1754 was Gov-Gen. of French India. See EAST INDIA CO (FRENCH).

DU PONT (1) Pierre Samuel (1739-1817), French economist and writer on free trade and politician, was financial adviser to Turgot and later Pres. of the French Constituent Assembly. A conservative, he migrated to the U.S.A. in 1799 where Thomas Jefferson became interested in his ideas. He played an important part in the Louisiana Purchase. From 1802 to 1815 he was again in France but died in the U.S.A. His son **(2) Eleuthere Irenée (1771-1834)** a chemist, built the powder mill near Wilmington, Delaware, in 1802 which founded the fortunes of the great armaments firm of Dupont de Nemours. His three grandsons **(3) Pierre Samuel (1870-1954), (4) Irenée (1876-1963)** and **(5) Lammot (1880-1952)** diversified the business into an immense chemical combine and Pierre helped to organise and finance the General Motors Corporation. In 1961 Du Pont was forced to sell its General Motors holdings under the Anti-Trust Laws.

DUPPA, Brian (1588-1662) an unobtrusive but influential churchman, became Dean of Christchurch in 1629 and, on Laud's recommendation, tutor to the future Charles II. In 1638 he became Bp. of Chichester; in 1641 he was translated to Salisbury and he was close to Charles I up to his death. Thereafter he laboured ceaselessly to maintain the morale of the expelled clergy and preserve the Anglican Church. In 1659 he negotiated its re-establishment with Sheldon and Hyde and this bore fruit at the Restoration. He died as Bp. of Winchester.

DUPPLIN. See HAY (KINNOULL).

DUQUESNE, Abraham (1610-88), originally a trader, joined the French navy and fought (1638-43) in five battles with the Spaniards. He then became a Swedish V-Adm. and twice defeated the Danes. In 1650 he returned to France and fitted out a private squadron to blockade the rebellious city of Bordeaux and drive away the Spaniards. After anti-piracy operations he took part in the Dutch war under d'Estrées and then commanded against the Dutch-Spanish fleets in Sicilian waters. Here he defeated and killed de Ruyter off Catania in 1676. In 1682 and 1683 he bombarded Algiers and in 1684 Genoa. A rare plebeian in such a high French post, he was made a marquis.

DUQUESNE, FORT. See PITTSBURGH.

DURAND, Sir Henry Marion (1812-71) as a subaltern blew in the Kabul gate at Ghazni in 1839 and became the Gov-Gen's private sec. in 1841. From 1844 to 1846 he was commissioner in Tenasserim and then served successively against the Sikhs and in political appointments in Gwalior, Bhopal and Central India. During the Mutiny he held Indore and reconquered Malwa. In 1859 he was appointed to the Council of India and was foreign sec. in India from 1861 until 1870 when he became lieut. gov. of the Punjab.

DURAND LINE, negotiated in 1893 by Sir Mortimer Durand, was the boundary between British Indian tribal areas and Afghanistan and so the frontier of Pakistan. It was a geographical and diplomatic, not an administrative or sovereign boundary, which included, on the Indian side, tribes whose members were never British subjects.

DURAS or DURFORT. See FEVERSHAM.

DURBAN, Sir Benjamin (1777-1849) after serving in the British and Portuguese armies, was Lieut-Gov. of British Guiana from 1821 to 1826, of Barbados from 1825 to 1829. In 1833 he became gov. of the Cape. His greatest problem was the settlement of the frontier, especially against the Zulus to the north and east. He thought that further annexations were essential to protect the settlers but was neither supported by the Home govt. nor by the Boers who began their great trek (1835-7) to Natal and established a precarious republic there. D'Urban occupied Natal and Durban is named after him (*see* SOUTH AFRICA). He became C-in-C in Canada in 1847 and died there.

DURBAR was a public assembly or court held by an Indian ruler or commander, at which he transacted public business, redressed grievances and, in the case of a political ruler, received homage from his vassals. Durbars were held also by British governors and local officials and by the British colonels of Indian regiments. They were conducted for the most part with remarkable outspokenness.

DURHAM, Bishopric, City, County and Palatinate (1) The modern county area was in the Benician part of Northumbria and in the diocese of Hexham, which was inferior in prestige to the See of St. Cuthbert at Lindisfarne. The Danish wars caused the abandonment of Lindisfarne in 875 and then the collapse of Northumbria. After wanderings with the preserved body of St. Cuthbert, the bishop and monks settled at Chester-le-Street (883), while behind them disorder and the consolidation of the Scots Kingdom interrupted contact with the Lothians and, after the cession of Cumbria to the Scots (945), with Cumbria too. St. Cuthbert's see was thus transferred bodily south. The last Danish Northumbrian ruler died in 954 and Saxon authority of a sort was re-established. Earl Uhtred helped to settle the bishopric, as the see of Northumbria, at the fortress town of Durham in 995.

(2) The lands from the Forth to the Tees were fiercely disputed between the rising Scottish monarchy and the English. The Scots unsuccessfully besieged Durham in 1006. In 1018 their victory at Carham on the Tweed settled that Lothian should be Scots: their claims further south, however, remained open. In 1035 they again besieged Durham; in 1061 K. Malcolm Canmore ravaged Northumberland. Norman authority, which arrived only in 1069 when Robert Cumin became E. of Northumbria, had a bad start. Malcolm launched his second raid to coincide with the northern revolt of that year and this combined with the Norman harrying of the North left Northumbria, in any case a poor land, prostrate. In 1071 **Walcher (?-1081) a** Lorrainer trained in Belgium, became bishop. He developed the monastic organisation at the expense of the secular clergy and from 1074 acted, too, as earl. A popular uprising in 1075 drove him away. Odo of Bayeux, then justiciar, restored him by force, devastated the Durham district yet again and erected parts of Northumbria into a regality vested in the bishop. Walcher was killed in a riot in 1081. **William of St. Carilef or St. Calais (?-1096),** who followed him, was more successful. The palatine status of the regality was established under him and he replaced the secular canons at Durham by the great Benedictine convent in 1083. He was, however, a persistent absentee as an adviser to William I and a national politician under Rufus. He was involved in the rebellion of 1090-1 during which K. Malcolm made his third raid, as far as the Tees. The bishop had fled to Normandy, but local forces drove the Scots back. William II, however, let him return to Durham, where he started work on a new cathedral and he later sided with William in the controversy with Anselm.

(3) In 1099 Rufus gave the see to **Ranulf Flambard (?-1128)** for managing his finances, but Henry I imprisoned him in 1100. He escaped to join Robert of Normandy; restored only in 1106, he lived at Durham only after 1109. The palatinate had thus been under royal control since 1096; this was the time when the outlying frontier castle at Norham was built, thereby involving Durham in a permanent military commitment close to Scotland. Ranulf continued to build the Cathedral and organised an effective central and local administration, but there was a five year interregnum before **Geoffrey Rufus (?-1141)** was elected in 1133. K. Stephen's disastrous reign opened with the strategically dangerous

cession of Cumbria to the Scots (1135). When civil war broke out, K. David wanted Northumbria too. In 1136 he stormed Norham: in 1138 he assembled a force of Scots, Galwegians, Cumbrians and Danes and began a slaving foray from Carlisle which was atrocious even by the standards of the time. Stephen could not stop them, but a popular movement headed by Abp. Thurstan of York and the northern magnates did. David refused arbitration by Robert Bruce and Bernard Balliol, great landowners in both countries, and was routed near Northallerton at the B. OF THE STANDARD, so-called because the English marched with a mast displaying the banners of the northern churches. The battle destroyed the predatory Galwegians, but in the prevailing disorder the K. of Scots was the closest authority. He acquired the lordship of Tynedale, remained in control of Northumbria and, after the fighting stopped, put his chancellor, Robert Cumin, in possession of the see. Neither the monks nor the Papacy would have him: in 1143 **William of Sta Barbara (?-1152)** was elected and fought a victorious local civil war with Cumin, ending in 1144. All the same Northumbria remained in Scots hands until 1153, the year of **Hugh de Puisets or Pudsey's (?1125-95)** election when David died. His younger son, William, a child, became Scottish E. of Northumbria but K. Malcolm (The Maiden) surrendered his north English possessions in 1157 for the honour of Huntingdon.

(4) William (the Lion) never accepted the loss of his earldom and when he succeeded Malcolm in 1165, he started to work for its recovery. The rebellion of Henry the Young King in 1173 seemed to present the opportunity, for Henry offered it for his support. The Scots invasion, accompanied by the usual devastation and atrocities, came, however, to an abrupt end when William was captured at Alnwick (1174). There was now a prolonged period of freedom from official war, in which recovery was aided by the length of Bp. Pudsey's reign. He bought Sedburgh and the north bank of the Tees in 1189 to strengthen the palatinate against the Scots in Tynedale, rebuilt the fortresses and pressed ahead with the construction of the cathedral. In his reign and that of **Philip of Poitou (?-1208)** Hartlepool began to develop as the Palatinate's chief port. After 1208 there was a long interregnum while royal guardians, notably Philip of Ulecote, milked the see of funds. This continued until the Scots invasion of 1216.

The Mediaeval Organisation **(5)** Within the Palatinate the bishop was King: in the rest of Northumberland he was only bishop, the secular authority being exercised by the usual shire officials. Frontier defence was the object of the arrangements but these were complicated by the existence of clans, mostly owing allegiance to the Percy family, and by the facts of feudal tenancy. In the palatinate the four greatest owners were the Convent of Durham, the Nevilles at Auckland, the Bruces at Hartlepool and the Balliols at Barnard Castle, but the Nevilles, Bruces and Balliols all had great estates under the Crown in Northumberland and the two latter, as Scottish landowners, also owed allegiance to the Kings of Scots. Hence the bishops relied upon their lesser tenants for defence: the knights were liable to *utware* or *servitium forinsecum* (external service) of 14 days at an hour's notice, but had to be paid if required to enter Scotland. All able-bodied men between 16 and 60 were similarly liable for border service and the inferior tenants of certain townships, known as *castlemen,* did garrison duty. The poverty of the land and the sparse population made it certain that these forces were seldom large, but 85 knights fought at Lewes (1264) and in 1313 1500 archers were raised.

(6) The four Saxon convents founded were 640 and 660, namely the double house at Hartlepool, the nunneries at South Shields and Ebchester and the monastery at Gateshead, perished in the Danish incursions of 867. The celebrated houses at Wearmouth and Jarrow survived, but in an attenuated form. The rich Benedictine convent at Durham, founded in 1083, came to dominate the scene, Wearmouth, Jarrow and Finchale being dependent upon it. Only the nunnery at Neasham, founded in the 11th cent., was independent, but there were Austin Canons at Baxterwood, friaries later at Hartlepool, Durham, Jarrow and Barnard Castle, and no fewer than 13 hospitals and six colleges.

(7) In the peaceful century after 1216 there was a series of contests between the bishops and their principal subordinates. The jurisdictional pretensions of the convent, encouraged by the long interregnum, were restricted in 1229. There was a running dispute about homage in Sedburgh with the Balliols from 1190; this culminated when John Balliol waylaid the bishop's retinue in 1255 and was forced by the King to give way. A quarrel about primer seisin of the Neville lands was settled by the King in the bishop's favour in 1271; and a long dispute with the Bruce's about port and other dues at Hartlepool was settled by arbitration in 1280.

(8) These heated disputes, and the later constitutional adjustments related to the palatinate's main sources of income, which even at this early date were industrial. In particular coastal salt making, the mining of lead and coal (exported by sea) and the winning and working of iron ante-dated the Saxon invasions; they created self-reliant bodies of workpeople and, if not interrupted, earned large profits. In the peaceful 70 years (mostly occupied by two scholar bishops) before the election of Anthony Bek (?-1310) in 1284 such interruptions were rare; but it is of the nature of feudal service to create such interruptions. In the long peace people forgot their military obligations. In supporting (as he was bound to do) Edward I's war in Scotland, Bek had perforce to call upon his men. No doubt their discontent was encouraged by the Bruces and Balliols, the principal contenders for the Scottish crown. Edward forfeited Tynedale in 1295 and when the Scots war broke out in 1296, the Balliol estates in Durham were forfeited to the bishop, but these accessions of strength were illusory because of the mutinous state of the palatine troops. In 1301 they refused to cross the Tweed, broke up and went home. In 1303 Bek had, on the analogy of Magna Carta, to issue a charter defining his and the tenants' rights. A dispute with the Convent ended in a royal forfeiture of the temporalities (1307) when Bek refused arbitration: papal action secured their return, but the Balliol estates, at royal insistence, were granted to the E. of Warwick and the forfeited Bruce estates to the Cliffords. Richard Kellaw (?-1313), elected in 1311, had to buy Robert the Bruce off when he raided Hexham and the palatinate in 1312, but after his victory at Bannockburn (1314) Bruce returned. Bp. Louis Beaumont (?-1333) was kidnapped by freebooters in 1317 and there were further Scots invasions in 1322 and 1327. He also quarrelled incessantly with the convent.

(9) The need for strong rule was answered in 1333 by the election of Richard Bury (?-1345) who had been a Durham Benedictine. He set about recovering the palatine rights from the crown, aided by the fact that he was a trusted crown servant, being Lord Chancellor (1334-5), a diplomat and Treasurer in 1337. Just after his successor's election (Thomas Hatfield ?-1381), the last full scale Scots penetration was defeated at Neville's Cross (1346). From 1349 to 1350, however, the Black Death raged in the north and English and Scots alike had other preoccupations, arising from the collapse of feudalism, the change to a monetary economy and the efforts of authority, in an age which knew nothing of economics, to regulate wages by feudal principles. Thomas Hatfield's reign, externally quiescent, was socially disturbed, but it took a generation to re-establish the population at an explosive level and then troubles

were provoked by an external factor: in the rivalry between the Houses of York and Lancaster the factions did all in their power to secure the valuable palatinate. The Nevilles and Cliffords, with their vast estates here and elsewhere, were ever more deeply involved. The episcopal throne became a major prize: the process began when Bp. Fordham, elected in 1382, was deposed in 1388 in favour of Walter Skirlaw (?-1405), a diplomat employed first by Richard II in Scotland, France and Flanders and later by Henry IV in France. Nevertheless, he found time and funds for building, especially the important bridges over the Tees and the Wear. Thomas Langley or Longley (?-1437) was elected in 1406 while Lord Chancellor. He gave up the Great Seal in 1407 but was employed, like Skirlaw, in diplomacy and in 1411 became a Cardinal. Another absentee, he was Lord Chancellor again from 1417 to 1424 and an important canonist, but he made little impact at Durham. Robert Neville (1404-57) translated from Salisbury in 1438, was the son of Ralph Neville, E. of Westmorland, warden of the West March. He understood both pastoral and border problems and took an active and locally useful interest in them as a truce commissioner (see MARCHES). In this way the palatine govt. became increasingly interested in the border peace rather than border war. Unfortunately his successor (elected 1457) Laurence Booth or Bothe (?-1480) was another national politician. He was suspended between 1462 and 1464, Lord Keeper from 1473 to 1474 and then became Abp. of York.

(10) By 1500 the original purpose of the palatinate (a frontier organisation shielding England from a savage half organised society beyond) was out of date. Wars were contests between states now infinitely stronger than the See. Border forays had long been the business of the Wardens of the Marches. In 1522 the Crown started to appoint military Lieutenants of the North. In 1536 the Act of Resumption compelled the bishop to issue all writs in the King's name. On the other hand, the dissolution of the monasteries ended the feud with the Convent. The new Cathedral chapter which replaced it was eventually made fabulously wealthy by coal. The area became, apart from a few peculiarities (such as a local Chancery Court) effectively an ordinary county, while Northumberland, so long a kind of *glacis* to the palatinate, now developed in fact as well as in name into an ordinary county too. The last vestiges of the military function disappeared with the union of the crowns in 1603.

(11) Mineral products and inclosures now became the preoccupation of a relatively peaceful zone. Lead, salt, iron and especially coal, were exported, coal in particular to London through Hartlepool and then in growing amounts through Newcastle. It was creating the notorious London fogs in the reign of James I, who issued a proclamation against it. Consequently the county became the politico-strategic objective of the Scots in the Second Bishops War. In 1640 they stopped the coal supply to London in order to bring pressure upon the parliament. The damage to the Durham economy was serious and because of the destructive habits of the Scots continued for some while; the civil war now supervened and royalist occupation again interrupted traffic with Puritan London and thereafter the Dutch wars of the Commonwealth threatened the coastal shipping. Apart from one case at Heighington in 1551, there were no inclosures until 1618. Between that year and 1700 about 25,000 acres were enclosed under agreements sanctioned by decree of the local Chancery Court (which proved its usefulness). The civil disturbances impeded this process too.

(12) The Restoration brought a hitherto unknown prosperity. Mining expanded and in the 18th cent. inclosure by Act began. After 1759 the rate of inclosure quadrupled. Between 1730 and 1801 the population rose

from 97,000 to 160,000. As Palatine, the mining rights belonged to the bishop or, by grant from him, to the Chapter. While his governmental functions fell into desuetude (the County was represented in parliament from 1668) the episcopal and capitular income from mining royalties were so inflated that the see was the most desired preferment after Canterbury, and Welsh bishops sometimes resigned their thrones to become prebendaries of Durham Cathedral. The rise of social discontent among labourers generally and miners in particular, coincided with conversions to Primitive Methodism. The righteous poor confronted the rich and worldly clergy, and their congregations became the foundation of a type of trade unionism. In 1827 Bp. **Van Mildert** of Llandaff was translated to Durham. He opposed R. Catholic emancipation but faced with realism the growing unpopularity of the Durham bishop and clergy. An act to empower chapters and impropiators to make voluntary endowments was really aimed at Durham. The likelihood of a parliamentary investigation into the affairs of the Chapter enabled him to persuade the reluctant prebendaries to obtain a private Act (1832) to create and then (1837) to endow a new university – with, however, professorships attached to prebends. When the Ecclesiastical Commissioners were set up, the greater part of the diocesan income and in 1840 most of its lands passed to them. The palatine rights were transferred to the Crown in 1836.

(13) Apart from other activities already mentioned, keel building was an ancient industry at Sunderland which developed towards small ship building in the later 17th cent. In and after the Napoleonic wars this developed into a speculative industry with a poor reputation. On the other hand iron ships and steam engines required capital, so that after the mid 19th cent. substantial and reputable builders were established not only at Sunderland but on the Tyne at Jarrow, South Shields and Hebburn (which flourished on Admiralty contracts) and even on the unnavigable Tees. These yards were prosperous until, and throughout World War I, after which international competition created increasing difficulties which were never resolved. Durham mining suffered similarly and was attacked even in its home markets by Asturian coal. The specialised economy could no longer support the population which had increased ten-fold between 1801 and 1921. In the great slump of 1929 unemployment reached disaster levels and brought on the celebrated "hunger marches" to London in 1933, when 34% of the workpeople were unemployed.

(14) There was the usual improvement in World War II but the expected decline after 1945 was arrested by govt. sponsored diversification. The iron and steel industry ceased to overspecialise in ship building (which nevertheless produced 40% of British ships), lighter industries came by way of new trading estates and there was an immense development of the chemical industry at Billingham.

DURHAM, E. of. *See* LAMBTON.

DURHAM REPORT. *See* CANADA-14 *et seq.*

DURIE (1) Andrew (?-1558) and his brother **(2) George (1496-1561)** were nephews of Abp. James Beaton, who appointed Andrew abbot of Melrose in 1526 against royal opposition and George second abbot of Dunfermline under himself. George became independent abbot when Beaton died in 1539 and Andrew Bp. of Galloway in 1541. Both were strong persecutors of protestants. George sat in the parliaments of 1540, 1542 and 1543, was a member of Arran's Privy Council in 1545 and tried to avenge Card. Beaton's murder in 1546. He was involved in the defeat at the B. of Pinkie in 1547 but became Lord Privy Seal in 1554. As such he was the R. Catholic party's representative at the French court in 1560 when Mary Q. of Scots husband died, and bore much responsibility for her return to Scotland.

DUROTRIGES. *See* BELGAE.

DÜRNSTEIN (Lower Austria). The castle where Richard I was imprisoned in 1192-3.

DUSTCHUCK. A certificate of tax exemption in Bengal.

DUTCH WARS (17th Cent.) GENERAL (1) The British war direction was unified under Cromwell and his Council of State or Charles II with his advisers. These laid down the major objectives and ensured supplies through one Admiralty. The Dutch had five navies, five admiralties and directed their wars through a States General where any one province had a veto. **(2)** The Dutch dominated the spice trade and its route round Africa; they had commercial and carrying centres in Guiana, the Caribbean and at New Amsterdam (New York) and their home based shipping engrossed most of the Atlantic, Baltic and Mediterranean traffic including that of England, France and Spain. Moreover they monopolised the North Sea herring fisheries; they exported cheese, salt fish and textiles, bought and resold Baltic timber, copper, hemp, tar, wheat and furs and made vast profits on warehousing. The province of Holland alone, with a resident population of only 260,000, supported 168,000 seamen and 10,000, mostly coastal, ships.

DUTCH WAR, FIRST (1652-4) (*see previous entry*) **(1)** Hostilities began with a flag incident at Dover between the Dutch Adm. Marten Harpertszoon van Tromp and Blake. A peace mission to London under Adriaan Pauw failed because the English were determined on extremities. Their objective was to seek victory by stopping the Dutch industries; this might be done by attacking either the merchant shipping or the forces defending it. They began by trying the first. Blake was sent against the Dutch fishery off the north of Scotland and to intercept an East India convoy coming north-about; Ayscue was sent to the Western Approaches to protect English and intercept enemy shipping using the Channel. Blake temporarily dispersed the fishermen but missed the convoy in a storm. Ayscue did still worse: de Ruyter's escort force beat him off (B. of the Lizard, Aug. 1652).

(2) A series of battles, on a rising scale with Dutch escorting squadrons, amounted to a progressive change of policy to that of destroying the Dutch fleet, to facilitate a blockade. For their part the Dutch war policy changed in the same direction: they would disable the British navy, blockade the Thames, interrupt the Baltic trade especially in naval stores, and free their seaborne trade from the attentions of a crippled enemy. In the first head on collision between the two policies, a fleet action off the Kentish Knock (28-9 Sept. 1852), Blake defeated Witte de Witt.

(3) The Council of State now detached 20 ships to the Mediterranean where British trade was at a standstill; the Dutch had driven the only British squadron into Leghorn, where the Tuscan authorities were threatening to impound it. The Council under-estimated the skill of Dutch shipwrights. Their losses at the Kentish Knock were more than made good before the 20 could be replaced. Blake with 42, had to fight Tromp's 85 (B. of Dungeness, 10 Dec. 1652) and was driven into the Thames. The port of London was closed; the Channel, perfectly safe for Dutch trade, became impossible for British. The King of Denmark seized British ships laden with timber and naval stores and the Dutch began to search neutral shipping for naval stores *via* Lisbon.

(4) The Council of State accordingly drew in the squadrons, put new ships into commission and concentrated for a decisive effort; the Dutch followed suit. The war was decided in a series of stubbornly fought fleet actions. In the Three Days Battle or B. of Portland (28 Feb.-2 Mar. 1653) Tromp had the advantage of Blake; at the Gabbard or Niuewpoort and at Wijk-aan-Zee, Monck drove Tromp within the Wielings (12-13 June) and at the decisive B. of Scheveningen or Ter Heijde or the Texel (10 Aug.) Monck defeated de Witt and Tromp, who was killed. The Netherlands could then be blockaded and the war was concluded by the T. of Westminster (15 Apr. 1654).

DUTCH WAR, SECOND (1665-7) (*See* DUTCH WARS-17TH CENT-GENERAL.) **(1)** Aggressive commercialism, which was focused in the City and had dominated the foreign policies of the Interregnum, pervaded Restoration society. James, D. of York, was the first gov. of the Royal African Co. chartered in 1663. The first three govs. of the Hudson Bay Co. were P. Rupert, James, and John Churchill (Marlborough). James later invested heavily in E. India stock. All the ministers and leaders of society were similarly involved. James, also, was Lord High Admiral.

(2) Thus private interest, commercial jealousy and public dislike of paying exorbitant toll to Dutchmen, combined with Charles II's personal hatred of the Republic. Moreover, Charles had always understood the need for power at sea and the royal navy was, at this period, better disciplined than the Dutch; its ships were more numerous, rather larger and more heavily armed but, being deeper of draught, could not penetrate the Dutch coastal shoals.

(3) Like Cromwell in the Spanish Main, Charles began with peacetime overseas aggression. In the winter of 1663-4 Capt. Robt. Holmes, in support of the R. African Co., took Goree, N. of the Gambia R. and Cape Coast Castle. In the spring Col. Richard Nicolls seized New Amsterdam and annexed the New Netherlands (29 May 1664). A Dutch force under De Ruyter recovered the African forts by the end of the year; meanwhile the D. of York and P. Rupert took a battle fleet into the Channel and started seizing Netherlands shipping and in Dec. 1664 Adm. Thos. Allin unsuccessfully attacked their Smyrna fleet off Cadiz. It was only in Feb. 1665 that the Dutch declared war.

(4) The fleet under Lord Sandwich now concentrated off the Texel to blockade Amsterdam, prevent a Dutch concentration and either intercept two great convoys (from Smyrna and the East) which were coming northabout, or force the enemy to fight at a disadvantage. The convoys took refuge in Bergen, and Sandwich had, after some weeks, to retire to Southwold for water, food and reasons of health. The enemy now concentrated and sailed under Opdam with orders to fight. At Lowestoft (13 June 1665) he lost 25 ships and was killed. Meanwhile the British had made a thieves' compact with the Danish rulers of Norway: De Ruyter's convoys in Bergen were to be attacked with Danish connivance, the Danish King to receive half the spoils. The operation went wrong. The Danish batteries were not warned and beat off the British with heavy loss. The embarrassed Dane hurriedly became the ally of the Dutch: the English humoured him by declaring a very nominal war. Smashed top hamper had prevented the British from clinching their victory at Lowestoft and De Ruyter had enough ships to bring the convoys into safety. English privateers, however, exploited Dutch preoccupations by reducing St. Eustatius, Saba and Tobago.

(5) As the general advantage was to England, France, an ally of the Dutch since 1662, was deterred from fulfilling her obligations. The Dutch might have fared worse but for the English Great Plague. It raged between June and Sept. 1665, disorganising every branch of administration, finance and commerce. The fleet was weakened too and in the next campaigning season the English, with about 80 capital ships, had to meet De Ruyter with about 100. Charles, however, on a mistaken report that the French fleet was coming out, detached 20 ships westward under P. Rupert. In June De Ruyter sailed for the Channel and anchored between Dunkirk and the Downs. At daylight Albemarle (Monck) saw them in the haze to leeward and in poor order; he decided to attack despite his inferiority in numbers. The resulting FOUR DAYS BATTLE (11-4 June 1666) surged back and forth

over the Straits; Albemarle gave ground westwards to get nearer to Rupert but slowly, in order to cover his more damaged ships. By the third nightfall he had lost several, but was united with Rupert and had done much damage. Nevertheless his inferiority was still marked and something like a defeat ended the fourth day with a loss of 17 ships altogether.

(6) The French now began to threaten; the fleet was refitted at desperate speed and achieved a strategic surprise; De Ruyter was severely mauled, with a loss of 20 ships, off Orfordness on 25 July; he suffered from the insubordination of Cornelis von Tromp and was driven eastwards. The British followed this up by burning the warehouses and 150 merchantmen at Terschelling. Again the Dutch were saved by chance: the Great Fire devastated London (2-7 Sept.) and for a second time British finance and administration were disorganised. The succour of victims and the diversion of resources towards reconstruction predisposed the govt. to rethink its war policy. The Dutch were wishfully believed to be *in extremis*. They might now be beaten to their knees merely by commerce raiding; the battle fleet was largely paid off; it was resolved to rely for safety upon local defences; and to send a force to the Mediterranean, where the commercial stoppage was causing distress in the English manufacturing towns. These Cromwellian miscalculations, and a decision to negotiate with France, was suddenly to end the war.

(7) The Dutch matured a plan for which they had taken soundings in the Thames in 1666. 80 sail raided the Firth of Forth in May 1667, cruised down the east coast stopping the trade and on 11 June they entered the Thames, occupied Sheerness and forced the Medway boom. The docks and ships at Chatham and Rochester were burned; the English flagship was towed away and the port of London closed for a month. France immediately became more active in her Dutch alliance. Charles could only sue for peace.

(8) By the T. of BREDA (31 July 1667) Britain gave up Surinam and the spice island of Polaroon, and had to admit goods in Dutch bottoms from Germany and the Low Countries as if they were Dutch. On the other hand she kept New York and New Jersey, thereby linking the two blocks of N. American colonies and giving them control of the Hudson-Mohawk route to the Great Lakes.

DUTCH WAR, THIRD (1672-4) (*See* DUTCH WARS-17TH CENT-GENERAL.) **(1)** The character of this war, though necessarily involving commercial issues, was primarily political. Louis XIV's designs on the Spanish empire were being frustrated by Dutch coalition-weaving. The Dutch must therefore be mastered. The French would attack them by land and the war would become predominantly a land war; but Charles II was involved partly for internal political reasons and he drove, in the T. of Dover (1670) a good bargain with Louis. There was to be a British seaborne invasion of Zeeland, but in the partition of the United Netherlands which was to follow victory, the British were to have the islands and territories on both sides of the mouth of the R. Scheldt and of both mouths of the Rhine. The prize was a glittering one.

(2) Louis was ready by the end of 1671. The English were to give the signal; they provoked a flag incident followed, in Jan. 1672, by a demand that all Dutch ships should salute even the smallest British man-of-war. Conciliation effected nothing and in Feb. the Dutch began to mobilise their fleet. On 23 Mar. Sir Robt. Holmes attacked the Dutch Smyrna convoy and Charles declared war on 29th. On 6 Apr. Louis followed suit. The Dutch republicans were strategically surprised. Louis easily overran their neglected outer landward defences; moreover the admiralty of Zeeland delayed manning its fleet and the Dutch were unable to concentrate before the British and French fleets met. Nevertheless De Ruyter surprised them (B. of Southwold or Sole Bay) on 7 June.

The English under the D. of York and the French under d'Estrées cut their cables and separated on opposite tacks. De Ruyter held off the French and fell upon the British. Both sides lost heavily but the advantage remained with the Dutch. More importantly De Ruyter escorted a necessary convoy home and the allies had to postpone their descent on the enemy coast for a month. This was the turning point: on 15 June the Grand Pensionary de Witt had got authority to negotiate a virtual surrender and on 20th some parties of French soldiers entered Muyden, which commanded both the sluices and the Zuider Zee port of Amsterdam. The Southwold victory activated a latent patriotism against de Witt's policies. Muyden and Amsterdam co-operated to expel the French. On 25 Amsterdam opened the sluices and other cities quickly followed. The French were flooded out. On 8 July a political revolution displaced the de Witts and brought in, in the shape of William III of Orange, a govt. determined to fight it out.

(3) The revival of the Netherlands gave time for European opinion to veer to her side during a winter when English local opinion became intensely suspicious of Charles' policy. There were obviously secret clauses in the T. of Dover, even if their exact nature was unknown. The Commons refused to pay for the war unless the King withdrew the Declaration of Indulgence and, still further, in Mar. 1673 passed the Test Act, which extended the principle of the Corporation Act, 1661 to all holders of civil and military office. This ousted the D. of York from the naval command, to which P. Rupert succeeded. The supplies, however, were voted and a vigorous prosecution of the war promised.

(4) In reply the Dutch posted their main fleet in the passage of Schoneveldt, S.W. of the Scheldt, so that no seaborne invasion could approach without an engagement; but De Ruyter used this difficult area of shoals as a base for tactical offensives. He began with a raid towards the Thames, which Rupert and the French stopped and when the combined allies appeared he sallied forth and fought two actions (7 and 14 June). In both the Dutch had 55 ships to 54 British and 27 French and concentrated on the British. The allies had to retire and refit, but reappeared carrying troops in Aug., when they were intercepted off Camperdown on 21. De Ruyter again held off the French and tried to crush the English. Tactically there was no decision because the odds were too heavily against De Ruyter, but the advantage was with the republic which, because the allies retreated, could open its ports. In the meantime the Dutch Adm. Evertsen had taken New York.

(5) On 30 Aug. Spain, Lorraine and the Emperor signed alliances with the Netherlands, while English opinion hardened against the war. Louis offered terms to the Dutch, which they rejected and French troops then withdrew so as to continue the war elsewhere. Thereupon Charles negotiated the P. of Westminster (19 Feb. 1674) whereby the Dutch returned New York, paid £180,000, acknowledged the English sovereignty of the seas and accepted the English view of the right of search.

DUTCH WAR, FOURTH (1780-4). (*See* AMERICAN REBELLION.) The only significant separate event of these Anglo-Dutch hostilities was a small Dutch victory at the Dogger Bank in Aug. 1781.

DUVAL, Claude (1643-70), daring highwayman known for his gallantry to women, was hanged at Tyburn. His epitaph in Covent Garden church reads:

Here lies Du Vall. Reader, if male thou art,
Look to thy purse. If female, to thy heart.

DUX BRITTANIARUM. See BRITAIN, ROMAN-21.

DWARKA (Kathiawar, India). A coastal place of Hindu pilgrimage with a great temple to Krishna, said to have been raised in a single night.

DYAKS or DAYAKS. Malay speaking river peoples of Borneo and Sarawak, who live mostly by fishing and cultivating rice and coconut palms. The Ibans or Sea Dyaks, representing about 80% of them, occupy the coastal and estuarial parts, the Land Dyaks live further inland but their respective customs and habits are much the same.

DYARCHY obtained in British India as a result of the **Montague-Chelmsford** reforms of 1919 based on the ideas of Lionel Curtis. Provincial administration was divided into **Reserved Subjects** (law, order, justice, police, land revenue and irrigation) administered by *executive councillors* responsible to the governors (i.e. the crown) and **Transferred Subjects** (local govt., education, public health and works) administered by *ministers* responsible to the local legislatures. The system worked where ministers could rely, as in the Punjab and the Madras Presidency, on the support of organised parties, but a major practical problem was that ministers wanted to milk the land revenue for projects in the transferred sector rather than finance them by new taxes. The system, though much criticised, trained a new body of Indian politicians and marked a definite step towards independence. It ended with the introduction of provincial autonomy in 1936.

DYES. Natural dyes derived mostly from plants were used until the mid-19th cent. In 1856 W. H. Perkins (then 18) discovered mauve, a synthetic dye, but British industrialists took very little interest and the idea was taken up by the Germans who rapidly developed (mostly through IG Farben) a vast dyes and then a derivative chemicals industry with a virtual world monopoly. This gave them an initial advantage in explosives production at the beginning of World War I, for the Allies had to build up their explosives industries virtually from the ground. The endless bombardments of that war created a vast demand and correspondingly rapid development. In 1919 the Allies decided to protect themselves against German importations and in 1920 such imports were prohibited in Britain. The courts held the prohibition illegal and it took until 1922 for the Dyestuffs Act to legalise it. In the interval the Germans, desperate for foreign currency during their wheelbarrow inflation, flooded every market which they could reach. Hence the peacetime redevelopment of the British dyestuffs industry did not start until 1923 but, heavily protected, it then made such strides that by 1939 it had 93% of the internal market and had quintupled its exports. Hence the Allies were not short of explosives or pharmaceuticals in World War II.

DYFED (Wales) a S.W. Welsh area occupied by the Demetae who were conquered by the Romans c. A.D. 60. Later it was dominated by Gwynedd and then taken over by the Normans in c. 1093. Since 1974 the name has been applied to a new S.W. Welsh county.

DYFRIG or DUBRICIUS, St. (?-550) Romano-British monk of Hereford and Gwent, founded monasteries in the area and was an associate of St. David.

DYMOKE (1) Sir John (?-1381) was M.P. for Lincolnshire in 1372-3 and 1377. He acquired by marriage the manor of Scrivelsby in right of which he claimed the office of King's Champion at the coronation of Richard II. The claim was upheld against Sir Baldwin de Freville and the right, exercised at every coronation until 1821, has belonged to his descendants ever since. Of these **(2) Sir Thomas (?1428-71)** was a Lancastrian leader beheaded after the B. of Tewkesbury. **(3) Sir Robert (?-1546)** was a professional soldier who distinguished himself at the siege of Tournai.

DYNAMITE was invented by Nobel in 1866.

DYNASTS, THE (1904-8) by Thomas Hardy, an "Epic-Drama of the War with Napoleon", is an immense work in verse and prose recounting the public fate and battles of statesmen and soldiers and the private sorrows of the humble, with glimpses from above through the eyes of impersonated abstractions or spirits, the whole centering on the tragic figure of Bonaparte himself. It impressed or elevated its relatively small readership which included Sir Winston Churchill.

DYRHAM PARK (Avon) classical mansion built between 1692 and 1698 by Talman and Hauduroy for Wm. Blathwayt, Sec. to William III. Thomas Povey, Blathwayt's uncle, entertained his literary friends such as Evelyn there. It is also in the area where Ceawlin won an important B. of DEORHAM over the British in 577.

DYSART. *See* MURRAY.

DYSENTERY, BLOODY FLUX or sometimes SURFEIT. This disease, which is dangerous primarily in warm climates, was rife during all the Crusades, but there were serious, more northerly incidents including a Scottish outbreak ("The Wame Ill") in 1439, a European-wide epidemic in 1539-40 and another in 1780-5. In the British

Is. there were, besides, some notable local outbreaks in 1624 (Whitechapel), 1629 and 1670-2 (London), 1689 (Londonderry), 1693 (Wales) and it was common in Scotland from 1693 to about 1736. Other outbreaks of diminishing virulence occurred in 1758-62 and 1825-6 in England and 1827-30 in Scotland. The British mortality was seldom high. *See also* YELLOW FEVER; EPIDEMICS, HUMAN.

DYVE, Sir Lewis (1599-1669) was with P. Charles (Charles I) in Madrid in 1620; M.P. for Bridport in 1625 and 1626 and for Weymouth in 1628. In 1642 during the Civil War he conspired to let the King's troops into Hull but was arrested. He escaped by way of Holland to the King's army. In 1644 as royal commander in Dorset, he took Weymouth. The parliamentarians imprisoned him from 1645 to 1647 when he went to Ireland and served with the King's partisans there. He retired to France in 1650.

E

EADBALD. See KENT, KINGDOM-4.

EADRERT. (King 757-58). See NORTHUMBRIA-8.

EADBERT PREAN or PRYN. See KENT, KINGDOM-5; WEST SAXONS, EARLY.

EADBURGA, St. (?-751) *d.* of Centwine, K. of the W. Saxons, became abbess of Minster in Thanet. She was a friend of St. Boniface.

EADMER (c. 1060-1130), an English monk of Christ Church, Canterbury, devoted to the glory of his house and the primacy of Canterbury, wrote a *Life of St. Dunstan*, some minor *Lives* of other English saints and a remarkable bipartite biography of St. Anselm comprising accounts of the saint's private, scholarly and spiritual life and in a *Historia Novorum* (Lat = History of Recent Events) of his work and the relations between Church and Crown under William Rufus and Henry I from c. 1098 to 1123. He was a member of Anselm's household. He quotes documents and conversations and was often an eyewitness e.g. at the Council of Rockingham (1095) Anselm 'leaned against the wall and slept peacefully while his enemies carried on their little conclaves for quite a time'. He was appointed to the see of St. Andrew's in 1121 but the appointment was cancelled because of his inconvenient insistence that he should render obedience to Canterbury.

E[A]DRED (r. 946-55). See AETHELSTAN'S SUCCESSORS-2.

EADRIC, LAWS OF (c. 685). A primitive Kentish code.

EADSINE, Abp. of Canterbury (1038-50), a chaplain of Canute, crowned Harthacanute and was a partisan of Godwin.

EAFA. See WEST SAXONS, EARLY-15.

EAGLE. Roman emblem affixed to the top of a pole. The Byzantine, Holy Roman (H.R.) and Austrian Emperors used a version with two crowned heads looking left and right, holding an orb in one claw and a sword and sceptre in the other; in the H.R. version the Emperor's family shield is on the breast and there was a large overall crown above the two crowned heads. The Russian Czars copied this but put the Russian shield (St. George and Dragon) on the breast and scattered the wings with shields of their other possessions. The RFSR has reverted to most of this. Electors and princes of the H.R. Empire (like the D. of Marlborough) and imperial cities put the double eagle, uncrowned, behind their arms. The Serbian kingdom used a white Byzantine eagle, Albania a black one. The Bonaparte Emperors of the French reverted to the single-headed Roman bird clutching horizontal thunderbolts. The Hohenzollern German Emperors' emblem was heavily crowned and single-headed but otherwise similar to the H.R. The German republicans simply removed the trappings. When the Austrians hoped to maintain their independence of Germany they reverted to a double-headed eagle, uncrowned but with the heads in haloes. The Nazis used a somewhat diminished eagle perched on a large wreathed swastika. Meanwhile the U.S.A. adopted a single-headed bald eagle with a thunderbolt in one claw and an olive branch in the other and the Mexicans revived an Aztec legend of the foundation of Tenochtitlan (Mexico City) with an eagle standing on a cactus. The Egyptian republicans, after the overthrow of their monarchy, adopted a black single-headed eagle. The Queens Dragoon Guards used the Austrian emblem as a specially conferred honour. Several, having captured French regimental eagles, used the Bonaparte eagle among their insignia.

EADRED or ALDRED (?-1069), abbot of Tavistock from 1027, became Bp. of Worcester in 1046. In 1054 he was in Germany negotiating for the return of the atheling Edmund of Hungary. In 1060 he became Abp. of York and in 1062 he gave up Worcester at the behest of Pope

Alexander II. He supported and probably crowned Harold in 1066 and wanted to crown Edgar the Atheling after Harold's death, but events proved too strong. He came over to William whom he crowned, probably in the hope of superseding Stigand at Canterbury.

EALHMUND. See WEST SAXONS, EARLY-16.

EAMONT BRIDGE (or EMMET) T. of (12 July 927) near Penrith (Cumbria). See AETHELSTAN.

EANFLAED (626-after 685), a Kentish baptised princess married K. Oswiu in 643. Her adherence, in opposition to her husband, to the Roman rite brought on the Synod of Whitby. After Oswiu's death in 670 she practised good works and in about 685 became, with her *d.* Aelflaed, joint abbess of Whitby.

EANSWYTH, St. (?-640), *d.* of K. Edbald of Kent, founded, at Folkestone, the first English nunnery.

EARDLEY-WILMOT. Legal and political family **(1) Sir John (1709-92)** who was educated with Dr. Johnson at Lichfield, was C.J. of the Common Pleas from 1766 to 1771. **(2) John (1750-1815)** besides being a master in chancery (1781-1804) was an M.P. from 1776 to 1796. **(3) Sir John Eardley (1810-92)** was a conservative M.P. from 1874 to 1885.

EAREMBERT. See KENT, KINGDOM-4.

EARL, EORL, JARL, EARLDORMAN. The Anglo-Saxon Eorl was at first simply one of a class of important gentry or nobles. The Scandinavian Jarl or Earl was a much rarer and more powerful person, who sometimes superseded a King. The Earldorman was an Anglo-Saxon local governor, sometimes related to the previous royal house of his area. He was bound to lead the forces of his jurisdiction and (with the bishop) hold its court. He was entitled to a third of the fines levied, and estates and rights of entertainment were attached to his office. There was a tendency for a particular earldormanry to run in the same family. In Wessex and probably Mercia, an earldorman's province was originally a single shire, but as the Anglo-Saxon kingdoms collapsed under the Scandinavian invasions, shires tended to be grouped under a single earldorman who thus became the equivalent of the Scandinavian Earl. This raised the status of the sheriff. With the unification of the country into an Anglo-Danish monarchy under Danish Kings, the Earldormen became known as Earls. Their circumscriptions under Edward the Confessor corresponded very roughly with the ancient Kingdoms. Consequently politics and family intrigues resulted in rather more Earls than earldoms and the Earls themselves were developing from officials into magnates. With the Conquest the Earl (*Count* or *Comes*) soon ceased (save in a palatinate) to have administrative functions. These were confided to the sheriff who was treated as a Norman *vicomte* (vice-comes). Earls now developed into grandees pure and simple and the title became hereditary by the 13th cent. They constituted the highest rank of the nobility until John of Gaunt was created D. of Lancaster in 1362; and their prestige has remained high and their numbers low. Clement Atlee was made an earl in 1955 and in 1995 there were only 175 of them including Countesses in their own right. See WERGILD.

EARLE, Giles (?1678-1758), M.P. for 32 years from 1715, was a supporter of the Marlboroughs and a boon companion of Walpole. He also chaired the highly political House of Commons disputed elections committees.

EARLE (1) Sir James (1755-1817) and his third son **(2) Henry (1789-1838)** together worked as surgeons at St. Bartholomew's Hospital from 1780 to 1837. They each separately held the position of Surgeon to the Hospital. Sir James was surgeon extraordinary to George III, Henry to Q. Victoria. They both held presidencies, Sir James of the R. College of Surgeons, Henry of the R. Medical and Chirurgical Society and each published learned and lasting books on their craft.

EARLE, John (?1601-65) as rector of Bishopstone (Wilts) became tutor to Charles, P. of Wales, in 1641 and in 1643 was appointed a reluctant member of the Westminster Assembly, with most of whose puritan members he (being essentially reasonable) disagreed. He then became Chanc. of Salisbury but at the victory of the parliament he was, not surprisingly, stigmatised as 'malignant' and deprived. He joined Charles, now King, in France, became his chaplain and Clerk of the Closet and, at the Restoration, Dean of Westminster. The Church's human character throughout the reign was strongly affected by his influence on church patronage in these first years of the Restoration. This influence diminished when he accepted the bishoprics of Worcester (1662-3) and Salisbury (from 1663). He opposed the persecution of dissenters, in particular the earlier bills comprised in the so-called 'Clarendon Code'.

EARL MARISCHAL David I of Scots (r. 1124-53) had marshals whose function, jointly with the Constable, was to keep order in the King's neighbourhood. Members of the Keith family held the office in the 13th cent. and it became hereditary to them by a charter of Robert I in 1308. Sir William de Keith was created Earl Marischal in 1458. George, 9th Earl Marischal (1693-1778) was a Jacobite attainted in 1716 but he escaped to France. He attempted to raise the Highlands in 1719 and entered the service of Frederick the Great of Prussia in 1747. They became great friends and he was Prussian Ambassador in Paris from 1751 to 1754, gov. of Neuchatel until 1763 and, as ambassador in Madrid, kept the English govt. informed of French and Spanish plans. Consequently he was pardoned in 1759 and recovered some of his estates but, disliking the Scottish climate, ended his life in Prussia. The title and office are possibly, but not certainly, extinct.

EARL MARSHAL originated in a court officer called the Master Marshal, a subordinate of the Constable's (i.e. the bunting dept.) in charge of the King's horses and in war a sort of asst. quartermaster. Gilbert the Marshal (?-1130) is the first known holder and from him the office passed to his son John (?-1165) and then to John the Marshal (?-1213). Under his brother, the famous William, E. of Pembroke, the importance of the office rose with the importance of the man. By 1236 he was described as Great Marshal of England and by 1300 he was considered the equal of the Constable. When the family died out in the male line, the office passed to the eldest co-heir and thence to the Bigods, Es. of Norfolk. The last of these surrendered the reversion and in 1306 it passed to the Crown and was granted in 1316 by Edward II to his half brother Thomas, E. of Norfolk. When he died in 1338 leaving only a daughter, it was granted successively for life to William Montague, E. of Salisbury, Thomas, E. of Kent (until 1385) and Thomas Mowbray, E. of Nottingham. He became D. of Norfolk in 1397 and hereditary marshal and thence the office came through a confusion of heirs to the Howard Ds. of Norfolk, who held it successively for life until 1672 when it was made hereditary again. The Earl Marshal is head of the College of Heralds and the Court of Chivalry, organises state occasions such as coronations and State funerals, but otherwise the functions of his office have long been ceremonial.

EARLS, FLIGHT OF THE (1607). *See* JAMES I AND VI-6.

EARLY CLOSING. *See* SHOPS HOURS.

EARLY ENGLISH. *See* ARCHITECTURE (BRITISH)-6.

EARTHQUAKE SYNOD (May 1382) at Blackfriars, London, was carefully packed with eminent anti-Lollard theologians to consider 24 propositions of Wyclif's writings on confession, transsubstantiation, papal and civil power and Grace. The proceedings were interrupted by an earthquake. It found 10 heretical and 14 erroneous propositions. Its critics found more comfort in the earthquake than the findings. *See* LOLLARDY-3.

EAST (1) Sir Edward Hyde (1764-1847) published *East's Pleas of the Crown* in 1803, was chief justice of Bengal from 1813 to 1822 and chief promoter of the Calcutta Hindu College. He was M.P. for Winchester from 1823 to 1830. His son **(2) Sir James Buller (1789-1878)** was M.P. for Winchester from 1830 to 1832 and from 1835 to 1864.

EAST (1) FAR. The countries and Indonesian islands east of the Bay of Bengal. **(2) MIDDLE,** formerly used of the countries between Syria and India, this term was confusingly re-used during World War II to mean the southern part of **(3)** the **NEAR EAST,** the countries eastward of the Aegean and Cyrenaica as far as Iraq of which **(4)** the **LEVANT** comprised the coastal territories from Antalya to Suez.

EAST AFRICA. This geographical expression includes Burundi, Kenya, Ruanda, Tanzania, Uganda and sometimes Mozambique. *For* EAST AFRICA PROTECTORATE *see* KENYA.

EAST AFRICAN COMMUNITY. In June 1967 Uganda, Tanzania and Kenya signed the T. of East African Co-operation which came into effect on 1 Dec. 1967. It replaced the East African Common Services Organisation which was a legacy from the British Commonwealth. It created arrangements for economic and service co-operation somewhat similar to the European arrangements under the T. of Rome. In subsequent years the three states drifted apart politically and co-operation deteriorated to a point of effective abandonment.

EAST ANGLIA. The E. Angles had a strong admixture of Frisians. The first known King was **(1) Wuffa,** whose successor **(2) Sebert (?-?616)** received Bp. Mellitus. Wuffa's grandson **(3) Raedwald (?-627)** received some Christian teaching at the court of his overlord Ethelbert of Kent and set up a Christian altar beside his other ones. When Ethelbert died in 616 Raedwald struck out on his own by helping Edwin of Deira to gain the Northumbrian throne from Aethelfrith of Bernicia at the B. of the Idle (617). Edwin, however, was the senior partner and converted Raedwald's son **(4) Eorpwald (?-?630)** who was soon killed in battle and succeeded by **(5) Sigebert (r. 631-7),** an exile baptised in Gaul. He accepted Celtic missionaries such as St. Fursey but obtained from Abp. Honorius the Burgundian missionary Bp. Felix, who established his see at Dunwich. The East Angles were then under constant attack by the Mercians under K. Penda, who slew Sigebert and his successors **(6) Ecgric** and **(7) Anna (?-654).** The splendid Sutton Hoo ship burial is probably associated with Anna. Its contents show that there was commercial and other traffic with the Continent and even with Byzantium. Anna's brother **(8) Aethelhere (?-654)** was, on the other hand, killed fighting for Penda at the B. of Winwaedsfield. Another brother **(9) Aethelwold (?-663)** reigned peacefully and converted K. Swithhelm of the East Saxons. A separate see for the North folk was erected at Elmham in 673. Aethelwold's nephew **(10) Aethelric** was still alive in 735. After 749 the Kingdom was divided between the North and the South Folk of the Angles and shortly afterwards its kings began to rule as Mercian under-Kings. The arrangement was not altogether happy for **(11) Aethelbert the Saint** was executed in 794 by K. Offa of Mercia where, presumably, his merits were less appreciated than among his own people. After the West Saxon victory at Ellendun in 825, however, Mercian rule collapsed and from 841 the East Anglians had to look after themselves against Danish invasions. Consequently in 854 **(12) Offa (?-?)** King of one Folk adopted **(14) St. Edmund (841-69)** son of **(13) K. Alkmund (?-855)** King of the other. The union effected when Edmund came to the throne at the age of 14 must have been less than complete for in 869 the Danes defeated him and used him as an archery target at Hoxne. Thereafter, when the East Angles were not under Danish rule, they had Eorldormen, of whom the most distinguished were **(15) Athelstan Half-King,** appointed c. 930 by K. Athelstan, and his sons **(16) Aethelwold** and **(17) Aethelwine; (18) Ulfcel (?-1016),** called SNILLING (The Gallant) by his enemies, inflicted severe casualties on the Danes at Thetford in 1004 and fought them again at Ringmere Heath in 1010. By his conduct East Anglia was long known in the north as *Ulfcel's Country.* He fell in the general defeat at Assandun. **(19) Harold Godwin's son,** later King of the English, was another Eorldorman and finally **(20) Aelfgar (r. 1051-62)** son of Earl Leofric of Mercia.

Domesday Book discloses a distinctive social pattern, with 40-45% being free or socmen. In the later Middle Ages the area had flourishing monasteries and from about 1400 many fine perpendicular churches were built from the profits of wool exported mostly through Lowestoft, Ipswich and Lynn. The special local human character was due to the isolating effect of the Fens to the west, but there was always some immigration from the Low Countries.

EASTER originally replaced the Jewish Passover. It was then transferred to the first Sunday after it, but when the Julian calendar was universally adopted, many churches used the Sunday after the full moon on or next after the spring equinox. The problems were raised at Nicaea in 325. In comparison with the Julian, the Jewish calendar was 11 days short and, while the Julian spring equinox had been arbitrarily fixed at 25 Mar. at Alexandria it was by then calculated astronomically as the 21st. In 457 the Gallic Church adopted a new set of paschal tables which did not correspond with the Roman and finally the Celtic Churches had a (now unknown) mode of calculation which differed from all the others. The Roman (Julian) method was adopted for Northumbria in 664 and for all England in 669. *See* WHITBY, SYNOD OF.

EASTERLING or ESTERLING. (1) *See* STERLING. **(2)** a term for a Hansard, *see* HANSE.

EASTERN ASSOCIATION was a union of the parliamentary county forces of East Anglia, Essex and Hertfordshire, formed in 1643 under the E. of Manchester. Its methods provided a precedent for the New Model Army, into which its cavalry, commanded by Cromwell, was incorporated in 1645. The members, notorious for their Independency, gave the London Independents their political clout. *See* CIVIL WAR-6 *et seq.*

EASTERN ORTHODOX CHURCH is a group of churches under 4 ancient patriarchates (Constantinople, Antioch, Jerusalem* and Alexandria*), 5 more recent ones (Moscow, Georgia, Serbia, Roumania and Bulgaria), 5 archbishoprics (Athens*, Cyprus*, Albania, Poland and Slovakia) and the Abbey of Sinai. The head of the West European orthodox diaspora is the Metropolitan of Thyateira. It recognises the first seven general councils of the Church and uses the Nicene Creed without the Procession of the Holy Ghost from the Son, and it gives communion in two kinds. It is in communion with the Anglican Church, having separated from the Roman Church in 1054. It worships mainly in the vernacular. It has always been markedly political since the Turks captured Constantinople and constituted its heads the representatives within their empire of the orthodox *millet.* The four heads marked * have been involved in British affairs in Egypt, Palestine, the Greek crises after World War II and Cypriot independence.

EASTERN QUESTION was the shifting group of problems generated by the slow break up of the Ottoman Empire between the Russian capture of Oczakov in 1776 and the settlement which ended World War I.

EASTER RISING (Dublin) (25-30 Apr. 1916). Augustine Birrell, the Sec. for Ireland, had not disarmed the Irish Volunteers, some of whose extremists, particularly Sir Roger Casement, sought German help. Casement tried (but unsuccessfully) to recruit an Irish Legion from prisoners of war in Germany and a rising with German help was planned for Easter Sunday (24 Apr.) 1916. The Germans went back on their half-promise and landed Casement from a U-boat on Good Friday to warn the conspirators off. He was captured but John MacNeill, the Volunteer Chief of Staff, cancelled the mobilisation and resigned. Hence the rising did not take place as planned, but on the Monday an undisciplined or unwarned Dublin group, unsupported anywhere else, seized the Post Office and proclaimed a Republic. This effort was suppressed in four days with the loss of 100 British and 450 Irish. The seven signatories of the proclamation and all the Volunteer commandants save de Valera were shot. *See* ASQUITH-A 8.

EAST FULHAM BY-ELECTION 1933. In Oct. 1933 Germany withdrew from the Disarmament Conference, which had been the hope of rising world wide pacifist opinion. The conference collapsed. Within a fortnight a Labour candidate turned a Tory majority of 14,000 into a Labour one of 5000 at East Fulham. The electors voted against conservative policies on unemployment, the means test and housing but the result was widely interpreted as a triumph for pacifism.

EAST HERTFORDSHIRE BY-ELECTION (Mar. 1916). Zeppelin raids, though ineffectual, caused alarm, outcry and demands for retaliation. Pemberton Billing successfully challenged the wartime electoral truce by demanding that the war should be directed against the guilty nation, i.e. indiscriminately against civilians. This was a novel idea.

EAST INDIA COMPANY (THE HONOURABLE, OR LONDON) (HEIC or Company Bahadur; nicknamed *John Company).* (*See* CHARTERED COMPANIES.) **(1)** was chartered in 1599 with 125 share holders and a gov. (Sir Thos. Smith) with a committee of 24, to trade for 15 years between the "Cape of Bona Esperanza and the straights of Magellan". Until 1612 the voyages were separate ventures financed by and profiting members privately (usually about 100%). The three-year round trips needed big ships, a large organisation and security. In 1609 the company opened its shipyard at Deptford and, subject to two years' notice, got its charter extended indefinitely. This made it possible to set up the first Indian factory houses in 1610-11 (Masulipatam, Pettapoli) and in 1612 the Indian H.Q. at Surat.

(2) The earlier voyages had penetrated to China for tea and silk and to Indonesia where they collided with Dutch spice interests. The Dutch EIC first proposed amalgamation and then took to violence. A number of HEIC merchants were killed at AMBOINA in 1623 and the Company tacitly retreated from the spice traffic in favour of the cottons and muslins of Bengal where, in the same year, it secured the necessary rights from the Great Mogul.

(3) There were always other bidders for this lucrative commerce and in 1635 Charles I licensed a rival partnership, the **Assada** merchants, to trade in the same seas. This annoyed the City, but in fact the HEIC scarcely suffered and in 1649, by an agreement to co-operate, the HEIC gently absorbed its rival. The main loser had been the govt., for two bodies were harder to tax and control than one; hence in 1657 Cromwell, in renewing its charter, insisted on a single joint Stock Co. and in 1661 Charles II followed suit. He also empowered the Co. to coin money for use in India.

(4) The HEIC shared in the commercial ebullience of the Restoration and for some while potential interlopers invested their money elsewhere. Its Indian status was, however, being transmuted by Indian disorders. The Surat factory, protected from the Portuguese by a mutual forebearance agreement since 1642, had, for example, to be defended against the Marathas in 1664. It was becoming impossible to trade without regard for Indian politics, but power politics require a base. It was a lucky coincidence that Charles II had acquired Bombay in sovereignty by the Braganza marriage and that, finding no use for it, he had given it to the Company. Thither the H.Q. was moved in 1668, the year when Fort William, the germ of Calcutta, was also founded. After hesitations and a local mutiny (Keigwin's Affair) the directors adopted a political, i.e. an aggressive, policy. In truth they had no option but it required concentration on India and involved abandonments elsewhere, notably the stations in the Persian Gulf and Java (1682).

(5) The HEIC now had to struggle through a difficult period. The French, organised in their own EIC, began a state-supported competition in India, where they had set up their first factory at Surat in 1668; the HEIC's rights were challenged in England (*Sandys Case*, 1683) and, worst of all, there was a collision with the Mogul power, not yet fully in eclipse. The factories at Cosimbazar, Masulipatam, Patna, Surat and Vizagapatam were destroyed; Bombay under Sir John Child was blockaded. The traders had to be evacuated from Bengal. Sir John's determination and the presence of a squadron capable of intercepting the *haj* enabled the company to save something in a humiliating peace. Trouble, however, continued. The company spent heavily on the war. Interlopers now competed illegally with it in English markets. It had had the expenses: they gained profits. It replied both to them and the French by improved organisation (the three presidencies of Bombay, Madras and Bengal dated from 1689) and staging (St. Helena was acquired). The interlopers began to meet regularly at Dowgate and organise parliamentary intrigue. By 1691 they were a company in all but name, with a predominantly whig complexion. In 1694 they got the Commons to resolve that all Englishmen should be able to trade in the East.

(6) The Commons resolution was connected with parallel operations in the Scottish parliament which had passed the first of the Darien Co. Acts in 1693. This was promoted mostly by English financiers, to give interlopers a legal standing. The Darien Co. was incorporated by Scottish Act in 1695. The HEIC managed to head off the English subscribers, to the fury of Dowgate, but the latter secured the ear of the govt. by offering a loan of £2M. The result in 1698 was the incorporation of an anomalous company (The **New** or **General EIC)** composed of the Dowgate traders under the title of the **English EIC,** and the HEIC which, however, retained the right to trade separately until 1701.

(7) The arrangement was unworkable. The New Company never functioned and its component bodies outbid each other in India and undercut in England, thus lopping off profits doubly. Their political policies were opposed and they obstructed each other's diplomacy. There were personal feuds. Indian rulers played off one against the other. The HEIC, however, had the advantage of established organisation and experience. By 1700 the likelihood of a French war resolved William III to end the *imbroglio.* He imposed an agreement for full amalgamation (1702) based on valuations to be settled personally by Godolphin. His award (1708) constituted the new HEIC which was to lend to the wartime govt. £3M at 8%.

(8) It was now by far the greatest private institution in Britain, yet thenceforward while its political importance grew steadily, its trading fell increasingly into deficit. Its great revenues were constantly burdened with the cost of policy and wars. Its servants, on the other hand, could, like interlopers, trade on private account, reaping huge advantages from their position and wide profit margins, while habitually entering into (by modern standards) corrupt dealings with local rulers and

businessmen. Hence they robbed the Company of earnings, influence and their own services, and its overheads rose as their wealth increased. The Co. got further extensions, in return for further loans, in 1730 until 1766 and in 1744 until 1780, but the interest simply financed the shield behind which private fortunes were amassed and the public saw with increasing jealousy the return of rich "nabobs" from ostensible employment in a bankrupt concern. It was not the fact of illicit private profit, but its extent which created hostility, for the HEIC's business ramifications penetrated far back into industrial and commercial life. Most of the great East Indiamen, for example, built to a specification, were hired from syndicates of builders entitled to replace them when worn out (usually three trips). Moreover HEIC patronage became important in Home politics just when its Asian activities were complicating Britain's foreign affairs. Prestige forbade Britain to repudiate the company's Indian imperialism, but it was not strong enough to fight the French alone and acts of govt. control thus pre-empted govt. support for the fortunes of men on the make. *See* WARS OF 1739-48; SEVEN YEARS' WAR.

(9) By 1763 the HEIC was an important Indian territorial power, and its ability to involve the govt. in foreign trouble made reform urgent. The first attempt occurred in 1766-7. The second enacted that all territories acquired belonged to the Crown and that the Co's servants might not appropriate their revenues (Lord North's Regulating Act 1773). This failed through the resistance of ingrained habit and the personal incompatibility of the casually corrupt Warren Hastings and the censorious Philip Francis, appointed to operate it. It had not been appreciated how dangerous a lack of co-ordination in the sub continent might be. Despatches between the three Presidencies took weeks and in the meantime they might follow opposed policies which the nominally supreme Gov. of Bengal needed strong powers to control even when his council was united. Fox's India Bill (1783) failed in parliament mainly on the patronage issue, but Pitt's India Act (1784) placed the Company under the supervision of a Board of Control whose President, usually a cabinet minister, had to be shown all political communications between the gov-gen. in Bengal, the Directors and the Secret Committee. This arrangement was easy to evade.

(10) It was still clear that control was inadequate, and in 1793 the gov-gen's powers of superintendance were strengthened. At the same time the charge of the East India Annuities was transferred to the Treasury. In 1813 the Indian monopoly was abolished and the Board was given oversight of the Company's trade. In 1833 the China monopoly was abolished as well, the shareholders being guaranteed 10% interest on stock redeemable at 200 in 1874. The HEIC had thus become a façade behind which India was (more or less) ruled. In 1853 the directors even became crown appointees. The Mutiny of 1857 resulted in 1858 merely in the demolition of the façade, though useful experience was retained by appointing half the new Council of India from the former directors.

EAST INDIA CO. COURTS. Within Calcutta, Madras and Bombay with their respective subordinate settlements and trading posts, the Co. set up an inefficient system of courts for settling disputes between Europeans by what passed for English law. In 1727 a charter transferred minor criminal jurisdiction to the governors and members of councils sitting as J.P.s, and major jurisdiction (save in High Treason) to them collectively as a Quarter Sessions. Civil disputes worth up to Rs. 15 were settled by a Court of Requests; others by a Mayor's Court, with appeal to the Gov. in Council and thence in cases worth over Rs. 3000 to the Privy Council. The Co's older **Zamindar's Court** at Calcutta and **Choultry Court** at Madras (for disputes between Indians) survived concurrently because of the Charter Courts' very restricted geography and lack of jurisdiction over Indians. This confusion, amplified by a further charter of 1753, survived until 1772, notwithstanding that the Co. had since 1757 ruled huge populations beyond the limits of the towns.

(2) In 1772 Warren Hastings set up town and district courts in Bengal, with civil appeals to a **sadar dewani adalat** (Chief Civil Court). The **sadar nazamat adalat** had power to call in and revise criminal judgments. The judges of the lower courts were mostly Co. servants: of the Sadar Courts, the governor and Council, but they all administered Hindu and Mohammedan law. Hence, each court had law officers (*Pundits* for Hindus; *Kazis* and *Moulvis* for Moslems) expert in the respective systems, to whom they publicly put questions to be answered in writing. These answers could be challenged. The courts habitually worked by such advice, unless it seemed against natural justice, or tainted with corruption or pressure.

(3) By 1801 (when the system was extended to the adjacent Ceded and Conquered Provinces and Saugor), overwork and the political need to separate politics from justice caused civil servants to be appointed as judges in the Sadar courts. They became effectively independent and, though English, conducted proceedings after 1803 in Persian.

(4) The Bengal system was copied for the Bombay Presidency in 1799 and for the Madras Presidency in 1802, but permanent judges were first appointed only in 1820. The chief criminal courts in these presidencies were called **foujdari adalat**. Sadar courts were established in 1832 at Allahabad for the Western Provinces.

(5) High courts superseded the Sadar courts in the three presidencies in 1862 and at Agra in 1866.

EAST INDIA CO. (AUSTRIAN). *See* GEORGE 1-12; OSTEND AND OSTEND CO.

EAST INDIA CO. (DANISH) was established in 1612 and after a prosperous period declined and was reconstituted as the ASIATIC CO. in 1732. It had a few Indian factories but, apart from tea, lost its Danish monopoly in 1772 and its Indian establishments between 1801 and 1807 through unavoidable Danish participation in the French Wars. The posts were returned in 1815 but failed commercially and were sold to the HEIC in 1845.

EAST INDIA CO. (DUTCH) (1602) was an amalgamation of 10 companies. These survived in 4 chambers for Amsterdam, Zeeland (Middelburg), the Maas (Rotterdam) and the North Quarter (Enckhuizen). Of its Council of Seventeen (XVII) Amsterdam, which subscribed half the original capital, had 8 and Zeeland, which found a quarter, four. The States-General leased its effective sovereignty and a monopoly of all Dutch trade between the Cape and C. Horn, to it for 21 years at a time. In return it took a large block of shares, 20% of all Spanish and Portuguese loot and certain customs duties, and it expected independent assistance in war. Only Dutchmen might take shares and small subscribers were numerous. Most of the nation was directly or indirectly involved and among the XVII would be found the leading members of the States-General, whose control, save at renewals, was minimal. By 1604 the Co. had seized Bantam, the Moluccas and Java, by 1608 Amboyna and Timor. By 1619 a gov-gen. and Council of India made Batavia (Jakarta) the overseas capital and had encouraged voyages to Siam and Japan, established factories at Pulicat and Surat (India) and occupied Formosa. They took Mauritius in 1638, Malacca in 1641 and, having lost Formosa, established a station at the Cape in 1650 and conquered Ceylon by 1661. This vast organisation was really the nation in aggressive commerce and the conquests represented investment and effort, in which there was little to spare for dividends before 1635. It was the biggest single threat to English commerce throughout

the 17th cent., its ships formed a substantial component of the fleets in the Dutch Wars, besides making the huge convoys which were a feature of the battles, and they brought a steady stream of Dutch migrants to the Cape. The Co. reached its peak in about 1690 and then declined slowly with the general decline of the nation, whose vitality was sapped in the War of the Spanish Succession. Its officials were corrupt and traded on private account. The HEIC monopolised India and engrossed the China tea trade. The Orange party forced their Prince upon the Co. as Director in Chief in 1749 and by 1779 overseas stations were heavily in debt. The final collapse came when the French revolutionaries occupied the Netherlands.

EAST INDIA CO. (FRENCH) was founded by Colbert in 1664. Its first Indian factory opened at Surat in 1668 and in 1673 its acquired Pondicherry (its H.Q.) and in 1690 Chandernagore, just upriver from Calcutta. Business declined during the Wars of the Spanish Succession and Surat was closed, but after the P. of Utrecht, the Co. obtained further encouragement and acquired Mauritius as a staging point in 1721, Mahé in 1725 and Karikal in 1739. Bitter and sometimes violent as the trading rivalry with Britain and Holland had been, it had generally kept to a commercial level. Dupleix, the gov. of Pondicherry, appointed in 1742 adopted a war policy conformably with the Anglo-French struggle in the Wars of 1740 to 1748. He took Madras (Sept. 1746) and held it after a great victory at St. Tomé over Anwar-ud-Din, Nawab of the Carnatic. It was returned to Britain by the T. of Aix-la-Chapelle, but the battles awakened Dupleix to the possibility of intervening with small, highly trained, forces in the politics of the S. Indian princes. French protected rulers had been installed in Mysore and Hyderabad and the Company was to be made self supporting militarily on the revenues of the Northern Circars to compensate for expected British interruptions of communications with France. In this undeclared colonial struggle with the British, the French failed to expel the HEIC, because the British, with dominant seapower, could copy their methods to greater effect. Dupleix was recalled in 1754 and in the Seven Years' War the British took the French settlements one by one. The decisive battle was Eyre Coote's victory over Bussy and Lally at Wandewash in 1760. By the P. of Paris (1763) Pondicherry, Chandernagore, Mahé and Karikal were returned solely as unfortified trading posts. These remained in French possession until handed to India in 1954.

EAST INDIA CO. (PRUSSIAN), planned between 1647 and 1652, was established at Emden in 1745 and chartered by Frederick the Great in 1750. An English Co. was also set up there in 1752. Both had gone out of business by 1765. An Emden financed Co. was launched in 1782 and failed in 1787.

EAST INDIA CO. (SWEDISH) was founded in 1626 and reconstituted in 1731. British competition prevented development in India but it maintained a profitable tea trade until its dissolution in 1813.

EAST INDIES. *See* INDONESIA.

EAST KILBRIDE. *See* NEW TOWNS.

EAST LONDON (S. Africa) at the north of the Buffalo River, was first settled as **FORT GLAMORGAN** by Capt. Wm. Baker in 1847. With the successive development of the port, rail terminal and oil storage, the population had reached 160,000 by 1970.

EAST PRUSSIA. *See* PRUSSIA.

EASTLAND COMPANY was founded in 1579 to monopolise and exploit the trade to Lithuania and Courland left open by the decline of the Hanse. It established a depot at Elbing (Elblag, Poland) and exported coarse cloth and salt in exchange for flax, hemp, furs, tallow and such naval stores as spars, pitch, tar, cables and ropes. It had, however, to endure competition from the Russia Co., which conducted (both ways) the same trade with the interior or intercepted it through Persia, and from foreign carriers, especially the Dutch. Moreover, it suffered after 1650 from a shortage of English shipping as required under the Navigation Acts. It failed in 1673. *See* CHARTERED COMPANIES.

EAST SAXONS. *See* ESSEX.

EATA, St. (?-686) one of 12 English monks trained by St. Aidan at Lindisfarne, became Abbot of Melrose where he trained St. Cuthbert. Between 657 and 661 he, Cuthbert and others founded the monastery at Ripon on land provided by K. Alcfrith of Deira. He accepted the Romanist system after the Synod of Whitby (664) and became Abbot of Lindisfarne with Cuthbert as his prior. In 678, when Theodore of Tarsus carved the see of Bernicia out of Northumbria, he became its first Bp. In 681, when Bernicia was itself divided, he took Lindisfarne, but in 685, when Theodore deposed his colleague Tunbert at Hexham, Eata went to Hexham leaving Cuthbert at Lindisfarne.

EBBSFLEET (A.S. = Shallow creek) (I. of Thanet, Kent) near Richborough at the Pegwell Bay entrance to the Wantsum channel. It was an accepted early mediaeval landing place, giving access by way of the Wantsum and the Stour to Canterbury. Hengist and Horsa landed there in 449 and St. Augustine in 597.

EBEDIW (Welsh) was a payment similar in type to a heriot, but unconnected with land, paid by a man who succeeded to the position of someone who had just died.

EBENEZER (Heb = Hitherto the Lord hath helped us – 1 Sam.vii v. 12). The name of many Baptist or Methodist Meeting Houses and thence any dissenting chapel.

EBORACUM. *See* YORK.

EBURY. *See* GROSVENOR.

ECCLESIASTICAL COMMISSION. *See* JAMES II AND VII-8.

ECCLESIASTICAL COMMISSIONERS. *See* CHURCH COMMISSIONERS.

ECCLESIASTICAL COURTS AND DISCIPLINE. (1) Lord Brougham's parliamentary commission (1830-2) on the ecclesiastical courts recommended the abolition of the York provincial courts, trial by jury and the transfer of the jurisdiction of the Court of Delegates to the Privy Council. The last of these few minor recommendations were effected in 1834. **(2)** In 1881 Gladstone and Selbourne secured a further parliamentary commission with similar terms of reference, mainly to find better ways of settling the ritual and doctrinal disputes then raging. In 1883 the radical ideas which emerged (including a highest court of Anglican laymen) were fully supported by only nine of the 25 members and nothing was done. **(3)** A Royal Commission on ecclesiastical discipline (1904-6) made exhaustive enquiries. It reported that the law on public worship was narrow and the machinery of enforcement unworkable. It recommended the regularisation of certain vestments, the reorganisation of dioceses, the adoption of the recommendations of the Commission of 1881 and the repeal of the Public Worship Regulation Act. The Letters of Business issued to Convocations as a result began a dilatory process of overhaul, including the Prayer Book revisions defeated in Parliament in 1927 and 1928, but nevertheless illegally authorised by Convocation.

ECCLESIASTICAL RESERVATION was a proviso to the P. of Augsburg (1555) that no ecclesiastical ruler should retain his lands if converted to protestantism.

ECCLESIASTICAL TENTH (1534) was a perpetual tithe payable to the Crown under statute as from Apr. 1535 upon the value of all church benefices in consideration of which the fifth (last) instalment of the fines of £118,840 imposed for breach of Praemunire in 1530 was remitted. *See* FIRST FRUITS.

ECCLESIASTICAL TITLES ACT, 1851. The papacy instituted a new R. Catholic hierarchy in Britain in 1850 and this Act was passed to prevent its members assuming territorial titles. A dead letter from the first, it was repealed in 1871.

ECCLESTON, Thomas of (?1216-after 1259), a London Franciscan studied at Oxford and knew the early English Franciscans, particularly William of Nottingham (Provincial from 1240 to 1254). To remind the friars of his time, of the simplicity and fervour of their predecessors, he meticulously composed *De Adventu Fratrum Minorum in Angliam* (Lat = The Coming of the Friars Minor to England).

ECGFRITH. *See* NORTHUMBRIA.

ECHELON. That part of a military force set aside for a particular function within the general scheme of its operations, e.g. the forward and rear echelons of its transport or medical services.

ECK, Johann Maier von (1486-1543) leading German R. Catholic controversialist and opponent of Luther, came to initial prominence at Leipzig in 1519 and fame or notoriety in his reply to Melanchon's *Loci Theologicales* (Lat = Theological Postulates) in 1525. He remained a leading R. Catholic intellectual throughout his life.

ECLIPSE, said to have been the finest racehorse ever, was foaled in 1764 and was unbeaten until put to stud in 1770. An ancestor of most modern English racehorses.

ECONOMICS. The many schools of economists have been so long and so much in conflict that unsurprisingly there is disagreement even about the definition and content of this "dismal science" itself. The following represents a cautious selection of definitions and descriptions: **(1)** The art of directing production, consumption, income and expenditure by a state; **(2)** The science of wealth and exchangeable values; **(3)** Man's relation to wealth; **(4)** Methods for the systematic alleviation of poverty; **(5)** The study of the social phenomena arising out of man's ability and activity in acquiring and using wealth; **(6)** The principles governing the application of scarce means with alternative uses to a multiplicity of ends; **(7)** A theory which furnishes no body of settled conclusions, but is a method or technique which helps its possessor to draw correct conclusions.

ECONOMIST, a weekly journal, was founded in 1843 with the encouragement of the Anti-Corn Law League. It survived the repeal of the Corn Laws (1846) to become a distinguished intellectual journal, covering all aspects of national and international affairs.

ECONOMY COMMITTEE of the Cabinet studied the situation in 1931 and made proposals to meet the crisis.

ECREHOUS and MINQUIERS (C.I.). Groups of islets and skerries in the bailiwick of Jersey, disputed because of their usefulness for fishing, for many centuries between Jerseymen and the French. They were awarded to Jersey by the International Court of Justice as late as 1953.

ECUADOR (*See* BOLIVAR.) Ecuador seceded from Colombia in Sept. 1830 and apart from two periods (1831-5 and 1839-45) of dictatorship under Gen. FLORES, by 1860 there was no effective central govt. at all. There followed the strongly ultramontane but modernising autocracy of GARCIA MORENO, who held office from 1861 to 1865 and 1869 to 1875. Under him communications and agriculture were much improved. His assassination during the election campaign of 1875 ushered in twenty years of disorder between the conservative and religious *serranos* (highlanders) and the more liberal *costeños* (coast dwellers). Eventually the *costeños* under ELOY ALFARO obtained power in 1895 and by 1916 the alternating liberal govts. of Alfaro and LEONIDAS PLAZA had disestablished the church, modernised the administration and built the Quito Rly. In 1916, the govt. fell under the domination of the Guayaquil (*costeño*) bankers who, in 1925, were ousted by the predominantly *serrano* army. Shortly afterwards the world depression supervened and between 1935 and 1940 the governing *juntas* had seven successive heads. In 1940 the liberal CARLOS ARROYO DEL RIO was elected president and in 1941 he was involved in an unsuccessful war with Peru, which annexed most of the Amazonian Oriente province. This seizure was confirmed by the Pan American Foreign Ministers Conference in 1942.

Arroyo del Rio, however, maintained himself in power until 1944, when the conservative JOSE MARIA VELASCO IBARRA seized the govt. with left as well as right-wing support. In the next three years he alienated first the left wing and then his own natural supporters and in 1947 was driven out by the army. After the elections of 1948 GALO PLAZA, son of Leonidas, formed a coalition and until 1960 govts. were constitutionally and, on the whole, peacefully elected. In 1960 Velasco Ibarra returned to power but was forced to resign in 1961. The Vice-President, Carlos Arosemena Monroy, tried to carry on but was removed in 1963 by the army which set up a military *junta*. This body promised constitutional govt. after stability had been achieved, but failing in its promises was driven from office by rioting and strikes in 1966. After further convulsions the armed forces agreed to establish constitutional govt. and at the 1968 elections under a new constitution Velasco Ibarra was elected president yet again. Further oscillations involving this erratic but wildly popular statesman ended with his fifth and last resignation in 1972 in favour of another military *junta*. This ruled until 1979 during an oil boom which created much development of the infrastructure but also an inflation which weighed heavily on the poor. In July 1979 the *junta* handed over to JAIME ROLD S AGUILERA, a constitutionally elected reforming social democrat, on a programme of greater equality and equity in the distribution of oil profits. He was killed in an air accident in 1981 but his successors, even if they had wished, could not carry on his policies because of declining world oil prices. Hence the rich, who were in politics, kept their gains while the poor, who were not, became poorer. By 1987 Pres. FEBREA CORDERO (who on one occasion was kidnapped by his own air force) had suspended payments on the foreign debt.

ECUMENISM is a movement of mainly protestant inspiration, which first became pronounced in the 1960s to reunite the Christian churches. The participants appeared by 1992 to have found some emotional common ground but to be intellectually at cross purposes.

EDDA. The Poetic or Elder or (erroneously) Saemund's Edda, is a collection made in about 1200 of Old Norse poems on mythology and traditions of Norse heroes. For PROSE EDDA *see* STURLASSON, SNORRI.

EDDYSTONE. A dangerous shoal and rocks visible only at ebb tide in the Channel fairway between the Start and the Lizard. Henry Winstanley's first (100ft) lighthouse (1696) was destroyed in a storm in 1703. John Rudyerd's second (92ft) (1706) was burned down in 1755. These were timber constructions on a stone base. John Smeaton built the third (85ft) of Portland stone and granite but the underlying rock proved unstable and it had, save for the ground floor, to be demolished. Sir John Douglass built the fourth (133ft) stone lighthouse in 1882.

EDEN. Family originating in Durham. Of the children of Sir Robert Eden, Bt. **(1) William (1744-1814) 1st Ld. AUCKLAND (Ir. 1789, G.B. 1793)** started brilliantly as a barrister and as a result of his book *Principles of Penal Law* became U.Sec. of State in 1772 and M.P. for Woodstock in 1774. He married Eleanor, *d.* of Sir Gilbert Elliot (later E. of Minto and gov-gen. of India) and in 1776 opposed transportation to America. In 1778 he was sent there as a negotiator and in 1780 he became the E. of Carlisle's Chief Sec. for Ireland and founded the National Bank for Ireland under Shelburne and Pitt. A strong Pittite, he resigned again when the Fox-North coalition assumed office in Dec. When Pitt returned to power Eden was sent to France in 1785 to negotiate the commercial treaty of 1786, the Convention of 1787, the settlement of the disputes between the English and the French East India Cos. and of the Dutch question (1787).

In 1788 he became ambassador at Madrid; in 1789 he went on a commercial mission to the U.S.A. and was ambassador at The Hague from 1790 to 1793; he retired from diplomacy, but exerted great political influence through his friendship with Pitt. As a result in 1798 he joined the govt. as postmaster-gen. but resigned with Pitt on the Irish issue in 1801. His brother **(2) Morton (1752-1830) 1st Ld. HENLEY (Ir. 1799)** was a diplomat employed as minister at Munich and Ratisbon (1776-9), Copenhagen (1779-82), Dresden (1783-91), Saxe Coburg and Berlin (1791-3), Vienna (1794), Madrid (1794) and finally Vienna again (1794-9). The second son of **(1)**, **(3) George (1784-1849) 2nd Ld. and E. of AUCKLAND (1839)** became M.P. for Woodstock in 1810 and attended the Lords as a consistently sensible Whig from 1814. Hence he entered the Cabinet as Pres. of the Bd. of Trade under Grey in 1830. He became First Lord of the Admiralty in 1834 but in 1835 succeeded L. William Bentinck as gov-gen. of India. He involved the govt. in the disastrous Afghan Policy (*see* AFGHANISTAN) and was recalled in Feb. 1842. He left, however, one enduring achievement, namely the famine organisation of the north west. His brother **(4) Robert (1799-1870) 3rd Ld. AUCKLAND,** was Bp. of Sodor and Man from 1847-54 and of Bath and Wells thereafter. Later descendants in the family include **(5) (Robert) Anthony (1897-1977) 1st E. of AVON (1961).** He became M.P. in 1923. He was U. Sec. for Home Affairs (1925-6), Sec. of State for Foreign Affairs (1926-9) and then U. Sec. of State in the National Govt. from 1931. He made a spectacular resignation over British policy towards Italian aggression in Ethiopia, but was brought back as Lord Privy Seal in 1934; Min. for League of Nations Affairs in 1935 and for Dominion Affairs from 1939 to 1940. When the Churchill govt. was formed in May 1940 he became Sec. of State for War, but in Dec. for Foreign Affairs again until July 1945 and from Oct. 1951 to Apr. 1955. He was Prime Minister from Apr. 1955 to Jan. 1957 when he was forced to resign over the Suez War (*see* EDEN GOVT.). His kinsman **(6) Sir John Benedict (1925-)** became M.P. for Bournemouth in 1954 and was Min. for Industry 1970-2 and for Posts and Telecommunications 1972-4.

EDEN GOVT. (Apr. 1955-Jan. 1957) (1) was a continuation of Churchill's Tory govt. elected in 1951, with Anthony Eden replacing Churchill, Harold Macmillan replacing Eden at the Foreign Office and Selwyn Lloyd replacing Macmillan at Defence. In Dec. 1955 there was a general reshuffle. R.A. Butler took the Privy Seal, Macmillan replaced him at the Exchequer. Lloyd moved to the Foreign Office. Sir Walter Monckton to Defence and Iain Macleod took Monckton's place at the Min. of Labour and N. Service.

(2) Budgets reduced income tax and increased purchase tax and a general election was called for in May. The Tories increased their majority to 344 seats against 277 Labour and 8 Liberal, but Butler's second budget marked a temporary end of the boom and this created a pretext for his removal from the Exch; his activism was distrusted by his party's traditionalists, who had muted their misgivings under Churchill. Their spokesman, the M. of Salisbury, advocated firmness and Britain's imperial mission. They were an embarrassment to Eden whose cast of mind was essentially liberal. The govt. acted firmly in the prevailing unrest in Kenya and Cyprus but newspapers began to suggest that Eden was a do-nothing. These jibes and Eden's false perception of the Egyptian Pres. Gamal Nasser as a kind of Hitler persuaded him to adopt the fatal course leading to war, after the Egyptians nationalised the Suez Canal. This involved collusive intervention in an Israeli-Egyptian war, in which nobody believed in British innocence; the military operations were bungled and the Russians threatened intervention by Inter-continental ballistic missile, while the U.S.A. refused to support Britain. The result was a humiliating retreat. Eden, who had long been in poor health, resigned. *See* EDEN-5; EGYPT-24.

EDEN TREATY 1786 between Britain and France provided for reciprocal duties on a most favoured nation basis. *See* EDEN-1.

EDFRITII, St. (?-721) Bp. of Lindisfarne from 698, was trained in Ireland. An accomplished scribe, he was the designer and artist of the Lindisfarne Gospels.

EDGAR, King (r. 959-75). *See* AETHEILSTAN'S SUCCESSORS-10.

EDGAR AFFAIR (1898). Tom Edgar, a British workman in the Transvaal, was killed by a Boer policeman who was tried by a packed Boer court, acquitted and commended. This provoked uproar among *Uitlander* workpeople and the Uitlander petition to the British govt. *See* SALISBURY'S THIRD GOVT.-11.

EDGAR the Atheling (?-1106) *s.* of Edward the Exile and born in Hungary, was canvassed for the English throne after Harold II's death at Hastings, but William the Conqueror moved too quickly and he submitted. William received him with honour. As a result of the English revolts of 1068 and 1069 and his Danish connections, he went abroad and lived successively at the Scots, Flemish and French courts, but returned to William, who liked him, in 1074. In 1086 he joined the Normans in Apulia and went thence to the court of D. Robert of Normandy. In 1097 he commanded the Scottish expedition which set his nephew Edgar on the throne. In 1099 he went on crusade but returned to Normandy where in 1106 he joined Robert against Henry I and was captured at Tinchebrai but released. *See* HAROLD II.

EDGAR (r. 1097-1107) K. of Scots. *See* SCOTS AND ALBAN KINGS. EARLY-22.

EDGCUMBE. W. Devon gentry **(1) Sir Richard (?-1489)** was M.P. for Tavistock and escheator of Cornwall in 1467. He supported the Buckingham rising against Richard III in 1484, was knighted for bravery at Bosworth Field in 1485 and became a privy councillor. In 1487 he was sheriff of Devon and in 1488 ambassador to Scotland and commissioner in Ireland. He negotiated a truce with Brittany where he died. His son **(2) Sir Piers (?-1539)**, another sheriff of Devon in 1493, 1494 and 1497, was knighted for bravery at the B. of the Spurs in 1513. His son **(3) Sir Richard** was also sheriff in 1543 and 1544 and a muster commissioner in Cornwall in 1557. Further descendants included **(5) Richard (1680-1758) 1st Ld. EDGCUMBE (1742).** He was M.P. for Cornwall in 1701 and subsequently for Plympton and a lord of the Treasury in 1716 and 1720. In 1724 he acquired (in absence) most of the effective offices in the Irish revenue. An adherent of Walpole, he later became the govt's manager of the Cornish boroughs. To ensure his silence in the suspected borough scandals, he was given a peerage and was from 1743 Ch. of the Duchy of Lancaster. **(6) Richard (1716-61) 2nd Ld.**, was M.P. for Lostwithiel from 1747 to 1754 and for Penryn in 1754. He was a friend of Horace Walpole and Reynolds. His brother **(7) George (1721-95) 3rd Ld., 1st Vist. (1781) 1st E. (1789)** became an admiral in 1778. His son **(8) Richard (1764-1839) 2nd E.**, was M.P. for Fowey from 1786 to 1795 and a privy councillor in 1806.

EDICTUM REGIUM (Lat = Royal Decree) (1195) issued by Hubert Walter, extended the Assizes of Clarendon (1166) and Northampton (1176). Knights were assigned in each shire to take oaths from all male adults to keep the peace and denounce or take peace breakers. *See* JUSTICES OF THE PEACE.

EDINBURGH (Scot). The castle rock was anciently a stronghold and the city is probably named after the 7th cent. Northumbrian K. Edwin. He built or garrisoned it as a northern protection for his kingdom, which then included Lothian. K. David I used it as an occasional royal seat. He founded Holyrood Abbey and chartered its burgh of Canongate; other kings followed his example,

but Edinburgh or its castle were intermittently disputed with the English. They held the castle in 1091-1113, 1327-38 and in 1356. It was James I (r. 1406-37) who made it his capital after his return from England in 1424. It was first walled under James II (r. 1437-60) but it was not the undisputed capital until the end of the 16th cent, by which time the Kings, since James IV (r. 1488-1513), had been using Holyrood House for some time. During the Jacobite rebellions of 1715 and 1745 English garrisons held the castle. No British monarch visited Edinburgh between Charles II in 1650 and George IV (who made himself popular in Highland dress) in 1822, but the exiled French K. Charles X lived at Holyroodhouse in the 1830s and Q. Victoria started to visit the city in 1842. The treaty of union of 1707 by expressly preserving Scottish institutions such as its law and courts and the Kirk, ensured that there would always be some sort of administration in Edinburgh, and this expanded considerably in the 20th cent. because of the rise of certain Scottish industries such as oil, engineering and shipbuilding and the natural Scots independent-mindedness. Hence Edinburgh began to recover most of the features of a capital city which had been lost in the upheavals of the early 18th cent. The important literary and musical festival was first held in 1947.

EDINBURGH, Dukedoms of, were held by **(1)** Frederick, a grandson of George I from 1726. The title merged in the Crown at the accession of Frederick's son as George III. **(2)** Alfred, 2nd son of Q. Victoria, from 1866. It became extinct when he died without a living son. **(3)** Philip Mountbatten from 1947.

EDINBURGH REVIEW A liberal journal from 1802 to 1829. It attracted attention by a mixture of classical literary standards and the championship of political innovation. In 1815 it was selling 14,000 copies per issue. The editor was Francis Jeffrey.

EDINBURGH, T. of (Mar. 1338) confirmed by **NORTHAMPTON, T. of (May 1338)** established Scots independence of England. *See* ISABELLA OF FRANCE-5; ROBERT I K OF SCOTS.

EDINBURGH, T. of (July 1560). *See* MARY Q. OF SCOTS-6, never ratified-8.

EDINBURGH UNIVERSITY was founded in 1583 by the burgh council as the Town's College, but its equivalence with a university was confirmed by Act in 1621. It developed a famous medical faculty in the 18th cent. but was, strictly speaking, erected into a university only in 1858.

EDINGTON, William of (?-1366) Bp. of WINCHESTER (1346-66) Chancellor (1356-63), a King's clerk in 1335, by 1340 was collecting the Ninth in the southern shires and in 1341 he reached high office as Keeper of the Wardrobe. From 1345-56 he was Treas. of the Exchequer and was much concerned in financing the French war during the years of English victories. He achieved the bimetallic currency reform of 1351 and restored the financial supremacy of the Exchequer over other depts., especially by 1356 over the King's Chamber. He then became Chancellor. His ascendancy as a minister coincided with a time when Edward III was content to govern with the advice of his council and to keep on terms with his parliaments. One chronicler calls him a friend of the Commons, whom he protected from royal extortion. His influence undoubtedly made for stability. In 1363 he asked to be relieved of royal office in order to pay more attention to diocesan affairs. He built and endowed a splendid collegiate church at Edington and began to recase the pillars of the nave at Winchester cathedral which enabled his successors, especially William of Wykeham, to transform the building into the spectacular perpendicular monument which it became. His own chantry chapel is a foretaste of this style. He sensibly declined the archbishopric of Canterbury just before his death.

EDISON, Thomas Alva (1847-1931) invented the phonograph in 1877; the incandescent electric bulb in 1879 and completed the first central power plant (at New York) in 1882. He took out over 1000 patents in the course of his life.

EDITH or EADGITHA (?-1075), *d.* of Earl Godwin, married Edward the Confessor in 1044. He secluded her for political reasons in 1051 but brought her back to court in 1052. Thereafter she played no significant role.

EDITH, St. (?962-84), *d.* of K. Edgar, built the church at Wilton.

EDLING. *See* WELSH LAW-2.

EDMONDES, Sir Clement (?1564-1622) married in 1598 an attendant of Lord Stafford and brought a victory despatch from Nieuport to court in 1600. By 1601 he was sufficiently noticed to become assistant to the City Remembrancer, to whose office he succeeded in 1605. As the main intermediary between the City and the Crown he became well known and in 1609 he secured a clerkship of the P.C. for life. He made a fortune through forfeitures for recusancy (1610-2) and was used in Dec. 1614 to negotiate the commercial disputes with the Dutch. An M.P. from 1620 to 1621 for Oxford University he became Sec. of State just before he died.

EDMONDSTONE (1) Neil Benjamin (1765-1841) was a govt. Persian translator with Mornington on the expedition against Tippoo Sahib in 1799, translating Tippoo's secret archives. In 1801 he became sec. of the foreign and political dept. and probably originated the policy of subsidiary treaties. In 1809 he became Chief Sec. to the govt. and was a member of the Council from 1812 to 1817. His son **(2) Sir George Frederick (1813-64)** was commissioner for the Cis-Sutlej states and sec. of the foreign and political dept. in 1856. He advised the annexation of Oudh, an important cause of the Indian Mutiny; he was lieut.-gov. of the N.W. Provinces from 1859 to 1863 and set up the new Central Provinces administration in 1863.

EDMUND OF ABINGDON, St. *See* HENRY III-8.

EDMUND, St. (841-69) King and Martyr. *See* BURY ST. EDMUNDS; EAST ANGLIA-14; VIKINGS-10.

EDMUND CROUCHBACK. *See* LANCASTER-FIRST FAMILY-1.

EDMUND I (r. 939-46). *See* AETHIELSTAN'S SUCCESSORS-7.

EDMUND "IRONSIDE" King (r. 1016). *See* ETHELRED II, THE UNREADY AND EDMUND IRONSIDE.

EDMUND OF LANGLEY (1341-1402) E. of CAMBRIDGE (1362) D. of YORK (1385) 5th *s.* of Edward III, was trained by him in the French wars and became an important aide to the Black Prince in Spain (1367) and at the storm of Limoges (1370) and for whose primary advantage he married Isabella *d.* of Peter the Cruel of Castile in 1372. In 1376 he became Constable of Dover and in 1377 a member of the regency for Richard II. In pursuit of his brother John of Gaunt's claim to Castile he commanded the ill-supported expedition to Portugal in 1381 and received his Dukedom during Richard's ineffectual Scottish invasion in 1385. In 1386 he was a member of the Commission for dealing with the King's favourites and household, but he was one of Richard's mediators in the crises of 1387 and attempted to save Sir Simon Burley, one of the King's most influential advisers, from the Appellants in 1388. In 1394 he acted as Keeper of the Realm during Richard's Irish Campaign. In 1399 he held the same position during another of Richard's absences and his ineptitude contributed to Henry of Lancaster's overthrow of Richard. He surrendered to Henry at Berkeley and retired after Henry's coronation.

EDMUND RICH OF ABINGDON, St. (?-1240) Abp. of CANTERBURY (1234) was one of the 13th cent. prelates who rose through the schools. Between 1190 and 1222 he studied at Oxford and Paris, lectured at Oxford, graduated in Theology at Paris and then taught at Oxford again. In 1222 he became Treasurer of Salisbury cathedral through his friendship with the learned bishop Richard Poore, and he became known for the moral inspiration of his preaching and the austerity of his life. On the death of Richard Grant, Abp. of Canterbury (1231) there was a long disputed election and the Pope recommended the chapter to elect Edmund Rich. Of great integrity but without any liking for administration or the temperament of an ecclesiastical statesman, he nevertheless helped to settle the political crisis which ended in the fall of Peter des Rievaux and showed much moral courage in his leadership of the bishops. Unfortunately he remained at odds with his own chapter throughout his primacy. He died at Pontigny on the way to Rome and his shrine became a place of pilgrimage. St. Edmund Hall (Oxford) is named after him.

EDMUND (?1430-56) E. of RICHMOND (1452) married the wealthy Margaret Beaufort, *d.* of the D. of Somerset. They were the parents of Henry VII.

EDMUND OF WOODSTOCK (1301-30) E. of KENT (1321) youngest *s.* of Edward I, was summoned to the Parliament of 1320 and supported his brother in the civil war of 1322, himself besieging Lancaster's stronghold of Pontefract and witnessing his execution. He then became Lieut. in the North and, after a diplomatic mission to Paris (1323), became Lieut. in Aquitaine (1324). He joined in the overthrow of Edward II, became a member of the council of regency for Edward III and was judicially murdered. *See* MORTIMER-9.

EDRIC OF KENT. *See* KENT, KINGDOM-4.

EDRIC STREONA (?-1017), self-seeking and notoriously unreliable ealdorman of the Mercians from 1007, married a daughter of K. Ethelred the Unready in 1009. He deserted K. Edmund Ironside for Canute, who put him to death. *See also* VIKINGS-22.

EDUCATION ACT 1496 (Scot) was inspired by James IV to ensure that those who might have to administer justice locally, such as lords of heritable jurisdictions, should (Scots law being based on Roman Law) have 'perfect Latin' and some legal knowledge to be acquired at the universities.

EDUCATION ACTS. That of **1870** was introduced by W. E. Forster, Vice-Pres. of the Privy Council for Education. It set up school boards for boroughs and parishes to be elected by burgesses or ratepayers and able to charge the rates. These were obliged to provide sufficient elementary schools accommodation: they had to charge fees, which could be remitted in cases of poverty and they could make byelaws requiring children to be sent to these schools unless the children were "under efficient instruction in some other manner". Since it took ten years to build the schools and train the teachers, attendance was not fully compulsory until 1880. The Schools received an annual parliamentary grant and a further grant where local rate resources were low. **1902** transferred the powers and properties of the school boards to councils of counties, county boroughs and boroughs with more than 10,000 inhabitants and empowered councils to assist education other than elementary by amounts not exceeding for counties the product of a 2d rate and for boroughs and urban districts a 1d. Each council had to set up an education committee and refer all educational matters to it. As education was supervised by the Board (later Min. and Dept.) of Education (or more especially by the strong-minded and ambitious Sir Robert Morant who drafted the Act), these committees tended to regard themselves as virtually independent of their parent councils and responsible to the central department. They even had a national association of their own. That of **1944** raised the school leaving age to 16, created a system of primary, secondary and further education into which existing voluntary schools was fitted, the whole being for the most part directly or indirectly centrally financed. Alongside this system, govt.-financed entry to universities made university places increasingly open to the new students, with a resulting expansion of existing universities and in due course increase in their numbers and the creation of many polytechnics.

EDUCATION, Central Depts. of. A Committee of the Privy Council to administer grants to educational societies was set up in 1839 and supplemented by an Education Dept. in 1856. Their functions were enlarged by the Elementary Education Act, 1870, which set up the School Boards and the system of inspection and they were superseded in 1899 by a Board of Education when secondary schools began to be created. The Board was replaced by an expensive Ministry under the Education Act, 1944. A Min. of Science was appointed in 1959 and the two were combined into a Dept. of Education and Science in 1964 under a Sec. of State. Welsh education, however, was administered from the Welsh Office from that date. These bodies were, since the advent of Sir Robert Morant, distinguished by their ambitions and tendency to encroach upon the daily work of the educational institutions. The Dept. was partly amalgamated with the Dept. of Employment in 1995.

EDWARD THE CONFESSOR (?1001-66) King (1042), *s.* of Ethelred the Unready and Emma of Normandy **(1)** spent his years from eleven, when K. Swein, K. Canute's father, invaded England, until he was forty in Normandy. When his mother in 1017 made her second marriage to Canute he continued under D. Robert's protection. He was called to England by Canute's son, K. Harthacnut, in 1041 and succeeded him a few months later.

(2) His position as King had serious weaknesses. He was really a foreigner. He was devout rather than strong. In a not wholly united country he lacked a secure power base because his ancestral Wessex had been granted by Canute as an earldom to Godwin. Canute could afford this because his authority was backed by his Scandinavian quasi-imperial power, but Edward did not have that either. Hence he had to depend on the ecclesiastical magnates and play the great earls, Godwin of Wessex, Siward of Northumbria and Leofric of Mercia against each other. Theoretically he could dismiss them; in practice their followings made this impossible. At the same time they had no habit of loyalty to him.

(3) His accession represented a change of balance in favour of the northerners as against the southern power of the house of Godwin, but the recent bad times had left the Crown without funds, which the earls were unwilling to supply. The northerners wanted to get rid of the twice widowed Q. Emma, who held most of the royal treasure at Winchester. They decided to seize it: a project in which Godwin could only concur. Stegan (Stigand), Emma's adviser and chaplain and Bp. of Elmham since 1038, was induced to go to his see for consecration. The three earls marched quickly from Gloucester to Winchester and seized the treasury for the King. Emma, unharmed, was deprived of her lands and thrust out of public life. Stegan lost his see and lands too.

(4) The political history of the reign centres on the question of the succession, for Edward was and remained childless, his brother Alfred was dead and Edmund Ironside's surviving son, Edward, was in Hungary. Of the remaining competitors, three had claims of equal weight by relationship through various married royal women. *See Table in Appendix where these are marked*.

There was a further complication: Magnus of Norway had been at war with the Danes and in 1038 had made a pact of mutual succession with K. Hardicanute when he was in Denmark. Hence he was at war with K. Sweyn. Magnus' son, the famous adventurer Harald Hardrâda ("ruthless") claimed that the pact applied to England.

(5) In England, Godwin's family was opposed by the other earls but he, as commander of the Thingmen (the only professional force) was the King's shield against Norwegian intervention. The King was determined not to be dominated by Godwin, but could not dispense with

him. He balanced the other earls against him and both sides competed to secure the great posts in state and church (with their properties and dependants) for their own supporters. In 1043 Siward, a neutral, became Abp. of Canterbury, but the King's chaplain, Heremon, secured Sherborne. In 1044 Stegan returned to Elmham and Edward married Godwin's daughter Eadgitha; on the other hand his Norman friend, Robert of Jumièges, became Bp. of London. In 1045 HAROLD (?-1066) Godwin's son, became E. of the East Angles but in 1046 Leofric, a King's chaplain, became Bp. of Crediton and in 1047 Heca, another Bp. of Selsey.

(6) Harald Hardrâda's accession in Norway raised the tension. He inherited his father's war and desired peace with England, but K. Swein of Denmark sent to England for help. When a Norwegian fleet raided the English coast, English help was refused. Harald's peace overtures were an important factor in the crisis which followed. Earl Swein, Godwin's vicious son, abducted the Abbess of Leominster, was outlawed and fled to Bruges. The Emperor was at war with the Count of Flanders and the English fleet blockaded the coast for him. E. Swein parleyed but the King had transferred his lands to Beorn, a relative, and Swein's brother Harold. On their insistence the King refused to reverse the outlawry. The fleet was now going home and Swein met Godwin and Beorn at Pevensey. His purpose was to persuade them to intercede with the King. Neither gave any undertakings but Beorn agreed to go with Swein, who kidnapped and murdered him.

(7) The disgrace of Godwin's family was complete. Swein again fled to Bruges. A council held by the King at London seized the opportunity to reduce the Thingmen. Godwin's partisan Eadsine, the Abp. of Canterbury, died 1050; the King nominated Robert of Jumièges. He sent him to Rome for his *pallium*, while Godwin's abbot of Abingdon, Sparhafoc, nominated to London, had to await consecration until Robert returned. The King's position was a strong one: he now offered to lift Swein's outlawry if the Thingmen were disbanded. The bargain was carried out. This not only weakened Godwin militarily, but the King got the credit for abolishing the unpopular *heregeld* out of which they were paid. In June 1051 Robert of Jumièges returned and refused to consecrate Sparhafoc.

(8) Godwin now had the opportunity to strike back. Count Eustace of Boulogne, who had married Edward's sister, visited Edward and had been temporarily granted some royal rights of purveyance. His retinue behaved badly and there was a bloody affray at Dover. The King called on Godwin, as Earl of Kent, to punish the men of Dover. Relying on local xenophobia and the unpopularity of purveyance, Godwin refused and summoned a secret family conference. This was betrayed to the King. It was clear that Godwin intended treason and Edward sent to the northern earls for help. Godwin raised the Wessex armies. The hosts confronted each other at Langtree in Gloucestershire. The King prevented a battle and it was decided to hold a great council at London.

(9) During the interval the ardour of Godwin's followers cooled. Before the council Godwin demanded hostages. When they were refused he, with his sons Swein, Tostig and Gyrth, fled to Bruges while the other sons, Harold and Leofwine, escaped *via* Bristol to Ireland. The council outlawed them all and Edward secluded the Queen, as Godwin's daughter, in a nunnery. Harold's earldom of the East Angles went to Alfgar, son of E. Leofric. Odda, a relative of the King, received Dorset, Somerset, Devon and Cornwall and William, another King's chaplain, became Bp. of London. This marked the summit of the King's fortunes. It was in this year that William of Normandy paid him a state visit and was probably designated heir to the English throne.

(10) Without a professional core, the King's forces could be kept on a war footing only for limited periods.

On the other hand many disbanded Thingmen had probably gone to Irish ports where Harold recruited his professional Housemen. In the spring of 1052 Godwin sailed from Bruges after the King's levies had dispersed. He met Harold at Portland and they sailed into London. The northern earls could not arrive in time. London surrendered, Robert of Jumièges and other Normans fled and Stegan arranged an accommodation. The council reversed the outlawry and restored the dignities of Godwin and his family. The Queen returned. E. Odda was relegated to the Hwiccas.

(11) Godwin, however, died in less than a year and Harold succeeded him as E. of Wessex. Respectful in outward forms to the King, he continued his family's pursuit of power. Stegan became intrusive Abp. of Canterbury. In July 1054 Siward of Northumbria defeated Macbeth at Dunsinane but his son and nephew were killed. In 1055 he himself died and the vacant earldom was conferred on Tostig, Harold's brother.

(12) He now felt strong enough to oust Alfgar from his old earldom of East Anglia. Alfgar was charged with treason but fled to Wales and, with the help of Gruffydd ap Llywellyn of Gwynedd and some Vikings, invaded the border earldom belonging to Ralph, a relative of the King. Alfgar's father, Leofric of Mercia, threatened to join them. Godwin's family came to terms. Alfgar was not only restored but his daughter was married to Gruffydd.

(13) Harold now approached the problem from the other end. A fighting priest, Leofgar, was put into the see of Hereford to strengthen Ralph, and military operations were begun against the Welsh. In 1057. however, Leofric died and the Mercian and East Anglian earldoms were united under Alfgar. Ralph, however, died and Leofgar was killed in a skirmish. In 1058 (when Stegan received his pallium from Benedict X) the border earldom, in so far as it was governed at all, was controlled by Harold. In 1063 he and Tostig, after intrigues with the south Welsh whom Gruffydd had conquered, invaded Wales. Gruffydd was murdered.

(14) Harold was now reckoned the chief ruler in the Kingdom, but two important events disturbed his progress. The first was that in 1064 he was wrecked on the Norman coast, captured and handed over to William, who forced him to swear an oath to him. The second was a northern revolt in 1065 against Tostig, who took refuge at Bruges. The earldom, on Harold's advice, was given to Morcar, son of Alfgar, whose sister (the widow of Gruffydd of Gwynedd) Harold now married. This compromise estranged Tostig. On 5 Jan. 1066 the Confessor died.

(15) The disorderly politics of the reign have obscured more solid developments evidenced by Edward's foundation of Westminster Abbey, consecrated just before his death and by administrative practices. The King's reputation for piety and his artistic taste were remembered. As his reign receded into the past, his life acquired a glow of sanctity in the minds of both English and Normans. In 1161, after much pressure from Henry II, Pope Alexander III canonised him. On 13 Oct. 1269 Henry III translated his body with great solemnity to a bejewelled shrine in Westminster Abbey, now rebuilt and embellished by a king who felt a personal reverence for his remote predecessor. The Translation became an annual national celebration.

EDWARD THE ELDER, King (r. 899-925). (1) K. Alfred left four daughters, of whom Aelswitha was married to Baldwin of Flanders and the able **Aethelfleda** (?-920) to Aethilred (?-911) alderman of the S.W. Mercians. His only son Edward, called the Elder, succeeded him but his title was disputed by his cousin Aethilbald, who fled from Wimborne (Dorset) and was received as a King by the Northumbrian Danes. They sent him abroad to gather reinforcements. In 903 he returned with a fleet to Essex, joined up with the E. Anglian Danish K. Jorik. In 904 they invaded Wessex together *via* the headwaters of the

Thames. Edward promptly cut in behind them by marching on Cambridge. Jorik and Aethilbald returned hurriedly and fell upon a slow moving Kentish force of Edward's. Both sides lost heavily in the ensuing battle, but Jorik, other Danish leaders and Aethilbald were killed.

(2) This crippling of the E. Anglian Danes facilitated the next moves. Alderman Aethilred fortified Chester in 906. In 909 Aethilfleda fortified Bramsbury. While Edward was in Kent, the Northumbrian Danes determined on a counter-attack. Under Halfdan and Jogisl they crossed into S.W. Mercia. Mercians and W. Saxons assembled in superior force. The Danes retreated but were overtaken at WEDNESFIELD near Wolverhampton where Jogisl, Halfdan and ten other Danish chiefs fell (910).

(3) This left only the E. Midland Danes in the field. Alderman Aethilred died in 911 and Aethilfleda succeeded to his authority, though Edward took over Oxford and London from her. Brother and sister now operated a joint, relatively peaceful policy of encroachment by means of a military frontier, which they extended from Whitham (Essex) to the Mersey and studded with fortresses, of which between 910 and 915 he built two and she as many as nine, ending with Runcorn. Under Alfred's treaty with the Danes, the English in the Danelaw were under English law. People near the frontier, which must have restricted Danish trading and grazing, began to renounce Danish allegiance as well. The Danish authority was crumbling away from within. In 916 a Danish attack on the line was beaten off with loss. They began to look for help.

(4) The Irish Ostmen had long had unmolested communication with the Northumbrian Vikings. The seizure of Chester and Runcorn threatened this. They prepared to move. In 916 Ragnvald O'Ivar became chief of the Ostmen at Waterford, while his brother Sigtrygg Gale O'Ivar became K. of Dublin. Their allies in Brittany now staged a premature naval raid against the Severn (917). Edward defeated this at Urchingfield (Herefords). This brought about a collapse of Midland Danish morale. The whole frontier could be advanced. Between 918 and 920 Edward destroyed the Danish power in E. Anglia and killed their king, Guthorm II, while Aethilfleda took two of the five boroughs. When she died in 920 Edward secured Mercia and removed her daughter Aelfwina to Wessex. In 921 Nottingham submitted and in 922 he built a new fortress at Manchester.

(5) In these circumstances Ostmen intervention came too late. Ragnvald O'Ivar and the Brittany Danes had landed in Cumberland in 918. Blocked to their north as a result of a furious battle with the Scots and Bernician English near Corbridge, they turned south and took York in 919. In 921 Ragnvald died and was succeeded in York by his brother Sigtrygg Gale, who had been turned out of Dublin by yet another brother, Guthfryth. Sigtrygg Gale's territory did not extend beyond the Vale of York itself. In 923 Edward advanced to Bakewell (Derbys) and the disunited northern rulers had to choose between catastrophe and surrender. At BAKEWELL a deputy of Edward's received the submission of Sigtrygg Gale, Constantine, K. of Scots, the Bernician English aldermen Edred and Uhtred, together with "all dwelling in Northumbria, English, Danish, Northmen and others". The exact significance of this event is uncertain, but it established as a recognised fact that Edward was the only King in England. Two years later he and Alfward, one of his sons, died at Farndon. Their burial at Winchester marked a stage in the rise of that city.

EDWARD THE EXILE (?-1059) a *s.* of K. Edmund Ironside went to Hungary after Canute succeeded his father. He was summoned back in 1057 by Edward the Confessor and died in England.

EDWARD THE MARTYR (?963-78) K. (975). *See* AETHIELSTAN'S SUCCESSORS.

EDWARD the BLACK PRINCE or EDWARD OF WOODSTOCK (1330-76) D. of CORNWALL (1337) by statute, **P. of WALES (1343)**, eldest son of Edward III, accompanied his father on his first invasion of France and early showed military promise, being knighted at La Hogue in 1345. At the B. of Crécy (1346) he commanded the van and carried his part of the field without help. He was active in the taking of Calais in 1346. In 1350 he was in the sea battle of Winchelsea with the Spaniards. On the renewal of the French war in 1355 he became Lieut. of Aquitaine. He marched north as part of a plan for reducing the French with simultaneous attacks in Normandy and Brittany, but his short autumn campaign degenerated into a profitable looting expedition. In July 1356 he set out again, intending to join his father in Normandy: he plundered and burned as far as Bourges, by which time the French King John had assembled an army to defend the Loire. The Prince therefore retreated by way of **Poitiers** where he was completely victorious (Sept. 1356) and captured K. John. This enabled him to impose a two year truce while he went home. In 1359 he returned to France and in 1360 he was nominally the chief negotiator for the T. of Bretigny.

(2) The second phase of his career now begins. He married his cousin, Joan of Woodstock, in 1361. In 1362 he was granted the Principality of Aquitaine and went to live at Bordeaux. He was one of the richest of the continental rulers and deeply involved in French and Spanish affairs (*see* AQUITAINE) but he was a poor administrator and politician.

(3) By 1370 Edward III was a sick man. In 1371 the Prince had to return to England to help deal with Welsh revolts, agrarian and parliamentary unrest. He was on particularly friendly terms with his younger brother John of Gaunt. The expense and lack of success in the French and Spanish wars after 1370 naturally made the court faction and John of Gaunt unpopular, while the public looked to Edward, the successful warrior, as their champion against overtaxation and corruption. In 1372 he resigned the principality of Aquitaine, which was mostly lost by 1375. In England he figured as a respected figure from whom much was expected at the time of the Good Parliament (Apr. 1376), during which he died.

EDWARD I (1239-1307) called **The Lord Edward** until he became King (1272), *s.* of Henry III and Eleanor of Provence **(1)** in 1254 he married Eleanor, half sister of Alfonso the Wise of Castile, at Burgos and his father endowed him with scattered English properties, Chester, Wales (apart from Gwynedd and the Marches) and all his overseas territories. The administrative centre of this complex based on seaborne communications was at Bristol. He gave Grantham, Stamford, Tickhill and the Castle of the Peak to Eleanor in dower and from 1255 she lived at Windsor until she grew up and he fell in love with her. *See* ELEANOR OF CASTILE.

(2) The marriage arose from the T. of Toledo. Henry's trickery over this embarrassed Edward, for though he enjoyed the revenues of his territories, his command of them was less than it seemed. He was, however, involved in a pressing difficulty. His new officials misunderstood the Welsh, who disliked their methods and were restive under their exactions. Llewellyn ap Gruffydd, the able and ambitious prince of Gwynedd, was happy to foment discontent and appear as champion of the oppressed. In Nov. 1256 he suddenly overran the Four Cantrefs of Perfeddwlad belonging to Chester. A general uprising ensued and in Mar. 1258 Llewellyn proclaimed himself Prince of Wales. During the contemporaneous English political confusion Edward sympathised with the baronial opposition to his father's decreasingly realistic policies and the social discontents which they caused and he supported the purposes, though not the methods, of the Provisions of Oxford (1258) and Westminster (1259). On the other hand he

had a common interest with the Marchers in defeating Llewellyn and in English policies in Wales generally. He and they alike opposed the repeated Welsh truces which kept Simon de Montfort in power while Llewellyn enjoyed Edward's and their lands. Still too young to exert a decisive role he went, early in 1260, to Aquitaine and, with brief intervals, stayed there until Feb. 1263.

(3) He returned with troops in response to his father's call. There were new Welsh wars and Henry III's intention to get rid of the Provisions was creating opposition and disorder. Louis IX's *Mise* (Arbitration) of Amiens (Jan. 1263) strengthened the moral resolution of Edward's lawyerlike mind. By 1264 he had emerged as the Crown's ablest military champion (*see* BARON'S WAR) and afterwards, from the Dictum of Kenilworth (Oct. 1266) with the legate Ottobuono, as an effective pacifier. He was winning a reputation for justice and perhaps because of it he was also put in charge of mercantile affairs.

(4) In 1270 he was able to go on a Crusade (*see* CRUSADES-20) uniquely financed by a general taxation. Still away at his succession, he reached home only in 1274, but he did much business on the way. His first major act was a truce in a Flemish trade war; the Countess Margaret of Flanders had in 1270 seized English and Gascon goods in requital for arrears of a pension from Henry III. In retaliation Edward forbade wool exports to Flanders save under licence. The Flemings had taken to piracy. Therefore Edward negotiated the Truce of Montrueil, whereby the Narrow Seas became less dangerous, but the dispute was not settled until 1280.

(5) Arriving home Edward found a depleted exchequer and many complaints. Once crowned (Aug. 1274) he instituted a general inquiry into local administration and the extent to which magnates had abused rights or withheld dues. The results, embodied in Ragman Rolls, formed the bases of the Stats. of Westminster I and on Distresses of the Exchequer (1275). Traders were pacified by substituting an export tax (The 'Ancient Custom') on wool, wool fells and hides for the New Custom of 1266.

(6) The new arrangements came into effect more slowly than had been hoped. There had been Welsh trouble since 1247. Another Welsh war broke out (Nov. 1276). *See* GWYNEDD, PRINCIPALITY OF-27-29.

(7) It had not been enough to investigate abuses, for such inquiries presupposed franchises which might be abused. Confusion arose, too, from challenges to lawful jurisdictions. There was now a general inquiry by *Quo Warranto* to get rid of unsupported franchises, which also ensured that those who could produce a charter or evidence of prescription as their warrant would be unchallengeable in the future. It also revealed incidentally many detailed defects in the law, and these Edward sought to remedy in the Stat. of Gloucester (1278). It brought into prominence too the growing problem of ecclesiastical ownership and the avoidance or evasion of feudal duties and dues, not only by churchmen, to which it could give rise. Magna Carta had already legislated against some of these. The Statute of Mortmain (1279) went further.

(8) Early in 1279 the dowager Q. Joan of Castile, Eleanor's mother, died. She was countess of Ponthieu, with its port of Abbeville at the mouth of the Somme, and the county now passed to Eleanor. Edward promptly arranged for her succession, paid the necessary relief to Philip III and set up an administration (T. of Amiens May 1279). The possession of this cross-channel port simplified the problem of the Flemish pirates, and when Guy of Dampierre succeeded the Countess Margaret in Flanders (1280) he was readier to co-operate. There was another reason for his friendliness. Disputes with the Hanse had caused the Hanseatic *Kontor* to be moved in 1280 from Bruges to Ardenbourg. The Hanse temporarily

lost some of the Anglo-French trade to local carriers but countered by transferring some business to its English houses, notably the London Steelyard, which received its definitive organisation in 1281. *See* HANSE-2.

(9) The Welsh aftermath of the T. of Conway was dominated by two main activities, litigation and castle building. Many disputes involved choices between English and Welsh law. In these, decisions were bound to give offence whichever way they went and meanwhile royal castles were rising and hemming in the northern Welsh. Legalism, with its delays, especially in an unfamiliar system of law, progressively alienated Welshmen. David ap Gruffydd made it his business to champion the discontented, probably to alienate his brothers' subjects as much as for any other reason. Edward was distracted by Scottish border problems, church disputes and European diplomatic difficulties. In Mar. 1282 David surprised Hawarden, raised the Four Cantrefs and the middle counties. Seven castles were destroyed by June. and Llewellyn felt obliged to join in. Edward counter-attacked methodically. Llewellyn fell in Oct. The last formed body of Welsh surrendered at Bere in Apr. 1283. David, taken in June, was executed in Oct. At Rhuddlan in Mar. 1284 Edward issued the Stat. of Wales for the govt. of the country. He also pressed on with his castle building. *See* EDWARDIAN CASTLES IN WALES.

(10) Abp. Pecham, elected in 1278, meant to strengthen the church, especially by abolishing pluralities and abuses of prohibitions and by ensuring the routine use of writs of *de excommunicato capiendo* (Lat = Arrest of excommunicates). He began at the council of Reading (1278) by imposing excommunications, but the clergy themselves throve on pluralities and, as much as laymen, sued out prohibitions to get their cases before the royal courts while writs of *de ex. cap.* were matters of royal discretion. Pecham was forced to withdraw in the Parliament of 1279 which enacted the Stat. of Mortmain, but jurisdictional quarrels continued and the Welsh war interrupted the progress of the settlement. Public order and jurisdictional reforms were much in Edward's mind at this period. The Stats. of Westminster II and of Winchester and the *Circumspecte Agatis* (q.v.) compromise of 1286 were the result.

(11) This period was the watershed of the reign. In Oct. 1285 Philip IV (The Fair) became K. of France. He had Angevin leanings and ambition. In Mar. 1286 the three-year old Margaret 'the Maid of Norway' became Q. of Scots. Edward was thus threatened with disturbances at opposite ends of his dominion. Margaret's father was K. Eric of Norway, where she was. The Scottish magnates appointed six guardians of the Kingdom, two of whom died. Edward's suzerainty over Scotland was tacitly assumed and then explicitly recognised in the ensuing tripartite negotiations; these culminated in agreements (q.v.) at Salisbury (Nov. 1289) and Brigham (Mar. and Aug. 1290) for the marriage of the King's son Edward with the Maid. The young Edward was to become K. of Scotland which was, however, to remain autonomous. During the same period the King's attention and resources had been much diverted by the Sicilian dispute, which involved the papacy and in which his southern neighbour Aragon and the French King were involved on opposite sides, together with cross claims and side issues in Provence and Aquitaine. He was until Aug. 1289 mostly in France establishing a peace, while Edmund of Cornwall and John Kirkby, Bp of Ely, administered England for him, and in 1287 he had to put down a Welsh rebellion.

(12) The external complications were matched by growing and new social problems. A money economy was developing, with its international trade routes, primitive mostly Italian banking, and exchange mechanisms based on the great fairs. The Straits of Dover where the coastal trade from the Baltic to Spain (*see* HANSE-4) intersected the Anglo-Flemish trade based on wool and hides had become the greatest cross-roads in Europe. It was becoming economically more convenient to pay professional soldiers than to disorganise agriculture by summoning feudal levies, but the money had to be found. Edward and the great lords needed a stable and reliable currency both for internal and for external operations. Commutation of services for cash was growing, but subinfeudation with its lengthening ladder of obligation could make it hard for a superior to get his money and might, indeed, make an inferior richer than the lord two or three stages above him. It was no coincidence that the Stat. *Quia Emptores* fell during a time (1279-1300) of active currency improvement.

(13) Despite Edward's vast reputation, energy and intellectual elegance, there were at this time signs of overstrain. Three deaths decisively unhinged his carefully built up and essentially pacific policies. In Sept. 1290 Margaret of Norway died in the Orkneys. In Nov. the death of Edward's adored Queen Eleanor oppressed his character, besides attenuating his important Spanish connections, and in June 1291 the death of Alfonso II of Aragon removed an important figure in Edward's southern diplomatic settlement.

(14) The Bp. of St. Andrews and John Comyn of Badenoch now attempted a *coup* to place John Balliol on the Scots throne, perhaps as a puppet. This provoked a violent reaction from two forces which soon coalesced: for it encroached on the privilege of the Seven Earls to declare a King's right at his coronation and it angered those who favoured the distinguished and personally more suitable Robert Bruce. Magnates and chiefs were levying troops; all parties, fearing a disaster, turned to Edward as mediator. In proceedings lasting until Nov. 1292 the Scottish crown was, on disputed but eventually agreed legal grounds, awarded to Balliol. Unfortunately Edward's legalism was a political error.

(15) Long standing English and Aquitainian trade disputes with the French evolved into a naval war and the B. of St. Mahé (May 1293) at the same period as Scottish appeals to Edward's court were creating further difficulties with the Scots. The parliamentary proceedings against John Balliol in *Macduff's case* were bound either to humiliate Balliol or to excite Scottish resentment. Edward included Scottish summonses in his mobilisation against the French. The anti-English faction at the Scottish court had to allow Balliol to obey them or force him into rebellion. Another Welsh revolt upset Edward's military preparations; French diplomacy was seeking allies everywhere including Scotland and Norway and the *Parlement* of Paris declared the forfeiture of Aquitaine. Edward defeated the Welsh at Conway (Jan. 1295) but in Oct. Philip of France and the Scots made an alliance at Paris (later called the 'Auld Alliance') against England. Scotland, behind a powerless king, was in rebellion.

(16) Measures to deal with the long ensuing crisis had far-reaching and permanent effects. While Edward sought allies in Flanders and Germany, his need for large funds was pressing. In Sept. 1294 he had summoned the clergy and astounded them by demanding half their revenues. In Nov. 1295 he summoned the Parliament, known to later generations as the "Model", because its composition and organisation was in principle copied for later assemblies. In this Parliament, clergy and laity were, in effect, associated for purposes of taxation. Philip of France was making levies on his clergy too. Boniface VIII reacted by combining a stroke of business with peacemaking. The bull *Clericis laicos* (Feb. 1296) sought again to block this source of royal revenue and power.

(17) Before this could provoke the inevitable quarrel, a great English army defeated the Scots at Dunbar in Apr. 1296; in July Balliol surrendered his crown to Edward and the coronation stone of Scone was removed to Westminster. In Aug. Edward triumphantly held a Scottish parliament at Berwick at which most Scots lay and ecclesiastical magnates and chieftains did homage and swore fealty. The Bruces and some leaders in Moray, however, held off.

(18) Edward was very willing to listen to papal offers of mediation. The French war was going badly; his allies were costing vast sums and beginning to desert; the Count of Holland had tried to change sides in 1295. In Jan. 1297 the ecclesiastical storm broke. In the spirit of *clericis laicos* Abp. Winchelsea and convocation refused money without papal consent; Edward outlawed the clergy. In the same month his Aquitainian seneschal, John of St. John, was defeated and captured. Then his ally Adolf of Germany, pressed at home, withdrew from the war; it was known that K. Philip was preparing to invade Flanders and Scottish unrest broke into rebellion in Balliol's name under Sir William Wallace in Lanarkshire (May 1297). A military operation in Flanders was essential for a favourable truce. Edward raised troops and demanded an eighth from the laity and a fifth from the towns (*see* MOVEABLES, TAXES ON). A powerful faction of lay magnates led by the Es. of Norfolk and Hereford refused to go or to pay and united with Abp. Winchelsea in opposition (*see* MONSTRAUNCES). Edward went to Flanders regardless, though with only a small force. The opposition forcibly stopped the exchequer. The country was now on the brink of civil war, but in Oct. came the news of Wallace's victory (11 Sept.) at Stirling Bridge. King, Church and magnates, faced with this crisis, agreed the important constitutional compromise called *Confirmatio Cartarum* (Lat = Confirmation of the Charters) (Oct-Nov. 1297). In this they were assisted by the bull *Etsi de Statu* (July 1297) which made an exception in *clericis laicos* for periods of emergency. By Oct. too Philip, faced by his formidable opponent in person, accepted a truce which in successive prolongations covered peace negotiations until 1303.

(19) Edward returned to England in Mar. 1298 and went north, transferring his administration and courts to York (where they remained until Christmas 1304), where also he completed his formal reconciliation with the magnates. By June he had assembled a powerful army of horse and Welsh archers at Roxburgh and in July destroyed Wallace's forces in a pitched battle at Falkirk. The Scots had already laid waste the country south of the Tay and for want of supplies the army retired to Carlisle. The campaigns of 1299 and 1300 were failures, but by the autumn of 1301 he had control of the Lowlands. In 1302 a five month truce was proclaimed at French insistence.

(20) One reason for Edward's military difficulties was that the war distracted or inhibited him from enforcing the charters confirmed in 1297. There was much malpractice, especially in connection with the Forests and prises, and the long delay made him suspect to the increasingly hostile magnates. The result was their *Articuli super Cartas* (Lat = Articles explanatory of the Charters) to which he assented in the Parliament of 1300.

(21) Boniface VIII had in June 1299 issued a demand that Edward should withdraw from Scotland on the ground that it was a papal fief. This reached Edward on the Scottish border in Aug. 1300 but he delayed his reply for the next Parliament summoned to Lincoln for Jan. 1301. The magnates were determined to enforce the forest perambulations which had been promised in 1297 and 1300. The parliament refused supply until the findings of the commissioners had been entered as verdicts. The result was further confusion in the raising of troops, but the parliament having won its point, then solemnly rejected the papal intervention (Feb.): a double campaign was launched from Carlisle and Berwick which overran most of the lowlands and ended in a truce early in 1302. By this time the peace negotiations in Paris were nearing completion, the French, defeated by the Flemings

at Courtrai (July 1302), had abandoned their Scottish allies and the Pope did not press his point; Bordeaux now rose against the French occupation (Dec. 1302). The prospect of continental peace freed resources for a final effort in Scotland. A great army and much castle building accomplished a conquest and many Scots lords came over to the new dispensation at a parliament at St. Andrews in Mar. Stirling Castle alone held out until July 1304.

(22) Edward now began to organise a Scottish constitution, based in part on the Irish model, and preparations for enacting it went forward. The Scots seemed co-operative and it was they who in May 1305 caught and handed over Sir Wm. Wallace. Amongst Edward's Scots councillors were Robert the Bruce and John Comyn. John of Brittany was to be Lieutenant and the new laws were to be presented by him and Scots parliamentary commissioners at Easter 1306. In the meantime the new atmosphere of peace and success weakened baronial vigilance and opposition, and a friendly Gascon pope (Clement V) was elected, and persuaded to release Edward from his oaths of 1297 and 1300 on the charters, as having been obtained under duress. Edward did not use these dispensations to annul the charters themselves, but only to suspend the new machinery for enforcing the perambulation. In Feb. 1306, however, Bruce murdered Comyn at Dumfries and on 25 Mar. had himself crowned at Scone. Rebellion was widespread, simultaneous and clearly planned. The Anglo-Scots reaction was ruthless and against formed troops successful. Defeated at Methven (June) and Dalry (July) Bruce went into hiding but reappeared in Carrick in Feb. 1307 as a guerrilla leader. Edward marched against him from Carlisle but died at Burgh-upon-Sands in July.

EDWARD II of Caernarvon (1284-1327) P. of WALES (1284) (q.v.) **King (1307),** son of Edward I and Eleanor of Castile **(1)** served in four Scottish campaigns before 1307. Early betrothed to Isabella of France, he scandalised the court and angered his father by his passionate attachment to Piers Gaveston (?-1312), a Bearnais with financier relatives at Bordeaux. Gaveston was banished in 1306 when Edward asked for one of the great earldoms for him. At his accession Edward made him E. of Cornwall and perhaps on his advice abandoned the current Scottish campaign, changed many of Edward I's ministers and recalled other exiles. The favourite was Keeper of the Realm while his friend fetched Isabella and in Jan. married her at Boulogne. She was twelve.

(2) Gaveston's elevation caused a political crisis. At the Parliament of Apr. 1308 the magnates forced Edward to promise to exile him. Edward did not mean to honour the promise. Gaveston was made Lieut. of Ireland and left England in that capacity, receiving considerable Gascon lands and rents at the same time. Thereafter the King strengthened his position. He won over his cousin, Thomas E. of Lancaster, by giving him the hereditary Stewardship, and others with other gifts and, at the Parliament of July 1309, enacted the Stat. of Stamford (a repetition of the *Articuli super Cartas* of 1300) (*see* EDWARD I-20) in exchange for Gaveston's return.

(3) Gaveston's greed and arrogance destroyed the settlement, in particular by alienating Thomas of Lancaster. He and four other earls refused to attend a council at York in Oct. 1309 as long as Gaveston was there. At the Parliament of Mar. 1310 they appeared in arms, demanding reforms and his expulsion. Their charges were that evil advice was causing the King to lose Scotland (where Robert the Bruce was rapidly extending his power) and to alienate too much crown property and in consequence to live by extortion. Edward was compelled to create a body of 21 ORDAINERS to reform the realm and the royal household. While this body was collecting evidence and drafting ordinances,

Edward and his friend went north taking the Chancery and Exchequer with them. The staffs were thus under their control, but funds grew progressively shorter and by Aug. 1311 Edward had to lodge Gaveston in Bamburgh Castle, face a parliament at Westminster and consent to the Ordinances (q.v.) which *inter alia* banished Gaveston, together with the Italian banker Amerigo dei Frescobaldi, receiver of the customs since 1304, Constable of Bordeaux and an associate of Bertrand de Calnan, one of Gaveston's financier relatives. The Ordinances thus cut off foreign credit and restricted the royal revenues at home. The Ordainers also took control of the major offices of state and when the King started to transact business through his Chamber and Wardrobe they demanded dismissals there too.

(4) Gaveston went first to France and then to Flanders, whence he quickly returned to England and openly appeared at Court until Christmas 1311. Since Edward had secured control of the Great Seal again, his lands were easily restored. It was clear that the Ordinances would lapse if the Ordainers did not fight for them. Preparations were made under cover of tournaments. In May 1312 Aymer of Valence, E. of Pembroke and the E. of Warenne, chased Gaveston into Scarborough where he surrendered on terms. On the way to Pembroke's Castle at Wallingford, Gaveston was seized by the E. of Warwick and, with Thomas of Lancaster's authority, decapitated on Blacklow Hill. The breach of faith caused Pembroke and Warenne to go over to Edward. The result was an unstable peace.

(5) Under cover of these distractions Robert the Bruce had been conquering Scotland piecemeal. Robert had to raise war funds, drive out his Scottish rivals and destroy the English garrisons. Lucrative raids into England went far towards achieving the first two objectives, since his main rivals had large estates in Northumberland and Durham. By the spring of 1313 Linlithgow, Perth, Roxburgh and Edinburgh had fallen. His brother Edward now laid siege to the important strategic castle at Stirling. In the summer of 1313 its constable, Sir Philip Mowbray, undertook to surrender if not relieved by 24 June, 1314. The civil peace now enabled all English parties to unite against the Scots. A large force under Edward's command concentrated to relieve Stirling. It was destroyed at BANNOCKBURN (24 June, 1314).

(6) Thomas of Lancaster, whose troops were still at Pontefract, was the leading Ordainer. The disarmed King was in his power. Parliaments at York (1314) and Lincoln (1316) reinforced the Ordinances in accordance with his will. The real ruler of England ruled at a time of great difficulty; the European harvests of 1315 were destroyed by rain and there was famine. At the same time Edward Bruce invaded Ireland. Unfortunately Thomas was not politically gifted, being almost as capricious as Edward. There were disorders and local rebellions and, of course, Edward was intriguing to regain his own. He had some support, especially among the administrators and some of the former Ordainers, who regarded Thomas' power as an intrusion into their orderly scheme of things. Their moving spirit was Pembroke and included in their number the Bps. of Ely and Norwich and E. Warenne, the Mortimers, Edward's half brother Thomas of Norfolk, Hereford, Arundel the Abp. of Canterbury, Walter Reynolds and some other prelates. Their object was to uphold the Ordinances as much against Lancaster as against Edward and compel them to co-operate. The effort failed because, though the Scots invasion of Ireland collapsed with Edward Bruce's death at the B. of Faughart (Oct. 1318), Robert took Berwick and defeated attempts to recover it by threatening the magnates' lands, especially Lancaster's, further south. In the resulting mistrust Lancaster refused to come to the Parliament at York (1320) because it was packed with his opponents.

(7) Among the King's friends were the Hugh Despensers, father and son. The elder Hugh had stood by Gaveston; the younger was the King's age and the object of a new infatuation. They were ambitious and set about building up a power in south Wales. Their attempt to acquire Gower led to a head-on collision with the Marchers (especially the Mortimers) for they persuaded Edward to escheat it (for regrant) but the Marchers denied the crown's power to do so. The Despensers were defeated in a short civil war from which Thomas of Lancaster stood aloof, but he was increasing his influence by holding assemblies resembling parliaments of his own in the north. The Despensers were officially banished (1321) and the younger took to piracy based, with Edward's connivance, on the Cinque Ports.

(8) In Nov. 1321 Lancaster and one of his assemblies issued a manifesto (*The Doncaster Petition*) charging the King with various illegalities including the Despenser piracy, and threatening redress by arms. Edward, who had a strong force at Cirencester, seized the pretext of threatened rebellion, with which he associated contacts between Lancaster and the Scots. He recalled the Despensers, subdued the Welsh Marches and, in Mar 1322, Sir Andrew Hartcla, his Warden of the West (Scottish) March defeated Lancaster at Boroughbridge (16 Mar. 1322). The ambitious earl was executed at York a week later and in May a Parliament at York repealed the Ordinances, hanged Clifford, Mowbray and Badlesmere and imprisoned the Mortimers.

(9) The Despensers were now supreme and rich with forfeited estates, but they had, as usual, to deal with a neglected Scottish war. Many northerners, despairing of their English allegiance, were seeking the protection of the King of Scots. These included some major abbots, the Bp. of Durham and Sir Andrew Hartcla., recently created E. of Carlisle. He was executed for treason, but the Despensers were realists. The war was clearly lost. To save face, the govt. negotiated a 13-year truce (Mar. 1323).

(10) The Despensers were competent in the economic field. They encouraged trade. They standardised weights and measures and their Ordinance of Kenilworth (May 1326) transferred the wool staple from Bruges to nine English, two Welsh and three Irish towns thereby safeguarding the customs. Their lack of political insight and their reputed or notorious greed steadily weakened their position, for a new faction was growing up around Q. Isabella (who had personal objections to them) and the greater magnates who were threatened by their interests. Moreover the Queen had become the mistress of one of them, Roger Mortimer of Wigmore.

(11) In the upshot, Mortimer went to France and she followed him and got P. Edward to join them. They moved to Holland and, in return for the betrothal of Philippa of Hainault to the Prince, secured an expedition through William II of Holland, Zeeland and Hainault. They landed at Walton-on-the-Naze. The King's and Despenser's supporters deserted. The Despensers were executed and in Jan. 1327 Edward II was deposed at Kenilworth. He was moved to Berkeley where he was temporarily rescued but recaptured. Fear of a further attempt decided Isabella and Mortimer to have him murdered. This was done, reputedly by the insertion of red-hot irons into his rectum in order to conceal the murder.

EDWARD III (1312-77) E. of CHESTER (1320), King (1327), *s.* of Edward II and Isabella of France. (*For his father's deposition see* EDWARD II-11 *and for the three-year govt. of his mother* (1327-30) *see* ISABELLA OF FRANCE AND MORTIMER, ROGER IV.) **(1)** Isabella and Mortimer's overthrow at Nottingham (Oct. 1330) and his execution marked the true beginning of the reign and was used by the King to break the disastrous trends of his father's reign and begin an era of achievement. This new start in practice amounted to a return to a military policy.

(2) Nobles disinherited of Scots lands by Robert the Bruce, who had just died, planned a return in the name of Edward Balliol, John's son. With royal connivance they landed a powerful force in Fife. The Scots regency was overthrown at Dupplin Moor (Aug. 1332); Balliol was crowned at Scone and, by the T. of Roxburgh, not only accepted Edward as his lord but agreed to cede Lothian (Nov.). The unwisdom of this was only partially obvious. Balliol stood forth as a crowned partisan. The cession offended nascent but as yet unperceived nationalist sentiment. The returned "Disinherited" dispossessed many families which had risen under Bruce and they had good reason to exploit this sentiment. Edward. determining upon a pre-emptive strike against Balliol's opponents, laid siege to Berwick and decisively beat a Scottish relieving force at Homildon Hill (July 1333).

(3) Negotiations had meanwhile been proceeding in Paris to achieve an Anglo-French agreement over Aquitaine (*see* ST. SARDOS, WAR OF) but these broke down when Philip VI insisted that David II of Scots, who had just taken refuge in France, be included in any treaty made (1334). In Scotland Edward and Balliol's forces overran the Lowlands and took Perth, but could not contain the Bruce guerrillas. The Papacy tried to negotiate a compromise, but French intervention became imminent when Philip IV transferred a fleet, originally meant for a Crusade, from Marseilles to Normandy. Edward looked for continental allies early in 1337. He failed with Flanders but succeeded with the Emperor Louis IV. In May 1337 Philip IV declared Aquitaine confiscate. Edward responded by claiming the French Crown (*see* HUNDRED YEARS WAR).

(4) Edward had united his people behind him in an aggressive foreign policy and also by magnanimity and generosity. His supporters in the *coup* against Mortimer had naturally been well rewarded: for example. Montague received a large portion of Mortimer lands and was summoned to parliament as Lord Montague and, in 1337 became E. of Salisbury. Richard Bury, William Clinton and Robert Ufford progressively received lucrative posts and high honours. But he neglected neither the old nobility, the Fitzalans, Beauchamps, Bohuns and Audleys. nor the House of Lancaster whose younger representative, Henry's son Henry of Grosmont. became E. of Derby (1337). He won over the former Mortimer partisans and employed them in high office; and the important Lancastrian ecclesiastical Stratford family received the highest preferments. John Stratford became Chancellor in Nov. 1330 and Abp. of Canterbury in 1333: Robert became Bp. of Chichester in 1337; Ralph, Bp. of London in 1340. It was thus feasible to maintain a proper govt. in England while the King was away opening his campaign in Flanders: but in practice the human and material resources were inadequate for a war on two fronts and there was constant administrative friction. Edward on campaign regarded the regency as a sort of military supply depot and had issued the Ordinances of Walton-on-the-Naze (1337) to ensure the necessary Exchequer conformity with his needs. But the regency had not only a kingdom to rule but the Scottish war on its hands and could not possibly meet all his requirements. Moreover Edward had acquired allies who demanded large subsidies, for which they gave little return, and he was neither a competent nor a particularly honest financier. By 1339 he was virtually hostage for the payment of his foreign debts.

(5) Edward attributed his difficulties to incompetence at home and decided to put a strong man, Abp. Stratford, in charge. It was a defective move, for mere ability could not conjure up funds which were not there and, besides, Stratford was beginning to doubt the wisdom of the war policy. As primate he had to pay heed to the papal excommunication of peace breakers (1337) and to papal objections to Edward's imperial alliance. All the same he

faithfully argued for additional supplies before the parliament of Oct. 1339. The funds reached Edward too slowly and his mind was, all too plausibly, poisoned against the Abp. The Oct. parliament dispersed to consult the people. That of Jan. 1340 made inadequate grants which also came in slowly. Edward's campaign languished; he borrowed heavily on the customs from William de la Pole and to come to England had to leave his family in Flanders as hostages for his debts. The parliament of Mar. 1340 extracted concessions, especially the eventual abolition of tallage and maltolts, but made large grants with which Edward built the fleet and won the great B. of Sluys in June 1340 in Flanders, just as French troops were overrunning Aquitaine.

(6) The victory revived Edward's flagging international prestige but did nothing for his finances. His Flemish creditors pressed him: the Hainaulters and Brabançons deserted. The war ground to a halt at Tournai. The truce of Espléchin interrupted it (Sept. 1340). The revenues of 19 counties had already been assigned to creditors. Only 18 remained to the King. His feeling of frustration and mistrust drove him to extremities. In Nov. he arrived suddenly at the Tower: ministers, the Constables of the Tower, five judges, the financiers John and William de a Pole and Reginald Conduit were arrested. Commissions of Trailbaston were issued and malversation alleged against officials of every degree. Six escheators, 12 sheriffs and all the coroners were deprived (Jan. 1341). Meanwhile Abp. Stratford, who had retired to Canterbury, was summoned to stand hostage for the King's debts at Louvain but, having secured a delay, denounced the King's proceedings from his pulpit on the Feast of St. Thomas à Becket (29 Dec.)

(7) Stratford, an able controversialist, widened the issues from matters of mere misconduct or incompetence. He issued excommunications against violators (other than the King) of the Charters, the public peace and ecclesiastical liberties: in other words against those who carried out Edward's rough and ready methods of dealing with public servants and raising funds. After further controversy, Edward's shortage of funds forced him to give way and summon a parliament for Apr. 1341. Here statutes gave legal force to Stratford's contentions and abolished the Eyres and Commissions of Trailbaston in return for a commutation of taxes for a large grant of wool. Edward and Stratford, who had never been hostile to him personally, were reconciled. Shortly afterwards K. David II, however, returned to Scotland: Edward Balliol finally left and there was renewed military activity along the Border.

(8) The improvement in the political atmosphere was due in part to a turn in the fortune of the French war which had spread to Brittany as a result of a disputed succession. Though the English claimant, John de Montfort, had been captured, his wife Joan carried on and Edward himself overran the duchy as far as Vannes by Jan. 1343. Then Sir Walter Manny and the E. of Derby were sent to Aquitaine, where they drove back the French as far as Angoulême and defeated them at Auberoche (Oct. 1345). One of the reasons for these successes was that Edward was no longer subsidising useless allies: thus, militarily more self reliant, the money was better spent. Moreover the population was being enriched by loot.

(9) A French offensive in Aquitaine drove Manny back to Aiguillon in the spring of 1346; the Scots were moving and, since James van Artevelde's murder in July 1345, the connection with the Flemish towns had become unreliable and, with the Bruges embargo on the English wool staple, hostile. Edward planned a brilliant counter stroke. The unsullied land of Normandy was to be invaded. The threat to Paris would draw all available French armies away from other theatres. The pressure in Aquitaine would be reduced; the pro-English factions in

Flanders encouraged. The army landed at St. Vaast in July 1346; on 26 Aug. Edward won the famous victory at Crécy (qv) and, in Sept., invested Calais. A month later an army organised by the Abp. of York and Q. Philippa defeated the Scots at Neville's Cross and captured David II. In June 1347 the English captured Charles of Blois, the French claimant to Brittany, at La Roche. Calais fell in Aug. 1347.

(10) The victories re-established the English position everywhere save in Flanders where the pro-French Louis de Mâle made up his quarrel with the cities. They also enormously enhanced the King's prestige in a cosmopolitan chivalric society and among the people. It was in 1348 that he inaugurated the Order of the Garter. Meanwhile, however, European society was being abruptly dislocated by the Black Death, which lasted from Aug. 1348 until Dec. 1349 and touched all areas. The immense mortality had, on a nationwide scale, the unpredictable effects of a famine and a battle: everyone was preoccupied with the personal changes it forced upon all. The scale of warlike operations naturally declined even if they continued. In 1350 a Spanish fleet (*Les Espagnols sur Mer*) was defeated off Winchelsea. In 1352 the Calais Pale was enlarged by the capture of Guines and a French attack on Brittany was repelled.

(11) The epidemic accelerated social tendencies already in evidence, especially the decline of villeinage. Money was converting the serf into a paid labourer or a leaseholder. The population fell but not the amount of money in circulation. The wage inflation damaged the prosperity of labour intensive cultivation. One attempt to remedy the difficulty was to regulate wages (Statute of Labourers, 1341), but there was no adequate enforcement machinery. A more effective adjustment was a change over to sheep farming, whose prosperity depended upon the rich export trade to Flanders and thus involved political issues. The King preferred that all wool should be sold at a single staple town, where it could be controlled and taxed and that the staple should be abroad, where its location could be used as a means of diplomatic pressure. Such a system, however, gave great advantages to large scale English monopoly financiers. The growers, on the other hand, preferred the staples to be dispersed throughout the Kingdom, whereby finance was purveyed through foreign buyers in competition. These growers were able to thrust their policy upon the crown through parliament. In 1353 the *Ordinance of the Staple* confirmed by statute in 1354 abolished the Bruges staple in favour of 10 English, 1 Welsh and 4 Irish towns. The immediate effect was greatly to increase wool exports but the profits were now transferred from English to foreign middlemen. In either event a difficult solution was finding increasing favour: to weave the wool into cloth and export it as such, thus avoiding the Flemish weavers' monopoly. This provided work for some driven from the land by conversion to sheep farming. It was much assisted by the spread of fulling mills which, incidentally, produced a relocation of the cloth industry from the old southern cloth towns to such areas as the Pennine rural foothills, where water power was available. Periodical embargoes on wool exports encouraged or forced Flemish weavers to migrate to England, where they taught their craft.

(12) By 1354 the War was reviving. The Franco-Scottish alliance was renewed and by 1355 the Scots were penetrating the Marches, where they won a victory at Nesbit (Aug.). In retaliation, the English early in 1356 laid most of Lothian waste (*The Burnt Candlemas*), while the Black Prince made a long distance raid northwards from Bordeaux. Intercepted by the French royal army near Maupertuis, the Prince won the spectacular victory of Poitiers (Sept. 1356) and captured the French King John II and his son Philip. With insurrection in the streets of Paris, the French regency was glad to conclude the

two years truce of Bordeaux (Mar. 1357) but this did not prevent the de Montfort claimant being established by the English in Brittany (July). In Oct. David of Scotland was released against a ransom under the T. of Berwick. The tide of fortune continued to favour Edward. Further Parisian insurrections were accompanied by peasant revolts (*The Jacquerie*). The prisoner K. John had to negotiate (Jan. 1358) and the peace T. of London (Mar. 1359) ceded all the old Angevin lands in sovereignty. This involved a partition of France. The Dauphin appealed to the French Estates (i.e. public opinion) who rejected it as unlawful, impossible and imposed under duress (Mar. 1359). This primitively nationalist event was the watershed of the long war and of the campaign. Edward launched an unsuccessful winter campaign towards Rheims and made an alliance (T. of Guillon Jan. 1360) with Philip of Burgundy, but the two sides were tired of war and negotiations between May and Oct. produced the victorious Ts. of Brétigny and Calais known as the P. of Brétigny.

(13) A new calamity now darkened the prospect. The second epidemic of plague, known as the *mortalité des enfants* (1361), had grave long term effects, for as its name implies, it attacked the younger generation, thus depressing the later rate of replacement. The population continued therefore to fall after it had spent itself. The related continuing inflation brought new conflicts. Edward, as usual pressed by creditors, compromised over the Staple question by moving it to English Calais (1362) but in 1363 Urban V extended papal rights of reservation and therefore financial exaction to all mitred benefices.

(14) The nine years after 1360 saw a gradual decline in English and a corresponding rise in French prestige and power. John II gave the Duchy of Burgundy to his younger son Philip (1363), but died in England in 1364 leaving the crown to his able son Charles V. The latter, having cleared his home territory by defeating Charles of Navarre (May 1364) invaded Brittany, of which he was Suzerain. He defeated the Anglo-Breton forces at Auray (Sept.) but Charles of Blois, his candidate for the Duchy, was killed there. As a result the English candidate John (IV) de Montfort was recognised as Duke (T. of Guérande, Apr. 1265) but the English troops had to leave. Meanwhile Edward and his parliament were involved in a dispute with the papacy which culminated in the passage of the second Statute of Praemunire (1365) and the refusal of the tribute to Rome in 1366. This coincided with the French expedition into Spain and the Black Prince's victory over them at Nájera (Apr. 1367) but also with Aquitainian unrest arising from the war taxation. The greater Aquitainian feudatories started to intrigue in Paris. Finally, the transfer of the staple to Calais had been designed to maintain English influence with Louis de Mâle, the Count of Flanders. He sought a marriage between his only child Margaret and Edward's son Edmund of Langley. Margaret was heiress, besides Flanders, to the Free County of Burgundy and to Artois. Charles was determined to frustrate this dangerous alliance and persuaded Urban V (already half willing to listen) to refuse the essential dispensation. He went further: in 1369, after much haggling, the great heiress married Philip of Burgundy. Thus Edward's direct and indirect influence in all the areas peripheral to the French King's dominions had, by 1369, sensibly diminished. Charles V now provoked a war: after taking high legal opinion he accepted appeals from the Aquitainian feudatories (Dec. 1368) and declared war in May 1369. Edward replied by resuming the title of King of France (June 1369) but at this moment he suffered a dangerous and personal tragedy: his beloved and popular Queen died.

(15) Edward lost his touch and aged rapidly. In this war the Flemings mostly supported the French, who opposed a new generation of able commanders to

Edward's ageing paladins. The English lost ground on all fronts, save a naval victory over the Flemings at Bourgneuf (1371). Robert the Steward as Robert II succeeded David II and the French hastened to renew their Scottish alliance (T. of Vincennes Sept. 1372). The Bretons came over to the French (1373). Two great raids across France damaged the countryside but yielded neither money nor military advantage. Parliament had to be asked for a tonnage and poundage. The truce of Bruges (June 1375) left the English in possession only of the Gascon coast from Bayonne to Bordeaux and Calais. Economic depression and social upheaval exacerbated public discontent with taxation and defeat. The old successes maintained public respect for Edward personally and for the Black Prince, who was now a sick man, but there was a demand for scapegoats, among whom London financiers and Alice Perrers, Edward's mistress, figured prominently. The Good Parliament of 1376 focused these demands while the Prince died. A year later Edward followed him, while the French raided the Channel coast. *See also* FOLVILLE.

EDWARD IV (1442-83) E. of MARCH. King (r. 1461-70 and 1471-83) (1) eldest *s*. of Richard D. of York, who was heir to the Mortimer Earldom of March, was born at Rouen. When his father, after his return from Ireland in Sept. 1460, was preparing to march north against Margaret and her Lancastrian supporters, he sent Edward to attack her supporter Jasper Tudor, E. of Pembroke and gain control of Wales (*see* ROSES, WARS OF). This he achieved at the B. of Mortimer's Cross (Feb. 1461) but in the previous Dec. his father had been killed at the B. of Wakefield. Margaret and the Lancastrians now marched on London. They won the B. of St. Albans (Feb. 1461) but the Londoners refused to receive her savage northern troops. On Edward's return to London the Nevilles and other Yorkists, who had refused to support his father's bid for the throne in the previous Sept., proclaimed Edward King. He pursued the Lancastrians north and defeated them at the bloody B. of Towton near Tadcaster (Mar. 1461).

(2) Edward's regime, temporarily dominated by the E. of Warwick, remained potentially unstable because Margaret, with K. Henry VI, retreated to Scotland, where they got quarters and troops in return for the surrender of Berwick, and sought to dominate Northumberland from the Scottish border and by occupying the three fortresses of Bamburgh, Dunstanburgh and Alnwick. Some of these changed hands several times, but eventually Henry VI was installed in Bamburgh and Margaret set off for Flanders to seek help (July 1463).

(3) The D. of Somerset, who had confirmed the cession of Berwick, had gone to Scotland with Margaret; but he had returned and made his peace with Edward who, because of his lineage and manners, held him in favour. The Duke was unpopular, especially in the Midlands, where Edward barely saved him from lynching. The web of Lancastrian relationships was nevertheless efficient and Lancastrian feeling still strong. Edward and Warwick were having difficulty in keeping conventional as well as political order. Their govt. seemed a temporary intrusion. Somerset rated his future more highly as a Lancastrian minister than as a Yorkist favourite or hostage. He joined a widespread Lancastrian conspiracy initiated in the autumn of 1463. At Christmas he rode, almost alone, for Alnwick. His arrival was the signal for revolt. Lancastrians from Alnwick seized Skipton and Norham. Jasper Tudor raised South Wales; there were risings in Cheshire and Lancashire.

Edward and Warwick were currently negotiating a truce between France, Burgundy, Brittany and themselves (June 1463). Margaret arrived in Flanders too late to upset the discussions but offered Calais, which she did not control, to Louis for 20,000 crowns. Immediately after the truce was signed, Warwick broached the possibility of a

French marriage for Edward. Thus Margaret had her French funds and the Lancastrian conspiracy was developing but the Scots, though they had Berwick, were already diplomatically isolated and embarrassed with a border war, directed by an English claimant from Scottish soil. They were ready to negotiate when Somerset fled to Alnwick.

(4) Warwick made short work of the Cheshire rising and sent Montagu to escort the Scottish ambassadors to York across Lancastrian Northumberland. Montagu dispersed Somerset's army at Hedgeley Moor, reached Scotland and brought the envoys safely back. The T. of York (June 1464) provided for a 15 year peace. The Scots undertook to expel the Lancastrians, the English to disarm the Earls of Douglas and Ross, whom they had been harbouring. The disheartened Lancastrians had finally broken at the B. of Hexham (May 1464). Somerset and their other main leaders were captured and beheaded. Henry VI, after wanderings, was discovered near Clitheroe and put into the Tower. Edward gave Montagu the Percy title of E. of Northumberland and most of the Percy estates. Alnwick, Bamburgh, Dunstanburgh and Norham surrendered by Aug.

(5) During these later months a difference of policy and outlook between Warwick and Edward began to show. Louis XI meant to absorb Brittany and as much as he could get of the Burgundian possessions. The autonomy of both, if for different reasons, was heavily supported upon English interests. The neutralisation of England was thus one of his prime objectives. Warwick had borne the burden of the war with France's ally Scotland and his family (which included George Abp. of York) had made vast gains on the border. A long Franco-Scottish peace was attractive to the Nevilles; but Edward was a southerner who knew the wool and other overseas trade and drew great revenues and personal profits from it. He was a trading King to whom the safety and prosperity of the realm and himself were closely related to Breton shipping, Flemish industry and other Burgundian markets. The French insisted upon a peace from which Burgundy, especially, would be excluded and relied upon Warwick to secure it. The Earl was an overbearing minister, determined to master his King whom the sacrifice of the Burgundian connection would impoverish and weaken. He underestimated Edward, for while Warwick was negotiating for a French royal marriage, Edward secretly married Elizabeth Woodville (May 1464).

Edward had fallen in love. She was a daughter of Lord Rivers and Jacquetta of Luxemburg, dowager Duchess of Bedford and widow of Lord Ferrers of Groby, a prominent Lancastrian killed at St. Albans. The event, when publicly known (Aug.), was personally obnoxious to Warwick, besides upsetting his private plans, yet he persisted in his French policy. In Jan. 1466 he, without authority, told Louis that England would not oppose his reconquest of the Burgundian held Somme towns and later in the year he was opposing Burgundian marriage proposals.

(6) The heir of Burgundy (Charles the Bold, Count of Charolais) sued for the hand of Edward's sister Margaret and Charolais' heiress Mary was to marry Edward's brother George of Clarence. International policy apart, Warwick had already marked out George as a husband for his own *d*. Isabel. In Apr. 1466 he met Charolais at Boulogne and made his opposition clear. In May he signed a truce with Louis until 1468: under this one-sided agreement Louis would not help the Lancastrians (now impotent), while Edward would not help Burgundy and Louis would find a husband for Margaret and pay Edward 40,000 crowns a year from the conclusion of a definitive peace. Edward, balancing between the Nevilles at home and the Franco-Scots alliance abroad, ratified the truce, but entertained ambassadors from Brittany and from Louis' brother Charles.

(7) Edward and the Nevilles were now heading for a collision. Edward persisted with his Burgundian negotiations, while George Neville, Abp. of York and Lord Chancellor, intrigued for a Cardinal's hat and a dispensation for the marriage between Isabel Neville and Clarence. Edward understood, as Warwick did not, that the English public much preferred the Burgundians to the French, but in the spring of 1467 Louis was already planning a *coup* in which Warwick should join with Q. Margaret and restore Henry VI, still living in the Tower. Meanwhile the Abp., in protest against Edward's Burgundian policy, absented himself from the parliament of June 1467, whereupon Edward felt strong enough to dismiss him. The factional drift was reinforced too by Edward's favours to the Woodvilles, who, to Warwick's fury, were acquiring powerful marriages and rich wardships.

(8) Edward had to make his determination and in 1468 he concluded 30 year alliances with Burgundy and Brittany supplemented by trade agreements opening the signatory states, subject to police regulation to each other's merchants, students, and pilgrims. To prevent military participation in the alliance, Warwick now claimed that a Danish seizure of English ships in the Sound was instigated by the Hansards, upon whom he demanded retaliation. In July Edward, under pressure, gave way. The ensuing unpopular naval war involved not only Poland but the Flemish subjects of the Burgundian (*see* BALTIC-14; HANSE-4,5). Meanwhile Warwick's French-Lancastrian conspiracy was going forward. If he would restore Henry VI and Q. Margaret, Louis might secure for him the counties of Holland and Zeeland. He planned to raise the north through the various Neville bailiffs, headed by Sir John Conyers, and to revive an old rumour that Edward was a bastard and that Richard of York's heir was really George of Clarence. While this was in progress the Nevilles with Clarence gathered at Sandwich; Abp. George Neville married Clarence and Isabel: Warwick fetched the Calais garrison and marched to London (20 July). Edward, in Nottinghamshire, was caught only partly prepared. His Woodville and Herbert supporters were dispersed by Sir John Conyers at Edgecot. Abp. Neville captured Edward himself at Olney and put him into custody at Middleham. Some Woodvilles and Herberts were put to death and Warwick, in the King's name, summoned a parliament to York for Sept.

(9) Widespread disorder, including a Lancastrian rebellion in Durham, forced the cancellation of the parliament, for Edward was more and Warwick and Clarence less popular than Warwick had calculated. Edward, too, satisfied his captors that he would change his policies and help to suppress the disorders. Released to Pontefract, his friends and supporters joined him. These included the Howards, Buckingham, Hastings and Richard of Gloucester, and John Neville, E. of Northumberland. They returned to London, cautiously followed by Abp. Neville. Summoned to London, Warwick demanded safe conducts under which he appeared in Dec., with Clarence. They were well received and Edward's daughter Elizabeth was affianced to Warwick's nephew George. In fact Warwick was outwitted. Edward was assembling overwhelming strength. In reply Warwick bade his agents foment local rebellions, under cover of which the French-supported Lancastrian restoration might be engineered. In Mar. 1470 there were outbreaks in Lincolnshire led by Sir Robt. Welles, and then in Yorkshire led by Conyers. But Welles was captured and gave away the details. Warwick and Clarence were summoned to answer charges of treason. They marched, getting no support, via Manchester and Warwick to Exeter, where they seized shipping and fought their way out. Denied entrance to Calais by Sir John Wenlock, they took passing Burgundian and Breton merchantmen and with their prizes reached Honfleur (May 1470).

(10) Since Louis was trying to maintain a truce with Burgundy and Brittany, the prizes were embarrassing and he did not want to meet Warwick publicly: on the other hand he could not engineer his desired reconciliation between Q. Margaret and Warwick without it. Eventually they all met at Angers. Warwick was to restore Henry VI with a fleet and army financed by Louis. In return Warwick was to bring England into an alliance against Burgundy and Henry VI's son Prince Edward was to marry Anne Neville. Q. Margaret, otherwise complaisant, refused to accept the last provision and would not leave France until England was mostly conquered (July 1470). The whole arrangement postponed and virtually destroyed Clarence's prospects of a throne.

(11) Edward was kept well informed by the Burgundians, whose fleet blockaded Warwick's expedition, but he had difficulty in taking the needful precautions. Worse still he had alienated John Neville, whom he had created Marquess of Montagu, by restoring most of his Northumberland estates to the Percies. A storm dispersed the Burgundians. Warwick's expedition landed at Dartmouth in Sept. and marched upon Coventry, where Montagu deserted to him. Thus weakened Edward had to flee. He reached Burgundian Flanders on 2nd. Oct. On 6th Warwick released Henry VI from the Tower and obtained his recognition or READEPTION by the citizens. He himself became Great Chamberlain, High Admiral, Capt. of Calais and Lieut. of the Realm. He was king without the title or the charisma. The exiles began to return when Parliament reversed the Yorkist attainders and resumptions (Nov. 1470).

(12) While Edward planned to some purpose with the Burgundians, Louis Xl denounced the P. of Péronne with Burgundy and set his troops in motion on the Somme (Dec. 1470). A French embassy arrived in London with this *fait accompli* at its back (Jan. 1471). Warwick was now to go to war with Burgundy. This revealed a fatal flaw in his position. He was short of cash and nobody wanted a Burgundian war. He could only undertake operations from Calais, where he controlled the customs, and this angered the City wool merchants. Thus when Edward with his small force landed at Ravenspur (Mar. 1471) the populace was ready to regard Warwick as the champion of interests other than their own. York opened its gates. Edward evaded John Neville at Pontefract. The Lancastrian magnates, Shrewsbury, Stanley and Jasper Tudor, who hated Warwick, would not move. The D. of Somerset and the E. of Devon went to London on the pretext that they were awaiting Q. Margaret and the Prince from France. Warwick's generals, Oxford and Exeter, fled to Newark. Edward bypassed Warwick's army at Coventry and seized Warwick castle. There he heard that Clarence had come over to his side. He reached London in Apr. and arrested Henry VI. Two days later he intercepted Warwick at Barnet (Apr. 1471). A confused engagement in thick fog ended in victory and Warwick's death.

(13) Q. Margaret and the prince landed at Weymouth the same day. They marched via Bristol, recruiting troops in Somerset, and then headed for Lancastrian Wales. Edward intercepted them at Tewkesbury, where the prince was killed and Margaret taken (4th May 1471). Edward now returned to London and by his order, his brother Richard, D. of Gloucester put Henry VI to death.

(14) Richard had always supported Edward, who now had excellent reasons for distrusting Clarence. Clarence, a husband to Isabel Neville, felt entitled to the greater part of Warwick's estates in Yorkshire and Cumberland. Edward sensibly gave them to Richard, who was proposing to marry Isabel's younger sister Anne. Clarence was still in touch with Louis XI, and various escaped Lancastrians, notably the E. of Oxford, were harrying the coast with French connivance; in Oct. 1473 they seized St Michael's Mount. A civil war between

Clarence and Gloucester seemed likely, but Louis' capacity for trouble making was limited by Oxford's lack of men. He surrendered in Jan. 1474 and joined Abp. George Neville as a prisoner in Hammes.

(15) A diplomatic revolution had changed the tactics of all the western powers. The Burgundian had become imperially ambitious and his resources were diverted from a westward and essentially commercial policy to an eastward-looking political one. Burgundian alliances were now less apt to restrain France. In 1474 Charles the Bold extended the Franco-Burgundian truce to 1475. Edward, meanwhile, got large war grants from Parliament: he and Charles agreed to a joint attack on France for which he began raising troops and in Oct. 1474 he procured the betrothal of Prince James of Scotland (aged two) to his daughter Cecilia (aged four). His hands were now free: but his ally was otherwise engaged in furthering (by the siege of Neuss) the claims of a pro-Burgundian Abp. Elector of Cologne. Edward's expedition reached France in July 1475. By itself it was inadequate to make headway against Louis though strong enough to give him concern. Edward, an able general who hated war, decided to treat and Louis thought it worthwhile to buy him off with a pension. The P. of Picquigny and the ransom of Q. Margaret was the result.

(16) Balked of the Neville inheritance and a widower, Clarence revived his old ambition to marry Mary, heiress of Burgundy. To this everyone of consequence, especially Louis, Gloucester, Edward's friend Lord Hastings, as well as Edward himself, were strongly opposed and the proposal was suppressed. Clarence took to absenting himself from court and affecting fear of poison when he came. Then two of his own retainers were condemned for treasonable witchcraft. This was getting near the bone. In June 1477, when an impostor posing as the E. of Oxford led a small rising in Cambridgeshire, Clarence was found to have some hand in it. Meanwhile Louis was feeding scandalous but plausible rumours about him to the English court. Suddenly Edward's patience gave way. He had Clarence arrested, condemned by attainder and drowned, possibly in Malmsey wine (Feb. 1478). Under the King, Richard of Gloucester was now the strongest man in the realm.

(17) Louis's purpose was to get Edward into war with Burgundy; Edward's to keep out of it while retaining his Picquigny pension. Just as Charles the Bold's eastward distraction had made Burgundy an unreliable ally for England, so Edward's Scottish preoccupation had a similar effect on Anglo-French relations; meanwhile Edward strengthened trade with Burgundy and in Aug. 1480 he and the Emperor Maximilian, confirmed the Anglo-Burgundian T. of Friendship of 1474 (*see* 15 *above*). For Edward planned to tame the Scots, who had threatened the stability of his throne and from Berwick, the integrity of the north. He put Richard of Gloucester in charge on the border and was in contact with the D. of Albany, James III's brother (Apr. 1481). This prince had been in France since 1478 and had sought his aid. Edward proposed to recognise him as King and help him to drive James III out, in return for which Albany would pay homage, cede Berwick and the Scottish West March, dissolve the 'Auld Alliance' and, if his existing marriage could be annulled, marry the princess Cecilia (already affianced to his opponent), or if not, marry his heir only in accordance with Edward's wishes.

(18) Gloucester, who had been besieging Berwick, now invaded Scotland, took Edinburgh (Aug. 1482) and met the Scots army at Haddington. He soon discovered that the Scots would not dethrone James in favour of Albany, who had already agreed to abandon his pretensions in return for his estates. Gloucester, the realist on the spot, accordingly let the engagement between Cecilia and James III stand, but made the Scots repay the advances on the dowry and surrender Berwick.

In the circumstances this was a considerable success, but one for which the more distant Edward did not thank him. One reason was that Edward was persuading parliament to make a grant for the war (Jan. 1483). But Edward was showing signs of decline. He had always been irresistible as man and King to women and exploited this facility beyond common prudence. He stayed in London (where the girls were) during the Scottish war, in theory to make the Emperor believe that he would meet him at Calais, for the Emperor was at truce with France and expected his support if no peace were concluded.

(19) The P. of Picquigny had been kept a secret. Louis now published it. Whereupon Maximilian came to terms with Louis (P. of Arras Dec. 1482), while in Mar. 1483 Albany came to the expected terms at Dunbar with James III. At this point Edward was suddenly taken ill and in Apr. died.

EDWARD V (1470-83) King (1483) *s.* of Edward IV by Elizabeth Woodville, was one of the murdered Princes in the Tower. *See* RICHARD III-4,5.

EDWARD VI (1537-53) King (1547) *s.* of Henry VIII and Jane Seymour, was clever, learned, inclined to Protestantism and unpleasant. Henry had named a council of regency which included Edward's maternal uncle Edward Seymour, D. of Somerset (1547) and John Dudley, E. of Warwick (1547). The reign was a struggle for power between these two; Somerset encouraged reformers who were mostly 'new men', but there were increasing peasant disturbances caused by depression, population growth and inclosure movements. His rival, now become D. of Northumberland, overthrew him in 1551. Northumberland tried to found a royal dynasty by marrying his son Lord Guilford Dudley to Lady Jane Grey, *d.* of the (Pole) Duchess of Suffolk who, under Henry VII's will, would inherit the crown if Henry's children were childless. As the princesses Mary and Elizabeth were both nubile, the only certain way of ensuring Jane's succession was to persuade Edward to disinherit them as illegitimates, to which he readily agreed when ill, by the *Kings Devise* of 1553. He died in July. Public opinion was prepared to accept such tampering from a mature and terrifying monarch such as Henry VIII, but not from a sickly minor bullied by an ambitious upstart. It favoured Mary's succession, leaving Northumberland without support and ensuring Lady Jane's execution. *See* DUDLEY, LADY JANE.

EDWARD VII (1841-1910) King 1901, (1) besides English and German, spoke French with exceptional fluency. His over-solicitous parents thought him frivolous. He was educated at Oxford, Cambridge, Edinburgh and in the Guards. His first major public service was a highly successful visit to Canada and USA in 1860. His father died in 1861 and thereafter the Queen exercised an ill-judged and oppressive tutelage. To escape he travelled, probably more widely than any other Englishman: before his accession he had, besides Canada and the USA, become well-known in France and Germany: he knew all the Scandinavian countries: he had travelled extensively in the Habsburg territories: he had visited metropolitan Turkey, Palestine and Egypt, had been to Greece and Roumania, had often visited Russia and had several times met the Pope. In addition he went regularly to Scotland and the Riviera, less often to Ireland and spent eight months in India. He married the beautiful but rather deaf and unpunctual P. Alexandra, *d.* of Christian IX of Denmark, in 1863.

(2) The Queen refused him access to state papers, on the pretext of an alleged lack of discretion. As she was in perpetual mourning after 1861, Edward and Alexandra, denied their proper place in the constitutional system, took over the social leadership which the Queen had denied herself. He had bought Sandringham in 1862 and his London establishment was at Marlborough House. He had full blooded and generally popular appetites. He appreciated good food, wine, cigars and pretty, not necessarily bedable, women. Three of his horses won the Derby, another the Grand National. He won yachting races and gambled heavily. His strong, somewhat larger than life personality, was reflected in an impressive physique, a large beard, and a very considerable public dignity. He was also personally considerate, especially to his hard worked entourage.

(3) If the Prince's social habits encouraged (as they did) the hedonistic reaction from mid-Victorian seriousness, this was due more to the qualities of his associates than his own. At home he took the leadership in charitable activity and in encouraging the arts and sciences. A long list of famous institutions owe their foundation, development or success to his interest: these include, by way of example, the R. Society of Arts, St. Bartholomew's Hospital. The Royal College of Music, the Imperial Institute and the Leprosy Fund. He was an active member of the R. Commission on Housing (1884). Abroad, his travels brought him into contact not only with foreign courts, where he was popular, but put him on terms of personal regard with many foreign statesmen, especially the French. By the 1890s it was impossible to ignore the abilities of this well informed heir to the throne and in 1892 Gladstone, with whom he got on famously, persuaded the reluctant monarch to show him papers and the M. of Salisbury, from 1895, sent him all the cabinet foreign dispatches.

(4) From his accession (Jan. 1901) he moved the Court to London and converted Osborne (I. of W.) into an officers' convalescent centre. His coronation had to be suddenly postponed because of an appendicitis operation. The pattern of his interests changed little and he is remembered, not entirely properly, for his work in foreign affairs. In fact his value in this sphere arose from his knowledge and geniality. He could create an atmosphere within which statesmen could work successfully. The best known case of this was the visit in 1903 to Paris, where he was booed on arrival and cheered ecstatically when he left, but his movements from capital to capital created similar effects elsewhere. On the other hand his work at home was increasingly burdensome. Apart from philanthropy and public causes such as new universities, he had to deal with growing embitterment in politics. He got on very well with men of liberal outlook such as Camphell-Bannerman and Haldane and did his best to dissuade the conservatives from throwing out Lloyd George's budget in the Lords which led, after his death, to the curtailment of the latter's powers. Indeed he raised no objection to Liberal plans for such curtailment, which had been mooted in 1902. He died unexpectedly in the middle of the crisis.

EDWARD VIII (1894-1972) King (1936), D. of WINDSOR (1936) was symbolically christened Edward, Albert, Christian, George, Andrew, Patrick David by his duty-conscious father. As P. of Wales he was popular, overworked and appealing. He was outspokenly interested in social problems and grew bored with royal protocol. He also acquired some, in the circumstances, suspect political acquaintances. At his accession he was already friendly with Mrs Wally Simpson, wife of an American millionaire and the only person who could arouse him. Though rumours circulated and the situation was known, the British press was more discreet than it has since become. At the time when Mrs Simpson was being divorced for the second time in Colchester, the King, on a visit to S. Wales, said publicly that something must be done about the miners' living conditions. Thereupon, with wide explicit and implicit support including that of the Abp. of Canterbury (Cosmo Gordon Lang) and of public figures, other than Churchill and Lord Beaverbrook, the prime minister (Stanley Baldwin) advised the King that because of the sacramental nature

of his office, he could not both marry the lady and remain King. She insisted on marriage. Six weeks after the divorce, the Bp. of Bradford referred to the King's morals in a sermon, the *Yorkshire Post* reported him and the press broke silence. Public opinion was deeply split. There were demonstrations both for and against the King. On 11 Dec. 1936 at Edward's request, Parliament passed a requisite Abdication Act in one day; his brother, the reluctant King George VI, made him D. of Windsor and he left the country. (For a contemporary popular view *see* CALYPSO.) He was discouraged from living in Britain. Mrs Simpson, whom he married in the summer of 1937, was not surprisingly refused the status of a princess and the style of Royal Highness. During World War II a safe place was found for him as Gov. of the Bahamas, to meet his wish to be useful yet avoid political embarrassments. There is some evidence that he may have been considered by the Germans as a possible King for a German occupied Britain, but none that he agreed with them. He lived out the post war years in Paris with his duchess for whom he collected jewels.

EDWARD (1453-1471) P. of WALES (1454) only son of Henry VI and therefore the hope of Lancastrian partisans after his father's breakdown, was disinherited by parliament after the Lancastrian defeat at Northampton in 1460 and was taken by Q. Margaret to Scotland and thence to Brittany and France in 1462. In 1470 Warwick's French-financed expedition in his favour had some success, but he sailed too late in support, was defeated at Tewkesbury (1471) and murdered after the battle.

EDWARD, L. (C. Africa) was visited in 1875 by Henry Stanley who, believing it to be part of L. Albert, called it BEATRICE GULF. He rectified the mistake on another visit in 1889.

EDWARD, E. of WARWICK (1475-99), eldest *s.* of George D. of Clarence, was imprisoned by Henry VII in 1485 as a potential rival for the throne. He was impersonated by Lambert Simnel in 1487 and by Ralph Wilford in 1499. After the failure of Perkin Warbeck's rebellion Ferdinand of Aragon pressed for Warwick's death so that Henry VII's position should be strengthened before he married Ferdinand's *d..* Catherine of Aragon, and he was entrapped in a contrived treasonable plot and executed.

EDWARDES, Sir Herbert Benjamin (1819-68) was Gough's A.D.C. at the Bs. of Moodkee (1845) and Sobraon (1846) and then became Sir H. Lawrence's assistant at Lahore. In 1848 he, on his own responsibility, twice overthrew the rebel Diwan Mulraj of Multan. In 1853 he founded Abbottabad and became (until 1859) Commissioner at Peshawar. It was on his advice that Sir John Lawrence made the mutual non-interference treaty with Afghanistan and raised mixed levies against the mutineers in 1857. He was Commissioner at Ambala (Umballa) from 1862 to 1865.

EDWARDIAN CASTLES IN WALES (*see* JAMES OF ST. GEORGE). Many e.g. Caerphilly (Glam.) or Chirk, mainly in S. Wales and in the Marches, were privately built before Edward I's time and there were some royal castles, e.g. Rhuddlan, Flint and Llanbadarn. The widespread damage in the later 13th cent. wars and the need to police the suppressed principality of Gwynedd led to impressive military building and garrisoning, especially at ports and estuaries. Some private owners rebuilt their own (Caerphilly), the crown rebuilt some private castles or built castles and handed them to feudatories for safe-keeping (Chepstow, Builth), but in N. Wales where new ground had to be broken, great fortresses were constructed, sometimes on older sites, as part of a co-ordinated design and often combined with fortified town complexes (marked *). The most important of these (in clockwise order) were Aberystwyth*, Bere, Harlech, Criccieth, Caernarfon*, Beaumaris, Conway*, Deganwy, Rhuddlan*, Flint*, and Denbigh. Caernarfon, Beaumaris and Conway were strategically the linchpin of the system, for they could cut off the Anglesey corn supply to Snowdonia. The towns, once settled, were chartered.

EDWI[G] (943-59) joint-King of the English (955). *See* A(E)THILSTAN'S SUCCESSORS-3.

EDWARD OF NORWICH (?1373-1415) E. of RUTLAND (1390), of CORK (1396), 2nd D., was a friend of Richard II and a leading opponent of the Lords Appellant. He acquired wide lands in Ireland and England and Richard made him D. of Albemarle. His support for the King was, however, inadequate and Henry IV deprived him of his dukedom and some of the later land grants, but left him otherwise unmolested. He was restored to the council and in 1403 was made Lieutenant in S. Wales. He commanded the right wing at Agincourt where he was killed. His brother **(3) Richard (?-1415), E. of CAMBRIDGE (1414)** married Anne Mortimer and was executed for his part in the plot of 1415 against Henry V. His son **(4) Richard (1411-60) 3rd D. (1415)** inherited the Mortimer possessions in 1425 and married Cicely Neville in 1438. In 1440 he became Lieutenant in France and on his return in 1445 became the head of the anti-Neville and Somerset faction. *See* HENRY VI and ROSES, WARS OF THE. He was killed at Wakefield. His eleventh child **(5)** was **Richard III (1452-85), King (1483-5).**

EDWIN (King 616-32). *See* NORTHUMBRIA-2,3.

EDWIN, Earl. *See* MERCIA, EARLDOM OF-4.

EFFECTIVE OCCUPATION. The diplomatic doctrine that a power which claimed a right to exclude another power from a colonial territory, must by occupation, exert a real control over it. The phrase became fashionable after the Berlin Conference of 1885 in relation to claims in Africa, but the concept is much older and was used to justify English, French, Dutch and other incursions into areas reserved, by the Papal bull *Inter Caetera* and the T. of Tordesillas, to Spain and Portugal.

EFFINGHAM. *See* HOWARD; ARMADAS-1.

EGBERT. *See* KENT. KINGDOM-4.

EGBERT or ECGBERT, St. (?-729) a Northumbrian hermit educated in Ireland, inspired the English missions to Germany and introduced the Roman Easter at Iona. *See* MISSIONS TO EUROPE.

EGBERT, King (r. 802-39). *See* ENGLISH MONARCHY. EARLY-1: WEST SAXONS, EARLY.

EGBERT of YORK (?-766) a cousin of King Ceolwulf of Northumbria was ordained at Rome and became Bp. of York in 732. On Bede's advice he applied for and received the pallium. In 738 his brother Eadbert became King. The two brothers were able to carry through reforms and improvements, of which the creation of the York Cathedral School was the most far-reaching. Egbert taught there himself and Alcuin was one of his pupils. He also wrote works on canon law, church discipline and liturgy and composed an important penitential.

EGYPT (*see* CRUSADES). **(1)** From 1250 Egypt was ruled by Mamelukes, freed military slaves self perpetuated by purchase, training and further manumissions. The Sultan was generally the leader of their strongest faction and came to office (and was sometimes deposed) by force. Despite this political instability, Egypt was powerful through the decline of her neighbours. She was also exceedingly prosperous through her entrepôt trade via Venice with Europe, with Genoese help to the Byzantine dominions and the Black Sea and through the Karimis, a sort of merchant guild, with India and Ceylon, the great mart for China. This trade, important to all Europe, reached its peak in the early 15th cent., but survived vigorously (as did the Mamelukes) the Ottoman Turkish conquest of 1517, and also the initial Portuguese efforts in the 16th cent. to control it from Indian bases.

(2) The Turks extended Egypt by conquering Nubia, and reasserted control of the Red Sea, especially against the Portuguese, by occupying the Yemen (1536), Aden (1546) and Massawa (1557). It was the confusion of Mogul India and the irruption of the Dutch, French and British into the Indian seas which diverted the trade from the Red Sea and caused economic stagnation in Egypt. Meanwhile the Turkish administrative constitution permitted the Mamelukes to penetrate military and civilian office, so that by 1768 their leaders had achieved a local autonomy recognised subject to a fluctuating suzerainty by the Sublime Porte. The Turks tried, but failed, to reassert a more direct authority in 1786-7. Bonaparte's invasion in 1798 was, however, to give them a further opportunity. *See* MEDITERRANEAN WAR.

(3) Bonaparte overthrew the Mamelukes at the Bs. of Shubrakhit and Imbabah (the so-called B. of the Pyramids) in July 1798. A week later Nelson destroyed his fleet and cut him off from France. French Egypt had thus to be self supporting, which required native loyalty. Bonaparte deceived himself that the overthrow of the Mamelukes would rally the rest to his revolutionary standards. The Egyptians disliked the new Unbelievers, the administrative changes, the cost of the military occupation and especially the new efficiency of tax collection. The Turkish Sultan declared War in Sept. A politic loyalty to their Padishah brought an insurrection, which Bonaparte the Gunner suppressed by bombarding Cairo. The resulting bitterness was never assuaged. His invasion of Syria was defeated by Ahmed Djezzar Pasha and Sir Sydney Smith before Acre (Mar-May 1799), and though he held off a Turkish seaborne counter-invasion in July, he deserted his troops for the delights of metropolitan politics in Aug. His successors Kléber and Menou held out until Sept. 1802.

(4) The French academics who had come with Bonaparte made little impression on the Egyptians, but they opened European eyes to Egypt. The Turkish gain was short-lived. In May 1805 Albanian regiments mutinied and elevated the famous MEHEMET ALI (1769-1848) to the pashalik. The Sultan Selim III confirmed him in office in Sept. In two respects the new Mameluke differed from the old. He depended upon new military immigrants and he founded a dynasty. One of his first acts (1807) was to frustrate a British attempt on Alexandria and Rosetta.

(5) Mehemet Ali's essential need was to take control of taxation (in the hands of the old Mamelukes) and land-holding (in the hands of the Mamelukes and the Ulema). By 1809 he had advanced far enough to be expropriating lands. In 1811 he ended the Mamelukes' opposition by massacring them, a precedent of which the reforming Sultan Mahmoud II took notice. The pasha and his family established monopolies of raw materials and of the textile industries, at a time when free exchange formed the ideal of European commercial dogma, and was upheld especially by British govts.

(6) With his suzerain's encouragement Mehemet Ali and his son IBRAHIM invaded Arabia to suppress the Wahabis (1811-3 and 1816-8) and, having conquered it, occupied the northern Sudan (1819-21). This put him in control of the rich Afro-Arabian slave trade. He could thus afford to comply with Mahmoud II's request to help suppress the Greek revolt. Egypto-Albanian troops subdued Crete (1822), and Ibrahim began a victorious campaign in the Peloponnese (1825). Here he came up against European romantic classicism. The western public mistook the Turko-Byzantine brigands of mainland Greece for the race of Themistocles and rallied to the cause. The govts., suspicious of each other, sent contingents to a combined French, Russian and British fleet, which sank the Turkish and Egyptian navy at Navarino (Oct. 1827). Ibrahim evacuated the Peloponnese in 1828.

(7) These events awakened European govts. to nascent Egyptian power while the Pasha's economic policies irritated their commercial public. Moreover he was modernising the country. Egyptians were being sent to Europe for education, the administration was overhauled; conscription had been introduced (1823). There were printing presses and books. Parallel reforms in Turkey were strengthening the suzerain, who might become a danger. In 1831 Mehemet Ali rebelled, invaded first Syria and then Anatolia, where he defeated the Turks at Konieh (Dec. 1832). Mahmoud II conceded the pashalik of Syria but bided his time. In 1839 Turkish troops entered Syria. The concentration required to defeat them at Nisibin, entailed weakness in Arabia. Rebellions drove Ibrahim from Nejd and the Yemen. Mahmoud, however, died (1840) and the western powers, fearing Russian intervention in the confusion at Istanbul, themselves intervened to restore order. They forced Mehemet Ali to evacuate Syria, and by way of *douceur,* the new Sultan Abd-el-Mejid I made the Egyptian pashalik hereditary. By now the Pasha, feeling the strain of his years, retired in favour of Ibrahim, who died within months. The new ruler ABBAS HILMI I (r. 1848-54) had, for some time, the advantage of his grandfather's wily advice.

(8) The modernisation of Egypt, as that of Turkey, was undertaken to support an autocracy against encroachments and had, for a while, parallel effects. Most of the economic surplus went into the court at Cairo and an inflated military establishment. The standard of living of the rising population rose hardly at all and the partly trained administration ran ever more deeply into debt. European civilisation had penetrated the country in a French form under Mehemet Ali. Abbas Hilmi I disliked the French and, realising that the British needed Egypt for their route to India, turned to Britain. He gave them a railway concession from Alexandria, via Cairo to Suez, upon which work began in 1851. It was completed in 1858 in the reign of SAID (r. 1854-63) who succeeded after his nephew's murder. Said, a younger brother of Ibrahim, thought that European support against the Porte was less necessary than a balance of predatory European powers. Accordingly one of his earliest acts was to grant, against Turkish opposition, a Suez canal concession to the French, led by Ferdinand de Lesseps. This stimulated not only railway building but Anglo-French mutual dislike, but the Crimean War, by a Franco-British-Turkish alliance against Russia, resulted in a diplomatic deadlock during which the French quietly began work (1859).

(9) The civil war shortage of American cotton (1861-6) caused a boom in the Egyptian long staple variety, originally introduced by Mehemet Ali. In the middle of riches, ISMAIL (r. 1863-79), Ibrahim's son, succeeded his uncle. He was extravagant, financially unsophisticated and committed to the canal. The boom collapsed in 1865, and he sought to blackmail the canal syndicate by cutting off compulsory labour and cancelling the sweet water concession, without which voluntary labour could not be recruited. Backed by their govts., the shareholders forced an arbitration: he had to pay £3M and pay for the shares with which he had been credited gratis. In return the works were legalised, under French pressure, by Ottoman *firman* (Mar. 1866). It was now in his interest to get his money back by pressing ahead with construction. The canal was opened in Nov. 1869.

(10) Other *firmans* established primogeniture as the rule of succession (1866), and confirmed the long assumed title of Khedive (Pers. = prince) (1867). These improvements of status had to be purchased at a high cost in bribes. A further and immense expense was the extension of nominal sovereignty to Suakin and Eritrea (1865), to Darfur and the Southern Sudan (1874), Harar and parts of Somalia (1875). The pretext (as represented to Western powers) was the need to suppress the slave trade. Europeans, such as Sir Samuel Baker and Charles Gordon, often commanded the troops. The outlay exceeded the advantages and simply increased the burden of taxation. Meanwhile a new body of European educated politicians and army officers had grown up to

challenge the Circassian and Albanian office holders and estate owners. They naturally adopted a nationalist tone and rejoiced when the Abyssinians resoundingly defeated Ratib Pasha, the Circassian *Sirdar* in 1876. By now the govt. was bankrupt. Ismail sold his canal shares to Britain in 1875. In 1876 the four main creditor powers, Britain, France, Austria and Italy imposed a kind of receivership. The *Caisse de la Dette Publique* (Public Debt Account), under their management, distributed the receipts. An Anglo-French *Dual Control* was supposed to manage the collection and disbursement of the revenue before passing the surplus to the *Caisse*. For these economies the supersession in 1875 of the old consular jurisdictions (under Turkish capitulations) by Mixed (i.e. partly Egyptian) Courts, patiently negotiated by Nubar Pasha, the Armenian Prime Minister, seemed only a minor compensation, and they embittered the unpaid troops.

(11) Since 1866 there had been an advisory Assembly of Delegates composed in practice of village headmen. In 1878 the Dual Control was breaking down through evasions at every level. An international enquiry concluded that the Khedive was at the root of the trouble and irresistibly advised him to establish a form of ministerial responsibility with some European ministers. In his weakness in the year of the Berlin Congress, he accepted the advice. In 1879 he joined with the nationalists, now led by Chérif Pasha, in overthrowing the ministers. The British and French retaliated at the Sublime Porte. A Turkish imperial *iradé* deposed Ismail in favour of his son TEWFIK (r. 1879-92); the Dual Control was imposed in a more stringent form with arrangements to pay half the gross revenue into the *Caisse*. Arabi and Chérif Pashas led a movement hostile both to Europeans and Turks, and twice revolted. By Sept. 1881 they controlled the govt. European intervention was deemed necessary, but only the British were prepared to go to extremes. In July 1882 the fleet bombarded Alexandria. In Sept. a British expeditionary force, which had occupied the canal, beat the Egyptians in a brilliant night action at Tel-el-Kebir. The British were now in possession.

(12) A rebellion had broken out in the Sudan in Aug. 1881. (*See* MAHDI; SUDAN.) Gen. Hicks and a few British officers with demoralised Egyptian troops were overwhelmed near El Obeid (Nov. 1883). Apart from Khartoum and a few isolated garrisons, the country was in the hands of the Sudanese. The Gladstone govt. advised the Khedive to abandon the huge province and this, after the fall of Khartoum and the death of Gen. Gordon, the Gov.-Gen., was, in 1885 done. *See* GLADSTONE'S SECOND GOVT.-8 TO 10.

(13) While the army, confined to frontier defence, was retrained, the British regenerated the govt. and the economy. The moving spirit was Sir Evelyn Baring (from 1891 Lord Cromer), the masterful British Agent and Consul-Gen., but he had the backing of the influential E. of Dufferin, now ambassador to the Porte. Dufferin visited Egypt in Nov. 1882 and reported on the prospects of reform. His conclusions implied a lengthy British presence, which the Gladstone govt. had, in the special circumstances of the withdrawal from the Sudan, to accept. The reforms were initially very unpopular, for they were begun in the atmosphere created by the trial and banishment of Arabi Pasha; but as sensible replaced corrupt finance, new irrigation fertilised the land, bridges and roads were built and new crops introduced, the bankrupt country began to prosper and evoke pride in a hitherto doubtful British public. It also created other problems. Egyptian public servants naturally disliked Baring's cadre of administrators, mostly drawn from India, and the British relationship, both internally with the Khedive and externally with the Porte and the European powers, lacked definition. As Egypt became more valuable, the French, especially, had increasingly strong reasons for meddling. Their part in revenue

collection (The Dual Control) had been abolished in Dec. 1882 but they continued to make trouble in the *Caisse de la Dette,* the British replied by involving other European powers. The Convention of London (1885) secured an international loan for the Khedivial Govt., and added German and Russian members to the *Caisse.* From 1889 onwards there was an annual budget surplus, but French manoeuvres continued and so publicly revealed their political character.

(14) In truth the Khedive Tewfik was a nonentity and his more strong minded, mainly French educated, ministers and courtiers had vested interests opposed to the reforms. The British demanded that their formal advice should be binding and compelled the now recalcitrant Chérif Pasha to resign (Jan. 1884). The cosmopolitan Nubar Pasha found the arrangement increasingly difficult to support and was forced out of office in 1888. Rias Pasha resigned in 1891 over differences in judicial administration. Thus, as the British steadily improved the administration and brought freedom and prosperity to the oppressed peasantry, they made themselves increasingly disliked by the educated or political public. Meanwhile there was always the nostalgic desire to avenge Gordon and in 1893 Milner's *England in Egypt* reawakened the British political public to achievements and possibilities. Sir Herbert Kitchener was now Sirdar. Reconquest of the Sudan or at least of Dongola, had long been accepted in both countries as a reasonable aspiration.

(15) Two events precipitated an early move: the conservative victory in the British election of 1895 and the Italian defeat at Adowa (Mar. 1896) by Abyssinians with French and Russian arms. On the principle of the Balance of Power, a pro-Italian demonstration seemed desirable. Moreover the Sudanese used the opportunity to threaten Eritrea. The British therefore proposed the recovery of Dongola for the Khedive, who applied to the *Caisse de la Dette* for funds. These were granted, but the French and Russian commissioners sued their colleagues before the Mixed Tribunal after the money had been spent and obtained a repayment order. It could not be obeyed, but the British govt. stepped in and repaid the money itself (Dec. 1896). The war was popular and French interference resented. The event virtually destroyed French influence.

(16) The reconquest took nearly three years (Mar. 1896-Dec. 1899) under Kitchener's command, by a force which was about 45% Egyptian, 25% Sudanese and only 30% British and it ended with the Sudan Agreement which (apart from capitulations and Mixed Courts) extended the salient features of the British Egyptian influence to the Sudan. In particular the new condominium was incorporated in the Egyptian economic zone. It had been created in the context of the French retreat after the Fashoda Incident (1898), and the *Entente Cordiale* of 1904 recognised the virtually free hand which the British had had since 1896. One effect was to deprive the nationalist cliques (mostly based upon small journalistic ventures) of their opportunities to intrigue with the French. Mustafa Kamil, the founder of the journal *al Liwa* moved, consequently, from an Egyptian nationalism centred on the new Khedive Abbas Hilmi II (r. 1892-1914) to the pan-Islamism now encouraged by the Porte. The Khedive secured the support of a Constitutional Reform "Party" led by Sheikh Ali Yusuf and his journal *al-Muayyad,* and in 1907 Christians and moderates, alarmed at Mustafa Kamil's pan-Islamism founded a new journal *al-Jaridah* and a National (*Umma*) "Party". None of these groups survived their founders, but political discussion in a widening educated public had stimulated an inchoate Egyptian consciousness.

(17) Sir Eldon Gorst succeeded Cromer in 1907 and the long tenure of the pro-British Mustafa Fahmi Pasha ended in 1908 with the succession of a Copt, Boutros

Ghali Pasha. The British by now were more interested in economic and political strategy and, as in India, were beginning to retreat from direct administration. Boutros saw advantages in this and he and Gorst agreed a gradual withdrawal of British advisers (which could be done administratively) and a 40 year extension of the Suez Canal concession. The deal misfired, for Gorst died suddenly, the Assembly threw out the concession and a Moslem murdered Boutros (1911). Kitchener was the new Agent and he, of course, knew Egypt well. Terrifying and autocratic, yet endowed with a liberal common-sense, Kitchener sought to dilute the Khedivial influence by encouraging constitutionalism. Thus by an Organic Law of 1913 a Legislative Assembly superseded the old Advisory Assembly, while the peasantry were given a more effective protection of their land tenure.

(18) How these reforms might have developed is unascertainable, for in 1914 war broke out between Britain and the Ottoman Sultan. ABBAS HILMI II, on good legal, political and economic grounds, refused to make war on his suzerain. The British on strategic grounds deposed him in favour of his uncle HUSSEIN KAMIL, suspended the new assembly and imposed martial law.

(19) Hussein Kamil took the sovereign title of Sultan. In Oct. 1917 he was succeeded by his brother FUAD. Some 250,000 British troops were stationed in Egypt to defend the Suez Canal: to act as a rear base for the Dardanelles operations and for the conquest of Turkish Syria. This brought considerable prosperity. The post-war recession as the troops were reduced in strength encouraged a local nationalism led by Zaghlul Pasha, a former minister of education, who was already demanding independence in 1919. The British govt. exiled him and his major supporters amid rioting, but appointed Lord Allenby (who knew Egypt well as British C.-in-C. during the war) as High Commissioner. He restored order and advised the British govt. to abandon the protectorate. Accordingly Egyptian independence was recognised (Feb. 1922) and ratified by parliament subject to four points reserved for negotiation viz.: (1) the security of British imperial communications (i.e. the Canal); (2) Defence; (3) Protection of European interests; and (4) The Sudan. The country became a western style Kingdom in Apr. 1923.

(20) The slowness of the negotiations arose mainly from the Sudan question, for the British intended to separate the two countries and maintain a powerful presence there, whereas the Egyptians wished to continue the condominium. There was much contrived nationalistic excitement, and extremists murdered the British Sirdar, Sir Lee Stack (Nov. 1924), but the tempo was increased by the rise of Italian imperialism in Africa with German Nazism in the background. In Aug. 1936 a 20 year T. of Alliance provided for British garrisons and for British special interests in the Canal, and in May 1937 the Convention of Montreux abolished the capitulations. This was both a long step towards independence, and the basis of the British military presence in the Middle East in World War II.

(21) The self-indulgent and Anglophobe King FAROUK had come to the throne in 1936. The Italians were driven away by Wavell's brilliant campaigns in 1940-1, but with the arrival of Rommel and the second retreat of the 8th army, the Japanese onrush in Asia and the Russian crisis at Stalingrad, Farouk's govt. showed an unmistakable hostility which might endanger the British bases. Accordingly, Sir Miles Lampson, the British ambassador supported by troops and tanks, demanded an audience and forced the King to appoint Nahas Pasha Prime Minister. Nahas was a strong nationalist but had signed the alliance. His administration was wholly beneficial to the war effort, until brought down in 1944 by a sensational corruption scandal.

(22) In Dec. 1945 the new govt. demanded the revision of the treaty and soon there was destructive anti-British rioting. Within a year it was demanding evacuation of troops not only from Egypt but the Sudan and the abrogation of the Sudan condominium. In Jan. 1947 it appealed for backing to the United Nations. It failed to get it, but British troops were moved out of Cairo and Alexandria.

(23) The Israelis now began to exercise a strong leverage in Mid-Eastern politics. As soon as the British mandate was terminated, Egyptian and Arab troops invaded Palestine from all sides (May 1948). A short truce was followed by a series of defeats, further truces and then further defeats, followed (Jan. 1949) by a general Armistice. These humiliations, jealousy of the King's luxurious habits, and Russian subversion, led to a *coup d'état* by left-wing army officers master-minded by GAMAL ABDEL-NASSER using the respected Gen. Mohammed Neguib as a front man. Egypt became a republic with Neguib as President (June 1953) but he gave way ultimately to Abdel-Nasser himself (Mar. 1956).

(24) There now occurred the events which destroyed Britain as an imperial power. In Dec. 1955 Britain and the U.S.A. undertook to finance the Assuan High Dam. Meanwhile Nasser was accepting Russian military advice and equipment. This communist penetration of the western position in the Middle-East was deemed a grave threat and it was unwisely thought that Nasser could be brought to heel by withdrawal of the High Dam finance. This was done in July 1956. Nasser, however, was made of sterner stuff. Within days he nationalised the Canal. Instead of enforcing their legal rights openly, the British and French (who were mostly concerned), followed a collusive and discreditable course. The Israelis attacked Egypt (Oct.). France and Britain intervened ostensibly to separate the combatants and protect the Canal. Actually they bombed the Egyptians and landed troops at Port Said from Cyprus. These operations (in which the Israelis used French aircraft) deceived no-one. They excited world-wide hostility and bellicose threats from Russia. They were conducted so slowly and incompetently that international opposition solidified and the Egyptians were able to block the Canal with sunken ships. Deserted by the Americans, who had instigated the withdrawal of the High Dam loan in the first place, the British and French had to withdraw and Sir Anthony Eden, the British Prime Minister, was forced to resign. This shame-faced British imperialist venture ended with Egypt dependent upon Russia, the confiscation of British property and investments and wholesale deportations of British subjects. *See* NILE.

(25) The prosperity generated by the High Dam after its completion in 1970, caused the population to grow by 1M a year.

EIGHTH ARMY, was the British formation created in Nov. 1941 under Gen. Sir Alan Cunningham, as the striking force in the Western Desert of the Egyptian garrison. It won a notable victory and relieved Tobruk (Nov. 1941-Jan. 1942) but was driven back to Alamein by Gen. Rommel (May 1942). Gen. Auchinleck then took command and held him until the force was reorganised and heavily reinforced for Gen. Sir H. Alexander with Gen. B. Montgomery as his field commander. After winning the defensive B. of Alam Halfa and the great victory of Alamein (Oct. 1942) it advanced continually until it joined up in Tunisia with the 1st Army, and forced the surrender of the Axis forces in Africa (May 1943). It then conquered Sicily (July-Aug. 1943) and in a reinforced and reconstituted form, invaded Italy (Sept.), captured Rome (June 1944) and Milan (Apr. 1945) when the Germans surrendered.

EIGHT-HOURS ACT of 1908, limited working hours for miners. It was the first legislation to regulate working hours for adult males and constituted an important precedent.

EGERTON. Cheshire Family. **(1) Sir Thomas (?-1540-1617) 1st L. ELLESMERE (1603) 1st Vist. BRACKLEY (1616)** bastard of Sir Richard Egerton, became sol-gen. in 1581 and att.-gen. in 1592, his fame as a practitioner having reached the Queen who, against Burghley's advice, made him Master of the Rolls in 1594 and Lord Keeper in 1596. He was employed in diplomacy with the Dutch in 1598 and with Denmark in 1600. He had always been a friend of Essex's, whose unwisdom he tried to restrain, but this did not prevent him doing his duty as Lord Keeper in presiding at one of his trials and taking part in the other. James I appointed him Lord Chancellor. As such he seemed a survival of the previous reign. He acted as the King's executive in opposing the puritans and enforcing penalties against Romanists. On the other hand he presided in the important *Case of the Postnati* (1609). He advised Whitelocke's committal for contempt in questioning the prerogative (1613), and acted as the King's adviser in the long quarrel with Coke, in which Coke was, incidentally, attacking the Chancery jurisdiction. He had been a patron of Bacon and he and Bacon together advised James on points of law. He swore in Coke's successor. He was widely admired. His son **(2) John (1579-1649) 2nd Vist., 1st E. of BRIDGEWATER (1617)** married his stepsister Frances Stanley through whom, as a coheiress, some of the Stanley fortune passed to the Egertons. He became Lord Lieut. of Wales and the Borders in 1631, and Milton's *Comus* was written for his ceremonial induction at Ludlow in 1634. After 1643 he withdrew from Wales and lived at Ashridge throughout the Civil War. His grandson **(3) John 3rd E. (1646-1701)** was a supporter of the protestant succession and died as 1st Lord of the Admiralty. His son **(4) Scroop (1681-1745) 4th E. and 1st D. (1720)** held minor court offices. He laid the plans and secured the local legislation for the Bridgewater canals, but it was left to his son **(5) Francis (1748-1803) 3rd D.** to build them, using James Brindley as his engineer. The first canal was opened in 1761 and was immensely profitable, but the building of some later canals taxed even his huge wealth and for a while he lived a penurious life in order to pay his workpeople. The dukedom became extinct at his death. Meanwhile his cousin **(6) John (1721-87),** Bp. of Bangor from 1756, was translated to Lichfield in 1768 and to Durham in 1771. He was the last Bp. who effectively ruled the palatinate, using the wealth of the see to build bridges, drain fens, abolish customary dues, improve the palaces and endow religious and educational institutions. His son **(7) John William (1753-1823), 8th E.,** a soldier, was a Tory M.P. from 1777-1803 and rebuilt Ashridge. He was succeeded by his eccentric brother **(8) Francis Henry (1756-1829),** a scholar and literary collector, who gave his manuscripts to the British Museum. He lived in a palatial house in Paris with many dogs and cats who were dressed as humans and taken for drives in his carriages.

EGLINTON. *See* MONTGOMERIE.

EGMONT, Earls of. *See* PERCEVAL.

EGREMONT. *See* WYNDHAM.

1848 – EIGHTEEN FORTY-EIGHT (*See* AUSTRIA-POST PRAGMATIC.) The popular insurrections of 1848-9 began in Sicily in Jan. 1848, incidentally overthrew the French July Monarchy in Feb. and broke out in mid-March almost simultaneously in Italy and Vienna, whence Metternich fled to England (15 Mar.). Mobs seized control in Berlin three days later and on 23 Mar. the opportunist Savoyards invaded Lombardy. In Apr. Prussian troops suppressed the Berlin outbreaks and helped to put down revolts in Russian Poland, while the hitherto liberal Pope, Pius IX, repudiated the Italian movements. The Emperor Ferdinand and the regency, by leaving Vienna for

Innsbruck, had freed their hands and in May loyal troops put down riots at Cracow and beat the Savoyards at Curtatone. In June they suppressed riots in Prague and the strong Archduke John replaced the weak Ludwig as regent. In Aug. after a triumph at Custozza (July) they drove the Savoyards to an armistice at Vigevano and the govt. returned to Vienna. In Sept. the Neapolitans recovered Sicily.

The insurrections, whether nationalist, liberal or merely personal, or motivated by half successful ambitions, represented no movement and exhibited a fatal lack of co-ordination. It was not until mid-Sept. that the Hungarians, after long argument, elected Lajos KOSSUTH as dictator, but they did not move while in Oct. the govt. suffered and suppressed another rising in Vienna. In Nov. a revolution drove the Pope from Rome to Gaeta, but in Dec. Louis Napoleon BONAPARTE became Pres. of France with R. Catholic help, and was preparing to restore him. Thus even though the neighbouring Habsburg D. of Tuscany was hounded from Florence (Feb. 1849), Mazzini's Roman Republic, proclaimed two days later, was doomed in advance.

The Archduchess SOPHIE, Ferdinand's sister-in-law, had held the court together throughout these upheavals and inspired it with aggressive courage. Men of strength and ability gathered round her. Jellacic, the Ban of Croatia, held Agram (Zagreb) and Radetzky beat the Savoyards, while Prince Windischgraetz bombarded Prague and then Vienna into submission. Now he set off against Hungary, offering his brilliant brother-in-law Prince Felix SCHWARZENBERG as head of the govt. Schwarzenberg would not serve without a new emperor. Sophie persuaded Ferdinand to abdicate and her own husband to renounce his rights (Dec. 1848). The Austrian (but not the Hungarian) crown thus passed to FRANZ JOSEPH (r. 1848-1916), her son, who, because he was only 18 was uncompromised by the contentions of the past. Schwarzenberg, a very modern man, assembled a powerful ministry which included the liberal Stadion, Alexander Bach the administrator and Bruck, the shipping magnate. Since the Hungarians were proving too much for Windischgraetz, he called for (Apr. 1849) Russian aid under the Münchengraetz treaties. By Aug. the Hungarians had capitulated to the Czar at Vilagos and their country was soon being fairly and incorruptibly administered by hated Austrians; but, first, some hangings created martyrs. Three years later Schwarzenberg was dead, but he had laid the foundations of an autocracy.

EIKON BASILIKE (Gr = Royal Image) or *The Pourtraicture of His Sacred Majestie in His Solitudes and Sufferings* was published on or about the day of Charles I's execution in Whitehall on 30 Jan. 1649. Widely believed to have been written by him, it passed through 47 editions in a year. The parliament felt obliged to commission a counter-blast; this was Milton's *Eikonoklastes* (Gr = The Image Breaker), a tedious and unsuccessful pamphlet which reached two editions. Dr John Gauden (1605-62), the editor of *Hooker*, claimed, plausibly, to have written the book.

EINHARD or EGINHARD (?770-840), courtier and friend of Charlemagne and Louis I, wrote several books including a life of Charlemagne, which are important sources for the period.

EINSTEIN, Albert (1879-1955) evolved his *Special or Restricted Theory of Relativity* between 1902 and 1909 and his *General Theory of Relativity* between 1915 and 1917. The special theory states broadly that natural phenomena move according to general laws which are the same for two observers one of whom is moving in a uniform rectilinear manner in respect of the other. This apparently conflicted with the accepted law that light is propagated *in vacuo* at a uniform speed, but the conflict could be resolved by abandoning the assumptions that the time interval between two events and the space interval between two points in a rigid body, are independent of the observer's motion; this enabled Einstein to find a formula whereby the quantities noted by the two observers would correspond in such a way that the law of propagation of light would hold good for both. The formula existed in the so-called Lorentz Transformations and led to the conclusion that relatively to a stationary observer a metre rod in the axis of a moving system is slightly shorter than a metre, and a second's interval between the beats of a clock slightly longer. This conclusion is confirmed by optical and electro-magnetic experience.

The General Theory starts from the assumption that the Special Theory is not an exception to the laws of nature and adopts a physical system consistent with it. This involved abandoning Euclidian geometry and postulating the curvature of space.

EIRE. See IRELAND, REPUBLIC OF.

EIRIC or ERIC BLOODAXE (?-952) K. of Norway (932) K. of Northumbria (946). *See* A(E)THILSTAN-2; A(E)THILSTAN'S SUCCESSORS-2.

EISENHOWER, Dwight (1890-1969) was one of Douglas MacArthur's aides in 1933, when MacArthur was U.S.C of S. In 1942 he became commander of U.S. troops in Europe and so commanded the U.S. invasions of N. Africa (1942) and Italy (1943). He was then Supreme Allied Commander for the conquest of Europe and between 1951 and 1952 Supreme Commander of NATO. He was republican Pres. of the U.S.A. from 1952-60. The so-called EISENHOWER DOCTRINE, enunciated in Jan. 1957, extended the TRUMAN DOCTRINE of U.S. support for Greece and Turkey against Russian pressure, to Middle Eastern countries which, as a result of the Suez crisis, were being supplied with arms by Russia.

EISTEDDFOD (Welsh = assembly). Sessions of bards and minstrels with contests are a very ancient Welsh custom. That held by the Lord Rhys at Cardigan in 1176 was perhaps the first on a large scale, but it was not the first. At the Carmarthen Eisteddfod of 1451 or 1453 the poet Dafydd ap Edmwnt settled the authoritative form of modern Welsh strict metre. In the 18th cent. the Caerwys Eisteddfod petitioned for a system of bardic licensing. By this time the practice of poetry had declined, and until 1789 eisteddfodau were mostly gatherings of poetasters composing impromptu. In 1789 Thos. Jones of Corwen with the support of the London Gwyneddigion held the first of the modern annual eisteddfodau at Bala. In 1792 Iolo Morgannwg established the Gorsedd of Bards in opposition, but in 1819 the two institutions were amalgamated at Carmarthen. In 1858 it was decided at Llangollen to form a national eisteddfod and since 1860 it has been held alternately in N. and S. Wales.

ELBA (Med.) was one of the chief sources of iron ore in W. Europe. Originally a Pisan possession, it passed to Genoa in 1290, and in 1399 to the Lords of Piombino. Piracy seriously affected production, until it was ceded in 1548 to the Tuscan Cosimo de Medici; he fortified Portoferraio. It was under Spanish control from 1596 to 1709, then under Neapolitan until 1802, when it was taken by France. Hence it became Bonaparte's principality from 1814 to 1815, when it reverted to Tuscany.

ELBE, R. has long been navigable by barge from Hamburg via Magdeburg and Dresden to Bohemia: by the tributary Moldau (Vltava) to Prague and by the Havel and its canal to Berlin; in 19th cent. it was connected to the Hanover Salzgiter area by canal and since 14th with the Baltic by a shallow canal from Lauenburg to Lübeck. The creation of the land-bound state of Czechoslovakia gave it a modern political importance and it was inter-nationalised from the confluence with the Vltava to the sea under the P. of Versailles (1920) which created a managing committee on which Germany, Czechoslovakia, Britain, France, Italy and Belgium were represented. The arrangement was in abeyance after the advent of the Nazis in 1933 but was resumed after World War II.

ELCHO. *See* WEMYSS.

ELDER, John (1824-69) in 1854 created the compound steam engine which by using the same steam twice reduced the coal consumption and raised payloads of ships. It became universal at sea until the appearance of diesels and the turbine.

ELDON, John Scott (1751-1838) 1st Ld. (1799) 1st E. (1821), became a Tory M.P. in 1783 and as Att-Gen from 1793-1799 was responsible for the anti-revolutionary govt. measures during the war with France. He was C.J. of the Common Pleas from 1799 and Lord Chancellor from 1801 to 1806 and from 1807 to 1827. Though exceedingly dilatory in legal administration, he led the development and systematisation of English equity (q.v.), in using injunctions and other equitable remedies to support and supplement the inadequacies of the common law. In particular he developed the law on trade marks and false descriptions. His politics were those of a conservative doctrinaire: he opposed R. Catholic emancipation and reform of the House of Commons. He also favoured imprisonment for debt and defended the slave trade, yet he had no political ambitions.

EL DORADO (Sp. = The gilded man). The Spaniards, Sir Walter Raleigh and half Europe believed that there was a country or city on the Amazon or the Orinoco called MANOA, which abounded in gold and was ruled by a 'golden king' whose Spanish sobriquet was soon transferred to his kingdom. Three Spanish expeditions sought it between 1540 and 1570. The legend was finally dispelled by Humboldt's surveys of S. America in the 1880s.

ELEANOR, ALIENOR or ÆNOR OF AQUITAINE (?1122-1204), the beautiful and enterprising daughter of Duke William X of Aquitaine, was married firstly to Louis VII of France in 1137. He was sexually unattractive; in 1146, while with her husband on crusade, scandal connected her with her uncle Raymond I of Antioch. On the way back Louis and Eleanor discussed nullification with Pope Eugenius III who, however, made them sleep together. The resulting child, born in 1152, was a girl. The marriage was then annulled for consanguinity. She retired to Poitiers and within two months married Henry of Anjou who, in Oct. 1154, became Henry II of England. Her seductive charm at this period earned her a verse in the *Carmina Burana*. Her great dominions in the South of France gave allegiance to her rather than him, but involved an extension of his ambitions over Toulouse and into Spain, Savoy and Northern Italy. Meantime their children received titular sovereignties: Henry in Maine, Richard in Aquitaine, Geoffrey in Brittany; John, by a marriage was to obtain Savoy. Eleanor in about 1167 quarrelled with the King and retired to her capital at Poitiers where she, with Richard, ruled from a famous troubadour court and stimulated her other sons' discontent with their ornamental but powerless situation. The Savoy treaty interfered with Geoffrey's lands and the sons conspired to rebel with French help. The King seized her before the rebellion broke out in 1173 and she remained in custody in England until her death in 1189. Richard had her released and she acted for him in securing his peaceful succession and defended his interests while he was on crusade and in Germany against John's intrigues; in 1193 the precautions taken by the justiciars on her advice frustrated John's French-supported rebellion. When Richard died in 1199 Aquitaine did homage to her, but she made it over, subject to her own life interest, to John. She defended the Duchy against French and Lusignan attacks and in 1202 was besieged by Arthur of Brittany and the Lusignans at Mirebeau where John rescued her. She died in Aquitaine.

ELEANOR OF CASTILE (c. 1244-90) was *d.* of Ferdinand III of Castile and Joan of Ponthieu. Her half-brother Alfonso the Wise succeeded in Castile in 1252. He claimed English Aquitaine through descent from Henry II and began to accept Navarrese and Bearnais homage. As part of an ensuing pacification, Eleanor was to marry the Lord Edward; he was to receive the revenues of Ireland and Aquitaine and large English estates (of which Grantham, Stamford, Tickhill and the Peak constituted her dower) while Alfonso renounced his Gascon claims. They were married at Burgos in Oct. 1254 when she was about ten and she lived at Windsor until the later consummation when they fell in love for life. During the Barons' War she took refuge in France. In 1271 she went with Edward on crusade. In June 1272 he was wounded by an assassin's poisoned dagger and she saved his life by sucking out the poison. In Sept. they left Acre; in Nov. he became King and from Feb. to June 1273 they were at the Papal court at Orvieto, after which Eleanor visited Alfonso at Burgos. The two then met in Gascony, where they settled local business before reaching England for their coronation in Aug. 1274. In 1279 Eleanor succeeded her mother as Countess of Ponthieu. Edward paid the feudal relief and gave the county an English administration. She occupied an important role in the Franco-Castilian succession disputes of 1279-82 because she understood the personalities and issues. Financially businesslike, even hard, she was respected for her fairness and moderation. In 1285, for example, she even arbitrated by invitation between her husband and the Vicomte de Fronsac. She was interested in books and Spanish tapestries and she exercised a calming influence on her strong-minded husband. Her early death robbed him of his happiness. He brought her body to Westminster, erecting at each night's resting place a monument. Several of these *Eleanor Crosses* survive, notably a large one in Northamptonshire and one in London after which Charing Cross is named.

ELEANOR OF PROVENCE (?-1291) *d.* of Ramon Berengar IV Count of Provence and Beatrix of Savoy, married Henry III at Canterbury and was crowned at Westminster in Jan. 1236. She was never popular in England because of Henry's favour (necessarily ascribed to her influence) towards her mother's relatives, notably her uncles WILLIAM, Bp. elect of Valence and BONIFACE OF SAVOY, who was made Abp. of Canterbury. In 1241, however, she did succeed in reconciling the King with the Earl Marshal. Her sister SANCHIA married Henry's brother RICHARD OF CORNWALL in 1243 and she and Richard shared the govt. when Henry was abroad in 1253-4. He and the King's continued financial support for the Savoyards during a recession in the 1250s contributed further to her unpopularity and his political difficulties. She is rumoured, after initial support, to have influenced the King and the Lord Edward against the Provisions of Oxford. This led to ill-treatment in London when she took refuge there in 1259. She remained abroad after Henry returned to England in 1263 and, after the B. of Lewes, hired a fleet from Sluys to make descents on the South Coast. The fleet dispersed when her money ran out. Activities such as this and her aid to her relatives combined with a magnificent life style left her poor when she returned to England in Oct. 1265. Henry died in 1272 and Edward I returned from Crusade in 1274. She then retired to a nunnery at Amesbury (1276) but kept control of her estates until she died.

ELECTIONS – MODE (1) Until 1872 those entitled to vote in a local or parliamentary election had to do so by mounting the raised hustings and, having identified themselves, openly naming the candidate for whom they wished to vote in the presence of a returning officer, who in a borough was the mayor and elsewhere the sheriff or his deputy, together with a large crowd of interested spectators. His name and vote were then recorded by the clerk. The electorate was sometimes very small and susceptible to private influences through bribes, pressure or drink and public influences through bystanders' lungs and missiles. In large electorates only the latter had much effect. Since the private and public influences were often opposed, elections were often riotous. They were not always as unfair as has been represented, for open voting enabled the unenfranchised to make their views felt.

(2) The Ballot Act 1872 required voting to take place by marking a printed list of candidates in the privacy of a booth, which no one was supposed to overlook. It was not invariably as private as the law required and after the enfranchisement of women, in particular, husbands were occasionally found in booths telling their wives what to do.

ELECTION PETITIONS. The House of Commons established the right to decide controverted elections in 1604. These were heard and decided by the whole house, which tended increasingly to vote along political lines, and wasted many days, especially at the beginning of a parliament. Defeat on an election petition in 1741 led to Walpole's resignation in 1742. In 1770 Grenville's Act transferred the decision to a committee of 13 chosen by lot. In 1868 the trial of election petitions was transferred to an Election Court under a judge.

ELECTOR (Ger: *KURFÜRST*). The Golden Bull of Charles IV (1356) laid down that the Holy Roman Emperor and his heir apparent, the King of the Romans (if any), should be elected at Frankfurt by a college of seven rulers viz: the Abps. of Mainz, Cologne and Trier, the Count Palatine of the Rhine, the Margrave of Brandenburg, the D. of Saxony, together with the King of Bohemia whose large state though an enclave within the Empire, was not part of it. The first six of these were called Electors, and ranked above all other non-royal personages. In 1623 the Palatine electorate was transferred to Bavaria. In 1648 the diminished Palatinate acquired a new, eighth electorate and in 1692 Brunswick-Hanover a ninth.

ELECTORATE. *See* REFORM ACTS; REDISTRIBUTION OF SEATS; REPRESENTATION OF THE PEOPLE.

ELECTRIC (1) Batteries. The first efficient ones date from 1836, the lead-acid accumulator from 1881. **(2) Generators.** A hand generator was first demonstrated in 1832, but efficient machines came into use slowly until the employment of Faraday's transformer in 1880. **(3) Light.** The carbon arc lamp was first tried out by Humphry Davy in 1810. The filament bulb was invented independently by Swan and Edison in 1878. **(4) Motors.** Faraday defined the principle in 1821 but the first commercial (direct current) machine was produced in 1873 and the first alternating current machine in the U.S.A. in 1888.

ELECTRICITY and MAGNETISM. (1) The 13th cent. Picard Crusader, Peter of Maricourt, observed the magnetic lines on a lodestone. The Englishman Wm. Gilbert published his seminal *De Magnete magneticisque corporibus et de magno magnete tellure* (Lat = The Magnet, Magnetic Bodies and the Earth as a Magnet) in 1600 and Stephen Gray discovered electrical conductors in 1729. In 1733 Louis XV's gardener, Charles Francois Dufey, distinguished between the attractive and the repulsive forces and these were further defined by Benjamin Franklin and Joseph Priestley. The mathematical work was done by Henry Cavendish and Poisson whose equation, published in 1813, summarises the laws of electro-statics. In the meantime Luigi Galvani at Bologna published his observations on the electrical effects of nerve on muscle in 1791, and Alessandro Volta of Pavia constructed the Voltaic pile in 1800.

(2) These various developments provided a bedrock for the further expansion of electrical theory. In 1820 the Dane Hans Christian Ørsted published the effect of currents in neighbouring conductors on compass needles and in 1821 the Frenchman André Marie Ampère demonstrated the nature of Dufey's attractive and repulsive forces. In 1827 the German Georg Simon Ohm

refined Cavendish's calculations into the well known Ohm's Law. In 1831 Faraday discovered electro-magnetic induction and in 1841 James Prescott Joule set out in quantitative form the heating effects of currents in conductors. Faraday also developed the idea of magnetic lines of force dimly discerned centuries before, and these led Sir James Clerk Maxwell to formulate his electro-magnetic equations in 1864 with the help of the Germans Weber, Kirchhoff and Kohrausch's comparisons between the speeds of electrical disturbances and of light.

(3) Between 1896 and 1898, but using the results of a generation of observation, Thomson and Townsend defined the cathode ray and the electron. During the same period the German Wilhelm Wien, with Lord Raleigh and Sir James Jeans, developed apparently partly conflicting views on thermal radiation, which were reconciled by Max Planck's formulation in 1900 of his theory of Quantum Mechanics. The Lorentz equations were published in 1909.

ELEVEN PLUS EXAMINATION was suggested in the Hadow report as a way of selecting children of that age for free places in grammar schools: then it was included in the abortive 1931 Education Bill, and finally applied nationally under the Education Act 1944. Parents disliked it, especially the intelligence test and often found the results inexplicable. It was a dangerous obstacle for late developers and non-conformers. Believing that long testing had established its reliability educational officialdom treated complaints as natural to the disappointed or the ill-informed. The Labour Party's proposals for comprehensive schools (motivated by social engineering) gained some support from those hostile to it. The changeover towards comprehensive education indeed marked the end of the examination, but after 1971 it was discovered that the educational conclusions of Cyril Burt (1883-1971) on which the intelligence test had been founded, were based on falsified research.

ELFRIDA (945-1000) second Q. of K. Edgar. *See* EDWARD THE MARTYR.

ELGAR, Sir Edward William (1857-1934) began composing in 1890 and became famous through his *Enigma Variations* (1899) and *Dream of Gerontius* (1900). He was the originator of a modern English style of composition. He published two symphonies (1908 and 1911) and his last major work was his cello concerto of 1919.

ELGIN MARBLES. *See* ACROPOLIS OF ATHENS.

***ELIOT'S CASE* (1629 and 1666)** (Sir John Eliot, Densil Hollis and Others) (3 St. Tr.294). In 1629 the defendants were convicted in the King's Bench of seditious speeches in the House of Commons and of assaulting the Speaker (they had held him down in his chair to prevent an adjournment). In 1666 the Lords reversed the judgement, holding that nothing said by a member as such in Parliament could be inquired into save in Parliament; that the conviction for sedition could therefore not stand, and that as the sedition and the assault were the subject of one judgement, the conviction for the assault could not stand either. They did not decide whether the King's Bench could have tried the assault separately. The case is the foundation of parliamentary freedom of speech.

ELIOT, Edward (1727-1804) 1st Ld. (1784) influential landowner in Cornwall and related to Gibbon the historian, inherited his lands and influence from his father in 1748. He controlled the constituencies of Liskeard (1768-75) and for the county (1775-84). He was politically associated with Shelburne and was a commissioner at the B. of Trade from 1760 to 1776. He initially supported Lord North, but resigned against employing Hessians in the American colonies.

ELIOT, George (1819-80), literary pseudonym (1857) of **Mary Ann EVANS** or **CROSS,** interpreter and propagandist of aesthetics and philosophy, began by finishing a translation of Strauss' *Life of Jesus* (1846) and was asst. ed. of the *Westminster Review* from 1851-3. She lived with George Henry Lewes from 1854 until he died. By 1860 she was a literary lioness with a reputation for profundity. Despite all these disadvantages her first batch of novels, *Scenes from Clerical Life* (1858), *Adam Bede* (1859), *The Mill on the Floss* (1860) and *Silas Marner* (1861) were highly successful and remain so. After a visit to Italy she published *Romola* (1862-3) and after another to Spain she wrote *The Spanish Gypsy* (1868), *Middlemarch* (1871-2) and *Daniel Deronda* (1874-6). There were also many essays, articles and poems. She married a banker called Cross just before she died.

ELIOT, Thomas Stearns (1881-1965) born in St. Louis (U.S.A.) settled in England in 1915. An influential critic and founder of the *Criterion* (1922) he was even more influential as a poet. In particular the *Waste Land* (1922) seemed to mirror ordinary people's loss of confidence in the promise of a bright post-war future and coloured the thought of the educated English of the time with pessimism. His *Murder in the Cathedral* (1935) was a successful but not imitated verse drama.

ELIOTT, George Augustus (1717-90) 1st Ld. HEATHFIELD (1787) became A.D.C. to George II in 1755, 2nd-in-C. of the Cuban expedition in 1763 and in 1775 Gov. of Gibraltar. From 1779 to 1783 he conducted a famous and successful defence of Gibraltar against powerful Spanish naval and land forces.

ELIZABETH, Q. of Henry VII (1465-1503) *d.* of Edward IV and Elizabeth Woodville. When Henry Tudor (later Henry VII) was conspiring in 1483 to win the throne, he undertook to marry the Princess Elizabeth, who was the sister of the princes murdered in the Tower, as soon as he obtained the Crown. To avoid any suggestion that his right to the throne might depend upon this marriage into the Yorkist line, he celebrated his own coronation, after his victory at Bosworth Field, in Oct. 1485 and his marriage to Elizabeth three months later in Jan. 1486. He sensibly extracted all the benefit which he could from this alliance and the queen's coronation was magnificently celebrated on 25 Nov. 1486. The so-called Tudor Rose, a combination of the white York and the red Lancaster rose, stems from this wedding. She bore him two sons, Arthur (d. 1502) and the future Henry VIII, and two daughters, Margaret and Mary. See *App: GENEALOGIES*.

ELIZABETH *d.* of James I (1596-1662). The so-called 'Winter Queen' of Bohemia married Frederick V, Elector Palatine, in 1613. He was elected K. of Bohemia in 1619 in the Protestant interest, but was defeated and driven out in 1620. Thereafter she lived a wandering life trying to raise funds or troops first for Frederick and after he died in 1632, for her children. She was a person of unusual charm, and though without dominions or much money, was seldom short of champions. Part of the Palatinate was restored to her son Charles Ludwig at the P. of Westphalia. She was pensioned by her nephew Charles II at the Restoration and died at Leicester House.

ELIZABETH I (1533-1603) Queen (1558) *d.* of Henry VIII and Anne Boleyn. **(1)** She was bastardised by the Act of Succession 1536 to make way for the expected offspring of Jane Seymour, but declared a lawful inheritor of the crown after Mary I by an Act of 1544. Committed to the care of Q. Catherine Parr, subsequently wife of Sir Thos. Seymour, Lord High Admiral and brother of the Protector Somerset, she was brought up a Protestant. The Admiral indulged in familiarities and, in the time of Edward VI, perhaps attempted seduction; this disposed her permanently against marriage. The Admiral, who was piratical and corrupt as well as ambitious, was eventually executed for treason as part of Northumberland's manoeuvres against Somerset in 1548.

(2) At Edward VI's death she avoided any public appearance during Northumberland's attempted *coup d'état* in favour of Lady Jane Grey, but rode out to meet her sister Mary who came to the crown on a wave of popular enthusiasm. She thus early identified herself with a popular movement; and this in the south was mainly Protestant in composition. At the same time she had to survive Mary's fanatical Romanist reaction to the Protestantism of the previous reign, the accompanying Spanish policy and the suspicion of Mary's Romanist advisers. She could not conform to Roman religious observances without losing public respect, nor reject them without mortal danger. Moreover her enemies at court tried to compromise her in Sir Thos. Wyatt's rebellion (1554), and for a while she was imprisoned in the Tower. Her behaviour had, however, been constitutionally impeccable and Wyatt himself repudiated the insinuation. Thereafter she lived in the country, mostly at Woodstock, in the custody of Sir Henry Bedingfield until Mary's death.

(3) The capacity, acquired in youth, for achieving great ends with minimal means was allied to a powerful and learned intellect, a handsome physique, a formidable character, linguistic and oratorical gifts. She once berated a Polish ambassador with 40 minutes of unrehearsed Latin invective. She also had an instinct for the nuances of public feeling. There was a consensus that the violent political and religious oscillations of the previous thirty years had to stop. This could be attained only by creating a balance in which her talent for political leverage could be asserted and this in its turn required the exploitation of the public longing for domestic peace. Her reign may be viewed as the establishment of a central compromise commanding the support or acquiescence of a great majority, its defence against internal and foreign enemies and its development as a base for economic and maritime expansion. It was done without a standing army, police or civil service and with tax resources which seldom sufficed even for modest exertions. The intellectual elegance of the Queen and her principal advisers had to make do.

(4) Her accession (*see* CECIL) put an end to the fears of many nobles and gentry that their titles to the vast former monastic properties might be called into question. A reform of the erratically debased coinage was begun and encouraged the mercantile community. Protestants of all degrees ceased to fear for their lives: by May 1559 the Acts of Supremacy and Uniformity had abolished Mary's oppressive religious laws, re-established Henry VIII's secular supremacy over the church and endowed it with a Prayer Book drafted to reflect the religious spectrum from the moderate Calvinists to the less intense Romanists. The settlement attracted the majority in the south and a minority in the sparsely populated north but, of course, it failed to satisfy the leaders of the contending religious factions. Fortunately they were, for the time being, powerless against the acquiescence of their flocks. Most bishops, for example, refused the oaths under the new Acts and were deposed; only one was willing to crown Elizabeth, but the Govt. carefully made no martyrs and the lesser clergy did not follow their superiors' example.

(5) Philip of Spain, Elizabeth's brother-in-law, moderated the developing conflict with Rome. To the Pope, the Catholic King woud have to be the sword of justice against the heretical queen, but in practice Spain, already suffering from inflation, was at war with Morocco, the Turks and France. His treasury was empty and could not stand an English assault on the communications with the Low Countries, Spain's richest provinces. Hence, while restraining the Pope from issuing the condemnation already prepared in 1559, Philip sought an accommodation with France. England had lost Calais in Jan. 1558 in a war as Spain's ally. Philip would like to have married Elizabeth, changed her religious policy and helped her to get Calais back, but she declined his price and accepted a face saving practical cession (P. of Câteau Cambrésis Apr. 1559). She knew, through Sir Thos. Gresham's Flemish intelligence, of Spanish financial confusion. Philip would be neither a dangerous enemy nor an effective ally.

(6) The official amity with France was short. In July 1559 the French crown passed to the weak Francis II, whose wife was Mary Q. of Scots. The Guise family now dominated the court, while one of them, Mary, was regent of Scotland. Her govt. was unpopular and, especially after the Calvinist John Knox's arrival, the country was in increasing disorder. By Oct. there was civil war, followed by French landings. With the Calvinists on the verge of defeat, the English council resolved to intervene. A naval stroke in the Forth (Feb. 1560) restored the position. By the T. of Edinburgh the French evacuated Scotland. The Scottish Reformers triumphed. Philip, however, was not deflected. He stopped the papal admonitory envoy Parpaglia on his way to England; though Elizabeth refused (1561) to be represented at the Council of Trent, he prevented her excommunication; and when the Council debated her in 1563, he and the Emperor ensured that nothing was done. These respites enabled the Anglican Church to settle down (albeit much despoiled) under Abp. Matthew Parker and it was in 1563 that Convocation issued and the Queen published the XXXIX Articles.

(7) The prolongation of the Edinburgh negotiations arose because Elizabeth wanted to include an indemnity and Calais. This was associated with a dangerous intrigue. She had fallen in love with Lord Robert Dudley, s. of the executed D. of Northumberland. Widely disliked, he cultivated the Spanish ambassador, Alvarez de Quadra, Bp. of Aquila. Outside support was necessary for England to secure Calais and for Lord Robert, who was married, to secure the queen. As early as Nov. 1559 it was rumoured that he meant to make away with his wife Amy Robsart. There was a two-fold danger. Elizabeth would be blamed for Amy's death and Calais plus Spanish support for this disguised 'Spanish marriage' meant the policy reversals which she had refused before Câteau Cambrésis. The English negotiator (Cecil) had, to Elizabeth's annoyance, conceded Calais and the indemnity. Then Amy Robsart was found with her neck broken (Sept. 1560). The sensation injured Elizabeth's international and domestic prestige. She made a great personal effort, perhaps reflected in a passionate sonnet, and gave Lord Robert up. The affair had been dangerous, too, in other fields, for it might have inhibited the development of alliances against Spain. The natural allies were Protestants, who were profoundly shocked.

(8) In fact the situation was changed overnight by the early death of Francis II (Dec. 1560) and the regency of Catherine de' Medici in the name of Charles IX. Mary Q. of Scots was now only queen dowager in France and her Guise relatives temporarily lost control of the govt. In Aug. 1561, however, Mary reached Scotland, and in Feb-Mar. 1562, with real or assumed Spanish collusion, the Guises staged the *coup d'état* which inaugurated the Wars of Religion (*see* HUGUENOTS). To ward off the mortal danger of a Franco-Spanish assault Elizabeth first offered mediation and then courted the Huguenots. She lent Condé, their leader, 140,000 crowns and 3,000 troops for the defence of Rouen and Dieppe: they accepted, in return, an English occupation of Le Havre as a pledge for the return of Calais (Secret T. of Richmond Sept. 1562). She told Philip that she was at war with the Guises not with France (which was true) and disingenuously invited him to help her with Calais! He, of course, was at war with the Huguenots, but his affairs were in decline. The Low Countries were disaffected and his troops could not move. To anticipate further English intervention (Rouen fell to royal troops in Oct.) he abruptly changed course and with equal disingenuousness offered Calais just as the Huguenots were beaten at the B. of Dreux (Dec.

1562). Catherine now appealed to French sentiment against the English. In Mar. 1563 the P. or Edict of Amboise halted the civil war while they were driven out. Le Havre fell in July. The T. of Troyes (Apr. 1564) ended the episode, and settled the Calais question, but the resumed Wars of Religion thereafter paralysed France as a power.

(9) The neutralisation of neighbouring countries by intervening in their internal politics, begun in Scotland against France and extended to France against Spain, was extended to the Spanish Low Countries; France, Spain and the Pope intermittently tried subversion in England and they nearly succeeded in Ireland, where Jesuit missions were heartening the treacherous Shane O'Neill, Captain of Tyrone since 1562. In Scotland the problem was to prevent Mary from making any dangerous marriage. In the Netherlands, urged on by English propaganda, the Calvinists, who had a working organisation by mid-1564, were taking on a nationalist colouring. In 1565 Mary married her cousin Lord Darnley and Philip's new catholicising policy was steadily uniting Dutch nationalists and Protestants. By now English traders were breaking the Spanish American monopoly: John Hawkins had made his first voyage in 1562-3 and his second, in which Elizabeth was a shareholder, in 1565. Anglo-Spanish undeclared friendship was giving way to undeclared dislike. In fact, the English meant to embarrass the Spaniard and since his reaction was likely to be dangerous, the more embarrassed he was, the better. More especially, O'Neill by 1566 had ousted all his Ulster rivals by murder and conquest, and was in touch with the Pope. He appealed for French help and attacked the Pale – Sir Henry Sydney, the Lord Deputy, advised major operations and carried them out brilliantly. By Nov. he had burned O'Neill's base at Benburb.

(10) 1567 was the decisive year. Mary Q. of Scots abdicated. Shane O'Neill's hereditary enemies, the O'Donnells, defeated him on Lough Swilly and in June the Scots of Clandeboy murdered him. The French Second War of Religion began. Philip sent Alva to Brussels to suppress civil disorder and provoked the armed rising in which until then, he had not believed. Elizabeth, whose throne was founded upon a Protestant southern public, could not now draw back without discredit among domestic or foreign Protestants nor gain from Catholics. It was thus inevitable that when Mary fled to England in 1568, she might be hindered from returning. Hawkins' efforts to break the Spanish monopoly of American trade had put the two countries at war on the other side of the ocean but his third expedition came to grief at San Juan de Ulloa in 1586, by which time Alva was making headway and encouraging English Romanist refugees. Some Spanish enterprise against England was obviously being planned. In anticipation, Elizabeth allowed Dutch refugees to send aid to Holland and Dutch corsairs under the Orange flag to load stores and sell captures in England. In Dec. (when Hawkins' disaster was known) these corsairs drove a Spanish treasure squadron into Plymouth and Southampton. Taking advantage of a convenient legality, she borrowed its 800,000 ducats herself. There was indiscipline among the consequently unpaid Spanish garrisons.

(11) The fanatical Don Guerau de Spes, Spanish ambassador since July, had made contact with the partisans of the secluded Mary Q. of Scots. At his urging Alva embargoed English property in the Low Countries (Dec. 1568) and the English retaliated (Jan. 1569). In the resulting trade stoppage Mary egged Don Guerau on. Her chances seemed to have brightened, for the Presbyterian Scottish regent Morton had just been overthrown. Don Guerau urged Philip to stop exports to England, to close Spanish ports and harry English shipping. He had been approached by a Florentine, Roberto Ridolfi, on behalf of

certain Romanist nobles, particularly Norfolk and Arundel (*see* NORTHERN REBELLION, RIDOLFI). There first ensued an abortive plot against Cecil; then another to marry Norfolk to the Q. of Scots and secure her rights of succession and finally, in 1569-70, the Northern Rebellion. Don Guerau thought that the trade stoppage would dispose the merchants and the City towards the plotters, especially as Huguenot corsairs had halted French trade as well. In this he was wrong; the trade simply switched to other ports in other bottoms.

(12) In May 1570 the papal bull of deposition (*Regnans in Excelsis*) was at last published in England: feeling over-isolated, Elizabeth called off the war (Sept.) and tried to negotiate for Mary's return to Scotland on conditions acceptable to herself; but Morton and the Scots would have her only as a private person and, since Elizabeth depended upon Morton's party for her influence in Scotland, she could not coerce them.

(13) As long as England and France were united against the danger from Spain, Mary's only hope of a crown lay in Elizabeth's elimination. In Feb. 1571, as Buckhurst and Walsingham negotiated in Paris for a marriage between Elizabeth and the D. of Anjou, Mary became involved in Ridolfi's assassination plot (q.v.). In Sept. Cecil had Norfolk arrested and parliament passed further anti Papal legislation. Condemned in Jan. 1572, the Duke was executed in July. The disclosures ruined Mary's reputation. The marriage negotiations were shipwrecked on religion but the politics led to the T. of Blois (Apr. 1572). France and England would support each other if attacked; there would be an English staple in France and they would jointly try to pacify Scotland. In practice this meant that the French, with some relief, abandoned the discredited Mary. The simultaneous outbreak of the Dutch revolution made the other clauses otiose.

(14) The Dutch rebellion was the unintended consequence of an act of Elizabeth's. The Prince of Orange's fleet (*The Sea Beggars* or *Gueux de Mer*) had been expelled from Dover because of its piratical habits (Mar. 1572). In Apr. it was welcomed by the Dutch port of Brill and by May the major Dutch cities had followed Brill's lead. Spaniards were expelled: the Prince was proclaimed Stadholder in four provinces, Protestant volunteers flocked in and thereupon a Franco-Huguenot army invaded Belgium. The Queen promptly sent troops to the Isle of Walcheren at the mouth of the Scheldt to deny it to the French (July) but Alva defeated the French and drove them out. These events (*see* HUGUENOTS 6-7) led to the Massacre of St. Bartholomew (24 Aug.) the seizure of power by the R. Catholics in Paris and renewed civil war. Mary's Scottish party now took Edinburgh Castle and expected French help. Huguenots were besieged in La Rochelle. Elizabeth had to support the Huguenots until her artillery battered the castle into submission (May 1573). By July the siege of La Rochelle had been called off.

(15) As Mary could now hope for support only from Spain, and the trade cessation was damaging the economy of London, Elizabeth sought accommodation with Alva. He was responsive: any reduction of tension would help him to cope with his rebels. In Apr. 1573 trade was reopened for two years pending negotiations. Under the T. of Bristol (Aug. 1574) a balance of losses was struck between rival confiscations. This turned out to be £21,000 in favour of Spain. Next, by agreement with Don Luis Requesens, Alva's successor, each side in Mar. 1575 expelled the other's rebels. William of Orange and his friends were forbidden English ports. Anglo-Spanish relations became so friendly that Spanish fleets put into Portsmouth and Dartmouth (Oct. 1575).

(16) This international equilibrium brought great commercial benefits. The next ten years were a golden age, but religious and political factors were liable to throw the mechanism out of gear. The Papacy of

Regnans in Excelsis represented, with its English Colleges, a threat to security, latent in England, patent in Ireland. Despite Mary and some Jesuit inspired increase in recusancy, the English R. Catholics were mostly quiescent, but common prudence after the northern rebellion dictated some repression and the govt. was under critical pressure from its supporters. Elizabeth refused "to make windows into men's souls" but she had already proceeded legislatively against papal secular pretensions. It was treason now to deny her title, to aver that she was heretic or schismatic, or to bring in, or act upon, certain papal instruments. *Praemunire* threatened importers of specifically Roman ceremonial objects and confiscation of property of those who had fled since 1553 and not returned by 1573. From the opposite direction Elizabeth ran into controversy with puritans, especially Calvinists. The latter's revolutionary notions of govt. were highly objectionable for they were seeking to replace the lawful church with a different body superior to the state. Rome and Geneva were too much alike, yet the Presbyterian Scots, Huguenots, and Dutch were essential to the queen's foreign policy.

(17) Unfortunately the defence of the middle ground in England was made to look like persecution in Ireland, where civilisation had to replace tribal barbarism to establish an ordered society at all. The people had been religiously apathetic, but resisted English efforts to alter their customs on land holding and succession, their distinctive hair styles and dress and, by shiring, to stop the endemic disorder. This combined with the unfortunate history of English invasion to create a seed-bed for newly planted Roman religious sedition. By 1566 (the time of O'Neill's revolt) Jesuits were beginning to offer the disunited septs and Anglo-Irish a unified purpose. Sidney's victory then had enabled him to proceed against the E. of Desmond in the south and though O'Neill's and Desmond's successors were as barbarous and recalcitrant as they, the way was more open to an extension of a civilising policy. In 1569 the Irish parliament had legislated against coign and livery. the foundations of chiefly power. Presidencies were established for Connaught under Sir Edw. Fitton (1569) and for Munster under Sir John Perrot (1571). They began to supersede the palatinates and enforce legislation. More important, they built roads, bridges and castles and established English colonies at strategic points. By a policy of enforced surrender and regrant they progressively substituted English land law for Celtic custom. The Romanist missions exploited the opposition to these secular policies.

(18) In the Low Countries the boot was on the other foot. Elizabeth wanted the Scheldt kept open because it was the best European avenue for English trade. Orange wanted to close it to starve the Spaniards out of Antwerp. She could hardly countenance a Protestant disaster, yet her attitude was driving Orange towards a French alliance – which might put the Scheldt under French control. Her proposed solution was a return to Spanish sovereignty subject to guarantees for the local liberties. This was unacceptable because Orange would not, with reason, trust Philip II and Philip insisted on unconditional submission before negotiation. She threatened to support Philip if Orange stayed Francophile, but the threat did not have to be put to the test. In 1575 Requesens moved against Ziericksee, the hinge of Holland and Zeeland. In Sept. the Spanish treasury suspended payment, but Requesens took the town and the Is. of Schouwen and Duiveland in Oct. In Mar. 1576 Requesens died and his troops started pillaging for lack of pay. At the same time Elizabeth repelled a special Dutch mission and the Zeelanders now began to seize English shipping. Spanish indiscipline culminated in the sack of Antwerp (*The Spanish Fury*) in Sept. Led by their provincial estates, the populations rose in self defence.

(19) Orange now saw his opportunity to unite the seventeen provinces. A States-General, which he summoned concluded the Pacification of Ghent (8 Nov. 1576), confirmed his Stadholderships in Holland and Zeeland and demanded a Spanish military evacuation. The new governor, Don John of Austria, was in difficulties. His secret instructions were directed towards an eventual attack on England, his public purpose towards a local settlement. The latter was impossible without an evacuation, the former with it. Elizabeth and the Dutch saw through the victor of Lepanto's offer to evacuate by sea, and the *Paix des Prêtres* (The Priests' Peace) or Perpetual Edict of Marche-en-Famine (Feb. 1577) reflected his helplessness. Forced to evacuate within three weeks and to acknowledge the ancient liberties of the Provinces, Don John was permitted to enter Brussels disarmed (May 1577). Orange, no party to the Paix des Prêtres, refused to trust Don John who, in July, justified his mistrust by seizing Namur. The war began again and in Jan. 1578 he and Parma defeated the rebels at GEMBLOUX and overran most of the southern provinces.

(20) This battle, the beginning of the modern Belgium, was overshadowed by the death in Morocco of K. Sebastian of Portugal (Aug. 1578) and the likelihood (*see* AVIS 8-9) that the rich Portuguese imperium and fleet would soon fall to Spain. Elizabeth alone could not prevent this, especially after Esmé Stuart's arrival in Scotland in Dec. 1579; and France, torn by civil wars, was a broken reed. In Jan. 1580 the Portuguese Cardinal-King died, and by Aug. the Spaniards had mastered the country. Only in the Azores was a rival claimant, the bastard Don Antonio proclaimed. This overthrow of the world balance of power made new policies urgent, especially as Spain would get control of the large Portuguese fleet. A French pacification and understanding became imperative even at the cost of a French presence in Flanders. In Sept. 1580 the Spaniards landed at Smerwick in Munster just as the D. of Anjou accepted the sovereignty of the United Provinces (T. of Plessis-les-Tours). Elizabeth tried and failed to mediate a peace within France, and Esmé Stuart overthrew the Anglophile Regent Morton (Dec. 1580). Then she turned again to marriage negotiations with Anjou. These began in London in Apr. 1581. The French wanted English support in a war with Spain which Elizabeth would not concede. In July the negotiations moved to Paris. Ideally she wanted an alliance without marriage or involvement in a present war so long as Anjou prosecuted his claim in the Low Countries. The French Court's attitude was "no marriage, no league", but Anjou wanted independently to enforce his sovereignty. In Sept. he invaded and took Cambrai, whereupon Elizabeth sent him £10,000. The French Court would not officially support or disown him. They sent him £4,000. Anjou put his troops into winter quarters and came to England to pursue his suit with the queen. She led him on to such purpose that he was persuaded (with another £10,000) to leave for Antwerp only in Feb. 1582. Incompetent and idle, his towns then fell progressively to Parma. The French Court had to act. A naval diversion was launched to support Don Antonio in the Azores. Twofold fortune smiled on Spain: Santa Cruz destroyed the French at Terceira, while Parma took Oudenarde and beat the Dutch at Ghent (July). The French Govt. at last sent troops where they were needed, but failed to stem the tide. Without money or proper authority Anjou now botched a *coup d'état* (*The French Fury*) against the obstructive Flemish Estates (Jan. 1583) and then left the country discredited. He died in 1584.

(21) The indirect war with Spain was accompanied by Scots complications. Esmé Stuart planned with the Jesuits to convert K. James VI to Rome and then, aided by Spain and the Guises, to provoke an English rebellion supported by military intervention. Guise and Spain were otherwise engaged and then the Gowrie conspiracy put the Anglophiles back in power (Aug. 1582). Esmé Stuart fled. The Jesuits and Guises now planned a direct invasion by Spanish troops from Flanders, which Philip refused again, but in July 1583 the pro-English party in Scotland was ousted once more. These almost farcical Jesuit plots were important because they had involved Don Bernardino de Mendoza, the Spanish ambassador in London. The Govt. had stumbled upon his secret communications with Mary Q. of Scots through Francis Throckmorton. As a result of Throckmorton's confessions, Mendoza was expelled (Jan. 1584). Anglo-Spanish hostility was now patent. It could not be otherwise; Parma continued to advance. In June Orange was assassinated: by Oct. Antwerp was isolated: in Jan. 1585 the Guise faction in France signed the secret T. of Joinville with Philip II and in Mar. launched the Holy League with Spanish money.

(22) Elizabeth had now to intervene directly in the Low Countries, for France was paralysed and the Dutch on the brink of defeat. Negotiations with them had begun in Nov. 1584. In May Philip seized English and Dutch shipping in his ports. By Aug. when agreement was reached at Nonsuch, Antwerp had fallen: but the Queen was to be protector of the States and provide an army in return for the cession of Cautionary Towns as security for her expenses. The campaign in which Leicester commanded and Sir Philip Sydney was killed was a discreditable and corrupt fiasco. Not so the naval reprisals. Sir Francis Drake raided Vigo, the Canaries and the Cape Verdes, crossed the Atlantic, attacked Hispaniola and Cartagena and returned via Roanoke with a vast booty at midsummer 1586. Another Scottish overturn had brought the Anglophiles to power and under the T. of Berwick (July) K. James became Elizabeth's pensioner. She could afford it. Leicester came home in Nov. defeated but none the worse, but Drake's triumph was electrifying. The monster could be attacked after all. Spanish credit fell: but more important, Philip's world wide sea communications could be protected only by destroying their attackers' bases. He became determined to launch the long contemplated "Enterprise of England".

(23) Philip had approached the Papacy for the finance in June 1585, but the sceptical Sixtus V promised the necessary crowns only in instalments beginning when the Spaniards landed in England (Dec. 1586). The expedition had to be financed on credit, but Spanish credit had just fallen. Next (Feb. 1587) Philip demanded a Papal brief declaring his right to inherit the English throne, in preference to the heretic James VI, failing Mary Q. of Scots (whose death at English hands he confidently expected). He intended to pass the throne to his daughter, the Infanta Isabella, but all French opinion feared Spanish supremacy in England, and the Guises, currently dominant at Paris, disliked the proposed treatment of their Scottish relative. The French attitude persuaded Sixtus to defer this decision until after the conquest. Meanwhile preparations at Cadiz moved slowly. The first Armada was to have sailed in the Summer of 1587, but in Apr. Drake raided the port, then from Sagres dislocated Spanish seaborne traffic and finally took an important treasure ship. The Armada had to be put off until 1588 and by Sept. its defeat had changed the political situation. The damage to Spanish prestige was immense, the encouragement to the Protestant and especially the Bourbon cause correspondingly great and the Papacy began to lose interest in reconversion by arms.

(24) Disaster challenged Philip II to redouble his efforts and rethink his war policy to some purpose. A drain on English resources was compounded by bad harvests and epidemics. Seaborne trade suffered not only from war but from rising competition from the successfully rebel Dutch. The first Armada had thus appeared as the climax of an Elizabethan golden age; many of whose leaders, Leicester (1588), Walsingham and Warwick (1590), Hatton and Shrewsbury (1591), Hunsdon (1596) and Burghley (1598) began to die off. Moreover the period of anti-climax was politically and militarily strenuous and engendered a crisis in crown finance. Rising taxation excited the political consciousness of the Commons, while large sales of crown property and foreign loans at 10% to meet urgent debts, reduced the crown's inherent power to withstand their criticism. Elizabeth could do it by force of her personality and lifelong love affair with the English, but the dangerous years from 1589 to 1603 gave birth to the financial troubles which destroyed Charles I.

(25) In Apr. 1589 a joint stock expedition under Drake and Norreys almost as big as the Armada, sacked Corunna, made an expensive and luckless attempt on Lisbon in support of Don Antonio and sacked Vigo on the way home. Elizabeth was not pleased. Meanwhile, in July, Henry III of France was assassinated. He was succeeded by the Protestant Henry IV (of Bourbon and Navarre) and shortly afterwards a further private expedition under Frobisher and Cumberland began to interrupt the Spanish Transatlantic trade. Temporarily crippled at sea, Philip counter-attacked by land; a Spanish supported insurrection by the Catholic League put Henry in desperate straits. Elizabeth had to help him with money, materials and men. The League openly appealed to Philip who offered troops, provided that all League-controlled ports were opened exclusively to his ships. This put naval bases in Brittany and Normandy within his reach, but Henry's victory at Ivry (Mar. 1590) and the investment of R. Catholic Paris dislocated his plans. Parma marched from Belgium successfully to the city's relief in Aug. and in Oct. a Spanish force in Brittany under d'Aguila threatened Brest. Strong intervention had become urgent; Norreys took an army to Paimpol while Sir Roger Williams occupied Dieppe (May 1591). The rising E. of Essex joined him in Aug. when Hawkins and Frobisher led an expedition against the *Flota*; but Philip had rebuilt his fleet and had set up a convoy system. An accidental contact between the escort squadron under Alonzo de Bazan and Hawkins at Flores brought about Sir Richard Grenville's famous defence of the *Revenge,* but the convoy system was a success, though the English continued to take single prizes, like the Portuguese *Madre de Dios* (1592) which yielded Elizabeth a 2000% return on her investment in Sir John Burrows. The combined Anglo-Royalist force failed to take Rouen (Oct.) and in Jan. 1592 Elizabeth recalled Essex. In Apr. Parma made another forced march from Belgium and broke up the siege; in May d'Aguila beat Norreys at Craon (Brittany) and then plague reduced the scale of operations throughout the summer. It did not, however, prevent Pope Clement VIII from sending James O'Hely, Bp. of Tuam, to the Ulster O'Donnells, who began to organise an anti-English movement among the clans.

(26) The Anglo-Huguenot combination in France could not quite match that of Spain and the Holy League. So in July 1593 Henry IV made his famous political conversion to Rome in order to detach the supporters, especially Paris, from the leaders of the League. It took some time to have this effect but meanwhile the O'Donnells' conspiracy was sufficiently advanced for him to appeal to Philip II direct and at the turn of 1593-4 d'Aguila tried to take control of Brest by building a fort at Crozon, and Spanish ships reconnoitred the Irish coast. Elizabeth saw her danger, the Irish their opportunity but Elizabeth got in first. Norreys and Frobisher stormed Crozon in Nov. 1594 when Frobisher lost his life.

(27) Elizabeth was, however, faced with a front in Ireland. The E. of Tyrone, at hereditary feud with O'Donnell, had held aloof from his movement, but now

that Philip meant business, he joined it, took the forbidden quasi-royal title of The O'Neill and assumed the leadership. Educated to a world outlook in England, he saw that the English could not be expelled without Spanish help. While he skilfully consolidated his power and nursed disaffection towards open revolt, Drake and Hawkins led another force against the *Flota*. The Spanish convoy system made it necessary to intercept at the American end, but they unsuccessfully attacked the Canaries first and when they reached the Caribbean their intentions were known. Hawkins died before Puerto Rico. Drake burnt some towns without realising much loot, was repulsed between Nombre de Dios and Panama, and died at Porto Bello. Sir Thos. Baskerville brought the survivors back in Apr. 1596.

(28) While this unfortunate squadron was still overseas, Essex, Howard and Vere had mounted a strong force to invade Spain. Vere, the English commander in Holland, withdrew some of his troops for it, whereupon Parma's successor, the Card. Archduke Albert, took advantage of their absence to descend upon Calais (Mar. 1596). Essex's expedition was held back while Elizabeth negotiated with Henry IV for the cession of Calais, should Essex relieve it, but Albert moved too quickly and Calais surrendered before he was allowed to intervene.

(29) There was now a Spanish naval base opposite Dover and Spanish troops in Brittany. Spanish money and armaments were reaching Tyrone. The latter, virtually an independent prince, was negotiating with the Lord Deputy at Dundalk, while demanding Spanish troops and proposing a visit from the Cardinal Archduke. A blow at Spanish naval power might dispose of Cadiz and Tyrone in one. In June Elizabeth unleashed Essex, Howard and Vere. They surprised and stormed Cadiz. The Spaniards hurriedly burned the *Flota* in the harbour. After sacking the city, Faro and Loulé, the English returned in triumph (Aug. 1596). The daring victory was incomplete. Spanish envoys reassured Tyrone and agreed landings with him. Another Armada, with a papal squadron, was assembling in Lisbon. Almost as big as its famous predecessor, this second Armada was dispersed and partly wrecked in storms (Oct. 1596). Nothing daunted, Philip set about organising a third, for in Tyrone he recognised his best ally and Spanish resources, though not inexhaustible, were increasing.

(30) The Queen's court, however, was witnessing the first acts in the political drama which arose out of Burghley's old age and the young Essex's ambitions. As far back as 1592 Essex, through Anthony Bacon, had organised a private foreign, especially Spanish, intelligence system to rival Burghley in supplying information to the Queen. He became a privy councillor in 1593. Burghley meant to pass his own influence to his hunchback son, Sir Robert Cecil; Essex meant to supplant him. In 1594 they quarrelled in council over the vacant attorney-generalship. Burghley favoured Coke, Essex, Sir Francis Bacon. Burghley won, as he did over the solicitorship in 1595. The court and the Inns of Court were now deeply divided. Burghley's tactics were to play against Essex's weak suits, his pride, irritability, militarism and demagoguery, all obnoxious to Elizabeth. While Essex was at Cadiz, Burghley jockeyed his son into the joint Secretaryship (with himself) and he even turned Essex's victory to his own advantage, for Essex's coadjutors were rewarded – Vere with the governorship of Brill, Howard, to Essex's fury, with the Earldom of Nottingham. Then, as a disingenuous sop, he was offered and could hardly refuse the E. Marshalcy, the one office, because military, which the Bacons had advised him against. The court factions now crystallised. The Knollys supported Essex and the Bacons, while Burghley led Raleigh and Cobham, lately appointed Warden of the Cinque Ports. Sir Robert Cecil already had a hold of his father's reins. A man of peace, he suited the Queen better

than his tempestuous rival who, apparently, took no account of her character at all.

(31) In 1597 Essex with his enemies Vere, Nottingham and Raleigh, were despatched against Philip's third Armada (in Ferrol) and the *Flota*. The absence of so many partisans from the council table gave Sir Robert a chance to strengthen his own position at home, but storms prevented any useful operations. Then the third Armada put to sea and, Essex having pressed on to the Azores, some of it caused a panic in England, but foul winds had already driven most of it back to Spain by Oct. This latest fiasco caused Philip to reduce his commitments and Tyrone to seek an accommodation. Henry IV's conversion at least made a Franco-Spanish peace respectable to Catholics and he needed peace. In May 1598 the T. of Vervins took Henry out of the war and Philip out of French internal politics. There followed a bitter dispute in the English council between the peaceable Burghley and the warlike Essex, who favoured an Irish campaign. Essex carried the day. Burghley (Aug.) and Philip II died shortly afterwards, but Essex's forebodings seemed justified. Tyrone suddenly took the strategic Blackwater frontier fort and destroyed Sir Henry Bagenal's relieving army at the Yellow Ford, while the Connaught O'Rourkes defeated Sir Conyers Clifford. These sensational disasters sparked off universal revolt. Irreconcilables everywhere superseded friendly chiefs. Celtic customs were revived; in Munster a new E. of Desmond drove out the English colonists. Defeat and massacre demoralised the English. The Pale itself was no longer safe or loyal and, at the height of the crisis, the military commander, Sir Richard Bingham, died in Dublin.

(32) There followed another wrangle. The Queen wanted to send Ld. Mountjoy, but many councillors, including Essex, favoured Essex. Some wanted him out of the way. He was appointed in Jan. and reached Dublin in Apr. 1599. The demoralised army lacked supplies and the essential draught horses, obtainable only from overseas. He and his council postponed an Ulster campaign until the summer and meantime in May he started to clear Leinster and Munster. This sensible decision was made to train his army, to secure the south against a fourth Armada and to anticipate any southward move by Tyrone to meet it. The campaign was a success and, as before, storms dispersed the Spanish fleet. This was a decisive conjuncture. No comparable native Irish opportunity was to appear until the 20th cent.

(33) Back in Dublin (July) Essex was now expected to deal with Tyrone, but the essential supplies and transport were still lacking and the council did not supply them. It was whispered that he had been prodigal of resources and knighthoods and unwilling to grapple with the decisive problem. Abrasive royal letters forbade him to leave Ireland until a northern campaign had been tried. Two forces were accordingly prepared; at Dublin under Essex and under Clifford to the west in the Curlews. Clifford was attacked en masse and destroyed. Essex and his council now represented that without supplies and reinforcements no campaign could succeed. The heedless or misinformed Queen would not listen, so in Sept. Essex made a frontier demonstration in force, which was as much as he could manage, but understandably felt that his career and honour were in jeopardy through court slanders which only his presence in London could dispel. He could not go without ending or interrupting the war; victory was beyond his reach, a truce with Tyrone the only seeming alternative. Thus for his own private purposes he met Tyrone at the Ford of Bellaclinthe on 8 Sept. 1599 and agreed a truce from six weeks to six weeks terminable on 14 days' notice. Worse still, part of the discussion took place without witnesses in midstream. Then he rode like a madman for London and burst into the Queen's apartment at Nonsuch on 28th.

(34) She was displeased. The council examined him and committed him to Sir Thos. Egerton's custody at York House. Ireland being without its general, Tyrone denounced the truce. The Queen was furious. In Oct. she called in his sweet wine monopoly, his main source of income. In June 1600 a special court deprived him of his offices. Released in Aug. he was still forbidden the court. He brooded and put it about that his enemies were plotting to put the Infanta Clara Eugenia on the throne instead of James VI. He counter plotted and made contact with James. His counter plot was betrayed and in Feb. 1601 he tried to raise the London mob against Cecil. He failed, was arrested, tried for treason and executed. *See* DEVEREUX-3.

(35) To avoid intrigues and keep the R. Catholics calm, the ageing Elizabeth refused to name an heir. The development of the Reformation and the war had divided the outlook of even devout Catholics who were increasingly ready to render to Elizabeth the things that are Caesar's while reserving a purely spiritual allegiance to the Pope. English patriotism and seamanship made nonsense of the Infanta's Lancastrian claims and English R. Catholic quasi-royalties such as the E. of Derby's daughter had no following. The only possible successor was the heretic James VI. He wanted to make certain by securing the Queen's nomination, or failing this, the support of the R. Catholic powers and since he followed both courses, English statesman had at least to speak with them as well as him. Both Cecils stirred up trouble in Scotland if only to prevent James from exerting too much leverage if the Spanish war went badly, and consistently with this, Sir Robert corresponded indirectly with Brussels about the Infanta. In this he was risking his head but not his country, for a serious Spanish claim would have brought France back into the anti-Spanish coalition and for that very reason the Pope opposed it.

(36) Essex's death cleared the way for the peacemakers, of whom James VI and Cecil were the leaders: it also simplified the politics of succession by destroying one faction in the debate. International amity would reduce England's need for confusion in Scotland. Between Essex's execution and May 1601 James and Cecil were reconciled. There were other reasons why this should happen. James had mistrusted Essex as an overweening magnate and for his patronage of Puritanism, a growing force whose Scottish equivalent, Presbyterianism, James detested. Cecil, like the Queen, was committed to the Anglican compromise: so, politically speaking, was James. Thus by 1602 it was certain that he would succeed: the only question was whether he would do it with some, probably Puritan, disorder or none.

(37) The able and dependable Mountjoy succeeded Essex in Ireland (1601). He had the confidence and material support of the Queen and the Council and he followed Essex's strategy of clearing the south before tackling the north; a fifth Spanish Armada was fitting out, while James and Cecil were moving together. It sailed in Aug. and at last Spanish troops under Aguila, landed at Kinsale in the south. It was too late. The south was cowed. In Oct. Mountjoy penned Aguila against the coast while Sir Richard Leveson's fleet drove away and later destroyed his supply fleet. By Dec. Aguila was desperate, but Tyrone and O'Donnell had collected forces and broken out of Ulster. They reached Kinsale, but a joint attack on the English lines was a disaster. O'Donnell fled to Spain; Aguila capitulated (Jan. 1602), Tyrone struggled back to Ulster; mercilessly harried by Mountjoy and Docwra, he surrendered in Mar. 1603. On the 24th of the same month the Queen died.

ELIZABETH II (1926-) (1952-Q.D.S.) married Philip Mountbatten, D. of Edinburgh, *s.* of Prince Andrew of Greece in 1947. She was in Kenya when her father died. Her reign was distinguished by conscientious performance of her duties, including many visits abroad and the use of the media. In 1992 various rival groups of overseas-owned British newspapers attempted to outdo each other in the course of a circulation war by indirect attacks on the monarchy through her children and by ill-informed demands that she should pay taxes.

ELIZABETHAN. *See* ARCHITECTURE BRITISH.

ELIZABETH WOODVILLE or WYDVILL (?-1492), Q. of Edward IV. Hostile propaganda has represented her as a parvenue but she was the eldest *d.* of Lord Rivers and the dowager Duchess of Bedford and widow of Lord Ferrers of Groby. She was intelligent and attractive and the King married her for love, but secretly, on 30 Apr. 1464. Naturally her family was enriched by new positions at court (her father became Treasurer) and by advantageous marriages, but these arrangements were part of Edward's plan to free himself from the power of the E. of Warwick (The Kingmaker) whose position was endangered and diplomacy also stultified. This was a factor in bringing about his rebellion of 1470. After Edward's restoration in 1471, he relied less on her family and at his death during the conflict between the Woodvilles and Richard III, she took sanctuary at Westminster. She later emerged, Richard III having invited her out to calm public suspicions about the princes in the Tower. She remained hostile to him and risked sanctioning the proposed marriage between the Lancastrian-supported claimant, Henry Tudor, and her eldest daughter Elizabeth. During his reign as Henry VII, when her daughter had become Queen, she was implicated in the Yorkist rebellion of 1487, deprived of her lands and put into the convent of Bermondsey, where she died.

ELLENBOROUGH, Lords. *See* LAW-4,5.

ELLERMAN, Sir John Reeves (1862-1933) Bt (1905) Ch (1921) had family connections in Hull and Hamburg, where he was born. He spent all his life in commercial shipping beginning with the Leyland Co. which he steadily developed into the Ellerman Lines by a series of take-over bids incorporating nine major and some lesser companies. He died one of the richest men in the world.

ELLESMERE, Earls. *See* EGERTON.

ELLICE. (1) Edward the elder (1781-1863) from 1803 a Canadian fur trader, amalgamated the Hudson's Bay, X Y Z and North-West Companies in 1821. M.P. in 1818 and 1820 and continuously from 1830 to 1863 he was a whip in Lord Grey's govt. of 1830 to 1832, and a founder of the Reform Club in 1836. His son **(2) Edward the younger (1810-80)** entered Parliament for Huddersfield in 1836 and was a strong advocate of free trade and Irish disestablishment.

ELLIOT (1) Sir Gilbert (1651-1718) Ld. MINTO (1705) helped in Argyll's rising in 1685, was forfeited but pardoned and in 1692 became Clerk of the Scots PC. He was an M.P. for Roxburgh in 1703 and became a Lord of Session in 1705, but opposed the Union. His son **(2) Sir Gilbert (1693-1766) Ld. MINTO (1733)** was also M.P. for Roxburgh from 1722 to 1726 and a Lord of Justiciary from 1733. An object of highlander animosity, he was hunted by the Young Pretender's men but narrowly escaped by the contrivance of his *d.* **(3) Jean** (1727-1805) the poet who wrote the celebrated *Flowers of the Forest* (1756) a lament for the fallen at Flodden, and which was movingly set as a pibroch. Her brother **(4) Sir Gilbert (1722-77)** was an M.P. in 1754 and from 1762-1777. He was a Lord of the Admiralty in 1756 and Treasurer of the Navy in 1770. Originally a supporter of Pitt, he went over to Bute and favoured the repressive policy against the Americans. His brother **(5) John (?-1808)** was Gov. of Newfoundland from 1786 to 1789. The son of **(4)**, **(6) Sir Gilbert (1751-1814) 1st Ld. MINTO (1798), 1st E. (1813)** was an M.P. from 1776 to 1784 and from 1786 to 1790. In 1787 he carried a motion against Sir Elijah Impey's activities at Madras. From 1794 to 1796 he was British Viceroy of Corsica and expelled Paoli from the island. From 1799 he was Minister at Vienna. He became Pres. of the Board of Control in 1806 and this led in 1807 to his becoming (until 1813) Gov.-Gen of India. As part of an aggressive defence against French penetration, he sent missions under Malcolm to Persia, Metcalfe to the Sikhs and Elphinstone with a subsidy to Shah Shuja in Afghanistan. The policy was not wholly successful in Afghanistan, but on the other hand he annexed the greater part of the Dutch E. Indies, and expeditions in 1810 and 1811 captured the French Is. of Bourbon and Mauritius. He also planned a system of Moslem colleges. His son **(7) Gilbert (1782-1859) 2nd E.** was a Whig M.P. from 1806 to 1814, Ambassador to Berlin from 1832 to 1834, 1st Lord of the Admiralty from 1835 to 1841 and Lord Privy Seal in 1846. He persuaded the Neapolitan govt. to create a separate, but largely ineffectual Sicilian Parliament. His grandson **(8) Gilbert John (1845-1914), 4th E. (1891)** after serving in Bulgaria, Afghanistan and Africa as a soldier, became Mil. Sec. to Lord Lansdowne the Gov-Gen. of Canada from 1883 to 1885. He was himself Gov-Gen from 1898 to 1904 and had to deal with sensitive problems, particularly the Alaskan frontier dispute with U.S.A., imperial preference and the use of Canadians in the Boer War. His success was due partly to contemporary Canadian prosperity, but also to his likeability and capacity for remaining on good terms not only with the Canadian politicians but with the Colonial Office and Joseph Chamberlain. These feats led naturally to his appointment by a Conservative Govt. as Viceroy of India (1905-10) but he worked well with John Morley, the now Liberal Sec. of State. (*See* MORLEY-MINTO REFORMS.) His practical spirit was useful in calming the excitement of Lord Curzon's flamboyant viceroyalty and in tidying up the administrative difficulties which that great man had created in the partition of Bengal. Meanwhile the nationalist movements expanded and became more heated but, though he established excellent relations with the Princes, they did not bemuse him and he dropped his own scheme for councils of notables when he realised the difficulties. He also dealt firmly and successfully with confusion in the Punjab.

ELLIS (1) Charles Rose (1771-1845) 1st Ld. SEAFORD (1826) leader of the influential W. India interest in Parliament in 1793, from 1796 to 1806 and from 1812 to 1826. He was also a friend of Canning. His *s.* **(2) Charles Augustus (1799-1868) 2nd L. and 6th Ld. HOWARD DE WALDEN** was Canning's Foreign U. Sec. of State in 1824 and held diplomatic posts, notably the legation in Lisbon from 1833 to 1841, when he strongly influenced Portuguese internal as well as external politics.

ELLIS, Thomas Edward (1859-99) became Liberal M.P. for Merioneth in 1886. He was a cultural and political Welsh nationalist, being one of the originators of the Welsh National Library and editor of the works of Morgan Llwyd. In 1989 he secured the Welsh Education Act and declared for a Welsh Assembly in 1890. This met with little support in Wales or elsewhere and in 1892 Gladstone made him Dep. Chief Whip. He became Chief Whip in 1894.

ELLIS (1) Welbore (?1651-1734) was Bp. of Kildare from 1705 to 1731 and Bp. of Meath and an Irish P.C. from 1731. His *s.* **(2) Welbore (1713-1802) 1st Ld. MENDIP (1794)** as a Foxite Whip was an M.P. almost continuously from 1741 until 1794. He was a Lord of the Admiralty from 1747 to 1755, Sec. at War from 1762 to 1765 and S. of State for America in 1782. From 1793 he supported Pitt because of the progress of the French Revolution. A cousin **(3) George James Welbore Agar (1797-1833) 1st Ld. DOVER (1831)** was an M.P. from 1818. He suggested the foundation of the National Gallery by the purchase of the Angerstein Collection in 1823 and became a P.C. and Commissioner of Woods and Forests in 1830.

ELMET was a British Kingdom of uncertain extent but

stretching from the marshes of the Humber westwards along Airedale and bounded on the south by the Pennine Forests about the headwaters of the Mersey. Difficult of access, it separated the Northumbrians from the rest of England and held out until cut off from the western British states by the Northumbrian crossing of the mountains. Its last and only known **King, Certic,** was driven away by K. Edwin (?-632) of Northumbria whose Mercian and Northumbrian colonists were known as Elmetsaetan. Sherborne-in-Elmet survives as the name of a suburb in Leeds.

ELMHAM (Norfolk) was the second see, after Dunwich, of the E. Angles and organised for their North Folk in 673. After the Danish disruptions the see of Elmham was alone revived. Under William I the Norman Bp. Herfast moved it to Thetford, but his successor moved it yet again, to Norwich and started to build the great cathedral in 1095.

ELMHAM, Thomas (1364-c.1428), monk of St Augustine's Canterbury, was from 1414 Prior of the Cluniac House of Lenton and from 1415 at Henry V's request, Cluniac Vicar-Gen. for England and Scotland. This promotion seems to have prompted him to write a *Liber Metricus* (Lat = Metrical Book) celebrating Henry's triumphs over French duplicity and the rising of the Lollard Sir John Oldcastle.

EL NIÑO **(Sp = The Little [Jesus]).** A reversal of Pacific currents, usually starting at Christmas, notably in 1891, 1925, 1941, 1957, 1965, 1976, 1982 (when the Mexican volcano Chichon erupted), 1986 and 1991 (eruption of Pinatubo in the Philippines). The cold Humboldt current normally flows northward up the S. American coast and generates a Pacific equatorial current flowing westward towards Indonesia, but in El Niño years, for reasons so far unknown, a warm eastward current from Indonesia turns south off C. America and overwhelms the Humboldt. This has global weather effects. Heavy rain in Britain occurred a year after 1982 and 1991 particularly. It also disturbs the breeding cycles of many Pacific creatures.

ELPHINSTONE. Leading Scottish lowland family. **(1) James (?1553-1612) 1st Ld. BALMERINO (1604)** an Octavian and James VI's Sec. of State from 1598, drafted a friendly letter to the Pope in 1599 and allegedly got the King to sign it unaware of its contents: Q. Elizabeth heard of it and was told that it was a forgery. In 1604 he became one of the Commissioners for the abortive union negotiations and in 1605 Pres. of the Court of Session. The King discovered the nature of the letter of 1599 and he was condemned for treason but later pardoned. His *s.* **(2) John (?-1649) 2nd Ld.** was a leading covenanter who advised calling in French help. **(3) Arthur (1688-1746),** Jacobite in 1715, escaped but was pardoned without his knowledge in 1733. He was Capt. of the Young Pretender's guards in 1745: captured after Culloden in 1746, he was executed.

ELPHINSTONE (1) George Keith (1746-1823) Ld. (1797) Vist. (1814) KEITH, M.P. in 1780 and 1790 and fighting Admiral, took part in the capture of Toulon in 1793, beat the Dutch in Saldanha Bay (S.W. Africa) in 1796 and occupied the Cape. In 1797 he was active and successful with Jervis in suppressing the naval mutinies and became C-in-C Mediterranean after Jervis (as St. Vincent) went home. As such he blockaded the Italian ports until Bonaparte's victory at Marengo in 1800. He refused to confirm the El Arish Convention and then joined with Abercromby in the amphibious operations which failed before Cadiz and succeeded in Egypt. He commanded at the Nore from 1803 to 1807 and in the Channel from 1812 to 1815. He became enormously rich. He married **(2) Hester Maria (1762-1857)** née **THRALE,** the learned Hebrew and mathematical scholar educated by Dr Johnson and their *d.* **(3) Margaret Mercer (1788-1867)** friend of P. Charlotte, married Bonaparte's A.D.C. the Comte de Flahault in 1817.

ELPHINSTONE, Mountstuart (1779-1859) spent most of his active life dealing with Maratha affairs. He began as Agent's Assistant at Poona in 1801 and, after a military interlude, was resident at Nagpur from 1804 and Ambassador to Shah Shuja at Kabul in 1808. From 1810 to 1816 he was Resident at the Peishwa's court at Poona. Here he tried, but only partly succeeded, in maintaining order among the turbulent Maratha rulers, but in 1817 he was ordered to annex Poona and as Gov. of Bombay from 1819 to 1827, had to deal with many of the consequences. He had acquired a strong hold on the Maratha mind by his courage, sense and justice and this enabled him to pacify the area with only minimal resources. He was offered, and refused, the Governor-Generalship in 1827 and retired leaving a legal and administrative code for the Bombay Presidency which became the model for many other such codes elsewhere.

ELPHINSTONE, William (1431-1514) was reader of Canon Law at Paris and in 1474 Rector of Glasgow University. He was then employed in Scots diplomatic missions to Louis XI (1479) and to Edward IV (1482 and 1484). He became Bp. of Aberdeen in 1488 and briefly Lord Chancellor. In 1491 he was again Ambassador in France and from 1492 Keeper of the Privy Seal. In 1494 he began the foundation of the University of Aberdeen which occupied much of his available time between episcopal and official duties. In 1507 he introduced printing into Scotland. *See* JAMES IV OF SCOTS.

ELTHAM (*see* LONDON) had a palace built mainly by Edward III but later extended. It was a favourite royal residence and Henry VII's family was brought up there. It was abandoned after Henry VIII's death.

ELTHAM ORDINANCES (1526) was a set of regulations framed by Cardinal Wolsey for the more efficient management of the royal household.

ELY, Abbey and Bishopric. St. Etheldreda founded the Convent in the 7th cent. and became its Abbess. She was succeeded by other members of her family. During the Danish invasions there was a break of at least a century in continuity, but St Ethelwold refounded the monastery with a large endowment and K. Edgar secured its position with a charter in 970. Between 970 and 1086, the Abbey greatly extended its lands first through Ethelwold's initiatives until his death in 984 and then through gifts, especially from the family of Ealdorman Brihtnoth, the hero of the B. of Maldon. According to Domesday (1086) Ely was, after Glastonhury, the second richest Abbey in England.

After troubles in the late 11th cent. with long vacancies (1075-81 and 1093-1100) and an inevitable involvement in Hereward's rising, for which it suffered reprisals, the Abbey rose to a different importance in 1109 when Henry I made it the Cathedral of a diocese for Cambridgeshire, carved out of the over-large diocese of Lincoln. The scheme, mooted by the aristocratic Abbot Richard (1100-7) was carried out for the Breton clerk Hervey, a refugee from his see at Bangor. In the division of the property between the see and the religious community (now a cathedral priory), the Bp. emerged in mid-century with the lion's share. Secular Bps. included Nigel (1139-69), Treasurer to Henry I; Geoffrey Ridel (1174-89) an opponent of Thomas Becket; and William Longchamp (1189-97), Chancellor of Richard I. There were also the monk-bishops John of Fountains (1220-25). Hugh of Northwold (1229-54) and Hugh of Balsham (1257-86) whose election the King hotly but unsuccessfully opposed, followed by the royal administrators John of Kerby (1286-90) and William of Louth (1290-98) but the see suffered financially from frequent vacancies.

The 12th cent. Norman church was embellished in 13th cent. by Hugh of Northwold so as to accommodate pilgrims to the shrine of St. Etheldreda. In 1322 the tower collapsed, and the sacrist, Alan of Walsingham, who came from a local family of goldsmiths, replaced it with the remarkable octagon and lantern. The Lady Chapel, planned before the octagon, was built immediately afterwards by John of Wisbech.

ELY, Isle of. *See* CAMBRIDGE, -SHIRE.

ELYOT, Sir Thomas (?1499-1546) *s*. of a judge, student of medicine, was clerk of the Privy Council from 1523 to 1530. At that time he wrote his well known *Boke called the Governor*, published in 1531. Full of classical allusions and partially inspired by Plato's *Republic*, it argues that under the Prince there must he governors and magistrates who require training from childhood up. This training should range from ordinary and advanced learning, to suitable sports, sedentary pastimes, dancing and archery so as to develop brains, character and physique in due proportion. The book marked a stage in the development of English prose and earned Elyot promotion. He was sent as Ambassador to negotiate with Charles V on Henry VIII's divorce in 1531 and again in 1535. He also published other works and translations, a Latin-English Dictionary and was M.P. for Cambridge in 1542.

EMANCIPISTS (Australia) were pardoned or time-expired convicts. Though mostly given land, they and their descendants were excluded from politics and started, despite immigrant opposition, to demand civil rights. By 1842 immigrants and emancipists were co-operating in an agitation for self-govt. In the course of this the objections to their civil rights gradually faded out.

EMBARGO (Sp. Embargar = to restrain) is a detention of any class of transport or goods by one state to prevent their movement to another. **Arrêt de Prince** is a temporary embargo, sometimes restricted to a single ship or object. A **Civil Embargo,** operates only on property of subjects of the detaining state e.g. the U.S.A. embargo of 1807 against France and Britain (*see* NON-INTERCOURSE). A **hostile Embargo** operates on property of foreign subjects e.g. the allied embargoes of 1914 preparatory to the exercise of angary. Either form can be used in pursuit of state policy, but a unilateral embargo against one side in a war is justly considered to be intervention. Embargoes have been among the few comparatively effective sanctions available to international agencies. Thus in 1934 embargoes by 30 countries against Bolivia and Paraguay (who were at war) were lifted for Bolivia when Paraguay refused to accept League of Nations mediation. In 1935 the oil embargo imposed by the League of Nations to defeat the Italian attack on Ethiopia failed because the U.S.A. evaded it. In 1951 in connection with the Korean war, 38 states embargoed strategic material and arms to Chinese and N. Korean territories and during the 1990-1 Gulf War most members of the U.N.O. imposed embargoes against Iraq.

EMBRACERY is the exercise of improper influence upon jurors by bribery or other means such as threats of violence. It is often committed by a person who is not on the jury, but communicates his influence through a member of it, who is with him equally guilty. Common in the 15th cent. there has been a notable increase in the later part of the 20th.

EMDEN (Ger.), capital of E. Frisia, dominated the trade of the Ems valley and, during the Dutch Wars of Independence, virtually replaced the Dutch ports as the entry for N.W. European seaborne trade, besides being a refuge for Dutch fugitives. It declined when the wars ended. In 1744 it passed, with E. Frisia, to Prussia and in 1757 the British occupied it to protect Hanover and help Prussia. The French annexed it in 1810 (*see* FRENCH COASTAL ANNEXATIONS) and it passed to Hanover in 1815. Until the fall of Hanover in 1866 it was thus always, and sometimes extensively, a port for British trade. It became the main port for Westphalia after the opening of the Dortmund-Ems Canal in 1899. *See also* EAST INDIA CO. (PRUSSIAN).

EMDEN a German cruiser of Adm. Count Spee's Pacific squadron was detached on 13 Aug. 1914 to raid commerce in the Indian Ocean. In Sept. she took British ships in the Bay of Bengal, bombarded Madras and raided the route to Aden. In Oct. she sank a Russian cruiser in the British port of Penang. These operations caused great excitement. She was sunk by H.M.A.S. *Sydney* in Nov. at N. Keeling.

EMERALD CHARTER (1328) conferred criminal jurisdiction and immunity from feudal service upon Good Sir James Douglas in respect of his many Scottish estates. Robert I invested him by putting an emerald ring on his finger.

EMERGENCY (1) The Emergency Powers Act 1920 was passed in the face of disturbances caused by demobilisation and unemployment. It empowered the govt. to proclaim a state of emergency if there was a threat to deprive the community or a substantial portion of it of the essentials of life. Parliament had to meet within five days of the proclamation, which could not remain in force for more than a month. During the emergency, orders in council might provide for or confer any power necessary to preserve peace or secure or regulate supplies of necessaries but not impose military conscription or make it an offence to strike. The powers were used during the General Strike of 1926 and at other times, e.g. to prohibit electric display signs during the 1970 electricity shortage.

(2) Wartime emergency legislation was passed in both World Wars to validate doubtfully legal acts in advance and particularly to deal with enemy trading and property and with civil defence.

EMIGRATION FROM UNITED KINGDOM

Population in the first year of each decennium (thousands)

	From UK	Canada	Australia	NZ	S. Africa
1821-30	250				
1831-40	702				
1841-50	1684				
1851-60	2287	2375	440	27	406
1861-70	1745	3206	1168	99	420
1871-80	1668	3688	1668	256	
1881-90	2558	4325	2253	490	1124
1891-1900	1743	4833	3175	627	2061
1901-10	2842	5371	3773	773	3519
1911	–	7207	4455	1008	3759

Emigration continued in later decades, with a pronounced increase between 1945 and 1970. By then, the proportion of Britons in the intake of the former "white dominions" had fallen. In 1980 emigrants from the UK amounted to 232,800 of whom only 103,000 were destined for the countries above. Net emigration was considerably less.

ÉMIGRÉS (Fr. = emigrants). The word commonly refers to nobles, ecclesiastics and other supporters of the French monarchy who left France during the Revolution. There were coherent groups of them in Belgium. Holland, Italy, Switzerland as well as Britain, but their main centre, until the French overran it, was at Coblenz and subsequently with Louis XVIII. Many took service in foreign armies against the French. They were amnestied by Bonaparte during his First Consulate but few took advantage of this until after 1815. They mostly lost and never recovered their estates.

EMIN, Eduard Schnitzer (1840-1902) Effendi (1875) Pasha (1878). German doctor under Hakki Pasha at Scutari, became a Moslem and worked in Egypt from 1875. Gordon made him medical officer of the Sudan Equatorial province and then Governor. He held it single handed until Stanley arrived in 1899, making extensive studies of its fauna, flora and languages. He left with Stanley but shortly returned in German service and was killed.

EMINENCE. The style of a Cardinal: for **Grey Eminence** *see* FRANCISCANS-4.

EMMA OF NORMANDY or AELFGIFU (?-1052) *d.* of Richard I of Normandy, married K. Ethelred the Unready in 1002. On Sweyn Forkbeard's invasion of England in 1013 she fled with her sons Alfred and Edward to Normandy. In 1017, after Ethelred's death, she married Sweyn's son Canute, now established as K. of England and on his death in 1035 she joined with E. Godwin of Wessex in supporting the claim to the English throne of her son by Canute, HARTHACNUT, then in Denmark. E. Leofric and others supported HAROLD HEREFOOT, Canute's son by Aelfgifu of Northampton. By a compromise reached at Oxford in 1036 it was agreed that Harold Herefoot should be regent, but that Emma should live at Winchester protected by Harthacanute's housecarls. By the end of 1037 Harold had made himself King and Emma took refuge in Flanders. Alfred, the younger of her two sons by Ethelred, had been savagely blinded by a group of Harold's partisans and died of his injuries. Harold died in 1040 and Harthacnut was invited to England, died after only two years and was succeeded in England by the second of her sons by Ethelred, Edward the Confessor. Emma, however, was suspected of scheming on behalf of Magnus, K. of Norway. The Earls supporting Edward seized her and confiscated her property in 1043.

EMMET (1) Thomas Addis (1764-1827). Irish barrister and propagandist for the United Irishmen of whom he became a director in 1797. Arrested in 1798 and deported to Holland in 1802, he helped to raise an Irish battalion in French pay. His brother **(2) Robert (1778-1803)** equally nationalistic, obtained a promise of assistance from Bonaparte in 1802, returned to Ireland and raised an insurrection in Dublin in July 1803. Horrified at the barbarities and incompetence of some of his followers he took refuge in the country and was caught and executed.

EMPEROR as a title. *See* ROMAN EMPERORS.

EMPEROR OF INDIA. The imperial title was taken in 1876 by Q. Victoria on Disraeli's advice to signify a sense of continuity with the imperial supremacy over the Princes. It was renounced by George VI on Indian Independence in 1947.

EMPIRE. Variously used term viz.: **(1)** The political constitution of Rome beginning with Augustus in 27 BC. **(2)** The Holy Roman Empire. **(3)** The First (French) Empire 1804-15, under the Bonaparte Napoleon I. **(4)**

The Second 1852-70 under Napoleon III. **(5)** The (British) Indian 1876-1948. **(6)** Any country whose ruler claimed a higher rank than King, notably Russia, Persia, Ethiopia, Brazil, China and Japan. **(7)** Any large area in submission to a smaller power nucleus.

EMPIRE TREE TRADE was an illusory ideal explored after World War I under which Britain was, in continuation of the war economy, to draw food and raw materials from the dominions and colonies in return for manufactures produced by an industry converted from the war economy. It involved a misreading of the facts. The dominions and many colonies had already developed industries which they wished to protect and to develop further with British capital (needed to convert British industry) while the conditions favourable to Empire food could be created in Britain only by taxing foreign food, to which the electorate objected. Lloyd George's 1921 London Conference of Dominion Prime Ministers was deadlocked in this complex because they insisted that it was politically impossible for Westminster to overrule the Dominion parliaments. This anticipated the Statute of Westminster by ten years. The cause, meanwhile, had been espoused by Lord Beaverbrook, who helped with the overthrow of Lloyd George (*see* CHANAK INCIDENT) in the hope that a Tory govt. would espouse it too.

It came up against the hard logic of facts, but the Beaverbrook press continued its campaign. During the 1929 slump he launched his Empire Free Trade crusade in conjunction with Lord Rothermere. It had many supporters including the tradition of the Chamberlain family. In 1932 an imperial conference was called to Ottawa, which struggled through 12 agreements on minor details but failed to agree on the major issues, even though the overseas countries were willing to raise their tariffs against some foreign manufacturers.

EMPIRE SETTLEMENT. *See* COMMONWEALTH SETTLEMENT.

EMPLOYMENT, DEPT OF. *See* LABOUR, MINISTRY OF.

EMPLOYER'S LIABILITY. At Common Law an employer was liable to an employee for his own personal acts, omissions, acts or omissions of other employees if specially authorised by him, for breach of his primary duties to provide a competent staff, adequate material, safe premises and a safe working system and for breach of any statutory duty, but he could not be made liable if the employee had accepted the risk, or was guilty of contributory negligence or (under the doctrine of common employment) for an injury caused by another employee not authorised by the employer. Sporadic voluntary insurance schemes had existed since the mid 18th cent. In litigation against employers, employees risked loss of jobs, expense and the possibility that the employer might be bankrupt. The Workmen's Compensation Act 1897 encouraged insurance schemes by imposing a wider liability on employers, but permitted them to contract out of the Act by setting up insurance schemes which had to satisfy the Registrar of Friendly Societies. Successive enactments widened the scope of such schemes. The doctrine of common employment was abolished in 1948. Industrial injuries insurance became compulsory in 1952.

EMPLOYMENT EXCHANGES (later JOB CENTRES) AND SERVICE. The service was set up under the Unemployment Workmen Act 1905. On the recommendation of the Royal Commission on the Poor Law (1905-9) Labour Exchanges were created by the Liberal Govt. under the Labour Exchanges Act 1909. This was largely due to Winston Churchill, William Beveridge and the latter's book *Unemployment* (1909). Beveridge was appointed to organise them. The MINISTRY OF LABOUR was created in 1916 to cope with the interlocking problems of wartime production and conscription. In 1939 it became the MINISTRY OF LABOUR AND NATIONAL SERVICE and during World War II all jobs had to be sought and allocated through its exchanges. After the war they reverted to their reserve function. The Ministry was absorbed into the DEPT. OF EMPLOYMENT (AND PRODUCTIVITY) in 1967.

EMPSON, Sir Richard (?-1510) lawyer, was M.P. for Northamptonshire (where he bought estates in 1476) and speaker of the Commons from 1491 to 1492. He was a financial civil servant associated with Sir Edmund Dudley and bore substantial responsibility for Henry VII's fiscal prosperity and for carrying it out, sometimes by ruthless, even brutal means. In 1504 he achieved the important office of Chancellor of the Duchy of Lancaster. It was his misfortune to reach high office near the end of the reign, for in the storm of complaints engendered by the publication of the King's Will, he was one of the main targets. Henry VIII sacrificed him and Dudley by having them executed upon false charges of constructive treason.

ENCEPHALITIS. The English sweating sickness of 1592 and the influenza outbreak of 1672 may have been encephalitis. The "A" variety, identified in 1916, was epidemic in France and England in 1918; the "X" variety in Australia in 1917-8, 1922 and 1926. The disease is often fatal. *See* EPIDEMICS, HUMAN.

ENCYCLICAL. *See* PAPAL CHANCERY.

ENCYCLOPAEDIAS. Organised *corpora* of information were published by Jean de Magnon (1663), Moréri (1674), Hofmann (1677), Furetiére (1690), Chauvin (1692) and Bayle (1697). The first in English was published by John HARRIS from 1708-1710, but the most influential of the early encyclopaedias was by Ephraim CHAMBERS (1728). This went through eight editions by 1752 and he also published it in Italian at Venice in 1748. Each of these drew to some extent on its predecessors. Chamber's was translated into French between 1743 and 1745, but quarrels prevented publication. Knowledge of the project was widespread among French intellectuals. D'Alembert was associated with it and in Oct. 1747 it was decided to amplify the now dormant project into the well known *Encyclopédie* under the direction of Diderot. The 17 volume text was finally completed after great opposition from the church in 1766. The 11 volumes of plates were issued between 1762 and 1772. The *Encyclopaedia Britannica* first appeared in 1771. The 10th edition (the last wholly under British control) in 1903. The German encyclopaedia now known as *Brockhaus* first appeared between 1796 and 1808. It influenced most subsequent encyclopaedias including Chambers' Encyclopaedia (1859-68) which is not related to that of Ephraim

ENDECOTT. *See* NEW ENGLAND.

ENDEMIC DISEASES (*See* EPIDEMICS.) Though most epidemic diseases are eventually endemic, emerging, so to speak, from ambush at intervals and remaining latent or relatively benign meanwhile, some are continually dangerous in particular territories, where they burden the economy, and sometimes inhibit civilisation or development together. Malaria, for example, seems permanently to have weakened the temporal power of the Papal states, and the once brilliant civilisation of the Two Sicilies and of Mediaeval Egypt. It inhibited the colonisation of the Isthmus of Panama and delayed the building of the canal, and it was one of a number of factors in delaying the development of West Africa. Tripanosomiasis stopped migration in many parts of tropical Africa and was long an obstacle to development of any sort in the Congo and Uganda. Yellow Fever made the W. Indies a death trap for European forces in the 16th to 19th cents. The study of the economic, social and political effects of endemic diseases has been confused partly because their nature has become apparent only in modern times and partly because previously they were taken for granted or were the objects of superstition. Moreover their effect being, in a sense negative, comparisons become possible only when the facts of a

previous disease-free era happen to be known or when a disease, such as malaria, is overcome.

ENFRANCHISEMENT means, in general, liberation from an inferior but not necessarily abject condition, in particular the conversion **(1)** of a villein into a free man; **(2)** of a copyhold into a freehold; **(3)** of a non-voter into a voter; **(4)** of an apprentice into a freeman of a guild or city; **(5)** of an unrepresented place into one entitled to elect an M.P. The legal setting free of a slave is called MANUMISSION.

ENGAGEMENT (26 Dec. 1647) between Charles I and the Scots, provided that a Scottish army should assist him and that in return all Independency should be suppressed and Presbyterianism established in England for three years. This Royalist-Presbyterian alliance precipitated the second Civil War and was the distant progenitor of the Restoration. *See* CHARLES II-28.

ENGELS, Friedrich (1820-95), of Rhineland origin, first collaborated with Karl Marx in 1844 with whom he published the *Communist Manifesto* in 1848. He also published his *Condition of the Working Class in England,* based on a two year study. From 1849 to 1869 he worked in his father's prosperous textile firm in Manchester and thereafter devoted himself to elaborating theoretical Marxism. *Anti-Dühring* appeared in 1878. His support, intellectual and especially financial, was essential to Marx who sponged on him. His *Dialectics of Nature* was not published until 1940.

ENGHIEN, MURDER OF D. OF (1804) *See* THIRD COALITION, WAR OF (1803-6).

ENGINEERING (1) CIVIL, concerned with communications such as roads, bridges, aqueducts and harbours, was practised on a vast scale by the Romans, revived in the 9th cent. and extended to dams, tunnels and canals in the 18th. **(2) MECHANICAL** concerned with large machines developed slowly because they were not envisaged until steam pumps in mines (in the 1780s) and then railways (1820s) came into use. (*See also* SHIPS, POWER-DRIVEN.) This created a need for, on the one hand boiler-makers with their allied trades, and on the other hand machine tools (for making other machines). Manchester, Birmingham, Glasgow and Newcastle-on-Tyne became specialised heavy engineering cities. Lincoln produced agricultural machinery; Coventry specialised in light engineering. These were slowly superseded by the motor industry at Oxford, Coventry and Dagenham. **(3) ELECTRICAL,** concerned with generation, transmission and switching of power and with telecommunications and electronics, developed on a large scale only after World War II while mechanical engineering declined partly through supersession and partly through foreign competition.

ENGINEERS, ROYAL (R.E.) consisting of officers only, were first formally constituted in 1716. MILITARY ARTIFICERS were raised in Gibraltar in 1772. By 1787 these were officered by R.E. officers and the Corps was constituted then. Military Artificers, for home service only, continued to be raised separately. In 1813 all these bodies were amalgamated as the ROYAL SAPPERS AND MINERS and the H.Q. moved from Woolwich to Chatham. In 1856 the Corps finally took the name ROYAL ENGINEERS and in 1869 the H.Q. became the School of Military Engineering. The Corps has fathered the military use of survey, signalling, cable and wireless telegraphy, aircraft, gas and anti-gas, motor vehicles and mines.

ENGLAND, i.e. the land of the Angles, was originally a term used by foreigners for the southern and eastern parts of Britain or for the territory ruled by the Kings of the House of Wessex. After the Danish invasions had destroyed the rival dynasties, the Wessex Kings called themselves Kings of the Angles (Rex Anglorum) but *Angle* and *English* were by then confused or nearly synonymous. After the Norman Conquest it meant simply the territory ruled by the K., which excluded Wales and Cumbria. The two Borders became accepted as the boundaries of England in the 13th cent., but whereas the location of the Welsh border was fixed early, the Scottish border, owing to disputes at each end, fluctuated and Berwick was considered a separate territory. In 1540 the Welsh Act of Union incorporated Wales into England even though it retained some special peculiarities. Neither the Union of the Crowns in 1603 nor the Act of Union of 1707 had this effect on Scotland. Berwick, however, was incorporated with England, and Wales began to be re-separated progressively with the Disestablishment of the Welsh Church in 1914 and was specially defined in the Local Government Act, 1972. *See* MARCHES.

ENGLAND, CHURCH OF (REFORMED) (*See also* ANGLICANISM; REFORMATION.) One may, with some caution consider the history of the reformed English Church in ten phases.

(**1**) Henry VIII's quarrel with the Papacy ended in the closure of England to Papal authority, the substitution of crown for Pope in supremacy over the Church, and the consequent submission of the convocations to the Crown (1539). Organisationally the attack on pilgrimages and the seizure of monasteries, chantries and their lands deprived the Church of immense endowments but enabled Henry to finance six new bishoprics. These were secular changes, for Henry countenanced no changes of doctrine, though he seems not to have appreciated the far-reaching probabilities arising from setting up the Great Bible in all churches.

(**2**) During the eleven years (1547-58) of his two successors, there was a violent doctrinal oscillation, first under Edward VI towards Protestant, even determinist doctrines exemplified by Cranmer's two *Prayer Books* (1549 and 1552), *Ordinal* and *42 Articles* (1553), then back under Mary to a persecuting Romanism and reconciliation with the Papacy. Many reformers fled abroad or were burned.

(**3**) Elizabeth, Abp. Parker, William Cecil, Sir Anthony Cooke and others established a compromise designed to occupy the middle ground. The more extreme Calvinism of the *42 Articles* was softened by the *39* which superseded them (1571). Papal supremacy was again repudiated, but the Crown no longer explicitly claimed headship of the Church and contented itself with the title of Supreme Governor. The service of Holy Communion continued strongly to resemble the Mass, but the sacrament was to be administered in both kinds, with words of administration which ingeniously alluded to the Real Presence and mere commemoration without denying either. This compromise of 1559 established a relative calm until, on the one hand the Papal bull *Regnans in Excelsis* (Lat: ruling on high) (1570) created a small permanent sect of papalists, and on the other, the victory over the first Armada (1588) made the more extreme reformers (later called Puritans) feel safe enough to resume controversy.

(**4**) Between 1588 and the death of Charles I (1649) the Elizabethan compromise was eroded by ceaseless criticism and attack from Presbyterian Calvinists and other reformers. The fall of Charles I and Laud entailed the eclipse of their Church.

(**5**) There was now another period of oscillation which lasted until the Revolution of 1689. When the Commonwealth was established the church soon ceased to exist as an organisation. The Scottish imposition of the Solemn League and Covenant effectively abolished episcopacy in 1643. In 1645 the usages of the *Book of Common Prayer* were superseded by those of the *Directory of Public Worship*. Holders of cures did either as they pleased or as their congregations demanded. In practice, the rule of the gloomy sectaries meant iconoclasm, whitewash, the suppression of cheerful customs, even music. The old inquisitorial curiosity about sexual habits, institutionalised under Puritan J.P.'s and archidiaconal courts such as those established in Essex in 1600, was now widely extended. The Restoration brought back (with pleasure) the church as a visible body, but with the difference that many of its members were sceptical or libidinous or both. The High Church, represented by Laud's successor, Wm Juxon, triumphed. A revised *Book of Common Prayer* was enforced by a new Act of Uniformity (1662). Over a thousand ministers resigned and became, in effect, independent non-conformists (*see also* COMPTON CENSUS) but the church came to be regarded as part of the machinery of a Protestant but aristocratic and monarchical regime ready to persecute other sects not for the good of souls, but in the interests of political supremacy. James II's attempted romanisation came to grief on the rock of politics rather than that of Peter. When, soon after, the nonconformists showed signs of flexing their muscles they too were excluded from politics by the Occasional Conformity and Schism Acts (1713 and 1714).

(**6**) The convocations, having lost their power of clerical taxation, had little to discuss. Indeed, after the Bangorian controversy (1717) they never discussed anything. A bench of Whig, mainly aristocratic Bps., presided over a motley lower clergy either sunk in the obscurity of pastoral care, or absent at universities or on travels or investigations of their own. In so doing they made a notable contribution to English civilisation, if nothing else.

(**7**) It was from the body of lower clergy that Methodism, first promoted by John and Charles Wesley at Oxford, made its way from 1740. The disruptive Methodist Church was regularised by John Wesley's trust deed in 1784 and the Anglican evangelical movement, whose representatives met regularly at Islington from 1827 onwards.

(**8**) The new seriousness revived the Convocations. The Canterbury one discussed business again from 1852, York from 1861. In 1885 a House of Laymen was associated with each convocation. Joint sessions began in 1900 and these developed into a General Assembly, established in 1920. Seriousness, however, was not enough. Some of the High Churchmen, dissatisfied with 18th cent. Latitudinarianism, were, like J.H. Newman, attracted by Rome while disgruntled ritualists and tractarians were trying, not without some success to evangelise the inner cities. Such enthusiasm was alarming to Bishops.

(**9**) Perhaps the biggest 20th cent. danger has been the decline of the Church's capacity to attract men of high ability. By 1920 Anglicans had largely ridden out the Anglo-Catholic and sectarian controversies, but the Church's financial security, underwritten by the establishment of Q. Anne's Bounty (1710) was virtually destroyed. The Bounty obtained administration of the tithes in 1925, but the Tithe Act 1936 bought out the tithes at an undervaluation. Already understaffed in the cities by reason of population growth and mobility, the rural base of the Church was eroded by the same factors working in reverse.

(**10**) The doctrinal doldrums of the mid-century were succeeded by a burst of superficial reformism, centred on the modernisation of the language of ritual, and adoption as nominally temporary expedients of new forms of service. At the same time discussions began with the Roman Church to find, as far as possible, common ground. A surprising amount was found by 1990, particularly in the matching together of the parallel Eucharistic theories (*see* TRANSUBSTANTIATION) but the growing intimacy was broken by the apparent assumption in 1994 by the Church of ability to alter its principles by vote.

ENGLISH COLLEGE, ROME, was founded as a pilgrim hospice in 1362 and converted into a priestly seminary in 1578. It was managed by the Jesuits from 1580 until their suppression in 1773 and then by Italian secular priests until closed in the French invasion of 1808. Reopened in 1818, it has ever since been under English seculars, of whom Card. Wiseman was one.

ENGLISH LANGUAGE. English was originally the dialect of the Angles which was the first to be written. The name eventually extended to all Anglian and Saxon dialects. OLD ENGLISH or ANGLO-SAXON is the English spoken up to about 1150; MIDDLE ENGLISH from then until about 1500. TUDOR ENGLISH, which followed it, was derived from the dialect of the East Midlands, especially London. This in its turn developed until about 1900 from the style and diction of the *Book of Common Prayer* and the Authorised (King James) Version of the Bible into a magnificent CLASSICAL ENGLISH. The early 20th cent. interest in material accuracy together with patronage of the under-educated eventually caused the abandonment of both books and the rise of an explanatory but, by the erosion of grammar, less accurate MODERN ENGLISH. This is being fragmented and destabilised by overseas variants communicated through media and a hugely expanded publishing industry, and by song. The number of words continues to be greater than that of any other language.

ENGLISH LAW (1) Unlike some Roman based systems, English Law is not codified but is primarily derived from three sources, namely Common Law, Equity and Statute. The **Common Law** is the ancient body of legal ideas and these were applied by the three Common Law courts to particular facts by a process of analogy and deduction from previously decided cases, on the principle that it is unfair to treat similar facts differently on different occasions. **Equity** (q.v.) is a powerful supplementary intellectual system developed by the Lord Chancellor's court to adapt the Common Law rules in circumstances where a rigid application might produce an over-rigid or unfair result. In general the Common Law acts by the award of compensation: Equity by physical compulsion where compensation by itself will not effect justice e.g. in a signed contract for the sale of a house, if the seller backs out the purchaser, instead of claiming compensation for breach of contract, can force the seller to hand the house over and accept the contract price. In the application of equitable rules the court uses the same process of analogy and deduction as it does at Common Law, and both systems have, since 1875 in any case been applied by the same courts. In the rare cases where Common Law and Equity conflict, Equity prevails. **Statute,** on the other hand, overrules the particulars of either system but is applied less by analogy and deduction and more by the interpretation of the words of a given statute itself.

(2) English law as described above, is applied with local adaptations in all countries and former countries of the Commonwealth unless it has not, for any reason, superseded an existing system of established law. Thus it does not apply in Scotland (whose system is Romano-Feudal); the Channel Is. (the Custom of Rouen of 1207); South Africa (Roman-Dutch); Quebec (The Custom of Paris of 1769); Mauritius (Code Napoleon) and in the Indian sub-continent and S.E. Asia there are local exceptions mostly concerned with status and inheritance.

(3) The longer the various countries of the Commonwealth have been independent, the further their basically English systems drift apart and in the meantime by joining the E.U., Britain has subjected her laws to E.U. legislation which overrules, in cases of conflict, any rule of domestic law. Since Britain ratified the T. of Maastricht (1993) the English system has been drifting, with the loss of independence, away more speedily from the American and Commonwealth systems than they have from each other.

ENGLISH MONARCHY, EARLY (*See* WEST SAXONS EARLY.) The Mercian weakness after K. Offa's death in 796

brought rebellions and civil wars during which **(1) Egbert (or Ecgbert or Ecgbryht) (?-839)** the West Saxon claimant fled in 799 to the court of Charlemagne; he returned with Frankish support at the death, possibly by poison, of K. Beortric in 802 and the Wiltshire men having held off the Mercians for him, he was recognised as K. of the West Saxons. Meanwhile the Vikings were beginning their raids which by 810 had reached the north Cornish coast. In 815 Egbert raided Cornwall, perhaps to extrude them. In 825 he overran Cornwall and overthrew the Cornishmen and Vikings at Camelford. The Mercians attacked Wessex in the rear and he beat them under their K. Bernwulf at Ellandun, Kent, and all England south of the Thames fell to him and he received the submission of Essex. The East Angles now asked for protection from the Mercians and Bernwulf was slain in a battle with them before Egbert's troops came up. This left Egbert without an equal in England. In 830 he enforced the submission of Mercia and pressed on into Northumbria where, at Dore, he was recognised as overlord. The English now had one King. By this time the Vikings had penetrated the Channel and in 835 they defeated him in an engagement at Charmouth. In 837 a combined Cornish-Viking host invaded Wessex, but he beat them decisively but in pyrrhic fashion at Hingston Down. In 838 he recognised the southern primacy of Canterbury as against claims of Lichfield. His *s.* **(2) Aethelwulf (?-858)** Bp. of Winchester, had been made sub-King in Kent and Sussex after the B. of Ellandun and succeeded his father as King of the English. A Danish force in northern France (845) having met disaster, stormed Canterbury and Rochester and defeated the Mercians at London. Aethelwulf, however, destroyed it at the B. of Ockley which secured peace for the rest of his reign. An attempt through Wales was foiled in 853, when Aethelwulf and Buhred of Mercia (who had married his daughter) jointly forced Rhodri ap Merfyn to hold the area against the Danes. In 855 Aethelwulf went on the first of his two famous journeys to Rome taking his youngest son Alfred, whom he apparently favoured, and in 856 he married Judith, *d.* of Charles the Bald, K. of the Franks. During his prolonged absences his elder sons laid claim to parts of the Kingdom, and Aethelwulf, to avoid a partition, settled the succession by his *Will.* He himself took Kent and the overkingship while his eldest surviving *s.,* Aethelbald, took Wessex. At his own death the overkingship was to pass to Aethelbald, and Kent to the next son Aethelbert, and so on from brother to brother. Accordingly **(3) Aethelbald (?-860)** succeeded him, married Judith, reigned uneventfully and was followed by **(4) Aethelbert (?-866)** in whose last months Hingwar, *s.* of Ragnar, arrived with a great Danish fleet off Thanet and invaded East Anglia. Aethilbert's death and succession by **(5) Aethelred I (?-871)** prevented immediate counteraction. *For the rest of this reign see* ASHDOWN, CAMPAIGN AND BATTLE.

ENGLISHRY, PRESENTMENT OF. *See* MURDRUM.

ENIGMA was an electro-mechanical enciphering machine incorporating movable drums and wheels adopted in the 1920s by the Germans who believed it to he impenetrable. Polish mathematicians partly mastered it in the 1930s but modifications and key changes prevented total success. Help was accepted from British and French intelligence and, after the fall of Poland and France, the work was carried out at Bletchley Park under the name of ULTRA. Early in the war the British sporadically deciphered German transmissions, but helped by the capture of two Enigma machines from a German U-boat, after mid-1941 they got immense amounts of information in advance of most German movements and initiatives. The continued German belief in its impenetrability was a major factor in their defeat.

ENLIGHTENMENT, AGE OF refers to a period commencing roughly with the English Revolution in 1688 and ending with the French Revolution of 1789. The term is a negative one signifying an intellectual toleration which superseded the passionate partisanship of the preceding 60 years, but it opened the doors for the discussions of the Royal Society, the publication of the first encyclopaedias, the researches and urbanities of Gibbon, George II's foundation of Göttingen University, and the social and philosophical speculations of Locke, Voltaire and Hume. In its middle years educated Europeans had confidence in progress and enlightenment and in the quarter-century before the French Revolution political power was often in the hands of monarchs or statesmen who believed that they had a duty to exercise power rationally. Leading enlightenment despots such as Frederick the Great of Prussia, Catherine the Great of Russia, the Marquess of Pombal in Portugal and Joseph II in Austria provided much of the inspiration for the French revolutionary doctrinaires.

ENNISKILLEN OR INNISKILLING (Fermanagh, N.I.) on an island at the important crossing between the Upper and Lower Lough Ernes was anciently a Maguire stronghold. In 1689 it held out for William III and thereafter became a garrison town at which the well known Royal Inniskilling Fusiliers (27th Foot) and the 6th Inniskilling Dragoons were long raised and quartered.

ENOSIS **(Gr = Union)** The Greek equivalent of irredentism, i.e. the union of all Greek speakers. The target varied with the seeming opportunities. Before 1912 it was aimed at mainland Greeks as far as Istanbul. After 1918 at Smyrna; after 1924 at the Dodecanese; after 1945 at Cyprus; and after 1992 at Macedonia.

ENROLMENTS, STAT. OF (1536) supplementary to the Stat. of USES, invalidated bargains and sales of freehold estates of inheritance unless made under seal and enrolled at Westminster or the relevant county. It was habitually evaded either by a covenant to stand seized in favour of a relative, or by a grant of a lease followed by a release. Repealed in 1924.

ENSA (Entertainments National Service Association) or less seriously "Every Night Something Awful" organised shows, varying from the very large to a couple of comics, for servicemen, factory workers and other depressed groups in World War II. Two examples of its enterprise may stand for the whole, which was widespread and free. Dame Myra Hess gave free classical recitals in the National Gallery for all comers every day throughout the war and ENSA put on *Desert Victory* with Dutch sub-titles in an Antwerp cinema while the Germans were still in part of the town.

ENTAIL. *See* LAND TENURE (ENGLAND)-4.

ENTENTE CORDIALE **(Fr = friendly understanding)** (Apr. 1904). The aggressive policies of William II's Germany had relied up to 1904 extensively upon Anglo-French mutual suspicions, arising from traditional attitudes and colonial rivalries. Moreover France's only ally (since 1894) was Russia with her divergent ambitions and internal difficulties, while Britain had only Japan (1902), then too distant to affect the European situation. The original motive of Theophil DELCASSÉ (1852-1923) the French Foreign Minister from 1895 to 1905, was to free France from commitments likely to disperse her power in a confrontation with Germany. The British side was becoming increasingly suspicious of German naval expansion, made vastly more dangerous by the improvements to the Kiel Canal (1895), so that Lord Lansdowne was sympathetic to the approaches of Paul CAMBON, the skilful French Ambassador in London. Moreover, King Edward VII was strongly Francophile. The method adopted was initially a series of compromises on overseas problems. Britain got a free hand in Egypt, France in Morocco. Britain ceded the Los Is., and some of her Nigerian and Gambian claims to France, in return for French fisheries claims in Newfoundland. Eastern Siam became a French zone of influence: Western Siam, a British one, and the settlers'

feuds in New Caledonia were suppressed. The agreement came only just in time, for the Russo-Japanese War of 1904-5 immediately embroiled France and discredited Russia. The Germans attempted to destroy the understanding by their claims at Tangier in 1905; this manoeuvre had the opposite effect and precipitated the Anglo-French military conversations which, beginning in 1906, slowly converted the *entente* into an unspoken but real alliance. This was confirmed by British support for the French at Algeçiras in 1906 and Agadir in 1911 as well as at the beginning of World War I. The word *entente* was commonly used in German to signify the coalition of countries which opposed the Central Powers in World War I. *See* ANGLO-RUSSIAN CONVENTION 1907.

ENTERTAINMENT DUTY introduced by the Finance (New Duties) Act 1916 was leviable at different rates on **(1)** live entertainment; **(2)** on racing, games and exhibitions and **(3)** reproduced entertainment. From 1950 the number of exemptions was steadily increased until 1960 when the whole tax was abolished.

ENTICK **v** *CARRINGTON* **(1765).** Entick was named as the author of a seditious libel in a Secretary of State's warrant requiring the seizure of him and his papers for examination. Carrington broke into his house under the warrant and seized the papers. In an action for trespass the Court of Common Pleas held the warrant illegal as unprecedented, based on mere suspicion, and tending to abuse of authority. *See* WILKES V WOOD.

ENTHUSIASM in the 17th and 18th cents. meant the introduction of emotion into properly intellectual, logical or reasonable processes. This was considered to be a disadvantage. Talleyrand once said with pride that he had purged his staff of the least trace of enthusiasm.

ENUMERATED GOODS under the Navigation Acts were colonially produced sugar, tobacco, ginger, cotton wool, indigo and logwood which could be shipped only to England (Britain after 1707). Later Acts added coffee, raw silk, naval stores and bar and pig iron. Rice was enumerated between 1706 and 1730: sugar only until 1739. The purposes were (a) to profit from the re-exports; (b) to provide the British population with cheap sources of these commodities; (c) to ensure the prosperity of commercial shipping and an adequate supply of prime seamen; (d) in the case of iron and ships stores, to ensure the basic needs of the navy.

ENZIE. *See* GORDON (HUNTLY)-5.

EOCHAID. *See* SCOTS OR ALBAN KINGS. EARLY-5.

EORL. *See* EARL.

EPATTICUS. *See* BRITAIN. BEFORE THE ROMAN CONQUEST-5.

EPIDEMICS – ANIMAL. *See* ANIMAL EPIDEMICS.

EPIDEMICS – HUMAN. *See* ENDEMIC DISEASES. **(1)** diseases commonly prevalent in an area will affect the theoretical level of its population graph but not its pattern, so that social adjustments can be made gradually and with foresight. On the other hand epidemics and pandemics, particularly those which are lethal or debilitating, being so far unpredictable, will produce sudden economic, and may precipitate social and political upheavals. The smallpox pandemic of A.D. 161-6 marked the downturn of the Roman Empire, that of 251-66 accelerated its decline. The world-wide plague of 542-600 frustrated Justinian's aggressive revival. The effects of the murderous Black Death have been studied in some depth in England and some European countries, but historians and economists have been backward in investigating the consequences elsewhere, or in relation to similar disasters such as the plagues of 1894-1938 or the Spanish Influenza of 1918-19. The otherwise surprising weakness of the vast Spanish American empire was due to a series of devastating epidemics.

Mortality figures, when known (e.g. the 22 million influenza deaths in 1918-19) disclose the extreme effects in a particular case, but they do not represent the full short term disorganisation. Of the survivors, many more will have been prostrate or involved in nursing or dealing with practical and social side effects. People are distracted from their work; normal business and production can be interrupted. In some cases there were panic flights from towns. Transport and shipping have been stopped. A state in such a condition may become a weak enemy, an unreliable ally or a valueless trading partner. Govt. policy may be confused or reversed through casualties among statesmen, administrators or armies.

(2) When the first crises are past there can be obvious longer term physiological effects (e.g. club-footed survivors from poliomyelitis), or others which are less easy to trace such as shortened life expectancy, reduced fertility or perhaps a reduction in the general stock of talent. In addition there may have to be a wholesale re-organisation of work and society, equivalent to a revolution. The process of readjustment will itself be distracting and wasteful. Price and market mechanisms are dislocated. If there has been a high rural mortality or debility, much land may have gone out of cultivation and may not, through shrinkage of demand, come back into use for many years. About 1000 Domesday villages no longer exist. The currency may be in confusion. In such circumstances vested interests and established govt. customs and taxes may be resisted or may simply vanish. Basic principles of behaviour or morality too, will change.

(3) The issues are complicated by the variation of age groups affected. The five 16th cent. English sweating sickness epidemics attacked strong adults and presumably affected the birth rate immediately. Diphtheria and the Mortalité des Enfants (see PLAGUE) attacked mainly young children and their effects on the balance of generations would be visible much later. Other epidemics affected all age groups at once.

(4) Finally there were great difficulties in the way of investigation arising out of the primitive state of medical science before the 20th cent. and the inadequacies of observation, description and nomenclature which obtained before that time. See CHOLERA; DENGUE; DIPHTHERIA; DYSENTERY; GAOL FEVER; INFANTILE DIARRHOEA; INFLUENZA; LEPROSY; MALARIA; MEASLES; PLAGUE; POLIOMYELITIS; RELAPSING FEVER; SCARLET FEVER; SWEATING SICKNESS; SYPHILIS; TRENCH FEVER; TRIPANOSOMIASIS; TUBERCULOSIS; TYPHOID; TYPHUS; YELLOW FEVER.

EPISCOPAL ORDINATION ACT, 1784. Until 1784 a Bishop could not ordain a priest who had not taken the oath of allegiance. When the U.S.A. became independent, English Bishops could consequently not ordain Americans, which disorganised the American Anglican churches. The Act abolished the need for the oath.

EPPILLUS. See BRITAIN, BEFORE THE ROMAN CONQUEST.

EPPING FOREST was part of the Forest of Essex, but successive Inclosures had reduced it to 5,600 acres by 1871 when the Epping Forest Act committed it to the care of the Corporation of London.

EPSOM (Surrey) a corruption of EBBISHAM, the manor in which it is. In 1618 a sulphate of magnesia spring was discovered, but the place never became a spa because Epsom Salts, a purgative, could be made from the spring by evaporation and sold at a distance. Instead Epsom became famous for its racecourse. See DERBY.

EQUAL FRANCHISE ACT, 1928 (properly the Representation of the People (E.Q.) Act, 1928) assimilated the voting rights of the sexes in parliamentary and local govt. elections.

EQUAL PAY AND OPPORTUNITIES as between the sexes. The Sex Disqualifications Removal Act 1928 removed most of the legal barriers to women's employment and most professions became open to them even if the process was in practice slow. The principle was incorporated in the original charter of the International Labour Org. and in the law of the U.K. by the Equal Pay Act, 1970. The Equal Opportunities Commission was set up under the Sex Discrimination Act, 1975, to keep the working of the 1970 Act under review and to eliminate differences of treatment. The combination of high taxation and equal opportunities has tended to relegate the upbringing of children to persons and institutions other than their families.

EQUERRY originally meant stables and then the officers in charge of the King's horses and, since 1526, an officer in attendance on the Sovereign.

EQUITY (see ENGLISH LAW) arose out of the deficiencies of the Common Law, e.g. at Common Law a plaintiff deprived of an heirloom could get compensation for the loss, but not (which he probably preferred) the heirloom itself. Plaintiffs aggrieved by such defects started as early as the 13th cent. to petition the Crown for supplementary remedies suited to their needs, especially in land disputes, and the Chancellor (through whose hands such petitions passed) began, initially by delegation to adjudicate upon them, originally as a matter of grace and then systematically as the various types of cases accumulated and became classifiable. His **Chancery** Court became a separate judicial organisation in which he, dispensing Equity, was the only judge. Equity naturally owed much to Roman and Canon Law because until Tudor times Chancellors were ecclesiasticals, but it was fully developed in 18th cent. (See ELDON.) It is based on principles of which four stand out: (1) it acts against the person through the threat of imprisonment for contempt; e.g. the Chancery court fixed the boundaries of Pennsylvania indirectly by threatening to imprison the defendant (Lord Baltimore) until he executed the necessary documents which would settle them; (2) it uses its powers to enforce trusts as obligations; (3) it provides remedies such as injunctions additionally to or in substitution for monetary compensation where the latter is inadequate; (4) it follows the Common Law. The Chancellor was distracted from his judicial work through being a politician, Speaker of the House of Lords, a cabinet minister and saddled with a multiplicity of other detailed duties. Hence as business increased, congestion in his court became serious. Moreover as Equity and Common Law were administered in different courts, the parties in a case with both aspects had to shuttle back and forth between the Common Law Courts at Westminster Hall and the Chancery Court in Lincoln's Inn. This compounded the delays and cost. Various efforts to alleviate the problems with additional judicial manpower broke down. In 1873, accordingly, the Judicature Act imposed a radical solution. All the various courts were turned into divisions of a single Supreme Court any of which might exercise the powers available to any other of them, with the proviso that where there was a (rare) conflict between Common Law and Equity, Equity should prevail.

EQUIVALENT, THE. A sum of £398,085 10s. sterling payable to Scotland under the Act of Union, 1707 to compensate Darien stockholders for their losses, to redeem the Scots national debt, which consisted of annuities and deferred payments, to reimburse those who might suffer from the recoinage contemplated by the Act, and to provide £2,000 a year for seven years to encourage Scottish fisheries and industry. It proved to be insufficient, and unpaid claimants were given 4% *Equivalent Debentures* charged on the Customs and Excise. These were not honoured, but after six years arrears of interest were added to the capital which was replaced by 5% *Equivalent Debentures* amounting to about £250,000. Though many Scots had, in the interval, sold out at a discount, this stock formed the basis of the capital of the Royal Bank of Scotland incorporated by statute in 1727.

ERASMUS, Desiderius (?1466-1536) s. of a priest of Rotterdam or Gouda became Latin secretary to the Bp. of

Cambrai in 1494; he went to Paris in 1495 and got to know the Blount family who invited him to England in 1499. He was patronised by Abp. Warham and John Fisher and became a friend of Grocyn, Colet, Linacre and Thomas More. In 1500 he began his travels in Europe, discovering at Louvain in 1504 Lorenzo Valla's *Annotations* to the New Testament. He returned to England and exerted much influence on English thought at Oxford and Cambridge through his contacts. He became Lady Margaret's Professor at Cambridge in 1511. He had by this time and at More's home finished the famous satire *In Praise of Folly*. The *Annotations* turned his attention to New Testament studies and led to the publication, from Basle of his *Greek Testament* in 1516. His two other major works, *Jerome* and *Institutio Principis Christiani* (Lat = The Ideal Christian Ruler) were also published from Basle. From 1517 to 1521 he was at Louvain; from 1521 to 1529 at Basle and from 1536 at Freiburg, but he died at Basle. His sensible influence, pervasive rather than combative, has tended to spread internationally with the centuries. *See* RENAISSANCE 10-11.

ERASTIANISM (from the Swiss theologian Thomas Erastus (1524-83)) is the subjection of the church to the state. He expounded this doctrine, which was also that of Grotius, in answer to Calvinism and though Richard Hooker owed much to him as early as 1594, his treatise was first published in English as *The Nullity of Church Censures* in 1659.

ERFURT (Ger.) a Saxon bishopric founded by St. Boniface in 742, was a great commercial centre until about 1600. It passed to the electorate of Mainz in 1664 and to Prussia in 1802. The **CONGRESS (Sept-Oct. 1808)** marked the apogee and downturn of Napoleon's empire. He summoned virtually all European rulers and the Czar Alexander I to co-ordinate military action against Austria. With Talleyrand's encouragement, Alexander refused. The DIET (Mar. 1850) was called by Prussia in an unsuccessful bid to form a German union, in which Prussia and Austria should have equal rights. The four second class states preferred the less aggressive Austrian leadership and the scheme collapsed.

ERGING (Welsh) IRCINGAFELD (A.S.) was the easternmost part of modern Gwent, held by the Welsh throughout the Anglo-Saxon period.

ERGOTISM (or St Anthony's Fire), an often lethal poisoning caused by a rye fungus, tended to follow famines when spoilt grain was eaten. It appeared mainly in France and Germany, but there were outbreaks in England in 12th cent. Ergot as an obstetrical drug was known in 1582 but used professionally only from 1777.

ERIC BLOODAXE. *See* YORK, SCANDINAVIAN KINGDOMS-B6.

ERICSSON, John (1803-89). *See* IRONCLADS.

ERIE, Lake and Canal. The British and Iroquois developed trading along the lake after its discovery by Jolliet in 1669 and the founding of the French fort at Niagara. Cadillac established the French fort at Detroit in 1701. The British took Niagara in 1759 and Detroit in 1760. The lake became international after the American revolution, when United Empire Loyalists settled the north shore. U.S.A. settlement did not begin on the south until 1796, Buffalo being founded in 1803. The lake was the scene of a British naval defeat in 1812. The U.S. Erie Canal, built between 1817 and 1825, formed a major vested interest against the construction of the St Lawrence seaway.

ERIN. Old name for Ireland.

ERITREA. *See* ABYSSINIA.

ERKENWALD St. (?-693) founded the great monasteries at Barking and Chertsey and became Bp. of the E. Saxons in 676.

ERLE, Thomas (?1650-1720) as an M.P. for forty years from 1678 was well known to contemporary politicians as a dependable Protestant, but was primarily a soldier. He supported William III's landing in England and fought in

his Irish and continental wars. From 1694 to 1712 he combined the Governorships of Portsmouth and the I. of Wight yet was sent to Spain where, in 1707, he commanded the centre with credit under Galway at the disastrous B. of Almanza. He then resumed his post at Portsmouth from which, with 7,000 troops, he was transferred to Ostend to organise allied supplies across inundations for the arduous siege of the great fortress of Lille. This he achieved, once with a huge wagon convoy and at another period by means of a sub-naval war with boats against galleys across the flooded countryside. Lille could not have been taken without his pertinacious but unsung ingenuity.

ERMENBURGA, St. (?-?700) niece of K. Erconbert of Kent, received the wergild from K. Ethelbert for her brother's murder and applied it in founding a famous nunnery at Minster in Thanet, of which she was the first Abbess (c. 670) and her *d.* St. Mildred the second. *See also* MILBURGA, ST.

ERMINE STREETS. The Saxon name, derived apparently from the Earningas, a tribal group settled near the R. Cam, of two Roman roads whose Latin names are unknown. **(1)** London, Ware, Godmanchester, Chesterton, Stamford, Great Casterton, Ancaster, Lincoln, Brough, York. **(2)** Silchester, Thatcham, Speen, Warborough, Cirencester, Gloucester.

ERNEST or ERNST AUGUSTUS. *See* CUMBERLAND, D'S OF-5.

ERNEST AUGUSTUS (1674-1728) a nephew of George I became D. of York and Albany and P. Bp. of Osnabrück in 1716. *See* HANOVER.

ERPINGHAM, Sir Thomas (1357-1428) an able and devoted Lancastrian, entered the service of John of Gaunt in 1380 and was with him in Spain in 1386. Thereafter he served John of Gaunt's *s.,* Derby, whom he accompanied to Lithuania in 1390 and 1392 and on his exile in 1398. When Derby became Henry IV in 1399, Erpingham became Warden of the Cinque Ports and Chamberlain of the Household. He was with Clarence in Ireland from 1401 to 1403, became Lord Steward in 1404 and having fought at Agincourt in 1415 represented the King in subsequent negotiations with the French.

ERROL. *See* HAY, FRANCIS.

ERSKINE, John, E. of Mar. *See* JAMES VI-5 *et seq.*

ERSKINE, Ebenezer (1680-1754) the redoubtable founder of the Scottish Secession Church, was deposed from his charge at Stirling in 1733 for protesting against the Assembly's censure of his views on elections to vacant charges. He promptly formed an Associate Presbytery, published in 1736 his *Judicial Testimony* against the Scottish Church and he, with his followers, was expelled in 1740. Nevertheless, he and they backed the right horse in 1745-6 against the rebels and their church was thereafter tolerated by the Govt.

ERSKINE, Sir James St. Clair (1762-1837) 2nd E. of ROSSLYN (1805), M.P. from 1781 to 1784 and from 1790 to 1805, was a manager of Warren Hasting's impeachment but also a soldier. He was Adj-Gen. at Toulon and in Corsica (1793-4) and military C-in-C in the Mediterranean in 1805. In 1806 he was sent on the special mission to Lisbon which decided the Govt. to send Sir Arthur Wellesley's expedition to Portugal. In 1834 he was briefly Lord President. *See* WEDDERBURN.

ERSKINE, William (1773-1852), an Indian lawyer and magistrate, helped to draw up the Bombay Code but in 1823 was driven from office by accusations of defalcation. He had made a study of Persian and published the valuable translation of Babar's *Memoirs* in 1826 when he settled in Scotland. He was provost of St. Andrews from 1836-39. His *History of India under Babar and Humayun* was published in 1854.

ERW (Welsh). *See* CANTREF.

ESCHEAT, -OR, -RY (1) If a feudal tenant died without heirs or was convicted of a felony, his land passed (or escheated) to the Lord, but in a case of felony the Crown first had the land for a year and a day and also took the movables; but the rules applied only to lands owned by him at Common Law, therefore if it was vested in trustees for his benefit, no escheat took place because his interest was not a Common Law interest and they were not the felons. In the disturbed state of politics this encouraged the development of the law of trusts.

(2) An escheator was an official appointed, respectively for the area north and south of the Trent, and in Munster from 1236 onwards until 1833. His duty was to extend (= survey) the lands of a tenant-in-chief at his death or during an episcopal or abbatial vacancy and to take them into the King's hand if he was without heirs; but since an extent would be needed to assign dower, establish a wardship, effect a division between heiresses or between heirs in gavelkind, or assess the incidence of a relief, it was convenient to commit the administration of these and other feudal incidents to him. This took much detailed legal and surveying work from the sheriffs and resulted in the work being organised by pairs of counties known as escheatries.

ESHER, Viscounts. *See* BRETT.

ESKIL, St. (?-1080). *See* MISSIONS TO EUROPE-5.

ESKIMOS or ESQUIMAUX, are N. American aboriginal nomads who live on the Arctic coasts and islands from the W. Aleutians to Greenland, where from the 10th cent. they had contacts with the Vikings. In 1970 there were roughly 50,000 who were beginning to live a more sedentary life.

ESPANIOLA. *See* HISPANIOLA.

ESPERANTO (= Hopeful). An artificial language intended for international use, combining features of several western languages with a phonetic spelling and without grammatical exceptions. It was launched in 1887 and has an organisation with branches in most countries including Britain and a considerable literature mainly in translations. Its logical perfection does not seem to appeal to most imperfect human beings, and so far it has been used mainly by its enthusiasts.

ESPRINGALE. A small mediaeval engine, the equivalent of the Roman *ballista* which threw spears or stones. It was operated by tension and a large bow.

ESQUIRE was originally an apprentice knight. When feudalism decayed the title was used as a minor honorific. William Camden and others drew up lists of those entitled to the distinction, which included most people of substance and the holders of most public offices. It also includes barristers, military captains or the equivalent in other forces (or higher) and anyone who has been addressed as 'trusty and well-beloved' by the sovereign in, for example, a commission or warrant.

ESSAYS AND REVIEWS (1860), on Anglican religious subjects were edited by Henry Bristow Wilson (1803-88) and the other contributors were C.W. Goodwin (1817-78) the Egyptologist and only layman, Benjamin Jowett (1817-93), Mark Pattison (1813-84), Baden-Powell (1796-1860), Savilian prof. and investigator of optics and radiation, Frederick Temple (1821-1902) later Abp. of Canterbury and Rowland Williams (1817-70). The authors had all reached their conclusions before Darwin published the *Origin of Species*. Applying commonsense and logic to the texts, they proposed a liberal interpretation of the Bible and the Fathers, doubted the Genesis account of the Creation and proposed a revision of doctrines hitherto based upon literal interpretations. They used strong language intended to shock. The publication attracted little attention until Bp. Wilberforce attacked it with his usual extremist fervour. A meeting of bishops condemned it in a pastoral letter (1862) and Wilson and Williams were condemned by the Court of Arches for heresy and deprived for a year. The Privy Council reversed the sentence, whereupon 11,000 clergy signed a declaration of their belief in the divine authority of the scriptures and Convocation issued a condemnation

which reflected their attitude but was otherwise without effect. The controversy excited much press comment and illustrated the obscurantism subsisting at the time.

ESSEX or EAST SAXONS, KINGDOM. This tribal state was ruled by **(1) Sledda** who married Ricula, sister of Ethelbert of Kent; their son **(2) Sebert, Saberet or Saba (?-616?),** dependent upon Ethelbert, was converted to Christianity at about the same time as his uncle and received Mellitus in London. He was succeeded by three sons as Joint-Kings: **(3) Sexred (?-626). (4) Saeward (?-?)** and **(5)** (perhaps) **Sigebert (?-?).** These refused baptism and eventually drove Mellitus out, but were killed in a W. Saxon invasion led by Ceawlin and Cwichelm. The son of (4), **(6) Sigebert or Sebert the Little (?-?)** reigned in dependence on the W. Saxon K. Cynegils. His kinsman **(7) Sigebert or Sebert the Good (?-654?)** followed him as a vassal of Oswiu of Northumbria, who had him baptised in 653 in Northumbria by Bp. Finan. Oswiu subsequently sent Cedd to preach in Essex but Sigebert was assassinated by two of his kinsmen and followed by another kinsman **(8) Swithelm (?-665)** who reigned as a Mercian vassal, jointly with his uncle **(9) Sebbi or Sebba (?-695)** who, in his turn brought in **(10) Sighere (?-710).** Sebbi and Sighere disagreed on religion, Sighere reverting to paganism during the plague of 664 and this provoked Sebbi to get Wulfhere of Mercia to send a mission under Erkenwald, who became Bp. of London. Sebbi died in the odour of sanctity. Sighere then shared the kingship with **(11) Sighard (-?710)** and his brother **(12) Suefred (?-?)** and they appear to have been used by Ethelred of Mercia as local viceroys in Kent until expelled by the Kentish K. Wihtred. They were succeeded by the son of (11), **(13) Sigemund (?-?),** his distant relative **(14) Saelred (?-746)** and then by a son of (13). **(15) Swithred (r. 746-98)** and the son of (14), **(16) Sigeric** and lastly **(17) Sigered,** by which time the area was a poor dependency of the kingdom which happened to be supreme.

ESSEX AFFAIR (1804-5). Britain, to stop the neutral trade between France and her W. Indian colonies, applied the 'Rule of 1756'. To evade this U.S.A. ships carried cargoes to home ports and then onward to France or the relevant colony. One of these, the *Essex,* was seized and condemned by the Admiralty Court because the voyage was really continuous. Thereafter the British operated more successfully against the trade. *See* ANGLO-AMERICAN WAR 1812-5; BLOCKADE.

ESSEX, Robert Devereux, E. of. *See* ELIZABETH 1-28 *ET SEQ.* AND DEVEREUX-2.

ESSEX, Es. of. *See* BOHUN; BOURCHIER; FITZPETER; GEOFFREY; MANDEVILLE; GEOFFREY OF.

"ESTABLISHMENT", THE. An alleged group or conspiracy of like-minded people in high places to maintain the existing British state of affairs. It was invented by Anthony Sampson and naturally attracted journalistic attention. There is no certain means of identifying its supposed membership, nor evidence of matters on which it is supposed to agree: on the contrary there is much evidence of fundamental disagreements on everything of any importance.

ESTAING, Charles Henri Theodat, Comte d' (1729-94), French Officer, commanded troops in India where he was taken prisoner and escaped. He then raided the Persian Gulf with a pair of ships and was again captured. During the War of the American Rebellion, he commanded a powerful French Fleet sent in 1778 to assist the rebels. His sluggish command resulted in the capture of Grenada and St. Vincent, an indecisive action against Sir John Byron and in 1779 a disastrous repulse from Savannah.

ESTATE DUTY. *See* DEATH DUTIES.

ESTATES OF THE REALM. In England the three estates were variously said to be crown, clergy and laity, or prelates, lords and commons. In Scotland they were prelates, lords and commonalty. The phrase was never of much legal importance, though Scots Conventions of Estates, assembled without royal authority, could be turned into Parliaments with it.

ESTLAND or EASTLAND. The northern part of Estonia.

ESTONIA. *See* BALTIC; BALTIC REPUBLICS.

ESTO PERPETUA (Lat = Remain for ever) CLUB (1784), a Foxite Club against Pitt, which in *Criticisms on the Rolliad* issued Whig political satires in the form of reviews of an imaginary epic on the adventures of a mythical ancestor of John Rolle, M.P., a supporter of Pitt. These were followed by *Probationary Odes,* directed at the poet laureate Thomas Warton and other miscellaneous political pasquinades. The authors are uncertain.

ESTRÉES, Jean d' (1624-1707), was a French general by 1668 but then transferred to the navy. In the Third Dutch War (1672-4) he commanded the French component in the Anglo-French Fleet at Solebay (May 1672), two Bs. of Schooneveldt (May and June 1673) and at the Texel (Aug. 1673). His 2-in-c, Duquesne and the English commanders strongly criticised his tactics and even his good faith. In 1676 he commanded a fleet against the Dutch W. Indies. He took Cayenne but wrecked the fleet. The influence of his relative Gabrielle, Louis XIV's mistress, saved him and he became a Marshal and Gov. of Brittany.

ÉTAPLES, Ts. of (3 Nov. 1492) between Henry VII and Charles VIII (q.v.) of France. Each side undertook not to support the other's enemies or to condone piracies; Henry agreed to hold his claim to France in abeyance and Charles VIII agreed not to help Henry's rebels (i.e. Perkin Warbeck) and to pay him 50,000 francs a year. It freed Charles for his Italian policies. The pension was paid until 1511. *See* HENRY VII-10, 15.

"ETC OATH" was enjoined by Art. XI of the canons of 1640. Schoolmasters, bachelors and doctors of divinity, law and medicine and church dignitaries had to swear not to alter the govt. of the church by "Archbishops, bishops, deans and archdeacons etc, now established."

ETHEL- (A.S. = noble or royal) for A.S. names beginning thus *see also* AETHEL-.

ETHELBALD, K. (716-57). *See* MERCIA, KINGDOM OF.

ETHELBERT II of Kent. *See* KENT, KINGDOM-5.

ETHELBERT, LAWS OF (c. A.D. 600). A Kentish list of ninety money penalties for particular offences including breach of a King's, Earl's and Ceorl's peace and offences against the Church.

ETHELBURGA, St. (fl. 666). Her brother Erkenwald, Bp. of the E. Saxons founded the double monastery at Barking and made her its first Abbess. Bede describes her as 'upright and constantly planning for the needs of her community'. Her memory was revered for many centuries in London and her church in Bishopsgate survived all vicissitudes until it was destroyed by an Irish bomb in 1993.

ETHELDREDA, St. (or ETHELFRYTH) (?-679) *d.* of K. Anna of E. Anglia was married, but as a virgin wife, to Tondberht E. of the Gyrwas until he died in 652. She then retired to the I. of Ely which she owned, but in 660 contracted a political marriage with the young K. Egfrith of Northumbria. It was agreed that she should remain virgin but when later he wished to consummate the marriage, she retired on St. Wilfrid's advice to Coldingham (672) and then founded the huge double monastery at Ely (673) which she ruled ascetically until her death.

ETHELFLEDA, Lady of the Mercians (?-918 or 920). *See* EDWARD THE ELDER.

ETHELFRID. *See* NORTHUMBRIA.

ETHELGAR or ALGAR (?-990) was Abp. of Canterbury from 988.

ETHELHARD or ADELARD (?-805) as Offa's nominee was elected Abp. of Canterbury in 791 but consecrated only in

793. A Kentish rebellion against Mercian ecclesiastical supremacy drove him out in 796, but he returned in 798. He visited Rome and under a compromise arranged with Leo III in 802, Lichfield was deprived of its archiepiscopal status and Canterbury was retained by Ethelbard. These arrangements and the supremacy of Canterbury were acknowledged at the synod of Clovesho of 803. He was a lifelong friend of Alcuin. *See also* ENGLISH MONARCHY, EARLY.

ETHELNOTH THE GOOD (?-1038) a relative of the Wessex King, was Canute's chaplain, became Abp. of Canterbury in 1020 and supported the claims of Hardicanute at Canute's death.

ETHELRED I (?-871). *See* ENGLISH MONARCH, EARLY-5; ASHDOWN; ALFRED.

ETHELRED II, THE UNREADY (r. 978-1016) (for the sobriquet *see para 10 below*) and his *s.* **EDMUND Ironside (r. Apr.-Nov. 1016). (1)** Ethelred aged ten, succeeded his half-brother Edward after the latter's assassination at Corfe and dishonoured burial at Wareham. Ethelred's mother Aelfthryth was implicated and nobody was ever punished. The whole episode horrified contemporary opinion. The reign began in contempt and discredit. The Mercian alderman Aelfgar demonstratively translated the body to the nunnery at Shaftesbury whence, of course, miracles were soon reported.

(2) The weaknesses revealed in the previous five reigns (*see* AETHILSTAN'S SUCCESSORS) had at least been compensated by the strong and disinterested influence of St. Dunstan. Now the power of the child King was being directed by a reputed murderess and aldermen who filched church property and got royal charters to confirm their thefts. Nor, as Ethelred grew up, did he have much opportunity to set things right. There were menacing developments in Scandinavia. Harald Bluetooth, K. of Denmark had built up a restless power which was shut off from Germany and impoverished, like everyone else by the great famine of 976. Some resented his autocracy and when Ethelred was twelve (980) dissenting Vikings appeared in numbers in the English seas for the first time for over 40 years. For two years they took much loot and slaves from the south coast and Cheshire. The King could not protect his people. The court camarilla was too busy feathering nests. During the quiet six years after 982, Swein Forkbeard succeeded K. Harald (985) and his ally Olaf Trygvasson made headway in Norway. Swein substituted royal direction of Viking activity for private enterprise. In 988 the raids were resumed on a formidable scale. Defence had devolved upon local initiatives. The thanes of Devon made a gallant and acclaimed stand but there was no resistance in Somerset. In 991 Olaf Trygvasson was heroically resisted at Maldon (Essex) by Alderman Brihtnoth in a battle made famous by a poem. By now Ethelred was 23, his mother was dead and the influence of churchmen was in the ascendant. Ethelred recognised Edward as a martyr and made apologetic references in public documents to his own misdeeds, that is to say, those of his mother's friends. The churchmen roundly asserted their belief in the incompetence (or worse) of the magnates. They had a policy.

(3) As no central force existed and local ones were now inadequate, the churchmen proposed to buy the Vikings off, by means of a national tax (*see* DANEGELD COINAGE). There was plenty of silver in England. The idea represented a form of national preventive insurance. The lay magnates at large would contribute most of the money instead of the men with whom most of them had so conspicuously failed to go to war successfully, and death, damage and the wholesale abductions of war would be avoided. The share of each would, of course, be much less than the burden of constantly calling out the men, perhaps for weeks, let alone losing them while the fields were untilled and cattle neglected, if not stolen.

As the arrangements took time to make, the plans must have been laid at the latest in 990. The first payment was made immediately after the B. of Maldon.

(4) The disadvantage was that the Vikings came back for more. Human nature apart, Swein needed the money to finance ventures against countries nearer home. In 993 Vikings ravaged Yorkshire. In 994 Swein and Olaf Trygvasson made a great joint assault on London and were bought off. The negotiations were conducted by the remarkable Bp. Alphege. In the next three years Olaf invaded Norway and began its Christianisation. This reproduced in converse the situation of 980. Danish Vikings were only supplemented by Norwegian dissidents. Nevertheless they attacked the south coast from Thanet to Lyme three years running (997-9).

(5) These Channel raids were to have a pregnant consequence. Many of the raiders used ports in Normandy with its Scandinavian population of kindred spirits. Diplomatic acrimony ensued. The loot enriched the Normans whose Duke could not or would not control them. In other raids the Vikings used Cumbrian or Manx havens. There was a revulsion against the Danegeld. It seemed time to take some of it back. English forces ravaged Cumbria and Man (1000) at a time when the Norman Duke was coming round. Thereupon Vikings attacked Normandy and there was an English foray into the Cotentin. The situation was rendered infinitely more dangerous by the defeat and death of Olaf Trygvasson at the B. of Svold (1000) for Norway passed under Danish control.

(6) The wars and disorders had loosened allegiances, as people, unable to rely on the King, fended for themselves or compounded with the enemy. Moreover the mixed population contained a self-conscious Danish element particularly around the Five Boroughs. At about the time when the King married Emma, d. of Richard, D. of Normandy, it seemed that Sweyn was organising a conspiracy. Ethelred's court evidently got wind of it and when Sweyn appeared off the I. of Wight with a small squadron, they launched a pre-emptive and sensational massacre of English Danes on St. Brice's Day (12 Nov. 1002). Sweyn landed and sacked Wilton and Sarum, but Alderman Aelfric in charge of the Wiltshire and Hampshire fyrd refused to take any action against him.

(7) After this failure at internal subversion, Sweyn resumed the policy of annual raiding until 1007, when Ethelred purchased a two year truce for £30,000. The respite was meant to be used to reorganise the defences and build a fleet. In 1009, the new fleet was concentrated at Sandwich to anticipate the expected arrival of the enemy. There were denunciations and recriminations among the leaders. A part of the fleet deserted and another part sent in pursuit, was lost in a storm. The King, with the depleted force retreated to London just before the Scandinavian invasion arrived. It was commanded by Thorkel, E. of the Jomsvikings, his brother Heming in charge of the Danes and Olaf Haraldsson (later St. Olaf) the Norwegian. Olaf attacked London unsuccessfully while Thorkel fortified a camp at Greenwich. They then devastated a wide circle of land round the city and routed the East Anglians near Thetford. The English defences collapsed and the King offered to buy Thorkel off. Before the negotiations ripened, Olaf stormed Canterbury and seized the Abp, Alphege (Alfheah). To everyone's surprise, Alphege flatly refused to pay any ransom. He was taken to Greenwich and spent the next months arguing with his captors. He probably converted Olaf to Christianity. At Easter the King's gafol of £48,000 was paid over. There was much contention between Olaf's following and the others. In the course of a great breaking-up party the Danes did Alphege to death. A few weeks later Olaf set off southwards, probably to recruit Normans for an attempt on Norway, but Thorkel took service under Ethelred. This

extraordinary fact seems explicable only if Ethelred needed protection against dissatisfied English, for when Sweyn appeared in 1013 with a great force he did nothing to oppose him. By the end of the year, Sweyn had exacted undertakings of submission from most of the north and west. London decided to surrender. Ethelred took refuge with his father-in-law in Normandy, where he met Olaf and made an agreement with him.

(8) K. Sweyn died suddenly in Feb. 1014 (slain, it is said, by St. Edmund of East Anglia in a dream.) His s. Canute was with the fleet at Gainsborough (Yorks) and the fleet instantly acclaimed him. The southern English magnates, on the other hand, invited Ethelred to return. The restoration was, however, effected by Olaf who landed at Charmouth with Ethelred's s. Edward (later the Confessor), marched unheralded up the Fosse Way and surprised Canute who was driven to his ships. The Danes evacuated England, whereupon Olaf moved into Northumberland and embarked on his long planned expedition against Norway.

(9) Two events now combined to make **Edmund Ironside** the real ruler. The English aldermen, led by Edric Streona, advised Ethelred to depose Sigfrith and Morcar, the leading lawmen of the Danish Boroughs. During a council at Oxford, Edric invited them to his lodging, murdered them and hustled Sigfrith's widow Aldgytha off to Malmesbury Abbey. Realising that nothing was more likely to set indigenous Danes and English against each other, Edmund took Aldgytha out of the abbatial custody and married her. Almost immediately Canute, who had only gone to the R. Scheldt to refit, returned to Dorset and marched across Wessex. In London Ethelred took to his bed. Edric raised the Wessex forces and Edmund joined him from the north. They quarrelled and Edric went over to Canute. Edmund did not despair but could not raise enough men to cope with the crisis without Ethelred's consent. Ethelred dragged himself from his bed to be present with the levy, but the delays had given Canute time in which to overrun Northumbria, kill its Aldermen and come round to London by sea. When he reached it, Ethelred was dead.

(10) Ethelred means royal counsel. Unred means not advised or no counsel. Ethelred Unred sounds like a wry soldier's joke (cf. 'order, counter-order and disorder').

(11) The Londoners and some of the magnates chose Edmund to succeed him, but many West Saxon nobles and churchmen submitted to Canute. Danish forces, however, were beaten by Edmund in a battle at Otford and withdrew from the siege of London to regroup. This opening success was partly reversed at the B. of Ashingdon (or Assendun) (S.E. Essex) where many English leaders, including Ulfcel Snilling, perished. Edmund and Canute then agreed to divide England, leaving Wessex to Edmund and the rest to Canute with, probably, a pact of mutual succession (T. of Olney), at least in England, for when Edmund died on 30 Nov. 1016 Canute became unopposed King of all England.

ETHELWIG (?-1077) an able churchman at Evesham, combined careful observance, commonsense, generosity and compassion. When Abbot Mannig of Evesham fell ill in 1059 he persuaded Edward the Confessor to entrust the govt. of the abbey to Ethelwig and he succeeded to the Abbey automatically at Mannig's death. William I entrusted far-reaching secular authority to Ealdred of York and Ethelwig. Ethelwig's covered the seven western shires of old Mercia. His fairness and wisdom were widely valued. In 1072 the abbey owed the service of five knights to the crown. In addition to Evesham, he administered Winchcombe and the two abbeys sent monks north to revive Benedictine monasticism in Anglo-Saxon monasteries destroyed by the Vikings. After William harried the north, Ethelwig made Evesham a haven for refugees and gave the care of some of the little boys among them to individual monks and servants of the Abbey. Later he gave timely help to Bp. Wulfstan of Worcester in defending the rights of his see against Thomas of Bayeux, Abp. of York. In admiration for his character and sense, the King ensured that the Abbey lost no property to Norman settlers and actually increased its lands.

ETHELWOLD, St. (c. 908-984) Bp. of WINCHESTER (963) a friend of St. Dunstan and St. Oswald, was born of a noble family at Winchester and was ordained with Dunstan by the heroic St. Alphege. He was a monk under Dunstan at the newly restored monastery at Glastonbury and was sent to restore the dilapidated house at Abingdon. It flourished under him and he despatched one of his young monks to the distinguished French house of Fleury to learn more of Benedictine practices. In 964, K. Edgar at his instance, arranged for the substitution of Benedictines for the secular clerks then in the Old and New Minsters at Winchester. The new communities achieved a high standard of observance and his energy and imagination inspired wider projects. He acquired derelict sites in the Fens and organised the rebuilding of monasteries at Peterborough (966), Ely (970) and Thorney (972). With monks from Ghent and Fleury, he drew up the *Regularis Concordia,* the monastic standardisation which emerged from the great Synod of Winchester in c. 970. This drew on continental practice but with English modifications, particularly regarding prayers for the King and Queen and the election of bishops in monastic cathedrals. This, by favouring monks, affected the tone and personnel of the episcopate even after the Conquest. An overwhelming personality, he was exceptionally versatile, acting as cook, mason, smith, bell-founder and organ-builder. He founded the Winchester school of vernacular writing, the Winchester style of illumination and originated the English musical polyphony. He also wrote a treatise on the circle.

ETHIOPIA. See ABYSSINIA.

ETHYLLT (fl.? 825). See GWYNEDD-9.

ETON COLLEGE was founded in 1440 by Henry VI, on the model of Winchester College and its link with a university college, and comprised 70 scholars supported by a large endowment drawn in part from suppressed alien priories, while scholars of King's College Cambridge (founded in 1441) had to have been on the foundation of Eton for at least two years. The first Provost, William of Waynflete, was headmaster of Winchester until appointed and brought half the first scholars with him from Winchester. Building was much interrupted by the Wars of the Roses and other upheavals and completed only in 1523. Its proximity to Windsor ensured royal interest and aristocratic patronage and it expanded more quickly than the other public schools, though like them it had its depressed period in the 18th cent. Its revival was due to George III's interest. The curriculum was wholly classical between 1500 and 1851 when modernisation began with the introduction of mathematics. By 1900 it was the largest of the public schools with 70 Kings Scholars and over 1000 oppidans.

ETRURIA (Staffs). The name of Josiah Wedgwood's pottery works and so to its district, when it was established in 1769 with its village for his work people.

ETRURIA. Bonaparte converted Tuscany into the Kingdom of Etruria in 1801 for Louis of Bourbon-Parma a son-in-law of Charles IV of Spain. His *s.,* Charles Louis, succeeded in 1803, under the regency of his mother Luisa. In Jan 1808 they were dispossessed so that Bonaparte's sister Elise could become Grand Duchess of Tuscany. The kingdom was not revived at Vienna, but Luisa was given the duchy of Lucca to compensate for Bonaparte's wife, Marie Louise's life tenure of Parma. *See* PENINSULAR WAR 1807-14 1-2.

ETSI DE STATU **(1297).** See CLERICIS LAICOS.

EUGENE OF SAVOY, Prince (1663-1736) *s.* of the exiled Countess of Soissons was refused a commission by Louis XIV, swore eternal enmity to him and entered imperial service. He displayed great courage and energy in the War of Devolution against France, became a field marshal in 1693 and in 1697, as C-in-C against the Turks, won the great victory at Zenta which led to the reconquest of Hungary. After a difficult campaign against the French he became Pres. of the Imperial War Council in 1703. He then campaigned brilliantly with or independently of Marlborough (*see* SPANISH SUCCESSION, WAR) but in 1712, after the British desertion of the alliance was defeated by Villars on the Rhine in 1716. When the Turks attempted a reconquest of Hungary he defeated them at Peterwardein (Petro Varadin), captured Temesvar and stormed Belgrade. He died in Vienna, where his Belvedere Palace commenced a new decorative style.

EUGENIUS III Pope. *See* CRUSADES-7.

EUGENIUS IV Pope. *See* RENAISSANCE-7.

EULOGIUM HISTORIARUM **(Lat = Praise of Histories)** written at Malmesbury (c. 1367) is a compilation from earlier authorities including William of Malmesbury and Geoffrey of Monmouth, but from 1356 to 1366 it is contemporaneous, and a continuation, valuable for the parliamentary proceedings under Richard II, was written in the first half of the 15th cent., possibly by John Trevor, Bp. of St. Asaph.

EUPEN and MALMÉDY were part of Austrian Limburg until 1801 and after a period of French rule were transferred to Prussia in 1814. Under the T. of Versailles (1919) they were ceded to Belgium in 1920. because the populations were predominantly Walloon, thus adding to the many real and imagined German grievances against the treaty. The two areas were reannexed to Germany during World War II and promptly returned to Belgium after it.

EURATOM *See* EUROPEAN UNION.

EUREKA STOCKADE (Dec. 1854). *See* BALL[A]ARAT.

EURO. The name given in 1995 to the projected European currency.

EURODOLLAR (E.D.) and EUROBOND (E.B.) MARKETS. The E.D. Market arose out of transfers by the U.S.S.R. of its dollar balances from New York to London during the Cold War. These were not subject to British banking regs. and could be manipulated as if they were off-shore funds. The E.D. Market expanded when European interest rates were substantially higher than U.S. and U.S. banks transferred dollars in search of them. Hence the Market became an extra-U.S. source of dollars and gave rise in 1963 to the E.B. Market for longer term investment.

EUROPE, COUNCIL OF, was set up at Strasbourg in May 1949. It had 15 member states and developed influential cultural activities but failed in its original purpose of political unification.

EUROPEAN COMMUNITIES AND UNION (E.U.) (*see also* EUROSPEAK) **(1)** The E.U. is the outcome of a movement towards political unification of mutually defeated continental countries, originally inspired by the Belgian Statesman Paul Henri Spaak, maintained by Jacques Delors, the French Pres. of the European Commission, and proceeding tactically by creeping accumulation of concessions by national govts. to common agencies. These, well spaced out, were unlikely, individually, to provoke much opposition, but cumulatively would in time neutralise such opposition as might eventually develop. The first was the creation by Benelux, W. Germany, France and Italy (T. of Paris 1951) of the "European" Coal and Steel Community to which was added a "European" Atomic Energy Community. These were calculated to exploit other European countries by a semi-monopoly of power and raw materials. A Defence Community (May 1952) collapsed (Aug. 1954) when France refused to ratify it.

(2) In the Second Stage (T. of Rome 1957) these six created a common market for themselves and **(3)** in the

Third (1967) the Market and Communities were merged into a "European" Economic Community (E.E.C.) designed to eliminate all obstacles to the movement of trade, capital and persons between the six signatory states. It was also intended to attract other countries by the threat of economic pressure and the inducement of participation in a new large protected trading system.

(4) It being politically risky to remove the internal obstacles all at once, the treaties set up machinery to do it slowly through harmonisation and approximation of national laws. The machinery comprised (a) the "European" COMMISSION, consisting of two commissioners nominated by each major signatory and one by each lesser. These must swear not to take orders from any govt. They with their staffs (not initially large) in Brussels constituted a permanent research body ostensibly to discover particular legal disharmonies and conflicts and make proposals for their elimination to (b) the COUNCIL, which had and has no permanent members, but consists of the national ministers responsible at home for the agenda items placed before them for a particular meeting by the Commission. These will have been debated during gestation by (c) the then nominated European "parliament" in Strasbourg and (d) the larger, also nominated expert Economic and Social Committee in Paris. The "Parliament" and Committee have consultative influence but no effective power. The initiative thus lay with the permanent Commission for the Council could consider nothing but its proposals, but the legislative decision lay with the politically variable Council. A Council meeting composed of heads of govt. is sometimes called a "Summit" by the media which equally often use this term for a meeting outside the ambit of the E.U. (e) Council legislation takes three forms. (i) REGULATIONS alter the law of member states. The many (ii) DIRECTIVES state the purpose for which given laws of member states must be altered but leaves them to make the changes themselves. These two types are conveniently called EUROLAWS. (iii) An Opinion binds only the Commission. Any Eurolaw overrides any national law and as a democratic national parliament cannot be trusted to obey a directive, the power to enact directed law is withdrawn from the parliaments and committed to the executives. (f) In addition a "European" COURT at Luxemburg resolves disputes in national courts about the interpretation of Eurolaw. These must be referred direct to Luxemburg by the court (no matter how inferior) where they arise, by-passing the national system of appeals. (g) The whole apparatus is financed by a percentage levy on VALUE ADDED TAX (V.A.T.) and consequently states must institute V.A.T. as a condition of admission.

(5) The British public knew nothing of the above and was not told.

(6) The territory of the Six approximated to that of Bonaparte's empire and the dominant partner in 1957 was France, as being larger than Benelux, richer than Italy, much less war-damaged than Germany and geographically better placed than any of them. Moreover she was headed by a Bonaparte type, Pres. Gen. Charles de Gaulle.

(7) In 1959 Britain formed E.F.T.A. (q.v.).

(8) In 1961 four E.F.T.A. govts. (Britain, Ireland, Denmark and Norway) applied for membership. In 1962 the E.E.C. instituted agricultural support through the Common Agricultural Policy (C.A.P.) which was the converse of the cheaper and better British system, but profitable to French and Italian farmers. Instead of withdrawing the application, the British allowed it to be publicly rebuffed by de Gaulle on the stated ground that the Special Relationship between Britain and the U.S.A. made her over-dependent on the U.S.A. The purpose of this insult was probably to defend C.A.P., but his policy was encapsulated in a private remark that "Britain will in the end have to come to the Council table naked".

(9) The govt. pressed its policy, which entailed dismantling Commonwealth preferences and the agricultural support system, and was again rebuffed in 1967. In 1969 the General resigned, but in 1973 Britain indeed came naked to the table and was admitted as from 1 Jan. 1973 together with Ireland and Denmark. A referendum kept Norway out. In 1975 as a manoeuvre related to British internal politics rather than the merits of the case (which had already been decided) the Wilson govt. invited the electorate to approve what had been done and it did so in a referendum.

(10) Even in 1958 the Commission was planning a Eurocurrency punningly called the E.C.U. (in French *ecu* means a coin of high value, and the initials stood for European Currency Unit) which was placed on the public agenda in 1969. Thus by accession in 1973 Britain was committed to *faits accomplis* including the constitution (*see* 4 above), major policies such as C.A.P. and negotiations for a single currency soothingly called European Monetary Union (E.M.U.). These needed administration in which the Commission was perforce, though unsuitable, involved. Plainly an administration had to be created or the Commission turned into one. The problem expanded with the accession of Greece (1981), Spain and Portugal (1986) and would expand further with expected further accessions. If the Market was to be more than a trading area it needed a govt; if only a trading area (on which the British referendum had been held) then the positive common policies would have, for lack of instruments, to be abandoned. National govts. with large agricultural electorates (France and Italy) could not face the latter, those with large financial concerns (Britain and Germany) the former. Moreover there had been a shift in the E.E.C.'s internal balance. By 1983, recovery had made Germany not France the leading continental power. The imbalance was to become very marked in 1990 with German reunification. The result was the Single European Act (1986) which made procedurally unworkable additions to the powers of the Parliament (elective since 1979), proclaimed that the movement towards unification was irreversible and initiated preliminaries towards a European Monetary System (E.M.S.) (q.v.).

(11) In Dec. 1991 heads of govts. agreed to negotiate revisions of the T. of Rome to conform with the Single European Act and this was done in the T. of Maastricht (1992). This converted the Commission into a govt., altered the voting balance in the Council by overweighting the votes of the smaller powers, allowed for non-economic Euro-functions such as the formation of an army and police force, and set in train the eventual creation of a European Monetary Institute or Bank able to lay down policies and fine govts. which did not conform with them. The implementation of the treaty was delayed by a Danish referendum (*see* below) and distorted by the German reunification (1990), for the degradation of the East under Russo-Communism called for vast investment. The German Federal Bank (*Bundesbank*) accordingly set high interest rates in order to attract foreign capital to finance the E. German substructure. These rates dragged German inflation well above the qualifying average rates for the creation of monetary union under the treaty.

(12) The nature of the Maastricht negotiations was not disclosed to the British public, no copy of the draft treaty being available through H.M. Stationery Office until 1992. The slow realisation that huge sectors of British sovereignty had been quietly bartered away to the Union provoked a movement called EURO-SCEPTICISM encouraged by a preliminary rejection in a well informed Danish referendum. On the other hand the Major govt's continued pressure to reduce the internal rate of inflation, while maintaining unemployment, lowered the average rate to which the *Bundesbank* would have to return to attain monetary union.

(13) Meanwhile by 1993 subsidy abuse (e.g. quick lorry turn-rounds across frontiers without delivery of subsidised goods), pointless public works (e.g. roads on the I. of Gomera), favouritism and ordinary corruption had become notorious. These issues surfaced in the "parliament" in 1998 over the activities of Mme Edith Cresson, E.U. Commissioner for Education and Science, but a motion to dismiss her failed of its necessary 2/3 majority. In Mar. 1999, however, financial and accountancy experts reported such outrageous manipulations and irresponsibility that the Commissioners resigned in a body to retain their pension rights rather than await dismissal. They continued, with doubtful legality as "caretakers" until July. *See* ACCESSION TO THE E.U.

EUROPEAN FREE TRADE ASSOCIATION (E.F.T.A.) of Austria, Denmark, Iceland, Finland, Norway, Portugal, Sweden and Switzerland was set up in 1959 under the T. of Stockholm and was associated with Britain as an organisation of states which did not wish to join the Common Market. When Britain and Denmark joined the Common Market in 1973 the Association slowly broke up.

EUROPEAN MONETARY SYSTEM (E.M.S.) involving ultimately a single currency was to be heralded by an EXCHANGE RATE MECHANISM (E.R.M.) designed to empty out the content of separate currencies by requiring the countries of Europe involved in it to intervene in money markets so as to maintain the exchange values within tolerances close to the relationships prevailing in 1988. Britain joined the E.R.M. in Oct. 1990 (just as Germany was reunited) and wisely left it in Sept. 1992.

EUROPEAN RECOVERY PROGRAMME was composed by 16 European countries in 1947 and set out how the aid promised by the Marshall Plan would be utilised.

EUROSPEAK comprises suspect linguistic usages in which familiar expressions convey different concepts from those generally understood. The most important cases are as follows (*fam* means the familiar meaning in English; E.S. the meaning in Eurospeak).

Council (fam) a local authority; (E.S.) the European legislature.

Directive (fam) an important rule requiring obedience enforced by a sanction; (E.S.) A direction to a member country to alter its law, but not in force until it does so.

European (fam) pertaining to the geographical European continent; (E.S.) pertaining to the area of the E.E.C. or E.U. for the time being.

Federalism (fam) the division of powers between a central govt. and local states; (E.S.) The concentration of the powers of the local states in central hands.

Parliament (fam) a sovereign legislature; (E.S.) An official discussion forum at Strasbourg.

Regulation (fam) a minor rule made under law; (E.S.) The most important kind of rule, superior even to an Act of Parliament.

Subsidiarity (no fam) The idea that power should be exercised by the most locally available authority but in subordination to those higher up. This un-English word has a French etymology.

EUSTACE of BOULOGNE. *See* EDWARD THE CONFESSOR.

EUSTACE (?-1215) Bp. of ELY and chancellor from 1197, was Richard I's envoy to Philip Augustus on the latter's infringements of the peace agreements. He was one of the bishops employed by Innocent III to force John to accept Langton as primate in 1208, or face an interdict. He pronounced the interdict and escaped.

EUSTACE s. of King Stephen. *See* STEPHEN-1.

EVACUEES were non-essential civilians, especially children, who were moved out of big cities likely to be bombed just before and during World War II and resettled with receiving families. Some were sent to Canada. The others tended to drift back.

EVANGELICALISM (1) A Reformation term for protestantism, in German speaking countries it came to mean Lutheranism as opposed to Calvinism. **(2)** In 18th century Britain the term meant a movement for religious regeneration within the Church of England led by the Wesleys and Geo. Whitefield (1714-70); it was distinguished by Calvinistic outlook, earnestness and austerity, combined with mass popular preaching and an addiction to good works. Among its most influential practitioners were the Clapham Sect. Evangelical fervour was behind the creation of the Church Missionary Society and many practical reforms, notably the suppression of the slave trade and slavery, the Sunday School movement and the Factory Acts. **(3)** In 1846 an interdenominational body called the Evangelical Alliance was formed in London to defend Protestantism ('against Popery and Puseyism') and to promote scriptural Christianity. It was eventually supported by protestant sects in most countries and remained influential until World War I. **(4)** The Evangelical Union was a mainly Congregationalist sect formed in Scotland in 1843.

EVANS and CHRISTIE. Timothy John Evans (?-1950) was convicted of murdering his infant daughter and hanged, mostly on the evidence of John Reginald Christie (?-1953). A charge of murdering his wife was not pressed. Later the bodies of six women, including Christie's wife, were found under the floor-boards. Christie was convicted of murdering her. Doubts about Evans' guilt now arose. A first inquiry, before Christie's execution, reported that there had been no miscarriage of justice. In 1966 after parliamentary pressure, Mr Justice Brabin, after an exhaustive public enquiry, reported that Evans had probably not murdered his daughter but probably had murdered his wife, for which he had not been tried. A posthumous pardon was issued.

EVANS or CROSS, Mary Ann (1819-80). *See* ELIOT, GEORGE.

EVANS, Adm. Edwards Ratcliffe Garth Russell (1880-1957) Ld. MOUNTEVANS (1945) ('Evans of the Broke') relieved Scott in the Antarctic in 1902 and 1904 and was with him on his last expeditions in 1912 and 1913. In World War I he commanded destroyers in the Dover Patrol and when in command of H.M.S. *Broke* fought a celebrated action in Apr. 1917 when he rammed a German destroyer. He was for a while Chief of Staff at Dover. He had various adventures as a Captain after the war and in 1929 became Rear-Admiral commanding the Australian squadron. He was spectacularly popular in Australia and also from 1931 as C-in-C on the African station. Here in the absence of the high commissioner, he was involved in the Tshekedi Khama affair. Tshekedi, regent of Banangwato, had a European flogged for seducing tribal women. Evans with a force of sailors suspended and expelled the European. This caused great excitement and controversy. He was C-in-C at the Nore from 1935 to 1939 and in World War II liaison officer to the K. of Norway during the German invasion and then Regional Commissioner in London until the end of the war.

EVANS, Sir George de Lacy (1787-1870) soldier in India, the Peninsula and the U.S.A. was M.P. for Rye in 1831 and for Westminster 1833. From 1835 to 1837 he commanded a British volunteer force in Spain against the Carlists. He was again M.P. for Westminster in 1846; and in 1852 he commanded a division in the Crimea in 1854 and was yet again M.P. in 1857 and from 1859 to 1865.

EVANS, Sir Evan Vincent (1851-1934) champion of Welsh Culture was Secretary of the Welsh National Eisteddfod from 1881 and of the Honble Soc. of Cymmrodorion from 1886. He retired in 1922.

EVAN'S SUPPER ROOMS (Covent Garden, London) from 1830 to 1880 was an early music hall, where the all-male performers and the patrons competed in blue entertainment and songs. Women could enter only on giving their name and address and had to sit behind a screen. The Prince of Wales was a frequent visitor in the 1860s.

EVAN-THOMAS, Sir Hugh (1862-1928) commanded the relatively fast 5th (15" gun) battle squadron at Jutland in 1916. His conduct aroused controversy and was criticised by, inter alios, Winston Churchill. Beatty, commanding the even faster battle cruisers, however, thought that he had been well supported. He was C-in-C at the Nore from 1921 to 1924.

EVELYN, John (the Elder) (1620-1706) joined Charles I in 1642 and from 1643 travelled the continent in learned pursuits. He married the 12-year-old daughter of the English ambassador in Paris in 1647. He returned home permanently in 1653, becoming, in due course a civil servant. With Wilkins and Boyle he had by 1660 evolved the scheme for establishing a 'Royal Society' to promote the extension of knowledge by experiment. In 1671 he became a member of the Council for Plantations; in 1672 Secretary of the Royal Society and from 1687 a Commissioner of the Privy Seal. Having moved to Wotton in 1694, his tenant at Deptford, Adm. Benbow sublet the house, Sayes Court, to Peter the Great, who wrecked it. He was an authority on architecture and landscape gardening, besides numismatics and published several learned works in his lifetime, but his well-known *Diary* was not published until 1818.

EVENING NEWS, founded in 1861, was bought up on the verge of collapse by the Harmsworths in 1894. In 1960, still flourishing, it absorbed the *Star*.

EVENING STANDARD founded as the *Standard* in 1827, became the *Evening Standard* by amalgamation in 1905 with the *St James' Gazette* founded in 1880. In 1923 it absorbed the *Pall Mall Gazette*.

EVEREST, Mt (Nepal), the highest mountain, is named after the Indian surveyor, Sir George Everest (1790-1866). It was first climbed in 1953 by Edmund Hillary and the Sherpa Tensing, members of a British expedition.

EVERTSEN. Dutch naval family. Four Evertsen admirals commanded against the English. **(1) Jan (1600-66)** commanded the Dutch reserve at the Battle of The Kentish Knock (Sept. 1652). He fought at Dungeness (Nov.), Portland (Feb. 1653) and took command when Tromp was killed at the Texel (July). He was killed at the Battle of St James' Day. **(2) Cornelis the Old (1610-66)** commanded a squadron in the Four Days Battle and was killed (June 1666). **(3) Cornelis the Younger (1628-79)** was Vice-Adm. under de Ruyter when he raided the Medway (June 1667) and fought at Solebay (May 1672) and the Texel (Aug. 1673). **(4) Cornelis the Youngest (1642-1706)** commanded a squadron against the American colonies, captured New York in 1673, escorted William III to England in 1689 and fought under Adm. Herbert against the French at Beachy Head (June 1690). Seven other members of the family died at sea fighting the English.

EVESHAM, B. of (4 Aug. 1265). In May 1265 William of Valence and William of Warenne landed in Pembrokeshire and on 29th the Lord Edward escaped from Hereford. Simon de Montfort summoned his military following across the Severn through Worcester but when Edward and the Marchers captured Worcester the troops had to be diverted to Hereford while Simon tried to get troops from Llywellyn, P. of Gwynedd. None appeared. Then Edward and the E. of Gloucester, by taking Gloucester, obstructed his line of retreat across the Severn. His outnumbered army, with Henry III in custody, managed to ford the river at Kempsey on 2 Aug. hoping to unite with troops raised by his son Simon around Kenilworth, but on 4th, Edward and Gloucester caught the father at Evesham where he and two of his sons were killed, another captured and Henry III rescued.

EVIL MAY DAY 1517. London apprentices under cover of traditional celebrations attacked foreigners and sacked their property, doing immense damage, as a supposed consequence of a xenophobic sermon preached by a Dr. Bole at St. Mary Spital a fortnight earlier.

EWART, William (1798-1869) free trader M.P. for Bletchingley (1828-30), Liverpool (1830-2 and 1835) and Dumfries Boroughs from 1841. Piloted an act for restricting capital punishment in 1837 and another which founded the public library system in 1850.

EWE. A Togoland tribe similar to the Ashanti, living partly in Ghana.

EXAMINER (Aug. 1710-June 1711) a Tory weekly started by Henry St. John (later Vist. Bolingbroke) to combat Steele's *Guardian*. It reflected a mood of war weariness and was very widely read. Jonathan Swift took over the editorship in November 1710 and accused the Dutch and Marlborough of protracting the War of the Spanish Succession in their own interests.

EXARCH in recent times was the special deputy of an orthodox patriarch.

EXCALIBUR (corruption of CALIBURN, perhaps related to or even confused with the Irish word CALADBOLG = Voracious). The name of King Arthur's sword given through Merlin by and returned through Sir Bedevere to, the Lady of the Lake.

EX CATHEDRA. *See* INFALLIBILITY, PAPAL.

EXCELLENCY in British and diplomatic practice is the style of a person who represents a sovereign, i.e. governors of dominions and colonies, heads of diplomatic missions and foreign ministers of govts. when addressed by diplomats.

EXCESS PROFITS (E.P.) TAXATION was taxation at a high rate on profits which exceeded the average profits of a given business during a standard period immediately before the tax came into force. Originally imposed in response to complaints of war profiteering, the E.P. DUTY (1915-21) varied between 40% and 80% on profits exceeding £200 above the average of any two years in the period 1911-1914. Farmers and professions were exempt. The E.P. TAX (1939-45) on all profits above the 1938-9 level was levied at 60% up to Apr. 1940, 100% until Dec. 1945 and then at 60% again. Professions were exempt and 20% for the 100% period was refunded (subject to Income Tax) to re-equip businesses in 1946. The E.P. LEVY (1954-6) at 30% was based on the amount by which profits after Jan. 1952 exceeded (by £5,000) the average profits of the years 1946-51. This taxation encouraged wasteful expenditure.

EXCHANGE CONTROL, modelled substantially on the system invented by Dr Schacht and the German Reichsbank in 1934, was introduced into Britain as a wartime measure under the Defence (Finance) Regs. 1939 and made permanent by the Labour Govts. Exchange Control Act, 1947. The world was divided into Scheduled Territories and the rest. The Scheduled Territories were the countries of the British Commonwealth and British Protectorates and Trust Territories plus Iceland, Jordan, Kuwait, Libya, South Africa and South Yemen. Foreign currency was defined as currency not issued by the govts. of any of the Scheduled Territories and it became illegal for any resident in the United Kingdom except an authorised dealer to deal in such foreign currency or in gold except with the permission of the Treasury and anyone with such permission had to offer currency or gold in his possession but not needed for his purpose, to an authorised dealer. United Kingdom residents were also forbidden in or outside the United Kingdom to make payments or transfers of securities for the benefit of foreign residents and there were elaborate related provisions about imports and exports. The permissions and orders under the Act put foreign exchange dealings into the hands of a narrow circle of banks and specialist dealers and resulted in due course in the creation of a system of Treasury spies abroad and in the opening of mail at United Kingdom points of entry.

EXCHANGE EQUALISATION ACCOUNT. When Britain went off the Gold Standard in 1932 this fund was established to regulate temporary exchange fluctuations, but in practice it was also used to prevent the pound rising.

EXCHANGE, ROYAL (London) was founded in imitation of the Amsterdam Exchange by Sir Thos. Gresham in 1556. It was burned in 1666 and its successor in 1838. The next building was opened in 1844. Its function as an exchange was eroded by the growth of more specialised exchanges such as the Baltic, The Stock Exchange, the great banks, Lloyds and the now defunct Coal Exchange. In 1982 it was occupied by small shops and offices.

EXCHEQUER (1) The Norman King's Council had a general secretariat, some of whose members specialised in finance and accountancy; to these taxes, rents and dues were paid and through them the King's debts were settled. This secretariat also dealt with such businesses as foreign relations, raising troops and swearing in high officers. The earliest indications of a separate Exchequer organisation date from Henry I (1100-35) when it was probably directed by Roger of Salisbury, his great Justiciar. In these early days the Exchequer was a session of the King's Court (see CURIA REGIS) to oversee financial business, that is to say, an occasion rather than a place or an institution. There were two great sessions each year, one at Easter and the other at Michaelmas when the sheriffs and other accounting officers rendered final account for the money collected for the King. This marked the end of the Exchequer year.

(2) The financial business tended to fall into three classes: routine collection and disbursement, revenue disputes and important dispositions. The two latter were initially decided by meetings of councillors at the Exchequer, but as law was elaborate, techniques and organisation improved. Two offices developed. In the lower, Exchequer of Receipt, money was received, tested and weighed: in the upper, accounts were settled between the Crown and its debtors, especially the sheriffs. By 1118 the tables here were covered with a chequered cloth, which together with counters and an abacus, were used for making the calculations. This cloth, the origin of the name, still covered the table in 1818. The Lower Exchequer was really a branch of the much older Treasury located at Winchester throughout the 11th cent. and most of the 12th.

(3) All the great officers were present at such settlements, which occurred twice a year, and the Justiciar commonly presided. It was convenient to hold Council meetings at such times and this maintained the connection between the Council and the Exchequer. Moreover records and the Great Seal were kept there. Revenue and business, however, increased and specialists knowledgeable in financial routines and revenue law were needed. The highest of these were the Barons of the Exchequer who already existed in 1179. The 12th cent. Exchequer was, however, more than a financial bureau. The court held in the Exchequer was in effect the court of the Justiciar, the King's alter ego and this was the age of the Justiciars especially when the King was abroad, and the Exchequer was the centre of Govt. where judicial and policy as well as financial decisions were made. The work had expanded so far, that it was virtually a permanent institution, settled after 1172 at Westminster. Then the disappearance of the Justiciar placed new burdens on the Chancellor, who developed in his Chancery a secretariat of his own. He became an increasingly political officer who followed the King whereas the Exchequer was settled for long periods at one place, originally Winchester later Westminster but with occasional excursions e.g. to Shrewsbury or York. He ceased to attend the Exchequer but left his clerk, later called the Chancellor of the Exchequer, to represent him. The latter eventually became the Head of the Exchequer staff, while the Barons by 1234 had developed into judges. By 1312 they had a Chief Baron.

(4) During the 13th cent. a contest developed

between the Exchequer and the Chancery which attained great bitterness in the period 1295-1316. In this the Exchequer was identified with the more autocratic policies of the Crown, the Chancery with the opposition. At the beginning of Edward II's reign, the Treasurer (Walter Langton) was deposed. He returned in 1312, was driven away and in 1315 was deposed again. The primary issue was the appointment of the sheriffs and so the ultimate control of local administration. The Lincoln Parliament of 1316 determined that they should be appointed through the Chancery, which henceforth also kept the Parliament Rolls.

(5) Thereafter, though it retained vestiges, some ceremonial, of its ancient political power the Exchequer developed on the one side into a financial bureau and on the other into a separate court (see EXCHEQUER, COURT OF). The financial business was ultimately limited to the control of receipts and payments. After 1688 the Exchequer ceased to be an executive organ and slowly became responsible to Parliament for the surveillance of the flow of funds into and out of the Treasury. These functions were transferred in 1866 to the Comptroller and Auditor General and 'the Exchequer' (otherwise called the Consolidated Fund) became the statutory term for the Govt. bank account at the Bank of England.

EXCHEQUER, COURT OF (see CURIA REGIS-6 *and previous entry*) **(1)** The separate Exchequer Plea Rolls began in 1236; the Barons of the Exchequer had an accepted senior by 1280 at which time the King still sometimes presided himself. Ordinances of 1270 and 1277 and statutes of 1282 and 1300 forbade the Barons to hear Common Pleas and in 1312 a Chief Baron was appointed. This marked the restriction, lasting until the 16th cent., of the court's jurisdiction virtually to revenue cases. Throughout this period, the Chief Barons were usually also judges of the Common Pleas and the Barons were considered inferior to the other judges. They had, however, become professional lawyers. They lost their technical knowledge of accountancy and by 1323 a Cursitor Baron who understood accounts was being appointed. He advised his brethren and examined the sheriffs' accounts until 1834.

(2) The court began in about 1560 to encroach on the Common Pleas in matters of contract and by way of the writ of Subpoena, upon the Chancery. Both these extensions were founded upon the fiction that the matter complained of made the plaintiff less (*Quominus*) able to satisfy a Crown debt. By 1579 the courts reputation had raised the reputation of the Barons who, henceforth, with the other judges, rode the circuits.

(3) Amalgamated with the High Court in 1875 it ceased to be a separate division of it in 1879.

EXCHEQUER, STOP OF (Jan. 1672-Jan. 1673). *See* CHARLES II-14.

EXCHEQUER TALLIES were primitive if foolproof receipts, consisting of a squared stick across one of the flat surfaces of which cuts and marks of varying sizes were made, each conventionally representing units of money from £10,000 down to pence. The accounting officer paid in his money; the tally was cut to correspond with the sum paid in. It was then split lengthways down the middle of the relevant surface, so that he and the Exchequer each had a cut and marked portion which tallied exactly with its counterpart when fitted together. The larger part with the handle or stock was kept by the Exchequer: the smaller by the payer. The stocks accumulated in enormous numbers in the cellars of the Palace of Westminster and became, as the sums represented increased, larger and larger, eventually as much as 8 feet long. They were also very dry. In 1832 it was decided to re-organise the system and burn the tallies. They generated so much heat that the Palace caught fire and was burned to the ground. Hence, Scott and Pugin's Houses of Parliament.

EXCISE, in origin a Dutch tax (excijs or accijs) was copied in 1643 by the Parliament whose ordinance created the Office of Excise or New Impost. The tax is charged upon home goods during manufacture or before sale but at that time it included certain duties imposed, in addition to Customs, upon foreign goods. The Restoration Parliament continued the tax: the main targets were beer, ale, cyder, perry, metheglin and mead, vinegar and spirits and there were higher rates upon these things if imported. Chocolate and coffee were also taxed. From 1697 to 1880 there was an excise on malt and from 1710-1862 on hops but between 1820-80 (when it was reimposed) there was no beer excise. These taxes were administered by Excise Commissioners who appointed their own gagers or valuers, hence Dr Johnson's definition of excise (1755) as 'a hateful tax levied upon commodities and adjudged not by the common judges of property, but wretches hired by those to whom excise is paid'. **(2)** At various times, other taxes were known as excise because they were collected through the excise machinery. These included 14 types of licence (e.g. guns, pubs, pawnbrokers, tobacconists) and the medicine stamp duty. **(3)** In 1827 the work was transferred to special commissioners and from them in 1849 to the new Board of Inland Revenue. In 1909 it passed to a still newer Board of Customs and Excise, which also administered motor vehicle, petrol and betting duties. Its work expanded enormously after the introduction of Valued Added Tax in 1972.

EXCISE CRISIS 1733. *See* WALPOLE'S EXCISE SCHEME.

EXCLUSION BILLS. *See* CHARLES II-21,23-26.

***EXCLUSIVA.** See* CARDINALS.

EXCOMMUNICATION (1) The mediaeval church used two sorts: the lesser involved only deprivation of sacraments; the greater amounted to expulsion from church and society and could, if supported by a powerful public opinion, bring about the fall of rulers or the flight of lesser persons. **(2)** An English bishop could not excommunicate a tenant in chief without the King's consent (*see* BECKET, THOMAS; CONSTITUTIONS OF CLARENDON). **(3)** Excommunications were rare before the Conquest but in 12th cent. Canon law developed and widened their scope. General sentences against particular classes of offences were first pronounced in the 13th cent. and publicly repeated 3 or 4 times a year. At the Council of Reading in 1279 Abp. Pecham publicly excommunicated infringers of Magna Carta. The use of ex-communication as a Papal political weapon, the mutual excommunications of rival Popes and finally their use to enforce even trivial ecclesiastical judgements eroded public support and proved self defeating.

EXE. This name, standing by itself, or in combination with other syllables is identical with AXE, ESK, USK; with ESCH or AIX on the continent and with ISCA in names of the Roman period. The old Celtic word means 'water' or possibly 'spring'.

EXECRABILIS (1460) Bull of Pius II excommunicating all who appeal from a Pope to a Council.

EXECUTION. This much misused word means the carrying out of any court order but has popularly been appropriated to the act of putting a criminal to death by some recognised means in an authorised place at an authorised time. Such a capital execution requires a warrant (directed to those responsible for carrying it out) signed by the Sovereign, otherwise it is murder. Some terrorist organisations try for propaganda reasons to whitewash some of their murders as 'executions'.

EXECUTION DOCK, near Wapping (London) was the place where convicted pirates were pegged down below high water mark and slowly drowned. From the 16th cent., however, it was more usual to hang them in chains from a high gallows.

***EXEQUATUR* (Lat = Let him be treated)** A direction by a govt. or one of its ministries to recognise the official standing of a Consul.

EXETER or EXON (Lat = ISCA DUMNONIORUM) (Devon). (1) Part of the site was already settled when the Romans came and it was the tribal capital of the Dumnonii under them. The Saxons reached it by c. 690 and they and the Britons apparently jointly shared and defended it, until Althilstan expelled the Britons in 928; he founded a large monastery in 932. The Danes sacked Exeter in 1003 and in 1017 Canute was taking action to have the monastery rebuilt and perhaps to repair the Roman walls, for in 1050 the see of Crediton was moved to Exeter for safety and the monastery became the cathedral. With London, Winchester and York, Exeter had a special status and paid geld only when they did.

(2) It sustained a short siege in 1067 and thereafter William I built Rougemont (= Red Hill) Castle to dominate it. The town, as a port, shared however, in the prosperity of its hinterland (*see* DEVON) and developed a flourishing wool trade and then a cloth working industry with influential guilds, some of which survive as livery companies. The cathedral was rebuilt (1112-c.1390) massively in externals and with splendour inside. Govts. courted rather than bullied the citizens and a long series of charters, beginning with Henry II, conferred guild organisation and fiscal and other privileges on the model of London. By 1537 it was a county of its own.

(3) The resources, attested by much surviving mediaeval secular building, were put under strain by increasing navigational difficulties in the R. Exe; these compelled ships, which in any case were becoming large, to unload further and further below the town quays and led to the building of the great 14th cent. Countess Weir, to improve the fisheries and enable merchandise to be floated instead of carted to the markets. This arrangement was not wholly successful and under Elizabeth I the town authorities built the first English locked canal over 5 miles long, round the obstacles to Topsham. Successive improvements to this kept Exeter in communication with seaborne trade into modern times.

(4) The city exhibited a kind of radical conservatism involving business enterprise combined with a dislike of political distraction. Hence it resisted Perkin Warbeck (1497) for which Henry VII conferred honours; it refused to countenance the Prayer Book rebels (1549) and it supported, perforce, the King in the Civil War. This attention to business and re-investment, made it one of the most beautiful cities in Britain, until the great German air-raid of 1942, which destroyed the central area. This was unworthily rebuilt after World War II.

EXETER BOOK, copied in about 975 was given to Exeter Cathedral by Bp. Leofric (?-1072). It contains many important Anglo-Saxon compositions, especially *Christ, Guthlac, Juliana, the Wanderer, the Seafarer, Widsith, Deor* and *Riddles.*

EXETER DOMESDAY is a survey of the five western counties which contains particulars, especially of livestock not contained in *Domesday Book.* It is very like the eastern counties volume of Domesday called *The Little Domesday* and is thought by some to be a local draft of which the entries in the Great Domesday are the final recension. *See* INQUISTIO GELDI.

EXETER HALL (Strand, London) was a religious meeting place which, from about 1825 became the main focus of humanitarian sentiment and activity, particularly on such issues as slavery and the protection of primitive races in the colonies. Many prominent liberals frequented it during the rest of the 19th cent. The so called Jamaica Committee for prosecuting Gov. Eyre was formed there and included such personalities as Darwin, Thomas Huxley and J. S. Mill.

EXETER, D. of. *See* BEAUFORT, HOLLAND-4,7.

EXETER, E. of. *See* CECIL-5.

EXETER, Ms. of. *See* COURTENAY-6.

EXETER, STATUTES OF (1286) regulated the coroner's duties especially those preliminary to an eyre (1292), and required money bargains and payments to be made in coin of the realm.

EXHIBITION, GREAT (1851) inspired by the Prince Consort, was housed in a huge glass building designed by Joseph Paxton (q.v.) in Kensington Gardens (London) on the site of the present Albert Memorial. Reputedly visited by 6M people, it assembled examples of most types of contemporary arts, crafts, machinery and engineering. Since most of these things were of British origin or invention, it was a vast shop window for British industrialism and imperial investment. Its influence was incalculable in scale and scope, since it introduced to people from all over the globe ideas about which many had never thought before. The considerable profits were invested and used to finance part of the complex of scientific, technical and musical colleges now existing in the neighbourhood, as well as the London Science Museum. The building, re-christened The Crystal Palace, was moved to Sydenham in 1854 and destroyed in a fire in 1936.

EXHIBITIONS, PUBLIC. (1) 18th cent. economic expansion, invention, industrial revolution and wars and colonisation engendered a curiosity which was unsatisfied by the primitive and haphazardly distributed educational bodies, but unorganisedly met by exhibition or public portrayal (with or without charge). **(2)** Among many examples the following, mostly London cases, seem representative. The **miscellaneous** British Museum was generated by the conditional bequest of Sir Hans Sloane's collection in 1753 and the related four times oversubscribed lottery which facilitated the purchase of other collections. **Artistic specialisation** inspired the R. Academy (R.A.) which first exhibited in Pall Mall (1771-9) and at Somerset House from 1780 to 1836. The watercolour painters broke with the R.A. and first exhibited separately from 1805. **Scientific specialisation** came forward with the building of the R. College of Surgeons' Hunterian Museum in Lincoln's Inn Fields in 1803. The miscellaneous habit continued widespread, for example (1820) at Nash's Woolwich Rotunda (developed from a vast ceremonial tent made for the Prince Regent in 1814) but scientific and learned interest grew with the British Museum's library and exotic stuffed animals, and then with the popularity from 1826 of the Regent's Park Zoo. In 1830 King's College next door to Somerset House was arranging public lectures in geology. **Practical science** was soon represented at the enterprising Adelaide Gallery (1832) where visitors began by firing a steam machine-gun and operated model ship-types in a 100-foot tank. It was copied by the Regent Street Polytechnic in 1838. **(3)** These various trends were synthesised in the Great Exhibition of 1851 (*see previous entry*) which, apart from its other effects, inspired the creation of provincial museum trusts supported, after 1892, by municipalities under the Public Libraries Acts. *See also* NATIONAL GALLERY; ROYAL SOCIETY OF ARTS; TATE GALLERY etc.

***EXIIT QUI SEMINAT* (1279) (Lat = "A sower went forth to sow");** Bull of Nicholas III enjoining silence in the Franciscan controversy over the apostolic poverty.

EXISTENTIALISM is an attitude towards moral problems rather than a doctrine, for the modern existentialist writers (Camus, Heidegger, Jaspers, Marcel and especially Sartre and Simone de Beauvoir) diverge wildly in their views. These are, however, mostly related to the unoriginal idea that individuals are responsible for their own acts and are what they choose to be. Hence, they can neither lament their misfortunes nor justify their actions by reference to circumstances; categories such as 'human nature' have no objective reality but are at the most verbal shorthand. The authentic existence is that of the self-conscious individual, as opposed to the human sheep responding to outside pressure or stimuli often arising from herd behaviour in society. Such responses are based on self-deception or even ill faith. Hence, independence, sincerity and conviction are the yardstick by which decisions are justified, and existentialists tend to dwell on extreme situations, not common in ordinary life. Existentialism caused great intellectual excitement in Europe after World War II, but the English public with its instinctive distrust of extremes, had by 1973, proved unreceptive.

EXMOUTH. *See* PELLEW.

EXOGAMY. A custom among tribal Africans and Indians which forbids marriage between members of the same clan, regardless of blood or adoptive relationship.

EXPANDED TOWNS. *See* NEW TOWNS.

EXPLANATION, ACT OF. *See* SETTLEMENT, ACTS OF 1662 AND 1665 (IR.).

EXPLOSIVES (1) Black (or gun) powder reached Europe via the Arabs in the early 13th cent. Roger Bacon left instructions on its manufacture in 1242 and guns were shipped from Ghent to England in 1314. The ingredients (sulphur, charcoal and saltpetre) were first crushed by hand but the first powder mill (water driven) was erected at Nuremberg in 1435. Uneven combustion due to uneven size of grains was eliminated by 'corning' in the 18th cent. William Bickford invented the safety fuse in 1831. **(2)** Nitroglycerine, discovered by an Italian chemist in 1846, was unsafe to use until Nobel invented the fulminate cap in 1865. **(3)** He invented dynamite, a mixture of nitroglycerine and a type of brick earth, in 1867, improved it with wood pulp and sodium nitrate in 1869 and **(4)** in 1875 developed blasting gelatine from it and also **(5)** the ammonium nitrate dynamites. **(6)** Picric acid, the main shell explosive in World War I, came into use in 1880; **(7)** T.N.T. (Trinitrotoluene) in 1904. **(8)** Plastic Explosives were first used in World War II along with **(9)** the armour piercing shaped charges. **(10)** Semtex, an extremely powerful explosive, capable of use in very small amounts, was made in communist Czechoslovakia and sold by way of Libyan finance to terrorists such as the I.R.A., in the early 1980s.

EXPLORATIONS AND 'DISCOVERIES'. (1) The Arabs maintained some memory of Greek cosmology and trading contacts with the Far East and had their own pilgrimages to Mecca, hence the Arab Yaqut compiled a geographical dictionary of 'Discoveries' in the early 13th cent. The Crusaders acquired their impressions from the Arabs and in 1160-73 a rabbi from Navarre travelled from Europe across Asia to Mongolia. In 1245-7 Carpini reached the Mongol court at Karakoram seeking alliance against Islam and so in 1253 did William of Rubruck. The brothers Polo made overland journeys to China in 1255-69 and 1271-88. The latter carefully recorded by the son of one of them Marco Polo. An archbishopric of Peking was established by Friar John of Montecorvino in 1289-1328. Despite these promising beginnings the period of persistent embassies and open trade was also one of rising discontent of the Chinese cultivators against their Mongol overlords and it ended by the rise of the Ming Dynasty in 1368. Already strained by the impact of the Black Death, the Ming ended foreign links with China at the same date as Timur the Great (Tamburlane) began his disruptive conquests in Persia. This ended the first age of modern European relations with Asia.

(2) In 1415 the Anglo-Portuguese P. Henry the Navigator (1394-1460) established his observatory and encouraged exploration and the mapping of the sea routes (1418-), to find those alleged Christian allies in Africa first sought by the Pope in 1316: he also wished to find a new spice route from India, first sought by the Genoese (Doria and Vivaldo) in 1291. In 1487 Bartholomew Dias rounded the Cape and Pedro de Covilham reached India via the Red Sea. Vasco da Gama reached India via the Cape in 1498. (*See* WEST AFRICA.)

(3) Almost simultaneously, but under Spanish patronage, the Genoese Christopher Columbus, reached the Caribbean in 1492 and had touched the American mainland by 1503 (*for the name see* VESPUCCI). De Balboa saw the Pacific by crossing at Panama in 1513. By 1540 the Spaniards had established the geographical outlines of Central and Mexican America.

(4) The first circumnavigation of the world, by the flagship of the Portuguese Ferdinand Magellan, in 1520-1, had the expected effect of fusing concepts that had been developing since 1493, for her east Indian landfalls were not far from areas in which his compatriots, sailing west to east, were already active (1509-1515). Antonio de Mota reached Japan from the west in 1542, the Portuguese establishing a new and regular trade with China from 1547. Their traders in the Spice Is. probably touched N.W. Australia in 1527.

(5) North American explorations lagged somewhat behind; Cartier had twice penetrated the St. Lawrence as far as Montreal by 1535 but little mapping was done until the time of John Davis (1585-7) and Henry Hudson (1610). No Frenchman followed Cartier until La Salle investigated the Great Lakes and floated down the Mississippi to its mouth in 1681. By then there was much colonisation of the western seaboard but the distant interior was little known. McKenzie explored British Columbia and the north in 1589. Lewis and Clark crossed the Oregon to the Pacific on Pres. Jefferson's instructions only in 1804-6.

(6) Vast efforts were needed to venture usefully into the Pacific. Spanish ships made the crossing and explored the Philippines between 1595-1607; between 1642-44 the Dutchman Abel Tasman touched Tasmania (van Diemens land), New Zealand and the Gulf of Carpentaria in a circumnavigation of Australia which still left the existence of that continent uncertain because the navigators thought that their landfalls were on scattered islands. Samoa and Easter Island were found by Jacob Roggeveen, a Dutchman, in 1722. The next great figure in Pacific exploration was James Cooke (*see* COOKE, JAMES and SCURVY) who added immensely to navigational and geographical knowledge between 1768-80 but had been preceded on the North American and Siberian coasts by the Dutchman Bering. Inland Australian exploration did not start until 1813 or end effectively until 1875.

(7) The African coast and north and east Africa had been known to Europeans for centuries or millennia and caravans crossed parts of the Sahara at least since the 10th cent., but inland exploration dates from the foundation of the African Assn. in 1788. The course of the Niger was not established until the Landers' journey in 1830-4; the relationship of the Nile with the Zambesi and the Congo was not mapped until 1880s and no systematic Saharan survey existed until the French made one between 1897 and 1939. In 1993 parts of the Brazilian interior were still only sketchily known.

EXPRESSIONISM was an artistic and literary movement of about 1885-1918, in which it was sought to portray the feeling which things and events arouse rather than reproduce the feelings and events themselves. Vincent van Gogh has been credited with the earliest statement of expressionism, but most of the practitioners were German. *See* IMPRESSIONISM.

EXSURGE DOMINE (Lat = "Let the Lord arise") (1520). *See* LUTHER, MARTIN-2.

EXTENT (1) A widely used type of survey, usually of a manor, setting out the value of a lord's demesne and what he was entitled to receive in rents and services. The names of tenants were commonly grouped by tenure beginning with the freeholders and proceeding down the scale. These extents are a valuable source from the 13th cent. onwards for social and economic history.

(2) Many of the above were in fact surveys and valuations made by a sheriff when preparing to enforce a judgement against a landed debtor. A writ of extent in chief was issuable by the Exchequer to a sheriff for the recovery of a debt to the Crown and directed him with the aid of a jury, to ascertain the debtors lands and goods and seize them. A writ of extent in aid could be obtained from the Exchequer by or against a debtor of a Crown Debtor.

EXTERNAL ECONOMIC FACTORS are those not under the control of a business, but which influence its efficiency e.g. improved communications may give access to wider markets, but pollution may increase illness in the workforce.

EXTRADITION. *See* FUGITIVE OFFENDERS.

EXTRATERRITORIALITY arises where the laws of one state are enforceable in a place within the apparent territorial jurisdiction of another. The most important cases were formerly the European concessions in Chinese ports and the Venetian, Genoese and Pisan quarters in Levantine Ports and at Constantinople and more recently American bases in the British West Indies, the Russian base at Hangö in Finland and the British enclaves in Cyprus. It is uncertain if embassies are extraterritorial or merely immune from the attentions of the local govt. Ships are subject to the law of their flag, but must also conform to the regulations of the foreign port where they happen to be and these, in case of conflict, supersede the law of the flag for the time being.

EYRE, Edward John (1815-1901) known as Gov. Eyre, was a masterful eccentric, *s*. of a Yorkshire vicar. He migrated to Australia, became a squatter on the Lower Murray and in 1841 set about proving the possibility of overland travel between south and west Australia by making the journey from Albany to Perth himself. It took him 5 weeks. He also became a stipendary magistrate and protector of Aborigines. He published his *Discoveries in Central Australia* in 1845 and caught the attention of the London Govt. which appointed him Gov. of New Zealand in 1846. In 1854 he was transferred as Gov. to St. Vincent and Antigua and in 1862 to Jamaica. In 1865 there was a negro uprising which he suppressed quickly and ruthlessly. In consequence he became the centre of a furious controversy. A committee under J.S. Mill was formed to prosecute him, another led by Carlisle and Charles Kingsley to defend him. After a sensational trial in 1867 he was acquitted and pensioned off.

EYRE (Scots. Ayre) JUSTICES in, ARTICLES of (1) (Lat. iter = journey). In 12th cent. Royal representatives were regularly deputed to travel the country. Some conducted judicial business (*see* ASSIZES; TRAILBASTON; KING'S BENCH) but others, the Commissioners or Justices in Eyre conducted mainly administrative investigations under judicial forms. They occurred at rather wide, generally irregular intervals, fixed by 1261 at not less than 7 years.

(2) The Commissioners began by summoning to the county town, at between 15-40 days' notice, all prelates, magnates, knights and freeholders of a county, with the reeve and four men of each township, 12 men from each borough and any others who might be liable to attend. Former sheriffs and executors of sheriffs dead since the last eyre were also summoned and had to bring all writs in their possession. All franchise holders had to bring in their title deeds, and a general proclamation was issued inviting complaints against officials. The issue of the general summons suspended all cases in or from the county before any court except the Exchequer and King's Bench. The sheriff surrendered his office and was re-granted it upon condition of taking an oath to do his duty loyally.

(3) Next the Commissioners conferred with the magnates, took the sheriffs and coroners rolls and pronounced on the franchises. Then the bailiffs of the hundreds were required to empanel juries, to whom the Articles were read. These consisted of a string of questions whose purpose was to extract such information as might enable the Commissioners to impose amercements or fines and they regularly increased in

number: those for London increased sevenfold between 1244-1321. In Kent in 1313 there were 142. They were concerned with neglect of administration, abuse of franchises, royal rights and properties and they enabled the Crown to supervise local administration and supplement its funds. Some strictly judicial business was also done.

(4) The juries were given a date by which to answer the Articles and proceedings would then be founded upon their answers (if true) against any person responsible or against them (if false), for their answers could be checked against the sheriffs' and coroners' rolls and private information.

(5) The eyres were exceedingly unpopular. The Cornishmen took to the woods in 1233 and there was an insurrection in Worcestershire in 1261. The commons petitioned against them in 1348 and obtained a general pardon save for pleas of land, *quo warranto,* treason and felony in 1397. By this time eyres were out of date as a means of augmenting revenue, now based on Parliamentary taxation and superseded by Parliament as a means of enquiry, while enquiries against officials had been conducted at Assizes since 1346.

Justices of Assize were thereafter considered to have the residual functions of the eyre and were rendering non-judicial reports to the govt. as late as 1715.

EYSTEIN, St. *See* MISSIONS TO EUROPE.

F

FABIAN SOCIETY founded in 1884 believed that socialism being inevitable, should not be pursued by revolutionary means. It took its name from the Roman General Quintus Fabius Maximus who avoided direct conflict with the enemy. It powerfully influenced the English Labour Party most of whose intellectuals belonged to it. **FABIAN ESSAYS (Dec. 1889)** by George Bernard Shaw, Sidney Webb, Sydney Olivier, Graham Wallas, Hubert Bland, William Clarke and Annie Besant, set out how socialism could be introduced in a country with free and parliamentary institutions. The Essays derived some publicity from their appearance shortly after the London Dock Strike and were widely read and influential.

FABYAN, Robert (?-1513) was Sheriff of London in 1493 and Master of the Drapers Co. in 1495-6 and 1501-2. His *Concordance of Histories* is from 1159 a chronicle of London and lists the mayor and sheriffs for each year. It has some independent value for the reigns of Edward IV and Richard III. The first edition, which ends at 1485 has later continuations. He probably compiled the second part of the *Great Chronicle of London* (1439-1512) which has contemporary value for 1485 to 1512.

FACTORY LEGISLATION. The first Act (1802) partially regulated the employment of pauper children in factories. Robert Owen's Act 1819, prohibited employment of children under 9, or of any child at night and limited hours for children between 9-16 to twelve. Enforceable only by local magistrates, often themselves employers, the provisions were much evaded. The next acts were concerned with hours in the textile industry as follows:

Year	Ages & Persons Affected	Permitted times pw = per week pd = per day
1833	9–13	48pw – 9pd
This Act instituted factory inspection		
	14–18	68pw – 12pd
1844	8–13	6½ days pw
	women	12 pd
1847	Under 16	10 pd
	women	10 pd
1853 Factories to be open only 12pd		

This type of legislation was extended to

1845	Calico printing	
1860	Bleaching & Dyeing	
1861	Lace	
1864	Pottery and Matches	
1874	Minimum	hours reduced
1875	age 10	to 57 pw
1891	Minimum age 12	
1895	Children	30 pw
	Women	60 pw
1937	Young persons	44 pw
	Women	48 pw
1961 onwards	Elaborate control provisions on hours, health & safety	

See DANGEROUS TRADES.

FACULTY, in canon law is a licence, usually from a Bp. or his consistory court, permitting something otherwise forbidden such as the alteration of a church or an ordination under canonical age. In 1534 the papal faculty jurisdiction was transferred to the Abp. of Canterbury and his specially created Court of Faculties. *See* DISPENSATION.

FAERO Is. became a Danish possession in 1380.

FAGEL'S LETTER (1688). Fagel was the Grand Pensionary of Holland. His *Letter* was a propaganda leaflet widely distributed in England against the policy behind James II's Declaration of Indulgence, which it condemned as intended to let R. Catholics into positions of power, while implying that William of Orange and Mary would persecute no one for conscientiously held beliefs.

FAGGOT VOTE. When a voter's qualification depended upon ownership of a small property, voters were sometimes artificially created by the transfer of small properties to them. These votes were called faggots or dummies.

FAHRENHEIT, Gabriel Daniel (1686-1736), German physicist who lived in England and Holland, introduced the use of mercury into thermometers and devised a temperature scale starting at the coldest thing then known (a mixture of ice and salt), with 180 degrees between the freezing and boiling points of water, on the analogy of the 180 degree half circle. This made the freezing point of water 32 degrees. His scale was still in popular use in Britain in 1990s despite metrication.

FAIRBORNE, Sir Palmes (1644-80) was Governor of Tangiers (1676-78) where he built the mole. He quelled a mutiny of the unpaid troops in 1677. Returning in 1680, he was killed while defending the city against the Moors.

FAIRBRIDGE, Kingsley Ogilvie (1885-1924), born in South Africa, studied forestry at Oxford from 1908-11 and as an amateur boxer made a name among young people. This led him to the idea of populating the empty spaces of the empire with young immigrants who should be trained in farm schools; he and his wife opened one at Perth, Australia in 1913. This was and is the model for the farm school movement.

FAIRFAX. Of this influential northern family the most important were **(1) Sir Guy (?-1495)** Recorder of York in 1476 and Chief Justice in Lancashire. **(2) Sir Charles (?-?)** who routed the Spaniards at Sluys in 1604. His brother **(3) Thomas (1560-1640) 1st Ld. FAIRFAX of CAMERON (1627)** was one of Q. Elizabeth's diplomatic agents with Scotland as well as a soldier, but returned to his Yorkshire estates. His eldest *s.* **(4) Ferdinando (1584-1648) 2nd Ld.,** was M.P. for Boroughbridge in 1622, 1624-26 and 1627 for Yorkshire in the Long Parliament. He took command of the Parliamentarians in Yorkshire in 1642, was defeated at Adwalton Moor in 1643, held Hull until 1644, commanded the infantry at Marston Moor and then became Governor of York. He retired in 1645. His brother **(5) Henry (1588-1665),** a friend of George Herbert, took part in the unsuccessful attempt to obtain a northern university. Ferdinando's *s.* **(6) Sir Thomas (1612-71) 3rd Ld,** a Swedish trained soldier, commanded against the Scots in 1639, became a Parliamentary General in 1642 and after serving at Adwalton and Marston Moors, became Parliamentary C-in-C in 1645. He helped Cromwell to remodel the army, defeated the King at Naseby, and took Bristol and Oxford in 1646. He then found himself balanced between his army whose just desserts he wished to defend and Parliament on whose behalf he commanded it. Moreover, he wanted to prevent further war. He pacified the army but the extremists seized Charles I against his will. He suppressed the Levellers, demanded pay for the army, and in 1648 presented the army's demand for the King's trial. As a member of the Court, he was against the King's execution. In 1649 he became a state councillor and C-in-C, but resigned against the Scottish war in 1650. In 1660 he represented Yorkshire in the Convention Parliament and was one of the commissioners who invited Charles II to return. His cousin (*s.* of 5) **(7) Brian (1633-1711)** acted as a confidential intermediary between Charles II and Gen. Monck in 1659 and was an equerry to Charles II and William III from 1670. **(8) Thomas (1692-1782) 6th Ld.** retired in 1747 to his mother's immense Virginia estates, where *inter alia* he trained George Washington. The surrender of Cornwallis in 1781 is said to have broken his heart.

FAIR MAID OF GALLOWAY. *See* JAMES II OF SCOTS-3.
FAIR MAID OF KENT. *See* RICHARD II.
FAIR ROSAMOND. *See* CLIFFORD.
FAIRS AND MARKETS (1) A market was 'the franchise right of having a concourse of buyers and sellers to dispose of commodities in respect of which the franchise is given' (*Downshire v O'Brien*, 1887). Markets were held at least weekly and mostly for retail dealings of local agricultural produce; fairs were held once or twice a year for traders from a much wider area dealing, often in large quantities or considerable values, and were used as a clearing opportunity to settle loans, debts and negotiable instruments (*see* CHAMPAGNE). In either case in England there was (a) a grant by charter (which might be inferred from immemorial or long user), or by statute; (b) the right to suppress a rival concourse within seven miles; (c) and to settle civil disputes between those attending, in a court of Pie Powder before the steward or mayor; (d) a duty after 1266 to enforce the Assise of Bread and Ale by fine, pillory and tumbrel. Lords of the view of frankpledge or of courts leet, could also punish market offences such as selling bad meat, using false weights or measures, engrossing or regrating and in addition, at certain important fairs local magnates might have special jurisdictions: thus at Winchester (St. Giles Fair) and Hereford the Bp. and at York the Abp. superseded the town authorities during the time of the fair.

(2) The CLERK OF THE MARKET conducted the market held at the King's gate to supply the royal household and laid down the weights and measures to be used there. This method of supplying the court had to be abandoned in about 1290 and the clerk then travelled the 12 mile verge around the court and, *inter alia,* enforced his weights and measures in his own court. A lord of the market's refusal to submit to his jurisdiction was a ground of forfeiture. The income of the clerkship from fines and bribes was very large and attracted Parliamentary protests in 1391-2. The King's court was constantly on the move; charters of exemption were frequently granted and infringed and in 1536 many rights thus assigned were resumed by statute. By 1640 the clerks had extended their jurisdiction beyond the verge and were leasing it county by county. An Act of 1641 restricted the jurisdiction to the verge and transferred the office beyond the verge to mayors and lords of franchise.

(3) By *Scire facias* a franchise could be avoided if inadvisedly made or improperly obtained; and forfeited for misuse, abuse or breach of the conditions upon which it was made. An illegal market could be stopped by *Quo Warranto*.

(4) Because of their obvious convenience to small growers and housewives, markets flourished in many towns and even villages, but there were noticeable inroads on their prosperity with the rise of multiple stores, shopping arcades and privately owned super- and hypermarkets in the late 20th cent. Fairs, however, began to lose their importance much sooner, particularly as clearing institutions, with the rise of banks, and their wholesaling functions withered away as improved communications and policing rendered merchant caravans obsolete. By the 1970s they had declined into travelling amusement shows.

FAIR TRADE (1) smuggling **(2)** reciprocal trading privileges with another country. A league of northern business men was formed in 1881 to press for this.

FAITH, in Christian theology is either *theological* meaning an intellectual act of assent guided by the will, to a truth established by God; or *fiducial* meaning trust in a person such as Jesus Christ. As the possible scope of these ideas is very wide, the use of the word in biblical passages has always to be closely scrutinised for context.

FALAISE (Normandy). The castle, built by Robert the Devil, was the birthplace of William the Conqueror who often resided there. It was taken by Philip Augustus in 1264, but reoccupied by the English from 1417 to 1450. It was the scene of desperate fighting during an Allied attempt to surround a large part of the German force holding Normandy in 1944.

FALA MUIR. *See* JAMES V OF SCOTS (END).
FALCONBERG or FAUCONBERG. *See* NEVILLE.
FALCONET (15-17th cents.). A light (2 pounder) field gun.
FALCONRY (*see* MEWS) is mentioned under K. Ethelbert (c. 760) and reached its highest development by 1600. There were two types: high level and low level using trained but different birds. The hawk was carried hooded on a heavily gloved right hand. The hood (or mew) was removed and the falcon launched at the quarry which was pursued until exhaustion, seized and killed and then dropped. Hunting dogs recovered the quarry. It was a favourite royal sport confined to persons of the highest rank but extended to all free men c. 1215.

FALKENHAYN, Erich v. (1861-1922) was German C.G.S. from Dec. 1914 to the failure of the Verdun offensive in Aug. 1916. He later acted as Turkish Commander against the British, but was recalled in Mar. 1918.

FALKIRK, B. of (22 July 1298). The Scots were led by Sir William Wallace who, after his victory at Stirling Bridge (1297), had been in control of the Scottish govt. Edward I had moved his own govt. to York to deal with him. His army, assembled at Roxburgh in June, comprised some 2400 horse and 10500 Welsh long-bowman. Wallace deployed his pikemen in four *schiltrons* (massed circles) behind a swamp, with Ettrick Forest archers in between. After a slow start, the English cavalry circumvented the swamp, scattered the small body of Scots horse and destroyed the archers. Under Welsh covering fire against the schiltrons, the English cavalry penetrated and broke them up. Edward could not follow up the victory on the day because he had been kicked by a horse the night before. His troops ravaged the countryside as far as Perth, but lost men through sickness and desertions. He withdrew south at the end of 1299.

FALKLAND. *See* CARY.
FALKLAND (Fife, Scot.) contained a Scots royal hunting lodge and favourite palace from c. 1400. The place became a royal burgh in 1458. James V completed the palace and died there in 1542. It ceased to be regularly used after 1603 but has been well maintained ever since.

FALKLAND, or MALOUINES (Fr) or MALVINAS (Sp) Is. (S. Atlantic) were discovered by John Davis in 1592. In 1690 Capt. Strong called the strait between the East and West I. Falkland Sound after his patron Lucius, Lord Falkland. The isles were unoccupied well into the 18th cent., but used for rest and careening by Malouin (= from St. Malo) fishermen and whalers. Bougainville, the French explorer, settled Port Louis in 1764 but in 1765 Capt. Byron garrisoned Port Egmont. In 1766 the Spaniards bought the French out, Hispanicised 'Malouines' as Malvinas and ejected the British, but did not themselves stay. The British claim was never abandoned. In 1829 Louis Vernet resettled Port Louis under the nominal protection of the evanescent republic of Buenos Aires, but in 1833 the British expelled Vernet and his protectors and annexed the whole archipelago. Port William, under the name of Port Stanley, became the capital in 1844 and there has ever since been a trickle of British, sheep-farming immigrants. The islands' peaceful life has been twice interrupted. On 8 Dec. 1914 Adm. Sturdee's battle cruisers surprised and sank Count Spee's armoured cruisers. In 1982 Argentinians invaded the islands and were defeated in a brilliant amphibious operation conducted at the end of communications (via Ascension I.) 8000 miles long.

FALLACY. Aristotle classified fallacies as **(1)** *material,* or misstatements of facts: **(2)** *verbal* or misuse of words: **(3)** *formal* or contrary to logic: or **(4)** *accidental* or proceeding from the general to the particular. This system made its way into Christian thought. J.S. Mill classified them into fallacies **(1)** of simple inspection including prejudices; **(2)** of observation; **(3)** of generalisation; **(4)** of ratiocination or induction; **(5)** of confusion including ambiguity. Close inspection suggests that the two philosophers were farther apart in time than substance.

FALMOUTH, Vist. *See* BOSCAWEN.

FALMOUTH (formerly Smithwick and Pennycomequick) was part of the Killigrew Manor of Arwenack and was a small port from earliest times. Smithwick was granted a parliamentary market charter in 1652 and this, with two fairs was confirmed in 1660. In 1661 the place was incorporated as Falmouth and in 1664 a local act converted it into a parish, thereby making it separately rateable. The corporation was thus one of the earliest to have the basic financial powers of a modern local authority. The local church rate was abolished in 1896. Penrhyn and Falmouth were together represented in parliament by two M.P.s until 1885.

FALSE DECRETALS (or Pseudo-Isidore) were compiled in about 850 and attributed to St. Isidore of Seville who died in 636. They consist of, mostly genuine, canons; some spurious letters of ante-Nicene Popes, and many papal letters from about 330 to 731, 35 of which (including the famous Donation of Constantine) are spurious. The object of the unknown compiler was to strengthen diocesan bishops against their metropolitans and to establish a foundation for papal supremacy. They were used for the latter purpose by Pope Nicholas I as early as 865 and particularly by Leo IX in 1054, and until the Reformation they were generally believed to be authentic, even though the true nature of the Donation was demonstrated at Naples by Lorenzo Valla in 1440. In The Donation, the Emperor Constantine, purported to confer upon Pope Sylvester I (r. 314-335) primacy over the other patri-archates, sovereignty over Italy and the Western Empire and supreme ecclesiastical Jurisdiction.

FALSE or (Sc) WRONGOUS IMPRISONMENT is the unauthorised detention of anyone against his will, even for the shortest time, so as to deprive him of his liberty. Release can be secured by Habeas Corpus and a civil action for damages can be maintained.

FAMILISTS. A mystical sect which held that all people are of one family and that religion is essentially love. It was founded at Emden by Hendrik Niclaes in 1540 and, despite persecution, secured a following in E. Anglia, where it survived until the 18th cent.

FAMILY ALLOWANCES, first appeared in provision for the dependants of those demobilised in 1919, and of the unemployed of 1921. There was controversy in the inter-war years about the need for a comprehensive system not related to unemployment, its champions basing their arguments partly on social principles and partly on the declining birth rate. Their case was conceded in 1945. It probably made no difference to the birth rate.

FAMILY BUSINESSES were the usual type of business organisation in W. Europe from c. 1660 until the rise of joint stock and limited companies gave access to capital markets in the mid-19th cent.

FAMILY COMPACTS. This phrase is most usually applied to **(1)** three treaties involving Bourbon powers (France, Spain, Naples, Parma and Tuscany). The First (1733) was a treaty of political and military co-operation whose main effect was to settle the War of the Polish Succession in favour of France and Spain. The Second (1743) was a renewal of the first but petered out as an influence in international politics at the accession of K. Ferdinand of Spain (1746). The Third (1761) was a secret treaty signed during abortive peace negotiations in the Seven Years' War. It arose from the succession in 1759 of the Anglophobe K. Charles of Naples to the Spanish throne on the death of K. Ferdinand and resulted in the entry of Spain into the war of 1762.

(2) The phrase is also applied to mutual succession

agreements, or other dynastic arrangements, for uniting scattered territories such as Brandenburg.

FAMINE AND DEARTH (1) In Britain and W. Europe between the fall of the Roman Empire and the age of steam, times of dearth (compelling changes of diet) and of local famine (involving rising mortality) were a disagreeable but common feature of life. The following table (applying to the British Is. unless otherwise noted) indicates the best and worst periods, though bad years occurred in good periods, and good in bad.

Good	Bad	Observations
325-515		
	525-30	B. of Camlan
550-90		
	600-6	See of Canterbury founded
610-50		
	695-706	
740-90		
	855-71	All W. Europe
	879	"Universal"
	887-90	Danish invasions
900-30		
	944-89	968 was European wide. **976 (The Great Famine)** a major European disaster. Hungarians invade Germany
	1036-58	
	1069	Northern revolt
	1120-56	Wars of K. Stephen
	1162	World wide
	1235	Especially London
	1252	
	1259	
	1286-1302	Mostly northern countries and Britain
	1321	Last serious English famine
1460-1520		
	1586-1603	Anglo Spanish wars 1600 devastated Russia
1610-89		
	1690-99	War of the League of Augsburg
	1709	Devastated France
1720-70		
	1780-91	French Revolution
1810-30		But Irish potato famine in 1822
	1840-50	Hungry Forties **Great Potato rot 1845-7**

(2) Though some European famines and dearths have been associated with unsuitable weather (too much or too little rain, unseasonable heat or frost) it has not by itself been the necessary or common cause. The persistence of several types in succession may produce famine, but this has been rare. Combination with other natural catastrophes has been more dangerous. Amongst these were the widespread earthquake of 543, the Great Storms which virtually flattened London in 944 and destroyed Glastonbury in 1274. "Locusts" were mentioned in 592, 862 and 1033. Sea flooding permanently engulfed large tracts of Holland in 1286 (which also destroyed Winchelsea), 1296, 1421, 1446 and 1575 and severely damaged the English east coast in 1762. The great Lisbon earthquake (1755) shook the whole Mediterranean basin. Animal epidemics ("murrain") were a factor in the dearths of the 1070s. The Irish famines of 1822 and 1845-6 were caused by plant disease.

(3) A further and important group of factors has been human misbehaviour or incompetence. Of these, lack of transport between glut and famine areas has been eliminated by various forms of mechanical transport, but the destruction, misuse or deliberate withholding of resources in wars, disorders and revolutions has remained potent e.g. in 1709, 1789-91; in Russia in 1921, the Ukraine in 1930-3 and in Ethiopia in 1988-91.

(4) There have also been instances where debility caused by successive dearths or epidemics has caused land to go out of cultivation. This happened during the Black Death.

(5) Outside the special case of India, famines have been occasional and have engendered no permanently established systems to combat them. In India the population depends upon the monsoons; the crop failures have always been frequent, notably however, in 1677, 1769-70, 1790-2, 1803-4, 1837-8 and 1866. As a result of the further disasters of 1868-70, and 1876-8 the British created a permanent famine administration which alleviated the famines of 1896-7 and 1899-1900. Until the coming of railways, the need of draft animals to consume the grain which they were drawing, severely limited the radius within which food could be sent. The later very considerable successes of the British famine administration were due partly to railway development.

FAMULUS (Lat = servant) was commonly landless but worked as a paid labourer on his lord's demesne. His work was undefined and might involve (for example) cultivation, shepherding, threshing, repairing buildings, ditching or dyking as required.

FAN VAULTING. See ARCHITECTURE, BRITISH.

FANE. A Kentish family. **(1) Sir Thomas (?-1589)** was involved in Wyatt's rebellion (1554) but was pardoned because of his youth. He came into favour in 1573 when he was knighted and he married **(2) Mary (1554-1626) Lady Le Despencer.** Of their many children **(3) Francis (?-1628)** became **ld. BURGHERSH and E. OF WESTMORLAND** in 1624. His *s.* **(4) Mildmay (?-1665) 2nd E.,** a royalist in the civil war, was heavily fined by Parliament and in 1660 became Lord Lieut. of Northants. His grandson **(5) John (?1682-1762) 1st Ld. CATHERLOUGH (1733)** a soldier and M.P. became **7th E.** in 1736. **(6) John (1759-1841) 9th E.** formed a lifelong friendship with William Pitt the Younger at Cambridge. He eloped with a Miss Child of Childs Bank in 1782. He was joint P.M.G. in 1789 and Lord Lieut. of Ireland from 1790. As he opposed Pitt's policy of R. Catholic Emancipation he was recalled in 1795 and was then Master of the Horse and from 1798 Lord Privy Seal with only one short break until 1827. His son **(7) John (1784-1859) 11th E.,** known as Ld. Burghersh until 1841 was M.P. for Lyme Regis from 1806-16. He was also Wellington's A.D.C. in the Peninsula from 1809-13 when he became Mil. Commissioner with the Austrians. In 1815 he negotiated the return of the Two Sicilies to the Bourbons. He was Minister at Berlin from 1841-51, and acted as mediator in the Schleswig-Holstein dispute of 1850. He was then heavily involved in the diplomacy preceding the Crimean War but retired in 1855. He was also a well known musician and patron of music and founded the Royal Academy of Music (1823). His kinsman **(8) Sir Henry (1778-1840)** was one of Wellington's most distinguished cavalry commanders in the Peninsula.

FANTI, a Ghanaian coastal fishing tribe related to the Ashanti.

FANTOSME, JORDAN (fl. 1170-5) wrote an Anglo-Norman historical poem on the revolt of 1173-4 which includes the best account of William the Lion's raids into N. England.

FARADAY, Michael (1791-1867) worked for Sir Humphry Davy from 1812; he published a paper on electro-magnetism in 1821; helped Davy to isolate chlorine in 1823; published papers on optics and electricity between 1831-36 when he became scientific adviser to Trinity House. By 1845 he had established the theoretical basis of the dynamo and adumbrated modern atomic theory.

FARM, -ER, FEORM, FOOD RENT. (1) Food rents were a pre-Norman burden upon land but especially an annual amount levied for the royal use upon a specific group of villages, rendered at the royal will and applied by the King's reeve. It was supposed to suffice to support the royal household for a night. Under the Laws of Ine ten hides were to provide 10 vats of honey, 300 loaves, 12 ambers of Welsh ale, 30 of clear ale, 2 cows or 10 wethers, 10 geese, 20 hams, 10 cheeses, an amber of butter, 5 salmon, 20 pounds of fodder and 100 eels. The King might grant the right away, or exempt land from it, if it became bocland. After the Conquest, the system declined but appears in Domesday as the *firma unius noctis* (one night farm) which was later sometimes commuted for a money payment of about £80. *See also* GWESTFA.

(2) Apart from the King's farm, food rents were part of the manorial economy before and after the Conquest, especially on monastic estates. (cf the French practice of *metairie*). The modern word 'Farm,- er' thus originated in two different ideas which became confused: **(1)** from O.E. *feorm* meant food or provision, and hence a meal; (b) from Fr *ferme* and med. Lat *firma* which meant a fixed (firm) periodical (usually annual) payment in kind or money and so, more technically an ascertained yearly composition for rents or taxes to be collected in a given area. A farmer was thus one who himself paid and recouped himself usually with profit, from those liable. This 'letting out' sense was ultimately transferred to the practice of renting land for agriculture.

(3) The FARM OF THE COUNTY or BOROUGH comprised the issues of the King's manors in the area together with the profits of justice in the shire and hundred courts. Until the reforms of 1236 a sheriff paid a fixed sum to the Exchequer and recouped himself in the process of exacting the money. He would make a large profit. Hence the Angevin Kings frequently demanded additional sums above the farm. Such additions were forbidden by Magna Carta (1215) but were exacted again after 1228 because of clipped coinage and inflation. In 1236 the whole system was revised. The royal demesnes were removed from the custody of the sheriffs, leaving only the profits of the hundred and shire courts and some small traditional payments such as 'sheriffs' aid'. Even these had now to be accounted for in detail. Throughout the 12th cent. royal boroughs were included in the sheriffs farm but the boroughs increasingly sought the privilege of paying their own farms, collected by their own officials and levied at a fixed sum in perpetuity direct to the Exchequer. An early case of the grant of such a 'fee farm' was that given by Henry I to London. This particular privilege was later abrogated and Henry II would never grant such privileges in perpetuity, but under his sons many royal boroughs gained this privilege at a price.

FARMER GEORGE. An unsuccessfully pejorative nickname for George III who was a progressive farmer and transformed the crown farms. Under the name of **Ralph Robinson,** the King also contributed to Arthur Young's *Annals of Agriculture.*

FARMERS' CLUBS to promote farmers' interests and social intercourse began with the Farmers' Club founded in 1843 during the Anti-Corn Law agitation. Overtaken politically, they made themselves technically and socially useful. In 1921 the United Dairies established one at Hemyock (S. Devon) which attracted Ld. Northcliffe's interest. In 1922 he reserved some space for them at an Ideal Homes Exhibition and a movement took off and established a Federation.

FARMER'S LETTERS (Properly *Letters from a Farmer in Pennsylvania*) were published by John Dickinson (1732-1808) a Philadelphia lawyer in the *Pennsylvania Chronicle* in 1767-8. They cogently set out the American arguments against British taxation of the colonies.

Dickinson was the draftsman of the Stamp Act Congress Resolutions of 1765 and the letters were published in reply to the Townshend Acts. As a member of both Continental Congresses he urged conciliation and refused to sign the Declaration of Independence. *See* AMERICAN REBELLION-11.

FARM SCHOOLS. *See* FAIRBRIDGE.

FARNBOROUGH. *See* LONG; MAY, ERSKINE.

FARNE Is. *See* ST. CUTHBERT; DARLING, GRACE.

FARNESE. International family which originated when Alexander Farnese, as Pope Paul III (r. 1534-49) gave the Duchy of Parma in 1545 to his bastard Pierluigi (1505-47). The third D. Alexander (1545-92) was the celebrated Spanish general and regent of the Netherlands. Elizabeth (or Isabella) (1692-1766) married Philip V of Spain. The ducal succession in Parma ended with the death of Antonio (1679-1731).

FARNHAM (Surrey) was a large Domesday manor belonging to the see of Winchester, at the junction of the Pilgrims Way and the London-Southampton road. A castle was built in about 1130. It had bailiffs in 1205 and in 1207 was a mesne borough. The Bp. of Winchester granted the first known charter in 1247 when the castle had been destroyed. It was soon rebuilt and became the chief episcopal residence. The borough sent an M.P. to Parliament in 1311 and 1460. The Charter was confirmed by Card. Beaufort in about 1410, but superseded by a new one in 1566. The grantor, Bp. Home, was a friend of Elizabeth I whom he entertained there. The corporation under his charter was a close body which slowly died out, the last survivor surrendering the charter to the Bp. in 1789. Hence Farnham was only an urban district between 1895-1974. Hops have been grown since 1597.

FARNLEY WOOD or DERWENTDALE "PLOT" (Oct. 1663) was an armed gathering of about 200 non-conformists and old Cromwellian officers at a place which had (perhaps evocatively) belonged to the Fawkes family. They scattered. The event resulted in widespread arrests and led to the passage of the Conventicle Act. *See* CLARENDON "CODE".

FARYNDON'S INN. The name, before 1484, of Serjeants Inn.

FARTHING (Silver). *See* COINAGE, *passim especially* 8-9.

FARQUHAR, Sir Robert Townsend (1776-1830) was Lieut. Governor, of Penang in 1802 and from 1812-23 as Governor of Mauritius, suppressed the slave trade there.

FASHODA INCIDENT (Mar. 1895-Mar. 1899). The British Govt. learned that the French meant to send a expedition from Senegal to the Sudan (then held by the Dervishes) and in Mar. 1895 Sir Edward Grey uttered a warning against it in the House of Commons. The expedition, under Maj. Marchand, nevertheless set off secretly in 1896. It marched 2,800 miles, encountering great hardships, and left a string of posts across the large Sudanese area of the Bahr-el-Ghazal, reaching Fashoda on the Nile in July 1989. Kitchener's methodical reduction of the Sudan from the north distracted the Dervishes from Marchand's activities. The French had for some while been intriguing with the Ethiopians to the east. Kitchener heard of the French presence three days after taking Khartoum (Sept. 1898), went to Fashoda, treated Marchand with courtesy but protested and left an Egyptian garrison at Fashoda. This was the "incident". Home popular opinion in Britain and France became heated because of the great efforts of the respective expeditions leading up to the encounter. The British refused to admit French claims in the Bahr-el-Ghazal because of the proximity of Ethiopia, and the French, getting no support from Russia or Germany, had to give way. The affair was settled by an agreement in Mar. 1899 whereby Britain and France accepted the Nile-Congo watershed as delimiting their respective territories and exploitation and the name of Fashoda was changed to Kodok. *See* SALISBURY'S THIRD ADMINISTRATION-9,10.

FASCISM (from *fasces,* a bundle of rods and an axe bound together to symbolise Roman state authority) was a term originated by Benito Mussolini to symbolise the views of his new political party. It has since been abused by communist parties, by whom it is sought to embrace a varying body of other parties with little in common, notably the German Nazis, the Spanish Falange, and pre-1940 Japanese, the Argentine *descamisados,* the Portuguese Govt between 1928-74, the Colonels' regime in Greece, occasionally, the republican Turks and other political bogeymen. There is no fascist philosophy in real terms; 'fascist' parties spring up as a reaction against the inefficiencies and muddles of democracies, or against the threat of social revolution. There is usually an administrative doctrine emphasising the importance of strong leadership, and a political bodyguard which imposes the will of the leadership without much regard for private rights, liberty or human dignity. Fascism, therefore, in so far as it exists, tends to be a machine for gaining power, and strongly resembles all other such machines, but especially communist parties. Many so-called 'fascists' have been socialists in their time. On the other hand they tend to fail to develop any coherent doctrine on the uses to which power should be put and for this reason they exhibit little policy in common and are apt internally to turn into increasingly corrupt bodies whose sole *raison d'être* is self preservation.

FASTNET. A rock 4 miles S.W. of C. Clear (Co. Cork, Ireland), long a navigational landmark and hazard, was crowned with a lighthouse in 1854.

FASTOLF, Sir John (?-1459) Shakespeare's anachronistic *Falstaff,* rose to military prominence at the end of the Hundred Years' War, although accused of deserting Talbot and Ld. Hungerford at the B. of Patay (1429). William Worcester and John Paston I were respectively his steward and legal adviser and he and his affairs appear a good deal in their jottings and letters; so that it has been possible to estimate something of his profits from the war and how he invested them. He endowed a college of secular priests near his fortified manor at Caistor. By his second will, made two days before his death, he left most of his estate to John Paston. This provoked nearly 20 years of litigation between the Pastons and other claimants.

FATAL VESPERS (Oct. 1623). A floor collapsed under a congregation listening to a Jesuit preacher in the French ambassador's house at Blackfriars and a hundred people were killed. God's judgement against Jesuits was, of course, assumed.

FATHERS OF THE CHURCH are some 28 early theologians regarded as doctrinally authoritative, together with a large number of others regarded as authoritative on particular issues. The earliest were St. Clement of Rome and Irenaeus in the 2nd cent; the most eminent were Sts. Athanasius (c. 296-373) and Augustine of Hippo (354-430) and the latest St. Gregory the Great, Isidor of Seville and St. John the Damascene with whose death (c. 750) the Age of the Fathers is considered to have ended. The term and idea was originated when the 5th cent. St. Cyril of Alexandria appealed to a consensus of the Fathers at the Council of Alexandria in 432 and accompanied his argument with an anthology of quotations from them.

FAULKNER, Brian (1921-77) was a moderate Unionist prime minister of N. Ireland from 1971 to 1972 and led the Unionists from 1972.

FAUST. The influential legend of Faust may have been oriental in origin, but the career of Johannes Faustus (i.e. Lucky John) (?1488-1541), a Swabian swindler, reputed to have learned astrology, divination, alchemy and other magic arts at Cracow, excited popular interest and envy; it prompted increasingly picaresque biographies, of which the first appeared at Frankfurt in 1587. The story, well known in England, provoked Marlowe's *Dr. Faustus* in 1588. Thereafter it attracted more interest on the continent than in Britain until the appearance of the first part of Goethe's famous play in 1798. By now belief in a personally satanic power had declined, and Marlowe's and Goethe's very different conceptions had become literary and philosophical monuments.

FAWCETT, Henry (1833-84), and his wife **Dame Millicent (1847-1929)**. He was blind. A Cambridge Prof. of Political Economy from 1863 he was a Liberal M.P. from 1865. She was a sister of Elizabeth Garrett Anderson. They were both interested in women's rights and married in 1867. She became his political sec. and campaigned on her own account after he died, becoming Pres. of the constitutional N. Union of Women's Suffrage Societies, and continuing her constitutionalism after the rise of militancy under the Pankhursts. With them she urged patriotic courses in World War I and her 1916 petition to parliament was the catalyst for the statutory admissions of women to vote in 1918.

FAWKES, Guy. See CATESBY, ROBERT.

FEAL AND DIVOT. The Scottish equivalent of turbary.

FEALTY was an oath of personal loyalty and good faith (*fidelitas*) made by a feudal inferior to a superior. It sometimes included personal service undertakings. "Without fealty there is no treason."

FEAR of the serious but improbable has long been induced, especially by insurers. After World War II, publicity specialists took to minimising the improbabilities to numb public scepticism into accepting hitherto undesired products such as cholesterol-free foods, smoke alarms and bicycle crash helmets. *See also* SECURITY.

FEBRUARY REVOLUTION (Mar. 1917). The overthrow of the Russian autocracy by liberals, themselves overthrown by Lenin in the October Revolution (Nov. 1917).

FÉCAMP (Normandy), a port developed by the Benedictine monastery founded in 660 and later devastated by the Vikings. In 1001 it was taken over by the learned Abbot, William of Dijon, a skilled administrator whose influence spread the Cluniac reforms to all the Norman Benedictine houses. The abbey had a fine library; a distinctive liturgical chant and became a pilgrimage centre. Three of its monks achieved distinction in England: Herbert of Losinga as Bp. of Norwich, Remigius as Bp. of Lincoln and Turold, Abbot first of Malmesbury and then of Peterborough. The port eventually became the main Norman fishing and smuggling centre, with trawlers going as far as Newfoundland.

FEDDAN. An Egyptian measure = 1.038 acres.

FEDERAL CONVENTION (U.S.A.). May-Sept. 1787 evolved the draft constitution of the U.S.A. which superseded the Articles of Confederation.

FEDERATION OF BRITISH INDUSTRIES (F.B.I), the largest employers' organisation in Britain, was founded in 1916 and incorporated in 1923. In 1965 it, the National Assn. of British Manufacturers and the British Employers Confederation merged to form the Confederation of British Industries (C.B.I.).

F[O]EDERATI **(Lat = allies)** were Germanic and other tribes settled in depopulated areas within the Roman frontiers to replace military units and provide local defence, in return for lands and annual subsidies. It is an open question whether the Saxons or Jutes were first established in coastal areas of Roman Britain in this way, from the early 4th cent. onwards.

FEE FARM, – RENT. Land held in fee simple, i.e. full ownership, for which a perpetual rent was paid in lieu of a lump sum down. Common in the North of England, fee farm rents were converted into 2000-year leases as from 1926 by the Law of Property Act, 1925.

FEE SIMPLE, FEE TAIL or ENTAIL. *See* LAND TENURE (ENGLAND)-4.

FEES, BOOK OF or *Testa de Neville,* a collection of returns

to special inquiries into knights fees, serjeanties, and alien actions, with financial documents for 1198 to 1293 collected and copied for the Exchequer in 1302.

FEET OF FINES were records of agreements (sometimes called final concords) of high authority made before royal justices in suits concerning land. From about 1170 they were made in chirographic form, and after 1195 in triplicate (two side by side and one across the foot) each party to the suit retaining one of the upper copies and the foot being kept by the court. They are a source of information about mediaeval land dealings. Subsequently they were found to be a convenient means of varying entails as between a life tenant and his heir, and from Tudor times were seldom used for any other purpose.

FEILDING. *See* DENBIGH.

FELIX, St. (?-?647) a Burgundian, was sent by Abp. Honorius of Canterbury to preach to the Angles. Sigebert, K. of the E. Angles, who was baptised in Gaul, helped him and encouraged him to introduce Gallic customs such as the schooling of boys in the Bp's household. He was the first Bp. of Dunwich from 630.

FELIXSTOWE (Suffolk) the tranquil existence of this small resort with its boarding schools on the Harwich estuary was interrupted in 1969 by a devastating tide, followed by redevelopment in the 1970-80s as the largest container port in the U.K.

FELLOW TRAVELLER. One who agrees with the Communist Party but is not, apparently, a member of it. The phrase is Leon Trotsky's.

FELONY (cf 'fell' = unpleasant or dangerous; Lat: 'fel' = gall or nastiness), originally a class of crimes striking at the roots of mediaeval society and justifying forfeiture of the property nourishing those roots viz: murder, wounding, rape, arson and robbery. A convicted felon was said to be 'in mercy' (*see* PUNISHMENT). Later any offence involving forfeiture was a felony. Serious ones became capital, but from 1660 to 1830 about 120 relatively minor offences were made capital felonies too. A felon might be appealed (*see* COMBAT, TRIAL BY) or he might abide the verdict of a jury. Since juries originally decided of their own knowledge, he could not, until mid 19th cent. give evidence. In either case he had to plead guilty or not guilty before proceedings could begin. If he refused to plead (stood mute of malice) he would be subjected to *Peine forte et dure* (q.v.). There were other procedural oddities. A bystander aware of a felony was bound to intervene and might arrest the offender and was bound to help the authorities. Forfeiture, save for treason-felony was abolished in 1870. The whole concept was abolished in 1967, the procedure in all cases being assimilated to that on misdemeanours, and offences were then un-grammatically classified as arrestable or non-arrestable.

FELTON, John (1595-1628). *See* BUCKINGHAM, D. OF.

FEMINISM is the urge to improve the status or increase the power of women relative to men. In this sense men as well as women can be and are feminists. Apart from widening the scope for the use of abilities which women have in common with men, such as intellect, strength of character, literary force and staying power, there appear (at the risk of over simplifying a complicated subject) to be two major types of feminism in each of which methods of attainment to some extent merge into the objects to be attained, namely **(1)** the pacific use of the traditionally feminine accomplishments to exert influence and bring feminine attitudes and methods into areas commonly regarded as masculine and **(2)** the belligerent repudiation of femininity to effect the desired social changes by essentially masculine techniques such as violence or strident propaganda. Pacific feminism has, historically, been very successful, as witness the careers of many women rulers, athletes, authors and social reformers and the wholesale entry of women into the universities and nearly all the civil professions. The word feminism in the sense of this article originated in 1895 by which time the desired trend (as evidenced by the Married Women's Property Act 1882) had already been set for some time. The successes of belligerent feminism such as suffragette violence before 1914 or efforts by the followers of Germaine Greer (1939-) to tamper with linguistic forms to which dead grammarians had attributed genders, seem harder to estimate because the outlook has arisen after the major successes had already been won. Suffragette window-smashing did not win the vote: war work did; and it was a whole generation later that the belligerent "Women's Lib" began burning brassieres. If it is true that pacific feminism wins its successes in adversity while belligerency makes headway afterwards, it may perhaps be hazarded that the main value of belligerency is as a preserver of gains rather than as a gainer. This is not the only seeming paradox. Pacific feminists such as the Czarina Catherine the Great (who murdered her consort) have often been very ruthless, while the Pankhursts, organisers of belligerency, were much admired by masculine opponents for their wit and femininity.

FENCE MONTH. A period of 15 days on each side of midsummer which was the close season for hunting in forests.

FENCIBLES were men fit and liable for defensive military service. The term is of Scots origin. Fencible units liable only for service at home were raised in N. America in 1775, and in Britain in 1795.

FENCING or SWORDSMANSHIP as a useful rather than a sporting accomplishment began when war armour was discarded in the 16th cent. and the sword (with or without a supplementary dagger) had to be used for both attack and defence. This changed the sword from the massive mediaeval cutting weapon through the balanced but still over-heavy rapier to the light thrusting epées which could be supported and controlled by the average practised wrist. Schools teaching the new quick and neat techniques sprang up in Germany and Italy. Henry VIII chartered a Corporation of Masters of Defence in 1540 and Italian fencing masters became part of the English social scene in the 1580s. The first prize fights were sword fights. The vogue lasted until the end of the 18th cent. when boxing superseded swordsmanship as a popular entertainment, and duelling (always illegal) was increasingly disapproved.

FENIANS were an Irish-American society with branches in other countries, founded in the U.S.A. in 1858 by John O'Mahony (1816-77) who had fled from the Irish rising in 1848. Its Irish wing was called the Irish Republican Brotherhood. In Nov. 1863 there was a convention in Chicago, which gave the movement considerable impetus. This was increased when many armed Irishmen were demobilised in 1865 after the U.S. Civil War. The Fenians now split; O'Mahony wanted to raise armed rebellion in Ireland: William Roberts (1830-97) to attack Canada. The British Govt. took very effective counter measures in Ireland where the movement petered out after a minor rising in Kerry and a spectacular explosion at Clerkenwell. Raids across the Canadian border were made in 1866, 1868, 1870 and 1871. These were driven off by the Canadians, except the last which was stopped by the U.S. authorities. The movement died down in 1877 but in 1883 there were attempts to cause explosions at London railway stations, at the Tower and at the Houses of Parliament.

FENTON. See STOKE-ON-TRENT.

FENWICK, Sir John (?1645-97) M.P. at intervals from 1675 for Northumberland, brought up Monmouth's bill of attainder in 1685 and became a major general in 1688. (*For the conspiracy for which he was himself charged with treason see* JACOBITES-5.) He induced one of the two necessary witnesses to go overseas and after prolonged investigations he was condemned by Act of Attainder.

FEN RIVERS. See SPORT AND COMMUNICATIONS.

FENS (Eng.) This low lying area, which drains north-eastward, consists of a broad belt of siltland on the north and west sides of the Wash and inland of this, irregularly shaped areas of peatland with islands at Soham, Ely, March, Thorney and Crowland. These and much of the siltland were cultivated in Roman times but for reasons unknown, the area deteriorated and by Norman times, the islands alone were cultivated (under monastic inspiration) but the rest was barely habitable marsh in which fenmen such as Hereward the Wake resisted invasions by fortifying Ely. Groups of rebel barons made similar resistance in 1139, 1142 and 1265. The first effort at drainage was Abp. Morton's Leam, a 12 mile cut from Stanground to Guyhirn in 1490. The dissolution of the monasteries did severe but temporary damage but in 1600 a drainage act was passed; it remained a dead letter until 1630 when the 4th Earl of Bedford formed a syndicate with 13 other fenmen and engaged a Dutch engineer, Cornelius Vermuyden (1590-1677), to drain the 95,000 acre Bedford Level in the south. This was completed in 1637 but royal interference and the civil war stopped further work which was, however, begun again by the 5th Earl in 1649. The Great Level was completed in 1652 for £40,000 and a General Drainage Act passed in 1663. The effect in the south was to lower the level of the peat so that water began to flow back on to the land. By 1700 it was on the verge of reinundation and it was necessary to protect it by sluices and windmill pumps. This increased the rate of subsidence and by 1790 fish and fowl were the common products of many southern fens. This situation was reversed only by the steam pump from 1820 and the diesel pump from 1913; but as the land continued to subside the care of embankments to contain the Wash and the rivers became increasingly costly and important. There were disastrous floods in 1862, 1937, 1947 and after the tidal surge of 1953. These resulted in the construction of further works and sluices, especially at Denver completed in 1964.

FEOFFMENT, strictly was the action of conferring a fief (for which homage and fealty would be due) upon a feudal tenant. It was accompanied or followed by a separate livery of seisin which placed the tenant fully in control. This livery was sometimes performed by handing over a sod. The statute *Quia Emptores* (1294) made it impossible to confer a fief by subinfeudation and consequently feoffment with livery of seisin were merged into a single concept, and later still evidenced by deed.

FEORM. See FARM.

FERDINAND, D. of BRUNSWICK-WOLFENBÜTTEL (1721-92), Prussian soldier was engaged by George II in 1757 as primarily Hanoverian C-in-C against the French. He was the victor of Crefeld (1758) and Minden (1759) and the captor of Cassel (1762).

FERGUS MOR. See DALRIADA.

FERGUSON, David (?-1598), an early Scots reformer, became minister at Rosyth in 1567. In 1572 he attacked the diversion of church funds to secular uses at the Leith Assembly and was Moderator in 1573. Thereafter he was always one of the moderator's assessors, employed on framing agendas and in political negotiations, where his wit and good temper prevented many quarrels.

FERGUSON, Patrick (1744-80) in 1776 invented the first breech loading rifle, used by the British Army, in America.

FERGUSSON. Scots legal family. **(1) Sir James (1688-1759)** was called **Ld. KILKERRAN (1735)** when he became a Lord of Session. His 8th son **(2) George (?-1827) Ld. HERMAND (1799)** when he too came to the bench. He is best known for his reply to an application to appeal a conviction of murder on the ground that the appellant was drunk. "If he will do this when drunk, what will he not do when he is sober?" His kinsman **(3) James (1769-1842)** was a Scots legal writer.

FERMANAGH (Ir) was included in James I's plantation of Ulster.

FERMANAGH. *See* MAGUIRE; VERNEY.

FERMOY, or ROCHE OF FERMOY (Ir). The prescriptive peerage of this Irish family was recognised by Henry VII in 1489; by 1585 they had audaciously and mightily advanced themselves to Viscounts. They were rich until implicated in the Irish rebellion of 1642. Their lands were then seized and they failed to get them back at the Restoration. The title became extinct in 1733. A distant and rich kinsman **Edmund Roche (1815-74) Ld. FERMOY (1856)** was M.P. for Co. Cork from 1837 to 1855 and a Liberal M.P. for Marylebone from 1859 to 1865. He had large Munster estates and was Lord Lieut. of Cork from 1856.

FERNANDO PO. *See* SPANISH GUINEA.

FERNS (Co. Wexford, Ir). The history of this place is a microcosm of mediaeval Irish social history. It was the seat of the MacMurroughs, Kings of the semi-nomadic Leinster tribes, and of their bishop. Grazing predominated over cultivation and safe buildings were so rare that churches, as elsewhere, were used for storing food under ecclesiastical protection. Though the Normans had been at Wexford, a few miles off, since 1160 there were none at Ferns when Maurice Fitzgerald died in 1177. In that year William FitzAudelin, Henry I's governor in Ireland, gave it to Maurice's sons in compensation for Wicklow, presumably to encourage a new colonisation. They hurriedly built a castle. Murtough MacMorrough in collusion with the Warden of Wexford, pulled it down, but other parts of the area were being colonised, and manors (and therefore their cultivation) being established. These encroachments on the grazing lands were the background of an early 13th cent. dispute between Albin O'Mulloy the last Irish bishop and the elder William Marshal who had taken some of the bishop's lands. Royal and Papal intervention settled in the bishop's favour, but when Bp. Albin died in 1222 a Norman, John of St. John was appointed. William Marshal built a new castle and John an impressive early Gothic cathedral. He obtained endowments and papal privileges. There was a distinct colonial prosperity and the Anglo-Normans were thin on the ground. The tribesmen were not driven out but tended to drift back individually or in organised offensives. In the 14th cent., notably in the long confusion begun by Edward Bruce's invasion (1315-8), they retook the castle and occupied much of the manors. The lay manor of Ferns had become almost valueless to the Normans by 1324 and a regular expedition under Anthony de Lucy was needed to recover the Leinster castles including Ferns. This was a military success but a social and economic failure. Hence, when the Anglo-Norman decline began after William de Burgh's murder in 1333, Irish tribal life was already mostly re-established, under an Anglo-Norman presence which was little more than a token police force. The land went back from arable to grazing, the cathedral gradually fell down.

FERRABOSCO, Alfonso (1) (?-1587), his son **(2) (?-1628)** and his son **(3) (?-1661),** musicians and composers, established the Italian style of music at the English Court.

FERRAR, Robert (?1508-55), convicted in 1528 of dealing in Lutheran tracts, became the last prior of Nostell in 1540, when he surrendered it and was pensioned. He was a friend of Somerset, and his consecration (as Bp. of St. Davids) in 1548 was the first to be performed in English. Deprived in 1554 under Q. Mary, he was burned at Carmarthen in Mar. 1555.

FERRARA, Andrea (16th cent.) Venetian swordsmith brought to Scotland by James IV or V to teach his craft. His name became synonymous with Broadsword, the favourite Scottish weapon until the B. of Culloden (1746).

FERRARS, Ld. *See* TOWNSHEND.

***FERRER'S CASE* (1543).** George Ferrers, M.P. for Plymouth and a page of the King's Chamber, was imprisoned by one White as a surety for a debt. The serjeant-at-arms failed to secure his release despite the order of the House of Commons. With the support of the Lords and Judges, they imprisoned the sheriffs, gaolers and plaintiff who had resisted the release. Henry VIII upheld their action on the ground that parliament was the highest court of his realm with which no lower court might interfere; "we at no time stand so highly in our estate royal as in the time of parliament". The case was the foundation of M.P.s' immunity from civil process.

FERROL. *See* ARMADAS; ELIZABETH I-29.

FESTIVAL OF BRITAIN (1951) at the centenary of The Great Exhibition was intended to raise morale after the austerities of the War and Labour administration. Concentrated at the South Bank in London, it failed in its main purpose but left legacies in the Festival (Concert) Hall and a coloured style of architecture.

FETTES, Sir William (1758-1836) Bt. (1804) and **College.** He made a fortune as an underwriter and military contractor in the Napoleonic wars and was Lord Provost of Edinburgh in 1800 and 1805. In 1830 he endowed the foundation for needy children which developed into the college.

FEU in Scots law is a land tenure. The Crown grants land to vassals who in turn feu it to others, who can in theory feu it to yet other vassals in an endless chain. The vassal plays a substantial annual feu duty (resembling a rent) and the holding can be forfeited if he fails to pay. Most Scots land is held in this way; it is distinguished from BLENCH, which involves making a nominal payment or service (e.g. a rose) to acknowledge superiority (cf. English serjeanty) and BURGAGE in a royal borough held for customary borough services (such as watch and ward) which have long since fallen into desuetude. *See* FEUFERME.

FEUDALISM. A. Theoretical Outline (1) Feudalism is a system of govt. likely to arise in the absence of a money economy. When a central authority cannot concentrate the funds for an effective army and administration, the need for public order compels the necessary instruments of govt. to be maintained in dispersion upon lands allotted for their sustenance. Routine operations then depend on the terms upon which the *overlord* allots the land to the *vassals* and upon, in addition, personal engagements between vassal and lord, strengthened by religious, superstitious, emotional or family ties. Within his own domain the vassal has considerable independence: moreover important non-routine state decisions each involve a process like mobilisation, but the number and extent of such mobilisations is equally controlled by set terms or accepted custom, because the vassals are involved in agriculture and their absence from home and the diversion of their work-force to non-agricultural activities leads to poor yields or famine. Hence a major decision of state policy can in practice be taken only with the consent of the chief vassals, who often exact their price, and they may themselves have to consult their own tenants too.

(2) West European Feudalism arose out of the collapse of the Roman Empire and monetary economy which the Carolingians were unable to replace. Carolingian officials and military dignitaries received lands appurtenant to their work. These *beneficia* were to be held, at the longest, for life. In fact as the Carolingians declined the disturbances caused by trans-Rhenanian and seaborne raids and invasions made continuity of command and therefore certainty in the succession vital. The rulers became hereditary because elections were fraught with danger and delay. The great vassals could urge the same case. Moreover many of them were locally too powerful to dislodge or military necessity made removal inexpedient. Thus a beneficium tended to pass inside the same family with the sometimes willing consent of the overlord. This developed into a regular

hereditary succession, recognised in France by Charles the Bald in the capitulary of Quierzy (June 877).

(3) Feudalism is not a tribal but a territorial institution and its posture is essentially defensive. In Britain the Anglo-Saxon invasions created a fluid situation in which it developed slowly, because the conquerors were on the offensive. Moreover they were themselves divided and often at war with each other and before society had time to settle, the Viking wars created further colonisations and the need for reconquests. The Saxon shires were debris of old tribal areas or new military districts convenient for assembling troops and administering justice under royal officials. They were never consolidated fiefs.

(4) A further difference between the Anglo-Saxon and the continental situations arose from this difference of posture. The English manor may be considered as a collective farm supporting a local organisation for justice and police, but it was often an island of cultivation in a sea of wilderness and forest. The Saxon grandee acquired manors as a source of income and otherwise left them largely to manage themselves. It was not necessary for his manors to be contiguous and indeed if he was much with the King, whose court travelled constantly, it might be convenient for his holdings to be scattered. On the continent the opposite was more true. The great vassals had consolidated domains and these tended to be parcelled among subtenants also with more or less consolidated holdings. The great English earldoms of 11th cent. with their tendency to melt and reform resembled the beneficia of the Carolingian decline more than the great Capetian fiefs.

(5) England and Normandy were influencing each other's public affairs for half a century before the Conquest. Norman feudalism was of the consolidated continental, rather than the scattered Anglo-Saxon type, but the Norman Dukes developed in the *Vicomte* a territorial official similar to, perhaps copied from, the English Sheriff. It was natural for him to govern through these nominees in England after the Conquest. They were as ready an instrument for preventing consolidation as the Vicomtes were for controlling it.

B. Asymmetry in Practice (6) The concept of a feudal pyramid with the King mounted upon progressively larger layers of tenants-in-chief, knights, undertenants, free cultivators and villeins was never wholly true. Seven major factors plus many minor and local ones distorted the picture. These were (a) the facts of economic and historical geography; (b) the church; (c) trade and the towns; (d) the survival of some currency and its expansion; (e) the pre-existence in England of a non-feudal order which never entirely succumbed to feudalism (*see* LAND TENURE – ENGLAND); (f) evasions; (g) households and retainers.

(7) Much land was thick forest or bog and generally impassable, or the configuration was such that cultivation had to be a minor activity. 25% to 30% of England was royal forest reserved for hunting, and besides in the large areas occupied by the Danes there were so many free farmers that there was little coincidence between the village settlements and the manorial organisations of feudalism.

(8) Though most estates granted to the church before 1070 were held by knight service, the church, already richer than any earl, was a growing institution composed of persons whose vocation in theory at least, lay outside the accepted purposes of feudal society. As a corporation it never died, and by the grace of the Cluniac Spirit it tended to withdraw its landed assets from the common feudal purpose.

(9) The basic farming units could never be self sufficient. In particular they had to get at the very least, metals and salt from outside. There were always demands for other, often decorative manufactured goods as well.

The itinerants who conducted the trade did not want to be paid in kind. The small manufacturing towns with their vociferous artisan and trading groups were soon too strong for their local lord and became independent. They needed money and so did their rural customers. The vast gafols raised by the Danes, and the many known Saxon mints, show that there was always some currency. From or very soon after the Norman Conquest, feudal services began to be replaced by money payments, notably the tax called Scutage (= shield money). This was encouraged by the crown, which preferred to hire soldiers, and became a practical necessity when estates liable to a feudal service were divided between different owners. Similarly agricultural services whether free or unfree were redeemed or commuted for rents, and this process had reached an advanced stage by 1200.

(10) There was a constant leakage of people from the obligations of society. The emptiness of the country and the absence of any police force conduced to this in any case, but in later times crusaders were exempted and there were two recognised bolt holes, namely, entry into the church as secular or regular, and escape to a chartered borough followed by residence there for a year and a day. The freedom of the city was freedom indeed.

(11) A lord had a household of personal servants and retainers not all of whom were necessarily tenants. Some of the greater Lords had small armies of them. Many of these had to be sustained with money and rations, not on land, if only because they had to be permanently mobile.

C. Types of Tenure (12) Knight Service was the grant of land subject to the condition that the vassal provided an armed horseman to serve the Lord in service to the crown. The amount of land (the Knights Fee) was seldom, if ever, less than 5 hides but might be as much as 24. The duration of service was 40 days a year in peacetime and probably 2 months in war. The system was introduced from Normandy by William I, but by the 13th cent. the fee was reckoned as land worth £20 a year or in some areas £10. The royal army raised by this means consisted of roughly 6,000 knights but as agriculture improved, a tenant in chief might enfeoff knights of his own, so that the amount of service owed to him (the *servitium debitum*) might far exceed his servitium debitum to the crown. A person who held by Knight Service might not be, indeed probably was not, a Knight by status. Knighthood implied the Lord's favour, the passing of tests and the undergoing of ceremonies and endowment by the Lord.

(13) Serjeanty, Grand or Petty, was any lay service other than Knight Service. Grand serjeanty was owed only to the crown and involved certain ceremonially menial tasks on great occasions such as serving the King at a banquet or carrying his sword. Petty serjeanties were owed to any Lord, and were endlessly variable: to provide foot soldiers, to act as naperer, to guard the court whores, to feed the King's zoo, to supply arrows.

(14) Socage was an agricultural service of work on the Demesne (home farm) owed by a free tenant to the Lord of the manor. Prefeudal in origin it was distinguished from Villeinage by the fact the villein was unfree and his service therefore not only heavy but indefinite in kind, and sometimes quantity.

(15) In Frankalmoign (free alms) (q.v.) an ecclesiastical tenant held land on condition of offering up prayer for the soul of the Lord and his descendants. Unknown before 1070, this tenure became increasingly common in 12th and 13th cents. The lightness of the burden tempted mediaeval rulers everywhere to resort to levies and other occasional extortions on church property, for the church's obligation to relieve the poor, the sick and the widow was, from time to time, all too obviously neglected.

D. The Incidents (16) A vassal owed homage, a ceremony of public acknowledgement of allegiance in which he declared himself to be the Lord's man (*homo* or *bara*) and bound himself to his service, and in which the lord accepted him. *Homage ancestral* was the homage paid by an existing tenant's forebear and in the terms of which the descendant held the land. *New Homage* was homage done by an alienee. Homage, however, was closely construed and as the lawyers narrowed its content to the actual service owed, lords usually demanded in addition an oath of fealty which was an oath of personal fidelity and good faith. "Without fealty there is no treason." On the continent, and so in the French fiefs of the English Kings, fealty was often replaced by an oath of non injury.

(17) The lord was morally bound to protect and help his vassal in difficulties and maintain him against unjust enemies. He was also legally bound to hold a law court for him. This court was partly a law court and partly a council or policy committee. It consisted of the lord and his tenants. The King's court or *Curia Regis* developed into the privy council, the law courts, and Parliament. The manors had a Court Baron for the free tenants and the Customary Court (where the steward presided) for the unfree. Civil justice of a minor sort was administered in these courts which also settled such matters as the crop rotation. There was also a Court Leet which had a minor criminal jurisdiction and mostly sat for a group of manors in the same ownership. It usually consisted of the Lord and the tenants of the head manor. Attendance at the appropriate court was in theory compulsory.

(18) In the case of a free tenant the lord was entitled in addition to the service to (a) *Relief* that is a succession duty when an heir took up his inheritance; (b) the *Three Aids,* viz: a contribution to ransom a Lord taken in war, a payment when the Lord's eldest son was knighted and another when his eldest daughter was married for the first time and (c) *Escheat,* that is return of the land on failure of heirs. In addition the lord was entitled to the (d) *wardship* of the land during a minority; he was bound to provide reasonably for the minor, but otherwise was entitled to the profits because in theory he would lose the feudal services during the minority. Lastly (e) no woman could be given or give herself in *marriage* without her lord's consent. In theory, again this was reasonable because marriages determined the devolution of a vassal's property. In practice Lords of all degrees from the King downwards abused wardships and marriages shamefully, stripping estates of their value and selling widows to the highest bidder.

(19) In the case of an unfree tenant the Lord was entitled, in addition to the very onerous services to (a) *Heriot,* a death duty consisting of the tenant's best beast and (b) *Merchet,* (q.v.) It was regarded as degrading, and proof of payment was later considered to be one proof of villein status. It was not necessarily large. (c) *minerals*; (d) *hunting and shooting.*

FEUFERME, FEUDUTY (1) was (and is) a Scottish heritable tenure in which the superior received on grant a large lump sum called grassum, and a rent fixed in perpetuity called feu duty. It originated in the 15th cent., the grassum reflecting the casual feudal incidents of wardholding tenure, the feu duty its obligations of knight service. These incidents and obligations were entirely superseded. The rise of feuferme was due to the desire for cash and its greater availability.

(2) Ferme was the lump sum payable by a burgh to the crown instead of collecting and accounting for the rents, issues of justice and tolls in detail. Burghs which might do this were said to hold by Feu Ferme. The first such charter of feu ferme was granted in 1319.

FEUILLANTS were French constitutional monarchists who seceded from the Jacobins in July 1791. They failed because the King would not work through them and they could not support the popular demand for war with Austria and Prussia focused by the extremists. They

disappeared in Mar. 1792. They included some distinguished figures such as Lafayette and Siéyès.

FEVERSHAM, Louis Duras or Durfort (?1640-1709) 1st E. of (1677), French Marquis de Blanquefort. A friend of Charles II, he was naturalised in 1665, became Col. of the D. of York's guards in 1667 and was created a peer in 1673. He was a negotiator at Nimwegen in 1675 and again in Paris in 1677. In 1680 he became the Queen's Chamberlain and in 1685 a privy councillor and commander of the royal troops at the B. of Sedgemoor.

FIANNA. A band or gang of young Irish warriors who hunted and made war away from home.

FIARS, TO STRIKE THE (Sc). To estimate the official local price of grain by means of a sheriff's jury. The figure thus obtained determined crown rents, ecclesiastical stipends, monetary teinds, and applied to contracts where the parties had not specified a price. It was a form of cost-of-living index. *See* CORN LAWS.

***FID DEF. See* DEFENDER OF THE FAITH.**

FIELD (1) Henry (1755-1837) was apothecary to Christ's Hospital from 1807. He was the foremost teacher of the subject in his time and was one of the first to establish effective means of combating cholera, especially in 1831. His son **(2) Barron (1786-1846)** a barrister friend of most of the main literary figures of the early 19 cent., published a devastating analysis of Blackstone in 1811, became advocate-fiscal in Ceylon in 1814, was judge in N.S.W. from 1817-24 and left many works of literary criticism.

FIELD, John (1782-1837) composer who inspired Chopin, and pianist admired by Spohr, was taken by Clementi to Russia as a piano salesman and demonstrator and in 1824 settled in Moscow, where he died. He devised the term *Nocturne* for a piece of a quiet lyrical kind representing night thoughts or habits.

FIELD, Adm. of the Fleet Sir Frederick Laurence (1871-1945) was C. of S. to Sir Chas. Madden from 1916-18, director of torpedoes and mines from 1918-20, C-in-C Mediterranean 1928-30 and First Sea Ld. from 1930-33. The pay cuts which led to the Invergordon Mutiny (1931) were made against his express advice.

FIELDEN, JOHN (1784-1849) radical Lancashire cotton manufacturer, and M.P. from 1832 to 1847, supported factory legislation, trade unionism and paid the highest wages while opposing the new Poor Law. He was largely responsible for the passage of the Ten Hours Bill 1847.

FIELD MARSHAL. Highest military rank, introduced into Britain from Germany in 1736.

FIELD OF THE CLOTH OF GOLD (1520). A place in the Calais pale between Guisnes and Ardres, where Henry VIII and Francis I of France had a splendid but abortive diplomatic meeting. Instigated by Wolsey, the object was to secure advantages out of the approaching Valois-Habsburg conflict, which would necessarily involve English interests in the Low Countries. It failed because the idea of alliance with the French was unpopular in England. Wolsey became involved in Habsburg politics from 1521 onwards. *See* FRANÇOIS or FRANCIS I-5.

FIELD PREACHINGS. Open air religious gatherings organised by those excluded for their convictions, from the use of a church, more especially **(1)** semi-clandestine gatherings sometimes of hundreds between 1662 and 1690 of covenanters in S.W. Scotland, Fife and Easter Ross and **(2)** the 18th cent. Methodist assemblies, often of thousands, in the English industrial midlands and Yorkshire and Lancashire.

FIELDING. *See* DENBIGH.

FIELDING (1) Henry (1707-54) celebrated social novelist, author of *Tom Jones* (1748) and friend of actors became chairman of Westminster quarter sessions in 1749 and published his influential *Inquiry* into effects of gin drinking in 1750. He proposed a scheme for providing county poorhouses in 1753 and originated the Bow Street Runners, the beginnings of the police, by which gangsterism was much reduced. His blind half brother **(2) Sir John (?-1780),** also a magistrate, carried on his work especially in the field of prostitution.

FIENNES (pron: Fines), ancient family divided between the border, where they held the lordship of Dacre, and Kent where other members had the lordship of Saye and Sele. **(1) James (?-1450) 1st Ld. SAYE and SELE (1447)**, a beneficiary of Henry V's wars, had lands in France and was sheriff of Kent in 1437 and of Surrey and Sussex in 1439. From 1447-49 he was Warden of the Cinque Ports and then became Lord Treasurer. He was attacked for the surrender of Anjou and Maine; also widely unpopular for alleged extortion, he was made a scapegoat and handed over by the Governor of the Tower to be murdered by Jack Cade's rebels. **(2) William (1582-1662) Ld. (1613) and 1st Vist. SAYE and SELE (1624)** "Old Subtlety" a puritanical opponent of Bacon's, refused to pay the forced loan of 1626 and discovered or invented the right of peers to enter protests in the Journals. He supported the Petition of Right (1628) and like others out of sympathy with contemporary political and religious policy, interested himself in colonisation. He helped to establish the Providence Co. (of which Pym was Secretary) in 1630, acquired land on the Connecticut in 1632 and in New Hampshire in 1633. He meant to emigrate but gave the idea up after his proposals for a colonial aristocracy were rejected in Massachusetts. In 1639 he obeyed the feudal summons to service in the Bishop's War, but refused the military oath which went beyond it. Long involved with Pym and other opposition leaders through his City connections, he was viewed with suspicion by the court. Charges of treason were contemplated against him, but prevented by Strafford's impeachment. He thus became a prominent parliamentarian and was a member from 1642 of the Committee of Safety, besides in 1643 of the Westminster Assembly. Having no military ambitions, he supported the Self Denying Ordinance and by claiming a proxy, saved Fairfax's list of commissions under it. He survived the Commonwealth and ended up as Lord Privy Seal after the Restoration. Of his sons **(3) John (fl. 1643-47)** was a col. of parliamentary horse and was summoned to the Protector's Upper House in 1657. **(4) Nathaniel (?1608-69)** as M.P. for Banbury in the Long Parliament led the attack on episcopacy in 1641 and became a member of the Committee on Church Affairs and in 1642 of Safety. In 1643 he arrested the treacherous Gov. of Bristol and directed the City's defence himself, until forced to surrender, for which he was condemned on grounds of cowardice but pardoned. In 1648 he was a victim of Pride's Purge but Cromwell made him a Councillor of State in 1654 and a Commissioner of the Great Seal in 1655. He was called to the Upper House in 1658.

FIERY CROSS was a wooden cross burnt at one end and (perhaps) dipped in blood, handed on from one household to the next as a signal to Scottish clansmen to mobilise for war.

FIFE (Scot.) (probably Jutish *fibh* = forest) so-called by 4th cent. Frisian settlers, who mingled with the local Picts and were themselves followed in the 8th-9th cents. by Danes. It long had a King and continued to be known as 'the Kingdom' after the royal line died out. The Earls had a recognised leading position symbolised by their right to crown the Scottish Kings at Scone. Kinross and Orwell were separated from Fife in 1426. Dunfermline, St. Andrews and Falkland played leading parts in Scots royal history; the Kings favoured Fife, creating eleven other royal burghs there, but the local public was always restless; it very early went over to the Reformation; it played a leading role in establishing the Covenant, and gave little support to the Jacobite risings of 1715 and 1745. The area always had important fishing industries; linen and silk weaving sprang up in the 18th cent., and coalmining at the beginning of 19th. Local self consciousness sufficed to inspire a campaign to preserve the county from Local Govt. reform as late as 1972.

FIFE, Es. of. *See* DUFF.

FIFE, Robert of (c.1340-1420) E. of MENTEITH by marriage (1361) E. of FIFE (1371) D. of ALBANY (1398), second *s.* of Robert II of Scots, succeeded the murdered Sir John Lyon, Thane of Glamis, as Chamberlain (finance officer) in 1382 (until 1408) and was appointed Guardian of the Realm by the Estates because of dissatisfaction with the poor health of Robert II and his heir. The appointment lapsed at Robert III's accession in 1390 and there ensued a power struggle with the King's eldest *s.* David, created D. of Rothesay also in 1398. In 1399 Robert was attacked in the Great Council for financial mismanagement at Rothesay's instigation and the latter also became Lieutenant of the Realm. In 1402, however, Albany and Douglas arrested Rothesay, who died mysteriously and Albany took over the Lieutenancy, which was annually renewed by the Estates. In 1406 as a result of the boy heir James (James I) being captured by the English, and the King's death, he was appointed Regent. He opened negotiations for the release of James I and his own son Murdoch, captured at the B. of Shrewsbury. These were allowed to drag on. Murdoch was ransomed for £10,000 in 1416 and James not at all, while Albany enjoyed the regency. He put his sons into major posts, giving up the Chamber to one, the E. of Buchan, while making Murdoch Lieutenant when he came home. On the other hand he restored order in the Highlands, whose administration had been neglected under Robert II and III, and if the English war was resumed in 1409 a six year truce was agreed in 1412, while he crushed an insurrection in 1411-12 by Donald of the Isles. After Murdoch's release Border forays began again but in 1419 Buchan took a Scottish force to France where, in 1421 he won the important B. of Beaugé and was rewarded with the Constableship of France. Albany, a popular ruler, died at Stirling leaving his authority and dukedom to Murdoch, who, eventually forced to secure James I's return, was duly executed by him.

"FIFTEEN, THE". *See* JACOBITES 10-13.

FIFTH COLUMN. In the Spanish Civil War (1936-9) Gen. Franco said of Madrid that he had four columns outside it and a fifth within. Hence, any organisation owing allegiance to the enemy.

FIFTH MONARCHY MEN were led by Maj-Gens. Overton and Harrison, with Christopher Feake and John Rogers. They held that the last of the five universal monarchies foretold by Daniel would replace the fourth (i.e. the Papacy) in 1656 and inaugurate a 1000 year rule of Christ and his saints including naturally, themselves. They supported Cromwell and the establishment of Barebone's Parliament and seemed influential because of the high military rank of their leaders. On the creation of the protectorate they turned against Cromwell, who promptly arrested the leaders. Insurrections were suppressed in 1657 by Cromwell and in 1661 by Monck. Thereafter they quickly died out.

FIFTH REPUBLIC. The French state instituted by a new constitution of Oct. 1958 with Gen. de Gaulle as its first Pres. as from Dec.

FIHTWITE A.S. fine for brawling payable in addition to other liabilities to the King if anyone was killed.

FIJI (Pacific) was visited by Tasman in 1643, Cook in 1774 and Dumont d'Urville in 1827. The main attractions for Europeans were sandalwood, sugar, and indentured labour. The chiefs of Mbau obtained firearms from them, and established an unpopular hegemony which seemed likely to be overthrown when Cakobau was driven back to Mbau in 1854. He became Christian, befriended the missionaries and through them got help from Tonga. A U.S. Consul was supposed to have been injured and in 1857 a British consul was appointed. The U.S.A. demanded compensation and Cakobau offered the sovereignty to Britain in 1863 to get protection against the Americans. It was rejected, but a group of settlers established a disastrous regime and in 1874 Cakobau made the offer again. This time it was accepted. In 1875 a third of the population died of European measles. The island enjoyed a high degree of local autonomy and in 1970 became independent within the Commonwealth.

FILI (Irish) were Gaelic professional poets employed often to keep clan memories (and feuds) alive or the Irish equivalent of bards or the Sennachies.

FILIBUSTER (1) a term of American origin, means a speech or series of speeches artificially prolonged to obstruct a decision in a legislature or disorganise a Govt.'s programme. An influential practice in the U.S. Congress, it is effective in the British Parliament only on days (in practice private members' days) where business is not timetabled. **(2)** A buccaneer (q.v.).

FILMER, Sir Robert (?-1653) a strong royalist, wrote *Patriarcha, or The Natural Power of Kings* which was published only in 1680, and attacked by Locke.

FINANCE ACT. The act by which Parliament legalises the annual budget.

FINANCIAL RESOLUTION is a minor Money Resolution in the House of Commons.

FINCH and FINCH-HATTON. Kentish family. **(1) Henry (?-1625)** was a successful lawyer whose *s.* **(2) Sir John (1584-1660) Ld. FINCH of FORDWICH (1640)** became M.P. for Canterbury in 1614 and was Speaker of the Commons in 1627-28. He was the last of the "King's Speakers" though he laid claim to the Commons privileges and when ordered by the King to adjourn the House (Feb. 1629) was held down in his chair so that the Three Resolutions might be passed. (*See* ELIOT'S CASE.) He became C.J. of the Common Pleas in 1634. He was notorious for his ferocity in the Star Chamber and was the principal author of the Shipmoney Judgements. Sworn of the privy council in Mar. 1639, he became Lord Keeper in 1640. The Long Parliament promptly impeached him and he fled to Holland whence he re-emerged as one of the court which tried the regicides in 1660. His elder brother **(3) Moyle (?-1614)** married Elizabeth Heneage who, as a widow was created **COUNTESS OF WINCHILSEA (1628)**. Their younger son **(4) Sir Heneage (?-1631)** was M.P. for West Looe in 1620 and opposed the Spanish match. He sat for London in later parliaments and was critical of some of the royal policies and in Feb. 1626 became Speaker. His nephew **(5) Heneage (?-1689) 2nd E.** was at Constantinople from 1661-69 as Ambassador and was later involved in speeding James II to exile. His cousin the *s.* of **(4)**, **(6) Heneage (1621-82) 1st Ld. FINCH (1674) 1st E. of NOTTINGHAM (1681)** M.P. for Canterbury in the Convention Parliament (1660) became Sol-Gen and was the chief court spokesman in the Commons. It was he who negotiated the compromise Act of Indemnity and Oblivion and opposed Hale's ecclesiastical bill. In the second parliament he proved a high Anglican in practice. He led the opposition to the Declaration of Indulgence of 1665; he pressed the Five Mile Act of 1665, but opposed Clarendon's impeachment of 1667. In 1671 he conducted the conferences which established the convention that the Lords should not interfere in money bills. He defended the legality of the Declaration of Indulgence of 1673 and was rewarded at Shaftesbury's fall with the Lord Keepership (Nov. 1673) becoming Lord Chancellor a year later. His skill as a lawyer and negotiator was generally appreciated and he remained part of the constitutional machinery, accepted by Parliament and court to the end of his life. His *s.* **(7) Daniel (1647-1730) 2nd E.** was a Tory M.P. from 1672 but after he succeeded to the peerage was gradually recognised as the Leader of those Tory Anglicans opposed especially to James II's religious policy but willing as a last resort only, to accept a change of dynasty. He was asked to co-operate in overthrowing

James II but, while refusing active help, kept the secret. Thus also he favoured a regency rather than William of Orange, but basing himself on the distinction in the law of treason, between a King in law and King *de facto*, proposed the compromise oath of allegiance which made William's accession possible. By Dec. 1688 he was a S-of-State and soon moving the unsuccessful Toleration Bill, which later became the model for annual acts of indemnity. His duties included the naval management of the French war and he was attacked in Parliament for the failure to follow up the victories at Barfleur and La Hogue (May 1692) and the consequent loss of the great convoy at Lagos (June 1693). He resigned and remained out of office until Q. Anne appointed him Sec. of State in Apr. 1702 but in 1704 he supported, but his whig colleagues disliked, the Occasional Conformity Bill. Demanding that Anne (who agreed on this issue) should choose between him and them, she chose them. He thus became an embittered opponent of the Govt. and of their ally Harley and so remained until 1711 when he struck a bargain for forcing the bill through in return for opposition in the Lords to the ending of the war. This was the occasion when 12 peers were created to defeat his motion on the war, but he carried his bill. On the other hand he opposed the Schism Act, and this alliance with whig opinion resulted, at George I's accession in his becoming Lord Pres. In Feb. 1716 however, he was deprived for supporting an address in favour of clemency for certain Jacobites. His brother **(8) Heneage (?-1647-1719) 1st Ld. GUERNSEY (1703) 1st E. of AYLESFORD (1714)**, Sol-Gen from 1679-86, appeared for the Seven Bishops at their trial, and was an M.P. in all the Parliaments, save that of 1698 until 1703. He seems to have been a Jacobite in 1703 but accepted the Hanoverian succession and minor office. Daniel's fifth *s.* **(9) Edward Finch-Hatton (?-1771)** was M.P. for Cambridge Univ. from 1727-64 and as a diplomat was accredited between 1723-42 successively to Sweden, the Diet of the Empire, the States-Gen., Poland and Russia. His grandson **(10) George William (1791-1858) 10th E. of WINCHILSEA and 6th of NOTTINGHAM (1826)** an extreme reactionary opposed every liberalising measure, no matter how small, which came before Parliament. His intemperate language and attitude, long a byword, even involved him in a duel with the D. of Wellington. (The Duke missed and he fired in the air.)

FIN DE SIÈCLE (Fr = end of century). The general atmosphere of moral exhaustion accompanying the end of an era.

FINE. *See* LAND TENURE (ENGLAND)-4; FEET OF FINES.

FINE GAEL or UNITED IRELAND. One of the two dominant Irish parties, was formed in Sept. 1922 under William Cosgrave from the members of the Dail who accepted the Treaty of 1921. In order to take office it usually sought allies among the smaller parties. They governed Eire from 1922-32 and were then in opposition under William Cosgrave until 1943 and thereafter under Richard Mulcahy until 1948. It then joined a coalition Govt. under John Costello until 1951 and again from 1954-57. James Dillon was leader from 1959-65 when he was succeeded by Liam Cosgrave.

FINGAL or FINE GALL was the Norse occupied territory around Dublin.

FINGERPRINTS. The individuality of fingerprints and their lifelong persistence have been known for centuries but methods of classification were first suggested at Breslau in 1823 and in 1858 by Sir William Herschell proposed a system in Bengal. The idea was elaborated by Henry Faulds (1844-1930) and Sir Francis Galton (1822-1911) but the modern numerical system was deduced from their work by Sir Edward Henry (1850-1931) who was Inspector-Gen of Police in Bengal from 1891 and Commissioner of Metropolitan Police from 1903-18.

FINLAND (locally SUOMI) (*see* BALTIC). **(1)** Her special position as a separate Duchy under the Czar was respected until the 1890s; assimilation with the Russian postal and monetary systems was followed in 1899 by the February Manifesto which confined the initiation of legislation to the crown i.e. the Russian Governor. In 1901 the army was disbanded and Finns became liable to Russian conscription. A nationalist agitation culminated in the assassination of the Gov-Gen, Prince Bobrikov (1904) but the outbreak of war with Japan prevented reprisals and led to liberalisation in 1906. By 1910 this had faded out and the right to legislate on major issues had been transferred to the Russian Duma. Full annexation was prevented by World War I. **(2)** The independence movement sought German help and in the February revolution of 1917 the Finnish Diet assumed all internal powers. In reply to the October Revolution it declared independence in Dec. 1917 but in Jan. 1918 the revolutionaries got control of the Social Democratic Party and seized the larger southern industrial towns. The Govt. moved to Åbo (Turku) and under Pres. Svinhufvud and Marshal Mannerheim organised a counter-attack which with German help, ended the civil war in Apr. A German prince was proposed for the monarchy but when Germany was defeated, Mannerheim secured the adoption of a republican constitution with a strong president. Agrarian reforms created a large body of smallholders and the Social Democrats had dropped their revolutionary programmes by 1926. The communists thus became a separate body. They were attacked by the authoritarian and militaristic Lapua movement, which helped Svinhufvud to power in 1931 but the Lapua was crushed by him in 1932 when they attempted a *coup d'état* (The Mäntsälä Rebellion). **(3)** There followed a Russo-Finnish defensive alliance (1932) which the Russians broke in Nov. 1939 after their annexation of the Baltic republics and Eastern Poland, by demanding in Nov. 1939 certain strategic islands and part of Karelia. The Finns under Risto Ryti decided to fight: their tiny army inflicted appalling casualties on the Russians, but Scandinavian neutrality and the German attack on Norway prevented a Western rescue and by the T. of Moscow (Mar. 1940) Finland had to cede Viipuri (Viborg), Petsamo and Hangö. After the Norwegian local capitulation, the Germans obtained military transit facilities, with the result that when they attacked Russia in June 1941 Finland was drawn into the war. By June 1944 the Russians were advancing towards Viipuri; Mannerheim, who superseded Ryti as President, demanded a German evacuation and in Sept. by an armistice, accepted the T. of Moscow and a liability to reparations. As the Germans had refused to leave, a devastating war had to be fought with them. The definitive peace was signed at Paris in Feb. 1947. **(4)** Under the leadership of Pres. Paasikivi (1946-56) and Kekkonen (1956-73) a careful policy of co-operation with Russia was pursued. This brought about the abandonment of Russian bases in 1955 but left the essential liberalism of the Finnish outlook untouched. **(5)** Finland's main economic importance to other countries lies in her vast but readily accessible forests. Culturally she has become influential through the compositions of composers of the school of Sibelius and through the highly original work of her schools of architecture, some of whose distinguished members such as the Saarinnens migrated to U.S.A. and other English speaking countries.

FINNIAN, St. *See* MISSIONARIES IN BRITAIN AND IRELAND-3.

FIRE has regularly done immense damage to the economy. London was wholly or mainly burned in 798, 982, 1212 and 1666; York in 1137; Carlisle in 1292; Leith in 1544; Cork in 1612 and 1622; Stratford-on-Avon in 1614; Northampton in 1675; Warwick in 1694. Systematic fire insurance began in London in 1680 at premiums calculated on the rent respectively of brick (2%) and wooden (5%) houses. The Royal Exchange Assurance started its fire brigade in 1722, other insurance companies soon followed suit and this originated the practice of identifying insured houses by insurers' fire marks. In 1833 several companies combined to form the London Fire Establishment whose ineffectiveness was demonstrated in 1834 by the destruction of the Houses of Parliament and in 1861 by the £2M Tooley St. fire. A parliamentary inquiry brought about the creation of the London Fire Brigade in 1865 to the expenses of which the insurance companies contributed and thereafter other cities gradually created fire brigades of their own. National standards and standardisation were imposed only in 1938; the 1,400 brigades were amalgamated into 140 during World War II, and further amalgamations continued after it. There were devastating crop fires during droughts (q.v.).

FIREARMS (1) Projectors of ballistic missiles propelled by explosives, became possible in Europe in 13th cent. when the formula for gunpowder (*see* EXPLOSIVES) reached the west, probably from China. Primitive cannon were used abroad by 1300 and in the Anglo-Scots war in 1327. The first hand guns appeared in Italy in 1364 and were being made at Augsburg by 1380. The match was applied by hand and they often required two men. The plain bored handgun fired bullets, the wrought iron banded conical type could also fire arrows, quarrels or anything else to hand, as first used in Britain by Flemish mercenaries at the second B. of St. Albans (1461). The mechanical lock for applying the match had been in increasing vogue since 1425, and was the essential feature of the Arquebus, with which half of Henry VII's guard was armed in 1486.

(2) Handweapons. The Wheel or Rose Lock came into use in about 1570. It was clumsy, expensive and its coiled spring was apt to go flabby. Little used in Britain, it was replaced by the Dutch Snaphance developed at the same time. This had a steel hammer which struck a flint. The Dog Lock was a variation capable of being half cocked. These weapons were nearly all made abroad, mainly in the Low Countries, because English iron was too impure for gun-making. Many arms of this sort were privately owned but the stock was insufficient for military purposes and both sides had to import weapons in the Civil War.

(3) The Flintlock musket, in which the flint was mounted on a hammer and struck a steel on the pan cover, originated in Italy in about 1640. It was soon used in pistols and carbines but British and Irish troops were not fully rearmed until about 1690 when the famous Brown Bess (effective battle range 60 yds) was issued. This flintlock with minor variations, remained the standard infantry weapon everywhere until about 1825, and some British units still had it in the Crimean war.

(4) Improvements began with the manufacture of high quality steel at Birmingham after 1660, combined with a rigid system of proof and a strong private market in which high prices might be paid for good fowling and sporting pieces and (for self protection and duelling) for light and accurate pistols. The latter reached perfection in about 1800. Other improvements, also due to private demand, included double barrelled weapons, and rifling, which was partially developed in the American colonies. Muzzle loading rifles (effective battle range 200 yds) were issued to the Rifle Brigade in 1800.

(5) The fulminate of mercury detonator was invented in 1810 by a clergyman and had developed as the percussion cap by 1820. Almost proof against bad weather, it made a reduced charge possible and, by eliminating priming, raised the rate of fire. It also eventually made possible a reliable cartridge, and so the Breechloader with a gas tight breach. The Prussian needlegun of 1848 was the first practical military breechloader: the sweeping Prussian victories of 1864 and 1866 led to a general rearmament. In Britain this began in 1867: but the Martini-Henry, the last black powder rifle, using metal cartridges, was adopted in 1871.

(**6**) As usual, the private sector encouraged the next improvement. This was smokeless (cellulose) powder, which creates much less recoil and fouling than black powder, and led to smaller bores and lighter ammunition. By 1890 foreign armies (and the Boers) were using Mausers and Männlichers; the British issued Lee-Metfords to the infantry in 1889 and Lee Enfields in 1899. The Boer War showed up the defects of the British cavalry carbine and the advantages of clip loading into a magazine. The result was that a single clip-loaded weapon, the Short Model Lee Enfield (effective battle range 600 yds) was developed for all units. It was self loading and remained the standard army rifle from 1908 until the middle of World War II.

(**7**) The revolver was introduced in 1880 but the search now began for automatic loading. The first successful automatics were the German Mauser and Luger pistols occasionally used by the Boers. Light automatic machine guns, notably the British Lewis came in World War I; in 1918 the Germans introduced the Bergmann, the prototype of all later submachine guns.

(**8**) The mass armies of World War II had to be trained quickly, and accurate shooting was superseded by the hopeful spraying of bullets. The withdrawal of skilled labour pointed in the same direction. Handweapons such as the sten submachine gun were roughly manufactured, since precision was no longer considered necessary. One consequence was the disappearance, after the war, of most of the small highly skilled British gunmakers. Cartridge making had been amalgamated after World War I into Nobel Explosives Ltd., which became part of Imperial Chemicals after World War II. Britain began to import weapons and the army was equipped with the Belgian F.N. rifle. *See* ARMY; MACHINE GUNS.

FIRMIN, Thomas (1632-97), a rich Unitarian clothier, raised funds in aid of protestant refugees from Europe and Ireland, but then went over to a business-like approach to charity. He advocated (in speech and writing) providing work for the poor and himself employed people ruined by the Great Plague and Fire of London (1665-6), and in 1676 set up a kind of hand-working factory called a "workhouse" to give employment in linen weaving. His propaganda, example and terminology survived him.

FIRST COALITION, WAR OF THE (Feb. 1793-July 1795). (*See* FRENCH REVOLUTIONARY WAR.) (**1**) Revolution had destroyed the discipline of the French navy and Parisian extremism had provoked provincial disaffection. Thus despite a late British naval mobilisation, the French did little harm to Britain and were pre-occupied with home difficulties. They set up the Revolutionary Tribunal just before the royalist revolt in La Vendeé and Dumouriez' defeat by the Austrians at Neerwinden (Mar. 1793) while the British signed a treaty with Russia excluding French trade from the Baltic. Spain and Savoy had promised assistance against France.

(**2**) In Apr. Dumouriez deserted to the Austrians, and the Spaniards advanced through the Pyrenees. The Convention replied by creating the famous dictatorial Committee of Public Safety. Fortunately for the revolution, Austria and Prussia were preoccupied with the Second Polish Partition and their consequent suspicions of each other and of Russia. They prosecuted the French war sluggishly, even though in May Lyons, the second city of France, broke into revolt. The immediate reaction at Paris was an extremist Jacobin coup against the more moderate Girondists (June) but this in its turn provoked provincial reactions against local Jacobins. The British, Austrians and Prussians took Valenciennes and then separated: the British attacking Dunkirk. There were outbreaks, too, in Normandy and Brittany and especially at Toulon, which hoisted the royal flag and invited the

British naval C-in-C, Lord Hood, to enter the port (Aug.). The British attack on Dunkirk was foiled (B. of Hondschoote) but in Sept. the French fleet at Brest mutinied; by now French maritime commerce had been swept from the seas, and labour troubles and bad weather brought the worst harvest for a generation.

(**3**) The Committee of Public Safety was indomitable. In Aug. it had decreed the *levée en masse,* a measure which would have been useless without an organised armaments industry. The Austrians were beaten at Wattignies (Oct.) and the siege of Lyons was pressed to victory. The wholesale drownings practised after the surrender were matched by the guillotining of Q. Marie Antoinette at Paris. In Nov. while troops sealed off Toulon, the Vendéan rebels were decisively beaten at Cholet.

(**4**) The expected famine had been partially anticipated by sending a purchasing mission to the U.S.A. and French W. Indian shipping to U.S. ports to await convoy. Sir John Jervis led a fleet to the W. Indies in Nov. Meanwhile at home the French penetrated the Toulon defences and threatened Hood's fleet with artillery commanded by one Napoleon Bonaparte. Toulon seemed too expensive to hold and Hood evacuated it with most of the royalist refugees (Dec. 1793). Sir Sydney Smith, in charge of the demolitions, burned only about a third of the French fleet, and did no permanent damage to the docks. The Toulon episode, however, involved the British in the ideological conflict to which Pitt had hitherto refused to commit the country. There was, too, mismanagement in the Channel, where Lord Howe, to save his ships, went into Portsmouth until May 1794. This enabled the French Admiral Van Stabel to sail from Brest for the U.S.A.

(**5**) Hood and Jervis, however, made good use of the winter. Profiting by an anti-French insurrection, Hood reduced Corsica between Feb. and May 1794, thus providing the fleet with an excellent central Mediterranean base at San Fiorenzo (St. Florent). The island assembly offered the crown to George III, and Sir Gilbert Elliott became the viceroy. In the Caribbean, Jervis took all the French islands except Haiti between Feb. and Apr. but lost Guadeloupe again in May. By now, however, the instability of French politics (Hébert and Danton were executed in Apr.) impressed an overriding importance upon the great American convoy. Van Stabel sailed with it from the Chesapeake in Apr. Villaret-Joyeuse sailed to meet it in May. Lord Howe emerged from Portsmouth to seek him out. In the B. of the Glorious First of June (which actually lasted three days) each side achieved its purpose: the British to neutralise the French fleet, most of which they severely damaged or captured; the French to preserve the convoy, which reached home unscathed.

(**6**) The Reign of Terror began in May 1792, reached and then passed its climax in the next two months. The Revolutionary Tribunal's powers were specially increased in June and it and Robespierre's Jacobin Govt. waged a murderous political warfare with their opponents. This had a bracing effect on the field armies which defeated the allies at Fleurus (June 1794) and reoccupied most of Belgium. The Austrian and the British forces parted company, the former eastwards, the latter north west, through Holland, which was becoming pro-French, and so north and east increasingly bedraggled, towards Bremen. Then political revulsion at Paris caused Robespierre's fall and execution (July). The reconstituted Committee of Public Safety could court both popularity and victory. In Nov. the Spaniards were driven across their frontier and defeated at Figueras. In Jan. 1795 Pichegru captured Amsterdam, and revolutionised the Dutch Govt., whereupon Pitt ordered the occupation of the Dutch colonies.

(**7**) The war was dying down through continental

intrigue and maritime torpor. In Jan. 1795 Austria and Russia signed their final Partition Treaty on Poland and with Austrian resources concentrated towards that area, and the other land allies defeated, Prussia felt isolated. The inefficient French fleet suffered severe damage in a winter cruise (Dec-Jan.) but the badly stationed British Channel Fleet failed to get to sea until the French had limped home. In Mar. the survivors of the British expeditionary force (including a Col. Arthur Wellesley) re-embarked at Bremen, while Carnot, the guiding strategic spirit of the French war direction was superseded under a rule of rotation of office. This might have been dangerous if Prussian negotiations had not been far advanced.

(8) Active and successful French diplomacy now coincided with a period of British naval languor in the Mediterranean, where Adm. Hotham had for some while been C-in-C. He fought an action (Mar.) off Hyerès with Commodore Martin, the indecisiveness of which had serious consequences later. In Apr. a Franco-Prussian peace treaty surrendered the Prussian possessions west of the Rhine to France and established a North German neutral zone under Prussian guarantee. In May, France and Holland signed a primarily naval alliance. In June the French occupied Luxembourg with its powerful fortress, and escaped, off Ile de Groix, a major naval defeat through Lord Bridport's neglect. In July the Spaniards signed a peace with France at Basel.

FIRST EMPIRE. Bonapartist France from 1804-14.

FIRST FRUITS AND TENTHS i.e. the first year's income of an ecclesiastical benefice and a tenth of subsequent years' were payable to the Pope, but annexed by Henry VIII in 1534. In 1540 a Court was set up to enforce payment, and this was merged in the Court of Exchequer in 1554. The dues were assigned to Queen Anne's Bounty in 1703.

FIRST OFFENDERS ACT, 1887, originated the system of probation orders which courts might impose in certain cases instead of custodial sentences. The scope of probation was widened by the Probation of Offenders Act 1907. Probation Officers were first appointed under the Criminal Justice Act, 1925.

FIRST READING, BILL. See BILL; TEN MINUTE RULE.

FIRST REPUBLIC. France from Sept. 1792 to May 1804.

FIRTH, The Rev. John D'Ewes (1900-1957), a descendant of Sir Simonds D'Ewes and grandson of Jesse Boot, as a boy at Winchester took ten wickets against Eton. A classicist, lawyer and theologian, he was a pervasive stylist and teacher at Winchester and liberalised an intellectual generation. He died as Master of the Temple.

FISHBOURNE near Chichester (Sussex) has the remains of the finest Roman Villa (or palace) so far found in Britain. It replaced an early villa in about A.D. 80 and was probably built for K. Cogidubnus.

FISHER, Geoffrey Francis (1887-1972) Abp. of CANTERBURY (1945-61) 1st Ld. (1961) became headmaster of Repton in 1914, Bp. of Chester in 1932 and of London in 1939 before being elected to Canterbury. Under his leadership the church embarked upon a functional and financial reorganisation and a more doubtful process of doctrinal revision which included approaches to other Christian churches, notably those with such differing outlooks as the Methodists and R. Catholics.

FISHER (1) The Rt. Hon. Herbert Albert Laurents, F.R.S., O.M., (1865-1940) studied history at Paris and Göttingen and from 1912 was a member of the R. Comm. on Public Services in India (until 1917) as well as V-Chancellor of Sheffield University. He did much to encourage the application of the arts to industry. In 1916 he was suddenly asked by Lloyd George to become President of the Bd. of Education and in consequence became an M.P. (Sheffield). In 1918 he introduced the

Education Act, often called after him, with its scheme of percentage grants for teachers' salaries, state scholarships at universities and School Certificate, and he championed part-time contribution schools to the age of 18. He left office with Lloyd George in 1922. In 1925 he became Warden of New College. His historical works include *Bonapartism* (1908), *James Bryce* (1927) and the *History of Europe* (1935). His brother **(2) Sir Warren (1879-1948)** became Chairman of the Board of Inland Revenue in 1918, and was Head of the Civil Service from 1919-39. He introduced the recruitment of the Treasury from other depts., combined the financial with the policy making responsibility of permanent heads of ministries, established the unitary concept of the Civil Service and championed independence and frankness of civil servants towards ministers. These attitudes and policies made him one of the strongest influences in 20th cent. British constitutional administration.

FISHER, John (1469-1535) St. and Card (1535) was Vice-Chancellor of Cambridge University in 1501, Chancellor in 1504, Chaplain to Lady Margaret Beaufort, and a friend of Erasmus. In 1504 he became Bp. of Rochester. He was also a famous preacher and became a friend of Henry VIII. He took the R. Catholic side against the reformers and helped the King to write his *Assertio Septem Sacramentorum* (Lat: Vindication of Seven Sacraments) against Luther. At this time he was Q. Katharine of Aragon's confessor, and soon protested frankly against Henry's plans for divorce. When Henry was to be declared Head of the Church in 1531, Fisher secured the insertion of the reservation "as far as the Law of God allows it" into the bill. By 1534 the King was his enemy and he was fined. Refusing to vote for the Act of Succession of 1535, he was put to death on trumped up charges.

FISHER, John Arbuthnot (1841-1920) Adm. of the Fleet, 1st Ld. FISHER (1909) O.M. was born in Ceylon. He served in H.M.S. *Warrior* (*see* IRONCLADS) in 1863, and from 1872-76 developed mines and torpedoes. He was director of ordnance and torpedoes from 1886-90. After being Third Sea Lord from 1892-97 he was from 1899-1902 C-in-C Mediterranean fleet, whose efficiency he greatly improved. As Second Sea Lord (1902-3) he introduced personnel reforms, notably a common entrance and training scheme for officers. In 1903-4 he was C-in-C Portsmouth, and also a member of the War Office Reconstruction Committee. During his memorable period as First Sea Lord from 1904-10 he redistributed the fleet to meet the German danger, inspired and carried through the production of the *Dreadnought* and other similar capital ships, and waged a ceaseless propaganda campaign to ensure that the navy could sustain a predominating world role. When the Conservative govt. fell in 1905 the Liberals reduced the building programme; this only caused him to redouble his efforts, involved him in politics and estranged him from a powerful body of service opinion which had never entirely supported his other policies. This manifested itself in a remarkable public feud between Fisher and Lord Charles Beresford who became C-in-C of the Channel Fleet in 1907. Meanwhile, the new First Lord, Reginald McKenna, had concluded with Fisher that German competition was increasing and that the Govt.'s policy had to be reversed. There was conflict in the cabinet, ending in the programme for eight new battleships in the budget year 1909-10; new taxes had to be raised to pay for them and this precipitated the constitutional crises of 1909-11. Fisher's policy also led to the resignation of Beresford who then addressed a formal memorandum of criticism to the Prime Minister. The cabinet supported McKenna and Fisher, who was made a peer. He resigned in Jan. 1910 but his influence still remained for he was chairman of the Committee on Oil Fuel (which eventually superseded coal as the basic motive power) and he was a friend of Winston Churchill who became First Lord in 1911. Accordingly, he returned to office at the outbreak of war in 1914. He was obsessed on the one hand with the routine of the war, and on the other with a scheme for occupying the Baltic route to Russia. As a result he gave insufficient support to the opening of the Dardanelles campaign and resigned when the cabinet persisted. The ensuing change of govt. ended his career.

FISHERIES (*see* WHALING). River and coastal subsistence fishing are very ancient, but commercial fishing had to await the first development of adequate boats in the 8th cent., and the presence of shoals accessible to British ports. In the 12th cent. Cornish and Breton fishermen were fighting for mackerel, pilchards and sardines migrating up Channel from the Atlantic. In the 14th cent. the herring suddenly deserted the Kattegat for the Dogger Bank where huge east coast fishing fleets began to fight equally huge Dutch fleets for them. The slow warming of the northern oceans caused fish to migrate at an earlier stage in their life-cycle and to go further north, so that Cornish ports lost their fish to the east coast, while the latter were replaced by Scots, and in due course by Icelanders. Cod fishing on the Newfoundland Grand Banks began in the 15th cent. possibly by Basques and Spaniards in pre-Columbian times. The visits of the Cabots soon brought the English and then the French and Portuguese in strong competition, of which the continuing French possession of St. Pierre and Miquelon is a survival.

FITCH, Ralph (fl. 1583-1606) sent by Sir Thomas Osborne with other Levant merchants in 1583, travelled via Aleppo and Basra down the Persian Gulf. He was intercepted by the Portuguese who imprisoned him at Hormuz and then at Goa. Released under surety he went to Akbar's court at Agra. He then sailed down the Ganges, stayed in Burma in 1586-7 and returned via the Malabar Coast and Mesopotamia. He reached London in 1591. He left a narrative of his travels and was associated with the Levant Company until the end of his life.

FITT, Gerard or Gerry (1926-) Ld. FITT (1983) was M.P. for W. Belfast (1966-83) and as a moderate R. Catholic formed the Social Democratic and Labour Party to oppose political terrorism.

FITTON (1) Sir Edward (1527-79) became President of Connaught (*see* ELIZABETH I-17) in 1569 and though wounded, successfully fought the Clanrickardes and the Burkes. Of his children **(2) Sir Edward (?1548-1606)** acquired a large part of the forfeited Desmond estates in Munster and **(3) Mary (f. 1600)** a Maid of Honour to Elizabeth I was mistress of William Herbert, 3rd E. of Pembroke. She was probably not the dark lady of Shakespeare's sonnets.

FITZ = 'son of', often implies bastardy.

FITZAILWIN, Henry (?-1212) was the first mayor of London; appointed possibly as early as 1189, he seems to have held office until his death.

FITZALAN (*see* STEWART, ROYAL) were Lords of Oswestry and Clun (Salop) to which by the 13th cent. they added Arundel in Sussex. **(1) John (1223-67)** styled **E. of ARUNDEL** originally supported Montfort in the Baron's War but changed sides when Montfort's policy prolonged the border war with Gwynedd, for he had a common local interest with the Lord Edward, for whom, at Lewes, he fought and was captured (1264). His grandson **(2) Richard (1267-1302) E. of ARUNDEL** was primarily a soldier. His son **(3) Edmund (1285-1332) 2nd E.** began as a determined opponent of Edward II. He was one of the Ordainers, supported Lancaster against Gaveston, and was present at Gaveston's murder. He refused to take part in the Bannockburn campaign, which put Lancaster into effective power, but was soon disenchanted with his feuds and self-seeking arrogance. He was not alone, and by 1317 he was trying to uphold Aymer of Valence's group, who were trying to uphold

the Ordinances within the framework of existing institutions, and so to reduce Lancaster's claims. Hence in the confusion which attended the rise of the Despensers and the civil war of Boroughbridge, Arundel was one of the several Earls who condemned Lancaster to death at York (Mar. 1321). Thus committed to the King and against his Mortimer neighbours on the Welsh March, he was murdered in Q. Isabel's and Mortimer's coup. He had married the sister of Earl Warenne, and their son **(4) Richard (1307-76) 3rd E. (1330)** married a daughter of Hugh Despenser. He recovered the family honours when Mortimer was overthrown in 1330, and inherited the Warenne honours too (1347). From 1334 he was justice of N. Wales but in fact he was a leading military and diplomatic servant of Edward III. He commanded the army in the north in 1334. In 1340 he led the attack at the B. of Sluys. He and his uncle Warenne were involved in Edward III's dispute with Abp. Stratford at the Parliament of 1341 and asserted the rights of the peers. In 1344 he was Lieutenant in Aquitaine, and Admiral of the West from 1345. He commanded a division at Crécy, and the siege of Calais (1346-7) and in 1350 was in the naval victory off Winchelsea (*Les Espagnols sur Mer*) over the Spaniards. He was enormously rich and lent large sums to Edward III, John of Gaunt and the Black Prince. In addition to his great estates, he left £60,000 in cash. His *s.* **(5) Richard (1346-97) 4th E. and E. of SURREY** was a popular figure. He was a member of the Council appointed by the Good Parliament and one of the regents and Governor of the King in 1380-81. He and the King disliked each other. In 1387 he won a naval victory over the French, Spaniards and Flemings off Margate. He lent his reputation in support of the opposition to Richard II, and was one of the Lords Appellant in 1388. Meanwhile his brother **(6) Thomas (1352-1414)** known as Thomas Arundel, Bp. of Ely since 1347, had become Chancellor in 1386 and was promoted to York in 1388. The quarrel with Lancaster isolated the brothers, and Thomas lost the Chancellorship but regained it in 1391. In 1396 he was elected to Canterbury which entailed resignation of the Chancery. Both brothers, with Gloucester and Warwick, were critical of the King's external policies and in 1397 in his revenge on the Lords Appellant, he seized them, and had them condemned in Parliament. Thomas was deprived and exiled, Richard was executed. Thomas went to Rome and was nominally translated to St. Andrews, currently in obedience to the anti-Pope, but at Richard II's fall in 1399 he was recalled by Henry IV whom he crowned. He served as Chancellor in 1399, 1407 and 1412 but was otherwise much concerned with rising Lollardy, which he persecuted. He was partly responsible for the stat: *de Haeretico Comburendo* of 1401. Richard's son **(7) Thomas (1381-1415) 4th E.** escaped to France, returned with Henry IV in 1399 and was restored to his father's dignities. Strongly partisan, he led some of the police operations needed to establish Henry on the throne. He died at the siege of Harfleur without heirs. A member of a different branch of the family **(8) John (1408-35) Ld. FITZALAN (1429) 5th E. (1435)** was a successful soldier in France and Duke (Viceroy) of Touraine until captured at Gournay. He died of his wounds.

FITZALDHELM, William (?-1198) was Henry II's steward and acted as his representative in Ireland. He succeeded Strongbow as justiciar in Ireland in 1176, and ruled the north-western counties of England from 1189.

FITZCLARENCE. William IV had two sons by Mrs Jordon **(1) George Augustus Frederick (1794-1842) 1st E. of MUNSTER (1831),** a soldier, as A.D.C. to the Marquess Hastings in the Maratha War (1816-17) and as President of the Asiatic Society, promoted Asiatic studies. He is said to have exercised a reactionary influence on his father.

He committed suicide. **(2) Ld. Adolphus (1802-56)** served in the navy.

FITZEUSTACE, Roland (?-1496) Ld. PORTLESTER (1461) was Irish Lord Treasurer from 1454 and Lord Chancellor from 1472-82. Though implicated in Lambert Simnel's rebellion in 1487, he was again Lord Chancellor from 1488.

FITZGERALD or GERALDINES (1) This remarkable and prolific southern Irish family is descended from Gerald of Windsor, an Anglo-Norman who became constable of Pembroke, and married, or had at least four children by, the seductive and gifted Princess Nest. Of these William of Carew (?-1173) Ld. of Naas (Co. Kildare) founded the Carew family, Lords of Idrone, who had extensive lands in Co. Cork and Pembrokeshire and the FitzGriffins, Lords of Knocktopher (Co. Kilkenny). David (?-1177) Bp. of St. Davids was the ancestor of the Fitzmiles family, Lords of Iverk (Co. Kilkenny). Angharat (?-?) who married William of Barry was the mother of Gerald the Historian and the ancestress of the Vists Buttevant (Co. Cork) who became Es. of Barrymore. Finally the great Maurice (?-1176), Ld. of Naas and Wicklow, had at least six children, of whom the eldest, William (?-?) founded the Fitzwilliam family, Lords of Naas; Gerald (?1204) was the ancestor of the Es. of Desmond (i.e. Co. Cork and Limerick) and Maurice (?-1176) founded the Fitzmaurice families, Lords respectively of Burnchurch and Kerry. Other descended clans included the FitzGibbons or White Knights; the Fitzgerald Knights of Kerry, principal tenants of the Fitzmaurices, and the Knights of Glinn (Co. Limerick).

(2) These families, with those of their more important followers (with whom they intermarried) were originally Welsh or trained in Wales and were distinct in outlook from the Anglo-Normans. They understood Celtic life and warfare and came to be on good terms with the Irish, whom they had no inhibitions about marrying. As a result they took root in Munster and Leinster and built up a powerful and lasting following. Their two main heads, the Earls of Desmond and Kildare, became semi-independent dynasts, who levied private wars and ruled their great, but somewhat discontinuous territories as Irish chiefs with feudal trappings.

(3) The Geraldines on the one hand and the Anglo-Norman Marshals, Lords of Leinster, de Burghs or Burkes, Lords of Connaught and Butlers, Lords of Kilkenny and Ormonde tended to be in enmity. This may be ascribed in part to differences of outlook but it was exacerbated by the way in which territories and jurisdictions were confused or intermingled. Moreover these families often had scores to pay off in Wales. The Geraldines might have attained even greater eminence, if they had had consolidated territories and fewer feuds.

FITZGERALD (Kildare) (1) John Fitz Thomas (?-1316) 1st E. of KILDARE (1316) tried by invasions of Leix, Offaly and Connaught to extend his already wide lands northwards but ultimately lost his Sligo and Connaught estates. He married his *s.* **(2) Thomas (?-1328)** to Joan, *d.* of Richard de Burgh, E. of Ulster, and he with the Burkes eventually repelled in 1316 Edward Bruce's destructive invasion from Scotland. He was Justiciar of Ireland in 1320-27 and a Mortimer partisan. His youngest *s.* **(3) Maurice Fitz Thomas (1318-90)** was Justiciar or Deputy almost continually from 1356 onwards. **(4) Thomas (?-1477) 7th E.** was Lord Deputy from 1455-59 and 1461-62. In 1463 he became Lord. Chancellor but was attainted and then restored in 1467. He was Lord Deputy again from 1468-75. His long tenures represented in reality the dependence of the English Govt. on the Geraldine resources. His *s.* **(5) Gerald (?-1513) the Great, 8th E.** was Lord Deputy from 1477-94 and (despite his partisanship for Warbeck and imprisonment) from 1496 onwards. During his time, insofar as Ireland was governed, it was ruled in quasi-independence by Kildare mainly because the Tudors were preoccupied

with establishing their position in England. His *s.* **(6) Gerald (1487-1534) 9th E.** was educated in England and became Treasurer of Ireland when he returned in 1504. From 1514, as Lord Justice or Lord Deputy he was the head of the Govt. and defended the Pale aggressively and with success, but the family feud with the Butlers blazed up at this time and as a result of their intrigues he was dismissed in 1520; reappointed in 1524 he was again dismissed in 1526 and put in the Tower. He returned in 1532, ousted Skeffington as Lord Deputy, was wounded and then summoned to England. He died in the Tower. His career illustrated the English change from reliance upon native Lords to a policy of strength. This provoked his five brothers and his *s.* **(7) Thomas (1513-37) 10th E.** into rebellion (while Lord Deputy) in 1534. Defeated by Lord Leonard Grey to whom they submitted, they were all executed at Tyburn. His *s.* **(8) Gerald (1525-85) 11th E.,** French educated, served with the Knights of St. John and St. Stephen against Barbary corsairs. He was restored to his properties under Edward VI and to his earldom by Mary I. Though he fought the Irish and their Spanish backers, he was arrested in 1582 on suspicion but released in 1584. The later history of the family, despite their promotion to the dukedom of Leinster in 1766 is unimportant. *See* IRELAND *passim*.

FITZGERALD, Lord Edward (1763-98) Irish M.P. from 1783-97. *See* UNITED IRISHMEN.

FITZGIBBON, John (1749-1802) 1st Ld. FITZGIBBON (1789), Vist. (1793), E. of CLARE (1795) became Attorney General of Ireland in 1783 and was a moderate nationalist Irish M.P. from 1778-83. He supported the Anglo-Irish Commercial Treaty of 1785, and opened the anti-terrorist policy with the Whiteboy Act of 1787. As Ld. Chancellor of Ireland from 1789-1802 he was simultaneously a law reformer and an opponent of R. Catholic emancipation. Immensely influential, he managed the Dublin end of the intrigues which ended in the Union of 1800.

FITZHERBERT (1) Sir Anthony (1470-1583) became a sergeant at law in 1510 and published the *Graund Abridgment* in 1514. This was the first renaissance attempt to expound the common law as a system. He became a judge of the Common Pleas in 1522 and as a Commissioner in Ireland negotiated the truce between Kildare and Ormonde. He advised on Wolsey's impeachment and was a member of the courts which tried More and Fisher. A grandson **(2) Nicholas (1580-1612)** was Secretary to Cardinal Allen from 1587. Another grandson **(3) Thomas (1552-1640)** assisted Parsons and Campion and in 1613 became a Jesuit. He was rector of the English college at Rome from 1618-39.

FITZHERBERT, Alleyn (1753-1839) 1st Ld. St. HELENS (Ir. 1794 Gt. Br. 1801) mainly a diplomat representing Britain at Brussels from 1774-82 and at St. Petersburg from 1783-87. He was chief secretary for Ireland from 1787-89 and then went to The Hague and thence to Madrid from 1790-94. Here he negotiated in the Nootka Sound dispute. In 1801 he negotiated the Russian Alliance.

FITZHERBERT, previously SMYTHE and then WELD, Maria Anne (1756-1837) a R. Catholic, went through an illegal ceremony of marriage in Dec. 1785 with George, Prince of Wales, later George IV and lived with him until 1803. During that period and for some time afterwards he regarded her as his wife. The royal family treated her with courtesy.

FITZHERBERT, William (St. William of York) (?-1154) was a nephew of K. Stephen and his influential brother, the ecclesiastical statesman Henry of Blois. At the King's request, he was elected Abp. of York in 1140 but the Cistercian abbots of the province bitterly opposed the election as simoniacal and procured his deposition by the Cistercian Pope, Eugenius III on the advice of St. Bernard, in 1147. He was replaced by Henry Murdac, the combative Abbot of Fountains and fled to Sicily. In 1153 both Murdac and Eugenius died, and Anastasius IV restored Fitzherbert, who, however died in the following year. Cures were later reported from his tomb, and he was canonised in 1226.

FITZJAMES. *See* BERWICK.

FITZJAMES (1) Richard (?-1522) a chaplain to Edward IV became warden of Merton College in 1483, Bp. of Rochester in 1497, was a negotiator of the Great Intercourse in 1499, Bp. of Chichester in 1504 and of London in 1506. He resigned Merton in 1507. He built Fulham Palace. He is hostilely remembered because one Richard Hunne, arrested for heresy, was found hanged in the episcopal prison. Fitzjames contended for suicide but the coroner's jury found murder against the gaoler and the Bps chancellor. His nephew **(2) Sir John (?1470-1542)** was Attorney Gen. 1519, Chief Baron of the Exchequer in 1521 and C.J. of the King's Bench in 1526. In 1529 he signed Articles of Impeachment against Wolsey, and was a member of the court which tried More and Fisher.

FITZMAURICE or MORRIS. Munster family at feud with the Geraldines. **(1) Thomas (1502-99) 16th Ld. KERRY and LIXNAW (1552)**, the youngest *s.* of the 10th Lord, succeeded by the death of all his brothers and their heirs, but had to fight for the estate, which was in the hands of a John Fitzrichard. He sat in the 1556 Parliament. He complained of the aggressive E. of Desmond while his sons Patrick and Edmund joined him. In truth, he was under pressure between the Govt. and powerful rebels, and suspect to both. He was said to have been the handsomest and strongest man of his time. His *s.* **(2) Patrick (?1551-1600) 17th Ld.** was in rebellion or prison most of his adult life. His *s.* **(3) Thomas (1574-1630) 18th Ld.** followed his father into rebellion in 1598; he was pardoned and restored to his lands in 1603, but his son was taken away and brought up a protestant with his uncle and the E. of Thomond. The son and father quarrelled, and Thomas was forced to make over much of his property to him.

FITZNEALE or FITZ NIGEL, Richard or Richard of ELY (?-1198) was a bastard of Nigel, Bp. of Ely, a member of the administrative family of le Poer and Treasurer to Henry I. His father had bought him the Treasurership in 1158 and he helped to reorganise the Norman Exchequer in 1176. He became Dean of Lincoln in 1186 and Bp. of London in 1189. The Treasurership became important under Richard I because of the huge sums raised for the Crusade. He remained in England and tried to compose the quarrels between Longchamp and P. John. At this time he was the Abp.'s delegate, and after Longchamp was deposed, he was in conflict with John over the latter's tendency to pillage the Church, and, as a practical financier, was very glad to act in raising Richard's ransom. He supported Richard's demand for knight service from the Bps. in 1197. He also served as a judge.

FITZOSBERN, William (?-1071) E. of HEREFORD (1067) *s.* of Osbern the Seneschal to D. Robert of Normandy, succeeded to his office after his father's murder. Osbern had maintained William the Conqueror as a child, and William Fitzosbern gave him loyal and energetic support. At the news of Harold Godwinsson's accession, Fitzosbern advised an invasion of England as practicable and likely to succeed. He commanded the Franks at the B. of Hastings. In 1067 he was entrusted with the I. of Wight, and then with the new earldom of Hereford. When K. William left for Normandy late in the year, his half-brother Odo of Bayeux and Fitzosbern exercised an effective regency. He performed a similar function in Normandy in 1070, so when trouble broke out in Flanders in 1070, the King sent him to protect the Norman interest. He was, however, killed in the B. of Cassel. An unsung architect of Norman England.

FITZPATRICK, Sir Barnaby (1535-81) Ld. of UPPER OSSORY. After actively fighting Wyatt in 1553 he settled in Ireland and was at feud with the Ormondes, who secured the abduction of his wife and daughter in 1573. In 1578 he put down Rory O'Mores' rebellion.

FITZPATRICK (1) Richard (?-1727) 1st Ld. GOWRAN (Ir. 1715) was distinguished as a naval commander against the French between 1687-1702 and was rewarded with estates in Queen's Co in 1715. His grandson **(2) Richard (1747-1813),** a friend of Fox, was M.P. for Tavistock in 1774, served in the army in America from 1777-78, was Chief Secretary for Ireland in 1782 and Secretary at War in 1783 and in 1806-07.

FITZPETER, Geoffrey (?-1213) E. of ESSEX (1199) began as an unordained clerk to Henry II's Justiciar Ranulf Glanville, who recognised his abilities, and he served as a sheriff and forest justice and then as an assistant justiciar in the administration created for Richard I's absence on Crusade. He had by good luck, married Beatrice de Say, originally a minor heiress, but through her he was able to claim the Mandeville earldom of Essex when the existing line died out in 1190. In Oct. 1191 he joined in the overthrow of the Justiciar William Longchamp. He was by now recognised as a coming man. In 1198 he succeeded Hubert Walter as Justiciar, and on Richard I's death (1199) acting with two envoys from the continent, he summoned the barons to Northampton and persuaded them to swear fealty to John. John confirmed his earldom and retained him as Justiciar until he died.

FITZROY (= King's son), a surname for royal bastards. In particular Henry VIII fathered upon Elizabeth Blount, Henry D. of Richmond (1519-36); Charles II upon Lucy Walter, James D. of Monmouth and Buccleuch (q.v.) and upon Barbara Villiers, Duchess of Cleveland (a) Charles (1662-1730) 1st D. of Southampton (1675) and Cleveland (1709) (b) Henry (1663-90) 1st E. of Euston (1672) and 1st D. of Grafton (1675) *see* FITZROY (GRAFTON) and (c) George (1665-1716) E. of Northampton (1674) and D. of Northumberland (1683).

FITZROY (1) Charles (1737-97) 1st Ld. SOUTHAMPTON (1780) was A.D.C. (i.e. British Liaison Officer) in the Seven Years' War to Ferdinand of Brunswick. His great-grandson **(2) Edward Algernon (1869-1943)** Tory M.P. for Daventry 1900-06 and from 1910 a respected Speaker from 1928-43.

FITZROY (Grafton) (1) Henry (1663-90) 1st D. of GRAFTON (1675) served as a French officer in Flanders in 1684 and with the royal army at Sedgemoor in 1685. He commanded H.M.S. *Grafton* at the B. of Beachy Head in 1690 and died at the S. of Cork. **(2) Augustus Henry (1735-1811) 3rd D. (1757)** as E. of Euston was M.P. for Bury St. Edmunds in 1756. Of radical opinions, he was a Pittite and supported John Wilkes in 1763, became a Sec. of State (Northern Dept) under Rockingham in 1765-6 and then, as 1st Lord of the Treasury was forced by Pitt's illness and Charles Townshend's death, to take the lead in Govt. Pitt resigned in 1768 and he became the real head until 1770 when he became Lord North's Privy Seal. He attracted much unpopularity during the Middlesex (Wilkesite) Election disturbances of 1768-70 but having no seat in the Cabinet, was not directly responsible for the American disasters. He resigned in 1775 and went into opposition. In Mar. 1782 he became Privy Seal in the second Rockingham Govt., but retired soon afterwards. Of his children **(3) George Henry (1760-1844) 4th D.** as E. of Euston was M.P. for Cambridge University for 1784 until 1811 and then became a Whig and **(4) Ld. Charles (1764-1829),** a general, was M.P. for Bury St Edmunds from 1784-90 and from 1802-18. His *s.* **(5) Sir Charles August (1796-1858)** was M.P. for Bury in 1837 and was then Lieut. Gov. of Prince Edward I. until 1841; as Gov. of N.S.W. from 1846-50 he resisted, with only partial success, the transportation of criminals there; but from 1850-55 he was Gov. Gen of Australia. His brother

(6) Robert (1805-65) commanded the celebrated voyages of H.M.S. *Beagle* to S. America from 1828-36 with Charles Darwin as naturalist from 1831. He was an M.P. in 1841 and an unpopular Gov. of New Zealand from 1843-45. Thereafter as chief of the Admiralty Meteorological Dept., he invented the Fitzroy Barometer, and the first weather forecasting system. *See* METEOROLOGY.

FITZSTEPHEN, Robert (?-1183) Norman Marcher Lord, castellan of Cardigan and half-brother of Maurice Fitzgerald (?-1176) was recruited by Richard Clare E. of Pembroke (Strongbow) for his attempt on Ireland. In 1169 Fitzstephen, with a small advance force seized Wexford, the nearest Irish port to Cardigan. Maurice followed in 1170 and Strongbow himself in 1171. In subsequent fighting, the Irish captured Fitzstephen and later still handed him over to the King, who soon released him. In 1171-2 Henry II made his own Irish expedition, imposed a superficial authority upon the Normans whose shallow power had spread westwards along the Munster coast. At a Council at Oxford in 1177, Henry devised a new scheme of Irish administration (actually subinfeudation of Munster) in which Fitzstephen and Miles of Cogan were jointly granted the principality of Cork for the service of 60 knights. They were defending it with some desperation when he died.

FITZSTEPHEN, William (?-1190) friend and secular clerk of Thomas Becket, sought to dissuade him from extreme courses, especially at the disastrous Council of Northampton in 1164. He was present at Becket's murder and later wrote a vivid *Vita Sancti Thomae* (Lat: Life of St. Thomas) which, *inter alia,* describes contemporary London (Becket's birthplace) with details such as the existence of take away cookshops on the river bank, horse fairs and amusements from ball games to miracle plays.

FITZWALTER, Robert (?-1235) Ld. of DUNMOW and BAYNARD'S CASTLE (1198), apparently related to the Clares, as castellan of Baynard's Castle in London, was a trader and owned wine ships. He married Gunnor, heiress of Valognes in Normandy. By 1202 he was also castellan of Hertford and in 1203 was in Normandy with K. John. He and Saer de Quincy surrendered Vaudreuil to the French (to their amusement) and in 1206 he witnessed the Truce of Thouars.

(2) Disillusioned with John, he now acted as a channel for French intrigues and from 1212 was known to be in opposition. When he and Eustace deVesci conspired with Llywellyn ap Iorwerth, John seized his lands and destroyed Baynard's Castle and Benington. Robert went into exile with the exiled Bps. After the settlement with the Pope he returned and his lands were restored, but he continued in opposition. He reinforced the revolt of 1215 with his own E. Anglian family connections and the northern barons elected him their marshal. Moderation eventually prevailed and he agreed to be one of the 25 executors of the Magna Carta. He was thus involved against the King in the ensuing Civil War and was excommunicated in Dec.

(3) Robert now felt forced to accept French assistance, and Prince Louis landed in May 1216. He was in great difficulty for the country was going over to the regency for Henry III and the French, perhaps remembering Vaudreuil, mistrusted him. The royalists captured him at the B. of Lincoln. In 1217 he was released and partly restored but in 1219 found it convenient to go on the 5th Crusade. He returned, probably in 1221 but played no further public part. He is the subject of several anecdotes, e.g. that John tried to force his daughter, and that he instituted the Dunmow Flitch.

FITZWARINE or FITZWARREN, FULK, was the name of eleven successive Shropshire nobles between 1150 and 1420. Of these **Fulk (III), Ld. (?-1256)** an opponent of K. John, was important enough to be specially

ex-communicated in 1215, but made his peace with the regency for Henry III. In 1245 he was responsible for enforcing the expulsion of the nuncio Martin. **Fulk (IV), Ld. (?-1264)** was killed at the B. of Lewes.

FITZWILLIAM. *See* HEREFORD.

FITZWILLIAM (1) Edward (1788-1852), his wife **(2) Fanny (1801-54),** their *s.* **(3) Edward Francis (1824-57),** and the latter's wife **(4) Ellen (1822-80)** formed a well-known family of London actors.

FITZWILLIAM, Ralph (?-1256-1316) Ld. FITZWILLIAM (1295) served in the Welsh wars of 1277, 1282 and 1287. In 1291 he was summoned to serve against the Scots and made his fortune on the border. In 1297 he became Captain of the Northumberland garrisons and of the Scottish March. In 1298 he levied troops in Yorkshire and in 1300-2 he was raising taxes and benevolences there. Under Edward II he joined the opposition, and was implicated in Gaveston's murder. In 1315, after Bannockburn, the local magnates made him a warden of the March. The extensive family estates in Cumberland, Northumberland and Yorkshire passed in 1487 to the Dacre family.

FITZWILLIAM, William (?-1542) 1st E. of SOUTHAMPTON (1537) was brought up with Henry VIII and became his esquire in 1511. In 1513 he was a naval commander against the French and was wounded. By 1518 he was Treasurer of Wolsey's household and in 1521 Wolsey used him as ambassador to the French court. On the outbreak of war in 1522 he became Vice-Admiral but as Capt. of Guisnes from May 1524 was employed as a diplomat at Malines, and then to the French court. In 1526 he became comptroller of the houshold and was employed in further French diplomatic business until 1529. In Oct. he became custodian of Wolsey's property and succeeded More as Chancellor of the Duchy of Lancaster. In 1533 he was briefly Lord Privy Seal. After a further diplomatic interlude in 1535 he was a member of the council which extracted Sir William Norris' confession of adultery with Anne Boleyn and a member of the court which tried him. In 1536 he became Lord High Admiral and helped to suppress the Lincolnshire insurrection and in 1538 he investigated the Countess of Salisbury's connection with the Nun of Kent. In 1539 he brought Anne of Cleves over to England and was accused by Thomas Cromwell of unduly raising the King's hopes. He helped to arrest Cromwell in 1540. He died on the march against Scotland.

FITZWILLIAM (1) William Wentworth (1748-1833) 2nd E. FITZWILLIAM (1756). His wife was a Bessborough related to the Cavendishes. He was a Whig opposed to Lord North. In 1782 he inherited the vast Rockingham properties and thereafter maintained a princely state at Wentworth Woodhouse. In 1794 he became Lord President, but in Dec. Lord Lieutenant of Ireland where he became involved in a political misunderstanding. He favoured R. Catholic emancipation and had been appointed as part of a bargain whereby Pitt secured Whig support. Before he arrived he wrote to Grattan announcing a change of system and asking for his help. This warned the diehards, especially in Pitt's cabinet. He agreed to use his first months observing the situation and reporting on it while adhering to his convictions, but one of his first acts was to dismiss John Beresford, head of the Irish Revenue Dept., and the second most important champion of English ascendancy. This was instantly taken as a declaration of policy and Grattan introduced an emancipation bill. The King objected and Pitt knew that some of the cabinet agreed with the King. He forced Fitzwilliam to resign. He went into opposition against Addington in Feb. 1801 and was Lord President again under Grenville in 1806. In 1819 he was dismissed from the Lieutenancy of Yorkshire for publicly condemning the magistrates in the Peterloo affair. His *s.* **(2) Charles William Wentworth (1786-1857) 3rd E.,** as Lord

Milton, was M.P. for Yorkshire from 1807-31 and from 1831-33 for Northamptonshire. He was slowly converted to Parliamentary reform even though the family owned several pocket boroughs. He was also a strong advocate of repeal of the Corn Laws, and like his father, condemned the Peterloo magistrates. He remained a Whig and then a Liberal all the rest of his life. He also published part of the correspondence of Edmund Burke.

FITZWILLIAM (1) Sir William (?1460-1534) Merchant Taylor, contested a London shrievalty in 1505 but was elected on the King's nomination in 1506. A fine for the 1510 shrievalty was remitted by the Star Chamber in 1511. He became Cardinal Wolsey's treasurer, sheriff of Essex in 1515 and of Northampton in 1524. He died very rich. His grandson **(2) Sir William (1526-99)** was related through his mother to the 1st E. of Bedford who presented him to court in 1547. By now he was buying land in Ireland. In 1555, he, though a protestant, supported Mary I against Lady Jane Grey and was temporarily a Keeper of the Irish Great Seal. In 1559 he became vice-treasurer of Ireland and in 1560 a Lord Justice in the absence of Sussex the Lord Lieutenant. He was then intermittently a Lord Justice until 1571 when he was sworn Lord Deputy and so continued until 1575. It was a stormy period. Reappointed in 1588 during the dispersal of the Spanish Armada, he was responsible for the massacres of its castaways. In 1589 he had to deal with MacMahon's rising and a violent quarrel with Sir Richard Bingham, President of Connaught; in 1590 with a mutiny of Sir Thomas Norrey's troops; in 1591 with border disputes at Dundalk; in 1592 with Maguire's rebellion in Cavan. He retired because of illness.

FITZWILLIAM MUSEUM (Cambridge) was founded in 1816 under the bequest of Richard, 7th Vist. Fitzwilliam (1745-1816) who gave (1776) his considerable collection of art and books and an endowment to Cambridge University. The buildings were constantly enlarged for pictures in 1931 and 1934 and for manuscripts (1925), coins (1934), prints (1936) and water colours (1955). It also contained in 1993 important representative collections of music, ceramics, antiquities, armour and textiles.

FIUME now RIJEKA (Y-S) (Both names mean 'river') the Hungarian port of the Austro-Hungarian Empire, was not promised to Italy by the allies for deserting the Central Powers in 1915, in case the Hungarians were minded to make a separate peace. They did not and to help make Balkan trade dependent on Italian shipping, Venetian business interests spurred the Italian Govt. to demand it at the peace conference. There, a protracted wrangle was cut short by d'Annunzio's expedition from Venice, which seized Fiume and the adjacent islands (1920). The conference half accepted this, and under the T. of Rapallo (Nov. 1920) Fiume, though dominated by an Italian militia, became a Free City embedded in Yugoslavia, and without the latter's consent useless to Hungary. In 1923 Mussolini's Fascist dictatorship (emotionally modelled on d'Annunzio's lifestyle and acts), annexed Fiume. This, distinction without a difference continued until Yugoslavia acquired it after World War II.

FIVE ARTICLES OF PERTH (1618 and 1621) James I announced that he intended five religious observances in the Scottish Church to keep it from drifting too far from mainstream Christianity viz: **(1)** kneeling at Communion (which might imply the Real Presence); **(2)** private communion in necessity (which might bring in secret extreme unction); **(3)** private baptism; **(4)** confirmation by a bishop (these two loosened the hold of the congregations over membership) and **(5)** observance of the great feasts (suggesting that some Sabbaths were less holy than others). In 1617 he came to Scotland to impose his will but the Parliament declined to increase the power of the bps. and a clerical assembly at St Andrews referred the issue to a General Assembly. This made reservations but another at Perth in 1618 accepted them, and in 1621 Parliament ratified them. They were not repealed in the subsequent upheavals but allowed to fall into desuetude at the Restoration. *See* SCOTLAND (PRESBYTERIAN) CHURCH.

FIVE BOROUGHS, THE. Five Danish armies settled between the Welland and the Humber and established fortified bases in the mid-9th cent. at Stamford, Leicester, Derby, Nottingham and Lincoln. These formed a confederation. K. Edmund reconquered the area in 942 but the Five Boroughs continued a distinctive part of the Danelaw. Their particular institutions and Scandinavian flavour are reflected in a code of Ethelred II which gave them royal authority. There was a Court of the Five Boroughs over which an earldorman or King's Reeve presided; there were lawmen who advised in the courts of the individual boroughs and wapentakes, and a sworn jury of 12 thegns might declare a man to be of ill repute or arrest him. All but Stamford became county towns.

FIVE KNIGHTS CASE. *See* DARNELS CASE.

FIVE MEMBERS, THE. For Pym, Hampden, Holles, Hesilrige and Strodes' attempted impeachment and arrest (Jan. 1642) *see* CHARLES I-22.

FIVE MILE ACT, 1665. *See* CLARENDON CODE 1661-5.

FIVE POWER NAVAL TREATY (1922). *See* WASHINGTON TREATIES-3.

FLAALD. See STEWART-1.

FLAGS, NATIONAL (1) On Land. Until 1603, England (St. George's) red cross on white; Scotland (St. Andrew's) white saltire on blue. English in Ireland, red saltire on white. 1603-1801. The first union flag, a combination of England and Scotland. Since 1801 the second union flag, a combination of all three. **(2) At Sea.** The Scots disliked the first union flag and James I ("Jack") while requiring it to be flown at the main, permitted the older flags to be flown at the foretop. Warships mostly flew a striped ensign of colours chosen by the Captain, with the St. George or St. Andrew in a canton at the top corner by the staff. Ships on war service usually wore a pendant. In 1661 the union flag was restricted to royal ships, but in 1674 merchantmen were given a red ensign with the canton. Meanwhile the fleet was divided into three squadrons flying respectively red, white and blue ensigns with canton. After England and Scotland were united in 1707 the union always occupied the canton, and the white ensign showed the St. George. It was, however, found that the multiplicity of flags could create confusion in battle especially at night, and Nelson adopted the practice of flying the white ensign and the union jack only in battle. Other navies (notably Imperial Germany and Russia) found white battle flags convenient too. In 1864 the squadron flags were abolished, the white ensign and the union jack becoming exclusive to the Royal Navy, the blue ensign to the Royal Naval Reserve.

FLAGS, Black (1) The emblem of piracy. **(2)** A threat, at sea, of no quarter. **(3)** Tonkinese rebels. **(4)** The Abbasid Caliphs. **Red (1)** Danger. **(2)** International socialism. **White (1)** Truce. **(2)** The Bourbon flag of France. **Yellow.** Ship in quarantine. **Upside Down (1)** Ship in distress. **(2)** Ship captured.

"FLAMBARD", Ranulf (?-1128) Bp. of DURHAM (1099) s. of a priest in Normandy became a hanger-on of the court and servant of Maurice, from 1081 Chancellor to William I. His nickname ('torch' or 'firebrand') perhaps reflects his disposition. His swift rise cost him enemies and in 1085 he was kidnapped and carried off by ship but escaped in the Thames. He had a temperamental affinity with Rufus, who, like himself was 'utterly secular' and with whom he built up a striking partnership. Ranulf applied his talent for organisation and legal chicanery towards financing Rufus' ventures. He exploited feudal rights and justice as sources of revenue, particularly wardships, reliefs and the revenues of vacant abbeys and bishoprics. In 1099 he was left in charge of the govt.

while Rufus was abroad. In 1100 the King was killed in the New Forest. Ranulf, as scapegoat for an unpopular King was imprisoned in the Tower. With characteristic resilience he escaped to Normandy and helped Duke Robert to invade England in 1101. Robert failed and made his peace with his brother Henry I. Henry, appreciating Ranulf's ability and cunning restored him to his see but sent him back to Normandy, probably to subvert the duchy. When Henry finally invaded (1106) Ranulf was waiting to receive him at Lisieux, the diocese which he had been administering for some years. He returned to Durham and threw his energies into organising and building. He laid the administrative foundations for the emerging palatinate of Durham. The fine church at Christchurch (Hants) exhibited his earlier talent for building and perhaps prepared the way for the remarkable cathedral at Durham. He also created St Giles' Hospital in a suburb of the city. Much reviled by monastic chroniclers at large for his financial exactions he was admired at Durham. 'His works...' wrote Lawrence of Durham 'declare that their author was a truly great-hearted man.'

FLAMBOYANT, was the latest type of French Gothic architecture, so-called for its curvilinear tracery in flamed (flambé) shapes, for example at St. Maclou in Rouen. In England the latest phase developed towards the more powerful lines of the perpendicular style, so that few English instances of Flamboyant can be found. *See* ARCHITECTURE, BRITISH.

FLAMMOCK'S or FLAMANK'S REBELLION (1497). For an imminent Scots war, Parliament granted two tenths and fifteenths and promised more. A force under Daubeny was got ready, but the Cornish led by Thomas Flamank, a lawyer, and Michael Joseph, a blacksmith, marched peacefully towards London to protest against the taxation, picking up the support of Lord Audley at Wells. The King's and Daubeney's forces blocked the way and in June 1497 after a fight at Deptford the Cornishmen were routed and the three leaders executed.

FLAMSTEED, The Rev. John (1646-1719) was appointed King's Astronomic Observator in 1675 to correct the tables of the heavenly bodies for the use of seamen. His *Historia Coelestis Britannica* (Lat.= British Account of the Heavens) published in 1725 though not wholly free of errors, was the basis of the great 18th cent. navigational advances.

FLANDERS (Dutch: VLAANDEREN) (1) At one time or another embraced most of the coastal area between the R. Scheldt and the R. Somme. During the Frankish invasions the sea level rose and flooded the Belgian littoral, but Flanders was established as a power by Counts Baldwin II (r. 879-918) and Arnulf I (r. 918-64) under the later Carolingians. Its southward expansion was halted just short of Amiens by the advent of the Normans. The Counts were allies of the Capetian Counts of Paris and when the latter became Kings they were no more than suzerains. The whole extent was in the royal ecclesiastical province of Rheims. Flemish, a dialect of Dutch, the common speech north of Calais, distinguished the population from the French and the Normans.

(2) Between 964 and 1012 there emerged four subordinate counties from whose rulers the French Ks. claimed homage or oaths of non-injury. These were St. Pol and Hesdin, together with Guines and Boulogne which later became English possessions. The frontiers were pushed eastwards to the gates of Antwerp and in some parts across the Scheldt towards Brussels. The latter areas were called Imperial Flanders as against Crown Flanders which was under French suzerainty, and later under the jurisdiction of the Parlement of Paris.

(3) Under the direction of immense, mostly Cistercian monasteries the coastal lagoons were reclaimed for horticulture and sheep farming in the 11th cent. Textile industries were early established in the towns, notably Ghent, Bruges, Ypres and Arras with their respective neighbours. These, the Four Members of Flanders, eventually wove English wool and exported the finished products to noble English households or to the rest of the west in Hanseatic or Venetian ships, or through the Champagne fairs. There was a Hanse of Flemish cities at the Dowgate in London. However, the Western *Kontor* of the German Hanse at Bruges was a European financial centre throughout the middle ages. The towns became precariously rich, depending mainly on English corn, wool and maritime goodwill.

(4) The Counts, however, were constantly faced with the need to resist French encroachments and to reduce Anglo-Norman power. Friction with France interfered with overland exports: friction with England could bankrupt the towns. This disharmony between urban economic and territorial political interests was the basic weakness of Flemish life.

(5) The direct line of the original dynasty died out in 1119, and the related Count Charles the Good (r. 1119-27) was murdered. Thereupon King Louis VI as suzerain tried to impose William Clito of Normandy who had a distant claim. But in the total absence of a ruler, the towns were able, partially, to fill the political vacuum. They rejected and killed Louis VI's puppet, installed Thierry (Dietrich) of Alsace (r. 1128-68) and forced Louis to accept him.

(6) During Thierry's reign a road was built from Cologne via Maastricht and Ghent to Bruges with its port on the Zwijn. This gave the Cologne entrepôt an alternative outlet besides the outward flowing Rhine and altered the axis of Flemish continental trade from south-east to east. The route is the true origin of modern Belgium, for it lent a cohesion of interest to the states in the zone through which it passed. Soon Thierry's daughter was married to his eastern neighbour the Count of Hainault.

(7) But the shifting of the route away from the Champagne provoked a reaction at Paris, especially when Thierry's *s*. Count Philip (r. 1168-91) acquired Vermandois by marriage. K. Philip Augustus himself made a bid for Hainault. In 1180 he married Isabel of Hainault. With a show of force and in the absence of his rivals on crusade, he took Vermandois and, by way of dowry, the south western Flemish area which, with St. Omer and the country about Arras became the subordinate county of Artois. This was actually, if not in theory, under his direct and masterful government. He secured it by the first T. of Arras (1191) as the price of the peaceful succession of Count Philip's sister, for she was married to Baldwin V of Hainault, who thus became the ruler of both Hainault and Flanders until 1195. Their *s*. Baldwin left for the Fourth Crusade in 1203 and his daughters Johanna (r. 1203-44) and Margaret (r. 1244-80) became wards of the French King.

(8) Since the reconquest of Lisbon in 1147 by an Anglo-Flemish pilgrim force, trade through the Straits of Gibraltar, was becoming a factor in Flemish economics. A Portuguese marriage might help to win the towns for French policy and establish a weak foreigner who might be expected to lean upon French support. So in 1212 Johanna was married to Ferrante of Portugal and Margaret to a kinsman, Burchard of Avesnes. K. Philip's calculations were, however, upset when his son Louis occupied Aire, and frightened the aristocracy and the towns into a joint alliance with England negotiated by Renaud of Dammartin, whose county of Boulogne was already occupied.

(9) The English naval victory at Damme (May 1213) relieved the towns: the French victory at Bouvines (1214) overthrew the feudality. The French King stepped nominally into the political shoes of the Counts, but found the town economy too strong for him. He could not even stop the baronial feuds. Margaret had sons by

Burchard of Avesnes, but the marriage was annulled in 1221. In 1225 she married William of Dampierre and had further sons. Dampierres and Avesnes fought over the inheritance even in the lifetime of the incumbent Johanna. In 1237 Louis XI tried partial disengagement by giving Artois in appanage to his brother Robert. In 1244, however, Johanna died and the King tried arbitration instead. He adjudged Flanders to the Dampierres and Hainault to the Avesnes, but the war promptly developed into a dispute about trade outlets and continued as a kind of feudal disorder. Robert I of Artois died in 1250. The towns, with their waterborne communications, fended for themselves and developed a certain (rather short sighted) political and military self sufficiency. They were also able to impose specialised forms of local peace in the countrysides through their influence in the drainage organisations, which the feudal lords dared not disturb. In 1299 however, the Avesnes acquired the counties of Holland and Zeeland, and the divided country seemed to be faced with the unpleasant dilemma of Avesnes domination, or loss of the English trade if it accepted French protection. The French were already extremely unpopular. In these circumstances Count Guy of Dampierre renounced his French allegiance, whereupon royal troops entered his lands. The townsmen of Bruges rose (*The Matins of Bruges*); the insurrection spread, and in 1302 the urban infantry routed the French chivalry at Courtrai (The B. of the Golden Spurs) where Robert II of Artois was killed. A French victory at Mons-en-Pevèle in 1304, however, disposed the Flemings to peace, and led to further attrition of the county: Lille, Douai and Bethune were pledged under the P. of Athis (1305) for a war indemnity. This proved an excessive burden on Flemish trade, and in 1312 the Count preferred to let the French foreclose the pledges.

(10) For a century the Flemish nobility had been moving over to French aristocratic standards and attitudes. The accession in 1322 of Count Louis of Nevers in Flanders represented its logical extension, namely the French royal policy against town privileges. In the P. of Paris (1323) the Count gave up his claim to Zeeland south of the Scheldt and the Avesnes theirs to Imperial Flanders. As the coastal ports were silting up, this put Flemish trade at the mercy of the master of the Scheldt. It was a bad bargain for Bruges and West Flanders which revolted. The Count called in his French overlord. The Flemish infantry fell before the royal troops at Cassel in 1328. Thus to the opposition of political and economic interests was added the bitterness of a species of class struggle, compounded by differences of language and outlook.

(11) For the impending fight for Aquitaine, which developed into the "Hundred Years' War", English diplomacy sought northern allies who could distract the French military effort. The Emperor and the rulers of the Low Countries were courted by magnificent embassies and it was natural to approach the Flemish towns now led, since the disasters to Bruges, by Ghent. The Gantois brewer JACOB VAN ARTEVELDE (?1287-1345) formed a League of Flemish Towns in 1336. His object was to stay profitably neutral: the Count, whose position depended upon French support, intended to fight the English. Mutual trade embargoes between England and Flanders brought matters to a head. In Nov. 1337 the English attacked the Count's ships at Cadsand. In June 1338 the French burned Portsmouth. In July Edward III landed in Flanders. Flemish urban neutrality was an illusion: there could be no trade with a hostile England; only England could clear the routes of French (and Genoese) interference. Thus the opening moves were naval operations in the Straits ending in the destruction of the French Fleet at Sluys (June 1340). A land campaign against France was less successful. In Sept. Edward and K. Philip concluded the Truce of Esplèchin.

(12) But the towns were not united. The commercial patriciates, who made vast profits as middlemen, led the prosperity still visible in the architectural elegance and burgeoning pictorial arts of the great cities, but the artisan guilds wanted cheap raw materials or higher prices for their finished goods. The patricians dealt in both. Moreover the English King could exercise authority over his unreliable princely allies only through an imperial vicariate conferred by the Emperor Ludwig IV under the T. of Coblenz (Sept. 1338) In Mar. 1341 Ludwig changed sides and the vicariate was withdrawn. In Apr. 1341 the war was renewed as a Breton war of succession, in less favourable circumstances, but English military efficiency everywhere maintained the balance until the truce of Malestroit in Jan. 1343.

(13) The brutal and arrogant Artevelde had personal enemies besides opponents. His association with English royalty had probably turned his head. Edward III planned a further diversion from Flanders but Artevelde was murdered (July 1345). A year later the diversion took the form of an invasion of Normandy: it culminated in the devastating victory at Crécy (Aug. 1346) where Count Louis of Nevers was killed. Then while Edward's Queen Philippa captured David II of Scots at Neville's Cross (Oct. 1346) Edward besieged Calais. In June 1347 the English captured Charles of Blois (the French claimant to Brittany) at La Roche, and in Aug. Calais surrendered.

(14) The immediate effect was to hasten the reorganisation of the Bruges Hanseatic *Kontor,* that vast financial centre, whose quasi-independence had been a source of international difficulty for a generation (*see* HANSE). In the long term it bound the economies of Flanders and England yet more closely together but not as before. In the bitter confusion of the towns, cloth production declined while English production stimulated by the water driven Pennine fulling mills (introduced in the 13th cent.) rapidly superseded it. The Flemish middlemen prospered and their European function as traders and bankers might have widened, but the artisans suffered and moreover, the Black Death (1347-51) supervened to disorganise policy, commercial dealing and economic relationships. The war continued desultorily and in 1353 the English wool Staple at Bruges was abolished in order to enable foreign buyers to buy in England at an enhanced price. In 1356 came the capture of the French K. John II at Poitiers and in Oct. 1360 the inevitable P. of Brétigny or Calais which left *inter alia* Calais, Guisnes and Ponthieu in English hands.

(15) For reasons connected with the royal finances and public objections to monopolies, a wool staple was established at Calais in 1363 (*see* CALAIS). Count Louis of Nevers was succeeded by his s. Louis of Mâle (r. 1346-84). In 1369 his daughter Margaret married Philip of Burgundy, who brought back Lille and Douai to Flanders. The bargain was designed to bring Louis into the French camp and the war resumed in 1369. A naval battle with the English off the saltpans at Bourgneuf (1371) was not encouraging, and the Gantois led by Philip van Artevelde (1340-82) (Jacob's son and Q. Philippa's godson) became restive, as French operations constricted the English holdings and interfered with trade. After the two year Truce of Bruges (1375) the French and their Castilian allies raided the English S. and E. coasts in 1377 (at Richard II's accession); the English retaliated by occupying Brest and Cherbourg (1378) and supporting a Breton rebellion (1379). In 1380 they defeated a Franco-Castilian fleet off Ireland.

(16) In 1381 there was a six year truce; both sides had their social troubles and religious doubts, exemplified by the English Peasants' Revolt (1381) and the French Maillotin risings in Paris and Rouen (1382). Above all, the political and economic regime in Flanders was breaking up; Louis of Mâle inherited Artois in 1382, and the towns were faced with an overmighty count and

indefinite prospects of policy detrimental to their foreign trade and local franchises. The reunion of Artois with Flanders was the signal for urban insurrection. The Count and his feudality, like their fathers, called in the French. A powerful royal army seized Ypres before the burgher infantry could concentrate. The forces of Ghent and its associates were wiped out at Roosebeke (Nov. 1382) and Philip van Artevelde killed. The English staged a counter attack. In the Great Schism, then in progress, the French supported Clement VII, the English Urban VI. An invasion of Flanders might be made in the form of an Urbanist crusade for which the Urbanist church, not the English taxpayer, would pay. The Crusade, mismanaged by the Bp. of Norwich, reached Flanders in May 1383 and retired in total discomfiture in Aug. The English however, managed to get Ghent included in the Truce of Leulighem of Jan. 1384.

(17) French supremacy was apparent, not real. In Feb. 1384 Louis of Mâle died and the united county, with Franche Comté passed in right of the Countess Margaret to her husband Philip the Bold of Burgundy. By this event he became one of the potentates of Europe, with interests which (like those of the English Kings) diverged sharply from those of any ordinary feudatory of the French crown. Moreover it altered the balance of Flemish economic interests: from the beginning the Burgundian Dukes sought to unify their large, if scattered, domains and encouraged the overland trade. English cloth exports were overtaking English wool, so that Flemish weavers either changed their occupations or migrated (in numbers) to England, or had to obtain their wool from Spain. In the Low Countries generally, banking, exchange, marketing and reconsignment began to over-shadow manufacturing, but the adjacent seas were lawless. All merchantmen turned pirate if opportunity served. Bretons and Flemings preyed on the English; the English were seeking to bypass the Bruges *Kontor* and sell direct to the Baltic, attacking Hansard ships as they went. The Biscay trade had to be organised in convoys.

(18) While conditions for an economic estrangement from England were beginning to develop, the triangular politics of England, France and Burgundy retarded the process. Flanders was the richest of the Burgundian possessions: its wealth had been made by the towns mainly on the English connection, and trading habits die hard. In the factional struggles in royal France and at court between Armagnacs (many of them southerners) and the Burgundians, most Armagnacs regarded war with England (in Aquitaine) as a normal condition of life, while Flemings were used to the opposite outlook. Both sides courted the English, but Burgundy with greater determination and success. *For later events see* BELGIUM; BURGUNDY; HUNDRED YEARS WAR; VALOIS.

FLANDERS GALLEYS were regular voyages of Mediterranean merchant fleets to Flanders, begun by the Genoese in about 1298, the Venetians and Catalans in about 1314 and the Florentines in 1421. They brought spices, silks, sugar and alum in return for cloth. From about 1380 they began to touch at English ports for wool, cloth and tin. They declined after 1515 and disappeared in about 1625.

FLANDERS MARE. Henry VII's term for Anne of Cleves. A reference to her figure.

FLAPPER, c. 1900-30, was a recently emancipated but not very responsible young woman, or bright young thing. The Flapper Vote was a derisive term for the women between the ages of 21-30 enfranchised under a Tory Govt. in 1928.

FLAXMAN, John (1755-1826) a child prodigy, exhibited at the Royal Academy in 1770, was employed by the Wedgwoods in 1775 and then gained a great reputation as a sculptor in Italy. He later returned and made many drawings, models and statues. He was the first Professor of Sculpture at the Royal Academy.

FLEET (London). The River or Ditch was the western outer defence of Roman London, being crossed in mediaeval times by a drawbridge at Lud Gate. Its wharves were the busiest above London Bridge and the area was notorious, partly for the debtors prison (on the east bank) whose damp and unhealthy state was caused by the river; partly for the criminals and whores who crowded the neighbourhood and could find safety in the local sanctuaries; and partly for the FLEET MARRIAGES which parsons in prison for debt were prepared, for a consideration, to solemnise, at one of the 40 local pubs, upon abducted heiresses. The river silted up slowly so that by the end of the 17th cent. it was fit only for small boats.

It stank and was liable to sudden floods. In 1735-5 it was partly covered over; the rest being finished in 1768. The **Street**, connecting the Strand with Ludgate bridge, assumed increasing importance or notoriety in the 18th cent. as journalists began to gather there, and in the 19th cent. the street and its neighbourhood was taken up with newspaper offices and printing works to such a point that the expression Fleet Street meant not only the whole complex of newspaper production, but a large adjacent area too.

The area began to acquire respectability when the prison was closed (1842) and the river properly sewered (1855) to become New Bridge St. This process was accelerated by the demolition of the brothel area called the Stews to the west, to make way for Kingsway and Aldwych, but the last notorious brothel was closed (and became a pub) only in 1911. The street remained the headquarters of the newspaper industry until after World War II, when the industry itself began to decline and major combines to move away. By 1973 it was occupied mainly by the London offices of provincial journals, and by 1990 half the pubs had closed.

FLEET AIR ARM. *See* ROYAL NAVAL AIR SERVICE.

FLEET IN BEING. A concept of naval strategy. The mere existence of a fleet will compel a power whose major interests might be threatened by it to maintain a larger one at a particular point; hence the threatening fleet needs only to remain in being to cause a significant diversion of enemy war potential or a neglect of other theatres or both. Generally considered a feature of German war policy in both World Wars.

FLEETWOOD (1) George (?-after 1660) was M.P. for Bucks. in the Long Parliament and one of the court which 'tried' the King in 1648-9. He was a member of the Council of State in 1653 and of Cromwell's House of Lords in 1657. He joined Monck in 1660 and was condemned to death but reprieved at the Restoration; he went to America. A relative **(2) James (1603-83)** was a chaplain to Charles II; he became Provost of Kings, Cambridge in 1660 and Bp. of Worcester in 1675. His nephew **(3) William (1656-1723)** was chaplain to William III, Bp. of St. Asaph from 1708 and was translated to Ely in 1714.

FLEETWOOD (1) Baron George (1605-67) a Swedish General, ennobled by Q. Christina in 1654, visited England as Ambassador in 1655. His brother **(2) Charles (?-1692)** commanded a regiment of Parliamentary horse at Naseby in 1645; became M.P. for Marlborough in 1646 and sided with the army in the controversies between the soldiers and the politicians. He was Lieutenant General of Horse at Dunbar in 1650, member of the Council of State in 1651 and C-in-C of the forces in England before the B. of Worcester. In 1652 he married Bridget Ireton, Cromwell's daughter and became C-in-C in Ireland. From 1654-57 he was also Lord Deputy, in absentia, as well as Major-Gen. for the Eastern district. In 1656 he was called to Cromwell's House of Lords, and at the latter's death supported his son Richard and became nominal C-in-C. He was incapacitated for further office at the Restoration.

FLEGEL, Eduard (1855-86) a Balt, ascended the R. Niger in 1879, reached Sokoto in 1880 and the source of the Benue in 1883. Only incidentally an explorer, his purpose was the largely successful furtherance of German economic imperialism in the region.

FLEMING, Sir Alexander (1881-1955) discovered lysozyme, an anti-microbial substance produced by bodily secretions such as tears and saliva in 1922. He became Professor of Bacteriology at St. Mary's Hospital in 1924, and had discovered Penicillin in 1928. The latter was developed and stabilised at Oxford as a revolutionary anti-bacterial agent by Howard Florey, joint winner with Fleming of the Nobel Prize for Medicine in 1945.

FLEMING, Sir John Ambrose (1849-1945) First Professor of Mathematics and Physics at Nottingham, became electrical engineer to the Edison Electric Lighting Co. in 1881 and introduced electric lighting on a commercial scale into the U.K. In 1885 he became Professor of Electrical Engineering at University College, London.

FLEMISH MIGRATIONS to ENGLAND. Spurred by warfare and civil strife and encouraged by good English wool, Flemish textile workers, especially weavers, migrated in numbers to E. Anglia in the 13th and 14th cents. and again because of religious persecutions in the 16th cent. There were further migrations to Yorkshire in the 18th cent. Common surnames such as Walker (Fl = Warp Maker), Gaunt (Fl = Ghent) and Mineer (= Mijn Heer = Mr) reflect them.

FLETA (= Fleet). A Latin text book (c. 1290) mainly on English law and in part an abridgement of Bracton, contains also a version of the tract on estate management ascribed to Walter of Henley. It was perhaps composed by a lawyer imprisoned in the Fleet.

FLETCHER of SALTOUN, Andrew (1655-1716) an opponent of Lauderdale in the Scots. Parliament, joined Monmouth in 1685 in Holland because of his opposition to James II. He was dismissed for killing one Dare, parted from Monmouth and entered Habsburg service. In 1688 he joined William III in Holland and returned to his Scottish estates. He was so strongly opposed to union that in 1708 he was absurdly suspected of complicity in a recent abortive Jacobite raid and briefly imprisoned. He introduced the Dutch barley mill into Britain. He uttered the dictum that 'a nation's ballads are more influential than its laws'.

FLETCHER, Giles the Elder (?1549-1611) was envoy to Russia in 1588. His book on Russia, suppressed in 1591, was not fully published until 1856.

FLETCHER (1) Richard (?-1596) chaplain to Q. Elizabeth I in 1581, and Dean of Peterborough in 1583, was chaplain at Mary Q. of Scots execution (which he recorded) at Fotheringhay. In 1589 he became Bp. of Bristol, in 1593 he was translated to Worcester and in 1594 to London, but his part in the Lambeth Articles annoyed the Queen, and later she suspended him when he married a second time. His *s*. **(2) John (1579-1625)** was the dramatist who collaborated with Beaumont.

FLETCHER, Sir Richard (1768-1813) a distinguished military engineer, served with the Turks against the French from 1799-1800 and in 1808 became Wellington's engineer in Portugal. *Inter alia* he built the lines of Torres Vedras between 1809-10, directed the siege operations at Badajoz (1811), Ciudad Rodrigo, Pamplona (1812) and at San Sebastian (1813) where he fell.

FLEURY, Cardinal. *See* WARS OF 1739-48 1-5; GEORGE II-5.

FLIGHT OF THE EARLS. *See* JAMES 1-6 & 7.

FLINT, -SHIRE, consisted of three disjoined areas forming part of the Palatinate of Chester. The town of Flint, on the Dee was never of much importance save to give its name to the three areas, the largest of which included it and Mold and was roughly ten miles wide along the south shore of the Dee estuary. It included the cathedral village of St. Asaph and was protected at its western end from the wild Welsh of old Gwynedd by Rhuddlan Castle. Roughly 10 miles away to the S.E. was a rectangular territory lining the Dee itself and based on Overton. The Stat, of Wales (1284) without separating these parts from the palatinate, and with the addition of a single manor-enclave between the two, shired them all together as a Welsh county whose sheriff soon moved from Flint to Mold. As Welsh administration became increasingly specialised to Wales, the Chester connection became nominal. The two Acts of Union (1536 and 1546) applied, and later the shire was under the Welsh Great Sessions. It survived in its curious territorial form until 1974 when it was amalgamated into the modern county of Gwynedd.

FLINTLOCK, FIRELOCK. *See* FIREARMS.

***FLORES HISTORIARUM* (Lat = Flowers of the Histories)** were extracts by the St. Albans historian Matthew Paris from the Creation to 1249 from his larger *Chronica Majora*; and from 1249 to 1265 by an anonymous monk of St. Albans who used the *Chronica Majora* to 1259, the rest being his own version of contemporary events. These have a pro-baronial bias but show some sympathy for Henry III as Simon de Montfort became more high-handed. At Westminster Abbey a copy was continued by an anonymous monk in a more royalist vein until 1307, and another copy was further continued to 1326 by the contemporary monk Robert of Reading.

FLORENCE (It) (locally FIRENZE) and FLORENTINES. (1) Florence owed its world influence to a combination of economic, social, political and artistic factors. Tuscany is exceptionally fertile. It long produced iron, lead, zinc, silver, mercury and copper. Its pastures produced excellent wool. It was close to the important Tyrrhenian maritime trade route and on the main road from Lombardy to Rome. It soon developed skilled artisan industries, and the manufacturers, mining and commerce needed capital and bankers. They also needed peace, which the Tuscan cities, led by Florence, imposed locally. Proximity to the immense international, religious and financial complex at Rome created a demand for exchange facilities and high art. The most distinguished of the bankers, the Medici, were also the richest and most interested in artistic patronage, and besides, the supple Tuscan dialect was capable, through practical and literary use, of being developed into a high art form on its own.

(2) It was initially important to England as an outlet for wool, but the political significance of the link grew in the later 13th and early 14th cents. when the Florentine bankers such as the Riccardi, Frescobaldi, Bardi and Peruzzi (q.q.v.) lent large sums to the Crown. This made them highly unpopular. The Ordainers attacked the Frescobaldi as early as 1311. Edward III's Govt. came to terms with the English wool merchants by which the wealth of the wool trade was channelled to the Crown by parliamentary grants. By 1345 Frescobaldi, Bardi and Peruzzi had all failed, but Florentine unpopularity continued long afterwards. In London in 1376 the citizens took swift advantage of a papal bull against the Florentines by sacking the warehouses. *See more particularly,* DUDLEY-7; HUGUENOTS; MEDICI; RENAISSANCE; TUSCANY.

FLORENCE OF WORCESTER (?-1118). One John, a monk of Worcester began the *Chronicon ex Chronicis* (Lat = Chronicle from other Chronicles) before 1095 using material collected by Florence whose death it records with acknowledgements. It begins with the creation and up to 1121 is mainly a compilation but from 1121-40 it is mostly original. It formed the basis of several other monastic histories.

FLORIDA (U.S.A.) The Spaniards first settled at St. Augustine in Sept. 1565 and for two centuries the territory was under their ineffectual sovereignty. It was ceded to Britain under the T. of Paris (1763), retroceded in 1783 and bought by the U.S.A. in 1821. Admitted to the Union as a state in 1845, it joined the Confederacy in the U.S.A. Civil War (1861).

FLORIN, GOLD. *See* COINAGE-10; **SILVER.** *See* COINAGE-22.

FLOTA and GALEONES. To protect the bullion annually shipped from the S. American mines to Spain, the Spaniards instituted a convoy system. There were two outward fleets: the *flota* to the Caribbean Is. and Vera Cruz (Mexico), the *galeones* to Cartagena and the Spanish Main. Great fairs were held at the principal ports of arrival. For their return they met at Havana in Jan. or Feb. and crossed the Atlantic together, their arrival in Spain being a major event. Instituted in the mid-16th cent. the system fell into disuse towards the end of the 18th cent. but in those 250 years they dictated a cyclical movement in Spanish finances and policy, and were a major factor in the foreign policy decisions of maritime trading powers such as France and Britain.

FLOTSAM. *See* DROITS OF ADMIRALTY.

FLOUR MILLING. The hand quern is very ancient and continued in use in remote parts of Ireland and the Hebrides down to the 1970s. Heavy hard grindstones between 4 and 6ft in diameter, driven by an animal, or wind or water power, came into use in the 14th cent. and were the ordinary means of milling until 1874, but a steam-driven roller mill was built in London in 1784 and vast mills, later electrified, at Budapest and Minneapolis concentrated production and drove most small firms out of business. Hence the many derelict wind and water mills.

FLOWER (1) Benjamin (1755-1829) a radical journalist edited the pro-revolutionary *Cambridge Intelligencer* from 1791-99 and the *Political Register* from 1807-11. His nephew **(2) Edward Fordham (1805-83)** founded a successful brewery business at Stratford-upon-Avon. Of his sons **(3) Charles Edward (1830-92)** was the first chairman of the Shakespeare Memorial Theatre at Stratford-upon-Avon and **(4) Sir William Henry (1831-1899)** was curator of the Hunterian Museum from 1861-84, Hunterian Professor of Anatomy from 1870-84 and from 1884 onwards Director of the National History Museum. A cousin **(5) Sir Archibald Dennis (1865-1950)** and his *s.* **(6) Sir Fordham (1904-1966)** were also chairmen of the Memorial Theatre.

FLOYD'S CASE (1621). The Commons punished Floyd, a R. Catholic barrister for a speech against the Elector Palatine. The Lords objected that the Commons could punish only for breaches of their own privileges. The Lords contention was admitted.

FLUSHING or VLISSINGEN (Netherlands), was a herring port at a controlling point in the approaches to Antwerp. Hence the strong effect of the anti-Spanish insurrection there in 1572 and the damage done by the insurgent Sea Beggars who made it their H.Q. Independence brought great prosperity especially as the terminus for the English trade, but it declined in the 18th cent. and did not revive until the establishment of the naval port and shipyard in 1875.

FLUTE. *See* SHIPS, SAILING.

FLYING BOMBS (or "V.1") were German pilotless jet propelled aircraft with a range of about 150 miles at a speed of 350-400 mph, carrying one ton of explosives. The Germans began development in 1942 at Peenemünde on the Baltic and this was noticed by the British in May 1943. They bombed and dislocated production there but the Germans dispersed subsequent production and in Mar. 1944 were observed building Channel coast launching ramps orientated on London. Launching began in June, just after the allied landings in Normandy, mostly in London. Of 8,000 fired at Britain only 2,300 reached London. The rest were erratic or destroyed by the defences. They damaged over 800,000 London houses and caused much indirect hardship, but ceased to be a menace when the coast was taken. The Germans then turned them on Liège and especially Antwerp between Oct. 1944 and Mar. 1945. Some 2,000 were fired at Antwerp but failed because of their characteristic inaccuracy, to interfere with the port.

FLYMENAFYRMTH (A.S.) the offence of harbouring a fugitive from justice, punishable by a fine which was sometimes paid to the local lord.

FOCH, Ferdinand (1851-1929) French corps and army commander in World War I, until Dec. 1916. He then worked out the contingency plans in case of a German offensive against Italy. In May 1917 he succeeded Pétain as Chief of Staff and in Oct. his Italian plans were brilliantly successful after the Caporetto debacle. He became allied Generalissimo on 26 May, 1918, five days after the last great German offensive had begun, and was made a Marshal in Aug. He successfully commanded the allies until the end of the war.

FOEDERA (Lat = Treaties). A collection of treaties and other, not necessarily diplomatic documents, from 1101 to 1654 by Thomas Rymer who worked from 1693 to 1713. The collection though not always accurate, contains much material since lost.

FOG. The burning of coal in open grates for room heating began in the early 17th cent. but only reached huge proportions at the industrial revolution. The frequent and disastrous winter fogs were caused, especially in London, by the depression of smoke from low altitude house chimneys by temperature inversions. Even as late as 1930 fog could cause total darkness at noon. The consequences, in terms of public health, aesthetic squalor and damage to the economy were never calculated, but the nation notoriously suffered from respiratory diseases (4,000 were said to have died in a three day fog as late as 1956), it cost over £1 million to clean St. Paul's Cathedral in 1969-72 and the annual damage to textiles alone in the 1950s was put at over £200M. The first clean air legislation was introduced in a local Act in the City of London in 1954; general legislation in 1956 and 1968; this was applicable in selected areas and forbade only dark smoke. The real improvements had, however, long been on the way through gas and electric fires, and central heating.

FOILLAN, St. (?-653). *See* MISSIONS TO EUROPE.

FOIX (Fr) was established as a semi-independent Pyrenean state by Bernard of Foix in 1012. Of his descendants Raymond Roger (r. 1188-1223) and Roger Bernard I (r. 1223-41) supported the Albigensians and the Counts of Toulouse against French encroachments and Roger Bernard II (r. 1265-1302) married the heiress of Béarn which he acquired in 1290. This created a long feud with the House of Armagnac and a preference for Navarre over France, which caused the magnificent Gaston III (r. 1343-91) to refuse French allegiance altogether. He fought with France at Poitiers (1356) but changed sides in 1358, until the French brought him back by the T. of Pamiers in 1360. This enabled him to pursue his Armagnac war with great success. Count Jean (r. 1426-36) finally dropped the English alliance and Gaston IV (r. 1436-72) married Eleanor of Aragon, Q. of Navarre. This led to disputes with Louis XI of France but Francis Phoebus (r. 1472-83) succeeded to the crown of Navarre in 1479. His sister Catherine (r. 1483-1517) married into the House of Albret through which Foix, Béarn and Navarre passed to the Bourbons in 1589.

FOKKERS were Dutch designed German biplane fighters much used in World War I.

FOLCLAND or FOLKLAND. *See* BOCLAND.

FOLEY (1) Thomas (1617-77) inherited a foundry using Swedish methods at Stourbridge and made a fortune, with part of which he founded the Old Swinford Hospital at Worcester. He represented Bewdley in the Convention Parliament of 1660. His *s.* **(2) Paul (?1645-99)** was Tory M.P. for Hereford and Speaker from 1695-98. His *s.* **(3) Thomas (?-1737) Ld. FOLEY of KIDDERMINSTER (1712)** was one of the twelve peers created to enforce the P. of Utrecht. A kinsman **(4) Sir Thomas FOLEY (1757-1833)** fought at Finisterre and Gibraltar in 1780; off Toulon in 1793 and at St. Vincent in 1797. In 1798 he led the British fleet into the attack at the B. of the Nile, and in 1801 was Nelson's Flag Captain at Copenhagen. Rear-Admiral in 1808, he was C-in-C the Downs in 1811 and as Admiral was C-in-C Portsmouth in 1830.

FOLIOT, Herefordshire family related to the Es. of Hereford. **(1) Robert (?-1186) Bp. of HEREFORD** from 1174 was an English representative at the Lateran Council of 1179. His kinsman **(2) Gilbert (?-1187) Abbot of GLOUCESTER (1139-48) Bp. of HEREFORD (1148-63) Bp. of LONDON (1163-87),** theologian, canonist and Roman lawyer, entered the Abbey of Cluny, where well-born young men of promise were trained for high appointments, in the early 1130s. He became Prior, and then superior of the dependent priory of Abbeville. In 1139, through the influence of Milo, E. of Hereford, K. Stephen secured his election to the great Benedictine Abbey of Gloucester. He safeguarded it during the civil war and won the confidence of Abp. Theobald, but seems to have accredited forgeries designed to protect some of the Abbey's acquisitions. Theobald secured his appointment to Hereford and Pope Eugenius arranged for his consecration at St. Omer. He discreetly supported the Angevin cause and welcomed the accession of Henry II but was hotly opposed to Thomas Becket's appointment to Canterbury in 1162, it being insinuated that he wanted the see for himself. The King, to placate him, proposed his translation to London in 1163; Gilbert accepted but protested against professing obedience to Canterbury (i.e. Becket). The Pope upheld him on the ground that he was already professed to Becket's predecessor but Gilbert now claimed that the Bp. of London should not be bound in obedience to Canterbury. At the same time, during Becket's exile, he was acting as administrator of the archbishopric. The mutual hatred of these two shepherds of Christ's flock reached a high level in 1166 when Gilbert addressed a virulent letter (known as *Multtiplicem*) to Becket for which he excommunicated him (1167). In 1169 he again excommunicated him for crowning the Young Henry at the King's request. The reconciliation between the Abp. and the King at Rouen was followed immediately by Becket's proceedings against Gilbert on his return to Canterbury and so to Becket's murder. Gilbert was not absolved until 1172 for he and the King were thought to be in some way jointly responsible. If the issue upon which he was held so long excommunicate brought about a considerable enlargement of papal jurisdiction in England, yet he was admired as an ecclesiastical judge delegate and was one of several lawyers-bps. who built up that jurisdiction. His many letters are a source for his personal interests and times.

FOLKESTONE (Kent) had a church in 630. It belonged to Earl Godwin in 1056 and to Odo of Bayeux in 1086 but it had early been a limb or associate of Dover and by 1330 it had a prescriptive corporation and defined rights in the Cinque Ports federation. The port was founded by royal licence in 1629. In the 18th cent. it became prosperous, especially for fisheries and in the 19th cent. it also became a flourishing health resort. The railway to Dover was built through it and so the harbour first developed importance in World War I as a staging post for troops, despite a cliff fall in 1915 which closed the railway until 1919. It became a prosperous ferry port after World War II.

FOLK SONGS. It had been thought (if anyone thought much about it at all) that England had no folk songs, until 1889 the Rev. Sabine Baring-Gould (1883-1924) novelist, author of *Onward Christian Soldiers* and Rector of Lew Trenchard (Devon) attracted great interest by publishing a collection of tunes and songs obtained from native Devonian singers. Other collections followed quickly, and were publicised through the writings of John Alexander Fuller-Maitland (1856-1936) who published one collection himself, and was music critic of *The Times*

from 1889-1911. The ENGLISH FOLK SONG SOCIETY was founded in 1898 and in 1904 the Rev. Charles Marson (1858-1914) Vicar of Hambridge (Som) having discovered some folk songs among his isolated parishioners, commissioned his musical friend Cecil Sharp (1859-1924) to record them. He and Marson eventually published five volumes of them, and this led Sharp to devote his life to folk songs and folk dance.

FOLVILLE. Six brothers, one a priest, of Ashby Folville (Leics) in the early years of Edward III formed a large gang which terrorised the county. Their crimes included the murder of Roger Bellers, a Baron of the Exchequer and the seizure of Sir Richard Willoughby, a royal justice, whom they held to ransom. Their associates included Sir Robert de Vere, castellan of Rockingham. Their activities illustrate the disorderly conditions of the time.

FONTAINEBLEAU, T. of (Apr. 1814) between the allies (Austria, Prussia and Russia) and Bonaparte. He renounced his thrones for himself and his family. The allies accorded him and Marie-Louise the imperial title for life, conferred on him the sovereignty of Elba and on her the Duchy of Parma, Piacenza and Guastalla with reversion to the King of Rome. He was to receive 2 million francs a year from France, and there were to be other large annuities for his family. The allies would protect Elba from the Barbary corsairs. Britain acceded only to the provisions on Elba and the Duchy.

FONTÉVRAULT (Fr) in 1100 Robert d'Arbrissel founded the Abbey and in 1115 converted it into a strictly ruled double order of monks and nuns under an Abbess, of whom the first was Petronilla. It attracted royal patronage: Henry II and Eleanor of Aquitaine were buried there and Isabel of Angouleme retired there after her final political fiasco. It had many French and a few English daughter houses.

FOOCHOW now MINHOW. *See* CHINA; CHINESE TREATY PORTS.

FOOD AND DRUGS, SALE OF 1875 prohibited compounding injurious substances or mixing them with other substances and provided for a progressive enlarge-ment of a system of public analysts. As the first compre-hensive measure on the subject, it remained in force until 1928 when further enlargements were enacted but the adulteration principles omitted. Hence, such practices as adding salt to beer to increase thirst received a new encouragement and were not unknown in 1941.

FOOD CONTROL AND RATIONING (1) save for military and naval supplies, was unknown save through the price mechanism until the U-Boat campaign against commercial shipping began to interrupt the N. American wheat trade in mid-1916. A royal commission was set up in Oct. and developed into an apparatus for controlling the wheat supply to the west European allies. On the advice of Lord Devonport the newly appointed Food Controller, the Ministry of Food was set up just in time to forestall serious unrest caused by shipping losses. The very mild rationing system mainly for fats, meat and sugar, settled the difficulties by ending the queues. The system was dismantled in 1918.

(2) The fear of impending conflict led to the establishment of reserves, control committees, registration of wholesalers and retailers and printing of ration books under the Essential Commodities (Reserves) Act 1938. After World War II broke out maximum prices were fixed for all stages of production; the Govt. held and released all imported stocks, and gave subsidies to keep prices down. Rationing dealt with meat, fats, milk and eggs. The Ministry of Food under Lord Woolton ensured reasonable shares for all, but the violence of the German war on shipping far exceeded that of World War I and civilian rations were sometimes very low so that people day-dreamed about food. There was also a substantial home production effort; much marginal land such as railway cuttings was used for allotments, and huge amounts of food remains were boiled down and fed to pigs.

FOOL. Licensed fools or jokers were kept in great houses. Entitled to ridicule anything or anyone without personal risk, they were sometimes valued as devil's advocates or advisers, or as companions and were not always of minor consequence. Thus Henry II's fool, Rahere, founded St Bartholomew's Hospital (London) and doubtless at the sitter's request Holbein included Patison, Sir Thomas More's fool in his portrait of More. The last Court Fool was apparently Muckle John, the Scottish Fool to Charles I, but the E. of Suffolk had one until at least 1728 when Swift composed an epitaph for Dickie Pierce in Berkeley churchyard. *See* JESTER.

FOOLS, FEAST OF. An indecent tumultuary burlesque of the mass and other offices, held in some cathedrals during the three days after Christmas. Popular in the middle ages, it was suppressed in the Reformation.

FOOT. *See* WEIGHTS AND MEASURES.

FOOT. Remarkable Plymouth family. **(1) Isaac (1880-1960)** *s.* of an undertaker, a solicitor in 1902 and a Liberal councillor stood unsuccessfully for Parliament twice in 1910 and in 1919 was defeated by Lady Astor, who became a lifelong friend. He was elected for Bodmin in 1922 and 1923, defeated in 1924 but held it again from 1929-35. He was distinguished by enormous learning, a photographic book memory, a strong sense of history and occasion and pre-eminent rhetorical talents as a politician, occasional speaker (e.g. at the *Mayflower* celebrations in the U.S.A. in 1920) and as a Methodist preacher. He was Secretary for Mines in the National govt. of 1931 but as a dedicated liberal resigned against the protectionism of the Ottawa agreements. This kept him out of Parliament after 1935. In 1945, out of universal local respect, he was elected Lord Mayor though not then a councillor. In 1953 he became Chairman of Cornwall Quarter Sessions and at his death the *Western Morning News,* always opposed to him in life, said 'Each of his major characteristics would have made a man outstanding in his time'. Of his seven children **(2) Sir Dingle Mackintosh (1905-76)** a barrister with the largest ever known Commonwealth practice and a special interest in human rights also became an M.P. He was Parly. Sec. to the Ministry of Economic Warfare under Churchill and then a member of the British delegation at the San Francisco meeting which framed the Charter of the UN and was Sol-Gen. in the Labour Govt. of 1964. His brother **(3) Hugh Mackintosh (1907-90) Ld. CARADON (1964)** was Capt-Gen and Gov-in-Chief of Jamaica from 1950-57, the last Gov. of Cyprus (1957-60) and permanent representative at the UN from 1964 to 1970. His brother **(4) Michael (1913-)** a distinguished journalist and M.P. for Devonport (1945-55), for Ebbw Vale (1960-3) and for Blaenau, Gwent (1983-92). He was Secretary for Employment (1974-6), Lord President (1976-79) and Leader of the Labour Party from 1980-83.

FOOTBALL (1) Association or 'Soccer' developed from informal games with unlimited sides played in villages and schools from ancient times.

'Brissit brawnis and broken banis,
Strife, discord and waistis wanis,
Crookit in eild, syne halt withal
Thir are the bewteis of the fute-ball'.
16th cent north-country rhyme.

The 11-a-side game was formalised in the 1850s, the Football Association of clubs being founded in 1863 to regulate it. The Football League dates from 1888. **(2) Rugby** developed from informal games at Rugby School, derived in part from an older game played at Winchester College, in 1823 and began to spread in 1841. The Rugby Union was formed in 1871. **(3)** After the establishment of

the English Cup in 1871 leading association clubs began to employ full-time players. Professionalism was officially recognised in 1885, in Rugby Union in 1995. One social result was that the English urban worker acquired a cheap form of Saturday winter entertainment. With the advent of television, football encroached increasingly on screen-time on other days throughout the summer as well.

FOOTE, Samuel (1720-77) Cornish actor, wasted two inheritances by 1752 and took to making money as a mimic and social blackmailer by staging scurrilous farces containing lightly disguised public personalities who would be omitted for cash down. Few called his bluff but the Duchess of Kingston did.

FOOTWAY. *See* HIGHWAY.

FORBES. Irish-Scots family. **(1) Arthur (1623-96) E. of GRANARD (1684)** served under Montrose and after two years in prison in Edinburgh went back to Ireland and thence in 1655 to join Charles II at Breda. An influential member of the Irish govt. he procured the *Regium Donum* for the Presbyterians. An opponent of James II, he helped William III to clear the W. of Ireland. His grandson **(2) George (1685-1765) 3rd E. (1733)**, soldier, sailor and diplomat was Gov. of Minorca from 1716-18 and undertook a diplomatic mission to Vienna in 1719. He took part in the defence of Gibraltar in 1726-27, was Gov. of the Leeward Is. from 1729-30 and negotiated the Russian T. of 1733. His second son **(3) John (1714-96)** an Admiral, was C-in-C Mediterranean in 1749 and resigned from the Admiralty in 1757 rather than sign Byng's death warrant. He was reappointed and held office until 1763.

FORBES. Brothers **(1) Edward (1815-54)** naturalist and palaeontologist, made pioneer studies of the relationship of plants and molluscs. **(2) David (1828-76)** geologist especially in the field of nickel, cobalt and silver, was one of the first to apply microscopy to geology.

FORBES, Sir Charles Morton (1880-1960) Admiral of the Fleet, was C-in-C Home Fleet from Apr. 1938 until Dec. 1940 and as such, though with losses, inflicted decisive damage on the German surface fleet in the Norwegian campaign. He became C-in-C Plymouth from May 1941 and was then concerned with Coastal Command of the R.A.F. in offensive warfare against German U-boats and surface raiders using French ports and German shipping in the channel. He also mounted the famous raid on St. Nazaire (26 Mar. 1942) which put that port out of action as a capital-ship base. He retired in Aug. 1943.

FORBES, John (1710-59). *See* SEVEN YEARS' WAR-5-6.

FORD, Henry (1863-1947) organised a petrol car in 1892, organised the Ford Motor Co in 1903 and started mass production of the Model T Ford in 1908, by novel factory assembly methods. In 1912 he inaugurated a high minimum wage policy which attracted an almost unlimited supply of labour. By 1927 15,000,000 Model Ts had been sold. His activities profoundly affected civilisation in three major respects: he revolutionised industrial methods, effected a vital change in attitudes to wages, and ended the older sharp contrast between urban and rural life.

FORDHAM, Bp. *See* DURHAM-9.

FORDUN, John of (fl. 1363-84) priest at Aberdeen and traveller, wrote the important *Chronica Gentis Scotorum* (Lat = Chronicle of the Scottish Nation) which was extended in 1437 by other hands.

FOREIGN ENLISTMENT. At Common Law an Englishman might fight for a power at peace with Britain, save in breach of a duty to the Crown. This led to international difficulties once govts. became strong enough to be held responsible for the actions of their subjects. The first English legislation, passed in 1736, against unlicensed foreign enlistment applied only to military service. There was an Irish Act of 1738. These acts were evaded by quibbles; in addition difficulties arose over the Scots

Brigade in Dutch service. In 1756 when war with France and possibly Holland was imminent, a further Act closed some of the legal loopholes and required members of the Scots Brigade to swear an oath of allegiance. Foreign and war policy was conducted with this defective legislation until Greek and S. American nationalists began to attack the liberal idealism or warlike cupidity of many trained English fighting men, especially seamen, surviving from the French wars and suffering from the post-war slump. The Act of 1819 forbade unlicensed military or naval service and the fitting out of warships and authorised the seizure of ships carrying persons contravening the Act. It was evaded almost as easily and was superseded by the Foreign Enlistment Act 1870 on the outbreak of the Franco-Prussian War. This dealt with all forms of unlicensed assistance by British subjects in foreign wars and, in the case, at least of the Spanish Civil War of 1936-9 was little more effectual than its predecessors. The same kind of difficulty arose with mercenaries in Africa after World War II.

FOREIGN SERVICE, still recruited by the Civil Service Commission; in 1965 it was amalgamated with the staffs of the Commonwealth Relations Office and the Trade Commission service of the Board of Trade to form the Diplomatic Service which in 1966 also absorbed the staffs of the former Colonial Office.

FOREST (1) "is a certain territory of woody grounds and fruitful pastures, privileged for wild beasts and fowls of forest, chase and warren to rest and abide in, in the safe protection of the King for his princely delight and pleasure... for the preservation and continuance of which said place together with the vert and venison there are certain particular laws, privileges and officers belonging to the same, meet for that purpose, that are only proper unto a Forest and not to any other place". (*Manwood's Forest Laws 1665*).

(2) The law, probably of Carolingian origin, was introduced into England at the Conquest and about 20% of the country was afforested by 1135 including not only the New and Epping Forests and the Forest of Dean but the whole of Devon, Essex and from 1154 Huntingdonshire, and administered by special justices. By Henry II's reign (1154-89) the forests were virtually foreign territory outside the ordinary law and administration.

(3) From 1238 there were two Justices of the Forest for those north and south of the Trent respectively, but they were obliged to act through local deputies. Each forest or group of small forests had a crown appointed warden, whose functions were similar to those of a sheriff, and generally four verderers elected in the County Court who were "gentlemen of good account". They like the warden, attended the Forest Courts and acted as a check upon him. Under the Warden there were *Foresters* who acted as gamekeepers and forest police. The Warden was supposed to pay them: in real life they paid him for the opportunities for blackmail and oppression which came their way. In addition each forest or group had four *Agisters* who collected the rents for agistment and pannage. Private owners subject to forest law appointed *Woodwards* to protect their property and the King's game. Purlieus, i.e. land disafforested at a perambulation but where game was still preserved, were under Rangers.

(4) The principal Forest Courts were, on the civil side the *Swanimote* which dealt on the analogy of a Court Baron, with agistments, pannage, fauning etc., and the triennial *Regard* held before 12 knights to inquire into assarts, waste, purprestures, mines, harbours, the export of Forest produce and the possession of things likely to harm the deer. On the criminal side the *Court of Attachment* sat every 40 days to deal with minor offences and *Special and General Inquisitions* might hand over serious offenders to the irregularly held *Forest Eyre* or *Justice Seat,* which could and did levy large fines, amounting in 1175 to over £12,000 and in 1212 £4,486.

The extent of the forests and the oppressiveness of the forest regime was a matter of constant political and other complaints, and violence. *See* FOREST CHARTER; HOOD, ROBIN.

(5) Population pressure and the inherent difficulty of patrolling these vast areas, made for constant encroachments and private settlements at which forest officials connived, so that much legally afforested land was in fact disafforested over the centuries. Charles I in pursuit of funds used the Forest Laws to make inexpedient reassertions of Crown rights, sometimes against large owners who had relied on old titles (some 200 years old) to wide acreages; and Justice Seats, unheard of for generations, imposed widespread and infuriating forfeitures. This was a factor in the adherence of the men of Essex and Huntingdon to the parliamentary cause.

(6) The system lapsed (save in the exceptional cases of the New Forest, Epping and Dean) in the Civil War, and Charles II's political tact made Manwood's treatise (*see* 1 above) of more antiquarian than practical interest. *See* NEXT ENTRY.

FOREST CHARTER 1225 (confirmed by *inspeximus* in 1299). This charter and the confirmation of Magna Carta were part of a compound settlement exacted from the govt. in 1225. It disafforested (c.1) new forests made by Henry II and (c.3) woods afforested by Richard I and John (c.4), legalised purprestures, wastes and assarts made between the Coronations of Henry II and of Henry III but forbade all others. Free owners of woods within a forest were to be entitled (c.12) to make arable ground, work mills, have springs and marlpits (c.13) fly hunting birds and take honey and (c.11) could keep pigs and drive them through the forest to and from their woods. Only (c.12) inhabitants of the forest were to be liable to forest summons. Enough (c.7) foresters were to be appointed but they were not to gather products save under the supervision of the rangers or (c.14) to take cheminage unless they were foresters in fee, and the amount of cheminage per half year was limited to 2d. for a cart and ½d for a draft animal. The rangers (c.5) were to make range every three years only, when dogs were to be clawed (have three claws of the forefoot cut) and owners of unclawed dogs fined 3s instead of losing an ox. Killing the King's deer (c. 10) involved a heavy fine or imprisonment for a year and a day, and the finding of sureties, but bishops and noblemen (c. 11) could kill a deer on the way to and from court. Forest pleas (c.16) were to be tried by itinerant Forest justices and not by royal constables or castellans.

FORESTALLING was intercepting goods and buying them at wholesale prices before they could reach a market for retailing. It was not always peaceful and forestallers were commonly put in neck-stocks so that their heads made an immobile target.

FORESTER or FOSTER, Sir John (?1520-1602) commanded the border castles at Harbottle (1542-49) and Bamborough from 1555. He was also warden of the Middle March from 1560-95.

FORESTER (1) Edward (1730-1812) a banker, and Gov. of the Russia Co., was Pitt's adviser on paper currency. His stepsons **(2) Edward (1765-1849)** and **(3) Benjamin Meggot (1764-1829)** were distinguished botanists.

FORESTRY COMMISSION. During World War I no pit-props were imported from Norway and huge quantities of wood were needed for hutments, ship decks etc. Hence there was wholesale felling of the woods. The Commission was set up in 1919 to grow timber. It had compulsory powers which it never used. Its reafforest-ations, especially before its timber matured, depended upon the supply of govt. funds which was never adequate to meet expected consumption. Timber imports rose steadily until World War II, when the rate of devastation was even greater than in World War I. Hence in 1943 the

Commission published proposals to plant 3 million acres and restock 2 million more in conjunction with private owners. This programme fell far behind schedule, and timber imports rose rapidly. In 1951 the Commission took power to control private felling but by 1958 timber imports had reached £500M while the Commission was planting only at a rate of 50,000 acres a year.

FORFAR, Es. of. See DOUGLAS. ("RED")-16-17.

FORFAR (Scot), county town of the former county of Angus or Forfarshire, was the royal centre of Malcolm Canmore and other early Scots Kings (who were much associated with the area) probably because of its inland position lacing the tribal highlands but protected from Scandinavian raiders. The Scots political centre of gravity moved slowly south so that by 1290 it had become no more than an occasional royal residence. The English took and held it until Robert the Bruce recovered it from them and dismantled the castle. Its royalist loyalty earned it a Cromwellian sack in 1651 and a new charter in 1665. By this time it had become a small market town, especially for cattle and for sheep which formed the basis of a cloth industry, to which later was added jute.

FORFEITED ESTATES COMMISSIONERS (Scot) were instituted in 1747 to manage the many and wide properties forfeited after the Jacobite Rebellion of 1745. The most important but not the only lands were in Perthshire, and the Lovat and Lochiel Estates. In 1752 they were annexed to the crown, but the Commissioners continued to manage them. The Commissioners were enterprising and successful and the profits were mostly spent in Scotland. They encouraged modern agricultural techniques and enormously increased profits and rents in the Highlands. They built roads, bridges and harbours, helped to finance canals and gave great encouragement to the important linen industry. The forfeited estates were restored to their owners in 1784.

FORGERS, LITERARY have imposed upon the gullibility or good faith of educated society for pleasure or profit. The principal ones so far exposed are: George Psalmanazar (?1679-1763) the inventor of a country called Formosa, its language and religion; James Macpherson (1736-96), an M.P. who created Ossian and deceived Gibbon with it; Thomas Chatterton (1752-70) whose verses by an alleged 15th cent. poet Thomas Rowley were published in 1777 and 1782; William Henry Ireland (1777-1835) whose many skilled Shakespearean forgeries included two complete plays; Thomas Wise (1859-1937) a celebrated collector and expert on books who forged many first editions for sale. See also JUNIUS; PARNELL; PIGOTT; PILTDOWN.

FORGLEN. See OGILVY.

FORLORN HOPE, in siege warfare, was the small leading or "pathfinder" party, perhaps 25 strong which made the first lodgement in a major assault. Its commander, a subaltern, if he survived and the assault had succeeded, was always promoted.

FORMOSA (locally TAIWAN) had for centuries a sketchy Chinese Govt. mostly confined to the coast. In 1895 under the P. of Shimonoseki it was ceded to the Japanese who reduced the barbarous tribes of the interior during the next 20 years. The Is. surrendered to the Chinese nationalist Chiang Kai Shek in Sept. 1945, and when the communists finally conquered mainland China in 1949, it became the H.Q. of the nationalist remnant. They nominally represented China in the United Nations until Oct. 1971 when, unjustly and against U.S. advice, they were expelled at the same time as communist China was admitted. See CHINA-31, 38.

FORSTER, Johann Georg(e) (1754-94) of Prussian origin was naturalist to Capt. Cook's second voyage.

FORSTER, William Edward (1818-86) was Liberal M.P. for Bradford from 1861 and in 1870 piloted the important Education Act through Parliament, as Vice-Pres of the Council (1867-74). He was Chief Secretary for Ireland from 1880-82 but resigned in opposition to Home Rule.

FORSTER, William (1) 1739-1808; **(2)** 1764-1824; **(3)** 1788-1824 and **Simon (1801-70).** A family of distinguished London violin makers.

FORSYTH, Sir Thomas Douglas (1827-86) was a special Commissioner at Umballa and later at Delhi during the Indian Mutiny (1857). As Commissioner in the Punjab from 1860-82 he promoted trade with Turkestan, negotiated a frontier settlement between Russia and Afghanistan and visited Yarkand. He was removed for severity in repressing Ram Singh's insurrection in 1872, but was sent to Kashgar to negotiate a commercial treaty in 1873 and then to Burma to obtain independent status for the Karenni states.

FORT AUGUSTUS formerly Kilcummin (Inverness) was erected in 1716 after the first Jacobite rebellion.

FORT DUQUESNE (Pittsburg). See CANADA-8; GEORGE III-15.

FORTESCUE, Sir John (?1385-1477) (1). A hard working lawyer of Lincoln's Inn was a King's serjeant by 1430. He gained experience as an occasional Justice of the Peace in 17 counties or boroughs, frequently served as a judge of assize and held many special inquisitions. He became C.J. of the Kings Bench in 1442. Politically he was a Lancastrian. He fought at the B. of Towton (1461) and was included in the subsequent attainder. Hence, between 1461-1471 he was with the exiled Lancastrian royal family first in Scotland and then in France. He returned to England with Q. Margaret and Prince Edward in Apr. 1471 but in less than a month was taken prisoner in the Yorkist victory at Tewkesbury. The Lancastrian cause being then irretrievable, he made his peace with the Yorkists. His estates were fully restored in 1475. He is buried at Ebrington (Glos).

(2) He wrote three books: *De Natura Legis Naturae* (Lat: The Nature of Natural Law) (1461-3) written in Scotland is a long pamphlet and parable in favour of the Lancastrian cause. It contains allusions to contemporary issues and habits, but is otherwise readable. The celebrated *De Laudibus Legum Angliae* (Lat: In Praise of the Laws of England) (1463-70) written in France is a dialogue between the author and Prince Henry designed to educate the Prince. It represents a confident distillation of Fortescue's vast legal and political experience in textbook form and describes in detail, yet in lay language, the main features of the Common Law and English legal institutions in his time. *De Monarchia* (Lat: Monarchy) better known in English as *The Governance of England* (1469 or 1475) was an analysis of the disorders and Lancastrian weaknesses which engendered the Wars of the Roses from the stand point of a legal intellect with much political experience. It contains practical suggestions such as the adaptation of the monarchy into an executive founded on the prerogative yet watched by Parliament. Both later books influenced Tudor and Stuart policies because Fortescue favoured associating laymen with Govt. through Parliament and the juries.

FORT GARRY. Winnipeg, see CANADA D.

FORT GEORGE (Inverness) was erected in 1746 after the second Jacobite rebellion.

FORT LAWRENCE (Nova Scotia). See GEORGE II.-15.

FORTRENN. See PICTS.

FORT St. GEORGE. See MADRAS.

FORT WILLIAM. See CALCUTTA.

FORT WILLIAM (Inverness) was erected in 1746 after the second Jacobite rebellion.

FORTH, R. and FIRTH of. The 107 mile river meanders and is navigable to Alloa for ships of 300 tons and of 100 tons to Stirling. It is of little importance save that in 1314 it obstructed part of the battle field of Bannockburn. It was connected with the Clyde by canal in 1790. The Inner Firth is 20 miles long and between 1 and 3 miles wide, the Outer 28 miles long and between 8 and 19 miles wide. The chief port is Leith, and in sailing days the sea approach was made dangerous by the Bass Rock and the I. of May. The whole Firth is a major obstacle of historical importance between Fife and the Lothians. There was an ancient ferry at Queensferry on the narrows between the two parts. This was supplemented in 1890 by the famous railway bridge. In 1936 a road bridge at the landward end was built, and in 1964 another at Queensferry.

FORTNIGHTLY REVIEW brilliant advanced liberal journal, founded in 1865 and edited successively by G. H. Lewis, John Morley (c. 1867-83). T. H. S. Escott, Frank Harris (e. 1886-94), Oswald Crawford and W. L. Courtney (e. 1894-1928). After a few years it appeared monthly. Under Morley, for example, it published articles and essays by every good English prose writer except Matthew Arnold, Froude and Newman, by foreigners such as Castelar, Mazzii, von Sybel, and many Frenchmen. It also published poems by Meredith and William Morris and a novel by Trollope.

FORTY-FIVE, THE. See JACOBITES-17-21.

FORTY SHILLING FREEHOLDERS (1429-1832). By 1400 suitors at county courts might be little known, or might come from afar to be impostors. In 1406 sheriffs were required to hold parliamentary elections in open court and to have the return, certifying unanimity, sealed by all the electors. By 1429 there were too many electors, not always of a law abiding kind. This act of 1429 restricted the county franchise to resident holders of freeholds worth 40s. a year. This was probably designed to exclude serfs, who, however had disappeared by 1620. Inflation and the political enfranchisement of copyholds steadily increased the county electorates.

FORTY-NINERS. Those, from all over the world, who took part in the California Gold Rush of 1849.

FORTY-TWO ARTICLES. See THIRTY NINE ARTICLES.

FOSSDYKE. See TRANSPORT AND COMMUNICATIONS.

FOSSE WAY, was a Roman military road designed to facilitate the rapid movement of the garrison of the *limes* (fortified frontier) laid out by the Gov. Ostorius Scapula c. A.D. 47. It ran from the mouth of the R. Axe near Exeter, via Bath, Cirencester, Leicester, Newark and Lincoln to Brough on the Humber with forts on or within reach to the west of it. It faced north and west, and probably had a ditch on that side (hence the name). It represented an intermediate stage in the Roman advance.

FOSTERAGE. A Scandinavian and Saxon custom of giving a son a second father who might be entirely responsible for him, especially during the father's prolonged absences on fishing, hunting, trading, piracy or politics. The relationship was created by the foster father taking the child onto his knee, and implied an admission that he was of lower rank than the father.

FOTHERINGHAY. See JAMES VI OF SCOTS, SCOTTISH REIGN-9.

FOUGASSE in 16th-19th cent. defences, an explosive mine sunk at an angle in the ground and filled over with stones or even grenades to be projected in the enemy direction. In World War II drums filled with petrol or other combustibles were similarly sunk into road cuttings for sudden projection against such German tanks as might get ashore in England.

FOUJDARI ADALAT. See EAST INDIA CO. COURTS.

FOULIS (1) Sir James (?-1549) of Colinton became a Lord of Session in 1526, private Secretary to James V in 1529 and a member of the Secret Council in 1542. **(2) Sir David (?-1642)** came to England with James I and eventually quarrelled with Strafford against whom he preferred charges over his conduct as Pres. of the Council of the North. He was overruled, fined and imprisoned. In 1641 he gave evidence against him on his impeachment. **(3) Sir James (?-1688) Ld. COLINTON (1672)** was M.P. for Edinburgh from 1645-48 and a member of the Committee of Estates in 1646-47 but was imprisoned as a royalist. At the Restoration he became a Lord of Session and a Lord of the Articles in each Parliament thereafter. In 1674 he became a privy councillor and Lord Justice Clerk in 1684.

FOULIS (orig. FAULIS) (1) Robert (1707-76) his brother **(2) Andrew (1712-75)** and Robert's s. **(3) Andrew the Younger (?-1829),** Glasgow booksellers and printers from 1741 printed many famous editions mainly of classical works.

FOUL RAID (1417). Henry V and most of the English troops being absent on operations in Normandy, James (7th) E. of Douglas and Robert Stewart, D. of Albany attempted to seize Roxburgh and Berwick but were badly beaten by the local English forces.

FOUNDLING HOSPITAL to prevent child exposure was founded in 1741 by Thomas Coram (?1668-1751) and built in 1745 on a large scale in Guildford Street, London. In 1760 admission was limited to illegitimate children by mothers of good character deserted by the father. It was transferred to Berkhamstead in 1928. Access to its large garden, called Coram's Fields in Guildford St, was still forbidden to adults as late as 1975 unless accompanied by a child. The **exhibitions** began because Hogarth had given a portrait of Coram. Other artists presented pictures and crowds came to see them. This was the seminal event of English public art exhibition. The Dilettanti Soc. met there annually. John Wilkes was its treasurer. See EXHIBITIONS; LANDSCAPE PAINTING.

FOUNTAINS ABBEY (Yorks) When monks fled from the moral laxity of the Benedictines of St. Mary at York in 1132, Abp. Thurstan gave them some uncultivated land, and secured them membership of the Cistercians and the protection of St. Bernard. After some years of poverty another secession from York brought endowments and manpower. The abbey became popular and active in the stormy ecclesiastical politics of northern England. After Thurstan's death the vacant archbishopric was heatedly disputed, particularly by the aggressive Abbot Henry Murdac. In 1147 he himself became Abp. The community meanwhile flourished on land reclamation, sheep farming and wool trading and from further benefactions, which led to the construction throughout the 13th cent. of splendid buildings. At the dissolution (1539) Henry VIII sold the estate to Sir Richard Gresham. His son Sir Thomas broke it up and sold the abbey to Sir Stephen Proctor, who treated it as a quarry from which to build Fountains Hall. After successive sales the abbey and hall passed to relatives of the M. of Ripon. It remains the most splendid church ruin in the Kingdom.

FOURAH BAY COLLEGE (Sierra Leone) was founded by the Church Missionary Soc. in 1827 as a training place for clergy, but was affiliated to Durham University in 1876. Thereafter it provided the first western type university education in W. Africa. Science was introduced in 1928. It became an independent college in 1960 and a univ. in 1967.

FOUR BURGHS, COURT OF THE. See BURGHS-4-5.

FOUR FREEDOMS defined by Pres. Franklin D. Roosevelt in a message to the U.S. Congress (Jan. 1941) were freedom **(1)** of speech, **(2)** of worship, **(3)** from fear, **(4)** from want. The method of achieving them was to lease-lend arms to Britain against the Germans.

FOUR MASTERS, ANNALS OF THE. A compilation of Irish historical events from the earliest times made in 1616 by Michael and Cuigcoigriche O'Clery, Cuigcoigriche O'Duigeanain and Faerfeasea O'Maolconaire and dedicated to Fergal O'Gara, Prince of Coolavin. It is one of the main source books of Irish history.

FOUR POINTS or VIENNA POINTS (1854) arose out of the Crimean War and were drafted with Austrian help. **(1)** A European guarantee for the Roumanian principalities was to be substituted for the Russian. **(2)** Navigational improvement of the Danube delta. **(3)** Revision of the 1841 Straits Convention in a wider European interest involving a reduction in the Russian Black Sea Fleet. **(4)** Abandonment of the Russian claim to protect the Millet-i-Rum. The peace negotiations broke down in 1855 on points **(3)** and **(4)** but were ultimately accepted as a result of the fall of Sebastopol, in the P. of Paris in Mar. 1855.

FOUR SEAS were the North Sea, the Channel, the Atlantic and the Irish Sea. "Within the Four Seas" however meant "within English jurisdiction".

FOURTEEN POINTS enunciated by the U.S. President Wilson in a message to Congress (Jan. 1918) set out his version of allied war aims in World War I. They were **(1)** open peace treaties and no secret diplomacy; **(2)** and **(3)** freedom of navigation outside territorial water and of trade; **(4)** reduction of armaments; **(5)** impartial adjustment of colonial claims, the interests of the inhabitants having equal weight with the claims of governing powers. The Germans were to evacuate **(6)** Russia; **(7)** Belgium and **(8)** France, which was to receive back Alsace Lorraine. **(9)** Italian frontiers were to be drawn on a basis of nationality; **(10)** the peoples of the Habsburg Empire were to be entitled to self determination; **(11)** Roumania, Serbia and Montenegro were to be evacuated, Serbia was to receive access to the sea, and Balkan boundaries were to be settled under international guarantees. This was partly related to **(12)** under which the non-Turkish nationalities of the Ottoman Empire were to be entitled to self determination and the Straits to be free to all shipping. **(13)** Poland was to be independent and to have access to the sea with boundaries to include areas with a Polish majority; **(14)** a League of Nations was to be formed to guarantee peace.

FOURTH COALITION, WAR OF (Dec. 1812 -May 1814). *See* MOSCOW DISASTER. 1812. **(1)** The Moscow disaster had destroyed the best of the French troops and Bonaparte's personal prestige. His Austrian and Prussian auxiliary armies were unscathed, but the Prussian Gen. Yorck von Wartenburg neutralised his force and the Tilsit area by the Tauroggen Convention (Dec. 1812) with the Russians. Technically treasonable, no act was more popular with crown and people. Prussia began to arm and move. Inspired by Stein, the Prussian Estates voted an army (Jan.). Silesia, led by a Prof., raised volunteers (Feb.). Austria played a waiting game but the Prussian King was in a difficulty. He wanted to recover Prussian Poland, currently occupied by Russian troops. With great good sense the Czar offered him as the price for changing sides, equivalents in a statistical, financial and geographical sense for the lands lost since 1806 and a proper territorial connection between Prussia and Silesia. (T. of Kalisch Feb. 1813). This fateful agreement carried with it the seeds of future Prussian supremacy in Germany. It was strongly approved by Lord Cathcart, the British Ambassador (Mar.) when the Prussians renounced all designs upon Hanover. Shortly afterwards Russia and Prussia defined their war aims (T. of Breslau, Mar. 1813) as the expulsion of the French from Germany, and the dissolution of the Confederation of the Rhine. The German rulers were to be summoned in aid and those who refused would lose their states.

(2) Bonaparte's call to arms from Paris raised 500,000 youthful conscripts by May and these were stiffened and might be trained by thinning the garrisons and bringing up troops from Italy and Spain. Time, however, was needed and meanwhile risings in Prussia, Hanover and Hamburg reopened N. Germany to British trade and submerged many local French authorities. The Austrians were raising troops and offering armed mediation. Bonaparte made impossible conditions; Castlereagh refused the offer because of these and because mediation might weaken and confuse Russia and Prussia (Apr.) Bonaparte offered Silesia to Austria for her alliance, and meanwhile his armies moved steadily across Germany towards the six Polish and Prussian fortresses still holding out for him. The Russians summoned the King of Saxony, who fled to Austria, and it was on his territory that the main collision took place at the indecisive Bs. of Lutzen and Bautzen (May 1813), while Davoust retook Hamburg

and cleared the R. Elbe. Both sides were in confusion and the Russians began to retreat into Silesia. Both sides wanted an armistice; Bonaparte to bring in the Austrians, the allies to reorganise and bring in the Swedes, whose troops under the Anglo-Swedish T. of Stockholm (Mar. 1813) were on their way. On 4 June 1813, an armistice until 20 July was signed at Poischwitz. In the middle of this period Wellington won his overwhelming victory at Vittoria.

(3) Bonaparte had misjudged. Austria had never intended to join him. Her conditions for mediation included the dissolution of Poland and the Confederation of the Rhine, the reconstruction of Prussia, the restitution of the Illyrian provinces and the re-establishment of the Hanse Towns. She agreed to join the alliance if Bonaparte refused these conditions (Secret T. of Reichenbach June 1813). Britain had already signed subsidy treaties with Russia and Prussia. Bonaparte temporised and wanted (26 June) to prolong the armistice into Aug. The 10th was agreed, but early in July the news of Vittoria leaked out. The allies now made the military convention of Trachenberg (July) while a nominal peace congress met at Prague. Here Bonaparte's negotiators could do nothing but prolong discussion while time ran out, for their master had determined to destroy the Prussians and Russians and then turn on Austria.

(4) By 14 Aug. the Prussians and Russians had linked up with the Austrians in Bohemia, so that Bonaparte's large forces were threatened from the south as well as north and east. In the north, outlying troops were beaten at Gross Beeren and Hagelberg (23 and 27 Aug); to the east they were driven headlong from Silesia at the B. of the Katzbach (26 Aug.) but meantime Bonaparte had won his last victory over the combined main force at Dresden (27-28 Aug.) in pouring rain which doused the muskets and made it mainly a hand-to-hand struggle. This was soon offset by Vandamme's defeat to the south at Kulm (29 Aug.) and Ney's at Dennewitz to the N.W. Bonaparte retreated to Leipzig where in a great two day battle (16-17 Oct.) he was irretrievably ruined. He reached the Rhine with barely 40,000 men (Nov.). Wellington had been in S. France for three weeks.

(5) The over-praised campaign now waged by Bonaparte both militarily and diplomatically in defence of Paris had already been lost in Saxony. The Germans rose everywhere. In Jan. Murat as King of Naples signed an alliance with Austria. The Danes made peace. The Dutch revolted. Bonaparte negotiated treacherously at Chatillon while Britain, Austria, Prussia and Russia pledged themselves to each other at the T. of Chaumont (9 Mar. 1814). This determined and decisive unity made a French victory impossible. On 30 Mar. 1814 the allied troops entered Paris. On 2 Apr. led by Talleyrand, the Senate declared that Bonaparte had ceased to reign, and on 11th he wrote his formal abdication, made an emotional farewell to his guard and hinted darkly that he would return when the violets were in bloom again.

FOURTH ESTATE. Edmund Burke's phrase for the press.

FOURTH INTERNATIONAL was the multinational body which sought to unify the communist sects owing intellectual allegiance to Leon Trotsky, as opposed to the Third International or Comintern. The idea was opposed in the 1920s by Trotsky but the ever closer links between Germany and Russia and their approval by the Third International showed that the latter was really a branch of the Russian Foreign Ministry, especially after Hitler's advent to power in 1933. Trotsky became convinced that a new international revolutionary movement was needed, and accordingly the Fourth International was launched at a conference at Périgny (Fr) in Sept. 1938, just as the Russians sacrificed Czechoslovakia to Germany. *See* BROCKWAY.

FOURTH PARTY was the name of the 'ginger group' in the

Parliament of 1881 consisting of Lord Randolph Churchill, A. J. Balfour, John Gorst and Sir Henry Drummond Wolff, all Tory party radicals who detested Sir Stafford Northcote and laughed uproariously at everything he said. They favoured selective social reforms, and were prepared to co-operate with the Irish.

FOWEY (Cornwall). *See* PIRACY.

FOWLER, Henry Watson (1858-1933) with his brother **Francis George (1870-1918)** produced the celebrated *King's English* (1906) and the *Concise Oxford Dictionary* (1911) and Henry published his most interesting work the *Dictionary of Modern English Usage* in 1926.

FOX, Charles James (1749-1806) was even more dissipated than his father (*see* FOX-2), but generous, fashionable and widely liked. By 1763 he had acquired on the continent his lifelong habits of wenching, drinking and especially gambling which embarrassed his finances. Nevertheless he was studious at Eton and Oxford. **(1)** M.P. for Midhurst in 1768 he began his career by opposition to John Wilkes, and was given a lordship of the Admiralty by North in 1770. He now began to feel his way towards the "Whig" philosophy associated with him and which foreran the later political liberalism. He was ready to risk unpopularity by opposing, on grounds of stability, the kind of subversive press liberty exploited by Wilkes, but opposition to the Royal Marriages Bill and resignation in 1772 indicated a penchant for dramatic yet superficial gestures and although he returned to office as a junior Ld. of the Treasury, he was dismissed in 1774. Thenceforth George III hated him.

(2) He now ran up huge gambling debts and after a short sojourn in Paris, became a member of Dr. Johnson's circle. Despite his reputation for preferring gambling, women and politics in that order, he returned zestfully to politics on the American issues. He championed the colonists' point of view on common sense rather than high constitutional grounds and savaged Lord George Germaine, the responsible Sec. of State; and he sensibly refused to deprive himself of the forum by seceding from the Commons when the Rockingham Whigs did so. In 1778 he was an accepted supporter of Rockingham, and an effective critic of North's war policy.

(3) From this position it was natural for him to advocate parliamentary reforms and R. Catholic relief, so that when Rockingham came to power (1782) he became a S-of-State and introduced the legislation for Irish parliamentary autonomy. Unfortunately, he was at logger-heads with Shelburne during the other Sec. of State during the peace negotiations (*see* GEORGE III-9-10) and resigned when with royal support Shelburne succeeded Rockingham in 1782. Efforts at reconciliation failed and in May 1783 he formed an unnatural coalition with North under the D. of Portland. Part of his influence arose out of a growing friendship with the P. of Wales but this only inflamed George III's dislike and helped to cement the alliance between the King and the younger Pitt.

(4) HEIC affairs and patronage had by now become a major political issue. He introduced an India Bill, but Pitt, who had become a possible alternative, and the King had it thrown out by the Lords and he was dismissed. His Commons following was strong enough, however, to defeat Pitt's rival measure and to maintain a dwindling influence by postponing supply and the annual Mutiny Act for three months.

(5) In Pitt's triumphant 1784 general election he was doubly returned for Kirkwall and Westminster; he took his Kirkwall seat while the Westminster returns were persistently adjourned by Govt. influence. This won him sympathy but not power. Pitt and the King represented national sentiment; Fox's allies were thought to represent faction. This was probably true of his allies: meanwhile Pitt's power grew steadily through hard work and attention to detail, while Fox's influence was primarily that of a public critic endowed with exceptional

oratorical gifts. The parliamentary duel between Pitt and Fox was one of the recurring excitements of the capital.

(6) Fox's difficulty was that Pitt was occupying more and more of the middle ground of opinion. Fox's principles made him support Pitt's reforms, but the need to build up a connection led him, with the business interests, to oppose the concomitant commercial arrange-ments with Ireland and France. It led his party up the blind alley of Warren Hastings' seven year long impeachment and it involved him, the champion of Commons' supremacy, in the inconsistency of demanding an inherent regency for his friend the Prince, against Pitt's statutorily regulated one (1788-9). Thus he seemed to represent a ragbag of attitudes whose main co-ordinating factor was opposition.

(7) When the French Revolution broke out, Fox consistently with his liberalism, favoured it but as France became aggressive, and popular unrest pronounced, his opposition to Pitt's treason and sedition (1795) bills could be represented as unpatriotic. He had however, enjoyed one previous relevant success: his Libel Act of 1792 saved many genuine political critics from the prisons. In 1795 the war had made his cause hopeless; for the next five years he concentrated on writing his *History of the Revolution of 1688* and seldom went to Parliament. During the short peace of Amiens (Mar. 1802-May 1803) he visited Holland and France where he met Bonaparte. He still favoured peace, retrenchment and reform and attacked the Addington Govt.'s declaration of war. The practical consequence was that the King would not entertain his inclusion in the Pitt-Grenville coalition when Addington resigned in 1804, and he achieved office again as Sec. of State only in the last year of his life. Characteristically, ten days before he died, he moved the latest of the long series of bills by which at long last, the slave trade was ended.

(8) The practical achievements of Fox's lifetime were, owing to his tactical misjudgements, not great, but his long years in opposition and support for progressive causes laid the foundations of that Whiggism which inspired the reformers of the early 19th cent.

FOX, George (1624-91) experienced in 1643 the conversion which led him to found the Society of Friends. He was often imprisoned between 1649-56. He made his H.Q. at Swarthmore Hall, near Ulverston and in 1669 married the widow of its owner Thomas Fell, V-Chancellor of the Duchy of Lancaster. He undertook a missionary journey to Ireland in 1669, the W. Indies in 1671 and Holland in 1677 and 1684.

FOX, (1) Sir Stephen (1627-1716) helped Charles II to escape after the B. of Worcester (1651) and then ran his household in Holland. A close associate of Clarendon, he visited England on confidential missions between 1658-60. In 1661 he became M.P. for Salisbury and paymaster-gen. He remained loyal to Clarendon on his impeachment in 1667. In 1679 he became M.P. for the popular Westminster constituency. With or through Nell Gwynn, he got Charles II to found the Chelsea Hospital to which he gave handsomely. He also endowed churches, almshouses and schools. Politically opposed to James II from whom he refused a peerage, he voted against the Army Bill. He had been a Treasury commissioner since 1679 and William III kept him in that post. He returned to Salisbury as M.P. in 1714. His *s.* **(2) Henry (1705-74) 1st Ld. HOLLAND (1763)** was brought up at Eton with the elder Pitt and Fielding, lost his fortune gambling, went abroad and returned as a protégé of Walpole's to become M.P. for Hindon in 1738 and surveyor gen. of works. Limited in his political ambitions, his passion was money with which to support expensive tastes. In 1741 he became M.P. for Windsor 1743-45 a Lord of the Treasury; in 1744 he made a sensational runaway marriage with Lady Georgina Lennox and from 1746 (during the Jacobite rebellion) to 1754 he was

Secretary at War, and so responsible for the unsuccessful two years before the P. of Aix-la-Chapelle (*see* WARS OF 1739-48; GEORGE II-13-14). By this time he had become a powerful but mistrusted House of Commons figure, and able to use the contemporary nuisance tactics to secure office. Though a member of the Govt., he attacked Hardwicke's Marriage Bill in 1754 with such ferocity that Newcastle, rather than dismiss him, raised him to the cabinet as Sec. of State (1755). In 1756 he resigned over the war and so manoeuvred himself into the long desired paymastership in 1757, where he made a huge fortune. He survived the fall of Pitt and Newcastle in 1761 to become Bute's manager in the Commons, and his principal agent for securing ratification of the P. of Paris in 1763. In return he had bargained for a peerage, but there was a dispute about the paymastership which he meant to keep. Eventually he compromised by accepting it until 1765. In 1767 he bought the estate upon which he built Holland House, where he (notwithstanding his unpopularity) and his wife maintained a literary and political salon. His famous third *s.* was **(3) Charles James (1749-1806)** (q.v.). His like-minded nephew **(4) Henry Richard Vassall (1773-1840) 3rd Ld.** from 1774, a prominent whig peer who had travelled the continent and like Charles James met Bonaparte, married **(5) Elizabeth Vassall** (1770-1845) who had divorced Sir Godfrey Webster. She dominated their later Holland House whig salon and he was Lord Privy Seal in 1806-7 and held minor office in the reform ministry of 1830.

FOX, Sir William (1812-93) resident agent for the New Zealand Co. from 1843 was Prime Minister for N.Z. in 1856 from 1861-62, 1863-64 and 1869-83.

FOX-HUNTING. Foxes, as vermin, were killed by any available means until the curious sport of mounted hunting with packs of hounds came into vogue between 1685-1700. Specialised packs were first introduced in Leicestershire and Northants in about 1750. Over 200 existed in Britain in 1980 besides some hundreds in other countries, notably India and N. America. Excellent as a test of human courage, fox hunting was increasingly a target for class based hostility. In 1995 there was an abortive Commons bill against it. Further efforts in 1997-2000 excited hostility as well as demonstrations against urban, and the Blair govt's, attitudes to rural affairs.

FOXE, John (1516-87) was the author of *Acts and Monuments of Matters Happening in the Church* usually called "Foxe's Book of Martyrs". First issued in English in 1559 it described, with illustrations, the sufferings and heroism of the protestant martyrs under Mary I. It long remained one of the most influential anti-papist propagandist works.

FOX-NORTH COALITION (Apr.-Dec. 1783) (*see* GEORGE III 9-10; SHELBURNE ADMINISTRATION). Seven in cabinet headed by the D. of Portland. It was formed only after a six weeks' interval because the King doubted the good faith of its leaders, former political adversaries, and the King's personal hatred of Fox and of North for deserting him over the American war. It abandoned Parliamentary, but continued administrative reform and it ratified Shelburne's American peace. The Indian problem brought about its fall for its theoretically ingenious solution was practically unworkable and raised widespread suspicion that Fox aimed permanently to engross Indian patronage (*see* FOX'S INDIA BILL). Thus after six months there was, yet again, no govt. able to deal with the crisis of the moment.

FOX TALBOT, William (1800-77) of Laycock Abbey (Wilts) published his invention of photography in 1839.

FRAMLINGHAM was granted to Roger Bigod, E. of Norfolk, in 1101. Henry II dismantled his earth and palisade fortifications in 1175-7 but Roger, the 2nd E., constructed the present thirteen towered fortress in 1190. K. John's troops took it in 1215. It escheated in 1306 and in 1312 Edward II granted it to Thomas of Brotherton, his half-brother, whom he created E. of Norfolk and it thence

passed by marriage in 1375 to Thomas Mowbray, 1st D. of Norfolk. It was the Mowbray's chief seat, though intermittently in crown hands during minorities until 1476 when, through another marriage, it passed to the Howard Dukes of Norfolk. They lived there in splendour until 1547 when it was forfeited. Edward VI granted it to his sister Mary who had her H.Q. there during Lady Jane Grey's rebellion in 1553. It was then returned to the Howards who, however, preferred other residences and allowed it to decay. In the 1590s it was a recusant prison; in 1636 it was bequeathed to Pembroke College, Cambridge, for purposes of a poor house into which the great hall was converted. This use continued until 1837. In 1913 the custody was passed to the Commissioners of Works.

FRANC **(Fr.) (1)** A gold coin first issued in France in 1360, the equivalent of the *livre* and divided into 20 sols (cf the pound sterling). **(2)** A unit of currency divided into 100 centimes which superseded the later *livre* in 1795 and whose value has fluctuated violently ever since.

FRANCHE COMTÉ. *See* BURGUNDY.

FRANCHET D'ESPEREY, Louis Felix Marie (1856-1942). French general, became C-in-C of the Allied Forces in Macedonia in June 1918. In the next three months he dispersed the Bulgarian army, threatened Constantinople and materially hastened the collapse of the Central Powers, a consummation which the bungled but strategically proper British attack on the Dardanelles had failed to do in ten months.

FRANCHISE (1) was a freedom from royal interference in a particular matter and correlatively a private jurisdiction over it. Franchises, held mainly by great ecclesiastics, existed before the Conquest but presented no serious political problems until after it, when the policy of the Kings was to press the assumption that any jurisdiction beyond the limits of manorial justice or feudal overlordship was derived not from tenure but from a special royal grant limited in scope and capable of interpretation by a royal court. This royal theory was resisted as late as the 14th cent. by the Welsh Lords Marcher who claimed, with some justification, that their exceptional rights came not from grant but *de conquestu* (by right of conquest).

(2) Most 13th cent. franchises amounted only to exemption from the sheriffs tourn. Some greater ones operated as if they were shires, as in the bailiwicks of the I. of Ely held by the Bps. of Ely and of West Suffolk by the Abbots of Bury St. Edmunds. These held courts of shire status. There were, however, some great franchises notably Tynedale, Redesdale, Hexham, some towns such as London, York and Norwich, and the palatine or quasi-sovereign lordships of the Bps. of Durham (comprising the modern county with detached areas at Bedlington and Norham) and of the Es. of Chester (comprising Cheshire and Flint). In Durham even the justices in eyre were excluded save during a vacancy of the see and the bishops held their own chancery court. Neither palatinate was represented in parliament.

(3) Edward I's *Quo Warranto* (= by what authority) inquiries served to emphasise the royal theory by forcing franchise claimants to state by what right they held their franchises. If they refused to answer, they were forfeited for contumacy; if they answered, the court adjudged whether the franchise was lawful. Not surprisingly, most holders were willing to pay for royal confirmation and such a transaction of course irrevocably admitted the royal contention.

FRANCIS, Sir Philip (1740-1818) (*see also* JUNIUS). It will here be assumed, without adding to the ink already spilled, that Francis was 'Junius'. After a short career as a well-connected amanuensis, he became First Clerk at the War Office in 1762 and contributed thereafter pseudonymously to the press. Barrington, Sec. at War, eased him out of his post and proposed him for the new Indian gov-gen's council. He arrived in India in 1774 where he deployed his talent for making trouble to the full. He, with his allies Monson and Clavering, had a majority of 3 to 2 against Warren Hastings, the gov-gen. On arrival they reversed his policy in Oudh; they disgraced his representatives; they abolished the bank which he had set up; they attacked the govt. salt and opium monopolies; they accused him of oppressing the zamindars and of personal corruption. In 1775 they brought trumped up charges of corrupt dealings with one of the Begums of Oudh, based upon information from a shady Brahmin money lender called Nuncomar or Nandakumar. Nandakumar was lawfully hanged for forgery. Francis falsely accused Hastings of judicial murder and meanwhile asked the govt. to replace Hastings with Gen. Clavering or himself. Monson died in 1776. After much confusion caused by delays in communication, Clavering in 1777 attempted an abortive *coup*. The govt. reappointed Hastings and Clavering died (1777). Hastings could for a while overrule Francis but meanwhile a French inspired Maratha war broke out in S. India. New councillors arrived to replace Francis' allies and Hastings made a compromise whereby Francis would not obstruct the conduct of the war if Hastings steady supporter Barwell retired. Francis broke the agreement: Hastings called him a liar. Francis called him out, was wounded in the subsequent duel, resigned and returned to England with a fortune. Here he used his contacts to become an M.P. (1784) and briefed Burke and probably Pitt to impeach Hastings, who sailed for England in Jan. 1785. Three years' political and personal intrigues brought Hastings to trial, which began in Feb. 1788 and ended with his complete acquittal in 1795. Meanwhile Francis was contriving both to help establish the Society of Friends of the People (1793) and to ingratiate himself with the Prince of Wales.

FRANCISCANS (FRIARS MINOR or GREY FRIARS). (1)
St. Francis of Assisi (1181-1226) underwent his conversion in about 1206 and gathered 12 disciples for whom he composed a rule based on poverty, approved by Pope Innocent III in 1210. The new Order spread rapidly in central Italy and in 1212 St. Francis founded the Order of Poor Clares for women and in 1221 a Third Order for those unable to withdraw from the world. The rule, twice revised, was finally approved by Honorius III in 1223. The orders were now spreading beyond Italy; in England the first houses were established at Canterbury, London, Oxford and Northampton, but there was confusion until the English Haymo of Faversham (Minister-Gen. 1240-4) organised the order into convents under wardens, provinces under a minister-provincial and a general chapter under the Minister-Gen. When St. Bonaventura was General (1257-74) its many members included such eminent scholars as Roger Bacon, John Peckham, William of Ockham, Duns Scotus and Adam Marsh. Robert Grosseteste, though not a friar, was their first lecturer at Oxford. Shortly afterwards the Order was split in a controversy between the *Spirituals* who stood for a simpler, more austere, inward looking life and the *Conventuals* who followed a more relaxed system better adapted to study and preaching. John XXII pronounced in favour of the Conventuals in 1323 and the extreme spirituals or *Fraticelli* rebelled. The fortunes of the Order now declined because the Great Schism lowered papal prestige and any large mendicant order was liable to be unpopular in times of scarcity and plague. There were quarrels with parish clergy over preaching, confession and even burial fees. Begging became importunate.

(3) The spiritual idea re-emerged in the *Observants,* organised as a special branch in 1415. They reached England in 1482 and became wholly separate in 1517. They openly opposed Henry VIII's religious and matrimonial policies and were liquidated by him.

(4) The separation of the Observants left room for a further movement of spiritual inspiration, austere and eremitical in character. In 1525 Matteo da Baseio founded the *Capuchins* who received papal confirmation and a vicar general directly under the minister general in 1535. They were harassed by the conventuals and their second vicar, Ochino, defected to protestantism in 1542. Nevertheless they prospered; they played, with the Jesuits, a leading role in the counter reformation and before the French Revolution some of them exercised great political and popular power, notably Father Joseph Francois Leclerc du Tremblay, the original "grey eminence" who, as Richelieu's confessor, strongly influenced French policy from 1624 until 1638 and Marco Cristofori who served the Austrians in the Turkish war of 1683-8. They were energetic preachers in Ireland and as Chaplains to London R. Catholic embassy chapels and the Queens Henrietta Maria and Catherine of Braganza they were often active in the English diplomatic underworld.

FRANCIS XAVIER, St. *See* JESUITS.

FRANC-MARRIAGE was a tenure under which a grantor gave land to a female relative and her husband quit of services save fealty, but so as to revert to the grantor or his heirs when the fourth degree of consanguinity between the issues of the grantor and the grantees was past.

FRANCO-AUSTRIAN WAR (July 1795-Oct. 1797) (*see* FIRST COALITION, WAR OF, 1793-5). (1) The treaties of Apr-July 1795 left Austria and Savoy to face the full French power on land but both sides were inhibited, the Austrians by the final Polish Partition expected in the summer, the French by political rioting in Paris, which culminated in Bonaparte's defence of the Convention and the establishment of the Directory (Oct.). All the same the French were driven back in Alsace, while their army won a spectacular success at Loano on the Riviera. British help to Austria should have been more effective, but until Adm. Hotham, the supine C-in-C was superseded by Jervis (Nov.) too little was done and when Jervis arrived it was too late. The Austrians and the French then agreed upon an armistice which lasted in Alsace until May 1796.

(2) The British war continued. The C. of Good Hope had been taken in Sept. 1795, Dutch Guiana in 1796. The British blockades had created such dearth in the French dockyards that the new Directory changed its naval policy from fleet action to commerce raiding. This was based upon a misunderstanding of British economics and was, though individually lucrative, quite ineffectual. British sea trade continued to grow: its losses from raiding never exceeded 2½%.

(3) Bonaparte was now given his chance. Appointed to the Italian command (Mar. 1796) he drove the Austrians and Savoyard-Sardinians apart in six days' fighting, made an armistice (Apr.) and then the P. of Cherasco with the latter (May) whereby they abandoned their allies and the counties of Nice and Savoy. When the treaty was signed Bonaparte had already beaten the Austrians at Lodi and the next day proclaimed the Lombardic Republic from their conquered Italian lands. The minor Italian principalities hurriedly changed sides. By June he had reached Verona and was negotiating with Naples and the Pope. French troops appeared in Leghorn and closed or confiscated the vast British commercial establishments there. The British promptly occupied Elba nearby (July).

(4) Though Bonaparte's army lived off the land it depended for reinforcements and military supplies upon the *Corniche* route along the Riviera beach. To proceed further he needed to take Mantua, now under siege. If the overstretched Royal Navy could prevent the use of the *Corniche,* Mantua would survive. If not, he might inflict new defeats upon the Austrians. The Directory saw its way to reinforcing the Toulon fleet (which Hotham had failed to destroy) by involving Spain, whose strategic position too might dominate the movements of Jervis and

Nelson's Mediterranean fleet. British blockades had interfered extensively with neutral shipping: Spanish bullion was entering France under the T. of Basel. The British were seeking to impede its arrival in Spain from America. The Spaniards were quick to resent British interference and easily persuaded to send a fleet into the Mediterranean. Jervis seized two treasure ships at a time when a Franco-Spanish alliance was being negotiated. The T. of San Ildefonso sealed it. Adm. Langara reached Toulon and Spain declared war (Sept.). Unfortunately at this point Jervis' fleet was well below strength by the misjudgement of Adm. Mann who, against orders, took five of its ships-of-the-line to England. Moreover it became known that the French were fitting out an expedition against Ireland. It was decided not to replace Mann's ships but since Jervis was now greatly outnumbered and in strategic difficulty, it was considered too risky to leave him where he was. Corsica and Elba were accordingly evacuated, peace negotiations opened and the Mediterranean abandoned (Oct.). The first result was Bonaparte's spectacular victory at Arcola, whereupon the French rudely ended the negotiations (Nov.).

(5) The great French-Irish expedition sailed in Dec. 1796. The Channel Fleet, still embayed at Portsmouth, failed again to intercept such a force, whose purpose was frustrated only by contrary winds. In Jan. 1797 Bonaparte defeated the Austrians decisively at Rivoli and Mantua capitulated in Feb. He now advanced steadily towards Vienna. Meanwhile, as part of the operations connected with the Irish expedition, Langara's Spanish fleet of 27 sail of the line passed into the Atlantic. There they were attacked off C. St. Vincent by Jervis and Nelson's 15, which took six and badly damaged the rest. The victory raised British morale and ensured British safety but it was too late to save Austria, which obtained an armistice at Leoben (Apr. 1797). By treaties with the Pope (Feb.) and Sardinia (May) Bonaparte began to redraw the Italian political map.

(6) It was as well that he had these distractions, for in Apr. the British fleet mutinied at Spithead and when this was settled a further mutiny broke out in July at the Nore. This period saw the revolutionisation of Genoa, now the Ligurian republic (June), the creation of the Cisalpine Republic (July) and the destruction of the ancient Venetian State. Bonaparte, with his Levantine schemes already forming in his mind, had appropriated the Ionian Is. and used the Venetian *Terrafirma* as a sop to Austria in the P. of Campo Formio (Oct. 1797). *See* MEDITERRANEAN WAR.

FRANÇOIS or FRANCIS I of France (r. 1515-47) cousin of Louis XII and D. of ANGOULÊME, was a huge, ill favoured but flamboyant, man, lacking common sense and given to the pleasures of the flesh, but he was well served by the political abilities of his mother, Louise of Savoy, and his minister Duprat.

(2) He took up Louis XII's Italian policy, negotiating a peace with Venice and a marriage treaty with Charles of Burgundy as a preliminary (24 Mar. 1515). Then he descended upon the astonished Milanese by chamois tracks and destroyed their Swiss mercenaries in the two day B. of Marignano (13-14 Sept. 1515). To Milan the Pope hastily added Parma and Piacenza (T. of Bologna, 14 Dec. 1515). Within weeks Ferdinand of Aragon was dead and Charles of Burgundy (*see 5 below*) succeeded to his Spanish rights; but these he could not enforce from the Netherlands without a safe passage to Spain.

(3) At Noyon and Brussels the temporal rulers talked world peace and a safe journey: at Bologna François extracted the celebrated CONCORDAT from the Pope (18 Aug. 1516). In return for the annates, the Pope conceded the appointment of all prelacies to the French crown; thus until 1790 the control of a quarter of all the property in France passed into the hands of Crown nominees, a vast patronage which could serve political uses and subsidise a nobility suffering the effects of inflation. The Concordat system was to be the object of savage hatreds; it virtually made the King the Pope's representative in France and identified the Crown with the church.

(4) By the P. of Noyon (Aug. 1516) Charles had his safe conduct but the event was dwarfed in 1517 by only slowly appreciated occurrences. Luther issued his XCV Theses and the Turkish Sultan, by conquering Egypt, adopted the Caliphate, took control of the Levantine spice trade and achieved suzerainty of the Barbary states. Then, while Turkish armies battered at the gates of Hungary and Moslem seamen harried the trade in the W. Mediterranean, the Imperial Diet refused subsidies for the defence of the east. In Oct. 1518 Wolsey achieved the much acclaimed P. of London which embraced the Papacy and all the major western states, but save as a means of raising English prestige, the treaty amounted to nothing. The European states continued to prey upon each other.

(5) In Jan. 1519 the Emperor Maximilian died and Charles of Burgundy succeeded to his Austrian inheritance. François stood as a candidate in the imperial election. He poured out money like water but Charles was elected (June 1519). The new Emperor seemed to be the most powerful European since Charlemagne: in reality his dominion was a flabby collection of scattered states with inconsistent interests, liabilities and internal troubles. France, centrally placed, prosperous, on the way to unification and with a strong army, was as powerful. Barbary piracy, German religious disorder and Spanish communal rebellion formed the accompaniment to diplomatic activity in which Charles visited England (May 1520). Henry VIII and François met on the Field of the Cloth of Gold (June) and Henry signed the (not very) secret T. of Calais (July). In Oct. Charles was crowned at Aix-la-Chapelle; by Apr. 1521 he had arranged to hand over the Austrian lands to his brother Maximilian and had defeated the Spanish rebels. In May his Edict of Worms condemned Luther, and the military T. of Bruges against France was made with the Pope (Leo X) and England (Aug. 1521).

(6) The new Habsburg constellation enhanced the strategic and economic importance of northern Italy as a corridor between their Mediterranean and Austrian territories. A seizure of Milan, previously motivated by greed, could now be justified by French and Habsburgs alike on grounds of self defence. The French were attacked and trounced at La Bicocca (Apr. 1522) and driven from Lombardy. For three years the powers including, in a very minor fashion, England and the Scots, were involved in a war whose principal theatre stretched from Verona to Marseilles (besieged in 1524), leaving the Reformation to secure a political base in Germany. In Jan. 1525 François led his great counter-attack against his weakening enemy. A tactical mistake brought disaster and capture at Pavia (Feb. 1525).

(7) In theory an ally since the T. of Windsor (June 1522) of Charles, England had hardly intervened, yet French envoys had been in London since June 1524. Pavia brought English demands in Madrid for the joint invasion and partition of France. Since Charles had won his victory without English help, he proposed to secure the gains without helping them. N. Italy became, practically, a Spanish province. The English were told to help themselves. In Aug. 1525 Louise of Savoy secured an English peace (of The More) with a bribe to Wolsey and increased pensions. By the T. of Madrid (14 Jan. 1526) the captive François undertook, *inter alia,* to restore Burgundy, surrender his Italian claims and the suzerainty of Artois and Flanders, marry Charles' sister Eleanor of Portugal and leave two of his sons as hostages. He formally but secretly denounced the treaty and when set at liberty (Mar.) received widespread

European advice to do so. The Pope, to maintain the Italian balance, absolved him of his oath on grounds of duress and, with the N. Italian states and France established the League of Cognac (May 1526) under English patronage, against Charles. It was not a success. England could not go to war with her Flemish economic partner: François wanted a rest.

(8) More importantly the Hungarians, isolated by Western parochialism, went down before the Turks on the decisive field of Mohacs (Aug. 1526) where the Crowns of Bohemia and Hungary fell vacant. For lack of an alternative the Bohemians elected Ferdinand of Habsburg (23 Oct.) but John Zapolya and his Hungarian remnant and Ferdinand indulged in the luxury of a savage quarrel, with Turkish armies within 30 miles of Vienna. The overstrained Habsburg finances could not support their Italian armies which, by Sept. 1526, had blockaded the Pope in the Castello St. Angelo in Rome. By 1527 the need for more effective Anglo-French co-operation was evident to both sides and on 30 Apr. the T. of Westminster provided for war if Charles did not release the French royal hostages and pay the English King's debts. Charles could not pay even his own debts and his mutinous army put Rome to a week-long sack (May). The Pope cowered but the English would not fight. By June 1528 there was a truce with the Netherlands but French generals drove the imperialists from Rome and besieged Naples. This time it was a political mistake which destroyed their hopes. François tried to divert Genoese trade to Savona; the Genoese possessed the ablest admiral and the strongest Christian fleet in the W. Mediterranean. The malaria ridden French were blockaded and then surrendered at Aversa (Sept. 1528).

(9) Meanwhile Zapolya, defeated by Ferdinand at Tokay (Aug. 1527) made a partial submission to the Turks (Feb. 1528) and an alliance with France (Oct. 1528). This was the catalyst for the coupling of France with Turkey. From Gibraltar to Pressburg the interests and clients of the Commander of the Faithful faced those of God's Viceregent on Earth, whose troops held Christ's Vicar in durance and who was at war with the Eldest Son of the Church. A new French army descended into Italy while an Ottoman host rolled towards Vienna. At Landriano (1529) the imperialists beat the French. The Medici Pope then made terms with the Emperor at Barcelona (June 1529). By now the *spahis* were looting in Upper Austria. Negotiations for a western peace were, however, in progress between Louise of Savoy and the Emperor's sister: this blossomed into the Ladies Peace signed at Cambrai (Aug. 1529). Charles abandoned his Burgundian, François his Italian, claims; François paid 2M crowns, assumed Charles debts to Henry VIII and ceded his remaining rights in Flanders and Artois. Henry knew nothing of this until it was made public, which degraded Wolsey in his eyes but he acceded (27 Aug.). Vienna repulsed the Turks (Sept-Oct. 1529).

(10) It was time for the Emperor to re-establish the pre-eminence of his office. He restored the Pope's relatives, the expelled Medici, to Florence (Aug. 1530) as he had promised at Barcelona. The Pope had consecrated him at Bologna with the crowns of Lombardy and the Empire (Feb. 1530), and the Two Swords would restore German religious order and drive back the Turk. With Pontifical blessing his Austrian brother Ferdinand would succeed him on the Imperial throne: his son Philip would become King of Spain.

(11) François maintained his alliance with the Turkish vassal Zapolya, but while the electors assembled at Frankfurt a new theme appeared in French foreign policy. The election of Ferdinand to the Kingship of the Romans (5 Jan. 1531) and the formation of the protestant League of Schmalkalden (31 Dec. 1530) were almost simultaneous. The latter was a direct reaction to the

coronation at Bologna. In Oct. 1531 the strongly Romanist ruler of Bavaria, for wholly political reasons, joined the League. On 26 May, 1532 François, by alliances at Scheyern with Hesse, Saxony and particularly Bavaria, became a supporter of the League as well, when a new Turkish army marched across Hungary. The idea that the Turks were dangerous had at last, however, got into thick German heads. The Religious Peace of Nuremberg (July 1532) to deal with them represented a check for François and when Ferdinand signed a peace with the Sultan (June 1533) the Habsburgs had reached the summit of their influence.

(12) The European revolutionary period from 1531 to 1535, when the English church was severed from Rome, saw also the foundation of religious bitterness in France. Calvin began work in Paris in 1532 where in 1534 the Jesuits also established themselves. These infections were eventually to destroy the country's international standing, but meanwhile François was rebuilding his military strength. His old ally Venice, his client Florence and even the Milanese looked to him for support. Clement VII had never recently ceased to do so. In Oct. 1533 he brought his famous niece CATHARINE DEI MEDICI (1519-89) to Marseilles and married her to François' second son Henry, an event which influenced French politics for many decades and French civilisation for centuries. François in return reimposed the persecution of heretics in France but this deterred him neither from supporting them in Germany nor from abetting the Barbary corsairs against Spain and Naples. Khair-ed-Din Barbarossa, their principal ruler, sent envoys to him at Marseilles; in Feb. 1535 François made the first formal treaty ("Capitulation") with the Sultan; so Charles V retaliated by seizing Tunis in June.

(13) François was nearly ready: in Feb. 1536 his troops seized the strategic Duchy of Savoy and in July he made a naval treaty at Lyons with the Portuguese. Charles was already advancing upon Marseilles, which he besieged. A scorched earth defence devastated Provence, but drove the Imperial army back in hunger and confusion (Sept.). The Portuguese treaty achieved little: co-ordination with the Turks was more efficacious and scandalous. By now, however, the Farnese Pope Paul III was working determinedly for a settlement, for the English schism was causing him serious concern. Thus in Feb. 1538 Ferdinand made peace with Zapolya (T. of Grosswardein); in June a Franco-Imperialist truce was signed at Nice and in July King and Emperor met at Aigues Mortes. Henry VIII tried to keep the two monarchs apart by suggesting himself as a husband for some close relative of each: but in Dec. 1538 Paul III ordered execution against Henry and in Feb. 1539 Charles and François in the T. of Toledo agreed to make no new alliance without mutual consent. Outside the Venetian dominions N. and S. Italy were (and until 1713 remained) firmly within a Spanish grasp which, in a further war begun in 1542, François could not shake. Henry VIII was involved as an ally of Charles and Scotland as an ally of France. The Italian war was finally settled at the P. of Crépy-en-Laonnais (Sept. 1544) which re-enacted the important principles of the Ladies Peace; the English war, by the P. of Ardres (June 1546) which left Boulogne in English hands until 1554 when it could be bought back for 2M crowns. At this point François I died.

FRANCO-PRUSSIAN WAR (July 1870-May 1871). (1) In the first six weeks the Germans drove the armies of Napoleon III and Marshal Bazaine apart, invested the latter in Strasbourg and in Sept. forced the Emperor to capitulate at Sedan. A revolution in Paris proclaimed a republic under Thiers. A fortnight later the Germans reached Paris, which resisted them and was besieged. Two days later the Italians seized Rome, no longer protected by France. Bazaine surrendered at the end of the month.

(2) Local French commanders raised field armies and the Paris garrison attempted a number of sorties. Consequently there was a heavy scattered fighting in many areas of France north of the Loire. German casualties were heavier in this later period than during the opening *Blitzkrieg*. Meanwhile Bismarck, who had negotiated alliances between the Northern and Southern German states (Nov.), persuaded the princes to establish a unified Germany under the K. of Prussia as Emperor. He was proclaimed at Versailles on 18 Jan. 1871. Next day the French were defeated at the major B. of St. Quentin, Paris surrendered on 28th and the French Eastern army was driven into Switzerland on 1 Feb. The new French Assembly met at Bordeaux next day and on 17th elected Thiers prime minister. On 26th this govt. signed peace preliminaries at Versailles, for Bismarck wanted peace quickly before other powers' concerted intervention.

(3) Power in Paris was seized (Mar.) by left wing extremists (*The Communards*) backed by the embittered and defeated population. The Germans tactfully stepped aside so that the French could fight each other and then Thiers' govt.'s troops besieged the city. On 10 May 1871 the Thiers' govt. signed the T. of Frankfort, ceding Alsace and Lorraine but not Belfort, and a war indemnity. Bismarck prevented his own extremists from demanding more and Thiers was now free to put down the insurrection in Paris, which surrendered on 28th.

FRANCO-RUSSIAN ALLIANCE, WAR OF (Aug. 1807-July 1809). (1) The Franco-Russian T. of Tilsit (July 1807) bound Russia to close the ports under her control to British trade. By secret articles that control was to be extended to the Baltic. Bonaparte was to close the Iberian and Italian ports and the two powers were ultimately to partition Turkey. The British, quickly informed, realised that attacks on Sweden and Denmark were imminent. The Russians, indeed, invaded Swedish Finland in Aug; the French, Swedish Pomerania with its important port of Stralsund in Sept. British troops were ferried from Stralsund to take part in a combined operation under Adm. Gambier against the Danish fleet. Copenhagen was bombarded into surrender (Sept.) and the ships carried off, whereupon Russia declared war on Britain (Oct. 1807).

(2) German nationalism was being organised and encouraged by many men and influences: by statesmen such as Stein, philosophers like Fichte, practical soldiers such as Scharnhorst and, not least, by the simultaneous effects of the emancipation of the Prussian serfs (Oct. 1807) and the Spanish rising (May 1808). Meanwhile Bonaparte and the Czar became mutually suspicious. Bonaparte declined, as he had promised, to evacuate Silesia on the pretext that the Russians were still in the Turkish Danube provinces. He also kept garrisons in the fortresses along the Oder and interfered in Prussian affairs. To the Czar it seemed that Turkish partition was being put off until Bonaparte was strong enough to take the major part. Meanwhile a scheme originated by Stein, for a German revolt in concert with Prussia, Austria and British intervention, was discovered. Stein took refuge in Austria. Bonaparte urgently needed a summit conference with the Czar to persuade him to hold Austria in check: for Austria too had carried out reforms, reorganised her forces and was arming. The summit conference (or Congress) took place at Erfurt (Sept. 1808). A social and literary event of great splendour, it only papered over the cracks in the Franco-Russian alliance, for Bonaparte had to concede Finland and the Danube provinces in return for the recognition of Joseph Bonaparte's shaky Spanish throne and a promise to come to France's aid if Austria attacked. The two also addressed a note to George III inviting him to make peace; this brought about an exchange of mutually abusive diplomatic manifestos in which Canning, writing for George III, had a clear advantage.

(3) Bonaparte then went to Spain (*see* PENINSULAR WAR-4) while the Tirolese rose, with some success, against the joint Franco-Bavarian occupation. With disaffection widespread in Germany, the Austrians went to war (Feb. 1809). Bonaparte returned and gathered enough scattered troops to defeat the Austrian Archduke Charles piecemeal in six days, culminating in the B. of Eckmühl (22 Apr.) and the fall of Ratisbon (23rd). In May he entered Vienna to find the Archduke in force on the other side of the Danube. An attempt to destroy his army brought on the second defeat of Bonaparte's military career at the B. of Essling (or Aspern) (21-2 May). The value of the Russian undertakings was now made plain. If the Czar was too entangled in his Swedish war to come to Bonaparte's aid, doubt of his intentions prevented others from aiding Austria while French reinforcements arrived. In July Bonaparte's augmented army, after a sanguinary struggle, drove the Archduke from his positions around Wagram but failed to annihilate him. The British, who meanwhile had been mounting an expedition against Antwerp, launched it too late. Delayed before Flushing, it found Antwerp ready and retired to the malarial swamps of Walcheren. The Archduke requested an armistice and the new European dispensation was established by the Russo-Swedish T. of Frederikshamn (giving Finland to Russia) (Sept.) and the T. of Vienna (Oct.) under which Austria lost Galicia to Poland and Russia, the Innviertel to Bavaria and above all her Adriatic coastline to Italy, whereby the Continental System could be enforced against her (*see* FRENCH COASTAL ANNEXATIONS). The remnant of the British Walcheren force was evacuated at the end of the year.

FRANC-TIREUR (Fr.). A guerrilla.

FRANKALMOIGN (Norman Fr. = free alms) was a tenure in which the Church held some of its lands by spiritual services only, such as saying masses for the grantor's soul. This prevented economic, military or personal services being rendered for the land and took it out of the system of secular administration because the church never died. In the Constitutions of Clarendon (1164) Henry II agreed that where both parties to a property suit agreed that the tenure was in frankalmoign, a church court might decide the dispute but that where they disagreed on this preliminary issue, it should be decided in the King's court by the assize *Utrum* (Lat = Whichever) (*see* POSSESSORY ASSIZES). In practice frankalmoign cases came to be tried in the royal courts anyway, because the latter were more reliable than church courts. *See* FEUDALISM-15.

FRANKING was the right, by signing the cover of a letter, to send it free of charge through the post. Many people possessed it including all M.P.s and it was barefacedly abused. It disappeared with other postal anomalies when the penny post started in 1840.

FRANKLINS in the 14th and 15th cents. were freeholders ranking next below the gentry. One appears as a respected figure in Chaucer's *Canterbury Tales*.

FRANKLIN, Benjamin (1706-90). This extraordinary man began as a printer's devil in Boston (Mass.) but at 16 discovered his own literary talent and ran away to Philadelphia. Under the patronage of Gov. Keith he visited England to buy printing machinery and from 1730 onwards (until 1766) published the influential *Pennsylvania Gazette*. He also organised a famous discussion group called the Junto Club. In 1732 he began to publish *Poor Richards Almanack* which owed its wide readership partly to his highly modern practice of issuing different editions with local material for the three groups of colonies. At the same time he was teaching himself languages and securing civic improvements, such as paving and police, in Philadelphia. By now he was a local personage; he inspired the foundation of the

American Philosophical Society in 1743 and the Univ. of Pennsylvania in 1751. He also had a passion for science; he began to publish the findings of his electrical experiments in 1751 and these were the basis upon which later electrical developments proceeded. He invented the lightning conductor.

Well known in and outside America, in 1751 he entered the Pennsylvania Assembly and in 1753 became Deputy P.M.G. for the Colonies. The experience gained in the field of communications convinced him of the need for federation and as a delegate to the Albany Congress of 1754 he drafted the Plan of Union which was the forerunner of the U.S. Constitution. In 1757 the Assembly chose him for his diplomatic talents to negotiate the termination of proprietory govt. knowing, however, that he would be received in the English literary and scientific world. The mission failed but Oxford made him a D.C.L. In 1764 he came to England on another mission to try and have Massachusetts turned into a Crown Colony and he also acted as Agent for Georgia, New Jersey and Massachusetts, who were lobbying for repeal of the Townshend Acts. While in London he got hold of private letters from the gov. of Massachusetts, Thos. Hutchinson, who advocated resisting the colonial demand for 'English' liberties. In 1772 these were read out (apparently without Franklin's connivance) in the Massachusetts Assembly; they created a political scandal in which Franklin lost his postmastership and became convinced war was inevitable. In 1775 he therefore returned to America where he served in the Continental Congress and in 1776 helped to draft the Declaration of Independence.

Congress immediately despatched him to France to secure recognition and an alliance. His enormous personal reputation did much to make good the decisive act of recognition in 1778. From then on he acted as U.S. Minister to the French Court and with Jay and Adams signed the T. of Paris in 1783. He returned home in 1785, became a member of the Constitutional Convention in 1787 and was one of the signatories of the U.S. Constitution.

FRANKLIN (1) Sir John (1786-1847) first went to the Arctic with Buchan in 1818. In 1819 he set out from Fort York, reached the Arctic Sea by 1822 and so continued east-about to Fort York again. In 1825 he headed another expedition from New York by way of L. Huron, Great Bear Lake and the Mackenzie R. to the Arctic Sea, returning in 1827 to Montreal. After a naval command on the Greek coast from 1830 to 1833 in 1845 he set out for the Behring Strait and disappeared. His wife **(2) Jane (1792-1875)** travelled much with him and fitted out expeditions to find him. One of these established that he died in 1847 after nineteen months in pack ice.

FRANK PLEDGE. Wergild, as a means of keeping order, broke down whenever a kindred was scattered or destroyed by the recurrent wars, migrations or epidemics. Kings, beginning with Athelstan (r. 925-40) therefore instituted *frithborh* (A.S. = peace pledge of which 'frank pledge' is a mistranslation). Households were grouped roughly by tens (tithings) all of whose adult men had to give pledges to present criminals, capture thieves and be responsible for each other's good conduct. The pledges were given publicly in the Court of the Hundred or Wapentake at shrieval sessions called the View of Frank Pledge. The system was confined to England south of Yorkshire and Lancashire and east of Cheshire, Hereford and Shropshire. It was liable to break down in troublous times when the King's officers were otherwise engaged; by the 13th cent. View of Frank Pledge had become a common franchise and by the 15th it was being replaced by Grand Juries, Quarter Sessions and Assizes. The head of a tithing was called the Headborough, Tithingman, Chief Pledge or Borsholder.

FRANKS. (1) This Germanic tribe had crossed the Rhine by

288. The **Salian** Franks pressed into modern Belgium where they settled by 358. They were in Flanders by 406 when the **Ripuarian** Franks began to encroach on Cologne, which fell to them in about 460. CLOVIS, King of both tribes (r. 481-511) defeated Syagrius, the last Roman representative, at Soissons in 486 and the Alemanni at Strasbourg in 496. He was then baptised into the R. Catholic church, on whose support he could then rely against the Alan Goths. At Vouillé (near Poitiers) he routed the Visigoths and annexed their territory as far as the Pyrenees. Regarded as the founder of the MEROVINGIAN DYNASTY, his territory was divided between four sons but essential unity was maintained leading to the conquest of Thuringia in 531 and of Burgundy between 532 and 534. After a brief reunion (558-561) under CLOTAIRE I the Kingdom was again quartered but family intrigue and rivalry brought confusion. In 567 the areas were reshuffled into **Austrasia, Neustria** and **Burgundy;** Austrasia was ruled from 575 to 613 by a famous queen regent BRUNHILDA in the name of a succession of minors; Neustria was ruled from 584 to 628 by CLOTAIRE II, only reputed to have been the son of his father. Austrasia and Burgundy were united in 613 but for reasons not now fully known the King had become a ceremonial cipher, the real power being wielded by the Mayor of the Palace, who was the leader of a cabal of magnates. This arrangement spread to Neustria when K. DAGOBERT I (r. 623-39) came to the throne (*see* CAROLINGIANS; CAPETIANS).

(2) The name 'Franks' was allegedly given by others because they used the *franca,* a kind of javelin, or the *francisque,* a throwing axe. The name is now represented by "Franconia" (Ger = *Franken*) and "France".

(3) The name is used by orientals, especially Levantines, for Europeans, because the Franks played a leading part in the Crusades. It now appears in the form *Feringi.*

FRASER, Bruce Austin (1888-1981) Ld. FRASER of the NORTH CAPE (1945) was captured and released by Bolsheviks at Baku in 1919. As C-in-C Home Fleet (1943-4) he conducted the operations which led to the sinking of the German battle-cruiser *Scharnhorst* off the North Cape (Christmas 1943). From 1944 to 1945 as C-in-C Eastern Fleet he had to endure American operational hostility but managed to fight the Japanese.

FRASER, James Baillie (1783-1856) and **William (?1784-1835).** William was Mountstuart Elphinstone's sec. at Kabul in 1811 and the brothers explored Nepal in 1815. In 1821 James travelled through Persian Kurdistan to Tabriz. In 1830 William became Resident at Delhi. In 1833 James rode from Semlin, *via* Constantinople to Teheran, which he reached in 1834. William was murdered at Delhi. James collected his papers and wrote a military memoir on Skinner's Horse, besides descriptions of his own travels.

FRASER, James (1713-54) lived in India from 1730, was an HEIC factor and made a distinguished collection of Sanskrit M.S. which he left to Oxford Univ.

FRASER, James Sturt (1783-1869) was a commissioner for the restitution of the French and Dutch possessions as a consequence of the P. of Paris, from 1816 to 1817 and then was successively Resident at Mysore (1834), Travancore and Cochin (1836) and Hyderabad (1839-52).

FRASER (1) William (?-1297), Chanc. of Scotland in 1276 and Bp. of St. Andrews from 1279 was, as a northerner and Scotland's leading churchman, one of the six regents appointed by the Estates when Alexander III died in 1285. He was primarily responsible on the Scottish side and against Bruce opposition for the Ts. of Salisbury (1289) and Brigham (1290) which failed with the death of the Maid of Norway, and he favoured the claims of the Balliols against the Bruce, but though he evidently respected Edward I he was not prepared to support English rule in Scotland and visited France to negotiate an alliance. He died there. **(2) Sir Alexander (?-1332)** was a Bruce partisan who fought for Robert at Methven in 1306 and against the Comyns. He fought at Bannockburn (1314), married a Bruce and was Great Chamberlain from 1319 to 1326. He was killed at the B. of Dupplin Moor. **(3) Sir Alexander (?1537-1623)** inherited the burgh of barony at Philorth and having built Fraserburgh at Faithlie on the coast a few miles away transferred the people and secured in 1592 a charter for a university college there. He was an M.P. in 1596 and began college buildings in 1597 but isolation, competition from Marischal College at Aberdeen and the royal dislike of local presbyterians ruined the college, which closed in 1601. The town, with its good harbour and prosperous fisheries, survived. The notorious **(4) Simon (?1667-1747) 12th Ld. LOVAT**, promoted his career by violence and treachery. He seized his cousin, the 11th Lord's property and forcibly married the widow. Meanwhile his Jacobite intrigues had been discovered. Outlawed for treason he visited James II at St. Germain in 1700 but got a pardon from William III. Meanwhile his enemies had taken further proceedings for the rape of Lady Lovat and he again went to France (1702) and, having affected a conversion to Romanism, undertook to assist the French invasion of Scotland. He returned with a letter from Mary of Modena and tried to set up, or compromise, some highland leaders in a Jacobite plot. They refused to trust him, he fled to France where he was now trusted even less and imprisoned. In 1713, however, he escaped to London where he was arrested but pleaded his long imprisonment as proof of loyalty and to earn his pardon called out his clan for the Hanoverians in the 1715 rebellion. He got the Lovat estates for life in 1716 and, after strenuous quarrelling and litigation, established his full title to them in 1733. He was now apparently respectable and Sheriff of Inverness, but in 1737 the Pretender offered him a dukedom to support another plot. This came to light and he was deprived of his posts. Not surprisingly he was seized by the govt. as a hostage for his clan's behaviour in the rebellion of 1745 but escaped, was retaken and executed for treason. He cheerfully married twice during his wife's lifetime. His eldest son **(5) Simon (1726-82)** Master of Lovat, led the Frasers for the Pretender in the 1745 rebellion, was pardoned in 1750 and became a successful advocate. In 1757 he raised the (78th) Fraser Highlanders, commanded them in America, was wounded at Quebec (1759) and, after leaving America in 1761, became both an M.P. and a Portuguese general and then in 1771 a British general. He recovered the family estates in 1777 and raised the 71st Highlanders for the American rebellion. Another **(6) Simon (1738-1813)** served under him in both American campaigns, raised the 133rd Foot in 1793 and served in Portugal as a general from 1797 to 1800. The half brother of (5), **(7) Archibald (1736-1815)** was consul in the Barbary State of Tripoli from 1766 to 1774, succeeded to the chieftaincy and estates in 1782 and was an M.P. from 1782 to 1796.

FRATERNITY. (1) The highwaymen's term for themselves. **(2)** One of the objects of the French Revolution. In neither case completely achieved.

FRAZER or FRA[I]ZER otherwise FitzSimon or Simson or Frizell. Scattered North Scottish clan living mostly in Inverness and Aberdeen lowlands. Its chief was called The MACSHIMI. The 24th Macshimi was the first Lord LOVAT.

FRATERNITY, DECREE OF (1792). *See* FRENCH REVOLUTIONARY WAR (APR. 1792-FEB. 1793)-2.

FRAZER, Sir James George (1854-1941) wrote his revolutionary *Golden Bough* with its seven loosely related disquisitions on myth and folk customs between 1890 and 1915 and many other later works on similar subjects. Starting from a narrow issue (to explain the ancient priestly succession at Aricia near Rome) he broadened

out into a stupendously learned series of theses which incidentally shook the authenticity of the Gospels and to which all social anthropology owes a major debt.

FREDERICK V. Elector Palatine. *See* THIRTY YEARS' WAR-1-8.

FREDERICK AUGUSTUS (1763-1827), 2nd son of George III, **D. of YORK and ALBANY (1784)**, administrator of the bishopric of Osnabrück from 1764; a soldier, he fought a duel with Col. Lennox for words spoken on the Regency Bill in 1789. He commanded the Flanders expedition of 1793 to 1795 and was C-in-C from 1798 to 1809 when he was removed because his mistress, Mrs. Clarke, was selling commissions. In the 1820s he was an opponent of R. Catholic emancipation. His somewhat indecisive operations in Flanders are commemorated in the rhyme:

> The grand old Duke of York,
> He had ten thousand men.
> He marched them up to the top of the hill
> And he marched them down again.

FREDERICK LUDWIG (1707-51) D. of GLOUCESTER (1717), EDINBURGH (1727), P. of WALES (1729) ("POOR FRED") mostly brought up in Hanover. He hated and was hated by his father, George II, and became a centre for opposition intrigue mostly at Norfolk House and Kew after 1737. Neither clever nor popular, his chief distinction was to father George III.

FREDERICKSHAMN, P. of (1809). *See* BALTIC-52.

FREE CHURCH OF SCOTLAND. *See* SCOTLAND, (PRESBYTERIAN) CHURCH.

FREE FRENCH was the name given to the Frenchmen led by Charles de Gaulle (q.v.) who developed an organisation to continue the fight against the Germans after the French surrender of June 1940. In so doing they repudiated the authority of the French govt., which had moved to Vichy. They were based in London and included not only fugitives from metropolitan France but whole provinces of the French African empire. In 1941 they set up a French National Committee which claimed the status of a pre-provisional govt. and organised non-communist branches of the French Resistance. In 1943, against U.S. suspicion, de Gaulle established his committee in Algiers and later it became a real provisional govt. with substantial forces. Its badge, the Cross of Lorraine, commemorated Joan of Arc.

FREEHOLD. *See* LAND TENURE (ENGLAND)-1.

FREEMAN, MRS. *See* ANNE, QUEEN.

FREEMASONRY (1) is described as "a peculiar system of morality, veiled in allegory and illustrated by symbols". In the English speaking world it is practised in a private rather than secret masculine body. It numbers about 600,000 in Britain. It is derived from mediaeval lodges or local guilds of English or Scots stonemasons engaged on large long-lasting projects such as cathedrals and castles. Like other guilds the lodges regulated admission to the craft and supported the members in trouble and celebration, but their itinerant nature called for private methods of recognition. **(2)** Demands for stonemasons' skills declined as these buildings ceased to be built and brick superseded stone. The lodges then began to admit outsiders (speculative masons). The ceremonies and rituals had differed little in purpose from those of other guilds, but as masonic lodges became decreasingly involved in stoneworking, their interest in social, ceremonial and mutually supportive customs increased. **(3)** By the 17th cent. there were three degrees. There was a tendency to elaborate, and many lodges began adding extra ones, giving rise to two rival associations known as Grand Lodges: the Moderns who kept to the three degrees, and the confusingly named Antient and Accepted Rite which is almost universal on the Continent. **(4)** In England the two Grand Lodges compromised and amalgamated in 1816 to form the United Grand Lodge of

England and Wales, which recognises masonry in three degrees only but allows those who have passed them to ascend the remaining 30 by joining separate recognised Chapters. Grand Lodge also recognises other kinds of side-orders in separate chapters and many foreign Grand Lodges (Antient or Modern) but no lodge which does not demand belief in the existence of God, normally by requiring initiates to swear allegiance on an open Old Testament, Koran or other sacred text. **(5)** Lodges which admit women are not recognised but female freemasonry has existed for over 200 years. In the 18th cent. its leading practioner was Elisabeth Chudleigh (*see* KINGSTON'S CASES). **(6)** Masons have included many people of high distinction including Sir Isaac Newton, most Presidents of the U.S.A. and Sir Winston Churchill.

FREETOWN. *See* SIERRA LEONE.

FREMANTLE (1) Sir Thomas Francis (1765-1819) served under Hood and Nelson in the Mediterranean especially at Toulon (1795), Leghorn and Elba (1796). He was wounded at Sta. Cruz in 1797, fought at Copenhagen (1801) and Trafalgar (1805) and, as flag officer in the Adriatic, took Fiume in 1813 and Trieste in 1814. His son **(2) Thomas Francis (1798-1890) 1st Ld. COTTESLOE (1874)** was a Tory M.P. from 1826 to 1846 ending as Chief Sec. for Ireland in 1845. From 1848 to 1875 he was V.C. and then chairman of the Board of Customs, whose management he greatly improved. He also took great interest in military welfare and training. His son **(3) Sir Edmund (1836-1929)** was C-in-C East Indies from 1888 to 1891 and commanded an expedition against Vito (E. Africa) in 1890. He was C-in-C China from 1892 and at Devonport from 1896 to 1901.

FRENCH. *See* LANGUE D'-O, L-OC.

FRENCH COMMUNITY was the successor to the French Empire and created under the Constitution of the Fifth Republic in 1958. By 1980, though French interests and connections including the language, were still influential, as a formal organisation it had ceased to operate.

FRENCH, Sir John Denton Pinkstone (1852-1925) 1st Vist. (1916) 1st E. of YPRES (1922) commanded the cavalry under Sir Geo. White in Natal in 1899, drove the Boers out of the Cape Colony, relieved Kimberley, forced Cronje's surrender at Paardeberg and took Johannesburg (Jan-Mar. 1900); was Inspector-Gen. in 1907 and C.I.G.S. in 1912. He resigned because of the Curragh Affair in 1914 and became C-in-C. B.E.F at the outbreak of World War I. He had the misfortune to have to carry out with inadequate means plans hitherto unknown to him, whose failure forced him to retreat; moreover, his relations with other Allied generals were never satisfactory. In the circumstances the British and French resistance to German invasion achieved a remarkable degree of instinctive co-ordination. He resigned in Dec. 1915 and thereafter he was, as C-in-C Home Forces, responsible for training until 1918. He was Lord Lieut. of Ireland from 1918 to 1921. A sensible soldier.

FRENCH COASTAL ANNEXATIONS (May 1809-Jan. 1811) (*see* THIRD COALITION, WAR, SECOND PHASE; PENINSULAR WAR-1,2; FRANCO-RUSSIAN ALLIANCE, WAR-3). Since states not under French rule enforced the exclusion of British trade against their own subjects very laxly, Bonaparte's continental system appeared to be failing to ruin Britain. Accordingly he brought the European coasts either under the control of persons whom he trusted such as Murat in Naples or directly under French rule, viz: May 1809; the Papal States; July 1810 Holland; in Dec. 1810 the German North Sea Coasts and Lübeck were occupied; in Jan. 1811 Oldenburg was annexed. *See* MOSCOW DISASTER.

FRENCH GUIANA. *See* GUIANA.

FRENCH GUINEA. *See* AFRICA, WEST (EX-FRENCH).

FRENCH OF STRATFORD [ATTE BOW]. An archaic court French of Norman origin, taught by the nuns of St. Leonard's convent, Bromley, to polite young women in Chaucer's time.

FRENCH REVOLUTION AND CONSEQUENT WARS (1787-1815). (1) The French Revolution is customarily dated from 1789, but the Assembly of the French Notables called in Feb. 1787 to consider Calonne's proposals for extricating the French Crown from bankruptcy took the irrevocable step; it rejected them, refused to concede any of the entrenched interests of the nobility and clergy or the tax farmers, and referred the difficulties to a States-General. Calonne was succeeded by Lomenie de Brienne. In 1788 a second Assembly proved equally irresponsible and in Aug. summonses for a States-General were issued. Necker succeeded Lomenie. Russia and Austria were at this time distracted by a major Turkish war and they, with Prussia, were scheming to dismember Poland.

(2) The States-General met in May 1789. The Third (Commons) Estate declared itself to be the National Assembly in June and the other Estates united with it. In July Paris rioters stormed the virtually empty Bastille and the Turks were beaten at Focsani. In Aug., while the French peasantry pillaged country houses (*La grande Peur),* their owners abdicated their privileges and the Assembly issued the Declaration of the Rights of Man. In Oct. the Paris market women forced the King to move from Versailles to Paris, the Austrians took Belgrade and simultaneously there was a revolution in the Austrian Netherlands. In Nov. the French provincial system was abolished in favour of territorial *départements.* In Dec. the Austrian Netherlands declared their independence as Belgium, and the French govt., tried to overcome its financial embarrassments by the issue of notes called *Assignats* secured upon crown and confiscated lands.

(3) By 1790 foreigners who had welcomed the revolution for its apparent liberalism or because it weakened French power were beginning to have doubts. A Convention (Britain, Holland and Prussia) on Belgium preceded the death of the Emperor Joseph II; his successor, Leopold, began to liquidate Joseph's liabilities. He concluded the T. of Reichenbach with Prussia (July) at about the time when the National Assembly enacted the Civil Constitution of the Clergy and decreed the People's Festival at the Champ de Mars. This was profoundly offensive to conservatives and R. Catholics everywhere and to most established govts. It was in Nov. that Edmund Burke published (and was ridiculed for) his forecast of revolutionary violence in his *Reflections.* The year ended with the Austrians suppressing the Belgian revolt while Britain, Holland and Prussia held the ring.

(4) In the general insecurity after Necker's resignation in Sept. 1790, increasing numbers of estate owners emigrated. Mirabeau's death in Apr. 1791 removed the one revolutionary politician of stature able to support the crown. The govt., unable to meet its debts, created an appalling inflation by wholesale issues of *assignats.* This destroyed public confidence and consumed both private and royal fortunes. The royal family was becoming a prisoner of the armed and uniformed Paris mob called the National Guard under the famous Marquis de Lafayette. It appeared that some of the provincial troops were still loyal to the throne and in June Louis XVI and his queen tried to escape to them. They were stopped at Varennes and returned in ignominy to the capital.

(5) The alarm which these events excited, especially eastwards of France, coincided with the approaching end of the Turkish War. Poland had reformed her constitution in May 1791 and the increase of strength which this might be expected to produce was most unwelcome to the three predatory powers. The liquidation of the Turkish War would enable them to pay attention to Polish affairs, and those of France. The Austro-Turkish P. of Sistova or Galatz was signed in the east while their rulers issued the Declaration of Pillnitz in the west (Aug. 1791). The

Russians ended their part of the war with the terrible storm of Ismail (Dec.) and the P. of Jassy (Jan. 1792).

(6) The French Assembly had repudiated any designs on foreign territory, but this was inherently a resolution which foreign statesmen were likely to discount. In any event the declaration of Pillnitz, only six weeks after the King's flight to Varennes, inflamed French political opinion. Southern radicals had been subverting the Papal enclave at Avignon. Some of its people were persuaded to demand incorporation in France and the Assembly accepted their word as the authentic voice of the territory. The Assembly passed the new constitution of France One and Indivisible in Sept. The next day it annexed Avignon. The new Legislative Assembly met in Oct. It was dominated from the start by the radical Girondists and their uncomfortable allies, the extremist Jacobins. The latter were not alone in observing the formal consistency between a policy of no annexations with one of "popular" voluntary accession. Moreover, if the Civil Constitution of the Clergy might in some quarters be thought France's private affair, the Pope had now, at Avignon, been directly attacked.

(7) A motley imperial army under the D. of Brunswick began to move towards France, in purported execution of the Declaration of Pillnitz, that is to say, in defence of the existing European Order. Before it had even reached Mainz the Legislative Assembly declared war (Apr. 1792).

(8) The wars which now began and continued almost without interruption until 1815 may be considered in fifteen phases which do not coincide exactly with every conventional name for them and which, also, occasionally overlap. These phases and, where appropriate, the treaty ending them are as follows and are separately described under the respective titles: **(i)** THE FRENCH REVOLUTIONARY WAR (Apr. 1792-Feb. 1793). **(ii)** THE REVOLUTIONARY CIVIL WARS (Feb-Dec. 1792) which were comprised in **(iii)** THE WAR OF THE FIRST COALITION until July 1795 (T. of Basel) and in which Britain took part. Thenceforth Britain was continually at war (including blockade and counter-blockade) with France and sometimes nominally or actually with other states, save from Oct. 1801 to May 1803 and from May 1814 to Mar. 1815. She co-operated or allied herself with other states whenever they were taking part against France. **(iv)** THE FRANCO-AUSTRIAN WAR (July 1795-Oct. 1797) P. of Campo Formio. **(v)** THE MEDITERRANEAN WAR (Oct. 1797-Mar. 1799). **(vi)** THE WAR OF THE SECOND COALITION (Mar. 1799-Feb. 1801) P. of Luneville. **(vii)** THE BALTIC WAR (Dec. 1800-Apr. 1801) (*see* BALTIC EXPEDITIONS-3,4). **(viii)** The Stalemate (Apr. 1801-Mar. 1802). P. of Amiens. **(ix)** FRENCH PEACETIME AGGRESSIONS IN ITALY AND SWITZERLAND (Oct. 1801-May 1803). **(x)** The British Declaration of War and the WAR OF THE THIRD COALITION which was in two parts viz:- **(a)** (May 1803-Feb. 1806) P. of Pressburg and **(b)** (Oct. 1806-July 1807) Ts. of Tilsit. **(xi)** THE PENINSULAR WAR (May 1808-Nov. 1812). **(xii)** THE WAR OF THE FRANCO-RUSSIAN ALLIANCE (Oct. 1807-Oct. 1809) P. of Vienna. **(xiii)** FRENCH COASTAL ANNEXATIONS in the Mediterranean, Adriatic and North Sea (May 1809-Jan. 1811). **(xiv)** THE MOSCOW DISASTER (May-Dec. 1812) and the WAR OF THE FOURTH COALITION (July 1812-May 1814) P. of Paris. **(xv)** THE WATERLOO CAMPAIGN (Mar-Nov. 1815) Second P of Paris.

(9) The sea being of central importance in these wars, the following are the figures of naval losses. Cols A = Ships of the Line: B = Ships not of the Line

	A	B	Total	Worst Years		
					A	B	Total
Royal Navy	32	110	142	1798	2	9	11
French	90	170	260	1793	15	18	33
Spanish	22	22	44	1805	12	0	12

In addition the Royal Navy inflicted heavy losses on the Dutch (B. of Camperdown 1797) and the Danes (Copenhagen 1801 and 1807). The above figures do not wholly justify the prominence accorded by historians to the seven major naval battles. At the height of these conflicts, the Royal Navy had over 600 ships in commission.

FRENCH REVOLUTIONARY WAR (Apr. 1792-Feb. 1793) (*see previous entry*). **(1)** The aggressive revolutionary majority in the Legislative Assembly saw, in the Declaration of Pillnitz and the movement of imperial troops, an opportunity both to spread its principles and destroy the monarchy. France declared war on Austria in Apr. 1792 and Prussia declared against France in July when the combined C-in-C, the elderly D. of Coburg, issued the Coblenz Manifesto threatening the destruction of Paris. This naturally provoked the Legislative to suspend the monarchy, detain the King (Aug.) and allow its partisans to invade the prisons and murder (in the so-called September Massacres) suspected aristocratic traitors.

(2) These French events created a revulsion in Britain where hitherto the govt. had seen good reason to stay neutral (*see* TALLEYRAND-4) and the opposition had welcomed the overthrow of monarchical despotism. Meanwhile the combined Germanic forces advanced over-cautiously into France and turned back after cannonading the French at Valmy (20 Sept. 1792). Next day the even more extremist Convention superseded the Legislative and proclaimed the Republic. Its leaders took ruthless command of the war; they drove the generals forward and, developing the Avignon precedent, appealed by the Decree of Fraternity (Nov.) to peoples over the heads of their govts. This changed the nature of the war, and Dumouriez' simultaneous victory over the allies at Jemappes emphasised its new character. A week later he took Brussels; a further week later, in extension of the ideological base of the Decree of Fraternity, the Scheldt was decreed open to navigation and a French squadron arrived to protect it against the Dutch. In Dec. the Austrian Netherlands were incorporated into France and the new French systems extended to them.

(3) The Decree of Incorporation coincided with the trial of Louis XVI, his condemnation and in Jan. 1793 his public execution. This was intended as a defiance and a way to commit revolutionaries irrevocably against opposition. Its most important effect was to unite British opinion, already alarmed by the proceedings in Belgium. The govt. increased the naval establishment (Dec.). The Portland whig opposition crossed the floor of the House and Pitt reconstructed his ministry so as to include them. Chauvelin, the French diplomatic agent, who had throughout been treated with high handed suspicion, was now expelled (Jan.) and the Convention replied by declaring war (Feb.). *See* DAGGER SCENE IN THE COMMONS.

FRENCH TRADE TREATY 1787. Adam Smith had persuaded Pitt that France would prove a better trading partner than the Americas, and France hoped to rescue her reeling finances by liquidating foreign, especially British, hostility. Hence Britain and France agreed to admit each other's hardware at a 10% duty; textiles except silk at 12%; and Britain agreed to accept wines at the lowest rate levied on other countries and halve the brandy duty. *See* PITT ADMINISTRATION, FIRST-6.

FRERE (1) John Hookham (1769-1846) was M.P. from 1799 to 1802, contributed to the *Anti-Jacobin* and in 1799 was U/Sec. of State for Foreign Affairs. He was British plenipotentiary at Lisbon from 1800 to 1802, at Madrid from 1802 to 1804 and with the Spanish Junta from 1808 to 1809. He was Sir J. Moore's political adviser. His nephew **(2) Sir (Henry) Bartle Edward (1815-84) Bt. (1876)** was Commissioner at Sattara in 1846 and 1847 and from 1850 to 1859 Chief Commissioner in Sind which he pacified and civilised. In 1859 he joined the Viceroy's council and from 1862 to 1867 he was Gov. of Bombay where he set up the city corporation. He then returned to England as a member of the Council for India and in 1872 negotiated the suppression of the Zanzibar slave trade. In 1877 he was appointed gov. of the Cape and High Commissioner for S. Africa. He found a belligerent cabinet in office and dismissed it so as to negotiate with the tribes. This failed and the ninth Kaffir War resulted (*see* XHOSA). He then tried to press his advantage with the Zulus, whose King Cetewayo rejected his demands. As a result of the Zulu war the govt. superseded him in the High Commission. Though he believed in firmness towards the Boers, he recognised the justice of some of their grievances and agreed to redress them in 1879. He was accordingly recalled.

FRESCOBALDI, Florentine merchants and bank took the place of the Riccardi when the latter went bankrupt in 1294, as the chief royal bankers. Between 1294 and 1311 they probably lent some £150,000 to Edward I and II, of which they were repaid only about £125,000. The Crown benefited from their international contacts and ability to pay across distances. They even once supplied grain during a Scottish campaign. In return they received favours, in particular priority for their actions for debt and, under Edward II, they were exempted from tallages, aids and liability for jury service and their clerical nominees had special preferences in presentation to benefices. Amerigo dei Frescobaldi had six manors in return for a nominal rent; in 1310 Bertus was appointed to the King's council. Such favours were a political miscalculation and in 1311 the Lords Ordainers expelled them from the country and their company collapsed.

FREUD, Sigmund (1856-1939) studied under the neurologist Charcot in Paris and then, with Breuer, investigated hysteria and neurosis as psychological phenomena. His findings led him to conclusions about the normal mind and the development of a technique of psycho-analysis, based on the assumed existence of a subconscious which influences the way in which the conscious mind functions. Within this subconscious he thought that important conflicts, notably those related to sexual matters, took place and that these conflicts were capable of producing conscious disturbances incapable of rational explanation, i.e. explanation in terms of logic, or material self interest. These ideas, though not new, were expressed in a new language with systematic clarity and frankness, at a time when the mentally repressive habits (particularly in sexual questions) of the 19th cent. were beginning to change. A skilful propagandist, he was already, by reason of his *Interpretation of Dreams* (1899) and *Psychopathology of Everyday Life* (1904) a controversial figure in the university world when his *Psychoanalysis* was published in 1910. Thereafter his views attracted widespread and fascinated interest, besides support, intelligent scepticism and abuse.

FREYBERG, Bernard Cyril (1889-1963) V.C. (1916) Ld. (1951). New Zealander, fought with Pancho Villa in the Mexican revolution in 1914, served in the R. Naval Div. at the Dardanelles and, at 27, became the youngest Brig-Gen. in the British army being much decorated, and wounded nine times. In 1925 and 1926, as a regimental soldier, he several times tried to swim the Channel. In 1934 he became a maj-gen; in 1937 he was invalided out but returned in 1939 to command the New Zealand forces. He commanded the desperate and gallant defence of Crete in May 1941 and went on to Africa and Italy. From 1946 to 1952 he was a well liked Gov-Gen. of New Zealand. He then retired to England as Deputy Constable of Windsor Castle.

FRIARS (Lat. *fratres* = brothers) were members of mendicant orders as opposed to monks who lived in communities. The principal mendicant orders were the Grey Friars (Franciscans q.v.), Black Friars (Dominicans q.v.), White Friars (Carmelites q.v.), Austin (Augustinian

q.v.) Friars, Red Friars (Trinitarian) and Crutched (Crossed) Friars.

FRIDESWIDE, St. (?-c. 735) well born lady who refused marriage to a Mercian earl and founded the large St. Mary's nunnery, possibly on the site of Christchurch, at Oxford and became its Abbess. Though little is known of her, she left a sustained impression and so became the city's patron saint.

FRIENDLY SOCIETIES (and the similar BENEVOLENT, CATTLE INSURANCE and OLD PEOPLE'S HOMES SOCIETIES and WORKING MEN'S CLUBS) sprang up in the late 18th cent. It was found necessary to encourage them and prevent abuses by legislation. The first Friendly Societies Act of 1793 required rules to be confirmed by the local Quarter Sessions. Since that time many Acts have been passed; a Register was set up in 1846 and registration was substituted for confirmation in 1875. The Registrar also registers building societies, co-operatives and trade unions. The Societies were an important feature of social and health institutions before the National Health and National Insurance legislation reduced their uses by substituting a state system.

FRIENDS, RELIGIOUS SOCIETY OF (QUAKERS). This influential sect was first organised when Geo. Fox drew up his *Rule for the Management of Meetings* in 1668. Though persecuted like other dissenters, their reasonable determination openly to live a godly life earned them the respect of fair-minded people. William Penn (1644-1718) became a friend of Charles II, who empowered him to found Pennsylvania, where Quakers could go in peace. The Society's leaders have ever since enjoyed a right of personal access to the sovereign on certain state occasions. The Toleration Act of 1689 enabled them to practise their religion openly but throughout the 18th cent. they lived a distinctive life of their own, rejecting 'frivolity', distinguished by peculiar modes of speech and dress and concentrating on hard work and philanthropy. Among their leading personalities were Elizabeth Fry (1780-1845) the prison reformer and Joseph Lancaster (1778-1838) the educational pioneer. As the disabilities of dissenters were progressively removed, the Quakers returned to the mainstream of ordinary life, but their pacifism and rejection of oath-taking continued to bring them into collision with state authority. On the other hand their integrity and devotion, especially to the relief of suffering in circumstances of danger, has attracted popular sympathy and in most countries they have become free to live in accordance with their conscience. They are organised into Preparative Meetings (single congregations), Monthly Meetings of representatives of Preparative Meetings, Quarterly meetings and at the apex the Yearly Meeting which governs the whole society. There is also a permanent *Meeting for Sufferings* set up in 1675 to deal with hardship. The clerk presides over a meeting and the Clerk of the Meeting for Sufferings is regarded as the senior member of the Society.

FRIENDLY Is. *See* TONGA.

FRIENDS OF THE PEOPLE was a society, formed in 1792, of young, often whig, aristocratic enthusiasts (*but see* FRANCIS, SIR PHILIP) for the French Revolution and particularly for Mirabeau. They disliked the ideas in Burke's *Reflections,* looked back to the expulsion of James II and were ineffective as an organisation, being in reality a debating group for liberals perplexed and dispersed by 1797 by French revolutionary violence and the British war effort against it.

FRIGATE. *See* SHIPS, SAILING.

FRISIANS IN BRITAIN. The 6th cent. Byzantine writer Procopius of Caesarea wrote that among the people living in Britain were the English and the Frisians. He probably learned this from some Englishmen who visited Byzantium with a Frankish mission to the Emperor Justinian. Linguistic evidence indicates a close connection between English and Frisian and there are archaeological parallels between Frisia, Kent, East Anglia and Northumbria. English missionaries went there without many second thoughts which suggests that they expected to be understood. *See* EAST ANGLIA; MISSIONS TO EUROPE.

FRITHBORH. *See* FRANK PLEDGE.

FROBISHER, Sir Martin (?1535-94), a seaman suspected of piracy as early as 1566, first sailed in search of the North West Passage in 1576 (when he discovered Frobisher Bay) and again in 1577 for the Cathay Co. In 1578 he took 15 ships to Greenland. He was V-Adm. in Drake's W. Indian expedition of 1586; commanded a squadron against the Armada in 1588 and was V-Adm. in Hawkin's expedition in 1590.

FROISSART, Jean (?1335-1410) of Valenciennes, early visited the English court, where his countrywoman Philippa, Queen to Edward III, became his patron and encouraged his studies. He gathered material in Scotland and through Jean le Bel of Liege, and so wrote his *Chronicles,* a history of the major European countries between 1307 and 1400, much of it based upon eyewitnesses. Despite shaky geography and chronology, the work is a major historical source, especially for the Hundred Years' War between 1361 and 1400.

FROGMEN. Swimmers who attached explosives to ships in enemy harbours. First used, with great success, by the Italians in World War I against the Austro-Hungarian fleet, and also against the British at Alexandria in World War II. The term originated in the latter war from their splay-footed rubber suits, then developed.

FROGMORE (Windsor Home Park) was a small royal residence used by Q. Victoria and her mother. The royal cemetery has a mausoleum erected by Q. Victoria for the Prince Consort, in which the queen was herself buried.

FRONDE. *See* LOUIS XIV-1,2.

FRONTENAC, Louis DE BUADE, Comte de. *See* CANADA-5.

FROUDE Three brothers **(1) Richard (1803-36)** was a friend of Newman and influenced the Tractarians. **(2) William (1810-79),** an engineer, propounded the railway adjustment curve, invented the bilge keel and investigated the nature of marine skin-friction. **(3) James Anthony (1818-94)** was the well known historian.

FRUCTIDOR, *COUP D'ÉTAT* OF (Sept. 1797). The French Directorate, threatened by royalist successes in the elections, purged the legislature.

FRY, Charles Burgess (1872-1956) reputed the handsomest man and most accomplished athlete of all time, captained Oxford Univ. at cricket, football and athletics, setting up a world record for the long jump. He then became a football international and captained the English cricket test team in 1912. He also ran a journal and, aided by his terrifying wife, commanded the boys' training ship *Mercury* in the R. Hamble from 1908 to 1950.

FRY (1) Joseph (1728-87) type founder and cocoa and chocolate maker of Bristol, removed to London in 1764. His son **(2) Edmund (1754-1835)** carried on the business and invented a raised type for the blind. His son **Joseph** married the quaker **(3) Elizabeth, née GURNEY (1780-1845)** who first became interested in prison reform on seeing the conditions of women in Newgate in 1817. She achieved world renown, persuading other govts. as well as the British to improve the prisons. Another relative **(4) Francis (1803-86),** also of the chocolate firm, campaigned all over the world against slavery. Further descendants of **(1)** included **(5) Joseph Storrs (1826-1913)** a quaker philanthropist; his brother **(6) Sir Edward (1827-1918)** a distinguished lawyer was a Chancery judge from 1877, a member of the Court of Appeal from 1883 to 1892 and was arbitrator between France and Germany in the Casablanca affair in 1908. His son **(7) Roger (1866-1934)** was a famous art critic.

FUEL CRISIS OF 1947. The early months of 1947 were unusually cold. Mines and railways could not meet the extra demands for fuel, factories closed or worked short time, housewives and old people suffered shortages.

Several newspapers launched a campaign to blame the Labour govt. The difficulties arose in part from low investment and restricted maintenance during World War II and were exacerbated by shortage of foreign currency to buy coal abroad.

FUGGER family, originally weavers of Augsburg. **(1) Andrew (?-1457)** founded the House of Fugger of the Roe which died out in 1586. His brother **(2) Jakob I (?-1469)** founded the famous family and business of Fugger of the Lily. His sons **(3) Ulrich (?-1510), (4) George (?-1506)** in partnership with **(5) Jacob II, called the Rich (1459-1525) Count (1514)** raised it to world importance. Jacob established a virtual European copper monopoly by acquiring the mines in Hungary, Carinthia, Tyrol and Spain and held a lien on the Tyrolese silver mines. By 1505 he was involved in the oriental spice trade *via* Venice and as banker to the Emperor and the Papacy he financed the imperial election of Maximilian in 1519. He left his immense fortune to his nephews **(6) George Raymond (1489-1535)** and **(7) Anton (1493-1560).** Spanish financial troubles created great difficulties and from 1548 they began to sever their hitherto fundamental connection with the Habsburgs. In this they were only partially successful but the mid-16th cent. wars caused them increasingly to give up large scale commercial and metal transactions in favour of banking. At the same time they began to buy lordships, a process which had begun almost accidentally in 1507. By 1595 the families of Raymond and Anton had amassed twelve. During its highest fortune the firm had representatives in most centres from Cracow to Seville but the Reformation broke up its effectiveness because Anton was a partisan R. Catholic, financed the counter-reformation and suffered protestant reprisals. Moreover, most of the Fugger mines were at the political mercy of the Habsburgs. From about 1600 the family concentrated increasingly on the management of its estates and in learned and aesthetic pursuits.

FUGGER NEWSLETTERS (1568-1605) were reports of occurrences likely to be interesting to the Fugger Bank. The 36,000-odd M.S. pages are mostly in German, Italian and colloquial Latin and occasionally in French and Spanish. English translations of 1924 and 1926 exist. They represent an illuminating quarry of materials on many public and private events of the time.

FUGITIVE CRIMINALS and EXTRADITION. If a person wanted for trial escaped from one country to another the possibilities of action depended on whether one country was foreign or another British possession. **(1)** If he was in a foreign country he could be secured and returned only by the govt. of that country. If he was wanted by a foreign govt. he could not at Common Law be secured in Britain. This became increasingly inconvenient as populations grew and transport improved, but the only way in which extradition could be made possible was by treaty confirmed by Act of Parliament. Arrangements of this kind were first made with France and the U.S.A. in 1844 and with Denmark in 1863. The Extradition Act, 1870, based on these precedents, empowered the crown to seize and surrender a fugitive criminal to the authorities of another country if there was a reciprocal treaty in force, provided that the offence was not of a political or revenue character, that it would have been an offence in Britain and that he is to be tried only for the offence for which extradition is sought.

(2) In British possessions the law depended on the local law modified by the Fugitive Offenders Act (F.O.A.) 1844 and generally the govts. could rely upon each other for necessary action. By 1880, however, there was confusion arising from imperial expansion and the multiplicity of local laws and jurisdictions. The F.O.A. 1881 set up a code for extradition as between the various British territories. The difference between this code and the practice under the Act of 1870 was that the code applied to offences by the law of the territory from which the suspect was a fugitive, whereas treaties with foreign states were drafted so as to apply only to acts which were offences in both countries. Since the Statute of Westminster, 1931, most of the territories have become independent states with diverging systems of criminal law. The *Case of Chief Enaharo* (1963) who was deported to Nigeria for basically political offences drew attention to the obsolescence of the 1881 Act; conferences of Commonwealth Law Ministers in 1965 and 1966 drafted a scheme for legislation which all the commonwealth countries agreed to enact. In Britain the 1881 Act was accordingly superseded by the F.O.A. 1967 which, with relevant modifications, adopted the rules in the Extradition Act, 1870, and the practice under it. In Britain extradition proceedings are held before the Chief Metropolitan Magistrate.

***FÜHRER* (Ger. = guide).** The title of Adolf Hitler as leader of the Nazi Party and ruler of Germany.

FULANI. *See* HAUSA.

FULHAM (London). The manor belonged to the Bps. of London from the 7th cent. until 1868. In 1141 a palace was begun which became and remained their residence until 1973 but the main existing part was built between 1510 and 1520. The area supplied London with vegetables from about 1650 and a pottery industry grew up after 1670. Its four villages were combined in 1892 into the metropolitan borough of Fulham, which became part of the London Borough of Hammersmith in 1965.

FULLER, John Frederick Charles ("Boney") (1878-1966) intellectual soldier, made himself famous by his development of tank tactics, soon after tanks first came into action at Cambrai in World War I. He became a maj-gen. in 1930. He wrote many learned and some prophetic books whose common theme was the relationship between military and political thought.

FULLING MILLS which saved much drudgery and were water driven, were first adopted in France but reached England in the 12th cent. Here they encouraged the movement of the cloth industry to hilly areas with fast flowing streams, especially Gloucestershire and later the Pennines.

FULL POWERS, DIPLOMATIC. *See* RATIFICATION OF TREATIES.

FULTON, Robert (1765-1815). American inventor of Irish parentage, studied mechanical engineering in England and lived in Paris from 1797 to 1804. Here he developed a flax-spinning machine but concentrated on maritime technology, including a dredger, a submarine and, in 1803, a small not very reliable steam-boat which ran on the R. Seine. Fortunately Bonaparte's govt. did not appreciate him and he went to the U.S.A. whose govt. employed him to build canals. Meanwhile he and Livingston revised their ideas on steam navigation and in 1807 launched the then spectacular paddle steamer *Clermont* which independently of the weather ran the 150 miles from New York to Albany in 32 hours. *See* SHIPS, POWER DRIVEN.

FULTON SPEECH was delivered by Winston Churchill in 1946. In it he used the phrase 'iron curtain' and proposed the creation of a U.N. International force.

FUNDAMENTALISM. An attitude traceable to a basic scripture, ignoring any other source of religious truth including continuously transmitted tradition in the organised religion possessing that scripture. It takes two major forms which have almost nothing in common.

(1) CHRISTIAN. A philosophical, mainly post-Reformation view that all truth must be consistent with the literal words of the Bible and that, therefore, scientists such as Charles Darwin or anthropologists such as Sir James Frazer, who published material at variance with them, were at best mistaken and at worst subversive or blasphemous charlatans. Occasionally this view was pressed beyond the confines of philosophy. Natal blacks, as Children of Ham, were held to be servants in accordance with Gen. c9.v25. In the Transvaal the Christian Separate Reformed Church rejected hymn singing in church because the Bible only mentions psalms.

(2) ISLAMIC. A powerful recurrent moral and political phenomenon arising from the simple austerity of Islamic origins and not confined to any one sect, comprising a generally violent reaction against current behaviour considered to depart decadently from the precepts of the Koran. This was the motor attitude of, for example, the mediaeval Spanish Almohads and Almoravides, the 19th cent. Arabian Wahabis and the Sudanese Dervishes. In the 20th cent. the target has been the usages (such as religious non-attendance, the emancipation of women and the drinking of wine) which have penetrated Moslem areas mainly by way of British, French and Russian imperialist civilisations. Hence the Sunni Wahabis expelled the post-Turkish pro-British rulers of Mecca; the Shia Ayatollahs of Qom overthrew the westernising Iranian Monarchy; Pakistan, reacting against British-imported liberalism, has become an Islamic Republic and similar movements have appeared in Nigeria, in the N. African (ex-French) states and in the central Asian parts of the ex-Russian atheist empire. Occasional demands for separate Moslem schools in Britain may be a symptom of, or a reaction against it. Unlike the Christian variety, Islamic fundamentalism is aimed at behaviour and can be physically enforced, for example by the veiling of women or the thrashing of wine drinkers.

FUNDS, THE. *See* CONSOLIDATED FUND.

FURNESS (Lancs). Savigny Benedictines were settled at Tulketh in 1124 by Stephen (later King) and migrated to Furness in 1127. Here they built a magnificent abbey, which was long the only English western monastery north of the Mersey. In 1148 they became Cistercian and obtained a virtually palatine lordship. It soon became one of the richest and largest English abbeys with daughter houses at Rushen (IoM.) and at Cartmel and was given by the Manx King the right to elect the Bp. of the Isles. The Abbot sat in Parliament from 1264 to 1330. At the dissolution the Abbot was charged with complicity in the Pilgrimage of Grace (1536). The House was surrendered in Apr. 1537 and the lands annexed to the Duchy of Lancaster, but James I granted most of them to a Scots family, the Prestons, through whom they passed to the Ds. of Devonshire.

FURSEY, St. *See* MISSIONS TO EUROPE.

FUR TRADE. Furs as luxury goods or marks of rank commanded high prices. Most of the prized varieties were supplied from the wilds by primitive huntsmen who could be paid very small amounts. The middleman's profits could therefore be large and the trade could support the cost of long distance transport. Squirrel and sables came from Siberia: marten from the Balkans: beaver and ermine from Scandinavia. They added a considerable cash surplus to Baltic and Mediterranean trade and represented a business consideration in forming bodies such as the Muscovy and Levant Cos. As civilisation encroached on the wild, supplies from the original sources declined and new fields and commercial organisations emerged, especially in N. America. The Hudson Bay Co. was formed mainly for the fur trade and beavers appear in its arms. Since World War II animal 'rights' champions have interfered and natural furs have been replaced increasingly by nylon or other substitutes.

FUSELI or FUESSLI, Henry or Heinrich (1741-1825) romantic painter of Swiss origin, was encouraged by Reynolds and in 1780 first exhibited at the Royal Academy where he was Prof. of Painting from 1799. He left hundreds of sketches; Haydon and Etty were among his pupils and his patronage helped to bring William Blake into prominence.

FUSILIERS were infantry originally armed with fusils or light muskets. Their function was to help and protect artillery.

FUSION BOMBS. *See* ATOMIC THEORY.

FUSTIAN (from FUSTAT = Cairo), otherwise VELVETEEN, CORDUROY or MOLESKIN is the cotton equivalent of velvet. The pejorative use of the word Fustian as 'pretentious' or 'turgid' arose because *silk* velvet (e.g. in a King-at-Arms' tabard) was a mark of high standing.

FYFE, Sir David Maxwell (1900-67) 1st Vist. KILMUIR (1953) 1st E. (1962) barrister, and from 1935 Tory M.P. for Liverpool, a portly man of superabundant energy at once in the courts and parliament. He became Sol-Gen. in 1942, Att-Gen. in 1945 and was a formidable prosecutor at the Nuremberg war crimes trials. He advocated a European Convention on Civil Rights and an early British entry (well before the T. of Rome) into a United Europe, a proposal killed by Eden. He was Home Sec. from 1951 to 1953 and Lord Chancellor from 1953. He strongly supported Eden's Suez policy in the Cabinet and was the prime mover in obtaining the succession to the premiership for Macmillan in 1957. His abrupt dismissal by Macmillan (with six others) in July 1962 naturally infuriated him; he left politics and legal affairs, gave up his parliamentary pension and went into business as Chairman of the Plessey Group.

FYRD was originally the Anglo-Saxon military array (existing more in the imagination than in life) of all able bodied free men and the obligation (more real) to serve in it. Inefficient through diversity of weapons and lack of training, such amateur mobs could not be kept on a war footing for long, or at certain key seasons, without disrupting agriculture. Later, the fyrd was more practically organised on the basis of one soldier for five hides of land or in the Danelaw, six carucates. It normally fought, as at Hastings, on foot.

FYZABAD or FAIZABAD, former capital of Oudh (India) includes the once splendid and holy city of Ayuthia. It was also the residence of the Begums of Oudh whom Warren Hastings was accused of despoiling, but its prosperity and importance diminished only after the death of Bahu Begum, the last of them, in 1816. There were Hindu-Moslem riots over sacred sites at Ayuthia in 1991.

G

GABERLUNZIE (Sc. pron. Gaberloony). A professional beggar. James V reputedly went among his people disguised as one.

GAEKWAR (more properly GAEKWAD) (BARODA). *See* MARATHAS-C.

GAELIC LANGUAGE. *See* CELTS.

GAELIC ATHLETIC ASSN. (1884) (Ir.) was designed to foster Irish nationalism by encouraging Irish games and preventing its members from playing any others.

GAELIC LEAGUE (Ir.) was founded under Douglas Hyde in 1893 to cultivate the then moribund Irish language. It was in theory not political, in fact fiercely nationalist. By 1913 the National University had had to make Irish a compulsory subject though it had hardly anyone qualified to examine in it. The League's meetings were prohibited as subversive in 1918 as a wartime measure. The British departure and the Irish govt's sponsorship of Irish drastically reduced the League's popular appeal in the 1920s.

GAFAEL. *See* WELSH LAW-6.

GAFOL, GAVEL (related to Ger. *Gebuhr* = fee or charge). A.S. (1) tribute (2) rent and later (3) interest on money. *See* DANEGELD and GAVELKIND.

GAGE. This versatile family included **(1) Sir John (1479-1556)** who was governor of Guines and Comptroller of Calais from 1522. In 1540 he was a commissioner for dissolving the monasteries and comptroller of the household and in 1542 he commanded against Scotland and later against Boulogne. Somerset dismissed, but Mary restored him and, as Constable of the Tower, he had the custody of Elizabeth. His great-grandson **(2) Sir Henry (1597-1645)** saw Spanish service in Flanders and held St. Omer for them in 1638. He joined the King in the Civil War, relieved Basing in 1644, became gov. of Oxford and was mortally wounded at Abingdon. His brother **(3) Thomas (?-1656)** was an explorer in Spanish central America who turned protestant and in 1642 joined the Parliamentarians. He published an account of his explorations in *The English American* in 1648 and also rules for learning central American languages. These were all later translated and much used by the French and Dutch. Sir Henry's half-brother **(4) Francis (1621-82)** was agent to the English Chapter in Rome from 1659 to 1661 and became pres. of the English College at Douai in 1676. His half-brother **(5) George (?-1640)** was employed by James I as a diplomat at Rome from 1621 to 1624. Their relative **(6) Count Joseph (?1678-1753)** commanded Spanish troops in Italy from 1743 to 1746 and became a Spanish grandee. His nephew **(7) Thomas (1721-87)** was Albemarle's A.D.C. in Flanders in 1747, served under Braddock in America from 1751, commanded the light infantry at Ticonderoga in 1758, and was gov. of Montreal from 1759 to 1760. From 1763 to 1772 he was C-in-C. in America and from 1774 gov. of Massachusetts, but in 1775 he was superseded and retired. His son **(8) Sir William Hall** (1777-1864) had an active, if conventional, naval career ending as Admiral of the Fleet in 1862.

GAIETY THEATRE (London) opened in 1868. Its beautiful "Gaiety Girls" became famous and some made distinguished marriages. George Edwardes specialised in and almost monopolised musical comedy from 1886 until the theatre was pulled down in 1901 to make way for the new Aldwych development. A new theatre replaced it nearby and continued the policy of the old, but with slightly reduced momentum. This functioned from 1903 until 1939.

GAINSBOROUGH (Lincs.), at the crossing of the North Road over the Trent, was a Saxon clan centre and then, under Canute, a Danish base. It was probably a borough by prescription. In the middle ages it was a busy inland port with, after 1296, a bi-weekly market and fair. It was first chartered in 1589. Local industries included malting, milling and brewing, timber and later engineering.

GAINSBOROUGH, Thomas (1727-88), landscape and portrait painter, first practised in London and then at Sudbury from 1746, moving to Ipswich in 1752. From 1760 to 1774 he worked at Bath. An original member of the Royal Academy in 1768, he settled in London in 1774 but ten years later quarrelled with Reynolds and refused to exhibit at the Academy any more. His pictures are important not only artistically but as historical records.

GAITSKELL, Hugh Todd Naylor (1906-63), educated at Winchester, was an academic economist and Labour Party adviser on finance before 1939. During World War II he was a senior civil servant in the Min. of Labour under Hugh Dalton. In 1945 he became an M.P. and in 1947 Min. of Fuel and Power. He persuaded the Govt. to devalue sterling in 1949. In Feb. 1950 he became Min. of Economic Affairs under Sir Stafford Cripps, whom he succeeded as Ch. of the Exch. in Oct., at a time when the international exchange problem dominated foreign policy. In his only budget he had to find money for the Korean War and he insisted on certain N. Health charges. This gave Aneurin Bevan and Harold Wilson a pretext for resignation. In opposition from 1951, he attacked the Labour left wing as well as the govt. and so defeated Bevan in 1953 and 1954 with trade union support. In 1955 he became leader of the parliamentary party, which was severely beaten in the 1959 election. As a result he persuaded the party to abandon the doctrine of total nationalisation; he lost the trade unionists, who forced upon him a policy of unilateral atomic disarmament. In 1960 he defeated Harold Wilson for the leadership. In 1961 he got the policy on disarmament reversed and in 1962 he formulated the earliest Labour opposition to entry into E.E.C. He died just before the Labour victory in 1964.

Both exceptionally able and ambitious, he thought that socialism concerned social justice and need not be related to class war and he was ready to risk his career for his principles. Courage of this kind naturally won him widespread respect, even in parties other than his own. Aneurin Bevan's jibe 'a desiccated calculating machine' did Bevan more harm than Gaitskell.

GALANAS (Welsh). A wergild paid by one Welsh kindred to another. *See* WELSH LAW (SOCIAL).

GALAPAGOS Is. (Ecuador) (Sp. Galapago = giant tortoise), discovered in 1535, were visited in 1835 by Charles Darwin in the course of the *Beagle* expedition. As a result of his observations here he began to form his coherent theory of evolution. In modern times the guano deposits formed the first basis of the international fertilizer trade.

GALE, Thomas (?1635-1702) active member of the R. Society from 1677, High Master of St. Paul's from 1672 to 1679 and then Dean of York. A pioneering mediaeval historian who published an edition of the *Antonine Itinerary* and other works. *See* SCRIPTORES.

GALEN[US] (c. 130-204). Polymath and physician to the Emperor Marcus Aurelius and his two successors. His 130 closely argued books on medicine, of which 83 survive, formed the foundations of all anatomical and physiological studies until Vesalius (1514-64) and Wm. Harvey (1578-1657), and presented his theories with such impressive authority that his largely erroneous humoral theory of disease dominated and obstructed western medicine for 1600 years. He also wrote on a similar scale on many other subjects.

GALICIA (Poland), is a forest region with important salt and oil deposits. From the fortress of Przemysl westwards (where the salt is), the population was Polish and R.

Catholic, eastwards including Lemberg (Lvov) it was partly Ruthene. The eastern end (where the oil is) was Eastern Orthodox in religion, the Orthodox Ruthenes being called Little Russians. Galicia was part of Poland until 1772 when it was annexed by Austria. It was the scene of desperate fighting in World War I and afterwards Carpathian Ruthenia passed to Czechoslovakia, the rest going to the new Poland. After 1945 the Russians, to get the oil, claimed and annexed the ex-Polish Ruthene areas to the Ukraine and erected the ex-Czechoslovak part into a Soviet Republic of Subcarpathian Russia.

GALICIA (N.W. Spain). Its four provinces have a population of Celtic origin which, as seafarers, had dark-age connections with the Irish Sea and its coasts and islands. It maintained a separate identity in the middle ages through its great pilgrimage centre at Santiago de Compostella and the need to defend it against the Moors. The overland pilgrim routes ran from Normandy, Burgundy and Provence to meet at Irun (Biscay) and so *via* Leon to Santiago. The sea routes from England, the Low Countries and the Baltic used the nearby North-West twin ports of Corunna and Ferrol: that from the Mediterranean, Vigo on the west coast. On the beaches sea-pilgrims picked up scallop shells, which became the accepted pilgrim's badge and often figure in the arms of families with names like Pilgrim or Palmer. All three ports were of great importance throughout the era of sailing ships, for which Capes Ortegal and Finisterre were important navigational landmarks.

GALILEE. A large porch, antechapel or small cloister where persons not allowed into a church as unshriven penitents, excommunicates, notorious adulterers or female relations of monks, might be allowed to wait. Durham cathedral has an impressive Galilee where the Venerable Bede is buried. His epitaph:

Haec sunt in fossa   Here in the drains
Bedae venerabilis ossa, Are the Venerable Bede's banes

has been derided for its rhyming latinity and thin sense.

GALILEO, Galilei (1564-1642) was Prof. of Mathematics at Pisa from 1589. Here he discovered the isochronism of pendulum oscillation and the equality of the velocity of falling bodies. In 1592 he moved to Padua, where he invented a thermometer and proportional compasses. He also applied the telescope to astronomy and so discovered many of the basic facts long since assumed. In 1610 he moved to Florence where he elaborated his astronomical views and tried to compare them with the Bible. In 1616 he was warned by the Inquisition, but in 1632 he published his defence of Copernican astronomy and was summoned to answer at Rome. Sentenced to recant his views, his sentence was not confirmed by the Pope (Urban VIII). *See* RENAISSANCE-14.

GALL, St. or CELLACH (?550-?645) was reputedly trained by St. Columba whom he followed to Gaul and then to Switzerland. His cell was said to be the nucleus of the great Abbey and state of St. Gallen.

GALLEONS. *See* SHIPS, SAILING-5.

GALLEY. *See* SHIPS, SAILING-3.

GALLIA. Latin for Gaul.

GALLICAN CONFESSION (1559) was a draft in 35 articles by John Calvin, revised by Antoine de la Roche Chandieu and adopted by the Synod of the French Reformed Church. With a preface it was presented to K. Francis II and his wife, Mary Q. of Scots, in 1560. It strongly influenced the organisation and doctrines of the later presbyterian Church of Scotland. It was revised into 40 articles at the Synod of La Rochelle in 1571 and this latter version is the guiding statement of faith of the French Reformed Church. *See* CALVINISM, WARS OF RELIGION.

GALLICANISM is the view that a national, particularly the French, branch of the R. Catholic Church should be free of papal control. The doctrine, widely held among

French churchmen, was long convenient to the Crown. In 1438 by the Pragmatic Sanction of Bourges the French clergy, with royal support, asserted their right to administer their property without papal interference and disallowed papal nominations to benefices. In 1516 it was replaced by a CONCORDAT conceding high nominations to the Crown. The constitutional doctrines of the Council of Trent (1545-63) were not accepted in France. In 1682 the French clergy affirmed the Four Gallican Articles, asserting royal independence of papal intervention, papal subjection to general councils and the privileges of the French church. These were rejected by Pope Alexander VIII in 1690 and withdrawn for political reasons at the instance of Louis XIV in 1693. There were Gallican provisions in Bonaparte's concordat of 1810.

GALLIPOLI EXPEDITION (1915-6) originated in a Russian request (Jan. 1915) for direct allied help in view of the Tannenberg disaster, Turkish Caucasian advances and inadequacies of military supply. The purpose was to overthrow Turkey by the capture of Constantinople and to re-establish communications with Russia *via* the Straits. There were five phases. **(1)** Feb. 1915. An inadequately supported bombardment of the outer batteries by a fleet under Adm. Carden. **(2)** Mar. 1915. Urged on by Winston Churchill, then First Lord of the Admiralty, a major purely naval effort to force the straits under Adm. de Robeck. This was prematurely recalled after some old battleships were sunk by mines. **(3)** Apr. 1915. An Anglo-French military assault on the Gallipoli Peninsula, without benefit of surprise, under Sir Ian Hamilton, made lodgements after heavy losses near C. Helles. **(4)** Aug. 1915. Heavily reinforced, a further attack from the Anzac beaches with landings at Suvla Bay under Gen. Birdwood, was frustrated by misdirected naval supporting fire and a timely counter-attack by Col. Mustapha Kemal, the future Atatük. **(5)** Aug. 1915-Jan. 1916. A stalemate ensued. In Oct. Sir Chas. Munro, an advocate of evacuation, replaced Birdwood. Meanwhile the govt. had decided to intervene at Salonika. The switch was carried out, the evacuations (Anzac Dec., C. Helles Jan.) being made without loss. Each side had about 500,000 troops involved from first to last and each lost about 50%. The campaign, which might have decisively affected world history, failed through military parochialism, incompetent logistics and poor leadership. *See* WORLD WAR I-4,5.

GALLOWAY (S.W. Scot.) comprises the old county of Wigtown and the stewartry of Kirkcudbright. The name is related to 'Wales' and the area with Cumbria across the Solway was predominantly Celtic. In Roman times the local tribe was the NOVANTAE. The last Celtic Prince of Galloway died in 1234 and thereafter the area was dominated by the rival Baliols and Comyns who were superseded after 1369 by the Douglas. Douglas power remained great until 1623 when most of their Galwegian property passed to the Crown. The tiny burgh of New Galloway was erected only in 1629. The area was strongly covenanter. In the early 18th cent. the tenant farmers suffered from evictions to make way for cattle ranching. In 1724 they formed a movement known as the GALLOWAY LEVELLERS. They issued a manifesto demanding justice and hacked the cattle. In reply to the Riot Act read at Kirkcudbright, they read the National Covenant. Troops were brought in; both sides avoided violent confrontation, but two levellers were transported.

GALLOWGLASS (Gael. *galaglach* = foreign youth or servant), were armed retainers of an Irish chief, commonly mercenaries from the Scots Western Highlands. In the later 13th cent. they were used especially by the O'Donnells of Tirconnell and the O'Connors of Connaught, but they continued to be hired well into the 17th cent. They fought on foot.

GALLUP POLLS. *See* PUBLIC OPINION POLLS.

GALMOY, Vist. (1652-1740). *See* BUTLER; PIERCE.

GALSWORTHY, John (1867-1933), moral or propagandist

playwright and social novelist. His plays, particularly *The Silver Box* (1906), *Strife* (about a strike) (1909) and *Justice* (a critique of the prison system) (1910) had a powerful effect on contemporary public opinion (*see for example* RUGGLES-BRISE). His long series of novels collectively known as the *Forsyte Saga* (1906-30) gives a telling picture of late Victorian, Edwardian and disillusioned Twenties life, which came into its own for the second time when televised in 1967.

GALTON, Sir Douglas Strutt (1822-99) was sec. of the Rly. Commission from 1847 and the Rly. Dept. of the B. of Trade from 1854. He investigated the feasibility of submarine cables between 1859 and 1861. He held high appointments in the War Office (1862-9) and Office of Works (1869-75) and in 1895 was Pres. of the British Assn.

GALTON, Sir Francis (1822-1911) invented finger-printing and his researches in this and related fields led him to build up a corpus of research on eugenics and the heritability of characteristics.

GALWAY ELECTION 1872. *See* KEOGH, WILLIAM NICHOLAS.

GALWAY, Henri Massue de Ruvigny, 2nd French M. de RUVIGNY (1648-1720) 1st E. of (1697). This Huguenot soldier served under Turenne. In 1678 he became Huguenot deputy-gen. Driven to England in 1688 by Louis XIV's persecutions, in 1692 he became William III's C-in-C in Ireland and in 1694 his ambassador in Turin. From 1697 to 1701 he was one of the Irish Lords Justices and after a mission to Cologne became English military commander in Portugal in 1704. After reducing Badajoz (where he was badly wounded) in 1705, Ciudad Rodrigo, Alcantara and Madrid in 1706, the failure of Peterborough's Catalonian campaign forced him to retreat into Valencia where, at Almanza in 1707, he was defeated by Berwick. In 1708 he re-established Portuguese safety by organising a new Portuguese army with which he fought a desperate battle on the R. Caya in 1709. He was recalled in 1710 and not re-employed until 1715 when, in view of the Jacobite rising, he was again briefly a Lord Justice in Ireland.

THE GAMBIA. *See* WEST AFRICA-6 *et seq.*

GAMBIER (1) V-Adm. James (1723-89) after an active naval career became C-in-C in North America from 1770 to 1773 and then 2nd-in-C to Howe. His nephew **(2) James (1756-1833 1st Ld. GAMBIER (1807)** as a Capt. broke the French line at the Glorious First of June (1794) and was a lord of the admiralty from 1795 to 1801, then gov. of Newfoundland and then from 1804 to 1806 a lord of the admiralty again. In 1807 he commanded at the bombardment of Copenhagen and the removal of the whole Danish fleet and from 1808 to 1811 the Channel Fleet. As such he made the much criticised attack on the Basque Roads. In 1814 he was one of the peace negotiators with the U.S.A. His nephew **(3) Sir Edward (1794-1879)** was chief justice of Madras from 1842 to 1849.

GAMBLING. *See* BETTING AND GAMING.

GAME LAWS. Game is any *wild* creature hunted for food except snipe, quail, landrail, woodcock and rabbits. The right to hunt or kill game outside a royal forest or free warren was usually vested in the lord of a manor. Hence the game, so long as it was within the confines, was the lord's temporary property and injury to it was a trespass against him. The right was also a separate right at common law; it could therefore be reserved on sale of land and usually was. By the 18th cent. a lordship might include little land, but game rights over vast areas long since sold. So long as the population remained small and the old forms of tenure and agriculture subsisted, this was tolerable: there was enough for all and lords could turn a blind eye to moderate poaching; but the inclosures and the population explosion created a hungry rural poor for whom poaching was one way out of starvation. Hence the coverts were depopulated and the rights

heavily reduced in usefulness and value. Breeding was little understood and the old summary and civil remedies were ineffectual, because the system of manorial courts had broken down. This led to the passing of oppressive Acts in 1829, 1831, 1848, 1860 and 1880. These made trespasses in pursuit of game criminal and forbade the sale of game except under licence.

GAME THEORY, apart from a few isolated analyses mostly concerned with chess, came into its own as the tool for a theory of decision making, with the publication of Neumann and Morgenstern's *Theory of Games and Economic Behaviour* in 1944.

GAMELIN, Maurice Gustave (1872-1958) was the allied C-in-C who in 1940 suffered the appalling defeat which brought France to her knees.

GAMING. *See* BETTING.

GANDAMAK, T. of (1879). *See* AFGHANISTAN-9; KHYBER PASS.

GANDHI (1) Indira (1917-84) as Jawaharlal Nehru's only and socialist daughter, was a member of Mahatma Gandhi's intellectually powerful political circle. She was not related to the Mahatma. She became a member of the Working Committee of the Indian National Congress (I.N.C.) in 1955 and was Min. of Information in the Shastri govt. At Shastri's death in 1966 she became leader of the I.N.C. and so also prime minister. She was distinctively ruthless, especially towards the princely order, with neighbouring states and with the law. In 1971 when Eastern Pakistanis set up a rebel state of Bangladesh, she protected them, and Indian troops fought Pakistan victoriously for Bangladeshi independence. She broke the constitutional pledges to the former princes by the use of presidential powers and when the Allahabad High Court pronounced against her and would have disqualified her for electoral malpractice, she declared a state of emergency, continued herself in office and imprisoned her political opponents. She remained in office until 1977, instituting a widespread programme of compulsory sterilisation. In 1977 she was defeated in a general election and was imprisoned for a while for corruption. Meanwhile she had been grooming her son Sanjay to succeed her, but he was killed in an aeroplane crash in 1980 just after she became prime minister for the second time. She now came into conflict with the Sikh separatists in the Punjab and employed her strong-arm methods on them. This culminated in June 1984 in a battle and many deaths in their Golden Temple at Amritsar. One of her own Sikh bodyguard murdered her soon after. She had summoned her son **(2) Rajiv (1944-91)** from private life to replace his elder brother. He became a member of the Lok Sabha in 1981 and succeeded her as prime minister. He was not a success and resigned in 1989. He too was murdered.

GANDHI[JI], Mohandas Karamchand (1869-1948) entitled **Mahatma (Hindi = great soul). (1)** This extraordinary man, almost as important to S. Africa as to India, was born in Kathiawar, called to the English Bar and started to practice at Bombay in 1892. In 1893 he went to S. Africa and set up a practice in Pretoria mainly to help oppressed Asiatic immigrants. In the next nineteen years he moved gradually from legal to political activity and developed his peculiar techniques of aggressive pacifism later called *Satyagraha* (= soul force). He organised an Indian Red Cross for the Boer War (1899-1902). He inspired the great Johannesburg demonstrations of Sept. 1906 against the Asiatic ordinances. During the African revolt in Natal in 1908 his corps of stretcherbearers tended the civilian casualties, that is, those who were injured by the police. He held public pass-burning meetings. He was often arrested and sometimes imprisoned and though violence was the occasional result of his activities, he would not countenance it and was as often the target for it from his own extremist supporters as from his opponents. In 1914 the ordinances were repealed.

(2) He now went to London by way of India and organised another Indian ambulance for World War I. He had hoped that the immense Indian achievements in the war (in which he did not believe) against the Central Powers, would have awakened a liberal response in the British govt. but the London govt. in 1918 had its eyes on Europe and knew too little of India, while the Indian administration was grappling with the provocative violence of nationalists led by Tilak. Exasperated by the British negative responses he exchanged his suits for a loin cloth and threw his powerful moral authority in with the nationalists. It was not, however, nationalism which interested him so much as relief of the oppressed, but as the British were the most obvious oppressors he made do with the Indian National Congress (I.N.C.). In Apr. 1919 he and his new associates called the great *Hartal* (strike) and supported Moslem agitation against allied treatment of Turkey. In 1920, however, Tilak died and Gandhi was, not unwillingly, pitchforked into the leadership. Despite his tumultuous S. African experience, he seems to have believed that the practitioners of *Satyagraha* incurred no moral responsibility if others behaved violently. He joined with the Moslems in *non-cooperation,* a system of tactics which was approved by an All India Congress at Calcutta in 1920. The govt. and its authority was to be denied and ignored and British industrial investment was to be undermined by home industries such as hand-spinning and weaving. In 1921 he was burning foreign goods. This was logically suitable for a saintly but secure ascetic, but others with more worldly desires and family obligations had to cope with the extreme uncertainties of the sprawling cities. As workers had nothing during a *hartal,* the temptation to loot was irresistible and official reaction to looting led to street battles. The I.N.C. was again dragged into the violence of Tilak's time, because it dared not seem to be on the side of the police. It proclaimed *Civil Disobedience,* which involved withholding taxes, and placed all decision making powers in Gandhi's hands. Civil disobedience led to widespread violence, where upon in 1922 he courageously called it off, but was convicted of sedition and sentenced to six years' imprisonment. He suffered an appendicitis operation in 1924, was released and remained quiescent until 1927.

(3) He restarted his public career with spectacular tours of Burma, then part of India, and Ceylon. He refused the presidency of the I.N.C., preferring an autonomous role. This developed into a new form of civil disobedience. In Apr. 1930 he led an imaginative mass march against the hated govt. salt monopoly from Ahmedabad to the sea and there proceeded to distil salt on the beach. He was detained near Poona but released in Jan. 1931 to take part in the Round Table conference. His contribution to the discussions was not great, but in Mar. he arranged the truce with the Viceroy. Violence, unfortunately, broke out again in 1933 and he was again detained and released. In 1934, when the Government of India Bill was in draft, he announced that he was retiring to his *ashram* at Wardha, but the I.N.C. leaders had become morally dependent upon him and consulted him so much that he remained their real leader. Meanwhile the Bill was enacted and elections were due for the provincial legislatures of British India which it had created. The I.N.C. leaders wanted to stand in the elections, which they were bound to win, but to paralyse the system by refusing office. With his usual common sense he changed their minds in 1937 on the ground that they could scarcely fit themselves for independence by refusing govt. experience.

(4) Within two years World War II broke out. Gandhi disingenuously held that Britain deserved Indian support but that it could be given fully only by a completely independent country. When a Japanese military invasion developed, his response was a demand that the British should *Quit India,* dissolve the Indian army and leave a pacifist country to negotiate with Japan. He must have known that no British and few Indians could stomach this, but the British refusal gave him and the I.N.C. the pretext, in Aug. 1942, to launch the organised obstruction of the war effort, which he called *Open Rebellion.* This was a long way from *Satyagraha* and he and the other I.N.C. leaders were interned.

(5) Gandhi had always been true to his hatred of oppression. He had intermittently championed untouchable castes, particularly in the South where high castes were peculiarly domineering and the untouchables numerous. He had intensified his public demonstrations of sympathy for them. No high caste Hindu had ever, in living memory, treated them with such respect and courtesy as he did and he renamed them *Harijans* (Children of God). This lost him much Hindu support and split the I.N.C. (a largely high caste body) on religious grounds. In May 1944 he was released so that negotiations could be resumed, but the situation had changed. Gandhi's high authority was very great when he chose to use it, but others were divided. Moreover, the Indian Moslems, who had been agitating for a separate state since 1938, had been virtually united by the violence associated with Quit India and Open Rebellion, for it had commonly degenerated into attacks on themselves as well as the British. 75% of the population of British India was Hindu. The Moslems felt unsafe without British protection unless the areas where they had a majority became defensible strongholds of their faith and people. The main areas were the Indus basin to the west and about two-thirds of Bengal in the east, to which they hoped to add Hyderabad, the greatest princely state in the south, because its Nizam was a Moslem. It became evident that these refuges could not be maintained within a united India; hence Mohammed Ali Jinnah, their leader, demanded partition and independence. There were protracted discussions between Gandhi and Jinnah, but their setting was confused, because Gandhi said that he spoke only for himself. It was true that he had not been a member of the I.N.C. Working Committee for several years, but he had always dominated it from outside whenever he chose. The negotiations drifted while extreme communal violence broke out and spread. Lord Pethick-Lawrence's cabinet mission had to settle arrangements for partition as best it could in discussions with both sides, with Gandhi, sometimes, behind the scenes.

(6) Independence and Partition brought appalling scenes of mass migration and slaughter in the west and rioting, with worse threatened, in Calcutta, Dacca and elsewhere in Bengal, which was about to be artificially partitioned. Gandhi, who hated partition and was preaching universal brotherhood in Bihar, went to Calcutta and started a fast, making it clear that he was ready to die if the violence did not stop (Sept. 1947). In four days it stopped and so, to widespread jubilation, did the fast. Four months later, however, a high caste Hindu murdered him in Delhi. Perhaps his greatest achievement now occurred. The dreaded outbreak of fanatical public fury did not happen. A stunned tranquillity lasted for several months while the new India was organised.

GANGES, R. (N. India) rises near Gangotri in the Himalayas as the Bhagirate and assumes the name Ganges after uniting with the Jahsari and Alaknanda. On leaving the mountains it turns S.W. and then curves slowly eastwards. At Allahabad it unites with the Jumna from Agra. This confluence is the holiest of places where Hindus come to wash away their sins. It flows windingly and in increasing volume past the sacred city of Benares until it joins with the Rs. Gumti and Gogra from the west and the Son from the south. At Patna it unites with the R. Gandak from the N.W. All these tributaries are themselves great rivers. About 220 miles from the Bay of

Bengal it begins to form an immense delta. The main river or **Padma** joins the **Brahmaputra** from Tibet at Goalanda and they together form the **Neghka** estuary, which is the most easterly delta channel. The most westerly leaves the Padma about 150 miles above Goalanda, passes through Murshidabad and, as the **Hooghli**, through Calcutta and so reaches the sea 150 miles to the west of the Neghka. The Ganges, sometimes over a mile wide, is wayward and changes condition and course, often without warning, because of the huge amounts of silt which it brings down. It has never therefore, been a great highway, though steamers in Victorian times penetrated to Allahabad. These were superseded by the railways. Its historic importance arises from its fertilising effects which have also made it the central object or symbol of Hindu religion.

GAOL DELIVERY. Mediaeval gaols existed mostly to detain suspects. A Commission of gaol delivery appointed certain persons, commonly serjeants-at law or judges, to bring out and try prisoners in a given gaol by the verdict of the locality (later by a jury). Otherwise prisoners might languish for years. Certain types of prisoner, such as a rebel, might be excepted. The commissioners were sometimes appointed for gaol delivery alone but more often in combination with eyres or assizes and latterly always with assizes. These commissions were a primitive form of *habeas corpus. See* ASSIZES-2.

GAOL FEVER. A generic but uncertain term. At the Cambridge Black Assize (1522) it killed judges, counsel, attorneys and others attending the court but left the prisoners untouched. At the Oxford Black Assize (1577) it attacked the well-to-do but not women or the poor and some 500 died in the area in six weeks. Many prisoners died at the Kings Bench prison, Southwark, in 1578. The outbreak at the Exeter Black Assize (1586) attacked court and prisoners and developed into a countywide epidemic lasting eight months. There were outbreaks at Newgate prison in 1583, 1595, 1597 and 1602 and at the Kings Bench in 1651. Some of these may have been typhus associated with pauperism and overcrowding. *See also* PRISONS.

GARDEN CITIES. The first in modern times was at Mulhausen (Mulhouse) in 1872. Port Sunlight on the Mersey was opened in 1890; Bournville 1891; the Garden Cities Association, which had been formed in 1887, laid out Letchworth (Herts) in 1903, Hampstead Garden Suburb in 1907, Gidea Park in 1911 and Welwyn in 1920. After 1898 the movement was dominated by the ideas of Sir Ebenezer Howard.

GARDEN SUBURB (1917-22). The private advisers of Lloyd George as prime minister and their staffs, so-called because they worked in huts in St. James's Park. They encroached progressively on the functions of regular govt. departments, caused some confusion and more jealousy and were plausibly perceived as an instrument of war cabinet and particularly Lloyd George's autocracy (cf KITCHEN CABINET).

GARDINER, James (1688-1745). A noted Scottish cavalry officer. Wounded and captured in heroic circumstances at Ramillies (1706), he headed a storming party at Preston (1715) and, having experienced a religious conversion (1719) after a dissolute life, became a colonel of dragoons. Deserted by them at the B. of Prestonpans (1745) he died of his wounds. His life was celebrated by Doddridge; his death by Sir Gilbert Elliot and in *Waverley* by Sir Walter Scott.

GARDINER, Stephen (?1483-1555) was master of Trinity Hall (Cambridge) from 1525 and from 1527 also sec. to Card. Wolsey for whom he negotiated the King's "divorce" business in Rome and obtained the second commission for the trial from Clement VII in 1528; in 1529 he became the King's Secretary and in 1531 Bp. of Winchester. A commissioner who declared the nullity of the royal marriage, he officiated shortly afterwards at

Anne Boleyn's coronation, but the protestant current was moving too quickly for him and, in visiting the doomed monasteries, he was not stern enough for Cranmer or Cromwell. His political position was thus precarious but in Feb. 1535 he renounced obedience to Rome. He published his *De Vera Obedientia* (Lat = True Obedience) in favour of royal absolutism in religious affairs and quarrelled with Cranmer, whose metropolitical authority he rejected as depending upon the renounced papal jurisdiction. From 1535 he was ambassador in Paris but in 1538 Cromwell had him superseded by Bonner. In 1539 he was on an embassy in Germany; his discussion with German theologians led to the issue of the Six Articles and his own dismissal from the privy council at Cromwell's instance. Cromwell, however, fell in 1540 and Gardiner returned to favour, becoming also Chancellor of Cambridge Univ. where the advance of reformist ideas caused him some concern. Accordingly, when Henry VIII died he was again expelled from his posts by the reformers and imprisoned and in 1552 he was deprived of his see. Mary I freed him and made him Lord Chancellor. As such he moved the legislation, including the reenactment of *de heretico comburendo,* which re-established papal authority and advocated a parlia-mentary declaration of the validity of Henry VIII's first marriage and consequently, of Elizabeth I's illegitimacy. He also took a leading part in the proceedings against heretics.

GARDINER, Sir Thomas (1591-1652) M.P. for Callington in the Short Parliament (1640), unsuccessfully contested London for the Long Parliament and was counsel for the defence in the impeachment of Sir Edw. Herbert in 1642. He held for the legality of ship money, for which he was impeached. In 1643 he became the royal sol-gen. and in 1645 att-gen. and one of the King's commissioners in the Uxbridge negotiations. Parliament fined him in 1647.

GARDNER (1) Alan (1742-1809) 1st Ld. (Ir.) 1800; (U.K.) 1806, a vigorous sailor under Hawke, Howe and Rodney, was commander at Jamaica from 1786-9, a Lord of the Admiralty from 1790 to 1795 and M.P. for Plymouth, he was nevertheless in the Glorious First of June (1794). M.P. for Westminster (1796-1806) he was noted for an outburst of ill-temper during negotiations with the Spithead mutineers (1797). Admiral in 1799. His nephew **(2) William Linnaeus (1771-1835)** an HEIC soldier, was employed by the Jeswant Rao, Holkar of Indore and married a princess, but in 1804 he escaped in disguise, joined Gen. Lake, raised irregular cavalry in Kumaon and Rajputana and ended his career by organising Gardner's Horse.

GARHWAL (India), part of Kumaon, an area on the Himalayan frontier west of Nepal. The British annexed the eastern half in 1815, the western, **TEHRI-GARHWAL,** remained a native state. The poor and hardy peasants of both areas provided many excellent soldiers for the Indian Army. *See* NEPAL.

GARIBALDI, Giuseppe (1807-82). The Robin Hood qualities of this transparently good man have made him a world hero and a major 19th cent. political figure. He joined Mazzini's abortive Young Italy insurrection in 1834, escaped to S. America and learned guerrilla tactics fighting against Brazil and Argentina for Uruguay (besides marrying a Uruguayan wife). He returned to take part in the defence of the Roman Republic against the French in 1849. In 1859 he fought for Savoy against the Austrians and then adventured with his famous red-shirted Thousand to the conquest of Bourbon Sicily and Naples. In 1862 he attempted Rome, but the Italian govt. would not support him for fear of Napoleon III. In 1866 he commanded irregulars briefly against the Austrians and in 1867 made another attempt on Rome which was again frustrated by the French. He was then retired, honoured but poor, to Caprera where he died. His name is kept alive by a type of biscuit, a blouse and a pomacentroid fish.

GARRAWAY'S COFFEE HOUSE (Change Aley, Cornhill, London) was a famous 17th and 18th cent. meeting place for stockbrokers, jobbers and auctioneers, notably at the time of the South Sea Bubble.

GARRICK CLUB (London) was founded in 1831 for the general patronage of the drama but has become mainly a literary and social club.

GARRICK, David (1717-79). Dr. Johnson's first pupil, first appeared on the stage in 1741. Well known socially, he made over the years a great fortune as an actor. He introduced concealed stage lighting in 1765 and retired in 1776.

GARTER, ORDER OF THE, was founded by Edward III in 1348, probably on St. George's Day, to fulfil a vow made at the end of the great Windsor tournament of 1344. St. George was held the patron of the Order and its badge was the blue garter. Its foundation legend is probably true:- the beautiful Countess of Shrewsbury dropped her blue garter as she was dancing with the King at a ball. Ladies at that time did not wear pants. Accordingly, the King stooped, picked up the garter and bound it round his own knee as a favour for the next day's tournament, silencing the sniggers of the bystanders with the words, long since the motto of the Order, *Honi soit qui mal y pense* (Fr = Evil be to him who thinks evil of it). Her husband was killed at the tourney and this placed the King under an irresistible moral obligation to fulfil the oath. The 26 knights include the sovereign and are pledged to one another 'in a lasting bond of friendship and honour' and are uniquely styled Knights Companions. There was a political advantage for the King in this idealistic fellowship with many of his greatest men, and membership came to be highly prized. Edward made the great Chapel of St. George at Windsor the church of the Order. The members still have their stalls and banners there and are supposed to pray regularly. This duty, however, is in their absence performed by deputies called Military Knights of Windsor, who live in the castle and are retired army officers of field rank distinguished for their gallant careers. At a demise of the Crown, the rehearsal of the dead monarch's titles always concludes with the words 'Sovereign of the Most Noble Order of the Garter'.

GARVIN, James Louis (1868-1947) became a leader writer on the *Daily Telegraph* in 1899 and editor and manager of Lord Northcliffe's *Sunday Observer* in 1908. By 1910 his frank and well argued journalism had converted the paper into a powerful organ of Conservative opinion. He urged the Lords to throw out Lloyd George's budget and so exacerbated the crisis of 1910, but advocated reform of the Lords. After World War I he supported international economic co-operation through the League of Nations and in 1931 he favoured a British political coalition and British re-armament, especially in the air, yet opposed the League of Nations sanctions against Italy when she invaded Ethiopia in 1935-6 and deprecated any policies which might lead to a military collision with Germany. In these apparently opportunistic attitudes, he reflected a common view that the T. of Versailles was unjust and required revision and an uncommon belief that Britain was militarily weak. Hence, like many others, he suffered a revulsion at Munich and thenceforth favoured resistance to further Nazi demands. Between 1932-4 he wrote three volumes of the *Life of Joseph Chamberlain* which pressure of international events prevented him from finishing. In 1942 Garvin published views on Churchill and Beaverbrook with which the owner of the *Observer*, W. W. Astor, disagreed and his editorship was terminated. Thereafter he wrote for the *Sunday Express* and the *Daily Telegraph*.

GAS, COAL, GAS COUNCIL, CORPORATION. Footpads by night in the unpoliced cities made lighting increasingly desirable to property owners, and the feasibility of gas lighting was understood by those who might pay for it by about 1800. Since powers were needed to dig up streets and erect obstructive standards in public places, there was a spate of private Acts beginning in 1803 with Alloa, Bradford, Chester and Doncaster, all close to coal mines. In the next three years Carlisle, Deptford, Plymouth, Bristol, Exeter and Boston followed suit. The invention in 1815 of the gas meter made commercial sales feasible. The significantly named Lighting and Watching Act, 1833, abolished the need for municipal acts by enabling vestries to "adopt" lighting or watching powers or both, while the Gas Works Clauses Act, 1847, simplified the procedure for setting up a gas undertaking. These developments led naturally to the use of gas for household and industrial heating and in 1875 urban sanitary authorities were empowered to supply gas for private consumption. Profits were raised by selling by-products notably coke, tar, ammonia, and benzol to other industries. Gas cookers were common by 1895. Most, even quite small, towns had a gas supply from either a municipal or a private undertaking by 1948. All these were vested in a Gas Council as from 1st May 1949 by the Gas Act 1948 which placed the management in 12 Area Boards. In the 1970s coal gas was superseded by North Sea (natural) gas. The 1972 Gas Act replaced the Gas Council with the British Gas Corporation which, in its turn, was privatised under the Thatcher govt.

GASCOIGNE, Thomas (1403-58), Chanc. of Oxford Univ. in 1434 and 1443-5, was an opponent of Lollardy, yet a sharp critic of Church abuses, especially Papal provisions, of which he said 'There are three things today which make a bishop in England: the will of the King, the will of the Pope in the court of Rome and the money paid in large quantities to that court'.

GASCOIGNE (1) Sir William (?1350-1419) became a King's serjeant in 1397 and attorney for Lancaster (then E. of Hereford) on his banishment. On Lancaster's usurpation as Henry IV, Gascoigne became C.J. of the Kings Bench in 1400. In 1403 he raised forces against the Percy rebellion and was with Henry in Yorkshire in the campaign which, in May 1405, ended Abp. Scrope's rebellion. He was appointed to preside at Scrope's trial and ordered to sentence him to death, but refused on the ground that the archbishop could not be sentenced by a secular. He resigned. His judicial integrity occasioned other, mostly apocryphal, anecdotes. His descendant **(2) George (?1525-77)** of Grays Inn was M.P. for Bedford from 1557 to 1559 and for Midhurst in 1572. He wrote many poems and plays much appreciated in his day and seems to have begun the long self-conscious association of the Inns of Court with literature. He was the stepfather of the poet Nicholas Breton.

GASCOIGNE-CECIL (or MODERN) CECIL FAMILY (1) Robert Arthur Talbot (1830-1903) courtesy Vist. CRANBORNE (1865) 3rd M. of SALISBURY (1868) spent two years pioneering in Australia and on his return in 1853 became a Fellow of All Souls and an M.P. His conservative brilliance was soon recognised through his hard hitting articles in the *Quarterly Review* and by his effective, sometimes satirical, criticism of the liberal govt. Hence he achieved cabinet office under Derby in 1866 as Sec. of State for India. In 1867, however, he resigned against Disraeli's Reform Bill but continued, after he went to the Lords, to attack Gladstone's policies. He was less a reactionary than a pragmatist, as competent in theology as Gladstone, much better educated in science and distrusting mass democracy as a threat to individual liberty. Outside politics he was chairman of the Great Eastern Rly. Co. (1868-72), Pres. of the British Assn. in 1894 and conducted practical experiments in electricity and magnetism.

His last speech in the Commons had been against Irish Church disestablishment. When the Bill came up from the Commons he persuaded the Lords to throw it out and await the verdict of a general election, and he propounded the major constitutional doctrine later enshrined in the Liberal Parliament Act, that the Upper House must secure for the country an opportunity to express its "firm deliberate and sustained conviction" whenever that opportunity was denied it by the Commons and must abide by that conviction once expressed. The general election returned a large majority for the Liberals; Salisbury therefore advised the Lords to pass the bill and voted for it himself. This set the tone of the next years when liberal bills of increasing radicalism (e.g. on Education and Irish Land in 1870 and abolishing university tests in 1871) came up and could not, on principle, be resisted; but meantime he practised a radicalism of his own, unsuccessfully supporting Russell's Life Peerage Bill and a measure on parliamentary procedure and achieving some reforms of university abuses.

By 1874 the Liberals had run out of steam. The Conservatives under Disraeli won the general election and Salisbury, despite temperamental differences, returned to the India Office. He was a sensible and enterprising administrator but Indian policy was overshadowed by Russian southward ambitions which, in the Balkans, affected the Foreign Office and, in Afghanistan, the govt. of India. He laughed at fears of a Russian invasion but thought that, to divert British energy from the Balkans, the Russians might encourage the Afghans to frontier violence: "Russia can ... offer the loot of India: We if we desired to make a competing offer, can promise nothing because there is nothing in Turkestan to loot". His local solution, pursued with some pertinacity through the E. of Lytton, his new Viceroy, was to resist Russian diplomatic encroachment at Kabul by counter-encroachment at Herat. He was now the cabinet exponent against the trend of Russian southward policy. Rebellions in the Turkish Balkans fomented by Russian intrigues, provoked by the Bulgarian atrocities and publicised by Gladstonian invective, suddenly brought the whole issue to a head. He was sent as a special plenipotentiary to the Constantinople international conference to secure both the integrity of the Ottoman Empire and the safety of its Christian subjects. To keep the Russians out he argued for a reorganisation of the Balkan provinces under Turkish sovereignty by an international commission supported by Belgian troops. The western powers and Russia accepted this. The Turks, understandably, did not. The conference collapsed (Jan. 1877) and war (Mar.-Dec. 1877) brought the Russians, despite stiff resistance, almost to the suburbs of Constantinople where they dictated the T. of San Stefano. This violated the Turkish integrity which Britain, Austria and France had guaranteed after the Crimean War. Salisbury persuaded the cabinet to insist upon the submission of all the Russian conditions to an international conference. The Russians demanded the right to exclude any they thought fit and the Fleet was then sent to the Straits. Derby, the Foreign Sec., unwilling to contemplate a war, resigned and on 1st Apr. 1878 Salisbury succeeded him. Next day he issued the *Salisbury Circular* to all the powers and this led ultimately to the open settlement of the issues at the Berlin Congress and Treaty (q.v.).

These diplomatic successes were, however, soon forgotten. The Conservatives lost the 1880 general election. In Apr. 1881 Disraeli died and in May Salisbury became leader of the opposition in the Lords and Sir Stafford Northcote in the Commons. This arrangement left their party temporarily without a real leader, but as Northcote was neither inspiring nor tactically clever, the main work fell on Salisbury, who succeeded in moderating the govt's Irish legislation by judicious amendments, and negotiated an electoral compromise (county household suffrage in return for redistribution of seats) without forcing an election. The Liberal govt.,

however, fell in June 1885. The Queen sensibly sent for Salisbury and there followed the remarkable 13 months during which Parnell and Irish issues dominated the political scene. (*See* SALISBURY'S FIRST GOVT. JUNE 1885-FEB. 1886; GLADSTONE'S THIRD GOVT. FEB.-AUG. 1886) and Salisbury found himself in power again (*see* SALISBURY'S SECOND GOVT. AUG. 1886-AUG. 1892).

Gladstone with a coalition was returned to power in the general election of 1892. He was 82 and accepted office solely to achieve Home Rule. His Bill passed all its stages in the Commons; in the Lords it was attacked by the D. of Devonshire, whom Salisbury supported, and thrown out. Gladstone retired in favour of Lord Rosebery and the Liberal govt. limped on, offering bills which the Lords threw out or mutilated. In view of Salisbury's opinions on the functions of an upper house (*see above*) it is hard to censure them, for there was no evidence of popular support for the govt. and when it resigned (over a shortage of cordite) and Salisbury came in (June 1895), the dissolution which he advised brought him a handsome victory, partly influenced by the current tide of imperial feeling (*see* SALISBURY'S THIRD GOVT. JUNE 1895-JULY 1902). From 1899 the govt. was occupied with the Boer War and with its difficult diplomatic effects. Salisbury's health was failing, but he thought it was his duty to see the war through. The Khaki Election (Nov. 1900) renewed his mandate but the Queen, to whom he was attached, died in Jan. 1901. The P. of Vereeniging was signed in 31 May 1902 and in July he advised the King to send for his brilliant nephew, Arthur Balfour, and resigned. He died at Hatfield a year later. His eldest son **(2) James Edward Hubert (1861-1955) 4th M.** and a major-gen. was an M.P. until he succeeded. He was a conservative U/Sec. of State at the Foreign Office (1900-3) and, under Balfour, Lord Privy Seal (1903-5) and Pres. of the Bd. of Trade in 1905. Under Bonar Law and Baldwin he was Lord President of the Council (1922-4) and Lord Privy Seal (1924-9). His brother **(3) Ld. Edward Herbert (1867-1918),** a soldier and diplomat, served in the Sudan, Ethiopia and S. Africa and in 1903 joined the Egyptian army. He became Dir. of Intelligence at Cairo and U/Sec. of State in the Egyptian Min. of Finance. He effectively ruled Egypt (1914-7) between Kitchener and McMahon. The eldest son of **(2)**, **(4)** the formidable **Robert Arthur James (1893-1972), Ld. CECIL (by writ 1941), 5th M.** was an M.P. from 1929 to 1934. He was S. of State for the Dominions (1940-2), Lord Privy Seal (1942-3), returned to the Dominions (later Commonwealth) Office (1943-5 and 1951-2) and was Lord Pres. (1952-7). **(5) Edgar Algernon Robert (1864-1958) 1st Vist. CECIL of CHELWOOD (1923)** 3rd *s.* of **(1)** above, was a Tory M.P. for E. Marylebone from 1906 to 1910 and Independent Conservative M.P. for Hitchin until 1923. He was 82 and Min. for Blockade from 1916 to 1918. His prominence in the formulation of the Covenant of the League of Nations and presidency of the League of Nations Union earned him a Nobel Peace Prize in 1937. Holding that Germany's aggressive outlook was a public danger which had to be reduced, he opposed a negotiated peace in World War I. World War II having destroyed the League, he transferred his influence to the furtherance of the aims of the United Nations Organisation.

A son of the 6th M. **(6) Robert Michael James (1946) Vist. CRANBORNE and Ld. CECIL of Essendon by writ (1992)** was M.P. for Dorset (South) from 1979 to 1987. Called to the Lords, he became Party U-Sec. for Defence from 1992 to 1994, and from 1994 to 1997 Lord Privy Seal and Leader of the House. On the change of govt. in 1997, he became Leader of the Opposition peers. *See* HOUSE OF LORDS BILL (1998).

GASCONY. The word is related to 'Basque' and represents that (approximately) quarter of Aquitaine (q.v.) occupied by or claimed for Basques along the coast south of the

Gironde. The word has long been unsatisfactorily used as if it were synonymous with Aquitaine.

GASCOYNE (1) Sir Crisp (1700-61) obtained an Act of the City Common Council in favour of orphans in 1748 and, as Lord Mayor in 1752-3, was the first to occupy the Mansion House. His son **(2) Bamber (1725-91)** M.P. for Malden from 1761 to 1763, Midhurst from 1765 to 1770, Weobley from 1770 to 1774 and from 1774 to 1786 for Cornish pocket boroughs, was also a receiver-gen. of customs. His son **(3) Isaac** (1770-1841) a soldier, was M.P. for Liverpool from 1802 to 1830.

GASKELL, Elizabeth Cleghorn (1810-65) née Stevenson, known as "Mrs Gaskell", social novelist of the Lancashire towns where she was brought up. Of her many books the famous *Cranford* (1853) was based on Knutsford. She was held to be hostile to employers who, however, read her works. In fact she had a practical sympathy for the poor. Her life of her friend Charlotte Brontë (1857) was challenged for accuracy and certain statements were withdrawn.

GASQUET, Francis Neil, in religion **Dom AIDAN (1846-1929), Card. (1914)** became prior of Downside in 1878 and enlarged and modernised the community and its school. He became Abbot President of the English Benedictines in 1900 and settled in Rome in 1914. As a Cardinal he inspired the establishment of a British legation to the Holy See in Dec. 1914.

GASTEIN CONVENTION (14 Aug. 1865) between Prussia and Austria, divided the administration of the Duchies occupied after the Danish War of 1864 provisionally: Holstein (within the German Confederation) to Austria, Schleswig (outside it) to Prussia, Lauenburg in full sovereignty to Prussia. The latter was adjacent to the independent Hanseatic ports of Hamburg and Lübeck which could now be easily pressurised by concentrations of Prussian troops. The frontier between Schleswig and Holstein followed much of the line of the later Kiel Canal. Bismarck referred to the Convention as 'papering over the cracks', an oracular statement indicating no doubt his own intention to open up the cracks if he could.

GASWORKERS' UNION. In 1888 gasworkers formed a general union and in 1889 demanded an 8-hour day without reduction of wages. Safety factors had created a respected body of workers and many of the employers were local councils which could pass the cost to their ratepayers. The union's case was conceded without a strike. This event was a landmark, for it encouraged peaceful unionism but did not raise employer's hackles.

GATES, Horatio or Horace (1728-1806), an active British regimental officer, retired in 1769 to America. At the outbreak of the rebellion he became Adj-Gen. to the rebel forces and in 1776 Commander of their Northern Army against Burgoyne in 1777. In 1777 he forced Burgoyne to surrender at Saratoga and this led to an unsuccessful attempt to make him C-in-C instead of Washington. He became Pres. of the Bd. of War instead. In 1780 he was soundly defeated at Camden (S. Carolina). A Congressional investigation having been cancelled in 1782, he resumed action until the end of the war.

GATESHEAD, opposite Newcastle-upon-Tyne, was chartered by the Bp. of Durham in 1164. The two towns were continually in dispute over fishing and trading rights. Gateshead became a parliamentary borough in 1832 but much of it was burned down in 1854. The rivalries between the two boroughs disappeared when bridges across the Tyne turned them into a single economic, if not official, unit after 1850.

GATHORNE-HARDY, Gathorne (1814-1906) 1st Vist. (1878) and E. of CRANBROOK (1892) became a conservative M.P. in 1856, held minor offices until 1866 and then joined Derby's third cabinet as Pres. of the Poor Law Board. In 1867 he became Home Sec. After the govt's resignation in 1868 he became a formidable debater and in 1874 he became Sec. of State for War in Disraeli's second govt. and had to complete Cardwell's reforms. On Disraeli's move to the Lords in 1876 he was baulked of the Leadership of the Commons by Sir Stafford Northcote; became briefly Sec. of State for India and had to deal with Lytton's policy in Afghanistan and the consequent wars. Like others he could not stand Northcote and in 1878 went to the Lords. He was Lord Pres. from 1886 to 1892 and, mainly concerned with education, maintained a very conservative position on the Education Act, 1891.

GAUDEN, John. See EIKON BASILIKE.

GAULLE, Charles de (1890-1970). French soldier and later statesman, was captured by the Germans in World War I, and between the wars was, though only of field rank, one of the few French officers who appreciated the new mobility of war conferred by the tank. Very tall, awkward and unconventional, he was only a *général de brigade* at the beginning of World War II. At the French debacle in 1940 he refused to surrender and, from London, issued a call to arms, robbed of some of its credibility by his low rank and lack of public status, but Churchill built up his image as the best available and some Frenchmen and colonial governors joined his Free French movement more out of anti-Teutonism than for the sake of the man himself. He thus had to impose his personality upon the Free French, some of whom had more distinguished careers than his own, and maintain assertively the integrity of the future France against all comers, allied or enemy. In due course his committee turned itself into a provisional Free French govt., despite widespread irritation (especially on the part of Churchill) and American distrust.

(2) In 1944-5 he made the Allies accept him as the head of a provisional govt. in Paris, where his most important preoccupations were the containment of the Communist Party which had infiltrated the Resistance movements, stolen their arms and was creating violent disturbances in the south, and the recognition of France as one of the victorious powers. This was symbolised by the creation of French zones of occupation in Germany and Austria and participation in the Nuremburg War Crimes Trials.

(3) After a period of grand retirement he returned in a quasi-coup in 1958. As President he conceded Algerian independence, put down a revolt, distanced France from N.A.T.O. and twice prevented British entry into the E.E.C. With many Frenchmen, he believed that the English speaking nations were inimical to France and, during an official visit to Canada, spoke publicly in favour of an independent French Quebec. After losing a referendum he retired in 1969.

(4) His language was often earthy, sometimes coarse, yet his public demeanour resembled that of Louis XIV, but in reply to an accusation of autocracy he said "You cannot dictate to a nation which has 200 cheeses".

GAULS. See CELTS.

GAULE, John (?1604-87). See HOPKINS, MATTHEW.

GAUNT. M.E. name for GHENT (Belgium). Families of this name are probably descended from Flemish immigrants. John of Gaunt was born there.

GAUNT, Elizabeth (?-1685) was burned at Tyburn for sheltering a Rye House conspirator, one Burton, who turned King's evidence against her, was pardoned and was later involved in the Monmouth rebellion. She was the last woman to be so executed for High Treason.

GAUNT, John of. See LANCASTER – SECOND FAMILY OR ROYAL HOUSE OF.

GAUNT or GANT, Maurice of (?1184-1230), a powerful landowning lord of Leeds (which he chartered in 1208), was one of the rebels captured at Lincoln in 1217. He later had lands in eight counties and in 1227 held the eyres of six mainland and southern counties, but he died in Brittany.

GAVEL. A small mallet used by some chairmen and American, but never British, judges.

GAVELKIND is a rule of succession in which land is divided equally between sons at the death of their father. Its elaborate jurisprudence was the Common Law of Kent and obtained in other areas of presumed Jutish colonisation such as south Hants, part of the I. of Wight and Kentish Town. In IRELAND, by the Gavelkind Act 1704, estates of R. Catholics were made subject to the rule unless the eldest conformed by taking the Test within a year or at majority. This pressed heavily where properties were too small to be divided economically and it steadily eroded R. Catholic ownership. It was repealed by Gardiner's Relief Act of 1778. English land was steadily disgavelled throughout the centuries and the Common Law status of what was left was ended in 1926 by the Law of Property Act. (*See also* WELSH LAW.) The name perhaps originated in a duty to a lord which could be discharged by a payment of Gafol (q.v.).

GAVESTON, Piers or Peter. *See* EDWARD II-1 to 4.

GAY, John (1685-1732), the author, was sec. to the Duchess of Monmouth from 1712 to 1714 and then to Clarendon on the deputation to George I at Hanover in 1714. In 1717 he similarly accompanied Pulteney to Aix. While a lottery commissioner from 1722 to 1731, he was offered a series of court posts. During all this time he was writing for the stage and the press and was a friend of Steele, Swift and Pope. His *Beggar's Opera* created a sensation in 1728 but its sequel *Polly* was suppressed. He also wrote the libretto for Handel's *Acis and Galatea* in 1732.

GAZA (Palestine), the scene of Anglo-Ottoman battles in 1917, was included in British mandated territory after World War I but was assigned to Egypt under the Israeli-Egyptian armistice of 1949. It, with the adjacent STRIP, was the resort of Palestinian Arab refugees; they used it as a base for guerrilla operations against the Israelis, who eventually occupied it at the 1967 war. It remained under their *de facto* rule which was challenged, in part effectively, by the uprising (*Intafada*) organised by the Palestinian Liberation Organisation, with which the Israeli govt. made a peace agreement involving progressive local autonomy in 1993.

GAZETTE, originally a small Venetian coin, the price of a gossip sheet. Such sheets became current in England after 1558. The term became associated with official news accounts, the *OXFORD GAZETTE* being founded in 1665 by the govt. at the time resident there to avoid the plague. It was renamed the *LONDON GAZETTE* in 1666. Although challenged in the era of the Popish Plot after 1688 it had few rivals. With the proliferation of periodicals in the 18th cent. it was confined to Court and official statements which formed the nucleus of such news in the press as a whole. It gained notoriety under the direction of William Knox during the American rebellion, by systematic printing of 'official', false or overoptimistic news. The *EDINBURGH GAZETTE* was founded in 1699.

GDYNIA. *See* DANZIG.

GEBUR (Lat *BURES* or *BURI*). Free but depressed rural labourers of Wessex and W. Mercia, some descended from manumitted slaves, others from freemen who had fallen on evil days. According to the 11th cent. *Rectitudines Singularum Personarum* (Lat = Rights of Individuals), they worked two days a week and three days in harvest on the lord's demesne and paid 10d in tribute at Michaelmas, barley and hens at Martinmas and a young sheep at Easter. This implies possession of a small plot of land. According to Domesday Book *coliberti* (collectively freed men), a considerable element in this population were otherwise known as *Bures* or *buri*.

GEDDES, (1) Sir Eric Campbell (1875-1937), dep. manager of the North Eastern Rly in 1914, became inspector of war transport in 1916, controller of the navy and then M.P. for Cambridge and First Lord of the Admiralty in 1917. From 1919 to 1921 he was Min. of Transport and effected the great railway amalgamation and from 1921 to 1922 he was chairman of the committee on national economy (*see* GEDDES AXE). In 1922 he returned to business as chairman of the Dunlop Rubber Co. and Imperial Airways. His brother **(2) Auckland Campbell (1879-1954) Ld. GEDDES (1942)** qualified as a physician in 1903 and then held academic posts, but in World War I he entirely reorganised the recruiting procedures, became M.P. for Basingstoke, Min. for National Service in 1917 and Pres. of the Bd. of Trade in 1919. In 1921 he joined A. J. Balfour and Lord Lee of Fareham as delegate to the Washington Disarmament Conference. In World War II he was civil defence commissioner in the S.E. region. In 1947 he went blind.

'GEDDES AXE' was a policy of retrenchment resulting from the report of Sir Eric Geddes' Committee on Public expenditure published in Feb. 1922. Five ministries, including those of transport and labour, were abolished and there were heavy cuts in manpower and pay of the forces, in teaching and in public health.

GEDDES, Jenny (fl. 1637) was the lady who, shouting "Ye'll no say the mass in my lug", threw a stool at Bp. Lindsay's head in St. Giles, Edinburgh, when he tried to read the Anglican communion, and started a riot which was the first act of the Civil War.

GELDERS. *See* JÜLICH.

GENDARMES properly **GENS D'ARMES (Fr = men at arms). (1)** An elite force of French royal cavalry created in 1445. **(2)** A French national (as opposed to local) police force created by Bonaparte.

GENEALOGY was important once the canon law on marriage and the validity of papal dispensations between forbidden degrees was accepted and in the devolution of entailed property. It became connected with heraldry and grants of arms because of the need to identify men disguised in coat armour. A warrior had to have the right arms or had to be granted some. On the continent it was socially important because access to certain courts (especially the Austrian) and membership of certain orders (e.g. the Knights of Malta) depended upon the correct number of quarters (usually 16), i.e. the right number of armigerous ancestors.

GENEAT (A.S. = companion) and RADCNIT (A.S. = riding servant) were mounted retainers of a lord to whom they owed rent and mainly non-agricultural services such as riding messages or setting fences when he hunted. The *geneat* possibly had the higher social status.

GENERAL is a military officer with a general authority, rather than one who commands a specialised unit. The rank is thus always high, involving direction rather than combat. In the 17th cent. a general's deputy was a lieut gen. (now a separate rank) and below him was the serjeant-major general (later major-gen.) who acted as a chief of staff or as a military gov. A brigadier-gen. (abolished 1920) commanded a brigade. In armies of the German tradition (including Russia) there is also a Highest Gen. (usually mistranslated Col-Gen.) who ranks above a gen. Most armies have a Marshal or FIELD-MARSHAL who is higher still. In armies of the Napoleonic tradition, generals are classified by the size of the formation they command.

GENERAL AGREEMENT ON TARIFFS AND TRADE-GATT (1947) was originally a collection of bilateral agreements between 23 western nations designed to free world trade from quotas, restrictions, controls and other protectionist devices. It provided for most favoured nation clauses between participating countries and obliged each to negotiate for customs reductions at the request of any other. It gave rise to an important component of U.N.O. and led to the establishment in 1964 of the G.A.T.T. Trade Centre to help the export trade of underdeveloped countries. By 1976 99 countries had agreed to adopt the rules: by 1994 111 with 22 others applying them *de facto*.

GENERAL ASSEMBLY OF THE CHURCH OF SCOTLAND is constituted under an Act of 1592 (The Charter of the Church) confirmed by Act of 1690, by the Act of Security which is contained *verbatim* in the T. of Union of 1707 and is a fundamental condition of that Union. It consisted of one minister for every four parishes in each of the 84 presbyteries and one elder for every six, with one commissioner for each university and royal burgh (95) and two for Edinburgh (total 735). The Crown is represented by a Lord High Commissioner who has quasi-royal status. He was no voice or vote but is the channel of communication with the Sovereign. The Crown and the Church both claim the right to convene and dissolve assemblies. Since 1695 the Moderator and the Commissioner have always agreed to summon the assembly for the same day and place. Within its own sphere, the Assembly is judicially and legislatively supreme and the courts cannot interfere. Legislation is commonly passed by the submission (by a member, a synod or a presbytery) of an overture (bill). If this is adopted it may be converted into an interim Act, valid until the next Assembly, but if it is to be converted into a Law of the Church it has under the Barrier Act, 1697 to be remitted to the presbyteries, a majority of whom must support it before it can be enacted.

GENERAL CHAMBER OF MANUFACTURERS (1785-7) under the chairmanship of Josiah Wedgwood was formed to protect Birmingham and Manchester manufacturers during the negotiations for an Irish trade agreement (*see* COMMERCIAL PROPOSITIONS; IRELAND D2-3; E1). The collective defensiveness of the otherwise enlightened members harmed Irish interests without much benefiting themselves. The Chamber broke up over disagreements on the French commercial negotiations of 1787, but its formation was probably premature.

GENERAL COUNCIL (Sc), a sometimes loose term, meaning usually a parliamentary assembly with a status lower than that of a full parliament through the absence of an accepted component such as the King or one of the estates, or the presence of persons not usually entitled to be summoned to parliament. Depending on its size, it might thus amount to an enlarged royal council or to an enlarged parliament.

GENERAL DEVELOPMENT ORDERS. *See* TOWN AND COUNTRY PLANNING-3.

GENERAL MEDICAL COUNCIL. *See* BRITISH MEDICAL ASSN.

GENERAL STEAM NAVIGATION CO. was formed in 1824 from a group of steamers which plied between London and Margate after 1820. It gradually extended its operations coastwise as far as Scotland by 1842 and then to the Continent and the Mediterranean. It became a limited Co. in 1902.

GENERAL STRIKE (1926) (1) the high cost of winning good British coal compared very unfavourably with that of the poor German and Polish, and its export price was further raised by the high level of sterling following the return to the gold standard in 1925. The advent, too, of oil fuel was constricting the market. Since World War I there had been trouble between miners' leaders, who saw themselves, in language borrowed from Russia, as the standard-bearers of the working class, and the coal owners who, for the most part, were greedy and unenlightened; their only solution to the problems was longer hours and shorter pay. The Baldwin govt., which saw that a clash was only too probable, regarded the miners as merely less stupid than the owners.

(2) In 1921 and 1925 strikes had been postponed by govt. subsidisation of wages, accompanied in 1925 by the appointment of the Samuel Commission to investigate. Meanwhile the govt., mindful that a conflict would affect the whole nation, prepared for the worst by enrolling volunteers for an Organisation for the Maintenance of Supplies. Early in 1926 the Commission reported that 75% of all coal was being produced at a loss; it recommended some mergers and strongly urged modernisation and re-equipment; it condemned the subsidies which destroyed the owners' incentive to modernise, but believed that modernisation could be financed by a short term cut in wages. The owners joyfully seized upon the last, ignored the rest and announced wage cuts for 1st May.

(3) The Trade Union Congress (T.U.C.) now intervened in support of the miners by calling a general strike for 3 May. On 1 May the miners rejected the proposals of the owners, who locked them out. The T.U.C. then tried to persuade the govt. to intervene before the general strike got under way. In fact it had begun sporadically; some newspaper printers had refused to print an article stigmatising it as revolutionary. On this ground or pretext the govt. broke off the discussion and in the ensuing stoppage it acted on the tenable, but inaccurate, belief that the T.U.C. was trying to override parliament. Churchill produced and edited the *British Gazette* to replace the strikebound press and, with the Russian revolution in mind, portrayed the strikers as subverters of liberty and constitutionalism. Not many people read the *British Gazette*, but many disliked the impacts of the stoppage; yet the affair was, on the whole, good tempered. Violence was very rare; the volunteer bus, train and food-convoy drivers enjoyed themselves; some police were found playing football with the unemployed and the T.U.C. safeguarded hospitals and the like.

(4) T.U.C. delegates headed by George Thomas called on Baldwin to discuss concessions but got none. They began to realise that the infliction of hardship on a whole nation in the interests of a small minority was making them unpopular. On the 9th day they called off the general strike. The isolated miners fought on in miserable poverty but in vain into the autumn. When work was resumed there were victimisations which, more than the stoppage, bred hatreds in and near the coal areas.

(5) This overrated but much discussed affair strengthened the moral muscles of the Labour Party when, after World War II, it won the general election on a programme of nationalisation. *See* BALDWIN'S SECOND CONSERVATIVE GOVT; TRADES DISPUTES ACTS.

GENERAL SURVEYORS OF THE KING'S LANDS were appointed in 1512 to manage the royal landed revenues. They were erected into a court in 1542 and in 1547 combined with the Court of Augmentations, which was absorbed into Exchequer in 1554.

GENERAL WARRANTS for the arrest of unspecified persons or the search of their property or both were issued by a Sec. of State in the 17th cent. and were authorised for the purposes of the Licensing Act, 1662 which, however, lapsed in 1692. (*See* WILKES V WOOD (1763).) Ultimately Camden C.J. held them illegal in *Entick v Carrington* (1765).

GENERAL WILL. The expression was borrowed from the jurist Gian Vincenzo Gravina (1664-1718) by Montesquieu (1689-1755) in *L'Esprit des Lois* (1748) and referred to legislative powers which expressed it. Diderot (1713-84), borrowing from Justinian, defined it as the sense of justice shown by all mankind: an objective rule or obligation to render to each his due. J. J. Rousseau (1712-78) thought that only mutual obligations in a limited civic body could be effective and concluded that the general will was a consensus of equals from which it followed that no man was free unless able to take part in the consensus.

GENERALITY, LANDS OF THE. *See* BRABANT, DUCHY OF.

GENEVA (Switzerland). The seat of the League of Nations, which offered the facilities of its *Palais des Nations* for major international conferences. Among these were the 1927 naval conferences and many meetings (besides its own sessions) arising out of the international crises of the 1930s. When the League was superseded by the United Nations after World War II, the latter's H.Q. was set up in New York to ensure the continuing interest of the Americans, who had never belonged to the League, but the *Palais des Nations* continued available for the meetings which proliferated with the growing post-war internationalism. Notable among these were the 1954 conference which, with British brokerage, ultimately ended French involvement in Vietnam, and the prolonged efforts of British and American negotiators to stop the partly sectarian tripartite civil war in Bosnia from 1991 onwards. *See* also CALVINISM; INTERNATIONAL LABOUR OFFICE, SWITZERLAND.

GENEVA CONVENTIONS. *See* RED CROSS.

GENEVA PROTOCOLS. *See* AUSTRIA (REPUBLICAN).

GENOA (Italy). This naval republic, long at odds with Pisa, developed the Levantine trade opened up after the First Crusade (1097). It established trading colonies in N. Africa, Syria and the Crimea and consequently fell foul of Venice. Hence Genoese eastern interests suffered from Moslem reconquest of Crusader states and from the Venetian-supported Latin conquest of Constantinople (1204). Its shipmasters therefore sought other markets and types of cargo. In the late 13th cent. they penetrated *via* the Channel as far as N W Europe The Byzantine recovery (1261) helped restore the eastern trade and was followed by victories over Pisa (1282) and the Venetians (1298). These were won mainly by noblemen with fiefs along the Riviera, who found Genoese service and politics profitable. Hence the republic's territory spread along the Riviera. They also liquidated Pisan claims, especially in Corsica. In 1307 the Genoese took the first direct shipment of English wool for their cloth industry. Thereafter they usually carried Papal alum westwards and wool back. The fatal duality of much Italian city politics now supervened. A revolution (1340) excluded the nobility from city office and established a plebeian dogeship. The nobles, however, strengthened their hold on the Bank of St. George, in reality an overseas trading company with extra-territorial rights. An attempt to repair the inherent disunity by attacking Venice (1379-80) ended in a major disaster. The republic could be maintained only by a partial liquidation. In 1396 the French Kings acquired a protectorate; in 1407 the Bank took over Corsica. The practical effect was that Genoa, whose commerce was related to that of Marseilles and Lyons, rose and fell with French influence. Her dependence went so far that in 1507 an insurrection, aimed at the nobility, was put down by French troops. In 1528, however, the great Doria family led many other nobles in a quarrel with the French and secured Habsburg backing. While Spanish power policed the E. Mediterranean, France fell into confusion. The new aristocratic govt. maintained a precariously balanced independence, despite wars and a general commercial decline, until French power revived under Louis XIV. He picked a quarrel in 1684 and bombarded the harbour. Genoa then became a French satellite and naturally attracted Austrian hostility when France and Austria were at war. The Austrians briefly occupied the city in 1746. During the French revolutionary wars the French first dominated, then revolutionised, and finally annexed the city. It passed to Savoy-Sardinia in 1815. *See* FLANDERS GALLEYS.

GENOA CONFERENCE (1922) was called to agree upon a rescheduling of German reparations which were, as usual, in arrears, persuade the U.S.A. to moderate or remit the war debts owed to her by her former allies and encourage communist Russia to trade with the outside world. The French would make no concessions on reparations, the Americans did not attend and the Russians and Germans made their own private deal 20 miles away at Rapallo. (q.v.)

GENTLEMEN-AT-ARMS. Influenced by the existence of a similar organisation at the court of Francis I of France, Henry VIII established a body of Gentlemen Pensioners in 1509. These were younger sons of noblemen who acted as personal bodyguards to the sovereign. This body was reorganised as the Gentlemen-at-Arms in 1862. The Captain is always a member of the govt. and acts as one of its spokesmen in the Lords.

GENTLEMEN'S MAGAZINE **(1731-1914),** a monthly founded by Edward Cave (1691-1754) a versatile printer (and also inventor of a spinning machine) who had previously acted as a kind of two-way news agency between town and country journals. His pseudonym *Sylvanus Urban* was a bid alike for rural and urban readers. He published political and other news, book reviews and essays. The word 'magazine', used in this context for the first time, successfully suggested a storehouse of all varieties and in the 18th cent. it was read by everybody who was anybody and many others.

GEOFFREY OF ANJOU (?1114-51). *See* HENRY I and STEPHEN.

GEOFFREY (?-1093) Bp. of COUTANCES (c. 1049) of the powerful Mowbray family, was notoriously a fighting as well as an able bishop. He improved the organisation of his church and diocese and was a munificent patron of building and the arts. His great cathedral was his memorial. He was also one of the ablest Normans in England. With Abp. Alfred of York he presented K. William to the Londoners after his coronation in 1066 and, as a leading and active conqueror, received wide lands, particularly in the west. He helped to put down the English rising of 1069 and the baronial rebellion of 1075 and was also active judicially, for example at Pennenden Heath (1072-6) and at Kentford (1080) concerning respectively a dispute between Lanfranc and Odo of Bayeux about lands in Kent and the estates of the Abbey of Ely. He and his nephew Robert Mowbray, E. of Northumberland, joined the short baronial resistance to William Rufus in 1088, when he held Bristol. When pardoned, he spiritedly defended ecclesiastical privileges against the King at a council at Salisbury. He died at Coutances.

GEOFFREY OF MONMOUTH (?1100-54) became Archdeacon of Llandaff in about 1140 and Bp. of St. Asaph in 1152. As such he witnessed the T. of Wallingford in 1153. His *Historia Britonum* (Lat = History of the Britons) based on Nennius, Gildas, Bede, William of Malmesbury and Breton traditions, was translated by Wace into Anglo-Norman and into English by Layamon. It is popular entertainment rather than history and some 200 mediaeval copies have been found. They contain, besides much else, the first elaboration of the Arthurian legend.

GEOFFREY OF NANTES or BRITTANY (?-1134). *See* HENRY II-4.

GEOFFREY RUFUS (?-1141). *See* DURHAM-3.

GEOFFREY (after 1143-1212) Abp. of YORK (1189), eldest bastard of Henry II, was destined for the Church. In 1173, after papal dispensation for his bastardy and uncanonical age, Henry secured him the bishopric of Lincoln, to which he was never consecrated and which he resigned on becoming Chancellor in 1182. Unlike his legitimate half-brothers, he remained loyal to his father, supporting him in his war with K. Philip Augustus at the end of his reign and was with him when he died at Chinon. Richard I permitted his election as Abp. of York but Hubert Walter tried with some success to prevent him getting possession of the see, so he retired to Normandy to get papal support and consecration while Richard was on Crusade. Forbidden to return before 1193, he defied the prohibition, but in obedience to it he was stopped by William Longchamp, the Justiciar, who unwisely had him dragged from sanctuary at St. Martin's Dover. This scandalous incident initiated Longchamp's fall. In 1193

Geoffrey, in support of the royal authority against P. John, joined with Bp. Hugh of Durham in attacking John's castle at Tickhill. He also became involved in a furious quarrel with his own canons over their respective contributions to Richard's ransom, and they tried to lock him out of York Minster. The Pope suspended him: Richard deprived him of the Yorkshire shrievalty, but in 1196 he successfully made his case at Rome and was reconciled with his Chapter. In 1200 he resisted K. John's carucage and in 1207 the levy of a thirteenth and was exiled. He died in Normandy.

GEOLOGY. James Hutton (1726-97) published his *Theory of the Earth*, based upon personal observations as a landowner in 1795. William Smith (1769-1839), a canal surveyor, published his great *Maps of the Strata of England and Wales* in 1815. The govt. Geological Survey was begun in 1831 and continues. Charles Lyell (1797-1875) discredited the biblical or catastrophic theories of geology in his *Principles of Geology* (1830-3).

GEORGE CROSS (GC) and **MEDAL (GM)** for conspicuous civilian gallantry were instituted by George VI in 1939. The Cross carries a small pension. *See* MALTA GC.

GEORGE, St. was legendarily a Christian born at Lydda (Palestine). As a soldier during Diocletian's persecutions he publicly declared his faith and was martyred at Nicomedia in 303. His shrine was established at Lydda by the mid 14th cent. and attracted crusaders, who disseminated the cult. The story of his battle with the dragon comes from that of Perseus and Andromeda, traditionally associated with the Lydda district. It is not found before the 11th cent. but was popularised by the 13th cent. *Golden Legend* because it appealed to warlike men in an age of chivalry. When Edward III gave the Chapel of Windsor to the Order of the Garter, St. George was associated with Edward the Confessor in the rededication and so almost imperceptibly became the patron of England. His feast is 23 April. It appears, however, that the Papacy abolished St. George in 1975.

GEORGE (1449-78), D. of CLARENCE (1461) *s.* of Richard, D. of York, and brother of Edward IV. *See* EDWARD IV-6 *et seq*; CLARENCE.

GEORGE I LEWIS (1660-1727) (King 1714) (*See* HANOVER and JACOBITES.) **(1)** First came to England to propose to the P. Anne in 1680. He took part in the relief of Vienna (1683) and in the Hungarian campaign of 1685 and also fought at Neerwinden (1693). In 1694 he divorced and imprisoned his wife. In 1698 he succeeded to the Electorate of Hanover and in 1701 joined the Grand Alliance, contributing considerable forces and forming with his mother Sophia a working understanding with Marlborough (who visited him in 1704) and the Whigs. He consequently commanded the imperial army on the Upper Rhine from 1707 to 1709. Meanwhile he made alliances related to the Northern War, with Poland (1709) and Denmark (1710) which enabled him in 1712 to occupy Verden, a Swedish possession. His main qualification for the English throne was his protestantism, and his preoccupations kept him out of English internal politics then dominated by the Tories. Also he never learned English.

(2) On Q. Anne's death (Aug. 1714) his ambassador, Bothmer, presented to the privy council a list of 18 Lords Justices who were to act, purely ministerially, for him until he arrived. This set the political and constitutional tone of the reign, for they were in fact his cabinet. 14 were Whigs and 4 Hanover Tories. Sunderland and his father-in-law, Marlborough, who occasionally corresponded with his nephew Berwick at St. Germain, were omitted. One of the earliest events was a royal instruction to dismiss Bolingbroke as S. of State and Ormonde as Capt-Gen. While George regulated his absentee rule of Hanover, such matters were settled mainly between Bothmer and George's able secretary, Jean de Robethon. Seven weeks after his succession, he disembarked at

Greenwich with the Baroness Kielmansegge (one of his three mistresses), Robethon, his Hanoverian ministers Bernstorff and Goertz and a shipload of courtiers.

(3) The govt. was now progressively reorganised. The only Tory left was Nottingham as Lord President. Shrewsbury, the last Lord Treasurer, was replaced in Oct. by a commission led by Halifax and became Lord Chamberlain. The rest were Whigs, headed by Townshend as S. of State for the North, with his brother-in-law Walpole as Paymaster. Marlborough was honoured but not trusted; Sunderland sent to Ireland as Lord Lieut; but Marlborough's soldierly friend Stanhope became S. of State for the South. This important appointment was a surprise.

(4) Parliament, with its Tory majority, was dissolved on 5 Jan. 1715 and the general election gave the govt. a majority of about 150. As soon as it met, impeachments were launched against the Tories Bolingbroke, Ormonde, Oxford and Strafford for their part in the Utrecht negotiations. These, the last wholly political impeachments, were unnecessary since the defendants did not enjoy royal confidence. Strafford's case was abandoned because he did not matter. Oxford, detained safely in the Tower until July 1717, was eventually acquitted for want of prosecution. Bolingbroke and Ormonde fled to St. Germain and were attainted. Their flight enabled the Whigs to get rid of the remaining Tories, Carlisle, Nottingham and three of his relatives and to smear the Tories with Jacobitism for a generation. Hence effective political opposition in leading circles came from factions among the Whigs themselves; these were held together for a while by the Jacobite rebellion of 1715. Walpole moved up from the affluence of the Pay Office to be First Lord of the Treasury and Ch. of the Exchequer, offices then less powerful than they have since become. The Whigs further attempted to establish themselves, on the pretext that a general election was inopportune in the disturbed state of the country, by extending the life of parliaments from three to seven years. The Septennial Act received the Royal Assent in May 1716. Its practical effect was to transfer politically effective action away from the hustings to the House of Commons where the Whigs long had an advantage.

(5) The Jacobite rebellion, a foreign interference, emphasised the international isolation into which the country had drifted, and which Stanhope and George were determined to end. The Emperor and the Dutch were still furious at their betrayal at Utrecht. Spain and the Emperor both had their eyes on Italy, with Savoy standing by and great English commercial interests at risk. In the Northern war Sweden was interfering with the vital trade in iron ore and naval supplies (*see* BALTIC) and a rising Russia might do so too. The Hanoverian connection was now entangling Britain's monarch with Baltic and N. European mainland concerns.

(6) The day after George's coronation Stanhope, an old friend of the Emperor's, set off to The Hague and Vienna to settle Austro-Dutch disagreements about the Barrier fortresses (which the Dutch were to occupy as a condition of the transfer of Belgium to Austria) and to get onto good terms with both. It was helpful that the Emperor expected war with Turkey. In Nov. 1715, at the height of the Jacobite rebellion, Stanhope agreed the Dutch-Imperial Barrier Treaty which gave the Dutch eight of the fortresses. In Feb. 1716 he renewed the Anglo-Dutch T. of Guarantee. In Apr. the Turkish war broke out and in May (T. of Westminster) the Emperor guaranteed the Hanoverian succession in return for a British guarantee of his gains (mostly Belgian and Italian) at the Ts. of Utrecht and Baden. Two agreements (Dec. 1715 and May 1716) with Spain disposed of some of the difficulties in the commercial clauses of Utrecht; and next a squadron under Adm. Norris escorted the Baltic trading fleet against the Swedes. This vigorous diplomacy culminated in Nov. 1716 in the Triple Alliance with France and Holland (*see* HANOVER-7; JACOBITES-11-13).

(7) Stanhope's common sense purpose was European peace, and the Triple Alliance was its effective foundation and of Walpole's long later prosperity, for it drove a wedge between the two Bourbon powers and enabled Britain and France to co-operate against those who wished to disturb the Utrecht-Baden-Rastatt settlement. In the short term, however, the negotiations broke up the govt., for Sunderland had led George to think that Townshend and Walpole had been currying favour in his absence with the P. of Wales, and the treaty had had to be signed in haste because of the Czar's occupation of Mecklenburg. Townshend (who disagreed with the Alliance) was degraded to the Lord Lieutenancy of Ireland (Oct. 1716) and then dismissed (Apr. 1717): Devonshire, Methuen, Orford, Pulteney and Walpole resigned with him. The ministry was re-formed under Stanhope and Sunderland; whereupon Townshend and his friends paid ostentatious court to the P. of Wales after all. The latter, provoked by the King's arrangements for the christening of his first child, ill-temperedly insulted the new Lord Chamberlain, Newcastle (Nov. 1717) and was turned out of St. James's Palace. This began the identification of the Prince's new establishment at Leicester House with the cause of Opposition.

(8) The new administration was internationally successful, but domestically mistaken in its tactics. P. Eugene had beaten the Turks and taken Belgrade (Aug. 1717) but the Spaniards nevertheless hoped to profit by Austrian distractions. The Triple Alliance, however, made the despatch of a British fleet to the Mediterranean possible. The Austrians made the favourable P. of Passarowitz with the Turks in July 1718 and the Quadruple Alliance was signed in Aug. Nine days later Byng fell upon the Spanish Mediterranean armada at C. Passaro and destroyed it. Curiously enough the war began technically only with the British declaration in Dec. and the French in Jan., by which time an alliance at Vienna between the Emperor, Saxony and Poland – and Britain and Hanover – had imposed peace in the Baltic. Shortly afterwards the French invaded N. Spain and the Spaniards equipped an ineffectual Jacobite incursion into Scotland (Apr-June). These were the circumstances in which Stanhope and Sunderland tried, firstly to establish a measure of religious unity by repealing the Occasional Confirmity and Schism Acts of 1711 and 1714, and even by approaching the R. Catholics (who refused to co-operate) and secondly, by analogy with the Septennial Act, to fasten a Whig permanence upon Parliament, by means of the Peerage Bill. In all these proposals they met Walpole's ingenious and sometimes apparently wayward opposition. In truth Walpole was determined to return to office: if he could not "join 'em" he would "beat 'em". By his defeat of the Peerage Bill he forced himself back into office (June 1720). By this time peace had been made with Spain (Feb. 1720) and war in the E. Baltic had ended with the Ts. of Stockholm (Feb.) and Fredricksborg (July).

(9) A new domestic excitement supervened. This was the speculation mania known as the South Sea Bubble (*see* SOUTH SEA CO.). This affair began in Jan. 1720. Walpole himself invested in South Sea stock but sold out at a loss in the summer. The collapse came in Sept. when the stock (which had reached a June peak of 1000) fell from 780 to 180. He tried but failed to bring in the Bank of England to support the South Sea Co. and then went off to his Norfolk estates. These tactics dissociated him from those who were being held responsible, while advertising his efforts to improve the position. By mid-Oct. he was thought to be the only person who might cope with the crisis. His scheme, drafted by Robert Jacombe his banker, was accepted by the South Sea and East India Cos., the Bank of England and Parliament. This

general approval restored confidence without the scheme having to be put into effect. It focused popularity upon Walpole at a moment when other ministers' images, save Stanhope's, were tarnished. Walpole could not attain his ambitions without crown support; as many of the chief offenders seemed to be close to the throne he declined to proceed against them – and besides, his own speculations might have come to light in the process. Early in 1721, however, he was lucky. Stanhope and both Craggs suddenly died. The administration had to be reconstructed anyhow. Sunderland, as author of the South Sea Scheme, could hardly retain the headship of the govt. Aislabie, also implicated, had resigned as Chanc. of the Exchequer; he was expelled from the Commons. Power simply fell into Walpole's hands, but it was not immediately absolute. Sunderland, a Groom of the Stole, retained the King's ear and control of the Secret Service Money, until he too suddenly died in Apr. 1722. Marlborough followed him in June.

(10) Nature, which by removing his rivals had given Walpole a pre-eminence, was supplemented by the Jacobites, who chose 1722 for one of their periodical conspiracies. Foreign support for this, the Atterbury affair, was compromised by Stanhope's Triple Alliance (1716) while Walpole's energetic and successful reactions raised his standing with the King. Walpole, however, believed that such commotions were best prevented by prosperity and contentment based upon a sound economy and rational public finance. This introspective or parochial policy presupposed peace, which Stanhope had secured: but already in 1723 the foundations of Stanhope's treaty system were showing cracks which Walpole took too little trouble to repair. Its stability depended upon the survival of the French Regent Orleans and his minister, Card. Dubois, and the presence in the British govt. of Stanhope's pupil Carteret as Sec. of State. In 1723 Orleans and Dubois both died. Walpole wanted to be rid of Carteret, who was the heir to Sunderland's political faction, and now saw no reason to keep him. An intrigue extruded him from Whitehall and sent him to Dublin as Lord Lieut. Foreign policy was put into the hands of Townshend, Walpole's much less able brother-in-law, while Newcastle took Carteret's place as Sec. of State (Apr. 1724). The govt. was now fully subservient to its leading minister.

(11) Walpole began his financial reforms (*see* WALPOLE'S FINANCIAL REFORMS) in 1723. It was typical of his commercialism that he was ready to provoke trouble over the Austrian East India Co., established at Ostend in 1722. The Emperor, freed from the Turkish war by the P. of Passarowitz, was also dragging his feet over the admission of the Spanish claimant, Don Carlos, to Parma and Tuscany. Townshend, always suspicious of Austria, started to organise a league. The first step had been the T. of Charlottenburg (Oct. 1723), a defensive military alliance with Prussia. At the diplomatic congress of Cambrai (Jan-July 1724) Anglo-French mediation between Austria and Spain seemed to achieve nothing: the Spaniards then tried secret negotiations with Vienna, through Ripperda, a renegade Dutch diplomat. He was to secure imperial agreement to Spanish garrisons in the Italian duchies and the marriage of Don Carlos and Don Philip to two Archduchesses. The Hofburg was not encouraging, but in Mar. 1725 the new French regent, the D. of Bourbon, clumsily insulted the Spanish King: Louis XV had long been affianced to a child Infanta who was being brought up at Versailles. Fearing that Louis XV, now marriageable, might die childless leaving the throne to the rival Orléans family, Bourbon suddenly announced that the Infanta would be sent back so that another bride could be found. The furious Spaniards broke off diplomatic relations and sought agreement with Austria at any price. By the end of Apr. accordingly Ripperda had signed three treaties. By the first (public) agreement

Spain guaranteed the Pragmatic Sanction; by the second the Emperor agreed to use his good offices (but not to fight) to get Minorca and Gibraltar back for Spain and by the third Spain conceded trading privileges and support for the Ostend Co. The nature of the two last was known only roughly, but Ripperda let it be thought that there were clauses in support of the Pretender.

(12) The French saw in these treaties a repetition of the old Austro-Spanish encirclement: Walpole a threat to British trading privileges with the Spanish possessions and especially interference with the *Asiento*. He probably found the rumoured Jacobite clauses useful rather than dangerous. Thus in Sept. 1725 Townshend was able to bring the French into his Prussian alliance (T. of Hanover): the three powers agreeing, in terms as vague as Ripperda's, to resist attempts on each other's possessions, including Minorca and Gibraltar, the activities of the Ostend Co. and the persecutions of German protestants; and to support the Prussian succession in Jülich and Berg. In reply, by a second series of Vienna Treaties (Nov. 1725), Austrian support on Gibraltar and Minorca was more sharply defined and a marriage between Don Carlos and Maria Theresa agreed, in return for renewed Spanish support for the Ostend Co. The two international factions now started to gather adherents. In Mar. 1728 the Hanover powers secured Hessian troops; in Aug. the accession of the Dutch. In the same Aug. the Emperor secured Russia and this led in Oct. to the defection of Prussia from Hanover to Vienna. Early in 1727 Sweden and Denmark sided with Hanover; the three ecclesiastical electorates, Bavaria and Wolfenbüttel with Vienna.

(13) Since May 1726 when Ripperda, dismissed by Spain, took refuge with the British ambassador, the exact nature of the Vienna accords had been known to the govt., which had already mobilised the fleet. Squadrons went to the W. Indies and the Spanish coast to intercept the American bullion without which the Austro-Spanish alliance could not finance its allies. The Spaniards promptly besieged Gibraltar (Feb. 1727). In the previous June, however, there had been a palace revolution in France: Louis XV had dismissed Bourbon and appointed his tutor, Card. Fleury who, at 73, still possessed much energy, as his chief minister and made the anti-English Chauvelin his foreign sec. English naval pressure and the changed atmosphere at Versailles had their effect. The Vienna powers were soon inclined towards peace. A French initiative brought it about. By the Preliminaries of 31 May 1727 the Emperor ended the Ostend trade, theoretically for seven years, and suspended the Ostend Co. The timing deprived Britain of too resounding a victory while achieving Walpole's object. It also rescued Walpole from Commons criticism of the Hanover treaty and of the generally anti-Austrian slant of Townshend's policy with which he was coming to disagree himself. Moreover, Townshend had neglected Portugal and annoyed the Russians. Walpole was therefore ready to accept the French peace. George I died a fortnight later in Germany.

GEORGE II (1683-1760) D. of CAMBRIDGE (1706), P. of WALES (1714), King (1727) *s.* of George I **(1)** *m.* the able and charming Charlotte CAROLINE (1683-1737) of Brandenburg-Ansbach in 1705 and fought with distinction at Oudenarde (1708). He was a friend of the 2nd D. of Argyll; Henrietta Howard became his mistress in 1715 but she and Caroline got on well enough.

(2) He acted as Guardian of the Realm during his father's first absence in Hanover (1716), but Sunderland told George I that his son was becoming popular and that Townshend and Walpole were intriguing with him. The usual feud between Guelph fathers and sons flared up and in 1717 the Prince became and thereafter remained a focus for dissident whig opposition. Turned out of St. James's in 1718 he set up his own court at Leicester House (formerly in Leicester Sq.). Then the govt. whigs, fearing the effect of his political leanings after his accession, introduced the Peerage Bill to cut down his future patronage. Walpole got the Commons to reject it. Thereupon the King deprived him of the custody of his children.

(3) In 1720 Walpole partially reconciled them as a preliminary to his own rise to office and thereafter became his father's minister, much to the Prince's annoyance. The Princess saw it otherwise and she and Walpole, despite differing tastes, remained in contact and friendship. This was to have far reaching consequences.

(4) While Caroline cultivated statesmen and savants George, perhaps in reaction against his alarming father, cultivated nonentities. Walpole, however, continued to rise and, since most of the ablest whigs were in the govt., the Prince was not fully in the political mainstream. This became obvious when George I died unexpectedly near Osnabrück. The new King in London began this most important reign by asking one of his nonentities, Sir Spencer Compton, to form the govt. The task was beyond Sir Spencer but, advised by Caroline, Walpole let him try and took over when he had failed. George was not, however, without character; he insisted on personal decisions in military and household appointments, the signature of death warrants and the creation of peerages and he had a strong influence on foreign policy; but Walpole managed him through Caroline, who usually induced him to believe that their policy was really his idea.

(5) She was, however, less successful in controlling Walpole who also had (apart from the Queen herself) a *penchant* for the second rate. Frederick, the new P. of Wales, set up his court at Leicester House in 1728, had the customary quarrel with his father and became the focus of a growing whig opposition, led by the Pulteneys and Sir Wm. Wyndham and inspired by the ex-Jacobite Bolingbroke. Bolingbroke had been excluded from Parliament, but his brilliant literary friends (whom he shared with Henrietta Howard at Twickenham) could speak powerfully and wittily for him. He was joined, as time went on, by the abler whigs whom Walpole drove from office. Carteret had already gone to Ireland in 1724; Macclesfield, Cadogan and Roxburgh had resigned in 1725; but in 1730, when Townshend retired to Norfolk, Carteret came back to Uxbridge, which his mother, the formidable Lady Granville, as well as Sarah, the great Marlborough's widow, had long frequented. There were to be further accessions.

(6) The T. of the Prado (Mar. 1728) ended the short Spanish War begun in the previous reign. It also foreshadowed disagreement between Walpole and Townshend. Austrian diplomacy was centred upon the Pragmatic Sanction of 1722, guaranteed *inter alia* by Prussia in Dec. 1728. Townshend's anti-Austrian bias led him to negotiate the T. of Seville (Nov. 1729) whereby Spain restored British trading privileges in return for support in a military occupation of Tuscany and Parma. France and Holland also joined this agreement. The treaty infringed imperial rights: the emperor would admit the troops only if the Seville powers guaranteed the Pragmatic Sanction, which the French refused. The Spaniards thereupon denounced the treaty. From the English point of view the real issue was whether the French were likely, under Fleury and Chauvelin, to become so hostile to Britain that Austria would be needed as a counterpoise. Townshend thought not. Walpole disagreed. In May 1730 Townshend resigned and was succeeded by the complaisant Lord Harrington (*see* STANHOPE, HARRINGTON-1). Walpole, now in charge of foreign policy, was immediately faced with a crisis: in Jan. 1731 with the extinction of the Farnese line in Parma, the Spanish queen's rights became vested. The essential decision had to be made. In another T. of

Vienna (Mar. 1731) Austria and Britain guaranteed each other's possessions; the Emperor undertook to abolish the suspended Ostend Co. and admit the Spanish garrisons. In return Britain, and eventually Holland, guaranteed the Pragmatic Sanction. In Oct. an Anglo-Spanish squadron convoyed the troops to Italy; in Dec. Don Carlos arrived there and in Jan. 1732 the German states other than Bavaria, the Palatinate and Saxony, guaranteed the Pragmatic as well.

(7) The Treaty, in expressing a retreat from Stanhope's policy of 1717, recognised the reality of French estrangement and a return to the policy of William III. Friction was growing. The French had not properly demilitarised Dunkirk or their Canadian establishments. They were touching a sensitive spot by recruiting troops in Ireland. There were disputes about the ownership of certain W. Indian islands and the activities of British traders there. Moreover the French were in fact contemplating an indirect aggression against Austria while Spain, having no more to gain from the British connection, was open to offers. All the same Walpole hoped that the French could be bluffed into quiescence while he, as a practical man of business, got on with his domestic administration and fiscal reforms (see WALPOLE'S EXCISE SCHEME).

(8) The internal effect was to strengthen the Uxbridge and Leicester House opposition, which was joined by the E. of Chesterfield, the D. of Bolton, Vist. Cobham (see TEMPLE) with his aggressive Boy Patriot relatives the Grevilles, and George Littleton and with the rising young William Pitt. The feeling was already abroad that however prosperous the home policy might make the country, a weak foreign policy might compromise the advantages. Wit, youth and fashion were deserting the govt. with its increasingly pompous and boring head. They launched an unscrupulous and noisy appeal to public prejudice against excisemen which, in defeating the excise scheme, ultimately triumphed over interest and common sense.

(9) The French now called Walpole's bluff. In 1733 a Polish constitutional dispute developed into the War of the Polish Succession, in which Austria and Russia supported Augustus III of Saxony, the French Louis XV's father-in-law Stanislas Leszczinski. In Nov. the Franco-Spanish alliance, known as the first Family Compact, was signed at the Escorial. French troops entered Italy with Savoyard help. Spanish troops from Tuscany moved upon Habsburg Naples. The hard pressed Emperor, with the Turks at his back, called for British and Dutch aid under the T. of Vienna. George II wanted to honour the treaty. Walpole and Caroline overbore him in the interest of trade. Italy was overrun, while Walpole boasted that not an English life nor an English shilling had been spent in the war. In the general election of 1734 he was able to assert his authority over the governmental machine by manipulating a brilliant success, despite his defeat in the previous year on the Excise Bill. The Uxbridge camarilla broke up. Meantime, however, Poland, the Austrian objective, slipped into Russian control. Britain had helplessly to watch the French redraw the European map (P. of Vienna 1735): the betrayed and furious Emperor, in his weakened condition, married the Archduchess Maria Theresa to Francis of Lorraine, now heir of Tuscany. He also faced a renewed and disastrous Turkish War (Apr. 1736) while, worse still, the French secured commercial and political capitulations with the Turks. For this Francis' succession in Tuscany (1737) was not much consolation. France politically supreme on the continent, seemed on the way to wresting by diplomacy the very commercial advantages which Walpole's policies were supposed to safeguard.

(10) The solid base of English development was being laid, little noticed at this time. The stocking frame, invented in 1589, was in common use in the Midlands by 1727. The Derwent silk industry was flourishing by 1730.

The flying shuttle, invented in 1733, raised woollen cloth production faster than spinners could make yarn for it. Cotton weaving and printing were developing at Manchester. Agriculture was booming, partly because Townshend and Walpole, as practical landowners were popularising the four-course rotation (barley, clover, wheat, turnips) already practised in Norfolk since the 1670s. It made the land more productive and, through winter feeding, hugely increased the stock and improved the quality of cattle. The population was rising, yet wheat could be exported. The harbours teemed with ships: merchantmen were small, but 2000 were counted on one day at the Pool of London in 1726. This represented a coastwise trade, for example in coal from Newcastle, a Baltic trade (see BALTIC), a European trade in wines, luxuries and alum, an oriental trade and the colonial produce of furs, sugar, tobacco, indigo and logwood and the vastly profitable triangular enterprises from Bristol and Liverpool with knickknacks to W. Africa, thence with slaves to the Caribbean and so back home with rum and sugar. The upsurge of energy inspired concomitant inventions. The mariners' compass had long been in use, but in 1729 Hall invented the acromatic lens, in 1731 Harley the navigational quadrant, the forerunner of the sextant and in 1736 came Harrison's chronometer. The new accuracy of navigation encouraged greater investment, bigger ships and lower insurance. The prospect of profits, especially on the Spanish Main, was the true Eldorado.

(11) The vast profits, rising to upwards of a 1000% on single lucky voyages and realised mostly in Spanish bullion, generated an aggressive commercialism which was too much not only for the Spanish colonial authorities but for Walpole. Spanish Law restricted the profits of the W. Indian trade to Castille, of the Italian trade to Aragon. The English, abetted by local merchants, cheerfully ignored these rules. The *Asiento* was a constant source of dispute. The Spaniards obstructed and the South Sea Co. abused the right to send a ship to the fairs of Vera Cruz and Cartagena. English traders were often piratical: the Spanish authorities retaliated by licensing privateer patrols (*guarda costas*) who were no better. Seaborne disorder, though endemic in Spanish waters, was apt to be exaggerated by the opposition. Between 1713 and 1731 the Spanish took, in fact, rather less than one ship per month. Walpole regarded such losses as minor overheads in a huge business, to be settled by negotiation and, anyhow, the long neglected forces were in no condition to fight. Moreover, Spain was allied with a triumphant France, only too likely to be attracted into a conflict, and the Spaniards, still resenting the British hold on Gibraltar and Minorca were themselves in an aggressive mood.

(12) Walpole's crumbling system now received a decisive blow. Q. Caroline had four times acted as Guardian of the Realm, especially during George's Hanoverian visit of nearly a year in 1736. In 1737 she died imploring George to marry again. His celebrated reply 'j'aurai des maitresses" was a mark of his odd but passionate relationship with her. Without her Walpole could no longer influence his antipathetic master effectively and, besides, the minister's vigour was being eroded by age while the King had found, in the attractive Countess Walmoden (Lady Yarmouth from 1738) another congenial but unpolitical bedmate. Thus it happened that the War of Jenkins's Ear arose because Walpole no longer had the support in palace or parliament with which to resist the public clamour (see PARDO CONVENTION), but the circumstances could hardly have been worse. France was increasingly menacing. A Franco-Prussian partition treaty of Jülich and Berg threatened Hanover (Apr. 1739). Under the pressure of French mediation, the Austrians had to give up Serbia and Craiova to the Turks (T. of Belgrade Sept. 1739), a

loss for which they legitimately blamed the treacherous British. The War had been in progress for some time in the Caribbean when it was declared in Oct. Britain had neither allies nor friends, nor a proper army nor an efficient fleet (*see* WARS OF 1739-48).

(13) George had military, but not naval, interests and experience and his people wanted naval, he military, success. Walpole's incompetent war direction irritated him and them in similarly divergent ways, by threatening his Electorate and their trade. Walpole fell in Feb. 1742. The King spent much time in Germany between 1740 and 1744 which, save when he commanded the victorious army at Dettingen (June 1743) did not add to his popularity. He was thus isolated from the political public by his continental interests and from the political leadership by his contempt for their incompetence. Only Carteret, whom he admired, was able, with George's advice, to conduct affairs so as to please both King and public; but Carteret could not manage the politicians and they turned him out when, in 1745, the Revolution was threatened by the Jacobites.

(14) Disagreement on grand strategy accounted mainly for George's antipathy to the rising Wm. Pitt. Pitt grasped the implications of sea power. His political method was publicly to accuse the King of sacrificing Britain's interests to Hanover's. He had denounced Carteret's arrangement for taking Hanoverian troops into British pay as a *quid pro quo* for Hanoverian re-entry into the war in 1742. The arrangement was a normal one distinguished only through the two countries sharing the same monarch. George naturally resented being portrayed as a traitor to one of them. Pitt, as the outcome showed, was right on the strategic issue but his tactless factionalism did not help the conduct of the war, at a time when the fleet was in no condition to fulful his vision. Moreover it delayed his own rise to power.

(15) There were important temperamental antipathies: George with his mistresses and love of money contrasted with Pitt's sanctimonious popular romanticism. A paymaster-general who refused the high perquisites of the office deserved to succeed in a popular appeal; but the King equally had cause to dislike the demagoguery involved. Moreover, by the time the Pelhams forced Pitt on the King (Feb. 1746) many of the deficiencies in naval strength had been made good and the war was already slackening. The opening phase of Pitt's career as a leading minister was occupied by a dying war and a peace so uninspiring that 'as silly as the peace' (*bête comme la paix*) was long a French proverbial expression. (Preliminaries and P. of Aix-la-Chapelle Apr. and Oct. 1748, supplemented by the Anglo-Spanish commercial T. of Aquisgran Oct. 1749.)

(16) The peace, moreover, was a truce enforceable only in Europe. The retrocession of Louisbourg had caused little trouble in America because, with British command of the seas, the colonists knew that they could retake it. The final defeat of Jacobitism and the subjugation of the highlands had made the base of English economic and naval aggression much less vulnerable. If French Canadian governors tried to subvert the largely French population of Nova Scotia, the British retaliated locally by building Halifax and Fort Lawrence (1748-9). British energy threatened the Bourbon powers at other points too. The Ohio Co. founded in Virginia and Maryland in 1748 was chartered in 1749. Its fur traders and land speculators were bound to collide with French interests in the Mississippi. In the south the Georgians had already fought the Florida Spaniards. In 1750 the *Asiento* and the annual ship to the fairs at Vera Cruz and Cartagena were abandoned in exchange for £100,000 and the renewal of trading privileges in the Spanish empire, but in practice British smuggling to the Spanish Main was more lucrative and, to the Spaniards, more damaging. In India, by the retrocession of Madras (in exchange for

Louisbourg) the French lost face with the native rulers of the Deccan but Dupleix, the French gov. and Bussy, his chief subordinate, were vigorous and determined. In 1749 they replaced the pro-British Mohammed Ali Subadar of the Carnatic, by Chanda Sahib, their own nominee, from whom they received cessions around Pondicherry. In 1750 they inserted another nominee Mozafar Jang and then his uncle Salabat Jang, in the subadarship of the Deccan. The ships of the rival companies carried on covert and sometimes open hostilities in the Indian and the African seas. Early in 1751 Bussy started to train a native army in Hyderabad. Thus military action, notwithstanding the peace, was unavoidable. Mohammed Ali was still holding out at Trichinopoly. The new gov. at Madras, Thos. Saunders, sent Robert Clive against Arcot, the capital of the Carnatic. He took it and held it and, by 1752, he had restored Mohammed Ali. The peacetime company war in India was soon paralleled by American hostilities. In 1753 the French built Fort Duquesne (later Pittsburgh) to check the British advance from the Alleghenies into the Ohio. In May 1754 a Col. Washington captured the place and was then himself captured there. In the meantime the French govt. had defaulted on its loans and their E. India Co. could not afford Dupleix's aggressive policies and recalled him. Henceforth the French had to maintain their colonial influence upon local resources.

(17) The course of the Pelham govt. thus continued that of Walpole's a generation earlier: largely uncontrollable overseas, commercial aggression was accompanied by successful financial management, an enlightened domestic policy (such as Hardwicke's Marriage Act 1753) and a dangerous weakening of the forces. The difference was that the Pelhams, like everyone else, expected a European war sooner or later and tried to construct their diplomacy to win rather than to prevent it. The drift was, however, slowed down by the obsolescence of established diplomatic habits. The Pelhams, particularly the D. of Newcastle, saw the old Triple Alliance with Holland and Austria as the best way to bridle France and they sought to strengthen it by collateral subsidies to German electors to secure votes for a Habsburg King of the Romans. The whole concept was a mistake, for the other allies now had different enemies. The Austrians wanted to fight Prussia for Silesia; the Dutch did not want to fight the French but had running quarrels with the Austrians about military and commercial rights in Belgium. The electoral subsidy treaties broke in 1750 against Prussian hostility, since Frederick the Great was trying to manoeuvre non-German great powers out of Germany. Hanover was thus at risk and, since nobody in England was willing to see George lose his electorate for a primarily English quarrel, Newcastle had to busy himself yet again with lesser German alliances, which were equally likely to fall before Prussian disapproval. Thus the only remaining available protection for Hanover was Prussia.

(18) One of the Bourbon powers, Spain, had begun to feel the change as early as 1751, when the P. of Wales died and the administration was remodelled to take in Granville as Lord President. In the Austro-Spanish T. of Aranjuez (June 1752) the two powers had guaranteed each other's possessions. Kaunitz, the new Austrian minister, was freeing the Italian front for the contemplated northern war. Thereupon George secured Bavarian and Saxon guarantees for Hanover. In Mar. 1754 the more important partner in the Pelham govt., Henry Pelham, died and his brother Newcastle had to reconstruct the govt. It was essential to take in or promote a House of Commons man, but the King's dislike of Pitt left Newcastle with only the initial choice of William Murray, the Sol-Gen., or Henry Fox, the most persuasive debater of his time. Murray hoped to be C.J. of the King's Bench and would accept only the (lucrative)

Attorney-Generalship on the way. Newcastle offered a Secretaryship of State with the leadership, but not the "management" of the Commons to Fox, who refused it. As a result Sir Thos. Robinson, an able diplomat but no orator, was given the post while Henry Legge, a Pittite, became Ch. of the Exchequer. The great Anson was First Lord of the Admiralty.

(19) In 1753 Bussy in Hyderabad had secured the financial independence of his army by the *jagir* of the Four Northern Circars of the Deccan. By 1755 he was threatening the British establishments there, even though in Dec. 1754 Godeheu, Dupleix's successor, had abandoned the French gains in the Carnatic. In America Gen. Braddock's force, sent to retake Fort Duquesne, was ambushed on the Monongahela (July 1755), and at sea Boscawen and Hawke were given no proper instructions about the various French convoys. As a result Boscawen captured two small ships on the way to America but missed the rest, and Hawke, having cruised off Brest from July to Dec., had to come into port for a long overdue refit and let a French fleet in. The reason for the ineffectual direction was that Newcastle was still hoping for alliances before declaring war. He got 6000 Hessians by a subsidy and in Sept. 1755, partly to preserve the vital Baltic trade and partly to restrain Prussia, he concluded a Russian treaty. The Czarina Elizabeth was to receive £100,000 a year in time of peace; in return she would station 55,000 men and 50 galleys on the frontier of Polish Courland (150 miles from E. Prussia). These would be set in motion if Britain or her allies were attacked and Britain would then pay £500,000 a year for the duration of the war.

(20) Both Fox and Pitt resented the politically incompetent Robinson; and the deplorable military events of 1754 forced Newcastle to reshuffle his govt. again. This time he secured Fox with a place in the outer cabinet, because he would be more acceptable at court than Pitt (Dec. 1754). Throughout the depressing year 1755 Pitt's demands for a change of policy and for control of it grew more pressing and popular. Newcastle responded by promoting Fox to a Secretaryship of State, for it was necessary to have a competent leader in the Commons (Sept.). When Parliament met in Nov. Pitt withered the govt. with a blast of invective. He was dismissed from the Pay Office and, a free man, became even more dangerous. He was appealing to the public against the system.

(21) The Russian treaty precipitated the so-called *Renversement des Alliances,* already partly effected in 1752 by the T. of Aranjuez and the Saxon and Bavarian guarantees. Frederick the Great, like every Prussian feared the attentions of the savage Muscovite and proposed an Anglo-Prussian treaty of mutual guarantee. This was signed at Westminster in Jan. 1756. Deprived of their only important German ally the French, who were planning an attack on Minorca, approached Vienna. Kaunitz, who had long been preparing Maria Theresa for this, made the Alliance of Versailles (May 1756) but the French had already put their own plans into action. They invested Port Mahon in Apr. and repulsed Byng's languid attempt at relief in May. Oswego, the only British stronghold on the American Great Lakes, fell and in June Minorca was lost. Pitt and his friends Legge, the Townshends and George Grenville, subjected the govt. to a flood of unanswerable criticism, mainly for public consumption. Ministers became alarmed at the clamour and decided to sacrifice Byng. Newcastle became panicstricken. Fox avoided answering the attacks in the Commons. Murray insisted on the Chief Justiceship of the King's Bench and left Parliament. In Oct. 1756 Fox resigned and Newcastle had to make a deal with Pitt.

(22) The King was still hostile to Pitt, who was reduced to communicating with him through the Countess of Yarmouth. He would neither work with

Newcastle nor take responsibility for his measures. It took a month for him to have his way. His first ministry, with the 4th D. of Devonshire replacing Newcastle and Temple at the Admiralty, still included Grenville as acceptable to the King and Holderness as the other S. of State. It lasted only four months, for the regular ministerial M.P.s would not support it in the absence of royal favour, the old whigs supported Newcastle, and Cumberland intrigued with Fox. Cumberland in fact brought it to an end by refusing to take up his Hanoverian command as long as Pitt headed the govt. and so in Apr. 1757 George dismissed Pitt. There followed nearly three months of political manoeuvring, during which the war had to be fought without an effective govt. In the end there was a four-sided compromise. The septuagenarian King had to accept Pitt as head of the ministry, but got back Newcastle as a coadjutor. Newcastle became the political manager, but subject to Pitt's policy leadership in the cabinet and parliament. Fox had to accept lucrative subordination at the Pay Office; and the new Leicester House clique headed by the M. of Bute, in return for lesser pickings, helped to win over the ministerial regulars. Pitt's power, not quite independent of the crown, was founded upon an upsurge of national sentiment and in one sense Cumberland's defeat at Hastenbeck and surrender at Klosterseven, by discrediting that prince with his ageing father, helped Pitt to settle into the saddle. The disasters which could be ascribed to previous incompetence continued to crowd in upon the new govt. and it was Frederick the Great, not Pitt, who, by the remarkable victories at Rossbach (Nov. 1757) and Leuthen (Dec.) turned the tide. All the same the govt. could now lead the nation, because it combined a unity of purpose with an inspired strategic insight and took the home and colonial public into its confidence. This represented a real change in the nature of govt.

(23) Pitt, having won over, or at least placated the King, could now afford to quarrel with Leicester House, where the P. of Wales and Bute (whom Pitt openly despised) were trying to organise an ill-timed peace party. By 1759, the *Annus Mirabilis,* the alliance had broken up on largely personal factors; but with news of victory pouring in from all quarters the Prince and Bute seemed unimportant. Yet suddenly and, despite his age, unexpectedly, the King died (Oct. 1760). The insignificant Bute suddenly rose to the status of a problem. *See also* SEVEN YEARS' WAR-1 to 10.

GEORGE III (WILLIAM FREDERICK) (1738-1820) P. of WALES (1751) King (1760) *s.* of FREDERICK, P. of Wales, (1) was dominated until 1756 by his unpopular mother, P. Augusta of Saxe Gotha, and then by the priggish and pacific 3rd E. of Bute, who introduced him to the works of Blackstone and Bolingbroke. He never visited Hanover and regarded himself as very English, but in 1761 he married P. Charlotte-Sophia from the nearby duchy of Mecklenburg-Strelitz.

(2) He disliked the corruption of his grandfather's reign and initially misunderstood the manipulations which kept govts. together. His accession during the expensive, if successful, Seven Years' War was expected to produce ministerial changes and he began with a proclamation against immorality. By May 1762 the disagreement of Newcastle, Bute and George with Pitt's policy of further war and expense drove Pitt from office. He was followed by the D. of Newcastle when Grenville and the Treasury board opposed further subsidies to Prussia. This made way for Bute. At this the political scene, unstable since 1754, degenerated further. No statesman of eminence could stand Newcastle and Newcastle could not work for long with anyone who had authority in the House of Commons. The country needed a royal conciliator. George was no such thing and Bute was no leader.

(3) Hence a ministry had to be cobbled together by Newcastle's methods from men of less talent. Henry Fox managed the Commons. Bute mismanaged and then wound up the war. The P. of Paris (1763) was heavily criticised for the supposed insufficiency of gains which it registered. Then Bute found that it was unexpectedly hard to taper off war costs: a new cider excise to meet the deficit caused indignation and riots. He tried to improve the govt's image by subsidising the *Briton,* a ministerial newspaper, and provoked Lord Temple's adherent, John Wilkes, into the savage and effective attacks on the govt. in the *North Briton* and the *Monitor.* Bute lost his nerve and resigned (Apr. 1763). Fox went to the Lords as Lord Holland and the bullying George Grenville (q.v.) succeeded Bute. He insisted on exclusive disposal of patronage and control of George's contacts. He, with Halifax, Sandwich, Egmont and Northington, took most of the major decisions, according peremptory treatment to the King. Their supremacy was, however, more apparent than real, for they had to cope with John Wilkes, whose celebrated or notorious *North Briton No 45* appeared just as Grenville took office. The govt. unwisely issued a general warrant. Spectacularly defeated by Wilkes in a court action (*see* WILKES V WOOD) the govt. narrowly averted an opposition resolution condemning general warrants. The effect was to drive Grenville and the King together.

(4) They had common ground in the need to reduce home taxation. Grenville sought to make every separate account balance by rigid economy, the exploitation of publicly inoffensive sources of funds and better tax-collection. The army was reduced to a mere *cadre,* the navy laid up, European subsidy treaties and allies abandoned. The Americans began to agitate at a time when Britain was friendless and ill-armed and yet Grenville wished to take a firm stand against France and Spain, who were preparing for revenge. The King appreciated the internal contradictions of the policy, but Grenville continued to bully. George now had a melancholic illness foreshadowing his later porphyriac seizures.

(5) When he recovered he wanted to set up a council of regency in case of his early death. To avoid a parliamentary scandal he agreed to a formula excluding his lascivious mother; but two followers of Bute moved, with opposition applause, to restore her. Ministers left the King, who had done it to please them, in the lurch. It seemed that the house understood his interests better than his ministers, for Grenville now chose to make even greater demands. Bute's brother-in-law Stuart MacKenzie was to be dismissed; Northumberland was to be superseded by Weymouth as Lord Lieut. in Ireland and Granby was to replace the King's uncle Cumberland as C-in-C. Granby decently refused the promotion, but George 'for the good of his people' (i.e. to gain time) accepted the rest (June 1765).

(6) The King now transformed the situation by asking Cumberland to engineer a new less domineering ministry acceptable to parliament. The Duke advised a return to the Pitt-Newcastle combination. Pitt insisted on office for his brother-in-law, Lord Temple, who wanted some independence by getting Grenville's support. Since Grenville could not accept Pitt's policy and neither the King nor Cumberland wanted him, Temple and consequently Pitt refused office. The result was a short, frail ministry of Newcastle's less experienced friends led by the young M. of Rockingham (July 1765).

(7) George refused to patch it up and, with the appearance of the non-party known as the King's Friends, was privately advised by Bute to call upon Pitt and Bute to arouse patriotic feeling. George knew, as apparently Bute did not, that Pitt would allow no dilution to his power. He became prime minister as E. of Chatham and Lord Privy Seal, taking over Grafton and Conway and Bute's friend Lord Shelburne. Cumberland being dead, Granby became C-in-C. Pitt's tactical purpose was to break up the opposing groups and attach fragments of each to himself. In this he failed. Moreover his policy of friendship with Prussia and the Americans failed too, for lack of co-operation. Disappointed at home and abroad, the great leader took refuge in nervous prostration and a darkened room in Hampstead (Apr. 1767). Ministers struggled on, uncoordinated, with a vacuum at the centre, unsuccessfully seeking support from Rockingham. In Sept. 1767 Chas. Townsend, the Ch. of the Exchequer, died and in Nov. Chatham at last resigned. Grafton, as First Lord of the Treasury, stayed on as head of the ministry. He appointed Lord North as Ch. of the Exchequer (Nov. 1768).

(8) With the ablest politicians dead, mad or in opposition, the Grafton ministry, harried by John Wilkes, wrestled with the gathering discontent of the Americans. They, especially Massachusetts, were now denying parliament's right to tax them, i.e. they disputed Rockingham's declaratory act and the hitherto undisputed right to regulate trade by customs duties, especially Chas. Townsend's. Grafton and Camden persuaded their less liberal colleagues to repeal these, save the Tea Duty which was to be symbolically retained. Hillsborough, the responsible S. of State, circulated the decision to colonial governors in harsh terms. Since the cabinet had agreed a conciliatory wording, Camden prepared to resign. Grafton, however, was inhibited because the public might think that he was running away from the flood of petitions and abuse generated by Wilkes' come-back and the Middlesex election. At the same time he was involved in the controversies of the Nullum Tempus Bill and subjected to Junius' informed invective. In Jan. 1770 Camden attacked his colleagues and was dismissed from the Woolsack. Philip Yorke was pressured into replacing him but died suddenly. This ended Grafton's tenure. He was replaced by general consent by Lord North. *See also* AMERICAN REBELLION-10 *et seq.*

(9) North's equanimity, application to the business of the hour and common sense gave England the pacifier she had lacked since 1760. Moreover, though he continued to neglect the Navy, he was a good financial administrator. His achievement was at home and in relation to the HEIC, whose chaotic affairs he brought under some sort of control by the Regulating Act of 1773. It was his misfortune to have inherited the inflamed relationship with the Americans. The Boston "Massacre" (Mar. 1770) occurred only two months after he took office and his peaceful talents were unsuitable for suppressing a Transatlantic rebellion, especially after the European powers had intervened. There was, however, no real alternative to his govt. Consequently, when he fell (Mar. 1782), through losing the war, the second Rockingham ministry (Mar-July) and then the Shelburne cabinet (July 1782-Apr. 1783) could only negotiate and even then not definitely. In particular, Shelburne's settlement, involving large territorial abandonments was meant to be complemented by free trade agreements with the U.S.A. and France as yet to be negotiated. At these, Shelburne would only hint. The Commons resented the cessions and preferred protectionism. Chas. James Fox and North united to overthrow him (Feb. 1783). The King, like everyone else, regarded this union of dissimilars as unnatural and refused for six weeks to send for the D. of Portland, its nominal head. In the end he had to give way and the new govt. had enough time to ratify the peace.

(10) North's Regulating Act had imperfections which the embittered disputes of Indian statesmen rendered intolerable. Fox introduced a bill to concentrate the HEIC's policy in the hands of permanent Commissioners appointed by the crown; Burke another to subordinate the authorities in India to the Commission. The proposals were attacked from many sides as subversive of the

constitution, since they would vastly increase royal, and Fox's, patronage, yet Fox's followers, who had voted for Dunning's resolution (q.v.), were now proposing to remedy their colleague North's legislation by increasing royal power. Dundas persuaded the younger Pitt, now 24, to make himself available for office. Robinson calculated the effects of a change in the Commons and in a general election and the results were passed to the King. It would be feasible to dismiss the Coalition. The bill having passed the Commons, the Lords were told through Temple that the King would regard those who voted for it as his enemies. The Lords rejected the bill, George dismissed Portland and sent for Pitt.

(11) Fox's friend still had a Commons majority of over 100. He induced the House to resolve that if parliament were dissolved it would be criminal to attempt to raise supplies. They then postponed the annual Mutiny Bill. This revolutionary challenge betrayed a sense of insecurity, since Fox ought to have had confidence in a general election. His majority began to fall. A new India Bill was thrown out by a majority of 8. Policy deadlock was causing alarm. Pitt and Portland were urged to come together. Pitt expressed willingness; Portland and Fox demanded his resignation first. This he refused. The Commons postponed supply by a majority of 12 and petitioned for the dismissal of the ministers; but this the King refused to do. Pitt was the popular support of the King against factions seeking to constrain him. The Commons now voted a reproachful representation by a majority of one. Whereupon Pitt brought forward the Mutiny Bill and got it passed (Mar. 1784). A fortnight later the King dissolved parliament for him.

(12) In the general election of 1784, electoral bargains and royal patronage gave Pitt the greatest electoral triumph of the century. It placed him unassailably in office so long as he stuck to administration. This he could do because the King would otherwise have to accept Fox or no govt. at all; but outside matters of administration, Pitt and George represented different forms of patriotism, to both of which the political public dimly subscribed. Pitt could not, in questions of policy, dominate the King save with united public support. Hence George backed Pitt's administrative improvements, but Pitt had to accept that he exerted no pressure in favour of his schemes for reform. The stability of this arrangement was reinforced by the independence of M.P.s, who were ready to keep Pitt in power, but insisted on a free hand in dealing with his legislation.

(13) Using the foundations laid by North, Pitt meant to rationalise the national finances. Confused by overlays of custom, habit, abuse and accumulated small scale solutions to particular problems, they were also burdened by debts incurred in a disastrous war. The interests which supported him expected lower taxes. George wanted a cleaner public life. The ending of abuses, the enforcement of economies and efficiency and the gradual elimination of sinecures suited both King and taxpayers. All the same they silently altered the balance of influence as between King and minister and as between the ministry and the House of Commons. The diminishing royal patronage slowly became less important in relations between the Crown and its advisers, and politicians had increasingly to be satisfied on issues, rather than cajoled by bargains and jobs. The alliance between George and Pitt began the modernisation of the constitution.

(14) But it was not plain sailing. Fox, as the opposition became more disunited, began to exploit the Guelph hatred between father and son. The P. of Wales hated the dull morality and formalism of George's court, whence he escaped with joy to the gambling salons, drinking tables and double beds of Fox's fashionable semi-public life. He could reign unchallenged there, if not at Windsor or Kew. He looked forward to being a

real King. From Nov. 1788 to Feb. 1789 George was in the depths of a violent, depressed and unpredictable porphyriac seizure. If the Prince became regent, Fox would come to power. Pitt, therefore, proposed a regency in which the royal patronage, especially on peerages, should be limited for the first year in case the King recovered. The limit could be imposed only by a statute to which, obviously, an insane King could not assent; therefore the Foxites argued furiously that the Prince had a vested right to all the royal powers. To such a limiting statute he, of course, would not assent. Thus Fox seemed to champion the Crown against his own best support in Parliament, while Pitt seemed to champion Parliament against George without whom he could not manage. At the height of the uproar George suddenly recovered as a result of gentle, rather than brutal, medication. Fox's and the Prince's mirage dissolved. The opposition, already bogged down since Feb. 1788 in Warren Hastings' impeachment, became increasingly futile and demoralised.

(15) With the outbreak of the French revolution the mirage seemed to return. The opposition welcomed it and sought to channel the new release of human energy into home channels favourable to itself. Pitt and the King were not alarmed. While other states manoeuvred and quarrelled over Polish partitions and Turkish annexations, it paralysed French power and left Pitt to get on with balancing his budget. As late as Feb. 1792 Pitt ushered in 22 years of war by predicting a durable peace. (See FRENCH REVOLUTIONARY WARS, ETC.)

(16) The war which Britain entered in Feb. 1793 strengthened both George as the national symbol and Pitt as the national leader. French excesses disgusted even liberal supporters of French ideas, while Pitt could exploit a wave of Francophobe and defensive patriotism; but depression, bad harvests and fervour were creating unrest in the country (see SPEENHAMLAND) while the French were trying with arms, money and ill-managed expeditions, to harness Irish disaffection. Pitt favoured R. Catholic emancipation, as advocated by Henry Grattan, and the Portland whigs, who had joined the govt., urged him on. One of them, E. Fitzwilliam, became Lord Lieut. of Ireland in Jan. 1795. He invited premature catholic agitation and Grattan introduced an emancipation bill into the Dublin parliament. Things had gone too fast and too far. George thought that the change was beyond cabinet competence, because it infringed his coronation oath. Much of the cabinet supported him and Pitt made Fitzwilliam resign. The effect was deplorable. The Irish, with hope deferred, were furious and violent; the English opponents of Irish reform encouraged. The rival parties, especially the nationalist United Irishmen, formed paramilitary organisations and fought. Ireland drifted from petty civil wars into (May-Oct. 1798) insurrections aided by a small French force.

(17) The Irish question had to be solved, if only for the sake of the French war. Pitt's solution was a package of parliamentary and commercial union with R. Catholic emancipation. With George's necessary co-operation, a liberal distribution of compensation and peerages secured the passage of union in the Irish Parliament. English politicians welcomed it but not emancipation. Pitt could not carry his cabinet, for most of them knew that George was still devoted to his coronation oath. The King doubted too if a war against revolution would be aided by introducing an Irish element into parliament based upon a R. Catholic electorate with alien sympathies. In Jan. 1801 he publicly pronounced against emancipation. Pitt could not dissuade him, for George knew that he could have an alternative administration. He was in touch with the Speaker, Henry Addington, who could secure powerful allies. In Mar., at George's persuasion, Addington formed a new ministry. Pitt resigned, after promising that, in the interests of a united war effort, he

would never raise the matter again. George, not Pitt, had accurately judged the country's mood.

(18) Addington also reflected the country's war weariness. He negotiated the P. of Amiens at any price (Mar. 1802) and disarmed recklessly to abolish Pitt's income tax. It was popular among the ignorant, but increasingly disliked by the knowledgeable, who saw France's continuing expansion excluding British trade. Addington's popularity was demonstrated by successes in the General Election of 1802, but by 1803 parliamentary criticism was embittered. The French were evidently arming for a naval war. In May 1803 the govt. declared war.

(19) Though the D. of York's military reforms had improved (if not enlarged) the army, the navy was in poor condition and undermanned. Nobody believed in Addington as a war leader. As the chorus of criticism mounted, George had another seizure (Feb. 1804) and nobody wanted to provoke a crisis until his permanent condition might be foreseen. His recovery (Apr.) was a signal for change. Pitt formed his last ministry in May.

(20) Pitt's war leadership was criticised and his frail physique succumbed about equally to overwork, the nation's grief at Nelson's death, the mainland allies' disasters at Ulm (Oct. 1805) and Austerlitz (Dec.) and to the transfer of S. Germany to French domination by the P. of Pressburg (Dec.). In Jan. 1806 he died. The Kingdom was at least safe, but George, faced with no obvious choice, had to make do with the mediocre coalition known as the Ministry of All the Talents headed by Lord Grenville, Fox and Addington (now Sidmouth) and including friends of the Prince. Most of the real talent, brought up by Pitt, was now in opposition and Fox was failing. In Sept. 1806 he too died. In the reshuffled ministry's general election (Oct.) the Foxite Whigs gained at the expense of Sidmouth's following. The govt. was now of a relatively liberal complexion, but the war blocked most liberal reforms. In the end they abolished the slave trade and tried to give R. Catholics the right to hold service commissions outside Ireland. George, by now nearly blind, was thought to have agreed to this *in toto*. The ministers were mistaken. When he understood the submission, he demanded that the ministry should defeat the proposal but stay in office. They complied. Then he demanded a written assurance that they would never raise the issue again. On this the whigs resigned (May 1807).

(21) The ensuing three years were a period of great anxiety. The new Tory administration under the D. of Portland and Spencer Perceval was unable to force an entry into Europe while Bonaparte and his (since the T. of Tilsit) new Russian ally tried to close the European ports to British trade. Their efforts met overt and covert internal opposition and forced Bonaparte to ever wider annexations, but the fact that the economic war with Britain was only a partial success did not prevent distress and bread rioting in Britain and severe losses of shipping. Even the opening of the Peninsular war (Aug. 1808) seemed a disaster in a disastrous atmosphere, for Sir John Moore's death (Jan. 1809) was followed by the defeat (July) and partial dismemberment (Oct.) of Austria. For this Wellesley's (Wellington's) victory at Talavera (July) had seemed small compensation, for Wellesley nevertheless retreated into Portugal. Portland had a stroke; Canning and Castlereagh fought a duel and resigned (Sept. 1809). In Dec. the British Walcheren expedition collapsed.

(22) Apart from the D. of Cambridge, all George's sons were dissolute and unpopular. In Jan. 1809 the D. of York, C-in-C, had been publicly accused of selling commissions through his mistress, Mrs Clarke. The fact of the sales was established, the Duke cleared of direct responsibility. The scandal coincided with a public hunt for political scapegoats, but Perceval endured. He tried,

but failed, to broaden the administration. He hung determinedly on while the Peninsula took a turn for the better. But the strain upon George was too great. The death of his favourite and youngest daughter P. Amelia (Nov. 1810) brought on a further and irremediable seizure. With the passage of the Regency Act, to which the Royal Assent was given by a commission of doubtful authority (Feb. 1811), George's effective reign was at an end. He lived quietly and in increasing public sympathy and affection at Windsor until he died.

GEORGE IV (1762-1830) P. of WALES (1762) PRINCE REGENT (1811) KING (1820) nicknamed "PRINNY" *s.* of George III and Q. Charlotte (1) was brought up with his brother, Frederick Augustus of York, in ineffectual seclusion at Kew. He was well educated, handsome, precocious and self-indulgent, entirely unscrupulous in pursuing his extravagant personal pleasures (whether at cards, with the bottle or in bed), lazy, yet with a certain charm, but with a sense of aesthetic style which left a lasting mark long after his public record, discreditable in other ways, had been forgotten. He probably suffered mildly from the porphyria which unhinged his father.

(2) He contracted his first mistress, Mary Robinson the actress, when he was 18 and by 1783 had run up large debts and set up at Carlton House. The need for money and the usual Guelph feud with his father led to an alliance with the whigs and Charles James Fox, whom his father hated. He shared Fox's devil-may-care tastes, helped him in his 1783 electioneering and, through him, got parliament to pay his debts (£30,000). George III gave him £50,000 a year, but by 1786 his newly discovered passion for building had (*inter alia*) run up his debts to £250,000. Meanwhile he had fallen for Maria Fitzherbert, a twice widowed R. Catholic, who refused, despite his tantrums and a staged attempt at suicide, to become his mistress. In Dec. 1785 he went through a secret Anglican marriage ceremony with her. If it had been valid it would have disqualified him from the throne, but as it was done without his father's knowledge, it was void under the Royal Marriages Act, 1774. It was enough for Maria and if it deceived her she was soon undeceived. She was now treated on all hands as his wife, but rumours of the marriage embarrassed the whigs, through whom he was trying to get another parliamentary grant. He authorised Fox to deny the marriage categorically in the Commons and then denied to Maria that he had instructed him to do so. He got his money, destroyed Maria's position and lost Fox.

(3) The resulting reconciliation with the King was overtaken by new waywardness. He was losing heavily at gambling, while simultaneously building not only at Carlton House but at Brighton where he was erecting the extraordinary Pavilion. Owing to his father's dullness and respectability he was now the centre of a raffish but entertaining and fashionable society. His interest created Brighton, hitherto only a coastal hamlet, and Bath, a minor, if historic, village because people with money to spend went where he did. It was from Brighton that he was called post-haste when George III had his first bout of madness in 1788. (*See* SPAS.)

(4) The first regency crisis (*see* PITT GOVT. - FIRST) arose because the Prince wanted the full powers of the crown and its money and patronage. Pitt's govt. doubted the convenience of this arrangement, or his suitability for it, and feared, reasonably, that he would supersede them if he took over the powers. The whigs, as opposition, had no reason to trust him and anyway he was wildly unpopular with the public, but they joyfully used his claims to embarrass the govt. and the Irish parliament, with similar motives, offered him an unrestricted regency in Ireland. Then, to the Prince's fury, the King recovered; the public thanksgiving for his recovery turned into a demonstration of popular affection for the father and dislike of the son, who was forbidden at court.

(5) Baulked of the obvious sources of funds, the prince now raised loans secured upon the bishopric of Osnabrück (of which he was administrator) and post-obits. Three years later when the bills were presented for redemption his agents repudiated them. By now, however, the French wars were beginning; little more was heard of these creditors, but possibly related negotiations for a marriage with the hoydenish Caroline of Brunswick-Wolfenbüttel, a Guelph relative, were soon on foot. The lady disgusted him but the wedding took place in 1795. The prince's current mistress had been Lady Jersey, but this event caused him to return to Maria. For some years he was now pursued by creditors who occupied some of his properties. He disbanded most of his establishments, sold his immense stable and lived at his friends' private houses, mostly in Dorset.

(6) This period of eclipse coincided with a change of opinion, due partly to the threat to monarchy posed by the French Revolution and the whig attitude to it, and partly to Lord Moira's advice to make overtures to Pitt. The prince was entitled to, but had never received, the income from the Duchy of Cornwall. These claims against his father were now compromised; he received another parliamentary grant and arrangements were made for gradually paying off his liabilities (1803). He was beginning to take a new interest in politics, but had yet another quarrel with the King, who deprived him of the custody of his daughter P. Charlotte. The King rather liked the Princess of Wales, with whom the prince had not been on speaking terms for some years. It was rumoured that she had had an illegitimate child and the cabinet had to appoint privy councillors to investigate the matter. This *Delicate Investigation* found no solid evidence of a child, but plenty about the Princess' dangerous follies. The King, hitherto her protector, changed his mind.

(7) The prince owed his new political interest (apart from money) to his reigning mistress, the M. of Hertford, whose Tory husband had been an M.P. from 1768 to 1794. Apart from Sheridan and Moira, he had practically broken with the whigs, so that when George III went incurably mad in 1811, the prince seemed in a weak position to deal with the restricted govt. Discussions with the whigs broke down. Lady Hertford convinced him, however, that he would have no interest in making major changes on assuming power and that, therefore, the restrictions in the first year were unimportant. On this basis the Regency Act was passed and given the Royal Assent by a commission of doubtful legal authority. The Regent celebrated his installation by an enormous banquet at which he publicly repudiated Maria.

(8) The Regency has given its name to a style, classically restrained in its architecture, more florid in its decoration, fashions and painting, which was inspired by his patronage and which has left its mark everywhere in the Kingdom and in many places abroad, such as Gibraltar. He refurbished the royal residences, notably Buckingham Palace and St. James's, and practically rebuilt Windsor Castle. He also added notably to Charles I's picture collection. He was an embarrassment to govts. because of his indiscretions and his rudeness and luxury at a time of widespread indigence. It was easy to seize upon his quarrels with his wife (who went abroad) and daughter to make political difficulties. In 1817 his carriage was stoned on the way to parliament.

(9) At his accession (shortly after Peterloo) there was a new scandal. Q. Caroline insisted on returning to be crowned with him. He insisted on the govt. introducing a divorce bill. Henry Brougham, her counsel, spectacularly destroyed the credibility of the witnesses against her in the Lords. The bill had to be dropped. For a moment she was a popular heroine. He forbade her to come to Westminster Abbey for the Coronation. She came but was refused admittance at the door. The crowd which

cheered her as she came, hooted her as she retreated. Then, a month later, she suddenly died.

(10) George now set off upon an extended and successful royal tour, visiting Hanover and Ireland in 1821 and Scotland in 1822. His London unpopularity did not follow him; his sense of style was valuable and he entered with more than graciousness into the local customs and clothes. When he returned to the bitterness of humdrum London politics he shied away, living at Windsor or Brighton with Lady Conyngham and never appearing in public. He was also, owing to his dissipations, intermittently ill. The result was that politicians began to capture the public attention while the crown lost much of its power. This process was accelerated because he had become stubbornly reactionary while opinion was moving ahead. His opposition to the recognition of S. American republics, to the repeal of the Corporation Acts and to R. Catholic Emancipation was no longer rooted in the realities and towards the end he suffered from delusions.

GEORGE V (1865-1936) D. of YORK (1892) D. of CORNWALL and P. of WALES (1901) KING (1910) was educated as a naval officer. He married Mary of Teck in 1893 and they brought up their children sternly. He visited all the future dominions and India while P. of Wales; his father showed him all state papers and he habitually attended parliamentary debates. He was also an acknowledged expert on yachting, shooting and philately. He had a strong religious streak and a somewhat alarming terseness and integrity.

(2) When he came to the throne he was faced immediately with a constitutional crisis. In Nov. 1910 Asquith secured a hypothetical understanding that he would create, if necessary, enough peers to vote the Parliament Bill through. The King then had to go to the coronation Durbar at Delhi while political excitement mounted at home. He was soon back and in Aug. 1911 the understanding was revealed in order to secure the passage of the Bill. He had been advised all along by Sir Arthur Bigge (Lord Stamfordham) his private secretary and concluded that the crown was now responsible when a bill was presented to him for assent under the Parliament Act, for deciding whether an appeal to the country was proper. The doctrine had instantly to be operated when the Lords twice rejected the Irish Home Rule Bill; he convened an all-party conference under the Speaker's chairmanship at Buckingham Palace to anticipate the difficulties (July 1914). The conference failed, but the issue was overtaken by World War I.

(3) His example during the war enhanced his prestige and popularity, which contributed to the country's stability in the difficult years afterwards and, in particular, his common-sense constitutionalism and talent for conciliation were trusted by politicians of all persuasions. In 1921 his intervention prevented a conflict between Lloyd George and the Irish Sinn Fein. In 1923, at Bonar Law's resignation, he settled the modern rule that the prime minister should be in the Commons by sending for Baldwin instead of the M. Curzon. He got on excellently with the members of the first Labour govt. (1924) and helped them in every way. He publicly urged an end to bitterness after the General Strike (1926), persuaded Ramsay MacDonald to form a coalition govt. to deal with the slump of 1931 and in 1932 instituted the Royal Christmas broadcasts with their annually renewed message of faith. By now, with his vast experience, he was his minister's best adviser and the acknowledged father of the country. His silver jubilee was an outbreak of national affection but was shortly followed by universal grief at his death.

GEORGE VI (1895-1952) D. of YORK (1920) KING (1936), second *s.* of George V, not expecting to become King, was trained for the navy and fought at the B. of Jutland (1916). After 1920 he took particular interest in the human and welfare problems of urban life and, as Pres of the Boys Welfare Assn., initiated the D. of York's camps, designed simultaneously to give boys of poor circumstances some country holiday experience and to bring together boys of different educational backgrounds. In 1923 he married Lady Elizabeth Bowes-Lyon. He succeeded Edward VIII in 1936 when the latter abdicated and was soon faced with World War II. He was bombed in Buckingham Palace, visited all the main war theatres, made broadcasts despite a slight stutter, and acted as friend and adviser to the statesmen and soldiers directing the war. He was immensely popular. In 1947 he visited S. Africa and in 1951 opened the Festival of Britain. A heavy smoker, he died suddenly.

GEORGE, Henry (1839-97), American land reformer and advocate of a single tax on land appreciation, published *Progress and Poverty* in 1879 and popularised it in Britain in 1887. His work inspired the early English Socialists, especially the Fabians.

GEORGE, P. of DENMARK (1653-1708) D. of CUMBERLAND (1689) married princess (later Q.) Anne in 1683. He was naturalised in 1689, but was kept out of office by William III. When Anne became queen in 1702 he became Lord High Admiral. She adored him and the Whig's criticism from 1704 on his conduct of the Admiralty did much to set her against them. His death made her more dependent upon Abigail Masham.

GEORGE, WILLIAM FREDERICK CHARLES (1819-1904) 2nd D. of CAMBRIDGE (1850) had a military career including a divisional command in the Crimea. He helped to found the Staff College; in 1862 became a F.M. and C-in-C. In 1870 his office was subordinated to the War Office but he remained a powerful, remote and very conservative figure opposed to such reforms as short service, the linking of battalions and the formation of a reserve. The inadequacies of military administration revealed by an inquiry held from 1888 to 1890 led to his enforced resignation in 1895 and the abolition of his office.

GEORGIA (Caucasia). This ancient Christian state was partly under Turkish and partly under Persian protection in 1774. In 1783 the last East Georgian King secured Russian interest and the resulting Persian pressure ended in his ceding his country to Russia in 1800. The West Georgian princes mostly followed suit in 1803 and 1804, though some survived until 1858. The result was a great increase in prosperity. Between 1918 and 1921 it was independent and later under British occupation. After the British evacuation it was overrun by the Russian communists against whom there was an uprising in 1924. Stalin was a Georgian. There was a more successful uprising in 1990.

GEORGIA (U.S.A.) was originally part of the 1663 grant to the Carolina Proprietors but remained undeveloped for some 60 years. Col. James Edward OGLETHORPE (1696-1785), an M.P. from 1722, was chairman of a parliamentary committee on debtors' prisons in 1729 and proposed colonising it with able bodied paupers of good character to relieve distress at home and protect the Carolinas against Spain. He secured a separate charter for Georgia in 1732 and in 1733 brought 116 debtors to Charleston and also founded Savannah. In early life John Wesley was chaplain to the colony. Oglethorpe prohibited slavery and spirits, which created administrative difficulties (*see also* METHODISM) but he organised systematic military training, built defences and was generally on good terms with the Indians. In the War of Jenkins's Ear (1739-48) he took the offensive against Spanish Florida, but was repulsed from St. Augustine in 1740. The Spanish counter-attack, however, was decisively beaten at the B. of Bloody Marsh (1742) and the colony's survival assured. He returned to England in 1743. At this period Georgia was only a string of coastal settlements. From June 1749 it was effectively ruled as a

Crown Colony: its proprietorial charter was surrendered in 1754. It remained the weakest and least developed of the southern colonies until the American rebellion and, for this reason, was the first to ratify the U.S. Constitution in 1788. Slavery was legally established shortly afterwards. It joined the Confederates in the American Civil War. *See* MISSISSIPPI.

GEORGIAN. *See* ARCHITECTURE, BRITISH-12.

GERALDINES. *See* FITZGERALD.

GERARD (1) Sir William (?-1581) was an M.P. in 1553 and from 1555 to 1572. Until 1561 he was Recorder of Chester and from 1562 V-Pres. of the Council of Wales. He became Lord Chancellor of Ireland in 1576 but next year returned to argue for an alleviation of Irish tax burdens. He failed and in 1580 he turned to the more lucrative and less troublesome post of Master of Requests in England. His cousin **(2) Sir Gilbert (?-1593)** was M.P. for Wigan and in 1553 and 1555, Att-Gen. in 1559 and drafted the reform of the Irish Exchequer Court in 1560. In 1563 he was a commissioner for the sale of crown lands and in 1567 a member of the High Commission. After 1570 he was engaged mainly in state trials, but was Master of the Rolls from 1581 and chief commissioner of the Great Seal from 1591 to 1592. His great-grandson **(3) Charles (?-1694) 1st Ld. GERARD of BRANDON (1645) and 1st E. of MACCLESFIELD (1679),** a royalist commander from the beginning of the Civil War, campaigned successfully in Wales but was removed for sternness towards the Welsh in 1645 after Naseby and became commander of Charles' bodyguard and a peer in compensation. He was badly wounded at Rowton Heath in Sept. 1645 and in 1646 went with Rupert to The Hague. After the King's death in 1649 he became one of the most active supporters of Charles II and so became commander of the Life Guards at the Restoration. He was also a gentleman of the bedchamber and these military and court appointments involved him in politics for which he had no talent. By 1679 he was conspiring to put Monmouth in James, D. of York's place as heir to the throne and in 1680 he protested against the rejection of the Exclusion Bill. By Sept. 1682 he had been dismissed and, at the beginning of James II's reign, was forced into exile, returning for the second time as commander of a King's Life Guard with William III in 1688. He was then appointed Pres. of the Welsh Marches. His son **(4) Charles (1659-1701) 2nd Ld. and E.,** was M.P. for Lancashire in 1679 and 1680. He was a member of the Westminster Grand Jury which presented James, D. of York as a Popish recusant in 1680 and was tried and acquitted of treason in 1683. In 1685 he was tried again and convicted but pardoned in 1687. From 1688 until his father's death he was again M.P. for Lancashire. His divorce in 1698 by Act of Parliament was the first in which the bill was introduced without a previous ecclesiastical decree. In 1701 be was ambassador to the Electress Sophia of Hanover.

GERARD or GIRARD (of YORK) (?-1108), Bp. of HEREFORD (1096-1101), Abp. of YORK (1101-8), was a nephew of Bp. Walkelin of Winchester and a Chancery clerk. He was appointed to Hereford as a reward for a successful diplomatic mission to the Curia. Later, Henry I, needing an Abp. of York, circumvented Anselm's refusal to consecrate royally invested bishops-elect, by translating Gerard, who was already a bishop, to York where he supported the King on the investiture issues and, naturally, refused canonical obedience to Anselm until ordered in 1107 to profess it by Pope Paschal II, but in terms which failed to resolve the long-standing dispute between the two archbishoprics.

GERBERT of AURILLAC (?-1003). Pope Sylvester II from 999 and a scientist. *See* CAPETIANS-6,7; CLOCKS.

GEREFA **(A.S. = Reeve).** A lord's estate manager, especially in the south and west, before the Conquest. SCIREGEREFA (= shire reeve i.e. sheriff) was originally as much the King's manager of royal estates in a county as a public official.

GERMAIN, George Sackville (1716-85) otherwise, until 1770, called Lord GEORGE SACKVILLE and then Lord GEORGE GERMAIN, **1st Vist. SACKVILLE (1782)** (*see* SACKVILLE). A professional soldier wounded in a daring charge at Fontenoy (1745), he subsequently served in Scotland and Ireland and then acted as executive commander of the absurd Cancale expedition of June 1758. He then took command in Hanover on the death of his superior and so served under Ferdinand of Brunswick at Minden (Aug. 1759). His conduct led to a prolonged, partly political, controversy with the M. of Granby, for Germain's refusal to charge prevented the victory from being total. The number of public houses still called The Marquis of Granby and the Sackville Arms commemorates public partisanship in the row. He was court martialled, cashiered (1760), became a politician in earnest and a supporter of Lord North. As such he gradually recovered his repute.

GERMAN EAST AFRICA. See TANZANIA..

GERMAN EMPIRE or SECOND REICH 1871-1914 (1) was founded upon the expulsion of Austria from Germany after 1866 and the combination of the North German Confederation under Prussian leadership, with the south German states to fight the French (July 1870). The victory at Sedan (Sept.) and the investment of Paris were accompanied by vigorous German interstate diplomacy. Formal alliances were re-concluded in Nov. Bismarck paid K. Ludwig II of Bavaria's debts from the expropriated *Welfenfonds* (*see* HANOVER), in return for which Ludwig publicly requested K. William of Prussia to assume the German Imperial Crown. The proclamation of the new Empire was staged in the *Galerie des Glaces* at Versailles (18 Jan. 1871).

(2) Prussia, itself a conglomerate, represented nearly two thirds of the Empire and the Emperor, as K. of Prussia, reigned from the Prussian capital with a govt. consisting mainly of Prussians. Moreover the General Staff was a Prussian organism and the states' armies automatically passed under Imperial, that is, Prussian command on a mobilisation. Though in the whole Reich only two other states, the Kingdoms of Saxony and Bavaria, counted for much (mainly for cultural reasons), a thirty year effort towards unification, especially in fiscal and legal fields, was needed.

(3) The French war was brought to a victorious and moderate, if resented, peace at Frankfurt (May 1871). Bismarck meant to maintain the peaceful European balance so that the unification processes could go ahead and the German economy would be free to expand. The balance had to be kept against potential French *revanchism* combined (or not) with competition for advantage in the area of the decaying, if still vast, Ottoman Empire. Here the opportunistic and unpredictable conduct of the major and minor powers made it possible to maintain a consistent line of policy only by tactical diplomatic agility which kept Foreign Offices busy, but had only temporary effects. The Berlin meeting of the Emperors of Austria, Germany and Russia in Sept. 1872 and their Alliance (*Dreikaiserbund*) of Oct. 1873 represented an imposing understanding, but did little to calm Russian aggressive sentiment, and it required the Berlin Congress of 1878 to reduce the Russian sponsored Greater Bulgaria of the T. of San Stefano and put an all too brief restraint upon Russian exuberance. Meantime Bismarck was encouraging the election of German princes to Balkan thrones.

(4) In the watershed year 1879 Bismarck had his first serious failure. The German economy was not developing as he had hoped and the industrialists demanded and got protective tariffs (July). With access to German markets obstructed, other economies began to turn towards colonisation. To remedy the defects of the

Dreikaiserbund, Bismarck far-sightedly negotiated the much less cloudy Dual Alliance with Austro-Hungary (Oct.). This was inconsistent with the *Dreikaiserbund* in fact if not in name, and though the latter was renewed in 1881 the inconsistency was made more glaring when Italy was persuaded, by joining, to convert the Dual into a Triple Alliance in 1882. By now non-German colonialism was in full swing with the French in the Pacific (1880), the British bombarding Alexandria and entering North Borneo (1882), the Italians colonising Eritrea and the French imposing protectorates in Indo-China (1883). Prestige pressure forced Bismarck to join in. In 1884 German troops landed in S.W. Africa, Togoland and the Cameroons. By now the further renewal of the *Dreikaiserbund* had become largely ceremonial. The new German colonialism was sowing the seeds of European conflict, but while they were yet germinating, there was still an opportunity for internal colonisation. In 1886 the Polish landowners of West Prussia and Posen were expropriated. In 1887 Bismarck negotiated his secret Reinsurance Treaty with Russia. This was, in effect, a counterpart to the Triple Alliance.

(5) In 1888 the waters of 1879 began to flow more steeply. Bismarck's Emperor William I died. Three months later his liberal successor Frederick also died, leaving an English Dowager Empress. To the All Highest Office and Supreme Warlordship there now succeeded a far-reaching inferiority complex in the person of William II, with his withered arm, aggressive self-regarding demeanour, suspicion, jealous Anglophobia and rich but socially inferior friends. Disliked by most and especially the best of his own aristocracy, he was bound to encourage the worst in his most powerful associates. Such a man had to assert himself. He began by putting in his private regiment to search his mother's correspondence. He sponsored an aesthetic and architectural style. In Mar. 1890 he dismissed Bismarck in favour of the mediocre Caprivi.

(6) There followed a series of events separated by years and under different Chancellors but in mutual relation, suggesting that the German govt. had decided in the first years of the reign upon international aggression. Three months after Bismarck's dismissal Caprivi persuaded Britain to accept the rich clove plantations of Zanzibar and Pemba for the barren island of Heligoland, which is strategically placed at the centre of a 40-mile radius from the entrances to the Elbe, the Weser and the Jade. For Britain the exchange was lucrative, but the Germans poured money into fortifying Heligoland. As nobody was likely to attack these estuaries, the fortifications were purposeless unless they were to shelter a fleet. A canal was being dug across the Danish isthmus from Kiel to Brunsbüttel at the mouth of the Elbe. Kiel was the base of the, as yet small, German navy. The Kiel Canal was completed in June 1895. In Nov. 1897 Germany occupied the Chinese naval harbour of Kiao-Chow. The Kiel base was enlarged. With scattered and unprotected possessions thousands of miles across the seas, the *Reichstag* perforce voted naval credits. North Sea bases at Cuxhafen, Bremerhafen, Emden and Wilhelmshafen were marked out. In 1899 the govt. bought assorted Pacific islands from Spain. It declared a protectorate of South-East Africa (Tanganyika) a few months later and then started to meddle with the near east and secured the Turkish-Baghdad railway concession. This virtually committed the Reich to the support of the Turks. Consistently with this, in July 1900 William II made his notorious speech at the new base at Bremerhafen in which he saw Germany as the champion of Europe against Huns and other conspicuous eastern races. The sensational words, though giving widespread offence, were not very important. The actions mattered. Further naval credits were voted. This was the year when Hohenlohe, who had succeeded Caprivi in 1894, was himself replaced by Bülow.

(7) As Chancellor, Bismarck had unintentionally left a legacy of misunderstanding. His clever and powerful personality had invested his office with an eminence which was more apparent, at least to the British, than real. In fact it had required strenuous effort to maintain his position against William I. His successors were lesser men, whereas the majesty of the royal and imperial office with its military splendour remained. The post-Bismarckian Chancellors were not prime ministers in the English sense but political technicians who shared the formation and execution of policy in fluctuating proportions with a varying group composed of the Kaiser and his business friends, the General Staff, the Navy with Adm. von Tirpitz's vociferous Navy League, other royalties, parliamentarians and anyone else with influence like Holstein, the charlatan at the Wilhelmstrasse. Between 1890 and 1914 it was never clear who (if anyone) ruled the Second Reich.

(8) Armed power required a successful economy to support it. Prussians had always and other Germans had now taken their army for granted and complained little about its growing expense, because after 1901 there was a boom. By 1904 the govt. was extending its economic zone by commercial treaties with contiguous states such as Russia, Belgium and Austria-Hungary and through them into the Balkans, Asia and Africa. This was the great era when the markets, whether free trading or diplomatically accessible, were flooded with cheap manufactures marked *Made in Germany*. The Reich was now not only in full commercial and colonial rivalry with Britain (*see* TANGIER, ALGEÇIRAS.) but had been seen for some time as a political and military threat. Britain and especially France had naturally protected themselves by colonial understandings (The *Entente* 1904) and Russian military agreements. In the "golden haze" of 1900 to 1914 the powers lurched through crisis after crisis towards polarisation, accompanied by seven wars and a multitude of assassinations. There was even, in SW Africa, a rebellion on German soil.

(9) In 1906 a maritime technical event, the launch of the British battleship *Dreadnought,* now supervened. This rendered all existing battle fleets obsolete, but in the case of Germany it had a special effect. Ships of Dreadnought size could not pass through the Kiel Canal. German industry depended on trans-Baltic supplies of Swedish iron and copper, which even a small Russian Dreadnought fleet might interrupt. Assuming a continuation of existing policy, the govt. was faced with the expensive task of building Dreadnoughts, and disruptive and time consuming canal engineering. The *Reichstag* wrong-headedly voted the money in 1906 and again in 1908 and so set the powers on a collision course. Very soon the British had no doubt that the new German navy was meant to be used against themselves. There was no other active purpose for so large a force.

(10) The younger Moltke had been chief of staff since 1906. Bethmann-Hollweg succeeded Bülow as Chancellor in July 1909. In these years the social and political pretensions of the forces, operating through the Supreme Warlord, expanded as the Zabern Incident was to show, into the gap left by the decreasingly articulate liberal politicians. In 1910 a new Bill to enlarge the army was in preparation. In Feb. 1911 it was passed and a crisis (*see* AGADIR) was provoked in Morocco (July) to blackmail France into central African concessions (Nov.). It also provoked a Franco-Russian military agreement. The European temperature was perceptibly rising. By May 1912 the *Reichstag* was passing further military and naval legislation. The Austrians matched them in June. The Russians began to enlarge their fleet, the Belgians their army and meanwhile the First Balkan War opened and closed (Oct-Dec.), whereupon Germany, Italy and Austro-Hungary renewed their Triple Alliance.

(11) If a policy based on threatened or actual aggression had been adopted as far back as the 1890s, it would be logical to abandon it or fix a date for war once threats could no longer yield dividends. By the winter of 1912 this position seems to have been reached. Clearly no war could be launched so long as the Kiel Canal was unfinished, but early in 1913, during the Second Balkan War, completion could be predicted for mid-June 1914. Several external facts suggest that war was intended. A detailed contingency plan (The Schlieffen Plan) for the invasion of France through Belgium had existed since 1905. Because of Russian military expansion there were political dangers in abandoning the east to even short term penetration during the time when the knock-out was delivered in the West. More troops were needed than Count Schlieffen (Chief of Staff from 1890 to 1905) had envisaged. In June 1913 yet another Army Bill passed the *Reichstag* and in Oct. a military convention with Turkey excited British and French suspicions. In fact it outflanked Russia. The Army Act drew in new classes of recruits whose training would reach its peak alongside the normal classes in July 1914. Special taxation was imposed to defray the cost of this military expansion, which was represented as temporary. Hence the murder of the Archduke Franz Ferdinand at Sarajevo three days after the Canal was reopened was, if it could be made to precipitate a conflagration, a convenient coincidence. *See* WORLD WAR I.

GERMAN LIBERTIES was a 16th cent. term for the constitutional rights of the individual rulers in the Holy Roman Empire.

GERMANUS or GERMAIN, St. (?-c. 449) Bp. of AUXERRE (418), was a former army officer as well as a professional advocate, scholar and perhaps a physician. Britain was hard pressed by raiders and Pelagian heretics, some of whom may have been raiders. In response to an appeal by British bishops, Pope Celestine I sent them Germanus in 429. He discussed doctrinal issues at Verulamium, stopped Pelagian preaching and apparently cured a girl of blindness. He also organised the local militia against invading or raiding Picts and Saxons. In the battle, known as *The Alleluia Victory,* the enemy fled before a thunderous shout of "Alleluia" which echoed from the surrounding hills. He gave thanks for the victory at the shrine of St. Alban. These combined events secured doctrinal peace for half a generation. He is said to have made a second visit to deal with a Pelagian revival in 447. The many French churches dedicated to him also show that he was a great and famous man and that there is no reason to doubt the outline of his story, which is evidence of the breakdown of Romano-British society well before 449 when the Anglo-Saxon invasions began in earnest. He also trained St. Illtud, St. Patrick and Paulinus at Auxerre.

GERMANY (Locally DEUTSCHLAND) (1) until 1815 was a variable geographical expression not in official use (save in the expression "Holy Roman Empire of the German Nation") representing the politically and economically disunited area linguistically and culturally dominated by Germans at any given time. This coincided until 1806 roughly, but only roughly, with the Holy Roman Empire which at its greatest extent included Slavonic Bohemia and Moravia and up to 1648 the Netherlands, Imperial Flanders and Switzerland, but never included East Prussia or Schleswig. The expression very often excluded the German speaking Habsburg territories, whether in the Empire or not, which were more usually called Austria. When the Empire disappeared, Bonaparte replaced it in 1807 with a Confederation of the Rhine which did not include Hanover, Prussia or other areas to the north. **(2)** After 1815 the word acquired a standing with the creation of the German Confederation, whose area coincided with the old Empire save that it extended across the Rhine as far as Luxemburg, but still excluded the much enlarged Prussian provinces of

E. and W. Prussia and Posen. This lasted until the divorce between the area of the Prussian dominated *Zollverein* (Customs Union) and the Habsburg territories in 1866 and the proclamation of the former as the German Empire in 1871. **(3)** From 1871 to 1920 Germany meant the German Empire or its republicanised area. **(4)** From 1920 to 1933 it meant the so-called Weimar Republic as defined by the T. of Versailles. **(5)** In the confused period between 1935 and 1945, owing to expansions and contractions, it reverted to a meaning analogous with that in para (1) above. **(6)** Between 1945 and 1990 the expression embraced the separated West and East Germany and, since 1990, the modern united Germany.

GERRYMANDER is the drawing of electoral boundaries so as to give an unfair advantage to a particular interest. Elbridge Gerry, Gov. of Massachusetts (1812-4) thus redrew them in his state and was left with an area shaped like the type of skillet called a salamander. "Gerrymander", he exclaimed. This jest by a notorious Anglophobe has passed into English on both sides.

GERTRUDE, St. *See* MISSIONS TO EUROPE-2.

GERTRUYDENBURG, P. CONFERENCES (1710) (*see* SPANISH SUCCESSION, WAR) were held in the aftermath of the allied victory at Malplaquet (Sept. 1709) and capture of Mons, but of French successes elsewhere, especially Spain. They failed because in order to remain allies, the allies had to demand collectively more than France could concede. They ushered in a change in French diplomatic tactics namely, at the cost of, if necessary, large concessions to buy off one major opponent, thus exposing the others to defeat in detail.

GERVASE of CANTERBURY (?-1210) entered Christ Church Canterbury in 1163 and later became sacrist. His *Chronica* is a history of Christ Church set against a background of general history. It contains the results of much research and a description of the contrast between the Norman choir burnt down in 1174 and the new one built by the master-builder, William of Sens. His *Gesta Regum* (Lat = History of the Kings) is a more political English history from the earliest times to 1210. He also wrote a series of *Lives* of the archbishops of Canterbury (to 1205) and the *Mappa Mundi* (Lat = Diagram of the World) which is, in fact, a list of English monasteries.

GERVASE of TILBURY (fl. 1189-1235) well educated and much befriended Englishman, who was present at the Venice meeting of the Emperor Frederick I and Pope Alexander III. He wrote a jest book for Henry II, worked for William of Champagne and became Otto IV's marshal of Arles. His *Otia Imperiales* (Lat = Imperial Diversions) is an historical geography with legendary embellishments.

GESITH (A.S. = personal friend or boon companion) was the primitive equivalent of the *thegn* immediately before the Norman Conquest. In Wessex his *wergild*, at 1200 shillings, equalled that paid for a Kentish 'earl' and was six times that of a Wessex churl. He is pictured in heroic poems such as *Beowulf* and *The Wanderer* as loyal to his lord in battle, his companion in the mead hall and the recipient from him of bright and costly gifts.

GESTA FRANCORUM (Lat = The Deeds or Achievements of the Franks) is a Latin chronicle of the First Crusade.

GESTAPO (Ger. portmanteau for *Geheime Staatspolizei* = Secret State Police) was developed, originally by Goering, out of the detective branch of the Prussian state police when he became minister president of Prussia in 1933. In Apr. 1934 Goering put Himmler (already head of the Bavarian police and of the S.S.) in charge as part of the intrigues leading to the overthrow of Röhm. The personal association of the three forces under a single headship led to the nationwide spread of Gestapo power in the Third Reich.

GEWISSAE. The original name of the West Saxons.

GHANA (*see* WEST AFRICA). **(1)** The inland Ashantis, deprived after 1866 of the profits of the slave trade, sought to recoup by a local imperialism which brought them into collision with the British occupied Gold Coast forts. A series of wars ended in 1874 with Sir Garnet Wolseley's capture and destruction of Kumasi and his Fommanah T. (July 1874) which freed the coastal tribes from Ashanti rule and made it feasible to establish the GOLD COAST COLONY. The provisions forbidding human sacrifice were broken by the Asantahene (King) and a punitive expedition under Sir Francis Scott occupied Kumasi again in 1886, but failed to enforce the prohibition. Eventually tribal treaties decomposed the Ashanti dominion and a protectorate was set up in 1894. This was annexed to the Colony in 1901 but given a separate identity in 1906. A strip of ex-German Togoland was attached in 1922 as a mandated territory but administered as an integral part. The building of the port of Takoradi between 1928 and 1931 brought great local prosperity, which was increased by wartime traffic as a staging point for Egypt.

(2) Increasing literacy and education, the experience gained abroad by soldiers returning from World War II and the rising cost of living brought dissatisfaction with existing chieftaincy rule and British administration. Moreover, swollen shoot disease was slowly destroying the important cocoa industry. Riots, partly instigated by the newly formed United Gold Coast Convention led by Dr. J. B. Danquah, led to the arrest of its leaders and the drafting of a constitution. In 1951 Kwame Nkrumah's (1909-72) Convention People's Party (C.P.P.) won the elections and the gov., Sir Chas. Arden-Clarke, summoned Nkrumah from prison to form the govt. The constitution came into effect in June 1954 and the country had, in effect, full internal autonomy with a purely African cabinet. The C.P.P. won a general election but meanwhile the Ashanti and liberal elements grew alarmed and formed respectively the National Liberation Movement under Prof. Busia and the National People's Party. In the 1956 elections the C.P.P. won an overall majority and its demand for independence within the Commonwealth was conceded (6 Mar. 1957).

(3) In 1958 Nkrumah arranged a combination with Guinea to form the basis of a West African organisation or, perhaps, empire and Mali joined it in 1960 but it failed to develop.

(4) Nkrumah, who was becoming increasingly dictatorial, now found it expedient to declare a republic with himself as president and in Jan. 1964 it was declared, after a virtually unanimous referendum, a one-party state. In Feb. 1966 a military coup overthrew him and he retired to Guinea. Thenceforth military and civilian govts. succeeded each other in not always bloodless coups. The civilian govts. were in power from 1969 to 1972 and from 1979 to 1981. In 1981 a military ruler, Jerry John Rawlings took power and set up a Provisional National Defence Council which in 1991 set up a group of experts to draft a constitution. This was agreed by a referendum in Apr. 1992. In Nov. 1992 Rawlings was elected president.

GHAZI. An oriental title meaning 'Conqueror'.

GHAZNI. *See* AFGHANISTAN-6.

G[H]EERAERTS or GARRARD, Marcus, painters **(1) Elder (?1510- 90)** fled from Bruges to England in 1586. His son **(2) Younger (1561-1635)** who came with him, painted a number of Elizabethan court portraits, the "Conference of English and Spanish Plenipotentiaries" and other works now lost and wrote a handbook on drawing.

GHENT. *See* FLANDERS-2 and *passim*.

GHENT, PACIFICATION OF (1576) was an agreement between the Dutch States-General and the powerful estates of Holland and Zeeland, negotiated under the urging of William of Orange, to give priority to the expulsion of the Spaniards and to deal with the religious problems of the XVII Provinces on a regional basis, allowing for the toleration both of Calvinists and of R. Catholics. The Spanish victory at Gembloux (1578) partially destroyed the arrangement.

GHENT, SIMON of (?-1315) was archdeacon of Oxford from 1284, Chancellor of the Univ. from 1290 to 1293, Bp. of Salisbury in 1297 and a Lord Ordainer in 1310. He was at once an ecclesiastical reformer, a resister of papal provision and a defender of the rights of his see, whose tallage at Salisbury he successfully maintained. He had a reputation as a scholar; he translated the *Ancren Riwle* into Latin and, whenever possible, collated scholars, including some former Chancellors of his university, to Salisbury prebends.

GHENT, T. of (1814). *See* ANGLO-AMERICAN WAR (1812-15)-6.

GHIBELLINE. *See* GUELPH.

GHIBERTI, Lorenzo. *See* RENAISSANCE-4.

G[H]URKAS. *See* NEPAL.

G.I. (= Government Issue) The American World War II nickname for a private soldier.

GIB, Adam (1714-88) became minister of a secession congregation at Bristo St., Edinburgh in 1741. He was an active champion of the Hanoverians in 1745 and, when extruded from his congregation, drew vast audiences at a new kirk built for him nearby. From 1747 he was the acknowledged leader of the Anti-Burgher Synod.

GIBBON, Edward (1737-94) became a R. Catholic at 16 and was sent by his father to Lausanne where he was reconverted. He stayed on at Lausanne until 1758 and had an affair with Susanne Curchod, later the famous Mme. Necker. From 1759 to 1763 he served in the Hampshire Militia. In 1764, while at Rome, he decided to write the famous *Decline and Fall of the Roman Empire*. While working on this he published critical essays and in 1772 returned to London. In 1774 he became prof. of ancient history at the R. Academy and also an M.P. The first volume of the *Decline and Fall* came out in 1776. In 1779 he was made a commissioner of Trade and Plantations. In 1781 the second and third volumes came out. He resigned office in 1782 and in 1783 retired to Lausanne where he finished the work in 1787.

GIBBONS, Grinling (1648-1720) the baroque woodcarver, was discovered by Evelyn in 1671 and introduced to Wren. Thereafter he never lacked commissions in churches (e.g. St. Paul's Cathedral) and great houses all over England.

GIBBONS (1) Orlando (1583-1625) the composer, was organist at the Chapel Royal from 1604. His brother **(2) Edward (?1570-1652)** also a composer, was organist at Bristol Cathedral from 1599 to 1611 and at Exeter from 1611 to 1644. Orlando's son **(3) Christopher (1615-76)** was organist at Winchester Cathedral in circumstances of great difficulty from 1638 to 1661 and thereafter at the Chapel Royal and Westminster Abbey.

GIBBS, James (1682-1754) distinguished architect trained in Rome. He designed *inter alia* St. Mary-le-Strand and St. Martin-in-the-Fields (London), part of Kings College, Cambridge and the Radcliffe Library at Oxford. He also published several architectural manuals.

GIBRALTAR was taken in 1704 by the Anglo-Dutch force under Rooke on behalf of the Archduke Charles, the allies' candidate for the Spanish throne. The cession to Britain was recognised at the T. of Utrecht (1713), but the Rock was offered to Spain in 1720 as a condition of joining the quadruple alliance (*see* GEORGE 1-13). It was refused. In 1726 the Spaniards made an unsuccessful attack and from 1779 to 1783 the Rock, under Eliott's governorship, endured a Great Siege which has become legendary. The place became a crown colony in 1830. It was demanded by Spain in 1880, when the Suez Canal made it even more important to Britain than before. Plans for attacking it were made in World War II, but came to nothing because Franco preferred to keep out of the war. The great scarcity of land and fresh water led to much tunnelling and reclamation beginning during the Great Siege and extending down to 1973. During World War II the spoil from the excavations sufficed to build an airfield projecting into Algeçiras

Bay, which visually speaking, is dominated by its rock. Spanish demands, accompanied by long closures of frontiers, continued after World War II. The population remained hostile to annexation by Spain and there was a pronounced trade shift from Spain to Morocco. *See Appendix of diagrams*.

GIBSON, Edmund (1669-1748) edited the *Anglo-Saxon Chronicle* (1692), Camden's *Britannia* (1695) and his long authoritative *Codex Juris Ecclesiae Anglicanae* (Lat = Law of the English Church) (1712). He became Bp. of Lincoln in 1716. Translated to London in 1720 he became Walpole's professional ecclesiastical adviser but opposed the Quaker Relief Bill in 1736, quarrelled with him and was passed over in 1737 for Canterbury. He refused it in 1747.

GIFFARD. Honour with, in 1208-13, 12 manors in Oxfordshire, Buckinghamshire and Berkshire.

GIFFARD, Bonaventure (1642-1734) was a R. Catholic chaplain to James II, who intruded him into the presidency of Magdalen College, Oxford in Mar. 1688. Ejected and imprisoned in Oct. he became a bishop *in partibus* and acted as a vicar apostolic in the west (1708-13).

GIFFARD (1) Walter (?-1279) became Bp. of Bath and Wells in 1265. He was an opponent of Simon de Montfort, whom he excommunicated, and after the B. of Evesham he was briefly Chancellor and one of the arbitrators in the Award of Kenilworth in 1266. He then became Abp. of York and was one of the regents from 1272 to 1274 and in 1275. His equally talented but less respected brother **(2) Godfrey (?1235-1302)** succeeded him as Chancellor in 1266, became Bp. of Worcester in 1268 and, having resigned the chancery in 1270, negotiated with the Welsh in 1272. Edward I employed him as a justice in Eyre and in diplomatic dealings with the Scots. A (possible) kinsman or brother **(3) John (1232-99) Ld. GIFFARD of BROMSFIELD (1295)** originally supported Montfort, but became attached to Gilbert of Clare and fought for the King at Evesham in 1265. Thereafter he served Edward I mainly as a soldier in Wales, Gascony and Scotland and in 1283 founded Gloucester Hall, a part of the modern Worcester College, Oxford. He was one of the regents in 1297.

GIFFARD, William (?-1129) Chancellor to William II, was nominated to the See of Winchester in 1100 by Henry I. He was a friend and supporter of Anselm and, on refusing consecration from Gerard of York, was banished and only consecrated to his See in 1107 when the investiture dispute had been settled. Until 1124 he had many disputes himself with the monks of Winchester Cathedral and in 1128 he founded the first English Cistercian house at Waverley.

GIFFORD, Adam (1820-87) a lord of session from 1870, founded the Gifford Lectures.

GIFFORD, Andrew (1700-84) asst. librarian at the British Museum from 1757 to 1784, was a distinguished numismatist, whose collection was acquired for the museum by George II.

GIFFORD, Gilbert (?1561-90) a R. Catholic, was a double agent used by Walsingham to penetrate the Babington conspiracy and to carry and copy Mary Q. of Scots' secret correspondence.

GIFFORD, John (alias GREEN) (1758-1818) a London police magistrate, edited the *Anti-Jacobin Review and Magazine* from 1798. *See* GIFFORD, WILLIAM.

GIFFORD, Robert (1779-1826) 1st Ld. (1824), a crown lawyer, as Att-Gen. prosecuted the Cato St. Conspirators and (before the Lords) Q. Caroline in 1820. In 1824 he became C.J. of the Common Pleas.

GIFFORD, William (1756-1826) edited the *Anti-Jacobin* (not the same as the *Anti-Jacobin Review*) and from 1809 to 1824 was the first editor of the *Quarterly Review*.

GIFLE were a small Middle Anglian folk in the Ivel valley (Beds.).

GILBERT, St. of Caithness (?-1245) archdeacon of Moray and, from 1223, successor to the murdered Bp. Adam of Caithness, he built the cathedral at Dornoch and hospices. He was an excellent preacher and a rare peacemaker in this violent diocese, which he did so much to civilise that his relics were used for swearing oaths until the Reformation.

GILBERT, Sir Humphrey (?1539-83), a step-brother of Sir Walter Raleigh, served under Sir Henry Sydney in Ireland and became Pres. of Munster in 1569. M.P. in 1571, he was attacked as a court sycophant. In 1572 he campaigned in Holland without success against the Spaniards and spent the next six years in retirement. Having obtained a charter for discovery and plantation, he made a voyage to North America in 1579 which was a failure and a second in 1583 during which he founded a colony in Newfoundland. He was drowned on the way back.

GILBERT, William (1540-1603) published his *De Magnete, Magnetisque Corporibus* (Lat = The Magnet and Magnetic Bodies) in 1600. In this, sometimes called the first major scientific work produced in England, he systematised the notion of magnetism and confirmed Copernicus' theory that the earth revolved.

GILBERT, Sir William Schwenk (1836-1914) and **SULLIVAN, Sir Arthur Seymour (1842-1900).** Gilbert published the *Bab Ballads* between 1866 and 1871. Sullivan was organist at St. Michaels, Chester Sq. from 1861 to 1872. They were introduced by Frederick Clay in 1871. Their Savoy Operas, beginning with *Trial by Jury* began to appear in 1875. *Patience* appeared in 1881, *Iolanthe* in 1882, *Princess Ida* in 1884 and the *Mikado* in 1885. All this time Sullivan was composing religious music as well. They quarrelled in 1890 but collaborated, with less success, again from 1893 to 1896.

GILBERT of SEMPRINGHAM, St. (?-1189) began as a clerk in the household of Bp. Chesney of Lincoln. Before 1131 Alexander, the next bishop, allowed him to instruct seven women in the strict religious life at his native Sempringham where he erected buildings. The community grew and he added some lay sisters and brothers. In about 1139 his feudal lord, Gilbert de Gant, granted a more suitable site for a larger priory. In 1147 St. Gilbert asked the general chapter of the Cistercians to make themselves responsible for Sempringham and a second house at Haverholme. They refused but St. Bernard helped him to draw up Institutes for his independent Order of Sempringham. In these Gilbert added canons to serve as priests to the nuns. The canons followed the Augustinian rule, the nuns the Benedictine and the lay brothers the Cistercian rule for *conversi*. Gilbert was Master of the order during his life. By his death the order had 12 houses, besides orphanages and leper hospitals in Lincolnshire and adjoining counties. He was canonised in 1202.

GILBERT THE UNIVERSAL (?-1134) Bp. of LONDON (1128), a Breton, studied under Anselm of Laon, became a schoolmaster at Auxerre and a canon of Lyons. He achieved European fame as an Old Testament commentator, theologian and philosopher. Abp. Thurstan retained his services to advocate before the Roman *curia* the rights of the church of York against those of Canterbury, but he changed sides against his employer. Perhaps as a bribe or reward for this, Henry I got him the Bishopric of London where, by miserly greed, he accumulated a vast treasure.

GILBERT AND ELLICE Is. (Pacific). Some Ellice Is. were visited by Spaniards between 1568 and 1595; and in 1781 others were sighted by whalers between 1807 and 1825. The Gilberts were visited by the British in 1765 and 1788 and by various traders between 1799 and 1824. Cook charted Christmas I. in 1777. Fanning discovered the Line Is. in 1798. A British protectorate was established in 1892 followed by annexation at local request in 1915. The Phoenix Is. were added in 1937. The islands were administered by local native authorities aided by visiting British officers under a British Commissioner. They became self governing in 1971. The Ellice Is., at independence in 1978, were renamed **TUVALU** and separated from the Gilberts.

GILBERTS ACT 1782, an adoptive act, created a procedure which permitted parishes to take power or unite for Poor Law purposes without having to seek a private Act of Parliament (*see* POOR LAW INCORPORATIONS). Passed at the moment when the industrial revolution made the workhouse system uneconomic, parish vestries were mostly reluctant to use it. Where it was adopted there was a slight administrative improvement as compared with the ordinarily degrading standard of rural workhouses, but important places such as Ipswich managed (badly) without any form of Poor Law incorporation until it was forced on them in 1835.

GILDAS (c. 497-570), a British monk, went to Brittany and in c. 540 composed the relatively short *De Excidio Britonum* (Lat = The Overthrow of the British) as a secular apocalypse and reminder of the divine retribution which follows sin. He was writing in the period of calm after the British victory at Mount Badon and hoped to warn the rulers and churchmen of his day against failings which might lead to further retribution. As it happens *De Excidio* is the only surviving narrative account of any sort for 5th cent. Britain.

GILDEROY alias Patrick MACGREGOR. A handsome Perthshire highwayman, who is supposed to have picked Oliver Cromwell's pocket and hanged an unspecified judge. He was hanged at Edinburgh in July 1638.

GILES, St., a very ancient cult makes him the patron of cripples, beggars and smiths. The centre was at St. Gilles near Arles (Provence) where he was a hermit. The Visigothic K. Wamba's hounds flushed out his pet hind and an arrow was shot after it. When the King caught up, he found Giles with the hind in his arms, himself wounded by the arrow and the hounds all cowering. This famous story does not wholly explain the European-wide mediaeval popularity of this saint, to whom in Britain alone over 150 churches are dedicated and on whose day (1 Sept.) several immense fairs, notably at Oxford and Winchester, were begun. The Winchester Fair lasted three weeks during which the bishop had control of the town. It has lapsed but the Oxford fair continues.

GILES, Ernest (1839-97) explorer of the Australian outback between 1872 and 1876, demonstrated that the interior west of 132° long was wasteland.

GILGIT (Kashmir). The ancient Trakane dynasty ended in about 1810 and, after a generation of disorder, the area was occupied in 1842 by the Sikhs. In 1846 Kashmir, with Gilgit, was ceded to Maharajah Gulab Singh of Jammu, but in 1852 his Dogras were driven out. They returned in 1860 and a further generation of disorder ended when the British established an agency to guard against Russian encroachments. In 1947 they handed it over to Kashmir, whereupon the Gilgit Scouts rose and claimed accession to Pakistan.

GILL, Eric (1882-1940), sexually extrovert yet religious sculptor and engraver, and a polemical typographer. He executed sculptures at, *inter alia*, the BBC, the *Palais des Nations* at Geneva and Westminster Cathedral. He formed a semi-religious craftsmen's guild and left well known new typefaces. A diffuse seminal influence in English 20th cent. art, he weakened it by overstrident advocacy on trivial issues.

GILLEVRAY, SIOL. See CLANS, SCOTTISH.

GILLRAY, James (1757-1815) issued about 1500, mostly savage, political cartoons between 1780 and 1811 when he went mad. His largest target was the royal family but Pitt, Fox, Sheridan, Burke, various radicals, Nelson, Bonaparte and the French revolutionaries were all impartially attacked.

GILT EDGED STOCK is any investment at a fixed periodical rate of interest whose payment may be safely expected because either the govt. is the borrower or the borrower (generally a local authority, public corporation, pension fund of foreign govt) is guaranteed by the British govt. or payment is secured (e.g. by mortgage or debenture) upon property which can be taken in default. The govt. is the biggest dealer in the GILT EDGED MARKET at the Stock Exchange because its needs and receipts seldom coincide, while its operations may be very large.

GIN was medicinally distilled at Leiden (Holland) in about 1650. British troops acquired the taste in Marlborough's wars and so under Q. Anne the customs duty was raised and the excise reduced. English distilleries flourished. Cheap and readily available in the 1720s and 1730s, gin became a popular palliative for miseries, poverty and urban squalor. The high related mortality led Walpole to raise the excise in 1736 and provoked riots, but by 1750 gin drinking ("drunk for a ha'penny, dead drunk for a penny") was the social menace portrayed in Hogarth's prints and by Henry Fielding who, as a magistrate was, with his brother John, directly concerned. Prosecutions under the Vagrancy Acts and religious exhortation alike failed to control this type of drunkeness, which was eventually reduced only by very high taxation.

GINKEL (1) Godert de (1630-1703) 1st E. of ATHLONE (1692), one of William III's generals, came to England in 1688 and, after fighting at the Boyne and at Limerick, was left as William's commander in Ireland. In 1691 he won the decisive B. of Aughrim and in Oct. ended the Irish war with the T. of Limerick. Subsequently he served in William III's campaigns and in 1702 was briefly Marlborough's 2-in-C. His son **(2) Frederick Christian (1668-1719) 2nd E.,** also a professional soldier, served as cavalry commander under Marlborough.

GIPPS, Sir George (1791-1847) and **GIPPSLAND.** After being wounded at Badajoz (1812) and superintending the Ostend fortifications (1815) he went to the W. Indies where he attracted govt. attention by sending home a long series of detailed reports. Ld. Auckland decided to try him out as his private sec. and, as a result, he became a joint commissioner in Canada (1835-7) and in 1838 gov. of N.S.W. He quickly appreciated the possibilities of development, especially of farming and grazing in the S.W. of Gippsland, later named after him, and encouraged them particularly by building roads, but the farming inclosures threatened the life of the aboriginals whom he was determined to protect and he had to keep the land revenue for the Crown to finance the public works. Both issues created conflicts with colonists and emancipists (a rough lot) which were not resolved before he came home in 1846.

GIRALDUS (de BARRI) CAMBRENSIS (?1146-1220), a Welshman of royal blood (*see* NEST) and ambitious to become Abp. of a metropolitan see for Wales, became Archdeacon of Brecon in 1175 and procured the excommunication of the Bp. of St. Asaph for infringing the rights of St. Davids. He was nominated for St. Davids in 1176 but Peter de Leia was elected instead. In 1180 he became a commissary for St. Davids, in 1184 a court chaplain and in 1185 he was with P. John in Ireland. At Henry II's death he toured Wales with Abp. Baldwin to preach the Third Crusade and then, after refusing four Welsh sees, he was elected to St. Davids, the leading see, in 1198. He now went to Rome to negotiate a *pallium,* but royal intrigues caused his own chapter to disown him and in 1202 he went into exile. Eventually he gave way to an intruder in the see and was pensioned. He wrote *Topographia Hibernica* (Irish topography), *Ex-pugnatio Hibernica* (The Conquest of Ireland); *Itinerarium Cambriae* (Journey through Wales), *De Rebus a Se Gestis* (Autobiography) and lives of St. David and St. Hugh of Lincoln.

GIRARDUS CORNUBIENSIS or GERARD OF CORNWALL (?14th cent.) is the alleged author of the lost *De gestis Britonum* (History of the Britons) and *De gestis Regum West-Saxonum* (History of the Kings of the West Saxons).

GIRIC. *See* SCOTS or ALBAN KINGS, EARLY-4.

GIRLS PUBLIC DAY SCHOOLS CO. (later TRUST). Frances Mary Buss (1827-94) started the North London Collegiate School as a private venture in 1850. She passed the property to trustees in 1870 (but continued to direct the school) and they and she together launched the G.P.D.S. Co. in 1871. This began founding girls' schools on the model of the North London Collegiate all over the country.

GIRONDINS. French moderate revolutionaries, originally led by Brissot and Vergniaud, who initially dominated the Legislative Assembly elected in 1791; they with Roland, his wife and Dumouriez formed a govt. in Mar. 1792. They were unable to maintain order in the face of a pro-royalist Austro-Prussian invasion and Jacobin organised extremism, though Dumouriez held off the invasion at Valmy (20 Sept. 1792). The Assembly suspended the monarchy; in Sept. it was succeeded by the Jacobin dominated Convention, which proclaimed the Republic (22 Sept.) and in Jan. 1793 executed Louis XIV, against Girondin opposition. The First Coalition against France, formed in Feb., resulted in the formation of a popular dictatorship and in Apr. its instrument, the Committee of Public Safety. The alarmed Girondins attempted a counter stroke by impeaching Marat, the most extreme of the Jacobins; the latter promptly organised a *coup d'état* which overwhelmed them (June 1793).

GIRTON COLLEGE opened at Hitchin in 1869 under Emily Davies as the COLLEGE FOR WOMEN. It moved to Girton (Cambridge) in 1872. In 1947 women were admitted to membership of Cambridge University, of which Girton became a college.

GISORS. London city aldermanic family from Normandy but with Gascon relatives. They flourished from 11th to 14th cents., mainly as spice and wine merchants and shipowners, with strong court connections. They also had estates in the city and Home counties.

GISORS, Ts. of (1113). *See* HENRY 1-10. **(1189).** *See* RICHARD I-1.

GLACIS. *See Appendix;* VALETTA.

GLADSTONE (1) Sir John (1764-1851) of the overseas trading firm of Corrie and Co. of Liverpool, acquired a very big interest in the East India trade after the end of the HEIC monopoly and also became a W. India merchant who consistently defended slavery. He was a Canningite M.P. for Liverpool in 1812, Lancaster in 1818, Woodstock in 1820 and Berwick in 1826. An opponent of the repeal of the Corn Laws, he was converted by Peel. He contrived to endow charities at Liverpool and Leith. His famous son **(2) William Ewart (1809-98)** became a Conservative M.P. in 1832 and his first important speech (1833) favoured progressive emancipation of slaves through intermediate stages of apprenticeship. Having a doctrinally sophisticated religious bent, he opposed the lay appropriation of Irish church property in the same year. He held minor office in Peel's first govt., wrote theological books and opposed the Opium War (1840) in opposition and began with minor office in Peel's second govt. His efficient handling of the Customs Bill (1842) created his opening. He became a member of Peel's Cabinet in 1843 as Pres. of the Bd. of Trade and, as such, managed the first general railway bill (1844). In 1845 his religious conscience got the better of him and he resigned over the Maynooth grant. He supported the repeal of the Corn Laws and succeeded Stanley (a protectionist) at the Colonial Office (1846) but having, as the rule then was, to vacate his seat, did not stand for re-election and was not in parliament during the repeal proceedings. Nevertheless, he was returned as a Peelite for Oxford Univ. in 1847, after the Conservative Party had split. At this period he was taking an interest in foreign affairs, which led to clashes with Palmerston over Greece in 1850. He also made the acquaintance of Giacomo (later Sir James) Lacaita, legal adviser at the British legation to Naples. Lacaita supplied information about Bourbon tyranny and induced Gladstone to make a visit. The result, in 1851, was a celebrated exposure of atrocities which discredited the Neapolitan govt. and was a milestone on the way to Italian unification. In 1852 he became Ch. of the Exchequer under Aberdeen (*see* TREASURY). His policy was to impose a succession duty so as to eliminate progressively the income tax. The plan failed because of the Crimean War and in 1855 he vacated office when Palmerston superseded Aberdeen. Bellicose policies did not appeal to his thrifty practicality and he was soon attacking the govt. for bombarding Canton. He also vigorously opposed the creation of a divorce court (1857) and then published some Homeric studies. This probably influenced Bulwer-Lytton, who sent him to the Ionian Is. to investigate the demand for unification with Greece (1858-9). In 1859 he supported Disraeli's reform bill and then became Palmerston's Ch. of the Exchequer. His most enduring measures at this time were the creation of the Post Office Savings Bank and, after a clash with the Lords, the repeal of the Paper Duty (1861) which was a form of indirect censorship. When Palmerston died in 1865 he became Leader of the Commons, in 1867 leader of the Liberal Party in succession to Ld. John Russell and in 1868 Prime Minister (*see next entry*.) He resigned the Liberal leadership in 1875. He was temporarily free to indulge his bent for knight errantry, this time at the expense of the infidel Turks. His denunciation of the Bulgarian massacres permanently injured Ottoman prestige and shook the foundations of British middle eastern policy. His advocacy of a Russian alliance to liberate the oppressed Christian subjects of the Porte broke down in the face of the hard realities, but his wholesale condemnation of Disraeli's imperialism sprang from the same source (*see* MID-LOTHIAN CAMPAIGN 1878-80). He became Prime Minister again in 1880 (*see* GLADSTONE'S SECOND GOVT. 1880-5) and for a third time in 1886 (*see* GLADSTONE'S THIRD GOVT. 1886). During much of this period he was engaged, not always successfully, in liquidating imperialism and it was the Irish Home Rule problem which brought him down, for the emotional public was against him in 1886 and again when he was prime minister for the last time (*see* GLADSTONE'S FOURTH GOVT. 1892-4).

GLADSTONE'S FIRST GOVT. (Dec. 1868-Feb. 1874). (15 in Cabinet under W. E. Gladstone. Lord Hatherley, Lord Chancellor; R. Lowe, Ch. of the Exch; H. A. Bruce, Home Sec; E. of Clarendon, Foreign Sec; Edw. Cardwell, Sec. for War; C. S. Fortescue, Chief Sec. for Ireland; J. Bright, Pres. of the Bd. of Trade. Clarendon died June 1870 and was succeeded by E. Granville. Bright resigned in Dec. 1870) **(1)** came into office after the electoral victory of Nov. 1868. This was fought on the new franchise which had increased the non-conformist vote and with Gladstone and Bright waging an oratorical campaign of a new kind, which Disraeli did not try to emulate. The outspoken issue was Irish reform and most of the voters showed no sympathy for the Irish Anglican Church. The less obviously canvassed issue was reform generally and this govt. was the most active reforming govt. of the 19th cent.

(2) Its first business was to disestablish the Irish Church and buy out the Canadian jurisdictions of the Hudson Bay Co. (both Mar. 1869). In 1870 it was busy with an unsuccessful attempt to protect Irish tenants (Irish Land Act 1870), with the inclusion of Manitoba in Canada, the grant of a constitution in Western Australia and with the important Education Act of 1870, which laid the foundations of the modern state educational system. By June 1870 most branches of the Civil Service were

opened to competitive examination and Cardwell was commencing his remarkable military reforms.

(3) This domestic work was carried on behind the screen of the Royal Navy which could overwhelm any seaborne threat, but without an offensive land potential. Thus the govt. took little interest in the growing power of Bismarck's Prussia until, with the rest of the German states, he attacked France in Aug. 1870. This affected British interests immediately at two widely separated points: Belgium and the Black Sea. Bismarck published a draft treaty (of 1866) for a possible French annexation of Belgium and the govt. promptly intervened to get France and Prussia to reguarantee the Belgian neutrality treaty of 1839, itself undertaking to join in the defence of Belgium against whichever side violated her territory. Meanwhile, to sidetrack possible interventions in the war, Bismarck induced the Russians to denounce the Black Sea neutralisation clauses of the T. of Paris (1856). This they did (Oct. 1870) after the surrender of the surviving major French army at Metz. Thus with Russia friendly, France desperate and Britain distracted in the near east, Bismarck could pursue his course. The event demonstrated again the limitations of British power, for the angry Turks could not move alone and Britain could give them naval, but not military, assistance. Hence the govt. took the general point that treaties should not be unilaterally denounced and at the London Conference (Jan. 1871) the powers agreed this principle, but signed a multilateral agreement conceding the Russian demand. A further side effect of the 1870 war was the seizure of Papal Rome by the Kingdom of Italy.

(4) These events shook simultaneously British complacency and the govt's prestige. They enabled Cardwell to carry his army reforms further, despite heated opposition within the army itself. They also impressed upon the public the contrast between Britain's technical, material and commercial pre-eminence and her apparent continental impotence and they bred an increasingly vociferous distrust of Russia. These were psychological changes which an imaginative opposition, led by Disraeli, was able to exploit with growing success, more especially as the govt. still seemed to be over-preoccupied with domestic reforms. In 1871 the University Tests Act opened Oxford and Cambridge to all denominations and the Local Govt. Board was set up. Lord Hatherley went blind and resigned the Woolsack in 1872. Lord Selborne, his successor, procured the passage of the important technical and yet parochial seeming reform of the legal system by the Judicature Act, 1873.

(5) The govt's grip on public opinion was also weakened by intangible factors. Its nonconformist support was eroded by the pro-Anglican compromises of Forster's Education Act, 1870. Its drastic Licensing Act, 1871, alienated not only the brewers and the publicans but their customers who, even if nonconformist, were not always as high minded as their pastors. From the summer of 1871 the opposition was gaining by-elections. All the same, successes at Westminster continued. The Trade Union Act, 1871, however left trade unionists unsatisfied. The Ballot Act, 1872 (for which there had been little demand) seemed to advance liberal ideals in a philosophical rather than a practical sense. Meanwhile the govt. had united Basutoland with Cape Colony and bought the Kimberley diamond fields from the Boers (Oct. 1871). In Feb. 1872 it acquired the Dutch Gold Coast forts in return for British claims in Sumatra, whereby it appeared to abandon potential wealth for an inevitable Ashanti War. In Oct. 1872 it conferred local self govt. on the Cape.

(6) These events, all very well in their way, seemed irrelevant to the wishes and circumstances of the voters, many of them now stricken by the world trade recession of 1871-2 and by the European agricultural collapse caused by the wholesale importation of cheap North

American grain. Gladstone's parliamentary power began to decline; he was attempting an instalment of Irish reform designed to create educational opportunities for the R. Catholics on the analogy of the University Tests Act. His Irish University Bill was defeated by the opposition in alliance with the Irish (for whom it did not go far enough) and the presbyterians and radical educationalists (for whom it went too far). Gladstone resigned and suggested that Disraeli should form a minority govt. Disraeli refused and Gladstone resumed office with a reshuffled cabinet, in which he himself took over the Exchequer. He continued to lose by-elections and was advised that under the law as it then stood he would have to face a by-election himself on accepting the Exchequer. Believing that he might lose his seat in a by-election but retain it in a general election, he advised a dissolution before parliament met again (Jan. 1874). The conservatives won the election and he resigned.

GLADSTONE'S SECOND GOVT. (Apr. 1880-June 1885)

(14 in Cabinet under W. E. Gladstone who was also Ch. of the Exch; Lord (from 1881 E. of) Selborne, Lord Chancellor; Sir Wm. Vernon Harcourt, Home Sec; Earl Granville, Foreign Sec; E. of Kimberley, Colonial Sec; M. of Hartington, Sec. for India; Joseph Chamberlain, Pres. of the Bd. of Trade; W. E. Forster, Chief Sec. for Ireland; John Bright, Ch. of the Duchy of Lancaster) succeeded Disraeli's second govt. after the general election of Mar. 1880 with an overall majority of 72, Parnell's Irish Home Rulers having 65 seats. (1) Hartington had previously led the liberals in the Commons and Granville in the Lords, but Gladstone's second Midlothian campaign had given him a primacy in public, especially radical, estimation which made his claim to the chief office incontestable but, except for Chamberlain and the now ineffectual Bright, all his chosen colleagues were whigs. This union of extremes which overthrew Disraeli was incapable of a steady policy in office in the face of the great difficulties it had to meet.

(2) Though business and industry were coming out of the 1873-9 depression, the agricultural decline, with its appalling Irish consequences, continued. The Afghan War was still in progress and there was a drift towards conflict with the newly proclaimed (Dec. 1879) Transvaal Boer republic. The French too were on the move in the Far East. At the very start of the new parliament a weak speaker (Brand) involved the Commons in the discreditable Bradlaugh affair, which brought the House into repeated collision with Bradlaugh's constituents. Then the govt's urgent Irish tenant compensation bill was introduced late, had a stormy passage through the Commons and was thrown out by the Lords. Thereupon the powerful Irish Land League, at Parnell's suggestion, organised boycotts of anyone taking a farm from which a tenant had been evicted. Boycotts spread all over Ireland, shaking the fabric of Irish society.

(3) By Sept. 1880 the Afghan War had been successfully liquidated, but in Oct. there was war with the Boers. The govt. meanwhile abandoned Irish conciliation. In Nov. it prosecuted Parnell and the Land League for conspiracy. The trial, protracted until 25 Jan. 1881, ended in a jury disagreement. While triumphant bonfires blazed in Ireland, the govt. introduced a Coercion Bill to suspend *Habeas Corpus* and give the Irish govt. powers of arbitrary arrest. Before it could be debated, the Boers defeated the army at Laings Nek (28 Jan. 1881). The Irish members obstructed debate for three days (31 Jan.-2 Feb.) and during entirely novel and disorderly closure proceedings, most of them were suspended. The closure rules were passed but even with their aid debate continued through Feb., while the army was defeated at Majuba Hill (26 Feb.).

(4) The govt's national and international prestige was by now very low; Gladstone disliked imperial adventures. In Mar. the Roumanian principalities proclaimed

themselves a single kingdom. In May the French seized Turkish Tunis, which Disraeli had promised them as "compensation" for the British occupation of Cyprus. Disraeli's policy of bolstering Turkey was thus thrown overboard. In July the Greeks annexed Thessaly. In Aug. the Pretoria Convention recognised the internal autonomy of the S. African Republic. These changes could not, in any event, be opposed because the govt. was obsessed with Ireland. Gladstone was determined to couple coercion with redress of grievances. In Apr. 1881 he introduced an Irish Land Bill to give tenants fixity of tenure, fair rents and rights of free sale (The Three F's). Far from welcoming it, Parnell redoubled his agitation, for he wanted to keep the support of the American extremists. The bill passed, but he provoked a scene in the Commons and was expelled. In Oct. he was interned in Kilmainham Gaol. His tactics ensured that coercion should fail.

(5) Trouble now arose in Egypt (*see* EGYPT – 10 TO 12). By Sept. Arabi Pasha had compelled the Khedive to dismiss the govt, establish a constitution and quadruple the army. Gladstone's govt. thought that Anglo-French joint intervention would be unworkable and favoured using a Turkish force. This the French govt. opposed but in Jan. the latter resigned and the new govt. opposed overseas adventures altogether. Thereupon Arabi made himself minister of war. While the govt. sought to attract the co-operation of other powers the Egyptian situation festered.

(6) Irish outrages grew in quantity and violence. In Apr. 1882 Parnell was given leave to visit a dying nephew in Paris and his dying daughter by Mrs O'Shea at Eltham. Through her husband, he communicated with Gladstone and Chamberlain. The result was the so-called Kilmainham T. They undertook to remit Irish arrears of rent; he to call off the violence. Forster, the Chief Sec. and Lord Cowper, the Lord Lieut. resigned and were replaced by Lord Frederick Cavendish (Hartington's brother) and Lord Spencer. A fair prospect of peace was, however, destroyed by the murder of Burke, the under-sec. and Lord Frederick while trying to defend him, in Phoenix Park, Dublin (May 1882). Parnell was not responsible and he and Gladstone tried to save the Treaty, but public opinion demanded new criminal legislation and the Arrears Bill was unfavourably amended. The Parnellites necessarily opposed both, and violence, now out of Parnell's control, reached new heights.

(7) Meanwhile in Egypt Arabi's followers were out of hand. British and French fleets went to Alexandria to protect European interests. In June rioters killed many Europeans, Arabi's guns threatened the anchorages and in July Adm. Seymour was authorised to destroy them. The French withdrew and the forts were bombarded into surrender (11 July 1882). The British were thus involved alone. Only on 18th did the govt. authorise an expeditionary force which landed under Sir Garnet Wolseley. The brilliant B. of Tel-el-Kebir destroyed Arabi's power. Cairo was seized. The Italians, baulked of Tunis, quietly occupied Assab in Eritrea.

(8) The anti-imperialist Gladstone govt. now found itself in possession of a bankrupt Egyptian empire which it did not want but, because of the Suez Canal, dared not abandon to any other power. The lower provinces were in disorder and the vast Sudanese territories in the grip of the Mahdist rebellion. The Khedivial govt. would not retreat and, determined to send an army of reconquest under a British officer, Hicks Pasha. The British Cabinet weakly let it go. It was overwhelmed in Kordofan (B of El Obeid Nov. 1883). It was now decided to abandon the area, but this meant gathering in many scattered garrisons depending on Khartoum. The famous, austere, but self-willed Gen. Gordon was sent to carry out this difficult plan (Jan. 1884). On arrival he changed his mind and

decided to hold on. In Mar. the cabinet vetoed this change but by May, with the Mahdists in Berbera, he was cut off.

(9) In the govt's. three first years, the political excitement had blocked all but harmless or uncontroversial legislation. In 1880 there were Acts on Seamen's wages and grain cargoes; in 1881 flogging in the services was abolished. In 1882 there were the far-reaching Married Women's Property and the Settled Land Acts. In 1883 came the important Bankruptcy and Patents Acts and an effective Corrupt Practices Act to prevent electoral abuses. But none of these could satisfy the govt's radical supporters, who were now restive. They wanted to assimilate the franchise in the country (their whig allies territory) to that in the towns. Gladstone was thus preoccupied with keeping his party together, while Chamberlain blew the trumpets of class war. The Franchise Bill passed the Commons, but whig and Tory peers held it up on the ground that it should be accompanied by a redistribution measure. The radicals shouted "peers against the people" and "mend them or end them"; politics reached a new level of bitterness and demagoguery, feared as much by the major leaders as by the court. Gladstone and the Queen worked to reduce the tension and compromises were laboriously reached behind the scenes. The gestation of the final enactments (*see* REPRESENTATION OF THE PEOPLE ACT, 1885 and REDISTRIBUTION ACT OF SEATS, 1885) thus occupied the time when decisions about Gordon's plight in Khartoum were needed. Rescue was not ordered until Aug. and could not start until Sept. The force fought its way gallantly south. It reached Khartoum at the end of Jan. 1885, two days after it had been stormed and Gordon killed.

(10) This popular hero's death due to procrastination, sealed the govt's electoral fate, but the British position in Egypt estranged Britain from France (hitherto the predominant local influence) while the French seizure of Tunis (convenient to Britain) had upset the Italians and driven them into alliance with Germany and Austria. Gladstone's anti-imperialism now created further difficulties. Against the advice of Sir Evelyn Baring, British agent and consul general since 1883, the govt. refused to guarantee the Egyptian loan of 1885 and it was guaranteed jointly by the six European powers, who were consequently all represented on the debt commission. Major decisions of Egyptian govt. policy needed the Commission's backing and, since the Russians and French were habitually hostile to Britain, the British had to lean upon the other three whose leading spirit was Bismarck. So Britain, having done all the work, became beholden to the Germans in Egypt.

(11) The govt., however, fell on an Irish issue. Cabinet disagreement over a devolution bill led to the radical Chamberlain's resignation, while the Tory, Lord Randolph Churchill, secured Parnellite support by offering an end to coercion. Hence on a Tory amendment to the budget (June 1885) the Tory-Irish combination carried the day by 12 votes because 76 liberals abstained. Gladstone then resigned.

GLADSTONE'S THIRD GOVT. (Feb.-Aug., 1886). (14 in Cabinet under W. E. Gladstone; Lord Herschell, Lord Chancellor; Earl Spencer, Lord Pres; Sir Wm. Vernon Harcout, Ch. of the Exch; John Morley, Ch. Sec. for Ireland; Joseph Chamberlain, Pres. of the Local Govt. Bd.) (*see* SALISBURY'S FIRST GOVT.). Hartington refused office. This govt., mainly concerned with Irish affairs, was a Liberal-Irish alliance. It decided to introduce a Home Rule Bill (q.v.) in Mar. whereupon Chamberlain resigned. The Second Reading was moved in Apr. Parnell's previous electoral pact with the conservatives had given the latter a number of additional M.P.s who would vote against a liberal Home Rule Bill. Hartington's whig and Chamberlain's radical dissentients (93 in all) voted against the bill, which was defeated on Second Reading after 16

days' debate by 343 votes to 313. In the resulting general election it turned out that the country was even more against Home Rule than the House. 316 Conservatives and 78 dissentient Liberals were returned against 191 Liberals and 85 Irish Nationalists.

GLADSTONE'S FOURTH GOVT. (Aug. 1892-Mar. 1894). (17 in Cabinet under W. E. Gladstone; Lord Herschell, Lord Chancellor; E. of Kimberley, Lord Pres. and Sec. for India; Sir Wm. Vernon Harcourt, Ch. of the Exch; H. H. Asquith, Home Sec; E. of Rosebery, Foreign Sec; M. of Ripon, Colonial Sec; H. Campbell-Bannerman, Sec. for War; John Morley, Chief Sec. for Ireland; H. H. Fowler, Pres. of the Local Govt. Bd.) (1) came to power with the support of 273 Liberals, 81 Irish and one independent Labour against 269 Conservatives and 46 Liberal Unionists after the general election of July 1892. Gladstone, though vigorous, was nearly eighty-three. Henry Labouchere, the radical who owned *Truth*, was excluded at Q. Victoria's request because of *Truth*'s treatment of the royal family. For the first time ministers had to resign their company directorships.

(2) While an Irish Home Rule Bill was being drafted, the govt. was faced with problems in Uganda. The territory had been passed to the Brit. East Africa Co., now in financial difficulties. Harcourt favoured abandonment; Rosebery retention (Sept. 1892). A decision was shelved by sending Sir Gerald Portal (and Lady Iris, his liberal and witty wife) to investigate.

(3) The Home Rule Bill was introduced in Feb. 1893 and after 85 sittings passed its Third Reading on 1 Sept. Its ablest critic was Chamberlain, but the debates founded the reputation of the Parnellite, John Redmond. Gladstone piloted the bill throughout these intense and exhausting days, during which the govt. had other calls upon its energies, for the French attacked Siam in May and obviously intended to annex it. Rosebery firmly stopped them and forced them to agree to make Siam a buffer state (July).

(4) A week after the Home Rule bill passed the Commons, the D. of Devonshire persuaded the Lords, on Second Reading, by 419 votes to 41, to throw it out. Gladstone wanted to dissolve, but British opinion supported the Lords and his colleagues dissuaded him. In the meantime popular imperialism was stirred by the operations of Cecil Rhodes, managing director since 1889 of the Brit. South Africa Co. and, since 1890, premier of the Cape. In Oct. and Nov. 1893, after long disputes with LoBengula, the much feared King of the Matabele, a Co. expedition armed with machine guns and led by Dr. Jameson, overthrew him. The memory of the Zulu wars made the exploit seem brilliant and distracted the people from the endless burden of Irish trouble.

(5) Despite the rising partisanship of a mainly conservative House of Lords, the govt's domestic policy was not wholly barren. In pursuit of the Newcastle programme a Local Govt. Bill and an Employer's Liability Bill passed the Commons. The former set up district and parish councils and distributed the functions of the 1875 sanitary authorities and the vestries among them. The parish council clauses caused controversy, for they loosened the squires' hold on village administration and appealed to nonconformists. The bill also contained a clear precedent for the political emancipation of women; it enabled them to become members of the proposed councils. The Lords amended both bills heavily. The spending powers of the parish councils were limited to a 3d rate and their members elected by show of hands. The employers were allowed to contract out.

(6) As the Lords had not dealt, thus drastically, with conservative legislation in previous years, the Liberals argued that their approach was purely factious. Though this was not wholly fair, it was inevitable that the Liberals should make the point. Gladstone, in his last speech (Mar. 1894) began the long process of raising the

temperature between the Houses by speaking of a state of things which "cannot continue" and a matter "when once raised, must go forward to an issue". Two days later he resigned.

GLAMIS (Pron: Glahms) (Angus). The castle was the ancient seat of the Es. of Strathmore. See LYON.

GLAMORGAN (S. Wales) (1) having been mostly part of Deheubarth, was later a vaguely delimited area of the equally vaguely delimited Morgannwg which embraced much of Gwent (Monmouth) as well. It was purely Welsh until the death of Rhys ap Tewdwr in 1093 when Robert fitz Hamon's expedition surprised the locals and built a castle at Cardiff. Welsh opposition soon crystallised and Norman civil administration was virtually eliminated a year later, but ecclesiastical penetration was more successful. In 1107 the Bp. of Llandaff submitted to Canterbury. Meanwhile Norman claims were attached to the earldom of Gloucester whose Earl, Robert, built Chepstow Castle as a point of entry. Other families colonised and fortified Kidwelly and Gower by 1135. The informal Norman influxes were, however, abruptly checked by a Welsh reaction and a Norman defeat at the B. of Swansea (1136). Robert of Gloucester, as the mainstay of the Empress Maud in the civil wars of K. Stephen, was too distracted to pay attention and Glamorgan reverted to a Welsh way of life, protected later and until 1190 by the strong and popular Rhys ap Gruffydd (The Lord Rhys).

(2) Now, as later, Glamorgan was fertile and prosperous and so, at Rhys's death, a goal of Gloucester ambition. K. John married Isabel of Gloucester to fill the local political vacuum and for a while drew Glamorgan and its resources back into Anglo-Norman politics with the dislikeable Falkes de Bréauté in charge; but his interlude ended with the baronial revolt in 1212 and the rise of Llywellyn ap Iorwerth, who conquered S. Wales and, by the Award of Aberdovey (1215), divided it equitably between the local Welsh chiefs. Hence Glamorgan remained under relatively peaceful Welsh rule.

(3) Glamorgan, with Carmarthen, was at this time a Welsh area which isolated the colonial Anglo-Norman shire of Pembroke from England. Since 1170 Pembroke had been no threat to Glamorgan because its lords and people had initiated and continued to be involved in the conquest of Ireland. One consequence was that the lordship of Gower had to be subordinated (1231) to Carmarthen to maintain its identity. This represented the high tide of Welsh resurgence and it was maintained at an artificially high level by Simon de Montfort's Welsh alliances in the Barons' Wars. Thus Edward I's conquest of N. Wales entailed the fall of the south and the firm establishment of marcher lordships which, with permutations, survived until the Acts of Union of 1536 and 1546, which also defined the county.

(4) The agricultural prosperity was supplemented as early as the 16th cent. by coal mining and later by the re-exploitation on a large scale of copper, lead, tin and ironstone mining. A tremendous industrial prosperity developed and fed the ports at Barry, Swansea and Port Talbot. This lasted down to World War I but afterwards the use of oil fuel by ships and the concession of the Saar coalfields to France destroyed the coal markets and brought prolonged depression and the migration of skilled labour to England, particularly Slough (Bucks).

(5) The county was abolished by division into three in 1974.

"GLAMORGAN TREATY" (1645). See CIVIL WAR-18,20,24.

GLANVILL, Gilbert (?-1214) Bp. of ROCHESTER (1185) was a member of Thomas Becket's household and a canonist; later in Henry II's reign he was a judge. As a bishop he helped the Q. Mother Eleanor to frustrate the unwelcome legatine visit of Card. John of Anagni and, in general, he supported the administration for the absent

Richard I. He was also an active judge-delegate valued by the Papacy and sat on the commissions which admonished K. John for his treatment of Abp. Geoffrey of York and he published the excommunication of royal officials who expelled the monks from Christ Church Canterbury in 1207. Nevertheless, he tried on the King's behalf to negotiate an end to the interdict in 1209. When John was excommunicated, Gilbert withdrew from England until the reconciliation of 1213.

GLANVILLE (1) Sir John the elder (1542-1600) was M.P. for Launceston (1585), Tavistock (1586) and St. Germans (1592). In 1598 he became a justice of the Common Pleas and was the first attorney to reach the bench. His son **(2) Sir John the younger (1586-1661),** an eminent barrister, was M.P. for Plymouth in 1614, 1620, 1623, 1626 and 1628 and led in Buckingham's impeachment between 1626 and 1628. In 1637 he became M.P. for Bristol and in 1638 recorder. He was speaker in the Short Parliament of 1640 and thereafter supported the King. From 1645 he was in parliamentary custody, but represented Oxford Univ. in the various commonwealth legislatures. His grandson **(3) John (?1664-1735),** a poet and barrister, translated Fontenelle's *Plurality of Worlds.*

GLANVILLE[E], Ranulf (?-1190), originally a northern administrator and landowner, was sheriff of Yorkshire from 1163 until dismissed after the inquest of sheriffs in 1170. He became sheriff of Lancs. in 1174 and as such captured William the Lion at Alnwick (1174), becoming also sheriff of Yorkshire again. These offices he held almost until his death. In 1177 he was also employed as ambassador in Flanders. In 1179 he became a member of the King's principal court and from 1180 he was justiciar and acted as the King's English vicegerent in all home and military business, as well as Welsh and French affairs and the problems created by the King's sons. Richard I disliked him and dismissed and fined him at his accession. Though by now elderly, he took the cross and died at Acre. A treatise *De Legibus et Consuetudinibus Angliae* (The Laws and Customs of England) was, without contemporary warrant, ascribed to him in the 13th cent. It was the first systematic attempt to describe the organisation and procedure of the law and its connection with the Exchequer.

GLASGOW (Sc) (1) There was a settlement on the R. Clyde connected with St. Ninian in the 4th cent. and St. Mungo set up his H.Q. here for the conversion of the Strathclyde Britons in about 543. The Clyde provided access for trade towards the Western Isles, Ireland and Scandinavia and the site was a nodal point for roads to the north and south and towards Stirling, Lothian and Fife. The fragmentation of W. Scotland retarded its development so that it was not until 1115 that a bishopric was permanently established and then by David, a Cumbrian prince, on the advice of John Achaius, the first regular bishop. His cathedral was burned down in 1176, by which time the King of Scots was in effective control and in 1178 William the Lion made Glasgow a burgh of barony. The new cathedral was financed in the 13th cent. by the Comyns of Kilbride.

(2) Glasgow naturally focused the ambitions and discontents of the West against the stronger focus at Edinburgh in the east. During the early Reformation this took the form of Calvinist church assemblies there in opposition to the R. Catholic govt. at Edinburgh. This type of rivalry died away with the union of the two Crowns (1603) which slowly opened trade (against English opposition) to the United Kingdom as a whole. Regular shipbuilding, for which the Clyde was very suitable, began. The town became a royal burgh in 1636. With the Union of the two Kingdoms, at first locally opposed and resented, commercial and industrial activity quickened. In particular access to America brought a vast increase in shipbuilding and the highly profitable importation of tobacco, sugar and rum. The capital accumulations financed, on the one hand, the Ayrshire coalmines (exporting through the Clyde) and tremendous extensions to the ancient but hitherto small university and in the 19th cent. school extensions which created an educated and enterprising work-force. In the new iron age, engineering was a natural development of shipbuilding, but lighter industries such as textiles (aided by the damp climate) followed on. The momentum continued with electricity and large water supply projects well into the 20th cent.

(3) In World War II Glasgow became exceptionally important as a strategic port with strategic industries and, therefore, suffered severely from enemy bombing, some 40,000 houses being damaged in Mar. 1941 alone. Nevertheless, these features of wartime life were a symbol of a real economic strength, which tended to ebb when the peace redirected overseas trade to other ports, other manufacturing centres restarted and the United Kingdom ceased to dominate the Commonwealth.

GLASGOW RIOTS, 1725, were caused by Walpole's malt tax. A very large organised crowd demolished the houses of all the known supporters of the tax and Gen. Wade's troops had to be called in to quell it.

GLASS (1) The ancient craft of glass making descended to modern times through the Roman Empire. There was a glass industry near Venice in the 7th cent. whose furnaces were moved to Murano in 1291. Egyptian glassmakers moved to Damascus and Aleppo in 1171. The crusades thus increased and spread the demand. Despite draconian Venetian regulations, Muranese craftsmen often absconded in the 16th cent. They probably expanded the Altare centre near Genoa. Muranese and Altarists spread the art to all Latin and German countries and from Antwerp they reached England and Scandinavia.

(2) Glass for windows was being made in England before their arrival, but vessel and bottle glass was imperfectly manufactured before the 1560s, when Huguenot as well as Italian craftsmen reached London. The industry was hampered after 1615 by govt. efforts to prevent the use of wood for firing and perhaps also by the monopoly conferred on Sir. Robt. Mansell in 1623. He was still in control in 1656 when he died. In 1664 Charles II rechartered the Glass Sellers Co., whose members were soon dissatisfied with Venetian supplies, and commissioned George Ravenscroft to experiment with English materials. His lead oxide glass, perfected between 1675 and 1700, revolutionised the industry, for it facilitated a high rate of production and produced a solid glass much demanded by continental engravers. Britain became a glass exporter. In 1746 an excise levied by weight led glassmakers to develop much lighter forms. Meanwhile the plainer English cutting style mainly ousted continental shallow cutting and, after the establishment of Anglo-Irish free trade in 1780, led to the development of the Irish style named after Waterford. The excise was abolished in 1845 and encouraged widespread development which the Great Exhibition of 1851 greatly assisted. English Victorian glass, made mostly at Birmingham and Stourbridge, created worldwide demand which has existed ever since. In 1959 British glassmakers began to market *float glass,* developed by Pilkington Bros. and made by allowing molten glass to flow over the surface of molten tin. This eliminated the need for grinding and polishing.

GLASSE, Hannah (1708-70), habit maker to the P. of Wales (*see* COOKERY). The phrase 'first catch your hare' at the beginning of a recipe is apocryphally attributed to her.

GLASTONBURY (Somerset). This ancient holy place attracted Celtic monks in the 7th cent. and there were traditional associations with St. Patrick and St. David and the Holy Grail (q.v.). Ine, K. of Wessex, refounded the monastery in 705, but regular monasticism had declined by the 10th cent. when St. Dunstan studied there. In 940 he became Abbot and introduced the Benedictine Rule, a turning point in English history, for St. Ethelwold was trained there and Dunstan was himself followed as Abp. of Canterbury by two other Glastonbury monks and at least seven others became bishops. Domesday Book records the Abbey as the wealthiest in England, owing a service of 40 knights to the Crown. It had, however, been unlucky in its first Norman Abbot, Thurstan of Caen, who tried to force unfamiliar ceremonies and the Dijon chant on the community. In a fight between the monks and his men-at-arms two monks were killed. Thurstan was returned to Caen, but the community was partly dispersed and went through troubled times until the era of Henry of Blois. Abbot from 1126 to 1171, he was also Bp. of Winchester from 1129 but this plurality did no harm, for the Abbey benefited from his administrative flair, patronage and power, by which he recovered many of the lost estates. He also modified the discipline along Cluniac lines. His immediate successor, Robert, was an excellent Abbot but died after nine years and hardships then ensued. In 1184 a great fire consumed most of the buildings and treasures and in 1192 the predatory Savary de Bohun, Bp. of Bath and Wells, challenged the Abbey's independence in the hope of converting it into a cathedral monastery for his see. Conflict and litigation ended only in 1234 when the Abbey regained its rights. It had, however, always been a popular, influential and lucrative pilgrimage centre. A 13th cent. golden age culminated under Abbot John of Taunton (1274-90), a scholar and theologian as well as a fine estate manager. Glastonbury's reputation stood high and at Easter 1277 he entertained Edward I and his court. During the later middle ages the House remained wealthy, influential and respected. Its Abbots were summoned to Parliament, though they did not always attend and many of the monks were educated at Oxford. The ecclesiastical visitors of 1535 found little to criticise. Nevertheless, when it was suppressed in 1539, it was found convenient to hang Richard Witing, the last Abbot.

GLEBE was land assigned to support the parish priest. He was customarily given twice as much as a villein but there might be very wide variations. It might be scattered over the Common Fields or consolidated. It brought the parson into close contact with the other villagers, who were engaged in agriculture alongside him, but with tithes and voluntary offerings it was not his only source of income.

GLEE. A peculiarly English form of unaccompanied setting for male voices, of good poems, in a series of short movements expressing the mood of each poem, the chords being harmonic rather than contrapuntal. The high period of glee composition ran from 1750 to 1830 and one of its features was the use of the adult falsetto. The London Glee Club existed from 1783 to 1857. Many catch clubs were or became glee clubs.

GLENCAIRN. *See* CUNNINGHAM.

GLENCOE, MASSACRE OF (13 Feb. 1692). This atrocity which long darkened Anglo-Scots and clan relationships arose as follows. Glencoe was an enclave in Campbell country. The Glencoe Macdonalds had raided the Campbell lands, especially Glenorchy, for many years. Campbell of Glenorchy, first E. of Breadalbane, and his superior chieftain the D. of Argyll, therefore had old scores to pay off. Alexander Macdonald of Glencoe, a Jacobite, had fought against the English at Killiecrankie (July 1689) and unrest in the western Highlands was maintained by the expectation of a French invasion. Breadalbane was employed by William III's govt. to pacify the clans and distributed large sums for the purpose. It was also decided to pardon chieftains who, before New Year's Day 1692, swore the oath of allegiance in the presence of a judge, but in anticipation of refusals Letters of Fire and Sword were drawn up in blank. The chiefs came in, unexpectedly, in large numbers but Macdonald of Glencoe delayed until the last day, when he rode to Fort William to take the oath before the Sheriff there. The Sheriff was away and before he could be found time had run out. At the insistence of Breadalbane, Vist. Stair and his son, the Master of Stair, the U. Sec. of State in London, decided to make an example of the Macdonalds who were reputed not much better than bandits. A Letter of Fire and Sword (a very long document) was presented to the King who signed it, possibly unread. The order was carried out treacherously. Soldiers of Argyll's regiment came amicably to Glencoe and were entertained by the Macdonalds for over a week. At dawn on 13 Feb. they turned on their hosts, murdered the chieftain, thirty-five adults and two children. The rest escaped. This sensational breach of the venerated laws of hospitality was magnified by the Jacobites and the non-Jacobite opponents of Stair. The Highlands seethed, William ordered an inquiry which was never held and protests grew louder. In 1695 a Scots parliament was due to meet and in anticipation William instituted a regular commission of inquiry. On the basis of its report Stair had to leave public life and Breadalbane was charged with treason, but was never in fact tried. *See* DALRYMPLE.

GLENDOWER, OWAIN GLYNDWR (?1354-1416) through his father had claims upon Powys and through his mother upon Deheubarth. He was also distantly connected with the almost extinct royal house of Gwynedd. He was brought up in London and accompanied the English Scottish expeditions of 1385 and 1387. He quarrelled in 1400 with his neighbour, Reginald Grey of Ruthin, assembled his kinsmen and attacked Ruthin and other English settlements. In 1401 they defeated an English force in the Plynlimmon area; he appealed for a general Welsh rising and took the title of Prince of Wales. In 1402 he captured Grey and Edmund Mortimer. He made an alliance with Mortimer, whose daughter Catherine he married, and they brought in the Percys, first Hotspur (killed at Shrewsbury in 1403) and then his father, the E. of Northumberland. In 1404 he took Aberystwyth and Harlech and in 1405 he executed with Mortimer and Northumberland a tripartite Indenture for the partition of England and Wales with French and Scottish support. In May 1405, however, he and his French ally were defeated at Pwll Melyn and his fortunes began to decline, as his allies were successively defeated. He lost Harlech and by 1410 was maintaining a guerrilla force in the mountains. After a great raid into Shropshire in 1412 he disappeared and apparently lived with his daughter at Monnington (Herefordshire) until he died.

GLENELG. *See* GRANT.

GLENORCHY. *See* CAMPBELL; GLENCOE, MASSACRE.

GLENROTHES. *See* NEW TOWNS.

GLOBE newspaper was started in 1803 by a syndicate of publishers and absorbed the *Courier* in 1842. Originally an advertising sheet, it became a Tory newspaper in 1852. It was acquired by Harmsworth in 1907 and ceased publication in 1920.

GLOBE THEATRES (London). (1) Burbage's theatre was built in Southwark in 1599, burned in 1613, rebuilt and finally closed in 1644. **(2)** Another was built in Northumberland St. in 1868 and closed for the building of the Aldwych in 1902. **(3)** Since 1906 there has been one in Shaftesbury Avenue. **(4)** The American millionaire Sam Wanamaker began to rebuild the Southwark theatre before he died in 1994.

GLORIANA. A name given by Spenser to Q. Elizabeth in the *Faerie Queene.*

GLORIOUS REVOLUTION. *See* JAMES II AND VII-4 *et seq.*

GLOSS,-ATORS. The gloss was an explanatory marginal note to a text originally classical or biblical, but developed by the 11th cent.-13th cent. Bologna jurists in connection with Roman law. They were known as the Glossators and their leading figures were Azo (c. 1150-

1230) who influenced Bracton, and Accursius (1182-c. 1260)

GLOUCESTER-SHIRE (Lat = GLEVUM, later CLAUDIA CASTRA) (*See also* WORCESTER.) **(1)** The area was occupied by the British Dobuni in whose territory the Romans built towns at Bath (Aquae Sulis), Cirencester (Corinium), Bristol (Abone) and Gloucester. Cirencester was the crossroad from the Forest of Dean through Gloucester into Hampshire and from Dorset to Bath and towards Leicester. These roads gave access to the W. Saxon Hwiccas; they sacked the towns between 577 and 586, when a Bp. Thomas fled to Wales with his clergy. The constant warfare between Britons and Saxons caused the failure of St. Augustine's conference with the British clergy at Aust in 603.

(2) By now the Hwiccas had fallen under Mercian domination and the people were mostly heathen, but after the death of the Mercian K. Penda at Winwaedsfield in 655 conversions became important. Monasteries were founded in the ruined towns, e.g. at Bath (676), Gloucester (681) and Cirencester. Trade and religion revived together. The new establishment of a bishopric at Worcester and the conversion of Ebba, the locally born Q. of the S. Saxons (both in 680), encouraged the process.

(3) At this time and for several centuries the Forest of Dean, which was in the diocese of Hereford, maintained through its defensibility, a separate Celtic character and an administration based on the timber and mines; when the Normans began to penetrate S. Wales, Tidenham and Woolaston in the angle of the Rs. Wye and Severn formed part of the Marcher Lordship of Striguil. In the rest of the shire there were the usual large royal forests, such as Malvern Chase, but 5/6ths of the exploited area was under the plough and most of the rest was woodland. Bristol and Gloucester, however, had developed as ports, Bristol having in the 11th cent. a lucrative slave trade. The religious were locally powerful: apart from hospitals and commanderies, there were large houses, Benedictine at Gloucester, Bristol and Tewkesbury, Augustinian at Bristol and Cirencester, seven Cistercian in the countryside; Gloucester had three friaries, Bristol five. In addition, there were alien priories and the abbeys of Westminster and St. Denis (Paris) had wide acreages.

(4) Monastic business example, followed by lay lords using the port facilities, led to a growing wool export trade in exchange for continental products such as Bordeaux wines. This began the conversion from arable land to pasture which slowly altered the landscape, particularly of the Cotswolds, and created the prosperous Wold villages, whose beauty has since attracted tourists. The surplus profits and 14th cent. invention of the fulling mill created a cloth industry, which disturbed the Flanders trade and developed the guilds of Merchant Adventurers (i.e. persons willing to risk capital) in Bristol and elsewhere. In some ways, however, the results of monastery-originated enterprise were less felicitous. Advowsons mostly passed to monasteries, which took the profits without making the appointments. Walter of Cantelupe (Bp. of Worcester 1236-66) complained in 1240 that heathenism was rampant and took stern measures to force the appointment of vicars and to ensure that they did their work.

(5) Apart from the sheep runs and the woollen industry, the Vale of Severn had flourishing dairies, cheesemakers, and orchards producing not only apples and pears but the famous cider and perry. All these activities continued when the monasteries were dissolved. Part of their property went towards endowing the new bishoprics of Gloucester and Bristol (1541) but the rest passed to the rising capitalists who were soon adding other new industries: broadcloth and in the 17th cent. silk weaving in the Stroud Valley, flax, rope and sailcloth and even, around Cheltenham, tobacco, which the major-generals of the Commonwealth suppressed. Much of this was related to the overseas trade. The discovery of Newfoundland soon resulted in the exploitation of the cod fisheries; the Bordeaux and Portugal trade led naturally to Brazil, the African coast, a renewed slave trade and the W. Indies. The profits poured in and were invested in a Baltic trade and in further local industries. Like Worcestershire, the county had a dissenting tradition whose first recorded manifestations, in Lollardy, occurred in the 14th cent. There were burnings of heretics under Mary I and Gloucester survived a famous siege by Charles I (see CIVIL WAR). Later Bristol became a great centre of the Quakers who led and disseminated the 18th cent. anti-slavery movement.

(6) By the 20th cent. the town and country had a prosperous mixture of agriculture and a diversified industry. This was as well because German bombing severely damaged Bath and Bristol, while American and European protectionism and the loss of imperial control was drying up the foreign profits from which capital investment was derived.

GLOUCESTER, Es. of. A title in the Clare family until 1314, but used also by Ralph de Monthermer (?-1325), the 9th earl's squire, in right of the earl's widow, whom he married in 1297. It was briefly revived for Thomas le Despenser (1373-1400) in 1397.

GLOUCESTER, Humphrey (1391-1447) D. of (1414) and E. of PEMBROKE (1414) ("Duke Humphrey"), youngest son of Edward IV, was made Chamberlain of England in 1413 by his brother Henry V, under whom he commanded one of the three divisions of the army at the B. of Agincourt (1415). He was rewarded with additional lands in Wales. He was also put in charge of the Channel coast defences as Warden of the Cinque Ports and Constable of Dover and Carisbrook castles and then took part in the King's second French campaign, being made gov. of Rouen in 1419. From Jan. 1420 to Feb. 1421 he replaced his brother John, D. of Bedford, as the King's Viceregent in England, then accompanied the King to France and resumed the viceregency from May to Aug. 1422. Earlier in the year he had married Jacqueline of Bavaria, heiress of William IV, Count of Hainault, Holland and Zeeland. This was the summit of his career.

Henry V could trust and supervise him in high office, but others mistrusted his character and feared his sadism and unreliability once supervision had gone. Henry V now died, naming him regent for the nine-month-old Henry VI in England, while Bedford was to govern France. The regency council, however, forced him to accept the lesser office of Protector. His difficulties and new political isolation were entangled with an antipathy which developed between him and the Beauforts, especially the Bp. of Winchester. He now sought (1424) to take his wife's great inheritance by force, but his expedition (1424-5), which proved personally expensive, was politically irresponsible, for it threatened the stability of the recent Anglo-Burgundian alliance and consequently Bedford's position in France. He also became involved in a further and self-indulgent inconsistency: he took Eleanor Cobham, one of Jacqueline's ladies, as his mistress and then destroyed the basis of his Netherlands' claims by moving for an annulment of his marriage. There was much public sympathy for Jacqueline. The annulment took place in 1428 and was shortly followed by the T. of Delft, whereby Jacqueline's rights passed to Philip of Burgundy. This attempt to shore up the Burgundian alliance and marry Eleanor Cobham left him without much credit in England, while Joan of Arc's intervention eroded the alliance itself. In 1435 Bedford died and, by the P. of Arras, Burgundy changed sides. Although appointed Captain of Calais in Nov. 1435, the

requirements of local defence ate into its great revenues. These were needed for the defence of the French Lieutenancy to which he was shortly appointed. Moreover the Council, mainly dominated by the financier William de la Pole, E. of Suffolk, was hostile and Edmund Beaufort was a military rival rather than a colleague.

Late in 1436 he abandoned the Lieutenancy and returned to England. He was not well received and with the proclamation of the end of Henry VI's minority in Nov. 1437, his Protectorate ended. As the Beaufort-Suffolk faction had the ear of the young King, his court influence was now negligible, even if his wider popularity, previously tarnished by his matrimonial problems, had risen by contrast with his enemies. He was even sometimes called 'Good Duke Humphrey'. This seemed to make him a potential threat (though holding no office of importance) to the dominant court party and plans were laid to ruin him. In 1441 Eleanor was arrested for witchcraft designed to encompass the King's death. He was now excluded from the royal presence while she continued in prison. He remained in this helpless condition until, finally, in 1447 he was summoned to come unattended to a parliament at Bury St. Edmunds and suddenly arrested. Three days later he died in custody. An Italianate renaissance nobleman, he was a great collector of books and a notable donor of manuscripts to Oxford University, where the mediaeval library is named after him and his faults forgotten.

GLOUCESTER, Miles of (?-1143) E. of HEREFORD (1141) under Henry I was sheriff of Gloucester and Staffordshire, an itinerant and a Forest Justice and Constable to the King. Stephen as King confirmed him in these offices together with the scandalous privilege of not being impeachable in the royal courts for his lands. In 1130 Miles, E. Robert of Gloucester and Brian FitzCount welcomed the Empress Matilda and admitted her to Gloucester. He made a treaty with E. Robert whereby each provided hostages for good faith towards the other. In the early stages of the civil war between the King and the Empress, Miles was an effective commander and established his authority in Herefordshire. In 1141 the Empress created him E. of Hereford, but later in that year when she was defeated at Winchester, Miles escaped in ignominy, reaching Gloucester weary, half naked and alone. He died in a hunting accident.

GLOUCESTER, STATUTE OF (1278) contained miscellaneous procedural enactments and **(1)** a requirement that suits for goods to the royal courts must exceed 40s in value. This was interpreted to restrict the county courts to that sum and led to their gradual extrusion from the processes of justice; **(2)** the rules on the effect of *Quo Warranto*.

GLUBB, Sir John Bagot (1897-1986) in 1932 took command and trained the Arab Legion of the Jordanian Army which formed the effective support of the Hashemite dynasty. He was dismissed in 1956.

GLYN (1) Sir Richard Carr (1755-1838) Bt. 1800, a partner in Halifax Mills Glyn and Mitton, bankers, was an M.P. from 1796 to 1802 and Ld. Mayor of London from 1789 to 1790. His grandson **(2) George Grenfell (1824-87) 2nd Ld. WOLVERTON (1873)** was also a partner and an M.P. from 1857 to 1873. He was a personal friend of W. E. Gladstone and was sec. to the Treasury from 1868 to 1873, Paymaster Gen. from 1880 to 1885 and P.M.-G. in 1886.

GLYNDEBOURNE FESTIVAL of opera was founded by John Christie in 1934.

GLYNNE, Sir John (1603-66) M.P. for Westminster in the Long Parliament, conducted part of Strafford's impeachment in 1641. In 1642 he was a member of the committee of privileges and became Recorder of London in 1643. In 1647, however, he was excluded from the Commons and later sent to the Tower, but was reinstated in 1648 and was one of the negotiators with the King that year. As a result he was a victim of Pride's Purge. He was returned for northern Welsh constituencies in the Protector's parliaments and was a judge of assize in 1654. From 1655 to 1659 he was a C.J. of the Upper (formerly King's) Bench and in 1658 spoke before Cromwell in favour of monarchy. He reverted to being a serjeant at law in 1660 and prosecuted Sir Harry Vane in 1662.

GNEISENAU. *See* COMMERCE PROTECTION, NAVAL-6.

GOA. *See* PENINSULAR WAR 1807-14-3; PORTUGUESE INDIES.

GOBIND RAI. *See* SIKHS-1,2.

GODDARD, Rayner (1877-1971) Lord GODDARD (1944), a Common lawyer, successively held three recorderships between 1917 and 1932 when he became a Queens Bench judge. He was promoted to the Court of Appeal in 1938, to the H. of Lords in 1944 and was Ld. Chief Justice from 1946 to 1958. Intellectual, vastly experienced and alarming as a personality, yet an entertaining speaker, he was a determined but, with a few lapses, fair upholder of the rigour of the criminal law. This earned him much, particularly posthumous, abuse by critics who exploited the lapses as a means of attacking the criminal legal system. In fact he inspired important reforms such as the abolition of the distinctions inherent in the doctrines of felony and misdemeanor.

GODDEN v HALES **(1686)** was a collusive test case against Sir. Edw. Hales (?-1695), a papist, by his servant Godden for not taking the sacrament and the proper oaths in accordance with the Test Act while acting as a col. of infantry. His plea of the King's dispensation was upheld in the King's Bench; this gave James II the legal precedent for commissioning further papists. Hales later became Lieut. of the Tower, but fled to St. Germain with James and in 1692 became Jacobite E. of *TENTERDEN.* The case was the last of a series upholding the dispensing power.

GODERICH GOVT. (Sept. 1827-Jan. 1828). 15 in Cabinet under Vist. Goderich, a friend of the late Geo. Canning, approached by George IV, who hoped to dominate him. Goderich resigned rather than have to manage without both Herries (Ch. of the Exch.), a friend of the King's, and Huskisson (S. of State for War and the Colonies) who had quarrelled with Herries. This govt. never met parliament. *See* ROBINSON.

GODESBERG MEETING (2-4 Sept. 1938) between Hitler and Neville Chamberlain, settled the preliminaries of the Munich Agreement.

GODFREY, Sir Edmund Berry (1621-78), knighted for his services during the Great Plague of 1665, was a popular and respected Justice of the Peace. In 1678 he received Titus Oates' first depositions and, doubting their credibility, referred Oates to the Council. He was found dead at Primrose Hill a month later and there were widespread rumours of murder by R. Catholics, leading to the conviction of three innocent men. *See* POPISH PLOT.

GODIVA (Godgifu), wife of Leofric of Mercia, one of the three great earls whom Edward the Confessor found in office at his accession, is remembered for the story attached to her name. She pleaded with her husband to remit a tax which he had imposed on the people of Coventry. He promised, no doubt in jest, that he would do so if she would ride naked through the streets at noonday. She took him at his word and nobody looked save, apparently, "Peeping Tom" who was struck blind.

GODLEY (1) John Robert (1814-61) a friend of Gibbon Wakefield's, planned Canterbury (N.Z.) in 1850 and became U/Sec. at War in 1853. His son **(2) John Arthur, 1st Ld. KILBRACKEN (1909) (1847-1932)** was a private secretary to Gladstone from 1872 to 1882 and then permanent U. Sec. of State for India from 1883 to 1909.

GODLY. A puritan's term for a puritan.

GODODDIN (i.e. VOTADINI) POEMS by the N. Welsh poet Aneirin, like those of Taliesin, are authentic 6th cent. compositions but now survive only in 13th cent. and later copies. Mainly elegies on particular heroes, they exhibit attitudes and ideals such as the code of loyalty to a heroic leader in return for his generosity also found in the A.S. poem *Beowulf.* Their value as evidence of personalities and events is as yet unknown.

GODOLPHIN (1) Sydney (1645-1712) 1st Ld. (1684) 1st E. (1706). A moderate Tory and M.P. for Cornwall boroughs from 1668 to 1681, he held a court office in 1679, became Sec. of State in 1684 and was Q. Mary of Modena's chamberlain under James II. Like most other prominent statesmen, he maintained a cautious correspondence with James II after the Revolution but was, with Marlborough, a friend of the P. Anne and supported her claims in succession to William III. He was First Lord of the Treasury from 1690 to 1696 and again in 1700 to 1701. At Anne's accession he became Lord Treasurer and his financial genius and experience were mainstays of the allied powers in the War of the Spanish Succession. He and Marlborough were on very close terms and he acted as the chief (sometimes called 'prime') home or civil minister of the wartime administration. As such he was directly concerned in such matters as the Union with Scotland, besides the shifts of party politics, but he was essentially an expert rather than a party man and ultimately became the target of both sides. Q. Anne dismissed him (with a pension which was not paid) in 1710, as a preliminary to the extrusion of the Marlboroughs from their offices in the next year. His financial administration was completely honest and he left office poorer than when he entered it. He introduced the Broad Arrow mark on govt. property and Robert Walpole was his disciple. (*See* EAST INDIA COMPANY-7.) His son **(2) Francis (1678-1766) 2nd E.** was George II's Groom of the Stole from 1727 to 1735 and Privy Seal from 1735 to 1740.

GODRIC, St. (?-1170) began as a champion and prospered to become a merchant and pirate with a share in voyages from E. Anglia to Scotland, Brittany, Flanders and Denmark. He made a fortune helping K. Baldwin I of Jerusalem on crusade. In due course he became a monk at Durham Cathedral and then set up as a hermit at Finchale. His hymns in honour of the Virgin and of St. Nicholas are the earliest Middle English verses known and survive with musical notation. He became a popular northern saint, the subject of several posthumous *Lives.*

GOD SAVE IRELAND. Anti-British hymn written by T. D. Sullivan. *See* MANCHESTER MARTYRS.

GOD SAVE THE KING. See HULL, JOHN.

GOD'S TOKENS. *See* PLAGUE.

GOD'S TRUCE. *See* ARMISTICE.

GODWIN, Earl (?-1053) and FAMILY. He was raised by Canute to the earldom of Wessex before 1018 and was responsible for the blinding and death of Alfred, younger brother of the future Edward the Confessor. Of his sons, four secured earldoms, **(1)** The unpleasant **Sweyn,** most of Somerset, Gloucestershire and Wiltshire; **(2) Harold** (later King), East Anglia with Essex and most of Oxfordshire and Bucks; **(3) Ralph,** the border area of Gwent and Herefordshire; **(4) Tostig,** who married Judith of Flanders, eventually Northumbria. **(5) Gyrth** and **(6) Leofwine,** though not landless, were without territorial jurisdictions. In addition his daughter **(7) Edith** married K. Edward; and his son-in-law **(8) Beorn Estrithson** became E. of East Mercia. *See* EDWARD THE CONFESSOR; GENEALOGY; HAROLD II.

GODWIN (1) Thomas (1517-90) became dean of Christchurch in 1565 and then of Canterbury in 1567. Appointed Bp. of Bath and Wells in 1584 he offended the Queen by marrying a second time. His son **(2) Francis (1562-1633)** became Bp. of Llandaff in 1601 and of Hereford in 1617. He wrote a *Catalogue of the Bishops of England* (1601), some *Annals* and *The Man in the Moone* (published 1638) from which John Wilkins and Cyrano de Bergerac borrowed. His grandson **(3) Morgan (?-1690)** was a liberal minister in Virginia.

GODWIN, William (1756-1836) who married Mary Wollstonecraft, the literary hostess in 1797, published his *Inquiry Concerning Political Justice* in 1793. In this book, long influential in the 19th cent. salons, he argued that human beings were emotionally neutral and reasonable and, therefore, perfectible by the elimination of bad ideas expressed in foolish institutions. Sensible instructional reforms, including the abolition of matrimony, would thus establish the good and peaceful life (cf MALTHUS).

GODWIN-AUSTEN (1) Robert Alfred Cloyne (1808-84) was an important pioneer of geology. His son **(2) Henry Havershal (1834-1923)** also a geologist, made the first survey of Kashmir in 1856 and of Kara Koram in 1861. He also served on Himalayan political missions, particularly in Bhutan in 1863 and did much pioneer surveying in the process.

GOEBBELS, Joseph Paul (1897-1945), an extreme German nationalist with socialist leanings, joined the Nazi party in 1925 and became Gregor Strasser's secretary. A debonair man of great courage and intelligence, his abilities were soon recognised by his appointment in 1926 to be provisional *Gauleiter* (Ger = district leader) in Berlin. Here he organised the Party public relations with much skill, but when it was banned in Prussia in 1927 he launched the weekly *Angriff* (Attack). By this time he had been drawn into the field of Hitler's personal magnetism and broke with Strasser, using *Angriff* against Strasser's radical faction and, in the interest of Hitler, who made him party propaganda chief in Nov. 1928. Goebbels thenceforth devoted his extraordinary talents and ruthless energy to the conversion or deception of the German people and foreigners too. After Hitler's take-over Goebbels became Min. for Public Enlightenment (*Volksaufklärung*) and Propaganda and his activities reached, on the communist model, into every aspect of intellectual life and aesthetic media. He became the champion of Nazi orthodoxy. The difficulty was that there was a wide ranging disagreement on the nature of Nazism on the one hand, while Goebbels' activities penetrated into the bailiwicks of every other party grandee. In particular Rosenberg and Dietrich had different ideas and rival, if less effective, machines and he had to defend his position against them. His methods were entirely unscrupulous; he combined lies, half truths, the perversion of language, the redeployment of emotional images and every other propagandist trick to mobilise the will of the German nation for any task decided by his *Fuhrer*. Even as late as 1944 he obtained a national commitment to war to the death. Designated as Hitler's successor in 1945 he, with his wife and daughters, committed suicide in May 1945.

GOEBEN and **BRESLAU,** a German battle cruiser and cruiser under Adm. Souchon, were in the Mediterranean in July 1914. They evaded the British before the Anglo-German declarations of war (4 Aug.) and reached the Dardanelles. The British seizure (angary) of two Turkish battleships fitting out in England created uproar among the Turks, many of whom had subscribed to their cost. The Germans seized the diplomatic opportunity and offered the *Goeben* and *Breslau*. After hesitations they were accepted with their admiral and crews, who now officially formed part of the Turkish navy, though Souchon actually took his orders from the German ambassador. As Germany was at war with Russia, the Germans wanted to involve Turkey. Accordingly Souchon bombarded the Russian oil ports of Batum and Novorossiisk and so helped to precipitate the Ottoman Empire into its final disaster.

GOERING, Hermann Wilhelm (1893-1946), intrepid and ebullient World War I fighter pilot, joined the National Socialists in 1922, took part in Hitler's beer cellar *putsch* at Munich in 1923 and fled the country. He returned in 1926, secured the support of industrialists with persuasive hints of important contracts, was elected to the *Reichstag*

in 1928 and, when Hitler took over power in 1933, developed into the administrative architect of the Third Reich. He began as prime minister of Prussia and Min. of the Interior. With this combination of offices he set up the enforcement machinery of the Nazi tyranny through the Gestapo. In 1934 he became prime minister of the Reich and disguised Min. of Aviation and began covertly to develop the German airforce forbidden by the T. of Versailles. He was next employed to reorganise and develop the economy through a 4-year plan based upon fraudulent devices such as the winter welfare collections and the Volkswagen business, as well as the confiscation and redeployment of Jewish assets. He trained his airforce partly against Spanish republicans and in 1939 he became chairman of the "Defence" Council. His slogan "guns before butter" was an actual, but unheeded, warning of the unbelievable (*see* WORLD WAR II). He was captured, tried and sentenced to death at Nuremberg in 1946 but escaped the rope by poisoning himself. In the latter years his enormous abilities were eroded by drugs. He died fabulously rich. Despite his remark that "whenever I hear the word 'culture' I reach for my revolver" he was found to have accumulated some £20M worth in works of art.

GOETHE, Johann Wolfgang von (1749-1832), German literary figure and scientist, was Minister of Prince Charles Augustus of Saxe-Weimar from 1776 to 1786 and the friend or acquaintance of many German statesmen. His moral and political insights, as well as his *Faust,* have established him as one of the most remarkable European intellects, yet one whose ideas were never easy to systematise. For example, the First Part of *Faust* is founded on the danger of surrender to the moment yet he recognised that the B. of Valmy (1792), at which he was present, was the beginning of a new era.

GOG AND MAGOG. Tutelary giants of London.

GOIDELIC. *See* CELTS.

GOLCONDA. *See* DECCAN STATES.

GOLD, mostly alluvial, was anciently found in Asia Minor, Persia and India, but these resorts being either worked out or cut off by barbarian invasions, gold was demonetised in the 9th cent. but returned to use as currency when Venice reopened trade with the gold-based oriental economies, and gold mining commenced in Saxony and Austria and, to a lesser degree, in mediaeval Spain. The Spanish Conquest of S. and Central America made a dramatic change. Between 1492 and 1600 some 8M oz. or 35% of world production crossed the Atlantic; between 1600 and 1700 the figure was 36.5M oz. (61%) and between 1700 and 1800 48M oz. (80%), mostly from Colombia. This supply was disorganised by the Napoleonic wars and the S. American revolutions and between 1823 and 1837 the main source was Russia. The major producers between 1850 and 1875 were Australia and California and between 1890 and 1915 Alaska, the Yukon and S. Africa. These five all experienced the notorious Gold Rushes. Production was enormously increased by the invention in 1890 of the Cyanide process, enabling even minute particles to be extracted. After 1920 the main developments were in Canada. By 1970 annual world production exceeded 18th cent. production a hundred-fold. Apart from routine wastage, the main permanent drain on gold supplies has, for many centuries, been the Indian demand for jewellery. In modern times industrial, electronic and dental applications have virtually demonetised it again. *See* GOLD STANDARD.

GOLD COAST. *See* AFRICA, WEST-3.

GOLDEN ACT (Scot. 1592). See JAMES IV-12.

GOLDEN HIND. *See* DRAKE, SIR FRANCIS.

GOLDEN LEGEND (*a misinterpretation of Lat: Legenda Aurea* = Golden things which ought to be read) was a mediaeval manual of church lore such as commentaries on church services, homilies suitable for particular saints' days and lives of saints. Caxton's version was his best seller and was the origin of later English versions.

GOLDIE, Sir George (1846-1925). *See* NIGERIA.

GOLD MARK. *See* COINAGE-4.

GOLD RUSH (1897). *See* CANADA-24; AUSTRALIA; SOUTH AFRICA.

GOLDSMID (1) Abraham (1756-1810) and his brother **(2) Benjamin (1753-1808)** started as bill brokers in 1777 and from 1792 dealt mainly in govt. business. Benjamin founded the R. Naval Asylum. Abraham overexpanded the business and committed suicide in the 1810 financial crisis. His nephew **(3) Sir Isaac Lyon Bt (1778-1859)** made a fortune in financial dealings in Portugal, Brazil and Turkey and helped to found University College, London in 1825 and the North London Hospital in 1834. His son **(4) Sir Francis Henry (1808-78)** became a Q.C. in 1858 and was M.P. for Reading in 1860; he was a successful campaigner for the removal of Jewish disabilities.

GOLDSMITH, Oliver (?1730-74) lived a wandering life in Ireland and Europe desultorily studying medicine until 1756 when he became a physician in Southwark and met Griffiths, the editor of the *Monthly Review*. He began to write for it in 1757 and his *Enquiry into the Present State of Polite Learning* attracted some attention in 1759 and got him opportunities in a variety of magazines. Hence in 1761 he became acquainted with Dr. Johnson, who in 1764 praised his *Traveller* and introduced him to Lord Clare, who became his patron. He published *The Vicar of Wakefield* in 1766 and *She Stoops to Conquer* in 1773 among many historical and critical works.

GOLD STANDARD was the free interconvertibility of paper money and gold at a predetermined rate. It acted as an automatic corrective to paper inflation. Gold sovereigns were the normal currency until World War I. In 1914 the Treasury started to issue £1 and 10s notes but the standard was not abandoned. In 1919 it was suspended by Act for six years. In 1925 Churchill (Ch. of the Exch.) refused to renew the Act but the renewed standard was applied only in international dealings (at a rate of £3-17s-10½d per ounce). In 1928 the issue of paper was confined to the Bank of England. Suspension was discussed and rejected in the financial crisis of 1929. The standard was finally abandoned by the National Govt. in Sept. 1931 because of speculation against Sterling. Thereupon the dollar value fell from 4.86 via 3.80, then to 3.23 and finally was stabilised around 3.40. These events made no difference to the internal purchasing power of the paper Sterling used since 1914.

GOLD STICK. The colonel of household cavalry through whom, since the time of William IV (who was a sailor), the sovereign communicates with the army. It is a monthly appointment.

GOLETTA or LA GOULETTE. The port of Tunis, in Spanish hands from 1535 to 1574.

GOLF, possibly of Flemish origin, was played among the sand dunes (links) of the Scots North Sea coast, mainly at Edinburgh and St. Andrews. In 1457 James II of Scots noted that golf and football interfered with the practice of archery. James VI, a keen player, brought it to England. The oldest documented club (1744) was at Muirfield in E. Lothian. The St. Andrews club existed in 1754 and became the ruling authority on the game. The spread of golf popularity dates from about 1860 when the Open Championship was instituted. The amateur championship dates from 1886, the Anglo-American Walker Cup from 1922.

GOLIAS or GOLIARDIC rhymes were 12th and 13th cent. satirical and profane poems, often macaronic or in Latin, such as those used by Carl Orff in *Carmina Burana*. They represent the desperately profligate under-side of the religious mediaeval outlook.

GOLLANCZ, Victor (1893-1967) left-wing publisher of Polish-Jewish origin, founded his successful firm in 1928 and started the Left Book Club in 1936, with its yellow jacketed books devoted to socialism, Marxism and their derivatives. They were briefly influential in the Labour party. His sympathy for Communist parties waned rapidly in the last decades of his life.

G.O.M. = Grand Old Man, i.e. W. E. Gladstone. The appellation is said to have been invented by Lord Rosebery.

GONDOMAR, Diego Sarmiento de Acuña, Count of (1567-1626), Spanish ambassador to James I, arrived in 1614 and soon established a leading personal influence at the Court. His instructions were to win the King for the Spanish side in the European wars or at least keep him neutral. He understood how to exploit James' vanity, timidity, dislike of persecution and increasing penury. He dangled a dowry of £600,000 before him for a Spanish marriage and James had Raleigh executed, and released recusant priests in response. The results were growing estrangement between James and parliament which neutralised England. This continued until the failure of the marriage negotiations, the Anglo-Dutch treaty of 1624 and P. Charles' French marriage, when Gondomar's influence disappeared. Meanwhile his mission had, from the Spanish point of view, been a distinct success.

GOOD FRIDAY "AGREEMENT" (Apr 1998). (1) The Blair govt. announced in June 1997 its intention to begin talks in Sept. with the Ulster parties, with or without Sinn Fein, and Sinn Fein and the IRA announced a cease fire in July. As this, by definition, involved no guarantee of disarmament, the loyalists refused to talk. Sinn Fein, which pretended not to control the IRA renounced the use of force for political ends in Sept. The Ulster Unionists (UU) and the govt, *faute de mieux*, accepted this but loyalists representing 40% did not. Mr Blair and Mr Gerry Adams, the Sinn Fein leader, then met in Dec., but Mr Adams said publicly that British involvement in Irish affairs must cease.

(2) Meanwhile an agenda for the talks was agreed between the British and Irish govts and presented to the Ulster parties in Jan 1998. The negotiations were chaired by the US Senator George Mitchell. After a flurry of murders, the Ulster Democratic Party (UDP) (related to the terrorist Ulster Freedom Fighters), and then Sinn Fein were suspended from them. The latter was invited back but delayed pending the agreement of a new agenda between the govts. This was presented through Senator Mitchell, and led eventually to a partial agreement.

(3) There was to be (a) an Ulster Assembly, a North-South Ministerial Council and a British-Irish Council drawn from Parliament, the Dail, the Scottish Parliament, the Welsh Assembly, Tynwald and the States of Jersey and Guernsey and (b) special arrangements to protect human rights, release prisoners, disarm and reduce policing.

(4) Violence now escalated, with 292 murders and "punishment shootings", 400 attacks on the police, and the "Real" IRA's Omagh bombing which killed or injured 329. Sinn Fein condemned it and again renounced violence. In response, the Sec. of State (Dr Margaret Mowlem) began to release prisoners and reduce patrolling.

(5) The agreement had specified no date for the commencement of disarmament. Sinn Fein refused to begin till an executive was formed; UU would not form one until it had begun. In Dec UU was overridden by an Anglo-Irish agreement on a ten-dept Executive and six north-south implementation bodies. Predictably, the IRA Convention rejected disarmament yet again. A Union between Eire and Ulster (anathema to loyalists) was now foreseeable, and violence, including murder inside the Maze prison broke out again and continued into the spring of 1999. In the summer, Mr Chris Patten, who had been investigating the R. Ulster Constabulary, recommended that it should be reduced and that its members should no longer take the oath of allegiance.

(6) An underlying war weariness, particularly among Ulster women, discernible since 1996, surfaced in 1999 in a political desire to curb all extremists. As disarmament would destroy their influence it was unacceptable to them but rank-and-file sympathy in Sinn Fein and UDP seemed to be ebbing The Dec. 1998 agreement had created a rudimentary disarmament apparatus. Mr David Trimble leading the UU, now persuaded his convention (Nov. 1999) to take Executive office with Sinn Fein on condition that disarmament was substantially achieved by Easter 2000. This potential alliance of centres against extremes was hesitatingly accepted. The Executive with Mr Martin MacGuiness of Sinn Fein as Min. of Ag. was formed in Dec. It seemed that by Feb. 2000 Sinn Fein could not or would not honour the bargain.

GOOD PARLIAMENT (Apr.-July 1376) was summoned in an atmosphere of discontent due to failure in war, poor harvests and economic depression. The unpopular John of Gaunt, as royal spokesman, demanded funds to prosecute the war and ordered the Lords and Commons to deliberate separately.

(1) The Commons began by drafting 146 petitions. Their grievances included the many ecclesiastical abuses, the trading advantages of foreign merchants, local administration and the household courts, public order, the cost of labour and the behaviour of beggars, defence of the marches and coasts.

(2) There followed a week-long debate, begun in the Commons by a universal pledge of secrecy and mutual support. It was decided to postpone discussion of supply and consider first how the kingdom might be better governed and the war won. The poor, it was said, could bear no more taxes, money was wasted or embezzled by unscrupulous favourites. The Staple should be settled permanently at Calais. It was agreed that reforms could not be made without the support of the magnates and that Sir Peter de la Mare, who had presided, should speak for the Commons before the whole Parliament. He is considered the first Speaker.

(3) Some of the Commons, as had been customary, had been excluded from the Parliament chamber but Sir Peter refused to proceed until they had been admitted. He then asked for the aid of 12 magnates to assist the Commons and named the Bps. of London, Norwich, Carlisle and St. Davids, the Es. of March, Stafford, Suffolk and Warwick, Lord Percy, Sir Guy Brian, Sir Henry Scrope and Sir Richard Stafford. These were known to be sympathetic. They were appointed and after further consultation with the Speaker said that the burden of taxation was the fault of certain royal councillors and servants who had enriched themselves. These included the London financier Richard Lyons, Lord Latimer and Edward III's mistress, Alice Perrers, and they demanded a reform of the council. Lyons was arrested, Alice was expelled from the court and new councillors (the Abp. of Canterbury, the Bps. of London and Winchester, the Es. of Arundel, March and Stafford, with Lord Percy, Brian and Roger Beauchamp) were sworn in Parliament.

(4) Lord Latimer demanded a trial and a named accuser and the Speaker stated that the Commons would maintain their accusations in Common (*see* IMPEACHMENT). After long proceedings against him, lesser offenders were also impeached.

(5) The crown's demands for a Tenth-and-Fifteenth were ignored and only a three-month wool subsidy granted, on condition that it should not be renewed for three years.

(6) This famous parliament left all the immediate problems unsolved and much of its proceedings were reversed or annulled at the instance of John of Gaunt in the next parliament.

GOODWIN, Charles Wycliffe (1817-78) barrister and Egyptologist, was acting judge in the court of China and Japan from 1868 and contributed the article on *Mosaic Cosmogony* to *Essays and Reviews.*

GOODWIN, John (?1594-1665), republican divine and propagandist who in γβριστοδικαι (Gr = Denunciation of pride) defended the trial of Charles I. He was an independent, equally opposed to presbyterians and bishops. Arrested at the Restoration, he was released as harmless.

GOODWIN v FORTESCUE (1604). James I directed by proclamation that parliamentary election returns should be made to Chancery. In Buckingham Goodwin, an outlaw, defeated Fortescue. The return was voided in Chancery and Fortescue was chosen at a by-election. The Commons sent for Goodwin, heard him and told him to take his seat. The King asserted that, as their privileges were derived from the Crown, they could not be used against the Crown. The Commons stood firm and James eventually conceded that the Commons were judges of their own returns. The Commons then issued a further writ as a gesture of conciliation.

GOODWIN SANDS. *See* TENTERDEN; DOWNS.

GOODWOOD (Sussex). Jacobean house much altered between 1780 and 1800. The seat of the Ds. of Richmond.

GOOSE BAY (Labrador) was the airport, completed in 1942 as the base and clearing house for the wholesale ferrying of heavy aircraft from America to Britain during World War II.

GORDON, Gen. Charles George (1833-85) 'CHINESE GORDON', decorated by the French and Turks for bravery at Sebastopol in 1855, was a commissioner for delimiting the Russo-Turkish frontier from 1856 to 1858. He served in the Anglo-Chinese war of 1860 to 1862 and then surveyed part of the Great Wall. In 1863 he was appointed Chinese field commander against the Taiping rebels and by Apr. 1864 had, after 33 battles, virtually suppressed them. He was made a Mandarin of the highest class. In 1871 he was British member of the commission for improving the Sulina mouth of the Danube. By now he was internationally famous. In 1874 he accepted the Egyptian gov-generalship of the Equatorial Sudan. His efforts to suppress the slave trade being thwarted by the Egyptian govt. he resigned and the ensuing international uproar brought him back with enlarged powers and territory in 1877. By 1878 he had conquered Darfur and put down slave trading, but his efforts in the direction of Abyssinia failed and he was, for a while, a prisoner. In 1880 he returned to England and then went to India briefly as the Viceroy's sec. After resigning, he went to China and persuaded the imperial govt. to come to an understanding with Russia. After routine appointments he became commander of the colonial forces in S. Africa, but in 1882 again resigned when his peace negotiations with the Basuto were used as cover for Boer treachery. He was in Palestine in 1883 and was about to go to the Congo for the King of the Belgians when he was urgently despatched by the British govt. to bring out the Sudan garrisons before its abandonment to the Mahdists. The Egyptians, however, made him Gov-Gen. with orders to set up a separate govt. Feeling that he could not abandon those who were faithful to the order which he had established, he defended Khartoum for 10 months against an immense Mahdist army, possibly calculating that the Gladstone govt. would be morally compelled to relieve him and continue the occupation. Popular agitation indeed compelled the despatch of a British relief force, which arrived too late.

Gordon had long been the model Victorian hero – a handsome, fearless and incorruptible evangelical who, in his spare time at home, taught in ragged schools and helped many poor boys. Not surprisingly, though, his own conduct was the main cause of his death, Gladstone was the target of measureless popular fury and

Q. Victoria, accurately judging the public mood, sent him an angry telegramme *en clair*.

GORDON. Anglo-Norman nobles often called ADAM who settled at Gorden 7 miles N.W. of Kelso on the border in the 12th cent. They had increasingly extensive property on both sides of the frontier. **(1) Adam (?-1333)** was faithful to the English crown and used by Edward II as a negotiator with the Scottish nobility until the B. of Bannockburn (1314) when he was welcomed into Robert the Bruce's allegiance. He acquired the neighbouring manor of Stitchel from Thomas Randolph, E. of Moray, and deployed his resources in fighting Bruce's enemies, the Comyns. In 1320 he was commissioned to take the Arbroath Declaration to the papal court at Avignon and to open *pourparlers* for reconciliation with the papacy and peace with England. As a reward Bruce gave him the former Atholl lordship of Strathbogie or Strabolgi (Aberdeen) and he renamed it Huntly after one of his Roxburgh villages. He was killed at the B. of Halidon Hill. A grandson **(2) Adam (?-1402)** a border fighter, was killed at Homildon Hill. His *d.* **(3) Elizabeth (?-1439)** married WILLIAM SETON (?-1440) of Edinburgh and brought him the Gordon and Huntly Baronies. Their son **(4) Alexander (?-1470) 1st E. of HUNTLY (?1445)** acquired Badenoch and wide estates in Inverness and Moray and inherited Aboyne and other lordships in Aberdeenshire. His descendants all took the name of Gordon and, as Es. and Ms. of Huntly and Ds. of Gordon, became mainly Highland Chieftains and, in the 16th and 17th cents. pronouncedly conservative and R. Catholic leaders. A younger grandson of Alexander **(5) Adam (?-1538) Ld. of ABOYNE,** married Elizabeth (?-1535) Countess of SUTHERLAND, in 1500 and in 1527 they resigned the earldom to their son **(6) Alexander (?-1530)** the ancestor of the Gordon Es. and Ds. of Sutherland. **(7) Charles (?-1681)** *s.* of the 7th E. and 2nd M. of Huntly, a strong royalist, was made **E. of ABOYNE** at the Restoration. *See succeeding entries.*

GORDON (HUNTLY) (*see* GORDON). **(1) George (?- 1502) 2nd E. of HUNTLY,** probably a supporter of the younger James IV at the time of the B. of Sauchieburn (1489) became Lieut. and a commissioner for forfeited estates in the north in 1491-2. He was Chancellor from 1498. His grandson **(2) George (1514-62) 4th E. (1524)** a blood relative and foster-brother of James V, also became Lieut. of the North (1537) and, in 1542, commanded the Eastern March force which staved off the English at Haddon Rig while James V came to disaster at Solway Moss. He was one of the four regents appointed under the King's allegedly forged will produced by Card. Beaton and helped that churchman to reassert his power against Arran in 1543. Appointed Lieut. in the North, he crushed a Cameron and Macdonald revolt and added considerably to the family properties. In 1546, after Beaton's murder, he became Lord Chancellor but also commanded troops against the English and was captured when his men ran away at the B. of Pinkie (1547). He was released on promising to further English interests but voted for a French marriage for Mary Q. of Scots at the Haddington Parliament of July 1548. By now he held the earldom of Moray, the hereditary bailiwick of the bishopric of Aberdeen and was virtually an independent northern prince. Not surprisingly, the Queen Regent, Mary of Guise, took steps against his excessive power on the pretext of laxity in suppressing a Macdonald uprising. In 1554 he was imprisoned until he had surrendered Orkney and also the functions of the chancery to a French vice-chancellor. The estrangement between him and the Regent had an important consequence, for he thought that she was trying to establish a French style autocracy with French troops. Hence, though a R. Catholic, he supported the Lords of the Congregation against her on political grounds in the decisive year 1560. Thereupon he reverted to his balancing policy by inviting Mary Q. of

Scots, after the death of her husband Francis II of France, to land at Aberdeen. She took other advice and put herself into the hands of the Lord James Stuart, who received the earldom of Moray (informally held by Huntly). The queen now made a northern progress which suspended the Lieut's authority. The Lord James publicly assumed the earldom and Huntly resolved to fight him for it. He died of a stroke during the B. of Corrichie (Nov. 1562) where the Gordons were routed. His son **(3) George (?-1576), 5th E.,** was deprived but nominally restored to his lands and dignities and made alliance with Bothwell. He escaped from Holyroodhouse on the night of Rizzio's murder (Mar. 1566) and, when Morton was attainted for it, succeeded him as Lord Chancellor. In 1567 Huntly got his estates back by helping Bothwell to divorce his wife (Huntly's sister) and witnessing the Queen's marriage to him. He remained a queen's partisan with a strong, but ill-organised following, until the Pacification of Perth (1572) when he retired from public affairs. His son **(4) George (1562-1636) 6th E. and 1st M.** (1599) took part in the counter-revolution which delivered James VI after the Ruthven Raid (1580) and in 1588 he married Lennox's *d.* Henrietta. He was widely regarded as the leading Papist and he corresponded with R. Catholic courts. Some of the letters came to light while he was Capt. of the Guard in 1589 and though James was friendly (the Armada having just failed) presbyterian Edinburgh drove him out. He went north, raised troops with Crawford and Erroll to rescue the King, who felt constrained to march against him. George submitted and after a short confinement went north to build a castle in Badenoch, provoking a clan war with the Mackintoshes, Grants, Athol and Moray. He killed Moray in a cave. This private war broadened out when George was implicated in and then cleared of complicity in the affair of the Spanish Blanks (1592-3) and given the choice of exile or conversion. He chose neither, was outlawed, but defeated the E. of Argyll (Oct. 1594) sent to enforce the judgement. He was thus involved in feuds with Clan Campbell, now supported by the King. The combination was too strong for him. In Mar. 1595 he left for Spain, was back in 1596 and (having been reconciled to the Kirk) was restored to his estates and earldom in Dec. 1597. Though much harried by the Kirk he remained thereafter a favourite at James' court until 1625. Charles I was less wise and deprived him of his northern Lieutenancy. Charles also, against Highland opinion, supported his enemies, the Crichtons. During his latter years his son **(5) George (?-1649) E. of ENZIE, 2nd M.** was brought up with Charles I as an Anglican. After the father's death Charles relied too much upon him, for he was irresolute, and set his personal enmities and friendships above policy; hence he would not co-operate with Montrose in his royalist rising (1645) and was eventually attainted and executed. The attainder was reversed in 1661 for his grandson **(6) George (1643-1716) 4th M. (1653) and 1st D. of GORDON (1684),** a R. Catholic who accepted office under James II & VII, but refused to enforce his policies, held Edinburgh Castle for him but would not bombard the town. Naturally he was suspect to both sides. The later dukes were mainly notable for their wealth.

GORDON-LENNOX. See LENNOX.

GORDON RIOTS (June 1780) began as a demonstration against R. Catholic influence, arising from the Relief Act (1778) and Lord North's commercial concessions to the Irish. Led by Lord George Gordon as a peaceful petition to Parliament by the new Protestant Assn., the supporters got out of hand and a week's looting in the city followed. Gordon was acquitted of treason but the general alarm increased support for North's govt. at the ensuing election.

GORDON-WALKER, Patrick (1907-80) Ld. (1974), Labour M.P. and Sec. of State for Commonwealth

Relations (1950-1) under Attlee. In 1964 he lost his seat in the general election but was appointed Foreign Sec. under Wilson. He was found a supposedly safe seat but contrived to lose it too and resigned the Foreign Office (Jan. 1965). He was eventually elected at Leyton (1966), was Mm without Portfolio in 1967 and Sec. of State for Education and Science (1967-8). He was fundamentally too decent.

GORDONSTOUN SCHOOL (Moray) was founded in 1934 when Kurt Hahn, the headmaster of Prince Max of Baden's school at Salem, escaped from Nazi Germany. It was conducted upon his educational principles, developed for the education of the Prince's son, involving participation in the life of local people and the substitution in part of real activities for the competitive sports usual in the English public schools which he admired. The D. of Edinburgh and Charles, P. of Wales, were educated there.

GORE, Charles (1853-1932) an influential Anglo-Catholic and, while Principal at Cuddesden (1880-3) and Librarian of Pusey House (1884-93), a leading Oxford figure. His advanced *Lux Mundi* (Lat = Light of the World) alarmed contemporary theologians and in 1892 he formed and until 1901 was Superior of the Community of the Resurrection at Mirfield. In 1902 he became Bp. of Worcester and in 1905 of Birmingham, whose diocese he founded with his private fortune and successfully managed until 1911. He was translated to Oxford where he was less successful, but resigned in 1919. He supported the Prayer Book Revisions of 1927-8.

GORE-BOOTH, Paul Henry (1909-84) Lord (LP 1969) nephew of the Countess Markiewicz and a talented musician, became a diplomat in 1933 and Director of Information in the USA in 1949. From 1953 to 1956 he was ambassador to Rangoon (Burma) and later gave a home to Suu Aung San when she was at Oxford. In 1956 he was put in charge of the new Economics Dept at the Foreign Office, and in 1960 helped to set up the OECD. He then became High Commissioner in Delhi during an active and difficult period. From 1965 to 1969 he was Permanent U/S at the Foreign Office.

GOREE (Senegal). This small I. off C. Verde was occupied by the Portuguese in the 15th cent. and then taken over by the Dutch (1617-77), who named it after one of their own Is. and made it the slaving base which it remained into the 19th cent. It was then successively French (1677-1758) and British (1758-63) when it was controversially retroceded. The French held it until 1800, then the British again (1800-15) and the French yet again from 1815 when it became their H.Q. for the commercial development of Senegal and originated the prosperity of Dakar.

GORHAM's CASE (1847). Henry Phillpotts, Bp. of Exeter, refused to institute the Rev. Cornelius Gorham to a living because he thought him unsound on infant baptism. The Judicial Committee overruled him.

GORING (1) George (1583-1663) Ld. (1628) E. of NORWICH (1644) accompanied P. Charles to Spain in 1623. He negotiated the marriage with Henrietta Maria in 1628 and became her Master of the Horse. He also acquired other offices, mostly related to the King's increasingly unpopular financial expedients: the clerkship of the Council for Wales, commissionerships for licensing the export of butter, the regulation of the manufacture of gold and silver wire and taverns, besides a large share of the tobacco monopoly. In 1639 he became a Privy Councillor and raised a squadron of cavalry for service against Scotland. The Long Parliament abolished his monopolies in 1640 but he remained wealthy and spent his fortune for the King, for he said "I had all from his majesty, and he hath all again". In 1642 he went to Holland with the Queen and helped her to raise funds. He returned in 1643 and then went to Paris to get money and support from Mazarin. His report of these negotiations was intercepted and articles of impeachment

were exhibited against him, while the King made him an earl. In 1647 he commanded the Kentish cavaliers in the second civil war but was captured at Colchester while trying to raise Essex. He was then tried for his life but respited, freed in May 1649 and joined Charles II, but played an undistinguished part at his court. His eldest son **(2) George (1608-57) Ld. GORING,** served in the Dutch army and was recalled by his father in 1639 to serve against the Scots. In 1641 he was involved in the "Army Plot" which he betrayed to the Commons, who placed him in command at Portsmouth; in Aug. 1642, however, he declared for the King; forced to surrender in Sept. he escaped to Holland. In Dec. he went to Newcastle, where the E. of Newcastle made him his gen. of horse, but after defeating Sir Thos. Fairfax at Seacroft Moor, he was himself captured at Wakefield. Exchanged for the E. of Lothian in Apr. 1644 he commanded cavalry at Oxford, Lincoln and under P. Rupert, whose right wing he commanded at Marston Moor. The King then gave him the cavalry command in the West, but when Rupert became C-in-C there, he became insubordinate and took to living off the land in Hants. and Dorset. By 1645 his disputes with the high command had paralysed the King's western war effort. He was eventually given the chief command in the west but, after Naseby, was defeated at Langport (July 1645) and in Nov. made off to France. He spent his later life in Spanish service.

GORST, Sir Eldon. *See* EGYPT-7.

GORT, John Standish Vereker (1886-1946) 6th (Ir.) and 1st (U.K. 1945) Vist. was commandant of the Staff College, Camberley from 1936 to 1937 and C.I.G.S. from 1937 to 1939 when he took command of the British Expeditionary Force to France. In May 1940 the force was almost enveloped by the Germans, when the French on his right were driven south from Sedan and the Belgians on his left surrendered. With great determination he prevented a break-through on either flank and got the force back to Dunkirk where it was successfully evacuated. From 1940 to 1941, as Insp.-Gen. Home Forces he organised the rebuilding of the army. In 1941-2, as gov. of Gibraltar, he prepared that fortress for its essential wartime function and, as gov. of Malta from 1942 to 1944, he organised its equally essential defence against naval and air attack. He was promoted Field Marshal in 1943 and was High Commissioner in Palestine from 1944 to 1945.

GORTON, Sir John Grey (1911-). Prime Minister of Australia from 1968 to 1971.

GOSCELIN OF ST. BERTIN (?-early 12th cent.), a monk at St. Omer in Artois, joined Herman, Bp. of Sherborne, from 1058 and as chaplain for Q. Edith's new church at Wilton became interested in the nun Eve. After the Conquest Herman's Norman successor expelled him from Sherborne and Eve became a recluse at Angers. In about 1080 he wrote his partly autobiographical *Liber Confortatorius* (Lat = Book of Encouragement) for her. In the 1090s he found a home at St. Augustine's. He disliked Norman clerical hostility towards the traditions of the old English Church and between 1078 and 1099 wrote many *Lives* of Anglo-Saxon saints, five being women (Sts. Edith, Wulfhild, Milburga, Etheldreda and Werburg), and possibly the *Life of King Edward*. William of Malmesbury borrowed from him and wrote 'He did research over a long period on many bishoprics and abbeys, and gave to many places monuments of his outstanding learning'.

GOSCHEN, George Joachim (1831-1907) 1st Vist. GOSCHEN (1900), grandson of a Leipzig publisher and son of a London banker, with an Anglo-German education, entered his father's bank and, at the age of 27, became a Dir. of the Bank of England. In 1861 he made a reputation with his *Theory of Foreign Exchanges* and, having become an M.P. for the City of London (1863), entered the Cabinet in 1866. His meteoric rise was due to a strong intellect, consistency, clear oratory and excellent social manners. He became Gladstone's Pres. of the Poor Law Board in 1868 and was then First Lord of the Admiralty from 1871 to 1874. He foresaw the European dangers which might follow the German victory over France in 1871 and his resolute refusal to reduce the naval estimates broke up the govt. In 1876 he conducted an investigation into Egyptian public finance. Losing his City seat he was elected for Ripon and went on a special mission to force the Turkish Sultan to carry out the Balkan provisions of the T. of Berlin of 1878. In 1882 he refused office; in 1883 the Speakership. By now he was out of sympathy with the new radicalism of Chamberlain and Dilke and with the foreign and Irish policies of Gladstone and Parnell. In 1885 he defeated a radical at E. Edinburgh and, with Hartington, formed the moderate Liberal Unionist Party with which they defeated Gladstone's Home Rule Bill. He then became Ch. of the Exch. under Salisbury (until 1892) and as such converted the National Debt from 3% to 1/2% and solved the Baring panic of 1890. He was for a second time First Lord (1895-1900) under Salisbury and began the great naval expansion against German colonial and naval policy. He retired in 1900.

GOSHEN. *See* STELLALAND.

GOSPATRIC (fl. 1067), a friend of Harold Godwinsson's brother Tostig, became E. of Northumbria in 1067 as part of William I's politic management of the north. Gospatric, however, joined the rising of 1068 and, with Danish allies, sacked York. His earldom was returned to him when he submitted but in 1072 he fell finally from grace and fled to Scotland where he received Dunbar.

GOSSE (1) Philip Henry (1810-88) was a distinguished (mainly marine) naturalist. His son **(2) Sir Edmund William (1849-1928)** worked on the catalogue of the British Museum (1865-75), introduced Ibsen to the British public and, from 1904 to 1914, was librarian to the H. of Lords. He wrote *Father and Son*, an anonymous biography of his father which relates the difficulties of a Plymouth brother in reconciling his religion with his scientific findings.

GOTHA (Ger.) capital of one of the former Saxe-Coburg states, was the earliest centre for printed maps and its factories produced a well known bomber in World War I.

GOTHENBURG, founded 1607, to evade the Sound Tolls. *See* BALTIC-24.

GOTHIC. *See* ARCHITECTURE, BRITISH-5 TO 8.

GOTHIC NOVELS involved a reaction against the emotional deficiency of the age of reason. They were commonly set in forests, castles, graveyards or wild country and included the occult, rape and deeds of horror. The genre was pioneered in Horace Walpole's *Castle of Otranto* (1765), became widespread by the 1790s e.g. in Ann Radcliffe's *Mysteries of Udolpho* (1794) and Matthew Lewis's *The Monk* (1798) and was cheerfully parodied by Jane Austen in *Northanger Abbey* (1818).

GOTHS formed a Kingdom on the Lower Vistula and in A.D. 150 migrated to the Black Sea. After wanderings in the Balkans they split into **Ostrogoths** (Eastern) and **Visigoths** (Western) in about 257. After further wanderings the Ostrogoths settled in Italy (about 395) where their rule lasted until 553. The Visigoths moved to S. France (415) and, having been converted to R. Catholicism in 589, settled in Spain which they ruled until the Arab invasion of 711 to 713.

GOTLAND. *See* BALTIC; HANSE-1, 5.

GÖTTINGEN (Ger.) has a famous Hanoverian university founded by George II in 1734.

GOUGH, Sir Hubert de la Poer (1870-1963), a controversial soldier, served bravely in India and S. Africa but, as a Brigadier-Gen., was the highest ranking officer involved in the Curragh "Mutiny" (Mar. 1914). He nevertheless enjoyed promotions via divisional and corps commands to the command of the 5th Army in front of Amiens. With defences uncompleted but having requested and been refused reserves against an expected attack, he had to endure the opening violence of the German Mar. 1918 offensive. The French uncovered his southern flank and, for lack of reserves unable to counter-attack, he retreated to save the ports and was instantly superseded. Critics held that his lesser misjudgments were used to cover major misjudgments by others. He published his justification only in 1931.

GOUGH, Sir Hugh (1779-1869) 1st Ld. GOUGH (1846) Vist. (1849), commanded the R. Irish Fusiliers under Wellington in the Peninsula and in 1837 went to India to command the Mysore division. From there he went to China where (May 1841) he stormed the forts at Canton and (July 1842) the fortress of Ching-Kiang fu. In Aug. 1843 he became C-in-C, India. He immediately took charge of the occupation of Gwalior and had to fight off the Marathas at Maharajpur (Dec. 1843). His tenure of the command was notable for the three victories in the First Sikh War and three more in the Second. He came home in 1849. He was a controversial figure. As Lord Ellenborough thought that he did not have "the grasp of mind and prudence essential to conduct great military operations", the govt. wanted to supersede him with Sir Charles Napier after the victory at Chillianwallah (Jan. 1849) but the troops adored him and he won more battles than any other contemporary general except Wellington.

GOULBURN, Henry (1764-1856), a practical Tory, was an M.P. from 1808. In 1810 he became U-Sec. of State at the Home Office and from 1812 to 1821 for War and Colonies. In 1821 he became Chief Sec. for Ireland and carried through legislation to compose for Irish tithes and suppress secret societies. As Wellington's Ch. of the Exch. he carried a reduction in national debt interest. He was briefly Home Sec. (1834-5) under Peel but, as his Ch. of the Exch., effected substantial fiscal savings by stock conversions.

GOULET, LE, P. of (May 1200). Philip Augustus of France secured Issoudun and Graçay for Blanche of Castile, who was to marry his heir. Arthur was to hold Brittany as K. John's vassal. The territory surrounding Chateau Gaillard was joined to France.

GOUT or PODAGRA. References to this disease are numerous and ancient, but it was probably confused with other diseases of an arthritic character. Widespread in England, it attacked mainly the well-to-do and seemed to run in families. It declined rapidly after 1780 but part of the decline must be ascribed to the assignment of symptoms, by better diagnosis, to other diseases. It could be distractingly painful. K. Frederick William I of Prussia, the philosopher Leibniz and the Younger Pitt were among many distinguished sufferers. It was virtually unknown in Scotland and Ireland.

GOVERNANCE OF ENGLAND. *See* FORTESCUE, SIR JOHN.

GOVERNMENT OF INDIA ACT, 1909. *See* MORLEY-MINTO REFORMS.

GOVERNOR (-GENERAL), represents the crown in a territory under British allegiance, outside Great Britain. Originally endowed with all the royal prerogatives, his powers were circumscribed by his Instructions which usually became an important feature of constitutional law and custom as it developed locally; hence the powers of no two governors were exactly alike. (i) Governors of some crown colonies ruled autocratically if with advice, assistance or interference from the Colonial Office. (ii) In some territories there was an executive council whose principal members were the Treasurer, the Colonial Sec. and the Attorney-Gen. and whose other members, if any, were usually colonial servants. He nominated them and they were responsible to him, but he had to listen to their collective advice, whose effect was known in the Colonial Office. (iii) There were territories with legislatures, of which such an Executive Council might form the upper house. In all these cases the governor was a working day-to-day ruler. (iv) The upper house might be a separate body or Senate and the Executive Council a cabinet, or the governor might be required to appoint local citizens to the Executive Council, thus making it partake of the features both of a Senate and of a Cabinet. Here the executive members, really ministers, were in theory responsible to him, but subject to local political pressures and influence. (v) The Executive Council might be a real Cabinet, perhaps appointed under his guidance but responsible to the legislature. In these cases the governor still had the power of witholding the Royal Assent: but he might exercise this in accordance with his Instructions or he might be required to refer certain classes of bills to the Colonial Office. (vi) There were large territories where the governor, in practice, behaved as if he were an ordinary constitutional monarch, though he was still appointed by the crown on the advice of the govt. of the U.K. (vii) Lastly, after the Statute of Westminster 1931, governors in dominions began to be appointed by the crown on local advice. Certain large territories such as Canada had governors-general, but since 1932 this title has been used for governors of independent dominions, regardless of size.

A LIEUTENANT-GOVERNOR is (as in Jersey) lower in rank than a governor, or governs a part (e.g. a Canadian province) of a territory under a Governor. *See* COLONIAL LAWS.

GOWER, Is. and Es. *See* LEVESON-GOWER.

GOWER, John (?1325-1408), poet and friend of Chaucer, wrote *Vox Clamantis* (Lat = The Voice of the Supplicant or The Voice of Grievance), a Latin elegiac account of the Peasants' Revolt and the *Chronica Tripartita* (Lat = Three Part Chronicle) on the reign and abdication of Richard II. His *Confessio Amantis* (Lat = Lover's Confession) is an important early English poem. He was well known at court where, in 1400, he went blind. He also wrote the *Miroire de l'Homme* (Fr = Mirror of Man) in French.

GOWRIE, Es. of. *See* RUTHVEN.

GOWRIE CONSPIRACY. See JAMES XI-12.

GRACE, Edward Mills (E.M.) (1841-1911) and his brother **Dr. William Gilbert (W.G.) (1848-1915),** known as Dr. Grace, Gloucestershire cricketers from 1862 until 1915, had an unrivalled influence on cricket and its popularity. E.M. was a forcible and ingenious batsman and an unsurpassed fielder. W.G., a large man with a large black beard, scored nearly 55,000 runs and took 2,876 wickets in first class cricket.

GRAF SPEE. This German raiding pocket battleship was attacked by Comm. Harwood with three British ships of half her power in the R. Plate and driven into Montevideo on 13 Dec. 1939. On 17 Dec. she was scuttled. *See* COMMERCE PROTECTION, NAVAL, C-1

GRAFTON, Ds. of. *See* FITZROY (GRAFTON).

GRAHAM CLAN. *See* MARCHES, ANGLO-SCOTS-9 *et seq.*

GRAHAM of CLAVERHOUSE, John (?1649-89) Vist. DUNDEE (1688) "BONNY DUNDEE", though a R. Catholic, served under William of Orange in Flanders and saved his life at Seneffe. William recommended him to the D. of York (later James II) and he served for a time under his kinsman, Montrose. Hence he was entrusted with the suppression of covenanters in Dumfries and Annandale in 1678-9 and in 1681 in Galloway. So long as they kept to the hills and made no formal stand the covenanters were safe. Defeating him at Drumclog, they foolishly tried a second time and were routed at Bothwell Brig. He was reputed stern towards leaders but affable to the common folk. In 1682 his influence, especially as a commander of newly raised regulars, secured the imprisonment of Sir John Dalrymple, a leading covenanter at Edinburgh, and in 1683 he became a Scots Privy Councillor. In 1684 he was actively hunting covenanters in Ayr and Renfrew but quarrelled with the more moderate M. of Queensberry, the head of the Douglas interest in S.W. Scotland, and briefly lost his

posts until James II put him in charge of the Scottish troops as maj-gen. in 1685. As such he was with James at Salisbury in 1688 and then escaped to Scotland, where he took command of the pro-Stuart clans at Lochaber. He and Cameron of Lochiel defeated Gen. MacKay at Killiekrankie but he was killed.

GRAHAM of DALKEITH. This lowland family received lands from David I of Scots and were the ancestors of the Grahams of Kincardine. *See below*.

GRAHAM of KINCARDINE. This lowland sept became prominent under Robert II of Scots as landowners and courtiers. **Sir Patrick** *m.* EGIDIA, the King's niece, and **Sir Robert** *m.* the P. Mary, *d.* of Robert III. These semi-royal Grahams represent the ancestry of the Grahams of Claverhouse (Dundee) and of Montrose.

GRAHAM, Malise, E. of STRATHEARN. *See* JAMES I OF SCOTS-5.

GRAHAM of MONTROSE. Scottish family **(1) Sir William (?-?)** received the Montrose lands in 1407. His son **(2) Patrick (?-1466) 1st Ld. GRAHAM (1445),** was a regent for James II of Scots. His grandson **(3) William (?-1513) 1st E. of MONTROSE (1488)** was a supporter of James III and fell with James IV at Flodden. His great-grand-son **(4) John (?1547-1608) 3rd E. (1571)** was a commissioner for receiving Mary Q. of Scots abdication in 1567 and supported the regent at the B. of Langside (May 1568). He was one of the regent Morton's commissioners at the Pacification of Perth (July 1572) and became one of James VI's councillors when the King took over the govt. at the Stirling parliament of 1578; he played an important part in Morton's final overthrow in 1581 but, as he did not intend to substitute Lennox and Arran for Morton, he was one of the conspirators in the Ruthven Raid (Aug. 1582) and helped to protect the King when he escaped from Falkland (1583). He now rose quickly in favour. In May 1584 he became a Lord of Session and Lord High Treasurer, but his rise was interrupted by Angus' *coup d'état* of 1585. He was not readmitted to office until 1591. In 1599 he became Lord Chancellor and in 1603, when James VI went to London, he and Lord Fyvie became effectively joint-viceroys and were appointed by the Perth parliament of 1604 to conduct the abortive negotiations for union. In Dec. 1604 he became sole King's commissioner, but Fyvie in practice carried on the administration because of Montrose's declining health. The family continued prominent and his grandson **(5) James (1612-50) 5th E. (1626) and 1st M. (1644)** brought up by the mathematical Napier family, travelled abroad but in 1636 returned and sought, but failed to obtain, court employment; in 1637 he joined the nationalist movement and in 1638 signed the Covenant, which he was deputed to enforce at Aberdeen. He did this by negotiation and in 1639 persuaded the Gordon M. of Huntly to send his anti-Covenanting forces home. He appears to have given Huntly a safe conduct and then repudiated it. Hence, while Huntly was taken, a prisoner, to Edinburgh the Gordons rose again and initiated the Civil War (May 1639). He reoccupied Aberdeen and beat them at Bridge of Dee. In the ensuing peace, however, he found himself driven away from the Covenant by the potentially anti-aristocratic policy of the Edinburgh presbyterians, in alliance with Argyll. The issue arose out of the abolition of the episcopacy and a proposed consequent reform of the Lords of the Articles, in which the nobles would be in a permanent minority. He crossed the Tweed with the Scots army (Aug. 1640) in the second Bishop's war, but meanwhile signed the Band of Cumbernauld (Aug. 1640) whereby he and others like-minded undertook to resist any dictatorship in the hands of subjects. By May 1641 he was corresponding with Charles I but the relationship came to light and Argyll had him arrested (June 1641); he was freed in Nov. By 1643 it was obvious to Montrose that a Covenanting army would invade England. He tried to persuade the Queen at York (May 1643) and the King at Gloucester (Aug. 1643) to forestall this by a royalist insurrection supported from Ireland. He was only allowed to implement the plan after the Scots had actually invaded. In Feb. 1644 he was appointed King's Lieut.-Gen. in Scotland. He was driven back in Apr. 1644 but in Aug. he crossed the border in disguise and commenced a brilliant campaign of small armies, based upon a body of Macdonnells sent over from Ulster by the M. of Antrim (*see* MACDONNELL). Supplemented by Athol highlanders he beat the Campbells at Tippermuir (1 Sept.); with local lowlanders he took Aberdeen (13 Sept.); with Scottish Macdonalds he routed the Campbells at Inverlochy (2 Feb. 1645); with Gordon cavalry he beat regulars under Sir John Urry at Auldearn (9 May) and under Baillie at Alford (2 July) and he took Glasgow after the B. of Kilsyth (15 Aug.). Here, however, his forces broke up, for each clansman had little interest in the wider issue and wanted to pursue his various clan feuds. His attenuated force was beaten by David Leslie at Philiphaugh (13 Sept. 1645) and the lowlands and burghs, enraged by his clansmen's ungovernable looting, rose against him. Collapse came as quickly as success and in Aug. 1646 Montrose escaped *via* Norway to the Queen's court at Paris (Feb. 1647). He got no support from her or the French, but the Emperor allowed him to recruit in Belgium. In 1649 he offered his services to Charles II, then at The Hague, who commissioned him to make a further attempt in Scotland. He raised 1200 men and some money in Sweden and Denmark and sailed for the Orkneys in Dec. 1649. 1,000 men perished in a shipwreck. With the rest he landed in the Dornoch Firth but was overwhelmed at Invercarron (27 Apr. 1650). Macleod of Assynt handed him over to the govt. and he was hanged at Edinburgh by act of parliament. His son **(6) James "the Good" (?1631-69) 2nd M.,** recovered the forfeited lands in 1652 but joined Glencairn's rising in 1653. This affair was confused because his hereditary enemies, the Campbells, led by Lord Lorne, also joined it and they quarrelled constantly. The rising collapsed in Mar. 1654 when he made terms with Gen. Monck. At the Restoration he refused to vote at his enemy's (now Argyll's) trial because "he had too much resentment to judge". Subsequent litigation with Argyll's heir was compromised and a formal reconciliation ended the feud. His grandson the handsome **(7) James (?-1742) 4th M. (1684) and 1st D. (1707)** bought the great Lennox properties and jurisdictions in 1702 and became Pres. of the Scottish Council in Feb. 1703. He was a convinced supporter of the protestant succession and of the Union. From 1709 to 1713 he was keeper of the Scottish Privy Seal. He was one of George I's Lords Justices at Q. Anne's death and Sec. of State shortly afterwards. His steadying influence was an element in the suppression of the Jacobite rebellion in 1715 but his overharsh land management caused the banditry associated with Rob Roy Macgregor. His grandson **(8) James (1755-1836) 3rd D. (1790)** was a Pittite M.P. from 1780 and held minor office until 1790 when he became Master of the Horse. He was Lord Justice-Gen. from 1795 and Pitt's Pres. of the Bd. of Trade from 1804 to 1806. He was again Master of the Horse from 1807 to 1830 and also Lord Chamberlain from 1821 to 1827 and from 1828 to 1830. He secured the repeal of the legislation against highland dress. His son **(9) James (1799-1874)** was a practical Tory who, as Postmaster-Gen. from 1866 to 1868, secured postal conventions or contracts reducing the cost of postage with the U.S.A., China, and India and placed the telegraph system under the Post Office.

GRAHAM, Patrick (?-1478), half brother of James Kennedy, Bp. of St. Andrews, was Bp. of Brechin from 1463 to 1466 when he succeeded Kennedy at St. Andrews. He went to Rome and stayed there while the Boyds were in power but returned in 1469, having laid the foundations for the erection of St. Andrews into a metropolitical see in 1472. James II, with the help of St. Andrews University and the highly political William Schevez, his archdeacon, procured his deposition for heresy in 1478 and Schevez succeeded him. He died in prison.

GRAHAM, Thomas (1748-1843) 1st Ld. LYNEDOCH (1814) was Whig M.P. for Perthshire from 1794 to 1807. British Commissioner at the Austrian H.Q. in 1796-7 and, after organising the defence of Sicily in 1800, was with Moore at Corunna and served also at Walcheren. In 1811 he went to Spain and won the B. of Barosa and thereafter served under Wellington until invalided home in 1814.

GRAHAM LAND (Antarctica) was discovered by John Biscoe in 1832 and thought to be a separate island until proved part of Antarctica by a British expedition in 1934-7.

GRAHAM-LITTLE, Sir Ernest Gordon (1867-1950), physician educated in S. Africa, was a very independent and respected M.P. for London University from 1924 to 1950. Apparently unable to understand people less self-reliant than himself, he combined a sturdy progressive individualism with implacable hostility to a national health service.

GRAHAME, Kenneth (1859-1932) author of *The Wind in the Willows* (1908), a classic alike of rural idealism, children's writing and prose style.

GRAIL, HOLY (ultimately from Gr = *Krater* = cup) the vessel used at the Last Supper, in which Joseph of Arimathea caught Christ's blood at the Crucifixion, figures in legends in many languages related to Arthurian cycles, the 12th cent. English one being compounded of at least two others. After various adventures Joseph leaves the Grail in the care of guardians and is imprisoned in N. Wales. Certain knights of the Round Table swear to find it, but are warned that only the pure will succeed. Some weary, others lapse into sin; attention is drawn to the libertine hedonism of Arthurian personalities such as Lancelot and Q. Guinevere; but in the end Galahad, Percival (Parsifal) and Bors see a vision of Christ and receive the Grail from him. There is a tenuous connection with Glastonbury where Joseph lived in a long preserved wattle hut and where tombs of Arthur and Guinevere were of course discovered in the 13th cent. Wagner's solemn and somnolent Knights in *Parsifal* represent a modern adaptation.

GRAMMAR SCHOOLS. In early English 'grammar' meant Latin grammar because Latin was the only language taught grammatically. Schools, mostly monastic, for teaching it existed throughout the middle ages. The dissolution of the monasteries and chantries (1530-47) made it necessary to replace their schools. Many grammar schools were attributed to Edward VI (1547-53) which in fact succeeded previously existing schools. Curricula differed little from those of the public schools which drew their pupils from a wider, rather than a local, catchment area. Ben Jonson (c. 1600) was apparently the first to speak of *English* grammar. Standards varied from the abysmal to the excellent. Dr. Johnson was educated at Lichfield Grammar School. The best habitually sent boys to the universities or developed into public schools. They were, however, charitably, not publicly, funded. The Education Act 1902 established new publicly funded grammar schools and assisted existing ones. Between the two World Wars a system gradually developed whereby children at about 11 took an examination which led to placements in Grammar, Secondary Modern and Technical Schools, the first leading mostly but not exclusively to the universities. Grammar School curricula had in any case considerably widened. After World War II there was widespread controversy (concerned more with social engineering than education) which led to many amalgamations of the three types into Comprehensive schools.

GRAMONT, Mémores de la Vie du Comte de, by Anthony Hamilton (?1646-1713) was published anonymously in 1713. Gramont was Hamilton's brother-in-law and probably dictated the first part dealing with his life down to his banishment from the French court. The second part, on the English court, was probably composed by Hamilton, whose grandfather was the E. of Abercorn. Though malicious and, in particular, untrustworthy, it is an important source.

GRAMOPHONE in the form of a rotating cylinder **PHONOGRAPH** was invented in 1876.

GRAMPOUND (Cornwall) was disenfranchised for corruption and its two parliamentary seats transferred to Yorkshire in 1821.

GRANADA (Spain), the last Moorish Peninsular state, was conquered by Ferdinand and Isabella in 1492. The beauty of the city and its Alhambra, and the intrigues of its leading Moorish families, inspired widespread romantic interest among Victorians.

GRANARD. *See* FORBES.

GRANBY. *See* MANNERS.

GRAND ALLIANCE (1701) of Britain, Austria and the Netherlands, to prevent the union of the French and Spanish crowns, was later joined by Portugal, Prussia and Savoy. *See* SPANISH SUCCESSION, WAR OF.

GRAND ASSIZE. *See* ASSIZES-1.

GRAND BANKS (Newfoundland), for five cents. the richest known fishery, was first reported by John Cabot in 1498 and soon attracted fishermen from all west European ports. Careening and drying grounds grew up wherever convenient and, in particular, the English colonised the W. coast of Newfoundland, while the French established themselves more dispersedly elsewhere in the island and on the neighbouring coasts. British sovereignty was recognised at the P. of Utrecht (1713) but the French kept and keep the small Is. of St. Pierre and Miquelon. Some other countries had customary or formally recognised fishing rights. Technical developments and the increase in the size and power of trawlers and the introduction of factory ships led to fear of over-fishing and Canada took over control of the Banks and renegotiated the agreements in 1977. Drilling for oil and gas began in 1980.

GRANDGORE (Sc.). *See* SYPHILIS.

GRANDI, Count Dino (1895-1988) was Italian representative to the League of Nations from 1925 to 1932 and Foreign Minister as well from 1929. He was ambassador to London from 1932 to 1939 and then Min. of Justice. His ingenuity and courage led to the overthrow of Mussolini in Apr. 1943.

GRAND JUNCTION CANAL. *See* TRANSPORT AND COMMUNICATIONS.

GRAND JURY. *See* JURY.

GRAND NATIONAL The principal national hunt horse race, was first run at Aintree near Liverpool.

GRAND REMONSTRANCE (Dec. 1641) consists of a petition by the House of Commons on three groups of issues, supported by the Remonstrance itself. The latter is in two parts. The first accuses "Jesuited Papists", bishops and evil councillors and courtiers, of a common design to subvert the fundamental laws. The second, in 204 paragraphs, provides supporting material and much propaganda which is sometimes strident and confused.

(2) The Petition requests (a) legislation to abolish episcopal votes in parliament and "immoderate" power over the clergy, for abolishing oppressions in religion, church government and discipline, including ceremonies; (b) the dismissal of corrupt or oppressive councillors and that "for the future your Majesty will vouchsafe to employ such persons ... as your Parliament may have cause to confide in"; (c) that Irish land forfeited or escheated as a result of the recent rebellion be not alienated.

(3) The First Part of the Remonstrance alleges that the conspirators against the fundamental laws act on four

common principles; (i) to "maintain continual differences and discontents between the King and the people upon questions of prerogative and liberty"; (ii) to "suppress the purity and power of religion"; (iii) to conjoin "parties most propitious to their own ends and to divide those who were the most opposite ... in church and state"; (iv) to make the King financially independent of Parliament.

(4) The Second *complains* (paras. 1-6) about the dissolution of the first parliament of the reign, mismanaged and misdirected war policy and consequent billeting of troops. Then (7-10) of the dissolution of 1626, the crown's efforts to raise money by forced loans, privy seals and excises and also of propaganda against the Petition of Right. Next (12-16) of the dissolution of 1629, the subsequent molestation of M.P.s and propaganda against parliaments generally. The next group (17-58) is concerned with events during the eleven years of Charles I's personal rule. Paras. 17 to 22, 44 and 45 deal with the exploitation of old crown rights for revenue purposes, 25, 26-30 and 48-50 with sales of crown assets and private restraints of trade, 34, 37-43 and 46-47 with judicial abuses, interferences or usurpations and 51 to 58 with objectionable church practices. Paras. 23 and 24 complain of the disbandment of trained bands and the impounding of gunpowder, while 33 castigates the seizure of bullion at the mint. The method and purpose of these activities is then alleged in paras. 59-64. It is to free the govt. from legal restraints and unite certain protestants with the papists in order to root out the puritans. For this (65-8) it was necessary to reduce Scotland to popery but the effort was foiled. Next the policy and tactics of Strafford, Laud and others are rehearsed and condemned (69-87) and it is asserted that with the inspiration of a papal nuncio, papists were being organised as an alternative govt. (88-94). Owing to govt. financial shortages, people were being bullied into forced loans (95-99) but fortunately (100-106) the Scottish occupation of the North and the T. of Ripon made possible the reform of these multiple evils and accordingly (107-137) the remonstrants proceed to congratulate themselves upon the payments to the Scots, the abolition of monopolies, the proceedings against Strafford, Laud and others, the destruction of the conciliar and ecclesiastical jurisdiction, the curbs on forests, stannaries and distraints of Knighthoods and the end of church ceremonial. Next it foreshadows (138-42) reforms in taxation, justice, foreign trade and fisheries. At this point the Remonstrance departs into self justificatory counter-propaganda on political and financial matters (143-79) and on ecclesiastical questions (180-90) and then propounds (191-203) a programme of claims to supremacy in church and state. There must be standing commissions to keep down papists and enforce the laws. The King must employ servants whom parliament can trust, admitting that crimes cannot always be proved against them or that what is proved is not always criminal such as favouring known papists or making contemptuous statements about either House. Councillors should swear to the public liberties and disclose their foreign pensions. The document's conclusion begins with an adjuration "that his Majesty may have cause to be in love with good counsel and good men...". Though in form addressed to the King, it was really a public manifesto. The most bitter debate in the House was on the motion to print it before sending it to the King who, in his reply drafted by Hyde, took notice of the discourtesy.

GRANDISON. *See* VILLIERS.

GRAND SERJEANTY. *See* FEUDALISM-13.

GRAND TOUR was a feature of the upbringing of most nobles and wealthy men of most countries, other than France, in the 18th and 19th cents., beginning with the P. of Utrecht (1713), though cases (e.g. Sir Philip Sydney between 1572 and 1573) occur earlier. At the age of 17 to 23 the young man, accompanied by a tutor and servants, would set off in his coach, armed (if English) perhaps with Jonathan Richardson's *Theory of Painting* and *Guidebook* (to art treasures). Italy was the initial goal, especially Florence, Rome and Venice; France, or rather Paris, and later Versailles were taken in on the way back. The more enterprising or moneyed might also visit Vienna, Salzburg, the Rhine cities and the Netherlands. The rediscovery of Herculaneum in 1719 and Pompeii in 1748 attracted these travellers south of Rome (though the Prussian Christoph von Blumenthal had visited Sicily, Malta and Gibraltar in 1655) and gave renewed stimulus to classical tastes. Lord Charlemont went further. In 1749 he visited Greece, then under Ottoman rule, while in 1752 James Stuart reached Asia Minor. Since execrable roads and lack of carriage springs made summer travel slow and winter travel mostly impossible, these tours usually lasted two or three years at least. The impression made upon the impressionable was necessarily great. They were at home at least in French and probably Italian as well as their native tongue and such educated men of all countries had a common background and corpus of experience. This accounts for the urbane familiarity of international gatherings at that time and, on a smaller scale, with the organisation of such bodies as the Dilettanti Society (1734). The French after 1792 and notably Bonaparte's unprecedented arrests of British subjects after the outbreak of war in 1803 created too many hazards for the practice to continue.

GRAND TRUNK ROAD (India) was built by Sher Shah (r. 1540-5) from E. Bengal to the Indus and extended in the 1860s to Calcutta and Amritsar by the British, who widened it. It had rest and post houses. Sher Shah built other trunk roads from Burhanpore through Agra to Jodhpur and Chitor and from Lahore to Multan.

GRANGE. A granary, or a house for which the rent was paid in grain and so, often, an isolated farm.

GRANT, CLANS. *See* CLANS, SCOTTISH.

GRANT family of lairds of Frenchie from about 1500. *See next entry.*

GRANT (1) Charles (1746-1823) made a fortune in the HEIC and became a member of the Calcutta Bd. of Trade in 1787. In 1804 (until 1818) he became an M.P. and from 1805 he was chairman of the Court of Directors of the Co. As such he was very critical of, and tried to restrain, the policies of the M. Wellesley (Gov.-Gen.) and supported his impeachment in 1808. He favoured Christian missions; had money set aside in 1813 for Indian education and instigated the foundation of Haileybury College. An earnest evangelical, he introduced Sunday schools into Scotland. His son **(2) Charles (1778-1866) Ld. GLENELG (1831)** M.P. from 1811 to 1835, was Irish Sec. from 1819 to 1823, Vice-Pres. of the Bd. of Trade until 1827 and Pres. until 1830. From 1830 to 1835 he was Pres. of the Bd. of Control and his HEIC Charter Act of 1833 vested the Co's. property in the Crown. As colonial sec. from 1835 to 1839 he carried through the emancipation of the slaves and also had to deal with the opening problems of the Great Trek. He was also heavily attacked for irresolution on Canadian policy. His brother **(3) Sir Robert (1779-1838)** was an M.P. from 1818 to 1834, a member of the Bd. of Control in 1830 and Gov. of Bombay from 1834.

GRANTHAM. *See* ROBINSON.

GRANTHAM (Lincs.) became rich in the Middle Ages through the wool trade and the operations of the Hall family. It was chartered under Edward IV and rebuilt its splendid church at that time. It was at an important cross roads and had a famous inn originating in the 15th cent. Its grammar school, founded in 1528, educated Sir Isaac Newton. With the building of the railway, it became a place for changing train crews and engines and acquired an engineering trade in consequence. It had two M.P.s from 1463 to 1885 and one thereafter. The original home of Mrs Margaret (later Lady) Thatcher.

GRANTMESNIL, Hugh of (?-1094) became abbot of St. Ernoul (Normandy) in 1059 but was exiled and went to Italy in 1065. He rejoined William in time to invade England in 1066 and became Sheriff in Hampshire in 1067 but returned to Normandy in 1068. A baronial opportunist, in 1088 he joined the opposition to William Rufus, but in 1091 he was involved in a private war with Robert of Bellême. He died a monk.

GRANVELLE, Antoine Perrenot de (1517-86) Bp. of ARRAS (1540) Card. (1561) became effective prime minister to Margaret of Austria, Regent of the Netherlands and, at the same time, Abp. of Malines in 1560. His abilities and local knowledge made him dangerous to the growing body of Dutch independent-minded opinion and, eventually, the intrigues of William the Silent and Counts Egmont and Hoorn secured his removal in 1564. He then served as Spanish viceroy of Naples from 1571 to 1575 and as Pres. of the Council of Italy from 1575 to 1579 when he became Philip II's Sec. of State and, as such, organised the Union of Portugal with Spain in 1580. This deprived England of an important market but exposed the Portuguese Empire to protestant attack.

GRANVILLE, Vist. and E. *See* LEVESON-GOWER.

GRANVILLE-BARKER, Harley (1877-1946), actor, minor dramatist and producer, revolutionised the English stage. From 1904 to 1907 at the Court Theatre, he produced many modern plays including some by George Bernard Shaw. Then, in his Shakespearian productions of 1912 to 1914, he abandoned the showman-melodrama tradition and the plays, virtually uncut, were produced with a minimum of scenery so as to concentrate attention upon the drama and stage picture. These plays were often, not always felicitously, spoken as verse.

GRAPHIC. *See* THOMAS, WILLIAM LUSON.

GRASSE[-TILLY], François-Joseph, Comte de (1722-88), French seaman, commanded the Brest fleet's American expedition in Mar. 1781, drove Hood off Martinique (Apr.), took Tobago, reinforced St. Domingo and then, in answer to an American appeal, sailed to intervene at Yorktown. United in the Chesapeake with Adm. Barras' squadron, he beat Hood and Graves and forced the British surrender (Aug-Oct. 1781). He then returned to the Caribbean intending to attack Jamaica; he took St. Kitts but could not prevent Hood uniting with Rodney. They brought him to action off the Saints (Apr. 1782), captured him and crippled his fleet.

GRASSUM. *See* FEU FERME.

GRATTAN, Henry (1746-1820) became an Irish M.P. for Charlemont by Lord Charlemont's patronage in 1775. His intellectual brilliance and fire impressed the House in 1776 and again in 1777. He attacked the British embargo on the export of provisions from Ireland and in 1777 he attacked govt. policy in America. In Feb. 1778 his motion for economic reform was defeated, but in Oct. 1779 one in favour of free trade was carried. The need was clear, for Ireland was in deep poverty, but it was the formation of the Irish Volunteers which forced the resolution through and made it safe to refuse new taxes or to underwrite new loans (Nov.). The British govt., embattled against the Americans and their allies, was forced by the tacit threat of armed mutiny, to act and most of the restrictions on Irish trade were repealed (1780) but Lord North had incautiously said that the concessions were resumable at pleasure. Grattan therefore, to safeguard them, demanded the legislative independence of the Irish Parliament. His motion, after a famous speech and a 15 hour debate, was adjourned (Apr. 1780) but he returned to the charge by trying to restrict the duration of the perpetual Mutiny Bill and in Nov. 1781 he attacked it as an Act. The resolutions of the armed Volunteers at the DUNGANNON CONVENTION (Feb. 1782) were now indirectly decisive. Grattan's motion for an Irish Declaration of Rights was again adjourned, but the North govt. fell and in Apr. 1782, at the third attempt, the

Declaration was passed *nem. con.* by both Houses; by the end of May the British parliament had repealed the Declaratory Act, the greater part of Poynings Law and the perpetual clauses of the Mutiny Act. The first act of the newly emancipated Irish parliament was to pass a bill for the independence of the judiciary; the second to vote £50,000 to purchase Grattan an estate.

Grattan saw that Irish political institutions would be weak and confused if the parliament were not reformed. It was not possible to clean up the jobbery of the Pension List (1786) or to get tithes (payable by the R. Catholic majority) to the Church of the minority) commuted (1787-9) or to inquire into the sale of peerages and seats in the Commons (1790-1) or to emancipate the R. Catholics (1792) or to promote commercial equality with Britain (1793) so long as those with vested interests could always control parliament. In 1794 he met Pitt, who indicated that the British govt. might not resist a R. Catholic Relief Bill if it were introduced, and in Jan. 1795 Fitzwilliam, the new Lord Lieut., arrived and indicated premature support for it. He was ahead of his time; the govt. had had its mind changed for it. Fitzwilliam was recalled (Mar. 1795) and the bill was defeated (May). Ireland was now in disorder and local insurrection. Grattan tried to resist the Insurrection Bill and the suspension of *Habeas Corpus* and in May 1797 he and his opposition colleagues seceded from the House because, in opposing the govt., they were encouraging the revolutionaries whom they equally disliked. At this point his health broke down. He took part in the very last days of the Irish parliament which corruptly voted its own extinction (1800) and did not return to politics until 1803 when Fitzwilliam found him a seat at Peterborough. In 1806 he was elected for Dublin, which he retained until his death. In every year except 1807 he took up the issue of R. Catholic Relief. His bill of 1813 passed its second reading but was amended to exclude R. Catholic's from the House of Commons, and he withdrew it.

GRATTAN'S PARLIAMENT (1782-1800) (*see* PARLIAMENT, IRELAND 1495-1800). This was the unreformed Irish parliament, accorded a slightly qualified legislative independence, by the Acts of Repeal and Renunciation (1782-3). The qualification arose from the method of certifying bills. These were certified by the Lord Lieut. to the Crown under the Great Irish Seal, returned under the Great Seal of Great Britain and then assented. Hence the London Privy Council could, and occasionally did, hold up bills by delaying their return. *See* GRATTAN; PARLIAMENT; IRELAND (1495-1800).

GRAVESEND (Kent), a Thameside manor belonging at Domesday to William I's half brother Odo, Bp. of Bayeux, was the highest point on the estuary which sea-going sailing ships could reliably attain, northerly winds moving the inward Newcastle colliers and the outward Channel bound shipping, southerlies vice-versa, easterlies the Dutch and Baltic inward, westerlies most outward shipping. It became the administrative stopping point for all shipping in and out of London, initially for the levy of the City coal dues, then for the customs and then for the Trinity House pilotage. Hundreds of ships riding at anchor daily in Gravesend Reach needed permanent protection. Hence the establishment of two forts and garrisons at Gravesend and another at Tilbury opposite. There was a miscellaneous nautical trade, such as green vegetables, for outward ships and other minor ships' stores. By 1560 the place had become substantial and busy. It was incorporated in 1562 and became the point of welcome for eminent foreigners. From the late 17th cent. it was the point of departure for the large E. Indiamen. The presence of many customs officers made it an easy target for crown electoral influence and it returned one M.P. Smuggling was also an important industry. By 1800 the borough was exceedingly prosperous and some of the accumulated capital was being invested in industries. This was as well, because steam driven shipping a generation later did not need to stop for long at Gravesend. The corporation sought to attract custom by building piers in 1834 and 1845 but the landings were mostly of local significance. Thus the town slowly changed from a primarily maritime settlement to a land based industrialism: in the 20th cent. it produced paper and cement and contained immense coal fired electricity generating stations. It was badly damaged in World War II.

GRAY (1) Andrew (?1380-1469) 1st Ld. GRAY of FOWLIS (1445) stood hostage in England for James I's ransom from 1424 to 1427 and was master of James II's household from 1452. His descendant **(2) Patrick (?-1582) 4th Ld.,** a supporter of Card. Beaton and Mary Q. of Scots, was a member of James VI's council from 1577. **(3) Patrick (?-1612)** Master of Gray and **6th Ld. (1609),** intriguer and possibly double agent, was on intimate terms with the Guises and Mary Q. of Scots' other French supporters, whose plans he reported to the Scots regency and James VI. He acted as go-between to Q. Elizabeth and James and secured Arran's deposition in 1585. He advised Mary's death in 1586 but was exiled by James in 1587. He returned in 1589 and was involved in 1592 in Bothwell's attempt on James at Falkland. His son **(4) Andrew (?-1663), 7th Ld.,** a soldier, was a member of Charles I's Scots Council of War in 1628; he supported him against the Covenant and was excommunicated and ruined in consequence.

GRAY (1) Sir James (?-1773) was British resident in Venice (1744-53), Naples (1753-61) and envoy to Spain in 1761. A keen antiquary, he and his brother **(2) Sir George (?-1773)** a soldier, together founded the influential Dilettanti Society.

GRAY, Robert (1809-72) Bp. of Cape Town from 1847 and Metropolitan of Africa from 1853, was involved in a doctrinal dispute with Bp. Colenso. He added five dioceses to the Anglican Church in S. Africa and proposed the establishment of the University Mission to C. Africa.

GRAY, Stephen (?-1736) discovered, in about 1729, the existence of electrical conductors (*non-electrics*) and non-conductors (*electrics*).

GRAY or GREY (1) Sir Thomas (?-1369), a soldier, served in France from 1338 to 1344, fought at Neville's Cross (1346) and became warden of Norham Castle where the Scots captured him in 1355. He became warden of the E. March in 1367. He wrote *Scalachronica,* an authority for the French and Scots wars of the time, especially the B. of Bannockburn in which his father fought. His grandson **(2) John (?-1421) E. of TANKERVILLE (1419)** fought at Harfleur and Agincourt in 1415, campaigned in the Cotentin in 1418 and became Chamberlain of Normandy in 1419, when he was a commissioner to negotiate the King's marriage. He was killed at the B. of Beaugé.

GRAY, Thomas (1716-71) friend of Horace Walpole and Prof. of History and Mod. Languages at Cambridge from 1768, began to write the celebrated *Elegy in A Country Churchyard* (that of Stoke Poges) in 1742 and published it in 1750. He left many works of scholarship, some lesser poems and his excellent *Letters.*

GREAT BIBLE. *See* BIBLE.

GREAT BRITAIN is the combination of England, Scotland and Wales, but does not include the Channel Is. or Man or N. Ireland. The term originated in 1603 as part of James VI and I's policy of uniting not only the crowns but the nations and their institutions. *See* MARCHES, POST NATI.

GREAT CHARTER. *See* MAGNA CARTA.

"GREAT CONTRACT" (1610) was an abortive financial negotiation between the Commons and James I and his Treasurer, the E. of Salisbury. After *Bates' Case* Salisbury had imposed prerogative merchandise duties which threatened to make the Crown financially independent of parliament. Parliament protested. Salisbury explained that £700,000 of debt had been paid off, that £300,000 was outstanding and that ordinary revenue was £50,000 a year short of needs. The Commons replied by demanding court economies and the abolition of monopolies, purveyance and wardship. After reflection they offered £100,000 for the abolition of the royal receipts from feudal incidents except aids. Salisbury demanded £200,000. They declined and began to debate grievances including uses of the prerogative. James forbade them to discuss the prerogative. The Commons then asserted their right to discuss anything affecting the subject. James retreated. Salisbury now induced them to offer £200,000; in return they wanted to abolish purveyance, all feudal incidents save £25,000 worth of aids, the exemption of the four English counties from the jurisdiction of the Council of Wales and a major inroad into royal Forests by making 60 year possession of land a good title against the Crown. The King answered in conciliatory language that he would consider their proposals. They wanted something more definite. He replied that they should pay all his debts and raise his income by £100,000. This evoked rude speeches about favourites and extravagance. James dissolved parliament.

GREAT COUNCIL or MAGNUM CONCILIUM was an assembly of magnates and priests, sometimes with judges in attendance, called by the crown for consultation or argument. Its precise constitution, if any, is unknown, so that tumultuary assemblies such as that which settled Magna Carta at Runnymede might be called Great Councils. When it became customary to summon an elected House of Commons, the Great Council slowly fell into desuetude because it resembled the House of Lords in most ways and that body was being regularly summoned anyhow. Occasional meetings, however, did occur and it was last summoned by Charles I to York in 1639. It refused to usurp the functions of Parliament but negotiated the T. of Ripon with the Scots.

GREAT DEPRESSION or SLUMP. *See* MACDONALD'S SECOND LABOUR and FIRST AND SECOND NATIONAL GOVTS.

"GREAT" FIRE OF LONDON (*for earlier fires see* LONDON). It raged from 2 to 6 Sept. 1666, consumed 80% of the City and destroyed St. Paul's. It was the second of three disasters affecting Restoration London, the others being the GREAT PLAGUE (1665) (*see* PLAGUE) and the incursion of the Dutch fleet into the Thames and Medway (1667) (*see* DUTCH WARS, SECOND-7). *See also* WREN, SIR CHRISTOPHER.

GREAT INTERCOURSE or MAGNUS INTERCURSUS. *See* HENRY VII-13.

GREAT or OLD CUSTOM was an old export tax, regularised in 1275, of 6s 8d per sack (364 lb) on wool and per 300 woolfells, 13s 4d per last (240) of leather and ⅓% *ad valorem* on lead and tin. The wool tax represented an average of about 5% on the price at London and the 13 other ports through which these goods were exported. It was abolished in 1311, reimposed in 1322 and died out with the Tudor prohibition on exports. It raised about £8,800 annually between 1278 and 1287 and £13,000 between 1303 and 1307. The takings on wool accounted for about 98% of the total. *See* CARTA MERCATORIA.

GREATER LONDON COUNCIL. The Commission on London Government (1957-60) recommended that a greater London county and council should be created comprising the old London County and Middlesex, together with some adjacent areas. This was enacted in 1963 with the significant amendment that the educational arrangements of the old London County Council should not be disturbed and should be administered for that area by a new Inner London Education Authority (I.L.E.A.). I.L.E.A. and the 32 London boroughs and the Greater London Council itself came into existence on 1 April 1965. It was soon captured by supporters of the left wing of the Labour Party and became the target of the animosity of the Thatcher govt. which abolished it and I.L.E.A. in Apr. 1986, leaving London and the other rather similar areas of the metropolitan counties to be administered by a confusion of *ad hoc* authorities and the boroughs. *See* LOCAL ADMINISTRATION-ENGLAND AND WALES.

GREAT EXHIBITION 1851. *See* ALBERT *etc.* PRINCE CONSORT.

GREAT NASSAU. William III.

GREAT OFFICERS OF THE REALM. In order of precedence under the Act for placing of the Lords (1539) were the *Lord Chancellor, *Lord Treasurer, Lord President of the Privy Council, Lord Privy Seal, *Lord Great Chamberlain, *The Constable of England, *The Earl Marshal, *Lord High Admiral, the Lord Steward of the Household, the Lord Chamberlain and the King's Secretary. Those marked * together with the Lord High Steward were the ancient Great Officers of State.

GREAT PLAGUE. *See* PLAGUE.

GREAT POWERS. A diplomatic concept, originating towards the end of the Napoleonic Wars, embracing originally those powers (Britain, Austria, Prussia and Russia) which had borne the burden of victory and felt entitled by that fact and their preponderance to make the decisions setting up the peace. Thus, lesser states had to protect their interests by negotiating with or through these powers. Talleyrand soon succeeded in inserting France into the circle, whose existence (though not its membership) has remained a fact of international politics ever since. In 1871 Germany superseded Prussia. At the end of World War I victory and stability qualified only Britain, France, Italy and the U.S.A. By 1938 Germany and Russia had almost elbowed their way back. At the end of World War II the concept received legal recognition by according permanent membership of, and a right of veto, on the decisions of the Security Council of U.N.O. to the U.S.A., Russia, Britain, France and China.

GREAT SCHISM. *See* SCHISM.

GREAT SEAL (1) is the seal of the sovereign and Kingdom. It shows the reigning sovereign enthroned on the obverse and mounted and armed on the reverse. During long reigns there may be several seals. An old seal is damasked with a hammer by the monarch and retained by the Lord Chancellor as a perquisite. Older seals were made of copper, modern ones of silver.

(2) The office of Lord Keeper of the Great Seal has mostly been held together with that of Lord Chancellor; the last separate one, Sir Robt. Henley, held office from 1757 to 1761 and then became Lord Chancellor himself. Lords Commissioners for holding the great seal were appointed after long Chancellorships, but this proved inconvenient and the last case was in 1850.

(3) The Great Seal is used to authenticate (a) royal proclamations; (b) for summoning a parliament or holding a by-election or conferring or confirming a peerage; (c) writs of *dedimus, mittimus* and *supersedeas;* (d) charters; (e) letters patent for confirming treaties; (f) for conferring dignities, franchises, offices and property rights and (g) for sealing a commission for the Royal Assent to bills.

(4) There were Great Seals for Scotland and Ireland, but the Great Seal of the United Kingdom superseded the former in 1707 and the latter in 1800.

(5) The procedure for affixing the Great Seal differed according to the subject matter, but in its most extended form involved successive authorisations and the payment of appropriate fees to a Six Clerk, the Clerk of the Crown in Chancery, the Solicitor and Attorney Gen., a Sec. of State and the Lord Privy Seal, besides the Lord Chancellor. The sovereign's sign manual was also necessary. In 1877 the press of business made wafer seals necessary. In 1884 the Great Seal Act abolished the Privy Seal and required simply that a warrant under the sign manual countersigned by the Lord Chancellor, a Sec. of State or two Treasury Commissioners was sufficient.

GREAT SESSIONS, WALES (*see also* UNION, ACTS OF WALES). In 1536 English law was applied throughout Wales. In 1543 the 13 counties of Wales and Chester were divided into three groups for which Courts of Great Sessions, having the powers of assizes, were established. Writs of Error lay to the King's Bench. Latterly they were held under two barristers who sat for 16 days in the year. By the end of the 18th cent. the courts at Westminster had established a concurrent jurisdiction. In 1830 Great Sessions were abolished and Wales was brought into the English circuit system.

GREAT STARVATION 1846-8. See IRELAND, E-5,6.

GREAT TAX (1532). See JAMES V OF SCOTS-5.

GREAT TREK (S. Africa) arose from exorbitant Boer land hunger, unsympathetic attitudes of British officials and missionaries to the Boer way of life and a rejection by the Boers of the British concept of equality before the law, which upset their labour relations. There was a large British immigration in the 1820s and slaves were emancipated throughout the Empire in the 1830s. In 1834 a COMMISSIE TREK reconnoitred W. Natal and the lands north of the Orange and Vaal. Acting on its favourable report the first party left the C. Colony under Louis Trigardt in Nov. 1835. Household equipment was packed in 16-span wagons: the huge herds of cattle were driven alongside. The movement was not organised *en masse*. Parties tended to wait upon the success or failure of those ahead and a limiting factor was shortage of gunpowder. In 1837 Hendrik POTGIETER crossed the Orange and defeated the Matabele, who moved north towards Rhodesia; Piet RETIEF, on the other hand, entered W. Natal over the Drakenbergs. The streams of VOORTREKKERS followed these two general directions, fanning out into territories which were either empty or emptied by the resulting wars. By 1845 about 12,000 Boers had left British territory and were haltingly developing republics in the Transvaal and between the Vaal and the Orange. In Natal British administration was catching up with them. It was annexed in that year. In the Cape, British immigrants had mostly replaced them on the abandoned lands.

GRECIAN COFFEE HOUSE (Devereux Court, Strand, London), was a 17th and 18th cent. literary rendezvous where Addison, Steele, Goldsmith and others from Will's Coffee House often met.

GREECE (1) The Turkish conquest, involving the fall of Constantinople (1453) and Mistra (1460) left certain, mostly island, territories in western hands viz:- Lesbos (Genoese) until 1462; Modon and Coron (Venetian) until 1500; Rhodes (Hospitaller) until 1523; Navplion (Venetian) until 1540; Chios (Genoese) and Naxos (Venetian) until 1566; Crete (Venetian) until 1645, except Candia until 1669 and the Ionian Is. (Venetian) until 1797.

(2) Turkish govt. mainly followed pre-existing Byzantine models, but tolerated non-Moslem religions; taxation was less oppressive than Venetian exploitation, and the septennial levy of children often opened up a brilliant career for an able child. The Greeks neither welcomed the Venetian reconquest of the Peloponnese in 1684, nor regretted their departure in 1718. Moreover, under the *millet* system, the Turks recognised the orthodox Patriarch of Constantinople as the representative of all orthodox Greeks, and Greeks living near the patriarchate (Phanariots) acquired privileges and wealth as assistants and interpreters (*Dragomen*) in the Turkish administration. By the 18th cent. Phanariots had a virtual monopoly of high office in the Sublime Porte and in the governorships of Moldavia and Wallachia.

(3) The growing weakness and corruption of the 18th cent. Ottoman central govt. to which the Greeks themselves contributed brought arbitrary behaviour by local Turkish officials. This provoked disorders and the formation of rural bandit gangs. Some of these *Klephts* (robbers) took on a romantic Robin Hood-like character

and attracted a sort of nationalist sentiment, but the first self conscious movement arose during the Russo-Turkish war of 1769-74. In Feb. 1770 Orlov's squadron landed marines in the Peloponnese and a widespread rising ensued. The Turks put it down with Albanian troops. This Russian presence caused a widespread development of Greek seaborne trading, smuggling and piracy and a permanent Albano-Greek feud.

(4) While Serbian and Albanian insurrections were shaking Ottoman rule, after 1797 secret societies were preparing rebellion in Greece. In 1821 there were two risings. Ypsilanti's relying on Russian support which never came, failed. That of Abp. Germanos of Patras succeeded. By May he had taken Athens. A provisional govt. was established. The affair caught classically educated western imagination. Greek liberation committees were formed, *inter alia,* in Britain, and volunteers, equipment and money, if much mismanaged, began to come in. The Constantinople govt. was in political crisis and unable to react. It called in the powerful gov. of Egypt, Mehemet Ali, whose son Ibrahim arrived with a fleet and army. By 1827 all the independent areas except the most inaccessible mountains had been overrun and Ld. Byron had died at Missolonghi (*see also* COCHRANE-6). The remnant of the leadership, mostly Klephts, elected Count Capo d'Istria, a Russian diplomat, to the regency. In the meantime the British, French and Russians had resolved to intervene jointly (T. of London, July 1827) each fearing to let the others intervene alone. A combined fleet destroyed the Egypto-Turkish armada at Navarino (Oct. 1827). While French and Russian troops pressed the Turks, by Sept. 1829 the Greeks had cleared the Peloponnese, Attica and Boeotia. The Russo-Turkish P. of Adrianople (Sept. 1829) was followed by the London Protocol (Feb. 1830) in which the great powers recognised a sovereign Greek Kingdom. Capo d'Istria was murdered in Oct. 1831; Leopold of Saxe-Coburg refused the dangerous crown, which was accepted for Otto of Bavaria, a minor, under a regency exercised by Count Armannsperg, with many foreign officials.

(5) The Greeks had no intention of accepting one group of foreigners for another and their appetite grew with eating. The first national govt. was established in 1837. The so-called GREAT PRINCIPLE of a Pan-Hellenic state centred on Constantinople, dominated public opinion. The foreign officials having failed to support the Cretan insurrection of 1841, they were driven out in 1843. A Franco-British occupation of the Piraeus put an end, during the Crimean War, to an invasion of Turkish Epirus. In 1862 the politicians dethroned K. Otto for his lack of foreign success. The Greek flag, in Bavarian blue and white, is his memorial.

(6) The new King George elected in 1865 was a Dane and Britain strengthened his position by handing over the Ionian Is. The govt. gave covert help to the Cretans; it took an unpopular stand in favour of neutrality in the Balkan War of 1875-6 and was stopped by Britain from invading Thessaly during the Russo-Turkish war of 1877. The Berlin Congress (1878) remitted the Thessalian question to direct negotiation, which meant that with pressure from the great powers the Greek frontier was advanced northwards to the line Arta-Volos by the Constantinople Convention of 1881.

(7) The next stage in Greek expansion occurred with their invasion of Crete in Feb. 1897. The Turks reacted victoriously. The Greeks were extricated by the great powers and had to buy back part of Thessaly, but the powers forced on the Porte a special Cretan regime with P. George of Greece as gov. under Turkish suzerainty. This could hardly last. In Sept. 1906 the prince resigned after persistent agitation and in 1908 a Cretan national assembly declared for unification with Greece. The Athens govt., however, dared not accept the gift.

(8) On the pattern of the Young Turk revolution of 1908, a Military League of young Greek officers staged a *coup d'état* in 1910 and put the Cretan Venizelos into power. Under his leadership Greece zestfully entered the Balkan wars and emerged by 1914 with its present territories save for the Thracian coast and the Dodecanese. In the ensuing World War I Greece was too weak to be involved; the Allies seized Lemnos and Tenedos as bases against the Dardanelles (Mar. 1915). K. Constantine I favoured neutrality; Venizelos, war against Turkey. He resigned but in Sept. 1916 staged a revolt at Salonika with Allied connivance, thus enabling northern Greece to become a base for an allied Balkan war. The King remained obdurate and was driven from the throne by allied threats (June 1917).

(9) The Great Principle guided Venizelos' policy, and the Bulgarian collapse (Sept. 1918) brought him Aegean Thrace. In Nov. 1918 the British and French occupied Constantinople and (May 1919), using Greek troops, Smyrna. They and Venizelos had gone too far, and Turkish opinion, violently aroused, was exploited by Mustapha Kemal (Atatürk) to form a nationalist govt. in opposition to that of the Sultan at Constantinople. The T. of Sévres (Aug. 1920) between the Allies and the Sultan's govt. awarded Smyrna and its hinterland and Thrace (to within sight of Constantinople) to Greece but the Turkish nationalists had consolidated and the French and the British had quarrelled. In Oct. a general election ended in Venizelos' defeat and the recall of K. Constantine. The Greek royalists had outbidden the Venizelists in nationalistic zeal; the Turkish nationalists had repudiated the T. of Sévres, but the French now supported Turkey. The Greeks struck first but in Sept. 1921 were repelled at the R. Sakaria and by Sept. 1922 driven, amid massacres, from Smyrna. Constantine abdicated a second time and the T. of Lausanne (July 1923) returned Smyrna and Adrianople to Turkey.

(10) Within a month Greece was involved in a quarrel with Italy, which used the murder of an Italian general as a pretext to seize Corfu. The League of Nations forced the Italians to leave, but the Greeks had to pay an indemnity. In these circumstances a right wing effort to overthrow the govt. not only failed but led to the abolition of the monarchy (1924). There followed a series of ineffectual govts. until 1925 when the monarchy was restored by plebiscite.

(11) By 1936 the older parliamentary generation had died out and Gen. Metaxas established an authoritarian but realistic regime which dissolved the many political parties and in Apr. 1938 signed a 10 year treaty of mutual non-injury with Turkey. Aimed at Italian aggression in the Levant, this emboldened him to reject the Italian ultimatum of Oct. 1940. The Greek army stopped an Italian invasion from Albania until Apr. 1941 but by this time the Germans were in a position to attack from Bulgaria. Despite British assistance the mainland was overrun by May 1941 and Crete succumbed to a pyrrhic airborne invasion in June.

(12) Greece was now placed under Italian occupation, while the govt. settled in London and a number of clandestine resistance organisations began to form. The most important were ELAS and EAM (communist), EKKA, a purely nationalist group, and EDES, led by the conservative republican Col. Zervas. When the Italians surrendered (1943) these groups seized local authority in a patchwork of mutually hostile areas while the Germans strove to maintain a military collaborationist administration. When, however, the Germans left (Oct. 1944) ELAS attempted a revolution in Athens. This was suppressed by loyal troops with British help but as the crown appeared to be a controversial institution, the British encouraged the creation of a regency under the respected Abp. Damaskinos. They, with the Americans, trained and equipped a modern

regular army, while the Yugoslavs supplied and trained ELAS in an uneasy and undeclared truce. In Mar. 1946 ELAS rose, but its atrocious conduct brought a public revulsion: and in Sept. K. George II was overwhelmingly recalled by a plebiscite. He and his successor, Paul, with their military leader Gen. Papagos, benefited by the triumphant peace (Feb. 1947) with Italy, which ceded the Dodecanese. Nevertheless, the last embers of the Yugoslav-supported ELAS revolt were only stamped out in Jan. 1950.

(13) The Great Principle, however, continued to work disorder. Marshal Papagos had formed a party, which won an overwhelming parliamentary majority in 1952 and brought Greece into N.A.T.O. in 1954, but Greek Cypriot nationalists had resorted to violence and, compelled by its right wing, the govt. felt bound to support them. The Karamanlis govt. which succeeded after Papagos' death (1956) obtained majorities mainly by not repudiating clandestine support for Col. Grivas, the invader of Cyprus. Few Cypriots wanted to be united with Greece and the Cyprus Agreement signed in London (Feb. 1959) gave them an effective independence which the extremists were determined to destroy. The result was an unholy alliance of extreme nationalists under Grivas and left wing parties under George Papandreou, determined to shake the western power in the Levant. Papandreou secured the govt. in 1964. Abp. Makarios of Cyprus had meanwhile secured a constitutional reform which balanced Turkish against Greek interests and consequently led to strained relations with Turkey. At this point K. Paul died (Apr. 1964) and his successor Constantine II, was publicly attacked by Papandreou, who was forced to resign. Civil administration was in confusion and the left wing parties were organising sporadic strikes. In May 1967 a group of colonels staged a *coup d'état*, established a mild dictatorship and drove both Papandreou and the King into exile.

(14) This **Junta** became increasingly oppressive as opposition in various colours developed despite the police. Eventually it took refuge in Bonapartism, namely an attempt to subvert the lawful govt. of Cyprus and achieve Cypro-Greek union **(Enosis)**. The Turks promptly invaded the island to protect the Turkish (20%) minority (1974). They occupied the 40% northern part and set up a republic while some 200,000 Greek Cypriots fled to the south or elsewhere. The Junta, knowing its unreadiness for war, fell apart.

(15) Constantine Karamanlis was recalled from exile and in Aug. 1974 re-established the constitution in a republican form and a new draft was promulgated in June 1975. By 1981 he and his New Democracy Party had run out of steam and in the elections the American educated Andreas Papandreou (s. of George), leading PASOK (The Pan-Hellenic Socialists) secured an absolute majority by uniting the unholy alliance led by his father.

GREEK FIRE. A liquid naphtha compound used in war. Its exact composition, now unknown, was a Byzantine state secret. Believed to be a vital element in Byzantine military and naval power, it played an important part in sieges and sea battles, especially in the 9th cent. Arab wars.

GREEK ORTHODOX CHURCH. *See* EASTERN ORTHODOX CHURCH.

GREEN CLOTH, BOARD OF. *See* STEWARD-4.

GREENLAND. *See* VIKINGS.

"GREENLAND FISHERY". *See* WHALING.

GREEN RIBBON CLUB was a group of M.P.s and London supporters of the E. of Shaftesbury formed at the King's Head tavern in Chancery Lane during the Popish Plot and Exclusion Bill excitements. It used green ribbons in memory of the Levellers, and organised noisy demonstrations such as pope burnings at the Statue of Elisabeth I at St. Dunstan's in the West. It fell apart when Shaftesbury fled (Jan. 1683). *See* CHARLES II-21 TO 27.

GREENSHIELDS CASE (1711) was the first in which the House of Lords entertained a civil appeal from Scotland.

GREENVILLE TREATY (1795) between the U.S.A. and 12 tribes in the N.W. territories, marked off Indian territory from white in such a way as to destroy British influence and encourage white settlement in Ohio and Indiana. The insatiable land-hunger of well armed settlers soon resulted in Indians being forced to part with lands and by 1809 the tribes had been mostly forced out.

GREENWAY, Francis (?-1837), Gloucestershire contractor and architect, was transported to N.S.W. for a forgery. Gov. Macquarie recognised his Regency architectural gifts, respited him from the chain-gang and employed him to lay out Sydney. He was eventually pardoned and became the local official architect but, bankrupt and quarrelsome to the last, he died destitute.

GREENWICH (London). Humphrey D. of Gloucester built the palace of Bella Court at this fishing village in 1428. This passed to Margaret of Anjou, Q. of Henry VI, who renamed it PLACENTIA. It was a favoured royal residence between 1485 and 1560. Inigo Jones built the beautiful Queen's House for James I's Q. Anne of Denmark in 1635 and his son-in-law John Webb enlarged the palace for Q. Henrietta Maria. Under the Commonwealth, however, it was sacked and ruinous and Charles II commissioned a complete rebuilding by John Webb, who died in 1672 with the work only partly finished. He also established the OBSERVATORY in 1676. In 1694 William and Mary gave the palace over for a naval pensioners hospital (cf Chelsea Hospital for Military Pensioners) and Wren designed buildings which were not all erected until 1824. Pensioners came into occupation in 1705 and it was then known as GREENWICH HOSPITAL. It was too the centre of the naval pensions administration (see also CHATHAM CHEST) which ultimately became so corrupt that it had to be dissolved. The last pensioners left in 1869; and in 1873 the Admiralty established the ROYAL NAVAL COLLEGE there. The nautical connection had also led to the foundation (1832) of the entirely different Seamen's Hospital and this eventually developed a famous school of Tropical Medicine. Meanwhile the town grew, took in neighbouring villages and was connected by a pedestrian tunnel and Blackwall tunnel to the opposite shore. In 1891 it was amalgamated with Woolwich as a London borough. The NATIONAL MARITIME MUSEUM, established in 1934, was moved to the Palace and the Observatory moved to Hurstmonceaux in 1948. A derelict site was appropriated in 1995 for the millennial exhibition.

GREENWICH, Ds. of. See CAMPBELL OF LOCHOW (ARGYLL).

GREENWICH, Ts. of (1543). See MARY Q. OF SCOTS-1,2.

GREENWOOD, Arthur (1880-1954) a respected leader of the Labour Party with a mixed record as a Minister. As Min. of Health (1929-31) his Housing Act aimed at slum clearance, did much to change the face of urban life by 1939. He was defeated for his Party leadership in 1935. In 1939 he launched a reasoned attack on govt. slowness in helping Poland and in 1940 entered the War Cabinet to represent Labour. His presence there was not very effectual and he resigned in 1942 and was placed in charge of post-war policy. On Churchill's advice he appointed William Beveridge to compose his famous Report on social welfare. He was in Attlee's cabinet of 1945-51, ending his career as Min. without Portfolio.

GREER, Germaine (1939-) Australian educated writer on the status of women. She leapt into fame on the publication of her 1967 Ph.D thesis, elaborated in 1970 as *The Female Eunuch*. She argued that the structure of the English language is calculated to depress the status of women, *inter alia* because its use of apparently masculine forms to express combined groups tends to eclipse the role of the women in a given group. It is not clear if the argument applies to other languages some of which have a different gender system or none, or how it would apply if renaissance grammarians had given other names to the grammatical genders.

GREGORY I (?540-604) Pope (590) and St. (The Great) had been (Civil) Praefect of Rome, papal ambassador (*Apocrisiarius*) at Constantinople and Abbot of St. Andrews at Rome. Through his width of experience he was uniquely equipped to become the founder of the mediaeval papacy. Government in Italy was collapsing under the pressure of flood, famine, epidemics and barbarian, especially Lombard, depredations. The imperial governor (*Exarch*) at Ravenna seemed powerless. Somebody had to do something and the only available centre of authority was the Pope. Gregory therefore undertook not only the spiritual leadership of the western church, but the political trusteeship of Italy and so unavoidably launched the papal entanglement with territorial politics which continued until 1870. In 14 years he achieved or was responsible for immense events. His political agreement with the Lombards involved the effective repudiation of Byzantine Imperial authority; it led logically to his assertion of the supremacy of the Roman See and to the quarrel with the Constantinople patriarchate which eventually divided Christendom. His inevitable temporal responsibilities required funds, properties and the making of political appointments throughout central Italy and laid the foundations of the Papal States. The Pope's contacts had led him to nourish a scheme for the conversion of England. He was still Abbot of St. Andrews, when he is said by Bede to have encountered English slaves whom he called "non Angli sed angeli" (angeli = messengers). In 596 he despatched the momentous mission to England under St. Augustine. Meanwhile the agreement with the Lombards ripened into their conversion in 603. This many sided man also compiled the *Liber Regulae Pastoralis* (Lat = Book of Pastoral Rule) which, translated by K. Alfred, became the text book of the mediaeval bishops. An enthusiastic promoter of Benedictine monasticism, he originated the system of monastic privileges which eventually brought the Orders directly under papal supervision; and he systematised church music and enjoined, if he did not create, the Gregorian Chant. His strong personality, humility and achievements caused him to be canonised by popular acclamation at his death.

GREGORY II, St. and Pope (r. 715-31) sent an English mission under St. Boniface to convert south Germany.

GREGORY VII (HILDEBRAND) (?1021-85) Pope (1078) and St. first became influential as chaplain to Gregory VI from 1045. From 1047 to 1049 he was at Cluny and then returned to become Administrator of the Patrimony of St. Peter (i.e. civil ruler of the Papal States) under St. Leo IX. From then until his death he was the effective guide of the church. He was largely responsible for the election of Popes Victor II, Stephen IX, Benedict X, Nicholas II and Alexander II and for the appointment of Adalbert of Bremen as Papal Vicar in Northern Europe. He had meanwhile in 1053 established the rule (destined to reduce secular influence) that the Pope should be elected by the Cardinals only and in the dispute with the Emperor over the antipope Honorius II, his diplomacy at the Council of Mantua in 1064 secured the recognition of Alexander II. It was on his advice that Alexander blessed the Norman invasion of England and appointed Lanfranc Abp. of Canterbury in 1070. This in its turn led to the reorganisation of the English church. On election as Pope he set about enforcing the reforming policy foreshadowed under previous reigns. The Church had been corrupted, in his view, by the intrusion of worldliness at too many points. At the lower levels sexual immorality and simony discredited the clergy with their flock and made them too dependent upon the whims of powerful laymen. At the top the episcopacy was entangled with feudalism. Most bishops were also tenants-in-chief. Monarchs reasonably exercised a power if not to appoint them, then at least to control the devolution of their feudal estates, by insisting on lay investitures through homage before consecration. Lay investiture had led to abuses particularly in the appointment of unsuitable or unqualified persons to ecclesiastical offices. Gregory now determined to sweep away the whole complex. In 1074 a decree against simony and clerical immorality was issued: in 1075 lay investiture, already condemned by Nicholas II at Gregory's prompting, was totally forbidden. Special Papal legates enforced the new dispensation; many simoniacal and immoral clerics were deposed, including nearly all the French bishops. In England William I enforced all the decrees with zeal except that on lay investiture, with which, in the special circumstances, Gregory was content. It was in Germany that the opposition was most strenuous. In the spring of 1076 at the synods of Worms and Piacenza, the Emperor Henry IV, declared the Pope to be deposed. Gregory in the autumn deposed and excommunicated Henry and released his subjects from their allegiance. Public opinion favoured reform and superstition reinforced the Papal thunderbolts. Henry's adherents left him and a rival for his throne, Rudolf of Suabia, appeared. In 1077 the Emperor submitted at Canossa and did penance but the political movement had got out of hand. The princes elected Rudolf despite the submission. Henry did not honour his Canossa undertakings. In 1080 Gregory recognised Rudolf and excommunicated Henry again. The cold war became a real one. At the Synod of Brescia Henry set up the excommunicated Abp. of Ravenna as Anti-Pope (Clement III) and marched on Rome which he took after a two year siege. Gregory called in the Sicilian Normans, who rescued him but behaved so badly that the Roman populace drove him out. He fled to Cassino and died at Salerno.

GREGORY IX Pope (r. 1227-41) was a nephew of Innocent III and a friend of St. Francis of Assisi. He spent the whole of his reign in political collision with the Emperor Frederick II, whose troops were besieging Rome when he died.

GREGORY X Pope (r. 1271-6) recognised Rudolf of Habsburg as Emperor and persuaded Alfonso of Castile to relinquish his imperial claims. He also introduced the secret conclave for papal elections.

GREGORY XI Pope (r. 1370-8). See AVIGNON POPES.

GREGORY XVI Pope (r. 1831-46) was elected after a conclave of seven weeks. A revolution was quelled only by foreign powers, mainly Austria and France, who demanded reforms. These were not properly carried out; the Austrians returned in 1832, whereupon the French occupied Ancona until 1838. He died leaving papal finances in disorder and a population seething with discontent, which broke into the open two years later.

GREGORY OF TOURS, St. (538-95). Bp. of Tours from 573, a prominent Frankish churchman and politician, wrote often from personal knowledge his important *Gesta Francorum* (Lat = History of the Franks) as well as religious works.

GREGORY OF UTRECHT, St. See MISSIONS TO EUROPE.

GREIG (1) Sir Samuel (1735-88) a British naval officer, entered Russian service in 1764, commanded a division under Orloff at Chesmé in 1770; he then became Grand Admiral and Gov. of Kronstadt and as such created the Russian fleet, which he commanded in the victory over the Swedes at Hogland in 1788. His son **(2) Alexei Samuilovich (1775-1845)** gained distinction as a Russian naval commander against the Turks in 1807 and 1828. He created the Russian Black Sea Fleet.

GRENADA (W.I.) was reached by Columbus in 1498. It was first colonised by London financed Europeans in 1609, but the local Caribs drove them out. The island was included in the E. of Carlisle's grant of 1627 but, owing to the previous experience, no commercial finance could be raised. In 1635 the French Crown granted it to the *Compagnie des Iles d'Amerique,* which sold its rights to the Seigneur du Parquet in 1650. He exterminated the Caribs. After two further sales the French Crown annexed the isle in 1674. The British captured it in 1762. It was ceded to them in the P. of Paris (1763) and became the seat of govt. of the British Windward Is. For practical reasons Lieut-Gov. Fitzmaurice allowed local French R. Catholics to sit on the representative council. In 1768 this caused press controversy and a Bd. of Trade report on the constitutional implications of allowing R. Catholics into office contrary to the Test Act and Coronation Oath. This episode foreshadowed a similar controversy related to Quebec. The French briefly reoccupied the island in 1780 but the Royal Navy recovered it. In 1795 there was a general uprising inspired by the French Revolution and led by Julien Fedor. Sir Ralph Abercromby put it down in 1796. Grenada became a Crown Colony in 1876 under the Windward Is., from which it separated in 1959 on joining the short-lived W. Indies Federation. It became a state in Association with Britain in 1967. In 1979 a Marxist People's Revolutionary Govt. seized power with Maurice Bishop as Prime Minister and began, with Cuban and Russian finance, to build a huge airfield. As no installation of that size could confer a purely commercial benefit on the island, it was deemed a military threat to the U.S.A. In Oct. 1983 Bishop was ousted by Gen. Hudson Austin and murdered. A fortnight later the U.S.A. landed an expedition in the island notwithstanding its membership of the Commonwealth and, without consulting the British govt., Gen. Austin and other members of his party were arrested and Cubans sent home. It is said that Q. Elizabeth II kept her prime minister standing throughout the subsequent audience. Elections were held in 1984 and the U.S. troops withdrawn immediately afterwards.

GRENADIERS. Originally two or three tall men armed with grenades were attached to each company. By the mid-18th cent. they were collected into a separate company for each unit because of the prevalence of siege-warfare, in which they were particularly useful. The *Grenadier Guards,* the 1st Foot Guards, are so-called because they defeated the French Grenadier Guards at Waterloo.

GRENTEBRYCGE. See CAMBRIDGE.

GRENVILLE (1) Richard Temple (1711-79) E. TEMPLE (1772) was an M.P. from 1734 to 1741 and from 1747 to 1752; he became First Lord of the Admiralty in 1756, at the opening of the Seven Years' War, but George II, who disliked him, was persuaded to remove him and he held the harmless Privy Seal from 1757 to 1764. He had early noticed Pitt's abilities and, being rich, financed him, but he offended both George II and III by patronising Wilkes and paying his legal costs. Like his brother George he was against conciliating the Americans, not only on legalistic grounds and so drifted away from Pitt, with whom he quarrelled in 1766. He three times refused the Treasury. His brother **(2) George (1712-70)**, M.P. from 1740, was one of the 'Boy Patriots' who thought like Pitt and was Treasurer of the Navy under the Pelhams. He resigned when they dismissed Pitt and Temple (1756) and resumed the office in the Pitt-Newcastle govt. of 1757. He joined the Cabinet in 1761. In 1762 he became Bute's S. of State for the northern dept. and First Lord of the Admiralty and from 1763 to 1765 Prime Minister (*see also* WILKES, JOHN; AMERICAN REBELLION-9) against George III's inclinations, for he insisted on ousting Bute from the King's confidence. His strong following made him dangerous in opposition. He defeated the budget of 1767 and, in the further Wilkes controversies, denied the constitutional propriety of expelling Wilkes and secured the transfer of the trial of election petitions from the whole house to a select committee. Of his sons **(3) George Nugent-Temple (1753-1813) 2nd E. TEMPLE, 1st M. of BUCKINGHAM (1784)** was an M.P. from 1774 to 1779. As a sympathetic Lord Lieut. of Ireland from 1782 to 1783 in the first years of Grattan's parliament, he procured the Irish Judicature Act, 1783, and the institution of the Order of St. Patrick, but on his return he helped to defeat Fox's India Bill in the Lords. He returned to Ireland as Lord Lieut. in 1787 and by 1789 was at loggerheads with the parliament. It was trying to make political capital out of the opposition between George III and the P. of Wales and he properly refused to transmit their addresses to the Prince. He retired sadder and wiser. His son **(4) Richard (1776-1839) 1st D. of BUCKINGHAM and CHANDOS (1822)** M.P. (known as **E. Temple)** from 1797 to 1813 held minor offices and made money. His son **(5) Richard Plantagenet (1797-1861) 2nd D.,** known as M. Chandos, was an M.P. from 1822 to 1839 and moved the so-called Chandos clause to the second Reform Bill. He was Lord Privy Seal in 1841 to 1842 and a strong protectionist. He had to sell much of the family property which was encumbered through incautious investment. His son **(6) Richard Plantagenet Campbell (1823-89) 3rd D.** was an M.P. (as M. Chandos) from 1846 to 1857, chairman of the L.N.W. Rly from 1853 to 1861, Ld. President from 1866 to 1867, colonial sec. from 1867 to 1868 and gov. of Madras from 1875 to 1880. He was Ld. Chairman of Committees from 1886 to 1889. A brother of **(3) William Wyndham (1759-1834) 1st Ld. GRENVILLE (1790)** was an M.P. from 1782, became Chief Sec. for Ireland in 1782, Paymaster-Gen. in 1784 and was Vice-Pres. of the Bd. of Trade from 1786 to 1789 when he was briefly Speaker. He then became Home Sec., then Pres. of the Bd. of Control from 1790 to 1793 but was also Foreign Sec. from 1791 to 1801. He was Pitt's main spokesman in the Lords, resigned with him in 1801, but refused office under him in 1804 because Fox was not included. He was the effective head of the ministry of All the Talents and in 1807 again resigned over the R. Catholic issue and deliberately stayed out of office as a sort of conservative guerrilla.

GRENVILLE'S ACT, 1770. *See* ELECTION PETITIONS.

GRE[Y]NVILLE, GRENFELL or GRANVILLE, large and influential family of West Country origin, which produced seamen, soldiers and politicians.

A. (1) Sir Richard (?1541-91) Devon landowner and cousin of Sir Walter Raleigh, was M.P. for Cornwall (1563), fought in Hungary against the Turks in 1567 and was M.P. again in 1571 and Sheriff in 1576. In 1585 he commanded a fleet for Raleigh's colonisation of Virginia and on a second voyage in 1586 took rich prizes and pillaged the Azores. He was by now very rich and able to find three ships for the Armada campaign, after which he commanded a squadron in Irish waters. In 1591 he was 2-in-C of a force sent under Ld. Thomas Howard to the Azores to intercept the *Flota* on its homeward voyage. The ship's companies lost heavily by sickness and a strong Spanish fleet had been sent to meet the *Flota* at the Azores. When this hove in sight, many of the seamen were recovering ashore. The squadron embarked its men but Grenville's ship, the *Revenge,* was behindhand. The others escaped. The *Revenge* was cut off and, after fighting the entire Spanish squadron single-handed for 15 hours, surrendered. Sir Richard was mortally wounded. His grandson **(2) Sir Richard (1600-58) Bart (1630)** left accounts of the Cadiz and Ile de Ré expeditions, in which he served, fought as a royalist in Ireland from 1641 to 1643 but was arrested by the parliamentarians at Liverpool. Offered a command by them, he accepted but joined the King at Oxford in 1644 and campaigned in Cornwall, where he quarrelled with the other royalist commanders. He was imprisoned in 1646 and then went abroad where, through Edward Hyde's hostility, he was not employed in the royalist cause. He died abroad.

B. (1) Sir Bevil (1596-1643), M.P. for Cornwall from 1621 to 1624, for Launceston from 1625 to 1640 and for

Cornwall again from 1640 to 1642 was a royalist who served against the Scots in 1639, defeated the parliamentarians at Bradock Down in 1643 and was killed at Lansdowne. Of his sons **(2) John (1628-1701) E. of BATH (1661),** another royalist, was wounded at Newbury in 1644 and held the Scilly Is. for Charles II from 1649 to 1651. Charles II made him Warden of the Stannaries and Groom of the Stole at the Restoration and gov. of Plymouth in 1661. He was belatedly instrumental in bringing Cornwall and Devon over to William III and became Lord. Lieut. of both counties in 1689. His brother **(3) Denis (1637-1703)** a Jacobite, dean of Durham from 1684, raised money in connection with the Fenwick conspiracy of 1691 and fled to St. Germain. James II nominated him Abp. of York in exile. His nephew **(4) Sir Bevil (?-1706),** a favourite of William III, was gov. of Barbados from 1702 to 1706. He was recalled after accusations of tyranny and extortion, which were rejected, but died on his way home. His brother **(5) George (1667-1735) 1st Ld. LANSDOWNE (1711)** was a Tory M.P. for Fowey in 1702 and for Cornwall in 1710, when he became Sec-at-War and therefore partly responsible for the abandonment of the French war. He was one of the twelve new peers created to force through the peace and in 1712 he became a P.C. and in 1713 Treasurer of the Household. As a leader of the party hostile to the Hanoverian succession, he was put in precautionary custody during the 1715 Jacobite rebellion, but released in 1717. He was also a minor poet and dramatist.

GRESHAM (1) Sir Richard (?1485-1549) mercer, and royal gentleman usher by 1516, was a confidant of Wolsey and Thomas Cromwell and a financier. He supported the benevolence of 1525 when he was Warden of the Mercers Co. and was a compiler of the *Valor Ecclesiasticus* which preceded the dissolution of the monasteries. As Lord Mayor he secured Barts, St. Mary's and St. Thomas' Hospitals for the city, while himself speculating on a huge scale in monastic lands. By 1540 he owned, *inter alia,* Fountains Abbey. He also initiated the planning of the Royal Exchange to compete with Amsterdam. His brother and partner **(2) Sir John (?-1556)** was a founder of the Russia Co. (1555) and in 1547 Lord Mayor. He founded Gresham's School, Holt (Norfolk). The son of **(1), (3)** the famous **Sir Thomas (?1519-79)** was apprenticed to Sir John and assistant to his father, on whose death he set up as a banker. In 1552 he became King's agent and merchant at Antwerp. He received land under Edward VI but, although a protestant and friend of Foxe the protestant martyrologist, his political and business success enabled him to survive under Q. Mary I. He also struck up a friendship with Cecil, for whom as ambassador in Brussels from 1559 to 1561, he set up a very successful intelligence service in the Spanish Netherlands. He also suffered a riding fall which lamed him for life. Henry VIII's expensive wars had eroded the financial gains made by the Crown in the break with Rome. Inflation and coinage debasements were major elements in the mid-Tudor recession. Gresham, acting on his famous dictum that "bad money drives out good", achieved a measure of control by restoring the coinage. In 1565 he set up the first English paper mills. Foreseeing the Hispano-Dutch crisis he abandoned his Antwerp business in 1567, and by 1569 had set up means for pledging English govt. credit with English bankers, notably himself. Of this the completion of his father's scheme for the Royal Exchange in 1569 was an important feature and it was at this time that he was a negotiator in the dispute over the seizure of the Spanish treasure. Increasingly infirm through his lameness, he retired in 1574 and founded Gresham College in 1575.

GRETNA GREEN (Sc.). *See* MARRIAGE.

GREVILLE (1) Sir Fulke (1554-1628) 1st Ld. BROOKE (1621) came to court with Sir Philip Sydney and was an uncontroversial favourite of Elizabeth I. From 1583 he held lucrative offices, was M.P. for Warwickshire from 1593 to 1620 and acquired Warwick Castle and Knowle. He was Chancellor and U/Treasurer of the Exch. from 1614. He adopted his cousin **(2) Robert (1608-43)** 2nd Ld.; he was speaker of the Commons in 1642, became a parliamentary general and was killed at Lichfield. Distant descendants included three brothers **(3) Algernon Frederick (1789-1864)** A.D.C. and private sec. to Wellington 1827-42; **(4) Charles Cavendish Fulke (1794-1865)** friend of the D. of York, Wellington and Palmerston and clerk of the Privy Council from 1821 to 1859. He left important, mostly political, diaries for the period 1817 to 1860. **(5) Henry William (1801-72)** also left mainly social diaries.

GREY (1) Charles (1729-1807) 1st Ld. GREY (1801) Vist. HOWICK and 1st E. GREY (1806), a successful soldier under Wolfe, Pr. Ferdinand at Minden (1759), in the Caribbean and against the American rebels, was made a Privy Councillor in 1795. His son **(2) Charles (1764-1845) 2nd E.,** a reforming Foxite Whig, was M.P. for Northumberland from 1786 to 1807 and (as **Vist. Howick)** for Appleby in 1807. He was a manager of the Warren Hastings impeachment. On behalf of the Society of Friends of the People, he attacked the French war and the concomitant Six Acts, seceded from the Commons in 1797, but returned in 1800 to oppose Irish union. He refused office under Addington but, favouring a resumption of the war, became First Lord of the Admiralty in 1806 and then Foreign Sec. but resigned in 1807 against the King's view of R. Catholic emancipation. In 1811 he and Grenville were together advising the Pr. Regent, but they disagreed, for Grenville favoured repressive legislation and opposed the independence of new (mostly S. American) nationalities. On the other hand Grey could not stand Canning with whom he might have agreed. Despite his tortuous political course, he approached office in 1830 because Tory internal policy was discredited and he was the only prominent surviving Whig. Hence he was able to take up his old reformist interests and became Prime Minister (see GREY GOVT.). He retired in 1834. His second son **(3) Charles (1804-70)** was private sec. to his father as prime minister; to the Pr. Consort from 1849 to 1861 and thereafter to the widowed Queen.

GREY. This great and widespread English house originated with **(1) Henry de GREY** of Grays Thurrock and an unknown relative. Henry married Iseude de Bardolf, the unknown relative a certain **Hawise.** Of the children of Henry and Iseude **(2) John (?-1266)** and his wife EMMA de Canz, were the parents of **(3) Reynald (?-1308) 1st Ld. GREY of WITTON (1290),** whose title and extensive marcher estates passed in the male line through ten generations to **(4) Thomas (?-1614)** who was attainted. Henry and Iseude's second child **(5) Richard** married Lucy de Humez; their son John was the father of **(6) Henry (?-1308) 1st Ld. GREY of CODNOR,** whose title and marcher estates passed through five generations to **(7) Henry (?-1496)** when, in default of legitimate children, the barony went into abeyance and the estates were dispersed. A grandson of **(3), (8) Roger (?-1352) Ld. GREY of RUTHIN (1325)** married Elizabeth of Hastings. He, besides marcher lands, had extensive properties in Essex and the Home Counties and the marriage brought to their grandson **(9) Reynold (?-1440),** as heir of the Hastings Es. of Pembroke, their properties in W. Wales and Munster in addition. His grandson **(10) Edmund (c. 1420-89) 4th Ld. GREY of RUTHIN (1440) E. of KENT (1466),** served in Aquitaine and was knighted in 1440. In the Yorkist-Lancastrian struggle he initially supported Henry VI and so continued, though occasionally under suspicion, until the

B. of Northampton in 1460 when he made his dramatic change of allegiance. As Lancastrian vanguard commander his 'timely treachery' ended the battle in half an hour with the King as prisoner. His reward was somewhat delayed but he received the great manor of Ampthill and was Treasurer of England from 1463 to 1464 before receiving his earldom. The bulk of the Grey and Hastings properties and titles passed thereafter through four generations to **(11) Charles (?-1623)** and thence through a series of female successions to the Longeville, Yelverton, Gould and Rawdon families. Meanwhile Hawise (see **1** above) had **(12) Walden de GREY,** Abp. of York, who acquired ROTHERFIELD and gave it to his brother **(13) Robert.** He was the ancestor of **(14) John (?-1359) Ld. GREY of ROTHERFIELD** from whom after three generations the title and properties passed to the Lovel family.

GREY or GRAY, Ld. Leonard (?-1541) Vist. CRANE (1535). His sister Elizabeth had married the 9th E. of Kildare, her husband's son being in rebellion when Grey arrived in Ireland. Grey naturally maintained Geraldine (Kildare) connections all his life and in 1535 had offered the 10th Earl (the same son) a safe conduct to London to end his rebellion. Henry VIII broke it and silenced Grey's complaints with lands and a viscountcy. Becoming Lord Deputy, he had both to deal with the 14th E. of Desmond's rebellion and preside over the Irish Reformation parliament in 1536. Meanwhile Irish councillors complained of his rapacity and attempts to restore the Geraldine interests, but he survived a royal commission of investigation, after which he made a precarious alliance with Desmond and the Kerry O'Briens. In 1540 he sought leave of absence to many, just as Kildare attacked the Pale. Anxious to depart, he concealed the disorders but news of them reached London ahead of him. He was arrested on suspicion of collusion with the Geraldines and was executed for treason.

GREY, Edward (1862-1933) K.G. (1912) 1st Vist. GREY of FALLODON (1916) became a Liberal M.P. in 1885, was Foreign U/Sec. of State under Rosebery from 1892 to 1895 and became Foreign Sec. in 1905. During his eleven years' tenure he was single-mindedly determined to maintain British and other powers' interests by preventing or settling conflicts. He was remarkably successful, as in the Algeçiras Conference (Jan-Apr. 1906); the agreements, with Italy on Abyssinia (Dec. 1906); with Spain on the Mediterranean (May 1907); with Russia on Persia, Afghanistan and Tibet (Aug. 1907); the renewal of the Anglo-Japanese alliance (July 1911); the exchange of letters with Cambon clarifying the scope of the *Entente* (Nov. 1912) and the T. of London (1913) which ended the Balkan Wars. It was his misfortune that the outbreak of World War I, engineered or allowed by men less cool or well intentioned than himself, swept these successes mostly away. They caused him a personal grief which was exhibited in a famous speech ("the lights are going out all over Europe"). Thereafter he devoted his considerable but calm energies to the diplomatic furtherance of the war, of which the conversion of Italy from a potential enemy to an active ally was the main achievement. He resigned with the change of govt. in 1916. In 1918, when it became likely that the thrust of Pres. Wilson's policy could not be pressed to its conclusion for lack of Senatorial support, he went to Washington as ambassador and argued by every available public means for support of an effective League of Nations. He failed, however, to win over the fundamentally Anglophobe and increasingly isolationist elements and the League, hamstrung without American support, was born, despite his efforts, in weakness and confusion. He returned in 1920 and led the Liberals in the Lords until 1924. He was an urbane and much liked Chancellor of Oxford University from 1928.

GREY FRIARS. *See* FRANCISCANS.

GREY. A semi-royal family **(1) Henry (?-1554) 3rd M. of DORSET (1530), 1st D. of SUFFOLK (1551)** was a vacillating and unreliable politician under Edward VI. He had three unfortunate daughters (qqv below). He refused to support Lady Jane, and was taken into favour by Mary I. In 1554 he joined the protests against Mary's proposed marriage to Philip of Spain and was executed. His daughter **(2) GREY, Lady Jane (1537-54)**. was bullied in 1553 by the D. of Northumberland into marrying his son, Ld. Guilford Dudley, and at Edward's death (10 July 1553) she was proclaimed queen. Public opinion rallied to Mary I, who was also proclaimed. Jane was seized (19 July). Mary intended to spare her, but when Northumberland supported Wyatt's rebellion, Jane and Ld. Guilford were executed (Feb. 1554). She was an accomplished scholar and a convinced protestant. **(3) Catherine (?1538-68)** married Henry Herbert, later 2nd E. of Pembroke but the marriage was annulled in 1554 after her sister's execution. In 1560 she secretly married Edward 2nd E. of HERTFORD (1539-1621) but when the marriage became public they were both imprisoned under an Act of 1539 forbidding marriage by persons of royal blood without Crown consent. She died, still a prisoner at Cockfield Hall. He was released in 1571. Her sister **(4) Mary (1540-78)** secretly married Thomas Keys, the Queen's serjeant porter in 1565. She too was detained, until 1573.

GREY, William (?-1478) Bp. of ELY (1454) was the King's representative in Rome from 1445 to 1454. As an experienced negotiator he acted as mediator in the English political crises of 1455 and 1460. He was also Lord Treasurer in 1469 and 1470 and then led the mission to settle peace terms with the Scots in 1471-2. He left 181 manuscripts and a printed book to Balliol College, Oxford, and was the patron of the humanist John Free whom he sent to Italy.

GREY GOVT. (Nov. 1830-July 1834). (13 in Cabinet under Earl Grey). **(1)** Nine members of this whig govt. were in the Lords. Palmerston, an Irish peer, but a highly confident Englishman, was Foreign Sec. Its main domestic activity was the passage of the Reform Acts 1832 and, after fighting the 1833 general election for the new reformed parliament, the investigation of the municipal corporations (1833) and the settlement of Irish grievances. **(2)** The introspective intensity of these preoccupations left Palmerston with virtual control of foreign policy at a time of European crisis. Charles X of France had been overthrown in July 1830. In Aug. the Belgians had risen against the Dutch. If there were a violent Dutch reaction, the Belgians would call in the French, the northern powers would support the Dutch and the result might be war. The dangerous negotiations began with a five power conference in London (Nov. 1830) and overhung the entire Reform Bill crisis; the Dutch, Belgians and French (through an intelligent understanding with Talleyrand) only accepted the practical settlement in Dec. 1832 (*see* BELGIUM).

(3) In 1832, too, there began a constitutional civil war in Portugal and Brazil, followed in Sept. 1833 by another in Spain. These would be important only if the French intervened. Palmerston's tactics both in Belgium and in the Peninsula were to secure French co-operation by alliances of local and western constitutionalists (including France) in order to keep the local and eastern authoritarians (including Prussia and Austria) away from the scene of action. Such a course had the merit of preventing the French acting separately. Palmerston carried his plans through the cabinet by surprise and by Aug. 1834 they had succeeded brilliantly (*see* BRAZIL-5,6; CARLISM-2; PORTUGAL-12).

(4) It was, however, the Irish problem which destroyed the govt. Daniel O'Connell, the Irish leader, tactically brilliant and inspiring, was not quite the master of his followers. He had secured civil equality for R. Catholics and supported reform. Most Irishmen blamed Irish economic backwardness (not wholly accurately) on the English and Scots connection. The 85% R. Catholic majority objected to paying tithes to the established church. O'Connell might be faced with defeat and loss of influence over tithes, which were an immediate issue, or insurrection against Britain and military defeat. In 1832 the govt. changed the method of tithe collection so that, without altering the total sums due or their incidence, far fewer were concerned in paying. This increase in efficiency was exactly the opposite of what the Irish wanted. The worse the system the better for them, but the fewer involved the more easily they could be victims of terrorism, now widespread. After the 1833 election the govt. decided upon simultaneous coercion and Irish church reform. For a year martial law and curfews were to be imposed in disturbed areas and rights of public meeting and *habeas corpus* were to be suspended. The bill passed the Lords and, after furious argument, the Commons. Meanwhile the Irish church was to be reorganised and the resultant savings appropriated to purposes which would not necessarily be defrayed by tithes. This Bill passed the Commons easily but the Lords only with difficulty and only after the govt. had given up lay appropriation of surplus church revenue. This alienated O'Connell and did little to reduce terrorism or discontent with tithes. It was now decided to convert the tithe into a land tax payable to the Crown but Ld. John Russell told the Commons that the proceeds might be diverted to other than church purposes and found himself at odds with four of his colleagues, Stanley, Graham, the D. of Richmond and the E. of Ripon, who all resigned (May-June 1834). The govt. could only appoint yet another commission of enquiry, which O'Connell called a wet blanket. Then the Coercion Act expired and in the renewal proceedings Littleton (Chief Sec. for Ireland) got O'Connell's support by telling him privately (as he believed) that the Cabinet would drop the clause against public meetings. The Cabinet did no such thing. O'Connell published the conversation and the govt. broke up.

GRIFFITH, Arthur (1872-1922) as editor of the *United Irishman* from 1899 to 1906 argued on the basis of much imaginary history and economics that Irish Home Rule could not be achieved by parliamentary action and in 1905, at a meeting of the self styled Irish National Council, advocated passive resistance. Sinn Fein adopted this but moved towards physical force. So did he and in 1910 he was Pres. of Sinn Fein and in 1913 a supporter of the Irish Volunteers. He tried to prevent Irish enlistments in World War I and his periodicals were suppressed. He took, however, no part in the Easter Rebellion (1916) but became increasingly active in Sinn Fein after it. As a result he was imprisoned several times between 1916 and 1921. For practical reasons he therefore resigned the presidency of Sinn Fein to de Valera in 1917. In 1918 he became an M.P. and was the first Irish (illegal) Min. for Home Affairs in 1919. He and Michael Collins negotiated the Irish treaty of 1921 and he was Pres. of the Dail Eireann in 1922. A selfless and cunning politician, he has claims to be regarded as the founder of the Irish Republic.

GRIMBALD, St. (?825-901) French scholar monk, was invited to Winchester by K. Alfred in 887 and helped him with his Latin translations, especially of the *Cura Pastoralis* of St. Gregory. In 889 he became dean of the Augustinian New Minster at Winchester, having refused the Archbishopric of Canterbury.

GRIMOND, Joseph (1913-93) Ld. GRIMOND of FIRTH (1983), barrister and politician, first elected liberal M.P. for Orkney and Shetland in 1950s was leader of his party from 1956 to 1967 and in 1976. He was personally popular with the general public so that the Liberals derived some reflected advantage during a long period of electoral difficulty.

GRIMSBY (Lincs.) was a settlement in Roman times. Legend and the placename indicate a Danish occupation. The 13th cent. poem *Havelock the Dane* recounts how Grim, ordered to kill his foster son Havelock, the heir to the Danish throne, flees with him instead to Grimsby and is suitably rewarded when the boy inherits the Kingdom and England as well. According to Domesday it was divided between Odo of Bayeux, Drew of Beruere and Ralph of Mortemer. It soon became the principal port of the Humber and received its first charter from K. John for 55 gold marks. A charter of 1319 set up two fairs but silting in the harbour caused a long decline, arrested in 1800 by the construction, by the Grimsby Haven Co. of the first modern dock. The Co. was amalgamated with the Manchester, Sheffield and Lincs. Rly Co. whose line reached Grimsby in 1848 and the Royal Dock was built between 1849 and 1852. This enabled a fishing industry with access to a substantial inland market to arise. Sixty trawlers despatched 97,000 cwt. of fish in 1860. Dock improvements were made in 1878 and by 1880 the figure had risen roughly tenfold. By 1909 there were 608 trawlers despatching 3,500,000 cwt. This immense expansion, which made Grimsby the biggest fishing port in the world, brought other at first ancillary industries such as ship building, ropes, paint, ice and cold storage, fish preserving, box making, cooperage and biscuit making and then other industries for the expanded population which included wood processing, bricks and tiles, castings and preserves. By 1912 it was necessary to extend the commercial docks to Immingham and a further fish dock was completed in 1934. There were set-backs in both World Wars because the North Sea became a major theatre of operations, and then northward movement of the herring shoals necessitated larger trawlers, an adaptation to cod fishing and in the 1970s a conflict with Iceland. By 1980 the industry was declining quickly.

GRIMSTON, Sir Harbottle (1603-85) M.P. for Harwich (1628) and for Colchester in the Long Parliament (1640 onwards). He led in the Isle of Wight negotiations with Charles I (1647), was excluded from the Commons in Pride's Purge and prevented from resuming his seat in 1656 but became a member of the Council of State when Richard Cromwell abdicated. He was Speaker of the Commons in the Convention Parliament (1660), a member of the commission which tried the regicides (1660) and thereafter Master of the Rolls.

It is uncertain how his mother addressed him.

GRINDAL, Abp. Edmund (?1519-83) a chaplain to Edward VI, went into exile under Mary I and at Frankfort tried to reconcile the extreme Calvinists with the supporters of the Book of Common Prayer. Bp. of London in 1559, Abp. of York in 1570, in 1575 he became Abp. of Canterbury. A moderate Calvinist, in 1577 he rejected Elizabeth's order to suppress Puritan extremist preaching and was suspended from his jurisdictional functions until 1582.

GRIPING IN THE GUTS. *See* INFANTILE DIARRHOEA.

GRIQUA-S,-LANDS. The Griquas had settled in Griqualand West where, after the discovery of diamonds in 1870, they were harried by the Orange Free State Boers. The British proclaimed a crown colony in 1871 and compensated the O.F.S. and in 1880 it was incorporated in the Cape Colony. Meantime Adam Kok, the tribal chief, led a Griqua 'Great Trek' over the Drakensbergs to Griqualand East and in 1875 came under British administration as a separate part of Cape Colony.

GRITHBRYCE (A.S.), was breach of the King's Peace or Protection, punishable with a fine.

GROANS OF THE BRITONS. See BRITAIN, ROMAN-28.

GROAT. *See* COINAGE-10.

GROCYN, William (?1450-1519) after various church and learned preferments, went in 1488 with Linacre to Italy.

They studied under Politian and Chalcondyles and became acquainted with Aldus Manutius the Venetian printer. He lectured in Greek and, with his friend More, was one of the earliest English renaissance intellectuals.

GROOM OF THE STOLE. MISTRESS OF THE ROBES. The Groom was a man of high rank, in theory the King's personal attendant, whose duties became formal and confined to state occasions under the early Hanoverians, save when the office was briefly held by the E. of Bute, appointed in 1760, who used the position as George III's favourite to direct affairs as virtual prime minister. The office is now in abeyance. For a queen the equivalent office is that of Mistress of the Robes which, however, was of such political significance under Q. Anne that it was considered necessary to change it with the govt. under Victoria; and though this has ceased to be the case, the office under a Queen regnant is important and more than formal.

GROSE, Francis (1754-1814). *See* AUSTRALIA-3.

GROSSE ISLE (Quebec). Notorious quarantine station for Irish fleeing across the Atlantic to escape the famine. Some 5000 died there.

GROSS AND FERNISON was the right to hunt deer. Gross was the summer hunting of males; fernison the winter hunting of females.

GROSSETESTE ("Big Head"), Robert (?-1253), Bp. of LINCOLN (1235), Franciscan of humble Suffolk origin, was a learned and powerful preacher, Oxford lecturer and administrator. At Lincoln he was a vigorous disciplinarian and reformer. In his first year he travelled the whole of this large diocese, composing an Oxford Town and Gown dispute and witnessing a confirmation of Magna Carta. During a monastic visitation in 1237 he removed eleven heads of houses. In 1239 he began a long and hilarious dispute about his visitatorial rights over his own chapter, which was settled in his favour only in 1245 by Innocent IV. He also had other ecclesiastical disputes on his hands and others with the King concerned with the abuse of church preferments to reward politicians or unworthy churchmen. He wrote many works on theology and philosophy and a treatise on *Light* and these were quoted for centuries. He knew Hebrew and Greek and during his episcopate made many translations and, like St. Dunstan, was an accomplished harpist. He was admired for his courage, his stern reasonableness and his efforts to make the barons and Henry III behave as statesmen. He publicly stood up to unjust judges and unreasonable monarchs including the formidable Innocent IV in a public confrontation at Lyons. He believed that the cure of souls was the supreme duty of every priest and had many friends both humble and distinguished, including Adam Marsh and Brother John of St. Giles.

GROSS NATIONAL PRODUCT is the money value of all goods and services produced in a year, or the national income added to depreciation. It is unlikely to be accurately ascertainable because of unadmitted but increasingly lucrative criminal activities such as the drug trade, overlapping, duplication and the movements in value of the money in which it is calculated, and in unrecorded transactions. A growth rate calculated upon it is likely to be equally unreliable.

GROSVENOR. Originally a Cheshire family which from about 1800 became the richest landowners in Britain. **(1) Sir Robert (?-1396)** the defendant in the heraldic case of *Scrope v Grosvenor* was sheriff of Cheshire in 1394 and the family was active as mayors of Chester, and M.P.s or sheriffs until **(2) Sir Thomas (1656-1700)** who was also many years M.P. for Chester, but married Mary Davies *d.* of a rich London scrivener and through her obtained most of the great Westminster estate. His son **(3) Richard (1731-1802) 1st Ld. (1761) and E. GROSVENOR (1784)** was also mayor in 1759 and M.P. from 1754. He combined successful horsebreeding with the patronage of the poor and talented William Gifford, (1756-1826) critic, editor of *Juvenal* and first editor of the *Quarterly Review*. His son **(4) Robert (1767-1845) 2nd E., 1st M. of WESTMINSTER (1831)** was an M.P. (under the name of Vist. BELGRAVE) from 1788, a lord of the Admiralty from 1789 to 1791 and a member of the Bd. of Control from 1793 to 1801. Through his marriage he added the bulk of the Egerton estates to the family inheritance. He laid out Belgravia (London) (q.v.) and rebuilt Eaton Hall (Ches.). Of his sons **(5) Richard (1795-1869) 2nd M.** M.P. for Cheshire constituencies intermittently from 1818 to 1835 was Lord Steward under Russell in 1850 to 1852. He began to lay out Belgrave Square (q.v.). His brother **(6) Ld. Robert (1801-93) 1st Ld. EBURY (1857)** was a whig M.P. from 1822 to 1857 and treasurer of the Household in 1846. He opposed Home Rule and favoured liturgical reform. The son of **(4)**, **(7) Hugh Lupus (1825-99) 3rd M., and 1st D. of WESTMINSTER (1874)**, a liberal M.P. from 1847, was Master of the Horse from 1880 to 1885 and another successful horse breeder and estate manager who built the greater part of Pimlico (London). His brother **(8) Richard de Aquila (1837-1912) 1st Ld. STALBRIDGE (1886)** was a liberal M.P. from 1861 and director (1870) and chairman from 1891 of the London and North Western Rly Co.

GROTE (1) George (1794-1871) a strong liberal, took part in the reform agitation, was M.P. for the City of London from 1832 to 1841 and a strong supporter of the ballot. In 1845 he retired to devote himself to history and the furtherance of a London University. He became President of University College in 1868. His wife **(2) Harriet (1792-1878)** was a friend of Mendelssohn and Jenny Lind.

GROTESQUE, a decorative painting style using portions of human, animal and plant forms fantastically interwoven, originally found in ancient buildings whose rooms were known in Rome as grottos.

GROTIUS, Hugh (1583-1645). See MARE CLAUSUM.

GROTTO or GROTTER DAY (c. 25 July) was an observance in Chelsea, Mitcham and on the Old Kent Road (the pilgrim road to Canterbury) which was related to the pilgrimages to St. James of Compostela. Internally lit grottos of shells and flowers on the roadside symbolised the saint's subterranean birthplace and passers-by were urged to contribute. The custom survived until World War II. See GALICIA.

GROUNDNUTS SCHEME (1947). A venture by the post-World War II Labour govt. to make a quick profit by obtaining vegetable oils from peanuts planted in hitherto unprofitable African land. Essentially speculative, it failed through mismanagement after £20M had been spent. The failure was greeted with joy by the Tory press.

GROYNE, THE. Tudor seaman's name for Corunna.

GRUB, St., otherwise Milton St., Cripplegate (London) was the venue of the archery trade but by 1598 mostly given up to bowling alleys and gaming houses. By 1730, when the *Grub Street Journal* was founded, it was associated with hack writing perhaps because its practitioners assembled at such places of amusement. Dr. Johnson used the term which became general for activities in journalistic areas such as Fleet St. and St. Paul's parish. The word 'grub' came to mean a hired or hireling writer and so the literary low life.

GRUFFUDD ap CYNAN. See GWYNEDD-23.

GRUFFUDD ap LLYWELLYN. See DEHEUBARTH-7; GWYNEDD-20.

GRUFFUDD ap MAREDUDD. See DEHEUBARTH-10.

GRUFFUDD ap RHYDDERCH. See DEHEUBARTH-8.

GRUFFUDD ap RHYS (?-1201) of Deheubarth, grandson of the Ld. Rhys, to whose lands in Dinefwr and Ystrad Tywi he succeeded in 1197. He married Matilda de Braose; he and his family were involved in the long destructive feud with his brother Maelgwn and his family,

which led to the ultimate fragmentation of the Lord Rhys' territories between 1207 and 1216.

GRUFFYDD LLWYD (ap RHYS ap GRUFFYDD) (?-1335) a powerful Welsh nobleman with lands mainly in Anglesey, Caernarvonshire and Denbigh, was a supporter of Edward I in the Welsh War of 1282-4 and was brought up in his household. He became a Knight of Edward II's household when P. of Wales in 1301. He acted as permanent and successful commissioner of array in N. Wales from 1297 to 1314, as well as sheriff in Caernarvonshire (1301-5, 1308-10), Anglesey (1305-6), Merioneth (1314-6 and 1321-7). In 1321-2 during a Mortimer rebellion, he seized a series of Mortimer Castles, including their H.Q. at Chirk, for the King and this gave rise to an apocryphal legend which made him the hero of a Welsh rebellion. He refused to take part in the parliament which deposed Edward II in 1327 and supported the overthrow of Mortimer in 1330.

GRUOCH. See SCOTS OR ALBAN KINGS, EARLY-15.

GUADALAJARA AIR CONVENTION 1961. See AVIATION RULES-2.

GUADELOUPE. See PARIS, P OF (10 FEB. 1763); SEVEN YEARS' WAR-7.

GUADALOUPE-HIDALGO, T. of (May 1848) transferred the areas of the later states of New Mexico, Texas, California, Nevada, Utah, Arizona with parts of Colorado and Wyoming from Mexico to the U.S.A. and ensured the penetration of the Pacific coast to the latter.

GUALO, Card. See HENRY III-1,2. He already had legatine experience when Innocent III sent him to England in 1215 to give papal support to K. John against P. Louis of France, who was about to invade England. Gualo arrived in May 1216 and within a week at a council of Winchester announced that the papacy regarded Louis' invasion as an attack on the Church as well as on K. John. Unable to achieve an early peace, he gave valuable support to John against Louis and the English rebels, in particular by bringing most of the clergy round. In Oct. 1216 John died, leaving Gualo as one his executors. The legate organised the crucial ecclesiastical support for John's nine year old heir. He had John buried at Worcester and the new King crowned as Henry III, in the abbey of Gloucester. He assisted in the restoration of civil administration and dealt with the ecclesiastical disputes and the filling of vacant bishoprics. He left England at his own request in Nov. 1218 and was succeeded as legate by Card. Pandulf.

GUAM (Pacific). An early Spanish possession, was ceded to the U.S.A. in 1898 and, because of its strategic importance, administered by the Navy. The Japanese took it within a week of Pearl Harbor (Dec. 1941) and its recapture became a major allied objective, achieved in Aug. 1944. In 1950 it was given a constitution and Guamanians for the first time became U.S. citizens.

GUARDIAN founded as the weekly *Manchester Guardian*, in 1821 it became a daily. It was the principal whig and later liberal organ, especially under the editorship of C. P. Scott, from 1872 to 1929. It dropped the name "Manchester" in 1960.

GUARDIANS OF THE PEACE. See JUSTICES OF THE PEACE.

GUARDS. Of the seven active Guards regiments, composing the Household Troops, two are cavalry and five infantry. *Cavalry.* The Life Guards were partly raised in Holland among gentry of Charles II's exiled court and fully recruited at the Restoration. The Royal Horse Guards originated in a troop raised in about 1650 by Gen. Monck and called 'Royal' to signify their new allegiance at the Restoration. They became part of the Household only in 1827. *Infantry.* The First or Grenadier Guards originated in a number of companies of royalists raised in Flanders in 1656 and amalgamated as a command in 1665. They acquired the title 'Grenadier' by defeating the Grenadiers of the French Imperial Guard at Waterloo in 1815. The Coldstream Guards were connected with Gen. Monck, who raised them under the Commonwealth and formed them as a regiment at Coldstream near the Scottish border immediately before he marched on London to restore Charles II. The Grenadiers recruit in the south of England, the Coldstreams in the north. The Scots Guards were inspired by a regiment raised by the M. of Argyll for service in Ireland during the Civil War. This ceased to exist after the B. of Worcester (1651) but at the Restoration a regiment was formed as part of the Scottish army. It became part of the British establishment in 1688 and was called the Third Foot Guards under George I. From 1815 to 1877 it was called the Scots Fusilier Guards. The Irish Guards were formed in 1900 to honour the gallantry of Irish regiments in the S. African War, the Welsh Guards in 1915 for similar reasons in World War I.

GUATEMALA was a member of the Central American Federation from 1821 to 1839 when it became an independent, but very unstable, republic in territorial dispute with Britain over British Honduras (Belize) and with Honduras and Salvador. The disputes with Honduras and Salvador were settled by boundary conventions in 1936. The claim against Britain had some local support when Guatemala acquired a left wing govt. under Jacobo Arbenz in 1951; this cooled off after an anti-communist coup in 1963 since when the country has been disturbed by externally fomented civil wars.

GUBBINS. Semi-savages who lived communally near Brentor (Devon) well into the 17th cent.

GUDEMAN OF BALLENDREICH, THE. A pseudonym or *nom-de-guerre* of James IV of Scots when wandering abroad among his people.

GUELPH, GHIBELLINE (Ital: versions of Ger. Welf and Waiblingen), were party faction titles after 1140. In Germany the Welfs supported the Saxons and Bavarians, the Waiblingen the Hohenstaufen. Hence the Italian supporters of the Hohenstaufen were called Ghibelline after c. 1150, their opponents Guelphs. In the struggle between Pope and Emperor, the papal party was the Guelph and supported guild democracy in the towns against imperial governors and so, subsequently, were the supporters of Charles of Anjou. The terms began to die out after Charles' victory in 1268, but were revived in northern Italy for the French in their 15th cent. struggle with the Habsburgs. The House of Hanover was Guelph.

GUERNICA (Spain), the ancient village capital of the Basques, was alleged to have been methodically destroyed by German and Francist bombers on 27 Apr. 1937. This was the first supposed example of aerial mass terrorism against civilians and provoked a lasting reaction exploited by communist parties against their opponents and commemorated in Picasso's symbolic masterpiece of hate. Internal memoranda in the German archives, discovered since World War II, expressed surprise at the press reports of this event, which was not expected in Berlin because it had no strategic or psychological purpose. This and the modern condition of the village seem to suggest that if bombs were dropped there, no systematically destructive operation ever happened.

GUERNSEY. *See* CHANNEL IS.

GUEUX DE MER. See ELIZABETH I-14; HUGUENOTS-5 *et seq.*

GUIANA or GUYANA. BRITISH, DUTCH, FRENCH. The English tried to settle Oapock in 1604, 1613 and 1627; the Dutch Essequibo between 1616 and 1621 and along the Bertrice R. in 1624, but the first permanent lodgement was made only in 1630 by the English Capt. Marshall. In 1633 Ld. Willoughby of Parham founded Surinam; sugar was introduced from Brazil in 1644 and by 1650 Surinam was permanently settled. French buccaneers from St. Christopher were also exploiting the eastern area and there were occasional Portuguese raids. In the endemic warfare the Dutch took Surinam in 1666 and it was definitively ceded to them in exchange for New Amsterdam (New York) in 1667. Throughout the 18th cent. its proximity, and that of its occasionally rebellious

slave population, was a source of friction with British West Indian interests. The British took and held Surinam from 1796 to 1802 and again from 1804, but in 1815 it was handed back to the Dutch. British settlement in Berbice, Demerara and Essequibo ensured that they were not restored to Holland, and the French interests were recognised by a territorial delimitation. The notorious French penal settlements existed there from 1854 until 1949. The three British settlements were united to form British Guiana in 1831 and governed as a crown colony with a local Court of Policy and a Combined Court. A legislative council was first introduced in 1928 and various constitutional amendments gradually established a bi-cameral legislature, but after much confusion and violence between 1956 and 1964, elections established a govt. The colony finally became independent in 1966. Since World War II there has been successful exploitation of mineral resources, especially bauxite, alumina and manganese.

GUICHEN, LUC-URBAIN du BOUÉXIC, Comte de (1712-90). As Capt. of the *Sirène* he captured British Caribbean privateers in 1748. In 1755 he was in the Canadian expedition intercepted by Adm. Boscawen and in 1780 he commanded a division in the B. of Ushant. In 1780, with a battle fleet, he escorted a large military convoy to the W. Indies, was joined by Adm. de Grasse and then fought Rodney indecisively off Martinique (Apr. 1780). In 1781 he lost part of another convoy to Adm. Kempenfelt and in 1782 he tried, but failed, to prevent Lord Howe from resupplying Gibraltar.

GUIDEBOOKS. The first printed guide book was Marianna Starke's *Information for Travellers on the Continent* (1820), published by John Murray (II). John Murray (III) (1808-92) published, as a result, a series called *Murray's Handbooks* which eventually covered much of the world and were copied by Karl Baedeker. The two parallel series were a model for the vast 20th cent. output of such books consequent on the growth of tourism.

GUIENNE or GUYENNE. *See* AQUITAINE.

GUILD or GILD (*cf* O.E. *geld* = payment) **(1)** signified a subscribing confraterity. Mediaeval guilds were mostly urban (though most towns were really villages) and, besides their primary objects, had certain incidental activities in common viz:- (a) mutual help in sickness; (b) members' funerals; (c) support of their families, widows and orphans; (d) education or apprenticeship; (e) commemoration of a patron saint and maintenance of his chapel or altar; (f) conviviality. Since they always needed a meeting place, they usually had a hall called, variously, the guild or hanse hall.

(2) Members (who often included women), on admission, usually paid an entrance fee called a *hanse*. In addition they paid their *scot,* an amount appropriate to each occasion laid down in the guild rules and bore their *lot,* i.e. their share of the guild's extraordinary obligations, which might arise from depression, siege, fire, pestilence, market manipulations or woodworm.

(3) The primary common purpose of a guild might be (a) religious or (b) charitable; (c) mercantile or (d) the practice of a craft, or more than one of these. (a) and (b) applied the profits of their properties to social purposes; (c) consisted of middlemen who dealt in goods, many of them produced by the practitioners of (d). Similarity of terminology and organisation tends to obscure fundamental differences, especially of interest; this similarity was caused partly by the use of precedents. In the north, charters often followed the pattern of the York guilds; in the south, Winchester was a common model, and its guild-controlled weights and measures so remained well into the 19th cent.

(4) The very numerous craft guilds existed in many places, as far apart as Abbotsbury, London, Cambridge and Preston. They were at once professional bodies (possessing disciplinary powers for maintaining standards) trade unions and area monopolists. They usually consisted of masters, journeymen and apprentices. Eventually Masters alone took in apprentices and so controlled entry to the guild. They also elected the head of the guild (called the Warden, Prime Warden, Master, Provost, Mayor or, in Scotland, Dean) and his assistants, who supervised affairs and discipline. A journeyman was one who had done his apprenticeship and, being free of the guild, might practice his craft within its area. A craftsman would seldom, but might be permitted to, belong to more than one craft guild.

(5) Craft guilds existed in Saxon times and sometimes, perhaps often, grew up in conflict with previously existing bodies (or guilds) of persons of local consequence, such as those mentioned in the *Laws of Ine*. These Thanes or "Knights" guilds probably originated in meetings to settle local affairs, or keep order.

(6) Merchants or chapmen's guilds were probably of 11th cent. origin. Essentially trading organisations with contacts outside their town, they increasingly handled capital. A member might have been a master craftsman, and some merchants' guilds were perhaps descended from thanes' guilds. Their premises might have not only a hall, but guest rooms and strong cellars. They entertained foreign colleagues and were more concerned with exchanges and policies than with parochial details. They sometimes (e.g. at Southampton) enforced a kind of internal partnership, or even traded collectively. They had an interest in acquiring control of, or supremacy over, local producers in or out of the craft guilds and aspired to govern their towns. Kings encouraged this because they had cash ready with which to pay the taxes or lend him money. By 1150, for example, the Winchester Guild Merchant was the Guild of the City and recognised until 1832 as its corporation.

(7) Conflicts between merchant and craft guilds were often violent in Scotland, where markets were generally restricted or stagnant. They were relatively peaceful in England whose markets, with some interruptions, expanded continually. The merchants' guilds could adventure profitably abroad. The craft guilds, on the other hand, declined from the mid-14th cent. as business organisations because the unity of the Kingdom rendered them superfluous. A journeyman could earn as good a living outside the town of which he was free, as in it. Moreover the practice of crafts became increasingly elaborate, requiring new equipment, techniques and even machinery. The successful master-craftsman became an investor and an employer. This altered the balance of influence within the craft guilds. Until the end of the 15th cent. guilds had proliferated by subdivision. Now they tended to coalesce and the new amalgamations acquired internal oligarchies, distinguishable by their livery, on ceremonial occasions. The number of liverymen became fixed by charters and, especially in London, the voting strength of the guilds (becoming known as livery companies) was limited in each case by this number.

(8) The merchant guilds, meanwhile, traded primarily in wool and leather and, especially the London Mercers, organised great export corporations such as the Staple at Calais (q.v.). Wool and hides were produced outside, often far from the towns. Their purchase, processing and transport required organisation and capital and most of this activity went on below the horizon of the craft guilds. In the 15th cent., when the Merchant Adventurers (involving especially the London Grocers, Drapers and Mercers) came forward to trade in cloth, the new water driven fulling mills drew producers away from the older towns too. Thus the rise of the merchant and the decline of the craft guilds represented opposed parallel rather than complementary movements. Moreover it became usual for merchant guilds to require a craftsman to abjure his craft as a condition of entry. In Tudor times this requirement cannot have been onerous for the ambitious

(already livened) master craftsmen, but it diminished the standing of his former guild.

(9) The merchant guilds, as international traders were transmuted or superseded after a 16th cent. brilliance, by the geographical discoveries and the difficulty of policing interlopers. Hence, by Stuart times, these and the craft guilds, though still numerous and often rich, were passing from economic to the sociable and charitable function which the City Companies, in London and a few other towns such as Exeter, still maintain. All the same habit dies slowly and the great companies such as the HEIC were in some ways merchant guilds writ large. *See* MERCHANT ADVENTURERS; STAPLE; EASTLAND CO; CHARTERED COMPANIES-2.

GUILDABLE or GELDABLE, THE. The part of a county which paid its taxes directly to the crown through the Sheriff, as opposed to a liberty where the sheriff's jurisdiction was ousted by a lord's bailiff. In particular the part of Suffolk not in the liberties of St. Edmund, or St. Ethelreda or the D. of Norfolk's liberty. The Suffolk Guildable comprised only nine of the 21 hundreds.

GUILDFORD (Surrey) was part of the King's land in Domesday, but was regarded as a borough in 1130. It soon developed as a trading centre for there were Jews in 1189. In 1257 the first charter coincided with a decision to establish the county court permanently there and a guild merchant already existed. The place was therefore the county town. It sent two members to Parliament from 1295. By 1367 the burgesses were responsible for their own fee farm. The town was incorporated in 1488 and given a quarter sessions of its own in 1603 and in 1626 its boundaries were extended to two small neighbouring areas. Charles I confirmed all these earlier grants but in 1686 they were surrendered and a new charter granted by James II. In 1688 the Charter of Charles I was restored and remained in force until a new charter under the Municipal Corporations Act, 1835. The M.P.s were reduced to one in 1867 and the borough was merged electorally in Surrey in 1885.

GUILDFORD, Lds. and Es. of. *See* NORTH.

GUILDHALL. A meeting place of the guilds or other popular assembly in a mediaeval borough, but especially in London where one existed in the 11th cent. It was replaced by a new one between 1411 and 1426; this was destroyed by bombing in Dec. 1940 and rebuilt in 1954.

GUILDHALL SCHOOL OF MUSIC (London) was founded in 1880.

GUILD SOCIALISM, a movement launched in 1906, sought to transform trade unions into guilds controlling the respective industries after nationalisation. A National Guild League was founded in 1915 and received some trade union support. In 1920 a building guild was organised to build and let houses. This collapsed in the post war slump and discredited the movement, which disappeared in 1925.

GUILLOTINE. *See* CLOSURE-(1) (a).

GUINEA CO. was formed in 1588 for Dom Antonio the Portuguese pretender, with a ten-year monopoly of African trade between Senegal and the Gambia. London and West Country merchants subscribed the capital and undertook to pay 5% of their profits and 25% of their prizes to him for the redemption of his English debts. This was a preliminary to the projected and ultimately abortive 1589 expedition to restore him to his throne and was really a political speculation. *See also* CHARLES II-9.

GUINEA, GULF OF (W. Africa). In the 18th cent. this area was a major source of negro slaves provided to slave traders by the native chiefs and exported *via* the dreaded Middle Passage to the American mainland and the W. Indies. *See* DAHOMEY GOREE.

GUINES. *See* FLANDERS-2; CALAIS-3.

GUINNESS (1) Sir Benjamin Lee (1798-1868) (Bt. 1867?) established the fame of this Dublin brewing family and their product and became publicly prominent on the proceeds. He was Lord Mayor of Dublin in 1851, became sole proprietor of the brewery in 1855 and developed it into a major exporting business. Between 1860 and 1865 he largely rebuilt St. Patrick's Cathedral and he was M.P. for Dublin from 1865. His son **(2) Edward Cecil (1847-1927) Ld. (1891), Vist. (1905) GUINNESS and 1st E. of IVEAGH (1919)** became chairman of the Co. in 1886. He was a large scale philanthropist, spending great sums in Dublin slum clearance and on housing in Dublin and London and in supporting the Lister Institute. He acquired Kenwood (outside London), amassed an art collection there and left both to the nation. His son **(3) Walter Edward (1880-1944) 1st Ld. MOYNE (1932)** was a conservative M.P. from 1907 and, after holding lesser posts, was minister for agriculture from 1925 to 1929, chairman of the R. Commission on the West Indies from 1938 to 1939, colonial sec. from 1941 to 1942 and the deputy minister and minister of state at Cairo where he was assassinated.

GUISBOROUGH or HEMINGBURGH, Walter of (fl. 1300) an Augustinian canon of Guisborough priory (Yorks), wrote a chronicle for 1066-1312 which is valuable for northern affairs, especially from 1301 to 1305. He often had access to good texts and sources of information through priories of his order such as Hexham and Carlisle. He also loved a good story even if it was not always fully authentic.

GUISE. See HUGUENOTS-1 to 13.

GUIZOT, Francois Pierre Guillaume (1787-1874) as prof. of history at the Sorbonne from 1812 was associated with the opposition to Bonaparte and was therefore made sec. gen. of the Min. of the Interior in 1814. He was with Louis XVIII at Ghent during the 100 days. From 1815 he held administrative judicial office and lectured and wrote so much in favour of the Charter that the extremists ejected him in 1820. He spent his time until 1830, when he became a deputy, in study and journalism. At the revolution he became Min. of the Interior and purged the ministries of legitimists. In 1832 he became Min. of Education and put through the legislation on primary education and teacher training, besides reviving the *Academie des Sciences morales et politiques*. After Thiers fell he became, in 1840, Marshal Soult's Min. of Foreign Affairs and virtually prime minister. He actually became prime minister in 1847. Temperamentally close to K. Louis Philippe, he rejected foreign adventures or political reform in favour of big business. He was dismissed in Feb. 1848 just before a bored Paris mob in an economically unbalanced society overthrew the regime and he went to England until mid-1849 and thereafter concentrated on writing. A rather slippery liberal royalist, his influence in French education and European culture has been lasting.

GUJARAT (India). (1) A linguistic area extending from Nasik to the Aravallis. **(2)** A part of it which was set up as a state in 1401. Its last Sultan was murdered by the Portuguese at Diu in 1537 and, after much confusion, the Moguls annexed it in 1573. In 1730 it passed to the second Peishwa (r. 1720-40). He conferred it on the Gaekwad, who made his capital at Baroda. After the Third Maratha War (1817-8) it was partitioned between the Gaekwad and the Bombay Presidency. Not to be confused with Gujarat in the Punjab.

GULISTAN, T. (Oct. 1813), named after a Persian imperial palace outside Teheran, was negotiated between Persia and Russia with British mediation. The Persian Caucasus including Baku was ceded to Russia.

GULLY, William Court (1835-1909) 1st Vist. SELBY (1905), a barrister, became Liberal M.P. for Carlisle in 1892 and Speaker in 1895. Exceptionally courteous and impartial, he was faced with persistent Irish obstruction and in Mar. 1901 was compelled to have the Irish M.P.s removed by force. He resigned the speakership in 1905.

GULS HORNEBOOKE **(1609)** by Thos. Dekker (?1570-

1632), a satirical book of manners, instructs fops and gallants on the art of giving offence in public places, e.g. Pauls Walk, the playhouse and the tavern.

GUMLEY (Leics) COUNCIL OF (?749) at which K. Ethelbald of Mercia, whose sexual morals were disapproved by the Church, released his churches from all burdens save the *trimoda necessitas*.

GUN. See ARTILLERY; FIREARMS.

GUNBOAT is a small shallow draught warship designed to engage land targets from coastal waters and rivers and therefore suitable for dominating comparatively primitive societies dependent on water communications. They were much used between 1880 and 1939 in W. Africa and China to protect commercial penetration, especially by the British and French. Hence the phrase "gunboat diplomacy". A **monitor** was a large slow gunboat armed with heavy guns used mainly against the German-held Flanders coast in World War I. A **motor gunboat** (M.G.B.) was a much smaller vessel with an entirely different function, so called to distinguish it from a Motor Torpedo Boat (M.T.B.), because it carried not torpedoes but guns. It was a very fast armed launch designed for English and other coastal and confined waters.

GUNDULF (?-1108) Bp. of ROCHESTER (1077) was an Italian monk at Bec when Abp. Lanfranc called him to Rochester. He was saintly yet able and practical, especially as an architect. He rebuilt his cathedral and built the White Tower of the Tower of London (1078). With Lanfranc's support he replaced the five canons of Rochester with a monastery which had over 60 monks at his death. He also founded a Benedictine nunnery at Malling (Kent). In 1089, with Bp. Walkelin of Winchester, he put down the riots against their Abbot which disgraced the monks of St. Augustine's at Canterbury and during Abp. Anselm's exiles he managed the Canterbury diocese on his behalf as well as his own.

GUNNER'S DAUGHTER. Any naval gun over which a midshipman was lashed for caning.

GUNNING, of Castlecoote, Roscommon. (1) Maria (1733-60) Countess of COVENTRY (1752) and her sister **(2) Elizabeth (1734-90) Duchess of HAMILTON (1752)** and then of **ARGYLL (1759)**, were two Irish girls whose staggering beauty was long the talk of London. Maria was once so mobbed by admirers that George II gave her a guard.

GUN POWDER. See EXPLOSIVES; RENAISSANCE-9.

GUNPOWDER PLOT. See CATESBY, ROBERT.

GUN WAR (1880). See BASUTOLAND-3.

GURKHAS. See NEPAL.

GURU **(Hindi = teacher).** This word is used especially of an exceptionally wise sage.

GUSTAVUS (II) ADOLFUS, K. of SWEDEN (1611-32). See BALTIC-24 TO 28; THIRTY YEARS' WAR-9 TO 13.

GUTENBERG, Johann. See BOOKS.

GUTHLAC, St. (c. 674-715) was the son of the Christian Penwalh, of Mercian royal stock who lived in Leicestershire. Guthlac led raids into British territory to the west but was careful, it was said, to return a third of his booty to its owners. In about 700, tired of banditry, he took the Roman tonsure at the monastery of Repton and in 702 got Tatwine, a fenman, to lead him to the remote island of Crowland where he lived as a hermit and, according to Felix his biographer and propagandist, wrestled, apparently in the manner of Beowulf with Grendel and his mother, with devils who sought him out in his den. It is not clear whether these bouts were of a physical or a spiritual kind.

GUTHRIE (1) Sir David (?-after 1479) was Scots Lord Treasurer in 1461, comptroller in 1466, Lord Treasurer again in 1467, Lord Clerk Register in 1468, Justice Clerk in 1469 and Justice General in 1473. A descendant **(2) John (?-1649)** was minister at St. Giles' Edinburgh in 1621 and royalist Bp. of Moray from 1623 until 1638 when he was deposed.

GUTHRIE, James (?1612-61) a covenanting divine, was a member of the Scots General Assembly from 1644 and in 1646 one of the Scots commissioners to Charles I at Newcastle. An extremist, he was hanged in 1661.

GUY, Thomas (?1645-1724) and **GUY's HOSPITAL (London).** He was M.P. for Tamworth from 1695 to 1707 and from 1704 a Gov. of St. Thomas's Hospital. He made a speculative fortune in South Sea stock and built and owned his hospital himself. It opened in 1725; the school of medicine and surgery in 1769.

GUYON, Richard Debeaufre (1803-56), KHOURSHID Pasha, became a General in the Hungarian army and won victories for the Hungarian insurgents during the civil war of 1848. After their surrender he took service with the Turks and distinguished himself against the Russians in the Caucasus from 1853 to 1855.

GWALIOR (India) an ancient city and princely state with a reputedly impregnable fort, passed to the Moguls in 1558. The Maratha Scindhia captured it in 1751 and made it his capital in 1771. Popham surprised and took the fort in 1781 but it was later restored. The Scindhias were driven out by the Rani of Jhansi and the garrison joined the Indian mutiny and, as a result, it was seized and retained by the British who, however, exchanged it for Jhansi in 1886. *See* MARATHAS-C.

GWANDO. *See* HAUSA.

GWARTHEKIG (Welsh) was an annual prise of cattle by a marcher lord from a Welsh community.

GWELY (Welsh) was the inner kindred to the fourth generation. *Cf.* Irish DERBFINE. *See* WELSH LAW-5,9.

GWENT or MONMOUTHSHIRE was a Roman military district based on the legionary fortress of Isca (Caerleon). The sparsely tribal hill culture remained Celtic, the valley areas and towns increasingly Saxon. Under Edward the Confessor it was combined with Herefordshire as a marcher earldom and subsequently the Normans built border castles at Monmouth and Chepstow. Its nature long remained uncertain but the non-Celts tended to be in the nature of garrisons rather than settlements. From 1534 the English govt. treated it as English and included it under the name Monmouthshire in the English judicial circuit system and excluded it from Great Sessions. In fact Welsh influence and language encroached steadily so that the position of the area in the English system became increasingly anomalous. The Local Government Act 1972 created the modern county, which excluded the Rhymney Valley but included Newport, by then a county borough, and it came into existence as part of Wales in 1974. *See also* WELSH LAW-2.

GWESTFA (Welsh) was an annual food levy payable by an occupier of free land to the lord and represented the freeman's obligation to entertain him. It was paid in two parts, the larger in winter, the lesser in summer and these two were together commuted for £1 per *maenol* per annum. This cash payment was called *tunc.*

GWYRDA (Welsh). A noble, or one who represented the free Welsh, at a commote.

GWRIAD. *See* GWYNEDD-10.

GWTHEYRN. *See* VORTIGERN.

GWYER, Sir Maurice (1878-1952) was a member of the committee which in 1932 investigated the financial relations between the states of India and the govt. He helped to draft the Govt. of India Act, 1935, which set up the Indian Federal Court and was the first C.J. of India form 1937 to 1943. As Vice-Chan. of Delhi Univ. from 1938 to 1950 he helped to draft the Constitution of India.

GWYN, Eleanor (Nell) (1650-87), prostitute ("orange-seller") at Drury Lane Theatre and, from 1665, a successful actress there until 1670, became the most charming of Charles II's mistresses and probably the only one he loved. Not unduly rapacious or political, she was well liked and her influence seems to have been benevolent. In particular she persuaded the King to found Chelsea Hospital in 1682. Charles on his death-bed asked his brother James 'not to let poor Nelly starve' and James honoured the request, though she had on one occasion publicly proclaimed herself "the *protestant* whore".

GWYNEDD, PRINCIPALITY OF (N. Wales) (c. 450-1283) (A) originated in the conquest of the citadel mountains of Snowdonia from the 'Irish' by a Christian **(1) Cunedda Whedig or Cunedag (fl. ?450).** He was the chief of the Votadii (Manau Gododdin), Berwickshire Celts who migrated south-westwards at the time of the Roman withdrawal (*see* MAP). His ancestors included Roman names. His grandson **(2) Cadwallon Lawhir (fl. ?500)** conquered the fertile grain growing I. of Anglesey, from which Snowdonia could be supplied. His successor **(3) Maelgwyn Gwynedd (?-?547),** a military ruler who briefly withdrew into a monastery, added the four Cantrefs (Rhos, Rhufoniog, Tegeingl and Duffryn Clwyd) east of the R. Conway and established Gwynedd on a more enduring footing than any state except Wessex. **(4) Cadfan (fl. 620),** the fourth in line from him, was the father of the well-known **Cadwallon (?-633)** who was driven into Irish exile by Edwin of Deira in 631. He made an alliance with Penda of Mercia and their combined forces killed Edwin at the B. of Heathfield or Meigen in Oct. 632. The victory was misused: the Welsh troops spending much of their time freebooting. Oswald of Bernicia, who had succeeded Edwin, surprised and killed Cadwallon at Cantysgol near Hexham in Dec. 633. His famous son **(5) Cadwaladr (?-664)** had to fight a usurper CADAFAEL, whom he ejected only after the B. of Winwaedsfield in 654. The rest of his reign was peaceful and he gave much encouragement to bards. Consequently many heroic and saintly tales were told about him and (like King Arthur) it was said that he would one day return. He died of the plague. His grandson **(6) Rhodri Molwynog (?-754)** had two sons **(7) Hywel (?-825)** and **(8) Cynan (?-816)** who were at war until Cynan were killed. Hywel, however, died childless and so brought the line of Cunedda to an end. Cynan's daughter **(9) Ethyllt (fl. ?825)** married a Manx chieftain **(10) Gwriad (fl. ?825)** who thus acquired the rights of her house, and their child **(11) Merfyn Frych (?-844)** succeeded first in Anglesey and then on the mainland. Merfyn married a daughter of the King of Powys and their son **(12) Rhodri the Great (?-877)** succeeded to Gwynedd in 844, to Powys in 855 and to his brother-in-law's Kingdom of Seisyllwg in 872. This temporary union of the two thirds of Wales coloured the policies of all Rhodri's Welsh successors: it also enabled the Welsh to hold off the growing threat from the Irish and Manx Norsemen. He apparently died in battle against the Mercians and his inheritance was divided between **(13) Anarawd (?-916)** and **(14) Cadell (fl. 930)** founders respectively of the houses of Aberffraw and Dinefwr, their territories becoming known as Gwynedd proper and Deheubarth (q.v.).

B. Anarawd in Gwynedd had to repel the Mercians and achieved victory on the Conway in 881. He tried to head off the Norse danger by an alliance with the Danish rulers at York but this policy, probably involving a Danegeld, proved unprofitable and in about 890, the Danish crisis being at its height, he turned to Alfred the Great and submitted to him as overlord; in later conflicts with his brother Cadell of Deheubarth he had English help. His son **(15) Idwal Foel (?-942)** also submitted to Wessex, but when at his death in 842 his sons **(16) Iago (?-979)** and **(17) Ieuaf (?-985)** attempted a change of policy, the English helped Hywel Dda (Howell the Good) of Deheubarth to expel them; the dominions of Rhodri the Great were thus briefly reunited. Iago and Ieuaf, however, returned after Hywel's death in 950 but quarrelled and, in the next 36 years, there was intermittent civil war between their families, and Iago eventually hanged Ieuaf. The last of Ieuaf's children died in 986, the year when the energetic Maredudd succeeded in Deheubarth. He immediately expelled the legal heir **(18) Idwal** (who died in exile in 996) and held parts of Gwynedd against Danish and Saxon attack until his death in 999. Civil war or usupation (or both) were now resumed save between 1018 and 1023 when Llywellyn ap Seisyll of Deheubarth ruled most of Wales. Eventually a son of the exiled Idwal **(19) Iago (?-1039),** came to the throne in 1033 but was murdered in 1039 at the instance of **(20) Gruffudd (?-1063)** of Powys (son of Llywellyn of Deheubarth) who supplanted him. Gruffudd's mother was a granddaughter of Hywel Dda; his father had already ruled most of Wales and he added to his claims much force of character and military ability. He sealed his usurpation in Gwynedd and Powys by a great victory over the Mercians at Rhyd-y-groes (Crossford) on the Severn in 1039. He then fought Hywel, King of Deheubarth, and eventually killed him and defeated his Danish allies in a battle on the Towy in 1044. Deheubarth, however, was unwilling to submit and Gruffudd turned his attention to the Herefordshire English. In 1052 he defeated them so heavily at Leominster that he was able in 1055 finally to conquer Deheubarth. Border warfare at this period amounted to civil war. Gruffudd, in alliance with Aelfgar, E. of Mercia, attacked Leofgar, Bp. of Hereford and a supporter of Godwin's family. Harold Godwin's son came to the rescue but in 1056 Gruffudd drove them back. In the subsequent peacemaking all Wales was, for a few brief years, united under Gruffudd, all parties swore allegiance to Edward the Confessor and Gruffudd married Aldgyth, Aelfgar's daughter. This kept the peace until Aelfgar died in 1062. Harold then renewed the war with a daring raid on Gruffudd's court at Rhuddlan and after scattered fighting all over Wales Gruffudd was killed, apparently by his own men. **(21) Cynan,** son of the murdered Iago, having already died in exile in 1060, the throne was usurped by **(22) Trahearn (?-1081)** son of Caradog, K. of Arwystii who, in 1078, overthrew Rhys ab Owain of Deheubarth as well; but Cynan's son **(23) Gruffudd (1055-1137)** grew up in Dublin, obtained Norse support, crossed to Wales with Norman help and in alliance with Rhys ab Tewdwr, Rhys ab Owain's cousin, eventually killed Trahearn at the B. of Mynydd Cam in 1081. In his absence the Normans pressed into central Gwynedd and across the R. Conway, building castles at Bangor, Caernarvon and Beaumaris. Ransomed in 1094 he retaliated by alliances with Rhys and the Norsemen, but was nearly cornered in Anglesey and driven to Dublin in 1098. Norman pressure was now suddenly reduced by the death of Hugh of Shrewsbury at a battle in the Menai Straits with K. Magnus of Norway. Gruffydd returned unmolested in 1099 and ruled Anglesey as tributary to Henry I. There followed a period of comparative peace. Gruffudd patronised the clergy and the poets and introduced the bagpipes from Ireland. He opposed the anti-Norman policies of the rulers of Deheubarth and supported Henry I's war with Powys. His son (24) **Owain Gwynedd (?-1170)** (q.v.) succeeded him peacefully in 1137 but took advantage of Stephen's weakness to storm Carmarthen, invade Powys and occupy Mold. His aggressions were brought to an abrupt halt by Henry II in 1157 and he did homage to him. Thereafter his policy was to maintain the balance of power: he supported Henry against Rhys ap Gruffydd from 1159 to 1164 but kept Normans out of Welsh preferments and from 1165 to 1167 was again at war with Henry II. At his death the succession fell to his son **(25) Dafydd I (?-1203)** who, having killed his brother Hywel, followed a policy of Norman alliances, particularly because his brother **(26) Rhodri (?-1195)** set up independently in Anglesey from 1175 to 1191. Dafydd was dethroned in 1194 by his nephew **(27) Llywellyn ap Iorwerth (The Great) (?-1240).** He had been brought up on his mother's lands in

Powys while his uncle held Gwynedd and had defeated him at the B. of Aberconway. By 1202 he had secured all Gwynedd. He was on good terms with K. John for most of the latter's reign and was seen as a useful counterpoise to Gwenwynwyn, the ruler of Powys. In 1201 he offered homage to John and performed it when he was betrothed to John's bastard Joan in 1203. He married her in 1206. With the King's connivance he overran much of S. Wales. In 1208, however, John, frightened by the threats of the Lords Marcher, changed his policy. His expedition of 1211 forced Llywellyn to surrender most of his conquests and give hostages, who were killed at the revolt of the Welsh princes in 1212. By 1213, however, he had recovered Gwynedd and briefly held Shrewsbury. His alliance with the barons had paid off. John undertook in Magna Carta to restore illegally taken Welsh lands. The English civil war then allowed Llywellyn to extend his conquests and take homage from other Welsh princes, notably Gwenwynwyn, whom he later expelled. At the P. of Worcester (1218) the English regency confirmed his conquests. Subsequently he fought wars with Lords Marcher, notably the Marshal William II in Pembrokeshire and Hubert de Burgh. The King's interventions in 1228 and 1231 proved ineffective and Llywellyn, taking advantage of a dispute between Richard the Marshal and Hubert, continued to extend his possessions, taking Builth in 1230. He had taken the titles of Prince of Aberffraw and Lord of Snowden and in 1238 the other Welsh princes recognised his son Dafydd's succession. He retired to the Cistercian abbey which he had founded at Aberconway, where he died a monk, having set up a Norman type of administration and court which **(28) Dafydd II (?1208-46)** inherited after a struggle with his half-brother Gruffudd. With the accession of Gruffudd's son **(29) Llewellyn II (?-1282)** the decline of the independent principality was rapid: Henry III intervened in family quarrels in 1247 to compel Llywellyn to surrender the lands west of the Conway and to hold the rest of the English crown. The distractions of the English civil wars led Llywellyn, after 1255, to try and recover his lands which had been conferred on the future Edward I. In time this naturally drove Llywellyn into alliance with Simon de Montfort; consequently when Simon was killed Llywellyn's position was insecure. By the T. of Montgomery of 1267 he was recognised as the Chief of the Princes of Wales, but there was no restraint upon the Marcher Lords (who were all of Edward's party) to enlarge their power. Moreover, Llywellyn's brother **(30) Dafydd** conspired to usurp his throne and in 1272 fled to England when discovered. At this point Henry III died and Llywellyn, suspicious of the protection given to the conspirators, refused homage to Edward I. After prolonged negotiations war began in 1277. South Wales was rapidly overrun, Anglesey occupied and, faced with starvation in Snowdonia, Llywellyn sued for peace; by the T. of Conway (Oct. 1277) while retaining the title of Prince of Wales, his frontiers were restricted to Snowdonia, Merioneth and Penllyn, with Edeyrnion and Anglesey in tail, and his brother received as fees of the crown half the surrendered lands east of the Conway. Llywellyn married Eleanor of Montfort. The disturbed condition of the country led to many disputes which had to be settled by law courts, but the treaty did not lay down whether Welsh or Marcher law was applicable. This created much discontent of which Dafydd took advantage. In Mar. 1282 he raised a revolt which Llywellyn (who had his grievances) felt forced to support. Edward counter-attacked Snowdonia and occupied Anglesey. An offer of mediation by Abp. Peckham failed and in Dec. Llywellyn was killed in a skirmish. Dafydd tried to carry on but by May 1283 Snowdonia had been overrun. In June Dafydd was taken and executed in Oct. This was the end. *See* WALES, STATUTE OF, AND WALES; WELSH LAW-2.

GYPSIES all speak dialects of a language (Romany) connected with Sanskrit. They originated in N.W. India, started a series of migrations perhaps in the 9th cent. and split into two streams in Persia; one (the Bosha) going by way of Armenia; the other (the Narwar, Caradji and Helebis) by way of Syria to Egypt. The Bosha probably reached Constantinople by the 11th cent., spread across the Balkans and by 1417 had reached Hamburg, having assimilated many itinerant metal workers or learned their crafts. They reached England and Scotland in about 1500, where they were popular at first. Surrey entertained them at Tendring in 1519 and they danced at Holyrood House in 1530. Opinion gradually changed and 5 men were hanged at Durham in 1592 and 4 at Edinburgh in 1611 for being within the Kingdoms. They continued to live a private tribal existence on commons and verges until the 1950s when their untidy habit of scrap metal trading (which had replaced metal working) drew attention to their social and educational problems. In 1968 local authorities were required to provide them with sites; in 1994 govt. support for the requirement was withdrawn and the offence of criminal trespass was created to drive them from their customary habitats.

GYRATION **(Feb.-Nov. 1387).** *See* RICHARD II-10.

GYRTH (?-1066) fourth son of Earl Godwin was E. of E. Anglia from 1057 to 1066 when he was killed at Hastings.

GYRWE were the Mercian Fenmen.

H

HABEAS CORPUS. *See* PREROGATIVE WRITS.
HABER-BOSCH PROCESS. *See* NITRATES.
HABSBURG or AUSTRIA, HOUSE OF. *See* AUSTRIA (AS EXPRESSION); AUSTRIA; AUSTRIA, POST PRAGMATIC; AUSTRO HUNGARY.
HACKNEY. *See* CAB.
HADDINGTON, Es. of. *See* HAMILTON (HADDINGTON).
HADDINGTON, T of (1548). *See* MARY QUEEN OF SCOTS-4.
HADDOCK (1) Sir Richard (1629-1715) commanded Sandwich's flagship at the B. of Solebay (1672). In 1682 he was commander at the Nore, joint C-in-C in 1690 and thereafter comptroller of the navy. His son **(2) Nicholas (1686-1746)** led the attack on the Spaniards at C. Passaro in 1718, became commander at the Nore in 1732 and, as C-in-C Mediterranean from 1738 to 1742 inflicted heavy damage on Spanish trade. He was M.P. for Rochester from 1734 to 1746. *See* WARS OF 1739-48-2.
HADDON HALL (Derbys.). William Vernon acquired Haddon under Henry III and commenced the building which over the centuries grew into an immense residence. Dorothy Vernon (?-1584), daughter of Sir George (?-1567), last of the male line, eloped with Sir John Manners and so in 1567 it passed to the Manners (Rutland) family.
HADHRAMAUT (Arabia), once the incense producing area of S. Arabia, consisted of the three unruly states of Shihr, Makalla and Seiyum. Its richer families often maintained trading concerns in Indonesia and Malaya and lived on the remittances. *See* ADEN.
HADOW REPORT (1926) proposed that the school-leaving age should be 15, that every child should receive a secondary education in either a grammar or a modern school, with the existing Eleven Plus examination for grammar school entry being retained. The report was pigeon-holed by the govt. because it did not satisfy the supporters of Church Schools but its recommendations formed the basis of future education bills, notably the Education Act 1944. *See* ELEVEN PLUS; GRAMMAR SCHOOLS.
HADRIAN or ADRIAN IV (Nicolas Breakspear) (c. 1100-59) the only English Pope (1154), became Abbot of St. Rufus near Avignon in 1137; he impressed Eugenius IV while on a mission to Rome and was retained there as Cardinal of Albano. In 1152 Eugenius sent him to Scandinavia where he reorganised the churches of Norway and Sweden and made Troodheim an independent Archbishopric. He asserted the highest claims of his office; he exacted homage from Frederick Barbarossa as a condition of his imperial coronation and claimed the Empire as a Papal fief. This precipitated a long quarrel between Empire and Papacy. An attempt to assert a more direct rule in Sicily led to a military debacle. He similarly intervened in French affairs by confirming action by the French crown against Burgundy. Consistently with this he authorised Henry II's expedition to Ireland in 1155 by the Privilege or Bull *Laudabiliter* (Lat = praiseworthily), which was later construed as a grant of Sovereignty over that island.
HADRIAN'S WALL was ordered by the Emperor Hadrian who visited Britain in A.D. 122 and mostly built under the Gov. Aulus Platorius (r. 122-6), though work and modification continued until c. 165. It extended across the width of Britain from Wallsend (Segedunum) on the Tyne, to Burgh-on-Sands on the Solway and was extended by a line of shore forts to Bowness. In principle it consisted of a wall 10 feet thick with a narrow berm, ditch and glacis to the north and it was intersected by a regular series of milecastles and larger forts, of which there are impressive remains at Housesteads and Chesters. To the south, at varying short distances, there was a parallel set of structures called the **Vallum**

consisting of a central ditch flanked by broad berms and two wide, flat earthen ramparts. The wall was the frontier and served to control traffic. The Vallum probably protected the civilian services from bandits. The whole complex was linked by military roads to depots, such as Vindolanda, further south. The design was not all carried out in full: for example at the eastern end the thickness was reduced by two feet possibly for speed of completion. The whole was garrisoned by auxiliary units of the army until about 383 after which, apparently, continuous occupation ceased. Twenty-eight miles of it were levelled by Gen. Wade to make a road in 1745. *See* BRITAIN, ROMAN-14.
HADRIANS, OTHER. *See* ADRIAN.
HAGANAH. *See* ISRAEL-3.
HAGUE AIR CONVENTIONS 1955, 1970. *See* AVIATION RULES.
HAGUE CONFERENCE 1929 endorsed the Young Plan, which reduced the amount of the German War Reparations and eased the details. Britain was represented by Philip Snowden. He thought that reparations were in principle wrong but nevertheless refused to reduce Britain's share in favour of the French who were predictably indignant. The decisions were overtaken by the Depression and the rise of Hitler in Germany.
HAGUE (PEACE) CONFERENCES. (1) 1899 on Russian instigation considered disarmament. It broke down on this issue because improved communications could offset reductions but it adopted rules of war especially those prohibiting aerial bombardment, gas and expanding bullets. It also created The Hague Permanent Court of Arbitration.
    (2) 1907 on Russian instigation again considered disarmament and again failed on it, but widened the statute of the permanent court and adopted a variety of other conventions of which the most durable related to the behaviour of neutrals during war.
HAIFA (Israel) the main Palestinian port under the British mandate, became the refinery terminal of the Kirkuk (Iraq) oil pipeline. After Israeli independence (1948) the pipeline was cut but in the 1960s a new one was laid from Eilat on the Red Sea. Haifa also developed substantial industries.
HAIG, Douglas (1881-1922), E. HAIG of BEMERSYDE (1919), of the Scotch whisky family, served in the cavalry in the Sudan (1898) and in the Boer War. In 1908-9 he was at the War Office involved in Haldane's reforms. He commanded a corps at Mons and in the initial stages of the Ypres battles and then, late in 1915, succeeded Sir John French as C-in-C in France. He was slow to depart from established orthodoxy and his earlier offensives, particularly the Bs. of the Somme and Paschendaele, gained little ground for vast casualties, but his victory at Amiens (1918) showed an unsuspected imaginative streak. He suffered much from Lloyd George's animosity, also voiced in his memoirs, but he was popular with fellow officers and, strong in adversity, was something of a hero to ordinary people. After the war he devoted himself to the British Legion and its fund-raising for disabled soldiers.
HAILE SELASSIE. *See* ABYSSINIA.
HAILEYBURY COLLEGE was founded in 1802 as a training school for the HEIC.
HAILSHAM. *See* HOGG.
HAINAULT. *See* FLANDERS-6 *et seq*.
HAIR. The first public stage show in which the actors appeared naked, began in London in 1968.
HAITI. *See* HISPANIOLA.
HAJ. The annual pilgrimage to Mecca obligatory once in a life-time to Moslems. Hence Hajji, one who has

performed the Haj and is entitled to wear a green turban. *See* CHOLERA.

HAKLUYT, Richard (?-1552-1616), a clergyman and chief adventurer (investor) in the South Virginia Company, held that self interest and protestantism alike imposed a duty of colonial expansion upon the English. In 1582 he published his *Divers Voyages*; in 1589 his *Principal Navigations, Voyages Traffiques and Discoveries of the English Nation* and in 1598-1600 an enlarged edition of the latter. It contained many first hand narratives. **SAMUEL PURCHAS (?1575-1626)** carried on his work in *Purchas, his Pilgrims*, the final version of which was published in 1625.

HALBERD. A long-staffed infantry axe with a rear and top spike, dangerous to cavalry.

HALDANE (1) Richard Burdon (1856-1928) 1st Vist. (1911) studied at Göttingen Univ. before becoming a successful barrister. He became liberal M.P. for E. Lothian in 1885. He had a practical interest in higher education, inspired or helped to set up several civic universities and in 1904 chaired the committee which recommended the fateful creation of the University Grants Committee. In 1905 he became S. of State for War. His understanding of the German outlook influenced his policies as such. Realising the need for wide-ranging military reforms, he overcame the Liberal party's indifference to the Army by careful study and application and, by getting the necessary legislation passed, was the refounder of the modern army. He turned the militia into a reserve, created Officers' Training Corps, strengthened the Territorial Army and established an Imperial General Staff (1909), together with permanent medical and nursing services. He maintained, nevertheless, his educational interests and in 1909 was chairman of the London Univ. Commission. After an abortive mission to Germany (which wrongly tinged him with a pro-German reputation), he became Lord Chancellor (1912) and by increasing the numbers of the highest judiciary raised the judicial reputation of the House of Lords and the Privy Council. In 1915 he was excluded from Asquith's first coalition because the Unionists affected to believe that he was pro-German. He became estranged, too, from Lloyd George's liberals and when the first Labour govt. took office (1924) he accepted the Woolsack again and afterwards led the Labour opposition in the Lords. His brother **(2) John Scott (1860-1936)** physiologist and philosopher, conducted the researches into gas and respiratory problems which brought about the modern safety arrangements both for miners and for deep sea divers and the introduction of gas masks in war. His sister **(3) Elizabeth Sanderson (1862-1937)** Liberal and coadjutor of Octavia Hill, was the first Scottish woman J.P. (1920) and an influential figure in Scottish universities and nursing, besides a Carnegie trustee from 1914 to 1937.

HALE, Sir Matthew (1609-76) was Abp. Laud's counsel on his impeachment in 1643 and later took on several other politically unpopular defences. In 1648 Charles I declined his proffered services. He took the oath to the Commonwealth, served on the committee for law reform in 1652 and in 1654 became a justice of the Common Pleas. He sat for Gloucestershire in the Convention of 1660 and became Chief Baron of the Exchequer. In 1666 he presided in the special court to adjudicate on the Great Fire of London and in 1671 he became C.J. of the King's Bench. His *Pleas of the Crown* and *Historia Placitorum Coronae* (Lat = History of the Pleas of the Crown) were long the standard texts on criminal and other Crown proceedings.

HALES, Sir Edward (1645-95) professed R. Catholicism in 1685 and having acted in the collusive case *Godden* v *Hales* (q.v.) became Lieut. of the Tower. He was with James II during his flight, but was taken at Faversham and detained. He reached the Jacobite court at St.

Germain in 1690 and received the Jacobite earldom of Tenterden in 1692.

HALES, Stephen (1677-1761), an innocent kindly polymath, was a parish priest and a man of affairs. He was a founder of the Royal Society of Arts, a trustee of Georgia and a temperance campaigner. He was also an enthusiastic scientist and as such defined (by experiments on a horse) arterial pressure and in his biochemical work *Vegetable Staticks* (1727) foreshadowed the identification of carbon-dioxide, nitrogen and the components of water. He also invented, for use on hot voyages, a type of ventilator, a water distiller and a method of preserving meat.

HALFDAN. Danish King of Northumbria. *See* ALFRED.

HALFDAN. *See* IVAR THE BONELESS.

HALIDON HILL, B. of (19 July 1333). Edward Balliol and the "Disinherited" landed in Fife and defeated the Scots regency at Dupplin Moor. He was then crowned at Scone (Sept. 1332) but a nationalist rising led by the E. of Moray and Archibald Douglas drove him into the Scottish East March. K. Edward III had moved his govt. to York and now came home. He and Balliol besieged Berwick, and Moray, Douglas and Robert the Steward marched from Duns to its relief with a superior force. The English were posted on Halidon Hill just north of Berwick, with swampy ground in front. A block of dismounted men-at-arms occupied the centre with archers diagonally on the wings. The Scots advanced, were impeded in the swamp and shot down in the archery cross-fire. Douglas, about 600 Scots lords and knights and some thousands of infantry were killed. The English loss was negligible. Edward III won the victory over the French at Crécy 13 years later by the same tactics.

HALIFAX. *See* DUNK; WOOD.

HALIFAX (Nova Scotia) was founded in 1749 with 2500 English settlers; the first Canadian legislature met there in 1758. The winter port for Eastern Canada when the St. Lawrence is iced up, it has always handled most of the commerce of the Maritime provinces. Hence with its docks it was long the chief British naval station in the N.W. Atlantic (especially in World Wars I and II) and it became the Atlantic terminus of the Canadian Pacific Rly. It was devastated in Dec. 1917 by an ammunition ship explosion followed by a blizzard. *See* GEORGE II-15.

HALIFAX (Yorks.) owed its first 15th cent. textile prosperity to ample soft water for fulling and later for powering spinning machinery; and its greater Victorian wealth to the discovery and mining of exceptionally good local steam coal. The place was never over-specialised and diversified into engineering, cotton and brewing. By HALIFAX or GIBBET LAW, thieves of cloth worth 13½d or more within the town liberty, might be tried by a jury of burgesses and executed on the Halifax Gibbet, a sort of guillotine. The custom lapsed in 1650.

HALL, Edward (?1499-1547), strongly protestant chronicler, was Common Serjeant from 1532 and M.P. for Bridgnorth in 1542. His *Union of the Noble and Illustre Families of Lancashire and York* (1542) is primarily an apologia for Henry VIII. It is politically unreliable but socially rewarding and Shakespeare based some of his plays on it.

HALL, Joseph (1574-1656). Cambridge scholar, became chaplain to Sir Edmund Bacon on mission to Spa (1605), then to Henry, P of Wales (1608), to Ld. Doncaster on a French mission (1616), and to James I and VI in Scotland in 1617. By now an experienced linguist and ecclesiastical diplomat, he represented the Anglican Church at the Synod of Dort (1618) and from 1627 to 1641 was Bp. of Exeter. He was a moderate Calvinist and a conciliatory but determined upholder of Anglicanism against presbyterians and other sectaries. In 1641 he was translated to Norwich at the centre of independency. He was impeached, imprisoned, deprived of his revenues. His cathedral was turned into a warehouse. In 1647 he was expelled from his palace and lived in poverty, never wavering, until he died.

HALL, Sir (William) Reginald (1870-1943) after an outstanding naval career became Director of Naval Intelligence in 1914 and effective head of British Intelligence in World War I and was largely responsible for its successes and international reputation. In particular he set up the establishments which deciphered German naval and diplomatic wireless traffic and developed the arts of counter-espionage to a high degree. Amongst other *coups* the most spectacular were the interception of the Zimmerman telegram and the capture of Sir Roger Casement. He was Tory M.P. for Liverpool from 1918 to 1922 and for Eastbourne from 1925 to 1929.

HALLAM or HALLUM, Robert (?-1417), unsuccessfully nominated to the Archbishopric of York by the Pope in 1405, was Bp. of Salisbury from 1407. He was an English representative at the Council of Pisa in 1409 and as leader of the English nation at the Council of Constance in 1414 opposed John XXII and demanded reform as a precondition of the election of a new pope.

HALLAM, John (?-1537) was a leader of the Pilgrimage of Grace and rebel gov. of Hull. He was pardoned for his involvement in the first series of risings but took part in the second series and was taken and hanged.

HALLAMSHIRE (Yorks.). The area about Sheffield within which the Sheffield Cutlers had a craft monopoly.

HALLÉ, Sir Charles (KARL) (1819-95) a Westphalian conductor and pianist, settled at Manchester in 1848 and instituted the orchestra named after him in 1857.

HALLEY, Edmond (1656-1742) observed a complete transit of Venus in 1677 and published Newton's *Principia* at his own expense in 1687. Between 1685 and 1693 he completed the first full description of the Trade Winds; in 1697 he settled the method of measuring height with a barometer and between 1699 and 1701 he drew up a general chart of magnetic variations (The Halleyan Lines) and made a tidal survey of the English coast. These practical and humanly influential activities have been obscured by his astronomical work. He predicted the solar eclipse of 1715, became Astronomer Royal in 1721 and by his prediction that the comet of 1531, 1607 and 1682 would return (as it did) in 1758 eventually caused it to be named after him. His important lunar and planetary tables were published in 1749. He was also a Latin poet. *See* NAVIGATION.

HALLMARKS. The Crown's interest in the purity of SILVER arose from the need to standardise the mediaeval coinage. The silversmith's craft was regulated from the 12th cent. and plate had to be tested and marked at permitted assay offices managed by the local guilds. The principal types of mark are **(1)** the MAKER'S mark, usually initials or a monogram; **(2)** the mark of ORIGIN of the assay office concerned; **(3)** the DATE LETTER. This was a single letter for the year from a 20-letter alphabet (A-I, K-U), each alphabet being distinctive in pattern; **(4)** the DUTY MARK (the sovereign's head) to show that duty had been paid from 1784 (England), 1807 (Dublin) and 1819 (Glasgow). **(5)** the ASSAY MARK (a) A lion was used in London from 1544 to denote sterling standard (92.5%) but in 1696 the standard was raised to 95.8%; this was denoted by the figure of Britannia and the ordinary lion's face mark of London was replaced by a lion's head erased. In 1719 Britannia standard became optional. London resumed its lion's face mark of origin and provincial offices began to use the sterling mark. The Britannia mark continued to be used when appropriate. GOLD was always rare and little used for currency until the discovery of America. From 1300 to 1477 the standard was 19⅛ carats and the ASSAY MARK was the lion's face. In 1478 the standard was lowered to 18 carats and date letters were added. In 1544 the lion replaced the lion's face and in 1575 the standard was raised to 22 carats. In 1798 an additional 18 carat standard denoted by a crown was introduced. From 1844 the crown was used for both standards. In 1854 15, 12 and 9 carat standards were added, the mark being simply the carat numbers and their decimal value. In 1932 the 15 and 12 carat standards were abolished and a 14 carat standard introduced. Assay offices were numerous. Of the 36 more important ones, those of Birmingham, Dublin, Edinburgh, London and Sheffield survive, and those at Chester (1962) and Glasgow (1964) were closed after World War II; nineteen were closed in 19th cent., the rest in the 18th.

HALLMOTE. A Saxon meeting corresponding to the later Court Baron.

HALLSTADT CULTURE. *See* IRON AGE.

HALSBURY, Harding Stanley Giffard (1823-1921) 1st Ld. (1885) 1st E. of (1898), was an enormously successful lawyer who led for Gov. Eyre (1867-8) and for the Tichborne claimant (1871-2). He became Sol-Gen. in 1875 and a conservative M.P. in 1877 and was heavily involved as a barrister and politician in the Bradlaugh case. He achieved his greatest triumph of professional advocacy in *Belt* v *Lawes* (1885). He was Lord Chanc. from 1885 to 1892 and from 1895 to 1905 and inspired important legal reforms including the Land Transfer Act 1897 and the Criminal Evidence Act 1898 and perhaps more importantly between 1905 and 1916 his great digest, *The Laws of England*, better known as *Halsbury*. He reduced his political reputation by leading the die-hard peers against the parliament bill in 1911 but his judicial capacity was never in doubt and he was still sitting as a judicial peer in appeals to the Lords in his 94th year.

HAMBURG (Ger.) started as an important Wendish commercial centre in the 12th cent; acquired customs privileges in 1189 and entered into an agreement with Lübeck in 1241 (*see* HANSE-2, 7 *and* WENDISH *references*). After the Reformation it gave refuge to Dutch and Huguenot protestants. It led Europe in developing whaling in the 17th cent. and the N. American trade in the 18th, when it took in further French immigrants. This prosperity was abruptly checked in the Napoleonic wars but revived after 1815 as the port of the N. German Confederation. In 1842 the railway reached the port but the city was devastated by a conflagration. By 1847, however, North American trade had been re-established and the city's development continued with the creation of the German Empire in 1871 and the establishment of its colonies in the next 40 years. It was the fourth largest European port when the British blockade halted its activities in 1914. The T. of Versailles (1920) indirectly compelled the surrender of all its long distance shipping but the merchant fleet was progressively rebuilt and promptly blockaded in World War II when much of the city was destroyed by fire-storm bombing.

HAMILTON, Alexander (1755-1804) was Washington's private sec. from 1777 to 1781, served in the Continental Congress in 1782 and 1783, in the Annapolis Convention of 1786 and in the Constitutional Convention of 1787. He then became Washington's Sec. of the Treasury. His centralising outlook was reflected in his economic policies which included federal assumption of state war debts, a national bank and a tariff to protect infant industries. His views found favour with New England business and shipping interests, whereas those of his colleague Thos. Jefferson, Sec. of State, favoured a less organised society, agrarian in outlook. These rival interests began to cluster into political parties: Jefferson's being called the Democratic Republicans, Hamilton's the Federalists. In 1795 he resigned when his tariff policy failed. In the 1800 election when Jefferson and Aaron Burr tried for Presidency, Hamilton used his influence in Jefferson's favour and in 1804 he prevented Burr from securing the governorship of New York. Burr provoked a duel and killed him.

HAMILTON, Anthony (1646-1720) a R. Catholic brought up at the exiled court of Charles II, at the Restoration raised Irish troops (The Regiment d'Hamilton) for the French service and fought under Turenne. James II made him gov. of Limerick in 1685 and a major-gen. He was badly beaten at Newtown Butler and fought at the Boyne. After the first S. of Limerick he went to James at St. Germain with dispatches and there remained. He wrote the well known *Mémoires de Grammont* about the bedroom intrigues at Charles II's court in 1662-4 and in 1696 published a description of James II's court in exile. He was with the Old Pretender on his abortive 1707 expedition.

HAMILTON (ARRAN). This powerful Scots family originated in about 1320 when K. Robert the Bruce gave the barony of Cadzow (Lanark) to his supporter **(1) Walter of Hameldone (?-?)** but its high fortune was founded by his descendant **(2) Sir James (?-1479) 1st Ld. HAMILTON** (1445). He was closely associated with the Black Douglas, for his wife was Euphemia Graham, widow of the 5th E. of Douglas; while her daughter, The Fair Maid of Galloway, successively married the 8th and 9th earls. He amassed large estates and, by 1445, a following. He went to Rome with the 8th Earl. He was also present when James II killed the 8th Earl in Stirling Castle in 1452 and felt bound to support the 9th Earl's subsequent rebellion, but after his submission felt free to go over to the King and in 1455 became Sheriff of Lanark and a Commissioner for the Peace with England. Euphemia having died, James III offered his sister Mary, former wife of Thomas Boyd, 1st E. of Arran; this marriage caused a permanent break with the Douglases and from it there sprang two rival lines of claim to the Scots throne (*see* JAMES III OF SCOTS-1 *et seq.*) namely of the Arran Hamiltons and of the Lennox Stuarts, for their daughter **(3) Elizabeth (?-after 1531)** married a Lennox Stewart who were son **(4) James (1477-1529) 2nd Ld. and 2nd or 1st E. of ARRAN (1503)** was a confidant of James IV, for whom he negotiated the marriage with Margaret Tudor and the favourable accompanying treaty in 1503. In 1504 he was prominent in the military reduction of the Isles and later in the restoration of James' cousin K. Hans of Denmark. He always favoured the French connection and furthered his family's presumptive claims. Hence he led the moves which ended in the French Albany becoming regent in 1515 and Margaret Tudor's reaction embroiled him with the Red Douglas (Angus). In 1524 he helped her to end the regency, but this was a miscalculation which paved the way for Angus' return. Consequently when James V escaped from Angus in 1528 Arran supported the armed measures which drove Angus into exile and was rewarded with the Douglas properties at Bothwell. His bastard **(5) Sir James (?-1540)** murdered Lennox after the B. of Linlithgow (1526) and was James V's architect at Linlithgow and Falkland. He was executed for treason. Another bastard **(6) John (1511-71)** was keeper of the privy seal and abbot of Paisley from 1543, Bp. of Dunkeld in 1545 and became Abp. of St. Andrews in 1548. Clever and strong minded, he was very close to his legitimate half brother **(7) James (?-1575) 2nd E. and 1st D. of CHATELHERAULT (1548)** who was a political protestant. Meantime a cousin **(8) Patrick (1540-78)** was a pupil of Luther and was the first Scots protestant martyr, being burned at St. Andrews. In 1542 Arran defeated Beaton for the regency for Mary Q. of Scots and conducted the govt. until the T. of Haddington in 1548 (*see* MARY, Q. OF SCOTS-3) thereafter, though still regent, he was overshadowed by Mary of Guise. In 1553 he was forced to resign and went to France. In 1559, though absent, he was made nominal head of the council of regency by the Congregation. His son **(9) James (1530-1609) 3rd E. of ARRAN** since 1553, had been proposed as a husband for Mary Q. of Scots as far back as 1543. Chatelherault, with Knox's support, now revived the project but the Queen evaded Hamilton power and the

English fleet by landing in Edinburgh, where at the beginning she took the advice of Moray and other moderates. She imprisoned the archbishop in 1563 for publicly celebrating mass and in 1566 banished Chatelherault for opposing the Darnley marriage, but he returned in 1569 after Mary's abdication and the defeat of Hamilton troops at Langside (May 1568). By this time Arran was insane and the birth of James VI had destroyed the Hamilton claims. In 1570 the archbishop arranged the assassination of the Regent Moray by a kinsman and a civil war between the Queen's Men (mostly Hamiltons) and the King's Men (mostly Lennox's) ensued. Lennox became regent with English help and his and English troops destroyed the Hamilton strongholds and in Apr. 1571 seized and hanged the archbishop. The leadership of the family now devolved upon two younger sons of **(7)**, **(10) John (1532-1604) 1st M. of HAMILTON (1599)** and **(11) Claud (?1543-1622) 1st Ld. PAISLEY (1587)**. Usually known as Lords John and Claud Hamilton, they had both been concerned in Mary Q. of Scots' escape and in Moray's assassination and Claud had led the sally from Edinburgh to Stirling which had ended with the death of the regent Lennox (1571). John negotiated the Pacification of Perth in 1573 when the family recovered its lands, but the reconciliation was unsound and after Morton's counter-revolution of 1579 Claud and John were forfeited but escaped abroad. John returned in 1584, Claud in 1586; Claud then joined Huntly's R. Catholic party and was a signatory of some of the Spanish correspondence intercepted in 1589 by the English. Like his brother Arran he became insane. John, however, remained in royal favour and joined in the campaign of 1594 against Huntly. He died just after the union of the crowns. His son **(12) James (1589-1625) 2nd M., E. of ARRAN (1609) and E. of CAMBRIDGE (1619)** was a Scots privy councillor from 1613 and high commissioner for the abortive Spanish marriage in 1623 but in 1624 quarrelled over French policy with Buckingham, by whom he was rumoured to have been poisoned. His son **(13) James (1606-49) 3rd M. and 1st D. (1643)** was Master of the Horse in 1628 and from 1630 to 1634 commanded a British force with the Swedes. He was a leading member of the Committee of Eight which advised Charles I on Scots affairs and in 1638, when the Covenant was being subscribed, he was High Commissioner to the Scots General Assembly which refused to disperse when he dissolved it. The Assembly abolished episcopacy, the Five Articles of Perth, the Book of Common Prayer and the Canons whereupon Hamilton, with Laud and Strafford, advised the holding of a Scots parliament. He commanded the King's troops in the peaceful First Bishops' War and then attempted to negotiate compromises. He was unsuccessful because of a general hardening of attitudes represented by the Covenanters on the one hand and Strafford on the other. In Scotland he tried to maintain a balance between the strongly royalist Montrose and the presbyterian Argyll and to prevent the Scots supporting the English parliament. Faced eventually with a demand to sign the Covenant (1643) he refused and joined the King at Oxford where, at Montrose's instigation, he was promptly arrested and remained in prison at Bristol until Fairfax captured the city in Sept. 1645. Shortly afterwards Montrose was defeated in Scotland and Hamilton made his way to Charles at Newcastle and advised an alliance with the Covenanters since they were the only effective Scots power left. He commanded the Scots invasion of 1648, was defeated at Preston and executed. His daughter **(14) Anne (1636-1716)** succeeded to his dignities; she married William Douglas, eldest son of the 1st M. of Douglas, and on her petition the dignities were conferred on him. *See* DOUGLAS and DOUGLAS-HAMILTON.

HAMILTON, Ds. of. *See* DOUGLAS (HAMILTON).

HAMILTON (HADDINGTON). (1) John (?-?1609) R. Catholic publicist, tutor to the Card. of Bourbon and in 1584 Rector of Paris Univ. He was a leading figure in the Catholic League. In 1594 he escaped to Brussels and thence to Scotland where he died in prison. His nephew **(2) Sir Thomas (1563-1637) Ld. DRUMCAIRN (1592), BINNING (1613), E. of MELROSE (1619), E. of HADDINGTON (1626)** was a lord of session, an Octavian and a favourite of James VI and I. He was pres. of the court of session and Sec. of State from 1616 to 1629 and largely responsible for the Five Articles of Perth. His son **(3) Thomas (1600-40), 2nd E.,** a royalist, died in an explosion. A descendant **(4) Thomas (1780-1858) Ld. MELROSE (1827) 9th E. (1828)** was a Tory M.P. from 1802 to 1827. He was Lord Lieut. of Ireland from 1834 to 1835 and First Lord of the Admiralty from 1841 to 1846.

HAMILTON-TEMPLE-BLACKWOOD, Frederick (1826-1902) Ld. CLANDEBOYE (Ir. 1850), E. of DUFFERIN (Ir. 1871), M. of DUFFERIN AND AVA (1888). Lord in waiting from 1849 to 1852 and from 1854 to 1858 had "all the best qualities of an Irishman and as a companion there was no one like him". Enormously knowledgeable in books, pictures and music, he was so handsome and captivating that the queen hesitated about his appointment as Lord In Waiting. According to Cromer he later "possessed in an eminent degree the qualities of statesmanship, political foresight and literary skill". He was at the Vienna negotiations of 1855 and Special Commissioner in Syria in 1859 to 1860. After secondary posts in govt. from 1864 to 1868 he was gov. gen. of Canada from 1872 to 1878 when federation was still new and untried, Pres. of the Royal Society for a year and then successively ambassador at St. Petersburg (1879-81) and Constantinople (1881-4) (*see* EGYPT-13). In 1884 he went to India as Viceroy and was then ambassador in Rome (1888-91) and in Paris (1891-96). He subsequently held ceremonial offices of various kinds. In his last years he was innocently involved in a dishonestly managed company, in which he had accepted a directorship and which caused him much trouble.

HAMILTON, Ld. George (1666-1737) E. of ORKNEY (1695) general, married Elizabeth Villiers, improbably supposed to have been William III's mistress in 1695. He had already served under William with distinction and was wounded at Namur in the same year. He commanded with great success in all Marlborough's major battles.

HAMMARSKJÖLD, Dag (1906-61), Swedish banker and politician, was the second Sec-Gen. of U.N.O. He took up office in 1953 in succession to Ld. Gladwyn and was killed in an air crash.

HAMMOND (1) George (1763-1853) was *Chargé d'affaires* in Paris from 1788 to 1790, the first British minister to Washington from 1791 to 1795 and U. Sec. of State for Foreign Affairs from 1795 to 1806 and from 1807 to 1809. His son **(2) Edmund (1802-90), Ld. HAMMOND (1874)** after accompanying Stratford Canning round the Mediterranean in 1831-2 became head of the Foreign Office Oriental Dept. and from 1854 to 1873 was permanent U-Sec. of State.

HAMMOND (1) John (1542-89). A delegate to the diet of Schmalkalden in 1578; one of the High Commissioners who examined Campion in 1581 and M.P. 1585-6. His son **(2) John (1551-1617)** was physician to James I. His son **(3) Henry (1605-60)** was chaplain to Charles I in 1647. His nephew **(4) Robert (1621-54)** served in the parliamentary army and, as a col. of foot in the New Model, took Powderham and St. Michaels Mount; captured at Basing he became gov. of the I. of Wight and so Charles I's custodian when he took refuge there in 1647.

HAMPDEN (1) John (1594-1643) was M.P. for Grampound (1621-5), for Wendover in the first three parliaments of Charles I and subsequently represented Buckinghamshire. He early opposed royal attempts to free the crown from the financial power of Parliament. He was a friend and supporter of Sir John Eliot, who was imprisoned for criticism of the royal foreign and financial policy in 1628-9. He was one of the original twelve proprietors of Connecticut in 1632. In 1635 he forced the issue of taxation by royal prerogative by refusing to pay the sum of £1 on the second writ of ship money and contesting the legality of the writ in the courts. The arguments of the two sides in the litigation crystallised the whole constitutional controversy in the mind of educated opinion. Judgment was given against him in the Exchequer Chamber in 1638 and it became clear to parliamentarians that the law had to be altered. In the Short Parliament of 1640 he therefore opposed the grant of twelve subsidies in exchange for the abolition of ship money and in the Long Parliament he was one of Pym's strongest supporters. He always, however, leaned towards the supremacy of justice and, though a manager of Strafford's impeachment, he opposed the attainder and in 1641 insisted on Strafford's right to be heard by counsel on it. He supported the Root and Branch Bill and the Grand Remonstrance, but was not a puritan nor against monarchy or episcopacy as such. As a dangerous opponent of the King he was one of the five members whom the King attempted to arrest in Jan. 1642. Thereafter, knowing that war was inevitable, he supported the Commons resolutions for taking control of the Tower and the militia and became a member of the Committee of Safety. He then virtually abandoned central politics, raised a regiment and was mortally wounded at Chalgrove Field. His son **(2) Richard (1631-95)** was a member of Cromwell's House of Lords and from 1660 until 1695 was almost continuously an M.P. He moved the Exclusion Bill of 1670 and in 1689 was Chairman of the Commons Committee which declared the throne vacant. He was Ch. of the Exch. from 1690 to 1694. His son **(3) John (?1656-96)** who was M.P. in 1679 and from 1681 to 1690, was imprisoned in 1683 for involvement in the Rye House Plot. In 1684 he was accused of plotting an insurrection and was fined. Re-imprisoned after Monmouth's rebellion (1685) he was condemned to death. Forced to plead for his life he was, surprisingly, pardoned. In the Convention Parliament of 1689 he was prominent as an extreme whig and later opposed Halifax. He committed suicide.

HAMPDEN CLUBS. The Corresponding Society and Society for Constitutional Information were destroyed by legislation against societies with branches. Each Hampden Club evaded the legislation by being in law a separate body but carried on their work. Sir Francis Burdett was chairman of the first of them in 1811. Their petitions and recruiting meetings were co-ordinated by the experienced agitator, Major John Cartwright, but membership was confined to people with £300 in land. They wanted to extend the franchise to all property owners, but their programme had insufficient fire to attract widespread support even after Wm. Cobbett injected greater sensationalism by personal attacks on the Prince Regent and criticism of govt. spending and debt management. Hence the clubs neither led popular agitation nor got support from established parties. In fact agitation against the Corn Bill of 1813 was spontaneous and in spite of the clubs, which slowly declined after 1815.

HAMPSHIRE (1) Roman Hampshire centred on Winchester (Venta Belgarum) from which roads radiated towards Southampton, Old Sarum and Mildenhall (Wilts.) and Silchester (Calleva Atrebatum). There was also a road from Southampton, inland of the various estuaries and harbours, to Chichester. The county was one of large villages and estates which in the 4th cent. exported wheat and wool to Gaul.

(2) The Jutes, who settled the I. of Wight, also penetrated in the 6th cent. across the great W. Hampshire harbours into the Meon Valley and probably settled in the New Forest area as well. The Gewissae or W. Saxons who ultimately made Winchester their capital and subdued the Jutes, did not arrive until the 7th cent. when Winchester and Silchester were in decay, probably through the severance of the continental trade. Winchester revived and became the episcopal see after the W. Saxons arrived and the establishment of the Frankish dominion in Gaul.

(3) By the Norman Conquest the county was agriculturally prosperous and the greatest landowner was the Church. The see of Winchester was and long remained one of the wealthiest in the country. There were also 31 royal manors scattered mostly around the periphery. The greatest private landowner was Hugh de Port. Lesser, or single manor owners, were confined almost wholly to the Itchen Valley and the New Forest, afforested in 1109. Of the 43 religious houses eventually established, 11 were in Winchester itself and 10 were alien. Of the 33 non-alien houses, 5 were Benedictine, 4 Cistercian, 7 Augustinian and there were five friaries. There was a substantial pilgrim (or tourist) traffic until the Dissolution of the Monasteries (see PILGRIM'S WAY).

(4) The loss of Normandy under John exposed the coast to piracy and French attacks and the population to the depredations of troops passing through or quartered on the way abroad. The I. of Wight assumed great importance in the naval defence of the coast and of Southampton and the fortune of the ports varied with peace and war. Ships were being built at Portsmouth Hard at the end of the 14th cent. but Portsmouth only began its important career as a naval base under the Commonwealth. By 1698 it had built as many of the larger ships in commission as Southampton.

(5) As elsewhere in the Kingdom the early export of wool gave way to cloth making in the later middle ages, but this in its turn gave way to coarse and sail cloth connected with the maritime industries. The strongly agricultural nature of the county supported the allied tanning and brewing and there were important saltpans down to the 18th cent.

(6) The railway reached Basingstoke in 1839 and Southampton in 1843. The population rose from 219,000 to nearly 800,000 between 1801 and 1901, the greater part after 1843.

HAMPTON COURT. Wolsey leased the manor from the Knights of St. John in 1514; he built the magnificent Tudor palace and surrendered it to Henry VIII in 1524 but continued to use it until his disgrace in 1529. It was refurnished for Anne Boleyn and for Jane Seymour, who bore Edward VI and died there in 1537. The unfortunate Katherine Howard lived there and the way in which she was prevented from seeing Henry VIII while awaiting execution gave rise to one of the many ghost stories about the Palace. It remained a regular royal residence until 1641 and in 1647 Charles I was in custody there. He had spent a great deal on pictures, furniture and hangings. These were partly dispersed after his death but Cromwell used it and prevented further depredations. Hence it was available at the Restoration and Charles II and William and Mary, especially Mary, laid out the park and gardens nearly in their modern form. They also commissioned Wren to rebuild it in a style more consistent with that of Versailles. Between 1699 and 1718 he pulled down half the Tudor palace, built the classical block and laid out most of Bushey Park. Fortunately his grandiose plans for the rest (which included a dome) never materialised. The palace remained in use as such until the accession of George III (1760) since when it has been mainly a public showpiece.

HAMPTON COURT CONFERENCE (Jan. 1604) was summoned by James I, who also presided, to reconcile the bishops and the puritans, whose Millenary Petition on church reform had just been presented to him. The puritans were led by John Rainolds (1549-1607) Dean of Lincoln; the bishops by Abp. Bancroft, who rejected the puritan demand for reduction in the authority of the bishops and was supported by James with the words "No bishop, no King". The conference failed politically but initiated the work on the Authorised Version.

HAMPTON COURT, T. of (1562). *See* HUGUENOTS.

HAMSOCN. Attacking a man in his house. It was regarded as a breach of the King's Peace.

HANAPER OFFICE, the department of the Chancery which received the fees for sealing and enrolling documents and accounted for the profits. It was established after the death of Ralph Neville in 1244 and replaced the earlier system by which the profits of Chancery were the perquisites of the Chancellor. Hence-forward he was almost invariably a salaried official. In Ireland it was combined with the Crown Office and its abolition in 1921 prevented further Irish peers being summoned to the House of Lords.

HANBURY WILLIAMS (1) John Hanbury (1664-1734) an early industrialist, developed estates and ironworks at Pontypool. He was whig M.P. for Gloucester from 1701 to 1715 and for Monmouthshire from 1721, when he became a director of the New South Sea Co. He was one of Marlborough's executors. His son **(2) Sir Charles Hanbury (1708-59) Williams (1729),** also M.P. for Monmouthshire (1734-47) and for Leominster from 1754, was Minister to Dresden in 1746, to Berlin and Dresden in 1751 to 1753, to Vienna in 1753 and Dresden again in 1754 and to St. Petersburg from 1755 to 1757.

HANDEL or HAENDEL, George Frederick (1685-1759) a Saxon, after conducting and composing operas in Hamburg and Italy, came to Hanover in 1710 and thence to England where he settled (1712). His *Te Deum for the Peace of Utrecht* gained him a royal annuity in 1712. He was director of music for the D. of Chandos from 1718 to 1720 and of the Royal Academy of Music from 1720 to 1728 and Court Composer from 1727. His immense output included the *Water Music* (1715), the *Anthems for the Coronation of George II* (1727) performed at coronations ever since, the *Messiah* (1741), the *Dettingen Te Deum* (1743) and the *Music for Royal Fireworks* (1750). His personal and musical popularity was enormous. The splendour of his choral settings for the language of the Authorised Version associated the majesty of royalty and religion in a form in which many people could take part and his oratorios, particularly *Messiah*, have been performed by massed choirs before mass audiences ever since.

HANDFASTING (Sc.) a temporary marriage for a year and a day, conferring legitimacy on children born during that period. **(2)** a form of betrothal practised on the Anglo-Scottish border. It sometimes created a locally recognised status which did not constitute border treason, or which evaded a canonical impediment.

HANDLOOMS. *See* TEXTILES.

HANKEY, Maurice Pascal (1877-1963) 1st Ld. (1938), became Sec. of the Committee of Imperial Defence in 1912, of the War Council in 1914, of the War Cabinet in 1916 (until 1918), of the Cabinet from 1919 and of the Imperial Conferences of the 1920s. In these various simultaneous capacities he strongly influenced all kinds of policy and created and developed the Cabinet secretariat. He retired from all these posts in 1939 but, at the outbreak of World War II, entered Chamberlain's cabinet as Min. without Portfolio. When Chamberlain fell in 1940 he retired again but was persuaded back into office as Ch. of the Duchy (1940-1) and Post-master Gen. (1941-2). He was against the policy of unconditional surrender and also against the trials of war criminals.

HANLEY. *See* STOKE-ON-TRENT.

HANMER, Sir Thomas (1677-1746), a Tory M.P. from 1701 to 1727 and a leader of the attack on Marlborough for malversation of military funds in 1712 and a champion of the peace with France, was Speaker in 1714-5. Though leader of the Hanoverian Tories, he got no favour from George I. He edited an edition of Shakespeare in 1743-4.

HANNINGTON, Walter (1896-1966), Marxist and inspirer of the disruptive shop stewards movement in World War I, he was a founder of the Communist Party of Great Britain in 1920 and in 1921 organised the Nat. Unemployed Workers Movement (N.U.W.M.) through which he organised violent demonstrations in 1922, 1925 and 1932 and was imprisoned. In 1932, 1934 and 1936 he was organising hunger marches and campaigning against the means test. His main purpose, in which he failed, was to engineer the Marxist Revolutionary Situation. His N.U.W.M. went into cold storage at the outbreak of World War II but from 1942 to 1951 he was national organiser of the Amalgamated Engineering Union.

HANOVER. ELECTORATE AND KINGDOM. (1) The much partitioned mediaeval Guelph duchy of Brunswick-Lüneburg had by 1634 coalesced into two: Lüneburg (capital Celle) the larger and Kalenberg (capital Hanover). In 1641 George of Kalenberg, who was also heir presumptive to Lüneburg, laid down that after his succession to Lüneburg, the duchies should be indivisible but never under the same ruler, the nearest heir having the option to chose Lüneburg. In 1658 Ernest Augustus of Kalenberg married Sophia of the Palatinate, a granddaughter of James I. This marriage eventually led to the Hanoverian succession in England.

(2) To frustrate the clause against union, Ernest Augustus persuaded his elder brother George William of Lüneburg never to marry. Hence George William took only a morganatic wife, Eleanor d'Olbreuse, and they had an only child, Sophia Dorothea. To make sure, Ernest Augustus married his son George Lewis (the future George I) to her in 1682. He gave her the future George II and Sophia, future Queen of Prussia, but made her miserable. Meanwhile Ernest Augustus, like other princes, had, for a consideration, helped the emperor in the Turkish wars of 1683 and 1685; as both a reward and a counterweight to Hohenzollern Brandenburg, the emperor created Lüneburg an electorate in 1692. In 1694 George Lewis divorced Sophia Dorothea and shut her up for life in the castle of Celle. In 1698 he succeeded in Kalenberg and in 1705 in Lüneburg. He kept the capital at Hanover. The electorate was known as the Electorate of Hanover from the start.

(3) Besides the two duchies, George ruled other adjacent territories including the counties of Diepholtz and Hoya, which gave him control of the upper Weser R. and put the inland trade from Bremen under his influence, and the duchy of Lauenburg, where he could interrupt the trade of Hamburg up the Elbe to Bohemia. In addition the episcopal principality of Osnabrück was ruled alternately by a R. Catholic bishop and a protestant member of his family; it straddled the Ems Valley and could influence trade from Emden and, of course, as more of the North Sea ports became susceptible to pressure collectively, the greater the pressure upon each. The Danes too had wrested Bremen and Verden from the Swedes; by 1714 these ports had almost fallen into George's hands. Thus Hanover could take profits from most of the German North Sea trade, in which British interests predominated.

(4) George took his seat in the electoral college in 1708. This made Hanover constitutionally important in the Empire. Otherwise Hanoverian foreign policy had been concerned mainly with the struggling Baltic powers, Denmark, Sweden, Prussia and Russia. An ambitious dynast in a small state (perhaps 600,000 people) without natural frontiers had to be agile, well informed and despotic to survive at all. The first two Georges knew more about European politics than their English ministers and disliked English politics because of the limitations of their constitutional position. They much preferred the deferential cosiness of the electorate to the strenuous life and criticism of London. They were absent from Britain for 19 periods of about six months between 1714 and 1760. Once George I appointed the P. of Wales as Guardian of the Realm and George II appointed his able queen Caroline four times. The other 14 times the whole cabinet were appointed Lords Justices as a collective regency with limited powers. When the King was in Hanover one of the Secretaries of State attended him. Since the regency could not, without reference to the King, decide questions of war and peace or dissolve parliament, create a peerage or deal with serious military matters, the attendant S. of State dominated policy, especially foreign policy.

(5) From the Hanoverians' point of view the ruler was an absentee. George I and II, however, reserved most, even trivial, decisions to themselves. Hence after the King the important personality was his Hanoverian minister attendant in England. In the first two reigns these were Hattorf (1715-37), Steinberg (1738-49) and Münchhausen (1749-62). These, being country gentry, were temperamentally suited to their master's paternalism. The govt. was enlightened; for example, in 1737 George II founded the Univ. of Göttingen, which soon attracted European-wide talent.

(6) As the English connection was liable to drag the peaceful electorate into international conflicts, the Elector-Kings reasonably wanted English policy to avoid the worst consequences. Conversely English statesmen found that Hanover in hostile hands might be a hostage against English overseas interests. The still powerful crown influence on foreign policy and the dictates of international prestige compelled an accommodation between the divergent views of the Elector and the King's English advisers, even though Westminster considered Hanover a foreign country (it was even represented, in addition to the King's Hanoverian Chancery, by a diplomatic resident). Britain could seldom help Hanover directly. She had to have allies who might protect the Electorate.

(7) George I arrived in Britain in Sept. 1714 when the Great Northern War was raging on the Hanoverian doorstep. Within a year he had a French-based Jacobite rebellion on his hands in Scotland. Louis XIV had died in Sept. 1715. His successor was a sickly child of five. The regent, Orléans, under the T. of Utrecht, was next in succession but the Spanish Bourbons still put French ambitions and Orléans was anxious for guarantees if the young Louis XV died. In secret conversations at The Hague and in Hanover between Orléans' confessor, Dubois, and Stanhope, the S. of State, a treaty of mutual guarantee was outlined (July 1716) but there were formal and bureaucratic delays. At this point the Czar, Peter the Great, who had been co-operating with Denmark and Hanover against Sweden, suddenly occupied the adjacent duchy of Mecklenburg, while the Swedes, to embarrass Hanoverian efforts to gain Bremen and Verden, were fomenting a Dutch-based Jacobite raid on England. Brandenburg was inclined to support the Russians. The French had powerful influence both at Stockholm and with the Czar. The Anglo-French negotiation thus became urgent both for Britain and for Hanover. The Elector-King saw to it that it was pressed through with speed. The Triple Alliance (for the Dutch acceded in Jan. 1717) was signed in Nov. 1716. It remained the foundation of British-Hanoverian policy until the 1740s. The French induced Peter to evacuate Mecklenburg, and Britain faced only minor Jacobite threats until 1745.

(8) Charles XII of Sweden was killed late in 1718. His death removed the main obstacle to peace in the Baltic, for Sweden was exhausted and Russia satisfied. Stanhope, with George, sought to profit from this but the touchy and jealous George was at feud with the equally touchy and jealous Prussian Frederick William, without whom nothing could be done. The Swedish oligarchy was desperate but hoped to salvage something by making peace with Russia or the western powers and using the first comer to help against the second. Stanhope feared that Russian domination in the Baltic might endanger trade and the Royal Navy. He decided to combine the western powers in a settlement with Sweden, leaving Russia to fend for herself. He talked George and Frederick William into committing their interests to the British ambassador in Sweden, who should secure Bremen and Verden for Hanover and Pomerania with Stettin for Brandenburg. Carteret now went to Stockholm (July 1719). He was just in time. The Russians were raiding the neighbourhood and the bankrupt Swedish court was ready to capitulate. He exuded confidence and common sense. He offered protection through the British fleet and a subsidy, and by treaties, signed in Aug., obtained *inter alia* the objects of Stanhope's Anglo-Prussian agreement. In 1720 he mediated the P. of Fredericksborg between Denmark and Sweden; the Baltic war moved eastwards and petered out in the P. of Nystad (1721).

(9) These Hanoverian influenced events had, too, beneficial effects in the Mediterranean by contributing to Spanish isolation and defeat in the Anglo-Spanish war of 1718-20. On the other hand Hanoverian interests were largely irrelevant to the T. of Hanover (q.v.) (Sept. 1725) negotiated by Townshend but so-called simply because George I was on holiday there.

(10) The maritime power's guarantee of the Pragmatic sanction (T. of Vienna July 1731) indirectly involved Hanover which, in common with most German states, made a direct guarantee in Jan. 1732. In the War of the Polish Succession (1733-5), however, Britain refused to support the Emperor, though bound by treaty to do so and in the War of the Austrian Succession the British support for Maria Theresa, forced upon Walpole by excitable public opinion, was initially qualified by Hanoverian neutrality when French troops threatened the electorate (Sept. 1741). George II even voted for the Bavarian candidate in the Imperial Election (Jan. 1742). By the summer of 1742, however, Carteret had persuaded him to abandon neutrality and, when the Elector-King professed poverty, took the Hanoverian army into British pay. Using this as a lever, Carteret persuaded Prussia to make peace with Austria (P. of Berlin July 1742) and to enter into an alliance (Nov.) which, it was hoped, would protect the Electorate from the French. Meanwhile he was organising a further composite alliance, ostensibly to support Maria Theresa's claims under the Pragmatic Sanction, but actually against French power in Germany. The combined "pragmatic army" (about 10% Hanoverian) was under George II's command. He defeated the French at Dettingen (July 1743) at a time when France and Britain were officially at peace.

(11) Hanover exerted little effect on, and was itself little affected by, the war which ended in the P. of Aix-la-Chapelle (Oct. 1748) but in Mar. 1751 Frederick, P. of Wales, who had spent much of his time there, died. His son George (III), who was brought up in England, never visited the Electorate. Meanwhile European diplomacy and colonial wars were moving towards the Seven Years' War, in which Britain's only ally was Prussia. The British declared war on France in May 1756. Frederick the Great attacked Saxony on the way to Bohemia in Aug. but by May 1757 Austria and France, by their alliance of Versailles, had consolidated the two wars into one. A French invasion of Hanover followed. The French defeated Cumberland at Hastenbeck (July) and forced him to capitulate by a Convention signed at Kloster Zeven which neutralised the electorate (Sept.). George II

and the Tories were furious and Cumberland was disgraced, but Frederick's spectacular victories over the French (Rossbach, Nov.) and the Austrians (Leuthen, Dec.) altered the situation. The British Hanoverian army was reconstituted under P. Ferdinand of Brunswick and the French driven back to the Rhineland. A French counter attack in 1759 led, however, to their crushing defeat on the Hanoverian frontier at Minden (1 Aug. 1759).

(12) In Oct. 1760 George II's death loosened the hitherto close personal English connection and the electorate was henceforth effectively ruled by its local gentry. On the whole they did it well.

(13) From 1763 to the French Revolution Hanoverian tranquillity was secured by the policy of Prussia, which was prepared to rely upon Britain to keep the French in check while she and Russia devoured Poland. The final Polish partitions (1792 and 1795) took place at the height of the revolutionary wars, in which Britain held her own at sea but her various allies were worn down or defeated, or deserted her. Of these Prussia was one. After the P. of Lunéville (Feb. 1801) the Prussians occupied Hanover (Apr.) but immediately after the short period of the P. of Amiens (Mar. 1802-May 1803) the French, by way of precaution, took over the electorate from them (June); then in 1805, after their victories at Ulm and Austerlitz, they ceded it to Prussia in exchange for Cleves, Neuchâtel and Ansbach (T. of Schönbrunn, Dec. 1805). By Oct. 1806 the pendulum had swung back again. After the Prussian disaster at Jena, Hanover was incorporated into the full Bonaparte system: the south in 1807 became part of the Kingdom of Westphalia, the north in 1810 an imperial province. The whole was liberated in 1813.

(14) The scheme for security against further French adventures inaugurated at Vienna involved, in the north and with British prompting, an enlarged Holland backed by a strengthened Hanover. Accordingly Hanover was re-established as a Kingdom: it lost Lauenburg to Prussia but received Osnabrück, Emden, East Frisia and some other minor territories. The rule of the gentry was consecrated in a limited parliamentary constitution vaguely resembling the British. In 1830 William IV appointed the D. of Cambridge as his viceroy: and in 1833 the remaining institutions of serfdom were abolished and the constitution considerably liberalised. This did not, however, last. In 1837 by operation of Salic Law, Ernest Augustus, D. of Cumberland, became King at Q. Victoria's accession to Britain and he immediately suppressed the constitution. He was succeeded by George V of Hanover in 1851. In 1866, as a result of the Austro-Prussian War in which Hanover supported Austria, the entire Kingdom was annexed by Prussia, of which it became a province. Prussia thereby added control of the North Sea ports to her Baltic influence in Schleswig- Holstein. The *Welfenfonds* (Guelph family trust) also passed under Prussian control and in 1870 was used to bribe Ludwig II of Bavaria. *See* BAVARIA; BISMARCK; PRUSSIA.

HANOVER, T. of (1725) or HERRENHAUSEN, T. of. Britain, France and Prussia guaranteed each other, Prussia against presumed threats from Austria and Spain. They were to resist attacks on Gibraltar or Minorca, encroachments by the Austrian Ostend Co. and the persecution of protestants in the Empire. As a special inducement to Prussia, K. Frederick William's claims in Jülich and Berg were to be supported: P. Frederick of Britain was to marry a Prussian princess and P. Frederick of Prussia a daughter of the P. of Wales. Holland acceded to the treaty in 1726, Sweden and Denmark in 1727. Prussia had already deserted in Oct. 1726 before the short and limited Anglo-Spanish war of 1727-8 broke out.

HANSARD (1) Luke (1752-1828) began to print the House of Commons Journals in 1774. His son **(2) Thomas Curson** (1776-1833) began to print Parliamentary Debates in 1803. *See* STOCKDALE.

HANSE, HANSA or (less properly) HANSEATIC LEAGUE. (1) *Merchant Hanses.* In the late 11th cent. north German merchants in foreign towns began to form guilds, called Hanses, which negotiated corporately with the local powers. Hanses from particular towns were widely established by the mid 12th cent; Henry II conferred privileges on the Cologne Hanse in London c. 1157, contemporaneously with the foundation of Lübeck. By this time Hanseatic operations extended from Russia, by way of the Baltic, to England. At certain places, which attracted traders from many towns, clearing houses (*kontors*) were established. The four great recognised *kontors* were at Novgorod, Bergen (Norway), Bruges and the Steelyard (*Stalhof*) in London. Life in these establishments was collegiate and, except at Bruges, enclosed. In dealings with local authorities the merchants naturally expected the support of their home towns. The *kontors,* however, being inter-urban if not international, had considerable independence. The risk that they might, unasked, embroil their backers in international complications led to demands at home for control. In 1161 a Hanse of Gotland merchants (mostly from Lübeck) at the fortified emporium of Visby, began to control the Russian trade and the Novgorod *Kontor.* Members of this Hanse founded Riga (1201) and Stockholm (c. 1250). These activities reflected the rapid rise of Lübeck, due to its advantageous position on the neck of Jutland, where at this time there was a canal. Danish claims on Holstein were related to this fact and a Danish attempt to divert all trade through the Sound led to war and a German victory at Bornhöved in 1227. This eased the westward commercial expansion of the Baltic cities and the Bergen *Kontor* fell under the control of Lübeck. In 1231 the Teutonic Knights began to conquer Prussia. They always admitted *bourgeois* to knighthood and many of them, at this time, were English; as much traders as soldiers, they were soon shipping timber to Britain. By 1237 they were in Livonia.

(2) *The Hanses of Cities.* The principal European marts were in Flanders. The Bruges *Kontor*'s demands for local privileges were angrily conceded by the count and the trading cities in 1253 but their maintenance was beyond its strength. Hence constant calls upon the political and naval resources of the home towns and the formation between 1256 and 1264 of a Hanse of the interested Wendish cities (Lübeck, Hamburg, Rostock, Stralsund with Wismar and Lüneburg to control as well as support the *Kontor.* By 1280 Flemish discontent brought trade to a stand-still and the Hanse imposed its first embargo by moving the *Kontor* of Bruges to the rival port of Ardenbourg, where it remained until 1282. This disruption also indirectly caused the definitive organisation of the London Steelyard in 1281. Flemish trade was now a major international issue and the struggle to dominate it gradually involved a widening circle of powers and trading cities. The Bruges' *Kontor* was moved to Ardenbourg again from 1307 to 1309 and its activities were regulated by a statute in 1347; but the problem of policy control remained.

(3) *Organisation of the League.* In 1356, therefore, Lübeck convoked the first Hanseatic Diet (*Hansetag*) which proclaimed the Hanse of Cities or "Hanseatic League". This amorphous commercial *entente* between the so-called *Seventy-Two Cities* embraced at one time or another 199 towns, the Teutonic Knights and the peasant republic of Dithmarschen. Most were N. German, but membership stretched outward as far as Tiel (Holland), Stockholm (Sweden), Reval (Estonia) and Cracow (Poland). Outside this area there were the four great *Kontors* and also factory houses at Pskov, Polotsk and Kovno in the East, Oslo and Tönsberg in Norway, Antwerp and Sluys in Flanders and in England at Ipswich, Yarmouth, King's Lynn, Boston and Hull. The Boston steelyard was controlled from Bergen, the rest from London. This great Hanse had certain peculiarities. Apart from Lübeck and the Knights its members were subject to different local princes whose divergent policies tended towards disruption. Secondly the commercial interests of the main groups of towns differed amongst themselves. Three, later four, such groups were recognised: these were Lübeck with the *Wendish* cities; the *Westphalians* led by Cologne included Dortmund, Osnabrück and Soest; the *Saxons* led by Brunswick and Magdeburg originally included all the rest, until the *Prusso-Livonian* cities led by Danzig broke away and formed a fourth. Local and regional diets met more often than the *Hansetag* and the Hanse as a whole never developed central institutions. The execution of common policy was left in practice and after 1418 in theory too, to the City of Lübeck. Loyalty even within the groups was partial. In all the Hanseatic wars some and often many members contracted out.

(4) *The Trade.* The Hanseatics introduced the cog, a roundship which, though slower than the Scandinavian longship, carried ten times the weight. A trade in bulk low-value cargoes now became possible in the north. Cereals were bought in Russia and Poland, butter in Sweden, timber in Livonia and Prussia (English bowmen were armed with Prussian Yew), salt herring in Scania, beer in N.W. Germany and to these were added high value consignments of Russian wax and furs, Prussian amber, and metals, especially iron and copper from Sweden, Germany and Transylvania. Wine was bought in the Rhineland. These goods were funnelled to Flanders and exchanged for manufactured goods, mainly English cloth and other, mostly Flemish, textiles, armaments, jewellery, and oriental products and spices brought north by the Italians. The low salinity of the Baltic ensured an immense northern market for salt and brought a 14th cent. extension to the saltpans of Bourgneuf (Brittany), Brouage and Portugal. Outward salt ships often carried pilgrims to Compostela and made contacts with Gascon wine growers on the way. After the English were expelled from Bordeaux in 1453 Hanseatic carriers intervened in the Bristol wine trade. The volume of trade is unknown but was large: in 1368, 858 inward and 911 outward sailings were recorded at Lübeck and about 2000 tons of butter, 80 of copper and 260 of pig iron were consigned there from Stockholm alone. The quinquennial average of English cloth exported by the Hanses was 1690 bolts in 1368, 5686 in 1418 and 20,400 in 1518, this increase coinciding with a decline in raw wool. In 1568 about 86,000 tons of rye passed the Sound, 68,000 from Danzig alone.

(5) *The Decline.* The ultimate Hanseatic sanction had been boycott and embargo; this depended on a near monopoly in sea-borne carriage of essentials, such as food and clothing, for which there was expanding demand. As long as the European marts of Flanders were in the hands of politically weak cities and govts. this could be effective, but from the mid 14th cent. Hanseatic operations were impeded by the organisation of territorial powers able to resist purely economic pressure and to sap the independence of the member cities within their confines. The decline, like the rise, began in the East. In 1361 the Danes sacked Visby, which never recovered. The war lasted until 1370. From 1375 the three Scandinavian powers were united under a common regency culminating in the Union of Kalmar (1397). In 1386 came the Jagellonian Union of Poland and Lithuania. Sporadic wars disrupted trade but peace in 1390 brought piracy at the hands of discharged sailors, the so-called *Vitalienbrüder.* In 1410 the Poles overthrew the Teutonic Knights at Tannenberg and the latters' system of state trading collapsed; and between 1408 and 1416 there were insurrections and revolutions, especially at Lübeck itself. There was a clash of interest between the local crafts and the trading patricians whose imports undercut local manufactures. High commercial profits had previously brought fringe benefits to the craftsmen but profits were no longer high. Patrician rule was however, re-established and in 1418 the *Hansetag* formally committed the management of Hanseatic affairs to Lübeck, to avoid the expense of frequent meetings. This sign of disunion was soon confirmed. In 1426 the Danes imposed a shipping toll on the Sound, never lifted until 1857. The Wendish cities blockaded the Sound regardless of the interests of the eastern or the western members, whose trade was diverted through Lübeck. This benefited neutrals, especially the Dutch, whose growing merchant fleet made inroads into old Hanseatic preserves. The peace of Vordingborg (1435) exempted Wendish shipping from the tolls and re-established their privileges in the Danish dominions, particularly Norway, to the detriment of other members. The Wends now turned on the Dutch and in 1438 blockaded the Sound against them. Since Dutch freight was lower than Wendish this collided with the cereals and timber interests of the Eastern membership which was openly hostile. A further Danish intervention ended the matter. The P. of Copenhagen (1441) opened the Danish dominions and the Baltic to Dutch trade. This, of course, weakened the *Kontor* at Bruges which ceased to be the exclusive Flemish exchange for products from these huge areas.

(6) If the English Merchant Adventurers are equated with the Dutch, an analogous situation was developing in the West. In the 15th cent. the country weavers, the Crown and the landowning nobility on the whole favoured the Hanse, whose support was needed during the wars and civil wars. These same wars, just as the Burgundian state was forming, diverted more and more of the cloth trade to the merchants, who sought to evade the Bruges' *Kontor* and sell direct in continental fairs; a merchant Staple was set up at Calais and by 1400 English factories were established as far afield as Danzig. Relations between the Hanse and English govts. deteriorated; even the Teutonic Knights closed the English factories in Prussia from 1420 to 1428. In 1449 the English seized a large channel convoy, half of which was Wendish, as part of the operations which ended the Truce of Tours. The nobility on the one hand and the Eastern and Western cities on the other restricted the conflict. By 1458 the war was a privateering feud between Lübeck and the Calais Staple. When, however, Charles the Bold succeeded in Burgundy in 1467, the situation deteriorated again. Commercial agreements between him and Edward IV opened his dominions to English trade. The Hanse supported Warwick. In 1470 he drove Edward overseas to Burgundian Flanders. In 1471 Edward returned with Burgundian help and Danzig shipping. A Wendish attempt to embargo English trade led not only to full scale war (ended only in 1474) but shook the Hanse to its foundations, for Cologne sided with the English and was excluded from the Hanse until 1476.

(7) Hanseatic privileges in England were eventually restored but English merchants abroad were not confined by Hanseatic regulation. Moreover, political and geographical considerations were eroding the organisation. In 1466 the Teutonic Knights had become vassals of Poland; in 1478 the Muscovite Ivan III captured Novgorod and in 1494 closed the *Kontor*. Consequently the Livonian cities stepped in, engrossed the trade and excluded the Wends. The great herring shoals moved from Scania to the North Sea where the Dutch could easily harvest them. The silting of the Zwiin after 1450 progressively diverted ships from Bruges to Antwerp, whither many Hanseatic merchants had moved by 1488. In 1508 the Danes abolished the privileges of the Norwegian factories. Hamburg and Bremen started fishing Icelandic waters and by landing the catches direct

in Britain evaded the Bergen *Kontor*, this not only damaged the interests of Lübeck but Bergen merchants ceased to frequent their steelyard at Boston.

(8) The Wends, though still prosperous as carriers, were losing the profits of international exchange. The south Germans, especially the Fuggers, were beginning to divert the Eastern trade overland towards Frankfurt. This created special interests among the inland Silesian and Polish cities. In 1518, on the eve of the Reformation, the *Hansetag* noted that the membership of 31 towns appeared to have lapsed. The Reformation loosened the solidarity of the Hanse still further. An attempt to re-establish some kind of unity by Jurgen Wullenwever, burgomaster of Lübeck from 1533 to 1535, foundered in a naval disaster against the Danes and in 1557 a *Hansetag* tried a further reorganisation centring on the appointment of a Syndic who was a common diplomatic official. Heinrich Sudermann's personal qualities, in this office until 1591, delayed the decline but English enterprise was too much for him. In 1563 the English (having lost Calais in 1558) moved their Staple to the non-Hanseatic town of Emden (which enjoyed a meteoric prosperity) but nearby Hamburg conferred privileges upon them in 1567. These were not renewed in 1578 whereupon the English returned to Emden and also set up at Stade. Frustrated at Danzig they also established a factory in 1579 at Elbing, which was promptly expelled from the Hanse, but suffered no inconvenience. The old commercial sanctions were ceasing to be effective. The Hanse accordingly appealed to the imperial diet which voted for the expulsion of the English. This was not confirmed by the Emperor, but in the war with Spain it was used as a pretext by the English, who accused him of aiding the Spaniards. Hanseatic convoys were seized in Lisbon and elsewhere in 1589. The London steelyard ceased to operate. Hostilities, however, remained informal and English trade continued to grow. In 1597 the Hanse at last obtained a ban. Q. Elizabeth now expelled the few merchants who remained and seized all Hanseatic property. Though restored in 1606 this practically ended Hanseatic activity in Britain. The collapse of the Hanse was now inevitable, hastened by the Thirty Years' War and the Swedish invasions of Livonia and Prussia. The last *Hansetag* was called for 1669 but adjourned for lack of numbers.

HANSE. A subscription or entrance fee to a guild.

HANSEN'S DISEASE. *See* LEPROSY.

HANSOM. *See* CAB.

HANWAY, Jonas (1712-86), an export merchant, made a practical rather than an emotional appeal to the rising post-1740 Methodist conscience on the difficulties of the young under developing industrialisation, partly as a writer on such issues as baby-farming, child chimney sweeps and prisons and partly by helping to found the Marine Society (1756) for apprenticing boys to seamanship, the Magdalen Hospital, a refuge for reformed prostitutes, and Sunday Schools. He was also a gov. of the Foundling Hospital.

HARALD HARDRAADA (c. 1015-66) K. of NORWAY (1047) half-brother of St. Olav, fought at the B. of Stiklestad (1030) (where St. Olav was killed) and fled to Constantinople where he became the commander of the Varangian Guard, lover of the Empress Zoe and a victor in various campaigns in Italy and N. Africa. He returned to Scandinavia rich and famous, marrying Elizabeth of Novgorod on the way and made an alliance with Sweyn of Denmark against his nephew Magnus. Magnus detached him from the alliance with half of Norway (1046). He took the other half as well when Magnus died. In 1066 he revived Magnus' claim to England and sailed, picking up men in Shetland and Orkney, with 200-300 ships to Scotland and united with Earl Tostig, brother of Harold II. *For later events see* HAROLD II; *see also* EDWARD THE CONFESSOR.

HARALD HEREFOOT, King (?-1040) *s.* of K. Canute. *See* CANUTE AND HIS SONS.

HARARE (Zimbabwe) formerly SALISBURY (S. Rhodesia).

HARCLA[Y] or HARTCLA, Andrew (?-1323) E. of CARLISLE (1322), sheriff of Cumberland and Warden of the West March, was a veteran of the Scottish wars. In 1322 he brought about the defeat of Thomas of Lancaster by Edward II at Boroughbridge through the deployment of his Border archers and pikemen. He was rewarded with his earldom. The elevation of the Despensers and wholesale forfeitures disorganised the northern defences when the Scottish truce expired at this time. The Scots ravaged the north-west. English retaliation in the Lothians failed and the pursuing Scots nearly captured Edward II between Byland and Rievaulx (Yorks). Heads of religious houses and even the palatine Bp. of Durham started to treat with the Scots. Harcla dismissed his troops and approached Robert the Bruce direct. They agreed that six representatives from each side should negotiate a peace on the basis that Bruce offered Harcla his daughter in marriage. Harcla, however, was seized at the instance of the Despensers, brought to London and hanged for treason.

HARCOURT (1) Edward (1757-1847) as **Edward VERNON** was Bp. of Carlisle from 1791 to 1807, became Abp. of York in 1809 and changed his name to Harcourt in 1831. Of his two sons **(2) William Vernon (1789-1871),** priest, carried on chemical experiments with Davy, was the first sec. of the British Association when it was founded in 1831 and its pres. in 1839. **(3) Octavius Henry Cyril Vernon (1793-1863),** an admiral, surveyed the coast of Central America between 1834 and 1836. William's son **(4) Sir William George Granville Venables Vernon (1827-1904),** originally an expert and professor of international law, served on commissions of neutrality (1869), naturalisation (1870) and extradition (1878). He became a Liberal M.P. in 1868 and was interested in practical reforms such as registration of voters (1871), abolition of university tests (1870) and purchase of commissions (1871) and the Judicature Act 1873, when he became Sol-Gen. In opposition he was a powerful critic of conservative foreign policy, particularly in Turkey, Afghanistan and S. Africa. In 1880 Gladstone made him Home Sec. and he had to deal with the Irish troubles of 1881-3. He tried, but failed, to reform London govt. in 1884 but found time to improve conditions in the mines. He accepted Gladstone's conversion to Home Rule and in 1886 was briefly Ch. of the Exch. In 1890 he persuaded Gladstone to repudiate Parnell and in 1892 was again Ch. of the Exch. in Gladstone's Fourth govt. Queen Victoria passed him over for the premiership because he had become intolerably arrogant in Cabinet. In 1894 he became Leader of the Commons under Lord Rosebery and his budget of that year introduced death duties calculated on the value of the deceased's estate. He resigned on the govt's defeat in June 1895. In early 1897 he was a member of the select committee on the Jameson raid and endorsed the acquittal of Chamberlain and the Colonial Office from responsibility. In Oct. when Rosebery resigned the leadership of the liberals, Harcourt accepted it but resigned at the end of 1898. Thereafter he held no important office.

HARDICANUTE or HARTHACNUT. *See* CANUTE AND HIS SONS.

HARDIE, James Keir (1856-1915), originally a Lanarkshire miner, was dismissed as an agitator in 1878 and took up journalism, left-wing liberalism and trade union organisation. By 1886 he was the first Sec. of the Scottish Miners Fed. He joined the new Labour Party in 1888 and founded the *Labour Leader* in 1889. From 1892 to 1895 he was an independent M.P. and in 1893 he became chairman of the independent Labour Party and, as M.P. for Merthyr from 1900, the first leader of the parliamentary Labour Party. Sometimes described as the

exponent of cloth cap socialism, he was a forceful speaker, much liked as a person and the true creator of the British political labour movement.

HARDINGE (1) Nicholas (1699-1758) was clerk of the House of Commons from 1731 to 1748, M.P. for Eye from 1748 and sec. to the Treasury from 1752. His son **(2) George (1743-1816),** a distinguished barrister and friend of Horace Walpole, was Tory M.P. for Old Sarum from 1784 to 1807. He adopted **(3) George Nicholas (1781-1808)** whose brilliant naval promise was prematurely cut off and rewarded with a monument in St. Paul's. His brother **(4) Sir Henry (1785-1856) 1st Vist. HARDINGE of LAHORE (1846)** was originally a competent quartermaster with the British and Portuguese armies in the Peninsular. He was Commissioner to the Prussians at Waterloo and in France (1815-8). From 1820 until 1844 he was a Tory M.P., being Sec. at War twice (1828-30 and 1841-4) and Irish Sec. twice (1830- and 1834-5). In 1844 he became gov. gen. of India and was involved in the 1st Sikh War. He tried to abolish suttee but refused to abolish flogging in native regiments. His son **(5) Charles Stewart (1822-94), 2nd Vist.,** was his father's private sec. in India, a conservative M.P. from 1851 and chairman of the National Portrait Gallery from 1876. His brother **(6) Sir Arthur (1828-92),** a court favourite and equerry to the Prince Consort and Queen, commanded the Bombay Army from 1881 to 1885 and was gov. of Gibraltar from 1886 to 1890. His son **(7) Charles (1858-1944) 1st Ld. HARDINGE of PENSHURST (1910)** served as a diplomat in eight capitals, became ambassador to St. Petersburg in 1904 and was permanent U/Sec. of State at the Foreign Office from 1906 to 1910 when he became Viceroy of India. His efforts to create some communal well-being were not wholly successful: he was injured by a bomb in 1912 and his background administration of the disastrous Mesopotamian expedition was subsequently censured. He returned to the Foreign Office in 1916 and was ambassador to Paris from 1920 to 1922. His son **(8) Sir Alexander (1894-1960) 2nd Ld. (1944)** was asst. sec. to George V and private sec. to Edward VIII. He warned Edward VIII in Aug. 1936 of the foreign newspaper scandals concerning his relationship with Mrs Simpson. In Oct. he urged the King to consult the Prime Minister (Stanley Baldwin) and in Nov. warned him of the ministerial meeting which Baldwin was calling to discuss the question and of the constitutional difficulties which might arise if the govt. resigned and a general election followed. The King resented his advice and made no use of him in the negotiations which led to the abdication. He believed that there was no conspiracy to drive the King from the throne. He continued as private sec. to George VI until 1943 when he retired.

HARDWICK HALL (Derbys.) renaissance mansion built between 1590 and 1596 by Bess of Hardwick and long in the Cavendish family.

HARDWICKE. *See* YORKE.

HARDWICKE'S ACT. *See* MARRIAGE.

HARDY. Of this naval family **(1) Sir Thomas (1666-1732)** and his cousin **(2) Sir Charles the elder (1680-1744)** both served under Norris in the Baltic in the period 1712 to 1715 while the latter's son **(3) Sir Charles the younger (?1716-80)** was gov. of New York from 1755 to 1757 and 2-in-C to Hawke at the B. of Quiberon Bay in 1759. He was M.P. for Portsmouth from 1774 and C-in-C Channel Fleet in 1779.

HARDY, Thomas (1840-1928). Dorset novelist and poet. The background feature of his novels is the struggle against the force which rules the world but which is largely indifferent to the result. Of his novels *Tess of the d'Urbevilles* (1891) has always been the most highly considered; *Jude the Obscure* (1896) the most controversial. The latter raised such an outcry that Hardy abandoned fiction and concentrated on his poetry.

HARDY, Sir Thomas Masterman (1769-1839) Bart (1806) was a friend of Nelson and his flag-captain from 1799 to 1805. Nelson died in his arms. He commanded on the S. American station from 1819 to 1824 and was First Sea Lord in 1830.

HARDYNG, JOHN. See HENRY V-4.

HARE, Hugh (1606-67) 1st Ld. COLERAINE (1625) a royalist Irish peer, supplied Charles I with a large fortune in the Civil War.

HAREWOOD. See LASCELLES.

HARFLEUR and LE HAVRE (Fr.) Harfleur on the Lézarde, a short tributary of the Seine, was the principal Norman port until the 17th cent. and consequently Henry V's main objective in 1415. The increasing size of ships and the silting of the Lézarde was already causing it to be superseded by Le Havre, downstream on the Seine. An English Havre Company was incorporated in 1409 and Louis XII (1498-1515) deliberately planned the new port. Le Havre was the seat of the Belgian govt. during World War I. See CHARTERED COMPANIES.

HARINGTON (1) John (?-1570) treasurer of Henry VIII's camps, married the King's bastard Ethelreda in 1546 and was imprisoned in the Tower with Pr. Elizabeth. His son **(2) Sir John (1561-1612)** a court wit and companion of Q. Elizabeth I, went to Ireland in 1598 with Essex, who deputed him to appease the Queen when he disobeyed her instructions. She would not hear him but he persisted in writing. He supported the succession of James VI and I and is said to have offered to go to Ireland both as Chancellor and Archbishop and to have invented the Water Closet. His cousin **(3) John (?-1613) 1st Ld. HARINGTON of EXTON (1603)** prevented the abduction of the Pr. Elizabeth by the Gunpowder Plotters in 1605. In 1613 he escorted her to her wedding with the Elector Palatine and died at Worms.

HARLECH. See EDWARDIAN CASTLES IN WALES.

HARLEIAN SOCIETY (1869) was established to publish heraldic visitations, pedigrees and related material.

HARLEY (1) Sir Robert (1579-1656) laid the foundations of the family fortune. He was M.P. for Radnor and Hereford and in 1626-35 and 1643-9 was Master of the Mint. In the Long Parliament he was a powerful opponent of Strafford and later organised the militia and lent money to Parliament. In 1648, however, he was imprisoned for voting to treat with the King. His son **(2) Sir Edward (1624-1700)** was parliamentary gen. of horse for Radnor and Hereford in 1645, as well as M.P. for Herefordshire in 1646. He was impeached in 1648 for supporting the Disbanding Ordinance. M.P. again in 1656 he was a member of the council of State in 1659. From 1660 to 1661 he was gov. of Dunkirk whose sale he opposed. Under Charles II he opposed legislation against nonconformity. A respected debater, he was an M.P. three times under William III. His son **(3) Robert (1661-1724) 1st E. of OXFORD (1711)** was M.P. for New Radnor from 1690 and at once became a commissioner for the public accounts. By 1693 he was reckoned the most formidable of parliamentary tacticians and in 1694 he embarrassed the court on the abortive Place Bill and secured the passing of the Triennial Act. By now he was a Tory leader, but his progress was retarded by the failure of his National Land Bank (1696) in opposition to the Whig Bank of England and by his opposition to the Fenwick attainder. In Dec. 1697 he secured the reduction of the army and in 1698 forced William III to dismiss his Dutch guards. His moderate Whig following added to his parliamentary stature and in 1701 when it became clear that he might become Speaker the King, in the hope of getting his support for the war, got Lyttleton, the previous Speaker, to withdraw. Harley was accordingly elected. In May 1704 when Marlborough and Godolphin obtained the dismissal of the high Tories, Harley became a S. of State but retained the Speakership until Apr. 1705. He was now a crypto-Tory in a Whig govt. and sought to

influence the Queen through Abigail Hill (or Masham) against the Whigs, by playing on her loyalty to the Church of England. She made episcopal appointments without reference to Marlborough and Godolphin and, by 1708, they had decided to get rid of him. An attempt to fasten the treasonable correspondence of a clerk in his office upon him in Jan. 1708 failed but in Feb. they compelled him to resign by refusing to attend councils until he did. He continued, however, in contact with the Queen through Abigail. The burden of his case was that the Queen could not exercise her proper functions so long as she was beholden to the Whigs. By 1710 the temperamental clash between the Queen and the Duchess of Marlborough had come to a head and in Apr. Abigail, prompted by Harley, obtained the Duchess' dismissal. Between June and Aug. most members of the govt. except Marlborough were dismissed and the Treasury was put in commission with Harley as Ch. of the Exch. He failed to convince the remaining Whigs and formed a Tory ministry with Rochester, St. John (Bolingbroke) and Harcourt and, having replaced the sheriffs and Lords Lieutenant, won a sweeping victory at the general election. He immediately opened secret negotiations to end the war while simultaneously funding the national debt in a body of stockholders who were incorporated as the South Sea Co. Immediately afterwards he was created a peer and Lord Treasurer and gov. of the South Sea Co. By Sept. 1711 he had initialled the peace terms but when the facts leaked out Marlborough and the Whigs carried a motion against him. Thereupon he persuaded the Queen to dismiss Marlborough and to create 12 peers to carry the treaty, which was signed at Utrecht in Mar. 1713. Harley's coalition now broke up. Bolingbroke and the Jacobite Tories, foreseeing the imminence of the Queen's death, wanted to get rid of him because of his Hanoverian propensities. In June 1714, through Abigail they secured his dismissal. The Queen died in Aug. At the beginning of the next reign he was impeached but in 1717 acquitted for want of prosecution. His son **(4) Edward (1689-1741) 2nd E.** was a collector. His "Harleian" manuscripts were sold to the British Museum in 1742. His grandson **(5) Thomas (1730-1804)** was M.P. for the City of London in 1761, prime warden of the Goldsmiths in 1762-3, as sheriff in 1763 burned No. 45 of the *North Britain*, was Lord Mayor in 1767-8 and was re-elected M.P. against John Wilkes in 1768. From 1776 to 1802 he was M.P. for Herefordshire.

HARLOW. See NEW TOWNS.

HARMSWORTH. Two brothers with a flair for journalistic popularisation and finance. **(1) Alfred Charles William (1865-1922) Bt. (1903) 1st Ld., 1st Vist. NORTHCLIFFE (1917)** and **(2) Harold Sidney (1868-1940) 1st Vist. ROTHERMERE (1919)** were self educated. Alfred began as a freelance journalist in 1882 and from 1885 to 1887 also gained publishing experience at Coventry; Harold had the financial acumen. By 1887 the brothers realised the potential of the growing semi-educated readership created through the Education Act, 1870. They launched their London publishing business (later Amalgamated Press) in 1887 and were soon buying up and refurbishing or issuing periodicals with increasingly popular features, beginning in 1888 with *Answers*. In 1894 they bought the *Evening News*. In 1896 they launched the *Daily Mail*, designed by its price (over 2d) superficial glitter and spectacular stunts to attract the new mass audiences. They employed skilled journalists, developed advertising revenues and prize competitions and stimulated reportable events such as inventions and exploration. They became very rich and by 1899 were moving into high society. In 1903 they launched the *Daily Mirror* and in 1908 Harold became chief proprietor of *The Times* and spent a fortune keeping it going. Their press empire reached its summit in 1914 and, though it continued to acquire properties and periodicals, it was slowly affected by wartime and subsequent attrition.

HARO, CLAMEUR DE. In the Channel Is. (and formerly in Normandy and elsewhere in N. France) a plaintiff can cry for justice by kneeling in public before witnesses and shouting *Haro, Haro, Haro. A l'aide, mon prince, on me fail tort.* (Help me, my prince, I suffer wrong.) The matter of the dispute is immediately referred to the court and the tort or trespass must cease until judgment. The equivalent of the English interim injunction.

HAROLD II Godwin's son (?-1066) King (1066) (For his career before he became King see EDWARD THE CONFESSOR) **(1)** He was crowned the day after Edward the Confessor's death (6 Jan. 1066). The uneasy consensus against outsiders was strengthened by the English church. William of Normandy supported the Cluniac reforms. Stegan, both Bp. of Winchester and Abp. of Canterbury, was a pluralist; he had been condemned as a usurper; and in 1064 the council of Mantua had, by implication, condemned Benedict X, from whom he had received his *pallium,* as schismatic. A Norman attack on England was not only a military, but an ecclesiastical, operation. In this it differed from the activities of Harald Hardraada, whose claim was supported only by his own professional troops. He had come over to Scotland. Tostig Harold's brother, having fitted out a fleet, sailed from Bruges on a freebooting expedition first against the I. of Wight, then against the east coast. Repulsed in Lindsey he joined Hardraada in Scotland.

(2) William's aggressive intentions were clear. It took him about six months to mount his expedition and when it was ready the winds were unfavourable. He and Hardraada each hoped that the other would have to fight Harold first. By Sept. Hardraada and Tostig in Scotland were on short rations and Harold's levies were having to go home for the harvest. His fleet dispersed just as Hardraada and Tostig sailed for the Humber. On 20 Sept. they met and destroyed the Northumbrians of Edwin and Morcar at the B. of Fulford. Harold was probably marching north already, relying on the wind to keep William in port. He marched faster than the news of his coming.

(3) On 25 Sept., as Hardraada and Tostig were setting out unarmoured to receive the surrender of York, Harold fell upon them at Stamford Bridge. They, together with 90% of their men, were killed. On 27 Sept. the wind in the Channel changed and William's army landed at Pevensey on 28th. Harold marched south as soon as he could after his victory and probably had the news on the way. He reached London with his Housemen on 6 Oct. and waited until 10th while the southern levies were raised again. He reached the neighbourhood of Hastings on 12th with some but not all of them.

(4) William, living on the country, would have had to move soon; and the later he attacked, the larger Harold's army would be. He offered battle on 14th. (*See* PLAN.) Both armies were very small. Harold occupied the crest of a ridge between forests. He placed his 2000 or 3000 professional axemen behind a breastwork and the levies, mostly with missile weapons, in mass formation behind the professionals. William, at the foot of the hill, drew up his mounted troops, Normans in the centre, Franks on the right, Bretons on the left with dismounted archers in front. The whole force began to mount the hill at about 10 a.m. The archers were mostly ineffectual. The knights charged through them. Harold's brothers, Gyrth and Leofwine, were killed on the right but the line was unbroken and, indeed, the Bretons fled. The English levies on the right, against orders and deprived of their higher commanders, broke ranks in pursuit. William rallied the Bretons and counter-attacked the disordered English, who had reached the valley. Many were killed. The attack on the weakened English line was resumed and, though it held, some progress was apparent. The Franks, on William's orders, now feigned flights and attracted further undisciplined pursuits, which were destructively counter-attacked. By the late afternoon Harold's professionals, tired and battered, still maintained their line but the levies were much thinned and unable to interfere with the Norman archers. These were now shooting high. The line of axemen was breached and Harold was killed. The rest fell fighting.

(5) In the special circumstances it was not surprising that the English did not at once accept the verdict. Abp. Stegan and the northern earls, Edwin and Morcar, proclaimed the rights of EDGAR the Atheling (?-1106), the young grandson of Edmund Ironside. William marched not directly to London, but round it, devastating much of Sussex, Surrey and Hertfordshire as he went. With the northern forces already destroyed at Fulford and the southern at Hastings, there was no power in Stegan's party. In Dec. Edgar submitted. On Christmas Day Stegan assisted in William's coronation.

HAR[R]INGTONS. Brass farthings, minted by the first Lord Harington, between 1613 and 1643 under a patent of James I.

HARRINGTON, Timothy Charles (1851-1910) founded the nationalist *Kerry Sentinel* in 1877, became Sec. of the Irish Land League in 1882 at the invitation of Parnell and an M.P. (Co. Westmeath 1883, Dublin from 1885). He originated the "Plan of Campaign" in the Irish land war and, having been called to the Irish bar in 1887, appeared for many Irish prisoners as well as being Sir Chas. Russell's junior for Parnell before the Parnell Commission (1888-9). He supported Parnell when the Irish Party split (1891) and joined Redmond after Parnell's death. He was Lord Mayor of Dublin from 1901 to 1904.

HARRIOT, Thomas (1560-1621), Oxford mathematician and tutor to Sir Walter Raleigh, who sent him to survey Virginia in 1585. His *Artis Analyticae Praxis ad Aequationes Algebraicas Resolvendas* (Lat = Practice of the Analytical Art of Solving Algebraic Equations) was the foundation of modern algebra. By his studies he invented and used telescopes contemporaneously with or perhaps earlier than Galileo and left records of sun spots (1610-13) and comets (1618) which he observed.

HARRIS, Arthur Travers (1892-1984) was C-in-C Bomber Command (1942-5) and Marshal of the R.A.F. (1945). His term as C-in-C coincided with a need to influence the war by the only available means, namely bombing, and he developed the atrocious fire-storm technique which was first tried out at the mediaeval port of Lübeck (Mar. 1942) and provoked the so-called Baedeker retaliatory raids on Exeter, Norwich, York and Canterbury. The technique was later used at Hamburg and, at Russian insistence, on the Baroque city of Dresden and involved enormous civilian casualties besides damage to the monuments of civilisation. He was not responsible for choosing the targets.

HARRIS, James Thomas ("Frank") (1856-1931) came *via* Ireland and the U.S.A. to London where he brilliantly edited the *Fortnightly Review* (1886-94) and the *Saturday Review* (1894-8) but later damaged his reputation by unreliability and social and sexual boasting. Bernard Shaw said of him "He is neither first-rate, nor second-rate, nor tenth-rate. He is just his unique horrible self".

HARRIS (1) George (1746-1829) 1st Ld. (1815), soldier, wounded at Bunker Hill (1775), captured Seringapatam in 1799 and subdued Mysore. His grandson **(2) George Francis (1810-72)** was gov. of Trinidad in 1846 and of Madras from 1854 to 1859. He kept his presidency so quiet during the Indian Mutiny that he was able to send troops to the Ganges Valley. His son **(3) George Canning (1851-1932),** an enthusiastic and successful cricketer, was U/Sec. of State for India from 1885 to 1886 and for War from 1886 to 1889. He was Gov. of Bombay from 1890 to 1895 and popularised cricket in India. He was president of the M.C.C. in 1895.

HARRISON (1) William Henry (1773-1841) was sec. of the U.S. North West Territory in 1798 and gov. of the Indiana Territory from 1800 to 1812. In the 1812 war he re-established the American position after Gen. Hull's defeat, retook Detroit and defeated the British and Indians under Proctor and Tecumseh at the B. of the Thames (Oct. 1813) where Tecumseh fell. This effectively broke Anglo-Indian co-operation, opened the North West permanently to U.S. penetration and made him a national hero. Subsequently a supporter of the American Whigs, he was elected 9th Pres. on his personality in 1841 but died a month later. His grandson **(2) Benjamin (1833-1901)** was a Republican Senator from 1881 to 1887 and 23rd Pres. of the U.S.A. from 1888 to 1892. Though honest and conscientious, this period marked a high point in the connection between government and business; policy was controlled largely by his associate, James Blaine, Sec. of State, and a high tariff (The McKinley Tariff Act) was accompanied by energetic American interest in the Pacific. *See* HAWAII.

HARRIS, -TWEED; CLOSED SHOP. Harris comprises the S. part of the large Outer Hebridean I. of Lewis and four adjacent Is. Its 3000-odd crofters and fisherfolk hand-wove a peculiar authenticated cloth from locally spun yarn or a similar unauthenticated cloth from cheaper imported mainland yarn. By 1941 most weaving was done by local mills but a few continued to hand-weave cheaper imported yarn. The dockers and mill-hands belonged to the Transport and Gen. Workers Union. To force the hand-weavers to join the union and raise spinners' wages, the union told the dockers not to handle imported yarn. The hand-weavers sued the union whose action was upheld by the House of Lords because the strike was not meant to injure the weavers but to improve conditions in the industry. This indirectly legalised the closed shop.

HARROW SCHOOL. John Lyon (1514-92) obtained a charter in 1571 and drew up the statutes in 1590. Opened in 1611 as a school for poor children, it developed into a major public school in the 19th cent.

HARRY, Blind (?-1492) poet in the Lothian dialect blind from birth, collected the traditions about Sir William Wallace and incorporated them into the popular, not invariably accurate, 12,000 line poem *Wallace*. This in its turn became a source of much Scots nationalist sentiment. James IV pensioned him.

HART, Sir Robert (1835-1911) became inspector-gen. of the Chinese Imperial Customs in 1863 and converted them into an honest and efficient organisation. He also acted as buying agent for the imperial govt. in its efforts to modernise, and also as its foreign affairs adviser, especially at the end of the Franco-Chinese War of 1884. The foundation of the Chinese Interpreters College in 1862 and the Chinese postal system were due to his inspiration.

HARTINGTON. *See* CAVENDISH (DEVONSHIRE)-21.

HARTLEPOOL. *See* DURHAM-5.

HARVARD UNIVERSITY (Cambridge, Mass.) was founded in 1636 with a grant from the Massachusetts legislature and large benefactions from John Harvard (1607-38). Its degrees were first bestowed in 1642 and it was chartered in 1650. The clergy were represented among the Overseers until 1851.

HARVEY, Beauchamp Bagenal (1762-98), presided at Dublin meetings of United Irishmen in 1793 and was elected insurgent commander in the 1798 rising. He was hanged.

HARVEY, William (1578-1657), studied anatomy at the then famous surgical school at Padua and, on his return to England, carefully dissected some 80 kinds of animals. He observed that the arrangement of arterial and veinous valves was consistent only with the flow of blood in a circle; and from the calculation that the human heart pumped in an hour a far greater weight of blood than the weight of a man, he inferred that the blood so flowed. This discovery, based on simple observation and logic, was made long before the microscope had revealed the capillary connection between arteries and veins. He first stated his theory of circulation in a Lumleian lecture in 1616 and published it in detail at Frankfurt in 1628. In 1633 he travelled with Charles I in Scotland and on the way back examined four Lancashire witches and concluded that witchcraft did not exist. He published a further work on the circulation in 1649. *See* BIOLOGY; RENAISSANCE-14.

HARWICH (Essex), a port for Holland, was fortified under James I and became the terminus of the Dutch packets under Charles II. There was a naval fight with the Dutch in 1666. During World Wars I and II it was an important naval patrol base.

HASTENBECK and KLOSTERZEVEN. *See* HANOVER-II; GEORGE II.

HASTINGS, M. *See* RAWDON HASTINGS.

HASTINGS, Sir Patrick Gardiner (1880-1952) began life in extreme poverty but saved enough by 1904 to be called to the bar. He took over Horace Avory's practice in criminal law and became a very busy K.C. in 1919. Labour M.P. for Walsall in 1922 he became Att-Gen. under MacDonald in 1924. He left politics in 1926 and was until 1939 the leading Common Lawyer of his day.

HASTINGS, Warren (1732-1818) went to India in 1750. He experienced imprisonment by the Nawab of Bengal while a member of the council at Cossimbazar in 1756, but Clive had him made Resident to the Dewani at Murshidabad in 1757. In 1761 he became a member of the Calcutta Council and after a mission to Patna in 1762 went to England in 1764. In 1766 he gave evidence on Indian affairs to a parliamentary committee. He impressed the authorities who sent him back as Second in the Madras Council in 1769. He became gov. of Bengal in 1772 and gov-gen. under the Regulating Act in 1773. His first care was to reorganise, as far as he could, the financial and judicial systems in Bengal, Bihar and Orissa. The development of the HEIC's investment required, in his view, territorial insulation from the warlike proclivities of the Marathas and Afghans by means of a strong buffer power in Oudh, and he helped its Nawab to strengthen his N.W. frontiers by conquering the Rohillas. His long experience and vast knowledge of Indian life and literature taught him to distrust grand gestures and general principles. He believed in personal arrangements and crisp decisions for each problem to suit the local conditions and he worked through friendships with English subordinates and Indian rulers with whom, for the most part, he got on famously. The members of the gov-gen's. council created by the 1773 Act now arrived and Hastings found himself in a minority of two against three led by Sir Philip Francis, who paralysed the administration and made false charges of corruption during the ensuing five years. In the meantime war with Mysore broke out in the Carnatic and added to his burdens. Further accusations ended in a duel in which Hastings wounded Francis, but the Mysore war went well and British troops took most of the French settlements. The council had interfered in the Oudh settlement and in 1781 Hastings had to intervene to secure arrears of troops' pay and tribute. This involved deposing Chait Singh, the intrusive ruler, and seizing part of the fortune of the Begums. These events occurred just before the final settlement of the Mysore War at the T. of Salbai and, as a result, the Directors approved his actions. He returned to London in 1785 and was impeached for corruption, high handedness and cruelty. The impeachment, which lasted from 1788 to 1795, ended in acquittal. He was treated with honour in his long retirement. *See also* FRANCIS, SIR PHILIP; MYSORE; OUDH.

HASTINGS, William (c. 1430-83) 1st Ld. HASTINGS (1462) was born of a traditionally Yorkist family. He gave real assistance to Edward IV in his struggle for the throne and was his closest friend and adviser throughout the reign. Sir Thos. More described him as 'an honourable man, a good knight and a gentle'. Edward trusted him and in 1461 made him his Chamberlain, which he remained until the King died. He became a member of the Council, Receiver-Gen. of the Duchy of Cornwall, Master of the Mint and Chamberlain of N.Wales. In 1462 he married the E. of Warwick's sister, Katharine Neville. During the 1460s the King enabled and encouraged him to build up a territorial power, especially in the midlands, through grants of large estates in Leicestershire, Lincolnshire, Rutland and Wiltshire, to which Hastings added by purchases. Hence he could recruit 3000 retainers to support Edward during the short civil war of 1471. As Chamberlain he had much control over access to the King and there are many contemporary references to his court influence which was not destroyed during the ascendancy of the Queen's relatives, the Woodvilles, but there were tensions, especially in 1471 when he was granted the lucrative Lieutenancy of Calais, which had been promised to her brother. Hastings' involvement in foreign policy resulted in his being much solicited abroad and in 1475, at the time of the negotiations for the P. of Picquigny, he was (as was customary) receiving substantial annuities from both Burgundy and France. His end was abrupt and violent, no doubt from jealousy or mistrust of his wealth. During the clash between the Queen's party and that of Richard of Gloucester he seems to have leaned towards reconciliation with the Queen and at a meeting of a Council Committee in the Tower of London on 14 June 1483, Richard charged him with treason and had him hustled out for summary execution.

HATAY, ALEXANDRETTA or ISKENDERUN (Turkey). This Sanjak which includes Antioch and its port was included in French mandated Syria in 1920 and transferred to Turkey in 1939.

HATFIELD (Herts.). The famous house, which includes parts of a palace belonging to the bishops of Ely, was completed by the 1st E. of Salisbury between 1607 and 1612. *See also* CECIL; NEW TOWNS.

HATFIELD, COUNCIL OF (679), held by Theodore of Tarsus, Abp. of Canterbury, at the request of Pope Agatho. Agatho was concerned to obtain a declaration of catholic orthodoxy from the individual churches of the West in preparation for a council in Rome which was to be convened to condemn the Monothelite heresy. Theodore, as a Greek, had seen the whole course of the controversy in the East and could understand the issues.

HATFIELD, Thomas (?-1381). *See* DURHAM-9.

HATTON (1) Sir Christopher (1540-91) patriot, friend and partisan of Q. Elizabeth, became one of her bodyguards in 1564 and soon received estates. In 1571 and subsequently he was an M.P.; in 1578 he acquired Ely Place, Holborn, through his influence with the queen and became her vice-chamberlain. In 1581 he opposed the French match, perhaps with the queen's connivance, and in 1584 Mary Q. of Scots accused him of being her lover. He was a member of the committee which tried Mary, spoke against her in parliament, and was one of those responsible for despatching her warrant of execution in 1587. Despite Elizabeth's fury on that occasion, he became Lord Chancellor soon afterwards but, though originally a lawyer, dealt with the legal business through assessors. He was a friend of Spenser. His kinsman **(2) Christopher (?1605-70) 1st Ld. HATTON (1643)** was M.P. also for Higham Ferrers in 1640 and was comptroller of Charles I household from 1643 to 1646. He was one of the royal commissioners at the Uxbridge negotiations. He went to France in 1648 but was allowed to return in 1656. In 1662 he became gov. of Guernsey.

HAU HAU. A 19th cent. sect of partly Christianised Maoris, whose most solemn sacrament involved eating Anglican clergymen.

HAUKSBEE, Francis (?-?1713) built the first electrical machine in 1706.

HAUSA were a negroid Moslem people enjoying, in N. Nigeria, the trans-Saharan trade focusing on their cities of Kano and Katsina. Early in the 19th cent. the pastoral FULANI, originally from Senegal, in the course of a war of religious reform, conquered the 14 Hausa states and established a federated empire of semi-independent Emirs, under rulers at the twin capitals of Sokoto (east) and Gwando (west). The Emirs carried on independent slave raiding and consequently wars, so that the Fulani circumscription was on the verge of dissolution when the British arrived under Lugard in 1907. The British policy of using institutions as they found them resulted in the Fulani retaining their aristocratic position, but they abolished slavery and tried to suppress the trade and raids associated with it.

HAVANA AIR CONVENTION 1928. *See* AVIATION RULES-1.

HAVANA CHARTER (1948) proposed the creation under U.N.O. of an International Trade Organisation. As the U.S.A. refused ratification it was a dead letter.

HAVANA DECLARATION (July 1940) of the Panamerican Conference as a result of the German victories in the Low Countries and France, threatened local intervention if European powers (i.e. France, Holland or Britain) attempted (i.e. were compelled) to transfer any of their American colonies to any other European power (i.e. Germany or Italy).

HAVELOCK and HAVELOCK-ALLEN. (1) William H. (1793-1848) was Elphinstone's military sec. at Madras from 1841 and was killed at Ramnagar in 1848. His brother **(2) Sir Henry (1795-1857)** after a very active military career was recalled from Mohammerah at the outbreak of the Indian Mutiny in 1857 and, after a march of 120 miles with four battles in nine days retook Cawnpore in July. In Aug. with Outram he relieved Lucknow and died shortly after relieving it a second time. His son **(3) Sir Henry Havelock-Allen (1830-97)** received the V.C. for his part in the defence of Lucknow in 1857. He fought in the Maori War of 1863. He became Liberal M.P. for Durham in 1874 and Liberal-Unionist M.P. from 1886 to 1892 and again in 1895.

HAVERFORDWEST (S. Wales) was settled by Henry I with Flemings. It became a county of itself by Act of 1528 and was the county town of Pembrokeshire.

HAVRE, LE. *See* HARFLEUR.

HAWAII (Pacific) or SANDWICH ISLANDS were discovered in Jan. 1778 by Capt. James Cook who was killed there in Feb. 1779. The islands were then divided between four principalities. In 1782 Kamehameha I came to the throne of Oahu; he had subdued the whole archipelago when Vancouver visited it in 1783 and received the cession of it to the British Crown. Kamehameha was modernising and centralising the government and despite a devastating cholera epidemic in 1804 he continued to make progress. The shadowy connection with Britain enabled him to resist Russia in 1816 and to get rid of Spanish Filipino pirates in 1818. He died in 1819. His successor Kamehameha II or Liholiho visited England in 1824 and died there. American, mainly Methodist, missionaries first arrived in 1820 followed by businessmen. Many of the King's relatives were converted including Kaahumanu, one of the wives, who acted as regent from his departure for England until her own death in 1832. The missionaries introduced schools and printing as well as Christianity during this decisive period which was one of controversy with the British. The latter considered that the cession of 1794, though never pursued, gave them a certain influence and their consuls mistrusted the missionary and business activities as unsuitable to the islander temperament and likely to lead to exploitation: whaling was established as an industry in 1820 and sugar in 1835. The missionaries on the other hand, continued to educate and interest the people and to intrigue with the chiefs. Kamehameha III succeeded to his mother's power in 1832. He brought American missionary advisers into the government in 1838 and with their help promulgated a Declaration of Rights and an Edict of Toleration (7 and 17 June 1839), a constitution (8 Oct. 1840) and a compilation of laws (1842). This imposition upon a tribal society of a western institutional framework laid the islands increasingly open to American entrepreneurs, who understood it better than the natives. The American recognition of Hawaiian independence in 1842 was really a half promise of protection.

Since 1845 the system of tribal and 'feudal' landholding had been progressively undermined by the introduction of Anglo-American common law ideas of private ownership. The main effect was to make it easy to sell land, which American businesses promptly bought. This eventually created a reaction. Tacit U.S. support enabled the King to resist French demands in 1851 but negotiations for a U.S. protectorate were broken off at his death and Kamehameha IV (r. 1854-63) and Kamehameha V (r. 1863-72) tried to resist the tide of American investment by angling for British support. The dynasty ended in 1872, however, and the subsequent, popularly elected, rulers, though increasingly anti-American, were insufficiently dextrous. Thus King Kalakaua (r. 1874-91) had to make the Reciprocity Treaty of 1876 with the U.S.A. and in 1887 not only ceded Pearl Harbor but promulgated a new constitution providing for ministerial responsibility — in other words American political intervention. Violent reaction in 1889 failed to change the course of events; Liliuokalani, his sister, succeeded him and her sympathy with it led to a *coup d'état* in Jan. 1893, the proclamation of a republic in July 1894, a further unsuccessful rebellion in 1895 and annexation by the U.S.A. in 1898. The construction of the great Pearl Harbor base began in 1908; this was the scene of the celebrated American naval disaster in 1941. The territory became the 50th state of the Union in June 1959 at the 23rd attempt.

HAWCUBITES. Nocturnal street bullies in London about 1711-13.

HAW-HAW, LORD. See JOYCE, WILLIAM.

HAWICK (Sc.) near Roxburgh and the English border, was an ancient market burgh on the Rs. Teviot and Slitrig, with a peel tower of the Douglas family by the river crossings. The combination gave it its importance; the market supplied the Douglas with a part of their income.

HAWKE, Edward (1705-81) 1st Ld. HAWKE (1776), commanded the *Berwick* at the B. of Toulon in 1744. He was specially promoted R-Adm. and captured the French squadron protecting the Rochelle convoy in 1747 when he also became M.P. for Portsmouth. From 1748 to 1752 he was C-in-C Home Fleet, from 1755 to 1756 of the Western Fleet and in 1756 in the Mediterranean. In 1757 he was naval commander of the Rochefort Expedition bungled by Sir John Mordaunt, the military commander, and in 1758 he delayed but failed to destroy the French American convoy. Admiralty criticism led him to strike his flag but on receiving assurances he resumed command, blockaded Brest throughout the summer of 1759 and in Nov. won the famous B. of Quiberon Bay during a violent storm. He was now a public hero and continued in command until 1762 after capturing a Spanish treasure fleet. From 1766 to 1771 he was First Lord of the Admiralty. His methods and determination put a permanent stamp on the character of the navy and most of the successful admirals of the Napoleonic wars served under or were trained by him.

HAWKESBURY. See JENKINSON.

HAWKINS. This family of Plymouth seafarers (related to the Drakes) included **(1) Sir John (1532-95).** He made

three slave trading voyages: in 1561-3 to Sierra Leone and Hispaniola; in 1564-5 to Rio de la Hacha and Florida and in 1567 to Sierra Leone, Vera Cruz and St. Juan de Ulloa where the Spaniards ambuscaded him. His activities and losses lost him official favour for a while but in 1570 he undertook clandestine missions for Burghley and Walsingham and in 1572 became M.P. for Plymouth and Treasurer of the Navy. As such he was responsible for great administrative improvements and a major change in the design of large warships which, under his direction, became units of sailing artillery rather than sea castles. These were the ships which fought the Armada in 1588. He also took part as a squadron commander. He was joint commander with Frobisher of the expedition to Portugal in 1590 and died on Drake's expedition to the West Indies in 1595 (*see* ELIZABETH I-1-10). His brother and partner **(2) William (?-1589)** was mayor of Plymouth in 1567 and 1578; commanded the West Indian expedition of 1582 and as mayor again in 1588 had an important part in fitting out the fleet. **(3) Sir Richard (?1562-1622)** son of Sir John, made a privateering expedition to Brazil and Chile in 1593-4 but was captured. Released in 1602 he became M.P. for Plymouth and Vice-Admiral of Devon in 1604. In 1620 he was Vice-Admiral of Mansell's expedition against Algiers.

HAWKSMOOR, Nicholas (1661-1736), Wren's deputy surveyor at Chelsea Hospital from 1682 to 1690 and clerk of the works at Greenwich Hospital, Kensington Palace and the Whitehall palaces, assisted Wren at St. Paul's and Vanbrugh at Castle Howard and Blenheim. He built on his own account much of Queen's and All Souls Colleges at Oxford and many London churches, mostly recognisable for their originality.

HAWKWOOD, Sir John (de) (?-1394) a mercenary, fought for the English in southern France until 1362, then put his force, called the White Company, at the service of a series of north Italian states including Monferrat (against Milan), Pisa (against Florence), Milan (against the Pope), The Pope (against Milan), Pisa (against Monferrat) and Florence. This son of an Essex tanner married a Visconti and is commemorated by an equestrian statue in the cathedral in Florence.

HAY, HAUGH (pron Ha); HAYWARD. (cf Fr. *baie* = hedge). A hedge or fence or the land or park enclosed by it. *See* HAYWARD.

HAY. Of the many lowland Scots of this name most are distantly or nearly related but some, e.g. the descendants of Gen. Alexander Leith who took the name in 1789, are not. The family includes the M.s of Tweeddale and the Es. of Carlisle, Erroll and Kinnoull, besides a number of Jesuits and judges.

HAY, Francis (?-1631) 9th E. of ERROL (1585) was a leading R. Catholic in Scotland. He, with Huntly and Crawford, raised the force which confronted James VI at Brig o' Dee (Apr. 1589) and he was suspected of complicity in Bothwell's attempt on the King at Falkland in 1592. The Assembly of the Kirk accused him and he was given a choice of exile or conversion. He chose neither, but with Huntly raised an army in Aberdeenshire. They defeated Argyll, but the King came up and demolished his castles. Errol fled to Zeeland but returned and compromised by signing a confession of faith (1597). The Kirk remained suspicious and in 1609 ex-communicated him. He remained in dispute, in and out of prison, with that body until his death.

HAY. (1) Sir George (1572-1634) Vist. DUPPLIN (1627) 1st E. of KINNOULL (1633) a judge and supporter of the Five Articles of Perth, was Scottish Lord Chancellor from 1622 to 1634. **(2) George (?-1758) Ld. HAY (1711) 7th E. (1719)** as Vist. Dupplin was M.P. for Fowey in 1710. He was suspected of Jacobitism on his brother's account in 1715 and in 1722 but served as ambassador to the Porte from 1729 to 1734. His brother **(3) John (1691-1740)** Jacobite **E. of INVERNESS (1725)** helped to prepare the Jacobite rebellion of 1715, for his brother-in-law, the E. of Mar, was the Old Pretender's master of the horse and succeeded Mar as Jacobite Sec. of State from 1724 to 1727. The son of **(2), (4) Thomas (1710-87) 8th E.,** was M.P. as Vist. Dupplin for Cambridge from 1741 when he became an Irish Revenue Commissioner. In 1746 he became a Lord of Trade, in 1754 a Lord of the Treasury, in 1756 Joint P.M.G. and in 1758 Ch. of the Duchy. He was ambassador to Portugal in 1759.

HAY (1) James (?-1636) 1st Ld. (1606), Vist. DONCASTFR (1618), E. of CARLISLE (1622), a courtier who came south with James I, received many grants of English land and was master of the Wardrobe from 1613. He was ambassador to the Emperor in 1619-20 and favoured war against him in support of James I's daughter, the Electress Palatine. Similarly he advised against the marriage with Henrietta Maria and favoured war against Spain and support for the Huguenots (qv). In 1617 he had married **(2) Lucy (1599-1660),** beautiful and clever *d.* of the 9th E. of Northumberland. She was a friend and patroness of poets, notably Herrick and d'Avenant; and an intimate at once of Q. Henrietta Maria, Strafford and Pym. She betrayed the King's intention to arrest the five members and in the civil wars both supported the presbyterians and sometimes acted as a intermediary between the English and the Scots. She was briefly imprisoned after Charles I's death.

HAY, John (1838-1905) private sec. to Pres. Lincoln (1860-5), diplomat and man of letters, was U/Sec. of State from 1879 to 1881 under Pres. Hayes; in 1897 Pres. McKinley's ambassador to Britain and from 1898 until his death S. of State. He inaugurated the Open Door Policy in China and concluded the **Hay-Pauncefote Treaty** of 1901 (superseding the Clayton-Bulwer Treaty of 1850) and secured British support for an American **Panama Canal** open to all ships on equal terms.

HAY (TWEEDDALE) (1) John (1626-97) 2nd E. (1654) and 1st M. of TWEEDDALE (1694), of covenanting persuasion but royalist loyalty, as a young man joined Charles I when he raised his standard at Nottingham in 1642 but later changed sides on the covenanting issue. He fought for the parliament at Marston Moor (1644), held a command for the Engagers in 1648 and was involved with the presbyterian extremism of James Guthrie. Consequently he was for a while suspect at the Restoration and spent some time in custody, but Charles II thought him a useful bridge between the restored moderate monarchy and the chastened and more moderate presbyterians and from 1663 to 1674 he held a variety of important Scottish posts, notably as Pres. of the Council Church Commissioner and extra-ordinary Lord of Session, where a compromising moderation could be pursued, particularly in policy towards covenanters. By 1674 Lauderdale, Charles II's Scottish adviser, thought that the policy had failed and got Charles to dismiss him. He was readmitted to only minor office in 1680 and to the council in 1682, but after the Revolution, which he strongly supported, he came into favour and in 1692 he became Scottish Lord Chancellor. It also fell to him to order the investigation into the Glencoe Massacre of 1692. By now, like all Scotland, he had invested in the Darien Scheme but, by his position, was its most conspicuous resident champion. In the clash of interest which followed he was dismissed. His son **(2) John (1645-1713) 2nd M.,** High Commissioner to the Scottish parliament and Lord Chancellor in 1704, led the so-called *Squadrone* mainly to secure good terms for the Union, which he thought inevitable. He was a Scottish representative peer from the union onwards. His second son **(3) Ld. John (?-1706)** was a cavalry commander under Marlborough. His nephew **(4) John (?-1762) 4th M. (1715)** was a representative peer from 1722 and, as S. of State for Scotland from 1742 to 1746, had to deal with the civilian

effects of the 1745 rebellion. He became Lord Justice-Gen. in 1761. His brother **(5) Ld. Charles (?-1760)** a soldier, was M.P. for Haddington from 1741. He was badly wounded commanding the First Guards at Fontenoy (1745). **(6) George (1787-1876) 8th M. (1804),** also a soldier, served in Sicily in 1806 and then continuously in the Peninsula from 1807 to 1813, during which time he was wounded at Bussaco (1810) and Vittoria (1813). He then went to Canada where he was wounded and captured at Niagara (1813). As a landowner he had become interested in agricultural improvement and reforms, especially in the Highlands, and he was a representative peer. In 1842, however, he accepted the governorship of Madras and held it until 1848. He ended as a field-marshal. His son **(7) Arthur (1824-76) Vist. WALDEN (1862),** 9th M., was a distinguished naturalist and traveller besides a soldier.

HAYEK, Friedrich (von) (1899-1992) CH (1984) Nobel Prizeman (1974). Austrian, British naturalised (1938) polymath and Whig. He was Tooke Prof. of Economics (1931-50) and taught at Salzburg (1968-77) before settling at Freiburg. He wrote some 200 works including *The Sensory Order: An Inquiry into the Foundations of Theoretical Psychology*, *The Road to Serfdom*, *The Constitution of Liberty*, *Law Legislation and Liberty*, and his last *The Fatal Conceit: the Errors of Socialism*. He rejected economic determinism and held that prosperity was possible only under individualistic economics where people were free to do what they could do best. Hence investment was to be derived from capital freely accumulated in free markets where govts should not intervene. Some of Margaret Thatcher's practical thought ran parallel with his, but through his influence her party was intellectually prepared for her policies, while her opponents were shaken to find that their doctrines were insecurely based. She recognised his British importance by recommending him for a Companionship of Honour. *See* INSTITUTE OF ECONOMIC AFFAIRS.

HAYMO of FAVERSHAM (?-1244), Franciscan who, as a lecturer in the Univ. of Paris, took the Dominican habit in 1225. He was a compelling preacher and after a sermon at St. Denis in 1225 he had to spend three days hearing the confessions of his auditors. In 1233 Gregory IX sent him to the east to try and organise a reunion with the Greek Church. In 1238 he took the lead in denouncing the scandalous behaviour of Elias, the Franciscan Min-Gen. Gregory deposed Elias and substituted Albert of Pisa, whom Haymo briefly (1239-40) succeeded as English Provincial Min. In 1240 he succeeded him as Min-Gen. He wanted to combine the simple life with theological study and encouraged priestly as opposed to lay authority within his Order. He also revised the Franciscan breviary to such effect that it was adopted by the whole church.

HAYWARD, a manorial foreman almost as important as the reeve. According to 13th cent. treatises on husbandry he was in charge of raising crops and hay and looking after the woods. He rounded up defaulters liable to regular 'week' work and irregular 'boon' work. He was often also the beadle and acted as a kind of local policeman. Like the reeve he enjoyed a reduced rent, an occasional measure of seed corn or some sheaves at harvest and sometimes a meadow of his own. He was sometimes elected, sometimes appointed by the Lord and the author of the *Seneschausie* said that he should be active and sharp and up and about early.

HAZARA (India) frontier district of the Punjab which was ceded to Britain in 1846, in lieu of part of the War indemnity payable under the T. of Lahore. Its gov. joined the rebellion of Jindan Kaur and Mulraj in Sept. 1848 but for the most part the people did not. It remained loyal during the Indian Mutiny.

HAZLITT, William (1778-1830) journalist and unfriendly critic of Wordsworth, Coleridge, Southey and Shelley. His

Principles of Human Action appeared in 1822. He divorced his first wife and his second ran away.

HEAD ACT, 1465 (Ir), authorised anyone in Meath to take any thief who was unaccompanied by a man of good name and fame in English apparel and cut off his head and present it to the portreeve of Trim upon whose certificate the taker would be entitled to levy 2d per ploughland. Illustrative of the appalling condition of Ireland at this time, it was repealed only in 1635.

HEADBOROUGH. *See* FRANK PLEDGE.

HEAD COURT was the court held by the Lord of an Honour or, sometimes, the Court Leet of the principal manor of a group, held by the Lord for all the manors of the group.

HEADMASTFRS CONFERENCE of headmasters of public schools was first organised by Edward Thring of Uppingham in 1869 when 37 were invited and 12 came. It was incorporated in 1909.

HEADS OF THE PROPOSALS (July 1647) offered by the Army to Charles I, then in their hands at Newmarket, suggested that parliament should name the day for its own dissolution and that there should thenceforth be biennial parliaments sitting for at least 120 days. Parliament should control the forces and appoint great officers for 10 years. No royalist should hold office for five years or be elected a member before the third biennial parliament. There should be a council of state whose membership should be agreed immediately and hold office for seven years; it would conduct foreign affairs subject, in the case of peace and war, to parliamentary consent. In a modified episcopal church the Book of Common Prayer was not to be enjoined; no one was to be required to sign the Covenant and ecclesiastical coercive power was to be abolished. Royalists were to be allowed to compound on easy terms. Drafted by Ireton, Lambert and Cromwell, this constitution envisaged retention of the House of Lords but did enshrine earlier attacks on Royal abuses of power (e.g. misuse of monopolies). It foundered amidst conflict within the army and due also to Charles' intentions merely to procrastinate.

HEALEY, Cahir (1877-1970), originally a journalist, joined Sinn Fcin in 1905 and was interned in 1922 but smuggled out articles to the *Sunday Express*. Elected M.P. for Fermanagh in 1922 he was not released until 1924 but held the seat until 1954. He was interned again between 1941 and 1943.

HEALEY, DENIS (1917-) Ld. HEALEY (1992) originally a Communist, became Labour M.P. for Leeds from 1952 and with responsibilities of office as Sec. of State for Defence in the First Wilson govt. and Ch. of the Exch. in the second and under Callaghan, moved steadily towards the moderate wing of his party.

HEALTH, MINISTRY OF was set up in 1919 to take charge of local govt. which had developed from the Public Health Acts from 1875 onwards. It acquired a variety of additional functions involving many matters not directly concerned with health, but in 1948 the Minister became responsible for the administration of the N. Health Service and related subjects and thereupon Housing and Local Government separated from it and was placed under a new ministry.

HEALTH, PUBLIC. (1) Provoked by sporadic cholera, the Public Health Act, 1848, set up a General Board of Health and empowered it, upon petition showing a death rate of 23 per 1000 or more in a locality, to make a local inquiry and recommend the creation of a local board of health which, in an area consisting entirely of a borough, would be the borough council but elsewhere would be elected by ratepayers. Such boards would be created by a parliamentary order; they were financed by the rates and they dealt with water, sewerage, drainage, paving, scavenging, burials, nuisances and pleasure grounds. Authorities for these purposes (singly or separately)

already existed under improvement acts in various places and these were sometimes, but not always, absorbed when new authorities were set up. The system spread slowly and only to certain towns.

(2) The Public Health Act, 1875, created urban and rural sanitary authorities. The former were all borough councils, improvement commissions and local boards of health; the rural sanitary authorities were the boards of guardians of the rural poor law unions. Their main function in practice was the provision of sewerage, though they had all their previous powers as well as others concerned with housing, infections, diseases, hospitals, highways, markets and slaughterhouses. *See* LOCAL ADMINISTRATION.

HEALY, Timothy Michael (1855-1931), self-taught Irishman, became parliamentary correspondent of the *Nation* in 1878 and impressed Parnell who got him to organise his Canadian mission. M.P. (Wexford 1880, Monaghan 1883, S. Londonderry 1885) and a barrister specialising in land (i.e. political) cases and he made himself an expert on parliamentary procedure and obstruction. He opposed Parnell after 1890 because he thought that Gladstone's support was essential to Home Rule. After sporadic disputes with his party he was expelled in 1902 but held his seats with R. Catholic support. By 1914 he was a critic of Redmond. In 1916 he declared in favour of Sinn Fein (save the use of force) and in 1918 resigned his seat in favour of a Sinn Fein prisoner. On the recommendation of Birkenhead and Kevin O'Higgins he became first Gov-Gen. of the Irish Free State. He retired in 1928.

HEARNE, Thomas (1678-1735), Oxford antiquary, had published many editions of Latin classics and Leland's *Itinerary* by 1715. In 1716 he was deprived of his academic posts as an extreme non-juror but published Camden's *Annales* and many English chronicles afterwards. His immense *Diaries* record Oxford politics and intrigues at their best and nastiest.

HEARTH MONEY or TAX at 2s. a hearth was imposed in 1662. It was highly unpopular and, though lucrative, was abolished in 1689 in favour of the Land Tax.

HEARTS OF STEEL (Ir). A protestant movement mainly in Ulster in 1772. Many of the M. of Donegal's leases fell in and he demanded £100,000 in all by way of renewal fines. The best tenants left for America. He and other similar landlords put in R. Catholic tenants. The dispossessed destroyed the cattle and burned the farms of the new tenants. The latter set up the CATHOLIC DEFENDERS as a counter organisation. Four years of terrorism followed.

HEATH, Edward Richard George (1916-) was educated at a grammar school at Ramsgate (Kent) and went to Oxford where he was Pres. of the Union. He became a Tory M.P. (Bexley 1950-74; Sidcup from 1974) and Chief Whip (1955-9) and was Min. of Labour in 1959-60. Then he was Sec. for Trade and Industry (1963-4) and succeeded in limiting restrictive practices and monopolies. As Macmillan's Ld. Privy Seal (1960-3) he was sent to negotiate Britain's entry to the E.E.C., which he did so skilfully that their failure in the face of Gen. de Gaulle's opposition actually enhanced Heath's reputation. He was the first person to be openly elected leader of the Conservative Party (1965). He then led the Opposition until he won power in 1970 (*see* HEATH GOVT JUNE 1970-MAR. 1974). Cool and unemotional in approach, he impressed in argument but was not a rousing speaker. His victory in 1970 was more a product of Labour's deficiencies than his own appeal. In 1974 he sought popular support against the miners in a general election but the public was unconvinced and an oil crisis supervened. He lost the election not, as was suggested, because he was a bachelor; but in any case he had a countervailing reputation for honest forthrightness. He then led the Opposition after the defeat but was defeated for the Tory leadership by Margaret Thatcher in 1975. Thereafter he wrote books about music and sailing and played the role of a not-quite-older statesman. He had always tempered his conservatism with a belief that free competition can go too far: his characterisation of one powerful private company's conduct as 'showing the unacceptable face of capitalism' has passed into the language. Margaret Thatcher's brand of revolutionary Toryism did not appeal to him nor, apparently, did she, and he refused to serve under her and was an occasional critic by implication as when, in 1981, he said that monetarism had 'no intellectual justification whatsoever'.

HEATH GOVT. (June 1970-Mar. 1974). The 1970 general election gave the Tories 330 seats, Labour 287 and the rest 13. Iain Macleod, as Ch. of the Exch. died in July and was succeeded by Anthony Barber. Sir Alec Douglas-Home, the former Prime Minister, became Foreign Sec., Reginald Maudling accepted the Home Office but resigned in 1972. William Whitelaw, Lord Pres. became Sec. for N. Ireland in 1972 but relieved Maurice Macmillan at the Dept. of Employment in 1973. Lord Carrington held the Dept. of Defence until 1974 and was then replaced by Sir Ian Gilmour. Margaret Thatcher was at Education and Science, Peter Walker created the Dept. of the Environment after a short spell at the Min. of Health, which was taken over by Sir Keith Joseph. Whitelaw's successor in N. Ireland was Francis Pym.

(1) The govt. entered office with a clear idea of its intention to let industries and people stand on their own feet without automatic resort to govt. help but was soon forced off course. The Industrial Reorganisation Corporation and the Prices and Incomes Board had been abolished as inconsistent with the intended competition, and taxation had been reduced, but unemployment and inflation rose markedly in the first two years and soon the govt. was helping what it had called 'lame duck' industries such as Rolls Royce and Upper Clyde Shipbuilders because of the social probabilities of not doing so. By 1972 they were establishing new industrial development and prices organisations which reflected the old. Meanwhile, to curb the trade unions the Industrial Relations Act, 1971, incorporated sanctions against unions which broke contracts, and imposed strike ballots and codes of conduct. This had wide support but there was a groundswell of industrial unrest due to an economic downturn. The 1973 oil crisis coincided with a struggle over miners' pay. Miners, electricians and railwaymen imposed overtime bans. A November state of emergency was followed in Jan. by the introduction of a three-day working week. The miners called a strike and Heath went to the polls on the slogan 'who rules Britain?'. Meanwhile the balance of payments was causing sporadic disquiet and the govt's. policy of expansion at all costs was coming to grief because of the world depression. Electoral disaster followed.

(2) The govt. did, however, have some achievements to its credit. Margaret Thatcher dropped universal comprehensivisation. A Fair Trading Act gave the consumer some more rights against sellers; steps were taken to retrain redundant workers and the Independent Broadcasting Authority was set up to organise the introduction of commercial broadcasting. The Local Govt. Act 1972 prepared the much criticised reorganisation of 1974 and a system of regional development grants was instituted. Unfortunately, in preparation for entry into the E.E.C. the currency was decimalised and this tipped the economy towards inflation. Rhodesia and N. Ireland, however, continued to consume time, energy and patience.

HEATH, Nicholas (?1501-78) accompanied Edw. Fox in 1535 on his mission to the league of Schmalkalden in connection with Henry VIII's divorce; he became the King's almoner in 1537 and Bp. of Rochester in 1539. In 1543 he was demoted to Worcester. In 1551, under Edward VI, he was deprived and imprisoned but restored in 1553 at Mary I's accession. He became Abp. of York in 1555 and Lord Chancellor in 1556 and was very active in recovering property alienated from the See. At Elizabeth's accession he was imprisoned but released on condition that he took no part in public affairs.

HEATH, Sir Robert (1575-1649) was M.P. in 1623 and 1625 and became att.gen. in 1625. He drafted the answer to the Petition of Right in 1628 and was much engaged in the Star Chamber prosecutions of 1629 and 1630. From 1631 to 1634 he was C.J. of the Common Pleas, but was dismissed on the ground of puritan sympathies. In 1641, however, he became a justice and in 1642 C.J. of the King's Bench. He tried a number of parliamentarians at Oxford and Salisbury and in 1645 was impeached and went into exile.

HEATHCOTE, Sir Gilbert (?1651-1733) was a principal refounder of the H.E.I.C. in 1693 and one of the first directors of the Bank of England in 1694. In 1700 he became Whig M.P. for London until 1710 when he was Lord Mayor. He was M.P. for Helston in 1714, for Lymington in 1722 and for St. Germans in Cornwall (1727) In 1732 he was one of the commissioners for Georgia. He was reputed the richest commoner of his time.

HEATHCOTE AMORY, Derick (1899-1981) 1st Vist. AMORY of TIVERTON (1963). Eton and Oxford educated Tory M.P. for Tiverton (1945-60) was Min. of Pensions (1951-3) then Pres. of the Bd. of Trade (1953-4) and Min. of Agriculture (1954-8). From 1958 to 1960 he was Ch. of the Exch. and as such persuaded the Cabinet to reduce taxation to encourage economic expansion. From 1961 to 1963 he was High Commissioner to Canada.

HEATON HALL (Prestwich) late Georgian mansion built by James Wyatt in 1772 for the Es. of Wilton.

HEBER, Reginald (1783-1826) first published his many hymns in 1811-12. He was Bp. of Calcutta from 1822, travelled all over India and completed the establishment of Bishops College, Calcutta.

HEBRIDES. *See* ISLES, LORDSHIP OF THE.

HECTORS were young bullies during the Interregnum. cf Mohawks.

HEDGEHOG or SCHILTRON (Med). A circular or oval formation of pike- or spearmen.

HEDGE SCHOOLS (Ir.). Acts of 1696 and 1710 forbade R. Catholics to teach or to send their children abroad for education. Accordingly the many illegal priests and teachers held schools in hidden places:-

"Still crouching 'neath the sheltering hedge,
Or stretched on mountain fern,
The teacher and his pupils met feloniously to learn."
John O'Hagan.

HEDGES (1) Sir William (1632-1701) after being the Levant Co's factor at Constantinople was gov. of Bengal from 1682 to 1684 and a director of the Bank of England from 1694. His cousin **(2) Sir Charles (?-1714)**, admiralty judge from 1689, was an M.P. for a variety of small boroughs from 1698 and Sec. of State from 1700 to 1706.

HEGIRA **(A.D. 622).** The flight of the Prophet Mohammed from Mecca to Medina and the date from which adherents of Islam commence their era.

HEIC Honourable East India Company (q.v.). Commonly found on its property and coins.

HEIMSKRINGLA. See SNORRI STURLASSON.

HEIR-AT-LAW. At common law real property passed at death (otherwise than for felony and treason) to the owner's **(1)** eldest son and his line, whom failing to **(2)** the eldest son's brothers successively in order of age and their respective lines, whom failing to **(3)** his daughters in equal shares, whom failing to **(4)** his father's descendants in like order, whom failing to the descendants in like order successively of **(5)** his grandfather, **(6)** his great-grandfather and **(7)** so forth until a point is reached where the LAST PURCHASER (i.e. the person in whom the property was last vested otherwise than by inheritance) is ascertained. If he had no eligible descendant, the property ESCHEATED to the Crown. This order of inheritance could be disturbed by sale or by will and it did not apply in areas of Gavelkind and Borough English. Consequently from about 1650 it applied only on intestacy of an unsettled estate. Since 1925 the list has been greatly limited. Apart from the rules on purchase, wills and escheat, a hereditary dignity passed in accordance with similar provisions unless otherwise limited in the patent of creation. Such limitation was normal.

HEJAZ. *See* ARABIA *passim*; CALIPHATE *passim*; LAWRENCE. T.E.; WORLD WAR I-8.

HELICOPTERS. Autogyros deriving propulsion from a propeller but their lift from unpowered rotors were invented in 1923. The modern helicopter, derived from them, was developed after 1940 by the ex-Russian Sikorski in the U.S.A.

HELIGOLAND (N. Sea). Danish from 1714, it was occupied by the British in 1806 as a base for smuggling goods into Bonaparte's continental system and ceded to Britain in 1814. In 1884 the Germans, who were about to open the Kiel Canal, suggested cession and in 1890 they received it in return for recognition of British protectorates over Zanzibar. They immediately fortified it and it became the key to their seaward defences in the Bight. Under the T. of Versailles the fortifications were destroyed in 1921 but after 1933 it was even more heavily refortified by Hitler. The fortifications were again destroyed in 1945.

HELL-FIRE CLUBS were early 18th cent. assns of wealthy young ruffians mainly in London. The FRANCISCAN or HELL-FIRE CLUB, founded in 1745 by Sir Francis Dashwood at Medmenham, was a society for drink, debauchery, mock witchcraft and other amusements under the Rabelaisian motto *Fay ce que voudras* (Do what you like).

HELOT'S DESPATCH. (*See* SALISBURY'S THIRD GOVT-11.) Sir Alfred Milner, High Commissioner in S. Africa, wrote to the British govt. (Apr. 1899) about conditions in the Transvaal. "The spectacle of thousands of British subjects kept permanently in the position of helots, . . . calling vainly to H.M. govt. for redress, does steadily undermine the influence and reputation of Great Britain and the respect for British govt. within the Queen's Dominions."

HELSINGFORS. Now Helsinki (Finland).

HELVETIC CONFESSION. *See* CALVINISM.

HELVETIC REPUBLIC. *See* SWITZERLAND.

HELY-HUTCHINSON (1) John (1724-94) a barrister, was an Irish M.P. in 1759 (Lanesborough) and from 1761 to 1794. He advocated Irish home rule, free trade, parliamentary reform and R. Catholic emancipation. By 1760 he was prime serjeant and one of the best known figures in Ireland. He became provost of Trinity, Dublin, in 1774 and founded the modern language school and in 1778 he was also briefly Sec. of State. Of his two sons **(2) Richard (1756-1825) 1st Vist. SUIRDALE (1797) and 1st E. of DONOUGHMORE (1800),** also an advocate of emancipation, supported the union (for which he received his earldom) and thereafter was an Irish representative peer. He was P.M.G. for Ireland from 1805 to 1809. **(3) John (1757-1832) 1st Ld. HUTCHINSON (1801)** and **2nd E.,** a soldier, was an Irish M.P. from 1776 to 1783 and from 1790 to 1800 and like his brother supported the Union but he was a divisional commander under Abercromby in Egypt and succeeded to the chief command in 1801. He cleared the country of the French. In 1806 he undertook a confidential mission to Prussia and Russia and in 1820 he was George IV's intermediary with Q. Caroline at St. Omer. A descendant **(4) Richard**

Walter John (1875-1948) 6th E. (1900) was U/Sec. for War from 1903 to 1905 and Lord Chairman of Cttees. from 1911 to 1931. He was also chairman of commissions on the Ceylon Constitution (1927-8) and on ministers' powers (1929-31).

HEMEL HEMPSTEAD. *See* NEW TOWNS.

HEMMING (fl.1080-1100). Sub-prior of Worcester, was commissioned by Bp. Wulfstan II (1062-95) to compile a cartulary, with historical notes, using the archives of the cathedral. *Hemming's Cartulary* consists of copies (1090-1100) of royal, episcopal and other charters. He also wrote a Life of St. Wulfstan shortly after the bishop's death.

HENDERSON, Alexander (?1583-1646) a political presbyterian divine who became minister at Leuchars in 1614. A forceful yet attractive personality with an unwavering belief in the dialectic of his faith and a discerning eye for the tactics needed to further it, he came into prominence over the failed opposition to the Five Articles of Perth in 1618. Thereafter he led or inspired the general shift of opinion against Laudian reforms. In 1637 he promoted the remonstrance against episcopacy which prepared the way for the National Covenant. The latter, with three coadjutors, he drafted himself and published at Greyfriars Church, Edinburgh, in 1638. He was now, in fact if not in name, the leader of the most important popular Scots urban movement. He was Moderator of Glasgow Assembly in that year and secured the adoption of the presbyterian organisation and in 1639 he was called to the Edinburgh High Kirk, which established him permanently at the centre of affairs. His services were in demand for secular issues. He was with the Scots army in the Bishop's Wars: was a Scots Commissioner at the Pacification of Berwick (1639) and then returned to persuade the Edinburgh Assembly to entrench the Glasgow reforms by passing the Barrier Act (1639). This presupposed that in Church affairs the Assembly was superior to Parliament or the estates, a position which lowland opinion accepted. He was thus powerfully placed when he returned to the army for the invasion of England and was able to negotiate the T. of Ripon (1641) which simultaneously solved the problem of Scots military finance and strengthened his potential Westminster allies. In 1641 he carried the church reforms a stage further by proposing to the St. Andrews Assembly the terms of a confession of faith and the publication of a Directory of Public Worship. He was soon in a way to imposing presbyterianism in England by means of the Solemn League and Covenant, yet he was posting incessantly between London, the King at Oxford and Scotland. His overstrained constitution broke down and he died an early death. His influence on Scottish life and religion was, however, pervasive and durable.

HENDERSON, Arthur (1863-1935) originally active in the Iron Founders' Union at Newcastle and from 1892 a member of the City Council, became Labour M.P. for Barnard Castle in 1903 and, save in 1932, was an M.P. until his death. In 1911 he became Sec. of the Labour Party and in 1914 its chief whip in the Commons. He was Pres. of the Bd. of Education from 1915 to 1916; a member of Lloyd George's War Cabinet from 1916 to 1917; Home Sec. under Macdonald in 1924 and Foreign Sec. from 1929 to 1931. Deeply respected in all levels of society, he was Pres. of the World Disarmament Conference from 1932 to 1935.

HENDERSON, Sir Neville Meyrick (1882-1942) a career diplomat with experience in senior posts in Egypt, France, Yugoslavia and the Argentine, became Ambassador to Germany in 1937, just before Hitler concluded the Axis agreement with Mussolini which destroyed Austria. He did not appreciate the fundamental treachery of Hitler's govt. and believed and allowed Chamberlain's govt. to think that Hitler's European appetite might be capable of satisfaction or that an accommodation with him might facilitate a defence of Europe against Communist Russian imperialism, or both. He thus bore an important share of the responsibility for the Munich agreement and for the advent of the war which seems, nevertheless, to have surprised him.

HENDON POLICE COLLEGE. *See* POLICE-4,5.

HENGIST (?-488) and HORSA (?-455) two, probably priestly, Jutish chiefs, traditionally brothers, who were employed as mercenaries by Vortigern, the British ruler of Kent. *See* HORSE MEAT; KENT-1.

HENLEY-ON-THAMES (Oxon). The regatta dates from 1839.

HENLEY, Walter of (fl. c. 1250). Dominican writer on agriculture. His French *Hosbondrie* survives in many copies including Latin, English and Welsh translations.

HENNESSY, Richard (1720-1800), originally an Irish soldier in French service, settled in the Cognac area in 1765 and founded the well-known distilling business named after him.

HENRIETTA or HENRIETTE ANNE ("MINETTE") (1644-70) fifth *d.* of Charles I, married Philip D. of Orleans in 1661. She was a person of great charm and a literary patron; she sometimes acted as a confidential intermediary between Louis XIV and her brother Charles II, particularly in connection with the secret T. of Dover (1670) when she introduced Louise de Kerouaille to him. She died suddenly.

HENRIETTA MARIA (1609-69) *d.* of Henry IV and Marie de Medicis, married Charles I in 1625, abstained from politics at first but her theatrical interests made her the target of Prynne's *Histriomastix* in 1632. Her activities until the beginning of the civil war were unimportant but from 1640 onwards she acted as Charles' intermediary with France, Holland and the Papacy. Money was needed and much was obtained as part of the marriage agreement with William of Orange. Some of this was used to finance the "army plot" to rescue Strafford, but the plot was betrayed and her activities became widely known. In Jan. 1642 she is said to have counselled the very similar *coup* which ended in the fiasco of the Five Members, and in Feb. she left for Holland where she raised large sums by pawning or selling plate and jewels. In Feb. 1643, after the civil war had begun, she ran the parliamentary blockade to Bridlinglon with the money and with a small force reached Charles at Edgehill in July. She was with him until Apr. 1644 when she escaped to France. Thereafter her political activity, though unremitting, was largely ineffectual as France declined into the Fronde. After the Restoration she lived until 1665 at Somerset House.

HENRY I (1068-1135) King (1100) (1) On his deathbed William the Conqueror left Normandy to his irresponsible eldest son Robert; England to his favourite William Rufus, but 5000 lb of silver to Henry who, though but 19, had the business sense to have it weighed out before his father expired. Robert's incompetence soon had Normandy in disorder and this suited William who wanted the Duchy but preferred to get it, if possible, by bribery or subornation. Henry determined to cut out a fitting lordship for himself by playing his brothers off against each other, while imitating William's tactics. In this way he acquired a Norman territory based on the fortresses of Cherbourg, Mont St. Michel and Domfront. In 1090, as a Norman feudatory, he helped Robert to put down a revolt in Rouen which William had instigated. Henry himself threw the leader of the revolt from a tower. William decided to come over himself (Feb. 1091) and he and Robert made a pact of mutual succession and aid in which Henry was expressly disinherited and Mont St. Michel and Cherbourg allotted to William. They then marched against Henry, who had to give them up.

(2) The three brothers then made peace and planned jointly to restore order in the Duchy, but trouble on the Scottish and Welsh borders supervened and they crossed the Channel and campaigned in the north. At this point Normandy was threatened from the east; Robert went back and denounced his agreement with William, who promptly hired Henry to fight for him there while William dealt with revolts in England. Thus Henry acted as William's military representative in Normandy with occasional interruptions by William.

(3) In 1095 Robert wanted to join the First Crusade and pledged his Duchy to William in return for a loan of 10,000 marks. He then left for the East. William cleared up some business in England and on the Welsh border and in 1097 crossed the Channel to defend Normandy against the future Louis VI. From this time Henry and William were much in each other's company and he was hunting with William in the New Forest when the latter was killed by Sir Walter Tyrel's arrow.

(4) Henry at 32 was well versed in the govt. affairs of Normandy and England. Whether William's death was an accident or murder and whether, if murder, Henry was implicated, is quite uncertain. No one suggested murder at the time. What is certain is that Henry understood what to do and that he immediately extended high favour to the Clare family who were relatives and patrons of Sir Walter Tyrel. He left the body lying, rode for Winchester, seized the Treasury, within 36 hours had himself recognised as King and within a further 36 hours was crowned at Westminster (5 Aug. 1100). He had reason for haste. Robert was nearing home with a new well-dowered wife, a better claim to the throne and the possibility of a son to inherit his rights and he could afford to repay the loan and claim the Duchy. To defend his inferior position Henry appealed to the public. He invited the exiled Abp. Anselm back and Anselm arrived in Sept. He arrested William's unpopular minister Ranulf Flambard. In his coronation charter he promised to revert to the 'Laws of King Edward', renounced William's 'unjust oppressions', remitted arrears, abolished reliefs for marriages and other incidents and freed the demesnes of knights' fees from the geld, and he issued a general pardon for certain offences. To please the English he married (Nov.) Eadgyth *d.* of the late K. Malcolm Canmore of Scots and Q. Margaret, a princess of the Wessex House of Cerdic. She took the name Matilda. At the end of the year Henry was able to get oaths of allegiance from all his subjects.

(5) This settling-in process took time and Henry could not be in two countries at once. Robert had reached Normandy within a month of William's death. He was well received and took possession without repaying the loan. He claimed the English throne, organised an expedition and built up a party in England. Henry mobilised. His fleet deserted him and Robert evaded his army at Pevensey by landing at Portsmouth (July 1101). Hence the two forces faced each other at Alton where they were so evenly balanced that they preferred a parley. The result was the T. of Alton. The brothers agreed that Henry should keep England; Robert, Normandy, subject to mutual presumptive succession; that Henry should pay Robert an annuity of 2000 marks and that each should pardon his rebellious vassals. Robert, thus defeated, returned home where his incompetence soon caused widespread complaint. Meanwhile Henry found lawful means to punish Robert's English supporters for reasons not covered in the treaty. By the time he had driven the house of Bellême (*see* BELLÊME OR TALVAS) out of the country he had destroyed the internal opposition (end of 1102).

(6) Meanwhile there was a postponed controversy with the Church over lay investiture. Anselm, on arrival, was asked to perform the usual homage for his temporalities, but on grounds of canon law refused to do so or to consecrate bishops who had received the staff and ring from Henry. As war with Robert was imminent, they agreed to consult the Pope (Paschal II) and that meanwhile Anselm should enjoy the temporalities *de facto*. Anselm, saintly logician that he was, then co-operated over the King's marriage and even at times took charge of the defences of Kent.

(7) Henry now laid foundations for the conquest of Normandy, where lay opinion was hardening against Robert for his misgovernment, and church opinion because of his simony. Moreover, unlike Henry, he had come to a rupture with the Papacy over lay investiture. The Normans had had experience of Henry's abilities and were comparatively easy to win over. The Bp. of Séez was his supporter. The pardoned Ranulf Flambard had effective control of the bishopric of Lisieux as Henry's agent, and Henry's diplomacy was depriving Robert of any hopes of support from his neighbours, the French King and the rulers of Brittany, Maine, Anjou and Flanders.

(8) The first step was to take an opportunity foolishly offered by Robert himself. He came to England to protest against the deprivation of Earl Warenne, one of his supporters, of the earldom of Surrey. Henry flatly refused to heed him, brought counter-accusations and forced him to surrender his annuity. This slap in the face enormously damaged the magnificent Crusader's prestige. In 1103 Henry went further. He sent Robert of Meulan to restore order in Robert's Duchy, as if the Duke could not do it himself. In 1104 he went to Normandy in person and made Robert surrender the homage of the Count of Évreux. In Apr. 1105 he invaded in earnest *via* his old possession in the Cotentin and with much local support took Caen and Bayeux. He met Robert and Robert of Bellême at Falaise (May) but they could not agree. In Aug. he had to return to England and they visited him with arguments during the winter. In June 1106 he resumed the offensive with his allies from Brittany and Maine. Robert's effort to relieve William of Mortain's castle at Tinchebray developed into a short decisive battle (28 Sept. 1106) in which Robert of Bellême fled the field and the rest were captured with most of their troops. Robert and William of Mortain never regained their liberty. The Bellêmes were reduced to impotence and Henry took over and reformed the Duchy.

(9) The period of the war also covered the negotiations establishing the Investiture Compromise which was ratified at London in Aug. 1106.

(10) Whatever its merits, the conquest of Normandy added a third frontier to Henry's possessions. The Duchy had to be policed and defended. Though Louis VI recognised Henry's possession in 1107, by 1109 he was at war and fomenting rebellion. This first war was mostly fought in the Vexin and sucked in Theobald of Blois on Henry's side and Anjou and Flanders on the other. It ended in 1113 (T. of Gisors) when Fulk of Anjou did homage to Henry, to whom Louis surrendered the homage and suzerainty of Maine and Brittany. Meanwhile Henry's d. Matilda was sent to Germany (1110) with a view to marrying the Emperor Henry V, which she did on attaining puberty in 1114. A second war was begun in 1115 by a quarrel between Theobald of Blois and the Count of Nevers. Henry supported his nephews of Blois. Louis, with Anjou and Flanders, supported the Count, and pro-French elements in Normandy tried to recognise Duke Robert's son William the Clito as Duke. In 1118 Baldwin of Flanders was mortally wounded. In June Fulk of Anjou decided to join a Crusade and visited Henry. In return for peace and funds he married his daughter to William the Aetheling (Henry's only legitimate son), settled Maine on her and, should he die on Crusade, Anjou as well. The climax of the reign now followed. Louis reacted by invading Normandy from the Vexin. He was routed at the B. of Brémule (Aug. 1119). The Pope (Calixtus II) negotiated a settlement advantageous to Henry, who was now the most powerful and stable ruler in Europe, father-in-law of the Emperor, distant cousin of the Pope and with further prospects of family inheritance.

(11) The wreck of the drunkenly manned *White Ship* changed everything. William the Aetheling, many nobles and members of the royal administration were drowned on a voyage from Harfleur to England. The only presumptive heir was now the Empress Matilda but there was no precedent for a female succession, much less by an Empress consort: therefore pretenders were bound to appear and Henry had to work very hard to resettle a stable future. Eadgyth having died in 1118, his first step was to remarry in the hope of an heir (Feb. 1121). His second wife was Adelaide of Louvain, a choice intended to strengthen his Flemish influence and bring it closer to Germany. Meanwhile the lapse of Count Fulk's settlement was followed by the reappearance of the Count himself (1121). He reasonably demanded the return of his widowed daughter. Henry refused. A third war broke out in 1123 accompanied by rebellions in the name of William the Clito, whom Fulk married to his second daughter Sybil. In Mar. 1124, however, Henry defeated and captured the chief Norman rebels at Bourgthérould. He then persuaded the Papacy to annul the marriage for consanguinity and the Emperor to invade France. This invasion (Aug. 1124) was a failure but distracted the French King. The war ended, nevertheless, in a distinct success for Henry.

(12) The scene was now transformed again with the Emperor's death (1125). Henry's second marriage was barren, but Matilda was now available. The dynasty might be re-established by a suitable marriage and an Angevin marriage might recover the loss in the *White Ship*. Matilda was summoned home. She came with an ill grace, having spent 14 of her 24 years in Germany in the highest social position in Europe, to the prospect of marriage to Geoffrey of Anjou, a mere count and a boy. She was strong and determined, but a termagant and essentially foreign, and she and the barons made a bad impression on each other. There were murmurings when she was presented to them as heir to the Kingdom (Dec. 1126) and the oaths had to be resworn when she married Geoffrey Plantagenet (June 1128), for neither the English nor the Norman barons had been consulted. Then in 1131 Geoffrey, finding her impossible, repudiated her and Henry brought her back to England where the oaths had to be resworn once more (Sept.). Meanwhile Geoffrey's father, Fulk, had been offered the crown of Jerusalem. Geoffrey needed support when Fulk left for the East and asked for her. She returned. It seems that he had grown up for in Mar. 1133 she bore him the future Henry II and in June 1134 another son, Geoffrey. The dynastic future now seemed secure, but at this moment Geoffrey demanded possession of Normandy. During the ensuing civil war Henry I died.

(13) Political events apart, the remarkable feature of the reign is that Henry had seen that in the two previous reigns govt. had depended upon the royal personality. The business of govt. was expanding geographically and in quantity and kind. An institution, however simple, was needed to stand beside the King and carry on his work no matter how busy or distant he might be. Henry was illiterate but he understood the value of literacy and the need for permanent records and accounts. In his reign the beginnings of a govt. machine may be discerned.

HENRY II (1133-89) King (1154) (*See* ANGEVINS.) **(1)** The death of Stephen's son Eustace cleared the way for Henry II's title, through his mother, to England and Normandy. Through his wife, Eleanor, he had the vast lands of Aquitaine and its dependent fiefs. A remarkable ruler in any age, Henry was clever, violent, imaginative, passionately addicted to hunting and hawking yet cultivated and intellectual, and possessed of a superabundant energy which enabled him to travel further and faster than other men, sleep with many women and comprehend the detail of great policies and the inwardness of the greatest issues.

(2) The territories from the Cheviots to the Pyrenees were held or claimed in different rights and governed by different customs. The one unifying factor was Henry and his travelling court. Consolidation and police were the first essentials. He quickly eliminated the surviving elements of the English anarchy. Aldulterine castles were reduced: masterless mercenaries rounded up and Stephen's Flemings sent home or despatched to colonise Pembrokeshire. This, however, was preliminary to absorption in the foreign issues raised by the geography of his dominions. The anarchy had presented opportunities to the Scots, whose King, precariously in occupation of the north as far as the Tees and the Ribble, was, however, in conflict with the Es. of Chester; but the distractions caused by these disputes had caused the Earls to give way before the well organised Welsh principality of Gwynedd, whose forces had crossed the Clwyd towards Flint. In S. Wales the Marcher Lords had supported Matilda in the civil wars and her defeat had weakened them too, in the face of resurgent Welsh princes in Powys and Deheubarth. Pembrokeshire, however, was considered safe and Welsh strength may have been exaggerated. In 1155 Henry was planning to invade Ireland from Pembroke and, though dissuaded from instant action by his mother, began to negotiate for Papal approval. Similarly the Scots threat was less pressing than at first it seemed. K. David I had left two grandsons, both children. The elder, Malcolm the Maiden, became a weak king: the younger, William, was only E. of Northumberland. This partition and the factions associated with regencies facilitated English recovery in the north.

(3) Across the Channel the pressing problem was Louis VII of France, his irreconcilable political and personal enemy. The spirit of the age disapproved direct assaults on a sovereign overlord, so that with all his worldly power, Henry was always at a moral disadvantage in a contest with the French King; conversely the latter had to find legal justifications for interfering in the dominions of one who had sworn to be his man. Thus Henry's tendency was to hold Louis in check through foreign alliances; Louis' to encourage internal disruption of Henry's territories. In parallel with these themes were the military and diplomatic activities concerned with particular frontiers and trade routes.

(4) The action equivalent to the pacification of England was the extrusion in 1156 of Henry's brother Geoffrey from Anjou, Maine and Touraine. This was vital to any unified policy because these lands divided Henry's northern from his wife's southern territories and marched with the French King's demesne. Geoffrey had been left them by his father. Henry forced him to accept a single castle and a pension and the French King was unable to intervene: legally because Geoffrey's possession infringed the local rule of succession, or politically because Henry was in diplomatic contact with the Emperor, Frederick Barbarossa. An opportunity for the brothers to act in concert appeared, however, within weeks: tired of rival claimants since the death of Count Conon II in 1148, Lower Brittany and Nantes chose Geoffrey as Count of Brittany. The opportunity to pacify Geoffrey and secure a foothold in Brittany seemed heaven sent. Better still, Geoffrey died in 1158 and Henry was his heir. Louis had to recognise the fact but Henry set about making double sure. Conon IV of Brittany was E. of Richmond and susceptible to pressure. Henry secured the betrothal of Conon's daughter Constance to his own son, also called Geoffrey, and so united the elective and hereditary rights. The Bretons, in general, were not pleased. Meanwhile, to the north the Norman border was stable even though the castles of the Vexin had passed into French hands during the Anarchy. In 1158 Henry arranged a child match between his son Henry (aged 3) and Margarite of France (aged six months). Her dowry was to be the Vexin which, pending the wedding, was to be in Templar trusteeship.

(5) The King, as was his habit, was making one purpose serve another. He was raising taxes and armaments for a great campaign in the south. The display of so much power had alarmed Louis and pleased the Pope (Adrian IV) who, anxious to reform the Irish church, approved the projected conquest of Ireland in the bull *Laudabiliter*. It was some years yet before it was put into effect. Meanwhile the great expedition moved against Toulouse (1159), to whose suzerainty Eleanor, as duchess, had an ill-defined claim.

(6) The Toulousaine campaign was an important event. Henry had allied himself with Count Raymond-Berengar of Barcelona, Regent of Aragon, and had raised great sums by accepting scutages, taking forced gifts and taxing the Jews and the boroughs. With this he had assembled many mercenaries. This was the first time that English statesmen became involved in Spanish politics. P. Richard (aged 2) was betrothed to the Count's daughter.

(7) The campaign itself failed, for K. Louis occupied Toulouse and so shielded it with his overlordship. During the blockade, however, there occurred a papal schism when, by Barbarossa's influence, Victor IV was elected against Alexander III and drove him from Rome The politics of Victor and his master were resented and when Henry and Louis made peace (May 1160) they agreed at Beauvais to recognise Alexander: but Henry separately got from Alexander a dispensation for the marriage of the children Henry and Margarite in return for the recognition and so helped himself to the Vexin. Louis was furious but Barbarossa could not afford to support him: Henry's influence in politics and Hanseatic trade was too valuable.

(8) One reason for Henry's success hitherto was that Thomas Becket's abilities were at his disposal, but from 1162, when he became Archbishop, these began to be used in a contrary interest. The English church developed into a source of political as well as social disorder but, as usual, there were compensations. The able and faithful Richard de Lucy became, as Justiciar for the next 17 years, the King's English Lieut., an office in which he was to relieve his king of much pressure of work. The continental balance, equally, remained stable for some years. Barbarossa, enmeshed in his Italian schemes, needed Henry to keep the French in check as much as Henry needed him for the same purpose. Friendly relations between the English and Imperial courts assumed a new dimension when Becket and Henry began to quarrel in 1163. By Jan. 1164 the dispute had developed into a full scale battle, brought to an issue by the Constitutions of Clarendon. Henry's determination to ruin Becket brought about his flight (Nov. 1164). Thenceforth Becket appealed for European public opinion and Alexander III's support. Since Barbarossa had an anti-Pope (now Paschal III) in his pocket, it was natural for he and Henry to come closer together. In 1165 Rainald of Dassel, Abp. of Cologne and Imperial Chancellor, led an embassy to Henry at Rouen where a marriage treaty was made. Henry's daughter Eleanor was betrothed to the emperor's infant son Frederick (an arrangement which was eventually abortive), and his 9-year-old daughter Matilda was betrothed to Henry the Lion of Saxony and Bavaria, a marriage with lasting consequences. Moreover Henry agreed to send a representative to Barbarossa's diet, called to Worzburg for May 1165, to discuss the unity of the church. This threat to Alexander's position undercut Becket's too, and immobilised the French King, just as Welsh affairs came to a head.

(9) The Lord Rhys (*see* DEHEUBARTH-16) invaded Cardigan and in concert with Owain of Gwynedd made a general attack on the Anglo-Norman lordships. Henry concentrated a large, mostly professional, army at

Shrewsbury and hired a fleet of Ostmen. Owain and Rhys barred his way at Corwen. Marshes, rain and the breakdown of supplies forced Henry to retreat without a battle and Breton troubles ensured that he would not return. Meanwhile the princes extended their conquests: by 1167 Owain had reached the Dee and Rhys had taken Cardigan castle.

(10) The Bretons disliked Normans as much as the Welsh did and, additionally, maritime rivalry raised the temperature. Henry had to conduct three successive campaigns (1166-8) to reduce them. Their example spread. In 1167 there was trouble in the Auvergne, this time fomented by Louis VII. The result was a destructive, if intermittent, war throughout 1168.

(11) A feature of Henry's methods was to delegate responsibility to men whom he hoped that he might trust. In the case of Richard de Lucy he was justified: in that of Becket mistaken. As long ago as 1166 Dermot McMorrough, exiled King of Leinster, had appealed to Henry for help; and Henry (then in Aquitaine) morally encouraged by *Laudabiliter* licensed Dermot to raise supporters. In 1168 Dermot recruited Maurice fitzGerald and Robert fitzStephen, half brothers and magnates in W. Wales, and agreed to marry his daughter Eva to Richard ("Strongbow") E. of Pembroke and Striguil and to make him his heir. Then he went to Leinster, became involved in further disputes and called for help. FitzStephen arrived first (May 1169) with a very small force and took Wexford. Even so, part of it under Maurice of Prendergast deserted to Dermot's enemies and the result was a compromise peace, instantly upset by FitzGerald's arrival. Dermot wanted to use his reinforcements to overthrow the High King of Ireland. The Normans, not averse, advised further reinforcements and between them they persuaded Strongbow to come.

(12) It was natural to attempt to solve some of the fidelity problems by delegation to royal children. Henry planned to confer Aquitaine on his second son Richard, Brittany on his third son Geoffrey, while the eldest, the Young Henry, was to receive Normandy, Maine and Anjou and be crowned as second King in England. In the French arrangements Louis VII, as suzerain, was necessarily involved and when the Auvergne war was settled (P. of Montmirail, Jan. 1169) Richard and Henry did homage to him for their proposed French fiefs. Geoffrey too was invested with Brittany in the summer. Young Henry's coronation then became urgent: for the brothers hated each other and delay in demonstrating his pre-eminence would jeopardise the long term unity of the Angevin dominions. The quarrel with Becket now became critical, for an archbishop of Canterbury was needed to crown a King. A papal legate had long been negotiating for a reconciliation but Becket knew his nuisance value and held out. Rather than risk further delay, the King had the coronation carried out by the Abp. of York and six other bishops in June 1170. In July, at La Ferté, he and Becket went through a form of general reconciliation. By this time Strongbow had assembled his Irish expedition and in Aug. he arrived in Ireland with 200 knights and 1000 light troops (say 2000 men). Waterford fell immediately and Dublin in Sept. This was more than Henry had intended and it weakened the Welsh garrisons. At the end of Nov., however, Owain Gwynedd died and the local dangers receded, but a week later Becket landed in England and started proceedings against the prelates who had crowned the young King. Their complaints and Henry's fury at Becket's breach of faith led to Becket's murder.

(13) The event shook Henry's throne and made the unsettled west a matter of urgency. He cut off reinforcements to Ireland just as Dermot McMorrough died (May 1171). Strongbow succeeded to his Leinster rights; but the Leinstermen would have none of him and joined with Rory O'Conor, the High King, in turning him

out. The Normans were besieged in Dublin all the summer, while at a council at Argentan in July Henry decided to come to Ireland himself. In fact Strongbow won a complete victory at Dublin while the royal expedition was forming. Henry now took advantage of his military presence to come to a settlement in Wales. Since the Normans were more interested in Ireland, it became necessary to rely on the Welsh. The Lord Rhys was taken into high favour and became, in effect, the King's delegate in Wales.

(14) Strongbow had come to England to treat with the King who forced him to cede Dublin, Waterford, Wexford and other fortresses and then enfeoffed him with the rest of Leinster. The impressive royal armament sailed for Waterford where Henry arrived in Oct., professing good will, protection and order for all. Apart from the chiefs of Connaught and the far north the provincial Kings came in to promise obedience and Henry built a palace at Dublin and entertained them. At Cashel he held a great ecclesiastical council during the winter, where reforming canons were promulgated and the bishops recognised him as Lord of Ireland. The proceedings were despatched to Alexander III.

(15) Henry's French dominions had, ever since Becket's murder, been under interdict and legates were on their way to dictate terms for his absolution. He was held up in Ireland for most of the winter by storms, but used the interval to enfeoff Hugh de Lacy with Meath. He got away in Apr. leaving Hugh (not Strongbow) as his delegate and reached Normandy in May 1172, when the formal reconciliation with the Papacy took place at Avranches (q.v.). Tempers had cooled in the interval and the Pope could hardly overlook the reform of the Irish church. The terms were light. In Sept. Alexander confirmed *Laudabiliter* and Henry's title as Lord of Ireland.

(16) The clash with the church had, personalities apart, been concerned with justice, finance and administration. This was to be expected, for these were the fields in which Henry, throughout his reign, carried out reforms. Wherever he could, he resumed royal properties alienated in Stephen's time. In 1157 he conferred privileges on the Cologne Hanse. In 1159 he accepted scutage for knight service. In 1166 his Assize of Clarendon improved the efficiency of criminal justice and, by the Inquest of Sheriffs of 1170, he improved local administration and tax collection. In the short term such measures were popular with the people and irritating only to the baronage. In the long run the greater efficiency of tax collection was bound to alienate all classes if the expense of govt. became burdensome. The cost of "foreign" policy was a major element in any such burden, for it involved the pursuit of ambitions in Ireland and Wales, the defence of the Scots border, the neutralisation of the French King, claims on Toulouse, the suppression of endemic disturbances in Aquitaine and Poitou, negotiations with the Emperor, dealings with the Pope, various involvements in Spain, especially since the Castilian marriage of his daughter Eleanor in 1170, and the increasing seaborne trade with which piracy constantly interfered. There was a diffusion of effort, too, which was shortly to leave the King weak everywhere; of this the Savoyard alliance was a further manifestation.

(17) The Pope and many Italian states were seeking allies against the ambitions of Barbarossa, who had invaded Italy six times since 1154. Henry had reasons for coming forward. There were personal relationships between the English and the Sicilian Normans. There were trading possibilities through Venice and the chance of becoming the Pope's chief protector. Henry spent large sums buying the goodwill of the Pope's Lombard citizen allies and in 1171 the impecunious and sonless Count Humbert III of Maurienne (Savoy-Piedmont) offered his daughter Alix and the succession to Henry for the four-year-old Prince John. Such an extension of his influence would give access to Italy, impede German access to the S. of France and isolate the County of Toulouse. When the marriage treaty was agreed at Montferrand in Jan. 1173, Raymond V of Toulouse also did homage to the two Henrys and to Richard as D. of Aquitaine.

(18) Since 1169 the Queen-Duchess Eleanor had not shared Henry's bed, but had held court with Richard and the southern troubadour knights at Poitiers. She encouraged her sons' opposition to their father. As they obtained the titles of power they became increasingly restive when Henry withheld its substance. The T. of Montferrand infringed the younger Henry's rights (*see* AQUITAINE). The long meditated rebellion was inspired by Louis VII, and Flanders and Scotland were involved, but Eleanor was seized before the outset (1173) and never regained her liberty until Henry's death. The younger Henry escaped to Paris where, with Louis' help, he offered lands and pensions to foreign allies: Kent and £1000 a year to the Count of Flanders, Northumberland to William the Lion of Scotland, Huntingdon to William's son David. Operations began in July. Imperfect enemy co-ordination, Henry's energy and his luck saved him. The Flemish attack on Normandy ended suddenly when Matthew of Boulogne, the Count's brother, was killed at Arques. Louis' advance was bogged down at Verneuil. The Bretons led by Hugh of Chester and Ralph of Fougères were scattered before they could fully assemble and the young Henry was taken at Dol. Thus the continental rebellion had collapsed before the young Henry's offer could be accepted by William the Lion. Henry II organised a peace conference and offered generous terms to his son which he, egged on by Louis, refused (Sept.). The rebellion had spread to Britain. Robert, E. of Leicester and Hugh Bigod, E. of Norfolk, had come out. Richard de Lucy and Ranulf Glanville were keeping order for the King and besieged Leicester. Strongbow and Hugh de Lacy were summoned from Ireland to Normandy, but after the abortive peace conference Earl Robert, with Flemish mercenaries, landed in Suffolk and marched for Leicester. The Constable, Humphrey Bohun, wiped out the Flemings and captured Earl Hugh; Norfolk hurriedly made a truce and sent his own Flemings home. Thereupon William the Lion started raiding across the border and crossed in force in the spring. Henry put down revolts in Anjou and Poitou and returned to find the midlands in arms and Flemish troops again landing in Suffolk. With Hugh Bigod of Norfolk they took Norwich, but Richard de Lucy and Humphrey Bohun were holding their own in the north; the King performed a desperate penance at Canterbury on 12 July. Next day they captured the King of Scots. The English rebel leaders quickly capitulated and Louis called off the Count of Flanders to concentrate for an attack on Rouen. Henry drove him back in Aug., forced P. Richard into submission in Poitou and imposed a generous peace on his sons and Louis at Montlouis (30 Sept. 1174). There was a general amnesty, but a wholesale demolition of private castles. Strongbow was rewarded with the Lieutenancy of Ireland. The T. of Falaise subjected Scotland and the Scots church to English supremacy.

(19) Great as was the physical damage, the war raised Henry's international stature while reducing the domestic prestige of even his greatest magnates. The work of institutional development could go forward in peace, while foreign potentates courted the formidable master of the west. Thus the Assize of Northampton (1176) supplemented the Assize of Clarendon by defining the circuits. The emperor Manuel Comnenus sought his aid. In 1177 Henry was invited to arbitrate between Castile and Navarre. The rapidly growing John, apple of Henry's eye, received great estates and the Lordship of Ireland. In 1178 Henry and Louis VII agreed to go on

crusade together (a promise which neither meant to keep). In 1179 Henry enacted the Grand Assize and in 1180 appointed Ranulf Glanville Chief Justice to carry out further judicial reforms. In 1180 he reformed the coinage; in 1181 enacted the Assize of Arms. During all these years Richard was busy acquiring his extraordinary military accomplishments putting down Aquitainian rebels.

(20) The years 1181 to 1183 reproduced on a smaller scale the rebellious years 1172 to 1174, but this time the victim of rebellion was Richard, the rebels were the Aquitainian baronage and their outside abettors were Henry the Young King, Geoffrey of Brittany, the Duke of Burgundy and the Count of Toulouse. Henry mobilised his troops but before he could intervene the young Henry died (11 June 1183). Richard, as heir to England, Normandy and Anjou, was expected to surrender Aquitaine for the benefit of his brother John, but this he reasonably refused to do. It was his homeland and he had ruled it himself for the past ten years. In 1184 and 1185 he beat off further attacks by Geoffrey and John and forced his father to reconsider John's endowment. Geoffrey died in 1186.

(21) In July 1187 Saladin defeated the forces of Outremer at Hattin and in Oct. took Jerusalem. The danger had been obvious for some time and an embassy had been in England from the Angevin King of Jerusalem since 1185. The shock caused a general resurgence of the crusading spirit. Richard took the cross at once. Henry and the new French King Philip (Augustus) did so later and with less enthusiasm. Richard needed assurance that his rights would be maintained in his absence. Henry refused them and by this, and immense enfeoffments, raised the overwhelming suspicion that he meant to replace Richard by John. He hindered the preparations for Richard's crusade and revolts broke out in Aquitaine and Toulouse. Richard put these down with such vigour that K. Philip made a diversion in Berry to save Toulouse itself. In July 1188 Henry took the field for the last time. During the desultory war Richard came to an understanding with Philip: at a peace conference at Bonmoulins in Nov. the two urged Henry to recognise Richard as his heir. Henry refused, whereupon Richard did homage to Philip for his continental lands, saving fealty owed to his father. This provoked another civil war, postponed by a papal legate in the interests of the crusade until May 1189 when, another conference having failed, Philip and Richard attacked. The combination was irresistible and the barons of Anjou, Maine and Touraine and even P. John deserted. Tours fell on 3 July. On the 4th Henry had to submit to a humiliating peace. On 6th he died.

HENRY III (1207-72) King (1216) (1) succeeded his father K. John in Oct. when Louis of France and baronial rebels controlled E. Anglia, the Home Counties and the south-eastern ports except Dover and Llywellyn ap Iorwerth was driving the Marchers from their castles. He was crowned, however, by a vigorous group of statesmen led by Card. Gualo, the papal Legate. It was arranged with the powerful Ranulf, E. of Chester, that William the Marshal, E. of Pembroke, should be regent (*bailli* or *rector*) and that Peter des Roches, Bp. of Winchester, should be the King's guardian and tutor. Hubert de Burgh (absent at Dover) was already Justiciar. These five, with John's nine other executors, formed a permanent council.

(2) In Nov. at Bristol they reissued Magna Carta slightly revised and swore not to alienate any crown property during Henry's minority, thus destroying the moral case for the already excommunicate rebels. K. Philip Augustus was by now only lukewarm in Louis' support. The Marshal took charge of operations and concentrated on Kent and the Channel. The Cinque Ports came over in succession to Philip Daubeny and his growing fleet. William of Kensham (Williken of the

Weald) organised a 'militia of God' in the Wealden *maquis*. The Marshal pressed outlying rebel strongholds and welcomed deserters. Louis divided his army, part against Dover, part to relieve Mountsorrel (Leics). The latter force marched on to help the northern rebels besiege Lincoln. Here, in May 1217, the Marshal captured most of them. Weakened, too, by desertions Louis parleyed but the negotiations broke down on the fate of his ecclesiastical supporters, whom Gualo would not absolve without reference to Rome. Meanwhile Louis' spirited wife, Blanche of Castile, with their admiral Eustace le Moine assembled a fleet. This was destroyed by Daubeny and Hubert de Burgh off Sandwich (Aug. 1217) and Louis had, at last, to accept terms (T. of Kingston Sept. 1217).

(**3**) Reconciliation could now begin. Mutual property restorations took about two years, during which Card. Pandulf replaced Gualo (Nov. 1218), the old Marshal died (May 1219) after transferring the King's interests to Pandulf who, however, was in a difficult position when Card. Stephen Langton, Abp. of Canterbury, returned. Langton thought that his own return rendered Pandulf's legation unnecessary. The King's tutelage was ending and his hero worship of Hubert de Burgh was creating friction with Peter des Roches. There had also been a quarrel among the baronage when Hubert forced Wm. de Foz to give up the castles in his possession (1219). Langton served notice to quit on Pandulf by ceremonially crowning Henry in May 1221, when the barons swore to yield up royal castles on demand. Pandulf left in the autumn but there was another dispute about the royal castles to which the oaths applied. This was related to jealousy of Hubert de Burgh, now E. of Kent, who had just married Margaret of Scots: but it was provoked by his removal of Peter de Mauley from Corfe. It created the first serious fissure in the council. Though the eyres had recommended them in 1218 the resumptions were bound to take time because so much was in the private hands of the faction which had won the war. The country was, however, experiencing the benefits of rest and routine and such competent men as Eustace of Fauconberg, treasurer, Richard Marsh, Bp. of Durham, and Ralph Nevil, successively Chancellors, and the judge Martin of Patteshull were developing an administration. Thus Hubert and Langton, with a papal brief recognising Henry's majority (Dec. 1223) save in the alienation of estates, were able to have most castles transferred to episcopal custody. An indirect effect was Fawkes de Bréauté's rebellion, for when he surrendered his castles (save Bedford) his many victims felt strong enough to sue him. His brother William kidnapped a judge and Fawkes was outlawed for failure to appear to various summons. The royal army promptly took Bedford and hanged William Fawkes escaped to exile (Aug. 1224).

(**4**) Owing to a failure to renew the Truce of Chinon (*see* AQUITAINE-5; LOUIS VIII) there was war in Poitou in 1224-7 which required a general tax. The magnates granted a 1/15th on movables but on Langton's insistence the Great and Forest Charters were reissued. This was farsighted for in Jan. 1227 Henry declared himself of age and able to alienate crown property. Encouraged by Hubert de Burgh he began a policy of rewarding his friends while recouping himself at the expense of the magnates through eyres and forest perambulations. A quarrel ensued with his brother, Richard E. of Cornwall, who had just successfully defended Poitou. Richard took refuge with William Marshal the Younger; they met other earls at Stamford and forced Henry to give way. The brothers were reconciled and soon Richard received grants which made him the predominant magnate on the Thames. The episode represented a weakening of Hubert de Burgh's position and in 1231 Richard made a further gain by marrying Isabel, *d*. of the Marshal and widow of Gilbert of Clare, E. of Hertford and Gloucester.

(**5**) The de Burghs tenaciously pursued their own as well as the King's interests. Like the Clares they were building up a body of related territories in south and central Wales and Ireland. Hubert had castles in Gwent, Montgomery and Cardigan: his nephew Richard was conquering Connaught. In 1230 Hubert got the wardship of Glamorgan. These enlargements crossed the interests of William the Marshal, who had been forced to give up Cardigan and Carmarthen, and of his ally Aedh, King of Connaught, and were hard to justify unless Hubert used them and his powers as Justiciar to reduce the Welsh. Hubert's friendship with Henry had been strained in 1229 when Henry's expedition to Brittany had been too ill-found to proceed, and by subsequent failure in Normandy and Poitou. There had, too, been an unsuccessful Welsh campaign in Ceri in 1228 against Llewelyn ap Iorwerth. In 1231 that able prince launched an offensive and carried all before him. A truce in Nov. left him in possession of his gains. Thus the Kingdom suffered while Hubert prospered.

(**6**) Peter des Roches had been abroad since 1226, mainly with the Emperor Frederick II. In 1231 Henry welcomed the return of this sophisticated childhood mentor. Papal provisions had been the object of a disorderly agitation, with which Hubert de Burgh sympathised, but the church was passing through a phase of centrally inspired moral regeneration, and the bishops, who had supported him in putting down disorder, disliked his provincial attitude to the new church. To his growing unpopularity with the King and magnates, was added the disapproval of the bishops. Peter des Roches got the treasurership of the Household for his able nephew the Poitevin Peter des Rivaux who, to effect thoroughgoing financial reforms, was given charge of wardships, escheats, the ports, the mint, the Jews and the Lesser Seal. The two Peters had become the most influential men at court and Henry's position was strengthened against Hubert by a three-year French truce. In Aug. 1232 Henry dismissed him *in absentia*; baronial protests prevented total forfeiture of his lands but, in fear of his life, he fled to sanctuary, from which he was forcibly taken. The bishops enforced respect for sanctuary but Hubert was put into custody at Devizes. The way was now open for further concentrations of power. Peter des Rivaux became Sheriff in 21 counties; he now controlled most of the financial administration.

(**7**) There was an early reaction. In form an outcry against Poitevins (of whom there were few), its substance was a demand that the King should govern with the counsel of his magnates and in conformity with the Charters, not through a royal bureaucracy. It was entangled with the affairs of the Marshal family, for William died childless in 1231 and his brother Richard, as a Norman feudatory, was a French vassal. Henry and Peter des Roches thought it dangerous that the vast inheritance should pass to such a man in time of endemic French conflict. They planned an expedition to Ireland for July 1233 which would pass through S. Wales. This might be used against the new marshal (who was suspicious) and the de Burghs. Henry assumed that they had come to an understanding. Gilbert Basset, a supporter of the Marshal, had a manor near Devizes from which Henry thought that Basset might rescue Hubert de Burgh. He forfeited the manor unlawfully. The Marshal supported Gilbert. Henry hired Flemish mercenaries and from the Whitsun court of Gloucester issued writs of Watch and Ward and summoned the feudal host for the end of Aug. It now appeared that Richard de Burgh was willing to maintain the King's Irish interests. Hence the force was employed to attack the Marshal's castle at Usk. There was a mutual renunciation of feudal obligations (*diffidatio*). The bishops, however, patched up a peace; there was to be a token surrender and return of Usk, and Basset's and other grievances were to be redressed. The

Marshal started for the court but Usk was not returned and, fearing treachery, he went back. He and his ally Llywelyn were now involved in a victorious war with the marchers, whom Henry could not help because the feudatories would not move. In Ireland, on the other hand, Richard de Burgh and the Irish Justiciar Maurice Fitzgerald wasted the Marshal's Leinster lands.

(8) The bishops' weakness had been a vacancy at Canterbury where, after several attempts, the monks elected the great St. Edmund Rich of Abingdon, who was acceptable to both Pope and King. Henry's English failure now presented the bishops with a second opportunity but it had been realised for some time that there could be no peace with Peter des Roches. The bishops negotiated a Welsh peace (Feb.-Apr. 1234); Henry, with St. Edmund's backing, announced his decision to replace Peter at the Apr. Council, when the Abp's election was confirmed. St. Edmund then went to Wales to finalise the settlement and the marshal to Ireland to negotiate with the King's supporters there. They murdered him at the Curragh. The news electrified the court. Peter des Roches was driven abroad and Henry proclaimed Peter des Rivaux and others traitors. St. Edmund, however, prevented extremities and in May there was a general reconciliation. The illegal outlawry and breach of Hubert de Burgh's sanctuary were reversed and Gilbert Basset's grievances set right. In June 1234 St. Edmund and Llywelyn made a definitive truce at Middle, not before time, because the French truce was due to end on the 24th. In fact Henry's ally, Peter of Dreux, Count of Brittany, went over to the French, taking his fiefs and Henry's castles. The war was tamely lost.

(9) The murder was an Irish affair. Apart from Peter des Roches most of the ministers returned, slightly chastened. The administrative reforms continued. In particular the appointment of escheators and wardens of royal demesnes (1234-6) took away work and influence from the sheriffs and paved the way for their temporary conversion from farming to salaried officials (1236). This involved new specialisations at the Exchequer and the need to settle points of law: the growth of the Court of Exchequer represents one aspect of this, the Statute of Merton (1236) another. These changes needed baronial co-operation.

(10) As the statesmen of Henry's youth retired or died he was ruling increasingly with contemporaries whom he overshadowed in rank. He became splendidly connected, in 1235 through his sister Isabel's marriage to the Emperor, and in 1236 through his own to Eleanor of Provence, sister-in-law to Louis VIII. Eleanor, though not ambitious, was vigorous and resourceful and her mother was a member of the enterprising House of Savoy. Important connections between the English and Savoyard courts began to develop. Provençals and Savoyards came to England and took small posts at court or in the church. Three important ones were the Queen's uncles: William, Bp. elect of Valence (?-1239) became a personal friend of Henry; Peter, Count of Savoy, became an important English political figure who acquired the Honour of Richmond; and Boniface succeeded St. Edmund as Abp. of Canterbury. The Savoy area in London represents the site of a palace built for them. Their interests and connections involved Henry in the politics of S. France.

(11) The rise of the Savoyards exemplified Henry's inclination to escape harmful baronial influence. In Apr. 1236 he had reconstituted the council under William of Valence and, along with the financial reforms, baronial liberties and local administration were being investigated. Henry had also obtained papal absolution from his oaths against alienation of crown estates and there were rumours that he meant to repudiate the charters. Hence when, in Jan. 1237, he requested an *aide* for his and Isabel's marriages, the magnates insisted, in return, on the admission of three of them to the council, some scrutiny

of expenditure and the reconfirmation, under ecclesiastical sanction, of the charters. Within a year Henry was evading these arrangements by permitting a private marriage of state between his French friend Simon de Montfort and his beautiful widowed sister Eleanor. This involved more south-French entanglements and was obnoxious to the church because Eleanor had vowed chastity before the archbishop. Led by Richard of Cornwall the magnates met under arms at Kingston. Henry, who had taken refuge in the Tower, was advised by Card. Otto, the new legate, to accept their demands. These included permanent means for maintaining the liberties through baronial conservators, who would be obliged to nominate a Justiciar and a Chancellor and so oversee their work. Richard now realised that such proposals encroached too far upon his brother's prerogatives and, anyhow, the marriage was irrevocable. The crisis subsided (Feb. 1238).

(12) The quarrel between the Emperor Frederick II and the Papacy, begun in 1236, spread westwards as Frederick revived old claims in the dismembered imperial shadow Kingdom of Arles, towards which French influence was moving. There was a general, if unorganised, desire to check French southern ambitions, which also cut across the ancient rights of the Kings of Aragon in Provence and Languedoc. Frederick was excommunicated in 1239 but to Henry it seemed as if the previous extent of the English Aquitainian dominions might be re-established through an international coalition with local support. The moment seemed to have come when his mother and Hugh of La Marche rebelled against Alphonse of Poitou in 1241. Henry raised money and troops but the barons would not support him; incompetent diplomatic preparation turned the expedition into an expensive failure and in 1242 the magnates refused a taxation to pay the debt on the ground that Henry had not accounted for the proceeds of 1237. They did not press their point to the limit: an *aide* was levied in 1243 ostensibly for Richard of Cornwall's marriage to Sanchia of Provence, sister of the queens of France and England. The marriage gave Richard an international standing. He was already very rich.

(13) Scutages could be levied only for war, and the special taxations and *aides* could be extracted only if they were earmarked. A King who wanted to develop a policy could, in theory, blackmail the Jews and tallage the towns, but these were only occasional expedients and apt to dry up. Greater efficiency was the only hope. Hence progressive improvements in the financial field and the recoinage of 1247 which Richard of Cornwall financed in return for half the profits of the mint; but there were two difficulties. The improvements, welcome in theory to the baronage, might collide with the interests of particular barons, and a general policy might tend towards a distant warlike issue, for which the community of the baronage would be unwilling eventually to raise the necessary tax. Co-operation between the King's govt. and the baronage was thus essential at all stages, but in practice Henry chafed against it and barons preferred not to be continually absent from their estates on the affairs of the Kingdom.

(14) The Gascon military fiasco of 1242-3 had left Henry's Aquitainian fiefs in disorder, which successive Seneschals had been unable to put down. Simon de Montfort returned from Crusade in the middle of it and his outspoken criticism led to a quarrel in 1242 which was made up. The Earl then settled at Kenilworth but in 1248 Henry asked him to become gov. of Aquitaine. He accepted provided that his office was an independent Lieutenancy to be held until 1255. The commissions resembled the terms of a treaty more than instructions to a local governor and this was a fatal flaw, for local conditions and finances made true independence impracticable and Henry could not be expected blindly to

support Simon if he had to pay for his policies. Simon's tactless efficiency soon grated upon the individualist Gascons and, besides, he had private local interests and claims which clashed with those of the greatest of the feudatories, Gaston of Béarn, the Queen's cousin.

(15) Henry's main objectives in appointing Simon had been the pacification of the Duchy as a fit appanage for his eldest son, the Lord Edward, the future Edward I (b. 1239) and peace with its neighbours, the Kings of Navarre, Aragon, Castile and France, so that he could join Louis IX on a crusade engendered by the rising Mameluke power in Egypt, for this appealed to his religious outlook. Louis was already on his way. Henry announced his intention of conferring Aquitaine on Edward in 1249. In 1250 he took the Cross and established a truce with Louis' govt. The worsening disorder caused by Simon's high-handedness was thus peculiarly objectionable. He was disposed to listen, despite his Lieutenant's angry protests and the Queen's disapproval, to the Gascon critics. His advisers advised concessions and a confrontation between them and Simon, combined with a truce, was arranged for May 1252. A furious debate ended in June. Henry imposed a further truce and stated that he or Edward would come in person in 1253. Opinion in general favoured Simon and he now returned to Gascony but continued the war. Not surprisingly Henry told the Gascons that they must obey their duke and observe the truce. This destroyed Simon's authority and he resigned. He was given compensation and appearances were maintained, but the long episode left a legacy of hate between the two men.

(16) Alfonso the Wise succeeded to the throne of Castile in June 1252; he promptly reopened his family's dormant claims in Gascony and received Gaston of Béarn a vassal. In July 1253 he claimed suzerainty over Navarre at the death of its King Theobald IV. Henry reached Gascony in Sept. and found turmoil with rumours of imminent invasion, which he communicated to the home regency. They acted energetically but had difficulty in raising men and money. This was the occasion when two knights were first ordered to be elected for each shire, to confer and agree collectively on a grant, because the magnates, though willing to help, professed to be unable to speak for their inferiors. It was also deemed necessary yet again to reconfirm the charters. It turned out, however, that Alfonso was feinting northwards but intended a crusade in Africa and he renounced his claims to Gascony in a treaty of friendship (Toledo, Apr. 1254).

(17) Simultaneously Pope Innocent IV had decided to set up a new King of Sicily (with Naples) which was a Papal fief, against Conrad, the excommunicate son of Frederick II. After trying Charles of Anjou and Richard of Cornwall he offered it to Henry who accepted it for his son Edmund (Mar. 1254). The Castilian treaty commit -ted Henry to a crusade in Africa: the Papal treaty contemplated the commutation of his crusading vows to the conquest of Sicily. Naturally Alfonso was not told. More still, in Feb. Henry had laid down the Lord Edward's endowment, which suggests that he never believed the rumours of Castilian invasion. Edward arrived in Aquitaine with Boniface of Savoy, Abp. of Canterbury, and under a treaty (July) he married Eleanor of Castile, Alfonso's sister, at Burgos (Oct. 1254). Such inconsistencies made Henry's magnates doubt his good faith or his competence or both.

(18) Under the treaties Alfonso had renounced his claims in Aquitaine, which helped to pacify the duchy. The next step was an accommodation with his fellow crusader Louis IX, now back from his Egyptian disaster. In Nov. and Dec. 1254 Henry and Louis were together at Chartres and Paris. Prospects in Sicily had brightened with Conrad's death (May 1254) and Innocent IV thought that there might be no need to commute Henry's vow; but Conrad's bastard half brother Manfred defeated the papal armies and

Innocent died (Dec.). The new Pope, Alexander IV, quickly confirmed the arrangement and Henry undertook either to send troops or assume the papal obligation in return for the commutation of the vow. So just as the chances of making his Sicilian claim good were receding he accepted a liability amounting to double the five year product of a crusading tithe (Jan. 1255). Nevertheless, discussions on the implementation of the T. of Toledo continued as if Henry was in a position to do his part. K. Alfonso was told the truth only in 1256, by which time Manfred had overrun most of the Sicilian Kingdom. Alexander now insisted that Henry should make a definitive peace with Louis and in 1257 negotiations opened in Paris. The negotiators were Peter of Savoy and Simon de Montfort. At about the same time the papal faction in Germany got Richard of Cornwall elected King of the Romans while their opponents elevated Alfonso of Castile. Thus the English royal house was elaborately involved as papalists in the Roman quarrel with the Hohenstaufen; and, it was at this point that the intrigues and then the commencement of war by Llewelyn ap Gruffydd became a serious danger in Wales and the Marches, now compounded by difficulties with the Scots. Since a treaty of 1237, when English claims to suzerainty had been effectively dropped, relations with his brother-in-law Alexander II had been generally cordial, but Alexander had died in 1249. His child successor Alexander III was Henry's son-in-law for whom Henry had been able to secure regents (1255) favourable to himself; but in 1257 they were overthrown in a *coup* and in 1258 the new regents concluded an alliance with Llewelyn.

(19) The constitutional struggles of the next nine years were provoked by Henry's unsuccessful efforts to extract the Kingdom from an involvement which it could not afford and the magnates' determination that, if he could not do it, they would. But this meant a basic change from royal govt. with baronial advice to baronial control of the growing administration. The change was naturally resisted by doubtful or interested parties, but there were policy cleavages among those who supported it. At a risk of over-simplification, there were three major attitudes. The French Simon de Montfort was primarily interested in a foreign policy of Christian unity, which would liquidate the problem by reconciling the Pope and the Emperor. Hugh Bigod wanted to cure financial and judicial abuses and reduce administrative costs. Earl Warenne, his Poitevin connections and marcher friends wanted to concentrate against Llywelyn and the resurgent Welsh with their Scottish sympathisers. Powerful factions supported these points of view. A unifying sentiment was a general dislike of Henry's young, favoured and arrogant Poitevin (Lusignan) half brothers and a common opinion, partly financial in origin, that Henry was too free with crown property. None of these groups was hostile to Henry himself. They wished to see him rightly advised. In the end the decisive question was whether the King should choose his own advisers, for if the answer was 'No', there was no agreement on who should choose them or whom they would choose. On this issue the Crown was steadfast: the others hesitant and disunited.

(20) In Mar. 1258 Llywellyn ap Gruffydd had assumed the title of Prince of Wales, but the decisive consideration in Apr. was that breach of the papal treaty would bring Henry's excommunication and an interdict. Nobody wanted the humiliation of the one or the inconvenience of the other. Hence Simon and Peter de Montfort, Peter of Savoy, the Es. of Gloucester and Norfolk, Hugh Bigod and John fitzGeoffrey swore together to force a change. Between 30 Apr., when they visited Henry, and 8 May they had their way. They offered to try and obtain a general *aide* on condition that the realm was reformed and foreign commitments reduced. This led, by short stages, to the Provisions of Oxford (q.v. June).

(21) The difficulties now began. The council of XV appointed at Oxford made a truce with Llywelyn until 1 Aug. 1259. This left him in occupation of his gains at the expense of the marchers, the Lord Edward and the Poitevins. The XV, logically enough, required the resumption of recently alienated royal estates but, as it happened, this affected the Poitevins especially. They left for Winchester, followed or pursued by Henry and the armed baronage. In July they went into exile. Their expulsion alienated Henry and removed a unifying factor among the magnates. The Pope (now Alexander IV) refused to send a legate as requested or to abate his treaty rights. The barons then declined to raise the general *aide* proposed in Apr. whereupon Alexander released the Lord Edmund from his Sicilian obligations and sought another candidate. This abolished Henry's main motive for co-operating with the magnates. The marcher's powerful advocate at court, the Lord Edward, favoured resistance to them and was placed under supervision.

(22) Then in the spring of 1259 there was a controversy about the subjection of private franchises (which included London and 358 out of 628 Hundreds) to the improved central jurisdiction. Many lords of franchises opposed the reformers, who had given undertakings to the lesser gentry. The momentum of reform had to be sustained by prolonging the controversial Welsh truce (June 1259). Those who suffered by it or by the threat to the franchises drifted together. There was an alliance between Edward, Richard of Clare (whom he disliked), Henry of Almain and other important nobles. Moreover Simon de Montfort was in France most of the year where his and his wife's interests were a clog in the peace negotiations. He returned for the routine October *parliamentum,* which enacted the compromise Provisions of Westminster (1259), came to an understanding with Edward which omitted Richard of Clare and returned to Paris. In Nov. the King, with Richard of Clare and Peter of Savoy, joined him to ratify the P. of Paris (Dec.) after which Simon returned to England; but Henry was detained by business and illness.

(23) At this point Llywelyn broke the truce, besieged Builth and raided Glamorgan. Henry wrote to the Justiciar from France to postpone the parliament due on 2 Feb. and take military action. Simon, in England, challenged his right to postpone the meeting and Henry believed that the Lord Edward was conspiring with him. Aided by K. Louis, the regents and the S.E. towns, Henry summoned and hired enough force to overawe Simon and the Lord Edward: Louis' envoy, the Abp. of Rouen, prevented a parliamentary trial of Simon; Henry and Edward were reconciled and Llywelyn was forced to another truce (Aug. 1260). In this incident a powerful baronial faction including Richard of Clare, Hugh Bigod and Philip Basset had sided with Henry. The reforming momentum disappeared. Hugh Bigod was succeeded as Justiciar by Hugh le Despenser, a lesser man. By Mar. 1261 Henry felt strong enough to allow one of his half-brothers (William of Valence) to return; and he issued a proclamation against his critics and presented to the magnates his detailed objections to the Provisions. They replied but the discussion was cut short by a bull of Alexander IV absolving Henry from his oath to maintain them. The Barons War ensued (q.v.).

(24) By its end Henry was tired and, by mediaeval standards, old. The war destroyed or converted most of the opponents of the Crown but transferred active manipulation of Crown affairs to others, notably the Lord Edward who had won the war and Ottobuono Fieschi (Legate from Dec. 1265 to July 1268) who established the English peace at Kenilworth and the Welsh peace at Montgomery (Sept. 1267) (*see* LLYWELYN AP GRUFFUDD). with Edward and the King he inspired the Statute of Marlborough (Nov. 1267) and he issued the Constitution

of London for the English Church (Apr. 1268). From a papal point of view his policy was directed towards a new Crusade and he induced many magnates and Edward to go to the Levant in 1270, allowing for this purpose a tax on the Church. Meanwhile Henry finished the 20-year building of the new Westminster Abbey, which was consecrated in 1269. This marked a retirement from affairs, which were carried on by Edward's nominees, the guardians of Edward's children, namely Richard of Cornwall, Walter Giffard, Abp. of York, Philip Basset, Roger Mortimer and Robert Burnell. When Henry died (Nov. 1272) there was no contest for the throne of the absent Edward.

HENRY IV, or of BOLINGBROKE (1366-1413) E. of DERBY (1377), D. of HEREFORD (1397) and LANCASTER (1399), King (1399), *s.* of John of Gaunt, D. of Lancaster **(1)** married Mary de Bohun, co-heiress of Hereford (1380) and was one of the Lords Appellant in 1387-8 (*see* RICHARD II-11-13). From 1390 to 1393 he acquired international experience on crusade in Lithuania and on pilgrimage *via* Bohemia, Austria, Hungary and Venice to Jerusalem. In 1395 he was one of the English council during the King's Irish absence and in 1397 he supported Richard's *coup d'état* and was given his dukedom in return but was shortly entangled in a quarrel with Norfolk, whom he appealed of treason. Richard stopped the trial by battle and banished him for six years (1398). He left proctors to receive moneys and inheritances but when his father died (1399) Richard sequestrated the Lancaster estates and increased the sentence of exile to life. Henry, in Paris, plotted a forcible return and when Richard was for a second time in Ireland sailed with the two Arundels and landed at Ravenspur.

(2) Though executing a carefully matured plan, his original intention was only to insist upon his inheritance, but when the northern magnates joined him his expedition turned into a movement and then into a revolution. By Aug. Henry had captured Edmund of York, Guardian of the Realm, who had called out the levies too late, together with most of his council and had taken Bristol, where he hanged Richard II's chief officials. He then quickly seized Chester. Richard, meanwhile, returned in haste. With both the southern and the northern routes into England barred against him and deserted by most of his magnates, his position was hopeless. He negotiated the surrender at Conway Castle with Abp. Arundel and the E. of Northampton, whom Henry may have duped. On the faith of the agreement Richard left Conway but was seized, brought to Chester and thence to Westminster, where he was compelled to abdicate (Sept. 1399).

(3) The Estates having declared Richard deposed and the throne vacant, Henry claimed it by right and by conquest, to which they agreed. Writs were then issued for an immediate parliament composed of those present. This body granted a tenth and fifteenth and a three year custom on wool. It then repealed the legislation against the Appellants and reaffirmed the Acts of the Merciless Parliament. Richard was consigned to perpetual custody and three of his dukes reverted to their previous rank. Finally, to secure Henry's dynastic future, his son Henry was created D. of Cornwall by statute and P. of Wales and invested with Aquitaine and Lancaster.

(4) In fact the new King has risen not so much on his own popularity as on the unpopularity of Richard. Rebellions occupied the next nine years. The first (Jan. 1400) by two ex-Dukes and other lords was quickly suppressed with the aid of the City. It led to Richard's murder or suicide at Pontefract. Henry now sought to anticipate French intervention by himself intervening in Scotland, where he had acquired an unexpected ally in George Dunbar, E. of the Scottish March. The invasion effected little but before Henry could return Owen Glendower rebelled in Wales (Sept. 1400). Hugh Burnell checked him at Welshpool but the N. Wales gentry rose in his support and by 1401 Owen controlled Anglesey and most of Gwynedd. Since Henry's council rejected his efforts at accommodation he began soliciting alliances with the K. of Scots and various Irish chiefs. Scottish raiders under the E. of Douglas penetrated the East March while their main army advanced on Carlisle. Douglas was beaten at Nesbit (June 1402) and thereupon the main army crossed the Pennines, reached Newcastle and was virtually destroyed at Homildon Hill (Sept. 1402). Here Northumberland, his son Henry Percy (Hotspur) and March took many French and noble Scots including Murdac, s. of the E. of Albany. The victory, however, did not simplify Henry's problems. The borderers, especially the Percies, had suffered severely and undertaken heavy responsibilities, but since 1399 compensation and pay had reached them too slowly. A Scottish counter-offensive with French and Welsh co-operation was probable, but the Percies would no longer defend the borders mostly at their own expense.

(5) While Henry was fighting his civil wars, he was trying to establish his position internationally in spite of the conditions which those civil wars created. The tax yield was well below average: expenses well above. He was always in debt. It was difficult, even in peaceful areas, to enforce public order so that, for example, English shipmasters took extensively to piracy. The French King Charles VI turned Henry's distractions to his own advantage, especially after Isabel, Richard II's widow, had been returned to him (July 1401). Henry naturally sought allies elsewhere. There were negotiations with Rupprecht of Bavaria, who had replaced Richard II's brother-in-law Wenceslas of Bohemia as King of the Romans. Henry's eldest daughter Blanche was to be married to Rupprecht's eldest son Ludwig, the Count Palatine, and in Apr. 1401 she was despatched with an embassy while Henry induced the D. of Guelders to recognise Rupprecht's title (Aug. 1401).

(6) Negotiations with the Baltic powers (of which Henry had some understanding) served a more mundane purpose. English shipping and exports were penetrating the Baltic to the displeasure of the Wendish Hanse. Henry proposed to make common cause with their rivals, the Scandinavian powers federated since 1397 under one crown at Calmar and the eastern Hanseatic cities led by Danzig. Eric of Pomerania was to marry Henry's daughter Philippa, while the P. of Wales undertook to marry Eric's sister (1402) but the eastern Hanseatics began to impose restrictions on English merchants who were making inroads upon their economic domination of Sweden and Norway. It would never in the long run have been feasible to please both the Hanse and the Scandinavians: but in fact the piratical infestation of the trade routes forced Henry into making a series of choices. The Western Channel was a battleground in which English, French and Bretons preyed on the shipping and each other: at the Straits of Dover the predators were mostly English and Flemish. While diplomatic missions passed back and forth to Flanders, Henry himself married the regent of Brittany, Jeanne, whose family had held the Honour of Richmond since 1176 (Feb. 1403). The marriage did not immediately stop Flemish piracy or set the Bretons to catch the French, but English pirates committed outrages of mounting ferocity on the Hanse.

(7) Helped by the threat of northern mutiny Glendower, a master of small war, meanwhile captured Edmund Mortimer (June 1402) and raised Glamorgan (Aug.). Then he contracted a marriage alliance with his prisoner (whose claim to the throne was better than Henry's) and a mutual pact to make Edmund King and himself Prince of Wales. This, in its turn, emboldened the Percies, who at the Parliament of Oct. 1402 refused, by way of financial pressure, to hand over Douglas to the King. Moreover they had a new grievance: their old opponent, the Scottish E. of March, was now a tenant of Henry's to the north of them and too high in his favour. They felt hemmed in as well as cheated and decided to throw in their lot with Edmund. Henry decided to go north in person to deal with the problems just as Hotspur began to move south-west towards Wales. At Nottingham Henry realised that the Percies had gone over to Glendower and Mortimer. Hotspur was raising men in Shropshire and Henry moved rapidly against him. In a day long battle at Shrewsbury (21 July 1403) Hotspur was killed. Northumberland surrendered in Aug.

(8) Again a war on two fronts prevented success on either. To secure the Percy country, troops had to be diverted to occupy the castles, but this left Henry too weak to overrun Wales and by Oct. he had been forced to retreat to Hereford. Glendower, meanwhile, had reached a working agreement with the French, whose ships began to land supplies. Hence by the spring of 1404 Henry had failed to occupy all the northern castles, for Alnwick and Warkworth still held out, while Glendower took the great fortresses at Harlech and Aberystwyth (Llanbadarn) and was able to summon a Welsh parliament (May 1404) to Machynlleth. From here he despatched ambassadors to Paris and concluded a formal treaty (July) which bore immediate fruit in French naval raids against S. Devon (Aug-Sept.) while Glendower consolidated his hold on S. Wales. To make matters worse, Danzig embargoed the annual sailings to England (Mar. 1404) and in Mar. 1405 the Hanseatic Diet stopped the cloth trade and Baltic exports in retaliation for English piracy.

(9) The weakness of Henry's northern military influence was now felt again. In Feb. 1405 Northumberland, Glendower and Mortimer entered into a league to partition the country between them: Wales and most of the Marches to Glendower, Norfolk, Leicestershire, Northamptonshire, Warwickshire and all parts northwards to Northumberland and the rest to Mortimer. By May the City of York, with Richard Scrope its archbishop and the Clifford and Cleveland interests, were in rebellion but Scrope's motley forces melted away and he was executed in June. The King thereupon set about the seizure of Northumberland's castles in earnest, while the Earl fled to Scotland (July). Within days a French force landed at Milford Haven (Aug.) and, having failed to take Haverfordwest castle or Tenby, captured Carmarthen and marched through Glamorgan and Brecon to the neighbourhood of Worcester. They were too late. The King was already mustering his host at Hereford. The French retreat began the decline of Glendower's fortunes and meanwhile Henry had a stroke of luck: James, heir of Scotland, on his way to France fell into the hands of Norfolk pirates who handed him over (*see* JAMES I OF SCOTS); by Aug. 1405 too an English embassy was with the Teutonic Knights and, though the Prince of Wales' Scandinavian marriage had been dropped, Philippa and Eric of Pomerania were married in 1406, when Blanche died in Bavaria.

(10) Northumberland heard that Albany, now Scots regent, intended to seize and exchange him for his son Murdac and he, with Bardolf, escaped to N. Wales (Feb. 1406) and thence to France (June) to seek help from the D. of Orleans. Their mission failed and later in 1407 they returned to the Scottish March where they raised a small force. At Bramham Moor (19 Feb. 1408) they were both defeated and killed. This left Henry's friends, the Nevilles, in undisputed control of the north and enabled him at last to concentrate on Glendower. Henry P. of Wales and the Talbots reduced Aberystwyth in Sept. 1408 and in Mar. 1409 Harlech, where Edmund Mortimer died and his children (Glendower's grandchildren) were captured. Glendower took refuge in the *maquis* and remained a hero and at large until 1416.

(11) The ending of the civil wars and the Flemish

truce (1407) did not bring peace. The controversies within the French royal house (*see* CHARLES XI OF FRANCE-5 *et seq.*) had not brought French Aquitainian penetration to an end and Henry had not been able to help the duchy, now much reduced by attrition. Worn by endless exertion, he lived on his nerves and was intermittently ill. The P. of Wales had had much experience in the Welsh campaigns and as a D. of Aquitaine favoured an aggressive policy. Peace, which the King understandably wanted, would help the Baltic and especially the wool trade, the City and the North Sea ports. A considerable decline in the Bordeaux trade since 1370 militated against Bristol and the west. The Prince had presided in the Council since 1408. A rift over policy between Henry and his son inevitably ended in the son's dismissal in Nov. 1411.

(12) The situation had been complicated by Burgundian bellicosity. John the Fearless had announced his intention to lead the French assault on Aquitaine, and forces had been raised to protect Calais against his adjacent bases. Henry was now forced into the war which his son wanted but as an anti-Burgundian (Armagnac) partisan. A secret agreement at Bourges seemed to put the Armagnac dukes at Henry's disposal and to make an expensive expedition necessary. Moreover the politicians hostile to the prince spread slanders about him. He was not summoned. As things turned out, the Bourges agreement was betrayed and the expedition turned into a foray which the French dukes bought off (Dec. 1412). Henry died in Mar.

HENRY V of Monmouth (1387-1422) King (1413), eldest *s.* of Henry IV and Eleanor de Mohun (for this part of the Hundred Years' War *see also* CHARLES XI AND VII OF FRANCE; AQUITAINE) (1) A powerful personality with much military and political experience in Wales (1400-9) and in France (1409-12), he succeeded in a period of civil and religious disorder to a usurped title which his father had not completely established. To achieve tranquillity he sought unifying factors:- (a) *reconciliation* by an instant amnesty; by public respect for Richard II's memory and the restoration of some of his less extremist supporters; (b) *precaution*, by taking security for good behaviour from possibly irreconcilable magnates; (c) following Sir John Oldcastle's Lollard rebellion (Jan. 1414) *legislation against heresy*; (d) *rewards* for his richest and strongest partisans. Henry Beaufort became Lord Chancellor and Arundel Treasurer; (e) *Overseas adventure*.

(2) He renewed the vigorous foreign policy which he had advocated as prince. In Sept. 1413 discussions, focused on the impending expiry (31 Dec. 1413) of the French truce began at Leulighem. The truce was, indeed, extended but Henry's representatives argued his right to the French Crown; the French denied his right to Aquitaine. The negotiations were transferred to Paris in Jan. 1414 and while they were in progress Henry reached an agreement with John the Fearless of Burgundy. Thereafter hollow haggling merely concealed the approach of a predetermined war and served to reconcile the Commons to the likely expense. Henry began to mobilise troops in May 1414; the army and fleet were assembled at Southampton in June 1415 and Anglo-French mutual insults exchanged in July. In these the French envoys finally rejected Henry's rights not only to the French but the English Crown. At this point Henry had to deal with Cambridge's conspiracy, despite which the expedition was able to set off for Normandy on 11 Aug. Harfleur surrendered on 22 Sept. and was annexed. The army, 6000 strong, marched for Calais, was intercepted by the French feudal host of 50,000 and, after several days manoeuvring, won an overwhelming victory at Agincourt in Artois (25 Oct. 1415). Much of the French chivalry was destroyed or, where captured, represented vast sums in ransom. On the triumphal return to London the Commons voted Henry tonnage, poundage and the wool custom for life (Nov.). Nobody in England doubted now that Henry meant to go on with the war, unless he could enforce the plenitude of his ambitions by other means.

(3) While Henry hoped to exploit the Armagnac-Burgundian feud which was dividing France others, notably the Emperor Sigmund III, were hoping to heal the greater Schism which was dividing Europe. Sigmund believed that the ability of the Council of Constance (summoned by John XXIII in Dec. 1413) to reduce the number of popes from three to one depended upon Anglo-French peace. In Feb. 1416 he journeyed from Constance westwards to offer or enforce mediation. He could get no satisfaction at Paris: the Armagnacs were heartened by their small counter-offensive and were besieging Harfleur with Genoese help. Sigmund accordingly moved to London where he was joined by the powerful Count of Holland, a relative by marriage of both the D. of Burgundy and the Dauphin (May 1416). Henry's purpose was to sell his influence at Constance for the isolation of the (Armagnac) French. For this he needed to convince Sigmund of their bad faith; by midsummer this was easy for French diplomatic missions talked interminably of peace while their masters tightened the siege. On 15 Aug. 1416 accordingly Sigmund signed a treaty of alliance with England at Canterbury. The same day the D. of Bedford defeated the Genoese in the Seine and revictualled Harfleur. The Armagnacs now changed their tune and obtained a truce until Feb. 1417 during which, however, their civil war with the Burgundians continued.

(4) Henry's diplomatic tactics won him other advantages. The Commons and the convocations voted him large sums with which he hired 12,000 professional soldiers and many ships. The new expedition set out in July 1417. Caen fell in Sept, but meanwhile the Burgundians were trying to isolate Paris. It was a delicate situation for Henry, as King of France, needed Paris himself, but an immediate attempt on it might drive John the Fearless into the arms of the Armagnacs. Hence Henry set about converting W. Normandy into a secure conquest. With the fall of Falaise (Feb. 1418) and Domfront (July) this was achieved but the Burgundians were following a like policy in E. Normandy. They had taken Rouen and Gisors by June; then a *coup d'état* in Paris left Armagnac a prisoner in their hands and Duke John entered the city. France now had two rival governments, both hostile to the English. Henry moved against Rouen which neither was able to save. The Norman capital fell in Jan. 1419.

(5) Henry's preoccupation with Rouen and their loss of Paris freed the Armagnacs, with the Dauphin, to reshape their thinking. They raised troops in the far south, consolidated a line of strongholds on the Loire, sought military help in Scotland, which was reconnoitred by John Hardyng from 1418 to 1421 and naval support from Castile. Henry controlled Nantes and Bordeaux but important if moderate succours arrived through Saintes and, especially, La Rochelle. A triangular stalemate developed into peace negotiations at Meulan (May-July 1419) centring on a marriage between Henry and the beautiful Catherine of France: these, however, broke down because the Dauphin was negotiating successfully at Pontoise with Burgundy and so felt able to resist English territorial and financial claims. An Armagnac-Burgundian treaty was made on 11 July. Henry's truce with Burgundy expired on 29th. Next morning Henry surprised Pontoise and though the garrison escaped he was now in a position to blockade Paris. The Dauphin and John the Fearless agreed to meet at Montereau to concert action against Henry but members of the Dauphin's entourage murdered the Duke (Aug.). (*For the T. of Troyes and events in France until Henry's death see* CHARLES VI OF FRANCE).

(6) Henry returned with Catherine of France to England in Feb. 1421, crowned her magnificently at Westminster and then toured the country. The T. of Troyes offered a hope of eventual peace and reduced taxation. It was only a matter of mopping up the Dauphin. The defeat and death of Clarence at Baugé (Mar. 1421), however, put an end to the hope of peace; it was impolitic to disappoint the Commons. Henry had to borrow heavily to prosecute the war. He bequeathed large debts to his child successor and had alienated Philip of Burgundy by protecting Jacqueline of Hainault when he died on campaign from dysentery.

HENRY VI of Windsor (1421-71) King (1422-61: 1470-1) (*for this part of the Hundred Years' War see also* CHARLES XII OF FRANCE, JOAN OF ARC; AQUITAINE) **(1)** *s.* of Henry V and Catherine of France, he lived first under the joint protectorate of his uncles John D. of Bedford and Humphrey D. of Gloucester. They shared power with the council but Bedford was mostly in France. From 1428 he was educated by Richard Beauchamp, E. of Warwick; in Nov. 1429 he was crowned at Westminster and in Dec. 1431 at Paris. He opened a parliament in person in 1432.

(2) By this time his fitness to rule was doubted, his moods and capacities being reported as varying from active and open intelligence to a sunny simplicity. He began to attend council meetings in 1436 when Bedford was already dead and the French had recovered Paris. The politicians disliked his interventions and he diverted his energies to founding colleges at Cambridge and Eton.

(3) His weakness encouraged faction and policy disputes between Gloucester and his Beaufort relatives. Gloucester, a cultured Renaissance prince, represented the policy, now in disarray, of maintaining Henry V's conquests but his marriage to Jacqueline of Hainault antagonised Burgundy. Card. Henry Beaufort, one of the richest men in Europe, regularly lent money to the court and council. Gloucester's policies and control of patronage necessarily irked him. Each faction sought to control the King, to sustain influence over the magnates and to discredit the other. Beaufort, attacked by *praemunire* for accepting his cardinalate in 1426, was in exile until 1428 and in 1432 had to fend off an attempt to deprive him, as a cardinal, of the see of Winchester. Truces with the Scots (1438-47) and Burgundy (1439-42) suited both sides for, despite the *Praguerie* (1440) the French War was not going well. Then the Beauforts hatched a peace plan: the D. of Orleans, a comfortably Anglicised prisoner since Agincourt, should be released to open the negotiations. To this Gloucester opposed weighty political and dynastic arguments. In 1441, therefore, the Beauforts dealt a destructive blow at his prestige, through Eleanor Cobham, the mistress whom he had married. She was convicted of witchcraft, publicly paraded in the streets and imprisoned for life. Gloucester went into retirement leaving the war to run itself and the Beauforts to bear the odium of expense and defeat, for their negotiations failed both directly through Orleans and indirectly through Armagnac.

(4) By 1444 the French, though at the gates of Bordeaux, were ready for a peace; the two year truce of Tours (May) inaugurated marriage negotiations, for by now it was time for Henry to marry. Beaufort's envoy was William de la Pole, E. of Suffolk. The discussions centred on Margaret *d.* of the Valois René of Anjou, titular King of Jerusalem and Sicily. "Good King" René wanted Maine next to Anjou. It was evident that a general peace was not possible but a marriage and a two year truce were agreed. Margaret and Henry were married by proxy in Mar. 1445, fully in Apr. and she was crowned in May.

(5) A French peace mission was to follow the Queen. It arrived (July) under the impression that England would cede Maine. It is uncertain if Suffolk had conceded this at Tours; but many came to believe that he had. Moreover the Queen was both beautiful and strong willed and she

wanted to please her father. The cession of Maine, certain to be opposed by Gloucester and the soldiers, became a precondition of peace upon which Henry gave way (Dec. 1445). It now became necessary to put Gloucester out of action before the deal became public, for he knew nothing of it. False rumours of rebellion were started. A parliament was summoned to Bury St. Edmunds (outside Gloucester's sphere of influence) and the unsuspecting duke was charged with treason. He died five days later of a stroke (Feb. 1447). Suffolk was now upon a dangerous eminence. As High Chamberlain he held the most powerful court office; a constellation of western offices included the Chief Stewardship of Lancaster and the Chief Justiceship of Chester and N. Wales. He had a great revenue as surveyor and steward of mines, and vast estates and following in E. Anglia. In the context of Beaufort policy he was responsible, as Captain of Calais and Warden of the Cinque Ports, for the defence of Channel shipping. In 1448 he became a duke.

(6) The cession of Maine would unhinge the defences of Normandy. As chief minister Suffolk would be blamed if he brought it about and discredited with his own party if he failed to do so. Either outcome would reflect upon the Queen and her simple-minded husband. The territorial magnates composing the govt. increased their local power at every opportunity, creating central weakness, endemic disorder and perverted justice. The court factions represented territorial powers. Matters were exacerbated by Crown insolvency. Parliamentary subsidies came grudgingly, with exemptions which reduced their yield and the King was under intermittent pressure to revoke grants of Crown lands. Suffolk and his friends devoted much energy to evading such revocations while tightening their grip on patronage and royal finances at the expense of Crown creditors. In 1443 the Treasurer resigned in protest and by 1449, with a Crown debt of £372,000, Henry was in no position to meet a French challenge to his continental possessions. Yet Maine was in the hands of Suffolk's opponents who declined to hand it over. The French resumed operations and forced the cession (1448). The English commanders retaliated on the Breton frontier and in July 1449 the French, fully mobilised, overran Normandy.

(7) Public opinion now focused on Richard D. of York, heir presumptive by descent from Edmund, 5th *s.* of Edward III and married to Anne Mortimer descended from Lionel his third son. Rich already, the marriage brought him wide Marcher lands. He had grievances, for his claims to office had been passed over in favour of his incompetent Beaufort kinsman, John D. of Somerset. Moreover, York had had great difficulty in recovering his expenses and Suffolk and Somerset excluded him from the sources of patronage. Discontent with Suffolk-Beaufort conduct of affairs crystallised about him. In Dec. 1447 he was made Lieut. of Ireland to get him out of the way, but he did not go until 1449. Defeat was filling the country with broken soldiers. There was a disaster at Formigny (Apr. 1450). The parliament which was to debate the resumption of the war preferred to consider public disorder and excessive taxation. The Commons impeached Suffolk. He went into exile and was murdered while crossing the Channel.

(8) Then in May came Jack Cade's Kentish revolt, directed at extortionate officials, corrupt justice and rigged elections. The rebels dispersed in June but gathered again in July, entered London and murdered royal officials including the Treasurer Lord Saye, a former Sheriff of Kent, and its present Sheriff William Cromer. Dispersed by a promised pardon they were savagely repressed.

(9) York had unwisely sent his troops home. He could make little impression on court or council and an M.P. who moved his recognition as Henry's heir was sent to the Tower (June 1451). Hence while the French overran Aquitaine, he retired to his territorial capital at Ludlow to re-emerge in arms in Jan. 1452. The armies confronted each other at Blackheath, where he got an undertaking that Somerset would be held in custody while certain charges which York made were investigated. Again he dismissed his men but he had been tricked and found himself in virtual custody. His son, the E. of March, saved him by threatening to come with 11,000 troops.

(10) In Apr. 1452, in response to a Bordelais appeal, a general pardon was issued as a preliminary to an Aquitainian expedition. This materialised in the inadequate form of 3000 men under Sir John Talbot (E. of Shrewsbury) who landed in Oct., whereupon the Gascon towns expelled their French garrisons. While three French armies assembled for the counterstroke, the English were preoccupied with factional struggles. Margaret and Somerset were too busy securing a compliant parliament to reinforce Shrewsbury properly. The Reading parliament of Mar. 1453 reversed the proceedings of the 1451 parliament, made life grants of tonnage, poundage, a tenth and fifteenth, and authorised 20,000 archers for six months. The court was fortifying itself against York while in July Shrewsbury was killed at Castillon and Aquitaine definitively lost.

(11) The Percy-Neville feud now broke out into a northern war, which the council tried to stop and then the stroke planned against York had to be postponed, for in Aug. Henry became insane. Once the fact was known York would be entitled to the protectorship, therefore Somerset and Margaret concealed it; but she was pregnant and in Oct. gave birth to a son, Edward. A Great Council had to be summoned. Somerset tried, but failed, to keep York away. While the magnates were now arming both in London and elsewhere York demanded the regency (Jan. 1454) but the Great Council replied (Mar.) by appointing York Protector and chief of the council during the King's incapacity, with Prince Edward to succeed him when he came of age. Somerset was imprisoned. York took over Calais and stopped the northern civil war by arresting the D. of Exeter, the Percy's main Holland supporter.

(12) York's authority was brief, for in Feb. 1455 the King suddenly recovered. The Queen again became the real head of the govt. Somerset and Exeter were restored. While York retired north to join the Nevilles and Lord Clinton, Margaret tried to win over the officials of his Welsh estates. A council had been summoned to Leicester. York and his allies marched south proclaiming that it would be unsafe for them at Leicester unarmed. They encountered the court and its army at St. Albans. After York's efforts to get his complaints heard by the King had been frustrated a short battle (22 May 1455) ended in the death of Somerset, Northumberland, Clifford and the E. of Stafford. Henry, wounded and again insane, was escorted with Margaret back to London. York resumed the protectorship. Warwick became Capt. of Calais and negotiated a settlement with the Company of the Staple for the pay of the garrison. This was a key event.

(13) York now encouraged the passage in Jan. 1456 of a resumption Act more drastic than that of 1451, designed to provide a Household income of £10,000 a year, but a month later Henry again recovered his sanity. This ended York's protectorship. The Queen put her nominees into all the high offices except Calais and secured a long list of exceptions which frustrated the purpose of the resumptions; she moved the court to Coventry (Sept. 1456-Nov. 1457) and began to build a faction among local officials by paying them direct from assignments on their local revenue collections, thus short-circuiting the Exchequer. York remained head of a council which was thus losing control of the revenues. Officially reconciled, the enmity between Margaret and

York (with Warwick) grew. She built up funds and intrigued with the Scots for the trial of strength; Warwick held up shipping and reached an understanding with Burgundy. There was fighting at court and Margaret encouraged the French to sack Sandwich. England had virtually ceased to be governed.

(14) In mid-1459 Margaret resolved to remove Warwick from Calais, and York treated this as the opening of civil war. Warwick marched through London towards York's H.Q. at Ludlow; the E. of Salisbury came down from Yorkshire. The Queen from her interior position in the Midlands and Cheshire failed to stop Salisbury at Blore Heath (23 Sept. 1459) but her Welsh diplomacy had prevented York from raising enough men to withstand her numbers. She routed him at Ludford Bridge (12 Oct.) and sacked Ludlow. York escaped to Ireland; March and the Nevilles *via* Devon to Calais. A quickly summoned parliament at Coventry atttainted the principal Yorkists, some of whom had been taken; but the Queen's writ could not reach Ireland or Calais. Her messengers were hanged at Dublin. The wool merchants ignored a parliamentary embargo on the Calais Staple. When the young Somerset fitted out an expedition against Calais at Sandwich, a Yorkist raid captured most of it and its commanders (Jan. 1460); and a second fleet under Sir Baldwin Fulford failed either to catch Warwick on a journey to Ireland and back or in Calais. The Queen's govt., to anticipate invasion, hanged or deprived Yorkist sympathisers, and York and Warwick used these evidences of oppression as material for propaganda.

(15) In June 1460 the Es. of March, Warwick and Salisbury landed at Sandwich with Francesco Coppini, a papal legate for raising a Turkish crusade. They quickly reached London which Warwick won over, and blockaded the Tower. Then, accompanied by Abp. Bourchier and four bishops, they marched upon the court at Northampton. After a bitter parley they stormed their enemy's flooded entrenchments in half an hour (10 July). Margaret escaped to Denbigh; Henry was escorted back to London where the Tower surrendered after bombardment. In these operations many of Margaret's supporters, including the D. of Buckingham, the E. of Shrewsbury, Lords Beaumont, Egremont and Scales, perished while the E. of Kendal and Lord de la Warr came over to York.

(16) York now landed at Chester (Oct.) and laid claim to the throne at a parliament at Westminster. To his surprise he got no encouragement but after much legalistic and theological haggling, in which the judges declined to join, it was, with Henry's agreement, decided that Henry was to keep the throne for life, that York and his heirs should succeed him and that the Coventry attainders should be reversed (Nov.). Meanwhile the northern Lancastrians were gathering. In Dec. York went north to deal with them. His inadequate force was attacked by Somerset and driven into Sandal Castle. Relieved by his son Edward of March York risked battle and fell at Wakefield (30 Dec. 1460).

(17) His claims descended to his more ruthless son. Coppini tried to negotiate a settlement but Margaret feared the consequences and sought Scottish help. Mary of Guelders, the Scots Queen Mother, a Burgundian, was inclined to the Yorkists. James Kennedy, Bp. of St. Andrews, favoured the French alliance. Margaret brought off a diplomatic *coup.* She offered Mary a marriage between the Prince of Wales and Mary, sister of James III, together with Berwick. This united the Scots and the arrangement was confirmed by an assembly at York (Jan. 1461) and notified to the French King, who promptly opened the Norman harbours to her supporters. While the Es. of Pembroke and Wiltshire landed with French and Bretons in the West, she marched swiftly upon London. Edward of March with Welsh troops, however, beat Wiltshire at Mortimer's Cross (3 Feb. 1461) and

himself marched for London. Warwick, having raised troops in the capital, marched to meet Margaret, who outmanoeuvred and defeated him at St. Albans (16 Feb.) and recaptured King Henry. But she lost control of her half-savage northerners, who looted the town. The Londoners who might have accepted her, wanted assurance against such treatment. In the short delay of negotiation Edward of March entered the City from the west (27 Feb.). The capital lost, Margaret retreated to York with her husband. She had no option. Her troops would have gone without her.

(18) The earls now had to choose; either they were in rebellion against their lawful King or a King had to be set up and lawfully defended. Edward of March was proclaimed and invested with the aid of the commonalty of London and the monks of Westminster (1 Mar.). His army then moved north and met the Lancastrians at Towton near Tadcaster. After a desperate all day struggle in a blizzard the Lancastrians were destroyed, Northumberland, Dacre and Neville among them, but Margaret, Henry and the princes escaped with Somerset and Exeter to Scotland where, by surrendering Berwick (Apr. 1461) they obtained a secure asylum and money from Mary of Guelders. *For remaining references to Henry VI see* EDWARD IV-6-13.

HENRY VII (1457-1509) E. of RICHMOND at birth, **King (1485)**, posthumous *s.* of Edmund Tudor, E. of Richmond, and Margaret Beaufort, **(1)** was brought up in Wales by his Lancastrian uncle Jasper Tudor, E. of Pembroke, and after his exile in 1461 by Lord Herbert. He inherited all the Lancastrian claims at the murder of Henry VI (1471) and Jasper got him to safety in Brittany where he remained, politely watched, throughout the reign of Edward IV.

(2) After the Princes in the Tower were murdered (1483) Henry became the focus of the revolutionary opposition to Richard III. Henry D. of Buckingham, a distant cousin, planned a *coup* in his favour (*see* RICHARD III) and proposed to Henry through his mother (now Lady Stanley) that he should strengthen his claims by marrying Elizabeth of York. The *coup* miscarried before Henry could land; Buckingham was beheaded and most of the surviving conspirators, especially Bp. Morton of Ely and prominent Yorkists such as the Woodvilles and the Bourchiers, again took refuge in Brittany. At Christmas 1483 they did homage to Henry as King and he swore to marry Elizabeth as soon as he had mounted the throne. Richard III reacted at once; he bribed Pierre Landois, the Breton duke's minister, to extradite Henry during Duke Francis II's illness; but Henry, urgently warned by Morton, escaped into French territory with an hour to spare (1484). The French court and Francis encouraged him with money and prominent Englishmen continued to join him, especially John de Vere, 13th E. of Oxford, and his gaoler James Blount from the prison castle of Hammes. Oxford advised boldness and with 60,000 francs and 1800 men borrowed from the French regency Henry landed at Milford Haven and, with the Stanleys, overthrew and killed Richard at Bosworth (Aug. 1485). Magnificently crowned in Oct. he summoned parliament in Nov. It confirmed his title, reversed the attainders of Henry VI and his supporters and attainted Richard III and his. To their forfeited estates, with the duchies of Cornwall and Lancaster, were added, by Act of Resumption, most of the crown lands alienated since 1455, a tonnage and poundage and a wool subsidy. These were the foundation of Henry's subsequent wealth, patiently and avariciously built up. In 1486, after stage-managed parliamentary entreaties, he married Elizabeth and in Mar. the marriage was approved and his title solemnly recognised by the Pope. He also created vested interests in his survival by granting lands and office to supporters. Jasper became D. of Bedford, (absent) Lieut. of Ireland and was given the hand of Catherine

Woodville; Oxford became High Admiral and Constable of the Tower; Lord Stanley was created E. of Derby and Constable, while Morton became Chancellor, Abp. of Canterbury (1486) and, at the King's request, a Cardinal (1493). Meanwhile a potential focus of trouble, Edward E. of Warwick (son of Clarence) was imprisoned.

(3) Safe at the centre Henry was insecure at the peripheries. Irish and northern opinion was hostile; so were powerful French courtiers and Margaret of Burgundy, the late King's aunt. Risings in Yorkshire and Worcestershire had to be put down (Spring 1486) and a false E. of Warwick appeared in Ireland. This was the boy Lambert Simnel, exhibited as "Edward VI" by John de la Pole, E. of Lincoln, with Richard III's friend Lord Lovel. With German mercenaries and Geraldine support they crossed to Furness, marched south and ended their adventure at the B. of Stoke-on-Trent (16 June 1487). Part of the royal army held back but the victory confirmed the effects of Bosworth. Henry sealed it by a progress in the north.

(4) The truce arranged with the pacific James III of Scots (July 1486) had envisaged negotiations in Mar. 1487 for marriages between James and two of his sons with the Queen Mother and two of her daughters. These were now renewed and the truce extended to Sept. 1489. Pacification and order were the themes of the moment. Henry had persuaded Innocent VIII to restrict the right of sanctuary (Aug. 1487); parliament, after attainting Simnel's main supporters, passed acts for maintaining good order among royal officials and for measures against murder, abduction and judicial delays. The peace-keeping powers of the Star Chamber were increased. While Henry celebrated a splendid coronation for his Queen, his trusted Sir Richard Edgcombe, with 500 men and a papal bull against rebels, landed in Ireland and bluffed or browbeat the Geraldines and other chiefs to swear allegiance. The Scottish negotiations, however, were more difficult: the Scots parliament (Nov. 1488) insisted on the cession or demolition of Berwick and then the Scots magnates revolted on the pretext of James' excessive Anglophilism and he was killed (June 1489). In Oct., however, James IV extended the truce until Oct. 1492. These events helped Henry to reduce disaffection in the North, though they did nothing to reduce the endemic brigandage of the Borders.

(5) Détente with France was to be delayed. The recovery of Normandy and Aquitaine might be used as home propaganda, but the real need was to contain the aggressive French monarchy's designs on Brittany and on the Flemish parts of the Burgundian inheritance. Flanders was in the Empire and the Emperor might be interested in it. Ferdinand and Isabella meant to recover French occupied Roussillon and Cerdagne for Aragon, besides bringing the Castilian crusade against Moslem Granada to victory. Something might be made of these disparate but anti-French interests. Henry tried to reduce French pressure on Brittany by a truce which, so far as Brittany was concerned, the French broke. Then a privately financed English expedition under Lord Scales, the Queen's uncle, landed in support of the Bretons and was involved with them in a disaster at St. Aubyn du Cormier (July 1488) where Lord Scales was killed. The old Duke acknowledged his French vassalage and undertook not to marry his daughter Anne without French consent (T. of Sablé, Aug. 1488). Within three weeks he was dead and Charles VIII claimed the wardship of Anne.

(6) Anne and her guardian, the marshal des Rieux, appealed to Henry who had just extended his French truce. The unavoidable war was not to be adventured alone. The parliament of Jan. 1489 made the necessary grants, but a northern insurrection impeded collection. Meanwhile Henry incited Maximilian, K. of the Romans, and the Spanish sovereigns. The T. of Medina del Campo (Mar. 1489), though never ratified, expressed a parallelism of English and Spanish interests which was to continue, with fits and starts, for 40 years. With Maximilian, however, the difficulty was the Flemish trade imbalance and piracy, and the Yorkist activity of Margaret of Burgundy: with the Spaniards, their impending attack on Granada. A three-handed war broke out on the Channel coast. While an English force landed in Brittany (Apr. 1489) there was a factional rebellion against Maximilian in Flanders and the rebels obtained French support. The confederates besieged Maximilian's town of Dixmude, whose loss would cut Calais off from Flanders. Lord Daubeney, Captain of Calais, with reinforcements from England and Guines, went to the rescue and won a resounding and lucrative victory (June 1489).

(7) In July the Imperial Diet at Frankfurt put a stop to Maximilian's war with France. By the T. of Frankfurt he ceased to support English policy in Brittany, Charles VIII renounced support for his Flemish rebels and four Breton towns were to be held in pledge by French and Imperial representatives. The Duchess Anne had to accept this and dismiss her English troops. With papal support Charles now proposed an Anglo-French peace which, of course, would leave him a free hand to absorb Brittany. Innocent VIII's interest was two-fold. He needed French troops against the Turkish threat to Italy and also in his quarrel with the Aragonese in Naples.

(8) Despite the siege of Granada some Spanish troops had been in Brittany. Henry disliked war, but peace at this moment might be worse: he would lose his only ally – Spain – forfeit his claims and pension under the T. of Picquigny (1475 *see* EDWARD IV), encourage émigré Yorkists and sacrifice Brittany. Characteristically he sought to revive the war while encouraging the developing British overseas trade, by supporting (on the balancing principle) the second trading powers against the greatest. In Aug. 1489 he had renewed the Portuguese treaty of 1387; in Jan. 1490 he amplified an agreement with Denmark which infringed the privileges of the Hanse; in Apr. he made a treaty with Florence at the expense of Venice. There followed a new military agreement with the Duchess Anne (July 1490). In Sept. Maximilian, having calmed the Low Countries, signed a new alliance with Henry who had made another with the Sforzas of Milan. The anti-French coalition seemed reborn, if in a different form, when in Mar. 1491 Maximilian married the Duchess Anne by proxy.

(9) Anne had had a French supported suitor, the Pyrenean Alain d'Albret, whom she had found repellent. The disappointed nobleman, currently gov. of Nantes, now betrayed this key post to the French (Apr. 1491) and by May they were overrunning the duchy. Neither Maximilian nor Henry could act in time. With a papal annulment and dispensations in his pocket, Charles VIII besieged Anne at Rennes and offered his hand. She married him in Dec. 1491. Granada fell in Jan. 1492.

(10) Perkin Warbeck, masquerading as the murdered D. of York, now appeared in Ireland and there were rumours of English Yorkist conspiracies. The Spaniards, no longer interested in Brittany and freed from their Moslem war, were negotiating for Roussillon and Cerdagne with Charles VIII direct. Without allies and facing a triumphant France, another Yorkist revolt could shake Henry's throne. The only solution was full scale war with France. The Irish magnates, however, did not support Warbeck for long and he escaped to France. Meanwhile Henry's powerful army, after taking Sluys, attacked Boulogne (Oct. 1492). But Charles VIII had already determined upon the fundamental reorientation of French policy towards Italy and was willing to buy Henry off, as Henry probably knew. French negotiators appeared and concluded the Ts. of Étaples (3 Nov. 1492), as a consequence of which Warbeck was expelled to Flanders. At the T. of Senlis (May 1493) Charles bought off Maximilian with Artois and Franche Comté and in the

summer of 1494 began his Italian adventure which took him to Naples by Feb. 1495.

(11) The P. of Étaples was not popular with military magnates in pursuit of loot but the European storm centre had moved from the Channel to the Mediterranean and Henry meant to stay out. He was strengthening his commerce and dealing with disaffection, for Warbeck had had a royal reception from Margaret of Burgundy and the Habsburgs and had attracted some distinguished English supporters. Among these were a Daubeney, Lord Fitzwalter, Sir Robt. Clifford and, above all, Sir William Stanley who had crowned Henry at Bosworth. Stanley was his mother's brother-in-law and very rich. Henry's intelligence system penetrated Warbeck's entourage; Daubeney and Fitzwalter were executed in the summer of 1494. Clifford, who was abroad, changed sides and on his evidence Stanley was executed too.

(12) The crown was moving from close association with landed noblemen to one with commerce. Warbeck was thus likely to attract the interest of some of the former, while his Flemish activities confused the latter. In the summer of 1493 Henry had sent Abp. Warham and Sir John Poynings to Philip of Burgundy to protest at Warbeck's activities. Philip declined to interfere with the Duchess Margaret in her own lands. Henry retaliated by an embargo on Flemish trade. The Hanseatic merchants stepped in and took the profits whereupon the London journeymen rioted at the Steelyard. Then Philip and Maximilian embargoed English iron and wool, the Hanse notwithstanding, and traders and manufacturers on both sides suffered. The Flemings, not surprisingly, wanted to get rid of Warbeck; Philip and Maximilian thought that he had a good chance if he invaded England. It suited princes and subjects to fit him out with an expedition which landed at Deal (July 1495) and was captured by the Men of Kent. Warbeck could not land and made for a second time for Ireland. This time his reception was less than enthusiastic. Poynings had enacted his celebrated reforms, brought in some competent civil servants and enlisted the support of the great E. of Kildare. Warbeck reached Waterford where the E. of Desmond brought him a following. Poynings and the Dublin bailiffs helped Waterford to beat him back with loss. Pursued to Cork and then Kinsale, he escaped along the west coast and helped successively by Burke of Galway, the O'Donnell and O'Neill of Clandeboy, reached Scotland (Nov. 1495). In his wake Kildare was again appointed Lord Deputy: the power of the Pale and his own outside it were enough to keep Ireland quiet if not, strictly speaking, to govern it during the rest of the reign.

(13) All the major powers hoped, for different reasons, for a quiescent Scotland: Henry to avoid trouble; Charles VIII to facilitate his southward policy; the Spanish sovereigns to attract Henry into war with Charles VIII. The young but able James IV was otherwise inclined. Since Robert the Bruce Scottish Kings had meddled with Ireland; James had helped Irish rebels and had been in contact with Kildare before the latter turned gamekeeper. In Sept. 1495 he prepared to attack the border in support of Warbeck. Naturally he had to treat him as a prince when he arrived as a fugitive. He pensioned him off and married him to a distant cousin of his own. The apparent threat to Henry magnified both Warbeck and James in European eyes but Henry was not perturbed. He as usual belittled the pretender and continued to work for peace with James (who could do little on his own) and meanwhile cut the ground from under the Flemish Yorkists, who had Scottish connections through the North Sea trade by negotiating local trade agreements. The *Magnus Intercursus* of Feb. 1496, though primarily a technical treaty, had this useful incidental effect, and when James in fact crossed the Border with Warbeck in Sept. 1496 the impostor attracted no support whatever.

(14) Henry's fondness for money was becoming

unpopular. He had profited greatly from Yorkist forfeitures, resumptions and fines. He had secured taxes from parliament to finance a war which had scarcely happened and he was now (Feb. 1497) voted more still for defence against the Scots. Parliament was out of touch with opinion. A Cornish rising against the tax led by Thomas Flamank and Michael Joseph (May 1497) supervened to interfere with the counterstroke against Scotland and was put down after a pitched battle at Blackheath outside London (17 June 1497). Meanwhile James, like Maximilian and Philip before him, was beginning to find Warbeck embarrassing and the Spanish sovereigns were urging James to abandon him. He settled the difficulties in much the same way: Warbeck was given an expedition and a rousing send off (July 1497). For the third time he appeared in Ireland but got no help. In Sept., with 120 men, he landed in Cornwall. His following had risen to 3000 when he reached Bodmin and to 8000 at Exeter but they were inadequately armed and Exeter resolute. Driven back and hemmed in at Taunton, Warbeck fled to sanctuary at Beaulieu and then surrendered and confessed his imposture (Oct. 1497). There were few executions but, as usual, large fines. By this time the Scottish war had been ended with the Truce of Ayton (Sept. 1497).

(15) If peace and trade had always been Henry's particular care, the new political orientations favoured them especially. A treaty similar to that of Medina del Campo was signed (Oct. 1496) and ratified (July 1497). Under it Arthur, P. of Wales, was betrothed to Katharine of Aragon (Aug.) but the Spanish sovereigns failed to involve Henry in war with France; he renewed the T. of Étaples (July 1498) and they settled with France at the T. of Marcoussis (Aug.). Thus the European Atlantic seaboard was politically tranquil at a time when for some years Henry had already been encouraging, with success, the development of the ports and of English or at least denizen traders and shipmasters. Initially (1485) he had used navigation legislation, confining the importation of claret and dyestuffs to English bottoms and forbidding exporters to use foreign ones unless none other were available. English shipping was slowly ousting foreign in the growing international traffic especially of the eastward facing ports from Boston to Winchelsea; Kings Lynn traded extensively with the Low Countries and Cologne, Sandwich with Caen and all these havens were stages in the movement of coastal shipping as far afield as Newcastle, which had long exported coal. Ships, however, were getting larger, sailing further and opening up wider prospects. Southampton had become the terminal of the Italian, mostly Venetian, trade in the 1460s. A long established Bristolian trade with Aquitaine, Iberia and the Celtic seas was extending to the Hebrides and Iceland and to the Azores and Canaries and speculating towards the unknown Brasils, "Cipangu" and the N.W. Passage. Bristol was a cosmopolitan mart where adventurers of diverse origins such as the Scottish Elliots, the Portuguese Joao Fernandez and the Genoese Cabots had their base. In Aug. 1497 John Cabot returned from his first N. American landfall and in May 1498 set out on his second, fatal, expedition but this discouraged neither Henry nor Bristol and in 1501 and 1502 he was granting charters for discovery and colonisation in N. America.

(16) But the English mercantile community needed more than encouragement against the still magnificent and ruthless organisations represented from the Baltic to Corunna by the Hanse and from the Levant to Antwerp by Venice. London's foreign trade had been mainly in foreign hands until 1485: English shipping had thriven elsewhere. The Hanse had privileges for their own products under the T. of Utrecht (1474) upon a basis of reciprocity, but reckoning upon English weakness during the Wars of the Roses habitually broke the treaty both by importing goods from third countries under privileges

and by failing to give the reciprocal facilities required. The unprivileged Venetians, whose trading galleys necessarily charged a higher freight than English roundships, imposed export duties on goods carried in English bottoms and so sought to drive the English from the wine carrying trade. Henry's counter measures against both monopolists were, in principle, the same: namely to make commercial compacts with rivals (Denmark and Florence 1490; Riga 1498) and then to manipulate regulations or tariffs to suit himself and the new partners. At the T. of Westminster (1498) he forced on the Hanse a strict adherence to the T. of Utrecht; the Mediterranean tariff war and the diversion of English wool through Florence continued until the League of Cambrai and the Turks forced the Venetians to relax.

(17) In Feb. 1499 yet another impostor, Ralph Wilford, pretending to be Warwick, was seized and hanged. The Spaniards, in the interest of the Aragon marriage, had been urging the real Warwick's elimination for some time and he, who had lived all his life in prison, together with Warbeck and Atwater, the mayor of Cork who had befriended Warbeck, fell victims of a trap which brought about their execution in Nov. The treason was alleged to have taken place in the summer when Edmund de la Pole, E. of Suffolk, of the one surviving family of Yorkist royal blood, suddenly fled to Calais and then to Flanders. He was, however, induced to return and he accompanied Henry to a meeting with Philip of Burgundy at Calais in May 1500.

(18) During these alarms Henry proceeded doggedly with his policy of pacification. A Scottish treaty of July 1499 provided for the truce beyond the lives of the two Kings; in Sept. Henry began negotiations for a marriage between his daughter Margaret and K. James, for which in July 1500 he obtained a papal dispensation on account of their common descent from John Beaufort, E. of Somerset. In Aug. 1501, however, Suffolk and his brother Richard fled once again, this time to the court of Maximilian and that winter Katharine of Aragon and the Scottish ambassadors arrived simultaneously. The Scottish negotiations were pressed ahead during the rejoicings which, organised on a tremendous scale, culminated in the marriage (Nov.) of Katharine and P. Arthur. Three Scottish treaties were signed on 24 Jan. 1502 and James and Margaret were married by proxy next day. Arthur, however, died at Ludlow in Apr. to Henry's desperate grief and the event unhinged some of his careful diplomacy, for a Yorkist pretender with imperial patronage was a real danger where Henry had only one remaining son. There was, too disaffection among the older families, perhaps unused to the new commercialism's threat to their status, and some doubtless horrified by the judicial murder of the innocent Warwick. In May 1502 executions included Sir James Tyrrell, Capt. of Guisnes, who was a friend of Suffolk's, and arrests included Suffolk's brother William and William Courtenay, son of the E. of Devon. In 1503 there were reports of conspiracies at Aachen (Maximilian's capital) and in 1504 of disaffection at Calais. Meanwhile Suffolk, after various adventures, fell into the hands of Philip of Burgundy. In Jan. 1506 Philip, however, was driven ashore at Melcombe Regis, conducted in splendour to Windsor and invited to surrender Suffolk before he left. So in Mar. 1506 Suffolk ended in the Tower.

(19) The Suffolk affair was entangled with Anglo-Burgundian commercial and political relations, which themselves had depended upon the long-standing wool trade with Flanders: Henry was by now actually and obviously rich: he began his chapel at Westminster in 1503 and the impecunious Habsburg rulers were hoping to be financed by him. He made some grants in exchange for promises not to support his rebels but in 1504 Isabella of Castile died and Philip decided to claim

her inheritance. With a Franco-Spanish conflict in prospect in the Mediterranean, French and Burgundian goodwill was more important to Henry than Spanish. He lent Philip large sums to embarrass Ferdinand of Aragon and it was the resulting expedition to Spain which was driven ashore at Melcombe. The Windsor Treaties (q.v.) into which Philip entered during his English sojourn, and commercial concessions (or *Malus Intercursus*), never came to fruition for Philip died before they could be ratified.

(20) Henry's character must have been strongly affected, especially in his caution and dislike of war, by his fugitive youth, and his tenuous claim to the Throne made him ruthless against pretenders. In a personal and religious sense mediaeval, he built upon or used existing institutions so much that contemporaries did not notice any pronounced changes, save those wrought by relative peace and prosperity. In fact he is recognisable as a modern type of statesman, more interested in economic than territorial expansion and using economic more than physical sanctions. He kept taxation low, yet maintained a calculated splendour without a standing military establishment; some of his methods, especially in the abuse of judicial fines and the sale of pardons, set a pattern for corruption which was widespread and he died unpopular, respected and rich.

HENRY VIII (1490-1547) King (1509) 2nd *s.* of Henry VII and Margaret of York **(1)** had, through his mother, a better right to the throne than his father who had, however, disposed of all, save very distant, other claimants. Red haired, of tremendous physique and agility, he was arrogant, hot tempered, unpredictable yet well educated, clever with a talent for poetry and music and in possession of a terrifying personality and an instinctive popular leadership which compensated him as a politician for his self indulgence, especially in sex. At an unknown moment he caught syphilis and declined into instability, disease and obesity.

(2) He inherited a fortune and most of his father's ministers remained in office; the most important were Abp. Warham, who was also Lord Chancellor, Richard Fox, Bp. of Winchester and Lord Privy Seal, Thos. Ruthall, his father's secretary whom he made Bp. of Durham, Lord Lovell and Sir Henry Poynings respectively treasurer and controller of the Chamber and Sir Henry Morney of the Duchy of Lancaster. They were anxious to carry on the existing peaceful policies.

(3) The late King had enjoined the marriage of Henry and his brother's widow, Katharine of Aragon. The dispensations were available. A month after Henry VII's obsequies he married her, in time for his own coronation. Ferdinand of Aragon, all flattery and helpfulness, judged it possible to make use of Henry, despite his energetic proclivities and doubtless his daughter described his character faithfully.

(4) There was a change of personal and political balance in the govt. Youth and fire had not only replaced wisdom and calculation at the head. Empson and Dudley, Henry VII's careful and competent financiers, had been sacrificed to public clamour on false charges of treason in a deliberate bid for popularity, and the soldierly Thomas Howard, E. of Surrey, had become Lord Treasurer. While the monarchy now ceased to invest and began to spend hugely on court establishments Fox, who feared Surrey's sympathy for his master's aggressiveness, brought in Thomas Wolsey as a counterweight. With the hard clarity of ambition, Wolsey saw that advancement lay in pleasing the King and that what pleased the King was glory. At the start there was plenty of it, in lavish spending and magnificence, in jousting and wenching and in popular acclaim, and in these Henry diverted himself while the decreasingly united council did the work.

(5) Henry confirmed the Scottish Treaties of 1502 (June 1509) and the French Treaties of Étaples of 1492

(Mar. 1510) with the concurrence of many W. European rulers and papal sanction, but his bullying temperament was soon used by others to suck England into the Italian whirlpool which his father had so determinedly avoided. Those interested in achieving this were Ferdinand of Aragon and the rapidly rising Wolsey. Sooner or later Henry would have had his war and since he claimed part of France, suzerainty over Scotland and sovereignty in the Narrow Seas, it was obvious that his martial glory would be won on French and Scottish fronts. Pretexts against Scotland were always on hand because of border reiving for which, however, machinery of redress existed if operated in good faith; moreover, Sir Edward Howard, commanding King's ships in the Channel gratuitously attacked two Scottish royal ships and Henry refused redress (Aug-Oct. 1511) contrary to the treaties and with insult. James IV saw what was coming and wrote to the Pope for absolution (Dec.).

(6) But the Pope, Julius II, was behaving like a bellicose Italian secular prince. Having invited the French in to help him partition the Venetian *Terra Firma,* he feared their too great success (B. of Agnadello, May 1509) and determined to extrude them. He made terms with Venice, formed an Italian confederacy and went to war at first unsuccessfully, then in person with greater advantage. In the first half of 1511 Louis XII replied by convoking with the aid of dissident cardinals a General Council to Pisa. Julius replied by creating eight new cardinals, of whom one was Christopher Bainbridge, Abp. of York and Henry's ambassador to the Holy See (Mar. 1511) and by himself convoking a council to the Lateran. The French tried to keep the northern peace and restrain the K. of Scots, but Ferdinand saw an opportunity to occupy Navarre with English help and egged Henry on. Small English semi-official expeditions went to help Margaret of Burgundy against the pro-French D. of Guelders and to Cadiz where Ferdinand refused their help. In Oct. 1511 Ferdinand, Julius and Venice set up the Holy League against France and in Nov. Henry joined it. His fleet made damaging raids on the French and convoyed his army to Fuentarrabia, where it distracted the main French army but suffered heavily from disease, while Ferdinand overran Navarre. The English army then mutinied and sailed home.

(7) With pyrrhic victories in Italy, Louis was hard pressed and now persuaded the Scots into the war. The papal defeats and the debacle at Fuentarrabia made Henry even more determined. With 25,000 men he crossed to Calais and invested Thérouanne. The French relieving army was routed at the B. of the Spurs at Guinegatte (16 Aug. 1513) and then James crossed the Border (24 Aug.). On 12 Sept. the Scots army was destroyed and James IV killed by the able E. of Surrey at Flodden. By this time Thérouanne had fallen and Tournai followed on 21st. Henry had his triumph in the service of Holy Church. The war was rounded off with a peace treaty (Aug. 1514) under which Henry kept Thérouanne and Tournai; his French pension was doubled and his sister Mary was protestingly married to Louis XII. She agreed only on condition that when the ageing Louis died she should choose her next husband herself. She had, in fact, already done so: he was Charles Brandon, the new D. of Suffolk who had one, if not two, wives already. Within a year Louis was dead and in 1515 she married as she intended.

(8) The impulse had been Henry's, but much of the organisation was due to Wolsey, who for the next 14 years dominated the scene. He had become Abp. of York in 1514 and a Cardinal in 1515. In the same year he became Lord Chancellor and galvanised the Star Chamber into a powerful activity which by 1516 had absorbed the work of the Privy Seal. He was thus supreme in parliament, in administration and in the law besides being, as a Prince of the Church, an international personality. In 1518 he was appointed legate a latere and, as the Pope's delegate, became supreme over the English Church. To this enormous concentration of power was added great private wealth derived from major and minor offices held *in commendam:* particularly the bishoprics of Bath and Wells, then Durham and finally Winchester and Tournai, together with the rich abbacy of St. Albans; he farmed the sees of Salisbury, Worcester and Llandaff on behalf of Italian absentees and used his legatine powers to override the ecclesiastical patronage of other bishops and the archbishop of Canterbury in favour of a vast retinue of followers. (*For the period of Wolsey's supremacy see* WOLSEY, THOMAS.)

(9) When Wolsey fell in Oct. 1529 he had shown Henry how a diverse and multiple society could be dominated by unification towards a centre, and his power, and most of his accumulated wealth, passed to the King. It included Hampton Court and York House which became the Palace of Whitehall. Henry, with adaptations suitable to his royal estate, took over the Cardinal's machinery. He proceeded to use it for purposes and in controversies which he had never contemplated when he came to the throne but his tactics were different. The cardinal was an autocrat: Henry a popular tyrant. Under Wolsey parliament met only twice: after his fall it met almost annually for Henry, whether as instrument or instigator, was carrying through a revolution and could not do without it.

(10) Henry's new minister was Thomas Cromwell, sworn of the council in 1531, but where Wolsey had been the King's Other Self, Cromwell was his instrument. Henry's manner of business resembled that of a modern prime minister: before each parliament met a schedule of business and drafts of most of the intended bills were settled in the council. Whatever the temperamental and external accidents and inducements, a continuous policy away from mediaeval secular particularism and ecclesiastical universality is discernible. The central idea may be found in Henry's repeated references to the Crown Imperial of England, meaning a self sufficient authority, sovereign within its territory, uncircumscribed in the rest of the world by doctrine or custom and at least equal to the emperor or pope. To the wearer of such a Crown, local franchises, tribal organisation, marcher lordships, palatinates, ecclesiastical privileges and the whole complex of papal influence in and over the church might exist because the Crown tolerated them, but not because they had an independent source of authority. Convenience dictated whether they ought to continue; expediency whether they should; political tactics how far they might but they had no rights.

(11) Such a view was convenient when the cost of govt. was everywhere rising, the King extravagant and foreign policy expensive. Apart from the endless Border fighting, patrolling and fortification absorbed large sums. So did the small navy. Ireland cost more, even in tranquillity, than it brought in. It was seldom tranquil. The bullion of America was creating a European inflation. The King's need for money was matched by ability to take it. But the Crown's new eminence made a settled succession even more important than before and Q. Katharine had produced a daughter, Mary, but no male heir. Wolsey's failure to secure an annulment for his master brought about his fall; but the problem survived him. It was seldom easy to annul a marriage already based upon a papal dispensation, especially a consummated one which had endured for 20 years and, anyhow, the pope was a virtual prisoner since 1527 in the hands of Katharine's nephew, Charles V.

(12) (*See* REFORMATION.) The English reformation thus began as a means to bring political pressure on the Papacy and financial profit to the Crown. The parliament which sat at intervals from 1529 to 1536 opened by passing popular measures against ecclesiastical abuses of probate and mortuaries; it strengthened public order by further restricting sanctuary. It increased the crown revenues by limiting ecclesiastical leases and it struck, in the name of greater holiness, at an important source of papal patronage by reducing pluralities and absenteeism (Nov. 1529). However, while Henry canvassed European university opinion on his marriage, the Pope crowned his captor (Feb. 1530). Henry now resolved to terrorise the English church. In Dec. he had the entire clergy indicted on a *praemunire* for submitting to Wolsey's legatine authority, but immediately afterwards the Pope forbade him to remarry pending a decision. The convocations hastened to procure pardons for £118,000 in cash (Feb.) but Henry kept up the pressure. The officially instigated *Supplication against the Ordinaries* brought about the SUBMISSION OF THE CLERGY (Mar.-May 1531) which put the convocations under royal control. Henry now procured the Act of Annates which he could put into force when he liked as a bargaining counter, enabling him simultaneously to extract more money and exclude papal control of consecrations.

(13) By mid-1532 Henry had allowed the universities to convince him that his marriage was void. The Emperor was threatened by Turkish fleets based on Constantinople and Barbary. Henry thus felt free to take his next step, assisted by the succession at Canterbury of Cranmer to the aged Abp. Warham. He confirmed the Act of Annates; in Jan. 1533 he married Anne Boleyn secretly and then procured the Act in Restraint of Appeals which enabled Cranmer to make the annulment which the Pope had refused. Anne then emerged as Queen. The movement for reformation thereby gained strength despite Henry's doctrinal conservatism, for her family had secular tastes. Meanwhile the King concluded the Truce of Newcastle with the Scots (May) and in Oct. came three important statutes: namely the ACT OF SUPREMACY, the Act which preserved Tenths and First Fruits to the Crown (another source of revenue) and an important amendment to the Statute of Treasons which, amongst other things, made even certain verbal criticisms treasonable.

(14) Henry's policy was being resisted. Many people agreed with the papal decision in favour of Q. Katharine (Mar. 1534) and mistrusted the incipient spoliation of the church, however corrupt it might be. There was trouble brewing in Ireland which broke into open rebellion under "Silken Thomas", son of the E. of Kildare (June), just as Henry managed to convert the Truce of Newcastle into a permanent peace. The Border, however, remained unpacified. Money was becoming short again.

(15) Henry now assumed the ecclesiastical supremacy (Jan. 1535) and the Pope prepared a Bull of Deposition but could find no ruler willing to execute it. The practical effect was that Cromwell became the King's Vicar-Gen. and controlled the church. This led by a sort of nightmare inevitability to More's execution under the amended Stat. of Treasons (July 1535) and to Cromwell's attack on the lesser monasteries (1535-6) but meantime Silken Thomas had been captured and put into the Tower. The proximity of Ireland to Wales drew attention to the confused and disaffected state of that country as well as its Celtic affiliations. There were recent memories of the important role which it and the marchers had played in the pre-Tudor Civil Wars and Henry himself was partly Welsh. The Welsh ACT OF UNION (Apr. 1536) began an administrative, judicial and legal reorganisation which in the end almost assimilated Welsh institutions to those of England. While Cromwell sold off English monastic properties, Lord Leonard Grey, as Lord Deputy, summoned an Irish parliament which imposed the English Church legislation there. Insofar as English rule was effective in the Pale it was greeted without enthusiasm; among the wild Irish with indifference; but the attack on the monasteries with their still important social role was another matter.

(16) By the autumn of 1535 Henry had convinced himself that there must be something sinful in his marriage with Anne Boleyn who, like Katharine, had produced a daughter, Elizabeth, but no male heir. Anne, the grand-daughter of the victor of Flodden, had entered court life as maid of honour to Q. Claude of France. She had not been chaste before her marriage and was imprudent afterwards. Her miscarriage (perhaps due to the King's syphilis) in Jan. 1536 seemed a sign of Divine anger. She was indicted for numerous adulteries, condemned without evidence and executed (19 May 1536). Two days later Cranmer declared her marriage void *ab initio* (making nonsense of the charges of adultery) whereby both Henry's daughters were technically illegitimate. On 30 may he married Jane Seymour but an Act of Succession (June) was clearly needed because the male heir presumptive, the D. of Richmond, was dying.

(17) These scandalous proceedings combined with the govt's religious and secular policies provoked the great northern rebellion, known as the PILGRIMAGE OF GRACE (Oct.-Dec. 1536) which in its turn led to the reform of the Council of the North, henceforth endowed with an efficient administration and strong judicial powers. The suppression of the rebellion also gave impetus to the attack on the greater monasteries, many of which had been implicated. By 1540 the last of them and the Houses of the Order of St. John had gone (*see* AUGMENTATIONS, COURT OF).

(18) Queen Jane Seymour died in 1537 giving birth to the future Edward VI. In Dec. 1538 the Pope (Paul III) issued the Bull of deposition prepared in 1535. The papal efforts at reform were beginning to take effect with a summons to a general council, originally at Mantua (1537), then Vicenza (1538) and finally to Trent. The Turkish threat was bringing Charles V and Francis I of France together and though Henry tried to keep them apart by offers of marriage to himself, they agreed in the T. of Toledo (Jan. 1539) to make no new alliance without the other's consent. There seemed to be a real danger of a crusade against England and Henry replied with a precautionary mobilisation (May 1539); the Act of Six Articles advertised that his quarrel was with the Papacy not with Christendom, while Hollanders were conciliated with a reduction in customs. All the same, Cromwell believed that a continental alliance was needed and negotiated a deal with D. William of Cleves (q.v.), a leading W. German prince of Erastian opinions (Oct. 1539). Henry was to marry the Duke's daughter, Anne, and the Duke, with French connivance, was to make trouble for the Emperor, who had a rebellion at nearby Ghent on his hands. The scheme turned out to be a fiasco. The French King and the Emperor quarrelled anyhow and the lady's charms did not suit Henry. All the same he married her (Jan. 1540), promoted Sir Ralph Sadler and Sir Thomas Wriothesley, protégés of Cromwell, to be joint secretaries and in Apr. made him E. of Essex and Lord Chamberlain. Yet at this moment the conservative Howards got the King's ear through Katharine, the D. of Norfolk's attractive daughter, who was much more charming than the Queen. The policy against papalism was still pressed: Bp. Simpson of Chichester was imprisoned. There were attainders for denying the royal supremacy. Then suddenly Cromwell was arrested. Convocation and parliament annulled the marriage; the Queen was packed off to the country with a fat pension and Cromwell beheaded. The same day Henry married Katharine (July 1540).

(19) Henry had sent Sadler to Scotland to persuade James V to dissolve his monasteries, a measure which might shake the power of the Francophile Card. Beaton (Apr. 1540). He failed but tried again in 1541 when Beaton was in France and persuaded James to meet Henry at York in Sept. Henry made the journey: James

did not and Henry resolved on war. It was during this journey that Henry received reports about Q. Katharine Howard which led to her trial and execution (Jan. 1542) for unconfessed premarital unchastity and adultery. In the course of the Franco-Imperial dispute both sides courted Henry and the French had proposed (Aug. 1541) a marriage between the D. of Orléans and Mary. In Feb. 1542 they suggested a meeting between Henry, James and Francis I. It was now obvious that Francis would not give the Scots any useful support and so Henry launched his war. His general, Sir Robt. Bowes, was defeated at Haddon Rig (Aug. 1542) and Norfolk, the late queen's father, commanded against, but failed to reach, Edinburgh. James V's counter-attack ended in a great disaster at Solway Moss (Dec. 1542) and his own death from the bitterness of defeat. His heir was the week-old Mary Q. of Scots.

(20) Henry's arrogance and aggression now led him into major errors. He began well enough by releasing the noble prisoners taken at Solway Moss under assurance to further his interest. He called off the war; the regent, the E. of Arran, and the reformist-dominated estates appointed ambassadors to negotiate (Mar. 1543). The T. of Greenwich provided for peace and a marriage between the P. of Wales and the infant Queen (July). The eventual union of two like minded Kingdoms now seemed certain. In fact Henry had agreed (Feb. 1543) to join Charles V in a war with France for which, despite a renewed French offer of the Orléans marriage, he was steadily mobilising. In the summer 6000 English troops served with the imperial army and in Dec. he made a military agreement at Hampton Court for a joint invasion. Meanwhile he was giving himself the airs of a Scottish suzerain and when this gave offence seized Scots shipping in the Thames. His alarmed Scottish allies were overborne by Beaton and the contentions of French diplomacy. The Estates revoked the Ts., renewed the Auld Alliance and legislated against heresy. Henry could have negotiated on both fronts since the French were anxious to keep him out of the war. He chose to fight on both. In May 1544 he launched the E. of Hertford on a destructive campaign (*The Rough Wooing*) which united almost all Scotland against him. In July, having married Catherine Parr, he crossed to Calais and thence besieged Boulogne, which surrendered in Sept. He had never meant to pursue his military obligations to the end and the emperor, finding himself alone, had negotiated. Henry refused to be included in the discussions and the P. of Crépy, on the same day as Henry's entry into Boulogne, left Henry to fight it out alone. The result was a desperate defence while the Scots defeated Hertford at Ancrum (27 Feb. 1545), a furious naval war which included battles in the mouth of the Seine and in the Solent (June 1545) and the ravaging of the Sussex and Norman coasts. The French, meanwhile, devastated the Calais Pale and landed an army in Scotland and in 1545 Hertford swept the Tweed and burned its five abbeys. The Scots, however, grew even more obdurate; in Mar. 1546 Beaton burned Geo. Wishart, protestant martyr and, possibly, English double agent and, with Henry's connivance, Beaton was murdered in his castle at St. Andrews in May. By now the govt. was virtually bankrupt and signed the P. of Ardres (7 June 1546). It was financially a bad bargain and it left the Scots protestants at the mercy of the French.

(21) Since 1540 the country had been more heavily taxed than ever in its history, but the vigorous foreign policy created a bottomless indebtedness. Six 15ths and 10ths, three subsidies, the new income from the church and confiscated property and four clerical subsidies failed to bridge the gap. In 1542 Henry raised loans by Privy Seal and was relieved of the obligation to repay in 1544. Benevolences, though illegal, were levied in 1545 and 1546. Monastic properties had to be sold wholesale but the quantity of land thus thrown on the market brought down the price and the profits. The coinage, partly to meet contemporary debasements elsewhere was debased both by raising the price of bullion and by alloy. The mint consequently prospered. Despite all these shifts Henry had to borrow (often at 14%) in the Netherlands and had a considerable foreign debt until the end of the reign.

(22) Henry, now corpulent and ill, was increasingly becoming the arbiter between the two major factions in court and council rather than the active head of the govt. On the one side were the reformers or protestants leaning on Abp. Cranmer, strengthened by Henry's marriage to Katharine Parr but weakened by the recent deaths of Suffolk and Poynings and by Hertford's and Lisle's absences on campaign. On the other were the conservative or Catholic Howards and Gardiner who, as Henry became more devout, intrigued against but failed to shake Cranmer's position. Norfolk and Gardiner, however, disagreed on foreign policy, for Norfolk was Francophile and Gardiner imperialist. After the P. of Ardres, however, Hertford and Lisle returned but in Oct. 1546 Lisle was excluded for hitting Gardiner and in Nov. Gardiner was excluded for refusing to exchange some lands with Henry. The last political crisis of the reign, caused by the rashness of Norfolk's son Surrey, now supervened. Surrey occasionally boasted of his descent from Edward I and now used the royal leopards and the arms of Edward the Confessor. He was denounced by Sir Richard Southwell and he and his father were tried for treason. Surrey went to the block. Norfolk, attainted in parliament, survived because Henry died on the day before his scheduled execution.

HENRY of ALMAINE (1235-71) *s.* of Richard of Cornwall and Isabella Marshall, a royal nominee for the drafting of the Provisions of Oxford (1258) came under the spell of Simon de Montfort and was put into custody at Boulogne in 1263 as a result. Here his friend, the Lord Edward, converted him; he fought with the royalists at Lewes and surrendered himself as a hostage. In 1265 he was in France negotiating with Louis IX but returned to command one of the mopping up expeditions after the B. of Evesham. He was a referee under Lord Edward's Dictum of Kenilworth (1267) and after settling a dispute between the King and Gloucester went on Crusade (1268). Two of de Montfort's sons murdered him in the church at Viterbo.

HENRY BENEDICT MARIA CLEMENT, Card. YORK (1725-1807). *See* JACOBITES AND PRETENDERS.

HENRY fitz EMPRESS (Henry II) "STATUTE" or PRIVILEGE (Ir.). This suppositious document was said to authorise the practice whereby the Lord Lieutenant or Deputy, with the Council's advice, filled the highest offices temporarily during a vacancy until the King's will was known. The appointee some times held office for years. The parliament of Trim in 1485 purported to confirm it but this was an expedient for ensuring that Richard III's govt. could function even if he were overthrown, for it also specifically confirmed the E. of Kildare and others in office.

HENRY FREDERICK (1594-1612) P. of WALES (1610) *s.* of James VI and I was the subject of one of James' Spanish marriage projects.

HENRY FREDERICK, Prince (1745-90) D. of CUMBERLAND and STRATHEARN, *see* CUMBERLAND, DS OF.

HENRY I of France (r. 1031-60). *See* CAPETIANS, EARLY-9.

HENRY II of France (r. 1547-59) (1) succeeded his father François I just after the Emperor Charles V had overthrown the Schmalkaldic League at the B. of Mülhberg (Apr. 1547) and had captured its leading princes. The changing fortunes in this mainly German religious war were to have strong effects in French internal history under Henry II with consequences in England. A major figure was Maurice of Saxony, head of

the Albertine house of Wettin, who coveted and by Charles' favour obtained most of the lands and the Saxon electoral hat belonging to the Ernestine house. This was not the limit of his ambitions and soon he was plotting with the Emperor's Lutheran enemies whom he had deserted before Mülhberg. During the decline of François I's last years the noble house of Montmorency had replaced the dead Duprat and had risen to eminence. Anne had become Constable in 1529 and with his nephews Châtillon (or Coligny) and Andelot formed a powerful Erastian influence which, on the whole, favoured rapprochement with the Emperor. The treasury was empty in 1547 and, especially in the south, the tax collectors were resisted. It was the Constable Anne's misfortune to have to use artillery against the awkward citizens of Bordeaux. Further north, in Saintonge, the young, personable and semi-royal D. of Guise, faced with an easier situation, won popularity and golden opinions on a similar errand. The Guise family, with its claims to the Kingdom of Naples and its ally the Cardinal of Lorraine, was strongly ultramontane. They favoured continued military intervention in Italy. The disagreements between these groups were to polarise into a bitter personal, political and religious feud. There was, in addition, a third group of Italians (The *fuorusciti* = emigrants) and Italian sympathisers attached to Catherine de Medici and deriving their influence from her. These tended to a nostalgic desire for Italian liberation from Spanish interference but favoured domestic concord in the interest of higher living standards. Franco-Italian renaissance architecture and the French cuisine are their lasting monuments. **(2)** In fact Henry II, youthful and bellicose, could find bellicose advisers. French guns reduced St. Andrews held by Calvinists with English help. The new English govt. mounted a major offensive, defeated the Scots at Pinkie (Sept. 1547) and occupied Edinburgh. The Scots Estates sent their young Queen, Mary, to France in a French galley; she arrived in Aug. 1548. Logically enough the French had begun (though still nominally at peace) to raid Boulogne. War with England was not inconsistent with Montmorency policy and, moreover, that family wished to divert attention from the Guises. The raids were led by Châtillon and English complaints were insolently rejected. The English withdrew from Scotland to fight the French and declared war (Aug. 1549). The ensuing French successes were due to inadequate provision by the govt. of Protector Somerset and contributed to his fall. The local English, however, maintained a stout defence in Boulogne itself and the war ended in the P. of Boulogne (Mar. 1550) which included Scotland, and the immediate cession of the town at a reduced price. **(3)** On the French side this peace, arising out of a Montmorency success, was desirable because an opportunity to follow a Guisard policy and make trouble for the Emperor was discernible in the activities of Maurice of Saxony. This prince had been refused Magdeburg, which he proceeded to besiege (Oct. 1550-Nov. 1551). Failure demonstrated his need for powerful patronage, for which he and his Lutheran allies secretly approached Henry II. By the fateful T. of CHAMBORD (Jan. 1552) they nominated him Imperial Vicar in Lorraine and, as such, protector of the three strategic bishoprics of Metz, Toul and Verdun. Leaving Q. Catherine (de Medici) in charge at home the King set off on a military promenade, ostensibly to inspect his new responsibilities, actually to impose his will on Lorraine in which the bishoprics were embedded. He was rapturously received by a population tired of paying for Charles V's wars. A French princess was offered to the young duke of Lorraine on whose behalf the King established a regency. Within weeks Lorraine had become a client state and the King had reached the Rhine. **(4)** All this was made feasible by collusion with

Maurice who suddenly turned on Charles V, seized Augsburg and nearly captured him at Innsbruck (May 1552). Charles fled; the end of his influence in Germany was marked by the T. of Passau (2 Aug.) (under which the Schmalkadic princes were released) but he counter-attacked in Lorraine. Francis of Guise held Metz against him (Jan. 1553) and made much of his success: a Montmorency force suffered a check at Thérouanne in Mar. The war now spread southwards. Protected by Turkish command of the sea the French seized Corsica as well as Piedmont and much of Lombardy and Tuscany. For this, however, the nearly simultaneous deaths of Maurice at Sivershausen (July 1553) and of Edward VI were compensations. **(5)** A Queen of Spanish ancestry and Roman convictions now ruled in England. She instantly sought the hand of Charles' son Philip of Spain. Thereupon (Apr. 1554) Mary of Guise took control in Scotland but Mary of England persisted and married her Philip (25 July). His interest in her as a person was minimal but, with his father's intended retirement looming ahead, Philip meant to involve her in the continental policies which he was about to inherit. In Apr. 1555 the Spaniards made headway in Italy where they took Siena and sold it to Florence. In Sept. the Diet of Augsburg led by Ferdinand established the Religious Peace and Philip renounced all Imperial claims; in Oct. the Emperor transferred his own rights and claims in Italy and the Low Countries to Aragon and Castile, and having thus prepared the ground, resigned the Spanish Kingdoms to Philip on 16 Jan. 1556. A truce between Henry and Philip, signed at Vaucelles (5 Feb.) followed but in May Paul IV, a Neapolitan Pope, signed an alliance for the transfer of Naples to a French prince. In Sept. Philip retaliated: the D. of Alva occupied the Papal states while his master intrigued with German protestants. Guise was sent, with inadequate forces, to rescue the Pope who had excommunicated Philip and had, incidentally, put a check to Mary's counter-reformation. In Mar. 1557 Philip came to England to arrange for English help. K. Henry had been welcoming English protestant exiles and fomenting conspiracies but the English govt. only reluctantly joined in the war (June 1557). On 10 Aug., however, a joint Anglo-Spanish force won a great victory at St. Quentin and captured the Constable de Montmorency. This was an event of great political significance. **(6)** It became necessary to recall Guise, to whose faction power and place increasingly fell. The Anglo-Spaniards, crippled by disease and poor administration, failed to pursue their advantage. In Oct. 1557 Guise reached St. Germain where he was invested with the Lieutenancy of the Realm. He now prepared a brilliant stroke. The Calais defences had been neglected since the death of Henry VIII. Despite a valiant local resistance Calais was stormed on 7 Jan. 1558 and Guines surrendered on 20th. In Apr. Mary Q. of Scots married the Dauphin and in June Guise took Thionville and Dunkirk. Only in July was the victorious Guisard career checked by Egmont at the B. of Gravelines. **(7)** Philip and Henry by now both wanted peace; Gravelines provided the opportunity and discussions were opened in Oct. Henry needed the captive constable as a counter-weight to the overweening Guises and nominated him as his plenipotentiary with the Guisard Cardinal of Lorraine. Mary of England died (Nov. 1558) and England was preoccupied with a protestant revolution. In these circumstances Philip and his minister Granvelle left Calais in French hands. The P. of CÂTEAU CAMBRÉSIS (Apr. 1559) was signed by the Constable. The Spaniards maintained their Italian positions and Corsica was handed to the Genoese. The French returned Savoy and Piedmont (but not Saluzzo) to its Duke who, however, married Henry II's sister Marguerite (1553-1615). Philip married Henry's daughter Elizabeth (1545-68). Above all France retained her hold on the Three Bishoprics and

consequently on Lorraine. Thus she kept the entrances both to Germany and Italy and brought off a victory of prestige over England. To mark the triumph King Henry organised a great ceremonial joust in which he took part and was killed in July 1559. For the remaining Valois rulers, FRANCOIS II (July-Dec. 1559), CHARLES IX (r. 1559-74) and HENRY III (1574-89) *see* HUGUENOTS.

HENRY of BLOIS (1100-71) Bp. of WINCHESTER. *See* HENRY I; STEPHEN.

HENRY of GROSMONT (1310-61). *See* LANCASTER, FIRST FAMILY-4.

HENRY of HUNTINGDON (?1084-1155), Archdeacon of Huntingdon from 1109, on a journey to Rome with Abp. Theobald met the Norman historian Robert of Torigny at Bec. As a result, perhaps, he wrote his own *Historia Anglorum* (Lat = History of the English) which is a useful source for the period 1120 to 1154.

HENRY of LANCASTER (?1281-1345). *See* LANCASTER, FIRST FAMILY-3.

HENRY of OATLANDS, D. of GLOUCESTER (1639-60), 3rd son of Charles I, refused to become a R. Catholic in exile but joined Charles II at Cologne and fought the Spaniards as a volunteer in the Low Countries in 1657 and 1658. He died of smallpox.

HENRY, St. *See* MISSIONS TO EUROPE.

HENRY THE NAVIGATOR. *See* AVIS.

HENRY THE YOUNG KING (1155-83). This gullible and spendthrift seeker after popularity was the second *s.* of Henry II and was his heir after the death of an elder brother. He was betrothed at the age of three and married at five to Margaret, *d.* of Louis VII of France, as part of territorial negotiations, and was educated in the household of Abp. Becket. At nine he received the homage of the bishops and barons but the quarrel between Becket and his father delayed his coronation which, at the hands of Roger Abp. of York, became the occasion of the final quarrel and Becket's death in 1170. Meanwhile Henry II had nominally assigned Brittany, Maine and Anjou to him (1169) and he had done homage for them to Louis, but Henry remained in tutelage while his abler younger brothers had a greater measure of independence. In 1173-4 he was persuaded into a revolt which failed but his father gave him a substantial pension afterwards. In 1182 he attacked his brother Richard, who had refused to do homage. In a war with Henry and Richard he was besieged in Limoges. He fell ill, was expelled from the city and died. *See* HENRY II.

HENRY, Patrick (1736-99) demagogue Virginian, was the leading orator of the American rebellion ("Give me liberty or give me death"). From 1776 to 1779 he was the first gov. of the State of Virginia and in 1788 opposed the ratification of the Federal Constitution as interfering with States' rights.

HENSLOW, John Stevens (1796-1861), the inspirer of Darwin, was a mineralogist and botanist who published *inter alia* a *Catalogue of British Plants* in 1829. *See* KEW GARDENS.

HENSON, Herbert Hensley (1863-1947) Bp. of DURHAM from 1920 to 1939, a champion of Church Establishment until Parliament rejected the Revised Prayer Books in 1927 and 1928, became convinced that church freedom was impossible without disestablishment of which, consequently, he became the foremost advocate. Eloquent and disinterested, he was also a leading liberal theologian.

HEPBURN. This Scots family, famous or notorious in the 16th cent., included **(1) Patrick (?-1508) 3rd Ld. HAILES, 1st E. of BOTHWELL (1488)** who defended Berwick against the English in 1482 and was a leader of the *coup* against James III in 1488 which culminated in the B. of Sauchieburn, after which James was constrained to bring the family into the centre of affairs by making Patrick at once Gov. of Edinburgh, Master of the Household and Admiral besides conferring the earldom.

In 1489 he received large grants in Orkney and Shetland and in 1492 most of Liddesdale. These later played significant parts in the family history. He was also a commissioner for the marriage treaty between James VI and Margaret Tudor in 1501. His brother **(2) John (?- 1522)** became Prior of St. Andrews in 1482 and Keeper of the Privy Seal. Patrick's son having died at the B. of Flodden (1513) his grandson **(3) Patrick (1512-56) 3rd E.**, as owner of Liddesdale, was heavily involved in border reiving for which he was imprisoned, and then offered his services to the E. of Northumberland in return for protection against his own govt. Naturally he was arrested and banished (1533). He returned to Liddesdale in 1542 and was recruited into the party of Card. Beaton and Mary of Guise, the Queen Regent, whom he protected at Stirling in 1543. He then divorced his wife in order to court the Queen Regent, who refused him, but in the meanwhile he arrested George Wishart, the protestant divine, for Beaton who burned him. Patrick's Liddesdale position led him into further English intrigues and he fled to England in 1548 but the Queen Regent recalled him in 1553 and he was her Lieut. (i.e. military commander) until his death. His son **(4) James (1536-78) 4th E.** and Mary (later Q. of Scots) were naturally acquainted when young and, as a political supporter of Mary of Guise and Beaton, was hostile to English policy. He came into prominence at first in 1559 when he intercepted English funds destined for the Lords of the Congregation. Their leaders, Arran and the Lord James, seized his castle at Crichton but (England being closed to him) he escaped to Denmark, nominally as an envoy of the Queen Regent and then went to Paris as a Lord of the Bedchamber to Mary Q. of Scots, then also briefly Queen Consort of France. In 1561, after K. Francis II died, she sent him to Edinburgh as her commissioner. The town was in political and social disorder; Bothwell's men had a brawl with the Hamilton following and Bothwell was driven out. John Knox at the time was trying to organise a front against the French-supported R. Catholic party and, acting on Bothwell's protestantism, arranged an unreal reconciliation with Arran (i.e. the Congregation) which broke down quickly because Bothwell's convictions were weaker than his attachment to Mary. Arran arrested him for plotting to abduct her (1561). Bothwell escaped (1562) towards France but was captured by the English. Mary secured his release to France to which, after another visit to Edinburgh, he retired. His retirement was short for she needed his support in the increasingly bitter disputes with the Lord James and the Congregation. (*For the remainder of his life see* MARY QUEEN OF SCOTS-11-14.) A kinsman **(5) Patrick (?-1573)** became Prior of St. Andrews (1522) and James V's sec. from 1524 to 1527. He was in part responsible for the burning of Patrick Hamilton (1527) and became Bp. of Moray and Abbot of Scone. He is alleged by the presbyterians to have been, like his relative, notoriously adulterous; the men of Dundee sacked Scone in 1559 and he was deprived of his abbatial properties ostensibly for protecting James on his flight to Denmark. In 1567 he was tried (without result) for being art and part in Darnley's murder.

HEPTARCHY (= seven govts.). An obsolescent and misleading term for a period (c. 7th-8th cent.) when seven Anglo-Saxon kingdoms were thought to have occupied most of England. These were Kent, Sussex, Wessex, Mercia, Essex, East Anglia and Northumbria. In fact the political map was volatile. Cornwall, Devon and most of the West Coast north of the Ribble had not been conquered; the calculation omitted Deira, Bernicia, the Hwiccas and the shifting tribal wars, intermarriages and political confusions, and the successive supremacies of Northumbria, Mercia and Wessex.

HERALD. (1) was a messenger of a great magnate or sovereign and bore his master's arms on the tabard which he wore. Royal heralds also superintended tourneys where participants were recognisable only by their coat armour; hence they became expert in coats of arms and ultimately supervisors of them. The chief royal heralds became known as *Kings of Arms*, the apprentice heralds *poursuivants*.

(2) In *England* there were two Kings of Arms, Norroy for North of the Trent, Clarenceux for South under Edward III. Henry V created a superior called Garter King of Arms and in 1484 these three, with six heralds (entitled Windsor, Chester, Richmond, Somerset, York and Lancaster) and four poursuivants (Rouge Croix, Bluemantle, Rouge Dragon and Portcullis) were incorporated into a College of Arms under the general control of the Earl Marshal. This body was rechartered in 1555. It manages state ceremonial, the tracing of genealogies (especially for peerages) and the grant of arms.

(3) In *Scotland*, the equivalent institution was the Court of the Lord Lyon (King of Arms) but this became an important court of law and developed a jurisdiction (in addition to those mentioned above) in matters relating to the chieftainship of clans and the enforcement (through Messengers at Arms) of court process.

HERALDRY, originally the corpus of knowledge of any herald, soon came to mean the science of armorial bearings. This is still a living science in Britain and follows two slightly divergent systems respectively in England and Scotland. The following is a brief summary of an immense subject.

(1) A coat of arms is granted or recognised by the Crown; its possession denotes gentility and it is heritable, subject to certain rules of differentiation.

(2) The principal part of a coat of arms is the shield, which bears the distinctive marks of its owner. Marriages in successive generations to gentlewomen without heirs may result in a person becoming entitled to place upon his shield the arms of other families in addition to his own. His will then appear in the top left hand part (*dexter chief*) of the shield. If there is only one other it will appear in the top right hand (*sinister chief*), the two being repeated the opposite way in the lower part (*base*). If a third family appears it will be in the left base (*dexter base*), a fourth in the right (*sinister*) base. Special arrangements beyond this number may have to be made but are uncommon in Britain. A married man places his own arms so as to occupy the left (*dexter*) half and (with one exception) his wife's arms beside them on the right (*sinister*). The exception is a wife without heirs. Her arms are placed in the centre of his shield. The arms of certain officers (such as bishops) are similar in appearance, the arms of office being on the left, the personal arms on the right. The arms of different legitimate sons of the same father are distinguished by *marks of cadency* in England, but by different types of border in Scotland. Bastards are distinguished in England by a short straight diagonal bar across the arms, called a *baton* (not bar) *sinister*, in Scotland by a wavy border. Corporations such as towns may have arms. NOTE: The technical terms *dexter* (right) and *sinister* (left) are used by heralds to denote the side of the shield from the point of view of the person holding it.

(3) Above the shield is the helmet with the crest on top and *mantlings* (representing a cloak slashed in battle) hanging from it.

(4) There are a large number of indicators of rank, office or honour which appear mixed in with a coat of arms. Peers and royalty are entitled to *supporters* (which in Britain are mostly animals depicted holding up the shield) and coronets or crowns of strictly regulated type. Orders of the highest degree encircle the shield, lesser decorations hang from the bottom. The insignia of office of certain people (e.g. archbishops, the earl marshal etc.) are placed behind the shield, usually crossed X.

(5) *Blazon* is the description of a coat of arms in a very precise, if archaic, language.

(6) *Royal Arms* or arms of sovereignty follow different rules, since they represent the Kingdoms over which the monarch reigns and consequently descend only to each monarch in succession. Moreover they vary with the Kingdoms under sovereignty rather than with family relationships.

(7) The arms of women are shown on a diamond shaped shield called a lozenge, without helmet, crest or mantlings, because they did not joust.

HERAT. *See* AFGHANISTAN; PERSIA.

HERBERT OF BOSHAM (c. 1120-94) had distinguished teachers at Paris and entered the service of Henry II and then of Thomas Becket, for whom he acted as secretary. He encouraged Becket's extremist stand at the Council of Northampton and went into exile with him. Provocatively refusing to take an oath of loyalty to Henry II, he remained in France after Becket's murder, probably in the service of Abp. William of Sens and Count Henry of Champagne, and also in the Schools at Paris. After 1184 he worked for William Longchamp before retiring to a Cistercian house in France. He wrote an eye-witness *Life* of Becket and edited Peter Lombard's *Gloss* on the Psalms and Pauline Epistles and, having doubted the foundations of Christianity, wrote a proof of God's existence.

HERBERT. Montgomery family. **(1) Edward (1538-1648) 1st Ld. HERBERT of CHERBURY (1629)** notorious or popular European duellist and roué, was also a friend of John Donne and Ben Jonson, who admired his learning and enjoyed his wit, and of John Selden and Richard Carew. In 1619 after an apparently casual introduction, Buckingham sent him as ambassador to Paris. It was in Paris that he wrote *De Veritate* (Lat = Truth). He was also entertaining learned men such as Grotius. He was entrusted, after the failure of the Spanish marriage project, with the impossible task of securing a French one on condition that Louis XIII intervened in the protestant interest in Germany (*see* THIRTY YEARS' WAR). James I dismissed him when he pointed out the difficulties (1624). In 1632 he began his life of *Henry VIII* based on original sources. He preserved a neutral position and most of his property in the Civil War. His brother was **(2) George Herbert (1593-1633)** the poet.

HERBERT, Arthur (1647-1716) E. of TORRINGTON (1689), kinsman of the Herberts of Cherbury, a very active ship's captain, campaigned four times (1669, 1671, 1673-5, 1678), the last two as vice-admiral, against Barbary, and then in Dec. 1679 became C-in-C and fought further campaigns from Tangier until it was abandoned in 1683. In 1688 he offered his services to William of Orange and commanded the Dutch fleet which brought him to England. In Mar. 1689 he became naval C-in-C and was involved in the inconclusive Bantry Bay action against superior numbers. The fleet as a whole was ill found and below strength and when he returned to the Channel he was to attack 80 French under Tourville with 56 English and Dutch off Beachy Head. The inconclusive battle was followed by a political court martial which acquitted him. He has been much traduced by Burnet and Pepys on grounds of arrogance, greed, dishonesty and licentiousness but his subordinates admired him.

HERBERT (POWIS) Welsh border royalist and R. Catholic family. **(1) William (1574-1655) 1st Ld. POWIS (1629)** held Powis Castle for the King until it was stormed in 1644. His son **(2) Percy (?-1667) 2nd Ld.** married ELIZABETH CRAVEN a daughter and grand-daughter of Lord Mayors of London and she acquired much London property. Their son **(3) William (1617-96) 3rd Ld., 1st E. (1674), 1st M. (1687),** a very tolerant Romanist, protected Quakers, was implicated in the "Popish Plot" and impeached in 1679. The impeachment was stopped but he remained in the Tower until 1684 while mobs burned his house. James II employed him to regulate (i.e. to purge) corporations and in due course he went abroad with James and died as his Lord Chamberlain at St. Germains.

HERCULES, PILLARS OF. Mts. Calpe (Gibraltar) and Abyla facing each other across the entrance to the Mediterranean. Hence the straits themselves. A number of public houses named after them commemorate the capture of Gibraltar. They inspired the pillars in the Spanish royal arms and so the two vertical strokes of the dollar sign.

HEREFORD, EARLS OF. The shire was one held by Swein Godwin's son. When Godwin was expelled in 1051, Edward the Confessor gave it to his Norman brother-in-law, Ralph, who continued to hold it after Godwin's return in 1052 and who built a castle in the town. At his death (1057) the shire passed to Harold Godwin's son, the later King.

(2) After the Conquest Hereford became a marcher lordship vested first in the Conqueror's steward William fitzOsbern until his death in 1071 and then in his second son Roger fitzWilliam but it was forfeited for his participation in the revolt of 1075 and he died in captivity.

(3) In 1141 the Empress Matilda revived the earldom for her supporter Miles of Gloucester. When he died it passed to his son Roger (1143) who died without heirs in 1155 when the earldom again lapsed.

(4) John Lackland revived the earldom in 1200 for Henry de Bohun who claimed the title through his grandmother, the eldest daughter of Miles of Gloucester. An unbroken sequence of earls of the Bohun family followed until Humphrey de Bohun died without heirs in 1373. In 1397 the earldom, now elevated to a dukedom, passed to his son-in-law Henry Bolingbroke and on his accession as Henry IV merged in the Crown.

HEREFORD (A.S. = army ford) SHIRE and CITY. The city on the R. Wye is close to a Roman road and the ford was the focus of a local road system for the tribal territory of the Mercian Hecanas. It was detached from the See of Lichfield in 676 when, according to a tradition, a cathedral was founded there. The Mercian Kings Ethelbald and Offa fortified it against the Welsh and like most fortified towns it acquired a mint. There was a market and prosperity was improved by the relics of Sts. Ethelbert and Guthlac. The local industries such as tanning, weaving, dyeing and milling were related to agriculture and after 1121 there was a fair. Until the conquest of Wales the shire set up by K. Athelstan was part of the march and its history follows marcher history closely. Its western boundary remained unsettled until 1535. Hereford was sacked by the Welsh in 1055. There were many castles, notably Wigmore, Weobley, Clifford, Hereford itself and Kilpeck, besides Richard's Castle and Ewyas Harold. The area was briefly a palatinate under William I and strong Mortimer territory in the 13th cent. when the city was rewalled so as to take in an enlarged population; but the city's military importance fell away with the progressive pacification of Wales, save in such emergencies as the Glendower revolt. It sent two M.P.s to parliament from 1295 onwards. Lollardy persisted in the area longer than in most parts but it was royalist in the Civil War and Lady Harley defended Brampton against the parliamentarians for six weeks in 1643. With beef cattle and Ryelands sheep there has always been a flourishing agriculture but the famous apple and pear orchards have been heavily reduced since 1970 by European Community policy. *For the Earldom see* HEREFORD, EARLS OF.

HEREGELD. *See* DANEGELD.

HERESY etc. (1) *Formal* heresy is the wilful adherence by a Christian to error in matters of faith and involves automatic excommunication. **(2)** *Material* heresy is the acceptance of heretical doctrines in good faith by a person who, never having accepted Christian doctrine, cannot have rejected it. This is neither a crime nor a sin. It is distinguished from (3) *Apostasy* which is the abandonment of Christianity by a Christian or the abandonment of orders or profession by a priest or monk and from (4) *Schism* which is formal separation or withdrawal from a church for reasons not involving doctrine and which does not, in the case of a cleric, involve loss of status.

HEREWARD the Wake (fl. 1070) was a partly legendary Saxon landowner who led an English insurrection at Ely and sacked Peterborough with Danish help in 1070. He was joined by Earl Morcar, Bp. Aethelwine of Durham and other northern dignitaries and held out in the Ely marshes for some time but eventually escaped to the Continent when the others submitted. He is said to have been killed by the Normans in Maine.

HERIOT (from O.E. meaning 'military equipment') was originally the return of arms or a mount provided by a lord for a tenant bound to some form of soldierly service, at the tenant's death. Later it was leviable only by manorial custom in respect of a copyhold and consisted of the best beast or chattel. In this form it survived until 1936, in one case developing into litigation about a racehorse.

HERITABLE JURISDICTIONS (Scotland). The rebellion of 1745 engendered a comprehensive effort to destroy the special institutions and features of Highland and clan life. Certain chieftains were attainted and the Act for Disarming the Highlands (1745) empowered Lords Lieutenant to seize all arms and (s.17) reserved the right to wear highland dress or the tartan to the army. In the following year the Heritable Jurisdictions Act transferred to the royal courts (subject to compensation) all heritable jurisdictions or justiciary constabularies, stewartries and sheriffships for parts of counties, except that of the High Constable of Scotland. In addition proprietary jurisdictions (other than those belonging to burghs) were abolished save in cases of minor criminal assaults, debts not exceeding 40s, actions for recovering rents and certain special cases concerned with fairs and mines. The rebellion had prevented the administration of justice and the wholesale abolition of these numerous and widespread jurisdictions imposed a new burden on the old machinery; hence the Act extended the circuit system to Argyll and Bute and created powers to reorganise the circuits in due course.

HERLEVA. See WILLIAM THE CONQUEROR.

HERM. See CHANNEL IS.

HERMANRIC. See KENT, KINGDOM-2.

HERRENVOLK. (Ger = master race.) A Nazi term.

HERRINGS, B. of the (Feb. 1429) was an unsuccessful French attempt to prevent the revictualling of the English besiegers of Orléans. The English used their barrels of herrings as barricades.

HERSTINGAS were a Middle Anglian folk who settled between the Nene and the Ouse south of Peterborough in the early 6th cent.

HERTFORD, Es. of. See CLARE and SEYMOUR.

HERTFORD, COUNCIL OF (673) convened by Abp. Theodore of Tarsus, was the first council of the English church as a whole. It was concerned mainly with organisation but forbade divorce except for adultery and fixed the date of Easter.

HERTZOG, James Barry (1866-1942) became Min. of Education in the O.F.S. govt. in 1907 and immediately tried to introduce compulsory Dutch into the schools. He was Min. of Justice in Botha's first Union Cabinet in 1910 but Botha got rid of him in 1913. He then formed his ultra-nationalist party. He opposed the invasion of German S.W. Africa in 1914. After the war he opposed the republicanisation of S. Africa as too hasty. In 1924 he became prime minister. He helped to draft the Statute of Westminster at the Imperial Conference of 1930. In 1939

he was forced to make way as prime minister for Jan Smuts.

HERVEY (1) John (1665-1751) 1st Ld. HERVEY (1703) 1st E. of BRISTOL (1714), wealthy Whig M.P., wine importer and supporter of Marlborough from 1694 to 1703. His youngest son **(2) John (1696-1743) Ld. HERVEY (1733)** by summons, was an M.P. from 1725. Originally a supporter of Frederick, P. of Wales, he became a friend of Q. Caroline and later of Lady Mary Wortley Montague. He was a pamphleteer for Walpole but is chiefly remembered for his often malicious *Memoirs of the Reign of George II.* His son **(3) George William (1721-75) 2nd E.** was minister at Turin from 1755 to 1758 and then ambassador at Madrid until 1761. He was Lord Privy Seal from 1768 to 1770. His cousin **(4) Augustus John (1724-79) 3rd E.** married the seductive Elizabeth Chudleigh (*see* KINGSTON'S CASES) in 1744. He was a naval officer of some distinction under Hawke in 1762. He was also an M.P. from 1757 to 1768, chief sec. for Ireland in 1766 and a Lord of the Admiralty from 1771 to 1778. His brother **(5) Frederick Augustus (1730-1803) 4th E., Bp. of Cloyne (1767-8)** and of **Derry** from 1768 (known as the Bishop of Bristol for short) reclaimed the great bog at Cloyne and spent huge sums on public works in his sees. He also travelled the continent in great state, leaving a trail of grateful "Bristol Hotels" wherever he went. Of a tolerant disposition, he favoured relaxing the laws against R. Catholics and admitting them to the Commons.

HERZEGOVINA. *See* BOSNIA AND HERZEGOVINA; AUSTRO-HUNGARY.

HERZL, Theodor (1860-1904) Jewish journalist and dramatist who lived most of his life in Vienna, launched Zionism in 1896 with a famous or notorious pamphlet *Der Judenstaat* (Ger = The Jewish State).

HESILRIG or HASELRIG, Sir Arthur (?-1661) as M.P. for Leicester, opposed Laud and introduced the Bill for Strafford's attainder, the Root and Branch Bill and the Militia Bill. He was one of the Five Members sought by Charles I in 1642 and distinguished himself in the Edgehill, Lansdowne, Roundway and Cheriton campaigns (1642-4). After the Self Denying Ordinance he became a leader of the Independents and in 1648 Gov. of Newcastle. He refused to sit on the Court for trying the King but commanded the reserve army for Cromwell in Scotland in 1650. Though a member of every Council of State he opposed Cromwell's authoritarianism and in 1657 refused to pay taxes or enter Cromwell's House of Peers. He was returned as M.P. for Leicester in 1654 but excluded in 1656 and again until 1658 and in 1659. He tried to get army support to prevent Richard Cromwell's succession in 1659 and when Richard fell he attempted to maintain a republican parliamentary govt. as member of the committee of safety. This failed when Lambert ejected the members and he then offered to help Monck in establishing some type of moderate parliamentary but, he hoped, republican govt. Persuaded to withdraw his troops from London he had to stand by and watch the monarchy restored. He was promptly arrested; Monck intervened to prevent further proceedings but he died in the Tower.

HESS, Rudolf (1894-1987) wounded as a fighter pilot in World War I, was a devoted and able colleague of Adolf Hitler from the early days of the Nazi Party and was designated third in succession to him in 1939. In 1941, without any authorisation from Hitler, a person calling himself Rudolf Hess parachuted himself into Scotland in order, apparently, to negotiate a peace between Britain and Germany through the Duke of Hamilton, whom he claimed to know. The British made him a prisoner of war and he was sentenced to life imprisonment at the post-war Nuremberg trial. The Russians affected to believe that he wanted a peace with the west because Hitler was about to move east. This Rudolf Hess died, allegedly by his own hand, in Spandau prison. It is uncertain, perhaps unlikely, that he was the real Hess. His chief British interrogator had doubts and he lacked the disfiguring and indelible wound scars which the real Hess had acquired in World War I.

HESSE(N) (Germany). This landgraviate on the roads from the Rhineland to Central Germany became rich and important under Philip the Magnanimous (r. 1509-67) who introduced Lutheranism and founded Marburg University (1527) but partitioned the state between his four sons and destroyed its power. After 1604 there were three states. H-Darmstadt, H-Homburg derived from it and H-Cassel. In the Thirty Years' War Darmstadt took the imperial, Cassel the protestant side. It was from Cassel that the British and Hanoverian govts. hired troops.

HEUSTON, Sean (1891-1916) trainer and commander of Irish nationalist volunteers, was one of the leaders of the 1916 rising. He was executed.

HEVENINGHAM HALL (Suffolk). Palladian mansion built by Sir Robt. Taylor and James Wyatt for Sir Gerard Vanneck between 1779 and 1784.

HEWART, Gordon (1870-1943) 1st Ld. (1922) 1st Vist. (1940) began as a journalist on the *Manchester Guardian*, but in 1902 was called to the bar where he had a reputation as a brilliant but fair advocate. In 1913 he became Liberal M.P. for Leicester; in 1916 sol-gen; in 1919 att-gen. and in 1922 Lord Chief Justice. He believed in the English based-on-law liberties which had been established in the 17th cent. and thought that these were being stealthily eroded by the executive and the civil service. His book *The New Despotism*, a well documented exposure of this trend, was respectfully ignored by those most concerned in govt. and achieved no popular appeal.

HEXHAM (Northumberland). St. Wilfred built the monastery at the junction of the N. and S. Tyne and in 678 Abp. Theodore of Tarsus raised it to a cathedral, which it remained until 824. Its sumptuous buildings had a vaulted crypt and Romanesque columns and porches. In 825 the Danes destroyed it. Later secular canons were established there until the foundation in 1113-14 of an Augustinian priory and a hospital. From 1296 both foundations were repeatedly sacked by the Scots and had ultimately to be rebuilt. They were dissolved in 1537 but the priory church remains. *See* DURHAM-1.

HEYTESBURY, William A'Court (1779-1860) 1st Ld. (1828) was a special envoy to Vienna in 1807 and after routine diplomatic appointments in Barbary (1813), Naples (1814) and Spain (1822) was ambassador to Portugal in 1824 and at St. Petersburg from 1828 to 1832. He was Lord Lieut. of Ireland from 1844 to 1846.

HIBERNIA = Ireland.

HIBERNIANS, ANCIENT ORDER OF (1905) (Ir.) A secret Society founded or at least led by Joseph Devlin to promote the material interests of R. Catholics. In practice it became a society for getting bad ones into jobs and was denounced by Card. Logue.

HICCE were a small Middle Anglian folk settled about Hitchin (Herts) in the 6th cent.

HICKES, George (1642-1715) expelled dean of Worcester and non-juring bishop devoted his later years, with a group of scholars to the compilation of his immense *Thesaurus* of northern languages (published 1703-5) which represents the foundation of English philological studies.

HICKS, George Ernest (1879-1954) became Pres. of the Nat. Fed. of Building Trades Operatives in 1919 and by 1921 had managed to unite the two bricklayers unions and the stonemasons into the Amalgamated Union of Building Trade Workers, of which he became gen. sec. Rabelaisian and left wing, as chairman of the T.U.C. in 1926 to 1927 he threw his influence on the side of industrial peace. In 1931 he became Labour M.P. for E. Woolwich. He gave up his union general secretaryship in 1940 and retired from parliament in 1950.

HICKS (and HICKS-BEACH) (1) Sir Michael (1545-1612) was the wealthy and influential secretary to Lord Burghley and Sir Robt. Cecil. His brother **(2) Baptist (1551-1629) 1st Vist. CAMPDEN (1628)** was a mercer and moneylender and from 1609 contractor for Crown Lands. He was an M.P. in 1620, 1624-6 and in 1628. A descendant **(3) William Hicks, Pasha (1830-83)** commanded the Egyptian army against the Mahdi and was killed in ambush at Kashgil. Another descendant **(4) Sir Michael Edward ("Black Michael") (1837-1916), Bart, Vist. (1906) and 1st E. of St. ALDWYN (1915)** became a conservative M.P. in 1864 (E. Glos) and was U/Sec. of State at the Home Office in 1868. He was Chief Sec. for Ireland from 1874 to 1878, entered the cabinet in 1876 and as Colonial Sec. from 1878 to 1880 was mainly concerned with African affairs. He was Ch. of the Exch. and leader of the Commons from 1885 to 1886 and then, in opposition, led the successful anti-Home Rule agitation in 1886. He was Irish Sec. from 1886 to 1887, Pres. of the Bd. of Trade from 1888 to 1892 and Ch. of the Exch. from 1895 to 1902.

HIDE (or PLOUGHLAND) and ACRE. A HIDE (O.E. probably = Household) was the amount of land needed by one family and was used as a measurement throughout England, save Kent, until the Danish invasions. In the Danelaw it was replaced as a unit under the name of CARUCATE by as much land as could be tilled by a heavy eight-ox plough (*caruca*) in a year. Each necessarily varied in extent with the soil and the configuration of the land. An ACRE was the amount of land which could be thus ploughed in a day. Allowing for sowing and growth, a hide was mostly reckoned at 100 acres, though 120-acre hides existed in Cambridgeshire and 40-acre hides in parts of Wessex. **HIDAGE** or **CARUCAGE** was the tax levied on each one and in due course each became a standard unit of assessment, particularly for the Danegeld, regardless of the numbers it supported.

HIGDEN, Ranulf (?-1363-4) a Benedictine of St. Werbergh, Chester, was probably born at Chester and does not seem to have travelled far. His *Polychronicon* (= Universal History) is in seven books. The first is geographical and the last deals, not very illuminatingly, with contemporary events. He drew, not always critically, on many earlier historians. The book, originally composed in c. 1340, was continually revised and extended to 1352. Higden was once summoned to Edward III's court at Westminster to exhibit it and it survives in over 100 MSS, some of which have independent continuations such as the *Westminster Chronicle* and the chronicles of Adam of Usk, Henry Knighton and Thomas Walsingham. It was twice translated into English, one of which was printed by William Caxton.

HIGH CHURCH. *See* ANGLICANISM.

HIGH COMMISSION, COURT OF. Ecclesiastical commissions began to be appointed in 1549 to enforce official forms of worship and to put down heresy. Their legality was recognised in the Act of Supremacy of 1559 but the term 'High' Commission only became usual after 1570 when the *ad hoc* commissions solidified into a permanent court with a fixed seat and litigation began to oust its visitatorial functions. It became the usual court of appeal in doctrinal and disciplinary matters. There was a permanent and very active local commission at York which was associated with the Council of the North. Disliked by common lawyers and puritans these courts were abolished by the Star Chamber Act of 1641 but James II briefly revived them in an attenuated form in 1686. They were finally declared illegal in 1689.

HIGH COURT. *See* COURTS.

HIGH FARMING. James Caird's (1816-92) name for a new developed farming believed to be able to overcome the effects of abolishing the protectionism of the Corn Laws in 1846.

HIGHLAND GARB ACT. *See* HERITABLE JURISDICTIONS.

HIGHLAND HOST (1678) was an assembly of some 3000 militia and 6000 Highlanders who were quartered on some of the lowland covenanting extremists as a method of episcopalian coercion. They went home after a month leaving a splendid grievance.

HIGHWAY or PUBLIC RIGHT OF WAY (1) is a place where all the lieges, regardless of the ownership of the soil, may pass and repass. The law developed out of the Roman roads, which were under the King's peace, and from the need to use navigable rivers to transport heavy goods. A footway was the right to pass on foot; a drove was a road along which beasts could be driven; a bridleway one on which horses could be ridden; a carriage-way one on which vehicles could go. The greater right included all the lesser. A landowner might *dedicate* or devote a right of way to the public and dedication might be presumed from his acts or behaviour but as it was irrevocable it was always construed, as far as possible, in his favour.

(2) From Tudor times all highways were repairable at the expense of the parish, whose inhabitants could be prosecuted for failure. Since most users of the high road came from outside a given parish, parochial reluctance caused the roads to decay, though they remained the best in Europe. With the industrial revolution, estate developers took advantage of the law to throw thousands of miles of unmade streets onto the ratepayers by simple dedication. The Highways Act, 1834, changed this. A dedicated highway still became public, but the parish did not have to maintain it until it had been brought up to private expense to a standard approved by the Highway Surveyor. These expenses generally fell upon the frontagers. Once approved the road was ADOPTED by the Surveyor and became publicly repairable.

(3) The surveyor's functions were transferred to the district councils in 1895; in 1929 County Councils became the responsible HIGHWAY AUTHORITIES for all rural roads and the most important urban ones except the long distance TRUNK ROADS assigned to the Ministry of Transport and minor urban roads claimed by urban authorities. The spectacular rise in the pressure on roads after World War II vastly increased their expense and led to a demand by the highway authorities for Exchequer contributions and by the public and the business interests for better roads and a much higher rate of expenditure. The result was the Special Roads Act 1949 which empowered the Minister to restrict or build roads for particular uses. The restriction powers were seldom, if ever, used. The building of the motorways was the principal result. The first motorway (M1), built to alleviate congestion between London and Birmingham, created as many problems in both areas as it solved; it was then realised that priority in peripheral motorway construction would bring greater advantages in the long run. The Great North Road (A1) was improved almost to motorway standard and the M1 was extended slowly to the West Riding: the Lancashire-Birmingham motorway (M6) was pressed towards Bristol and Cardiff while the London-Bristol-S. Wales motorway (M4) was built mainly from the western end, except for the London-Maidenhead portion, mistakenly given priority to serve Heathrow Airport; this should have been connected to the adjacent London Underground railway system, for by 1971 rush-hour traffic was at a standstill and work had to begin on the Underground extension through force of circumstance. By 1992 motorways radiated from London to the West Riding, Carlisle, S. Wales, the West of England, Winchester and Canterbury and joined Carlisle with Bristol.

***HIGHWAYMAN'S CASE. Everet v Williams* (1725) [1893] 9 LQR 197.** Everet brought an equity bill in the Exchequer against Williams for refusing to come to a fair accounting in a partnership. They were in fact highwaymen and the fair accounting a division of the spoils. The court held the bill to be scandalous, fined the solicitors and hanged both parties.

HILDA, St. (614-80) was daughter of Hereroc, nephew of K. Edwin of Northumbria. Baptised in 627 by Paulinus, she sought to join a sister in the nunnery of Chelles (near Paris), was restrained by St. Aidan and became abbess of a religious house at Hartlepool. In 657 she founded the abbey of Whitby for both men and women and presided over it as abbess. At the Synod there in 664 she defended the Celtic practices but accepted the Synod's decisions in favour of the Roman ones. *See* MISSIONARIES IN BRITAIN AND IRELAND-5,8.

HILDELITH, ST. (?-712) second Abbess of Barking from 675. She was a visionary and an accomplished Latinist.

HILL, Abigail. *See* MASHAM.

HILL, Octavia (1838-1912) taught in Marylebone and being appalled by the housing problems turned her energies to their solution. She interested John Ruskin and bought the first houses for improvement in 1865. From 1874 she was able to devote herself to housing reform because funds raised by friends had placed her undertakings on a business footing. From 1884 she managed the Ecclesiastical Commissioners' Southwark estates. She was also a founder of the Society of Women Housing Managers and the National Trust and was a strong influence in the Charity Organisation and Commons Preservation Societies.

HILL (1) Richard (1655-1727) a trusted diplomat employed in difficult situations, was envoy to Bavaria in 1696, ambassador to The Hague and Lord of the Treasury in 1699 and minister to Savoy from 1703 to 1706. A grand nephew **(2) Sir Richard, Bart (1732-1808)** was M.P. for Shropshire from 1780 to 1806 and a noted debater. His nephew **(3) Rowland (1772-1842) 1st Ld. (1814) 1st Vist. HILL (1842)** was one of Wellington's ablest divisional generals in Spain and at Waterloo and was C-in-C in England from 1825 to 1839.

HILL, Sir Roderick Maxwell (1894-1954) air chief marshal, commanded No. 12 Fighter Group from July-Nov. 1943 and then became C-in-C Air Defence of Great Britain. As such he planned the defence against the flying bomb attack which began in June 1944 and, by redeploying the entire defence in July, defeated it.

HILL (1) Thomas Wright (1763-1851) an ingenious Birmingham schoolmaster, invented *inter alia* a system of phonetic shorthand. Of his two sons **(2) Matthew Davenport (1792-1872)** was a founder of the Soc. for the Diffusion of Useful Knowledge in 1826, M.P. for Hull from 1832 to 1835, first recorder of Birmingham in 1839 and counsel for Daniel O'Connell in 1844. He was also a successful law and prison reformer. His brother **(3) Sir Rowland (1795-1879)** invented a rotary printing press and revolutionised postal communications by inventing the postage stamp. The Penny Post was introduced in 1840 but he was dismissed from the Post Office in 1842. He then became chairman of the Brighton Rly. and introduced express and excursion trains. In 1846 he became sec. to the P.M.G. and from 1854 to 1864 he was Sec. to the Post Office. He was also a member of the railway commission and in a minority report advocated state ownership, with companies holding leases.

HILL FIGURES, cut, with four exceptions, in chalk are numerous. The oldest is the White Horse of Uffington (Hants.), possibly a Belgic cult object or totem dating from 50 B.C.-A.D. 50. The Vale of the White Horse was already named after it by the 14th cent. The ithyphallic Cerne Giant (Dorset) may be a Herculean figure related to a fertility cult revived in the 2nd cent. by the Emperor Commodus: maypole and less respectable celebrations were associated with it until the 1930s. The Long Man of Wilmington has lately been supposed to be a 14th cent. sign to guide travellers to the Wilmington priory guest house. The Westbury Horse (Wilts.) was cut in 1778 on the site of an older horse. The Cherhill Horse (Wilts.) was cut in 1780 and the Osmington Horse and Rider (Dorset) commemorates George III's visits to Weymouth. These three are Hanoverian badges. A series of military badges were cut at Fovant (Wilts.) in 1916 and the New Horse at Pewsey commemorates the coronation of George VI in 1937.

HILLSBOROUGH (N. Ireland). A small market village with the residence of the gov. of N. Ireland.

HILTON, Walter (?-1396) an Augustinian of Thurgarton (Notts.) wrote, allegedly for an ancress, the *Scala Perfectionis* (Lat = Ladder of Perfection) in which, stage by stage, he analyses the contemplative life. Influenced by the writings of Richard Rolle and the *Cloud of Unknowing*, it probably in turn influenced Juliana of Norwich. It was widely diffused in translation.

HINAYANA. *See* BUDDHISM.

HINCHINBROOKE (Lincs.). Former 13th cent. nunnery, became the house of the Cromwell family in 1529 and in the 17th cent. of the Montagus.

HIND. A Scottish lowland ploughman. A whole hind brought a servant to work with him. A half hind worked with a man provided by the landowner.

HINDENBURG, Paul v. (1847-1934). German First World War hero who, with Ludendorff his C-of S, saved Germany from Russian devastation by his victories at 'Tannenberg' (Aug. 1914) and the Masurian Lakes (Sept.). He then commanded the Austro-German offensive and for his victory at Kutno (Nov. 1914) was made a F-M. He commanded the Eastern Front until Aug. 1916 and then became C-in-C of the German army until June 1919 when he retired. He emerged to become Pres. of the Republic in Apr. 1925. From then on his prestige lent respectability to the increasingly reactionary movements of German politics, though it is not likely that he fully understood what was happening. In Apr. 1932 he was re-elected just as the Nazi campaign was reaching its climax. Hitler's Enabling Act (*Machtübernahme*) was passed in Apr. 1933. On 30 Sept. Hindenburg was forced to agree to Hitler becoming Chancellor, on an oral promise that no extreme legislation would be enacted without his consent. Hitler, by virtue of the Enabling Act, was by then the legislator. His death (Aug. 1934) thus removed the only baffler to Hitler's perfectly legal tyranny.

HINDI, a group of north Indian dialects spoken from Bihar to the Sutlej, took a poetic form in the 15th cent. and a literary prose form in the 19th. Its use for official purposes by the British aided standardisation and in 1922 the Congress resolved that it should be the national language, which it became in 1965.

HINDUISM has a 3,500 year history and a vast literature. **(1)** The oldest scriptures are the *Vedas*, notably the *Rig Veda* and *Tajur Veda* (1500-900 B.C.) which are compilations of Aryan sacrificial hymns and incantations and the *Atharva Veda* which possibly reflects an even earlier time. To these were added appendices of commentary and amplification called *Brahmanas* (800-600 B.C.) and to these were added further sub-appendices, mystical in character called *Aranyakas* and *Upanishads* (650-400 B.C. but many are later). This Vedic corpus is not now fully intelligible but is still widely studied and venerated. It reflects ideas which, however, were substantially different from those of modern Hinduism. In particular the great population of Hindu divinities was largely masculine and dominated by Indra, the war and weather god, Varuna, a kingly omnipresent figure notable for justice, and Rudra, a god of disaster and plague.

(2) The fundamental doctrine of transmigration of souls first appears in an Upanishad: all forms of life are part of a single system, the soul passing from one form to another (better or worse) as a result of 'infection' by its *Karma*, i.e. its behaviour in a given life; in this way a cosmic determinism was combined with some individual freewill. Escape from this eternal and tedious round was the motive behind many heterodoxies, of which Buddhism and Jainism were the most important. They spread the idea of a universal soul or godhead into which it might be feasible to absorb the individual personality and so put an end to movement. The converse notion also gained currency that the universal godhead was present everywhere and things and people and gods were therefore its manifestations (*Avatars*).

(3) By the 1st cent. B.C. the Vedic literature was studied only by Brahmins so that **brahmanism** has become a specialised, learned and esoteric branch of Hinduism. Popular religion developed a system compounded of Vedic elements, the doctrines already mentioned and legendary histories and epics. Thus the western Indian gods Vasudeva and Narayana became identified with the Vedic god Vishnu, who was closely connected with the tribal heroes Krishna and Rama and the latter in turn came to be identified as (divine) avatars of Vishnu. This was the basis of **vaishnavite** Hinduism, whose principal scriptures are the *Puranas* ('Ancient Stories'), the *Dharma Sutras* (Sacred Laws) and the Epics, especially the *Ramayana* and the *Mahabharata*. These, originally secular, texts acquired religious interpolations of which the most famous is the utterance of Krishna called the *Bagavadhgita* ('Song of God'), the only known revelation to have occurred during a battle.

Simultaneously Shiv or Siva, a god of procreation, meditation and destruction developed from the Vedic Rudra. In this **saivite** Hinduism the notion of the avatar is unimportant, the cosmic continuity being much closer to nature. Siva is represented by a phallus (*lingam*) and there is death even in heaven.

(4) Both these later versions of Hinduism have been strongly influenced by an ancient cult of the Mother Goddess into which many local feminine deities have been absorbed; the gods acquired wives or consorts who are thought to represent the strength and practicality of their transcendent and inactive lords. Though Lakshmi, Vishnu's wife, is important they form as might be expected a more important element in Saivite Hinduism, where Siva's wife appears under many names and forms, notably the kindly Parvati, Mahadevi or Annapurna and the fierce and terrible Kali or Durga.

(5) The main Vedic act of worship was sacrifice, which has since been mainly replaced by adoration; but a communal service in the western sense is not practised save perhaps in the curious cult of **tantrism.** The Tantric sects worship female divinities and their 'initiates' use co-operative ceremonies. These are remarkable because they involve otherwise ritually unclean acts including the consumption of alcohol, meat and fish and the performance of copulation, while creating no ritual pollution between participants of different castes.

(6) Apart from worship, Hinduism is said to contain six systems of Doctrines conducive to Salvation. Of these **yoga,** the specialised practice of self discipline, is the best known in the west, while **vedanta** is the most important and has virtually superseded the other four. It is an intellectual system based upon the 1st cent. philosopher Sankara which attempts to reconcile the inconsistencies and paradoxes of Hinduism by recourse to the Buddhist method of varying standards of truth or reality. At the highest level all phenomena are *Maya*, an illusion, the only reality being *Brahman*, the World Soul.

The immense ramifications of Vedanta have led towards, on the one side, trinitarian doctrines (Brahma, Vishnu and Siva) and on the other to the modern schools of Indian philosophy associated with Vivekananda and Radhakrishnan.

HINDU MAHASABHA was an advanced and sometimes extremist Hindu political and social organisation founded in 1907 in the Punjab but operating within the Indian National Congress. It expanded rapidly in the years 1925 to 1927. It was violently anti-Islamic, advocating reconversion of Mohammedans and unified electorates within which Hindus would naturally have a majority. Consequently it denounced the communal award of 1932 and broke with Congress in 1937. It was apparently implicated in the murder of Gandhi in 1948. Its influence declined thereafter.

HINGWAR. *See* ASHDOWN, B. OF.

HINSLEY, Arthur (1865-1943) Card. (1937), widely experienced churchman, was educated, *inter alia*, at the English College in Rome, and was Headmaster of St. Bede's Grammar School, Bradford from 1889 to 1904. After 13 years as a parish priest, he became in 1917 Rector of the English College, and in 1930 as a titular Archbishop, Apostolic Delegate in Africa. In 1934 he succeeded Card. Bourne as Abp. of Westminster.

HIRE PURCHASE AND CREDIT SALE, though always possible, became common from the 1880s onwards when people with regular wages but no capital began to wish to buy expensive mass produced objects such as furniture. Partly regulated by the Factors Act, 1889, and Sale of Goods Act, 1893, the volume of such transactions increased astronomically when motor cars, gramophones and wireless sets came onto the market after World War I. The law was accordingly recast in 1938.

HIROSHIMA. *See* ATOMIC THEORY AND ENERGY.

HISPANIOLA or ESPAÑOLA; (HAITI, SANTO DOMINGO, DOMINICAN REPUBLIC) (Carib). A. (1) The history of this large mountainous neighbour of the British sugar islands was dominated by the Trade Winds which blow steadily hereabouts from the North-East in winter and from the East and South-East in summer.

(2) Christopher Columbus discovered it in Dec. 1492 and his brother, Bartholomew, founded Santo Domingo in 1496. This was the first permanent European settlement in the New World and, for 60 years, the centre from which the Spaniards colonised and conquered their American empire; sugar cultivation was introduced in 1506 but the kidnapping of the Taino and Arawak tribesmen as slaves led to depopulation and from 1512 African slaves were imported especially to the western part. Santo Domingo became legendary for its wealth and the *Audiencia* for the Spanish Antilles was established therein in 1526.

(3) Despite its advantages the Spaniards tended, after the discovery of the Peruvian and Mexican precious metals, to bypass Hispaniola where consequently their power was not securely founded. From about 1625 buccaneers, mostly French, began to settle on the North and West coast, particularly at the island of Tortuga; they spread into the western interior and in the 1640s were joined by the first companies of proper French colonists. The west thus became a largely French area governed, if at all, by the influence of the French gov. of Tortuga.

(4) The realities were recognised at the P. of Ryswick (1697) when Spain ceded the west to France. In 1728 the French introduced coffee cultivation and many more slaves but the boundaries between the French and Spanish spheres remained in dispute until the T. of Aranjuez (1777). By this time the French west was a country in which a prosperous white planter aristocracy ruled over a black slave labouring population with a small class of, often mulatto, freedmen mostly at Port au Prince in between.

(5) The French Declaration of the Rights of Man brought revolution in the west in 1791. The white landowners were killed or driven into the towns and in 1793 slavery was formally abolished by the home govt. In 1795 Spain was forced to cede the east to France at the P. of Basel but the power of the British navy prevented the exercise of any real authority there and the French gov. of the west was by now a former slave called Pierre Toussaint L'Ouverture, who had risen to the rank of general in the French army. In May 1801 he convened an

assembly which voted him governor for life and drew up a constitution. In 1802 he invaded the east and captured Santo Domingo. Thus the temporary reunion of the island was achieved by a local rebel who, however, was captured in 1803 by a Napoleonic expedition. The rebellion, however, continued under the leadership of the negro Jacques Dessalines and the mulatto Alexandre Pétion. The French, with supplies interrupted by the British and disease killing their men, conceded independence on 1 Jan. 1804. Dessalines, the new head of state, quickly proclaimed himself emperor but was killed at Port au Prince in an insurrection in 1806.

(6) The new mainly Afro-French republic under the presidency of the negro Henri Christophe, the army commander, exerted only minimal authority in the Spanish east for schism broke out in 1807 between the northern, mainly Negro, Haitians and a southern mulatto-led faction which elected Pétion president at Port au Prince. Consequently in 1809 a Dominican rebellion broke out with British assistance and led to a Spanish reassumption of sovereign rights.

(7) In the north west Henry Christophe proclaimed himself King of Haiti in 1811. A brilliant but tyrannical administrator, he instituted a nobility, developed agriculture, schools and roads and constructed the fabulous castle of La Ferrière. Pétion died in 1818 and was succeeded in the South West by Gen. Pierre Boyer who, when Christophe committed suicide during an officers' mutiny, reunited the west in 1820. He was able to go further. The Spanish American revolt was gathering strength and in Dec. 1821 the Dominicans expelled the Spanish authorities. In the ensuing confusion he seized Santo Domingo, annexed it and proclaimed the united Republic of Haiti. The French recognised the republic in 1825 and in 1838 gave commercial preference in exchange for compensation for the lost plantations. Boyer's govt. established a modern administration and judiciary but was never able to pacify or dominate the Dominicans. In 1843 a revolt in the south west overthrew him and the Dominicans seized the opportunity to declare their independence in Feb. 1844 and to establish a republic under Pedro Santana in Nov. They could not be reduced because the west was the victim of five successive *coups* ending in Mar. 1848 by the election of Gen. Faustin Soulouque as life president at Port au Prince. The generally weakened condition of his country resulted in his invasion of the east being repelled in 1849. In 1849 he proclaimed himself Emperor while political squabbles between Santana and Buenaventura Baez (1810-84) kept the east in turmoil. Nevertheless another western invasion in 1855 was successfully defeated.

(8) In 1859 Faustin's empire was overthrown and a republic established under Gen. Nicolas Geffard, while in 1861 Santana retroceded Santo Domingo to Spain with himself as gov. gen. Geffard in reply obtained a treaty of recognition and commerce with the U.S.A. in 1863. When an insurrection broke out against Spain in the East in 1864, he formally renounced all claims to Santo Domingo and negotiated its independence with the relieved Spaniards at Madrid in 1865. This established the present political geography of the island. He was driven from office in 1867.

B. Dominican Republic. (1) Baez, the new president, was faced with economic, social and financial problems beyond his abilities. In 1869 he even suggested annexation by the U.S.A. but the U.S. Senate rejected the proposal. Anarchy continued until 1882 when Gen. Ulises Heuraux established a dictatorship. He kept order at the expense of increasing indebtedness. His assassination in 1899 was followed by four *coups* and American intervention. In 1905 the Dominican republic became a U.S. protectorate in which the U.S. managed the customs and kept 55% of the proceeds to pay off the debts. The other 45% amounted to more than the whole previous revenue but American activities did not quell the disorders and occasional border disputes. By 1916 the approach of war with Germany and the endless revolts was thought to necessitate military control and the republic was occupied by American troops. In 1924 they were withdrawn but the customs control was continued.

(2) An interval of peace ensued under the presidency of Horacio Vasquez, but in 1920 there was a revolt under Gen. Rafael Leonidas Trujillo who was made president. Immediately afterwards the island was struck by a great hurricane which devastated cities and plantations alike. The crisis gave Trujillo the opportunity to take strong emergency action and to fasten, in the process, a tyranny upon the republic. Order as usual brought some prosperity and the regime promoted some industrial development. On the other hand in 1935 it perpetrated an atrocious massacre of resident Haitians. In 1961 Trujillo was assassinated. Free elections were held in Dec. 1962 but within nine months the new govt. was deposed. After a brief period under a junta, civil war broke out in 1965 which was only stopped by U.S. intervention.

C. HAITI. Haiti had five govts. between Geffard's overthrow in 1867 and the election of Louis Salomon in 1879. He lasted until 1888 when, after a short but violent civil war, power was seized in 1889 by Gen. Florvil Hippolyte, who established a dictatorship, spent much money on public works and in 1891 successfully resisted a U.S. demand for naval bases. His death in 1896 ushered in a period of financial and administrative confusion. This ended in a civil war which brought Gen. Nord Alexis to power in 1902. He preferred to finance his govt. by inflation rather than foreign loans and was overthrown in 1908 by Gen. Antoine Simon, who did the same. Another revolt in 1911 brought his overthrow but both heads of succeeding liberal regimes died in quick succession and this was followed by four *coups*. In July 1915 U.S. troops landed at Port au Prince. American military occupation remained, in circumstances of increasing unpopularity, until 1934. Stenio Vincent, elected under the occupation, was succeeded in 1941 by Elie Lescot who then brought the republic into World War II and claiming a national emergency sought to extend his own term of office. In 1946 he was expelled by a military junta and after four years of political confusion a constituent assembly adopted a new constitution. Eugene Magloire was elected president in 1950 and began to pursue the usual programme of public works accompanied by efforts to extend his own term of office. A general strike compelled him to resign in 1956 and in Sept., after an interval which enabled Francois Duvalier ("Papa Doc") to organise his armed party, the electors were cajoled or terrorised into electing him. His govt. survived on a basis of superstition, corruption and terrorism until his death in 1971 when, on a similar basis, his son Jean-Claude ("Baby Doc") succeeded him. By 1986 the Haitian population was one of the poorest in the Americas but U.S.-fomented popular and military unrest then forced Jean-Claude into exile and a military govt. took over.

HISTORICAL SOCIETY, ROYAL (1868) was founded to deal with biographical and chronological investigations outside the field of archaeology but which present difficulties for private investigators.

HISTORICISM is the view that a predictive science of history can exist. Examples include Marxism, Rosenberg's form of Nazism and, perhaps, Toynbee's theory expounded in his *Study of History.*

HISTORIOGRAPHY. The earliest major works of history, rather than annals or chronicles, in the Atlantic west were *Bede's Ecclesiastical History of the English* and Einhard's *Life of Charlemagne.* The 11th cent. Sigibert of Gembloux wrote the largest of many *Universal Histories* and the Crusades stimulated historical writings such as Villehardouin's *Life of St. Louis.* Probably the ablest

mediaeval work was Snorre Sturlasson's *Heimskringla,* for Snorre was a public figure and explained his use of sources. The Renaissance slowly refocused historical writing from the co-ordination of accepted matter to criticism of it. The process began in Italy with humanists such as the 15th cent. Lorenzo Valla but moved westwards through Jean Bodin's *Method for the Easy Comprehension of History* (1566) to Sir Henry's Spelman's (?-1641) learned compilation of documents on the English church. Meanwhile English writers went, mostly, to the continent for their outlooks or, like Clarendon, wrote highly authoritative apologias. In the 18th cent. renaissance classicism had become absorbed into the background of all the well educated, and classical antiquities were subjected to new and enterprising scrutiny. One result was Gibbon's splendid and penetrating *Decline and Fall of the Roman Empire* (1766-88) which probably discouraged the efforts of lesser men with a sense of style. The Germans, however, were less inhibited and, beginning with Ranke, were soon imposing upon the learned communities a scholarship of indiscriminate detail and bulk. Anglo-German connections were close through Hanover, Göttingen University and the royal families. Early 19th cent. English historians such as John Motley were trained in such methods and some managed to maintain their detachment. Acton, however, thought that history was a science from which it seemed to follow that a definitive history could be written. If the *Cambridge Modern History* which he planned was to be such a definitive history, he wrote little of it. His achievement, however, was to attract many people of scholarly mind into an interest in history and to precipitate the creation of university historical faculties. In the 20th cent. the writing of history in the English language has developed to an enormous volume which will in due course require several Historiographical schools to analyse it. A monumental work on German historiography was written by Xavier von Wegele in 1885. In 1940 J.W. Thompson and others published a two volume *History of Historical Writing* in New York.

HITLER, Adolf born **SCHICKLGRUBER (1889-1945)** German FÜHRER (Leader or Guide) was born at Linz (Austria) and spent five years as a drop-out in Vienna. He became a corporal in the Bavarian infantry in World War I and later established the N.S.D.A.P. (National Socialist German Workers Party or Nazi Party) with a hate-based farrago of disjointed ideas which he set out in the book *Mein Kampf* (Ger = My Struggle). The Versailles grievances and depression attracted votes. Terrorism and lies ensured success with an unsophisticated electorate. Denunciation of the Versailles Treaty, rearmament-based industrial expansion, territorial aggrandisement and imperialism followed. The rest of his career and suicide in summarised in the course of World War II in the direction of which he took an increasingly personal part, his mind being clouded at the end by nihilism and syphilis.

HLOTHTHERE. *See* KENT, KINGDOM-4.

HOADLY, Benjamin. *See* BANGORIAN CONTROVERSY.

HOARE-LAVAL PACT (Dec. 1935). The League of Nations was trying to end the Italian attack on Abyssinia and rescue what was left of international law by imposing oil sanctions. Hitler had repudiated existing treaties and so threatened French security. Laval, the French Prime Minister, feared to provoke Mussolini, Hitler's friend, and refused, in the interests of realism, naval co-operation in enforcing sanctions; the British had to negotiate with him and he was in touch with Mussolini. The British would not accept Mussolini's full demands but a diplomatic deadlock favoured the advancing Italian troops. Accordingly, Sir Samuel Hoare, the British Foreign Secretary, met Laval and they agreed that Italy should receive the Tigre, already conquered, and an exclusive economic sphere of interest over two-thirds of Abyssinia, which would be given an outlet to the sea and that the rest of Abyssinia should be guaranteed by the League of Nations. It is doubtful if Mussolini would have accepted it but in any case the pact was leaked to the French press; British public opinion, already hardening against appeasement, was outraged and Eden replaced Hoare at the Foreign Office whereupon the English outcry abated. The incident marked the moment when the League of Nations was seen to have lost all credit.

HOARE, Samuel John Gurney (1880-1959) 1st Vist. TEMPLEWOOD (1944), Harrow and Oxford educated Tory M.P. for Chelsea (1910-44) was one of those who attained ministerial rank at once in the Bonar Law administration, which was the first Conservative govt. for nearly 20 years and thereby assured themselves of a status enabling them to dominate the political scene of the 1930s. For most of the 1920s he was Sec. for Air, then for India (1931-5) before becoming Foreign Sec. under Baldwin (1935). He resigned after six months in response to the outcry over the Hoare-Laval Pact but returned as First Lord of the Admiralty (1936-7) and Home Sec. (1937-9). He then joined Chamberlain's War Cabinet and was also Lord Privy Seal and Sec. for Air. Churchill sent him to the embassy at Madrid, a difficult post in which he acquitted himself with considerable success. He retired in 1944.

HOBART (1) John (1723-93) 2nd E. of BUCKINGHAMSHIRE (1756), a lord of the bedchamber from 1756 to 1767, was ambassador to the Czarina Catherine the Great from 1762 to 1765 and Lord Lieut. of Ireland from 1777 to 1780. In the latter capacity he prepared the ground for the free trade and autonomy achieved for Grattan's parliament. His nephew **(2) Robert (1760-1816) Ld. HOBART (1798), 4th E. (1804)** was Chief Sec. for Ireland from 1789 to 1793 and favoured the Ascendancy. In 1794 he became gov. of Madras, then at the storm centre of S. Indian politics, and provided the base for the Mysore War. He was recalled in 1798 and summoned to the Lords so that he could assist the govt. in the elaborate and corrupt operations for uniting the British and Irish Parliaments. In 1801 he became Addington's Sec. of State for War and Colonies until 1804. He briefly held minor offices until 1812 when he became Pres. of the Board of Control. Hobart, Tasmania, was named after him. He was killed in a riding accident.

HOBART (-HAMPDEN) Brothers (1) Vere Henry (1818-75) 1st Ld. (1872), a clerk in the Bd. of Trade from 1840 to 1861, reported to such effect on Ottoman finance that he became dir-gen. of the Ottoman Bank. He was gov. of Madras from 1872. **(2) Augustus Charles (1822-86) Pasha (1869)** as a naval officer hunted slavers off the U.S. coast, was promoted for courage in the Baltic during the Crimean War and retired as a Capt. in 1863. He then became a N. Carolina blockade runner for the Confederates in the U.S. Civil War and, in 1867, naval adviser to the Ottoman Sultan by his brother's recommendation. He commanded the Turkish Black Sea fleet in the Russian war of 1877 and reduced the rebellious Cretans in 1881.

HOBBES, Thomas (1588-1679), twenty years a tutor in the Cavendish family, met Galileo in Italy and was a friend of Harvey and Ben Jonson. In 1651 he published his *Leviathan* which later influenced Leibniz, Rousseau and the Utilitarians. In his political philosophy he held that the state was formed as the alternative to anarchy or a natural condition of war, and that its claims were absolute since it could absorb the energy of all its subjects. Since this necessarily set aside the claims and, perhaps, even the theological and moral doctrines of the church he, not surprisingly, also expounded a form of psychological determinism in *Questions Concerning Liberty, Necessity and Chance* (1656) and in 1666 his

views were censured as atheistical by the Commons. He had been mathematical tutor to Charles II, who intermittently pensioned him and afforded him some protection against his own unpopularity with the High Churchmen but intervened to hinder him from writing on current political and religious issues. *See* RENAISSANCE-14.

HOBHOUSE (1) Sir Benjamin Bt. (1757-1831) was M.P. for Bletchingley in 1797, Grampound in 1802 and Hendon from 1806 to 1816. Sec. of the Bd. of Control in 1803 he was chairman of Committees in 1805. His son **(2) John Cam (1786-1869) 1st Ld. BROUGHTON DE GIFFORD (1851)** travelled with Byron in the Peninsula and the Middle East, contested Westminster as a radical in 1819 and was elected in 1820. He was an active member of the Greek Committee. In 1832 he became Sec. at War and in 1833 Chief Sec. for Ireland, but resigned on the house and window tax issue. In 1834 he was returned for Nottingham and, after a short time as Commissioner for Woods and Forests, was Pres. of the Bd. of Control until 1841 and again from 1846 to 1852. He is said to have invented the phrase 'His Majesty's opposition'.

HOBILAR or HOBLER (Med.). An unarmoured horseman armed with spear or bow, usually used in Europe as a scout or messenger.

HOBSON, Bulmer (1883-1969) a leading organiser and developer of Sinn Fein and its guerrilla tactics after 1907, was the first Sec. and one of the founders of the Irish Volunteers in 1913. He opposed the 1916 Rising because he thought that the Volunteers should be used to back Irish claims after the end of the war and withdrew from revolutionary politics.

[H]OCCLEVE, Thomas (fl. 1430-50) long a clerk to the Privy Seal, wrote *De Regimine Principum* (Lat = The Conduct of Princes), an English verse translation of Aegidius and, *inter alia, La Male Regle* (Fr. = The bad example), a self deprecating autobiographical poem petitioning for his salary.

HOCK. *See* WINE TRADE.

HOCKTIDE, the second Monday and Tuesday after Easter, was a period of sports, festivities, ancient mimetic performances and other amusements connected with the collection of funds for church and charitable objects.

HODSON, William Stephen Raikes (1821-58) was Asst. Commissioner with Sir Henry Lawrence in the Punjab in 1849 and commander of the Guides from 1852 to 1854. He raised Hodson's Horse in the Indian Mutiny and captured the last Mogul emperor. When a rescue was attempted he shot some of the princes. He was killed at Lucknow. An inspired cavalry leader, he was idolised by the British and execrated by the Indians.

HOFMEYR, (1) Jan Hendrik (1845-1909) formed the Cape Farmers Assoc. in 1878 and amalgamated it with the political Afrikander Bond in 1883. He sat for Stellenbosch in the Cape Parliament from 1879 and was the recognised leader of constitutional nationalism, refusing the premiership in 1884. In 1887 he sought a form of imperial preference at the London conference; in 1890 he negotiated the Swaziland convention with Kruger, while giving all support to Rhodes until the Jameson Raid of 1893. In 1899 he attempted to prevent war by initiating the Bloemfontein conference with Milner and Kruger and after the Boer War he advocated conciliation and federalism. His nephew **(2) (1894-1948),** a successful academic, became M.P. for Johannesburg North in 1929 and held ministerial office until 1938 when he resigned from the Cabinet over native representation and from the United Party caucus over the Asiatics Bill. Nevertheless, he remained in office and became deputy prime minister in 1948.

HOGARTH, William (1697-1764) began with engraved illustrations to *Hudibras* in 1726. He issued the 'Harlots Progress' (c. 1731), 'Rakes Progress' (1735), 'Marriage a la Mode' (1742-4), 'Industry and Idleness' (1747), 'Four

Stages of Cruelty' (1751); his last plate 'Bathos' appeared in 1764. Between 1726 and 1764 he also painted many works celebrated in their day as well as issuing many other prints.

HOGEN MOGEN, a derisive corruption of *Hoogmogend-heiden,* (Dutch = High Mightiness), a title of the Dutch States General, used of Dutchmen or other important persons.

HOGG, (1) Douglas McGarel (1872-1950) 1st Ld. and then Vist. HAILSHAM (1928), successful barrister and conservative politician, was invited in 1922 to become Att-Gen., though not yet an M.P. He found an uncontested seat at St. Marylebone and, after the Labour govt. of 1924, became Att-Gen. again, this time in the cabinet. He was Lord Chancellor from 1928 to 1929, Sec. of State for War from 1931 to 1935, Lord Chancellor again from 1935 to 1938 and then briefly Lord President. He was a lawyer's lawyer rather than a politician. **(2) Quintin McGarel (1907-) 2nd Vist.** (disclaimed 1963), **Ld. HAILSHAM of ST MARYLEBONE (LP 1970)** was a conservative M.P. from 1938 to 1958, First Lord of the Admiralty from 1956 to 1957, Min. for Education in 1957, and Lord Pres. 1957 to 1959 and from 1960 to 1964, during which time he disclaimed his peerage to be able to compete for leadership of the Tory party, but on his first appointment as Lord Chancellor (1970-4 and 1979-87) he was created a life peer.

HOHENSTAUFEN. (*See* HOLY ROMAN EMPIRE; SAXON AND SALIAN EMPERORS.) **(1)** The hatreds bred in Germany by the struggle between the Papacy and the Saxon and Salian monarchs were not assuaged by the Investiture Compromise (Concordat of Worms 1122) but lived on in party strife. A large faction rejected the quasi-hereditary claims of the Saxon house of Henry V (husband of Matilda, *d.* of Henry I) when he died childless in 1126. They elected LOTHAR of Supplinburg (r. 1125-37) and he married his only child, Gertrude, to Henry the Proud, the Welf (Guelph) D. of Bavaria. The prospective aggregation of the Saxon and Bavarian duchies alarmed the princes and when Lothar died they elected **Conrad III (1138-52),** son of Henry V's sister Agnes (i.e. Matilda's sister-in-law) and Frederick of Hohenstaufen, D. of Swabia. The supporters of this return to family succession became known as the Ghibellines: their opponents the Guelphs. Conrad tried to deprive Henry the Proud of the two duchies; in further civil wars he upheld, with difficulty, his Babenberg half-brothers (for Agnes had married again) in Bavaria. In Saxony, however, he conceded defeat to Henry the Proud's son Henry the Lion (1142) and when he died the latter revived his Bavarian claims.

(2) Conrad's brother Frederick of Swabia, who died in 1147, had married a Guelph. Their son was the famous **Frederick Barbarossa (1152-90).** In 75 years of civil war the German world had changed. The secular functions (*regalia*) of smaller ecclesiastical rulers had passed into the hands of lay advocates (protectors). Many new nobles had illegally engrossed imperial rights. Frederick came to terms with the realities. Firstly he settled with the Guelphs and his Babenberg relations. Henry the Lion was confirmed in Saxony and Bavaria proper. For the Babenbergs the Bavarian East March was erected into the new Duchy of Austria for the defence of the frontier against the Magyars (*The Privilegium Minus* 1156). Henry the Lion was thus left free as a sort of north-eastern viceroy to colonise the Slav lands, destroy Baltic pirates, encourage seaborne trade and found ports and cities. By contrast in the south and west, notably along the Rhine where an English trade had already grown up, Frederick balanced his power by confirming usurpers in return for valuable feudal obligations and quietly but persistently building up a demesne.

(3) Frederick's German policy was designed to free his hand in Italy, now divided into four zones: the rich and dangerous Norman-Sicilian state whose rulers long kept contact with the Anglo-Normans; the Papal territories, the Tuscan area and the multiplicity of Lombard cities. While the cities, lately grown rich in the 12th cent. trade boom, were subduing local nobles and ousting imperial officials, Papal policy had played off the Normans and the Empire against each other. Pope Hadrian IV (r. 1154-9) was currently on bad terms with the Normans. Frederick meant to enforce the highest and oldest imperial claims as if he were a Roman, but with a new philosophy based on Roman legal analysis of common life, i.e. upon scientific method rather than deduction from revelation. The Emperor, as successor to Justinian, would be the great legislator, authorised by God equally with the Pope. It was he who first spoke of his Roman Empire as Holy. In Bohemia he created a King, thereby exercising a prerogative hitherto held to be ecclesiastical. There were, too, within the church imperialist and Norman factions which clashed at the death of Hadrian IV and produced another schism between Card. Octavian as Victor IV (r. 1159-64) and Card. Roland as Alexander III (r. 1159-81). Frederick called a council at Pavia (1160) to decide between them but the Hildebrandine doctrine that no Emperor could sit in judgment on a Pope had taken firm hold. Alexander III appreciated the philosophical as well as material reasons for refusing to submit and, by that fact alone, was recognised throughout Europe, save Germany. Naturally he made an alliance with the Normans.

(4) Simultaneously Frederick was embroiled with the Lombard cities led by Milan. Vigorous, rich, corrupt, plebeian and in mutual hostility, their disorders and impositions obstructed travel and raised the cost of trade across the Alpine passes. The restoration of imperial rights would make order and economic sense. He captured Milan; at the Diet of Roncaglia (1159) he forced the cities to restore the imperial rights and imposed upon each a governor (Podestà: Lat = power) to ensure order. In 1062, following a Milanese insurrection, he demolished Milan and dispersed its people. The cities were cowed but resentful.

(5) He next planned to overthrow the Norman-Papal military alliance with the aid of Pisan and Genoese fleets. His grip on Lombardy was, however, too weak and some of the cities were secretly negotiating alliances. His army occupied Rome and then the Campanian malaria withered it away. Alexander III incited the Lombards, who expelled their podestàs and set up the sixteen-city Lombard League, which instantly rebuilt Milan (1167). Frederick had to raise more troops. During the ensuing six years in Germany he had constant difficulties with Henry the Lion who married Richard Coeur de Lion's sister Matilda in 1168. The League, meanwhile, secured the passes and protected its western flank with a new fortress called, after Alexander III, Alessandria. When Frederick returned in 1174 all Lombardy rose in its defence. He appealed to Henry the Lion for reinforcements and was refused. In May 1176 he was overwhelmed at Legnano.

(6) His realism took over. He abandoned his anti-Pope, restored all church property (P. of Anagni, Oct. 1176) and made a formal submission to Alexander at Venice (July 1177). Left in the lurch, the Pope's late allies accepted truces. Frederick's *volte face* was designed to free his hands for revenge upon the Guelph. A dispute between the Bp. of Halberstadt and Henry the Lion created the opportunity. Arraigned before the princes he was deprived of his fiefs (1179). After a two-year civil war (1180-1) he went into exile at the English court. Apart from his enlarged western demesnes, the resources which enabled Frederick to overthrow so powerful a prince included control of the trade routes with new castles and by taking the great trading towns under his protection. But when it came to the crisis he had to buy the support of the nobles. The Guelph inheritance had to be partitioned into five new duchies for his mightier supporters and the lay princes had to be recognised as a closed and exclusive corporation of tenants in chief. Henceforth the King could, outside his demesne, enfeoff nobody without the agreement of a prince.

(7) If it now needed active and ever present monarchs to maintain the royal power, after 1184 they were too often absent. Frederick had made peace with the Lombard League (T. of Constance 1183) and an alliance with Milan. In 1186 he married his son Henry to Constance, the Norman heiress of Sicily. Then the fall of Jerusalem (1187) drew him towards the ancient imperial military leadership usurped by the Papacy. He was drowned in Asia Minor (June 1190). (*See* CRUSADES, THIRD.)

(8) Henry VI (r. 1190-7) inherited trouble on all sides. Henry the Lion returned from England. Henry VI had already claimed Sicily in right of his wife (1189) but the Normans preferred the illegitimately descended Tancred of Lecce, whom they put in possession. The Papacy naturally preferred Tancred. Thus Henry's Sicilian business meant a Neapolitan civil war and a renewed quarrel with the Pope. In addition there was a rebellion in the northern Rhineland. In all these England was somehow involved. There were now strong Anglo-Rhenish commercial links. The Guelph had his English princess and English money. Tancred had the Queen Dowager Joanna, another sister of Richard Coeur de Lion, in custody and Richard, on the way to the Palatinate, made a financial and matrimonial treaty with Tancred involving Joanna's release (T. of Messina 1190). In 1186 there had been abortive negotiations for an Anglo-Magyar royal marriage and then at Acre Richard insulted Leopold, Henry VI's Babenberg cousin. So when Richard fell into Henry's hands on the way home the latter made the most of it. Apart from the ransom and the surrender of England as a fief of the Empire, the essential result was a change in English policy. Richard and Henry got on famously and had commercial and anti-French interests in common. Richard returned home with a network of Rhenish alliances, but then Henry died.

(9) Frederick, his heir, succeeded in Sicily at the age of three and the princes passed him over. Other candidates were a powerful Ghibelline, Henry's brother PHILIP of Swabia (king 1198-1208) and a Guelph, **Otto IV** (Emperor 1209-1218), son of Henry the Lion. Innocent III, of course, supported Otto but he was unable to establish himself in the ensuing civil wars until Philip's murder in 1208. Then he disappointed Innocent by invading Italy. As suzerain of the Norman Kingdom Innocent had protected the orphan Frederick, though he had neither made his acquaintance nor arranged for his training. He now risked supporting this unknown sixteen-year-old Sicilian King's imperial claims.

(10) The Norman Kingdom and its King were the astonishment of the world (*stupores mundi*). It was vastly rich through its textile, metal, jewellery and food exports, its entrepôt trade and its state industries (fisheries, mines, quarries, salt). Trained Greek civil servants carried on the administration. Arabs managed the finances and the Court, where Englishmen such as the Chancellor Walter of the Mill also found a welcome. The Norman dynasty was intellectually outstanding. Roger II (r. 1130-54) supported al Idrisi, the Libyan geographer; William I's (1154-66) officials translated Plato; the architects developed a composite Norman-Byzantine-Moslem style more splendid than any in Europe. Salerno had the first western medical school. Frederick had inherited his ancestors' abilities. He had educated himself under this cosmopolitanism, which was protected by its power and riches from the relative barbarism of the west. His outlook was independent (as befitted a King), inquisitive (as one who associated with scientists) probably agnostic but, as it turned out, cold. When Innocent III promoted his claims he mistook his man.

(11) The Ghibellines thus elected him as **Frederick II (r. 1212-50, Emperor 1220).** His intelligence and youthful vigour soon gained him a lodgement which his ally Philip Augustus converted, at the B. of Bouvines (*see* JOHN-14; PHILIP (II) AUGUSTUS-7) into a throne. He was crowned King at Aachen in 1215. Otto IV, worn down by failure, died in 1218. In 1220 Frederick was crowned Emperor at Rome by Honorius III (r. 1216-27). He had been careful to conciliate the German churchmen. In 1216 he had renounced the primer seisin of abbeys and bishoprics; in 1220 he confirmed the church princes in their temporalities. This could not establish his rule in Germany, though it might maintain a temporary *status quo*. In Italy he sought to exploit his Norman Kingdom, with its huge navy and excommunication-proof (because Moslem) army, as a new power base. He warred down rebel Sicilian Moslems and resettled them in mainland military colonies. He founded the university of Naples to train more civil servants and men of affairs. He helped the church by enjoining his civil authorities to root out heresy.

(12) He had several times promised to go on Crusade and found excuses to evade the obligation. The Curia had spiritual and moral, as well as worldly, reasons for insisting. In the end, under threat of excommunication, he promised to leave in Aug. 1227. His friend Honorius III died in Mar. The new Pope, Gregory IX (r. 1227-41) had the unbending nature of his 86 years and the vigour and versatility of a man in his prime. A plague broke out in Frederick's ships and he returned. Gregory excommunicated him. Unabsolved he set out again. Gregory renewed the excommunication. Frederick, having renewed his suzerainty over Cyprus, married the heiress of Outremer, persuaded the Sultan to cede the Holy Places and crowned himself King of Jerusalem in the Church of the Holy Sepulchre. All to no avail. Gregory believed, correctly, that Frederick had no concern for the welfare of souls. This strengthened his resolve when he came to think that Frederick's ability to threaten the seat of the Papacy from all directions endangered the Church. He released the Sicilians from their allegiance and invaded the Norman state (1228). Forced to make peace in 1230 he intrigued with the Lombard cities, assisted the formation of a new Lombard League and suborned Guelph factions everywhere.

(13) The war which broke out in 1237 was fought between cities and within them as well as in the field and between a modern, organised, but essentially impersonal power and a church inspired by the propagandist enthusiasm of the new friars. It began with Frederick's victory at Cortenuova (1237). In the middle, the struggle was transferred at Gregory's death to the conclave, for Frederick needed a pope to absolve him. Innocent IV (r. 1243-54), a Ghibelline, was elected and promptly transferred his allegiance to the whole church. He fled to Lyons and at the council mainly attended by English, French and Spanish bishops, pronounced Frederick's deposition (July 1245). Frederick prepared to march on Lyons but was held up and then overthrown near Parma. Two years later he was dead.

(14) His son **Conrad IV (r. 1250-54)** and then an illegitimate son **Manfred (1254-66)** carried on the struggle but the Papacy was now in a position to invite French participation. By 1266 Charles of Anjou had conquered the Norman Kingdom. In 1268 Conrad's handsome young son **Conradin** attempted to recover it, was beaten at Tagliacozzo and publicly beheaded at Naples. *See* RICHARD OF CORNWALL.

HOHENZOLLERN. *See* BRANDENBURG; PRUSSIA.

HOLA (Kenya) was a detention camp during the Mau Mau revolt of the 1950s where terrorists were alleged to have been beaten to death and the deaths attributed by the authorities to contaminated water.

HOLBEIN, Hans, the younger (1497-1543), originally of Augsburg, was already an established painter at Basel when he came to England with an introduction to Sir Thomas More in 1526, and by 1528 had executed many portraits of members of Henry VIII's court including More and Warham. He returned to Basel but came back in 1532 and did most of his remaining work in England. This included religious paintings, title pages for protestant books such as Coverdale's and Cranmer's Bibles and further court portraits. He was also one of the earliest miniaturists; his miniatures of Catherine Howard and Anne of Cleves survive.

HOLBORN (London), named after the upper part of the R. Fleet, there called the Holebourne, was a business and professional suburb of the City. It grew up around Lincoln's and Gray's Inn, the complex of Inns of Chancery, the jewellery trade of Hatton Garden and the franchise of Ely Place belonging to the Bps. of Ely. It also contained the Rookery and other slums. The smallest Metropolitan borough, it was amalgamated with Camden in 1965.

HOLDSWORTH, Sir William (1871-1944) O.M. (1943) Vinerian prof. of English law at Oxford from 1922 to 1924 and a member of the committee on ministers' power from 1929 to 1932, wrote a famous 13 vol. *History of English Law* published between 1903 and 1952.

HOLIDAYS, as something more than a pause from work (such as the eight hanging days) or a church festival, developed with the railways (*see* COOK, THOMAS) which created opportunities to see the world, engendered the demand for time to do it, and eventually brought in shorter working hours and higher pay to make saving for holidays possible. By 1920 1.5M people already had paid holidays; by 1939 the figure was 12M; by 1995 virtually the whole workforce.

HOLINSHED, Raphael (?-1580). His *Chronicles* of England to 1575, Scotland to 1571 and Ireland to 1547 were published in 1578. They are a continuation of a chronicle begun by Reginald Wolfe. Shakespeare, Marlowe and others made much use of them in their historical plays.

HOLKAR (INDORE). *See* MARATHAS.

HOLKHAM. *See* COKE, THOMAS WILLIAM.

HOLLAND (before 13th cent. RIJNLAND) COUNTY and PROVINCE. (1) The volume of seaborne trade and Anglo-Dutch trade rivalry has made this area of prime importance to England for nearly a thousand years. Many Englishmen, especially in E. Anglia, are of recent Dutch descent. The name 'Holland' in English common speech means the Netherlands and the adjective 'Dutch' (i.e. 'Deutsch' = German) reflects Holland's position on the way to Germany. The people were called Frisians until the area became known as Holland.

(2) Its lord Gerulf (?-889) expelled the Normans and his son Dirk I acquired the protectorship of the Abbey of Egimond in 922. This was a seminal event, for Egimond became both the administrative and the cultural centre. Dirk I having extended his lands across the mouths of the Rhine, Dirk III (r. 993-1039), the first Count, levied tolls on the Rhine trade, already used by the English, and provoked a war with traders led by D. Godfrey of Lorraine. Godfrey's defeat in 1018 converted the county into a major western state which could force Robert I of Flanders to invest Dirk V with Zeeland in 1076. This enabled the Counts to levy tolls on the Scheldt as well and so to cream off profits from the European trade to and from the Atlantic, and set off disputes with Flanders and, ultimately and in one form or another, with England, France, Burgundy, Germany and other European powers. These were not resolved until after World War II.

(3) The county expanded northwards; by 1287 Floris V had conquered W. Frisia but the storms which created the Zuider Zee and the Jade inhibited eastward progress, separated the combatants and fixed the frontiers for the next 500 years.

(4) The reign of Floris V (1256-96) had been prosperous. His murder ushered in growing disorder. When his successor Jan I died in 1299 Holland passed to his cousin Jan (or John) II of Avesnes, Count of Hainault, a country interested in free navigation of the rivers. His son William II (r. 1304-37) secured Zeeland as a separate county in 1322. There was now acute economic and political controversy between the rising industrialised capitalists with their workpeople and the small traders and farmers. The former wanted a freer system of international commerce in which raw materials (such as English wool) were imported, worked into manufactured goods and resold, often abroad. The latter sought markets for their own raw materials and an increasing carrying trade. At the death of William IV of Avesnes (r. 1337-45) these interests formed rival parties called respectively Cods and Hooks, who disputed the succession between William's sister Margaret (r. 1346-54), Empress to the Bavarian Louis IV, and her son William V (r. 1356-8). The party conflict divided the nobility, the towns and even the townsmen in the towns. The Bavarian counts (1356-1417) tried, and partly succeeded, in maintaining a precarious balance through border aggression but this was not open to the Countess Jacoba (or Jacqueline) (r. 1417-33) (*see* HENRY V-6; GLOUCESTER, HUMPHREY D. OF). She had to depend upon the Hooks, while the next claimant, Philip of Burgundy, intrigued with the Cods. **(5)** Rising Burgundian power and subversion together with destructive inundations were too much. By the T. of Delft (1428) Philip succeeded at her death. Thus from 1433 the county was part of the Burgundian economic complex. The English were increasingly making their own cloth but this did not prevent a spectacular economic revival based upon maritime expansion. The Hanse was driven from the North Sea fisheries and the Hollanders annually encroached further upon the Baltic carrying trade. They won increasing privileges from their rulers notably in 1477. After the fall of Lübeck (1537) they dominated the Baltic and began to take over the former Hanseatic routes to Bourgneuf (salt), Bordeaux (wine) and Portugal (Pilgrims and wool). **(6)** The Reformation now confused the economic and political relationships. Lutheranism made rapid strides in Holland between 1520 and 1560 and Calvinism between 1560 and 1567. By now the Count was Philip II of Spain who faced a dilemma. His Burgundian lands were the richest part of his dominions but religiously and temperamentally they were becoming estranged from his rule. Coercion and resistance might ruin the Burgundian economy. Failure to coerce, apart from questions of religious conscience, might lead to its fragmentation. The Prudent King temporised as long as he could but militant Calvinism forced his hand. In 1567 he commissioned the D. of Alba to put down heresy and subversion as, respectively, mortal sin and treason. **(7)** The economic consequences followed. Holland could not and would not support his troops and he was progressively shorter of Spanish and American bullion; the American bullion created a European inflation so that more of it was needed with each season. Hence Alba's hated and ragged troops were half beaten before the Sea Beggars (pirates with commissions from the Prince of Orange), driven from the Downs by Q. Elizabeth, seized Brill in Apr. 1572. In the ensuing revolution all the Dutch towns and provinces except Amsterdam took part. Garrisons and pro-Spanish administrations were expelled. In July representatives of the Hollanders, united in the STATES OF DORDRECHT, recognised William of Orange as Stadholder and permitted freedom of worship. They also established a confederation of north and south Holland with Zeeland. Romanist public services were forbidden in Feb. 1573. Alba now launched an organised counter attack which came to a standstill before the desperate resistance of Alkmaar and Leiden. In 1576 the Confederation was formalised at the Union of Delft. The Pacification of Ghent (Nov.) brought in the dissatisfied towns, especially Amsterdam. The riches and populace of Holland made the Dutch Republic virtually a Hollander dominion. It contributed and could threaten to withdraw 58% of the budget; through its Advocate (from 1618 the Grand Pensionary) it conducted the Republic's foreign affairs; through the independent Admiralties of Holland and Zeeland it dominated maritime policy and because of its overwhelming influence in the States-General it indirectly controlled the large Lands of the Generality. *See* ELIZABETH I-9,14 *et seq.*

HOLLAND. This able and later prominent family was descended from **(1) Sir Robert (c. 1270-1328) Ld. HOLLAND (1314).** He was an adherent of Thomas of Lancaster but deserted him in the final struggle with Edward II and was later murdered by the earl's adherents. His second son **(2) Thomas (?-1360) Ld. HOLLAND (1353) E. of KENT (1360)** distinguished himself at the B. of Sluys (1340), the siege of Caen and the B. of Crécy (1346). He was a founder Companion of the Garter and successively Lieut. of Brittany (1354), Gov. of the Channel Is. (1356) and Capt-Gen. in France (1359). Just before he died he married the royal Countess of Kent, Joan *d.* of Edmund of Woodstock and took her earldom. Immediately after he died she married the Black Prince, thus eventually making his children half-brothers to Richard II. The family now played a major role in English politics and war. The eldest **(3) Thomas (1350-97) E. of KENT (1381)** was Earl Marshal (1380-5). His brother **(4) John (c. 1352-1400) E. of HUNTINGDON (1387) D. of EXETER (1397)** meanwhile married Elizabeth *d.* of John of Gaunt, took part in the latter's Spanish expedition and became Chamberlain of England and Admiral. With his nephew, the son of **(3), (5) Thomas (?-1400) E. of KENT (1397) and D. of SURREY (1397)** he was a leading supporter of Richard II in the struggle with the Lords Appellant and rewarded with their dukedoms and a large share of forfeited estates. Thomas also became Marshal of England. This prosperity was brief. At the accession of Henry IV they were deprived of the dukedoms and new acquisitions. In Jan. 1400 they rebelled. John was executed, Thomas lynched by the men of Cirencester. His brother **(6) Edmund (?-1407) E. of KENT (1403)** took no part in the rebellion. He helped the King to suppress the Percy revolt, became Admiral in 1407 but was mortally wounded at St. Briant (Brittany). The eldest son of **(4)**, **(7) John (1395-1447) E. of HUNTINGDON (1316), D. of EXETER (1443)** distinguished himself at the B. of Agincourt (1415) and the earldom was consequently revived for him. He was a very successful commander, of the fleet against the Genoese at Harfleur (1417), at the surprise of Pontoise (1419), at Fresney and Melun (1420) but was captured in 1421 and not exchanged until 1425. He became Gov. of Aquitaine in 1440 and his dukedom was restored thereafter. His son **(8) Henry (1430-75)** a prominent Lancastrian soldier in the Wars of the Roses, shared Henry VI's exile after 1461 and was attainted by the Yorkists. Captured at Barnet (1471) he was held captive until 1475 but was recruited for Edward IV's French expedition of 1475. He was drowned on the return crossing.

HOLLAND, Henry (1745-1806) architect, who in partnership with Lancelot (Capability) Brown left his mark on English life. He built or altered many important houses beginning with Brook's Club. This brought him to the notice of the Prince Regent for whom he refashioned the Marine Pavilion at Brighton and Carlton House (1783-5). Among his other designs were Cardiff Castle, Luton Hoo, Nuneham Courtney, Woburn Abbey, Althorpe and Broadlands. As a speculative builder he laid out, *inter alia*, Sloane St. (London) and the adjacent parts of Chelsea.

HOLLAND, Ld. *See* RICH-6 *et seq.*

HOLLAND. *See* LINCOLNSHIRE.

HOLLAND HOUSE (Kensington, London) originally called COPE CASTLE, was a splendid Jacobean mansion built for Sir Walter Cope (?-1614) by John Thorpe (fl. 1570-1610) in 1607. Sir Henry Rich, first Lord Kensington and then E. of Holland, inherited it and in 1769 Henry Fox. In the 18th cent. it was the scene of a great literary and political salon of the Fox family and its literary influence continued until the end of the 19th. It was destroyed by bombing in World War II.

HOLLES (Pron. HOLLIS). (1) John (c. 1566-1637) 1st Ld. (1616), 1st E. of CLARE (1624) fought the Spaniards of the Armada (1588) and the Azores (1597), and the Turks in Hungary and from 1610 to 1612 was comptroller to P. Henry. He was also, in 1604 and 1614, an M.P. and he pleased James I by supporting Somerset and opposing Coke. On the other hand he disliked Buckingham but favoured a compromise on the Petition of Right. His eldest son **(2) John (1595-1666) 2nd E.** was of a similar cast of mind being, as **Ld. HAUGHTON,** an M.P. from 1624 to 1629. He negotiated with the Scots in 1640 and sided with the 'popular' peers, but defended Strafford, his brother-in-law, in 1641. He tried to steer a middle course in the Civil War unlike his brother **(3) Denzil (1599-1680) 1st Ld. HOLLES of WIELD (1661),** an M.P. in 1624, 1629 and in the Long Parliament, one of the group which held down the Speaker in his chair in 1629. He was imprisoned and fined and fled abroad. In 1641 he, like his brother, tried but failed to help Strafford. He led in Laud's impeachment. In Jan. 1642 he was one of the Five Members and in July joined the Committee of Safety. As a presbyterian he fell foul of the Independents, the army and Cromwell in turn and eventually fled to France where his extremism mellowed. Monck made him a Councillor of State in 1660 and he went to the Hague as a parliamentary commissioner. He was ambassador at Paris from 1663 to 1666 and helped to negotiate the P. of Breda in 1667. By now he had returned to the family middle road. He entered a protest against the Test Act of 1675, favoured Danby's impeachment in 1678 but voted against the Exclusion Bill in 1679. A grandson of **(2), (4) John (1662-1711) 4th E. (1689)** married Margaret Cavendish, co-heiress of the D. of NEWCASTLE, and was created **D. of NEWCASTLE** in 1694. He was Lord Privy Seal from 1705 to 1711. *See* PELHAM and PELHAM-HOLLES.

HOLLOWAY (London) the first British purpose built women's prison, opened in 1852.

HOLLOWAY, Sir Charles (1749-1827), a royal engineer, helped the Turks to reorganise their army against Bonaparte in 1798 and commanded their troops in Syria and Egypt in 1801 and 1802.

HOLLOWAY, Thomas (1800-83) made a fortune from a patent medicine and endowed Holloway Women's College, Egham, and a Lunatic Asylum at Virginia Water.

HOLSTEIN. *See* BALTIC *passim.* PRUSSIA.

HOLSTEIN, Friedrich (self styled Baron) (1837-1909) entered the Prussian diplomatic service in 1860 but after giving evidence against the Ambassador in Paris on a charge of stealing state papers, was socially ostracised; an embittered charlatan, he took part in the intrigue which in 1890 induced William II not to renew the Russo-German reinsurance treaty of 1887 and to dismiss Bismarck. Thereafter he strongly influenced German policy in its threatening attitude to France, which drove that country into alliance with Russia and isolated Germany. Bülow sensibly dismissed him in 1906 after the Algeçiras conference.

HOLT, Harold (1908-67). *See* AUSTRALIA-15.

HOLT, Sir John (1642-1710) a distinguished Common Lawyer, appeared as counsel for Danby in 1679 and for Russell in 1683. He became a Serjeant-at-Law in 1686 and an M.P. in 1689. As such he managed the conference with the peers on the vacancy of the throne. He then became C.J. of the King's Bench. He presided in the case of *Ashby* v *White* in 1701. He discouraged prosecutions for witchcraft and for failure to attend church and leaned against standing armies and their use in times of riot.

HOLY ALLIANCE (1815) (1) was a personal agreement between the rulers of Austria, Prussia and Russia that their relations should be based on "the sublime truths which the Holy Religion of Our Saviour teaches". It declared that "justice, charity and peace" should influence and guide the Councils of Princes, that they would be united "by bonds of a true and indissoluble fraternity" and would regard themselves as "fathers of families towards their subjects and armies". Other rulers were invited to sign and most did so. The Pope refused because so many signatories were heretics, the Sultan of Turkey because all of them were infidels, the Prince Regent because constitutionally he could not personally sign without committing the govt. Castlereagh called it a "piece of sublime mysticism and nonsense" and preferred the arrangements based on the Quadruple Alliance and the congresses planned to follow it.

(2) In practice it declined into an understanding between the rulers of Russia, Prussia and Austria against changes of frontier and constitutional concessions after 1815. Its existence and the movements to which it was opposed resulted in meetings or congresses of these rulers or their ministers together with English and French observers at Aix-la-Chapelle (1818), Troppau (1820), Laibach (1821) and Verona (1822). The general understandings received approximate definition in the Münchengraetz Ts. of 1833. The system fell apart after the rebellions of 1848-9. *See also* CONGRESS SYSTEM.

HOLY Is. *See* LINDISFARNE.

HOLY KINSHIP. The cult of Jesus Christ's grandmother, the thrice married St Anne was brought from her shrine at Sephoris (Palestine) by crusaders to the west, where it inspired interest in the family origins of Christianity, for through her, He was John the Baptist's second cousin, and cousin to the five apostles Simon, Jude and James the Less (sons of Cleophas) and James the Great and John the Evangelist (sons of Zebedee). The joint upbringing (**TRINUBIUM**) of Jesus with the five by their mothers, the three half-sisters Mary Cleophas, Mary Salome or Zebedee and the Virgin Mary at Jerusalem, became widely represented in art. Maries Cleophas and Salome with Mary Magdalene and her Egyptian slave Sarah fled with St Anne's relics by sea to Les Saintes Maries de la Mer (Bouches du Rhône) where gypsies ("egyptians") still hold a festival for Sarah on the beach. Mary Magdalene became the patroness of the Oxford and Cambridge colleges of her name. St Anne was, and is associated with teaching.

HOLY LEAGUES were, with two exceptions, international alliances to which the Papacy was a party. There were five **(1) 1495** organised by Alexander VI against France; **(2) 1511** by Julius II against France; **(3) 1520** by Leo X to establish the authority of Charles V against protestant and other disorders; **(4) 1571** by Pius V with Spain and Venice against the Turks. The combined fleet won the naval victory of LEPANTO (Oct. 1571) at the mouth of the Adriatic. The League then fell apart because Venice, for commercial reasons, made peace whereas Spain wanted to continue operations along the African coast. These ended in 1574 with the Turkish recapture of Tunis. **(5) 1683** by Innocent XI with the Habsburgs, Poland and Venice against the Turks. The Polish King John Sobieski broke up the Turkish siege of Vienna (1683). In 1686 the imperialists recovered Buda and in 1687 most of Hungary. The Venetians conquered Sta Maura, the Peloponnese and Athens but Polish invasions of the Danubian principalities failed. The War of the League of Augsburg (1689-97) then distracted imperial efforts and the momentum into the Balkans was not maintained. The war ended with the P. of CARLOWITZ (1699) whereby the Habsburgs and Venice kept most of their gains.

The two exceptions mentioned above were the Holy Leagues of 1576 and 1585. These were French R. Catholic political alliances during the Wars of Religion. They were encouraged and subsidised by Spain. *See* HUGUENOTS.

HOLY OFFICE. *See* INQUISITION.

HOLY ORDERS. *See* CLERKS.

HOLY PLACES (18th-19th cent.) included the Churches of the Holy Sepulchre, of the Virgin (Jerusalem), of the Nativity including the Grotto of the Holy Manger (Bethlehem) and Golgotha (outside Jerusalem). The French claimed to protect them under Capitulations of 1740; the Russians under later Ottoman firmans and the T. of Kuchuk Kainardji of 1774. After the Revolution French pilgrims fell off while Orthodox greatly increased and so the Russians tended to exaggerate their relatively minor rights; but this expansion represented a practical reality. Hence the revival of French interest in 1852 (Napoleon III was trying to curry favour with his own clericals) was regarded by the Russians as a diplomatic aggression. Meanwhile, as the powers argued, the buildings fell down and, on British suggestion, were repaired by the Turks.

HOLY ROMAN EMPIRE (OF THE GERMAN NATION) (*see also* AUSTRIA; HABSBURG; HOHENSTAUFEN; ELECTORS; THIRTY YEARS' WAR) **(1)** This curious confederation, ascribed to the coronation of Charlemagne at Rome in A.D. 800, was a large eastern remnant of the Carolingian dominions arising from the election as German King of Conrad I (r. 911-18) when the German Carolingians died out. His successor, Henry the Fowler (r. 919-36) was primarily concerned with Slavonic and Danish wars. His son Otto the Great (r. 936-73) defeated the Huns, established the marcher fiefs and twice intervened as papal protector in Italy. The second of these interventions resulted in his imperial coronation at Rome in 962. Otto II (r. 967-83) was so crowned in 967. At the death of Henry II (r. 1002-24) the Saxons were succeeded by the Salians, whose most distinguished member was Henry III (r. 1137-56). Germany was peaceful and prosperous: Bohemia became a fief of the Empire which expanded eastwards (so that Hungary and Poland acknowledged an indeterminate suzerainty) and the Emperor appointed and sometimes deposed Popes and, *a fortiori,* bishops within his own realm.

(2) The imperial position was degraded in a struggle with Hildebrand (Gregory VII) who, seeking independence for the Papacy, intrigued temporally and used excommunication to subvert the German princes. Henry IV (r. 1056-1106) was humiliated at Canossa (1077) and was deposed by his son Henry V (r. 1106-25) who married Matilda or Maud of England. The so-called Investiture Compromise (Concordat of Worms 1122) reserved the conferment of spiritualities in church appointments, and therefore nomination, to the Papacy. Many of the church positions were rich or even important territorial states. The Papacy had won the Compromise by encouraging the independence of the lay princes. The Emperor became, not a paramount ruler but the greatest (especially after the Habsburgs became Kings of Bohemia) of local rulers over whom he presided and amongst whom his political power varied as the comparison between their local power and his own. Thus, among the many scattered small states, imperial free cities and imperial knighthoods, he had real powers but *vis-à-vis* large states he had to rely on the shifts of diplomacy.

(3) In theory the Emperors had always been elected but in practice members of a dynasty had been elected successively until extinction. Henry V was the last Salian. Encouraged by the Papacy the princes asserted electoral rights which created a series of disputes in an interregnum until 1152. For this reason Matilda, socially at the European summit, had no German support in her wars with Stephen. In 1152 Frederick I of Hohenstaufen was elected and the Hohenstaufen were occupied with a variety of struggles whose general feature (apart from Mongol incursions in the 1240s) was an unsuccessful effort to reassert imperial authority wherever (particularly in Italy) it was thought deficient. It ended effectively with the death of Frederick II in 1250 and his son Conrad IV in 1254. There followed a complicated interregnum until 1273.

(4) In this *Great Interregnum* various candidates appeared including William of Holland, Alfonso of Castile and Richard of Cornwall. In 1257 three Electors elected Alfonso, four Richard, who was crowned at Aachen. In fact neither became Emperor or exercised any real authority and Germany declined into confusion.

(5) In 1273 Rudolf of Habsburg was elected King. This did not inaugurate a Habsburg monopoly of the office for, able as he was, he was poor and after his death in 1291 the elective throne was occupied for only 20 years out of the next 147 by a Habsburg; but the family achieved a cohesion and patiently built up a large composite holding in the S.E. whose size and prosperity made some measure of pre-eminence inevitable. This came with the election of Albert of Austria in 1438. After that year, with the sole exception of the Bavarian Charles VII (r. 1742-5), the imperial office was in Habsburg hands until the dissolution of the Empire in 1806. During this period it suffered further transformation arising out of the Reformation and the Turkish wars. North Germany, protestant from the mid-16th cent., came to regard it as a secular institution. Moreover, from 1648 (P. of Westphalia), the Low Countries, Italy and Switzerland ceased to be part of imperial territory.

(6) After 1125 the Empire seldom had much direct political power as an Empire because the Emperors could not raise an imperial tax or, therefore, raise an efficient imperial army, but its importance has been over discounted because of the political antics of its major princes, particularly Bavaria, Saxony, Brandenburg and Bohemia, and the jibes of Voltaire ("neither Holy, nor Roman not an Empire"). In fact its head had a distinct and useful precedence which lent prestige and colour to its holder. It maintained a certain likemindedness and consciousness of German identity through its roads, trade channels, currency exchanges and financial institutions, besides its travelling guildsmen and students. It had a postal system based on Brussels and as late as 1794 when it was thought (with hindsight) to be moribund, it was regulating such socially useful matters as quarantine.

HOLYROODHOUSE (Edinburgh), originally an Augustinian monastery founded by David I in 1128, was used, like other monasteries, with increasing regularity by Scots Kings as a residence. The palace buildings begun by James IV in 1498 were completed by James V. The monastic buildings were mostly destroyed in 1570 and there was a fire in the palace in 1650. Charles II had the palace rebuilt by Sir Wm. Bruce between 1671 and 1679 but no sovereign used it until 1822.

HOLYWELL ST. or BOOKSELLERS ROW (London) an alley comprising the northern side of the present Strand from St. Clement Danes to Lancaster Place. It had an excellent spring in the 12th cent. and became the mart of the secondhand book trade in the 17th. It was pulled down for the Aldwych.

HOLYWOOD, Christopher (1562-1616), Jesuit professor of theology at Dôle and Padua, came to England and was imprisoned in 1599. He was Jesuit superior in Ireland from 1604. *See* NAG'S HEAD CONSECRATION.

HOMAGE. *See* FEUDALISM-16.

HOME (pron. HUME) Scottish East March family and clan strongly influential in the Merse, especially from Hume Castle and around Kelso. The family was already well established in the 14th cent. **(1) Sir Alexander (?-1456)** was warden of the March from 1449 but went to Rome with William, E. of Douglas, in 1450. He later founded the collegiate church at Dunglass. His son **(2) Sir**

Alexander (?-1491) 1st Ld. HOME (1473) had been an associate of Arran and other Boyds and he, with the Hepburns, joined to drive the regent Albany, who had superseded the Boyds, from the Kingdom (1484). The Homes had long held the Priory of Coldingham (a cell of Durham) and were provoked, when James III appropriated its revenues, into joining a rebellion which had been brewing for other reasons for some while. This culminated in James' murder after the B. of Sauchieburn (1488) and, in the first parliament of the 15-year-old James IV, Sir Alexander became Great Chamberlain, Warden of his March, Baillie of Ettrick, Steward of Mar and Keeper of Stirling Castle. His Hepburn ally, Hailes, became E. of Bothwell, Master of the Household, Warden of the other Marches and Keeper of Edinburgh Castle. Each had the guardianship of a prince. By this exact division of power the crown was dominated by the Home-Hepburn alliance until Sir Alexander died. His grandson **(3) Alexander (?-1506) 2nd Ld.,** became Lord Chancellor at the same time, thus balancing some other Hepburn appointments. He so remained until his death but combined the office with much border reiving and invaded Northumberland in Perkin Warbeck's interest in 1496. His son **(4) Alexander (?-1516) 3rd Ld.,** was Great Chamberlain and Warden from 1506. He invaded Northumberland in 1513, took charge with Huntly of the Scots' van in the disaster at Flodden, whence he was one of the few high ranking survivors. He assumed the function of Justice-gen. south of the Forth and proposed the recall of Albany from France to act as regent for the year-old James V. He probably meant to dominate the foreign regent. In fact Albany meant to rule himself and Home was defeated in a intrigue with Q. Margaret, the queen mother and Henry VIII and attainted. His brother **(5) George (?-1547) 4th Ld. (1522)** by restoration was loyal to James V and supported him in asserting his independence of the Douglas in 1528 and in pacifying the Border in 1529 and 1530. In 1542 he successfully held his March against the English when the royal army was beaten at Solway Moss in the west but was unable to withstand Lord Grey of Wilton's advance which ended in the defeat at Pinkie (1547). His son **(6) Alcxander (?-1575) 5th Ld.,** retook Hume in 1548, helped the French expeditionary force before Haddington, became Warden of his March and in 1561 a councillor to Mary Q. of Scots, whom he supported until the public outrage at her marriage with Bothwell in 1567. He remained politically committed against the Queen until Moray's death in 1569, rejoined her party and was Kirkcaldy of Grange's 2-in-C in the defence of Edinburgh Castle. He died in prison. His son **(7) Alexander (1566-1619) 6th Ld. (Sc.) and 1st E. (Eng.) of HOME (1605)** was involved in the Raid of Ruthven (1582), was warden of his March from 1582 to 1599 but was nevertheless in prison from 1583 to 1584 as a result of a fight with the 5th E. of Bothwell, a bastard of James V. He subsequently helped Bothwell against Arran. In 1593 he came into collision with the Kirk, was excommunicated as a R. Catholic, but signed a confession of faith and was absolved. James VI regarded him as an ally and made him captain of his guard. He was a Lord of the Articles in the parliament of 1594. In 1603 he came to London with James and became Lieut. of all the Scottish Marches. **(8) Sir James (?-1666) 3rd E. (1633)** originally a covenanter, went over to the royalists in 1641 and fought at Preston (1648). Consequently his estates were seized but only partially returned at the Restoration. He was a member of the Scots Privy Council from 1664. Thereafter the family was unremarkable as landowners until the 20th cent. when **(9) Sir Alexander (Douglas-Home) (1903-95) 14th E. (1951-63)** disclaimed his peerage and became prime minister in 1963.

HOME GOVT. (Oct. 1963-Oct. 1964). When Macmillan resigned, the 14th E. of Home, the able and well liked

Foreign Sec. announced that he would stand for the leadership of the Tory Party and, if elected, would disclaim his peerage and stand for the House of Commons. He then defeated Quintin Hogg and R. A. Butler, accepted the prime ministership, remained for a few days in the Lords while the administrative processes were completed and then found a safe Tory seat. Save that Butler took the Foreign Office and Iain Macleod and Enoch Powell refused to serve, his administration was composed of the same people in the same offices as Macmillan's. A general election was due at latest in 1964 so Sir Alec Douglas-Home was seen by the media as on probation. Important decisions were postponed until the last moment including the need to retrench the aircraft industry and a settlement for Rhodesia, because Indonesian aggression against the new Malaysia had to be prevented (as it was). In the upshot the election was lost by 317 (Labour) to 303 (Tory) and 9 (Liberal), a bored electorate voting seemingly at random. Sir Alec then returned to the Lords as a life peer.

HOME, Sir George (?-1611) Ld. HOME (Eng.) (1604) E. of DUNBAR (Sc.) (1605), an early favourite of James VI, was his Master of the Wardrobe from 1590 and later an ally of Maitland of Lethington. He became Lord Treasurer of Scotland in 1602 and, as Border Commissioner for both Kingdoms from 1606, pursued James' policy of uniting the two countries, meanwhile also acting as one of the King's most important representatives in Scotland. In particular he was paving the way for a new episcopacy and managing the Glasgow Assembly just before his premature death.

HOME FLEET, centred at the Nore, was organised by Fisher in Oct. 1906 as a permanent deployment against possible German naval threats. *See* CHANNEL FLEET.

HOME GUARD, originally **LOCAL DEFENCE VOLUNTEERS** was created in 1940 after the fall of France as a sort of *levée en masse* for a desperate stand if the expected German invasion made a real lodgement. About a million enrolled. Uniforms and weapons were at first very short. Its main military value was that it provided for guards and similar static duties while the army reorganised and was retrained for other purposes. Its uses in the event of an invasion have never been certain but it would undoubtedly have been supported by the whole (unenrolled) population and would have inflicted guerrilla casualties.

HOME RULE BILLS properly GOVERNMENT OF IRELAND BILLS. (1) Gladstone's Bill of **1886** was to set up an Irish single chamber parliament of two orders who might vote separately and could veto each other for three years or until the next dissolution. One order would consist of 204 M.P.s, the other of the 28 representative peers plus 75 members elected for 10 years on a higher property qualification. Irish representation at Westminster would disappear. The parliament would control the existing and unaltered executive and would eventually control and pay for the police and it would be able to legislate for any internal matter save that it could not create or endow a religious body or legislate on the Crown or its devolution. It would have had no authority in overseas or armed service matters and would have remained under the existing prerogative. A Land Purchase Bill was introduced with it and dropped when the Home Rule Bill was defeated. (*See* GLADSTONE'S THIRD ADMINISTRATION.)

(2) Gladstone's bill of **1893** was to set up an Irish parliament consisting of a Legislative Council of 48 members elected for eight years by electors with a £20 rating qualification and a Legislative Assembly of 103 members. 80 Irish M.P.s were to remain at Westminster with the right to vote only on Imperial and Irish affairs. The Council's veto on bills might last two years but then the issue had to be settled by a vote in joint session. The parliament's powers were similar to those proposed in 1886 except that land legislation was to be reserved to

Westminster for three years and customs and excise permanently.

(3) A. J. Asquith's Bill of **1912** was to set up an Irish parliament consisting of a Senate of 40 originally nominated by the Crown but thereafter by the Irish executive and a lower house, elected on the ordinary franchise, with exclusive control of money matters. In other cases of difference between the houses the issue was to be settled in joint session. Land Purchase, Pensions, National Insurance, Post Office Savings and, for six years only, the Police were reserved to the Westminster parliament.

HOMILIES, BOOKS OF. In Jan. 1542 Convocation agreed to issue prescribed homilies for use instead of sermons by disaffected or tongue-tied clergy. The First Book had been written by Jan. 1543 but Henry VIII would not approve it and it was authorised only in July 1547. Of its 12 homilies Cranmer wrote four and Harpsfield and Bonner one each. The first is an exhortation to read the Bible; the next five are theological expositions of the Fall, Salvation, Faith, Good Works and Love; two deal with obedience and strife and the rest with conventional morals. The Second Book, containing 21 homilies mostly by Jewel, was ready by 1563 and published (with a homily against rebellion) in 1571. It was explicitly approved in the XXXVth Article.

HOMOSEXUALITY. *See* BUGGERY.

HONDURAS. This fertile, mainly agricultural, Central American republic became independent in 1821. It has had 16 constitutions and its economics have been dominated since about 1900 by two U.S. fruit companies.

HONG KONG, (1) with its splendid harbour and creeks was a desolate pirate refuge before 1841 when the British occupied it as an offshore base and trading station analogous to Macao. The island was ceded to Britain by the T. of Nanking (1842) and operated as a free port with freedom of access and departure for all Chinese. British oriental trading concerns soon provided capital and opportunities which converted it into a powerful magnet as well as a safe place for the products of South China, then in a disturbed state.

(2) The population rose very quickly. The terrain was largely uncultivable and the only significant primary product was fish. Disturbances on the mainland as well as piracy increased, and to improve the colony's self sufficiency and reduce the harbour to order, the mainland KOWLOON peninsula and the Stonecutters Is. were acquired under the T. of Pekin (1860). Growth and mainland troubles continuing, a need for further expansion was repeated in a generation. Under the Pekin Convention of 1898 the NEW TERRITORIES were taken on a 99 year lease. This mainland district, part of which is agriculturally productive, together with some 200 associated islands was over 10 times the area of the rest.

(3) The collapse of the Manchu empire (1908), the civil wars of the early republican era (from 1911) and the Japanese intervention (from 1931) all contributed to Hong Kong's expansion and prosperity as the only dependable and impartial refuge where traders could salvage something from the surrounding military and political confusion under the protection of the British China squadron (*see* GUNBOATS).

(4) These conditions led to a considerable increase, both natural and migrant, in the population and to the rise of relevant industries and employments such as ship repairing and husbandry, deep sea fishing, as well as banking and commercial ancillaries. This, in its turn, brought building, road construction, shore line reclamation and occasional terrace cultivation. In 1941, however, the colony was attacked by the Japanese and fell after a short but bitter resistance. Occupied for four years, its liberation by the British in Aug. 1945 was greeted with real joy and relief and once the more obvious war damage had been made good, the advance was resumed in conditions which were an accentuated version of those previously prevailing. The Chinese civil war had attained a new level of sanguinary and ideological fury. Refugees poured in and had to be found employment. Of the 1963 population of 3.6M, 2M had arrived or were born between 1945 and 1956. It was necessary to establish and continue a type of strong govt. and this was done but in such a way that the authorities had access to and habitually listened to local advice. Paternalistic in form, the govt. has very largely followed policies proposed by the inhabitants.

(5) The result was a tremendous light industrial development; for industries related to shipping and commerce indeed expanded, but could not contain the demand for jobs, and some 9000 small factories arose producing textiles, clothes and such things as cameras, radios and plastics. The building industry naturally expanded too: high rise accommodation in addition to offices, factories and reclamation was being completed for 80,000 people a year. The old problem of dependency now arose in a new form. South China (apart from the disturbances of the Cultural Revolution) was relatively tranquil and so Hong Kong could not improve its position by further territorial acquisitions. China by 1963 was supplying 20% of all imports and this included nearly half the food. Above all the territorial water supply was inadequate despite immense construction and when the colony had to be helped by the Chinese in the 1964 drought the precarious nature of its economic, as well as its military, position was thrown into sharp relief. In 1979, after a break of 30 years, the railway service to Canton was reopened. The trade provided China with valuable foreign currency and the Chinese govt. was interested in stability but in negotiations during the 1980s it became clear that when the leases of the New Territories expired in 1997 the Chinese expected a transfer of sovereignty of the island as well and would cut off the water supply if it were refused. In addition it became clear that whatever special arrangements Hong Kong might subsequently enjoy would be mere concessions, not rights, and would not in any case endure beyond 2047. In the meantime the Chinese began to develop a special economic development zone just on their side of the frontier and raised continuous objections to democratisation of the constitution. *See also* LUGARD.

HONITON. *See* LACE.

HONORIUS I Pope (r. 625-38) sent Birinus to preach in Wessex and gave the pallium to Honorius of Canterbury and Paulinus of York. Later involved in a doctrinal indiscretion, he was condemned posthumously as a heretic in 681.

HONOUR was the term for a major collection of mostly dispersed fiefs held in chief by laymen (not ecclesiastics) after the Conquest. Honours might be divided between co-heirs or joined with other honours in the same hand but they represented, in view of the scattered situation of the lands, surprisingly stable organisations. Some owners held private courts for an honour. These were mainly concerned with tenure and succession, judgment being normally given by the vassals. The effectiveness of these courts was limited by three factors: the rise of co-existent royal courts, especially after the reign of Henry II, the scattered geography of many honours which might make it hard to convene a court, and the difficulty, inherent in a private system, of enforcing judgments. *See e.g.* HUNTINGDON.

HONOURABLE ARTILLERY CO. (H.A.C.). *See* ARCHERY.

HONOURS, SALE OF. *See* LLOYD-GEORGE.

HOOD brothers **(1) Samuel (1724-1816) 1st Ld. HOOD (Ir. 1782) 1st Vist. (1796)** after successfully commanding small ships, was commander on the N. American Station from 1767 to 1770. He was with Rodney at St. Eustatius in 1781; held off a French fleet while blockading Martinique and then commanded the rear of Graves's force off the Chesapeake in Sept. 1789. Early in 1782, in Rodney's absence, he defeated de Grasse's larger fleet at Basseterre and he was Rodney's 2-in-C at the B. of Dominica in Apr. He was a Sea Lord from 1788 to 1793 and then as C-in-C Mediterranean took Toulon, destroyed the French fleet there and brought away the royalist refugees. In 1794, after occupying Corsica, he was recalled for political reasons. Not to be confused with the much less distinguished Admiral Sir Samuel Hood (1762-1814). **(2) Alexander (1727-1814) 1st Ld. BRIDPORT (Ir. 1794; Br. 1796) 1st Vist. BRIDPORT (1801)** served under Hawke in 1759. A captain at the controversial B. off Ushant in 1777 he gave evidence for Palliser against Keppel in the subsequent court martial. He assisted Rodney in relieving Gibraltar in 1782. In 1794 he was Lord Howe's 2-in-C at the Glorious First of June and in 1795 captured three French ships from Adm. Villaret-Joyeuse. From 1797 to 1800, as C-in-C in the Channel, he maintained the continuous blockade of Brest. Not to be confused with the Capt. Alexander Hood (1758-98) who was chased out of his ship by the Spithead mutineers in 1797.

HOOKE, Robert (1635-1703) experimental scientist and polymath, designed the Bethlehem Hospital, discovered the fifth star in Orion (1664), established the nature of combustion (1665), applied the spiral spring to watch making, elaborated the theory of the elasticity of gases (1678), invented the marine barometer and a system of telegraph (1684). He was sec. of the Royal Society from 1677 to 1682.

HOOKER, Richard (?1554-1600) the leading advocate of Anglicanism, published the first four books of his *Treatise on the Laws of Ecclesiastical Polity* in 1594 and the fifth in 1597. Book VI (possibly spurious) and Book VIII appeared only in 1648 and Book VII in 1662. He held that there is a natural law whose 'seat is the bosom of God and her voice the harmony of the world'. This is the expression of God's reason and everything including scripture must be interpreted in accordance with it. Human law must conform with it or it is bad. The Bible therefore is not an infallible code of rules because many good things are not directed by it. Law, the church and state similarly are not static but can develop according to circumstances. The Church of England, therefore, is a reformed branch of a continuing Christianity and able to control its own legislation. Hooker's views were set down in conscious opposition to puritanism. Stated in a cogent and beautiful prose they provided the intellectual backbone of the defenders of Anglicanism throughout the 17th and 18th cents.

HOOKWORM or ANCYLOSTOMIASIS. A debilitating, mostly tropical, disease. The worm infests the soil, penetrates the soles of unshod feet and after leading a parasitic existence in the body is excreted to reinfect the soil. It creates extreme lassitude and anaemia so that the sufferer cannot work. Of ancient origin, it was reported in Brazil in 1611, in the Caribbean in 1663 and 1745. It was common among slaves (*see* SLAVERY) in the American colonies and was identified as a major scourge of the Egyptian population in 1853. In 1880 an outbreak among miners working on the St. Gotthard tunnel (Switzerland) spread to all the mines in Europe including Britain. It was not eliminated until 1914. In 1965 500M people were said to be sufferers and the disease was possibly the greatest single burden on the world economy. *See* EPIDEMICS, HUMAN.

HOOLE, Charles (1610-67), was master of Rotherham School until sequestrated in 1642 by the parliament, when he moved to London and in 1650 published a Latin text book. In 1660 he published the influential *New Discovery of the Old Art of Teaching Schoole* on grammar school education.

HOOLIGAN. This word, which has passed into other languages including Russian, originated with an Irish family of that name who disturbed Southwark at the end of the 19th cent.

HOOPER, George (1640-1727) as almoner to Princess Mary, confirmed her in her anglicanism. He was Dean of Canterbury from 1691 and in 1703 became Bp. of Bath and Wells.

HOOPER, John (?1500-55) fled abroad in 1539. He reached Zürich in 1547 where he adopted the views of the Zürich reformers. He became chaplain to Somerset in 1549, denounced Bonner and in 1550, after imprisonment, became Bp. of Gloucester and in 1552 of Worcester as well. He reorganised these sees on Zürich principles. He opposed the usurpation of Lady Jane Grey in 1553 but, at Bonner's insistence, was deprived by Mary and burned for heresy.

HOOVER, Herbert (1874-1964) was head of the U.S. Allied Relief Operations at the outbreak of World War I and also the Commission for the Relief of Belgium. After American entry into the war he was national food administrator. In none of these activities was he very successful. From 1921 to 1929 he was U.S. Sec. for Commerce and in 1929 he became Pres. of the U.S.A. where his belief in *laissez-faire* prevented him from dealing with the economic disasters of the time and led to his resounding defeat by F. D. Roosevelt at the elections of 1932.

HOOVER, John Edgar (1895-1972) was chief of the U.S.A. Federal Bureau of Investigation from 1924 onwards. Research since 1990 suggests that he was dangerously corrupt.

HOPE. Several distantly or recently related Scottish martial and legal families. One group produced seven generals or admirals including **(1) Sir John (1765-1823) 4th E. of HOPETOUN (1816),** the general who organised the evacuation of Corunna after Sir John Moore's death; **(2) Sir Henry (1787-1863)** who, while commanding H.M.S. *Endymion,* captured the more powerful U.S.S. *President* off Sandy Hook in 1815 and **(3) Sir James (1808-81)** the admiral who took the Taku forts in 1860 (*see* CHINA-22). The lawyers included two Lords Advocate, two Lords of Session, a Lord Justice-clerk and two Lords Justice-Gen. **(4) Sir James (1614-61)** Lord of Session from 1649 was a member of Cromwell's Council of State from 1653.

HOPE (1) Thomas (1770-1831) of Amsterdam, settled in England in 1796. He was a discerning collector and a patron of Canova, Thorwaldsen and Flaxman. He also wrote on household furniture. His son **(2) Alexander (1820-87) BERESFORD-HOPE** (from 1854), a Tory M.P. (1841-52, 1857-9 and from 1865) was politically somewhat reactionary but inherited some of his father's interests. He was a trustee of the British Museum and the National Portrait Gallery, built All Saints Church, Margaret St. and, besides novels, wrote on architecture and established the *Saturday Review* (1855). He was also Pres. of the Inst. of British Architects from 1865 to 1867.

HOPE, James Fitzalan (1870-1949) 1st Ld. RANKEILLOUR (1932), Conservative M.P. from 1900 to 1906 and from 1908 to 1929, was a whip from 1916 to 1919, Parl. Sec. to the Min. of Munitions from 1919 to 1921 and deputy speaker from 1921 to 1929.

HOPKINS, Matthew (?-1647) East Anglian witch hunter, procured with John Godbolt, a special judicial commission in 1645 under which some 200 miserable women were hanged at Colchester, Bury, Norwich and elsewhere. He was denounced as a charlatan by John Gaule (?1604-87), the courageous vicar of Great Staughton, and hanged for sorcery.

HOPPNER, John (1758-1810) was a boy chorister in the Chapel Royal who was given an allowance by George III to study painting at the Royal Academy Schools. He exhibited at the Royal Academy from 1780 and the circumstances of his early promotion led to unproved and unlikely rumours that he was the King's son. He was patronised by the P. of Wales and, commercially

speaking, was the chief rival of Thos. Lawrence who was patronised by his supposed father.

HOPTON (1) Sir Arthur (?1588-1650) was sec. to Ld. Cottington's embassy in Spain in 1629 and was ambassador there from 1638 onwards. His nephew **(2) Ralph (1598-1652) 1st Ld. HOPTON (1643)** served in Mansfield's army and was a middle of the road Anglican M.P. from 1625 onwards. He voted for the Strafford attainder and presented the Grand Remonstrance to the King in 1641 but opposed the militia ordinance in 1642 and was expelled from the House. He then joined the King and, as one of his generals, won victories in Cornwall and at Lansdowne and directed the defence of Devizes in 1643. He was briefly deputy gov. of Bristol and in 1644 was defeated at Cheriton. Thereafter he was sent to the West to reorganise the troops but, defeated at Torrington, had to surrender at Truro in 1646. He left England with Prince Charles in 1648 but was involved in policy disagreements at the fugitive court and retired.

HORDER, Thomas Jeeves (1871-1955) 1st Ld. HORDER of ASHFORD (1933) consultant physician at Barts Hospital and physician to the royal family, made a tremendous reputation as a teacher and medical writer between 1912 and his death, particularly in the dangerous communicable diseases and was personally revered by the medical staffs of the many institutions where he worked.

HORE-BELISHA, Leslie (1893-1957) 1st Ld. (1954) became Liberal M.P. for Devonport in 1923 and in 1931 organised the Liberal National Party to support the national govt. of Baldwin and Ramsay MacDonald. In 1932 he was made Financial Sec. to the Treasury, especially to manage the political side of the Ottawa agreements and in 1934 he became Min. of Transport. As such he instituted pedestrian crossings (with 'Belisha beacons'), driving tests and the Highway Code and took over responsibility for and built many miles of trunk roads. He joined the Cabinet in 1936 and became Sec. of State for War in 1937. He achieved a minor revolution in the army, which included the introduction of battle dress, the amalgamation of officer training schools and a great advance in mechanisation. His methods and temperament, however, made him unpopular in the army and the War Office. When the British Expeditionary Force was established in France in World War II he became anxious about the state of the defences along the Belgian frontier and the Prime Minister (Chamberlain) asked him if he wanted to change the C-in-C (Lord Gort) or the C.I.G.S. Hore-Belisha refused to do either but continued to warn the Cabinet of the dangers. The soldiers and the French insisted that he was wrong, though supported by Casey and Reitz, and a combination of generals and politicians forced him to resign in Jan. 1940. Thereafter, save briefly as Min. of National Insurance in 1945, he held no office.

HORMUZ. *See* BANDAR ABBAS.

HORNE. *See* TOOKE.

HORNE, Robert (?1519-80) an extreme reformist churchman, as dean of Durham destroyed St. Cuthberts tomb in 1551 and, as Bp. of Winchester from 1560, destroyed much ornamentation in churches and colleges. He assisted in drafting the *Book of Advertisements* and the canons of 1571 and collaborated in the revision of the 'Bishop's Bible'.

HORNIMAN, Annie (1860-1937) a rich friend and secretary to W. B. Yeats who built the Abbey Theatre, Dublin, in 1903 and the Manchester Repertory Theatre in 1908. She was a generous patron and organiser of the modern repertory movement.

HORNING (Scots.). A sentence of outlawry.

HORNWORK. *See* APPENDIX *plan* of VALETTA.

HORSE GUARDS was built on the site of the guard house of Whitehall Palace in 1751-3 to house the dept. of the Commander-in-Chief, an office abolished in 1904.

HORSE MEAT. The English visceral dislike, not shared by the French, of eating it may, apart formerly from personal relationships with horses, arise from superstitions related, perhaps, to the White Horse of Uffington (*see* HILL FIGURES), Hengist and Horsa and the prancing horses in Kentish symbolism.

HORSE RACING is doubtless an immemorial sport, but the earliest recorded English race meetings were held at Chester in 1540. There was a track at Doncaster in 1595; James I visited races at Newmarket in 1607 and Charles II's interest gave Newmarket its later prominence. He himself rode there in 1671. The first Ascot meeting was in 1711. The sport developed rapidly and in 1750 the Jockey Club was formed to control Newmarket Heath. The St. Leger was first run at Doncaster in 1776, the Oaks at Epsom in 1779, the first Derby in 1780, the first Ascot Gold Cup in 1807, the first 2000 Guineas in 1809 and the first 1000 Guineas in 1814. Races were local events until 1836 when Lord George Bentinck sent a colt to Doncaster in the first horsebox, but this practice only became common with the development of the railways, which also brought nationwide audiences.

HORTHY de NAGYBANYA, Miklos Prince (1868-1957), Admiral, a brilliant destroyer commander in World War I, became the last C-in-C of the Austro-Hungarian Navy which consequently remained a threat to the Allies until 1918. He led the *coup* which overthrew the communist revolutionary regime in Budapest in 1919. He then took the Regency of the Kingdom until World War II, when he was manoeuvred and forced into alliance with Hitler, who played on Magyar irredentism by transferring a large part of Transylvania to Hungary. He tried to protect the Jews but the Nazi police apparatus had taken too firm a hold by 1943. He put out feelers to the British for an armistice with the approaching Russians but was betrayed and arrested. As a result most of Budapest was destroyed in the Russian assault. He died in Portugal.

HOSPITALLERS, KNIGHTS or KNIGHTS OF ST. JOHN or OF MALTA. The Order was founded in 1070 as an Amalfitan pilgrim hostel at Jerusalem dedicated to St. John the Almsgiver and under Benedictine supervision. After the crusader conquest in 1099 it acquired endowments and in about 1118 a military establishment, but it remained famous rather for its hospital and generosity to the poor. Its patron soon turned into St. John the Evangelist and it acquired vast estates in the Levant and in Europe and many crusader castles. It was the richest of the three crusading orders. After the fall of Acre and the destruction of Outremer it was moved to Cyprus and between 1306 and 1308 expelled the Byzantines from Rhodes, which became the H.Q. In 1344 it helped to take Smyrna, which it held until 1402 when it was driven out by the Mongols. The Order's substantial English estates were seized by Henry VIII as part of the Dissolution of the Monasteries. *For later history see* MALTA GC.

HOSTE, Sir William (1780-1828) served under Nelson and from 1808 onwards, though only a Capt., commanded a frigate squadron which dominated the Adriatic, defeated a French force at Lissa (Vis) in 1811 and enabled the Austrians to take Cattaro (Kotor) and Ragusa (Dubrovnik) in 1814.

HOTHAM, Sir John (?-1645) levied shipmoney as sheriff of Yorkshire, but after removal from the governorship of Hull in 1639 went, as M.P. for Beverley, into opposition; he was the moving spirit behind the Yorkshire petition and then became parliamentary gov. of Hull in which capacity he prevented the King's entry in 1642. In 1643 he was discovered in negotiations to change sides and executed.

HOTHAM (1) William (1736-1813) 1st Ld. HOTHAM (1797) served as Commodore on the American station in 1778, under Rodney in 1780 and under Howe at Gibraltar and C. Spartel in 1782. In 1795, as C-in-C Mediterranean

his sloth and incompetence twice prevented a victory over inferior French forces. His brother **(2) Beaumont (1737-1814) 2nd Ld.,** was M.P. for Wigan from 1768 to 1775 and a commissioner of the Great Seal in 1783. His son **(3) Sir Henry (1777-1833)** was an energetic and successful cruiser commander from 1805 to 1812 mainly in the Bay of Biscay, his local knowledge of which prevented Bonaparte's escape to America in 1815. His nephew **(4) Beaumont (1794-1870) 3rd Ld.,** was a Tory M.P. for Leominster (1820-41) and the East Riding (1841-68).

HOTSPUR (Sir Henry Percy 1364-1403). *See* PERCY; HENRY IV- 4,7.

HOT TROD. *See* MARCHES; ANGLO-SCOTS-5.

HOUSEBOTE. *See* LAND TENURE (ENGLAND)-3.

HOUSE OF CORRECTION. The Poor Law of 1600 required a parish to provide only for those of its legally settled poor, but social dislocations, the existence of nearly 800 extra-parochial places and post-war demobilisations threw onto society sturdy unsettled (and therefore unsupported) vagabonds whose gangs sometimes terrorised countrysides. In 1610 county magistrates were directed to set up houses of correction into which they were to be driven, whipped on admission and set to work as quasi-public slaves, but at least they were fed and sheltered. From this it was a short step to thus treating the merely idle, bad workers, small thieves and prostitutes, and sometimes detaining them pending trial. By 1780 gaols (i.e. places of detention) were being used too, so that the functions of the two types of institution were becoming inter-changeable. In 1866 the functions were merged and they were all called *local prisons*.

HOUSE OF INDUSTRY A large workhouse belonging to a Poor Law Incorporation.

HOUSE OF LORDS BILL (1998) (1) was to abolish the right of all hereditary peers to be summoned to the House, but arising out of criticism of the govt's lack of proposals for a Second Chamber and private negotiations with Vist. Cranborne, Leader of the Tory peers, and in return for the passage of the five times rejected European Elections Bill, a modification was contrived to deal with the, as yet unpublished proposals, for a second stage reform by a R. Commission under Lord Wakeman. Wm Hague, the Tory party leader disapproved of Cranborne's manoeuvre and dismissed him, but Cranborne said that he had behaved outrageously but would do it again, and he carried his modification regardless.

(2) Accordingly under the **ACT 1999**, the positions of the Lord Great Chamberlain and the Earl Marshal were preserved; 14 hereditary peers were to be elected to various offices by the whole House; and 75 more were to be elected proportionally by party groups. The Act came into effect at the end of the session (Nov. 1999) and in the new session the, perhaps provisional House, previously consisting in theory of 1296 peers (of whom 134 were without writs or on leave of absence) had been reduced to 571 viz: 214 Tories, 161 Labour, 46 Liberal Democrats and 148 Cross-Benchers.

(3) The Act destroyed the access of many non-political and public bodies (such as universities and professional associations) to parliament through honorary offices conferred on hereditary peers, deprived parliament of a body of independent and specialist talent, and ignored the hitherto represented heredity of all human beings.

HOUSING (1) In London, Bristol, Norwich and York and some mining villages, badly built, overcrowded and insanitary quarters with water fetched from shared wells, had bred disease and caused short life expectancies since time out of mind. Until the 18th cent. the main palliative had been that most people in similar living conditions avoided town life "like the plague" (significant phrase). There was an old dislike for city life amounting almost to a moral attitude, vestiges of which can still be found, but most towns outside London were really villages, with the advantages of country air and amenities.

(2) Industrialisation changed all this in two generations (1780-1830). There was a population explosion and migrations towards new haphazardly placed factories whose neighbourhoods were soon occupied by hastily built potential slums. These were often of slightly better material quality than heretofore, but degraded by coal-based pollution, without a sanitary substructure or drained and paved roads and, in the absence of proper local authorities, unregulated to accepted standards. The problems were noticed as early as 1815.

(3) The Highways Act 1834 made the first improvements by raising the standard and drainage of new roads, and the nearly simultaneous Municipal Corporations Act introduced in some places, permanent authorities which, if they could do little, could at least observe trends. A public opinion grew and was initially focused in a Commons select committee inquiry into Town Health (1840). For the first time knowledge of the full extent of urban slums was assembled and exposed. Outbreaks of cholera (q.v.) from the 1840s emphasised the need for action. In 1851 the still scattered local councils were empowered (not required) to provide worker's houses. Urban sanitary authorities were being created sporadically where no authorities existed and in 1868 the authorities which existed were empowered to force owners to demolish or improve insanitary dwellings. In 1875 the great Public Health Act established sanitary or port health authorities everywhere and another Act reinforced that of 1868 by enabling them to take areas unfit for human habitation by compulsory purchase. The obstacles to rapid improvement were, however, the substructure costs compared with the poor taxable (or rather rateable) resources of the authorities.

(4) Expectations had, however, been raised particularly through the work of businesslike social improvers such as Octavia Hill, and practical visionaries such as John Ruskin, and the Salvation Army. An outcry in 1884 about destitution in London caused the appointment of the 1885 R. Commission on the Housing of the Working Classes, which made an assemblage and exposure similar to that of 1840 and led to the Housing Act 1890. This consolidated existing law and concentrated on sanitation, building standards and new provision. A new era seemed about to open in 1894 with the creation of a rationalised system of local govt.

(5) Unfortunately the erosion of rural local govt. by 50% derating of agricultural land began as a result of the farming slump, in 1896. No alternative source of funds was then provided and, rural substructure costs being, per head, anyway far higher than urban, rural improvements ceased. The derating also introduced new factors: in the long run central subsidisation of local authorities became morally inevitable, especially with further derating.

(6) World War I was a landmark. As the people moved out to battle or into war production, house building ceased and rents threatened to rise. With millions of soldiers being paid 1s. a day at the front, this might have created impossible, perhaps war-losing, conditions for their families. The Increase of Rent and Mortgage (Restriction) Act 1915 ("The Rent Act") froze rents and mortgage interest and, complementarily prevented evictions (see RENT RESTRICTION). By 1919 inflation had gravely reduced landlords' real incomes (from 1915 rents) and taxation, especially death duties occasioned by vast war casualties, had destroyed their other resources. Demobilisation created a clamant need for new houses which private owners could no longer afford to build, yet with successive electoral enfranchisements, it was politically impossible to return

to the 1914 free market in rents. The period 1919-39 was thus a time of legislation (1919, 1923, 1924 and 1933) designed to encourage the untaxed local authorities to provide houses, but total derating of agriculture and industry in 1929 called for govt. subsidies. There was also some limited raising of rents, as old tenancies fell vacant, but pre-1914 houses were accordingly often ill-maintained.

(7) World War II repeated, but in worse form, the difficulties of World War I. Rents were again frozen but bombing destroyed 1M buildings and damaged another 2M, and many undamaged houses were badly run down pre-1914 stock. Moreover the temper of politics had sharpened since left-wing politicians had imbibed post-1917 notions of class struggle. An Act of 1946 revived the flagging housing powers of local authorities with new subsidies, but meanwhile furnished lettings had become the resort of demobilised service people and their families. In 1947 furnished rents were placed under the control of lodger-sympathetic tribunals. In 1949 a further Act empowered tribunals to determine reasonable unfurnished rents on application by tenants but not landlords. The Labour govt. plainly intended by obstructing private housing and encouraging public to effect a creeping replacement of system. Meanwhile justice was at least done to the rural areas by the annual provision of large central funds to install piped water and sewerage.

(8) The policy broke down on bad organisation. Replacement houses were not being built quickly enough. Accommodation became a major source of discontent. The first solution was undertaken by Harold Macmillan as Tory Min. of Housing and Local Govt. He got more houses built than electorally promised by increasing the supply of bricks (1951-4) and between 1954 and 1957 landlords could be allowed to raise rents firstly to take account of repairs and improvements (now possible) and then more freely on changes of tenancy. In 1958-9 they became eligible for improvement grants. In 1961-7 there was a return to Labour doctrine: there were new forms of rent freezing and secure tenancies.

(9) By now the steam had gone out of the national, if not the local, controversies and housing began to be entangled with planning, especially in the rising New Towns, and with social issues. If Labour preferred public housing and secure tenancies as against private landlords, the Tories catered for security by encouraging private ownership. From 1978 first-time buyers could get advantageous finance. From 1980 local authority tenants of three years' standing could at any time buy their house at discounts between 33% and 50%. These rights were extended in 1984 and to the private sector.

(10) In 1977 local authorities had been required to accommodate the homeless. The events of 1978 to 1984 severely reduced both the local authorities' housing stock and the demand for their houses. These they began to demolish. The problem of homelessness was a compound of immigration, unemployment, especially in the terrible slump of 1989 onwards, and a youthful restlessness and social dissatisfaction. Groups sometimes seized houses scheduled for demolition and one High Court judge refused to evict such a group because "any roof is better than none". For the first time since 1914 people slept rough in central London. There were 60 squatters' tents in Lincoln's Inn Fields when the local council shut them out in 1990. There was a recrudescence of some of the diseases (e.g. tuberculosis) associated with bad housing and where the homeless had young children or were otherwise vulnerable, the authorities sheltered them, at great expense, in bed and breakfast accommodation.

HOVEDEN or HOWDEN, Roger of (?-1201) a royal clerk and justice under Henry II and Richard I, wrote a

Chronicle for the period 732-1201 which is a useful source for the reigns of these two Kings.

HOWARD. The fortunes of this aristocratic dynasty was indirectly based upon a kinship between John, the last Mowbray D. of Norfolk who died in 1476, and the competent John Howard, whom he employed and who succeeded to much of his influence. John Howard became the first Howard **D. of NORFOLK** and Earl Marshal in 1483 but was killed commanding Richard III's van at Bosworth. His son Thomas (I) became **E. of SURREY** in 1483 and his father's Dukedom was revived for him in 1514 as a result of his victory at Flodden. The dukedom and the earl marshalcy were still in the family in 1993. These Howards also amassed many Mowbray estates and many other peerages; the following is a summary of the eight which descended in collateral lines (NB. Thomas (I) was the father of Thomas (II) who was the father of Thomas (III)).

A. Thomas I's younger son William became the **1st Ld. HOWARD of EFFINGHAM** and William's son Charles became the **1st E. of NOTTINGHAM.**

B. Thomas II's son Henry, courtesy E. of SURREY, predeceased him but his son was Henry, **1st E. of NORTHAMPTON.**

C. Philip's younger son was William, **Vist. STAFFORD.**

D. Thomas III's younger son Thomas became **1st Howard E. of SUFFOLK** and **1st Ld. HOWARD DE WALDEN** and was the father of the **1st Ld. HOWARD of ESCRICK.** His eldest son was **Philip E. of ARUNDEL.** The influence of such a noble clan in the Upper House which, until the 18th cent. seldom mustered as many as 50 at meetings, was diminished by the fact that some of its members, particularly the dukes, were R. Catholic and unable to take their seats until 1829.

HOWARD of EFFINGHAM, Ld. *See* ELIZABETH I-28 *et seq.*

HOWARD, Henrietta neé **HOBART (1681-1767) Countess of SUFFOLK (1731),** lived with Charles Howard, later E. of Suffolk, at Hanover, followed George I to England and became one of the household of the P. Caroline. Mistress of George II, she remained on good terms with the Queen. Her house at Marble Hill, Twickenham (not far from Bolingbroke's house at Uxbridge) was a literary *salon* frequented by John Arbuthnot, his friend Jonathan Swift, Alexander Pope, Wm. Fielding, John Gay and other opposition literateurs. Her position made her an obvious target for the ambitious, the ill natured or those merely hostile to Walpole. She retired in 1734 and took Geo. Berkeley as a second husband in 1735.

HOWARD (NORFOLK) (1) John (?1430-85) (*see* HOWARD; MOWBRAY-9) **1st Howard D. of NORFOLK (1483)** M.P. for Norfolk in 1455, was Edward IV's sheriff of Norfolk and Suffolk and constable of Norwich from 1461 and generally operated against the Lancastrians, but his first peerage was a Lancastrian dignity which he accepted during Henry VI's restoration. He was in fact too influential in E. Anglia to attack. Consequently, on Edward IV's return, he took command of the fleet and the Lieutenancy of Calais and from 1475 to 1480 was employed there and on four missions to France. Richard III made him Admiral of England and Ireland and commanded that King's van at Bosworth where he was killed. His son **(2) Thomas (1443-1524) E. of SURREY (1483) D. of NORFOLK (1514)** like his father fought for Richard III and was, for a while, in custody in the Tower; in 1489 he had recovered his estates but Henry VII preferred to employ his developing military talent in the north. He put down a Yorkshire rising in 1489, drove back a Scots invasion in support of Warbeck in 1497 and agreed a seven year truce during which he helped to negotiate the marriage of 1503 between James IV and Henry VIII's daughter Margaret. From 1501 until 1522 he was Lord Treasurer, but left most of the work to others

and in 1510 Henry VIII made him Earl Marshal. Owing to Wolsey's increasing influence this might have been the summit of his career but for the Scottish war of 1513 in which he won an overwhelming victory at Flodden, returned in triumph and was rewarded with his dukedom. He disliked Wolsey and his policy but, though high in prestige, could not withstand him and so became a peripheral presence in the politics of the period, now increasingly dominated by the King's suspicious personality. This led him to over-assert himself in putting down the London apprentices in the Evil May Day riot of 1517. He was flattered when appointed guardian of the Kingdom during Henry's absence at the Field of the Cloth of Gold (1520). His final humiliation came in 1521 when Henry compelled him to preside over the trial and condemnation of his friend the D. of Buckingham on false charges of treason. His sons **(3) Thomas (1473-1554) E. of SURREY (1514) and 3rd D.** and **(4) Sir Edward (1477-1513)** served together at sea and captured the Bartons, Scottish corsairs, in 1511. Edward commanded the fleet against Brittany and the French with success in 1512 but was killed on a cutting-out expedition at Whitsand Bay. Thomas became Lord Admiral in 1513 and also fought at Flodden and like his father disliked Wolsey and his policy. He was Irish Lord Lieut. in 1520, commanded raids on the French coast in 1521 and 1522 and, as Warden-gen. of the Scottish March, faced Albany's miscarried invasion of 1522 and his discredited attack on Wark in 1523. He became High Treasurer in 1522 on his father's resignation. In 1525 he put down the Suffolk insurgents. During the next years he mainly managed his estates. Hans Holbein came to court and left a famous portrait drawing of him. His credit with Henry VIII rose steadily and when Wolsey fell, though he did not succeed to his great position, he was the splendid leader of the most influential group at court, to which his niece Q. Anne Boleyn belonged. He was also Lord President. Such prosperity could not last and in due course he had to accept her execution (1536). Essentially a moderate or compromiser he was now caught between the R. Catholic Pilgrimage of Grace, which he put down, and the policies of Thomas Cromwell, which he opposed. To further his views and the Howard interest his attractive but poor niece **(5) Katherine (?-1542)** was brought forward. She met the King at Lambeth Palace and their short, tragic, marriage ensued in Aug. 1540. Her attainder and execution damaged the duke's position but he had almost immediately to take command against the Scots (1542) and then in France (1544) and consequently fell and was attainted as a result of an intrigue by Hertford. Henry's death the night before his execution was due saved his life but he remained in the Tower through Edward VI's reign. Mary I restored him. He presided at Northumberland's trial and put down Wyatt's rebellion. His son **(6) Henry (?1517-47)** courtesy **E. of SURREY,** translator, poet and soldier, introduced the sonnet from Italy. He was executed on trivial pretexts designed to enmesh his father. His son **(7) Thomas (1536-72) 4th D. (1554)** a pupil of John Foxe, was employed in the important Scottish transactions of 1559-60 and became a member of the council in 1562. He and Leicester disliked each other and, perhaps, were motivated by the Howard-Dudley feud of the previous generation. The Queen maintained a balance, even though in 1565 they nearly came to blows in her presence, and in 1568 he was sent to York to investigate the quarrel between Mary Q. of Scots and her subjects. The Queen trusted Leicester in preference to him and Norfolk was apparently fascinated by Mary. This lent some plausibility to his alleged project for marrying Mary, connected with the Northern Rebellion, and he was imprisoned. In 1572 he was implicated in Ridolfi's plot and executed. He always denied being a Papist. His monument is Magdalene

College, Cambridge, which he richly endowed. After him the dukes lived a quiet life, managing their always extensive estates.

HOWARD, Thomas (1586-1646) 2nd E. of ARUNDEL and SURREY (by reversal of attainder 1604), a R. Catholic, was Pres. of the Lord's committee on Bacon's case in 1621, imprisoned from 1626 to 1628 as an opponent of Buckingham, commanded against the Scots in 1639 and presided at Strafford's trial in 1641. In 1642 he escorted Q. Henrietta Maria to the continent and thereafter lived at Padua. He is noted for having formed, at Arundel House, the first great English art collection, the marbles in which were given to Oxford Univ. in 1667.

HOWARD DE WALDEN, Thomas Evelyn Scott-Ellis (1880-1946) 8th Ld. (1899) and 4th Ld. SEAFORD, inherited huge London estates and acquired others and also in Wales and Kenya. He was engaged in ceaseless, often successful, dispute with the Revenue authorities but meanwhile benefited the arts and charities; supported the Turf and sailing; practised falconry; edited and financed the *Complete Peerage* and collected modern paintings.

HOWE (1) Scrope (1648-1712) 1st Vist. (Ir.) HOWE (1701), a whig politician, was M.P. for Notts. from 1673 to 1698 and from 1710 to 1712. An active protestant, he was groom of the bedchamber from 1689 to 1702. His brother **(2) John Grubham (1657-1722),** also a whig, was Q. Mary's vice chamberlain from 1689 as well as a Gloucestershire M.P. from 1689 to 1705. Dismissed by the Queen in 1692, he became a Tory and denounced William III's partition treaty of 1698. He was joint clerk of the Privy Council under Anne. **(3) Richard (1726-99),** the admiral, **4th Vist. (Ir.) 1st Vist. (British) (1782) and 1st E. HOWE (1788)** was M.P. for Dartmouth from 1757 to 1782. He took a distinguished part in the Rochefort expedition of 1757, the attacks on St. Malo and Cherbourg in 1758 and at Quiberon Bay in 1759. He was Lord of the Admiralty from 1762 to 1765 and treasurer of navy from 1765 to 1770. He was C-in-C of the American Station in 1777 but resigned against the govt's war policy and remained in retirement until 1782 when he commanded the relief of Gibraltar against heavy odds. As First Lord of the Admiralty from 1782 to 1788, he developed signalling and improved the sailing qualities of line-of-battle ships and the welfare of the crews. In 1790 he became C-in-C in the Channel and in 1794 won the hard fought Glorious First of June. He retired in 1797 but was promptly recalled to pacify the Spithead mutineers. His brother **(4) Sir William (1729-1814) 5th Vist.,** was M.P. for Nottingham from 1758 to 1780 and after a distinguished junior career in America, took command of the troops there in 1775. Though defeated at Bunker Hill in 1775 he held his own. He and his brother both favoured conciliation but their efforts were unsuccessful and he was forced to military action, winning successes on Long Island, White Plains and the Brandy-wine and taking New York in 1776. His successful defence of Germantown at the end of the year was his last engagement, the rebels thereafter sensibly refusing battle. He resigned command in 1778 just after his brother, and his speeches in the Commons on American affairs forced a committee of inquiry in 1779.

HOWE, Joseph. *See* CANADA-13.

HOWEL in Welsh names, *see* HYWEL.

HOWITZER. *See* ARTILLERY.

HOWLEY, William (1766-1848) was Prof. of Divinity at Oxford from 1809 to 1813, Bp. of London from 1813 and supported the proceedings against Q. Caroline in 1820. He became Abp. of Canterbury in 1828. Rigidly conservative, he opposed R. Catholic emancipation in 1829, the Reform Bill in 1831 and Jewish Relief in 1833. In 1839 he carried a vote of censure on Lord John Russell's education scheme.

HUBERTUSBURG, P. of (15 Feb. 1763) between Prussia,

Austria and Saxony, re-established the territorial boundaries of those states as at the beginning of the Seven Years War. *See* PARIS, P. OF 1763.

HUBERT, WALTER (?-1205), a chancery clerk educated in the household of his mother's brother-in-law, Ranulf Glanville, became Dean of York in 1186 and in 1188 founded W. Dereham Abbey for his patron's soul. It is possible that he wrote the *De Legibus et consuetudinibus regni Anglie* (Lat = The Laws and Customs of the Kingdom of England) and ascribed it to Glanville after whom it is known. He was also elected Abp. of York but was considered too junior for the post and in 1189 Richard I made him Bp. of Salisbury instead. He went with Richard on Crusade, distinguishing himself in Syria, visited Jerusalem and visited Richard during his captivity. By this time his abilities were widely known.

(2) Baldwin, Abp. of Canterbury, died at Acre in Nov. 1190. In Mar. 1193 Richard obtained the see for Hubert. In Jan. 1194 he made him Justiciar. He reached England in Apr. and in Mar. 1195, with his pallium, Pope Celestine III sent him a legatine commission. He was the chief executive of the realm. His main functions were to keep civil and ecclesiastical order and to raise funds for Richard's foreign policy. Neither devout nor scholarly, he achieved public stability in church and state by an unusually careful adherence to law, which he understood better than most. His first action was to investigate crown rights and official corruption through an Eyre. In 1195 he set up the peace keeping machinery by the *Edictum Regium* (Lat = Royal Decree) and in 1196 he promulgated standard weights and measures. Meanwhile the taxes which he had to levy made him increasingly unpopular. He had to put down William fitz Osbern's London insurrection in 1196 and smoked him out of sanctuary in order to hang him. The bishops of Lincoln and Salisbury denied liability for overseas knight-service in order to evade scutage. There was widespread opposition to a survey in preparation for a new Danegeld. The papacy, too, was becoming uncomfortable at the incompatibilities (as evidenced by fitz Osbern's fate) between the Justiciarship and the Primacy. In Aug. 1198 he resigned the Justiciarship.

(3) In May 1199, however, he accepted the Chancellorship from K. John. He had inherited and was still involved in a furious quarrel with the monks of his cathedral but his capacity for practical administration now found important use. He had, as Justiciar, introduced the Common Pleas system of triple indenture (Fines). From June 1199 the Chancery fees were reduced and the Charter, patent and other Chancery rolls begun. The Chancery became a regular secretariat. In 1200 he and John quarrelled briefly and in 1201 he had to give way to the monks but meanwhile he was holding legatine councils and extending, with John's encouragement, the practice of calling in suits from private jurisdictions by the writ *praecipe*. By the time of his death the technical machinery of uniform justice was in existence.

HUDSON, George (1800-71) the 'railway king' made a fortune as a York draper by 1830, when he founded a bank. He was Lord Mayor of York in 1837 and became manager of the York and N. Midland Rly in 1839. He cashed in on the speculative fever for promoting railways, mostly in the N.E., and launched many shaky railway companies. He was M.P. for Sunderland from 1845. His dishonest prospectuses brought in large sums but public disquiet grew progressively louder and in 1854 he left the country. The negotiations to settle his affairs without entirely ruining his shareholders lasted until 1868. A few of his amalgamations benefited the public, particularly the Midland Railway.

HUDSON, Henry (?-1611) searched on behalf of the Muscovy Co. for a northern passage to the Orient in 1608. In 1609 the Dutch East India Co. employed him first in an attempt North-Eastwards (which reached

Novaya Zemlya) and then North-Westwards. His survey from Nova Scotia to Sandy Hook discredited the belief in a strait across America at a low latitude and his ascent of the Hudson River as far as Albany founded the Dutch claim to that area. Finally in 1610 he commanded an English attempt to find the Passage and entered Hudson's Bay, where mutineers set him adrift.

HUDSON, Robert Spear (1886-1957) 1st Vist. HUDSON (1952), a diplomat, went into politics and became Conservative M.P. for Whitehaven from 1924 to 1929 and for Southport from 1931 to 1952. After minor ministerial posts he was Sec. for Overseas Trade from 1937 to 1940 and then, after two months as Min. of Shipping, became, to everyone's astonishment, Min. of Agriculture and Fisheries. It was a brilliant appointment. By setting up a system of agricultural supervision manned by thousands of volunteers (whom he constantly visited) from agriculture itself and by guaranteed markets and prices he had, by 1944, raised the arable area by 69% and convinced the country of the need for a balanced economy. This agricultural revolution saved vital shipping during World War II and profoundly affected the balance of payments until Britain joined the E.E.C.

HUDSONS BAY, COMPANY and TERRITORY (Canada). The bay, which is shallow and icebound for nine months in the year, has rich salmon, walrus and whale fisheries which enabled Henry Hudson to penetrate it in 1610. The fur bearing animals of the adjacent forests attracted exploitation and brought the foundation of the Co. under Prince Rupert in 1670. The French recognised the Co's monopoly as part of the Utrecht settlement (1713) but its turnover remained low because of the geographical difficulties, until the Baltic powers began to threaten the vital British trade in naval stores and timber and the shipbuilders turned perforce to Canadian sources. The sparse trapping population was now supplemented by lumberjacks and other timber workers; Co. ships grew in size and began to call in other areas — especially after the victorious Seven Years War opened up the St. Lawrence and the Great Lakes. The territory and Ontario prospered hand in hand with the Co. until the mid 19th cent. The winding up of the HEIC after the Indian Mutiny formed a precedent for similar proposals when there were social disturbances in Canada and in 1863 the Co. was deprived of its monopoly and quasi-sovereign functions. It retained, however, its immense properties which became important with the discovery of rich mineral deposits and later of oil. The Co. then developed from a primarily British trans-Atlantic exporting agency into a Canada-wide multi-purpose business and shopping concern, with the exploitation of natural resources for a mainly Canadian market as a Co-equal enterprise. *See* CHARTERED COMPANIES.

HUE AND CRY, the pursuit (as noisily as possible) of criminals, the pursuers having the right of arrest. Under the laws of Edgar and Athelstan it was obligatory on the men of each hundred and this was reinforced in subsequent legislation, notably the Statute of Westminster. Those who failed to join in were liable to a fine; so were those who displayed a misplaced enthusiasm or raised one maliciously.

HUFF-DUFF. See COMMERCE PROTECTION, NAVAL c-8.

HUGH OF AVRANCHES (?-?), *vicomte* of Avranches, a leading supporter and possibly a nephew of William I, played a major part in the Norman Conquest. He was given many scattered properties and in 1071 the Marcher Earldom of Chester. He extended this over much of northern Wales and built a castle in Anglesey but most of these gains were permanently lost again to the Welsh in 1094. He had been loyal to William II during the English revolt of 1088 and so, unscathed, supported the King's brother Henry (later Henry I) when William and Robert of Normandy deprived him of Cherbourg and Mont St. Michel in 1091. It was at his invitation that St. Anselm

came to England to install monks from Bec at St. Werburgh's, Chester, a visit which ended with Anselm becoming Abp. of Canterbury.

HUGH OF CYFEILIOG. See CHESHIRE.

HUGH OF GRANTMESNIL (?-1094) became either abbot or protector of St. Evroul (Normandy) in 1059 but was exiled and went to Italy in 1063. He rejoined William I in time to invade England in 1066 and became sheriff in Hampshire in 1067 but returned to Normandy in 1068. A baronial opportunist, in 1088 he joined the opposition to William Rufus but in 1091 he was involved in a private war with Robert of Bellême. He died a monk.

HUGH OF LINCOLN or AVALON, St. (?1135-1200), burser of the Grande Chartreuse, was invited by Henry II in about 1175 to become head of the Charterhouse at Witham (Som.) and was one of his most respected advisers. He was liberal to the poor and sick but sceptical of alleged miracles. From 1186 he was Bp. of Lincoln where he enjoyed great popularity as a defender of ordinary folk against the exactions of powerful and royal officials. All the same he represented the King on an embassy in 1188. After Richard I's accession he joined the opposition to the Justiciar Longchamp but in 1194 opposed and excommunicated John. In 1198 he led the opponents of a money grant to the crown but had no difficulty in pacifying Richard at a personal interview. He partly rebuilt Lincoln Cathedral, establishing the Guild of St. Mary for the purpose.

HUGH OF LINCOLN, Little St. (?1246-55) was falsely supposed to have been crucified by a Jew of Lincoln. The impossible story became a focus for anti-semitic feeling.

HUGHENDEN MANOR (Bucks). Disraeli needed a landed estate in order to be a credible leader of an essentially land-owners' party, besides liking the life which such a possession made possible. With £35,000 lent him by the Bentinck family he bought Hughenden, built most of the Victorian mansion and lived there from 1848 to 1881.

HUGHES, William Morris (1864-1952). See AUSTRALIA-11.

HUGH (?-1235) and JOCELYN (?-1242) of WELLS were brothers. **(1)** Hugh was archdeacon of Wells from 1204 and Bp. of Lincoln from 1209, but as a follower of Stephen Langton lived in exile until 1213 when he returned and supported John against the baronage. For his dealings with the French party he was heavily fined in 1217. Chiefly memorable for his pastoral activities, he established vicarages in parishes appropriated by monasteries: with Grosseteste he carried out visitations in his large diocese and he continued the building of the Cathedral. He and his brother **(2)** Jocelyn reorganised Wells Cathedral, which Jocelyn largely built. He was Bp. of Bath and Glastonbury from 1206, witnessed Magna Carta, was a justice in Eyre in the West in 1218 and supported Langton against Fawkes de Bréauté in 1224.

HUGUENOTS were French Calvinists, first organised militarily and politically at the SYNOD OF PARIS in 1559, when the accession of Francis II brought the R Catholic Guises to power at court. These seized the opportunity of a political demonstration against themselves to call it a conspiracy against the throne and engineered the judicial murder of several hundred notables, mostly protestants, at Amboise. This TUMULT OF AMBOISE made civil war inevitable.

(2) Francis died within a year and Catherine dei Medici became regent for Charles IX. She favoured compromise, and in 1562 armed negotiations (The Colloquy of Poissy) ended in the *Edict of St. Germain* which gave legal recognition to the practice of Calvinism. Not only religion was at stake; there were old geographical, dynastic and international involvements. Huguenot strength was in the south and its leaders included the Princes of Condé, most of the royal family of Navarre (*see* BOURBON) and the great house of Montmorency and Coligny, soon allied by marriage to the House of Orange. The Catholic League was based on

Paris and the East. Its Guise leaders included three cardinals, the Dukes of an autonomous Lorraine, and Mary, Dowager Queen and Regent of Scotland, where she was supported by French troops. Her daughter Mary Q. of Scots had been married to the King, Francis II, himself but her mother having died in 1560 she returned to Scotland in 1561.

(3) The alliance of the French and Scots R. Catholics threatened the new protestant England of Elizabeth. She worked with the Scots protestants, who in 1560 had secured power at the Queen Regent's death, and had sent the French troops home. In Mar. 1562 the Duke of Guise's retainers massacred some Huguenots at Vassy. This inaugurated the ferocious 37-year long civil war known as the **Wars of Religion.** It consisted of eight military struggles each patched up by an insincere agreement, which failed to end the intrigues, riots and murders in between.

(4) The Huguenots sought foreign aid. On the analogy of her Scottish policy, Elizabeth responded. By the Hampton Court treaty (Sept. 1562) she occupied Le Havre as a lien for Calais from Oct. until July 1563. Meantime the contestants had fought an indecisive battle at Dreux and Guise had been murdered. In Mar. they made the *Peace* (or Edict) *of Amboise*. The war ended in Apr. 1564 with the Anglo-French T. of Troyes.

(5) France was hemmed in by enemies, of whom Habsburg Spain with its Italian and Flemish possessions was the most threatening. A divided France might, so it seemed to Catherine dei Medici, fall to a Spanish intervention. She sought to placate Philip II's oppressive regime by anti-Huguenot interpretations of the Edict of Amboise. In June 1565 during a routine progress she met the Duke of Alba at Bayonne.

(6) The Second and Third Wars arose out of the beginnings of the Dutch Protestant rebellion, which was then confined to piracy under the flag of the House of Orange and civil commotions in the towns. The pirates (*'Gueux de mer'*) were based on English waters and the commotions were fanned by English propaganda. In 1566 Alba was sent by way of Italy to put down the Dutch. In 1567 Catherine raised troops against Alba but countermanded operations. The Huguenots suspected that the troops might now be used against themselves and rose. William of Orange joined them; defeated in battle they could not, however, be suppressed. In Aug. 1570 they were amnestied at the *P of St. Germain* and were given four fortresses including La Rochelle as security. This precedent had important consequences.

(7) Complicated diplomatic twists followed. The Huguenots Henry of Navarre and Coligny joined Catherine's council. Their policy was anti-Spanish. Elizabeth, through Murray's assassination, had lost the principal support of her Scottish influence. By the T. of Blois (Apr. 1572) the French and English agreed to support each other against Spanish attack and the French abandoned the Scots R. Catholics. Meantime Elizabeth was seeking a settlement with the Spanish govt. in the Netherlands, which had embargoed English commerce in reprisal for English unofficial support of the *Gueux de mer*. An accommodation was reached and the *Gueux* expelled from English waters. They promptly crossed to Holland, seized Brill and kindled the Dutch revolution. The enmity between the Huguenots and the R. Catholics however continued. Coligny proposed that the parties should co-operate against Spain (which in the summer was making headway against the Dutch rebels) and that the Protestant Henry of Navarre should marry the R. Catholic Margarite of Valois. The marriage was agreed, but not the attack on Spain because the Guises would not help the Dutch protestants (currently besieged in Mons).

(8) In July 1572 a compromise was reached. A Huguenot force was to relieve Mons, but there was to be no war with Spain. The force accordingly set out but was annihilated on 17 July. This shook Huguenot influence and decided Catherine in favour of peace.

(9) Meantime everyone of importance was converging with their armed retainers on Paris for the wedding, and Catherine apparently thought of ending the anti-Spanish movement and the political deadlock by assassinating Coligny. The festivities began on 17 Aug. On 22 Aug. Coligny was shot and wounded; the angry Huguenots, who blamed Guise, threatened reprisals. It seemed as if a fourth War of Religion would break out in the streets of Paris. Catherine therefore decided to strike the first blow; she overbore the characterless King Charles IX and secured the use of the royal guard and the support of the Paris mob.

(10) The signal (*Tocsin*) was given early in the morning of 24 Aug. (St. Batholomew's Night) by the bells of St. Germain l'Auxerrois. The massacre lasted for three days and spread to some other R. Catholic towns in the provinces.

(11) The consequences were not those expected by the Queen. She had her Fourth War just the same. The massacre gave the survivors a desperate strength and the sympathy of decent opinion. It also brought to leadership Henry of Navarre who, as a King and Prince of the Blood, had escaped. In the ensuing years Huguenotism owed its life to his soldierly abilities, personal brilliance and statesmanship. Moreover, when Charles IX was succeeded in 1574 by the homosexual Henry III, Navarre became not only the presumptive but the probable heir to the French throne. Meantime the Huguenots held on grimly in La Rochelle; English ships under such men as Sir Walter Raleigh brought them unofficial succour and Elizabeth financed a Palatine army to threaten the frontier. The Fifth War ended in May 1576 with the *Edict of Beaulieu*. The short Sixth War of 1577 ended with the *Peace of Bergerac*, which enabled the Huguenots to practise their religion everywhere save in Paris.

(12) The peace lasted, with a minor intermission in 1580, until 1586. The parties were merely gathering strength. The Dutch war of liberation was at its height. R. Catholics and Huguenots each thought that the victory of their Dutch sympathisers would usher in the downfall of their French opponents. Each struggled to commit the crown to war in the interest of its friends. Moreover the Guises and Don John of Austria, the new Spanish Governor of the Netherlands, had agreed to establish R. Catholic supremacy not only in their respective countries but in England. Since a French occupation of the Netherlands by either party endangered English interests as much as a Spanish victory, Elizabeth sought to re-establish the ancient Dutch privileges under a weakened Spanish suzerainty. In June 1578, however, the Spaniards won the B. of Gembloux and the Dutch seemed to be *in extremis*. They called in the Huguenots headed by the royal Duke of Anjou. His intervention was largely ineffectual but shortage of money and the plague (which killed Don John) frustrated the Spaniards until 1584 when, under Parma, they resumed their advance. By then William of Orange had been assassinated and Anjou was dead.

(13) To the Guises this seemed the moment of opportunity. In Jan. 1585 they came to a secret agreement at Joinville with Spain and in Mar., with Spanish subsidies, they proclaimed the Holy League to prevent the succession of Henry of Navarre. In Aug. Parma sacked Antwerp. Elizabeth replied by sending, for the first time, a military expedition to Holland under Leicester. Militarily a failure, it had some value as a distraction. Meantime the Spanish govt. was preparing the Armada which was to sail to Belgium, embark Parma's troops and land them in England. For this a R. Catholic or at least a neutralised France was necessary but in Oct.

1587 the forces of the Holy League had suffered a serious defeat at the hands of Henry of Navarre at the B. of Coutras; accordingly a Spanish-Guise conspiracy was organised which overpowered the govt. of Henry III at Paris in a coup known as the Day of Barricades (May 1588). The Armada was defeated in July and Aug. and in Dec. 1588 Henry III managed to kill Guise and his brother, the Cardinal of Lorraine, at Blois. These events averted the threat to England, Holland and the Huguenots.

(14) Henry of Navarre came to the French throne in 1589 as Henry IV on the murder of his predecessor and defeated the League at Ivry. He then pacified the country by embracing R. Catholicism while issuing the famous *Edict of Nantes* in Apr. 1598, which legalised Calvinist practices and gave the Huguenots certain fortified strongholds for their protection.

(15) He had married Marie dei Medici and she became regent for Louis XIII when he was assassinated in 1610. Her policy of friendship with Spain alarmed the Huguenots who in 1615 supported Condo's armed protest against it. In 1620 an attempt to restore R. Catholic property in Navarre (not technically subject to the Edict of Nantes) caused a revolt led by the Duc de Rohan and the subsequent *P. of Montpellier* (Aug. 1622) deprived the Huguenots of all their strongholds except La Rochelle and Montauban. In 1624 Card. Richelieu came to power. His anti-Habsburg policy suited the Huguenots but his military and naval preparations in southern French ports alarmed them. The treaties of Madrid and Monçon (1626) ended the conflict with Spain and Austria and left him face to face with the Huguenots who sought help from Charles I and his minister Buckingham. Their shortlived uprising ended in a compromise in 1626 but in 1627 they assisted Buckingham's attack on the Ile de Ré. The Cardinal now mobilised fully against them and despite English efforts at relief, La Rochelle capitulated in 1628 after a year's siege. The *P. of Alais* of 1629 retained the religious settlement of the Edict of Nantes but abolished all its military and political provisions. This situation was confirmed in Louis XIV's name in 1642 and maintained by Card. Mazarin until his death in 1661.

(16) But the Huguenots were defenceless and Louis XIV fanatical and totalitarian. The church demanded successfully that the operation of the Edict should be restricted to its most literal interpretation. Violent encroachments upon Huguenot privileges went unpunished and from 1681 they were persecuted by the quartering of dragoons upon protestant households. This led to mass "conversions". In 1685 the Edict was formally revoked and there was a mass migration of Huguenots to Hamburg, Prussia and England, where they still have a church in London, a chapel in Canterbury cathedral and their recognisable surnames in many places.

HULKS were old moored warships originally used as temporary prisons pending transportation and later used in substitution for transportation. They and transportation were abolished in 1853.

HULL (1) was founded by the Holderness Abbey of Meaux as WYKE-UPON-HULL (c. 1190) and bought and rebuilt by Edward I as KINGSTON-UPON-HULL in 1293 (when the lordship of Holderness escheated) as a base for Scottish wars. Its prosperity was already in wool (later cloth) exports in return for Rhenish and French wine and Baltic products but its development was partly due to the decline of Hedon and eventual inundation of Ravenspur. Edward I chartered it as a free borough in 1299 and he built quays and established a ferry. The town was fortified in 1322 because of the defeats in Scotland. It became a county of its own in 1440 and its area, slightly enlarged in 1447, remained the same until 1835.

(2) The northern trade dominated the town's economy but was supplemented from the 18th cent. by whaling and since 1850 by North Sea fisheries. The Humber, though an excellent haven, obstructed southward movement by land so that Grimsby grew up as a port for Lincolnshire. Its late 15th cent. trade was the foundation of the de la Pole family's power; the customs were the main financial support of the northern military establishments. The town's rejection of Charles I at the opening of the Civil War was a major royalist set-back and they acknowledged its importance by besieging it twice. Nothing, however, held Hull back and the industrial revolution stimulated it still further by diversifying its trade. It acquired a growing ring of suburbs and in the 19th and 20th cents. constantly enlarged its boundaries by private legislation. It also extended its docks, storage and processing industries and established engineering industries originally related to shipbuilding. It was badly damaged in World War II.

HULLE, Robert (?-1442), distinguished Oxford mason and architect, succeeded William Wynford at Winchester in 1400 and finished the cathedral nave and most of the college.

HUMAN-ISM-ISTS (1) This 16th cent. term (*see para 3 below*) related to the influence of Greek and Latin writers. In the middle ages Greek authors were known, very incompletely, through Latin ones and their main influence, being pre-Christian, was literary and historical. Virgil, Horace, Lucian, Sallust, Cicero and Seneca were the best known before the end of the 12th cent. and were admired for their style and pungency more than the values which they represented, partly because they were often read in collections of excerpts. They inspired an elegant Latinity and an interest in human personality, exemplified in the works of the 12th cent. Walter Map, Giraldus Cambrensis and John of Salisbury, whose *Policraticus* influenced later writers such as John of Wales.

(2) The 13th cent. rediscovery and circulation of Aristotle and the increased concentration of the universities on theology and law effected an accidental reaction against such an approach to the classics (though John of Wales and the chronicler Thomas Walsingham stood in the earlier tradition) but in the 15th cent. classical studies advanced as improved proficiency in Greek and the length of Aristotle's primacy in the universities were supplemented by the westward migration of Byzantine scholars. This stimulated appetites for other classical (including Hebrew) authors but, above all, Plato. Greek was taught in England by visiting Italians, notably Poggio Bracciolini, Piero del Monte and Frulovisi, attracted by patrons such as Card. Beaufort and D. Humphrey of Gloucester and by the mistaken belief that English libraries contained classical writings awaiting discovery. In reply some of their pupils such as Adam de Moleyns and John Free visited Italy to look for unknown works or continue their Greek studies. Considerable libraries were assembled, particularly by D. Humphrey; a school of neo-Platonism developed and also, now, an ornate involved style of writing and oratory.

(3) By the mid 15th cent. the mediaeval theocentric concentration of thought, which long co-existed with the rising humanism, was seen to leave many practical questions of philosophy, science and morals unanswered, while itself being practised too often by ecclesiastics whose behaviour was open to criticism. Humanism was not a body of doctrine but an attitude to the contemporary scene, shared by rising numbers of Renaissance intellectuals, who tended to direct their attention away from the mysteries of the divine to the difficult but possibly soluble problems of the human. This initial humility was inspired and sustained by the revived classical studies earlier in the century.

(4) The greatest of the humanists is considered to have been Erasmus of Rotterdam who, with his friends Fisher, More, Grocyn and Warham, ultimately caused a classical revolution in English education and profoundly influenced the cast of European thought.

675

HUMANE SOCIETY, ROYAL (R.H.S.) to encourage bravery or enterprise in the preservation and restoration of life, was founded by Dr. Wm. Howes (1736-1808) and friends in 1774 and acquired permanent royal patronage in 1783. Its medals were permitted to be worn (on the right hand side) in 1869.

HUMAN RIGHTS, UNIVERSAL DECLARATION OF (1948). The Nazi and Japanese atrocities were already known in outline in 1941 when reference to a need for such a declaration was inserted in the Atlantic Charter and debated at Dumbarton Oaks (1944). It also appeared in the preamble to the United Nations Charter adopted at San Francisco (1945). The Tokyo and Nuremberg trials revealed the full horror of these barbarities but not those committed by the Russians. The Declaration was adopted by the General Assembly of the United Nations, the three Russian member states, Poland, Czechoslovakia, Yugoslavia, S. Africa and Saudi Arabia (i.e. the forced labour states) abstaining. Its 31 Articles, not being binding, had little effect, for in countries which already observed them there were unnecessary and in the others they could not be enforced. Even the moral influence of the articles is doubtful because few people know what they contain other than precepts which people of decency observe without thinking.

HUMBLE PETITION AND ADVICE (Mar. 1657). *See* COMMONWEALTH AND PROTECTORATE-14.

HUMBOLDT, von (1) Karl Wilhelm (1767-1835), celebrated liberal philosopher and statesman, became head of the Prussian dept. of Education in 1809 and effective founder of Berlin Univ. He was a Prussian rep. at the Congress of Vienna but, being in opposition to the policy of Hardenberg and Metternich, was sent abroad (Minister in London 1816-7) and dismissed in 1819. The even more celebrated **(2) Friedrich Heinrich (1769-1859)** geologist and naturalist explored America from Peru to Mexico as well as Central Asia and his Berlin lectures of 1827-8, published under the title *Cosmos,* were the foundation of scientific advances in many fields.

HUME, David (1711-76), philosopher and historian, was a Scots lawyer and lived in France from 1734 to 1737. His anonymous *Treatise of Human Nature* appeared in 1739 but he came to prominence with his *Essays Moral and Political,* published in 1741 and 1742, which attracted the powerful patronage of Bp. Butler and the M. of Annandale. As an indirect result he became Gen. St. Clair's Judge-advocate on the Lorient Expedition (1747) and his sec. on the military mission to Vienna and Turin (1748). During this period he also wrote his *Philosophical Essays.* In 1751 he published his *Enquiry Concerning Morals* and in 1752, when he became Keeper of the Edinburgh Advocates Library, his *Political Discourses.* He also became Sec. of the Edinburgh Philosophical Society. He now began to write his works on English history, the last of which was published in 1761. In 1763 he accompanied Lord Hertford's embassy to Paris where he was an enormous social and diplomatic success and procured an English pension for Rousseau. He came to London in 1767 and was Seymour Conway's U/Sec. until 1768, after which he returned to Edinburgh. Charming, famous, influential in England, his native Scottish universities always treated him with reserve because of his reputed scepticism. As a political economist he partly anticipated Adam Smith in his doubts of the validity of mercantilism.

HUME of POLWORTH (1) Sir Patrick (1641-1724) 1st Ld. POLWORTH (sc. 1689), 1st E. of MARCHMONT (1697), a Scots M.P. in 1665, was a strong opponent of Lauderdale and of Claverhouse's actions (*see* GRAHAM) against the covenanters in 1675 to 1679. He was imprisoned for organising a petition against them and became a public supporter of Monmouth. In 1685, suspected of complicity in the Rye House Plot, he fled abroad and, eventually, under the name of **WALLACE** practised as a surgeon at Utrecht and became an adviser on Scottish affairs to William of Orange, whom he accompanied to England. William made him a Scottish peer and privy councillor but he also had legal talents and training and he was sheriff of Berwickshire from 1692 to 1710, a Lord of Session from 1693 and Scottish Lord Chancellor from 1696 to 1702. He was largely responsible for incorporating the establishment of the Church of Scotland in the Act of Union (1707) and he proposed the Hanoverian succession. His son **(2) Alexander (Campbell) (1675-1740) 2nd E.,** was minister in Denmark from 1715 to 1722 and at the Cambrai congress of 1722. His son **(3) Hugh (1708-94) 3rd E.,** horticulturalist and horseman, was an opponent of Walpole as an M.P. from 1734 to 1740, a friend of Bolingbroke and Chesterfield and an executor of the Duchess of Marlborough and Alexander Pope.

HUMPHREY, DUKE. *See* GLOUCESTER.

HUNDRED (Eng.) WAPENTAKE (Dan.) or WARD (Border) (1) Assemblies (or *Gemots*) for only part of a shire were a necessary, probably spontaneous, feature of early life to deal with disputes, disturbances or outside incursions. The wapentake was an armed assembly in the Danish occupied areas, possibly held in part to ensure that everyone who should had weapons. The border ward often had to deal with matters of vigilance. The catchment areas for these assemblies were a matter of common knowledge. In Wessex they were later settled at a round 100 hides for the assessment of public obligations and taxes. The earliest reference to Hundreds appears in the Laws of Edmund (939-46) in which their existence is assumed. Hundreds spread from Wessex across England with the Saxon reconquest and Wapentakes (which were on average smaller) were absorbed into the Hundred system as the reconquest progressed. The figure 100 soon had little relevance to the purpose of these areas.

(2) The main function of the Hundred came to be to adjust taxation, to settle local disputes and to act as a police unit. Since taxes were assessed on the hundred but land ownership changed and land itself was constantly going in and out of cultivation, many disputes originated from these assessments but whatever the dispute the *gemot* or court consisted of the local suitors under the presidency of the King's Reeve. Many hundreds were based on royal manors or grouped round them and the president was usually the reeve of this manor. The court met every four weeks in the open air and early acquired the functions of the local peace guilds which existed to put down theft; and since it was ready to function as a peace keeping body, it was natural to make the hundred liable for *murdrum* and the basis of the frank pledge system. It also had miscellaneous work: land transfers might be made and there might be small cases of defamation, debt and presentments for bad ale or bread.

(3) After the Conquest the reeve turned into a bailiff; about a 100 hundreds were in private hands but by 1272 358 out of 628 hundreds were. Suit of court had become appurtenant to particular holdings and for the ordinary meetings the suitors arranged to attend by rota. The sheriff, however, held a six-monthly "law hundred" or tourn which everyone attended and the Stat. of Winchester made the hundred liable for robberies. By this time, however, Edward I's judicial reforms were removing the real judicial work from shire and hundred courts alike and though particular, especially private, hundreds such as Salford and Wirral continued to function actively until the 19th cent. the rest slowly died out.

HUNDRED ASSOCIATES, CO. *See* CANADA-3.

HUNDRED DAYS (Mar-June 1815). The period between Bonaparte's escape from Elba and his surrender after Waterloo.

HUNDRED ROLLS survive from royal inquests of 1255,

1274-5 and 1279, intended to recover royal rights and demesnes and to check abuses by officials. The principal abuses discovered were failure to execute writs, the manipulation of jurors and peculation. One of the chief fruits of the inquest of 1274-5 was the Statute of Westminster of 1275.

HUNDRED YEARS WAR. This unfortunate expression, consecrated by habit, is common to text books in all languages. It relates conventionally to a period from 1328 to 1453 when England and France were said to be at war. In fact there were wars of a similar kind before 1328 and this series continued after 1453. Moreover, other countries were involved. Apart from the wars before 1328 there were five main groups of hostilities each consisting of comparatively short, mostly summer, campaigns interrupted by more or less sanguinary truces, some lasting for many years. It is perhaps convenient to name each group of hostilities thus: **(1)** THE FIRST WARS OF THE FRENCH SUCCESSION 1328-60 (*see* PHILIP VI; JOHN II OF FRANCE; EDWARD III), **(2)** THE WARS OF AQUITAINE 1364-82 (*see* JOHN II; CHARLES V OF FRANCE AND AQUITAINE), **(3)** THE SECOND WAR OF THE FRENCH SUCCESSION 1415-35 (*see* CHARLES XI AND XII OF FRANCE; AQUITAINE; JOAN OF ARC), **(4)** THE WARS OF FRENCH UNIFICATION 1436-75 (*see* CHARLES VII; LOUIS Xi; AQUITAINE), **(5)** THE WAR OF THE BURGUNDIAN SUCCESSION 1477-92 (*see* LOUIS XI AND CHARLES VIII).

HUNGARY (1) Magyar nomads under Arpad and his family settled the present area and parts of Transylvania in the 9th cent. and came into collision with the Germans in the 10th. Istvan or St. Stephen (?-1038) gave them institutions suitable for a territorial state namely a monarchy at Buda, an endowed church centred on Esztergom and a local administration. He obtained political recognition from the Byzantine Emperor but, in return for Papal support, the Church was a Latin-speaking western church. Magyar was a central Asiatic language intelligible only to Magyars and amounting to a barrier between them as a ruling caste (*populus* or people) and the indigenous peasantry (*plebs*), until the plebs learned to speak it. Similarly it represented a potentially dangerous isolatory factor in the wider world. Hence Latin, the Church language of the West, was embraced as the second language of the populus and govt. This linked them psychologically with Rome and the Papacy against German colonising aggressions while tribal and eventually Mongol pressure from the N.E. linked them militarily with the Byzantines.

(2) These essentially unstable balances of a minority populus over a majority plebs and a populus-based state between greater powers to the East and N.W. remained a feature of Hungarian politics and history into modern times. Latin was still being taught as a spoken language in 1939.

(3) Through trade and diplomatic interplay between Germany, Hungary and Rome western connections developed. Two sons of K. Edmund Ironside went there in the time of Canute. One died; the other, Edward the Aetheling, married a daughter of Istvan and Gisela, a niece of the Emperor Henry II. As the survivor of the House of Cerdic he was Edward the Confessor's heir and in 1054 Bp. Ealdred of Worcester went abroad to negotiate his return. He arrived in England in 1056 but died before he reached court. Of his two children, one was Edgar the Aetheling (?-?1106) (q.v.), the other, St. Margaret (?-1093) was a splendid and luxury loving Queen to Malcolm Canmore of Scots. They Romanised the Scots church and developed a Scottish overseas trade. Matilda or Maud, who married the Emperor Henry V, was her grandchild.

(4) These events and the track of the earlier crusades show that land routes from the west across Hungary to the Byzantine Empire were in persistent use. Hungary was closer to the west than it since became. In 1186 K. Bela III approached Henry II, for example, for a marriage treaty and Richard I's roundabout route from Acre to England *via* the eastern part of his enemy's Austrian duchy is explicable if he meant to visit Bela, with whom he had diplomatic relations.

(5) The Arpad dynasty died out in the male line in 1301 and was followed successively by Angevin, Luxembourg, Transylvanian and Polish rulers but in 1353 the Turks crossed over into Europe. They took Adrianople in 1357, Sofia in 1382 and overthrew the Serbs on the Kossovo Polye in 1389. In response to Hungarian appeals a crusade was organised and disastrously defeated at Nicopolis in 1396. The Turkish onrush was however, halted by the Mongol invasion and capture of Bayazid I at Ankara in 1402. In the breathing space K. Sigismund was elected Emperor (1411) and he and his Hungarian diplomats were much involved in far-sighted efforts to unify the West by mediating between France and England, which he visited in 1416, and through the Council of Constance to settle controversies between Romanists, Orthodox and Bohemian Hussites.

(6) The Turkish resurgence began in 1429. Thenceforth Hungary was in the front line of European defence until the B. of Mohacs and the Turkish conquest of 1526 of all save the western march.

(7) This was disputed between the Habsburgs and local claimants. Pressburg (Bratislava) was the Royal capital: Buda the Turkish, and the area was the scene of endless minor and major Turkish wars complicated by religious and political revolts against the Habsburgs and by the quasi-independence of the Transylvanian princes. A Turkish army broke through to Austria in 1583. There was a Hungarian revolt from 1604 to 1606. The Turks besieged Vienna in 1683 but Buda was taken in the counter offensive of 1686. From 1703 to 1711 there was a major (protestant inspired) rebellion. These events gravely weakened Austrian participation in the wars of the League of Augsburg and the Spanish Succession. The Turkish threat continued almost to the end of the century. The French revolution, however, sowed new nationalist seeds and eventually resulted in Kossuth's great uprising of 1848. This was suppressed only with Russian help, but Hungarian stubbornness remained a feature of European politics because the Italian irredentists, especially Cavour, were prepared to subvert the Hungarians to weaken Austrian power in Italy. The Italian Kingdom came into existence in 1866. Hungary obtained equal status (*Ausgleich*) with Austria in 1867. Thereafter, because of the memory of 1848, the Hungarians were in foreign affairs the predominant influence in Habsburg policy. *See* AUSTRO-HUNGARY; HORTHY DE NAGYBANYA.

HUNGERFORD (1) Sir Thomas (?-1398) M.P. (Wilts and Somerset) and from 1357 to 1390 John of Gaunt's steward, was speaker of the Commons in 1377. His son **(2) Sir Walter (?-1449) 1st Ld. HUNGERFORD (1426)** was M.P. for Wilts. in 1400, 1404 and 1407, for Somerset in 1409 and again for Wilts. in 1413 and 1414 when he became speaker and later in the year English representative to the Council of Constance. He then served in the war at Agincourt in 1415, against Rouen and as commander of the fleet in 1418. He was one of Henry V's executors and a member of Gloucester's council and became steward of Henry VI's household in 1424 and Treasurer from 1427 to 1432. His son **(3) Robert (1409-59) 2nd Ld.,** acquired large estates in Cornwall through marriage. His son **(4) Robert (1431-64) Ld. MOLEYNS (1445)** in right of his wife and **3rd Ld. HUNGERFORD** maintained a feud with the Norfolk Pastons over the ownership of Gresham and, after being in prison in France from 1452 to 1459, returned as an active Lancastrian. After the B. of Towton in 1461 he accompanied Henry VI to the north and then went to France to negotiate help. On his return he was captured and beheaded at Hexham. His son **(5) Sir Walter (?-**

1516) was M.P. for Wilts. in 1477, fought at Bosworth and was a privy councillor to Henry VII and Henry VIII. His grandson **(6) Walter (1503-40) 1st Ld. HUNGERFORD of HEYTESBURY (1536),** one of Henry VIII's Esqs. and sheriff of Wilts in 1533, was executed with Thomas Cromwell. His son **(7) Sir Walter (1532-96)** got his father's attainder reversed in 1554. Of his three grandsons **(8) Anthony (?-1657)** was a royalist in Ireland. His half-brother **(9) Anthony (?-1657)** was a parliamentary colonel in Ireland and **(10) Sir Edward,** M.P. for Chippenham in the Short and Long Parliaments, was a local parliamentary commander in Wiltshire. The son of **(8)** above, **(11) Sir Edward (1632-1711)** was M.P. for Chippenham from 1660 to 1681. He was dismissed from the Lieutenancy for opposing the King in 1681 and from 1685 sat for Sussex boroughs, Shoreham (until 1690) and Steyning (1695 to 1702). From 1682 onwards he built and managed Hungerford Market (London) on the site now occupied by Charing Cross Station. Hence the name of Hungerford Bridge.

HUNSDON, Lords. *See* CAREY.

HUNT, George Ward (1825-77) was M.P. for Northants. from 1857, Ch. of the Exch. in 1868 and First Lord of the Admiralty from 1874 to 1877.

HUNT, Henry (1773-1835) "Orator Hunt" was active in radical politics in Wiltshire from 1800. He contested Bristol in 1812, took part in the Spa Fields demonstration in 1816, contested Westminster in 1816. He presided in 1819 over the Manchester 'Peterloo' demonstration and was sent to prison for two years as a result. He contested Somerset in 1826 and was at last elected for Preston in 1830-33.

HUNT (James Henry) Leigh (1784-1859) began to edit the *Examiner* in 1808, was unsuccessfully prosecuted for an article against army flogging in 1810 but was imprisoned for two years in 1813 for some reflections on the Prince Regent. He continued to edit the *Examiner* in prison where he was visited by the leading radicals of the time. In 1816 he introduced Shelley to Keats and made their work public. He launched the *Indicator* in 1819 and carried on the *Liberal* with Byron in Italy from 1822 to 1825. He also wrote a great many articles and works of his own. He appears as Skimpole in Dickens' *Bleak House.*

HUNT, William Holman (1827-1910). *See* PRE-RAPHAELITES.

HUNTINGDON,-SHIRE AND HONOUR. (*See also* CAMBRIDGE.) **(1)** The area had a poor soil and a sparse population under the Romans who first placed it in touch with the world by building Ermine Street (London-York). This crosses the Ouse from Godmanchester to Huntingdon. Occupied by the Middle Angles in the 6th cent., the area was absorbed into Mercia in the 7th. Between 870 and 874 the Danes overran the northern half and Ceolwulf's treaty of 877 ceded the southern to them too. They garrisoned Huntingdon but abandoned it in 921 when Edward the Elder defeated them at Tempsford. He repaired the town and the **SHIRE** developed around it.

(2) The English policy of converting the Danes led Aylwin, K. Edgar's foster brother, to endow the great Benedictine Abbey at Ramsey in 969. St. Neots, another Benedictine house under Ely, was endowed in 972. The priory of St. Ives, under Ramsey, was established a generation later.

(3) The shire had an earl only intermittently and was part of Mercia from about 970 until 1017. The second Danish invasions again brought it under Danish control, and Canute (r. 1016-35) expelled most of the English landowners, built a road from Ramsey to Peterborough and gave much of the land to Fenland monasteries or to Danish magnates. This represented a policy of reclaiming the fens, but the gifts to Thorkil, the most prominent Dane, were the germ from which sprang the important landowning complex later known as the **HONOUR** of

Huntingdon. There were Danish earls between 1017 and 1049 when the shire was briefly part of Harold Godwin's son's E. Anglia.

(4) By 1052, however, the Earldom had gone to Siward, E. of Northumbria. This set in train the events which associated the earldom and the future Honour with the Scottish crown. Siward died in 1055 and Harold's brother Tostig took over his power. A Northumbrian revolt drove him away and the property and titles came back to Waltheof, Siward's heir, in 1065. He married Judith, the niece of the Conqueror, who gave him Thorkil's lands, together with extensive properties in Northamptonshire and seven other shires and in Middlesex and London. This large scattered grant to Waltheof comprised the Honour.

(5) Waltheof was executed in 1076. His daughter Maud married Simon (I) of Senlis, who became Earl. They had two sons, Simon (II) and Waltheof (II). Earl Simon died in 1113 and K. Henry I then married Maud to K. David I of Scotland, to whom he granted the earldom and the honour with virtually extraterritorial immunities. David continued to hold them after Maud's death (1131) notwithstanding Simon (II's) prior right. They thus became an issue in the civil wars of Stephen, for Simon occupied the honour with Stephen's connivance and David supported Stephen's rival, the Empress Maud, in consequence. Stephen, however, bought David off in 1136 with an agreement whereby, *inter alia*, Northumberland and the honour were to go to David's son Henry.

(6) There was now a dispute at Ramsey. Abbot Walter had alienated many of the estates to his relatives. The monks, led by one Daniel, deposed him. He went to Rome for redress (1142) and thereupon Geoffrey de Mandeville, assisted by Earl Henry, revolted, seized the abbey and expelled the monks. Daniel set off for Rome too while Mandeville fortified Ramsey and raided the countryside as far as Cambridge. Walter won his case at Rome and returned to find the abbey a den of thieves. Ecclesiastical thunders did not move Geoffrey de Mandeville until, faced with a mortal illness, he instructed his son to give the abbey up. Walter got it back, much impoverished, in about 1146. This notorious local war (mentioned in the Peterborough Chronicle) devastated much of the shire.

(7) Earl Henry died in 1152. Simon (II) succeeded him but died in 1153. His son Simon (III) being under age K. Henry II gave the earldom and honour to Malcolm IV (The Maiden) of Scotland, from whom it passed in 1165 to his brother William the Lion. This prolonged the dispute between the Kings of Scots and the Senlis. In 1174 William supported the rebellion of Henry the Young King and Simon (III) took charge of the siege of Huntingdon, took it and demolished the wooden castle. He was recognised as earl for his services but died without issue in 1184 whereupon the earldom and the honour were regranted to William the Lion, who promptly (1185) resigned them to his brother David.

(8) K. David made Fotheringhay the *caput* because of the destruction at Huntingdon. He was followed (1219) by John the Scot who died childless in 1237 when the honour was partitioned between his three sisters. These each married into families which later competed for the Scottish crown, namely the Bruces, Balliols and Hastings. Hence, as a result of Edward I's Scottish politics, the Balliol part was forfeited in 1296 and the Bruce part in 1304. The Balliol part was granted to John of Brittany, E. of Richmond, in 1306 and reverted finally to the Crown in 1341. With the escheat of the Hastings part in 1389 the honour was permanently united under the Crown. It was maintained as a distinct entity with baron's motes at Fotheringhay, Earls Barton and Tottenham Court. Its rents were assigned for at least two queens' dowers. Katharine of Aragon, after her divorce, was settled first at Buckden and later at Kimbolton. Fotheringhay was the place of Mary Q. of Scots imprisonment and death and was consequently demolished by her son James I.

(9) Meanwhile the monasteries, including Norman and Angevin foundations, besides acquiring many manors, had impropriated many livings. Richard Williams (otherwise Cromwell), nephew of Thos. Cromwell's wife, bought up the property of the dissolved monasteries and the convents of Ramsey, Sawtry and the Austin Canons at Huntingdon and Hinchinbroke. He also became sheriff. The Cromwells now dominated the shire, much of which they owned until they impoverished themselves at the end of the century; they then parted with some of their power and property to the Kimbolton Montagues. The great Oliver Cromwell was born at Huntingdon in 1599 and had the family influence at his back but the shire's parliamentary loyalty was never absolute.

(10) At the Restoration the influence of the Montagues and their kinsmen the Wortleys became very strong. M.P.s for both the town and the county being drawn from that family or elected on their nomination, but there was an internal family feud: some Wortleys were whigs, some Montagues Tory; hence politics revolved around the interest which a party had with the appropriate branch of the family. Between 1660 and 1832 there were 39 general and 11 by-elections (11 and 3 contested) for the county and 39 general elections and 2 by-elections (8 and 3 contested) for the borough. The family patronage was maintained with the aid of the new party organisations as late as 1868. The town lost a member in that year and the other in 1884 when the county was divided into two single member constituencies, amalgamated into one in 1918. In the period after 1868 the county representation was generally Tory, though Liberals were returned in 1885 and 1906.

(11) As the area was entirely agricultural the effect of inclosures and fen drainage was particularly important, especially after the dissolution of the monasteries. Reclamation began in the 1550s and greatly increased the productive land: the large scale 18th cent. inclosures had converted about 74% of the land then available to pasture by 1800 but the population had increased by about 16% since 1750. The general prosperity continued until the repeal of the Corn Laws in 1846 placed the county at the mercy of movements in world food prices and involved it in the long agricultural depression (interrupted by two World Wars) after 1870.

HUNTLY, Earls and Marquesses of. *See* GORDON.

HURONS were a confederacy of Indian tribes which originally inhabited Ontario. They were at feud with the Iroquois, who obtained firearms and almost destroyed them between 1648 and 1650. Their main remnants, known as Wyandots in Michigan and Ohio, were allied with the British in the wars of the 1770s and 1812. They bred a type of chicken named after them.

HURON TRACT. A triangular area fronting for 60 miles on L. Huron, bought in 1826 by the Canada Co. from the Crown.

HUSBAND -LAND (Sc.). An owner of two oxen and the land able to support two oxen.

HUSCARLS or HOUSE CARLS (Old Norse = Household servants) were the military retainers of a King or great Earl, organised as a guild. The word first appears under Canute. Maintained until 1051 from the *heregeld,* they formed the professional nucleus of English armies. By the Conquest many of them no longer lived at court but on estates and resembled, if they were not actually, English *thegns.*

HUSKISSON, William (1770-1830) lived in Paris from 1784, witnessed the French Revolution and helped the Gov. of the Tuileries to escape a mob. Dundas employed him in 1793 and in 1795 he became U/Sec. for War. Save in 1802-4 he was an M.P. from 1796 until his death. He was a clever, Benthamite economist, serving as Sec. to

the Treasury from 1804 to 1805 and from 1807 to 1809. He advocated moderate Corn Laws in 1814 and 1815 to ease the transition to a peacetime economy. In 1819 he devised a method of reducing the debt and resuming gold payments and the modified Corn Law of 1821 was due to his influence. He entered the Cabinet in 1823 as Pres. of the Bd. of Trade and his tenure was memorable because he secured the virtual repeal of the Navigation Acts, some obsolete labour legislation, and the repeal or reduction of many excises and import duties. In 1827 he became Colonial Sec. under Goderich but resigned in 1828 over the East Retford Affair. He was run over by the engine at the opening of the Liverpool and Manchester Rly.

HUSS, John and HUSSITES. *See* BOHEMIA; RENAISSANCE-3.

HUSSARS were light cavalry, originally raised from the estates of Hungarian nobles, well horsed and suitable for scouting. They were armed only with sabres. Of the 13 British hussar regiments 10 were converted from light dragoons between 1805 and 1861; three in 1861 from Indian cavalry regiments.

HUSTING(S) (from O.E. = indoor assembly) (1) The supreme court of the City of London held before the Lord Mayor, Recorder, Sheriffs and Aldermen at the Guildhall, or a similar court in a borough. **(2)** The platform on which it was held. **(3)** The temporary platform (not necessarily indoors) where parliamentary candidates formerly stood for nomination and from which they addressed the electors and on which they endured the electoral catcalls and ordure; and hence, the proceedings at a parliamentary election.

HUTCHINSON, John (1615-64) and his wife **Lucy (1620-after 1664).** Both extremely learned, they were married in 1638. He joined the parliament in the Civil War, held Nottingham against the King and in 1646, as M.P. for Nottinghamshire, joined the Independents and then, having accepted a place on the court which tried Charles I, signed his death warrant. Nevertheless he supported Monck in his demand for a free parliament and co-operated with him and Heselrigg in maintaining order. As a regicide he was condemned to death but she and others, including Monck, secured a conditional pardon and avoided the usual forfeitures. He died in prison. She wrote his biography, which was not printed until 1806, and some devotional works. The *Life* vividly records the life and sentiments of the puritan gentry of the time.

HUTCHINSON, Thomas (1711-80) was speaker of the Massachusetts House of Representatives from 1746 to 1748 and, as a commissioner at the Albany Congress in 1754, drafted, with Franklin, the plan for the union of the American colonies. In 1760 he became chief justice of Massachusetts. In 1769 he became acting and in 1771 actual governor, but when in 1773 Franklin published his correspondence with Whately, the legislature petitioned for his dismissal and in 1774 he left for England. George II and his ministers consulted him on American affairs but paid little attention to his advice.

HUTTON, James (1726-97) chemist and geologist, originated the theory of uniform development of the earth's crust and also first manufactured salammoniac from coal soot.

HUXLEY. This gifted family is descended from **(1) Thomas Henry (1825-95)** who began his tropical biological researches as surgeon in H.M.S. *Rattlesnake,* became an F.R.S. in 1851 and was a friend of Darwin, whom he encouraged to publish the *Origin of Species* (1859). His vast capacity for work made him widely known not only as an intellectual but as an executive and he combined in the 1860s research into such subjects as taxonomy and ethnology with the Hunterian Professorship, the presidency of the R. Geological Society and the principalship of the S. London Working Men's College. In the 1870s he dominated the new London School Board and so exerted a lasting influence on public education generally while as a fellow of Eton he developed science teaching in the public schools. He was also teaching at the School of Mines. Of his children **(2) Leonard (1860-1933)** married Julia Arnold, a granddaughter of Arnold of Rugby, niece of Matthew Arnold and sister of Mrs Humphrey Ward, and of their children **(3) Sir Julian Sorrell** (1887-1975) became a famous zoologist and biologist, reorganiser of the London Zoo and organiser of Whipsnade open air zoo and the first gen-sec. of UNESCO. His brother **(4) Aldous (1894-1963)** was the morally revolutionary author of *Antic Hay, Point Counter Point* and *Brave New World*.

HWICCE were a group of tribes consisting partly of Middle Angles who colonised the middle Severn and the Gloucestershire Avon, and partly of West Saxons who, under Ceawlin, conquered the Bristol Avon from the Britons in 577. In 628, after a battle at Cirencester, the West Saxon K. Cynegils ceded this southern part to the Mercians under Penda and he apparently organised the area into one unit in which the Mercian Kings appointed or tolerated an underking. In about 680 the diocese of Worcester was established for them but about 980 the area was divided between Gloucestershire, Worcestershire and a shire based upon Winchcombe, which was annexed to Gloucestershire in 1017. The name of the Hwicce now survives only in Wychwood Forest.

HYDE, Douglas (1860-1949), learned Erse from old people around his father's rectory in Roscommon. He was a distinguished philological scholar and in 1893 inspired the foundation and became the Pres. of the Gaelic League to revive the ancient customs and language of Ireland. It was successful but became, against Hyde's will, entangled with nationalist politics and in 1915 he resigned from it and continued his universally respected scholarly pursuits. He was Pres. of Ireland from 1937 until 1945.

HYDE (1) Sir Nicholas (?-1631), a barrister, became an M.P. in 1601 and was prominent in opposition until 1626 when he was retained for Buckingham's defence. He became C.J. of the Kings Bench in 1627. A nephew **(2) Sir Robert (1595-1665)** was an M.P. in the Long Parliament but was imprisoned by the Commons in 1645; he sheltered Charles II after the B. of Worcester (1651). In 1660 he became a judge and in 1663 C.J. of the Kings Bench. Another nephew **(3) Edward (1609-74) 1st Ld. (1660), 1st E. of CLARENDON (1661)** was the famous constitutional statesman. He first became an M.P. in 1640; he led the attack on the Star Chamber and helped to prepare Strafford's impeachment in 1641; but, refusing to support the Root and Branch Bill against episcopacy, composed the King's reply to the Grand Remonstrance. Though manager with Colepeper and Falkland of the King's parliamentary affairs he was kept in ignorance of the plan to arrest the Five Members. On the outbreak of civil war he became the King's principal political adviser. He secured the assembly of the King's Oxford Parliament in 1643 as a bid for constitutional opinion and as Ch. of the Exch. he raised substantial loans. He was one of the King's Uxbridge negotiators and then became Prince Charles' adviser and so virtually the King's Lieut. in the west. In 1646 he escaped with the Prince to Jersey and argued the Queen out of her plan to use foreign troops. Eventually he reached the Hague and after a mission to Ireland became Charles II's Sec. of State (1651-4), Lord Chancellor in 1658. In these capacities he advised alliance with the main body of English moderates and opposed concessions to extremists of any persuasion. From 1660 a member of Charles' secret committee, he was effective head of the govt. and was responsible with the King for the mildness of the civil measures against the upholders of the Protectorate. He was less successful in the ecclesiastical sphere; after parliament passed the Corporation Act (Dec. 1661) and the Act of Uniformity (May 1662) he opposed efforts to water them down and

became, though a minister, a pronounced opponent of Charles' policy of indulgence. In consequence he had to support the Commons in the Conventicle Bill (1664) and the Five Mile Bill (1665), professing to think the nonconformists a danger to the state. Intimately acquainted with James, D. of York, he may have foreseen the dangers of an alliance between the puritan and R. Catholic extremes against the centre, which that Prince later encouraged as King. Since his policy was essentially one of peace and economic development, Clarendon took great interest in colonial affairs. He was from the beginning a leading member of the Council for Plantations and the Privy Council Committee on New England. He encouraged religious equality in the American colonies as a safety valve against repression at home. He favoured crown control through governors and appeals to the Privy Council and sought to weaken the American colonies by encouraging local separatisms. He was also feeling his way towards a mercantilist policy for them by enforcing the Trade and Navigation legislation. The short term effects were too much for the commercial interests which wished to enlarge the colonial domain, if necessary by force. Clarendon wanted peace with the Dutch and in 1662 had negotiated a treaty to settle existing disputes, but James D. of York instigated raids on Dutch African settlements and on New Amsterdam (New York) in 1664. Dutch reprisals led to open war in Feb. 1665 (*see* DUTCH WAR, SECOND). In June 1667 the Dutch burned the fleet in the Medway. The govt. was forced to negotiate the P. of Breda (July 1667).

Although the Commons had for some time been trying to control the royal finances, Clarendon opposed an appropriations proviso in 1665 and a bill to audit the war accounts in 1666. Saddled with much of the blame for the Medway disaster, he advised a dissolution: he had, in any case, fallen out temporarily with the King to whom he was didactic and whose mistress (Barbara Castlemaine) hated him. He was dismissed in Oct. 1667 and parliament was recalled, whereupon the Commons, led by Edward Seymour, exhibited seventeen articles of impeachment in support of a general charge of treason. The Lords would not commit him without a specific charge and, in the ensuing conflict between Houses, Clarendon first issued a vindication and then, hearing that Parliament might be prorogued (leaving him to the mercy of a High Steward's Court), fled to Calais. This was construed as an admission of guilt and he was banished by Act (Dec. 1667). He wrote two famous works: *The History of the Great Rebellion* (1646-8) and his *Life* (1668-70). The two were combined in the *History of the Rebellion* (1671) and published in 1702-4 by the Oxford Univ. Press to its great profit and the annoyance of the Whigs.

Of his children **(4) Anne (1637-71)** met James, D. of York (later James II) at Breda in 1659 and married him in 1660. Her father disliked this union and later regarded it as the cause of his fall. Their children were Mary II and Q. Anne. **(5) Henry (1638-1709) 2nd E., as Vist. CORNBURY** was M.P. for Wilts from 1661 to 1674 and from 1662 Sec. to Catherine of Braganza. He was Lord Privy Seal in 1685 and Lord Lieut. of Ireland from 1685 to 1686. As a supporter of James II he was briefly imprisoned in 1690 and again, in connection with the Preston Plot, in 1691. His younger brother **(6) Laurence (1641-1711) 1st E. of ROCHESTER (1681)** was M.P. for Newport (Cornwall) in 1660 and for Oxford University from 1661 to 1679 when he became Tory first Lord of the Treasury; in 1681 he negotiated the secret French Treaty to make the crown financially independent and so, by making Parliament unnecessary, prevent a return of the Whigs. In the course of the next four years he quarrelled with his colleagues (particularly Halifax and Sunderland) but maintained himself in office though accused of peculation. When James II, his brother-in-law, succeeded he became Lord Treasurer but was soon faced with a choice between the King's catholicising policy, against growing popular opposition, or the King's enmity. Meantime he corresponded with William of Orange (whom he advised to get rid of Monmouth) while Sunderland was intriguing against him and his brother. To alleviate his difficulties he accepted, in the Autumn of 1686, a post on James II's new Ecclesiastical Commission but James pressed him to take R. Catholic instruction. Rochester, now certain which way the wind was blowing, refused and was dismissed in Jan. 1687 not without a *douceur* of £4000 a year for two lives. When William of Orange landed, Rochester was among those who urged James to call a Parliament but though he crossed over to William's side in Dec. 1688, he would not support a transfer of the crown to William, preferring, with Abp. Sancroft, a regency. He was thus out of favour but, unlike his brother, took the oath of allegiance in Mar. 1689. Though a witty and drunken libertine, he was a friend of the Burnet's and became influential in the circle of Q. Mary II, who instigated his readmission to the Privy Council in Mar. 1692. He was now a powerful figure again through the support of the high churchmen and by 1700, when he became Lord Lieut. of Ireland, he and Harley were virtually heads of govt. He spent little time in Ireland, being too intent on English politics, which he largely mismanaged. William dismissed him just before his death but Anne continued him in office until the Marlboroughs secured his dismissal in Feb. 1703. He remained out of office until Sept. 1710 when he was briefly Lord President.

HYDE PARK (London), common of the manor of Hyde, owned by Westminster Abbey, was seized by the Crown in 1536 and opened to the public by Charles I. The Westbourne was dammed in 1733 to form the Serpentine and the Great Exhibition was held in it in 1851. The northwest corner at Marble Arch was the site of the Tyburn execution ground and, now called Speakers Corner, is a place of decreasingly effectual public oratory.

HYDERABAD (India) CITY and STATE. The city was founded in 1589 by a local Moslem dynasty. In 1713 Chin Qilich Khan was appointed Subadar of the Deccan with his capital there and the title Nizam-ul-Mulk (Lieutenant of the Realm). After confused Mogul intrigues he defeated his court enemies in Berar (Oct. 1724) and, under the title of Nizam-ul-Mulk Asaf Jali, was recognised as the ruler of a large, virtually independent, state. He died in 1748 and his successor, a Moslem ruler over a Hindu population, was threatened by dynastic strife encouraged by the British, the French, Hyder Ali of Mysore and the Marathas. By 1752 the French had military trainers in the City and these had to be expelled by Col. Forde in Mar. 1759. The French defeat, sealed by the P. of Paris (1763) left the Nizam Ali exposed to Maratha and Mysore pressure and he concluded an alliance with the British (Nov. 1766) whom he deserted and then rejoined in 1768 (T. of Masulipatam). Under the latter agreement the HEIC was to pay 9 lakhs of rupees annually for the Northern Circars but a dispute arose over one of them, the coastal district of Guntur. This was eventually ceded in 1788 but the Nizam demanded help in recovering some southern areas currently occupied by Mysore and fought with the British in the Third Mysore War. In the ensuing distractions and devastation the Marathas acquired an ascendancy which they asserted in 1795 by defeating the Nizam at Kharda. He sought first French and then British protection and submitted to the first of the subsidiary alliances (1798); he thus took part in the partition of Mysore and supplied the British armies in the Maratha Wars. The final, rather diminished extent of the state, was settled by treaty in 1822 (*but see* BERAR). At this period the area was in confusion because of the govt's inability to police the many demobilised cavalry. It was still much the largest of the Indian princely states and, apart from a number of administrative interventions, maintained its own administration until 1948. *See also* GEORGE II-15.

HYDERABAD. *See* SIND.

HYDER ALI or HYDAR ALI or HAIDAR ALY (?-1783). *See* MYSORE.

HYDROGEN BOMB, first exploded by the U.S.A. (1954), Britain and Russia (1957), France and China (1970).

HYE WAY TO THE SPYTTEL HOUSE, probably by Robert Copland (fl. 1508-47), is a dialogue describing the beggars and other poor people who visit an almshouse.

HYMN SINGING. *See* BAPTISTS.

HYTHE (Kent) small port and limb of the Cinque Ports. The Army School of Musketry (later Small Arms School and then School of Infantry) was established here in 1854. It has been responsible for the development of most British small arms.

HYWEL DDA (Welsh = The Good) LAWS OF. In about 945 Hywel Dda held a conference of six men (4 lay, 2 clerical) from every Commote (about 1000 men in all) at Whitland. After ascertaining the local customs of each commote and their points of resemblance they agreed upon abrogations and amendments and commissioned BLEGYWRYD, a famous lawyer, and 12 laymen to codify the results. They are said to have been confirmed by the Pope. Three copies were made: for Gwynedd (the book of Cyfnerth or the **Venedotian Code**), for Powys (the Book of Iorwerth or the **Gwentian Code**) and for Dyfed (the Book of Blegywryd or **Dimetian Code**). When Hywel's dominions broke up these became the basis of three slowly diverging systems. Apart from minor changes they remained in full force until the Statute of Rhuddlan (1284) and parts of them until Tudor times. The Dimetian Code is believed to be the closest to the original. Though greatly respected, the Codes were adaptable. In particular they allowed departures (i) in favour of other proven customs provided that they were reasonable and supported by precedent and (ii) in favour of parties who contracted outside the Code. No copies now exist but in 1841 ANEURIN OWEN published reconstructions based upon apparent excerpts made by 12th and 13th cent. practitioners, together with their notes and commentaries. *See* DEHEUBARTH-1; WELSH LAW.

HYWEL ab EDWIN. *See* DEHEUBARH-6.

HYWEL ap RHODRI. *See* GWYNEDD-7.

I

IAGO ab Idwal (?-1039). *See* GWYNEDD-18.
IAGO ab Idwal Foel (?-?979). *See* GWYNEDD-15.
IBADAN. *See* NIGERIA.
IBERVILLE, Pierre Lemoyne Sieur d' (1661-1706) a French settler in Canada commanded French squadrons against British trading posts in the Wars of Louis XIV (1689-97 and 1702 onwards). In 1699 he established a colony at Mobile (Louisiana) and in 1702 took St. Kitts.
IBN (Arab = son of) e.g. Ibn Saud, son of Saud. *See* ABU.
IBN BATUTA (1304-60) set out from Tangier in 1325 on a series of adventurous journeys to Egypt, Persia and Iraq, then down the Red Sea and African coast as far as Kilwa (1327); to Anatolia and the Crimea (1328); to the Caucasus and Constantinople (1329-30); to India (1330-42); to Ceylon (1345); Sumatra and China (1346-7); he saw the Black Death in Syria in 1348 and reached Fez in 1349. In 1352 he visited Nigeria across the Sahara. His valuable accounts of these journeys, composed after 1352, throw much light on the trade routes and on conditions in those countries with which Europe was, directly or indirectly, establishing trading relations.
IBN KHALDUN (1332-1406), a Tunisian statesman and judge under various North African, Moorish and Egyptian rulers after 1359, wrote a famous history, the *Kitab al-Ibar* (Book of Examples) to illustrate a theory of politics. The theory is expounded in the Introduction, followed by four books of East Islamic history and two of West. He held that the rise and fall of states is due to the relative strength of corporate feeling in the ruling body: a feeling liable to be sapped by success.
IBN SAUD. *See* ARABIA.
IBO. *See* NIGERIA.
IBRAHIM PASHA (1789-1848), the son of the celebrated Mehemet Ali, pasha of Egypt. His abilities and strength of character led his father to entrust him with the highest commands in Arabia and elsewhere. In 1824 he became his father's deputy and C-in-C in the Peloponnese and it was the destruction of his combined Turkish-Egyptian fleet at the B. of Navarino (1827) which laid the foundations of Greek independence. From 1832 to 1841 he was Gov. of Syria and thereafter effective ruler of Egypt. A ruthless but honourable man, he was much traduced especially by Princess Lieven, who ascribed to him the non-existent "Barbarisation Project", whereby the Greeks were to be exterminated and replaced by Mohammedans.
IBSEN, Henrik (1828-1906), Norwegian playwright, was a theatre director from 1851 to 1864 when he left Norway and lived in Italy and Germany until 1891. His dramatic output, already vast in Norway, developed after 1869 into iconoclastic, widely influential, social and political criticism and much of it was translated into all major languages. He inspired and was a better playwright than George Bernard Shaw and influenced Edmund Gosse and John Galsworthy. His willingness to deal with inhibited subjects such as hereditary disease (as in *Ghosts*) made him the effective leader of a modernism whose influence stretched far beyond the stage and the confines of Europe. Many of his plays are still performed in English.
ICE BREAKERS, to prolong the annual trade flow in cold climates, could be introduced only with the coming of propeller driven metal ships. The earliest were 'ice rams built at Stettin in 1871 for use on the Baltic coast. The first spoon-bowed 'ice crusher' was the *Yermak* (7,900 tons) built in England in 1898 to the design of the great Russian Adm. Makaroff. She was still in service in 1956. The Russian 16,000 ton atomic ice-breaker *Lenin* was completed in 1961.
ICELAND (*see* VIKINGS) **(1)** Ingolf Arnesen, from Norway, was the first settler in about 875. Norwegian and Ostman colonisation continued for about 80 years, the earlier

settlers such as Ingolf himself and Aud, the widow of Olaf the White, K. of Dublin, obtaining large areas. The Parliament (*Althing*) was first called in 1000. When the tithe was imposed in 1096 the population had already reached 70,000.

(2) Power originally resided in 36 (later 39) chiefs (*Godhar*) whose virtually hereditary office was theoretically related to jurisdiction within one of the island's four quarters. Actual power depended upon the size of a chief's following and a man could, regardless of quarter, transfer allegiance from one chief to another. Hence chiefs suborned each other's followers in order to dominate the local quarter assemblies. The *Althing* met mainly to settle disputes and in the year 1000 a court of appeal was created from the *Althing* in an effort to overcome the growing instability of the chiefly factions.

(3) In the late 12th cent. feuds and Norwegian church influence grew side by side. The Norwegian Archdiocese of Nidaros at Troodheim (*see* BREAKSPEARE), established in 1156, included Iceland which had two bishops, but the archbishops interfered constantly. The murderous intrigues of 13th cent. Icelandic politics led to a deadlock in which the churchmen urged and the population in 1262 accepted, submission to the Norwegian Crown.

(4) In the four centuries after the Union (1380) of Norway and Denmark, Icelandic prosperity declined steadily under the impact of Danish commercial interference, epidemics and later (1783-4), the great Skafta eruptions. The population fell to 40,000. Some action was necessary. In 1787 the royal trading rights were thrown open to all Danish subjects but in 1800 the *Althing* was abolished.

(5) The blockades of the Napoleonic Wars cut Iceland off from Denmark and in 1809 the govt. was overthrown by an adventurer called Jorgen Jorgensen with the help of Samuel Phelps, an Englishman. At the request of the Law Speaker Magnus Stephensen the British repudiated Phelps and suppressed the revolt; but this demonstrated that the fate of Iceland was no longer in the hands of the Danes.

(6) Thenceforth there was orderly but determined agitation for local autonomy. This was achieved in stages; Frederick VI (r. 1818-39) set up provisional consultative assemblies in 1834 and provoked agitation for the revival of the *Althing*. Icelandic nationalism found a leader in Jon Sigurdsson, who from 1841 devoted all his energies to it. In 1845 the *Althing* was given consultative powers; in 1854 trade was opened to all nations, in 1875 the *Althing* again became a legislature; in 1903 local parliamentary responsibility was recognised and in 1918, under a 26 year treaty, Iceland and Denmark became independent countries under one crown. In 1937 the *Althing* asserted its intention not to renew the treaty but in 1940 the British occupied Iceland to protect it from Germany and communications with Denmark were cut. Accordingly in May 1942 the *Althing* resolved that the treaty should not be renewed and that Iceland should become a republic. These resolutions were confirmed by plebiscite in Feb. 1945.

(7) In 1949 Iceland joined N.A.T.O. In 1952 the govt. extended the Iceland fishery and territorial waters. The extension was not recognised by the British and in 1953 the first of the so-called COD WARS broke out when British trawler owners refused facilities to Icelandic trawlers in British ports. As a result the Icelanders sold their fish to the U.S.S.R. under annually renewed trade agreements and Britain ceased to be Iceland's main customer. In 1958 the Geneva Congress on territorial waters supported a general extension and the Icelanders promptly claimed a 12 mile limit. This was finally accepted subject to a three year transitional agreement by the U.K. in 1961. In 1971 Iceland claimed a 50-mile limit and a further consequent dispute with Britain was settled in 1973; there was little that the Royal Navy could do, short of firing on Icelandic vessels, and in due course an Icelandic claim for a 200-mile fishing limit was respected if not accepted by the British.

ICENI. A wealthy British tribe inhabiting Norfolk and Suffolk at the time of the Roman Conquest. Their chief town was Caister-by-Norwich. Their King, Prasutagus, submitted to Aulus Plautius but apparently failed to carry all his people with him: for some rebelled and were suppressed in A.D. 48. Prasutagus died in A.D. 59 leaving half his fortune to the Emperor and a quarter each to his daughters. The Roman fiscal authorities seized more property than the Iceni thought right and in the ensuing dispute the daughters were raped and their mother, the famous BOADICEA (Boudicca), whipped. A revolt followed and spread to the neighbouring Trinovantes. Colchester (Camulodunum), St. Albans (Verulamium) and London were stormed (A.D. 61). Suetonius Paulinus, the Roman C-in-C, was in North Wales at the time and his troops had to be brought southwards from Chester. The tribesmen were defeated in a pitched battle near Coventry. Boadicea died or took poison shortly afterwards, the tribal territory was laid waste and the Iceni ceased to exist as an organised society.

ICH DIEN **(Ger = I serve).** It was long thought that this was the motto of John of Luxemburg, K. of Bohemia, found on his helmet after the B. of Crécy (1346) and adopted by the victor, the Black Prince, together with his triple-feathered crest and used by Princes of Wales ever since. In fact the Prince used the motto in his arms for peace before the battle.

"ICHTHYS" formed from the initials of the Greek phrase for 'Jesus Christ, son of God, Saviour' is also the Greek for 'fish'. Thus drawing a symbol ⊂> vaguely resembling a fish was a kind of encoded confession of faith. The symbol appears frequently in the decoration of romanesque and gothic churches.

ICONOCLASM ("Image breaking") is the doctrine, controversial in the Mediterranean world, that representations (icons) of Christ and the saints should not be venerated or even exhibited. Sometimes legally enforced in the East; condemned by the Papacy, it widened the hatreds between east and west and weakened resistance to Islam (which forbids representations of human or animal forms).

ICONOCLAST. See BRADLAUGH.

ICKWORTH (Suffolk). Eccentrically designed mansion built by Francis Sandys between 1794 and 1830 for the E. of Bristol.

ICKNIELD WAY. An ancient and unromanised route (mostly avoiding towns) running from Avebury (Wilts) in a general north-easterly direction. The first part or **ridgeway** mainly follows the tops of the ridges, crosses the Thames at Streatley and continues by way of Royston, Newmarket, Thetford and Swaffham to Brancaster near the Norfolk coast. The north-eastern half of it is crossed at intervals by earthworks, particularly Fleam Dyke and the Devil's Dyke in Cambridgeshire. Most of these face southwest, are post-Roman and must be defences against penetration from the Thames Valley; but whether they are Anglo-Saxon defences against the resurgent British who had reoccupied the middle Thames after the B. of Mount Badon (c. 500) or British defences against Saxons who had outflanked East Anglia, is unclear.

ICOLMKILL (Iona) STATS. OF (1609). A bond forced upon the Scottish western chiefs, particularly the Macdonalds (q.v.), to obey the law, eschew feuding, build churches, reduce feudal burdens on their tenants and send their children to be educated in the lowlands. The bond was not honoured. *See also* IONA.

IDA the Flamebearer (Bernician King 547-60). *See* NORTHUMBRIA-1.

IDDESLEIGH, 1st E. of (1818-87). *See* NORTHCOTE.

IDENTITY CARDS were instituted in Britain in Sept. 1939 partly to facilitate military and industrial conscription. They were abolished in 1950, the numbers being retained for National Insurance purposes. Proposals to reintroduce them were being discussed and resisted in 2000.

IDIOT or FOOL NATURAL was one who from birth was incurably of unsound mind. Under the *Stat. De Praerogitiva Regis* of 1324 the King had the custody of an idiot's lands, taking the profits without waste or destruction, funding his necessaries and returning the lands to his heirs. This shut out the mesne lord and prevented alienation. *See* LUNATIC.

IDLE, R. *See* TRANSPORT AND COMMUNICATIONS.

IDLEMEN (Ir.). Armed retainers or liveried robbers.

IDOLATRY was initially the worship of images forbidden by the Second Commandment and by Islam, leading sometimes to a total prohibition on representation, even in art, of human and animal forms. As Christianity is based upon an incarnation of God in a human and visible form, it could scarcely maintain such a prohibition but some heretical sects such as the 7th cent. Iconoclasts and more recent puritans did. In modern theology idolatry is the concentration upon temporary things (e.g. wealth) rather than upon eternal things (e.g. goodness).

IDWAL FOEL (?-942). *See* GWYNEDD-14.

IDWAL ab Meirig (?-997) defeated the usurping Meredydd, grandson of Hywel Dda, and became a King in Gwynedd in 995 but was killed by the Danes in 997.

IEUAF ab Idwal Foel (?-985). *See* GWYNEDD-16.

IFE. *See* NIGERIA; YORUBA.

IFOR BACH or MEURIG (?-?1169) Lord of Senghenydd, a barony of Glamorgan, captured William of Gloucester and his family at Cardiff in 1158 and compelled William to cede him much territory.

IGNATIEV, Nikolai Pavlovich, Count (1832-1908), brilliant, charming and brave Russian diplomat, was involved in Russian frontier negotiations as well as Mil. Attaché at the Paris Congress of 1856. In 1858 he undertook a daring mission to Khiva and Bokhara and in 1859 he was rewarded with a special mission to Pekin to offset the Anglo-French advance. They burned the Summer Palace. He convinced the Chinese of Russian friendliness. By the T. of Pekin (1860) they recognised the Russian occupation of the left bank of the R. Amur and of the area between the Ussuri and the Pacific, allowing for the building of Vladivostok and eventually of the railway to it. By 1864 he was ambassador to the Porte and fomenting national separatism within the Ottoman Empire. He was too successful. The Russo-Turkish war of 1877 ended with the virtual partition of the empire's European territories at the T. of SAN STEFANO which he negotiated. The powers took fright and forced Russia to abandon the treaty. Ignatiev was moved to the ministry of the interior.

IGNATIUS LOYOLA (1491-1556) St. (1622), a Spanish nobleman and soldier, underwent a conversion during convalescence from a wound in 1521 and swore at Montserrat to become a soldier of Christ. He wrote most of the *Spiritual Exercises* at Manresa (1522-3). Until 1528 he travelled to Rome, Jerusalem, Barcelona and Salamanca subsisting on alms. Then, until 1535 he studied at Paris. In 1534 he and seven others (who included St. Francis Xavier) together vowed poverty, chastity and a pilgrimage to Jerusalem. They set out by way of Italy but the pilgrimage having become impracticable, they offered their services to the Pope; this decision was confirmed by a vision. The offer was accepted by Paul III, who sanctioned the Society of Jesus in the bull *Regimini Militantis Ecclesiae* (Lat = For the regulation of the Church Militant) with Ignatius as its first General. He drew up its constitution between 1547 and 1550 and continued to organise and spread its influence until his death. *See* JESUITS.

IGNATIUS, Father (LYNE, Joseph Leycester) (1837-1908) famous preacher, attempted without authority to introduce Benedictine practices into the Church of England and, for the purpose, founded a community at Llantony. After his death, Llantony passed to the Benedictine community at Caldey, most of whose members became R. Catholic in 1913.

IGNORAMUS **(Lat = "we do not know").** In theory a grand jury was empanelled to report of their own knowledge accusations which were then tried before a petty jury. The declaration of ignorance was, therefore, a refusal to prosecute. *See* INDICTMENT.

IGRAINE, IGERNE or YGERNE, the legendary mother of King Arthur.

ILCHESTER. (Lat = LINDINIS) (Som.) had a royal mint by 959. John confirmed a town charter in 1203 but the mint was discontinued in about 1220. From 1298 it was represented in Parliament and in the 14th cent. it became the county town. A new charter of incorporation was granted in 1556. Assizes and quarter sessions ceased to be held there in 1875.

ILCHESTER, Es. of. *See* FOX-STRANGWAYS.

ILE DE FRANCE (1) The (Frankish) region about Paris. **(2)** The former name of Mauritius.

ILFRACOMBE (N. Devon) was a substantial port involved in the mediaeval wine trade and supplying men and ships for royal expeditions, notably Calais (1347). It remained moderately prosperous as such and was sufficiently well known to attract a devastating French naval attack as late as 1797. Since then it declined as a port but has become a resort.

ILIFFE, Edward Mauger (1877-1960) 1st Ld. ILIFFE (1933) inherited some specialist magazines and the *Coventry Evening Telegraph* from his father and in the twenties became associated with the Berry brothers of Merthyr Tydfil. In 1923 he became a Tory M.P. In 1924 they formed Allied Newspapers Ltd. The company took over most of Rothermere's newspaper group including the *Sunday Times* and in 1927 it bought the *Daily Telegraph* from Lord Burnham. They halved the price and doubled the circulation. Meanwhile Iliffe also became a leader of the Assoc. of British Chambers of Commerce and a powerful figure in insurance. In 1939 the three partners divided their publishing interests. Iliffe took over Kelly's Directories and in 1943 the *Birmingham Post* and *Birmingham Mail*.

ILK. A Scottish word meaning "the same" used sometimes in the titles of the highest clan chiefs. Thus "Maclean of that Ilk" means "Maclean of Maclean" i.e. the chief of all Macleans, but "Maclean of Ardgour" means chief only of the Macleans of that place. *See* CLANS, SCOTS.

ILLEGITIMACY. A child is illegitimate if born out of wedlock and in general was deemed to have no father and to be entitled to inheritance only from the mother. Unfortunately wedlock is defined differently in different systems of law, the inconsistencies between canon and secular law being particularly wide. Thus P. Arthur's precontract with Katharine of Aragon rendered, according to some canon lawyers, his brother Henry VIII's marriage to that lady void on the grounds of incest and so made her daughter Queen Mary I illegitimate. According to secular laws and practices, on the other hand, the marriage was valid and Henry's second marriage to Anne Boleyn was therefore void on grounds of bigamy — which made Mary I legitimate and Anne's daughter, Elizabeth I, illegitimate. Since the two princesses were respectively R. Catholic and Protestant in an age of reformation, the issue was of supreme political importance. Henry VIII characteristically cut the Gordian Knot by declaring them both capable of inheriting the throne.

ILLINOIS (U.S.A.) was visited by French Jesuits in 1673 and the first French settlements were established at Kaskaskia in 1703 and Fort Chartres in 1719. The area was ceded to Britain in 1763 and mostly incorporated in Quebec by the Quebec Act of 1774. The Illinois French were generally loyalists in the American rebellion and the Indian tribes sided with the British; the territory was consequently overrun by the Virginians. This eventually resulted in cession to the U.S.A. under the T. of Paris of 1783. The territory became a state of the Union in 1818; it was carried by Abraham Lincoln in the election of 1860 and remained loyal to the Union in the Civil War.

ILLITERACY. *See* LITERACY.

ILLTYD, St. (450-535) a Breton, came to Britain in about 470 and was converted to Christianity in about 476, having been spared when an entire hunting party fell victim to divine wrath. He founded a monastery, probably that of Llantwit Major, and is said to have taught St. David and to have introduced improved ploughing techniques into Wales. *See* MISSIONARIES, BRITAIN AND IRELAND-3.

ILLUMINATION OF MS. (1) Post 7th cent. Byzantine models influenced the N. Italian illuminators who in their turn affected or even taught the early mediaeval Roman styles; these were handed on into Britain by St. Augustine's mission; his Gospels (Corpus Christi, Cambridge) survive. Thus an Anglo-Saxon style developed from the aesthetic commerce between the English cathedral monasteries and those of Italy and especially Rome.

(2) Italian styles also spread through and were adapted in Provence and Languedoc, N. France and Burgundy; they had achieved considerable variation when they arrived in England, where the Anglo-Saxon styles were already far advanced.

(3) The foregoing represented scribes' rather than painters' arts, concerned with the honour due to the Word of God and confined mainly to the embellishment of the page or the initial letter. Figures, if still or hieratic, tended to naturalism. In Ireland, for reasons unknown, an entirely different style suddenly appeared. Irish manuscripts had an abstract splendour (more akin perhaps to Moorish or Arabic illumination) whose riotous colouring and sheer expanse attracted attention away from the text but created such astonishing works (all c. 700) as the Book of Durrow, the Book of Kells (both at Trinity College, Dublin) and the Lindisfarne Gospels (British Museum).

(4) Charlemagne's writing reform naturally gave birth to new 9th cent. styles of illumination, originating at the Palatine school at Aachen and deliberately related to ancient and Levantine art. Other Frankish schools existed, of which the best known were at Rheims and Tours. The English, Irish and Frankish illuminators influenced each other both on the continent and in England, where in the mid 10th cent. the first great Winchester School, inspired by St. Ethelwold, held the field. His Benedictional (British Museum) survives. Another major centre, naturally, was Canterbury, from which Saxon artists migrated to N. France and which remained active until about 1100.

(5) The need for books and the Norman invasion created, in time, Anglo-Norman scriptoria under Romanesque influence. The earliest major centre was at Bury St. Edmunds but in mid-century there arose the second great Winchester school. The productions of these scriptoria were mostly very large gospels and psalters capable of being read at a distance and illustrated in flat opaque tints. Later they returned to intricate and extraordinary initials in an Anglo-Irish style; later still they were influenced by Byzantine models and produced such works as the Winchester Psalter (British Museum).

(6) In about 1250 Gothic architecture began to influence the illuminators, especially at Paris, whence interest was disseminated through the patronage and prestige of St. Louis and his queen Blanche of Castile. These manuscripts were notable for their remarkable miniatures which remained a feature of illumination until the appearance of printing. The new style very soon elbowed out its predecessors in France and England so that the products of the Salisbury scriptorium are difficult to distinguish from those of Paris or Tours. Naturalism, like the growing scepticism, became more pronounced so that this later method became as well a representational as an ornamental art. Thus by the 15th and 16th cents., when printing intervened, the illuminators had crossed over to the art of miniature painting especially in Flanders, France and Italy.

ILLUSTRATED LONDON NEWS, the first illustrated journal, was founded by Herbert Ingram, a Nottingham bookseller and printer, in 1842.

IMAGIST POETRY was practised mostly by Americans of whom Ezra Pound was the most conspicuous. It represented a reaction against the less disciplined forms of romanticism and its adherents claimed to pursue description and objectivity through orderly and concise expression It later influenced T.S. Eliot. The length and obscurity of some of Ezra Pound's *Cantos* and T.S. Eliot's longer poems indicate the difficulty in achieving the objectives.

IMAM (Arab = leader). A supreme Moslem ruler according to the tenets of a given Moslem sect, e.g. the rival Abbasid and Omeyyad Caliphs were Imams and so is the Aga Khan as leader of the Ismailis. The ruler of the Yemen used the word as a title. A lesser Imam is the prayer leader in a mosque. *See* CALIPHATE-4.

IMBROS. An island within distant sight of the Gallipoli peninsula used by the Allied Dardanelles expedition as a base in 1915 and 1916.

IMMACULATE CONCEPTION. The ancient idea that from the first moment of her conception the Virgin Mary was by the Grace of God and the merits of Jesus Christ free from all stain of original sin. The Feast of the Conception was celebrated in Ireland in the 9th cent. and in England in the 11th. The Paris theologians led by St. Bernard opposed the doctrine. Duns Scotus, the Oxford theologians and the Franciscans supported it. The Council of Basle in 1439 and the Sorbonne in 1449 pronounced it a pious and proper opinion. The Council of Trent (1545-63) declared that its decree on original sin did not include the Virgin Mary and in 1708 the Feast became one of Obligation. In 1854 Pius IX raised it to the status of a dogma by the bull *Ineffabilis Deus* which created an important obstacle to reunion between the Roman and the Protestant churches.

IMMANENCE and TRANSCENDENTALISM. Immanence is the doctrine that God pervades the universe and that His activity is expressed solely in its development; Transcendentalism, that He has a separate existence from the universe which is therefore a subsidiary expression of his activity.

IMMEDIACY. The status enjoyed by those territorial rulers in the Holy Roman Empire who owed direct allegiance to the Emperor without intervention of a feudal superior; they were entitled to a seat in the Imperial Diet and the Emperor could not confer the status without its consent.

IMMIGRATION. (1) Influxes of strangers upon a settled population after 1066 began with Flemish and Dutch weavers on the E. Anglian coast and in the W. Riding of Yorkshire in 13th-14th cents and have left their traces in surnames such as Gaunt and Mineer. There was also some Welsh immigration because most professional archers were Welsh. Their civilian migrations began mostly after Henry VIII's Acts of Union. Scots movements into the northern counties and English into Lothian are attested by the respective local prevalence of surnames such as Scott and Inglis but large Scottish migrations into England came after the abolition of the frontier at the accession of James VI as James I in England.

(2) From the late 17th cent. until the 1960s immigrants were usually political or religious refugees and were regarded as beneficial. The Huguenots in the 17th cent. and the Sephardi Jews from the Peninsula brought new skills; migrants from Ireland provided 19th cent. Britain of the steam age with badly needed unskilled labour, while the Ashkenazi Jewish inflow from Russia around 1900 brought gifts and talents.

(3) Thus far immigrants, whatever their background, customs or language were visually little different from anybody else and were easily absorbed. Foreign names were often anglicised (e.g. Ricci into Ritchie; Poitevin into Portwine). There was now a change to types which were instantly distinguishable by their appearance. So long as the numbers were small nobody minded or even thought about it. There had been an inflow from the Caribbean into S. Wales after the W. Indian sugar slump. In the 1950s West Indians began to take over unpleasant jobs everywhere and they were followed by a wave from India and from S. Africa. Kenyans of Indian origin were mostly driven from Africa in the late 1960s and in 1972 there was a mass exodus of Asians from Uganda. The British govt. coped, with difficulty, with the latter movement by persuading other countries to take some and freely accepting the rest.

(4) As the new migrants tended to concentrate in certain areas of particular towns they seemed omnipresent to some indigenous people while remaining invisible to others. In the areas of dense immigration competition for housing and later for jobs created animosities which sometimes developed into racial hostility, notably in midland industrial cities. The gifted Tory politician Enoch Powell called attention to the threat of racial conflict in ill-chosen, if arresting, words in 1968; in 1964 a Tory candidate with an anti-immigration programme had won the apparently safe Labour seat at Smethwick. In truth an enormous change towards multiracialism had been unexpectedly made without democratic consultation or popular approval and some people did not want this. A succession of immigration and race relations acts was passed, the former to control the inflow, the latter to ease the lives of those who got in. In 1980 about 3% of the population was coloured. Its rate of increase was higher than the indigenous average, though lower than the Irish, mainly because of its youth, a characteristic which could be expected in time to change. There was some racial friction but this resulted less from numbers than from the increased proportion of British born coloured citizens who were less tolerant of discrimination than their parents and by the very existence of the institutions such as the Race Relations Commission which were designed to alleviate their difficulties. A clash of civilisations was also apparent sometimes between those who wished to adapt to British life and those who preferred to maintain their customs, tradition or religion. Mosques and gurdwaras began to rise beside the synagogues in the country of the legally established church. Less often there were disagreements between racial groups within the immigrant population.

(5) The media were also inclined from time to time to excite racial controversy, not so much by propaganda against the new minorities as by overstressing their rights. For the most part, however, the indigenous populations remained remarkably tolerant, being by the 1990s accustomed to thousands of Chinese, Indian and other Asiatic restaurants and shops.

IMMUNIZATION. *See* EPIDEMICS.

IMPEACHMENT. (1) A process, judicial in form, whereby ministers and other powerful persons are accused by the lower house of a legislature in Britain and the U.S.A. and tried by the upper house for high crimes and misdemeanours committed in office. There were a number in mediaeval England beginning with **Simon Beresford** in 1330 and including the D. of Suffolk in 1450, but they were for long superseded by Acts of Attainder and were revived only in 1620. From then until 1688 some forty took place of which that of **Strafford**

failed and was replaced by an Attainder. The question whether a royal pardon could be pleaded in bar of impeachment was debated in the case of **Danby** but determined only by the Act of Settlement in 1701. Fifteen took place between 1688 and 1721 but between 1721 and 1760 only one – that of **Lord Lovat** for treason in 1746. The last of the English impeachments were those of **Warren Hastings** (1788-95) and **Lord Melville** in 1806, though Thomas Anstey tried unsuccessfully to move against Lord Palmerston as late as 1848, by which time the procedure was regarded as too cumbersome, expensive and severe.

(2) Just as impeachments were dying out in Britain they began to be instituted in the U.S.A. where the first (against Senator Blount) was dismissed on a point of law in 1797 and that against Pres. Nixon, abandoned in 1974 because he resigned office. One reason for the continuance of this apparently obsolete institution in the U.S.A. is that British impeachments if successful could lead to punishment but in the U.S.A. they can lead at the most to deprivation of office. A further difference is that British impeachments have mostly been launched against politicians but of the 14 American cases 10 have involved judges. The most notable American case was the impeachment and acquittal by one vote of Pres. Andrew Johnson in 1868.

(3) The procedure is that the lower House votes Articles of Impeachment one by one and these are then exhibited to the Upper House. The accused having been brought before the Upper House, the trial proceeds in the same manner as a criminal trial but the verdict on each article is taken openly and the Upper House does not pass sentence on the conviction unless the Lower House moves for it. In this way the Lower House has a right of pardon. Though a pardon cannot be pleaded in bar of an impeachment, the offence may be pardoned by the Crown or executive after conviction.

IMPERIAL CHEMICAL INDUSTRIES LTD (I.C.I.) was founded in 1926 by the amalgamation of British Dyestuffs, Brunner Mond & Co., Nobel Industries and United Alkali. It rapidly expanded into every field of industrial chemical production from acids to insecticides and from synthetic fibres and resins to explosives. It was still much the biggest British industrial business in 1994.

IMPERIAL CITIES of the Holy Roman Empire were not subject to a territorial prince and were considered to have the status of immediacy. Hamburg and Bremen are the only modern survivors of this once numerous class.

IMPERIAL COLLEGE OF SCIENCE AND TECHNOLOGY. This is a federation of several institutions. The Davy College of Chemistry was founded in 1845: the Govt. Schools of Mines and of Science applied to the Arts were both founded in 1851. These were amalgamated in 1853 and combined with the City and Guilds College in 1907. The capital finance was found in part by the Commissioners for the Exhibition of 1851 and in part by the Corporation of London and the City Livery Cos. The College became a chosen instrument for increasing the number of available scientists in 1953 and has expanded steadily ever since.

IMPERIAL and COMMONWEALTH CONFERENCES. (*See* COLONIAL CONFERENCES) **(1)** The **Colonial** conferences between 1884 and 1902, comprised only the self governing colonies. The hope of the enthusiasts was that the series might be institutionalised perhaps into a Council of Empire. Their weakness was that the institution might be dominated by an industrialised Britain relying on cheap free traded imports, whereas the major overseas territories hoped to develop their own industries protected by local tariffs. They also were becoming self conscious. Hence in 1907 the Conferences were renamed **Imperial** Conferences, but this strong term connoted no stronger association then or in 1911 when the German naval threat began to be noticed

outside the UK. Imperial cohesion in fact depended on political and traditional rather than economic factors, and on Britain's willingness to interpose her naval shield between the colonies and European dangers.

(2) World War I altered the character of the Empire and of the conferences. Overseas troops (mostly volunteers) and resources were employed extensively in the main theatres of war and in liquidating the German colonies. This created a weight of opinion which changed the Empire from an imperially dominated confederation with consultative habits to an expanding group of countries each with a mind and outside relationships of its own. India, though not self governing, was included in the War Conferences of 1917-18. During the 1921 Conference several colonies signed the P. of Versailles and joined the League of Nations in their own right. Redefinition of imperial relationships was in the air, and this was supplied by the Balfour Definition and the Statute of Westminster (1931, q.v.).

(3) The worldwide slump had meanwhile set in and prompted the Canadians to inspire the 1932 Ottawa economic conference. This revealed in a magnified but different form the difficulties which had beset the Colonial conferences between 1894 and 1907. The overseas countries wanted economic protection but now so did Britain. This enabled participants to negotiate a series of bilateral agreements of small compass which were helpful but never solved the major issue.

(4) The goodwill exemplified in a commonalty of language, education, laws and ideologies nevertheless proved as strong as the economics to pull the Commonwealth through World War II. On the other hand the sacrifices which Britain had to make towards American economic imperialism to keep alive, eroded the hold which she had upon the overseas territories, and this process was supplemented by the policy of imperial liquidation pursued by the post-war Labour govts. The **Commonwealth** conferences no longer, in a constitutional sense, advised a decisive centre and the institution as such was mainly superseded by a Commonwealth Secretariat, while Britain, by joining the EEC progressively distanced herself from her brethren, particularly through immigration policies. The refusal of a Tory govt. to continue to finance the Royal Yacht *Britannia* was a repudiation of the Sovereign's right to make her presence felt in her overseas territories at no cost to them. Henceforth Commonwealth consultation was conducted *ad hoc.*

IMPERIAL DEFENCE COLLEGE was founded in 1927 on the 1922 recommendations of a Cabinet Committee under Winston Churchill (then Colonial Sec.) to train a body of senior officers and civil officials from Britain and Commonwealth countries in the broadest aspects of imperial strategy and occasionally to examine concrete problems referred to it by the Chiefs of Staff. Closed in World War II, it was reopened in 1946. The courses last a year and the Commandant is a service officer of the highest rank.

IMPERIAL DEFENCE COMMITTEE, as proposed by Lord Esher's War Office Reconstruction Committee, was set up with a secretariat in 1904. The Prime Minister was Chairman and entitled to select and vary the members. By Aug. 1909 it had investigated the whole of the ground covered by a possible war with Germany.

IMPERIAL FEDERATION LEAGUE, founded in 1884 by W.E. Forster, was supported by many influential figures including James Bryce, J.A. Froude, the E. of Rosebery, J.R. Seeley, W.H. Smith and prominent colonial politicians. It was briefly the leading source of imperial thought and made seminal suggestions for the Jubilee of 1887, particularly that the prime ministers should consult when together in London. After the Jubilee its members never agreed on a policy and the league broke up in 1893. *See* COMMONWEALTH CONFERENCE.

IMPERIAL GENERAL STAFF. The Hartington Commission (1890) reported while the extremely conservative D. of Cambridge was still C-in-C. It proposed to abolish his office when he retired, devolve the duties of a local commander to a separate officer; create a General Staff whose Chief, with the Adjutant-Gen., the Quartermaster-Gen., the Dir. of Artillery and the Insp-Gen. of Fortifications would be responsible directly to the Sec. for War. The proposals were opposed by the Duke and by Campbell-Bannerman, who feared that greater military efficiency might be dangerous. Hence when the Duke was superseded by Wolseley in 1895 nothing was done. It took the disasters of the Boer War (1899-1902) and the advent, in J.B.S. Haldane, of a Sec. for War (1905-12) educated in Germany, familiar with German military thought and supported by all the professionals, to overcome Campbell-Bannerman's opposition. The Staff was set up in 1907. The notable wartime chiefs were:

Sir William Robertson 1915-18
Sir Henry Wilson 1918-22
Lord Gort 1937-39
Lord Ironside 1939-40
Sir John Dill 1940-41
Sir Alan Brooke 1941-46

IMPERIAL INSTITUTE. See COMMONWEALTH INSTITUTE.
IMPERIALISM. This word has two very different meanings. (1) Kipling, Curzon and others of like mind attached to it a sense of obligation by an imperial power to govern colonial territories well and justified further acquisitions by the belief that European imperial powers could manage the territories of non-European races better than they did themselves. Since slave-trading, thuggery, widow burning and similar abuses were largely suppressed under these imperial regimes this view was not without justification. (2) Lenin, on the other hand, used "Imperialism" as a specialised term in his theory of colonialism. Colonialism to him was the subjection of under-developed territories to capitalist exploitation; imperialism was simply the imposition of colonialism upon theoretically unwilling territories by the armed power of capitalist states; and since, by definition, a socialist or communist state was not capitalist, no such state could be imperialistic. This convenient alteration of meaning converted the word into a term of one-sided abuse and partially disarmed the opponents of Russian territorial expansion. See BANDOENG.
IMPERIAL PREFERENCE. See CANADA; COMMONWEALTH PREFERENCE.
IMPERIAL TOBACCO CO LTD was formed in 1901 as a joint venture by W.D. & H.O. Wills, John Player & Sons, Ogden, Churchmans and Player & Wills (Ireland) Ltd to resist American attempts to capture the British market, the constituent bodies remaining independent. The developing attack on cigarette smoking led to diversification so that tobacco became only part of the group's activities in 1964 when divisions were created to deal in Paper and Boards; to take part in the distributive trades and deal in a variety of goods such as textiles, plastics and potato crisps. The H.Q. has always been at Bristol.
IMPERIAL WAR CABINET. See CABINET.
IMPERIAL WAR MUSEUM was originally a miscellaneous collection of mostly World War I materials founded by the War Cabinet in Mar. 1917 and housed in a gallery of the Imperial Institute. It suffered neglect until a more fitting building was found in Lambeth where it rapidly expanded, especially after World War II, into a wide-ranging museum of modern war.
IMPEY, Sir Elijah (1732-1809) became first C.J. of Bengal in 1774 and was promptly involved in the affair of Nuncomar, an enemy of Warren Hastings. Nuncomar was fairly convicted of forgery and, the court having refused to reprieve him, he was hanged. Francis and other enemies of Hastings accused Impey of being a tool of Hastings because they wanted Nuncomar as a witness in impeachment proceedings. They moved for, but failed to secure, articles of impeachment against Impey in 1788. In 1789 he resigned and was an M.P. from 1790-6.
IMPHAL. See MANIPUR.
IMPI. A regiment of Zulu fighting men. They were strictly disciplined and well trained in their special tactics, especially of distraction by envelopment. Each impi was distinguished by the colour of its shields and the offensive weapon was a standardised spear. Impis could move great distances at speeds which often took opponents by surprise. Hesitation in action was often punished capitally: conspicuous courage rewarded by being invited to dance before the King. Service was compulsory and warriors were not allowed to marry until it was over.
IMPORT DUTIES REPORT (1840) by a Commons Select Committee discovered that of 1150 dutiable articles, 16 realised £22M out of £22.9M. See CORN LAWS.
IMPORTUNING. See SEXUAL OFFENCES.
IMPRESSIONISM was originally a derisive name for a French painting style in which objects are seldom directly represented, but the effects of light from them upon the painter are. In this sense J.M.W. Turner was an impressionist but was never classified as such, because the critical controversy centred upon the Paris group originated by Claude Monet (1840-1926). The American James Abbott WHISTLER (1834-1903) was trained among them and exhibited in London between 1874 and 1877, when he sued Ruskin for libel for his attack on his *Falling Rocket*. The action was a sensation which speeded the conversion of a hitherto hostile English public but bankrupted Whistler; but he continued to work and by 1886 was pres. of various English and international artists' societies and almost respectable.
IMPRESSMENT is the crown's right to take persons or property for the defence of the realm. Regularly used for manning warships (whose men once abroad could not escape) and occasionally for taking merchantmen, it could also be used as a form of military conscription and requisition, e.g. of transport. In practice military impressment was early found ineffectual and impressment of ships dislocated trade. Impressment for naval crews continued until 1815 and was then abandoned but never abolished. Other forms were superseded by statute in 1939.
IMPRIMATUR (Lat = "Let it be printed"). The certification that a book has been passed for publication by the appropriate religious authority. (1) In the R. Catholic church the word is printed in a book on theological or moral subjects after it has been passed by an episcopal power. (2) The Licensing Act, 1662, prohibited books contrary to the Christian faith, the doctrine or discipline of the Church of England or tending to scandalise the govt. All books had to be entered at Stationers Hall and licensed according to their subject by the Lord Chancellor, a Sec. of State, the Earl Marshal, the Abp. of Canterbury or the Bp. of London. The licence was called "the Royal Imprimatur". The Act expired in 1679, was renewed in 1685 and finally expired in 1695.
IMPRISONMENT FOR DEBT. See BANKRUPTCY.
IMPROPRIATION. See ADVOWSON AND TITHE-6, 7.
IMPROVEMENT COMMISSIONERS. A common but mostly unofficial term for local bodies (mostly in towns) set up with varying constitutions to pave, light, cleanse or otherwise improve streets or rivers, repel encroachments and remove obstacles. They could levy rates. Most of them were created between 1720 and 1834 by local Acts of Parliament. See LOCAL ADMINISTRATION.
IN BEING. See FLEET.
IN CAPITE. Lat = in chief (q.v.).
INCEST was made an offence in 1908.

IN CHIEF. A feudal tenant who held his lands direct of the Crown was said to be a tenant-in-chief. cf IMMEDIACY.

INCHTUTHILL (Scot). Site of Roman legionary H.Q. begun in A.D. 83 but, owing to a change of policy abandoned in A.D. 86.

INCITEMENT TO DISAFFECTION, MUTINY. The Incitement to Mutiny Act, 1797, passed as a result of the Nore and Spithead naval mutinies, made such incitement a capital felony and was extended to the Royal Air Force in 1918. The Incitement to Disaffection Act, 1934, created lesser offences.

INCHIQUIN. *See* O'BRIEN.

INCIDENT, THE (Sept.-Oct. 1641) was an intrigue by Will Murray (later E. of Dysart), Charles I's favourite groom of the bedchamber, to induce certain professional soldiers, notably Lord Crawford and Cols. Cochrane and Urry, in the King's retinue, to stage a *coup* against the rising Covenanters. The Ds. of Argyll and Hamilton were to be kidnapped from the royal apartments at Holyroodhouse on the night of 11 Oct. 1641. The King knew of an intrigue, but it has never been proved that he knew the details. On 29 Sept. the royalist Lord Ker called out the D. of Hamilton and when the Estates forced him to apologise he came with several hundred armed men. The Covenanters counter-armed. Then Col. Cochrane set about tampering with the troops but Col. Urry betrayed the plot to the covenanting Gen. Leslie on the morning of 11 Oct. Argyll, Hamilton, with his brother Lanark, withdrew to Kinneil 20 miles away and published the conspiracy. In the subsequent parliamentary private inquiry Will Murray distracted attention from himself by producing a letter which apparently implicated the long imprisoned M. of Montrose but actually referred to a different series of events. This saved the conspirators and blackened Montrose but the whole affair was joyfully used by the Covenanters to destroy the King's short-lived Scottish popularity.

INCLOSURE (less technically ENCLOSURE) (1) is to be distinguished from three other similar operations involving consolidation or alteration of English land holdings; these others are ASSART which is the reduction into cultivation of royal forest (which was illegal) or of manorial waste; APPROVEMENT which is the inclosure of common land by a lord of a manor in exchange for other land to be thrown open to the commoners; and the LEASING OF ADJACENT TENEMENTS by lords or tenants so as to produce unity of management. Inclosure, on the other hand, is the rearrangement of holdings and their appurtenant or appendant rights of common pasture so that for the many intermingled parcels of the mediaeval open field and those rights there is substituted a few compact farms spreading not only over the former open fields but often over the more valuable parts of the local common or waste.

(2) Inclosures were mostly carried out for the behoof of the comparatively small number of Lords and tenants who had common law interests in their previously existing tenements, but they were impracticable unless they involved extinguishing customary rights or tolerated practices of the much larger number of squatters, cotars, servile tenants, tenants at will or for short periods, and others whom the common law did not protect. All these were often deprived of their mode of life with inadequate or no compensation and mostly had to seek a living as unsheltered wage earners on the new farms or in a neighbouring town.

(3) All four processes tended to produce similar visual results on the ground and to raise productivity and so have been lumped together by later observers under the title of an "inclosure movement", but actually they were different in their technique and social results. Assarts (which were facilitated by statutes of 1235 and 1285) would benefit lords without necessarily harming existing tenants and might benefit future tenants by bringing more cultivable land into the market. Approvement left the economic position of the tenants unchanged. Lease of adjacent holdings was necessarily voluntary and was an important means of social promotion in the later middle ages.

(4) By contrast inclosure was usually forced upon villagers against their will; but the scope of the method was limited (speaking generally) to areas where the other methods had not been much tried and then only where the circumstances were not inherently unsuitable. The open field system was fully workable only in better drained parts of the inland plain and could not be worked at all in the Kentish Weald, the great moorland tracts of the north and west, the mountainous areas or in fowling, fishing, hunting or cattle raising districts such as the Fens or the New Forest. Moreover, in some parts where it was workable it was not in fact worked because of the survival of ancient local customs mostly of Celtic origin. Inclosure is found mostly in open field areas, seldom elsewhere.

(5) Nevertheless the two great inclosure periods produced enormous, if sometimes exaggerated, social and economic consequences. They changed the face of half the country. The first period began in the middle of the 15th cent. and was spent by the end of the 16th; the second commenced at the opening of the 18th cent. and ended a few years after Waterloo. Each had its characteristic causes and features.

(6) By the late 15th cent. most of the exploitable land was being exploited. The older landed aristocracy was almost destroyed by civil war and the export boom in wool and cloth was enriching the merchants. The inclosures of this period represented not capital improvement or investment but a change of land use from arable to sheep farming. It was effected mainly by a commercial class with social pretensions anxious to buy land and make quick profits. The land came onto the market in vast quantities through confiscations during the civil wars and on the dissolution of the monasteries. Land speculation and inclosure were contemporaneous and interconnected. The usual method was simple eviction, either at the end of a lawful term or violently before it ended, and many were driven from their homes to make room for sheep runs who would later have been protected by the royal courts. The govt. denounced evictions in the parliament of 1484; the first statute against inclosures was passed in 1489; and Tudor rulers, strong though most of them were, struggled ineffectually against the current. Both Wolsey and Somerset took measures against inclosures and roused the hostility of powerful interests able to contribute to their downfall.

(7) The time between the end of the first period and the opening of the second was marked by civil and constitutional struggles on the one hand and by the increasing willingness and ability of the royal courts to protect manorial, especially copyhold, tenants. The commercial and industrial revolutions were beginning: the rising population raised the demand for food; the machines devoured more raw materials, especially wool. The second inclosure movement represented not so much a mere change of land use as a reorganistion for greater efficiency and capital investment. The prizes were larger than before; but the legal difficulties were also much greater. Thus the characteristic method of this second period was to override all legal interests by means of a private Act of Parliament. The first such was passed in 1709; by the period 1765 to 1785 they were averaging 47 a year. In 1801 the Inclosure Consolidation Act facilitated this process to such an extent that in that year parliament passed no fewer than 119. Not surprisingly the rate of enactment began to decline soon afterwards as the amount of uninclosed land dwindled. By the time social and aesthetic opposition to the process began to develop, with the passing of the general

Inclosure Act of 1845, the movement was already almost exhausted. Nearly 4000 inclosure acts were passed before 1845; less than 200 have been made since.

(8) The Act of 1845 codified the common practices which had grown up over the years. The private bill having been passed, commissioners or surveyors were appointed to carry out its terms. These, after inquiry, issued an award which set out the boundaries of the new properties, the compensation, if any, to be paid by the new owners to the dispossessed, the public and private roads and the village greens to be laid out and the liabilities for maintaining them and the land drainage. These awards were and are "land charters" fundamental to life in at least 5000 villages, for they are the starting point of the local public and private rights. Moreover, because the new holders were habitually required to plant quickset hedges as a condition of taking up their holdings, the inclosures created a landscape which until recently has been regarded as typical of the English countryside. *See* LAND TENURE, ENGLAND-3.

INCOME TAX (1) In 1797 Pitt faced a war deficit of £17M with a direct taxation system based upon an unalterable land tax. He therefore introduced land tax redemption combined with a tax (called PROPERTY TAX) on "unearned" incomes above £60 a year, graduated up to a maximum of 10% on incomes above £200. The survey of 1798 showed a national income of £102M and a taxable income of £79M. The tax was first levied in 1799 but yielded about £6M until Addington abolished it in 1802 after the P. of Amiens. When war broke out in 1803 Addington reintroduced it in a simplified and more efficient form at 5% and it yielded £4.5M until 1815 when it was again abolished at the peace.

(2) By 1842 Peel had inherited a succession of deficits with a revenue 75% of which was drawn from indirect taxation. To raise customs and excise duties might discourage consumption and lower taxation yields. He decided to reduce the duties and tide over the probable revenue gap by an income tax (so-called) at 7d in the pound (2.9%) and then, as rising consumption raised the yield, use any surplus to finance further reductions in indirect taxes. This process continued until 1845 when the tax was renewed. Though Peel was overthrown in 1846 the tax continued and in 1852 Disraeli, in seeking to compensate the great vested interests for Free Trade by repealing duties on malt, shipping and sugar, proposed to extend it to PRECARIOUS ("earned") income above £100 a year and to "unearned" income above £50. Gladstone succeeded him; he avoided taxing earned income and hoped, by extending the legacy duty to land, to abolish the entire tax by 1859. In the meantime he continued to reduce indirect taxation but the yield of legacy duty was less than expected and the Crimean War (1854-5) interfered with his plans. Consequently the rate on unearned income was raised to 1s. 2d. in £ (5.8%) in 1854 and this decisively established it as a permanent tax, though the abatement level was raised and the rate of tax lowered to 7d. (2.9%) in 1863, 6d. (2½%) in 1865 and 4d. (⅓%) in 1874.

(3) The tax was levied (with exemptions and abatements at the bottom) on total income, but when rates began to rise and the increased electorate began to contain a significant number of manual workers, demands for personal allowances and a distinction between "earned" and "unearned" income arose and from 1907 it became a two part tax; child allowances and a supertax on high incomes were added in 1909. During World War I the standard rate of income tax was 30%, in World War II 50%, with surtax rising by stages to 95%. In the period from 1946 to 1976 it varied around 30% with surtax up to 80%. From 1979, when surtax was abolished, the lower levels on taxable income were set at 25%, the higher at 40%. A narrow 20% band was introduced in

1992 but otherwise this remained, with detailed variations, the pattern as late as 1995.

IN COENA DOMINI **(Lat = In the house of the Lord).** A papal bull, first issued in 1364 and annually republished, listing the heresies, schismatical actions, infractions of papal claims and temporal offences subject to papal censure. Republication was discontinued in 1770 in response to pressure from national govts.

INCOGNITO **(Ital = unrecognised).** An unofficial identity assumed by a high state personality to avoid the ceremony and protocol surrounding his office, e.g. the Czars sometimes travelled as "Counts of the North".

INCOMES POLICY was a euphemism for govt. efforts from 1948 to 1978 to limit pay rises negotiated between trade unions and employers. The object was to control inflation.

INCREMENT VALUE DUTY was a discriminatory capital gains tax by which Lloyd George as Chanc. of the Exch. proposed to pay for the increased naval estimates of 1909 while provoking a successful battle with the predominantly property owning House of Lords. It was to be £1 for every £5 by which the value of land increased after 30 April 1909, leviable on sale or long lease or on death, or every 15 years in the case of a corporation. Agricultural land was exempt unless on sale (e.g. for building) the price exceeded the market value as agricultural land. Effectively a tax on urban and industrial properties, the feature most offensive to property owners was that the Inland Revenue would need to survey and value all land in the country and thus pry into owners' affairs to make the tax work.

INCUMBENT in England means the rector, vicar or curate in charge of an ecclesiastical parish. In Scotland it is the holder of a similar office in the episcopal church.

INCUMBERED ESTATES ACT, 1848 (Ir.). Partly as a result of the Irish famines, many estate owners needed to borrow on their lands but lenders were backward because emigration had reduced income from rents and the complications of tenure and mortgage law made it difficult to sell the land upon which loans might be secured. The act made it possible with court approval to sell property clear of any such incumbrance and then impose the lenders rights upon the fund represented by the purchase money, which had to be paid into a special account with the Bank of Ireland. The Act did not bring the intended benefits. Potential English buyers feared that as improving landlords they might be murdered by their tenants. Hence there was little money in the special account.

INCUNABULA are books printed at a period when European printing was still primitive, especially books printed before 1500.

INDECENT EXPOSURE, originally dealt with in the Star Chamber, was held to be a misdemeanour in 1663.

INDECENT PUBLICATIONS were originally punishable only in the ecclesiastical courts. The first successful prosecution in the temporal court occurred in 1727.

INDEMNITY, ACTS OF. In emergencies such as war or insurrection it may be necessary for servants of the Crown to take speedy action of whose legality they are not certain. The Crown probably has a prerogative to act in such extreme cases but it is normal to pass Acts of Indemnity afterwards to protect persons who have acted in good faith. Such Acts were passed in the Cape of Good Hope in 1900 and 1902 after the South African War; and in Britain in 1920 after World War I but not after World War II.

INDEMNITY AND OBLIVION, ACT OF (1661), in principle pardoned all otherwise criminal acts committed between 1 Jan. 1637 and 24 June 1660 by persons acting under direct or indirect authority of the crown, parliament, the Lord Protector or chief magistrate of the Commonwealth. It annulled court proceedings before 1 May 1658, arising out of such acts but not so as to restore property awarded under such judgments and it protected all *bona fide* purchasers of property. It then created (a) certain excepted acts. These were major crimes (especially murder, buggery, rape, bigamy and witchcraft) not committed under such authority; and embezzlement of royal personal property. (b) certain classes of excepted persons, viz all Jesuits, Romish priests and Seminarists; those who plotted the Irish rebellion of 1641; anyone who betrayed the King's trust and (c) it named certain excepted individuals, viz 49 living and 4 dead regicides but required that 19 of them should, if condemned, not be put to death without a further Act of Parliament because they had surrendered in response to a royal proclamation. It also forfeited the properties of certain named individuals and disqualified others from office by name or, in the case of persons serving on illegal courts, as a class.

INDENTURES were a form, said to have been of Byzantine origin, of solemn agreement written out twice or three times on the same sheet of parchment, the third copy, if any, being written below the bottom of the other two and known as the FOOT OF THE FINE. The copies were then cut apart along fortuitously indented lines so that the parts could be seen by their fit to belong to each other. Indentures were used particularly for personal service agreements and military hirings but even for humble affairs such as apprenticeships. *See* SERVICE INDENTURES.

INDENTURED LABOUR. *See* CHINESE LABOUR QUESTION.

INDENTURED SERVANTS in particular were recruited for the American colonies to work for colonists in return for the cost of passage, maintenance and an eventual gratuity. This 17th cent. practice ended, save in New England, with the 18th cent. importation of slaves.

INDEPENDENCE, DECLARATION OF (1776). *See* AMERICAN REBELLION-16.

INDEPENDENT LABOUR PARTY (I.L.P.) was founded in 1893 to secure working class representation in Parliament independently of the existing parties. Initially unsuccessful in 1900, it formed the Labour Representation Committee with the trade unions and various socialist groups and this, in 1906, became the Labour Party with J. Ramsay MacDonald, an original member, as Sec. It then formed an extremist wing of the Labour Party with a strong anti-liberal bias and since the Liberals and most of Labour supported the war effort in World War I, it lost influence. This recession was confirmed by the Labour Party constitution of 1918, after which the I.L.P. became largely Scottish based. It disaffiliated from the Labour Party in 1932 and thereafter ceased to matter.

INDEPENDENTS. *See* CONGREGATIONALISTS.

INDEPENDENT TELEVISION AUTHORITY. *See* BROADCASTING-8.

INDEX LIBRORUM PROHIBITORUM (Lat = "List of prohibited books") was instituted by the Inquisition under Pope Paul IV in 1559. From 1571 to 1917 it was supervised by a special Congregation. From 1897, however, this control was exercised mainly by diocesan bishops, since 1917 under advice from the Holy Office. The supplementary INDEX EXPURGATORIUS contained books which might be read after certain passages had been purged. Never very efficiently maintained, both were abolished in 1966.

INDIA ACT 1784, PITT'S set up a joint govt. of the HEIC and the Crown over the British possessions in India. The Court of Directors was left in control of commerce and patronage but the Court of Proprietors was deprived of all powers except that of electing the Directors. A BOARD OF CONTROL was set up of six privy councillors, one of whom was the president with a casting vote. No despatch was to be sent by the Directors to India without the Board's previous approval and all despatches from India were to be laid before it. It could also send orders to India without the consent of the

Directors. The Crown also could recall the Gov.-Gen. The membership of his council was reduced from four to three, of whom the C-in-C was one. The Governor-General-in-Council was given theoretically fuller control over Bombay and Madras in matters of war, revenue and diplomacy but could not declare war or enter into any aggressive design without the explicit authority of the Court or of its Secret Committee in agreement with the Board of Control. An amending Act passed in 1786 gave him the right to overrule his Council when he thought it essential. In addition the original Act made British subjects amenable to the English courts for wrongs done in India and required returned 'nabobs' to declare their fortunes.

INDIA BILLS, FOX'S (Nov. 1783) were drafted by Edmund Burke to do away with, as he thought, corrupt and oppressive direction in the HEIC and to restore its profitability yet reduce its distorting influence on national policy and the London money market. The **first bill** named seven commissioners to manage the territory and policy for four years. They were to be removable only on the address of either House, by the Crown which would appoint their successors. Under them were to be 9 named assistant commissioners each with at least £2000 of HEIC stock whose successors were to be elected by the stockholders. These nine were to manage the commercial business. The **second bill** subordinated the three governors (Bengal, Bombay and Madras) directly to the seven commissioners, who were to control their actions and investigate and remedy abuses. Despatches took several months between India and Britain. Of the 16 with security of tenure, the seven were partisans of Fox and North and the nine pro-Fox stockholders. The bills passed the Commons but, once George III knew that Pitt was ready to form an alternative govt., it was thrown out by the Lords at George's request.

INDIA HOUSE (properly East India House). The H.Q. in Leadenhall Street, London, of the Honourable East India Co (HEIC) built in 1726 and demolished in 1861.

INDIAMEN were vessels owned by the HEIC. They were the largest trading ships of their time and were armed as weak frigates against pirates but sometimes painted in line-of-battle ships to bluff national enemies. They lasted about three round trips. The expression POSH stood for Port out, Starboard home, because the coolest and most expensive cabins were thus located.

INDIAN MUTINY (1857-8) was confined to the Bengal Army but some, especially Maratha, notabilities became involved. **(1)** Its complicated origins go back to a time before the disastrous Afghan War of 1839. The mutual trust of British officers and sepoys was beginning to be replaced by psychological barriers due to the beginnings of evangelical intolerance, a waning linguistic competence among officers, a social isolation at big cantonments as more English wives replaced Indian mistresses, a certain arrogance among English women and new officers and a steady increase in the proportion of British to Indian officers. The latter were promoted by seniority but their responsibilities necessarily decreased and this bored them and wounded their pride. Moreover, unlike the Madras and Bombay Armies, caste was an essential feature of the Bengal force and made it inherently difficult to manage. It was, in fact, cemented together until 1839 by an unbroken record of victory which fed its pride and terrified the civil population.

(2) To this the Afghan disaster administered a jolt. The British reputation for invincibility vanished and this gave comfort to disaffected but hitherto cowed rulers and others interested in British decline. There were too a number of specific grievances which disseminated both indiscipline and civil unrest. The sepoys customarily received an allowance (*batta*) when on service outside British territory. *Batta* amounted to more than the ordinary pay and enabled a sepoy to send back more money to his family. Troops were raised in particular districts and among farming families and their friends so that groups of villages had strong personal ties with certain units, a close interest in their adventures and depended upon them for their cash surplus. The difficult war in the appalling climate of Sind (1843-4) led to the annexation of that territory and, logically enough, to the end of *batta* there. Thus the reward of victory was loss of income in camp and village. Certain units refused their orders unless *batta* was paid. The danger from the neighbouring Sikhs was great. It was necessary to pardon most of the mutineers. A just grievance had been remedied by mutiny.

(3) The financial authorities learned nothing. The two Sikh wars (1845-6 and 1848-9) included seven of the fiercest battles fought in India and ended with the annexation of the Punjab. In June 1849 *batta* in the Punjab was stopped retrospectively to Apr. There were mutinies at Rawalpindi, Wazirabad and Govindgarh and sporadic unrest elsewhere. Sir Chas. Napier's efforts to deal with another grievance related to the cost of living led to a public quarrel with Dalhousie, the new gov-gen. Napier resigned. The English were now publicly disunited.

(4) The new atmosphere of civil administration was also disturbing. The sepoy came from the upper stratum of a village society based on land holding and religion. The new, Haileybury trained progressive administrators arrived in increasing numbers determined to impose their ideas on social justice, to regularise the confusion of land titles and ancient (or modern) privileges and anomalies. This involved the wholesale examination and questioning of property rights and of the Hindu and Muslim religious endowments which the new muscular Christians held in horror. To sepoy suspicions about pay were now added worries about the security of family homes and ancestral religion.

(5) There was also a complementary trend in high politics; it was becoming axiomatic that British rule should be extended because it was good for Indians and that Indian states were corrupt, oppressive and should be abolished. Dalhousie proposed to annex seven states either for misgovernment or on the basis of the doctrine of *lapse* and to extinguish 4 hereditary titles with their pensions. He had his way with three of the latter including the Nana Sahib's, and with four of the states: Satara (1848); Nagpur (1853) (*see* MARATHAS), Jhansi (1853) and most importantly Oudh (1856).

(6) More than anything else the annexation of Oudh brought northern India to the brink of catastrophe. Its Kings had been faithful allies for a century yet the royal widows were humiliated. Most of the Bengal army was recruited there. A sepoy in Oudh was privileged: through the British Resident he could obtain a hearing from the King's officers which other subjects of the King could not. Annexation ended the Residency and the privilege. Again sepoys felt threatened in their homes and downgraded.

(7) To Dalhousie's uncomprehending arrogance was added rumours of Crimean disasters. Certain castes in the Bengal army were polluted by crossing the sea or the Indus. Men remembered the unsuccessful effort to send Bengal troops by sea to Burma in 1852. If everyone was a polluted outcast, could he be sent on campaign to the other end of the earth? Missionaries, difficult to distinguish from govt. chaplains, preached openly and offensively against Hinduism and Islam. The false belief grew up that there was a British conspiracy against religion. Moreover the western scientific outlook was bound to undermine the Brahmin-dominated hierarchical structure of society. Brahmins had every motive for fomenting discontent.

(8) In this potentially hysterical atmosphere the authorities at the Dum Dum arsenal began issuing a new tallow greased cartridge. Such cartridges were normally opened by biting. It was rumoured that there was pigs' fat (unspeakable to Muslims) and cows' fat (a profanity to Hindus) in the tallow (Jan. 1857). Orders were published to withdraw the tallow and let the men grease the cartridges themselves but it was too late. Suspicion fed on suspicion. In Feb. there was a mutinous outbreak at Barrackpore; this was suppressed and the regiment concerned disbanded. Other disbandments followed. On 10 May, however, the cavalry and then the infantry mutinied at Meerut and marched for Delhi, the seat of the Great Mogul. Energetic action at Meerut might have averted the trouble but the generals were old and inert. The news spread (despite the absence of electric telegraphy) at great speed. It was known at Lahore on 11th and John Lawrence disarmed his Bengal troops on 13th. The unpursued Meerut mutineers crowded into Delhi on 11th and 12th and the troops there joined them. British were hunted down; a British party defending the magazine, despairing of rescue, blew it and themselves up. The Delhi mutineers proclaimed the unwilling and powerless Mogul as their leader. Mutinies now occurred at minor and major stations, especially Lucknow (30 May), Sitapore (2 June), Cawnpore (4 June), Allahabad (6 June).

(9) By mid June British garrisons (all including Indian troops) were besieged at Lucknow, Cawnpore and Agra, while a British and Indian force, assembled mostly from the Punjab, was attacking a much larger garrison of mutineers in Delhi. There were notorious outrages such as the massacres of Europeans at Delhi and Cawnpore and many murders in isolated stations. The British were enormously outnumbered but they had a single purpose, the suppression of the rebellion, a single emotion, vengeance which served that end, a co-ordinated command and a single military objective, Delhi, whose fall would decide everything. Their opponents never had a concerted policy, command or plan. Many gravitated to the Mogul because he seemed a useful symbol; the Nana Sahib at Cawnpore represented a Maratha hope, inconsistent with the Mogul's position and only sporadically supported by other Marathas. The dispossessed Rani of Jhansi stood for the rights of rulers but was herself an anomaly, and in many areas the breakdown led only to brigandage or the settling of private scores between Indians.

(10) Considered geographically the reconquest falls into three major sections. The mutinous heartland was pressed from the West and North at Delhi and from the east around Cawnpore (retaken in July) towards Lucknow, which was finally relieved in Nov. 1857. The British acted with speed and ferocity, burning villages and hanging people with little discrimination, their blood-lust fed on false, as well as true, reports of murder and rape. While this heartland was being overrun a second, more properly rebellious movement had had time to form to the adjacent south around the romantic and vigorous genius of the Rani of Jhansi, to whom Tantia Topee (the Nana's nephew) escaped with the best of the mutineer cavalry. It was necessary to mount a separate Central Indian Campaign under Sir Hugh Rose. Jhansi was besieged and taken, the Rani dying in battle at the head of her cavalry. Tantia Topee was captured a little later. By Sept. 1858 the mutineers had been dispersed, hunted down or driven to starvation in the Himalayan foothills. *See* PALMERSTON'S FIRST ADMINISTRATION-8 and for the British generals involved CAMPBELL, SIR COLIN; HAVELOCK, SIR HENRY; LAWRENCE, NICHOLSON, BRIG-GEN. JOHN.

INDIA. NORTH'S REGULATING ACTS. Those of 1773:- **(1)** (c.9) forbade the HEIC for six months after 7 Dec. 1772 to appoint commissioners to superintend business in India "while their affairs are actually at this time under immediate consideration in parliament". **(2)** (c.44) opened the colonies to HEIC tea free of duty thereby upsetting American contraband dealers (*see* BOSTON TEA PARTY). **(3)** (c.63) (a) required annual election of the HEIC directors by fourths in rotation, raised the voters qualification from £500 stock to £1000 and forbade collusive share transfers or instructions to influence voting. (b) created a gov-gen. and council of four in Bengal, subjected the presidencies of Bombay and Madras to them and named Warren Hastings as first gov-gen., Lieut-gen. John Clavering, George Monson, Richard Barwell and Philip Francis as the first councillors. (c) created a supreme court for Bengal; (d) forbade the gov-gen. and council to accept presents or engage in trade.

(4) (c.64) required the Co. to accept a treasury loan of £1.4M; forbade it to issue bills of exchange without treasury consent and required it to export to India in 1773-4 £308,037 worth of goods.

The Act of **1774:- (5)** (c.34) extended the drawback on re-exported tea (*see* **2** *above*) but allowed others to import it if the Co. did not keep the English market supplied.

The Act of **1775:- (6)** (c.44) continued the compulsory export provisions of **(4)** above until 1778.

The Act of **1776:- (7)** (c.57) gave greater latitude to the Co. in re-exports because of the interruption of trade due to the American Rebellion.

INDIA OFFICE was created in 1858 on the abolition of the HEIC and abolished in 1947 on Indian and Pakistani independence.

INDIAN ASSOCIATION was founded in Calcutta in 1876 for the creation of a strong public opinion in India and for the unification of Indian races and peoples upon the basis of common political interests and aspirations. From its inception it was an organisation of moderates.

INDIAN NATIONAL CONGRESS was founded in 1885 on the initiative of a retired British civil servant, ALLAN OCTAVIAN HUME (1829-1912) who convened its first meeting to Bombay and was its gen-sec. until 1908. Initially it was encouraged by the Viceroy (Lord Dufferin) and its resolutions were presented to the govt. as petitions. It soon began to feel that its demands were not being taken seriously and in 1888 it established an agency and a weekly journal in London. After the Indian Councils Act, 1892, an extremist party led by Bal Gangadhar TILAK (1857-1920) began to form within the Congress. At the Benares meeting of 1905 a resolution demanding a govt. which should be "autonomous and absolutely free of British control" was narrowly defeated. In 1906 at Calcutta a compromise was patched up but the Surat meeting of 1907 came to blows. At Allahabad in 1908 a new constitution declared that the Congress' first object was "the attainment of a system of govt. similar to that enjoyed by the self governing members of the British Empire by constitutional means". This ambiguous formula enabled the moderates to retain control until 1916, especially in view of the Morley-Minto reforms of 1909 for which they could take some credit. In the 1920s and 1930s the Congress was led by the Mahatma Gandhi as a movement for non-co-operation with the British. In 1939 Congress refused to support the war effort unless India was granted full independence, so the war was carried on without its help. Held together largely by opposition to the British, it slowly fell apart after they left. *See* GANDHI AND NEHRU.

INDIAN PRINCELY STATES (1) Between 1858 and independence in 1947 they comprised 40% of the area and 35% of the population. Their numbers varied slightly around 560 with dynastic alliances. Their several areas and the nature of their sovereignty were settled and guaranteed by individual treaties with Great Britain. These treaties were the juridical and moral bedrock of their existence. They were classified into **Salute States,** whose rulers were entitled to a salute of guns varying from 9 to 21; **Second Division States** not so entitled and over 300 small states where the civil and criminal jurisdiction was exercised on the ruler's behalf by Political Agents of the govt. of India. The most important was the 21-gun state of Hyderabad (about half the area of Sweden but with twice the population), the smallest salute state, Sachin, was about 7 miles square. The smallest of all, Vejanoness, had 200 people in 22 acres.

(2) The Nizam (of Hyderabad), Nawabs, Mehtars, Walis and Mirs were Moslem, for these titles were derived from the Mogul administration. The rest (a vast majority) were born by indigenous Hindu dynasties, some of great antiquity. 66 rulers of salute states were Rajputs. The Nizam was styled His Exalted Highness and the rest down to 11-guns and at the end 9 guns were Highnesses. The Maharana of Mewar or Jaipur, though entitled to only 19 guns, was revered as the senior of all Hindus and was never summoned to Delhi.

(3) They were also organised for political convenience into another hierarchy of groups. In 1931 five 21-gun states (Hyderabad, Mysore, Baroda, Jammu and Kashmir and Gwalior) enjoyed direct relations with the govt. of India. So did the 15-gun states of Bhutan and Sikkim but these were not Indian and had relations with other govts. 336 states enjoyed such relations indirectly through the following Agencies:

Agency	Number of Salute States	Senior State (& guns)	Number of Non-salute States
Rajputana	19	Mewar (19)	2
NW Frontier	1	Chitral (11)	4
Baluchistan	1	Kalat (19)	1
Western India	16	Kutch (17)	185
Madras	4	Travancore (19)	1
Central India	28	Indore (19)	61
Punjab	13 *82*	Patiala (17)	– *254*

213 enjoyed relations with provincial govts:

Province			
Bombay	20	Kolhapur (19)	132
United Provinces	3	Rampur (15)	–
Central Provinces			15
Bihar & Orissa	4	Patna (9)	
Bengal	2	Cooch Behar (13)	–
Assam	1	Manipur (11)	15
Punjab	1 *31*	Bashahr (9)	20 *182*

(4) The rulers (mostly men but a few women) were autocrats but their rule was tempered by five powerful influences. (a) Indian morality enjoined a parent and child relationship between ruler and ruled. He was expected to act as father and mother (Ma-Baap) in accordance with accepted parental practices and was entitled to filial respect. (b) Most rulers held regular public durbars attended as of right by certain vassals and ministers and were expected not merely to consult them but to listen to the often frank speeches made not merely to them but within the hearing of the bystanders. This informal and traditional arrangement for bringing public opinion to bear was undoubtedly real. (c) The British govt. had developed a doctrine of paramountcy by which it regulated successions and, in cases of grave misrule, intervened to control or even depose a ruler. Through this doctrine many very small states were to some extent administered in the name of the ruler by Agents of the British govt. (d) The Paramount power persuaded most rulers by argument or pressure to limit the amount of their Privy Purse to a fixed percentage (ideally 10%) of the state revenue. (e) An Agent, if not resident in the state, was never far away.

(5) The average standard of princely administration roughly equalled, perhaps slightly exceeded, that of British India. There were deviations above and below this average. Some states had well developed systems of public education. By 1944 Gondal was industrially developed, without taxes and had a unique system of compulsory education for women as well as men. Mysore was reckoned an administrative model throughout Asia. On the other hand Alwar, almost alone, was so misruled in the 1920s that the peasantry rebelled and the Paramount Power deposed the Maharajah Jay Singh. The populations, ruled by their own people rather than foreigners, were for the most part more tranquil than those across the border. Political or communal violence was rare.

(6) In Bengal, Bihar and Orissa there were landowners called *zamindars* who held and paid a tax-rent for sometimes enormous tracts and had, like the Maharajab of Burdwan, personal titles. These men were mostly richer than the rulers of smaller or even medium sized states but they represented the debris of former states whose ruling families had kept their properties but had been deprived of their powers.

(7) Some states maintained forces of infantry and cavalry (but not artillery) which they placed at the disposal of the Paramount Power in time of war.

(8) When the issue of partition and independence was agreed between the Indian National Congress, the Moslem League and the Attlee govt. the latter announced that the transfer of power would be made not later than June 1948 and Lord Mountbatten was sent to India as Viceroy to make it. He arrived in Mar. 1947 and announced in June that the date was to be advanced to 15 Aug. 1947. If the States' treaties lapsed with the disappearance of the Indian Empire, they would become independent. To prevent this a States' Dept. was created under Sardar Patel in July. They were given deceptive assurances that if they joined India or Pakistan their interests would be respected. They were rushed into situations where they had no time to organise and hustled into signing Instruments of Accession which guaranteed their sovereignty and the continuity of state govt. Relying as royalties on the word of a royal Viceroy, as they had hitherto relied on the treaties, they signed with varying doubts, seldom realising until too late that these instruments did not bind the Indian and Pakistani successor govts. Only the Nizam, the Nawab of Junagadh and the Maharajah of Jammu and Kashmir refused to sign because they preferred to join Pakistan. Indian troops attacked Junagadh within days of independence. Hyderabad was overrun in Sept. 1949. Jammu and Kashmir became a battleground and was de facto partitioned.

(9) The drawn-out *coup d'état* was now complete. The politicians of the successor govts. never intended to respect their interests and abolished the princely states in return for constitutionally guaranteed Privy Purses. In Dec. 1971 even this guarantee was broken.

INDIANA (U.S.A.). The area was explored and exploited by the French until they ceded it to Britain in 1763. Britain ceded it to the U.S.A. at the T. of Versailles in 1783. It was admitted to the Union as a state in 1816.

INDICTION. A Roman 15-year tax assessment period instituted under Constantine I and widely used in the middle ages for dating, by indiction number and year, alongside regnal and Christian dating. A Papal indiction beginning with 1 Jan. 313 survives.

INDICTMENT is an accusation of serious crime made by the Crown. Formerly it had to be laid before a grand jury when it was called a 'bill of indictment'. Proceedings could not go forward until the grand jury (by a majority)

had agreed. This was called 'returning a true bill' (*see* IGNORAMUS). Grand juries were abolished in 1933 and these preliminary proceedings are now held before magistrates. An indictment may be disposed of (1) by the Crown entering a *nolle prosequi* (refusal to prosecute); (2) by the Crown granting a free pardon; (3) by the accused successfully pleading that he has already been acquitted or convicted or pardoned for the same offence (4) by the accused successfully moving to quash the indictment on the ground that it is bad in form or discloses no offence known to the law; (5) by trial before a jury ending in a verdict of guilty or not guilty.

INDIES, EAST. A geographical term meaning, at first rather vaguely, the inhabited land from the west coast of India eastwards, including the Spice Islands and other fabled places, with adjacent territories. As European knowledge and penetration of these areas developed after the Portuguese reached India, the term became increasingly specialised until it eventually meant the Indonesian Archipelago.

INDIES, LAWS OF THE, were the decrees, especially on mining, labour and trade which the Spanish crown issued in the Spanish-American possessions. The latter were considered to be separate kingdoms from those of Spain and their laws differed from those of Castile which had the trading monopoly. In particular they were meant to protect the natives against maltreatment by Spaniards (who flouted them for economic reasons) and to protect Castilian trade against foreigners (who similarly flouted them).

INDIRECT RULE was an inexpensive technique for governing those British colonies which already had existing indigenous (often tribal) authorities, by leaving the internal administration to them subject to supervision and sometimes with the aid of a subsidy. This sometimes had the unintended effect of encouraging local sentiment and particularism. It was prevalent in the Indian princely states and in many of the African colonies. It was the opposite of the principle in French colonies, often intermingled in Africa with British, of encouraging colonial inhabitants to become citizens of France by accepting French law.

INDIVIDUALISM. This much abused word has many accepted or implied meanings of which the following seem to be the commonest, viz (1) The New Testament notion of the supreme value of the individual person. (2) The direct approach to God without mediation of priest or church. (3) The renaissance idea of self development. (4) Self direction or independence of judgment. (5) Moral anarchy. (6) Freedom of a person from interference by others or society. (7) The adaptation of societies so as to respond to the needs or demands of those composing them. (8) The limitation of political authority to purposes sufficient to achieve individual purposes. (9) The explanation of social phenomena in terms of facts about individuals. (10) Economic *laissez-faire*. (11) The acquisition of knowledge through experience.

INDO-CHINA. (1) Under the T. of Versailles (Nov. 1787) French officers helped Nguyen phua Anh, King of COCHIN CHINA, against the so-called Tay Son rebels. He established himself, reigned as Gia Long (r. 1802-20), founded the Nguyen dynasty and ceded Tourane and Pub-Condor to France. His successors were less Francophile and in 1859 a joint Franco-Spanish expedition intervened against persecution of Christian priests. It reached Saigon, was besieged by the Annamites and relieved in 1861. A treaty (June 1862) ceded three eastern provinces of Cochin China to France. In Aug. 1863 the French established a protectorate over CAMBODIA; in 1867 they annexed the three western Cochin-Chinese provinces. They were now ready to interfere further north and in Nov. 1873 Francis Garnier, who had already explored the Mekong, took Hanoi but was killed by

Chinese Black Flag troops. In fact the Annamite rulers soon played off France and China. A treaty conceding rights of passage to Yunnan and a virtual protectorate (1874) was rendered nugatory in 1880 when the Annamite govt. reaffirmed an ancient, long obsolete, Chinese overlordship. French troops landed in Tong King while French fleets appeared off Hué, the Annamite capital. In 1883 ANNAM accepted a French protectorate, but war with the Chinese-supported Black Flags continued. The French destroyed a Chinese squadron on the Min and bombarded Foochow. In June 1885 the Chinese recognised the French protectorate (T. of Tientsin) and the French created a largely administrative UNION INDOCHINOISE in 1887 but local resistance continued until 1895. The French extended their protectorates to Laos in 1893 and there were further encroachments and exchanges of territory on the Siamese frontier in 1904 and 1907. Two seldom articulated features of, particularly, Laotian affairs were firstly the physical and linguistic similarity of Laotians and Thai which made border control, especially in the northern jungles, virtually impossible, and secondly the beauty of Laotian women who provided many Frenchmen with mistresses.

(2) The French allowed Adm. Rozhestvenski's fleet to use the ports on its way towards Japan in 1905. In 1940 the Japanese occupied Tongking and in 1941 the rest. They ceded the W. Cambodian provinces to Thailand but otherwise the Vichy French administration stayed until 1945 when they dissolved the *Union Indochinoise*. This was replaced by the three Associated States of CAMBODIA, LAOS and VIETNAM.

(3) In the latter the Viet-Minh, a communist party under Ho Chi-Minh exploiting national sentiment, proclaimed independence (Sept. 1945) and provoked the violent revolution and war with the French which ended in the French defeat at Dien Bien Phu (May 1954) and the Geneva Agreement (July) under which the French left and the country was divided at the 17th Parallel between the communist north and a U.S. supported conventional south. The north never tried to honour the agreement but gave material, moral, financial and manpower support to communist rebels. This provoked powerful and mostly misguided U.S. intervention. The resulting VIETNAM WAR ended, after doing fearful damage, in U.S. withdrawal in 1973-4. The communists then resumed operations against the lawful govt. This was overthrown in 1975 and in 1976 the two parts of Vietnam were united under Ho Chi-Minh.

(4) Meanwhile in 1953 Cambodia became independent under its ex-king, Prince Norodom Sihanouk who, while professing neutrality, permitted the communists to use Cambodian territory for their tactical purposes in the Vietnam War. Right wing officers deposed the Prince in Mar. 1970 and he went to Peking. In May the U.S. and S. Vietnamese entered Cambodia to root out the communists but encountered the ferocious primitive agrarian communism appealing, under the name of Khmer Rouge, to Cambodian sentiment led by Pol Pot. They launched a civil war which carried them to the occupation and depopulation of the capital (Phnom Penh). They slaughtered over 1M people and were attacked (Jan. 1979) by the more conventional communist Vietnamese. They set up a govt. at Phnom Penh which was ineffectual because it could not control the countryside.

(5) Laos achieved a step-by-step independence by 1954 and until 1962 control oscillated between neutralists on the Sihanouk pattern and right-wingers analogous to those who deposed him but meanwhile a Marxist party called Pathet Lao ("Laotia") grew up and the head of the royal house, Prince Souvanna Phouma, formed a coalition which included them. With Viet Minh help, however, they subverted the system and took over the whole country in 1975.

INDO-EUROPEAN. The term, denoting a linguistic group, apparently originated in an article by Thomas Young in the *Quarterly Review* of Oct. 1813. The languages in the group are often classified by their use of the k or s sound in the word for *hundred*. The k (centum) languages are Greek, Latin and Italian languages, Celtic languages such as Gaelic and Welsh, Teutonic including Norse and English. The s (satem) languages are Sanskrit, Zend, Slavonic and Albanian.

INDONESIA (1) Though Indonesian spices (mostly pepper and cloves) had long been imported into Europe by the Venetians through Egypt the first direct contacts began through the Portuguese early in the 16th cent. Afonso de Albuquerque took and fortified Malacca, the main emporium, in 1511 in pursuit of Portuguese crown policy of controlling this lucrative trade at its source. At this time Indonesia was mainly Hindu and still dominated by the declining Kingdom of Majapahit, but in 1520 the Portuguese made an alliance with the Moluccan (Spice Is.) principality of Ternate, which was at war with the neighbouring Tidore allied with Spaniards coming from America. In 1525 Moslems overthrew Majapahit. In the disturbed condition of the area military weakness and corruption prevented the Portuguese from completing their control but the initial profits were vast until 1570 when there was a revolt in Ternate. When Drake visited the islands in 1579 the Portuguese were in difficulties but the union of Spain and Portugal put Spanish power in Tidore on their side but opened Portuguese possessions to raids by Spain's enemies, the English and Dutch.

(2) An English expedition under Lankester visited the islands in 1591 but it was the Dutch who seized the opportunity, first with a visit in 1595 and then with fully organised operations by the Dutch East India Co. (founded in 1602) which drove the Portuguese out of Amboina, their main establishment in the Moluccas, in 1605. Meantime in the spice trade the English and French East India Cos. remained in commercial and piratical rivalry with the Dutch and Portuguese. The French never established themselves: the Dutch destroyed the English settlement at Amboina in 1625 ('The Amboina Massacre'), took Ceylon, the essential staging post, from the Portuguese in 1638 and Malacca in 1641. Thenceforth the Dutch, who had moved to Jakarta (renamed Batavia), controlled all the islands save Portuguese Timor.

(3) Save in the Ommeland or Pale about Batavia, Dutch control was exercised indirectly through native rulers who were supposed to export their produce through the Dutch East India Co. In practice, like the Portuguese, the company was militarily weak and its representatives corrupt. Disorder was never overcome: the Co. sank into debt while its servants made fortunes.

(4) A new era opened with the French revolutionary wars. The bankrupt Co. was taken over by the republican state and so fell under French control. The British accordingly attacked the islands and ousted, between 1800 and 1810, what remained of Dutch authority. In 1811 Sir Stamford Raffles, the founder of Singapore, became Gov. of the archipelago. English opinion was already turning against indirect rule in India and Raffles, to cure the prevailing confusion, tried to impose direct rule in Indonesia. He made progress but under the T. of Paris (1815) Indonesia was returned to the Dutch (against Raffles' passionate opposition) as part of a wider British policy of strengthening them against the French. They were not, however, to extend their influence north of Singapore. Save in parts of Java and Sumatra they inherited the British system but the British, against Dutch protests, continued to penetrate North Borneo. Thus James Brooke became Rajah of SARAWAK by cession from the Sultanate of BRUNEI in 1841, and SABA was acquired from Brunei by a business syndicate in 1878 and transferred to the British North Borneo Co. in 1882.

(5) Piracy, always endemic in these waters, in mid-19th cent. centred most strongly in Achin, whose position on the Malay Straits made it peculiarly obnoxious. Under the Sumatra T. British and Dutch agreed to co-operate and the Dutch undertook the conquest of Achin in 1871. This proved difficult and when in 1888, in part-pursuit of a similar policy, the British took Sarawak, Brunei and Saba under their protection, the Dutch were still at war. The area was finally pacified as late as 1898.

(6) Though the Dutch had claimed western NEW GUINEA (or IRIAN) in 1848 and the British and Germans had agreed to divide the Eastern part in 1884, it remained largely uninfluenced by Europeans until 1898 when, in reply to increased German interest, the Dutch bought off the claims of the Sultan of Tidore. This rounded off the Dutch dominions and with the arrival of Van Heutsz as governor-general (until 1909) a rigorous period of administrative consolidation began. One of the results was to make Indonesians more conscious of their identity and it was at this time that nationalism began to take root.

INDONESIA, REPUBLIC. Dutch prestige was destroyed by the Japanese occupation from 1942 to 1945 when the Nationalists proclaimed a Republic. The Dutch then tried to establish a series of autonomous units and there followed a period of disorder ending with a compromise transfer of Dutch sovereignty save in West Irian (W. New Guinea) to a Federal Republic in Dec. 1949. In Aug. 1950, however, this was nominally converted into a unitary state which had to put down a series of local revolts. These sanguinary local civil wars lasted until 1958, when the Republic was able to take up the Irian Question again. Diplomatic relations with Holland were broken off in 1960 and a further local war was ended by the U.N.O. which secured the transfer of the territory to the Republic in 1962.

The endemic insecurity caused the govt. of Pres. Soekarno to seek another foreign distraction in the form of claims against the Malaysian territories in N. Borneo. Communist guerrillas in Malaya were assisted with supplies across the Malacca Straits but the British and Malaysian authorities successfully ended the communist troubles and in 1966 a military council under General Suharto took over Soekarno's effective powers and ended this anti-British episode.

INDORE. See MARATHAS.

INDUCTION. See ADVOWSON.

INDULF (r. 954-62). See SCOTS OR ALBAN KINGS, EARLY-9.

INDULGENCE, DECLARATIONS OF. (1) Charles II issued the **Declaration of Breda** in Apr. 1660; he expressed his readiness to grant liberty to tender consciences in religious matters not affecting the peace of the Kingdom. After he had been restored he confirmed this in the **First** Declaration of Indulgence (Oct.), granted indulgence in certain minor ceremonial matters and announced his intention to call a conference on the whole question (see SAVOY CONFERENCE). **(2)** In Dec. 1662 he issued a Second Declaration confirming the policy of Breda and announcing his intention to seek powers to suspend the penal laws against dissentients. In Feb. 1663 the Commons petitioned for full enforcement of the penal laws and the King's bill was defeated in the Lords. **(3)** In Mar. 1672 he issued the **Third** Declaration suspending the penal laws against nonconformists and recusants by virtue of the royal prerogative of mercy. In 1673 Parliament resolved that this was unconstitutional and it was withdrawn. **(4)** In Apr. 1687 James II issued the **Fourth** Declaration according full liberty of worship, suspending the penal laws, permitting peaceful meetings of nonconformists and remitting penalties for ecclesiastical offences. More significantly he dispensed with the requirements of the Test Act and the need to take the Oaths of Supremacy and Allegiance for those in royal service. His object was to buy nonconformist support for a policy of filling the govt. with R. Catholics. The Declaration was republished in Apr. 1688 and was required to be read in churches. Episcopal opposition provoked the arrest in June of the Seven Bishops, their trial (see SEVEN BISBOPS) and the movement which brought about the King's downfall.

INDULGENCES. In R. Catholic theology sin is considered to be visited by a period of punishment for the individual who, though pardoned or reconciled with God, will not normally be admitted to the Beatific Vision until the period is over. Such punishment can consist of discipline or penance during life and expiation in purgatory afterwards. But the church possesses a treasury of the infinite merits of Jesus Christ, his Mother and the saints, which is available for the relief of the faithful. The Church is entitled to administer the benefits of these merits to the faithful in consideration of prayer or good works. An indulgence is thus the remission not of sin but of the punishment arising from it. General indulgences (i.e. those applying automatically to all who undertake a certain course) have not been certainly traced before the First Crusade and particular indulgences (i.e. those granted in relation to certain places or events) a little later, but the practice grew rapidly and led to abuses. Chaucer's pardoner is an example of the petty rogues who throve in the later middle ages as a result, but when the Church itself began to raise funds by the sale of indulgences, many decent people were revolted. The mission of Johann Tetzel, a Dominican, to Magdeburg and Halberstadt, to raise funds for the building of St. Peters, Rome, by this means and the commercialism of his methods sparked off the explosion of the Reformation, for it led Martin Luther in Oct. 1517 to issue the Ninety-Five Theses with which the movement began. The logic of the situation drove Luther first to condemn abuse of indulgences by the church, then the issue of them at all and so finally the whole basis of Papal authority. The activities of pardoners were prohibited by Pius V in 1567 but indulgences continue to be granted as an encouragement to good works.

INDUNA. A Zulu officer or Matabele military chief. See IMPI.

INDUSTRIAL ACCIDENTS. See FACTORY LEGISLATION, EMPLOYER'S LIABILITY.

INDUSTRIAL COUNCILS AND COURT represent efforts to resolve industrial disputes. The Councils originated in a national joint council set up in 1911 representing employers and employed. It failed to function properly and was replaced in World War I by compulsory arbitration. In 1917 the WHITLEY Committee recommended that each industry should have a joint industrial council to consider general problems. In practice these only functioned if they degenerated into wages negotiating bodies. Since many industries already had established negotiating machinery, the coverage by these "Whitley" councils was only partial, the best known being in teaching. In 1919 the Industrial Court was created, the Minister of Labour being empowered to refer disputes to it with the consent of the parties or to appoint an inquiry without it. During World War II a NATIONAL ARBITRATION TRIBUNAL had powers of compulsory arbitration: these powers were reduced in 1951 when it became the NATIONAL DISPUTES TRIBUNAL. In 1959 this was abolished, leaving the Industrial Court to hold the field until 1971 when a new Industrial Relations Act established the National Industrial Relations Court.

INDUSTRIAL DEVELOPMENT CERTIFICATES. See DEVELOPMENT AREAS, DISTRICTS-2.

INDUSTRIAL REVOLUTION (1) is an accepted name or misnomer for a convergence of inventiveness, intellect, capital accumulation and reinvestment and natural exploitation which, between 1780 and 1850, radically changed both organic (primarily agricultural) and inorganic (primarily industrial) production. People noticed the leap forward in inorganic production because the new machines were different in kind from the method of the change in a familiar agriculture which sustained the rest. Yet the leap forward in the rural economy was, and had to be, equally great.

(2) The revolution produced or was accompanied by social changes which included (a) the creation of resources and their development and control by new people, not necessarily beholden to, or part of, the older rural polity; (b) the movement of people to and their subsequent multiplication in towns where they became divorced from natural events and rural assumptions; (c) an enormous increase in the population fed from the new agriculture; (d) dissemination of material goods previously accessible to few; (e) a multiplication in the speed and capacity of communications; (f) an educational revolution; (g) a change from village, county and state horizons to town-region, national and trans-marine outlooks. At the beginning of the period parishes maintained the roads; at the end millions were migrating across the oceans.

(3) These developments were preceded or accompanied by intellectual upheavals as great as those of the Reformation. If the proper study of mankind was "man" by the beginning of the 18th cent. the study of nature, meaning physical and applied sciences, was well launched and continued by interaction with events.

(4) The inventions which multiplied human dexterity came into being in the agricultural and industrial fields in step with each other and many were known long before 1780. The fulling mill, an early application of (water) power to production, was mediaeval. Large scale sheep run inclosures occurred in Tudor times. The stocking frame was also a Tudor invention. The four course crop rotation started in E. Anglia and large scale land drainage in the Fens after the Restoration. In the 18th cent. the need for bulk carriage encouraged waterways and seagoing ships. The felling of woodland for clearance, shipbuilding, housebuilding and furniture created a demand for other fuels; more coal was required also for foundries, which throve by wars and which themselves encouraged the iron mines.

(5) If a single (but complex) circumstance can legitimately be called the originating impulse, it is the response of a widespread woollen and linen industry to the influx of cotton, mainly from the Americas, India and Egypt and the adaptation of older techniques to it. John Kay's flying shuffle (1733) doubled the productivity of a hand loom weaver. There was soon a bottleneck in spinning. In 1764 James Hargreaves invented the spinning jenny and Richard Arkwright the water frame. The two, combined in 1779 by Samuel Crompton in the so-called mule, ensured mass production of yarn under a factory organisation. There was now a bottleneck in weaving. In the meantime steampower had come upon the scene and Dr. Cartwright patented his power loom in 1785.

(6) Steampower was inspired by the need to pump water out of the growing mines. Savery's steam pump dates from 1696; Newcomen's piston engine from 1711. It was James Watt's piston engine with the separate condenser, introduced in 1769, which changed the situation. It not only facilitated deep mining but through successive adaptations, especially his double acting engine of 1782, could be used for other purposes.

(7) An important element in the revolutionary combination was the country's prosperity through the mid 18th cent. development of overseas trade. English enterprise and warlike skills had attracted or engrossed a high proportion of Indian, American and W. African commerce, which included the unimaginably lucrative slave trade. Capital, as the many semi-palatial houses of the time still testify, was being accumulated rapidly and was seeking investment. The man who would risk fortune and life in the storms, diseases, piracies and other

hazards of distant ventures was likely to take investment in a new invention or a new agricultural method at home in his stride. Moreover in England the aristocracy, kept small by primogeniture, was not closed. Ambition, agility and money could make any man a lord, or a clever and beautiful orange girl a mother of dukes. Social eminence was an important part of the return on investment. Money invested meant, too, money distributed. The spectacular fall in the price of finished goods was bound to expand industry but rapidity of expansion was due to the numbers who could afford to buy.

(8) Most of the new inventions required metal and within a few years there were inventions in the iron industry. Cort's puddling process, begun at Fareham for naval supplies, dates from 1783. Both the making and the operation of the machines required more coal which in any case, had lately been in large farming demand for the burning of lime. The bulk transport of ores, lime, coal, and tiles for land drains demanded canals, improved rivers and better roads to act as capillaries of the distribution system. The macadamisation of roads, however, began extensively only after 1820 by which time improvement, through turnpike trusts, was well on its way. Road improvement also meant bridge building and bridges were being constructed in thousands. In the meanwhile the pressure upon the cloth finishing industry encouraged bleaching, dyeing and printing and the two former, in particular, became the foundation of a new and enormous chemicals industry. The bleaching powder works at St. Rollox became the biggest chemical works in the world. The accessibility to potential users of these bulk supplies was constantly leading to new developments. For example, more lime in the Scottish lowlands created a new abundance of barley and expanded the distilling industry, but in the south it expanded the breweries, created a demand for Kentish hops and originated the East End Londoners' hop-picking country mass holidays. It also made Barclay Perkins' brewery in Westminster one of the tourist sights of the metropolis.

(9) The new industrial methods did not at once, or sometimes for a long while, displace the old. There was enough demand for both. For example the linen industry continued to grow alongside cotton. One reason was, perhaps, an initially understocked market, another that the population grew at a rate of over 1% a year and real wages also rose. This growth, the surest index of real prosperity, was due to a better and more varied diet and a better understanding of the factors in public health. The benefits of sewering and paving towns were coming to be recognised as well as the advantages of vaccination. Infant survival and expectation of life were rising together.

(10) The revolution continued in full swing during, but was distorted by, the twenty-year French wars. These partly separated Britain from her continental markets; special, primarily naval and political, measures, such as the enormous Baltic convoys in defiance of Bonaparte's continental system had to be taken to promote her goods, and the demand for foodstuffs had to be satisfied by the increased tempo of inclosure and the cultivation of marginal lands. Moreover the economic war from time to time upset the delicate and, so far barely comprehended, structure of production. A major wartime depression occurred, for example, in the period 1810-12. There was urban unemployment, indigence and in some parts machine smashing. In the post war slump, conversely, the price of corn, despite the Corn Laws, fell. There was rural unemployment and cereal growing ceased in marginal lands. The business cycle was beginning to be established.

(11) The fact that the revolution began in Britain and that the wars retarded other countries put Britain for a while far ahead of the rest in the exploitation of virgin

resources and the harnessing of primitive economies. This was the opening period of investment in S. America, the solid establishment of rule in India, the colonisation of the Cape, the expansion of Canada. The acquisition or settlement of colonial possessions was not, however, a part of any programme. On the contrary the defection of 13 American colonies was a warning against it. The acquisition of the 19th cent. empire was a haphazard and often reluctant process arising out of the special circumstances of particular cases.

(12) If there is a sense in which the industrial revolution has never ended, an important turning period was reached in the years 1825 to 1856. The Stockton and Darlington Railway successfully applied steam power to transport. In 1828 Neilson's invention for exploiting the special Scottish iron ores made possible the great foundries and shipbuilding industries of the north while the railway boom suddenly ended the 6000 year supremacy of the horse. When in 1856 the introduction of Bessemer's conversion process inaugurated the age of steel, the govt. was already trying to control its ambassador at Constantinople by the electric telegraph.

INDUSTRIAL SCHOOLS were set up under an act of 1866 as boarding schools for child vagrants, destitute orphans and children with parents in prison, where they could be sheltered and taught a trade.

INE, DOOMS OR LAWS OF (c. 694). A West Saxon code which is thought to owe something to the Kentish codes of Ethelbert and Wihtraed but includes provisions on agriculture and trade.

INE (?-726). See WEST SAXONS, EARLY.

INEFFABILIS DEUS. See IMMACULATE CONCEPTION.

INFALLIBILITY, PAPAL. A R. Catholic doctrine that in matters of faith and morals the Pope cannot err in a formal pronouncement made *ex cathedra* (Lat = From the Throne), that is, with proper solemnity after all proper consultation and prayer. The idea is ancient but was first defined authoritatively as a dogma by the First Vatican Council held in 1870 under Pius IX at the moment when the Papacy lost its temporal possessions by the unification of Italy. The doctrine is concerned with the ascertainment of the nature of a subject and implies no claim to change it.

INFAMOUS CONDUCT is conduct, not necessarily criminal, which is considered to unfit a person practising a profession (especially medicine) from continuing in it. The service equivalent was "conduct unbecoming an officer and a gentleman".

INFANGTHIEF and OUTFANGTHIEF. The ancient right of a Lord of a Liberty to seize and condemn respectively his own tenant or serf and some other lord's if caught in the act of crime within his jurisdiction; outfangthief was also sometimes the right to pursue a criminal beyond the boundary of the jurisdiction.

INFANT. See MAJORITY.

INFANTE or INFANTA. The title of a Spanish or Portuguese royal personage other than a ruling sovereign, panicularly (in the case of women) of a King's sister.

INFANTILE DIARRHOEA, "GRIPING IN THE GUTS", "CONVULSIONS" OR BILIOUS COLIC. This often lethal disease of young children is commonest in the heat of summer and in crowded industrial towns. In Britain the heaviest incidence was originally in London. In 1669, for example, there were 6,000 deaths there, in 1670 5,200. Similar mortalities were reached in 1675, 1678-81. There was a tendency to increase even in good years so that average *annual* mortalities in London exceeded 6,000 from 1693. In 1718, a bad year, nearly 9,000 died. Sir Wm. Fordyce associated the disease with a rickety condition and asserted that 20,000 were ill in 1750 because of improper food, lack of fresh air and neglect. Thereafter it began to decline in London but increased elsewhere as other big towns grew up. By 1847 there were 4,200 deaths in a much enlarged London but the national figures were, in 1868 31,000, in 1879 11,000, in 1893 29,000. The fluctuations were connected with the weather. The disease declined after 1900. *See* EPIDEMICS, HUMAN.

INFANTILE PARALYSIS. *See* POLIOMYELITIS.

INFANT SCHOOLS arose from a desire to rescue small children from the squalor, exploitation and moral degradation to which they were exposed in the early industrial revolution and were, if at all, only remotely concerned with teaching. The first were founded by the Swiss Jean Oberlin (1740-1826) on the continent in 1769. Robert Owen opened the first in Britain at New Lanark in 1816. James Buchanan, the headmaster, took charge of another at Westminster in 1818 and his co-adjutor, Samuel Wilderspin, opened yet another at Spitalfields in 1820. He superintended the creation of many more on behalf of the London Infant School Society, founded in 1824, and his friend David Stow formed the Glasgow Society in 1826. These and the DAME SCHOOLS were for children under six and they spread rapidly. PAROCHIAL and SUNDAY SCHOOLS and schools based on a monitorial system (q.v.) began to cater for children over six at this period and taught reading, writing and arithmetic. This haphazard but enthusiastic movement was the base from which popular universal education started when the Education Act, 1870, made school attendance compulsory from the age of five.

INFEFTMENT or SASINE. The Scots equivalent of delivery of a conveyance of land, performed ceremonially before 1845, and also the instrument originally recording the ceremony and now taking its place. This is recorded in the Register of Sasines upon which a purchaser or lender upon heritable security is entitled to rely as against any unrecorded transaction. The ability to make an infeftment depends (save in the case of Udal land in Orkney and Shetland) upon ability to trace title ultimately to a Crown grant.

IN-FIELD, OUTFIELD FARMING was till about 1700 a northern English, and till about 1800 a Scottish practice as the margin where arable land was limited and livestock consequently the main source of profit. The smaller in-field near home comprised the best arable and was manured constantly and cropped regularly for subsistence, while in the sometimes very large outfield, a different part was ploughed and cropped each year (not necessarily in rotation), the rest being used as pasture. The method exploited the cattle as a source of fertiliser, but tended slowly to exhaust the outfield.

INFLATION and DEFLATION. A. Though there are four commonly used descriptions of the nature of these it seems likely that the truth partakes of elements of all four.

(1) QUANTITY THEORY starts from a basic moment when the amount of currency and the solid and productive assets and production (S.P.P.) of the area of that currency's circulation are known. Prices may then be expected to rise if the ratio of currency to S.P.P. rises (either because the amount of currency increases or because S.P.P. falls, or both) and to fall if it falls. Over long periods this "theory of a seller's market" may be fairly accurate but human mental inertia delays the reaction to short term movements and the unexpected (e.g. gluts, disastrous harvests or epidemics) may distort them.

(2) KEYNES'S THEORY assumes that people spend an ascertainable part of any increase which they receive in their incomes. In this "theory of a buyer's behaviour" a gap between national income and consumption expenditure can be predicted and the difference may be filled by private investment as long as rates of interest make such investment attractive. On this view, if private investment is unattractive, the govt. must step in and invest, e.g. by public works programmes.

(3) PRICE-WAGE THEORY assumes that prices are determined by the total cost of production plus amortization plus desired profit but that money supply responds to demand. There is competition between wage earners and profit takers, whose incomes together add up to more than the total value of production. Hence when wage earners obtain, by means of some threat, wage increases these are made at first at the expense of profits. Then prices are raised to raise profits and this in its turn sets up a new demand for wage increases. On this theory one might expect wage demands to move inversely with the rate of unemployment; this has not always accorded with modern experience, which tends to the possibility that there are significant numbers employed in economically neutral or even negative activity.

(4) STRUCTURAL THEORY is a kind of sociological approach to economics concerned with obstacles to price movements which may be, but are not necessarily of economic origin. It is a matter of common observation that resistance to money-wage cuts is so strong that they seldom happen, therefore cuts must be made (if essential) by raising prices (price inflation) or by taxation which has the same effect. Historical experience shows that primitive countries run into debt because their exports of primary goods seldom pay for their imports of manufactures and machinery and this leads to excessive borrowing and further outgoings which widen the gaps still further.

B. These theories tend to disregard factors of great importance but which happen to be incommensurable. The general level of honesty affects not only the quality of production and the cost of police, administration and accountancy but also the ascertainable level of incomes. Taste and prejudice, whether inherited or artificially created, do irrationally reduce or inflate markets or inhibit or over-stimulate activity.

C. Despite the construction of many different types of price indices, fine comparisons of prices are unreliable and seldom mean what they seem to mean, if only because in different eras and places different types of currency (e.g. metallic, bimetallic, trimetallic, token clipped, weighed, paper and supplemented by sometimes very large amounts in negotiable instruments) have been in use. (*For movements in corn prices see* CORN LAWS.) In the 1520s Cardinal Wolsey estimated £500 for building Magdalen Tower, Oxford. In 1981 it had already cost £826,000 to rebuild half of it. One would hesitate to assume an inflation in excess of 165,200% between the two periods.

INFLUENZA (or perhaps AGUE) (1) Despite problems of description and identification it seems that (as distinct from the common cold) this annually or biennially recurrent disease, which is always epidemic and often pandemic, has caused many deaths, notably in England in 1173, in Flanders in 1404 and in France in 1411. There was a Europe-wide epidemic in 1510 and another which sought out the well-to-do in 1557-8 and spread to Scotland in 1562, That of 1580 was world-wide. The epidemic of 1593 affected all Europe, those of 1627 and 1655 had catastrophic effects in the Americas. There were dangerous English outbreaks in 1658, 1675 (also in France), 1688 (also in Ireland) and 1693 (also in France and Flanders). A terrible European-wide visitation accompanied the famine of 1709 and there was a German outbreak in 1712. The epidemic of 1729-30 affected all Europe and was, perhaps, the source of the World pandemic of 1732-3. In 1737-8, 1742-3, 1757-8 and 1761-2 English outbreaks were shortly duplicated in North America. The two last affected France and the last also Ireland and Germany. In 1767 there was another pandemic, in 1772 a serious outbreak in North America, in 1775-6 one in Europe and in 1780-1 a European (but not British) epidemic grew into the pandemic of 1781-2.

After a short interval all Europe was again attacked in 1788, the Americas in 1789-90, northern Europe in 1799-1800, all Europe, but especially Britain, in 1802-3 and Britain again in 1807-8. After the Napoleonic wars, North America had serious epidemics in 1815-6 and in 1824-6 and Russia in 1827. There was a pandemic in 1830-2 which continued throughout the Eastern Hemisphere in 1833 where it was repeated in 1836 and 1847-8. There was then a hitherto unexplained forty years of quiescence followed by a spectacular pandemic in 1890-2. This caused great excitement and a large mortality all over the world. A further interval of a quarter of a century ended in the appalling so-called Spanish Influenza of June 1918 to Feb. 1919. This was first observed on the same day in northern India and the American mid-west, spread everywhere with astonishing velocity, especially among the contending armies, and is estimated to have killed 22M people, especially persons in the prime of life.

(2) The Spanish 'flu disappeared as suddenly as it came but it has been followed by sporadic epidemics ever since. It prompted a considerable research effort. This led to the isolation of the biennial influenza Virus A in 1932 and in 1940 to that of Virus B whose periodicity, being longer and less regular, sometimes coincides with outbreaks of Virus A. The "Asian 'flu" of 1957-8 attacked mainly younger people. Between 1962 and 1973 annual man-days claimed for sickness benefit due to influenza varied between 6.6M and 14.6M but in the peak of the "Hong Kong 'flu" (Dec. 1969-Mar. 1970) 25M days were claimed.

(3) It is perhaps not over imaginative to observe that some of these incidents preceded or accompanied important political events. The epidemic of 1557-8 preceded the overthrow of R. Catholic rule at Elizabeth I's accession; that of 1658 the collapse of the Protectorate; that of 1688 the overthrow of James II; those of 1772 and 1775-6 the American Revolution; that of 1788 the French. There were major epidemics before the revolutionary years of 1830 and 1848. Influenza is notoriously depressing. The progress of the Spanish influenza has provoked distinguished speculation that its origin might have been extra-terrestrial. *See also* SWEATING SICKNESS (ENGLISH); EPIDEMICS, HUMAN.

INFORMERS, COMMON, were persons who, under a variety of statutes (notably those concerned with Sunday observance and religion) were entitled to a proportion (usually half) of any fine levied upon persons convicted on information laid by them. Generally disliked by public opinion, they became obsolete after the creation of effective police forces in the 1840s but their rights were not repealed until 1951 when the activities of the Lords Day Observance Society drew attention to them. **Qui tam** (Lat = who moreover) was the technical term for a proceeding begun by a common informer.

-INGAS NAMES. The suffix -ingas in Old English (now shortened to -ing or -ings in English place names) represented a group of people. Thus Hastings is the place occupied by Haesta's people and Loddon (from Lodningas) is the place of the people living by the river Loddon. These names point to a time when groups of people were more important or memorable than the local place name (if any previously existed) and are evidence of the progress of Anglo-Saxon colonisation. They are common but the majority are found east of a line running from Portland Bill to the mouth of the Tees. *See* PLACE NAMES.

INGE, Dean William Ralph (1860-1954), 'The Gloomy Dean', after studying philosophy as a fellow of Hertford College, Oxford, was offered the deanery of St. Paul's to his surprise in 1911. He was an active and successful preacher and much discussed journalist who was efficiently critical of popular fallacies such as 'progress' and wrote many works of liberal theology. Consequently he was at odds with lay and clergy alike and generally regarded as a controversial figure. His nickname came mainly from his articles.

INGEBJORG OF ORKNEY, first wife of Malcolm III Canmore (r. 1058-93). *See* ALBAN KINGS, EARLY-19.

INGENOHL, Friedrich von (1857-1933) Adm. and C-in-C of the German High Seas Fleet at the outbreak of World War I. His prestige, shaken by the successful British raid on the Heligoland Bight (27-8 Aug. 1914) when three German cruisers were sunk because the tide kept the battlefleet in port, did not survive the loss of the *Blücher* in the B. of the Dogger Bank (24 Jan. 1915) when he failed to support his battle-cruiser squadron. He was superseded by Adm. von Scheer.

INGHILD brother of Ine. *See* WEST SAXONS, EARLY-13.

INGULF (?-1109), sec. to William I, was made Abbot of Croyland by him. The *Historia Monasterii Croylandensis,* attributed to him, is spurious.

INHABITED HOUSE DUTY on houses above the annual value of £20 was substituted for Window Tax in 1851 and abolished in 1924.

INHERITANCE. *See* HEIR-AT-LAW.

INHIBITION. An episcopal order suspending an incumbent from his parochial duties.

INJUNCTION. At common law the remedy for a civil wrong (tort) was pecuniary damages, which in certain types of case was unsatisfactory. The Lord Chancellors from early times began to reinforce the common law by compelling a party to desist from the wrong complained of, upon pain of imprisonment for contempt, if damages were inadequate. This type of order was called an injunction. It was used, *inter alia,* to fix the boundaries of Pennsylvania. Its Scots equivalent is called **INTERDICT**. *See* EQUITY.

INJUNCTIONS, ROYAL were five series of Tudor proclamations on church affairs. Henry VIII **(1)** in 1536 required the clergy to observe existing anti-papal legislation, abrogated certain festivals and ceremonies; discouraged miraculous beliefs and pilgrimages; required clergy to teach religion in English and provided for them to be taxed for the benefit of the poor and the maintenance of churches; **(2)** in 1538 he ordered the Great Bible to be set up in every church and regular religious instruction for the laity and enjoined the maintenance of parish registers of births, marriages and burials. Under Edward VI **(3)** in 1547 regular sermons had to be preached against Papal authority and superstition and in favour of royal supremacy, and pulpits were to be provided. Mary I reversed the reformist trend of the Injunctions and **(4)** in 1554 the Oath of Supremacy was abolished and all previous canon law not repugnant to statute was required to be enforced. This involved the repression of heresy, the re- ordination of clergy and the removal or divorce of married clerics. **(5)** In 1559 Elizabeth I returned to the pre-Marian policy; the injunctions as at 1547, shorn of their more offensive anti-Roman provisions, were substantially restored and a number of new ones added. These included an ineffectual effort to discourage marriage of clergy and a more successful attempt to encourage church music and hymn singing.

INLAND NAVIGATION. Anciently any river was a public right of way. Subsequently extended by Acts of Parliament to canals, the term was much used in the canal boom of 1770 to 1820; and labourers employed to dig canals were jestingly called "navigators", hence "navvies". *See* TRANSPORT; RIGHTS OF WAY.

INLAND REVENUE, BOARD. Commissioners of Stamps were appointed in 1694; of Taxes in 1719. The two were amalgamated in 1834 and in 1849 they absorbed the Board of Excise and adopted their present title. In 1908 the Excise was transferred to the Board of Customs.

IN-LAW when attached to a noun of relationship refers to Canon law, which treated relationships created by marriage as if they brought about a physical consanguinity.

INNER LONDON EDUCATION AUTHORITY. *See* LONDON (GREATER) LOCAL GOVERNMENT.

INNING. An old word for the process of reclaiming land from the sea, especially at Romney Marsh and the Wash.

INNIS, INIS, INNISH or YNIS, in place names = island.

INNISFAIL. A poetic name for Ireland. The Fail is the stone which served Jacob as a pillow and which, by way of Tara and Scone, ended up under the Coronation Chair at Westminster.

INN, -KEEPER. Monasteries commonly had guest houses or hospices for travellers, and inns along main routes existed from early times. The *Fighting Cock* at St. Albans is said to date from the 9th cent. The ancient moral obligation to protect and comfort the wayfarer developed, in the case of inns, into a legal obligation to provide such food and lodging as was available, to any wayfarer who offered the reasonable price, and the innkeeper had to keep the guest's property safe against all hazards except the guest's negligence or dishonesty. Innkeepers were already an important social body by 1500. The London Innholders Co. was chartered in 1514; after the Dissolution, monastic hospices often came into private hands. Improved communications and especially the increased movement of trade after the Restoration brought prosperity which the coming of the 18th cent. stage coach and macadamisation greatly increased. The older inns in large towns were substantial establishments capable of dealing with the convoys necessary for self protection *en route*; the stage coach and the hard road brought into being smaller, but still quite large inns like the Grosvenor Arms at Stockbridge, capable of accommodating nobility and their servants. These often declined when the railways took away the road traffic in the 1840s but revived when the motor car brought it back after World War II. The innkeepers strict liability was modified, as a result of frauds, by the Innkeepers Liability Act, 1863, replaced by the Hotel Proprietors Act, 1956.

INNOCENT III (Pope 1198-1216), an Italian noble, was not a priest when he was unanimously elected but he immediately began to assert the papal supremacy over temporal authority. He exploited the rival claims to the imperial throne following the death of Henry VI and anti-German feeling in Italy, to expel imperial officials from the papal states and to reassert papal overlordship of Naples and Sicily. He became the guardian of Henry VI's Sicilian son Frederick. At the same time he was engineering the defeat of the republicans in Rome (achieved by 1205), securing the homage of Aragon (1204), the tribute of Portugal and organising the 4th Crusade. This was diverted by the Venetians to the storm of Constantinople, an act which this highly political pope denounced with indignation, even if he had to accept the results which included the local establishment of the Latin Church. The Albigensian Crusade of 1208 to 1214, on the other hand, combined a stroke against an armed heresy with a temporarily French oriented policy. It brought French authority to the frontier of Aragon and unhinged the strategic defences of S. Aquitaine, where English Kings reigned as Duke. It was natural that with such (expensive) preoccupations, Innocent would pursue a policy of ecclesiastical centralisation. He meant to raise the standard of the higher clergy, to prevent the diversion of church resources to secular uses and to assure himself of a powerful influence and public opinion within each state. The key was to make bishops dependent upon himself for their appointment, ambitions and obedience. *See* INVESTITURE CONTEST.

INNOCENT IV (?1200-54, Pope 1243) member of a powerful papal family and canonist was elected after an 18 month interregnum caused by the manoeuvres of the excommunicate Emperor Frederick II. Innocent negotiated with him but fled to Lyons and French support when Frederick tried to enforce his rights in Lombardy. He called a General Council and then proposed impossible conditions to Frederick before it met. This being refused, the Council pronounced a further excommunication and deposition against Frederick, who held a rival diet at Verona. Innocent then induced the princes to elect (May 1246) a new emperor but he died seven months later. Frederick now prepared to move against Lyons but was stopped by a Lombard rebellion. Efforts by St. Louis to compose the quarrel were rejected by Innocent and in 1250 Frederick died still excommunicate. While Innocent's diplomacy secured widespread recognition for Frederick's rival and successor William of Holland in Germany he was also concerned to re-establish papal overlordship of Naples and Sicily and for this purpose offered the Sicilian throne successively to Richard of Cornwall in 1252 and Charles of Anjou in 1253. Both refused the privilege of fighting the Hohenstaufen, in Richard's case because Henry III could not persuade parliament to find the money. In Dec. 1254 Manfred, Frederick's bastard, raised a highly popular rebellion and Innocent is said to have died of shock. As a canonist Innocent published his *Commentaria super Libros Quinque Decretalium* (Lat = Commentary on Five Books of Decretals) in which he set out, with some qualification, the extreme papal claim to be the Father of Princes. His essentially political outlook on the functions of his office began the long decline into papal worldliness, ended by the Counter-Reformation.

INNOCENT VI Pope (r. 1352-62). *See* AVIGNON POPES.

INNS OF COURT AND CHANCERY (*for the main topic see* BARRISTERS-AT-LAW). The four Inns of Court were and are Lincoln's and Gray's Inns and the Inner and Middle Temples and in addition there were 14 Inns of Chancery which were primary institutions for the four main Inns. They occupied a tract between London and Westminster (between the business men and the politicians) stretching a mile and a quarter northwards from the Thames and, because the only two universities were in obscure provincial towns and biased towards church education, they attracted those who wanted some form of higher but secular education. They developed a strong social life, in which dancing played an important part, and considerably more influence than the universities. At the same time the length of the training meant that only a minority attended them in order to be called to the practising bar.

IN PETTO **or** *IN PECTORE* **(Ital and Lat = In the breast)** in papal practice, a nomination of a cardinal which has not been published.

IN PLACE OF STRIFE. White Paper on Trade Unionism in 1969 issued by Barbara Castle (q.v.).

INQUEST. An official inquiry into disputed or uncertain, especially crown, rights and the conduct of royal officials, conducted through a sworn group or jury of lawful men of the area, assumed originally to know the facts; it was occasionally used in Anglo-Saxon times, generally in private lawsuits, and from Norman times it became the principal means by which Crown rights were defined and tax obligations imposed. Investigations of this type were used, for example, to compile Domesday Book and bring to light official misdeeds. *See* CORONERS; SHERIFFS, INQUESTS OF; INQUISITIO COMITATUS CANTABRIGIENSIS; INQUISITIO GELDI; INQUISITIONES POST MORTEM.

INQUISITION (HOLY) is the prosecution of heresy before special ecclesiastical courts. Until the 12th cent. heresy was investigated by diocesan bishops and punishment confined to excommunication though lay rulers sometimes joined in. It was the mid 12th cent. Albigensians who drove the church to seek secular aid. The Inquisition as an organisation was founded in 1232 when the Emperor Frederick II decreed that heretics were to be pursued by state officials. By way of counterblast Gregory IX appointed Papal inquisitors, who were mostly Franciscans and Dominicans. Innocent V authorised

torture in 1252 and in 1542 Paul III established the Holy Office as a final court of appeal.

The **Spanish Inquisition** had special features. Set up in 1479 by Ferdinand and Isabella with Papal approval, it was in fact, if not in theory, a state department staffed by ecclesiastics with oversight of Marranos (Jewish converts) and Moriscos (Moorish converts). Later its powers were used against protestants. Its head was the Grand Inquisitor who, from 1483, appointed his own councillors only after consultation with the Crown. The Grand Inquisitor (1479-98) Torquemada, has passed into folk mythology. It was established in Mexico and Peru against strong local church opposition only in 1570 and on the Spanish Main as late as 1610; native Indians were always exempt from its jurisdiction. It was abolished in Spain by Joseph Bonaparte in 1808, reintroduced in 1814 and finally abolished in 1820. In America it simply faded away. *See* AUTO-DA-FE DE HAERETICO COMBURENDO.

INQUISITIO COMITATUS CANTABRIGIENSIS **(Lat = Inquiry into the County of Cambridge)** is a 12th cent. copy (at Ely) apparently recording proceedings before sworn juries of eight men as a preliminary stage in the inquiries leading up to the compilation of Domesday Book, but it is arranged by hundreds and vills not, as in Domesday, by honours and manors. The reason for copying it many years later is unknown.

INQUISITIO GELDI **(Lat = Inquiry into the Danegeld)** is a survey of the five western counties showing the amount of geld for each hundred, those free of geld and the amounts of which they are free and the arrears. The document, preserved at Exeter, probably dates from 1083-4.

INQUISITIONES POST MORTEM **(Lat = Inquiries after death)** were records of enquiries made by escheators on the death of tenants-in-chief to ascertain what goods and lands they held and the name and age of the heir. They were theoretically conducted before a jury but it seems that the returns were mostly agreed in advance between the escheator and the deceased's steward. Hence the surviving returns (dating from Henry III) presumably understate the value of the deceased's property as modern probate valuations do.

INQUISITIONS. *See* FOREST-3.

INSANITY. *See* IDIOT; LUNATIC.

INSEMINATION, ARTIFICIAL of a married woman with semen given by a donor not her husband was held adulterous by the Church and the English courts but in 1958 not adulterous by the Scottish courts.

INSKIP, Sir Thomas Walker Hobart (1876-1947) 1st Visct. CALDECOTE (1939) became a Tory M.P. for Bristol in 1918. He was a law officer in all Tory administrations from 1922 to 1936. He opposed Prayer Book revision in 1927 and in 1928 piloted the Govt. of India Act. In 1936 he became Min. for the Co-ordination of Defence, an anomalous appointment because service depts. retained their autonomy and he could get co-operation only by his powers of persuasion. There was no time before times grew dangerous internationally for this laborious method to take effect. In 1939 he became Sec. of State for the Dominions and then Lord Chancellor, but from 1940 to 1947 he was Lord Chief Justice. He had strong religious convictions and many friends.

INSPEXIMUS **(Lat = we have inspected).** A charter in which the grantor states that he has inspected a previous charter which he now confirms, thus estopping himself or anyone claiming under him, from denying the previous charter.

INSTALLATION. *See* CATHEDRALS.

INSTITUTES OF JUSTINIAN. A Byzantine law students' text book inspired by the Emperor Justinian in about 532. Its brevity and compression have ever since made it an immensely influential source of legal ideas, especially in Scotland, Europe, Ceylon and S. Africa. Though required reading for every English bar student down to 1960, its

English influence was confined to canon law and its derivatives in divorce and probate. When Britain joined the E.U., whose member states other than Eire have Roman law inspired legal codes, the book was not restored to the bar curriculum.

INSTITUTES OF POLITY. An analysis for the avoidance of sin and the maintenance of order, of the duties and rights of all social ranks by Abp. Wulfstan of York (q.v.).

INSTITUTION. See ADVOWSON.

INSTITUTE OF ECONOMIC AFFAIRS (I.E.A.) was set up in 1957 for politically orientated economists who rejected determinism and socialism, were critical of the welfare state and favoured free will and free markets. In the 1960s it caused much surprise by proposing the reversal of the hitherto thought irreversible trend towards state ownership, management and provision and, in particular, advocated privatisation even in the National Health Service and Education and propounded ways of making the equivalents available through private enterprise. Never powerful, its ideas were catching once it began to demonstrate that revolutionary anti-socialism might, as a matter of practice, create workable, not merely Utopian, political and social institutions. One of its founders was Friedrich v. Hayek (q.v.).

INSTITUTIONAL WRITINGS in Scots Law are works by legal commentators whose authority enjoys a weight comparable to that of a judgement of the Inner House of the Court of Session. The works on Civil Law are: *Jus Feudale* (1655) by Craig; *Institutions of the Law of Scotland* (1681) by Vist. Stair; *Institute of the Law of Scotland* (1773) by Erskine; *Commentaries on the Law of Scotland* (1800) and *Principles of the Law of Scotland* (1829) by Bell. On criminal law the works are: *Laws and Customs of Scotland in Matters Criminal* (1678) by Mackenzie; *Commentaries on the Law of Scotland respecting Crimes* (1797) by Hume and *Principles* (1832) and *Practice of the Criminal Law of Scotland* (1833) by Alison.

INSTRUMENT OF GOVERNMENT (16 Dec. 1653-25 May 1657), vested legislative and taxation power in a Lord Protector (Cromwell) and a parliament, and executive authority in him and a Council of fifteen members named in the instrument. The parliament was to have 400 English, 30 Scots and 30 Irish members elected by voters worth £200, in constituencies of roughly equal population. Parliament was to be summoned every three years and to sit for at least five months. All who fought against parliament were debarred from standing or voting for the first four parliaments. R. Catholics were debarred permanently. Christians other than papists and prelatists were protected in the exercise of their religion. There was to be a permanent revenue sufficient for an adequate navy, an army of 30,000 men and £200,000 a year for other expenses. This ensured that parliamentary control over the executive would be confined to new legislation only. During parliamentary sessions the forces were to be under the control of the Protector and parliament; in the intervals under the control of the Protector and Council. His legislative veto was to last only 20 days but he and the Council could make ordinances between parliaments. There was no provision to amend the Instrument. *See* COMMONWEALTH AND PROTECTORATE-9.

INSTRUMENT OF INSTRUCTIONS. *See* COLONIAL LAWS, VALIDITY-7.

INSURANCE. The idea is very ancient, the three earlier and primitive mediaeval forms being the subdivision of the ownership of ships and cargoes, the protection of a maritime borrower on a bottomry bond against repayment if the ship were lost and the practice of maritime average. In England marine insurance grew with the gigantic expansion of British mercantile shipping after about 1680 and with the development of Edward LLOYD's (c. 1688-1726) coffee house as a resort for brokers and underwriters. This was opened in Great Tower St. London in 1687; Lloyd supplied his customers with shipping information and in 1696 founded *Lloyd's News*. Thomas Jemson (?-1733) the fourth master laid the foundations for *Lloyd's List,* launched in 1734. By 1750 Lloyd's was virtually a society and a shipping register was being compiled from 1760. This was formalised as *Lloyd's Register of Shipping* in 1834. By that time Lloyd's was in fact a society with a governing committee and established customs and commercial practices. Of these the most important were the subdivision of risks among underwriters, the total commitment of an underwriter's private fortune and the restriction of direct dealings to brokers but the classification of ships by their design and condition and the introduction of Lloyd's salvage arbitrations had a powerful influence on shipping design and safety.

The habit of underwriting proportions of risks spread to other types of risk, of which the most obvious in an era of combustible towns and disorder were fire and theft. Insurance (then Assurance) Cos., however, mushroomed after the Great Fire of London (1666) because they were prepared to seek customers rather than wait for them to come to Lloyds. Many of these were fraudulent but some of those which survived the South Sea Bubble (1721) such as the Royal Exchange Assurance and the Sun were still in business after World War II. In their earlier days they sought to reduce their losses by maintaining fire brigades and marking the houses entitled to fire assistance.

INTELLIGENCE, i.e. information on rivals, has always depended mainly on public or semi-public sources such as the accounts of travellers and ships' captains, the use of reference works and directories, the compilation of statistics and latterly aerial and space photography and directional wireless. The political and martial intentions of states can often be inferred from the jigsaw puzzle of such variegated facts so long as there is a centre where that puzzle is put together. Under primitive conditions much depended, too, on the relative speed with which information, often of an ordinary kind, could be transmitted. Secret intelligence (i.e. the penetration to matter which is being deliberately concealed) and counter-intelligence (the protection against hostile intelligence operations and sometimes their deception) were first practised in some detail by the Venetians. The English, reputedly very skilled, seem to have undertaken them spasmodically. Under Elizabeth I, Walsingham and Burghley were well informed through Sir Thomas Gresham of confidential political and financial matters in the Spanish Netherlands and they also frustrated several conspiracies and brought Mary Queen of Scots to the block. In the War of the Spanish Succession Marlborough, mainly through Cadogan, organised a very effective network which even had an agent (identity unknown) of high standing at the French court. Daniel Defoe is also thought to have been concerned in counter-intelligence. In the French wars of 1793 to 1815 the British, mainly through the Foreign Office and the Admiralty, were very well informed on the state of Europe because the oppressed peoples were glad to supply or transmit information. It is said that the secret terms of the T. of Tilsit were known in London before they had reached Paris. It was at this period that the regular censorship of ordinary mail (as opposed to the clandestine opening of diplomatic mail) became an important feature of intelligence practice. It was to dominate other sources in World War I. *See* CIPHER; M.I.

INTELLIGENCER. *See* L'ESTRANGE, SIR ROGER.

INTER-ALLIED DEBTS. *See* REPARATIONS.

INTER CUNCTAS (1418) bull of Martin V condemning Lollardy.

INTERCURSUS MAGNUS or GREAT INTERCOURSE (Feb. 1496). Anglo-Burgundian treaty of political and commercial co-operation. The two powers undertook not to assist each other's rebels, Philip of Burgundy undertaking especially to restrain Margaret Tudor from maintaining Henry VII's enemies. The elaborate commercial clauses enabled each side to impose proper dues and customs but otherwise required each to promote free intercourse, to prevent causes of dispute and to ensure that individual delinquencies did not lead to war. This involved minute regulations about maritime jurisdiction of all kinds and the application of maritime law on piracy and wreck, fisheries, contraband and carrying arms, treatment of debtors, scrutiny of cargo and carriage of bullion. There was a supplementary treaty in July 1497. The treaty formed the precedent for much subsequent maritime practice but failed to settle the economic problems and gave rise to much English dissatisfaction. When Philip was wrecked on the English coast in 1506 he was coerced into signing a supplementary so-called MALUS INTERCURSUS (Evil Intercourse) enabling English cloth to be sold free in Philip's Netherlands territories other than Flanders but he died before ratification and the Great Intercourse was renewed by Margaret, his successor, in 1507.

INTER CAETERA **(May 1493).** *See* TORDESILLAS, T. OF (1494).

INTERCOMMUNING, LETTERS OF (Sc.) were a state-enforced interdict against individuals considered contumacious in religion. They required a boycott and were used in the presbyterian lowlands against R. Catholics and later sometimes in episcopalian areas against presbyterians.

INTERDICT. (1) The equivalent in Scots and Roman law of an injunction in England. **(2)** A papal order forbidding the clergy to exercise religious ministration or have other dealings with a class or body of people defined in the order. In the superstitious middle ages the consequences could be serious; laymen could be denied baptism, confession, absolution, communion, extreme unction and Christian burial, with all the spiritual consequences. There were far-reaching practical effects as well: the churches could not be used for their many non-religious uses. The people were denied access to the majority of clerks and canonists. Church courts might refuse to deal with matrimonial disputes or grant probate to wills. Mystery plays could not be performed. Charity might be refused to the needy. See JOHN.

INTERESTS, PECUNIARY. Neither an M.P. nor a local councillor may vote on an issue in which he has a direct (other than trivial) pecuniary interest and when speaking on such a matter he must declare his interest. Councillors have always been able to register their interests. M.P.s have been required to do so since 1975.

INTERIM DEVELOPMENT CONTROL. *See* TOWN AND COUNTRY PLANNING-1.

INTERLOPERS were English merchants who traded in the East in breach of the HEIC's and the Dutch E. India Co's respective monopolies. The word is of Dutch origin.

INTERMEDIATE EDUCATION (Ir.). *See* NATIONAL EDUCATION SCHEME.

INTER MERSHAM ET RIPAM **(Lat = Twixt Mersey and Ribble).** *See* LANCASHIRE.

INTERNATIONALE Revolutionary song written and composed in 1871.

INTERNAL COMBUSTION (*see also* DIESEL). Several inventors had proposed the use of volatile fuels between 1794 and 1850 but the first commercial gas engine was built by the Frenchman Lenoir in 1860. In 1862 Nicolaus August Otto (1832-91) defined the thermodynamically efficient cycle and various other inventions led to the patenting in 1883 of Gottlieb Daimler's (1834-1900) high speed petrol engine, from which most petrol reciprocating engines are derived. The gas turbine idea was conceived as early as 1791. Parsons suggested its modern form in 1884 and a hot air engine was exhibited in 1900, but development did not begin seriously until 1935.

INTERNATIONAL COURT OF JUSTICE. The Conventions for the Pacific Settlement of International Disputes signed at The Hague Peace Conference of 1899 and 1907 established the PERMANENT COURT OF ARBITRATION which was in fact a panel of jurists to whom disputes might or might not be submitted. The T. of Versailles (1919) envisaged the creation of a genuine court as part of the machinery of the League of Nations and the PERMANENT COURT OF INTERNATIONAL JUSTICE was set up at The Hague in 1921. It possessed compulsory jurisdiction only in cases, or classes of cases, where both parties in a dispute had accepted its jurisdiction. In fact only 29 countries ever did so. It was superseded by the International Court of Justice, which was created as part of the U.N.O. after World War II and first sat in 1946. This court similarly possesses compulsory jurisdiction only between parties who have accepted it. Rather more states had accepted by 1973 but as the Iceland fishing dispute of that year showed, the court's practical ability to enforce its judgments was limited even in cases where the jurisdiction is accepted.

INTERNATIONAL, FIRST (1864) was founded by Karl Marx, with a deliberately vague programme, to draw together all so-called working class societies in Europe. Only seven countries were represented. Bakunin and his anarchists joined in 1869; but the authoritarian majority expelled them in 1872. It was defunct by 1876. **SECOND (1889)** arose from a socialist assembly in Paris to celebrate the French revolution. Anarchists, of course, were excluded. It held a long series of well managed congresses and in 1910 established the International Socialist Bureau at Brussels. There was the usual controversy between those who favoured participation in national politics, and revolutionaries. As most of the members rallied to their national govts. in 1914 this International collapsed leaving one memorial – May Day became Labour Day. **THIRD.** *See* COMINTERN. **FOURTH.** *See separate entry.* TROTSKY.

INTERNATIONAL LABOUR ORG. (I.L.O.) was set up at Geneva under the T. of Versailles in 1920. Its directors were Albert Thomas (French, 1920-32), Harold Butler (British, 1932-8) and John G. Winant (American, 1938-41). Winant moved the office to Montreal in 1940. He was followed by Edward Phelan (Irish, 1941-8) who brought it back to Geneva and David Morse (American). It is primarily concerned with poverty, unemployment and the mobility of labour.

INTERNATIONAL LAW, PRIVATE or CONFLICT OF LAWS. That part of the *internal* law of any country which regulates legal situations containing a foreign element, e.g. a foreign marriage or a contract made abroad. With the rise of international institutions such as the General Agreement on Trade and Tariffs, the European Union and improvements in communications, its scope has greatly widened since World War I.

INTERNATIONAL LAW, PUBLIC is a group of so-called rules regulating the conduct towards each other of international personalities, that is sovereign states or persons or bodies which are treated as their equals. The identification of international personalities is its basic problem: thus the United Kingdom and the United Nations are universally accepted international personalities but the Knights of St. John are only locally accepted. The rules depend on (a) TREATIES and other express agreements such as the United Nations Charter between international personalities, (b) COMITY, namely the willingness of any sovereign to accept and enforce within his dominions a convenient practice similarly accepted and enforced by some other sovereign, (c) FORBEARANCE, namely the willingness of a sovereign not to interfere with an established practice in international circumstances (e.g. the high seas) and (d) SANCTIONS namely the expectation that the infringement of an established mode of behaviour will attract retaliation from other international personalities. The rules are formulated and interpreted partly in treaties, partly by international tribunals and partly in international arbitration awards but in the end they all depend for their enforcement upon consent of governments.

INTERNATIONAL MONETARY FUND was set up under the Bretton Woods Agreement (1944) and began operations in Mar. 1947. Its object was eventually to abolish exchange control and multiple exchange rates, a task in which it had by 1973 been only partially successful against largely political opposition. By 1995 102 members contributed to its resources.

INTERNATIONAL RED CROSS. *See* SWITZERLAND.

INTERNET was invented in the U.S.A., originally to store and distribute militarily useful information at the speed of light. By 1994 civilian and business interest had caused it to spread worldwide, so as to be cheaply and unrestrictedly available to any computer owner. On a world scale it resembles the nervous system within the human brain. Its phenomenal growth was partly related to the production of cheap computers; in 1995 there were 635,000 users in the U.K., in 1996 2,500,000.

INTERNMENT is non-punitive deprivation of liberty. A neutral state may for its own safety intern forces of a belligerent which enter its jurisdiction and in both World Wars all belligerents so treated enemy subjects caught within their boundaries at the onset of war. The internment of persons suspected of organised violence designed to overthrow a regime or society has long been practised (e.g. by Britain in India and Northern Ireland and France in Algeria) where these persons' activities have amounted to quasi-war, but is both more questionable than the internment of belligerents and less so than wholesale interventions by armed police or troops (e.g. by Russia in Czechoslovakia, Hungary and Poland). An internee is entitled to the same treatment (so far as possible) as he would receive if he were free.

INTERPOL (International Criminal Police Organisation) began in Vienna in 1923 but its H.Q. was seized by the Nazis in 1938. After World War II it was revived under Belgian inspiration but with its H.Q. in Paris. The T. of Maastricht provides for the creation of a Europolice.

INTERREGNUM. In later English law a monarch began to rule at the moment of his predecessor's death and therefore no interregnum was theoretically possible. This view replaced an earlier view that a King had to be accepted or chosen and his position confirmed by a solemn act. Thus Harold II was killed on 14 Oct. 1066 but William I reckoned his reign from his coronation on 25 Dec. This precedent led to interregna at all accessions until Edward I whose interregnum, begun on 16 Nov. 1272, was ended by his proclamation on 20th. As all commissions conferring public authority lapsed at a demise and parliaments automatically ended, interregna had become inconvenient and on Edward I's death in 1307 the modern rule was applied with some practical and theoretical exceptions. The first demise which did not dissolve a Parliament was that of Q. Victoria on 22 Jan. 1901. *For further particulars see* APPENDIX ON REGNAL YEARS.

INTERVENTION and NON-INTERVENTION. The first is armed support by one nation in favour of one of the parties to a civil war in another. The second, according to Talleyrand, is 'a metaphysical and political word which means almost the same as intervention'. *See* CARLISM for the context of this observation.

INTIMIDATION, in the context of industrial relations, is the bullying of those who wish to work by those who wish to strike.

INTRINSEC (inner) as opposed to **FORINSEC (outer) (1)** The services and dues owed to a mesne lord were intrinsec to him: his obligations to a higher lord, usually the crown, were from his point of view forinsec. **(2)** In some English honours a manor court (usually a court leet) with jurisdiction confined to the manor where it sat was intrinsec but if it extended to other manors the jurisdiction was forinsec. There is a village in Dorset called Ryme Intrinseca. **(3)** In a Welsh lordship the words meant respectively the English settled areas and the Welsh inhabited areas.

INVENTORY DUTY. *See* DEATH DUTIES.

INVER- in, mostly Scots, place names = mouth or estuary of a river.

INVERGORDON MUTINY (Sept. 1931) was an orderly refusal of duty in protest (led by a communist) against naval lower-deck pay cuts imposed by the "National Government" in the economic crisis. It resulted in all cuts for public servants being restricted to 10%, thereby helping the teachers who had been cut by 15%.

INVERNESS-SHIRE (Scot). Brude, K. of the Picts, lived at a fort near the town when Columba visited him c. 565 and the place had a royal castle for centuries. With the gradual formation of the Scots Kingdom the area formed part of the old province of Moray but Norse influence was strong. In the 12th cent. the eastern part was colonised by clans Mackintosh and Bisset; in the 14th by Frasers, Chisholms and Grants. The Chisholms established themselves at Erchless Castle; the Grants at Castle Urquhart. The west, however, was held by Macdonalds, Camerons and Macleods; they owed allegiance to the independent Lords of the Isles who later held the earldom of Ross. Early royal efforts to control the area had to be confined mainly to the town itself, which was chartered by William the Lion (c. 1209). In the 15th and 16th cents. the Crown tried, without much success, to rule through clan chiefs who were coming frequently to Edinburgh but Donald of the Isles burned the town in 1411 and later disorder was compounded by religious disagreements. Hence the shire never existed as a unit of govt. until the revolution of 1688 brought the forts (George, Augustus and William), the pacification of 1716 which brought Wade's military roads (1725-36) and the pacification of 1746 when the heritable jurisdictions of the chiefs were abolished. The population in this large area has always been sparse. 72,000 in 1801, 98,000 in 1841 but by 1961 it had fallen to 83,000. The main economic activity was sheep farming with its complementary woollens industry in the town, which also had distilleries. The west coast herring fisheries were always important. Since World War II hydro-electricity has developed with associated aluminium smelting.

INVESTITURE CONTEST (*see* ANSELM) **and COMPROMISE.** In the 11th cent. prelates had important properties totalling perhaps a quarter of the land of England. These owed feudal service and dues. Kings generally nominated these churchmen, invested them with ring and staff and took homage for the lands before consecration. The church reformers led by Pope Gregory VII (r. 1073-85) disliked these arrangements because they made for worldly prelates. The contest with the Emperor over this issue prevented the proposed reforms reaching England until the Lateran Council of 1099 anathematised laymen who performed and clerks who accepted such investiture. Anselm in exile was present. Churchmen were not united on this, which involved a breach of tradition and greater centralisation of the church. Adela of Blois and Ivo of Chartres negotiated a compromise in 1107 which seems to have been recorded in the Constitutions of Clarendon (1164). Elections were to be free and the ceremony of lay investiture abandoned. In return prelates were not to be denied consecration because they had done homage. In practice elections were always held in the Kings' courts, where they were less than free, and the Kings always exacted homage before consecration.

INVINCIBLES (Ir.). Another name for, or perhaps an exceptionally fanatical sect of, the Fenians.

IONA or ICOLMKILL (Columba's I), a small island close to Mull (Argyll) where St. Columba came from Ireland to found a celebrated monastery and mission centre in 563. This became the mother church of Christianity in Scotland and for long the seat of its leading bishop. The isle contains the tombs, supposedly, of 4 Irish and 8 Norwegian Kings and also 48 Scots Kings (whose life expectancy must have been short) from before Malcolm Canmore. The numbers and energy of its emissaries made it a predominant religious and educational influence and a disseminator of Irish scholarship and art throughout Scotland, E. Ireland and N. England until it was sacked by Vikings in 795, 802 and 806, but its prestige enabled it to revive after the slaughter so that the Norwegian King Olaf Cuaran (in 981) and the 11th cent. Ostman Sigtrygg, K. of Dublin, died there as monks. Its useful function and the existence of its community declined after other authorities, particularly newly organised churches in Scotland, Ireland and N. England, took over its work. *See also* ICOLMKILL, STATS OF (1609).

IONIAN Is. (Med.) became Venetian in the late middle ages and the French took them in 1797 on the dissolution of the Venetian Republic. In 1799 a Russo-Turkish force took brief possession and they were formed into a picturesque but nominal republic of the Seven Islands which was extinguished and given to Bonaparte under the T. of Tilsit (1807). After Waterloo they were again formed into a United Republic under British protection. In 1849 the people, or some of them, asked for union with Greece. Palmerston refused because he had a low opinion of Greeks and their methods of dealing with British grievances. In 1858 Gladstone went there as High Commissioner to discover the islanders' wishes. He did not advise union but the agitation continued. In 1862 the islands were offered to Greece and ceded by treaty in 1863. The Cathedral of St. Michael and St. George at Corfu is the original seat of the British Order of Chivalry so named; the British planted cumquat orchards, and cricket (under local rules) is still played there.

IORWERTH ap BLEDDYN. *See* POWYS.

IPSWICH (E. Suffolk) was already busy in the 6th cent. and pottery kilns demonstrate much prosperity from the 7th to 12th cents. despite Viking raids. They sacked it in 991. From the 11th cent. it was also an important trading port for E. Anglian textiles such as kersey. It had its first charter in 1200 and was incorporated in 1446. It was still prosperous in the time of Thos. Wolsey, who was born there, and who tried to create a dual foundation for Ipswich and Oxford similar to Wykeham's Winchester and New College. The Ipswich college was dissolved. When the cloth trade declined in the 17th cent. Ipswich, by now extremely corrupt, declined too but the resurgence of E. Anglian agriculture stimulated by post World War II subsidies brought new prosperity and other industries. The city was a County Borough from 1888 to 1974. *See* CORPORATIONS, MUNICIPAL, PRE-1834.

IQBAL, Sir Muhammed (1876-1938) of Kashmiri convert origin, educated in Europe and an English barrister, wrote in Persian and Urdu, particularly *Secrets of Self*, a seminal best seller among his younger Moslem contemporaries. He became a member of the Punjab legislature in 1927 and Pres. of the All India Muslim League in 1930 when that body first adopted a separate Moslem Indian state as its objective. As a result the ultimate creation of Pakistan is, perhaps not entirely accurately, associated with him. He represented the Moslems at the First Round Table Conference (q.v.).

IRAN. *See* PERSIA.

IRAQ (1) was ruled by the Turks until the British expelled them in 1917 to 1918. There were disputes about its future arising from Shiite movements in the south, tribal disorders, Kurdish demands, Arab nationalist propaganda from Damascus and the ambitions of the city intellectuals and politicians of Baghdad and Mosul. When the British

troops began to withdraw in 1920 the town politicians and certain sheikhs raised a revolt which had to be put down with some severity. In Oct. 1920 Sir Percy Cox and Gertrude Bell returned to enforce the policy of local autonomy under British advice, settled after the San Remo conference had awarded the mandate to Britain. Cox inaugurated an all Iraqi govt. and a Hashemite King in the person of the Emir Feisal who had just been turned out of Syria by the French. There followed a period of joint Anglo-Iraqi state building which was terminated (by a Treaty of 1930) in 1932. King Feisal I died in 1933 to be succeeded by Feisal II, a child of three, under the regency of the Emir Abd-ul-Ilah.

(2) The Kirkuk oil fields had been discovered in 1927 but development went slowly because of declining standards of order and Kurdish revolt. Politicians tended to encourage tribal forays against their rivals and in 1926 there was a short military *coup d'état*. World War II brought the expected German intrigue but the govt. officially broke off relations with Germany. The result was another *coup* by Rashid Ali el Gailani in Mar. 1941 with the support of anti-British generals. The regent fled and the British airbase at Habbaniya was besieged for a month in May until reinforcements from Britain and India restored the legitimate govt. British troops remained until 1945. The Syrian oil pipeline was opened in 1953.

(3) The govt. meanwhile was western in its outlook and depended for support increasingly upon right wing elements. This might not have mattered if the rise of the State of Israel had not united Arab nationalist opinion with the Iraqi left against the western powers. In July 1958 the monarchy was violently overthrown by Gen. Abd-ul-Karim Kassem with strong left-wing support. Disorders and the Kurdish war, however, continued and in 1963 a right wing *coup* led by Col. Arif led to the death of Kassem and many communists. It was followed by an attempt to set up a political union with Egypt. The attempt failed; in July 1965 Arif got rid of the pro-Nasser ministers who then tried and failed to raise another military insurrection. In Apr. 1966, however, Arif was killed in an accident and succeeded by his brother, who was overthrown in another *coup* in July 1968.

(4) There followed an unstable so-called Revolutionary Govt. established by the Ba'ath party under Saddam Hussein. It conducted a form of national totalitarian socialism, using the oil revenues to industrialise and arm and to suppress the large minorities, namely the Kurds in the N.W. and the Marsh Arabs of the S.E. The Iranian missionising but confused Islamic govt. of the Ayatollah Khomeini was seeking to subvert the Iraqi Shiite majority and Ba'ath was accordingly driven steadily towards secularism and military adventures against neighbouring states. Ideology apart, Iraq's immense oil output, if supplemented by those of Iranian Kuzistan and Kuwait, would give her a powerful, decisive leverage in the world oil markets while, more locally, control of their areas would free the Shatt-el-Arab and other outlets for Iraqi shipping.

(5) Expecting a walkover, Saddam launched a surprise attack on Iran in Sept. 1980. The army advanced about 75 miles into Kuzistan but was stopped by fanatical resistance. At the end of 1982 it withdrew to Iraq and Saddam sought peace which the Iranians would not concede because they hoped that success would bring the overthrow of the Ba'ath govt. Iraqi resistance in turn solidified and there was a sanguinary entrenched frontier war during which Iraq received much finance from Saudi Arabia and Kuwait until Aug. 1988 when Iran, faced with economic collapse, accepted a U.N. mediated armistice.

(6) The Iraqis then redeployed and in Aug. 1990 seized and annexed Kuwait. The support which the U.N. had not given to Iran was now accorded to Kuwait. A mainly Anglo-American combined force under the U.S. Gen. Schwarzkopf operated from Saudi territory and, after a month's aerial bombardment, drove the Iraqis out. Their casualties and damage were huge, those of the U.N. negligible, save that the Iraqis fired some 800 out of 1300 Kuwaiti oil wells (23-7 Feb. 1991). Schwarzkopf would probably have achieved a Cannae on the Iraqi army but suddenly had orders to stand fast. The Saddam govt. survived and continued to maltreat its minorities.

IRELAND, ENGLISH LEGISLATION IN. (*See* PILKINGTONS CASE; MERCHANTS OF WATERFORD, CASE or.) In one of Poyning's Laws (1495), the Irish parliament enacted that English statutes *so far made* applied in Ireland. In 1640 the Irish House of Lords, on the advice of the judges, declared that the English parliament could not legislate for Ireland but in 1641 the English parliament by the Adventures Act purported to dispose of Irish land in favour of anyone willing to advance money to put down the Irish rising. This precedent was followed under the Commonwealth when the Irish parliament was ignored and, under the Instrument of Government (1653) Irish members were admitted to the new parliament. At the Restoration the English parliament did not interfere in the Irish land settlement but it did uphold the Cromwellian prohibition on growing tobacco (1661, 1664 and 1680) and in 1690 it declared King James II's parliament of 1689 an unlawful assembly and its enactments void. In 1695 the Irish parliament did the same. Another English Act of 1690 suspended an Irish Act of 1666 and this was apparently not noticed by the Irish parliament which seemed to be allowing English claims by acquiescence. There were public but not parliamentary protests against the English Woollens Act of 1699. In 1700 and 1702 English acts disposed of Irish lands. In 1718 there was a dispute on appellate jurisdiction: the Irish and the English House of Lords each asserting the finality of their judgements in Irish cases. Thereupon the English parliament unilaterally enacted (1719) not only the supremacy of the English over the Irish House of Lords but the right of the English parliament to legislate for Ireland. This act was either unnecessary or required Irish assent. In fact the Irish parliament did nothing at all. This Act commonly called THE SIXTH OF GEORGE I remained in force until repealed in 1782. *See* REPEAL AND RENUNCIATION, STATS. (IR).

IRELAND, NORTHERN (1) comprises six of the Ulster counties (Antrim, Armagh, Down, Fermanagh, Londonderry and Tyrone), the others (Cavan, Donegal and Monaghan) being part of Eire. The large but shallow Lough Neagh is in the centre. Belfast is the capital and main port but Lough Foyle and the Strangford and Carlingford Loughs provide other sea accesses. It is within sight of the Scottish coast. Most of all Irish industry, primarily textiles, engineering and shipbuilding, is concentrated around Belfast. The farms are fertile and produce about 20% root crops and 80% grains, and animal husbandry and poultry thrive. On average 75%-80% of the trade is with Britain, 6-8% with Eire. There are about 5 R. Catholics to every 8 Protestants, of whom about half are of Scots origin. The area has been developed almost wholly by English and Scottish capital. Strategically it is important to the sea defence of N.W. Britain. Not surprisingly it is coveted by Irish republicans for it would subsidise the comparatively primitive economy of Eire and its possession would, especially in wartime, increase Eire's diplomatic and economic leverage on Britain.

(2) The area's definition and retention in the United Kingdom emerged from the complex of Irish and English politics between 1910 and 1922. The Liberal policy of Home Rule for all Ireland would put the relatively sophisticated and economically developed Ulster Protestant minority at the mercy of the poorly educated and under developed R. Catholic mass electorates of the south. This simultaneous threat to pockets and religion called forth a leader in the ruthless and charismatic Sir

Edward Carson. In the current state of English parliamentary policies the Liberal govt. saw no possibility of English stability without concessions to Ireland as a whole, probably leading to the withdrawal of the Irish element at Westminster. Such concessions seemed to involve the sacrifice of the Ulstermen. The latter refused to be sacrificed; they flocked to join Carson's armed Ulster Volunteers and threatened to defend Ulster by force against the rest of Ireland and, if necessary, the British. The British ability to force Home Rule on Ulster was now called in question by the Curragh "Mutiny" (1914) and in any case Carson was reckoning that British electorates would oppose an Irish war in alliance with Britain's enemies in Dublin against her friends in Ulster.

(3) The issue was postponed by World War I, for the huge majority of the Irish joined in condemning Germany and in shelving differences until the war was over. Large Irish forces were raised voluntarily for all fronts. There remained, however, a small closely knit body of enraged irreconcilables who staged the farcical and tragic Easter Rebellion in 1916. These rebels may in one sense be seen as the Irish republican equivalent of Carson's Ulster Volunteers but with the difference that because of their minute numbers they had to achieve their ends by conspiratorial war rather than open processes. Given the extremism and immutability of their objectives, they were probably correct. The result was that the political nationalists (Sinn Fein) acquired (and overlapped with) the Irish Republican Army (I.R.A.), a clandestine military force which, in the years 1918 to 1923, burned country houses and murdered opponents both English and Irish even after Eire became independent.

(4) The prospect of union in 1920 with an Irish state whose ability to control its extremists was in doubt, commended itself to Ulster protestants no more than the prospect of being outvoted in 1914, but the southern Irish M.P.s elected in 1920 never came to Westminster: they turned themselves into an Irish parliament (or *Dail Eireann*). Consequently the political difficulties which their presence at Westminster had created since the 1880s had vanished. There was now no internal British reason to sacrifice the Ulster protestants and anyhow experience since 1916 disposed British statesmen to sympathise with them. It was, however, important that "British Ulster" should be large enough to be viable but small enough for the protestants to be in a comfortable majority. Thus the three R. Catholic counties were ceded to Eire (which helped to cool heated relations with Dublin) leaving the six to form Northern Ireland with a parliament, govt. and governor of its own.

(5) These arrangements worked tolerably well between the wars because the civil disorders in Eire, and world economic problems distracted attention from the (soluble) difficulties. The I.R.A., whose professional gangsters found themselves with too little to do, remained unreconciled to what, for propaganda among the Irish diaspora in America, they chose to call 'Partition'. They represented it as being forced upon Ireland by the overbearing descendants of George III from whose yoke the Americans had so successfully liberated themselves in the 18th cent. This mixed virus of lies and unhistorical emotionalism gradually infected important sections of Irish-American opinion and obtained for the I.R.A. a good deal of innocently subscribed finance.

(6) World War II, however, interrupted the smooth development of I.R.A. ambitions for after Pearl Harbor Irish Americans and the British were on the same side, while Eire not only stayed neutral but permitted an enemy legation in Dublin. The British, however, trained their troops for the Normandy invasion in the Sperrin mountains, thereby having large forces locally available in case of a German airborne attack on Eire which, without an army, was quite unable to defend herself.

(7) The war eclipsed but did not destroy Sinn Fein and the I.R.A., which resumed their previous policy in the 1950s. Funds were built up from Irish American and Libyan sources and weapons and explosives (notably Semtex) bought from Russian satellite states such as Czechoslovakia. Terrorism or the War of Unification was launched in Northern Ireland in 1964. It was sporadically maintained and occasionally spread to Britain in the ensuing 30 years. The physical effects, which included the murder of Earl Mountbatten and an attempt to blow up the Prime Minister in a Brighton hotel, though nasty, were small, the casualties amounting to about 250 a year; but the publicity effects were more serious. The British press lovingly exaggerated the details so that Irish Americans were led to think of the events (many trivial or ridiculous) as a war of liberation and continentals sometimes believed that a civil war was in progress. The physical effects were also much extended by the police which, in anticipation of press outcries against casualties, closed wide areas of public services to the public whenever a bomb exploded or was rumoured.

(8) By 1992 the N. Irish public (especially the women) was disillusioned with this dangerous nuisance and even the Dublin govt. doubted the value of operations which, while expensive in ill will, seemed to bring their objective no nearer than it had been in 1922. Moreover, the I.R.A. was a dangerously headstrong body not under proper govt. control. There had been private and semi-public discussions for some years and in 1993 these culminated in the joint Downing Street Declaration by the British and Irish Prime Ministers which set forth the way in which Britain, N. Ireland and Eire might co-operate in solving the difficulties. Sinn Fein and the I.R.A. received this with bombs. In 1994 a truce was set while all concerned debated the conditions for further discussions. The British insisted on previous I.R.A. disarmament. In Feb 1996 there were further explosions in London.

IRELAND. A. OLD AND EARLY MEDIAEVAL (to 1318)

(1) Christianity came initially through the importation of Romanised Christian captives (of whom the most important was St. Patrick) by Irish slave raiders during the collapse of the Roman regime in Britain and the opening Anglo-Saxon invasions. A very successful, classically erudite and artistically creative Gaelic Church was based upon a monastic rather than a diocesan organisation (though bishops existed for sacramental purposes). Gaelic paganism disappeared quickly and in the late 6th cent. Irish monks turned their superabundant energies to conversion in Scotland, northern England and central Europe. The Angles, who were converted from Rome, were taking political hold of northern England where Roman and Irish religious practices rather than doctrines conflicted inconveniently, especially on the dating of feasts and fasts. As is well known, the crisis and resolution came at the Synod of Whitby (664) after which Irish practices slowly disappeared, leaving an Irish church in distant communion with Rome.

(2) Though a High King reigned at Tara and accepted superstitious deference from provincial Kings and tribal chiefs, there was no unity. Apart from one Viking raid in 620 the country was undisturbed by foreign enemies from the 5th to the 8th cents. and the Irish happily fought each other. Hence when the Vikings began to raid in earnest (c. 794) no systematic defence was possible. By 825 the country's plunder was exhausted and the Norsemen (or Gall) began to set up fortified trading settlements at any suitable haven, most importantly at Dublin, Wexford, Waterford, Cork and Limerick. They acquired little territory but (apart from competition amongst themselves) monopolised overseas trade notably in silver from Munster and in slaves, cattle and hides. This provoked two centuries of wars but because the Gall became in that time a part of the local society, these ended not as straightforward contests between Gael and Gall but between shifting factions of each with other factions of each being drawn in.

(3) Two widely separated cases of Irish factions involving the Gall or their foreign cousins strongly influenced later history. In 1014 Brian Boru, a usurping High King, defeated the adherents of the Tara dynasty and their Gall allies at Clontarf (now a suburb of Dublin). He was murdered in his tent after the victory and his army was unable to storm the walls of Dublin. This affair nevertheless sowed the seed of an Irish spirit in later Irish minds. In 1155 Henry II had obtained Papal approval for the acquisition of Ireland (The bull *Laudabiliter*). In 1166 Dermot McMorrough, King of Leinster, sought the help of Pembrokeshire Normans and their overlord Henry II to recover his kingdom from a usurper. A reconnaissance arrived in Wexford in 1169. Strongbow, E. of Pembroke, followed having been promised the hand of Dermot's daughter and the succession to his Kingdom. Norman military equipment and prowess overbore opposition: he took Waterford and Dublin and succeeded to Leinster in 1170. The possibility of power straddling the Irish Sea from Pembroke to Wexford was unwelcome to Henry II who reactivated the dormant bull and came to Ireland himself (1171). He imposed fealty and allegiance on the Normans and was acclaimed by many Irish chiefs. It is improbable that they and he understood each other. These events began the long piecemeal Anglo-Norman conquest. The execration later heaped on Dermot as a traitor to Ireland is probably misconceived. There was no idea of Ireland and he was merely calling in Normans as Irish factions had called in the Gall.

(4) Henry went home and the Normans, freed from royal supervision, began the unplanned attrition whereby the country was imperfectly taken over with irregular additions of English immigrants. Even where they dominated there remained free Irish enclaves. In Leinster where they began, their power was long confined to the coast and the western periphery: they scarcely touched the Wicklow mountains. Then they spread along the south coast and feudalised Munster, less Kerry or Clare. Connaught remained untouched. In the third stage they achieved similarly patchwork effects in Meath and Ulster but these were accentuated by a trend towards absorption into the more numerous and prolific Irish population. Incomers often married Irish girls, dressed as their in-laws and in later generations became indistinguishable from the Irish. There was, too, an irreconcilable conflict over land. Under Brehon law land belonged ultimately to the clan, and the chief was no more than a life manager, unable to alienate it. Under feudal law land was held in full heritable ownership and could be alienated at any stage. Irish chiefs who alienated lands to the Normans were, in effect, repudiating or dissolving their clan. Feudalism as such was a mortal threat to Irish society but weakened because Norman barons, at odds with each other, often sought clan alliances.

(5) The rough balance between the rival civilisations reached at the end of the 13th cent. was disturbed by the Scottish wars of Edward I and II. After the English debacle at Bannockburn (1314) Robert the Bruce sent his brother Edward against Ireland. His political purpose was not achieved, for the behaviour of Edward's barbarous soldiers turned many of his Irish allies against him. He was killed in 1318 but the damage which he had done injured the English superiority and accelerated the absorption of 'degenerate' English into Irish society. Irish land could no longer be taken for colonisation: it supported a self-conscious population capable even of converting isolated colonies to its own customs. The English areas began to shrink by a counter-attrition which continued for nearly half a century. *For a local case see* FERNS.

IRELAND. B. DYARCHY 1318-1556. (1) The shrinkage of the English areas after 1318 was causing concern in Dublin and Westminster by 1360 when the Anglo-French war was interrupted. Edward III sent his son, Lionel of Antwerp, D. of Clarence, over in 1366 as a special Lieutenant; he summoned a parliament to Kilkenny. The defensive character of its famous Statutes demonstrate the extent of English decline. They recognised a tacit partition between the ten obedient shires and the rest, inhabited by Irish enemies, and sought to regulate daily behaviour in the ten so as to keep the Irish at arm's length. The Statutes were not a success. When Richard II came to Dublin in 1394 he had to recognise a distinction between Irish land (under Brehon law) and enclaves of English (under Common Law) which were mostly found in the Pale around Dublin. He determinedly had the Pale marked out, partly fortified and recolonised. His foresight was rewarded. Though Irish chiefs flocked to his court to have their holdings and jurisdictions confirmed, they resumed their encroachments once he and his army had gone. The solid English core in the Pale preserved the nucleus of English influence.

(2) Had the Irish been united they might have taken the Pale too, but they were not. The country was governed, if at all, for the next 120 years by an Anglo-Irish dyarchy. The greatest families outside, especially the Geraldines, though Irish to English eyes and supporting their influence by attention to Irish culture, were of Anglo-Norman extraction and took part in English politics. James, E. of Desmond, and his son Thomas attracted both English and Irish loyalty, encouraged Irish customs, music and language, enforced Brehon law when it suited them and brought Irish chiefs to parliament. They and their kinsmen, the Es. of Kildare, supported York in the Wars of the Roses and exploited the weakness of the Lancastrian Crown to extend their influence. Richard of York, a popular Lieutenant at Dublin, found them useful allies and when he was attainted in England, maintained his Lieutenancy with Desmond and Kildare Deputies and the aid of a parliament hostile to English parliamentary interference. He was killed at the B. of Wakefield (1460). From 1463 Thomas of Desmond was Deputy until executed in 1468, whereupon Kildare stepped in and, as George, D. of Clarence's Deputy, established so stable a govt. that his son, the 8th Earl, known by the Gaelic appellation Garret More (Gerald the Great), succeeded him as a matter of course and the parliament ejected Edward IV's nominee. By this time the Gaelic revival begun by the Desmonds had gone so far that Irish M.P.s normally spoke Gaelic and the Speech from the Throne had to be translated for them.

(3) Garret More's larger than life personality impressed all his contemporaries but his policy was a disaster. Mindful of Thomas of Desmond's fate, he sought to secure a friendly occupant of the English throne in alliance with the Yorkist Margaret, Duchess of Burgundy, by crowning the impersonator Lambert Simnel at Dublin as Edward VI (1487). The necessary but expensive war entailed English-style taxation and Irish-style impositions such as coign, which were violently enforced but to no avail. Lambert's defeat diminished Garret More's prestige and established Henry VII's. When the latter was free to deal with the Irish question in 1494, a small well found expedition under the able and faithful Sir Edw. Poynings (as the child P. Henry's Deputy) accompanied by some civil servants, was rapidly successful, largely by promising justice and ending exactions. In 1495, moreover, he repulsed an attempt on Ireland by the impostor Perkin Warbeck. Garret More was attainted, his vast possessions seized and he was put into the Tower. POYNINGS' LAW subordinated the Irish parliament to the English administration.

(4) Henry understood that contemporary Ireland could not be held down by a force as small as Poynings' nor could he afford a larger one. Only a native ruler could do it and the only suitable native was the prisoner in the Tower. A chastened and less wealthy Garret More was returned as Lord Deputy to Dublin where he ruled in semi-autonomous prosperity until mortally wounded in the Wicklow Mountains in 1513. He was succeeded as 9th E. and Lord Deputy by his son, known as Garret Oge, who ruled until 1520.

(5) The autocratic revolutionary Henry VIII had by now been King for eleven years and affairs were moving towards a totalitarianism needing new sources of finance. He dismissed the Deputy in order to rule more directly through a Lord Lieutenant with an army. His father had known better. The policy (for it was no experiment) failed because it cost too much. The King reverted to Deputies but, consistently with his own suspicious nature, changed them frequently to prevent them becoming too powerful. The distant royal autocracy broke the Geraldines and badly weakened the Irish administration. To wear away clan society (*see above* A-4) attempts were made to get chieftains to surrender lands and obtain them back by regrant, while the simultaneous dissolution of the monasteries, though pursued with less vigour than in England, did great damage in a society with a monastically orientated church. The Dyarchy was abandoned.

IRELAND. C. THE AGE OF PLANTATIONS 1556-1690. (1) Henry VIII's abandonment of dyarchy ushered in a period resembling that of an alien invasion. The dourly protestant and corrupt intriguers of Edward VI's protectorates did nothing to mend matters. The protestant England and the obstinately R. Catholic Irish drifted into smouldering hostility exacerbated by religious controversy.

(2) The train was fired by clan risings in Offaly and Leix. Mary I's govt. took the secular view that the Irish were incorrigible and their promises worthless. In 1556 an alternative solution was proposed. The English should abolish the Irish. The disorderly septs of Offaly and Leix were to be cleared off their land, which was to be repopulated (or Planted) with armed English settlers in the newly reconstituted Queen's County and King's (i.e. Philip of Spain's) County. Thus began an intensified resumption, called Plantation, of the Norman policy which had been abandoned in the Statutes of Kilkenny, but this time it was the lesser cultivators rather than the ruling families who were replaced. It caused terrible misery and outcry. Its geographical course resembled that of the Norman attrition (*see* IRELAND A). Beginning on the western edge of Leinster, it spread along the south to Munster and then *via* Meath towards Ulster. Connaught and Clare again were scarcely touched. It was brutally enforced by such grantees as Sir Walter Raleigh and provoked local risings, of which the greatest under Elizabeth I occurred in Munster in 1579. A Spanish expedition sent to succour it failed to make contact. The Munster rising merely accelerated the clearances.

(3) At this stage there were broadly three groups in Irish society, namely the Irish themselves with their remaining leaders all living under Gaelic customs and law: the Anglo-Normans or old English, mostly a bilingual aristocracy who had great lands and lordships and lived under English law yet enjoyed affinities by friendship, marriage, concubinage, culture or sympathy with the Irish and seemed to an outsider much like them: and thirdly, the New English colonists who ranged from lordly grantees of wide plantations to small tenants whom they had recently implanted on land from which the Irish had been dispossessed. In Leinster, Munster and Meath the New English were advancing but the groups were intermingled. In Ulster the Irish predominated; in Connaught Irish and Anglo-Normans shared a poor but not disagreeable heritage. The Irish hated their New

English despoilers who returned their hatred with fear and violence: the Anglo-Normans mistrusted the New English as a threat to their estates.

(4) Plantation enabled royal authorities to acquire bases further from Dublin than before. For the first time, if sporadically and inefficiently, they reached every part. The killing of Armada survivors on the west coast would not otherwise have been possible. In Ulster the govt's writ ran only when the local Irish magnates were not hostile. As the planters became more ambitious the hostility developed. Hugh O'Neill, the greatest and ablest of the Ulster chiefs, had been educated at the English court. Events in Munster convinced him that in the end the English had to be defied. He unified Ulster opinion, recruited an Irish army and publicly took the Irish title (long in unofficial use) of The O'Neill. The Queen did not want to fight him for wars were expensive. The planters and the local authorities did. They launched an offensive in 1597 which was beaten back and a second attack was routed at the B. of the Yellow Ford in 1598. This Ulster war also had a strange side effect, for it was entwined with the tragic fall of the Queen's friend and favourite, the E. of Essex.

(5) The O'Neill was now the accepted champion of the Irish, who rose in many places. They overwhelmed the Munster plantations but were ill armed and, outside Ulster, uncoordinated. Good English troops under Mountjoy defeated them in detail: one after another The O'Neill's allies deserted. A Spanish force came too late and just before James I mounted the English throne the Spaniards and Irish were beaten at Kinsale. The O'Neill submitted.

(6) In 1607, despairing of any respite, The O'Neill and other Ulster chiefs quitted Ireland. This FLIGHT OF THE EARLS was a major event. It deprived the Irish of their greatest natural leaders whose vast estates became available for new plantations. Because of the Union of the English and Scottish crowns, Scotland could no longer be a refuge for dissident Irish but, *per contra*, became a new source of plantation colonists. Their Calvinism widened the religious chasm and the policy of social revolution was broadened too. There were to be no more voluntary changes from Brehon to Common Law. A parliament of 1613 abolished Brehon Law, set up English courts and conformably repealed the Statutes of Kilkenny. Insofar as the sketchiness of a thinly manned administration permitted, Gaelic customs and overt habits were suppressed but the Irish lived on as tenants or squatters because it was neither humanly nor economically possible to drive them out. The Ulster Plantations, however, added a fourth influential and cohesive group to the three mentioned in para (3) above, namely the presbyterian, hard working Scots whose land management over the years made visible changes in the Ulster landscape. They were no more popular with the Irish than the New English.

(7) The later 17th cent. English controversies, especially the campaign fought in Ireland, were devastating and divisive (*see* CIVIL WAR; COMMONWEALTH AND PROTECTORATE; JAMES II; WILLIAM III AND MARY II). Some of the English, Old and New, maintained a loyalty to the Crown; others favoured parliament because of Charles I's unreliability and a hope of wringing concessions and, after the appalling Ulster Rebellion of 1641, a further division appeared between the royal C-in-C, the E. of Ormonde and the Lords Justices in Dublin who nominally represented the royal civil power but actually opposed it. These wrangles seemed irrelevant to the aspirations of the Irish who were beginning to think of a free Ireland and who received Papal encouragement and, in the formidable if wrong-headed Rinuccini, a Papal delegate. Their quasi-govt., known as the Confederation of Kilkenny, was at first dominated by the Old English, to whom Rinuccini was hostile, and Ormonde negotiated an

agreement between the Confederation and the King (Mar. 1646). This was nugatory, for shortly afterwards the King surrendered to the Scots. Then the Irish general Owen Roe O'Neill beat the Scots at Benburb (June) and Rinuccini repudiated the agreement with the King, whereupon Ormonde left and abandoned Dublin to the parliamentarians. This purgation failed: the Confederates still quarrelled while the Parliamentarian New Model troops gathered. In Aug. 1649 Cromwell stormed Drogheda and slaughtered the whole population. In Oct. he did the same at Wexford. The terror ended the Confederation. It was followed by wholesale clearances and replantations conducted with greater ruthlessness and efficiency than ever before. Most of the Irish proprietors lost their estates. Over half the land was cleared and the people driven into Connaught. These events burned an abiding hatred into Irish minds.

(8) The Cromwellian colonists were quick to welcome the Restoration and re-establish the parliament which Cromwell had abolished. Charles II had to do something for his supporters in exile but, for the sake of peace, had to leave the colonists mostly alone. Hence he let the anti-Romanist laws be laxly enforced. The Old English filtered into office: even by 1688 they had frightened some of the colonists into flight. Under James II they flocked in, and his 'Patriot Parliament' dispossessed protestant absentees against his wishes, for he knew what the effect would be in England. Their stories lost nothing in the telling. Dutch William came to Ireland as an avenging protestant. He was assisted by the dilatory incompetence of James' commanders. The local apprentices held Derry against them. The Jacobites had as much time as William to prepare for the conflict but he used it properly and the B. of the Boyne (1690) was a debacle. In the ensuing year the Jacobites under Patrick Sarsfield could not fight for victory, only for clemency. William III, always with his eye on Europe, was glad to end the struggle. The T. of Limerick (1691) permitted the Jacobites to emigrate. As these were for the most part Old English, the event repeated the Flight of the Earls. The Irish lost their remaining leadership to French and Austrian military service.

IRELAND. D. THE ERA OF MANIPULATION (1691-1800)

(1) England was in mortal danger for many years from the Caesaro-Papal aggression of Louis XIV and was thereafter in intermittent if less dangerous conflict with his successors. The first aim of English policy was, with Irish protestant applause, to prevent Ireland from being useful to the enemy and, accordingly, PENAL LAWS debarred R. Catholics from politics, civil and military office and education. The second aim, against Irish protestant opposition, was less respectable, namely to subject the Irish economy to the British. No products could legally be exported if they competed with the British. Both aims required British supremacy which was achieved at a legal level through the Declaratory Act 1719; this without repealing Poynings' Laws, affirmed the right of the Westminster parliament to legislate for Ireland; and at the political level by systematic corruption. All substantial posts in Church, State and Law were in practice reserved for the protestant colonists and their descendants (the ANGLO-IRISH) while parliament and the executive, thus manned, were managed by UNDERTAKERS, ready to deliver majorities in favour of suitable bills in return for control over patronage. For nearly half a century Ireland was ruled in the British interest by a self-perpetuating Irish protestant oligarchy while those outside the privileged circle broke the law (especially by smuggling) whenever they could.

(2) The Irish being leaderless, the first stirrings of open opposition arose among the protestant traders against the economic policy. Then came the appearance in mid-century of a Patriotic Party, whose very name implied hostility to Britain rather than opposition to a

current policy. It was led by Charles Lucas, physician, writer and flamboyant M.P. for Dublin from 1761 to 1771 and Henry Flood (1732-91) a more sophisticated politician who entered the Irish parliament in 1759 and was sufficiently effective to have a money bill thrown out in 1769. He held office from 1775 to 1781 and then joined Grattan and the E. of Charlemont (1728-99) in leading the Patriot Party again.

(3) The American rebellion presented them with a surprising opportunity. Much of the English garrison was sent to America. To replace it the govt. raised Volunteers among the more articulate Anglo-Irish, whose rank and file were mostly traders. Once armed and organised, it dawned on them that political leverage had been put into their hands. The habit of covert law-breaking was now extended to open law-changing. They demanded commercial parity with Britain and the govt., defeated in America and at sea, conceded Anglo-Irish free trade. Emboldened, they demanded political reforms and at their DUNGANNON CONVENTION (1782) threatened force. The Declaratory Act and most of Poynings' Laws were repealed.

(4) Events had outrun Grattan, who had refused office, while Flood, with whom he quarrelled, became a Westminster as well as a Dublin M.P. The English retreated to new defences. It was in any case for the Lord Lieutenant to commission the govt. which then controlled parliament partly through patronage but especially through the pocket boroughs which elected about two-thirds of the Commons. Save in the economic field, the political machine of 1788 was producing much the same results as before. Prospects brightened along with a material prosperity which created Georgian Dublin, but the political system, after a short Whig interval, was steered along a repressive course which, *inter alia,* included the dissolution of the Volunteers.

(5) The French Revolution profoundly influenced all the world. Wolf Tone's potentially revolutionary Society of United Irishmen (1791) was formed from Volunteers and their friends, less the aristocrats but *plus* the Ulster Scots who launched the Belfast *Northern Star* as its mouthpiece; but the French course of events split the Society between those who, with Grattan, wanted parliamentary reform and thereafter to use the reformed parliament to obtain their religious, commercial and political demands and those who, with Tone, meant to frighten or bully the govt. into concessions at once. Jacobinism and the guillotining of Louis XVI destroyed Tone's hopes, for many of the Society's activists crossed over to the side of moderation, and govt. repressive measures jeopardised the others and drove Tone abroad. In 1795 he persuaded Lazare Carnot, the French Min. of War, to send an expedition to Ireland under Gen. Hoche. This arrived with Tone on board at Christmas 1796. It was driven back by appalling weather and provoked further police measures, especially in Munster. This did not prevent the Society planning a general rising which was to be led by Arthur O'Connor and Lord Edward Fitzgerald, but the plans had been penetrated by govt. agents, of whom O'Connor was probably one. He and Fitzgerald obtained promises from Hoche but most of the leaders, including Fitzgerald, were rounded up and Tone was taken on a French frigate. The rising, of ill-armed and uncoordinated Munster peasants, nonetheless took place but was put down with ease (1798).

(6) The abolition of the Irish parliament had been mooted intermittently for some time. The 1798 rising convinced many Westminster politicians that it should be done. This required an Act of the Irish parliament but the necessary Bill of 1799 met opposition, each for their own reasons, from Patriots, placemen, borough owners and traders. It was thrown out. In 1800 the govt. mounted a determined and expensive campaign to force it through. Pocket boroughs were bought; placemen compensated;

new peerages conferred and the R. Catholics promised emancipation. This time the bill was passed and the Dublin parliament ceased to exist. *See* PITT'S FIRST ADMINISTRATION.

IRELAND. E. POVERTY AND STARVATION 1800-51. (1) The Irish had hoped that the Anglo-Irish parliamentary union of 1800 would at least open a combined market to Irish manufacturers. Unfortunately in Britain the Industrial Revolution had taken off 18 years earlier and British steam-driven industry using native coal could undersell the Irish, who had to import coal from Britain before they could start up. To start they needed some form of protection. The new and disunited hundred Irish members at Westminster in a House of 700 were quite unable to secure this. Southern Irish industries, being mostly hand operated, went out of business. Urban unemployment might have been alleviated by migration into the countryside if agriculture had remained moderately prosperous but southern Irish agriculture suffered upheavals even more violent than the British. The high wartime corn profits had caused multiple subdivision of holdings for the labour-intensive work of growing cereals. When the French wars ended in 1815 the bottom fell out of the cereals market and outside Ulster landlords began to evict their unprotected tenants and pull down their cabins in order to go over to the 'dog and stick' economy of animal husbandry. The urban and rural poor were not only destitute but shelterless. Three Commissions, Thomas Drummond, the Under-Sec. for Ireland, local correspondents and visitors such as the Frenchman Gustave de Beaumont, the German traveller Herman Kohl and Karl Marx's Manchester friend Friedrich Engels, were united in testifying to the horrifying starvation level of poverty in Leinster, Munster and Connaught, which surpassed even the oppressed and depressed levels of rural Calabria and Courland.

(2) Improvement was hindered in other ways. It was natural for working people to try to combine to protect their interests. Such combinations were illegal and therefore clandestine, conspiratorial and, in Ireland, violent. As British competition reduced southern industrial wages, industrial violence became endemic: agricultural violence, as cattle replaced corn. This was sharpened by the rising birthrate. Potential investors would not invest because Irish labour had acquired a reputation for unpredictability. Even the great Dublin families invested their capital in England.

(3) There were further causes of hatred. The precarious rural tenant at least lived under a roof but he had to pay rent to a generally alien absentee through an immediately present rent-farming agent whose sole function and interest was to screw it out of him. Already close to the starvation line, the R. Catholic southern tenant in addition had to pay tithes to the representative of an equally alien and, to him, heretical Anglican church. Thus in the three provinces an economic grievance was multiplied by religious animosity, kept alive by R. Catholic priests in the background. There was altogether quite enough vexation and violence in southern life to constitute a civil war: the reason why there was no organised war was that there was nobody to organise it.

(4) In Ulster conditions were notably different. The vast growth of British shipping encouraged Belfast shipbuilding and the rise of such yards as Harland & Wolff. The unique linen industry, combining a local agricultural base with a local industrial process, had survived. The Scots colonists were not only better farmers than those further south but the Ulster Tenant Right, which had come with them, required an evicting landlord, unlike his southern colleague, to pay for improvements. This was a practical protection which enabled the tenant cultivators to exploit their skills in relative security. Ulster production had been financed

largely from Britain and was exported to Britain. Moreover, in the solidly protestant six counties closest to Belfast if tithes were paid in sorrow they were paid without religious anger. The province, though not rich, was neither desperate nor violent.

(5) Poverty led to dependence on the cheapest sort of food, namely the potato, and the staple, if not very nutritious, diet in the three provinces varied from potatoes with a little milk and meal in the east to potatoes and water in Connaught and Connemara. As a crop the potato was never reliable, being subject to local bouts of blight in most years. In 1822 there was a famine but this was as nothing compared with the Great Starvation. The continental Potato Rot reached the West of England and Munster in 1845. It created a hungry, but not a starving, winter. In 1846, however, it destroyed 75% of the Irish crop. Starvation set in and the weakened population often succumbed to epidemic diseases such as typhus. Appalling accounts reached England. Three measures were debated: charity, an embargo on the export of food and the repeal of the Corn Laws. Embargo was not tried and would probably have failed. Repeal was relevant to English politics but scarcely to Irish conditions for, as the D. of Wellington (himself brought up in Ireland) pointed out, the Irish were so poor that they could not afford even corn. On the other hand the British charities mounted a tremendous effort which saved many lives through soup kitchens, and the govt. followed suit. In 1847 they were feeding daily 3M out of 8M people.

(6) It was now obvious that the hungry of 1845-8 had no future in Ireland. 250,000 crossed to Lancashire, Cheshire and Glasgow where, as cheap R. Catholic labour, they undercut the locals and created social and religious problems. Over a million sailed for N. America, sometimes in unseaworthy, often in insanitary, ships. About 140,000 of these were lost by disease or by foundering on the voyage. Over 1M died prematurely at home. By 1851 the population had fallen from 8M to 5.5M.

(7) The migration to, in particular, the U.S.A. did incalculable injury to Britain. Many believed erroneously that British ill-will had caused the famine, whereas in truth once it had started the British were not mentally equipped by the outlook of their time to alleviate it systematically. Hence the migrants exported grievances and created, besides the natural Anglophobia of the U.S.A., an enduring and powerful hate lobby. *See also* FAMINES AND DEARTHS; CORN LAWS; PITT'S FIRST ADMINISTRATION; PEEL'S SECOND ADMINISTRATION.

IRELAND. F. NATIONALISMS 1815-1921. (*See* IRELAND, E. POVERTY AND STARVATION) **(1)** Before 1815 Irish separatism had been mainly a protestant led, commercially orientated, movement not, despite rural outbreaks, hostile to the English connection as such but seeking by nuisance value to eradicate its undesirable features. Between 1815 and 1848 it changed to a more broadly based and R. Catholic supported nationalism born of long memories, a tendency to react against authority and sharpened by the horrors of the Great Starvation of 1846-8 and the fluctuating effect of subversion especially among the homesick and resentful diaspora in the U.S.A. The British have forgotten their own losses in the dreadful Ulster rebellion of 1641; the Irish have not forgotten the massacres at Drogheda and Wexford only eight years later and the Cromwellian plantations. Similarly the British saw such affairs as the insurrections of 1798 and 1803 as minor, if troublesome, incidents in a bigger war and hardly even knew the names of Wolfe Tone, Edward Fitzgerald and Robert Emmett, their leaders who have become Irish heroes. Save at extremes the differences of attitude have never, all the same, been clean cut. The British have not forgotten their sympathy in the Great Starvation which, in a disorganised but important fashion, they tried to alleviate: and Irishmen in great numbers from private soldiers to field-marshals have fought for Britain in all her wars.

(2) In 1842 Thomas Davis, John Dillon and Charles Gavan Duffy had launched the quickly influential and exciting *Nation*. They appealed to liberals and nationalists against the Union and bracketed them as Young Ireland (q.v.). They were young men advocating an Irish nationhood regardless of ancestry or religion. Young Ireland developed powerfully but its ideas were at variance with the older nationalisms and Davis, a protestant and its main inspirer, died in 1845 aged 33. By then nationalists were divided not along religious but along tactical lines between the constitutionalist or peaceful and the revolutionary. In 1848 the latter, tempted by contemporary European rebellions, provoked a minor and easily suppressed insurrection which had its importance because the Young Irelanders took part and so identified with the active and rebellious. This was to have important effects at Westminster.

(3) There were differences in perspective between the Irish as seen from Ireland and their impact on British political mechanisms. In 1800 nobody in either country foresaw the effect of injecting 100 self-conscious Irishmen into an Anglo-Scots House of Commons, a prospect obscured by the fact that not all of them were Irish; and statesmen, who in 1800 thought of Ireland as one, did not foresee the possibility of a territorial and political backlash against a sectarian nationalism as yet unborn. They were, for one thing, preoccupied with a twenty-two year war with France.

(4) There was a reversion to constitutionalism after the 1848 failure but it was difficult to attract mass support for action which was out of sight at Westminster. Charles Gavan Duffy proposed a solution in a Tenants' League against clearing landlords, which was to support only those Irish M.P.s who would refuse office and eschew other party ties. This failed on a point of character. Enough Tenants' League M.P.s were elected in 1852 to help eject the Tories from office, but their leaders, John Sadleir and William Keogh, accepted office under the Whigs. The Tenant Leaguers broke up and the despairing Duffy went to Australia. Rebellion and constitutionalism were alike discredited in Ireland.

(5) The political vacuum was filled from the American diaspora. Many emigrants had imbibed Young Irish ideas and American republicanism as well as grievances (*see* IRELAND. E.). To them revolution on the American pattern meant a triumphant return to their distantly radiant home. The Fenians and the Irish Republican Brotherhood were secret, overlapping oath-bound American bodies and the leaders, whose main personality was John O'Leary, were mostly of urban stock. They thought in terms of war, organised murderous outrages in England and prepared an Irish rising. Internal disagreements prevented arms shipments and the Brotherhood was penetrated by agents. The govt. suppressed the 1867 rising as easily as that of 1848 but certain incidents made a lasting impression, particularly the blowing up of part of Clerkenwell Gaol (London) and the hanging of three Fenians at Manchester for the murder of a policeman (both in the course of attempted rescues). The three were promptly dubbed the *Manchester Martyrs*. The Brotherhood's propaganda treated English law as no more than a declaration of war policy.

(6) These events caused another swing, this time to a constitutional Home Rule movement under the barrister Isaac Butt and the passionate English country gentleman, Charles Stewart Parnell, who had been aroused by the Manchester executions. Butt advocated a kind of Commonwealth federalism which made progress among Irish but not English M.P.s. He was helped in Ireland by the Ballot Act 1872 which protected tenants against pressure by their landlords and brought him and 58 other Home Rulers to Westminster. The Irish population, however, had more personal concerns. The repeal of the Corn Laws had not brought prices down in 1846 but from the 1860s it left the farmers of the United Kingdom defenceless against mass importations, by increasingly efficient steamships, of cheap N. American soft wheat. In England tenants left the land on the hands of ruined landlords to work in the industries. In southern Ireland there were few industries. There were renewed hostilities between southern landlords and their tenants.

(7) The Gladstone govt. of 1868 had reacted to Fenianism by an effort to remove two of its major causes. In 1869 they disestablished the Church; tithes ceased to be payable and it became easy for church tenants to buy their holdings. In 1870 of 680,000 farms the mainly southern 525,000 were occupied by tenants at will who had to provide buildings, fencing, implements and seed, yet had no right to compensation for these or for any improvements which they made in fertility. The govt's. Irish Landlord and Tenant Act 1870 effectively extended the Ulster Custom, or Tenant Right, to the three provinces. In prosperity this might have worked but N. American importations had already depressed prices for several years and the harvest failures of 1877 and 1878 merely created a vacuum into which still more American cereals poured. Landlords and tenants were involved on opposite sides in an economic disaster. The landlords could not or would not pay: tenants thought of them as parasites who should be eliminated. In 1879 the Fenian Michael Davitt, whose parents had been evicted after the Great Starvation, launched a tenants' Land League in Co. Mayo where poverty made landlordism unprofitable without rackrenting and the population was large enough to ensure candidates for tenancies after evictions. Nearly all evictions were for failure to pay rent yet prices were so low that most tenants could not afford to pay. People flocked to the League. In Oct. 1879 it became National with Parnell as President. He and Davitt, who respected but did not like each other, agreed that action not persuasion might achieve their purposes. The renewal of the land war and the simultaneous systematic obstruction of business in the House of Commons were the result.

(8) In the southern land war landlords, their agents, bailiffs, police and the army were on the side of the law; the tenantry, covertly banded together, sought to frustrate its operation by silent, moonlight terrorism. Animals were maimed, houses and byres burned; women shaved; agents beaten or done to death. Naturally the police and army retaliated. In 1879 Butt died. In these circumstances in 1890 Parnell combined and garnered the gains of violence and the benefits of peace by the invention of the boycott (q.v.).

(9) The Liberals, returned in 1880, were determined both to fight disorder by a Coercion Bill (to suspend Habeas Corpus) and to eliminate its causes by a new Landlord and Tenant Act. The former created a heaven-sent opportunity for obstruction and was fought with such ferocity that at one stage all the members of Parnell's party were suspended. This gained them widespread Irish popularity. It reached the statute book in 1881 and Parnell and other leaders of the Land League were detained. This raised their popularity still more and the Leaguers began to withhold rents. The govt. decided that some kind of deal was needed and the compact known as the KILMAINHAM TREATY with the released Parnell was the result (early May 1882). The govt. would forgo further coercion, declare an amnesty and relieve tenants of arrears: Parnell would call off terrorism. Unfortunately, within days The Invincibles (q.v.) murdered Lord Frederick Cavendish and T. H. Burke in Phoenix Park and shook public faith in Parnell's ability to carry out his side of the bargain. An Irish Land Law Act

had already been passed (Aug. 1881). English opinion would allow nothing more.

(10) Parnell now reorganised his M.P.s and converted the Land League which had served most of its purposes into an Irish National League dedicated to Home Rule. In 1885 he helped the Conservatives to turn out the Liberals and after the 1886 election had 86 M.P.s in a House where the Liberals had 86 more seats than the Conservatives. Gladstone accordingly promised Home Rule, formed a govt. with their support and introduced his first Home Rule bill. It split the Liberals: Chamberlain formed the Liberal Unionists and defeated it. The govt. resigned and lost the general election. Consequently Parnell, though able to press Salisbury's conservatives (who hated him) for further land reforms, could do nothing about Home Rule and had trouble restraining violence in the National League. In 1887, opportunely for the Conservatives, the Piggott (q.v.) forgeries were published in The Times.

(11) A special commission (The Parnell Commission) was set up to investigate (1888-90). Piggott was discredited but the Commission, not unreasonably, reported that the Phoenix Park murders arose out of the agitation and terrorism caused by Parnell's party. This increased English suspicions of him but made no difference to his Irish reputation. His downfall came with the O'Shea divorce in Nov. 1890 (see PARNELL) for the Irish R. Catholic bishops denounced his adultery and Gladstone, who had known for years of the affair, would no longer co-operate with the Home Rulers as long as Parnell led them. The Home Rulers deposed him (Dec. 1890) by 45 votes to 22. Ten months later he died.

(12) In many ways the 1892 election reproduced the conditions of 1886. The Conservatives would not concede Home Rule: the Liberals could not rule without it. Gladstone's Second Bill passed the Commons but was rejected by the Lords in Sept. 1893. The Liberals acquiesced and a Conservative victory in the elections of 1895 postponed the Home Rule issue for ten years. The Conservatives were, however, willing to make administrative and social concessions. They made govt. funds available to subsidise tenant purchasers to levels which would tempt landlords to sell. A Congested Districts Board (set up in 1891) encouraged public works and domestic industries in the poor and primitive West. As a combined result, a rural social revolution gathered momentum. Ultimately (i.e. in 1922) 400,000 tenants had become owners.

(13) These kindnesses did not kill the Home Rule movement but it could secure no constitutional concessions so long as the Conservatives and their now indistinguishable Liberal Unionist allies were in power. Hence, under John Redmond, it organised itself for the next opportunities. The M.P.s learned to act cohesively while the Order of Hibernians was created to combat the Orange Order. This reintroduced R. Catholic sectarianism into nationalism. The first great opportunity came with the 1906 Liberal victory and the parliamentary crisis of 1909-10. After both the general elections in 1910 the 82 Home Rulers held a balancing position. They supported the Parliament Bill in return for a Third Home Rule Bill which passed the Commons and was rejected by the Lords for the first time in Jan. 1913. The govt. now prepared to drive it through under the Parliament Act.

(14) At this point a sudden change surfaced in Ireland. To several southern Irish groups the Bill did not go nearly far enough. These included the Gaelic League, Sinn Fein, a Socialist Republican Party, the Irish Labour Party and the Irish Transport and General Workers Union. Ulstermen feared that these activists would operate Home Rule against Protestant interests. The recruitment of Carson's Ulster Volunteers for armed resistance, and promises of Conservative support (see IRELAND, NORTHERN) brought sharp southern reactions.

Nationalists and Sinn Fein started to recruit (Nov. 1913) Irish Volunteers (armed from the U.S.A.) against the Ulster Volunteers (armed from Germany). The govt. passed the Bill a third time in May 1914 and promised an amending Bill to except areas which refused submission to an all-Ireland parliament. Before the latter could be passed World War I broke out. The Bill received the Royal Assent immediately after the outbreak. Carson and Redmond offered the services of their respective Volunteers in the war and a suspensory Act was passed pending the amending Act.

(15) The political truce was unreal. A minority of Redmond's Volunteers, with Sinn Fein and other extremists, planned a rebellion for which they tried to create an armed organisation. Some of the arms were American: Sir Roger Casement went to get more from Germany. The rising was planned for Easter 1916 and so as to grow out of the routine Easter Volunteer manoeuvres. German help was intercepted by the Royal Navy. Casement was landed from a U-boat determined to postpone the rising to avoid failure, but was arrested next day. The manoeuvres were cancelled but the rising took place in Dublin and was put down. Sixteen of its leaders and Casement were executed and added to the Republican martyrology. Many others were imprisoned but releases began at the end of the year. By July Lloyd George could move towards conciliation by organising a convention of Irish notables, but Sinn Fein would not come and the Ulstermen would not accept an all-Irish parliament. Simultaneously republicanism with nationalism triumphed and with the election of Eamonn de Valera as M.P. for East Clare, Sinn Fein and the Republican Brotherhood organised a mass republican movement necessarily committed to further rebellion. De Valera was in any case head of the Volunteers.

(16) The slaughter on the Fronts now decided the govt. to introduce Irish conscription (Apr. 1918). This ill-timed idea discredited Constitutionalism. In the 1918 elections Sinn Fein won 73 out of 79 southern seats. The Republicans refused to take their seats, constituted themselves an Irish legislature (or *Dail Eireann*), proclaimed a Republic with de Valera as President and the Volunteers as an army. They began to set up their own organs of govt. while the population ignored the official ones, and they canvassed for international recognition. Some of the revolutionaries attacked the army and police. Martial law was proclaimed and the *Dail* proscribed. It went underground. The nationalists fired country houses and drove off cattle. The govt. recruited volunteer auxiliaries (later called *Black and Tans*) who naturally retaliated, and the Ulster protestants started to attack their local R. Catholics. Again civil war was real but not organised as a formal war. Meanwhile a fourth Home Rule Bill had passed by Nov. 1920. This allowed for legislatures at Dublin and Belfast with Irish representation at Westminster. The Ulster Unionists had doubts but accepted. The Republicans rejected it.

(17) In the May 1921 elections the Ulster Unionists won 40 out of 52 local seats, the Republicans all but four in the south. They, with 6 Ulster Republicans, constituted themselves a second all-Irish *Dail* at Dublin but meanwhile, though southern civil authority was wholly in republican hands, the republican army was losing the war. English public opinion, however, had had enough of this prolongation of the World War, and Americans were vocal. Lloyd George arranged a truce (July 1921) and, after hesitations, Arthur Griffith and Michael Collins, as Irish delegates, started discussions with the British. These lasted until Dec. during which Michael Collins, unknown to the British, organised the murder of Sir Henry Wilson, formerly C.I.G.S. and now an Ulster M.P. A treaty was signed and approved by parliament and the *Dail* in Jan. 1922. Many republicans promptly rose against it. The British threatened to use troops against them if the

Free State did not, and a civil war ensued during which Griffith died and Collins was killed. William Cosgrave took Griffith's place and got the *Dail* to pass the Free State Constitution in Oct. but the civil war ended only in Oct. 1923. *See* IRISH FREE STATE etc.

IRETON, Henry (1611-51), associate of Cromwell and his deputy at Ely in 1642, became Manchester's Q.M. Gen. in Yorkshire and at the second B. of Newbury. After a successful fight the night before the B. of Naseby (1645) he commanded the left wing and was wounded and captured by P. Rupert but escaped, became an M.P. and took part in the 1646 operations around Bristol and in the west. By now he was an important figure in the anti-Royalist side and attempted to reconcile the army with the Commons and, through his *Heads of the Proposals,* both with the King. Consequently he was a hot opponent of the Levellers, whose views seemed to him to be subversive of society and property. He had in 1646 married Cromwell's daughter Bridget. The Second Civil War disillusioned him with Charles I and thenceforth he advocated deposition in favour of one of his children. In 1648 he, with Ludlow, arranged Pride's Purge. By now he was something of an extremist. He took part in the King's trial and signed his death warrant. He then served under Cromwell in Ireland and when Cromwell left was Lord Deputy. He died before Limerick. As a regicide his body was gibbeted at the Restoration.

IRISH ARTICLES. In 1615 the Irish Church adopted 104 articles of faith, which were much more Calvinistic than the English 39 Articles; they were drawn up by James Usher, Prof. of Divinity at Dublin, who was Abp. of Armagh in 1625-6. In 1635 an Irish Convocation under Strafford replaced them by the 39 Articles. He required adherence to both sets until 1641 when he left Ireland.

IRISH CHARITABLE TRUSTS ACT (1844) vested the Irish charitable jurisdiction in a Board of Control composed equally of R. Catholics and Protestants. It worked without friction.

IRISH CONFEDERATION. *See* YOUNG IRELAND.

IRISH COUNCIL BILL (1907), introduced by Austin Birrell, was to create a council of 82 elected and 24 nominated members to exercise the powers of the eight most important Irish govt. depts. viz: those dealing with local govt., congested districts, public works, education and registration. The nationalists forced its withdrawal.

IRISH EMIGRATION 1651-4. The Commonwealth Government encouraged Irish ex-rebels to take military service abroad. 34,000 were recruited for France, Spain and Poland.

IRISH FREE STATE (EIRE). REPUBLIC OF IRELAND. (1) The Treaty (*see* IRELAND F-17) set up a constitution in which, to ensure a minority (i.e. protestant) voice, there was proportional representation in both Houses of the *Dail* and it conferred an international status for Ireland equivalent to the, later invented, Dominion status under the Crown. In addition the British retained naval bases in three Atlantic ports. The Civil War of 1922-3 had left unassuaged hatreds and destroyed much property. De Valera had waged it against the treaty and called it off when it seemed unlikely to succeed, but he and *Fianna Fail* remained determinedly hostile to it. Irish political history between the wars deals mainly with the destruction of the treaty by means short of violence.

(2) Initially De Valera and *Fianna Fail* demonstrated their rejection of the constitution by refusing to take the Oath of Allegiance. This manoeuvre carried with it the intended consequence that they could not take their seats in the *Dail*. Thus while the Cosgrave govt. prosaically set up the organs of the new state, his opponents agitated. Their flamboyance steadily attacted support which by 1927 created a dilemma. To achieve their objects outside the constitution meant the uncertainties of a new civil war: to act within it held out better prospects of success but involved eating their words. They called the Oath a

mere formality, took it and their seats. At the 1932 election they achieved a majority.

(3) The new govt's first act was to abolish the Oath, and the British Crown ceased to have any constitutional place save for the accreditation of diplomats. The govt. then witheld the annuities due under the Irish Land Acts (*see* IRISH LAND PURCHASE). This provoked a tariff war, for Britain imposed duties on Irish farm produce to recover the amounts due (about £3M). The De Valera govt. in any case meant to diversify the economy and imposed selective tariffs to protect tillage and nascent industries. These failed in their purpose, but by 1938 the Chamberlain govt., anxious in the period of appeasement to have a not unfriendly Ireland at its back, offered to end the tariff war and forgo the annuities for a lump sum of £10M and offered the three bases as well, perhaps as an indication to Hitler that Britain did not intend to fight Germany. De Valera leapt at the offers which would bring back some agricultural prosperity and enable the country to keep out of the approaching war. The B. of the Atlantic in consequence had to be fought without the bases. De Valera declared that his defenceless republic would not become a base for attacks on Britain but the Germans maintained a legation in Dublin throughout the war.

(4) The Cosgrave govt's Public Safety Act 1927 had made revolutionary societies treasonable. It was invoked against the Irish Republican Army (I.R.A.) and in 1933 against Cosgrave's own Blue Shirts. Between 1948 and 1990, with *Fine-Gael*-headed coalitions alternating with *Fianna Fail*, one of the few stable elements was the continued survival of the small *Sinn Fein* and its illegal terrorist force, the I.R.A., which, financed and supplied from outside, habitually inflicted outrages in Ulster. In 1965 these had become serious enough to warrant a meeting between the Irish Prime Minister (*Taoseach*) Sean Lemass, and the N. Ireland Prime Minister, Terence O'Neill. In 1970 another *Taoseach*, Jack Lynch, dismissed two ministers for complicity in arms smuggling and in 1973 there was an abortive Anglo-Irish agreement to set up a Council for Ireland. In 1976 the British ambassador in Dublin was murdered. In 1981 yet another *Taoseach*, Garret fitzGerald, campaigned to make Unification more attractive to Ulstermen and in 1985 the British and Irish govts. agreed (for the second time) that it could not happen without the consent of the majority of the Irish electorate.

(5) In 1987 *Sinn Fein* failed to win any seats in the general election but terrorism and loyalist counter-terrorism continued. From 1989, however, foreign supplies and finance (from U.S.A., Russia and elsewhere) began to fall off. Hence in 1994 the I.R.A. was brought to a truce on the basis that if it showed signs of actually surrendering its arms, discussions with the British govt. might be opened. Its leader, Gerry Adams, continued with great skill to keep controversy with the British going while avoiding compliance with the condition. In the previous thirty years over 3000 people had perished but in Jan. 1996 the truce still held. In Feb. however, there were explosions in London for which Adams blamed the British.

IRISH LAND LEAGUE. *See* LAND LEAGUE.

IRISH LAND PURCHASE. The advance of public monies to facilitate land purchase began with Bright's amendments to the Land Act 1870 and the Glebe Loan (Ir.) Acts, 1870 to 1875. Under these the Board of Works could advance sums to tenants to purchase their holdings, not exceeding two thirds of the purchase price, repayable by annuity over thirty five years. The Land Law (Ir.) Act 1881 constituted the Land Commission which could advance up to three-quarters, and the condition was annexed to every holding, while subject to an annuity, that the Commission might sell it if the land were sub-divided or sub-let without its consent, or if the proprietor became

bankrupt; and these conditions applied to holdings sold under any of the subsequent Purchase Acts. The Purchase of Land (Ir.) Act 1885 (*The Ashbourne Act*) was the first with the definite object of creating a peasant proprietorship. Over 67,000 purchasers took advantage of it before the Irish Land Act 1903. The Commission could advance the balance of the purchase money if one fifth of it were provided for. The guarantee deposit was either lodged by the purchaser or retained out of the purchase money and held until he had paid a sum equal to it. Under the Act of 1903, upon the sale of an estate or a holding for which a fair rent had been fixed by the Court, or by agreement if the price agreed was within certain limits, the Land Commission had to make an advance repayable by an annuity which was less and often much less than the fair rent. The Commission could also purchase untenanted land for redistribution. To encourage landlords to come in and take advantage of the Act, the Land Purchase Aid Fund was established out of which a bonus of 12 per cent upon the purchase money of estates was paid to the vendors. This fund was raised by the issue of guaranteed stock. The bonus was also payable on untenanted land sold to the Commission or the Congested District Board. Under the older Acts, all arrears of rent were wiped out when the purchase agreement was signed whether the sale was by the owner or the Land Judge, though the payment of all arrears could be required as a condition precedent to the signature of the agreement. Under the 1903 Act, one year's arrears only could be required. The Act was very successful and worked perfectly until 1932 when the Free State govt. intercepted and appropriated the annuities.

IRISH LAND TENURE. English tenures were gradually extended to the districts outside the Pale by the inclusion of portions of the land subject to the custom of "Irishry" in Shire land, viz: where there was a sheriff, the king's writ ran and the common law could be executed. No statute was needed as the Crown created Irish counties under the prerogative. In Munster, Leinster and Connaught extension of the English system was gradual. Sometimes, however, the "custom of Englishry" was extended to clans and the Statute 12 Eliz c. 4 empowered the Crown to receive surrenders of land from "the pretended lords, gentlemen and freeholders of the Irishrie, and the men of degenerate English name" in order that the lands might be re-granted to hold under the common law. The introduction of the English system into Ulster arose mainly out of the plantation grants to private settlers and companies under James I. The *Case of Gavelkind and Tanistry* (1606) put an end to the descent of lands by an Irish custom similar to gavelkind, viz, the division on the death of a tenant of the lands of the sept among the heads of families, without distinction between legitimate and illegitimate issue. Under James I it came to be regarded as finally settled that all lands are held of the Crown and the assimilation of English and Irish tenures and estates date from that period, but the old customs to some extent survived, e.g. in the West the holding in Rundale: a division of the arable lands annually, the pasture being held in common. The Crown claimed the right to create manors notwithstanding the Statute *Quia Emptores,* but doubts having been raised as to the validity of these grants, they were confirmed by statute. The Irish Statute of Tenures 1661 like the English converted knight's tenure into socage. There was, however, no copyhold. *See* GAVELKIND, IRELAND.

IRISH LEGISLATION (*see* POYNINGS' LAW). Neither House could initiate a Bill, so legislation would be suggested by either house in the form of Heads of a Bill. This was submitted to the Irish Privy Council which examined, revised and submitted the revised version to the King and Council in England. The English council made further examination and, if necessary, revision and returned the result in the form of a bill, which went through all the usual stages in both houses, beginning with the House which had proposed the original Heads. It could be thrown out but not amended.

IRISH MASSACRE (Oct. 1641). This event, decisive in Anglo-Irish relations and appalling after all exaggeration has been discounted, occurred in the following circumstances.

Laudian bishops had driven Ulster presbyterian ministers from their parishes back to Scotland, where they had a loud voice in the revolution. The Lord Deputy Wentworth (later E. of Strafford) had also been deporting unlanded Ulster Scots to Scotland. This was equally infuriating to Scots but because of the migratory connection between Ulster and Scotland, not wholly effective. During the Bishops' Wars he had imposed the Black Oath on all substantial persons save R. Catholics and had severely punished those who refused it. At the same period he had managed to alienate the Irish and also the Connaught landowners by manipulating the Crown inquests, ostensibly to extend the plantation system, but actually to raise revenue. The Castle Chamber, the Irish equivalent of the Star Chamber, had functioned in like manner, while actual Star Chamber proceedings had been launched against the Corporation of London for failures at Coleraine, which ended in forfeiture and a fine of £70,000. The analogy with the abuse of forest proceedings in England (*see* CHARLES I-8) was obvious. The difference was that the basic population was R. Catholic, secretive and Gaelic speaking. Moreover, when Strafford's Irish army was disbanded and paid off at less than half its entitlement (May 1641) the mostly R. Catholic soldiers joined the underground malcontents.

Strafford's policy had thus antagonised large sections of society in all parts and could be pursued only by Strafford himself. When he had gone there was aimlessness at Dublin Castle, for puritan Lords Justices exasperated the R. Catholics still further, while those whom Strafford had terrorised began to pluck up courage. A conspiracy was set on foot, directed and partly led by a group of R. Catholic notables, particularly Emer MacMahon, Bp. of Clogher, who was its brain, Sir Phelim O'Neill, Lord Maguire of Fermanagh, Philip O'Reilly, Hugh MacMahon Emer's brother and Roger Moore of Leix. The main places, especially Londonderry, Carrickfergus, Newry and Dublin Castle, were to be surprised and the Ulster Irish were to rise, drive out and strip the English and Scottish settlers and their families. Captured arms were to be distributed. R. Catholic priests acted as preliminary organisers. The date fixed was 23 Oct. 1641, when crops were stored but taxes yet unpaid, and when strong westerly winds might be expected to deter reinforcements from England. The attempts at Dublin and Enniskillen miscarried because the garrisons were forewarned but the rest succeeded and the naked colonists, if not murdered, died in thousands in the cold between Oct. and Mar. 1642. Contemporary R. Catholic priests returned their parish casualties at 154,000. Cooler, later protestants estimated them at 37-40,000. Some escaped, mainly to Dublin, and when the risings spread south, put them down, especially in Wexford. The massacre reminded all good protestants of the Parisian St. Bartholomew's Night and rekindled the hysterical anti-Romanism of English opinion for two generations. *See also* CHARLES I-20.

IRISH NATIONAL FEDERATION was the anti-Parnellite faction formed in Mar. 1891 after Parnell's adulteries became publicly known.

IRISH NATIONAL VOLUNTEERS (1913-14). The project was originated by Prof. John McNeill, a founder of the Gaelic movement, in Nov. 1913 and launched at a meeting of 13,000 people at the Rotunda in Dublin. Drilling proceeded, unobstructed by the govt, but as there was a risk that the Volunteers might be

manoeuvred against John Redmond's Irish parliamentary party, he forced the committee to accept nominees from him. By June 1914 there were 65,000 volunteers but the tension between Redmond and the Sinn Fein-orientated McNeill rose when World War I broke out. *See* IRISH VOLUNTEERS (1914).

IRISH REBELLION 1798. *See* UNITED IRISHMEN.

IRISH REPUBLICAN ARMY (I.R.A.) is descended from the secret Irish Republican Brotherhood formed in the U.S.A. in 1858 and associated with or overlapping the Fenians. It acquired great influence among the Irish Volunteers formed in 1913 against Carson's Ulster Volunteers and, with Sinn Fein, took part in the 1916 Easter Rising. In 1919 it fought the British but after the Anglo-Irish treaty (1921) it split into the Free State Army and the private force of Sinn Fein opposed to the treaty. By 1926 it had been defeated but in the 1930s and 1970s some of its members reappeared as anti- British terrorists. *See* IRELAND, NORTHERN; IRISH FREE STATE *etc*.

IRISH SOCIAL HISTORY (MEDIAEVAL). *See* FERNS.

IRISH VOLUNTEERS (1777 onwards) were originally raised to replace troops sent to America to cope with the American rebellion. These, the so-called UNITED VOLUNTEERS, were mostly protestant, though R. Catholics were not excluded, and they included most of the residents of distinction. They elected their own officers and paid for their own arms. By 1779 some 8,000 had been trained. They were vociferous, especially when the Irish parliamentary opposition began to stir them up: they were in a good position to organise boycotts of English goods and with their support Grattan demanded and got free trade with the empire. *See* DUNGANNON CONVENTION.

IRISH VOLUNTEERS (1914). John McNeill's secessionary minority from the Irish National Volunteers (q.v.) were nationalist activists who circulated many small sedulous journals in the towns, designed to hinder the generally successful recruiting companies, in the opening months of World War I. They amalgamated with the Citizen Army in Nov. 1915. Many belonged to Sinn Fein.

IRON. Iron was originally produced in fires built against a bank exposed to the prevailing wind and later in rock furnaces blown by bellows, followed by hammering to drive out impurities. In the 14th cent. tall or blast furnaces came into use and the material could be melted and cast. Rolling started in the 16th century. These processes were each started in Germany and imported into Britain a little later. Sporadic experiments in the 17th cent. led Abraham Darby to introduce smelting using locally available coking coal in 1709. Huntsman produced steel at Sheffield in 1740. Cort's various processes came into use after 1767. The steam engine, by powering both blast and processing, raised temperatures, speed and scale of production. Pig iron production in the U.K. rose from about 20,000 tons in 1700 to 70,000 in 1790, to 2,250,000 in 1850 and to a peak of just over 10,000,000 in 1910. The principal ancient source of commercial iron was the I. of Elba but the ores, of one sort or another, are fairly common and since at least the 14th cent. it has been mined in quantity in Spain, Sweden, in the Cleveland area of Yorkshire and, since the mid-19th cent., in Lorraine, the Belgian border and Luxemburg. The U.S.A. developed a very large output after 1854.

IRON AGE in W. Europe began with the EARLY HALLSTADT culture of 7th cent. B.C. This, apart from the use of iron artefacts instead of bronze, was distinguished by cremation rites and was succeeded by the two phases of LATE HALLSTADT ending c. 500 B.C., when a new culture in three phases known as LA TÈNE, marked by inhumation, appeared. Each of these reached Britain some considerable time after they had been established on the continent, through the medium of invaders from the Low Countries and France, who used ploughs, sickles and swords of iron and made increasingly fine pottery.

Being agricultural, they lived mainly in low lying villages with storage pits for food, and fortified hill tops only against emergencies. Early La Tène lasted from about 500 to 300 B.C.; the Middle coincided with the beginning of the so-called British Iron Age B (c. 280 B.C. to about 120 B.C.). The Late La Tène slowly merged with that of the Roman Conquest.

IRONBRIDGE (Salop). Called after the first iron bridge: built in 1770, it is preserved as an ancient monument. There is a museum at Telford.

IRON CHANCELLOR. *See* BISMARCK.

IRONCLAD. (1) Sir William Congreve, the inventor of the war rocket, proposed armoured floating batteries for use against coastal forts in 1805. American designs for armoured warships were drawn up in 1836 and Dupuy de Lôme submitted plans to the French govt. in 1845. The real impetus was, however, provided by the B. of Sinope (Nov. 1853) when a Turkish squadron of wooden ships was destroyed, it was believed, by Russian shellfire: both the French and the British, now committed to war in the Crimea, built ironclad floating batteries and three French ones bombarded Kinburn, a Russian fort at the mouth of the Dnieper, on 17 Oct. 1855. **(2)** The poor seakeeping quality of these batteries led to much rethinking and the first seagoing ironclads were the French *Gloire,* laid down in 1858 and the British *Warrior* in 1859. The hulk of the *Warrior* was recovered in 1975 from use as a coal store in the Falkland Is. and reconstructed as an exhibition ship at Portsmouth. **(3)** Meanwhile the American Civil War broke out and the earliest ironclad contest took place on 9 Mar. 1862 between the Confederate *Merrimac,* a broadside ship, and the Federal *Monitor* which had a turret. They did each other little harm even at point blank range. **(4)** The apparent superiority of armour over guns led navies to try the ram, and the Austrian Adm. Tegetthoff, despite the fact that his ships did not have rams, rammed the Italians at the B. of Lissa (Vis) (July 1866) and sank their flagship. This affected armoured ship design, notably by the inclusion of rams for the next 40 years, by which time steel had long superseded iron.

IRON CROWN. The Crown of Lombardy kept at Pavia.

IRON CURTAIN. The barrier with barbed wire, minefields and watch towers, erected in 1960-1 by communist states from the Baltic to Yugoslavia to prevent the escape of their populations to the west. It had four police-obstructed crossing points in Berlin and only six elsewhere in Germany. Several thousand were shot or blown up trying to escape before the system was demolished amid rejoicing in 1989. 200 crossing points were opened thereafter in six weeks.

IRON DUKE. The first D. of Wellington.

IRON LADY. (1) Mrs Margaret Thatcher. **(2)** An instrument of torture.

IRON MAIDEN. An instrument of torture and slow death.

IRON PUDDLING PROCESS. *See* CORT, HENRY.

IRONSIDE, William Edmund (1880-1959) 1st Ld. IRONSIDE (1941) fought in World War I, becoming Commandant of the Machine Gun School and then a brigade commander. In Sept. 1918 he went as Chief of Staff and then commander of a composite allied force at Murmansk and Archangel. This had to be withdrawn in the autumn of 1919 owing to communist aggression, disaffection amongst his Russian units and political irresolution at home. In 1920 he was chief of a military mission to Adm. Horthy's Hungarian govt. and then commanded the Ismid and North Persian forces against Turkish and communist penetration. It was his support for Trenchard which brought about the Air Control scheme in Iraq in 1921 but he broke his legs flying there and was invalided home to become, from 1922 to 1926, commandant of the Staff College.

After various more conventional appointments he was Q.M.G. in India from 1933 to 1936 and then returned to the English Eastern Command. Much perturbed by lack of direction, shortage of resources and men, and obsolescence of equipment he met Hitler, Goering, Mussolini and Badoglio at the 1937 German army manoeuvres but neither Hore-Belisha (Sec. of State) nor Chamberlain, the Prime Minister, would listen to his experiences. After various inactive posts he unwillingly became C.I.G.S. at the beginning of World War II. He found no world-wide, or even proper European, plan; he correctly predicted that the Germans would use a combined air-ground attack *via* the Ardennes to force a victory. The French thought that the blow would come *via* Brussels. He planned for 20 divisions in France, 12 in the Middle East with a reserve of 18 at home but this took time, the war direction machinery was not adapted to quick action, the three services were uncoordinated and he and his Sec. of State (Hore-Belisha) were temperamentally at odds. Hence he could not carry out his plan to seize the Gällivare iron mines during the Russo-Finnish war; the Germans anticipated him at Narvik; Churchill, despite his protests, redirected the Norwegian expedition to Trondheim and Namsos and, as the French failed to support his intended counter-attack against the northern wing of the Germans in the Ardennes, the British in Belgium had to be evacuated. Appointed C-in-C of the Home Army in May 1940, he had to build it from nothing out of defeated and demoralised troops. He was superseded by Sir Alan Brooke, made a Field Marshal and retired in July. An unconventional and honourable soldier, his active career was cut short through the failings of others.

IRONSIDES. Cromwell's cavalry.

IROQUOIS, also called THE FIVE or the SIX NATIONS, were Amerindian tribes, of whom five, the Seneca, Cayuga, Onondaga, Oneida and Mohawks, were federated in about 1560 and were joined in 1715 by a sixth, the Carolina Tuscaroras. They were bound by an agreement that no one of them would make aggressive war without the consent of the others so long as the perpetual Council Fire burned. They are alleged not to have exceeded 15,000 at any one time but in the 17th and much of the 18th cents. they ruled a rough triangle of lands from the Ottawa R. (Canada) and including most of the inland parts of the modern coastal states of Maine, New Hampshire, New York and Pennsylvania, together with Michigan, Ohio, Indiana, W. Virginia, Kentucky and Tennessee, and kept the English and French in check. Their council of chiefs aimed to keep the hunting grounds west of the Alleghenies open and so helped the English against the French, who were operating from the west. At the outbreak of the American rebellion they were neutral for a while but in unexplained circumstances the Council Fire, which was in the custody of the Onondaga, was doused and the confederacy broke up. The Mohawks and Cayuga under the leadership of Joseph Brant joined the English and eventually moved to Canada. See JOHNSON, SIR WILLIAM; NEW ENGLAND.

IRRAWADDY RIVER (Burma). This great river is a mile and more wide along the 500 miles before it reaches the sea.

IRREDENTISM. From *Italia irredenta* ("Italy unredeemed"). An Italian nationalist doctrine which grew up after 1878 advocating the recovery, if necessary by war, of "Italian" areas still forming part of other states. Language was the main, but not always the only, criterion. The word is often applied to similar movements elsewhere, especially Roumania with regard to Transylvania and post-Versailles German irredentism was an important part of Hitler's political stock in trade. Under the name "Great Principle" it has long been an important element in Greek politics, particularly in relation to Cyprus, Constantinople and Macedonia.

IRREMOVABILITY. A pauper's right, acquired by a year's residence in a parish, not to be removed to his parish of origin.

IRVINE. *See* NEW TOWNS.

IRVING, Sir Henry (born John Henry BRODRIBB) (1838-1905) acted in London from 1866 and achieved popularity in 1870. In 1874 he played Hamlet for 200 nights and in 1878 he became the manager of the Lyceum Theatre with Ellen Terry as his leading lady. He dominated the Shakespearean stage until 1895 when financial mismanagement and a fire drove him to go on tour. He remained a famous, if less influential, figure until his death.

IRWIN. *See* WOOD.

ISAACS, Rufus Daniel (1860-1935) M. of READING, became a Liberal M.P. in 1904 and sol-gen. and then att-gen. in 1910. He joined the Cabinet in 1911. There now followed the Marconi scandal, an affair in which Isaacs' brother Godfrey secured a Post Office contract for the Marconi Co. of which he was a director. When the *Titanic* disaster occurred in 1912 the need for ships' wireless was demonstrated. Godfrey gave Rufus some American Marconi shares which Rufus promptly sold at a huge profit. Furious accusations of corruption followed. An investigation showed that there had been no corrupt, but some unwise, dealing but in Oct. 1913 Rufus became Lord Chief Justice. This provoked Kipling's angry poem *Gehazi*. In Jan. 1918 he became Ambassador to Washington where he remained until the end of World War I, competently co-ordinating the British and U.S. war efforts. From 1921 to 1926 he was Viceroy of India at a time of rising nationalist agitation and the first Indian parliament. In 1931 he was briefly Foreign Sec. in Ramsay MacDonald's National Govt.

ISABEL of ANGOULÊME (?1185-1246) was daughter and heiress of Audemar, Count of Angoulême and claimant, against Hugh le Brun of Lusignan, to the county of La Marche. Eleanor of Aquitaine reconciled the rivals and in 1199 Isabel was affianced to Hugh. This would have created a dangerously strong fief in English Poitou. King John dissuaded Audemar from the match and married Isabel himself: thereby incurring many years of Lusignan hostility. She scarcely influenced him. In 1214 the quarrel with the Lusignans was made up during the Bouvines campaign and their daughter Joan was affianced to Hugh, the son of Hugh le Brun. John, however, died in 1216 and after the coronation of Henry III, Isabel returned home and in 1220 married the younger Hugh herself. She and he paid no attention to her son's interests but tried to play off England and France against each other. In June 1224 Hugh agreed to support the French King in return for Saintes and Oléron (Isabel's dower) and French troops occupied Poitou. This decisive event resulted, in 1241, in the investiture by King Louis IX of Alphonse, his brother, with the County of Poitou and Hugh and Isabel were called upon to do homage. They now rebelled and asked Henry III and other French potentates for support. The combination never functioned. The English, Poitevin and other forces were defeated in detail. Hugh was forced to submit. Isabel retired to a convent. Their children mostly migrated to England where they became a burden to Henry III.

ISABEL of BAVARIA (?-1435) queen (1385) of Charles VI of France (q.v.).

ISABEL of ENGLAND (1214-41) daughter of King John, married the Emperor Frederick II in 1235. He kept her in oriental seclusion.

ISABEL of ENGLAND (1332-79) eldest daughter of Edward III and Philippa of Hainault, was proposed as a wife seven times to continental magnates with whom her father was seeking alliance against France. The prospective swains were Peter, son of Alfonso XI of Castile (1335), Louis of Flanders (twice, 1338 and 1347), John III of Brabant (1344), the Emperor Charles IV (1349) and Bernard, son of the Lord of Albret (1351). Only one of these proposals came near to solemnisation, namely that to Louis of Flanders, who evaded the marriage and

alliance by flight. Finally in 1365 she married Enguerrand VII of Coucy who was created E. of Bedford. She bore him two daughters but his loyalty to France eventually caused a separation.

ISABELLA of FRANCE (c. 1294-1358) Queen to Edward II (1308) and MORTIMER, Roger (1287-1330) Ld. of WIGMORE (?1304), E. of MARCH (1328), RISE, RULE AND FALL. (1) Roger acquired large Irish estates by marriage in 1308 and was in Ireland, first pursuing a feud with the Lacys; then as Lieutenant defending the country against Edward Bruce's invasion and then as Justiciar. He was already highly experienced when he returned to Wales in 1320 to help his uncle Roger (III), Lord of Chirk, to strengthen the Mortimer position against the encroachments of the King's favourites, the two Despensers. Edward II's victory at Boroughbridge (1322) destroyed the political balance and when he came west Roger had to submit and was sent to the Tower.

(2) The resulting political grievance was matched by Isabella's personal one. She had been affianced to Edward as part of Anglo-French truce negotiations since she was four and was married to him at Boulogne at the age of twelve. Her complaints of poverty to her father when she reached England may have been an early symptom of her remarkable later greed but at the time Edward's affections were engaged to Piers Gaveston. Her relatives at the coronation said that Edward loved the arrogant base-born Gaveston more than his modest high-born wife and later Thomas of Lancaster wrote to her that he would not rest until he had rid her of him. Such a letter could never have been written if her hatred for Gaveston had not been well-known. It is not, however, likely that she helped to engineer his fall for she was only sixteen and her eldest son, Edward (later III) was born at this time. She evidently tried to get closer to her peculiar husband after Gaveston's death for she was in Paris with him in 1313 and she bore him three other children between 1316 and 1321. She also showed a talent for negotiation and in 1318 and again in 1321 acted on his behalf with the barons. The Despensers were by now in the ascendant and she was faced with another homosexual infatuation but this time she had rivals in greed. In 1324 she was forced to surrender her estates and the revenues of Ponthieu and Montreuil which she had had since 1308 in exchange for an allowance. Nevertheless she undertook, at papal suggestion, a diplomatic mission to her brother Charles IV in 1325, perhaps for some such human reason as desire to get away from the atmosphere of Edward's court and company to a place where women were appreciated. Her mission was a diplomatic success. Roger meanwhile had already escaped from the Tower to Paris (1324) and joined a group of influential exiles which included three earls and two bishops. There she and Roger met.

(3) They shared a mutual sexual attraction and grievances against the King. Their bedfellowship was as notorious as his less regular affections but she was royal and he was an experienced politician. They conspired against the Despensers and Edward. Chance dealt them a trump card. She and Charles IV had agreed that Aquitaine should be returned intact to Edward who should do homage for it in person. The Despensers feared to let him out of their sight and adopted a proposal by papal diplomats that P. Edward should be invested with Aquitaine and do homage for it instead. Accordingly the prince did homage at Bois de Vincennes (Sept. 1325). She now announced that she and the prince would not return until the younger Despenser had been dismissed. The Paris exiles had some armed men in their service and there were rumours of impending invasion all the winter in England.

(4) The *liaison* was now internationally scandalous. The Pope urged Charles IV to countenance it no longer; she and most of the exiles accordingly moved to Hainault

where she negotiated a bargain with Count William II whereby P. Edward should marry Philippa, the Count's daughter, in return for a force of 700 troops. In Sept. 1326 the expedition sailed from Dordrecht to Orwell in Suffolk. Isabella was rapturously received. The royal govt. collapsed. She pursued the elder Despenser to Bristol where he was hanged. Henry of Leicester caught the King and the younger Despenser at Neath. The King was put in Kenilworth Castle. At the end of Nov. the younger Despenser was beheaded at Hereford. The magnates having appointed the thirteen-year-old P. Edward Keeper of the Realm, he summoned a parliament to Westminster for 7 Jan. By 25th Edward II had been deposed. Roger had him removed from Kenilworth to Berkeley Castle (Glos.) in Apr. There were two attempts to rescue him and in Sept., after the second, he was done to death.

(5) The joint govt. of 'the she-wolf of France' and Roger was conducted through representatives, especially Orelton, on the council of regency. They obtained a settlement in Aquitaine by paying a large sum as well as the usual relief on homage; an act to limit the forests by reference to the perambulations of Edward I was passed to settle rural grievances in 1327 and the Despensers' English Staples were suspended in order to gain mercantile support. They also entered into negotiations for a definitive peace with Scotland. These superficially sensible policies were, however, suspect because of Isabella's extraordinary rapacity and Roger's acquisitiveness or ambition. Isabella obtained an enormous dower. Roger secured the property of his father, of his uncle of Chirk, the Despenser lordship of Denbigh and other of their lands, some lordships belonging to Arundel, and the Irish palatine jurisdictions of Louth, Meath and Trim. Like his uncle, he became Justice of Wales. During the negotiations ending in the recognition of Scottish independence at the T. of Northampton (1328) Roger became E. of (the) March. His power, as a kind of marcher viceroy of lands on both sides of the Irish sea, with Isabella's influence over Edward III, was becoming a danger to other elements in the state. Henry of Lancaster, the chief of the council of regency, with his supporters recognised this; they refused to attend the Parliament of Northampton and gathered troops, which led to a brief conflict and agreement in Leicestershire in 1329.

Amongst Henry's supporters had been the King's uncle, Edmund of Kent, but the agreement was forced on Henry by Edmund's last minute defection. Roger and Isabella now decided to strike at Edmund, who was condemned and executed at the Winchester Parliament of 1330 on charges of conspiracy with agents provocateurs. This warning had the opposite to its intended effect. Lancaster determined to gain access to the King, which was done through Richard Bury, the Keeper of the Privy Seal and William Montague, a yeoman of the household. Montague explained the King's difficulties to the Pope (John XXII) at Avignon. At the Nottingham Great Council in Oct. 1330 Roger and Isabella seemed to be seeking pretexts for action against unidentified magnates and Montague advised the King that he was in danger. They secured entry to Nottingham Castle, overpowered Roger's guards and hustled him off to London where he was attainted and executed.

(6) Isabella was thrust out of public life and made to disgorge her illegitimate gains, but lived a comfortable life on an ample allowance, mostly at Castle Rising, hawking, reading and collecting relics. She took the habit of the Poor Claires just before she died but whether this represented a form of fire insurance or a change of heart is unknown. She was a much tried woman of extreme appetites.

ISABELLA, Infanta. *See* ELIZABETH I-22.

ISABEY, Jean Baptiste (1767-1855), designer, lithographer and portrait painter of European celebrities,

from the Court of Louis XVI to that of Napoleon III, but especially at the Congress of Vienna (1815). After 1830 he directed the artists' studios at the Sèvres porcelain factory.

ISCA or CAERLEON (Gwent) was founded in A.D. 74 as a legionary base against the Silures. It was in military use until the Romans left and inhabited thereafter. As a site of some strength and strategic importance it acquired a powerful castle just after the Norman Conquest. It was held successively and extended by both Welsh and Norman lords but always under the English crown. It also had one of the principal Cistercian monasteries in S. Wales. Its legendary history was more colourful: it was believed to have been the capital of King Arthur, with an archbishopric held successively by Dubricius and St. David.

ISCA DUMNONIORUM (Exeter). *See* BRITAIN, ROMAN-2.

ISHBOSHETH (*see* 2 SAM iv). King Saul's ineffectual and quickly deposed son. In Dryden's *Absalom and Achitophel* he stands for Richard Cromwell.

ISIDORE of SEVILLE, St. (?560-636) was Bp. of Seville from about 600 onwards. His immense learning is preserved in his works which are the main sources for the history of the Vandals, Suevi and Visigoths. He presided over the fourth Council of Toledo in 633 and within a generation was virtually recognised as a "Doctor of the Church". *See* FALSE DECRETALS.

ISLAM (Arab = 'resignation') is the corpus of religious doctrine founded by the Prophet Mohammed (570-629). The principal text is the KORAN, a book of 114 suras or chapters said to have been revealed to the prophet and written originally on palm leaves, but arranged and codified under the Caliph Othman (r. 643-56). It is supplemented by the SUNNA or 'customs' of the prophet and his orthodox successors. The main doctrines are the unity of God (Allah) and universal predestination to which man must submit. At long intervals God has sent prophets to announce the truth. The last but one of these was Jesus of Nazareth (whose divinity and crucifixion are denied) and the last, Mohammed himself. The main religious practices are confession of faith in God and in Mohammed as his prophet, circumcision, prayer five times a day, fasting during daylight hours in the month of Ramadan and pilgrimage to Mecca. The main social practices are almsgiving and the establishment of religious charities, the prohibition of wine and pork, occasional (but not very common) polygamy restricted to a maximum of four wives, and easy divorce. The early political programme is summarised in the alternatives habitually offered to hostile states: "either believe, or pay tribute or fight". The prophet, however, accepted that People of the Book, i.e. Christians, Jews and possibly Zoroastrians, whose religion was based on a written canon, were superior to 'idolators' and if they paid tribute (i.e. the jhizya or tithe) should not be molested in the exercise of their religion. In practice this meant forcible circumcision for 'idolators', a matter of great importance in India. *See* CALIPHATE.

ISLANDSHIRE (Northumberland) with Norham and its castle, was a triangular territory just south of the Tweed and was administered from Holy Island (Lindisfarne). It was long a military outwork of the palatinate of Durham.

ISKENDERUN. See HATAY.

ISLES, LORDSHIP OF THE (*see also*, MAN I. OF). The Western Isles and Argyll were colonised by and owed a distant allegiance to Norway from about 794. Norwegian overlordship was strengthened by an expedition of K. Magnus Barefoot in 1098 to secure the recognition of his rights and by treaty with Edgar, K. of Scots. In 1156 the local ruler or lord **(1) Godred, Gutbfrith or Godfrey** was defeated in a sea battle by a raider known as **(2) Somerled (?-1164)** who took the isles south of Ardnamurchan. In 1158 he drove Godred out of Man and refused allegiance to the King of Scots but in 1164 he was defeated and killed at Renfrew by K. Malcolm IV. Of his sons **(3) Dougall** took Morvern, Lorne and Mull and was the ancestor of the chiefs of CLAN DOUGALL and **(4) Ranald** took Kintyre, Cowall, Islay and the islands of the Clyde. He had two sons **(5) Donald (?-1247)** of Kintyre and Islay, ancestor of the chiefs of CLAN DONALD and **(6) Rory (fl. 1212)** of Bute and Arran, ancestor of the chiefs of CLAN RORY. These two clans tended to act together and their chiefs became important virtually independent rulers who intervened in Scotland to assure their position or get support against rivals. By 1299, however, the MacDougalls were at feud with the MacDonalds, perhaps in connection with the Dublin trade. Thus **(7) Ewen MacDougall (fl. 1315)** commanded the fleet at Dublin against Edward Bruce's invasion of Ireland in 1315 while **(8) Angus Og MacDonald** and **(9) Lachlan MacRory** supported Bruce and were both killed with him at the B. of Faughart in 1318. K. Robert the Bruce, in return, drove Ewen from the Isles and gave them to the son of **(8)**, **(10) Ewen or John MacDonald of Islay (?-1387) 1st LORD OF THE ISLES** who married Margaret, daughter of Robert the High Steward and later King of Scots. Ewen's policy was to maintain his own independence by a balance of power on the Scottish mainland. He supported Edward Balliol in 1335 and David II in 1341. His descendants, being semi-royal, were ambitious **(11) Donald (?-1420)** married **(12) Mary or Margaret Leslie** after 1402 and through her claimed the earldom of Ross. When she died he married the niece and heiress of **(9)**, **(13) Anna or Amie** and united the Isles under his rule. By this time loosely federated MacDonald Clans were occupying much of the Outer Hebrides, as well as lands on either side of the Great Glen, almost as far as Loch Ness. In 1411, however, their mainland advance was checked by Donald's defeat at the hands of the E. of Mar in the desperate B. of Harlaw (Aberdeen) and he swore allegiance in 1412. His son **(14) Alexander (?-1449) 3rd Ld. and 10th E. of ROSS** was one of the chiefs briefly imprisoned by James I at the Inverness gathering of 1428. Released with a caution, he returned in strength and burned the town. James defeated him at Lochaber (June 1429) and imprisoned him until Nov. 1431, after the collapse of another rebellion by a relative **(15) Donald Balloch.** Alexander remained quiescent but powerful for the rest of his life, being employed as Justiciar N. of the Forth from 1438. His son **(16) Ewen or John (?-1498) 4th Ld. and 11th E.** had just succeeded when James II was called south by persistent trouble with the Douglases. He rose in 1450 and sacked Inverness and then came to terms with the King but immediately made a *band* with Crawford and Douglas, which was the occasion of Douglas' murder by the King at Stirling in Feb. 1452. The fall of the Black Douglas in 1455 made alliances between west coast magnates even more necessary to their survival than before, even though Ewen obtained some Douglas lands and a Douglas wardenship of the Marches in 1457. Nevertheless Ewen's troops fought with James II at Roxburgh in 1460 where the King was killed. The minority of James III and the emergence of a more settled English monarchy under Edward IV created new opportunities. Under the T. of Westminster-Ardtornish (1462) Douglas, Ewen and Donald Balloch agreed to help Edward IV to conquer Scotland in return for which Douglas would receive back his lands in the S.W. under the English crown while the Highlands N. of the Forth were to be divided between Ewen and Donald Balloch. Edward's object was to neutralise the Lancastrian policy of James III's regents. Meantime Ewen set up his capital at Inverness but by 1464 the Lancastrians had been finally beaten; the regency came to terms with Edward and the whole ambitious scheme collapsed. Immediately afterwards James III created the Earldom of Arran for the Boyds, at MacDonald expense, but the turmoil of the years after 1467 tempted Ewen to try for a quasi-independence in other directions. The Norwegian cession of the Orkneys to Scotland in 1469, however, placed the trade between Scandinavia and the Isles at the royal mercy and in 1475 James III was strong enough to turn on Ewen. Attainted in the parliament of that year, he was forced to surrender the Earldom of Ross with its mainland influence. This set-back destroyed Ewen's authority. A bastard **(17) Angus (?-1490)** made himself independent but was eventually killed. A nephew **(18) Alexander of Lochalsh** also set up on his own and in 1491 forcibly laid claim to the lands of Ross, sacked the Cromarty lands intermingled with them, seized Inverness and raided the Mackenzies of Kintail, who retaliated. James IV would not tolerate such disorders and, since the Lord of the Isles could not keep his people in order, he decided that the Crown should do it. After a series of campaigns the Lordship was annexed to the Crown in May 1493. Ewen died a monk. The spirit of the Isles was not, however, crushed. In 1494 a kinsman **(19) Ewen or John of Islay** hanged the King's governor but was himself seized by Maclean of Ardnamurchan; and in 1504 a grandson of **(16)**, **(20) Donald Dubh (?-1504)** raised a rebellion together with the Macleans, Macleods and Camerons. This was crushed only after hard-fought combined operations. Ross was now given a separate sheriff with deputies in the Isles but the new arrangements were too sketchy and authority was wielded mainly by local magnates acting as royal Lieutenants. In 1530 these were the Es. of Argyll (Campbell) and Moray (Stewart) who attempted, in concert, to enlarge their interests at MacDonald expense. The ensuing civil war was composed by James V in person. He deprived the Lieutenants and left the MacDonalds of Islay to keep order in the southern isles. In the north the MacDonalds of Sleat with the Macleods of Lewis tried to recover the Ross lands in 1539 but were repulsed before Ellandonan. A royal sea progress of 1540 pacified the Isles. Feud violence (especially between MacDonalds and Campbells) lasted into the 18th cent.

ISLINGTON, ISENDON or ISELDON (London). This area, embracing the manors of Barnsbury, Canonbury, Highbury and Holloway, was mostly agricultural until the 16th cent. though a suburb of London had developed in Finsbury. The dissolution of the monasteries released building land and the Great Fire of 1666 drove many into temporary shelters in Moorfields which were later permanently rebuilt. At this time medicinal springs such as Sadler's Wells attracted fashion, and pleasure gardens grew up. Until 1800 the area was a favoured place of amusement but the City Road had already been built in 1761 and the New North Road followed in 1812. This encouraged urbanisation which was further accelerated by the new Regents Canal (1814), the Islington-Bow railway (1850) and the Metropolitan railway (1863). The amusement habit continued in the form of music halls down to 1914.

ISLIP, Simon (?-1366), canon lawyer, was Edward III's chaplain and privy seal and acted as negotiator in France in 1342. He was Abp. of Canterbury from 1349 by royal recommendation and papal provision. The Black Death was raging and he showed courage and good sense in dealing with its effects. He tried to regulate the wages of the clergy to prevent them being lured away from their cures. He founded a priests' training college (Canterbury College) at Oxford and in 1356 he led the clergy in refusing the six-year clerical subsidy. At the same time he ended the ancient dispute with York about precedence and he was not prepared to claim clerical immunities contrary to the justice of cases.

ISMAILIS. *See* CALIPHATE; AGA KHAN.

ISMAY, Hastings Lionel (1887-1965) 1st Ld. ISMAY (1947), a soldier, served with distinction in Somaliland and India. After World War I he became Sec. at the Committee of Imperial Defence. From May 1940 he was

Chief of Staff to Winston Churchill and his personal representative to the Chief of Staffs Committee and as such was one of the most powerfully influential personalities in the direction of World War II. He held this post until 1946. From 1951 to 1952 he was Sec. for Commonwealth Relations and from 1952 to 1857 Sec. Gen. of N.A.T.O. A modest man with a powerful mind.

ISMAY (1) Thomas Henry (1837-99) a self made man acquired the White Star Line of Australian clippers in 1867. With William Imrie he formed the Oceanic Steamship Co. in 1868 and began running steamships from Liverpool to North America in 1871. His son **(2) Joseph Bruce (1862-1937)** was chairman of Ismay Imrie and Co. from 1899 and of the International Mercantile Marine Co. from 1904 to 1912.

ISOLATIONISM. An American attitude to world politics based upon the belief that the rebellion freed the U.S.A. from foreign entanglements and that its population and resources enable it to thrive without exerting itself in the international field. Foreigners are apt to regard it as a convenient position from which the U.S.A. can make money by the world's misfortunes. The U.S.A.'s isolationist posture was abandoned in 1798 in favour of hostilities with France; the U.S. attempts to break the British blockade of Bonapartist France brought war with Britain in 1812; in 1898 there was the U.S. attack on the Spanish colonies; and in 1903 the political foray which deprived Colombia of Panama. Isolationism was thus a very limited concept; it was based in reality on the Atlantic which protected America from the upheavals of European politics and was policed until 1920 by British naval power. In World War I the German U-boat campaign made the premise unsafe and the U.S. entered the war after two years and promptly returned to isolationism when the war was won. This included contracting out of the League of Nations which the U.S. govt. had sponsored. By 1939 politics had become global and the U.S. was again driven into the war by the inability of Britain and her allies to dominate the oceans. This time, however, the U.S.A. was the victim of a surprise attack. Thus global politics and the disadvantages of the passive military posture which isolationism engendered killed it. By the end of World War II the U.S.A. was not only a leader in the United Nations but insisting that its H.Q. should be in New York.

ISRAEL, STATE OF (*for previous events see* ZIONISM) **(1)** Jewish migration into Palestine is mainly the result of millennia of Jewish religious, literary and poetic tradition well understood by other biblically minded nations. "If I forget thee, O Jerusalem, let my right hand forget her cunning." It is secondarily due to the persecutions which Jews have from time to time suffered but which did not necessarily drive them to Palestine and, most recently, to the moves by the remnant of West European Jewry surviving from the systematic Nazi massacres sometimes called the *Holocaust*. The immigration is, however, the fundamental fact of modern Israel and enshrined in her constitution which, in the Law of Return, gives all Jews everywhere an unqualified right to settle in Israel at will.

(2) In the particular circumstances this was bound to create insoluble difficulties. Palestine, even empty, is too small to hold all the Jews entitled to settle there. It is partly barren even where it is not mountainous and at Acre there is the only, and not very good, natural port. It is much smaller than the biblical Land of Israel which included most of the modern Jordanian Arab state. The country was not, however, empty. It contained large indigenous populations mostly of Arab stock but with Moslem or various types of Christian convictions. Initially the immigrants pushed aside the Palestinian Arabs.

(3) There had always been a military minded undercurrent in Jewish colonisation (cf *The Book of Joshua*). A secret armed organisation (Haganah = Defence) had been formed as far back as 1921;

prolonged violence had provoked the Peel inquiry and recommendation that Palestine should be partitioned. The more aggressive Irgun Zvai Leumi was set up in 1937; the Stern or Star Group (or Gang) in 1941. In 1948, just as the British mandate was about to be surrendered and the State of Israel proclaimed, Irgun staged an atrocity, the storm and massacre of the village of Deir Yasin, to terrorise Arabs into leaving. This was very successful. Within a year land abandoned by Arabs constituted a large element in the resources available to the much increased Jewish immigration. On the other hand, the *émigré* Arabs became a vocal and justifiably malcontented element in the countries to which they fled.

(4) The second stages of the conflicts soon followed. As the Jewish population rose, Israel was tempted or driven by population pressure to expand territorially at the expense of neighbouring states, usually under the pretext of strategic necessity. The history of the Palestinian Middle East between 1948 and 1993 has been one of continuous conflict between, on the one hand, Israelis and indigenous Palestinians largely led and organised by the Palestinian Liberation Organisation based outside the country and, on the other hand, between Israel as a state and her neighbour states in the form of short formal wars of extreme savagery, in 1956 (*see* SUEZ CRISIS) which marked the end of British world power, 1967, 1973 and 1982. The intervals between these high points were not, however, peaceful but, especially after the outbreak of the Palestinian uprising (*Intafada*) in 1987 almost as sanguinary as the wars themselves. This was ended in 1995.

ISTANBUL. *See* BYZANTIUM.

ITALIAN SOMALIA. *See* SOMALIA.

ITALY – KINGDOM 1870-1945 (*see* ITALY, UNIFICATION OF) **(1)** Social and climatic differences between Sicily, Naples, the ex-Papal states and Lombardy delayed, and still hinder, the consolidation of Italy. In 1878 K. Victor Emmanuel II was succeeded by Umberto I and Pope Pius IX by Leo XIII, but the disagreement with the Papacy over territorial sovereignty remained unresolved. The internal problems created a natural tendency towards colonisation which was diverted by the govt. to Somaliland (after 1880) and Eritrea (after 1882) where aggressive expansion soon led to conflicts with Ethiopia; but meanwhile inherited distrust of France resulted in an alliance (1882) with the other two Central Powers, Germany and Austro-Hungary, and an implied renunciation of predatory claims in the Tyrol, Istria and in the Balkans, to which the Turkish decline was a temptation. In 1896, however, the govt. provoked a war with Ethiopia and suffered a resounding defeat at the B. of Adowa. Italian imperialists had to look elsewhere.

(2) In 1900 K. Umberto was assassinated and succeeded by Victor Emmanuel III whose reign covered the remaining history of the Kingdom. It opened with an intensification of naval construction and moves towards a rapprochement with France. The object was to achieve an opportunist freedom. In 1911 Italy supported France against her own ally Germany at Agadir in return for which in 1912 France held the ring while the Italian fleet attacked Turkey. Libya and Cyrenaica were annexed and soon colonised from Sicily, and the Dodecanese was also taken so as to threaten Asiatic Turkey and the Greek Aegean.

(3) These adventures had been launched because industrialisation was creating difficulties in the northern cities where cheap immigrant southern labour was creating resident unemployment and provoking the rise of left wing parties; but World War I had internally calming effects, for Italy, contrary to her alliances, held aloof and offered her services for sale to the highest bidder. From Austro-Hungary she demanded the Trentino, Istria, Dalmatia and Albania and was naturally refused. The Allied powers naturally agreed, since these areas were not theirs to give and threw in a loan of £50M as well. Under the secret T. of London (Apr. 1915) Italy went to war against her allies (May).

(4) Save that it distracted Austro-Hungarian and later German troops and attention from other fronts and simplified the war against the Austrian navy, Italian intervention was only marginally helpful to the western powers who had to come to her military rescue after the Caporetto disaster (Oct. 1917) and carry her on their backs to the final victories in the autumn of 1918 (see WORLD WAR I).

(5) The ignominy of these proceedings did not restrain Italian appetites; the nationalists sought to make the Adriatic an Italian lake with an Albanian protectorate at the exit and the eastern coasts, particularly Trieste and Fiume, annexed. This conflicted with the ambitions of the Serbs who had provoked the war in the first place and were creating a new South (Yugo) Slav state at the expense of Austria, Hungary and Turkey. The conflict focused on Fiume for, with Trieste already in Italian hands, it was the only port accessible westwards from the middle Danube and the north Balkans. Italy had lost 400,000 men in the war; her finances were in disorder and her politicians corrupt; demobilisation and industrial conversion had created large unemployed masses. The hope was that control of the Adriatic ports would enable her to milk the hinterland. Gabriele d'Annunzio, air ace and romantic poet, with a force of volunteers seized Fiume in Sept. 1919 and proclaimed the Regency of the Quarnero but he reckoned without international sympathy for Serbia. Negotiations at Rapallo ended in a treaty (Nov. 1920) which gave Dalmatia to Yugoslavia, leaving an enclave at Zara to Italy and converting Fiume into a free port and city.

(6) This solution offended the nationalists and did nothing for the urban poor. Extremists exploited sentiment and hunger. In May 1921 twenty-nine of Benito Mussolini's new blackshirted Fascist party were elected to parliament. Mussolini was a flamboyant, left wing journalist who neatly advocated a redistribution of benefits combined with appeals to Roman glories and quick (that is, strong arm) solutions likely to anticipate the advocates of class war. The possessing classes subscribed to his funds. The unemployed were invited off the streets, promised work and given black shirts. People flocked to him. In a year he was ready. In the coup d'état known as the March on Rome (Oct. 1922) Mussolini (who actually arrived by train) intimidated the King into dismissing the ministers and appointing a combined Fascist and Popular Party govt. By June 1924 he had dissolved all parties save his own and had driven out the opposition deputies from the Chamber while the Black Shirt militia broke up the trade unions. Only two other sources of power remained: the Papacy and the Crown. In 1929 Mussolini's Vatican T. and Concordat created the extraterritorial Vatican State in the centre of Rome and a privileged Church, while the Papacy at last recognised the Italian Kingdom. The King seemed compliant.

(7) The govt. now set the people to work through corporative organisations on great engineering projects, particularly the railways, the autostrade, the Venetian sea defences and the reclamation of the maremma and the great Pontine Marshes. The mass of the people supported these programmes which made for internal peace and a modest competence. The Blackshirt hierarchy provided a corrupt but useful ladder of promotion for the socially humble, and welfare included public entertainment. The violent suppression of opposition, the creation of a police apparatus and the incarceration of some 2,000 political prisoners were held to be a small price for the general improvement in life for the many, evidenced also by a rise in the birthrate. Mussolini took the title of Duce (Leader).

(8) Thus far Mussolini had been distinctly successful, but he inherited the appetites of earlier political generations; and four considerations caused him to place special emphasis on their satisfaction: (a) Any dictatorship without a parliamentary mechanism has to distract its masses from its own shortcomings, which in practice means an exciting Bonapartist foreign policy. (b) The armaments needed for Bonapartism created employment. The govt. built a very large navy and a Dodecanean fortress-base at Leros; created, for the period, a powerful airforce; increased and re-armed the army. (c) Roman history, to which the Duce habitually referred, represented a pattern for a Mediterranean empire. Mare Nostrum (Lat = our sea) became implicit in foreign policy. This could not be achieved as the Romans had done but the tools to hand, notably the African possessions, might be picked up and used. (d) The Defeat at Adowa, unavenged, continued to rankle.

(9) The main obstacles to a vigorous policy were British interests in the Mediterranean and Red Sea as the main (east-west) artery of imperial communication, protected by bases at Gibraltar, Malta, Alexandria and Aden; British investments in Egypt; and a long-standing friendliness which most Italians felt for the British. A secondary difficulty was the interest of Britain's French ally in North Africa and her (north-south) communications from Marseilles and Toulon to Algerine and Tunisian ports.

(10) It was decided to attack Egypt. As a preliminary step a war of conquest would be launched against Ethiopia. This would not upset the French but would threaten the Red Sea and, via the Sudan, Egypt from the south. The war was provoked (The Wal-Wal Incident) in May 1935 and then, while Ethiopia was being devoured (the annexation was proclaimed in May 1936), civil war broke out in Spain (July 1936) and with covert Italian help distracted French govts. and British opinion.

(11) Italian Fascist methods had partly inspired the rising (if dissimilar) violence of Nazism and by 1937 Mussolini had to recognise the existence north of the Alps of a dangerous competitor of Austrian origin who openly intended to unify the German speaking peoples. Thus Mussolini's imperialism was impeded by the need to defend the Austrian buffer state to the north. On 1 Nov. 1936 he proclaimed the Rome-Berlin Axis, an attempt to influence German policy by association. On 18th the two govts. recognised Franco's govt. in Spain. Actually the Axis was a diplomatic failure for other powers recognised the truth, that Germany, not Italy, was its leading member and its Spanish manoeuvre openly, and contrary to Italian intentions, threatened France. Mussolini set about trying to save something from the drift towards shipwreck. There was a pact with Yugoslavia in Mar. 1937, a conference at Venice with the Austrian Chancellor, Kurt von Schuschnigg in Apr. and a treaty with Austria and Hungary in Nov; the signature of the anti-Comintern Pact with Germany and Japan was mere lipservice to the Axis, for the Italian Communist Party had already been destroyed.

(12) These cobwebs were blown away in Mar. 1938 by the German seizure of Austria, which potentially put Italy at Germany's mercy. Mussolini could still rely for a while on the defensibility of the Alpine frontier and the under-developed state of the German airforce but the seizure led automatically to the Czech crisis (see WORLD WAR II) and the September conferences with Hitler at Godesberg (22-3) and then at Munich (29) where Mussolini participated with Chamberlain and Daladier and tried to moderate Hitler's demands; by Dec. the Italian Chamber of Deputies was demanding Nice, Corsica and Tunisia from France as a final demonstration before the Duce abolished it but his last serious efforts to strike out an independent line were the Good Friday seizure (Apr. 1939) of Albania as a jumping-off base for Greece and his declaration of neutrality at the start of World War II.

(13) (*See* WORLD WAR II-5-7,9,12-15) Two basic misjudgements brought the Fascist regime to its ruin. The first was the Duce's unjustified belief in the martial reliability of his modern Roman army. The second was the complementary decision (repeating 1915 in reverse) to pick up advantages on the side while someone else won the war. The airforce was obsolescent; the army had been fought to a stand-still by the Greeks and much of it did not want to fight the British, to whom it surrendered in thousands (Dec. 1940-Feb. 1941). The gallant battle-fleet was savaged at Taranto (Nov. 1940) and at the B. of Cape Matapan (Mar. 1941). By July 1941 Ethiopia, Eritrea and Somalia had been lost and the Germans had had to be called in to save Cyrenaica and Libya. In Jan. 1941 Mussolini placed the forces and increasing parts of Italian life under German direction.

(14) The fall of Fascism was precipitated by the German surrender at Tunis (May 1943) and the rapid allied occupation of part of the Italian homeland, namely Sicily. King Victor Emmanuel III, still surrounded by Fascist organisations and increasingly beset by Nazi police agencies, had at great personal risk opened secret communications with the Allied govts. On 25 July 1943 he, with Count Grandi, the D. of Acquarone and Marshal Badoglio arrested Mussolini. They dissolved the Fascist organisations the next day. The Marshal became prime minister and signed a secret armistice to come into effect when the Allies made landings in mainland Italy. These took place at Reggio (3 Sept.) and at Salerno (9 Sept.). On 11 Sept. the Badoglio govt. declared war on Germany and the Italian war was henceforth fought by the Germans in hostile territory.

(15) In June 1944 Rome fell and the King, having appointed Crown Prince Umberto as Lieutenant of the Realm, retired. Badoglio retired in favour of Ivanoe Bonomi, a pre-Fascist politician. Meanwhile the anti-German partisan movements had acquired a prestige from the similarly named movement in Yugoslavia, and Moscow-supported Communists took unwarranted credit for their activities and convinced incautious western opinion of their representative credentials. In Apr. 1945 they murdered Mussolini, his mistress Claretta Petacci and others from the so-called Fascist Republican govt. at Salo and hung their naked bodies from the eves of a Milan garage. When the Germans surrendered (May 1945) Bonomi resigned in favour of a coalition which established a consultative assembly. A wave of left-wing terrorism created a body of 'progressive' opinion in northern Italy which, as a preliminary to revolutionary designs, put the monarchy in issue and, through the assembly, bullied the govt. into providing for a plebiscite on its future. In May 1946 the Lieutenant succeeded as Umberto II on his father's abdication. The plebiscite was held in June amid scenes of fraud and malpractice. The Supreme Court, required by law to pronounce the result, never did so but the new King, swayed by probably false accounts of a hostile majority and threats of civil war, went into exile. *See* ITALY, REPUBLIC.

ITALY, REPUBLIC (1946 onwards) (1) The doubtful legitimacy of the republic (*see* ITALY, KINGDOM-15) was compounded by electoral manipulations for a Constituent Assembly (designed to give the Communists their own medicine), wartime devastation, widespread breakdowns in services, public disorders and private revenges. Apart from public order the govt's opening task was to negotiate the Peace Treaty (Feb. 1947). Under this Yugoslavia advanced to the Isonzo, taking in Istria; Trieste became a free port; the African colonies were formally given up and the Dodecanese was ceded to Greece. Much Italian influence and investment in these ex-colonies remained. In addition, reparations were to be paid to Ethiopia until 1954 and there were forces' limitation and demilitarisation clauses. The treaty created an artificial uproar which soon died.

(2) A new constitution came into effect on 1 Jan. 1948 by which time the govt. had learned to rule without the left wing by leaning heavily on the slowly progressive Christian Democrats and in 1949 by joining N.A.T.O. and helping to found the Council of Europe. By 1970 an Italian admiral was commanding the N.A.T.O. Mediterranean force.

(3) These events were anathema to the Communists who, if not their doctrines, continued to attract a large following but successive govts. kept ahead of them by strengthening the welfare system, widespread land reforms and especially by promoting the T. of Rome (Mar. 1957) which placed Italy squarely in the wide markets of the European Economic Community. The ensuing rise in prosperity frustrated the Communists but also created vast on-going opportunities for corruption, drug dealing and social scandals through the organised violence of the Sicilian *mafia* and the Neapolitan *camorra*, besides the furtive methods of private business. Italian political rottenness was, however, to a remarkable extent countered by the courage and integrity (despite murders and assassinations) of the police and the magistracy. By 1992 on the one hand the influence of the *mafia* and the *camorra* had been much confined and on the other many Ministers and about a third of the deputies were under investigation.

(4) The far left opposition had difficulty in exploiting this because of the catastrophe of Communist Russia and her satellites after 1988 which deprived them of moral and, especially, material support. Italy was acquiring a political vacuum in a prospering economy while the British withdrew from Egypt and their Mediterranean bases east of Gibraltar and the French gave up north Africa. Thus the conditions which Mussolini failed to create developed of themselves while Italy was no longer equipped to exploit them.

ITALY, UNIFICATION OF. (1) Italy, despite the vast scope of influence radiating from particular places in it, and the writings of the occasional propagandist was, from the fall of the Roman Empire to about 1820 only a geographical abstraction.

(2) The French imported the notion of nationality with the Italian campaigns of Bonaparte, whose first language was Italian. They culminated in the subjection of the peninsula (but not Sicily) to a partially standardised French-type administration. The educative effect continued when Italy was redivided after 1815 under a number of dynasts (and the territorial Papacy) all in varying degrees under Habsburg influence. If the Kingdom of the Two Sicilies and the Papal States represented psychological realities (marred by misgovernment), North Italian fragmentation was artificial. 19th cent. local history is, on the one hand, one of French efforts to return where they could and, on the other, of the decreasing patience of the North Italians with the political irrelevance and practical inconveniences which, under Habsburg surveillance, they had to endure. The revolutionaries of the period all originated or lived in the north. The discontents were associated with liberalism in opposition to Habsburg and Papal conservatism and, consequently, insurrections in 1830 and 1848 combined nationalist and liberal flavours.

(3) The Foreign Office was initially exercised about the French and Neapolitan Bourbon restorations because of the importance of Naples and Messina in Mediterranean strategy. In fact the two dynasties had little in common: the Neapolitans being unambitious, corrupt and overshadowed by Austria, the French more interested in Algeria. The advent of Napoleon III changed the focus. He knew something of Italy, having in his youth been associated with the semi-secret and revolutionary *carbonari* but he supported the weak Papal govt. against local insurrectionaries to please his powerful R. Catholic lobby. From its inception to its fall the Second Empire maintained a garrison in Rome.

(4) Central to Italian politics, if geographically on the periphery, was Savoy which straddled the Alps from Chambéry to Turin and possessed Genoa and Sardinia. Tactically defensible, with a small hardy army, its greatest asset was the long term ambition of its dynasty with its ancient skill in playing off the greater powers against each other, but at a crisis in Italo-European affairs it also possessed in Camillo, Count Cavour, a minister of inspired opportunism and far-sighted duplicity which passed for statesmanship. The coincidence of liberal sentiment in the minds of nationalist Italians was convenient to the Savoyard rulers who habitually provided a haven for political refugees from the police of other Italian states. English opinion, shocked by Papal and Neapolitan misgovernment, was favourable on this account to Savoy which also, through Genoa, admitted British goods to northern Italy. The Savoyards also drew attention to themselves by entering (Jan. 1855) the Crimean War with the British and French against Russia with whom they had no conceivable quarrel. Thus by the adroit use of other greater powers' goodwill they played a larger role in European affairs than their power by itself warranted.

(5) This was strikingly evident when they succeeded, with the promise of Chambéry and Nice (The Plombières Agreement June 1858) in inveigling Napoleon III into a war with Austro-Hungary. The Bonaparte hoped to extend his considerable influence at Rome at Austrian expense to other parts of the peninsula. The hard-fought Bs. of Magenta and Solferino (June 1859) destroyed Habsburg influence and knocked away the Austrian buttresses of the other non-liberal regimes, but Napoleon III did not step into their shoes. The nationalists, already heartened by revolutions in Tuscany, Modena and Parma (May 1859) believed, or affected to believe, that he was their champion. When he concluded the truce of Villafranca with the war, in their eyes, only half fought, he was represented as a betrayer who had taken his territorial payment and not finished the work.

(6) Cavour's maxim "Italy will make itself" now assumed vast importance. France and Austria were temporarily off the stage. Britain smiled. Plebiscites in the revolutionised areas were organised (Mar. 1860). The Savoyards connived at the voyage of Garibaldi (a Nizzard) and his Thousand from Savona near Genoa to Marsala in Sicily (Apr. 1860). The British carefully failed to intercept them. Under his leadership and with popular acclaim the Kingdom of the Two Sicilies collapsed like a house of cards. Popular enthusiasm also precipitated the smaller states into the Savoyard net. King Victor Emmanuel swept up a child and with her on his saddle-bow rode through the delirious crowds into his new countries. The Papal army had to be defeated (B. of Castelfidardo Sept. 1860). French intervention saved Rome and the Campania (The Patrimony of St. Peter) for the Pope. The rest of the Papal States went the same way as the rest of Italy. The provisional capital of the new Italian Kingdom was fixed at Florence (Feb. 1861) and everyone knew the connotation of the epithet 'provisional'.

(7) Italy, apart from the Patrimony, Venice and the Southern Tyrol, was now united. In 1866 Italy joined Prussia in her attack on Austria and, though defeated on land at Custozza (June) and at sea at Lissa (July), received Venice as her reward for the Prussian victory at Koniggraetz (July). In 1870 the French defeat at German hands entailed the withdrawal from Rome which was annexed (Sept.) and became the capital. The major part of the Tyrol, including a large non-Italian area, was acquired (July 1920) after World War I. Istria, acquired at the same time, was, apart from Trieste, lost after World War II.

ITCHEN, R. See TRANSPORT AND COMMUNICATIONS.

IVAR THE BONELESS (fl. 858-73) and his brother **HALFDAN (fl. 858-77)** were sons of Ragnar Lothbrok. They commanded the great Viking invasion of England which began in 865 but Ivar left the army some time before 870 and perhaps commanded and died in Ireland in 873. Halfdan was the principal leader until about 875 when apparently he too went to Ireland and was killed near Strangford Lough in 877.

IVEAGH. See GUINNESS.

IVO of CHARTRES, St. (?1040-1116) was educated under Lanfranc at Bec. He became prior of Beauvais in 1078 and Bp. in 1090. Philip I imprisoned him in 1092 for denouncing the King's lechery. A vastly learned canonist, his *Collectio Tripertita, Decretum* and *Panormia* exercised great influence in the development of and, particularly, the principles of interpretation in the Canon Law. *See also* ADELA OF BLOIS; ANSELM; INVESTITURE CONTEST.

IVORY COAST. See AFRICA, WEST (EX-FRENCH).

IZMIR. See SMYRNA.

IZVOLSKI. See AUSTRO-HUNGARY-13 *et seq*.

J

JACKANAPES, a rude nickname for William de la Pole, D. of Suffolk whose badge was a clog and chain, such as was attached to a tame ape.

JACKEROO (Austr). In 19th cent. a newly arrived Englishman, learning to farm. A JILLEROO was a World War II land girl.

JACK IN THE GREEN. A gigantic leaf-clad mummer, generally a chimney sweep, who, with clowns and cacophony, paraded through the streets on May Day; perhaps a survival of tree worship, the ceremony, once widespread, was still observed at Cheltenham in 1892

JACQUERIE. *See* JOHN II of France.

JACKSON, Sir George (1785-1861), a diplomat was chief commissioner for the abolition of the slave trade at Rio-de-Janeiro from 1832 to 1841, then at Surinam until 1845 and finally at Loanda until 1859.

JACK THE RIPPER. Between Aug. and Nov. 1888 at least eight women, mostly prostitutes, were murdered and mutilated by an unidentified killer who has gone down in history under this sobriquet.

JACOB (1) Sir George le Grand (1805-81), was political agent in Kathiawar from 1839 to 1843, in Sawantvadi from 1845 to 1851, and in Cutch from 1851 He suppressed the mutiny in Kolhapur in 1857 and was also special commissioner for the S. Maratha area. He returned in 1861. His famous cousin **(2) John (1812-58),** was given political charge of E. Cutch by Outram in 1841, fought with great distinction at Meeanee in 1843 and as superintendent of Upper Sind from 1847 pacified that riotous country by force of his personality, so that Dalhousie named Jacobabad after him in 1851. He negotiated the T. with the Khan of Kalat in 1854 and became acting commissioner in Sind in 1856. In 1857 he commanded Outram's cavalry in Persia and in 1858 raised Jacob's Rifles, armed with a rifle of his own devising, for the defence of Sind.

JACOBEAN STYLE, was named after James I whose reign occupied the middle of the period when the style was in use. *See* ARCHITECTURE, BRITISH-10.

JACOBINS, were a French club called the *Society of Friends of the Revolution,* originally of Breton deputies at Versailles, who took over the Jacobin monastery in Paris after the National Assembly moved there in Oct. 1789. Essentially a debating society for public figures, affiliated provincial societies sprang up which took their lead from the Paris club. By 1791 the Jacobins had developed into a party. In June 1791 there was a schism arising from the King's flight to Varennes and the moderates moved to the FEUILLANTS, leaving only the extremists led by Robespierre and Pétion. They converted it into the left wing of the revolution, especially after the declaration of the republic in Sept. 1792. In June 1793, it organised the risings which expelled the Girondins from the Convention, and from then Robespierre and the Club dominated France until their common overthrow in the *coup d'état* of Thermidor (July 1794). The club was suppressed in Nov.

JACOBITES and their PRETENDERS. (1) The Pretenders after James II's death (1701) were his son JAMES (Francis) EDWARD (1688-1766), "JAMES III" or the Chevalier de ST. GEORGES or the OLD PRETENDER; his son CHARLES EDWARD (CASIMIR) 1720-88, BONNIE PRINCE CHARLIE, The YOUNG PRETENDER, or "CHARLES III" who also used at least ten aliases; and his brother HENRY BENEDICT MARIA (1725-1807) Card. of YORK, "HENRY IX".

(2) The main British supporters of Jacobitism were some Scots R. Catholic highland clans particularly Gordon, Macdonald and Cameron, some Dumfriesshire and Cumbrian clans, about 25,000 in all, spiritually knit but scattered, together with some English R. Catholic squires and politicians and a minority of the Tories. English Tory Jacobitism was strongest in Lancashire and the West country: it depended on traditionalist attachment to the ancient royal continuity, and a belief that adequate safeguards for Anglicanism could be secured, if not from James II, then from his son who was in a weaker position. In Ireland opinion was initially hotly anti-English so that even the R. Catholic majority was more concerned with reversing English policies than with the rights of the Lord's Anointed.

(3) Thus after James II's departure, Jacobitism was kept alive only by small, if enthusiastic minorities and had to depend for real vigour upon foreign support and finance. It was at its most active in wartime when it suited hostile powers (mainly France) to encourage it. Wars were common between 1689 and 1746 and the Jacobites were feared more than their small hold on public opinion might justify, because they always seemed, and often were, ready to organise *coups de main.* The Jacobite court was constantly in touch with English and Scottish personalities by messenger and in peacetime by letters in foreign diplomatic bags. At the beginning many of these, Shrewsbury, Clarendon and Marlborough (half brother to the D. of Berwick) were known personally to the ex-king. Plots, real, imaginary, dangerous, or ineffectual, were being hatched continuously, and were a major govt. distraction. Counting James II's Irish Campaign at least *eight* of these were dangerous, six of them leading to operations in Britain or the Four Seas.

(4) The first, in the winter of 1690, was Lord Preston's affair. He had been a Sec. of State to James II and was arrested with letters proposing a restoration if he should turn Protestant. Since this occurred at the height of the War of the League of Augsburg while French troops were still in Ireland, the main effect was to reinforce William III's distrust of English statesmen.

(5) Secondly, after Q. Mary's death (Dec. 1694) had removed one element of stability in the revolution settlement, there was Sir John Fenwick's affair. William III was to be assassinated and a French army was to cross the Channel and restore James II. French troops concentrated in the Pas de Calais and James joined them, but the govt. got wind of the conspiracy; William announced it from the throne. Some of the participants were taken. The Association was set up and Fenwick was condemned by attainder.

(6) In the P. of Ryswick (Sept. 1697) Louis XIV recognised William III as K. of Great Britain and the Protestant Succession after his death, but James II continued to maintain an attenuated court at St. Germain under a personal guarantee. There now ensued the Partition negotiations which were ultimately rejected by Charles II of Spain. He appointed Philip of Anjou, Louis XIV's grandson, as his sole heir (Oct. 1700) and died a month later. Louis recognised Philip as K. of Spain and occupied the Spanish Netherlands. The stroke made a European war inevitable, but not necessarily whole-hearted British participation. In Sept. 1701, however, James II died and Louis, believing too much in Jacobite reports of British disunity, recognised the Old Pretender as James III. This precipitated a united Britain into the war, immediately before William III himself died.

(7) Q. Anne's succession was peaceful and peculiarly dangerous to Jacobitism since she was protestant, utterly opposed with her friends Marlborough and Godolphin, to Louis' ambitions and yet a true Stuart. Against such a combination the Jacobites could make little headway (especially with a 12-year-old Pretender) without resounding French victories; but in fact their war went wrong. Marlborough was steadily reconquering the

Netherlands. There was a protestant rebellion in France; in Aug. 1704 the Franco-Bavarian army was overthrown at Blenheim; in Oct. 1705 a Habsburg claimant, with British help, invaded Spain and in 1706 the French were beaten by Marlborough at Ramillies, and by P. Eugene at Turin. Hence, despite a French revival in 1707, Louis had little to spare for Jacobite adventures.

(8) The power (as opposed to influence) of Jacobitism in the Scottish Highlands arose from the heritable jurisdictions of clan chiefs. Where a chief was a Jacobite, the Jacobites controlled a territory which was accessible by way of a sea loch. This special weakness in the Hanoverian defences was compounded by recent events. Nobody had forgotten the Glencoe massacre of 1692 or the drawn out agony of the Darien scheme (1695-1700) in which many beggared Scots laid the blame, with partial truth, on the English. Measures against English non-conformity were interpreted as a threat to Scots presbyterianism. The two countries were drifting into a dangerous state of mutual separatism, yet the statesmen saw that this condition of affairs, however favourable it might be to the Pretender, would be far more likely to end in the subjection of the British Is to the French. The accession, in the person of Anne, of a Stuart was a favourable moment for reversing the drift. Both parliaments petitioned for commissioners to discuss a project of union. By Oct. 1703 these discussions had failed, and thereupon the Scots parliament began to pass separatist legislation: the Act for the Importation of Foreign Wines, the Acts anent Peace and War and Security (in 1703) and, by refusing supply, forced through the Scottish Militia Act in 1704.

(9) The project of union had, out of political and military necessity, to be taken up again, especially as it was known in 1707 that James Edward's entourage was preparing a Scottish expedition. The Union became effective in May 1707, but by now the Pretender was eighteen, a man, and determined to try his luck. As Scottish discontent with the Union was at its noisiest, the moment (Mar. 1708) was politically well chosen, but English intelligence and the fleet frustrated the venture. The pursuit came up with the Pretender's expedition waiting for the tide in the Forth; it escaped but the French admiral would not land. They returned, humiliated, to Dunkirk, and soon afterwards (July) the Pretender was with the French at the B. of Oudenarde. These events reunited the quarrelling English so that the Tory party soon had a strong section favouring the Hanoverian succession.

(10) James Edward's prestige was further damaged by his own character. He was neither inspiring nor persistently energetic; his devotion put him in the hands of charlatans and prevented him from recognising the British religious compromises; and worst of all, he was no judge of character. He had important correspondents in Britain, and distinguished English leaders were Jacobites, notably Francis Atterbury, Bp. of Rochester, the D. of Ormonde, the E. of Mar and Vist. Bolingbroke. At Q. Anne's death, Atterbury wanted to attempt a *coup d'état* but the others knew that it was hopeless. George I, on arrival, chose whig ministers, who instantly impeached the leading Tories for their part in the T. of Utrecht. Bolingbroke fled to Paris in Mar. 1715; Ormonde in Aug. By then, in accordance with the T., the Pretender had been refused support and quarters in France. He was at Commercy in the technically foreign state of Lorraine, 100 miles from Paris, while his queen-mother presided over a Jacobite court at St. Germain financed, at Louis XIV's request by Spain. Bolingbroke became the Pretender's Sec. of State. He found preparations for an invasion of Britain far advanced.

(11) Bolingbroke knew more of British conditions than anyone at the Pretender's court and in his view the Jacobite main effort should be devoted to winning over a powerful section of English popular opinion. He came up against the Pretender's bigotry and the ignorant flattery of his entourage. His efforts to modify Stuart propaganda so as to conciliate the protestant churches were frustrated. James Edward simply published his own manifestos from Lorraine: he had given private undertakings to the Pope. Evidently he meant to rely upon the known Jacobites especially in Scotland to conquer the rest. The distance between Commercy and St. Germain made it difficult for the Sec. of State to consult his master and easy for Lord Stair, the British ambassador, to discover Jacobite plans. The Royal Navy began to watch French ports. Then in Sept. 1715 Louis XIV died and Orleans, the new regent, was unenthusiastic. Before this change was known in Scotland the E. of Mar raised the revolt at Perth. Ormonde set sail in Oct. and tried to land in Devon, but got no support. But the North East English Jacobites, led by Thos. Forster and Lord Derwentwater, tried and failed to surprise Newcastle and then retired into the Scottish march for reinforcements.

(12) There were now two simultaneous campaigns. Forster, reinforced in Scotland, tried for Lancashire while Mar, also reinforced marched from Perth to Dunblane. On 13 Nov. Forster, surrounded at Preston, capitulated. On the same day Mar fought Argyll indecisively at Sherrifmuir and retired to Perth. At this point the Pretender took ship (Dec.) and found Mar's disintegrating army at Perth. The govt., by now, had imported Dutch troops (under the Barrier T. of 1713) and some Swiss. The energetic Cadogan superseded Argyll and advanced with overwhelming force. Mar and the Pretender took ship for France in Feb. 1716 and the revolt was over by Apr.

(13) The failure had important results. The Pretender dismissed Bolingbroke, his one competent adviser, against whose advice the enterprise had been undertaken and appointed Mar in his place. Orleans refused to permit the Pretender to live in Lorraine and he had to move to papal Avignon and, in 1717 as a result of the Triple Alliance, was driven into Italy. George I took the opportunity to dismiss his remaining Tory mins. The Jacobite danger was so much reduced that the govt. was able to use politic mercy towards the rebels. Only three peers and 26 officers were executed. By an Act of Grace of 1717 all those still in confinement were released.

(14) Foreign powers nevertheless still had a use for the Jacobites. The Swedes, through Count Gyllenborg their ambassador, were intriguing with them in order to embarrass George in his Hanoverian claims on Bremen and Verden; Gyllenborg's papers were seized and published at about the time of the Act of Grace. The Russians were distantly involved in this affair and so too was Alberoni, the Spanish chief Min., who was organising his naval smash and grab raid in the interests of his Queen's Farnese relations and his King's Sicilian claims. The Spaniards occupied Sardinia in Aug. 1717. The Emperor, Britain and France formed the Quadruple Alliance a year later when the principal Spanish armada had sailed for Sicily. They had been anticipated. Adm. Byng destroyed the armada, officially in time of peace, at C. Passaro (11 Aug. 1718). Anglo-French declarations of war followed (Dec. 1718 and Jan. 1719) whereupon the Spaniards fitted out and escorted a Jacobite expedition under Ormonde. Much reduced by storms, his force reached Scotland in Apr. 1719. It got little support and was brought to battle and dispersed at Glenshiel. By Jan. 1720 the Spanish sovereigns had dismissed Alberoni, accepted terms and added another item to the lengthening tale of Jacobite defeats.

(15) When Walpole began his long rule in 1721 he was almost at once faced with another widespread conspiracy, revealed through the Abbe Dubois, Orléans' diplomatic agent. This was a plot to seize power in Apr. 1722 as the King was starting for Hanover. The news

leaked out and there was a run on the Bank of England. Walpole persuaded George to stay, called up the troops to Hyde Park and watched the mails, which soon yielded most of the details. They involved Lords North and Orrery, the D. of Norfolk and the learned and popular Francis Atterbury, as well as Ormonde in Spain and others. The English ringleaders were soon in custody, and a heavy special tax was clapped upon R. Catholics and non jurors. As Atterbury's treason could not be formally proved, he was driven into banishment by means of a bill of pains and penalties (May 1723). Evidence subsequently unearthed shows that he was substantially guilty.

(16) The Pretender was in Madrid during the Spanish interlude but settled in Rome, where he married Maria Clementina Sobieska, in 1719. The Jacobite court was riven by faction, jealousy and treachery, while Walpole took care to ensure that every significant Jacobite was watched. As a result his govt. had nothing to fear throughout its peacetime life, while, from 1727 the Pretender had to subsist on a Papal pension.

(17) The outbreak of the Spanish war in 1739 quickened the life of the Jacobite world, more especially because Bonnie Prince Charlie, at nineteen, was far more personable than his father had ever been. But Jacobite resources had declined so far, that it was not until the undeclared hostilities of 1743 with France that the Prince's activities became dangerous. The able marshal Maurice de Saxe made secret preparations with him at Dunkirk for an invasion, which was to be covered by the Brest squadron. News of the sailing of the latter and of the Prince's arrival in France reached the govt. together (1 Feb. 1744), and three weeks later the French anchored off Dungeness. By this time a powerful English force was at sea; a furious tempest destroyed most of the Dunkirk transports, drove the French out of the Channel, and dispersed the English. The prince had to try again.

(18) Mutual declarations of war followed in Mar. 1744; Saxe, having beaten Cumberland at Fontenoy (May 1745), overran Flanders. This redirection of French effort left little available for the Jacobites, but Charles Edward believed that there were advantages in not being tied too closely to the French and, with his father's and friends' help, collected enough money to hire two small ships, the *Du Teillay* known as the *Deutelle* for himself and his "seven men", and the privateer *Elizabeth* for the arms and equipment. They met H.M.S. *Lion* off the Lizard and she forced the *Elizabeth* into Brest. The *Deutelle* sailed up the E. Coast and north about Scotland, reaching Eriskay (off S. Uist) on 23 July. Charles, his brother Henry, and his seven men landed at Moidart in Macdonald country on the highland W. Coast opposite Eigg on 25th. After a suspicious reception, Macdonald of Clanranald and Cameron of Lochiel the Younger joined him with 900 men. On 16 Aug. the Macdonalds won a psychologically important success by waylaying half a company of Royal Scots near Fort William. The Royal Standard was solemnly raised at Glenfinnan on 19th.

(19) The 3,000-odd troops in Scotland were mostly dispersed in small garrisons and Sir John Cope, their commander, first searched for the rebels near Fort Augustus and then, finding the country hostile, marched his few men to Inverness. The prince, gathering reinforcements from the Stewarts of Appin, Frasers and Macdonalds of Glengarry, reached Perth and proclaimed his father King. On 16 Sept. at Coltbrigg he dispersed the dragoons and Town Guard of Edinburgh, which he occupied next day. Meanwhile Cope had sailed south from Inverness to Dunbar and marched upon Edinburgh from the east. He was routed in the ten minute B. of Prestonpans (21 Sept.) which put most the Lowlands at the prince's disposal. By Nov. he had recruited 4,500 foot and 400 horse, financed by the tribute of captured towns.

(20) The British army (with 6000 Dutch troops) could not be withdrawn from Flanders until Oct. but the govt. was recruiting in England. Marshal Wade was at Newcastle, reputedly with 18,000 men. The prince decided to invade England by the western routes, hoping for Lancashire Jacobite support. Wade, snowbound at Hexham, could not prevent the fall of Carlisle (17 Nov.) and the prince, despite contrary advice, marched on via Preston. On 4 Dec. the Jacobites reached Derby: on 6th, faced by the mutiny of his officers, the prince ordered a retreat. He had gained no English supporters and lost some deserters, but neither Cumberland nor Wade could seriously hinder his northward march. In Jan. 1746 he joined up with some 400 newly raised highlanders, besieged Stirling and defeated Gen. Hawley at Falkirk (17 Jan.) He then moved further north, seized Inverness and by March had cleared the Great Glen and taken Fort Augustus. Cumberland matched this guerrilla-style movement methodically. He retook Aberdeen (27 Feb.), marched slowly up the coast while cruisers took French ships and stopped a French fleet from landing reinforcements, and on 14 Apr. reached Nairn. The Jacobites were posted on Culloden Moor and here, two days later, he destroyed their army.

(21) He followed up his victory by a ruthless pursuit which lasted all the summer and penetrated remote hamlets. Numbers were shot and their shielings burned. Some 80 leading prisoners were tried and executed for treason in the next two years. These included Lords Balmerino, Kilmarnock and Lovat, the last. The Prince wandered starving but always protected, despite the enormous price on his head, by poor, sometimes destitute crofters and fishermen until he got away to France in Sept. The clan standards were burned; the heritable jurisdictions abolished; the wearing of highland dress and tartan setts forbidden. Despite his romantic aura the prince's defeat was total. Under the P. of Aix la Chapelle he was expelled from France. He took to the bottle and a mistress, Clementina Walkinshaw (1726-1802), whom he had met in Scotland. Many Jacobites began to fear contact with him because of his drunkenness and a belief that Clementina was betraying his plans, through her sister Catherine, to the British govt. He was reputed to have visited London in 1750, 1752 and 1754, and in 1756 he lived in Basel. By 1760 his violence caused Clementina to leave him but she was pensioned by his father and brother.

(22) The Jacobite cause was by now moribund. The Old Pretender died in 1766 and George III commissioned a memorial over his Roman grave. The Young Pretender married Louisa von Stolberg in 1772 but she could not control his drinking and they parted in 1780. He too died at Rome. His brother Henry, a curial Cardinal, lived mostly at Frascati until the French sacked it in 1799. He fled to Padua and then to Venice, where George III helped him with money. At his death he left the crown jewels, carried off by James II, to George IV.

JACOBSEN, Theodore (?-1772), large scale architect who designed the Foundling Hospital, London and Haslar Naval Hospital, Gosport.

JACOMBE, Robt. *See* GEORGE I-9.

JACQUELINE or JAKOBA OF HAINAULT (1401-36) *d.* of D. William of Bavaria and Margaret of Burgundy exercised a major influence on English continental policy in the years 1421-5. In 1420 her husband, John D. of Brabant, against her bitter opposition, made over much of her dower including Holland, Zeeland and Frisia to a rival. In 1421 she fled to the English court where she was championed by Humphrey D. of Gloucester. The Anti-pope Benedict XIII was persuaded to annul her marriage and she married D. Humphrey in 1422. In 1424 they gravely injured good relations with D. Philip of Burgundy, whose co-operation was vital to the English in France, by launching an expedition to Hainault to recover her lands, upon which Philip had claims. It began successfully but then Humphrey, moved by the attractions of Eleanor Cobham (whom he later married) and perhaps by a belated awareness of the repercussions of the foray, withdrew. Jacqueline was captured in 1425 but escaped. Her appeals to England for help were unheeded and after a series of decreasingly successful risings whe was forced to cede her lands to Philip in return for a pension.

JACTITATION, was the ecclesiastical offence of falsely boasting that one was married to a particular person. Proceedings for jactitation were of some importance as long as divorce was impossible, because a decree in jactitation was sometimes the only means of facilitating a marriage to a different person. See DIVORCE; KINGSTON'S CASES.

JAENBERT or LAMBERT (?-791), became abbot of St. Augustines, Canterbury in 760 and Abp. in 766, but the brief erection of Lichfield into a metropolitical see deprived him of much of his power.

JAFFA or JOPPA (Palestine), was occupied by the crusaders from 1126 to 1187 and from 1191 to 1196. The town was rased and the harbour filled by the Egyptians in 1345 to forestall another crusade. It began to redevelop as a port in the 17th cent. In 1950 it was incorporated in Tel Aviv.

JAFFNA. See CEYLON.

JAGAT SETH ("banker of the world"), was the Mogul title from 1723 of **FATECHAND,** who had inherited a Bengal banking business from his uncle **MANICKCHAND.** The bank's H.Q. was at Murshidabad with branches at Dacca and Patna and it acted as a central bank for the govt. of Bengal. It established the Murshidabad mint, controlled gold sales, regulated rates of exchange, received the revenue and remitted the Delhi tribute. The second Jagat Seth who succeeded in 1744 and his cousin and partner, eventually quarrelled with Suraj-ud-Dowla and their financial support of Clive in the Plassey campaign was a major element in his fall. The Bank prospered until 1763 when hostilities between the Nawab Mir Kassim and the British led to Mir Kassim murdering the partners. The confusion of the period, the transfer of the govt. financial administration from Murshidabad to Calcutta in 1773 and the repudiation of some of the HEIC's debts to the bank, led to its decline in the early 19th cent., and the later holders of the title were mostly govt. pensioners.

JAGIR was originally a method of paying an Indian official from the revenue of an estate, also called a *jagir.* Jagirs tended to become hereditary and divorced from the efficient conduct of the office, which deprived govts. both of revenue and service, and led to the decline of many native Indian administrations.

JAIL FEVER. A virulent form of typhus prevailing in English prisons from 16th to the 18th cents. The death of Judge, Jurors, prisoners, counsel and court officials at the Oxford Black Assize (1577) and at the Old Bailey (1750) caused those assizes to be abandoned. Hygiene eliminated it in 19th cent.

JAINS are members, still several million strong, of a wealthy casteless sect of N.W. India, where they have a sacred hill covered with shrines at Palitana near Diu. They hold that every single living creature has an immortal soul and that to kill one causes improper as well as unforeseeable effects upon it. Hence, for example, they will not use disinfectants. Jainism is older than Buddhism and perhaps inspired it. It developed a remarkable architecture but was regarded as a heretical Hinduism and persecuted by the Brahmins.

JAIPUR (India). In the 16th cent. the ruler of this ancient state submitted to Akbar and married his daughter. Two of their descendants became famous Mogul generals, while Rajah Jai Singh II was a celebrated astronomer. Towards the end of 18th cent. dynastic confusion,

Maratha interference and Pindari raids led the Rajah to seek British protection which was accorded by the T. of Jaipur in 1817.

JAISALMIR or JEYSALMIR (India). The Rajput Rawal Jaisal founded this oasis city and named the state in 1156. The slow desiccation of the area led to loss of peripheral territories, but in 1818 the Rawal Mulraj entered into treaty relations with the British. They re-established the old boundaries, which remained until Indian independence in 1949. *See* RAJPUTS.

JAMAICA (Carib.) (Span: SANTIAGO), was discovered in 1494, settled by the Spaniards in 1509 and captured in 1655 by the British under Venables and Penn, who expelled all the Spaniards in 1660. The I. was legally ceded under the T. of Madrid in 1670 and the British suppressed the local buccaneers in 1672, when the Royal African Co. was established to manage the slave trade. Jamaica then became an immense slave mart and smuggling base for Spanish America. It also exported sugar, indigo and cocoa, and from mid 18th cent. coffee.

(2) In 1678 an attempt was made to impose crown govt. and English taxation, but local privileges were restored in 1682. In 1692 Port Royal was wiped out in an earthquake and Kingston was founded. Meantime the taxation issue continued controversial, the home authorities arguing that the vast local fortunes depended upon protection by the Royal Navy. By a compromise of 1728 Jamaica paid only £8,000 a year to the home govt., but English legislation was to become binding there. Many Jamaica planters actually lived in England.

(3) The I. was not seriously threatened until the American Rebellion, but was saved from French attack by Rodney's victory at Dominica (The Saints) in 1782. Trafalgar (1805) ended the French danger, but an attack was staved off by Duckworth in 1806. This was the moment when Jamaica's prosperity reached its zenith, for the coffee plantations yielded immense profits from the blockade of Europe; but it coincided with the abolition of the slave trade and thereafter costs began to rise. Moreover prices fell when the war ended in 1815; slaves were emancipated (with compensation at £19 a head to owners) in 1833 and fully freed in 1838; in 1846 the British abolished their preferential tariffs and the bottom fell out of the sugar market.

(4) There followed 20 years of dispute, mainly on public expenditure and administration of justice, between liberal minded governors from Britain such as Sir Chas. Melcalfe and Elgin, and the planter dominated assembly. The situation had been complicated by the compromise importation of Indian labour. By 1865 declining wages, rising taxes, land hunger, judicial maladministration and over-population were creating serious trouble. In Oct. 1865 Gov. Eyre suppressed a riot at Morant Bay by martial law and panicked the Assembly into voting its own extinction. Eyre was recalled, but Crown Colony Govt. was established by Act of Parliament in 1866.

(5) The new dispensation under Sir John Grant was an immense improvement. The planter J.P.s were replaced by stipendiaries and an efficient constabulary. A savings bank was set up. A new public works department irrigated the Kingston plain. Education was improved and a public health service created. Capt. A.W. Baker founded the valuable banana trade, and in due course the United Fruit Co. Jamaicans also began to find employment improving plantations in Central America and Cuba. In 1884 and 1895 a measure of local representation could be re-established. In 1907 however Kingston was destroyed in an earthquake.

(6) There followed the usual oscillations of colonial prosperity arising from World Wars. The boom of 1939 to 1944 was equally followed by demands for local autonomy made more vociferous by the weakening of the Imperial power. The new constitution of 1944 was followed by autonomy in 1947. Again a natural disaster,

this time a hurricane, interrupted progress in 1951, but British colonial development funds and private capital created new opportunities notably in citrus growing, bauxite and the tourist trade. This was important because openings for Jamaicans in Central America and Cuba were disappearing. From 1958 to 1962 Jamaica was part of the abortive W. Indies Federation whose collapse was precipitated by her withdrawal; on 6th Aug. 1962, the I. became independent within the Commonwealth and in June 1969 a member of the Org. of American States.

JAMES I of SCOTS (1394-1437) King as prisoner (1406), released and crowned (1424). (1) The Scone parliament of 1371 assured the Crown to Robert (Bruce) II's children, of doubtful legitimacy, by Elizabeth Mure whom he had married after their birth, rather than his undoubtedly legitimate children by his second wife Euphemia Ross. This started a royal feud. Elizabeth's *s.* John succeeded to the throne as ROBERT III (r. 1390-1406). He had been permanently and gravely injured by a kicking horse in 1388, and his brother ROBERT D. of ALBANY conducted the govt. till 1393. By 1399, however, Robert III's infirmities forced him to appoint his eldest son DAVID D. of ROTHESAY (1378-1402) as Lieutenant of the Realm. The Highlands were in chronic rebellion and David succeeded only partially in putting them down. He repudiated his wife, Elizabeth of March, and antagonised her powerful relatives. His second wife was Margery of Douglas but her relatives were defeated by the English at Homildon Hill (1402). The isolated Lieutenant was overthrown by his uncle Albany and perished by starvation in Falkland Castle. K. Robert, suspecting Albany's designs, sent his only other son JAMES (the subject of this entry) to France, but the English intercepted him and held him until 1424. These were the circumstances of his accession, and he lived at the English court and was educated there during eighteen of the first thirty years of his life, while his uncle and then his uncle's son made no efforts on his behalf. He was, however, on friendly terms with Henry V, whom he accompanied on campaign, and he married JANE OF SOMERSET (?-1445) for love.

(2) The Albany regencies were not successful. They necessarily depended on the Estates, which were dominated by the Douglas' in the SW and by the Macdonalds of the Isles, whom, however, the elder Albany defeated at Harlaw in 1411. To keep the factions in the Estates quiet he continued the dangerous habit of alienating crown lands and revenues to buy a little spurious peace. He also in 1416, when Henry V was campaigning in France, had recourse to the distractions of war. Demanding the return of James, he made a refusal the pretext for a disastrous invasion (*The Foul Raid*) in 1417. When he died he was succeeded in the regency by his son MURDOCH (?-1425) 2nd D., who had been justiciary north of the Forth from 1392. Captured at Homildon Hill in 1402, he was a prisoner in England until exchanged in 1415. His regency was overthrown in 1424 with accusations of corruption, but mainly because of its weakness.

(3) James I returned and was crowned in 1424. Apart from a ransom (technically maintenance expenses) the condition of his release was the withdrawal of Scottish troops from France, which he could not enforce, and prevention of further French recruitment, which he could.

(4) His policy of 'peace retrenchment and reform' was initially popular, but the treaty clauses on French recruitment ran counter to the interests of the Albanys. Dumbarton, the port for France was in the hands of the Duke's son WALTER (?-1425) who was seized and executed. With this demonstration of the will to orderliness the Perth parliament of 1424-5 established the statute book, forbade private war, created a central court, confirmed ecclesiastical privileges and punished heresy, provided for registration of land titles and made a

permanent grant of customs to the crown. The Albanys saw their danger but before they could act, the King arrested and executed him and his supporters. Only Sir Robert Graham, a descendant of Euphemia Ross, escaped.

(5) In 1427 James overawed the highland chiefs at an Inverness parliament and he deprived Malise Graham, 2nd E. of Strathearn, and sent him as a hostage to England. Malise's mother was the 1st Earl's daughter. At the same time James reorganised the administration of the revenue, stopped alienations and resumed as many grants as he could. Thus internally strengthened he could improve his international position. In 1428 he agreed to marry his daughter MARGARET (?1425-45) to the Dauphin (later Louis XI). This manoeuvre helped to prolong the English truce in 1429 and he also made a commercial treaty with Burgundy, whence in 1430 he imported guns which only the crown could afford and which strengthened him again. In 1433 a Scots mission attended the council of Basel and in 1436 Margaret was married as arranged. The monarchy was now strong at home and respected abroad. Moreover the King encouraged the arts, conferred benefactions on St. Andrew's univ. and was himself a poet. It was too good to last. Sir James Graham and other conspirators in his household, acting in the interests of the Atholl Stewarts, also descendants of Euphemia Ross and hoping for the support of "oppressed" magnates, murdered him. Jane, the Queen, however, rallied popular opinion against the assassins and the Atholls, who were put to death.

JAMES II of Scots (1430-60) King (1437) (1) became the centre of a power struggle when the Grahams and Atholls murdered his father James I. A govt. was set up consisting of Q. Jane as guardian of the King, Bp. Cameron of Glasgow as Chancellor, and Archibald 5th E. of Douglas as Guardian of the Realm. Sir William Crichton, Keeper of Edinburgh Castle, attempted to take charge of Jane and the King. She moved to Stirling by a ruse, but the castle there was seized by Sir Alexander Livingstone. He and Crichton bid for Douglas's support against each other and both were refused. They then joined forces against Douglas, Livingstone becoming guardian of the King and Crichton replacing the bishop as chancellor. Early in 1439 Douglas suddenly died and immediately afterwards the Queen married Sir JAMES STEWART (*The Black Knlight of Lorne*), (?-after 1447) a distant and personable relative, possibly with ambitions. In Aug. Livingstone entered the Queen's rooms at Stirling, put her in custody and put the Black Knight in irons in the dungeon. He then extorted the legal guardianship of the King and a parliamentary pardon from her in exchange for her husband's liberty. This ended her political career if not her dynastic importance.

(2) In 1440 James was willingly kidnapped by Crichton, but Livingstone persuaded Crichton to return him by a reference to the growing power of the sixteen-year-old William, 6th E. of Douglas. William had a French dukedom and vast territories astride the border, and was of royal descent on both sides, his mother, especially being EUPHEMIA (?-1415), a sister of MALISE GRAHAM (?1407-?85), E. of STRATHEARN (*see* JAMES I). William was in fact a semi-independent prince. He came to Edinburgh with a great following, was entertained in the King's name in the castle and then seized with his brother and murdered by Livingstone and Crichton (*The Black Dinner*). They were abetted by his great-uncle 'James the Gross': he inherited the earldom, but not the French dukedom, nor Annandale (which passed to the Crown), nor Galloway which passed to the murdered Earl's sister Margaret (*The Fair Maid of Galloway*).

(3) The accomplices controlled the govt. until 1443, when James the Gross died and was succeeded as 8th E. by his son William. He set about reuniting and enlarging the Douglas patrimony by marrying the Fair Maid and securing Balveny for his brother John. Two other brothers became earls and another Bp. of Aberdeen. At the same time he divided the Crichtons from the Livingstones by encouraging the ambitions of the latter. Livingstones occupied the keeperships of four castles, the justiciarship and the financial posts of chamberlain, comptroller and Master of the Mint. Crichton kept Edinburgh castle but his chancellorship went to the redoubtable Bp. James Kennedy of St. Andrews (1406-65). As a son by the second marriage of James II's aunt Mary, Kennedy was the King's cousin; as the leading churchman of the kingdom he was interested in peace and good govt. Moreover, Douglas had made a band (alliance) with the E. of Crawford (in the N.E.) who had a grudge against Kennedy. Thus Kennedy's policy was to support Crichton and strengthen the crown against the centrifugal tendencies of the magnates. There were widespread, loosely connected private wars in which Douglases, Crawfords, and the Livingstones fought Kennedys and Crichtons. These were complicated by border fighting. Kennedy and Crichton, however, held the balance, and Douglas beat the English in 1448 at Gretna. By 1449 when the King came of age, the country was tired of disorders.

(4) Douglas and Crichton saw an opportunity to end them. The King was to marry the wealthy MARY of GUELDERS (?-1463), assume power and liquidate the Livingstones. This suited Kennedy; it was accompanied by commercial treaties with Burgundy and the Flemish states which suited the burghs. The Livingstones were dismissed from their many offices, and the Crown and Douglas shared the spoils, but Douglas by his band with Crawford and Macdonald of the Isles (Ross) sought to maintain his quasi-independence. James II now took firm hold. In 1450 a parliament proclaimed a general peace and re-enacted the legislation of James I.

The Fall of the Douglases (5). The King secured the powerful support of the Gordons and in 1452 summoned Douglas to Stirling and in a fury, when Douglas would not break his band with Crawford, stabbed him to death; the Gordons defeated Crawford at Brechin. James, 9th E. of Douglas, submitted, surrendering Wigtown and Staverton, and undertook to keep the ward of the English March in person. John of the Isles was brought over by subsidies and diplomacy.

(6) In 1453 Douglas went to London on a mission to extend the truce. Here he secured the release of Malise Graham, former E. of Stratheam (*see* JAMES I OF SCOTS-5). when Douglas returned, the King marched against him: Douglas fled to England, his brothers were defeated at Arkinholme, and in 1455 the Earl was attainted. The western lowlands fell directly under the Crown.

(7) The English were anxious to retake Bordeaux, lost in 1453. Consequently a threat of joint action with France in 1456 quickly brought a three year truce and left the King free to deal with the Highlands. Here in 1457 he married his sister ANNABEL (?-1494) to the Gordon E. of Huntly. But when the truce was due to expire England was torn by feud and James seemed to see an opportunity to recover Roxburgh and Berwick. Margaret, Queen of Henry VI, arrived to seek help against the Yorkists. James was killed by a bursting gun at Roxburgh, which nevertheless fell.

JAMES III of SCOTS (1451-88) King (1460) (1) succeeded on the accidental death of his father James II at the siege of Roxburgh. His mother Mary of Guelders and his relative Bp. Kennedy acted as Regents and began with an apparent success. The combined army of northerners and Scots under Margaret, Queen of Henry VI, after a victory at St. Alban's, was defeated at York in Mar. 1461. In return for further aid she and Henry surrendered Berwick and promised Carlisle. In reply, the Yorkist King Edward IV agreed, in the so-called T. of Westminster-Ardtornish (1462), to partition Scotland with

John of the Isles, Crawford and Douglas. The conspiracy failed after fighting on the Border and in the glens, but achieved Edward IV's purpose of distracting the Scots govt. Mary of Guelders died (Dec. 1463) and Bp. Kennedy, having made a fifteen year truce with England, died in May 1465. Bereft of reliable supporters, the lonely young King was seized in 1466 by a faction of lesser nobles led by the Boyds of Kilmarnock. In Oct. he confirmed Lord Boyd as Governor of the King and Keeper of all fortresses. At his behest his *son* Sir Thomas Boyd, was made E. of Arran in 1467 and married James's sister MARY (1457-86), while James in 1469 married Margaret *d.* of Christian I of Denmark, who pledged Orkney and Shetland for her dowry, whereby through non-payment these islands passed to Scotland. Moreover while Arran was absent in Denmark and his father in England, others secured the, probably homosexual, King's favour; the Boyds fled and in Nov. 1469 were attainted. When Arran died in 1474 Mary was married to James, Ld. HAMILTON (?-1479). From this union two major families, the ARRAN HAMILTONS and the LENNOX STEWARTS had strong claims to the crown. Between the death of James III's brother Alexander, D. of ALBANY (?-1485), and the birth of Mary, Q. of Scots in 1542, the heir presumptive was always a Hamilton.

(2) Meanwhile James's govt, estranged from most of the great houses and the main group of minor nobles, was through debasement of the coinage alienating the market towns too. Parliamentary complaints of weakness, injustice, inflation and disorder accompanied a revival of private wars. The King's aesthetic tastes and peaceable habits were derided and unfavourably contrasted with the martial and athletic disposition of his brothers Albany and John (?-1479), E. of Mar. Suspecting conspiracy, the King put his brothers in custody in 1479. Mar accidentally died: Albany escaped first to France, then to England. The upshot lends colour to James's suspicions. By the T. of Fotheringhay (1482), Edward IV recognised Albany as King, subject to English suzerainty, the cession of Berwick, and the other borderlands and marriage to Edward's daughter Cecilia. He and the ageing Black Douglas made their way towards Berwick with an English army. James mobilised, but the nobles, led by Archibald (*Bell the Cat*), E. of Angus (a Red Douglas), not only refused to march, but hanged the King's favourites at Lauder Bridge and imprisoned James. Berwick was lost for ever. Albany briefly became Lieutenant of the Realm, but his undertakings at Fotheringhay were too much for him. Rather than submit to the English, the nobles, urged by the citizens of Edinburgh, restored James. Albany fled to England in 1483 and was forfeited. A foray with Douglas raised no support even in Douglas territory. Douglas was captured and became a monk. Albany died in exile. Richard III, with trouble at home, preferred peace on the border. There was trouble of another kind, however, with the Humes over the properties of the suppressed priory of Coldingham. 'Bell the Cat', with Argyll, other western magnates, the Bp. of Glasgow and the Hepburns supported the Humes and seized Prince James. The northerners with the archbishop and the Bp. of Aberdeen supported the King. A skirmish, followed by a pacification at Blackness, left the Prince in the hands of the rebels. Dissatisfied, the King insisted on a meeting at Stirling, where he was killed before his northern supporters could come up. The embarrassed rebels finding themselves with a new King James IV (1473-1513) who could claim the support of both parties, alleged an accident.

JAMES IV of SCOTS (1473-1513) King (1488) (*For his succession see end of previous entry.*) **(1)** Despite his youth, he was a strong and skilful politician. He encouraged mercantile and other urban interests, establishing Edinburgh as the permanent seat of an increasing number of govt. institutions. The coinage was improved (but not restored). Parliaments extended the legislation of James I, and made the King less dependent on the noble factions which had betrayed his father; but he was careful to repay his political debt to the latters' northern supporters by curbing and between 1490 and 1493 destroying the power of their enemies, the hitherto independent Macdonalds of the Isles. He established Crown rule where it had never obtained before. This type of action, repeated on the Border, represented the King's obedience to the demand of his loyal Estates to 'hold the law to the people'. It also filled his coffers with fines and forfeitures, eroded the local power of magnates, simplified and cheapened administration and brought back locally intercepted revenues. Another facet of the same policy was the establishment of superior courts to which all men could resort, and their permanent location in Edinburgh together with efforts, through an Education Act (1496) to improve local legal knowledge.

(2) Some of these policies were inspired by the King's Min., Bp. Elphinstone of Aberdeen, where in 1495 James established yet another, somewhat embryonic Univ. The Bp. was also to encourage printing: Walter Chepman, a clerk in the King's household from 1496, financed the importation of Andrew Myllar's press from Rouen in about 1506 and procured a monopoly especially of Elphinstone's works in 1507.

(3) Meanwhile relations with England were confused by the Perkin Warbeck affair, the Scottish chapter of which began with Warbeck's arrival in 1495 under recommendations from Margaret of Burgundy. In 1496 his supporters and Scottish troops invaded England, but the allies quarrelled and no local English support was forthcoming. Warbeck, however, had married Katharine Gordon, a daughter of the E. of Huntly (see JAMES II OF SCOTS) and James would not repudiate him. In July 1497, however, Warbeck left Scotland, and in Sept. a seven year truce was signed through the good offices of the Spanish sovereigns, who opposed Warbeck because their daughter, Katharine of Aragon, had been betrothed to Henry VII's son Arthur. Henry now proposed a treaty of marriage and perpetual peace.

(4) By his mistress, Marion Boyd, James had a son ALEXANDER STEWART (1493-1513), who was Chancellor from 1510 and Abp. of St. Andrews from 1512. By another mistress, Janet Kennedy, he had JAMES STEWART (1499-1544) E. of MORAY (1501). Finally he fell deeply in love with Margaret Drummond and had, perhaps, married her secretly. Thus James was unenthusiastic about marrying Henry VII's daughter MARGARET TUDOR (1489-1541), but in 1500 Margaret Drummond and her two sisters died of poisoning and the unhappy King felt constrained to enter into negotiations seriously. The obstacles were diplomatic: Henry wanted an alliance with Spain and Scotland against the growing power of France, whose ambitions were directed towards Spanish dominated Italy. James did not want to sacrifice political stability by abandoning the special relationship with France. He secured his point. The treaty was ratified in Feb. 1502 and the wedding took place in Aug. 1503. Exactly a century later it engendered the union of the English and Scots crowns. The perpetual peace was less durable.

(5) Scotland enjoyed some of the economic and cultural benefits of the Renaissance boom, encouraged by Elphinstone's and the King's policies. Statutes were passed to enlarge the fishing industry and tenants were induced to improve their land by being given security of tenure. The King practised surgery and founded the College of Surgeons in 1506, and by getting Damion the abbacy of Tungland, financed experiments in alchemy and chemistry. He erected important buildings at Falkland, Linlithgow and Sterling, and built the Palace of Holyroodhouse.

(6) International problems led him also to build a navy with the advice of his Captain, Sir Andrew Wood (?-1515). These arose from French power which threatened English trade in the Channel and, after the Venetian defeat in the War of the League of Cambrai (1509), from Spanish territorial interests in Italy. Just after the bellicose Henry VIII's accession (1509), Pope Julius II, to prevent French domination of the Papal States, began to form a coalition in which Spain figured. James had feared this development (which would probably involve him in the end) and as early as 1508 had proposed a general pooling of resources for a crusade against the Turks who were approaching Hungary and raiding Italy. Unfortunately the crusading idea was discredited; the Pope was too interested in Italian politics and the lay rulers in parochial affairs. The anti-French coalition developed into a Holy Alliance (1511); Henry VIII naturally joined it and adopted a minatory attitude towards James. A French defeat would bring about demands for Scottish submission. James used every diplomatic resource to prevent war, but when Henry VIII agreed with the Emperor Maximilian (T. of Malines) in Apr. 1513 to attack France, self interest as well as the French alliance forced him to deliver an ultimatum. In his reply Henry indeed revived the English claim to Scotland. The Scots fleet, mishandled by Arran, achieved nothing. In Sept. 1513 at Flodden Field, K. James and half the Scots nobility perished.

JAMES V OF SCOTS (1512-42) King (1513) (1) came to the throne at the age of 17 months, in the confusion following the appalling disaster at Flodden (see JAMES IV). His pregnant English mother, Mary Tudor, took over the tutelage, which parliament confirmed, but her birth and opinions made her suspect as a ruler. The Hamiltons, led by Arran, James Beaton the Abp. of Glasgow and Lord Home the High Chamberlain favoured and sent an invitation to James IV's cousin JOHN (1581-1536) 2nd D. of ALBANY, who had lived all his life in France. The Queen's reply in 1514 was to marry Archibald Douglas, 6th E. of Angus, grandson of Bell the Cat, to secure the support of the Douglas. She was considered by the remarriage to have forfeited the tutelage and in May 1515 Albany arrived and was installed as regent. Though naturally pro-French he favoured peace with England and his integrity soon overcame Douglas and English efforts to capitalise on the reputation of his treacherous father. He began by seeking Q. Margaret's help and when repulsed besieged her at Stirling (Aug. 1515) and secured the royal children. After failing with the help of Ld. Dacre, Henry VIII's Warden of the March, to abduct them, Margaret fled to England where she gave birth to MARGARET DOUGLAS (1515-78). A Home rebellion possibly connected with these events was put down in 1516, and Albany had Home executed. He then went to France where he negotiated the important T. of ROUEN (Aug. 1517) but in his absence the pro-English party of Margaret and Angus came to blows with the pro-French led by Arran. But Margaret and Angus were themselves at odds, each wanting to secure the power and Margaret decided to try and get a divorce. Henry VIII, her brother, would not help so she applied to Albany who was related by marriage to the Pope. In 1520 Angus' partisans defeated Arran's at a pitched battle in the streets of Edinburgh (Cleanse the Causeway). Albany, who had been kept in France as a consequence of an Anglo-French rapprochement, was able to return in 1521 when the friendship broke down. He pleased Margaret by sending Angus to France, but Francis I wanted him to invade England. Margaret betrayed his plans to Dacre and in any case the nobility followed Albany to the border only with reluctance. Dacre offered and Albany gladly accepted a truce (Aug. 1522). Albany then went to France to get French military support, and thereupon Henry VIII offered his d. Mary in marriage to James V. This was refused because under the T. of Rouen, ratified in 1521,

James was contracted to a French princess. The purpose of Henry's offer was soon apparent: the English ravaged Kelso and Jedburgh and Albany's return with French troops in Sept. 1523, was welcome. Nevertheless the Scots were as reluctant warriors as before and a siege of Wark had to be abandoned. This damaged Albany's prestige and in the spring of 1524 he finally left for France.

(2) Immediately Margaret, helped by Arran, seized control of the King and proclaimed him of age (he was twelve). This put a formal end to Albany's regency, but by the same token permitted the return (with Henry VIII's help) of Angus, from whom in 1525 Margaret obtained her divorce. Angus soon dominated the council and in Nov. 1525 seized the King. He kept him at Falkland Castle, deprived of a proper education but deliberately spoiled and debauched him to destroy his interest in public business. Meanwhile Douglases occupied all the chief offices.

(3) Angus' policy broke on the King's strength of character, for he developed a wily ruthlessness which strained and finally overthrew the power of the Douglases. In 1526 his cousin JOHN (?-1526) 3rd E. of LENNOX twice attempted rescue and was brutally murdered after the B. of Linlithgow which ended the second. In May 1528 James organised his own escape to Stirling. He raised support without difficulty and drove Angus into Tantallon Castle. With him safely invested, James started to tame the highlands by authorising the extermination of Clan Chattan; Angus surrendered in Nov. and was permitted to retire to England; under a five year peace signed with Henry VIII in Dec. (Henry being then embroiled in the diplomacy leading to Wolsey's fall), Angus was allowed to live at the English court and James promptly took advantage of the absence of the principal Douglas to bring order to the Scottish March. In 1529 he hanged the reivers Scott of Tushielaw and Cockburn of Henderland; in 1530 the famous John Armstrong of Gilnockie.

(4) In the Highlands James reverted to the policy of favouring the Gordons against the Crawfords but in the Isles, the Macdonalds and Macleans had risen in self-protection against the rapacity of Argyll, the Lieut. and the King's bastard half-brother Moray, Lieut in the North. When Argyll died in 1529 the area was in civil war. Accordingly the Lieutenancy of the Isles was transferred from the Campbell family to Macdonald of Islay when James threatened to come in person with his army in 1531. Moray was moved south in 1532 where he was Warden of the East and Middle Marches until 1536.

(5) The King's determination to keep the peace endeared him to common folk. So did his habit of wandering abroad *incognito* as the *Gudman of Ballengeich*, an easily penetrated disguise in which he was reputed to have had many adventures and seduced many wenches. Six well borne mistresses, singly or simultaneously (Elizabeth Beaton, Elizabeth Carmichael, Euphemia Elphinstone, Margaret Erskine, Elizabeth Shaw and Elizabeth Stewart) shared his favours and gave him children. Of these Margaret Erskine, the acknowledged favourite, was the mother of Ld. JAMES (1531-70) E. of MAR and MORAY (1562). Moreover James took practical steps to strengthen the govt. without alienating the public by taxation. The members of the court called the session became paid judges through the foundation, in 1531, of the College of Justice, and James used Henry VIII's anti-papal manoeuvres to extort, through the Pope, large sums (*The Three Teinds* 1531-33 and *The Great Tax* 1532) from the Scottish church, some of which was used to endow the College. An orthodox R. Catholic, involved, through the commendation of royal bastards, in some of the temporal abuses of the church, he was prepared to profit from the church without aiding the protestant reformers. Indeed in 1528 the first Scots protestant martyr, Patrick Hamilton, had already been burned.

(6) By 1532 the bachelor King was being courted by all Europe, for the struggles centred on the rise of France were complicated by the Reformation, especially in Germany, and by the Turkish conquest of Hungary in 1526. James, still bound by the T. of Rouen, was anxious for its fulfilment. The French Princess, Madeleine, was young and in poor health; understandably Francis I was not in haste. The English peace treaty of 1528 was due to expire. As part of a new treaty Henry VIII again offered Mary Tudor, no longer a fitting match because she had been bastardised on the birth of Elizabeth. James politely declined but acknowledged Henry's marriage to Ann Boleyn. The peace treaty was to last for the joint lives of the two Kings and a year beyond. Then James put further pressure on Francis by entertaining marriage proposals from Hungary, Denmark, Portugal and Catherine de Medici. In 1535 Francis offered Marie of Bourbon, *d.* of the D. of Vendôme, with a large dowry in place of Madeleine, and James accepted. In Sept. 1536 he visited the lady informally at St. Quentin. Alarmed at her ungainly figure, he made his way to the French court at Lyons and swept the princess Madeleine and her father off their feet. The marriage was celebrated at Paris in Jan. 1537, the bride reached Leith in May and died in July. The Scots embassy which went to France to announce her death was also to find another bride. Francis, still impressed by James, offered MARY OF GUISE (1515-50) widow of the Duc de Longueville, a member of the Orleans branch of the royal house, with yet another dowry.

(7) James peace-keeping policies and popular habits were likely to create friction with the nobility who were the biggest disturbers of the peace. Moreover, affable to the lowly and charming to strangers as he was, the King was never comfortable with the Lords and consulted them with decreasing application as time went on. In 1526 his mother had married a distant relative HENRY STEWART (?-1495-1551) Ld. METHVEN (1528) but when he returned from France he found that she was trying to divorce him in order to re-marry Angus, whose recall from England was being plotted by other nobles. He feared the return of the Douglas faction and sent her back to her husband: but he went further in compassing the execution of the Master of Forbes, Angus' brother-in-law, and the beautiful Lady Glamis, Angus' sister, on inadequate and different charges of conspiracy to murder him. Lady Glamis was burned: the discontented nobility to a man sympathised with the Douglas. Thus by the time of his marriage to Mary of Guise by David Beaton (who soon became a Cardinal) in May 1538, the nobility were against him and he relied increasingly on the French connection, the leaders of a worldly church and the ability of his handsome and clever wife, who gave him two children. Heretical, especially Calvinist doctrines were becoming current and brought anti-clericalism with them. Moreover the King's declining health perhaps, warped his judgment: he did not seem to know how weak his position was becoming. In 1541 Henry VIII mobilised to forestall movements by a projected papal alliance of France, the Empire and Scotland against him, and James sent Beaton to France to negotiate military help. The alliance never materialised, so Henry made overtures to the Emperor against France, and proposed a meeting with James at York. Meanwhile both James' young sons had died. James agreed to the meeting, kept Henry waiting and then found a pretext for backing out. The easily enraged Henry went south to be involved in the affair of Katharine Howard. Card. Beaton now returned without any French guarantees and in Nov. 1542 an English army under Katharine Howard's uncle the D. of Norfolk (anxious to curry favour with Henry) ravaged the Scottish March. He had to retreat for want of supplies, but the noble commanders of James' army encamped at Fala Muir and took their revenge by disbanding. A new force raised by Beaton and Moray was routed by a tenth of its number at Solway Moss. The King, too ill to take part, despaired and died.

JAMES VI of SCOTS (and I of England) (1566-1625) K. of Scots (1567), of England (1603) SCOTTISH REIGN. He was the son of Mary Q. of Scots by Ld. Darnley and succeeded when his mother, a prisoner in Lochleven, appointed the E. of Moray regent and abdicated. The baby James was crowned immediately, but in May 1568 the indomitable Mary escaped, revoked her abdication, headed west, gathered Hamilton support, was defeated at Langside near Glasgow and crossed into England.

(2) The reality of the English protectorate over Scotland was now apparent. The Queen of Scots charged her subjects with rebellion; Moray and his friends replied that she was unfit to rule. Both sides were content to submit the issue to the Queen of England, whose commissioners heard the evidence at York; it tended to incriminate Mary in Darnley's murder and included copies of the notorious *Casket Letters* (q.v.). Genuine or forged, the evidence ruined Mary's reputation in Scotland. In Jan. 1569 Elizabeth, through Cecil, declared that nothing derogated from the honour of either party; that Moray might resume his regency and that Mary might remain as her guest. In the autumn the rising of the Northern Earls showed that Elizabeth was wise to consider Moray the safer neighbour, but in Jan. 1570 a Hamilton shot him dead from the steps of Abp. Hamilton's house at Linlithgow. A civil war between Hamiltons (*Queen's Men*) and Lennoxes (*King's Men*) broke out. Hamilton forces were let loose and one raided England. The English retaliated.

(3) The new regent, elected with Elizabeth's approval, was the King's grandfather Lennox, whose troops combined with the English to destroy the Hamilton strongholds. The Abp. was captured and hanged in Apr. 1571, but the Queen's men under Kirkaldy of Grange and Maitland of Lethington based in Edinburgh Castle, and the King's Men based in Leith fought each other in the partly abandoned city. In Aug. the Regent held a parliament at Stirling. Grange planned to surprise and kidnap its most prominent members, but the prisoners were rescued by a sally from the castle; Lennox, however, was killed in the melée. The parliament promptly filled the regency with the rescuer, JOHN ERSKINE (?-1572) E. of MAR who died in the following summer and was succeeded in Nov. by MORTON. He was a nephew of Margaret Tudor's E. of Angus, but held his earldom in right of his wife. His first act was to offer terms, embodied in the Pacification of Perth, to the Hamiltons; his second to get Elizabeth's help. In May 1573 an English force with artillery under Sir William Drury forced Grange to surrender. Lethington was already dead, Grange was hanged. Elizabeth and Morton had made sure that Mary would never reign in Scotland so long as they lived.

(4) Mary fought to reign again and in England too. To achieve this Morton and Elizabeth would have to die and the rights of her own son would have, at least temporarily to be set aside. Deprived of useful internal support she had to rely upon the intervention of foreign powers with whom she intrigued as best she could from her increasingly strict custody (*see* ELIZABETH 1-9 *et seq*).

(5) Meantime Morton kept the peace from Edinburgh, while the Erskines educated the King at Stirling. There were two parallel churches. Mar had agreed in Jan. 1572 (*Concordat of Leith*) that Bishops should be nominated by the crown, but examined and admitted by chapters of Kirk ministers. Morton made his nominations conditional on most episcopal revenue being paid to the crown. The old church supplied by way of taxation, commendation, or assignment nearly half the revenue of the govt. It had

the property but was forbidden to preach its own doctrine. The Kirk, on the other hand, could agitate as it pleased, but remained poor. Andrew Melville who succeeded in the Kirk leadership when Knox died (Nov. 1572) demanded the end of episcopacy and a transfer of the endowments to the Kirk for its own and educational purposes. The govt. refused. It could not accede to the first demand without endangering its own ecclesiastical influence, nor to the second without doubling lay taxation.

(6) While Morton's policy would have agreed with the King's later views, the King was tutored by the Calvinists George Buchanan and Peter Young as well as others. Their first object was to inculcate hatred of his mother; their second to enjoin a wholesome respect for the highest claims of the Kirk. They failed in both. On the other hand the whole household (except the young E. of Mar) was increasingly hostile to Morton. To this James was susceptible and Morton did not try to reverse this trend. The truth was that the Regent was not much liked by anyone.

(7) In 1578 Morton summoned the feuding Es. of Athol and Argyll before the council for levying private war and disobeying his mandate to keep the peace. They joined forces and Argyll, admitted by the Erskines to Stirling, persuaded the flattered King (then twelve) to summon a meeting of the nobility before whom the quarrel might be settled. Morton demanded that his powers as regent be respected or that he be allowed to resign. On Athol and Argyll's advice James accepted the resignation and "accepted the govt." (Mar. 1578). Morton assembled troops and with the help of Mar captured Stirling and the King. A threatening civil war was composed by the English ambassador, Robert Bowes; the regency was displaced by a council in which Morton had the first place and Athol the second, but in the spring of 1579 Athol suddenly died leaving Morton apparently supreme. He spent the summer harrying the Hamiltons: their castles were destroyed, and Lds. Claud and John Hamilton were forfeited for their part in Moray's murder. Unintentionally this left the way open for a new development, for in the autumn the King's handsome and charming cousin ESME STUART (?1542-1583) Ld. D'AUBIGNY and 1st. D. of LENNOX (1581) arrived from France. He was the son of the deceased John, younger brother of the regent Lennox; and the regent's estates and claims having passed to Robert Stuart, Bp. of Caithness, D'Aubigny was now in Scotland to secure his heritage. He treated James with respect: James reciprocated with love. He persuaded the Bishop to resign the earldom of Lennox to D'Aubigny (1580), gave D'Aubigny the great Hamilton property at Arbroath, and command of his guard. Lennox was ambitious. A distant kinsman, JAMES STEWART of BOTHWELLMUIR (?-1596) E. of ARRAN (1581) was moved in Dec. 1580 to secure Morton's arrest for complicity in Darnley's murder. He was executed in June 1581, despite diplomatic intervention from England. Lennox was made a duke, James Stewart an earl.

(8) Lennox, through James, was *de facto* ruler but as a Romanist foreigner without alliances he was in a weak position. He tried to placate the Kirk by a conversion to protestantism (which the Kirk disbelieved) and by signing and circulating the Negative Confession (Jan. 1581) condemning practices contrary to the Confession of 1560 (*see* COVENANT-ORS-1). Mary's Guise relatives, backed by Spain were at this period negotiating the farcical 'Association' to restore her as joint sovereign with her son, and they canvassed Lennox. Though the idea was obviously against his and James' interests the Kirk chose to work up a theological xenophobia. Consequently when the extreme protestant Es. of Mar and Gowrie kidnapped James in Aug. 1582 and held him at Ruthven Castle (*The Ruthven Raid*), the Gen. Assembly applauded them and Lennox was driven abroad (Dec. 1582). This

turned James permanently against presbyterianism. Like James V the furious King escaped from Falkland in July 1583, and with the help of the northern earls established Arran as his Minister. Melville and Mar fled to England: Gowrie was hanged. In May 1584 Erastian legislation (*The Black Acts*) declared James head of the Kirk which was to be governed through bishops, forbade meetings of the Gen. Assembly without royal permission, discharged judgements of the Kirk unless approved by the King or Parliament, and forbade preaching in contempt of the King or his Council. At this time Elizabeth wanted an alliance with a peaceful and isolated Scotland and doubted Arran's reliability as a peacemaker or ally. In the autumn of 1585 Ld. Russell, a son of Bedford, was killed at a Border day of trew (truce). She demanded the surrender of Arran who was ultimately responsible; when this was refused she armed the exiled lords and let them loose. In Nov. they appeared at Stirling and drove Arran out. He was forfeited in 1585, and the King formed a coalition consisting of them, the northern Es., of Huntly, Crawford and Montrose, with Maitland of Thirlestane, Lethington's brother. They negotiated a new compromise with the Kirk: Bishops were to be presented by the crown for election by the Gen. Assembly, to which they were to be responsible. At the same time James made an alliance with Elizabeth, denouncing the Association in return for a subsidy of £4,000 (sterling) (= £40,000 Scots). The money was not enough for the extravagant and financially incompetent King who, on Thirlestane's advice, annexed the revenues of all the prelacies but not the manses (*Act of Annexation* 1587) to the crown; this rendered the crown's rights of presentation practically valueless, and eventually destroyed the episcopate.

(9) James was simultaneously faced with the crises provoked by the conspiracies of his mother. They had never known each other: their political interests were partly, their religious convictions wholly opposed. He was bound to benefit from her death, yet he tried most means short of war to save her life. She was beheaded at Fotheringhay in Feb. 1587 and, apart from Elizabeth's equivocations, James was now the best and the protestant claimant to the English succession.

(10) Possible hostilities with Spain required special action: R. Catholic nobles were discussing the King's conversion and an attack on England. James, in case of a Spanish victory, let them talk, but he strengthened the constitution of parliament; the Franchise Act of 1587 authorised the 40s freeholders of the shires to elect commissioners who were to have equal representation in the committee of the Articles with the burghs. He was also negotiating for a protestant bride, hesitating between Catherine of Navarre, a Calvinist, and the Lutheran ANNE OF DENMARK (1574-1619) with whose country Scotland had commercial ties. His real interest lay in the defeat of the Armada. He confirmed the league with Elizabeth, mobilised and awaited the outcome. The English victory was followed by the Danish marriage by proxy in 1589, but not before the English govt. had intercepted letters from Huntly, Maxwell and Ld. Claude Hamilton to Philip II regretting the English victory and suggesting a landing in Scotland next time. The King's reaction to Calvinist and English indignation was very mild, whereupon the offenders made a band with Crawford, Errol, Montrose and Bothwell to seize his person. James forestalled them and forced them to surrender at Brig o'Dee, but merely put them in custody for a few months.

(11) In Oct. 1589 James went to Denmark to fetch home his bride, and met with appalling storms. On his return (May 1590) witches were accused of raising the wind and confessed under torture that Bothwell (nephew of Mary's Bothwell) had paid them; but Bothwell was an ally of the Kirk: he was arrested, escaped early in 1591 and was outlawed (*put to the horn*). With the connivance of the lowland congregations and the English he carried

on a daring guerrilla war and even attacked Holyroodhouse in Dec. 1591. James Stewart of Doune, E. of Moray by marriage to the regent Moray's daughter and a Calvinist, was said to be in league with him. He had inherited the feud with Huntly engendered by the B. of Corrichie. The King commissioned Huntly to take Moray, but announced that he would settle the feud. The two were to meet in Feb. at the royal estate of Doniebristle on the Forth. Here the R. Catholic Huntly murdered Moray. Public indignation was fanned by the Kirk, as a means of discrediting the King.

(12) In the summer, parliament enacted and the King, on Thirlestane's advice, assented to the *Golden Act* which permitted the Kirk to assemble as it pleased, save that the King's commissioner to the Gen. Assembly might name the time and place of the next meeting. In return for this long range ecclesiastical concession, James got a short term *quid pro quo*: The Kirk's disreputable ally Bothwell was forfeited, its Romanist enemy Huntly was not. But Huntly, with Errol and Angus, was deep in a Spanish plot which seems to have been a continuation of the correspondence discovered in 1589. George Ker, brother of Ld. Newbattle, was arrested just as he was about to sail from the Clyde to Spain: he bore letters and blank parchments (*The Spanish Blanks*) signed by the three earls and admitted, under torture, that instructions to help Spanish operations against England were to be filled in on the blanks. In the face of this overt treason James, nevertheless, resisted the Kirk's more bloodthirsty demands: Bothwell, who had attacked Falkland in Jun. 1592, forced his way into James's bedroom at Holyroodhouse in Jul. 1593. His activities were discrediting the Kirk, so that when Huntly and Errol appeared for judgment in Oct. 1593 they were offered the alternatives of abjuration or exile. Accepting neither, they were forfeited, but remained in armed defiance in the north. After an unsuccessful raid on the court, Bothwell joined them in the spring of 1594, and so provoked a brief alliance of King and Kirk. In the ensuing campaign Huntly and Errol defeated Argyll in Glenlivet (Oct. 1594) but when the King's combined forces came up they surrendered and were exiled. Bothwell never returned. The others came back in 1596 on condition that they submitted to the Kirk. They remained R. Catholic in fact, but took no further part in Spanish intrigues, probably because of the English sack of Cadiz (1596) and the failure (by bad weather) of two Spanish expeditions against England immediately afterwards.

(13) James's policy was dictated by the desire for peace and unity and a need to counterbalance the growing influence of the power-hungry Kirk. Moreover Huntly was married to Lennox's daughter and James had educated Lennox's children himself. But he also had an eye to the English succession, calculating that his willingness to compromise with both sides would win the moderate opinion of both sides in England. Meantime Cecil and Elizabeth remained mindful of a danger of the Spanish landing: James's Queen, Anne of Denmark, was received into the Roman church in 1600. The English intrigued with the Kirk. James replied by intriguing inside it. In 1597 he persuaded the Kirk to let him appoint ministers to vacant bishoprics with seats in parliament. They remained technically only ministers within the Kirk and he appointed the first three in 1600. This, of course, made the Kirk party to legislation and brought Kirk and state together: but a Minister could hardly be a bishop for lay purposes without some of the episcopal aura affecting his sacred function. Soon the Assembly was tolerating episcopacy as part of Kirk institutions. This favourably impressed the Anglican Church, for whom Hooker had begun to publish his *Ecclesiastical Polity* in 1594. With the King evidently at peace with the controversial parties in Scotland, those like Cecil who expected to outlive Elizabeth, saw no reason to prevent his succession in

England. Nevertheless Aug. 1600 saw one alarming event namely the death of the Ruthvens at Gowrie (*The Gowrie Conspiracy*) when James visited them, and apparently thought that they were about to kill him. No elucidation of this affair has survived, for James' account alone exists. Queen Elizabeth died in Mar. 1603; James was calmly proclaimed King of England and Ireland, and entered England in April. Scotland was at peace with Spain, England at war. *See next entry* -2, 3.

JAMES I (r. 1603-25) and VI – ENGLISH REIGN (*and see* SCOTLAND 1603-25). **(1)** The great Ulster rebellion ended with the O'Neill's submission on 20 Mar. 1603. Elizabeth I died on 24th. James, who as a purely Scots King, had sympathised with the Irish, was proclaimed on 10th Apr. He spent a month *en route* to London making himself liked by his courtesy, zeal for hunting and profuse distribution of knighthoods. Sometimes grossly familiar and foul mouthed, he was a learned and amusing conversationalist but homosexual, conceited, pacifist and without royal dignity.

(2) His first and best decision was to retain Sir Robert Cecil (whom he ennobled) as his chief adviser as Sec. of State and Ld. Privy Seal. His second was to end English maritime operations in the war with Spain, for Scotland was neutral, and there had been a Spanish invasion of Ireland only a year before. Consistently with this, he dismissed (with compensation) Sir Walter Raleigh (a leading planter in Munster) from the captaincy of the Guard, but Raleigh became guiltlessly implicated in Cobham's Main Plot to supplant James by Arabella Stuart; convicted of treason, he was reprieved and confined.

(3) By the Anglo-Dutch alliance of 1598 against Spain, the Dutch had acknowledged a debt of £800,000, had taken the English troops into their pay and had handed over the CAUTIONARY TOWNS (Flushing, Brill and Ramekens), and these were still in English occupation. The Dutch were now safe, and anyhow James disliked them as rebels. Thus the outstanding issue with Spain was trade and its concomitant, freedom from molestation by the Inquisition. Cecil wanted trade with the Indies — a Castilian monopoly; Madrid could not concede to Englishmen what it would not concede to Aragonese. In the end both freedoms were granted but only in the European Spanish possessions which included much of Italy (T. of Madrid 1604).

(4) In the same year (when he published his *Counterblast to Tobacco*), James summoned and provoked his first English parliament, and in the cases of *Shirley*, and *Goodwin* v. *Fortescue* was defeated on privilege issues. The emboldened Commons began to discuss grievances, particularly abuses of wardship and purveyance, both of which provided pickings for court favourites and officials. Some of these were Scots.

(5) On his way from Edinburgh, a puritan deputation had presented the Millenary Petition, whose main contentions James rejected at the subsequent Hampton Court Conference. The Commons also discussed the Petition and, to James's irritation, mentioned the subject in their APOLOGY. The enforcement of recusancy laws, like other religious matters was, he thought, especially within his province, as was Ireland. He was unwilling to enforce them uniformly because he hoped for a reunion of Christendom, or to relax them completely in the face of strongly protestant English opinion. Priests and papist gentry were harried, insufficiently to gain popular support, but enough to drive some towards extremism; moreover a new Irish policy against recusancy was beginning to emerge under Sir Arthur Chichester, the new Ld. Deputy, and seemed to foreshadow the King's real intentions.

(6) The result was the GUNPOWDER PLOT to blow up the second session due for 5 Nov. 1605; this engendered a fellow feeling between King and Parliament who made a generous grant and extended a commission from the previous session to treat for Anglo-Scottish union. The possible subjection of Ireland to a protestant joint govt. containing a large admixture of Calvinists disturbed Irish opinion, already hostile to Scots presbyterian penetration in Ulster. The Old English Lords and gentry of the Pale, headed by Sir Patrick Barnewall, petitioned the Ld. Deputy in 1606 against interference with private use in religion. Barnewall was prosecuted. In the meantime the shiring of Ulster and the imposition there of English land law was undermining the status of the great chiefs by ending their tribal and customary rights and promoting their vassals, The beginnings of a major conspiracy involving the O'Neill (E. of Tyrone) and Rory O'Donnell (E. of Tyrconnell) were known to Sir Richard Nugent (Ld. Delvin) who had a quarrel with the govt. over a revoked grant. Nugent was arrested, and fearing that the details might be betrayed, the earls with some 90 other Ulster chiefs took ship (14 Sept. 1607) for France and found their way *via* Spanish territory to Rome.

(7) This FLIGHT OF THE EARLS, a decisive Irish event, occurred when the third session of the English parliament was debating Anglo-Scots union. The Gunpowder honeymoon was over. James's generosity to his Scots favourites was inflaming the ancient dislike of Scotsmen; free trade was exaggeratedly held a threat to English commerce and naturalisation to land ownership. The project had to be dropped, though in the matter of naturalisation James fell back on the Common law by which, in *Calvin's or Colville's Case* he was usefully vindicated. The govt. meanwhile prepared the Plantation of Ulster by wholesale confiscations in Armagh, Cavan, Derry, Donegal, Fermanagh and Tyrone and the plan (*Articles of Plantation*) was published in May 1609. With its offers of cheap land to be sold in parish sized lots to business men, it was a sop to the Scots and the City which in due course acquired an immense territory from Derry to Coleraine. The English and Scots exploited the Irish while the King alternately mitigated and gave way to their demands. There were other lesser Plantations too: mainly in central Ireland.

(8) It had been natural to govern England in accordance with established law and to use the courts to define that law when applied to new situations. The Commons cited much law in their complaints on purveyance and their objections to Union with Scotland. The King paid them in their own coin. He was short of money and court extravagance made him shorter. The royal right to grant monopolies and to impose duties on foreign merchandise were an accepted but irregular source of influence and revenue. In *Bates Case* (1606) an imposition arising (incidentally) from a surrendered monopoly was pronounced lawful and thereupon Cecil (now E. of Salisbury), who had just given up the privy seal for the Ld. Treasurer's staff (1608) framed, in consultation with city interests, a book of rates creating new impositions. These were to be as light as possible but the new revenue, £70,000 a year, was substantial, and capable of development. This unparliamentary change stored up trouble.

(9) James had frequently expounded his views on the pre-eminent character of monarchy, and new interests were arising which feared his policies, particularly in religion and the now unpopular peace with Spain. The very competent *entrepreneurs* and financiers now in the Commons did not take kindly to lectures on English state-craft in a strange thick accent from a foreign King. The respectful temper of the Commons slowly changed to an irritable desire to curb him. This change of mood might have been forestalled if James had not neglected Elizabeth's precautions and ensured that enough influential privy councillors (with their precedence in speaking) were members of the Commons. Deprived of such leadership they listened to others, able to excite the suspicion that the royal income from the older sources plus impositions might make the King independent of parliament altogether. In the 1610 parliament impositions, monopolies, grants of wardships and purveyance were all attacked, together with court prodigality and Scots favourites. Salisbury tried to negotiate a permanent settlement, (THE GREAT CONTRACT) (q.v.), but failed because his master was unwilling permanently to bind himself. Parliament was then gleefully dissolved and the King celebrated the event by more largesse to his Scotsmen, and the elevation of his favourite, Robert Carr, to an English peerage as Vist. Rochester.

(10) The Hispano-Dutch war masked a latent rivalry with Holland which became explicit after the truce of 1609. The English peace with Spain had not worked well since 1604 (with English ships being frequently seized by the Castilians) so that in the interval after the 1610 dissolution, rivalry with Holland in the carrying trade began to obtrude upon existing difficulties with Spain. Moreover the Dutch began to trespass in the English and Dogger Bank herring and cod fisheries, and there were local skirmishes over the whales of Spitzbergen which both powers claimed (*see* WHALING).

(11) In 1612, also, Salisbury died and James, with a sigh of relief, put the Treasury in commission under Northampton (his Privy Seal) and became his own Sec. of State. The arrangement was not happy, for James had no taste for routine, and the Treasury, in debt in 1612, became still more indebted. Moreover he was enamoured of Rochester (whom he made E. of Somerset in 1613) and blinded to the man's appalling character, relied too much upon him. By 1613 Somerset was acting Sec. of State: he had also fallen in love with the wife of the E. of Essex, Frances, who as a Howard, was related to Northampton and to Nottingham, the Ld. High Admiral. He began to quarrel with and hector James who supported Frances' outrageous nullity suit against Essex, and which incidentally strengthened the Howard, pro-Spanish, court faction. It was in these circumstances that an Irish parliament was needed to confirm the Plantations and attack recusancy, and an English one to deal with the usual financial stringency. The govt. ran into storms in both countries. Papists were not excluded from the Irish parliament, and attempts to pack it by creating rotten boroughs were defeated by a combination of Catholic M.P.s and the old Anglo-Norman nobility. Thus the plantations were confirmed but anti-Roman legislation was defeated.

(12) In England the Addled Parliament (1614) was asked to provide subsidies first and then bring in individual constituency petitions. Instead the mistrustful Commons debated a bill against impositions and asked for a conference upon it with the Lords. This was refused by a narrow majority of bishops and courtiers over the older nobility. The Bp. of Lincoln (Neile) accused the Commons of sedition. They debated his speech and him. James ordered them to desist, whereupon they attacked royal favourites and pensioners. James lost his temper and dissolved. The Treasury commission was, however, superseded, Suffolk (another Howard) becoming Ld. Treasurer.

(13) The govt. was no richer and efforts to raise benevolences mostly failed. In the meantime the young and personable George Villiers, a Leicestershire gentleman, appeared at court. He attracted James who knighted him in Apr. 1615. Relations with Somerset now became strained and James tried to placate him by expedients related to Somerset's affair with the countess, and these progressively eroded public respect for the monarch. Somerset's fall, however, was caused by his new wife. Sir Thomas Overbury was an old friend and had helped him in the original affair. He now tried to prevent Somerset marrying the Countess after the annulment of her marriage with Essex, and she, through

Somerset, had procured his imprisonment in the Tower where he had died in 1613. Ugly rumours began to circulate and in 1615 it emerged that Overbury had been poisoned. The countess was rightly and Somerset probably wrongly convicted; this put an end to his power at court, where Sir George Villiers now superseded him in the King's favour, but James foolishly pardoned them both and attracted public suspicion to himself.

(14) This was the background to James' running quarrel with some of the judges. Since Sir Edward Coke had become C.J. of the Common Pleas in 1606, the Common Law Courts had been allowing writs of prohibition against the ecclesiastical court of High Commission; and this body was part of a complex of organisation and doctrine which James regarded as peculiarly his own. The writs confined ecclesiastical courts within progressively narrower definitions of spiritual jurisdiction, so that, e.g. even incidental questions touching property had to be removed into the civil courts. The quarrels with parliament and compensating successes at law encouraged the King to hope for more favourable treatment of royal principles from lawyers than they received from politicians, but to this the uncompromising demand of Sir Edward Coke for a virtual monopoly of law speaking presented a serious obstacle. Matters came to a head when James proposed to intervene in legal proceedings himself (*Peachams Case*) and dismissed Coke in 1616 for resistance to the royal determination. The morally discredited King, by securing a sycophantic judiciary did little to strengthen his constitutional and political position, because his action robbed the judge's opinions of moral appeal. That Coke's private life too was disreputable, was not noticed, but the drift of the King's policy became increasingly clear in the next few years: he sold the Cautionary Towns back to the Dutch for £215,000 in 1616; this simultaneously gave him money and disentangled him from involvement with their anti-Spanish stance. In 1617 the famous Sir Francis Bacon became Ld. Keeper and Villiers was made E. of Buckingham.

(15) These appointments had widespread effects. Buckingham owed his rise, apart from his courtly accomplishments to his advocacy of the Spanish peace and was an intimate of Gondomar the influential Spanish ambassador since 1613. The parvenus of James' court were on bad terms with the Howards, namely, Suffolk (Ld. Treasurer) and Nottingham (Ld. High Admiral) – that same puritanical Ld. Howard of Effingham who had commanded the fleet against the Armada. Buckingham seems to have had a talent for ferreting out guilty secrets. Suffolk was convicted of taking bribes (1618), and succeeded at the Treasury by another commission whose leading member was Lionel Cranfield, E. of Middlesex, originally a city business man. This happened just at the outbreak of the Thirty Years' War, in which James' son-in-law Frederick V of the Palatinate was deeply involved. Public opinion favoured Frederick (whom neither Buckingham nor James meant to support) but an inquiry into the readiness of the navy served to side-track public opinion and, when the report was hostile to Nottingham, to get rid of him (1619). Buckingham took over the Admiralty and he and Cranfield effected many useful reforms in their respective departments.

(16) But greater govt. effectiveness was purchased at the expense of further alienation from the public, for Buckingham not only ruled but exacted a hateful deference at court, while his pro-Spanish policy (now to be reinforced by a marriage) was unpopular with the masses; and besides, 1619 saw the commencement of a five year economic depression. The situation rapidly worsened as Frederick (seen as a protestant champion) was driven from Bohemia and the Palatinate in 1620 (*see* THIRTY YEARS' WAR-1 TO 5) and the chronic shortage of money made a parliament essential. This met in Jan. 1621.

(17) It was in every way hostile to the govt. Having voted two subsidies to equip an army for the Palatinate, it debated monopolies, and after a procedural false start impeached and secured the conviction of two monopolists, Sir Francis Mitchell and Sir Giles Mompesson. It then unearthed evidence against Bacon (since 1618 Ld. Verulam and Ld. Chancellor) of accepting presents from suitors, and he made a general admission of guilt. The King had requested funds to rescue his son-in-law, but continued to pursue the **Spanish Match,** namely, a Spanish marriage for the P. of Wales in return for Spanish support in the Palatinate. News of the Amboyna massacre (1619) reached England in 1620, but though it raised much anti-Dutch feeling it did little to encourage the Spanish policy; the Commons did not believe that Spain would side with a Protestant prince and when asked for more money naturally wanted to know whom the army was to fight, and said firmly that it should fight Spain. The King denied their right to discuss the question and the Commons then voted the Protestation (18 Dec. 1621) which provoked another dissolution.

(18) The Commons' suspicions were correct. The Spaniards were drawing out the negotiations to embroil James with his parliament. Buckingham, on excellent terms with the Prince (the future Charles I), did not suspect this and the two went to Madrid to accelerate matters (Mar.-Aug. 1623). This move, sometimes represented as farcical, was in fact sensible, for it set a limit to Spanish procrastination: it was Charles who finally drove Olivares to admit that Spain would never fight the Emperor for the Palatinate. This ended the Match. The country rejoiced. James, by now was tired: Buckingham and Charles now virtually ruled the Kingdoms (*see* CHARLES I).

(19) Elizabeth's economical habits had checked the rising power and ambition of those estates of the realm represented in the House of Commons, but James' extravagance gave these troublesome and argumentative people their opportunities. As he said to the Spanish ambassador in 1614 "I am surprised that my ancestors should ever have permitted such an institution to come into existence. I am a stranger, and found it here when I arrived . . . I am obliged to put up with what I cannot get rid of". His view of the standing of a King appears in his writings especially *The True Law of Free Monarchies* (1603) and the *Declaration due Roy Jacques I ... Pour le Droit des Rois* (1615).

JAMES II and VII (1633-1701) D. of YORK and ALBANY King (1685-8) (*see also* SCOTLAND 1668-89). S. of Charles I and Henrietta Maria of France. **(1)** Served under Turenne (1652-5) and with the Spaniards in Flanders (1657-8). He was largely French educated but married his protestant mistress, Anne Hyde, *d.* of the E. of Clarendon in 1659 at *Breda.*

(2) Appointed Ld. High Admiral at the Restoration, he organised the fleet and his Instructions remained the basis of fleet management for nearly 150 years. In 1663 he became Post Master Gen. and in 1664 Gov. of the Royal African Co. He had also a patent for the plantation of the New Netherlands which were seized at the outbreak of the Second Dutch War and renamed after him (1664). In 1665 he commanded at the naval victory of Solebay. Rich, competent, successful, the King's brother and heir presumptive, his influence and prestige were enormous, but as a known papist in the era of the aggressive Louis XIV, he was suspect to a nation in which patriotism and protestantism went hand in hand. There were, too, grounds for personal dislike: he was tactless, domineering, obstinate and untrustworthy.

(3) (*See* CHARLES II-10,24.) By Anne Hyde he had two

daughters, the future Qs. Mary II and Anne. Charles II, aware of James' defects and unpopularity, had them brought up as protestants so that the probability of an ultimate protestant succession might make James' Catholicism more acceptable. But it deranged his family life, especially when Anne Hyde died in 1671; and his marriage to Mary of Modena, an Italian R. Catholic (1673) made him no more adaptable. In the political storms which raged about him before his accession, his brother protected him mainly by keeping him out of the way, and in 1680 after Monmouth had put down the Cameronian rising and Lauderdale had been removed, Charles sent him to Scotland where he persuaded the parliament to declare that no religious difference could disqualify a rightful successor to the throne (1681). He had thus secured his future when he returned to England in the spring of 1682. It was safer for him to resume his place, particularly as Shaftesbury's flight (1682) and the Rye House Plot had discredited the old Cromwellian sectaries. Charles released R. Catholic peers and commoners and began packing the bench. In 1683 courts so manned were ready to forfeit municipal charters attacked by *Quo Warranto* so that Charles could replace them with remodelled parliamentary franchises. But these were mainly technical victories which disposed the governing machine more towards James, and perhaps deceived him, but they did not win over the public. Moreover since 1681 there had been a recession; bank failures late in 1682 heralded a five year depression and much unformulated discontent, and besides, there was Louis XIV's religious policy. While Charles relaxed the law against papists and enforced it against dissenters, Louis' dragonnades were driving Huguenot refugees *inter alia* to England. There were widespread apprehensions about religious policy after James' succession.

(4) In this atmosphere of superficial success and lurking doubt James mounted the throne (Feb. 1685). He proclaimed no desire for arbitrary power and called his battle record to witness that he meant to preserve the nation in its just rights and liberties. He made few changes of ministers. Yet he instantly began to attend mass in public and it was soon clear that by "just rights and liberties" he meant something other than those established by law. All those imprisoned on religious grounds were released. The bishops were told to restrain their clergy from preaching against popery, and he informed the French ambassador that he intended freedom of worship for Catholics and, eventually, the repeal of their legal disabilities. His policy was based upon the erroneous belief that R. Catholics and loyal Anglicans were close to each other and that they and the crown were alike threatened by the dissenters. In truth the Anglicans were not willing to cede some of their privileges or contemplate a threat to their property while the R. Catholics united behind their crowned champion. He was advised by hasty and over-zealous converts, whose wisdom was doubted alike by the English old Catholics and the Pope. Royal rashness, by alarming the protestants, endangered the precarious extra-statutory toleration of the previous reign.

(5) A parliament was needed to renew the taxes voted only for Charles II's lifetime. That the honeymoon was not quite over is shown by its complexion (May 1685) which was more favourable to the court than any since 1661. James repeated his earlier proclamation and the taxes were renewed without trouble, but his innate opportunism was now given a fatal opportunity by his bastard nephew the D. of Monmouth. While the E. of Argyle raised a futile insurrection in the western Highlands, the Duke landed from Holland at Lyme Regis with a band of extremist exiles (June) and raised his own rebellion. It was put down (B. of Sedgemoor 6 Jul. 1685). Monmouth, having abased himself before his pitiless uncle, was executed nine days later. Titus Oates had just been so cruelly punished that even he attracted sympathy. In the aftermath of rebellion the troops hanged the peasantry in dozens. Such atrocities eroded the loyalty which the rebellion had excited. Ld. Chief Justice Jeffreys held his Bloody Assizes in the West Country (Sept.) and people started to remember "Bloody Mary". At this period women convicted of treason were normally burned. Then in Oct. Louis XIV revoked the Edict of Nantes and the irregular arrivals of Huguenot refugees developed into a stampede.

(6) James now demanded (Nov.) a standing army to replace the useless militia. It was to be composed of troops which he had already enlisted against the rebellion. The demand seemed reasonable but they included officers who had not taken the tests. When pressed he said that in view of their past services and his possible future needs, he meant to retain them. This simultaneously raised two constitutional issues: the legality of a standing army and of the now overworked royal dispensing power. The Houses were disposed to compromise; the Commons offered the large sum of £700,000 for a reformed militia instead of the standing army and they were prepared to allow statutory exemptions from the tests. James, however, preferred on his own authority to confer any office on a R. Catholic, and decided to part with the money and the parliament, which he prorogued. It never met again.

(7) The forum of criticism thus closed, James advanced by his own interpretation of existing law. He could in any case legally recruit R. Catholic private soldiers, and he steadily altered the military balance by doing so, and by dismissing Irish protestant officers and drafting Irish R. Catholics to England in their place. The judges held (see GODDEN V. HALES) that a dispensation to hold a commission was valid. Thereupon many R. Catholics were installed. Sir Edward Hales became Governor of the Tower; the E. of Tyrconnell commander and then Ld. Lieutenant in Ireland and Sir Roger Strickland, replaced Vice-Admiral Herbert at sea. The policy soon spread to civil offices. Jeffreys became Ld. Chancellor; Ld. Arundell of Wardour, Privy Seal. The E. of Sunderland, ambitious and energetic, was converted to become joint Sec. of State and James' inner council included Nicholas Butler, another convert and Edward Petre, a Jesuit from an old family of Essex R. Catholics. A papal nuncio was received; apostolic delegates were appointed, and bishops consecrated according to the Roman rite.

(8) From the particular to the wholesale. Peers, mayors and office holders began to announce their conversion in increasing numbers. The army, brought each summer threateningly near London to a training camp at Hounslow, had a chapel tent. Friaries were opened at Lincoln's Inn Fields; a Benedictine monastery at Clerkenwell; a Jesuit school at the Savoy and a girls' school in St. Martins Lane. Inns of Court and Livery Companies were pressed and generally agreed to admit papists. Bp. Compton of London was suspended for refusing to discipline his clergy as the King required. When this erosive process was judged to have sufficient momentum, an Ecclesiastical Commission was set up to govern the church. Composed of the Abp. of Canterbury, two bishops, three councillors and one of the chief justices, it had extensive powers of deprivation and censure. Ostensibly innocuous, it was dominated by the Romanists: the aged Abp. Sancroft ceased to attend. It was seen to be a device for using the Royal Supremacy (which doctrinally James could not exercise) in the Roman interest. It began to interfere with the Univs. (see MAGDALEN COLLEGE, OXFORD) which resisted with sullen determination.

(9) James became aware of widespread Anglican alarm. In Apr. 1687 he sought to unite the wings against the centre by a Declaration (in Scotland, Letters) of Indulgence suspending the laws against both Papists and non-conformists. The prorogued parliament was dissolved and he prepared to pack the next one. Neither wing was tolerant enough to support, or strong enough to enforce a general tolerance. James sent a questionnaire to deputy-lieutenants and J.P.s which produced such adverse answers that it became necessary to postpone parliament for the year. The questionnaire advertised his intentions to every corner, but the non-conformists were not gained over because the attempt to indulge them was patently tactical, contrary, once again, to the King's own convictions and so certain to be reversed when opportunity offered.

(10) In Holland, James' son-in-law, William of Orange, was making precautionary contacts with leading English politicians through Dykeveld, a Dutch ambassador in London between Feb. and May 1687. The Prince's concern was the growingly aggressive intentions of Louis XIV in W. Europe and against Holland in particular. With the Emperor distracted by the Turks, who had besieged Vienna only four years ago, an understanding between Louis and James, the ruler of the other maritime trading power, might be mortally dangerous to the Dutch. As James became increasingly unpopular in England his apparent (but perhaps unreal) dependence on Louis increased. When the high Anglicans began to evince a desire for James' removal, that very desire increased William's need to abet them. James, meanwhile strengthened his army and recalled (Jan. 1688) the English regiments in Dutch pay. The Dutch let the officers go but not the men, and they began naval preparations, to which (Feb. 1688) James responded by ordering his own. The latter became known to the Dutch at about the time (May) when James issued his Second Declaration. This repeated the substance of the first and promised a parliament in Nov.

(11) Though a flash point had been reached and though William was being widely considered for the leadership against James, he was determined not to repeat Monmouth's mistakes and make an overt move, unless responsible English statesmen risked their necks by inviting him. Two events now precipitated the explosion. In mid-May James ordered the second Declaration to be read twice in all churches: the machinery of the Anglican church was to be used for its own destruction. The church naturally refused to comply: in London, with six exceptions, the clergy obeyed Compton, their suspended bishop and refused to read. Abp. Sancroft and six others respectfully petitioned that the order be withdrawn, on the ground that the Declaration represented an illegal use of the dispensing power. James decided that the church must be coerced. The Seven Bishops were arrested and tried for publishing a seditious libel. This act of aggression against the spiritual majority decided the principal statesmen to risk all. The E. of Danby, Adm. Russell, Henry Sidney, Bp. Compton, the Ds. of Shrewsbury and Devonshire and Ld. Lumley drafted their formal invitation to the Prince on the day that the Bps., amid crowd hysteria, were acquitted. But a second event ensured that the planned uprising would succeed. On 20 June James' Queen gave birth to a prince and it now seemed that the rule of James and his friends, instead of ending with his life, might be prolonged for ever. The dismissed Adm. Herbert brought the invitation and the allegiance of the fleet to William (July), who immediately started to recruit troops in N. Germany. The States-Gen. were persuaded to pay them (Sept.). In England panic seized the govt. James dismissed Sunderland and replaced Strickland with the protestant E. of Dartmouth. Compton was reinstated in his seat: all charters granted since 1679 were cancelled: Lds. Lieut: were dismissed and the Ecclesiastical Commission dissolved. It availed James nothing.

(12) William set sail and the wind which favoured

him held up James' fleet. The protestant army landed at Torbay on 5 Nov. without hindrance: of its 11,000 men only about 4000 were English or Scots. It began its slow but orderly advance through rain and mud next day. Ten days later Louis XIV declared war on the Dutch. James moved towards Salisbury which he reached by 29th. His system was collapsing behind him. Some western magnates had already joined William. Now Danby seized York; the Delameres raised Cheshire and Devonshire raised Nottingham. The next night James' best soldiers, Churchill and the D. of Grafton went over; the night after, P. George, husband of the Princess Anne. Finally Anne herself left Whitehall in disguise and with Bp. Compton took refuge at Chatsworth.

(13) James returned to London where, at a conference of peers, he promised a new parliament at once, a free pardon to William's supporters and negotiations; but in fact he had decided to seek the support of Louis XIV, and had already sent the baby P. of Wales to Portsmouth. His commissioners, Halifax, Nottingham and Godolphin, who met William at Hungerford (18 Dec.) were thus negotiating in the air. While William replied with military conditions for the impending election, James was ordering the E. of Dartmouth to take the P. of Wales to France. The Earl, however, refused, and the baby was brought back to London. On the night of 20 Dec. the family embarked at Sheerness: James having disbanded his army unpaid. The London streets were riotous: twenty-nine lords proclaimed their allegiance to William and took over the task of keeping order. Unfortunately some fishermen caught James before they discovered who he was, and brought him back. He proposed a conference which William refused. The Dutch guards now took over Whitehall where James was lodged, and next morning he left openly via Rochester and crossed over to France.

(14) Louis XIV helped him with money and manpower to raise a force. With this he reached Ireland in Mar. 1689.

(15) The effect of James' reign and that of Tyrconnel, his Lieutenant, had been to put the Irish governmental machine into the hands of the R. Catholics and to establish religious liberty by prerogative. The Irish regarded James as useful in their feud with those who had stolen their land. He thought of Ireland as a physical base for the recovery of England. They thought of him as a legal base for the recovery of their estates. Thus the Irish ("Patriot") parliament which James summoned (May) was a counter revolutionary body dedicated to sweeping away the Ascendancy, while James fought their war for them with French troops, Irish irregular levies and no artillery. The matter was serious because the Protestant strongholds in Ulster, Londonderry, Enniskillen, Crom, and Bangor held out and gave his enemies a dangerous foothold. They had to be blockaded because they could not be stormed, and in Aug. William's Gen. Schomberg landed with a regular army (mostly Dutch, Danish and Huguenot) and moved to Dundalk, while Col. Kirke broke the blockade of Londonderry. The two sides, however, were unwilling to risk a decision and sat down opposite each other in the rainy winter. So matters continued in military suspense while politicians enjoyed their revenge in Dublin and alienated the Anglo-Normans, until William landed at Carrickfergus in June 1690. James retired to the line of the R. Boyne and there, without delay, William defeated him (11 July 1690). James fled through Dublin to Kinsale and France; the army retired methodically south-westwards to Limerick and the Shannon, where it held out for almost a year.

(16) James disillusionment and early despair raised protestant moral but his supporters continued to fight openly both in Ireland and in the Scottish highlands until the B. of La Hogue (29 May 1692) ended their military hopes.

(17) Miscellaneous support for his cause, however, continued to be, both apparently and actually strong, and the court which Louis XIV maintained for him at St. Germain was frequented by some statesmen of repute as well as by malcontents, and adventurers. James was thus a French military or political asset because of his ability to foment discontent or disunity (*see* JACOBITES AND THEIR PRETENDERS).

JAMES (1499-1544) E. of MORAY, bastard of James IV of Scots by Janet Kennedy.

JAMES, The LORD (1531-70). *See* MARY Q. OF SCOTS-5 *et seq.*

JAMES EDWARD. See JACOBITES.

JAMES (FRANCIS) EDWARD the OLD PRETENDER (1688-1766). *See* JACOBITES.

JAMES OF ST. GEORGE (fl. 1261-98), Savoyard military architect and town planner, built Yverdon (Switz) and became known to Edward I on his way home in 1273. Edward employed him from 1277 to 1298 as Master of the King's Works in Wales. He built the combined town and castle complexes at Aberystwyth, Caernarvon, Conway, Flint and Rhuddlan, and the castles at Beaumaris, Builth, Criccieth, and Harlech of which he was constable. He also built additions to Linlithgow Castle (Scot.) His flair influenced building in Gascony, directly or through Bertrand and Bernard of St. George, probably his sons, who were employed there.

JAMES, American brothers **(1) William (1842-1910),** Prof. of physiology at Harvard, became interested in psychology and published his *Varieties of Religious Experience* (as Gifford lectures) in 1902 on the psychology of religion, with widespread controversial results. **(2) Henry (1843-1916),** lived in England from 1876 and was eventually naturalised. He became a novelist of the impact of Americans in Europe and the English social scene. Some of his works were widely acclaimed, but his later stylistic elaborations have attracted more professional critics than readers. Mark Twain preferred to be condemned to John Bunyan's Heaven than read a James novel.

JAMESON RAID (1895-6). (1). The *uitlanders* (non-Dutch Europeans) in the Boer republics (especially the Transvaal) represented the enterprise and capital, paid the taxes but had no rights. Numerous and noisy, they conspired (autumn 1895) against the Boer Govt. of Paul Kruger. The British and Boer Govts. knew this and Joseph Chamberlain (Colonial Secretary) planned to send a mediator to Johannesburg as soon as rebellion broke out. Cecil Rhodes, however, secretly prepared a small force under Dr. Jameson, in Bechuanaland, to invade the Transvaal in support of the conspirators.

(2) Before the mine could explode, a bitter dispute broke out with U.S.A. Venezuela claimed most of British Guiana, and had given a concession in the claimed area to an American syndicate. A U.S. presidential election was due in 1896 and Pres. Cleveland, to harness the anti-British vote, suddenly announced (17 Dec. 1895) that he would appoint a commission to settle the Guiana boundary and impose its award, if necessary by force, upon Britain. Kruger had been angling for German support, which was being offered in Oct. and there had been a tart exchange on the subject between the Foreign Office and the Wilhelmstrasse. France and Russia, for imperialist reasons, were hostile to Britain. Cleveland's announcement revealed Britain's diplomatic isolation. To the many American and German uitlanders, a British victory over the Boers seemed problematical. At the brink the uitlanders quarrelled on whether to hoist the British or the Transvaal flag. Jameson was due to move on 29 Dec. The conspiracy was paralysed, but nobody stopped Jameson. Chamberlain publicly repudiated him, ordered him back, but he went on, and was rounded up by the Boers at Doornkop (2 Jan. 1896). Rhodes resigned. Next day the German Kaiser William II sent a notorious telegram of congratulation to Kruger, and ordered E.

African troops to Delagoa Bay for transit by rail to Pretoria. The Portuguese, however, refused transit.

JAMESTOWN. See VIRGINIA.

JAMMU. See KASHMIR.

JANE or JOAN of SOMERSET (? -1445), queen of James I of Scots.

JANISSARIES (Turk: 'Yeni sheri' = new troops), were a regular Turkish force recruited from boy prisoners from 14th cent., and after about 1430 by a septennial levy of Christian children. They soon became a praetorian guard: their first revolt occurring in 1446 against the child Mehmet II. In 1481 they exacted the ruinous precedent of pay increases at imperial accessions; meantime they remained the most advanced field force in the world, but it paid Sultans to keep them safely and destructively at war. Many, e.g. were killed at Malta in 1565.

Though technically slaves, their privileges and wealth generated pressure to admit Turks, and the children of Janissaries themselves. This was done under Murad III (r. 1574-95). Numbers increased, efficiency declined, and the tendency to stay at home and make politics was accentuated. They overthrew Osman II in 1622, and Ibrahim I in 1648. Under Mohammed IV (r. 1648-87) they became of great importance to western powers because they monopolised power and trade, and the Turkish element elbowed out the rest. The child-levy was discontinued in 1700 and they deposed Mustafa II in 1703. They were now unpopular, besides no longer victorious. Ahmed III was deposed in 1730 against them, and there followed a long period of slow reform which they resisted. In 1807 they dethroned Selim III. His principal successor Mahmud II (r. 1808-39) was a match for them. He patiently created an alternative force, and in May 1826 slaughtered them all.

JANJIRA. See DECCAN STATES.

JAN MAYEN I, was claimed for a Dutch whaling Co. in 1614, but whales were exterminated by 1642 and it ceased to be occupied. It was occasionally visited after 1840. A weather station was established in 1921 and it was annexed by Norway in 1930.

JAPAN (1) traded regularly with S.E. Asia before 1636 but for political reasons Christian missions and books were banned in 1614; the HEIC ceased to come in 1623, and by 1636 foreign travel, and foreign contacts and publications, save through a tiny Dutch community on Deshima I. in Nagasaki harbour, were illegal. Under Yoshimune, the Eighth **Shogun** (1716-45) of the Tokugawa dynasty, the law against importing books (if not Christian) was repealed and by 1800 literate Japanese had a fair knowledge (through a Dutch filter) of western politics and science and there was a considerable trade in European specialities from telescopes to velvet. Confucianism of a sort being the official ideology of the **Bakufu** (the govt. of the Shoguns or hereditary Cs-in-C) there was a great aesthetic and philosophical dependence on China. Rumours of the British victory over China in the Opium War (1840-2) thus caused a sensation, but the visit in 1853 of the U.S. commodore Perry with an irresistible squadron caused interest at large and consternation at the Bakufu. The U.S.-Japanese T. of Kanegawa (1854) opened two ports to U.S. ships; in 1863 six more became treaty ports and the British bombarded Kagoshima.

(2) These events served to discredit the already shaken Bakufu. Japan was ready for a change. The 15th and last Shogun abdicated in 1868 after a short civil war, and the emperors, after centuries of impotence, resumed power **(The Meiji Restoration).** The shogun's vassals surrendered their fiefs; a modern administrative pattern was created, and missions of inquiry were sent to Europe and U.S.A. The leaders of the Restoration laid the foundations of a modern economy, created an army (and, after false starts, a navy), and in 1889 a parliamentary constitution.

(3) With industrialisation Japanese statesmen encountered a dominating problem, namely how to support a hardy, energetic and growing population in a group of mountainous islands virtually without natural resources. The apparent solution was to control nearby mainland sources of raw materials which could be imported, converted into manufactures and exported in exchange for secondary imports. The military outlook of the Bakufu lived on. It seemed natural to use force. The first such use, the seizure in 1879 of the Lu-Chu or Ryu-Kyu Is passed almost unnoticed. The victorious direct attack on China in 1894 was another matter. The western world became conscious that these people had leapt from feudalism to technology in a generation.

(4) Russia, France and Germany, however, combined to deprive the Japanese of most of the fruits as required by their first T. of Shimonoseki (Apr. 1895). By the second treaty (May 1895) they kept only Formosa (Taiwan). The dangers of diplomatic isolation were thus thrust upon them when the British were experiencing the same dangers at the other side of the world. There was a romantic sympathy between two crowded offshore island nations. There were commercial calculations too. The Japanese were buying British industrial equipment, railways and shipping. They also, before and after the Anglo-Japanese Alliance (Jan. 1902) bought battleships and cruisers and were taught how to build more.

(5) The govt. thought that control of Korea was vital both to defence and to expansion. On either assumption Japan was willing to fight Russia if that country continued to develop her hold on Manchuria and the Maritime Province. The object of the alliance with Britain was to ensure that the French fleet could not intervene in a Russo-Japanese War. The British, like everyone else, thought that the Japanese could not win and there-fore would not attack. They underestimated Russian incompetence and the difficulties of the Trans-Siberian railway, or the morale of the Japanese German-trained army and British equipped fleet. The RUSSO-JAPANESE WAR of 1904-5 was a debacle for Russia. It destroyed her fleet, and brought her to the verge of revolution. It also exhausted the still under-developed Japanese economy. It was a close run affair, but this time Japan had friends. The American-mediated T. of Portsmouth (Sept. 1905) put her firmly in control of Korea and Southern Karafuto (Sakhalin).

(6) The struggle with Russia was, however concerned with the fate of China; the war had been fought in the native territory of China's ruling Manchu dynasty. Japan needed to recuperate, but could not afford repose if she was to profit from the Chinese imperial collapse. Thus she avoided foreign controversies, built up her strength and fastened a purely colonial regime upon the Koreans. The morally powerful **Meiji Emperor** had died in 1912. The new **Taisho Emperor** was mentally unstable. World War I seemed a heaven-sent opportunity for the now untrammelled military and industrial groups to develop an aggressive policy against China while the world's back was turned. Japan paid lip-service to the Allied cause (and took Kiao-Chow, and the various German Pacific Is), but in Jan. 1915 issued her TWENTY-ONE DEMANDS to the struggling new Chinese republican govt. These revealed her intentions with great clarity, for they would, if enforced, have converted China into a political and economic protectorate. The move was, however, premature. The whole world's back was not turned, for the U.S.A. was not yet in the war. The demands were reduced and re-presented with an ultimatum whose effect was postponed by the diplomacy of the U.S.A., with whom a limiting agreement was concluded in Nov. 1917.

(7) To the Chinese the Twenty-One Demands had been a bitter insult which they did not forget. To the Japanese the modifications of the Versailles settlement (1920) introduced at the Washington Conference (Nov.

1921-Feb. 1922) created the same sense of frustration as the Second T. of Shimonoseki in 1902. The Allies handed back the ex-German possessions in China to the Chinese and Japan had perforce to do the same. This left the others with their many treaty ports and the Japanese with nothing. Much worse still, the British alliance was merged in a T. between Britain, France, USA and Japan to maintain the Pacific *status quo* and a Nine Power treaty to guarantee the independence of China, while the Naval Disarmament T. required Japan to limit her capital ships to 9, against the British and American 15. Behind the courtesies of diplomatic usage (not extended to Germany at Versailles) these were real impositions on Japan. At the same time (1922) the Taisho Emperor's eccentricities had forced the institution of a regency under the Crown Prince who became, as **Hirohito,** Emperor in 1926.

(8) The policy dilemma already mentioned (para 3) was now underlined in internal politics. There were too many people with nowhere to go and industrialisation was not raising the standard of living because raw materials could be imported only at high prices. Mob violence and depression were exacerbated by two particular events: in 1923 a furious earthquake devastated many of the cities, and from 1924 the U.S.A. refused to accept any Asiatic immigrants. Hence mainland imperialism, hitherto the policy of militarily trained intellectuals, acquired a popular appeal. Two successive pacific and civilian minded Prime Ministers (Hamaguchi 1930 and Inukai 1932) were murdered. The iron convention that the service Mins. must be officers was used, by threats of resignation, to force aggressive policies upon the cabinet. Moreover the sluggishness of the Taisho Emperor's reign had reduced the calming influence of the Throne.

(9) Inukai's murder was the result of his efforts to restrain the armed Manchurian adventure launched in 1931 by the local Japanese so-called **Kwantung Army.** The Japanese had invested heavily from their privileged position since the Russian war, in Manchurian primary resources, especially mines. This was thought to be under threat from Chinese railway and port development. The Kwantung Army without consulting the home govt. seized the railways and disarmed the Chinese garrisons. The Chinese appealed to the League of Nations, which set a timetable for Japanese withdrawal. The govt. accepted this but insisted on direct negotiation. This was a face-saver, for the Kwantung Army ignored the time-table, and the govt. could only prolong the negotiations while the army broadened its conquests. In truth the Kwantung Army was a species of independent state. By 1932 it had overrun most of South Manchuria including the Chinese military H.Q.

(10) Its success converted or silenced opposition. The watershed was the turn of the years 1931-2. A fleet and army from home attacked Shanghai, while the last Chinese (i.e. Manchu) Emperor (Pu-Yi) was set up as a puppet in a new Manchurian state called **Manchukuo.** The League of Nations had sent a commission to Manchuria under Ld. Lytton which, in Oct. 1932 proposed the usual compromises: there were to be safeguards for Japanese so-called rights in a Manchuria still under Chinese sovereignty. Events had anticipated this nonsense. The Japanese needed no safeguards and had recognised Manchukuo. They also observed that China (with which they had insisted on negotiating direct) had no effective govt. capable of making an agreement. Western powers, with their treaty ports and gunboats on Chinese rivers, knew that this was true but could not say so. The home govt., now committed to the Kwantung Army, reinforced it, resigned from the League and occupied the coal-rich province of Jehol, which was incorporated in Manchukuo in 1933. In 1934 it denounced the Washington naval limitation treaty and became free to build as many warships and of whatever

size and design it pleased. In 1935 it bought out the Russian share of the Chinese Eastern Rly, and a pro-Japanese splinter govt. was set up in the W. areas of N. China. In 1936 a similar regime appeared in Chahar and an anti-Communist pact was signed with Germany. Meanwhile warship building was accelerated, particularly aircraft carriers. Western powers took no serious precautions against the obvious.

(11) In 1937 there was full-scale war (called the **China Incident)** beginning with a staged incident in July, the seizure of Peking in Aug., of Shanghai in Nov. and of Nanking in Dec. The Chinese govt. escaped to Chungking. In Oct. 1938 the Japanese occupied Canton and Hankow. By 1939 their main objective was to stop supplies to Chungking through British and French territory. They seized the I. of Hainan and their troops appeared on the Kowloon frontier of Hong Kong and along the frontiers of Tong-King.

(12) The occupation of Chinese ports and cities had not brought victory. There had always been a school which favoured southward moves against the tropical and oil producing areas of Indonesia and S.E. Asia, and now that further Chinese campaigns might be costly and protracted, a quick profit, mainly at Dutch expense, might be a better investment. The European war was a welcome distraction: the French and Dutch debacle an unexpected bonus. A southern offensive thus presented no serious military and naval problems and would further isolate Chungking (to which the British had reopened the Burma road) and engross the immense Siamese rice-bowl, but it would certainly bring in the U.S.A. which was growing restive about its interests and investments in the area. It was decided to deal a knockout blow at the U.S. fleet just as or just before the southern attacks were launched (*see* WORLD WAR II). In fact the knock-out blow was only a very partial success. The services had miscalculated, and lost the war well before the atom bombs were dropped on Hiroshima (6 Aug. 1945) and Nagasaki (9th). It was on that same 9th that the Russians hurriedly invaded Manchuria in order to have a place at the peace settlement. The ruined Japanese accepted the Allied demand for unconditional surrender under the Emperor's moral pressure on 14 Aug. and actually surrendered aboard the U.S.S. *Missouri,* on 2 Sept. 1945.

(13) Between 1945 and 1951 the Americans, under Gen. MacArthur ruled Japan and tried, but partly failed, to introduce their ideas. The Japanese enacted an American style constitution; the main war leaders were tried by a War Crimes Tribunal, the armed forces were dissolved and millions of Japanese driven from S.E. Asia and the former colonies such as Taiwan. On the other hand the Imperial institution (theoretically shorn of its divinity) remained, as did the Meiji structure of govt. and the bureaucracy. Economic reconstruction, however, proceeded very quickly with huge American subventions and investment converting the great armaments firms to peaceful uses and great landed estates being divided up between small farmers. This second industrial revolution brought the usual difficulties of which urban immigration was the most spectacular, and if the standard of living apparently rose, it brought, too, a recurrence of the original dilemma, but without the warlike means to solve it. The 1950s saw many strikes. An alternative was accordingly tried in the international post-war effort to reduce the obstacles to trade and capital movement. The profits of the revitalised industries were invested abroad in a new 'investment colonialism'. While reparations treaties signed with Burma (1954), the Philippines (1956) and Indonesia (1958) imposed new if expected burdens, the policy of industrial development and foreign investment had gigantic successes. Throughout the 1960s the economy expanded at about 11% a year. Japan became a world industrial power and could demand where previously it had been able only to negotiate. The

U.S. war in Vietnam had become increasingly unpopular and the govt. used huge student demonstrations to secure the return of the Bonn and Ryu-Kyu archipelagoes.

(14) The fertile atmosphere of headlong growth bred scandals which rocked the reputations of politicians. It also resulted in economic halts and even setbacks being acutely felt. Moreover the Showa Era ended with the death of the Emperor Hirohito (Jan 1989) and the commencement of the Heisei era of his son Akihito. There was a feeling of *fin-de-siècle* despite the new affluence. In truth the country, as the world's greatest trader had become sensitively vulnerable to world economic movements, and from 1989 there was a world recession.

JARROW. *See* BEDE; BISCOP. In the 19th cent. the town became a coal and shipbuilding port whose prosperity continued until the end of World War I. Unemployment was disastrous in 1930s and led to the hunger marches on London. *See* DURHAM- 13.

JATS are Hindu cultivators scattered throughout northern India. They entered politically organised life in 1681, when they rebelled against Aurungzeb's religious intolerance. The rebellion petered out in 1721. In the 1740s their leader, Baden Singh, established the state of Bharatpur, and others set up Mursan and Patiala. Bharatpur was stormed by the British in 1826 and became a subsidiary ally. This, and the Patiala treaty ended Jat separatism.

JAVA. *See* INDONESIA.

JAY'S TREATY. John Jay (1745-1829) was American Minister to Spain from 1780 to 1782, a peace commissioner to Britain in 1783 and Secretary of Foreign Affairs to the Continental Congress from 1784 to 1789 when Washington appointed him first C.J. of the U.S. Supreme Court. In this position he was sent specially to Britain in 1793 to solve residual difficulties arising from the aftermath of the Rebellion. The British had not (as they had agreed in 1783) evacuated their military posts in the old North West: their claim to seizure and impressment at sea was endangering American trade, and the settlement of pre-revolutionary debts remained unsolved. Under *Jay's Treaty* of 1794 they undertook to give up the military posts by 1796, to allow a limited U.S. trade to the West Indies, and to give the U.S.A. most favoured nation treatment in trade. The pre-revolutionary debts were to be settled on their merits by mixed commissions and the problem of impressment was sidestepped. Though criticised on both sides of the Atlantic, the treaty lowered the temperature.

JEDBURGH (Scot). The Augustinian priory was founded by David I in 1118 and in 1147 became an abbey. It was burned in border warfare in 1523 and suppressed in 1559. The lands passed to the crown and in 1637 were granted to the Es. of Lothian. Its people were said to hang suspects first and try them later. This was called JEDBURGH JUSTICE.

JEDBURGH, Lord. *See* KER OF FERNIEHURST-6.

JEFFERSON, Thomas (1743-1826), (1) became a member of the Virginian House of Burgesses in 1769. He supported the view that Virginia owed allegiance only to the Crown, and that Parliament had no authority there. His *Summary view of the Rights of America* (1774) gave him the intellectual leadership of the rebels, and was the distant origin of the 20th cent. British doctrine of Dominion status. As a member of the continental Congress he drafted the Declaration of Independence. He then returned to Virginia politics and was Governor from 1779 to 1781. In 1783 he re-entered the Congress. He was chairman of the committee on the Peace Treaty; he drafted the plans for the decimal coinage and also the principles behind the great Ordinances of 1784, 1785 and 1787 which regulated the settlement of the Public Domains (i.e. the territories outside the existing states) and the method by which territories should acquire

statehood. In 1784 he went to France with Adams and Franklin to negotiate the commercial treaty of 1784, and remained there as Min. until 1789 when he became Sec. of State.

(2) His differences with Alexander Hamilton (Sec: of the Treasury) in cabinet and, through partisans, in the public press eventually generated the American party system. Jefferson's *Democratic Republicans* favoured an educated individualistic society based upon agriculture; Hamilton's *Federalists* a more complex organism based upon mercantile and industrial development. During the Wars of the French revolution, those who thought of revolution as essentially a movement against tyranny supported the Democratic Republicans, while those who saw it as an economic struggle joined the Federalists. Jefferson resigned in 1793, and Jay's Treaty may be regarded as a Hamiltonian victory.

(3) In 1796 he became vice-president and in 1801 after an electoral tie he was selected (with Hamilton's help) for the Presidency by the House of Representatives after 35 ballots. He appointed Madison as his Sec. of State. In 1803 he made the Louisiana Purchase and followed it up in 1804 with the Lewis and Clark Expedition. His policies towards the European Wars were less effective and the self denial principles of the Non-Intercourse Act, 1806, and the Embargo of 1807 damaged his political position without protecting American trade. After his retirement in 1808 he was much consulted by his successors, Madison and Monroe, whose international policies continued his own. Thus, after Washington, he was the strongest influence in forming the international status of the U.S.A.

(4) Monticello, his beautiful Virginia house contains many examples of his inquiring and scientific mind and his interest in useful contrivances.

JEFFREYS, George (1648-89) 1st Ld. JEFFREYS OF WEM (1685) (known as 'Judge Jeffreys') was sol-gen to the D. of York in 1677 and Recorder of London from 1678. He showed his well-known savagery in the 'Popish Plot' cases (1679) but was forced to resign in 1680 for obstructing petitions for the reassembly of parliament. He successfully pressed *Quo Warranto* proceedings against the City of London in 1682 and became C.J. of the King's Bench, though Charles II thought little of him. James II used him as one of the most ruthless of his executives and consulted him frequently. In 1685 he held the 'Bloody Assize' (q.v.) in the west country after Monmouth's rebellion. Soon after, he became Ld. Chanc. and in 1686 Chief of the Ecclesiastical Commission. Active in reforming municipal corporations in the R. Catholic interest in 1687, he was also a member of the Council of Five during James II's absence with the army in 1688. At the Revolution he was arrested at his own request to protect him from mob violence and died in the Tower.

JEHANGIR (1587-1627). *See* MOGULS.

JELLICOE, John Rushworth (1859-1935) Vist. (1918) E. JELLICOE (1925), had a varied naval career including presence in the *Victoria* when she was sunk by the *Camperdown* (1893) and the conversion of Wei-hai-wei into a British naval base (1900). He was also C-of-Staff of the International naval brigade in the Boxer rising (1900), and Director of naval ordnance (1905-7) besides holding increasingly important admiralty and sea-going appointments. In Aug. 1914 he took command of the Grand Fleet. He was in personal command in the great B. of Jutland (June 1916) where, despite considerable losses, he was able, with cautious tactics, to maul the German High Seas Fleet to such purpose that it never challenged battle again. In Dec. 1916 he became First Sea Ld., but was dismissed in Dec. 1917, as lacking in energy in dealing with the submarine crisis. Nevertheless his reputation stood high. He was acclaimed during a naval tour of the Commonwealth and his findings led to the establishment of Indian and New Zealand navies, and the foundation of the base at Singapore. He was Gov-Gen. of New Zealand from 1920 to 1924.

JENA (Ger.) The Univ. was opened in 1558. Hegel, Schelling, Schiller and Schlegel taught there, and Karl Marx obtained a degree there.

JENKINS, Sir Leoline (1623-85), exerted a lasting influence on the development and organisation of English Law. He became Principal of Jesus College, Oxford, from 1661 to 1673, was dep. prof. of civil law from 1662, Judge of the Admiralty Court from 1665 and of the Canterbury Prerogative Court from 1669. He was an M.P. from 1673. He represented England at the Congresses of Cologne (1673) and Nymwegen (1676-9), as a mediator between Denmark and Brandenburg and between Sweden and Holland. He was also concerned in drafting the Statute of Frauds (1677) and the much less permanent Statute of Distributions (1678). In 1680 he became a Secretary of State and privy councillor and led the opposition to the Exclusion Bill. He retired in 1684.

JENKINS, Robert (?-?). This master mariner's **EAR** was either cut off by a Spanish captain at Havana in 1731, or lost in the pillory later. In either case he appeared as one of the opposition's witnesses before a Commons Committee on Spanish behaviour in the Caribbean and inflamed their passions with the ear and the observation that, 'he committed his soul to God and his cause to his country'. Hence the name of the war of 1739. *See* WARS OF 1739-40.

JENKINS, Roy (1920-) Ld. JENKINS of HILLHEAD (1987) son of a Welsh M.P., become an M.P. in 1948. He was Home Sec. under Wilson in 1965-7 and Ch. of the Exch. till the Labour defeat in 1970. He returned as Home Sec. in 1974 but when Callaghan took the Labour Party leadership in 1976, Jenkins became Pres. of the European Commision. Returning from Brussels in Mar 1982 he, with David Owen, William Rodgers and Shirley Williams launched the Social Democratic Party which, after various electoral pacts with the Liberals, was swallowed by them in 1987.

JENKINSON, Anthony (?-1611), explorer for trade, got permission to trade in Turkey from Suleiman the Magnificent in 1553 and in 1558 commanded the Muscovy Co's Russian expedition. He rounded the North Cape, sailed up the Northern Dvina, sledged to Moscow, where he was well received by the Czar, went down the Volga to Astrakhan and penetrated to Bokhara. Failing to gain entry to Persia he came home *via* Moscow in 1560. In 1561 he nonetheless returned bringing letters both to the Czar and the Shah, but again failed to open up trade with Persia. In May 1565 he sent a memorial to Elizabeth I about the possibility of a northabout passage to China, fortunately without result. In 1567 he obtained a Russian grant of trading rights for the Muscovy Co. and this was reconfirmed in 1572. In 1577 he went on a special mission to Emden to treat with the Danes on navigational rights in the Baltic. *See* HANSE.

JENKINSON (1) Charles (1727-1808), 1st Ld. HAWKESBURY (1786), 1st E. of LIVERPOOL (1796), a royal friend like Bute, was master of the mint in 1775, Sec. at War in 1778 and Pres. of the Board of Trade in 1786. His *s*. **(2) Robert Banks (1770-1828) Ld. HAWKESBURY (1803)** by acceleration, was in Paris on Bastille day (1789) and was an M.P. from 1790. He became a member of the Board of Control in 1799, was Foreign Sec. under Addington in 1801 to 1803, and Home Sec. under Pitt from 1804 to 1806, and from 1807 to 1809. He was Sec. for War and Colonies from 1809 to 1812 when he became Prime Min. *See* LIVERPOOL'S GOVT 1812-27.

JENNER, Edward (1749-1823), a Gloucestershire country doctor, was unaware of the Turkish method of inoculation against small-pox but, noticing the immunity of milkmaids to the disease, elaborated vaccination as a preventative in 1796, and published his findings between 1798 and 1800. He received parliamentary grants in 1802 and 1806 and founded the National Vaccine Establishment in 1808. He had interviews with Czar and the King of Prussia in 1814 and vaccination became compulsory during the next 20 years in several German and Scandinavian states. It was made compulsory in Britain in 1853.

JENNINGS, Sir Ivor (1903-65) K.C. (1949), initially lecturer and reader in Law at London Univ. He was principal of the Ceylon Univ. College from 1940, and as Vice-Ch. of the Univ. of Ceylon from 1942-55, was an influential adviser of Ceylonese ministers on steps toward independence. He drafted the Pakistan Constitution on 1955 and that of Malaya in 1957. During the period 1955 to 1958 he was also chairman of the R. Commission on Common Lands, from 1957 Master of Trinity Hall, Cambridge and Vice-Ch. of Cambridge Univ. from 1961 to 1963. At once one of the most distinguished and least assuming public servants of his day, he died in considerable pain. He wrote four famous books, *The Law and the Constitution* (5th Ed. 1959), *Cabinet Government* (3rd Ed. 1958), *Parliament* (2nd Ed. 1958), and *Party Politics* (1962).

JENYNS, Soame (1704-87), politician, poet and moralist was an M.P. from 1742-1780 and a Commissioner of Trade from 1753. His *Free Inquiry into the Nature and Origin of Evil* (1757), reviewed by Dr. Johnson, is still remembered.

JERBOA or DESERT RAT, a leaping rodent very common in Cyrenaica, was taken as a badge or nick-name by the British 8th Army in World War II.

JERMYN (1) Henry (?-1684) Ld. JERMYN (1643) E. of St. ALBANS (1660), became M.P. for Liverpool and Vice-Chamberlain to Q. Henrietta Maria in 1628. A skilled courtier and gallant, he became her Master of the Horse in 1629 despite amorous scandals, and took a leading part in the first army plot which raised much suspicion against the Queen. He fled to France and returned only in 1643 to escort her to Oxford. He was personally brave, but his activities were more diplomatic than military. In particular he proposed a Dutch marriage for the Prince of Wales, raised French finance for the Queen and suggested abandoning the Anglican church for Scottish support. His political influence declined after Charles II's first Scottish failure, though he remained a conspicuous court figure under the Restoration. He was Ld. Chamberlain from 1671 to 1674. His nephew **(2) Henry (1636-1708) 1st Ld. DOVER (1685)** obtained a post in the D. of York's exiled household in 1652 and remained one of the latter's supporters in the Exclusion controversies, and during his reign as James II. James even committed his children to his care at the Revolution. In 1690 he submitted to William III and was pardoned. Like his cousin he was notoriously amorous. He was also an exceptional horseman, once riding 20 miles in an hour for a bet.

JEROME, St. (?347-?420). *See* BIBLE; DAMASUS.

JERSEY. *See* CHANNEL IS.

JERSEY. *See* VILLIERS.

JERUSALEM. *See* CRUSADES; OUTREMER; PALESTINE; WORLD WAR I-12.

JERUSALEM CHAMBER. This 14th cent. room in the Deanery of Westminster Abbey was called after tapestries portraying Jerusalem which once hung there. Henry IV died there in 1413. The Crown is lodged there on the night before a coronation.

JERVAULX ABBEY (Yorks.) was a Cistercian house founded in 1156. Implicated in the Pilgrimage of Grace, the last abbot was hanged in 1537.

***JERVIS BAY*, H.M.S.,** a converted merchantman, saved most of a convoy in Nov. 1940 by engaging single-handed the powerful German pocket battleship *Adm. Scheer* and keeping her away for two hours before she was herself sunk.

JERVIS (1) John (1735-1823), 1st E. of St. VINCENT (1797) rose from the lower deck, and being much trusted by Gen. James Wolfe in 1759 led the advance transport squadron past Quebec, and carried the despatches to Ld. Amherst in 1760. He visited the Baltic ports in 1774 and the western French ports in 1775 and commanded the *Foudroyant* at Ushant (1778) and at the three reliefs of Gilbraltar (1780-1782). He was an M.P. in 1783 and 1784. In 1794 he and Sir Chas. Grey took Martinique and Guadeloupe. He began his victorious period as C-in-C Mediterranean in 1795. He defeated the Spaniards at St. Vincent in Feb. 1797 and sent Nelson to win the spectacular victory at Aboukir (The Nile) (1 Aug. 1798). After suppressing a mutiny, ill health forced him to go home in 1799 where, after an interval, he took command of the Channel Fleet. In 1801 he became Addington's 1st. Ld. of the Admiralty, but supported the naval policy against the Armed Neutrality which culminated in Nelson's victory at Copenhagen in Apr. 1801. He strengthened the system of inshore blockade (*see* BLOCKADE, SAILING, NAVAL FEATURES), but drifted into a quarrel with Pitt over the peculation's of Pitt's friend Dundas (Vist. Melville). The commission of inquiry which resulted in Melville's impeachment also resulted in reforms at the Admiralty. Pitt retaliated by accusing St. Vincent of not building enough ships, and the admiral then refused to serve under him. He resumed command of the Channel Fleet after Pitt's death. He retired in 1807. His second cousin **(2) Sir John (1802-56)** was liberal M.P. for Chester from 1832 to 1850; he was Att. Gen. under Russell from 1846 to 1850 when he became Pres. of the Common Law Pleadings Commission and C.J. of the Common Pleas. His work strongly influenced the development of modern legal practice.

JESSEL, Sir George (1824-83), a chancery barrister, was liberal M.P. for Dover from 1868 to 1873, and Sol. Gen. from 1871 to 1873 when he became both Master of the Rolls and working head of the Patent Office. He was one of the greatest equity lawyers.

JESSE WINDOWS displayed, commonly in stained glass, the descent of Christ from King David son of Jesse, and were teaching diagrams of Old Testament history. There are such mediaeval windows at Chartres and Wells Cathedrals, a 19th Cent. copy of a huge one at Winchester College, and a Gothic sculptured one at Dorchester on Thames.

JEST BOOKS, were collections of jokes (practical or spoken) ascribed to an individual such as James I's notoriously humorous Calvinist tutor George Buchanan, or anthologies such as *Westminster Drollery or a Choice Collection of the Newest Songs and Poems both at Courts and Theatre* by a Person of Quality (1671). They flourished between 1525 and 1740. Though collectively they illustrate the ephemeral and fragile nature of humour, it is still possible to find something amusing in most of them.

JESTER (Lat: Gestum = a happening, plur: Gesta = deeds, hence historical events and Fr: *Chanson de Geste,* a ballad or epic). A jester was not necessarily a funny man but, at first, a kind of public historian who in an illiterate age relied on his memory, which was often assisted by versification. He rehearsed his lord's merits, achievements and lineage. Accuracy was desired but some plausible embroidery was doubtless acceptable. His function sometimes involved comment or wit and so he might become a FOOL (q.v.). Alternatively his mode of expression might make him a poet (A.S.), Saga Man (Scandinavian) or Bard (Celtic). Sometimes he was a singer.

JESUITS or SOCIETY OF JESUS (*see* IGNATIUS LOYOLA, ST.), was founded, with the aim of supporting the Pope and the Church against heresy and converting the heathen. To the normal religious vows was added another to go instantly wherever the Pope might require for the salvation of souls. The society was organised under an elected *General* whose power, under the Pope, was absolute, and its members were forbidden to take any ecclesiastical dignity save one imposed under pain of mortal sin by the Pope himself.

The society began by teaching, and by St. Ignatius' death (1556) had missions in America, Africa and Asia, besides establishments in Europe. It began to acquire a formidable reputation for scholarship, under Diego LAYNEZ (Gen. 1558-65) and St. FRANCIS BORGIA (Gen. 1565-72). In 1578 Jesuits reached England where they were held in abhorrence as advocating the papal right of deposition and the assassination of excommunicated rulers, or disliked for being too clever. To underpin their subversive plans, they maintained an English College at Douai whence graduate seminarists were sent to England. Some 40 of these including Edmund Campion and Robert Southwell died in the hands of the Elizabethan govt.

By 1599 they had elaborated their educational system based on the classics and formalised a teaching method embodied in the *Ratio Studiorum* (Lat = systematised studies). By 1650 their missionaries were found all over the globe. They had a marked habit of associating with the great, the powerful or the rich through whom they expected (not without reason) to influence the masses. They were thus widely, and correctly, believed to be involved in politics and this tended to obscure their other achievements as educators, social workers and historians. In the area now covered by modern Paraguay they administered a virtually independent welfare state (The Misiones) for over two cents.

By the 18th cent. many rationalist statesmen of R. Catholic background nonetheless disapproved of them. In 1759 Pombal expelled them from Portugal; in 1764 Aranda from Spain and Louis XV from France. These events naturally involved their wide overseas dominions. To prevent all missionary work being opposed by civil authority, Clement XIV suppressed the society by the bull *Dominus ac Redemptor* (July 1773) but left its execution to the bishops. The result was that Jesuits survived in or migrated to non-R. Catholic countries, notably Prussia and Russia whose rulers appreciated their intellectual gifts, and Austria where Papal encroachments were never tolerated. They gradually revived, and in 1814 the Society was officially reanimated in Pius VII's bull *Sollicitudo omnium ecclesiarum* (Lat: The care for all churches). It was during their period of official non-existence that they acquired their first English base at Stonyhurst (Lancs.).

JETHOU. See CHANNEL IS.

JET PROPULSION. Frank Whittle patented certain relevant inventions in 1930, but the first jet aircraft was the Heinkel 178 which flew in 1939. Whittle's Gloster E 28/29 first flew in 1941. The Germans had an operational squadron of Messerschmitt 262 fighters. These predated the British Gloster Meteor but were less reliable. The first commercial jet aircraft was the British De Havilland *Comet* in 1952. The gas turbine, the basic element of jet propulsion was also used in the very successful Vickers *Viscount* to turn its propellers, but thereafter the British aircraft industry slowly lost its lead in this general field.

JETSAM. See DROITS OF ADMIRALTY.

JEUNE (1) Francis (1806-68), was Secretary to Sir J. Colborne in Canada in 1832, Dean of Jersey from 1838 to 1843, Master of Pembroke College Oxford from 1843 to 1864 and then Bp. of Peterborough. His *s.* **(2) Francis Henry (1843-1905) 1st Ld. St. HELIER (1905)** was counsel for the Tichborne claimant in 1871 and became Pres. of the Probate Divorce and Admiralty Division of the High Court in 1892.

JEWEL, John (1522-71), Oxford theologian, Public Orator and fellow of Corpus Christi, resigned at Q. Mary's accession and fled to Frankfurt in 1555 where he associated with Richard Cox, and then moved to Strasbourg at the invitation of Peter Martyr. On learning at Zürich of Queen Mary's death, he returned to England. A protestant disputant at the Westminster Conference of 1559, he became one of Q. Elizabeth's new bishops (of Salisbury) in 1560. In 1562 he issued his *Apologia pro Ecclesia Anglicana* (Lat = Case for the Anglican Church), a foundation statement of the Anglican position against Rome. He encouraged and protected Richard Hooker whom he educated in his house and sent to Oxford. He also re-established a major library at Salisbury. In 1571 he was appointed to supervise the revision of the XXXIX Articles but died before anything could be done.

JEWS, before 1120, being religious and civil aliens were hated and regarded as chattels belonging to nobody, but because their abilities as merchants, financiers and physicians made them valuable they were partially protected by the Kings. William I introduced them from Rouen. Henry I allowed them to settle in important towns notably London, Oxford, Canterbury, York and Lincoln and gave them trading rights and a certain autonomy. Their average lending rates were about 44% (cf. the 24% of the modern credit card co.) and they could retain land which had been pledged to them for a debt. In return the Kings imposed loans and later tallaged them, besides acquiring their debts when they died. They were thus a species of royal indirect financial agents and collectors and correspondingly unpopular. For the Saladin Tithe of 1188 they were assessed at only one quarter of their wealth. In the generally anti-semitic atmosphere of the Third Crusade there were, not surprisingly, serious anti-Jewish riots which damaged the royal interests, so that a special Exchequer of Jews was set up to deal with their affairs and those of their debtors. Associated with this were local *Archae* (eventually 29) or registries of Jewish bonds where receipts and *starra* (assignments) had to be enrolled. Guardians for them were appointed in 1198; these were effectively specialist Exchequer judges.

Protected as useful to the revenue, the protection was seldom in practice complete. In 1144 the Norwich Jews had to take refuge in the castle when accused of murdering a boy (Little St. William) for some ritual purpose. This was the earliest of a continuous series of harassments which frightened and impoverished them. An attempt to abolish usury was made in Magna Carta (1215) but had to be repealed in 1216 because of its effect on the revenue. Meanwhile Crusades, religious prejudice and racism bore upon them with increasing weight despite the royal interest. Ordinances against them were issued in 1153 and 1211. Usury was prohibited again in 1295. In 1290 they were all expelled.

For four centuries almost the only Jews in England were connected with foreign embassies. The memory of them disappeared and with it anti-semitism. A few *marranos* reached England from Spain after the Spanish expulsions of 1492 and they tried to secure permission to return from the Commonwealth (when it was refused) but after the Restoration they began to settle, especially *Sephardim* from Portugal after Charles II's Braganza marriage. In 1674 he issued a prerogative order in Council to protect them, and this remained the foundation of their status until their religious disabilities were abolished by statute in 1846. Their political status remained inferior until 1858 when the Jewish Relief Act permitted them to take oaths of office in their own manner. *See* AARON OF LINCOLN.

JEW, WANDERING. An anti-semitic 13th cent. anecdote of a pitiless Jew who told Jesus Christ when resting on the way to his crucifixion to 'get on with it' and was condemned to find no rest till the Second Coming.

JEX-BLAKE, Sophia Louisa (1840-1912), a mathematician, began to study medicine in Boston (Mass) in 1866 and matriculated at Edinburgh medical faculty in 1869. She founded the London School of Medicine for Women in 1874, qualified in medicine at Dublin in 1877 and in 1878 opened a dispensary for women and

children in Edinburgh in 1878. Eight years later she opened another school for women there. Her remarkable career exemplifies the contemporary obstacles to women's medical practice in England and some ways of surmounting them.

JHANSI (India). This small Maratha state passed under British protection in 1819 and was annexed by Dalhousie in 1854 under the doctrine of lapse. The dowager Rani, Lakshmi Bai, joined the mutineers in 1858, defended Jhansi and Kalpi against the British, drove their ally Scindiah from Gwalior, and proclaimed Nana Saheb, Peishwa. She was killed fighting as a lancer at the B. of Kotah on 17th June, 1858 and is an Indian national heroine.

JIBUTI. *See* SOMALILAND; SOMALIA.

JINGO-ISM. In 1878 certain Tories favoured sending the fleet to Turkey to resist the Russians and a song became current in the music halls:

We don't want to fight, but by Jingo, if we do
We've got the men; We've got the ships and we've got the money too.

A 'jingo' was thus an aggressive patriot.

JINDAN KAUR. *See* SIKHS-4,5.

JINNAH, Mohammed Ali (1876-1948), Qaid-i-Azam (= Great Leader) opposed the Moslem League's campaign for separate Indian electorates in 1906, became a member of the Imperial Legislative Council in 1910, but joined the League in 1913. He was pres. of it in 1916, when it concluded the LUCKNOW PACT with the Indian National Congress. This was momentous. Congress agreed to separate electorates and the League to more radical constitutional reforms than it had previously contemplated. The former provision ensured that the gap between Hindus and Moslems would remain open: the latter that Moslem political security would gradually weaken. The formation of Pakistan as a place of refuge was the only eventual possibility. Jinnah, however, did not seem to see this; he was a leading nationalist spokesman in the Montague-Chelmsford discussions; he resigned from the Council in 1919 against the Rowlatt legislation and for a while lost influence because he would not support Congress' tactics, nor give way to the more conservative Moslems. He slowly reached the conclusion that Moslem safety depended upon a separate strong organisation which could bargain with the Congress on equal terms, but in 1923 entered the Legislative Assembly as an opposition spokesman. This fundamental contradiction led to a decline in Moslem influence, so that by the 1927 All Parties Conference he was having to make sweeping Moslem demands in order to keep the League alive. Since Congress could not accept his demands and he had kicked away his British 'prop', the Moslem League became increasingly ineffectual. In 1929 Jinnah left India for England where, though he took part in the Round Table Conference (1930-2), he remained until 1934.

The League was moribund when he returned, and he had to rebuild it, and meanwhile co-ordinate its policies with Congress. By 1937 he had an organisation and an opportunity. Congress insisted on merger rather than alliance, and some Congress Hindu provincial govts. excited Moslem suspicions by their actions. His appeal to communal prejudice won thousands of adherents and saved the independence of his party. It also encouraged the first open demands (1938) for PAKISTAN i.e. a Moslem homeland. When the Congress ministries resigned (Dec. 1938) against the war, the Moslem League celebrated a Day of Deliverance. Partition was now a major issue. In the Lahore Resolution (Mar. 1940) the League demanded a handover of political power to independent Moslem states in the N.W. and N.E. and cast eyes on Hyderabad. The war put these aspirations into abeyance, but Jinnah ensured that they would not be forgotten, and after the cabinet mission's proposals of 1946, organised Direct Action Day (Aug.), won all the Moslem reserved seats, and got the right to nominate all the Moslem Mins. in the interim Govt. Since it was not his intention now to help to govern a united India, their presence was a mere wrecking device. Civil war had already broken out, and communal divisions were encouraged in army and police, which were often unable to cope with the disorders. Vast numbers died in fighting or migration or of starvation or disease, but Pakistan was formed, and Jinnah took the post of Gov-Gn. with Mins. who were merely his advisers. He was not able to enjoy his pre-eminence for long.

J[H]IZYA. A poll tax levied by Moslem rulers on non-Moslem men capable of bearing arms, at a rate varying with the productivity of their land. Its late imposition (1660) by Aurungzib in India emphasised the widening gap between Moguls and the Hindu subject majority.

JOAN or JOANNA of ACRE (1272-1307) *d.* of Edward I, after five years in Spain was betrothed to Hartmann of Habsburg in 1279, but in 1290 married Gilbert of Clare. After the latter's death she married Ralph of Monthermer in 1297.

JOAN (THE FAIR MAID OF KENT) (1328-85), *d.* of Edmund of Woodstock., E. of Kent, was widely adored for her beauty and charm. She was brought up by Q. Philippa, contracted and cohabited with Sir Thomas Holland, and then contracted with William 2nd E. of Salisbury. A papal arbitration followed in which she was awarded to Holland (1349) and in 1352 she succeeded to the earldom and in 1360 Sir Thomas died. In 1361 she married the Black Prince who had courted her in 1348. The couple lived in Aquitaine until 1371 where she bore Richard II. She acted as his guardian after the Prince's death in 1376 until his accession. In 1378 she intervened in proceedings against Wyclif; some of her entourage being Lollards. During the Peasants' Revolt she escaped with kisses and in 1385 she posted back and forth between Wallingford and Pontefract in successful efforts to prevent a conflict between Richard and John of Gaunt. She is said to have died of grief at Richard's determination to slay her son John Holland.

JOAN or JOANNA (1165-99), *d.* of Henry II, married William II of Sicily in 1177. He died in 1189 and the new King Tancred secluded her. Her brother Richard I rescued her on his way to Palestine in 1190. She went with him and in 1196 married Raymond VI of Toulouse. *See* CRUSADES-13.

JOAN or JOANNA (1210-38), *d.* of K. John was betrothed to Hugh of Lusignan, but in 1221 married Alexander II of Scotland. She died, however, in England.

JOAN or JOANNA, ANNA or JANET (?-1237), a Princess of N. Wales and reputed *d.* of K. John, married in 1206 Llewelyn ap Iorwerth. She acted as a mediator between him and John in 1211 and between him and Henry III in 1225.

JOAN of NAVARRE (?1370-1437), third wife of John IV, D. of Brittany (?-1399) was regent for John V until 1403, when she married Henry IV of England, and committed her children to Burgundian wardship. She lost all influence in Brittany and when Henry died in 1413 she became the object of much hostility in England too, being even imprisoned for witchcraft from 1419 to 1422. Thereafter she lived in retirement.

JOAN OF THE TOWER (1321-62), *d.* of Edward II was married to David Bruce, also a child, in 1327, and went to France with him when Baliol seized the crown in 1332. She lived at Chateau Gaillard from 1334 to 1341 and returned with David to Scotland in 1341. He was captured in 1346 and she visited him from time to time, eventually settling in England because of his infidelities.

JOAN of ARC, St. (1412-31), called LA PUCELLE (Fr = virgin) or the MAID OF ORLEANS, **(1)** was the pious daughter of a peasant of Domremy in the Champagne. From 1425 and with increasing frequency she had visions described by her as voices accompanied by bright light, and she identified the voices of St. Catherine, St. Michael and St. Margaret, who by 1428 had convinced her that she must save France from the victorious English. Her first approach to the French garrison commander at Vaucouleurs was received sceptically, but when some of her prophecies were fulfilled in 1429, he sent her (with fanfares) to Charles the Dauphin at Chinon where she recognised him in disguise, told him things which he believed were known only to him and convinced him, and a committee of theologians, that her mission was genuine.

(2) The last great French city holding out against the English was Orleans, which, for the last seven months had been under blockade. Moreover, Charles seriously doubted his own legitimacy and so his own claim to the French crown, and these doubts were shared by many even among his sympathisers. Joan's recognition swept these doubts away. A dauphinist force set out in Apr. 1429 along the Loire to relieve Orleans. Joan made the soldiers take vows against robbery and fornication. She entered the city; on 3 May she led the historic capture of the English blockading fort of St. Loop, and by the 8th the siege was raised (*see* PLAN). Fired by her determination the offensive was continued. On 12 June the E. of Bedford (the English regent of France), was forced to surrender at Jargeau. On 18th she defeated Fastolf and captured Talbot at Patay.

(3) The eight weeks military miracle justified the Dauphin's confidence in Joan's recognition. She now insisted that his Kingship should be publicly proclaimed. Together they marched to Rheims, the towns on the way joyfully opening their gates. On 18 July, 1429, Charles was crowned at Rheims, the ancient coronation place, with Joan at his side. This directly challenged the English claims under the T. of Troyes, and the authority of the captured regent Bedford and put in issue the Burgundian allegiance. Charles at one stroke had become the palladium of France, but his treasury had run low and there was dissension among the second-rate personalities of his magnates. A demonstration march and an unsuccessful attack on Paris ended in disbandment for the winter.

(4) In Apr. 1430, the English and Burgundians attacked Compiegne. Joan left the court and rushed to the rescue. On 24 May the Burgundians captured her and in Nov. 1430 sold her for 10,000 crowns to the English. In Feb. 1431 she was charged before the court of Pierre Cauchon, Bp. of Beauvais, sitting at Rouen, with witchcraft and heresy. After flagrantly one-sided proceedings she signed a recantation on 23 May 1431. Six days later she was sentenced to life imprisonment, repudiated her recantation, and on 30 May, 1430, was burned as a relapsed heretic at Rouen.

(5) In 1456 a papal court reversed the decision of the Rouen court, on grounds of English pressure upon the court and its officials, of the use of agents provocateurs and of suppression of evidence. Joan was canonised in 1920.

JOAN, POPE. This mythical lady was supposed to have been the daughter of an English missionary and educated at Cologne. She travelled to Athens disguised as a man in the company of a monk. When he died she opened a school in Rome, was ordained, and was elected Pope as John VIII (c. 855) but died in the ensuing procession, probably as a result of Divine displeasure. Blondel exploded the story in 1647 but Döllinger had to explode it again in 1863.

JOCELIN of BRAKELOND (fl. 1200), monk of Bury St. Edmunds wrote a chronicle of St. Edmunds Abbey from 1172 to 1202.

JOCELYN (1) Robert (?1688-1756), Ld. NEWPORT (1743), Vist. JOCELYN (1755) entered the Irish parliament in 1725, was Sol. Gen. in 1727, Att-Gen. in 1730, and Ld. Chanc. of Ireland from 1739 to 1756. His *s.* **(2) Robert (1731-97) 1st E. of RODEN (1771)** was auditor-Gen. of Ireland from 1750 to 1797. His *s.* **(3) Percy (1764-1843)** was Bp. of Ferns from 1809, and of Clogher in 1820, but was deposed for scandalous crime. His nephew **(4) Robert (1788-1870) 3rd E. and 1st. Ld. CLANBRASSIL (U.K.) (1821)** was M.P. for Dundalk from 1810 to 1820 and grandmaster of the Orange Society.

JODHPUR or MARWAR (India), submitted to Akbar in 1561 and its Rajput rulers married Mogul princesses, but Aurungzeb's Islamic religious fanaticism led to a victorious military alliance between Jodhpur, Jaipur and Udaipur. Then dynastic disputes arose in the three states, because of a condition of the alliance that the offspring of an Udaipur princess married in the ruling families of the other two states should have preference of inheritance over all other offspring. This gave the Marathas ready pretexts to intervene on behalf of pretenders and eventually to Maratha domination, only ended by the British in 1818. *See* RAJPUTS.

JOFFRE, Joseph Jacques Césaire (1852-1931), as a young officer fought in China and, to extend French rule in Africa, led a column to Timbuktu in 1893. By 1914 he was French C-in-C on the Western Front. His massive calm, very suitable to the alarming German invasion across Belgium, made the victorious counter-attack on the Marne possible, and he thought, unlike nearly everyone else on both sides, that the war would not be short; but he was not successful in overcoming the murderous difficulties of trench warfare. In 1917 he was replaced on the Front by the more optimistic Nivelle, perhaps because he kept Deputies and journalists away from the front. His relations with British generals were good, and he secured their co-operation in several operations which, as it turned out, were costly failures. He was the first officer to be made a Marshal of France since the fall of the Second Empire.

JOGISL. Danish K. of Northumbria. *See* EDWARD THE ELDER-2.

JOHN of BEVERLEY, St. (?-721), after training at Canterbury, became a monk at Whitby and in 687 Bp. of Hexham. He ordained Bede. In 705 he succeeded Bosa as Bp. of York while St. Wilfrid succeeded him at Hexham and then founded the monastery in the forest at Beverley to which he retired in 717. His talents were mostly those of a social worker and physician.

"JOHN BULL" was John Arbuthnot's (1667-1735) character representing England in a series of anti-war pamphlets. The first (1712) was called *Law is a Bottomless Pit,* exemplified in the Case of Lord Strutt, John Bull, Nicholas Frog and Lewis Baboon, who spent all they had in a Law Suit. John Bull is represented as solid, independent and irascible. By 1803 his symbolic figure was widely understood as the image of the nation — honest, a trifle vulgar, generous and kind, but apt to explode under a sense of injustice. His decreasingly pejorative use by foreign cartoonists as the battered symbol of imperialist sentiment owes much to the newspaper of his name, founded by Horatio Bottomley in 1906. The name had no connection with Dr. John Bull who composed the National Anthem.

JOHN DOE and RICHARD ROE, were fictitious tenants of different persons who needed a court judgement (rather than a contract or conveyance) to establish title in a property. They appeared mostly in actions to bar (break) an entail which would otherwise prevent the land from being sold. The real purchaser and seller agreed on a price and deposited the money with their attorneys as joint stakeholders. The non-existent Doe, relying on a lease from the purchaser, sued the non-existent Roe who relied on a lease from the seller. Roe's counsel then 'craved leave to imparl' i.e. to negotiate a settlement out

of court. Both parties then left the court but only Doe's counsel returned. Judgement was then given in favour of Doe in default of further defence by Roe. The legal implication was that the purchaser could lawfully grant his lease and was therefore the owner by virtue of the judgement, which predominated over the entail, rather than by a private transaction which would not. The purchaser's attorney would then release the money to the seller's. The procedure became so conventional that it acquired a name (COMMON RECOVERY) and was in the end merely recorded with no physical action being taken in court. It probably reflected a real situation in the time of Edward IV which was quickly exploited for tenants in tail who needed to raise funds. It lasted till 1852 when the substance of the law thus developed was enacted so as to dispense with the fiction. As between purchaser and seller the procedure was voluntary since it depended upon their respective refusal to deny the facts alleged by the other side. As between the seller and his children or other beneficiaries under the entail, the latter could bargain for a share of the money by threatening to intervene in the action. The procedure immensely increased the liquidity of the market in land, without resort to legislation.

JOHN OF GAUNT. *See* LANCASTER — SECOND FAMILY *or* ROYAL HOUSE OF.

JOHN "LACK-LAND" (1166-1216), E. of CORNWALL (1173); Ld. of IRELAND (1185), Count of MORTAIN (1189) King (1199) (1) Youngest *s.* of Henry II, was brought up at Fontevrault; in the household of his eldest brother Henry the Young King; and by Ranulf Glanville. His sobriquet (also used in French) arose during abortive marriage negotiations for the daughter of C. Humbert of Maurienne. The King's attempt to remedy this at the expense of the Young King was a cause of the latter's revolt in 1173. John was then betrothed to Isabella, heiress of Gloucester. In 1185 he was refused permission to accept the throne of Jerusalem. He then visited his new Lordship of Ireland where his tactless behaviour alienated Irish and Normans alike.

(2) Under Richard I he encouraged the opposition to William Longchamp, and during his brother's imprisonment, sought the throne for himself. He was forgiven.

(3) Richard I's sudden death removed from the English side in a French war the ablest general and one of the most experienced diplomats in Europe, leaving disunion, incompetence and discredit, which the French King Philip Augustus knew how to exploit. Richard had nominated John as his universal heir and he secured England and Normandy (Apr-May 1199) while Aquitaine swore allegiance to his mother Eleanor, but Anjou, Touraine along with the Bretons did homage to the youthful Arthur of Brittany. Richard's Flemish allies hurriedly made peace (Péronne Jan. 1200). By May (P. of le Goulet) John had secured the recognition of his overlordship of all the lands, if on humiliating terms.

(4) John now provoked opposition in a series of irresponsibilities. First he carried off and married Isabella of Angouleme (his earlier marriage having been annulled), and having thus humiliated her betrothed, Hugh of Lusignan, failed to compensate him for the loss of her inheritance. Naturally he appealed to the French King. Refusing to do justice to Hugh, John also refused a summons to Paris to answer for his conduct. Hence, in July 1202 Philip declared his fiefs forfeit under feudal law and recognised Arthur as their Lord, save in Normandy which was escheated to the French Crown. In the ensuing war John captured a number of his opponents at Mirebeau in July 1202 including Arthur, whom he later murdered; but he continued to offend his supporters, while the Normans would not tolerate the misbehaviour of his mercenaries, unpaid through English reluctance to provide the necessary funds. By June 1204, the continental lands apart from Aquitaine had been lost.

(5) The conspicuous feature of John's reign, the great rebellion which led to the charters, has been distorted with contemporary and later propaganda. No wholly adequate explanation of the events has ever been offered, but some factors stand out and must have been somehow relevant. (a) John was a bad character. His countries had already had some years' experience of his self-centred double dealing. Nobody with sense trusted him. It followed that his unsanctioned promises were worthless. (b) A money economy was replacing feudalism but had not wholly done so. Armies were partly supported from taxation at a time when royal and baronial incomes were also being eroded by inflation. This was just tolerable if, as under Richard I, there was confidence in the royal foreign policy, but between 1199 and 1204 it had been a wasteful debacle; moreover the Anglo-Norman lords, with estates on both sides of the Channel, usually willing to serve or pay scutage for a Norman war to protect their properties, were reluctant to do so after those properties had been lost and still more so when later campaigns were launched in Poitou where they had no interests. (c) If in some ways, Henry II's govt. was the imposition of an embryonically bureaucratic order upon the feudal licence of the Anarchy and the rebellion a reaction against it, John's taxation was imposed through the abuse of his feudal rights, and as the reign progressed, he sought to force the baronage into indebtedness which made it liable to distraint, or coerce individual barons by manipulating justice, taking hostages and appointing mercenary leaders to sheriffdoms and castellanies from which malcontents could be watched. The power of the great lords might have been overborne by new citizen and commercial interests (which John encouraged by chartering towns), but the general negotiation of his govt. was too low for such support to rally effectively. (d) This reputation was severely damaged by John's quarrel with the Church, which lasted for too long for the Papal *volte face* towards the end of the reign to make much difference while he lived. (e) The rebellion came at the end of a long strenuous time represented by the foreign enterprises of Henry II, the Third Crusade, the ransom and French wars of Richard, and John's own wars and disputes.

(6) There was a panic, unjustifiably encouraged by the govt. after the fall of Rouen (June 1204). Heavy taxes were imposed. By 1205 a large army was concentrated at Northampton, a large fleet at Portsmouth, all to repel a logistically imaginary danger. Philip's objectives had to be more limited. He wanted to mop up the Loire. At a council in Mar. the barons, led by Hubert Walter and William the Marshal, refused to support a grand counter-stroke. More modest reinforcements were sent from Dartmouth to La Rochelle under John's bastard Geoffrey and the E. of Salisbury. In June 1206 John followed with a substantial armament. The Poitevin barons welcomed him and a two year truce at Thouars in Oct. temporarily secured the northern frontier of Aquitaine.

(7) Hubert Walter died in July 1205. Besides removing the ablest administrator of the period, a disputed election precipitated a conflict with and within the church. The electors were the monks of Christchurch, Canterbury, but the bishops wished to have their say and John wanted the post for his secretary John de Grey, Bp. of Norwich. John persuaded the monks to postpone the election until Dec. 1205 while monks and bishops appealed to Rome for a settlement of their respective rights. With the connivance of the bishops, John sent messengers to Rome to get Innocent III to instruct the monks to elect Grey. A majority of the monks then secretly made a provisional election of Reginald, their prior and sent him to Rome. There he revealed all and sought papal confirmation, which was postponed at the request of the bishops' proctor. John heard of it and in Dec. bullied the monks into repudiating their choice and

electing Grey, whom he invested with the temporalities. Innocent quashed this uncanonical election in Mar. 1206 and summoned plenipotentiaries from the monks, the bishops, and John. From June to Oct. John was on campaign in Poitou and in Dec. Innocent quashed Reginald's election, decided for the monks, and persuaded their plenipotentiaries to accept Card. Stephen Langton, a distinguished scholastic.

(8) At about this time John quarrelled with his half-brother, Geoffrey Abp. of York, who fled overseas. Langton was consecrated Abp. at Viterbo in July 1207, but John refused confirmation, and seized the temporalities of both Abps. Until 1213 the English church was without a metropolitan. Innocent retaliated by appointing the Bps. of London, Ely and Worcester as his commissioners, with power to pronounce an interdict. The threat, uttered in Aug. 1207, left John unmoved. Accordingly in Mar. 1208 the three issued the interdict and fled the country, followed by the Bp. of Hereford. With three sees (Lincoln, Chichester, and Exeter) vacant and two bishops dying (Durham and Lichfield), only six out of 17 diocesans remained. John had the revenues of eleven at his disposal and he also began to confiscate the property of ecclesiastics who obeyed the interdict, selling it back to them for considerable sums.

(9) John needed the money. In the spring of 1208 Llewelyn ap Iorwerth (who had married his bastard daughter Joan) overran Powys (*see* GWYNEDD-27) and in the spring of 1209 the Scots began to raid the border. Llewelyn and John came to an understanding and the Welsh prince sent a contingent on John's Scottish campaign. They overran Lothian and forced William the Lion to a humiliating peace and in Oct. Llewelyn and his followers did homage to John at Woodstock. Meanwhile, however, John's position was deteriorating elsewhere: the Albigensian crusaders were devastating Languedoc and flooding into the territory of John's ally the Count of Toulouse. In Nov. John's excommunication was published in France.

(10) The excommunication, as the news spread, was more damaging than the interdict. Churchmen hitherto willing to serve him, left his side. He was regarded by many with superstitious horror; moral restraints on treason and aggression were loosened. He was vilified in contemporary chronicles as he was to be in tradition. He redoubled his exactions on the church: amounts taken after 1209 exceeded K. Richard's ransom. By relieving taxation, they helped to mitigate John's unpopularity. The industrious pursuit of the business of kingship also helped in this direction and, like Henry II after Becket's murder, he decided to go to Ireland.

(11) Certain common elements in John's actions suggest that he was already seeking allies against the baronage, particularly among the Celts and in the towns. Favours to Llewelyn were not likely to endear him to marcher lords and he had already (1208) driven the most powerful of them, William de Braose, away. In Ireland his behaviour conformed to a similar pattern. He was there with a powerful force from June to Aug. 1210 theoretically to hunt down de Braose, who had been sheltered by William the Marshal and the de Lacy lords of Meath and Ulster. Marching north from Waterford, he received the Irish chiefs with favour and they helped him to drive his enemies into Carrickfergus. Hugh de Lacy of Ulster and de Braose escaped, but many baronies were confiscated and either ransomed or given to his own adherents. Much of eastern Ireland was shired and Irish towns were chartered; so too were some English towns, such as Liverpool, which was connected with the Irish trade. Londoners had been appointing a common council since 1206. There was a noticeable growth of municipal self management related to the continental trade.

(12) In the German civil war John's nephew, Otto IV (K. of the Romans) was driven out and came to England

in 1207. In June 1208 his rival, Philip of Swabia, was murdered; Otto returned and he, and his brother the Count Palatine, interceded in 1209 in the English ecclesiastical quarrel. This led to a Palatine alliance. In Oct. 1209 Otto was crowned Emperor, but began the Neapolitan enterprise which led to his excommunication and the appearance of Frederick II as papal anti-King in Sicily (1211). The Christian conscience could stand one royal excommunicate, but not two. John and Otto had their supporters from Dublin to Magdeburg. In the Low Countries they were organised into an active alliance through Renaud of Dammartin, Count of Boulogne, and Count Theobald of Bar. The T. of Lambeth (4 May 1212) bound John and Renaud not to make a separate peace with the French King. The Palatinate, Brabant, Limburg, and Flanders as well as Otto, adhered. Philip naturally replied with counter-intrigues. John and Llewelyn had quarrelled in 1210 and so John, with English and Welsh forces, had made war in north Wales in 1211. Llewelyn had had to surrender the Four Cantreds west of Conway while John's mercenary, Falkes de Bréauté, built a castle at Aberystwyth. Falkes provoked a united Welsh revolt in 1212. Innocent III capitalised on the situation by releasing the Welsh from their allegiance and lifting the interdict in Wales. John's alliance was mobilising against Philip who, in Aug. offered an alliance to Llewelyn. Consequently the army for foreign service had to be diverted to Wales. It was assembled at Nottingham but failed to move, paralysed by treason among its commanders; Robert FitzWalter and Eustace de Vesci fled to France and Scotland. Almost immediately Philip made an alliance with Frederick II (T. of Toul 19 Nov. 1212) and on 5 Dec. Frederick was elected anti-King in Germany. The excommunications seemed to be having insidious effects.

(13) Accordingly the Abbot of Beaulieu headed a mission to Rome to discuss terms. Innocent demanded that Langton should be accepted as Abp; that the exiled clergy be readmitted and the church recompensed for all its losses and that FitzWalter and Vesci be restored. On his own initiative, John offered England and Ireland as fiefs of the Holy See. These terms were agreed, but Innocent wrote in Feb. 1213 insisting upon ratification by June, on pain of deposition. In April Philip, at a council at Soissons, decided to invade England. The connection between these events was loose, but strong enough in John's mind to compel submission. The surrender and re-grant (for a 1000 marks a year to the Holy See) was made at Temple Ewell by Dover on 15 May, 1213.

(14) The immediate effects were to divert Philip's attack to Flanders, where it met disaster at the B. of Damme (28 May 1213), and a truce with Llewelyn (3 June). John's efforts to mount a counter-offensive were, however, frustrated by further baronial obstruction on the over-suspicious ground that he had not been formally absolved. Langton, however, came to England, and at the absolution at Winchester on 20 July, John promised to maintain the ancient laws. He now tried to set out again, but this time the northern barons objected to serving overseas. John therefore marched north to punish them, but Langton, after councils at London and St. Albans, overtook him and effected a reconciliation at Wallingford (1 Nov.). John could now reanimate the twice frustrated offensive in Poitou. This was launched in Feb. 1214 but failed when Otto and his allies were routed at BOUVINES (27 July 1214), but John was able to negotiate a truce, due to last until 1220.

(15) He returned in Oct. 1214 to face a perfectly logical refusal by the northern barons to pay a scutage and this developed into a controversy about the restoration of the ancient laws and indeed, about what they were. Some of their demands are known from a so-called *Unknown Charter*. At Epiphany a settlement was postponed until Easter with the bishops and magnates standing surety for the northerners. Both sides appealed

to Innocent as the overlord and John took the cross in a vain attempt to win a crusader's immunity. On 19 Mar. 1215 Innocent wrote forbidding conspiracies against the King, but it was too late. The northerners, now joined by adherents from Essex and E. Anglia had assembled in arms at Stamford. In April they renounced their allegiance (*Defiance*) at Brackley. Repulsed from Northampton, they came *via* Bedford towards London. They were in touch with Philip who sent them siege engines by his piratical admiral Eustace le Moine. On 9 May John offered arbitration by a court composed equally from both sides with the Pope as superior, and formally granted trial by peers in the King's Court pending a decision; on 12th the northerners, unsurprisingly, refused this loaded offer, and John ordered the sheriffs to seize their property. On 17th, however, a faction admitted them to London and many other barons joined the rebellion. On 27th a truce was made.

(16) MAGNA CARTA was the product of a triangular negotiation related to the Coronation Charter of Henry I between an arbitrary King, a selfish and undistinguished but large group of barons from the north and east, and a group of elder statesmen and court administrators headed by Abp. Langton, the Marshal's uncle and nephew, Hubert de Burgh, Alan Basset Ld. of Wycombe and Hugh de Neville, John's chief justice of the Forests. Its underlying principle was that there was a law, that a King might be bound by it if only it were defined, and that it was necessary to set up enforcement machinery in the case of John. On 15 June the parties met at Runnymede and agreed the ARTICLES OF THE BARONS, but some of them left before the charter was drafted and sealed on 19th. They refused to give security for the peace as they had promised at Runnymede; they began to fortify themselves and raid royal manors and they stayed under arms for tournaments. The bishops, who protested against their behaviour, arranged a conference at Oxford on 16 Aug. but John refused to attend it. In truth neither side believed in the other's good faith. Moreover John was negotiating for Innocent's support and on 24 Aug. the Pope condemned and quashed the Charter. Since the papal attitude was known by mid July, after his sentence of excommunication on the rebels had arrived, the behaviour of the northerners was understandable. Civil war now broke out. They appealed to Philip for help, but John had occupied the Kentish coast where his mercenaries reached him. In Oct. he besieged Rochester Castle which fell on 30 Nov. In Dec. thirty of the northerners were excommunicated and John moved *via* Nottingham and York to Berwick, whence he raided Lothian. Then he turned south, ravaging and levying extortions. By Apr. he had subdued the north and east. Meanwhile, Philip had decided to invade, alleging a fictitious condemnation of John for Arthur's murder in 1203. Storms dispersed John's fleet; the French led by Philip's son Louis who claimed the throne in right of his wife, John's niece Blanche, landed in Thanet and reached London on 21 May. John retreated westwards gathering reinforcement, mainly Welsh, and then advanced into Lincolnshire. He crossed, thence, to Kings Lynn, but returned losing his baggage in quicksands near Long Sutton. He died of dysentery at Newark (19 Oct. 1216) and was succeeded by his nine-year old eldest son, Henry III.

JOHN OF LANCASTER (1389-1435), D. of BEDFORD (1414), E. of RICHMOND (1425), 3rd *s.* of Henry IV, received lands and offices in N. England, many forfeited from the Percy family. From 1403 he was Constable of England and nominally warden of the East March, but later he was active in it and in repelling Scottish incursions and renewed Percy conspiracies. He resigned the March in 1414 because he was inadequately reimbursed for his expenses. He was also granted the reversion of Richmond.

(2) During his brother Henry V's absences in 1415, 1417-19 and 1421-2 he acted as Guardian of England, inflicting on the Scots the sharp defeat which led to one of their invasions becoming known as The Foul Raid. He presided over the trial and execution of Sir John Oldcastle and he also secured parliamentary financial support for his brother's French War. He joined the King from time to time in France and distinguished himself in 1416 by defeating a French fleet off Harfleur.

(3) On Henry V's death in 1422, D. Philip of Burgundy having declined the regency for Henry VI, Bedford accepted it and became Protector of England, but this office was mostly exercised on his behalf by his younger brother Humphrey, D. of Gloucester, for Bedford spent most of his remaining years in the difficult task of defending Henry V's French gains. He formed a triple alliance with John D. of Brittany and Philip D. of Burgundy, and in 1423 married Philip's sister Anne. In 1424 he beat the Dauphin's troops at Verneuil, but it proved hard to maintain the alliance, for Bedford refused to give the Bretons any important military command and Philip was offended when Bedford failed to stop Humphrey of Gloucester attacking Holland in the interests of Jacqueline of Hainault (q.v.) (1424). Moreover disputes between D. Humphrey and the Beauforts were threatening the conduct of the war so that in 1424 and 1426 Bedford was obliged to come to England to compose them. In 1429 a quarrel with Philip about the division of booty caused the Burgundian contingent to be withdrawn from the siege of Orléans and materially assisted Joan of Arc's victory there. From then on nothing went well. The trial and burning of Joan of Arc had the opposite effect to that which he intended, and the coronation of the infant Henry VI in Paris was derided by the French because they already had a crowned adult King miraculously certified by her. His Burgundian ties were further eroded by Anne's death in 1432, and in 1433-4 another Gloucester-Beaufort dispute brought him back to England to neglect the war at a period of military crisis. Burgundy's defection in Sept. 1435 was due mainly to Bedford's lack of success but it equally deprived the English of any real hope of victory. Similarly Bedford's efforts to create a common interest in trade and to reform the French coinage came to grief because the shortage of English money forced him to tax the French heavily.

(4) He was a munificent patron of illuminators and a collector of manuscripts. His splendid illustrated Book of Hours commissioned from Paul of Limburg as a wedding present for his first wife, is in the British Library.

JOHN the SCOT. *See* CHESHIRE-4.

JOHN II of France (r. 1350-64), surnamed THE GOOD, for his knightly but rash quality, succeeded Philip VI at a time of disaster. The rot continued. He executed his own High Constable for surrendering Guines to the English: the Black Prince raided the provinces marching with Aquitaine, and Charles of Navarre (a grandson of Louis X) laid a claim to the throne. He had large estates around Paris and had to be fended off. The taxation system broke down and to finance the army the King summoned the Estates General. Led by the Parisian provost of merchants, Etienne Marcel, they demanded control of finance. Anarchy in the capital frightened the noble and ecclesiastical estates, which acquiesced in a dissolution. With inadequate funds, the King had to depend upon the reconstituted feudal host. The Black Prince routed it and captured him at Poictiers in 1356. The Dauphin CHARLES (later V) took over the govt. as the King's Lieutenant-Gen., at the age of eighteen. In the confusion, the Estates had to be reconvoked. The popular estate ignored the condition of the Kingdom and, with the support of the Paris mob, sought to wring concessions. They forced the Lieutenant to free Charles of Navarre, who became the master of the capital. Two of the govt's principal members were murdered in the presence of the Lieutenant, whose life was saved by Etienne Marcel. In 1357 the estates voted the *Grande Ordonnance,* a parliamentary constitution based upon the power of Paris.

Disorder now spread to the rural peasantry north of Paris. (*The Jacquerie*). This coincided with a further Estates General summoned to Compiegne far from the Paris mob. In this depleted assembly the popular estate was overborne. With rural as well as urban revolution staring them in the face, the aristocracy came to their senses. Etienne Marcel had made overtures to the peasants: Charles of Navarre (whose estates were affected) deserted him and started to reduce them. Marcel appealed to the English, but he and his supporters were crushed by the royal forces in July 1358. This did not end the disorders, for the countryside remained at the mercy of wandering unpaid military gangs called Free Companies.

Edward III proposed to his royal prisoner that about two thirds of France, including the entire Atlantic seaboard, should be transferred to him in full sovereignty. The condition of France now prompted him to try for the highest prize, and have himself crowned at Rheims. He came just too late. In a winter campaign (1359-60) he was repulsed before its walls, and his army suffered in appalling weather. Moreover the Lieutenant was assuming direction of the war. Privateers interfered with cross Channel communications: guerrillas harassed the English troops. In May 1360 peace negotiations were opened at Bretigny near Chartres, and a humiliating treaty was ratified at Calais in October. John was comforted at that moment by the escheat of Burgundy, but proceeded to create three appanages for Charles' younger brothers:- to JOHN (?-1415) the duchy of BERRY which escheated at his death; to LOUIS (?-1364) ANJOU which escheated only at the death of his grandson, RENE (?-1480); and to PHILIP THE BOLD (?-1404) the duchy of BURGUNDY around which a dangerous political constellation was soon to form, and which escheated only in 1477, leaving much of the constellation in Habsburg hands.

John II was not long at liberty: one of the royal hostages broke his parole: the King returned to England and died in luxurious custody.

JOHN SCOTUS ERIGENA (9th cent.), reached the court of the Emperor Charles the Bald from Ireland in about 845, and at the instance of Hincmar of Rheims completed his *de Praedestinatione* in 851. This was condemned by councils at Valencia (855) and Langres (859) but Charles induced him to translate the *Corpus Areopagiticum,* a powerful neo-Platonist mystical work which influenced his own *De Divisione Naturae* (c. 866). This work was one of the foundations of scholasticism. He may, later, have gone, at Alfred's request, with Grimbald to Malmesbury.

JOHN XXII. *See* AVIGNON POPES.

JOHN XXIII (1881-1963), Pope (1958), was apostolic delegate in Bulgaria from 1925, and to Greece and Turkey from 1934. In 1944 he became nuncio in France. Elected Pope as an elderly compromise between the long reign of Pius XII and the expected election of Paul VI, he astonished the world by his regard for frailty and suffering, reformist energy, and active interest in the reunion of churches. In 1962 he summoned the Second Vatican Council, which *inter alia* enjoined the use of the vernacular in the liturgy.

JOHN OF AUSTRIA, Don (1545-78), was a bastard of the Emperor Charles V by his mistress Barbara Blomberg, and so half-brother to Philip II of Spain. Handsome, charming and able he was the victor of Algiers at the age of 21; of Granada at 25; of Lepanto, the biggest sea battle of the millennium at 26, and of Tunis at 27. His fame has echoed down the centuries, being the subject even of an English poem (*Lepanto* by G.K. Chesterton). His headlong

Mediterranean career was now checked by the difficulty of supporting him, for Philip was beset by Atlantic enemies, Dutch rebels and inflation. Accordingly he was appointed Viceroy of the Netherlands in 1576 (aged 31) to save something from the wreck of his predecessors' misgovernment. Short of funds, with ragged and mutinous troops and an entire population against him, he courageously advised Philip to accept the defeat embodied in the Pacification of Ghent (1577). A year later (at 33) he was dead. King Philip has been traduced for allegedly frustrating his ambitions, but as Don John was entrusted with the highest commands, it is hard to see why. It seems certain that the long episode which culminated in the Armada of 1588 would have had a different outcome if this brilliant realist had lived a full life-span.

JOHN OF AUSTRIA, Don (1629-79), bastard of Philip IV, a Gen. rather than an admiral who, as gov. of Flanders was defeated by Turenne at the B. of the Dunes in 1658 and unsuccessfully commanded against England's ally, the resurgent Kingdom of Portugal from 1661 to 1664. He headed a successful *pronunciamiento* against the Spanish queen-mother's adviser, Nithard, and became Viceroy of Aragon. In 1677 he drove her out altogether, and became a popular but not a competent chief minister.

JOHN (?-1479), E. of MAR. *See* JAMES III OF SCOTS-2.

JOHN OF SALISBURY (?1115-80), a pupil of Abelard and a protégé of St. Bernard, came to England in 1150 and was Sec. to Abps. Theobald and Becket until 1170. He wrote the *Historia Pontificalis* (History of the Popes) in about 1166 at Rheims. He was with Becket when he was murdered and wrote his life. In 1174 he became treasurer of Exeter and from 1176 was Bp. of Chartres. He took an active part in the Third Lateran Council (1179). An early Aristotelian, his works include the philosophical *Metalogicus, Entheticus*; a Life of St. Anselm; and *Policraticus*, a handbook for rulers.

JO[H]NSON or JANSSEN VAN CEULEN, Cornelius (1593-?1664), English born artist began as a small portraitist (c. 1618) but later painted on a larger scale. He was celebrated for his portrait of Lady Bowyer, family groups of the Rushouts and Lucys, but his best works were probably the portraits of Sir Ralph Verney (1634) and Henry Ireton (1640). Migrating to Middelburg, Holland in 1643, during the Civil War, he subsequently moved to The Hague, painting the leading citizens of that town. Faces staring out from gloomy shadows, his pictures often need cleaning to reveal the subtlety of their subdued colouring.

JOHNSON, Lyndon Baines (1908-72) democratic Pres. of U.S.A. from the assassination of Pres. Kennedy in 1963 until 1969. Liberal at home, and willing to defend western interests against communist aggression in Viet Nam, he fell foul of right wing and left wing extremists whose activities his liberalism naturally encouraged. His 'Great Society' involved channelling many millions of dollars to the deprived sections of the population.

JOHNSON or MOLLISON, Amy (1903-41), flew solo to Australia in 1930, and made record flights to Tokyo in 1931, Cape Town in 1932, Karachi in 1934 and to the Cape and back in 1936.

JOHNSON, Dr. Samuel (1709-84), s. of a Lichfield bookseller took pupils, including David Garrick, with whom he came to London in 1737. He assisted William Guthrie in compiling parliamentary debates, and from 1741 to 1764 did so himself. The contacts he made combined with his learning and force of personality soon got him other employments. He catalogued the Harleian Collection in 1742. In 1744 he issued his *Life of Savage* and so made the acquaintance of Sir Joshua Reynolds. In 1747 he began his seminal *Dictionary*, from 1750 to 1752 he wrote most of the *Rambler*, and through it made the acquaintance of the Burneys. His *Dictionary* was completed in 1755. He first met Goldsmith and Burke in 1761. In 1762 Bute gave him a pension and in 1763 he

met Boswell, and formed his Literary Club which met at the Turks Head in Gerrard St., until 1783. He was now received everywhere and knew everyone. Boswell's celebrated *Life* appeared in 1791. The first English lexicographer, he described a lexicographer as 'a harmless drudge'.

JOHNSON, Sir William (1715-74) came to America to manage the lands of his uncle, Sir Peter Warren, in the Mohawk Valley where he set up a trading post in 1738. He won the affection of Indians, who gave him huge tracts of land and treated him as their champion and protector. By 1750 he was the greatest American landowner and the richest colonist of his time. He lived in "baronial if untidy splendor", wore Indian clothes and allowed Indians the run of his house. In 1756 he became Superintendent of Indian Affairs, and Iroquois loyalty, which he had engendered, was a vital factor in the defence of the colonies against the French. He was the only successful British commander in 1755, when Braddock was killed at Ft. Duquesne.

JOHNSTON, Archibald (?1610-68) Ld. WARRINGTON (1641) was a leading Scots Calvinist and associated with Alexander Henderson in drafting the Nat. Covenant (1638). He represented the Scots in the Ts. of Berwick (1639) and Ripon (1640) and then became a Lord of session. He favoured intervention against Charles I in his disputes with the parliament, was a prominent member of the Westminster Assembly (1644) and of the Committee of Both Kingdoms, resisted the Engagement and as draftsman of the Act of Classes (1649) and an amateur but powerful advisor to Gen. Lesley had a major responsibility for the disaster at Dunbar (1650). Driven into retirement, he emerged as Cromwell's Lord Clerk Register (1657) and a member of the Upper House. He joined those trying to save the Commonwealth as a member both of the Council of State and of the Committee of Safety. Now hopelessly compromised with republicanism he fled at the Restoration to Rouen where he was arrested and deported to Scotland. Tried before the Scots parliament he was hanged.

JOHNSTONE CLAN. *See* MARCHES; ANGLO SCOTS-9.

JOHORE. *See* MALAYA.

JOINVILLE, Jean Sire de (1224-1317), marshal of Champagne and Romania, a friend and biographer of Louis IX. His writings are an important source for mediaeval French life and crusader politics.

JOLLIET, Louis. *See* CANADA.

***JOLLY GEORGE,* S.S.** was a munitions ship whose cargo in 1920 was destined for Poland, then being invaded by the Red Army. London dockers refused to load her.

JOLY DE LOTBINIERE, Sir Henry Gustave (1829-1908), became a liberal member of the Canadian House of Assembly in 1861 (where he opposed federation) and of the Quebec assembly in 1867 until 1874. He headed a Quebec Govt. from 1878 to 1879 and was lieut. gov. of British Columbia from 1900 to 1906.

JOMINI, Henri (1779-1869). Marshal Ney's chief of staff, wrote several important treatises on military affairs, and devised a less satisfactory system of map draftsmanship, sometimes called Jomini's caterpillars.

JONES, Earnest (1819-69). *See* CHARTISM.

JONES, Edward (1641-1703), had Swift as a pupil at Kilkenny School and became Bp. of Cloyne (1683) and at St. Asaph (1692), but was deprived for simony and maladministration by appointing laymen to Irish cures.

JONES, John (?1597-1660), was brought up by his kinsman Sir Hugh Middleton, who in 1644 raised troops for the Parliament in which he was commissioned. An able soldier, he became a Col. of Horse in 1646 and an M.P. for Anglesey (in 1649), having twice conquered it. As a member of the Court of Trial he signed Charles I's death warrant. He was a commissioner for civil govt. in Ireland from 1650 to 1654. In 1656 he married Oliver Cromwell's sister, Katherine Whetstone, and became a member of the Council of State. He had strong differences with Oliver and disapproved (more in theory than practice) of his Protectorate. In 1657 he became a member of the Upper House and Governor of Anglesey. At the collapse of the Commonwealth he supported the Rump and was again sent to Ireland (1659). At the Restoration he was executed as a regicide. *See* DESBOROUGH, JOHN.

JONES, John Paul (1747-92), originally JOHN PAUL, a Scot, began in the slave trade, killed one of his seamen and disappeared, and then took a commission in the rebel American navy in 1775 under the alias of Jones. In 1778 he burned the fort at Whitehaven and captured the small frigate *Drake*, and in 1779 with a small squadron he captured the frigate *Serapis*. The reputation built upon these minor exploits is an example of hyperbole. He soon left American service, joined the French and then the Russians. A dance in which partners are changed is named after him. He died unemployed in Paris.

JONES (1) Lewis (?1550-1646), was Dean of Cashel, whose Cathedral he restored, from 1607 to 1633, and Bp. of Killaloe from 1633 to 1646. His *s.* **(2) Michael (?-1649)** enlisted against the Irish rebels in 1641 but went over to the parliament as a result of the truce of 1643. A successful parliamentary col. of horse in North Wales he was sent as C-in-C to Ireland in 1646. Here he defeated the royalists at Dangan Hill (Aug. 1647) and made Cromwell's landing feasible by his crushing victory over Ormonde at Rathmines (Aug. 1649). He died of fever.

JONES, Philip (1618-74), was a parliamentary col. in South Wales when with Col. Horton, he defeated the royalists. Governor of Cardiff and M.P. for Brecon he became a leading figure in the Interregnum and a war profiteer, through his wide and detailed knowledge of Welsh affairs. As a member of the Committee on Compounding he made a fortune on land transactions. In 1653 he was a member of the Council of State and then of the Upper House and comptroller of Oliver Cromwell's household. Never a political extremist, he concentrated on making money and by the Restoration had amassed an income of £3000 a year, which he maintained after it by buying up depressed reversions. He was sheriff of Glamorgan in 1671.

JONES, Robert Thomas (1874-1940), was a moderate and successful sec. of the N. Wales Quarrymans Union from 1908 to 1933 and M.P. for Caernarvonshire in 1922-3.

JONES, Sir William (1566-1640), was a very learned C.J. of the Irish King's Bench from 1617 to 1620, a justice of the English Common Pleas in 1621 and then of the English King's Bench from 1624. His reasoned judgements in favour of the Crown in *Eliot's Case* (1630) and in the *Case of Shipmoney* (1638) were models of the legal deductive method, even if politically inexpedient.

JONES, Sir William (1631-82), Sol-Gen. from 1673 to 1675, and Att-Gen. from 1675 to 1679, directed the Popish Plot prosecutions. As M.P. for Plymouth from 1680 to 1682 he managed the Stafford impeachment and was a champion of the Exclusion Bill (q.v.).

JONES (1) William (1675-1749), mathematician and tutor to Philip Yorke (E. of Hardwicke) and the Es. of Macclesfield, was a friend of Newton and Halley. His *s.* **(2) Sir William (1746-94)** tutor to Ld. Althorpe, was called to the bar in 1774, published a famous legal treatise on Bailments in 1781 and was judge of the Calcutta High Court from 1783. Meantime he had also pursued oriental studies beginning with a French translation of a Persian royal biography in 1770 and a Persian grammar in 1771. In 1773 he published a version of the Arabic *Muallaqat*, founded the Bengal Asiatic Society in 1784, and having mastered Sanskrit, published translations of, *inter alia*, *Sakuntala*, extracts from the Vedas and the Laws of Manu.

JONSON, BEN [JAMIN] (?1573-1637) was well educated at Westminster and possibly Cambridge, but ran away to the army in Flanders. He returned in 1592, found work with the Admiral's Men (actors) in 1597, killed one of them in a brawl and escaped death by benefit of clergy in 1598. He was for about twelve years a R. Catholic. His *Everyman in His Humour*, played by the Lord Chamberlain's Men at the *Globe* in 1598 launched him on his seminal career as a playwright and he turned out plays until 1605 when he seems to have invented, with the aid of Grinling Gibbons' scenery, the court masque. Plays, actors, masques and courtiers, and a walk to Edinburgh, now occupied the rest of his life. He was well known to statesmen, Kings, writers and poets. Not a writer of genius, he inspired other writers and equally importantly their potential patrons. His *Volpone, The Alchemist* and *Bartholomew Fayre* are still played.

JORDAN, HASHEMITE KINGDOM OF THE (before 1949 TRANSJORDAN). In World War I the local Arabs, stirred by T. E. Lawrence and his sherifian friends, rose against the Turks, and ABDULLAH, son of the Hashemite Sherif of Mecca, was installed as Emir under a British held League of Nations mandate. He ruled as a benevolent autocrat with British advice and formed a well-trained Arab Legion under Gen. Glubb which helped the British in World War II against the Vichy French in Syria and German intrigues in Iraq.

(2) In 1946 the mandate ended, the emirate, now a Kingdom, joined the Arab League and soon became involved as a principal in Levantine politics. These embraced the new Israel, the older Islamic conservatism of the Hashemites opposed by the newer urban quasi-revolutionary Arab attitudes of the Fertile Crescent, Egyptian enterprise and a culture clash between desert and settled Arabs. All mistrusted Britain, namely the Egyptians as an imperial power, the Syrian Arabs because the Balfour Declaration had given away too much, the Israelis because it offered too little.

(3) Jordan joined the Arab attack on Israel, seized much of central Palestine and Jerusalem, and so bid for the leadership of the Palestine Arabs, but in 1951 Arabs assassinated the Anglophile King. His unstable son Talal made way in 1952 for the able and politically agile 17-year old Hussein. Personally well disposed to Britain (in 1961 he married an English second wife), he asserted his Arab nature by dismissing Gen. Glubb (1956) but when Egypt and Syria formed the United Arab Republic (U.A.R.), he formed an Arab Federation with his kinsmen of Iraq. Revolutionary volatility in the Fertile Crescent ended both combinations. Having failed to overthrow the Jordanian Hashemites in 1951, it succeeded in Iraq in July 1958, caused Syria to abandon the U.A.R. in 1961, and in 1964 created among the Palestinian Arabs Yasser Arafat's Palestine Liberation Organisation (P.L.O.) and its allied terrorist Al Fatah ("Victorious") organisation based in Syria. Both were hostile to the Hashemites as well as the Israelis.

(4) The resulting new phase combined a struggle between K. Hussein and Arafat for Palestinian Arab allegiance with joint hostility to Israel. Hussein tried to prevent Al Fatah infiltrating Palestine via Syria but naturally had to support the Arab side in the disastrous war of June 1967, when Jordan lost more heavily than other Arab states, especially in territory, and ended up with 200,000 refugees. In this potentially revolutionary situation Al Fatah and some new Marxist friends tried to subvert the army, but Hussein single-handedly put down the mutiny and drove them into Syria. Violence continued until the next Arab-Israeli war in Oct. 1973.

(5) Hussein joined in, but in view of the course of the previous war, opened no front on the Jordan. Consequently the P.L.O., supported by other Arab states claimed the Palestinian Arab leadership. At the Rabat conference he agreed, in return for a large sum in dollars from Saudi Arabia and the termination of his anti-Israeli obligations.

(6) The Israeli-Egyptian Sinai accord of 1975 brought Jordan and Syria briefly together, and Hussein began to cultivate the P.L.O. The friendship with Syria was so brief that Hussein was diplomatically isolated. In 1980 the Iraqi-Iranian war began. Hussein had nothing in common with the Ba'ath govt. of Iraq but strong doctrinal objection to the Ayatollahs. Moreover, his support for the P.L.O. brought American hostility; so he supplied Iraq with French and Russian arms but in 1988 calmed the Americans by surrendering his Palestinian West Bank claims and withdrawing Jordanian citizenship from the Arab residents. Nevertheless he kept up the relationship with Iraq, and in the Gulf war (1991) identified with Fertile Crescent opinion by continuing to supply Saddam.

(7) Hussein died in Feb. 1999.

JORDAN, Mrs Dorothea (1762-1816) actress, was the publicly acknowledged mistress and wife in all but name of the D. of Clarence (later William IV) from 1791 to 1811. They had ten children (*see* FITZCLARENCE) and lived at Bushy Park.

JORDANS (Bucks.), an early, possibly the earliest regular Quaker meeting place. The Quaker burial ground dates from 1671, the Meeting House from 1688.

JORIK (?-904), Danish K. of E. Anglia. See EDWARD THE ELDER-1.

JOSEPH II. See AUSTRIA, POST-PRAGMATIC.

JOUGS or JUGGS. A Scottish pillory, consisting of an iron collar locked round the victim's neck and chained to a post or wall.

JOULE, James Prescott (1818-89), a pupil of John Dalton, published his papers on the relationship between heat and electricity and on the thermodynamic qualities of solids, between 1840 and 1878.

JOURNALS OF THE HOUSES OF PARLIAMENT. The *Commons Journal* was begun in 1547, treated as authoritative from 1580, interrupted from 1584 to 1601 and was printed from 1742. Portions of the *Lords Journal* date from the 15th cent. and it is continuous from 1510. It was treated as official from 1620. The two Journal Offices which prepare the Journal from the records of Minutes and Proceedings kept by the clerks at the table.

JOURNEYS and VOYAGES – PRE-INDUSTRIAL REVOLUTION, TIMES OF. Merchant caravans might take 7 days from London to Chester and 8 or 9 to Edinburgh. The voyage from the Wash to Copenhagen took 7-8 days, that from Poole to St. Malo was reckoned at 4. The Transalpine route from Turin to Lyons (closed most winters) took 12 days: the parallel but longer sea route from Genoa to Marseilles two, if lucky. More goods could be carried by water and, in favourable conditions, at far greater speed than overland, but winds could play havoc with calculations, e.g. there was no reliable coastal service between the Thames and the Forth before 1780 because winds set for a long time in one direction hindered return; a mistral might blow a ship from Genoa bound for Marseilles as far as the Algerian coast and fleets from Portsmouth bound down-Channel could be prevented from rounding St. Helens (I. of W.) for three weeks at a time.

In 1798 Nelson's fleet made the voyage from Syracuse to Aboukir in 7 days; in 1805, with foul bottoms, the passage from Gibraltar to Barbados in 29. East Indiamen usually took 5 to 6 months from the Thames to the Hooghli, but in 1866 three tea clippers made the run from Foochow to London in 3 months and 6-8 days.

JOURNEY WEIGHT. The number of coins which could be minted in a day. This was reckoned at 15 lb troy of gold, minted into 701 sovereigns, or 60 lb troy of silver minted into 3,960 shillings. The unit is used in the Trial of the Pyx.

JOUSTING or TILTING, was introduced from France as a feudal warlike exercise. A meeting for such a purpose was called a **Tournament. (1)** The apprentice knight (or Esquire) was trained by tilting at a **Quintain** which was a bar pivoting freely by its centre on an upright timber. At one end the bar had a figure with a shield, at the other a bag of stones hanging by a three-foot rope. A lancer riding at proper speed and striking the shield accurately would escape the bag as it came round; otherwise it would unhorse him.

(2) Tournaments were originally dangerous and disorderly mock battles between rival, supposedly friendly bodies of knights using blunt (and not so blunt) weapons in open areas without boundary or focus. They were a detestable nuisance and were roundly denounced by the Church, for they did much damage and were occasionally a cover for murder or political conspiracy.

(3) Richard I's justiciars took them in hand in 1194. They confined private ones to five grounds near permanent royal garrisons respectively at Wilton, Kenilworth, Stamford, Brackley and Tickhill. They required every tournament to be licensed and each participant to pay in advance a large fee, graduated from 20 marks for an Earl to 2 marks for a landless knight. This ensured that even lawful tournaments were infrequent, and that unlawful ones could be easily identified and dispersed.

(4) As armies became professionalised, there was less need to train the feudality, and jousting declined into a pastime or occasionally a mortal duel called a joust *à outrance*. It was conducted before stands for courtly audiences and with ceremony regulated by heralds or for royal events, by Kings of Arms. Encased in their armour, the knights were unrecognisable save by their armorial bearings which it was the business of heralds to know and proclaim. For this purpose they developed an accurate terminology call Blazon (*see* HERALDRY).

(5) At a full tournament each participant had a tent facing the ground (called the **Lists**) and hung his shield outside it on a frame (such as it still seen on the Portuguese flag). A challenge was made by going openly across the lists with a lance and striking the shield with the butt for a friendly challenge (with blunted or boarded lance) or the point for a challenge *à outrance*. The squires of the two concerned then made the necessary arrangements. Supporters of particular knights wore favours in their colours, and sometimes a knight dedicated his arms by offering his colours on the point of his lance to a lady of his choice, or a lady dropped her colours into the lists and he wore then.

(6) The lists were usually a field with the court stand along one side and the other left open for other fans. In the middle and parallel with the stand was a stout wooden fence 5 feet high. The lance (a heavy affair) was used right-handed with the butt in a rest, and the knights charged each other along the fence from opposite ends each keeping as close to it on his right as he could and with his lance projecting across it. His prime target might be his opponent's head (which led to heavily reinforced helmets) or the often embossed 'honour point' just above the middle of his shield. Geometrically the lance held at the acute angle across the barrier would meet its target first and if accurately laid would unhorse the opponent. Simultaneous contacts might unhorse both. An inaccurate contact usually broke the lance. After an indecisive course the contestants returned to their own end to rearm. Three courses were usual, and if neither or both had been unhorsed, the lord of the tournament consulted the ladies and declared the winner.

(7) Despite all the rules, precautions and increasingly well made armour, this rich man's sport remained dangerous. The E. of Shrewsbury was killed in 1344 (*see* GARTER, ORDER OF THE) and King Henri II of France in 1559.

JOWETT, Benjamin (1817-93). The academic career of this pugnacious, learned but heterodox scholar was impeded until the cessation of Univ. religious tests in 1869. In 1870 he was elected Master of Balliol. He was an influential educational reformer with a wide political acquaintance.

> "Here come I, my name is Jowett;
> There's no knowledge but I know it.
> I am master of this College;
> What I don't know isn't knowledge."
> *Balliol Rhymes*

He was one of the greatest of teachers and was invariably willing to help men of ability regardless of their background.

JOWITT, William Allen (1885-1957), Ld. (1945), Vist. (1947), E. (1951) called to the bar in 1909, by 1922 when he became a K.C. he was recognised as one of the ablest of jury advocates and common lawyers. He entered politics as Liberal M.P. for the Hartlepools, but supported the Labour Govt.; lost his seat in 1924, and became a member of the R. Commission on Lunacy (1924-6), but was re-elected as a Liberal in 1929. The Labour Prime Minister (Ramsay MacDonald) invited him to cross the floor and become Att-Gen., which he did. This caused great indignation: all but one of the members of his chambers moved elsewhere, but Jowitt resigned his seat and was re-elected as Labour M.P. for Preston in July 1929. In 1931 he supported the National Govt., kept the attorney-generalship and was expelled from the Labour Party. In the Oct. 1931 election he stood as National Labour candidate for the combined universities (whose franchise he wished to abolish) and failed. He then resigned office. In 1936 he was re-admitted to the Labour Party, and in 1939 became M.P. for Ashton-under-Lyne. He was sol-gen. in 1940, paymaster-gen. in 1942, Min. without Portfolio in 1943 and Min. of N. Insurance in 1944. When the Labour Party won the General election of 1945, he became Ld. Chanc., and as such was responsible for the form and much of the content of the far reaching legislation of that period. He relinquished office in 1951 on the fall of the govt.

JOYCE, George (?-after 1670), a London tailor, as a Cornet of parliamentarian horse, seized Charles I at Holmby House in 1647, took him to the Army at Newmarket and subsequently advocated his trial, against the orders of Sir Thos. Fairfax, the C-in-C. In 1650 the Council of State made him Gov. of Portland, but in 1653 Cromwell imprisoned him for 'carping and conspiring' about the Dissolution of the Long Parliament. In 1659 he was employed against the royalists but escaped to Rotterdam at the Restoration. William Lilley claimed that he was the hooded figure who beheaded Charles I. Sir William Temple tried to negotiate for his extradition in 1670 but the Rotterdam magistrates were obstructive enough to enable him to escape without trace.

JOYCE, James (1882-1941) Irish novelist who left Ireland in 1902 and lived mostly in Paris. Dublin provided the background of much of his work, which included *Ulysses* (1922) and *Finnegan's Wake* (1939). These are written in a semi-poetic, often beautiful sub-concious monologue, vastly intriguing to critics, intellectuals and the linguistically curious, but unreadable to most others and so only indirectly influential.

JOYCE, William (1906-46), otherwise 'Lord HAW-HAW', was born in New York of a naturalised Irish father. He spent much of his early life in Britain and obtained a British passport by false pretences. He broadcast from Germany to British listeners during World War II. The effect was minimal, for his enunciation was poor and his claims were at variance with British news releases and with common sense. He was tried and executed for treason after the war, on the ground that, as he had claimed British status by obtaining a British passport, he was sufficiently in allegiance to be capable of treason and therefore a traitor by reason of his broadcasts. The correctness of the judgement cannot be doubted and was upheld on successive appeals, but it is arguable that this trivial and ineffectual offender's sentence should have been commuted.

JOYNSON-HICKS, William ('Jix') (1865-1932), Vist. BRENTFORD of NEWICK (1929), a conservative M.P. was P.M.G. in 1923 and Min. of Health in 1923-4. An evangelical, as Home Sec. (1924-9) he tried to impose his own concept of morality. The period featured prosecutions for obscenity, police interest in courting couples and raids on night clubs. He was also concerned in the ARCOS raid, which was intended, but failed, to produce evidence of Bolshevik plotting. He also, more sensibly, opposed the introduction of the Revised Prayer Book.

JUAN FERNANDEZ Is. (Pac.) were discovered in 1563. *See* SELKIRK, ALEXANDER; DAMPIER, WILLIAM.

JUBILEE. (1) A special Papal indulgence granted to those making a pilgrimage to Rome during a particular year, visiting its major shrines and making confession. First instituted for 1300, it was intended to be centennial, but in 1342 a jubilee was decreed for 1350, in 1389 the interval was reduced to 33 years and since 1470 it has remained fixed at 25.

(2) Of the modern British jubilees, Q. Victoria's Diamond Jubilee (1897) represented the triumphant summit of the British empire, the Silver Jubilee of George V (1935), a sort of patriotic relief after the passing of the 1929-32 depression and that of Elizabeth II was a cheerful national get-together.

JUDGES. The three Common Law Courts each had four judges (called *Justices* in the King's Bench and Common Pleas, *barons* in the Exchequer) who often sat together. All the judges of any two of these courts sitting in the Exchequer Chamber, acted in certain cases as a Court of Appeal from the third; the judges too were habitually consulted in the 17-19th cents. by the judicially weak House of Lords sitting as a final court of appeal, and also they habitually travelled as commissioners of assize on circuit. Their number, twelve, remained constant despite changes in population and volume of business until 1873. To alleviate the growing congestion, serjeants-at-law were often used as additional commissioners of assize, and an increasing volume of lesser criminal business was assigned to Quarter Sessions and magistrates courts and on the civil side to county courts created in 1846.

In the Court of Chancery the congestion was still worse. The only judge was the Lord Chancellor, a politician with many other calls on his time, but his Master of the Rolls gradually took over the lesser business. Mid-19th cent. experiments with a Vice-Chanc. and Lords Justices in Chancery were not entirely successful.

The problem of congestion was only solved with the amalgamation of these courts in 1875, and the progressive creation of enough judges thereafter.

Judges were originally appointed by the Crown during pleasure (*durante beneplacito*) but after 1689 during good behaviour (*quamdiu sese bene gesserit*); High Court judges can be removed only on addresses from both Houses of Parliament or on automatic retirement. Their salaries are charged on the consolidated fund.

JUDGES' RULES, on the conduct of police inquiries and the questioning of suspects, originated in 1906 in a letter of Lord Alvestone C.J. to the Chief Constable of Birmingham in response to a request for advice. The King's Bench judges agreed some rules in 1912 and further rules in 1918. A new set was similarly agreed in 1964. Their general effect is that a suspect must be put on his guard if he is to be questioned, and formally cautioned when charged or told that he may be prosecuted. If the rules are not observed, a court may refuse to admit an accused's statements in evidence; otherwise their effect is persuasive, but, if observed, will usually protect the police against criticism in the conduct of a particular case.

JUDICATURE ACTS 1873, 1875. The Act of 1873 set up a Supreme Court of Judicature of which the old Court of Chancery, the old Common Law Courts of Queen's Bench, Exchequer and Common Pleas, and the Courts of Admiralty Probate and Divorce were to become divisions. There was to be a final Court of Appeal and the jurisdiction of the House of Lords was to be abolished. Before it came into effect the Act of 1875 restored the jurisdiction of the latter because otherwise there would have been no unifying court for England and Scotland. By 1881 the Common Pleas and Exchequer had been amalgamated into the Queen's Bench Division, and Probate, Divorce and Admiralty formed one other. Legislation of 1971 set up a Family Division to which the family business of the Chancery Division and the Divorce jurisdiction were transferred. Probate was transferred to the Chancery Division, while commercial and Admiralty business went to the Queen's Bench.

JUDICIAL COMMITTEE (Sc), was instituted in about 1367 to exercise the appellate functions of parliament. It was merged in the Court of Session in 1532.

JUDICIAL COMMITTEE OF THE PRIVY COUNCIL. *See* PRIVY COUNCIL, JUDICIAL COMMITTEE.

JULIANA of NORWICH (?1342-1416), an anchoress at Conisford (Norfolk), composed in 1393 sixteen *Revelations,* considered the finest mystical writings of the time.

JÜLICH. William of Jülich, count from 1328, mediated at the beginning of the 100 years' war between the German princes and Edward III, who made him E. of Cambridge. He became D. of Jülich in 1356. His descendants acquired Gelders in 1371 and Berg with Ravensberg in 1423. The male line died out in 1511, when Jülich and Berg passed by marriage to John III of Cleves; his successor William the Rich got Gelders back. A leading protestant, he married his sister Anne to Henry VIII. The 16th cent. international importance of the three duchies straddling the Rhine arose because their people were mostly protestant and their rulers could interrupt and tax traffic on the Rhine between R. Catholic southern Germany and the North Sea. William's diplomacy, however, failed to save him in a war with the Emperor Charles V and at the T. of Venlo he had to renounce Gelders and protestantism. He died in 1592 and his son John William died childless in 1609. There were four claimants through four sisters but two, John Sigismund of Brandenburg (Protestant) and Wolfgang William of the Palatinate-Neuburg (R. Catholic) occupied the duchies jointly and partitioned them at the T. of Xanten (Nov. 1614). Brandenburg got Cleves, Mark and Ravensberg. A pact of mutual succession was made in 1666, but was never implemented (*see* BRANDENBURG), probably because by now brown coal (lignite) had been found in vast deposits and the area began to supply Germany with most of its fuel and, from the end of the 18th cent., most of its industrial fuel.

JULIUS CAESAR, GAIUS. *See* BRITAIN, PRE-ROMAN-2.

JULIUS FRONTINUS, SEXTUS. *See* BRITAIN, ROMAN-11.

JULIUS II, Pope (1503-13). *See* RENAISSANCE-11.

JULLUNDUR DOAB. *See* SIKHS-5.

JULY MONARCHY (1830-48). The reign of Louis Philippe of the French.

JUNIOR CARLTON CLUB. *See* CARLTON CLUB.

JUNIUS was the pseudonymous author of some 61 letters contributed to Woodfall's *Public Advertiser* between Jan. 1769 and Jan. 1772. They attacked with skilful and ferocious invective the administrations of the D. of Grafton and Lord North, and the royal association with them. Bedford, Bute and Mansfield were especially singled out. His identity is unknown: but the most probable candidates are Sir Philip Francis, and Laughlin Maclean, Lord Shelburne's under-sec.

JUNKER (Ger), meaning, strictly, a young German nobleman, came to mean an overbearing Prussian military minded landowner.

JUNOT (1) Andoche (1771-1813), Duc d'ABRANTÉS (1808), Bonaparte's A.D.C. in Italy from 1794 to 1796, was with him as a Gen. in Egypt in 1799. In 1805 he was ambassador in Lisbon, and in 1807 commanded the French invasion of Portugal (*see* PENINSULAR WAR). Bonaparte distrusted his competence, and in Russia publicly blamed him for the failures at Smolensk. In 1813 he was relegated to Illyria and committed suicide. In 1800 he had married **(2) Laure (1784-1838)** who was friendly with many *émigrés* and other suspect persons; she published her remarkable *Mémoires* between 1831 and 1835.

JUNTA. A council, committee, cabal or conference. In Spanish-speaking countries it has come to mean a collective body which has assumed the govt. Sydney and Beatrice Webb used the word for the group which guided the policy of mid-Victorian trade unions.

JUNTO (from Sp. *Junta*) was a close group of five whig lords who supported Marlborough and Godolphin in prosecuting the War of the Spanish Succession, and who gradually replaced Tories or less wholehearted politicians in office. They were the E. of Sunderland, Marlborough's son-in-law, who replaced Sir Chas. Hedges as S. of State in 1706; the E. of Wharton, a powerful political manager, especially in Buckinghamshire, who became Ld. Lieut. of Ireland in 1708; Lord Somers, a former Lord Chancellor, who replaced the E. of Pembroke as Ld. President; the E. of Orford, a Russell and a successful admiral, who became First Lord of the Admiralty in 1709; and Lord Halifax, a Montagu, and inventor of exchequer bills who ranked, with Godolphin, as the ablest financier of the time. This was virtually a party Govt., but it was eroded by the intrigues of Harley through Abigail Masham; and its members gradually lost office or resigned in 1710, leaving Marlborough alone in the field. *See* ANNE-6,7.

JURATS are **(1)** the equivalent of aldermen in the Cinque Ports or **(2)** in the Channel Islands, members of the Royal Court sitting judicially under the Bailiff.

JURY, originated in England in the Norman practice of establishing facts by inquiry (*inquest*) of a body of local sworn men (*recognitors*). In problems of landownership 12 Knights might be chosen in the county court to declare on oath who had the better or best right. Theoretically this body spoke of its own knowledge, and in case of disagreement the number would be increased (*afforced*) until 12 were of one mind. They developed into the Grand Jury which customarily consisted of 23 persons, later mainly J.P.s.

Meanwhile the idea that the 12 should be disinterested arbiters of evidence laid before them, rather than themselves witnesses to the facts, was encouraged by the withdrawal of ecclesiastical support in 1215 for trial by battle. The King's Bench now offered a defendant the right to *put himself upon the country,* i.e. to choose trial by a Petty Jury of 12 instead.

The institution of itinerant justices to inquire into what felonies and crimes had been committed and deliver the gaols imported these arrangements into criminal practice. It was natural to inquire of the Grand Jury, which then presented the names of suspected criminals by means of Bills of Indictment (*see* IGNORAMUS). The latter were then given the opportunity to put themselves upon the country (*see* PEINE FORTE ET DURE).

The private consideration of bills by a Grand Jury was considered an important safeguard against frivolous or vexatious accusations. It was abolished in 1933 and an investigation before magistrates substituted. In 1949 special (petty) juries composed of more substantial householders were abolished.

Though not formally abolished, juries in civil cases have been confined almost entirely to defamation cases since World War I. In criminal cases they have long been confined to the 3% minority of serious charges. In 1971 the rule of unanimity was eroded by statute, and it became possible for two dissentients to be overruled by the rest.

Trial by jury in criminal cases was introduced into Scotland in 18th cent., but the system was radically different. *See* JUSTICIARY.

JUS GENTIUM (Lat = The law of nations). A technical term meaning either **(1)** the proper law applicable to strangers, or **(2)** the legal rules common to the law of all nations, or **(3)** international law.

JUSTICE SEAT. *See* FOREST-3.

JUSTICES OF THE PEACE (J.P.) (1) probably developed from knights or substantial persons appointed as keepers of the peace in a county. There is a possible reference to these in the *edictum regium* (q.v.) of 1195, and to inquiries by them in 1263. By 1277 they were accepted and the Stat. of Winchester 1285 assumes their existence. They were specifically given powers of arrest in 1314 and of inquiry into felonies and trespasses in 1316. Commissions of the peace were issued in 1332 and 1338 but the keepers were being supervised by crown appointed magnates at this time.

(2) With the conferment of statutory powers of *oyer and terminer* (to hear and determine cases) in 1344 the keepers were more approximated to Justices of the Peace and began to be ordinarily known as such. Some were appointed on account of their legal knowledge, and with these so-called *justices of the quorum* they could try felonies. After 1350 it became usual to commission them in this form. The Justices of the Peace Act, 1361, seems to have recognised an accomplished fact. It also enjoined the quarterly meetings later called Quarter Sessions. These justices dealt with routine judicial matters which were not too difficult or because there was not too much business. The difficult cases were reserved to the various itinerant justices (e.g. the Eyre, Trailbaston, Assizes or the King's Bench travelling with the King), the latter in troubled times such as the Peasants Revolt (1381-2) and Jack Cade's rebellion (1452) to special commissions.

(3) By 1416 the J.Ps were also beginning to acquire administrative work such as the care of rivers. In 1438 their judicial commissions were standardised to require or empower them to keep the peace, hold inquiries, hear and determine cases, return juries and keep records, but after some hesitations they began to administer such matters as trade legislation, weights and measures and after 1371 the Statutes of Labourers. In 1388 their numbers were fixed at 6 per county, increased to 8 in 1390. In 1414 they were required to reside in their county and in 1439 to have land worth £20 a year in it. By the 16th cent. their business was increasing so much that the limitation on numbers was abandoned.

(4) By 1640 they had become virtually the backbone of the constitution. They had, in addition to functions already mentioned, a wide range of miscellaneous powers. They supervised the poor law and the levying of rates; they were supposed to ensure that the roads were mended. They maintained houses of correction, built bridges, supervised land drainage, gave testimonials to wrecked seamen, licensed ale houses and ensured that people went to church. This and their judicial experience not only trained them as politicians but made them the effective local administration. From their ranks came most of the House of Commons which they could support if the crown defied it.

(5) In theory appointed by the crown, the JPs were in practice recommended by the Lord Lieut. who, as Custos Rotulorum (Keeper of the Records) was not only one of themselves but appointed their clerks and other officials. Once appointed they were in practice irremovable and consequently independent. Parliament continued to heap work, mostly of an administrative kind, upon them right down to the Local Govt. legislation of 1888 and 1894 which transferred to elected councils their administrative functions except the licensing of public houses and the control of the police. *See* POLICE; STIPENDIARY MAGISTRATES; QUARTER SESSIONS.

JUSTICIAR (1) was originally the title of William I's deputy or viceroy during his absences in Normandy. His authority lapsed on his return. The office was held by Odo of Bayeux and William FitzOsborn in 1067, William of Warenne in 1073, Abp. Lanfranc in 1078 and by Odo again in 1087.

(2) William II made the office permanent, beginning with Ranulf Flambard, Bp. of Durham (1088-1100). The justiciar remained the King's Deputy in his absences but otherwise was a kind of royal supervisor, issuing his own writs to judges and taking a leading part in treasury and council business. The office was a difficult one to sustain, for it involved judicial, financial and political ability, a capacity for dealing with the strong and ambitious, and a liability to royal repudiation. The importance of the Justiciar varied, as might be expected, inversely with the royal influence: being at its highest during long royal absences, e.g. under Richard I, and during the minority of Henry III. Its ablest holders were, under Henry I, Roger of Salisbury (1107-8) but Henry also experimented with local Justiciars; under Henry II, Richard de Lucy (1154-79) and Ranulf Glanvil (1180-89); under Richard I, Glanvil's relative Hubert Walter (1193-8); under John, Hubert Walter's pupil Geoffrey FitzPeter (1198-1214). Hubert de Burgh (1215-9), the last great Justiciar was appointed by the baronage because Henry III was a child. The office ceased to be filled permanently with the fall of Stephen Segrave (1232-4) or at all after 1267. The practical reason for this was that it was safer to concentrate power in the hands of a body such as the Council than in the hands of a possibly dictatorial individual.

JUSTICIARY is the Scots criminal jurisdiction. The High Court of Justiciary, the supreme criminal court, consists of the Lord Justice Gen., the Lord Justice Clerk and the Lords Commissioners of Justiciary. These, in fact, are also all Lords of Session. Circuit courts of justiciary consist of a Commissioner with a jury of 15; verdicts of guilty may be made by a majority of at least 9, but a middle verdict of non-proven can also be given and enables the panel (accused) to be pursued (prosecuted) again. The accused has since 1926 been able to appeal from the circuit court to the High Court sitting with a quorum of at least three judges.

JUSTUS. *See* MISSIONARIES IN BRITAIN AND IRELAND-4.

JUTE. Jute was virtually exclusive to India, where jute cloth was made by 16th cent. The raw jute was first imported into Britain (Dundee) in 1838. Large scale operations began in India (Bengal) only in 1855, but Dundee production was overtaken only after the great expansion between 1894 and 1908. The industry had a profound social and physical effect in Dundee where many Irish were employed in slum conditions, but the town profited heavily from the demand for military supplies, such as sandbags in both World Wars. The industry was important to E. Pakistan and subsequently to Bangladesh.

JUTES (A.S. = YTE), a Germanic people speaking a language akin to Frisian, inhabited Schleswig and were perhaps northern neighbours of the Angles, with whom they (or some of them) and the Saxons invaded Britain in the 5th cent. The Frankish Merovingian K. Theudebert (r. 534-48) called himself ruler of many nations including the Jutes, who are also described as trembling before Chilperic I (r. 561-84) K. of Neustria which included the Rhine delta. This and certain farming practices suggest that they had been settled in the Rhineland for some time, and that some were still there. When St. Augustine arrived in Kent (596) the local Jutish King Ethelbert was married to a Frankish Christian princess Bertha. The Jutes occupied Kent, the I. of Wight, parts of Hampshire including the New Forest and some enclaves. Their settlements can be detected by place names, and the presence of the land law called *gavelkind* under which land was divided equally between sons. It was in force throughout Kent, in parts of the I. of Wight, the Meon Valley (Hampshire) and in Kentish Town. It had certain technical features in common with the Welsh law of *tir cyfrif* which suggests that the Jutes learnt from their Kentish victims (*see* WELSH LAW, SOCIAL).

In Kent the Jutes seem to have been divided into two tribes or circumscriptions evidenced by the division between the dioceses of Canterbury and Rochester, and the surviving distinction between 'Men of Kent' east of the Medway and 'Kentish Men' to the west. The probability that they comprised tribes of different origin is suggested by the fact that their settlers along the Thames estuary cremated their dead whereas the others buried theirs. *See* HENGIST AND HORSA.

JUTLAND, B. of (31 May 1916). Following the interception of German radio signals, the British Grand Fleet under Adm. Sir John Jellicoe met the German High Seas Fleet under Adm. von Scheer off Jutland. Six battle-cruisers under V-Adm. Beatty encountered the advance force of five German battle-cruisers under V-Adm. Hipper and lured them in a running fight towards the main Grand Fleet of 24 Dreadnoughts, besides five fast battleships under R-Adm. Evan-Thomas.

Hipper was simultaneously trying to lure Beatty towards his own battle fleet of 16 Dreadnoughts and 6 pre-Dreadnoughts. Two of Beatty's ships blew up, and just as the main battleship action began, a third exploded. In the early evening Jellicoe deployed into line of battle north of and across the head of the German battle line. The latter being in an inferior tactical situation reversed course together, but to reach an unmined passage to their bases they had to re-reverse towards the guns of Jellicoe's battleships and then reverse a third time screened by a destroyer torpedo attack. Jellicoe turned away but not before inflicting heavy damage on Hipper. The mist and nightfall prevented further fleet contact although, as the German battle fleet slipped past the British in the darkness, a destroyer torpedoed a German pre-Dreadnought.

Though the Germans lost only one modern capital ship against three British, others had been so mauled as to make it clear that in daylight fleet encounters the Germans could not win.

The loss of the British battle cruisers was due to lack of protection against fire-flashes down magazine hoists; a defect first suspected at the B. of the Dogger Bank, but not made good. The battle disappointed the British public who were not informed of the need for caution by a Grand Fleet commander, who in Jellicoe's words, "might lose the war in an afternoon". *See also* WORLD WAR I-7,10,11.

JUVENILE COURTS AND OFFENDERS. At Common Law a child under seven was conclusively presumed incapable of committing an offence. This age was raised to eight in 1933 and to ten in 1963. Up to 14 a child was presumed to be incapable of guile but the presumption is rebuttable, and a male was conclusively presumed impotent. Juvenile courts were first statutorily recognised in 1908, though magisterial benches had for some years informally constituted themselves in a manner suitable for dealing with children. In juvenile courts at least one magistrate must be a woman, the public are not (but the press are) admitted, and the names of persons before the court cannot be disclosed without the court's permission. These courts hear charges against the applications concerning persons under seventeen, and care proceedings.

JUXON, William (1582-1663), unfairly called 'Laud's constant acolyte' became Pres. of St. John's Coll., Oxford (Laud's college) in 1621; on Laud's recommendation he was made Clerk of the Closet in 1632, and when Laud was translated to Canterbury, Bp. of London in 1633. In truth Laud recognised in him the tact and abilities which he did not himself possess, and which enabled Juxon to restore St. Paul's and enforce a measure of conformity in his diocese. He added to his functions those of a Lord of the Admiralty from 1636 to 1638 and of Lord High Treasurer from 1636 to 1641. Though summoned as a witness against Strafford, he advised Charles I not to betray Strafford by assenting to his attainder. He nevertheless attended the King throughout his 'trial' and on the scaffold. He was then deprived of his see, and lived during the Interregnum unmolested at his manor at Little Compton (Glos) where he enjoyed the hunting. Charles II made him Abp. of Canterbury at his Restoration.

K

KABUL. *See* AFGHANISTAN.

KACHINS and KACHIN STATE (*see* BURMA). The Kachins, a mountaineer people of N.E. Burma speak six varieties of Tibeto-Burmese. Their territory, which was divided among small chieftains, contains jade mines and so has been intermittently claimed by Chinese govts. since 18th cent. From 1885 the area was administered by the British who divided it into the three districts of BHAMO, MYITKYINA and PUTA-O. Here the Kachins occupied the heights, and the valleys were mostly held by Shans. When the British left in 1947 the Burmese constitution united the three districts into the Kachin State.

KAFFIR, KAFFRARIA. *See* XHOSA.

KAIMAKAM (Turk "Deputy"), was an Ottoman Lieut-col., or Lieut-gov., or a deputy of the Grand Vizier, especially the civil gov. of Istanbul.

KAISER. *See* ROMAN EMPERORS-1.

KAISER WILHELMS LAND. *See* NEW GUINEA.

KALAHARI DESERT (S. Africa), was first crossed by Livingstone and Oswell in 1849. The central part was, and is, inhabited by primitive bushmen.

KALAT. Formerly the leading princely state of Baluchistan.

KALGOORLIE (W. Australia). Gold was discovered in 1887, and there was a Gold Rush in 1892 to 1894. It reached its highest prosperity and population in 1903, remained steady until 1920 and declined until 1929. The rise in gold prices and modern machinery raised the local prosperity thereafter.

KALININGRAD formerly KÖNIGSBERG, renamed after a titular head of the U.S.S.R.

KALISCH, CONVENTION of (Feb. 1813), between Prussia and Russia. Russia was to continue the war against Bonaparte with 150,000 men. Prussia was to desert him and join Russia with 80,000 in return for restoration "to the material power which she possessed before the war of 1806", including a corridor between E. Prussia and Silesia. The implication was that Prussia would abandon Warsaw and receive unstated, but unavoidably German, territories elsewhere.

KALMAR or CALMAR, UNION of (1397). As a result of dynastic marriages and disputes between Swedish factions, the regencies of Denmark and Norway, already in the hands of Margaret of Denmark, were combined with the regency of Sweden in 1389. She was childless and nominated her great nephew Eric of Pomerania as her successor. He was crowned King of the Three Countries in 1397 and Kalmar became the most important political centre of the Union. She died in 1412. The union was not strong: Sweden and Denmark kept their own institutions and Danish commercial rivalry with the Hanse brought naval wars in which Sweden suffered. Eric was deposed in 1439. In 1448 Christian I of Oldenburg was elected in Denmark, but Karl Knutsson Bonde in Sweden. Christian reigned, however, in Sweden from 1457 to 1464. Danish influence in Sweden was decisively ended with the B. of Brunkeberg in 1471, and Sweden maintained a regency of its own under the Sture family (related to Karl Knutsson) until 1520 when most of them were massacred at Stockholm by Christian II of Denmark. Their most important supporter, Gustavus Vasa, however, secured the crown with the help of the Hanse in 1523, and thus brought the Union formally to an end.

KAMBA. A Bantu speaking Kenyan tribe.

KAMIKAZE (Jap = divine wind). The hurricane which wrecked a Mongol Armada, applied by the Japanese to their own suicide pilots in World War II.

KAMPALA. *See* UGANDA.

KANARIS, Konstantinos (1790-1877), was an audacious Greek naval commander against the Turks in the War of Independence. He later opposed King Otto, was prime minister in 1848 and 1849 and a member of the govt.

which deposed Otto in 1861. He was then one of the regents until 1863, prime minister again in 1864, 1865 and 1877.

KANDAHAR. *See* AFGHANISTAN-6,9; ROBERTS.

KANDY. The Sinhalese capital. *See* CEYLON-2-7.

KANGAROO. *See* CLOSURE.

KANO. *See* HAUSA; LUGARD; NIGERIA.

KAPUDAN PASHA. Turkish Lord High Admiral, who after the 16th cent. decline of the fleet, acted as a supplementary foreign Min.

KARACHI (W. Pakistan), was first developed as a port by Hindus in 18th cent., when other ports of the area silted up. The Mirs of Talpur acquired it from Kalat in 1795 and fortified Manora. The British captured and rebuilt the fort in 1839, and in 1843 Sir Chas. Napier made it the capital of Sind. It was then only a village. It developed rapidly after the opening of the Suez Canal, and was capital of Pakistan from 1947 to 1960.

KARAULI. *See* RAJPUTS.

KARENNI STATES (Burma), were the four adjacent principalities of Kantarawadi, Kyebogyi, Bowlake and Mongpai to the S. of the Shan states on the E. Frontier of Burma. From 1922 they were administered, if at all, by the British Commissioner for the Shan states. In 1947 they were merged, and the Karens demanded, and in 1952 got equality of status in the Union of Burma.

KARIBA DAM (between Zambia and Zimbabwe), was built between 1955 and 1959. The hydro-electric scheme was opened in 1960 and the great lake was filled by 1962.

KARLSKRONA (Sweden), was founded as Sweden's chief naval base in 1679.

KARS (Turkey). This important Turkish fortress repulsed the Persians in 1731 and the Russians in 1807. It surrendered to the Russians in 1828 and 1855 and they stormed and annexed it in 1878. It was returned to Turkey in 1921.

KASHGAR (China) CITY and PROVINCE, is at an ancient cross-roads of C. Asia. The city was an important political, religious and commercial centre supported by a fertile agricultural area, and it had strong trading links with E. Afghanistan, Kashmir and N. India. Hence it was coveted by the Russians and the Chinese, and its affairs were watched with concern by British Indian govts. It was under Chinese rule from 1755 to 1862 and then intermittently under Moslem and Russian influence until 1908, when Chinese Govs. returned. In 1928 there was a Moslem rising, eventually put down with Russian help, and from 1937 Russian influence predominated until the Chinese returned in 1943. Chinese communists took over in 1949.

KASHMIR was under Afghanistan from 1757 to 1819 when the Sikh Ranjit Singh conquered it. When the British defeated the Sikhs in 1846, the latter sold it to Gulab Singh, Raja of Jammu to raise one crore of rupees towards the war indemnity of 1½ crores. He obtained British recognition and also conquered LADAKH. Thus this largely Moslem area was misruled by a Hindu dynasty until 1947. At the Indian partition, the Raja Han Singh wished to establish an independent neutral state, but in Oct. 1947 Pakistani tribal and Indian regular troops invaded the territory from opposite directions, and in Jan. 1948 it was effectively partitioned along U.N. imposed cease-fire lines, never legally recognised by India or Pakistan.

KATANGA. *See* ZAIRE.

KATHARINE OF ARAGON. *See* HENRY VIII-3, 11 TO 14.

KATHIAWAR (India), divided in later Mogul times into many small principalities, came under British paramountcy in 1820.

KATRINE, LOCH (Scot.), became the principal source of Glasgow's water when the dam was finished in 1859.

KATTEGAT. *See* BALTIC-6.

KAUNDA, Kenneth. *See* ZAMBIA.

KAVANAGH, Cahir Mac Art (?-1554) MACMURROUGH (until 1550), Ld. of St. MOLYNS (1543), Ld. BALLYANN (1554), a Leinster chief, supported the rising of the Leinster Geraldines in 1538 but shortly submitted and sat in St. Leger's parliament of 1541. He was then involved in a dispute with his kinsman Gerald Kavanagh whom he defeated in a fight at Hacketstown (1545). As a result of the govt's. surrender and regrant policy he renounced his clan title of Macmurrough, but received a barony as a reward for good behaviour in 1554.

KAVANAGH, Arthur MACMORROUGH (1831-89), crippled from birth, was a conservative Irish M.P. (Co. Wexford 1866-68, Co. Carlow 1868-80), but is remembered as an enlightened estate owner who rebuilt villages, subsidised the local railway, and, though a protestant, built an R. Catholic chapel for the Roscommon poor house. As an M.P. he opposed Irish disestablishment but favoured the Land Bill of 1870.

KAY and KAY-SHUTTLEWORTH (1) Sir James PHILLIPS K-S (1804-77), was the first sec. of the committee of council on education from 1839 to 1849 and an originator of the system of public education. He was well qualified for this work, having practised as a physician in the poorer parts of Manchester, and been a Poor Law Commissioner. He also founded the Battersea training college in 1840. His brother **(2) Joseph K. (1821-78),** was an economist who also investigated educational conditions in Britain and abroad.

KAY, John (?-1764), invented the flying shuttle in 1733.

KAZI **(India).** The principal Moslem law officer attached to a Sadar Court. *See* EAST INDIA CO'S COURTS.

KEAN. The principal members of this acting family were **(1) Edmund (1787-1833),** who became a celebrity overnight as Shylock in 1814, and specialised in villainy. His second son **(2) Charles John (1811-68),** started at Drury Lane in 1827 and played all over the English speaking world. Father and son only played together once: in Mar. 1833 Edmund as Othello collapsed into the arms of Charles as Iago and died a few weeks later. In 1842 Charles married **(3) Ellen Tree (1806-80),** who had also begun at Drury Lane, and acted with him until his death.

KEARLEY, Hudson Ewbank (1856-1934), 1st Ld. DEVONPORT (1910), Vist. (1917) was Liberal M.P. for Devonport (1892-1910). He was an U. Sec. in Asquith's first govt. and worked on Lloyd George's Bill to reorganise the London Docks, becoming the first chairman of the resulting Port of London Authority in 1910. In 1912 he successfully stood firm against the second London Dock strike. In Lloyd George's coalition he was the first Min. of Food (1916-17), but preferring advice to compulsion, he did not impose rationing, which Lloyd George thought politically desirable, so the latter replaced him after a few months.

KEBLE, John (1792-1866), fellow of Oriel Coll. Oxford from 1811, joined his father as a parish priest in the Cotswolds in 1823. Here he wrote *The Christian Year* (1827). He was elected Prof. of Poetry in 1831. He and his Oxford friends were increasingly conscious of the dangers of reformist and liberal movements to Anglicanism, and on 14 July, 1833, he preached a sensational sermon before the University on **National Apostasy** and so became one of the leaders of the Oxford Movement (*see* ANGLICANISM). From 1836 he was primarily a parish priest at Hursley (Hants), but he collaborated with Newman (until 1845) and others in the production of the Tracts. Widely admired for his saintliness, he refused preferment. Keble Coll, Oxford was raised in his honour.

KEDAH. *See* MALAYA.

KEDLESTON (Derbys), immense Georgian mansion built by Robt. Adam between 1757 and 1765 on the site of 12th cent. Manor belonging to the Curzon family.

KEELING. *See* COCOS; EMDEM.

KEEP. *See* MILITARY ARCHITECTURE, MEDIAEVAL-4.

KEIGWIN, Richard (?-1690), as naval commandant at Bombay defeated the Maratha fleet in 1679, and led a revolt against the HEIC in 1683. He ruled Bombay in the King's name until 1684 when he surrendered it on receiving the King's orders and a pardon. He was killed attacking St. Kitts (W.I.).

KEITEL, Wilhelm (1882-1946), field marshal, became chief of the German Armed Forces High Command under Hitler in 1938 and so remained until the end. He was hanged for war crimes.

KEITH. *See* ELPHINSTONE.

KELANTAN. *See* MALAYA.

KELLAW, Richard (?-1313). *See* DURHAM-8.

KELLERMANN (1) François Christophe (1735-1820), Duc de VALMY (1808), took command of the French troops at Metz in 1792 and under Dumouriez resisted the Prussians at Valmy in Sept. After various adventures he became an inspector of troops in 1797, and was employed by Bonaparte as commander of reserves until 1814. He took no part in the 100 days. His cunning and ugly son **(2) François Etienne (1770-1835),** a famous French Cavalry commander, fought at Marengo, signed the Convention of Cintra (1808) and commanded a cavalry corps at Waterloo.

KELLOGG PACT (1928), KELLOGG, Frank Billings (1856-1937), was a U.S. Senator from 1916 to 1923, ambassador to London from 1923 to 1925 and Pres. Coolidge's Sec. of State from 1925-1929. Isolationist in attitude, he attempted to reduce naval armaments at Britain's expense at the abortive London Conference of 1927, and with Aristide Briand sponsored the Kellogg Pact or Pact of Paris, under which adherent powers undertook to renounce war and pursue their policies by peaceful means. 62 nations signed it, calculating that, as it contained no sanctions, adherence would improve their image without practical commitment. The Pact was, however, cited by Justice Robert H. Jackson, the U.S. prosecutor as, in part, a basis for the legality of the Nuremberg War Crimes trial of 1945-46.

KELL, Sir Vernon George Waldegrave (1873-1942). In 1907-9 the Committee of Imperial Defence (of which Kell was asst. sec.), prompted by the Metropolitan C.I.D., set up a Secret Service Bureau, both for offensive and defensive secret intelligence against the Germans. He became one of its two directors and then its only one, and was the real founder of MI5. On the first night of World War I he rounded up 21 German spies; and by the end of the war 35 more. These successes ensured the continuance of the service, which he directed until 1940.

KELLS (Meath), originally a royal residence, was granted to St. Columba in 6th cent. and became a bishopric in 807. The splendidly illuminated BOOK OF KELLS, written partly there and partly at Iona, dates from 8th cent.

KELLY, George (1688-1762), alias **John JOHNSON,** an adventurous Irish Jacobite, preached in favour of the Old Pretender in Dublin in 1718, went to Paris and became involved with John Law and his Mississippi Scheme, and then became Francis Atterbury's Sec. in his correspondence with St. Germains. Arrested for treason in London in 1722, he made a spirited defence and was imprisoned. In 1736 he escaped and joined the Young Pretender. He was one of the Seven Men of Moidart in 1745, but escaped after Culloden and became the Young Pretender's Sec.

KELLY, Ned (1855-80), was an Australian bushranger. With Joe Byrne and Steve Hart he roamed the Victoria N.S.W. border from 1878 to 1880, when he was captured (in a suit of home-made armour) at Glenrowan and eventually hanged.

KELSEY. Lincolnshire family. **Robert (?-1335)** a lawyer who migrated to London, became an alderman in 1315 and amassed a large fortune as a financial and property speculator.

KELVIN, William Thompson (1824-1907), 1st Ld. (1892) became Prof. of Natural Philosophy at Glasgow in 1846 and expounded the Second Law of Thermodynamics in 1851. In 1854 he elaborated the mathematics of signalling by cable; in 1867 he patented his mirror galvanometer and siphen recorder. Between 1873 and 1880 he redesigned the mariner's compass, invented a sounding apparatus and the tide predictor. In politics, as an Ulsterman, he spoke at meetings in favour of maintaining the Union. He was also a man of piety, opposed to ritualism and sacerdotalism, and he publicly professed his belief in a Creative Design.

KEMAL, Mustapha (1880-1938), entitled **ATATÜRK** (Father of the Turks), was a Turkish regimental commander at Gallipoli, whose presence of mind defeated the British in their last offensive operation. The resulting prestige raised him in Turkish politico-military affairs. In 1919 he began to organise resistance to his country's economic and political dismemberment after World War I. This involved the creation of a patriotic army out of Allied naval reach at Ankara (which became the capital), westernisation, including a Latin-based alphabet, and secularisation including abandonment of all Ottoman imperial claims outside Anatolia and Roumelia and the incidental abolition of the Sultanate and Caliphate. The Greeks were expelled from Smyrna and Roumelia, and this led to the Chanak Incident (q.v.) and eventually to Lloyd George's overthrow. He proclaimed the Turkish Republic in Nov. 1922 and obtained international recognition for it at the T. of Lausanne (July 1923) where France, Italy and Greece renounced their various claims. He remained an extremely popular dictator and teacher until his death.

KEMBLE. See SIDDONS.

KEMP, Margery (c. 1373-c. 1439), of a prosperous King's Lynn family, incurred a puerperal illness from which she thought herself cured by Christ's direct intervention, and persuaded her husband that they should live in continence while she went on pilgrimages to Jerusalem, Rome, Compostella and holy places at Danzig and elsewhere in Germany and Holland. She wrote *The Book of Margery Kemp,* a forthright if sometimes banal work of devotion and autobiography. She criticized the clergy so fiercely that she was sometimes suspected (but never convicted) of Lollardy.

KEMPE, John (?1380-1454) Card. (1439), Abp. of YORK (1426), Abp. of CANTERBURY (1452), a canonist, administrator and politician who drew more income than inspiration from the Church. He became Dean of the Arches in 1415, Chancellor of Normandy in 1418 and in 1419 Bp. of Rochester, whence he was translated to London in 1421. He was an influential supporter of Card. Beaufort as against Humphrey D. of Gloucester during Henry VI's minority, and in 1426 became Lord Chancellor, but was made to resign in 1432 because he could not control D. Humphrey during the King's and Beaufort's absences. He favoured a French peace, even at the cost of renouncing all rights to the French crown, and was active in the Arras (1435) and Calais (1438) negotiations. In 1450 he became Chancellor again and was responsible for much of the action against Jack Cade, and later, the Yorkists. His tenure of Canterbury was undistinguished.

KEMPENFELT, Richard (1718-82), as a R-Adm. won a brilliant victory against odds over de Guichen off Ushant in 1781. He introduced the divisional system into the navy, reformed the tactical system, and introduced the long-used signal book. He went down with the *Royal George.*

KEMSLEY. See BERRY.

KEN, Thomas (1637-1711), taught at Winchester College from 1672 to 1679 and there wrote two celebrated hymns as well as a devotional book for schoolboys. In 1679 he became chaplain to Mary, wife of William of Orange, whom he admonished for his treatment of her. Charles II made him one of his own chaplains and as such Ken refused to receive the King's Mistress (Nell Gwynn) at Winchester. Charles respected men of principle and in 1684 made him Bp. of Bath and Wells. He gave Charles his deathbed absolution. He was one of the Seven Bishops acquitted in 1688; in 1691, true to form, he refused allegiance to William, and was superseded. Though he made common cause with other non-jurors, he opposed the perpetuation of a non-juring church through the consecration of new non-juring bishops and lived a quiet ascetic life until he died.

KENDAL (Cumbria), had a Roman fort and was a Northumbrian royal burgh. William I gave the barony to Ivo de Taillebois and eventually part of it passed to an ancestor of Q. Katharine Parr who was born there. There was an ancient burgess organisation which secured market charters in 1472 and 1484. The town was incorporated in 1575. The huge parish church testifies to the prosperity of its long established wool and leather trade.

KENDAL, Ebrengard Melusina von der Schulenburg (1667-1742), Duchess of MUNSTER (1716) and of **KENDAL (1719)** became one of George I's mistresses in 1690. Fat, ungainly, rapacious and hated, she made a fortune in bear and bull dealings in South Sea Stock and acted as a broker to titles, jobs, and patents, one of which led to the scandal of *Woods Halfpence.*

KENILWORTH (Warwicks), was given to the Clintons by Henry I and they commenced the huge fortress palace. It was released to K. John in 1207. Simon de Montfort became Castellan in 1258 and his supporters stood a six-month siege after his death at the B. of Evesham in 1265 (*see next entry*). It was the scene of Edward II's deposition in 1327. A Lancastrian possession until the accession of Henry IV, it then passed to the Crown, but Elizabeth I granted it to the E. of Leicester in 1562. He considerably embellished the already grandiose buildings. It reverted to the Crown in 1588. The Hydes defended it for the King in the Civil War and the Roundheads dismantled it. The ruins are still impressive.

KENILWORTH, DICTUM OF (Nov. 1266) (1) dealt with warlike offences committed between 4 Apr. 1264 and 16 Sept. 1265, the period of the Barons' War, by those rebels whose lands had been seized under the Ordinance of Winchester. Breaches of the peace not committed in pursuance of the war were treated as peacetime offences. The Dictum amounted to articles of surrender and conditional indemnity for the Montfortian supporters after the B. of Evesham a year before, but rebels were still in arms elsewhere. Separate articles were agreed with them, and these, so far as they were concerned, extended the war period to the date of their surrender; at Kenilworth this was 14 Dec. 1266, at Southwark June 1267, at Ely Aug. 1267, in Wales Sept. 1267.

(2) The Dictum as an act of pardon and resumption, laid down the terms upon which ex-rebels might redeem their property, whose capital value was reckoned at 10 years purchase. Robert Ferrers, E. of Derby, lost almost all his lands; Henry of Hastings, the commander of the Kenilworth garrison, and those who mutilated a royal messenger had to pay seven years purchase; others who fought openly on Montfort's side paid five; those who merely persuaded others to join him, or who failed the King when summoned paid two; unwilling adherents who left him when they could, paid one; and those at Northampton who did not resist the barons but took sanctuary paid half a year.

(3) The Dictum had to incorporate much detail, for many of the lands had already been granted away or had otherwise come lawfully into the hands of third – or later – parties, and some innocent persons had suffered as rebels or been illegally disseised. Justices were specially commissioned to travel four circuits to enforce the Dictum and disentangle these complications. In practice most cases were settled direct with the crown or privately, and approved by these courts. Nevertheless the litigation and absorption of the rebels into a peaceful society was hardly completed in 1275 and a few cases lingered until the next century.

(4) The Dictum did not apply to Simon de Montfort's son or widow who, accordingly, left the country.

KENILWORTH, ORDINANCE (1326). See EDWARD II-10; STAPLE B-1.

KENNEDY. Violent, influential, S.W. Scottish family and **Es. of CASSILLIS. (1) Gilbert (?-1527), 2nd E.,** a partisan of Arran against Angus, changed sides and was killed in Ayr. His son **(2) Gilbert (?1517-58), 3rd E.,** a pupil, in Paris, of Geo. Buchanan, was a member of James V's council from 1538. He was captured at Solway Moss in 1542 and became one of "The English Lords". On his return he became Lord Treasurer (1554). He witnessed Mary Q. of Scots' wedding to the Dauphin in 1558 but died on the way home. His son **(3) Gilbert (?1541-76),** was a gentleman of the bedchamber to Henri II of France and a partisan of Mary Q. of Scots, for whom he fought at Langside in 1568. He had a powerful following in Carrick and was sometimes called the King of Carrick. Lennox imprisoned him in 1570, ostensibly for pursuing his land claims with too much violence, but Morton released him in 1571 and thereafter he became a comparatively respectable privy councillor. His son **(4) John (?1561-1615), 5th E.,** Treasurer of Scotland from 1598, was equally energetic in pursuing his claims and murdered a kinsman from Bargany in Ayr in 1601. His nephew **(5) John (1598-1668) 6th E.,** a covenanting Lord Justice-Gen., was one of the Scots commissioners to treat with Charles II in 1649 and 1650, and a member of the Scots Privy Council from 1661. His son **(6) John (?1646-1701) 7th E.** was a bitter opponent of Lauderdale's rule in Scotland, and at one stage was outlawed, but his fortunes were reversed under William III, who had him sworn of the council and made him a lord of the treasury.

KENNEDY, James (?1406-65), as Bp. of Dunkeld from 1438 to 1441 was present at the Council of Florence (see LAETENTUR COELI), and as Bp. of St. Andrews from 1441 was a prominent politician under James II of Scots., and under James III, for whom he was regent. He also founded St. Salvator's College.

KENNEDY, John Fitzgerald (1917-1963) ("JFK") U.S. Pres. (Democrat) (1961-3) son of the millionaire Joseph F. Kennedy, an anti-British U.S. ambassador in London (1937-40) who was withdrawn at British request, had spent much time in Britain. His first book *Why England Slept* dates from this period. He was frenetically promiscuous but he and his wife (whom he loved) had, with the aid of a powerful public relations machine, an enormous attraction for younger Americans. The word "Charisma" was reinvented for him. He had a friendly relationship with Harold Macmillan but this masked the decline of the so-called special relationship with Britain in favour of a more rigorous pursuit of the Truman Doctrine. He was assassinated in circumstances which have not been fully explained, but in 1993 it was suggested with circumstantial evidence that the murder was organised by J. Edgar Hoover, the corrupt head of the Federal Bureau of Investigation. See also KHRUSHCHEV, NIKITA SERGEYEVICH.

KENNET, R. & KENNET AND AVON CANAL. See TRANSPORT AND COMMUNICATIONS.

KENNET. See YOUNG.

KENNETH I (MacAlpine), II and III. See SCOTS OR ALBAN KINGS, EARLY.

KENNEY, Annie (1879-1953). Heroic disciple of Emmeline and Christabel Pankhurst, was several times imprisoned before 1912, and when Emmeline was sent to prison she took over the management of the Women's Social and Political Union under the direction (from Paris) of Christabel. An exponent of extreme militancy, she was imprisoned for 18 months in 1913 and underwent a series of hunger strikes and forcible feedings. She maintained her gallant militancy until 1914 when she helped the Pankhursts in their war work.

KENSINGTON and PALACE (London). Holland House was begun in 1605 but only acquired by the Es. of Holland in 1624. Nottingham House was begun in about 1626, bought by William III in 1689, and converted into Kensington Palace by Wren and Wm. Kent. The Palace gardens were open to the public from the first. The borough was amalgamated with Chelsea in 1965.

KENT, Es. of. See BURGH, HUBERT DE; EDMUND OF WOODSTOCK; ODO; GREY, EDMUND; HOLLAND FAMILY.

KENT AND STRATHEARN, Edward Augustus (1767-1820) D. of (1799) 4th son of George III, became C-in-C in N. America in 1799. Prince Edward I is named after him. In 1802 he was Gov. of Gibraltar where his severity caused a mutiny. In 1818 he married Victoria Louisa of Leiningen, who in 1819 gave birth to the future Q. Victoria.

KENT, KINGDOM OF (1) According to Bede, a Vortigern (British paramount ruler) decided to employ a force of Jutes against raiders. They arrived c. 449 at Ebbsfleet (Thanet) under two chiefs entitled **Hengist** (Stallion) and **Horsa** (Horse), settled on Thanet and soon attacked their host. In 455 they killed the Vortigern but were themselves defeated at Aylesford on the Medway, where Horsa was killed. A victory at Crayford in 456 drove the British administration to London. It then seems that the Vortigern was superseded, perhaps by Ambrosius Aurelianus. A counter-attack apparently pushed the Jutes back into Thanet, but they defeated their attackers in 456 at an unidentified place called Wippedesfleot. Hengist went to Holland where he became the legendary founder of Leyden, returned with reinforcements and established a stable dominion in Kent after a victory at an unnamed site in 473. When Hengist was succeeded by **Oisc** or **Aesc,** said to be his son, after whom the Kentish Oiscings were called in 488, Jutish rule was protected by the sea, by bogs and the Weald. The Western Jutes who penetrated to Rochester seem to have been regarded as a separate force.

(2) The detailed resemblances between Kentish Gavelkind and the comparable parts of the Welsh Laws of Hywel Dda, and the probability that Christianity existed in Kent before as well as after the coming of the Jutes, suggest that the Kentish population was largely British and survived the invasions. The leadership or throne of both Eastern and Western forces descended through Aesc, **Octa** and **Hemanric** to **Ethelbert** (r. 560-616), a powerful and rich ruler who by 568 was engaged in an unsuccessful war with Ceawlin K. of Wessex (B. of Wimbledon). In about 572 he married Bertha, *d.* of Ingeborg and Charibert of Paris. The marriage treaty provided that Bertha should have her own chaplain. He was a bishop called Liudhard, and Ethelbert gave them the existing St. Martin's church at Canterbury for their use.

(3) Ceawlin died in 592 and Ethelbert took advantage of the confusion in Wessex to seize London and extend his rule over Essex. He seems, too, to have achieved a pre-eminence over the other Anglo-Saxon rulers up to the Humber. Thus Augustine's mission which arrived in 597 had a peaceful landscape in which to work, and in 604 it was possible to go forward and establish a bishopric at Rochester. This was also the time when Ethelbert recorded the laws of Kent, mainly in the form of a table of fines.

(4) Of Ethelbert's children Ethelburga married K. Edwin of Northumbria and took Paulinus' mission with her. **Eadbald** (r. 616-40) a pagan at his accession, was

later converted. He had, however, to contend with the E. Anglians under K. Redwald. The nationwide influence was lost (and Essex and London) but independence was preserved, mainly because Edwin defeated the other Saxon states but, perhaps on his wife's advice, left Kent alone. Eadbald was followed by **Earembert** (r. 640-64), a fanatical Christian who destroyed pagan shrines and enjoined the strict observance of Lent, but after his death Kent ceased to be an independent or at any rate an effective political entity. Kings **Egbert** (r. 664-73) **Hloththere** (673-8) and **Edric** (686-6) apparently shared the power with, or were subject to, the Essex Kings Oswine and Swaffheard. In 686 Ceadwalla of Wessex imposed his brother Mul by force, but Mul was burned in an insurrection in 687. By 690, after much confusion, the Govt. was shared between the Kentish **Wihtred** (r. 690-725) and the Essex Swaffheard who died in 694 leaving Wihtred in sole possession. His first act was to submit to Ine of Wessex, and pay a heavy wergild for Mul's death.

(5) Wihtred was succeeded jointly by his sons **Ethelbert II, Eadbert** and **Alric,** but under them Kent was fragmented among a number of princelings under the protection of adjacent rulers. The Archbishop was in fact the only universal authority and was issuing his own coinage, but in 774 K. Offa of Mercia invaded and defeated the local forces at Otford. When Offa died in 796 the possibly royal Eadbert Preen (r. 796-9) was made King but the archbishop turned against him and secured a papal bull condemning him as an apostate priest. Cenwulf of Mercia then invaded Kent, mutilated him and imposed his own brother Cuthred as under-King.

(6) Mercian domination lasted about 20 years when Egbert of Wessex claimed Kent by hereditary right through his father **Ealmund** (an otherwise unrecorded Kentish King) and expelled **Baldred** the last King. Kent was already in rebellion against Mercia and it readily submitted to Wessex. In 838 Egbert came to an understanding with Abp. Ceolnoth which safeguarded both sides. The practical effect was that Kent became a kind of appanage of Wessex and in 860 at the accession of Ethelbert of Wessex, its crown was merged with that of Wessex.

(7) This political merger did not, however, result in the disappearance of Kent as a name, or unit or its peculiar institution gavelkind, or its special local organisations all of which survived into the 20th cent.

KENT, William (1684-1748), a Yorkshire coachbuilder's apprentice, was sent by friends to Rome and in 1716 attracted the attention of Richard, 3rd E. of Burlington who befriended him. He was a jack (and sometimes a little more) of many trades: portrait painter, decorator, landscape gardener, sculptor, engraver and monumental architect of such buildings as the Horse Guards and Holkham; he also designed women's dresses and servants' liveries, and probably originated the naturalistic style of English garden layout, developed by Capability Brown.

KENTIGERN or MUNGO, St. (?518-603), probably of British royal descent, was educated by St. Serf at the monastery school of Culross, and became a missionary and eventually bishop to the Strathclyde Britons. Driven out, he preached in Cumberland and in Wales where he founded the monastery later dedicated to St. Asaph. After c. 573 he returned to Strathclyde and died near Glasgow. See CUMBERLAND-2.

KENTISH FIRE. Prolonged and organised applause, or the reverse, said to have originated at public meetings in Kent in 1828-9 on the R. Catholic Emancipation Bill.

KENTISH PETITION (1701), urged Parliament to co-operate with William III in providing funds to re-arm against Louis XIV. Suspecting a whig plot, the Tory Commons imprisoned the petitioners who were automatically released at prorogation.

KENTUCKY. See VIRGINIA.

KENWOOD (London), neo-classical mansion built by Robert Adam in 1764 for Lord Mansfield and converted to house the Iveagh Bequest in 1929.

KENYA (1) highlands were inhabited partly by agricultural tribes of which the Kikuyu (much the biggest), the Luhya and the Kamba were Bantu speaking, and the Luwo Nilotic. The Rift Valley was occupied mainly by Nilo-Hamitic pastoral tribes of which the most prominent were the Masai, Kipsigi and Turkana. The coastal tribes were agricultural and much affected by Islam through contact with the Sultanate of Zanzibar, where European traders and squadrons touched for water on their way to and from India, or for cloves and slaves sold there in abundance.

(2) The interior was first penetrated by British and German missionaries, and then prospected in 1880 by the East Africa Co. In 1895 the 10 mile coastal strip was forcibly leased from the Sultan and became known as the EAST AFRICA PROTECTORATE. Europeans now began to penetrate the highlands, where they took grants of land from the Kikuyu and started lucrative coffee and tea plantations. The whole area was placed under Colonial Office protection in 1905 and both protectorates were collectively known as Kenya from 1920. Jubaland was ceded to Italian Somaliland in 1924 and some Ugandan territory was annexed in 1926.

(3) Prosperity brought some diversification, mainly into sisal, pyrethrum, hides and cereals and it attracted Indian immigration but simultaneously raised a form of local nationalism. The cession of lands had been attended by serious misunderstanding: the settlers had accepted grants from Kikuyu chiefs as acknowledgments of ownership. The Kikuyu regarded land as common to their tribe and incapable of permanent alienation. Moreover in 1922 Jomo KENYATTA (?1889-1978), educated at the London School of Economics, had become sec. of the Kikuyu Central Assoc. and began to preach an independent African Kenya. This led to a govt. compromise (1923). Kenya was to be primarily an African country, but the European holdings in the White Highlands were confirmed. This strengthened the morale of Africans in general and the sense of grievance of the Kikuya in particular: meantime, however, production and prosperity had a calming effect, which was deceptively increased by rising prices and increased employment in World War II.

(4) The rise in African prosperity created a power base on which a nationalist movement could be built. In 1944 Kenyatta launched the Kenya African Union which immediately fastened, as a grievance, upon the influx of Europeans from the confusion attending the independence of India and Pakistan: the Home and Colonial Govt. stuck to the compromise in 1952. The extremist Kikuyu formed the secret terrorist MAU MAU organisation which committed numerous atrocities against settlers and Africans loyal to them. This organisation was managed by Kenyatta, who was arrested and sentenced to life imprisonment (1955) and a state of emergency was imposed which lasted until 1957, by which time Mau Mau had been effectually suppressed. The Union, however, had attracted support in other tribes and decolonialisation was in the air. Informal talks with African leaders led in 1961 to elections in which the Union, now the Kenya-African National Union (K.A.N.U.) gained the largest number of seats, whereupon Kenyatta was released, and as Min. for constitutional affairs led discussions in London (Feb.-Apr. 1962) for Dominion status. In the May 1963 elections K.A.N.U. won an overwhelming victory which made independence certain; in Oct. Zanzibar ceded the coastal strip; in Nov. 1962 the country became a one party state, and independence was proclaimed as a republic within the Commonwealth with Kenyatta as president. Wholesale expropriations of European lands followed.

KENYON (1), Sir Frederick George (1863-1952), was a classical scholar and from 1909 to 1930 a pioneering Director of the British Museum. He understood the need to cater for a relatively uninstructed public and stimulated a wider interest with guided tours and picture postcards, and other expedients now regarded as commonplace. His daughter **(2) Kathleen Mary (1906-78), Dame (1973)** was Principal of St. Hugh's College, Oxford from 1962 to 1973 and a distinguished archaeologist.

KEOGH, John (1740-1817) led a R. Catholic Irish delegation to London in 1791, organised the Catholic Convention in Dublin (1792) and secured the R. Catholic Relief Act, 1793.

KEOGH, William Nicholas (1817-78), elected as a R. Catholic conservative M.P. for Athlone in 1847, opposed Russell's Ecclesiastical Titles Bill, in 1851 was a founder of the Catholic Defence Association, and a leader of the Irish tenant-right movement. He became sol-gen. for Ireland under Aberdeen in Dec. 1852 and att-gen. in 1855 under Palmerston. Irish extremists furiously attacked him for accepting such offices, even though he had resigned on an issue of Irish principle in 1852. In 1856 he became a judge of the Irish Common Pleas and in 1872 he had to try the Galway election petition and found (with a jury) that three R. Catholic bishops and 31 priests had been guilty of religious intimidation, and unseated Capt. Nolan the Home Ruler in favour of Capt. Le Poer Trench the Conservative. His summing up to the jury was fair if forthright. He has been held up as an arch traitor to Ireland ever since.

KEPPEL, Alice Frederica (1868-1947), *née* Edmondestone, married Lord George Keppel in 1891. They had two children but in 1898 she met and became the mistress of Edward, P. of Wales, and so remained after his accession as Edward VII. She was known as *La Favorita*, and was a conspicuous and respected leading member of the Court through her charm, tact, skill as a hostess and ability to keep the King, who did not suffer fools gladly and had a deaf wife, amused. She also had a flair for speculation and made money. When Edward lay dying, her famous tact for once deserted her and she forced an uninvited entry and made an embarrassing scene in the death chamber. In World War I she helped Lady Sarah Wilson to run a hospital at Boulogne, and from 1927 until 1939 she dominated the society of Florence.

KEPPEL (1) Arnold Joost van (1669-1718), 1st E. of ALBEMARLE (1696) came to England with William III and returned to Holland when he died in 1702. He served under Marlborough at Ramillies (1706) and Oudenarde (1708) and was Gov. of Tournai in 1709. His son **(2) William Anne (1702-54) 2nd E.** was Gov. of Virginia in 1737, and after a conventional military career was briefly ambassador in Paris in 1748 and then C-in-C in Scotland. Of his sons **(3) George (1724-72) 3rd E.**, also a soldier, was Gov. of Jersey in 1761 and served in the Havana expedition of 1762. His brother **(4) Augustus (1725-86) 1st Vist. KEPPEL (1782)** sailed with Anson round the world in 1740; was in charge of relations with Algiers from 1748 to 1751; commanded the North American station in 1754, and sat on Byng's court martial in 1757, recommending mercy. From 1765 to 1766 he was a Sea Lord, in 1778 Admiral and C-in-C in the Channel, where his operations against Brest excited accusations pronounced groundless by a Court Martial in 1779 which the opposition celebrated with enormous publicity. In 1782 he became First Lord of the Admiralty. His brother **(5) Frederick (1729-77)** was Bp. of Exeter from 1762. The great-grandson of **(3)** was **(6) William Coutts (1832-94) 1st Ld. ASHFORD (1876)** and **7th E. (1891).** He was superintendent of Indian Affairs in Canada from 1854 to 1857 and then M.P. for Norwich in 1857 and 1859, when he became Treasurer of the Household. M.P. for Wick from 1860 to 1865 and for Berwick from 1868 to 1874, he was U/Sec. of State for War from 1878 to 1880 and again from 1885 to 1886.

KEPPLER, Johannes (1571-1630). *See* RENAISSANCE-14. He published a work on cosmography in 1596 which procured him the friendship of Tycho Brahe and Galileo. He became the former's assistant in 1600 and succeeded to his post as imperial mathematician in 1601. His *De Motibus Stellae Martis* (Lat = The Movement of Mars) was the earliest demonstration of the Copernican thesis. His *Harmonia Mundi* (Lat = Harmony of the World), dedicated to James I, set forth the three laws of planetary motion now called after him, and later inspired the studies whereby Newton developed his *Principia*.

KER of KERR (pron: Car). This Scottish border sept consisted of loosely related families at Cessfurd and Ferniehurst, and the descendants of Mark Ker, Abbot of Newbattle. *See below.*

KER or KERR (pron: Car) Scots landowners. **(1) Mark (?-1584)** Abbot of Newbattle from 1546, renounced R. Catholicism in 1560 but kept the abbacy, in right of which he continued to sit in the Scots parliament. He became a Privy Councillor in 1569 and was one of the lords who carried on the regency after Morton's fall in 1578. His son **(2) Mark (?-1609) Ld. KER (1587), 1st E. of LOTHIAN (1606)** was a friend of James VI and I. He was Scots Master of Requests from 1577 to 1606 and Chancellor in 1604.

KER or CESSFURD (1) Sir Andrew (?-1526), a powerful Border Chieftain, fought at Flodden (1513) and was Warden of the Scottish Middle March from 1515. He died after a victorious clan battle with Scott of Buccleuch. His son **(2) Sir Walter (?-?1584)** carried on the blood feud. He was implicated in the murder of Sir Walter Scott of Buccleuch and banished in 1552, but pardoned in 1553. He became, and remained, a supporter of the factions hostile to Mary Q. of Scots.

KER of FERNIEHURST (1) Andrew (?1471-1545), a Border chief taken by the English in 1523, escaped, but agreed to serve the English interest. His grandson **(2) Sir Thomas (?-1586)**, succeeded as laird in 1562. A Marian privy councillor, he was implicated in Darnley's murder and helped the Queen after her escape from Lochleven. In 1584 he became Warden of the Middle March, but his anti-English or perhaps anti-protestant proclivities aroused govt. suspicion, and he died in prison. His cousin **(3) Robert (1578-1654) 1st E. of ANCRUM (1633)** succeeded as laird in 1590. A courtier and Master of Charles I's privy purse from 1625 to 1639, he retired in 1641 and died in Amsterdam. His son **(4) William (?1605-75) 3rd E. of LOTHIAN (1631)**, having served with Buckingham at the Ile de Ré (1627), and in the Spanish expedition of 1629, became progressively disenchanted with Charles I and took the Covenant in 1638. As a leading Scottish moderate, he was naturally accused of treachery by extremists when in Ireland in 1643. He joined Argyll's forces against Montrose in 1644, and in 1647 was a commissioner to Charles I and was with him at Holmby House. He then became Sec. of State and led the Scottish commissioners sent to protest against the trial of the King in 1649. In 1662 however, he refused to abjure. His *s.* **(5) Robert (1636-1703) 4th E. of ANCRUM (1690), 1st M. of LOTHIAN (1701)** became Ld. Justice-Gen. at the Revolution. His son **(6) William (?1662-1722) Ld. JEDBURGH (1692), 2nd M.**, favoured the Union and was a Scottish representative peer in 1708 and 1715. The brother of **(5), (7) John, 5th E. (1696) and 1st D. of ROXBURGHE (1707)** was Scottish Sec. of State in 1704 and four times a representative peer. From 1714 he was a privy councillor and he was one of the Lords Justices during George I's absences in 1716, 1720, 1723 and 1725. His grandson **(8) John (1740-1804) 3rd D. (1755)** was the bibliophile after whom the Roxburghe Club is named. At his death the dukedom was claimed, eventually with success by **(9) James (1738-1823)** who was awarded it in 1812. A descendant of **(6)**, **(10)** **Schomberg Henry (1833-1900), 9th M. (1870)** was a diplomat until 1870 when he became a politician. He was Scottish Privy Seal from 1874, and Salisbury's Sec. of State for Scotland from 1892. His grandson **(11) Philip Henry (1882-1940) 11th M.**, originally a protégé of Milner, was editor of the *State* in 1908 to 1909 and of the *Round Table*, which he founded, from 1910 to 1916, when he became Lloyd George's private sec. As such, he played a powerful role in dealings between the U.K. and the emergent dominions, and was the principal draughtsman of the preamble to the P. of Versailles (1920). He was an intelligent liberal supporter of the National Govt. of 1931, and in 1932 chaired the committee on the Indian franchise. He became ambassador to Washington in 1939, and died there, much respected.

KERN. A lightly armed, or relatively poor, Irish Tudor foot soldier or a band of them. The word was sometimes applied in Scotland to a highlander.

KEROUALLE, Louise Renée de, (1649-1734), Duchess of PORTSMOUTH (1673) and **AUBIGNY (1674)** was maid of honour to Henriette (Minette) duchess of Orleans, sister of Charles II on her visit to England in 1670 and became one of Charles' mistresses. She was naturalised in 1673, and seems to have exerted some not very important pro-French influence over Charles (*see* FITZROY). He called her Fubbs.

KERRY (Ireland), fell to the FitzGeralds at the Anglo-Norman invasion and remained Geraldine until their fall in 1580. It then became part of the Plantation of Munster (begun in 1586) and much of the land came to the Browne family, later Es. of Kenmare.

KERSEY was a twilled smooth woollen cloth, exported from Suffolk from 14th cent. onwards.

KESSELRING, Albert (1885-1960) Field Marshal (1940), commanded the German air attack on Poland and in the West in 1939 and 1940 and became C-in-C in Italy. He eventually relieved Rundstedt on the Western Front in 1945 and after the surrender was imprisoned for war crimes.

KESTEVEN. *See* LINCOLNSHIRE.

KETCH, John ('Jack') (?-1686), was common hangman from 1663 to 1686. A by-word for barbarity, his name long remained synonymous with his office and a bogeyman for children.

KETT'S REBELLION (1549). An inclosure dispute at Wymondham (Norfolk) developed into a riot in July and then into a major demonstration. In Aug. the people, led by Robert Kett (?-1549) a small landowner, and his brother William, blockaded and then, despite an offer of amnesty, seized Norwich. Three weeks later Warwick's troops scattered them and Kett was executed.

KEW GARDENS, a 15 acre dell laid out by Capability Brown, was much extended by Sir Wm. Chambers who built the pagoda in 1761. Its 10 dragons on the roofs and other orientalisms have disappeared. Sir Wm. Hooker between 1841 and 1865 extended the gardens to some 650 acres, imported plants from all over the world, founded in 1847 with John Henslow the important museum of botanical economy and the plant breeding station, and opened the whole to the public. It provided, *inter alia*, the original Malaysian rubber trees.

KEYES, Robert John Brownlow (1872-1945), 1st Ld. (1943) adventurous naval officer, first came to notice during the Boxer War in China (1900). From 1910 he was effectively in charge of submarines, which he commanded in the North Sea in 1914-5. In 1915 he was C-of-Staff at the Dardanelles, and, passionately but unsuccessfully, advocated a determined naval effort to force them. He was briefly Dir. of Plans at the Admiralty (Oct. 1917 to Jan. 1918) and then, as C-in-C Dover Patrol, planned and led the daring attempts to block Zeebrugge and Ostend (Apr. 1918). During conventional post-war appointments he established naval control of its own air

service (1925) and became Admiral of the Fleet in 1930. From 1934-1943 he was Conservative M.P. for N. Portsmouth, and in 1940 he was, first, liaison officer to the King of the Belgians, and then until 1941 director of Combined Operations.

KEYNES, John Maynard (1883-1946) 1st Ld. TILTON (1942), a prize winner in philosophy and economics at Cambridge, joined the India Office in 1906 and became editor of the *Economic Journal* in 1912 besides being chairman of the National Mutual Investment Society and making a fortune running his own investment company. He was interested in the stage, a member of the intellectual 'Bloomsbury Set' and married the ballerina Lydia Lopokova (1925). He was the main Treasury representative at the Paris P. Conference (1919) but resigned from that disastrous assembly to write the stylistically brilliant *Economic Consequences of the Peace*, in which he held up the P. of Versailles and particularly its reparations clauses as impracticable, vindictive and morally wrong. By 1925 he had returned to the Treasury in search of means to stem the rising tide of unemployment, and this remained the guiding principle behind his *Treatise on Money* (1930) and its more fully developed successor the *General Theory of Employment, Interest and Money* (1936) which made him the most famous economist since Adam Smith. He argued for the timing of public expenditure to coincide with the onset of the recession so as to provide employment otherwise made unavailable. This involved rolling investment programmes and unbalanced budgets. It also, more doubtfully and in the hands of his less competent disciples, led to ill-conceived efforts to control inflation by taxation. In 1940 he published *How to Pay for the War* and became a director of the Bank of England, and from 1943 he led the British negotiations with the U.S.A. on wartime finance and the transition to peace, and in 1944 to the Bretton Woods Conference. He settled (as far as the Americans would let him) the terms of the American Loan Agreement in 1945 just before he died. His ideas dominated British politico-economic policy until about 1978 when Mrs. Thatcher's conservatives started to advocate the return to private ownership of the excessive amounts of property progressively acquired by public authorities since 1939. This dragged in the entirely different concept of a change from a controlled economy to one dominated by the market, subject only to controlled interest rates. The adoption of the latter amounted to an abandonment of Keynes' solicitude for the unemployed, who increased from under 1M in 1980 to nearly 3M in 1993.

KEYS, HOUSE OF. *See* TYNWALD; I. OF MAN.

KEYS, POWER OF THE. *"Thou art Peter and upon this rock will I build my church ... and I will give unto thee the keys of the Kingdom of Heaven; and whatsoever thou shalt bind on earth shall be bound in heaven; and whatsoever thou shalt loose on earth shall be loosed in heaven"* (AV St Matthew 16 vv 18–19). This passage was the foundation of the doctrine that by apostolic succession from St Peter, the Popes can admit or refuse to admit a person to the beatific vision. Its authenticity is uncertain because *Peter* and *rock* constitute a pun in Greek and Latin, but not in Aramaic in which the words, if spoken at all, must have been uttered. The Latin version of the italicised words, in letters nine feet high, decorate the dome of St Peter's in Rome. The keys (golden to bind, silver to loose) appear in church heraldry and on public house signs.

KHAIRPUR (Pakistan), was part of Sind until 1783 when the Baluchi Talpur family overthrew the Kalhora rulers of Sind, and obtained a grant (*sunnud*) of the province from the Amir of Afghanistan. Sohrab Khan, one of the Talpurs, set himself up as Mir of Khairpur, and in 1813 his successor ceased to pay tribute to Afghanistan. In 1842 the British forced the Mirs of Sind to pay tribute to

Shah Shuja, their nominee in Afghanistan, but when British Afghan policy collapsed, the Baluchis attacked the British but were put down by Sir Chas. Napier. Khairpur thus became tributary to the British, and so remained until 1947 when the state acceded to Pakistan. *See* KARACHI.

KHAKI (Urdu = dust coloured). Twilled cloth for military use was tried by Lumsden and Hodson in India in 1848. The War Office adopted it for active service in 1884.

KHAKI ELECTION (Oct. 1900). *See* SALISBURY'S THIRD GOVT.-15.

KHALIFA. *See* CALIPHATE; SUDAN-5.

KHALSA. *See* SIKHS-2.

KHAN. A Tartar or Persian chief or ruling prince.

KHANPUR or CAWNPORE. *See* INDIAN MUTINY.

KHARAN. *See* BALUCHISTAN.

KHARTOUM. *See* GORDON; SUDAN.

KHASSADARS. *See* KHYBER PASS.

KHEDIVE (Pers: 'Prince'), was the title confirmed by the Ottoman Sultan to the hereditary Pasha Ismail of Egypt in 1867 and used until 1914.

KHYBER PASS (Pakistan), the usual invasion route into India, was first penetrated by the British when Wade escorted an Afghan notability to Kabul in 1839. The Khyber tribes came under British control as a result of the T. of Gandamak in 1879, after the Second Afghan War. In 1897 British officers were withdrawn, whereupon the Afridis seized the pass and closed it. The Tirah expedition of 1897 eventually defeated them, and thereafter the Khyber Rifles were formed under British officers to hold and police the pass with military support from Peshawar. After the Third Afghan War the Rifles were disbanded in 1919, and replaced by British subsidised tribal levies called *Khassadars*.

KIAOCHOW. *See* CHINESE TREATY PORTS.

KID[D], William (?1645-1701), emigrated to America when young. In 1696 he was commissioned by the Gov. of Massachusetts and members of the British govt. to clear the pirates from the Eastern Seas. He reached Madagascar in 1697 and promptly joined them, but on his return to Boston in 1699 he was charged with piracy by taking the *Quedagh Merchant* belonging to the Great Moghul, and with murder. He was hanged in London. Q. Anne gave his considerable effects to Greenwich Hospital. He buried treasure in various places but little has been recovered.

KIDDERMINSTER (Worcs.). *See* CARPETS.

KIEL and KIEL CANALS. Kiel was a Hanseatic port from 1264. The shallow medieval **Stecknitz canal,** built between 1381 and 1398, silted up in the 15th cent. The city became part of Denmark in 1773 and the 10ft. deep **Eider Canal** was cut between 1777 and 1784. This was made obsolete by the rapid growth in the size of ships. The present (1996) 60-mile **Kaiser Wilhelm, Nord Ostsee** or **Kiel Canal** was built between 1887 and 1895 for naval as well as commercial reasons and enabled the German battle fleet as then designed to dominate the Baltic without reducing the defence of the North Sea coast. The launch of the British H.M.S. *Dreadnought* in 1906 rendered the canal as well as all other battleships strategically obsolete, and immense and urgent works to deepen and widen it (besides raising bridges and rebuilding locks) were completed only in June 1914. International freedom of navigation was established by the T. of Versailles in 1919 but lapsed when Hitler denounced the treaty in 1936. It was reimposed in 1945. In 1992 it was the world's busiest waterway.

KIKUYU. *See* KENYA.

KILBRACKEN. *See* GODLEY.

KILDARE. *See* FITZGERALD (KILDARE).

KILDARE ST. SCHOOLS (Ir.), represented a multi-denominational effort to educate the Irish poor. The Kildare Place Society (Dublin) was started in 1812, began receiving govt. grants in 1814 and opened its first model schools in 1817. Scripture was read without comment and no other religious instruction was given. This ultimately provoked the hostility of the R. Catholic hierarchy, which petitioned against the principle in 1824.

KILIMANJARO, Mt. (Tanzania), was first reached by the German missionaries Rebman and Krapf in 1848.

KILKENNY (Ireland), consisted from Norman times of two towns. Irishtown was chartered by the bishops of Ossory, Englishtown by the Earls Marshal. The castle was acquired by the 3rd E. of Ormonde in 1391. The place surrendered honourably to Cromwell in 1650. The two towns were at last united in 1843.

KILKENNY, CONFEDERATION OF (1642-6) This political, R. Catholic and military organisation approximated to an Irish govt. outside Ulster and Dublin from its formation in May 1642 until the Cromwellian reconquest of 1646-50. *See* CIVIL WAR-9,18,23,24; COMMONWEALTH AND PROTECTORATE-2.

KILKENNY (Ir.) STATS. OF (1366). (*See* LIONEL OF ANTWERP.) Distinguished between the *King's Lieges* living in the ten obedient shires (i.e. Louth, Meath, Dublin, Kildare, Carlow, Kilkenny, Wexford with the Liberties of Trim, Waterford and Tipperary) and *Irish enemies,* the native Irish, living elsewhere. The lieges were forbidden to parley with, marry or sell armaments to them; there was to be no recourse to Brehon law, and they were not to have or entertain Irish minstrels or story tellers, or indulge in Irish sports, e.g. hurling and quoits. Only English was to be spoken and English dress worn, and all, whether English or Irish dwelling in the obedient shires, were to use English surnames, follow English customs, and practice the longbow. The statutes, often confirmed until 1495, failed to prevent the English from "going native" or their gradual retreat to the Pale. Licences to break the law had habitually to be given, especially for admission of Irish monks to monasteries; noblemen such as the 3rd E. of Desmond were renowned Irish poets; Brehon law was generally followed, and in 1541 a Speakers' Address had to be translated into Irish so that parliament could understand it. The statutes were repealed in 1613.

KILLEARN. *See* LAMPSON.

KILLIGREW. Cornish family. **(1) Sir Henry (?-1603),** was M.P. for Launceston in 1552 and an exile under Mary I. Elizabeth I employed him as a diplomat in France and in Scotland in 1566 and 1572. His nephew **(2) Sir Robert (1579-1633),** was a courtier and financier, and a shareholder in the drainage of the Bedford Level. He was intermittently imprisoned, partly for his links with Sir Thomas Overbury, with whose death he may have been connected. Of his sons **(3) Thomas (1613-83)** and **(4) Sir William (1606-95)** were poets and Restoration playwrights while **(5) Henry (1613-1700)** got the Mastership of the Savoy (out of which he made a fortune) because his sister was one of the King's mistresses. A son of **(3), (6) Charles (1655-1725)** was Master of the Revels from 1680, while his half-brother **(7) Thomas (1657-1719)** was yet another court playwright. A son of **(5), (8) Henry (?-1712)** was an unsuccessful admiral.

KILLING TIME, THE (1679-82). The period, so-called, by Covenanters, after the failure of their 1679 rising, when numbers of lowland covenanters were hunted down. *See* MACKENZIE-SEAFORTH-3.

"KILMAINHAM TREATY" (Apr. 1882). *See* GLADSTONE'S SECOND GOVERNMENT-6.

KILMARNOCK, E. of. *See* BOYD.

KILMUIR, David Patrick Maxwell Fyfe (1900-67) 1st Vist. (1954). *See* FYFE.

KILVERT, Francis (1840-79), a country clergyman, left diaries of which only about 10% survive. These relate to life at Clyro (Radnor) and Langley Burrell (Wilts) where he was a curate. They convey with sensitive acuity the village life about him and provoked intense public interest as a television series in 1977.

KILWA. *See* PORTUGUESE INDIES.

KILWARDBY, Robert (?-1279), after teaching in Paris, became English Provincial of the Dominicans in 1261. Gregory X nominated him Abp. of Canterbury in 1273; he became a Cardinal Bishop in 1278 and took some of the Canterbury judicial records with him. They were never recovered.

KIMBERLEY, E. of. *See* WODEHOUSE.

KINCARDINE (Sc.) (Gael. Head Field i.e. the cultivation closest to the mountains) or **MAERNS,** coastal **COUNTY** and **TOWN.** The Romans built camps at Raedykes, Normandyke and the ford under the Dee at Perculter. The area was originally Pictish, but at some early period the Scottish Kings occupied it, built a castle in the town and created a county of 19 parishes. That it continued to be a disputed area may be inferred from the number of castles. Besides Kincardine, Dunnottar and Fetteresso there were at least six others. The area was strongly Jacobite in 1715 and 1745 and suffered from depredations by Cumberland's army, but is rich agriculturally, and there have always been excellent sea fisheries (from Stonehaven) and river fisheries in the Avon, Dee and Feugh.

KINDLY TENANTS were Scottish customary tenants common, mostly on ecclesiastical estates, up to the middle of the 16th cent. when they mostly lost their holdings.

KINDERSLEY, Robert Molesworth (1871-1954) 1st Ld. (1941) a merchant banker, who held many important directorships, was from 1916 to 1946 chairman of the War (later National) Savings Committee through which the govt. was able to raise some £12,000M at low rates of interest.

KINEL or CINEL (Ir.). A group of associated or allied clans.

KING (1) from A.S. *cyning* (cf German König) which is said to be related to *cynn* = Kin, and explained as 'scion of the kin' or 'scion of one of noble birth' or more plausibly is 'one who personifies the kin'. The title was always very high, and until 12th cent. used in relation to the nation rather than the territory. This usage continued in Scotland until 1603.

(2) Though inferior in precedence to an Emperor, a King was always regarded as sovereign, independent and obliged to no other ruler save of his own free will. Bohemia was thus considered not to be part of the empire even though its King had a vote in imperial elections. The Elector Frederick of Prussia's anxiety to be King in Prussia was due to his desire to be rid of Polish suzerainty over that part of his dominions.

(3) English and French Kings were anointed at coronation. The special symbols of Kingship are an arched crown and a sceptre. In continental heraldry only kings may use angels as supporters, or enclose their arms in a pavilion.

KING, Mackenzie. *See* CANADA-27.

KINGHORNE. *See* LYON.

KINGLAKE, Alexander William (1809-91) wrote *Eothen* in 1844, accompanied St. Arnaud's column in Algeria in 1845, and went to the Crimea in 1854. At Lady Raglan's request he published his 8 vol. *Invasion of the Crimea* between 1863 and 1887. He was also M.P. for Bridgwater from 1857 to 1865.

KING PHILIP'S WAR (1675-76). The American name for a devastating war between the New England colonists and the Mohawks. King Philip was the English nickname of Metacomet (c. 1640-76), chief of the Wampanoag clan. The settlers did not recover the lands lost in the fighting for 45 years. *See* NEW ENGLAND; WAMPANOAG.

KING'S BENCH was a common law court held in the King's presence and, therefore, originally peripatetic. In 1268 it acquired a Chief Justice of its own and by 1300 it was sitting without the King. By 1400 Kings seldom sat in person, and never gave judgments; by 1500 they never

sat, but the fiction was maintained in the documents until the unification of the judicial system in 1875. The Court was said to have a supreme jurisdiction throughout England. It could deal with all pleas of the crown (i.e. crime) and matters touching the King, all errors of fact and law in other courts, extra judicial errors tending to a breach of the peace, and trespasses. Its Chief Justice was considered the highest common law judge.

KING'S BENCH PRISON (Southwark), established in the 13th cent. became increasingly a prison for debtors who, for a consideration, might live in the adjoining area called the *Rules.* It was rebuilt in 1754 and abolished, along with imprisonment for debt, in 1869.

KING'S BOOK (1543). *See* TEN ARTICLES.

KINGS BOOKS. *See* VALOR BENEFICIORUM.

KING'S CONFESSION. *See* COVENANT.

KING'S COUNTY (Ir.) (before 1556 and after 1921 Offaly). *See* IRELAND C-2.

KINGS COLLEGE (1) CAMBRIDGE was chartered in 1441, but building finished only in 1515. It was a royal peculiar and until the university reform it was largely independent of the University too. **(2) LONDON** was chartered in 1828. It developed faculties (engineering 1838, hospital 1839, theology 1846, Civil Service classes 1856, Higher Education for women 1885 etc.) and by 1908 was performing most of the functions of a London university, into which it was amalgamated in 1908.

KINGS CUP. British aviation trophy awarded between 1922 (120m.p.h.) and 1938 (236m.p.h.).

KING'S (or QUEEN'S) COUNSEL (K.C. or Q.C.). The increase of legal business under the Tudors over-whelmed the King's Attorney who took to appointing 'Kings learned counsel' to advise in difficult or important matters, on permanent retainer. By 1590 there was a recognised body of them and in 1604 Francis Bacon was appointed by royal patent. This precedent was followed, and until about 1700 they were royal advisers, and could not appear against the crown without permission (a rule which still technically survives). Thereafter they were simply leading practitioners. Until after World War II they had to be accompanied in court by a junior barrister who had to be paid a fee of two-thirds of the fee paid to his leader.

KING'S EVIL or scrofula, a form of tuberculosis, was thought to be curable by the royal touch. The power of healing it, was claimed by the English and French royal houses and was connected with the use of chrism at the Coronation. The custom of touching sufferers was maintained intermittently from the time of Henry III until the accession of the Hanoverians and by the Stuart Pretenders. The practice was nourished by almsgiving which attracted real or simulated sufferers and by the manner in which this self-limiting disease cures itself.

"KINGS FRIENDS" (1766 *et seq.*), were an unorganised body of important but second rank politicians who, in the political instability of the years after 1760, thought that the executive, i.e. the King, should, in the absence of strong leadership, be supported so as to obtain at least effective administration. The term connoted an attitude, not a connection with the court; many of them were not placemen, and their affiliations differed widely. They included high aristocrats such as Lds. Granby and Strange who had been associated with Grenville and favoured a strong policy towards America, Hans Stanley a diplomat, and the ambitious lawyer Sir Fletcher Norton. They agreed in disliking the existing parties or factions of Rockingham, of Bedford and Grenville, and of Pitt, and thought of themselves as a fourth and largest party which had "always hitherto acted upon the sole principle of attachment to the Crown". In the absence of a great name to lead them, they thought that "His Majesty should have the free choice of his servants ..." The supporters of the factions used the phrase 'Kings Friends' as a term of political vilification which misled many, then and later.

KINGS INNS (Dublin). There was originally an association of Irish judges and barristers which gave no degrees. **Colletts Inn** was founded outside Dublin as a training body under Edward I, but was sacked by marauders and driven within the walls. Sir Robert Preston C.B., of the Exchequer in Ireland then accommodated the inn at his house (c. 1340) and it became known as **Preston's Inn.** When the courts were moved from Dublin Castle to the dissolved Dominican monastery in 1542, the Inn also moved there. As Henry VIII had just proclaimed himself King of Ireland, it changed its name to King's Inns. To achieve legal uniformity, its barristers had always to be called to the bar by one of the four London Inns. By 1607 it had declined to a point where self conscious revival under gubernatorial patronage was necessary and the reconstituted Inn enrolled attorneys as well. Corruption and incompetence reduced it to virtual bankruptcy by 1782, and the Irish parliament allowed attorneys to be admitted without training. In fact barristers without an English training had been intermittently, if covertly, admitted since 1706. In 1782, however, the society was chartered and the new governing body took power to make its own rules. These provided for call by an English Inn after training in Ireland. These arrangements remained theoretically valid until 1920, but the English call had by then long been a nominal requirement.

KINGSLEY (1) Charles (1819-75), Vicar of Eversley (Hants), published *Westward Ho!* in 1855 and was Prof. of Modern History at Cambridge from 1860 to 1869. He published the *Water Babies* in 1863. (*See* CHRISTIAN SOCIALISM; NEWMAN, CARD. HENRY.) His brother **(2) George Henry (1827-92),** a courageous medical specialist on cholera, was best known as a world traveller. His brother **(3) Henry (1830-76),** a novelist and journalist, edited the *Edinburgh Daily Review* from 1864 and was present at the B. of Sedan (1870). George Henry's daughter **(4) Mary Henrietta (1862-1900)** explored the west coast and western rivers of Africa from 1895.

KING'S LORDS. *See* RESTORATION-4.

[KING'S] LYNN (Norfolk), owed its early importance to a position facing the North Sea and Baltic, a rich agricultural hinterland and the complex of tributaries to its river, the Great Ouse, which facilitated transport of heavy cargoes over a wide area. Of Saxon origin, it belonged to the Bps. of Thetford and passed, after the Conquest to the Bps. of Norwich, who granted it to the Cathedral in about 1118 but resumed it in about 1200. John de Gray, a friend and supporter of K. John, followed John's municipal policy. He obtained a borough charter in 1204 and a merchant charter in 1206. It naturally attracted the Baltic trade, and the Hanse had a steelyard. It was one of the foremost medieval English ports, and churches, colleges and an elaborate guildhall survive from that period. In 1524 Henry VIII incorporated it and in 1537 added "King's" to its name because it resisted the rebellion of 1536. It was royalist in the civil war. Its commercial prosperity continued into the 18th cent., from which many merchants' mansions survive. The export of wool and cloth gave way to other more industrialised products, in 19th cent., but railways and, later, metalled roads attracted major activity to other ports while silt in the Wash diverted the growing ships elsewhere. Hence it remained prosperously static, while other ports overtook it. The years after World War II, however, saw a new development in the use of the many picturesque yet under-used buildings for an increasingly successful annual arts and music festival.

KING'S MEN (Scot). *See* JAMES VI (SCOTTISH REIGN)-2.

KING'S PEACE originally (a) reigned in the precincts of royal residences and the four great Roman roads; (b) protected children, lunatics, foreigners and persons without kindred; (c) was involved in certain crimes which so grossly affronted the moral or religious sense that they could not be atoned in money. Such criminal acts were considered an injury to the King and amenable to the jurisdiction of his court. There was a tendency for the King's Peace to grow at the expense of other protections and jurisdictions. In particular more trade meant more foreigners. There were more offences which could not be atoned in cash (e.g. in Henry I's time secret homicide, robbery, coining, rape, arson, forcible entry). There were more people (e.g. manumitted slaves) without kindred. The state became better organised and there were more public duties whose breach was a contempt of the King. This in due course extended to disobedience of royal commands and legislation. Moreover the greater power and efficiency of royal justice tempted litigants to extend the King's Peace, as it were, themselves, and ultimately any allegation of breach of the King's Peace immediately took the case to the King's Bench. This led slowly to the supersession of local private jurisdictions by the royal courts.

KING'S or QUEEN'S PRINTER. The person to whom the crown delegates its right to publish statutes, proclamations and other public documents. Since 1845 documents evidently printed by him are considered true copies of the original. He shares with Oxford and Cambridge Univs. the monopoly of the Authorised Version of the Bible and the Book of Common Prayer until the year 2040.

KINGSTON. *See* PIERREPONT.

KINGSTON (Jamaica), laid out rectangularly in the late 17th cent., became the capital in 1692 when an earthquake engulfed Port Royal. It was almost destroyed by fire in 1780, but quickly recovered through the prosperity of the sugar trade. There was a damaging earthquake in 1907. It has been the most important Caribbean city since about 1750.

KINGSTON'S CASES, THE DUCHESS OF. The seductive Elizabeth Chudleigh (1720-88) secretly married Augustus Hervey, later E. of Bristol in 1744 and bore a short-lived baby in 1745. He was mostly abroad on naval service and she was riotously promiscuous at Court. She became the D. of Kingston's mistress. Hervey suggested collusive divorce proceedings, but as these involved a private bill in parliament she settled for a suit of jactitation. She then married the vastly rich Duke (1769). He died in 1773, leaving her his personal property and a life interest in his huge estates. To destroy her rights, the husband of the Duke's rapacious niece charged her with bigamy. This led to four leading cases: **(1)** though a woman, she successfully claimed privilege of peerage; **(2)** at her trial in the Lords she pleaded the ecclesiastical decree in jactitation, involving a finding that she was single, as a bar to the prosecution for bigamy, but it was held that as the Crown was not a party to the jactitation proceedings it was not estopped from prosecuting at Common Law. She was found guilty and **(3)** pleaded privilege of clergy, and (having previously loaded her cash, pictures and valuables onto her private yacht) fled the country because the niece's husband was preparing proceedings which (she being a convicted felon) might end in outlawry and the seizure of her fortune. She travelled the Continent, acquiring a villa in Rome, another near Paris and building a distillery near St. Petersburg, and always calling herself the Duchess of Kingston. **(4)** She was then sued (on the basis of the conviction) in the King's Bench for using someone else's title, but the court held in her favour that in her case it was a mere name and that there was no property in a name. Her activities and character were lampooned in the press, but she forced Samuel Foote (q.v.) to withdraw a scurrilous play about her. The foregoing is a very pale summary of a singularly rumbustious career. *See* FREEMASONRY.

KINGSTON, T. of (Sept. 1217) (*see* HENRY III-2) between Louis of France and the English Council, provided for a gen. amnesty for the English rebels, the restoration of their lands, and their exemption from all ransoms other than those already agreed. The late Eustache le Moine's brothers were to give up the Channel Is., and Louis undertook never again to support English rebels and perhaps also to procure the restoration of Normandy and other French fiefs. The Council paid him 10,000 marks to hasten his departure.

KINGSTON UPON THAMES (Surrey), on the best ford into Middlesex west of London was an ancient manor, where the W. Saxon Kings were crowned and established upon a stone (which still exists). NORBITON and SURBITON, the northern and southern outlying farms were part of the manor. Royal and Church councils, notably that of 836 under K. Egbert, were held there, and the town's prosperity grew rapidly after the bridge was built, perhaps in 11th cent. John granted the earliest known charters in 1200 and 1209 and there was already a grammar school in 1264. This was reformed in 1561. The bridge had to be rebuilt in 1828, by which time Kingston was becoming a market with small industries for the district, and Norbiton and Surbiton were becoming residential. The arrival of the railway with stations in all three places in the 1840s hastened these developments, and after 1888 Kingston, though not the County town, became the county administrative centre. Surbiton became a separate district in 1894.

KING'S TOWN (Ir.), before 1821 **DUN LEARY,** after 1921 **DUN LAOGHAIRE,** was a fishing village converted between 1817 and 1859 into an outport for Dublin and station for the Holyhead packets.

KINGSWAY. *See* FLEET (LONDON).

KING'S WIDOW was the widow of a tenant in chief. She could remarry only with the King's licence or forfeit a year's dower. This was a useful source of royal revenue. The Master of the Court of Wards and Liveries was empowered to compound such forfeitures.

KING WILLIAM'S ILL YEARS. In Scotland the four famine years of 1695-99.

KINLOCH, CLAN. *See* CLANS, SCOTTISH.

KINLOSS, Edward (1549-1611), 1st Ld. (Sc.) (1603), had been a judge of the Edinburgh Commissary Court until 1583 when he was given Kinloss Abbey *in commendam.* He was ambassador to Elizabeth I in 1594, 1598 and 1601, being also appointed a Lord of Session in 1597. His judicial standing and legal knowledge made him an acceptable envoy to Burghley and his supporters who wanted a quiet succession. James VI & I made him a peer before taking him to England where he was appointed to the then inferior office of Master of the Rolls.

KINNOULL. *See* HAY (KINNOULL).

KINROSS-SHIRE (Scot.), originally consisted of three parishes detached from Fife and depending upon Loch Leven Castle. Some small parts of Perthshire were added in 1685. The area was progressively enclosed between 1705 and 1845.

KINSHASA or LEOPOLDVILLE. *See* ZAIRE.

KINTAIL. *See* MACKENZIE (SEAFORTH).

KIPLING (Joseph) Rudyard (1865-1936), returned to India in 1882 after an unhappy education in England and worked until 1889 as a journalist. He married an American and lived in Vermont until he quarrelled with his brother-in-law. Thereafter he had a home in England, but travelled much in S. Africa. The greater part of his prose writing took place between 1886 and 1909 and his fame rests on his short stories and ability to conjure up atmosphere in them, but they are distinguished by the conscientious imperialism of the better colonial administrator, and in his Indian pieces, by an acute ear for the native temperament. Maligned on account of his versification, his finest work, *Kim,* shows an understanding sympathy with Indians of all kinds. Attempts have been made by modern critics to rehabilitate his verse.

KIPSIGI. *See* KENYA.

KIRK (Sc.). *See* SCOTLAND, PRESBYTERIAN CHURCH OF.

KIRKALDY OF GRANGE. (1) Sir James (?-1556), Lord Treasurer of Scotland and a political and religious opponent of Card. Beaton was privy to Beaton's murder at St. Andrews (1546) in which his son **(2) Sir William (?1520-73)** took part. Besieged in St. Andrews Castle, he was taken by the French and condemned to the galleys, but on Francis II's accession with Mary Q. of Scots as his consort, he was released and entered French military service. He subsequently returned to Scotland, still a protestant and opposed those about Mary, whom he considered a victim of evil men. He opposed the Darnley marriage, was party to the Rizzio murder, and joined the rising against Bothwell. He accepted Mary's surrender at Carberry Hill and was himself mainly responsible for her defeat at Langside. He protected her from the Edinburgh mob, however, and was converted to her party as a result of her sufferings. He and Maitland of Lethington held Edinburgh Castle for her until forced to surrender, when he was hanged.

KIRKBY'S QUEST (1284-5), was an investigation by Edward I's treasurer John Kirkby into Knights' fees held in chief, and debts owing to the crown in certain areas.

KIRKCALDY (Scot.), a possession of the bishopric of St. Andrews, was given in 1240 to the Abbey of Dunfermline. When it became a royal burgh in 1450, the Abbey transferred the lands to the corporation. By this time it was growing into a port for the Netherlands, and in 1644 it became a free port. After the union it declined in the face of English competition and, in the American War of Independence, of rebel piracy. Its fortunes were, however, restored in 18th cent. by the establishment of linen weaving. It was united with Dysart in 1930.

KIRKCUDBRIGHT, SHIRE or STEWARTRY of (Scot.), grew up around a chapel associated with St. Cuthbert. The area, part of Galloway, was ruled by Ostmen between about 800 and 1100 and they prevented the spread of Roman law and left the local magnates much to themselves. Local criminal and revenue jurisdiction was from 13th cent., exercised by a steward under the Lordship of Galloway or the Crown, whichever happened to be the stronger. The stewartry became a Balliol possession in 1245, but passed to the Black Douglases on the victory of Robert Bruce (early 14th cent.). The Douglas power was broken when James II stormed Threave Castle in 1455. The stewartry ceased to function in 1708, but the term was still in use in 1972.

KIRKE, Percy (1646-91), a relative of the Cornish Killigrews, son of a court official, and a professional soldier, served with the French army and was Gov. of Tangier from 1682 to 1684. The Tangier Regiment which he commanded, was known ironically as Kirke's Lambs, from Catherine of Braganza's paschal lamb badge which they used. He and they were particularly brutal in suppressing the Monmouth rebellion in 1685.

KIRKWALL. *See* ORKNEY.

KIROV, Sergei Mironovich (1886-1934). In 1920 was Russian agent in Georgia whose govt. he subverted. In 1921, as Sec. of the Azerbaijan Communist Party, he made the acquaintance of Stalin. In 1926 he succeeded Zinoviev in a similar post at Leningrad and in 1930 became a member of the politburo. He was murdered in 1934 and Stalin, who probably instigated the murder, used it as a pretext for murdering his own political opponents in increasing numbers.

KIRSET (Scot), or PEACEFUL SETTING was a period, usually a year and a day, during which a new settler in a burgh had to build a well secured tenement and during which he paid no rent. In isolated or dangerous places such as Dingwall or Dumbarton the rent free period might be ten or five years. *See* BURGH.

KIRTON. *See* CREDITON.

KIT CAT CLUB. A pro-Hanoverian society which met at Christopher (Kit) Cat, the pastry cook's house in London. Founded in 1700 by Jacob Tonson the publisher, its 39, eventually 48 members included Walpole, Vanbrugh, Congreve, Addison and Steele. Each member gave Tonson a half length portrait of himself by Kneller, and portraits of this kind are known as *Kitcats*. It was dissolved in 1720.

KITCHEN CABINET (1964-70 and 1974-6), was the journalistic nickname for Harold Wilson's semi-private advisers as prime minister, prominent among whom was Marcia Williams (later Lady Falkender). Its political influence seems to have been less than was supposed at the time (cf. GARDEN SUBURB).

KITCHENER, Herbert Horatio (1850-1916), 1st E. KITCHENER of KHARTOUM, fought in the French army in 1870, did survey work in Palestine (1874) and Cyprus (1878), became a major of Egyptian cavalry (1883) and Gordon's intelligence officer (1884). In 1886 he returned to the Sudan and then secured a job reorganising the Egyptian police (1891). From this point of vantage he used his talent for intrigue to become Sirdar (1892), and as such he rebuilt the Egyptian army (1892-6) and reconquered the Sudan (1896-8), of which he became Gov. Gen. He replanned Khartoum. In 1899 he became Lord Robert's Chief of Staff in S. Africa and planned the system which ended guerrilla resistance there. He then became C-in-C in India (1902-9) where he quarrelled endlessly with Curzon, reorganised the Indian Army, and eventually forced Curzon to resign. He was unemployed for two years but in 1911 he became, as British Agent, Consul-Gen., and Min., virtual ruler of Egypt. He was in the process of putting a land reform into effect when World War I broke out, and he became Sec. of State for War. The appointment had been made by the public rather than the cabinet, in which his position was rather that of an independent potentate than of a member of a group. The Cabinet deferred to his conduct of war policy with an ill grace. He had arrived too late to influence the resistance to the opening stages of the German western offensive (whose course he guessed rightly) but correctly foresaw that the war would last years rather than weeks or months. The First B. of Ypres (Oct-Nov 1914) marked the final consolidation of the trench-front from Switzerland to the North Sea. He drew the conclusion that only great violence by masses of men and material would overthrow the enemy. He therefore launched his great recruiting drive, which netted 1,000,000 volunteers by the end of the year, and insisted on wholesale conversions of industry. He early realised that proper communication and co-operation with Russia was essential, and that the enemy cordon between Russia and the western allies had to be broken through. He thus contemplated overthrowing Turkey through Alexandretta (Iskanderun) from Cyprus and Egypt, but a Russian appeal for help diverted attention and resources to the navally sponsored attack on the Dardanelles (q.v.). The failure of these operations was not his fault, but anxiety about continued Russian disasters then induced him to consent to diversions on the Western front as the only available spot where pressure could be brought. The resulting allied frontal attacks, the British at Loos (Sept. 1915), the French further south, were expensive failures in which they lost three times as many men as the Germans. Meanwhile the latter had temporarily shot their bolt against the Russians who were organising ripostes. The first of these, on the Beresina (Mar. 1916), was vast in apparent scale but ineffectual. There were, too, disquieting political reports. The Cabinet, which wanted Kitchener out of the way, persuaded the great man to go on a fact-finding mission to Russia. He sailed for Archangel in June in the cruiser *Hampshire* which struck a mine. He was drowned.

KLAIPEDA. *See* MEMEL.

KLÉBER, Jean Baptiste (1753-1800), with Marceau defeated the Vendean army at Savenay in Dec. 1793; had a variety of commands under Jourdan between June 1794

and 1797 and then went to Egypt with Bonaparte who left him in command when he himself deserted to France in Aug. 1799. He was assassinated.

KLEPHTS (Gr. = Thieves). Those who would not submit to Turkish rule in 18-19th cent. Greece, or bandits.

KLIP RIVER REPUBLIC (1846-7), was set up by migrating Natal Boers west of the Klip and Buffalo Rivers across the present boundary between Natal and the O.F.S. Sir Harry Smith, Gov. of the Cape, found most of the other Natal Boers trekking miserably nearby over the Drakensberg Mountains and offered them land. Some accepted. Some returned to coastal Natal, others went on with Pretorius some 200 miles to Potchefstroom. The Klip River republicans, now unsupported, returned to Natal or crossed the Buffalo. Their republic dissolved.

KLONDIKE (Yukon, Canada), was the scene of the notorious **gold rush** of 1896, later hilariously portrayed by Charlie Chaplin in a film of the same name.

KLOSTERZEVEN, CONVENTION OF (1757). *See* BALTIC-48; GEORGE II; HANOVER-11; SEVEN YEARS' WAR.

KNATCHBULL-HUGESSEN, Sir Hughe Montgomery (1886-1971), already an experienced diplomat, was Min. at Nanking from 1936 to 1938, when he was severely wounded by the Japanese. After a year's recuperation he became Ambassador at Ankara. He held that the Turks were so unprepared for war that it was in Britain's interest to keep them neutral, which, despite diplomatic conflicts with Franz von Papen the German ambassador, he did. Ankara, as the neutral capital closest to enemy territory, was an echo-chamber for secret intelligence in both directions, and between Nov. 1943 and Feb. 1944 the embassy security was penetrated and his secret papers copied for von Papen by his valet (whom the Germans code-named Cicero). These included accounts of the Moscow, Cairo and Teheran conferences. Though not of military importance, Cicero caused a huge unwarranted press sensation later. From 1944 to 1947 Sir Hughe was ambassador to Brussels. He then took, on retirement, the Court post of Marshal of the Diplomatic Corps, but meanwhile his eye had been caught by the similarity of the chalklands of the Downs and Champagne. He took French viticultural advice and planted vines. His vineyard flourished and was producing good and profitable wine by his death. His example inspired others and led to the revival and expansion of the English wine industry which had languished since 14th cent.

KNEBWORTH (Herts.). Mansion built by Sir Robert Lytton between 1492 and 1540 and Victorianised by 1st Lord Lytton in 1843.

KNELLER or KNILLER, Sir Godfrey (1646-1723), came from Lübeck (Germany) and established himself as an English portraitist in 1672, when Charles II sat for him. He was appointed chief court painter with John Riley in Dec. 1688. Even allowing for his long working life, the number of his ascribed portraits is so large and the similarity of the sitters, especially the women, so marked that he must have used mass production techniques and professional models. *See* KIT KAT CLUB.

KNIGHT OF THE CHAMBER. A knight bachelor created in peace time.

KNIGHTHOOD, DISTRAINT OF. A landowner worth a certain minimum amount per year could collect an aid from his tenants on the knighting of his eldest son and might have to pay an aid on the knighting of his lord's eldest son. He would, in theory, have to lead his men into battle, and would have to be a knight to do so. Hence he was liable to be compulsorily knighted. When professional armies replaced the feudal host, fines made on distraint of knighthood became, in effect, a tax supplementary to scutage. Henry III and Edward I particularly tried to oblige landowners to accept the obligations of knight service, the qualifying income level varying according to the King's needs. Under Henry III it was £20; under Edward I £40, though he admitted that an income of £100 was really needed to support a knight. In 1279, however, he levied amercements on those with over £20 who had evaded knighthood and again tried to demand the service on this basis in 1297, thereby adding to the discontent of the time. Thereafter knighthoods became increasingly honorific rather than military, and distraint fell into desuetude until Charles I revived the practice in 1629 to raise money, with high rates of fine. Inflation had brought into the distrainable class many middle-sized landowners who had not been in it before, and the measures, though very profitable, alienated many of them. Distraint was abolished in 1641.

KNIGHTHOOD, and KNIGHT SERVICE. See LAND TENURE; FEUDALISM; KNIGHTHOOD, DISTRAINT OF.

KNIGHT MARSHALL. An officer of the Marshalsea with jurisdiction over offences committed within the royal household and verge, and over contracts to which a member of the household was a party.

KNIGHT v WEDDERBURN (1778). See SLAVERY IN BRITAIN.

KNIGHTON, Henry (?-1396), a canon of St. Mary's Leicester, wrote an unfinished continuation of Ranulf Higden's *Polychronicon.* Much of the earlier part comes from Walter of Hemmingburgh and there is a gap between 1366 and 1377, but the part dealing with the years 1377 to 1395, a major source for the period, is almost entirely original. At St. Mary's he could secure eyewitness accounts, such as that of the B. of Radcote Bridge.

KNOLE (Kent). A huge mansion begun by Abp. (later Card.) Bourchier in 1456, passed to the crown and was granted by Elizabeth I to Thos. Sackville, 1st E. of Dorset, who was a relative of her mother. He made Jacobean style extensions in 1605, and later members of the family made more classical additions. They also collected pictures, furniture, carpets and tapestries during the 17th and 18th cents. The house was given to the National Trust in 1946.

KNOLLYS (Pron: "Noles"), a London family descended from Sir Thomas Knollys (? -1435) Ld. Mayor in 1399 and 1410. **(1) Robert (?-1521),** a royal usher and dogsbody, married Lettice Penyston (?-1557) and she, after his death, married successively Sir Robert Lee of Burston (?-1537), and then Sir Thomas Tresham (?-1557) Prior of the Hospitallers under Mary I. Of the children **(2) Henry (?-1583),** a popular protestant at court under Edward VI and Elizabeth I, was employed in diplomacy with the German Protestants in 1562 and as gaoler of Mary Q. of Scots at Tutbury, and of the D. of Norfolk in the Tower. His brother **(3) Francis (?1514-96),** married Catherine Carey, whose mother, Mary Boleyn, was Elizabeth I's aunt, and briefly Henry VIII's mistress. The brothers were thus prominent at court and Francis became a friend of the Princess Elizabeth. Under Mary I, Francis and Catherine fled to Strasbourg, and returned in 1558 when he became Elizabeth I's vice-chamberlain and she a woman of the privy chamber. They were rich, having inherited Rotherfield Greys and acquired Caversham, Cholsey (Berks) and Taunton (Somerset). He first became an M.P. in 1559 and, as a friend of Cecil, was a regular govt. spokesman in the Commons until his death. Despite his increasingly extreme Protestantism, the Queen trusted him as a relative, and employed him in awkward tasks, especially in equipping the Havre expedition at Portsmouth in 1562, and in trying to control the cost of Sir Henry Sydeney's Irish wars in 1566, when he became Treasurer of her Chamber. In May 1568 he was sent to Carlisle to share the custody of Mary Q. of Scots with Ld. Scrope. He achieved a certain intimacy with his fascinating but hysterical and demonstrative ward, whom he tried to convert. Mary naturally kept on good terms with him until he left her, on account of his wife's death at court, at Tutbury in Feb. 1569. She had, however, failed to shake his allegiance, for in 1571 he supported

the legislation for protecting Elizabeth's life and in 1572 she made him Treasurer of the Household, even though she disliked his religious zeal: he much encouraged persecution of recusants and by 1584 was quarrelling with the bishops. Meanwhile his daughters **(4) Lettice (1540-1634),** one of the beauties of her day, married Walter Devereux, 1st E. of Essex, and after his death became the mistress and then the wife of Robert Dudley, E. of Leicester, and finally married Sir Christopher Blount. Three other daughters made court marriages, and of his seven sons five were M.P.s. One son **(5) William (1547-1632) 1st Ld. KNOLLYS (1603) 1st Vist. WALLINGFORD (1616) 1st E. of BANBURY (1626),** was also a court personality but though well rewarded, refused to support Charles I's policy of personal rule. *See* BANBURY PEERAGE CASE; ELIZABETH I-28 *et seq.*

KNOX, John (1505-72), began preaching the reformed religion in Scotland in 1547. He was caught in St. Andrews Castle when the French invested it, and was sent as a prisoner to France in 1548, but released in 1549, at English intercession. He came to England and preached at court, but fled to France at Mary I's accession and made his way to Calvin's Geneva in 1554. Thence he became Min. of the English Calvinists at Frankfurt, but after a brief recall to Scotland returned to Geneva in 1556. There he published against Mary Q. of Scots the *First Blast of the Trumpet against the monstrous regiment of Women* which offended other women rulers including Elizabeth I and Catherine de'Medici. He then made his way, with English connivance, to Edinburgh, where his fiery eloquence was serviceable both to Elizabeth and to the Lords of the Congregation. In 1560 he published his *Treatise on Predestination* and he, with his political and English allies, forced the French forces to leave. The next stage, in the virtual interregnum before Mary Q. of Scots could arrive, was to stampede parliament. This "Reformation Parliament" of 1560 abolished papal jurisdiction, adopted a Calvinist Confession and passed enactment's against monasteries. In 1561 (when Q. Mary arrived) Knox's *Book of Discipline* (q.v.) appeared; in 1564 his *Book of Common Order,* the church service book. Parliament enacted a Presbyterian church constitution in 1567, which was not as thorough-going as the *Book of Discipline.* In furtherance of his political programme for establishing Calvinism in Scotland he repeatedly denounced the sexual morals of Q. Mary and her husbands and alleged lovers.

KNYVET, Sir Henry (?1537-98), had court connections through his grandfather and father. He was an important Wiltshire personality and three of his daughters married into comital families. He became a gentleman pensioner (bodyguard) to Elizabeth I in 1560, when he was wounded at the siege of Leith, and was M.P. for Wootton Basset or Malmesbury from 1571 to 1597. His interests were mainly concerned with military, as opposed to naval, defence and how to pay for it, and for this reason his views conflicted fundamentally with those of the sea-orientated govt. He seems, however, to have been trusted enough to have been able to make a fortune by embezzling crown forest rents.

KOHIMA (Manipur q.v.) on the Indo-Burmese frontier. *See* WORLD WAR II-10.

KOH-I-NOOR, a huge Mogul diamond seized by Nadir Shah when the Persians sacked Delhi in 1739, fell at his death to the Afghan Ahmed Shah Durrani. The British-supported Afghan pretender Shah Shuja had it until he was driven into the Punjab, where he had to surrender it to Ranjit Singh. The British acquired it in 1849 when they annexed the Punjab, and it became a British Crown Jewel. It was recut in 1852.

KOKAND (C. Asia). The Khanates' subjection in 1865 and annexation in 1876 marked a distinct stage in the Russian southward advance from Siberia.

KOLA PENINSULA. See ARCTIC EXPLORATION.

KOLHAPUR (India), was a small Maratha coastal principality founded by the second son of Shivaji. Its piratical ships provoked British naval expeditions in 1765 and 1792; in 1819 it was taken by land in the Third Maratha War, and became tributary. It was merged when India became independent in 1948.

KÖNIGSBERG (KALININGRAD). Capital of the Duchy and early Kingdom in Prussia.

KÖNIGSMARCK, Count (?-1694), lover of Q. Dorothea, wife of the Elector George (later George I) of Hanover. He was murdered in Berlin and she divorced.

KOOPS, Mathias (fl. 1789-1805), a Pomeranian naturalised in 1790, invented important processes for recycling paper and for making it from straw and wood. He set up the biggest paper mill in the Kingdom at Millbank (London) in 1801, but his business capacity was unequal to the size of the enterprise and it failed in 1804.

KORAN. *See* ISLAM.

KORDOFAN (Sudan). This large area was disputed between Sennar and Darfur in 18th cent. After a war beginning in 1784, it fell to Darfur, which held it until 1821. The Egyptians then conquered it in pursuit of their slave-trading policies and it remained under their tyranny until the 1882 Mahdist revolt, which began there. In 1883 a British-led expedition under Hicks Pasha was wiped out at Kashgil. It was Mahdist territory until the B. of Omdurman in 1899, when it remained part of the Anglo-Egyptian Sudan.

KOREA, became independent of the Mongols in 1392 under its own dynasty which ruled (under nominal Chinese suzerainty) with varying efficiency until modern times. A treaty with Japan in 1876 was followed by others with U.S.A. in 1882 and Britain in 1883. The Japanese invaded it without warning in 1894 and so brought on their victorious war with China. Western intervention resulted in the Japanese, at the second T. of Shimonoseki, obtaining only Formosa and an indemnity, Korea being declared fully independent. Hence in 1897 the King assumed the title of Emperor. Independence was based in fact on a balance of international interests and the Russian presence at Vladivostock and Port Arthur. The latter was captured in the general Russian defeat of 1904-5, in which Japanese operations were conducted largely from Korean soil. By the T. of Portsmouth which ended this War, Korea consequently became a Japanese protectorate. In 1910 the Emperor was dethroned, and the country became a Japanese colony. In 1919 it was incorporated in Japan. At the Cairo Conference (Nov. 1943) it was agreed that it should again be independent, and in 1945 Russian and American zones of occupation were established N. and S. of the 38th parallel. The two powers failed to agree upon the form of govt.; in 1948 a republic was set up under Syngman Rhee with its capital at Seoul, while a communist state was set up at Pyong-yang. In June 1950 communists including so-called Chinese volunteers invaded the Republic but were driven back by American and other western troops acting under the authority of the United Nations Security Council, in which the Russians, because of a political absence, were unable to impose their veto. This fighting included a famous stand by the Gloucester Regiment. In Oct. they took Pyong-yang, whereupon the Chinese intervened and drove them back to the sea, but by July 1951 a counter attack had retaken most of the South and devastated much of the North. The truce of 1954 left the country divided as before. With American aid and an authoritarian Govt., the Republic became a successful exporter of industrial goods, while maintaining strong forces. Save for a military Govt., between 1961 and 1963, presidential rule prevailed. North of the 38th parallel the People's Republic developed more slowly, and followed doctrinaire communist models. The two republics first spoke to each other at a Red Cross meeting at Pyong-yang in 1972.

KOREISH. *See* CALIPHATE-3.

KOSSOVO POLYE (Serb = Field of Blackbirds). A Balkan battlefield where the Moslem Turks overwhelmed Christian Serbs (1389) and Magyars (1448). The adjacent province, named after it, was heavily colonised by Moslem Albanians. Hence Albania claimed it on racial, the Serbs on emotional, grounds. There was also oil at the Serbian end. The province became the scene of a bloody conflict (1995-9) culminating in an American-led N.A.T.O. attempt to impose peace by force, in which British troops participated. Serbia was bombarded from U.S. aircraft carriers and submitted in June 1999, whereupon Russian troops from Bosnia intervened.

KOTAH. *See* RAJPUTS.

KOTTE. *See* CEYLON.

KOWEIT or KUWEIT. The as-Sabah dynasty was established in 1756. The Ottoman Turks tried to take control in the 1890s: the Sheikh accepted British protection in 1899, and so was able to resist the termination of the Berlin-Baghdad railway there. In 1914 the British recognised Koweit as an independent protected state, and this played some part in their operations against Mesopotamia in World War I. Saudi hostility brought intermittent raiding, which was ended by the creation of a neutral zone on the southern frontier under the T. of Uqair (1922). The Iraqi boundary was settled in 1923. In 1934 oil prospecting began, and oil was found in 1938; development began only in 1946 (after World War II) and was exceedingly rapid. In 1961 the treaty of 1899 was mutually revoked, whereupon Iraq claimed Koweit as part of her territory, and attacked. British aid stopped this, and in 1963 Iraq again recognised Koweit, which joined U.N.O. Koweit supported Egypt in the Israeli War of 1967, but for the most part was preoccupied with problems of wealth. In 1989 it was suddenly attacked and overrun by the Iraqis who were driven out by western forces including a large British component. The Iraqis systematically fired the hundreds of oil wells. They burned for several months, causing perceptible worldwide air pollution. *See* GULF WAR.

KOWLOON. *See* CHINA-32; HONG KONG.

KREMLIN (Russ: *Kreml*), is the citadel or 'forbidden city' of a number of capitals of old Russian principalities, most importantly at Pskov, Novgorod, Smolensk, Suzdal, Yaroslavl and Nizhni-Novgorod. The Moscow Kremlin was the largest and when Moscow again became the Russian capital after the Revolution, the word became synonymous with the Russian govt.

KRIO. An Anglo-African composite language spoken by West African Creoles.

KRONSTADT (Russia), was captured by Peter the Great from the Swedes in 1703, and converted by him into a fortress, naval base and commercial harbour for St. Petersburg. It lost its trade when the channel was dredged to the city in 1885. This also made it possible for warships to come inland and permitted one of the dramatic events of the Russian Revolution, the mutiny of the Cruiser *Aurora* and her bombardment of St. Petersburg. In 1921 the Kronstadt sailors mutinied again, against the Bolshevik regime.

KRUGER TELEGRAM. *See* JAMESON RAID-2.

KRUPP. Of this family of German steel millionaires **(1) Friedrich (1787-1826),** founded the firm at Essen in 1811. His son **(2) Alfred (1812-87)** extended the business by manufacturing for the railway boom and from 1856 by selling armaments. His son **(3) Friedrich Alfred (1854-1902)** acquired works at Magdeburg, the Germania shipyards at Kiel and built the Rheinhausen steel works. The business was now heavily involved in armaments. It was inherited by his daughter **(4) Bertha (1886-1957)** who married **(5) Gustav v. BOHLEN und HALBACH (1870-1950)** in 1906, and the name **KRUPP v. BOHLEN** was thenceforth appropriated to the head of the business. Though accused of war crimes in World

War II, ill health prevented his trial, but his son **(6) Alfried (1907-67),** was condemned and imprisoned for employing slave labour. An order to liquidate most of the undertaking, could not be enforced and he died still managing it.

KHRUSHCHEV, Nikita Sergeyevitch (1894-1971). *See* U.S.S.R. 12-16.

KSHATRIYA. *See* CASTE.

KUALA LUMPUR (Malaysia), was founded as a Chinese tin mining village in 1857. It superseded Klang as capital of Selangor in 1880. In 1882 Sir Frank Swettenham became resident. He persuaded the Sultan to rebuild the town in brick and build a railway. Between 1882 and 1895, when it became capital of the Federated Malay States, the population had grown from 5,000 to 25,000. In 1957 when it became capital of Malaya it was 316,000, only 15% of whom were Malay. In 1963 it became capital of Malaysia.

KUBLAI KHAN. *See* MONGOLS. He is the subject of a famous unfinished poem by S. T. Coleridge beginning:

In Xanadu did Kubla Khan
A stately pleasure dome decree,
Where Alph the sacred river ran
Through caverns measureless to man
Down to a sunless sea ...

Coleridge, who took opium, composed it in his sleep after reading *Purchas His Pilgrimage* on Mongolia, and started to write it down when he awoke, but was interrupted by a gentleman on business from Porlock, and when the gentleman had gone, Coleridge found that he had forgotten four fifths of the poem.

KULTUR **(Ger. =** *Culture***).** A term used ironically in allied World War I propaganda to mean German tyranny.

KUNWAR SINGH (?-1858). Rajput rebel leader in Bihar during the Indian Mutiny.

KUOMINTANG. *See* CHINA-37,38.

KURDS, favoured the development of a series of feudalised principalities among these border people, and in the 1830s five survived on Ottoman territory and two in Persia. They were all suppressed leaving much unrest, which turned into nationalism parallel with that of other Ottoman minorities. The first Kurdish newspaper appeared in 1897, and Kurdish delegates attended the peace conference of 1919 when the T. of Sévres created a Kurdish state. The treaty was never ratified because of the Turkish military revival under Atatürk. Turkey, Iraq and Persia opposed the creation of such a state whose area and location might be used to control the headwaters of the Mesopotamian rivers and interrupt oil supplies, and the frontiers fixed by the later Ts. of Lausanne (1923) and Ankara (1926) divided Kurdistan between them. The area was now convulsed by Kurdish rebellions which intermittently occupied nineteen of the years between 1920 and 1990. Three were against Iraq, three against Turkey and two against Persia. After 1989 the Iraqis attempted systematic elimination using, in some villages, a type of nerve gas, but were frustrated by the United Nations.

KURILE Is. (Pac.), were annexed by Japan in 1875, and ceded to Russia in 1945 as a result of the Yalta agreement. They are important for fishing, whaling and their strategic position across an oceanic approach to the Siberian Pacific ports.

KYLSANT. *See* PHILIPPS.

L

LAAGER (S.A. Dutch = camp). (1) A camp protected by a temporary fortification consisting often simply of wagons. **(2)** In World War II a similar formation of tanks encamped for the night.

LABEL, in heraldry is a mark thus ⊓⊓⊓. Superimposed upon a shield it denotes in the case of a commoner, an eldest son. For royalty, labels of different colours and ornamentation, denote different junior branches.

LABOUCHÈRE, Henry Du Pré (1831-1912), a wealthy and witty radical, entered politics in 1864, became part proprietor in 1869 of the *Daily News* to which in 1871 he sent celebrated dispatches from the besieged city of Paris. In 1877 he launched *Truth* which specialised in exposing frauds, and in 1880 he became M.P. for Northampton. He wanted to abolish the House of Lords, destroyed Pigott's reputation on the Parnell Commission and helped to secure, and took part in, the Jameson Raid Inquiry. He was as much a critic of Rosebery, his nominal leader, as of the Tory Chamberlain. He retired in 1906.

LABOUR (AND NATIONAL SERVICE) MINISTRY OF, was created in 1916 under war pressure although employment exchanges (q.v.) and trade boards had been functioning for seven years. In 1917 it was concerned in certain kinds of wage fixing; from 1919 it promoted industrial conciliation and arbitration. The first National Insurance Act was passed in 1919. The Act of 1934 which required the means test for uncovenanted benefits, was administered by the Unemployment Assistance Board independently of the Minister. From 1939 the Ministry administered the deployment of labour (mostly by compulsory direction) in the interests of defence, added the words 'and National Service' to its name, and created the necessary registration and identity card system. Wartime dislocation and the entry of vast numbers of women into industry involved the Ministry in welfare activities, in professional appointments, and (jointly with the Home Office) in factory inspection. In 1944 however, it lost its national insurance functions to the new Ministry of National Insurance; the end of conscription terminated its connection with defence in 1959, and its functions were transferred to the Dept. of Employment in 1968.

LABOUR DAY. 1 May.

LABOUR ELECTORAL ASSOCIATION (1887) was the successor of the Labour Representation League.

LABOUR EXCHANGES. *See* EMPLOYMENT EXCHANGES.

LABOUR PARTY (1900) was formed after a Trade Union congress resolution of 1899 to summon a special congress of 'co-operative, socialist trade union and other working-class organisations' to establish means for securing 'an increased number of labour members to the next parliament'. The resolution was inspired by Keir Hardie and his Independent Labour Party (I.L.P.). The congress met in Feb. 1900. It represented trade unions, the I.L.P., the Fabians and the Social Democrats, and it set up the Labour Representation Committee (L.R.C.), which was instructed to establish a distinct Labour group in parliament. The L.R.C. had instantly to fight a general election: it contested 13 seats and won 2. By 1903 it had won 3 more at by-elections. The *Taff Vale* case, however, increased trade union interest, which had been hitherto more theoretical than real, and in 1906 the L.R.C. took the name *Labour Party*. In the election of that year it secured 30 seats. There was no mention of socialism in its manifesto at all. In fact it was preoccupied with trade union legislation, for no sooner had it secured the sweeping Trades Disputes Act, 1906, than the *Osborne Case* invaded its financial stability. The effect was removed by the Trade Union Act, 1913.

LABOUR REPRESENTATION LEAGUE (1869-82). A trade union sponsored organisation for securing the election of working men to parliament as Liberals.

LABOURERS ACTS 1883-1906 (Ir.) enabled a labourer without a proper home to claim half an acre and have a cottage built on it and to occupy it at a nominal rent. The object was to reduce the extent to which farmers exploited their labour in tied and substandard accommodation.

LABOURERS, STAT. OF (1349), passed after the Black Death, required labourers on pain of imprisonment to work for those who required their labour, at the wages current between 1340 and 1346, a lord having a prior right over his own man. Consequently servants were to be paid at similar rates; deserters were to be imprisoned; beggars were not to be supported. Lords who paid above the rate were to forfeit thrice the value. Employees accepting wages above the rate were to be imprisoned. As a complementary provision, food was to be sold at "reasonable" prices. In 1350 the difficulty of proving the level of wages several years before was met by a tariff: e.g. haymaking 1d. a day; mowing 5d. per acre; reaping 2d. a day in the first week of Aug. and 3d. thereafter, but the price of leather goods was fixed by the older principle. In 1361 the legislation was confirmed and applied to masons and carpenters, masters at 4d. a day, others at 3d. or 2d., and forbade 'alliances or covines' among them. It was reconfirmed in 1368. In 1388 parliament lamented that labourers would not serve without "outrageous and excessive hire" and laid down a tariff for particular jobs, e.g. a bailiff 13s. 3d. a year plus clothing, a carter 10s., a swineherd and a woman labourer 6s. In 1389 the previous legislation was confirmed, but J.P.s were empowered to fix wages and prices annually by proclamation. In 1402 it was forbidden to engage labourers by the week. In 1427 the Act of 1389 was confirmed with detailed improvements, and in 1429 this was reconfirmed. Under an act of 1444 bailiffs got 23s. 4d. a woman labourer 10s. Further detailed legislation, passed in 1494, was repealed in 1497. Thereafter galloping inflation ended the enforcement of these never well enforced acts, which, however, remained on the statute book until the Statute Law Repeal Acts of the late 19th cent.

LABRADOR and UNGAVA were first sighted by Bjarni Herjolfsson driven off course for Greenland in 986, and Leif Ericsson landed colonists there in about 1000. These events were not wholly forgotten in northern Europe for Snorre Sturlasson, who died in 1241, mentioned them in *Heimskringla*. Jon Scolp and J.V. Corte-Real may have reached there in 1472, John Cabot certainly did in 1497, followed by Caspar Corte-Real in 1500 and Jacques Cartier in 1534. 16th cent. exploration, mostly concerned with the N.W. Passage, neglected Labrador, and the first settlements, consisting of Portuguese, Basque and English fishermen, were established only at the opening of the 17th cent. The east coast was charted reliably for the first time by James Cooke between 1763 and 1767, but the interior remained unknown until the Hudson Bay Co's., penetration under John Maclean from 1825 to 1850. Even after the geologist A.P. Lowe's journeys in the 1890s only sketch maps existed until the aerial survey of 1945. Labrador formed part of Newfoundland, the boundary with Quebec being fixed in 1912. *See* NEWFOUNDLAND.

LABUAN (Borneo) was only a casual pirate hideaway until 1846, when Sir James Brooke persuaded the Sultan of Brunei to cede it to Britain. A crown colony from 1848, it functioned mainly as a staging post and warehouse for Brunei and as an anti-piracy base. It was administered from 1889 to 1906 by the British North Borneo Co., and from 1907 under the Straits Settlements first as part of Singapore and from 1912 separately. Japanese occupied from 1942 to 1945, it began to acquire electric installations in 1946. In Sept. 1963 it was transferred to Sabah.

LACAITA, Sir James Philip (1813-95), an Italian lawyer, legal adviser to the British legation in Naples, helped Gladstone to get the facts upon which he was able to denounce the Neapolitan Govt. In 1852 he came to England, was naturalised in 1855, and in 1858 made sec. to Gladstone's Ionian mission. He became an Italian deputy in 1861 and a senator in 1876.

LACCADIVE Is. (Indian Ocean). The Portuguese held these Moslem islands from 1498 to 1545, when the inhabitants drove them out and put themselves under the protection of the Rajah of Cannanore. From 1792 they became tributary to Britain, but, the tribute being often in arrears, the British took them over in 1877. After 1956, with Minicoy and Amindivi Is. they became an Indian Union territory named LAKSHADWEEP.

LACE. Needle point lace was made in Paris in the 13th cent., and extensively in the Low Countries by the end of the 15th. Bobbin lace is not recorded before 1520. There are records of English needlepoint in 17th cent. and Flemish refugees brought bobbin lacemaking to England at that time, settling at Honiton and elsewhere in Devon. It languished, but was revived in the 19th cent. The introduction of machines did not prevent hand-made lace thriving until 1914, when the wars dispersed or killed most of the craftsmen.

LACE'S CASE. See MAN. I. OF-9.

LACKLAND. See K. JOHN.

LACY, Peter (1678-1751), Count. Irish Jacobite, entered James II's service in 1691, French service in 1692 and Russian service in 1697. He had a distinguished career against Charles XII of Sweden in the Great Northern War, and by 1728 he was a Gen. and Gov. of Livonia. In 1733 he commanded the Polish expedition to impose Augustus of Saxony on the throne. He became field-marshal in 1736 and after commanding yet again against the Swedes and then the Turks, retired, rich and respected to Livonia in 1743. He immensely improved the morale and efficiency of the Russian army under Peter the Great and Catherine the Great.

LACY FAMILY (MEDIAEVAL). At the Conquest or shortly after, two brothers **(1) Ilbert (fl. 1070)** and **(2) Walter (?-1085)** arrived as vassals of Odo of Bayeux and William fitz Osborn and were established respectively at Pontefract (W. Yorks) and Weobley (Herefords).

A. The PONTEFRACT branch became Tenants-in-Chief and a leading northern family at Odo's fall in 1088. There was an unexplained fall from favour under Henry I, and exile, but there followed a recovery under Stephen, and **(3) Ilbert (II) (?-1194)** fought at the B. of the Standard (1193). **(4) Roger (?-1212)** the son of a female cousin succeeded to the barony in 1194. He spiritedly defended Chateau Gaillard in Normandy for K. John in 1203-4 and was Justiciar in 1209, but after his death the King characteristically imposed a heavy relief upon his son **(5) John (?-1244) E. of LINCOLN (1232),** which was remitted only in 1214 when he campaigned for K. John in Poitou. He supported the opposition to the King but not implacably and was reconciled in 1216 and pardoned by the regency for Henry III in 1217. The family reached its greatest English position when he took his earldom in right of his wife. Allegedly a strong opponent of Peter des Roches, he is said to have been bribed to change sides, but witnessed the Confirmation of the Charters in 1236. He was certainly a leading figure at court by the end of his life. The male Pontefract line ended with his grandson **(6) Henry (?-1311),** a leading soldier and diplomat in Wales, Gascony, and France. He was affronted under Edward II by the taunts of Piers Gaveston and became a Lord Ordainer but died before the outbreak of civil war.

B. The WEOBLEY branch became Tenants-in-Chief after E. Roger of Hereford's rebellion and forfeiture in 1075, during which Walter opposed his Lord and reaped the advantages. The honour passed to successive sons after the eldest had unwisely supported Robert Curthose against William II, and part of it then passed to Payen Fitz John. The result was a tangle of claims and allegiances under K. Stephen, but these were resolved by 1155 when **(7) Gilbert (fl. 1150)** recovered most of the lands. From the 1170s the Weobley branch were mainly interested in Ireland. Gilbert's son **(8) Hugh (?-1186)** went there with Henry II in 1171 and received the Lordship of Meath. He became increasingly formidable, notably by marrying into the ruling family of Connaught, and Henry began to regret his generosity, but then Hugh was assassinated. His two elder sons **(9) Walter (II) (?-1241)** and **(10) Hugh (II) (?-1242)** were amongst the most turbulent of the Irish baronage. Hugh seized Ulster from the rebel John de Courcy in 1201-4 and K. John invested him with the earldom, but both brothers earned his displeasure by sheltering William de Braose. Walter fled to France in 1210 when John launched his attack on Ireland. His exile was shorter than Hugh's who went to France *via* Scotland, joined up in 1221 with Llywellyn ap Iorwerth and returned only in 1227. With the deaths of these brothers the Weobley branch also became extinct.

LADO ENCLAVE. *See* SUDAN.

LADRONE or MARIANNE Is. (N.W. Pacific) (Main islands Guam and Saipan) were under a sketchy Spanish rule from 17th cent. but Guam was ceded to U.S.A. in 1898 after the Spanish-American War, and the rest were sold to Germany in 1899. Consequently in 1919 the islands passed to Japan under a League of Nations mandate whose terms, especially on demilitarisation, were mostly ignored. Guam fell to Japanese attack partly based on neighbouring islands 16 days after Pearl Harbor (Nov. 1941). It was recovered in Aug. 1944. The islands have since been under U.S. trusteeship.

LADY. *See* LORD.

LADY CHAPEL. A cathedral chapel dedicated to the Virgin Mary and usually built to the east of the ambulatory behind the High Altar.

LADY DAY (25 Mar.) was until the Calendar Act 1752 the first day of the English (and Venetian) year and of the fiscal year. The Act shifted the first day back to 1 Jan. but the fiscal first day stayed at the same point in time and therefore became 6 Apr. where it still remains.

LADY MARGARET. *See* BEAUFORT.

LADAKH. *See* KASHMIR.

LADY CHATTERLEY'S LOVER (1928) was a novel about the sexual act suggested by Middleton Murry to D.H. Lawrence. The errant Lady's husband is a war crippled baronet and her lover a gamekeeper. It was banned in Britain but published in France, whence copies filtered easily across the Channel. The book was one of several in which Lawrence demonstrated an uncorroborated belief that the working classes were more potent than others. In a celebrated prosecution in 1960 the judge summed up in favour of the book and the jury refused to convict.

LADY CLARES. Similar to WHITEFEET.

LAENLAND. See BOCLAND.

LAET. A man of low rank in Kent, probably descended from a freedman.

LA FAYETTE. Internationally significant French family. It included **(1) Gilbert (?1380-1463)** marshal and supporter of Joan of Arc. **(2) Louise (1618-65)** mistress of Louis XIII. **(3) Marie Madeleine (1634-93)** whose "Blue Salon" revolutionised French and so European manners and literary tastes, and who wrote *The Princesse de Cleve,* the first modern psychological novel. **(4) Marie Joseph Paul Motier, M. de (1757-1834)** French subaltern sailed to America in 1777 and helped Washington as adviser and commander. He became a maj-gen. in 1781 and returned to France at the P. of Paris. In 1787 as a member of the Assembly of Notables he demanded the convocation of the States General, to which he was elected in 1789. When it converted itself into a national assembly, he, as one of its vice-presidents, introduced a Declaration of Rights based upon the U.S. Declaration of Independence. He also suggested the tricolour and took command of the National Guard. Too moderate for the Jacobins and too reformist for the court (which he tried to protect) he had to flee abroad and was imprisoned by the Austrians. Bonaparte released him, and at the restoration he reappeared in France and was a prominent opposition leader from 1825 until the revolution of 1830 when he again tried, unsuccessfully, to control the National Guard.

LAFONTAINE. Sir Louis Hypolite (1807-64), Lower Canadian statesman, opposed the union of the Canadas in 1840, but then sat in the united legislature for both upper and lower constituencies. In 1842 he became att-gen. and leader of the French Canadians, and in 1849 as premier (since 1848) of Lower Canada he introduced the Rebellion Losses Bill. He left politics in 1851 and became C.J. of Lower Canada in 1853.

LAFOREY. Of this Huguenot family **(1) Sir John (?-1729-96) 1st Bart. (1789)** was Navy Commissioner at Barbados in 1779; C-in-C Leeward Is. 1789 to 1793, and as admiral and C-in-C Leeward Is. from 1795 to 1796 captured Demerara, Essequibo and Berbice. His son **(2) Sir Francis (1767-1835)** was present at Trafalgar and also C-in-C Leeward Is. from 1811 to 1814.

LAGAN. See DROITS OF ADMIRALTY; SALVAGE.

LAGGAN ARMY consisted of protestant settlers in Ulster who united for self protection in 1642 under Robert Stewart. They founded the tradition of Londonderry and Enniskillen being safe protestant refuges.

LAGOS. See NIGERIA.

LAGUERRE, Louis (1663-1721), French painter, assistant to Verrio, and employed on his own account to decorate, *inter alia,* Burleigh House, Blenheim, Chatsworth and Marlborough House.

LAHORE (Pakistan) was a Mogul centre, and a place of magnificence until 1765 when the Sikhs took it and made it their capital. In 1849 the British captured it and it became the capital of the Punjab and after Independence remained capital of the W. Punjab.

LAHEJ (S. Arabia), agricultural Sultanate, was part of the Aden protectorate.

LAIBACH (LJUBLJANA), CONGRESS of (1821). See HOLY ALLIANCE.

LAING, John (?-1483), was the Scottish King's Treasurer in 1470 and wrote the earliest extant treasury rolls. He became clerk of the rolls and register in 1472 and Bp. of Glasgow in 1474 where in 1476 he founded the Greyfriars. He was briefly Lord Chancellor in 1482.

LAING, (1) Samuel (1780-1868), translated *Heimskringla* from the Icelandic in 1844. His son **(2) Samuel (1812-97)** was sec. of the railway dept. of the Bd. of Trade from 1842 to 1846, member of the Railway Commission in 1845 and managing director of the London Brighton and South Coast Railway from 1848 to 1852 and from 1867 to 1894. Liberal M.P. for Wick from 1852 to 1857 and in 1859, he was financial sec. to the Treasury in 1859 and 1860 and financial minister in India in 1860. He was M.P. for Wick from 1865 to 1868, and for Orkney and Shetland from 1872 to 1885.

LAINGS NEK (Natal) is a pass in the Drakensberg Mountains essential to communication between Durban and Pretoria and a scene of operations in the S. African wars of 1880-1 and 1899-1902. The railway was opened in 1891.

LAIRD. See CLANS, SCOTTISH.

LAISSEZ-FAIRE, -ALLER (Fr. = Leave it alone, or let things run). The political doctrine that govts. should not intervene in economic affairs and, in its extreme form, that the health, safety and status of individuals should be determined exclusively by their function and success in a free economy. It was a late 17th cent. reaction against the remains of state interference in trade and the regulation

of manufacture through guilds or monopolies. Though it influenced many philosophers and politicians, it was never established anywhere in practice because of the pressure of foreign affairs, the disputes between the champions of direct and of indirect taxation, the increasing difficulty of making machinery and transport safe, and the need for vast public capital works such as roads and sewers. Even 19th cent. free trade could be represented as a temporary expedient for correcting world imbalances.

LAKE (1) Sir Thomas (?1567-1630), was James I's Latin sec. from 1603, became a privy councillor in 1614 and was Sec. of State from 1616 to 1619, when he was dismissed as a result of an action for libelling the Countess of Exeter. His brother **(2) Arthur (1569-1626)** was Warden of New College from 1613 and V-Chanc. of Oxford Univ. and Bp. of Bath and Wells from 1616 to 1626. A descendant of Sir Thomas **(3) Gerard (1744-1808) 1st Ld. (1804) and Vist. (1807) LAKE** served in N. Carolina in 1781, was M.P. for Aylesbury from 1790 to 1802, became C-in-C in India in 1800 and in 1803 gave Wellesley (later Wellington) the backing necessary for his victorious Maratha Campaign.

LAKE DISTRICT (Eng.). Nobody had noticed its scenic beauties much until Celia Fiennes drew attention to them in 1698. Interest was first widely aroused by Thos. Gray in 1769, but William Wordsworth lived there from 1799 to 1850 and made the area famous. Since then it has been a refuge of literary figures. It became a national park in 1951.

LAKH or LAC (Anglo-Indian derived from Hindi) = 100,000.

LAKSHMI BAI, Rani. See JHANSI; INDIAN MUTINY.

LALLANS. The Lowland Scots language.

LALLY, Thomas Arthur Comte de Lally, Baron de TOLLENDAL (1702-66), son of Sir Gerald O'Lally, an Irish Jacobite, was the Young Pretender's A.D.C. during the '45 and was promoted *maréchal de camp* on the capture of Maastricht in 1748. In command of the French expedition of 1758 to India, his cruelty, arrogance and French insularity gained him the detestation of his own troops and the dislike of his Indian allies. Hence, otherwise competent though he was, he was no match for the British. Forced by their fleet to raise his blockade of Madras in Dec. 1758, he was defeated by Sir Eyre Coote at Wandewash in Jan. 1760, and in Jan. 1761 he had to surrender Pondicherry, the French local capital. The French executed him.

LALOR, (1) Peter (1823-89) became a leader of the Ballarat insurgent miners in 1854 (*see* EUREKA STOCKADE). Having been appointed to the Victoria legislative council in 1859, he became an inspector of railways. Elected in 1856 to the parliament, he was P.M.G. in 1878 and speaker from 1880 to 1888. His even more energetic brother **(2) James Finton (?-1849)** was a leading Irish revolutionary and contributor to the *Nation* and edited the *Irish Felon,* a satirical anti-English occasional journal. He had a profound influence on the Young Ireland group.

LAMB, Charles (1775-1834) and his sister **Mary Ann (1764-1847).** He was a friend of Coleridge. They were both somewhat unbalanced: she murdered her mother in a fit of insanity while he was in a lunatic asylum in 1796, but this did not prevent his being employed as a clerk in the HEIC from 1792 to 1825, and after his release he looked after her all his life. He was an essayist and humorist, and they collaborated in a well known *Tales from Shakespeare* (1807). His *Essays of Elia* were published in 1820-1822.

LAMB, (Henry) William and Lady Caroline. See MELBOURNE.

LAMBARDE, William (1536-1601), wrote his *Peram-bulation of Kent* in 1570 and collected material for a general History, which he abandoned in favour of

Camden, on discovering that he was similarly engaged. In 1581 he published *Eirenarcha*, a practice manual for magistrates, based on his experience at Lincoln's Inn and as a J.P.

LAMBART (1) Sir Oliver (?-1618), 1st Ld. LAMBART of CAVAN (1618) fought the Spaniards in the Low Countries from 1585 to 1592 and was in the Cadiz expedition of 1596. In 1599 he went to Ireland with Essex and spent the rest of his life as an administrator there. His son **(2) Charles (1600-60) 2nd Ld. and 1st E. of CAVAN (1647)** was a royalist M.P. for Bossinney in 1625 and 1627. **(3) Richard Ford William (1763-1836), 7th E. (1818)** was in the Egyptian expedition of 1801 and became its commander. **(4) Frederick Rudolph (1865-1946), 10th E. (1900)** commanded the Guards Division at Loos in 1915, the XIV Corps on the Somme and at Ypres from 1916 to 1917 and became British C-in-C in Italy in Mar. 1918. In 1921 he headed the War Office section of the British delegation at the Washington Conference and from 1922 to 1926 was C.I.G.S.

LAMBE, John (?-1628), a fashionable crystal gazer, patronised by, amongst others, Buckingham. He was believed to have assisted the duke's erotic propensities with charms and, incurring the duke's political unpopularity as well as puritan hostility, was beaten to death by a London mob.

LAMBERT, John (1619-83), a parliamentary soldier, was Fairfax's commissary-gen. in 1644 and took a regimental command in the New Model. He had a radical cast of mind besides being a competent soldier and in 1647 helped Ireton to draft the *Heads of the Proposals*. As a commander in the north he resisted the Scottish invasion and fought at Preston (1648) and later was 2-in-C at Dunbar (1650) and Worcester (1651). He was briefly deputy-lieut. of Ireland in 1652 and then led the officers who offered the Protectorship to Oliver Cromwell. He became a member of Cromwell's council and a major-gen. and began to enrich himself by buying up private soldiers' warrants of arrears at a discount. He hotly opposed the offer of the crown to Oliver, for whom his radicalism and prolonged absenteeism was now excessive. He was dismissed. He re-emerged with Oliver's death to support Richard Cromwell as an alternative to a monarchy. In 1659 he profited from the govt's. difficulties and was restored to his commands, and the recalled Long Parliament appointed him to the Committee of Safety, but his furious temperament and ambitions created tensions and led to his coercion of the House. Failure to stop Gen. Monck's advance led to another dismissal and confinement in the Tower, whence he escaped, tried to raise troops, was insufficiently supported and was retaken and again confined. After the Restoration he was tried and condemned to death, but not being a regicide, the sentence was remitted and he was exiled variously to Guernsey and St. Nicholas. He died in prison.

LAMBETH. The manor was acquired from the see of Rochester by Abp. Baldwin in about 1187, and soon became the principal residence of Abps. of Canterbury. The 'Lollards' tower was built by Abp. Chichele in 1434. The library was founded by Abp. Bancroft in 1610. Previously known as Lambeth House, it was styled a palace at the Restoration, because the Canterbury palace had become uninhabitable. The great hall was built by Abp. Juxon in 1663.

LAMBETH or TIIREE or SIX ARTICLES (1583) were six paragraphs containing three principles viz: **(1)** that the Crown is supreme in matters ecclesiastical; **(2)** that the B.C.P. and the Ordinal contain nothing contrary to the Scriptures; and **(3)** that all the XXXIX Articles are agreeable to the Word of God. Drawn up by Abp. Whitgift who required all clergy to subscribe to them without reservation, they formed the principles underlying the activities of the Court of High Commission and caused the immediate suspension of over 200 clergy in the eastern coastal counties.

LAMBETH ARTICLES (1595) were nine strongly Calvinistic propositions drawn up by Abp. Whitgift's committee. Acceptable to the many puritans, they were strongly disapproved by Elizabeth I and never authorised.

LAMBETH CONFERENCES are approximately decennial assemblies of bishops of the Anglican communion under the presidency of the Abp. of Canterbury. Their opinions and declaration are not binding, but have strong persuasive authority within the communion. The first (1861) was held in response to Canadian requests arising out of the Colenso case, and the publication of *Essays and Reviews*. The original proposal to hold a council to define doctrine, was abandoned. It was attended by 76 out of a possible 144 bishops. Since then attendances have steadily increased, but the decision of the Church of England to 'ordain' women priests has placed difficulties in the way of further growth.

LAMBETH DEGREES, in Divinity, Law, Arts, and Music are conferred by the Abp. of Canterbury in virtue of the transfer to him of papal rights under the Statute 25 Henry VIII c.21, (1534).

LAMBTON, John George (1792-1840) 1st Ld. DURHAM (1830) and 1st E. (1833), of a wealthy Durham family, was M.P. for Co. Durham from 1813 to 1828. As whig Lord Privy Seal in 1830 he helped to draft the Reform Bill and then did a tour as ambassador to St. Petersburg, Berlin, and Vienna. After the bill was passed and the subsequent elections held, he accepted posts abroad first as permanent ambassador to St. Petersburg (1835-7) and then as Gov.-Gen. and Commissioner in Canada. Attacked as high handed, he resigned, but his famous and liberal *Report on the Affairs of British North America* (1839) (The Durham Report) set the precedent for British imperial development which guided all British govts. until the liquidation of the colonial empire after World War II.

LAMMAS LANDS were cultivated in the summer until 1st Aug. (Lammas) and then thrown open to common pasture.

LAMPETER or LLANBEDR PONT STEFFAN. (*See* CARDIGANSHIRE.) The college was founded in 1822 mainly to educate Welsh clergy, and its Charters of 1852 and 1865 made it the first Welsh College with Univ. status.

LANARK-SHIRE (Scotland). The town became a royal burgh and the area an administrative unit under David I (r. 1124-53), and it was the centre of Sir Wm. Wallace's rebellion. In later times it was dominated by Glasgow, and growing industrialisation brought about a strong movement of political radicalism. Local political figures included Robert Owen and Keir Hardie.

LANCASHIRE. (1) The area south of the Ribble appears in the Domesday return for Cheshire, under the heading *Inter Mersham et Ripam* (Lat. = Twixt Mersey and Ribble). It had been transferred from Northumbria to Mercia in 923. To its north Amounderness, Lonsdale, Cartmel and Furness still mostly belonged to Tostig, E. of Northumbria, and then to Roger of Poictou, whose honour was forfeited in 1102, and conferred upon the Counts of Mortain. The honour was not partitioned and became the foundation of the county, as well as the later Duchy, but meanwhile development was retarded because in 1139 K. Stephen invested the K. of Scots with Northumbria and the lands north of the Ribble passed with it. There was an administrative reunion of the two parts in 1149 and a sheriff was shortly established at Lancaster. This is the origin of the geographical shire but true establishment probably dates from its importance to K. John in connection with his Irish ambitions. He founded Liverpool.

(2) For a while "Lancashire" was prosperous until the defeat at Bannockburn and the confusion of Edward II's reign. The Scots devastated the area north of the Ribble in 1316 while govt. broke down to the south. It had not been brought to order when the Black Death (1349-50) supervened. It was in these unpropitious circumstances that the Duchy of Lancaster was created. Disorder aggravated by piratical French and Scots raids continued into 15th cent. The Duchy was annexed to the crown in 1461. The practical consequence was that Lancashire had, for the first time, an ordinary crown administration (garnished with some unimportant peculiarities) with the crown as the most important landowner. It was from crown grants, however, that the Stanleys obtained their influence in the 16th cent. and both they and the area benefited from the virtual end to organised Scottish incursions after the B. of Flodden (1513).

(3) As with other northern counties, R. Catholicism survived strongly in Lancashire. (*See* PRESTON.) There was an Elizabethan persecution, and the area being conservative, was strongly royalist in the civil war and Protectorate. A royalist rising in 1659 anticipated the Restoration. Its following was almost all R. Catholic, and the Jacobite armies in the 1715 and 1745 rebellions could obtain no other volunteers.

(4) The area had never been well provided with wood, and the digging of peat for fuel in the wastes was of great importance, and led to occasional disputes between mediaeval landlords, such as Furness Abbey, and their tenants. These became fiercer as Tudor prosperity raised the population. They were soon compounded by the discovery of minerals, particularly slate, freestone and then huge beds of coal. Coal mining developed quickly after 1526 and brought furious controversies between owners and customary peat diggers, all the more because the climate is exceptionally wet.

(5) There had always been a village cloth industry and the combination of Irish linen and local wool brought in the early manufacture of fustian. When cotton wool began to be imported, the wet climate became an advantage, especially after the introduction of the spinning jenny in 1764. The Lancashire cotton industry became the principal support of the British economy at the start of the industrial revolution. Since it depended on imported cotton, the port of Liverpool suddenly expanded. Its income from port dues trebled between 1818 and 1833. The enormous profits were due to the presence of cheap coal, but this also stimulated an important iron industry, especially after 1796 when iron mining at Barrow began large scale production. The combination of iron and coal created secondary manufacturing industries including hardware, armaments and shipbuilding, while the continuing development of textile techniques not only increased the profits but brought diversification. Besides wool, cotton and linen, there was silk, calico, printing and dyeing, chemicals and soap, potteries and glass.

(6) There was in consequence throughout the 19th cent., a large prosperous partly immigrant population with a tendency towards radicalism, matched by indigenous conservatives. Industry and mining, though they attracted concentrations of people, left large rural areas untouched. Many of the towns became county boroughs after 1888 and had separate, often radical administrations, but the separation tended to leave the conservatives in a majority in rural areas.

(7) The county ceased to exist in 1974, the area being divided, with aggregations from other counties.

LANCASTER, CHANC. OF THE DUCHY and COUNTY. **(1)** The first duchy Chancellor was William Burgoyne (?-1402), appointed at the coronation of Henry IV in 1399. He was the head of the Duchy administration. From 1402 the two offices were generally held by the same man. The Chanc. was long appointed for life, though politics sometimes interfered with the prospects. Thus Sir Richard Empson, appointed in 1505 was executed in 1510, Sir Thos. More appointed in 1525, relinquished the office on

becoming Lord Chancellor in 1529; Sir Wm. Paget, appointed in 1547 was forfeited in 1552. Other distinguished Tudor holders included Sir Ralph Sadler (1568-87), Sir Francis Walsingham (1587-90), Sir Thomas Heneage (1590-5), Sir Robert Cecil (1597-9) and Sir John Fortescue (1501-7).

(2) The office originated as a kind of head clerkship, but developed in 15th cent. into a judicial and administrative post of prestige; for the holder was habitually associated with the monarch. In the 16th cent. statesmen began to be appointed, and chancellors. commonly became privy councillors from 1600 onwards. The Duchy had developed a smoothly organised administration leaving little for the Chanc. as such to do. Hence the office was soon conferred as a form of pension (e.g. Sir Thomas Ingram 1664-72), or to increase a minister's emoluments (Sir Robert Carr 1672-82), or to secure an unburdened office holder for the Govt. (e.g. Ld. Mulgrave 1804-5). With two exceptions, it was held during pleasure after 1682. The last attempt to make a life appointment (in 1807 for Spencer Perceval) had to be abandoned against parliamentary opposition. The first Chanc. who was, as such, in the cabinet, was Charles Bathurst (1812-23). Twenty-two others followed him (out of 47) before 1914. Since World War I the office, which is virtually devoid of duties, has been used as a means of paying a politician for some quasi-ministerial or emergent ministerial function so far not in official existence e.g. as Min. for the Arts under the Thatcher Govt.

LANCASTER, DUCHY OF. (1) This organisation began in 1351 when Edward III granted palatine powers in Lancashire to his kinsman Henry of Grosmont (?1299-1361), E. of Lancaster since 1345, whom he made a duke. He had only two daughters. John of Gaunt, son of Edward III, married Blanche, the younger, in 1259. Her father and sister died in quick succession, so the whole inheritance came to John, who was also created duke in 1362. He died in 1399 and Richard II partitioned the inheritance, most of it going to his friends Aumale, Exeter, and Surrey. This provoked the *coup d'état* engineered by Lancaster's exiled son and heir, who seized the throne as Henry IV, using the duchy resources and loyalties as the mainspring of his movement, and as the nucleus of the royal administration. He revoked Richard's grants and issued the Great Charter of the Duchy, constituting it a separate holding not merged in the crown, but held by him as Duke.

(2) In 1461 the Yorkist Edward IV in his first parliament forfeited the property of major Lancastrians including his predecessor's; the enormous extent of the duchy and its well developed separate administration made it convenient to leave it in existence as an entity, though now merged in the Crown. There was a Chancery Court which sat at Preston until 1970 and a Duchy Court sitting in London until 1873.

(3) The name of the institution has always been misleading. Though it included the palatine County of Lancaster, the bulk of the property was elsewhere viz: in Yorkshire, it included in the North Riding, from the Tees and Westmorland border to Knaresborough (excluding Ripon); in the East Riding Scarborough and the Vale of Pickering; in the West Riding, the greater part of Wharfedale and Airedale including Leeds, Pontefract, Goole, Doncaster, and Sandal; in Nottinghamshire it included the northern third of the county; in South Wales the honours of Kidwelly, Ogmore, and White Castle. There were also scattered possessions, e.g. part of the Strand in London.

LANCASTER – FIRST FAMILY (1) Edmund Crouchback (1245-96), E. of LEICESTER (1265) and LANCASTER (1267) 2nd son of Henry III and Eleanor of Provence (*see* SICILIAN AFFAIR). In the troubled years 1258-65 he enjoyed his father's confidence, though very young, to a high degree. He was sent back to England as Capitaneus (military commander) when Henry was ill in Paris in 1262. In 1263 he took charge of Dover castle and surrendered it to Montfort's party only on the King's orders. At the end of the baronial revolt (1265) he became Seneschal of England and received Montfort's and Derby's estates. He was now the richest and most prestigious man in England after his elder brother, the Lord Edward, with whom he went on Crusade in 1270. He served his brother as King as loyally as his father. From 1267 to 1278 (when the lands passed to the Crown) he held Carmarthen and Cardigan. In 1275 he married Blanche, Countess of Artois, and did homage for her lands to the French K. Philip III. From 1266-9 he was regent and, already familiar with Wales, suppressed the revolt of Rhys ap Maredudd in the south. On several occasions he acted as negotiator on Edward I's French rights including the disastrous discussions, conducted by Philip in bad faith, which ended with the break between Edward and Philip IV, and the Gascon war which broke out in 1294. Two years later he died on campaign in Gascony. Of his sons **(2) Thomas (c. 1278-1322) 2nd E.**, with three earldoms in his own right and two (Lincoln and Salisbury) by marriage to Alice of Lacy (who left him in 1317), was a leading as well as the most powerful opponent of his cousin Edward II. He led the attack on the hanged Piers Gaveston (1308-12). In 1314 he refused to join Edward II's Scottish expedition and after Bannockburn found himself effectively in control of the govt., a position confirmed in 1316 when the Parliament of Lincoln appointed him Chief Councillor, but his attempts to control the royal govt. and restore its finances by resuming alienated lands were vitiated by his political failure to deal with the Scots, combined with the disastrous famine of 1315-6 and his own inertia and unpopularity. In 1316-7 his power ebbed and at the T. of Leake (1318) he had to accept a diminished authority. By the siege of Berwick (1319), which he deserted, and the rise of the Younger Despenser he was moving towards treasonable courses which finally broke into rebellion in 1321-2, with Thomas a somewhat indecisive leader of a coalition of Marcher and northern opponents of Edward and the Despensers. Defeated at Boroughbridge, he was summarily executed at Pontefract (1322).

He based his policies on a strict adherence to the Ordinances and an appeal to the work of Simon de Montfort and he tried to revive or create powers for the hereditary Stewards of England, but he was vindictive, greedy and cruel, and lethargic when presented with real power after 1314. He treated his tenants badly, had few allies or friends, was left by his wife, and seldom ventured out of his estates. Somewhat surprisingly he gained in some quarters an almost saintly posthumous reputation. His brother **(3) Henry (1281-1345), 1st E. of the second creation (1324)** inherited his father's holdings on the Welsh side of the Severn and the Lordships of Monmouth, Kidwelly and Carwarthlan in 1296. He served with Edward I in Flanders and Scotland in 1297-8, 1299-1300, 1303 and 1305, and by 1299 was attending parliament. He was one of the Ordainers in 1310 and supported his brother's murder of Gaveston, but he helped to suppress the Welsh revolt of 1315 and served against the Scots in 1318. His hostility to the Despensers is well attested, but he was not involved in his brother's rebellion because by marriage he had acquired lands in France, and was abroad at the time. Hence two years later he was able to succeed to his earldoms and the stewardship of England but was regarded with suspicion at court, for, *inter alia*, he erected a cross to his brother outside Leicester. The suspicion proved justified, for in Sept. 1326 he joined Q. Isabella's revolt and co-operated in the condemnation of the elder Despenser, and in Edward II's deposition.

He was named Guardian of Edward III, and as a prominent member of the ruling council procured a grant from the clergy to the Crown at the Leicester parliament, but he failed to provide effective defence against the Scots in 1327. By this time he was on bad terms with the Queen and Mortimer. They kept him away from the King. He refused to attend the 1328 parliament. With the King's uncles, the Es. of Kent and Norfolk, he formed a confederacy against Mortimer whose prompt reaction and seizure of Leicester led to its dispersal and collapse. He was fined 11,000 marks, but later in the year was sent on an embassy to France. He was probably involved in Mortimer's overthrow on his return but thereafter, owing to blindness played no further part in politics. He founded a hospital at Leicester in 1330, and long before he died his role as one of the chief magnates had been taken over by his only surviving son **(4) Henry of Grosmont (1310-61) E. of DERBY (1337), E. of LIN-COLN (1349), 1st D. of LANCASTER (1351), E. of MORAY (1359).** He was a distinguished soldier and diplomat and an internationally respected prince. Under Edward III he was with the King in France in 1331 to negotiate with Philip of Valois, and in 1333 distinguished himself against the Scots. In 1334 his father gave him Kidwelly and Carwarthlan. In 1336 he commanded against the Scots and was rewarded with the Earldom of Derby and a grant from the customs. In the Flemish campaigns, he fought in 1337-9, stood surety for the King's debts in 1340, fought at Sluys in the same year. In 1341 he moved to the Border and commanded against the Scots. He was by now the King's "second personality". He became Lieut. of Aquitaine in 1344 and visited the courts of Castile and Portugal and the *Curia* at Avignon as an envoy. During his Aquitainian campaign of 1345-6 he gained much territory including Bergerac (with which his father enfeoffed him), defeated the French at Auberoche and tied down the D. of Normandy's army during Edward III's Crécy campaign. After further French campaigns and a victory in the sea-fight off Dymchurch known as *Les Espagnols-sur-Mer* (The Spaniards at Sea) (1350), and further diplomacy with the French and Flemish courts, he was made one of the first knights of the Garter, and in 1351 the earldom of Lancaster was elevated to a Palatine Duchy for him. In the next twelve months he went crusading with the Teutonic Knights in Prussia. This was in reality the first of the major govt. commercial trading missions into the Baltic (*see* BALTIC; HANSE-). He alleged that Otto of Brunswick had attempted to abduct him on the way and fought a judicial duel with him at Paris. This visit gave him a useful knowledge of the factions at the French court and this was one reason for his later frequent visits as ambassador in the abortive peace negotiations. In fact, the English side never seriously contemplated peace but his very high rank gave credence to the opposite belief while he approached potential allies such as his cousin Charles of Navarre and in 1354, the *Curia*. On the resumption of war in 1355 he commanded first against the Scots and then in Normandy and Brittany, but his siege of Rennes was ineffective save to extract a large indemnity for a truce. It was at this time that he was given the Scots earldom of Moray by K. David II, probably as one of the conditions of that King's release from captivity. After the failure of the siege of Paris (1360) through lack of provisions, he advocated peace and led the English side in the Brétigny negotiations. He is said to have built his London palace at the Savoy in 1349 from the profits of his Aquitainian campaign but as the Crown was a slow payer he probably financed his career from his extensive English revenues which amounted to about £8,400 a year (*for his estates see* LANCASTER, DUCHY OF). He made large public benefactions, being a joint founder of Corpus Christi Coll., Cambridge and he enlarged his father's hospital at Leicester. During 1354 he wrote his devotional *Livre des Seyntz Medicines* (The Book of Holy Cures). He died without male heir and his lands passed to his son-in-law John of Gaunt. *See next entry.*

LANCASTER – SECOND FAMILY or ROYAL HOUSE OF. John of GAUNT (or GHENT) (1340-99), 1st D. of the second creation (1362), 4th son of Edward III, had married Blanche, daughter of Henry of Grosmont, 1st D. of the first creation in 1359. Through her all the Lancaster lands came to him. By reason of his huge wealth, following and rank, he was a powerful English figure, but in fact he spent about half his adult life intermittently abroad as a soldier, governor or diplomat, or pursuing private ambitions. In none of these activities was he particularly successful, and his home reputation suffered accordingly. He commanded part of the Black Prince's army at the victory of Najera (Spain) in 1367, became Capt. of Calais in 1369, helped the Black Prince to sack Limoges in 1370 and was briefly Lieut. of Aquitaine in 1371, but he resigned and, Blanche having died, he married Constance, co-heiress of the Castilian throne in 1372.

His Castilian claims were now the spring of a personal policy. He had conducted two unsuccessful campaigns in France (1370-3). English resources should be mobilised to gain him a Spanish Kingdom, which would be friendly to the English in Aquitaine. This meant peace with other powers, notably France and Scotland and greater access to the hoarded riches of the church with, as a corollary, a reduction of ecclesiastical power in politics. He espoused the views of John Wyclif on church poverty. Meanwhile the war, and his negotiations in Flanders to end it, went badly. There was much slander, especially in the City, of Alice Perrers, Edward III's mistress, and other figures. Gaunt himself had acquired a mistress in Katherine Swynford, his children's governess. He returned to England for the Good Parliament (1376) to find his father and the Black Prince seriously ill and had to preside in their stead. He thus attracted much of the unpopularity of the govt. to himself. Moreover he was caught in a dilemma: it was necessary to re-establish the royal prestige in the interests of his family and himself, but his own interests required the co-operation of the govt's. critics. The Black Prince and Edward III died within a few months.

He was now the uncle of a young King, not the son of an old one. He stage-managed a magnificent coronation for Richard II and some public reconciliations, but the French attacked the coast and a counter-offensive, which he led, on St. Malo was an unpopular disaster (1378). He was at feud accordingly with the wealthiest interests in the state, namely the City and the bishops who had, in his association with Wyclif, a handle against him. His property, especially the Savoy palace, was gutted in the Peasants' Revolt (1381). His opposition to court extravagance now involved him in quarrels with royal favourites and the King himself: nevertheless his attempts to liquidate existing wars by success or negotiation served their interest as well as his. Unfortunately Richard II had become, as a result of his magnetic success in the Peasants' Revolt, uncontrollable and unreliable. It was mainly his fault that the great Scottish offensive of 1385 failed and since French troops had been in Scotland (and gone), Lancaster now organised the long cherished Castilian expedition. Richard was glad to get rid of him. The expedition failed because Lancaster was no soldier or statesman, but thought too much in terms of private interest. He married his daughter to his rival, allowed himself to be bought off and returned to Aquitaine as Lieut. until 1389, when he returned to attempt mediation between the King and the Lords Appellant. There was a series of French truces, and the Kingdom was in increasing disorder. In 1393 Lancaster had to put down a rebellion in Cheshire, while yet managing French negotiations. These resulted in a four year truce in 1394, when he departed again for Aquitaine until 1396. The 28 year truce and marriage treaty of the latter year was the origin of Richard II's fall, but Constance died and Gaunt now married Katherine Swynford and had her children, the formidable Beauforts, legitimated.

Meanwhile Gaunt was placed in another dilemma, when his son Henry joined the growing opposition to Richard II, for too open support of activities, which might be construed as treasonable, could jeopardise Katherine and the Beauforts as well as himself and his heir. Thus after Henry was exiled (1397) Gaunt retired from public affairs. *For the descendants of John of Gaunt see* BEAUFORT AND HENRY IV, V AND VI; ROSES, WARS OF THE; JOHN OF LANCASTER.

LANCASTER, Thomas (?-1583), Bp. of Kildare from 1549, being married, was in 1554 deprived by Mary I; he became treasurer of Salisbury in 1559. He went with Sir Henry Sydney to Ireland in 1565 and Sydney and Cecil procured him the Archbishopric of Armagh in 1568. He was a strong and controversial protestant, described as a 'lusty good priest' by his friends, but said to have been gluttonous and to have died of red herring and much sack. He worked very hard to reorganise his province with a protestant clergy, and was one of the few Irish archbishops who made headway in this task.

LANCASTER HOUSE AGREEMENT (1979) sponsored by Ld. Carrington the Foreign Sec. ended the Rhodesian civil war with provision for free elections on the basis of one man one vote.

LANCELOT was a brave and lecherous knight of the Arthurian legends.

LANCERS. The lance as a shock weapon was ineffectual until the invention of stirrups in the 6th cent. Organised lancer squadrons were introduced to counter pike protected and bayonet armed musketeers, but only on a large scale after the formation of Polish lancers in 1807. Their performance impressed other nations, which raised lancer regiments after 1815. Prussian lancer regiments (Uhlans) were mowed down in 1914.

LANCET. *See* ARCHITECTURE, BRITISH-6.

LANDAU (Ger.), a powerful Palatine fortress, 15 miles N.W. of Karlsruhe, blocked the northern approach from Germany to Alsace and was occupied by the French from 1680 to 1815. *See also* CARRIAGES.

LAND COMMISSIONERS. Commissioners were appointed to administer the Tithe Act, 1836. These were given functions under the Copyhold Act, 1841, the Enclosure Acts of 1845 onwards, and the Settled Land Act, 1882, which gave them their title. In 1889 they were merged in the new Board of Agriculture.

LAND LEAGUE (Ir.), began in Apr. 1879 at a protest meeting against a particular eviction at Irishtown, Co. Mayo. The meeting had been called by Michael Davitt who had been planning a land movement with American Irish extremists of the Fenian Brotherhood and the Clan-na-Gael. The formation of the Mayo Land League was thus no accident. The movement spread rapidly: the Irish Land League with Parnell as Pres. and Davitt as one of the Secretaries established itself at Dublin in Oct. In Dec. Parnell, John Dillon and Timothy Healy went to U.S.A. to drum up support. The American Land League was founded in May 1880, and was soon finding more than half the money for the Irish League. Parnell's sister founded the Ladies Land League in Mar. 1881. By then there were branches everywhere with a system of private "courts" enforcing its orders by terrorism. Agrarian outrages rose from 236 in 1877 to 2590 in 1880. These involved cattle maiming, arson and murder. The victims of violence were tenants who paid rents higher than the local League "court" thought proper, and persons who accepted a tenancy of land from which someone had been evicted. In addition, the League organised the eponymous *boycott* in Mayo, and many others, and in 1881 issued its 'no rent' manifesto. The crimes and intimidation continued after the Irish Land and Arrears Acts, 1881 and 1882, had dealt with most of the grievances, because the objects of the leadership were in fact political and only incidentally concerned with land.

LANDOR, Walter Savage (1779-1852), a quarrelsome and unbusinesslike person, was a Jacobin in youth, but went to Spain to fight in the rebellion against the French in 1808. He lived in Italy from 1815 to 1835. A considerable prose stylist admired by contemporary writers, his *Imaginary Conversations* appeared between 1824 and 1829, *The Pentameron* in 1837. He lived at Bath until 1848 and then returned to Florence, where Robert Browning helped him.

LAND REGISTRY. *See* LAND TRANSFER ACT 1875.

LANDROST, LANDROS or LANDDROSTE. A sort of Boer sheriff.

LANDSKNECHT (Ger: literally 'country servant') **LANSQUENET** (Fr.) **LANCEKNIGHT** (Eng: corruption). A mercenary footsoldier (usually a pikeman) from imperial rather than Swiss territory in the 16th and 17th cent.

LAND RECLAMATION (*see* SEWERS). The main continuous areas of English land reclamation were Romney Marsh (from Saxon times to about 1250), Hatfield Chase (1626-31), Malvern Chase, Sedgemoor (1627-35), and the Fens (q.v.), but there were many smaller undertakings, substantial in aggregate, in river valleys all over the flatter areas. These were mostly recovered under the inspiration of Dutch engineers such as Vermuyden, employed under Charles I, and their pupils.

LAND TAX, enacted in 1688 to supersede all other land taxes e.g. 10th-and-15th, tallage, scutage and hidage, was (where not redeemed) payable by beneficial owners. It was abolished as late as 1963.

LAND TRANSFER ACT, 1875, created a Land Registry and empowered owners to register their title to land voluntarily, with the consequence that it also contained provision for unregistered dealings in registered land. This tentative beginning avoided the vast survey costs of a universal imposition of compulsory registration. Voluntary registration was suspended in 1967 pending the creation and extension of compulsory registration areas. By 1993 the cost had mounted to vast figures.

LANDSCAPE PAINTING, ENGLISH. In this vast and complicated subject the following features seem to stand out. The earlier English interest in Dutch marine painting bred such marine and landscape artists as **Samuel Scott (?1710-72)**; the interest in animals such painters as **George Stubbs (1724-1806)**; and the dislike of town life, the feeling for the countryside and the power of French culture, **John Wootton (?1668-1765)** animal and landscape painter, and imitator of the Poussins. These were contemporaries of Hogarth, who knew most of the significant artists and patrons of his time, and, though no landscape artist, set an overpowering example by his technical competence. **Richard Wilson (1714-82)**, originally a portraitist, painted landscape in Italy and made an English reputation after 1756. The brothers **Sandby, Thomas (1721-98)** and **Paul (1725-1809)** learned their profession as military draftsmen and teachers under the patronage of the D. of Cumberland, and Thomas became an architect and the landscape expert who laid out Windsor Park and formed Virginia Water. **Thomas Gainsborough (1727-88)** was brought up in rural Suffolk. Since patrons and purchasers congregated in London artists gravitated there too. They generally knew each other and with the influential portrait painters such as Sir Joshua Reynolds formed the Royal Academy, of which Wilson, Thomas Sandby and Gainsborough were founder members in 1768. This was immensely important. It brought those who could afford pictures into annual contact with the latest painting, and provided financial incentives for generations of artists to come. These included the water colourists **Alexander Cozens (?-1786)**, Russian-born reputed son of Peter the

Great, and his son **John Robert Cozens (1794-1842)**. These overlapped with **Thomas Girtin (1775-1802)**, the water colourist **Edward Dayes (1763-1804)**, and the three **Cotmans, John Sell (1782-1842)** and his son **Michael Edmund (1810-58)** and **Joseph John (1814-78)**, and with the famous **John Constable (1776-1837)**. Partly because of the artistic stagnation of early 19th cent Europe these painters formed the leading school in the western world and paved the way, through **Joseph Mallord William Turner (1775-1801)**, for the unknown and so far unnamed Impressionists (q.v.).

LAND TENURE – ENGLAND. The contrasting terms *freehold* and *copyhold* concern the status of tenure, *fee Simple* and *Leasehold* its duration and *Fee Tail* or *Entail* devolution.

(1) **FREEHOLD** originated in feudal services (*see* FEUDALISM) of a free and honourable kind rendered to a superior in return for an inheritable property. The principal types of service were KNIGHT SERVICE (military), SERJEANTY (civilian service), and FRANK ALMOIGN (prayer in the case of an ecclesiastical holding). In addition, tenants by knight service and serjeanty were bound by the **feudal incidents.** The many free Saxon cultivators already on the ground had to be fitted somehow into this scheme, and so there arose a fourth free tenure of paramount ultimate importance called SOCAGE to which the incidents usually applied, but in which the services were of an agricultural but strictly defined sort. All freeholders owed homage and fealty to their lord and were bound to attend his court, over which he presided. The free status very soon attached to the land, as more people became personally free. By 1400 most people were. An owner of freehold land was entitled and theoretically bound to attend the County Court, and if his land was worth 40s. a year he had, after 1432 a vote in parliamentary elections outside the parliamentary boroughs. A freeholder might also have rights of common (*see* para-3).

(2) Knight service soon ceased to be an efficient basis for a military system, and it became normal to levy a tax called **scutage** ('shield-money') in wartime upon those liable to it. Serjeanty at this level was usually so honourable as to be honorific. From the point of view of mesne lords and the crown, the system had two defects. Firstly, any tenant could enfeoff another, who would be bound to him by a similar nexus as he was to the original lord and so *ad infinitum*. As this "feudal ladder" grew longer it became harder for the superior lord to exact the services and incidents, because though the land was burdened, the only person who could be called upon to discharge the burden was the tenant who had done him homage. This state of affairs was slowly reduced to order by the Statute **Quia Emptores (1295)** which laid down that henceforth a feoffee should always hold of the feoffor's lord. Secondly a lord lost most of the services and incidents if land came into the ownership of a corporation, because a corporation had no natural attributes appropriate to them. The greatest of these, and an increasing threat to the crown, was the church. Hence the 15th cent. Statutes of **Mortmain** forbade the conveyance of land to corporations without royal licence. The whole system of feudal tenure with its constraints and irregular forfeits was obsolete by Tudor times and might have been ended then, had not the dissolution of the monasteries thrown huge quantities of land onto the market. By Stuart times it had become merely an infuriating source of revenue to the crown, and so in 1661 after the Restoration all freeholds were converted into socage, service other than the picturesque ceremonial serjeanties and incidents except **escheat** were abolished, and the crown compensated by the grant of a hereditary excise (*see* CIVIL LIST).

(3) **COPYHOLD** originated in servile economic services rendered by a villein to the lord of a manor in

return for a holding. The mutual obligations were sooner or later crystallised by manor custom. The services originally included labour on the lord's **demesne** ('home farm') and he was entitled to certain **copyhold incidents** (*see* FEUDALISM-19). The tenant had to attend the lord's **customary court** where his steward presided. This court governed the agricultural management of the holdings and its rolls were the sole evidence of a tenant's title. It is from the tenant's copy of the court roll that the word 'copyhold' is derived. The holding usually consisted of enough land to support a tenant and his household, but it was broken up into several scattered portions interspersed (for equality) with other similar portions belonging to the other copyholders in **common** or **open fields.** There were normally three such fields, two in cultivation and one, in rotation, fallow. In addition, a copyholder had varying RIGHTS OF COMMON in the unenclosed common lands of the manor: the most important of these were *pasture, pannage* (the right to pasture pigs), *piscary* (fishing), *turbaty* (the right to take turf or peat for burning) and *housebote* (wood for household repairs) (*see* INCLOSURE).

As with freehold, the servile status soon attached to the land rather than its owner, and by the 14th cent. the service was beginning to be commuted for a rent charge. This process of commutation was speeded up after the Black Death, and was virtually complete by Tudor times. The incidents, however, remained valuable to lords who could always **enfranchise** a copyhold (i.e. convert it into a freehold), but who seldom did so. Enfranchisement could have political consequences (*see para-1*) and with the industrial revolution the minerals became enormously valuable. Hence copyholds survived until 1925 (electoral law had long since ceased to be relevant) when they were all enfranchised.

(4) FEE SIMPLE, is the right, subject to the laws of inheritance, of absolute ownership for a period which is theoretically of infinite length. It thus includes the right to dispose of the land for an equally infinite period. A **LEASEHOLD** is a defined period of time within which the tenant in fee simple (the landlord) grants to the leaseholder certain rights in return usually for a rent. The period extending from the end of the lease to infinity is called the **landlords reversion.** An **ENTAIL** or **FEE TAIL** is theoretically an infinite right which, however, descends in a defined family. On the failure of heirs it reverts to the original grantor or his descendants. The fee tail was consequently unsaleable. English law has always leaned against perpetuities of this kind, and from the 15th cent. it became established that entails could be broken (barred) by fictitious legal proceedings called respectively FINE (which barred the collaterals) and RECOVERY (which ended the entail altogether). *See* LEGAL FICTIONS. By the 17th cent. it was established that an entail could not hold for longer than a life in being plus 21 years. Thenceforth, apart from a few statutory entails, all long standing family entails were maintained by periodical barring and resettlement.

In the 19th cent. the notion of the **TRUST** created further flexibility and eventually in 1922 an entail ceased to be capable of impeding a disposal of land, for the terms of the entail were simply applied to the proceeds of sale as if it were a trust. This rule applied in gen., to any land regardless of its status.

(5) The foregoing rules applied generally, but were subject to a number of exceptions, for local tenures existed which had distinct jurisprudences of their own. Of these the most important were Gavelkind, Borough English and Ancient Demesne.

LANE, Jane (?-1689) (later Lady FISHER) rode with Charles II disguised as a manservant, across England after the B. of Worcester in 1651 and ensured his escape. She later entered the service of the Princess of Orange, was pensioned at the Restoration and married Sir Clement Fisher.

LANE, Sir Ralph (?-1603), became gov. of Sir Richard Grenville's Virginian settlement at Wokokan in 1585, but on its failure returned with Drake in 1586.

LANE, Sir Richard (1584-1650), was Att-Gen. to the P. of Wales in 1634, defended Strafford in 1641 so energetically that the Commons abandoned the impeachment and used a Bill of Attainder. Appointed to defend the Twelve Bishops in Jan. 1642, he joined the King and was knighted in Jan. 1643. In 1644 he became Chief Baron of the Exchequer, and in 1645 Lord Keeper. He followed Charles II into exile.

LANERCOST (*see* CUMBERLAND). The *Lanercost Chronicle,* written at Carlisle, is an authority for the period 1201-1346.

LANFRANC of PAVIA (?1010-89) son of a judge, gained a great reputation as a teacher at Avranches (1039 onwards) and in 1045 became prior of Bec, to whose school scholars and pupils came from all Europe, including Ivo of Chartres, St. Anselm and the future Pope Alexander II. A skilful disputant, he confuted the doctrines of Berengar of Tours at papal councils notably at Tours (1055) and the Lateran (1050) and was well known at the *Curia.* He was also notably strong willed, (*see* WILLIAM I-II), but he and William I built up a friendship of mutual respect. He became abbot of St. Stephen's Caen in 1063 and was William's main ecclesiastical adviser, while Stigand still held the see of Canterbury. When William deposed Stigand in 1070, Lanfranc succeeded him, and with the King's co-operation put through a major reorganisation of the church. The province of York was increased in size but subordinated to Canterbury. The creation of the great sees of Lincoln and Salisbury changed episcopal geography from the Humber to Weymouth. Bishops' seats were moved (e.g. Selsey to Chichester). Corrupt monasteries were reformed and from 1077 Cluniac houses began to be founded. He also brought the church into closer contact with the reforming continental church by substituting Normans (often trained by himself) for Saxons in higher preferments. Lanfranc also found time to rebuild Canterbury Cathedral and wrote books on transubstantiation, the Benedictine Rule and Canon Law. In accordance with the Conqueror's wishes he crowned William Rufus in 1087.

LANG, Cosmo Gordon (1864-1945), Ld. LANG of LAMBETH (1942) first achieved prominence as vicar of Oxford Univ. Church (1894-6), of Portsea (1896-1901) and as a chaplain to Q. Victoria. He was Bp. of Stepney from 1901 to 1908 when he became Abp. of York. In 1928 he was translated to Canterbury. He was influential in political and court circles and was a successful ecclesiastical diplomat and practical church reformer, but he became involved in the issues surrounding Edward VIII's projected marriage and was suspected of lending himself to the intrigues of the King's enemies. He resigned in 1942.

LANGHAM, Simon (?-1376), Abbot of Westminster from 1349, became Treasurer of England in 1360 and Bp. of Ely in 1361. As Lord Chancellor from 1363, he was the first to deliver official parliamentary orations in English. In 1366 he became the last monk to be Abp. of Canterbury. He dismissed Wycliffe from Canterbury Hall, Oxford. In 1368, on becoming a Cardinal, he resigned from Canterbury. He died at Avignon.

LANGLAND, William (?-1330-?1400) wrote his long alliterative poem, *The Vision of Piers Plowman* apparently in three forms: *A* c. 1370; *B* c. 1378; and *C* c. 1395. Its moral fervour and realist if rather pessimistic, picture of his time, won great popularity. Fifty contemporary copies exist. The only evidence of his life is in the poem. He was a shepherd brought up near Malvern, learned Latin and moved to London where he supported his family by chanting the office. The poem is an allegory in which Piers sees the world as a fair field full of folk between a high Tower of Truth and the Dungeon of Wrong. The people go about their variously described business guided or misled by temptations or good impulses. Then a 1000 men seek St. Truth, but the way is obscure and Piers offers to help them if they will help him to plough his half-acre. Some help, some do not. In the last *passus* of the poem there is a search for Do well, Do Bet, and Do Best who cannot be found in the Church or in Scripture. In a series of new visions Piers and Christ blend together. The poor receive their Heavenly reward but the House of Unity (*see ps.* 50) is assaulted by Pride and Anti-Christ, and mankind by Death.

LANGLEY or LONGLEY, Card. (1411) Thomas (?-1437), brought up in the household of John of Gaunt, became dean of York in 1401, privy seal in 1403, Lord Chancellor in 1405 (to 1407) and Bp. of Durham in 1406. In 1409 and 1410 and 1414 he was employed on diplomatic missions, and was again Lord Chancellor from 1417 to 1429.

LANGRES PROTOCOL (Jan. 1814), embodied discussions at Basle between Castlereagh and Metternich, and at Langres between them and the Czar. They agreed that after Bonaparte's defeat, France should be restricted to her 'ancient' frontiers; that a strengthened Kingdom of Holland should be constituted, and that subject thereto, all questions, except that of Maritime Rights, should be settled at a Congress to be held at Vienna.

LANGTOFT, Peter of (?-1307), an Augustinian canon of Bridlington (Yorks), wrote a French verse history of England to the death of Edward I (1307). It is mostly derivative but the concluding parts are useful sources for contemporary events, particularly the Scottish wars of Edward I and northern affairs generally. It was widely circulated, and translated into English by Robert Mannyng.

LANGTON, Stephen (of) (?1157-1228) Card. (1206). (1) Academic theologian at Paris from c.1170 to 1206, was also a poet and a famous preacher. In 1206 Innocent III summoned him to Rome to teach theology as a cardinal, and then, on the disputed election to Canterbury following Hubert Walter's death, got him elected in place of both rivals. K. John's proctors refused assent, but in June 1207 Innocent consecrated him nonetheless. John objected because he was, though born in Lincolnshire, virtually a Frenchman, knowing little of England, and because his royal rights of patronage had been invaded. He expelled the electing monks and demanded security for his loyalty and papal recognition of his rights. In Mar. 1208 Innocent replied with an interdict.

(2) Langton stayed in France until June 1213 when John surrendered England to the Papacy and received it back as a fief. Restoration of church property would need a year-long accountancy exercise, but meanwhile Langton and Innocent, through his legates Nicholas and Pandulf, pursued divergent courses. At councils in Aug. 1213 Langton, French trained casuist without political or administrative experience, encouraged discussion of Henry I's coronation charter and was becoming identified with baronial opposition. The legates, on the other hand, were helping the King to secure acceptable bishops by influencing electing chapters, and the King was preparing for a French war. With his background, neither activity was likely to please Langton. He began to obstruct the legates and the King in pursuit of his view of justice and the remedy of abuses. In Jan. 1214 Pandulf returned to Rome and complained. In Feb. the war began. In July, at the time of its disastrous climax at Bouvines, the interdict was lifted.

(3) In the Magna Carta crisis (June 1215), therefore, Langton sympathised with the barons, but as head of the church in a papal fief and, by tradition, the King's First Adviser, he could not lead them. Moreover three months

earlier Innocent, while urging K. John to do justice, and the barons to keep quiet, had instructed Langton to keep order, and immediately after Runnymede he had instructed Langton to excommunicate barons who had not submitted within eight days. In the disorders which soon broke out, Langton took no action. He was peremptorily ordered to do his duty (July) and suspended (Sept.) by papal commissioners when he failed. He then set out for Rome but Innocent confirmed the suspension (Nov.).

(4) He returned in 1218 to a changed England. John was dead. The most respectable magnates had united with the church under the legate Guala to protect the child King, to repel a French invasion, and to restore order. He could co-operate in such a unity, but he recrowned Henry III (May 1220) and got rid of Pandulf, Guala's successor (Autumn 1221). In 1222, at the Council of Oxford, he issued canons modelled on the pronouncements of Innocent III. His prestige was now very high.

(5) Most of the rest of his life was spent in co-operating with Hubert de Burgh in governing the country during the King's minority. In the troubles (1223-4) involving E. Ranulf of Chester and the mercenary castellans, he arranged for Henry III's conditional majority and redistributed the castles impartially himself (Jan-Apr. 1224). In the summer of 1224 he helped to suppress Falkes de Bréauté's dangerous insurrection and in 1225 he summoned the first clerical assembly to make a grant to the crown as part of the arrangements for reissuing Magna Carta. The King declared himself fully of age in Jan. 1227. A year later Langton died.

LANGTON, Thomas (?-1501), canonist, undertook diplomatic missions to France in 1467, 1476 (when a royal chaplain), 1477, 1478 and 1480. By 1483 he had acquired several prebends and was Bp. of St. Davids. In 1485 he was Bp. of Salisbury and from 1487 to 1495 Master of Queen's Coll., Oxford. From 1493 he was Bp. of Winchester. He died just after election as Abp. of Canterbury.

LANGTRY, Lillie (1852-1929), the beautiful daughter of W.C.E. le Breton, dean of Jersey, became a stage celebrity overnight in 1881 and was later much associated with Edward VII as prince and king. She died very rich.

LANGUE D'-OÏL,-OC. The Latin 'hoc ille' meant 'yes'. In N. France the emphasis was on 'ille'; in the south on 'hoc'. Thus 'oïl' and 'oc' became the distinguishing signs of mediaeval N and S French. The users of the two languages had difficulties of mutual comprehension and there are still visible differences of outlook and culture. The Langue d'oïl was the language of the **Trouvères**, composers of courtly, comic, dramatic, lyric, narrative and satiric verse at the northern courts such as Paris and Troyes. The **troubadours** composed similarly in the Langue d'oc and Provençal, but with greater stylistic elaboration, and an interest in courtly love, crusading and the Virgin. The more skilled used esoteric poesy (*trobar clus*) and elaborately strict versification (*trobar ric*). The poems were accompanied by but not always sung to an instrument. Trouvères and troubadours were drawn from all levels of society: e.g. K. Richard I, his minstrel friend, Blondel de Nesle and Arnaut Daniel were troubadours; trouvères included Theobald, Count of Champagne, the Cleric Chrétien de Troyes and the poor travelling minstrel Colin Muset.

The Troubadour poetry spread to Spain and Italy, but was destroyed as a literary influence by the Albingensian crusades. Of the Langue d'oïl dialects Norman, Picard and Francien (spoken in the Ile de France) maintained some literary independence until the 14th cent. when the growing importance of Paris tended to elevate Francien into the standard language and so the ancestor of modern French.

French was the natural language of most ruling

Englishmen after 1066, but the dialect used depended upon family traditions and connections, and particularly the location of their French estates. The lawyers used the Norman which became increasingly debased after the loss of Normandy (1204-6). The fragmentation of French, as well as the need to speak English with tenants and servants, accelerated the use of English at high levels, but French was a very common accomplishment until the mid 15th cent. and Norman French remained the legal jargon until 1707.

LANKA, SRI. *See* CEYLON.

LANNES, Marshal Jean, D. of MONTEBELLO (1769-1809) was a republican gen. in 1796 when he supported Bonaparte in the *coup d'état* of Brumaire. In June 1800 he won the B. of Montebello and he took a leading part in major French victories from Marengo to Friedland. In 1808 he defeated Castaños at Tudela (Spain) in Nov. and captured Saragossa. He rejoined the Grand Army in May 1809 in time for the defeat at Essling, where he was mortally wounded.

LANSBURY, George (1859-1940), lived originally in the East End of London. He migrated to Australia in 1884 but returned in 1885 and entered Liberal politics. In 1889 he demanded an eight-hour day at the Manchester National Liberal Conference but, unable to make headway, joined the new Labour Party. He was always sensitive to people's daily cares and became a poor law guardian in 1892 and a borough councillor in 1903. In 1910 he was elected M.P. for Bow and Bromley largely on a personal vote, and from 1912 edited the *Daily Herald*. As mayor of Poplar during the unemployment period of 1919 to 1920, he led the council's refusal to honour precepts issued to it (*see* POPLAR) and his and other councillors' triumphant imprisonment for contempt. He returned to Parliament with an overwhelming majority in 1922, and was one of the parliamentary Labour Party's most powerful members. He gave up the editorship of the *Daily Herald,* but in 1925 launched *Lansbury's Labour Weekly* which failed in 1927. He was First Commissioner of Works in the Labour Govt. of 1929-31 and made popular improvements in the London parks. One of the few survivors of the electoral debacle of 1931, he became leader of the Labour Party, but his unrealistic pacifism slowly eroded his influence and in 1935 he gave way to Clement Attlee. Nevertheless in 1937 he tried personally to convert Hitler and Mussolini to his views. His kindly idealism and integrity gave him a special place in the affections of all parties and persuasions.

LANSDOWNE. *See* GRENVILLE B-5; PETTY; PETTY-FITZMAURICE.

LANSING, Robert (1864-1928), became Pres. Wilson's Sec. of State in 1915. He tried to uphold the U.S. right to trade with both sides in World War I, but foresaw the probability of belligerence and prepared for it by signing accommodations with Mexico and acquiring the Danish W. Indies. After U.S.A. entered the war, he signed the disastrous Ishii agreement recognising the special interests of Japan in China. When the war ended he disagreed with Wilson on priorities. Wilson believed that the establishment of the League of Nations should precede a Peace treaty; Lansing the reverse. Wilson's illness left the conduct of foreign policy in his hands and he had his way, but was dismissed in Feb. 1920 when Wilson recovered. By this time the damage had been done. He was an uncle of John Foster Dulles, Sec. of State from 1953 to 1959.

LAODICEAN (Rev. 3 vv 14-22). A lukewarm supporter of any cause.

LAOS. *See* INDO-CHINA.

LA PLATA. *See* ARGENTINA.

LAPSE, DOCTRINE OF (India). *See* PARAMOUNTCY.

LA ROCHELLE (Lat. RUPELLA = Little Rock), (1) capital of the prov. of Aunis, was loosely a part of Aquitaine until it passed to the French crown in 1271. With its good fortified haven, it then rose to prosperity as the main port of Aunis and Poitou (*see* WINE TRADE-2). In 1360 it passed to the English Kings under the P. of Brétigny and was the destination of their reinforcements when war broke out again. In June 1372 these, under Pembroke, were destroyed by a Castilian fleet just off the port, and in Aug. the corporation, by a trick, disarmed the garrison. During the wars of 1402 onwards, the port was long the only French base and a refuge for fugitive Norman and Breton seamen. These, with the Castilians, sharply defeated the English in Dec. 1419.

(2) The general confusion of the period resulted in a state of maritime quasi-independence. From 1425 the Breton Plusquellec family built and commanded private fleets, issued letters of marque and protection and established a sort of unofficial admiralty. The French govt., still weak, tried conferring admiralty commissions in 1439 on their Breton rivals the Coetrivy, four of whom were distinguished Rochellais seamen. In practice the Rochellais did as they pleased for over two centuries. They traded overseas regardless of crown policy, building up strong commercial links with the British Isles, Spain, Portugal and, in due course, the Americas. Most French Canadians have Rochellais ancestry. They also habitually preyed on passing shipping. Not surprisingly they became church-sacking Puritans in reply to the Catholic centralising monarchy and in 1570 they, with Hawkins, destroyed the royal fleet and took the last Catholic base at Brouage (Mar-July) with its valuable saltpans.

(3) La Rochelle was now the accepted Huguenot capital and was besieged from Aug. 1572 to June 1573, unsuccessfully because of the English supplies. French statesmen regarded the city's commercial and naval power as the mainstay of political Huguenotism in its final form as established by the Edict of Nantes (Apr. 1598). Hence it became the centre of operations in the civil wars renewed in 1621. After naval defeats off the Ile de Ré (Oct. 1622) and in the Pertuis Breton (Sept. 1625), the Rochellais were blockaded, and when Card. Richelieu took over naval and military affairs, besieged. This was the desperate affair in which three English expeditions failed to relieve the city and led to Buckingham's assassination and the financial collapse of the English crown. When the alderman-Admiral Jean Guiton surrendered the city (Oct. 1628) 80% of the population of 29,000 had perished.

(4) After Louis XIV revoked the Edict of Nantes (1689) most of the protestant population moved to Britain, Canada, and Germany. The rest maintained as American traders and, in war time, as privateers, a lucrative activity reflected in their opulent surviving architecture. *See* ELIZABETH I-14; HUGUENOTS.

LARREY, Dominique Jean (1766-1842), Baron (1809) Bonaparte's fearless chief military surgeon, took part in over 400 engagements and was wounded three times. The greatest of all military surgeons he invented first aid, devised many operations including amputation at the hip, and described trench feet. His teaching has saved many thousands of lives in all armies then and now.

LA SALLE, Robert Cavelier, Sieur de (1643-87), settled in Canada in 1666 and, with royal encouragement, completed a journey down the Mississippi to the sea. He named its basin Louisiana in Apr. 1682 in honour of Louis XIV. His second expedition in 1684 from the south was designed to harass Mexico with Indian aid. It landed by mistake in Texas and La Salle was killed by his own disappointed men.

LAS BELA. See BALUCHISTAN.

LASCAR, -I, -INE (Urdu = army or camp), meant originally a kind of Indian military labourer (e.g. for manhandling guns) and then a deck hand recruited for European ships from the Moslem seamen of Kathiawar.

LAS CASAS, Bartolomé de (1474-1566), Spanish missionary in America from 1513 to 1547 advocated the abolition of slavery, and in 1552 published *A Very Brief*

Account of the Destruction of the Indies to arouse Spanish opinion on the subject. Translated into many languages, the atrocities described in this pamphlet became the foundation of protestant anti-Spanish propaganda.

LASCELLES. Yorkshire family, whose head became **E. of HAREWOOD** in 1812. **Henry George (1882-1947), 6th E.** inherited a fortune from the M. of Clanricarde in 1916, and married Mary, the Princess Royal in 1922. Their son **George Henry (1923-) 7th E.,** was an important patron of music.

LASKI, Harold (1893-1950), of Polish origin, was Prof. of Political Science at the London School of Economics from 1926 until he died. Personally liked and respected, especially in the Labour Party, his efforts to adapt Marxism to the British socialist movement were largely ineffectual. During World War II he was Clement Attlee's assistant and he became Chairman of the Labour Party in 1945. He was a favoured target for right-wing vituperation of a not very respectable kind.

LASTINGHAM ABBEY (Yorks.) was founded by St. Cedd and later ruled by St. Chad. It was converted from Irish to Roman practices at the end of the 7th cent. and moved to York in the 1080s.

LATAKIA or LATTAKIEH (Syria) became an important port of the Frankish Principality of Antioch until the expulsion of the crusaders in 1187 when Saladin's troops sacked it. The French established a trading factory there in 16th cent. and their interests were specially protected by the Ottoman authorities. It became a French mandated territory in 1922, and was a separate state until merged in Syria in 1926. It has long grown and exported a peculiar type of black tobacco.

LA TÈNE CULTURE. *See* IRON AGE.

LATERAN (St. JOHN LATERAN) is the Cathedral Church of Rome; the palace attached to it was the Papal residence from 4th cent. until 1308 when it was burned down. The Popes moved to Avignon in 1309, but settled at the Vatican when they returned in 1377.

LATERAN COUNCILS were church councils held in Rome. Five of these are regarded as ecumenical. The First (1123) was summoned by Callixtus II to confirm the Concordat of Worms which ended the Investiture dispute. The Third (1179) by Alexander III confined papal elections to a two-thirds majority of the college of cardinals and provided for the creation of cathedral schools. The Fourth (1215), by Innocent III, defined transubstantiation, required annual confession and forbade priests to countenance judicial ordeals.

LATERAN TREATY (11 Feb. 1929). By this treaty the Papacy and the Italian state recognised each other as sovereign international personalities and the Vatican City became a sovereign state.

LATHE. One of the five districts, each administered by a lathe reeve and containing several hundreds, into which Kent was divided.

LATIFUNDIA **(Lat. = wide estates).** A pejorative term denoting estates so large that a dangerously high proportion of the land is in a few hands, and incapable of proper or liberal management. Used of the properties of English landlords in Ireland, and of estate ownership in the southern American colonies.

LATIMER, Hugh (?1485-1555), eloquent champion of the New Learning and social reform, was one of 12 licensed to preach anywhere in England by Cambridge Univ. in 1522; in 1525, on refusing to attack Luther, he was forbidden to preach within the diocese of Ely (i.e. Cambridge) but Wolsey, having heard his defence, quashed the prohibition. His witty and intelligible style made him the most popular and influential publicist of his time and when he preached before Henry VIII in 1530 against his habitual use of force to defend religion the King smiled. All the same he was censured in Convocation in 1532 for his extremism, but submitted; but when the break with the Papacy came, Henry VIII

relied much on his advice and made him Bp. of Worcester (1535). Here he continued to preach against social injustice, to denounce many accepted Roman doctrines and to support the Dissolution of the Monasteries and some of Thomas Cromwell's unpopular and violent acts such as the execution of the Pole family and the condemnation of R. Catholics and heretics. In 1539 he resigned against the Six Articles and was forbidden to preach. At first imprisoned and in fear of execution, he lived obscurely until 1546, when he was confined but released at Edward VI's accession. In 1548 he preached a famous sermon *Of the Plough* and afterwards became one of Somerset's ablest propagandists. Not surprisingly he was arrested under Mary I and he and Ridley were convicted of heresy after a debate at Oxford. They were burned together, Latimer remarking with his usual wit as the flames tormented them "Have courage Master Ridley, we shall this day light such a candle, by God's grace in England as shall never be put out".

LATIMER AFFAIR (Apr. 1384). John Latimer, a Carmelite, told Richard II during the Salisbury Parliament that John of Gaunt (D. of Lancaster) was plotting his death. Richard wanted to have Lancaster condemned out of hand but was persuaded by the peers to have Latimer detained pending inquiries. On his way to prison Latimer was seized by John Holland, Richard's half brother, and other Lancastrians and murdered. Richard's uncle Thomas of Woodstock threatened to kill anyone, including Richard, who imputed treason to Lancaster. The incident demonstrated the growth of a Lancastrian party and led to a dissolution of the Parliament.

LATIMER originally a Yorkshire family of which **William (1) (?-1304) 1st Ld. LATIMER** was a wealthy household knight of Edward I. He served in the Welsh campaigns of 1276 and 1282 and in Aquitaine. Edward employed him on the draconian judicial inquiry of 1289 and he subsequently commanded on the border and in Scotland, being present at the Bs. of Stirling (1297) and Falkirk (1298). His son **(2) (?1276-1327) 2nd Ld.,** also held commands in Scotland and was captured at Bannockburn (1314). He at one time supported Thomas of Lancaster but later went over to Edward II. His grandson **(3) (?1329-81), 4th Ld.,** served in Aquitaine and Brittany in 1359-60. He became King's Chamberlain in 1369 and warden of the Cinque Ports in 1374. A corrupt courtier, he suffered the first known impeachment, in the Good Parliament (1376), for peculation, but was saved from serious consequences by the Lancastrian reaction. In 1377 he was appointed Capt. of Calais. He died on campaign in France.

LATIN, always the regular speech of the R. Catholic Church, was reinspired in the barbarous west by Pope Gregory the Great (r. 590-604) and by the isolated Irish church, especially the school of Bangor, whence St. Columbanus' first and second generation disciples carried a new style across Europe. In England the pioneers were Aldhelm of Malmesbury (c. 640-709) and Bede of Jarrow (c. 673-735), while St. Boniface (680-755) went to Germany and the great Alcuin of York (735-804) founded the Carolingian schools. The re-creation of this international language attracted great interest and emulation. A substantial and widely read literature circulated throughout western Europe and provoked in its turn such exhibitionism as the language of K. Athelstan's charters. Scholarship, generally speaking, suffered setbacks in the barbarian incursions of the 8th to 11th cent revival. By this time, however, a parallel development of vernacular literature was confining the use of Latin to the educated, the scholarly and the official. In these levels it remained normal, though progressively eroded, until the Reformation emphasised liturgies "understood of the people" and led to wholesale abandonment of Latin by national churches. In

England, though spoken business was conducted in English, court pleadings, if not in Norman French, were in dog-Latin until 1707 and Latin remained a compulsory subject in some public schools as late as 1940. The long period of compulsory school Latin was dominated by two text books: the much criticised and sometimes altered *Brevissima Institutio* of Wm. Lily (?1468-1522), High Master of St. Paul's and the *Latin Primer* of Benjamin Hall Kennedy (1804-89) a famous classical scholar and Headmaster of Shrewsbury. *See* LITERACY.

LATIN EMPIRE. *See* BYZANTINE EMPIRE-8,9.

LATIN (MONETARY) UNION (1865-73) was a bimetallist union of Belgium, France, Italy and Switzerland to which some minor Balkan and S. American states adhered. The object was, by coining a fixed quantity of new silver annually, to protect members from the relative appreciation against gold caused by the Gold Rushes in Australia and America.

LATITAT. *See* LEGAL FICTIONS.

LATITUDINARIANISM. *See* ANGLICANISM.

LATVIA, was substantially ruled and its economy managed by a minority of German origin until 1917, when the Lettish majority claimed Latvian independence on the Russian March Revolution of 1917. This claim amounted to a social revolution which it was imperial German policy to prevent. Hence in Mar. 1918 Latvia was ceded to Germany under the P. of Brest-Litovsk. In Nov. 1918 when Germany collapsed, a Lettish national assembly at Riga again claimed independence, but the Russians set up a rival communist govt. at Valmiera. In Jan. 1919 the Russians took Riga, but German "free companies" counter-attacked from Libau (Liepaja) and in May recaptured it, but their further advance was defeated at Cesis by an Estonian-Latvian army whose leader, Ulmanis, returned to Riga in July. By 1920 the indigenous Germans were mostly driven out with Anglo-French naval help, and the Russian invaders by a combined Lettish-Estonian-Polish force. Under the Peace of Aug. 1920 the Russians renounced their claims. With a multiplicity of parties, parliamentary govt. proved virtually unworkable and Ulmanis, the prime minister most often in office, proposed constitutional reforms which were hotly opposed by the communists and the rising Nazis. He therefore declared a state of siege. In Aug. 1939, Germany traded the Baltic States to Russia in return for help against Poland. In 1940 the Russians again invaded, arrested Ulmanis, began the deportations which reduced the Letts to a minority in their own country and incorporated Latvia into the so-called Union of Soviet Socialist Republics (U.S.S.R.). In 1987, with the rise of the Gorbachev govt. in Moscow, the Letts, with other Baltic nations, claimed their independence, but the large proportion of Russians now in the country and its economic and transport links with Russia and White Russia confused the political situation, and so Latvia began to set up trading links with western powers through the port of Riga. A juridical independence was achieved in 1991.

LAUD, William (1573-1645) was Pres. of St. John's Coll, Oxford in 1611, archdeacon of Huntingdon in 1615, dean of Gloucester in 1616 and Bp. of St. David's from 1651 to 1626. He was a determined, maddening, sometimes witty Arminian with a penetrating eye for detail. He was already well known at court at Charles I's accession and became Bp. of Bath and Wells in 1626. In Charles' second parliament he preached a detailed exposition of his and the court's view of politics. "A royal command must be God's glory, and obedience to it the subjects honour." He championed ceremonial uniformity and the exclusion of puritans, especially from the pulpit. As Dean of the Chapels Royal he was the King's closest religious adviser and early recognised as an influential enemy of the gradually coalescing opposition. In 1627 Charles made him a privy councillor, thus confirming his political

status. In 1628 he was translated to London, whose merchant patriciate was becoming hostile to the court. He had a genuine sympathy with the poor, which did not endear him to the alderman. He had a real interest in education and learning. In 1629 he became Chanc. of Oxford Univ. and instituted practical reforms in its statutes and management. He instituted the professorship of Arabic still named after him. He sent agents to Turkey to rescue Greek and Persian manuscripts.

He became Abp. of Canterbury in 1633. As such he was associated with the King's long period of personal rule, while himself attempting to exercise an even more authoritarian influence in the church. Bearing in mind his view of royal supremacy, his constant meddling in everything raised up enemies, not only of the church, but within it. His metropolitical visitations disturbed ancient abuses. His association in the public mind with the equally efficient Strafford did him no good either, and his authority was linked to the Church courts and the Star Chamber where his association with the harsh sentences upon Leighton (1630) and Prynne, Burton and Bastwick (1631) made him deeply unpopular. He was a member of the committee on foreign plantations. He always moved in splendour and was wrongly assumed to favour Rome. He was a public irritant. Since it was his influence which made Charles try to introduce the Book of Common Prayer into Scotland he had a major responsibility for the Bishops' War and the King's ultimate downfall.

The parliamentary opposition found it necessary to attack him as part of their programme to dismantle the royal absolutism, but it was politically convenient to do so because they gained popularity thereby. Articles of impeachment were voted against him in 1640, and he was committed to the Tower early in 1641. His colleague Strafford went to the block in May and at the same time the archbishop's principal instruments of authority, the High Commission and the Star Chamber, were struck down. Laud, safely in custody, was no longer a danger. Moreover he was difficult to impeach because there was no evidence directly in point. All his major activities had been lawful. He asserted that he and the King were and always had been protestant. An attempt to represent numerous administrative misdemeanours as a cumulative treason, was met derisively by his counsel: "I never understood before this time that 200 couple of black rabbits would make a black horse". The impeachment was abandoned in favour of an attainder and he was brought to the block in Jan. 1645. He roundly reasserted his and Charles' Protestantism and declared, rightly, that he was undeserving of death "by any known law of this Kingdom". The attainder, not having the royal assent, was itself unlawful.

He summed up his attitude to church policy at his trial: "I laboured nothing more than that the external public worship of God might be preserved ... being still of the opinion that Unity cannot long continue in the Church, when Uniformity is shut out at the Church door."

***LAUDABILITER* (1155).** Bull by Pope Adrian IV, granting the lordship of Ireland to the English Crown. *See* HENRY II; IRELAND-A.

LAUDER (Berwick). At the bridge of this otherwise undistinguished place Archibald Bell-the-Cat, E. of Angus, hanged the E. of Mar and other supporters of James III in 1482.

LAUDERDALE. *See* SCOTLAND 1660-89-3 TO 6.

LAUDIBUS LEGUM ANGLIAE, DE. *See* FORTESCUE, SIR JOHN.

LAUENBURG. *See* BISMARCK; HANOVER; SCHLESWIG-HOLSTEIN.

LAUGHARNE or LACHARNE (pron: Larn) (Carms) is an ancient borough whose unreformed corporation continued after the Municipal Corporations Act, 1834, as a property trust. The poet Dylan Thomas lived there and it inspired his *Under Milk Wood* under the reversible name Llareggub.

LAUGHARNE, Rowland (?-after 1660), became parliamentary C-in-C for Pembrokeshire in 1642 and for the four western Welsh counties in 1646. In 1648 he came over to the King. The royalist cause being then hopeless, he was captured and court marshalled, but successfully cast lots with others for his life. Charles II gave him a pension.

LAUNCESTON or DUNHEVED (Cornwall), an ancient settlement was acquired in Saxon times by the canons of St. Stephen. At the Conquest it seems to have been divided with the Count of Mortain, who seized the market and built the castle. It became one of the county towns, but its isolated position made it necessary to hold additional sessions and assizes elsewhere. The castle was ruined in the course of a parliamentary siege in the Civil War.

LAUREATE, POETS are officers of the Royal Household who receive a stipend for the, now nominal, duty of writing odes for state events. Edmund Spenser performed this function from 1591 but the title was first used by John Dryden from 1670. His successors down to the reign of George VI were Thomas Shadwell (1688), Nahum Tate (1692), Nicholas Row (1715), Laurence Eusden (1718), Colly Cibber (1730), William Whitehead (1757), Thomas Warton (1785), Henry Pye (1790), Robert Southey (1813), William Wordsworth (1843), Alfred Tennyson (1850), Alfred Austin (1896), Robert Bridges (1913) and John Masefield (1930).

Starting with Shadwell and Tate, respectively the subject of Dryden's *Mac Flecknoe* and Pope's *Dunciad,* many of the laureates have been the target of satire, not invariably good natured. Q. Victoria is said to have refused to offer the post to Rudyard Kipling because of his poem on the *Widow of Windsor.*

LAURENCE, Henry. *See* SIKHS-5 *et seq.*

LAURENTIUS. *See* MISSIONARIES IN BRITAIN AND IRELAND-4,5.

LAURIER, Sir Wilfrid (1841-1919) was Liberal prime minister of Canada (1896-1911) and the first French Canadian to occupy that post. He sent troops to the Boer War and supported their dispatch to the Western Front in World War I but opposed conscription. *See* CANADA-23-25.

LAURENCE OF LUDLOW. *See* STAPLE B-1.

LAUSANNE CONFERENCE and T. (Nov. 1922-Apr. 1923). The Kemalist Turks repudiated the T. of Sèvres which gave Thrace and Smyrna to Greece. They drove out the Greeks and then signed an armistice at Mudania (Oct. 1922) to which the British and French were parties. The final settlement was reached at Lausanne. The western powers recognised the Kemalists as the govt. of Turkey, which abandoned its old Ottoman claims and the Aegean Is., in return for Smyrna and Thrace. The Mesopotamian frontier was settled by an Anglo-Turkish-Iraqi T. signed at **Ankara** in June 1925. The Lausanne T. also guaranteed the freedom of the Straits and demilitarised them; but the Turks regained the right to fortify them in the **T. of Montreux (1936).**

LAW, Andrew Bonar (1858-1923), Ulster Presbyterian born in Canada and brought up by rich relatives in Glasgow, became a Conservative M.P. in 1900 and soon made an impression by his lucidity and command of facts. He held minor office in 1902 and after Joseph Chamberlain, with whom he agreed, died, he became the ablest parliamentary expositor of Tory tariff reform. In 1911 he was unexpectedly elected to succeed Balfour as leader of the Conservative party by votes against Austen Chamberlain and Walter Long. He ably led the party in the Home Rule and Ulster controversies and supported the govt. in declaring war in 1914. In the wartime coalition he was Colonial Sec. and then served under Lloyd George as Ch. of the Exchequer and (from 1919 to 1922) as Privy Seal. Ill health forced him to resign as prime minister only seven months after gaining the post.

LAW (1) James (?1560-1632) was Chaplain to James VI in 1601 and moderator of the Scots General Assembly in 1608. A convinced supporter of James' ecclesiastical policy he was Bp. of St. Andrews from 1611 to 1615 and Abp. of Glasgow thereafter. A grandson **(2) Robert (?-?1690)** was a subversive covenanting preacher in the years 1662 to 1674. Another descendant **(3) John (1671-1729)** was sentenced to death for murder by duelling in 1694, but escaped abroad and in 1701 and 1709 published pamphlets on Scottish finance. He wandered Europe for some years seeking patrons for his financial schemes and made influential friends in France by his charm and quick wit. By 1716, through the influence of the Regent he had established the *Banque General,* the first French bank issuing a paper currency. This had many noble backers who also supported his scheme for exploiting the Mississippi basin through his *Banque de l'Ouest* which became an over-inflated investment company. In 1720, just after he had been appointed Controller-Gen. of Finances, the Company crashed dragging down the Bank. This was the French equivalent of the South Sea Bubble. Law fled into obscurity and died in Venice. His grandnephew **(4) James (1768-1828) Comte de LAURISTON** was a French general, A.D.C. to Bonaparte and a marshal under Louis XVIII.

LAW. (1) Edmund (1703-87), a tolerant intellectual divine, was master of Peterhouse, Cambridge, from 1756 to 1768 and Bp. of Carlisle thenceforth. Of his many remarkable descendants his son **(2) John (1745-1810)** was successively Bp. of Clonfert (1785-7), Killala (1797-95) and Elphin (from 1795); **(3) George Henry (1761-1845),** was successively Bp. of Chester (1812-24) and of Bath and Wells (from 1824); and **(4) Edward (1750-1818) 1st Ld. ELLENBOROUGH (1802)** a barrister, became famous as Leader for the defence of Warren Hastings from 1788 to 1792. He became Att-Gen. in 1793, and M.P. for Newtown (I. of W.) in 1801. From 1802 he was Lord Chief Justice; he was also Speaker of the Lords in 1805, and a member of the Ministry of All the Talents in 1806. His son **(5) Edward (1790-1871) 2nd Ld. and 1st E. ELLENBOROUGH (1844)** was Lord Privy Seal in 1828 and Member of the Board of Control from 1828 to 1830. He retained his interest in Indian affairs and in due course became, in 1841, an aggressive gov-gen. of India. Having dealt with imbroglios in China and Afghanistan, he was responsible for the conquest of Sind and Gwalior. He was, however, disliked by the civilian administrators, and his Indian policy was suspect at home. Recalled and placated with an earldom in 1844, he remained formidable and was First Lord of the Admiralty under Peel in 1846. He was the last president of the Board of Control in 1858. His brother **(6) Charles Ewan (1792-1850),** was recorder of London from 1833 and M.P. for Cambridge Univ. from 1835.

LAW, William (1686-1761), mystic and author of the *Serious Call* (1728) was also a tutor in the family of Edward Gibbon, grandfather of the historian.

LAW CODES, INDIA. The Charter Act, 1833, set up an Indian Law Commission of which T.H. Macaulay was the leading member. He drafted the highly successful Indian Penal code between 1834 and 1837, before returning home in 1838. Further codes on Civil (1859) and Criminal (1861) Procedure, Succession (1865), Evidence, and Contract (1872), Trusts and Transfer of Property (1882) followed. These codes later influenced the law of the Sudan and Nigeria.

LAW DAY was a session of a sheriff's court or court leet.

LAW REPORTS. *See* ABRIDGMENTS; YEAR BOOKS.

LAWES, Henry (1596-1662), a gentleman of the Chapel Royal from 1626, was the first English composer to study the pointing of psalms. He suggested *Comus* to Milton and wrote the music for it (1634). He also produced many other local compositions.

LAWS, Sir John (1814-1900). *See* ROTHAMSTED.

LAW MERCHANT is that part of the general custom of merchants of all nations which English courts will enforce.

LAWN TENNIS. The Wimbledon Lawn Tennis and Croquet Club instituted the first championship in 1877. The Lawn Tennis Assoc. was founded in 1888.

LAWRENCE, D. H. *See LADY CHATTERLEY'S LOVER.*

LAWRENCE, John. *See* SIKHS-5 *et seq.*

LAWRENCE, Sir Thomas (1769-1830), painter, was already famous as a child prodigy in Bath by 1781. By 1787 he had the patronage of George III, whom he painted in 1792. He executed most of the Waterloo Chamber portraits at Windsor and was Pres. of the Royal Academy in 1820. He had great learning as well as skill in his art.

LAWRENCE (or SHAW) Thomas Edward (1888-1935) "LAWRENCE OF ARABIA" knew Syria and learned Arabic during student travels gathering material for a thesis on crusader castles. In World War I he joined the Arab Bureau in Cairo and was sent to the Hejaz. By combining Arab tribal unrest and desire for loot, with the prestige of the Grand Sherif of Mecca and adequate supplies of dynamite, he raised a revolt against the Turks, permanently wrecked the Hejaz railway, carried the Arab movement to Damascus and made himself famous. Intellectually brilliant yet in some ways perverse and unreliable, his ornately written *Seven Pillars of Wisdom* was a best seller. He joined the R.A.F. as Aircraftsman Shaw, possibly to escape public attention, and was killed in a motorcycle accident.

LAW'S CONSERVATIVE (Oct. 1922-May 1923), and **BALDWIN'S FIRST GOVT. (May 1923-Jan. 1924)** were two phases of one govt. and had 12 cabinet ministers in common, of whom the leaders were Vist. Cave, Lord Chanc., the M. Curzon, Foreign Sec. and the D. of Devonshire Colonial Sec., but in the first, Andrew Bonar Law was prime minister with the M. of Salisbury as Lord Pres. and Stanley Baldwin as Ch. of the Exchequer and in the second Stanley Baldwin was prime minister and Ch. of the Exchequer with Lord Robert Cecil as Lord Privy Seal; and in Aug. 1923 Neville Chamberlain took over the Exchequer.

(1) The election of Dec. 1922 was a 'plebiscite against Lloyd George' in which Bonar Law promised economies, a tranquil foreign policy and free trade. Baldwin went to Washington with Montagu Norman, the Gov. of the Bank of England. Law had briefed him to settle Britain's war debt to the U.S.A. on the basis that Britain should pay only what she received from others. Norman persuaded him to pay interest at 3% for 10 years and 3½% for 52 with a 1% sinking fund. He did so without consulting the Cabinet. Law was overruled by his own cabinet. Thus Baldwin was the real leader from the start. In May 1923 Law was found to have cancer of the throat and resigned.

(2) Law declined to advise the King who his successor should be. He expected that it would be Curzon but suggested that the King should consult Salisbury who, through Ld. Stamfordham, the King's Sec., recommended Curzon. Stamfordham, however, had been given a memorandum supporting Baldwin. This had been written by Davidson, a friend of Baldwin's, but had been represented by Law's own private secretary as 'practically' representing Law's views. Stamfordham also consulted A. J. Balfour, the only other living conservative prime minister, who recommended Baldwin. The King accepted the view in Davidson's paper because he thought that it represented Bonar Law's. Bonar Law mistrusted Curzon. The existence of the paper was unknown to Bonar Law, but it probably expressed his real opinion.

(3) Baldwin accepted office and the leadership of the conservative party at the end of May, but had to wait until Aug. to find a Ch. of the Exchequer, when he appointed Neville Chamberlain, and so began a long political association based on a common dislike of Lloyd George. Chamberlain introduced a Housing Act so geared that the poor could get only second-rate new houses, and

then Baldwin declared for Protection (25 Oct.). As this was against Bonar Law's election pledge, a general election had to be held, in which the vote-losing Housing Act played its part. The govt. was defeated in the Commons on 22nd Jan. and resigned.

LAWSON, Sir John (?-1665), parliamentary admiral, served under Blake, but was dismissed for Anabaptist and republican leanings, and was perhaps wrongly implicated in the Fifth Monarchy conspiracy in 1657. In 1659, however, he commanded the fleet and in 1660 co-operated with Monck to restore the monarchy, and himself brought the King to England. He then served in the Mediterranean campaign against the Algerines, but was recalled to take command of the centre (Red) squadron against the Dutch and was killed at the B. of Lowestoft.

LAW TERMS. From the earliest times there were four law terms (Michaelmas, Hilary, Easter, and Trinity) in a year regulated by the church prohibition on oath taking between Advent and Epiphany, Septuagesima and 14 days after Easter, Ascension and Corpus Christi, plus the need for a long summer vacation to avoid urban epidemics, collect harvests, and settle the annual accounts. They were thought to be a major source of legal delays, for a party in a case might, if he wished, take one step in the originally spoken but later written pleadings, each term. They were abolished in 1873, and thereafter pleading could be carried on to a less loosely defined timetable. This reform does not seem to have made much difference.

LAW SOCIETY, originally a Society of Attorneys, Solicitors, and Proctors was founded in 1825, chartered in 1831 and known from 1860 to 1903 as the Incorporated Law Society. It qualifies, disciplines and represents solicitors, maintains a compensation fund to relieve clients against solicitors' malpractice, regulates solicitors' accounts and has, since 1951, administered the legal aid system. A similar body was set up in Scotland in 1949. Since about 1960 it has adopted policies in some ways more appropriate to a trade union than a professional body and its disciplinary function where clients are involved has sometimes been criticised as less than impartial.

LAWS AND ACTS OF PARLIAMENT **(Sc).** Two collections of Scottish statutes respectively for **(1)** 1424-1597 by Sir John Skene; **(2)** 1424-1681 by Sir Thos. Murray of Glendook, much of it copied from Skene.

LAWS OF ENGLAND, HALSBURY'S, represented a statement of English law as it had developed in a world of accelerating change through centuries of judicial decision and legislation. Each edition was produced under the editorship of an ex-Lord Chancellor, with the advice of the highest judges, and the articles were written by the ablest practitioners in their subject. The editions so far are:- **(1)** 1907-17 by Ld. Halsbury. **(2)** 1931-42 by Vist. Hailsham. **(3)** 1951-4 by Vist. Simonds. **(4)** 1973- by Ld. Hailsham of St. Marylebone.

The far reaching interventions of statute in legal development made it desirable to publish separate annotated editions of the statutes. These were **(1)** 1928-30; **(2)** 1947-50; **(3)** 1968-72. The changes between each were so vast as to justify a total overhaul. Over 1100 public Acts, for example, were passed between 1930 and 1947. By 1949 the amount and scope of subordinate legislation by way of Statutory Rules and Orders (before 1949) Prerogative Orders, and (after 1948) Statutory Instruments (S.I.s) was so vast that the foregoing encyclopaedic compendia gave a significantly patchy account of the law. About 2000 S.I.s were being made annually. By 1976 the average was nearer 3000, by 1994, 3300 covering 7000 pages and so, from 1951, editions of S.I.s were published as a companion to the statutes and revised on a current basis. As from British adherence to the European Community, the rate of change was accelerated by direct legislation in European Regulations, but mainly by the importation of European Directives through the medium of S.I.s. These S.I.s, though made by authority of an initial Act of Parliament of 1973, actually repeal or otherwise overrule or amend Acts inconsistent with them and are thus a clear threat to parliamentary sovereignty.

LAWSON, James (1538-84) fanatical successor to John Knox at St. Giles, Edinburgh from 1572.

LAYER, Christopher (1683-1723), well known barrister, went to Rome in 1721 to propose an elaborate Jacobite plot to the Old Pretender. Townshend's intelligence, perhaps through Mar, traced the plot. Layer was arrested on his return in 1722 and executed.

LAYAMON or LAWEMON (Anglo-Saxon 'Lawman') **(fl. 1200),** a priest of Emley (Worcs.), wrote a *Brut* or verse history of England from the arrival of the legendary Brutus to Cadwalader (A.D. 689). It is based on Wace's French version of Geoffrey of Monmouth's *Historia* with Norman and Breton additions, and contains the earliest English versions of the history of Arthur, Cymbeline and Lear.

LAYARD, Sir (Austen) Henry (1817-94), travelled in Turkey and Persia from 1839 with Emil Botta, the first excavator near Mosul; he was employed by Stratford Canning, ambassador to the Porte, to report on the state of the country and in 1845 to search for Nineveh. He started with Nimrud (later identified as Calah) and in 1846 worked at Ashur for the British Museum. He supposed that Nimrud was part of Nineveh. From 1849 to 1851 he was attaché at Constantinople, but continued his archaeological investigations. In 1852 he became liberal M.P. for Aylesbury (until 1857) and in 1860 for Southwold. He was U/Sec. for Foreign Affairs in 1852 and from 1861 to 1866, and chief commissioner of works from 1868 to 1869. He was then minister at Madrid until 1877 and at Constantinople until 1880.

LAYER MARNEY (Essex), Italianate Tudor mansion built in 1520 for Ld. Marney.

LAY READERS were reintroduced into the Anglican Church in 1866.

LAZZARONI were ruffianly layabouts so numerous in Naples that no govt. between 1750 and 1859 could survive without consulting their wishes. They created problems for Sir John Acton, Nelson and Garibaldi.

LEAD. Its malleability made it useful for roofs and piping; its density for crossbow and musket ammunition, and its association with silver in mines encouraged speculation and pewter. It was intensively mined in the Mendips, Derbyshire and Wales from Roman times, and between the 16th and 19th cents. Britain and Spain were the largest exporters. Discovered to be a slow poison in the water supply but an insulator against radiation, vast mileages of lead piping were removed after World War II and re-used in atomic power stations. George Washington, who however used lead dentures, died at 67, an advanced age for his time.

LEAGUE, THE. *See* HUGUENOTS.

LEAGUE OF AUGSBURG, WAR OF 1688-97 (*See* JAMES II; WILLIAM III-6,7.) **(1)** This great war, misnamed in the interests of French propaganda, opened with unheralded French aggressions in the Palatinate and in southern Germany (Sept-Oct. 1688) and the Whig-Dutch *riposte* which overthrew James II (Nov-Dec.). William III, on arrival in London, expelled the French ambassador and the T. for the League was signed at Vienna (12 May 1689) Louis having, additionally, declared war on Spain (Apr.). Europe west of Poland was ranged against France whose important ally Sweden, however, kept Denmark semi-neutral and threatened the equipment of the allied fleets. (*See* BALTIC-35,36.) The Turks continued to distract Austria. Subject to this, the war was fought in seven land theatres, the Danube, the Rhine partly linked with the Low Countries, N. Italy, partly lined with Catalonia and the independent areas of Ireland and Scotland. James II had reached Ireland in Mar. 1689, but the Scottish Jacobites

were decisively beaten at Killiecrankie (July 1689) and the pacification of the Highlands, hand in hand with the Irish reconquest, was dependent on command of the sea. The French failed to exploit an advantageous battle off Beachy Head (July 1690) and the protestant relief of Londonderry and Enniskillen was followed by James' defeat at the R. Boyne (July 1690), the destruction of his field army at Aughrim and the capitulation of Limerick (July 1691). The British naval victory at La Hogue (May 1692) ensured that no French counter-attack on this side was possible and that the British could support William's indecisive Flemish campaigns, despite the political uproar caused by the Massacre of Glencoe (Feb. 1692).

(2) The pressure of the war upon the national, especially financial, resources brought important institutional effects. The earliest was the generation of a marine insurance market at Lloyd's coffee house (1692), quickly followed (1693) by the establishment of the National Debt. The service of debt and war required annual parliamentary sessions so that William's veto of the Triennial Bill (Mar. 1693) was an irrelevance remedied in the next year (Dec. 1694), but the way was clear for the simplified creation of debt through the foundation of the Bank of England (July 1694). These four interlocking devices enabled much capital to be channelled towards the support of govt. policy. It was consistent with them that the HEIC was remodelled in 1693. All the same the war was unpopular because expensive and, in the west, unsuccessful. Jacobitism became rampant, and 1695 saw the most dangerous of the plots against William III. The D. of Berwick came secretly to England to investigate the Jacobite strength which he thought considerable, while independently there took shape a plan to murder William at Turnham Green in Feb. 1696. His death was to be the signal for a French invasion. French troops moved to the Channel ports and James II to Calais. The conspiracy was discovered and announced to parliament. William was suddenly popular and his person protected by an Association. The plot, in fact, was futile, for Q. Mary's death (Dec. 1694) had ensured the succession of the P. Anne who, with Marlborough, was identified with the same foreign policy as William.

(3) On balance the war was moving towards an end advantageous to Louis' opponents, while the English economy was strengthened by a currency reform (1696). Moreover the French, having abandoned their maritime policy after La Hogue, left overseas expansion to the English at the expense of the Dutch. The year 1696, when the Board of Trade was set up, was also the year when the HEIC founded Fort William at Calcutta. The overseas events had no effect, however, on this long and widespread war itself, which was ended by the Ts. of Ryswick (Sept-Oct. 1697) because other and immense issues connected with the Spanish Succession were appearing upon the international horizon. Under the treaties Louis recognised William as King but fatefully refused to expel James. *See* JACOBITES AND THEIR PRETENDERS.

LEAGUE OF NATIONS was set up at Geneva by the T. of Versailles (1919). It consisted originally of 28 states which had made war on Germany, and 14 neutrals. The U.S.A., which invented the idea, refused to join. Britain, the five Dominions, Ireland and India counted as separate members. It was governed by an Assembly (representing all the members) whose decisions on matters of substance had to be unanimous, and a council in which great powers had permanent seats and could be outvoted by the 12 others elected in rotation. There was an International Labour Office at Geneva and a Permanent Court of International Justice at The Hague.

Its main purpose was to prevent war and members covenanted not to go to war until every other recourse had been exhausted and then only after nine months; they also covenanted to discontinue financial and economic relations with any state which broke the covenant (SANCTIONS), and to register for publication all treaties which they made. They also undertook social action in the field of labour relations, health, communications, economic and financial issues and the shadier traffics such as arms, drugs and prostitutes. These social activities were more persistent and successful than the political ones but some international disputes (e.g. between Finland and Sweden on the Aaland Is. in 1920) were settled and two wars (Yugoslav-Albanian 1921 and Greco-Bulgar 1925) were stopped. The real difficulties arose when vital interests or major ambitions of great powers were involved, for there was nothing to stop a member from withdrawing from the covenant. Russia joined in 1934 but Italy attacked Ethiopia, and Japan, China with impunity in 1935 because the member states knew that if they applied sanctions the Americans would step in and capture their markets. Japan and Germany left the League in 1935; Italy in 1937. Thereafter it was, in a political sense a moribund organisation, though useful work in the social and economic fields continued until World War II.

LEAKE (1) Richard (1629-96) was a parliamentary naval commander, but in 1677 became Master Gunner. His son **(2) Sir John (1656-1720),** seaman in command of the 40 gun ship *Dartmouth*, forced the boom at Londonderry to revictual the besieged garrison (July 1689), fought at Barfleur (1692) and, after the capture of Gibraltar was heavily engaged in its defence (1701-6) and in the relief of Barcelona (May 1706). After Sir Clowdisley Shovell was drowned, he became C-in-C in the Mediterranean. On his passage from England he captured a fleet of French victuallers from which he again supplied Barcelona (Jan. 1708). He then conquered Sardinia (Aug. 1708) and with Stanhope mounted the important expedition which seized Minorca (Sept. 1708), though he sailed for England before the final surrender, because of the approaching winter storms. He ended as a Lord of the Admiralty. An underrated officer. His adopted heir **(3) Stephen Martin (1702-73)** was Garter King of Arms from 1754. His grandson **(4) William Martin (1777-1860)** instructed Turkish troops in 1799; he then travelled and reported on the state of the Ottoman Empire from 1800 to 1807 and lived in Greece until 1810. He presented marbles to the British Museum and his other collections went to Cambridge.

LEAMINGTON (Warks.) owed its rise to the salt springs; baths were opened in 1786 and the Pump Room in 1814. In 1825 the parish committee was superseded by Improvement Commissioners. The stage coaches ceased to run in 1839, the railway (from Coventry) only came in 1844. The Commissioners were superseded by a Board of Health in 1852 and the town was incorporated from 1875 to 1974. During this period manufacturing, mainly of agricultural machines, became the main industry.

LEANDER CLUB (Henley on Thames) originally for London oarsmen, became the "oarsmen's Atheneum" after it was reorganised and made an open club in 1862. It is the prime inspirer of the Henley Regatta.

LEAR was a legendary pre-Roman King of the Britons, perhaps invented by Geoffrey of Monmouth. He allegedly founded Leicester and ruled for 60 years. He divided his kingdom with his daughters Goneril and Regan to the exclusion of his youngest daughter Cordelia, but he quarrelled with the elder daughters and had to seek help from Cordelia and her husband, the King of the Franks. With their forces he returned and ruled for a further three years and was succeeded by Cordelia. The story gained wide currency and the Tudors used it and cognate legends to support the belief in their British origins.

LEASEHOLD. *See* LAND TENURE (ENGLAND)-4.

LEASEHOLD REFORM ACT, 1967 (with later amendments) enabled resident tenants of houses of a low rateable value to acquire the freehold compulsorily, if they had been in possession for over five years.

LEBANON with its large Christian population was separated from the rest of Ottoman Syria under a Christian gov. in 1868. In 1920 it was proclaimed a state but the French, who had the League of Nations mandate, remained in control until 1941 when the British expelled them. The country became an independent republic in 1946 and joined in the anti-Israeli war of 1948. Thereafter Druze separatism, Syrian intrigues and occasional Israeli invasions and occupations of the south turned the area and particularly Beirut into a battleground, which it still was in 1992.

LEBENSBRAUM (Ger. = living space). The term used by German, especially Nazi, politicians for the territory which Germany was alleged to need to support her population.

LEBWINE or LIAFWHINE, St. *See* MISSIONS TO EUROPE-2.

LECLERC (DE HAUTECLOQUE) Philippe François Marie (1902-47), one of the most attractive Free French leaders, joined Gen. de Gaulle in 1940 and after acting as his gov. successively of Chad and the Cameroons in 1942, led a force across the desert, subduing Italian garrisons on the way, to join the British in Libya. He held divisional commands in Tunisia and France and in 1945 briefly commanded the French troops in Indo-China. He was killed in an accident while military inspector-gen. in N. Africa.

LEE, Arthur Hamilton (1868-1947), 1st Ld. (1918) and 1st Vist. LEE of FAREHAM (1922), retired from the army in 1900 and became conservative M.P. for Fareham. From 1903 to 1908 he was Civil Lord of the Admiralty. In 1915 he became mil. sec. at the Min. of Munitions, in 1916 he was personal mil. sec. to Lloyd George and from 1917 to 1918 director of food production. It was at this time that he presented Chequers for the official use of prime ministers. From 1919 to 1921 he was Pres. of the Bd. of Agriculture and as 1st Lord of the Admiralty from 1921 to 1922 he was second British delegate at the Washington Conference on Naval Disarmament. With Samuel Courtauld he founded the Courtauld Institute and he also established the Warburg Inst. in London.

LEE, Edward (?1482-1544), controversial opponent of Erasmus in 1519 and 1520, became Abp. of York in 1531. He was inclined to Roman usages but his position was compromised by the Pilgrimage of Greece. Fear of the King made him retract and he survived by the influence of his friend Thomas Cromwell.

LEE, Sir Henry (1530-1610), a nephew of Sir Thos. Wyatt, was clerk of the armoury in 1549, M.P. for Bucks. in 1558 and 1572, became Queen's Champion in 1559 and was Master of the Ordnance from 1590. He was a wealthy sheep farmer and courtier.

LEE, Sir Richard (?1513-75), surveyor of the King's Works, fortified Berwick and other border places between 1557 and 1565. *See* ACONTIUS.

LEE. Distinguished American family. **(1) Richard (?-1664),** migrated from Shropshire to become a successful tobacco planter in Virginia, where he served in the legislature and council, and became Att-Gen. and Sec. of State. Among his descendants were four brothers: **(2) Richard Henry (1732-94)** and **(3) Francis Lightfoot (1734-97)** supported Patrick Henry and Jefferson and were members of the Continental Congress. Richard Henry, an early anti-slavery campaigner, agitated against the Stamp Act and organised the Westmoreland Association in 1766. He instigated Washington's appointment as C-in-C, and introduced the motion which brought about the U.S. Declaration of Independence. **(4) William (1739-95)** and **(5) Arthur (1740-92)** went to London where they supported John Wilkes. William, a merchant, became an alderman of London in 1775. Arthur, a doctor and lawyer, gained some notoriety as the writer of the *Junius Americanus* letters in the London press (1769-74). The brothers undertook to raise foreign support for the American Continental Congress. William tried the Dutch, but his draft treaty fell into the hands of the British who used it as one pretext for the Anglo-Dutch war of 1780-4. He also unsuccessfully approached Austria and Russia. Arthur was more successful with the French. In 1776 and 1777 he got arms from the French govt. through its secret agent, the playwright Beaumarchais. He was then joined by Deane and Franklin with whom, despite quarrelling with both, he negotiated the decisive Franco-American alliance. In 1777 he acted unsuccessfully as commissioner to Spain and Prussia. He was recalled in 1779. A cousin **(6) Henry (1756-1819)** ('Light Horse Harry') was the ablest rebel cavalry general and eventually became gov. of Virginia. His son **(7) Robert Edward (1807-70)** was the celebrated Confederate C-in-C in the U.S. civil war. His nephew **(8) Fitzhugh (1835-1905)** was a Confederate cavalry general, later gov. of Virginia. He then served as U.S. Consul-Gen. at Havana from 1896 to 1898 and by his reports had some responsibility for the outbreak of the Spanish-American War, after which he was Gov. of Havana until 1902.

LEE, William (?-?1610), invented the stocking frame in 1589. The English govt. disapproved of it and he accepted an invitation from Henry IV of France and settled at Rouen.

LEE (1) Sir William (1688-1754) King's Latin Sec. from 1718 to 1730, was M.P. for High Wycombe in 1727, Prince of Wales' att-gen. in 1728 and C.J. of the King's Bench from 1737. His brother **(2) Sir George (1700-58)** was an M.P. for four successive boroughs from 1733. From 1751 he was also Dean of Arches. He became a P.C. in 1752.

LEE or LEGH, Rowland (?-1543) was employed by Wolsey to suppress small monasteries in 1528 and 1529. In 1534 he became Bp. of Lichfield and Lord Pres. of the Council of Wales, and as such was responsible until 1540 for suppressing disorder there. *See* LEGH, SIR THOMAS.

LEECH, John (1817-64), Punch cartoonist from 1841, gave an entertaining record of the social life of his time.

LEEDS, Ds. of. *See* OSBORNE.

LEEDS (Yorks), in Norman times was a hamlet. It achieved its first growth as a collecting centre for Airedale wool exported abroad. In the 14th cent. it acquired, secondly, settlements of Flemish weavers and began manufacturing and exporting cloth (*see* MERCHANT ADVENTURERS). The Black Prince is traditionally credited with this. It was chartered in 1626. In 1718 its importance was attested by the foundation of its first newspaper, the *Leeds Mercury*. In the late 18th cent. (when the population was 17,000) the new canals connected it with Liverpool and the Humber, by which time the local coal and iron mines were being exploited and it developed engineering and metals industries alongside garment making as well as a position in international trade. With the coming of the railways the population increased steeply. It became a county borough in 1889 and diversified in one direction into other industries such as chemicals and in another into services such as banking and insurance. By World War II the population was 500,000 but the smoke-blackened houses and cobbled streets of the industrial revolution created an impression of indigence, and the slump of 1929 had affected the balance of wealth. It was heavily bombed in World War II and afterwards its textile industries lost ground to the new artificial fibres industries elsewhere, and after seven centuries textiles ceased to be the mainstay of employment.

LEET. In E. Anglia, a subdivision (about a 12th) of a Hundred.

LEET, COURT. *See* FEUDALISM-17; MANOR.

LEEWARD Is. (BRITISH) were constituted a single colony in 1871 consisting of the presidencies of Antigua, St. Kitts-Nevis, Anguilla, Montserrat, Dominica and the British Virgin Is. Dominica became a separate colony under the govt. of the Windward Is. in 1940. The other five were made separate colonies in 1956, under a single govt. abolished in 1959. All these islands became independent members of the British Commonwealth, St. Kitts-Nevis in 1983 being the last.

LEFT BOOK CLUB. *See* GOLLANCZ.

LEFT and RIGHT as political terms originated in the semi-circular chamber of the French National Assembly during the Revolution. Those inclined to defend the existing situation sat to the right of the presidential platform, as viewed from the chair: those who favoured further change, to the left. Hence a tendency to edge round the semi-circle as successive events changed opinion or successive elections altered the complexion of the House. The English parliamentary system, with govt. supporters on the Speaker's right facing an opposition on the Speaker's left, made little room for these gradual shifts; and distinguished politicians not by the intensity (or lack) of their convictions, but by their willingness to support or oppose a programme. The terms are obsolescent because of the modern rise of mutually hostile yet revolutionary parties wishing to alter an existing situation in opposite ways.

LEGACEASTER. *See* LEICESTER.

LEGACY DUTY. *See* DEATH DUTIES.

LEGAL AID in the form of Poor Persons Defences in criminal proceedings, and the "Dock Brief" for one guinea was available since the mid 19th cent. but the systematic aid to all persons of moderate means both in civil and in criminal cases was instituted in 1952 since when as a result of the method of assessing means, the very rich and the very poor have been at a considerable advantage over those in between. In 1993 the qualifications were considerably raised, because the cost of the system originally estimated at £1M per annum, had risen to over £1,000,000,000 and the govt. of John Major wished to encourage private litigation insurance.

LEGAL FICTIONS represent a primitive method of adapting the law to new circumstances where there was no legislature able or willing to alter the law. Every trial in a court is a form of syllogism in which the major premise is a rule of law, the minor an established fact and the verdict or judgement the conclusion. Hence if the rule cannot be altered, the consequences of immutability can be mitigated by altering the facts; this is done by bringing forward evidence which is unchallenged, e.g. a pregnant girl could not sue her seducer because she was a willing partner in her seduction; but a master could sue someone for depriving him of the services of his servant. Thus a father could sue his daughter's seducer if he could prove that he had been deprived of her services. Soon fathers were permitted simply to prove services, such as making a cup of tea, which were so slight as to be fictional. For the law on the barring of entails (*see* JOHN DOE AND RICHARD ROE). Procedure by Bill of Middlesex and writ of *Latitat* was used both as a jurisdictional and as a property device. The defendant was alleged to be in Middlesex, where the courts of Record sat, and a writ to arrest him was issued, alleging that he lurked (latitat) elsewhere. Naturally the sheriff replied that he could not be found, and judgement would then be given in default. 19th cent. legislation enacted the effect of these manoeuvres into substantive law.

LEGATE (Lat: legatus = ambassador), is a papal representative. There are six classes:-

(a) *Legatus natus* (literally = born) was an ex-officio status of the metropolitans of certain churches, particularly Canterbury, Rheims, Seville, Cologne and Venice and gave them effective papal temporal and diplomatic jurisdiction within their province. This is now only an honorary title. (b) A *Legatus missus* (= sent) may be either (i) a Legate *a latere* (from the Pope's presence). Always a cardinal, he is charged with some special weighty matter and supersedes all other papal diplomats in the relevant issue during the currency of his commission in the province. **(ii)** *Nuncio* (ambassador); **(iii)** *Internuncio* (Minister Plenipotentiary): **(iv)** *Apostolic delegate* (chargé d'affaires): **(v)** *Envoy extraordinary.* Legates *a latere* were naturally rare and sometimes resented by the rulers and metropolitans of the countries to which they were sent; nevertheless by representing a full interpolation of the papal power they were able sometimes to perform services of the highest value, e.g. in the case of the Legate Erminfrid in the deposition of Abp. Stigand (1071), Guala and Pandulf in Henry III's minority and Ottobuono after the Barons' War.

LEGATIONS, THE. A part of the Papal states notoriously misruled in 19th cent.

LEGATUS. *See* BRITAIN, ROMAN-5,7.

LEGES EDWARDI CONFESSORIS (Lat. = Laws of Edward the Confessor), was a Latin and unreliable account of Anglo-Saxon Law made c. 1130 by a French clerk.

LEGES HENRICI PRIMI (Lat. = Laws of Henry I) (c. 1100-18) was an anonymous account of Anglo-Saxon law as amended under the first three Norman Kings. The first mediaeval European legal textbook, it draws on some continental sources, the Winchester *Quadripartitus* and the *Panormia* of Ivo of Chartres, but virtually no Roman texts.

LEGGE (1) William (1609-70), a royalist and alleged leader of the army plot in 1641, became gov. of Oxford in 1645 and was imprisoned from 1649 to 1653. He was rewarded at the Restoration. His son **(2) George (1648-91) 1st Ld. DARTMOUTH (1682)** combined court life with active service in the forces. Naval capt. In 1667, he was groom of the Bedchamber from 1668, Lieut.-gov. of Portsmouth from 1670, master of the horse to the D. of York in 1673 and commander in Flanders in 1678. In 1682 he became Master-Gen. of the Ordnance and in 1683 and 1684 he commanded the Tangier expedition. In 1688-9 he was C-in-C of the Fleet, but because of a personal attachment to James II, incurred William III's disfavour. He died in the Tower. His son **(3) William (1672-1750) 1st E. of DARTMOUTH (1711)** was a commissioner of Trade and Plantations in 1702, but was out of office until the policy revolution of 1710-11. He was Sec. of State from 1710 to 1713 and Lord Privy Seal from 1713 until the Hanoverian accession. Of his sons **(4) Heneage (1704-59)** was a baron of the Exchequer from 1747. His brother **(5) Henry Bilson (1708-64)** M.P. for E. Looe in 1740 and for Oxford from 1741 to 1759, was a Lord of the Treasury from 1746, special envoy to Prussia in 1748 and Ch. of the Exchequer, with short breaks from 1754 to 1761. His financial abilities helped to raise the status of the office. His brother **(6) Edward (1710-47)** was with Anson in the Pacific from 1740 to 1742 and then became naval C-in-C in the Leeward Is. **(7) William (1731-1801) 2nd E.,** a Methodist, was Pres. of the B. of Trade from 1765 to 1766. In 1769 he endowed Dartmouth College, New Hampshire. Reputedly pro-American, he did not act as such when colonial sec. From 1772 to 1775 and Lord Privy Seal from 1775 to 1778. His son **(8) George (1755-1810) 3rd E.** became pres. of the Board of Control in 1801 and was Lord Chamberlain from 1804.

LEGH, Sir Thomas (?-1545) was ambassador to Denmark from 1532 to 1533 and in 1535 inspected monasteries. He was involved in Anne Boleyn's trial (1537) and in the suppression of the Pilgrimage of Grace. He then obtained a lucrative Chancery mastership and was employed in suppressing religious houses from 1538 to 1540.

LEFEBVRE, François Joseph (1755-1820), Duc de DANTZICK (1807) became a Gen. in 1793 and, until 1799, was an energetic divisional commander on the Rhine and in Westphalia. Bernadotte then gave him the Paris command, and his support ensured the success of the *coup d'état* of Brumaire (Nov. 1799) and the favour of Bonaparte. He was a marshal in 1804 and carried the sword at the imperial coronation. His uninhibited wife was the well known "Madame Sans-Gene" (Fr: care free).

Preferring active service he took Danzig in 1807, won the B. of Durango in Spain in 1808 and directed the campaign against Andreas Hofer in the Tyrol in 1809. He voted for Bonaparte's deposition in 1814 and retired.

LEGIONS, ROMAN, II Adjutrix. *See* BRITAIN, ROMAN-11-13; **II Augusta** *See* -1: **VI Victrix** *See* -13; **IX Hispana** 1-14; **XIV Gemina** *See* -1-10; **XX Valeria Victrix** *See* -1-25; **XXX** *see* -20.

LEGHORN or LIVORNO (Italy) was bought from Genoa by Florence in 1421 as an outlet to the sea, but became a proper port only when Cosimo I built the Medici harbour in 1571. He established the Knights of St. Stephen on the analogy of the Knights of Malta, and these waged a holy piracy on Mediterranean shipping. At the same time he encouraged Jewish financiers and subsequently protestant traders, amongst whom first the Dutch and then, after about 1590, the English predominated. Leghorn became a mart for legitimately carried and piratically stolen goods and Ferdinand I (r. 1587-1609) settled refugees of all religions there to start the industries. The port was free and neutral (save for a French interruption in 1796) from 1691 to 1867 when it was incorporated into the new Kingdom of Italy and it was the most important point of entry for British commerce into central Italy until then. *See* DUDLEY-7; FRANCO-AUSTRIAN WAR (1795-7)-3; PENINSULAR WAR (1807-14)-1 2.

LEGITIMACY. (1) A child is *legitimate* if begotten in lawful wedlock, or between parents who, in good faith, believed that their wedlock was lawful. A child born of a married woman is *presumed legitimate* if her husband was within the four seas at any time during a year and a day before the birth. A child born of unmarried parents can in Scotland since 1371 and in England since 1926 be *legitimated* by their marriage, but a child born of adultery cannot. Wedlock, however, is defined differently in different systems of law, the inconsistencies between canon and secular law being particularly wide. Thus Prince Arthur's precontract with Katharine of Aragon rendered, according to some canon lawyers, his brother Henry VIII's marriage to that lady void on grounds of incest, and so made her daughter Q. Mary I illegitimate. According to secular laws and practice, on the other hand, the marriage was valid, and Henry's second marriage to Anne Boleyn was therefore void on grounds of bigamy — which made Mary I legitimate and Anne's daughter, Elizabeth I, illegitimate. Henry VIII characteristically cut the Gordian Knot by declaring them both capable of inheriting the throne.

(2) An illegitimate child was regarded as nobody's child. At Common Law a woman's property belonged to her husband, therefore her child could inherit nothing save under a will. The word 'child' in a will or grant was presumed to mean 'legitimate child'. The importance of these rules was much diminished in recent times by the increasing disuse of entails and the powers conferred on the courts to order provision for widows and children out of deceased estates. In 1969 illegitimate children were put on a level with legitimate children.

LEGITIMISM is a political doctrine that the representative of the oldest or original dynasty (usually in exile) is entitled to the headship of the state as against some other dynasty. Jacobites might have claimed to be legitimists had the word then been in use. *See* DIVINE RIGHT OF KINGS.

LE GOULET, P. of (May 1200), between K. John and Philip Augustus of France. John ceded Evreux, whereby Chateau Gaillard became an enclave in French territory; Issoudun and Graçay (in Berri) were to go with Blanche of Castile (John's niece) as a dowry on her marriage with Philip's heir, and Prince Arthur was to have Brittany as John's vassal.

LE HAVRE (France) was founded in 1517 by Francis I and fortified under Louis XIV. The basins were built between 1850 and 1880.

LEICESTER. *See* TOWNSHEND-11.

LEICESTER-SHIRE (Lat. RATAE CORITANORUM, A.S. LEGACEASTRE). The town was a substantial Roman settlement on the Fosse Way, but there is little evidence of Roman civilisation elsewhere in the county. A Saxon bishopric, established there, was moved to Dorchester-on-Thames in 874 when the Danes came, and place names indicate extensive Danish colonisation. The town was one of the Five accepted Danish boroughs after the P. of Wedmore (878) and fell under Saxon domination under Edward the Elder. At the Conquest it was allotted to Robt. of Beaumont, Count of Meulan, who built the first castle. At that time the population of the town was about 2000. The Beaumonts ruled the area until late in 12th cent., enlarging the Castle and building several abbeys and churches, but Robt., 2nd E. of Leicester, joined the rebellion of 1173 against Henry II who stormed and burned the town. Meanwhile the countryside was developing as pasture, and became well known for wool and cattle, so that cloth and leatherworking grew up in the town as well as the market. The hand knitting frame established it as the leading hosiery centre in the Kingdom in 16th cent. Sheep and cattle strains were much improved in the 18th cent. and an extensive dairying industry grew up as well. Surplus labour and the wealth of the local landlords began to be employed in exploiting local minerals, notably coal, ironstone, limestone and granite which was much in vogue for paving. By the 19th cent. the city was turning out machinery, originally connected with the established industries but soon branching out into types ranging from cranes eventually to turbo-generators, while the more skilled operators began to be employed in precision work, such as surgical instruments and watches. A University college was founded in 1918 and chartered as a university in 1950.

LEICESTER, EARLDOM OF, was created in 1107 for Robert de Beaumont, and remained in his family until the childless death of his great-grandson in 1206. It was then held by the latter's sisters as coparcenors and was taken into the hands of K. John until 1215 when he assigned the lands to Ranulf, E. of Chester. In 1229 Simon de Montfort claimed the earldom and lands as son of one of the Beaumont sisters and by 1231 he had reached an accommodation with the other claimants and recognition by Henry III. On his death (1265) it was forfeited and granted to the King's second son, Edmund Crouchback, E. of Lancaster, and thereafter to other earls and dukes of Lancaster until Henry Bolingbroke, D. of Lancaster, took the throne as Henry IV, when it merged with the Crown. Elizabeth I granted the title and some of the lands to Robert Dudley in 1564, but at his death in 1588 they escheated. The title was subsequently granted separately from the lands, between 1618 and 1696 to three successive members of the Sydney family and in 1784 on George Townshend, eldest son of the Marquess Townshend so that the marquessate superseded it when he inherited it in 1807.

LEICESTER HOUSE PARTY. The house at Leicester Square, London, was originally built for the Sidney Earls of Leicester. It became the London residence of the P. of Wales from the accession of George I until the future George IV moved to Carlton House. The name commonly meant the political opposition which centred on each P. of Wales in turn.

LEICESTER, SEE of. In c. 679 Abp. Theodore of Tarsus divided the Mercian diocese into five sees, of which Leicester was one. Its bishops included St. Wilfrid during his expulsion from Northumbria and the see survived (though sometimes held by neighbouring bishops) until the 9th cent. when its bishop fled to Dorchester before the Danes.

LEIGH (1) Charles (?-1605), sailed the St. Lawrence for fish and Spanish pillage in 1597 and in 1604 tried, but failed, to establish a colony in Guiana, where he died. He

seems to have been financed by his brother **(2) Sir Oliph (1560-1612)** who prudently stayed at home and made money.

LEIGH or LEE, Wealthy Anglicans, **(1) Sir Thomas (?1504-1571)** was thrice master of the Mercers Co., Alderman of London from 1552 to 1571 and Lord Mayor in 1558, when he was knighted by Q. Elizabeth I. His second son was **(2) Sir Thomas (?-1671),** royalist, **1st Ld. LEIGH of STONELEIGH (1643),** whose nephew or great nephew **(3) Francis (?-1653), 1st Ld. DUNSMORE (1628) and 1st E. of CHICHESTER (1644)** also a royalist, was M.P. for Warwick in 1625 and a privy councillor in 1641.

LEIGH MALLORY. See MALLORY.

LEIGHTON (1) Alexander (1568-1649) studied at St. Andrews and Leyden; in 1628 he published a tract against prelacy for which he was condemned to mutilation and life imprisonment by the Star Chamber in 1630. The Long Parliament released him in 1640 and he became Keeper of Lambeth Palace. Of his sons **(2) Robert (1611-84)** was a famous preacher. He became principal of Edinburgh Univ. in 1653, Bp. of Dunblane at the Restoration and Abp. of Glasgow from 1669 to 1674. His brother **(3) Sir Elisha (?-1685)** joined the royalists abroad on the King's death, became a colonel and in 1650 was Charles II's sec. for English affairs in Scotland. He went to Ireland as sec. to the Lord Chancellor in 1670 and in 1675 was a notoriously corrupt member of the embassy to France. He was a R. Catholic convert.

LEINSTER. See FITZGERALD (KILDARE).

LEINSTER or LAIGHIN, S.E. Irish Kingdom or Province. The principal town was Wexford; the principal Irish clan was the MacMorrough, whose quarrels led to the Norman invasion. The metropolitical see was at Dublin, originally just outside the province. When Meath province was partitioned, it was added, apart from Cavan and Monaghan to Leinster, which thus acquired Dublin. The area seldom had any practical unity, because a varying area formed part of the Pale and it was seldom possible to tame the O'Byrnes and O'Tooles in the Wicklow Hills.

LEINSTER HALL MEETING (Ir.) (Nov. 1890) of the Irish National League, reaffirmed the League's support for Parnell after his adulteries became publicly known.

LEITH, CONCORDAT. See JAMES VI-5.

LEIX (Ir.), LAOIS, LAOIGHIS formerly **QUEEN'S COUNTY** was shired in 1556 and named after Mary I. Maryborough (Portlaois) was the county town. It is primarily agricultural where not boggy but has some coal, limestone and ironstone. See IRELAND-C2; OFFALY.

LELAND or LEYLAND, John (?1506-52) had become Henry VIII's librarian by 1530 and his antiquary in 1533. His tour of England between 1534 and 1543 bore fruit in his *Itinerary* (9 vols.) and *Collectanea* (6 vols.) published respectively in 1710 and 1715 at Oxford. He became insane in 1550.

LELY, Sir Peter (1618-80), painter, born and trained in Holland, was introduced to Charles I in 1647, was also patronised by Cromwell and was in high favour with Charles II, many of whose courtiers and commanders he painted.

LE MANS. See MAINE (FR.).

LEMASS, Sean Francis (1899-1971), a founder of the Fianna Fáil party, was Irish Min. of Industry and Commerce under de Valera from Mar. 1932 until he became deputy prime minister in 1945. He was prime minister from June 1959 until Nov. 1966.

LEMNOS (Aegean). Turkish I. from 1478 until 1914 when the British seized it and made its harbour at Mudros their base against the Dardanelles. In 1918 the Anglo-Turkish armistice was signed at Mudros and the island was transferred to Greece.

LEND-LEASE. Britain had placed large armaments orders in U.S.A. but these could not, by the operation of the U.S. Neutrality Act, 1939, be honoured until Nov. when the

Act was amended to allow deliveries for cash payment. By 1941 British cash was running out, and purchases would have had to fall to the level represented by the British Commonwealth's gold production and greatly reduced exports. The U.S. Lend Lease Act permitted the President to lend or lease defence materials and equipment upon such terms as he might agree to any nation whose defence he considered vital to the U.S.A. This enabled arms and other things to be provided on a vast scale until 1 Oct. 1945 without monetary return and helped to change U.S. industry over from peace to wartime production before the U.S. was involved directly in the conflict. In fact Britain made return services (so-called Reverse lend-lease) and had to open markets to U.S. economic penetration. The U.S.A. provided altogether about $43,000M worth of materials (about $30,269M to Britain) and British Reverse lend-lease amounted to about $4,000M, and ultimately the ending of Commonwealth preference and the beginning of the break-up of the Commonwealth.

LENIN or ULYANOV, Vladimir Ilyitch (1870-1924). (1) This famous or notorious revolutionary was born at Simbirsk of German, Kalmuck and Russian ancestry. In 1887 his elder brother was hanged for conspiring to assassinate Alexander III; Vladimir subsequently graduated in law, and in 1893 moved to St. Petersburg where he became active among the younger Marxists. Arrested in 1895, he was banished to Siberia until 1898; here he wrote *The Development of Capitalism in Russia*. On his return he published his ideas on the formation of a revolutionary party in the clandestine but influential paper *Iskra* (The Spark), and in 1900 he left Russia.

(2) He was now a professional politician, and deployed all his energies in forming his new party in the safe exile of the liberal west. He had no other interest in life, and subordinated his moral sense, intellectual ability and health to building it up and shaping it as he wished. Time being short, the party played no significant part in the Russian revolutionary riots of 1905 – though Lenin briefly visited Russia twice soon after. Meantime he converted the party into a sort of political priesthood or missionary force devoted to himself, through which he became the best known but not the best liked, left wing prophet in Europe. The creation of this *elite* had fateful consequences. It was the instrument through which the Marxist revolutions were carried out. It was inconsistent with the deterministic basis of the Marxist doctrines which Lenin himself professed, and it developed into the political bureaucracies by which communist states have since been ruled. Lenin's practical character ensured that the goals of Marxist idealism could not be reached. Socialists of the period believed that the overthrow of the Czarist regime would be followed by a phase of democracy and economic liberalism, during which society would become ripe for the socialist revolution. Lenin's experiences in 1905 and the creation of the political priesthood made a telescoping of these processes seem possible. With a sort of opportunist logic he favoured the defeat of Russia and her allies at the outbreak of World War I because their political collapse, and consequent civil wars would bring about the desired revolutionary situations. In this he opposed contemporary social democrats who favoured victory for the allies because they were less reactionary than the Central Powers. The result was a permanent split between his own Bolshevists and other socialists which has tended to widen with every year. Lenin believed in world revolution where the others expected the transformation of society within the framework of national states. As it turned out both were wrong. Revolution broke out in Russia in 1917, but it was not a Bolshevik revolution. Lenin was expedited to St. Petersburg by the Germans to increase the confusion. He overthrew the new parliamentary govt. and so precipitated the country into a devastating civil war. Not surprisingly Fanny-Dora Kaplan, a non-Marxist revolutionary, shot (but only wounded) him in Aug. 1918.

(3) The establishment of order out of chaos required a ruthless despotism which Lenin created during the three year civil war. The establishment of a working economy proved more difficult and in 1922 he inaugurated the so-called New Economic Policy, which was an artificial reversion to that economic liberalism which other socialists believed to be a prerequisite of revolution. When private enterprise had thus been called in to avert the worst consequences of revolutionary economics, it was to be discarded; but by now Lenin was a sick man. He died after a long illness.

(4) He is credited with or blamed for a number of aphorisms e.g. '60 fools, 39 knaves and one communist', 'public control plus electricity equals socialism', and (while signing death warrants) 'politics are a dirty business'. He laid down that communist parties should have two co-equal and mutually suspicious committees, the central committee and the 'control committee'. LENINISM is a doctrine ascribed to him after his death, that capitalist states will seize markets by force if they cannot do it in other ways.

LENINGRAD. The communist name for St. Petersburg or Petrograd. *See* BALTIC; RUSSIA.

LE NÔTRE, André (1613-1700), the designer of Louis XIV parks and gardens and populariser of the European-wide French formal style of decorative garden, visible, e.g. at Hampton Court.

LENNOX, Es. of. *See* JAMES IV, V AND VI OF SCOTS *passim.*

LENTHALL, William (1591-1662), a barrister, was nominated Speaker on Charles I's behalf when the Long Parliament met in 1640, but revolutionised the nature of his office by acting as the servant of the House rather than of the King, especially in the affair of the Five Members. He became, in addition, Master of the Rolls in 1643, a Commissioner of the Great Seal in 1646 and Chancellor of the Duchy in 1647. These lucrative offices compensated him for the occupation of his estates by the royalists. In July 1647 when the army and parliament quarrelled, the House was so menaced by Presbyterian mobs that on Sir Arthur Hesilrige's advice Lenthall left for Fairfax's H.Q. Only after signing the Engagement at the Hounslow army review (Aug.) did he return to the chair, and secure the annulment of ordinances passed under duress in his absence. His actions thereafter seem to support his later claim that he was a man of moderate views opposed to the overthrow of the monarchy. He did not protest against Pride's Purge (1648) because it would have been useless, and he presided, if with reluctance, at the proceedings on the Ordinance for bringing the King to trial. On the other hand he used his casting vote twice in favour of condemned royalist grandees. As Speaker he was under the Commonwealth formally the Head of State. When in Apr. 1653 Cromwell forcibly overthrew the Long Parliament, he refused to leave the chair until compelled. He went into retirement but was elected for Cromwell's first parliament (1654-5) and became Speaker again. When it was dissolved he became a commissioner of the Great Seal, and was involved in a quarrel with the Protector about the reforms of the Court of Chancery. His two colleagues objected to the reforms, but he submitted behind their backs. He was elected to the parliament of 1656 but not made Speaker, and argued strongly for the offer of the crown to Cromwell. He was subsequently summoned to the Upper House as a peer. When Richard Cromwell fell and the restoration of the Long Parliament became a political issue, Lenthall as its Speaker became a key figure and in Dec. 1659 he with some of the London garrison took control of the City and the Tower. Thereafter he acted in concert, if not in direct agreement, with Monck especially in obstructing republican efforts to have the monarchy abjured and the membership of the

House filled by co-option. He was not elected to the Convention Parliament and was included in the liability to pains penalties, but the punishment was limited (on Monck's insistence) to disqualification from public office.

LEO I THE GREAT (?-461), as Pope from 440 during the collapse of the Western Roman Empire, was the most powerful exponent of the doctrine of papal primacy and his pronouncements have ever since been the fountainhead on the subject.

LEO X. See RENAISSANCE-11.

LEOBA or LIOBA, St. See MISSIONS TO EUROPE-3.

LEOFGAR (fl. 1056) Bp. of HEREFORD. See EDWARD THE CONFESSOR-11.

LEOFRIC (?-1057). See GODIVA; MERCIA, EARLDOM OF.

LEOFRIC (?-1072), educated in Lorraine, became Edward the Confessor's secretary or chancellor and in 1046 Bp. of Crediton. The see included Devon and Cornwall and was difficult to manage from Crediton, then an open and inconveniently situated village. In 1050 he moved the see to Exeter which was populous, fortified and accessible by ship, and he conferred large endowments upon it, including the *Leofric Missal* and the *Liber Exoniensis* (The poetical *Book of Exeter*). He was left undisturbed at the Conquest.

LEOFWINE (?-1066), son of Earl Godwin, for whom he deputised in Kent from 1049. He was involved in Godwin's disgrace in 1051, fled to Ireland and was reinstated with his father in 1053. From 1057 he was E. of the Home Counties. He was killed at Hastings. See EDWARD THE CONFESSOR-7.

LEOMINSTER (Herefords) grew up round a Mercian monastery and fortification (destroyed by the Welsh in 1055) and became a wealthy wool trading centre. It was represented in Parliament from 1295 and chartered in 1556, but declined in the 18th cent.

LEON. See CASTILE AND LEON.

LEOPOLD of AUSTRIA. See CRUSADES-12.

LEPROSY or HANSEN'S DISEASE was often confused with Yaws, Syphilis and Pellagra. Lepers were sometimes called the POOR OF CHRIST. The disease was widespread in Europe by the 6th cent. A leper hospital was founded at Canterbury in 1084, six more in the vicinity of London by 1105 and by 1184, when the great hospital at Bury St. Edmunds was established, there were about 100 in England. Thirty are evidenced by charters. Lepers were a common sight. In 1346 they were expelled from London by proclamation. The disease declined, save in Scotland and Scandinavia, very rapidly after the Black Death, partly no doubt through mortality among lepers, but also through a widespread increase in pulmonary tuberculosis and a rise in the vitamin C content of diet, both of which strengthen resistance to leprosy. Nearly all leper hospitals had been converted to other purposes by the Reformation.

LEROS (Aegean) Is., acquired by Italy from Turkey in 1912 and so heavily fortified that it was not attacked in World War II, but passed to Greece afterwards.

LESBOS or MYTILENE. Large Aegean island and home of many Greek poets including the homosexual poetess Sappho. Hence 'Lesbianism'. The island was disputed between the Seljuks and the Venetians between 1091 and 1224 when the Byzantine empire recovered it. From 1354 to 1462 it was held by the Genoese, from 1462 to 1912 by the Turks, and from 1912 by Greece.

LESLIE, Alexander (?1580-1661) 1st E. of LEVEN (1641) served with great distinction from 1605 to 1630 in the Swedish army, acted as Hamilton's sergeant-major gen., in the English expedition to N. Germany in 1630 and in 1638 offered to lead a force to recover Bohemia for the Elector Palatine. He was, however, a Presbyterian and when the Bishops' Wars broke out he came to Scotland with a shipload of Swedish arms, and took victorious charge of the Scottish forces. After the T. of Ripon (Aug. 1641) Charles I visited Scotland where Leslie, as Lord

General received him in state and Charles, at parliament's request, made him E. of Leven. In July 1643 he took command of the expedition against the royalists in England; by Apr. he was besieging York and in July he was driven off the field of Marston Moor. After the victory and the surrender of York he assembled his troops, invested Newcastle and in Oct. stormed it. At the end of this war he returned in triumph, determined to resign on account of his age and health. He was, however, too well liked and trusted, and the parliament rejected his resignation. Hence he had to raise an army against Cromwell in Aug. 1648 and command another with David Leslie as his active subordinate in 1650. This force was beaten at Dunbar (Sept. 1650). In Aug. 1651 he was captured and was in intermittent custody until May 1654 when he retired, to his restored Scottish lands.

LESLIE, David (?-1682) 1st Ld. NEWARK (1661) was trained in the Swedish army and became Leven's major-gen. (chief of staff). His handling of the parliamentary cavalry reserve on the left wing decided the B. of Marston Moor. After York surrendered, he took Carlisle (June. 1645). In Sept. he was summoned urgently to deal with Montrose, whose army he surprised and destroyed at Philiphaugh. He captured Montrose in May 1647. After Charles II's Scottish accession he became the effective commander of Leven's army and was mainly to blame for the defeats at Dunbar (Sept. 1650) and Worcester (1651). He was in intermittent custody during the Interregnum, retired at the Restoration and was granted a pension.

LESLIE, John (1571-1671), the fighting bishop, was Bp. of the Isles from 1628 to 1633 and then of Raphoe until 1661. He led the rebellion of 1641, defended Raphoe against the parliament, and was the only Anglican bishop to remain during the Commonwealth and Protectorate. He was Bp. of Clogher from 1661.

LESLIE or LESLEY, John (1527-96), a theological opponent of John Knox, was a chaplain to Mary Q. of Scots in France, and after various employments in Scotland became a privy councillor (1565), Bp. of Ross (1566) and her principal adviser on ecclesiastical questions. In 1569 he became her ambassador in London, but was imprisoned and eventually expelled in connection with Ridolfi's plot (1571). He represented her interests in Paris in 1574 and in Rome in 1575.

LESLIE, Walter (1606-67). Count, Scottish mercenary and one of Wallenstein's murderers (1634), became imperial *Feldzeugmeister* (Ger: Master of Ordnance) in 1646, vice-pres. of the War Council and Keeper of the Slavonian March in 1650, and in 1665 imperial ambassador to the Porte.

LESLIE (ROTHES) (1) Norman (?-1554) Master of Rothes, sheriff of Fife from 1541, chief murderer of Card. Beaton in St. Andrews Castle in 1546, was besieged and taken a prisoner to France, whence he escaped to England and was pensioned by the Protector. At Mary I's accession he returned to France and was killed at Cambrai. His great-nephew **(2) John (1600-41) 6th E. of ROTHES** was a royalist but opponent of episcopalianism in Scotland. He organised opposition to Charles I's ecclesiastical policy but disliked the military consequences and remained with the King after the end of the Bishops' Wars. His son **(3) John (1600-81) 7th E. and D. of ROTHES (1680)** fought for the King, was captured at Worcester in 1651 and not released until 1658. At the Restoration he became a commissioner of the Scots Exchequer, in 1663 Scots Lord Treasurer besides an English privy councillor, and in 1664 Keeper of the Privy Seal. He was Lord Chancellor of Scotland from 1667. He was one of Charles II's more reasonable and influential advisers on Scottish affairs. The dukedom became extinct at his death. The earldom passed by marriage with his daughter Margaret to **(4) John Hamilton (1679-1722) 8th E.,** who took the surname of Leslie. He was a supporter of the protestant succession and of the union of 1707, and a representative peer from 1707. He fought against the Jacobites in 1715. His son **(5) John (?1698-1767) 9th E.**, also a representative peer, was a soldier who fought at Dettingen (1743) and was C-in-C in Ireland from 1765.

LESSEPS, Ferdinand Vicomte de (1805-94). *See* SUEZ CANAL.

LESTER, Sean (1888-1959) was League of Nations High Commissioner at Danzig in 1936 when the Germans annexed it, and as last sec-gen. of the League from 1940 wound it up in 1947.

L'ESTRANGE, Sir Roger (1616-1704), royalist and early journalist, wrote monarchist pamphlets and in 1663 became surveyor of printing presses and licenser of the press; until 1666 he published the *Intelligencer* and *The News,* both outdistanced by Muddiman's *Newsletters* and *London Gazette.* He had to go abroad on account of the "Popish Plot" in 1680 but from 1681 to 1687 published *The Observator* which attacked the dissenters, Titus Oates and the Whigs. He also published many translations especially of Erasmus, Josephus, and Quevedo. In 1685 James II knighted him, but at the Revolution he was disgraced.

LE SUEUR, Hubert (?1595-?1650) probably Parisian, executed in 1630 the Charing Cross equestrian statue of Charles I set up in 1674.

L'ETAT? C'EST MOI (Fr = The state? That's me). The 17 year old Louis XIV's reply to the First President of the Paris *parlement,* which objected to registering a new fiscal decree on the ground that it was against the interests of the state.

LETH CUINN (Celt. = Conn's Half). The northern half of ancient Ireland, as opposed to LETH MOGA NUADAT (Mug Nuadat's Half) in the south. The dividing line, if any, is unknown.

LETTER OF SLAINS (Sc.). A petition from the relatives of a murdered man that, having received satisfaction, they desired the crown to pardon the murderer.

LETTERS CLOSE. *See* CLOSE ROLLS.

LETTERS OF MARQUE. *See* PRIVATEERS.

LETTERS PATENT are letters under the Great Seal enabling a person to do acts or enjoy privileges otherwise not available to him. They are open and ready to be shown to anyone requiring confirmation of the authority conferred. Copies are written out on a continuous roll called the Patent Roll which is therefore a record of grants of liberties, privileges, lands, peerages and offices.

LEVANT CO. represented an effort to regularise the penetration of the Mediterranean by piratical Dutch and English merchants, arising out of the Dutch rebellion and the undeclared hostilities with Spain. Their ships came as raiders but brought cargoes of wool, cloth and tin, and often revictualled at Barbary ports. In 1578 Sir Ed. Osborne and Richard Staper, London merchants, sent Wm. Harborne to Constantinople where in 1580 he secured a *firman* from Murad II for trading privileges throughout the Ottoman Empire. This infringed the Venetian monopoly. Elizabeth I then imposed heavy duties upon Venetian cargoes, and in 1581 chartered the **Turkey Co.** An ambassador was accredited to the Porte at the expense of the Co. which set up factory houses at Aleppo, Alexandria, Damascus, Tripoli and Tunis and began to trade, despite prohibitions, with the Venetian dominions and Venice itself. Venice retaliated with counter tariffs and in 1582, under a new commercial agreement, the Venetians resumed trade to England.

Despite this and Spanish privateers, the Co. prospered through the Tuscan free port at Leghorn and because English cloth was much desired and came much more cheaply to the Levant in English ships than through Venetian middlemen. In 1583 Osborne and Staper sent John Newbery and Ralph Fitch to India *via* Aleppo and Basra. They reached the Mogul court and went on down the Ganges to Burma and Malacca. At the same time the **Venice Co.** was formed to export grain, sugar, salt, fish and tallow in return for sweet wine, currants and oil. In 1582 the Venice and Turkey Cos. were amalgamated as the **Levant Co.** Its large well-armed galleons habitually defied Venetian controls and often seized Venetian ships. The short distance eastern Mediterranean carrying trade as well as English exports thus enabled the Co. to trade profitably until the Civil War. *See also* CHARTERED COMPANIES; RUSSIA CO.

LEVANTER. East wind, liable to endure for 2-3 days at a time, in the straits of Gibraltar; if it did not delay ships for that period, it often forced them to tack within range of the Barbary pirate harbours on the African side.

LEVÉE was a ceremony at rising, when great men received their dependants. It then developed into a court for men only, held by the sovereign or the Speaker of the House of Commons. Levées were discontinued at the beginning of World War II and not revived.

LEVELLERS (1) were disunited Civil War radicals, whose views emerged from discontent, in 1647-8, with parliamentary dictatorship, and came variously to be based upon natural human rights and rights of freedom, supposedly based on Common Law. They rejected the existing constitution, for they held that a parliament derived its authority from the people. Hence they mostly proposed to abolish the monarchy and upper house, and to call biennial parliaments based upon a widened franchise and redistributed constituencies. Some advocated law and tax reforms, and even religious toleration. They were led by John Lilburne (?1614-57), Richard Overton (fl.1641-63) and Wm. Walwyn (fl. 1647-51), and in order to attract political support, they added demands for military pay arrears and indemnities. Mostly of obscure origin, they appealed primarily to small masters and journeymen in London and to other ranks in the army, whose representatives (or Agitators) co-operated with them to draft the "Agreement of the People", a sort of counter manifesto to the Heads of the Proposals. Their opponents naturally represented them as far more subversive of politics and property then they perhaps were, for their definition of their proposed franchise and based upon those who could dispose of their own labour. There were Leveller mutinies in Nov. 1647 and May 1649 but their suppression ended their military influence. Thereafter the leaders disappeared into their previous obscurity.

(2) DIGGERS or self-styled TRUE LEVELLERS, a small but noisy sect led by Gerard Winstanly (1609-1660), espoused the cause of paupers and labourers in 1649-50. They demanded that crown lands, forests and commons be opened to communal ownership, and that the purchase and sale of land should be prohibited by law. Because of the likely agricultural dislocation, this unsophisticated programme never had a hope.

LEVEN, E. of. *See* LESLIE, ALEXANDER.

LEVEN, LOCH (Kinross) has seven Is. The ancient priory of St. Serf was on one. The castle where Mary Q. of Scots was detained in 1567 was on another. It is now a well-known nature reserve and trout fishery.

LEVER, William Hesketh (1851-1925) 1st Vist. LEVERHULME (1917), wholesale grocer, bought a soap works at Warrington to combat the existing soap makers and in 1888 founded Port Sunlight, where the employees received subsidised housing and payments in kind from his firm, Lever Bros. Ltd. He was Liberal M.P. for the Wirral from 1906 to 1910. In 1918 he acquired most of the Is. of Lewis and Harris; he attempted but failed to develop them and handed over much of his property there to the inhabitants. By his will he founded the Leverhulme Charitable Trust comprising most of the Lever Bros. assets.

LEVESON, Sir Richard. *See* ELIZABETH I-35.

LEVESON-GOWER (pron: "Lewison-Gore"). Originally a Yorkshire and Staffordshire family, they were prolific, influential and rich. **(1) John (1675-1709) 1st Ld.**

GOWER (1703) was Ch. of the Duchy of Lancaster from 1703 to 1706. His son (2) John (?-1754) 2nd Ld. and 1st E. GOWER (1746), six times a Lord Justice during George II absences, was Privy Seal from 1742 to 1743 and in 1744. His son (3) Granville (1721-1803), 2nd E. and M. of STAFFORD was an M.P. from 1744, a Lord of the Admiralty from 1749 to 1751, Privy Seal from 1755 to 1757, Master of the Horse from 1757 to 1760, Keeper of the Wardrobe from 1760 to 1763, Lord Chamberlain from 1763 to 1766, Lord Pres. from 1767 to 1779 and from 1783 to 1784 and Privy Seal again from 1785 to 1794. He married an Egerton. His son (4) George Granville (1758-1833), Ld. GOWER (1798), 2nd M., 1st D. of SUTHERLAND (1833) was an M.P. from 1787 and Ambassador to Paris from 1790 to 1792, where he reported understandingly on the progress of the revolution. In 1799 he became joint Postmaster-Gen. (until 1810). In 1785 he had married the Countess of Sutherland, thereby acquiring her family's vast, if poor, Scottish estates. The rich Egerton estates and those of his own family came to him in 1803 by the death of his uncle, the last D. of Bridgwater, and of his father. He was now one of the country's richest men and sought to improve the depopulated highland properties by using the profits of the others to build over 400 miles of roads with their many bridges. His brother (5) Granville (1773-1846) Visct. GRANVILLE (1815), E. GRANVILLE (1833) was an M.P. from 1799 to 1815, ambassador to St. Petersburg in 1804 to 1805, and to Paris from 1824 to 1841. His son (6) Granville George (1815-91) 2nd E. was a whig M.P. from 1837 and foreign U/Sec. of State from 1840 to 1841. In 1848 he was Ld. John Russell's Vice-Pres. of the Bd. of Trade; from 1851 to 1852 Foreign Sec., from 1852 to 1854 Lord Pres. and in 1854 Ch. of the Duchy of Lancaster. From 1855 to 1858 and from 1859 to 1866 he was Lord Pres. again, and leader of the Lords. He was Gladstone's Colonial Sec. From 1868 to 1870, Foreign Sec. From 1870 to 1874 and from 1880 to 1885, and returned to the Colonial office in 1886. During his active political life he also had a strong interest in higher education and was Ch. of London University from 1856. Meanwhile his cousin's wife (7) Georgiana (1806-68) Duchess of SUTHERLAND, a great friend of Q. Victoria was Mistress of the Robes under the liberal govts. of 1837-41, 1846-52, 1853-8 and 1859-61, and his brother (8) Frederick (1819-1907), a well known society figure, was a liberal M.P. in 1846, 1852-7 and 1859-85.

LEVIATHAN. See HOBBES.

LEWES (Sussex), in the middle of an anciently inhabited zone, was first settled in Saxon times and was a trading centre to 1050. William I granted the lordship to the Warennes who built the castle to control the Ouse gap in the Downs. They also built an immense Cluniac priory and school and, after the B. of Lewes (1264) walled the town, and built a barbican in the 14th cent. The priory, the Warennes and the gap encouraged trade and there was a market, a fair and a harbour nearby. The principal trade outward was in South Down wool, inward in Norman products such as Caen stone and provisions. The Grammar school was moved to Southover in 1512; the priory blown up at the dissolution. It had an ancient charter under which it was governed by a Society of Twelve and Constables, but these were slowly superseded by a Court Leet, and meanwhile the trade sought other outlets. It was still a sleepy place when first incorporated in 1881. Lewes, B. of *see* BARONS' WAR-3.

LEWIS FAMILY of VAN (Glam.), acquisitive landowners in Glamorgan and Wiltshire, bought the Keynsham Abbey estates c. 1535, then property in Cardiff and at the beginning of the 17th cent., St. Fagan's Castle. They then acquired further lands in Wiltshire and still more by marriage. Eventually Edward (1650-74) entailed the estates to his uncle Richard (1623-1706) who added Corsham and dismantled Van. His son Thomas (?-1736)

acquired further property through his wife, but died leaving only a daughter Elizabeth, through whom the immense inheritance passed to the Es. of Plymouth.

LEWIS, Sir John Herbert (1858-1933), chairman of Flint County Council in 1889 and Liberal M.P. for the Flint boroughs from 1892 to 1906, was a friend of David Lloyd George and an important advocate of the claims of Welsh culture, being mainly responsible for establishing the Welsh National Library. He was M.P. for Flintshire from 1906 to 1918 and for the Univ. of Wales from 1918 to 1922.

LEWIS, Owen (1532-94), a distinguished clerical academic, left England in 1561. A great friend of Card. Allen he was with him responsible for the establishment of the English colleges at Douai and Rome.

LEWIS (1) Sir William Thomas (1837-1914) 1st Ld. MERTHYR of SENGHENYDD (1911) was born of a coal trading family and in 1864 became mineral agent for the Bute estates. He made money and by 1895 had acquired control of most of the Rhondda and Rhymney Valley mines. He also expanded the Bute docks in Cardiff and organised the local coal owners associations in opposition to the trade unions. He probably originated the sliding scale payments for miners, and was much respected as a mediator and public adviser. His grandson (2) William (1905-77) 3rd Ld., suffered as a prisoner in Japanese hands but never ceased to work for good public causes. He was Chairman of the Magistrates Association, President of the National Assoc. of Local Councils and Chairman of Committees in the House of Lords. He was justifiably considered the finest chairman of the century.

LEWIS (1) Sir Thomas Frankland (1780-1855), was Tory M.P. for Beaumaris from 1812 to 1826, for Ennis until 1828 and for Radnorshire until 1834. He was chairman of the Poor Law Commission until 1839 and M.P. for Radnor Boroughs from 1843. His son (2) Sir George Cornewall (1806-63) a noted linguist, was sucked into politics by carrying out some distinguished investigations on behalf of the govt., notably on the Irish poor in Lancs. and W. Scotland (1834), the Irish Poor Law (1837), Maltese affairs (1838); in 1839 he succeeded his father as a Poor Law Commissioner and was involved in the quarrel between the Commission and (later Sir) Edwin Chadwick, its secretary; this led to the reconstitution of the Commission and Lewis's resignation in 1847. He then became liberal M.P. for Herefordshire, held a number of minor govt. posts and attempted twice to abolish the Turnpike trusts. Defeated at the general election of 1852 he became editor of the *Edinburgh Review*. From 1855 he was M.P. for Radnor Burghs, and in that year became Palmerston's Chanc. of the Exchequer and so responsible for financing the Crimean War. In 1859 he became Home Sec. and from 1861 Sec. for War.

LEWIS AND CLARK EXPEDITION. The U.S. Pres. Jefferson appointed his Sec. Meriwether Lewis (1774-1809) to lead a transcontinental exploration, and Lewis co-opted his friend William Clark (1770-1838). They started from St. Louis up the Missouri late in 1803, wintered in North Dakota and in the autumn of 1805 reached the Rockies. With Shoshone help they then crossed through Idaho and reached the Pacific in Nov. They returned to St. Louis in Sept. 1806. Their scientific and anthropological observations created a sensation, and their reports led directly to the settlement of the Oregon.

LEWIS GUN. See MACHINE GUN.

LEWKNOR'S LANE, now Charles St., Drury Lane was in the 17th and 18th cents. a particularly disreputable haunt opening off the Stews.

LEX (Lat = either Law, or the Law or a Law) (1) *Lex Fori* (Lat: the law of the court), is the legal system administered by a given court. (2) (e.g.) *Lex Calpurnia de repetundis* a Roman statute against extortion. (3) (e.g.) the reversible saying *Rex est Lex* (The King is the Law).

LEXINGTON. *See* AMERICAN REBELLION-15.

LEY (1) James (1550-1629), 1st Ld. LEY (1624), 1st E. of MARLBOROUGH (1626) lawyer and M.P. in 1597, 1604, 1644, 1609-11 and 1621 became C.J. of the Irish King's Bench in 1604. In 1608 he was at once a commissioner for the plantation of Ulster and attorney to the Court of Wards and Liveries. In 1622 he became C.J. of the English King's Bench and in 1624 Lord Treasurer. He ended in 1628 very rich and Lord President of the Council.

LEYBURN, LEYBOURNE, LEMBURN or LEEBURN, Wealden ironmasters and armourers. **(1) Roger (?-1271),** was 'warden' (perhaps royally appointed naval commander) of the Cinque ports fleet. He went to Aquitaine with Henry III in 1253; brought a fleet to the Welsh coast against Llewelyn in 1256, joined the Barons in 1258 and lost access to his industries as a result. He became a bandit, joined Simon de Montfort in 1263 but rejoined the King and fought for him at Evesham. His son **(2) William (?-1309),** a Baron of the Cinque Ports, served in Wales in 1277 and then became Constable of Pevensey in 1282. In 1297 he was naval commander ('Admiral') and he served against the Scots in 1299-1300, and in 1304. He seems to have been the first high English professional naval commander.

LEY FARMING is the cultivation of land, long used for one purpose for another, e.g. the laying down of arable to grass. It was pioneered in the 1880s when a great deal of arable land had gone out of cultivation through the fall of corn-prices (*see* CORN LAWS). It came into extensive use in World War II when it was a major element in milk and meat production.

LEYDEN JAR, the earliest accumulator, was invented in Holland in 1745, but improved to its modern form by John Smeaton and Sir Wm. Watson (1715-87) in 1747.

LIBEL and SLANDER. *See* DEFAMATION.

LIBEL OF ENGLISH POLICY, written between autumn 1436 and early 1438, urged greater expenditure on the control of the Channel and defence of Calais, the use of wool exports to win over the support of the Flemings, and the expulsion of Italian merchants who had come to enjoy a preferential position. Each of these contentions was opposed to the policy of the ruling council, but agreed with the views of D. Humphrey of Gloucester, the Staplers and the cloth exporters. Its author may have been John Lydgate, patronised by Gloucester and the London merchants.

LIBERAL ARTS. Varro, in the 1st cent. B.C. mentioned nine of them as subjects of study but, as his enumeration shows, used the term 'art' as a fascicule of related subjects of intellectual rather than imaginative application. The nine were grammar, rhetoric, logic, geometry, arithmetic, astronomy, music, medicine and architecture. By the 5th cent. A.D. the last two had been excluded from general education as technical or specialised, and of the remaining "arts" the first three were termed the *trivium* (cf. trivial) and the others the *quadrivium*. Until the 12th cent. "secondary" education (for men often went to universities in their early 'teens) concentrated on the *trivium* with logic as the junior partner, and was thus concerned mainly with the means of human communication, but from then on logic grew in importance, while the study of the *quadrivium* (save for "music") was increasingly regarded as a foundation for specialist studies such as law, medicine, or as a stage in the approach to theology. The meaning of the word "music" had slowly changed from the practices protected by the nine muses (history, four types of poetry, sacred song, dance, comedy, tragedy and astronomy) to the more modern usage related to the emission of organised sound. These studies, in either sense, came to be neglected as such in the universities because they were conducted or practised in monasteries, cathedrals and at court.

LIBER ALBUS. *See* WHITE BOOK.

LIBERALISM is a Reformation attitude to social life, based upon the ideas of toleration, freedom, and equality. It was adumbrated in 16th cent. rejections of religious persecution, but could not become a political programme until religious violence was assuaged towards the end of 18th cent. It is bedevilled by a practical dilemma. If the object of policy is to reduce state interventions in individual freedom, then individuals may be free to encroach upon each other's; but if the state chooses the fields within which freedom is exercisable, it is by the mere definition limiting freedom. Hence liberal parties can take popular initiatives when there are obvious abuses to overcome, but once the doctrinally correct political balance has been achieved, the public gets bored. "The greatest feasible happiness of the largest practicable number" is seldom a trumpet call. Moreover the main principles of liberalism carry the seeds of their own destruction; toleration eschews force and may create weakness in defence against the intolerant. The nature of liberal equality is hotly disputed, since people are in fact seldom equal in any respect. Thus liberalism tends to become less an organised movement and more a tacitly respected ideal, sometimes called 'liberalism with a small L.' In this form, despite episodic inefficiency, it remains potent as a yardstick of political institutions.

LIBERAL NATIONAL PARTY. In 1931, 23 Liberal M.P.s supported the National Govt. After the Woolton-Teviot agreement in 1947 the National Party moved closer to the Conservatives and after a period when it called itself the National Liberal Party, the Conservative absorbed it.

LIBERAL PARTY was inspired by or claimed inspiration from Jeremy Bentham, Charles James Fox, J.S. Mill and Adam Smith. It was an alliance of independent minded, often Whig, aristocrats and ambitious often non-conformist professional and business men, who saw that industrialisation would end the old political system which the Reform Act, 1832 and the repeal of the Corn Laws had already wrenched out of shape. Their purpose was to guide society through an educated and noticeably high-minded group in alliance with a much wider and therefore poorer electorate, which would keep it in power in order to press the reforms in which it was interested. These reforms were seen as practical increases in the general liberty, or freedom of action for the individual, or as providing an atmosphere in which anyone might develop his talents without irrelevant obstruction.

The party was formed in the 1860s and its first and most spectacular period of office was Gladstone's govt. of 1868 to 1874. This founded the modern educational system and abolished the university tests. It reformed the army and the civil service. It also legalised trade unions and introduced the secret ballot. Though its programme for widening the electorate was twice pre-empted, it cleaned up elections and, more questionably, introduced single member constituencies of roughly equal population. In foreign policy the desire to increase liberty meant reducing govt. expenditure and the foreign commitments which caused it. It also meant free trade, which the world's most industrialised nation was to afford by buying cheap grain and ruining its agriculture.

In 1877 the party established the first regular British party organisation but in 1886 it split over Home Rule, losing most of the Whigs and Radicals who became **LIBERAL UNIONISTS,** and had to make a basic change in its philosophy to attract the growing electoral poor. Hence the party of free enterprise became the party of social responsibility and, helped by the need for expensive battleships against the Germans, set out, under the leadership of Lloyd George, to make the rich pay. The Labour Party was, however, already competing in this very field. Hence though the Liberal govt. of 1906 to 1915 created, through the new govt. organisations, the machinery of the welfare state (pensions, national insurance, labour exchanges, trade boards and minimum wages) Labour, in the end, reaped the benefit. Similarly it passed the Parliament Act, 1911, and put the Trade Unions on the pedestal from which they have dispensed largesse to the Labour Party every since.

LIBERATION was the term used of the recovery by the united allies of the territory of allied states overrun by the Nazis and the Japanese in World War II. In the case of areas occupied by the Russians the term was ironical or propagandist. Some govts. have since used it as a euphemism for invasion or occupation, and left-wing or professedly left-wing revolutionary organisations have used it to describe their actual or intended imposition of minority rule.

LIBER CENSUUM (Lat. = List of Contributions) (1192). *Census* was an annual rent payable by many ecclesiastical and lay bodies all over Europe for papal protection as a result of the Carolingian collapse. The *liber*, which includes monarchs, cities, churches and even hostels, was compiled for the use of the Apostolic Chamber.

LIBER FEODORUM. *See* TESTA DE NEVILL.

LIBERIA and MARYLAND (W. Africa) were acquired in 1821 as a refuge for freed negro slaves, who began to colonise in 1822. The two coalesced in 1857. From 1909 the finances and administration were supervised by American advisers. The trade, however, was always in German hands until 1917.

LIBER LXXIV TITULORUM. *See* DICTATUS PAPAE.

LIBER REGIS (Lat. = The King's Book) (1) a name for Domesday Book. **(2)** *See* VALOR ECCLESIASTICUS.

LIBERTY (1) The ability to do that which is forbidden. **(2)** Self rule. **(3)** A privilege or exceptional right of an individual or corporation. **(4)** A property or domain exempt from some or all of the burden of royal or local police or administration. **(5)** A collective term for the properties and rights of a great lord.

LIBERTY SHIPS were 11 knot, 7100-ton mass-produced American cargo ships. 200 were built as part of the Lend-Lease policy to Britain in 1941. After U.S.A. was attacked by Japan some 2700 were built. Over 400 of the 18-knot variety (VICTORY SHIPS) were built after 1943. These ships were a major determinant of World War II.

LIBERUM VETO, a phrase derived from the old Polish constitution, under which any single senator could prevent a decision of the Diet.

LIBER WINTON[IENSIS] (Lat = The Winchester Book). Two surveys of Winchester bound together. One (1103-15) deals mainly with royal rights. The other (1148) for Henry of Blois, with episcopal ones.

LIBRARIES, PUBLIC. (1) From 1850 borough councils with over 10,000 inhabitants might, if a majority were in favour, spend up to a ½d. rate in providing a public library. The procedure was simplified and extended by later Acts, so that by 1895 any borough or urban district council, or parish meeting might adopt public library powers without financial limitation. County Councils acquired the power in 1908 for areas where the Acts had not been adopted. Progress was slow, and authorities sometimes adopted the powers solely to prevent the County Council from levying a library rate in their area.

(2) By 1920 duplication and lack of inter-library exchange facilities was obviously a source of expense and inefficiency and the Carnegie Trust set up a supplementary series of libraries to provide an exchange service. By 1933, when the slump had destroyed many subscription libraries, rising educational standards had created a demand which led county councils to set up a nationwide system, which, after World War II even included mobile libraries for remote areas. This gradually squeezed the small public libraries out by 1960.

(3) In 1979 a limited fund and computerised sampling system was established to give authors a very small payment for each library loan of their books.

LIBRARY ASSOCIATION, the librarians' professional body, was founded in 1877.

LIBYA (*see* BARBARY) was under Ottoman rule until 1912 when the Italians seized Tripoli. The T. of Ouchy (Oct. 1912) was in form a Turkish grant of autonomy, the Sultan as Caliph reserving the right to appoint a *naib* or religious vicegerent. Despite Libyan resistance, the Italians overran the country by 1914, but withdrew to the coast during World War I. The Libyans offered their throne to the Senussi Emir Mohammed Idris. Under Fascism Graziani conquered Tripolitania in 1923, Fezzan in 1929, and Cyrenaica in 1932; and some 30,000 Sicilian colonists were introduced. After the Axis forces had been finally driven out in World War II, there was a series of British military governors and the status of the country was referred to the United Nations.

A federal constitution was created under the supervision of a U.N. Commissioner and the crown was offered to Mohammed Idris, as Idris I. Independence was proclaimed in Dec. 1951, and Libya joined the Arab League in Mar. 1953 and began to export oil in 1961. In 1969 a group of army officers overthrew the monarchy, and Col. Muammar Gaddafi, an admirer of the Egyptian Pres. Nasser instituted a personalised and moslem socialist regime based on a philosophy contained in his mass-circulated *Green Book*. He accomplished a number of valuable reforms financed from the oil revenues, which however, he also used to finance political terrorism in other countries notably the Baader-Meinhof Gang in Germany, the Basque Euzkadi Ta Askadasuna (E.T.A.) in Spain and the Irish Republican Army (I.R.A.) in Britain.

LICENSING (1) LIQUOR. Wine trade licensing, though not under that name, was first enacted in 1494. Licensees other than free vintners had to have served a proper apprenticeship. The growth in the tavern trade led in 1551 to the first attempt to restrict hours of opening (not before 11 a.m. on Sundays or during evensong) and numbers (London 40, York 8, Norwich 7, Bristol 6, nineteen other towns 4, the remaining boroughs with Gravesend, Sittingbourne, Tuxford and Bagshot 1 or 2).

(2) These enactments were partly revenue enactments and, though not repealed, were not enforced. The crown's licensing power was lucrative. In 1570 the power was leased for £500 a year to Sir, Edward Horsey; in 1585 for £1200 to Sir Walter Raleigh; in 1605 for £2768 to the E. of Nottingham; in 1617 for £2281 to Sir Lionel Cranfield; in 1624 for £3032 to John Williams; in 1627 for £2700 to Sir George Goring (not Devon or Cornwall) for 31 years. The licensing requirements were basically a method of raising revenue. The legislation was all superseded or consolidated in the Alehouses Act, 1828, which provided that the Justices should grant or withhold licences annually at the so-called Brewster Sessions, which were held in Mar. in Middlesex and Surrey and in Aug. or Sept. elsewhere. An Excise Licence could not be got until a justices' licence was produced. Possession of a Justices' licence was thus valuable and its scarcity value raised the value of a public house. Much of the difficulty of subsequent reform has arisen from this fact, but the Licensing Act 1903 helped to solve it by compensating for voluntarily surrendered licences from a fund levied on the trade. Strict limitation of hours was introduced by regulations under the Defence of the Realm Act, 1914 (D.O.R.A.) and then permanently enshrined in the important Licensing Act 1921. An Act of 1961 allowed greater flexibility in restaurants and clubs, and in 1967 the excise licence was abolished and the justices' licence itself became the authority for the sale of liquor. This removed bureaucratic difficulties but enhanced the value of the justices' licence. On the other hand in 1987 licensed places certified as restaurants were allowed to sell liquor at any time between morning opening and night closing.

(2) CLUBS were first licensed in 1902.

(3) PLAYS. *See* CENSORSHIP.

(4) CINEMATOGRAPHY EXHIBITIONS were first licensed in 1909 mostly for fire safety.

(5) BILLIARDS licensing was first required in 1845 and abolished in 1964.

(6) MUSIC AND DANCING were always controlled under local legislation. Most of the provisions date from 1890, but from 1964 no licence was needed for reproduced music or television entertainment or for performances by less than three performers. *See* STAGE CARRIAGES.

(7) HEAVY GOODS VEHICLES. *See* TRAFFIC COMMISSIONERS.

LICHFIELD (Staffs) became the bishopric of the Mercians in 656, and St. Chad (Ceadda) was its bishop c. 670-2. K. Offa had it raised to an archbishopric in 787 but this lapsed in 802. The city was captured by the Danes in 9th cent. but the see was re-established in 10th. In 1075 the see was moved to Chester, but it returned to the midlands a century later and, thereafter, shared the headship of its large diocese with Coventry. Hence there were frequent disputes between the electing bodies of the two cathedrals with episcopal *interregna* and even schisms, and papal and royal co-operative interventions leading to regular provisions (*see* ADVOWSON AND TITHE).

The great triple spired cathedral was built in 13th cent. and there was a major Norman castle-palace and a late 15th cent. Grammar School, which survived the Reformation. Human and natural disasters retarded the town's growth. Most of it was burned down in 1291; there were at least three plagues soon after the Black Death; a great storm ruined half the houses in 1593; another plague carried off 30% of the people a year later and much of the town was wrecked in the parliamentary siege of 1643. In 1801 the population was only 4700 and only 10,000 by the end of World War II. Nevertheless it has produced more than its share of English worthies, including St. Chad, Elias Asmole, Dr. Johnson, Erasmus Darwin and Anna Seward.

LICHFIELD HOUSE COMPACT (Feb.-Mar. 1835) was an agreement between the mainly whig political groups opposed to or estranged from Peel to overthrow his govt. Irish support led by O'Connell enabled them to achieve their purpose.

LIDDELL, Henry George (1811-98) with Robert Scott compiled the famous Greek *Lexicon* between 1834 and 1843. He was headmaster of Westminster from 1846 until 1855. Then until 1891 he was Dean of Christchurch, Oxford. His daughter was the Alice of *Alice in Wonderland*.

LIDDERDALE, William (1832-1902) of a family of Russian merchants born at St. Petersburg, became dep-gov. of the Bank of England in 1887. He was Goschen's adviser in the reduction of interest in the National Debt in 1888 and became Gov. of the Bank in 1889. Almost immediately he had to deal with the first Baring's Crisis (Nov. 1890), caused by over-speculation in the River Plate area, where public debts were mounting but the funds so raised were not being re-invested. Using his many foreign and also his home banking contacts, he raised £11.5M in 20 hours to guarantee Barings (q.v.), and then reconstructed that company, so that all its advances from the guarantee fund were paid off by 1894. Public confidence in him thus made his advice on the Bank Bill of 1892 virtually irresistible.

LIE, Trygve (1896-1968), politician and min. of foreign affairs in the Norwegian govt. in exile in London from 1941. He was sec. gen. of U.N.O. from 1946 to 1952.

LIEGE. *See* NATIONALITY; HOMAGE.

LIÈGE (Belgium) was an ecclesiastical principality from 980 onwards. Quarrels between the City and the Prince-bishop were continuous and often violent until Charles the Bold sacked the city in 1467. Under Bp. Erard de la Marck the principality recovered its prosperity, and from then until 1792 it kept its neutrality and independence being often held in plurality with its electoral Archbishopric of Cologne though occasionally overrun by the armies of the other powers at war with each other. *See* BERTHA, BIG.

LIEVEN, P. Dorothea (1784-1857) b. Benckendorf. A vivacious and intriguing Balt, married P. Christoph Lieven in 1800. He was Russian ambassador to Berlin from 1809 to 1812 and to London from 1812 to 1834. She was a leading figure in the London social and political scene until her husband died in 1838. She then moved to Paris. She knew everybody who mattered and was believed to know more state and private secrets than most politicians. Her letters and diary are a quarry of information and, sometimes, malicious gossip.

LIFEBOATS. The first English unsinkable lifeboat was built in 1785. In 1789 as a result of the *Adventure* disaster off the Tyne, a self-righting boat was commissioned by a voluntary group. The line throwing mortar was invented in 1807. The National Institution for the Preservation of Life from Shipwreck was founded in 1824 and was renamed the ROYAL NATIONAL LIFEBOAT INSTITUTION in 1854. The crews remain volunteers but may claim salvage if successful.

LIFE EXPECTANCIES from birth were between 35 and 45 years on average until about 1860. They have since risen to 72 for a man and 76 for a woman and continue to rise. A major factor has been the decline in infant mortality.

LIFE PEERAGE. Though most peers were hereditary the first life peerage was granted in 1377 and they continued to be granted at intervals down to 1856 when the Govt., to strengthen the House of Lords with men of ability who might not wish to sustain a hereditary peerage, called Ld. Wensleydale, a distinguished judge, to the House for life in order (unnecessarily) to create a precedent for further such creations. In defiance of precedent and the prerogative, the House held that he could not take his seat without a writ; and that a summons by writ without patent created a hereditary barony if the person summoned took his seat. This effectively abolished the creation of life peerages by prerogative, though bishops had long resembled life peers in practice, and Irish representative peers had held their seats for life since 1800 under the Act of Union. The Appellate Jurisdiction Act, 1876, enabled the judicial functions of the House to be strengthened by the creation of life peers who have held high judicial office. Their number at any given time was about nine.

From 1958 it became possible in addition to create life peers under statute, and without qualification, save that a hereditary peer who had renounced his peerage could return to the House only as a life peer. Thereafter, few peerages outside the Royal Family were created save for life, and the average age of the House rose markedly. *See* HOUSE OF LORDS ACT 1999.

LIGHTHOUSES. Leghorn (1304), Venice (1312), St. Catherine's Isle of Wight (1323), Dieppe (1389), Spurn Point (1427), Tynemouth (1540), Cordouan (1550), Heligoland (1630), Isle of May (1636), St. Agnes, Scillies (1680), Eddystone (1698-1703; 1708-55; 1755-1880; 1881). The succession of towers on the Eddystone provided the experience which led to the design of modern towers. The first oil burner was introduced in 1784, electricity in 1862. *See* TRINITY HOUSE.

LIGHTING. Oil and tallow were used until the mid-18th cent. when the whaling industry brought spermaceti. The spermaceti candle is the origin of the measurement of light by *candlepower*. Gaslight was first tried in England at Redruth by Wm. Murdoch in 1798, and public gas lighting was introduced in London in 1807. The police advantages were deemed so great that in 1834 the Lighting and Watching Act enabled all parochial authorities to install lighting at the public expense, and many hundreds did so. The first successful electric arc lamp was at Dungeness Lighthouse in 1856, but electric lighting on a commercial scale had to wait until 1879.

LIGHT INFANTRY was trained to march and manoeuvre at speed with the minimum of commands; given light equipment, and armed with rifles instead of muskets. Their skirmishing tactics encouraged self-reliance and tactical concealment, for which reason they wore predominantly green or black uniforms and never carried colours.

LIGONIER (1) Jean Louis or John (1680-1770), a Huguenot, migrated to Ireland in 1697 and fought under Marlborough until 1709. By 1739 he was gov. of Kinsale and fought at Dettingen in 1743. He commanded the infantry at Fontenoy in 1745 and for the next two years was C-in-C in the Austrian Netherlands. In 1748 he became M.P. for Bath; in 1757 C-in- C; as Master-Gen. of the Ordnance from 1759-1763 he had much technical responsibility in the Seven Years War. With a variety of Irish and English peerages he eventually, after 1766 became known as Field Marshal **Earl LIGONIER of RIPLEY.** His nephew **(2) Edward (?-1782)** fought at Minden in 1752 as a Lieut-Gen., inherited an Irish Viscountcy from his uncle in 1770 and in 1776 became an Irish **Earl LIGONIER.**

LIGURIAN REPUBLIC, was the republic of GENOA reconstituted by Bonaparte in June 1797 as a French client state. It was annexed by France in June 1805. *See* FRANCO-AUSTRIAN WAR (1795-7)-6.

LILBURNE. Two brothers. **(1) Robert (1613-65),** a parliamentary colonel, was a member of the military opposition to the parliament, promoted the Petition of the Officers and encouraged mutiny in 1647, but submitted. He was one of the regicides of 1649. In 1651 he served against the Scots. He was M.P. for the E. Riding in 1656. Opposed to Cromwell's possible Kingship, he supported Lambert in 1659. He was sentenced to death at the Restoration but died in prison. **(2) John (?1614-57)** a pamphleteer and awkward character, was imprisoned by the Star Chamber from 1638 to 1640, fought for the parliament and was captured in 1642. Exchanged in 1643, he continued to fight until he resigned in 1645 to avoid taking the Covenant. He engaged in bitter argument with the Presbyterians Prynne and Bastwick, and wrote pamphlets against the army leaders and Cromwell. He was arrested but acquitted in 1649. He then attacked chartered companies, monopolies and other profiteers, but was driven from England by the influence of Sir Arthur Heselrige, who had bought the property of the See of Durham. He returned in 1653 to further publicity and trial. On refusing to be of good behaviour he was confined until 1655 when he became a Quaker and, committed to peaceable works, was released.

LILLE (France) was sacked by Philip Augustus in 1214 but was rebuilt by, and obtained communal privileges from, the Flemish counts. Attacked by Philip the Fair in 1297, it was ceded to France in 1312. Charles V of France gave it to Louis de Male whose rights passed to the Burgundians and so to Austria and Spain.

It was claimed and taken by Louis XIV in 1667; it was regarded as a key prize of his policy and Vauban was commissioned to fortify it regardless of cost. Marlborough and Eugene retook it in 1708, but it was returned to France under the T. of Utrecht (1713). *See* CAPETIANS; VALOIS *passim.*

LILLIBURLERO and *BULLEN-A-LAH* were passwords used by the Irish in their massacre of Protestants in 1641. In 1687 Ld. Wharton used them as the refrain of an ironical political song discrediting Tyrconnel's Irish administration for James II. It became enormously popular, especially the lines referring nominally to Tyrconnel but actually to William of Orange:-

"O, why does he stay so long behind?
Ho! by my shout, 'tis a Protestant wind".

"Singing", according to Wharton "a deluded prince out of three Kingdoms", the contemporary Bp. Burnet said that "perhaps never had so slight a thing so great an effect".

LILLY, William (1602-81), professional prophet and physician, published the first annual astrological almanac from 1644 and other astrological writings. He also wrote a *True History of K. James and K. Charles I* (1651).

LIMBURG, a Burgundian possession from 1430, passed to the Habsburgs in 1482. **Maastricht** became part of it in 1530. At the P. of Westphalia (1648) the northern part with Maastricht were ceded to the Netherlands, and became one of **Lands of the Generality.** The rest remained with the Spanish Habsburgs and so devolved to the Austrian Habsburgs at the P. of Rastadt in 1714. It then shared the fate of the Belgians until the 1830 revolution, when all Limburg except Maastricht sided with the Belgians. In 1838 however a new partition left parts of it and Maastricht with the Netherlands, but placed the parts under the German Confederation as well. This German connection was severed in 1867.

LIMEHOUSE DECLARATION (1981), was issued by Roy Jenkins, David Owen, Shirley Williams and Will Rogers to launch the Social Democratic Party and set up the Council for Social Democracy. They were four members of the Labour party who were temperamentally estranged from Harold Wilson and had come to believe that the party's policy was becoming bureaucratic and sterile.

LIMEHOUSE SPEECH (30 July, 1909) by Lloyd George at a meeting of 4000 at the "Edinburgh Castle", Limehouse, (London), was a demagogic but effective defence of his budget. The City, he argued, wanted a large navy, but though the workmen of the country were willing to contribute, the rich were not. The poor needed retirement pensions to which the rich were refusing to contribute. The new land taxes were being attacked with great fury by landowners such as the D. of Northumberland who was selling land rented at 30s. an acre for £900 for a school. If landlords as monopolists ceased to discharge their duties, the conditions of landowning should be reconsidered. The speech was widely reported and greatly raised the electioneering temperature which preceded the passage of the Parliament Act, 1911.

LIMERICK (Verse form) first appeared in 1820. Lear's *Book of Nonsense* started a British craze which has never ceased. The Germans caught the idea after World War II. This is thought to show that they have a sense of humour.

LIMERICK (Ireland) was a Norse Kingdom from 812 until about 1000. From 1106 to 1174 it was capital of Thomond and then until 1195 it was disputed between Normans and Irish. It was chartered in 1197, and English Town was fortified. In 1609 it was constituted a county of a city and a staple. It held out for Charles II in 1651 and was stormed by Ireton. In 1690 it repulsed William III and surrendered only to treaty. The fortifications were demolished in 1760.

LIMES **(Lat = a balk, path or track).** A Roman fortified frontier commonly composed of a lateral road for troop movements, covered by a series of fortified camps and posts, or a wall (e.g. Hadrian's) or a natural obstacle. The Fosse Way (from near Exeter to the Humber) was a *limes* with the Fosse or ditch on the northern or enemy side and outlying posts beyond it.

LIMITATION OF LEGAL ACTIONS. (1) "Time does not run against the crown", therefore there was originally no limitation of time on criminal proceedings or for the recovery of crown property or debts (e.g. arrears of taxes). **(2)** In civil proceedings between subjects the period was limited (with some exceptions) to 12 years in cases of land and six in others in 1623; since 1939 the period is restricted to three years for personal injuries, and 30 years in actions by the crown. In certain restricted cases an Act of 1769 known as the *Nullum Tempus Act* also barred the crown.

LIMITED LIABILITY. In a partnership every partner is equally liable to outsiders for all the debts of the business. This rule dominated the organisation of business, apart from a few chartered or statutory companies, until the mid-19th cent. and discouraged investment. After several attempts to alter the law had failed, the Limited Liability Act, 1855, conceded the principle and the Joint Stock Companies Act, 1856, filled out the details. The Companies Act, 1862, consolidated and improved these provisions which required all companies, except those operating under statute or charter, to register, and created a simple procedure for creating them and winding them up. Limited companies sprang up in dozens, and this in its turn greatly increased the importance of the Stock Exchanges, especially that in London. Companies legislation has been several times amended and consolidated, but the principles remain the same.

LIMOGES, LIMOUSIN. The early county was divided into the viscounties of Limoges (well known for ceramics and enamel), Aubusson (carpets), Bridiers, Comborn, Rochechouart (wood) and Turenne, and formed part of Aquitaine but was partially isolated from neighbouring counties by hilly forests. After Eleanor of Aquitaine's marriage to Henry II it became, in effect, a marcher territory with the French royal sphere, and the scene of intermittent warfare, dispute and northern immigration as French pressure grew. It thus became divided (but not on coinciding boundaries) linguistically between the northern *Langue* d'oïl and the Aquitainian *Langue d'oc*, and legally between northern customary and southern written law. Its political boundaries also tended to fluctuate and the fusion of viscounties created powerful lordships such as La Marche which, under the Lusignan family was virtually separate. By the 13th cent. Anglo-Aquitainian power had thus been largely eroded but the T. of Brétigny (1360), restored the area to Aquitaine. Consequently the French had no great difficulty in recovering it when war broke out again and this exposed Limoges to the Black Prince's (q.v.) unwisely vengeful sack in 1370. The area was lost by 1374.

LINACRE, Thomas (?1460-1524) was educated at Oxford and became a doctor of Medicine at Padua where he also acquired a classical education. He returned to England in 1492 and in 1509 became Henry VIII's physician. He received many benefices and in 1518 he was the prime mover in founding the College of Physicians, of which he was the first President. From 1523 he was also Latin tutor to Princess (later Queen) Mary. He translated Galen and wrote on Latin grammar.

LINCHET. A terrace formation along chalk downs caused by Celtic hillside ploughing. It is an infallible sign of Celtic settlement.

LINCOLN (Lat = LINDUM or LINDOCOLINA). Its prosperity was based on its position on the R. Witham, giving access to the R. Trent and the North Sea and upon two roads, the Fosse Way and Ermine Street. It became the H.Q. of the Roman IXth Legion in A.D. 47 and in about A.D. 100 a walled *colonia* covering, however, only 40 acres; but in the 3rd cent. the walls were extended to the river to double it. There is a tradition of fighting there in 475. Paulinus built a church in 628. In 877 it became one of the Danish Five Boroughs and its Danish 12 Lawmen with their heritable franchises continued to govern it well into the 12th cent. William I built a powerful and often disputed castle in 1068. The need for a castle was commensurate with the town's importance, due partly to its long continuing commercial connections with Scandinavia and Frisia. There was a 12th cent. Jewish colony (*see* AARON OF LINCOLN). The bishops, as diocesan after 1072 of the biggest see in England, brought much wealth and work, and the shrine of St. Hugh, the strong minded bishop who died in 1200, brought flocks of pilgrims. The oldest surviving hostelry in England, *The*

Trip to Jerusalem, remains. Much wool, skins and leather came through Lincoln; cloth, in particular a kind of scarlet, was exported. Its importance as a financial centre is evidenced also by its being made a staple in 1291 and by the grant of fairs in 1327 and 1409. Parliaments were held there in 1301, 1316 and 1328. The trade in fact began to decline after 1350, not perhaps because of controversies over the location of the staple, as through failure to develop a cloth industry when the export of cloth was superseding that of raw wool. Successive Charters have the air of subsidization. Thus from 1327 the burghmanmote held all the crown pleas (and took the fees); from 1409 the borough was a county with its own sheriff and escheator; in 1466 the boundaries were enlarged to make it easy to pay the *ferme*, in 1546 it was given 4 advowsons, and in 1554 the markets were declared toll free. The Reformation of course had destroyed the pilgrim traffic. By the 17th cent. Lincoln was a sleepy county town with a vast Cathedral. It elected two M.P.s from earliest times to 1885 and thereafter one. *See also* LINCOLNSHIRE; LINDSAY; ROMAN BRITAIN.

***LINCOLN or DR. KING'S CASE* (1889).** *See* BENSON-3.

LINCOLNSHIRE represents a coalescence of four areas namely LINDSEY (q.v.), centred in Lincoln, which was long virtually an island between the sea and the Witham and Trent marshes, HOLLAND (= low land) an area of fens debouching on Boston, KESTEVEN, a wooded area around Sleaford, and the smaller ISLE OF AXHOLME. Lindsey was long disputed between Northumbria and Mercia, the rest were Anglian. It was the Danish invasions which artificially brought the areas together, for Torksey was a favourite camping ground, and in 878 Lincoln and Stamford became Danish boroughs and the many Danish place names attest widespread settlement. The invaders were probably used to meeting each other before they arrived, and arranged to continue the practice at Lincoln. The Parts of Lindsey, Kesteven (with Axholme) and Holland remained identifiable and had their own reeves, but the Lincoln meetings turned into a shire court for the whole of Lincolnshire, held every 40 days and composed later of the Lords of the small Lincolnshire manors or their stewards, sometimes afforced by village reeves with four good men. Water was a dominating feature — Domesday lists over 2000 fisheries, 361 salt works and over 400 mills — and this created uncertainty of boundaries; that between Kesteven and Holland was settled after four centuries of acrimony in 1816. Land reclamation, both from the marshes and from the sea was also an important and continuing feature of life which, incidentally, created the remarkably elongated parishes in Holland. Such work was first undertaken by the many monasteries notably at Barlings, Sempringham, Thornton, Kirkstead, Crowland and Spalding. Grazing and sheep were lucrative through the overseas wool and cloth trade via Lincoln and Boston, and the disafforestation of Kesteven in 1230 recognised a fait accompli: the pressure on the land was irresistible.

As however, the foreign trade declined in the 15th cent. cultivation increased, for the soil was fertile especially where recently reclaimed, and the market, set back by the Black Death, was expanding. Hence huge planned reclamations were made in the 17th cent. (*see* FENS) which, *inter alia*, created two thirds of Holland, and by exterminating most of the wild fowl, altered the eating habits of London. The area also produced large amounts of gravel, clay, ironstone and chalk.

Though Lincolnshire always had one Lord Lieut. and apart from Lincoln, one sheriff, the ancient Parts became individually more important as their populations grew. As a result in 1889 they acquired separate county councils. These were superseded by a single county council in 1974 when a northern strip (including Grimsby and Immingham) was detached to form the southern part of the new county of Humberside.

LINCOLN, Abraham (1809-65) (Pres. of U.S.A. from 1861). See U.S.A-11-15.

LINCOLN, EARLDOM OF. K. Stephen, with whom it originated, seems to have thought of it as an appointment rather than a dignity. **(1)** He gave it first (c. 1139) to William D'Aubigny, husband of Henry I's widow, but in so doing, offended Ranulf de Gernons and his half-brother William of Roumare (?-?1161) who seized Lincoln and made Stephen captive (1141). On his release he sought to appease them by translating D'Aubigny to Arundel and recognising Roumare as Earl. When Roumare again opposed him, the earldom was given to a third baron, Gilbert de Gant (1147).

(2) These grants gave rise to conflicting claims based upon the assumption that they had created hereditary dignities and these continued into the 13th cent. Roumare was succeeded by a childless grandson William (?- 1198). The earldom then remained vacant till 1217 when P. Louis of France conferred it on Gilbert of Gant's nephew Robert, but when Louis was defeated in 1217 it passed to Henry III's supporter E. Ranulf of Chester, who resigned it in 1230-1 to his sister and thence in 1232 to his son-in-law John de Lacy (1232). The Lacys held it until 1311 when it passed to Thomas of Lancaster in right of his wife (see LANCASTER, FIRST FAMILY) and so to the Lancastrian royal house, and was merged with the Crown in 1399 at the accession of Henry IV. It was revived by Edward IV in 1467 for John de Ia Pole, subsequently a supporter of Richard III, who was killed in 1487 leading the Lambert Simnel rebellion against Henry VII. He was attainted and the earldom became extinct. See CLINTON; LACY; POLE; ROUMARE.

LINCOLN ELECTION. Dick Taverne, Labour M.P. for Lincoln, disagreed with his party about its change of mind on the Common Market and incomes policies. He resigned his seat in Oct. 1972 and, as an independent, resoundingly defeated the official Labour candidate on 1 Mar. 1973.

LINCOLN'S INN. See INNS OF COURT AND CHANCERY.

LINDBERGH, Charles A. (1902-72) made the first Transatlantic flight (from New York to Paris) in May 1925 in 33 hours. In 1933 he flew from the Gambia to Port Natal in Brazil in 19 hours. These events inaugurated the era of Transatlantic air traffic which was the main factor in turning the London airports into the biggest in the world. The kidnap and murder of his child and the trial and execution of the murderer (1932-6) also kept him in the public eye. A known pacifist, he was invited to inspect the German airforce in 1938. Its powerful technology converted him into an international and dangerous exponent of appeasement and isolationism, of which he later repented.

LINDEMANN, Prof. Frederick Alexander (1886-1957) Ld. CHERWELL (1941), Vist. (1956) son of Adolphus Lindemann, a rich naturalised German astronomer **(1)** was born accidentally in Baden-Baden; educated at Darmstadt and then at Physico-Chemical Institute in Berlin under Prof. Nernst. He was a brilliant and versatile pupil and researcher. He was also a tennis player of Wimbledon standard. His wealth and attributes gave him access to high English political society. His scientific abilities early won him the respect of the famous scientists of his time. He became an F.R.S. in 1920. He had by then published papers or made inventions in the fields of physics, electronics, astronomy, geophysics, and chemical reactions.

(2) His association with defence problems began in 1915 at the R. Aircraft Factory at Farnborough where he learned to fly, worked out the theory of aircraft spin and its cure, and risked his life in order to prove it. In 1919, partly through the influence of Sir Henry Tizard, he became Dr. Lee's Prof. of Physics at Oxford and head of the moribund Clarendon Laboratory, which he transformed into a leading physics institute, with a large

intake and output of subsequently distinguished scientists, some recruited among German Jewish refugees. Meantime, through Sir John Masterman he had made friends with Ld. Birkenhead and in 1921, through the D. of Marlborough, with Winston Churchill. Extremely conservative in politics, he helped Churchill to publish the *British Gazette* during the Gen. Strike of 1926, but like Churchill he early foresaw the danger of Nazi Germany, and was alarmed at Britain's lack of preparedness.

(3) Accordingly in 1934 he and Churchill pressed for urgent consideration of the problem by a high level committee, but the Air Ministry set up an advisory committee of its own under Tizard. Lindemann and Churchill thought this inadequate, and in 1935 bullied the govt. into creating, under Sir Philip Cunliffe-Lister and with themselves as members, an air defence sub-committee of the Committee of Imperial Defence. The sub-committee was a side track, but one outcome was that Churchill had Lindemann appointed to the Tizard Committee. Here his actively political character brought him into collision with his more passively scientific and service colleagues. He was prepared to agitate covertly and in the press for executive power: they were not. A lifelong feud with Tizard began. In June 1936 half the committee resigned, and the ministry reconstituted it without Lindemann, who accordingly tried (and failed) in 1937 and 1939 to enter parliament through Oxford Univ. on a programme of air defence.

(4) When war broke out, however, Churchill took him to the Admiralty as his personal assistant and head of his statistical section, functions which he continued to perform under Churchill as premier. In particular he rendered an inestimable service by his gift for accurate summarisation of bulky memoranda, and as a statistician he exercised the essential, if unpopular function of criticising other people's figures. In 1940 he discovered that the Air Ministry was grossly over-estimating the German bomber strength; in 1941 that British bombing was only one-third as effective as the Air Ministry claimed; and in 1942 (when he became paymaster-gen.) that British shipping on the Middle Eastern and American routes could be cut by over half. These each led to major shifts in warlike economic policy. At the same time he pursued his scientific interests. He supported Dr R.V. Jones's striking invention for bending German navigational radar beams, which had important consequences at sea and in the air, and Derek Jackson's researches into micro-wave radar which produced "H25", the pathfinder's navigational ground scanner. The latter invention, because of Lindemann's over-estimate in 1942 of the effects of carpet bombing, turned out to be less important than was thought. Another issue on which Lindemann was wrong was the V2 in whose existence he refused to believe until very late.

(5) He returned to Oxford with the fall of the govt. in 1945, but continued in the shadow cabinet and was the opposition spokesman on economics in the Lords. From 1951 to 1953 he was a member (as Paymaster-Gen.) of the Churchill Cabinet in which he defeated the Treasury's proposals for floating sterling, and managed to get the control of Atomic energy transferred from the Min. of Supply to an *ad hoc* authority. He retired in 1956.

LINDISFARNE or HOLY I. (Northumberland) was the site of the important monastery and of a bishopric founded by St. Aidan in 635, as a centre from which to convert Northumbria, which then extended from the Humber to the Forth. Its influence also extended over Cumbria. It was abandoned in face of Danish raids in 875. See MISSIONARIES IN BRITAIN; DURHAM; VIKINGS.

LINDISFARNE GOSPELS, a set of Latin Gospels in an Anglo-Saxon writing style with Celtic illumination similar to that in the Books of Kells, was splendidly written and ornamented by Eadfrith (?-721), Bp. of Lindisfarne in memory of St. Cuthbert his predecessor. The next bishop, Ethelwold, had it enriched by the hermit Bilfrith and bound with gold and jewels. In about 970 Aldred interlined the text with a Saxon translation.

LINDSEY (*see* LINCOLNSHIRE) was an Anglo-Saxon kingdom. It was Christian from the time of Paulinus and had a separate bishopric from 678 when Theodore of Tarsus appointed Eadheath to it. The overlordship was disputed between Northumbria and Mercia during the 7th cent. and fell, after the death of the last King, Aldfrith (786) to Mercia. The bishopric survived until the 9th cent. Danish invasions but when Wessex regained it in 954 it was placed under the see of Dorchester-on-Thames, which was itself transferred to Lincoln after the Norman Conquest.

LINDSEY, E. of. *See* BERTIE.

LINDSEY, Theophilus (1723-1808), clergyman of Unitarian persuasion, held a number of Anglican livings and took part in the agitation against clerical subscription. He resigned when the petition against it was rejected in 1773 and set up the Essex Street Unitarian chapel in London. He was a dogmatic theologian of considerable power and expounded his views in his *Apology* (1774) and *Sequel to the Apology* (1776).

LINDUM (LINCOLN). *See* BRITAIN, ROMAN-2.

LINE, St. Anne (?1565 1601) kept house for the Jesuit John Gerard in London as a regular place of meeting and hospitality for R. Catholics and their priests. After Gerard's arrest and escape she calmly moved her activities to another house, where she in due course was arrested during a well attended mass, and eventually executed.

LINEN. Flax, though cultivated in N. Ireland, Scotland and parts of N. England, played little part in the local economics until some Huguenots established a colony at Lisburn (Ulster) and William III got the Crommelin brothers (q.v.) to investigate it. By 1725 they had set up an organised industry but the technical means for mass production were invented late and the cotton industry outdistanced linen by adopting the 18th cent. weaving and spinning inventions. The first effective linen spinning machine was patented by Kendrew and Porterhouse only in 1787 and power looms came into extensive use in Scotland only in 1821. Flax cultivation is labour intensive and declined steadily after World War I when alternative better paid employments became available. By World War II linen was, though very durable, something of a curiosity.

LINE OF BATTLE (SHIPS). *See* SHIPS, SAILING.

LINER. Any merchant ship plying on a fixed route to a scheduled timetable. Passenger liners have been superseded by aircraft since 1973.

LINGAM. The common phallic emblem of the god Siva, widely venerated among Hindus, especially by the Lingayat sect.

LINGUA FRANCA (Lat = Frankish tongue). A mediaeval pidgin language compounded of French, Greek, Arabic and Turkish long used in commerce and diplomacy in the Levant and N. Africa.

LINLITHGOW (1) John Adrian Louis Hope (1860-1908) 7th E. of HOPETOUN and 1st M. (1902), a Lord in Waiting (1885-6 and 1886-7) was Gov. of Victoria (1889-95), Paymaster-Gen. (1895-8), Lord Chamberlain (1898-1900), Gov-Gen. of Australia (1900-2) and Sec. of State for Scotland (1905). His son **(2) Victor Alexander (1887-1952)** was Dep. Chairman of the Unionist Party, Chairman of various banks and insurance cos. and of the Medical Research Council. He became Viceroy of India in 1936 and sustained that difficult office with success throughout much of the independence and civil disobedience agitation and the opening of the Japanese onslaught which had reached the Indian frontier by mid-1942. He left India in 1943.

LINLITHGOW (Scot), was an important Scots royal residence from early times as well as county town of West Lothian, and from 1389 a royal burgh. The palace remained in use after the union, and the Scots parliament met there (during an Edinburgh epidemic) as late as 1646. Hawley's dragoons burned it in 1746 and it remains a ruin.

LINLITHGOW, M. and E. of. *See* LIVINGSTONE.

LINOLEUM was invented by Frederick Walton in 1860.

LIOBA, St. *See* MISSIONS TO EUROPE-3.

LIONEL OF ANTWERP (1338-68), E. of ULSTER (1347), D. of CLARENCE (1362), third son of Edward III, was titular regent in 1345-6 during Edward III's absence on the Crécy Campaign. Thereafter he was designated for an Irish career. In 1352 he was married to Elizabeth, heiress of William de Burgh, E. of Ulster and Connaught, who was assassinated by Irish relatives in 1332. This gave him the honour of Clare as well as the two nominal Irish earldoms. He was appointed Lord Lieut. in 1361 and allotted a force, which was inadequate, to re-establish English rule in the lost areas, including most of his earldoms. His wife died in 1362. He made no impression in Connaught; in Ulster he recovered most of Co. Down only. He had to rely mainly on the towns and lesser men of the ten obedient shires, for the magnates, for all their protestations, held aloof. Just before he left in 1366, however, he held a famous parliament at Kilkenny whose Statutes (q v) laid down the gen. trend of English policy until their repeal in 1613. He then went to Milan, where he married Violante, daughter of Bernabò Visconti, for a huge dowry, but died very soon. For his daughter PHILIPPA *see* MORTIMER-11; *see also* CLARENCE.

LIONNE, Hugues de, M. de BERNY (1611-71), diplomat trained by Mazarin, whom he effectively succeeded in 1661 in the French dept. of Foreign Affairs, and as an influential member of Louis XIV's Council.

LIPSON, Ephraim (1888-1960), economic historian, published the first three volumes in his incomplete *Introduction to the Economic History of England* between 1915 and 1933. He held that there was no such industrial revolution as might constitute a breach with the past, and that there were cyclical movements of free enterprise and collective control.

LIPTON, Sir Thomas Johnstone (1850-1931), Bt. (1902) opened a grocery in Glasgow in 1871 and made himself a millionaire, mostly in tea, by 1880. He spent lavishly between 1899 and 1930 in attempting to recover the America's Cup in his yachts, successively called *Shamrock*.

LISBON (Port.) was taken from the Moors by a partly English force in 1147 and its remarkable harbour gradually attracted Mediterranean and Atlantic traffic. The important local products were wine, raisins, cork, fruit, ships' stores, and salt. The Portuguese court moved there from Coimbra after Alfonso III had conquered the Algarves in 1251; a University was founded in 1290 (but moved to Coimbra in 1308), and the primatial see in 1393. In the middle ages trade was largely in the hands of the Genoese, who established strong connections to England through the Gascon wine trade and from England by exporting wool. These links were strengthened during the Hundred Years War, when England needed Peninsular allies against Castile. Thus in 1353 Edward III granted a safe conduct and partial toll-exemption to the merchants of Lisbon, while from 1373 a series of alliances was made between England and Portugal against Castile. These were particularly close during John of Gaunt's attempts to win the Castilian throne.

The eastern spice trade round the Cape which commenced at the beginning of the 16th cent. brought immense prosperity which was continued with the development of the East Indies and Brazil. The English connection (*see* AVIS) was eroded though not wholly broken during the Spanish occupation (1580-1640), but Portuguese independence was effectively supported on

British guarantees after 1660, and the city became a great British trading centre. This was one of several reasons why the destructive earthquake of 1755 caused such a sensation in Britain. It also caused rationalist philosophers to doubt the justice of divine providence. Pombal rebuilt the lower city in rectangular fashion and after Bonaparte's wars many of the spectacular ecclesiastical buildings were taken over for govt. offices. A shipbuilding industry grew up in the 19th cent. and textiles, pottery, paper and chemicals followed.

LISKEARD, ancient Cornwall stannary borough.

LISMORE (Co. Waterford), had a powerful monastery founded by St. Carthach in 633, but its tactically strong position on a headland caused K. John to build a castle there in 1185.

LISLE. *See* DUDLEY.

LISLE (1) John (?1610-64), M.P. for Winchester in the Short and Long Parliaments and extreme opponent of Charles I, took a prominent part in his trial and signed his death warrant. As President of the High Court he swore Cromwell in as Protector and, an enthusiastic supporter of his judicial reforms, tried to reform the Chancery. In 1657 he became one of Cromwell's peers. At the Restoration he escaped to Lausanne where an Irishman shot him dead. His wife **(2) Dame Alice (?1614-85)** was executed for unwittingly sheltering a rebel after the B. of Sedgemoor (1685). The trial was the most notorious of Jeffreys' judicial murders during the Bloody Assize and helped to discredit James II.

LISSA. *See* VIS.

LISTER (1) Joseph Jackson (1786-1869), originally a wine merchant, devised the modern (achromatic) microscope in 1830 and first described mammalian red corpuscles in 1834. His son **(2) Joseph (1827-1912) 1st Ld. LISTER (1897)** became celebrated as a surgeon in 1853 when he first used an antiseptic in the form of carbolic. The principle revolutionised medicine.

LITERACY (1) Roman law and literature show that most Romans of both sexes and many of their slaves read and wrote, but the western literates were heavily diluted by barbarous immigrants, so that by K. Alfred's time literacy, save among churchmen, was unusual. It spread only slowly from the clergy because their letters expressed Latin, by the 10th cent. a foreign language to everyone else.

(2) Nevertheless the making of translations in the 9th cent. proves that there were readers, and that they were increasing with time is evident from the many contemporary copies of vernacular writings such as *Piers Plowman* and the works of Chaucer (14th cent.) and the rapid development of printing in the 15th and 16th cents. In 1539 Henry VIII would not have required the great expense of putting English Bibles in every church, if they could not be read. The emergence of handbills and flysheets later in the century points in the same direction. There are no statistics, but there must have been many readers by 1700, and it seems that they were not all concentrated at any particular level of society.

(3) Writing, a time consuming skill, lagged behind because most people did manual work which inhibited it or engaged in pursuits where it was not needed. Ploughmen cannot plough, poachers cannot catch rabbits and their women cannot cook or spin, and write at the same time, nor was it necessary for them to be able to write at all. 18th cent. ragged and Sunday schools taught many to read but gave lasting writing skill to few. In 1800 there were only 24 accountants in London, and the tendency of reading and writing to be out of step continued with the rise of mass education in state elementary schools after 1884. The new popular press had vast readerships by 1914 but until 1939 soldiers were paid weekly before witnesses because they could not necessarily write their names.

(4) All the same, reading ability dragged writing

ability with, if behind, it, and the post-Second World War schools were very successful in both fields, as the vast university expansions prove. On the other hand there seem to have been later set-backs. Changes in teaching methods were often confusing and if the mechanics of literacy continued to be absorbed, the misuse of words, syntax and grammar percolated upwards throughout society, encouraged by pictorial presentations in so-called 'comics' and television, which reached everyone but made virtually no use of the written word at all. By the 1990s too, the manual ability to form letters of the alphabet was being superseded by the use of word processors.

LITERARY FORGERS. A number of persons have imposed upon the gullibility or good faith of educated society for pleasure or profit. The principal ones so far exposed are:- George PSALMANAZAR (?1679-1763), the inventor of a country called *Formosa*, its language and religion; James MACPHERSON (1736-96), the creator of Ossian; Thomas CHATTERTON (1752-70), whose verses by an alleged 15th cent. poet *Thomas Rowley* were published in 1777 and 1782: William Henry IRELAND (1777-1835), whose many highly skilled Shakespearean forgeries included two complete plays; Thomas WISE (1859-1937), a celebrated collector and expert on books, who forged many first editions for sale. *See also* JUNUS; PARNELL; 'PIGOTT'.

LITHOGRAPHY was invented by the Austrian Aloys Senefelder in 1796. but a flat machine process came into use only in 1852 and a metallic rotary process in 1905.

LITHSMAN. A paid sailor under the Danish Kings (cf Sw. *Ledung* = fleet).

LITHUANIA. *See* BALTIC-59.

LITTLE ENTENTE. *See* CZECHOSLOVAKIA.

LITTLETON, Thomas (?-1481), King's serjeant from 1455, became a judge of the Common Pleas in 1466. His book on *Tenures* was the earliest systematic exposition of English land law, the first English legal text book and legal work to be printed (1481). It ran to over 70 editions by 1628 when Coke published his *Commentary* on it. The book summarised the state of the law as it had been developed in the middle ages, but before it was re-modelled by later developments.

LITTLETON, Sir Thomas (1647-1710), a whig, was M.P. for Woodstock from 1689 to 1702 and Speaker from 1698 to 1700 when he became Treasurer of the Navy. He was later M.P. for Castle Rising (1702), Chichester (1707) and Portsmouth (from 1708). His career is one of many examples of the combination of stability of conviction yet interchangeability of function among politicians of the period.

LITVINOV, Maximilian (1876-1952), a charming Jewish revolutionary who married an Englishwoman, was the Russian Foreign Affairs Commissar from 1930 to 1939. He tried to uphold the League of Nations and to work for better relations with the democratic west because of the need to keep the western powers quiet while they were subverted, but when Stalin signed an open alliance with Hitler he was relieved of his post and, after an interval, became ambassador in Washington (1941-3). He died a natural death.

LIUDHARD. *See* KENT, KINGDOM-2.

LIVERIES were uniform clothes worn by guildsmen (*see* LIVERY COMPANIES) or given by lords to their following. They were a chief means by which the Crown and nobility exhibited their power, and to exaggerate this power a lord might clothe not only his armed retainers but his domestic, administrative and professional servants. Thomas of Lancaster had five hundred. The main abuse was the immunity which lords and disorderly retainers might forcibly secure for each other in defiance of the law. Despite an Act of 1372 the Lancastrians had maintained considerable private uniformed armies and so had other magnates with whose support Henry IV usurped the throne. The giving of livery amounted to a promise of protection to the wearer; its acceptance an expression of support for the protector. Not surprisingly legislation against livery was mostly Lancastrian. An Act of 1400 forbade private, other than ecclesiastical, liveries and restricted the wearing of royal liveries to the King's presence and to the retinue of the Constable and marshal on campaign. An Act of 1405 made a still valid, exception for guilds. The legislation was largely ignored and had to be re-enacted with simpler penalties in 1468.

LIVERPOOL The manor was bought by K. John, then E. of Mortain, with an eye to Irish affairs in 1191, and he founded the borough in 1207. As expected, it became the main English commercial and military depot for central and northern Ireland and Anglesey too. Hence it always had Welsh and Irish settlers. Its prosperity depended on peace in Ireland and the Irish sea and the steady development of Lancashire. All these were disturbed in 14th and 15th cents. and especially in the Wars of the Roses. Tudor rule, however, brought a revival which was supplemented by the first beginnings of Transatlantic voyaging. All the same when Charles I sold the borough to a London consortium in 1628, its value was not high for they resold it to the Molyneux family for £450. It was held for Parliament in the Civil War and only briefly taken by P. Rupert in the course of the Marston Moor campaign. The aggressive American trade increased under the Commonwealth and Charles II, and this combined with Irish peace brought enough prosperity to enable the corporation to buy out the Molyneuxes in 1672. The slave trade also began to bring large profits, and in 1709 the corporation started to build the docks. The Mersey now developed very rapidly, its tidal scour maintaining deep water while the neighbouring open estuary of the Dee was silting up. By 1750 Liverpool had thus mainly superseded Chester as the port for Ireland and it was acquiring a sugar and tobacco trade with the Caribbean. To this, with time, was added North American products such as timber, and the export of a growing number of northern English goods including woollens and salt. The rise of the Lancashire cotton industry at the turn of the century brought an enormous stimulus which entirely replaced the slave trade, abolished in 1807, and by 1843 the overcrowded docks were being extended to BIRKENHEAD on the other side of the Mersey. This was timely because the repeal of the Corn Laws (1846) brought a new and soon very large trade in Canadian grain. The old docks organisation broke down and in 1857 their administration was unified under an independent MERSEY DOCKS AND HARBOUR BOARD.

The flood of trade and capital engendered secondary industries such as sugar refining, cattle food processing, pottery, and engineering. The early connection with the railways (the Mersey railway tunnel was opened in 1886) made Liverpool a national as well as an international port, and the development of the steamship opened up a further trade to Australia and New Zealand. The population expanded immensely and this led to a demand for extensive educational facilities. A univ. college was founded in 1881; the university in 1903.

In World War I the port was one of the principal entry points for supplies from overseas and the shipping suffered heavily from German submarine attack. The decline of the cotton industry, though serious, was partly offset by a growing trade in fruit. Nevertheless the strain in the local economy was enough to create political friction between the R. Catholic Irish of immigrant origin and other population elements. Developments such as the Mersey road tunnel (1934), however, continued. In World War II Liverpool played a vital role; its shipping suffered correspondingly and it attracted sustained bombing which destroyed large sectors. After the war the shipping business declined steadily with the corn trade and the rise of air transport, and by 1990 industrial and tourist redevelopment and the Beatles had virtually turned the city's back to the water.

LIVERPOOL *See* JENKINSON.

LIVERPOOL GOVT. – WARTIME PHASE (June 1812-Dec. 1815). (13 in Cabinet. The leading figures under the E. of Liverpool were the E. of Eldon, Lord Chanc; Vist. Sidmouth Home Sec., Vist. Castlereagh Foreign; E. Bathurst War and Colonies.) (*See* PERCEVAL ADMINISTRATION; MOSCOW DISASTER; FOURTH COALITION, WAR.)

(1) Perceval's assassination unleashed personal animosities which the Prince Regent, representing the general patriotism of independent M.P.s and gentry, could not assuage. He first tried to persuade Canning and Wellesley to join the govt. but Canning hated Castlereagh and thought Liverpool's views on R. Catholic emancipation unworkable. Then, on the motion of Stuart Wortley, an independent, the Commons voted an address for an efficient administration; on a further resolution that it should be presented to the Prince by Wortley and Ld. Milton (21 May 1812), Liverpool and the govt. resigned. Wellesley was now approached alone, and he tried the whig Lds. Grey and Grenville who eventually refused. Then the whig Lord Moira, a friend of the Prince's, attempted discussions but these broke down because Prince and whigs mistrusted each other. By June it was obvious that Liverpool would have to return; he had been successful at the War Office and, in spite of the uncertainties, home affairs would have to take second place.

(2) The economy was barely improving after the 1811 crisis and there were occasional riots and outbreaks of machine smashing. Britain and her important trading partner the U.S.A. were drifting towards war and Bonaparte had just begun his spectacular invasion of Russia (May). The main rift in the clouds was in Spain, where Wellington had cleared the frontier by taking Ciudad Rodrigo and Badajoz. Meanwhile it was hoped to prevent an American war by revoking the Orders in Council (under which Britain was intercepting U.S. trade with Europe), but this proved to be an irrelevance for it did nothing to head off Henry Clay and his war party, who were interested in continental conquest rather than maritime expansion. Indeed, the traders most affected by the orders opposed the war, which Congress and Pres. Madison declared (18 June 1812) five days before they were revoked. This was a sideshow (*see* ANGLO-AMERICAN WAR 1812-15) but meanwhile the important events were happening first in Spain, then in Russia. Wellington won his great victory at Salamanca in July and entered Madrid in Aug. Bonaparte entered Moscow in Sept. The conflagration there, and the Russian refusal to negotiate now indicated for the first time that the balance was turning against the enemy. While the govt. did its best to support the Peninsular campaign, it tried a measure of pacification at home and for Ireland. A new Toleration Bill repealed the, now largely symbolic, Conventicle and Five Mile Acts. By Dec. the extent of the French disaster was known in London, but meanwhile Wellington had had to retire from Burgos to Portugal.

(3) By Mar. 1813 the Russians had reached the North Sea but Bonaparte had raised another army. It assembled near Jena and by June it dominated N. Germany and had entered Saxony. The reply was a triple alliance signed at Reichenbach (June). Britain was to provide £2M to keep 150,000 Russians and 80,000 Prussians in the field and no party was to negotiate with France without consulting the others. Britain's ability to hold her allies to the bargain was created by Wellington's sweeping victories, culminating in Vitoria (June) and the invasion of S. France. The other allies, nerved to hold on, redeemed their defeat at Dresden (Aug.) by five local victories and the great decision in the three-day B. of Leipzig (Oct.). By Nov. all non-French Europe had come over to the allies.

(4) The Austrians had cleared Dalmatia and Istria and were ready to advance into Italy but Metternich, with reason, feared Russian ambitions and diplomacy. The Czar was proposing to partition the Polono-Saxon complex with Prussia: he to have all Poland, Prussia all Saxony. Russian armies would line the Carpathians and Bohemia be permanently threatened on two sides by Prussia. Hence Metternich wanted a quick western settlement, where Austria had no interests, in order to free her hands in S. Germany, Saxony and Poland, Italy and E. Europe. His allies were easily persuaded that the war might still be long and could be doubtful and besides, Bonaparte was his master's brother-in-law. At Frankfurt he rushed those of his allied colleagues who were present (the Russian Nesselrode and the E. of Aberdeen) into offering France, for quick acceptance, her so-called 'natural' frontiers (The Pyrenees, the Alps and the Rhine) including Antwerp. External issues were left vague, but Aberdeen agreed that Britain might recognise such liberty for trade and navigation as was properly claimed by France. Bonaparte, who was determined to keep Italy and Holland, delayed accepting this sacrifice of British to Austrian interests.

(5) By 1814, when Castlereagh reached allied H.Q., the offer had lapsed and allied armies were invading France. Castlereagh's position, fully supported by the cabinet and Wellington's victorious northward advance was strong. He ensured that the maritime (essentially wartime) issues should be separated from European territorial (essentially peacetime) questions, where Britain had no ambitions. He was prepared to offer colonial sacrifices to make the European settlement durable and he argued initially that the French must be kept currently informed. Of French control outside France, Britain would reject that of Belgium or, *a fortiori* Holland; Prussia that of S. Germany; Austria that of Italy. A united front would therefore require the reduction of France to something less than the so-called natural frontiers. Metternich, who knew Bonaparte well, rightly did not believe that he would accept this. A fight to the finish was thus inevitable and in this the three allies were strengthened by the Czar's determination to get rid of Bonaparte himself. The Czar disliked the Bourbons and proposed the suspect Bernadotte as an impossible alternative. For the time being there thus seemed to be no alternative to Bonaparte, with whom consequently, during the spring campaign of 1814, negotiations were attempted at Chatillon from 5 Feb. to 19 Mar.

(6) Metternich and Castlereagh were agreed that if Bonaparte's were to be replaced by any other regime, the change would have to be made by the French themselves. Castlereagh, with an eye to Hanover, assured Metternich that Britain would oppose the total elimination of Saxo-Poland by Russia and Prussia. Metternich, for his part, favoured a regency by the Archduchess-Empress Marie Louise but could reply that family considerations would not be opposed to a Bourbon restoration. Actually Wellington, in the south, was solving the riddle. His troops were becoming more popular with the local French than their own, and Bourbon sentiment was mounting there. Bonaparte on the other hand was spinning out time. By the T. of Valençay (Feb.) he agreed to restore Ferdinand VII if that miserable Bourbon got the British out of Spain. His Spanish armies thus released for northern spheres, Bonaparte could fight on more equal terms. These calculations left both Wellington and Spain out of account. Even if the Cortes had not promptly repudiated the treaty, the southern armies would still have had to reckon with Wellington's forces supplied from the sea.

(7) Castlereagh now repeated, in a treaty at Chaumont (Mar) on a greater scale, the manoeuvre of the T. of Reichenbach. With their overwhelming numbers, Bonaparte's only hope had been to divide his enemies.

Now he was lost; Paris fell. By the end of Apr. he was in Elba and Louis XVIII was King of France.

(8) Under the Ts. of Paris (30 May 1814) Britain returned her French conquests except Mauritius, Tobago, and St. Lucia; Belgium was ceded to Holland from whom Britain bought (for £6M) the Cape, Demarara and Curaçao. Meanwhile the unliquidated conflict with U.S.A. led to minor mutinies when the govt. decided to send the forces released from Europe to America. It soon petered out for nobody wanted to conquer the U.S.A. which could not conquer Canada. In Dec. the *status quo ante* was restored by the P. of Ghent, but the news travelled too slowly to prevent the British attack on, and defeat at, New Orleans in Jan. 1815. The Congress of Vienna had already opened in Nov. *See* WATERLOO, BAND CAMPAIGN.

LIVERPOOL GOVT. – PEACETIME PHASE (*see previous entry*) **1815-Apr. 1827.** (13 in Cabinet. Leading figures under the E. of Liverpool: Ld. Eldon, Lord Chanc; Vist. Sidmouth, Home Sec; Vist. Castlereagh, Foreign Sec; from June 1816, George Canning, Pres. Bd. of Control; from Jan. 1819 the D. of Wellington, Master-Gen. of the Ordnance; from Jan. 1822, Robert Peel, Home Sec; from Sept. 1822 after Castlereagh's death, Geo. Canning, Foreign Sec; Oct. 1823, Wm. Huskisson, Pres. of the Bd. of Trade.) **(1)** Until the war issues had been settled at the Congress of Vienna and the 2nd T. of Paris, and Bonaparte had been safely packed off to St. Helena, this Tory govt's attention had been focused on great foreign and warlike affairs while overwhelming industrial developments (*see* INDUSTRIAL REVOLUTION) and social changes had grown up at home. These were, of course, noticed but not understood. The existing institutions had been rendered obsolete as instruments of home govt. yet they had apparently been adequate to fight the greatest war in British history and they sheltered important interests. Reinforced by natural human inertia and a reasonable horror of the excesses of the French Revolution, there was an inclination to defend the existing dispensation, which was at variance with developing opinion and the facts of life.

(2) The Whig opposition was unorganised. Between 1815 and 1821 it had no recognised leader in the Commons and from 1821 to 1830 no leader at all, and its members were in public life by the same political mechanisms as the Tories. It contained individuals capable of expounding the emergent social, economic and moral considerations but no coherent policy. In fact the differently orientated Tory party had such individuals too. The two sides were likened by Wm. Hazlitt to two rival stage coaches which splashed each other with mud but went down the same road to the same place.

(3) Thus home politics took on the aspect of an embattled two-party aristocracy having reformist notions thrust upon it by rising industrial plutocrats on the one hand and on the other by the poverty-stricken, often hungry mobs in the post-war slump. At this period electorates, however constituted, voted openly and might therefore be influenced by uproar, as illustrated by Hogarth, and the missiles of the un-policed voteless. These were the conditions under which Liverpool's Govt. saw post-war problems in terms of the protection of property and trade. Without public order, nothing was safe. Creditors, traders and investors were at risk with an unstable currency when peace brought a sudden contraction in public expenditure. Farming, still the greatest interest and the biggest employer had to be protected to prevent economic and social disaster, for in wide areas the agricultural labourers' wage was supplemented through the rates paid by the landowners who employed most of them. (*See* SPEENMAMLAND.) Rural employment and Poor Relief rose and fell together, yet it was difficult to protect farming without, through the Corn Laws, seeming to tax the food of the poor.

(4) These three complexes of problems – order, credit and agriculture – arose contemporaneously and had to be solved simultaneously, but they had their influence on a fourth problem, that of international tranquillity. This, as such, was not controversial, since a trading nation needed firstly peace, secondly freedom of the seas and thirdly a European balance under which British power could be thrown against any potential disturber of the continent. British diplomacy under Castlereagh succeeded admirably in the first two of these tasks. Peace was made. Britain had off-shore European bases from Heligoland to the Ionian Is, Caribbean bases between the U.S.A. and the nascent Spanish-American states, together with the Cape and Mauritius on the sea route to India and the E. Indies. The initial European balance was achieved as against France by the enlargement of Savoy, the union of the Low Countries and the Confederation of Germany; as against Prussia by combinations first with Russia and then with France and Austria; and as against Russia by the strengthening of Austro-Hungary. On the other hand the maintenance of that balance was a strenuous exercise because of local instabilities and great-power ambitions. It was to cost Castlereagh his life.

(5) The economy had barely recovered from the slump of 1811 when the peace of 1815 disturbed it again. Overseas demand slackened and industrialists laid off labour. To the ranks of the unemployed were added tens of thousands of discharged soldiers and sailors, and there was a bad harvest. People were alarmed by disorderly occurrences such as Orator Hunt's Spa Fields demonstration (1816), by sporadic hunger riots and the stoning of the P. Regent on his way to parliament. The govt. considered suspending *Habeas Corpus* but the good harvest of 1817 brought down farm prices which calmed the towns but disturbed the countryside. The war had reduced trade with Europe but, by cutting off the Spanish monopoly, had increased it 14-fold with Spanish America where there was much speculative investment. Oscillations in paper currency value created investment difficulties and a business-man's demand for a return to gold; the govt. set up a committee to investigate the question shortly after the so-called Peterloo Massacre at Manchester (1819) which caused widespread indignation. Upheaval and overreaction were in the air. Arthur Thistlewood's absurd Cato Street conspiracy came to light while rebellions broke out in Spain, Portugal and S. Italy. While the Govt. secured the passage of the Six Acts, the powers of the Holy Alliance proposed for themselves an in a sense correlative right to police rebellious countries, and called a congress at Troppau (1820) to consider it. The appalling Ferdinand VII of Spain was asking for their intervention. British political opinion, though favouring repression at home, was hostile to him personally and feared a re-establishment of the Spanish colonial monopoly. Hence Castlereagh had from an insecure moral base and without personal conviction to argue against intervention. The other powers thought that they could bring him round and reassembled at Laibach (Ljubljana) in Jan. 1821, where they announced a major congress at Verona for Oct. 1822.

(6) The gold committee now recommended that gold payments be reintroduced in stages between Feb. 1820 and May 1823 (*see* COINAGE). Its violently deflationary effects created widespread new unemployment, just as old George III, mad but beloved, died, and the self-indulgent and dislikeable P. Regent became King as George IV. He had long ago quarrelled with his hoyden Queen Caroline, who in June 1820 returned to Britain from a long and not wholly innocent stay in Italy. Whig politicians and hungry rioters seized upon her as a means to embarrass the ruling powers. On her way to London, she became an undeserving heroine. George's self-centred disregard for public susceptibilities was never worse exhibited than in the episodes of his abortive divorce bill and his coronation, which for a while injured the repute of the institutions which he represented (*see* CAROLINE OF BRUNSWICK).

(7) Further disasters now supervened upon the shaken political scene. Within nine months farm prices collapsed, which helped the urban unemployed (who had no money) only a little, but created destitution in the villages, and simultaneously deflation and urban unemployment rose hand in hand. Then the speculative investment in the newly or potentially independent Spanish American states (*see* BOLIVAR) began to turn sour. The banks, looking for easier gains then seemed available at home, had invested (not for the last time) in 'banana republics'. This coincided with the Greeks' rebellion against the Turks. Public opinion romantically favoured them, but Castlereagh feared Russian warlike intervention, her possible domination of Turkey and threat to British interests in the Mediterranean and on the land route to India. As long ago as 1770 a Russian fleet had sailed from the Baltic to the Aegean. He therefore worked to bring the issue to Verona and to go there himself. He drafted his own instructions for Cabinet approval for a preliminary meeting at Vienna and then, deranged by overwork, he killed himself (Aug. 1822). Canning replaced him and the D. of Wellington went to Vienna at 48 hours' notice.

(8) Castlereagh had relied upon his personal standing with European statesmen to use the European congresses as the fora for his diplomacy. He was orientated towards continental issues and adopted an analogous attitude to dealings with the U.S.A. Essentially geographical problems had been settled by the demilitarisation of the Canadian frontier (*see* RUSH-BAGOT AGREEMENT) and the joint opening of the Oregon. Canning had a different priority. His eyes were fixed on the Spanish American seaborne commerce, with which European intervention in Spain might interfere. In Sept. 1822 it became clear that French troops (ranged along the Pyrenees ostensibly for sanitary reasons) were about to enter Spain. At Verona Wellington protested and walked out. Canning asked for an increase in the Navy, spoke publicly of the dangers of war and announced that Britain would allow no permanent military occupation of Spain, no violation of Portuguese territory and no seizure of any Spanish colony. The French tried to call his bluff; and, unresisted, overran Spain (Sept. 1823) but their operations and influence ended at the sea-shore, for the sea was in British hands. Canning thereupon invited them, through their ambassador, the Prince de Polignac, to state their intentions. The agreed Polignac Memorandum (q.v.) (Oct. 1823) anticipated the similar Monroe Doctrine (Dec.) (in any case inspired by Canning). The difference was that the Royal Navy could enforce it, the Americans could not.

(9) The U.S.A. had already recognised some of the Spanish American republics. There was now no pressure from traders, Lloyds, the banks and other investors to follow suit. The Polignac-Monroe doctrine protected their speculations from European but not American intervention. Accordingly at the end of 1824 Canning persuaded the Cabinet to insert recognition in the Speech from the Throne. George IV avoided reading this recognition of new republics himself by losing his false teeth. The recognition did nothing to assist the Spanish American speculations which were reaching the dimensions of a South Sea Bubble. There was no limit on the banks' power to issue notes. In Mar. 1825 Liverpool warned speculators against the risks. In Nov. came the crash. Sixty-six banks failed. The real reason, bad judgement, was obscured by the technical reason. The Bank of England's monopoly had kept the other English banks small. Govt. and opposition legislated in 1826 to permit joint-stock banks to be set up outside a radius of 65 miles from London and to issue notes for £5 and over.

This was the administration's last important act. In Feb. 1827 Liverpool resigned after a paralytic stroke.

(10) The Liverpool peacetime govt. presided in an important period of modern history where it had to cope with largely unprecedented problems. Where it failed, as in Spain, the damage was less than it feared. Where it succeeded, as in Spanish American commerce, the commercial interests reaped smaller profits than expected, while its defensive inertia at home was soon overtaken by events.

LIVERPOOL, BANK OF, founded in 1831, became a limited co. in 1882, changed its name to Liverpool and Martins Bank and to Martin's Bank in 1928.

LIVERPOOL *DAILY POST*, *ECHO* and *MERCURY*. The *Liverpool Mercury* was founded as an independent weekly journal in 1811; the *Daily Post* in 1855 after the repeal of the newspaper stamp duty. The *Mercury* became a daily in 1858 but was absorbed by the *Daily Post* in 1909. The Echo was the *Daily Post*'s companion evening paper.

LIVERPOOL IRISH. Between Jan. and Nov. 1847 278,000 people, mostly hungry, landed at Liverpool from Ireland and 123,000 left for foreign countries. Thirteen relief stations were set up. Most of the balance of 155,000 settled in the city.

LIVERY (Ireland). *See* ELIZABETH I-17.

LIVERY COMPANIES, LONDON were guilds or 'mysteries' originating as associations for regulating and improving the principal means of their members' livelihood. In some cases they were local so that several guilds (e.g. of Butchers) practised the same mystery in different parts of the City. The subsoil of the hall of the Sadlers Co., associated with the Saxon foundation of St. Martin the Great, contains pre-Saxon evidence of leatherworking, and as under Henry II (1154-89)18 guilds were amerced as adulterine, the existence of more can be inferred by that time. The head of such a body was usually called the Alderman, but by the reign of Henry III Warden or Master. In 1355 36 guilds made gifts to Edward III and in 1363, as a result of Commons' petitions, artificers were required to confine themselves to one mystery of their choice. Edward III started to incorporate guilds (most of them already ancient) by charter, and in 1376 the Common Hall of the City transferred the right to elect the members of the Common Council to the 48 guilds or companies then recognised. The number continued to increase and under Richard II (1377-99) companies were required to enrol their charters.

By this time the distinctions between the twelve GREAT or commercial, and the LESSER or craft companies were becoming important and were expressed in the precedence accorded to the great companies, the customary reservation of the mayoralty until 1724 to members of them and to the fact that they mostly bore the military and administrative expenses of the City. It was by now recognised that the mayor was the person through whom the King addressed the Companies, and consequently that the mayor had a very wide authority to enforce his mandates. By 1435 he was being addressed as 'sovereign', and later still as 'master of all the companies'. His authority was worth gifts, which the Companies showered on him.

The practice of wearing livery is probably ancient. It consisted of a coat, surcoat, mantle and hood, and though it was uniform within a particular guild it was not unchanging. It became important when voting rights in Common Hall were confined at the end of the 15th cent. to those entitled to wear it, i.e. those admitted to the number of livery laid down in a given company charter. The practice of chartering also had the effect of controlling the numbers of companies. The old self-formed and appointed guild was a thing of the past but the numbers continued to grow. Henry VII chartered three, Henry VIII five.

By Tudor times the Great Companies were rich. In 1544 they lent Henry VIII over £21,000 for the Scottish war, and were becoming objects of royal rapacity. The Chantries Acts of 1547 and 1548 compelled them to compound for any sums chargeable upon their property for the maintenance of masses. This amounted to some £19,000. In 1557 Mary I raised a compulsory loan of £20,000 at 12% and required them to provide soldiers. In 1558 she raised £65,000. Elizabeth I made a practice of raising loans and imposing obligations by mandate which the mayor transmitted, duly apportioned, by precept. These were very diverse: in 1566 for setting the poor to work; in 1573 for overseas expeditions to La Rochelle and Virginia; between 1562 and 1596 there were large precepts for military and naval armaments (e.g. £7,400 in 1591 for ships) and for troops (e.g. 3,000 men in 1579) besides provision for the defence of the City. In addition the City had to look after itself. There were precepts in 1565 for building the Royal Exchange; in 1569 fo cleansing the City ditch and in 1665 for storing coal and releasing it in times of shortage. There was a similar older custom of storing grain to cure price fluctuations: common granary was erected at Leadenhall in 1435, but the methods for supplying it broke down and in 1521 precepts for a compulsory loan were issued in a time of famine. Such loans (which the City was often slow in repaying) became a regular feature, until 1578 when the companies undertook to provide grain themselves and store it in the City's Bridge House which had mills and ovens. From 1567 Elizabeth I also used the Companies to raise money by lottery, but when it came to monopolies, especially of inspection, she met with effective opposition. Her habitual interferences could on the whole be tolerated, but the efforts of her alien successors could not, and were a major cause of the Civil War. The companies fell out of the frying pan into the fire. In 1642 parliament demanded a loan of £100,000, in 1643 £50,000 besides weekly gifts and the livery halls were in constant use for govt. business.

The Great Fire of 1666 inflicted great damage on these, by now essentially financial, institutions by destroying their rents and melting their plate. It took a considerable time to re-establish their position, and by then the channels of trade and finance had shifted, hence the *Quo Warranto* inquiries of 1684, which affected the composition of parliament and ended in surrenders and re-grants of Company Charters, had less effect upon the public functions of the Companies than might have been expected. They were already mostly declining into convivial and charitable bodies.

Livery and Common Hall. Common Hall, the assembly of the London liverymen had important functions which in 1996 still included the election of the Lord Mayor and the Chamberlain. The company charters by laying down the number of liverymen in each company controlled their respective voting strengths in Common Hall. Votes were counted by companies in order of precedence, and a particular trend among the companies at the head of the queue, most of whose members were employers or merchants, would decisively influence the rest. The following list shows the precedence.

Great Companies		Existing	Chartered
1. Mercers		1172	1393
2. Grocers		1315	1428
3. Drapers		1180	1365
4. Fishmongers		1321	1384
5. Goldsmiths		1180	1327
6. Skinners		1272	1327
7. Merchant Taylors		1267	1328
8. Haberdashers		1372	1448
9. Salters		–	Edward III
10. Ironmongers		1364	1463
11-12. Vintners		1282	1437
12-11. Clothworkers		1480	1528

Lesser Companies		Existing	Chartered
13. Dyers		1188	1471
14. Brewers		1345	1438
15. Leather-sellers		1372	1444
16. Pewterers		1358	1473
17. Barbers		1308	1462
18. Cutlers		1285	1416
19. Bakers		1155	1486
20. Waxchandlers		1358	1483
21. Tallowchandlers		1363	1462
22. Armourers and Braziers		Edward II	1453
23. Girdlers		1180	1448
24. Butchers		1180	1605
25. Saddlers		1216	1395
26. Carpenters		1333	1477
27. Cordwainers		1272	1439
28. Painter-Stainers		1466	1581
29. Curriers		1272	1606
30. Masons		1356	1677
31. Plumbers		1365	1611
32. Innholders	as Hostelers	1327	1515
33. Founders		1365	1614
34. Poulters		1345	1504
35. Cooks		1311	1482
36. Coopers		Edward II	1501
37. Tylers and Bricklayers		1502	1568
38. Bowyers		1488	1621
39. Fletchers		1371	None
40. Blacksmiths		1325	1571
41. Joiners		1309	1571
42. Weavers		before 1272	Henry I
43. Woolmen		?14th cent.	Unknown
44. Scriveners		1357	1617
45. Fruiterers		1416	1606
47. Stationers		?1403	1556
48. Broderers			1561
49. Upholders		14th cent	1626
50. Musicians	as Minstrels	1350	1604

		Existing	Chartered
51. Turners		1310	1604
52. Basket-makers		1422	?None
53. Glaziers		1328	1638
54. Horners		1376	1638
55. Farriers		1272	1645
56. Paviours		before 1479 (withdrawn)	1683
57. Lorimers		1260	1711
58. Apothecaries		1511	1617
59. Shipwrights		1456	1605
60. Spectacle-makers		?1628	1629
61. Clockmakers		1627	1631
62. Glovers		14th cent.	1638
63. *Combmakers*			*?1650*
64. Feltmakers		1180	1667
65. Framework Knitters		–	1657
66. *Silk-throwers*		–	*?1629*
67. [Silkmen]		–	–
68. *Pinmakers*		–	*?1636*
69. Needle-makers		Henry VIII	Common-wealth
70. Gardeners		1345	1605
71. [Soap-makers]		–	?1638
72. Tinplate Workers as Wiredrawers		1469	1670
73. Wheelwrights		–	1670
74. Distillers		–	1638
75. [Hatband-makers]		–	?1638
76. Patten-makers		14th cent.	1670
77. Glass-sellers		–	1664
78. *Tobacco-pipe Makers*		–	*1663*
79. Coach and Coach-Harness Makers		–	1677
80. Gunmakers		–	1638
81. Gold and Silver Wyre Drawers		1423	1623
82. *Longbow-string Makers*		–	–
83. Playing-card Makers		–	1628
84. Fan-makers		–	1709
85. [Woodmongers]		–	–
86. *Starchmakers*		–	*?1632*
87. *Fishermen*		–	*?1632*
*88. Parish Clerks		1233	1442
89. Carmen		1516	1524
90. *Porters*		–	–
*91. Watermen and Lightermen		Unknown	None
92. Surgeons		–	?1308
Not numbered { *Solicitors		1908	None
Master Mariners		1926	1930

* = no livery
Italics = extinct
The Vintners and the Cloth-workers took precedence over each other in alternate years.

LIVERY COS. OF LONDON IN IRELAND. In 1609 James I offered forfeited lands in the County of Derry to the City of London, which set up the IRISH SOCIETY to treat with the crown and deal with the matter. This body raised £60,000 from the Twelve major livery cos., some of which had minor cos. including the Poulters, Butchers, Joiners, Basketmakers, Musicians and Scriveners in partnership. The money was paid to the Crown, the Society was incorporated and the land conveyed to it. The Society divided the area into 12 parts of equal value for which the 12 companies drew lots and for which they paid, and sometimes still pay, a ground rent. They then set about colonising and improving the area. The Society's Charter was forfeited by Star Chamber decree under Charles I for non-performance of the Charter (*see* ULSTER CUSTOM) but restored in 1662. Some of the cos. sold out later, e.g. Merchant Taylors in 1727, the Goldsmiths in 1730, the Vintners in 1737 and the Haberdashers in 1741.

LIVINGSTONE. *See* NEW TOWNS.
LIVINGSTONE (1) Robert (1654-1728) migrated from Scotland to New York in 1673, married an heiress and acquired immense wealth and estates through the fur trade. He was the most powerful man in the colony. Of his grand-children **(2) William (1723-90)** commanded the New Jersey militia against the British in 1776 and was Gov. of the state from 1778 to 1790. **(3) Robert R. (1746-1813)**, helped to draft the U.S. Declaration of Independence and from 1781 to 1783 was U.S. Foreign Sec. From 1801 to 1804 he was Min. in Paris and negotiated the Louisiana Purchase.
LIVINGSTONE, Dr. David (1813-72) self educated, was sent by The London Missionary Society (L.M.S.) to the Cape in 1840. He explored the interior until 1843 and in 1849 discovered L. Ngami and followed the R. Zambezi far inland. In 1852 he started on his great exploration from the Cape, through west central Africa *via* Loanda

back to Quelimane which he reached in 1856. He then made a sensational return to England, published his travels, received high academic honours and quarrelled with the L.M.S. The govt. appointed him consul at Quelimane to enhance his status and thence he made further expeditions in E. and C. Africa, notably Ls Shirwa and Nyasa (1859). In 1864 he came home, published *The Zambezi and Its Tributaries* (1865) and returned to investigate the origins of the Nile. He reached L. Bangweolo in 1868 and Ujiji on L. Victoria in 1869 and, having travelled the neighbourhood in hardship and sickness, was found in 1871 by H.M. Stanley, an American journalist out for a scoop, who reputedly greeted him with the words "Dr. Livingstone, I presume." He died during further explorations among the source areas of the Nile.

LIVINGSTONE of CALLENDAR, Lowland Scots family. **(1) Sir Alexander (?-?1450)** was a leading politician of his day; in 1439 he compelled Q. Jane to surrender the young James II and Stirling Castle to him, but the Crichtons kidnapped the King to Edinburgh and it was not until 1443 that Livingstone, with the help of the E. of Douglas, recovered him. By 1449 he was Justiciary of Scotland but James, as his character and influence formed, regarded him as a danger to the state. In 1450 Livingstone was accordingly disgraced and executed. **(2) William (?-1592) 6th Ld. LIVINGSTONE (1553),** a supporter of Mary Q. of Scots, fought for her at Langside, went with her to England and acted as her agent there for some years. He and his son **(3) Alexander (?-1622) 7th Ld., 1st E. of LINLITHGOW (1600)** were rewarded for their faithfulness and Alexander became a Lord of the Bedchamber in 1580, one of Octavians in 1594, and a guardian of the P. Elizabeth from 1596 until the Union. A younger son **(4) James (?-1674) 1st E. of CALLANDER (1641),** though he accepted office with the Covenanters, was a supple minded politician who in fact favoured the King; he became lieut-gen. of the Engagers and fled to Holland when their venture failed. He was an active parliamentary royalist after the Restoration. His nephew **(5) George (1616-90), 3rd E. of LINLITHGOW (1655)** an anti-covenanting M.P. for Perthshire in 1654, became Lord Justice-Gen. in 1684, but was deprived at the Revolution. His son **(6) George (?-1652-95),** of similar opinions, tried to prevent the revolution but was nevertheless appointed to the Scots privy council in 1692.

LIVONIA or LIVLAND. See BALTIC-10 *and thereafter passim.*

LIVRE (Fr. = pound). The primary unit of the old French currency, divided, similarly to the English pound, into 20 *sous* of 12 *deniers* each, but there were two types of *livre,* the *livre tournois* (i.e. of St. Martin's at Tours) and the *livre parisis* (i.e. of Paris). The latter with its subdivisions stood at 5:4 in relation to the former, but was abolished in 1667. The *livre tournois* was always the commoner unit and often used in international trade and subsidy treaties; it generally stood at approximate parity with the pound sterling. In 1795 it was superseded at 80:81 by the *franc.*

LLAN (Welsh). The syllable in a Welsh place name initially signified a holy place or site (often pagan) and then the place of a church, and finally but not always the church building itself. It seldom stands alone, being usually qualified by a reference to a saint e.g. Llanbedr = St. Peter's.

LLANCARFAN (Glam.). See MISSIONARIES IN BRITAIN AND IRELAND-3.

LLANDAFF (Glam.), a bishopric close to Cardiff of controversial origins. The Norman Bp. Urban (r. 1107-1133/4), who had had at least one predecessor, built the cathedral. To define the diocesan boundaries (mainly against Hereford), to support episcopal claims over the monasteries and their dependent churches and to resist the primatial claims of St. Asaph and Canterbury, a collection, called *The Book of Llandaff* of saints' lives and early documents was made c. 1124-50. The lives, which

are mostly legendary present three 6th and 7th cent. saints as Abps. of Llandaff, and the documents, mostly forged, represent occasional *acta* of the bishops and gifts to the church. The forgeries are sometimes based on gifts to or by other churches. No Welshman was appointed to the see after 1323. Under the protection of the Clares it suffered little during the Welsh wars until the revolt of Owain Glyndyr, when the cathedral was damaged and the palace destroyed. The see was always poor and after the Reformation held *in commendam* with one of the rich canonries of Windsor.

LLANILLTYD FAWR or LLANTWIT MAJOR. *See* MISSIONARIES IN BRITAIN AND IRELAND-3.

LLEWELLYN, Martin (?1565-1634), the earliest British cartographer, drew charts of the sea from the C. of Good Hope to Japan and the west coast of New Guinea, probably as a member of the Dutchman Cornelis de Houtman's trading expedition in 1597-99.

LLEWELYN. *See* LLYWELYN.

LLOYD FAMILIES. Of the many, six stand out viz: **(1)** of **Bodidris** in Denbigh. These were prominent protestants under the Tudors and **Sir John (?-1606)** was a regular supporter and contact of Essex, for whom he recruited troops for Cadiz and Ireland, suffered Star Chamber proceedings and raised money for his revolt.

(2) of **Dolobran** in Montgomery (q.v.) **(3)** of **Leighton** in Montgomery, who were influential in that county from 1430 until about 1700. Of these **Humphrey** was one of the earliest Welsh M.P.s and **Sir Charles (?-1678)** was a strong local parliamentarian in the Civil War. **(4)** of **Maesyfelin** nr Lampeter, Cardigan. **Sir Marmaduke (1585-1650)** was King's Attorney for Wales and the Marches from 1614 to 1622 and then a Welsh judge. He and his son Francis (?- 1669) were both active royalists in Carmarthenshire. Another **Francis (1655-1704)** was M.P. for Ludlow from 1691 to 1695 and also a Welsh judge. In 1750 their properties passed to their relatives **(5)** of **Peterweil,** Cardiganshire. **John (?-1755)** was M.P. for the county from 1747. He was a friend and supporter of Henry Fox. His son **Herbert** was M.P. for Cardigan boroughs from 1761 to 1768. A man of imperious character and powerful presence, he led a number of riotous gatherings, and has remained a legend for deeds of violence. He committed suicide and so ended the line. **(6)** of **Rhiwaedog,** Merioneth. The family was established near Bala by 1395; it provided 13 sheriffs of the county between then and 1941, and was notable for the patronage and support which it gave, especially in the 16th and 17th cents. to wandering bards. At least 22 poets wrote poems to members of the family.

LLOYD FAMILY of Dolobran, Montgomery. This ancient Demetian family settled in Dolobran in 15th cent. and took the name in 16th. Two brothers **Charles (1637-98)** and **Thomas (1640-94)** became Quakers. Charles shared with William Penn the cost of a settlement in Pennsylvania; Thomas went there and in due course became Penn's deputy-gov. The descendants of Charles were Birmingham iron masters by 1733 and used their wealth to found Lloyds Bank and to campaign against slavery. **George Ambrose (1879-1941), 1st Ld. LLOYD of DOLOBRAN (1925)** was of this family. He was a special commissioner to inquire into British middle eastern trade in 1907 and became a Conservative M.P. in 1910. In World War I, however, his oriental contacts made him useful at the British middle eastern H.Q.s in dealing with the Arabs. In 1918 he became sec. of the British delegation to the Inter-allied Council, but was shortly afterwards appointed gov. of Bombay. He encountered great political and economic difficulties, but inaugurated the Bombay development scheme and the great Indus barrage. In 1925 he became High Commissioner in Egypt but was soon at loggerheads with the Foreign Office and Sir Austen Chamberlain, the Foreign Sec., who started negotiating behind his back. In

1929 the Labour Govt. forced him to resign. He, Winston Churchill and Ld. Salisbury now became outspoken critics of govt. policy on India, armaments and European policy. Consequently he was included in Churchill's 1940 cabinet as Colonial Sec. He died suddenly.

LLOYD GEORGE FUND was created mainly from the sale of honours during Lloyd George's prime ministerships, "to promote any political purpose approved by him". About £3M went to each of the parties in his coalition. In Nov. 1918 it bought the *Daily Chronicle* for £1M in order to get rid of its editor Robert Donald, who was sacked overnight. In Dec. 1923 it gave £160,000 towards Liberal election expenses: in Oct. 1924 only £50,000. In 1926 it sold the *Daily Chronicle* for £3M. In 1926 when Asquith resigned the leadership of the impecunious Liberal Party it elected Lloyd George. He paid them £300,000 in 1929. In 1935 it spent some £400,000 on unsuccessful Action Councils. Whether he appropriated any of the money is uncertain, but much was spent on entertainment and pretentious offices. *See* POLITICAL HONOURS SCRUTINY.

LLOYD GEORGE, David (born George) (1863-1945) E. LLOYD GEORGE of DWYFOR (1945) ("Ll-G"), Welsh solicitor **(1)** became Liberal M.P. for Caernarvon Boroughs in 1890. The Liberals were in opposition till 1892 and from 1895 until 1905 and he became a leading liberal figure by his fiery personality, Welsh nationalism and opportunist rhetorical gifts. He made his first mark by attacking, as inadequate, his own party's Welsh Disestablishment Bill in 1895 and he was the most eloquent opponent in 1902 of Balfour's Education Bill because it was proposed to finance Anglican Church schools from rates which in non-conformist areas would be paid by non-Anglicans. His speeches gave him great power in his party, and when, led by Sir Henry Campbell-Bannerman, it came to power, Ll-G had a cabinet post as Pres. of the Bd. of Trade (Dec. 1905).

(2) Most of this govt's bills were mutilated or thrown out by a partisan House of Lords but Ll-G managed to get badly needed legislation through by keeping to technical rather than political issues such as Merchant Shipping, Patents, a Census of Production and the creation of the Port of London Authority. He also settled a threatened railway strike. He was thus winning the respect due to a statesman rather than the following of a demagogue, yet strengthening the influence of the radical liberals whose ideas he articulated.

(3) This became obvious when Campbell-Bannerman fell ill, resigned and died (Feb-Apr. 1908) and his successor H.H. Asquith appointed Ll-G to succeed himself as Ch. of the Exch. and Winston Churchill to succeed Ll-G at the Bd. of Trade. The great constitutional storm of the ensuing three years began to gather momentum for, prompted by the liquor trade, the Lords rejected a very necessary Licensing Bill against the advice of the King and the votes of the ablest peers and bishops. (*See* PARLIAMENT BILL CRISIS.) In the ultimate defeat of the Lords Ll-G played the decisive roll, for his land value and undeveloped mineral duties in his 1909 budget required a valuation of all land, and the revelation of its often noble owners' wealth. The peers' resistance could be made to appear suspect, even sinister, and Ll-G's witty and rabble rousing oratory (*see* LIMEHOUSE SPEECH) against their rejection of his budget put them in a hopeless tactical position. When George V called a constitutional conference (June-Nov. 1910) of four representatives on each side to try to resolve the difficulties, it was natural to send Ll-G with Asquith, Augustine Birrell and the E. of Crewe. His position as a leading liberal seemed clear.

(4) His political stance (if not his convictions) at this time was that of any conventional liberal. He supported the aims of the suffragettes, sympathised with the poor and was prepared to tax the rich for their benefit, but preferred to raise the money by saving on armaments. Consistently with this he had been pro-Boer in the Boer

War and was to oppose entry into World War I. It was the pressure of German policy in 1909 and the need to build battleships which underlay his famous budget. It was German aggression which turned him into a war leader, but besides this he was village educated, a man of the people, one who enormously enjoyed demagoguery, the artistry of political manipulation – and the pleasures of the bed, and besides, he had connections with the new Lords of press vulgarity, particularly the unprincipled Ld. Northcliffe.

(5) It happened that Sir John French, C-in-C in France, fought three unsuccessful battles between Mar. and May 1915 and sought to excuse himself by complaining of a shortage of shells. Northcliffe set about whipping up a shells scandal which would sell his papers. It might drive Kitchener from office and sell even more. The Unionist opposition wanted to get rid of the Liberal free trade ministers, and meanwhile Ll-G was bringing the trade unions into the war effort (*see* TREASURY AGREEMENT). Shell production depended on manpower and required a dilution of labour, to which the unions had to be brought to agree. Ll-G seemed to know how. Thus when the shell scandal broke and became a political crisis as well as a demand for a Ministry of Munitions, Ll-G was obviously the man for the job. In Asquith's coalition (May 1915) he took the office. He made it brilliantly his own, developed a huge and successful organisation and became virtually the leader of the civilian war effort.

(6) There was an inherent contradiction in a liberal govt. committed to freedom of trade and behaviour, having to defend it by imposing the disciplines and restrictions of war. The Ministry of Munitions represented a negation of liberal principles and also an imposed social revolution, even if much of its work was done through negotiation. This did not worry Ll-G. He had acquired some favour with conservative protectionists who needed an apparatus to achieve their purposes. Ll-G's political allegiance had become nominal. He was on his own and though, or because, he was attractive to women he had few friends. His ambitious momentum had now to be maintained by tactical manoeuvres rather than statesmanship and by seizing opportunities presented by govt. conduct of the war, which in 1916 was going badly. This was the time of the B. of the Somme, of unrestricted U-boat warfare and the Dublin rebellion. In July he got himself transferred to the War Office.

(7) Liberals had reached a point of no return: they had either to abandon their principles or leave office or negotiate a peace. The public, however, wanted to win the war, and therefore a better war direction. Ll-G had provided the war materials and could manage the trade unions. By Nov. he had experience in the War Office, where Sir Wm. Robertson (C.I.G.S.) was keeping the war direction to himself. Ll-G claimed the direction and proposed a War Council of three with himself in the chair, intending this as a means of overruling Robertson, but Asquith insisted that the council should be subordinate to the Cabinet and that he, Asquith, should chair it. His supremacy had depended upon a tacit front bench agreement to avoid parliamentary controversy. Hence Ll-G with the nation at his back, confronted the front benches. The, especially Tory, backbenchers and Bonar Law now took a hand. Asquith's support crumbled. He accepted the War Council without consulting his liberal colleagues. When they found out, they angrily demanded a fight. Asquith changed his mind. Ll-G resigned. Asquith, believing that no alternative to himself could be found, made a tactical resignation. The King sent for Bonar Law who would form a govt. only with Asquith, but was in touch with Ll-G. Asquith pettishly refused. Bonar Law advised the King to send for Ll-G who gathered Labour, backbench Liberal and Tory support. Only the Liberal ex-ministers stayed out. He kissed hands (Dec. 1916).

(8) For the period Dec. 1916 to Oct. 1922 *see* LLOYD GEORGE'S WAR CABINET; LLOYD GEORGE'S COALITION GOVT; CHANAK INCIDENT; CARLTON CLUB MEETING; VERSAILLES SETTLEMENT.

(9) Forced by the Carlton Club Meeting to resign in Oct. 1922, Ll-G never held office again. As a man without a party, he was suspect to all parties. Known at Westminster as 'The Goat', he was the first prime minister for over a century to live openly with a mistress. His dealings in honours and the Lloyd-George Fund (q.v.) laid him open to plausible charges of corruption and dishonesty. He left office much richer than he entered it. He was a disloyal and unscrupulous colleague. Not surprisingly his qualities as a war leader were discounted with some relief when the crises were over. His influence after his resignation rested upon his Fund and little else. It was not enough.

LLOYD GEORGE'S COALITION GOVT. (Jan. 1919-Oct. 1922)

(1) The War Cabinet (*see next entry*) continued to exist at first, and consisted under Ll-G of Bonar Law, Curzon, George Barnes and Austen Chamberlain as Ch. of the Exch. 18 other "Cabinet Ministers in waiting" existed among whom the leading figures were A.J. Balfour Foreign Sec; Vist. Milner Colonial Sec; Winston Churchill Sec. for War and Air; C. Addison, Pres. of the Local Govt. Bd. (later Min. of Health); H.A.L. Fisher Pres. of the Bd. of Education; Edwin Montagu Sec. for India; Sir Robt. Home, Min. of Labour. In Oct. 1922 the full Cabinet of 22 began to operate as such and the War Cabinet disappeared. Balfour then became Ld. Pres. and Curzon Foreign Sec. In Jan. 1920 Barnes resigned. In Feb. 1921 Churchill became Colonial Sec. In Mar. 1921 Bonar Law retired; Chamberlain took his place and Stanley Baldwin became Pres. of the Bd. of Trade. In Apr. 1922 Montagu resigned and was replaced by Vist. Peel.

(2) The British part of this 'khaki' election (*see* COUPON ELECTION) which brought the govt. to power, had been fought round Ll-G with his enlightened legislative record to support his fame as a war leader. It was certain that whoever supported him and his coalition would win. Of such supporters 339 Unionists and 136 Liberals were returned as against 36 orthodox Liberals and 59 Labour. The Irish part was different. Sinn Fein swept the board and their 73 M.P.s, instead of coming to Westminster, proclaimed themselves the Dail of an Irish Republic in Dublin. As the Unionists had an unshakable absolute majority at Westminster, Ll-G might be their prisoner.

(3) The first task was peace. Three members of the War Cabinet, Ll-G, Bonar Law and Geo. Barnes with A.J. Balfour went to Paris with enormous staffs of diplomats and civil servants, while two, Curzon and Chamberlain, stayed in London. Hence the War Cabinet never met, the full Cabinet was not summoned and Ll-G settled every important matter, and not only peace but domestic reconstruction and Irish and Imperial issues. In Paris, however, he had to contend with the other three members of the Big Four (Wilson, Clemenceau and Orlando). He hoped to keep his potential gaolers quiet (as well as at a physical distance) by achievements, or decisions which could be represented as achievements for which he could claim personal credit, but his habitual opportunism and improvisations were tinged with an arbitrariness which his war successes and world stature turned towards arrogance. He listened decreasingly to home, especially Unionist, opinion and was not always well informed, especially, and surprisingly for a Welshman, on coal, the fundamental commodity of industrial power. He eventually permitted a settlement of the Silesian coal mines without knowing exactly where they were, and by allowing the French cheap coal from the Ruhr, ruined S. Wales.

(4) Ll-G and his supporters began to be estranged for

reasons of external policy which were creditable to him, but a post-war boom (with squalls) provisionally took the edge out of controversy and enabled the enormous demobilising forces to get jobs. The Irish sidled quietly towards independence, while the statesmen at Paris debated the future of the world. War had brought territorial disintegration (Bulgaria apart) from the Red Sea and Persian Gulf to L. Constance, but debate focused too much on Germany because Clemenceau ("The Tiger") and the French were fear-stricken and vengeful. The Boche were to be made to pay (so-called Reparations) in cash, in territory, in military restrictions. They were to admit guilt for the war. Their representatives were made to wait till the treaty was ready, and were treated with brutal insolence. This attitude had its counterpart in the "Hang the Kaiser" agitation in Britain and Unionist pressure for a hard peace.

(5) Ll-G, with the ablest economists like J.M. Keynes, on the other hand favoured magnanimity and reconciliation. The Armistice had suspended only the fighting: the blockade, the prohibition on intercourse, travel, business and social contacts and the absence of diplomatic and consular exchanges continued. Thus the Allies and their press were ill-informed about the state of Germany. Two communist revolts in Berlin, others in Bremen and Bavaria, the widespread breakdowns of transport, food supply and power made no impact in Paris. If they had, it might have been easier to persuade the French that they had little to fear. Ll-G, then, had to seek other means to restrain them.

(6) In the cloudy and even worse informed idealism of the Americans, there figured a world organisation to end all war. The British fastened on this and, as a matter of priority, drafted the Covenant of the League of Nations, over which Pres. Wilson became enthusiastic. To Ll-G the League was to be a means of bringing the defeated back into comity; to the French, a further guarantee against Germany. To please them it was inserted into the Versailles Treaty with Germany. (*See* VERSAILLES, P. OF 1919-20.) The helpless German representatives were handed the document (June 1919) and ordered to sign it. Their distress is on record. Brockdorf-Rantzau refused to stand, and thus began the universal German repudiation before the ink was even on the paper. In the German world it was called *The Diktat*, to be defied no matter how. Peace, in German eyes, became war carried on by other means. This was an unsteady foundation for the League of Nations. The treaty came into force in Jan. 1920.

(7) The Unionists, who disliked but supported Ll-G., were confused. They were dully displeased with the break-up of imperial unity evidenced by the separate representation of the major colonies (now called Dominions) in Paris, and the rapid strides of the Irish towards Independence, and they did not yet grasp the advantages of Britain's new and powerful Levantine position, based on Egypt with Palestine, among Arab client rulers and the oilfields of S.E. and N.W. Iraq. They were more familiar with the old rich commerce with the Far East where, however, China was in turmoil. Turmoil also extended through Siberia and Russia, where the Revolution had reached an imperialist phase and was threatening the Versailles settlement through Poland and Hungary. In Britain there were strikes by railwaymen, transport workers and miners, which the govt. managed to encounter serially rather than simultaneously, and then, in the winter of 1920-1 the boom broke and unemployment soared. The Versailles settlement was widely criticised. The victorious statesmen were attacked for not bringing prosperity. There was general discontent and war weariness.

(8) With the ground quaking under its feet, the govt. saw a need to defend Europe against Communism, the Straits against the new Turkish nationalism and the Far

East against the Americans. The Allied Supreme War Council agreed to intervene in Russia, but because of demobilisation and trade union opposition, help for the anti-Communists had to be confined to torpedo-boat raids on Riga and Kronstadt, Gen. Dunsterville's occupation of Baku, and material, with some volunteers, for Gens. Denikin and Yudenich and Adm. Kolchak. In fact the Roumanians, having seized Transylvania as their reward for joining the Allies, marched on to Budapest in Aug. 1919 and expelled the Communist Govt. which had ruled there since Mar., and the Poles, by Pilsudski's victory over the Russians near Warsaw (Aug. 1920) established the short life of their republic. Communist military conquest was prevented without British help.

(9) The Far Eastern problem turned, so Ll-G thought, on outbuilding the U.S. Navy and, with Japanese help, resisting American penetration. He received a sharp slap in the face from Canada, which would not antagonise the Americans, and from Australia which already mistrusted the Japanese. The potential erosion of the British Far Eastern predominance had to be accepted with as little fuss as possible. The Washington Conference and Treaty (Nov. 1921- Feb. 1922) (q.v.) saved resources by restricting warship building among the five great powers, but was otherwise a face-saving device.

(10) The atmosphere of imperial and domestic decline was thickened by the outbreak of the Irish trouble on the doorstep and by difficulties in British India where, led by Mohandas Gandhi, the Indian National Congress was exploiting the Amritsar "massacre" (q.v.) (Apr. 1919) to move over to a programme of civil disobedience not unlike the practices growing in Ireland. The "recessional" had been predicted as far back as 1897 by Rudyard Kipling. It was due in the 1920s, locally specialised reasons apart, to the exhaustion, human, economic and moral caused by the War. The power and will to sustain a great dominance was no longer there, but people tended to blame the govt. because since 1914 a govt. had supposedly governed and was, therefore, responsible for failures.

(11) The T. of Sèvres (1920) with the Sultan at Istanbul had neutralised the straits under Allied garrisons and divided Asia Minor into French and Italian zones of influence while ceding a large province around Smyrna to Greeks. The Turkish nationalists under Mustapha Kemal (later Atatürk) built up a govt. and army at Ankara. The French and Italians read the signs, gave up their zones and made friends with him and he made an alliance with communist Russia. The Greeks, apart from British support, were isolated, and in Britain nobody but Ll-G supported them. Edwin Montagu resigned against his attitude. Mustapha attacked the Greeks, destroyed their army, took Smyrna amid massacres, and turned north to the Straits where a British garrison under Gen. Harington held Chanak on the Dardanelles. Ll-G wanted to fight and asked the Dominions for help. Dominion autonomy now became independence. Save for Newfoundland and New Zealand, the least considerable, they said 'no'. Harington was told to deliver an ultimatum to the Turks all the same. They did not intend to fight for what they knew that they could get by negotiation. The well informed Harington sensibly omitted to deliver it and within a fortnight the Turks agreed to respect the neutral zone pending peace negotiations (Pact of Mudania). The coalition govt. was less well informed than Gen. Harington. They hoped to catch a non-existent mood of public belligerence and renew their hold on the country in a Gen. election. The conservative M.P.s led by Bonar Law and Baldwin, in deciding to fight the election separately, ended the coalition and the Govt. Ll-G resigned. See CARLTON CLUB MEETING.

LLOYD GEORGE'S WAR CABINET (Dec. 1916-Oct. 1919). Originally 5 in Cabinet: under D. Lloyd George ("Ll-G"), Earl Curzon, Lord Pres; A. Bonar Law, Ch. of the Exch; Arthur Henderson and Vist. Milner, Mins. without Portfolio, to whom in June 1917 the S. African J. Smuts and in July Sir Edw. Carson were added. In Aug. George Barnes replaced Henderson. In Jan. 1918 Carson resigned. In Apr. Milner went to the War Office and was succeeded by Austen Chamberlain. Only Bonar Law had departmental duties. Maurice Hankey provided (for the first time) a secretariat from the Committee of Imperial Defence. It met about six days a week. (For a general account of the war see WORLD WAR I.)

(1) The war cabinet was intended as a means to enforce Ll-G's will to win the war. In practice the War Office and the Admiralty, being long established and controlling huge forces outside the Kingdom, became more not less independent because their ministers were not in the Cabinet. On the other hand the civilian backing for the warlike operations was easier to control. Traditional departments were simply given orders. The new Min. of Munitions and five additional ministries (shipping, food, food production, labour and national service) were created in parallel with them to administer an aptly named 'war socialism', run voluntarily by industrialists and landowners for patriotic reasons.

(2) External affairs, as always in a great war, dominated thought. It was necessary to devise an idealism whose dynamic or crusading zest would carry the nation to victory. It was essential however not to split the Allies by enunciating objectives which trenched on their particular aspirations, nor rob the idealism of its dynamic by admitting the possibility of mediation, as proposed by the American Pres. Wilson. Hence War Aims were expressed in terms of self-determination (a distant appeal to the American Rebellion) to be applied strictly in enemy territories only. The crusade was to redeem Jerusalem and free the vaguely defined Arabs from the Turks. By analogy the nationalities subject to the Habsburgs were to be liberated willy-nilly, and their empire dismantled. The Habsburg Italians were mentioned as fit for freedom, the Yugoslavs, at Italian prompting were not. The Americans were attracted. Jewish agencies, Arab rulers and Czechs seeking cheap Slovak food, climbed onto the bandwagon. It followed logically that Germany too must be forced to surrender and to give up non-German territories. These ideas sowed the seeds of most of the post-war disasters, but American enthusiasm and power germinated the seeds.

(3) Ll-G, who trusted every general but his own, meant to have a unified Allied war direction under a foreign C-in-C. At a conference in Rome (Jan 1917), which coincided with the resumption of the German U-boat offensive, he failed to persuade the powers to launch a combined offensive in Italy under Gen. Cadorna but was himself persuaded by Gen. Nivelle, the new French C-in-C, to back a scheme of his own. There were to be surprise ruptures of the western front at two pincer points 150 miles apart, and the destruction of the German forces in between. By surreptitious intrigues he placed Nivelle in command of the British as well as the French armies. Sir Wm. Robertson (the C.I.G.S.) threatened to resign. Gen. Haig (C-in-C) forced a right of appeal to the govt. and the appointment was limited to the operation itself. Apart from Ll-G and Nivelle every responsible British and French authority was against it, and wrangles, delays and inadequate security destroyed the element of surprise. The two attacks, made just after the Feb. (O.S.) Revolution in Russia, were located too far apart for mutual support. The result was disastrous. The Canadians took Vimy Ridge but lost twice as many men as the enemy (9-14 Apr. 1917). The French failed in Champagne (23-9 Apr.) with such losses that some of their armies mutinied. Russia was virtually if not formally out of the war, France was crippled until Gen. Pétain, Nivelle's successor (May) could restore order.

(4) The German onslaught on shipping also

threatened total defeat. Apart from the Grand Fleet and the colliers to France, ships still sailed without convoy and between Jan. and the end of Apr. (the month of Nivelle's disasters) 2M tons were sunk, 1.2M being British, while only 240,000 tons were built. The Admiralty alleged (with massaged figures) that convoys were statistically impossible and anyway that merchant captains could not keep station in them. On 30 Apr. Ll-G and Curzon went to the Admiralty and compelled it to institute convoys. The first sailed from Gibraltar on 10 May. Convoyed shipping eventually rose to 80% of the total, sinkings fell from 25% to 1%. This was Ll-G's greatest single wartime service. (*See* COMMERCE PROTECTION, NAVAL B-4.)

(5) The Nivelle failures left Haig free to propose a great Flanders offensive from Ypres, intended to cut off the Belgian coast and then roll up the German armies to the South-East. Service and ministerial opinion was sceptical but Haig argued the war cabinet down. The operation was launched on 31 July. Strategically promising, it was tactically catastrophic. By its last phase, known as Passchendaele (Nov.), a third of a million had died (as the October Revolution took place in Petrograd) swallowed in machine-gun dominated barbed wire and mud, before they ever reached open country. The mud had prevented the use of tanks. Haig now decided to try them. The tank command chose hard ground at Cambrai and on 20 Nov. burst through into the open in six hours. The infantry for the follow-up was not available. The Germans re-closed the gap.

(6) The Russian Feb. (O.S.) Revolution had been casting its shadow. In May Arthur Henderson visited Russia. The Independent Labour Party and the (Marxist) British Socialists set up a United Socialist Council which organised a grand conference at Leeds for June. Henderson returned convinced that Labour should send delegates to a conference of Allied, neutral and enemy socialist parties in Stockholm. He carried the Labour Party Conference in this sense. The seamen refused to transport the delegates, and in Aug. Henderson was driven from the War Cabinet. He swore never again to join a govt. in which Labour did not predominate. Thus, before the Oct. Revolution, he set about creating an effective national organisation with constituency associations, a party programme written by Sidney Webb and even a foreign policy. At the Oct. Revolution (Nov.) the Bolsheviks signed an armistice with Germany. These events and murderous Bolshevik violence established the Labour Party and its moderation.

(7) Some light now appeared in the gloom. In Mar. 1917 British troops had taken Baghdad. By mid-year the Turks had been driven from the Hejaz. In Nov. with some confidence, Balfour promised the Jews a home in Palestine. In Dec. Allenby entered Jerusalem. Turkey was obviously going down hill. Ll-G got rid of Robertson in order to enforce his belief that the Central Powers might be overthrown from a flank. Before he could do anything the German March 21 offensive blew the western front apart. Two days later Ll-G intervened at the War Office and put the machinery into high gear. The reserve (120,000 men) and the men on leave (88,000) were got over to France in a week and meanwhile he telegraphed Pres. Wilson for the use of American troops, and raised the issue of Irish conscription.

(8) In Feb. 1918 Ll-G had set up a ministry of information under Beaverbrook, ostensibly to influence overseas opinion and shake German morale. Almost accidentally, it committed Britain in foreign eyes to self-determination because there was little else to say. At this time the convention which had been trying to find solutions at the Irish question, reported failure, and political opinion at Westminster and Dublin was against Irish conscription. Ll-G proposed a new solution. Conscription was to be brought in (to fend off the

Unionists), but only when (to please the Irish) Ireland received Home Rule. This was the first great occasion when the Welsh Wizard's statesmanship was seen to be tricky. Either British conscription would be a major derogation from Home Rule inconsistent with Irish self-determination: or a true Home Rule Govt. would never enforce British conscription. In hoping to attract both sides, he repelled both. This was the moment when his political credit began to decline. It was marked by spectacular events. At the height of the Western Front crisis the Irish Nationalist M.P.s seceded from the Commons and joined up with Sinn Fein. The Irish R. Catholic Church, hitherto politically disengaged, pronounced for resistance to conscription. That very Sunday all the congregations at Mass swore to resist it. On 23 Apr. a one-day strike closed everything save in Belfast. The Govt., alleging a German plot, arrested the leading Sinn Feiners, instituted military rule and withdrew the combined proposals. The Irish remained unshaken. They had seceded in their hearts. It remained only to make secession a physical reality.

(9) Within a fortnight Ll-G had a paradoxical parliamentary triumph in the 'Maurice Debate'. Sir Frederick Maurice (Director of Operations at the War Office) had publicly accused him of lying to the Commons about British strength in France. Asquith challenged a debate and a division. Ll-G got his majority because the Unionists voted against Asquith, the Liberals split and the Irish had gone. The debate revealed the insecurity of a popularist leader without a party. His lease of power had become a tenancy at will.

(10) By the beginning of Aug. 1918 the German offensives were spent and their morale and that of their allies broken. The speed of their ensuing collapse did not take Ll-G and Bonar Law by surprise. They decided to maintain the coalition and hold a "khaki" election. George V, who had duties to all his subjects, was understandably reluctant to dissolve parliament in the interests of party chicanery, but the case for dissolution was strong on its merits. Parliament had outlasted its statutory term by three years and franchise reform had created a large electorate which had never voted before. Parliament was dissolved in Dec. *See* COUPON ELECTION.

LLOYD, (John) Selwyn (Brooke) (1904-78) Ld. SELWYN-LLOYD (1976). (1) Methodist Cheshireman educated in Scotland, stood for parliament unsuccessfully as a Liberal in 1929, but was converted to protectionism by the 1929 slump. Called to the bar in 1930, he served on the Hoylake Urban District Council and became its chairman in 1936. He joined the army as a gunner in 1939 and rose to brigadier on the General Staff by 1944. From 1945 he was Tory M.P. for the Wirral. As a member of the Beveridge Committee on broadcasting he advocated, in a minority report (1951), competitive television financed by advertising.

(2) In the Churchill govt. of 1951 he became Anthony Eden's Min. of State at the Foreign Office. He negotiated the Sudan independence agreement and the military withdrawal from Egypt and during Eden's absences and illnesses he was in charge of the Office. Hence Churchill promoted him Min. of Supply in Oct. When Eden succeeded Churchill (Apr. 1955) Lloyd entered the Cabinet first as Min. of Defence and in Dec. 1955 as Foreign Sec.

(3) Very soon he faced the Suez crisis when the Egyptians seized the canal. He got 18 of the 22 user countries to agree to a new regime under Egyptian sovereignty, and a mission was sent to Cairo. It was stultified by Pres. Eisenhower's sudden hostility. Lloyd then proposed reference to the Security Council but the U.S. insisted that their eventually abortive Canal Users Association should be tried first. Meanwhile the French and Israelis were entering into secret military collusion, to which on 16 Oct. Lloyd and Eden adhered at a meeting

at Sevres. The Israeli invasion began on 26th, and a bungled British intervention began on 5 Nov. but was called off the next day in the face of Russian military and U.S. economic threats. As Eden took responsibility and was blamed by the public for the debacle, his resignation did Lloyd no harm, and as Foreign Sec. under Macmillan until July 1960 he, with Macmillan, was engaged in mending fences, particularly at discussions with the Americans at Bermuda (Mar. 1957) and with the Russians in Moscow in 1959, at the end of which he also opened the first negotiations for entry into the E.E.C.

(4) Lloyd's intellectual grasp of almost anything which came to his hand, had involved him in the foreign policy of economics. He now naturally accepted the Exchequer (July 1960) where he had to deal with rampant inflation. His solution was a "pay pause followed by public sector increases not exceeding 2½%. There was an outcry focused on the conscientious services such as nursing and teaching where pay had always lagged behind. He also set up the National Economic Development Council, but meanwhile there was trouble in local and by-elections. The problems for a Tory running a socialist-created machine were virtually insoluble. Suddenly, in the "Night of Long Knives" Macmillan dismissed a third of his Cabinet including Lloyd. The event created deep scars.

(5) Lloyd now conducted a nationwide inquiry into the Tory party which gave him wide contacts among the rank and file. When Macmillan resigned in Oct. 1963, Lloyd's influence tipped the scale in favour of the E. of Home who disclaimed his peerage to succeed Macmillan. He and Lloyd were friends and Lloyd returned to the govt. as Leader of the Commons until 1964, and after the defeat of that year he remained a Tory front bencher until 1966. He then, while retaining his seat, spent the next five years in business.

(6) In 1971, against some opposition which contended that his political record would make him less than impartial, he was elected Speaker. He rapidly established the opposite and took pains to give fair openings to all points of view. Naturally he was criticised for over-countenancing parliamentary exhibitionists. He retired in 1976.

LLOYDS. See INSURANCE.

LLOYDS BANK, originated in Taylor and Lloyds banking partnership in 1765. This operated mostly in the midlands. It became a joint stock bank in 1865, changed its name to Lloyds, Barnetts and Bosanquets in 1884, and settled on the present name in 1889, by which time it had moved to London. See LLOYD FAMILY OF DOLOBRAN.

LLOYD'S PATRIOTIC FUND. In 1782 £6,000 was raised at Lloyds for the widows and orphans of the *Royal George*, in 1794 £21,281 for widows, orphans and wounded arising out of the Glorious First of June. Further subscriptions were raised in 1797 (Bs. of C. St. Vincent and Camperdown), 1798 (The Nile) and 1801 (Copenhagen). The fund was incorporated in 1803 and £123,000 was collected in one day at services held all over the country in thanksgiving for Trafalgar.

LLYWELLYN ap IORWERTH or Llywelyn Fawr (The Great). See GWYNEDD-27.

LLYWELYN (II) ap GRUFFUDD. See GWYNEDD)-29.

LLYWELYN ap SEISYLL. See DEHEUBARTH; GWYNEDD-18.

LLYN CERRIG BACH (Anglesey). A lake into which, between c. 150 B.C. and the Roman conquest of Anglesey in A.D. 61, sacrificial offerings were thrown. A huge quantity of cauldrons, chariot parts, chains, slave collars, and weapons have been recovered.

LOANS, FORCED. In the late 14th and most of the 15th cents. the Crown sometimes raised compulsory loans from wealthier subjects, particularly Richard II in 1396-9; Henry V and VI to pay for French wars and Richard III to meet the cost of preparations against Henry of Richmond. Considerable amounts were levied: some £14,000 in

1435-49, and perhaps £29,000 under Richard III. It seems that, at any rate in intention they were raised, like modern Exchequer bills, in anticipation of revenue and repaid when the proceeds of a tax were received. Occasionally they were not repaid, especially if a change of monarch had intervened. The Petition of Right (1627) hopefully if inaccurately cites Acts of Edward III and Richard II against forced loans, and of Richard III against benevolences, but then declares them illegal without parliamentary consent. A speculative tax assessment is in effect a statutory forced loan.

LOAN SOCIETIES originally represented a kind of philanthropy. Well disposed people pooled and invested funds so that money could be lent in small amounts at low rates to the poor. The movement began during the depression after the Napoleonic Wars and the societies were, subject to conditions, protected by statute in 1835. Loans were limited to £15. This limit was still in force in 1980.

LOANGO (S.W. Africa), an important source of slaves for America in 17th and 18th cents., was divided between France, Portugal and the Congo by the Berlin Conf. of 1885.

LO-BENGULA (1833-94). See MA-TABELE.

LOBITO BAY (Angola). Good harbour and terminal of the Benguela Rly.

LOCAL ADMINISTRATION – ENGLAND AND WALES. (A) Before 1888 (1) Local administration, as distinct from feudalism, was based upon the ancient Counties, but began to emerge as part of a modern state system only with the appointment of justices of the peace to keep order in 14th cent. The key event in England is the dissolution of the monasteries (1527-29) which dislocated the system of unemployment relief. In 1550 the Swiss protestant states adopted the principle of poor relief by the parish of the pauper's birth; the English statute of 1600 which required Overseers of the Poor to be appointed in each parish and authorised the levy of rates to defray their expenses, adopted the same principle. Henceforth until 1888 the country was locally administered by parish assemblies called VESTRIES which appointed the parochial officials namely the Overseers, the Guardians and the Churchwardens, and these in varying combinations administered functions and funds under the general supervision of the Justices in Quarter Sessions.

(2) This simple picture was, however, immensely complicated by fragmentation, historical accidents, local franchises, charters and local enactments. In mid-18th cent. there were, e.g. about 13,000 vestries and at least 700 places forming no part of the system at all. Many areas had special commissions of the peace of their own. The boroughs had charters exempting them in varying degrees and these charters conferred different and widely varying constitutions and privileges. Moreover, the technical developments of the 18th cent. and the growth of the towns led to demands for unforeseen improvements and to the setting up of Select Vestries, Local Boards and Commissioners for lighting, cemeteries, paving, sewerage and improvements. The powers of these bodies varied and their boundaries ignored existing administrative geography.

(3) The Municipal Corporations Act, 1834, converted the boroughs into Local Authorities with elected councils (*see* below under 1888-1974). The Poor Relief Act of 1835 authorised the amalgamation of parishes for poor law purposes into Unions for which proper poor houses were to be built. These enactments did something to reduce the numbers of bodies and increase their efficiency, but did little to reduce the confusion, which was in due course increased again by the need for sewerage. The Public Health Act, 1875 extended throughout the country a system of urban and rural sanitary districts which had, as before, been growing up under local or locally applied

enactments. These became the basis of the urban and rural district councils.

(B) 1888-1974 (4) Local administration was carried on by four types of bodies, namely: (i) local branches of central ministries; (ii) (later) local sub-managements of nationalised industries (coal, electricity, gas, public transport and the post office); (iii) specialist authorities such as the police and water conservation; and (iv) the system of **Local Government** described below. The phrase 'local government' came to mean that diminishing part of the local administration conducted through elected councils.

(5) Outside London there were six types of councils, namely, parish, rural district, urban district, municipal borough, administrative county and county borough councils. Councillors were elected for three years: in boroughs annually by thirds: in counties and parishes triennially *en bloc*. In districts it was possible to have one system or the other. In addition, the councillors of counties and boroughs elected aldermen. Their number was one-third of the number of councillors and they held office for six years, half retiring at three-yearly intervals. Otherwise they had the same rights as councillors. The annually elected Chairman of the borough council was called the mayor, or in a famous or large place the Lord Mayor. The presiding officers and aldermen had to be qualified as, but did not need to be, councillors.

(6) On the eve of the 1974 reforms there were 83 county boroughs with populations ranging between 1.1M and 33,000. These were surrounded by administrative counties but were not part of them. The County populations varied from 19,000 to over 2 million. Within the 58 counties there were 259 boroughs and 522 urban districts; their populations varied from 120,000 to 500; save where several of them were clustered together they were embedded in, but were not part of the 469 rural districts, which covered 90% of the area of most counties, and had populations of between 106,000 and 1,500. Every rural district was divided into parishes. There were 10,000 of them. Their populations varied from nil to 34,000, and only the 7,600 larger ones had parish councils.

(7) A council had only those powers specified by statute. The relationship between the different types of authority was therefore one of specialisation, depending upon the powers deemed by parliament to be appropriate to its type, and not upon any hierarchical principle: each authority was in theory free within the ambit of its own powers to make what decisions it liked. In practice this legal freedom was restricted by the need after 1947 to get consents from the planning authority for most works of importance, but in certain planning cases there was a right of appeal to the govt. which could also publicly inquire into complaints. Moreover, govt. sanction was required to borrow money and sell land.

(8) Councils were kept within the law by a system of public audit and in the last resort could be restrained from overstepping their powers by the courts.

(9) Disregarding a few exceptions (such as the unclassified roads in urban districts and municipal boroughs) local govt. functions could be grouped into parish, rural district and county functions. In urban districts and boroughs (which contained no parishes) the council exercised the combined functions of the parish and the rural district. In county boroughs (which contained neither districts nor parishes) the council exercised all three types. The following is the threefold grouping: *Parish functions.* Allotments, burial and cremation, halls and meeting places, facilities for exercise and recreation, public lighting, footpaths. *Rural District Functions.* Aerodromes, civic restaurants, entertainment, housing, markets, refuse and sewerage. *County functions.* Welfare of children, old people, the physically handicapped and the infirm; primary, secondary, further

education and libraries; animal diseases; fire; consumer protection; public health; highways (other than trunk and motorways); vehicle registration; smallholdings; and, most important of all, land-use planning. County Councils often delegated functions or parts of them to district and non-county councils.

(C) Finance (10) The councils since World War II had been financed in roughly equal proportions by Treasury grants, loans, rents and rates, but the grant element tended to rise. Grants and loans were wholly controlled by the govt., which also partly controlled rents. The **Rate** was the only local tax. The total expenditure of the councils in 1966-67 was £5,032M., of which £1411M was on capital account.

(11) The system had been criticised since 1943, and by 1994 no fewer than six commissions had investigated it. The *Local Govt. Boundary Commission* of 1947 found that it could not safely alter boundaries without having powers over the distribution of functions and finance. Its request for these powers led to its dissolution in 1952. The two *Local Govt. Commissions* for England and for Wales of 1958 had powers to deal with these matters in certain conurbations but had to work under so many procedural safeguards that by 1966 significant territorial changes had been made only in the Fens, Birmingham and Tyneside and in only one county (Salop) had the districts and parishes been reorganised. In 1966 the Commission was replaced by Ld. Redcliffe-Maud's Royal Commission on Local Govt., which could only make recommendations. Its sensational report (June 1969) recommended that all local authorities except parishes should be replaced by a uniform system of so-called **unitary** authorities, on average smaller than counties but exercising all the functions of the previous county and district authorities, and that these powerful bodies should be supported by "Local councils" representing communities, with power at their discretion to do what was needed for their people. The change of govt. in 1970 caused an abandonment of these recommendations which turned out to be temporary.

(12) The Conservative 1972 Local Govt. Act came into force in 1974. It amalgamated county borough areas into counties and these, with the other boroughs and districts were formed into enlarged non-metropolitan districts whose councils acquired enhanced functions. In England three new counties (Avon Humberside and I. of Wight) were created but the total number was reduced by mergers to 45 outside London, including six metropolitan counties for the urban agglomerations. Welsh counties were reduced to eight. Small boroughs and districts became parishes or, in Wales, communities. Demographic changes caused these smaller units to increase slowly to 8000 in 1993. Following these changes, central govt. despite protestations to the contrary increased its interference, particularly by controlling expenditure and by removing functions and handing them to specialised bodies concerned, e.g. with water, sewerage and education. The Thatcher govt., being at variance with the left wing Greater London Council (G.L.C.), abolished all the metropolitan county councils including the G.L.C. (Apr. 1986). In 1988 it abolished the Rate and substituted a Community Charge (dubbed a Poll Tax by the opposition) which caused riots and payment strikes through which over £1000M remained uncollected in 1993. In that year it substituted a council tax which was remarkable for the dilatoriness with which valuation appeals were settled. Moreover it set up other Local Govt. Commissions for England (1993) and for Wales (1994) to substitute Redcliffe-Maud's unitary authorities for its own creation of 1972, and these began to operate in 1996-7.

LOCAL GOVT. ACT, 1898 (Ir.) vested Irish local govt. in elected councils similar (except for parish councils) to those in England.

LOCAL GOVERNMENT and LOCAL GOVERNMENT COMMISSIONS. *See* LOCAL ADMINISTRATION.

***LOCAL GOVT. BOARD v. ARLIDGE* (1915).** The House of Lords held that those whose duty it is to decide an administrative appeal must act judicially, but not necessarily that they must conduct their proceedings in the same manner as a court of law. So long as they act in good faith and listen to both sides, they may discover the facts in their own way. *See* NATURAL JUSTICE.

LOCAL GOVERNMENT, SCOTLAND. (A) (1890-1975). In 1890 the powers exercised by Commissioners of Supply, the Justices and the Road Trustees in counties were mostly transferred to county councils. An Act 1894 established a Local Govt. Board for Scotland and a parish council in every parish, mainly to administer the Poor Law and in addition powers similar to those of parish councils in England. In 1919 there were 869 of them. The functions of the Board passed to the new Scottish Board of Health and thence in 1928 to the new Dept of the Sec. of State for Scotland. In 1962 the Scottish Development Dept took over responsibility for local govt. affairs, and the Home and Health Dept responsibility for "social" services e.g. Health, police and fire.

Each burgh had a town council consisting of a provost or Lord Provost, bailies and councillors. The provost presided and held office for three years. Bailies were selected by the councillors from among their own number; they acted as magistrates in police courts. There were three principal kinds of burghs, numbering altogether 201: **(1)** royal burghs, i.e. burghs created by royal charter; **(2)** parliamentary burghs, which had statutory constitutions almost identical with those of the royal burghs; **(3)** police burghs, constituted under general Police Acts. "Police" in this context means "public improvement". Burghs were classified according to functions as counties of cities; **(4)** other large burghs (21) and small burghs (176). In 1929 the parish councils were abolished and their functions transferred to counties and large boroughs, but partly elected district councils were established for the rural parts of counties. These had only minor powers and very limited spending rights. In 1948 the Poor Law was repealed and responsibility for aid to the needy was moved to the Dept. of Health and Social Security; hence County Councils and large burghs had a duty to provide only residential and temporary accommodation for the aged and welfare services for the blind and the crippled.

(B) Since 1975. The previous system was entirely superseded by nine Regions divided into 53 districts all with councils. Of the Regions, Strathclyde contained nearly half the population. Special Island Councils were also created for the Western Is, Orkney and Zetland.

LOCAL OPTION, i.e. the right to decide locally what drinking facilities should be available, was introduced into Scotland in 1920. Septennial polls on Sunday opening hours were introduced in Wales in 1961.

LOCAL AND PUBLIC WORKS LOANS (P.W.L). The Public Health Act, 1875, set up a system of sanitary authorities (later district councils) which needed large amounts of capital. Acts of 1875 enacted a code of borrowing procedure by authorities able to levy or precept for a rate, and created under the Treasury, a Board of P.W.L. Commissioners through whom the authorities could borrow from the govt. Large sums were progressively made available to the Board, but most big authorities borrowed on the money market. Between 1945 and 1954 borrowing otherwise than from the Board was forbidden.

LOCAL GOVERNMENT BOUNDARY COMMISSION. *See* LOCAL ADMINISTRATION – ENGLAND AND WALES.

LOCAL SUBSIDIES (Ir). *See* ASSENT AND DISASSENT.

LOCARNO TREATIES (1925), ostensibly an attempt to supplement the defective peace keeping machinery of the League of Nations, consisted of arbitration agreements between Germany and, respectively, Belgium, France, Poland and Czechoslovakia (i.e. countries in possession of former German territories as a result of World War I) plus a treaty of mutual guarantee between Germany, Belgium, Britain, France and Italy. The arrangements were meant to satisfy the French demand for security and the British suspicion of undefined obligations. The structure depended upon the supremacy in Germany of liberal-minded parties willing to accept the Versailles territorial settlement, which the treaties were meant to bolster, but these parties were themselves fatally weakened by the ex-Allies contempt for Germans and their policy on reparations. The Nazi bid for power based, *inter alia*, on disguised *irredentism*, succeeded in 1933 and made denunciation inevitable. The pretext for denunciation was the Franco-Russian negotiations of 1936, but the purpose was to clear the way for the resumption of full German sovereignty in the Rhineland.

***LOCHLANNACH* (Irish = Northerners).** Vikings.

LOCHABER (Scot.), a mountainous refuge for the disaffected down to the end of the 17th cent. Since 1926, however, the scene of an immense hydro-electric scheme which, *inter alia*, has brought an aluminium processing industry to Fort William.

LOCHIEL. *See* CAMERON.

LOCKE, John (1632-1704), became Sec. to Lord Ashley (later Shaftesbury) in 1666 but pursued intellectual interests alongside his employer's tumultuous political business and began work on his famous *Essay Concerning Human Understanding* in 1671. From 1672 to 1675 he was Sec. to the Board of Trade, where he drafted a curious constitution for the Carolinas, but after Shaftesbury's fall he lived in France until 1679 and then in Holland from 1682 until 1689. It was here that he completed the *Essay*. It was published in 1690 and immediately followed by his *Civil Government*, generally regarded as the classical defence of the English revolution. From 1691 he lived with Sir Francis and Lady Masham near Epping. Here he wrote his *Second and Third Letters on Toleration* (1690 and 1692) and his still read *Thoughts on Education* (1693). The *Essay* has been a major element in academic philosophy ever since. The treatise on Civil Government, by formulating a theory of property, set out a base for individual liberties and much influenced the draftsmen of the U.S. Declaration of Independence and the Constitution of the U.S.A.

LOCKHART (1) Sir James (?-1674) Laird of Lee, a gentleman of Charles I's privy chamber, represented Lanarkshire in the Scots Parliaments of 1630 and 1633 when he was a Lord of the Articles. He again sat in Parliament in 1645, became a Lord of Session in 1646 but, having fought for the King in 1648, was deprived of office in 1649. He organised the levy of troops for Charles II's attempt in 1651, and was later imprisoned. In 1661 he was restored to office and from 1671 was Lord Justice Clerk. His son **(2) Sir William (1621-76)** commanded Lanark's royalist regiment in the Civil War; deserted to the Parliamentarians and became a Scots Commissioner of Justiciary in 1652. He was also M.P. for Lanark in 1653-8 and ambassador in Paris in 1656-8. He then commanded the capture of Dunkirk and became Gov. of it. In 1660 he was deprived of his offices but returned to diplomacy after 1671. His brother **(3) Sir George (?1630-89)** was also M.P. in the Protectorate Parliament in 1658 and 1659, and in the Scots. Parliament in 1681 and 1685, when he became Ld. Pres. of the Court of Session. In 1686 he also became a Commissioner of the Exchequer and a privy councillor. He was murdered by a dissatisfied litigant. He had two Jacobite sons **(4) George (1673-1731)** and **(5) Philip (?1690-1715).** George was M.P. for Edinburgh from 1702 to 1707, and 1708 to 1710, and for Wigton burghs from 1710 to 1715. Implicated in the rebellion of 1715 George was released for lack of evidence; Philip was shot. From 1717 George was the Pretender's confidential agent in Scotland until detected in 1727 and forced to flee. He was allowed to return in 1728 and was killed in a duel. His Papers on the *Affairs of Scotland* are a source of Jacobite history.

LOCOMOTIVES (1) STEAM. Richard Trevithick built a very awkward steam engine for a Welsh plateway in 1803 and John Blenkinsop a rack and wheel engine in 1812. George Stephenson's *Rocket,* which ran on the Stockton and Darlington railway in 1829, had all the essential elements viz: the multiple tube boiler, draught fire box and condenser. The pistons drove a single pair of large driving wheels. A pair of small wheels supported the driving platform. It was soon found that if an engine was to haul heavy weights at higher speeds, it would need a longer boiler for the additional power and more than one pair of driving wheels for adhesion. Driving wheels were increased to two, three, four (and in other countries five and six) pairs. The fire-box came to be carried on bogey wheels behind them: the forward elongation of the boiler usually on a two axle bogey in front. Despite better condensation, mainline engines had to carry several tons of water in a tender which also carried the coal. By the time that the railway system was fully developed locomotive designs were being adapted to the type of coal mined in the area of the company concerned: hence the differing silhouettes of the engines on the various systems. Steam engines might be fast and powerful, hauling trains for 700 passengers at speeds up to 100mph but they were thermally inefficient (94% loss) accelerated and decelerated slowly, needed constant maintenance and a permanent crew and their pounding motion damaged the rails.

(2) ELECTRIC GROUND RAILS. To combat these disadvantages, companies experimented with electricity. The first working electric locomotive was exhibited in Berlin in 1879. Switzerland and Italy had them in regular use by 1902. Such developments were retarded in Britain by the abundance of cheap coal and it was only the Southern Railway in 1929 which began to use electricity transmitted through ground rails, mainly in self-propelling sets of carriages rather than separate locomotives.

(3) DIESEL propulsion came in after World War II.

(4) OVERHEAD ELECTRICITY to supply self-propelled train-sets and goods engines came in the midlands in 1970s.

LOFOTEN (S. Norway) immense cod fishing centre since the 1850s. The British raided and destroyed the fish oil plants in Mar. and Dec. 1941.

LOFTUS (1) Adam (?1533-1605), a spectacular pluralist, became Abp. of Armagh in 1563, Dean of St. Patricks in 1565 and Abp. of Dublin in 1567. He was also Irish Lord Keeper from 1573 to 1576 and in 1579 and 1581 after which he was Lord Chancellor until his death. He assisted with the foundation of Trinity Coll. Dublin, of which he contrived to have himself made Provost in 1590. His nephew **(2) Adam (1568-1643) 1st Vist. LOFTUS of ELY (1622),** after a conventional legal career, became an Irish P.C. in 1608, an M.P. in 1613 and Irish Lord Chancellor in 1619. He was one of the Lords Justices (Regents) in 1629. A great-grandson of **(1), (3) Dudley (1619-95),** also a lawyer, was a distinguished orientalist.

LOG N-ENECH. The Irish equivalent of wergild. It was reckoned in cows, based upon the status of the injured man, and paid by the kin of the attacker. Cf *Sarhad* and *galanas, see* WELSH LAW (SOCIAL)-8.

LOLLARDY (1) John Wycliffe (?1329-84) of a Yorkshire landowning family was educated at Balliol College, Oxford and became Master of Canterbury Hall. He resigned when the hall was reformed in 1367 and obtained a series of livings ending, in 1374 by becoming vicar of Lutterworth. In fact he was an absentee until 1381 when he was forbidden Oxford, being employed in the Bruges negotiations on papal provision and reservation in 1374, and otherwise spending most of his

time at Oxford. He was thus well known both in intellectual and political circles.

(2) At Oxford he was a controversial philosopher, beginning with an attack on the fashionable nominalism of Duns Scotus and Occam. He then attracted political attention by his two books *De Dominio Divino* and *De Civili Dominio* (Divine and Civil Property) in which he argued that the right of property depended upon grace. Since the church was in an obviously sinful condition it should be disendowed, while anyone in a state of grace was entitled to it. The only guide to Christian action, which indicated a state of grace, was the Bible, which every humble man should be entitled to read and interpret for himself. Unsurprisingly Gregory XI condemned these doctrines in bulls of 1377. Wycliffe retaliated in *De Potestate Papae* (1379) (The Pope's Authority) by arguing that papal authority had no scriptural foundation and that the validity of his acts depended upon his moral character. This led to an attack upon transubstantiation, and other characteristics of doctrine and practice, including the invocation of saints, and pilgrimages, as well as pluralist and non-resident clergy (he was himself both). His most important practical measure at this time was to start translating the Bible. By now the Great Schism had begun and scandalised devout opinion as much as Papal pecuniary claims annoyed the propertied. Wycliffe became perhaps unintentionally, a figure in court politics.

(3) His and similar views were propagated by 'Poor Preachers' some of whom were unfrocked priests. Their combination of simplicity in doctrine and condemnation of a wealthy and unholy church spread quickly, especially in Kent and the Midlands. Many participants in the Peasants' Revolt (1381), which he did not incite, were attracted so that his doctrines were part of the revolutionary jargon of the time. The revolt had the effect of discrediting him with his courtier friends, while his academic friends condemned his heresies at the Blackfriars "Earthquake Synod" (1382). Thus in high places the tide mounted against him, but among ordinary people Lollardy, as Wyclifism was abusively called at the Synod (Dutch = mutterings), continued to spread, and he was never excommunicated.

(4) These processes continued after his death. The Statute *de haeretico comburendo* (on burning heretics) was passed against Lollardy in 1401; the burning of Wm. Sawtrey (?-1401) led to the recantation of most of the academic Lollards; the burning of Sir John Oldcastle in 1417, suppressed them at court, but popular Lollardy continued to spread until about 1450 when it slowly ebbed away.

(5) The doctrinal similarity of Lollardy and Lutheranism has led to a belief that there was a direct connection between the Lollards and the English Reformation. This is improbable, but Lollard ideas certainly survived in Central Europe (*see* BOHEMIA). In any case a controversialist intent on rooting out ecclesiastical abuses protected by the Pope was bound in the end to challenge the doctrinal basis of Papal authority and, in their turn, the central propositions upon which those doctrines rested. Circumstances and the violence of their opponents drove Wycliffe and Luther in the same fundamentally political and Erastian direction.

LOLLIUS URBICUS, QUINTUS. *See* BRITAIN ROMAN-14.

LOMBARDIC REPUBLIC. *See* FRANCO-AUSTRIAN WAR (1795-7)-3.

LOMBE, Sir Thomas (1685-1739) and his half-brother **John (1693-1722).** *See* SILK.

LONDON AIRPORT, from 1922 at Croydon, was already overused by 1939. During World War II there were military airfields (*inter alia*) at Heathrow and Gatwick and after the war these were converted to civil use. By 1969 aircraft were landing and taking off at an average of one a minute and generating traffic congestion on the ground. A third airport was proposed for Stansted or on the marshes of the Essex coast, but increasing size of aircraft and difficulties of air control, together with the financial contraction of the 1975 slump prevented progress. In 1985 the Stansted project was taken up again and a relatively modest but sophisticated airport operated there from 1989. London air traffic was also influenced by the creation of an airfield for the City in the Docklands, and the slow but steady increase of traffic at Luton.

LONDON BOROUGHS. *See* LONDON (GREATER) LOCAL GOVERNMENT.

LONDON BRIDGE was wooden from Roman times until 1209 when a stone bridge was completed. with a drawbridge between the 13th and 14th arches counting from the north, and a fortified gate at the Southwark shore, where criminals heads were exhibited. The piers soon had to be protected by piling filled with rubble, making the apertures narrow and the bridge a partial barrage which, save at slack high tide, prevented navigation for all save the most adventurous (and small) downstream boats. There was a chapel, many wooden houses and shops and a sufficient population for the bridge to be a ward of the City with its own alderman. In the 16th cent. barges with pumps worked by tide-paddles brought water up from the river. The houses were damaged in the Great Fire of 1666 and partly rebuilt, but all were removed in 1758. The alderman thenceforth was appointed by the Court of Aldermen from amongst themselves. The old bridge finally became unsafe as well as a bottleneck, and was replaced by a new arched structure a few yards to the west in 1831. By 1965 this too had become a bottleneck and it was sold to an American city and replaced by a three-arched concrete bridge completed in 1971.

LONDON CHARTERS 1327 granted by Q. Isabel and Mortimer, gave Southwark to the City. It forbade markets within seven leagues and confirmed the City's control over aliens. Its farm was reduced. It was freed from the prise of wine, and was henceforth to be taxed only with the rest of the Kingdom. No royal wardens were to be appointed in the future to take over the City Govt. *See* CONSTITUTIONS OF LONDON 1319.

LONDON, CITY AND VICINITY (pre 1550). (1) The Romans occupied pre-existing settlements, built the first bridge and, probably after the sack in Boadicea's rebellion (A.D. 60), fortified them. The position, at the lowest crossing of the biggest river with the best haven on the route from the North Sea to the Channel determined its future. The Roman walls long governed its form.

(2) The place, almost but not wholly, deserted after the collapse of Romano-Britain, had some prestige and probably markets in the 6th cent. when the E. Saxons took it. Gregory the Great meant it for the southern English archbishopric, but Mellitus, the first bishop (from 604) was bishop of the E. Saxons only. On the establishment of the Mercians' hegemony, they took London over (c. 770) until they in their turn fell before the Danes. From 871 to 886 Danish armies used it as a base. In 886, however, Alfred took it and ended two and a half centuries of disputed possession, which had retarded its development. He handed it over to his son-in-law Ethelred, earl of the Mercians.

(3) By 918, when Edward the Elder effectively united Mercia with Wessex, it had become English, yet cosmopolitan. Its population was big enough to be formidable. The Street pattern dates from this time. In 994 it repulsed K. Olaf Trygvasson and Swein Forkbeard. In 1013 it resisted Swein because K. Ethelred and Thorkil the Tall were there. Between 1014 and 1016 Ethelred made it the centre of his influence and when he died councillors, with London support, elected Edmund Ironside King against Canute, who had been acknowledged at Southampton. The city's economy had expanded. Wine was being imported in 1012. In 1017, of

Canute's great *gafol* of £82,500, London provided £10,500. Much of the prosperity came through Viking fur and slave traders. The Scandinavian influence is attested by six church dedications and, perhaps, by the glottal stops of the Old Cockney accent.

(4) After Canute died (1035) London was a power in the state. The Vikings were gradually replaced by Flemings (Cloth), Normans and Frenchmen (Wine), and especially Rhinelanders (linen, wine and oriental goods). There was a royal palace. The London shipmen assisted Harold Herefoot to the throne in preference to Harthacnut and the city constituted the popular backing for Edward the Confessor's successful claim in 1042. In 1052, however, they or a faction of them such as the *Cnihtengild,* helped to force a compromise upon the King during the fighting between his forces and Godwin's on the Thames. The Confessor then moved to Westminster, and thereafter concentrated much skill and finance on building the Abbey.

(5) Rural devastation, the threat of storm, bribes, and promises won the city to William I and made his coronation possible, but he took no chances. He built three castles within the walls. Gundulf's White Tower (of Caen stone), the core of the Tower, provided protection against seaborne attack at the eastern end and together with Baynard's Castle and Montfichet at the west controlled the population. All three survived the great city fires of 1077 and 1087. (*See* ST. PAULS CATHEDRAL.)

(6) William Rufus showed his interest in Westminster by adding the vast Hall to the palace there. Meanwhile London, though cosmopolitan, kept its English leaders to a proportion unknown elsewhere. It was a non-Norman, relatively free, commercial enclave of 20,000 people in a feudalised agricultural hamlet-society now duminated by a Franco-Norman aristocracy. Its leaders were commercial patricians based upon wards already defined by 1127. By 1130 it was electing its own sheriffs. Despite the set-back of another conflagration in 1133, Stephen in 1135 recognised as an established privilege the Londoners right to elect a King and they supported him powerfully until he was captured (1141). Negotiations between them (now organised as a *commune*) and Matilda broke down in tumult. She reinforced the notorious Geoffrey de Mandeville in the Tower; they prevented her coronation, for the Strand as far as Westminster was by now already mostly built up. Their well armed militia assisted Stephen as far away as Winchester and Faringdon (1145). Hence Henry II, learning from Matilda's errors, took care not to encroach upon their freedoms, and they supported him in most of his controversies.

(7) The London-Westminster-Southwark complex was developing a metropolitan character. The regular presence of the courts at Westminster was attracting professional men. Magnates were building town houses. Norman, Aquitainian and the new Mediterranean trade was activating the wharves. The great businessmen were making money and lending it not only in commerce but to the crown. A money market managed by the Jews, by financiers such as the Cades, and by the Knights Templar was growing up alongside the mints. Traffic was too heavy for the wooden bridge which was rebuilt in stone between 1170 and 1209. In the domestic crisis (1191) of Richard I's reign, the City helped to overthrow Longchamp. P. John and other magnates, by a charter, granted or recognised the commune. The activity of Henry fitz Ailwin, the first mayor (c. 1193 to 1212) in raising Richard I's ransom made the charter and mayoralty respectable, but they had to await final confirmation until Magna Carta (1215), when fitz Ailwin and his policy of co-operation with the crown were dead. Baynard's Castle was occupied by Robert fitz Walter, a major baronial leader.

(8) The City proper had now approximately attained its present boundaries, which are some distance outside the walls, and its area of about one square mile. One effect of Magna Carta was, indirectly, to incorporate these boundaries in the public law. Within them and under its shelter, apart from merchants and financiers there were other major interests. The rising population needed the catering crafts commemorated in The Shambles, Fish and Friday Streets, Vintry, Bread Street, and Milk St. St. Paul's Cathedral owned a brewery. The trade, however, also supported growing manufacturing crafts. The leather working lorimers, saddlers and cordwainers, essential to transport, settled together between St. Pauls and St. Mary le Bow; the Mercers and Drapers further east, the Goldsmiths nearby. These groups were developing guilds.

(9) Extreme overcrowding, partly created by the work centres, was compounded by church establishments which interrupted lay settlement. There were 104 parishes within the walls alone, each with its church, and St. Paul's had its walled close. Besides Westminster Abbey, there were too, the Collegiate sanctuary of St. Martins le Grand, the priories of Bermondsey, Southwark, Aldegate and St. Bartholomew's (with its hospital), several nunneries, several other hospitals and the great barracks, properties of the crusading orders. Friaries came later. The crown too, besides the Westminster palaces and the castles, owned the Wardrobe. The streets, in which pigs roamed, were unpaved. There were regulations, however, on the rearing of cattle in houses. In the 13th cent. serious and on the whole successful efforts were made to combat fire risks. The City Assize of Building required redevelopment of wooden thatched houses with stone and tile. This led to a rapid rise in the building crafts and in even greater overcrowding. Prosperity attracted country-born apprentices even from E. Anglia and the North. Despite the high death rate, the mid-14th cent. city population at 40,000 was three times that of the next biggest, York and Bristol. The populations of Westminster, Southwark and other suburbs is unknown.

(10) The City constitution was developing under property owning but commercial dynasties, which provided many of the aldermen and owned some of the aldermanries. These were mostly drapers and vintners with some goldsmiths, mercers and pepperers, much interrelated, e.g. in the period 1216-1263 eight inter-married families produced 45 aldermen. The oligarchy influenced wages and prices through banking, overseas trade and as employers, but differences with the growing bodies of craftsmen and retailers became increasingly marked. The main points of contention were taxation and purpresture. The crown levied its demands upon the City as a whole, leaving the city authorities to assess the actual amount upon the payers. A patrician who obtained an exemption shifted his burden to his less fortunate neighbours, and a patrician could often do so through his influence with the exchequer or upon the sheriffs whom he helped to elect. Purprestures, similarly, might be licensed to the inconvenience of the citizens, and this particular type of encroachment upon the public domain rankled whenever anybody happened to encounter it.

(11) Henry III's sustained efforts to constrict the city's power initiated two generations of turmoil and civic revolution. He tried to regain influence over the shrievalty (a royal and financial office). He demanded and eventually imposed tallages, and he capitalised on the rivalry with Westminster by granting a market to the abbot, who thus became entitled to close the city shops. He took the city into his own hand ten times between 1239 and 1257. The aldermen resisted with some success. In 1258, however, he found their weak spot. John Mansell, on his behalf, proposed to investigate aldermanic corruption by juries of presentment. The aldermen refused to co-operate, so Mansell summoned a Folkmoot to empanel the juries, and when the latter

made their presentments, further Folkmoots compelled the aldermen to answer and deposed some of them. Hence at the opening of the Barons' Wars the City was divided between some royalist aldermen supported by a mob, and a silenced but rich group of aldermen leading, as far as they could, the many useful craftsmen and lesser shopkeepers. These naturally gravitated to the baronial side. Furthermore, the crown's use of the Folkmoot destroyed the supremacy of the Court of Aldermen. When Henry's govt. collapsed, a mass meeting overrode it and accepted the Provisions of Oxford (July 1258). Hugh Bigod's eyre disregarded many local property customs upon which aldermanic claims were based. This disruption put the City into the hands of whomever seemed likely to hold the govt.: it was Monfortian by 1263. Its rioting apprentices had looted most of the Strand. It provided most of Montfort's infantry in the Lewes victory (1263).

(12) Large assemblies, especially if led by demagogue mayors such as a Walter Hervey, naturally encouraged craft guilds; they were chartered on a large scale after Lewes, but not discouraged by Montfort's defeat or, until 1270, by a period of royal wardenship. The leaders of this new trend were entrepreneurs seeking to control their (mostly Baltic) trade by institutional creation. They were fish and iron-mongers, skinners, dealers and workers in leather, that byproduct of agriculture, limited in amount, which preceded modern plastic, corders who dealt in rope, canvas, pitch and other maritime stores, and potters. These traded or went into partnership with Hansards, whose Steelyard, by 1266, had superseded the Rhinelanders' Guildhall, and who began to maintain Bishopsgate in 1282 (*see* HANSE). An important stabilising element was the Great Wardrobe, the Crown's purchasing agent, to which these partnerships resold.

(13) The earlier years of Edward I saw growing estrangement between the tumultuous, and lately corrupt Montfortian City and that tidy-minded but wily ruler, who, with his queen, had south European commercial interests and was in debt to Cahorsin and Italian bankers. City privileges obstructed his financial operations. Gascons and Italians began to replace Londoners in the greater royal financial posts. Royal officials penetrated to the aldermanries. In 1281 Henry le Waleys, a royalist mayor, instituted reforms which, beginning with acceptable police measures, trenched increasingly upon common urban privileges, particularly the interests of the victuallers. In 1284 the aldermen replaced him. In 1285 the King took the City once again into his hand and kept it until 1298. His wardens enforced policies hostile to the old patrician monopolistic order. By 1298 it had been practically overthrown.

(14) The local free trade from 1285 became a national system of unregulated trade under the *Carta Mercatoria* of 1303. The fall of the retail monopolies led to expansion and proliferation of crafts, such as barbers, brewers, carpenters, chandlers, coopers, and fruiterers. The chartering of such guilds made room for a new immigration. In the first years of Edward II new citizen enrolments were twice and thrice the annual average. The public assemblies were increasingly moved by new men. Moreover the Great Wardrobe was taking much of its custom elsewhere and causing confusion in the City economy. The attack by the magnates, transformed into the Lords Ordainers, upon the mishandled system of Edward I, was fed by xenophobia, itself the product of commercial factors. The City supported the Ordainers because Gascons were obstructing the finances of the Baltic trade. One of the major Ordinances (1310) abolished the *Carta Mercatoria* and restored the City franchises, while Richer de Refham the mayor, instituted administrative reforms. He, however, was overthrown and in 1311 the commonalty seized administrative control by dictating annual election of all executive officers. In

1312 they enacted that letters were not to be sealed nor aliens enrolled without their prior consent. In 1313 they were expelling Gascons and Italians. The domination of the commonalty by the crafts was, however, short, for it alarmed not only the aldermen but many pro-Lancastrian business interests. Thus the B. of Bannockburn (1314) had its effect in the City, for Lancaster's return to power brought conservatives and the new class of administrators into power in the City and this in its turn provoked a further reaction and compromise in the great Charters of 1319 known as The Constitutions. The primary concern of the effective city leaders was, until Edward III's assumption of power in 1337, to defend this position against all comers. The first assault was by way of an Eyre in 1321 which virtually suspended the Constitutions and committed the City to opposition to Edward II and the Despensers. Hence it offered its support to Isabel and Mortimer in return for concessions. The Charters of 1327 (q.v.) emancipated the City, but nothing else, from royal interference.

(15) The stabilisation of the City thus effected gave it the confidence necessary for an alliance with Edward III, whose bellicose policy it approved and helped to finance. Its activities were by now closely connected with the staple and once the Staple was established at Calais a systematic movement of shipping (outward wool, inward continental goods) developed. Calais was an outport of London: the mayors were sometimes simultaneously mayors of the Calais and Westminster Staples. The expansion which this facilitated was however abruptly checked by the Black Death which reached London in 1348 and recurred in 1361 and 1368; it was never fully suppressed and lingered on, with at least eleven other major outbreaks, into the 18th cent.

(16) Epidemics, French wars and the encroachment of cloth upon wool exports wrought important changes. Unskilled immigrants were replacing skilled residents. Mob rule threatened, during the period before the Peasants Revolt, to reverse the trend, so the great guilds secured a limitation of the ward franchise to liverymen (1374). This excluded not only unliveried guilds, but most of their own members, and, since livery was in the gift of the Court of Aldermen, it gave that body control over the composition of the electorate. It gave livery prestige, and permanently entangled the livery companies with the constitution. Not surprisingly the disfranchised mobs gave dangerous sympathy to the rebellious peasants, especially in the suburbs (1381). London remained disorderly until 1399 when the Lancastrian revolution engendered a compromise. The ward franchise was returned to the freemen, who should elect aldermen for life, and common councilmen in proportion to the number of freemen, annually. Sheriffs were to be elected by the Livery in Common Hall, who also were to offer two candidates for the mayoralty, of whom the Aldermen should select one.

(17) Though mayors were often mayors of the Calais and Westminster Staples too, they encouraged the cloth trade. The famous Richard Whittington established the London Cloth Market (1397) during his first mayoralties at Blackwell Hall, and as a mercer did much to further the interests of the Merchant Adventurers. Despite all setbacks, political, military and sanitary, prosperity grew. By 1419 there was a public water supply, and rudimentary paving and lighting. Nevertheless the concept of the mediaeval city as a trading and manufacturing state within the state was already out of date, and the guilds, at the moment when they became intimately enmeshed in the City's institutions, were ceasing to exercise their economic function. The future lay in mercantile and financial operations on the highroads of the world and in the treasuries of government.

(18) An indication of changing attitudes is to be found in the location of the population which, within the very limited City boundaries increased to only about 70,000 by Tudor times. Many people were living in the nucleated areas of Westminster and Southwark and in the roadside linear settlements of Clerkenwell, Islington, Hoxton, Shoreditch, Wapping and Whitechapel and in the liberties (see SANCTUARY) and connecting suburbs. These areas were beginning to be loosely considered as part of "London" though the City authorities had, save in Southwark, no jurisdiction over them. See other LONDON entries and LIVERY COMPANIES WESTMINSTER.

LONDON CLAY which is impermeable, underlies most of the London basin from Reading to the Essex Coast and is an important element in the London economy. It caps the artesian basin, is the cheap raw material for London stock bricks, used in building most of the houses in the 19th cent., forms good foundations for buildings and, being easily worked, facilitated the construction of the underground railway and sewerage network.

LONDON CO. See VIRGINIA.

LONDON CONVENTION (Feb. 1884) between Paul Kruger, Pres. of the Transvaal, and the E. of Derby revised the Pretoria Convention of 1881. The British abandoned suzerainty over the Transvaal, which changed its name to The South African Republic. The British veto on native legislation was abolished, the Resident became effectively a consul. All Europeans were to enjoy equal civil rights and taxation. There were to be no prohibitive tariffs or exclusions of British goods. The Republic could make treaties with the O.F.S. and neighbouring tribes, but with other states only with British approval.

LONDON CONVENTION, 1885. See EGYPT-13.

LONDON COUNTY COUNCIL. See LONDON (GREATER) LOCAL GOVT.

LONDON, DECLARATION OF (1909). See DECLARATIONS OF PARIS AND LONDON.

LONDON DEFENCES 1889-1906. In 1889 Gen. Hamley MP and Lord Wolseley (Adj-Gen), unsure that the R. Navy could prevent hostile landings, persuaded Edw. Stanley (Sec. of State for War) to create sets of linear defence positions comprising redoubts and trenches. There were 8 on the North Downs from Guildford to the Darenth Valley (Kent), and 4 north-about from Laindon (Essex) to North Weald, with a floating bridge near Tilbury protected down river by batteries. Volunteer units were to hold the systems, while the regulars fought the battles. Haldane had them dismantled in 1906.

LONDONDERRY. See STEWART.

LONDONDERRY, DERRY, CO. DERRY. Over the centuries a considerable settlement gathered round the port and the monastery which St. Columba founded in 546. Ostmen several times raided it, but it always recovered and the Abbot O'Brolchain, the first bishop, was able to build a cathedral in 1164. The town was granted to Richard de Burgh in 1311. The surrounding country was O'Neill territory but an understanding between the de Burghs and the O'Neills brought a fairly peaceful time, during which agriculture flourished, notably cattle, sheep, oats, barley, root crops, and linen for which the climate was suitable and which could be exported via the port. This lasted until the disastrous O'Neill insurrection of 1566; moreover the town was badly damaged by an accidental explosion and temporarily abandoned in 1568. The area now fell on evil days through civil disorder and intermittent rebellion, culminating in the forfeiture in 1609 of the O'Neill lands (i.e. most of the county) and the Jacobean Plantation. The lands were made over to the City of London, which created the Irish Society (q.v. and LIVERY COMPANIES OF LONDON IN IRELAND). This managed the City properties (principally Derry and Coleraine) as trustee, the rest being divided between the leading livery companies. The Irish were to be transported to Connaught and replaced by protestants, mostly of Scots and English origin. In practice many remained because of shortages of labour; but by 1633 (when the protestant cathedral was begun) the protestant immigrants were in a majority and the town was an important English stronghold. In 1688 it resisted a siege by the forces of James II. The relief and subsequent succours from London caused the change of name to Londonderry. Peace now supervened and the town developed a cottage linen and shirt making activity, which assumed an industrial character towards the end of the 19th cent. Later still various engineering industries arose, partly connected with the uses of the port as a naval station in World War I. As the southern Irish bases had been given up, this naval role became vital in World War II and the port was the principal British base in the B. of the Atlantic (q.v.).

LONDON DOCK STRIKE OF 1889, a landmark in British trade unionism, was the first successful large scale union action with unskilled workpeople, and was supported from Australia. See also SALISBURY'S SECOND GOVT.

LONDON HIBERNIAN SOCIETY (Ir.), protestant educational body, had, in 1825, 653 schools containing 61,000 children, mostly in Ulster.

LONDON (GREATER) LOCAL GOVT. (1) The metropolitan population explosion after 1800 caused a reappraisal of the local administration, beginning with the creation of the Metropolitan Police in 1829. In 1848 a Board of Sewers replaced eight commissions of sewers which dealt, in addition with flood protection. In 1855 some 300 authorities, mainly open and select vestries and commissioners for paving or lighting, were replaced by elective vestries for large parishes and local boards for groups of small ones. These new boards and vestries appointed the members of an overall Metropolitan Board of Works whose area was much smaller than the Metropolitan Police District. By the Local Govt. Act, 1888, the Board was superseded by a **London County Council (L.C.C.)** and in 1899 28 Metropolitan Boroughs replaced the vestries and local boards outside the City. In 1902 a Metropolitan Water Board superseded the water companies. The division of functions between the L.C.C. and the boroughs was different from that which obtained elsewhere (see LOCAL ADMINISTRATION − ENGLAND AND WALES-B). In particular the boroughs maintained the streets. This lasted until 1965 when the London Govt. Act, 1963, using the Metropolitan Police District (population 7.88M) as its base, abolished the L.C.C., the Middlesex County Council and the other authorities in London and Middlesex and created a **Greater London Council (G.L.C.)** for the whole area (except the City), an **Inner London Education Authority** to preserve the excellent educational system for the area of the old L.C.C., which was divided into 12 Inner London Boroughs without educational powers, and a ring of 16 outer London Boroughs with them. The other functions were differently divided between the G.L.C. and the boroughs; in particular, the G.L.C. dealt with large-scale planning, major roads, ambulance and fire services, refuse disposal and major sewerage.

(2) The City was in most respects independent of the surrounding system under both dispensations. It had an ancient constitution and powers respecting sanitation, police, bridges, justice, etc. and, in the investments represented by the City's Cash, an additional source of finance.

(3) Londoners elected majorities of old style Labour members to the G.L.C. and may not have foreseen that Kenneth Livingstone was far to the left of them when he secured control by a series of well-contrived votes. Thereafter the Labour majority pursued a generally Marxist or destabilising line. The Thatcher govt. accordingly abolished the electors' opportunities to turn them out by abolishing the G.L.C.

LONDON GROUP, of English post-impressionist painters associated with William Sickert (1860-1942), was founded in 1913.

LONDON LIBRARY, the largest subscription library in the world, was founded by Thos. Carlyle in 1841.

LONDON MISSIONARY SOCIETY. See CONGREGATIONALISM.

LONDON NAVAL TREATY. See NAVAL LIMITATION.

LONDON PROTOCOLS 1830. See GREECE; WELLINGTON ADMINISTRATION.

LONDON, SEE OF probably existed in later Roman times and ended with the Saxon conquest. When Pope Gregory I sent St. Augustine to convert the English, he intended that London should become, with York, one of two equal archbishoprics, but political conditions in Kent being better settled and propitious than London, Augustine established his see at Canterbury. This step proved justified in about 616 when his nominee to London was expelled and there was no subsequent bishop until 668. There was a second gap in the continuity during the last quarter of the 9th cent. under the Danes. The see was always a suffragan of Canterbury but there were three attempts to raise its status. In 798 K. Cenwulf of Mercia sought to secure his new archbishopric of Lichfield by transferring it to London. Pope Leo III quashed this in favour of Canterbury. In 1108 Bp. Robert and in 1169 Bp. Gilbert Foliot made short-lived initiatives but Abp. Becket's murder in 1170 effectively extinguished London's claims. It has, however, been recognised as the senior English diocese from 1072 at the latest. The seat of the bishopric was at St. Paul's Cathedral (q.v.) but the bishops made their residence at Fulham, where they owned the manor from 1141 to 1869. The considerable property was early divided between the bishop and the canons of St. Paul's, who were often absentee royal servants.

LONDON, SECRET T. of (1915) between Britain, France, Russia and Italy. See ITALY, KINGDOM OF-3.

LONDON STONE, possibly a Roman mile stone and then, conjecturally, a Saxon ceremonial stone, was originally on the south side of Cannon St. It was then built into the wall of St. Swithin's Church opposite. The church was bombed in 1940 and the stone was later built into the side of a Chinese bank.

LONDON, T. of (1604). See JAMES I AND VI, (1641) see CHARLES I.

LONDON ULTIMATUM (1921). See REPARATIONS.

LONDON UNIVERSITY. The earliest proposal for a London Univ. was made by Richard Mulcaster (?1530-1611) but the real impetus arose from dissenters, who were excluded from Oxford and Cambridge, and from disquiet at the state of medical education. Thos. Campbell and Henry Brougham raised funds for a non-sectarian college which, as Univ. College, was opened in Gower St., London in 1828. A rival Anglican college was opened as King's College in the Strand in 1831. As a result of agitation for a right to give degrees, a Univ. of London was chartered in 1836. This gave degrees but left teaching to the Colleges and any other bodies which it might recognise. By 1858 it was examining candidates residing in nearly 140 Colleges and Schools, some of them overseas. In 1858 the residential requirement was dropped and in 1878 degrees were made available to women. By 1885 there was an agitation for a teaching Univ. and the issues were examined by R. Commissions in 1889 and 1894. After much argument the London Univ. Act, 1898, brought six colleges, three theological colleges and 10 medical schools together as a teaching Univ. in 1900. Over the years many new institutes, colleges and schools have been added and the original ones are vastly expanded.

LONG, Walter Hume (1854-1924) 1st Vist. LONG of WRAXALL (1921) became a conservative M.P. in 1880 and as Parl. Sec. to the Local Government Board (L.G.B.) from 1886 to 1892 framed the Local Govt. Act, 1888 and piloted it through the Commons. He was in the cabinet as Pres. of the Board of Agriculture from 1895 to 1900 and made himself unpopular by his successful but ruthless antirabies measures. As Pres. of the L.G.B. from 1900 to 1905 he again made himself unpopular by creating the Metropolitan Water Board (1902). In 1905 he became Chief Sec. for Ireland and from 1906 to 1910 represented Dublin in the Commons. He established the Union Defence League in 1907. During World War I he was Pres. of the L.G.B. again from 1915 to 1916 and Colonial Sec. from 1916 to 1918.

LONGBOW. *See* ARCHERY.

LONGCHAMP, William of (?-1197) Bp. of ELY (1189), a Norman and worldly but probably weak civil servant became Chancellor to Richard I when D. of Aquitaine and helped to block peace negotiations initiated by William Marshal with K. Philip Augustus. On Richard's accession he became Chancellor of England and Keeper of the Tower. When Richard went on crusade he was left as joint Justiciar with Hugh, Bp. of Durham (Mar. 1190) but put his colleague in custody and forced him to resign. In June Clement III gave him a legatine commission. He was thus precariously supreme in state and church, but in difficulties because of the presence of P. John and his illegitimate half-brother Geoffrey. Longchamp's main concern was to defend Richard's interests (with which his own were bound up) against John's encroachments and violence. Interested yet plausible complaints about Longchamp's arbitrary conduct and arrogance reached the King at Messina in Feb. 1191 and he sent Walter, Abp. of Rouen to England to act as additional Justiciar. He found John at war with the govt. and arranged a short truce. This hopelessly undermined Longchamp's authority particularly over those magnates with whom John had tampered. In Oct. the bishops excommunicated him and a council of barons obliged him to surrender his castles and offices and leave the Kingdom. During visits to England in 1192 and 1193 he failed to recover even his diocese. Nevertheless he acted as the King's agent at home and with foreign rulers until Richard came home in 1194, notably in the matter of the King's ransom and in negotiations with K. Philip Augustus (1194) and the Emperor Henry VI (1195). In 1196 he went to Rome to appeal against an interdict imposed by Abp Walter but died at Poitiers on the way back.

LONGFORD. *See* PAKENHAM.

LONGFORD, TOWN and COUNTY (Ireland). The small town grew up round the bishopric and the county attached to it was by reason of its hills and marshes a sparsely populated farming area.

LONGESPÉE. *See* LONGSWORD.

LONG I. (U.S.). The W. end was settled by the Dutch in 1635; the E. by Connecticut puritans. The whole passed to New York colony in 1674.

LONGLEAT (Wilts.). Immense Renaissance mansion built between 1567 and 1580 for Sir John Thynne from whom it descended in the family of the Ms. of Bath until modern times.

LONG PARLIAMENT (1640-53 and 1659-60). *See* CHARLES I; COMMONWEALTH; PROTECTORATE; RESTORATION.

LONG SHIPS. *See* SHIPS, SAILING.

LONGSWORD (1) William (?-1226) E. of SALISBURY (1198), bastard of Henry II, traditionally by Fair Rosamond (Rosamond Clifford), was a military administrator. He was Lieut. of Aquitaine from 1202 to 1204, Warden of the Cinque Ports from 1204 to 1206 and warden of the Welsh Marches from 1208. He supported his half brother K. John, yet advised him to grant Magna Carta in 1215; but in the confusion after John's death he for a time supported the French but was persuaded to return to his allegiance in 1217 and took an active share in the subsequent pacifications notably against William de Forz (1220) and Falkes de Bréauté (1224). In 1225 he was Richard of Cornwall's adviser in Aquitaine. His son **(2) William (?1212-50) 2nd E.** went on crusade with Richard of Cornwall in 1240, accompanied Henry III to Aquitaine in

1242, and went crusading again in 1247. He died in Egypt. His brother **(3) Roger (?-1295)** was Bp. of Coventry and a supporter of Simon de Montfort.

LONSDALE and LONSDALE BELT. *See* LOWTHER.

'LOO', for WC, popularly derived from 'Waterloo' may be related to the Edinburgh housewife's cry *gardie loo* (Fr: *gardez l'eau* = mind the water) when emptying slops out of a window.

LOOS, B. of (Sept.-Oct. 1915) was a British offensive, largely using Territorial Army troops, in support of a French offensive in Artois. Both failed. Haig used gas, but the wind blew much of it back onto the British who, nevertheless, made a breakthrough but their reserves came up too late to exploit it and lost heavily against the German re-occupied trenches. Sir John Haig, the C-in-C, was replaced soon afterwards.

LOPES, Henry Charles (1828-99) 1st Ld. LUDLOW (1897) became a tory M.P. for Launceston in 1868, Q.C. in 1869 and M.P. for Frome in 1874. In 1876 he became a Judge and in 1885 a member of the Court of Appeal.

LOPES, Sir Manasseh (1755-1831) Bt. (1805) Spanish Jew born in Jamaica was M.P. for Romney (1802) and Barnstaple (1812). In 1819 he was convicted of bribery, but was M.P. for Westbury in 1823 and from 1826 to 1829.

LOPEZ, Roderigo (?-1594). Portuguese Jewish physician, came to England in 1559 and became Q. Elizabeth's physician in 1586. He was probably falsely implicated in a plot to murder her and executed in 1594.

LORD like **LADY** had two syllables. In both cases the first was the A.S. *hlaf* (= loaf), but the second in *Lord* was *weard* (= keeper, *cf* warder) and in *Lady dige* (=kneader, *cf* dough). Thus the original idea was of a provider of food, with a suggestion of worldly benevolence.

Lord was used informally for any peer below a Duke and especially of any baron; *Lady*, in addition, for the wife of a baronet or knight. In this work it is used to distinguish a British baron from the much commoner and less important foreign variety.

LORD CHANCELLOR is a member of the cabinet, Speaker of the House of Lords, both in its legislative and in its appellate capacity, President of the Judicial Committee of the Privy Council, head of the Judiciary and adviser on the appointment of judges, chief legal adviser to the Crown and Keeper of the Great Seal. He also advises the Crown on lesser church appointments and advowsons; he is ultimately responsible for enrolling commissions and treaties and at one time was responsible for the guardianship of infants and lunatics, for the issue of all writs and for proceedings in bankruptcy. As the senior cabinet minister in the Lords he is responsible for defending the govt's policy there. When presiding in the Lords he sits on the Woolsack. When speaking as a min. he stands to the left of it. As speaker of the Lords he has no power to call a Lord to order or to expel him or to suppress irrelevance, but his opinion on procedure carries great weight.

LORD CHANCELLOR OF IRELAND. After the loss of Normandy, the office of the Justiciar who issued the writs became redundant in England. After the fall of Hubert de Burgh, writs were issued by the Chancery but in 1232 Ralf Neville, Bp. of Chester, already Chancellor in England, was granted a separate Irish Chancery which was managed for him by a deputy, the Archdeacon of Dublin, and then by one Robert Luterel. When Neville died in 1244 Luterel was recognised as Irish Chancellor. The office was from about 1290 second in precedence after the Justiciar's, but holders were seldom persons of independent social consequence and were often not given a peerage.

LORD CLERK REGISTER. A Scottish officer of State originally Clerk and Keeper of the records of parliament, other important courts and councils, and of the Court of Session, of which he was often a Lord. Later he was a member of parliament and council by virtue of his office. After the Union of 1707 most of his functions disappeared, but in 1817 the office was amalgamated with the Keepership of the Signet. After 1879 the office was titular, save for the conduct of elections, which ceased in 1958 (*see* PEERAGE) of Scottish representative peers.

LORD DUNMORE'S WAR (1774), consisted of two Virginian expeditions by Lord Dunmore (the governor) and Gen. Andrew Lewis, which drove the Shawnees from their land S. and E. of the Ohio.

LORD JUSTICE-CLERK, originally clerk of the Scottish Justiciars' court, rose in importance as a permanent official and assessor to the Lord Justice General. By 17th cent he was always a councillor and a member of the Court of Justiciary. After 1672 he became the second judge in it, but its working head. In 1808 he became pres. of the Second Division of the Inner House of the Court of Session.

LORD JUSTICE-GENERAL. This Scottish title superseded that of Justiciar (i.e. chief criminal judge) in the 15th cent. The office became hereditary in the Es. of Argyll in 1514 but, save for Argyll and the Isles, was surrendered to the crown in 1628. It was then granted, mostly for life, to various lay nobles, who had to rely for their law on the Lord Justice-Clerk. When the Court of Justiciary was set up in 1672 the Lord Justice-General had to preside if present. Under an Act of 1830 the office was amalgamated with that of Lord President of the Court of Session on the death in 1836 of its last lay holder.

LORDS, HOUSE OF. *See* PARLIAMENT; PEERAGE.

LORDS, HOUSE OF, PROTECTOR'S or CROMWELL'S OTHER HOUSE. As a result of the Humble and the Additional Petitions and Advice of 1657, it was decided to create a second chamber of between 40 and 70 members and 62 were actually summoned. It was not intended to create hereditary peerages, but some thought that it did. It was a failure because on the one hand eleven previous peers, though summoned, refused to attend because by so doing they might compromise their rights as peers, and on the other because the two houses wrangled incessantly about their powers.

LORD or KING'S LIEUTENANT. (1) Originally one who acted for the King when the latter was not personally present.

(2) Commissions of Array, for raising special forces in addition to the levy, were issued as early as the reign of Edward I, in particular in (usually border) counties. Such county forces were each commanded by a Captain, but in the north, under the Yorkists and Henry VII, there was a King's Lieutenant or local C-in-C; Henry VIII's commissions against the rebellion of 1536 placed them under three such and this was thought an innovation. In 1547 Somerset created a North and a South Lieutenancy, with Lieutenants for groups of counties in the South and in 1549 Lieutenants were appointed for 21, mostly county, areas. In 1551 Northumberland appointed his own partisans. Mary I disliked them, but found it necessary to follow suit because of rising protestant discontent. Thus the Lieutenants drifted into permanency.

(3) Being military officers their jurisdiction was not (unlike that of the sheriffs) excluded from honours, liberties or boroughs, and it was thus convenient for them to take control of the sheriff's forces. Under Elizabeth I they were mostly privy councillors and usually peers (i.e. with govt. loyalties), with estates in their county, and they were fairly often changed. The system reached its permanent geography at the Armada crisis which also called forth the appointment of many Deputy Lieutenants, sometimes by the principals themselves, sometimes by the crown direct, but after 1589 there was a tendency to leave vacancies unfilled and by 1601, 17 southern counties had Lieutenants and 12 had commissioners instead. The local difference was small in practice for the Lieutenant was always expected to co-operate with and consult the local justices.

(4) Apart from their growing military and police duties Lieutenants were expected to raise funds and loans for the crown, to supervise the enforcement of recusancy laws, to supply the navy with victuals and to supervise miscellaneous economic regulations especially in times of dearth. By James I's time they were generally the leaders of their respective counties and after the Restoration they held the separate office of *Custos Rotulorum* (Lat. = Keeper of the Rolls), save in Durham, the North Riding of Yorkshire, Westmorland and Herefordshire. This remained the invariable practice after the Revolution.

(5) The growth of regular forces led to the disuse of the musters and commissions of array, and the Lieutenants' military functions gave way to social and administrative work mainly by recommending persons for appointment as J.P.s. Since the latter dominated local administration as well as petty justice and the Lord Chancellor had few other sources of information, the Lieutenant's indirect influence was very great and continued until the creation of county and district councils.

(6) Lords Lieutenant are still connected with the management of territorial army and reserve formations and still, in consultation with a committee, recommend J.P.s. The Clerk of the Lieutenancy was commonly the Chief Executive of the County Council.

LORD MAYOR. Title used by the mayors of London and York intermittently from 13th until 16th cents. and from about 1545 regularly. Subsequently conferred by the crown on the chief magistrates of a number of larger cities.

LORDSHIP. *See* FEUDALISM.

LORDS OF THE COMMITTEE. The members of the cabinet council under Q. Anne, when she was not present.

LOREBURN. *See* REID.

LORIENT (Biscay), originally L'ORIENT was founded by the French E. India Co. in 1664 and passed to the crown in 1782. The republican and imperial govts. developed it into the main fishing port and naval shipyard which it remained. Consequently it was a dangerous German submarine base in World War II. Largely destroyed by allied bombing, it had to be completely rebuilt.

LORNE, a Campbell area in Argyll. The heir to the chief of clan Campbell (The E., M. or D. of Argyll) takes his courtesy title (Master, Lord E. or M.) from it.

LORRAINE originally **LOTHARINGIA** (= Lothar's Lands), created in 870, was a German duchy divided into Upper and Lower parts in 960. The Upper retained the name and was conferred in 1048 on Gerard, grandson of Eberhard IV of Alsace and Eadgifu, an English princess. His dynasty struggled until 1431 with recalcitrant vassals and the Bps. of Metz, Toul and Verdun which had important W. European fairs. Violence and confusion destroyed the credit of the fairs, which moved to Champagne. The T. of Bourges (1301) transferred Bar from Lorraine to the French King. The impoverished citizens of Metz obtained communal privileges against their weakened but autonomous bishop but the 14th cent. decline of the Champagne fairs brought the exchanges back, this time to St. Nicolas de Port.

(2) Isabel, daughter of D. Charles II, married the amiable Rene I of Anjou, (titular K. of Naples, Sicily and Jerusalem) whereby the duchy had an Angevin dynasty from 1431 to 1473, but a rival claimant under Salic succession in Antony Count of Vaudemont and Guise. His family combined male descent from D. Charles II, with female descent from the original Gerard. In 1431 Remi ceded part of the duchy to Burgundy to buy support against Antony, and married his daughter Margerite to K. Henry VI of England but, at the death of his grandson D. Nicolas, the duchy passed to the

Vaudemonts (1473-1737) in the person of D. René II, grandson of Antony. This had important effects; he acquired Bar by marriage, and in 1506 conferred upon his fifth son Claude all the Lorraine fiefs (Guise, Aumale, Elboeuf, Mayenne and Joinville) in French royal territory. Claude was naturalised French in 1506, while his elder brother Antony (r. 1508-44) succeeded in Lorraine and Bar in 1508.

(3) This founded the association of the Guise family power with Lorraine (see HUGUENOTS; JAMES V OF SCOTLAND; MARY OF GUISE) and involved France and Lorraine even more closely in each other's politics; D. Antony married a Bourbon and his grandson D. Charles III (r. 1545-1608) married a daughter of Henry II of France. Such alliances were safe so long as the greater neighbour remained weak through internal feuds and civil wars; but Antony had similar troubles. He kept his independence by an imperial grant of allodiality (1532) and he and his three successors edged away from the main stream of European politics and maintained the Duchy as a prosperous enclave in a war-torn west, until the rise of Richelieu threatened to revive French power. D. Charles IV (r. 1624-75) tried to check the cardinal's political advance, and had his states occupied for his pains.

(4) Thereupon the Swedes entered and devastated the area (1645-7) and Charles recovered only part of his inheritance under the Ts. of the Pyrenees (1659) and Vincennes (1661). The French power increased still further under Louis XIV, who offered a protectorate in 1670 and again occupied the duchy when it was refused. The ducal court, such as it was, took refuge in Vienna.

(5) Here its curious association with Poland and Tuscany began, when D. Charles V (1643-90) who never ruled, married Eleanore Maria of Austria, widow of the King of Poland. Their son Leopold (1679-1729) was allowed to return under the P. of Ryswick (1697) and married Elizabeth Charlotte of Orleans, sister of the future French regent. She acted as regent for her son D. Francis III (1708-65), whereby France and Lorraine had in effect the same govt. from 1729 until 1738. In that year the P. of Vienna settled the War of the Polish Succession. Francis, on his mother's advice, ceded his rights in the duchy to the dethroned Polish King Stanislas Leszczynski (1738-66), Louis XV's father-in-law, in exchange for Tuscany; he had already married the great Archduchess Maria Theresa, and in 1745 became Holy Roman Emperor. Under the treaty France had the reversion to Lorraine and Bar, and Stanislas left the administration to a French civil servant who became intendant when he died. The union with France was thus practically effected over 30 years and nothing but legal formalities remaining in 1766.

(6) The area, apart from the Saar, remained French until 1871 when about 40% of it was annexed by Germany. The French in consequence strengthened the now artificial frontiers at Toul, Epinal and Verdun which played an important part in World War I.

LORRIS, PEACE OF. See AQUITAINE-7.

LOST GENERATION. Those, particularly the well educated, who lost their lives in World War I.

LOTHARINGIA. See CAROLINGIANS; LORRAINE.

LOTHIAN, Es. and Ms. of. See KER OR KERR.

LOTHIANS, THE were originally the former English Eastern lowland part of Scotland from the Cheviots to the Forth, but subsequently came to mean the Counties of Haddington (East Lothian), Midlothian, and Linlithgow (West Lothian), with the City of Edinburgh. The "Heart of Midlothian" was the Edinburgh Tollbooth.

LOT, PARSON the pseudonym of Charles Kingsley.

LOUDOUN. See CAMPBELL (LOUDOUN).

LOUGHBOROUGH. See WEDDERBURN.

LOUGHREA COMMISSION. See TRANSPLANTATION (IR).

LOUIS VII, K. of FRANCE (r. 1137-80) had been married to Eleanor Duchess of Aquitaine some years before his accession (see CAPETIANS OR ROBERTINES, EARLY-12). Aquitaine

and Eleanor presented problems which he could not solve. The ancient duchy was eight times the size of the royal domain and had its own customs. Its unruly baronage paid court to the Duchess, not to the King. Moreover, their marriage was sexually maladjusted. Eleanor's contempt for her monkish husband was deepened by the King's military defeats in Champagne. There were scandals when both went on the Second Crusade (1147-8) and when they returned Suger and the Pope failed to reconcile them. In 1152 he repudiated her. His calculated match with Aquitaine's southern neighbour was equally unlucky, for Constance of Castile died childless. Eleanor, meanwhile, had married Henry Plantagenet who, with her, now controlled the Atlantic seaboard from Flanders to Navarre. In 1154 he became King of England too. In the course of an energetic and stormy marriage she gave him four sons. There was no doubt that the Capetians were in danger.

Louis' reaction suited his temperament. He courted the church and used it to undermine his eastern vassals. In 1153 he supported the Bp. of Langres against Burgundy; in 1160 the Abp. of Rheims in Champagne. In 1165 his position was strengthened when his third wife, Alice of Champagne, gave birth to a son. In 1166 he protected the Chapter of Vézelay against Nevers, and the Abbey of Cluny against Châlon, which he annexed. Soon he was intervening at Macon and then defending the bishops of le Puy against the Polignacs. Involved in southern ecclesiastical politics since 1161, by 1170 he had secured the allegiance of Bourbon, Beaujeu and Forez. An alliance with Toulouse followed but, true to form, Louis tampered with the important Toulousain subfeudatory at Narbonne.

He could now make trouble for Henry Plantagenet, who had quarrelled with Eleanor, with Becket and with his own sons. By 1173 Louis had edged the Plantagenet fiefs into civil war. Moreover, the ecclesiastical politics were paying off. In the Second Investiture Dispute between the Empire and the Papacy, Louis supported Alexander III against the Emperor Frederick Barbarossa. The Pope became a devoted son of France and took up residence at Sens. Becket's murder was a major diplomatic event. Henry had to bow to Becket's Pope. In 1177 Alexander's diplomacy prevented an English alliance with Barbarossa.

LOUIS VIII, K. of FRANCE (r. 1223-6) and his Q. Blanche of CASTILE, Regent of FRANCE (r. 1226-36) (see PHILIP II AUGUSTUS). Louis' first major independent work was to command the Languedoc expedition of 1219 and during his short reign he overran Poitou and all Languedoc except Toulouse. When he died, his remarkable widow had to act as regent for their infant son Louis IX (St. Louis). She was faced with disruption, for Philip Augustus and Louis VIII had both left appanages for younger sons, and Philip's son, Philip Hurpel, disputed the regency. The great feudatories tried to exploit these difficulties, but were united by no principle, each being ready to betray another. In 1227 Blanche overawed the Poitevins. She allied herself with Paris, the 34 privileged towns and the Church, and at the T. of Meaux (1229) compromised advantageously in the South. This success alarmed the English, who, taking advantage of Franco-Breton hostilities in 1230, intervened militarily; but in 1231 Blanche purchased a truce until 1234 which included Brittany. She could now concentrate upon the dangerous house of Champagne with its fiefs both east, and on the Loire, west of the royal domain. By 1234 she had forced the Count to cede the westward Chartres and Blois, thereby strengthening the royal hold on Poitou. On the other hand, the Count, by marriage acquired the crown of Navarre.

The cession of Chartres and Blois also represented a threat to Brittany, held by Peter (Mauclerc) of Dreux as a vassal of England, then temporarily powerless through political disturbances. Peter's methods were causing unrest, and a French army was assembling for the end of the truce. Despairing of English help, Peter deserted to the French, who left him as regent of Brittany until his son should come of age.

In 1236 Louis IX came of age and superseded his mother.

LOUIS IX, St., K. of FRANCE (r. 1226-70) (1) Succeeded Louis VIII as a child under the regency of his mother (*see* previous entry). He came of age in 1236. A great warrior, he was also famous for the arts of peace, and for his justice and piety.

(2) He inherited the Albigensian troubles. There was too, a popular movement against French penetration in the south. This was entangled with imperial claims in the Kingdom of Arles (*see* BURGUNDY) and with disputes between the Emperor and the Pope. The Emperor might help the Count of Toulouse to re-establish himself against both the Pope at Avignon and the French. In fact imperial policy went awry; the County got no support, and a popular rising, led by the exiled Viscount of Béziers, collapsed early in 1241. Meanwhile further troubles had been brewing. Louis invested Alphonse, his brother, as Count of Poitou in July. The Lusignans, summoned to do homage, rebelled and Henry III of England (whose mother, Isabel, was married to their head) supported them. A dangerous looking combination of Gascons, Toulouse and England came, however, to nothing through the incompetence or sluggishness of its members.

(3) By 1243 Louis had subdued Poitou and brought Toulouse to heel. The Lusignans migrated to England, and Isabel became a nun. In 1249 Raymond VII of Toulouse died and his lands passed to Alphonse.

(4) During an illness in 1244 Louis vowed a crusade. In 1248 he conferred the regency on Blanche and in Aug. sailed with most of his principal feudatories; they wintered in Cyprus and attacked Egypt in June 1249. He and his army were captured in Apr. 1250. Released for a huge ransom, he stayed in Outremer to protect it from the consequences, and to get the other prisoners released. He was *de facto* ruler of Outremer until he returned to France in May 1254.

(5) Blanche kept the peace until she died in 1252. The regency then devolved jointly on Alphonse and his ambitious brother CHARLES OF ANJOU (1227-85), who had just been offered the crown of Sicily (a papal fief) by the Pope, and had been ordered to refuse it by Louis. Charles, through his wife Beatrice, had been ruler of Provence since 1246 and of Anjou and Maine since 1247. He now embroiled the crown in a Flemish civil war, by supporting Margaret of Flanders militarily against her son John of Avesnes, for which she made him Count of Hainault and Warden of Flanders. When Louis returned he made Charles renounce these positions and in 1256, in an arbitral award he gave Hainault to John of Avesnes. The justice of the award added immensely to the King's prestige and to Charles' disappointments. The truth was that Louis, driven by necessity to negotiate even with the infidel, had learned the advantages of peace to the Levant. Peace had also brought prosperity in France. The recent enlargements of the royal domain demanded peace, consolidation, and the settlement of old disputes.

(6) Alphonso the Wise, King of Castile since 1252, threatened to become a major factor in Gallic affairs by claiming suzerainty over Navarre (connected with Champagne) and the overlordship of Gascony. Henry III of England wanted peace for his Sicilian plan, which in Oct. 1255 was to lead him to accept the Sicilian crown from the Pope for his young son Edmund. A crusading treaty (Apr. 1254) against the Moors (never implemented) disembarrassed Henry of Castilian claims, but, of course, did nothing for Louis. The key factor was the rich and powerful James I of Aragon who could neutralise Castile.

Negotiations with England and Aragon proceeded simultaneously and were concluded in May 1258. By the T. of CORBEIL Louis abandoned the ancient Gallic claims in Catalonia and Roussillon, and James his more modern rights in Languedoc and Provence. By the T. of PARIS (ratified in Nov. 1259) Henry abandoned the Plantagenet claims to Normandy, Maine, Anjou and Poitou, and Louis acknowledged his lordship in Gascony, but as a French vassal and so necessarily committed to oppose Castilian pretensions. There were other territorial provisions (*see* AQUITAINE-8) and Louis also undertook to support for two years the Sicilian venture with 500 knights.

(7) At this period the King was at the summit of his moral prestige and England was distracted by the Barons' war. The papal grant of Sicily to Edmund had been cancelled in Dec. 1258. The Pope again approached Charles of Anjou, who alone seemed able to oust Manfred, the Emperor Frederick II's bastard, from his hold on Italy. In July 1263 Charles accepted, this time with Louis' blessing. He invaded Italy, killed Manfred at Benevento in Feb. 1266 and defeated Conradin, Frederick II's grandson, at Tagliacozzo in Aug. 1268. He had become protector of the rising Guelph faction in the north Italian cities, and as Senator of Rome and (Papally appointed) Imperial Vicar of Tuscany, he was the civil ruler of central Italy as well as King of Naples and Sicily.

(8) When he beheaded Conradin in Oct. 1268, his Italian dominion seemed secure, but it was to be only the starting point. He planned a Mediterranean empire by the restoration of the Kingdom of Arles, and the overthrow of the Greek Empire, re-established since 1261 at Constantinople. Preparations went ahead, but Louis was preparing another (the Eighth) Crusade, to Outremer. Charles persuaded Louis to divert it to Tunis (opposite Sicily) where, in 1270 the King and other notables died of fever.

LOUIS X of FRANCE. *See* CAPETIANS, LAST.

LOUIS XI of FRANCE (r. 1461-83) (for previous life *see* CHARLES VII) **(1)** was in Burgundy, whither he had fled after an unsuccessful insurrection, when he came to the throne. His situation was exactly the converse of that which had obtained during the Hundred Years War. A unitary French power with a potential enemy (Burgundy) at its back, was exploiting an English civil war in which the two sides angled for outside help. As Dauphin, Louis had favoured the Yorkists. As King he wanted to keep England weak. The Yorkists being in the ascendant, he lent support to the French Lancastrian queen. Meanwhile (1462) he acquired Roussillon in pledge from Aragon and took steps to divert the trade of the Rhône Valley from Geneva to Lyons. This struck simultaneously at Burgundy and Savoy.

(2) Papal diplomacy was still intent on a crusade against the Turks, who were raiding N. Italy. Louis made a truce with the Yorkist Edward IV at Hesdin (Oct. 1463) in formal deference to Papal wishes, but actually to tighten his administration. Determined to recover the Somme towns ceded by Charles VII to Burgundy at the T. of Arras (1435), he imposed heavy taxation to get the necessary war-funds. He forced the old D. of Burgundy to surrender the towns in 1463 but raised a second noble revolt or *Praguerie* (*see* CHARLES VII) called The League of the Public Weal, this time against himself. Most of the higher nobility, led by the D. of Berry joined, but the inspiration came from the Count of Charolais, CHARLES THE BOLD (1433-1477), heir to Burgundy, in alliance with Brittany. Defeated at Montlhéry (16 July 1465) the King had to retrocede the towns and confer Normandy in appanage upon Berry (Ts. of Conflans and St. Maur Oct. 1465).

(3) Edward IV had leaned towards the Burgundians in his struggle with the Lancastrians. Warwick, his essential supporter, sought to ally him with Louis. Warwick's base was Calais, now a wealthy enclave in

Burgundian territory. A French alliance would simultaneously protect Calais and increase the King's dependence upon him. Edward understood this perfectly well; moreover his love match with Elizabeth Woodville (Apr. 1464) had frustrated Warwick's project for a French royal marriage and displeased many of the English nobility. The Yorkist party was splitting and Louis resolved to support Warwick (1466). The Franco-Burgundian struggle was thus, at Charles the Bold's accession (June 1467), already extended to England.

(4) Louis now tried to reverse the treaties of 1465 by an appeal to the Estates General which resolved that the King could not by himself cede territory. With this Louis tore up the treaties, mobilised against Brittany, forfeited Normandy and suborned Liège to rebel against Charles the Bold. Brittany had to accept the humiliating T. of Ancenis (Sept. 1468). Charles was made of sterner stuff. He and Louis met to discuss the new situation at Peronne (Oct.) and there learnt of the Liègeois rebellion and of Louis' part in it. He calmly put the King in custody. The King's policy had revived the League of the Public Weal. He could get no help and had to submit to Charles' demands. He had to help to suppress the Liègeois, to confer the strategically dangerous appanage of Champagne on Berry, to re-enact the treaties of 1465. Almost immediately too the duke also acquired Ghent.

(5) There now occurred a decisive change in the slant of European affairs. Sigmund of Tyrol visited Charles and at the T. of St. Omer (May 1469) pawned Upper Alsace to him. He also ceded or promised rights in Breisgau and suggested that he might support Charles' candidature for the Kingship of the Romans. The greater part of the Burgundian territories lay in the Empire: the prospect of imperial power to unite and promote them was overwhelmingly attractive. From then on Charles' ambitions were diverted towards Germany. The pressure upon Louis was reduced, just as Charles reached the summit of his power.

(6) One consequence was that Louis' friend Warwick was not hindered from defeating Edward IV (July 1469), who took refuge in Flanders in Oct. 1470. During the diplomatic and military confusion Louis had again persuaded the Estates General to repudiate the treaties: Berry was given the richer but innocuous duchy of Guyenne instead of Champagne and Louis occupied the Somme. This time, honours were more nearly even. Edward IV returned (see HANSE), killed Warwick at Barnet (Apr. 1471), murdered Henry VI (May) and finally established a Yorkist govt. but in 1472 a resuscitated League of the Public Weal gave only enfeebled support to Burgundian efforts which, because of the German distraction, were weak. In 1473 Charles was busy acquiring Zutphen and Gelders, and negotiating vainly (at Trier) with the Emperor himself. France and Burgundy signed a truce which in 1474 was extended to May 1475.

(7) In Jan. 1475, however, Edward made an offensive alliance with Charles for the recovery of the French crown. Charles' principal (but not only) reward was to be Champagne, which would ensure the territorial continuity of his dominions. He was already pursuing the Roman dignity by other means than through the Emperor: a majority of the Electorates (three ecclesiastical, one lay) were in the Rhine Valley within his reach. He intervened in a disputed election to the electoral archbishopric of the Cologne and laid siege to Neuss. Consequently when Edward IV's expedition landed from Burgundian ships, it was without Burgundian military support. By Aug. he was negotiating with Louis. The T. of PICQUIGNY (29 Aug. 1475) was the result. In 1476, moreover, Q. Margaret renounced in favour of Louis her maternal rights in Lorraine, then in the possession of Charles the Bold, and those which she would inherit from her father René over Anjou, Bar and Maine, and Provence.

(8) In Jan. 1477 Charles was killed at Nancy (see BURGUNDY; SWITZERLAND). The French duchy of Burgundy escheated and Louis occupied Artois; René recovered Lorraine. The other of Charles' immense territories passed to his daughter Mary (1457-82) by his second wife Isabel of Bourbon. Louis occupied Franche Comté and tried to lay his hands on the rest. In the ensuing WAR OF THE BURGUNDIAN SUCCESSION, the Germanic policy of Charles the Bold was shown not to have been wholly unwise. Mary won the support of the Dutch by the timely grant of the *Great Privilege* to their numerous Estates (Feb. 1477) and in Aug. 1477 she married the son of the Emperor Frederick III, the Archduke Maximilian, heir to all the disunited Habsburg states. His military resources and her money were too much for Louis. The distraction prevented him from intervening against the effects of the fateful marriage of Ferdinand of Aragon with Isabella of Castile (Jan. 1479). In Aug. 1479 his troops were beaten at Guinegatte. 1480 was the year when the centralising Spanish inquisition was set up, and, by the T. of Toledo, Portugal had to give up her claims to the Canary Is. in exchange for illusory concessions in Morocco.

(9) For these dangerous developments, the death of René, the consequent escheat of Bar, Anjou and Maine (July 1480) and the acquisition in 1481 of Provence were, however, some compensation but meanwhile Edward IV, Louis' pensioner, signed an alliance with Maximilian and Mary in Aug. 1480 (designed by Edward to protect his Flemish cloth trade) and thereupon they made a truce with Louis. In Apr. 1481 a Scots invasion gave Edward the pretext for not honouring his military engagement to Mary and Maximilian, who in Dec. 1482 signed the P. of ARRAS with Louis. This partition T. turned out more advantageous to Maximilian than to Louis: he kept the Low Countries, and Luxembourg which were to descend to his son Philip the Handsome, while his daughter Margaret was to many the Dauphin, bringing to France Franche Comté and Artois as her dowry. As the two were children, the fate of these provinces had to remain in suspense: in fact, the French remained in occupation.

(10) From Apr. until July 1483 England was convulsed by Edward IV's death and Richard III's usurpation. In Aug. Louis XI died, leaving three children, ANNE (1464-1522), wife of Pierre de BEAUJEU (?-1503), who in 1488 became the head of the House of Bourbon; the ugly JEANNE (1464-1505), wife of LOUIS D. of ORLEANS (see CHARLES VIII) and the fourteen-year old CHARLES VIII.

LOUIS XII of FRANCE (r. 1498-1515) (1) previously D. of Orléans (see CHARLES VIII) was initially intent on internal pacification. He reduced the *Taille,* reorganised the judicial system, confirmed the privileges of Burgundy, divorced Plain Jane (whom he pensioned), married Anne of Brittany as agreed at the T. of Langeais (1491) and confirmed the special position of her duchy. It was a happy marriage.

(2) The internal policy was however, designed to facilitate Italian adventures which ultimately had disastrous effects in Scotland. He began in 1499 by seizing Milan from the Sforzas. In execution of the T. of Granada (11 Nov. 1500) he and Ferdinand conquered and partitioned Naples (July-Aug. 1501). By the P. of Trento (13 Oct.) the Emperor recognised his claims in northern Italy. The Spaniards were alarmed and changed sides. They drove the French from Naples (Bs. of Seminara, Cerignola and the R. Garigliano). Venice joined in, and when Pope Alexander VI was succeeded (after the three weeks of Pius III) by the warlike della Rovere (Julius II 1503-13) so did the Papacy. A counter-offensive in Roussillon so far failed that the Spaniards threatened Narbonne and forced a truce. Under the T. of Lyons (Mar. 1504) Naples passed under Aragonese control. Under the complementary T. of Blois (Sept.) Louis' daughter CLAUDE (1499-1524) was to marry Charles of Burgundy (the future Charles V) bringing with her Burgundy and

Milan and, if Louis died without an heir, other French provinces. Louis knew that his restive subjects would not let him keep this bargain, but it isolated the dangerous Spaniards. The latter, however, fell out among themselves for Q. Isabella died in Nov. having nominated her husband Ferdinand of Aragon regent of Castile, but the Castilians, who hated the Aragonese, recognised the mad Joanna as their queen and supported Philip of Burgundy's claims on her behalf. Thus France and Spain were simultaneously threatened with civil wars. The two Kings decided to prop each other up. Ferdinand paid a million gold crowns in return for a beautiful French bride, Germaine de Foix, to whom was ceded the Angevin claim to Naples (Second T. of Blois Oct. 1505). Spanish control of Naples became permanent. In a neatly managed Estates General at Tours (May 1506) Claude's hand was transferred from Charles to François, D. of Angoulême (*see* FRANÇOIS I), Louis' heir presumptive; the compact was further strengthened when the two Kings met at Savona. There had been uprisings in Genoa and Milan connected with the ambitions of Maximilian Sforza. Milan was to be left to Spain: French troops occupied Genoa (May 1508).

(3) Thereupon the Emperor, to support his Milanese claimant announced his intention of coming to Italy for his coronation. Franco-Venetian forces resisted his advance and imposed a truce in which he had to abandon Friuli and Istria to Venice. The Venetians took their share without consulting Louis and simultaneously quarrelled with the Pope about church appointments. The two Kings now seized upon growing public concern at Venetian acquisitions (which controlled all the East Alpine trade routes), and at a diplomatic congress at Cambrai, a military league comprising the Emperor, the Pope and the two Kings was established to despoil Venice (10 Dec. 1508). The French overthrew the army of the excommunicated republic at Agnadello (14 May 1509), much of her Italian possessions were partitioned and the French even tried to bombard the city.

(4) The Pope thought that they had gone too far. The loyal population of the Venetian mainland harried the French army. Julius II came to an agreement with Venice in Feb. 1510 and established a league with Ferdinand and the new English King Henry VIII against France (Oct. 1511). Defeated at Ravenna (11 Apr. 1512) the French evacuated Italy and called upon their Scottish ally against England. The League renewed its compact at Malines (Apr. 1513) but the combined Franco-Scots offensive was launched. The French met disaster at Novara (6 June 1513) and at Guinegatte (16 Aug.); the Scots at Flodden (9 Sept.); the Castilians were in Navarre.

(5) The victorious Henry VIII was now closest to the heart of France and the greatest danger. He wanted the profits of a quick peace, especially as his allies had made a truce without consulting him. Tournai was in his hands. Secret negotiations ceded it to him, together with a large pension. Under the peace of 7 Aug. 1514 Henry's sister Mary married Louis XII (1st Jan. 1515). He was twice her age: celebrations and conjugal efforts brought on a stroke.

LOUIS XIII (1601-43, K. of FRANCE 1610) (1) a nonentity, succeeded on Henri IV's murder, under the regency of his mother Marie dei Medici with her Italian lover Concino Concini, the Maréchal d'Ancre. She had been a cruel and rapacious mother and the Princes of the Blood, Bouillon, Condé and Soissons objected to Concini's predominance in a not very effective govt. Their political manoeuvres, however, tended to cancel each other out and the regent bought them off with huge bribes from the state treasury. In 1612 Louis was betrothed under the Franco-Spanish peace treaty to Anne of Austria, daughter of Philip III of Spain, and they were married in 1615, but meanwhile through his obsession with field sports he had befriended the royal falconer,

Charles M. d'Albert, later D. of Luynes. They organised Concini's murder (Apr. 1617) and banished Marie dei Medici to Blois.

(2) Luynes' administration was no better. In 1618 the outbreak of the Thirty Years War created international problems with which he was unfitted to cope, and he was no more popular with the Princes than the Concinis. The rising personality of the time, however, was Richelieu, then a protégé of Marie dei Medici, with whom he arranged a reconciliation, after a series of noble plots allied to Huguenot risings in 1620. Richelieu impressed the King who relied increasingly upon him. Marie dei Medici's corruption and incompetence did not impress Richelieu, who rightly became her main opponent. Since the King hated his mother, this was an easy partnership after Luynes died in 1621. From 1624 Richelieu, with Louis' support, was the effective ruler, but he needed that support to remain in office in the face of at least six major conspiracies. Marie dei Medici fled after the second (The Day of Dupes, Nov. 1630) to Brussels and for a while to England. The reign was characterised by the Huguenot problems in which the English, inspired by the D. of Buckingham, meddled, and the opening of the Thirty Years War in Germany. Louis and Richelieu died within a few months of each other. *See* CHARLES I; HUGUENOTS; THIRTY YEARS WAR.

LOUIS XIV (1638-1715, K. of FRANCE 1643) (1) succeeded under the regency of his Spanish Habsburg mother, Anne of Austria, who soon shook off the council appointed to limit her powers. On Richelieu's recommendation, Louis' father had made the Italian Giulio Mazarin (1602-61) a member of this Council; Anne and Mazarin, who became a Cardinal though never ordained, were lovers and believed to be secretly married. They managed the govt. against opposition from the Princes of the Blood and the nobility who objected to a single minister, and the *Parlement* of Paris and the Parisian population who disliked the Spanish regent. The new govt. had inherited the Thirty Years War, which Mazarin had no idea how to finance. By 1648, though the war was ending, there was widespread European insurrection or revolution, notably in Naples, Portugal and, closer to home, in Catalonia and Britain. The contagion spread to France, where the disorderly rebellions known as the *Two Frondes* (Aug. 1648-Mar. 1649; Jan. 1651-Oct. 1652) paralysed public business and twice drove the court from Paris.

(2) Louis declared himself of age in Sept. 1651, but continued Mazarin in office until his death in 1661. He apprenticed himself to the Minister and slowly took over the reality of decision. One landmark in the process was his coronation in June 1654; another his marriage to the Infanta Maria Theresa in 1660. However administratively misguided Mazarin was, he was a diplomat of genius, while Louis had learnt the horrors of political impotence in the childhood terrors of the Frondes. He was determined to establish order through an internal autocracy. In this he felt that he had, like Richelieu, to put down the princely factions, an anarchic nobility and the Huguenots. Like Richelieu's too, his purpose was to establish a base from which to make France internationally dominant and so to glorify her monarchy.

(3) During the earlier years of his rule, when he was still relatively modest, he recruited men of outstanding ability. Mazarin had already found him Turenne, Le Tellier and Lionne. Le Tellier's secretary Colbert, and his son Louvois followed on. These great public servants set diplomatic norms, reorganised the army, built a navy, established colonies, built roads and canals, and encouraged old, and established new, industries. The main inhibiting factor, which a long peace might have discounted, was a system of unsound finance and taxation. This had been progressively degraded by corrupt or incompetent rulers and ministers since Henri

IV's death. Fouquet's arrest and sequestration (1661) advertised without curing the problem. Probably Louis was misled by the glamour of the surroundings which he had created. Possibly he thought that aggression would pay its way. In any case, with Mazarin's advice he was at war with Spain a year after the end of the Second Fronde, allied with Cromwell's England. The P. of the Pyrenees (Nov. 1659) gave him notable gains at Spanish expense, which threatened the Dutch, and meanwhile (Aug. 1658) a Rhenish League of German states was created under French protection. Aggression seemed to be paying when Mazarin died.

(4) From then on a certain excess began to show in his character. The grandiose palace at Versailles was commenced in 1662, though Colbert advised rebuilding the Louvre. During the disastrous Anglo-Dutch War of 1665 to 1667 a secret Anglo-French treaty (Mar. 1667) left Louis with a free hand against the Dutch, and he promptly used it to invade the adjacent Spanish possessions (*see* DEVOLUTION, WAR OF, 1667-8) and secure the Belgian fortresses (P. of Aix la Chapelle, May 1668). By the end of 1669 he was reaching into eastern Germany with a Brandenburg treaty. In Aug. 1670 (fortified by the Secret T. of Dover) he had occupied Lorraine. In Mar. 1672 a joint Anglo-French attack on Holland began.

(5) Louis' fortunes passed their watershed when William of Orange (P. Mary's husband) reclaimed the Dutch Stadholderates in July 1672, overthrew the Dutch peace party and opened the dykes to keep the French out. There were henceforth to be few cheap aggressions. It took until the P. of Nymegen (Aug. 1676) to establish the next gains. The disturber of the peace, however, continued his career. His Chambers of Reunion, by casuistry, fraud or force, absorbed most of Lorraine into France. In Sept. 1681, he seized Strasbourg and Casale in full peace time.

(6) Europe was becoming alarmed, more especially as Louis now began to systematise the hitherto sporadic persecution of Huguenots by the Dragonnades and exclusion from guilds and public office, while pursuing a furious quarrel with the Pope about the rights of the French church. In 1683, while the Turks besieged Vienna and Colbert died, the European powers edged into mutual understandings, not strong enough to prevent an attack on Spain or an occupation of Luxemburg and Trier, but significant for the future. It was at this point that Charles II was succeeded by the openly Romanist James II.

(7) The Anglo-French understanding now broke down. Since the death of Louis' queen in 1683 he was too strongly influenced by the devout Mme. de Maintenon who, with the church, urged him to complete the conversion of the Huguenots by revoking the Edict of Nantes. This he did (Oct. 1685). He had now no first-rate advisers to resist his increasingly arrogant self-reliance. The damage to the French economy was very great; that to French diplomacy even greater. European states were flooded with hardworking respectable refugees and resounded with their complaints. The English public suddenly realised where James II's policies might lead. In July 1686 the Emperor, the major German rulers, Sweden and Saxony drew together in the League of Augsburg which he attacked (*see* LEAGUE OF AUGSBURG, WAR OF 1688-97). The war ended with the P. of Ryswick, in which Louis recognised the English protestant succession but acquired potentially rich colonial territories. His eye, long on Spanish affairs, now discerned the possibility of immediate and great Spanish gains. (*see* SPANISH SUCCESSION, AND WAR OF 1701-14). In the upshot he failed to establish the gains and ruined his country.

(8) The political failure has left the artistic and literary achievements as the now outstanding feature of this long reign. Though Versailles is the largest monument, it is one of many. The French theatre and its dramatists (e.g.

Molière and Racine) flourished. André Le Nôtre (1613-1700) originated the widely copied formal vista gardens. Charles Lebrun (1619-90) led the new glorification of royal absolutism in painting, and Jean Baptiste Lully (1632-87) in music.

(9) The Great King, whose sign was a sun in splendour, was a small man who increased his stature and dignity by wearing high heels and a tall peruque. Described as a professional King "who loved nobody and whom nobody loved", he nevertheless excited passionate devotion among many women (whom he bedded), many of his closer attendants and a personal terror which had nothing to do with his power. He mistrusted and undermined every source of authority other than his own, particularly the Church, the provincial institutions and the nobility which he reduced to languid impotence at the expensive 'pleasure prison' of his endlessly ceremonial court. This combined with the economic damage of his wars, left the monarchy isolated and vulnerable in the hands of his less savagely determined successors.

LOUIS XV (1710-74) (K. of FRANCE 1715) tactfully called the Well Loved, succeeded under the regency of Philip D. of Orléans, who had him educated eventually by (the later Card.) Fleury. He came officially of age in 1722, but in practice the D. of Bourbon acted as quasi-regent from Orléans death in 1723. It was Bourbon and his minister Paris-Duverney who broke off the Spanish match in order to spite the Orléans family and married him in 1725 to Maria Leszczynska. Of their ten children, seven survived. In 1726 he took over real power by exiling Bourbon and appointing Fleury as his Minister. Fleury was a skilful diplomat with peace at heart, for the country needed rest after Louis XIV's disasters and Orléans extravagance, and it was necessary to allow the newly stabilised currency (1726) to work its effects. In 1730 Orry became *contrôleur des Finances* and succeeded, despite the War of the Polish Succession (1733-8), in balancing the budget by 1738, mainly by a graduated tax. Fleury's and Walpole's pacific and commercial outlook were alike, and their understanding maintained the peace until the War of Jenkins' Ear. Even the Polish War was turned to account, for under the Vienna treaties of 1738 France acquired the reversion of Lorraine and Bar (annexed in 1766). Disenchantment with his Polish queen set in 1737. His taste for the chase had always been inordinate. His first four permanent mistresses were the daughters of the Marquis de Nesle (1732-44). His fifth (until 1764), a Mlle Poisson, was celebrated as the Marquise de Pompadour, who created or inspired the architectural and decorative style called after him. She also acted as his private sec. and, since Fleury had died in 1743, was his most influential adviser on foreign policy. This was not an easy assignment, for considerations of balance of power resulted in Prussia in 1740 and Britain in 1756 forcing France into war. (*See* SEVEN YEARS WAR; WARS OF 1740-8). The second of these wars was disastrous: the first only slightly less so and both were a major drain on the economy.

During this period the Crown was also in constant dispute with the church, the lawyers, and, as taxation rose, with public opinion. The period 1763-1765 marked a watershed. The Seven Years War ended badly; the Marquise and the Dauphin died; there was discontent and bad harvests. In 1768 the Queen died and the King took the last of his permanent mistresses, the luxurious and greedy Mme. du Barry. In 1769 Louis abolished the monopoly of the French East India Co. In 1771 the internal disputes reached crisis level with the exile of the *Parlements*. The country was in disarray when he died of smallpox.

LOUIS XVI (1754-93, K. of FRANCE 1774-91), grandson of Louis XV and locksmith, was a good husband to his wife the Archduchess Marie Antoinette, and father. He was interested in the welfare of his people: abolished torture in judicial proceedings and admitted protestants to the protection of the law. He encouraged science and exploration. Unfortunately this excellent man lacked the decisive touch or any interest in politics. Moreover he inherited a virtually bankrupt and exceedingly corrupt administration. Attempts by ministers such as Turgot (1774-7) and Necker (1777-81) invariably created an opposition so noisy that the King abandoned rather than supported them. Meanwhile, tempted by the mirage of easy victory, France plunged into the War of the American Rebellion (1778-83) and emerged successful but altogether bankrupt. Calonne (1783-7) attempted the only alternative when vested interests are too strong for the govt. and borrowed large sums for expenditure on public works. Financial reform was now the only way to pay off the accumulated debts, but Calonne's successor Lomenie de Brienne could not find a way, and the recalled Necker advised the calling of the Estates General. The Revolution, in whose long course Louis met his death, followed.

LOUIS XVII (1785-95) so-called by French royalists after Louis XVI's execution in Jan. 1793, died of tuberculosis and malnutrition in the custody of one Simon, a shoemaker.

LOUIS XVIII (1755-1824) K. of FRANCE (1815) escaped to Brussels in 1791, was recognised as regent only, by the Czarina at Louis XVI's death in 1793, moved to Coblenz and in 1794 to Verona where he took the royal title. There was a royalist network in France and he was in contact with the Vendean resistance and also with members of the French govt., particularly Pichegru. Expelled from Verona in 1796, he moved to Jelgava (Mitau) on the Baltic, where, with a brief interruption, he remained until compelled under the T. of Tilsit to leave Russia. He made his way to England in 1809 *via* Sweden and was called to the throne in 1814 by a rather tired French public opinion represented by Bonaparte's senate. Conservative, mountainously fat, but shrewd, he could not hold the loyalty of the new France with its recent diet of histrionics, or even the affection of his court. Bonaparte easily drove him to Ghent in 1815, but on his return, despite his desire to restore the ancient monarchy, he had the sense to appoint recently trained statesmen such as Fouché and Talleyrand and, though unenthusiastic about the semi-bourgeois constitution, mistrusted the ultra-conservatism of his foolish brother the Count of Artois (later Charles X) whom he disliked. Consequently when the ultra conservatives won the elections of 1820 he found himself without support for the rest of the reign.

LOUISBOURG (C. Breton I.) the strongest French fortress in N. America, controlled the approaches to the St. Lawrence R. and also the rich cod fisheries. Massachusetts troops and a British squadron took it in 1745 but it was restored at the P. of Aix-la-Chapelle (1748). Amherst took it again in June 1758 as an essential preliminary for the capture of Quebec in 1759. *See also* CANADA; SEVEN YEARS WAR; WARS OF (1739-48)11.

LOUIS PHILIPPE (1775-1850) (Louis Philippe ÉGALITÉ), King of the French 1830-48, son of the D. of Orleans, known as Philippe Égalité, escaped with Dumouriez to the Austrians in 1793, and after wanderings in Scandinavia and America was reunited with the exiled Louis XVIII in 1800 and settled in Twickenham. In 1809 he went, *via* Malta, to Sicily where he married Maria Amalia, daughter of Ferdinand IV of Naples and returned to France after Bonaparte's defeat. Louis XVIII endowed him with the remaining Orléans estates, which made him very rich, and with the Palais Royal in Paris which became a liberal bourgeois *rendez-vous*. This earned him two years more at Twickenham, but meanwhile he courted further popularity by sending his children to state schools. When Charles X was forced to abdicate in 1830,

the liberals, headed by Thiers and Lafitte, offered him the throne, because they calculated that a republic would awaken European suspicion. He accordingly took the quasi-Bonapartist title of King of the French. His position, however depended upon internal political opinion of his external policies, for the French public found him otherwise uninteresting. Hence his close connections with England, cultivated through his son-in-law, Leopold I of Belgium, pleased the liberals who had brought him to power. The affair of the Spanish Marriages, however, alienated the Court of St. James and the liberals, and when in consequence he sought the support of the reactionary monarchies his throne collapsed in the 1848 revolutions directed against them. *See* SECOND REPUBLIC; BONAPARTE (CHARLES) LOUIS NAPOLEON.

LOUISE, Princess (1848-1939) Duchess of ARGYLL (1900) was a sculptress who kept open house for artists and was the first pres. of the Union for the Higher Education of Women.

LOUISIANA and LOUISIANA PURCHASE. The area was named by La Salle after Louis XIV. The name covered the entire tract, then of unknown extent, W. of the Mississippi (from source to mouth) to the Rockies. It became a French Crown colony in 1731 and received thousands of Acadians expelled from Nova Scotia by the British in 1755. In 1762 it was ceded to Spain, which closed the river to commerce. In the French revolution it became a refuge for French royalists. In 1801 it was retroceded to France (*see* SECOND COALITION, WAR OF 1799-1801-3). This cession to Bonaparte's aggressive and more efficient empire alarmed the U.S. Pres. Jefferson. He opened negotiations with Talleyrand for irrevocable navigation and trading rights. In Jan 1803 James Monroe was sent with authority to buy New Orleans and W. Florida. Meanwhile Bonaparte had provoked another war with Britain, and feared the trouble and expense of defending Louisiana against the dominant Royal Navy. In Apr. Talleyrand offered to sell the whole area and the bargain was struck at $15M. The territory was transferred in Dec.

LOVAT. See FRASER.

LOVEL[L] (1) Philip (-1259) was King's Treasurer in 1253 and an itinerant justice in 1255. From him were descended the Lords **LOVEL OF TICHMARSH** (Northants) of whom **(2) Francis (1454-87) 9th Ld. and 1st Vist. (1483)** was a supporter of and much enriched by Richard III who made him a privy councillor, Ld. Chamberlain and K.G. at his usurpation. He was a leading but not popular member of govt. In the jingle, nailed to the door of St. Pauls in July 1484:

The Cat, the Rat and Lord our dog
Ruleth all England under a Hog.

which refers abbreviatedly to William Catesby the Speaker and Sir Richard Ratcliffe; the dog was Lovel's well-known badge, the Hog that of Richard. He fought with Richard at the crisis of the B. of Bosworth from which he escaped to his house not far off, where he died. A kinsman **(3) Sir Thomas (?-1524)** fought on the other side and was rewarded by Henry VII with the chancellorship of the Exch; for life. He was a Northamptonshire M.P. and Speaker from 1485 to 1488. In 1502 he became Pres. of the Council, but in 1509 Constable of the Tower. He was not in favour with Henry VIII and retired to his estates in 1516.

LOVETT, William (1800-77). See CHARTISM.

LOW, James (?-1852), colonel and scholar, published a grammar of Siamese and works on Siamese literature in 1828.

LOW (1) Sir John (1788-1880), was resident or political agent successively at Cawnpore, Jaipur (1825), Gwalior (1830), Lucknow (1831) in Rajputana (1848-52) and Hyderabad (1852). He took a distinguished part in suppressing the Indian Mutiny in 1857-8. His son **(2) Sir Robert Cunliffe (1838-1911)** was director of transport on Roberts' march to Kandahar in 1880, C-in-C of the Chitral expedition in 1895 and of the Bombay Army from 1898 to 1909.

LOW, Sir Sydney (1857-1932), editor of *St. James's Gazette* from 1888 to 1897, was one of the main publicists for the imperial ideals of Cromer, Curzon, Milner and Rhodes.

LOW CHURCH. See ANGLICANISM.

LOW, David Alexander Cecil (1891-1963), a New Zealander who came to Britain as an established political cartoonist and is best remembered for his work in the *Evening Standard*. His thirstily awaited symbols included the lumbering cart-horse of the Trade Union Congress and the spluttering moustachioed Colonel Blimp of the Tory right, who has passed into the language.

LOWE, Sir Hudson (1769-1844) (1) This much traduced infantry officer, commended by Sir John Moore, had a remarkable career. Beginning in the Mediterranean, he held Capri with a scratch force of Maltese from 1806 to 1808 when he was forced to surrender. In 1809, after operations against the Ionian Is, he became Gov. of three of them until 1812. In that climacteric year he went with a mission to Sweden and continued to Finland to inspect a legion of German deserters from Bonaparte, after which he was the only British officer to accompany the various Allied H.Q.s in the victorious campaign through Saxony into France, across which he rode alone (Apr. 1814) to bring the first news to England of Bonaparte's abdication. Knighted and promoted maj-gen., he became C-of-Staff of the Allied forces in Belgium. When Bonaparte's return from Elba was reported, he directed the Prussian troops to concentrate near Brussels, but was immediately sent to take command at Genoa, which he reached the day after the B. of Waterloo. Marching west, he took Toulon and Marseilles, where he heard that he was to take charge of the surrendered Bonaparte.

(2) Appointed Gov. of St. Helena by the HEIC, who owned it, in Apr. 1816, he was to make Bonaparte and his people comfortable and as free as possible but, in view of Elba, to take no security risks. They hoped to obtain their release by creating popular sympathy and intriguing with such British politicians as they could reach. They insinuated that Bonaparte's life was being deliberately shortened by the rigours of the (quite mild) climate. By calculated insults, he tried to goad Sir Hudson into indiscretions. He failed. There were false accusations of insults, food shortages, miserable accommodation and needless restrictions. After Bonaparte's death (May 1821), in furtherance of the Napoleonic Legend (or myth) there were rumours, and even a book, that Sir Hudson had somehow, poisoned him. He was also said to be stiff and pedantic, which, if true would hardly have been surprising in the circumstances. Other events belie it. The Ionian Greeks gave him a sword of honour on leaving: the Toulonnais a silver bowl in gratitude for his treatment of their town. His later career included a mission to Constantinople and a command in India. On the way back he stopped at St. Helena and the islanders feted him.

LOWE, Robert (1811-92), Vist. SHERBROOKE (1880), migrated to N.S.W. in 1842 and was a member of the legislative council from 1843 to 1850, when he returned to London, became a leader writer for *The Times* and from 1852 a Liberal M.P. He held a series of offices with more influence than display at the Board of Control (1852-5), the B. of Trade, and was Vice-Pres. (for Education) of the Privy Council from 1851 to 1864. Among his little publicised achievements was competitive entry into the Indian Civil Service; the statutory creation of the limited liability Co., and the payment by results system in schools. His enormous but rather insidious influence was directed towards establishing the principle

of the educated democracy, i.e. the dependence of suffrage on educational qualifications, and he caused the overthrow of his own party by opposition to the Reform Bill of 1866. All the same he was Gladstone's Chancellor of the Exchequer from 1868 to 1873 and Home Sec. from 1873 to 1874.

LOWER CANADA (QUEBEC). See CANADA-11 *et seq.*

LOWER PROVINCES (India). Another name for Bengal especially after the reorganisation in 1833.

LOWESTOFT (Suffolk), an ancient settlement and minor 18th cent health resort, began its rise as a fishing harbour when L. Lothing was connected with the sea in 1831. The Trawl Basin (1846) and the railway connection (1847) greatly extended the fisheries and the market for them and led to further docks extensions in 1883 and 1906. The German fleet bombarded it in 1916. In World War II it was a naval base and H.Q. of the North Sea mine-sweeping operations.

LOWTHER. Of this north country family, the best known were **(1) Sir Richard (1529-1607),** Warden of the W. March from 1591. His son **(2) Sir Gerard (?-1624),** an Irish judge from 1610. His bastard nephew **(3) Sir Gerard (1589-1660),** was C.J. of the Irish Common Pleas from 1634. **(4) Sir John (1655-1700) 1st Vist. LONSDALE (1636),** was a strong Orangeman. His son **(5) Henry (?-1751), 3rd Vist.,** who was Privy Seal from 1733 to 1735. **(6) James (1736-1802), 1st E. of LONSDALE (1784)** M.P. for Cumberland or Westmorland constituencies from 1757 to 1769 and from 1774 to 1784. **(7) William (1757-1844) 1st E. of LONSDALE** of the second creation (1807) was the patron of Wordsworth and built Lowther Castle. **(8) William (1787-1872) 2nd E.,** M.P. also in Westmorland and Cumberland constituencies from 1808 to 1832 held various minor ministerial posts and then was Pres. of the Board of Trade from 1834 to 1835 and Lord President in 1852. **(9) James (1840-1904)** was a Tory protectionist M.P. from 1865 to 1885 and from 1888 to 1904. He and his relative **(10) Hugh Cecil (1857-1944) 5th E.** were celebrated sportsmen and horse breeders; the latter instituted the Lonsdale Belts which are presented to the champion in each boxing weight. They are highly ornamental.

LOWTHER, James William (1855-1949), 1st Vist. ULLSWATER (1921) was Conservative M.P. for Rutland in 1883 and for Penrith from 1886. In 1895 he became Chairman of Ways and Means and was speaker from 1898 to 1921.

LOYOLA. See IGNATIUS LOYOLA, ST.

LOZI. A tribe which provided the rulers of the group of tribes occupying Barotseland (Zambia).

LUBBOCK, Sir John William (1803-65), 3rd Bart. (1840) was an astronomer and mathematician and a distinguished academic, whose combination of detailed tidal observations with astronomical theory was of immense value in commercial navigation.

LÜBECK. See HANSE *passim;* BALTIC-8 *and thereafter passim.*

LÜBECK, P. of (1629). See BALTIC-28.

LUBLIN, UNION OF (1569). See BALTIC-20.

LUCIUS. A mythical British King supposed to have been converted to Christianity by missionaries from Rome. The story is said to arise from a legend about a K. Lucius of Edessa (Syria), a city also said to have had a letter in Christ's handwriting guaranteeing its safety against the heathen.

LUCKNOW. See OUDH; INDIAN MUTINY-7 *et seq.*

LUDDITES are said to be named after Ned Ludd, a Leicestershire half-wit who destroyed some stocking frames in a fit of temper in 1779. They were organised bands of unemployed manual workers who ascribed their miseries to machines and in 1811, 1812 and 1816 systematically smashed them in the Midlands and Yorkshire.

LUDENDORFF, Erich (1865-1937) was chief of staff to Hindenburg in 1914 (*see* WORLD WAR I-2 for 'TANNENBERG') and they together succeeded Falkenhayn as chief of staff in 1916. They soon virtually controlled as well as military policy and brought off a number of remarkable victories including the conquest of Roumania and the B. of Caporetto. The failure of his spring offensives in 1918 (*see* WORLD WAR I-14) has been attributed to his failure to stick to his own plans, but he also had a nervous breakdown. In Nov. 1918 he fled to Sweden. He took part in Hitler's Beer Cellar Putsch in 1923.

LUDGATE (O.E. ludgest = postern). A gate half way up Ludgate Hill (London), representing a gap in the Roman Wall. It was long used as a prison. Damaged and rebuilt in 1586, it was demolished in 1762.

LUDGER, St. *See* MISSIONS TO EUROPE-3.

LUDLOW (Salop). This little fortified town had a huge castle founded in 11th cent. and progressively extended as a royal fortress and palace. There was a grammar school from c. 1280 and there were corn mills and a clothing industry. Roughly equidistant in time from the northern and southern extremities of Wales and from Westminster, it became the seat of the Council of Wales and the Marches in about 1490 and so a provincial sub-capital, until the outbreak of the Civil War. Milton's *Comus* was first presented there in 1634. The castle was ruined, but the Council was revived in an attenuated fashion from 1661 to 1689. After its dissolution Ludlow relapsed into a local market village, but began to expand again after World War II. *See* PLAN

LUDLOW, Edmund (1617-92) was a Wiltshire M.P. in 1646, a promoter of Pride's Purge in 1648 and a regicide. From 1650 to 1655 he was a Commissioner for the civil govt. of Ireland but refused to acknowledge the Protectorate or give security for good behaviour. He was impeached in 1660, gave sureties on release and escaped to Switzerland. He returned in 1689 but fled again on finding that he was unwelcome. The MS of his memoirs has lately come to light.

LUFTWAFFE. *See* BATTLE OF BRITAIN.

LUGANO CONVENTION was enacted into United Kingdom laws in 1991. It abrogated, as between Britain and the seventeen other European Union and Free Trade Area countries the convenient Common Law rule that a plaintiff could sue a foreign defendant in the court of the plaintiff's own country and, apart from some exceptions, inconveniently forces him to sue in the defendant's country. It does not affect the law by which the court will settle the dispute.

LUGARD, Frederick John Dealtry (1858-1945) 1st Ld. LUGARD (1928) after a conventional military career defended Karongwa for the African Lakes Co. against slave raiders in 1888 and was then sent by the Imperial British E. Africa Co. to Uganda in 1890. These events began his remarkable career as a colonial administrator. *See* HONG KONG; NIGERIA; UGANDA.

LUHYA. *See* KENYA-1.

LULACH (r. 1057-8). *See* SCOTS OR ALBAN KINGS, EARLY-18.

LULL, St. *See* MISSIONS TO EUROPE-3.

LUMOR ALBUS. *See* TUBERCULOSIS.

LUMSDEN, Sir Harry (1821-96), a pupil of Henry Lawrence, commanded the brilliant Hazara expedition of 1846 and then raised the well known frontier corps of Guides, sometimes called Lumsden's Horse, from the most desperate bad-hats he could find. They made themselves famous especially before Delhi during the Mutiny, while he was on a mission to Kandahar. He commanded the Hyderabad contingent from 1862 to 1866 by which time, though probably the most famous soldier in India, he was only a colonel.

LUMLEY, Richard (?-1721) Ld., 1st E. of SCARBOROUGH (1690), educated a R. Catholic, became a protestant in 1687, supported the Seven Bishops in 1688 and signed the invitation to William III. He was influential in Co. Durham and seized Newcastle for him.

LUNAR SOCIETY (c. 1765-92) was a scientific, philosophic and intellectual club at Birmingham, to which Boulton, Erasmus Darwin, Galton, Priestley, Watt and Josiah Wedgwood belonged. It met at the full moon.

LUNATIC was one who became insane after birth and whose condition might be temporary or intermittent. MADNESS was a similar but permanent state. Lunatics were first legislatively mentioned in an act of 1542. In the ancient writ *de lunatico inquirendo* (Lat = For the need to inquire into a (case of a) lunatic) the word connoted any kind of unsoundness of mind. *See* IDIOT.

LUNDY, Robert (fl. 1688-9) was the gov. of Derry, now Londonderry, in 1688 who wanted, probably from lack of courage rather than conviction, to surrender to the Jacobites and was deposed by the apprentices. His effigy is annually burned there.

LUNDY I. (Bristol Channel) was outside English territorial waters and, until incorporated in Devon in 1972, not part of any county. Hence the courts had no jurisdiction and it was for centuries a smugglers' haven, despite lighthouses and a naval signal station.

LÜNEBURG (Ger), originally capital of the Brunswick duchy which developed into the electorate of Hanover, was a Hanseatic town. After the Prussian annexation of Hanover in 1866 its Heath became the main training ground of the Prussian and later the German army. The British took the German surrender there in May 1945.

LUNETTE. *See* APPENDIX ON FORTIFICATIONS.

LUNÉVILLE, P. of (9 Feb. 1801) between the French on the one hand and the Emperor as such and as ruler of Austria and his relatives on the other. France took the west bank of the Rhine. Austria and the Habsburg princes ceded their Italian lands west of the Adige to the Cisalpine Republic or the new Kingdom of Etruria, which was to be under the Infante Louis of Parma. France and Austria guaranteed the independence of the Cisalpine, Dutch, Ligurian and Swiss Republics. The Empire undertook to compensate within itself the rulers dispossessed by the various cessions.

LUSATIA (Ger. LAUSITZ). *See* THIRTY YEARS' WAR-4.

LUSHINGTON (1) Stephen (1782-1873), M.P. from 1806 to 1808 and from 1820 to 1841, was Admiralty judge from 1838 to 1867. A distinguished Civil and Canon lawyer, he was also an important practical reformer. His brother **(2) Charles (1785-1866)** worked for the HEIC from 1800 to 1827; and was an M.P. from 1833 to 1841.

LUSIGNAN. A Poitevin family which acquired considerable prestige and sometimes power as Kings of Jerusalem, Cyprus and Armenia in various combinations between 1129 and 1474, while other members built up substantial estates in Poitou under Henry II and his sons. From the 1170s they claimed the county of La Marche. K. John recognised the claim but in 1200 abducted and married Count Hugh IX's betrothed, Isabel of Angoulême. Hugh naturally or collusively appealed to K. Philip Augustus who seized the opportunity to forfeit John's French possessions. In the subsequent war, Hugh was captured at Mirebeau but soon released. He resumed the revolt and was not reconciled until 1214. It was proposed to marry his son Hugh X to John's daughter Joan, but in 1220 he married John's widow Isabel instead, and the family naturally became important in the plans of Henry III's govt. to regain the lost French lands. During Henry III's campaign of 1242-3, however, they deserted him and made terms with Louis IX.

Isabel died in 1246 and Hugh X soon joined his royal kinsmen in Outremer. Henry III adopted a policy of generosity towards Isabel's children, his half-brothers, because of their potentially royal independent rank and to secure their influence in Poitou. William was married to the heiress of Pembroke. Guy benefited from several escheats and wardships, while the youngest, Aymer, though under canonical age, became Bp. of Winchester.

Such enrichment and family influence attracted bitter

hostility from the English baronage generally and from the baronial reformers in particular. On refusing to observe the Provisions of Oxford, they were driven into exile, where Aymer died in 1261. William, however, was able to return on undertaking to observe the Provisions but fought as one of the King's leading supporters at the Bs. of Lewes and Evesham. This laid the foundations of a close association with Edward I, who as a crusader himself, had known the oriental Lusignans, and William, as E. of Pembroke took a prominent part in Edward's Welsh campaigns. He died in Gascony in 1296. Guy, the last of the Poitevin male line, died in 1308 and his daughters surrendered their rights to the French Crown.

LUSITANIA. An ancient name for Portugal.

LUSITANIA, **S.S.**, a Cunard liner was torpedoed by the German U-boat U.20 off the Irish coast on 7 May 1915. The German consulate in New York had warned U.S. citizens not to sail in her. Because of the speed with which she sank, nearly 1600 civilians including 128 Americans were drowned. The fact, suppressed at the time, that she was carrying munitions, had no bearing on the speed of the sinking, which was caused by a secondary coal dust explosion in an empty bunker. *See* WORLD WAR 1-7.

LUTHER, Martin (1483-1546), LUTHERANISM. He was an Augustinian and became a lecturer on philosophy at the new Univ. of Wittenberg in 1508. He was influenced by Occam's methods and had already begun to abandon formal scholasticism when he went to Rome in 1510 on the business of his order. The profligate Rome of Julius II shocked him. In 1511 he returned to Wittenberg to be Prof. of Scripture. Between 1512 and 1515 he reduced his religious duties to a minimum and underwent a revelatory inspiration known as the *Turmerlebnis* (The Tower Experience) in which the justification of works exclusively by faith was demonstrated as the essence of the gospels. His eloquence at this time drew crowds, and in 1515 he became a vicar (district administrator) of his order, though his revelation necessarily denied the need for priestly mediation between God and Man and contradicted parts of the New Testament.

(2) The event which made him the foremost figure of the Reformation now occurred. To raise funds for the new Basilica of St. Peters at Rome, indulgences had been proclaimed in 1507. In 1514 Leo X conceded the right to sell them in Germany to the Fugger bank at Augsburg and in 1516 Johann Tetzel, a Dominican, was appointed as local agent to preach these indulgences. His commercialism brought together all the strands of Luther's mistrust. On 31 Oct. 1517, Luther nailed NINETY FIVE THESES against the sale of indulgences to the door of Wittenberg church. Translations spread rapidly throughout Germany, and he became nationally celebrated. In the same year he published his *Expositions* on the Seven Penitential Psalms, the Ten Commandments and The Lord's Prayer and in 1518 his *Resolutions*. He was beginning to find that it was impossible to attack the sale of indulgences without attacking indulgences themselves, and thence it became necessary to question other central doctrines of the Church including the functions and authority of the Papacy. This he did in his most important works *The Liberty of A Christian Man*, the *Address to the Christian Nobility of the German Nation* and *The Babylonish Captivity of the Church*, all published in 1520. The Bull *Exsurge Domine* (Lat: Let the Lord arise – June 1520) showed even by its title, the extent of papal alarm. It condemned forty-one of his propositions as heretical, ordered the destruction of his writings and required recantation within 60 days. He publicly burned the bull, having already secured powerful princely support. Excommunicated in Jan. 1521 and summoned before the Imperial Diet at Worms, he refused to recant, but, fearing for his safety, his friend the Elector of Saxony spirited him away to the fortress of the Wartburg. Here

during an eight months' seclusion he translated the Bible into a luminous and popular German, which made it the cornerstone alike of north German religious thought and of literary development.

(3) Meantime there was great social and religious excitement and disorder, which he had himself unintentionally provoked. In 1522 he returned to Wittenberg to put down disturbances, but the peasantry was getting out of hand. The result was the Peasants War of 1524-5, in which Luther supported 'order' and the ruling princes, and forfeited much popular support. He and his supporters were now and henceforth identified with govts. and this led, through political convolutions, after his death to the Religious P. of Augsburg (1555). Meanwhile the Diet of Speyer (1526) resolved to allow the Romanists and Lutherans to preach freely, but in 1529 the powerful ecclesiastical Electors secured an amendment to the effect that no religious body might be deprived of its ecclesiastical revenues. The Lutheran princes who had seized church properties instantly protested (hence the word *Protestant*) and the dispute now became largely political. The former had also fallen out amongst themselves, with the result that three rival confessions of faith were sent to the Imperial Diet at Augsburg in 1530. Of these the most famous was the AUGSBURG CONFESSION drafted mostly by Luther himself, though he did not attend the Diet. The Emperor Charles V now felt strong enough to issue the imperial ban against the Lutherans; the protestants in reply formed the political and military LEAGUE OF SCHMALKALDEN. Luther had already begun his slow abdication of leadership into political hands, but he continued to write polemical and other works until his death.

Lutheranism. **(4)** Luther's doctrines were never systematically developed, but are to be found in his writings, in the Articles of Schmalkalden (1537), the *Formula of Concord* (1577) and the *Book of Concord* (1580). The scriptures are considered to be the sole rule of faith, the creeds being mere historical records of belief; original sin deprives man of the freedom to do good, but faith in Christ enables him to be accounted righteous (though still a sinner) by God without any co-operation on his part. There being no room for a priesthood in such an intellectual scheme, the doctrine of the Real Presence at communion (in which Luther believed) was modified from the Romanist Transubstantiation in favour of Consubstantiation, and all worship was to be conducted in the local language. *See* RENAISSANCE-11; REFORMATION-7.

LUTINE, originally a 32-gun frigate captured from the French, sank in a gale off Holland in Oct. 1799, with much bullion belonging to London merchants, insured with Lloyds underwriters. Her bell was salved in 1858 and hung in Lloyds, where it is sounded for important or disastrous announcements.

LUTON HOO (Beds.), mansion commenced by Robert Adam in 1767 but internally rebuilt in the French style in about 1820.

LUTTERWORTH. *See* WYCLIFF.

LUTTERELL, Henry (?1765-1851) bastard of the 2nd E. of Carhampton; Byron called him "the best sayer of good things and the most epigrammatic conversationalist I ever met", Lady Blessington "the one talker who always makes me think".

LUTTERELL PSALTER, written and illustrated in about 1340 with scenes of contemporary life was commissioned in E. Anglia by Geoffrey Lutterell, but found its way into the hands of the Dorset Weld family, who sold it to the British Museum in 1929.

LUTYENS, Sir Edwin Landseer (1869-1944) English romantic architect, built country houses from 1888 to 1900, was consultant for Hampstead Garden Suburb in 1908, and joint architect with Sir Herbert Baker for New Delhi from 1913 to 1930. They hated each other.

LUWO. See KENYA.

LUXEMBOURG (locally LETZEBURG). The ruler of this country became, as Henry VII, Holy Roman Emperor in 1308; his grandson Charles IV made it a duchy in 1354. It came to the House of Burgundy in 1443, remained R. Catholic during the Reformation, and passed to the Spanish Habsburgs in 1596. The city became an important fortress. In 1713 it was allotted, with the rest of the Spanish Netherlands, to Austria and so was annexed by France under the T. of Campo Formio in 1797. The Congress of Vienna (1815) divided it, creating the Grand Duchy out of the eastern part; the King of the Netherlands was to be Grand Duke, but it was part of the German Confederation. Hence when Belgium became independent of the Netherlands under a separate dynasty in 1830 the connection with the western province of Luxemburg was severed. By this time the large iron ore deposits were being worked. The Prussian victory over Austria in 1866 converted North Germany into a Prussian economic area, but the Grand Duchy's neutrality and independence were guaranteed in 1867 by the T. of London. In 1890 the ducal rights passed to the Nassau branch of the Dutch royal house.

The Germans occupied Luxemburg in World War I and so it was specifically freed from German ties by the T. of Versailles. In 1921 it entered a currency and economic union with Belgium. After a second German occupation in World War II, during which the iron industry was further developed, it entered the BENELUX customs union with Holland and Belgium in 1948, and abandoned its unarmed neutrality. The Grand Duchy was a founder member of the E.E.C. whose court is located in the City.

LYDD (Kent), a limb of the Cinque Port of New Romney, had experimental ranges where much of the work on military explosives was done in and before World War I.

LYDENBURG (Transvaal) (Du = place of sorrow), so-called because of the wholesale death of Voortreckers there from malaria. From 1857 it was a small republic on its own.

LYDFORD LAW. Lydford castle (Devon) contained the Stannaries prison, where conditions were so bad that prisoners often died before trial. Hence to punish without trial. *Cf* JEDBURGH JUSTICE.

LYGON (1) William (1747-1816), 1st Ld. BEAUCHAMP (1806), 1st E. BEAUCHAMP (1816) was M.P. for Worcester from 1775 to 1806. **(2) Frederick (1830-91), 6th E. (1866)** was M.P. for Tewkesbury from 1857 to 1863 and for Worcestershire from 1863-1866. He was Lord Steward from 1874 to 1880 and Paymaster of the Forces from 1885 to 1887. He was a founder of Keble Coll. Oxford. His son **(3) William (1872-1938) 7th E.,** was Gov. of N.S.W. from 1899 to 1902, Lord President in 1910, first commissioner of works from 1910 to 1914, Lord President again from 1914 to 1915 and Liberal leader in the Lords from 1924 to 1931.

LYME (1689) REGIS (Dorset). This small borough returned two M.P.s to parliament from early times until 1832 and was incorporated under Elizabeth I. In 1644 it beat off a royalist siege; in 1685 Monmouth landed there and so, in 1689, did William of Orange. It had one M.P. from 1832 to 1868 when it was merged electorally in Dorset. The municipal corporation survived until 1974. It was notoriously corrupt.

LYMPNE (Kent). Lat. PORTUS LEMANIS, once a port, is now well inland. A military aerodrome was established in 1915, converted into an air staging post between the wars and into a fighter station in World War II. In 1949 it reverted to civil use for charter flights.

LYNCH LAW, the killing of alleged criminals by mobs without lawful authority, is probably called after Charles Lynch (1736-96) a Virginia J.P. who encouraged it against the local loyalists during the American Rebellion.

LYNDHURST, Ld. See COPLEY.

LYNEDOCH. See GRAHAM.

LYNN LAW. See TRANSPORT AND COMMUNICATIONS-2.

LYON, John (?1514-92). See HARROW SCHOOL.

LYON. Scots lowland family who became Lords GLA[M]MIS and Es. of KINGHORNE (1606). **(1) John (?1510-58) 7th Ld.,** whose mother was burned on a fabricated charge of treason in 1537, acquired Kinghorne in 1548 after the Kirkcaldy forfeiture. His son **(2) John (?-1578) 8th Ld.,** after some doubts, supported Morton's regency against Mary Q. of Scots, became Lord Chancellor of Scotland in 1573 but joined in the intrigue which forced Morton to resign. Described as 'learned, godly and wise', and of a conciliatory disposition, he was killed in a brawl with the Lindseys. His brother **(3) John (?-1608),** was a leader of the Ruthven Raid (Aug. 1582), fled to, and returned from, Ireland and in Apr. 1584 was driven into England with his adherents. They returned in Oct. 1585, overthrew Arran, and he became Scots Lord Treasurer. The Lindsey feud continued and John fought them and their Huntly allies until 1590. He refused to resign when James VI appointed the Octavians and had to be bought out. **(4) Patrick (1642-95) 3rd E. of KINGHORNE (1646) and 1st E. of STRATHMORE (1677)** succeeded to an inheritance wasted by covenanters and defaulters, and slowly rebuilt the family fortune. He supported the Crown in the Argyll insurrection of 1685, was rewarded and duly fell under William III's suspicion. He abandoned public life in 1690. See BOWES-LYON.

LYONESSE was a legendary land, later submerged, between Cornwall and the Scilly Is. where the Arthurian Sir Tristram was born. The legend perhaps refers to some small sunken lands in the Scillies themselves.

LYON KING OF ARMS, The LORD, combines the offices of a mediaeval herald, a *sennachie* or bardic historian, by whom a new King was proclaimed, and a judicial functionary. The jurisdiction (both civil and criminal) of his court over matters of genealogy and heraldry was important because of the position and powers of chiefs in relation to their clans. It was supplemented by Acts of 1592 and 1672 and reserved in the Act of Union. Though the Heritable Jurisdictions Act, 1746, abolished the formal powers of chiefs, their social prestige still maintained the court's importance, which was later continued by the genealogical interest of the Scottish diaspora.

LYONS (1) Edmund (1790-1858) 1st Ld. LYONS (1856) combined a naval career with diplomacy, being Min. to Athens in 1835 when a commander, Min. to Switzerland from 1849 to 1851 as a r-adm., then minister to Stockholm from 1851 to 1853. He was C-in-C Mediterranean from 1855 to 1858. His *s.* **(2) Richard Bickerton Pemell (1817-87) 2nd Ld. and 1st Visct. (1881) and 1st E. (1887)** was attaché at Athens from 1839; at Dresden from 1852 and at Florence from 1853. He was Minister at Washington from 1858 to 1865, ambassador to the Porte from 1865 to 1867, and at Paris from 1867 to 1887.

LYONS (Fr.) (Lat. LUGDUNUM), at the junction of the Sâone and Rhône and of main roads from Germany, and northern and central France, Marseilles, Provence and Toulouse was easy to fortify, and stood at the meeting point of three Gallic provinces. It became an important Gallic religious centre. The Romans established a permanent garrison to control and a mint to supply the immense markets and fairs, especially for wine. It became the seat of a bishopric but in the 3rd and 4th cent. its administrative and commercial importance gave way to Trier and Arles. In 457 the Burgundians took it and later it became a secondary city of the Carolingian empire. Its recovery was due to its establishment as a powerful archiepiscopal principality and then to French annexations between 1307 and 1347. This made it the centre of a unified S. French economic area, for which it was made the staple for the Mediterranean traffic. It had an enterprising merchant commune which developed major trades in cloth, furs, wool and spices besides wine.

There were lead, silver and copper mines nearby, and the banking and exchange houses, operating in the re-established and expanding fairs, were able to supersede the Lombards and Cahorsins because the Levantine trade was being diverted from the Languedoc and Alpine routes up the Rhône. The Genoese-Venetian wars affected these developments. By 1420 when the fairs were reorganised, German and Tuscan finance was coming in. In 1467, silk weaving was established, in 1473 printing. This was the period when the Medici, the Gondi and other Italian firms established branches there, and these were soon enmeshed in French royal finances, for during the long Italian wars, Lyons became the French effective capital, as well as the military base, and the military demands encouraged the metal and cloth industries. This somewhat artificial prosperity declined with the settlement of the wars, but silk took the place of armaments and Lyons became the major silk supplier of W. Europe. At the same time Huguenot penetration estranged the city from N. France and left a legacy of political distrust. This exploded into a series of revolts and massacres during the French Revolution (1793, 1796) and these influenced allied strategy, especially in the seizure of Toulon.

LYONS, Richard (?-1381), a bastard of obscure origin, became a London alderman and sheriff in 1374. His great wealth was founded on the wine trade and upon a series of advantageous loans to the Crown repayable by licences to evade the Staple and an effective monopoly on customs levies. He was successfully impeached in the Good Parliament (1376) for these practices and for acting as a broker in Crown debts. His fortune, which included £2500 in London alone, was forfeited but in the Parliament of 1377 the conviction was reversed and he recovered most of his assets. Though he did not again hold civic office, he served as a knight of the shire for Essex in 1380. He continued unpopular and was murdered in London during the Peasants' Revolt.

LYTTON REPORT (1933). When Japanese troops entered Manchuria in Sept. 1931, China appealed to the League of Nations whose most influential member was Britain. Inaction would have destroyed the League's credit, but no member state would face imposing instant military sanctions. Accordingly a commission under Ld. Lytton was sent to investigate, but meanwhile a Japanese Manchurian puppet state (*Manchukuo*) was set up and the Japanese attacked Shanghai in Jan. 1932, and in Dec. invaded Jehol. The Report was confined to Manchuria and could only condemn Japanese aggression. The assembly of the League adopted it on 24 Feb. 1933, the day after the Japanese extended their operations to China north of the Wall. Having no further use for the League they resigned from it.

LYTTON, Lady Constance, alias Jane WARTON (1869-1923). Lady Constance joined the Suffragettes in 1908. She was imprisoned after a demonstration, refused food and was released under the "Cat and Mouse Act". "Jane Warton, a seamstress" was imprisoned after an identical demonstration, refused food and was forcibly fed. The Home Sec. having refused an inquiry into the inequality, the experiences were published in 1914, by which time the issue was dead.

M

MAAS or MAES R. (1) The Flemish Meuse. **(2)** The northern mouth of the Rhine.

MAASTRICHT or MAESTRICHT. Strategic, now industrial, city on the west bank and at a major crossing of the R. Maas (Meuse) and occasional capital of Brabant. It sustained a number of sieges notably by the Spaniards in 1579 and by the French in 1673. It was an important allied base in the War of the Spanish Succession. The French again besieged it in 1748 and yet again in 1794 when they annexed it. In 1815 it became part of the Netherlands but was not included in Belgium at the partition of 1830. This had the effect of strategically entangling Belgium and the Netherlands. Its existence restricted the swing of the German turning movement through Belgium in 1914. *See* also MAASTRICHT, T. OF.

MAASTRICHT, T. of (1991-93), designed to convert the European Single Market into a federal political state dominated by a bank, was the subject of controversial negotiations between the European powers and the Commission of the European Community. A Danish adverse referendum blocked the ratifications in 1992 but a further referendum reversed the decision in 1993. In Britain the Parliamentary Bill embodying the necessary law had the longest committee stage in the House of Commons in the 20th cent.

MABILLON, Jean (1632-1707) Benedictine author of *De re Diplomatica* (Lat = On Ancient Documents) which founded the study of mediaeval archives and settled the principles of Latin palaeography.

MABINOGION (1) The 14th-15th cent. Red Book of Hergest contains *inter alia* four interlinked *mabinogi* by different hands dating from c. 1050-1120. These *Tales of Youth* deal with the adventures of Pwyll, Prince of Dyfed, Branwen, daughter and Manawyddan, son of Llyr; and Math, son of Mathonwy. In the first, Pwyll exchanges shape with the King of Hades and by a trick gets Rhiannon to wife, though she is already promised to Gwawl, the Sun God. Their son Pryderi vanishes for a while but reappears in the last two legends. In the second, Matholwch, King of Ireland marries Branwen, but is insulted in Dyfed and consequently ill-treats her. In the ensuing war the Irish and most of the Welsh fall, while Branwen's brother Bran, mortally wounded, orders that his head be buried as a talisman against invasion at the White Mount (perhaps the Tower of London). In the third, terrible evils befall Manawyddan and Pryderi for the treatment of Gwawl and in the fourth the nephews of Math, the wizard, trick Pryderi out of some supernatural pigs and in the ensuing feud Pryderi is killed.

(2) In 1838-49 Lady Charlotte Guest published a *Mabinogion* which includes the above and seven others from the Red Book, five being Arthurian.

MAC, Mc., M'. Scots and Irish Gaelic = son. For the main Scottish clans whose names begin with this prefix besides some which do not, *see* CLANS, SCOTTISH AND TARTANS.

MACALISTER, Arthur (1818-83). Immigrated to Queensland in 1850 and entered its first Parliament in 1860. He was Premier from 1866-67, Speaker from 1870-71, Premier again from 1874-76 when he became Agent-Gen in London until 1881.

MACANWARD. Irish sept which boasted eight poets between 1587-1696. Of these Hugh Boy (?1580-1635) was the first Prof. of Theology at the Irish College at Louvain, from 1616 and made collections for an Irish martyrology.

MACAO (China) first reached by the Portuguese in about 1520 was granted to them subject to tribute in 1557. It was the summer residence of foreign merchants established at Canton, from the mid 17th cent. until the Anglo-Chinese war of 1841 and the subsequent rise of British Hong Kong. In 1857 the Gov. expelled the Chinese officials and was himself assassinated; the tribute ceased to be paid and the merchants moved away. China recognised Portuguese sovereignty in 1887. In 1974 Macao became a substantially autonomous Portuguese territory. China having failed to provoke riots, changed to a tolerant regard for stability but considered Macao to be Chinese territory which happened to be under Portuguese administration.

MAC- [or Mc] ARDELL, James (?1729-65) mezzotint engraver well known for his many engravings of Reynolds pictures.

MACARIUS the Scot (?-1153) left Scotland for Germany in 1139 to become Abbot of St. Jacobs near Würzburg.

MACARONI. Late 18th cent. term for a young man who had made the grand tour and affected the more exquisite of the continental fashions observed on the way.

MACARTHUR. Australian founding family **(1) John (1767-1834)** went to N.S.W. as a soldier, became commandant at Parramatta from 1793-1804 and occupied his time lucratively improving agriculture and sheep breeding. He was one of those unsuccessfully tried in connection with illegal rum dealing in 1808; he settled as a farmer and by 1817 was planting vines. He was a member of the first N.S.W. legislative council from 1825-31. His enormous wealth and influence was inherited by four sons and a nephew. The nephew **(2) Hannibal Hawkins (1788-1861)** immigrated to N.S.W. in 1805 and became a wood grower and politician. **(3) Sir Edward (1789-1872),** a professional soldier, fought in the Peninsula and became C- in-C Australia (1855-60) and Governor of Victoria in 1856. **(4) John (1794-1831),** a lawyer, became C.J. of N.S.W. in 1831. **(5) James (1789-1867)** was a member of the N.S.W. legislature in 1839; explored Gippsland in 1840, and was again a member of the legislature in 1848 and 1857. **(6) Sir William (1800-82)** was also a member of the legislature in 1849 and 1864.

MACARTHUR, Douglas (1880-1968) was U.S. Chief of Staff from 1930-35 and military adviser to the Philippine Govt. from 1935-37. Recalled to service in 1941 he escaped the fall of Manila, became C-in-C U.S. Far Eastern Forces and in 1942 Allied Supreme Commander for S.W. Pacific where he was largely responsible for the defeat of Japan. From 1945 he commanded the occupation of Japan and in 1950 was Commander of the U.N. war forces in Korea. He publicly disagreed over Korean war policy with Pres. Truman who dismissed him whereupon he lent his reputation as a war hero to support the president's political (Republican) enemies.

MACARTNEY, George (1737-1806) 1st Ld. MACARTNEY (Ir. 1776) E. (Ir. 1792) was Envoy at St. Petersburg from 1764-67, an Irish M.P. from 1769 and Chief Sec. for Ireland from 1769-72. He was Gov. of the Caribees from 1775-79 and then of Madras from 1780-86. He then led the first British embassy to Pekin (*see* CHINA) from 1792-94 and from 1796-98 was Gov. of the Cape.

MACBRUAIDEDH, Tadhg (1570-1652) poet, *Ollamh* to the Es. of Thomond, and in 1605 Pres. of Munster. A grantee under the Cromwellian plantation flung him over a cliff.

MACCARTHY. Irish chiefs of Muskerry between Bantry Bay and the R. Blackwater in Munster **(1) Fineen or Florence (?1562-?1640)** sided with the crown against his neighbour Desmond in the rebellion of 1588 and was suspected of Spanish intrigue and imprisoned. He was periodically in custody from 1589-1626. **(2) Justin (?-1694) Vist. MOUNTCASHEL (1689),** Jacobite commander under Tyrconnel, disarmed the protestants of Cork in 1689, was captured at Newtown Butler but broke his parole and escaped to France where he commanded the well known Irish Brigade. He was responsible for the conversion of his nephew **(3) Donough (1668-1734) 4th E. of CLANCARTY (1676)** to Romanism. The latter was also a Jacobite, captured at Cork in 1690. He escaped from the Tower to St. Germains in 1694, returned and was arrested in 1698 but was pardoned. He died in Germany.

MACAULAY. (1) Zachary (1768-1838) managed a Jamaica estate and was horrified by the condition of the slaves. From 1793-99 he was Gov. of Sierra Leone and from 1799-1808 Sec. of the Sierra Leone Co. From 1802-16 he edited the anti-slavery *Christian Observer* and from 1807-12 he was Sec. of the African Institute. He was a founder of the Anti-Slavery Society in 1823. His son **(2) Thomas Babington (1800-59) 1st Ld. MACAULAY (1857)** wrote regularly for the *Edinburgh Review* from 1828 and became a Liberal M.P. in 1830. In 1832 he became a member, and in 1833 Sec. of the Board of Control and from 1834-38 was a member of the Council for India. His successful advocacy of English as a medium of higher education in India was a turning point in Indian history. As Pres. of the Commission he composed the Indian Criminal Code (which eventually became law in 1860). From 1839-47 and from 1852-56 he was M.P. for Edinburgh and from 1839-41 Sec. for War. His *History of England* was published between 1848-55 and has been much attacked, especially in relation to Marlborough, by Winston S. Churchill, who accused him of fabrication.

MACBETH (?-1057) was chieftain of Moray and Commander of K. Duncan of Scots army. In 1040 he rebelled, slew Duncan in battle and became king, possibly in right of his wife. In 1050 he visited Rome, to secure absolution and became celebrated for his almsgiving. On his return, Duncan's son Malcolm, who had become King of Cumbria in 1054, attacked and killed him with Northumbrian support, and took his throne. The politics of Shakespeare's drama thus represent a true tradition. *See* SCOTS OR ALBAN KINGS, EARLY.

MacBRIDE (1) John (1865-1916) militant Irish nationalist, helped raise funds in U.S.A. for the Irish Republican Brotherhood and fought in the Boer War in an anti-British Irish brigade. He married in Paris in 1903 but returned to Dublin. He did not join the Irish Volunteers but offered his services in the 1916 rising and was executed. **(2) Maud Gonne (1866-1953)** was a dedicated Irish Nationalist to whom W.B. Yeats had proposed in 1891. She made a sensation in one of his plays and continued to agitate mainly in France. Her marriage to John was not a success and when he went to Dublin she stayed in Paris until 1917 and then went to Dublin where she was briefly gaoled. From 1922 she spent her energies in helping republican prisoners and their families. Their son **(3) Sean (1904-)** was Irish Minister for External Affairs from 1948-1951 and received both the Nobel (1974) and the Lenin (1977) Peace Prizes.

MACCLESFIELD, Es. of. *See* GERARD; PARKER.

MACCONMIDHE. A family of hereditary poets and historians to the O'Neill. GILLABRIGHDE flourished in 13th cent; others between 1420 and 1583.

MacDERMOTT, Hugh Hyacinth O'Rorke (1834-1904). THE MACDERMOTT and **PRINCE OF COOLAVIN (1873)**, a well known practitioner at the Irish Bar, was Liberal Sol-Gen. for Ireland in 1885 and 1886 and Att-Gen. from 1892-95.

MACDIARMID, Hugh (or Christopher GRIEVE) (1892-1978) a poet mostly in Scots, began in the Scots National Party (SNP) in 1928, but slowly moved over to Marxism. In 1934 he was expelled from the SNP and joined the Communists.

MacDIARMADA, Sean (1884-1916) a friend of Bulmer Hobson, became full-time organiser of Sinn Fein in 1907 and set up branches all over Ireland. He fought in the 1916 rising and was executed.

MacDONAGH, Thomas (1878-1916) poet and director of training of the Irish Volunteers from 1913 he joined the Irish Republican Brotherhood in 1915, signed the Proclamation of the Irish Republic at the 1916 rising and was executed.

MACDONALD CLANS. *See* ISLES, LORDSHIP OF THE; MACDONELL CLANS.

MACDONALD, Alexander (1821-81) miner and mine manager was Secretary of the N. Union of Miners from 1863 and M.P. from 1874.

MACDONALD, James Ramsey (1866-1937) educated at Moray Board School, became a pupil teacher, worked on a farm and then came to London where he secured employment first as a clerk and then as a laboratory assistant. In 1888 he became private secretary to Thomas Lough M.P. and thereafter wrote for the Liberal press but joined the Independent Labour Party (I.L.P.). He stood unsuccessfully for Southampton in 1895 and Leicester in 1900 but from 1901-04 he was a member of the London County Council.

In the General Election of 1906 he was elected at Leicester and became, until 1909 Chairman of the I.L.P. By 1911, however, he had moved away from continental socialism and helped to set up and became Chairman of the fledgling Labour Party. He hotly opposed entry into World War I, sympathised with the Russian revolutionaries and apparently also with the Bolsheviks, with the consequence that he was defeated at W. Leicester in Dec. 1918 and at E. Woolwich in Mar. 1921. In 1922 he returned to the Commons and became Leader of the Labour Party and of the Opposition. After the General Election of Dec. 1923 he formed the first Labour Govt. (*see* MACDONALD'S FIRST LABOUR GOVTS) which lasted only nine months. He was then leader of the opposition against Baldwin's Govt. until the General Election of May 1929 when he was elected for Seaham Harbour (Durham) and took office again. He was Prime Minister continually until 1935 in three different govts. (*see* MACDONALD'S SECOND LABOUR GOVT and his FIRST AND SECOND NATIONAL GOVTS). Throughout this strenuous time he was faced with the British slump of 1929. This was a phase of a world recession in which dictatorial govts. were imposed successively on Italy, Russia and Germany. In Britain the immediate problem was high unemployment and social misery, such as he had experienced as a young man. He now disliked the revolutionary socialists, whose politics would precipitate the poor into even greater present distress with only a hope but no certainty of a better future. His mind had been captured by a conscience stricken Fabianism in the light of which, matters being what they were, it was necessary to preserve the existing social and economic order until it accumulated enough resources for further social advance. He and many of his Labour supporters drifted apart and he, not they, reflected the public mood. Hence, when his Govt. resigned over financial and fiscal problems in 1931, he was returned to office with little personal support in his own party but with widespread support everywhere else. He and Philip Snowden had formed a National Labour Party (N.L.P.) to fight the election. He, but not it, won the greatest landslide victory in history, but with apparent futility the Labour Party expelled him and all other N.L.P. members.

As the country came through the slump, people felt that they could afford the political luxuries of factionalism or (as the case might be) extremism. His national Govts. had been supported upon the shoulders of a profound conservatism represented by the large number of conservative M.P.s in the House. By 1935 he was 71 and no longer robust. Accordingly he resigned in favour of Stanley Baldwin their leader but stayed on under him as Lord Pres. In the 1935 election his expulsion from the Labour Party was seen to be less fatal than it had appeared. He was heavily defeated at Seaham Harbour and a seat had to be found for him for the Scottish Universities. His health, meanwhile, was failing. On medical advice, he went on a cruise to S. America but died at sea.

MACDONALD'S FIRST LABOUR GOVT. (Jan.-Nov. 1924).

Twenty in cabinet under J. Ramsay Macdonald, Prime Minister; and Foreign Secretary, the leading personalities were Vist. Haldane, Lord Chancellor; J. R. Clynes, Lord Privy Seal; Philip Snowden, Ch. of the Exch; Arthur Henderson, Home Sec; J. H. Thomas, Colonial Sec; Vist. Chelmsford, First Lord of the Admiralty; J. Wedgwood, Chancellor of the Duchy of Lancaster; Sydney Webb, Pres. of the Board of Trade; C. P. Trevelyan, Pres. of the Board of Education; J. Wheatley, Minister of Health.

(1) The election of Dec. 1923 had been fought on the single issue of the Conservative demand for protection; the result was Conservatives 258; Labour 191; Liberals 159. Defeated in the Commons, the Conservatives resigned. George V held that Labour, never before in office, must, as the next largest party, be given a fair chance and sent for Macdonald. Only Henderson and Haldane had been cabinet members before; only three others had ever held any office. The Govt. depended on Liberal support. Nevertheless its achievements in its nine months were considerable.

(2) At home, Snowden cut expenditure and the remaining wartime tariffs. Wheatley's Housing Act required district councils and boroughs to build houses for rent and raised the building subsidy and by thus settling the direction of the national housing policy until 1932, quietly established the principle that housing was a social service. Trevelyan's Education Act created an English secondary school system between the ages of 11-14 (with the intention of raising it later) and so established another principle, namely that everybody is bound to undertake at least some education beyond the elementary stage.

(3) In foreign policy the Govt. sensibly sought to assuage the post-war Franco-German animosities. It believed that the French had less to fear from Germany than they believed and that therefore a British guarantee could be usefully given because it would never have to be honoured, and would calm French nerves. On the other hand Macdonald was riding a tide of pro-German sentiment, well known to the Germans, and he negotiated a Reparations policy (*The Dawes Plan*) under which the Germans paid less than before, the French accepted less and Britain got enough to pay interest on Baldwin's War Debt settlement with the U.S.A.

(4) With all the information of office, Macdonald had ceased, unlike his left wing, to imagine that Bolshevism was simply an extreme colour in the socialist spectrum. He recognised the Communist Govt. of Russia and demanded repayment of part of the pre-war British Russian loans. The Russians refused unless Britain made them a Govt. guaranteed loan. In Aug. at the start of the summer recess, negotiations broke down. The Labour left wing mediated a compromise: there was to be, first, a commercial treaty, then a debt settlement and finally a loan. The Russians accepted this. It was, of course, attacked by the Conservatives, but more importantly, Lloyd George turned the Liberals and bullied Asquith into opposing it. It was obvious that when Parliament reassembled the Govt. would fall. It was defeated at the end of Sept. by 364 to 191, not, however on the treaties issue but on the *Campbell Affair* (q.v.). The course of the subsequent election was slightly influenced by the Zinoviev Letter (q.v.).

MACDONALD'S FIRST NATIONAL GOVT. (Aug.-Nov. 1931).

Ten in cabinet viz: J. Ramsey Macdonald (Lab), Prime Minister; Lord Sankey (Lab), Lord Chancellor; Stanley Baldwin (Con), Lord Pres.; Philip Snowden (Lab), Ch. of the Exch; Sir Herbert Samuel (Lib), Home Sec; The Marquess of Reading (Lib), Foreign Sec; Sir Samuel Hoare (Con), Sec. for India; J. H. Thomas (Lab), Dominions Sec; Sir Philip Cunliffe-Lister (Con), Pres. of the Board of Trade; Neville Chamberlain (Con), Minister of Helath (*see* PREVIOUS ENTRY).

(1) This 'Govt. of co-operation for a specific purpose', namely 'to deal with the national emergency which now exists' was, on the War Cabinet model, kept small. The Liberal M.P.s with one dissentient and the Conservatives unanimously supported it. Macdonald failed to win over the Labour rank and file, nearly all of whom supported by the Trade Union Congress, went into opposition. There were rowdy accusations of cowardice and treachery when Parliament met on 8 Sept. to deal with Snowden's emergency budget.

(2) The budget raised income tax to 25% and cut all persons paid by the state from Ministers to the unemployed by 10% except the police (5%) and the teachers (15%). The King voluntarily gave up 21%. French and American bankers provided credits. The euphoria lasted only a few days. Foreign short term lenders still wanted their money and (correctly) doubted the ability of the City to get all its long term money back from Germany. Reasoned Labour opposition created reasoned doubts and on 15 Sept. the sailors of the fleet at Invergordon refused duty, for some lower-deck cuts exceeded 10% under the published Admiralty scheme. The result was a general limitation to 10% which benefited seamen and teachers without hurting the police.

(3) The damaged image of the greatest naval and trading power created a foreign sterling holders' panic. On 19 Sept. the foreign credits were exhausted. On 21st the Govt. rushed through an act to suspend the gold standard. Sterling fell against the dollar from $4.86 to $3.80 , then to $3.23 and finally settled around $3.40. This helped exports but made no internal difference because gold had not been internally used for half a generation.

(4) There were now calls for a General Election 'to strengthen the National Govt.' which was supposed to have saved the nation. The Cabinet for once decided upon it. The Prime Minister was to explain the general reasons for it, the parties to put forward their own programmes. It was held on 27 Oct. The electors overwhelmingly confirmed the Conservative capture of Macdonald.

MACDONALD'S SECOND LABOUR GOVT. (June 1929-Aug. 1931)

Nineteen in Cabinet. Under J. Ramsey Macdonald the main personalities were Lord Sankey, Lord Chancellor; J. H. Thomas, Ld. Privy Seal; Philip Snowden, Ch. of the Exch; J. R. Clynes, Home Sec; Arthur Henderson, Home Sec; Lord Passfield, Colonial and Dominions Sec; W. Wedgwood Benn, Sec. for India; C. P. Trevelyan, Pres. of the Board of Education; Margaret Bondfield, Min. of Labour; Arthur Greenwood, Min. of Health; George Lansbury, First Commissioner of Works.

(1) In the General Election of May 1929, owing to population movements since the 1911 census, the Liberals won 59 seats, Labour 288, the Conservatives 260. Labour took office with Liberal support. Margaret Bondfield was the first woman cabinet minister. Lansbury, the spokesman of the Labour left got on splendidly with the King, but because the Govt. could be turned out at any time by the (mostly Asquithian) Liberals, no socialist or even very radical programme was possible.

(2) The Govt., having inherited prosperity and social tranquillity at home, addressed the more pressing foreign issues which had been allowed to slide. In Aug. 1929 The Hague Conference settled the Young Plan for German reparations. This reduced Germany's payments and relieved her of allied control; and while Snowden maintained the previous British share, Henderson got rid of the cost of the other allies by getting Allied troops withdrawn, to the pleasure of the Germans, five years ahead of time, from the Rhineland. International conciliation was in the air. This happy compound result laid the foundation of Henderson's rise as a briefly leading figure in the League of Nations, which suffered

from the death of the German Gustaf Stresemann in Oct., and the slow withdrawal of Aristide Briand. Henderson understood the French better than Macdonald and his record at The Hague had made him popular with the Germans. He was thus able to steer the Preparatory Commission on Disarmament, which had been in the doldrums, to the summoning of a World Disarmament Conference for Feb. 1932, and in the meantime Macdonald began the naval negotiations with U.S.A., Japan, France and Italy which ended in the useful T. of London.

(3) In Oct. 1929 came the great American Wall Street Crash. American capital exports and current account purchases stopped. The primary producer countries could not afford foreign (including British) goods and no longer needed British shipping. Merchant ships were laid up: exporters, having lost their markets, laid off their workpeople. Unemployment rose from 1 million to 2 million in eight months: to 2.5 million by Dec. 1930. Other countries were in similar difficulties. This was the background against which foreign policy initiatives, begun in happier times, had to be continued. Naturally the issues, such as disarmament, involving financial savings were easier to resolve than those where hitherto dominant powers were resisting, with weakened resources, the demands of rising independence.

(4) In the same month as the crash the Viceroy, Ld. Irwin, made a public promise of Dominion status for India. Not for nothing were the Indian political intellectuals educated in a Britain where "England's difficulty is Ireland's opportunity". The Indian National Congress (I.N.C.) declared independence and Ghandi led a march across India to the sea to distil salt, defy the tax system and institute civil disobedience. These moves by the apostle of non-violence naturally led to bloodshed. He was arrested. In June 1930 the Simon Commission recommended provincial responsible govt. and further negotiations on the form of the central Govt. A Round Table Conference was convened in Nov. The I.N.C. refused to attend. The princes agreed to enter a future Indian confederation. Thereupon the I.N.C. expressed interest after all. Ghandi was released from his comfortable custody and after discussions with the Viceroy, agreed to attend a second session.

(5) The considerations which enabled the parties to agree on armaments' reduction (see BALDWIN'S SECOND GOVT) made attacks on the Suez Canal unlikely. Moreover, France and Italy were friendly and the Ottoman Empire had vanished. To replace the British political and military presence in the Middle East by treaty relationships should not jeopardise this vital imperial link, but the efforts to achieve it failed, in Egypt because the Egyptians (weaker than the Indians) demanded by the proposed treaty to regain their hold, lost in 1924, over the Sudan whereas the British preferred an autonomous but client stage; and in Palestine because the British had accepted a Mandate in which rising Jewish immigration was irreconcilable with the rights and needs of the indigenous populations.

(6) In other imperial relations the effects of conciliation were strikingly disparate and sometimes unexpected. The Balfour definition of the Commonwealth was turned into legal shape by the Statute of Westminster 1931. This freed Eire and S. Africa to get rid of their entrenched constitutional clauses by whatever means were locally available, but the Canadian provinces and minorities preferred that their rights should continue to be protected under Westminster-enacted law.

(7) The British depression was uneven in its effects. The terms of overseas trade rose by 20% and its volume fell by nearly 60%. The latter caused the unemployment, but the wages of those in work remained stable. Moreover unemployment was not spread throughout the country but concentrated in ports, shipyards, the textile

districts of Lancashire and Yorkshire and the coalfields of S. Wales, E. Kent, the N. Midlands and northern counties, and Lanark, all far from London. Geography screened off those in power, stable wages those in work, from those in trouble. This made for unreality in the discussion of solutions. The only original ideas were offered by Sir Oswald Mosley who, like Dr Hjalmar Schacht of the German Reichsbank, advocated an extreme *dirigisme* in the form of planned foreign trade, direction of industry and the use of credit to promote growth. Such ideas offended Snowden, the conscientious free-traders, socialists and libertarians. In May 1930 the Cabinet threw them out. Mosley resigned his minor office and took the fight first to the Parliamentary Labour Party and then to the Party Conference. His speeches were admired but the inertia of party loyalty smothered his influence. He founded his New Party and slowly drifted away into alien extremisms.

(8) The side effects of unemployment, not the problem itself, brought the Govt. down. Mounting expenditure on unemployment relief had to be met from falling tax-yields. Snowden increased income and super-taxes and accepted a liberal proposal for an economy committee under Sir George May. He produced an interim budget (Apr.) and expected from the committee a report with which he could bully Labour into accepting economy, and the opposition, higher taxes. Another report, however, had previously drawn attention to the effect of the slump on the invisible earnings which had always closed the perennial trade gap. The City had been trying to re-establish itself as a world financial centre by accepting short-term deposits from victorious countries at 2% and making long term loans to defeated countries at 8% or even 10%. The system depended on a steady flow of short term money. The French now started to withdraw their deposits, because of tension with Germany. Austrian and German banks started to collapse because English banks could no longer support them. Then there was a run on the pound. Macdonald, recalled from holiday, met bankers who feared a European wide collapse of credit and trade. They insisted that a balanced budget could alone restore confidence. The May committee had proposed further taxes and a 20% cut in unemployment relief. Fearing still more foreign trade-generated unemployment and faced with the false analogy of the earlier European wheel-barrow inflations, the Cabinet quarrelled. Clynes, Henderson and seven others were not impressed by May. Neither were economists like J. M. Keynes. The nine (out of 19) threatened to resign against unemployment relief cuts. The Liberals suggested a temporary, all party Govt. for the duration of the crisis. The King liked the idea. Macdonald resigned in order to form it. *See* NEXT ENTRY.

MACDONALD'S SECOND NATIONAL GOVT. (Nov. 1931-June 1935).

Twenty in Cabinet. Nine of the ten members of the previous cabinet remained, with some changes in office viz: Philip Snowden as Lord Snowden became Lord Privy Seal; Neville Chamberlain, Ch. of the Exch; Sir Philip Cunliffe-Lister became Colonial Sec. and was replaced at the Board of Trade by William Runciman (Nat. Lib). The M. of Reading left the Govt. and Sir John Simon (Nat. Lib.) became Home Sec; Sir Archibald Sinclair (Lib) became Sec. for Scotland.

(1) In the General Election of Oct. 1931, the Conservatives took 473 seats, their allies the (Simonite) National Liberals 35; Macdonald's National Labour 13 making 521. The Labour opposition 52; Lloyd George's Liberals 4. All the Labour leaders lost their seats except George Lansbury who found himself, to his surprise, leader of the opposition. Despite the immense conservative preponderance, the electorate had voted to continue a 'national' i.e. a co-operative Govt., and so, though the Prime Minister was virtually a prisoner of the Conservatives, they had to let him allot cabinet posts to

the other parties as well as themselves. Raising the cabinet from 10 to 20 made more posts available.

(2) The Govt. had to take up the unemployment problem at once. Industry generally was to be revived by a degree of protection and in 1932 Chamberlain brought in an Import Duties Bill. The Commonwealth Conference at Ottawa was not a success. There were some bilateral but no general preferential agreements because the dominions wanted to protect their own industries. The Govt. also got some uncompetitive businesses to close in order to clear the way for help for the distressed areas (*see* MACDONALD'S SECOND LABOUR GOVT-7) through the Special Areas legislation (1934) and a new Unemployment Insurance Act provided help for the poor, subject to a much criticised means test. Unfortunately all these beneficial measures needed time to take effect and meanwhile there was misfortune, discontent and demonstrations such as the march of the Jarrow shipbuilders to London.

(3) Meanwhile the international outlook darkened. The Japanese invasion of the Manchuria preceded (1932-3) Hitler's accession to power in Germany (May 1933). The former was too far off to interest British public opinion much and British Chinese interests were mostly much further south. The full beastliness of the Nazi regime was initially masked by the lawful means which brought it to power; it took some time to establish and afterwards people could not believe what was happening. The only clear-sighted personality was Winston Churchill who made himself unpopular. 1932 had been, too, a bad year for the enormous British overseas investments. In S. America they were put in jeopardy by revolutions in Chile and Brazil, wars between Peru and Colombia and between Paraguay and Bolivia and civil disturbances in Mexico. Moreover, in Nov. Persia cancelled the Anglo-Persian Oil Co's concession.

(4) Disillusionment with the League of Nations was growing. Having investigated Japanese Manchurian aggression through the Lytton Commission (*see* MANCHURIA) it was defied by Japan which resigned. Other symptoms of instability included Adolf Hitler's murderous *coup* by means of a violent elite against his own mass support in the *Schützabteilungen* (S.A. or Brown Shirts). In Europe small countries huddled together like sheep sensing a wolf. There was a tendency for powers to negotiate regional or specialised pacts instead of relying on the League. Of these the most noticeable was to be the Franco-Russian Treaty of mutual assistance of May 1935. The collective security which the League was supposed to enshrine was seen to be weak when shaken by a single determined power. Then in June 1934 Germany suspended cash transfers abroad and effectively ended reparations. At the end of the year Japan, which had been evading the Washington naval agreement since 1931, came out into the open and denounced it.

(5) 1935 opened with the plebiscite in the Saar, where the population, over-exploited by the French and overwhelmed by Nazi propaganda voted almost without dissent to rejoin Germany (Jan.). The British thought that this was only just. It postponed yet again the moment of revelation. The Saar was returned to Germany on 7 Mar. On 16th Germany, which had long been evading the military provisions of the Versailles T., took a leaf out of Japan's book and repudiated them. Representatives of Britain, France and Italy met ineffectually at Stresa to consider the consequences. In these circumstances of drift, disbelief and delayed economic recovery, the Labour Ramsey Macdonald, who was unwell, retired by the expedient of exchanging offices with the Conservative Stanley Baldwin.

MACDONALD, Flora (1722-90) met Prince Charles Edward in 1746 at the Clanranalds in Benbecula and helped him to escape to Skye. She was imprisoned but released in 1747 and from 1774-79 lived in N. Carolina.

MacDONNELL, Anthony Patrick (1844-1925) 1st Ld. MACDONNELL of SWINFORD (1908), the principal draughtsman of the Bengal Tenancy Act 1885, was Lieut-Gov. of the United Provinces from 1895-1901 and then in 1902 Permanent U/Sec. to the Govt. of Ireland. His Irish Land Act, 1902 dealt with analogous problems to those of Bengal. He tried to get more authority devolved upon the Dublin Govt., but ran into opposition from the nationalists who feared that it might weaken their case. He was more successful with higher education: the National University of Ireland and Queen's University Belfast being directly attributable to his work. He resigned in 1908.

MACDONNELL CLANS. These are offshoots of the Macdonalds of the Isles and of Argyll, split, through Campbell pressure, so that part was confined to Glen Garry (Inverness), while the rest were migrating to Antrim (Ulster) in the 15-16th cent. These have an unclear relationship with the O'Donnells further west. **A.** The **GLEN GARRY CLAN** was Jacobite until their chief **(1) Alastair Ruadh (1725-61)**, employed by Jacobite chiefs on secret missions to the Young Pretender, was captured by the English and converted into a double agent under the cover name of Pickle the Spy. The Jacobite defeat and his activities induced them to let him return to Glen Garry in 1754. **(2)** The remarkable **Alexander (1762-1840)** was ordained a R. Catholic priest in Spain in 1787, and when on mission helped to form R. Catholic Highlanders into the Glengarry Fencibles. These were disbanded at the P. of Amiens. He obtained land in Canada for them and re-formed them in 1812 to play a notable part in the defence against the Americans (*see* ANGLO-AMERICAN WAR 1812-15). Afterwards he simultaneously helped to organise the colony and to carry on his religious mission. In 1819 he became Vicar Apostolic of Upper Canada, in 1826, Bp. of Regiopolis (Lat = Kingston, Ontario).

B. The **ANTRIM CLAN** led by **(1) Sorley Boy (1505-90)**, chief on both sides of the water and Lord of the Route, was migrating into O'Neill country and its position depended on English support. They made him Constable of Dunluce but in the 1560s their policy changed and by 1565 the Macdonnells were mostly driven back into Scotland. He then made his submission to the English and returned as Common Law grantee as opposed to the O'Neill tribal possession. His son **(2) Sir Randal (?-1636) 1st Vist. DUNLUCE (1618) 1st E. of ANTRIM (1620)** having joined the O'Neill revolt of 1600, submitted in 1602 and thereafter helped the Lord Deputy to keep the O'Neill in check. This became relatively easy after the Flight of the Earls (1607) and he eventually filled much of the void by becoming an Earl himself. The clan, thus originally Scottish, became Anglo-orientated and eventually protestant, but the Earls after 1696 mostly concentrated on land management.

MACE was originally a heavy metal club for battering in chain mail. Later, because of its resemblance to a sceptre it was used to symbolise high rank and was then ornamented with an arched crown at the head, and often made of a precious metal. In this form it symbolised the presence and delegation of royal authority, and is consequently carried covered or reversed in the Sovereign's presence; hence its place in the House of Commons, its use by the Lord Chancellor and by Lord Mayors of major cities and at the other end of the scale, in the small handy often iron variety used by parish constables. Because of their association with influential bodies, many escaped the melting pot during the 17th cent. political crises and now represent the largest class of surviving ancient plate.

MACEDONIA. *See* BULGARIA.

MACE[G]GAN, Owen or Eugene (?-1603), Irish priest and agitator secured Spanish help for Tyrone's rebellion of 1601. He returned and, as Vicar Apostolic, animated the rebels but was killed in a skirmish.

MACHIAVELLI, Niccolo (1469-1527) held various offices in Florence and from 1502-03 was the republic's most influential adviser. He is famed for his political writings. These include *The Prince* (1513, Eng. Tr. 1640), *The Art of War* (1520, Eng. Tr. 1562), and the *Florentine History* (1525, Eng. Tr. 1595). *The Prince* was known in England under Henry VIII and is said to have influenced Thomas Cromwell and Cecil. It is a clear sighted and therefore disagreeable description, based upon Italian habits, of the methods of statesmanship and earned him a reputation for double-dealing. The book has always been controversial: in 1739 Frederick II of Prussia, then Crown Prince, published a refutation.

MACHICOLATION. See BRATTICE.

MACHINE GUNS. The *mitrailleuse*, invented in 1851, was introduced into the French army in 1865. Mounted as an artillery piece and organised in batteries it failed in 1870s through bad tactical handling. The Gatling was used in the American Civil War. In the Russo-Turkish War of 1877 the Russians used it while the Turks used the Nordenfelt. The first British use was the Royal Navy's Gatlings in the Zulu War of 1879. So far these were all crank operated and, except the Gatling, multi-barrelled.

The first recoil-operated gun was invented in 1883 by the American Hiram Maxim and it, and its lighter version, the water-cooled Vickers, was adopted by the British in 1891. It revolutionised military tactics, giving great advantage to the defence and soon spread to most countries. Combined with barbed wire and the gas-operated light machine guns (Lewis or Hotchkiss) it brought the western and southern fronts in World War I to bloody stagnation until the coming of the tank.

Air cooled machine guns were first introduced into aircraft in 1916. They fired slowly, but water cooled guns were too heavy. As aircraft speeds rose, research to combine the advantages of both without the disadvantages led to the air-cooled Browning, operated by gas-assisted recoil, which, mounted in eights in fighter aircraft, won the B. of Britain in 1940.

MACINTOSH, Charles (1766-1843) industrial chemist, patented his waterproof cloth in 1822.

MACKAY. Sutherlandshire clan frequently at feud with the Es. of Sutherland, especially under Mary Q. of Scots **(1) Sir Donald (1591-1649) 1st Ld. REAY (1628)** chief of the clan (1614) settled the feud in 1620, and in 1626 was commissioned to raise troops to serve under Mansfeld in the Thirty Years' War but Mansfeld having died, he transferred to Swedish service. He returned to London in 1631. In the Scottish religious controversies he seems to have had, like many others, serious doubts: he was a member of the commission to secure signatures to the National Covenant in the North but in 1643 he raised troops in Denmark for the King's service and gallantly helped to hold Berwick with them in 1644. After Montrose's campaign ended in Sept. 1646, he lay low and eventually went to Denmark where he died. He had children by all his five wives. His eldest son **(2) John (fl. 1650) 2nd Ld.** took part in various Scottish royalist risings under the Commonwealth. His grandson. **(3) George (?-1748) 3rd Ld.** was an active Hanoverian supporter in the Jacobite troubles of 1715, 1719 and 1745. His brother **(4) Aeneas (?)** settled in Holland as commander of the Dutch Mackay regiment and was naturalised. Ultimately the peerage came to his descendant **(5) Aeneas (?-1876)** Baron Mackay d'Ophemert, **10th Ld.** a Dutch Minister of State. Hen **(6) Donald James (-) 11th Ld.** resumed British domicile and allegiance and was Gov. of Bombay from 1885-90.

MACKEAY. Australian founding family. **(1) Alexander (1767-1848)** entomologist and expert on prison administration, was Colonial Secretary in N.S.W. from 1825-37 and Speaker of the first legislative council from 1843-46. Two of his sons and a nephew followed his example. **(2) William Sharp (1792-1865)** went to N.S.W. in 1839 and extended his father's distinguished entomological work. **(3) George (1809-91)** explored S. Australia. The nephew **(4) Sir William (1820-91)** also went to N.S.W. in 1839, was a member of the legislature from 1854. He developed the entomological museum and gave it to the state.

MACKENZIE and MACKENNETH. Two Caithness and central Highlands clans. Colin of Kintail (?-1278) is the ancestor of the first; his son Kenneth (?-1304) of the second and of the Es. of Seaforth and of Cromarty. See *following entries.*

MACKENZIE (CROMARTY) (1) Sir John (?-1654) of Tarbat was a nephew of Kenneth Mackenzie of Kintail. His son **(2) George (1630-1714) 1st Vist. TARBAT (1685) 1st E. of CROMARTY (1703)** joined Glencairn's royalist rising in 1653, migrated abroad and returned at the Restoration. He became, as Ld. Tarbat, a Lord of Session, besides a member of the Estates. He was dismissed from the bench in 1664 for his part in an attempt to oust Lauderdale but appointed Ld. Justice Gen. in 1678 and readmitted to the Court of Session in 1681. When Lauderdale fell in 1682, he succeeded to his political position and he smoothed the way for William III in 1689 by disbanding the militia. Employed to negotiate with the Highlanders, in whose politics he had become well versed, his advice was only partly followed with dangerous results. At Anne's accession be became a Secretary of State but returned to judicial office in 1704. He was an able advocate of the Union. His grandson **(3) George (?-1766) 3rd E. (1731)** was a prominent Jacobite commander in the rebellion of 1745 and condemned to death but pardoned. His *s.* **(4) John (1747-89), Swedish Baron MACLEOD and Count CROMARTY,** was captured, condemned and pardoned with his father, but forced to hand over his estates to the Crown. In 1749 he took service with the Swedish Crown, but returned in 1777 and raised the 73rd (later 71st) Foot from his clansmen. With these he campaigned successfully in India. In 1780 he became M.P. for Ross (his home ground) and in 1784 the family estates were returned.

MACKENZIE (SEAFORTH). Highland Clan Chiefs **(1) Kenneth (?- 1611) 12th Chief, 1st Ld. MACKENZIE of KINTAIL (1609)** greatly enlarged the clan territory, particularly by acquiring the I. of Lewis. His second son **(2) George (?- 1651) 14th Chief, 3rd Ld., 2nd E. of SEAFORTH (1633)**, a 'covenanting royalist', helped to prevent Huntly's attempt on Inverness (Feb. 1639) (*see* GRAHAM OF MONTROSE-5), offered to join Leslie's covenanting army (May) and then persuaded the Gordons to go home by disbanding his own troops. In July he was image-breaking, but later, with Montrose, he signed the band of Cumbernauld. During Montrose's celebrated campaign he started neutral. Then, professing adherence to the Covenant, he was involved in Hurry's defeat at Auldearn; and finally he came over to Montrose and was excommunicated for apostasy. After Charles I's death (1649) he joined Charles II who made him his Scottish Secretary. He died in Holland. His nephew **(3) Sir George (1636-91)**, a very professional lawyer, known to Covenanters as 'Bloody MacKenzie', came to eminence by his determined defence of the covenanting M. of Argyll at his trial before the Estates in 1661. He entered the Scots Parliament in 1669, and after a period of opposition to Lauderdale became, as Ld. Advocate (1677) one of his ablest supporters. His first act was to release many prisoners long detained without trial; yet, after the rising of 1679 he prosecuted covenanters with relentless ingenuity. They threatened assassination; he secured legislation imposing summary death for refusal to disclose the possession of arms. It was during this time that he founded the Advocates Library. He resigned in 1686 when James II abrogated the laws against R. Catholics and as a private practitioner defended covenanters. In Feb. 1688 he was reappointed, and opposed James's deposition to the Estates in 1689. After the revolution he went, publicly, to England and entered Oxford University. He was a famous party wit, detested religious extremism and prevented the torture of witches. His kinsman, a grandson of **(2)**, **(4) Kenneth (?-1701) 16th Chief, 4th E. (1678)** was a Jacobite who was imprisoned intermittently between 1690-97 and died in Paris. His son **(5) William (?-1740) 17th Chief and 5th E.** called 'The Black' also a Jacobite, raised 3000 men for the Pretender in 1715, escaped to Paris and was attainted. His clansmen continued to send him rents, but in 1725 on Gen. Wade's advice he was relieved of the penal effects of the attainder but not the forfeitures and was given an allowance out of his forfeited estates, to relieve the clansmen. He died in Lewis.

MACKENZIE, Murdoch (?-1797) originated a scientific method of survey by triangulation by which he mapped the Orkneys between 1742-50. The Admiralty commissioned him to survey the coasts of the British Is., and by 1770, when he retired, he had finished Ireland, and Britain as far as Pembroke. He nephew **Murdoch the Younger (1743-1829)** carried on his work.

MACKENZIE KING, William Lyon. See CANADA-27.

MACKINNON, William Alexander (1789-1870), Tory M.P. from 1830-52, Liberal from 1852-65. He was a practical legislator who sponsored bills on patents, turnpikes and rural police and against urban burials and pollution.

MACKWORTH, Sir Humphrey (1627-1727), son of a Cromwellian colonel from Shropshire, started developing collieries and copper smelting near Neath, after his wife became the sole heiress of the Evans property in Glamorgan. By 1698 he had bought the Price mines and he then transferred the whole to a Company of Mine Adventurers with the Duke of Leeds as Governor and himself as Deputy Governor. He raised large amounts by lottery to build docks and canals and became an M.P. Neighbouring rivals objected and in 1709 the members of the Co. quarrelled. His opponents in the Co. got him declared guilty of fraud by the House of Commons, but failed to get a bill restraining his activities passed. He was also a founder and one of the largest subscribers to the S.P.C.K. and wrote many religious and political pamphlets. These, particularly one of 1705 accusing the Whigs of designs on the Church, probably occasioned the attack on his business.

MACKY, John (?-1726), British spy on the Jacobite court in France, brought timely warning of the planned French attack in 1692. He had probably traced the communications of Jacobite agents, for from Oct. 1693 he was inspector of the coast from Harwich to Dover and in 1696 he discovered the proposed plan of attack in connection with Sir George Barclay's plot. He published a best selling pamphlet on the Jacobite court at this time. After Sept. 1697 he changed his cover and became director of the packets between Dover and Ostend, Calais and Boulogne. These were discontinued at William III's death (1702) and he went to the I. of Zante where he had property. They revived when the French wars began again. He returned in 1706 and in 1708 reported on aggressive preparations at Dunkirk. This type of work necessarily involved double agency; he fell under suspicion and was imprisoned until 1714. His *Memoirs* are a valuable source for the period.

MACLAINES, James (1724-50) gentleman highwayman who between 1748-50, *inter alios*, robbed Horace Walpole and passed in London society as an Irish squire. A "famous kept mistress" was found at his lodgings when he was arrested and great ladies shed tears at his trial.

MACLEAN. See BURGESS.

MACLEOD, Iain Norman (1913-70) journalist and progressive Tory M.P. from 1950, was Minister of Health (1952-5). The M. of Salisbury once described him as 'too clever by half'. His dislike of the Suez Affair in 1956 may

have helped to change the Govt.'s mind. He became Colonial Sec. in 1959 to introduce multiracial solutions for the serious political problems in Kenya and began to abandon the Central African Federation in favour of majority regimes in an independent Nyasaland (Malawi) and N. Rhodesia (Zambia), thereby facilitating the rise of local tribal factions disguised as political parties. From 1961-63 he was Leader of the Commons as well as Chairman of the Conservative Party Organisation and from 1963-65 he was editor of the *Spectator*. In 1970 he was appointed Chancellor of the Exchequer but died suddenly.

MACLAURIN, Colin (1698-1746) Professor of Mathematics at Marischal College, Aberdeen at the age of seventeen and F.R.S. at 21, brilliantly developed Newton's calculus in his *Geometrica Organica sive Descriptio Linearum Curvarum Universalis* (Lat. = Organic Geometry or Principles of the Curve) (1720) and *A Treatise of Fluxions* (1742). He died of dropsy and exertions in organising the defence of Edinburgh against the Jacobites in 1745.

MACMAHON. Irish sept mostly in Monaghan. **(1) Heber (1600-50)** an active conspirator was heavily involved in the Irish rebellion of 1644 and was appointed R. Catholic Bp. of Clogher in 1642. He was popular and influential in his diocese and a partisan of, and adviser to, the Papal legate Rinuccini and his basically Spanish policy. While the Irish quarrelled, the Parliament took Dublin in 1647 and in 1648 MacMahon tried to reconcile Ormonde and O'Neill in Ulster. As the Parliamentarians were making dangerous headway in Munster, the reconciliation was effected in 1649, but only at the expense of MacMahon (who had no military training) becoming general of the combined forces. He was captured at Scariffhollis in June 1650 and executed. His cousin **(2) Hugh Oge (?1606-44)** was the indiscreet conspirator with Ld. Maguire and others who accidentally gave away the plan to seize Dublin Castle in 1641. After adventures, including an escape from the Tower, he was executed at Tyburn.

MACMAHON, Marshal Marie Edmé Patrice (1808-93) of Irish Jacobite origins, was Gov-Gen. of Algeria from 1864-70 and held the highest commands under the Emperor against the Prussians in the disastrous campaigns leading to the surrender at Sédan. Released after the peace he suppressed the communard revolts and in May 1873 became Pres. of the Republic. Suspected of royalism, he resigned in 1879.

MACMILLAN, (Maurice) Harold (1894-1986) E. of STOCKTON (1984) a member of the publishing family educated at Eton and Oxford, served in the trenches of the Western Front in World War I. He entered politics as Conservative M.P. for Stockton-on-Tees (1924-9 and 1931-5) and then moved to Bromley (1945-64). His experiences at Stockton during the slump, gave him an abiding sympathy with the difficulties of the ordinary man. After holding minor offices, he was sent to N. Africa as Resident Minister with the Allied H.Q. in the Mediterranean area. He had to deal with a multiplicity of problems including those posed by the adherents of Adm. Darlan, the rivalry between Gens. de Gaulle and Giraud. He had to establish a co-operative framework for the Allied commanders under Gen. Eisenhower, manage Italian anti-Fascist politicians and deal with Tito's Yugoslav Partisans. Though he consciously surrendered the Yugoslav Chetniks into the murderous hands of their Partisan enemies, he carried through his tasks otherwise with credit. He left in 1945 to become Sec. of State for Air in Churchill's caretaker Govt. When the Conservatives returned to power he became Minister of Housing and Local Govt. (1951-4) and gained much credit by promising to build 300,000 houses a year and then, by organising the brick industry, doing so. He was Minister of Defence in 1954-5 and Foreign Sec. in 1955 and then Chancellor of the Exchequer (1955-7). A witty speaker, as Prime Minister from 1957 (*see* MACMILLAN GOVT.) he was the obvious dominating personality in the Commons. His affection for the British past did not prevent him looking forward: as a young M.P. he had championed the unemployed; a little later he foresaw and urged precautions against the rise of Nazism, and as Prime Minister he made notable reforms in the House of Lords and told the white S. Africans to heed the 'wind of change'. Later still, as Chancellor of Oxford University, he described ex-Prime Ministers as 'a small and unpopular species'.

MACMILLAN GOVT. (Jan. 1957-Oct. 1963) (1) On Eden's resignation after the Suez Affair, the Conservatives preferred Harold Macmillan to the Dep. Premier, R. A. Butler, who became Home Sec. Selwyn Lloyd stayed at the Foreign Office. Peter Thorneycroft moved to the Exchequer. Duncan Sandys, who in 1954 was Minister of Housing under Churchill, went to the Ministry of Defence and in 1959 to Aviation. The right-wing M. of Salisbury remained Lord Pres. There were several major later changes. In 1958 Thorneycroft and a few junior ministers resigned when Macmillan would not countenance a restrictive budget. Heathcote Amory then went to the Exchequer but was replaced by Lloyd in 1960 with the E. of Home moving from the Commonwealth Relations to the Foreign Office and Duncan Sandys replacing him. In 1962, in a remarkable reshuffle called the *Night of Long Knives,* Reginald Maudling, expected to be more amenable to expansionist economics, replaced Lloyd; Peter Thorneycroft replaced Watkinson at Defence. Sandys moved to the Colonial Office, Edward Boyle replaced Eccles at Education and Henry Brooke replaced Butler, who became First Sec. of State without specific responsibilities. Edward Heath, Lord Privy Seal to handle the Common Market negotiations since 1960, remained in place.

(2) This new govt. enjoyed rising living standards, but the stop-go economic sequence was not overcome. 1957-8 was a period of restraint with restrictions on credit and high interest rates but in 1958 the Govt's refusal to give in to a London 'bus strike created confidence and there was fast growth in the next year. This helped Macmillan, who supervised foreign policy, to improve relations with Pres. Eisenhower who was hostile to Britain but personally friendly to Macmillan. Macmillan's sympathy with ordinary people led him to promote legislation to encourage industries to move to areas of unemployment, and Govt. spending increased, particularly on motorways, higher education and forces' pay. All this helped to win the 1959 General Election with 365 seats in a House of 615.

(3) Decolonisation proceeded, Ghana and Malaya leading the way, but there were complications in Kenya and Central Africa. Some Mau Mau terrorists were said to have been beaten to death in the Hola camp (Kenya) and there were accusations that a diluted police state was being imposed in Nyasaland. The appointment of the liberal minded Iain Macleod to the Colonial Office (1959-61) was a response and in 1960 Macmillan made his celebrated reference to the 'winds of change' in a speech to S. Africans. In 1961 S. Africa became a republic, but its application to remain in the Commonwealth was scouted by most heads of Commonwealth Govts. Britain accepted the majority decision without herself voting, in order to preserve the Commonwealth.

(4) Defence policy, transformed by atomic weapons, reacted on European policy while permitting the end of conscription. The essential, if expensive missile systems required money which the Govt. could not find. The Blue Streak programme was cancelled in favour of the U.S. Skybolt. When this was cancelled Macmillan agreed to take the Polaris from the U.S.A. This angered the French.

(5) There was a significant programme of home legislation. The Rent Act halted the decline of the housing stock by permitting landlords to raise some very low rents. The Peerage Act of 1959 started a creeping revolution in the House of Lords. The Street Offences Act 1959 made life harder for prostitutes, the Betting and Games Act easier for bookmakers and there was the first of several acts against immigration, but the 1962-3 winter was exceptionally cold, so that unemployment rose to almost 880,000 and the Polaris (Nassau) agreement caused Gen. de Gaulle to veto Britain's entry into the Common Market on the pretext that Britain was dominated by the U.S.A. Meanwhile newspaper sensations alarmed the public. In 1963 the Vassall and Profumo cases shook the Govt. The former involved the sale of secrets to the Russians; the latter was not a spy case at all but (despite media efforts to say otherwise) was no more than a salacious intrigue. At this time, Macmillan had to have an operation and sensibly resigned.

MACMILLAN and MAY COMMITTEES (1929-31) were set up by Philip Snowden, the Labour Chancellor of the Exchequer, Macmillan to discover what was wrong with the financial system, May to propose remedies for the budgetary deficits. The former thought that the exchange rate should be managed rather than fixed, and indicated that Sterling was overvalued. This shook international confidence in the pound, which began to desert London. The latter recommended large expenditure cuts, which threatened even more unemployment. Torn by internal dissension, the Labour Govt. collapsed.

MACNAGHTEN'S CASE. *See* DRUMMOND, EDWARD.

MACNAGHTEN, Sir Edward (1830-1913) Ld. MCNAGHTEN (LP 1887), was a Conservative M.P. for Antrim from 1880 and for N. Antrim from 1885. A respected court practitioner, he became at one bound a Lord of Appeal in 1887 and his judgements were widely known for learning, clarity and humour.

MACNAGHTEN, Sir William Hay (1793-1844), learned in Indian languages and law, was Secretary to the Governor General from 1830-33 and then until 1837 was in charge of the secret and political department. He was with Ld. Auckland in the N.W. and became resident at Kabul in 1838. It was on his advice that Shah Suja was supported against the Dost Mohammed. He was then appointed Governor of Bombay but stayed on to help deal with the Afghan insurrection in which he was a victim of the incompetence of the military, and of the treachery of the Dost's son Akbar, who shot him during a parley.

MACNEILL, Eoin (1867-1945) Professor of Early Irish History, met the Sinn Fein leaders through the Gaelic Society and became C-of-S of the Irish Volunteers in 1913. As he was against a rising, because it was unlikely to succeed, the Irish Republican Brotherhood plotted behind his back. He learned of the plan three days before the date fixed for the Easter Rising, agreed to it, but on hearing of Casement's capture countermanded it. The others went on. He was imprisoned but released in 1917 and became an M.P. He supported the Anglo-Irish T, became Irish Minister of Education and represented the Free State on the Ulster Boundary Commission. He was bitterly attacked when the two Govts. agreed to the present boundary and in 1927 returned to academic life.

MACNEILL, James (1869-1938) was Irish High Commissioner in London from 1923-28 and the last Governor General of Ireland from 1928-32.

MACONS BILL No. 2. *See* NON-INTERCOURSE-4.

MACPHERSON, James (?-1700) wandering Scottish bandit, eventually executed.

MACQUARIE, Lachlan (1762-1824). *See* AUSTRALIA-4.

MACWILLIAM. These descendants of William *s.* of K. Duncan II of Scots claimed the throne. The attempts of **(1) Donald (?- 1187),** his sons **(2) Guthred (?-1212)** and **(3) Donald (?-1215)** all ended in their execution. A fourth attempt by an unidentified Macwilliam in 1230 ended at Forfar in the murder of his baby daughter.

MADAGASCAR first sighted by Europeans in 1500 had Portuguese missions between 1600-19 and an English settlement at Nosi Bé in the 1630s. The French garrisoned Fort Dauphine from 1642-74. At this time the Malagasy states were still primitive but the Hovas of Antananarivo and the Sakalavas in the south overshadowed the rest. The west coast swarmed with European pirates (including William Kidd) who preyed on the busy East India and Arab shipping in the Mozambique Channel, which the French tried to police. They annexed Ste Marie in 1750, tried to reoccupy Fort Dauphine in 1768 and Antogil in 1786. The Sakalava remained fiercely tribal and disorganised but the Hova King Andrianampoinamerina (r. 1787-1810) established the kingdom of MERINA.

The later Napoleonic Wars inaugurated a long period of local Anglo-French rivalry. There was a French agent at Tamatave from 1803-11 but King Radama I (r. 1810-28) came to an understanding with Sir Robt. Farquhar, Gov. of Mauritius; he received arms in return for abolishing the export of slaves and this enabled him to conquer most of the island. From about 1820 Christian missions began to arrive. When he died his chief queen, Ranavalona I (r. 1828-61) seized power. She was, not without reason, suspicious of European practices: from 1835 Christianity was illegal and from 1845 the island was closed to foreigners. Though outlying provinces were in constant revolt, the Hovas beat off an Anglo-French attack on Tamatave in 1845. Radama II (r. 1861-3) reversed his mother's policy, opened the country to foreigners and granted concessions to a French Co. Before the treaty could be ratified the previously ruling faction led by Rainilaiarivony, the chief minister, murdered him. He proceeded to marry each of the last three queens Rasoherina (1863-8), Ranavalona II (1868-83) and Ranavalona III (1883-96). He made treaties with Britain, France and the U.S.A. and permitted Christian missions from many different sects, so as to play off the powers against each other. Imerina was ruled directly, with the eastern and north eastern states as tributary. The army, however, had declined and the Sakalavas, with whom the French intrigued, remained independent. The British continued to improve the army.

In 1883 the French demanded the protectorate of the Sakalavas as the price of recognising the new Q. Ranavalona III. When this was refused they occupied Tamatave and by a treaty of 1885 obtained the cession of Diego Suarez and the conduct of Hova foreign relations. The British conceded the special French position in return for Zanzibar in 1890. In 1894 the French occupied Antananarivo and in 1896 abolished the monarchy.

The island was developed rapidly until 1940 when it declared for Vichy after the French surrender. The British occupied it in 1942 and handed it over to Gen. de Gaulle in 1943. The damage to French prestige was irreparable and a rising in 1947 eventually led to autonomy in 1958 and independence within the French community in 1960.

MADAME (Fr.) standing alone, was the title of princesses of the French Royal House and particularly of the eldest daughter of the King or Dauphin. Under Louis XIV it was used exclusively by the wife of **MONSIEUR**, the King's eldest (or in this case only) brother. **MADEMOISELLE** was the latter's eldest daughter.

MADDEN, Sir Charles Edward (1862-1935) O.M. (1931) one of the ablest, most versatile and least known of modern Admirals began as a torpedo expert and became Fisher's naval assistant at the Admiralty during the reforms 1906-7. He was the first Captain of the *Dreadnought* as well as Chief of Staff to the Home Fleet (1907-08) and 4th Sea Lord (1910-11). From 1914-16, during the opening decisive years of naval aspects of World War I he was C. of Staff of the Grand Fleet. From 1916-19 he was 2-in-C to Beatty and commander of the first Battle Squadron. After further conventional service in a shrinking navy he became First Sea Lord in 1927 and in

that capacity correctly but unsuccessfully advised against the reduction of the cruiser strength to fifty at the London naval conference of 1930. He retired after the conference.

MADEIRA (Atl.) possibly known in 14th cent. was uninhabited until 1420 or 1425 when the Portuguese settled at Porto Santo. Sicilian sugar cane was planted and by 1445 sugar was being exported. The islands were granted by Prince Henry the Navigator to the Order of Christ in 1460 but in 1479 Madeira was given to the Braganza family. By 1492 Madeiran sugar had so reduced European sugar prices that production was restricted. It was the principal source until the settlement of W. Indies, but its prosperity was continued on Malmsey, whose stock had also come from Sicily. The islands were useful besides as outward stopping points between Portugal and Brazil. The British occupied them from 1807 to 1814 and during World War II. *See* PENINSULAR WAR 1807-14 − 3; WINE TRADE.

MADELEINE OF FRANCE (?-1537). *See* JAMES V OF SCOTS.

MADHAVA RAO. *See* MARATHAS.

MADHYA PRADESH. *See* CENTRAL INDIA AND BERAR.

MADISON, James (1751-1836) 4th (Democratic-Republican) Pres. of U.S.A. (1809-17) was Jefferson's Sec. of State from 1801-09. He was faced in both offices with problems created for American trade by Anglo-French hostilities and the British policies on blockade and impressment. These combined with American clamour for more British territory eventually led to the unsuccessful War of 1812. *See* ANGLO AMERICAN WAR 1812-15.

"MAD MULLAH". *See* SOMALIA-4.

MAD NUN OF KENT. *See* BARTON, ELIZABETH.

MADOG ap LLEWELYN (fl. 1277-95). His father, an opponent of Llewelyn ap Gruffydd, had been deprived of Meirionydd in 1256 and subsequently lived as a pensioner in England where Madog was brought up and continued in favour after his father's death in 1263. The crown recognised his claim to Meirionydd in 1277 and in 1278 he sued Llewelyn ap Gruffydd for its recovery. He received lands in Anglesey in 1280 and in 1294 he came forward as a leader of the revolt and claimed to be Prince of Wales. He was surprised at Maes Mydog in Mar. 1295 and surrendered in Aug. He died in London.

MADOG ap OWAIN GWYNEDD (1150-?80) was a legendary discoverer of America.

MADOG. *See* POWYS.

MAD PARLIAMENT (1258) was the meeting which produced the Provisions of Oxford.

MADRAS or FORT ST. GEORGE. Francis Day (?-1642), chief of the HEIC factory at Armagaon, procured a site for a new fortified factory from the local ruler in 1630. Conformably with the Golden Firman of 1632, which permitted free trade in the Golconda ports, the rulers of Chandragiri and Golconda confirmed the grant and in 1642 the Co. replaced Masulipatam as the chief British settlement on the Coromandel Coast. It became an independent and prosperous agency by 1653 and received a charter in 1688 and a civil (mayor's) court in 1726. Though taken by the French in 1746, it was restored in 1748 under the P. of Aix la Chapelle. Madras troops under Clive and Watson recovered Calcutta from Suraj-ud-Daula in 1756. The Regulating Act, 1773, placed the Presidency, which by now had acquired considerable, if scattered territories, under the legal but actually nominal control of the Governor General, who was also Governor of Bengal. This led to difficulties and policy divergences, for the Madras presidency had always conducted its foreign relations itself and its Governors understood these questions better than the Govt. of Bengal. Pitt's India Act, 1784, made the subordination explicit but could not control the native powers or the French. The result was that Madras had in practice to conduct most military and political affairs in S.E. India whenever, as often happened, it was or could say that it was attacked. This marcher status continued in effect until the partition of Mysore in 1799 and the annexation of the Carnatic in 1801. Madras had by then become the capital of a huge province embracing the Coromandel Coast from Orissa to C. Comorin and including even part of the Malabar Coast. The wars had left great administrative confusion especially in the land titles and taxation, partly because the various territories had been annexed from different states with different laws. In the north the *Mirasdari* system was adopted. In the south, under the Governorship of the great Sir Thos Munro (r. 1820-7), who understood the disadvantages of the Bengal zamindari system, *ryotwari* was gradually elaborated and introduced. The resulting generation by generation security of tenure did much to settle the country. By 1857 a university could be founded at the city. The presidency remained in its then existing form until Indian Independence. *See* GEORGE II-15.

MADRID, hitherto an unimportant upland village, was made capital of Spain by Philip II in 1561 because of its central position. He was increasingly at Escorial, a day's journey away, where accommodation was inadequate even for his court. Ambassadors made shift at Madrid. Administration and diplomacy was thus much impeded during his reign by the physical inconveniences and distances.

MADRID CONVENTION (29 Jan. 1801) between Lucien Bonaparte and the Spanish Govt. provided that if within 15 days Portugal did not renounce her British alliance, expel British shipping, open her ports to French and Spanish shipping and cede part of her territory to Spain, France and Spain would consider themselves at war with her and France would aid Spain with 15,000 infantry and the necessary communications troops – whose presence would then facilitate a French occupation of Spain. Portugal rejected the demands, was invaded by a Spanish force and surrendered after a three week campaign.

MADRID, T. of (21 Mar. 1801) between Lucien Bonaparte and Godoy (Prince of the Peace) created the Kingdom of Etruria by adding French Piombino to it in exchange for Elba, and vested it an Infante.

MADRID, T. of (1526) between the Emperor Charles V and Francis I of France, a prisoner after his defeat at Pavia (Feb. 1525), whereby Francis was released in return for heavy territorial concessions which were not carried out.

MADRIGAL. This originally Flemish form, consisting of pastoral or amatory poems set contrapuntally for up to six male voices was imported from Italy in about 1588 and soon absorbed into English, especially family life. The high period of this delicate art ended with the civil war. The Madrigal Society, founded in 1741, represented a conscious (and very private) revival.

MAEATAE. *See* BRITAIN, ROMAN 15-17.

MAELGWN GWYNEDD. *See* GWYNEDD-3.

MAELGWYN ap RHYS. *See* DEHEUBARTH-18.

MAELRUAIN, St. (?-792) was founder and abbot of Tallaght (Co. Wicklow) and reformer of the Culdees. He insisted on settlement rather than wandering, encouraged ascetic observances, work and spiritual direction.

MAENOL, MAENOR **(Welsh).** *See* CANTREF.

MAER. *See* WELSH LAW-9.

MAER DREF. The Welsh royal demesne. *See* WELSH LAW- 3.

MAFEKING (Bechuanaland) was the starting point of the Jameson Raid in 1896. In the Boer War it was defended by Baden-Powell against Cronje in a siege lasting from Oct. 1899 to May 1900 when Plumer and Mahon relieved it. This relief caused hysterical rejoicing in Britain.

MAGDALEN COLLEGE, OXFORD, EXPULSIONS FROM. These notorious uses of the dispensing power arose at the death of the College President in Mar. 1687. James II sought to impose the Bp. of Oxford, Samuel Parker, by dispensing with the fellows' right of election. They challenged the legality of the dispensation at Common Law. James cited them before the High Commission which expelled most of them. The resulting vacancies were filled after further dispensations, mostly by R. Catholics. Parker died in 1688 and after a third dispensation, James appointed the Jesuit Bonaventure Giffard. When William III's invasion was already on its way, James withdrew the dispensations and the fellows returned amid rejoicing. In 2000 the College repelled a govt. attempt to impose on unsuitable students.

MAGDEBURG, SACK of (1631). *See* THIRTY YEARS' WAR.

MAGELLAN, Ferdinand (?1480-1521) sailed from Spain in Aug. 1519, rounded the Horn in Nov. 1520 and reached the Philippines in Mar. 1521 where he was killed. One of his five ships crossed the Indian Ocean, rounded the Cape and arrived in Spain in 1522. This first global circumnavigation revolutionised geographical thought, by demonstrating that the American Continent was distinct from Asia and much further from it than had hitherto been believed.

MAGIC was a false science, based upon the assumption that phenomena are influenced by divinities who can themselves be influenced or even compelled. Such operations can be achieved by securing control of things associated or mystically identified with the appropriate divinity, for example his secret and most personal name, or with a person, for example, an image of him or a lock of his hair. *Black* Magic (i.e. for personal advantage) might bring misfortune by compelling a powerful divinity (often called up by name) to inflict some disaster upon the object of animosity, represented by his image or possession. Such spells sometimes worked through neurotic effects, or seemed to work by coincidence, enough to perpetuate a fear of witches from century to century. Since magic is pre-Christian, the churches naturally equated it with demonology. *See* WITCHCRAFT.

MAGINOT LINE. André Maginot, Min. of War in several French govts. from 1922 onwards originated a defensive strategy which relied upon a 200 mile system of mutually supporting forts, barbed wire and tank obstacles along the German frontier. Built between 1929 and 1936, it was then weakly extended along the Belgian frontier. The German armies penetrated France through this weak section near Sédan and Malmély in May 1940.

MAGISTRATE. (1) In older usage anybody charged with a function of govt. **(2)** Less anciently, inferior judicial officers with a summary jurisdiction over crimes or quasi-crimes. J.P.s are unpaid magistrates, but usually at least two must act together. Stipendiary (paid) professionally qualified magistrates have been appointed in London since 1792, in Manchester since 1813 and in other populous places since 1834. A stipendiary can do alone things for which two ordinary J.P.s are required.

MAGNA CARTA or GREAT (or LARGE) CHARTER (*see* JOHN 12 AND 13) was granted by K. John in 1215 and reissued or confirmed in 1225 under Henry III. This confirmed version is the accepted text printed, for example, as the first statute in *Statutes at Large*. It has been confirmed altogether 33 times. The traditional numbering of its chapters is printed below in parentheses. They may, with caution, be classified as follows. Some, however are interdependent (e.g. No's 35, 3 and 30) or are mutually repugnant (e.g. No's 2 and 30).

I Liberties

(1) (cap 1) The Church of England to have 'all her whole rights and liberties inviolable'. **(2)** (cap 9) London to have 'all the old liberties and customs which it hath used to have', and all other cities, boroughs, towns the Barons of the Cinque Ports and all other ports to have 'all their liberties and free customs'. **(3)** (cap 30) Foreign merchants to be able to enter and leave the Kingdom unless previously prohibited and to buy and sell by the 'old and rightful customs without any evil Tolts except in time of War'. Enemy merchants to be given the same treatment in England as English merchants get in an enemy country.

II Justice

(4) (cap 29) No freeman to be taken, imprisoned, disseised, outlawed, exiled 'or any otherwise destroyed' 'nor will we pass upon him nor condemn him save by the lawful judgement of his equals or by the law of the land. We will sell or deny or postpone justice or right to no man'. (5) (cap 26) Writs of inquisition of life or member to be free of charge. (6) (cap 28) Wager of law not to be imposed without a witness.

(7) (cap 34) A woman to have an appeal of death for her husband only. (8) (cap 8) Sureties for debts to the King not to be charged unless resort to their principal is impossible. (9) (cap 10) No distress to be taken for more service than is due for a Knight's fee or a freehold. (10) (cap 18) the goods of a dead crown debtor may be seized and sold, and any balance remitted to the executors. (11) (cap 14) A freeman to be amerced only for a great fault, saving his living; a merchant saving his merchandise; another's villein saving his wainage. Such amercements to be assessed by the oath of lawful men of the neighbourhood, or in the case of peers by their peers. Churchmen to be amerced only to the value of their lay tenement.

III Legal Administration

(12) (cap 11) The Court of Common Pleas not to follow the King. (13,14) (caps 12 and 13) Assizes of Novel Disseisin and Mort d'ancestor to be taken on circuit and of Darrein Presentment before the King's Bench. (15) (cap 17) Sheriffs, constables, escheators, coroners and royal bailiffs not to hold pleas of the crown. (16) (cap 24) The writ *Praecipe* not to be granted so as to deprive any freeman of his court. (17) (cap 35) County courts to be held monthly; sheriffs tourns only at Easter, and at Michaelmas for the view of frankpledge. The sheriff only to take the fees, on these occasions, which were customary in the time of Henry II.

IV Rivers

(18,19) (caps 15 and 16) No one to be required to build or maintain bridges and banks save those customary in the time of Henry II. (20) (cap 23) All fish weirs on the Thames, Medway and elsewhere (except coastal ones) to be destroyed.

V Feudal Incidents

(21) (cap 2) The relief of an heir of full age of a Tenant in Chief on succession limited to, Earls £100; Barons 100 marks; Knights 100s. (22) (cap 3) A lord must not take a wardship without taking homage from the ward. The ward comes of age at 21 and is then entitled to his inheritance without relief. (23) (cap 5) The guardian must maintain the lands of the ward and must not commit waste. (24) (cap 4) Similar rules to apply to ecclesiastical benefices. (25) (cap 6) Wards must be married without disparagement. (26) (cap 7) Widows entitled to stay 40 days in her dead husband's house during which a third of his property is to be assigned to her for life or until coverture. She must not be compelled to marry but must give surety that she will not marry without the consent of her lord. (27) (cap 27) Royal wardship not to extend to lands not held of the King by the royal ward. (28) (cap 22) Felons' lands to pass to the lord subject only to the King's right to hold them for a year and a day. (29) (cap 31) Escheat to a barony to be upon the terms of the barony, when the barony is in the King's hands. (30) (cap 32) A freeman must not sell so much of his land, that he cannot perform the services.

VI Mortmain

(30) (cap 36) Gifts to religious houses followed by a regrant of a lease to the giver are void and accrue to the lord of the fee.

VII Castle and Purveyance

(32-34) (caps 19-21) Purveyance, horses, carts and wood for castles and other services to be paid for. Castleward may be performed by deputy.

VIII Weights and Measures

(35) (cap 25) Measures of wine, ale, corn and cloth to be standardised.

IX Subsidy

(36) (cap 37) In consideration of the above and the Charter of the Forest a subsidy is granted to the crown of a 15th of all movables. *See also* CONFIRMATIO CARTARUM.

MAGNETIC POLE. *See* ROSS, SIR JAMES CLARK.

MAGNUS INTERCURSUS. *See* HENRY VII-13.

MAGNUS MAXIMUS. *See* BRITAIN, ROMAN-25.

MAGONSAETAN were an Anglian tribe, with a dynasty of their own, who in the 6th cent. settled about the R. Wye and the Upper Severn, but abandoned their lands west of the Wye as a result of Welsh opposition, when Offa built his dyke. They early became a part of Mercia, but in about 676 the diocese of Hereford was established for them. In about 980 the northern part of this area was thrown into the new shire of Shropshire but their name remained in use in the 11th cent. St. Milburga was of this tribe.

MAGRATH, Meiler (?1523-1622) papal bishop of Down, from 1565-80 and Anglican Abp. of Cashel from 1571 (together with three other sees) was an Irish balancing churchman or double agent of remarkable agility. He even died in his bed.

MAGUIRE. N. Irish clan in Fermanagh and about Enniskillen. **(1) Hugh (?-1600) Ld. of FERMANAGH** was a very independent minded chief and ally of Tyrone, who kept the English and Anglo-Irish out of his country all his life. He and Sir Warham St. Leger killed each other. **(2) Connor or Cornelius (1616-45) 2nd Ld. ENNISKILLEN (1634)** was fatally involved in the Irish rising of 1641. He was captured and barbarously executed for treason.

MAHAN, Alfred Thayer (1840-1914) U.S. Rear-Admiral published *The Influence of Sea Power on History* (1660-1783), *The Influence of Sea Power upon the French Revolution* (1793-1812) and *The Life of Nelson* between 1890 and 1895. Their deep scholarship and stylistic brilliance strongly influenced strategic and political thought among all the major powers of the day.

MAHARAJAH. *See* RAJAH.

MAHAYANA. *See* BUDDHISM.

MAHDI or MEHDI. *See* CALIPHATE-4; SUDAN-3 TO 5.

MAHICANS were Algonquian Indians, of whom the Mohicans or Mohegans formed a part. In the 17th cent. they occupied the Hudson Valley until mostly driven out by the Mohawks and the Dutch. The Mohicans remained, but were destroyed by disease and massacre.

MAHON, Charles James (1800-91). THE O'GORMAN MAHON, helped O'Connell to win the Clare Election (1828). Himself elected for Clare in 1830, he was unseated on a petition. In 1831 O'Connell supported his opponent (who won) and the quarrel with O'Connell was never healed. He then travelled Europe, the East and S. America, returning to become an M.P. (Ennis 1847-52) but set out again. He fought with high rank in the Russian army, travelled in India and China and fought in the Turkish and Austrian armies. In the 1860s he was a Uruguayan General, a Chilean Admiral, a Brazilian Colonel and fought for the Union in the U.S. civil war. After returning to France he became a colonel of Chasseurs yet managed to be on good terms with Bismarck, whom, like everyone else, he knew. He returned to Ireland in 1871 and became a Parnellite M.P. (Clare 1879-85, Carlow from 1887). It was he who introduced William O'Shea to Parnell. He was the aggressor in all his thirteen duels. Many of the stories about this extraordinary man are doubtless apocryphal.

MAHOMET or MOHAMMED. *See* CALIPHATE; ISLAM.

MAHON, PORT. *See* MINORCA.

MAHOUND, corruption of Mohammed. In the mediaeval west often imagined as a demon, or to be worshipped as a god.

MAHRI. *See* SOCOTRA.

MAHSUDS, a tribe of N.W. Indian Pathans who, led by the Mullah Powindah and his son Fazl-el-Din, constantly raided neighbouring territories and were as constantly attacked by the British between 1860-1920.

MAIDEN CASTLE (Dorset) was settled in 3rd and 2nd millennia B.C., but after 1800 B.C., when it was deserted, a neolithic bank barrow was built there. The site was then intermittently occupied until about 350 B.C. when a fortified Iron Age Village was established and extended. The Veneti took it and elaborated the vast earthworks between 100 B.C. and A.D. 44 when Vespasian's 2nd legion stormed it. The population was moved to Roman Dorchester in A.D. 70.

MAID OF KENT. *See* BARTON, ELIZABETH

MAID OF NORWAY. *See* MARGARET (1283-90).

MAIDSTONE (Kent) (A.S. MAEIDESTANA) lies at a Roman crossing over the Medway. From ancient times the manor belonged to the Abps. of Canterbury, who had a palace there from about 1200 until 1537. It was the county town of Kent. The adjacent Penenden Heath was used for shire moots, executions and other great county meetings down to the 19th cent. In 1260-1 Abp. Boniface built the Newark, a hospice for poor travellers and also received the grant of the Thursday market. In 1356 Abp. William Courtenay built the palace, a college of secular canons and his stables all in a single complex about the rebuilt church of All Saints. In 1537 Abp. Cranmer exchanged the manor with the King; under Edward VI, Somerset granted it to Sir Thomas Wyatt, and incorporated it in 1549 with four fairs, at which time the grammar school was founded and endowed with local ex-monastic property. The charter, however, was forfeited after Wyatt's rebellion (1554) but Elizabeth I granted a new one in 1559. The town began to experience a renewed prosperity with the settlement of Walloon Huguenot weavers in 1561, soon followed by paper makers financed by Gresham. There was also extensive quarrying and fruit growing. James I granted further charters in 1603 and 1619 but all the old charters were replaced by a new one in 1682. This was itself forfeited in 1740 and replaced in 1747. The place was a borough under the Municipal Corporations Act, 1835 until 1974.

MAILDULF or MAILDUB (?-?675) Irish teacher who founded the school at Malmesbury and taught Aldhelm.

MAILLOTINS **(Fr = mallet men)** French urban insurrectionaries contemporary with the English peasants' revolt. *See* CHARLES VI OF FRANCE.

MAINE, Sir Henry James Sumner (1822-88) regius Professor of Civil Law at Cambridge from 1847-54, published his *Ancient Law* in 1861. He was legal member of the Council of India from 1862-69 and as Corpus Professor of Jurisprudence at Oxford from 1869-78 published his *Village Communities* in 1871. In 1875 he published his *Early History of Institutions* and in 1883 *Early Law and Customs*. From 1877 he was master of Trinity Hall, Cambridge. One of the earliest to apply historical and sociological ideas to the study of human institutions, he in some ways anticipated Sir James Frazer.

MAINE (Fr). A scrubby woodland country with its capital Le Mans was held together with Anjou from 1110, and so passed under the rule of the English Kings until they lost them both in 1204. As a result of a grant by Louis IX to Charles of Anjou in 1232, it remained in his family until 1328 when it returned to the French Crown. In 1356 K. John II of France gave it to his own second son Louis I of Naples. The English occupied it from 1425-48 and it finally reverted to the French Crown in 1481, when the Naples line failed.

MAINPAST. Collective word for the inferior adherents, not necessarily tenants, of a great lord who would extend his protection in return for their loyalty.

MAIN PLOT (1603) Ld. Cobham's plot with Sir Walter Raleigh and others to substitute Arabella Stuart for James I. They were tried together with the conspirators in the Bye Plot.

MAINTENANCE, CHAMPERTY, EMBRACERY were ways of perverting justice common in the middle ages. Maintenance was intermeddling (e.g. by financing one of the parties) in a suit in which one had no lawful interest. Champerty, an aggravated form of maintenance, was a bargain whereby someone carried on a suit for a party and divided the spoils if successful. For embracery *see* separate entry. All were offences at Common Law, but legislation was in addition passed against champerty in 1275 and 1285, and against maintenance generally in 1377 and 1540. The institution of legal aid in 1953 made the law against maintenance and champerty obsolete, since a legally aided party was maintained and engaged in proceedings otherwise champertous. Hence in 1967 they were abolished as offences. *See* LIVERIES.

MAINWARING (pron: Mannering) Sir Henry (1587-1653), soldiered in Flanders between 1608-10 and in 1611 was commissioned against the Bristol Channel pirates. Inspired by Sir Robert Shirley, he acquired a ship and letters of marque against Spain, and from a base on the Barbary coast, operated lucratively against all save British shipping. He came home in 1618 and James I made him a Gentleman of the Bedchamber, but he instantly set out again in order to frustrate the Spanish plot against Venice. On his return he became Lieutenant of Dover Castle. In 1626 Buckingham made him a member of the commission then inquiring into naval abuses and in the next years helped to reorganise the ship money navy, besides serving at sea. In 1641 he was a Vice-Admiral. He joined the royalists. He wrote a practical treatise on the suppression of piracy for James I, and in 1620 the *Seaman's Dictionary*, the first English exposition of seamanship.

MAINWARING, Sir Philip (1589-1661) was M.P. for Boroughbridge (1624-6) and Derby (1628-9), became Strafford's Secretary in Ireland in 1634 and was M.P. for Morpeth in 1640. Imprisoned in 1650, he became M.P. for Newton (Lancs) in 1661.

MAINZ or MAYENCE (Ger.) (*See* MISSIONS TO EUROPE.) The Abps. became primates of Germany and, from 1356 Electors; in later times they were strongly under French influence. The see was abolished in 1803 when its lands were partitioned among neighbouring states.

MAITLAND, Frederic William (1850-1906). Downing Professor of English Laws from 1888, founded the Selden Society in 1887, and published important works on Bracton, Canon Law, Constitutional History and his well known *Domesday Book and Beyond*

MAITLAND, Sir Thomas (?1759-1824) an M.P. from 1794-96 and from 1800-06, became C-in-C in Ceylon in 1806 and in 1813 Governor of Malta. From 1815 he was Ld High Commissioner to the Ionian Isles where he left a considerable mark. A rude, drunken, authoritarian but kindly Scot with an eye for style, he built fine public buildings, laid out the town of Corfu, introduced cumquats and cricket and through an ingenious constitution hobbled the local politicians. The Corfiotes, other than the intellectuals, adored him.

MAJOR. In the early 17th cent. the serjeant, sergeant-major and serjeant-major-general were responsible for the drill and administration of a company, a regiment and an army respectively; by 1660 the word *serjeant* had been dropped in the two latter cases and they acted as seconds in command and chiefs of staff. The appointment of adjutants and adjutants-general in 18th cent. relieved them of administrative functions and converted those posts into ranks, but a 'brigade major' is still the chief of a brigade staff. Non commissioned serjeant-majors were introduced early in the 18th cent. They became warrant officers in 1881.

MAJOR-GENERALS. *See* COMMONWEALTH AND PROTECTORATE-12.

MAJORITY, AGE OF, was originally the age at which a boy could perform the tasks allotted to his station in life e.g. when a ploughboy could plough a straight furrow (about 14), or a gentleman's son could ride in coat armour (21). The coat armour rule had become general by 1600. The age was attained on the day before the 21st birthday. It was changed to the day of the 18th birthday in 1969.

MAJOR, John (1943-) (1) Tory M.P. since 1983, Govt. whip in 1984-5, Minister of State at the Department of Health and Social Services in 1986-7; Chief Sec. to the Treasury (1987-9), Foreign Sec. in 1989, Ch. of the Exch. (1989-90) and Prime Minister (1990-7) in succession to Mrs Thatcher who was ousted from the Tory leadership in a party intrigue.

(2) His **GOVT,** only nominally Conservative, was in fact revolutionary, if in senses other than those lately understood by the term. There was scarcely anything with which it did not interfere e.g. local govt. geography, finances and functions, the courts, prisons and criminal law, education at all levels, health services, transport, power, shipbuilding, harbours, mines and trade unions. Even minor matters such as copyright details, and the sealing of deeds received meddlesome attention. A principle behind these activities was the dismantling of the post-1939 partly socialist institutions in favour of the kind of materialism, private enterprise and competitive market forces favoured in Europe. In fact, it did not always prevent take-overs and cartelisation contrary to its proclaimed principles, particularly where powerful banking and insurance interests were involved. The complementary economics and loans policies were accompanied by bankruptcies, liquidations and house-repossessions on an unexampled scale, by unemployment at the highest levels ever recorded and a general sense of insecurity, by persistent rises in taxation, by alarming frauds (e.g. the Bank of Credit and Commerce International and the Robert Maxwell scandal), crime of every sort, and a lowering of the tone of public life. It is however, uncertain, whether these features of the period can be ascribed to the Govt. itself or to its inability to control them. On the other hand the Govt. established in 1994 the extraordinarily successful National Lottery, and with the collapse of Russian communism and the decline of politically financed international terrorism, it began the process of bringing order to Ulster.

By committing Britain to the T. of Maastricht (1991) (with reservations on the European Social Chapter and the future of Sterling) the Govt. permitted decisive inroads into the sovereignty of Parliament and British independence in favour of a bankers-dominated European Union, while further eroding (partly through frontier and citizenship policies) the declining solidity of the Commonwealth.

MAJOR, Thomas (1720-99) engraver trained in Paris, was briefly interned in the Bastille at the outbreak of war in 1746. He settled in England in 1753 where he generated a new respect for his art, was elected A.R.A. in 1770, and became a royal and govt. engraver.

MAJOR ORDERS are the episcopal, priestly and diaconal grades of ordination. *See* CLERKS.

MAKARIOS. *See* CYPRUS.

MAKRAN. *See* BALUCHISTAN.

MALABAR CHRISTIANS, probably of 5th cent. Syriac origin, are traditionally ascribed to St. Thomas. Mostly settled near Madras (India) they maintained a connection with the Nestorian patriarchate at Baghdad until 1490. Regarded as R. Catholic by the Portuguese, they abjured Nestorianism in 1599, broke with Rome in 1653, but most

returned in 1661. Some, however, developed a link with the Syrian Orthodox Patriarchate at Antioch, others became Monophysites and so in friendship with the Anglican church.

MALACCA. *See* MALAYA.

MALACHY or MAOL, St. (1094-1148) Irish Gregorian reformer whose life illustrates the intermixture of family successions and clan politics in the old partly reformed Irish Church. He came to fame as vicar gen. of Armagh (1111) where he enforced canon law and marriage as a binding contract, and reintroduced Roman practices. In 1121 he studied the Gregorian reforms under Malchus, a former monk at Winchester, then Abp. of Cashel. In 1123 he accepted the deserted Bangor Abbey from his uncle, but refused most of the endowments and with help from Armagh built a church. In 1124 he became Bp. of Connor and Down, though continuing to live at Bangor, but was driven away by a local chief in 1127. He then founded a centre for Austin Canons, from which he propagated reforms in many parts of Ireland. In 1129 Cellach, Abp. of Armagh died, leaving the succession to him not to a relative, but with the help of a local chief and Cellach's clan, one Muichertach was intruded. Malachy did not assert his rights until 1132, when the papal legate Gilbert of Limerick persuaded him to try. He took over the rural areas but not the town or cathedral, until Muichertach's successor Niall abandoned them in 1134. Until 1137 the province was divided in allegiance; then Malachy and Niall both resigned in favour of Gilla, Abbot of Derry. He returned to Down and thence went to Rome *via* Clairvaux to secure papal confirmation of the reforms and metropolitical status for Armagh and Cashel. At Clairvaux he met St. Bernard who inspired him to found Mellifont Abbey in 1142. He set out for Rome again in 1148, but died in St. Bernard's arms.

MALAGROWTHER, Malachi, pseudonym of Sir Walter Scott in 1826 when writing letters to the *Edinburgh Weekly Journal* on the Scottish paper currency.

MALAKAND (N.W. Frontier, Pak.), a pass between the Kabul and the Swat Rs. was the scene of a Swat rising, indirectly connected with the Khyber rising in 1897. This provoked a British expedition, the subject of an early work of Winston S. Churchill who served on it.

MALAN, Daniel François (1874-1959), from 1906 a predikant in the Dutch Reformed Church, became a promoter of Afrikaans and from 1912 increasingly interested in politics. In 1915 the Nationalists offered him the editorship of their own new Cape Town newspaper *Die Burger,* in which he preached *apartheid,* republicanism and secession and attacked Botha and Smuts as traitors. In Sept. he presided over the first congress of the Cape Nationalists. Twice defeated in Parliamentary elections, a safe Africander seat at Calvinia was resigned for him by his father-in-law in 1919. He held it until 1938 when he moved to Piketburg. In 1924 he supported the Hertzog-Labour Pact which ousted Smuts, and took office as a reforming Minister of the Interior, Health and Education. He substituted Afrikaans for Dutch as a second language. He altered the electoral laws, reformed the Senate, recruited nationalists into the civil service, imposed a new S. African flag and tried, but failed to repatriate Indians. Meanwhile he falsely averred that he had never contemplated the abolition of the monarchy or policies contrary to the interests of the English population. Too many of the latter were fooled. As a result, after the political confusion between 1932 and the end of World War II, Malan was able, in alliance with N. C. Havenga to gain a majority of five in the elections of 1949.

He used this small majority with cunning ruthlessness. S.W. Africa was given seats in both houses, and these increased his majority. The abolition of dual citizenship for Commonwealth immigrants cut off the supply of new English voters. When his act to abolish the Cape

Coloured franchise was declared unconstitutional by the Supreme Court, he brought in packing legislation. His Group Areas Act separated the living areas of whites and the rest. Future mixed marriages were declared void: sexual intercourse between whites and others criminal. *Apartheid* was enforced on railways, buses, govt. offices and elsewhere. The death penalty was widely imposed. The prisons were overcrowded.

The onset of physical frailty forced him to leave politics in 1954, but not before he had fastened an unjust dispensation upon his country.

MALAN, François Stephanus (1871-1941) S. African nationalist, entered politics as a member of the 1908 national convention and was Minister for Education from 1910-21, Agriculture from 1919-21, Mines and Industries from 1912-24 and for Native Affairs from 1915-21. He became a senator in 1927 and Pres. of the Senate from 1940.

MALARIA (QUARTERN and TERTIAN AGUE). This debilitating and often lethal illness arises through the development and cyclic passage of *Plasmodium* parasites through *Anopheles* mosquitoes and human beings. It probably began in Central Africa and was well established by the Middle Ages, perhaps through the agency of wind blown mosquitoes and later in association with human migrants on the Nile, and then in the fluvial civilisations of Mesopotamia, the Punjab, the Ganges Valley and S. China. It may have reached America in pre-Columbian times. Natives of malarial districts resist it more strongly than immigrants. Conversely an irruption of malarial mosquitoes or humans into an uninfected area may create a lethal epidemic and will establish an endemic condition. In Britain it was endemic from 7th cent. in the marshes of the Humber, the Fens and the Thames Estuary. It was common in Europe as far north as Denmark and had infested the W. African coast by the 15th cent.

A European epidemic in 1557-8, coincided with an outburst of influenza. James I and Oliver Cromwell probably died of malaria. The English outbreak of 1661-4 may have been imported from W. Africa. There were European epidemics in 1678-82, 1718-22, 1748-50, 1770-72, 1806-11, 1855-60 and 1866-72. The disease was the main obstacle to the settlement and development of W. Africa, the Caribbean and N. American colonies and the Isthmus of Panama. The use of quinine bark in combatting it, once contracted, was known to native Peruvians, from whom the Jesuit Juan Lopez learned it in about 1600. It reached Spain in 1637 and Rome in 1643. Regular supplies were reaching Europe in 1647.

The name *malaria* (Ital: = bad air) reflected a belief that "unhealthy air" of marshes and wet warm climates caused it. This notion was first discarded in favour of an insect vector by Beaupertuy in 1854, but it took until 1900 to demonstrate the manner of transmission and incubation. Eradication has, since 1900, been attempted mainly through the laborious destruction of the vector mosquitoes, usually by draining or sterilising the breeding grounds. Europe, save Greece and Turkey, was clear in 1972, but most of non-desert Africa, the Amazon basin and C. America, the Arabian coasts, northern India, the Irrawaddy, Chow Phya and Mekong basins and Indonesia were still infested. Modern outbreaks can still be grave: in Uruguay in 1966, of 100,000 cases, 14,000 died and in 1985 the Anopheles mosquito was re-establishing itself even in some European habitats which had been clear in 1972. *See* EPIDEMICS, HUMAN.

MALAWI. *See* NYASALAND.

MALAYSIA. (*See* INDONESIA.) **(1)** In 1511 the Portuguese Afonso de Albuquerque conquered MALACCA, whose Sultan died in exile. After years of debilitating involvement in local wars, the Malayan Portuguese were attacked by the Dutch East India Company which from 1607 was intercepting their shipping from bases in Java.

The Dutch took Malacca in 1641. JOHORE claimed and sometimes exercised suzerainty over the rest until 1699 when its last Malacca ruler was murdered; the BUGIS from Celebes established themselves in SELANGOR; a group of Menangkabau princes from Sumatra settled in NEGRI SEMBILAN and by 1722 the Bugis and tributary princes were in Johore and PAHANG.

(2) Endemic feuds, piracy and Siamese invasions kept Malaya in confusion, and prevented the Dutch trading monopoly from being wholly effective. In 1786 the HEIC leased PENANG from the Rajah of KEDAH and broke the monopoly completely. In 1791 a military treaty was made with Johore. In 1792 the British took Malacca but returned it to the Dutch in 1815. In 1824 Sir Stamford Raffles took a lease of SINGAPORE from Johore, and by the T. of London (1824) the Dutch gave up their claims in Malaya and ceded Malacca. Malacca, Penang and Singapore became known as the STRAITS SETTLEMENTS. In 1826 Siam recognised the independence of PERAK and Selangor and in 1858 the India Office took over the Straits Settlements from the defunct HEIC. In 1862 Sir Orfeur Cavenagh, Governor of Singapore, prevented the Siamese from deposing the Sultan of TRENGGANU.

(3) In 1873 the British, to curb the incessant warfare, began to offer official residents. These were accepted in Perak, Selangor and one of the Negri Sembilan states in 1874 and by the rest of those states and Pahang in 1888. In the states with residents law and land titles were rationalised and slavery abolished, and, with foreign capital and the researches at the Botanical Gardens at Kew, rubber plantations soon produced a boom. In 1896 these four states were FEDERATED.

(4) Meanwhile, Sir Frank Swettenham, Governor of Singapore, in 1902 pressed further British claims in the northern states against the Siamese. In 1904 *entente cordiale* removed the risk of French compensations in Siam in return for British advances northwards, and in 1909 the Siamese K. Chulalongkorn ceded Kedah, Perlis, Kelantan and Trengganu in return for a loan to build the Bangkok-Singapore railway and the surrender of British extraterritorial rights in Siam.

(5) British protection and indirect rule brought immense prosperity until the Japanese occupation of 1941-45. The British then attempted, and failed to turn Malaya into a unitary state, and the MALAYAN UNION was set up in 1948. Thereupon a communist revolt broke out and was not suppressed until 1954. In 1957 the Union became independent and Britain surrendered her sovereignty of the Straits Settlements to it. SARAWAK and SABAH joined the Federation, renamed MALAYSIA in 1963. SINGAPORE left Malaysia in 1965 and British military protection was withdrawn in 1971.

MALCOLM I, II, III and IV. *See* SCOTS OR ALBAN KINGS, EARLY.

MALCOLM. Two brothers, both Admirals. **(1) Sir Pulteney (1768-1838)** served under Nelson in the Mediterranean (1804-5) and was C-in-C Mediterranean from 1828-31 and from 1833-34. **(2) Sir Charles (1782-51)** was superintendent of the Bombay Marine (later Indian Navy) from 1827-37.

MALCOLM, Sir John (1769-1833) one of the ablest Indian administrators and diplomats, originally studied Persian (the language of diplomacy) and became Persian interpreter to the Nizam in 1792. From 1795-98 he was Secretary to two successive Cs-in-C and in 1798 he returned to Hyderabad as assistant to the Resident. The M. Wellesley sent him on a diplomatic mission to Persia (1799-1801) and then made him his private Secretary. In 1803 he passed him to his brother Arthur Wellesley (later Wellington) as political agent during the Maratha War. It was among the Marathas that his main work was done, and after further missions to Persia (1808-10) he was again in demand for the Maratha War of 1817-18. After organising land reclamation schemes in Malwa he went home in 1822 but returned as Governor of Bombay from

1826-30. He found time to write a *Political History of India* (1811), a *History of Persia* (1815), a book on the *Administration of India* (1833) and a posthumously published *Life of Clive* and was M.P. for Launceston from 1831-32.

MALDON, B. of (11 Aug. 991) was a desperate stand by a force under Byrhtnoth, ealdorman of Essex, against a powerful Viking army. It was fought mainly on a causeway connecting an off-shore island with Maldon (Essex). Byrhtnoth and most of his men perished. The event was narrated in a famous Old English poem by an eye-witness or from eye-witness evidence. The Vikings suffered heavily, but were able to exact a large *gafol*.

MALET. Family of Norman origin **(1) William (?-1071)** performed deeds of daring at the B. of Hastings and as Sheriff was captured in York in 1069. His *s*. **(2) Robert (?- ?1106) Ld. of EYE** was killed fighting against Henry I at Tinchebrai. His nephew **(3) William (fl. 1195-1215)** was Lord of Shepton Mallet. Modern descendants include **(4) Sir Charles Warre (?1753-1815) Bt. (1791).** Resident at Poona from 1785-91 and then acting Governor of Bombay until 1798. His *s*. **(5) Sir Alexander (1800-86) 2nd Bt.** Minister to the Germanic Federation from 1849-66. His *s*. **(6) Sir Edward (1837-1908) 4th Bt. (1904)** also a diplomat, negotiated the meeting between Bismarck and Jules Favre at Plombières in 1870, and after various routine appointments was British Agent and Consul General in Egypt and so the country's indirect ruler from 1879-83. As such he instigated most of the financial and administrative re-organisation of the period. From 1884-95 he was a very successful ambassador in Berlin where he negotiated the settlement of the Anglo-German disputes over Rabaul and the Congo. He was a member of The Hague International Court from 1899.

MALI, a central Sudanese empire from 1200-1670 was divided between the fluctuating native states of Segan, Kaarta, Masina and Yatanga which were successively subjected by the French between 1880 and 1895. They detached the Chad-Niger area in 1911 and the Upper Volta in 1919. It became the Sudanese Republic within the French community in 1957 and after a 15 month union with Senegal, became an independent republic in 1960. *See* AFRICA, WEST (EX-FRENCH).

MALIGNANT. A puritan's term for his political opponent.

MALINES. *See* STAPLE B-1.

MALL (London) was laid out by Charles II. *See* PALL MALL.

MALLORY and LEIGH-MALLORY (1) George Leigh M (1886-1924) a famous mountaineer, took part in the Everest expeditions of 1921 and 1922 and died in that of 1924. His brother **(2) Sir Trafford Leigh L-M** commanded No 11 Group RAF in the B. of Britain and after was A.C.C. Fighter Command from 1942-43 and C-in-C Allied Air Forces in 1943-44 during the Normandy invasion.

MALLOW (Co. Cork) was originally a tribal centre of the McCarthys but after the ruin of their castle it declined until about 1780 when it began to develop as a small but fashionable Anglo-Irish spa, somewhat similar to Bath. This lasted until after the famines of the late 1840s when it declined rapidly as such but after World War I it developed again as an agricultural market and fishing centre.

MALMÉDY. *See* EUPEN.

MALMESBURY ABBEY, a Benedictine house, grew out of a school founded by the Irish hermit Maildulf or Maildub (?-675) whom Aldhelm succeeded. Aldhelm was charming, learned yet strong and austere. He became famous and attracted large endowments and this continued under his successors, especially from Alfred and Athelstan. It remained an important centre of learning throughout the Saxon period. The house was sufficiently important for a long line of Norman abbots to be imposed after the Conquest, and sufficiently endowed to be involved in a fifty year long dispute with the Bps.

of Salisbury from 1118. In the anarchy of Stephen it was fought over. Its late mediaeval history was undistinguished but it was still fairly rich at the Dissolution.

MALMSEY or MALVOISIE (named after the Peloponnesian port of MONEMVASIA) was a sweet Greek or Cretan wine imported from 14th cent. into England mostly by the Venetians, despite intermittent obstruction from vintners with interests elsewhere. It cost about twice as much as Bordeaux and even more when Henry VII briefly raised the duty on it from 13s 4d to 18s a tun but as a luxury it was favoured by the wealthy; hence the story that Clarence was drowned in a butt of it at court. The foundation of Richard Lyon's ill-gotten fortune was a monopoly over the three London taverns where it could be sold. *See* WINE TRADE.

MALORY, Sir Thomas (fl. 1469) (1) completed the famous *Morte d'Arthur* in 1469-70 while in prison. He drew on English and French works but added much of his own. Caxton printed it in 1483. **(2)** Much ink has been spilled on the question of whether the author of *Morte d'Arthur* was **(i)** an unidentified Welshman born at Maelor; **(ii) Sir Thomas Malory of Papworth St. Agnes (Hunts) (1425-69)** who has not been connected with it save by the period of his life-span; **(iii)** Based on some northern words in the text, **Thomas Mallory of Studley and Hutton (Yorks)** a frequent rebel against Edward IV who was excluded from pardon in 1468 but is not known to have been imprisoned. **(iv) Sir Thomas Mallory of Newbold Revel (Warwicks) (1393-1471)** who was often charged with theft and once with rape, served at Calais with the E. of Warwick and was M.P. for Warwickshire in 1445. He was imprisoned several times in the Marshalsea and Newgate but not certainly at the right time.

MALTA G.C. (1) The Turks drove the Knights of St John from Rhodes in 1522. After wanderings their Grand Master (G-M) Villier de l'Isle Adam obtained the Maltese Is. and Tripoli from the Emperor Charles V as King of Sicily. The Knights moved in in 1530; Tripoli was lost to the Turks, and Dragut, one of their commanders landed briefly on Malta in 1551. This caused G-Ms d'Homedes and La Sengle to press the fortification of Birgu, St. Angelo and St. Elmo despite shortage of resources. In 1565 the Turks under Piali and Dragut mounted a siege (*The Great Siege*) repelled by G-M La Vallette. The evident inadequacies of the defences led to new building on the other side of Grand Harbour at Valletta the new capital, under the direction of the Italian engineer Laparelli. These fortifications, completed in 1570, formed the nucleus of one of the greatest architectural as well as military concentrations in Europe. Further Turkish threats led G-M de Paule to build the great Floriana fortifications in 1634. There was a Turkish invasion in 1641 and when Crete fell to them in 1670 further scares resulted in more fortifications. Meantime civil and ecclesiastical Baroque flourished under Maltese architects using the resources of the Order's widespread European estates and encouraged by a succession of sophisticated French, Spanish and Portuguese G-Ms.

(2) Internationally the Knights carried on their function as champions of Christendom. In practice this meant permanent hostilities with the Barbary states (*see* BARBARY), piracy at the expense of Moslem shipping and the seizure of non-Christian owned goods in Christian ships. In the 17th cent. knightly piracy was no better than any other and the Knights wholly failed to protect Christian shipping. Later Malta was occasionally used by other navies as a base against the corsairs; the Venetian Admiral Angelo Emo, for example, died there in 1786. An important side effect was that in the 17th and 18th cents. many French naval officers, as Knights, received active training in the Maltese navy, the most famous being Suffren. A further more lasting result was that the

Hospital of the Order became the best centre of practical surgery in Europe.

(3) The rule of the Order was abruptly ended by Bonaparte on his way to Egypt in June 1798 (*see* SECOND COALITION, WAR OF THE, 1799-1801, 3-4), but the immense loot was lost when the flagship *Orient* blew up at the B. of the Nile in Aug. In Sept. the Maltese revolted against the French, who surrendered to Anglo-Maltese forces in Sept. 1802. The British undertook as part of the T. of Amiens to restore it to the Knights. The settlement of which the treaty was a part, having been broken by Bonaparte, the British, much to Maltese relief, retained Malta as a naval base. The Maltese eventually offered the sovereignty to the British Crown in 1809: the offer was accepted in 1813, and the transfer was ratified by the T. of Paris in 1814.

(4) Malta had been subsidised for a strategic purpose from 1530-1798 through the Knights, and this situation was unchanged by the British, whose fleet used it as their principal Mediterranean base. The first Governors used their absolute powers to reform the law and administration. An advisory council was created in 1835, a legislative council with an elected minority in 1849 and an executive council with an extended franchise in 1881. By this time the Suez Canal had been open for 12 years and had brought additional prosperity. The defence of the official status of the Italian language became the focus of a so-called nationalist party, headed by Fortunato Mizzi. Since most inhabitants spoke Maltese, a semitic language, not Italian, this represented an attempt by a professional and enfranchised minority to preserve their status. In 1887 a new constitution established a legislature with an elected majority, all of whom originally supported Mizzi, but heated disputes on language, taxation, and marriage laws brought govt. to a halt and in 1903 the official majority was re-established. This lasted until the end of World War I. Unemployment and constitutional agitation led in 1919 to the calling of a national assembly and in 1921 to the granting of a bicameral constitution, with a linguistic compromise preserving Italian exclusively in the law courts and making English the language of administration. This worked fairly well even though the majority spoke Maltese, but in 1930 there was a series of disputes with the church. Twice suspended, the constitution was revoked in 1936 and the privileges of Italian abolished. In 1939 the islands entered the war under a Governor and a council without responsibility.

(5) When Italy entered the war in 1940 Malta was directly in the path of the Axis supply route to Africa and it became a major enemy war objective. The result was a second Great Siege which lasted until 1943. It was conducted mostly by aerial attack against a determined defence which earned for the island the unique collective award of the George Cross. The physical damage (37,000 buildings) was relatively much greater than the casualties (5000). The British paid £31M as war compensation.

(6) In 1947 there was a return to constitutional government with English and Maltese as the official languages. Governments of Labour or Labour dominated complexion were returned under the leadership of Dom Mintoff who in 1955 began to negotiate for integration with Britain and representation in the House of Commons. The Nationalists led by G. Borg Olivier claimed eventual dominion status, and in 1958 Mintoff resigned after financial disagreements with the British Government. Constitutional government broke down and in 1959 the constitution was once more revoked. Public protests brought a commission, and in Oct. 1961 a new constitution was promulgated. In the ensuing elections Borg Olivier obtained a large majority and formed a government. He then went to London to demand additional financial aid. This being refused, he demanded independence. On 21 Sept. 1964 accordingly Malta became independent within the Commonwealth, and the

British then became tenants at a rent of the warlike installations. In 1971 Dom Mintoff returned to power and after protracted negotiations, raised the rent. Anglophobia continued to mount as the British reduced their service establishments, and the Labour govt. sought alternative support in the economic difficulties which this created by special agreements with China and especially Libya. One connection with Britain was terminated when the islands became a republic (Dec 1974). In 1979 the British base was closed, but in 1987 a new Nationalist govt. moved for membership of the E.U.

MALTHUS, The Rev. Thomas Robert (1766-1834), political economist, published his celebrated *Essay on the Principal of Population as it Affects the Future Improvement of Society* in 1798. He argued that any rise in productivity would be followed by an increase in population, and that as population would increase in geometrical ratio but subsistence only in arithmetical, there would always be a return to previous levels of prosperity or worse. The balance was maintained by misery and vice which were nature's corrective, or Malthus parsonical concession to original sin. The doctrine appealed to the new businessmen, for it pandered to their self-satisfaction, but it contained major miscalculations. Subsistence levels are to some extent matters of fashion, altering from generation to generation. Moral restraint and contraception were and are capable of preventing fecundity from outstripping production and rising standards have tended to diminish the rate of population increase. In the second edition of the *Essay* (1803) Malthus, influenced by a perceptible improvement in standards, admitted the possible effectiveness of moral restraint. He became Professor of History and Political Economy at Haileybury in 1805 and published *The Nature and Progress of Rent* in 1815.

MALT TAX was first imposed in 1713 and continued at varying rates until abolished in 1880.

MALTOLTE (Fr = Evil Toll), an export tax on wool first levied in 1294 by Edward I in addition to the Ancient Custom, from the first provoked opposition of such strength that in 1297 he conceded that it should not be levied without the consent of the merchants, must not be excessive, and could be levied only when the common benefit was at stake. There were further levies in 1322. Their frequency, the confusion which they created in the international markets and the burden on the growers led to consistent demands that the Commons alone should authorise it. This was conceded in 1340 by Edward III, though he twice went back on his word, and was finally confirmed in 1351.

MALTRAVERS. *See* MAUTRAVERS.

MALUS INTERCURSUS. *See* HENRY VII-19.

MALVERN (Worcs.). This area was a wilderness until the 12th cent. but in 1085 the large Benedictine priory of Great Malvern was established as a cell of Westminster and became a bone of contention between the Abbot and the Bp. of Worcester. The quarrel, which occasionally erupted into violence lasted until 1283. The smaller priory of Little Malvern was founded in 1171 as part of Worcester Cathedral. It was always subject to the bishop and the Worcester establishment used it as a house of correction. The manor belonged to the church of Worcester and the area was only slowly developed. It was still shepherds' country in Langland's time and remained a scattering of hamlets until mid 19th cent., when a spa and Malvern College (founded in 1863) developed. The place housed many govt. departments during World War II.

MALWA or MALAVA (India). This state whose capital, the Holy City of Ujjain, was a famous centre of Hindu learning and literature, was annexed by the Moguls in 1573 and passed to the Maratha Sindhia in 1738.

MALYNES or MALINES, Gerard (de) (fl. 1586-1641) a capitalist and economist, was sent to the Low Countries on exchange negotiations in 1600. He also tried but failed to develop English silver and lead mines, and mint farthings. He wrote an early treatise on so-called scientific economics.

MAMELUKES (Arab = slaves) (1) Middle eastern Moslem rulers formed slave armies, which tended to usurp or dominate the govt. In Egypt Saladin organised the first slave regiment in about 1170 and under the Ayyubids the practice grew until the death of Al-Malik-as-Salih in 1249; the Mameluke generals murdered his heir and set up one of themselves as Sultan. This sultanate was a military aristocracy recruited by purchase and training. It lasted until 1517 and is usually considered in two periods viz: the "Turkish" (1250-1382) when the Bahri regiment dominated and the Circassian (1382-1517) or Burji regimental period.

(2) The Bahri destroyed the crusader states and by 1350 had established a brilliant dominion which included modern Egypt with Palestine and Syria as far as the Taurus. The Black Death and factionalism caused its collapse after the death of an-Nasir (r. 1293-1341) by preventing effective policing of the long frontiers against Bedouin raids.

(3) Under the Burji, the Sultans were men of mediocre talent, and recruitment and promotion tended to depend upon (Circassian) race rather than ability. The capture of the spice trade with Venetian help, only delayed the decline which had already begun. The Asiatic territories were lost in the Mongol invasion of 1400 but Cyprus was conquered in 1426 and held for a generation. High taxes compounded the govt's difficulties and the Portuguese began to interfere in the Indian trade after 1500. The collapse under Ottoman attack in 1517 was, however, due to inferior generalship and artillery.

(4) The Ottomans at first left the mameluke system undisturbed and appointed Mameluke Governors until 1551. Thereafter Governors with troops and administrative staffs were sent from Constantinople. These displaced the Mamelukes in the important offices but they continued to be recruited as before and still formed the bulk of the army. Sons of the mamelukes, however, became eligible for recruitment. Consequently the old military factions were confused by new family loyalties to so-called 'houses'.

(5) As Ottoman imperial power declined within the empire, the Mamelukes filtered back into the ruling Egyptian positions. The Ottoman Sultan eventually had to compound with local autonomy, by conferring the viceroyalty on the head of that house which would pay the annual yield of certain taxes to Constantinople. Hence when Bonaparte invaded Egypt in 1798 he had to deal with a Mameluke state and army, which he shook but, owing to British intervention, could not destroy. The destruction was effected in 1811 by Mehemet Ali.

MAN, ISLE OF: MAN AND THE ISLES (1) Oghma inscriptions and church dedications show that Man was strongly influenced from Ireland until the 8th cent. The main religious centre was the Celtic monastery at Maughold but every substantial estate (*treen*) had its chapel, and there were many standing crosses.

(2) From 798 the Vikings used Man as a staging point on their autumn return from Irish Sea campaigns. Permanent colonisation started in about 900. Their north-about route included settlements in the Hebrides and these became associated with Man, which achieved a primacy for its strategic position and relative fertility. Under K. GODRED CROVAN (or King ORRY r. 1079-95) the first monarch of whom much is known, the kingdom consisted of 32 parts, of which Man counted as 16, while the island groups of the Outer Hebrides, Skye, Mull and Islay each counted as 4. Godred came from Islay but also ruled in Dublin.

(3) Man was long divided along the S.W.-N.E. watershed into "northern" and "southern" areas. The

Vikings settled in the more fertile North and the two parts were distinguished by differences of dialect, custom and affiliation. After Godred's death there was a conflict between Ottar, the northern chief and Macmarus, the southern. Victory went to the North at the B. of Santwat (?1098) but both chiefs were killed and made way for the Norwegian K. Magnus Barefoot (r. 1098-1103). He was killed in Ireland and was succeeded, after a period of confusion, by Godfred's son Olaf I (r. 1113-53). He had been brought up at the court of Henry I, and his diplomacy maintained a prosperous peace throughout most of his reign. It was through his grant of Rushen to Furness Abbey that the Cistercians came. He was murdered by his Dublin nephews when his son Godred II (r. 1153-87) was doing homage on his behalf to the King of Norway. Godred II drove out the nephews and seized Dublin, but left the Hebridean chiefs unsatisfied. His brother-in-law Somerled seceded with the Mull and Islay groups and established his independence by a naval victory off Colonsay (1156). In this partition, the foundation of the Lordship of the Isles, Man retained the Outer Hebrides and the Skye Group, but in 1158 Somerled tried to oust Godred altogether. The King fled to Norway, but returned quietly after Somerled's death in 1164.

(4) Reginald or Rognvald I (r. 1187-1228) was a premarital son of Godred II but elected in preference to his legitimate brother Olaf (the Black) who received Lewis. Reginald soon collided with the Munster English who were approaching Dublin and claiming the Lordship of Ireland. K. John rejected the Manx habit of interfering in Dublin, and demanded homage in 1206. To pay the traditional homage to Norway Reginald voyaged there in 1210 whereupon John sent a destructive expedition against the Isle (1210). Thus weakened, Reginald had difficulty in resisting Olaf the Black who wanted more territory. Intermittent fighting ended in full civil war. The North supported Olaf and the Hebrideans; the South, Reginald, who was killed at Tynwald Hill. This affair alarmed the English, for Olaf had Norwegians with him. Henry III consequently forced him to undertake to defend the Irish Sea, which excited Norwegian suspicions. Olaf died on the point of departure for Norway. His fourteen year old son Harold I (r. 1257-48) was equally entangled in this Anglo-Norwegian struggle which led to a Norwegian occupation (1238-9). He was drowned in the Shetlands returning with a new Norwegian wife. His brother Reginald II was assassinated a few weeks later and after further confusion Magnus, son of Olaf II (r. 1252-65) was recognised as King. In 1263, however, K. Haakon of Norway was beaten by Alexander III of Scotland at the B. of Largs. Magnus, though Haakon's ally, was elsewhere, but retired to Man, pursued by Alexander's much superior forces. By the T. of DUMFRIES (1263) Magnus abandoned all the Hebridean Is. and did homage for Man. In 1266, after his death, all Norwegian claims were ceded to Scotland, and the Isle's future became a matter of Anglo-Scottish dispute. (T. of Perth).

(5) Godred, s. of Magnus, rebelled against the Scots but was killed at Ronaldsway in 1275. He was the last male descendant of Godred Crovan. There were two female claimants, but in practice Man became part of the subject matter of the Competition for the Scottish crown. After Balliol's deposition (1296) Edward I appointed Bp. Bec of Durham Governor of Man and in 1310 Edward II appointed Piers Gaveston. In 1313 Robert the Bruce descended upon the Isle, destroyed Castle Rushen and conferred Man on Thomas Randolph, E. of Moray. His victory at Bannockburn (1314) briefly confirmed the gift, but Man was then involved in Edward Bruce's Irish expedition and Anglo-Irish reprisals. By 1333 the English were in possession. Edward III granted the Kingship to William Mantacute E. of Salisbury whose son William sold it to William Scrope, E. of Wiltshire, in 1392. After Scrope's execution (1399) it was conferred on Henry Percy, 1st E. of Northumberland, but after his attainder in 1405 it was granted to Sir JOHN STANLEY, in whose descendants it remained until 1765.

(6) During the 14th cent. troubles ecclesiastical power had grown by default. The bishop and his courts exercised great power in moral and ecclesiastical causes. The bishopric, the abbey of Rushen, itself subject to Furness, the Nunnery at Douglas, the Irish abbeys of Bangor and Sabhal, the Scottish priory of Whithorn, the English one at St. Bees, and the Franciscans, established at Arbory in 1373, held civil and criminal jurisdictions and enforced sanctuary on their wide lands. All these bodies levied tithes which were heavier than in neighbouring countries. Sir John was too distracted to pay much attention, and began the tradition of appointing separate, and usually competent Lancastrian Governors, through whom, with usually short interruptions caused by some crisis, the sovereignty was exercised.

(7) The most important of these interruptions was that of Sir John (II) (r. 1414-32) who re-established the royal power and regulated the governorship: the first required an operation against the church. He forbade sanctuary, and then summoned all the tenants to acknowledge him at the Tynwald (1415). The Abbot of Furness and the Priors of Whithorn and St. Bees failed to attend and were deprived. The second was achieved by writing down the laws, hitherto remembered by the Northern and Southern Deemsters and the Keys. He also abolished trial by battle and standardised weights and measures.

(8) The Stanleys rose steadily (r. 1504-21) in the convolutions of English politics. Thomas (II) (Ld. Stanley) was stepfather to Henry VII and crowned him on Bosworth Field. His grandson Thomas (III) (1st E. of Derby) substituted the title of Lord for that of King in 1504 and visited Man in 1507 to put down a tumult occasioned by a Scottish raid. His son Edward (1521-72) succeeded young, and Card. Wolsey acted as guardian of the lordship. When the Cardinal died, Edward resumed the sovereignty in the developing Reformation. The Reformation statutes were never applied to Man, but Edward enormously enriched the family by taking over all the monastic property by virtue of his prerogative. The Manx reformation, nevertheless, proceeded far more slowly than the English. There were no prosecutions for prayers to the dead until 1594 nor were the clergy allowed to marry until 1610.

(9) The Lords Henry (r. 1572-98) and Ferdinando (1598) left only daughters. Q. Elizabeth I took the lordship during the resulting abeyance and James I continued to appoint governors until 1610 when he returned it jointly to William Stanley, 6th E. and his Countess Elizabeth, who actually ruled the island. When she died, William's son James, Ld Strange, became Governor, and as 7th E. from 1642-51, Lord James was known, even in his lifetime as The Great Stanley, as much for his personality as for the results of his rule. As a royalist he raised troops and ships for Charles I but had also to deal with discontent, mainly arising out of tithes, of which as owner of the old monastic lands, he was the principal recipient. These were reduced, but he substituted a system of leases for three lives instead of the traditional system of straw tenure. (*See* SETTLEMENT ACT (1704) MAN). Meanwhile the burden of war weighed heavily upon the islanders and when the Great Stanley was taken and executed in 1651 they put up no further resistance.

(10) The leader of the trouble under the Great Stanley had been William Christian (or Illiam Dhone) who led the surrender to Parliament, and was Parliamentary Governor from 1656. He was condemned and shot for treason in 1663 but K. Charles II ordered all

his property to be returned to his family. The new Lord, Charles (r. 1660-72) and Bp. Barrow acting as his Governor contrived to embroil themselves with the inhabitants over the land tenure problem originally raised by the Great Stanley. The issue, in essence, was whether the Lord was a true owner or only the ultimate sovereign of the land and it was brought to a head by Barrow's seizure of John Lace's farm at Hangahill. Lace appealed to the Keys, who twice pronounced in his favour, but gave way under threats. This conflict between Lord and legislature continued for a generation and was exacerbated by poor harvests and fishing seasons, but in 1699 the Lord William (II) (r. 1672-1702) visited the island and appointed Bp. Wilson to receive proposals. The result was the Act of Settlement of 1704.

(11) In 1736 the existing branch of the Stanleys died out with the Lord James (II) and the lordship passed to James (IV), D. of Athol (r. 1736-64) his kinsman. An Act of Tynwald of 1737 thenceforth required that the customs duties could be fixed only with its consent. The customs issue was thus brought into commercial prominence, for the greater the difference between British and Manx rates the greater the temptation to smuggle. Smuggling had become the most lucrative Manx activity and a major source of loss to the British revenue. Accordingly the British Govt. brought pressure to bear upon the Lord John, 3rd D of Atholl, to sell the sovereignty and this was effected in 1765 by the REVESTMENT ACT. The Duke's other rights were progressively bought out at Manx expense by 1828, a last payment being made in 1866. The fourth Duke was Governor from 1793-1830.

(12) After 1796 customs receipts exceeded the total cost of administration but the London Govt. failed to plough back the surplus. Tynwald would not raise further revenue because the London Govt. could appropriate it. It began to create boards with rate raising powers instead. These boards became the basis of much of the later administration. The Keys, however, remained effectively self perpetuating. By 1863 the anomalies had become intolerable in an island now strongly affected by reformist agitation. The new Governor, Lord Loch, concluded that Man must control most of its own revenues to be able to develop its trade and tourist industry but that for this purpose the Keys must be reformed. Hence in 1866 the Keys became an elected body and though the harbours remained under British control, most of the revenue was applied as Tynwald directed. Though the detailed method of calculating the proportions of the revenue due to Britain and Man have varied, the principle of the arrangement has continued.

MANAGING AGENCY SYSTEM. An important British overseas trading habit in the 19th and 20th cents. especially in India. British firms requiring managers with local knowledge, employed local firms on commission as managing agents. The effect was to develop colonies commercially rather than industrially.

MANASSEH ben ISRAEL (1604-57) a friend of Grotius, established a Hebrew press at Amsterdam in 1626 and published *Spes Israelis* (Lat: The Hope of Israel), a tract urging readmission of the Jews to England, in 1650. In 1652 his petition to this effect was rejected, against Cromwell's views, by the Council of State, but in 1655 he petitioned Cromwell again. They were tacitly admitted and built a synagogue. He was pensioned.

MAN-AT-ARMS. An armoured horseman.

MANBOTE. Compensation for homicide payable to the relatives or in the case of a serf, to the Lord.

MANBY (1) Aaron (1776-1850), Wolverhampton ironmaster founded the Charenton (Paris) iron works and began the gas lighting of Paris in 1819. He built the first iron steamship to put to sea in 1822, and bought the Le Creusot ironworks in 1826. His *s.* **(2) Charles (1804-84)** was Secretary to the Institution of Civil Engineers from 1829-56.

MANCHESTER. Edward the Elder repaired the ruined Roman hill fort in 923 against the Danes and by 1086 it was a recognised manor. The barony, a larger area in S. Lancashire, was held by the Grelley family but the head or forinsec manor of the Hundred was Salford, which had an early 13th cent. charter and acquired its well-known Court of Record. Manchester received a seigneurial charter in 1301 by which time it had corn and fulling mills, a weekly market, an annual fair, a fortified manor and a church, which in 1421 acquired a college of priests to serve the very large parish. The lords retained some judicial and fiscal rights including a monopoly of milling and baking. The Free Church School founded by Hugh Oldham in 1509 became the celebrated Grammar School in 1515. Chetham's Hospital was endowed from the property of the priests' college after the Dissolution of the Monasteries. The wool trade made Manchester prosperous in 16th cent. and weaving added in 1620. The material woven was fustian whose cotton weft began the Lancashire cotton industry connected with America through Liverpool. The decisive stimuli to this development were the completion of the Bridgewater Canal to Worcester in 1762, assuring a cheap coal supply and to the Mersey in 1776 assuring cheap cotton. Factories and population now multiplied but administration remained strictly manorial until a local constabulary was formed in 1792. By 1801 the population exceeded 70,000 but the place was not represented in Parliament until 1833 nor chartered until 1838.

Meantime cotton manufacture was giving way to the general financing and exchange operations necessitated by the cotton industry, and the capital accumulations served to finance an engineering industry which had grown out of the need for textile machinery. The result was the 19th cent. diversification into machine tools, armaments and locomotives. A second decisive stimulus was the **Manchester Ship Canal** (*see* TRANSPORT AND COMMUNICATIONS), opened in 1894 which brought oceanic trade to the heart of the city. Hence when electrical engineering began to develop in the U.S.A. it found a natural home at Manchester or Salford.

By 1970 the area was a conurbation consisting at the centre, of Manchester, Salford and Stretford with suburbs in all directions and surrounded by the cotton spinning towns of Bolton, Bury, Rochdale, Oldham, Ashton and Stockport. The population of this area was about 2.5M.

MANCHESTER, EARL AND DUKES OF. See MONTAGUE (MANCHESTER).

MANCHESTER GUARDIAN. See GUARDIAN.

MANCHESTER "MARTYRS" (Ir. 1867). To frustrate a Fenian attack on the arms depot in Chester Castle, two Irish Americans, Kelly and Deasy, were arrested under the Vagrancy Act and remanded to Bellevue Prison, Manchester. Three men, Allen, Larkin and O'Brien held up the prison van, and in trying to shoot out the lock, killed a police sergeant inside. These three were correctly convicted of murder, but hanged. Their death created a furore in Ireland and provoked T. D. Sullivan to write *God Save Ireland*.

MANCHESTER SCHOOL was a group of liberal politicians and economists which survived the success of Cobden and Bright's Manchester based Anti-Corn Law League after 1846. It favoured freedom of the seas, free trade, and peace keeping arrangements and opposed exploitatory colonialism. It had considerable influence in France and even in Germany and its principal achievement was the Cobden commercial treaty with France in 1860.

MANCHURIA, MANCHUKUO. This international trouble area which had given a non-Chinese dynasty to China in 1644, was heavily colonised by Chinese in the 19th and 20th cents. but remained loosely organised and bandit ridden. Russia acquired the left bank of the R. Amur by

the T. of AIGUN (1858) and the territory east of the Ussuri by the T. of PEKIN (1860). In return for diplomatic support against Japan after their defeat in 1894, the Chinese granted a railway concession to Russia in 1896. The CHINESE EASTERN RAILWAY connected Siberia with Vladivostok. It in effect became a Russian extra-territorial area. In 1895 the Russians bullied China into ceding Port Arthur, with which the railway was connected by 1900. They then occupied the whole country on the pretext of keeping order after the Boxer War. They constantly delayed evacuation in order to enlarge their influence, and so clashed with Japan.

The Japanese victories in the RUSSO-JAPANESE WAR of 1904-5 were gained on Manchurian soil, and in the waters adjacent to Korea, and Port Arthur with the Russian interests in S. Manchuria were ceded to Japan, but thereafter by secret agreements of 1907, 1910, 1912 and 1916 the two powers co-operated to exclude outsiders. The territory remained, however, part of the Chinese empire which was steadily introducing modernised Chinese troops alongside the older fashioned local Manchu forces.

At the Chinese revolution of 1911 Chang Tso-Lin with the loyalist Manchu army expelled the revolutionaries and having allied himself with Yüan Shihkai became effective Chinese ruler of Manchuria. In 1915 the Japanese extorted 99 year leases of Port Arthur and the S. Manchurian railway, and privileged status for Japanese in the province; and the Russian revolution enabled them to extend their interests in the north.

The Japanese continental or KWANTUNG ARMY became, in 1919, a separate command and virtually a separate state more imperialist than the home Govt. Chang Tsolin represented an obstacle to its ambitions. By 1926 he dominated the Chinese Govt at Pekin, but in 1928 retired, on Japanese advice, before the advancing Kuomintang armies from the south. The home Govt. offered to guarantee him in Manchuria. The Kwantung army thought otherwise and murdered him. The *coup* failed to create an excuse for military occupation and Chang's s. Chang Hsüeh-Liang succeeded him.

Chang Hsüeh-Liang inconveniently supported the victorious Kuomintang, whereupon in Sept. 1931 the Kwantung army staged a series of incidents at Mukden and used them as a pretext to invade Manchuria. The Chinese relied on the League of Nations which sent out the LYTTON COMMISSION to investigate. It pronounced the Japanese guilty of aggression but made no constructive recommendations. The U.S.A. decided to take no action; the League followed suit. The Japanese over-ran the rest of the province, and the Chinese accepted the inevitable at the TANGKU TRUCE (May 1933). The Japanese then established the last Chinese emperor on the throne of their new puppet state of MANCHUKUO. These events discredited the League.

The Japanese now bought out the Chinese Eastern Railway (1936) and converted Manchukuo into an agricultural and industrial war base for the Kwantung army's further attempted conquest of N. China. It so remained until the Russians attacked Japan in Aug. 1945 They then plundered it and obstructed Chinese reoccupation so as to give time to recruit the banditti into a revolutionary force. By 1948 communists of a Russian type were in control and Russian privileges were conceded until 1952. Sporadic disputes and frontier incidents continued until the collapse of Russian communism from 1988 onwards.

MANCUS. A money account = 30 pence.

MANDAMUS. See PREROGATIVE WRITS.

MANDATE (1) ELECTORAL. At a modern General Election each party issues a manifesto which is intended to attract votes. The winning party then attempts to carry through a series of legislative and administrative measures which it defends on the ground that, as they were fore-shadowed in the manifesto, it has the mandate of the electorate for them. The opposition, besides questioning the wisdom and expediency of these measures, usually tries to show that they are not in accordance with the electoral mandate. Since manifestos upon which the notion of mandate is founded tend to be expressed in pleasing rather than precise terms, the discussions involve nice problems of interpretation.

(2) INDIVIDUAL. In certain organisations, notably trade unions, a delegate is often *mandated*, i.e. required by those who appointed or elected him, to vote in a particular way on particular issues. Where the mandate is STRICT he must vote as instructed regardless of circumstances or the outcome of the discussion. Where it is CONDITIONAL, he must put the point of view of his mandators but may vote otherwise if so convinced.

(3) LEAGUE of NATIONS. The committal of a colony conquered from Germany and the Ottoman Empire in World War I to the administration of a victorious power which was technically, if lightly responsible for it to the League. Such territories were renamed Trust Territories after World War II. *See* DECOLONISATION.

MANDEVILLE (1) Geoffrey (?-?) a companion of William I secured the large forfeited estates of Asgar the Staller in Essex. His son **(2) William (?-?)** was constable of the Tower. He allowed Ranulf Flambard to escape and lost the Constableship, several manors and was heavily fined. His son **(3) Geoffrey (?-1144) E. of ESSEX (1141)** succeeded to a depleted inheritance with much of the fine outstanding. Nevertheless he had castles at Pleshy and Saffron Walden and in the civil wars of Stephen, joined the Empress Maud in return for the hereditary shrievalty and then deserted her for a higher bid from Stephen, who made him Sheriff and justice in Herts, London and Middlesex. He then offered himself to Maud for an even higher bid, but the intrigue was discovered and he was suddenly arrested at court and forced with a halter round his neck to surrender his castles. On his release, he seized Ramsey, devastated the Fens and was ultimately killed. His activities provoked the horror-struck Peterborough chronicler's account of the period. His *s.* **(4) William (?-1189) 3rd E. (1166) and Count of AUMALE (1179)** was a powerful and intelligent supporter of Henry II in England and France from 1166 until he took the cross in 1177. He was in Palestine until 1179 and then returned to his duties with Henry II. He secured Aumale by marriage but also had Flemish fiefs which involved him in Flemish politics. He assisted Richard I to ascend the throne and died just after Richard had appointed him Justiciar.

MANDEVILLE, Sir John alias, perhaps Jean de Bourgogne or Burgoyne (?-1372) was probably the Chamberlain of John Ld de Mowbray who was executed in 1322. He fled to Flanders and composed in French in the name of Mandeville a book of travels drawn from William of Boldensele, Odoric of Pordenone and Vincent de Beauvais.

MANDUBRACIUS. *See* BRITAIN BEFORE THE ROMAN CONQUEST-2.

MANGALORE, T. OF (1784) between Tippoo Sahib of Mysore and the HEIC ended the second Mysore War by restoring the *status quo ante bellum*, including the restoration of Balaghat to Mysore.

MANGONEL (Med.) A large siege engine, whose arm was operated by torsion. It could throw 300 lb some 400 yards.

MANHATTAN. *See* NEW YORK.

MANHATTAN PROJECT was the cover name for the joint U.S.-British-Canadian establishment at Oak Ridge, Tennessee, which between Aug. 1942-46 developed the atom bomb.

MANICHAEISM. *See* ALBIGENSIANS.

MANIFEST DESTINY was a 19th cent. American slogan describing the continental imperialism of the U.S.A.

MANILA. *See* PARIS, P. OF (10 FEB. 1763); SEVEN YEARS' WAR-12.

MANILA INCIDENT (Aug. 1898). The local British flag officer prevented German interference with American operations by placing his ships between the German and American squadrons. *See* SALISBURY'S THIRD GOVT.-8.

MANIPUR. The Rajah requested British help against the Burmese in 1762 and 1824. The British ruled, and reformed the Govt. during a minority from 1891-99; after 1907 the President, under the Rajah, of the Durbar was an Indian Civil Servant. After 1917 the subdivisional officers were drawn from the Govt. of Assam. The capital, IMPHAL, was a vital strategic centre in the war with Japan, and was desperately and successfully contested. The state acceded to India in 1947.

MANITOBA. *See* CANADA.

MANLEY, Mrs Mary de la RIVIERE (1663-1724), a disreputable friend of the Duchess of Cleveland, later published her *Letters* (1696) and the scurrilous *New Atlantis* (1709) in which the Whigs and others were traduced. Arrested but released in 1709, she published *Memoirs of Europe* (1710) and *Court Intrigues* (1711). Having been attacked by Swift in the *Tatler,* she succeeded him as editor of the *Examiner* in 1711 and they collaborated for some time. She also wrote successful plays.

MANN, Sir Horace (1701-86) 1st Bt. (1755), a friend of Horace Walpole was at Florence from 1737-86 as assistant to the minister and then as minister. His main business was to watch the Young Pretender who lived there but he has also left a voluminous correspondence with Horace Walpole.

MANNERS (*see* ROS) **and MANNERS-SUTTON. (1) Thomas (?-1543) 13th Ld. ROS (1513) 1st E. of RUTLAND (1525)** received much favour from Henry VIII who made him warden of the E. March in 1525. He was very active against the northern rebellion of 1536. His son **(2) Henry (?-1563) 2nd E.,** campaigned against Scotland but was a protestant extremist. Hence Mary I forfeited his offices and imprisoned him, but Elizabeth I made him Pres. of the Council of the North, as well as Lord Lieut. of Rutland. His son **(3) Edward (1549-81) 3rd E.,** was Lord Lieut. of Nottinghamshire and Lincolnshire, and a member of the court which tried Mary Q. of Scots. His descendant **(4) John (1638-1711) 9th E. (1679) and 1st D. (1703)** raised midland troops, especially in Nottinghamshire for William III, and was given his dukedom for helping to ensure George I's succession. **(5) John (1721-70) Marquess of GRANBY,** eldest son of the 3rd D., was the cavalryman after whom many public houses are named. His advance at Minden (1759) was halted by Ld. George Sackville (of opposite political persuasion) and the ensuing challenges and controversy caused great public agitation. He became commander of the British contingent a few months later, and won a succession of victories in Germany. In 1763, he became Master General of the Ordnance and in 1766 Commander in Chief, in which offices he was hotly attacked by "Junius". His son **(6) Charmes (1754-87) 4th D. (1799)** was M.P. for Cambridge from 1774 and opposed the Govt.'s American policy. In 1783 he was Lord Steward, but in 1784 took the Privy Seal briefly under Pitt. Thereafter he was a successful Lord Lieut. of Ireland until his death. Of two of his cousins **(7) Charles Manners-Sutton (1755-1828)** was Bp. of Norwich from 1792-1805 and then Abp. of Canterbury. He succeeded in being both a favourite of royalty, and a religious revivalist. His brother **(8) Thomas (1756-1842) Ld. MANNERS (1807)** was M.P. for Newark, Sol-Gen. from 1802-05 and Irish Lord Chancellor from 1807-27. He was strongly opposed to R. Catholic emancipation and also active in the proceedings against Q. Caroline. The archbishop's son **(9) Charles (1780-1845) 1st Vist. CANTERBURY (1835)** was Speaker of the Commons from 1817-35 when he was defeated on allegations of partisanship. His son

(10) John Henry (1814-77) 3rd Vist. (1869) was U/Sec. of State at the Home Office under Peel from 1841-46 and then governed New Brunswick (1854-61), Trinidad (1864-6) and Victoria (1866-73). A grandson of **(6) (11) Charles Cecil (1815-6) 6th D. (1857)** completed the Gothick reconstruction of Belvoir Castle begun by his father, but was mainly known as a protectionist M.P. His brother **(12) John James (1818-1906) 7th D. (1888)** was a brilliant and radical Disraelian M.P. who advocated factory reform, allotments and Irish disestablishment but parted with his colleagues over free trade. He was out of Parliament as a result from 1846-50, but sat as a Tory for various places until he succeeded to the dukedom. During this period he was in the cabinet as first commissioner of works in 1852, and from 1858-59 and from 1866-68. From 1874-80 and from 1885-86 he was a successful working Postmaster-Gen. and from 1886-92 Chancellor of the Duchy of Lancaster.

MANNING, Henry Edward (1808-92) Card. (1875) Archdeacon of Chichester from 1840 published *The Unity of the Church* in 1844, visited Pius IX in 1849 and became a R. Catholic in 1851. After much preaching and literary work, he was appointed a papal domestic prelate in 1860 and R. Catholic Abp. of Westminster in 1865. Strongly ultramontane, he defended the temporal sovereignty and the infallibility of the papacy. He was also a social reformer, much concerned with alcoholism, housing and education.

MANNINGHAM-BULLER, Reginald Edward (1905-80) 4th Bart; 1st Vist. DILHORNE (1964) became an M.P. without opposition under the wartime electoral truce in 1943. He was Sol-Gen. under Churchill in 1945, and Attorney-General from 1954-62 when he became Lord Chancellor in the 'Night of the Long Knives' (*see* MACMILLAN GOVT.). After an interval out of political office, he became a Lord of Appeal in Ordinary in 1969. Not suspected of any transcendent ability, but of intimidating size, he nevertheless delivered some notable judgements as a Law Lord.

MANNINGHAM STRIKE 1891. The defeat of a five-month strike at Manningham Mill, Bradford, arising out of wage reductions during a wool trade slump, led to the formation of the Bradford Labour Union and, in 1893, to the inauguration of the Independent Labour Party at Bradford.

MANNY or MAUNY, Sir Walter de (?-1372) Ld. (1345) came from Hainault as squire to Q. Philippa. He was given lands in Merioneth and became Governor of Harlech in 1334. In 1337 he commanded a fleet in the Scheldt and having taken Thuin l'Éveque with a token force in 1339, distinguished himself at Sluys in 1340. In 1342 he commanded the expedition to Brittany: and then served under Derby in Gascony. He was field commander at the S. of Calais in 1345-6 and acted as one of the peace negotiators in France in 1348 and in Holland in 1351. In 1355 he managed the S. of Berwick and in 1359-60 he was with Edward III in France. He was one of the negotiators at Brétigny in 1360. In 1368 he was briefly in Ireland and then went to France with John of Gaunt. In 1371 he founded and endowed the London Charterhouse.

MANOA. *See* EL DORADO.

MAN OF STRAW. *See* LEGAL FICTIONS.

MANOR. *See* FEUDALISM-4 *et seq.*

MANSABDARS **(Hindustani = holders of a command)** consisted of 33 ranks required, in theory, to lead horsemen to the service of the Great Mogul. The horses were owned by the govt., and the ranks distinguished by the number (10 to 10,000), the kind of horses and the number of months per year during which the *mansabdar* was entitled to pay. *Mansabs* of 1,000 and over conferred nobility. Pay was made by assignments of revenue upon particular lands, but these were often changed and the relatives were liable for advances outstanding at the

Mansabdar's death. In practice this created a body of public servants many of whom performed purely civil functions. About half were Hindus.

MANSE originally enough land to support a family came to mean the residence of a minister of a Scottish parish.

MANSEL or MAUNSELL, John (?-1265) counsellor and diplomat of Henry III became Keeper of the Great Seal in 1246. He was employed on missions to Brabant, Scotland, France and Brittany and negotiated the Lord Edward's marriage to Eleanor of Castile, the election of Richard of Cornwall as King of the Romans and the abandonment of English claims to Normandy in 1258. He was responsible for the manoeuvres which neutralised the London oligarchy at the start of the Barons' reforms. As one of the 25 and 15 set up under the Provisions of Oxford, he vigorously defended the royal interests. He was much traduced, being alleged to have accumulated 300 benefices. In 1261 Henry had to dismiss him, but this did not prevent him from negotiating the papal bull releasing Henry from his undertakings. He escaped to Boulogne when the Barons' War broke out in 1263 and was present at the Mise of Amiens in 1264. He died a poor man.

MANSELL, Sir Robert (1573-1656) was a corrupt naval administrator from 1604-18. As Treasurer of the Navy, he made a fortune. He was also an unsuccessful admiral against the Algerine pirates in 1620-21.

MANSFIELD (orig. MANFIELD) (1) Sir James (1733-1821) called to the bar in 1758 advised John Wilkes in 1768; became a K.C. in 1772, M.P. for Cambridge University in 1779 and solicitor-general from 1780-83. From 1804 onwards as C.J. of the Common Pleas, he made persistent but in the long run unsuccessful efforts to import principles akin to equity directly into the Common Law. His grandson **(2) Sir William Rose (1819-76) 1st Ld. SANDHURST (1871)** gained military distinction against the Sikhs in 1849, was military adviser to the British Ambassador at Constantinople in 1855 and served against the Indian mutineers in 1857 and 1858. He was Commander in Chief Bombay in 1860; of India in 1865 and of Ireland from 1870.

MANSFIELD. *See* MURRAY, WILLIAM (1705-93).

MANSION HOUSE, originally the principal residence of a nobleman, came to mean the official residence of the Lord Mayors of London and York. The London Mansion House, built by George Dance the Elder between 1739-53 is remarkable as the last functioning palace of Govt. with a residence for the Lord Mayor at the top, state rooms and offices below it, and a court of justice and prison underneath.

MANSLOT (Dan = man's share). A landholding a little less than an oxgang, in Lincolnshire, Norfolk and Nottinghamshire representing an ordinary Danish soldier's holding.

MANUMISSION. The formal act, commonly by charter or deed and the handing over of a weapon by which a slave, or later a serf or villein was made free, as opposed to the informal method of taking freedom by escaping to a town or royal manor and remaining there for a year and a day, which involved the risk of recapture. A pre-Conquest slave could not purchase his freedom because he had no property of his own with which he might do it, but a post-Conquest serf or villein could own chattels and could therefore build up savings. The post-Conquest implications of manumission were initially unclear, but the study of Roman law (which has a detailed jurisprudence on the problems) helped to clarify such difficulties as the effect of the act on a man's status outside the manor, and whether he owed his manumitting lord any duties after the event. *See* ENFRANCHISEMENT.

MANWARING or MAYNWARING, Roger (1590-1653) as a Chaplain to Charles I from 1627, was an extreme advocate of the Divine Right of Kings; he asserted the royal power to tax without consent of Parliament, but being arrested and sentenced, retracted. He became Bp. of St. Davids in 1635 but was deprived by a vote of the House of Lords in 1640, and was later imprisoned.

MANWOOD. Kentish family **(1) Sir Roger (1525-92)** held various legal appointments in the Cinque Ports and was M.P. for Hastings in 1555 and for Sandwich from 1558. He was a friend of Sir Thomas Gresham and of Abp. Parker who helped him to found Sandwich Grammar School. A judge of the Common Pleas in 1572 and C.B. of the Exchequer from 1578, he was strongly partisan in his treatment of those suspected of treason, and was a member of the commission which tried Mary Q. of Scots in 1586. In 1591 he was accused of corruption in selling offices and was summoned to the Star Chamber just before he died. His son **(2) Sir Peter (?-1625)** was a learned antiquary.

MANX. *See* CELTS; MAN, I. OF

MAORI. *See* NEW ZEALAND.

MAO TZE-TUNG (1893-1976) a professional revolutionary, developed ideas on raising and development of revolutionary movements among rural dwellers and in 1927 took refuge with a few hundred followers on the Ching Kang Shan. Here with Chu Teh he developed a technique of rural guerrilla warfare until 1930 when he went to Kiangsi and in 1931 founded a "Chinese Soviet Republic" with himself as chairman. In 1934 this body, driven by the Kuomintang, made its Long March to the north-west, during which, especially at the Tsunyi Conference, Mao established his position as leader. He appealed to the nationalistic spirit by calling for a united front against Japan, thereby making it hard for the equally nationalist Kuomintang to attack him. In 1937 when the Japanese attempt at conquest really began, Mao's guerrillas used their technique as much to get control of the rural population as to fight the Japanese, leaving the business and losses of more formal operations to the Kuomintang. His strength thus grew while the Kuomintang patriotically wasted theirs. When the Japanese had surrendered he promptly turned on them and by Apr. 1949 had taken their capital at Nanking. By Dec. the Chinese People's Republic was established (*see* CHINA). Later as Chairman of the Council of Ministers, Mao, both as figurehead and initiator of successive drastic policies was the object of compulsory adulation, but after his death his omniscience was publicly doubted, especially on the shaky economics of the Great Leap Forward and the disastrous Cultural Revolution.

MAP, Walter (fl. 1190) a Herefordshire man was a clerk of the household of Henry II with whom he went abroad in 1173. He was sent to Rome in 1179 and travelled with Henry II abroad again in 1183. He received a plurality of ecclesiastical preferments and became archdeacon of Oxford in 1197. A satirist and wit, he wrote an interesting collection of anecdotes called *De Nugis Curialium* (Lat. = Courtiers' Trifles).

MAPLEDURHAM (Oxon) late Elizabethan mansion of the Blount family.

MAPS. *See* CARTOGRAPHY.

MAQUIS (Fr.) were thickly overgrown areas of Corsica in which fugitives could easily hide; it became the common term for the French active resistance to the Germans in World War II.

MAR, Es. of (A) Mar, comprising modern Aberdeenshire and Banff, was the one of the seven Scots Earldoms. **(1) Roderick (fl. 1115)** is the first known earl. There followed **(2) Morgund (1141-82) (3) Gilchrist (c. 1182-1211) (3) Duncan (c. 1228-44)** and **(5) William (1244-81)** their inter-relationships being mostly unclear. William's *s.* **(6) Donald (?-1297)** played a leading part in the succession crisis after the death of the Maid of Norway, and in the Scots revolt against Edward I. Captured at Dunbar, he died in captivity. His son **(7) Gratney (?-1305)** and grandson **(8) Donald (?-1332)**

who was educated at Edward II's court, vainly led Scots forces on his behalf in 1327 and was killed when Regent by adherents of Edward Balliol. After a long abeyance or minority, his *s.* **(9) Thomas (?-1373)** succeeded him and was briefly Scots Great Chamberlain (1358-9) but spent much of his time at Edward III's court and for this reason was arrested by David II in 1361, and died in prison leaving no male heir.

(B) There was now a long period of conflicting claims, but his brother-in-law **(10) William E. of DOUGLAS** and **(11)** the latter's daughter **(c. 1390) Isabel** successively followed but she contracted marriages to an Erskine and then, after rape, to **(12) Alexander Stewart,** to whom she was forced to cede the earldom in 1404. There were now contests between Erskines and Stewarts interrupted in 1479 by the appointment of the low-born royal favourite **(13) Thomas Cochrane (?-1482).** He was murdered by a group of nobles who resented his influence. The earldom then passed back to the Stewarts and remained with them until the heirless death of **(14) John Stewart** in 1503, whereupon the Earldom fell vacant until 1562. *See* JAMES VI-3.

MARAT, Jean Paul (1744-93) of Swiss origin, practised medicine in London until the French Revolution when he published the extremist *Ami du Peuple*. He had to flee to London in 1791 but was elected to the Convention in 1792. In May, 1793, he was accused of treason before the Revolutionary Tribunal for attacking the Girondins. His acquittal gave the signal for their fall, but in July he was assassinated.

MARATHAS or MARRATTAS of the Maratha and Kubi castes form most of the population of MAHARASHTRA (W. India).

(A) Rajas of Satara. They were first welded into a powerful state by **(1) Sivaji I (1627-80)** an adventurer of genius who, beginning as a bandit in 1646, had taken most of the forts about Satara in 1660; he was confirmed as Rajah by the Emperor Aurangzib, and set himself up as an independent monarch in 1674. By his death his dominions covered the W. Carnatic from Belgaum to the R. Tungabhadra. His son **(2) Sambuji (r. 1680-89)** held the Kingdom until surprised and killed by the Moguls at Samgameshwa. His brother **(3) Raja Ram (r. 1689-1700)** maintained the family position and so did his widow **(4) Tara Bai (r. 1700-07)** until 1707 when the *s.* of **(2)**, **(5) Shahu or Sivaji II (r. 1707-49)** returned from the Mogul court where he had been held since his father's capture in 1689. Shahu seems to have had little taste for govt. and relied increasingly upon the dual system which Sivaji I had set up. In this there were eight Brahmin ministers, six of whom held military commands, while an army of light infantry and light cavalry, partly regular and partly irregular, was under a hierarchy of Kshatriya officers headed by a senapati or C-in-C.

(B) Peishwas of Poona. The ablest of the ministers was the Peishwa **(1) Balaji Viswanath (r. 1713-20)** who made his office pre-eminent by considerable feats of arms and diplomacy. Shahu accordingly conferred it upon his *s.* **(2) Baji Rao I (r. 1720-40)** who proposed to replace the crumbling Moguls with a Hindu empire, and with Rajput allies had conquered Malwa and Gujarat by 1724. At this point he was opposed by the Senapati Dhabade whom he killed after a civil war, and in 1731 he agreed with the Nizam of Hyderabad that in return for a free hand in the south, the Marathas should have a free hand in the north. By 1737 he was at the gates of Delhi, when the Emperor Mohammad Shah summoned the Nizam (his subordinate) to the rescue. The Nizam's defeat established Maratha supremacy over the greater part of India and in 1739 the Portuguese were expelled from Salsette and Bassein.

(C) The **Confederacy.** But trouble with Kshatriya leaders now arose again and Baji Rao was constrained to establish a kind of feudalism by conferring large circumscriptions upon his ablest military supporters. These were BHONSLA of NAGPUR, who was related to Shahu, SINDHIA of GWALIOR, HOLKAR of INDORE and the GAEKWAD of BARODA. The families of these four rulers together with the PEISHWA, whose capital was at POONA, constituted the five main dynasties of the Maratha Confederacy. The Peishwa himself owed nominal allegiance to the Rajah of Satara: Shahu ended his days as a religious recluse and his successors were expected to emulate him.

Baji Rao I died immediately after this major reorganisation and his s. **(3) Balaji Baji Rao (r. 1740-61)** succeeded him. The Afghans had just captured Delhi and this Peishwa, less intelligent than his father, saw an opportunity to establish an empire which should be Maratha, rather than Hindu. The Marathas had for some time been collecting the *Chauth* from lands under Mogul or other alien control. The army now included heavy artillery and even more expensive, large numbers of Pathan mercenaries (PINDARIS). Outside their homelands the Marathas were beginning to be regarded as predators, especially as Balaji sometimes failed to control freebooting by his more exalted confederates. When in 1761 the Mogul called upon him for protection against the Afghans, the latter had Indian allies. The greatest Maratha army was bloodily defeated at the Third B. of Panipat, with the loss of many high Maratha personalities; Balaji died of a broken heart.

(4) Madhava Rao (1761-72) had a shaken inheritance for the defeat had fallen most heavily upon the resources and prestige of the Peishwaship; the great feudatories began to assume a posture of independence or disunion. Before he could rebuild his power he died. He was succeeded by his brother **(5) Narayan Rao (r. 1172-3)** at whose death **(6) Raghoba (brother of (4))** seized the office, but was driven out in the same year when a posthumous s. **(7) Madhav Rao Narayan (1774-92)** was born and a council of regency was formed.

The First Maratha War. Raghoba now approached the British at Bombay and offered them Salsette and Bassein in return for their support. By the T. of SURAT (1775) they agreed and a discreditable war culminated in the surrender of a British force at Wargaon in 1779. The commander undertook to hand Raghoba over, but Warren Hastings, the Governor General, repudiated him and the war continued. Despite Leslie and Goddard's march from Bengal to Surat in 1779, and Popham's capture of Gwalior in 1780 neither side was able to inflict much damage on the other and in 1782 negotiations through Sindia ended in the T. of SALBAI. Raghoba got a pension: the British kept Salsette and there was mutual restoration of other territories.

Raghoba's principal Maratha opponent had been the NANA FADNAVIS (?-1800) who, not without opposition from Mahadji Sindia, became chief minister during the minority, and managed the war against the British. In 1784 he turned his troops against Tippoo Sultan of Mysore, from whom he retook some territory and in 1789

he with the British and the Nizam, joined against Tippoo in the Third Mysore War and recovered further territory. After Mahadji Sindia died in 1794 he was able to employ a united army against the Nizam, whom he defeated at Kharda (1795). At this point the Peishwa Mahav Rao Narayan committed suicide and the Nana, for the rest of his life, had to deal with a deadly enemy **(8) Baji Rao II (r. 1796-1819)** son of Raghoba. In these circumstances the Peishwaship was guided against the will of the Peishwa by the acknowledged abilities of the minister.

Second Maratha War. When he died Sindia and Holkar quarrelled over the right to control the Peishwa: in 1801 they fought a pitched battle at Poona, during which Baji Rao II escaped to British protection. By the T. of BASSEIN (Dec. 1802) they agreed to restore him in return for a subsidiary alliance. In the ensuing war the Gaekwad sided with him and the British, against Bhonsla, Holkar and Sindia, but Holkar would not co-operate with his allies. Sir Arthur Wellesley (the future Wellington) thus defeated the latter at Assaye (Sept. 1803) and Argaum (Nov.) and imposed a subsidiary treaty at DEOGAUN on Bhonsla. Lake defeated Sindia at Laswari and imposed a similar treaty at SURJI ARJANGAON (Dec. 1803). It was only then that Holkar moved and was beaten at Deeg (Nov. 1804). His treaty was imposed in 1806. All these rulers forfeited substantial territories and their defeat meant that relations between the British and the Peishwa were regulated by the T. of Bassein.

The Pindari or Third Maratha War. The British did not wish to interfere inside the Maratha states nor did they have enough troops to police the frontiers. The Marathas mostly went home. The Pindaris, in large or small organised forces, roamed Rajputana and the Deccan from their bases in the Narbada valley. For over 10 years there was fire in the villages and death on the roads everywhere, encouraged by Maratha chieftains great and small. Hence, when Ld Hastings determined in 1817 to round the Pindaris up, a Maratha war became likely. Baji Rao II organised it. The British troop movements began and the Peishwa with Holkar and Bhonsla attacked the cantonments at Kirkee (Nov. 1817). The Gaekwad was held in check and Sindia bullied into joining the British. By 1819 it was all over. The Pindaris vanished. Holkar lost half his lands, Bhonsla some further territory. The Peishwaship was abolished and Poona became a British cantonment. The Raja of Satara was set up in a small demesne of his own. Baji Rao was pensioned off and lived near Cawnpore where his adopted s. **(9) Nana Saheb (?-?1856)** was, in due course, to play a sinister part in the Indian Mutiny.

Later History. Satara lapsed when the last Rajah died childless in 1848; the Bhonsla (Nagpur) lands for the same reason in 1853; Sindia (Gwalior) and Holkar (Indore) continued to rule in oriental splendour and scandal. A Gaekwad had a major crisis in 1875 when he was deposed for misrule but the last Gaekwad, Sayaji Rao (r. 1875-1939) made Baroda a model state. All three were absorbed into the Indian Union at independence.

Independent Maratha Confederate Rulers

Sindia (Gwalior)		Bhonsla (Nagpur)		Holkar (Indore)		Gaekwad (Baroda)	
Ranoji	1730-50	Raghuji I	1743-88	Malhar Rao	1736-64	Pilaji	1721-32
Mahadaji	1750-94	Raghuji II	1788-1816	Malle Rao	1764-6	*Civil War till 1800*	
Daulat Rao	1794-1819	Raghuji III	1816-53	Ahalya Bhai	1766-95	Anand Rao	1800-19
				Tukoji	1795-7		
				Jaswant Rao I	1798-1811		
				Malhar Rao II	1811-33		

MARAVEDI. A Spanish gold coin worth 14s. sterling in 17th cent.

MARCH, English Es. of. *See* MORTIMER; MARCHER LORDSHIPS.

MARCHER LORDSHIPS (Wales). The Lords Marcher held their jurisdictions by a kind of crown forbearance combined with conquest. Save for a duty to serve the crown for 40 days within Wales, they owed nothing and were absolute over their people who, despite royal encroachments, had no appeal to the royal courts. Their essential purpose was war; Welsh resistance and mutual relationships determined their true extent so that their boundaries before 1284 generally expressed hope rather than reality.

The Norman invasion of Wales began soon after the conquest of England. By 1086 there were palatinates of Chester (which included the area of Flint) and Shropshire (which included Ruthin); most of later Denbighshire was the regality of Deganwy; Mathraval in central Wales covered most of the later Montgomeryshire except Montgomery itself which belonged to Shropshire; on the border of Hereford was Ewyas; and much of Gwent was already being parcelled out. From this southern base, the March was progressively extended along the coast especially by the Clares, for here the Normans had the advantage of naval support from Bristol to the estuaries of S. Wales, and of weak Welsh opposition in comparison with the well organised N. Welsh principality of Gwynedd. By 1111 they were established in Pembroke and were striking northwards beyond Cardigan.

In north and central Wales the frontier of the March swayed back and forth. The Palatinate of Shropshire was suppressed in 1102 after Robert of Bellême's rebellion, though the associated Lordships of Bromfield and Yale, Ruthin, Chirk and Oswestry survived in other hands. Welsh leaders occupied Deganwy, Mathravel and the area from the southern march to Aberdovey and Edeyrnion, but much of Radnor and Brecon was occupied by Norman lords. The central area was thus a debatable land.

After 1168 the Clares devoted most of their strength to the Irish invasion and Richard of Clare (Strongbow) died in 1176. Pembroke with Striguil passed to the Marshall family by the marriage of his daughter in about 1190. Pembroke became a palatinate. At its greatest extent (1214-40) the principality of Gwynedd reached to the modern Welsh border most of the way from the Dee to the Brecon Beacons, claimed the allegiance of all the Welsh and absorbed all the north and central March except Chirk, Oswestry, Montgomery, Clun and Wigmore. During the royal wars in N. Wales which ended the principality, the March advanced again, and some Welsh leaders fell or were bribed away from their allegiance. Thus when Anglesey, Caernarvon, Flint, Merioneth, Cardigan and Carmarthen were shired (Statute of Wales 1284) there was a Welsh baronial area between the central and northern March and the shires.

By the 14th cent. the situation, if turbulent, was no longer fluid and the March was becoming important not so much as a system for reducing the Welsh, as bases for the power of certain political families in English politics, even if these seldom acted in concert. There was never a Marcher Party. The families with their lordships were as follows:

Family	Lordship
Arundel	Chirk
	Ruthin
	Oswestry
	Bromfield & Yale
Bohun	Brecon
	Hay
Clare	Glamorgan
	Usk
Clifford	Cilgerran
The Crown	Builth
	Emlyn
	Haverford
Lacy	Ewyas
Lancaster	Carnwallon
	Kidwelly
	Iscennen
Marshall	Pembroke
	Striguil
Mortimer	Radnor
	Wigmore
	Maelienydd

Other lordships in single ownership or less permanently associated together were:

Abergavenny	Narberth
Blaenllyfni	Pebidiog
Cemaes (Kemes)	Perfedd
Dysterlow	St Clears
Elfael	Tallacharn
Gower	Tuddenham
Llan Stephan	White Castle

The great Mortimer holding in central Wales gave that family not only undue power but exceptional knowledge of Marcher habits. Thus when Roger Mortimer (IV), Lord of Wigmore became the Queen's lover and through her the ruler of England he sought to ensure a monopoly of Welsh power by having a special EARLDOM OF (the) MARCH created for himself in 1328. This powerful organisation stood between the March proper and the Hereford and Shropshire borders. It included not only the original Mortimer lordships but most of the Bohun territory to the south and Montgomery and Welshpool to the north. The earl could interfere with most traffic in and out of Wales. His attainder in 1330 probably reflected public apprehension of the dangerous eminence of such a position and the inheritance was withheld from his grandson Roger (V) until 1354. He died in 1360 and thereafter the Earls were minor or entangled in Irish affairs until the last of the Mortimer Earls died in 1425.

Henceforth the earldom was held by a member of the royal house, but the March proper continued to be a political problem until the accession of Henry VIII who by the Acts of Union of 1536 and 1543 abolished it.

MARCHES, ANGLO-SCOTS or NORTHERN. (1) Before the 1290s the Border was simply the wavering line between those professing English and Scots allegiance. Cumbria was intermittently in Scottish hands and the unity of the Border was interrupted at its centre by the franchise of Tynedale. Northumberland, though an English shire, was held primarily by great lords such as the Percies, Greys and Balliols (also strong in Durham) who did much as they pleased. On the Scottish side magnates such as the Homes were prominent in the east, and the Douglas' in the west but both sides had a markedly tribal society, which however, was stronger and survived longer in the Scots areas. The population was sparse, especially on the English side and the Scots land was much more fertile.

(2) Edward I's and II's attempt and failure to conquer Scotland brought Tynedale into the hands of the English crown (1297) and the later recognition of each crown by the other. Edward I began to set up a march and the Scots soon followed. The result was a curious international institution which operated under conditions of endemic brigandate, feuding and the intense hatred of the Scots for the English. *See* PLAN.

(3) On each side there was a warden for each of the three Marches. His functions were to keep order; in wartime to mobilise and command the levies, for which he could muster the able bodied tenants of his March and dispose of a system of hilltop beacons; and in peacetime to administer, in conjunction with his opposite number, a kind of international justice called the Laws of the Marches. For this purpose there were recognised Trysting Places where they met. Apart from Land and Water Serjeants, their men, messengers and other minor staff, the wardens had important officials who acted as their deputies for certain special or difficult areas. In the English Middle March Redesdale and Tynedale (after they fell to the crown) had Keepers, and in the West March Bewcastle had a Captain. The Scottish Middle March had a Keeper of Liddesdale, and the West March one in Annandale after 1452. In the early 16th cent. the English East March could raise about 2200 footmen; the Middle 5300; and the West 7700, with mounted men adding roughly 5%. The Scottish figures are unknown. Technically the palatinate of Durham was not part of the Marches, but a Scots invasion across the Tweed was bound to involve it; the Bishop's forces invariably co-operated with the English wardens and garrisoned Norham Castle.

(4) Each truce included an agreement to appoint Conservators of the Truce from each side, to settle, as far as possible, points of principle or new rules which might be helpful but would not infringe the sovereign stance adopted by each side. This standing conference met irregularly at Berwick or Carlisle.

(5) The Laws of the Marches were originally the customs of an area which had a common life but a divided sovereignty. First codified by a jury of 12 knights from each side in 1249 (before the Wardens were established) they developed spasmodically and were supplemented by agreements in 1449, 1464, 1533, 1549, 1553, 1563 and 1596. A victim of a raid might instantly pursue across the border and execute vengeance or retake his property himself (*The Hot Trod*) or if he could not do this, he might cross the border within six days of giving notice of his purpose to the local watchers (*The Cold Trod*). In default of either remedy, a *bill* was filed with the warden. When enough bills had accumulated, a *Day of Truce* was arranged with the opposite warden, and the wardens then held a *Border Meeting* or *Tryst*. Customarily these were held in the open air just inside Scots territory and were large assemblages, each warden bringing not only his own men but most of the local gentry with theirs. The Truce lasted from the moment that each warden signalled his agreement to it (by raising his arm) until sunrise next day and was considered sacred. The wardens then settled the bills ("Attempts") as far as they could by private agreement, the rest being tried by compurgation or battle. Evidence in a trial was not allowed and pledges for restitution could be admitted only from the opposite side. Pledges were always volunteers and difficult to get, but if a pledge broke his word, his warden was expected to pledge himself.

One important feature of border life was the emphasis on good faith. An agreement, a pledge given, a bargain struck on a Day of Truce had a special status which was heinous to violate. Quarrels about faith always led to bloodshed and often to mortal feud. Hence a man aggrieved might denounce a breach of faith at a Tryst only with the permission of both wardens, for otherwise the denunciation would turn the Day of Truce into a battle. The arrest of Kinmont Willie in 1596 was scandalous because he was leaving a Tryst, and Buccleuch with the Grahams who rescued him from Carlisle Castle could justify their action by the Laws of the March.

(6) The system had serious weaknesses. Feuds existed not only across the frontier but between clans on the same side (e.g. the Scottish Maxwells against the Johnstones, and the English Reeds against the Halls) so

that there was inherent uncertainty about the identity of raiders. There was a system of watches by day and night during the winter, the great raiding season, at all the passages and fords on the boundary, which palliated but did not solve the problem. Secondly bills could be settled only at a Tryst, which could not be held unless both sides agreed to come. Internal disturbances, changes of office, illness, accidents, bad weather or obstruction might delay a Tryst for years. Thirdly, though the Scottish March was richer than the English, it was less orderly, so that Scottish wardens could offer or enforce satisfaction less easily than the English. Hence a perpetual temptation for the English to prefer raiding to filing bills.

(7) The position of the English and Scots wardens differed in important respects. The English ones were crown officials with their own courts, and though ordinary offences were supposed to be tried by the ordinary courts, the warden himself dealt with Border Treasons such as bringing in raiders or illegally marrying a Scot. The Scot's wardens were weaker because the local magnates prevented encroachments on their private jurisdictions, to which all offences had consequently to be referred. Moreover the Scots warden's office tended to become actually if not theoretically hereditary in the very families which he might have to control. Before 1456 the Warden of the West and Middle March was always a Douglas; most Wardens of the East were Homes. Hence strong Scottish monarchs sometimes intervened in person. Moreover the English wardens were close to Edinburgh, the Scots far from London. Hence the English had important intelligence functions on behalf of the London govt., and were sometimes concurrently appointed ambassadors in Edinburgh.

(8) Both sovereigns occasionally appointed a Lord Warden General e.g. the 2nd Ld. Dacre of Gilsland (1467-1525) under Henry VII, primarily a military C-in-C, who sometimes superseded the ordinary wardens. In practice, even the purely military work was too much for one man, and the civil and police business had to be committed to deputies. Sometimes two wardenships were held by the same man, especially on the Scottish side.

(9) The most notorious and unruly of the Border clans were the Scottish Grahams who had lost most of their lands to other Scots clans, particularly the Johnstones. A landless clan had to steal cattle to live at all. In the Debatable Land cattle could be pastured from both sides by day only; buildings, especially stalls were unlawful, and liable to demolition by the Warden of the other side. The landless Grahams naturally encroached and built, in order to house their stolen cattle. Hence endemic warfare between them and the English Warden, with the Scots Warden or a Keeper of Liddesdale, like Buccleuch, joyfully intervening from time to time. The Liddesdale Keepers seldom obeyed their Warden unless it suited them, and were really brigand chiefs under an official title. In the mid 16th cent. the Liddesdale people were even raiding the East March.

(10) As Elizabeth I's reign wore on, and James VI's succession became more probable, the March institutions became increasingly provisional. James did not want a war over Kinmont Willie, no more did Elizabeth with a Spanish War on her hands. The so-called T. of Carlisle (1597) was really an enlarged Conservators' meeting with amplified powers, under the chairmanship of the Bp. of Durham. It was agreed to raise the ecclesiastical preaching strength on both sides; to set up border councils to register notorious thieves and execute them after first conviction; to make blackmail (kidnapping) a felony; to abolish the borderers' idle retinues; and to forbid Wardens and Keepers to make foray without a special royal authority. James came in person to co-ordinate these measures.

(11) After the Union of the Crowns, the Wardens

were superseded (1605) by a strengthened Commission for the Middle Shires, as the Marches were renamed. This controlled peacekeeping from both sides until 1616. One of its first acts was to deport the Grahams wholesale to the Dutch Cautionary Towns.

(12) The Civil War, however, had specialised local consequences. The two kingdoms drifted into separate political dispensations, but since neither the Wardenships nor the Border Commission now existed there was no machinery for peacekeeping. The recrudescence of feuding and mosstrooping early engaged the attention of Restoration Parliaments, more especially as the abolition of feudal incidents had indirectly abolished the Coinage problem (see CUMBERLAND). Under an Act of 1662 against mosstrooping which had degenerated mostly into cattle lifting, special justices were appointed together with 30 *Country Keepers* for Northumberland and 12 for Cumbria. These commanded flying squads and were responsible for the value of unrecovered stolen cattle; their work was assisted by *Bookkeepers* at cattle markets, who registered brands and ownership. Such a system was required because a crime committed on one side of the border, could not be punished by a court on the other. It had to be maintained until 1756. Mosstrooping survived in Borrowdale as late as 1760.

MARCHES. See WALES AND THE MARCHES, COUNCIL OF.

MARCHES, LAWS OF. See MARCHES, ANGLO-SCOTS-3-5.

MARCHMONT. See HUME OF POLWARTH.

MARCONI, Guglielmo, Marquese (1874-1937) pioneer of radio, migrated to England. He established a radio link with France in 1899 and another with Newfoundland in 1901. He was Italian plenipotentiary at the Peace Conference of 1919-1921.

MARDYCK. French fortified privateering base near Dunkirk, which was required to be demilitarised under the P. of Utrecht in 1713 and the Triple Alliance 1717. The French habitually evaded the provision.

MARE CLAUSUM **(Lat. = Closed Sea).** The 16th cent. doctrine that a country could assert sovereignty over the high seas. England claimed the Channel and the North Sea, Spain the Pacific and the Caribbean. John Selden wrote a book under this title, asserting that the seas could be privately owned. This was published in 1635 as a reply to *MARE LIBERUM* **(Lat. = The Sea Free [to All])** published by Hugo Grotius (1583-1645) the celebrated Dutch jurist in 1609. It asserted that the sea was common to all. The English and the Spanish claims were inconvenient to the Dutch, who were developing their carrying trade.

MAREDUDD ab EDWIN. See DEHEUBARTH-5.

MAREDUDD ap OWAIN (fl. 990). See DEHEUBARTH-3.

MAREDUDD ab OWAIN See DEHEUBARTH-9.

MAREDUDD ap RHYS GRYG. See DEHEUBARTH-20.

MARGAM (S. Wales) coal mining centre, was amalgamated with Aberavan in 1921 to form Port Talbot (now Afan).

MARGARET (1240-75), eldest *d* of Henry III, married Alexander III of Scots in 1251. Both were children. The Scots regents, being hostile to English influence, at first treated her badly, but the birth of her children strengthened her position and the English link.

MARGARET (1283-90) *The Maid of Norway, d.* of Eric II of Norway. Her mother was Margaret of Scots, *d.* of Alexander III and she was recognised heiress of Scotland in 1284. Alexander III died in 1286. Her grandmother was Margaret *d.* of Henry III and for the sake of peace she was engaged to her cousin Edward (later K. Edward II). She died on the voyage from Norway to Scotland.

MARGARET (?1425-45) *d.* of James I of Scots, was sent to France in 1436 to marry the Dauphin (later K. Louis XI). He treated her badly.

MARGARET (1446-1503), sister of Edward IV, married Charles D. of Burgundy in 1468. She became the mainstay of the Yorkists after 1483 and financed Lambert Simnel and Perkin Warbeck.

MARGARET OF ANJOU (1430-82) *d.* of René of Anjou and brought up by her grandmother Yolande of Aragon, was married to Henry VI in 1445 (see HENRY VI AND EDWARD IV). Her adventurous career as a politician and military commander ended at the B. of Tewkesbury (1471) after which she remained in custody until ransomed under the T. of Picquigny (1476). Louis XI pensioned her, but forced her to resign all rights in French territory. She lived thereafter in relative poverty at Saumur. See also ROSES, WARS OF THE.

MARGARET OF DENMARK (?1457-86) *d.* of K. Christian I of Denmark, Norway and Sweden, married James III of Scots in 1469. Her father pledged the Orkney and Shetland Is. for her dowry and as they were never redeemed, the Is. remained under the Scottish crown. In 1945 a Christmas Note was delivered to the Court of Christiansborg in Latin, proposing the settlement of the debt with accumulated compound interest. This note was received with all the gravity proper to the occasion.

MARGARET, St. (c. 1045-1093), granddaughter of Edmund Ironside and sister of Edgar the Atheling, was brought up mostly in Hungary before returning to England about 1057. With her brother she fled to Scotland in 1068 and married K. Malcolm III of Scots. Despite the tensions between William I's court and her husband's, she corresponded with Lanfranc, securing his help in founding a Benedictine monastery at Dunfermline. Her daughter, Matilda, was the first wife of Henry I. Renowned for her charity and piety, she was canonised in 1250. See SCOTS OR ALBAN KINGS, EARLY-19.

MARGARET TUDOR (1489-1541) eldest *d.* of Henry VII, married James IV of Scots in 1503 after ten years of negotiations designed to prevent James from supporting Perkin Warbeck. On his death at the B. of Flodden (1513) she became Regent for her son James V and was drawn into the struggles of rival and violent factions (see JAMES V), contracting in the process secret and shaky marriages with Angus in 1515 and Henry Stewart in 1527 and having occasionally to take refuge in England. See GENEALOGY.

MARGESSON, Henry David Reginald (1880-1956) 1st Vist. MARGESSON of RUGBY (1942) was the influential and well liked Conservative Chief Whip from 1924-40. His capacity for work was not restrained by being gassed in World War I and his interventions in the Parliamentary crises of the interwar period were invariably sensible. He became Churchill's Secretary for War in 1940 but was given a peerage after the defeats in N. Africa and Singapore. A politician rather than an administrator.

MARGRAVE. (Ger: MARKGRAF = Count of the March) the title of certain important princes of the Holy Roman Empire notably the rulers of Brandenburg and Baden.

MARIANNE. The familiar personification of Republican France, originated as the name of a revolutionary society, some of whose members were imprisoned in 1854.

MARIANNE IS. See LADRONE IS.

MARIE GALANTE. See PARIS P. OF (10 FEB. 1763); SEVEN YEARS' WAR-7.

MARINES, ROYAL, a corps of sea soldiers, was established in 1664, originally to make good a shortage of seamen. It was sometimes called the Lord Admiral's Regiment and was raised or disbanded according to need. It became a permanent part of the naval establishment in 1755. Trained to seamen's as well as military duties, they manned part of a ship's armament as well as providing landing forces and were divided into artillery (R.M.A.) and Light Infantry (R.M.L.I.) in the 19th cent. In the crowded hardship of a sailing navy manned by pressed men, they were important to the maintenance of discipline because they were set apart from the sailors. Detachments in each ship were never below platoon size, and only larger frigates and ships of the line or in modern times, cruisers and capital ships carried them. The marines established their reputation at the capture of

Gibraltar in 1704 and since that time they have been employed everywhere in the nautical world. Their numbers have generally amounted to about 10% of the naval establishment. The R.M.A. and R.M.L.I. were amalgamated in 1923.

MARISCO, Geoffrey de (?-1245) a relative of the Comyns, landowner in Munster and Leinster overran Connaught and was Justiciar of Ireland from 1215-21, 1226-28 and from 1230-34. During his many private forays, he attacked the Marshal lands with the Lacys, and instigated Richard Marshal's murder. Suspected of treason in 1238, he fled to Scotland whence he was expelled in 1244. He died in France.

MARISCO or MARSH, Richard (?-1226) adviser and executive of K. John, was Justiciar from 1213-14, Chancellor in 1214 and Bp. of Durham from 1217.

MARISCHAL, EARL. David I of Scots (r. 1124-53) had Marshals whose function, jointly with the Constable was to keep order in the King's neighbourhood. Members of the Keith family held the office in the 13th cent. and it became hereditary to them by a charter of Robert I in 1308. Sir William de Keith was created Earl Marischal in 1458. George, 9th Earl Marischal (1693-1778) was a Jacobite attainted in 1716 but he escaped to France. He attempted to raise the Highlands in 1719 and entered the service of Frederick the Great of Prussia in 1747. They became great friends, and he was Prussian Ambassador in Paris from 1751-54, Governor of Neuchatel until 1763 and as Ambassador in Madrid kept the English Govt. informed of French and Spanish plans. Consequently, he was pardoned in 1759 and recovered some of his estates but disliking the Scottish climate ended his life in Prussia. The title and office are possibly but not certainly extinct.

MARJORIBANKS (pron: Marchbanks) Edward (1849-1909) 2nd Ld. TWEEDMOUTH (1894), Liberal M.P. for N. Berwicks (1880-94) was Chief Whip under Gladstone in 1892, Lord Privy Seal under Rosebery (1894-5), married Lord Randolph Churchill's sister and, as First Lord of the Admiralty, maintained the policy of naval supremacy over Germany despite the financial and political crisis which it was likely to induce. He became Asquith's Lord Pres. in 1908, but died suddenly.

MARK or MERK (Scots.). A money of account equal to 13s. 4d. in both currencies i.e. the Merk was worth 13½d. sterling. *See* COINAGE.

MARK BANCO. A Mark of variable standard, based on the currency of Hamburg, in which Hanseatic commercial accounts were kept and which were thus unaffected by variations in rates of exchange or in bullion prices.

MARKET HARBOROUGH (Leics) became in the 15th cent. a wealthy cattle market for the fertile grazing of the Welland Valley, as is attested by a splendid church and grammar school. The meat industry continues alongside lighter activities mostly connected with rubber and plastics.

MARKETING, AGRICULTURAL. The rural depression (1860-1914) was interrupted by World War I, after which farmers, to avoid a return to pre-war poverty, sought to strengthen their bargaining power through voluntary co-operatives for particular products to which they bound themselves to sell and which then negotiated a price with the wholesalers; this provided more regular supplies but at the expense of restrictive price maintenance. It could work only in the absence of serious foreign competition such as obtained in cereals and was concerned mainly with milk (affecting butter and cheese), hops (beer and ale), potatoes and pigs (bacon and lard). It broke down in the 1929 slump. This was mistakenly attributed to the voluntary nature of the co-operatives and Acts of 1931 and 1933 permitted marketing monopolies through statutory boards empowered to buy farm products compulsorily. To the old products were added wool and eggs and there were price-fixing non-trading boards mainly for perishables. Co-operatives continued in other fields with steadily increasing memberships. World War II distorted the system, for subsidies were needed to prevent rising prices from imposing price rationing rather than fair shares, and the subsidies were politically difficult to withdraw. The result by the '60s was a managed market incompatible with the objects of the T. of Rome and in the twenty years after Britain joined the E.E.C., the system was dismantled in favour of the much less efficient Common Agricultural Policy (C.A.P.) (q.v.).

MARKETS for the sale of goods, mostly food, held at the same place generally weekly, often attracted settlements which served as the nuclei of towns. More than 50 date from before 1086. Many had a customary origin but Edward I held that owners of markets who claimed a monopoly within a given radius (commonly seven miles) needed a royal charter. Such charters were and are saleable. Until the reign of Henry III many markets were held on Sundays but pressure from the Church caused them to be shifted to other days. Boroughs later began to promote legislation to regulate their local markets and in the 19th cent. they and urban district councils had general powers to regulate them mainly in the interests of hygiene.

MARKHAM, Sir Clements (1830-1916) explorer and geographer, wrote biographies of explorers and a Quichua Dictionary, but instituted a health revolution in India to which he brought the Peruvian Cinchone (Quinine) tree, and an economic revolution in Malaysia by introducing (*via* Kew) the Brazilian Rubber plant.

MARKHAM (1) John (?-1400) Judge of the Common Pleas from 1396-1408 was one of the judges who advised Henry IV on the manner of deposing Richard II. His son **(2) Sir John (?-1479)** became a Judge of the King's Bench in 1444 and though well known for his impartiality, was popular with the Yorkists and superseded Fortescue as C.J. at the elevation of Edward IV in 1461 (until 1469).

MARKIEVICZ. *See* GORE-BOOTH.

MARLBOROUGH, D. of (1702) John Churchill (1650-1722) Ld. CHURCHILL (Sc.) (1682) Eng. (1685) E. of MARLBOROUGH (1689). (1) Handsome, charming and remarkable, he distinguished himself as a regimental officer in the French service, was introduced by Monmouth to Charles II in 1674 and had a daughter by that King's mistress, the Duchess of Cleveland (*see* VILLIERS). In 1676 he fell in love with and in 1678 married Sarah Jennings, an attendant and close friend of the Princess Anne, in the household of the Duchess of York. He got on well with the Yorks and was with them in the Hague (1679) and in Scotland (1681) even though they were bigoted papists and he an Anglican. He became one of York's gentlemen of the bedchamber when he succeeded as James II. He was Major-General under Feversham in putting down Monmouth's rebellion (1685) but could see the trend of James' policy and had already determined to oppose it. In May 1687 he told William of Orange through Dijkveld that he, like the Princess Anne, would risk death rather than change his religion, and in Nov. 1688 he went over to William and was one of the group of Lords who organised a provisional administration after James fled. He and Sarah persuaded Anne not to press her rights.

(2) He took an active part in William III's wars. He was one of Q. Mary II's council while William was in Ireland. He then proposed and effected the capture of Cork and Kinsale (Sept. 1690). He had, like most people of consequence, had correspondence with James II and in Jan. 1691 some of this came to light. He was dismissed from his employments, and put briefly (on the basis of forgeries) into the Tower. Anne, however, stood by the Marlboroughs even though she had to quarrel with Mary II to do it. After the Queen died (1694) Anne and William III were reconciled and the Marlboroughs were permitted to return. In 1701 he became Commander in Chief of the

English troops in Holland. Anne made him Captain General immediately after her accession in 1702, and Sarah became Mistress of the Robes. He then returned to Holland to prosecute the French war which was declared in May. (*For his active career see* SPANISH SUCCESSION, WAR OF; BLENHEIM.)

(3) His opponents, in attacking his political associates at home had, by 1711 steadily undermined his standing. Then they fabricated charges of malversation, as a pretext for getting rid of him. These were never pressed and were later positively disproved. He spent the years 1712-14 abroad and returned to England on the day Q. Anne died. The rest of his life was spent as that of a great man in retirement.

MARLBOROUGH. *See* LEY.

MARLBOROUGH HOUSE (London) was built by Wren for the 1st D. of Marlborough in 1709-10. After his Duchess died in 1744 it was sold to the crown and became a residence for royalty of the second rank e.g. P. Leopold (1817-31); Q. Adelaide (1837-49); Edward P. of Wales (1863-1901) and George P. of Wales (1901-10). In 1960 it was converted into the Commonwealth secretariat with permanent accommodation for commonwealth prime ministers.

MARLBOROUGH HOUSE SET. The friends, some raffish, of Edward (later VII) as P. of Wales in the period 1860-80.

MARLBOROUGH, STATUTE OF (1267) a part of the settlement following the Barons' Wars, dealt with many details and technicalities in the law of distress (c 1-4, 15, 21), wardship (6-7), suit of court and sheriff's tourn (9-10), procedure (11-14, 16-24, 26-29) and some miscellaneous matters; and (c 5) confirmed Magna Carta and the Charter of the Forest.

MARMION (1) Robert (?-1143) a Norman freebooting lord, waged private war under Stephen and was killed at Coventry by the E. of Chester. His grandson **(2) Robert (?-1218)** Sheriff of Worcester in 1186, attended both Richard I and K. John in Normandy, but supported the baronial party against the latter.

MARNE, B. of the (Aug. 1914) (*see* WORLD WAR I). The Germans were swinging through Belgium and encountered the British Expeditionary Force at Mons. It retreated. Then, instead of enveloping Paris on the west, the Germans changed to a more direct approach, exposed their right flank and were counter-attacked by the French and British at Marne.

MAROONS were fugitive negro slaves and their descendants living wild (Sp. *Cimarron*) in the forests of Guiana and the larger W. Indian islands.

MARPRELATE TRACTS, published in 1588 and 1589, under the pseudonym of Martin Marprelate, were sarcastic and sometimes coarse attacks on episcopacy. Seven survive. The authors were probably Job Throckmorton (1545-1601), John Udall or Uvedale (?1560-92) who both denied it and John Penry (1559-93) who was executed for it. Published at a succession of places beginning at Molesey (Surrey) and ending near Manchester, their stylistic brilliance attracted a widespread but not always friendly readership.

MARQUESAS Is. (Pac.) were acquired by the French in 1842.

MARQUIS, Frederick. *See* WOOLTON.

MARRIAGE could originally be contracted between boys of 14 and girls of 12. The parties had to be outside the forbidden degrees of kinship. They had freely to consent and be able to understand the nature of the contract. In Christian regular marriages the parties were themselves always the ministers of the sacrament and needed only to exchange vows before witnesses. This made it possible for marriages to be too easily, even inadvertently contracted and much matrimonial litigation in church courts was initiated to force reluctant spouses to honour their contract. Accordingly the Council of Trent decided

that, without detracting from the principle of ministration vows should be exchanged before four witnesses, one of whom should be a priest (*per verba de praesenti*). In post-Reformation England a priest or deacon was sufficient if episcopally ordained. In Scotland four types of irregular marriages were also lawful viz: (i) by exchange of written consents or (ii) by verbal consents before two witnesses or (iii) by promise followed by sexual relations on the faith of the promise, or (iv) by habit and repute (*see* HANDFASTING). In feudal areas the consent of the lord was necessary to the marriage of a tenant's widow or daughter lest the rights and services escape from his control. No other consent was necessary.

It being only too easy to marry secretly (*see* FLEET), Lord Hardwicke's Act 1753 required in addition that in England all marriages had to be solemnised either in a church or chapel of the Church of England after banns had been proclaimed on three successive Sundays in the parish of at least one of the parties, or after the grant of an ordinary licence dispensing with banns, or a special licence dispensing also with the need for a church. Since this did not apply in Scotland, Gretna Green, the nearest Scottish place across the border from Carlisle became notorious for runaway irregular marriages by English couples.

In 1837 civil marriages before a registrar, after a procedure analogous to banns, became feasible in England. In 1852 a slight control was placed upon runaway marriages by requiring a party to have been resident in the parish for at least 21 days. This was easily evaded in practice. In 1940 methods (i), (ii) and (iii) of Scottish irregular marriage were abolished and the romantic traffic at Gretna Green ended. *See* DIVORCE AND NULLITY; FEUDALISM-18.

MARQUESS, MARCHIONESS. *See* PEERAGE.

MARRIED WOMEN'S PROPERTY. Since at common law the husband and wife's property belonged absolutely to the husband from the moment of marriage, the husband was, however, under a corresponding duty to maintain his wife, and consequently she had an implied authority to pledge his credit. The duty of maintenance was suspended if she left him unjustifiably and without his consent and ceased altogether if she committed adultery. In the 18th cent. however, lawyers devised ways of holding property separately in trust for the wife and by 1790 a woman carrying on a separate trade might, by agreement with her husband, enjoy any business and profits for her separate use. For the limited purpose of protecting a wife under a separation order, legislation of 1857 and 1870 created proprietary rights for a wife in property acquired after the commencement of the grounds of the Order. The Married Women's Property Act 1882 enabled women married after 1 Jan. 1883 to hold and deal with property separately, and women married before that date to acquire and deal with property accruing to them after it. Hence the "subject wife" slowly died out. In 1935 the transition was completed by an enactment that wives were to hold property in all respects as if they were unmarried.

MARROW OF MODERN DIVINITY an extreme predestinatarian tract first published in 1646 was republished at Selkirk in 1718 and caused furious controversy within the Kirk, leading ultimately to the secession of the Associate Presbytery. *See* ERSKINE, EBENEZER.

MARRYAT, Frederick (1792-1848) an adventurous and versatile naval officer who served under Cochrane, commanded the *Larne* in the Burma War of 1824 and became Senior Naval Officer, Rangoon in 1825. He received the R.H.S. gold medal for saving life at sea; adapted the naval signalling system for mercantile use; published the *Naval Officer* in 1829, *Peter Simple* in 1834, *Mr Midshipman Easy* in 1836; these give a lively picture of contemporary naval life.

MARSALA (Sicily). For several generations before 1860 the Marsala wine trade had been in the hands of four firms, three of them English. The Bourbon Govt., suspecting that Garibaldi might land there, had disarmed the people and the English, who complained to the Royal Navy. As a result, two British warships were there on 11 May 1860 when Garibaldi's force in three merchantmen appeared. Neapolitan warships also appeared and could have sunk them if they had not been under the false impression that the Royal Navy might intervene. When they had ascertained the facts, most of Garibaldi's force was safely ashore. This hesitation was the key event in the Bourbon overthrow.

MARSDEN, Samuel (1764-1838) a chaplain in the N.S.W. in 1793 obtained in 1807 an audience with George III. The King gave him five Spanish sheep with which he founded the Australian flocks. Thereafter he visited N.Z. where he encouraged settlement and sound morality.

MARSDEN, William (1754-1836) originally in HEIC service and Govt. secretary in Sumatra, established an agency in London in 1785 and then became successively second secretary (1795) and first secretary to the Admiralty (1804). He was also a distinguished member of several learned societies. With his *Dictionary and Grammar of the Malayan Language* (1813) he founded the study of Indonesian philology, and with his large collection of coins (presented to the British Museum) oriental numismatics.

MARSEILLES (Fr.) This ancient port was a minor mediaeval republic which first acknowledged outside sovereignty to Charles of Anjou in 1245. It was sacked by the Aragonese in 1423 and came, with Provence, to France in 1481. Fanatically R. Catholic, it resisted Henry IV until his conversion and supported the Frondes in 1648-53. It was subdued in 1660 when its walls were breached. It supported the French Revolution but opposed the Convention and was put down by force. The destruction of its trade in the Napoleonic wars made it anti-Bonapartist and therefore pro-Bourbon in 1815 and anti-Napoleon III from 1849-70.

MARSEILLAISE, the French Revolutionary hymn, was written at Strasbourg by C. J. Rouget de Lisle, an engineer officer, and got its name because some extremists from Marseilles sang it in Paris in 1792.

MARSH or DE MARISCO, Adam (?-1259) Somersetshire Franciscan, nephew of a Bp. of Durham, and friend of Grosseteste, whom he accompanied to the Council of Lyons (1245). He was offered a chair at Paris, but preferred Oxford, where from 1247 he was Regent of the Franciscans. Well known and trusted for his intellect and sense, he was much sought by, *inter alia,* Henry III, Simon de Montfort, and Boniface of Savoy, and his learning gained him the admiration of Roger Bacon.

MARSH, Herbert (1757-1839) vigorous Anglican controversialist at Cambridge and Leipzig. His widely read *History of the Politics of Great Britain and France* (1799) earned him a govt. pension and a Napoleonic proscription. His anti-Calvinist and anti-nonconformist sermons drew large audiences at Cambridge. In 1816 he became Bp. of Llandaff; in 1819 he was translated to Peterborough where he tried to exclude evangelical clergy by his LXXXVII Questions. He was denounced by Sydney Smith and attacked in the Lords, but gave as good as he got. He also opposed R. Catholic emancipation and, more surprisingly, hymns.

MARSH, Narcissus (1638-1713) provost of Trinity College, Dublin (1672-83) encouraged the study and maintenance of Erse; as a mathematician he contributed an essay on *Sound* to the foundation proceedings of the R. Dublin Society (1683) and he was a learned orientalist. He became Abp. of Cashel (1691) and then of Armagh (1703). Not to be confused with Francis Marsh (1627-93) Abp. of Dublin in 1692.

MARSHALL, Alfred (1842-1924) published his seminal *Principles of Economics* in 1890. This was the most influential work on the subject between Adam Smith and Keynes. He held that economics can be based on its own internal logic and is therefore separable from political economy and economic history.

MARSHALL, George Catlett (1880-1959) U.S. soldier and statesman first attracted attention as a divisional and then Army Staff Officer in France in 1918. He helped to reorganise the peacetime U.S. Army and became Chief-of-Staff in Sept. 1939. He then converted the army into an organisation capable of expansion when war came and subsequently went to China to try, against communist intransigence, to unite the Chinese war effort against Japan. His efforts here failed. In Jan. 1947 he became U.S. Secretary of State and as such promulgated the Marshall Plan for European post-war economic rehabilitation. He retired in 1949.

MARSHALL, Henry (1775-1851) military surgeon from 1806 by his researches, laid the foundations of military medicine, especially in the tropics. *See also* LARREY.

MARSHALL, Stephen (1594-1655) "the best preacher" according to Scottish presbyterians "in England" and an extreme presbyterian himself, who nevertheless was sufficiently reasonable for Baxter to remark upon it. He was one of the most influential parliamentary advisers in all the ecclesiastical aspects of dealings with Scotland.

MARSHAL (1) William the Marshal (?1146-1219) fighting for Henry II against his rebel sons had unhorsed Richard Coeur de Lion, who instantly took him into favour as King and married him to Isabel of Clare. He increased his wife's huge holdings. He supported the lawful Govt. against John's intrigues but therefore persuaded the Abp. and magnates after Richard's death to accept John upon whom he was a moderating influence. He spent 1207-13, however, in Ireland. He returned to fight a Welsh revolt at John's request and was one of his representatives at Runnymede and an executor of his will. Widely respected, he was chosen Regent for the infant Henry III in Nov. 1216 and in 1217 beat the French and rebels at Lincoln and agreed the T. of Lambeth for the evacuation of the French. At his death he committed the care of Henry III to the Papal Legate. His son (2) **William (?1190-1230)** one of the executors of Magna Carta, joined the rebels in 1216 but changed sides and fought with his father at Lincoln. He built up a power in Ireland, with which in 1223 he was able to put down another Welsh rising. He was justiciar of Ireland from 1224-26. He died on campaign in Brittany. His brother (3) **Richard (?1190-1234)** acquired his father's Norman lands in 1220 and became by marriage Lord of Dinan in Brittany in 1222. He acquired his brother's English and Irish honours in 1231. Despite his cosmopolitan background he led the magnates against the King's Poitevin advisers – was driven into rebellion and maintained himself in Wales, but his Irish lands were attacked by the Lacys, and when he went over to recover them he was captured and murdered. His brother (4) **Gilbert (?-1241)** was granted Glamorgan and Carmarthen in addition to the inheritance. His sister married Richard E. of Cornwall and he married Margaret, illegitimate *d.* of K. William the Lion. He supported Cornwall against Henry III's foreign favourites. He was driven to take the cross but stipulated for a reconciliation with the King before he went. This was granted, but he was killed in a tournament. His brother (5) **Walter (?1199-1245)** who had supported Gilbert, secured investiture with difficulty, and supported Cornwall in his later quarrel with Henry III. His brother (6) **Anselm (?-1245)** died before he could be invested. *See* PEMBROKE, EARLDOM; CLARE; VALENCE.

MARSHAL, John (1755-1835) as C.J. of the U.S.A. from 1801-35 raised the Supreme Court of the U.S.A. to its eminence in public affairs and practically created the legal concept of the constitutional superiority of fundamental laws over governmental institutions.

MARSHAL, Is, discovered by the Spaniards in 1526 were rediscovered by the British in 1788. In the 19th cent., there was much miscegenation between the inhabitants and western traders and convicts, but from 1862 a Hawaiian evangelical mission exercised some influence. In 1878 the Germans established a coaling station at Jaluit and from 1886 with British agreement a German Co. the *Jaluitgesellschaft* ruled the islands, until 1906 when they came under direct German Govt. control and thence in 1922 under a Japanese mandate. As Japan militarised the islands, there was heavy fighting in World War II. They were placed under U.N. trusteeship in 1946 with U.S.A. as trustee, and the latter held H-bomb tests at Bikini (1946) and Eniwetok (1958).

MARSHALSEA, a prison in Southwark from 14th-19th cent., was used originally for those convicted before the Steward of the Royal House and the Marshal, and later for pirates. From Elizabeth I's time it was used mainly for debtors.

MARSHALSEA COURT (not related to the Marshalsea Prison) was held by the Steward and Marshal of the Household to administer justice between royal servants, and to deal with trespasses within the Verge. Abolished 1849. *See* PALACE COURT.

MARTELLO TOWERS, called dyslexically after a tower on C. Mortella (Corsica) which resisted British naval bombardment, were coastal artillery towers about 40 ft. high, garrisoned by about 30 men, erected along the south coast as a precaution against French invasion.

MARTEN (1) Sir Henry (?1562-1641) was judge in the Admiralty from 1617 and a member of the High Commission from 1620. He was M.P. for St. Germans in 1625 and 1626 and for Oxford University in 1628. He supported the criticism of Buckingham, and figured prominently in the debates on the Petition of the Right. In 1630 he appealed unsuccessfully to the King to stop Common Law courts from interfering in the Admiralty jurisdiction. He was an M.P. for St. Ives in 1640. His *s.* **(2) Henry or Harry (1602-80)** firebrand M.P. for Berkshire in 1640 urged on Strafford's attainder and then raised a regiment of Parliamentary horse and became a member of the Committee of Safety. The King regarded him with special and justifiable animosity for he seized royal private property and professed extreme republicanism. His excitable factionalism led him to persuade the Commons to vote the incompetent Waller an independent command instead of supporting the starving but competent Essex. He greatly embarrassed Pym who in 1643 had him expelled from the Commons for advocating the extermination of the Royal family. Employed in provincial military tasks for a while, he was readmitted to the House in 1646; here he led the extremists against Scottish claims and further negotiations with the King. In 1647 he proposed the Vote of No Addresses. In 1648 he was industriously preparing for the King's trial. In 1649 he was a member of the Court. He signed the death warrant. He was commissioned to destroy the ensigns of royalty and public statues. He was teller in the motion to abolish the House of Lords and member (Feb. 1649) of the first Council of State. Though in alliance with the Levellers he rather mediated for than led them, but their suppression weakened his position. In general his short entertaining speeches were more suitable and influential in a larger body such as the Commons than in the Council to which he was re-elected for the second and fourth occasions. When Cromwell expelled the Rump, Marten was left without a forum. He openly paraded a mistress in that puritanical society, and his extravagant life resulted in outlawry for debt. He is said to have been fetched from prison to make a quorum when the Long Parliament was re-established (May 1659). This body elected him to its two councils of state. At the

Restoration he surrendered voluntarily and defended himself with humour and courage. He died in prison.

MARTIAL LAW is limited to the law necessary to administer the crown's armed forces. The supersession of ordinary law and the govt. of an area by military courts is illegal at Common Law and was prohibited by the Petition of Right 1628. Hence acts done under "martial law" have to be covered by an Act of Indemnity. Martial Law was imposed by statute in Ireland in 1803, 1833 and 1920. In Jamaica it was illegally imposed by Governor Eyre in 1865 but he was indemnified by a Jamaican Act. **MILITARY LAW** is that part of Martial Law which is directly concerned with the discipline and administration of troops.

MARTIN, Sir Thomas Byam (1773-1854) rose from the lower deck to frigate commands and between 1796-1808 captured two French frigates, a Russian ship of the line and many privateers. He took part in the defence of Riga in 1812, was comptroller of the navy from 1816, and M.P. for Plymouth from 1818, both until 1831.

MARTIN. Two admirals of this name **(1) William (?1696-1756),** a linguist and classical scholar, commanded the fleet in the Mediterranean (1742) and later off Lisbon and at the Nore. His grand-nephew **(2) Sir George (1764-1847),** mainly a successful ship captain against the French between 1778-1805.

MARTINEAU, Unitarian family of Huguenot origin. **(1) Harriet (1802-76)** left destitute after illness in 1829 began to publish writings on social questions viz: *Illustrations of Political Economy* (1832-4), *Poor Law and Paupers Illustrated* (1833), *Illustrations of Taxation* (1834). Arrived in London in 1834, she was lionised in literary circles and consulted by ministers. She then went to the U.S.A. about which she published *Society in America* (1827) and *Retrospect of Western Travel* (1838). In 1848 she went to the Middle East and published *Eastern Life,* and then *History of England during the Thirty Years Peace* (1849). Her brother **(2) James (1805-1900)** was unitarian pastor at Paradise St. Liverpool from 1835-57 and held a series of philosophical professorships at Manchester and London. He was pastor at Little Portland Street, London from 1859-1872. He was a close friend of R. H. Hutton and Walter Bagehot. His son **(3) Russell (1831-98)** was a celebrated Hebraist.

MARTINIQUE (W. Indies) was colonised by the French in 1635. Sugar planting began in 1654. The island passed to the French in 1674. It was occupied by the British in 1762, and from 1794-1802 and from 1809-14. It has had a troubled history of slave and ex-slave revolts and volcanic eruptions. Sugar remains the principal product. *See* SEVENS YEARS' WAR-10-13.

MARTIN'S BANK. *See* LIVERPOOL, BANK OF.

MARVELL, Andrew (1621-78) of Hull, became tutor to Mary, Lord Fairfax's daughter in 1650 and so became well known in republican circles. In 1653 Milton tried to have him appointed as his assistant at the Council of State but he became tutor to Cromwell's ward William Dutton instead. In 1657 however he became Milton's colleague in the Latin Secretaryship to the Council. He had already written a number of poems. From 1660 he was an incorruptible republican M.P. for Hull, yet was popular at court and much liked by Charles II. In 1663-65 he was the E. of Carlisle's secretary as Ambassador to the northern states but after 1669 he became a vigorous pamphleteer against court politics and intolerance. One pamphlet, the *Growth of Popery and Arbitrary Government in England* (1677) became famous. His later reputation, however, rests on his lyrical gifts especially *Thoughts in a Garden.*

MARWAR (India). *See* JODHPUR.

MARX, (Heinrich) Karl (1818-83) a Rhinelander was initially inspired by Feuerbach's materialist critique of Hegelian idealism in his *Nature of Christianity* (1841). He married in 1843 and moved to Paris where he made friends with Friedrich Engels the left-wing son of a Manchester industrialist. They collaborated on the *Holy Family* (1845), a long attack on one Bruno Bauer, the *German Ideology*, an exposition of Marx's *Historical Materialism* (not published until 1932) and the *Poverty of Philosophy*, an attack on Proudhon. In 1847 some German immigrant craftsmen in London invited the two to join them. They gave themselves the new name of the Communist League, and it was for them that they composed the *German Ideology-based Communist Manifesto* published in Jan. 1848. The continental uprisings of 1848, upon which it had no influence, began within weeks. Marx and Engels went to the Rhineland, suppressed the Manifesto and when Andreas Gottschalk, the leader of the Rhineland Workers Union was arrested, Marx took his place. Himself tried for sedition, he made a political defence and was resoundingly acquitted. He returned to Paris, was expelled and moved permanently to London.

Here he lived in poverty, ruthlessly pursuing his studies for *Das Kapital* while his family hungered, children died and Engels supported him financially and intellectually. After 1864 he was less poor because Engels became a partner in his father's business. *Das Kapital* was still unfinished at his death. Engels, whose researches contributed much to it in the first place, published it. *See* MARXISM.

MARXISM (In this article expressions used technically by Marxists are printed in italics. They do not necessarily have their common meaning.) **(1)** Marxism is a conglomerate of ideas derived by Karl Marx from others, notably Feuerbach and St. Simon. It assumes that society is founded upon the means of material production, the sum of which constitutes the economic structure, and that intellectual, legal and political institutions merely reflect the features of that structure. This *historical materialism* is supplemented by a *dialectical* materialism. The structure of post-feudal society consists of three *classes,* the *capitalists* who own and, by force of deception, control the means of production; the *workers* or *proletariat* who actually do the work; and a *middle class* which, in distributing the results, skim off part of the profits. There is little left for the *workers,* whose individual share is reduced to tiny proportions by their numbers. The latter always get poorer as their numbers increase but the others get richer through their means of control.

(2) The *proletariat* is eventually alienated from society, and as its condition approaches the intolerable it becomes rebellious. Lenin added the idea of *imperialism,* which he considered to be the forcible imposition of the products of capitalism upon foreign markets as a means of maintaining capitalist predominance at home. *Imperialism* is therefore a symptom of capitalist decay. Human history being a *dialectical* (i.e. logical) process of political determinism, is seen as a series of *class struggles,* which inevitably end in *revolution.* Such revolutions occur first in industrial societies.

(3) The process of *revolution* begins in a *revolutionary situation* where the disorderly condition of a capitalist society is such that the workers, having by a general strike seized the levers of power, set up a *Dictatorship of the Proletariat.* This ruthlessly *liquidates* all preceding institutions, censors all ideas emanating from the previous dispensation, and *re-educates* the *masses* in the new ideology which, in the sense that the capitalist and middle classes and their ideas have been eliminated, has become socialist in a *classless* society. With the advent of this golden age, the *Dictatorship of the Proletariat* becomes unnecessary and the organs of the state wither away to make room for the *communist society*

(4) These ideas are elevated into dogmas by Marx's abuse of words and by an enormous superstructure of doctrine. They depreciated the role of the individual yet like other deterministic sects (e.g. Calviists and Islam) communists under Lenin's influence everywhere developed a *Bolshevik* outlook on political organisation in which their *party* was actually a small body of activists (or secular priesthood) dedicated to the furtherance of their dialectically inevitable revolution. This internal and double contradiction was supplemented by a misreading of history. The social revolts to which Marxists attached importance, such as the Spartacist rebellion, the Jacquerie and the English Peasants' Revolt did not begin in industrial but in agricultural societies and when this was repeated in the backward E. European states in 20th cent. they were without exception launched not by proletarian action but by *elitist* opportunism during, not a *revolutionary situation* but a period of military defeat. These revolutions ended (in Milovan Djilas's (q.v.) analysis) by substituting a *new class* of Party Bureaucrat which acquired under socialism the same role as that attributed to the capitalists and middle class before the revolution. This class, having no traditional but only material roots was boring (e.g. in abandoning such part of an artistic heritage as did not suit their doctrines), parasitic in engrossing economic privileges, tyrannically heedless of ordinary humanity (e.g. by mass deportations) and apt to conceal its shortcomings by police secrecy and lies through controlled media, or by policies involving natural exhaustion (e.g. the shrinkage of the Sea of Aral) or excessive risks such as fluvial pollution and the Chernobyl atomic disaster. Its rise actually depressed the condition of the working class to levels lower than those which obtained before the Russian Revolution.

MARY I (1516-58) Queen (1553) only surviving child of Henry VIII and Katharine of Aragon **(1)** was well educated especially by the semi-royal (*see* PARA 7 BELOW) Countess of Shrewsbury, mother of Reginald Pole (late Cardinal) and was the subject of betrothal negotiations to the Dauphin and to the Emperor Charles V. In 1525 she was made nominal Princess or Governor of Wales.

(2) She was separated from her mother on her parents' divorce (1552) but publicly sided with Q. Katharine and refused to give up the title of princess. In 1533 she and the P. Elizabeth were put under Ann Boleyn's aunt Lady Shelton at Hadfield. She was bullied and threatened but attracted public sympathy besides the protection of her cousin Charles V. After Anne Boleyn's execution (1536) Jane Seymour reconciled her with the King and she had to acknowledge his supremacy and in view of the second Act of Succession, her own illegitimacy; moreover, in the aftermath of the Northern Rebellion, close friends like the Countess of Salisbury were executed. Nevertheless, in 1539 she was proposed as a wife for Philip D. of Bavaria and later there were other such proposals. In 1544 she was declared capable of succession. By now she was on friendly terms with both P. Edward and with Elizabeth.

(3) Under Edward VI she diverted herself, mostly at Hunsdon, with literary pursuits, and rejecting proposals from Thomas, Lord Seymour who was making more than proposals to Elizabeth at Hatfield. In 1559 she refused despite the Act of Uniformity, to forgo the mass, and her resolution won respect not only from R. Catholics. Pressure from Protector Somerset and later from Northumberland was checked by a threat from her imperial relatives. Moreover by 1552 Northumberland realised that her accession would endanger him and reverse the religious settlement, and that only a well organised coup could prevent it. She realised this too; summoned to Edward VI's death bed, she disappeared from Hunsdon and rode for the Howard country of E. Anglia, where she was gathering adherents by the time that her enemies reached Hunsdon. It took a fortnight to overthrow Northumberland and his Queen Jane. She had a rapturous welcome in London. Only the Duke with two supporters were executed; Jane and Abp. Cranmer were condemned but imprisoned. Her leniency astonished all.

(4) The new council was composed partly of Henry VIII's existing councillors, with some of her friends. As the first queen regnant, there were new problems particularly her marriage and the jealousies which it might occasion if she married a subject. Moreover there was the legacy of corruption and economic mismanagement from both previous reigns, and the incompatibility and incessant quarrels between the factions. She spent much time arguing at her council with, she said, little effect. In fact she had her own solutions: she would marry a Spaniard and cleanse the realm. She has been remembered for the savagery of her religious persecutions and forgotten for her improvements in financial management and trade, and her restoration of the currency which benefited everyone. Moreover there was a case for the Spanish-Habsburg-Burgundian alliance to counterbalance French power at Boulogne, and influence at Edinburgh. A Spanish match, however, was suspect at court and disliked by the people, all the more since Dutch opinion was hardening against the Spanish connection. In Oct. 1553 she promised the imperial ambassador (Simon Renard) that she would marry Philip of Spain and despite a joint deputation from Parliament, the treaty was concluded at Westminster in Jan. 1554.

(5) Preaching had been prohibited since Aug. 1553, whereby the opposition was deprived of its principal medium, and Bp. Gardiner had been empowered to license preachers which put it into the hands of the Romanists. Bp. Ridley as a supporter of Northumberland, was already in prison. On various pretexts, Bp. Hooper and Abp. Cranmer had followed him. Wyatt's rebellion broke out (prematurely) within days of the marriage treaty; it was suppressed by the beginning of Feb. but used as a pretext to execute Lady Jane Grey, Lord Guildford Dudley her husband and her father the D. of Suffolk. P. Elizabeth was sent to the Tower in Mar. and Renard pressed for her execution but juries were turning hostile and when Sir Nicholas Throckmorton was acquitted in May, the Govt. doubted the wisdom of severity and sent her into country seclusion at Woodstock. An attempt in Parliament to exclude her from the succession failed as also did a bill to make offences against Philip high treason (Apr.-May 1554). Despite all these warnings Mary pressed ahead. On the excuse of irregularities, the vital bishoprics of London, Winchester, Durham, Exeter and Worcester were returned to previous Romanist holders. There was no difficulty about persuading her first Parliament to abolish the religious legislation of Edward VI, for it was sufficiently unpopular, but Parliament would not go back further. The process of replacing bishops continued (mostly on grounds of marriage) and injunctions of Mar. 1554 ordered the new bishops to deprive about 1500 married reformist clergy.

(6) The same Parliament understandably refused to revive the laws against heresy, or especially since many Romanists were involved, to restore church property, but convocation was slightly more pliant and appointed delegates to dispute with Cranmer, Latimer and Ridley. In Apr. 1554 they found them to be heretics, but since their findings could not be enforced, the three were returned to prison. The general trend of the govt.'s intentions was however, clear and foreign reformers began to leave or were expelled. Thus the process of Romanisation was far advanced when Philip arrived with a large fleet at Southampton. The marriage took place at Winchester on 25 July 1554 and after a royal progress, Philip and Mary entered London in Aug. with *inter alia,* cartloads of Spanish gold.

(7) Reginald Pole's mother was a niece of Edward IV and Richard III. He had gone to Rome, became a

Cardinal and as an extremist associate of reforming churchmen such as Caraffa and Contarini had attended at the opening of the Council of Trent. He longed to redeem England from heresy but his ability and judgement did not match his faith. Mary was willing to let him come but preferred to complete her campaign first. The emperor, suspicious of his statesmanship put obstacles in his way but he persevered. He was due to arrive on 20 Nov. Parliament was summoned for 12th and duly sweetened. His attainder was reversed. After a passionate address from him as legate, the houses petitioned for the return of the Kingdom to the church. An impressive ceremony of absolution and readmission engendered a devotional atmosphere, in which the anti-papal legislation of Henry VIII was repealed, and the laws against heresy re-enacted (Dec. 1554).

(8) Mary put it into effect at once. Church courts could condemn but not burn; for burning her warrant was needed. The first, of John Rogers, editor of *Tyndale's Bible*, took place at Smithfield on 4 Feb. 1555. Thereafter, save during Parliamentary sessions, burnings (about 300) occurred regularly. They had unintended effects, for reformism of an English patriotic tinge had gone so far, that these people, who bore their sufferings gallantly, were regarded as martyrs of a foreign-imposed cult. Personally respected, unpopularly married and now hated, the unhappy Queen presently suffered too from an indifferent husband (who left for Flanders in Sept. 1555) and delusions of pregnancy associated with cancer of the womb. Philip was making insistent demands for money for Spanish policies and using Mary's inability to satisfy them as an excuse for remaining among the gaieties of Brussels, for Parliament voted only one subsidy and refused to restore the church revenues except at the expense of the crown. There was a furious quarrel between the Govt. and the Commons in which they were locked in, like a jury, on one bill, and locked themselves in on another. As a good tactician Philip disassociated himself from Mary's policy of persecution and worse still, Bp. Gardiner, Lord Chancellor and the brain behind Mary's policy, died (Nov. 1555). The much less able Nicholas Heath, Abp. of York, succeeded him on the woolsack and Mary had to depend yet more on the unworldly and undersophisticated Cardinal, whose position however, was becoming insecure. In May 1555 the Neapolitan Cardinal Caraffa had become Pope as Paul II. In his desire to exclude Spanish power from Naples he made an alliance with France (Dec. 1555). Moreover, he suspected Pole who had been a friend of the renegade Ochino, of heresy. In Jan. 1556 Philip became K. of Spain and lost interest in Mary and in English internal affairs; by Sept. he was at war with France and the Pope, and excommunicated and wondering how he could turn his English crown to account.

(9) Mary's Spanish marriage had brought on a hostile French policy. Henry II tried to get the Scots to attack; he sheltered English exiles, let them prey on English shipping from French ports and helped their ineffectual conspiracies in favour of Elizabeth. Hence Philip could come to England (Mar. 1557) to induce Mary to go to war. Paul II at this point withdrew his representatives from Philip's dominions and cancelled Cardinal Pole's legatine commission. Mary, was now in a dilemma: should she follow the head of her religion or her lawfully wedded husband? In practice she could give little military help, and the country was against war, but French support for Thomas Stafford's attempt on Scarborough (Apr. 1557) brought it on (June). An Anglo-Spanish army routed the French at St. Quentin (Aug.) but Philip would not press his advantage and the winter dispersal of the troops gave the French time to assemble. In Jan. 1558 Guise pounced upon the undergarrisoned Calais territory and conquered it in three weeks. Parliament refused adequate supply to get it back but by various expedients enough money and forces were raised to send troops to Flanders with whose aid Philip won a victory at Gravelines (July 1558); but it was Spain which profited for it enabled Philip to begin negotiations and sign a truce (Oct.) in the absence, even, of the English ambassadors. Since Aug. however, Mary had been mortally ill. In Nov. she and Pole both died.

MARY II (1662-94) Queen (1689) eldest child of James II and Anne (Hyde) was by Charles II's direction brought up a Protestant, mostly with her grandfather, the E. of Clarendon. In 1677 she reluctantly married William of Orange to whom, despite his unprepossessing characteristics and suspect preferences, she became devoted. She was popular in Holland and became a focus of English Protestant sentiment under James II. At the revolution she became in name joint sovereign with William. He was the ruler, but she managed the important ecclesiastical patronage with discernment and moderation. She also relieved the condition of the non-juring clergy and acted as William's mouthpiece during his European absences. Her influence was considerable enough to make grave difficulties for her sister Anne and her political friends (Marlborough, Godolphin etc.) when they were estranged in 1690. A patron of the arts and architecture, she lived at Kensington Palace and Hampton Court where, in both places she rebuilt much of the structure, laid out the gardens and threw them open to the public. William was grief-stricken at her death.

MARY OF ENGLAND AND ORANGE (1631-60) clever and beautiful daughter of Charles I married William son of Frederick Henry, P. of Orange in 1641 and provided an initial refuge for Charles II and James when their father was put to death. William died in 1650 and she bore his posthumous son, later William III. She returned to England at the Restoration and died of smallpox.

MARY "of FRANCE" (1496-1533), *d.* of Henry VII, was from 1508-14 betrothed to Charles of Castile (Charles V) and then married by Henry VIII to the elderly Louis XII. She acquiesced on condition that thereafter she might marry whom she pleased. In 1515 he died and she married (in France) Charles Brandon D. of Suffolk. This angered Henry VIII who had to be bought off. *See* BRANDON.

MARY of GUELDERS (?-1463) married James II of Scots in 1449 and when he was killed at the S. of Roxburgh in 1460, she personally pressed the siege to success and acted thereafter as Regent for the child James III. She sheltered Henry VI and Margaret in 1461 after the B. of Towton.

MARY of GUISE or of LORRAINE. *See* ELIZABETH I-6. MARY Q. OF SCOTS-1 *et seq.*

MARYLAND (U.S.A.). The coast was partly charted by John Smith in about 1610. Promised in 1632 by Charles I to George Calvert 1st Ld. BALTIMORE (1580-1632) the charter was actually granted to his son Cecilius, 2nd Ld. (1604-75). The Calverts were R. Catholics and hoped to make Maryland a refuge for them. The first Governor from 1634 was Cecilius' brother Leonard Calvert (1606-47) and he divided the land into manors on the English pattern. The supply of R. Catholics being insufficient for the land available, many grants were made to protestants and after the establishment of the English Protectorate, the puritans obtained control in 1654. At the Restoration the Calverts were able to reassert their rights. The boundary with Pennsylvania was at this period unsettled, and the Marylanders began to encroach. This led to the celebrated Chancery case of *Penn v Lord Baltimore* in which the boundaries were protected by injunction through an assertion of the chancery jurisdiction *in personam*. After the revolution of 1689 the Baltimore rights were transferred to the crown, and the Church of England was established. The result was a compromise society very similar to that of contemporary England; and sensitive to outside interference. The province asserted its statehood, adopted its own constitution in 1776 and enthusiastically joined the rebellion. In the civil war it was deeply divided but remained in the Union.

MARY of MODENA (1658-1718) became the second wife of James D. of York (James II) in 1673 through the influence of Louis XIV. Though friendly with his protestant daughters, she shared James's unpopularity as a R. Catholic. Her first five children all died young. In 1678 her secretary Edward Coleman was involved in the Popish Plot which implicated James but she remained faithful to him then and in spite of his infidelities, after he came to the throne. In 1688 she gave birth to a son and so became a victim of the 'Warming Pan' rumour. After the flight to France she took effective charge of James's affairs because she made a good and he a bad impression at the French court.

MARY, Queen to George V (1867-1953) *d.* of the quick tempered Francis, D. of Teck and the popular and unpunctual P. Mary Adelaide, a cousin of Q. Victoria. They were not interested in her education, which she pursued determinedly in spite of them. She became fluent in French and German, an expert in certain fields of art and tapestry-making and had a wide knowledge of European history and German internal politics. Engaged to the D. of Clarence, who died suddenly in 1892, she was married to George, D. of York in 1893. It soon became a love match. Her difficulty was that her intellectual interests differed from the social interests of the late Victorian and Edwardian court but her strong character, alarming charm and robust constitution upheld her husband in the arduous tours (1898 Ireland, 1902 Australia and other colonies, 1905-6 India, 1906 Spain and Norway, 1911-12 after his succession again to India and state visits to Berlin in 1913 and to Paris in 1914). Moreover she had always had besides an enquiring mind, an empathy with ordinary people. Margaret Bondfield, the Labour politician, liked and respected her. During World War I she compelled and organised attention to the problems of the employment of women, supervised the austerity of the palace, inspected hospitals and convalescent homes in France as well as Britain in considerable detail and came to know many leading members of the Labour movement. Consequently she and the King quite naturally received and looked after the members of the first Labour Govt. in 1923. She also had another merit: she never discussed politics, but political and other confidences were known to be safe with her. Hence, after the King's illness in 1928, which unfitted him for about half his work, she was able to supply his deficiencies until his death in 1936.

She did not retire but had first to cope with the abdication crisis and then, though partly blinded in a motor accident in 1939, she worked tirelessly almost until her death. She has been described as having "a golden sense of what was fitting not alone for . . . a monarchy but for men and women in every rank of life" and "blazingly truthful", feeling sympathy with the East End delinquent but none for the liar. She could also swear like a trooper.

MARY Q. of SCOTS (1542-87) Queen (1542-67) Scottish Reign. (1) Mary, celebrated *d.* of James V, began her reign at the age of one week when her father died on campaign. Her mother, Mary of Guise, naturally brought her up but in a short struggle for the regency, the second E. of Arran defeated and imprisoned Abp Beaton, who with the Queen Mother, was identified with the disasters at the end of the previous reign. Moreover, the French policy which they represented was compromised by the rise of a Protestant movement unwilling to fight English protestants. Arran was a half-hearted Protestant himself. Henry VIII now took pledges from Angus, two earls and four lords who had surrendered at Solway Moss (1542) (*The English Lords*). In return for their release and pensions, they were to further a marriage between the baby Queen and P. (later King) Edward. They prevailed upon Arran who in July 1543 signed the Greenwich peace treaties, whereby the children were to be betrothed and Mary sent to England at the age of ten to be educated. Arran's Parliament also took the important step, on Henry's advice, of permitting the circulation of translated Bibles. The movement against the old church was growing.

(2) Cardinal Beaton, however, was released from prison and soon changed Arran's policy by playing on his family ambitions. An English marriage if fruitful, would end the Arran-Hamilton claims. Moreover doubts about the marriage of Arran's parents placed his claim at the mercy of the church courts. Finally MATTHEW STUART (1516-71) 4th E. of LENNOX whose father had been murdered after the B. of Linlithgow, appeared from France and sued for the hand of Mary of Guise. He too had claims to the Crown. In Dec. 1543 Arran repudiated the Greenwich treaties, whereupon southern Scotland suffered destructive English invasions under Hertford in 1544 and 1545 (known as *The Rough Wooing*) in which Edinburgh, Holyroodhouse and the Border abbeys were burned. The revulsion caused by these operations played into the hands of Beaton and the Q. Mother, and the English lords changed their tune and began to advocate a marriage between the Queen and Arran's son, the Master of Hamilton. This isolated Lennox who agilely allied himself with the Tudors by marrying Margaret Douglas. *See* JAMES V OF SCOTS.

(3) Henry VIII regarded Beaton as his chief opponent and encouraged murderous attempts on him. In May 1546 one of these succeeded and the murderers (Norman Leslie of Rothes and William Kirkaldy of Grange) were besieged in Beaton's castle at St. Andrews and appealed for English help. A French force captured them and their chaplain, John Knox.

(4) Henry died, but Hertford, now D. of Somerset and Regent for Edward VI, continued the policy of coercion, won a resounding victory at Pinkie (Sept. 1547) and left garrisons in the Lowlands. It was now Arran's turn to suffer the consequences of English victory. The marriage between his son and the Queen had to be dropped, and Mary of Guise, to secure French help contracted her to the Dauphin (T. of Haddington). The Queen was brought from a hiding place in the Lake of Menteith and shipped from Dumbarton to France with Arran's son as a hostage for his father's good behaviour (July 1548). The Hamilton prestige was, however, sustained, for Arran was awarded the French Dukedom of Châtelherault and his half-brother John, Abbot of Paisley and Bp. of Dunkeld became Abp. of St Andrews. A French regular force arrived and made Mary of Guise the strongest person in Scotland. Her combined forces took Haddington and cleared the Lowlands. In Mar. 1550 Scotland was included in the P. of Boulogne whereby England ceded Boulogne to France. Mary of Guise could now visit France, cautiously bringing the lords who might make trouble in her absence. Her recent successes combined with the splendour, courtesy and presents of the French court dazzled the recalcitrant lords. On the way back in 1551 they all visited the sickly K. Edward VI. He died in July 1553 and England now acquired a persecuting R. Catholic Govt. seeking Spanish support and on worsening terms with France. The moment was propitious for Mary of Guise's next move.

(5) In Dec. 1553 when the Queen was eleven, the *Parlement* of Paris, on request pronounced that the Queen might during her twelfth year choose a *curator* instead of a *tutor* (guardian). Châtelherault's regency and *tutela* were held together. Bribes and threats induced him to resign and in Apr. 1554 the regency passed to Mary of Guise in the presence of the Estates. Frenchmen now began to hold high office and French troops to garrison major centres. The Queen-Regent, however, took steps to calm opposition. She sheltered English religious refugees and referred demands for church reform to Abp. Hamilton for his provincial council; from 1555-56 she allowed John Knox to come from Geneva to preach; but such toleration multiplied the reformers while the French made themselves unpopular. Calvinist protestantism became identified with an urge to expel the French. The French took Calais from the English in Jan. 1558 but Mary of Guise understood the danger; when the Queen married the Dauphin (Apr. 1558) the Scots commissioners had publicly stipulated for Scots autonomy, but in fact the Queen had assigned her rights in Scotland and her claims in England to the French Crown if she died childless. This undertaking, which infringed the rights of the Hamiltons, was understandably kept secret, for the nucleus of a noble Calvinist party had already been formed under the leadership of the Lord James, a bastard of James V, and E. of Mar.

(6) *The Crisis.* The Scots crisis was precipitated by a series of unpredictable deaths. Mary Tudor died in Nov. 1558 and when her protestant half-sister Elizabeth succeeded her, the Scots Calvinists understood that she might be a political ally. But Elizabeth, her domestic authority still weak, wanted peace abroad and was willing to recognise (with face saving devices) the loss of Calais to obtain it. This was effected as part of the Franco Spanish P. of Câteau Cambrésis (Apr. 1559) which included England and Scotland. In May the Acts of Supremacy and Uniformity established a compromise protestantism in England and John Knox returned to Scotland. His thunderous eloquence and the armed support of the Calvinist lords (now called *The Lords of the Congregation*) brought rioting and church sacking in most of the principal towns. In July Henry II of France was killed in a tourney and Mary, Q. of Scots suddenly became Queen Consort of France. Her mother's Guise brothers seized power, and in the so-called Tumult of Amboise (*see* HUGUENOTS) did many French Calvinists to death. It was essential to restore order in the Scottish towns, but the govt. had to use French troops, and their moves were plausibly represented as a sinister Guise plot. The Lords of the Congregation, who originally intended a religious compromise now felt constrained to greater extremism. In Oct. they proclaimed the demission of Mary of Guise, transferred the regency to a council nominally headed by the absent Châtelherault, and drove her out of Edinburgh. She fortified herself in Leith and called for French reinforcements. The Congregation called for English help and by the T. of Berwick (Feb. 1560) they and Q. Elizabeth agreed upon mutual aid against France. English troops and warships helped to isolate Leith, but it was resolutely defended until June, when Mary of Guise died. By this time the French Guises, for internal reasons, wanted peace and under the T. of Edinburgh (July) French and English troops were evacuated, and France sacrificed her Queen-Consort's claims by recognising Elizabeth's title to the English throne.

(7) Scotland had become an English protectorate, under cover of which the Lords of the Congregation, in a Parliament summoned in Aug. in their R. Catholic sovereigns' names, put through a protestant revolution. They abolished Papal authority, forbade the Mass, adopted Knox's *Confession of Faith* and condemned practices inconsistent with it; but they refused to adopt the Calvinist *Book of Discipline* which proposed a new ecclesiastical and educational system to be financed by the entire assets of the old church. Their reasons were mixed; some had possession of assets which they did not wish to disgorge: others had religious scruples or feared political extremism. Nevertheless, the revolution was real, involving abandonment of the French connection and increasing identification with English interests. The Reformation Parliament laid the foundations for the Union.

(8) Four months later (Dec. 1560) Francis II of France died, and Mary Q. of Scots found herself as Queen-Dowager, without a future in France. The Hamiltons led by Châtelherault (whose son had taken the earldom of Arran) hoped that she would stay there, so that they could acquire the reality of power and perhaps the crown itself. As Mary was, to most intents and purposes French, and Elizabeth's lineal successor in England, Elizabeth hoped so too. Mary never ratified the T. of Edinburgh. She evaded the Queen's ships and the Hamiltons and landed at Leith in Aug. 1561. She was nineteen and considered beautiful. Her carriage and athleticism, and her social energy impressed all beholders, some more favourably than others. This physical side of her character was to be important.

(9) On the advice of the Lord James 'to press no matters of religion', she had refused offers from the Gordon E. of Huntly to raise a R. Catholic army and impose a counter reformation by force, and Hamilton proposals that she should marry Arran and become a Protestant. While insisting on her right to maintain her own chapel as she pleased, she forbade infringements of the religious settlement just made. If ever a R. Catholic ruler tried to reach an accommodation with Calvinists, it was Mary. The old church was still in possession of its properties and revenues: unlike the Reformation Parliament she conceded some of this (about one sixth) to the Kirk (1561). She made the protestant Lord James, E. of Moray, at the expense of the R. Catholic Huntly, who had been administering the Moray lands, and let Moray crush Huntly at the B. of Corrichie (Oct. 1562). In 1563 Abp. Hamilton and some other clergy were imprisoned for publicly celebrating mass outside her court. Yet none of this availed against the obdurate misogyny and religious extremism of John Knox, the greatest demagogue of the age.

(10) Moreover Knox could capitalise on a political issue. The Queen was one of the most desirable matches in the world. She would probably marry a R. Catholic and if she were to marry an equal the result would be an alliance with one of the great houses (Spain, Austria, France) identified with the Counter-Reformation. There was recent Scots experience of such foreign intervention. Elizabeth, not unreasonably, feared such a prospect. She threatened war. Mary invited her to propose a candidate. Perhaps Elizabeth already understood something of Mary's sexual frustrations. She suggested her own favourite Robert Dudley, newly E. of Leicester, whom Mary naturally refused. In the autumn of 1564 Elizabeth got Mary to allow Matthew (1516-71), the forfeited 4th E. of Lennox, to return to Scotland, and in Feb. 1565 his tall handsome R. Catholic son HENRY STUART (1545-67) Ld. DARNLEY followed him. Elizabeth hoped that Mary and Darnley would fall in love; their marriage would admittedly unite the two best claims to the English throne in a R. Catholic family, but the power of the Lennox Stuarts was not to be compared with that of the continental great families, and their English estates would be at the mercy of English govts. By April Mary was hotly infatuated.

(11) The result was disaster. Marriage meant supersession of the personally applied influence of Moray and Lethington and their moderate supporters; a Lennox Stuart husband would end Hamilton hopes; a Papist union gave new pretexts to the religious fanatics. She proclaimed that she would not molest her subjects in matters of religion, but in return for a papal dispensation for consanguinity, undertook to defend the Roman faith to the utmost. Protestant lords in arms at Stirling naturally demanded assurances before they assented to the marriage. She promptly married Darnley before the dispensation could arrive (July 1565) and assembled her supporters. The lords, led by Moray, Argyll and Glencairn entered Edinburgh (Aug.) but the Queen in person

chased them all over the Lowlands and into England (*The Chase-about Raid*).

(12) At this moment she discovered that Darnley was a jealously spiteful, craven, arrogant and promiscuous drunk. She had sensibly refused him the Crown Matrimonial (with its right of succession in the absence of offspring). Unable to get advice from him, or from the alienated nobility, she had in her isolation to rely upon members of her private household, especially the modest Italian musician-Secretary, David Rizzio (or Riccio), who assumed an importance beyond his or her intention. To the Lords he was an upstart; to the extreme protestants a papal spy; to Darnley an adulterous rival. A Parliament was due for 12 March, 1566 to forfeit the lords defeated in the Chase-about Raid. They attracted Darnley into a conspiracy; an act of terrorism was to secure for him the crown matrimonial and for them pardon; and he would lend his authority to discharge the Parliament. The act of terrorism would be the killing of Rizzio. The Queen, being six months' pregnant, might miscarry or even die of the shock, leaving the way open for Darnley.

(13) Darnley, JAMES DOUGLAS (?1516-81) 4th E. of MORTON, with Lords Ruthven and Lindsay of the Byres murdered Rizzio at supper with the Queen on 9th. On 10th Parliament was discharged and Moray and the other lords arrived. On the 11th Mary, under duress, pardoned them. The same night she terrified or seduced Darnley into changing sides. On 12th they escaped to Dunbar, which belonged to an unstable adventurer, JAMES HEPBURN (?1536-78) 4th E. of BOTHWELL, and assembled her supporters, notably Athol and the Gordons. The murder had revolted public opinion. With the help of the pardoned lords she returned victoriously to Edinburgh within a week, and Darnley's co-conspirators fled to England. He pretended not to know that Rizzio's murder was intended; Mary doubted this, but co-conspirators, in revenge for his treachery, made sure. All the lords hated Darnley for his insolent arrogance, and besides, he had contracted syphilis.

(14) Hate now dominated events. In June 1566 Mary gave birth to JAMES VI (1566-1625) K. of Scots (1567) and of England (1603) and publicly asserted Darnley's paternity. He withdrew from the court and Bothwell became the Queen's lover. In Dec. she pardoned Rizzio's murderers; in Feb. Kirk o'Field, a house outside Edinburgh where Darnley was staying, was blown up and he was found strangled in the garden. Who did this is not known, but the public had no doubt that Bothwell was responsible. In Apr. he abducted the willing Queen and took her to Dunbar. In May his very recent marriage to Lady Jane Gordon was dissolved in the Commissary Court, at her instance on grounds of adultery, at his on grounds of consanguinity. Within a week the pregnant Queen married the murderous adulterer at Holyroodhouse. A storm of indignation and rebellion followed. The great families, already in control of the P. James at Stirling, called out their followers. In June Mary surrendered at Carbeny without a fight. Bothwell died insane in Danish captivity.

(15) In July, Mary now a prisoner at Lochleven, appointed Moray Regent and abdicated. James VI was crowned immediately, but in May 1568 still indomitable, she escaped, revoked her abdication, headed west, gathered Hamilton support, was defeated at Langside near Glasgow and crossed into England (*see* JAMES VI OF SCOTS, SCOTTISH REIGN, for later career).

MARY (?1450-88) sister of James III of Scots. *See* JAMES III OF SCOTS-1.

MASAI. *See* KENYA.

MASARYK (1) Thomas (1850-1937). *See* CZECHOSLOVAKIA-1 *et seq.* For his son **(2) Jan (?-1948)** *see* CZECHOSLOVAKIA-7.

MASHAM née HILL, Abigail (?-1734). This important and elusive figure was a cousin both of Robert Harley and of Sarah, Duchess of Marlborough, with whom she was brought up and by whose influence she became bedchamber woman to Q. Anne. She sympathised with the Queen in her personal concerns and gradually replaced Sarah in her affection, at a time when she was tiring of the Whigs. In 1707 she married Col. Samuel Masham, groom of the bedchamber of P. George of Denmark, Anne's husband, in a ceremony kept secret from Sarah but graced by Anne. She had already been acting as a channel of private communication between the Queen and the opposition, particularly Harley.

The Queen now habitually took their clandestine advice through her, and organised the intrigues which destroyed the Whig govt. at home. In 1711 she secured Sarah's dismissal as Mistress of the Robes and herself became Keeper of the Privy Purse. Her husband was one of the twelve Tory peers created in 1712 to ensure the ratification of the P. of Utrecht; she and Harley made a corrupt bargain to share some of the profits of the Asiento (conceded by Spain in the treaty) but they quarrelled over it and she refused to help him any more with the Queen. The Whigs were Hanoverian and hated her; Harley had gone over to the Hanoverian persuasion; she was left with no choice but to further Bolingbroke's Jacobite machinations. The Pretender, however, refused to change his religion (1713) and thenceforth Abigail's influence and even safety could last no longer than Anne's life. When the Queen died she retired to country obscurity.

MASHONAS. A group of Bantu speaking tribes who inhabited approximately the northern quadrant of S. Rhodesia centred on Salisbury, and represented the largest single body in the area.

MASON, Sir John (1503-66) diplomat, was for some time Sir Thomas Wyatt's secretary; from 1542 he was clerk of the Privy Council, and from 1544 Master of the Posts and French Secretary. In 1550-51 he was Ambassador in Paris and then became Clerk to the Parliaments. He was also an M.P. from 1551-53 when he became Ambassador to the Emperor Charles V whose abdication he witnessed in 1556. At Elizabeth's accession he became one of her expert advisers and negotiators until 1564.

MASON. See NEW HAMPSHIRE.

MASON-DIXON LINE, the southern boundary of Pennsylvania, was surveyed between 1763-67 by two English astronomers Charles MASON (1730-87) and Jeremiah DIXON (1733-79) to settle a boundary dispute with Maryland. It and its extensions came to mean the line between free and slave territory.

MASQUES or MASKS were dramatic entertainments, possibly of Italian origin, popular among English courtiers in the 16th and 17th cents. They depended on music, song, dance and disguise rather than plot or character, but many distinguished dramatists composed them, including Beaumont, and especially Ben Jonson under whom they reached their fullest development, often with stage machinery and effects devised by Inigo Jones.

MASSACHUSETTS (*see* PLYMOUTH COLONY). The MASSACHUSETTS BAY CO, a group of puritan businessmen, was chartered in 1629 to colonise between the Rs. Charles and Merrimack. A first party of about 1000 led by John Winthrop, arrived in 1630 at Boston, joined up with the Salem colonists and set up the Massachusetts Bay Colony. This and the Plymouth Colony remained separate, electing their own Governors annually. Harvard College was founded in 1636. The two organisms, of which the Bay Colony was much the bigger and growing rapidly, were intolerant puritan theocracies; pursuing their way regardless of the home Govt., which by now was becoming embroiled in political controversies. After the Restoration, London began to take an interest. An investigative commission reported in 1664 that the colonies were breaking the law, by coining money, denying freedom of worship and ignoring the Trade and Navigation Acts. A second commission of 1676 reported similarly but in stronger terms. As the colonists took no notice, the Co. Charter was forfeited in 1684, but its govt. continued to function without it, until both colonies were amalgamated into the DOMINION OF NEW ENGLAND (q.v.). After the Revolution of 1689 a new charter was granted in 1691. This combined the two colonies as the PROVINCE OF MASSACHUSETTS, under a royal Governor with a legislature (The General Court) which controlled taxation and paid his salary. Between 1692 and the rebellion of 1775 there were 23 Governors and three *interregna*. Only one Governor Jonathan Belcher (r. 1730-41) ruled as long as eleven years or two others for more than five. This partly accounts for the weakness of the royal representatives in the face of local independents, who refused to finance policies which they disliked, or enforce the law if it did not suit them. The disputes set in motion the disagreements which developed into the Rebellion. See WARS OF 1739-48.

MASSACHUSETTS CIRCULAR. See AMERICAN REBELLION-11.

MASSASOIT. See WAMPANOAG.

MASSÉNA, André (1758-1817) Marshal (1801) D. of RIVOLI and Prince of ESSLING, after brilliant service at Wagram in 1809, was given the Spanish command against Wellington, who defeated him in May 1811 in Fuentes d'Oñoro. He was superseded and faithfully supported the Bourbons after their restoration in 1814. Probably the ablest of Bonaparte's marshals, Bonaparte called him the 'spoiled child of victory'.

MASSEREENE. See SKEFFINGTON.

MASSEY, Sir Edward (?1619-?74) originally a royalist, joined the Parliamentarians in 1642 in the Civil War, and by his heroic and successful defence of Gloucester in 1643 deflected the course of the war decisively against the King. He helped Fairfax to reduce the west, became M.P. in 1646 and in May 1647, commander of the London troops and a member of the Presbyterian Committee of Safety. The army impeached him and in 1648 he fled briefly to Holland, but after his return he was a victim of Pride's Purge. He and Waller were then imprisoned, but he escaped and joined the royalists in Holland. Hence he fought for Charles II, was wounded at Upton Bridge (1651) and captured, but escaped from the Tower in 1652 and fled again to Holland. He was one of the King's intermediaries with the Presbyterians in 1654, 1655 and 1660. Charles made him Governor of Gloucester for which he sat as M.P. from 1661. He was subsequently appointed absentee Governor of Jamaica, and fought in the Dutch war of 1667. His remarkable career illustrates the doubts and difficulties of honest men of the time.

MASSINGHAM, John. Father (fl. 1409-50) and son (fl. 1438-78) were noted sculptors, wood carvers and polychromists in S. England.

MASTERMAN, Charles Frederick Gurney (1873-1927) was considered a talented politician yet somehow failed to make much of his talents as such. A brilliant and inspiring speaker, he could not win difficult elections. He was Liberal M.P. for West Ham (1906-11) and as Financial Secretary to the Treasury did much of the work on the Insurance Bill. He was unseated on an election petition because of malpractices by his agent, but took Bethnal Green in 1911. In World War II he was Director of Propaganda and in the Cabinet, Chancellor of the Duchy of Lancaster but without a Parliamentary seat. He was forced to resign because no constituency party organisation would adopt him. He was elected again only in 1923 but held the seat for only a few months.

MASTERS. See CHANCERY-8 *et seq.*

MASULIPATAM (Bay of Bengal, India) had an HEIC factory from 1611 and a French EIC one from 1669. The French took the city in 1746; the British captured it in 1758 and annexed it in 1759.

MASULIPATAM, T. (1768) The British conceded Balaghat to Hyderabad.

MA-TABELE, a branch of the Zulus, found in 1835 by D'Urban's representative Dr A. Smith, under their King Msilikazi (?-1867) just north of the R. Vaal. They signed a treaty (1836) but Voortrekers under Potgieter and Uys coming from the S.W. invaded their area and defeated them without loss on the R. Marico (Nov. 1837). The Matabele then moved north across the R. Limpopo, conquered the Mashonas and settled in (modern) Matabeleland. They remained undisturbed until the discovery of gold at Tati (1867) which the Transvaalers tried to annex. In 1885 in connection with the activities of Cecil Rhodes and the British South African Co, a Protectorate was proclaimed over the neighbouring Bechuanaland (Botswana) and prospectors began asking K. Lo Bengula (r. 1867-94) for concessions. A first treaty was signed with Piet Grobler on behalf of the Transvaal (July 1887). Then Lo Bengula agreed with J. S. Moffat on behalf of the British Govt. not to cede land without British consent (Feb. 1888). Rhodes negotiated the Rudd concession in Oct. 1888 and then promoted the Cape-Cairo railway project. This would have to cross Matabeleland but meanwhile his company was in financial difficulties and needed to show prospects by 1894. Border incidents were provoked in July 1893 and a mixed force of volunteers and Bechuanaland police with machine guns overthrew the Matabele army and seized Bulawayo. Lo Bengula died. After the failure of the Jameson Raid (Dec. 1895) the Matabele and the Mashonas rose (June 1896), mainly driven by the seizure of gold bearing, but fertile land. Unable to reduce them in the Matopo Hills, Rhodes himself settled the trouble direct with the Chiefs. See RHODESIA, SOUTHERN.

MATCHES. Sulphur matches were invented at Stockton in 1827. Phosphorous matches came from Germany in 1833.

MATCH GIRLS PROTEST (1871) was a march from Bryant and May's match factory to Westminster against a proposed (but already rejected) tax on matches. Apart from shaking the credit of the first Gladstone Govt., it set an early precedent for women's agitations. In 1888 a strike at Bryant and May's secured recognition of the union and better pay. See BESANT, ANNIE.

MATERIALISM, DIALECTICAL AND HISTORICAL. See MARXISM-1.

MATHER (1) Richard (1596-1669) a puritan divine, migrated from Lancashire to Massachusetts in 1635 and as pastor at Dorchester was the main founder of New England Congregationalism. His son **(2) Increase (1639-1723),** pastor at Boston (Mass.) from 1664, was elected Pres. of Harvard in 1684. He was the first 'American' diplomat; at the English revolution of 1688 he represented Massachusetts in London and obtained the replacement of Governor Andros by Phipps, and a new charter. He retired from Harvard in 1701. His son **(3) Cotton (1663-1728)** a learned and temperamental person, also pastor at Boston, on failing to obtain the Presidency of Harvard, supported the foundation of Yale. He published the first account of plant hybridisation in 1716, and gained credence for smallpox inoculation, against mob prejudice, in 1721 but shared the contemporary New England belief in witchcraft.

MATHIESON CLAN. See CLANS, SCOTTISH.

MATILDA, EMPRESS (1102-67) d. of K. Henry I and Matilda of Scots, was betrothed as a child to Henry V of Germany in 1110, went to Germany to be educated and was crowned as his Queen. The marriage followed in 1114. It was childless, but henceforth she was at the summit of the European social world until he died in 1125.

(2) Her elder brother William had drowned in 1120 and, widowed, she was now her father's only surviving legitimate child. In Jan. 1127 Henry secured the assent of the English magnates to her succession if he died without a male heir, but later in the year, in order to deny an Angevin alliance to his nephew and rival William the Clito, he married her off to Geoffrey, eldest son of the Count of Anjou. Geoffrey was much younger than she and much beneath her in rank. This fateful step was (as it happened) rendered unnecessary by the death of the Clito. The Angevin court harboured a number of supplanted English and Norman barons and this naturally made the prospect of Matilda's succession unwelcome to their supplanters. Their dislike hardened during quarrels between her and her husband in 1129-31 and between the couple and the King just before his death in 1135. This hindered her natural adherents, especially her half-brother Robert of Gloucester, from ensuring her succession against a majority of the magnates, who decided to disregard their oath of 1127 (renewed in 1131 and 1133) on the reasonable ground that her marriage had discharged them. Moreover, it was alleged that the late King had designated Stephen, upon whom, accordingly the barons' choice fell.

(3) In the ensuing civil war, Matilda and Geoffrey initially campaigned in Normandy but were hampered, she by pregnancy, he by a wound. An effort to get support from Pope Innocent II failed, for Stephen was in possession of England, and his agents asserted her illegitimacy (see MATILDA 1090-1118). In 1139 however, Stephen was faced by a series of revolts in England from her supporters and other opportunists. She landed in Sept. and was foolishly allowed to join Robert of Gloucester. Negotiations during 1140 failed but Stephen's capture at Lincoln suddenly (Feb. 1141) brought her in sight of success and the submission of most of her opponents including Stephen's brother Henry of Blois and other bishops.

(4) Her success was precarious. The baronage was divided in its pursuit of rival expectations and claims so that a smooth transfer of power was unlikely. At Winchester she had been recognised as *domina* (Lady) and in June she proceeded to London, possibly for coronation. It is not now, and perhaps was not then clear if she meant to rule in her own right, or on behalf of her eight-year old son Henry. An arrogant termagant, harsh with opponents and ungenerous with supporters, she rejected, contrary to her promise, Henry of Blois' advice on episcopal elections, and denied to his nephew the lands which his father Stephen had held in his own right. He joyfully withdrew his support when the *domina* was driven from London at the end of June. In the ensuing war, fought mostly in and near Winchester, Robert of Gloucester was captured and she had to free Stephen in exchange (Nov.).

(5) In the consequent protraction of the civil war, Matilda suffered further setbacks in England while Geoffrey was increasingly successful in Normandy, but when Stephen besieged her at Oxford in the winter of 1142, she had to escape over the ice to Wallingford. The war was now continued indecisively until she left England in 1147 to rejoin Geoffrey in Normandy. Her able son Henry took over the Duchy in 1150 and succeeded to Anjou when his father died in 1151. He effectively replaced her as leader of the opposition to Stephen until his own succession was agreed in 1153.

(6) Matilda spent the rest of her life in Normandy and in her later years was improbably credited with a moderating influence on her son. On her deathbed she reinsured her misspent life by taking the customary veil, and was buried at Bec.

MATILDA (?-1083) d. of Baldwin V of Flanders, was forbidden by the Council of Rheims (1049) to marry William the Conqueror but married him in 1053. They received *ex post facto* dispensations from Nicholas II in 1059 on condition that they built the two great abbeys at Caen. She superintended Norman affairs during William's many absences and he remained faithful to her all her life.

MATILDA (1090-1118), though daughter of St. Margaret, Q. of Scots, was brought up in Romsey or Wilton nunnery and spent little of her life in Scotland. In 1160 she married Henry I after Abp. Anselm had assured himself that she had taken no conventual vows. This assurance was important later, because K. Stephen's adherents alleged that her daughter, the Empress Matilda, was illegitimate. She also bore Henry a son, William, who was drowned in the White Ship in 1120. She was a woman of some piety and as her correspondence shows, learning. She founded a hospital and a house of regular canons in London, besides adding to the endowments of existing foundations.

MATILDA of BOULOGNE (?1103-52) *d.* of Eustace III of Boulogne married Stephen of Blois before 1125 and was one of his ablest partisans in the Civil War ensuing on his seizure of the throne in 1135. She negotiated for him with Scotland in 1139 and with France in 1140. In 1141 she won over London for him and then rescued him from the Empress Matilda's besieging army at Winchester.

MATTHEW, Theobald (1790-1856) Irish R. Catholic priest and from 1838 highly successful temperance agitator.

MATTHEWS BIBLE. *See* BIBLE.

MATTHEWS, Thomas (1676-1751) after a minor naval career became the C-in-C Mediterranean and Minister to the Italian states in 1742. While blockading Toulon he was frustrated in his efforts to defeat the enemy fleet by the insubordination of some of his officers. He was subsequently the victim of a political court marshal and in 1747 dismissed.

MAUD, MAHALDA, MAHAUT or MOLD were alternative mediaeval versions of the name Matilda.

MAUDE, Sir Frederick Stanley (1864-1917) was Military Secretary to the Governor General of Canada from 1901-05 and after staff appointments commanded 13th Division at Gallipoli in 1915; he then took command in Mesopotamia, where he restored the position after the surrender at Kut el Amara. He took Baghdad and died of cholera.

MAUDLING, Reginald (1917-79) Tory MP from 1950 to 1972, was Pres. of the Board of Trade (1959-61) and Colonial Sec. (1961-2) under Macmillan and then Ch. of the Exchequer. He tried to check rising unemployment by tax reductions on income and potential investment, but in 1964 balance of payments deficits frustrated the policy, and this led to the return of Labour under Harold Wilson after a general election. In 1965 he was defeated for the Tory leadership by Edward Heath under whom he was Home Sec. from 1970 to 1972, but then left public life after unsubstantiated charges that he had accepted a bribe from an architect.

MAUDSLAY. Engineering family **(1) Henry (1771-1831)** invented the carriage lathe in 1797 and various screw cutting machines and improved existing marine engines. His son **(2) Thomas Henry (1792-1864)** carried on the business and built naval marine engines for over 25 years. His brother **(3) Joseph (1801-61)** built the first engines for a naval steamer.

MAUGHAM (1) Robert (?-1862) originated and formed in 1831 the Law Society, of which he was the first Secretary. He also owned and edited the *Legal Observer* and promoted the Attorneys Act, 1843, and the Solicitors Act, 1860. His grandson **(2) Frederick Herbert (1866-1958) 1st Vist. MAUGHAM,** mathematician and chancery barrister, became Q.C. in 1913, a High Court judge in 1928 and a Lord Justice of Appeal in 1934. Though he had no political experience he was offered and accepted the Woolsack in 1938 but on the outbreak of war gave way willingly to Ld. Caldecote and became until 1941 a Lord of Appeal in Ordinary. During his short period as Lord Chancellor, he played an important part in the passage of the Coal, and the Law of Evidence, Bills. In 1951 he wrote *U.N.O. and War Crimes* which challenged the view that the Charter of Nuremberg was founded in

international law. His brother **(4) William Somerset (1874-1965)** was the celebrated novelist and essayist.

MAUGHOLD. *See* MAN. I. OF-1.

MAULE. Scots royalist and Jacobite family **(1) Patrick (?-1661) 1st E. of PANMURE (1646)** tried to reconcile Charles I with the Covenanters. His grandson **(2) James (1659-1723) 4th E.** was a councillor to James II in 1686-7 and proclaimed the Old Pretender at Brechin in 1715. He and his brother **(3) Harry (?-1734)** fought at Sheriffmuire where James was captured and Harry rescued him. They both escaped abroad and James estates were forfeited in 1716. He refused to accept them as the price of swearing allegiance and died in Paris. An indirect Kinsman **(4) Fox (1801-74) 2nd Ld. PANMURE (of a U.K. creation) 11th E. of DALHOUSIE (1860)** was an M.P. from 1835 to 1852 and Sec. at War 1846-52 and 1855-8. As such he bore some responsibility for the poor contempory state of the army.

MAULE, Sir William Henry (1788-1858) a Senior Wrangler at Cambridge, refused the Haileybury Professorship of Mathematics while a pupil at the Bar and became a leading commercial lawyer. Witty and satirical, he held a poor opinion of the judges and as a judge himself, lit the fuse which led to the creation of the Divorce Court by explaining to a poverty stricken prisoner the steps which he should have taken at a cost of £1,000 ('but the Law knows no distinction of rich and poor'), to avoid a charge of bigamy, and then sentencing him to one day's imprisonment.

MAULÉON. *See* SAVARY.

MAU MAU. *See* KENYA.

MAUNDY THURSDAY the day before Good Friday was the day when, in commemoration of Christ's action, English Kings washed the feet of 12 poor men, and gave food and clothing to as many poor men and women as their own age. Charles II added specially minted silver coins (Maundy Money). William III delegated the foot washing to the Lord High Almoner, who ceased to perform it in 1750. Money was substituted for the food and clothing in 1833. Maundy money is still minted.

MAURICE AFFAIR (1916) General Maurice was Director of Military Operations when Lloyd George was under parliamentary attack for the gloomy situation on the Western Front in the Spring 1916. In a letter to *The Times*, he wrote that the figures which Lloyd George had quoted for British troops in France had been padded. Asquith pressed his attack to the vote, but Lloyd George showed that his figures had actually come from Gen. Maurice's office.

MAURICE, Prince. *See* PALATINE PRINCES.

MAURITIUS (1518-1710, 1810 onward) or ILE de FRANCE (1715-1810) (Indian Ocean) was discovered by the Portuguese in 1507 but colonised by the Dutch in 1598. They abandoned it in 1710. The French came in 1715. In the Napoleonic Wars it was a base for French corsairs (notably Robert Surcouf) who raided the HEIC's communications between India and Britain. Consequently it was seized by the British in 1810. Their possession was recognised at the T. of Paris (1814) but the island remained French speaking. It became independent within the Commonwealth in 1968. *See also* MADAGASCAR.

MAUROIS, André (pseud. of Emile Herzog) (1885-1967) French writer attached as liaison officer during World War I to the British for whom he conceived an affectionate understanding which appears in his French and English works.

MAURITANIA. *See* AFRICA, WEST (EX-FRENCH).

MAUTRAVERS or MALTRAVERS family had wide lands in Dorset, Gloucestershire, Somerset and Wiltshire under William I, but all held of mesne lords. They served in various high ranking capacities without rising much in rank until **(1) John (?1290-1364) 1st Ld. (1330)** a supporter of Thomas E. of Lancaster was involved in his defeat at Boroughbridge (1322), escaped overseas and returned with Q. Isabel and Roger Mortimer. He and Thomas of Berkeley had custody of the deposed Edward II, and Mautravers was responsible for his murder and the manner of it. He was well rewarded with properties, and called to Parliament. Outlawed on Mortimer's fall, however, he lived obscurely in Germany. In 1334 he made his peace with Edward III, on whose behalf he acted in negotiations with Jacob van Artevelde. His outlawry was annulled in 1351. By the marriage of his granddaughter **(2) Eleanor (?-1404)** to Richard Fitzalan, E. of Arundel the barony passed to the Fitzalans and ultimately to the Howards.

MAXIM. *See* MACHINE GUN.

MAXIMUS, MAGNUS. *See* BRITAIN, ROMAN-25.

MAX MÜLLER, Friedrich (1823-1900) of Dessau settled in England in 1846 and was commissioned by the HEIC to bring out an edition of the Sanskrit *Rigveda*. He taught modern European languages at Oxford from 1850, becoming Professor in 1854 and Professor of Comparative Philology from 1863. His writings were influential in many fields including ancient oriental languages, comparative mythology and philology, philosophy and biography. He was widely honoured both abroad and in Britain, even becoming a privy councillor.

MAXTON, James (1885-1946) pacifist schoolteacher and member of the Independent Labour Party was imprisoned in 1916 for inciting a strike or mutiny among munition workers. He became M.P. for Bridgeton, Glasgow in 1922 and Chairman of the I.L.P. in 1926. He published a study of Lenin in 1932. His views were founded upon a widely recognised compassion which, together with his winning charm, made him personally the most popular member among M.P.s themselves.

MAY COMMITTEE. *See* MACMILLAN AND MAY COMMITTEES.

MAY, Sir Thomas Erskine (1815-86) 1st Ld. FARNBOROUGH (1886) entered the service of the House of Commons in 1831 and was Clerk from 1871-76. From 1866-84 he was Pres. of the Statute Law Revision Committee. His book, now simply known as *Erskine May* has in successive editions ever since been the standard authority on Parliamentary law and procedure.

MAY DAY was formerly celebrated with customs descending from ancient Celtic rites including the decoration of houses with branches, the crowning of a May Queen at sunrise and maypole dancing. There were permanent maypoles in London streets. The festivities, denounced as idolatrous and immoral, were stopped in 1644 by the Puritans, revived in 1661 but slowly disappeared. *See* LABOUR DAY.

MAYFAIR (London) had a May fair from Charles II's time. This was gradually superseded by the permanent Shepherd Market built at the time (c. 1730) when the area was filling up with fashionable residences. It was also notorious for 'Mayfair marriages' of abducted heiresses celebrated by the Rev. William Keith until his imprisonment in 1743.

MAYFLOWER. *See* MASSACHUSETTS.

MAYNOOTH COLLEGE (Ir.) a R. Catholic training college established by Irish Act of Parliament in 1795. *See* PEEL'S SECOND GOVT-5.

MAYO (Ireland) sparsely inhabited cattle raising county, anciently dominated by monasteries. In the 19th cent. the population had grown to more than the land would support, and the slump of the '60s impoverished the tenants, who suffered wholesale evictions for failure to pay their rent. They flocked to Michael Davitt's Mayo Land League in self protection and his success in Mayo caused him to convert the Land League into a national body.

MAYOR (*cf* major) of uncertain origin, this is one of the words which denote the leader, headman or primary notable of a group with a public status. The Merovingian mayor of the palace was chamberlain, then chief minister and finally ruler of the state. The mayor of the Staple,

especially at Calais, was a powerful public officer elected by the Staple to regulate the trades in which the Staple dealt. The mayor of a corporation was the head of the municipality. He acted as its chairman; represented it on public occasions and often (especially but not only in London) held his own civil and sometimes criminal court. Since 1974 the title is conferred by charter upon the chairman of district councils, and by resolution on the chairman of Parish and Community Councils.

MAYORS COURT (at Yeovil). *See* COURT OF RECORD, BOROUGH.

MAZZINI, Giuseppe (1805-72) conspiratorial Italian republican was exiled from Savoy in 1830. He lived in Marseilles until 1848 writing and preaching Italian unity and republicanism. After the suppression of the 1848 revolts, he continued his overrated activities in London until 1859. Thereafter he pursued them in Italy.

MBOYA, Thomas Joseph (1930-69) a Luo leader in Kenya but initially tolerant of the rival Kikuyu Mau Mau rebellion, he was Secretary of the Kenya Federation of Labour. He was elected to the Legislative Council in 1957 in opposition to British policy but was eclipsed when Jomo Kenyatta (the leader of the Mau Mau) was released from prison in 1961. He was Minister of Justice in 1963, then for Constitutional Affairs and finally for Economic Development from 1964, all under Kenyatta. He was murdered, just before Kenya was declared a KANU (predominantly Kikuyu) one-party state.

McADAM, John Loudon. *See* TRANSPORT AND COMMUNICATIONS (BRITAIN).

M'CARTHY, Justin (1830-1912) a journalist was M.P. for Co. Longford in 1879 and for Londonderry in 1886. In 1890 he became Chairman of the Anti-Parnellite Nationalists. In 1892 he became M.P. for N. Longford. He lost the chairmanship in 1896 and his seat in 1900.

McAULEY, Catherine (1787-1841) founded the later internationally famous R. Catholic Sisters of Mercy at Dublin in 1827.

McCANN AFFAIR (Ir. 1911). Owing to alleged clerical pressure a Mr McCann, a Roman Catholic, deserted his protestant wife and made no provision for her or the children. The papal bull *Ne Temere* (Lat = Do not, defiantly) had just pronounced mixed marriages void unless previously dispensed. The affair, much discussed in Parliament, increased the determination of anti-Home Rulers, who feared that an Irish Parliament might enact laws based on *Ne Temere*.

McCAUGHEY, Sir Samuel (1835-1919) built up a huge N.S.W. sheep breeding business after 1860 and greatly improved the merino breeds.

M.C.C. *See* CRICKET.

McGRATH. *See* NEWFOUNDLAND.

McGILL UNIVERSITY (Montreal, Can.) is named after James McGill (1744-1813) who left money to endow a university. A charter was obtained in 1821 but the University did not prosper until about 1850.

McILWRAITH, Sir Thomas (1835-1900) migrated to Victoria in 1854, became a Queensland sheep farmer and entered the legislative assembly in 1869. He was Premier from 1079-83 and annexed New Guinea in 1883. He was again Premier in 1888 and 1893 when he returned to England.

McKENNA DUTIES were World War I taxes introduced by Reginald McKenna at 33.3% on so-called luxury goods such as motor cars and clocks, in order to save shipping. The Labour Philip Snowden abolished them only in 1931 but Winston Churchill restored them in 1932 to finance the extended contributory old age pension scheme.

McKENNA, Reginald (1863-1943) educated in France, at Cambridge and at the Bar was Liberal M.P. for N. Monmouthshire (1895-1918). He was First Secretary to the Treasury (1905-7), President of the Board of Education (1907-8) and then First Ld. of the Admiralty (1908-11) at the height of the naval race with Germany. He determinedly supported the Admirals in cabinet but deferred to the strong-minded Fisher in his aversion for a naval staff, and on the Army's proposals for sending six divisions to France on the outbreak of war. Asquith resolved the conflict by exchanging him with Churchill. As Home Secretary (1911-15) he had to deal with Suffragettism (*see* CAT AND MOUSE ACT). He was Chancellor of the Exchequer (1915-16) and to finance the war raised income tax, imposed a heavy excess-profits tax and prepared to let the National Debt rise to a limit set only by the govt.'s ability to pay the interest plus a small sinking fund contribution. As a Liberal he opposed govt. interventions and conscription. There was no place for such a man under Lloyd George, and he became chairman of the Midland Bank (1919-43). In 1922 he was offered the Chancellorship of the Exchequer, refused, but accepted in 1923, but could not find the necessary Parliamentary seat.

McKINLEY, William (1843-1901) 25th (Republican) Pres. of U.S.A. (1897-1901) was a representative of American extremist capitalism. In 1890 he had sponsored the McKinley Tariff Act to foster American products, regardless of consequences, by bounties and prohibitory tariffs, while allowing economic penetration of other American countries through reciprocal agreements. It caused the collapse of the Hawaiian sugar industry and led directly to the coup which brought about Hawaiian annexation. As Pres. he was pushed into the Spanish War by press hysteria and demanded and got the Philippines and the control of Cuba as a result. He also authorised the Open Door Policy towards China. He was assassinated.

MEADE (1) Richard Charles, 3rd E. of CLANWILLIAM (Ir. 1805) Ld. CLANWILLIAM (U.K. 1828) was Castlereagh's assistant in Vienna in 1814, his private secretary from 1817-19. U/Sec. of State at the Foreign Office and with Wellington in Verona in 1822 and then Minister to Berlin until 1827. His son **(2) Sir Robert Henry (1835-98)** entered the Foreign Office in 1859, accompanied the P. of Wales to Palestine in 1861 and became his Groom of the Bedchamber in 1862. From 1864-68 he was Granville's Private Secretary and in 1868 he went to the Colonial Office where he was Assistant U/Sec. of State from 1871-92 and Permanent U/Sec. until 1896. As such he had a considerable influence in the development of late Victorian colonial policy.

MEADOWS (1) Sir Philip (1626-1718) became Cromwell's Latin sec. in relief of Milton in 1653. He went as negotiator to Lisbon in 1656, then to Denmark for the T. of Roskilde in 1658 and finally as Ambassador to Sweden. He published a book on the Danish-Swedish wars in 1675 and another on marine jurisdiction in 1689. He was employed as a commissioner of public accounts in 1692 and thereafter at the Board of Trade. His son **(2) Sir Philip (?-1757)** Knight Marshal in 1700 was minister to Holland in 1706 and to the Emperor in 1707.

MEAL TUB PLOT. *See* DANGERFIELD, THOMAS.

MEANS TEST to determine the proper amount of transitional unemployment benefit by reference to the applicant's means, was introduced in 1931. In 1934 the basis of the test was changed to the means of his household as a result of pressure from the TUC. The system was replaced by the National Insurance Act, 1946, and the provision of many services out of taxation rendered the issue less important.

MEASLES. Anciently confused with smallpox and sometimes with leprosy, was sometimes fatal among European children but not on a disastrous scale, because, the disease being endemic, Europeans developed resistance to it. It was otherwise in countries to which they brought it for the first time. In particular, outbreaks devastated Spanish America in the years 1529-31, carried off most of the Maoris of New Zealand South I. in 1834-6 and of North I. in 1854 and in 1874 killed 20% of the population of Fiji. *See* EPIDEMICS, HUMAN.

MEATH (Ir.). (The Middle) was the territory of the High Kings of Ireland whose seat was at Tara. It consisted of the present counties of Meath, Westmeath with parts of Longford and Cavan. The county came into existence as an earldom conferred in 1172 upon Hugh de Lacy, who fortified Trim and Kells, and created a number of baronies which collectively with his demesne defined the county on a somewhat smaller scale. This area remained within the Pale throughout the latter's history, and so was always under English rule.

MEATH ELECTION (1892). In the 1892 general election violence and clerical intimidation of Parnellites were rampant in Ireland. Michael Davitt and his colleague Fullam were unseated on an election petition in which the judge, O'Brien, J., a devout R. Catholic said that "the Church became converted for the time being into a vast political agency, a great moral machine moving ... to a single will in a certain way".

MEAUX, T. of (1229) between Blanche of Castile as regent of France and Raymond VII of Toulouse. He kept Toulouse and Albi, but ceded the eastern half of his county to the French crown, and Agenais, Rouergue and Quercy as a dowry for his only child on marriage with Louis IX's brother Alphonse. On failures of direct heirs, the lands were to pass to the French crown. The treaty settled the eventual end of Toulouse as an autonomous power.

MECHANICS INSTITUTES. John Anderson started evening classes at Glasgow in 1760 and left property to endow Anderson's Institution there. George Birkbeck, Professor of Science there, invited his instrument mechanics to his lectures. In 1823 there was a dispute with Anderson's Institution and the mechanics set up on their own. Birkbeck, in London since 1804, with Brougham and Francis Place opened the London Mechanics Institute in 1824. By 1860 there were 610 institutes with about 100,000 members, but as a result of inadequate teaching methods, they were changing into recreational and social bodies.

MEDALS (MEDALLIONS) were struck by Roman rulers, and the idea was revived in Italy in the 15th cent. where one of the earliest commemorated the Council of Florence (1439). The French began to strike them c. 1451, the Germans in 1453 and Spaniards in 1503 and the Danes in 1516. The earliest known English medal portrayed Henry VIII's supremacy over the church (1545). Coronation medals have been struck ever since Edward VI and also medals for great, or at least public events such as the Armada, the appointment of James D. of York as Lord High Admiral, and the B. of Waterloo.

MEDESHAMSTEDE. *See* PETERBOROUGH.

MEDICAL COUNCIL, GENERAL was set up by statute in 1858 to maintain a *Medical Register* of qualified practitioners. Its power to strike names off the register for infamous conduct in a professional respect has made it the controlling professional medical organisation. Members are appointed by the crown, medical faculties and corporations and the profession as a whole. The Medical Act, 1950, transferred its disciplinary powers to a committee of the council, and created a right of appeal to the Privy Council. The Council also maintains the *British Pharmacopoeia*.

MEDICAL OFFICERS OF HEALTH (M.O.H.), originated in London where a Metropolitan Association of M.O.H.s was founded in 1856. The Society of M.O.H.s was founded in succession in 1873 and its advice helped to form the Public Health Act 1875, which, in its turn greatly increased the numbers of M.O.H.s. As the most effectual practitioners of preventive medicine, their influence has been incalculable.

MEDICI family, connected with the lesser (popular) Florentine guilds, sprang into prominence with the international banking activities of **Giovanni (1360-1429)** who made fortunes financing govts. represented at the

Council of Constance (1414-18). His son **Cosimo the Elder (1389-1464)** revolutionised the city in 1434. He was the famous patron of Brunnelleschi, Donatello, Ghiberti and Della Robbia. He persuaded the church council for reunification to be held at Florence (1439-44) and made yet another fortune. He also attracted and patronised Byzantine refugees and scholars. His grandson **Lorenzo the Magnificent (r. 1449-92)** ruled the City with an iron (but polite) manner and meanwhile trained his second son **Giovanni (Pope Leo X r. 1513-21)** and his nephew **Giulio (Pope Clement VII r. 1523-34)** because the domination of Rome was the mainstay of his politics. He too patronised famous artists (e.g. Michelangelo) and revived the languishing literary Italian. Leo X put Lorenzo's grandson, another Lorenzo in possession of Urbino and it was the latter's daughter **Catherine (1519-89)** who married Henry II of France. She brought Italian culture to Paris, and was at the storm centre of the Wars of Religion. (*See* COOKERY: HUGUENOTS.)

The legitimate line of Cosimo the Elder meanwhile died out and the line of **Lorenzo (1395-1440)**, his younger brother, came forward. There had been a series of confused and violent interregna ended by **Cosimo I (r. 1537-74)** the first Grand Duke of Tuscany, who massacred his political rivals and subdued neighbouring small states by violence. The Medici political character had changed from that of educators of the world to that of petty local politicians, but the family prestige was still good for another royal marriage **Francesco's (r. 1574-87)** daughter **Marie (?-1642)** married Henry VI of France. His brother, the unconsecrated **Cardinal Ferdinand I (1587-1609)** built the Villa Medici in Rome. He also reverted some way to the more lucrative and civilised habits of his house. He revived trade, tolerated foreign and even heretic banks and capitalists, built the free port of Leghorn (*see* DUDLEY-7) and developed, in the Order of St. Stephen, a sort of sea police. Protestant, especially English, traders congregated at Leghorn which became a mart for northern commerce threatening to circumvent Venice. This ceased at his death, when Tuscany became a stagnant area ruled with deepening incompetence and intolerance by Ferdinand's mother and wife as Regents for **Ferdinand II (r. 1609-70)** then by him in person and then by his son **Cosimo III (r. 1670-1723)** and grandson, the spectacularly drunk **Gian Gastone (r. 1723-37)**. At his death Tuscany passed to the House of Lorraine.

MEDINA DEL CAMPO, T. of. *See* HENRY VII-6,15.

MEDINA SIDONIA. *See* ARMADAS-1.

MEDITERRANEAN AGREEMENTS (1887) were undertakings based on exchanges of notes between Britain, Italy and Austro-Hungary: **(1) (Feb.-Mar.)** to maintain the Mediterranean, Adriatic and Aegean *status quo* with Britain and Italy co-operating diplomatically as to their respective ambitions in Egypt and Tripoli; **(2) (Dec.)** to maintain peace and the *status quo* in the Near East and especially freedom of the Straits, Turkish authority in Asia Minor and her suzerainty over Bulgaria. The first was aimed at France, the second, which was secret and unworkable without French neutrality, at Russia.

MEDITERRANEAN WAR (Oct. 1797-Mar. 1799) (*see* FRANCO-AUSTRIAN WAR). **(1)** Admiral Duncan frustrated a second French attempt, to be convoyed by the Dutch, on Ireland, by his great victory at Camperdown (Oct. 1797) and in Dec. a sham peace conference was opened at Rastadt. In Jan. the Dutch set up a Directory on the French model. In Feb. the French engineered a revolution in Rome. In Mar. they annexed all the territories to the left of the Rhine. Their preparations against Britain were on a spectacular scale but they were intended to cover their true objective which was Bonaparte's attempt upon Egypt.

(2) Apart from Egypt's own economic value, the project had at least two other purposes, namely the dismemberment of the Ottoman Empire, then thought to be further advanced in decay than it actually was and the control of a short route to India for the sustenance of Britain's enemies there. The expedition left Toulon in May 1798 and seized Malta by a mixture of subversion and blackmail. A garrison was established and the fleet disappeared (loaded with loot) into the open. Jervis, now E. St. Vincent, from his H.Q. at Gibraltar sent Nelson into the Mediterranean to destroy it. There was reason to think it might be part of another Irish expedition or of an attack on Naples. Elimination eventually showed whither it had gone. The troops had already landed at Alexandria when Nelson found Admiral Bruey's squadron in Aboukir Bay (The B. of the Nile) and destroyed it (Aug. 1798). With Bonaparte now isolated in Egypt, the Ottoman Sultan screwed up courage to declare war (Sept.). More important, the British now had a permanent presence in the Mediterranean. They invested Valletta and took Minorca (Nov.) Their allies took heart. The Austrians began to mobilise: the Neapolitans, against Austrian advice, prematurely attacked the Roman Republic and were chased out by the French in Dec.

(3) In Feb. 1799 Bonaparte, having overthrown the Mameluke Govt. of Egypt, set out to conquer the Ottoman Empire. He came up at Acre against a determined Turkish resistance under Djezzar Pasha, Governor of Syria supported by a small squadron under the conceited but brilliant Sir Sydney Smith. In Mar. Austria re-entered the war, and inflicted a sharp reverse on the French at Stockach, and by May, Acre had been relieved and Bonaparte had retreated to Egypt. *See* SECOND COALITION, WAR OF 1799-1807.

MEDMENHAM. *See* DASHWOOD.

MEDWAY LETTER (1948) settled the liability of landowners to pay drainage rates on the basis that those who benefited from the protection should pay for it.

MEDWAY R. (Kent) is the boundary between Men of Kent (to the east) and Kentish men (to the west) and (with some departures) of the bishoprics of Canterbury and Rochester. *See* DUTCH WARS, 17TH CENT. THIRD; TRANSPORT AND COMMUNICATIONS.

MEERUT. *See* INDIAN MUTINY.

MEHEMET ALI (1769-1849). *See* EGYPT-4 TO 8; TURKEY.

MEIGHEN, Arthur. *See* CANADA-27.

MELANCHTHON (or SCHWARTZERD) Philipp (1497-1560) whose mother was the niece of Johannes Reuchlin (1455-1522) the humanist, became Professor of Greek at Wittenberg in 1518 when he met Luther and through him became a major figure of the Reformation. In 1521 the leadership was forced upon him while Luther was in confinement; his *Loci Communes* (Lat = Common Positions) of that period represents the first systematic statement of Reformation doctrine. He next wrote a translation and commentary on the Bible. He opposed the Zwinglians at the Marburg Colloquy. He was a conciliatory personality at the Diet of Augsburg in 1530 and was mainly responsible for the Augsburg Confession. As late as 1537 he was ready to accept a reformed Papacy. His generally peaceful habit of mind was in public affairs overborne by the follies of statesmen and fanatics, but in the field of learning he left a lasting mark for he taught that archaeology and history were necessary to an understanding of scripture, and his commentaries and textbooks were used in universities well into 18th cent.

MELBOURNE (Victoria) first settled by John Batman and Pascoe Fawkner, Tasmanian sheep farmers in 1835, became a bishopric in 1847 and expanded rapidly with the gold rush to Ballarat and Bendigo. In July 1851 Victoria was separated from N.S.W. and Melbourne became its capital. The University was founded in 1853 and the Parliament permanently established there in 1856. The port was now flourishing. The cattle and sheep raising hinterland created a market, and varied food, leather and wool processing industries as well as trades connected with building created employment. A mint, to reduce gold exports, was opened in 1872 and became the exclusive Commonwealth mint when that at Sydney closed in 1926. Two further universities, Monash (1958) and Latrobe (1967) were founded and by 1970 the population just exceeded 2M.

MELBOURNE (1) (Henry) William Lamb (1779-1848) 2nd Vist. (1829), a courtly aesthete as well as politician, as William LAMB, a Foxite Whig, was an M.P. from 1806 to 1812 and from 1816 to 1829. He was Chief Sec. for Ireland under Canning and Wellington, and then Home Sec. under Grey in 1830, and in 1834 reluctantly prime minister. He wanted to take in Lord John Russell as Ch. of the Exch. but when the King objected he happily resigned (Dec. 1834) but returned within a few months. Though a whig, he resisted Chartist popularism and the anti-Corn Law agitation. He was unsuccessfully cited in matrimonial proceedings by George Norton, husband of Caroline Norton, the novelist, in 1837. He was still prime minister at the accession of Q. Victoria who liked and admired him, and he remained in office until defeated in 1841. In 1842 he had a stroke and retired. He had in 1801 married **(2) Caroline (1785-1828)** *d.* of the 3rd E. of Bessborough, known as **Lady Caroline LAMB.** A spoiled darling, she became publicly infatuated with Lord Byron in 1812 but he ejected her in 1813 and thereafter she remained in a furiously delicate state, writing novels, of which the first, *Glenarvon* (1816, later called *The Fatal Passion*) was a revenge on Byron. Her social eccentricities resulted in a judicial separation from Melbourne in 1825. Her husband's brother **(3) Frederick James Lamb (1782-1853) Ld. BEAUVALE (1839) 3rd Vist.,** a diplomat from 1811, was head of missions in Munich (1815-20), Madrid (1825-7), Lisbon (1827-31) and finally to Vienna (1831-41).

MELBOURNE'S FIRST GOVT. (July-Nov. 1834) (16 in cabinet under Vist. Melbourne). This mainly whig Govt., succeeded that of Grey during an Irish crisis and included eight of his ministers. Palmerston continued at the Foreign Office. Melbourne had accepted office on condition that Althorpe should lead the Commons. Althorpe succeeded to the Spencer earldom in Nov. 1834 and Melbourne offered to resign or have Ld. John Russell (Paymaster Gen.) as Leader of the House. William IV disliked Russell and accepted the resignation.

MELBOURNE'S SECOND GOVT. (Apr. 1835-Sept. 1841). 13 in cabinet. Cottenham was Lord Chancellor from Jan. 1836. Ld. John Russell was Home Secretary; Palmerston Foreign Secretary.

(1) This Whig govt. took power after the Tamworth manifesto had failed to convert the electors to the new Conservatism, and as a result of the Lichfield House Compact. Internationally there was a lull; the Govt. could begin by concentrating on home affairs. It carried the Municipal Corporations Act 1835 which in a political sense, complemented the Reform Act 1832, and also revolutionised the constitution and purpose of town authorities. This long term measure had few immediate effects but there were pressing problems, namely, as before, the Irish in and out of Parliament, and the rise of Chartism encouraged by the reduction of the newspaper tax in 1836.

(2) As Chartism seemed to threaten the aristocratic Whigs and the new Reform Act electorate alike, the Whigs, despite their radical fringe, were liable to be driven into a defensive or 'conservative' posture. The Irish demands represented a different challenge with similar results. The first encountered religious prejudices; the cost of the second would have to be defrayed by the Anglo-Irish landowners; the third would alter the Irish political balance permanently against the English. Thus the govt., truly representing ordinary English opinion, procrastinated. The tithe issue was settled only in 1838.

(3) Meanwhile in 1837, Q. Victoria succeeded to William IV. The crown's influence had been much diminished by the growth of popular ideals and practices, and by the short-comings of her two predecessors. It now passed to an unknown princess of 18. This was bound to change the relationship between politicians and the throne still further, but Melbourne's urbanity and constitutional caution ensured that changes would be painless. It disposed of the rabidly reactionary D. of Cumberland, for the Salic Law made him King of Hanover, and incidentally deprived the crown of its independent Hanoverian resources.

(4) There was renewed colonial interest. In 1836 a new colony had been founded (at Melbourne) in S. Australia. In 1837, while Papineau raised his French Canadian rebellion, Dutch Voortrekers tried to assuage their dislike of the British by escaping to ungoverned land. By 1838 Papineau had been defeated, but the Dutch had slaughtered Zulus in thousands at the Blood River (Dec.). Meanwhile in Oct. the British Indian establishment was fighting the First Afghan War (*see* AFGHANISTAN), and involving Britain in Chinese troubles, culminating (July 1840) in the Opium War and (Aug.) in the seizure of Hong Kong. Nor was this all. 1839 was the year when New Zealand was proclaimed a colony as a result of growing trader pressure for protection. Events, such as these, forced British statesmen to reconsider their traditional distrust of colonialism. The developments were mostly brought on by uncoordinated local enterprise. The difficulties created calls for help to the home govt., and considerations of prestige seemed to forbid withdrawal.

(5) The growing investment in the Far East brought Egyptian affairs again into prominence at the same time as the Belgian negotiations were concluded. The policy of supporting Turkey to prevent Russian penetration to the Mediterranean sea routes, was now threatened from the opposite direction. Syria had the ship timber, manpower and money which Egypt lacked, besides a strategic position central to any threat from the north. Mehemet Ali's armies advanced to secure it. The Turks were utterly defeated just as the strong Sultan Mahmoud II died (1839). The Egyptians soon reached central Anatolia. There now seemed to be a danger that Mehemet Ali might ally himself with Russia, or that France and Russia might agree to divide the protection of the Ottoman Empire along the frontier. Hence in July 1839 Palmerston negotiated a Quintuple Alliance with France, Russia, Austria and Prussia to settle the problems jointly, and when the French tried to negotiate privately with the Porte, he replaced it with a Quadruple Alliance which omitted them. A compromise (July 1840), giving Mehemet Ali Egypt as a hereditary possession and S. Syria for life, was forced upon him by the bombardment of Acre.

(6) These immensely important events were partly masked from domestic attention by spectacles nearer home. The People's Charter was published in 1838 and was brought to parliament with a monster petition. While economic depression led, in Sept. 1838, to the foundation of the Anti-Corn Law League, the establishment of the first Transatlantic steamship service attracted widespread attention. To this the Irish Poor Law (1838) seemed a very uninteresting thing, soon eclipsed by the new penny post (Jan. 1840) and the Queen's marriage (Feb.) to Albert of Saxe-Coburg-Gotha.

(7) In truth this useful govt. lacked political energy and eschewed panache at a time of mounting economic trouble and political excitement. In the twelve months after Jan. 1839 its composition, even, was in doubt. Seven offices changed hands: one of them twice. The govt. doggedly carried on with the business in hand. There was the Waitangi Treaty with the New Zealand Maoris (Feb. 1840); there was the Union of Upper and Lower Canada by the British America Act, 1867 in the aftermath of the Papineau affair, which was greeted with interest as perfunctory "as that accorded to a private bill to unite two or three parishes". In July 1841 the Mehemet Ali affair was tidied up with the Straits Convention. In Aug. the govt. at last passed a mutilated Irish Muncipal Corporations Act. It resigned the same month.

MELDRUM, Sir John (?-1645) a soldier administrator, was employed between 1610 and 1617 in the plantation of Ulster. He then served in the Low Countries and in the Rochelle expedition. At the beginning of the Civil War he joined the Parliament allegedly for profit. He was at the B. of Edgehill and the S. of Reading in 1642, and in 1643 relieved Hull. After other successful operations, he was forced to capitulate to P. Rupert at Newark in 1644, but by the B. of Marston Moor (Aug.) he was back in service. He was subsequently mortally wounded.

MELFORD HALL (Suffolk) Tudor mansion built for Sir Wm. Cordell, Speaker, and acquired by the Parker family in 18th cent.

MELFORT. See DRUMMOND-8.

MELLIFONT ABBEY (1142) near Drogheda (Louth, Ir.), the first Irish Cistercian foundation.

MELLITUS. See MISSIONARIES IN BRITAIN AND IRELAND-4.

MELLON, Harriot (1777-1837) socially mobile actress, played many parts at Drury Lane Theatres from 1795 to 1815 when she married the banker Thomas Coutts. When he died in 1827 she married the 9th D. of St. Albans.

MELO, Sebastian Jose de Carvalho, Count of OEIRAS (1759) and M. of POMBAL (1770) is referred to as Pombal in this work. See PORTUGAL AFTER 1640-5.

MELODRAMA, a type of early 19th cent. romantic and sensational stage play interspersed with songs and music. The musical element gradually gave way to increasingly naive emotional appeal. Melodrama, especially as a vehicle for Henry Irving's (1838-1905) declamatory talent, virtually monopolised the London stage between 1840 and 1890, reaching its highest development in such moral dramas as *The Bells, The Lyons Mail* and *The Silver King* (which has *two* black cloaked villains).

MELROSE ABBEYS (Roxburgh). Of the two **(1)** was a Celtic foundation at Old Melrose dating from c. 650 where St Cuthbert became a monk and later Abbot. Sacked by Kenneth MacAlpin in 839, it was revived but abandoned in 1070. **(2)** 2½ miles away, a Cistercian house was founded from Rievaulx, under the patronage of K. David I. It became one of the most important Scottish monasteries and inspired the early agricultural improvements in the Tweed Valley. Burned, perhaps incompletely, by the English in 1322 and 1385, it was quickly rebuilt and remained prosperous. By the 16th cent. it had become virtually a crown estate. The English burned it in 1544 and again in 1545 during the foray called 'The Rough Wooing' and this time it was not re-established. The chancel was re-used as the parish church from 1619 until 1810. The monks wrote an important **Chronicle** starting as a continuation of Bede's Ecclesiastical History. It extends to the year 1275 and includes a lengthy and favourable account of Simon de Montfort.

MELTON MOWBRAY (Leics.). This small market town became famous in the late 18th cent. as the centre of the Quorn fox hunting country and for its pork pies and cheese.

MELVILLE. See DUNDAS.

MELVILLE, Andrew (1545-1622) learned Scots extremist presbyterian taught at Poitiers but in 1568 fled, for political reasons to Geneva where Theodore Beza secured him a Professorship. In 1574 he returned to Scotland to become Principal of Glasgow University and in 1580 he moved as principal to St Mary's College St Andrews. Here he drafted the *Second Book of Discipline*. He was driven into a period of exile in England (1584-5) but returned and in 1590 added the Rectorship of the University to his principalship. A powerful teacher, his

advocacy virtually eclipsed episcopacy in Scotland and James VI and I rightly feared him. When Calvinist divines were summoned to London in 1606 he came too and was put into the Tower until 1611 while James matured his plans for restoring bishops to Scotland (1610). He was then released but refused permission to go to Scotland and became Professor at Sedan where he died.

MEMEL or KLAIPEDA (Lithuania). This port, founded in 1253 by the Teutonic Knights, was long important for its timber and fisheries. Though in E. Prussia, its hinterland was Lithuania and after that country's independence in 1918, Memel was assigned to it (subject to Polish transit rights) under the P. of Versailles, as the only available access to the Baltic, notwithstanding its German majority. It was seized in Mar. 1939 by the Germans who thus acquired an economic stranglehold on Lithuania. In 1940 Lithuania was seized by the Russians and Memel by them in 1945. It became of great importance to Lithuanians when they reaffirmed their independence in 1990.

MEMORANDUM of 1831. This was a joint document presented by the powers after the Italian revolts of Feb. 1831 proposing detailed reforms in the Papal states. Half-heartedly accepted by Gregory XVI (r. 1831-46), his failure to implement it was a direct cause of the convulsions of 1848-9.

MEMORANDA ROLLS (1199-1848) were records of letters and cases prepared by the King's Remembrancer for the barons of the Exchequer.

MENAI BRIDGES. The road bridge was built in 1826; the railway bridge in 1850 and closed by fire in 1970 and rebuilt.

MENDELANISM. Gregor Johann Mendel (1822-84) Abbot of Brünn from 1860 experimented with plant breeding in his monastery garden and founded the modern theory of genetics. His principles only won general scientific acceptance after 1900.

MENDICANT ORDERS are those whose members, like Buddhist monks, are supposed to rely for their daily living on begging. The main such orders consist of friars viz: Augustinians or Austins, Carmelites (White Friars), Dominicans (Black), Franciscans (Grey) and the Servites.

MENDOZA, Don Bernardino de. See ELIZABETH I-20.

MENINGITIS, EPIDEMIC was described among Michigan Indians in 1670. There were Irish outbreaks between 1837-50. The incidence of the disease is world wide with high infection rates in crowded conditions such as military barracks; there were severe outbreaks in World War I and II. Until the introduction of modern chemical therapy in World War II it was usually lethal, especially among the young. See EPIDEMICS, HUMAN.

MENSHEVIK. See BOLSHEVIK.

MENTEITH, Sir John of (?-after 1329) apparently a friend of Sir William Wallace was appointed Sheriff and castellan of Dumbarton by Edward I in 1304. As such he captured Wallace and delivered him to London. He was for a while English created E. of Lennox, but abandoned the dignity and in 1307 became a faithful supporter of Robert the Bruce and so remained until his death. He has suffered the execration of hindsight after the Wallace affair.

MENZIES, Sir Robert Gordon (1894-1978). See AUSTRALIA-16.

MERCANTILE MARINE, MERCHANT NAVY, though unseen by most people was of paramount importance to a trading island. **(1)** Seamen were engaged by the voyage, which under sail might be of uncertain duration, and congregated at ports to seek work. Until Henry VIII's reign there was no clear distinction between naval and merchant shipping but the King occasionally demanded merchant ships for warlike uses. Henry VIII built royal dockyards at Woolwich, Deptford and Portsmouth and established a naval and in Trinity House a pilotage organisation. If the specialist warships which began to appear could not be fully manned through the casual labour market, the shortfall was made up by impressment, even from ships at sea. Conversely royal ships might be navigated (but not commanded) by merchant officers who would return to merchant shipping. These customs remained virtually undisturbed as long as overseas wars, trade and piracy continued to expand, for there was seldom any difficulty in getting work.

(2) The 20 year long French wars till 1815 created quasi-permanent employment in the vast Royal Navy and a commensurate casual demand for distant rather than short commercial voyages. Peace suddenly threw many naval seamen onto the casual market and created a slowly realised need for regularisation. The Register of Shipping and Seamen was set up in 1835 and successive Merchant Shipping Acts defined the qualifications of officers and the ways in which ships should be manned (*see also* PLIMSOLL, SAMUEL).

(3) Until the advent of steam, merchant ships were small, the biggest (the East Indiamen) being no more than 700 tons. They had to be numerous to handle the traffic (a 1000 ships were often seen together in the Port of London in the 1840s); they were slow, so that a voyage, say to Calcutta might take six months; and being at the mercy of the weather needed considerable crews to handle the sails. Steam made the industry less labour intensive, for ships became bigger, faster and more reliable on regular routes where coaling ports were available. Officers and seamen often came to be employed for many years by the same owners. Some of the older habits continued, such as tramp traffic to areas such as Russia and S. America which had no transoceanic shipping of their own, but the enormous pre-1914 merchant navy was gravely damaged by sinkings in World War I and then by the development of rival fleets. In the slump of 1929-31 millions of excess tons were laid up and the trade revival was interrupted by World War II with its even bigger sinkings.

(4) After that war aviation creamed off the passenger and light goods traffic; the decline of the British coal industry destroyed a major customer and vast oil tankers superseded the smaller means of moving oil. Meanwhile, with the decline of the Empire, the British authorities became decreasingly able to enforce their own stringently enlightened regulations which were now habitually evaded by transfers of ships to 'flags of convenience', i.e. to registration in countries where regulations imposed a lower burden on owners. Hence many ships in most respects, including crews, British, sailed under the flags of countries (often Panama) which they never visited. The safety and welfare problems of flags of convenience remained a subject of international dispute throughout the latter half of the 20th cent. It also distorted the apparent, as opposed to the real, size of merchant fleets.

MERCANTILISM was a primitive economic theory which estimated a country's wealth by the amount of bullion it contained. This, a rationalisation of private greed, prevailed from 16th to 18th cents. as the commercial policy of the Spanish American Empire and of those who sought to force their way into its commercial system. In England, its principal exposition was in *England's Treasure by Forraign Trade* by Thomas Mun (1571-1641) and Locke assumed its truth. The balance of trade was said to be favourable when it led to net imports of bullion and unfavourable in the reverse direction. Hence six classical measures of trade policy were:

(1) Restraints by prohibition or customs duties upon the importation of consumer goods which could be produced at home; **(2)** Restraints of importation from countries with whom there was an unfavourable balance of trade; **(3)** Encouragement of exports by drawbacks on dutiable goods purchased at home and on dutiable foreign goods intended for immediate re-export; **(4)** The payment of bounties to encourage nascent exporting industries; **(5)** The regulation of trade by treaty; and **(6)** The acquisition of colonies and the regulation of their trade so that their raw materials were exported to the imperial power in exchange for the latter's manufactures.

The S. Americans operating within this framework soon created an inflationary crisis first in Spain and then, especially in the Thirty Years War, in Europe. The English Trade and Navigation Acts immensely developed the merchant navy and ruined the Dutch, but deprived England of cheap Dutch fish, and raised the price levels of English exports to the American colonies to a point where illegal local manufacture and efforts to suppress or tax it brought rebellion.

The most successful critique of mercantilism was Adam Smith's *Wealth of Nations* which denied the basic premise and identified wealth as the product of land and work, but in an increasingly competitive world statesmen became obsessed with neo-mercantilism after World War II, related to imbalances between exports and imports in which the ability to print currency replaced the mines of Peru.

MERCATOR. *See* CARTOGRAPHY.

MERCHANT(S) ADVENTURERS (1) were men who risked (adventured) capital in commerce at some distance, especially abroad. Such overseas traders were operating on a sufficient scale to be given Flemish privileges in 1358. They were probably an offshoot of the Staplers but they concentrated on cloth, and their eventual supersession of the Staplers (who had a wool monopoly) was connected with the rise of the English cloth industry and the complementary decline of wool exports. Their first separate charter was granted in 1406 and confirmed in 1430.

(2) They were a loosely bound company of 'all the merchants of the realm' which anyone might join on paying the proper dues (or *hanse*). The members were wealthy and came particularly from Newcastle, York, Hull, Norwich, Ipswich, London, Bristol, Southampton and Exeter. Many were Mercers. The recognised limits of their trading area were the R. Somme (France) to the R. Eider (Schleswig-Holstein) and the practice was to set up one or more *Marts* where they brought and bought all their goods but they had dealings and establishments (factory houses) in Germany and Scandinavia as well. Before the mid-16th cent. their mart was at Antwerp or Middleburg, depending on the political situation, but Hanseatic competition drove them from Scandinavia and the Baltic, and they concentrated increasingly and at the expense of the Hansards, on the Low Countries.

(3) Besides cloth, much of it unfinished or undyed, they exported or sold woolfells and leather, lead, tin, spices, rabbit skins, tallow, alabaster, corn, beer and other special products. In return, they bought from the Dutch and the Rhinelanders metal and metal goods, armour, wine, fustians, hemp and linen, worked leather, saltpetre and gunpowder, and Nuremberg knicknacks. Italians supplied silks, the Portuguese spices and drugs; the Baltic merchants naval stores, fur and soap.

(4) The Adventurers developed English organisations, some of which became locally powerful. They had halls at York and Bristol, and at York they took over the City government in 1430. In London they met at Mercers Hall and set up 'courts' (Committees) or fellowships within, at least, the Mercers, Drapers, Skinners and Grocers Companies. The Mercers took the lead, and the London Adventurers had a preponderant influence which was generally exercised at the important meetings held at the Mart itself. The control, however, was never complete. The well known Bristol Merchant Adventurers had an independent organisation after 1467. In 1474 the York Adventurers managed to impose their own scale of fees for the right to trade in Flanders, Brabant and Zeeland. Those at Hull intercepted the northern trade and in 1497 almost provoked a civil war, exacerbated by the

Londoners, who tried to exclude other ports by a high fine. Henry VII interfered to cut the fine to £6-6s.-8d.

(5) In 1504 the Merchant Adventurers tried to absorb the Staplers, but were ordered to respect them by the Star Chamber. This was only the latest incident in a history of disorderly ambition which resulted in the Charter of 1505 (confirmed in 1513). By this the Adventurers were to regulate their affairs through a governor and court of 24 assistants which sat at the Mart. In practice the London Mercers dominated the Court and others sought their own salvation. In 1519, for example, Newcastle won the right to compound for the fees of its members and by 1552 Bristol had its own charter. The Flemish markets, however, were expanding or being vacated by rivals, so that these internal quarrels mattered little. The Venetians ceased to come after 1533; the Hanse and the Staple were already in decline, and when Antwerp became the W. European financial centre, the Merchant Adventurers shared spectacularly in its prosperity. In 1550 they were said to be employing 20,000 people there, and 30,000 elsewhere in the Low Countries. They were fully incorporated for the first time in 1564.

(6) Development was interrupted in 1568 first by the Spanish embargo and seizures at Antwerp and then by religious persecution and the difficulty of revival in the face of (almost Hanseatic) competitors re-established under cover of it. The mart was transferred to protestant Emden and Stade which benefited the east coast ports at the expense of Bristol and the Channel. Meanwhile, the Hanse was itself divided and Hamburg offered facilities. These were enjoyed until 1597 when the practical independence of the Netherlands made the Low Countries, if not the exact location within them, attractive again. The mart oscillated between Middleburg and Dordrecht and when the Hanseatic *Kontor* at Bruges collapsed, there was talk of Bruges. The important Hamburg factory house was, however, maintained with important results.

(7) The Thirty Years' War created a European recession which was slightly reflected in new charter restrictions. In 1634 Charles I was persuaded to exclude shopkeepers. In 1643 Parliament (in return for £30,000) raised the admission fines generally. By 1651 however, the war had finally ended. It had destroyed the prosperity of Antwerp, and isolated the Spanish Netherlands from the general European trading area. On the other hand the Hanse was in virtual dissolution. Germany was now wide open. The mart was finally moved to Hamburg, where it remained, a slowly declining institution, which ended in the middle of the 19th cent. as an English dining club.

(8) The concentration upon the continental North Sea coast forced Bristol and the Channel Adventurers to fend for themselves. Exeter unsuccessfully attacked the London Adventurers in Parliament in 1661 but the traditional southern trade of these ports was carried on and survived the political vicissitudes of the Low Countries. As a result, the wealthy Bristol Adventurers laid the foundations of the African and Iberian trade, and eventually of the enormously lucrative commerce in slaves and sugar, and of the N. American discoveries. Hence when trade ceased to be carried on by the great chartered companies, the Bristol Merchant Adventurers survived as a wealthy charitable guild responsible in part for the foundation of Bristol University. *See* CHARTERED COMPANIES.

MERCHANT CHARTER. *See* CARTA MERCATORIA.

MERCHANT SHIPPING ACTS 1850, 1876 and 1877 regulated shipping safety. *For the Act of 1876 see* PLIMSOLL.

MERCHANTS, STATUTE OF (1283) provided a simple method whereby merchants, especially foreigners, could recover their debts. If a debt had been acknowledged before a mayor and enrolled, the creditor could get the debtor's movables sold when the day for payment had passed, by producing the acknowledgement to the mayor. This turned all mayors into small debt courts. *See* ACTON BURNELL.

MERCHANTS OF WATERFORD, CASE OF (1484). Ignoring the English Staple Act, Waterford Merchants consigned wool not to Calais but to Sluys. The Calais authorities seized it and on the owners' petitioning for release, the English Exchequer Chamber held that the Act did not bind Ireland because she had a Parliament of her own and was not represented in the English Parliament. It then apparently changed its mind at the instance of Hussey, C.J., on grounds now unknown. *See* POYNINGS' LAWS.

MERCHET (Norman Fr = market). A payment, seldom large, which a villein had to make for his lord's permission to give his daughter in marriage. It is improbably said to have been in redemption of the lord's *jus primae noctis* (Lat = right to the first night), of which there is no trace in Britain. The name suggests a more plausible compensation for the lord's loss of fees at his hirings' market. The existence of the liability, if proved, was conclusive that the father was a villein. *See* FEUDALISM-19.

MERCHISTON. *See* NAPIER.

MERCIA (A.S. tribal name MIERCE = a marchman) KINGDOM (1) originated in penetration of the midlands by Anglian war bands *via* the R. Trent and settlement along its valley. The war leaders claimed descent from Woden through Offa, K. of Angeln in Schleswig and his great grandson Icel, the first to reach Britain (c. A.D. 500). By the 7th cent. the Mercians had reached the vicinity of Lichfield and Tamworth, respectively the main ecclesiastical and royal centres of the later Kingdom, and migrants could colonise the northern midlands direct from the Humber because of the erosion of the British Kingdom of Elmet.

(2) To the south the Mercians incorporated or conquered most of the Middle Angles (who never had a unifying head), the Kingdom of Lindsey behind them to the east and the Magonsaeton westwards towards Wales. In addition, they pressed upon the West Saxons in the valley of the Gloucestershire Avon. The Fens obstructed their influence in E. Anglia.

(3) From about 628 this confederacy experienced the determined leadership of the family of PENDA (?577-655 King 642) and his brother EOWA (?-641). The Britons held up the westward advance, and after limited expansion into Gloucestershire at the expense of the West Saxons (B. of Cirencester 628) Penda turned southeast. London became a Mercian port and the East and Middle Saxons tributaries. The predatory character of a Teutonic warrior court enjoined further aggression. Penda was soon fighting the Northumbrians in alliance with Cadwallon, K. of Gwynedd. In 632 they killed K. Edwin of Northumbria in Hatfield Chase and began to pillage his kingdom. Edwin's family was destroyed but Cadwallon was killed in 633 in a Northumbrian revival. Without their ally a loosely knit Mercian confederacy was too weak. Penda ensured unity and efficiency and had to accept Northumbrian superiority until 641 when, in a war whose origins are unknown, he killed K. Oswald at the B. of Maserfield at or near Oswestry (Salop). This second victory was no more decisive than Hatfield. Oswald's brother Oswiu of Bernicia rebuilt Northumbrian power despite Penda's efforts to catch him. In 654 Penda organised a great alliance of Welsh princes and Aethelhere, K. of the E. Angles and led the combined army north. Despite the odds, Oswiu was victorious at Winwaedsfield near Leeds. Penda and Aethelhere were killed (655).

(4) Penda's son PEADA (?-655) K. of the Middle Angles, died within months and for about a year Mercia was a Northumbrian possession, until three earldormen proclaimed WULFHERE (?-675) another son who had been kept in hiding. The move was successful and the new King able. By 670, when Oswiu died, the Mercians were supreme in Essex and the Thames Valley. In 674 Wulfhere led a southern host into Northumbria, where, however, Ecgfrith, son of Oswiu defeated him. The alliance broke up and the Northumbrians took over Lindsey until 678 when Wulfhere's brother AETHELRED (r. 675-704) in beating Ecgfrith by the Trent ended Northumbrian southward pretensions altogether.

(5) Like Wulfhere but unlike Penda, Aethelred was a Christian. He sympathised with St. Wilfrid in his ecclesiastical controversies and they were personal friends. They established new churches and foundations and the King also supported Theodore of Tarsus in founding new bishoprics at Hereford, Worcester, Leicester and in Lindsey. After nearly 30 years of incessant activity he retired to Bardney Abbey (Lindsey) and was succeeded by Wulfhere's son CENRED (r. 807-9) who had to face frequent incursions from North Wales. In 709 he retired to Rome. His cousin CEOLRED (r. 709-16) was less well disposed to the church; St. Boniface calls him dissolute and records that he died, the last of Penda's descendants, insane.

(6) The throne passed to the line of Eowa now headed by AETHELBALD (r. 716-57) who had been in exile. Powerful but tyrannical and vicious, he rose to supremacy over the southern English because the death (725) of Wihtred of Kent and the retirement (726) of Ine of Wessex had left those states in the hand of incompetents. He used the title "King of Britain", ruled large parts of Wessex directly and completed the transfer of Middlesex and London from East Saxon authority, but his violence and self indulgence raised widespread internal opposition among both church and laymen. In 749 he placated the church by freeing it from public burdens, except the maintenance of fortresses and bridges, but in 757 his own bodyguard murdered him. The southern English confederacy dissolved while a Mercian civil war was fought out between one BEORNRED (?-?) and the late King's nephew, the great OFFA (r. 757-96).

(7) Offa re-established his southern supremacy by stages, beginning (764) with Kent which was breaking up after its dynasty died out and Sussex (770) but in 776 the Kentishmen asserted their independence at the B. of Otford, and Offa's overlordship was not re-established until 785. Offa and the Kentishmen were at enmity for reasons (other than personal ones) unknown, but which were probably connected with his foreign, ecclesiastical and commercial policies. He and Abp. Jaenberht had superseded the old *sceat* coinage by the silver penny approximating to the Carolingian coinage, just before the B. of Otford: Offa negotiated, in the end successfully (788) for the division of the province of Canterbury by the establishment of an archbishopric at Lichfield; and in 789 royal marriage negotiations with Charlemagne broke down and resulted in the Franks closing their ports to English trade. All these events must have disturbed Kentish life (*see also* COINAGE) and the latter events were perhaps related to the flight of Egbert son of K. Ealhmund, the West Saxon ruler of Kent between 776 and 785 to Gaul for in 789 there was a West Saxon civil war between one Beotric and Egbert in which Offa supported Beortric and secured the overlordship of Wessex (789).

(8) Offa attempted, further to consolidate Mercian peaceful supremacy by having his son Ecgfrith consecrated King in his life time (787). This formal decision on the succession also associated the church with Mercian monarchy. On a physical level the construction of Offa's Dyke against the Welsh represented a similar line of policy. A peaceful but strong land was to supply the royal wants by farming and trading rather than tribal forays. The policy was a partial failure. A Kentish revolt broke out just before his death,

and K. ECGFRITH (r. 796) survived him by only five months. The new King CENWULF (796-821) was a distant kinsman who had to establish himself. It took time to overcome the Kentish men, and in Wessex when Beortric died (802) Egbert was immediately acclaimed and could not be expelled. Kent was only subdued in that year in which also Cenwulf accepted the suppression of the archbishopric of Lichfield but failed to secure the transfer of the reunited metropolitical see from Canterbury to London. He was not, and never claimed to be, overlord of all the English.

(9) Cenwulf's reign witnessed a decline. There had been a Northumbrian invasion in 801 in which a peace was patched up by the bishops and nobles. In 816 aggression against the Welsh was resumed but in 817 Cenwulf had a major quarrel with Wulfred, Abp. of Canterbury since 805. The dispute lasted throughout the Welsh wars during which Cenwulf harried Dyfed, and penetrated to Snowdonia. A forced reconciliation took place just before he died but his brother CEOLWULF I (r. 821-3) carried on the war, stormed Deganwy and established some kind of rule in most of Powys. He, however, was deposed in favour of a certain BEORNWULF (r. 823-5) who immediately sought ecclesiastical support by settling the problems remaining after the reconciliation with Wulfred. Beornwulf had not fully established himself when Egbert of Wessex attacked and beat him decisively at Ellendun (nr Swindon) in 825. The West Saxons immediately secured the allegiance of Kent and the other Saxon states, and Beornwulf was killed attempting to suppress an East Anglian revolt. The event was decisive. No Mercian authority was ever exercised outside Mercia again. The kingship passed to an earldorman LUDECA (r. 825-7) and then to WIGLAF (r. 827-9, 830-7). In 829 Egbert overran Mercia and enforced a nominal submission of the Northumbrians at Dore near Sheffield beyond it but this campaign had only limited effects. Wiglaf returned in 830 and maintained his independence. BEORHTWULF (r. 840-52) his successor followed suit but had to cede Berkshire to Wessex (c. 848) while in 850 the Vikings stormed London and routed him. Viking activity provoked Welsh intervention and Beorhtwulf's successor BURGRED (r. 852-74) had immediately to ask for Egbert's help in resisting him. The Mercian might be the West Saxon's equal but he was no longer self sufficient. He married Egbert's daughter and in 866, when a Viking host occupied Nottingham he called upon Aethelbert, his brother in law, for help. The West Saxons arrived but the enemy declined battle and harried the countryside until Burgred bought them off. In 872 they returned and raided the countryside from Torksey until bought off again when they moved to Repton. Worn down by disaster Burgred went to Rome where he died. His place was filled by one of his thanes CEOLWULF II (874-?883) who was a Viking nominee appointed on condition that he should be ready to serve them with his following and that the kingdom should be at their disposal whenever they chose. In 877 they returned and took half. Ceolwulf's fate is unknown. From at least 883 his part was ruled by West Saxon earldormen. *See* MERCIA, EARLDOM.

MERCIA EARLDOM (1) This is a misleading term. After the partition with the Danes along Watling St., the western, West Saxon part was shired into military commands of roughly equal size each centred upon a burgh, while the Danish part was divided into areas occupied by the various Danish armies. In the western part Mercian law (which differed only slightly from the W. Saxon) obtained. The eastern, soon known as the Danelaw, was governed according to the very different Danish laws.

(2) In the west AETHELRED (?-911) appears as earldorman of the Mercians in 883; in 886 London was added to his circumscription and in 889 he married K. Edward the Elder's sister AETHELFLAED (?-918). They carried on warfare with the Danes until his death, when she was declared Lady of the Mercians and continued the war until she died in 918. Then K. Edward seized Tamworth and in 919 carried off their daughter Aelfwynn to Wessex. The shiring, which took little account of the ancient Mercian divisions then took place and the country was ruled by the West Saxon Kings who, when they appointed earldormen, appointed them for these sub-units of groups of them. Meanwhile the boundaries of the "Mercian" area varied with the fortunes of the Danish wars to the east and the Welsh wars to the west.

(3) With the establishment of relative peace in the midlands from the accession of K. Edwy, an earldorman, AELFHERE (?-983) was appointed (956). Welsh wars mostly fought in Wales, occurred in the middle 60s but when Aelfhere died his son AELFRIC (?-1016) became earl only of the Danish part. He was banished between 986 and 991 and was notorious for his Danish sympathies. Hence in 1003 K. Ethelred appointed the unreliable EDRIC STREONA (?-1017) who was a supreme earl with, in some cases, other earls (e.g. LEOFWINE (?-1024) of the Hwicce under him.

(4) After Canute put Edric to death there was an interval, but between 1024 and 1032 he appointed LEOFRIC (?-1057) son of Leofwine and husband to the legendary Lady Godiva. He, his son AELFGAR (?-1062) and grandson EDWIN (?-1071) were known as Earls of the Mercians down to the Conquest, but the area of their jurisdiction fluctuated very widely as shires were transferred back and forth in the course of the political upheavals e.g. at one period Monmouth and Hereford were a separate earldom for Ralph, Gloucestershire belonged to Sweyn Godwin's son, while Harold and Beorn Godwin's sons had Danish Mercia between them. As an administrative entity Mercia did not survive the Conquest though the peculiarities of Mercian law did for two centuries.

MERCIER, Honoré (1840-94) was premier of Quebec from 1887-92 when he was dismissed on charges of peculation, for which he was acquitted on trial.

MERCILESS PARLIAMENT (Feb.-June 1388) tried Richard II's advisors and favourites, accused of treason by the Lords Appellant. The Abp. of York, the D. of Ireland (*see* DE VERE) and the E. of Suffolk (*see* POLE, DE LA) were attainted *in absentia* and the Chief Justice, Robert Tresilian, and Sir Nicholas Brembre were executed. Various knights of the King's Chamber were also impeached and executed. The impeachments formed the precedent for those used under Charles I.

MEREDITH, George (1828-1909) educated at the Moravian school at Neuwied, married T. L. Peacock's widowed daughter and was a friend of the pre-Raphaelites. As Chapman and Hall's publisher's reader from 1862-94, he was one of the most influential figures in contemporary literature. He was also a prolific but initially unsuccessful writer. *The Ordeal of Richard Feverel* appeared in 1857, *The Egoist* in 1879 but *Diana of the Crossways* in 1885 was the first to achieve popularity.

MERFYN FRYCH. *See* GWYNEDD-11.

MERGER TREATY (1965) merged the European Coal and Steel and Economic Communities and the European Atomic Energy Authority under a single Council and Commission of the European Economic Community.

MERGUI, a port of Tenasserim. *See* BURMA; SIAM.

MERINO. *See* SHEEP.

MERIONETH (Wales) mountainous sparsely populated area and county, notable for its sheep and black cattle. It had some gold, lead and copper and in the 19th cent. slate was extensively quarried at Dolgellau and at Ffestiniog, where a nuclear power station was built in the 1950s. In 1974 it became part of the new county of Gwynedd. *See* GWYNEDD; WALES, STATUTE OF.

MERIT, ORDER OF, was founded in 1902 to confer the highest possible distinction without carrying precedence. Membership is limited to 24.

MERKLAND (Scot). Land assessed at one merk for taxation purposes.

MERLIN two legendary figures. **(1)** A Welsh bard who composed a lament for the fallen in the B. of Arderydd in 573, in which year he is recorded by the *Annales Cambriae* as having gone mad. He is known in the Welsh tradition as Merlin Wyllt (= Wild Merlin).

(2) A creation of Geoffrey of Monmouth, possibly developed from **(1)**, an enchanter and bard at the court of Vortigern and advisor to Ambrosius. He was associated with Arthur and his story more fully developed by Malory.

MERMAID TAVERN in Bread St. and Friday St., London was the venue of the Friday St. Club started by Sir Walter Raleigh and to which Shakespeare, Selden, Donne, Beaumont and Fletcher, Carew and Jonson belonged. The tavern dated from 1529 and was destroyed in the Great Fire in 1666.

MERRIVALE. *See* DUKE.

MEROVINGIANS. *See* FRANKS.

MERRY ANDREW. A clown or buffoon. 'Andrew' was a common servant's name in plays. A merry one had a farcical part.

MERSA MATRUH. Small Egyptian port on Libyan frontier much disputed in the Western Desert Campaigns of World War II.

MERSE, THE (Scots = March) Actually part of the Scottish East March.

MERS-EL-KEBIR (Algeria) Naval port of Oran, where the Royal Navy put the local French fleet out of action in 1940.

MERSEY – NAVIGATIONS. *See* TRANSPORT AND COMMUNICATIONS; LIVERPOOL.

MERSEY, Vist. *See* BIGHAM.

MERTHYR TYDFIL. An inconsiderable village, it developed after the Dowlais ironworks opened in 1757. In 1759 the Guest family began smelting and in the next 20 years ironworks were opened at Cyfarthfa, Penydarren and Pentrebach. Iron was being exported to America by 1780, facilitated by a new canal, and there were railed roads by 1804 when Trevithick tested his first locomotive. Brunel built the mainline railway to Cardiff by 1855, and the coal and iron of the area advanced together. By 1856 Bessemer steel was being rolled and Cyfarthfa was converted into a steelworks in 1884. The rather specialised prosperity continued until the post World War I slump, locally aggravated by the Saar cession of cheap coal to France.

MERTON, STATUTE OF (1236) represented a settlement of everyday legal problems which had arisen in the experience of the judges during Henry III's minority. Caps 1 and 2 protected widows against seizure of their dower; Cap 3 protected successful litigants against a further disseisin of the property in issue; Cap 4 permitted inclosure of common and waste by lords only if there were enough land to satisfy the common rights of tenants; Caps 5 and 7 prevented the exaction of the interest on a father's debts during the minority of his heir and compensated guardians if their ward were unwilling to enter into an assigned marriage. Under Cap 8 writs of right could no longer be brought for disputes arising before 1154. Cap 10 permitted suit of court by attorney and thereby recognised the decreasing importance of personal services. Copies of the statute were widely circulated and sent to Ireland.

MERTON, Walter of (?-1277) pupil of Adam Marsh, protégé of Robert Grosseteste and royal clerk, had amassed numerous livings and properties by 1259 when he was employed as negotiator with the Pope in Henry III's Sicilian Business. He was Chancellor from 1261-63 and then appears to have endowed a college at Maldon to educate his 'nephews'. This developed into **Merton College,** Oxford. He resume office after the baronial defeat in 1265 and was Bp. of Rochester from 1274. The college contains the oldest academic library in England.

MESOPOTAMIAN CAMPAIGN (1914-17). The British landed at Basra in Oct. 1914, repelled a Turkish counter attack in Apr. 1915 and by Sept. had advanced to Kut-el-Amara. In Nov. they were defeated at Ctesiphon and in Dec. they were besieged in Kut, where they capitulated in Apr. 1916. The Turks were now diverted into an invasion of Persia which enabled the British to reinforce Basra and recommence offensive operations in Dec. In Feb. 1917 the Turks were forced to abandon Kut, Baghdad fell in Mar., and by Apr. the Turks were in full retreat to the north. *See* IRAQ.

MESSENGERS (1) Queen's (or King's) messengers carried important official, mostly diplomatic documents and sometimes made arrests for treason. They became part of the Foreign Service in 1955. **(2)** The Messenger of the Great Seal was responsible until 1874 for ensuring that Parliamentary writs reached the sheriffs. **(3)** The Messengers of the Exchequer were supposed to act as enforcement officers for the Lord Treasurer and the Court of Exchequer. **(4)** The Messenger of the Press was an 18th cent. Stationer's Co. official appointed to search for unlicensed printing. **(5)** Messengers at Arms (Sc) appointed by the Lord Lyon King of Arms, execute writs issued by the Courts of Session and Justiciary.

MESSINES, B. of (21 May-7 June 1917). In this brilliant limited operation, Gen. Plumer and his Chief of Staff Gen. Harington punched out a German salient which deeply outflanked the British at Ypres on the south. Some 2300 guns suddenly bombarded a nine-mile front. On the last day 19 enormous mines were exploded under the German positions and in 13 hours the infantry had seized and so effectively consolidated every objective, that all German counter-attacks failed.

METACOMET. *See* WAMPANOAG.

METAGE. The Corporation of London's prescriptive right to *measure* merchandise, latterly only grain, and levy dues called fillage and lastage accordingly. Abolished in 1872.

METCALFE, John. *See* BLIND JACK OF KNARESBOROUGH.

METCALFE. Family of prominent colonial servants. **(1) Charles Theophilus (1785-1846) Ld. METCALFE (1845),** industrious, honourable and good humoured Indian and colonial administrator, made his first success beside Generals Smith and Dowdeswell, with whom he was political agent in 1806. He negotiated the treaty with Holkar; in 1808 persuaded Ranjit Singh to withdraw behind the Sutlej and signed the T. of Amritsar with him in Apr. 1809. In 1810 he became acting Resident with Scindiah and from 1811 as Resident in Delhi until 1819 he developed the resources of and settled central India. After a year (1819-20) as private secretary to the Gov. Gen., he was appointed Resident at Hyderabad and it was here that he attracted the hostility of the Gov. Gen. because of the report and proposals for dealing with the Palmer loans to the Nizam. His proposals were ultimately adopted. In 1827 he was appointed to the Gov. Gen.'s council and by reason of absences, resignations and other delays, he became acting Gov. Gen. (1835-36). During this time he abolished press censorship, was passed over for substantive promotion by the Directors and in 1838 resigned. He was promptly appointed Gov. of Jamaica and having acted as a peacemaker in that disturbed colony, he resigned in 1842 and became Gov. Gen. of Canada, then equally disturbed by the ambitions of nationalistically minded politicians to reduce the Gov. Gen. to a cipher. When he refused to admit their right to be consulted on appointments, the executive council resigned and he carried on the Govt. single handed for a year before a general election enabled him to find more moderate ministers. He then retired through ill health. His nephew **(2) Sir Theophilus John (1828-63)** was joint magistrate at Meerut during the Indian mutiny. His nephew **(3) Sir Charles Herbert Theophilus (1853-1928)** civil engineer and friend of Cecil Rhodes designed the Rhodesian and Benguela railway systems.

METEOROLOGY, vital to a nation with a large seaborne trade, rested on personal experience and guesswork until the essential instruments were invented: the first thermometer by Galileo (end of 16th cent.) and the barometer by Toricelli (1643). English weather maps showing trade winds and monsoons were drawn from 1688 onwards. Fahrenheit's mercury thermometer simplified observation after 1800 when the French began to establish weather stations. In England much of the theory had been developed in the Royal Society, but meteorology assumed its modern form as a result of the interest of Alexander Dalrymple (1737-1808) first Hydrographer of the Navy from 1795-1808, Sir Francis Beaufort (1774-1857), Hydrographer from 1829-55, the studies of the Dutch meteorologist C. Buys Ballot, and especially the work of Admiral Robert Fitzroy (1805-65) who had gained a reputation as a practical meteorologist through his voyages in command of (Darwin's) H.M.S. *Beagle* between 1829-36. Fitzroy left the navy in 1850 and was appointed superintendent of the new Meteorological Department set up under the influence of the British (now Royal) Meteorological Society by the Board of Trade in 1854. Here he compiled the first synoptic charts for forecasting. He set up the telegraphic gale warning system, invented visual warning storm cones, and the Fitzroy barometer. He also published books, long used as standard works, on forecasting. By this time maritime traffic was becoming less dependent on wind.

He collected daily telegraphic data from 1860 and issued daily printed maps from 1868. The office, transferred to the Royal Society in 1867, promptly suspended the issue of bulletins and warnings. These were only resumed after public protests in 1874. The use of wireless after 1900 facilitated the employment of weather ships. The development of aviation in World War I bought a new urgency, and in 1919 the Met. Office was transferred to the Air Ministry. Electrical storm interference in communications and television and crop-damage in an increasing industrialised agriculture added new types of interest. After the U.N.O. was set up, a World Met. Organisation was created to pool information from the widespread national networks of observatories, crop weather stations, weather ships, satellites and through the new radar techniques.

METHODISM is a system of religious attitude and practice first promoted in 1729 by JOHN WESLEY (1703-91) a clergyman and son of a clergyman at Oxford where he was a fellow of Lincoln College. He was joined by his brother CHARLES (1707-88) and by GEORGE WHITEFIELD (1714-70). The unexplained term 'methodist' was used at the time.

(2) In 1735 they went to the new colony of Georgia. Charles became Governor Oglethorpe's secretary and all three preached against the slave trade and gin and Whitefield founded an orphanage. They were not popular and returned despondent in 1737. The Wesleys now came under Moravian influence, and after a visit to Herrnhut experienced conversion in London in May 1738. Whitefield, however, had been preaching independently in the open air to raise money for his orphanage. One of the greatest preachers of modern times, he had immense success in S. Wales and Scotland but held Calvinist views which steadily parted him from the Wesleys.

(3) They began field preaching to the Kingswood colliers in 1739 and soon had to create a body of lay preachers to share the work. John discovered a talent for organisation, while Charles, less austere and more mystical, took to writing hymns. He wrote over 5,000 many of which remain famous.

(4) Their problem was that they wished to remain Anglican, but could not persuade any bishop to consecrate a Methodist bishop. Hence the preachers and pastors for want of ordination could only be laymen. By 1742 methodist activity was spreading to the whole kingdom and the problem was becoming urgent. In 1744 John held his first conference of preachers, and this soon became an annual event. It eventually supplied the lack of a provincial and diocesan organisation.

(5) By 1762 when DANIEL ROWLANDS (1713-90) built his meeting house at Llangeitho, the movement was slowly dividing between two connections neither of which, as yet, wanted to leave the Church of England. These were the CALVINISTIC METHODISTS who published a Welsh Bible in 1770, reached Wales in 1784 and became increasingly presbyterian in outlook; and the ordinary Methodists later known as Wesleyans. The Calvinistic Methodists became a strongly Welsh movement to which Welsh literature and national consciousness owe much. In 1823 they were Methodist only in name.

(6) In 1784 the Bp. of London refused to ordain a Methodist for service in America, where there was a shortage of priests of Methodist persuasion. John Wesley thereupon instituted three himself and this marked the break with the Anglican church.

(7) In the same year, John Wesley created the permanent METHODIST CONFERENCE, and the already partly developed system of local synods, circuits and societies was fully established in the years afterwards.

(8) Secessions and Reunifications. The Conference of 1795 agreed to the administration of the Anglican sacraments. Thenceforth internal differences related to discipline and organisation only. These, however, were extensive. The METHODIST NEW CONNEXION (M.N.C.) seceded in 1779; the north of England INDEPENDENT METHODISTS in 1805; the PRIMITIVE METHODISTS (originally a small independent parallel sect) in 1810; and the BIBLE CHRISTIANS in 1815. The WESLEYAN METHODIST ASSOCIATION was formed in 1835 and the WESLEYAN REFORMERS in 1849. These two last united as the UNITED METHODIST FREE CHURCHES (U.M.F.C.) in 1857. Sectarian good feeling, however, gradually reasserted itself, and in 1811 all the sects joined with the main 'Wesleyan' METHODIST CHURCH in a first of a series of decennial conferences. In 1907 the M.N.C., the Bible Christians and the U.M.F.C. combined as the UNITED METHODIST CHURCH and in 1932 this, with the original Methodist Church and the Primitive Methodists, was further combined in the METHODIST CHURCH OF GREAT BRITAIN.

(9) Methodism began as a reaction against indifference and moral laxity, and its principal characteristics have been fervour, good behaviour and good works, rather than doctrinal development. Hence the possibility of reunion with the Anglican Church has always been held open. See MORAVIANS.

METHUEN. Of this Wiltshire family **(1) Paul (?-1667)** made and traded in drugget but in 1659 obtained Dutch spinners who trained his people in fine spinning and weaving so that he became the greatest clothier of his time. For his son **(2) John (?-1650-1706)** see METHUEN TREATY. His son **(3) Sir Paul (1672-1757)** accompanied his father in the negotiation of the treaty and succeeded him as Ambassador to Portugal when he died. He came home in 1708 and was elected M.P. for Devizes, and in 1709 became a Lord of the Admiralty. In 1710 he was elected on a double return, but unseated by the Commons and in 1713 he stood for Brackley but was again unseated. In 1714 he was elected and became Ambassador to Spain, and in 1716 he acted as Sec. of State for Stanhope but resigned with Townsend and Walpole. When they returned in 1720 he held household appointments until 1730 and thereafter remained out of office and increasingly in opposition. He left the Commons in 1747. A descendant of **(1)**, **(4) Paul Sanford (1845-1932) 3rd Ld. METHUEN (1891)** a soldier, served in the Ashanti War (1873-4), Egypt (1882) and Bechuanaland in 1884 and 1885. Here he

commanded mounted rifles. At the outbreak of the Boer War he took command of a division, and though checked at Magersfontein was the only General to distinguish himself in the first months of the war. Buller trusted and supported him. After the completion of regular operations, Methuen was left to chase the Boer guerrillas and though he won a victory over de la Rey at Klerksdorp in Feb. 1901, he was captured badly wounded in Mar. 1902. After the war, he took over Eastern Command and was an important trainer of troops. From 1908-12 he was Commander in Chief in S. Africa, as well as Governor of Natal from 1910. He became a Field Marshal in 1911. In World War I he held the important post of Governor of Malta from 1915-19. *See also* GEORGE I-7.

METHUEN TREATY (16 May, 1703). Portugal was a nominal ally of Louis XIV, and had closed her ports to British and allied shipping. She was not enthusiastic for a Bourbon on the Spanish throne; an allied landing at Cadiz and the threat of blockade, by cutting off her colonies easily persuaded her to change her policy. The result was two agreements. By the political agreement Portugal offered 28,000 troops, half of which were to be paid by the allies, and the use of the port of Lisbon; the allies offered to support the claims of the Archduke Charles, brother of the Emperor, to the Spanish throne. The commercial or Methuen T. was negotiated by John Methuen (*see previous entry*) former M.P. for Devizes, who had been to Portugal as a diplomat in 1691 and had since 1697 been Lord Chancellor of Ireland. The treaty provided that English woollens should be admitted free to Portugal and her colonies, and that Portuguese wines should be admitted to Britain at 66.6% of the duty levied on French wines. Since a Portuguese cloth industry hardly existed, and Britain was at war with France, there was no short term loss to either side, and the long term advantages were considered sufficient to keep the treaty in being until 1836. See GEORGE I-7.

METHVEN, Henry Ld. (?1495-1551). See JAMES V OF SCOTS-7.

METIS were semi-nomadic Canadian huntsmen, boatmen and traders of mixed French, Scottish and Indian descent and R. Catholic religion. Mostly illiterate, they spoke a compound of old French, English and Cree with invented expressions. They carried on a kind of compromise life between that of the tribal Indians and the European fur traders in the great Assiniboine area of S. Manitoba, but their principal settlement was at Pembina, just across the U.S. frontier, with another at Fort Garry in Canada. Their numbers perhaps reached 20,000. They maintained their energetic, roistering way of life until 1870 when they were forcibly suppressed and settled as a result of the creation of Manitoba. See RIEL.

METRICATION was first introduced in France in 1799 and superseded the more natural if confused British measures in 1963 by which time the binary computer had made it obsolescent.

METROPOLITAN BOARD OF WORKS. See LONDON (GREATER) LOCAL GOVT.

METROPOLITAN BOROUGH. See LONDON (GREATER) LOCAL GOVT.

METROPOLITAN POLICE. See LONDON (GREATER) LOCAL GOVT.

METROPOLITAN WATER BOARD (1902). See LONDON (GREATER) LOCAL GOVT.

METTERNICH-WINNEBURG, Clemens Wenzel von, Prince (1773-1859). See AUSTRIA, POST-PRAGMATIC-12-17.

MEULAN. Important fief in the French Vexin. Its counts, of the Beaumont family, particularly Robert (?-1118) and his son Waleran, were friends of Henry I and K. Stephen and had two castles on the Seine and three on the Risle, besides fiefs in Warwickshire. They were notable upholders of the royal interests in Normandy until Waleran went on crusade in 1147.

MEWAR (UDAIPUR) (India). The capital of this Sisodia Rajput state was moved to Udaipur by the Rana Udai Sinha after the Moguls stormed Chitor in 1567. His son the Rana Pratap Singh (the Rajput national hero) was overthrown at the B. of Haldighat (Apr. 1576) but he maintained a guerrilla force and had recovered part of Mewar by his death in 1597. In 1614 his successor Amar Singh submitted as a privileged vassal, but Mewar joined the sister state of Marwar in the risings against the religious policy of Aurungzeb (1679-81) and in return for minor cessions secured effective independence. The state submitted to British protection by the T. of Udaipur in 1818.

MEWS. The Royal Mews at Charing Cross was originally the place where the royal hawks were *mewed*. They were demolished in the 17th cent. to make way for stables for the palace of Whitehall. The word was then applied to any stables round a court or in an alley, and so to the many London roads running along the back of residential houses.

MEXICO was in a state of rebellion from 1808 until the last Spanish viceroy recognised independence in 1821, whereupon Agustin de Iturbide, the army commander, made himself Emperor (1822). He was overthrown by Antonio Lopez de Santa Anna (1823) who proclaimed a republic but after ten years of confusion made himself dictator. Under his rule, Texas seceded (1836) and joined the U.S.A. (1847) and after the consequent war, New Mexico and California were lost to U.S.A. as well (T. of Guadaloupe-Hidalgo 1848). Santa Anna was overthrown in 1855. There followed a period of anti-clericalism propagated in the interests of the Indian cultivators by the famous Benito Juarez. This led to a civil war (1858-61) after which the victorious Juarez expropriated the church and when the Govt. finances collapsed, he suspended payment on foreign loans. The British, French and Spaniards mounted a joint expedition (Dec. 1861) but only French troops pressed the war. Mexico City was taken and the Austrian Archduke Ferdinand Maximilian was offered and accepted the Mexican crown. Juarez and his partisans were, however, only dispersed in the countryside and when by reason of the end of the American Civil War, Washington was (*see* MONROE DOCTRINE) able to make its displeasure effective, French troops were withdrawn and the archduke shot (June 1867).

Juarez died in 1872 and from 1876-1911 the country was under the violent and oppressive but modernising tyranny of Porfirio Diaz, who hunted down bandits and tribesmen, imported much foreign capital and foreign businessmen, built railways and ports, encouraged industry and expanded the towns. A rebellion in Nov. 1910 drove him overseas and unleashed a ten year civil war and social revolution. A new, federalist and democratically orientated constitution was adopted in 1917 but the Institutional Revolutionary Party monopolised power, sometimes violently, while encouraging, not always perceptively, industrial development with the incidental result that the lakes at Mexico City dried up and an enormous migration towards the capital made it one of the biggest and sleaziest cities in the world.

MEYRICK, Sir John (?-1638) was agent for the Russia Co. at Jaroslavl in 1584 and at Moscow from 1592. In 1602 he became Ambassador to the Czar and secured English trading concessions from successive rulers until he became Governor of the Co. in 1628.

MEZZOTINTS. The method invented in the Palatinate by Ludwig von Siegen, was brought to Britain by P. Rupert. It was soon taken up by English artists and became known abroad as 'engraving in the English manner'. Its earliest leading exponent was John Smith (1625-1742), followed by James MacArdell (1729-65).

MFECANE **(Zulu = The Crushing).** A period in the 1820s when the Bantu tribes broke up and destroyed each other.

MI = MILITARY INTELLIGENCE (Dept). MI5 is the branch which by secret means defends the internal security of Britain against spies and saboteurs. MI6 is responsible for secret intelligence and counter-intelligence outside Britain including deception.

MICHELL, Sir Francis (fl. 1603-21) financier, bought the reversion to the clerkship of the market in 1603. In 1618 with Sir Giles Mompesson, he had acquired the right to licence gold and silver thread. In the angry agitation against monopolies of 1621, the Commons illegally and without a hearing, sentenced him to degradation and imprisonment. He was subsequently released and an irregular impeachment then confirmed the sentence, which was not carried out.

MICHELANGELO. *See* RENAISSANCE-11.

MICHIGAN (U.S.A.) was first visited by French Jesuits in 1622; Marquette founded the first permanent settlement at St. Ignace in 1668 and Antoine Cadillac founded Detroit as a fur-trading post in 1701. Ceded to Britain in 1763, it passed to the U.S.A. in 1783. Detroit and MacKinac were not actually handed over until 1796 by the British who reoccupied them in the War of 1812. Michigan entered the Union as a state in 1837 and supported the Union in the Civil War.

MICKLEGARTH (O.N. = Big Town). The Scandinavian name for Constantinople. *See* BYZANTIUM.

MICMAC (Algonquian) Indians were probably encountered by the Cabots in the 15th cent. They later acted as middlemen between Europeans and other Indians, particularly in Acadie (Nova Scotia). When Nova Scotia became British in 1713 their Francophilism caused difficulty until 1779. In 1973 they were still occupying their original lands.

MICROSCOPE The achromatic lens was invented in 1752 and great advances were made by Lord Lister's father. The optical microscope advanced greatly between 1873-81 as a result of the joint researches of E. Abbe and B. Schott, respectively German optical and glass experts. The electronic microscope came into use in 1951.

MIDDLE AGES. A vaguely defined period between say 9th-10th cents. and 15th-16th cents. according to taste.

MIDDLE ANGLES were a large group of small tribes who colonised the midlands *via* the Wash and settled between the East Anglians and the Mercians. The principal tribes now known were the North and South Gyrwe of the Fens, the Gifle in S. Bedfordshire, the Hicce around Hitchin, and the Cilternsaetan against the Chilterns. They had no common ruler until Penda of Mercia imposed his son Peada who, in 653 was baptised by Finan from Lindisfarne and they remained simply a part of Mercia after Peada's death in 656. Their conversion appears to have been rapid, but they had to wait until 737 for a bishopric which was then established at Leicester. Their dialect became the foundation of the West Midlands form of Middle English.

MIDDLEBURG (Zeeland). *See* MERCHANT ADVENTURERS, STAPLE B-3-7.

MIDDLE EAST. *See* EAST.

'MIDDLE PARTY'. *See* EDWARD II-6.

MIDDLE PASSAGE. *See* SLAVE TRADE-3.

MIDDLE SHIRES. James I's name for the Anglo-Scottish marches.

MIDDLESBROUGH. Anciently, Yarm was the local port on the R. Tees but as it silted up Stockton-on-Tees nearer the sea superseded it. Middlesbrough owes its rise to John Pease the railway promoter, who started building a coal port in 1830 to rival Stockton and extended his Stockton and Darlington Railway to it. He laid out the town and started an iron industry in 1841. There were nearly 8,000 people by 1851 when ironstone, discovered in the Cleveland Hills, gave the place further encouragement. There were 31 blast furnaces by 1856 and 50 by 1861 but this rapid expansion was really made possible by the establishment in 1892 of the Tees Conservancy to build and dredge the port.

MIDDLESEX. The name first appears in 704 and seems to indicate the Saxons between the East and the West Saxons. Apart from London, the main place was Brentford which had a good crossing over the Thames. The area never had a dynastic ruler or King probably because it was dominated by London which lived on its agricultural produce. Administratively, it was treated as an appendage of the City, which down to 1888 appointed the Sheriffs and held the assizes and it is as the scene of much of the nation's political history that Middlesex has a history at all. By 1888 most of Greater London had grown over it and the northern part of the County of London was detached from it, but it had a county council whose functions became increasingly attenuated as boroughs and urban districts were filled with growing London suburbs. The county was abolished and its area incorporated in Greater London in 1965.

MIDDLESEX CASE OF THE SHERIFFS **(1840)** 11 Ad and E. 273 (*see* STOCKDALE *v* HANSARD). Stockdale obtained judgement against Hansard by default in another action based upon the previous libel and by authority of a Queen's Bench writ, the sheriffs levied execution. The House of Commons committed the sheriffs for contempt. A writ of *habeas corpus* against the serjeant at arms was returned that he had detained the sheriffs under a warrant from the Speaker, which stated that the sheriffs had been guilty of contempt of the House of Commons; it did not specify the contempt. The Queen's Bench refused to issue the writ because "it would be unseemly to suspect that a body acting under such sanctions as a House of Parliament, would, in making its warrant suppress facts which, if discussed, might entitle the person committed to his liberty". (per Lord Denman C.J.).

MIDDLESEX, E. of. *See* CRANFIELD.

MIDDLESEX ELECTION (1779). *See* WILKES, JOHN-6.

MIDDLETON, Sir Charles. *See* BARHAM.

MIDDLETON, John (1619-73) 1st E. of (1656) was a prominent covenanting officer in the first civil war but commanded the Scottish cavalry at Preston and joined Charles II in 1650. He commanded the cavalry at the disaster at Worcester (1651) was captured, but escaped from the Tower to France in his wife's clothes. He was in charge of the Highland rising in 1653-4 and then remained abroad until the Restoration when he returned with the King and became his Commissioner to the Scots Parliament. He was over-enthusiastic in pressing for episcopacy in Scotland and procured the expulsion of some hundreds of ministers from their livings. Lauderdale secured his dismissal, for Charles II wanted peace and thought that Middleton had misled him. He ended as Governor of Tangier.

MIDLAND BANK was founded as the BIRMINGHAM AND MIDLAND BANK in 1836. It began its policy of branch multiplication and predation in 1888. In 1891 it acquired the Central Bank of London; in 1898 the City Bank. Banks in Belfast and the London Joint Stock Bank followed in 1918, banks in Scotland in 1920-4 and in Ireland in 1958. By 1967 it had over 3,000 branches in the British Is.

MIDLETON. *See* BRODRICK.

MIDLOTHIAN. *See* EDINBURGH; LOTHIAN.

MIDLOTHIAN ELECTION CAMPAIGNS 1879, 1880. Disraeli had at the Berlin Congress of 1878 overturned the T. of San Stephano and protected British interests against Russia by returning large areas, including most of Bulgaria to Turkey. Bulgaria had been the subject of Gladstone's atrocity campaign in 1876. The disastrous Afghan and Zulu wars occurred in 1879. Gladstone challenged the sitting M.P. in Midlothian, the E. of Dalkeith, son of the D. of Buccleuch, the greatest of the Scots Tory landowners. By associating Turkey and these wars with imperialism, Gladstone gave a moral edge to his campaign at a time when the voters were feeling the effects of a recession. The result was an electoral

triumph. In a general election early in 1880, Gladstone's second Midlothian campaign resulted in the return of a Liberal govt. Hitherto politicians of Gladstone's standing had seldom been active in electioneering.

MIDSHIPMEN were teenage trainee naval officers who were originally quartered amidships with a mess in a gun room. Their mark of status was a white patch on the collar and a dirk instead of a sword. They were liable to, and often suffered corporal punishment. They were abolished in the 1970s.

MIDSUMMER FIRES were lit on Midsummer Eve (24 June) in public streets; and house doors were decorated with flowers and lamps. The custom (still common in Scandinavia) died out in the South of England as a result of the Civil War, but persisted all over Cumberland down to about 1760 and at Whalton (Northumberland) as late as 1879.

MIGRATION. (1) Save in time of war, there was no control over a person wishing to enter the country unless he could be regarded as criminal by English legal criteria. The Aliens Restriction Act 1914 arising out of World War I imposed controls and was amended in 1919 and 1953. These were aimed at intending alien settlers, and did not affect British subjects who, at least in the case of countries in allegiance to the Crown, were entitled to come and go as they pleased. Controls on Commonwealth citizens were first imposed in 1962 and 1968. The Immigration Act 1971 treated them and aliens together, permitting freedom of movement to those with **a Right of Abode** in the United Kingdom, and requiring all others to obtain leave to enter.

(2) Between 1881 and 1931 Britain was regularly a net exporter of population. From 1931-46 European persecutions and wars reversed this process. From 1946-56 Britain became an exporter again mainly to Canada and Australia, but from 1956-61 there was a net gain, mainly from Pakistan and the New Commonwealth. The balance was roughly even until 1971; then until 1981 there was a net annual loss of about 39,000 and between 1982-90 a net annual gain. In 1991 it was 28,000; in 1992 of 52,500 immigrants, 27,710 came from the New Commonwealth.

(3) The figures do not support the statistical necessity for the Act of 1971 or its effectiveness as a control but they suggest a fact commonly observed, that migration in both directions is altering the ancestral composition of the population especially in larger towns.

MIHAILOVICH, Draza (1893-1946). *See* YUGOSLAVIA-4. The communists shot him.

MIKADO. A title for the Japanese Emperor used almost exclusively by Europeans. *See also* GILBERT AND SULLIVAN.

MILAN was ruled by the Visconti from 1311-1447 and by the Sforza from 1450-1535. It became a duchy in 1395. Of great strategic and economic importance, its possessor might dominate all Italy north of Naples. Hence Louis XII's seizure of the city in 1500, the Franco-Spanish controversies over it and its final passage in 1534 to the Habsburgs under a treaty of 1524. Charles V conferred it on Philip, later K. of Spain, and from 1540-1713 it was the linchpin and H.Q. of Spanish power in Italy. In 1713 somewhat diminished by cessions to Savoy, it passed to Austria and further small areas were ceded in 1738 and 1744. Despite the abolition of its local autonomy, Austrian rule was benign, and liberal and scientific ideas flourished. It was accordingly ready to be the centre of French revolutionary influence and became the capital of the successive French puppet states. In 1815, with Venetia it passed again to Austria which ceded it to the New Kingdom of Italy in 1859.

MILAN DECREE (17 Dec. 1807) by Bonaparte ordered armed French ships to arrest as a vagrant any ship which had been searched by a British cruiser, declared any ship sailing to or from a British port to be lawful prize and forbade residents in territories under his control to trade with Britain or use any article of British origin. The first part was indiscriminate, the second contrary to international law and both unenforceable, while the third was ineffectual because European countries wanted the goods, and the British had means to smuggle them in. *See* BERLIN DECREE; FRANCO-RUSSIAN ALLIANCE, WAR OF; PENINSULAR WAR 1807-14-2.

MILBURGA (?-715) *d.* of K. Merewath of Mercia and St. Ermenburga. He founded Wenlock nunnery in 670 and she became its second abbess. *See* CHELLES.

MILDENHALL (Suffolk). A huge hoard of Roman and Byzantine silver ware was found here in 1942. There was an important R.A.F. airfield nearby in World War II.

MILE. *See* PACE AND MILE.

MILESIANS. The people of a fabulous Spanish King called Miledh, whose sons are said to have invaded Ireland in about 1300 B.C. They probably stand for the first Gaelic invaders of that island and drove the Fir Bolg, another traditionally Iberian tribe into the Hebrides.

MILFORD HAVEN (Dyfed). This magnificent natural harbour was originally developed by Massachusetts Quakers as a whaling base and then became a naval base; the latter, moved to Pembroke Dock, was important in both World Wars and was extended after 1957 and developed as a tanker terminal with oil refineries.

MILFORD HAVEN, 1st M. of. *See* BATTENBERG OR MOUNT BATTEN.

MILITARY ARCHITECTURE, MEDIAEVAL. (1) The Saxons mostly adapted or repaired existing and so usually Roman walls though sometimes they dug ditches, threw up an earth bank on the inner side and crowned it with a palisade. They thought in terms of protecting towns and villages such as the original Bamburgh (c. 550). Alfred repaired London Wall in 886. There is little evidence of the castle or private fort. The policy of burgh building (e.g. Towcester 921, Thelwall 923) as part of the reconquest after Alfred's death was based upon similar principles. The strategic purpose was to control the waterways along which Vikings moved. The Vikings in England were similarly inclined; the great Danish boroughs were repaired Roman towns, but they sometimes made temporary fortified camps.

(2) The Normans imported the castle i.e. the private fort which, given subinfeudation and the need to hold down large populations with small forces, spread far and wide. Based on French models its main feature was the *motte*, a steep sided mound covered with turf and surrounded by a ditch. Such mottes could be massive as at Thetford, and were difficult to climb. Unless stone was the only available material, the buildings were of wood. The motte was topped with a palisade, occasionally broken by towers, and it contained the owner's house. There was sometimes a palisaded platform in front of the gate and this was approached by a steep removable ladder or board across the ditch. Below, there was commonly an enclosure (bailey) which might, but in early days seldom did surround the motte. It was fortified by ditch and bank with a palisade or thorn hedge. This accommodated the garrison and their animals. These wooden castles could be elaborate structures and they were still being erected at the end of the 12th cent. Richard I built one at Messina. (*See* APPENDIX.)

(3) Stone fortifications came in with larger armies and siege techniques aimed at the fortifications rather than the men defending them. A great impetus was given to methods both of attack and defence by the crusaders who saw immense Byzantine fortresses and acquired much siegecraft from Byzantine armies. Palisades and gates were vulnerable to fire. Earth could be dug away under cover of mobile sheds (*penthouses*) and fences (*mantlets*) and great damage could be done to the motte enclosure by heaving stones thrown by beam engines (*ballistae*) or by slingshot from even larger beam engines (*trébuchets*). Wooden towers, sometimes mobile, and

covered with skins against fire, might be raised to dominate the bailey walls.

(4) The motte and bailey plan continued in use but stone walls began to replace the bailey palisades and there were more elaborate gates. The *portcullis,* an oriental introduction, was a protection against fire, since the garrison could shoot attackers and heave away combustibles through it. The motte became a citadel: but artificial mounds would bear only a fairly light weight of construction (*shell keeps*) and new castles tended to have either a *tall keep,* such as the White Tower (London) or the great keep at Rochester, requiring solid ground. These were square in plan (tower keeps) or rectangular (hall keeps); they were commonly placed on the side from which most danger was expected and served as the Lord's residence, storehouse and prison. If built in a town, they were usually on the wall (Porchester). Baileys were enlarged and often there was more than one (e.g. Chepstow). Sometimes the keep was virtually surrounded by one (e.g. Alnwick and Dover). Such fortresses were virtually military towns. (*See* APPENDIX.)

(5) These castles mostly suffered from the same defect. Each line of defence could offer a largely passive resistance only alone, and in the direction reciprocal to that of the attacker. This defect was first reduced by the addition of square towers or bastions projecting from the outer or *curtain walls* and capable of flanking an attacker, who then tended to concentrate his attack on these towers themselves. Since square towers are vulnerable on their face, round towers, which are harder to batter were soon substituted (e.g. Scarborough). Secondly galleries were built outwards from the tops of walls and towers so that the enemy could be assailed from directly overhead. It now became the object of the besieger to smash these galleries by bombardment before his miners and battering rams approached the wall and so wooden galleries (*hourds*) were replaced by stone (*machicolation*).

(6) By the 13th cent. the bailey had become, in a military sense, the vital part of the castle, for it supported most of the garrison and its resources and its loss would make the surrender of the keep inevitable. This led to a design revolution. In some cases (e.g. Caernarvon) the curtain was strengthened by high, *self contained towers* each of which had to be separately taken before an enemy who had penetrated to the bailey could stay there. In others (e.g. Harlech and Beaumaris) a *concentric plan* was adopted in which the outer curtain was comparatively low while close within, an inner bailey with towers far over-topped it so that an attacker had to engage both sets of fortifications at once, while most of the resources were in the inner bailey. Moreover some castles had protected *sally ports* for counter attack. To storm such castles before relief arrived involved a major battle; hence they were seldom attacked and hardly ever taken in the middle ages.

(7) Artillery, initially very inefficient, influenced military architecture only slowly. Late mediaeval castles were solidly built and could stand much battering, as the parliamentarians discovered in the Civil War. But it was eventually realised that high velocity, low trajectory guns would fell high buildings from the top downwards and that distant siege guns would have to be countered by fortress guns of equal range but whose recoil would shake any high walls on which they were placed. The first low profile artillery castles were built by Henry VIII at Deal and Walmer to control the Downs and at Yarmouth (I. of Wight).

(8) Meanwhile there had been changes of another kind. Strong King's destroyed castles or occupied them and would not permit new ones without *licence to crenellate*. Moreover, life became more settled and castles from 14th cent. onwards ceased to be minority strongholds in a hostile countryside. Royal castles (e.g.

Windsor) remained fortresses even if they were adapted as palaces but private ones developed into fortified houses (e.g. Maxstoke) proof against gangs but not intended for military purposes. The fierce independent baron was being replaced by the country gentleman and civil wars were fought in the open field.

MILITARY CROSS (M.C.) AND MILITARY MEDAL (M.M.). The M.C. was instituted in 1914 for officers below the rank of major and warrant officers for distinguished service in war; the M.M. in 1916 for warrant officers and below for bravery.

MILITARY KNIGHTS OF WINDSOR. See GARTER, ORDER OF THE.

MILITARY POLICE. Mounted military police were raised in 1855; foot police in 1885. They were amalgamated in 1926. Though always responsible for extra-regimental discipline, under modern conditions their most important wartime role is control and direction of the huge and vulnerable mass of military traffic.

MILITIA (1) The power (*posse*) of the county could not be required for service outside the county save in case of necessity or sudden invasion, and the townsmen could not be mustered outside their towns. These half-organised bands were replaced outside London by a militia. An Act of 1662 made Lords Lieutenant responsible for mustering and training. Individuals had to provide or pay for their own arms but might find a substitute for personal service and could not be required to serve outside England. In 1663 service was limited to 14 days a year i.e. the crown had to pay for more. It had been granted £70,000 a year for three years for expenses. In 1714 special arrangements were made for emergencies and insurrections. These expired in 1719 but were revived from 1722 to 1729. An elaborate militia act of 1757 attempted to re-animate the semi-moribund system because of the Seven Years' War. It fixed the numbers to be raised county by county to a total of 30,650 men and required half-company (20 men) training on the first Monday in the month from Apr. to Oct., company training on the third Mondays and regimental (7 companies) training from Tuesday to Friday in Whitsun week. The law was codified and amended in 1761. Militias of this type remained in actual or half hearted existence until 1921 but were fortunately never required to fight.

(2) The term was also used for part-time compulsorily raised troops in the French wars of 1793-1815. It was possible to escape service by paying for a substitute. Standards and discipline were low.

(3) In 1921 the previous special reserve was renamed the militia and the word was briefly used for the conscripted force raised just before World War II.

MILL, John Stuart (1806-73) was over-systematically educated from the age of three by his father, **James Mill** (1773-1836) a political economist, and he devoted much time to editing and publishing his father's work. He later regretted his missed childhood. From 1823-58 he worked in the India Office. He joined a utilitarian circle in 1823 and in 1825 the Speculative Society, but in 1826-7 he had a moral crisis or nervous breakdown and emerged convinced of a kind of converse utilitarianism, in which happiness is to be secured by pursuing some moral objective and the cultivation of the mind and feelings. He was naturally attracted by Wordsworth's poems and was soon a feared and admired literary critic. In 1830 he made friends with Mrs John Taylor, a radical scholar (whom he married in 1851) and he called her, probably with truth, the part author of his best works. Amongst them the most notable are his *System of Logic* (1843), an exposition of inductive science, *Principles of Political Economy* (1848), *On Liberty* and *Thoughts on Parliamentary Reform* (1859), *Representative Government* (1861), *Utilitarianism* (1863), and *The Subjection of Women* (1869). He was an M.P. from 1865-68 and his advocacy of women's franchise in print and on the 1867 Reform Bill originated the movement for women's rights.

He built much on his father's work and that of Bentham, Ricardo, and Malthus but in his writings he informed the aims of utilitarianism with a humane and moral quality, and offered for human problems radical solutions which were not always practicable.

MILLAIS. See PRERAPHAELITES.

MILLENARY PETITION (1603) was presented to James I by puritan ministers claiming support from over 1,000 others. Moderate in tone, it requested that certain practices (e.g. the sign of the cross at baptism and the use of the ring at weddings) be abolished and others (mostly related to vestments) made optional. See HAMPTON COURT CONFERENCE.

MILLENNIA. If the Star of Bethlehem was Halley's Comet, then Halley's periodicity falls in A.D. 16 or A.D. 2. Chinese astronomers recorded it in 87 B.C. which puts an appearance at 11 or 10 B.C. The gospel interpolation (Luke ii v 2) that the taxation (census) which caused the journey to Bethlehem took place when Cyrenius (Quirinius) was Gov. (procurator) of Syria points to 6 or 7 B.C. The first year of the Christian era was deferentially numbered at 1, not arithmetically at 0. Thus the date of the Nativity is as yet unproved, but the available evidence disproves the accepted one; and the millennial human disturbances of the years before A.D. 1000 and 2000 occurred in the wrong years. (2) Christians regarded A.D. 1000 as an approaching doom, and a reason for gravity, self abnegation and repentance. Such chiliasm, of course, meant nothing to the non-Christian world majority. The futuristic hedonism encouraged by British govts and hardly criticised by the churches, in the approach to A.D. 2000, and the construction at Greenwich of a domelike commercially managed temple to materialism (at a cost of £758M) represented the opposite outlook. Science was to guarantee a Brave New World (for those who could afford the entrance fee) while all the world and especially E. London could enjoy the artfully stimulated boom, the rejuvenation of some derelict Greenwich lands and the extension of the London transport system. The Dome celebrated the New Year 2000 with a show of unexampled vulgarity.

MILLET SYSTEM classified the Turkish subject peoples by their religion, made the religious head responsible for law and behaviour, and applied the law of the religious group (*millet*) to its members. In disputes between members of different *millets*, the law of the defendant applied. The enormous extent of Ottoman jurisdiction left the system embedded in the social outlook of many countries from the Danube to Aden and from Algiers to Basra. The Millet-i-Rum ("of the Romans") was the millet of the Orthodox Christians.

MILLING (FLOUR). Primitively a pestle and mortar was used, and then the (stone) hand quern, sometimes, if large, operated by two women. Grindstones, operated by slaves or quadrupeds, and later by wind or water were common in the middle ages because communal milling required quantity production. Such querns and grindstones were still occasionally used by the end of the 19th cent. but meanwhile steam mills were introduced in 1784 and in 1838 steamdriven roller mills were built at Budapest which acquired, as a result, a world wide flour trade. In 1880 powered roller milling was universal and wind and water milling out of business. See WINDMILLS.

MILNER, Alfred (1854-1925) Vist. MILNER (1902) was partly German, and educated in Germany and Oxford where he won every possible honour. In 1882 he joined the *Pall Mall Gazette* but meanwhile was strongly influenced towards public social service by Canon Barnett and Arnold Toynbee, whom he helped in 1884 to found Toynbee Hall. He became G. J. Goschen's private sec. in 1884 and learned imperial ideas and policies from him. The association continued when Goschen was

Chancellor of the Exchequer and in 1889 he became Director General of Accounts in Egypt, rising to U/Sec. for Finance in 1890. In 1892 he published a famous book *England in Egypt*. He then became Chairman of the Board of Inland Revenue and mainly devised the technicalities of Harcourt's death duties. From 1897-1905 he was High Commissioner in S. Africa. By then the Jameson Raid (1896) had inflamed the Boers and discredited Rhodes. He concluded that reform, meaning guarantees for *Uitlander* rights in the Transvaal, was essential or war was unavoidable. He encouraged *Uitlander* agitation and hardly tried to placate Paul Kruger. His activities were not wholly approved in London and he was thus spurred to justify them. Hence war broke out too early when the country was inadequately defended. When it was over he set about reorganising the conquered republics, repatriating deported Boers, improving farming and settlement and introducing English as the medium of instruction. One of the main problems was shortage of labour in the mines, which were needed to re-establish the economy quickly. He persuaded the Govt. to permit the introduction of Chinese indentured labour (1904). The proposal, on the face of it sensible if insensitive, was politically disastrous and involved the London Govt. in trouble at home and with J. C. Smuts, the rising Transvaal politician. He came home in 1905, and after much work in the City, committed the remarkable solecism of advising the Lords to reject Lloyd George's budget of 1909. He also opposed the Parliament Act of 1911 and Home Rule. From 1916 he was an important member of Lloyd George's war cabinet and his post-war govt. (1918-22).

MILNES, Richard Monckton (1809-85) 1st Ld. HOUGHTON (1863) became a conservative M.P. in 1837. He was pompous but sensible and kept up an extensive acquaintance with continental statesmen while promoting measures such as the Copyright Act and reformatories. He joined the Liberals in 1846 after the repeal of the Corn Laws. After 1849 he dropped politics and devoted himself to the literary scene which had always interested him. He had secured a pension for Tennyson in 1844, and had written *The Life and Letters of Keats* in 1848.

MILTON, John (1608-74) a scholar and writer by the age of ten, was producing poems while a Cambridge undergraduate. He wrote his lyrical poems between 1632-38 when he visited Grotius in Paris and Galileo in Florence. By now established as a protestant stylist, he began publishing political works, beginning with *Of Reformation, Touching Church Discipline* (1641) which earned him the dislike of the court. In 1643 he married and quarrelled with Mary Powell, daughter of a cavalier, and in the *Doctrine and Discipline of Divorce* advocated divorce for incompatibility which made him unpopular with everyone. He had also taken up the cudgels against censorship and in 1644 published his *Tractate on Education* and *Areopagitica*, the English *locus classicus* of the case for a free press. Reconciled with Mary in 1645, he wrote the *Four Chief Places in Scripture which Treat Marriage*. His commissioned *Eikonoklastes* against Gauden's *Eikon Basilike* was a well deserved failure, because his heart was not in it but his defences of the King's execution in *Tenure of Kings and Magistrates* (1649) and his *Pro Populo Anglicano Defensio* (1650) earned him a European reputation, and in 1650 the Council of State made him its Latin (Foreign) Secretary. He was already beginning to go blind, and Andrew Marvell was appointed to help him. Mary died in 1652, leaving him three daughters.

In 1654 he published his second *Defensio* which was even better known than the first and in 1656 he married Katherine Woodcock. She gave him a daughter in Oct. 1651 but both died in 1658. He was by now increasingly disenchanted with public affairs, blinder, driven more in

on himself. He began his long planned religious epic *Paradise Lost* in 1658. His last political work, the *Ready and Easy Way to Establish a Free Commonwealth* was written during the confusion after Oliver Cromwell's death. He was deprived and went into hiding at the Restoration, but Marvell and d'Avenant secured him a pardon.

By 1663, quite blind and rather helpless, he got his friend Paget to recommend a wife and, like K. David in his declining years, took Elizabeth Minshull who was 25. With her help he finished and published *Paradise Lost* in 1664. This, the greatest English classical poem, was instantly acclaimed even by those who disliked Milton's opinions or disapproved of his religion. *Paradise Regained* and *Samson Agonistes* appeared in 1671.

MILTON KEYNES. *See* NEW TOWNS.

MINCING LANE (London) so called from the nuns (mincheons) of St. Helen's, Bishopsgate which owned it, was used by Mediterranean importers to store their goods and later, by importers from the colonies especially for tea and sugar.

MIND **(1876)** periodical founded by Alexander Bain (1818-1903) was one of the earliest exponents of a physiologically based psychology.

MINDELHEIM. The Emperor Leopold offered the D. of Marlborough a principality while the latter was marching to Blenheim in 1704. In 1706 the new Emperor Joseph had possession of the Bavarian principality of Mindelheim as a result of the B. of Blenheim and conferred it on Marlborough. The lands reverted to Bavaria under the P. of Utrecht in 1712. The title is still born by the Dukes.

MINE ADVENTURERS. *See* MACKWORTH.

MINERAL AND BATTERY WORKS, CO of, was founded by William Humfrey and chartered in 1568. He had isolated zinc in 1566 and so could produce brass, then replacing bronze. The Co. mined for precious metals and also lead and copper which was converted from ingots into plates at its Nottingham Battery Works and into wire at Tintern. As a crown co. it was attacked for monopoly under James I, and the Civil War disrupted its operations. *See* CHARTERED COMPANIES.

MINES ACT 1842 (EMPLOYMENT). In 1840 the public was shaken by the report of a Royal Commission that in nearly every district, small sub-contractors or individual coal miners employed children of six or even five underground to draw trucks in the lowest or narrowest passages or to look all alone after ventilation doors in total darkness. In Scotland, S. Yorkshire, Yorkshire and Lancashire girls and women were also used to draw and carry coal in conditions verging on the bestial. The Act forbade the employment of females altogether and boys under ten underground and created an inspectorate to enforce this.

MINES ACTS 1850-72 (SAFETY). (1) 1850 legislated for safety in coalmines and created an inspectorate, to train which the Royal School of Mines was founded in 1851. The school, inspectors experience and reports created a better understanding of the industry as a result of which in **(2) 1860** boys under 18 were forbidden to run the engines; in **(3) 1862** every mine was required to have at least two shafts and in **(4) 1872** (which overhauled and consolidated the regs.) mine managers had to have certificates of competence. In addition, experience and its dissemination brought into use many technical improvements including large-fan ventilation, wire ropes and safety lamps.

MINES (NAVAL). *See* COMMERCE PROTECTION, NAVAL B(1), C(1).

MINES ROYAL, SOCIETY OF, a Crown Co. for mining precious metals started in 1564 by a patent to Thomas Thurland and Daniel Hochstetter an Augsburg miner and smelter. Mining began in Cumberland. In 1566 on the analogy of treasure trove the Court of Exchequer held that a base metal containing substantial amounts of gold or silver was a mine royal. The charter followed in 1568. Mining operations were moved to Devon and Cornwall and smelting to Neath in 1580 and a supplementary charter was obtained in 1605. Acts of 1689 and 1693 ended its monopoly. *See* CHARTERED COMPANIES.

MING. *See* CHINA.

MINING. *See* COAL.

MINISTER originally meant any servant. Its use for *diplomatic agent* and for an *important crown adviser* dates from the early 18th cent.; for *non-conformist clergymen* from the mid 19th cent. for a *political subordinate of a Sec. of State* from the mid 20th cent.

MINNESOTA (U.S.A.) reached in 1655 by French explorers, was not intensively organised or exploited. Part was ceded to Spain in 1762, and the rest to Britain in 1763. The British part passed technically to the U.S.A. in 1783 but the British North West Co. continued there as if nothing had happened. In 1803 the Spanish part was acquired by the U.S.A. under the Louisiana purchase and in 1806 the Americans explored and hoisted flags all over the area but the British North West Co. was not expelled until 1816. Organised as a territory in 1849, and admitted to the Union as a state in 1858, it sided with the Union in the Civil War.

MINIMUM LENDING RATE. *See* BANK RATE.

MINORCA or MENORCA (Med.). Balearic Catalan populated I. Its capital, Port Mahon, has a fine sheltered natural harbour. This was of great strategic and technical importance in the sailing era because ships could beat out of it against the prevailing N. Westerly winds. Thus a fleet could blockade the French and Spanish Mediterranean coasts, protect, in conjunction with Gibraltar, the trade route from the Atlantic to the E. and Central Mediterranean (which ran further south) and intercept shipping on a southerly wind. Accordingly the British seized it in 1713, developed the base, and held it until Admiral Byng lost it in 1756. It was recovered at the P. of Paris (1763) and lost again in 1781 and then held from 1798-1802. By that date the British possession of Malta made its recovery unnecessary (*see* GEORGE I-13; MEDITERRANEAN WAR 1797-9-2). The island has some red-haired descendants of Scottish troops. Mahon is named after Hannibal's brother Mago. Mayonnaise, invented by the French C-in-C's cook during the siege of 1756 is named from Mahon.

MINORITY TREATIES were meant to guarantee the special rights of minorities, such as Magyars in Roumania, in Central and Eastern European states, as part of the post World War I peace settlement. As the Govts. of the countries concerned knew that the guarantor states would in practice be apathetic, they did what they liked.

MINOR ORDERS. *See* CLERKS.

MINQUIERS. *See* CHANNEL IS.

MINSTRELS (10th-14th cents.) were musicians and occasionally rhymesters, originally servants of troubadours or trouvères, who acted as accompanists on the harp or pipes. Their inferior status clung to them even when they were independent strollers.

MINTO. *See* ELLIOT.

MINTON, Thomas (?-1836) and his son **Herbert (1793-1858)** began making porcelain at Stoke-on-Trent in 1790 and white-bodied earthenware with printed designs in 1825.

MINTS, FRANCHISE. *See* COINAGE *PASSIM*-7.

MINUET a fairly simple dance, capable of elaboration, for a couple who always had the floor to themselves.

MINUIT, Peter (1580-1638). *See* NEW YORK.

MINUTEMEN were Americans who kept arms and equipment in their houses and held themselves available to arm at a minute's notice to fight Indians or the British.

MIQUELON. *See* ST. PIERRE; NEWFOUNDLAND; PARIS, P. OF (10 FEB 1763); SEVEN YEARS' WAR.

MIRACLE PLAYS were mediaeval dramatic shows illustrating biblical history or saintly legend. The earliest surviving in English dates from about 1300, though much older French ones exist. The four great cycles of English plays are those of Chester, Coventry, Wakefield and York and they reached their fullest development in the early 16th cent. Performances were a public benefit or duty (cf the Oberammergau Passion Play) supervised by the corporation, different episodes being distributed among the several guilds. They mostly took place on the great festival days. They were acted on wheeled stages which were sometimes drawn, like modern floats, in processions. *See* MORALITY PLAYS.

MIRASDAR (India) was one of a group of co-owners of villages in N. Madras. Each share was heritable and the principal members of the group collected the village tax and paid a lump sum to the Govt.

MIR JAFAR (?-1765) the greatest noble at the Court of the Nawab Suraj-u-Dowlah of Bengal, conspired with the Jagath Seth to depose him and secured the HEIC's help by promising large sums of compensation for his seizure of Calcutta. Naturally the HEIC agreed and so Mir Jafar's troops stood aside, while Clive defeated the Nawab at Plassey. On elevation he granted the *zamindari* of the XXIV Parganas and undertook an offensive and defensive alliance with the HEIC. Extravagance and the onerous financial terms of his agreements drove him towards bankruptcy and he entered into an intrigue with the Dutch which came to nothing. Meanwhile Clive had gone to England and Mir Jafar's son had died. The British accordingly deposed him in favour of **MIR KASIM (?-?1767)** his son-in-law, who ceded the three districts of Burdwan, Midnapore and Chittagong but was a more efficient and sensible administrator than Mir Jafar. In particular to regularise the wholesale abuses of private trade by HEIC officials he agreed a new tax regime (9% *ad valorem* on the officials, 40% on the rest) with the Pres. of the Calcutta council but the council demanded 2% and on salt only. Thereupon he remitted all duties, which enabled the industrious Bengalis to undersell the British. War followed. Mir Kasim was driven into Oudh where he, with the Nawab of Oudh, were defeated at Buxar (Oct. 1764). Mir Jafar, was meanwhile reinstated upon financial terms which were much more onerous than before, for he had to pay for the war against his son-in-law, restrict his duty on European trading to 2% and pay out enormous sums in presents.

MIRROR OF JUSTICES, THE. A Latin legal treatise compiled in c. 1285 printed in 1642 and translated in 1646. It deals with offences, considered as sins against the Holy Peace, actions, defences, judgement and abuses. The unknown author claimed to have been wrongly imprisoned, denounced contemporary judges for corruption and the law for uncertainty. He sought a return to an idealised Anglo-Saxon past. The work was uninfluential until Sir Edward Coke C.J. used it to support his view that Anglo-Saxon liberties had been subverted by the Normans.

MISDEMEANOUR, in English law was any offence for which lands and goods were *not* forfeitable. It was generally triable by jury, the accused could give evidence and bystanders were not bound to prevent the commission of the act. *See* FELONY; PUNISHMENT.

MISE was an expense, payment or concession in connection with an important matter, and so a settlement. In Wales and Chester a mise was paid by the people to a Lord Marcher, Earl, Prince or King at his succession and accepted as a token of mutual security. The Mises of Lewes (1264) and Amiens (1265) were settlements involving arbitration. *See* MONTFORT-4.

MISL. *See* SIKHS-3 *et seq.*

MISSAL or MASS BOOK began to appear as a combination of earlier incomplete liturgical books in the 10th cent.

MISSIONARIES IN BRITAIN AND IRELAND (1) Christianity was well established in parts of Britain when

St. ALBAN was martyred at Verulamium (c. 287). It spread to Ireland perhaps through fugitives from Diocletian's persecutions which began in 303. St. NINIAN, a Cumbrian, consecrated Bp. at Rome in 394, was a friend of St. Martin of Tours to whom he dedicated a church at Whithorn in about 400. CALPURNIUS, a priest's son, was a deacon somewhere on the West Coast of Britain when his son St. PATRICK (?385-461) was born. Patrick was kidnapped in 401 in the upheavals before the collapse of Roman Britain and was a slave in Antrim until 407 when he escaped to Brittany. He is said to have become a disciple of the great St. GERMANUS (?378-448) at Auxerre. This saint (an ex-officer) visited Britain as a papal commissioner to deal with PELAGIANISM and incidentally organised a British force which won the "Halleluja Victory" over invading Picts and Saxons. He consecrated Patrick bishop and sent him to Ireland in 432. Patrick, a powerful preacher, spread the Gospel in Meath, Ulster and Connaught and even secured a hearing before the High King at Tara.

The year 444 was crucial. Germanus visited Britain again and this time got the Pelagians expelled by the local authorities, while in Ireland Patrick set up his see at Armagh, and with many priests and teachers, whom he had trained, began systematically to organise the Irish Church. Consequently when the heathen invasions of Britain began in earnest, the British and Irish Christians were doctrinally in unison with Rome.

(2) Though Britain reverted to heathenism, the invasions did not wipe out British Christians. Pockets of them remained behind but most were driven westwards to Cornwall, Wales, Galloway and possibly Cumbria. These (and the Irish) were cut off from the rest of the Christian world. From Cornwall some went to Brittany. Isolated too by parallel developments on the Continent, Ireland being spared invasions if not raids, soon developed a powerful church in comparative security. These scattered bodies all maintained some mutual contact but their isolation and the political peculiarities of their situation led them to diverge from the Roman church in ceremonial, the calendar and above all organisation. In the Celtic churches the effective centres were monasteries; the paramount authorities were abbots; bishops became lesser monastic officials with the power of consecration derived from their apostolic succession but without jurisdiction or a territorial cure.

(3) These developments began in the generation after St. Patrick. Thus St. ILLTYD (?460-?540) founded a great monastic school at Llantwit Major (Glam.); his pupil St. SAMSON (?490-?565) abbot and bishop, visited Ireland, preached in Cornwall and founded the monastery at Dol in Brittany. His contemporary St. CADOC (?-?) founded a monastery at Llancarfan near Cardiff and preached in Cornwall and Scotland. St. BRIGID or BRIDE (?450-?523) was abbess of a famous nunnery which she founded at Kildare. The Irish monastic movement was launched by St. FINNIAN (?-549) another Abbot-Bishop who knew St. Cadoc and established at CLONARD in Meath an influential convent based on his ideas. This was a momentous event, for his pupils at Clonard included four famous men. These were St. CIARAN or KIERAN (?516-49), who founded the great abbey at Clonmacnois, St BRENDAN (486-578) the founder of Clonfert, who visited Scotland and probably Britain, St. COLUMBA or COLUMCILLE (?521-597) and his colleague St. CANICE or KENNETH (?-?600). In 563 Columba moved to the Scottish Isle of Iona, established the monastery there and began with his colleagues and followers to strengthen the Irish (i.e. Scots) Christians in Argyll, and to preach among the mainland and island Picts; he converted Brude, the Pictish King and doubtless helped by further Scots immigration, established Christianity as a majority religion in Western Scotland, with Iona as its focus. He trained St. AIDAN (?- 651) from 574, and missions soon crossed into Lothian where they came into contact with the Northumbrians. (*See* DALRIADA.)

(4) In the south there were important developments inspired from Rome. There were Christians in Kent, including Bertha wife of K. Aethelbert, and in 597 the year of Columba's death St. AUGUSTINE (?-605) prior of Pope Gregory's monastery of St. Andrew, landed on Gregory's instructions with LAURENTIUS (?-619) and 40 monks in Thanet. The King was baptised on 1st June. In 601 a second mission arrived with MELLITUS (?-624), JUSTUS (?-627) and PAULINUS (?-644) and Augustine went to Arles to be consecrated first Abp. of Canterbury. He failed to win over the Celtic churches of Wales and the West but pressed his work successfully among the Anglo-Saxons. In 604 he established Justus as first Bp. of Rochester, and Mellitus in Essex as Bp. of London. He also founded the great monastic institution at Canterbury later named after himself.

(5) Laurentius succeeded him, and had to deal with a serious crisis at the end of his rule. Mellitus had converted Sebert, K. of the E. Saxons, but not his family. Sebert and Aethelbert of Kent both died in 616. A heathen or perhaps political or personal reaction drove Mellitus and Justus to France. Laurentius, however, converted or cajoled Aethelbert's son Eadhald into having them back and when Laurentius died, Mellitus was able to succeed him. At this period, Paulinus acquired his intimacy with the Kentish Royal family and when Justus became fourth Abp. negotiations for a marriage between K. Edwin of Northumbria and Ethelburga of Kent were set on foot. Paulinus, consecrated Bp. by Justus went north with her in 625 and in 627 staged a spectacular baptism of the King and most of his court including St. HILDA (614-80) Edwin's daughter. He travelled much in Yorkshire and Lindsey and was recognised as Abp. of York in 632, just as Edwin fell in battle with the Mercians. Paulinus escaped with Ethelburga to Kent and ended his career at Rochester.

(6) Romanist activity in the south, especially that of HONORIUS (Abp. of Canterbury from 627-53) and of St. BIRINUS (?-650) whom he made Bp. of Dorchester in 635, remained unabated but the military disaster left the northern missionary field open to the Celts. St. OSWALD (?605-42) a royal exile had been brought up at Iona. In 633 he returned as King to Northumbria with Aidan, expelled the occupying Welsh and Mercians and set up Aidan as Bp. of LINDISFARNE in 635. Aidan created a monastery and training school through which Celtic Christianity was disseminated in the north of England. He spoke Saxon badly, and the King often interpreted for him at important assemblies. This close relationship with royalty continued after Oswald fell at the B. of Maserfield and was succeeded by his cousin OSWIU (?- 651). Aidan also trained St. CEDD (?-664) and his brother St. CHAD or CEADDA (?-672) at Lindisfarne where the next bishop was St. FINAN (?-661) from Iona. Finan was a determined missionary; he encouraged St. Hilda to found the great double convent at Whitby which she ruled until her death. He baptised Peada, the Mercian King and Sigebert the King of Essex and set up missions in their territories. The head of the Essex mission was Cedd who became Celtic Bp. of the East Saxons in 654. There was already the Roman bishop based in London but Cedd established monasteries at Maldon and Tilbury. For reasons now uncertain he withdrew to Yorkshire where he founded and became abbot of Lastingham.

(7) By now the inconvenience of two missionary churches in competition was becoming intolerable. The laity were confused by differing rites; the conflicting calendars caused the scandal of simultaneous feasts and fasts; and the jurisdictional claims of Roman bishops clashed with the pre-eminence of the Celtic abbots. In the north there now arose St. WILFRID (634-709) who began his training at Lindisfarne but went in 653 to Rome

and Lyons whence he returned in 658 as a convinced champion of Roman methods. He was not alone. K. Aldfrid of Northumbria had founded Ripon Abbey with Celtic monks from Melrose; K. Oswiu required them in 661 to adopt Roman customs. The King then made Wilfrid abbot. This year was the year when St. COLMAN (?-676) another Iona monk became Bp. of Lindisfarne.

(8) With Wilfrid's aggressive personality and a half convinced King a confrontation was arranged at St. Hilda's convent. At this SYNOD OF WHITBY (664) the Celtic party was led by Colman, Cedd, Chad, and Hilda; the Romanist by Wilfrid. K. Oswiu settled the issue himself in favour of Rome, because it was said, if St. Peter had the Keys of Heaven he might otherwise not open the gate to the King. Cedd, Chad and Hilda accepted the ruling. Colman retired to Iona (and thence to Ireland) and Chad took his place at Lindisfarne. Wilfrid, who seemed to have annoyed the King, went to France and was consecrated Abp. of York at Compiègne. He was prevented from exercising his jurisdiction which was wielded from Lindisfarne by Chad. It seems likely that Chad's position was part of a compromise package which Oswiu imposed and which Wilfrid rejected.

(9) Wilfrid went to Ripon and carried on episcopal business in Mercia. He also kept in touch with affairs in Kent where DEUSDEDIT, the first Saxon Abp. of Canterbury had died in 664, leaving the see vacant. Wighard, the successor-elect died in 667.

(10) Pope Vitalian twice offered the post to the African St. ADRIAN (?-710) who suggested the Cilician THEODORE of TARSUS (?602-690). Vitalian despatched them both, the Greek as Abp. the African as Abbot of St. Augustine's. Their remarkable partnership revolutionised the English Church. Theodore began with a general visitation. He ingeniously disposed of the controversy between Chad and Wilfrid by discovering a defect in Chad's consecration. In 669 Wilfrid thus took his place at York, while Chad returned to Lastingham and was then (properly) consecrated Bp. of the Mercians, with his see at Lichfield. Here he died. Wilfrid by introducing the Benedictine rule in all the northern monasteries, stamped out the remaining Celtic influences; and in 673 at Theodore's COUNCIL OF HEREFORD, all the ecclesiastical authorities submitted to Canterbury.

(11) The new unity was however fragile. In about 677 K. Egfrith of Northumbria and Theodore attempted to divide the see of York and Wilfrid went to Rome to appeal against them. Theodore promptly put Bosa (?-705) a monk of Whitby, in possession of York. Wilfrid returned in 679 with bulls restoring him to his position. Egfrith arrested him and kept him in custody until 681.

(12) Wilfrid now went to Sussex, then still heathen. He is reputed to have built Selsey Abbey, converted the South Saxons and taught them how to fish.

(13) When Egfrith died in 686 Wilfrid was reconciled with Theodore who allowed him to oust Bosa from the reduced see of York. In 691 just after Theodore's death, he quarrelled again with a Northumbrian King (Aldfrid), resigned the see to Bosa and accepted the Bishopric of Leicester from Ethelred of Mercia. The result was further conflict with BRIHTWALD (?650-731) the new Abp. who disapproved of Wilfrid's anti-Celtic fanaticism and excommunicated him at the Council of Estrefeld in 702. He again appealed to Rome, was again upheld but resigning his see for Hexham, died at Ripon.

(14) By Brihtwald's death the English Church had assumed a formal unity, weakened by the seeds of the long feud between Canterbury and York; it had achieved an organisation into 17 tribal bishoprics which survived with minor changes until the Norman Conquest; and it was in full subjection to Rome to which appeals had become customary. It was the only nationwide organisation and though there was much teaching and preaching to be done, heathenism had ceased to be respectable.

MISSIONS TO EUROPE. (1) Central Europe. St. COMGALL (517-603) founded the monastery of Bangor near Belfast in 559. It had many colonies: he trained hundreds of monks and himself helped Columba in Inverness. Two of his pupils, St. COLUMBAN (540-615) and St. GALL (550-645) with eleven others travelled up the Rhine Valley founding monasteries, particularly at Luxeuil, in 590. Their obstinate adherence to Celtic customs made them ecclesiastical enemies and their denunciation of ducal morals caused their expulsion from Burgundy, but they went to L. Constance and separated at Bregenz. Columban founded a famous house at Bobbio in 614. Gall remained near Bregenz. The abbey of Corbie in Picardy was founded from Luxeuil in about 660 and that at St. Gallen in about 750. The Corbie foundation had a further colony at Corvey in Germany. By the 9th cent. Irish missionaries were working as far afield as Vienna.

(2) Low Countries. The Carolingian Pepin of Landen and his wife Itta were Christian. In 630 St. FURSEY (?-648) with his brothers St. FOILLAN (?-655) and St. ULTAN (?-686) founded a Celtic monastery at Burgh Castle (Essex) and in 640 Fursey went to Gaul, being succeeded at Burgh Castle by Foillan. With the help of Erchinwald, mayor of the palace of Austrasia, he founded a monastery at Lagny. Fursey's apocalyptic visions influenced mediaeval thought and art and even Dante's *Inferno*. Meantime, Mercian raids drove his brothers abroad. After Pepin's death (640) Itta had founded a convent at Nivelles, of which her daughter St. GERTRUDE (625-59) was abbess. Itta and Gertrude encouraged missionary monks and gave Foillan land for a convent at Fosses. Gertrude's sister St. BEGGA (?-693) was the mother of Pepin of Herstal.

The Carolingians were thus inspired to recruit preachers and teachers (*see* ALCUIN) extensively in the British Is. Possibly for linguistic reasons the English soon became prominent among them. St. Wilfrid preached in Frisia from 678-79. His mission there was locally ineffectual, but his pupil at Ripon St. WILLIBRORD (658-739) after training at Rathmelsigi (?Mellifont) in Ireland, headed a mission in 690. His followers, the two EWALDS (?-695) penetrated and were martyred in Westphalia. He visited Rome in 693 and 695 when the Pope made him Abp. of the Frisians. With papal backing he obtained grants from Pepin of Herstal for a cathedral at Utrecht (695) and an important monastery at Echternach (698). He was driven from Utrecht in 714 by a local potentate. Another Ripon monk St. LIAFWHINE or LEBWINE (?-773) started work at Deventer in the 740s.

(3) Frisia and Germany. St. BONIFACE or WYNFRITH (?675- 755) a monk for 40 years at Exeter and Nursling, went unsuccessfully to Frisia in 716 perhaps to succour Willibrord; and like him, visited Rome to get papal authority. He was a man of powerful intellect, character and charm. He and Willibrord re-established the Low Country missions and created a system of circuit bishops. By 722 he was operating in middle and south Germany where he hewed down Thor's Oak at Geismar, and soon after he began from Mainz to create a permanent ecclesiastical organisation. In this he was helped by many born or trained in England, including his relatives St. WINEBALD (?-761) first Abbot of his dual foundation at Heidenheim, and St. WILLIBALD (?-786) whom he consecrated Bp. of Eichstatt in 742. He was now given a legatine commission to reform the Frankish church, which he effected through a series of councils; he also appointed his most important pupil, the Carolingian St. CHRODEGANG (715-66) Bp. of Metz. The German work, however, went on. In 743 he founded the great abbey at Fulda and in 748 he established a nunnery at Bischofsheim under the abbess St. LIOBA (700-80) from Wimborne. He was eventually murdered while preaching in Frisia and was succeeded at Mainz by St. LULL (?-786) another Saxon trained at Malmesbury. In 761 St. WALBURGA (?-779) succeeded her brother Winebald as head of the double convent at Heidenheim. Because her festival happens to be on May Day (*Walpurgisnacht*) her name is associated in German folklore with witchcraft. Boniface's work in Frisia was continued by his pupil St. GREGORY of Utrecht (707-75). He had trained several Englishmen of whom one, St. LUDGER (744-809) went to York, studied under Alcuin, and in 775 started work at Deventer, where Lebwine had recently died. In 795 Charlemagne sent him to Westphalia. He founded Münster of which he became the first bishop and its abbey. WILLEHAD (?-789), a friend of Alcuin, also preached in Holland and Frisia (766-80), then among the Saxons until 782, and after Widukind's revolt became Bp. of Bremen in 787.

(4) Interlude. This powerful western influence upon the Continent was interrupted by the Viking Wars which blocked the regular sea routes, particularly by the creation of the Duchy of Normandy. The establishment of the Cluniac-influenced Anglo-Norman state and the subsidence of Scandinavian migrations brought about a new orientation in English missionary effort.

(5) Scandinavia. The attempt of St. ANSKAR (801-65) trained at Corbie and Corvey, to convert the Scandinavians first from Hamburg and then from Bremen was frustrated after his death by wars and not resumed until the conversion of the Norwegian K. Olaf Tryggvason. From about 995 he encouraged Christianity, probably using English priests encountered during his English campaigns, but employing much cajolery and violence too. His Danish contemporary K. Swein Forkbeard acted similarly using missionaries mostly from Hamburg. In the next generation St. Olaf was converted in England and brought many English missionaries when he conquered Norway in 1016. His methods resembled those of Olaf Tryggvason. Swein's son, Canute the Great, was already Christian, and missionary activity continued under his patronage in Denmark and in Norway after he conquered it in 1030.

The constant intercourse of the Scandinavian lands with each other and north Germany imported the new ideas into Sweden, and probably with Canute's encouragement, an English mission from York under St. SIGFRID (?-1045) worked from Växjö in southern Sweden and baptised the Swedish K. Olaf Skotkonung, while Sigfrid's relative St. ESKIL (?-1080) the martyr, established a centre at Strängnäs on L. Malar. By the end of the 11th cent. the history of Scandinavian missioning and German political problems made it necessary to separate Scandinavian from the always weak authority of Hamburg. In 1104 a bishopric was set up at Lund then in Danish territory.

In another generation the Scandinavian church organisation had proved too primitive and the crusading Pope Eugenius III despatched the English cardinal NICHOLAS BREAKSPEARE (later Pope Adrian IV) to effect a reorganisation. In 1152 he gave Norway its own metropolitical see at Nidaros (Trondheim) and brought forward St. EYSTEIN (?-1188) who was elected Abp. in 1157. At the same time the Englishman St. HENRY (?-1160) became a bishop of the leading Swedish see of Uppsala. He accompanied the Swedish King St. ERIC (?-1160) in his forcible conversion of the Finns, by whom he was murdered. Abp. Eystein at Trondheim waged a ceaseless campaign to spiritualise the Norwegian church; this involved him in the sanguinary politics of the time, but he continued to press missionary activity. In particular he supported St. THORLAC (1133-93) an Icelander trained at Lincoln and Paris who returned to Iceland to give shape to the unorganised Christianity of that island's colonists. Thorlac became Bp. of Skalholt in

1178; but meanwhile in 1181 Eystein had to flee Norway and spent two years at Bury St Edmunds. Here he wrote a *Life of St. Olaf.* He returned to Norway in 1183.

Henceforth Scandinavian church development is part of the domestic history of the countries concerned.

MISSISSIPPI, RIVER, STATE AND TERRITORY. De Soto crossed an inland reach of the river in 1541 but its possibilities as a highway were only appreciated after Marquette and Jolliet had explored it in 1673.

The nameless area between the river and the present state of Georgia had been granted to the Carolina proprietors by a Charter of 1662 as far south as Lat. 31°, extended to 29° in 1665. On the other hand in 1682 La Salle following in the steps of Jolliet, claimed the riparian territories for the French crown. Forts were built and from 1699 Iberville began to settle and administer the western end which thus, according to the French ideas was part of the Louisiana, and according to English part of Carolina. Neither side colonised at all vigorously here, and local conflicts remained insignificant. When the colony of Georgia was formed in 1732, it succeeded to the local Carolina claims; English settlement did not reach far inland even in Georgia proper but the possibility of conflict remained. Consequently, its cession to Britain was imposed by the T. of Paris (1763) at the end of the Seven Years War. Some English coastal colonisation followed and the areas south of Lat. 31° was constituted a separate province called West Florida. It was occupied by Spanish troops in 1770 during the American rebellion and formally ceded to Spain by the T. of Paris in 1783. Spain, however, continued to claim the area up to Lat. 33° against Georgia, now part of the U.S.A., until 1795 when she gave up these claims by Pinckney's T. In 1798 the area was organised as the MISSISSIPPI TERRITORY of the U.S.A. and Georgian claims were given up in 1802.

In 1812 the western part of East Florida was annexed by the new state of Louisiana and in 1813 the rest was added to the Mississippi territory. In 1817 the western half of the territory became the STATE OF MISSISSIPPI, the eastern becoming the TERRITORY OF ALABAMA, which was itself constituted a state in 1819. The cession and liquidation of East Florida was recognised by Spain in the Adams-Onis T. of 1819. Mississippi and Alabama both supported the Confederacy in the American Civil War.

MISSISSIPPI SCHEME (1717-20). John Law launched the French *Compagnie des Indes* for colonising the Mississippi basin. Reports of gold and silver caused the shares to appreciate and the company by securing control over the Paris mint and the farm of the Govt. revenue was effectively in control of the national finances. Its main asset, the Mississippi, was unexpectedly hard to develop and no gold or silver appeared. The debts could only be paid by further extensions of control, and Law tried to acquire the *Banque Royale*, but public suspicions brought a run on the Company, the shares fell from 40 times par to below par and in the ensuing crash Law fled.

MISSOLONGHI (Greece). Where Byron died during the Greek War of Independence in 1824.

MISSOURI. *See* LOUISIANA PURCHASE.

MISSOURI COMPROMISE (1820) admitted Missouri to the U.S.A. as a slave state and Maine as a free state keeping the numbers even. It divided the Louisiana territory along Lat. 36° 31' so that the greater part north of the line was free in compensation for the probability that Florida and Arkansas would enter the union as slave states. It put off the civil war for a generation and encouraged the mid-century westward expansion of the U.S.A.

MISTERY (related to *Master*) is a skilled craft or the body or guild whose Masters regulated it, and which exhibited the mystery plays.

MISTRAL. A strong summer north wind, which blows for 3 or 4 days at a time in the Gulf of Lions, creating great difficulties for shipping under sail and interrupting commercial traffic.

MISTRESS OF THE ROBES. *See* GROOM OF THE STOLE.

MITCHELSTOWN. When William O'Brien was summoned to a court at Mitchelstown for conspiracy, a densely attended meeting was addressed by John Dillon in the square. The police were squeezed out and fired from their barracks. A coroner's jury pronounced a verdict of murder against the police.

MITFORD and FREEMAN-MITFORD Of this articulate family **(1) William (1744-1827)** wrote a well known *History of Greece* at Gibbon's suggestion and was an M.P. in 1785-90, 1796-1806 and 1812-18. His brother **(2) John (1748-1830) 1st Ld. REDESDALE (1802)** became an M.P. in 1788, Attorney General in 1799, Speaker of the Commons in 1801 and from 1802-6 an unpopular Lord Chancellor of Ireland who opposed R. Catholic emancipation. He wrote learned legal works and favoured the Corn Laws. His son **(3) John Thomas (1805-86) 2nd Ld. and 1st E. (1877)** became Lord Chairman of Committees from 1851 because of his grasp of legislative detail. He also engaged in public controversy with Cardinal Manning, opposed Irish disestablishment and the institution of divorce. The peerages died with him but his relative **(4) Algernon Bertram (1837-1916) Ld. REDESDALE (1902)** of the second creation, was a diplomat and civil servant and a conservative M.P. from 1892-95. He wrote, inter alia, an autobiography and a book on Japan. Of his children **(5) Nancy (1904-73)** was a witty and influential writer of novels (e.g. *The Pursuit of Love*), essays (*Noblesse Oblige*) and biographies (*Madame de Pompadour* and *Voltaire in Love*). She coined the phrases "U or non-U".

MITRE. This curious episcopal hat symbolises the tongues of fire which hung over the heads of the Apostles at the first Whitsun. It was first recorded in the west in 1049. Anglican bishops did not wear them between the Reformation and the late 19th cent.

MITTIMUS **(Lat: 'we send'). (1)** A writ to remove the record of a case from one court to another; **(2)** A warrant committing a person to the custody of the keeper of a prison.

MOD (Sc. related to A.S. *moot*) Anciently a meeting for summary justice in Scotland; more recently a Gaelic literary and musical gathering equivalent to an Eisteddfod.

MODS. *See* ROCKERS.

"MODEL" PARLIAMENT. Edward I's Westminster parliament of Nov. 1295 is sometimes so-called because it was organised in two houses, one of lords spiritual and temporal, the other of two knights per shire and burgesses from towns, and it was thought to be the model for later parliaments down to 1834. Diocesan clergy, however, sent proctors, a number of lords spiritual were abbots, and nearly a century later the commons were inviting lords to sit with them.

MODENA. *See* HABSBURGS.

MODERNISM. *See* ANGLICANISM.

MODUS TENENDI PARLIAMENTUM **(Lat. = Manner of Holding a Parliament or How to hold a Parliament),** a treatise written between 1316-1324 by William Ayreminne, a royal clerk and later Bp. of Norwich. A version on the Irish parliament was written 70 years later.

MOGULS or MOGHULS. This word, a corruption of 'Mongol', signifies an Indian imperial Moslem dynasty.

(1) Babur its founder was a Barlas Turk descended from Genghis Khan. Using Kabul as his base, he defeated Ibrahim Lodi at the decisive first B. of Panipat (1526), established his capital at Delhi, overthrew the Rajputs at Khanua (1527) and in 1529 conquered Bihar. He was succeeded by **(2) Humayun (r. 1530-56)** who in 1542 was driven into exile in Persia by Afghan rebels. He made a recovery and by 1555 had retaken Delhi and Agra. His famous son **(3) Akbar (r. 1556-1605)** crushed

a Hindu rebellion at the second B. of Panipat in 1556. Between 1556-71 he extended his rule over Northern India and by 1601 it was widened northwestwards to Kashmir and Kandahar and southwards into the Deccan. He established religious toleration and with the aid of a Hindu minister established the Land Revenue Settlement. His son **(4) Jehangar (r. 1605-27)** an extravagant incompetent, lost Kandahar to the Persians and spent most of his father's reserves. He was the first Indian emperor visited by an English ambassador, Sir Thomas Roe.

His son **(5) Shah Jahan (r. 1627-58)** outwardly the most splendid of the Moguls, built the Taj Mahal at Agra. His other building activities, the wars with the Persians inherited from his father, and above all unrest created by his religious bigotry thrust the empire rapidly on a downward path and weakened the authority of the throne. During an illness in 1657 his sons **(6) Dara Shirkuh** and **(7) Aurungzib (1658-1707)** rebelled and fought each other. Aurungzib defeated his brother, assumed the empire and imprisoned his father at Agra until his death in 1666. He had considerable military success and under him the empire nominally reached its greatest extent. His policy of high taxation and religious persecution, however, divided the empire which Akbar had striven to unite, between an oppressive dominant moslem military minority and a discontented Hindu majority, and the government found it impossible to enforce its policies fully in the outlying provinces. Meantime, three factions, the so-called Turanis, Iranis and Hindustanis had grown up at court. When Aurangzib died in 1707 the structure virtually collapsed. The Marathas revolted; viceroys, particularly in Hyderabad, Bengal and Oudh set themselves up as local dynasts, while the three factions ignored the real problems and fought for the throne. A civil war between his sons led to the triumph of **(8) Bahadur Shah (r. 1709-12).** Seven years of chaos and war between his relatives ended in the accession of **(9) Mohammed Shah (1719-48).** The collapse of central power was now completed by invasions. In 1737 the Marathas defeated the Moghul forces at Delhi and in 1739 Nadir Shah of Persia defeated them again at Karnaul and sacked Delhi. From this time onwards, the Moghul throne was a nominal or ceremonial sovereignty centred on a small tract of country around Delhi and controlled mainly by the Marathas. In 1761 **(10) Shah Alam** was involved in war with the British who defeated him at Patna, and in 1764 at Buxar. He was then moved to Allahabad but restored to a nominal position in 1805. The Moghul monarchy was extinguished by the British after the Indian mutiny.

MOHAMMEDANISM. *See* CALIPHATE; ISLAM.

MOHARREM, DECREE OF. *See* OTTOMAN PUBLIC DEBT.

MOFFAT, Robert (1795-1883) this powerful, indeed heroic, personality worked very successfully as a missionary in Namaqualand from 1816-19 and then among the Griquas and Bechuanas until 1869 not only as a missionary but as a general protector to whom the Botswana tribes owe their survival.

MOHAWKS were a tribe of the IROQUOIS confederacy (q.v.) MOHICANS or MOHEGANS were a different family of clans of MAHICAN (q.v.) affiliation. MOHOCKS were aristocratic young ruffians who terrorised the London streets. A proclamation was issued against them in Mar. 1712.

MOHUN a Norman family whose first member William was settled by William I in Somerset, where the family was powerful and founded and maintained connections with, Bruton and Dunster priories until the later 14th cent. **John (?1270-1330) Ld. of DUNSTER** was an influential personality under Edward I and II. His grandson **John (1320-76)** was a soldier in France and Scotland. Later descendants included **John (1592-1640),** a royalist ennobled as **1st Ld. MOHUN (1628)** and **Charles**

(1675-1712) 4th Ld., a duellist acquitted by the Lords of murder at the age of eighteen, who killed many men and ended in a duel with the D. of Hamilton in which he and his antagonist were both mortally wounded. The event figures in Thackeray's *Esmond*

MOHUR. Indian gold coin worth, under British rule, 16 rupees (£1) at Calcutta and 15 at Bombay and Madras (18s. 9d.). As it was minted at Madras, this resulted in a northward drift of gold and a southward drift of silver. It was superseded by the gold sovereign at 16 rupees to the £1 in 1899.

MOIDART, SEVEN MEN OF (*see* JACOBITES-18) were the Young Pretender's seven friends, George Kelly (1688-?) formerly Atterbury's secretary, Sir John and Aeneas Macdonald, Sir John O'Sullivan the Prince's Adj.-Gen., Thomas Sheridan (?-1746) his tutor, Sir John Strickland, and William Murray, M. of Tullibardine (?-1746) the attainted son of the first D. of Atholl and a commander in the Jacobite expedition of 1719.

MOIDORE. A Portuguese 17th and 18th cent. coin worth 27s. sterling.

MOIRA. *See* RAWDON HASTINGS.

MOLASSES ACT (1733) to encourage colonial distillers, taxed foreign rum brought into British colonies at 9d. a gallon but molasses at 6d. *See also* SUGAR.

MOLESWORTH (1) Robert (1656-1725) 1st Vist. (1719) an Irish supporter of William III in 1688 was sent on unsuccessful missions to Denmark in 1689 and 1692. He was an Irish M.P. in 1695 and from 1703-05 and an English M.P. from 1705-08 and from 1714. His *s*. **(2) John (1679-1726) 2nd Vist.** was Ambassador in Tuscany and Turin and from 1715 a commissioner of Trade and Plantations. His brother **(3) Richard (1680-1758) 3rd Vist.** fought at Blenheim (1704) saved Marlborough's life at Ramillies (1706) and after further conventional military service, became an Irish M.P. in 1714. He was an Irish privy councillor in 1735, C-in-C in Ireland in 1751 and died a Field Marshal.

MOLEYNS. *See* HUNGERFORD.

MOLL CUTPURSE (?1584-1659) originally a London pickpocket, became a well known dealer in stolen goods. She wore men's clothes, mixed in moneyed society and, surprisingly, died in her bed.

MOLLY MAGUIRES. Similar to Whitefeet.

MOLUCCAS or SPICE Is. *See* INDONESIA.

MOLTENO, Sir John Charles (1814-86) wool trader in the Karoo and commandant in the Kaffir War of 1846, became M.P. for Beaufort in the first Cape legislature (1854) and became the first Cape Premier in 1872, but came into conflict on virtually all issues with the Governor, Sir Bartle Frere, who dismissed him in 1878.

MOMBASA. *See* KENYA.

MOMPESSON, William (1639-1709) rector of Eyam (Derbys.) in 1665 is remembered for the successful quarantine action which he took during the plague. He persuaded the people to confine themselves to the village and to receive supplies in return for money placed in running water.

MON, MONA or ANGLESEY. *See* GWYNEDD.

MONACO, with the detached ports of Roquebrune and Menton, was a Genoese dependency from 1215 but was acquired by the Grimaldi family in 1297. It passed by marriage to the Matignon family (who changed their name to Grimaldi) in 1731. During all this period the ports were useful for smuggling and water. They were annexed by France in 1793, but placed, after 1814 under Savoyard-Sardinian protection. In 1848 Menton and Roquebrune declared themselves free towns, and during the Italian upheavals which preoccupied Savoy in 1860, they were induced to join France while Monaco itself was transferred to and remains under French protection.

MONARCHIST LEAGUE, founded in 1943, started to publish a journal and by 1995 was corresponding with some 200 similar bodies worldwide. It enlarged its membership considerably during press attacks on the Crown in 1994-6 and in 1995 formed an allied CONSTITUTIONAL MONARCHY ASSOCIATION for those specially interested in the British monarchy. This too expanded quickly.

MONASH, Sir John (1865-1931) Australian, brilliant as a soldier and as an educator, commanded a brigade at Gallipoli, a Division and then the Australian Army Corps on the Western Front (1916-18) and opened the Allied counter offensive in Aug. 1918. From 1923 he was Vice-Chancellor of Melbourne University, and from 1924-26 Pres. of the Australian Association for the Advancement of Science.

MONASTERY BUILDINGS. The example was set in design by the Benedictines. They evolved a standard plan, which of course, was locally adapted. The largest building was the cruciform church, built along the north side of the complex to give protection against the winter cold and situated suitably far from a stream so that it ran near or under the south side of the complex. A square cloister with sides roughly as long as the nave of the church was built into the angle between the nave and the south transept. Along the western (i.e. the outermost or worldly) side of the cloister was the cellarer's building, a kind of warehouse and barn conveniently accessible for carts. The lay brothers dormitory was over it. On the eastern side (partly overlapped by the transept) the Chapter House was next to the end of the transept, and the various monk's quarters, with their dormitory above came next. The south side was occupied by the refectory and kitchen: this drew its water from the stream which also served to flush the conveniences. The cloister was thus a passage connecting all parts of the monastery, but it often contained washing facilities against the kitchen wall, and cubicles (carrels) for study in summer. Its walks were also used for contemplation and its green (garth) as a burial ground. The abbot had a separate establishment sometimes associated with a guest house and an infirmary. There were also separate buildings for a novice's school and workshops.

Cistercian houses were built on variants of this layout, but commonly had a second lesser cloister opening to the library, lecture rooms and studies while their infirmary and novices quarters usually formed part of the total complex.

The Carthusian houses (Charterhouses) were entirely different. The church lay along the west side of the cloister together with the Chapter House and Refectory. Along the other three sides were alleys on which were a series of cottages (cells) each containing a living room and a work room for a monk and each with its own small garden.

MONASTERIES, DISSOLUTION (1518-47) (*see* VALOR ECCLESIASTICUS). **(1)** There were precedents for the redirection of religious endowments. Winchester College was founded (1382) upon properties belonging to a declining hospital; Jesus College, Cambridge, with the buildings and funds of St. Radegund's Nunnery, whose religious were expelled for immorality (1497); St. John's College similarly from the proceeds of two nunneries suppressed for misconduct by Bp. Fisher of Rochester (1499).

(2) Chantries apart, in 1518 there were 606 religious establishments in England and Wales. Of these, 43 belonged to the Knights of St. John and the remaining 563 supported about 7000 monks, friars and regular canons, 2,000 nuns and some 35,000 lay people. Their net annual income was £136,000, £110,000 of it from land, representing about 35% of the income of the church. They had been variously estimated to have owned 2,000,000 acres or between 35% and 18% of the cultivable land, but the higher figures do not seem to tally with the returns of taxable income.

(3) Monasticism had lost much of its force and usefulness. Monastery schools which now mainly trained novices, did little for other education. There were few monastic writers or chroniclers. Few scholars were sent to the universities. Perhaps 5% of the income went in charity, but much of this to undeserving connections. The excellent hospitality served tourists rather than wayfarers. Too many inmates were allowed, and sometimes forced, to take vows without vocation, in order to maintain unenthusiastic prayers. Nunneries were sometimes used to dump unmarriageable daughters or as rest homes for dowagers. The abbots and cellarers tended to be businessmen and their establishment to become safe deposits and banks. There were often old understandings with founders' families and other local landowners who protected monasteries, managed their property or contracted with them and, of course, they had much legal business. Thus their relationships with their neighbourhoods were increasingly material rather than spiritual, a fact emphasised rather than diminished by their acquisitions of rectorial tithes. (*See* ADVOWSON.) There was bound to be some immorality and corruption but such imputations are too convenient for a govt. pressed for money to be taken literally. Their sins were more often sloth and gluttony than lust.

(4) Cardinal Wolsey suppressed 12 houses in 1518 to endow Christchurch, Oxford and his college at Ipswich. In 1532 an Austin house in Aldgate, London was suppressed and in 1534 seven Observantine houses (*see* BARTON, ELIZABETH). Having learned the technique, Thomas Cromwell, now the King's Vicegerent in Spirituals, obtained a commission of visitation (Jan. 1535) which superseded the episcopal powers. Having formed commissions of common and canon lawyers, armed them with the articles and injunctions usual in the bishop's triennial visitations, and rehearsed them in the usual methods, the visitations began in July. It was not the methods but the motives which mattered. The object was to obtain, if not a surrender, at least discreditable admissions. By Feb. 1536 half a dozen smaller houses had been driven to surrender and the reputation of many others blasted. On the basis of the reports and royal influence, Parliament passed bills to set up the Court of Augmentations and to enforce the surrender to the crown of monasteries with under £200 a year. There were 304 of these. 220 were suppressed at once; the rest in the next three years. Heads of houses were mostly well pensioned. Some religious were transferred to the larger houses praised in the preamble, others allowed to take livings as secular clergy. Valuables were taken into the Jewel House. Between Apr. 1536 and Nov. 1538 property worth £37,000 was sold; about £10,000 a year in rents retained.

(5) In 1538 there was a lucrative attack upon pilgrimage centres and shrines. This helped to discourage superstition and pay the cost of putting down the Pilgrimage of Grace. Some abbeys had been implicated in the latter, so that between Mar. and May 1537 the superiors at Barlings, Bridlington, Fountains, Jervaulx, Kirkstead and Whalley had been hanged and the Abbot of the great house at Furness had escaped execution by surrender. In Nov. Lewes had surrendered too; in Dec. Warden (Beds.). In this atmosphere of terror new visitations began. The abbot of Woburn and the prior of Lenton were hanged for criticising the royal supremacy. The Commissioners were armed with ready-made documents of surrender and other superiors realised that the less they resisted the better it would be for them. Since they had no authority to effect such surrenders, Parliament validated past and future ones (Apr. 1539) made in this way. In the autumn the abbots of Colchester, Glastonbury and Reading were hanged, the two latter for implication in the Pole conspiracy. Rochester and Christchurch (Canterbury) were still resisting when commissions dissolved them in Mar. 1540.

Waltham Abbey, the last, surrendered in the same month. Later in 1540 an Act took over the properties of the Knights of St. John.

(6) The members of the cathedral monasteries were transmuted into secular chapters. Six new bishoprics (Westminster until 1550, Peterborough, Oxford, Bristol, Chester and Worcester) were endowed. Some superiors eg. at Peterborough became bishops, others were pensioned. Other monks and friars were pensioned or took secular livings or both. Nuns were permitted to abjure their vows and even to marry. *See* AUGMENTATIONS, COURT OF; CHANTRIES.

MONBODDO, James Burnett (1714-99) a Lord (1767) of Session, of unusual outlook who foreran Darwin by demonstrating the affinity of men and apes, wrote a book on philology, rode stirrupless and gave learned (if ridiculed) suppers. On an appeal against conviction for murder on the ground that the appellant was drunk at the time he observed "if he will do that when drunk, my Lards, what will he not do when he is sober?"

MONCK. Devonshire family related to the Grenvilles. **(1) George (1608-70) 1st D. of ALBEMARLE (1661)** thrashed an under-sheriff in 1625 and hurriedly took service in the Cadiz expedition. In 1627 he brought a royal letter to Buckingham at the Ile de Ré at hazard of his life and was commissioned. In 1629 he entered Oxford's (later Goring's) Regiment then in Dutch pay and was distinguished for courage and good discipline especially at the S. of Breda in 1637. After a dispute, he left Dutch service.

(2) In 1640 he was a Lieutenant Colonel in Newport's regiment in the Bishops' War and saved the English guns in the rout at Newborn. He was offered an Irish commission by the Ld-Lieutenant, his kinsman the E. of Leicester and raised a regiment with which he campaigned with distinction, mostly in Leinster and Munster. By June 1643 Leicester had (unsuccessfully) nominated him for the Governorship of Dublin.

At this point he came under suspicion of intending to change sides, and was sent in honourable custody to Oxford, where he satisfied the King on all points. He then joined his regiment, now in Cheshire, was captured at Nantwich (Jan. 1644) and sent by the Commons to the Tower. Everyone agreed that Monck was the best expert on Ireland. The royalist Ormonde wanted to secure his release for Irish service. The Parliament offered to employ him there. Distinguishing between service against the King and service against the Irish, he accepted the latter and went to Ireland in Feb. 1647 as Ld. Lisle's Adjutant General.

(3) His Irish operations were now mostly conducted in Ulster where, despite his many successes, his position was decreasingly secure. It was only by brilliant *coups de main* at Belfast and Carrickfergus (Sept. 1648) that he negated the effects of the desertion of Monro's Scottish troops and captured Monro himself; but after the King's execution the local Scottish Colonists rose and with the O'Neills drove him and his ill supplied force down to Dundalk. Realising that if O'Neill, the Scots and Ormonde linked up, the Parliamentarians might be driven from Ireland, he concluded a three months' armistice with O'Neill to gain time, well knowing that the Parliament would not ratify it. In fact his own troops would not stand it either; they went over to Ormonde and forced him to surrender Dundalk. On his return to England (July 1649) Parliament disapproved the armistice but declared its belief in his good faith.

(4) In July 1650 Monck was in Scotland with Cromwell, who left him there as Lieut-General and Local C-in-C in Aug. 1651. He took Stirling (Aug.) stormed Dundee (Sept.) and secured so many Scottish leaders that the conquest of the country was well advanced when his health broke down. From Feb. to Nov. 1652 he was thus at Bath or fortifying Yarmouth.

(5) In Nov. 1652 Monck, Blake and Deane were appointed joint commanders of the fleet. His part in the three days B. of Portland (Feb. 1653) was a minor one, but in the two day B. of the North Foreland (June) Deane was killed and Blake came up late, so that Monck had to command alone. Blake now fell ill and in July Monck became acting C-in-C and, as such, defeated and killed Tromp. It is likely that his military experience, adapted by the advice of able subordinates such as Penn to naval tactics, mainly achieved this result. After the expulsion of the Rump (Apr. 1653) Monck secured the Fleet's loyalty to Cromwell on purely patriotic grounds.

(6) In Apr. 1654 he was commissioned to deal with another Scottish rising, which he put down with conciliation and a minimum of bloodshed but the work was almost jeopardised by a military conspiracy, involving the Parliamentary opposition (to Cromwell) and the Levellers who were circulating seditious literature among the unpaid troops. Monck purged his army of these subversives and meantime set about organising with justice and efficiency, the Scottish administration. Peace, good order, and his invariable courtesy combined with judicious transportations of moss troopers and other brigands, made him locally popular. He was on excellent terms with the Lord Protector, whose viceroy he really was. After Oliver's death his status became yet more significant. He was almost the uncrowned King of the Scots, with a faithful and uniform army at his back. England, by contrast was confused, disorderly and aimless, a condition which was repellent to his temperament.

In these circumstances, Ld. Colepepper pointed out to Hyde (Charles II's Secretary of State) that Monck's allegiance to the existing English dispensation had been only professional (as a warrior) and personal (to Oliver). Accordingly, in Aug. 1659 Charles approached him through his brother Nicolas Monck and Sir John Grenville. These assurances had a distant but not immediate effect. His attitude was that England would no longer endure arbitrary government, but that he would not be responsible for a civil war which would result if he crossed the Border while the southern army was still in substantial control. By Oct. this army was riven by factions and some of it had expelled the parliament again. Monck could now act. He declared for a free parliament and secured the Scottish fortresses. Between Nov. and Dec. his supporters in the south had brought over the fleet in the Downs and the garrison of Portsmouth. The London garrison restored the Parliament after Christmas. He entered England on 2 Jan., bloodlessly dispersing or disbanding opposition troops on the way, and reached London triumphantly on 3 Feb. (*See* RESTORATION.)

(7) The English Restoration settlement was not quite as moderate as Monck (now D. of Albemarle) had hoped but its main features were the direct and indirect result of his advice. He was absentee Lord Lieutenant of Ireland until Nov. 1661. The Scottish settlement was less to his liking because the Govt., against his opposition, withdrew the English garrisons, with long lasting effects.

(8) Meanwhile, as the regime's chief fighting man, his advice was much in demand on foreign policy. He had always adhered to the Cromwellian view that England should have a proper share of world trade. It followed that Dunkirk should remain in English hands and Dutch competition be put down. The sale of Dunkirk is the measure of his diminished influence after 1661 in home rather than foreign affairs, but the Govt. used his organising and naval talents in the Dutch Wars. The D. of York, as Lord High Admiral, deputed his authority to Albemarle who could thus run the Admiralty and keep order in London during the year of plague (1665). In Apr. 1666 he was sent to sea, with P. Rupert.

(9) He held his own against great odds in the Four Days Battle (June 1666) and shared in the victory of Orfordness a month later. Almost immediately afterwards he was summoned to take charge of London after the Great Fire and then to Chatham to try, with dismantled defences, to stop the Dutch (Oct. 1667). This was his last public service.

MONCKTON COMMISSION under Vist. Monckton of Brenchley recommended that the Central African Federation be dissolved and so opened the way for the individual independence of its constituent countries as Malawi, Zambia and Zimbabwe.

MONCKTON, Walter Turner (1891-1965) 1st Vist. MONCKTON of BRENCHLEY (1957) first came to public, as opposed to professional, notice as K. Edward VIII's legal adviser during the abdication affair; and after early forensic successes was taken into Churchill's conservative Govt. as Minister of Labour. His conciliatory and understanding technique removed some of the suspicious animosity among defeated Labour supporters, but some Conservatives ascribed the high wages which the trade unions were demanding and getting in the period (1951-5) to his approach. In 1955 he was moved to the Ministry of Defence and was consequently involved in the Suez operation, which he disliked. Once it was over he accepted non-departmental office as Paymaster General (1956-7). *See* MONCKTON COMMISSION.

MONCREIFF (1) Sir Henry (1750-1827) and his son **(2) Sir Henry (1809-83)** were distinguished Scottish divines. **(3) Sir James (1776-1851)** his son **(4) Sir James (1811-95) 1st Ld. MONCREIFF** and his son **(5) Henry James (1840-1909) 2nd Ld.** were even more distinguished Scottish judges.

MOND (1) Ludwig (1839-1909) began his inventive and lucrative career by successive developments in the production and use of alkalis and ammonia derivatives and with Sir John Brunner, founded the Brunner-Mond business with its work near Northwich (Cheshire). His experiments in the use of nickel to purify producer gas led to the discovery of methods for extracting nickel from ores and the foundation of the Mond Nickel Co. with Canadian mines and works near Swansea. He gave large sums to charity, an art collection to the National Gallery, and large foundations for scientific research. His son **(2) Alfred (1868-1930) 1st Ld. MELCHETT (1928)** a director of many enterprises, amalgamated into the vast Imperial Chemical Industries Ltd. in 1926. He was also a Liberal M.P. in 1906, First Commissioner of Works from 1916-21 and Minister of Health from 1921-22. He was a powerful and enthusiastic Zionist.

MONETARISM. The technique of controlling an economy exclusively through the money supply which is to be influenced by the manipulation of interest rates. The method was a central tool of Tory policy under the Thatcher govt. which (on the whole) eschewed physical controls. Its full application was discredited in the first months of the Major govt. when an attempt to raise interest rates to 15% had to be abandoned after a few hours because it threatened wholesale bankruptcies, repossessions and a political catastrophe. The Govt. then deemed it necessary to restrict the money supply by taxation.

MONEY BILL is a Public Bill to impose or alter taxation or authorise expenditure. Under the Parliament Acts a Money Bill is one which is endorsed by the Speaker as dealing only with taxation and charges on the Consolidated Fund. The Lords cannot amend such an endorsed bill nor delay it for more than a month. In practice such bills, even sometimes Finance Bills, are often not endorsed because they contain provisions which may be conveniently considered by the Lords. *See* MONEY RESOLUTION.

MONEYLENDERS. *See* USURY.

MONEY RESOLUTION in the House of Commons may be introduced on a bill involving expenditure at any time before the Committee Stage and its passage amounts to confirmation that expenditure, ultimately necessitated by the bill, will be met from public funds. Such a bill cannot proceed without a money resolution which is always moved in Committee of the whole House. The budget is a series of money resolutions.

MONGOLS a great military confederacy formed under Jenghiz (?-1227) attacked China between 1211-1215 conquered central Asia and Persia between 1218-1224, and N. India in 1221. His successor Ughetai or Ogodai (r. 1229-41) conquered Russia between 1237 and 1240 and his armies were invading Poland and Hungary when he died. A nephew Batu established a separate Khanate (The Golden Horde) in Russia in 1242, and in 1258 took Baghdad. In 1260 Kublai (r. 1260-94) conquered China. Marco Polo served at his court from 1275-92.

These immense efforts led to a period of quiescence if not exhaustion, and the loosening of central authority, but in 1363 Timur (Tamberlane) a Prince of the imperial dynasty began to re-establish authority and reigned as supreme ruler from 1369-1405. He took Herat in 1381, sacked Kandahar 1392 and Delhi in 1398. In 1400 he turned West again, seizing Baghdad and Damascus in 1401. In 1402 he overwhelmed the Turks at Ankara, thus delaying the Ottoman conquest of Constantinople for a generation but he had meanwhile lost China. The last great ruler was Shah Rokh (1405-47) after whom the empire broke up.

MONGREL PARLIAMENT. The Oxford Parliament of 1681.

MONIER-WILLIAMS, Sir Monier (1819-99) given a writership in the HEIC, went to Haileybury in 1840 but went to Oxford instead of to India and set about encouraging academic oriental studies. He was Prof. of Sanskrit, Persian and Hindustani at Haileybury from 1844-58 and of Sanskrit at Oxford from 1860. He published a Sanskrit English Dictionary in 1872 and founded the Oxford Indian Institute in 1883.

MONITOR. *See* GUNBOAT.

MONITORIAL SYSTEM. A early 19th cent. teaching method developed simultaneously in England and India by Joseph Lancaster (1778-1838) and Andrew Bell (1752-1832) to overcome the need for mass education under a shortage of funds and teachers. A group of the ablest pupils (the monitors) was taught by a teacher. The monitors then taught groups of other pupils. This was an efficient way of conveying elementary information and seemed to create leadership abilities. It was initially adapted to state elementary schools until adequate numbers of teachers became available.

MONK, Maria (?1817-50) published her *Awful Disclosures* in 1836. The book, a prurient classic which made a fortune, told of unseemliness in R. Catholic convents, from one of which she was supposed to have escaped. The story was wholly false.

MONMOUTH, E.s of. *See* CAREY; MORDAUNT-6.

MONMOUTH and BUCCLEUCH, James Scott or Fitzroy or Crofts (1649-85) D. of. Bastard of Charles II by Lucy Walter. Handsome and worthless, save perhaps as a soldier, he served against the Dutch in 1672 and 1674 and the French in 1678 and put down the Scots covenanters after Abp. Sharp's murder in 1679. Helped by scattered rumours since 1662, the exclusionists put him forward as a protestant candidate for the throne in place of James D. of York, but the King would neither admit a marriage to Lucy nor allow an alteration in the line of succession. After some reckless progresses designed to court popularity, an act of manslaughter (or murder) and some conspiracies, he went to Zeeland, met the P. of Orange (who did not like him) and thence mounted the West Country rebellion known after him. He declared himself King at Taunton, was defeated at Sedgemoor by Feversham and Churchill, and executed in July 1685. See JAMES II-5.

MONMOUTH, -SHIRE or GWENT. This border area possessed a legionary fortress at Caerleon and a Roman town at Caerwent. In late Saxon times it was combined with Hereford in a border earldom. It was turbulent and ruled piecemeal after the Norman Conquest by marcher lords from castles at Monmouth, Raglan, Chepstow, Caldecot or from the abbeys at Tintern and Llanthony. There were always fisheries but as S. Wales was pacified it became increasingly possible to exploit the coal mines. It was converted into an English county by the Act of Union of 1536. The demand for coal in the industrial revolution and especially the development of the steamship led to a sudden increase in the prosperity and population which lasted with occasional set-backs until about 1920. The mines were liable to flooding and heavily dependent on pumping. Much of the coal was exported in small colliers to France and this trade was ruined beyond recovery because German reparations coal, exploited by France under the T. of Versailles, forced the closure first of marginal mines at the top of the valleys thus imposing a mounting burden of pumping on each mine successively lower down. The govt.'s failure to provide alternative local employment led to great misery in the 1920s and 30s and the migration of many of the enterprising to Slough.

World War II brought a revival which was strengthened by the creation of non-coal based industries, such as nylon and aluminium smelting. It was renamed Gwent and declared part of Wales again in 1972.

MONMOUTH PURCHASE an area in New Jersey between the Raritan and Sandy Hook was settled by Long I. and Newport Quakers and Baptists under a charter of Governor Nicholls issued in 1665. They exercised virtually complete self government. The charter, being repugnant to an earlier grant, was recalled in 1672.

MONOPHYSITES or EUTYCHIANS hold that the incarnate Christ had a single and divine nature as opposed to the Orthodox view that his nature was both divine and human. The logical consequences were considered to be so far reaching that they split the Byzantine Empire and provided doctrinal backbone for other political, economic and linguistic schisms. Monophysitism became an organised body of opinion after the Council of Chalcedon (451). It was especially strong in Egypt in the 6th cent. and contributed to the collapse of local resistance to Arab invasion in 640 and 642. Three important Christian churches are monophysite viz: the Coptic and Abyssinian, the Jacobite and the Armenian. *See* MALABAR CHRISTIANS.

MONOPOLIES (*See* STAPLE; MERCHANT ADVENTURERS) **(1)** to encourage export trades, especially in wool and leather, date from the early 14th cent. The complementary grant of protection to foreigners who brought in and taught a craft hitherto unused in England, began as early as 1331 with Flemish weavers, dyers and fullers who were sometimes further encouraged by the prohibition of imported cloth. Industrial monopolies apparently began in Italy in about 1500 and spread to Holland and thence to England. Acontius (q.v.) first suggested an inventors' monopoly in 1559. Manufacturing monopolies, to protect a new manufacturing process hitherto unknown in the country, began to be granted in 1561. These differed from the older guild and foreign trade monopolies in that, the grant once made, the crown did not supervise the conduct of the grantee.

(2) Once launched, the idea was abused in favour of those whom otherwise the crown was too impecunious to reward directly, and grants were soon being made to persons who had not introduced anything new (e.g. making paper from rags, to the Queen's jeweller (1592)) and even for purposes not of a manufacturing nature (e.g. Candler's grant for the sole registration of mercantile documents). These grants were issued under the prerogative and enforced in the Star Chamber. Parliamentary criticism was rebuked in 1571. Though the number of grants steadily increased, the prosperity of the next 20 years cushioned their deleterious effects.

(3) The recession at the end of the century provoked further discontent. Monopolies impeded commerce, raised prices, circulated shoddy goods, created ancillary abuses and corruption and put people out of work. In 1597 the Queen promised that all patents should "abide the trial and true touchstone of the law", but little was done. In 1601 a public outcry caused a House of Commons committee to investigate. It found that while meritorious inventors were being denied protection, courtiers were controlling necessaries such as salt, near necessaries such as wine, and tavern licences and that there were dispensations to traffic in forbidden articles, to do things prohibited by penal acts and even grants of the royal power to dispense with a given statute. The list of new patents covered, *inter alia*, aniseeds, ashes, calamine, cards, cloth, currants, iron, lead, oil of blubber, oxshin-bones, pilchards, saltpetre, sea coal, train-oil and transportation of leather. The Queen gave way and undertook, in a famous speech, that none be "put in execution but such as should first have a tryal according to the law for the good of the people". Shortly (1603) in *Darcy* v *Allen* (11 Co. Rep. 846) a case on the importation of playing cards, the judges held that all monopolies are illegal save those which will increase or improve trade (e.g. a new process) or are necessary in the interests of the state (e.g. armaments).

(4) James I ignored this tolerably clear statement of the law and continued Elizabethan patents or issued new ones. The main object was neither to fill the Exchequer nor to gratify the courtiers, but they were suspected of both in the corrupt atmosphere of his court and some courtiers certainly made some money out of them. They created the same difficulties as before: they were numerous and pervasive, including such matters as licensing taverns and alehouses, salmon fisheries and gold and silver wire. Enforcement involved many irritations and private interferences. In 1610 an attempt to include a charge for licences for the benefit of the Exchequer had to be withdrawn in the face of protests that it amounted to a tax. The Parliament of 1621 found that many new ones had been created since 1610. The issue was entangled with the political future of Bacon and pursued heatedly for that as well as other reasons. In the end one Statute of Monopolies (1624) declared them all void save patents for 14 years to inventors and ancient franchises, and cast the rules into the statutory form which has been, save for the 20th cent. nationalised industries, the basis of the law and practice ever since. *See* COMMON INFORMERS.

MONOPOLIES AND MERGERS COMMISSION (until 1973 MONOPOLIES AND RESTRICTIVE PRACTICES COMMISSION) investigates major company mergers, existing or suspected monopolies in commerce, industry and services, and unfair competitive action such as predatory pricing. Where it discovers a practice which is contrary to the public interest it mostly acts by requiring undertakings from guilty businesses, but in serious cases or cases of broken undertakings it may take action leading to a dispersal of assets. The Board of Trade may, and occasionally does, prevent an investigation for reasons which are not always clear.

MONROE, James (1758-1831) (Pres. of the U.S.A. 1817-25) U.S. Senator from 1790-94 became Minister to France in 1794 but was recalled by Washington in 1796 for suggesting that a new U.S. Govt. might repudiate the Anglo-U.S. Jay T. In 1803 however, Jefferson sent him to France to assist the resident Minister Livingston in the Louisiana Purchase and in 1804 he reached London to negotiate on impressment with the British Govt. In this he was unsuccessful and in 1807 went home. In Nov. 1811 he became Pres. Madison's Secretary of State and in 1814 Secretary for War as well. He thus had to conduct the war with Britain.

Under his presidency U.S.A. acquired the Floridas from Spain (1819-21) and recognised the independence of the Central and South American colonies in 1822. It was the latter event which was complemented by the so-called Monroe Doctrine. This originated in a proposal by Canning, the British Foreign Secretary that the British and Americans should jointly assert their opposition to interference by European powers but Monroe rejected the British proposal and then announced the same proposition unilaterally in a message to Congress (Dec. 1823). Since the U.S.A. had no fleet or army, the doctrine was dependent on British power, and in any case should be called the Canning-Monroe Doctrine.

MONS, B. and RETREAT from (Aug. 1914). The French 4th Army with the British Expeditionary Force (B.E.F.) under Sir John French on its left awaited the thrust of the three German armies wheeling though Belgium. The French held Charleroi, the B.E.F. Mons. Against massed frontal attacks the well-trained British riflemen at first inflicted heavy losses but the weight of German numbers and the French strategic withdrawal from further to the right compelled Sir John and the French 5th Army to retire. The B.E.F. fought successful rearguard actions at Mons and Le Câteau. Moving southward, they were preserved for the B. of the Mârne. These operations had a great effect on popular imagination. It was said that angels were seen fighting for the British.

MONSIEUR. *See* MADAME.

MONSOON Any wind which blows regularly at fixed seasons but especially the Indian S.W. Wind. This blows from Apr. to Oct. and brings heavy rains which cause floods and stop travel. If it fails (as in 1895) the result is commonly famine. It is thus a major feature of Indian life.

MONSON. Lincolnshire family. **(1) Sir Thomas (1564-1641)** was M.P. for Lincolnshire in 1597 and for Castle Rising in 1603. In 1611 he became master of the Tower and Greenwich armouries. In 1614 he was M.P. for Cricklade, but from 1615-17 he was in custody for alleged complicity in the Overbury case. From 1625 he was clerk of the King's Bills to the Council of the North. His brother **(2) Sir William (1569-1643)** a naval commander, was a prisoner in Spain from 1591-93 and served under Essex in the Cadiz expedition in 1596 and was Sir Richard Leveson's Vice Admiral at the taking of the rich carack *St Valentine* in 1602. He then became Admiral in the Narrow Seas and started to accept a Spanish pension to favour Spanish against Dutch ships and to help smuggle Romanist priests. In 1611 he caught Lady Arabella Seymour who was fleeing to France and in 1614 he put down the Irish pirates of Broad Haven. The Spanish pension came to light in 1611; suspected with his brother of complicity in the Overbury affair, he was dismissed in 1615 and put briefly in the Tower. He was not re-employed until 1635 when he served as Vice Admiral under Lindsey in the Channel. He wrote the *Naval Tracts* (first printed in 1682) which are the earliest practising seaman's critical account in English of naval warfare. The son of **(1)**, **(3) Sir John (1600-83)** was M.P. for Lincoln in 1625 and began to reclaim part of the Fens (1635-8). In 1646 he negotiated the surrender of Oxford and in 1652 signed the Engagement. This did not prevent him from resisting the decimation tax of 1655 for which he was under house arrest until 1657. His brother **(4) Sir William (?-1672) Vist. MONSON of CASTLEMAINE (Irish 1628)** was M.P. for Reigate in 1640 and was nominated to try the King in 1649, but attended only three sessions. Deprived under an Act of Pains and Penalties in 1661 he died in the Fleet Prison. A grandson of **(3)**, **(5) Sir John (1693-1748) 1st Ld. MONSON (1728)** was M.P. for Lincoln in 1722 and 1727 and a Commissioner for Trade and Plantations in 1737. His sons were **(6) John (1727-74) 2nd Ld.,** a minor supporter of the Rockingham administration and **(7) George (1730-76)** was M.P. for Lincoln from 1754-68 and a groom of the Bedchamber to the P. of Wales from 1756. In 1758 he went to India as a soldier and served with distinction against Pondicherry (1760) and Manila (1762). In 1773 he became a Member of the Council of Bengal and joined Francis in opposition to Warren Hastings.

MONSTRAUNCES, THE were the formal grievances of the barons delivered to Edward I at the height of the crisis in 1297, immediately before his expedition to Flanders. Arising out of the expedition, they asserted that the writs for the military service were insufficiently specific, that service in Flanders was unprecedented, that insufficient thought had been given to the security of the realm, that the community had been too impoverished by prises, maltoltes and tallages to be able to provide the services, and that in general a sense of grievance existed because the King had persistently flouted Magna Carta.

MONSTRELET, Enguerrand de (1390-1453). Chronicler in the service of John of Luxembourg, and continuator from 1400-44 of Froissart. He was at Compiègne when Joan of Arc was taken.

MONTACUTE (Somerset). Tudor mansion, built between 1588-1600 for Sir Edward Phelips, Speaker and Master of the Rolls.

MONTAGUE-CHELMSFORD REFORMS (1919). See DYARCHY.

MONTAGUE, Edwin Samuel (187?-1924) Liberal politician, was Chancellor of the Duchy of Lancaster in 1916, and Minster of Munitions later in the year. Though Jewish, he disliked the Balfour Declaration. He became Secretary for India in 1917 and brought in the Montague-Chelmsford Reforms, but resigned in 1922 against Lloyd George's pro-Greek stance in the days before the Chanak Incident.

MONTAGU. Distinguished and versatile Northamptonshire family claiming descent from the Es. of Salisbury. **(1) Sir Edward (?-1557)** acquired many ex-monastic estates in the county and became C.J. of the King's Bench in Jan. 1539. In Dec. 1541 he assisted in the preliminaries for Katherine Howard's attainder. In Nov. 1545 he was demoted to the Common Pleas and in 1547 was a member of the Council of Regency. He would not attest Somerset's patent as Protector, but attested its limitation (Dec. 1547) and his deposition (Oct. 1549). In June 1553 he at first refused to draft the clauses in Edward VI's will altering the succession in favour of the Dudleys, but was finally induced to do it by a commission and promise of a pardon. He signed the will as guarantor and consequently lost his post and some of his estates at Mary I's accession. Of his grandsons **(2) James (?1568-1618)** was first master of Sidney Sussex College, Cambridge (1596-1608) and Bp. of Bath and Wells from 1608-16. His principal activity was to restore Bath Abbey which was in ruins. He died as Bp. of Winchester. His brother **(3) Edward (1562-1644) 1st Ld. MONTAGU (1621)** was an M.P. in the Parliaments of 1601, 1603-4, 1611, 1614 and 1620. Was a strong but puritanical royalist. His son **(4) Edward (1616-84) 2nd Ld.** was M.P. for Huntingdon from 1640 and from 1644 a Parliamentarian peer, concerned in the proceedings against Laud. He received Charles I from the Scots, put him in Holmby House and attended him until 1647, but took no part in his trial. He was summoned to Cromwell's Upper House in 1651. His eldest son **(5) Edward (1635-65)** M.P. for Sandwich from 1661-65 was killed at the B. of Bergen. His brother **(6) William (?1639-1706)** became C.B. for the Exchequer in 1676. He was a somewhat passive member of the court which under Scroggs C.J. tried the supposed Popish plotters, and he was assessor at Stafford's impeachment in 1680. James II hoped for the support of his legal authority on the issue of dispensation. He refused it and was removed from the bench. He was assessor to the Convention Parliament in 1688-89. See MONTAGU-MANCHESTER; MONTAGUE-SANDWICH; MONTAGUE-HALIFAX.

MONTAGUE (Halifax) Charles (1661-1715) Ld. HALIFAX (1700) E. of HALIFAX (1714) a grandson of the first E. of Manchester, was a friend of the E. of Dorset and Matthew Prior. He became M.P. for Maldon in the Convention Parliament of 1689 and showed extraordinary skill as a debater and committee chairman. By Mar. 1692 he was a Lord of the Treasury and was raising money by a type of national Tontine. In 1694 he introduced the bill establishing the Bank of England, and was given the Chancellorship of the Exchequer. In Dec. 1695 he with the advice of Halley, Locke, Newton and Somers introduced legislation to remedy the depreciation of the currency, which was reaching inflationary proportions. The recoinage was originally financed by a new window tax which long survived him. The new currency was milled; and clipped coins were no longer to be tender. The recoinage took four years and to tide over the shortage of govt. credit, Montagu invented Exchequer bills. In 1696 he set up the consolidated fund and also enlarged the capital of the Bank of England. By Nov. 1697 he was First Ld. of the Treasury. Repeated charges of peculation were made against him and dismissed in 1697 and 1698 and political libellers continued to harass him until he resigned in 1699.

In June 1701 the Commons impeached him for corruption and for his part in the Partition Treaties. The Lords dismissed the impeachment and he, for his part, in 1703 prevented the Commons from tacking the Occasional Conformity Bill to a Land Tax Bill. His views on religious legislation did not agree with those of Q. Anne and he held no major office under her. He became First Ld of the Treasury at George I's accession. For **George Montague, 2nd E.** see DUNK.

MONTAGU (MANCHESTER) (1) Henry (?1563-1642) Vist. MANDEVILLE (1620) 1st E. of MANCHESTER (1626) became recorder of London in 1603 and M.P. from 160?-1611 and in 1614. In Nov. 1616 he was made C.J. of the King's Bench in supersession of Coke, and presided at the sentence of Sir Walter Raleigh in 1618. He was also involved with Bacon in the golden and silver wire monopoly in 1620. In return for £20,000 to Buckingham he exchanged the chief justiceship for the Lord Treasureship and a peerage in 1620. He was a member of the joint investigation into Bacon's case but in Sept. 1621 became Lord Pres. to make way for Lionel Cranfield in the Treasureship. In May 1624 he acquired the lucrative but unpopular office of Master of the Court of Wards and was made Pres. of the Virginia commission. He became Lord Privy Seal in 1628 and as such an assiduous member of the Star Chamber. An active supporter of royal policy, he subscribed large sums for it, campaigned to raise City loans and collected arrears of ship money. His son **(2) Edward (1602-71) 2nd E.** married into the puritanical Rich family, was called up to the Lords in 1626 and known until 1642 as **Ld. MANDEVILLE.** He took the opposite side to his father, signed the Petition of the Peers (Aug. 1640) and negotiated the T. of Ripon with the Scots. (see CHARLES I-15). He was in close accord with Pym, led the opposition in the Lords and was the only peer whom Charles I joined with the Five Members. He cheerfully accepted the King's articles of impeachment and had himself cleared by a bill (Mar. 1642). He was occupied thereafter in raising money and troops until appointed Major General of the Eastern Association with Cromwell in command of the Horse. They campaigned successfully in the area and he commanded the Parliamentary forces at Marston Moor (July 1644). Thereafter his military activities became increasingly sluggish, either from dislike of war or for reasons of health and he expressed despair at an eventual Parliamentary victory. The army slowly moved south, and the campaign centring on the second B. of Newbury (Oct. 1644) petered out, the army starving and depleted by desertion. In Nov. Cromwell laid charges before the Commons, but this was part of a more general campaign for the Self Denying Ordinance. Manchester resigned his commission the day before it was passed in Apr. 1645.

He now worked mainly in the Committee of Both Kingdoms and as Speaker of the Lords. With other presbyterian peers he tried but failed to get a reasonable compromise with the King and in Jan. 1649 he opposed the ordinance for the King's trial. Thereafter, during the interregnum he was politically inactive, even though Cromwell summoned him to the House of Peers in Dec. 1657. He confined himself to his duties as Chancellor of Cambridge University. On the other hand he was active in procuring the Restoration, welcomed the King as Speaker of the Lords, and was given many resounding if not very profitable honours.

His famously handsome grandson **(3) Charles (?1660-1722) 4th E. (1682) 1st D. (1719)** was one of the earliest adherents of William of Orange whom he visited as early as May 1685. He was with William in Ireland and from Aug. 1699 until Louis XIV recognised the Old Pretender as King (Sept. 1701) he was Ambassador in Paris. He made various other diplomatic journeys. His grandson **(4) George (1737-88) 4th D.** was a consistent champion of the American colonies from 1774 onwards and a Rockingham Whig. He was Lord Chamberlain from 1782. His s. **(5) William (1768-1843) 5th D.** was a liberal and competent Governor of Jamaica from 1808-27.

MONTAGUE or MONTACUTE, William (1301-44) 3rd Ld. MONTACUTE (1319) 1st E. of SALISBURY (1337) *See* EDWARD III-4; ISABELLA OF FRANCE (c. 1294-1358)

MONTAGUE or MONTAGU (SANDWICH). (1) Sir Henry (?-1644) brother of Edward 1st Ld. Montague, was a Master of Requests. His son **(2) Edward (1625-72) 1st E. of SANDWICH (1661)** on the inspiration of his cousin the 2nd E. of Manchester became a parliamentary regimental commander. A personal friend of Cromwell, he was appointed to the Council of State in 1653. He became Blake's colleague in command of the fleet in Jan. 1656. He was reputed never to have seen the sea before but soon learned the business and commanded the expedition to the Sound in 1659. Approached by the King through his second cousin, Ld. Montague, he brought the fleet home in accordance with the King's wishes. He resigned but in Feb. 1660 was reappointed and in May he brought the fleet over to the King and brought him to England. A year later he commanded the Mediterranean fleet which brought Catherine of Braganza and took over Tangier.

In June 1665 he fought as Rear-Admiral at the B. of Lowestoft. In Aug. he was C-in-C of the attack on Bergen and shortly after was involved in a furious quarrel over an irregular prize distribution with Albemarle, the D. of York the HEIC and even the King. There was talk of impeachment, which Clarendon side-stepped by sending him as Ambassador to Madrid. It was a successful and popular negotiation and afterwards (1670) Sandwich became Pres. of the Committee on Trade and Plantations. He returned to the fleet as the D. of York's Second in Command in 1672 and was blown up at the B. of Solebay. His g-grandson **(3) John (17178-92) 4th E.** (1729) entered politics in 1739 and became a member of the board of Admiralty in Dec. 1744 under the D. of Bedford. By 1746 in Bedford's absence he was the effective political head of the Admiralty and wisely held to Anson's reforms particularly the Naval Discipline Act of 1749 and the regular system of dockyard inspections. Political changes forced his dismissal in 1751. He held Irish sinecures from 1755-63. He was then briefly First Lord again and then a Secretary of State. Under George Grenville he became a prominent govt. spokesman against John Wilkes when he was prosecuted for his blasphemous *Essay on Woman*. Sandwich had been an

associate with Wilkes in the Hellfire Club and this change of front gained him much obloquy and the nickname (derived from the betrayer of Macheath in the *Beggar's Opera*) 'Jemmy Twitcher'. Moreover, in provoking Wilkes and his journalist friends he became a butt for the fashionable anti-ministerial calumny of the time. His deplorable appearance, unsavoury reputation and Wilkes' enmity all contributed to a bad press.

All the same he was a formidable parliamentary manipulator; he built an effective following in the rising HEIC where his men of business intervened chiefly in Clive's interest; by employing anonymous apologists he manipulated the press and as several printers found out, he would retaliate against libels. He was out of office during the Buckingham and the early Chatham govts. but returned as Postmaster General under the D. of Grafton in 1768. He became Secretary of State under Ld. North in Dec. 1770 and from 1771-82 was First Ld. again.

With Grafton and North he suffered from the exhaustive and savage journalism of Wilkites, Junius and Burke over imperial policy and also the Middlesex election, failures in the American war and the inefficiency of the fleet together with, after 1783, alleged corruption and jobbery in the Navy and the Victualling Office which had been attributed to him. In fact the bad ships, lack of stores and of spars which affected the Navy were the fault of the previous regime under Ld. Hawke, while the intervention of the powerful French and Spanish fleets resulted from administrative and diplomatic failures. Further blows to his reputation arose from opposition defence of the court-martialled Adm. Keppel in 1778 and the murder, in 1779, of his mistress Martha Ray by a madman. With the end of the war he went out of office with North and so remained until 1782.

He was personally charming, his subordinates at the Admiralty greatly respected him and he commissioned the voyages of Captain Cook. He was industrious and a discriminating patron of arts, especially of music. He was ugly to the point of repulsion and his walk was described as 'walking down both sides of the street at once'. His brother **(4) William (?1720-57)** ("Mad Montague") was a brilliant, if eccentric, naval captain.

MONTAIGNE, Michel D'Eyquem, Sieur de (1533-92) learned in classics and philosophy, practised as a lawyer until he retired to Montaigne in 1570 and there wrote his first two books of *Essays*, published in 1580. After travels in the Alps and in Italy he was mayor of Bordeaux from 1581-85. In 1588 he published his third book of *Essays*. He was a professing but moderate R. Catholic and a respected acquaintance of Henry of Navarre (Henry IV) for whom he acted as an occasional intermediary with the southern warring factions. In his essays, written in a time of violence and fanaticism, he originally proposed a kind of Neo-stoicism, but subsequently became increasingly sceptical and under the motto *Que sais-je?* (Fr. = What do I know?) presented Epicurean doctrines strongly tinged with Renaissance humanism as ethical systems independent of religion: the good life, he held, consisted in the fair development of the entire person or personality. Bacon derived the idea, though little of the substance, of his *Essays* from Montaigne, who though widely appreciated in his lifetime, exerted little real influence in England until new generations had suffered from revolution.

MONTCALM DE ST. VERAN, Louis Joseph, Marquis de (1712-59) a distinguished French soldier, was given the Canadian command in 1756 and was much hindered at first in his defence of Canada against the British by interference from Vaudreuil, the Gov, but he took Oswego in 1756, Fort William Henry in 1757 and made a successful and brilliant defence of Ticonderoga against heavy odds in 1758. When Wolfe's expedition appeared before Quebec in 1759 he defended the city with difficulty and he and Wolfe were both mortally wounded at the Battle after Wolfe's escalade to the Plains of Abraham above the town.

MONTE CARLO. *See* MONACO.

MONTE CASSINO (Italy). (*See* BENEDICTINES.) The abbey was destroyed in the fighting of May 1944 and rebuilt after the War. The destruction represents a crux in the doctrines on the protection of important human monuments in time of war for it was ancient, of admitted sanctity, and occupied by troops of one foreign power who were attacked by troops of others, none of those engaged having any sovereign or political interest in it.

MONTEFIORE, Sir Moses Haim Bt. (1784-1885), stockbroker, had amassed a huge fortune by 1824 when he retired and devoted himself to the welfare of the Jews. In 1840 he persuaded the Sultan to abolish their disabilities in the Ottoman empire. In 1846 he got the Czar to revoke the Ukase requiring their removal inland. In 1864 he secured equality for them in Morocco, and in 1867 he intervened on their behalf in Moldavia.

MONTENEGRO, CRNAGORA or KARADAGH (= Black Mountain) a strategically important high mountainous wooded area, sparsely inhabited by tough slavic Orthodox Christians engaged in raising pigs, sheep and goats. It survived all Turkish attacks. In 1516 the Prince transferred his power to a *Vladika* or Prince-Bishop whose office became hereditary until 1851, when the Vladika Danilo I ended the episcopal connection and ruled as Prince again. Its position, close to the entrance of the Adriatic, gave it an interest to European powers which led to their intervention against a determined Turkish onslaught in 1853. This amounted to a customary guarantee, but the Montenegrin outlook remained warlike and the Princes joined enthusiastically in the Balkan alliances and military conspiracies against the Ottoman Empire which preceded World War I. In 1910 Nicholas I proclaimed himself King and in 1913 occupied but had to abandon Scutari. He joined the Serbs against the Austrians who in 1916 took Cetinje, the capital. He fled and as a result the dynasty was unable to maintain itself in public esteem. Hence when the defeat of Austria led to the formation of Yugoslavia, the National Assembly decided to join it.

MONTESQUIEU, Charles Louis de Secondat, Baron de (1689-1755) distinguished French lawyer and member of the Parlement of Bordeaux until 1726, published his *Lettres Persanes*, a critique of French Society, anonymously in 1721. His *Esprit des Lois* (1748) published at Geneva was an attempt to rationalise the function of law in an organised state and owed much to English example.

MONTEVIDEO. *See* URUGUAY.

MONTEZ, Lola (GILBERT, Marie Dolores Eliza Rosanna) (1818-61) Irish actress, Baroness von Rosenthal and Countess of Lansfeld, mistress of Ludwig I of Bavaria. *See* BAVARIA.

MONTFICHET with Baynard's Castle, was one of the two Norman castles at the western end of the City of London. It was probably demolished to provide materials for the debtors' prison. *See* FLEET.

MONTFORT. International family which originated at Montfort L'Amaury in the Ile de France. Through marriages, migrations and participation in Crusades it had property and branches in England, Normandy, Languedoc, the Vorarlberg and Outremer. **(1)** In 1204 **Simon (IV)** became heir through his grandmother to the last Beaumont E. of Leicester. K. John recognised his rights in 1206, but with other Anglo-Normans he was forced to choose between his French and English allegiances. He chose the former and John forfeited his Leicester estates in 1207. In 1215, on papal intervention, Simon's nephew, Ranulf E. of Chester was given a life interest in them. At his death at the siege of Toulouse during the Albigensian crusade in 1218, the family regained the English estates by allotting the rights and

titles in Normandy and England respectively between the two heirs **(2) Amaury** and his younger brother **(3) Simon (V) (?1208-65).** Even with royal support the recovery of the lands from the palatine E. of Chester took a long time, but meanwhile Simon regained his hereditary office of Steward of the Royal Household in 1236, and with the friendship of Henry III he married the King's sister Eleanor in 1238, after a papal dispensation from a vow of perpetual widowhood had been obtained. He accordingly acquired her unsettled claims to dower from her first marriage to William the Marshal the Younger (?-1231) but the couple received no marriage portion from the King, with whom in consequence Simon quarrelled. Further quarrels over money continued until he went on Crusade in 1240-2, but good relations were restored when he returned, and he went with the King on campaign in Poitou. In the controversies of 1244 (*see* PETER DES RIEVAUX) he acted as a parliamentary mediator on Henry's behalf.

In May 1246 he and Richard of Cornwall led the opposition to papal demands and in 1247 he planned to go on Crusade again but did not go. Instead, in 1248 he went with a seven year commission to Gascony as Governor. In 1252 the Gascons complained to the King about his harshness and exactions. As before, Simon quarrelled with the King about money. He resigned in return for his expenses and withdrew to France, though persuaded to return to Gascony in 1253. For the rest of his public career *see* HENRY III; BARONS' WAR; OXFORD, PROVISIONS OF. Of his children, **(4) Henry (1238-65)** represented his father at the Mise of Amiens in 1264, led the baronial army at Lewes, and held Dover and the Cinque Ports. He fell at Evesham. **(5) Simon the Younger (1240-71)** was captured at Northampton in 1264 but released after the B. of Lewes. He arrived too late for the B. of Evesham, was besieged in Kenilworth and escaped abroad in 1266 with **(6) Guy (?1243-88)** who also escaped; he wantonly murdered Henry of Cornwall in the cathedral of Viterbo in 1271.

(7) Eleanor (1252-82) was married by proxy to Llewelyn ap Gruffyd, P. of Gwynedd in 1275 but was captured on the way from France to Wales and only fully married to him when he submitted to Edward I in 1278.

MONTGOMERIE. Lowland Scots of Norman origin. **(1) Sir John of Eaglesham (?-1398)** obtained Ardrossan and Aglinton by marriage. His grandson **(2) Sir Alexander (?-1470)** Lord of Parliament in 1445 was much employed in diplomacy with England. His grandson **(3) Hugh (?1460-1545) 1st E. of EGLINTON (1506)** was a guardian of James V and one of the regents in 1536. His great-grandson **(4) Hugh (?1531-85) 3rd E.** a R. Catholic and supporter of Mary Q. of Scots, was opposed to her marriages but fought for her after she escaped from Lochleven and subsequently tried to secure toleration for R. Catholics. **(5) Alexander (1588-1661)** a cousin originally called Seton, **6th E. (1612)** by settlement from the childless 5th E. and royal confirmation, helped to draft the National Covenant. He was a Scots Privy Councillor, commanded cavalry for the Parliament and fought at Marston Moor, but after Charles I's murder supported Argyll and the recall of Charles II. After the defeat at Worcester in 1651 he was taken, and detained but ultimately included in Cromwell's Act of Grace. His son **(6) Hugh (1613-69) 7th E.,** a relatively junior officer, though opposed to Charles I, was excepted from Cromwell's Act of Grace for being implicated in the Engagement. A descendant **(7) Hugh (1739-1819) 12th E. and 1st Ld. (U.K.) ARDROSSAN (1806)** built Ardrossan harbour. His grandson **(8) Archibald William (1812-61) 13th E. and 2nd Ld., 1st E. of WINTON (1859)** was a Tory politician and pro-Corn Law Whip in 1846. He was Ld Lieut. of Ireland under Derby in 1852 and 1858-9.

MONTGOMERY, -SHIRE (Welsh SIR DREFALDWYN). The area arose from the 12th cent. division of Powys and corresponded with POWYS WENWYNWYN. Roger of Montgomery built the first castle above the village in 1072 to cover his Shropshire territories, but the Welsh name commemorates Baldwin of Boller who built the more imposing second castle under Henry I. The third castle was built in 1223 just before a charter was granted to the village, which was walled. The local marchers were the Mortimers to the west, and in the east the Charltons who had married into Welsh princely families and were really claimants to Powys Wenwynwyn. The area was Yorkist in the Wars of the Roses. It was first shired in 1535, by which time the village, now dignified as a borough, and castle were passing to the Herbert family. Hence as royalists, they surrendered it in 1644 to the Parliamentarians who blew up the fortifications. They retained their properties in and shared influence and parliamentary seats with the Vaughans of Llwydiarth and their heirs, and Wynns down to 1832. The village remained the smallest borough as late as 1974.

The area was richly agricultural but was an important source of navy oak, and at one time, lead.

MONTGOMERY, Bernard Law (1887-1976) Vist. MONTGOMERY of ALAMEIN (1946) and **F.M.,** commanded the 8th Army in N. Africa from Aug. 1942, won the expensive victory at Alamein in Nov. and drove the Italo-German armies in N. Africa to surrender at Tunis in May 1943. He conquered Sicily in July and commanded the operations in Italy until called to take over command of the Normandy invasion in June 1944. On this front his only major failure was the Arnhem operation. Eventually the Germans were driven into Germany by combined Anglo-American-Canadian forces and surrendered to him at Lüneburg in May 1945. He was subsequently C.I.G.S. (1946-8) and Deputy Commander of N.A.T.O. from 1951-8. A soldier of great ambition and some talent, he won his victories through the enormous resources which he, but not others, was supplied with but they brought comfort to a war-depressed British public.

MONTGOMERY (1) Roger the Great (?-?) was a cousin of William the Conqueror and his son **(2) Roger (?-1093) E. of SHREWSBURY (1071)** and **ARUNDEL** was one of William's most trusted men. He contributed a substantial force for the invasion and was then sent back to Normandy to act as its joint-warden. He built castles and founded monasteries all along the Welsh border. In 1088 he and his eldest s. **(3) Roger the Poitevin (?-after 1102)** fought on opposite sides in the civil war with Rufus. The third son was **(4) Robert of Bellême** (q.v.) and Roger the Poitevin shared his policy and exile. The second son **(5) Hugh (?-1098)** succeeded to the earldoms and was killed fighting the Ostmen in Anglesey.

MONTGOMERY, T. of (1267). See GWYNEDD-28.

MONTHERMER, Ralph of (?-?1325) a squire of Gilbert of Clare, married his widow in 1297 and bore her titles as **E. of GLOUCESTER and HEREFORD.** He campaigned much in Scotland between 1298-1306 when he was made **E. of ATHOL** but surrendered the title in 1307. He was Edward II's Lieutenant in Scotland in 1311 and 1312 and was taken prisoner at Bannockburn in 1314.

MONTMORENCY. See HUGUENOTS.

MONTPELLIER (S. France) was a fashionable resort for English people in the 19th cent. Hence the streets and other places named after it in English towns.

MONTREAL (Canada) was visited by Cartier in 1535-6 but founded by Paul de Chennedey de Maisonneuve in 1642. He became Governor in 1644. The place developed very slowly until it surrendered peacefully to the British in 1760 as a result of the fall of Quebec the year before. American rebels occupied it in 1775 but retreated when their attack on Quebec failed. It developed rapidly after the British unification of Canada so that by 1871 the population was 133,000, by 1900 it was 270,000, and by 1971 1.3M. It was the world's third largest French speaking city.

MONTREAL AIR CONVENTION 1971. See AVIATION RULES-2.

MONTREUX CONVENTION (1936) at Turkish request modified the Straits provision of the T. of Lausanne and was signed by countries adjacent to the Bosphorus and Dardanelles and by Britain and France. The Turks feared Italian expansion into Anatolia. It allowed them to refortify the Straits and permitted Russia to send warships through them other than capital ships and submarines while confining other powers to small warships and it limited the number of foreign warships at any other time in the Straits to one. The Russians exploited this after World War II for several years, by ensuring that one of theirs was always in the Straits.

MONTROSE. See GRAHAM.

MONTSERRAT (W. Indies) named by Columbus in 1483 after the monastic mountain near Barcelona was colonised in 1632 by Sir Thomas Warner who introduced a mixture of English from Britain and Irish from St. Kitts. The French attacked it in 1667 and the Irish went over to them, but it was restored in 1668 and heavily fortified. It grew sugar and later limes and cotton under African slave labour until 1782 when the French took it again, but it was again restored after a year and remains part of the Commonwealth. The population of mainly African ancestry, speaks English with a marked Irish brogue.

MONUMENT, THE (London) to the great fire of 1666 was completed from Sir Christopher Wren's design in 1677.

MOORE, Sir Francis (1558-1621) learned law reporter and conveyancer, invented the lease and release, by means of which the Statute of Enrolments was habitually evaded.

MOORE (1) John (1729-1802) an able Glasgow physician and writer, travelled Europe originally with the D. of Hamilton after 17721 and was in Paris during the French revolution of which he published an account. His brilliant soldier s. **(2) Sir John (1761-1809)** was commissioned at 15, saw service in the American War in 1779, was a Scots M.P. from 1784-90 and with Paoli cleared the French out of Corsica. In 1796 he went as a Brigadier General under Abercromby to the W. Indies. Abercromby put him in charge of St. Lucia which he rapidly reduced to order while maintaining his troops in unusually good health by sensible hygiene and food and well cut uniforms. In 1799 he was sent to Holland where he was wounded. In 1800-01 he distinguished himself in the Mediterranean and Egypt. In 1801 as colonel of the 52nd Foot at Shorncliffe (Kent) using his experience, he began to revolutionise the British military outlook by creating a light infantry based on the rifleman's personal responsibility and adaptation of equipment to an open style of warfare. By 1805 he was a Lieut. General and had created the Light Division and his ideas were reaching into every branch of the army. In 1808 he was sent to the Peninsula under the egregious Sir Harry Burrard but became C-in-C when that worthy was recalled. He advanced into Spain towards Madrid at the request of the Ambassador and joined up with Baird at Mayorga (Dec. 1808). In an effort to thwart Bonaparte's invasion by cutting into the French communications, but finding that the French were in overwhelming force, he made (in order to save the only British field army) his famous retreat across the mountains to Corunna, which he reached in 13th Jan. 1809. He fought a victorious battle there to cover the embarkation (16th) but was mortally wounded.

MOORE, Thomas (1779-1852) between 1807-34 preserved many old Irish melodies which were edited musically by Sir John Stevenson. By 1813 when he issued his collected lampoons on the Prince Regent as the *Twopenny Postbag*, he was a friend of Byron and Leigh Hunt. In 1817 he had a European-wide *succès de scandale* in his best known novel (partly in verse) *Lalla*

Rookh. Meanwhile as sinecurist Admiralty Registrar at Bermuda he was made liable to the public funds by his deputy's dishonesty, and went abroad, travelling in Italy with Ld John Russell and, at Venice, meeting Byron, who gave him his memoirs. He returned to England in 1823. In 1830 he destroyed Byron's memoirs and wrote a *Life* (1830) of him instead, perhaps to protect his friend's already tarnished reputation.

MOORE-BRABAZON, John Theodore Cuthbert (1884-1964) 1st Ld. BRABAZON of TARA (1942) was ploughed at Cambridge and then followed his mechanical bent by working for C. S. Rolls and becoming a racing driver. He turned to aircraft, flying a heavier than air machine as early as 1909. He later took a pig as a passenger to prove that pigs can fly. In World War I he specialised in air photography. He was twice a Conservative M.P. (1918-29 and 1931-42) and Churchill's parliamentary private secretary at the War Office. In 1940 he was Minister of Transport and then Minister of Aircraft Production. In 1942 he expressed the hope (entertained by most informed people) that Germany and Russia would tear each other to pieces and was forced to resign.

MOORGATE (London) opened onto Moorfields, a fen north of the City caused probably by the damming of the water courses by the walls.

MOPLAHS, Moslems of seafaring origin, living as small tenants and agricultural labourers in S. Malabar (India), staged several fanatical uprisings in the 19th cent. and a particularly violent one in 1920-21 which temporarily took over the administration and attacked Hindu landlords and bankers. The rising, suppressed by the army, exacerbated communal feeling throughout India.

MORAL REARMAMENT. *See* OXFORD GROUP.

MORAN, Patrick Francis (1830-1911) Card. (1885) R. Catholic Abp. of Sydney from 1884, a militant churchman was also prominent as an advocate of Australian federation and home rule.

MORANT, Sir Robert Laurie (1863-1920), as tutor to the Siamese Crown Prince, became an influential educational adviser to the Siamese govt. from 1888-93. This perhaps trained him in the art of intrigue by means of which he became Secretary to the new Board of Education in 1903. He strengthened the primary school system and teaching and orientated the secondary school towards entry into universities and professions, probably because he believed in educational co-ordination and was dealing with material ready to hand. In any case his eight-year tenure came to an abrupt end in 1911 when, as a result of some criticism of teachers in a circular, he was hurriedly transferred to the Chairmanship of the National Health Commission. Here his extraordinary intellectual clarity and ruthlessness were well employed in laying, despite the four years of World War I, the foundations of the modern welfare services and in creating the new Ministry of Health, of which he became the first permanent Secretary in 1919.

MORAVIANS, a Hussite off-shoot formed in 1467 to revive the austere spirit of the Apostles and to practice good works. The 18th cent. Count Nicholas Zinzendorf set up, despite persecution, a Moravian community at Herrnhut whence in 1731-4 a still existing teaching colony was built at Fulneck (Yorks.). Its orders were recognised by the Anglican Church in 1737. Moravian emphasis on preaching, hymns and a simplified communion ("Love Feast") influenced evangelicalism and, especially, the Wesleys.

MORAY (pron. Murry). An ancient eastern province of Celtic Scotland. According to legend it was ruled by a King. He, it is surmised, became or was replaced by a Mormaer, who in turn developed, apparently, into one of the Seven Es. Whatever the facts, the later earldom had high precedence and a special, quasi-royal repute.

MORAY, Es of. *See* RANDOLPH; STEWART.

MORALITY PLAYS were late mediaeval allegorical performances in which characters represented vices, virtues and other abstractions: eg, in the 15th cent. *Everyman.* Everyman is summoned by Death and finds that of his friends, Kindred, Goods, Knowledge, Beauty, Strength and Good Deeds, only the last will go with him. Sir David Lindsay's *Pleasant Satyre of the Three Estaities* begins with the temptation of Rex Humanus by Sensuality, Wantonness, Solace etc., while Good Counsel is thrown out, Verity is put in the Stocks and Chastity is shouted down. *See* MYSTERY PLAYS.

MORCAR or MORKERE (?-after 1087) 2nd son of E. Aelfgar of Mercia with his brother Edwin stirred up a Northumbrian revolt against E. Tostig Godwin's son in 1065. The rebels expelled Tostig and made Morcar E. of York. Having Mercian and Welsh support he was accepted in the position by Kings Edward the Confessor and Harold II. The brothers were defeated at the B. of Fulford (Sept. 1066) by the Norwegian K. Harald Hardrada and Tostig and so neither took part in the B. of Hastings. In the aftermath, they failed to persuade the Londoners to accept one of them as King and submitted to William I at Berkhamstead. Both were involved in short rebellions in 1068 and again in 1071 when Morcar was taken at the surrender of Ely. He spent the rest of his life in prison.

MORDAUNT. Bedfordshire family. **(1) Sir John (?-1504)** a commander at the B. of Stoke (June 1487) and M.P. for his county was elected Speaker in Nov. He was a King's serjeant from 1495 and C.J. of Chester from 1499. His son **(2) John (?1490-1562) 1st Ld. MORDAUNT (1532)** a court sycophant, attended Henry VIII at the Field of the Cloth of Gold, and the Emperor Charles V at Gravelines and Canterbury. A friend of Thomas Cromwell, he inquired into Wolsey's fortune, was present at the Submission of the Clergy (1532) appeared both as a supporter of Anne Boleyn's marriage and in her trial and helped to put down the Pilgrimage of Grace. His g-grandson **(3) John (?-1642) 1st E. of PETERBOROUGH (1628)** was a parliamentary general under Essex but died of tuberculosis. His *s.* **(3) Henry (?1624-97) 2nd E,** deserted from the Parliamentary army (Apr. 1643) fought for the King at Newbury (Sept.), raised a regiment, and after a period in France compounded for his estates in 1646. In 1647 with Buckingham and Holland he tried to raise Surrey for the King but was beaten at Kingston, wounded and escaped to Holland. He recompounded in May 1649.

Shortly after the Restoration he became Governor of Tangier but resigned the impossible task for £1,000 life annuity. During later service afloat, he became friendly with the D. of York and acted as his matrimonial negotiator both for the Archduchess Claudia, and for Mary of Modena, whom he brought to England (Sept. 1673). He was a P.C. from 1674 until 1680 when he was dismissed in connection with the Popish Plot. He attended the Duke in Scotland (Oct. 1681), was recalled to the P.C. in Feb. 1683 and became James II Groom of the Stole. In 1687 he was received into the Roman church. At the Revolution he was impeached but released when Parliament dissolved. His brother **(4) John (1647-75) Vist. MORDAUNT (1659)** an adventurous royalist, organised unsuccessful risings in Surrey in July 1648, in Sussex in Jan. 1658 and again in Surrey in July 1659. In Apr. 1660 he took royal messages to London to General Monck. By Elizabeth, née Carey, his spirited and beautiful wife, he had a son **(5) Charles (1658-1735) E. of MONMOUTH (1689) 3rd E. (1697)** who served afloat from 1674-80 in the Mediterranean and in 1680 ashore at Tangier. He then entered politics as a supporter of Shaftesbury and as an opponent of James II. He went to Holland after the prorogation and is said, or perhaps claimed, to have been the first to suggest to William of Orange that he might overthrow the King. He made several journeys to England on William's behalf and also commanded a small Dutch squadron in the W. Indies where he was probably sent to suborn Admiral Narbrough. He landed in Torbay with William, raised Dorset and Wiltshire ahead of his advance and was soon a P.C., gentleman of the Bedchamber, and in Apr. 1689 First Lord of the Treasury, under whom Sidney Godolphin did the work.

He was perverse, vain, unreliable and over-clever. In 1690 while William was in Ireland, secret letters describing Mary II's council deliberations were intercepted on the way to a French agent in Antwerp. He was the most probable originator, but he said that they were written in the offices of Nottingham a political opponent. William did not at that time withdraw his confidence, but in Feb. 1694 he was advocating triennial parliaments and deprived of his preferments. Reinstated in Apr. 1695, he tried to persuade Sir John Fenwick to incriminate other opponents, viz Marlborough, Russell and Shrewsbury. The Lords committed him to the Tower for planting forged papers on Fenwick but by 1697 he had made up the quarrel save with Russell but was, through his son John, M.P. for Chippenham, trying to impeach Somers.

From Anne's succession he lived quietly until appointed joint C-in-C of the Peninsular expedition of 1705, with Admiral Sir Clowdisley Shovell. (*See* SPANISH SUCCESSION, WAR OF.) As a result of his conduct he was recalled in Feb. 1707 but made a circular tour of European powers instead, visiting in turn Turin, Vienna, Charles XII of Sweden at Leipzig, Hanover and Marlborough's H.Q. near Brussels. At each of these he urged action at variance with British policy. Not surprisingly his arrest was contemplated but in fact the Lords instituted an inquiry in which he, a radical whig attacked the Whig Govt. and was supported by Tories. The Tory accession to power simplified the situation. They sent him as Ambassador to Vienna and then to the Imperial Diet at Frankfurt. At both places his activities were self indulgent and useless. George I's accession and the triumph of the whigs ended his career.

MORE, Hannah (1745-1833), poet, playwright and friend of Dr Johnson and David Garrick, became interested after 1779 in moral reform. She was befriended by William Wilberforce and later introduced to the Clapham Sect, and became interested in Friendly Societies and Sunday Schools, especially in Somerset.

MORE (1) Sir John (?1453-1530) was a judge from at least 1518. His famous son **(2) Sir Thomas (1478-1535) St. (1935)** was placed in the household of John Morton, Abp. of Canterbury, and at Oxford was taught by Grocyn and Linacre. In 1496 he was called to the bar. He was a friend of Colet, Erasmus and Lily who often stayed with him. Later he was a generous patron of Hans Holbein the Younger. In 1499 he experienced a spiritual trauma and considered ordination, but after four years of austerity and contemplation returned to the world in 1503. He was spectacularly successful at the bar and became an M.P. in 1504. Recognised as one of the ablest rising men, he was nominated for the Burgundian commercial negotiations of 1515 and those with the French on Calais in 1516. During these absences he wrote *Utopia*. He is said to have impressed Henry VIII with arguments against the Crown in a Star Chamber case against a papal ship. In 1518 he became a Master of Requests and councillor.

Charming and intellectually supple, he was treated by Henry VIII as a companion rather than a favourite, and was often employed as speaker at functions, such as Cardinal Campeggio's reception in 1518 and the Field of the Cloth of Gold in 1520. He even managed to stay in Cardinal Wolsey's good graces. In 1521, as Under Treasurer of England, he was administratively responsible for the King's finances, yet was able to go with Wolsey on his journeys to Bruges and Calais. In 1523, as Speaker he presided over a House which refused to be bullied by Wolsey. By 1525 he was Chancellor of the Duchy and High Steward of Cambridge University but he and Wolsey were still together in the Amiens negotiations of 1527. In 1529 he was Wolsey's obvious successor as Ld Chancellor and carried out the legal duties with unrivalled expedition, partly because in Norfolk there was a separate chief minister.

It was at this point that Henry discovered that More was a man of principle, for he would neither countenance the divorce of Katherine of Aragon as being against the doctrine of the church, nor be a party to changing that doctrine by legislation. His parliamentary position as Speaker of one of its Houses was incompatible with his conscience, and in 1532 he resigned. The resignation of so universally admired a man was a grave blow to Henry's repute and though More lived in retirement, Henry, already showing signs of derangement, was determined to re-establish himself. Moreover, the protestant factions were complaining of More's severity when in office against the potentially seditious heresies. In 1533 he was attacked through a bill of attainder as a result of the affair of the Holy Maid of Kent, but public pressure secured the deletion of his name. In 1534, however, he was attacked for refusing an oath impugning papal authority or (which went together with it) the propriety of Katherine of Aragon's divorce. He was committed to the Tower, and periodically questioned without effect. In July 1535 he was convicted of treason on the perjured evidence of Richard Rich, possibly at the instance of Thomas Cromwell, and executed. The event profoundly shocked contemporary opinion everywhere, and has been the subject of debate ever since. He left a considerable number of English and Latin works, of which only *Utopia* is now remembered.

MOREAU, Jean Victor Marie (1763-1813) became a French General in 1793, fell into revolutionary disfavour in 1797, saved the retreating French army in Italy in 1799, helped Bonaparte to overthrow the Directory in Brumaire (Nov.) 1799 and in Dec. 1800 defeated the Austrians at Hohenlinden. This success was too much for Bonaparte who accused him of treason. He left France; he eventually (1812) joined the Austrians and was killed at the B. of Dresden.

MORGAN, a Gwent family descended from **Cadifor Fawr (?-1089)** whose third son **(1) Bledri (?-1120)** received land from the Normans in Gwent. His descendant **(2) Llewelyn ab Ifor (fl. 1375)** married Angharad, daughter of Sir Morgan ab Maredydd, and so acquired the Morgan Tredegar estates. The family flourished and was strongly Lancastrian. **(3) Sir John (?-1492)** was a military supporter of Henry VII who rewarded him with offices in Gwent and took his s. **(4) Thomas** as one of his squires. A family of kinsmen headed by **(5) William (?-1582)** had meanwhile arisen and acquired some former monastic lands at Llantarnam. The result was a division into a Protestant family descended from Thomas, and an actively R. Catholic family descended from William. The latter family did much to keep recusancy in being for a century. Both families were royalist in the Civil War until 1645, when **(6) Thomas (?-?1660)** an M.P. in the Short Parliament, who had fought for the King at Naseby, was arrested for hindering the King's cause. He became an M.P. in the Protector's Parliament of 1654. **(7) William (?-1680)** a successful barrister, bought large estates in Gwent which created a Morgan power base in South Wales. As a result, Monmouthshire, Brecon and Brecknock were never without a Morgan M.P. between 1701-1875, while in 1859 **(8) Charles (1792-1875)** became **1st Ld. TREDEGAR.**

MORGAN, Sir Henry (?1635-88) a privateer, was elected Admiral of the Buccaneers in 1666. In 1668 the Jamaicans commissioned him to ward off a rumoured Spanish attack. This he did, in anticipation, by sacking Porto Bello on the Spanish Main, which ensured Spanish hostility and caused a quarrel with the trade-conscious Jamaicans. In 1669 he forced L. Maracaibo by an ingenious ruse and pillaged its towns, and then descended on the Mexican and Cuban coasts. In 1670 he stormed and sacked Panama, then an important emporium. This success was spoiled by the drunken cruelty and indiscipline of his irregular followers and much loot was lost, but the Governor and Council publicly thanked him and he was sent to England to explain why he had exceeded his commission. Diplomatically and briefly disgraced, he was knighted in 1675 and returned as Lieut. Governor and C-in-C to Jamaica where in due course he died in riches and respectability.

MORGAN, William (?1540-1604) single handedly made a complete translation of the Bible into Welsh, published in 1588. This had as profound an influence on Welsh as the Authorised Version had on English a generation later. His work was enthusiastically supported by Abp. Whitgift. He became Bp. of Llandaff in 1595 and was translated to St. Asaph in 1601.

MORGANATIC MARRIAGE. A type of marriage unknown in England save in a solitary partial case, between persons of unequal rank, in which the inferior and the children of the union are excluded from the dignities and property of the (usually royal) superior who is commonly but not always the husband. Conspicuous examples include Louis XIV and Mme de Maintenon, and the Archduke Franz Ferdinand and Sophie, Duchess of Hohenberg (both murdered at Sarajevo in 1914). By act of Parliament the children, if any, of the Duke of Windsor (formerly Edward VIII) were excluded from succession to the Throne.

MORGANNWG (S. Wales) roughly coterminous with the diocese of Llandaff, comprised the tribal area of the Silures, and embraced Gwent and Glywysing, later Glamorgan. Its purely Welsh history is now obscure. The Normans led by Robert fitzHamon invaded it by sea, seized Cardiff and assisted by a discontented local chief called Einion, spread up the valleys from the coast. Iestyn ap Gwrgan, the last Prince, retired into a monastery and his sons Caradoc and Rhys and their descendants became vassals in eastern Glamorgan. Robert fitzHamon's rights passed to his daughter Mabel who married Henry I's bastard Robert of Gloucester, and then through another female succession to the Clare family.

MORGENTHAU PLAN (after its author Henry Morgenthau, U.S. Secretary of the Treasury) envisaged that after World War II Germany should be reduced to a pastoral country without industries, incapable therefore of further aggressions. The plan was urged by Morgenthau and Pres. Roosevelt at the 1944 Quebec Conference and sidetracked as impracticable and unjust by the British.

MORIER. Of this oriental diplomatic family **(1) Isaac (1750-1817)**, born at Smyrna and naturalised in 1803, was Consul General for the Levant Co. at Constantinople from 1804. This post was converted into a British Consulate General in 1806. Of his sons **(2) John Philip (1776-1853)** reported on the fighting in Egypt in 1800. In 1803 he was Consul-General in Albania and in 1810 he went to the Legation in Washington. Briefly U/Sec. for Foreign Affairs in 1815, he was Minister to Saxony from 1816-25. His brother **(3) James Justinian (?1780-1849)** a Persian diplomat from 1807 was the author of *Hajji Baba of Ispahan*. His brother **(4) David Richard (1784-1877)** served between 1804-12 in the Ottoman dominions, and then at Vienna in 1814-15. He then entered French service and was Minister to Switzerland from 1832-47. His son **(5) Sir Robert Burnett David (1826-93)** held diplomatic posts at German courts from 1853-76 and became the acknowledged expert on German affairs. He was Minister to Lisbon from 1876-81; to Madrid from 1881-84 and then until 1893 Ambassador to Russia, where he exhibited exceptional talent.

MORISCO, MOZARAB, MUDEJAR. These terms refer to relations between Christian and Moslem in Spain. A *mozarab* was a Christian who had given allegiance to a Moslem ruler. *Moriscos* were conquered Moors in a Christian state, especially after 1492. Much persecuted, they were expelled in 1609 and 1610 except for the *mudejars* who had been converted to Christianity. The expulsion seriously weakened the Spanish economy. *See also* BARBARY-2.

MORISON, Sir Richard (?-1556) was ambassador to the Hanse in 1546 and with Ascham as his secretary to Charles V from 1550-53.

MORISON, Robert (1620-83) King's botanist from 1660 revived the languishing study of systematic botany, especially at Oxford where he was Professor from 1669.

MORLAND, dynasty of painters **(1) George Henry (?-?1789)** a genre painter whose works were engraved by Watson. His son **(2) Henry Robert (?1730-97)**, a portraitist. His son **(3) George (1763-1804)** was a prolific genre and animal painter who died in a sponging house, leaving as his own epitaph: "Here lies a drunken dog."

MORLEY, John (1838-1923) Vist. MORLEY (1908) a Gladstonian but agnostic liberal began as a freelance journalist in 1860 and became a friend of J.S. Mill, George Meredith and Frederic Harrison. He was editor of the *Fortnightly Review* from 1867-82 and made it an influential forum of Liberal ideas. He published his *Voltaire* in 1872 and *Rousseau* in 1873. By now he was working with Joseph Chamberlain and Sir Charles Dilke on their schemes for disestablishment, secular education, land reform and progressive taxation, and his views took a pronounced pacifist turn. In 1880 he became editor of the *Pall Mall Gazette* and changed its conservative imperialism to radicalism overnight. In 1881 he published his well known *Life of Cobden* and after attempts in 1869 and 1880, he at last became M.P. for Newcastle on Tyne in 1883. A poor speaker, but respected as a man, he could be both influential and independent. He broke with Chamberlain over Irish affairs, became Chief Secretary for Ireland (1886) but promoted the discussions to reconcile Chamberlain. In opposition he was a powerful critic of conservative coercive policies and meanwhile published his *Walpole* (1889). In 1892 he returned to the Chief Secretaryship and bore an important role in carrying Gladstone's second Home Rule Bill in the Commons. He disliked and opposed the Boer War. In 1900 he published *Oliver Cromwell* and in 1903 his monumental *Life of Gladstone*. In the Liberal Govt. of 1905-10 he was Secretary of State for India (*see* MORLEY-MINTO REFORMS). He went to the Lords in 1908 and piloted the Parliament Act, 1910, through it. In 1914 he with John Burns, resigned against entering World War I.

MORLEY, Mrs. *See* ANNE, QUEEN.

MORLEY-MINTO REFORMS (1909) the usual name for the effects of the Government of India Act, 1909. Indians were to be associated on a larger and more important scale with Govt. decision making and accordingly the Viceroy's and Governor's councils were enlarged to four so that an Indian could be appointed to each. Legislative councils were much enlarged so that they could include a substantial number but not a majority of elected members. These were to be chosen upon a communal basis. The partition of the subcontinent is sometimes ascribed to this.

MORMAER. (Celt: possibly Great Steward or Chief of the Sea). A title possibly of Pictish origin, first found in the *Annals of Ulster*. The ancient Scots Kingdom of Alban was traditionally supposed to have seven of these high officers, who were responsible for the defence or sea defence of Angus, Atholl, Strathearn, Fife, Mar, Moray and either Caithness or Argyll. There is historical evidence of *mormaers* in Angus, Buchan, Lennox, Mar, the Mearns, Moray and Morvern. The word was also used to translate the Norse title 'earl' and it is supposed that the *mormaers* were the seven Earls who raised Scottish Kings on to the coronation stone. The office became hereditary and some probably developed into the great Celtic earldoms. *See* MORAY.

MORNING ADVERTISER (1794) is the licensed victuallers' organ.

MORNING CHRONICLE (1769-1862) founded and, until 1789, edited by William Woodfall (1746-1803), was a Whig journal. James Perry (1756-1821) bought it and edited it until 1821. He employed Henry Brougham, Thomas Campbell, Charles Hazlitt, Thomas Moore and David Ricardo. His successor John Black (1783-1855) held the post until 1843, and employed J.S. Mill, Dickens and Thackeray. He resigned because of declining energy and the paper continued to decline thereafter.

MORNING HERALD, a popular London paper specialising in crime which originated in about 1780 and merged with the *Daily Express* in 1800.

MORNING POST (and DAILY ADVERTISING PAMPHLET) was founded in 1772 and developed a conservative but robust style after 1795. *See* DAILY TELEGRAPH.

MORNINGTON. *See* COLLEY OR COWLEY; WELLESLEY.

MOROCCO (*see* BARBARY). The Spanish territory under the Almoravides and Almohades was part of a Moroccan empire which began to disintegrate after the B. of Navas de Tolosa in 1212. By 1230 Castilians were intervening in dynastic wars in Morocco proper and after 1269 Moroccan rulers made their influence felt in Spain only through sporadic expeditions. On the other hand the seamen controlled or levied toll upon Christian commerce in the Straits, and from about 1400 began to molest Portuguese traders along the Atlantic coast, especially after the opening of the Guinea gold mines. The Portuguese seized Ceuta in 1415, Arzila and Tangier in 1471, Safi in 1508 besides other places. The Spaniards after the fall of Granada, occupied Melilla and Peñon de Velez in 1497. The Marabout reaction unified the country and by the 1540s most of the Iberians had been driven from their outposts. On the other hand the Turks were advancing from Algiers, and by 1550 there was a Hispano-Moroccan alliance against them. By 1560 the Turks had abandoned their ambitions but in 1578 the Sultan Saad the Victorious (r. 1578-1603) destroyed an ill-considered invasion by K. Sebastian of Portugal and killed him. Subsequently Moroccan armies, by reaching (1591) the Niger controlled the slave, salt and gold trades of W. Africa and as English merchants were now common, Saad opened an official trade with England. The 16th cent. generally transformed Morocco, for the expulsions from Spain brought in a huge Hispanic immigration and the slave trade many blacks. It was with a black army that the Sultan Mulay Ismail (r. 1672-1727) recovered Tangier from the English in 1684. He never conquered the High Atlas and after his death, dynastic and tribal disputes fragmented the country until the reign of Muhammad ibn Abd Allah (1757-90). He signed commercial treaties with Britain in 1760 and 1765, and in 1765 founded Mogador as a centre for European trade. Other protestant states were brought in, accepted capitulations similar to those in Turkey, and opened eight other ports. Between 1790-1822 rebellions and civil wars reduced the trade but thereafter the French and Spaniards sought to extend their influence. The war with France on the Algerian frontier (1844-5) and with Spain (1859-60) thus represented indirect aggression against the hitherto commercially predominant British, but the Moroccan defeats encouraged a general desire to expel the infidel. It was on the crest of this xenophobia that Sultan Mulay Hassan (1873-94) secured the alliance and nominal submission of the Glaui, the leader of the Atlas clans. His successor, Mulay Abd-el-Aziz (1894-1908) was less statesmanlike. Westernised in outlook, he was soon the

target of a dynastic rebellion. The French now resolved to intervene in the name of order and commercial good sense. The Fashoda affair had already left them with a recognised leading interest in W. Africa. By the *Entente Cordiale* Britain bowed out of Morocco while France signed a partition treaty with Spain. It was not to be as simple as it seemed, for at this point Germany intervened at Tangier, nominally to support the Sultan, actually to extort African concessions. The resulting Algeçiras conference (Jan. to Apr. 1906) internationalised Moroccan trade and recognised the predominant political role of France and Spain. After a further quarrel with the Germans (the Agadir Incident 1911) France and Spain acquired a free hand. Tangier under a Moroccan *Mendoub* became an international free port under joint Franco-Spanish administration; the Rif and Ifni, under the *Khalifa*, were to be administered and policed by Spain; the rest by France, whose Resident General was to be the Sultan's foreign minister. In practice the Spaniards did not penetrate the Rif until 1927 nor the French beyond the Atlas until after World War II but a post-war independence movement resulted in the creation of a new monarchy in 1956, which included Tangier and from 1969 Spanish Ifni. Most of the Spanish Sahara was annexed in 1976 but this provoked a strong local movement called Polisario.

MORRELL, Lady Ottoline Violet Anne (1873-1938) vivacious half-sister of the 6th D. of Portland, married the wealthy brewer Philip Morrell in 1902. They attracted and she inspired a literary and artistic salon from 1913-24 at Garsington Manor (Oxon) and then at Gower Street London, where most of the best English writers, critics and artists fought well tempered intellectual battles.

MORRIS, William (1834-96) originally an architect and then a painter, helped Rossetti and other pre-Raphaelites to establish their well-known interior decorating business, and also the *Oxford and Cambridge Magazine*. From 1858 he published poems; in 1875 a translation of the *Aeneid* and in 1876 some Icelandic stories. He became interested in socialism and in 1888 he published the *Dream of John Ball* and in 1891 *News from Nowhere*. In 1890 he had also set up the Kelmscott Press for which he designed his own very distinctive type and decoration. His versatile idealism was directed to the overthrow of ugliness by beauty, and his socialism was a reaction to the aesthetically squalid aspects of the industrial revolution.

MORRIS, William Richard (1877-1963) Ld. NUFFIELD (1934) Vist. (1938) started a garage and turned it into a light engineering works at Cowley in 1903. He designed, built and started the mass production of the *Morris Oxford,* a small popular car, in 1913. The *Morris Cowley* and MG were developed after World War I. There followed mergers with Wolseley, Riley and in 1952 Austin, which formed the British Motor Corporation and revolutionised the British motor industry. He applied most of his immense wealth to benefactions to Oxford University.

MORRIS, MORRICE or MORES DANCE. The name (= Moorish) indicates a southern origin and it was probably brought to England in the 13th cent. in the entourage of Edward I's Q. Eleanor of Castile. It was popular in rural areas and its mimes were entangled with the Robin Hood myth and ancient survivals like the hobby horse. Suppressed under the Commonwealth, it lingered in a few places until self consciously revived by Cecil Sharp.

MORRISON, Herbert Stanley (1888-1965) Ld. MORRISON of LAMBETH (1959) after an elementary education began his political career as Mayor of Hackney (1919) and went on to be a Labour member of the London County Council (1922) which, against Govt. opposition, rebuilt Waterloo Bridge. He was its leader from 1934-40. With two breaks, he was also M.P. for S. London seats from 1923-59. As Minister of Transport

(1929-31) he introduced a bill to combine the London bus and underground systems. This was later passed under the National Govt. He unsuccessfully contested the leadership of the Labour Party with Attlee in 1935 but his absence from the Commons between 1931-35 told against him. During World War II after a short time as Minister of Supply (1940) he became Home Secretary until 1945 in the War Cabinet. In the Attlee govt. he was Dep. Premier throughout and briefly a not very competent Foreign Secretary (1951) when he was attacked for failing to frustrate Persian seizure of the British oil installations at Abadan. In fact he was frustrated by Attlee. A capable administrator, he was partially blind and his grasp on the Foreign Office was perhaps weaker than elsewhere. Thus, when Attlee retired, he again failed to win the leadership against Hugh Gaitskell.

MORSE CODE was adopted as an international telegraphic language at a European conference in 1851.

***MORTALITÉ DES ENFANTS.** See* PLAGUE.

***MORTE D'ARTHUR.** See* MALORY.

MORTEFONTAINE T. of (Sept. 1800) between France and the U.S.A. settled outstanding differences and joined the two countries in asserting that neutral merchantmen should be exempt from search by belligerent powers and that the flag covers the cargo, ie. that the Americans should prolong the wars for their own profit. Naturally the British did not accept the principle, which, in any case, neither High Contracting Party could enforce.

MORTGAGES are loans secured on a defined property which, according to the wording, can be taken by the creditor if the debtor defaults. At an early stage the Chancery intervened to prevent oppressive repossessions as long as the debtor paid the interest and obeyed the other conditions. Mortgage finance was a feature of 18th cent. agricultural and industrial development and, in debenture form, of company finance in the 19th. Since World War II it has become a dominating aspect of housing finance.

MORTIMER FAMILY. Bp. Hugh of Coutances had a son **(1) Roger (I) (?-1074)** who was named after Mortemer-en-Brie, where he defeated K. Henry I of France in 1054. His son **(2) Ralph (?- 1104)** was a member of William the Conqueror's court and became seneschal of the Shrewsbury palatinate. Amongst other estates in the Welsh marches he was given Wigmore (c. 1074) and later large parts of the considerable Montgomery lands after the fall of Robert of Bellême in 1102. From his lands at Caux in Normandy he assisted Henry I's conquest of the Duchy. His son or grandson **(3) Hugh (?-1181)** continued the Mortimer advance in the Welsh Marches despite feuds with Jocelin of Dinant, Lord of Ludlow and the Es. of Hereford. The disturbed reign of Stephen created opportunities for lords such as Hugh; he seized the royal castle of Bridgenorth to add to his castles at Cleobury and Wigmore but Henry II besieged him there (May-July 1155) and he had to give it back. In 1174 he founded a priory at Wigmore. His son **(4) Roger (II) (?-1214)** was suspected of conspiring with the Welsh by the Justiciar William Longchamps who besieged and took Wigmore in 1191 and exiled him until the return of K. Richard I. Under K. John, like other Anglo-Norman families the Mortimers had to choose between their Norman and their English lands and allegiances and Roger gave up his Norman possessions in 1204 and became more involved in Marcher affairs. His son **(5) Ralph (II) (?-1246)** married Gwladys Ddu, daughter of Llewelyn ap Iorwerth and their son **(6) Roger (III) (c. 1231-82)** married in 1247 Matilda de Braose, co-heiress of William de Braose. She brought him much of the Marshal family inheritance in Brecon and Radnor, besides other estates in England and Ireland. He was the leading and also a widely influential Marcher who combined with his own possessions the office of castellan for the Lord Edward (later Edward I) in Builth. The ambitions of

Llewelyn ap Gruffydd of Gwynedd consolidated Mortimer's loyalty to Edward, for Llewelyn overran many of Edward's lands between 1256 and 1258. After the Provisions of Oxford (1258) the Marchers and Edward demanded action in Wales. Simon de Montfort, however, persuaded the King to accept a truce. This left Llewelyn in possession at their expense; they naturally became hostile to Montfort. Mortimer played a decisive part in the escape of Edward to Wigmore and in the operations leading to Montfort's death at Evesham (1265). Builth had, however, to be left to Llewelyn in the T. of Montgomery (1267). In the Welsh war of 1276-7 Mortimer held the frontier and was in 1278 rewarded with extensive lands in S. Powys. He died during Llewelyn's last rebellion and two of his sons **(7) Edmund (V) (?-1304)** and **(8) Roger (IV) (?1256-1326)** were in the B. of Orewin Bridge (1282) where Llywellyn fell. Edmund succeeded at Wigmore. Roger took the new lordship of Chirk, enlarged by annexations from Llewelyn's principality. He was a successful commissioner of array and raised strong bodies of Welsh infantry for the Aquitainian wars of 1294 and 1297 and for Edward's Scottish campaigns. This helped to keep order in Wales. In 1307 he became the King's Lieutenant and Justice in Wales and an opponent of the Despensers. Edmund's famous *s.* **(9) Roger (V) of WIGMORE (1287-1330) 1st E. of MARCH (1328)** had acquired large Irish properties through his wife Joan of Genville. He went to Ireland in 1308 and became involved in a long feud with the Lacys. The latter sided with Edward Bruce in his Irish invasion after Bannockburn, and Roger with the English. Defeated at Kells in 1316, he maintained resistance, became the King's Lieutenant and in 1317 after driving out the Scots, put down the rebels of Ulster and Leinster. In 1319 he became Justiciar of Ireland. He supported his uncle of Chirk with troops against the Despensers but they both had to submit at Shrewsbury (1322) and were imprisoned in the Tower afterwards. Roger of Chirk died there. Roger of Wigmore escaped in 1324 with the help of his protégé Adam of Orelton, then Bp. of Hereford. He went to Gascony and offered his services to Charles IV of France but when Q. Isabella reached Paris on her diplomatic mission, Roger joined her there and became her lover and chief adviser. Between them they devised the plan for getting the young P. Edward (later Edward III) away from the Despensers on the pretext of doing homage for his father for Aquitaine, but their scandalous liaison and papal intervention, worked against them, and they moved to Holland, whence they launched their successful invasion (1326) leading to Edward II's deposition and murder (1327). (*For the rest of his life see* ISABELLA OF FRANCE (1294-1358).)

His grandson **(10) Roger (VI) (?1327-60) 2nd E. (1355)** was a military companion of Edward III who gave him Radnor in 1342 and returned Wigmore in 1343. He was knighted before Crécy (1346) and given a Garter and the rest of the older Mortimer lordships afterwards. In 1348 he was summoned to Parliament as a peer; his grandfather's attainder was reversed in 1354, and steps were taken to restore the other lands, including Denbigh, in the next years. His son **(11) Edmund (1351-81) 3rd E.** married Edward III's granddaughter Philippa of Clarence, Countess of Ulster, and as marshal from 1369-77 led embassies to France and Scotland in 1373. He was one of the leading opponents of John of Gaunt in the Good Parliament of 1376 and after a mission of inspection and diplomacy in the north and Scotland became from 1379 Lieutenant in Ireland. Here he established a brief settlement in E. Ulster but was drowned at Cork. Of his sons **(12) Roger (VII) (1374-98) 4th E.** and **E. of ULSTER** was recognised as heir presumptive to the throne in 1385, and married Eleanor Holland, the King's niece in 1393. He acquired control of his inheritance in 1393. Some of it had been dispersed to friends of Richard II who by appointing Robert de Vere C.J. in North Wales and Chester, and D. of Ireland threatened the Mortimer position in both countries, until de Vere's death in 1392. Thus Roger was hostile to the King until Richard had to rely upon him in Ireland and appointed him Lord Deputy in 1395. The hostility was not developed because Roger was killed at the second B. of Kells. His brother **(13) Edmund (III) (1376-1409)** a supporter of Henry of Lancaster, first helped to suppress a revolt by Owen Glendower and then when captured by him in 1402 changed sides and married his daughter. The son of **(12)**, **(14) Edmund (IV) (1391-1425) 5th E. of MARCH and 3rd E. of ULSTER** was recognised as heir presumptive at his father's death but was kept in honourable custody by the Lancastrian Henry IV until 1413 when Henry V released him. They became friends: he refused to be used as a claimant to the crown, and informed Henry V of the 'Southampton Plot' to place him on the throne. They fought together in France until 1421 when he was appointed Lieutenant of Ireland. Compelled to go there in person in 1424, he died of the plague, childless. His accumulation of estates and titles passed, with his claim to the throne, to Richard, D. of York, and his house. *See also* ISABELLA OF FRANCE (C. 1294-1358) AND MORTIMER, ROGER.

MORTMAIN i.e. the giving of land to a religious house, was suspect to the crown because of the immense power and wealth of the church; it was constantly abused, because the permanence of the church deprived it of incidents depending upon death or marriage. Magna Carta (c 36 of 1225 version) consequently enacted that land granted in mortmain and leased to the grantor should accrue to the Lord of the Fee. The Statute of Mortmain 1279 so awarded *all* land granted in mortmain, and required lords to resume the land within a year or risk a resumption of their superior lord, and so on; it also forbade future grants in mortmain without royal licence. This implied the existence of a legal policy against perpetuities. *See* CHARITIES.

MORTON, Es. of. *See* DOUGLAS (MORTON).

MORTON, John (?1420-1500) successful canonist and Lancastrian supporter, was attainted but made his submission after the B. of Tewkesbury (1471) and having become Master of the Rolls in 1473 was employed on an embassy to Hungary and then in the T. of Picquigny (1475). In 1479 he became Bp. of Ely. An intimate of Edward IV, he was openly hostile to the usurpation of Richard III who imprisoned him first in the Tower and then at Buckingham's Castle in Brecon, where he persuaded the Duke to revolt. It was a failure but Morton escaped via Ely to Flanders and thence to Henry, D. of Richmond (later Henry VII) in Brittany. His warning saved Henry from surrender to Richard III. When Henry took the crown Morton came home and became Abp. of Canterbury (1486), Lord Chancellor (1487) and a Cardinal in 1493. A vigorous builder and engineer he left Morton's Dyke in the Fens. *See* MORTON'S FORK.

MORTON, 4th E. of. *See* JAMES VI-3 *et seq*; ELIZABETH I-11.

MORTON'S FORK was the dilemma with which Cardinal Morton (*see above*) was said to have faced well-to-do persons in soliciting contributions to benevolences. A handsome way of life betokened wealth; wealth must have been accumulated by modest living. Either way the victim could afford to pay. The idea was probably the brain child of Bp. Foxe.

MOSCOW (Russia) first became important when the patriarchate was established there in 1326. It was the political capital from the time of Ivan II (1462-1505) until 1703 and again from 1918.

MOSCOW DISASTER (July-Dec. 1812) (*See* FRENCH COASTAL ANNEXATIONS 1809-11; PENINSULAR WAR). **(1)** Apart from the inherent likelihood of collision between two expansionist autocrats, the Franco-Russian quarrel of 1812 arose from three main and interlinked causes. On a personal level

the Czar Alexander's mother was hostile to Bonaparte and when the latter had inquired after the hand of the Czar's sister, she had promptly affianced the Grand-duchess to the D. of Oldenburg (Sept-Oct. 1808). Sixteen months later, when Bonaparte inquired, somewhat peremptorily, after the Czar's other sister, the Czar discovered that much more serious matrimonial approaches were at that very moment being made at Vienna. Secondly Alexander had designs on Poland and therefore wished to keep the Napoleonic grand-duchy of Warsaw weak. The Austro-French P. of Schönbrunn (Oct. 1809) enlarged the grand-duchy. Bonaparte's subsequent marriage with the Archduchess Marie-Louise suggested a Franco-Austrian combination to hold Russia in check. Thirdly adherence under the T. of Tilsit to Bonaparte's economic war with Britain was creating severe stress both in W. Europe and in Russia. The Czar, mindful of his murdered predecessor, dared not enforce the ban on British and colonial goods to the utmost, for this destroyed the lucrative Russian export trade to Britain. He excluded British ships, but not cargoes (mostly falsely certified) arriving in neutral vessels. Many of these flew the Oldenburg flag. Neither could he continue to give preference to goods, chiefly French luxuries, arriving overland, since this would disorder his foreign exchange. Bonaparte's North Sea Coastal annexations (including Oldenburg) (Dec. 1810) represented simultaneously an attack on the prosperity of the Russian landowners and a personal insult to the Czar's sister. Before the Oldenburg annexation was known at St. Petersburg, however, the Czar had formally admitted colonial goods in neutral bottoms and imposed a tax on luxury imports. Since both Bonaparte's and the Czar's actions broke the T. of Tilsit, that treaty was now implicitly abandoned as the regulator of their relationship.

(2) The economic war and the oppressive and violent ways of enforcing it, were making the French execrated throughout Europe, yet failing in their purpose, for forbidden goods were still coming in from all sides including especially Russia. At the same time the Spanish war was giving the European populations hope and encouraging local anti-French outbreaks (e.g. in the Tirol and Westphalia). So long as Russia remained powerful and independent Bonaparte had to keep his forces in the east, whereby neither Europe nor Spain could be properly pacified, nor British trade excluded. The logic of facts and his own intentions towards Britain precipitated the Russian war. The decision to attack was made in Aug. 1811 and Prussia was bullied into promising supplies, passage for troops and a contingent in Feb. 1812. Meanwhile Sweden, now ruled by Bernadotte as Prince Royal, had refused to enter the Continental System, and in Jan. Bonaparte had occupied Swedish Pomerania. Thereupon Bernadotte offered help to the Czar in return for Norway, the possession of Bonaparte's ally Denmark (Mar. 1812), and the Czar cleared his southern frontier by negotiations with the Turks. At the end of Apr. he demanded that French troops should evacuate Swedish Pomerania and Prussia, that Bonaparte should recognise the Russian trade with neutrals and reduce the garrison of Danzig. He offered in return to negotiate on Oldenburg and reduce his customs dues on French goods. He did not expect a favourable reply and left for the army a week before the demand was delivered.

(3) Bonaparte's reaction was to assemble a huge international army in Prussia, Poland and Saxony and to gather his vassals at Dresden. The force of 600,000 men consisted of 200,000 French, 147,000 Germans, 60,000 Poles, 80,000 Italians with Swiss, Dutch and Croats; an Austrian force was to cover the southern flank in Volhynia; a Prussian the northern in Courland (June 1812). Alexander was unimpressed. Bonaparte himself moved to the R. Niemen and issued a belligerent proclamation to his troops. Alexander appealed to the religious patriotism of his own. On 23 June 1812, invasion began near Kovno (Kaunas).

(4) Heat and disease in that wasteland were soon killing the horses and preventing the transport of supplies. The huge army had to live by plundering a wide swathe of land. It suffered losses by desertion, exhaustion and local trouble before the first battle, at Smolensk (Aug.) added 12,000, and nearly 40,000 at the desperate drawn B. of Borodino (Sept.). Then the army toiled into the deserted city of Moscow which promptly caught fire and burned for six days. By now the organised major force was reduced to 200,000 men and food had to be plundered from increasingly distant areas, where foraging parties were cut up by the enemy cavalry. In mid Oct. it became clear that the military state of Spain and the politics of France made it impossible to winter in Moscow. Moreover Murat had been defeated near Kaluga in a great cavalry battle. The retreat by a southerly unplundered route began with 115,000 men. At Malo-Jaroslavetz, after a furious battle the way was blocked. There was nothing but to retreat hungrily along the more northerly and already devastated line of advance. Though the weather was still good, the sickly troops, weakened by dispersal in the search for food, were increasingly hunted down. The army was reduced to about 60,000 when the first, rather late, winter storm struck on 6th Nov. Discipline now largely dissolved and staff work became sketchy. Some 12,000 were lost at the R. Beresina because the bridges were not fully used. Early in Dec. Bonaparte abandoned his troops at Smogorni for Paris; a fortnight later 20,000 starving men struggled into Kovno. Bonaparte's propaganda invented an exceptionally severe winter to account for a disaster, most of which had already happened before its onset.

MOSHESH. See BASUTOLAND.

MOSLEM or MUSLIM LEAGUE (India) was founded in 1906 to defend Moslems in British (as against princely) India against feared encroachments by the Hindu 3:1 majority. It originally favoured the British raj as likely to defend the Moslem minority simply as a byproduct of keeping order, while the British encouraged it as a divisive influence likely to weaken growing Indian nationalism. In 1913, however, the League adopted the objective of Indian self-govt. and its leader, by now Mohammed Ali Jinnah (q.v.) continually argued for Hindu-Moslem unity in the interest of independence. He was too idealistic. Escalating communal violence eventually convinced the League that moslems could not be safe in a Hindu dominated state. In 1939 they issued their first demand for a separate Pakistan, which was to consist of the Punjab with the territories west of it, Bengal and Hyderabad. Their object at Partition in 1947 was only partly realised. The Punjab and Bengal were divided. Hyderabad was lost.

MOSLEY, Sir Oswald Ernald Bt. (1896-1980) was M.P. for Harrow from 1918-22 as a Tory, from 1922-24 as an independent and from 1924-30 as a socialist, acting from 1929-30 as Chancellor of the Duchy of Lancaster in the Labour Govt. He and some followers seceded from the Labour Party early in 1931 because of the need to develop economic policies to deal with unemployment. His new party, the British Union of Fascists, never won a seat in Parliament but provoked occasional riots and affrays. He was interned with some others under Defence Regulations in May 1940 and thereafter ceased to have any effective influence, though he proclaimed the launching of a Union movement 'beyond Fascism and democracy' in 1948.

MOSQUITO COAST (C. America) was a British protected sphere from c. 1665 until it was abandoned in 1786.

MOSSTROOPING. Cattle lifting by mounted gangs on the Boarder. See MARCHES, ANGLO-SCOTS-12.

MOSTYN (1) Sir Roger (?1625-90) Bt. (1660) raised the Cheshire and Flint royalists for the K in 1642 and 1643

and recruited for him in Ireland in 1645. His grandson **(2) Sir Roger (1675-1739)** was Tory M.P. for Cheshire in 1701 and for Flintshire or Flint from 1705-34. Of his sons **(3) Savage (?-1757)** though censured by a naval court-martial in 1745, was M.P. for Weobley in 1747, controller of the navy in 1749 and Second in Command in N. America in 1755. His brother **(4) John (1710-79)** was M.P. for Malton in 1747, 1754 and 1761 and Governor of Minorca in 1768.

MOTOR INDUSTRY (1) was commenced at Coventry in 1896 by the German-licensed Daimler partnership. Lanchester and Austin set up their Birmingham workshops at about the same time. The Red Flag Act, which restricted speeds to 4 m.p.h., was repealed in 1896 and by 1900 there were some 80 makers, mostly in the W. Midlands. Permitted speeds were raised to 20 m.p.h. in 1903 when registration and licensing were introduced. In 1904 there were about 8,500 registered cars, all hand-built.

(2) In 1911 Fords began to turn out their mass produced Model Ts at Manchester, and then World War I created an enormous emergency demand. From 1920 smaller manufacturers were being forced out by new production techniques (e.g. Morris's welding and pressed steel bodies) or by mass appeal. The Austin Seven caused great excitement at the Motor Show of 1929. The great Ford plant at Dagenham was opened in 1931.

(3) World War II created a further huge demand for the heavily motorised Commonwealth armies and though there was bomb damage, the post-war industry emerged with much convertible plant which, in the absence of German or Japanese competition, supplied an expanding domestic market stimulated by road building and hire purchase, and also an international, especially Commonwealth, demand. New factories (e.g. Vauxhall at Ellesmere Port; Ford at Halewood) rose to underpin innovative design and technical improvement, but the advances were retarded by a militant trade unionism. Mergers were concentrating the industry progressively into fewer conglomerates (e.g. Morris and Austin combined as the British Motor Corporation which was itself merged with Leyland to become British Leyland (B.L.), and militancy spread with the mergers. Dagenham became a storm centre of restrictive practices related to the old habits of the original component firms. Hence Japanese, French and Americans could undersell in British markets. The manifest decline of B.L. became a pretext for nationalisation. Foreign firms soon dominated the British mass markets.

(4) By 1996 the 26M vehicles on British roads were causing concern for the pollution which they created, while the immense road building programmes to accommodate them were being challenged on grounds of expense and environmental damage.

MOTORWAYS. See HIGHWAY.

MOTTE. See MILITARY ARCHITECTURE, MEDIAEVAL-2.

MOTTISTONE. See SEELY.

MOTU PROPRIO. See PAPAL CHANCERY.

MOULVI (India). A Moslem law officer. See EAST INDIA CO. COURTS.

MOUNTBATTEN OF BURMA, Louis (1900-79) Vist. (1946) E. (1947) s. of Admiral of the Fleet the M. of Milford Haven and Princess Victoria of Hesse, entered the R. Navy in 1913 and became a signals specialist between the wars. He took part as a destroyer Captain in the desperate defence of Crete in May 1941 where he was sunk. He became Chief of Combined Operations in 1942 and Supreme Commander in S.E. Asia in 1943. As such he was responsible for the defeat of the Japanese western forces. In 1946 he reverted briefly to the command of the 1st Cruiser Squadron. He had long been known for his radical political opinions and in 1947 the Attlee Govt. appointed him Viceroy of India in order to liquidate the British raj, which he did with devious expedition (*see*

INDIAN PRINCELY STATES). He did his best, and once risked his life, to prevent the slaughter which accompanied the Partition. In 1948 he left India (by then divided) to become C-in-C Mediterranean. He was First Sea Lord from 1955-59 and Chief of Staff to the Ministry of Defence until 1965. The brilliant career of this gifted man was ended by murder at the hands of Irish extremists.

"MOUNTAIN". The left or Jacobin wing of French politics during the Revolution. *See* PLAIN.

MOUNTCASHEL. *See* MACCARTHY.

MOUNTJOY. *See* BLOUNT; ELIZABETH I-30, 35.

MOUNT PLEASANT (London). The name humorously given to the City rubbish dump, survived in the appellation of the great post office establishment built on the site.

MOURIE or MAOLRUBHA, "ST". A disguised Celtic god worshipped with pre-Christian rites including bull sacrifices, in Wester Ross (Sc) as late as 1656.

MOVABLES, TAX ON, was the first form of parliamentary taxation. It gradually replaced the profits of justice and feudal dues as the main source of royal revenue. In 1290 Parliament granted the King a 1/15th on movable property to discharge his foreign debts. It was assessed by two or four people chosen in each vill to value the goods of all inhabitants, certain items such as clothing, weapons, tools and gold and silver vessels being exempted. The results were enrolled. At first the rates of tax varied: in 1294 it was 1/6th for inhabitants of boroughs and royal demesne, 1/10th for the rest; in 1297, 1/5th and 1/8th. By 1327 the rates were becoming standardised at 1/10th and 1/15th, though parliament might grant multiples of a tenth and fifteenth e.g. 1½, 2 or 3. The administrative process was now reversed: a standardised total valuation replaced the individual assessments so that from 1334 the 1/10th and 1/15th was valued at £38,170, which was apportioned, not always equitably, between the towns and the shires. Inflation, especially after the Black Death, and rising govt. expenditure eventually rendered this tax inadequate as a basis of govt. finance, and led to experiments with new forms of taxation such as the disastrous poll tax. From 1381 increasing reliance was placed on indirect taxation. *See* TONNAGE AND POUNDAGE.

MOWBRAY. This powerful family's fortunes arose out of kinship with William I's talented supporter Geoffrey Bp. of Coutances, who was the uncle of **(1) Robert (?-1125), E. of NORTHUMBERLAND (c. 1080)** a perverse nobleman who sided with D. Robert against William II in 1088, introduced Benedictines at Durham, surprised and killed K. Malcolm Canmore at Alnwick in 1093 and was detected in a conspiracy in 1095. He was forfeited and imprisoned or became a monk. **(2) Roger (?-1188) 2nd Ld.** went on crusade in 1147 and in 1164 he returned to the north and joined the Scots in the rebellion of 1174. As a result, Henry II demolished his Yorkshire castles. He died on a further crusade. His grandson **(3) William (?-1222) 4th Ld.** was a leading opponent of K. John and a named executor of Magna Carta. His great grandson **(4) John (1286-1322) 8th Ld. (1298)** was set at enmity with the Percys in 1312 but acquired the Lordship of Gower through his wife. This was claimed by the Despensers and a local private war resulted. This ended with the Despensers' fall in 1312 but when they were recalled he joined the opposition, was captured at the B. of Boroughbridge and executed. His son **(5) John (II) (?-1361) 9th Ld.** was imprisoned, but released after the death of Edward II (1327). When not fighting the Scots, he was involved in constant quarrels over his mother's inheritance. He fought at Neville's Cross in 1346. His grandson **(6) Thomas (?1366-99) 12th Ld., E. of NOTTINGHAM (1383) and 1st D. of NORFOLK (1397)** was a moving spirit in the Merciless Parliament (1388) but changed his views shortly afterwards and became Warden of the Scottish Marches (1389) and then Captain

of Calais (1391). He was with Richard II in Ireland (1394), negotiated his French marriage (1396) and acted for the King in arresting Gloucester, Arundel and Warwick. He probably murdered Gloucester at Calais and he received some of the Arundel estates. Accused by Hereford of treason, he fell as Richard II's Govt. collapsed, forfeited his estates and died in exile. His son **(7) John (III) (1389-1432) 2nd D. (1425)** was a loyal military supporter of Henry V's wars and a member of the Protector's Council when Henry V died (1422). He recovered the Dukedom and estates in 1425 and assisted in the pacification between Gloucester and the Beauforts in 1426. His son **(8) John (IV) (1415-61) 3rd D.** after some routine posts and a pilgrimage in 1446, became involved in the policies of Richard, D. of York. He remained a Yorkist, though he quarrelled with the Nevilles, and in 1459 swore to the Lancastrian succession, and was rewarded by Edward IV after his victory. His son **(9) John (V) (1444-76) 4th D.,** not a national figure, consolidated his East Anglian influence by exchange of his Gower and Chepstow lordships for Herbert estates in Norfolk and Suffolk. The Mowbray dukedom ended with him. *See* HOWARD AND HOWARD (NORFOLK).

MOYLE, Sir Thomas (?-1560) Chancellor of the Court of Augmentations from 1537, became M.P. for Kent and Speaker in 1542. He was the first Speaker to claim the privilege of freedom of speech.

MOYNE. *See* GUINNESS.

MOZAMBIQUE. From the 16th cent. this large Portuguese colony was no more than a string of intermittently held ports at Lourenco Marques, Beira, Mozambique itself, Inhambane and Quelimane sustained by a passing trade to India and by piracy and a slave trade. It was not until the 1860s that there was serious development and in 1875 the MacMahon Award gave the Portuguese unchallengeable sovereignty at Delagoa Bay. This created a non-British outlet for the Transvaal Boers; and a railway to Pretoria was slowly built between 1875 and 1890. Under the first Anglo-Portuguese convention (1890) a railway was also built from Beira into Rhodesia. In addition, the colony was the main source of labour for the S. African mines. It was thus part of the British African economy and so remained until civil wars broke out in 1967. It became nominally independent if highly disturbed from 1975 onwards.

MOZARAB. *See* MORISCO.

MUDALIYARS. Sinhalese district officials of ancient origin ultimately transformed under the British into local social leaders.

MUDANIA ARMISTICE. *See* CHANAK INCIDENT (1921).

MUDDIMAN, Henry. *See* NEWSLETTERS.

MUDIR was in Turkey the headman of a village or neighbourhood, in Egypt the Governor of a Province.

MUDROS. *See* LEMNOS.

MUFTI. An Islamic canon lawyer. *See* ULEMA.

MUIR, Thomas (1765-89) helped to found an Edinburgh society for securing parliamentary reform, and in 1793 was sentenced to 14 years' transportation. He escaped in 1796 and after many adventures was wounded aboard a Spanish frigate. He died in France. *See* CORRESPONDING SOCIETY.

MUKALLA. A tribal sultanate which was part of the British Aden protectorate.

MULATTO is the offspring of a European and a negro; a QUADROON, of a European and a mulatto; an OCTOROON, of a European and a Quadroon. The terms were used mainly in the Caribbean.

MULBERRY HARBOURS were two mobile floating harbours towed from Britain and set up on the Normandy coast as bases for the allied invasion (*see* WORLD WAR II. 14-15) in June 1944. The British one at Arromanches had to support most of the operations because the U.S. one further west was wrecked by storms. At one period it was delivering 25,000 tons a day.

MULE, CROMPTON'S. *See* INDUSTRIAL REVOLUTION-5.

MULGRAVE. *See* PHIPPS; SHEFFIELD.

MULLAH or MOLLAH (Arab = one who is near) originally any close associate e.g. master, servant, freedman or relative: then any non-Arab Muslim: then a polite form of address and so eventually a scholar or judge.

MULTURE (Sc). The toll paid to a miller for the compulsory grinding of grain.

MUN, Thomas (1571-1641) trader to Italy and the Levant, became a director of the HEIC in 1615. He wrote two works on economics. *A disclosure of Trade from England unto the East Indies* (1621) was designed to explain and defend the export of bullion involved in the company's activities. For *England's Treasure by Forraign Trade* (1630, published 1664) *see* MERCANTILISM.

MÜNCHENGRÄTZ TREATIES (Sept.-Oct. 1833). (1) An Austro-Russian agreement to maintain the status quo in Turkey was balanced against **(2)** mutual guarantees against Polish rebellions and **(3)** Austria, Russia and Prussia declared against the doctrine of non-intervention, wherever an independent sovereign appealed for help against (liberal) disorder.

MUNDBRYCE. A.S. = Breach of the King's protection.

MUNDELLA, Anthony John (1825-97) a Nottingham hosier, set up in 1866 with Nottingham conciliation board for the hosiery industry, which became the model for other industrial conciliation boards. He was a radical M.P. from 1868; procured the passing of the Education Act, 1870, the Factories Act of 1874 and as Vice-Pres. of the Board of Education from 1880, the Compulsory Education Act, 1881. As Pres. of the Board of Trade in 1880, he created the Labour Dept. which eventually became the Ministry of Labour. He was Pres. again from 1892-94.

MUNGO, St. *See* KENTIGERN ST.

MUNICH AGREEMENT (29 Sept. 1938) (*see* WORLD WAR II-2) As a result of a Czechoslovak crisis provoked by the demands of the Sudeten Germans in Bohemia, orchestrated from Germany, for separate rights, Neville Chamberlain on 15 Sept. flew to Adolf Hitler's house at Berchtesgaden where he conceded that in principle some Czech territory might be transferred to Germany. As the French had little offensive strength he easily persuaded them to forget their guarantee to Czechoslovakia. A week later he met Hitler at Godesberg near Bonn, to work out the details, but Hitler now raised his demands to include tactically important territory where the Czechs were in a majority. On his gloomy return, Chamberlain had the Navy mobilised and in addressing the Commons began firmly, but announced that he would fly to Hitler once more. There ensued the Munich Conference with Hitler, Benito Mussolini and the French premier, Edouard Daladier. Czechoslovakia was not invited. It was agreed that Germany might take over most of the claimed territory immediately. This included the Bohemian fortified zone and put Czechoslovakia at Hitler's mercy. Hitler signed a letter expressing a wish never to go to war with Britain. Chamberlain waved this to reporters on his return and called it 'Peace with honour . . . Peace in our time'. The event was celebrated with relief by most people in Britain but not by the more far sighted. One minister, the later famous Duff Cooper, First Lord of the Admiralty, resigned. When Hitler seized the rest of Czechoslovakia in Mar. 1939, Chamberlain realised that he had been cheated and within a few weeks British guarantees were given to Poland, Roumania and Greece (which ultimately obliged Britain to enter World War II) and conscription was instituted. The shame of this episode now penetrated the public mind, which accepted the inevitability of war.

MUNICIPAL BOROUGHS. *See* LOCAL ADMINISTRATION – ENGLAND AND WALES-3 *et seq.*

MUNICIPAL CORPORATIONS ACT, 1840 (Ir.) Of the 48 Irish boroughs subsisting in 1840, the Act preserved but reformed 10. Of the rest (which were all dissolved) 18 had no property, but arrangements were made in the others for poor law and improvements. In the ten reformed boroughs the boundaries were extended and the franchise widened to residents with property worth £10. The Act transformed not only the system but, in the 1841 elections, the entire political complexion of the councils, where Tories were nearly all superseded by Whigs or Repealers.

MUNICIPIUM (Lat = one who receives a duty or right) under the Romans was a settlement which already existed before they conquered the area, as opposed to a *Colonia* which was a self-governing and deliberately laid-out settlement originally for Roman military colonists. The Romans conferred upon a *municipium* a measure of self-govt. modelled in miniature upon Rome itself. It had a *territorium*, an often large adjacent farming area, and its govt. was expected to do for its people what the municipal authorities did for the Roman population, including the construction of public works, the maintenance of temples and the orderly regulation of the imperial cult. Verulamium (St Albans) was probably a *municipium*.

MUNITIONS, MINISTRY OF, was set up in June 1915 under D. Lloyd-George who was followed in July 1916 by Edward Montagu. It created the British war economy of World War I, and starting from nothing, ended with 3,000,000 workers under its direction. Apart from supplying the vast bulk of material it equipped the forces with enough machine guns, and developed the light mortar and the tank against War Office opposition. It was dissolved in 1921.

MÜNSTER (Ger.) a bishopric since the 9th cent. covered most of the Ems Valley, an important trade route from the North Sea into W. Germany, and the city was a prominent member of the Hanse. The trade was mostly in timber, grain and beer. The bishops early acquired princely rights. Immensely prosperous in the middle ages, its security was disturbed during the Reformation, when it became the centre of the Anabaptists and suffered in the consequent persecutions. It was also much devastated in the Thirty Years War, but the city was the seat of part of the negotiations leading to the P. of Westphalia. A university was founded there in 1773. The principality was abolished by the Diet of Ratisbon in 1803, and along with other western ecclesiastical states was seized by Prussia. The annexation was confirmed in 1814.

MÜNSTER, PEACE OF (1648). *See* THIRTY YEARS' WAR.

MUNSTER, MUMHA or MOMONIA, Irish Kingdom or Province comprising the areas of Cos. Clare, Limerick, Tipperary, Kerry, Cork and Waterford. The old political and church capital was Cashel. The main clans were MacMahon, O'Sullivan, O'Donovan and O'Brien. The area was the earliest to be subjugated by the Anglo-Normans who entered via Waterford, Youghal and Cork, drove these clans towards the coasts, and settled down as clans (Butlers, Fitzgeralds, Fitzmaurices and Clare) themselves. These families had immense feudal possessions and the province was, under Tudor times, much fragmented by palatinates and liberties. The Tudors imposed a council with a Pres. who remained a foremost official figure in Ireland until the revolution of 1689. *See* ELIZABETH I-17.

MURAGE. A toll on goods for the upkeep of town walls.

MURAT. *See* NAPLES AND SICILY; BONAPARTE-9.

MURDAC, Henry (?-1153) third abbot of Fountains from 1143 founded five daughter houses, and in 1147 was elected Abp. of York on the deprivation of William fitzHerbert, K. Stephen's nephew. The citizens of York kept him out until 1151 when there was a reconciliation. In 1153 Hugh of Puiset, treasurer of York since 1143, was elected Bp. of Durham against Murdac's wishes, and this precipitated a quarrel cut short by his death.

MURDER was a felony at Common Law, and by statute under the offences against the Person Act, 1861. The Homicide Act, 1957, confined the death penalty to repeated murders and certain serious types of murder. An act of 1965 abolished it altogether.

MURDRUM. Secret killing for which, under Anglo-Saxon customary law, a fine graduated by the rank of the deceased, was payable to the relatives. After the Conquest, a corpse found in a Hundred was presumed to be Norman and the Hundred liable to the King for the *murdrum* fine unless it was proved to be English. This *Presentment of Englishry* was made before the sheriff in the Hundred Court. By 1340 it was impossible to tell a Norman from an Englishman and the *murdrum* was abolished by statute.

MURE, Elizabeth. *See* STEWART OR STUART, ROYAL HOUSE, EARLY-11.

MURIMUTH, Adam (?1275-1347) was educated at Oxford and often served at the papal court at Avignon between 1312-23 as agent for his university, the Abp. and Chapter of Canterbury, and K. Edward II. In 1323 he was the King's envoy to K. Robert of Sicily. He was vicar-general to Abp. Reynolds in 1325 and later held benefices in the West Country. Sometime after 1325 he began a *Continuatio Chronicorum* (Lat. = Continuation of the Chronicles) for the Exeter Chronicle from 1303 and for the Westminster Chronicle from 1305, in three successive versions to 1337, to 1341 and to 1347. An anonymous compiler continued them to 1380. He seems to have been close to the regime of Q. Isabella and Roger Mortimer of 1327-30.

MURMANSK. *See* ARCHANGEL.

MURPHY or O'MURPHY, Marie Louise (1737-1814) an Irish shoemaker's daughter born at Rouen, was a mistress of Louis XV at the Parc aux Cerfs from 1753-55. Boucher painted a famous nude of her.

MURRAY, Andrew Graham (1849-1942) Ld. MURRAY (1905) Vist. DUNEDIN (1926) Scottish Conservative M.P. from 1891-1905 was Scottish Sol-Gen. from 1891-92 and from 1895-96. He then became Lord Advocate and from 1903-5 Sec. of State for Scotland. Thereafter until 1913 he was Lord Justice General and subsequently a Lord of Appeal.

MURRAY, Sir Archibald James (1860-1945) a successful trainer of troops from 1907-14, was C.G.S. of the British Expeditionary Force to France for the first five months of World War I. He was then successively Dep. C.I.G.S. and C.I.G.S. from Feb. to Dec. 1915 and then C-in-C in Egypt. He was checked twice at Bs. near Gaza (Mar. and Apr. 1917) and superseded by Allenby.

MURRAY, Charles Adolphus (1841-1907) 7th E. of DUNMORE, explored Kashmir and Tibet in 1892 and published his findings in *The Pamirs* in 1893.

MURRAY (1) Thomas (1564-1623) was Sec. and tutor to Charles I as P. of Wales from 1617 and Provost of Eton from 1622. His son **(2) William or Will (?1600-53) 1st E. of DYSART (1643)** was educated with Charles and became a gentleman of his bedchamber after his accession. Charles used him to negotiate with the Covenanters and he played a leading, yet uncertain role in The Incident (q.v.) and apparently passed confidential information about the King's plans to Pym just before the attempted arrest of the Five Members. He also negotiated with Scottish R. Catholic leaders, the French and the Pope. In 1646 he was arrested as a spy, but he joined Charles at Newcastle, and Charles II at the Hague in 1649. His role has long been disputed, but Burnet (a good judge) thought him double faced. His daughter **(3) Elizabeth (?-1697) Countess of DYSART (1650, confirmed 1670)** was a well known court beauty, who married Sir Lionel Tollemache in 1647 and John Maitland, D. of Lauderdale, in 1672.

MURRAY, William (1705-93) 1st Ld. MANSFIELD (1756) became M.P. for Boroughbridge and Sol-Gen. in 1742. He was an exceptionally able debater but his ambitions were legal rather than political and in 1754 he became Attorney General in order to secure the customary

reversion of the next Chief Justiceship. In 1756 he began his celebrated career as C.J. of the King's Bench, using his immense learning to support mainly liberalising or reformist judgements. He also encouraged important improvements in legal procedure, the law of evidence and mercantile law. His attitude to public affairs and his continuing private influence earned him Macaulay's not unjustified title of the 'father of modern toryism'. He retired in 1788.

MUSCAT (Arabia) was occupied by the Portuguese in about 1515 as part of their policy of blocking the Arab spice trade. It was lost to the Omanis in 1650 and became an independent sultanate in 1741. *See* BANDAR ABBAS; TANZANIA.

MUSCOVY (*see* RUSSIA, KIEVAN OR VARANGIAN). **(1)** The Russian state built up, under Mongol domination around Moscow, challenged her disunited Mongol overlords at the B. of Kulikovo (1378). The victory was important for prestige, but not overwhelming. The victor, **Dimitri Donskoi,** died in 1389. His successor **Basil I (1389-1425)** doubled the size of the patchwork principality. There followed, however, a dynastic civil war which was not settled until 1455.

(2) The ambitious and able **Ivan III (The Great) (r. 1462-1505)** married Zoë or Sophia, a niece of the last Byzantine emperor. Ivan cultivated grandeur and began by seizing Novgorod (1465). He repudiated Mongol overlordship, adopted the title of Czar (Caesar) of All the Russias and distanced himself from his subjects by introducing Byzantine court ceremonial. While thus laying the foundations of an autocracy, he represented Russia as the third Roman Empire. He asserted its economic independence of the Hanse by closing the Hanseatic *Kontor* at Novgorod (1496), but maintained the aspect of a crusading state. His son **Basil III (r. 1505-33)** continued his line of policy with determination and recovered much of the old Water Road by ending a century of Polish rule in Smolensk. These two rulers left Muscovy a great landlocked power, with a weak governmental structure. This was immediately obvious when Basil died. His son, the famous or notorious **Ivan the Dread (or Terrible) (r. 1533-84)** was three. For thirteen years Moscow was distracted by intrigue, murder and riot while friendly Mongol rulers gave way to hostile Tartar Khans, and the southern frontiers dissolved into confusion. In 1547 fires virtually destroyed Moscow. The 17 year old Ivan took control by a policy of "Bonapartism". He used popular discontent against the nobility; he was crowned emperor; and he launched great wars, firstly against the Tartars of Kazan which fell in 1552. By 1566 he had annexed Astrakhan. This safeguarded the way to Siberia, gave access to the Caspian, and outflanked the Tartar Khanate of the Crimea. Many Cossacks transferred their allegiance to Poland. He was in touch with Persia, and the Princes of the Caucasus.

(3) He was also developing contacts in the opposite direction. He established a route through Archangel to the White Sea. This was due to the Willoughby and Chancellor expedition of 1553, Richard Chancellor's visit as Ambassador in 1555, and Nepey's return mission to England in 1556. Chancellor secured capitulations on the Ottoman model for English traders, and Nepey reciprocal concessions in England. Ivan already understood the need for modernising western talent and had, since 1547 been attracting Germans. From England he got miners, chemists and physicians through Anthony Jenkinson and the Muscovy Co., but he now learned clearly the colossal advantages of unobstructed world trade. There is too much ice at distant Archangel. He wanted the Gulf of Finland and the Baltic states. From 1558 he was at war with the Teutonic Knights and other Baltic powers. In 1569 he was seeking a political alliance with England, whose merchants were equally interested in a short icefree and toll free route. Such approaches were premature. Elizabeth I was distracted by dangers nearer home, and the Muscovy Co's. White Sea monopoly had to be confirmed in 1572. By 1582 truces with Poland and Sweden proclaimed Ivan's failure to break into the Baltic. *See* TIME OF TROUBLES; RUSSIA, PETRINE, ETC.

MUSCOVY CO. founded in 1555, sent a ship under Stephen Burrough to try the N.E. passage to China in 1556 and Anthony Jenkinson overland in 1557 *via* the Russian rivers and the Caspian. He reached Bokhara, found that the Asian trade was in the hands of the Venetians (through Turkey) and the Portuguese in the Indian Ocean. In 1561 he reached Persia, and until 1581 English cloth went to Persia *via* Astrakhan. The Co. also secured concessions in N. Russia and established an H.Q. at Rose I. in the White Sea, and factories at Cholmogory, Moscow, Jaroslavl, Vologda, Kazan and Astrakhan. The main English exports were salt and coarse cloth in return for ships' stores, wax, tallow, hides and furs. A further attempt on the N.E. passage was made in 1580. The Co. eventually failed through navigational hazards, plunder of caravans, competition from interlopers and the Dutch, and the transfer of the Asian trade to the Mediterranean after 1581. *See* LEVANT CO. MUSCOVY.

MUSEUMS. *See* BRITISH MUSEUM; EXHIBITION, PUBLIC

MUSGRAVE, Sir Anthony (1828-88) a colonial servant with a remarkably varied career, began as an administrator in several Caribbean Is. until 1864. He then became successively Gov. of Newfoundland, British Columbia (1869), S. Australia (1872), Jamaica (1877) and Queensland (1888).

MUSGRAVE (1) Thomas (?-1384) Ld. MUSGRAVE (1373) was a border magnate and warden of the Marches and the ancestor of the following. **(2) Sir Philip (1607-78)** an M.P. twice in 1640 and Governor of Carlisle for the King. He joined Charles II after the death of Charles I and helped him in the Preston campaign. His *s.* **(3) Sir Christopher (1632-1704)** mayor of Carlisle, and Governor of its castle was an M.P. for various places conitnuously from 1661 until his death. He was a High Tory opposed to James II's catholicising policy yet refused to vote for the resolution declaring the Throne vacant when James fled. In 1696 he was heavily bribed to support William III's war finances, but the money-bags burst and the fact provoked a malign verse from Pope. **(4) Sir Richard (1757-1818)** was a strongly loyalist Irish M.P. from 1778 until the Act of Union, which he hotly opposed, abolished the Irish Parliament in 1800.

MUSIC (*see* OPERA and ORATORIO). **(1) English.** Literary evidence and the 13th cent. *Summer is i cumen in,* suggest the existence of native folksong, but troubadours, of whom K. Richard I was one, were influential in S. England in 12th and 13th cents. Friar Simon Tunsted (?-1369) provincial of the Minorites from 1360, left a theoretical treatise, *Quatuor Principalia Musicae* (The Four Main forms of Music). The earliest identified English composer was John Dunstable (?-1435): he was internationally known, and English choirs, at least, had already developed considerable sweetness and sophistication, admired by Rozmital, a Bohemian visitor in the 1480s. Unaccompanied chorales remained a leading feature of English musical life throughout the 16th and 17th cents., but instruments were not neglected and by the time of the composer William Byrd (1542-1623) English players were being sought by foreign courts. The Puritan reaction, especially under the Commonwealth, seems to have broken the continuity and originality of English musical thought and when the exiles returned they brought continental, especially Italian, ideas with them. Nevertheless, the tradition continued for a while with Humfrey Pelham (1647-74) and Henry Purcell (1658-95) but from the reign of Anne there was a steady decline in interest and performance, resisted, however, by the cathedrals, the

growth of the many, largely social glee clubs and the influence of Handel. This continued into the 19th cent. when a new interest began to be aroused partly through such figures as William Sterndale Bennett (1816-75) and Gilbert and Sullivan, and partly by the introduction of German musical influences begun by Haydn and encouraged through the Hanoverian and Coburg connection. The effects were soon apparent in instrumental performance, but they led to the rise of a new school of English composers. Sir Edward Elgar (1857-1934) himself an astonishingly versatile player, published his *Enigma Variations* in 1899; and composers, with players and orchestras to match, have increased in numbers and interest ever since, enormously encouraged until 1993 by the publicity and patronage given to young musicians orchestrally and as soloists by the BBC.

(2) Scots. Scots folksong certainly flourished before the 15th cent. when James I (r. 1406-37), James II (r. 1460-88) and 'Blind Harry' (fl. 1490) composed. Bagpipers, however, had to be imported from England. From 1695 Edinburgh became, and remained, the centre of musical culture.

MUSIC HALLS. Floor shows and crude dramatic performances known as saloon theatre were a sub-legal feature of London taverns in the 1820s as an encouragement to smoking and drinking. The standard remained low until the patent monopolies of the theatres were abolished by the Theatres Regulation Act 1843. It then became more profitable to specialise. Saloons became either more nearly theatres or relapsed into places where the price of drink was higher than in the public bars. Eventually the first Music Hall as such (Charles Morton's *Canterbury* in Lambeth) appeared with stage, orchestra, singers and 'lions comique'. Admission was cheap; light refreshments and drinks being the main source of profit. (Sometimes entrance was by 'wet money', cash paid at the door entitling the customer to free drinks.) Such music halls rapidly increased; by the mid-1860s there were more than 300 registered in Britain. By 1875 there were more than 200 in London alone, and large numbers in the provinces, particularly Yorks and Lancs mill towns. Performers became full-time professionals, and writing music hall songs a lucrative profession. Audiences were often young, vocal but better-behaved than they had been subsequently depicted. In the 1890s it began to fade and there were already revivals of 'old time' music hall. Larger theatres (e.g. the London Coliseum, and the national Empire circuit) presented a more professionally-packaged kind of 'variety' bill, a form which lasted until cinema competition killed it in the 1950s. The old 'Music Hall' however continued to be revived on stage and on television (albeit in a sentimentalised style, and with a loquacious chairman, neither of which had much historical justification). But many music hall songs are remembered, and sung in their original form.

MUSKERRY. *See* MACCARTHY.

MUSKET. *See* FIREARMS-3, *et seq.* and ARMY.

MUSSOLINI, Benito (1883-1945) was expelled as a socialist revolutionary from Berne in 1903 and from the Austrian Tyrol in 1911, having meanwhile founded a socialist newspaper in Forli and become editor of *Avanti!* (Forward!) in Milan. At the outbreak of World War I he advocated neutrality but was then abruptly converted to intervention against Austria. Hence the Socialist Party expelled him in Nov. 1914, just as he had founded the later influential *Popolo d'Italia.* Injured during military training, he resumed the editorship as a furious opponent of pacifism and defeatism. This led logically to his recruitment of the *Fasci di Resistenza* or *Fasci di Combattimento* (Resistance or Battle Squads) which formed the nucleus of his Fascist Party. *For his political rise, fall and murder see* ITALY, KINGDOM-6 *et seq.*

MUSTANGS were Arab horses which escaped from the American Spaniards, formed wild herds and were domesticated anew by Indian buffalo hunters. The Cayuse Indians of Oregon bred them: hence a *cayuse* is a broken Indian pony; a *bronco* is unbroken. They revolutionised the life of the plains Indians.

MUSTARD GAS, YPERITE or YELLOW CROSS, first known in 1854, is a viscous liquid producing enormous blisters on skin contact, blindness in even minimal eye-contact and, in spray form, dangerous respiratory effects. The Germans first used it as a chemical weapon at Ypres in July 1917. Mainly a ground contaminant, its primary use was defensive, but fear of delivery by aircraft placed a strain on military industries in World War II which had to produce much remedial and preventive equipment.

MUSTER BOOK. The ancient register of royal forces kept in Tudor times by the Muster Master General whose office by 1802 had become a sinecure.

MUTESA I and II. *See* UGANDA.

MUTINIES, NAVAL 1797 (1) Spithead (Apr.) This was a well organised strike. It originated in a misunderstanding in Feb. when genuine seamen's petitions for pay rises were left unanswered because the Admiralty believed them to be forgeries. The plans and signals were well laid and on 15 Apr. the Channel Fleet concertedly refused to weigh anchor. Thirty-two seamen's delegates drew up respectfully worded petitions to the Admiralty and Parliament expressly stating that they would sail if the French fleet put to sea and requesting pay rises, healthier food, an end to the practice of paying pursers by a deduction of one eighth from the rations, better treatment of the sick and short leaves to visit families. There was widespread sympathy from the public and the C-in-C, Lord Bridport. The requests were conceded to the whole Navy, the necessary pardons were issued and the seamen returned to their duty on 22 Apr. **(2) St. Helens (7-15 May)** Violent outbreaks in three ships of the line against certain oppressive officers were supported by seamen of the whole fleet who feared that the Spithead settlement might not be honoured and turned some hated officers out of their ships. On 15th, Ld. Howe, the previous C-in-C, arrived from the Admiralty with an Act of Parliament confirming the settlement, and after amicable explanations the seamen again returned to their duty. The expelled officers were mostly tacitly accepted back, but some of the Captains were replaced. **(3) Sheerness and the Nore (10 May-13 June).** This was a sedition led by one Richard Parker, inspired by news from St. Helens. The Admiralty explained the nature of the Spithead settlement, but Parker and the mutineers (whom he apparently misled) would have none of it and tried to blockade the Thames. Public opinion was hostile. Then some of the crews came to their senses and deputed Capt. The E. of Northesk, of the *Monmouth* to negotiate with the Admiralty on their behalf. The mutiny collapsed quickly once it became clear that the grievances had already been met. Parker and some others were hanged. **(4) Cape of Good Hope (Sept.).** The mutiny of a whole squadron was inspired by news from England but soon suppressed. **(5)** There were some mutinies against tyrannical captains, notably Pigot of the *Hermione* (32). He and most of his officers were murdered and the ship taken into the Spanish Caribbean port of La Guaira. *See* BLIGH.

MUTINY ACT authorised the Crown to maintain a standing army by providing for the enforcement of discipline mainly through courts martial. First passed in 1689 it had to be renewed annually as a constitutional safeguard. From 1715 it authorised the Crown to frame Articles of War to maintain discipline in peacetime. They were incorporated in the Army Act, 1881, which itself had to be annually renewed until 1955 when it was replaced by an Army and an Airforce Act. These were continued annually by orders made under the Armed Forces Act 1971. This represents a major change, albeit quite unnoticed, in the constitution.

MUTTON. An old slang word for a prostitute or illicit sexual intercourse.

> Here lies our mutton loving King
> Whose word no man relies on,
> Who never said a foolish thing
> Or ever did a wise one.
>   Rochester on Charles II

The accuracy of the first line is attested by the King himself; the unreliability of the rest by a cloud of witnesses – but Rochester preferred neatness to truth.

MUTUUM **(Lat = loan).** In mediaeval govt. finance was either a payment of a customs due before it was legally required, or a loan or advance to the Crown out of the Exchequer.

MYANMAR is the local name for BURMA.

MYDDLETON, Welsh and London capitalist brothers **(1) Sir Thomas (1550-1631)** and **(2) Sir Hugh (?1560-1631)** had mining interests in Denbighshire, helped to finance the New River Co. and had various investments in the Virginia Co. and HEIC. Sir Thomas was Lord Mayor in 1613 and parliamentary Sergeant Major General in North Wales. There was also a brother **(3) William (?1556-1621)** who was a Welsh poet.

MYLNE (1) Alexander (1474-?1548) became Abbot of Cambuskenneth and James V's master mason in 1517, and in 1532 a Lord of the Articles (until 1542) and Pres. of the Court of Session. A great nephew **(2) John (?-1621)** was a master mason (architect and engineer) and from him was descended a remarkable line from father to son in eight generations, of architects and engineers at Dundee, Edinburgh and London. These were **(3) John (?-1657), (4) John (1611-67), (5) Alexander (1613-43), (6) Robert (1633-1710), (7) William (1662-1728), (8) Thomas (?-1763), (9) William (?-1790), (10) Robert (1734-1811), (11) William Chadwell (1781-1863), (12) Robert William (1817-90).**

MYNGS, Sir Christopher (1625-66) in command of the *Elizabeth* in 1653, single-handedly captured a Dutch convoy escorted by two warships. In 1655 he was appointed to the mutinous battleship *Marston Moor* and brought her under control. After the Restoration he was Vice Admiral at the B. of Lowestoft (1665) and was killed in the Four Days Battle. Admired by Pepys, he was adored by the sailors, some of whom, after his funeral applied for a fireship to avenge his death.

MYSORE (S. India) This ancient state fell, after the collapse of Vijayanagar in 1610, under the rule of a local Hindu dynasty which with its ruling Dalwai or chief minister, was overthrone by Hyder Ali (?-1783) a Moslem *condottiere* in 1761. His frontier aggressions rapidly brought him into collision with the British and his other neighbours, and in 1767 he fought the Nizam and the British with enough success to secure a promise of British support against third parties, and a mutual restitution of conquests. British assistance was not given against the Marathas in 1771, but meanwhile Hyder Ali was reconstituting his army with French assistance, and in 1779, he with others, tried to take on British embarrassments arising from the American rebellion and French, Spanish, and Dutch intervention in it. With Hyderabad, the French and the Dutch, he invaded the Carnatic in July 1780 on the pretext that the British had seized Mahé, a French factory within his jurisdiction. After a devastating war he stopped at Porto Novo (1782) and died of cancer while the British seized all the local Dutch possessions. His son Tippoo Sultan (?-1799) fought the war to a standstill and agreed another mutual restitution (T. of Mangalore Mar. 1784). Like his father he reorganised his army and sought alliances, for he was determined to dominate S. India. By 1787 he was sending ambassadors to Versailles and the Sublime Porte. In Dec. 1789 he invaded the HEIC's ally, Travancore. The British in concert with the Marathas and the Nizam reacted in Mar. 1792 and dictated peace before the walls of Seringapatam, the capital. In addition to an indemnity, Tippoo had to make cessions to the Marathas, Hyderabad and the British, keeping only about half. Undeterred he continued to seek foreign alliances and rearm. His intentions being quite clear, and in view of the dangers from the French revolutionary wars, the M. Wellesley called upon him to accept a subsidiary alliance and attacked him when he refused. The conquest was effected by Wellesley's brother, later the D. of Wellington. Tippoo was killed, and the old Hindu dynasty restored. In practice this meant indirect British rule because the new rajah was 5 years old, and then when he grew up, his rule was so disorderly and tyrannical that in 1831 they had to rule it themselves directly until 1867. They then returned it to the dynasty, which achieved a model administration. A university was established in 1916.

MYSTERY. *See* MIRACLE PLAYS; MISTERY.

MYSTICISM, CHRISTIAN is said to be an immediate knowledge of God attained through personal experience. It is sometimes associated with physical or psychological phenomena such as dreams, visions, trances and ecstasies, but the surest proof of true mysticism is its tendency to increase the personal goodness of the mystic, while the physical concomitants usually disappear as the process advances. The power of mystics thus tends to be based on example. Christian mysticism in some form has always been common: there are traces in the New Testament as well as early writers. Among English mystics there were the Yorkshireman Richard Rolle (?1295-1349), the unknown author of the *Cloud of Unknowing* (?14th cent.), the Augustinian writer Walter Hilton (?-1396), Juliana of Norwich (?1342-1414), the lyrical poet Richard Crashaw (?1613-49), George Foxe (1624-91) the founder of the Society of Friends, and Henry Vaughan (1622-95).

MYTENS, Daniel (?1590-1642) of The Hague worked in England between 1617-30; Charles I appointed him his official painter in 1625.

MYTH is a story often, but not necessarily, fictitious, which symbolises a popular belief or idea, eg the story of Alfred burning the cakes at Athelney, suggests the low ebb of English fortunes and the King's intense concentration on his problems. He may or may not have burned the cakes; he was undoubtedly at Athelney.

MYTTON, Thomas (?1597-1656) the leading Shropshire parliamentarian, slowly overran the county from Wem and Oswestry between 1643-45 when he became C-in-C in N. Wales. He was M.P. for Shropshire in Cromwell's first parliament.

MYXOMATOSIS, an epidemic virus, wiped out most Australian rabbits between the wars and was introduced into Britain via France in 1953. By 1960 it had destroyed most English rabbits. Everywhere the epidemics caused a major rise in farm production (e.g. in Anglesey 30%) and benefits such as the preservation of coastal sand dunes, but a minority of rabbits developed immunity and by 1970 were breeding proverbially. *See* ANIMAL EPIDEMICS.

MZILIKAZE. *See* MA-TABELE.

N

NABOB, NAIB, NAWAB (Urdu = Deputy) originally a Moslem Lord Lieutenant of an Indian province under the Moguls, then the Governor of a district and finally an independent prince descended from such a Governor. In the form *nabob*, the word came to mean a very rich man, particularly one who at the end of the 18th cent. had returned from India with a fortune. *See* EAST INDIA COMPANY.

NAGANA. *See* TRYPANOSOMIASIS.

NAGAS, NAGALAND. The disorders caused in Assam by the head-hunting Nagas led the British in 1866 to create a frontier district to deal with them. This was annexed in 1880. At Indian independence a Naga nationalist movement sprang up, and a separate state was set up within the Indian Union in 1961, but a dissident movement continued.

NAGASAKI. *See* ATOMIC.

NAGLE, Sir Richard (?-after 1691) became Attorney General of Ireland in 1686, and was regarded by the Govt. as the principal representative of R. Catholic opinion there. An extremist, he used his position to abolish many protestant corporations and pulled down protestant churches. In 1689 he became Speaker of the Irish House of Commons and against the policy of James II secured the repeal of the Irish Act of Settlement and the passing of the great Act of Attainder against the 2400 protestant landowners who had fled the country, thereby ensuring that every protestant would be an Orangeman. As James' Sec. of State, he advised his departure to France and followed him after the fall of Limerick.

NAGPUR (India) was founded by a Gond prince from Deogarh in the 18th cent., but dynastic disputes after his death in 1739 led to Maratha interference and by 1743 the Maratha Bhonsla dynasty had taken over. The latter lost territory to the Peishwa and to Hyderabad and in 1803 were defeated with Scindiah by Wellington at Assaye and Argaum. This shook their govt. and from 1811 they were so far unable to deal with Pindari raids, that the villagers fortified themselves. When the Raja Raghuji III died without an heir in 1853, the British annexed Nagpur.

NAG'S HEAD CONSECRATION. A false rumour put about by a Jesuit, Christopher Holywood (1562-1616) in about 1604, that because the only bishop available after the Act of Uniformity 1559 had refused to consecrate Abp. Parker, he had been irregularly consecrated in a Cheapside tavern by John Scory, the Bp. of Chichester, deprived by Q. Mary I. In fact, Parker was consecrated at Lambeth by four bishops. The matter is important in the history of Anglican Apostolic Succession.

NAHAS PASHA. *See* EGYPT-21.

NAIDU, Mrs Sarojini (1879-1949), poet and politician, joined the Indian Congress in 1912 and was Pres. at the Cawnpore Meeting in 1925. A disciple of Ghandi, she organised the Salt March of 1930 and acted as his staff officer at the Round Table Conference of 1931. From 1947 she was Governor of the United Provinces.

NAIK (Urdu = leader). An Indian Gov. or military officer, and later a corporal of native infantry.

NAINI TAL (India). The hot weather capital of the United Provinces.

NAIRNE, Carolina (1766-1845) (*née* Oliphant) published many mostly Jacobite poems anonymously. These were collected under her name in 1846 as *Lays from Strathearn* and include *Land o'the Leal, Caller Herring*; and the famous *Charlie is my darling* and *Will ye no come back again?*

NAIROBI. *See* KENYA.

NAMAQUALAND is named after the Namas, a branch of the Hottentots. Great Namaqualand, a part of S.W. Africa is mainly desert. It was occupied by the Germans in 1885 and remained relatively undisturbed until diamonds were found in 1927 since when it has suffered much prospecting. It is divided from the Cape Province district of Little Namaqualand by the Orange R.

NAMIBIA. *See* SOUTH-WEST AFRICA.

NANA FADNAVIS. *See* MARATHAS-7.

NANA OF EBROHIMIE (?1852-1916) was a palm oil monopolist in the Western delta of the Niger. He signed a protection treaty with the British in 1884 but refused a free trade clause and molested his rivals. He was exiled in 1906.

NANA SAHIB. *See* INDIAN MUTINY; MARATHAS-9.

NANFAN or NANPHANT (1) Sir Richard (?-1507) was sent on a mission to Portugal in 1489, was Deputy at Calais and the patron of Wolsey. A descendant **(2) John (?-1716)** was Lieut. Gov. of New York from 1697-1702.

NANTES (S. Fr) at the lowest ford, 30 miles inland, on the R. Loire, was the greatest of the Breton cities and a usual residence of the dukes who between 1466-1500 built the fortress palace. By then it virtually monopolised the Breton coastal tramp-trade and was the focus of the Loire valley economy. It exported wine, salt and linen in exchange for oil and Flemish cloth. In the 16th cent. as profits accumulated, its trade extended to England, the Baltic and Spain and by 1700 it was exchanging its exports at Bilbao for silver, leather, steel and woollens, which were in turn sold in Africa for slaves; they were carried to the Caribbean and exchanged for tropical goods. Nantes became the centre of the French slave trade and by 1730 was fabulously rich with, too, a shipbuilding industry and its ancillaries besides other local manufacture. It was also the centre of a thriving Irish contraband industry, which was connected with the collection of recruits for the French Irish regiments. The trade of Nantes contributed about 30% of the French national product at this time and it provided much of the finance for the French East India Co. (FEIC) and for the Jacobite court. Its prosperity was accordingly violently interrupted by the 18th cent. wars with Britain (1756-63, 1776-82, 1792-1815) because of the British blockades, especially that of 1756-63 which eroded the finances of the FEIC and hastened the collapse of French power in India. The Nantais were in general hostile to the Bonapartes who had done much to harm them. The city did not recover until the industrial redevelopment of the 20th cent.

NANTES, EDICT OF. *See* HUGUENOTS: JAMES II & VII-5; LOUIS XIV.

NANTWICH. *See* SALT.

NANSEN. *See* ARCTIC EXPLORATION-4.

NAPIER, Macvey (originally MACVEY, Napier) (1776-1847) was editor of the *Edinburgh Review* from 1829.

NAPIER. Able Scots family, primarily **lairds of MERCHISTON** or related to them **(1) Sir Alexander (?-1473)** was comptroller of the Scots household from 1449-61 and also Ambassador to England. He negotiated James III's Danish marriage in 1468 and was engaged in Flemish and Burgundian missions in 1472-3. Of his many descendants or kinsmen **(2) John (1550-1617)** the inventor and mathematician experimented in manures, designed a screw mining pump, invented the notation for decimal fractions, logarithms, the calculating rods known as Napiers Bones and designed the first calculator (*see* RENAISSANCE). His son **(3) Sir Archibald (1576-1645) 1st Ld. NAPIER (Sc 1627)** came with James I to England, became a P.C. and Treasurer Depute of Scotland and was with his son **(4) Archibald (?-1658) 2nd Ld.**, a supporter of Montrose. **(5) Sir Robert (1560-1637)** Bt. was a rich Turkey merchant. **(6) Sir Charles James (1782-1853)** as a Major-General quelled the northern Chartists in 1839 by inviting their leaders to an artillery exhibition. In 1841 he was put in charge of the operations against Sind, and after winning the desperate B. of Meeanee (Feb. 1843) against 8:1 odds, he subdued the country and organised its administration. He disapproved of the policy and is said to have reported success in the single word Peccavi (Lat. = I have sinned). His extraordinary character and energy gained him a place in the Hindu pantheon and a sect of worshippers (whom he tried violently to restrain) in his lifetime. He resigned the Governorship of Sind in 1847 and from the service as a result of a disciplinary dispute in 1850. He also wrote books on Indian and colonial administration, military tactics and the Cephallonian roads. **(7) Sir Charles (1786-1860) Conde de Cabo St. VINCENTE (1834)** a naval officer, unsuccessfully promoted iron steamers (on the Seine) and in 1833 commanded the Portuguese fleet in its victory (against odds) over the Brazilians, and later secured the northern Portuguese provinces. In 1839 as Commodore he reinforced Stopford in the Mediterranean and took charge of the Turkish land forces at Beirut against the advancing troops of Mehemet Ali. Ordered to retire and hand over his command, he offended the Turks by victoriously driving the Egyptians from Beirut, after which, without authority or consultation, he signed a convention with them. This, though repudiated, served as the basis of more official negotiations, but meanwhile all the European powers showered honours upon him. In 1841 he became M.P. for Marylebone. He commanded the Baltic Fleet in 1854. His brother **(8) Sir William (1785-1860)** fought with distinction as a regimental officer in the Peninsular War and subsequently wrote (1828-40) his classic *History of the Peninsular War* besides defences of his brother. **(9) David (1790-1849)** and his cousin **(10) Robert (1791-1876)** were marine engineers, shipbuilders and successful pioneers of steam ships. **(11) Sir Joseph (1804-82)** was Lord Chancellor of Ireland from 1858-59. **(12) Robert Cornelis (1810-90) 1st Ld. NAPIER of MAGDALA (1868)** originally a military engineer, built the E. Jumna irrigation canal (1831), laid out Darjeeling and built the roads to it (1838-41) and the well known Sir Hind Cantonment in 1842. He distinguished himself as an engineer in the Sikh wars (1846-49) and then built the road from Lahore to Peshawar, and the Doab canal. In 1857 he was in the relief of Lucknow and then directed the mining operations during the second siege. He later joined Sir Hugh Rose before Gwalior and was largely responsible for the victories over Tantia Topee and his allies. In 1860 he played an important part in the China War for which, at last, in 1861 he was promoted Major-General. After four years as Mil. Member of the Viceroy's Council he became C-in-C Bombay (1865) and thence C-in-C of the Abyssinian expedition of 1867 in which he destroyed the Ethiopian army at Magdala. In 1870 he became C-in-C in India, and in 1876 Governor of Gibraltar.

NAPLES AND SICILY were Spanish possessions from 1529 and contributed four powerful galleasses to the Armada. At the P. of Utrecht (1713) Naples and Sardinia passed to the Habsburgs; at the P. of Rasstadt (1714) Sicily to Savoy. In 1720 Sardinia and Sicily were exchanged. The Habsburg administration was on the whole enlightened: seaborne trade was developed with N. Africa, and the local institutions were respected. In 1738 under the P. of Vienna, Naples and Sicily were ceded to the Spanish Bourbons, and its Kings were the heirs to the other Spanish thrones. The reign of Ferdinand IV, his strong minded wife Maria Carolina and their Minister Acton represented an uneasy period of conflict between the modernising movements of the enlightenment and a conservative and somewhat obscurantist church and nobility. Despite the efforts of Nelson and the Hamiltons, the French overthrew the mainland Kingdom in 1799. While the Court escaped to British protected Sicily, the puppet mainland PARTHENOPAEAN REPUBLIC was

established on the contemporary French directorial model. This was converted into a monarchy for Marshal Murat, who ascended the new throne as Joachim I in 1808. The enlightenment and efficiency of his rule might easily have established a Muratist dynasty and changed subsequent Italian history, but unfortunately he supported Bonaparte during the Hundred Days, and was in due course taken and shot.

Under the P. of Vienna the Spanish Bourbons returned, but as a local dynasty. Their unprincipled and tyrannical rule rapidly made the double kingdom, renamed **The Two Sicilies**, notorious for moral, physical and intellectual squalor. Rebellions were put down with Austrian help in 1821. In 1849 Messina was bombarded into submission an event which earned Ferdinand II the sobriquet of *Bomba*. The regime staggered on without justification or support until the house of cards collapsed at the touch of Garibaldi and 1000 men between May and Oct. 1860, and the Kingdom was incorporated in the new Savoyard Kingdom of Italy.

NAPLES SICKNESS. *See* SYPHILIS.

NAPOLEON I. Following the contemporary British practice, this ruler is called 'Bonaparte' throughout this work.

NAPOLEON II. *See* BONAPARTE-3 (b) (iii).

NAPOLEON III. *See* BONAPARTE-6 (a) *and separate entry.*

NAPOLEONIC WARS. This popular collective expression is too often confusingly used for the fifteen conflicts listed in the entry FRENCH REVOLUTION AND CONSEQUENT WARS (1787-1815). Napoleon Bonaparte played no significant part until 1796 and then only as a local general until he returned from Egypt and seized power in Nov. 1799. Thereafter, he dominated French policy, and his responsibility is undoubted, but he became Emperor and officially Napoleon I only on 2 Dec. 1804.

NARBROUGH, Sir John (1640-88) commanded the D. of York's flagship at B. of Solebay in 1672. In 1674 and again in 1677 he was C-in-C against the Barbary Corsairs, and from 1680-87 was a commissioner of the Navy.

NARES, Sir George (1831-1915) explorer and hydrographer (*see* CHALLENGER). He also commanded the *Alert* and the *Discovery* expeditions (1875-6) and did the fundamental research on the Mediterranean and Equatorial currents.

NARVIK (N. Norway) was connected with the N. Swedish iron mines by rail in 1903 and were their main outlet. In Apr. 1940 the Germans seized it in a surprise attack. The nearest British force, a weak destroyer flotilla under Capt. B. W. Warburton-Lee VC, was sent in. In a first fight it sank two and damaged three German destroyers; in a second it was overwhelmed and the Captain killed. Two days later a powerful British force came in and sank eight German destroyers and a U-boat, but the German troops were by that time well established ashore and allied troops did not dislodge them until the end of May. Strategic defeats further south made it necessary to evacuate Narvik on 10 June with the important consequence that all Swedish mining production was at German disposal through World War II.

NASH, John (1752-1835) the most elegant of the regency architects, laid out Regents Park, London and designed the splendid terraces facing onto it in 1811 and the *enfilade* from Carlton House via Lower and Upper Regent Streets and Portland Place to Regents Park between 1813-20. He also repaired and enlarged Buckingham Palace, but his entrance gateway, the Marble Arch, was removed to Tyburn in 1851 and most of the *enfilade* south of Regents Park has been destroyed by architectural vandals. His habitual use of stucco, an inexpensive material, made large scale effects (which have been criticised for monotony) financially possible.

NASH, Richard ("Beau") (1674-1762) established the Assembly Rooms, etiquette and dress at Bath, whose society he organised from 1705-45 when his popularity slowly waned.

NASMYTH, Charles (1826-61) was *Times* correspondent to Omar Pasha's force at Shumla (Bulgaria) at the beginning of the Crimean War and helped to organise the successful defence of Silistria against the Russians; after which he became a Major in the British Army.

NASMYTH, James (1808-91) in 1839 invented a steam hammer originally to forge a wrought iron paddle shaft for the admiralty, but it was then found to overcome difficulties generally in the production of very large iron bars. He also invented a steam pile driver and a hydraulic punch.

NASSAU AGREEMENT (Dec. 1962). U.S.A. agreed to provide Britain with Polaris missiles (without warheads) provided that the submarines in which they were mounted should be available at all times for the purposes of the Western Alliance except where supreme British national interests were at stake. The U.S.A. offered similar terms to France which were refused. British acceptance probably convinced Gen. de Gaulle of Britain's subordination to U.S.A. and led in Jan. 1963 to the French veto on British entry into the Common Market.

NATAL (S. Africa). British settlers founded Port Natal in 1824 on coastal territory depopulated by the Zulus. Voortrekers came over the Drakensberg Mts. in 1837, defeated the Zulus at the Blood R. in 1838 and established a republic. The British annexed the area in 1843 and many of the Dutch left and were replaced by British, so that Natal became, as against the Dutch, predominantly British. Zululand was annexed after the Zulu War of 1879, the lands to the Buffalo R. in 1902. The Boers invaded Natal from the north in 1899. The colony became a province of S. Africa in 1910.

NATION. This vague and dangerous word appears to refer to a *relatively* large group of people who believe themselves to have a common bond justifying permanent political cohesion, and marking them off from other groups, not all of which may be nations in that kind of sense. By way of illustration the Twelve Tribes of Israel were a confederacy which seems to have been considered collectively as a nation with a common religion and political and military direction. The Iroquois were considered as a confederacy of six nations created for reasons of expediency. The mediaeval German *Reich* was called the Holy Roman Empire of the German Nation, though many of its outlying territories were not German. The French have been a nation since the 16th cent., their most obvious common bond being their language, yet French is spoken in Belgium and the Val d'Aosta, while significant numbers of Frenchmen in Brittany and Alsace speak other languages. The citizens of the Swiss Confederacy speak four languages and live in 26 states but are undoubtedly a nation.

There is also a difference between the way in which such groups regard themselves and the way in which they are regarded by others. The foreigner is apt to speak of Spaniards where, until recently, there were only subjects of the disparate Spanish Kingdoms. The word *British* in English usage covers the whole or part of four self-conscious groups but the continental is apt to lump them together and ask why some English troops wear skirts.

The idea of the NATION STATE is, therefore, indefinable and Pres. Wilson's doctrine of SELF DETERMINATION was an arbitrary concept probably connected with his American anti-royalism.

NATIONAL AFRICAN CO. *See* ROYAL NIGER CO.

NATIONAL ANTHEM. *See* BULL, JOHN.

NATIONAL ARBITRATION TRIBUNAL. *See* INDUSTRIAL COUNCILS AND COURT.

NATIONAL ART COLLECTIONS FUND (1903) is a chartered society for organising public opinion behind the retention of works of art in the U.K.

NATIONAL ASSEMBLY. On 17 June 1789, the Third Estate of the French States General proclaimed itself the *National Assembly* and in July the *Constituent Assembly*.

NATIONAL ASSISTANCE was, after 1949, the equivalent of the previously given Poor Relief (or Dole) for the virtually destitute. It was progressively overlaid by supplementary and housing benefits, family means supplements and emergency cash grants. These made improvements but complicatated administration. The Social Security Act 1986 renamed them.

NATIONAL COUNCIL FOR CIVIL LIBERTIES (since 1990 **LIBERTY**) was founded in 1834 and refounded in 1945, mainly to observe police action.

NATIONAL COVENANT, SCOTS (27 Feb.-9 Mar. 1638). This landmark in 17th cent. history set up the Scots nation as a body united in Presbyterianism and Calvinist theology, but associated these systems with the law and liberties of Scotland and with an undertaking to uphold the King in their defence. It restated the *Confession* of 1580 which the boy King James VI and I had been forced to sign. The practical inconsistency within the document, which nearly every adult Scot signed, became increasingly glaring as time went on, and ultimately caused dissension between England and Scotland, between the Scots parties themselves, and between the English army and parliament. *See* CHARLES -12; SCOTLAND. PRESBYTERIAN CHURCH OF.

NATIONAL DEBT. Before 1664, govts borrowed by means of non-negotiable interest-free Exchequer tallies; from 1664 to 1696 by interest bearing or discounted orders of repayment (later called Exchequer Bills). Until 1694 this was all very short term debt. The first funded loan £1.2M was raised in 1694 but short term borrowing dominated financial habits for some years, before giving way to ordinary or perpetual loans or annuities. Most of the £14.5M debt in 1697 was short term. Most of the £36.2M debt in 1714 was long term and this became habitual. The following were the amounts of the national debt at later significant dates:

	£m		£m
1745	75	1914	650
1793	245	1923	6657
1815	834	1938	7111
1899	635	1945	21,237
1903	798	1965	30,550

Borrowing by local authorities made little appreciable difference until after World War I when the totals borrowed rose steadily and interest rates with them.

NATIONAL DEBT COMMISSIONERS. *See* SINKING FUNDS.

NATIONAL DEMOCRATIC PARTY, led by George Barnes existed from 1918-23. He had been the Labour representative in the War Cabinet. It favoured trade unionism and mild socialism and derived much of its support from Labour supporters of Lloyd George's coalition who refused to resign in 1918. It won 15 seats in 1918 but most of its M.P.s drifted back to Lloyd George.

NATIONAL DISPUTES TRIBUNAL. *See* INDUSTRIAL COUNCILS AND COURT.

NATIONAL ECONOMIC DEVELOPMENT COUNCIL (N.E.D.C., or popularly NEDDY) was set up in 1961 and represented a Conservative Govt.'s movement towards central planning, being designed for discussion, research and advice but without powers; but its target of an annual growth rate of 4% was accepted by Labour and Conservatives alike until the slump of 1989.

NATIONAL EDUCATION SCHEME (Ir.) was set up in 1831. The grants hitherto made to the Association for Discountenancing Vice, and the Kildare Place Society, were transferred to a multi-dimensional unpaid National Education Board. Anyone could apply to have a school placed under the Board, provided that the site was worth at least a third of any building cost and had been locally found. Applicants were usually clergymen (of any denomination) who became the patron or manager, and employed the teachers. The Board inspected schools and could dismiss but not appoint teachers. Thus in practice every school was denominational but the Board set up teacher training schools. By 1843 the Board, despite heated Protestant opposition, had 2721 schools attended by around 320,000 children and in 1914 about 7,500 attended by 650,000. Cavour thought it the best elementary system in Europe and far ahead of the English. Intermediate (i.e. secondary) education was started in 1878 by an Act which applied funds from the Irish Church surplus to it.

NATIONAL FRONT a small but noisy body, founded in 1966, resembled the pre-war British Union of Fascists, save that it was primarily hostile to non-whites. It contested elections unsuccessfully and its demonstrations were a pretext for attention-getting violence from its extreme or more determined enemies. A small and equally noisy counter-movement, the Anti-Nazi League was spawned. Both organisations attracted more media than real interest.

NATIONAL GALLERY was opened in Pall Mall, London in 1824 and moved to Trafalgar Square in 1838.

NATIONAL GOVT. (1) replaced the second Labour Govt. in Aug. 1931. Under Ramsey MacDonald (Labour) with ministers from all parties, it undertook a programme of retrenchment to restore foreign confidence. Arthur Henderson, the former Labour Foreign Secretary, refused to join and led a Labour opposition. In Oct. when foreign confidence had been restored the National govt. held a general election asking for 'a doctor's mandate'.

(2) In the ensuing landslide the Labour opposition was virtually destroyed but the govt. was Tory dominated. MacDonald resigned in 1935 and **(3)** in Nov. a new National govt. under Sir Neville Chamberlain was again returned with a very large majority. This was overthrown to make way for Churchill's Wartime Coalition of 1940.

NATIONAL HEALTH SERVICE (N.H.S.). See SOCIAL SECURITY.

NATIONAL INSURANCE. See SOCIAL SECURITY.

NATIONALISATION. (1) is the process by which sectors of the economy are put under the ownership or at least control of public authorities. The first public service was the Post Office created under Charles II.

(2) In 1934 the Labour Party declared for 'public ownership and control of the primary industries and services' and listed them under 14 headings. Between then and 1945 for practical reasons its opponents created the Central Electricity Generating Board, the London Passenger Transport Board and British Overseas Airways, and in World War II almost every part of the economy was controlled and a kind of war socialism practised in the interests of national self-preservation. When Labour came to power in July 1945 much experience and much of the required administrative apparatus were already available. The necessary legislation had initially a more theoretical than practical impact.

(3) The following was the Attlee Govt's first programme.

Bank of England	1946
Civil Aviation	1946
Coal	1947
Cable & Wireless	1947
Public Transport	1948
Land Development Rights as part	
of Town and Country Planning	1948
Electricity	1949
Gas	1949
Iron and Steel	1951

Agriculture was exempted from planning controls but farmers were to be supervised and if found incompetent, evicted. This political compromise did not work because civil servants were unqualified to supervise farmers, and supervisory committees of farmers (the ex-War Agricultural Committees) would not evict their own kind. The italicised item was not part of the programme but was an agreed bipartisan measure.

(4) Six of the 14 headings were not reached in this period viz: chemicals, engineering, insurance, shipbuilding, shipping and textiles and in 1953 the Conservatives denationalised some road transport and iron and steel undertakings but in 1967 Labour renationalised them. Later nationalisations, sometimes amounting only to purchases of majority shareholdings included the British Oil Corporation (1976), British Shiphuilders and British Aerospace (1977) together with Rolls Royce and British Leyland, the lorry builders.

(5) These various industries were operated not by ministries responsible to parliament, but by nominated boards to which ministers could give only general directions. This attracted growing criticism for daily grievances could not be aired in parliament and the profits did not enure to the state but to the employees whose trade unions habitually held up production in order to extort benefits, so that capital accumulation and investment were dangerously reduced, the industries tended to obsolescence, while public direction, if not bureaucratic or obstructive (e.g. the Attlee Govt.'s refusal to allow new hotels over railway termini) was incoherent. This ultimately provoked a new Conservative commitment not to respect nationalisation as a principle, but to challenge it root and branch. See PRIVATISATION.

NATIONALISM (*see* NATION) is diverse in its actual or attributed forms. It must be distinguished from **(1)** *racialism* which is concerned with distinctions (often of doubtful validity) between particular groups and the subjugation or oppression of some by others, usually within the frontiers of a country and **(2)** from *patriotism* which is a spirit of primarily defensive championship of a people and **(3)** from *imperialism* which involves conquest of other nations. Nationalism hardly antedates the French Revolution (1789 onwards). It is essentially popular and presupposes identification of a nation with a territory. It is characterised by a certain aggressiveness or over-reaction to actual or supposed aggressions by others. One of its major forms is *irredentism,* i.e. the 'redemption' of territories whose people resemble or are supposed to resemble those of a mother country but are under another govt. e.g. the Tyrolean Italians or from the Greek point of view, successively the Aegean Is. Cyprus, Constantinople and Macedonia. The Scots, Welsh and Irish, each by reaction against the English, entertain nationalism. Amongst its other features is a self-conscious attention to symbols e.g. a flag or the semi-deification of a hero such as Robert the Bruce or William Tell and the popular celebration of a national festival such as 4 July (U.S.A.) or 17 May (Norway). It may involve the deliberate propagation of the main national language or the attribution of national characteristics to a branch of an art (e.g. music, painting or architecture) which is not necessarily related to group psychology. For uncertain reasons the English are so little touched by it that few of them know the date of Commonwealth day or St George's Day or can describe the Union Jack accurately.

NATIONALITY (1) The Anglo-Saxons shared a sense of common identity before the Norman Conquest, as did the people of the Danelaw; and it seems that the whole population could be embraced in such a term as *Gens Anglorum* (Lat: The Race of the Angles). The Conquest connected England with the spreading continental dominions of the Norman and Angevin Kings and substituted feudal landholding and fealty for notions of racial or tribal unity. K. John's loss of Normandy forced some of his barons to choose between their English and their continental properties and this focused attention in the mid-13th cent. on the need for legal definition of those who 'belonged' and those aliens who did not.

Edward I held that aliens could not acquire land, and enemy aliens could not sue in the King's courts without a licence but the Crown could by letters of denization enable an alien to hold land and office.

(2) At Common Law a person born within the Realm was held always to be in allegiance to the Crown. Save that a woman might lose or gain allegiance by marriage, it could be lost or gained only by Act of Parliament. A person physically present in the realm was also in temporary allegiance. A person under allegiance was amenable to the law of treason. Procedures for naturalisation without special Act were introduced and elaborated in 1844 and 1870. In 1914 the law was codified. The principal requirements were ability to speak English, five years' residence in British territory and taking the Oath of Allegiance. The Act of 1914 created a common nationality for the whole of the British Empire. In 1949 Britain and the seven other major Commonwealth countries agreed on a common code of local citizenship within the general category of British Subject.

(3) In 1971 public excitement about coloured immigration led to the Immigration Act of 1971 which denied a right of abode in Britain to all persons who were not patrials. In principle a patrial was a citizen of the U.K. by birth, adoption, naturalisation or registration or who, if a citizen by descent, had been settled for at least 5 years there. This virtually destroyed the concept of common subjection to the crown. *See* CALVINS CASE; DOMICIL.

(4) As states define their nationality by different criteria to suit themselves, naturalised individuals who conform with the criteria of more than one state, have more than one nationality, unless there is a subsisting contrary treaty between those states, and may have conflicting rights and duties; e.g. the P of Versailles (1920) abolished such dual nationality as between the U.K. and Germany, but Hitler's denunciation of it in 1935 for 1936 re-established it, and the German State Treaty of 1955 abolished the re-establishment. Thus between 1936 and 1955 Germano–British naturalised persons (including the present author) could not seek diplomatic protection in their other country, and might be hanged under the law of one, if captured while serving against it in the forces of the other.

NATIONAL LABOUR PARTY comprised those members of the Labour Party who, led by Ramsay MacDonald, supported the National Govt. of 1931 and were expelled from their own Party. It did reasonably well in the 1931 election, badly in 1935 and was reduced to two M.P.s by 1940.

NATIONAL LIBERAL PARTY (1) This was the name assumed by Lloyd George's faction of the Liberals (that is, the Coalition Liberals) in the 1922 election. **(2)** *See* LIBERAL NATIONAL PARTY.

NATIONAL MARITIME MUSEUM (Greenwich) was established in 1934 with Sir Geoffrey Callendar (1875-1946) as its first Director. It covers all aspects of maritime, especially British, history.

NATIONAL PARKS (N.P.) and **AREAS OF OUTSTANDING NATIONAL BEAUTY (A.O.N.B.).** N.P.s grew out of the same post World War II reaction to urban squalor and sprawl as the Town and Country Planning movement but they represented a far-sighted attempt to preserve unspoiled areas (some large) for public enjoyment by forbidding in advance any, or much, development. The principles were focused by John Dower the Elder in a govt. memorandum of 1945 and the N.P. and Access to the Countryside Act 1949 set up an N.P. Commission which between 1951-59 designated ten N.P.s in Northumberland, the Lake District*, North Yorkshire, the Yorkshire Dales*, the Peak*, the Pembrokeshire Coast, the Brecon Beacons, Snowdonia*, Exmoor, Dartmoor, and many A.O.N.B.s especially along the coasts of the

Solway, Lleyn, Gower, Devon, Cornwall and Dorset and the I. of Wight but including A.O.N.B.s in the Forest of Bowland, Shropshire, Cannock, Malvern Hills, the Quantocks and the North Downs. In the 1990s the unbuilt character of some of the N.P.s marked attention the attention of road planners as a source of cheap land for new or widened roads and motorways.

NATIONAL PARTY was formed by Henry Page-Croft from dissatisfied Conservatives in 1917 and proclaimed distrust of foreigners and belief in Britain's imperial mission. At the 1918 election its members, save for Page-Croft, and one other rejoined the Conservatives.

NATIONAL POLITICAL UNION, a radical organisation formed 1831, advocated withholding taxes in support of parliamentary reform, and hoped to unite all political unions, but failed because the wilder spirits broke up its meetings.

NATIONAL PRESS **(Ir.)** Anti-Parnellite journal started in 1891 and amalgamated with the *Freeman's Journal* in 1892 to make the *Daily Independent*.

NATIONAL REFORMER. *See* BRADLAUGH.

NATIONAL SAVINGS MOVEMENT a joint organisation comprising a national committee, the National Savings Bank (formerly the Post Office Savings Bank) and the Trustee Savings Banks. It was launched in World War I to tap the resources of patriotic small savers in aid of war finance, through the low-interest but tax-free savings certificates. The movement developed a large voluntary organisation which was continued between the wars. In Nov. 1939 Defence Bonds with conversion rights were also introduced for World War II. In 1956 Premium Bonds in which the interest was allotted in the form of lottery prizes were introduced and in 1965 Development Bonds, with terms similar to those of Defence Bonds. The movement's exploitation of wartime patriotism to secure low-interest finance was continued by its own momentum and with less respectable results in peacetime, for it depended largely on small savers' ignorance of more profitable forms of investment. The commercial changes in the constituent banks effectively ended it.

NATIONAL SCHOOLS, SOCIETY (FOR THE EDUCATION OF THE POOR). This Anglican organisation was founded in 1811. It took over many charity schools and raised funds to provide others called National Schools. From 1833 a school received a 50% govt. grant provided that the other 50% was raised by subscription. In 1841 it established its teachers training college at St. Marks, Chelsea and its secular teaching was subjected to Govt. inspection. The schools became eligible for grants from school boards under the Education Act, 1870. It still provides many schools.

NATIONAL SERVICE was compulsory war service imposed between 1939-60. *See* CONSCRIPTION.

NATIONAL SOCIALISM. The farrago of doctrines, wrongly equated with 'Fascism' by which Adolf Hitler attracted German allegiance. There was to be a corporate state with a single political hierarchy, open to all Germans, with the Führer (= Guide) at the top. Such a system was hostile to older interests, particularly the aristocracy and the R. Catholic church. Every German was to receive a competence proportionate to his rank. This was hostile to established capitalism and labour organisations. The resources of Weimar Germany could not supply this competence; therefore, in the absence of colonies, the German territory had to be enlarged, if necessary by violence. This was justifiable because Germany was crowded but other countries to the east were under-populated and because the so-called Aryan races, of which the Germans were the best examples, were the standard bearers of a civilisation which would benefit the world. Aryanism was transmitted by heredity and breeding and had to be safeguarded from non-Aryan, especially Semitic (mainly Jewish) admixture. Racially mixed marriages and copulation were therefore criminal. The Semites, especially the Jews, were hostile to the Aryans and had by commercial and conspiratorial methods consistently frustrated their destiny. The Jews had therefore to be destroyed rather than merely enslaved. This tribal predation, disguised as a philosophy, had all the ingredients of mass appeal: to egalitarianism, to national pride and disappointment, to greed, and to the German militaristic spirit. It also created a highly profitable scapegoat.

Within the German hierarchy, apart from the cynics who only paid lip service and took the loot, there were a number of differing theoretical opinions. The extreme racialists held that all power and resources should be vested in the Aryans and that all Aryans were blond, blue eyed and tall. This classic description of Celts, apparently confined the rule of the world to Germans, and to some Scandinavians and Anglo-Saxons. Others, who included the political realists such as Himmler and Rosenberg, believed that anyone within reason (i.e. not a Semite) could by loyalty and honour enter the charmed circle. There were many (racially) non-German S.S. men.

NATIONAL SOCIETY FOR THE PREVENTION OF CRUELTY TO CHILDREN (N.S.P.C.C.). See CHILDREN etc.

NATIONAL STUD. In 1916 Lord Wavertree, foreseeing the inroads which motor transport might make on the stability of horse breeding, gave his bloodstock and stud farm at Tully (Co. Kildare) to the nation. It was transferred to Gillingham (Dorset) in 1943 and later extended to West Grinstead. By 1963 it was obvious that breeding for sport was the only purpose of breeding at all, and management was transferred from the Ministry of Agriculture to the Betting Levy Board which ceased breeding and concentrated on stallions, while the Jockey Club set up its own stud at Newmarket.

NATIONAL THEATRE. Though there was much 19th cent. talk, the first practical steps towards its creation was taken in 1904 by Harley Granville-Baker and William Archer, who published estimates. An appeal was launched in 1908 under Sir Israel Gollancz, but World War I suspended progress, which was resumed in 1919. By 1938 there was enough money to buy a rather small site opposite the Victoria and Albert museum. After World War II this was exchanged for a much bigger site on the South Bank in connection with the Festival of Britain and the buildings were completed in stages after 1963.

NATIONAL TRUST was founded by Octavia Hill in 1895 to preserve places of historic interest and natural beauty by acquiring them. A National Trust for Scotland was formed in 1926.

NATIONAL UNEMPLOYED WORKERS' MOVEMENT was a front organisation to exploit the post-World War I indigence in the interests of the Communist Party. Against Labour, trade union and conservative opposition, it organised hunger marches and campaigned against the means test. This actually helped the unemployed but not the Communist Party. It was wound up in 1939 when Russia and Nazi Germany attacked Poland.

NATIONAL UNION OF CONSERVATIVE AND CONSTITUTIONAL ASSOCIATIONS was founded in 1867 by Henry Raikes and other younger Tory M.P.s to attract worker support (see CONSERVATIVE CENTRAL OFFICE). These associations sometimes called Conservative Working Men's Associations existed in many but not all constituencies, and not all were affiliated to it. They were the product of the 1867 extension of the franchise, but some were formed in anticipation of it. Lord Randolph Churchill attempted between 1880-84 to influence Conservative policy by gaining control of its council, but failed because he had no coherent policy himself. Between 1903-5 Joseph Chamberlain and the tariff reformers took control but the conservative defeat of 1910 brought about a reorganisation in which the Central

Office, the N. Union and the Liberal Unionists were placed under a Chairman of the Party Organisation.

NATIONAL UNION OF WOMEN'S SUFFRAGE SOCIETIES. See FAWCETT.

NATIVUS Lat: One who is native to the land on which he lives, i.e. a serf.

NATIVITY, CHURCH OF THE. See PALESTINE; CRUSADER PILGRIMAGE CHURCHES; HOLY PLACES.

NATURA LEGIS NATURAE, DE. See FORTESCUE, SIR JOHN.

"NATURAL" FRONTIERS OF FRANCE. Controversial expression in 18th-19th cent. diplomatic parlance meaning the Alps, the Pyrenees and the Rhine and including therefore Alsace, Lorraine and Belgium in France. See ANCIENT FRONTIERS OF FRANCE.

NATURALISATION. See NATIONALITY-3.

NATURAL JUSTICE, RULES OF as administered by the courts require that any body (whether a club, committee or a minister), which has to reach a decision affecting an individual's rights, must ensure that he knows the nature of the complaint against him, that he has a proper opportunity to make his defence, and that it should act in good faith and not on the basis of matters irrelevant to the issue. See LOCAL GOVT. BOARD V ARLIDGE.

NATURAL LAW was said to be that part of the law based upon natural reason or instinct, discoverable because it is observed by all nations, and originating at the beginning of mankind. It is to be distinguished from civil or local law (of which it may form a part) since the latter depends upon local legislation, and also from divine law which depends upon revelation.

NATURE CONSERVANCY was established in 1949 for the scientific study and conservation of British wildlife.

NAU, Claude de la BOISSELIERE (?-after 1605), Sec. to the Guise Cardinal of Lorraine, he became Mary Q. of Scots Sec. in 1574. He managed her finances and also went to Scotland for her in 1579 and 1581. Accused by the English of being a principal in the Babington Plot and by the French and the R. Catholics of betraying her in 1586, he vindicated his loyalty to her and was released in 1587. He wrote a *History of Mary Stewart*, first published in 1883.

NAUNTON, Sir Robert (1563-1635) a fellow of Trinity College Cambridge, from 1592 acted as a travelling tutor and intelligence agent for the E. of Essex. He was an M.P. in 1606-14, became a Master of Requests in 1616 and Sec. of State in 1618. As such he was involved in the events leading to the execution of Sir Walter Raleigh. He tried to influence James I into intervention in the Thirty Years War in favour of the Elector Palatine Frederick V and clashed with the Spanish Ambassador Gondomar. He resigned against the Spanish marriage negotiations in 1623, and became Master of the Court of Wards. He was an M.P. again in 1621, 1624 and 1625.

NAURU or PLEASANT I. (S.W. Pacific) was discovered in 1798 and annexed by the Germans for its large phosphate deposits. Australia took it in 1914 and save for a Japanese occupation between 1942-45, it was under Australian administration under joint mandate or trusteeship to Britain, Australia and New Zealand, until the Australian Nauru Act 1965 led to independence in 1968.

NAUTICAL ALMANAC was first published in 1766.

NAVAL DISCIPLINE was long regulated by the accepted custom of the sea with rare statutory incursions. An Act of 1378 punished desertion and another of 1562 extended to seamen the legislation against deserting soldiers. Such legislation was needed to empower land authorities to act against escaped seamen. The Navy continued to be regulated by Articles made by the Admiralty under the prerogative and even 19th cent. Naval Discipline Acts preserved the prerogative.

The often savage discipline was not invariably adequate and had to be supplemented by frequent acts against abuses of pay and impressment, and using warships for private trading (1722) on the one hand and on the other for payment of bounties for destroying or taking enemy ships (1740-44) and for ensuring prize money (1762). (*See* PRIZE.) The system was codified in 1957.

NAVAL LIMITATION post WORLD WAR I. (1) The WASHINGTON CONFERENCE (1921-22) was called to reduce tension in the Far East and to limit naval armaments; to induce Japan to co-operate, Britain and U.S.A. fatefully agreed not to strengthen fortifications between Singapore and Hawaii. Two Naval Limitation Treaties were signed in Feb. 1922 between Britain, U.S.A., Japan, France and Italy. One limited the size of capital ships to 35,000 tons and that of naval guns to 16 ins. Britain and U.S.A. were limited to 15 such, Japan to 9 and France and Italy to 5. The other contained pious rules on the use of submarines, and outlawed poison gas.

(2) The LONDON NAVAL CONFERENCE (1930) and TREATIES 1930 and 1936 continued the work of the Washington Conference of 1921. In 1930 Britain, U.S.A. and Japan agreed to limit their numbers of capital ships to 15, 15 and 9 respectively; to limit battleship-tonnage to 35,000 and guns to 16 ins. and for cruisers 10,000 and 8 ins. and to limit total tonnages of cruisers and destroyers to 489,000 for Britain, 475,000 for U.S.A. and 313,000 for Japan. No capital ships were to be built for six years. The treaty was signed by Britain, the Dominions, U.S.A. and Japan; France and Italy signed but did not ratify. The 1936 treaty reduced new capital ship guns to 14 in and laid a moratorium on cruiser building. The treaties worked to Britain's disadvantage since she had to maintain world-wide responsibilities with her force while the others had only local commitments with theirs. Moreover she observed the tonnage limitations whereas Japan, in particular, did not. The treaties placed no limitations on aircraft carriers.

NAVAL RACE, ANGLO-GERMAN (1898-1914). Colonial ambitions inspired Germany's Navy Law of 1898 and showed that she might wish to challenge Britain at sea. It took until 1904 for her naval building combined with the Kiel Canal (q.v.) to become a threat. In 1905 the British decided secretly to build the revolutionary *Dreadnought*. (launched 1906) (q.v.). As she outclassed every ship afloat, it was thought safe to reduce the building programme (by the so-called Cawdor Programme) to save money and to take credit for it at the Second Hague Conference. The Germans replied by secretly building Dreadnoughts themselves. These were better protected but more lightly gunned than the British. In 1908 the Admiralty discovered that 4 German battle ships were being started against 2 British. McKenna, the First Lord of the Admiralty, proposed 6 for 1909. The cabinet were split and Asquith compromised on 4 with 4 to come if needed. There was public agitation ('We want eight and we won't wait'). The Govt. promised 8 with 5 in each of the next 2 years, but the cost required additional taxes and provoked the Parliament Bill crisis. Meantime the Germans pressed the widening of the Kiel Canal so that even if their fleet were inferior to the British, it could dominate the Russians. The British replied by getting the French to take over most Mediterranean responsibilities so that the modern British units could be concentrated in Home waters. The relative operational strengths were revealed at the B. of Jutland (1916):-

	British	**German**
Modern Battleships	28	16
Battle Cruisers	9	5
Cruisers	26	9

NAVARRE was a west Pyrenean part French, part Spanish speaking kingdom, but with a large Basque population. It was associated at one time with the Albret house of Champagne, and later with the Bourbons. Spain annexed Spanish Navarre in 1512. By the accession of Henry of Navarre as Henry IV to the French throne in 1589, French Navarre became effectively part of France, but retained its own customs and privileges until the Revolution. Both parts, but especially the Spanish, have remained self conscious down to modern times, and Navarrese sentiment played a part in the Spanish civil war of the 1930s.

NAVICERT (*see* BLOCKADE). A method of controlling neutral shipping in time of war. Orders in Council declared ships and cargoes liable to seizure if on unnavicerted voyages to or from ports through which goods might reach or come from enemy territory. British consuls in neutral countries were empowered to issue the navicerts and the effect of the arrangement was to force shipowners to apply to, and therefore to submit to, inspection by the consuls or risk total loss.

NAVIGATION by methods other than unaided observation of landmarks, probably started with the use of soundings and a wind-rose, but guidance by the Pole Star was practised in the 3rd cent. B.C. and celestial navigation was steadily improved in the middle ages, until the publication (at the behest of K. Alphonso X of Castile) of the Alphonsine Tables in 1252 and the *Sphaera Mundi* (Lat: The Earth's Sphere) by John Holywood at about the same time. The lodestone was also known from early times but the magnetic principle could be put to little practical use until the invention of the **mariners' (card) compass** in about 1282. This made navigation possible in bad, mainly winter, visibility and doubled Mediterranean annual traffic in a generation. The new freedom created a demand for charts which developed from the old portolans and both chart making and chart use led to the development of navigational aids and surveying instruments. Majorcan pilots had the **astrolabe** by 1295 and Chaucer later wrote a treatise on it. The Cross or Jacob's staff for measuring the altitude of a heavenly body was invented at about the same time but seldom used in navigation until the 16th cent. These were superseded in their turn by the Backstaff or Davis's **quadrant** (invented in about 1580) which made it possible to observe the sun without being blinded. Such instruments had become necessary for oceanic navigation but until the 20th cent. most developments other than chronometrical ones were really refinements. These, however, included 15th cent. improvements in the Alphonsine Tables, the development of the Azimuth compass to observe magnetic compass error in about 1514 and the foundation of **Greenwich Observatory** in 1674 with its development of lunar tables in the ensuing century. The main remaining problem was a practical way of establishing longitude and in 1714 a Board of Longitude was set up to encourage research and development. This culminated in the invention in 1764 of John Harrison's (1693-1776) **Chronometer** (q.v.).

The need for accurate navigation of rapidly moving aircraft led between 1940-42 to the development of navigation based upon the reception of radio waves from **radio beacons** (hyperbolic navigation). The post World War II need to navigate nuclear submarines without surfacing brought about **inertial navigation** which is a sort of computerised dead reckoning.

NAVIGATION ACTS were intended to encourage shipping or seamen by manipulating the carrying trade. **(1)** The first model was an Act of 1381 which required English traders to ship their goods (both inwards and outwards) in English ships upon pain of seizure of their goods in other vessels, the crown taking two thirds, the relator one third. An Act of 1382 created an exception where no English ships were available. These statutes were re-enacted in 1390 with the significant addition that ship owners were to take reasonable gains. There was in fact a shortage of English ships. The law was ineffectual or only intermittently enforced throughout the 15th cent. In 1485 Gascon wines were required to be imported in

English ships but only two years later this rule was extended to Toulouse woad by a statute which repeated the two original acts. In 1531 this legislation was confirmed but in 1534 Henry VIII took power to repeal and restore it during his lifetime. This did not prevent him from securing a parliamentary confirmation in 1540.

(2) The system was repealed in 1558, the first year of Elizabeth, as a diplomatic sop to Spain, but in 1562 there was a new departure. The statute of 1487 was revived (save in the case of wines imported into Wales or through Chepstow). Foreign ships were not to carry between English ports and cereals were now to be exported solely in English ships. There was also a prohibition on small English ships ('hoys and plates') sailing to European ports east of Caen. In 1570 the prohibition became total. In 1581 an attempt was made to encourage the fisheries by forbidding fish imports by English merchants, but far from English fishermen catching more fish, foreigners simply captured the fish trade and the act was repealed in 1597. In 1605 an attempt was made to encourage the export of beer in cask, since this took up four times as much room as cereals.

(3) Matters remained in this posture, while the Dutch steadily took over a world-wide carrying trade, until the Commonwealth imposed a stringent ordinance (1651) intended to injure them. This required all imports to arrive in British bottoms, or, if from Europe, in those of the country of origin, and all exports to be shipped in British bottoms. Since Britain was the most important foreign area of call for Dutch shipping the result, naturally, was war. It is remarkable that one of the first acts of Charles II, who arrived from Holland, was substantially to re-enact the Cromwellian ordinance. The Act of 1660 restricted raw imports from the colonies, Africa, Asia and America to British ships, and goods and manufactures of any provenance to British ships or ships from the place of origin. It also confirmed the Turkey and Russia trade to British ships. All outward ships had to deposit a bond that they would return with foreign goods. This Act was confirmed in the Cavalier Parliament of 1661 which in 1663 extended the monopoly to European goods and coal for colonial ports, except for curing salt to Newfoundland.

(4) By now navigational policy had become entangled with mercantilist colonialism. The machinery which existed to maintain the merchant marine dovetailed, in theory, with the exchange of the correct goods between the plantations (including Ireland) which supplied raw materials, and the imperial power which replied with manufactures. The Act of 1660, for example, included the Cromwellian ban on English tobacco growing. The trouble was that the system was difficult to enforce, expensive and maddening. Goods might be rotting on a quay with an empty foreign ship offering lower freight alongside, while British ships in the offing were held by foul winds. Outward as well as inward smuggling from creeks was endemic and forms the background of the prohibitions on trading by small ships. The transatlantic voyage was much more expensive than one from the Caribbean to the American colonies so that a huge illicit trade grew up. Local difficulties, famines or depressions made constant tinkering necessary; exceptions, were made for Irish linen in 1704, for the loading of sugar for European ports direct in 1739, for southern rice to the other colonies in 1764 and to Europe in 1766. Foreign retaliation could result in all the shipping between two points sailing empty in one direction, and finally an uncontrollable occasional shortage of British shipping created an artificial shortage of necessary goods or a local glut of unsaleable goods, which might have been moved in foreign ships. During the American rebellion and the French Wars of 1793-1845 so many exceptions had to be enacted as virtually to dismantle the

system: for example, in 1780 alone exceptions were made for corn exports, all Mediterranean goods, all Irish trade with the colonies and all Irish wool and glass for foreign destinations. The long wars of 1792-1815 created habits and vested interests which could not be ignored and in any case British shipping released after the wars soon acquired a world predominance which made Navigation law unnecessary. Repeals in 1814, 1823, 1846, 1849 and 1854 effectively ended them.

NAVY BOARD (1546-1832) responsible for the supply and administration of the navy was set up under the Ld High Admiral, to free him for his operational tasks. It was originally supervised by the Lieutenant of the Admiralty and comprised the Treasurer of the Navy, the Comptroller, the Surveyor, the Master of the Ordnance for Ships and the Clerk of the Ships. The Lieutenancy soon lapsed, and the Treasurer became the head of the Board, while the Clerk, as Clerk of the Acts, became the effective Secretary. Samuel Pepys held this important office. Meanwhile the Admiralty had acquired a board of its own in the shape of the "Lords Commissioners for exercising" the Lord High Admiral's office. The two boards, one administrative, the other operational, co-existed not without overlapping, friction or scandal until 1832 when the Navy Board was merged with the Admiralty. The 18th cent. Navy Board was never very efficient, save in the provision of guns, canvas and cordage, and ship design was usually behind the best contemporary practice. *See also* VICTUALLING BOARD.

NAVY LEAGUE was founded in 1895 to promote a two-power standard navy, i.e. one which was as strong as any two other powers. Initially only a parliamentary lobby, it soon bid for public support especially after the German Navy Law of 1898. Its *Navy League Journal* had an influence disproportionate to the size of its circulation and later it was involved in the Sea Cadet Organisation. Its German counterpart, the *Deutscher Flottenverein* was launched in 1898 and soon all aspiring naval powers had their own navy leagues. Russia even had two. *See* NAVAL RACE. ANGLO-GERMAN.

NAVY, ROYAL (1) as a permanent specialised fighting institution dates from Henry VIII's wish to clear the Four Seas of foreign and English pirates. He created a permanent Admiralty (q.v.) for operational control and a Navy Board (q.v.) for administration and *matériel,* and encouraged industries such as gun-founding at the Tower, ropemaking and hemp (q.v.) cultivation in Dorset, and he built dockyards at Deptford, Chatham and Portsmouth. The Navy, however, remained small; in the Armada crisis (1588) royal ships, though mostly much larger than the rest, represented numerically less than 10% of the fleet.

(2) Warship design remained pragmatic within a broadside-gunned galleon type until Charles I launched *The Sovereign of the Seas* of 100 guns in 1628 (*see also* SHIP-MONEY FLEETS). The Navy then began to standardise ship-types and guns to cut costs and simplify logistics for large fleets against the Dutch, the Barbary Corsairs and later the French. Though design was never static, by mid-19th cent. the major English types were the 74 gun two decker *line-of battle* ship, with a few 100 gun three deckers as flagships, and the *frigate* which mounted 32 to 36 guns on a single deck and was used for all purposes except fighting in the line. Smaller ships were used in numbers for supplies, despatches, tenders and so forth. By this time too, dockyards developed at Plymouth and Falmouth and also bases at Tangier, Gibraltar and Minorca to support the strategy of the French wars.

(3) In the absence of a flexible signalling system, the Admiralty evolved *Fighting Instructions* whereby officers would know what was expected of them in most foreseeable situations. Their rigidity led to Matthews' court-martial and indirectly to Byng's loss of Minorca (1742). It was not until Kempenfelt's flag-signal book was promulgated in 1782 and the Admiralty telegraph (q.v.) was set up, that fleets could be properly controlled. Signalling played a major role in the victorious prosecution of the French Wars of 1792-1815. Even then, admirals expected in the battle smoke and uproar to order a manoeuvre by example rather than signal.

(4) A sailing navy can function without fuel (save for cooking) but needs food, ammunition, careening, refitting, hospitals and finance. The Navy kept pace with the spread of empire and established bases from Trinidad, St. Lucia and Jamaica to Cape Town, Trincomalee (Ceylon), Bombay, Madras and the Hooghly, but Gibraltar by itself could not support Mediterranean campaigns, and without Minorca, bases had to be improvised in the ports of allies (if any) and of complaisant or overawed neutrals. At various periods fleets depended on Leghorn (Tuscany), Naples, Messina and Palermo (Two Sicilies), San Fiorenzo (N. Corsica) and the Maddalena Is. (N. Sardinia) and supplies, notably N. African cattle, brought to them. Eventually a virtually impregnable base was acquired at Malta in 1800 which remained the pivot of British Mediterranean supremacy until 1950.

(5) The advent of steam propulsion enabled fleets to disregard the wind, but tied them to coaling stations. Coaling at sea was possible, if difficult, in good weather. Admiralty and diplomatic policy became concerned to secure or develop harbours with large coal-yards at suitable bunkering intervals. After the Suez Canal opened, these included Port Said and Aden; on the Atlantic Coast of Africa, Freetown and Lagos; in the Far East, Singapore and Hong Kong. The govt. encouraged colliers to bring the famous Best Welsh Coal upon which the Admiralty insisted from Cardiff and Swansea. The refitting of metal, especially armoured ships also revolutionised dockyards themselves and the sort of people employed in them.

(6) From the B. of Trafalgar (1805) to about 1890, the Royal Navy could rely on its prestige and numbers to maintain international respect but its technology developed more quickly, especially after 1860 than the minds of its seaman officers. As one idea overtook another, e.g. breach-loading guns, barbettes, turrets and their ammunition hoists, hull subdivision, rams, mines, torpedoes, quick-firing secondary armaments, search lights, radio, smokeless powder, triple expansion engines, the fleet became increasingly heterogeneous. There was also much, mostly single-ship activity suppressing pirates and slavers, coping with epidemics and volcanoes, gunboat diplomacy, exploration and hydrography, but little development, because little needed, of strategic doctrine. Admirals became captains writ large. There were no naval staffs.

(7) All this changed when the Germans decided to dispute the seas after 1898 (see DREADNOUGHT; NAVAL RACE). Functionally by 1914 the Admiralty had developed a naval staff; strategically the fleet was concentrated near home; technically it reverted to standardisation and, by changing from coal to oil, had extended its political interests to oil fields, notably the Persian Gulf. World War I, however, brought an unexpected U-boat war which had to be fought by many small ships (see DOVER PATROL). The shipbuilding emphasis changed from a few large and expensive capital ships to many smaller ones. Despite post-war shrinkage this trend continued: so-called sloops were built to patrol the Gulf, and flat bottomed river gunboats to protect inland trading communities in China and Africa, but high level thought seemed nevertheless to concentrate on capital ships and cruisers and these were the subjects for debate in the international naval limitation conferences (q.v.) which took little notice of air power.

(8) Air power had not, however, been ignored. In a controversy about the merits of a unified RAF. as against a separate naval air service, the Admiralty got its way.

Some light battle cruisers were converted to aircraft carriers with a Fleet Air Arm to man them. The U.S.A. and Japan had some specially designed, which took time to come into service. Meanwhile the Washington Treaty capital ship ratio (Britain 15, U.S.A. 15, Japan 9) seemed to be disadvantageous because the Royal Navy had to spread its strength over the globe while its rivals could concentrate in limited areas, but British aircraft carrier strength for some years gave Britain an advantage unappreciated save by the Japanese. The British global problem was also well illustrated by the decision to build the fast county class cruisers which had the most powerful permissible treaty armament mounted on hulls designed to carry a battalion of infantry.

(9) The first distinct phase of World War II had two peaks, namely the defeat of the German surface fleet mostly in Norwegian seas by June 1940, and of the Italian battle fleet at Taranto (Nov. 1940) and C. Matapan (Mar. 1941). This had divergent effects. The Germans switched to U-boat warfare (see ATLANTIC, B. OF) against merchant traffic in the Atlantic, while the British from Malta waged a similar war on the route between Italy and Libya against convoys escorted by light Italian forces. The B. of the Atlantic lasted until the end of the war: the Mediterranean campaign until Oct. 1943 when Italy changed sides.

(10) These campaigns required vast numbers of small ships and aircraft which, with the replacement of merchant losses absorbed most of the maritime manpower and production. Potential Japanese aggression was however, anticipated. A new secret base at Addu Atoll, 600 miles south of Ceylon supported Colombo and Trincomalee. Admiral Somerville brought a big but elderly battle fleet to the area, while two modern battle cruisers under Admiral Philips went to Singapore. These, though unsuitable, were all that could be spared. The disaster which overtook Philips three days after Pearl Harbor (Dec. 1941) was the indirect but real consequence of the Atlantic and Mediterranean Wars. It entailed the loss of Hong Kong and Singapore, and when the Japanese bombed Ceylon, Somerville withdrew to Kilindini in E. Africa, thus abandoning the Indian seas. The defence of Ceylon had, however, mauled the enemy carrier-borne airforce. The expected further offensive did not materialise because Japanese fleets, already overstretched, were still engaged in Indonesia. Scratch combined Dutch, British, Australian and US squadrons under the Dutch Admirals Helfrich and Doorman fought to the death in the Straits of Macassar, the Java Sea and the Sunda Strait (Feb-Mar. 1942). Indonesia was lost but time was gained. The Japanese were soon defeated in carrier battles with the Americans in the Coral Sea just east of Indonesia, and at Midway I. in the Pacific (May-June 1942).

(11) It was necessary to leave the potentially powerful Americans, pitch-forked into the Pacific War as they had been, to recover the Far Eastern position, but they were inexplicably unprepared for shipping disasters in the Atlantic where they had already been part-committed for some months. In the absence of a U.S. convoy system, mere handfuls of U-boats sank 3,000,000 tons between Venezuela and Newfoundland in the first seven months of 1942. The main weight of defending U.S. Atlantic interests fell upon Britain. British anti-submarine trawlers were handed over to the American Navy and German Shipyards were bombed. This latter had less effect than had been hoped. On the other hand, two German battle cruisers (see SCHARNHORST AND GNEISENAU) with other ships emerged from Brest, passed Dover and, heavily damaged, reached Germany. This sensational affair improved the naval situation, because the southabout approaches to the Atlantic were no longer menaced by capital ships. The only similar threat now arose from the immense *Tirpitz* at Trondheim (Norway).

As she could not temporarily be attacked, the only dock on the Atlantic seaboard where she could be repaired (at St. Nazaire) was brilliantly raided and the dock gates destroyed.

(12) The Atlantic War dominated the whole war between Jan. 1941 and the Italian surrender (Sept. 1943) after which ships could be redeployed in the invasion of Europe and the counter-attack against Japan. German naval interference in the cross-channel traffic turned out to be trivial. The Japanese war, though primarily a trans-Pacific U.S. operation, was powerfully seconded from the Bay of Bengal under British command.

(13) Peace saw the natural reduction of the fleet and also something quite new, namely govts. ready to abandon the empire. They deprived the Royal Navy of all its overseas bases except (for a while) Hong Kong, and Gibraltar. On the other hand new designs, new weapons and electronics greatly raised the ratio of efficiency to tonnage. One combined result was the extraordinary Falklands campaign (1982) when the Argentinians had to be fought and were defeated at a distance of 8,000 miles from the home ports. The shrinkage of the fleet, however, continued and the Admiralty was absorbed into a larger Ministry of Defence obeying the limited strategic concepts of govts. determined to merge home sovereignty in a European federation. By 1992 all the naval home dockyards had been closed except Portsmouth, and there were hardly any private shipbuilders left. The Navy was reputed to have more surviving admirals than modern ships. *See also* BALTIC; various BATTLES; BLOCKADE; CINQUE PORTS; IMPRESSMENT; FLEET IN BEING; MERCANTILE MARINE; NAVIGATION; PIRACY; SHIPS.

NAWAB. *See* NABOB.

NAYLER, James (c. 1617-60) a parliamentary soldier, became a successful Quaker preacher in 1651. He travelled widely and was imprisoned at Appleby (Cumbria) in 1653 and briefly at Exeter in 1656, after which he made a triumphal Palm Sunday entry into Bristol riding a donkey, was convicted of blasphemy and severely punished. He resumed preaching just before his death.

NAZIMUDDIN, Khwaja (1894-1964) Bengal Moslem educated in England, became a prominent figure in the Muslim League and Ministry of Education (1929-34), Home Minister (1937-41) and Premier (1943-5) of Bengal. After Pakistani independence he became Premier of E. Bengal. He succeeded Mohammed Ali Jinnah as Governor General of Pakistan in Sept. 1948, resigned in 1951 to become Premier in succession to Liaqat Ali Khan, who had been murdered, and retired in 1952.

NEALE, John Mason (1818-66) a founder of the strongly Anglo-Catholic Cambridge Camden or Ecclesiological Society which, by its researches in mediaeval religious practices, powerfully influenced the style and arrangement of the many 19th cent. churches.

NEAR EAST. *See* EAST.

NEATH (Glam) being accessible by river, had a Roman auxiliary fort, a Norman Castle and an Abbey founded in 1130. It developed only slowly until the end of the 19th cent. when the metal and chemical industries were established.

NEBRASKA. *See* LOUISIANA PURCHASE.

NECHTAN, K. of the Picts (r. 706-24), accepted the conclusions of the Synod of Whitby (664) and was on good terms with Northumbria, but not, it seems, with his relatives with whom he was in constant dispute. Eventually he retired to a monastery, whence he occasionally emerged to do battle.

NECK, CRYING THE. A doll called "the neck" was made from the last stalks of the harvest. The reapers let out a melodious triple cry of "The Neck" followed by a triple "Way yen". This was often audible for several miles in still air. The bearer of the neck then ran to the farmhouse where girls, armed with pails of water, tried to drench him before he could get the neck inside. The winner in this contest was rewarded. The custom, with variations, lasted down to about 1890 in Devon, Pembroke and Shropshire.

NECK VERSE. *See* BENEFIT OF CLERGY; SANCTUARY AND ABJURATION.

NEEDLEWORK was, until about 1900, probably the most important single piece of training for all women, who habitually made or mended their own and their family's clothes. The annual output of work from plain sewing to high embroidery is unknown, but was undoubtedly enormous, forming a major element in the clothing and appearance of every family and therefore in the textile and clothing economy. All girls were taught, and the elaboration of their teaching is demonstrated by the vast numbers of surviving samplers. These were practical samples of types of sewing from darns to elaborate conversation pieces, made or assembled as working notes for future use, and as proof of skill. The art contracted rapidly with rise of mass produced throw-away garments. *See* CLOTHING.

***NE EXEAT REGNO* (Lat: Let him not leave the Kingdom).** At Common Law the King could forbid a subject to leave the Kingdom because every man in allegiance was bound to assist in its defence, but the writ in these terms came to be used in Chancery proceedings and for the recovery of debt, and is still so used.

NEGLIGENCE consists either in doing something carelessly e.g. baking a bun with a stone in it, or since the snail in the ginger beer case (*Donohue* v *Stevenson* 1934) the independent breach of a duty of care resulting in damage. This concept, which has spread to all the Common Law countries of the world, has had a vast effect on ordinary behaviour, business and insurance and because of a deadening effect on responsibility and enterprise, not always for the good.

NEGRI SEMBILAN. *See* MALAYSIA.

NEHRU (1) Pandit Motilal (1861-1931) Indian nationalist lawyer at Allahabad and founder of the *Independent*. His famous, charming and intellectual son **(2) Pandit Jawaharlal (1889-1964)** also an Allahabad lawyer, was educated in England, and launched his political career at the Indian National Congress at Bankpore in 1912. He was its Pres. in 1929-30 and 1936-7. A convinced socialist who flirted with Marxism in the 1920s, his purpose was to achieve an egalitarian industrialised India by extruding the British, destroying the princely states and abolishing the caste and most of the religious system. Naturally, he encountered internecine as well as anti-govt. violence and spent a total of 13 years in prison, yet entertained no animosity towards the British as British. At Partition he became Premier and instigated military subversion in order to increase the Indian and weaken the emerging Pakistan forces and though the Princes were supposed to have a free choice as to the country which they might join, he used force to coerce Hyderabad and Junagadh and provoked a long war in Kashmir. He also attacked the French and Portuguese settlements. Meanwhile, he pursued his policy of industrialisation and economic planning but attempted to interfere in the buffer states of Nepal and Bhutan and more distantly in Tibet. In 1962 this provoked a Chinese war in which the Indian army was defeated. A self-appointed spokesman of the non-aligned countries, he preached a non-violence which he did not practice. He died in office. His daughter **(3) Indira Ghandi (1917-84)** using methods of demagoguery also became Prime Minister. Inheriting her father's anti-sectarianism without his tact, she fell foul of the Sikhs and was murdered by a Sikh member of her own bodyguard.

NEILE, Richard (1562-1640) was an influential High Churchman who, as Bp. of Rochester (1608-10), gave Laud, his chaplain, valuable preferments. He was then successively Bp. of Lichfield (1610), Lincoln (1614) and Durham (1617). He became a Privy Councillor in 1627 and Bp. of Winchester in 1628 and was then an active member of the Star Chamber and the Court of High Commission. From 1631 until his death he was Abp. of York. *See* ADDLED PARLIAMENT.

NEILSON, Samuel (1761-1803) originator in 1791 with Henry McCracken of the United Irishmen. He and Wolfe Tone established the first branch at Belfast in 1792 and launched the republican *Northern Star*. Arrested in 1796, released but arrested again while reconnoitring a rescue of Lord Edward Fitzgerald, he was ultimately deported.

NEJD. *See* ARABIA.

NELSON, Horatio (1758-1805) Ld. (1798) Vist. (1801) Sicilian D. of BRONTE (1799) (1) a Norfolk man was related through his mother, a Suckling, to the Walpoles, and her brother, Captain Maurice Suckling gave him two decisive chances in early life. Charm and a gift for friendship supplemented his seamanlike genius and readiness to learn. Between 1770 when he first went to sea and Jan. 1793 when he was offered the command of his first line-of-battleship, the *Agamemnon* 64, he had had detailed experience in the Thames and Channel, in the Arctic, in the E. Indies from Bengal to Basra, in the W. Indies, the Baltic and North Sea, the N. Atlantic and N. American coast; he had also served in a merchantman, had commanded every sort of war vessel below the Line, and had been in charge of expeditions and garrisons ashore. He was probably the best trained captain of his day. His courage was famous. His subordinates of all ranks adored him; he had won the professional respect of his superiors particularly Hood, and the friendship of royalty in the shape of Prince William Henry, the future William IV, who was a colleague. These factors served to sustain an independence of naval conduct which was seldom otherwise tolerated in that age. Physically slight and temperamentally nervous and passionate, this maritime paragon's weakness was a tendency to fall headlong for the wrong women. His marriage was not a success. His affair with Lady Hamilton, the flamboyant demi-mondaine wife of the British minister to the Two Sicilies, has some, still disputed, historical importance.

(2) He first met her in Aug. 1793 on reaching Naples in the *Agamemnon* but almost immediately Hood, C-in-C Mediterranean, detached him to help conquer Corsica, and he commanded guns and landing parties (and lost an eye) in the capture of the key fortress of Calvi (1794). After employment as Commodore, in harassing French Riviera communications to Italy in 1796, in Feb. 1797, he took a decisive initiative under Sir John Jervis in the victory of Cape St. Vincent. This action was opportune. With half the navy mutinous, he and Jervis knew that the country needed victory; but his daring capture of two huge Spanish battleships, one across the deck of the other, fired public imagination.

(3) Promoted Rear-Admiral, he met his only repulse and lost an arm at Santa Cruz in the Canaries (July 1797) and in Apr. 1798 was sent to blockade the French Toulon squadron. It escaped in thick weather with Bonaparte aboard, took Malta, and landed him with an army in Egypt. A week later (1 Aug. 1798) Nelson fell upon the French squadron in Aboukir Bay and annihilated it (*see* MEDITERRANEAN WAR).

(4) He returned in triumph to Naples whose court decided to go to war in alliance with the Austrians. Ordered to co-operate with the latter he went to Leghorn (Nov. 1798) but the French, aided by local traitors overran the country, Nelson, having seen the Court and the Hamiltons safely to Palermo. The Neapolitan commander, Cardinal Ruffo had, meanwhile, secured a conditional capitulation of the rebels because Austrian troops in Lombardy had forced the French to retire. Nelson returned to Naples, annulled the capitulation, hanged the deserting Neapolitan commodore P.

Caracciolo, and re-established the Royal Govt. As however, the Court resolutely refused to leave Palermo, the Hamiltons naturally had to be there, so Nelson set up his H.Q. at Palermo and directed from there his operations in Maltese and (somewhat incommoded by Sir Sydney Smith) Egyptian waters. (*See* ACRE, EGYPT.) He returned with the Hamiltons overland to England in 1800, separated from his wife and became a Vice-Admiral in 1801, and was sent under Sir Hyde Parker to Copenhagen to demand the surrender of the Danish fleet. It was here that he fought and won the sanguinary battle against floating and pile batteries and turned his blind eye to Sir Hyde's signal for recall. He then returned, bought a house at Merton and set up there with the Hamiltons. In 1803 he was given the Mediterranean command and kept two years at sea blockading the French Toulon fleet. He was shot by a sniper at the B. of Trafalgar (q.v.).

NELSON'S COLUMN. *See* TRAFALGAR SQUARE.

NELSON, Sir Hugh Muir (1835-1906). Queensland minister and treasurer 1888-98 opposed to federation.

NELSON, Thomas (1822-92) established a branch of his father's publishing business in 1844, invented the rotary press for newspapers in 1850 and went into partnership with Bartholomews' the map engravers. One of the most important figures in 19th cent. publishing.

NENNI TELEGRAM (Apr. 1948) While the British Labour Party was supporting Italian right wing socialists in an Italian general election, John Platts-Mills, Konni Zilliacus and others telegraphed support for Signor Nenni, the left wing socialist leader. Platts-Mills and Zilliacus were expelled from the party.

NENNIUS (fl. 796) lived in Brecon or Radnor and was a pupil of Elbod, Bp. of Bangor. He is traditionally the author of the *Historia Britonum*.

NEO-CLASSICISM. The term was first used by William Rushton in 1863 and signifies either an adaptation of classical Greco-Roman models to modern purposes, mainly in architecture, or a modern revival of 18th cent. classicism. In either case a certain humourless "nobility", "grandeur" or "austerity" is associated with it. *See* ARCHITECTURE, BRITISH.

NEO GOTHIC. *See* ARCHITECTURE, BRITISH.

NEOT, St (?-?877) diminutive Glastonbury monk who settled as a hermit near Bodmin Moor and founded a small monastery at the place later named after him. In about 875 E. Leofric founded a priory at Eynesbury (Cambridgeshire) which obtained most of Neot's relics, and Eynesbury has since been called St. Neots too.

NEPAL, as a result of a mediaeval partition, consisted in the early 18th cent. of three major states (Katmandu, Patan and Bhatgaon) and a number of small hill principalities ruled by Hindu dynasties which had fled before the Moslem conquest of India. In 1769 one of these, under the Gurkha King Prithvi Narayan Shah, conquered the country and set up his capital Katmandu. Unification proceeded, despite minorities between 1775-1832, because leading noble families established regencies, particularly the Thapas from 1806-37 and the Ranas from 1846 onwards. The Ranas indeed became hereditary Maharajahs, relegating the King to a purely religious function.

The Nepalese advance along the Himalayas was checked in wars with the Tibetans from 1788-92, with the Sikhs in 1809 and with the British from 1814-16, but the Thapas realised that the British might be a rival threat and by the T. of Sagauli (1816) they ceded Garhwal and Kumaon, withdrew from Sikkim and agreed to accept British advice on foreign policy. In fact, as a renewal of Tibetan war in 1854-6 after the accession of the Ranas proved, this advice was only sketchily given or heeded.

Nepalese internal policies were conspiratorial and dominated by family interests. The Ranas felt no safer than the Thapas had been but they reinsured by a series of agreements with the British. The British now guided

Nepalese foreign policy and were allowed to recruit Gurkhas regularly within Nepal. In return they guaranteed the Ranas against their domestic as well as foreign opponents. But after the British withdrew from India the guarantee was no longer workable and was replaced by the opposite circumstance namely Indian republican pressures which were resented as much by the Nepalese as by their rulers. The British continued to recruit Gurkhas as troops, of whom 10,000 were serving in the British army in the 1980s, by which time Indian Govts. appreciated the function of Nepal as a buffer state.

NE PLUS ULTRA (Lat = No further). (1) A sticking point in negotiations. (2) The name of the French defensive lines from Avesnes le Comte *via* Arras to Bouchain which were ingeniously forced by Marlborough in Aug. 1711.

NEPTUNE. 18th cent. expression for a marine Atlas. Such collections of charts were mostly compiled by the British Admiralty.

NESS (related to *nose* and similar words in European languages) when part of a place name signifies a promontory or cape (as in Orfordness) and is generally considered to be evidence of a Scandinavian settlement.

NESSELRODE, Karl Vasilievitch, Count (1780-1862) was Russian Foreign Minister from 1814-56, and took part in all the international congresses of the period including the P. of Paris (1856) which closed the Crimean War.

NEST (?1088-?) was the daughter of Rhys ap Tewdwr, last independent prince of South Wales. Strong minded and seductive, she figures, legitimately or otherwise in the ancestry of most of the Norman Irish families. (1) Her son HENRY by her lover K. Henry I left three children of whom MEILER was justiciar of Ireland from 1199-1208. (2) In about 1202 she married GERALD of WINDSOR, Constable of Pembroke. Of the four children believed to have sprung from this union, WILLIAM of Carew was the ancestor of the Carews and the Lords of Knocktopher; MAURICE FitzGERALD was the ancestor of the great Geraldine houses of Naas, Kildare, Desmond and Burnchurch; DAVID was Bp. of St David's; ANGHARAT married William de Barry and was the mother of GIRALDUS CAMBRENSIS the historian, and through another son PHILIP, ancestress of the Es. of Barrymore. In 1108 Nest was willingly abducted by (3) STEPHEN, Constable of Cardigan, by whom she had a son ROBERT, who settled in Cork.

NESTORIANS hold that the incarnate Christ contains two Persons, one human, one divine. *See* MALABAR CHRISTIANS.

NETHERLANDS (1) The mediaeval seven parts (Holland, Zeeland, Utrecht, Overijssel, Gröningen, Drenthe and Friesland) were feudalised mainly under the Counts of Holland and ecclesiastical princes such as the Bp. of Utrecht. Divergent economic interests and Franco-Burgundian politics prevented political cohesion, though the many communities became very rich through the wool and cloth trades and shipping and they invested the profits in land reclamation.

(2) This reclamation and five other factors provoked a common self-consciousness. These were, firstly, the accident that the Burgundian inheritance, of which the Low Countries, since 1364 were a part, fell to the Habsburgs and so to the Habsburg rulers of Spain; secondly, this occurred during the period of the American and E. Indian explorations; thirdly Spanish Habsburg policy restricted colonial trade to Castilians and so thwarted the ambitions of Dutch enterprise with capital to spare; fourthly, the Reformation, particularly the Calvinist doctrines began to spread after 1550 and led to a tremendous outbreak of church vandalism in 1566; lastly there was stiff R. Catholic opposition to the Reformation, but its seventies were mitigated in the first half of the cent. during the Governorships of two understanding Burgundian princesses.

(3) If the people were forbidden to trade or worship as they pleased, the religious riots of 1566 proclaimed to all the world that Madrid's law and policy were being flouted. Covert congregations flourished, and beyond the horizon the shipmen of Holland and Zeeland, sometimes in squadrons, attacked Castilian ships, sold their booty in English ports and even sailed to the Americas. These so-called *Beggars,* congregated in the Downs off Deal, where Q. Elizabeth's govt. turned a blind eye.

(4) K. Philip II determined to enforce the law. In 1567 the existing govt. was replaced by a ruthless D. of Alba. The *alcábala,* a 10% sales tax, was imposed to finance his enlarged army. Executions by axe and fire rose ten-fold and claimed in 1568 the popular Counts of Egmont and Hoorn. Such measures did not cow the people, they merely gave enormous offence, while the *alcábala* was a daily irritation in an artificially restrained economy. The population became accustomed to secret resistance and wholesale tax evasion. Alba's methods ashore were quite inadequate to their purpose and at sea he was at a hopeless disadvantage. The Beggars by now amounted to a floating republic. In 1572, with local Calvinist help they seized the strategic port of Brill and so could partially control the oceanic trade of the Rhine delta. In the same year the States of Holland met at Dordrecht and made William the Silent, P. of Orange (?-1584) stadholder (regent) of Holland and Zeeland.

(5) William held a patchwork of lordships and offices in five of the seven areas. As stadholder it was his duty in K. Philip's eyes to enforce the royal policy. In his own it was to enforce the will of the King as a local not a Castilian ruler. Moreover, William was a Calvinist, and Hollanders and Zeelanders were doing most of the damage to Castilian trade. He did not stop them; indeed, as sovereign of Orange he commissioned them as privateers.

(6) The influx of Spanish-American bullion created an inflation which, combined with piracy and rebellion, made it hard to pay the Spanish troops. In 1576 they sacked Antwerp for their pay (*The Spanish Fury*). It now became clear that the disorders, hitherto legalised as efforts against the King's evil representatives, had to be transformed into a political revolution. In 1579 most of the country subscribed to the essentially military Union of Utrecht in which the princes of Orange figured as military commanders. In everything except name, this was a declaration of independence.

(7) The Union ushered in 80 warlike years, divided between 1609-21 by a truce. William the Silent was assassinated in 1584 but other princes of his House conducted the campaigns. The period was one of great prosperity, especially after 1609, for no other nation had as yet developed a large-scale merchant navy and the country not only exported its manufactures but carried most of the European water-borne trade from Finland to the Levant and Indonesia (*see* EAST INDIA CO – DUTCH). The Spanish seizure of Portugal (1580) encouraged the Dutch to attack the Portuguese spice trade and their E. Indian spice colonies which, save in Timor, they largely took over. The profits were fabulous. The period 1609-1713 was the Dutch Golden Age, which created the famous townscapes and the rural dykes and windmills of further land reclamation.

(8) The P. of Westphalia (1648) gave the Netherlands their modern territorial extent, but it was the product of deep war weariness which had been increasingly asserted by the rising burgher traders in opposition to the House of Orange. William of Orange II died of smallpox in 1650. William III was a child. Five of the seven provinces discontinued their stadholderships, but in 1652 the country was involved in war with Cromwellian England (*see* DUTCH WARS – FIRST). This ended in a collusive peace whereby the House of Orange, as representing a war party, was legally excluded from public office (*The Act of Seclusion*) for the benefit alike of the Dutch and English republicans. This *Stadholderless Period* continued under

the leadership of the brothers de Witt through the Second Dutch War (q.v.) until 1672.

(9) A new threat had now developed from France. The wars of 1672-1713 began with a sudden French invasion. The Dutch turned to William III, lynched the de Witts and opened the dykes (*see* DEVOLUTION; LEAGUE OF AUGSBURG; SPANISH SUCCESSION; WARS OF). From this time until the P. of Utrecht (1712) the foreign political history of Britain and the Netherlands was inseparable, more especially as between 1689-1702 William III was King of England, Scotland and Ireland in right of his wife Mary II (who died in 1694). By the accession of Q. Anne (r. 1702-14) this arrangement ceased to be institutional but was continued as an alliance; the Stadholdership lapsed and Marlborough and Godolphin who conducted English war and policy until overthrown, dealt with a confused but friendly oligarchy led by Heinsius, the Grand Pensionary of Holland. A prime Anglo-Dutch purpose was to interpose a BARRIER of fortresses in the southern Netherlands to safeguard the Seven Provinces from French ambitions. This barrier had been held since 1579 by the Spaniards, but when Spain joined France in the wars, it was taken over by the French, and much of Marlborough's Anglo-Dutch war effort was devoted to its reconquest. The P. of Utrecht put it into the hands of the Austrian Habsburgs.

(10) The internal triumph of the commercial oligarchies was political rather than economic. The wars had cost much in lives and money and the English had superseded the Dutch in the cloth and the carrying trades. Economic stagnation, a balance kept boringly stable by the Indonesian colonies, supervened. This was not expected by the commercial oligarchies. Hence when new wars threatened there was a reversion to the House of Orange. In 1747 the Stadholderate was made hereditary for William IV of Orange. The Republic now had an uncrowned constitutional regent. William V succeeded him in 1751. He was of no consequent but his courageous wife Wilbelmina (sister of Frederick the Great of Prussia) upheld the family position at home (with Prussian help) and abroad in yet another war with Britain (1775-83).

(11) The shaky structure continued until thc Frcnch revolutionary wars. It was then overthrown. A French army imposed the BATAVIAN REPUBLIC (1795-1806) which was converted into a KINGDOM OF HOLLAND (1806-10) for Louis Bonaparte and then (*see* FRENCH COASTAL ANNEXATIONS) incorporated into his brother's empire in 1810. This lasted only until 1813. Between 1795-1813, the English with their dominant sea power, took over and exploited the Dutch colonial empire.

(12) The Dutch part of the Vienna settlements (1815) was based on the widely accepted need to make French northward expansion impossible. This was as much a British interest as a Dutch. To this end the former Austrian (P. of Utrecht) Netherlands was incorporated in the new KINGDOM OF THE NETHERLANDS to which Britain returned the colonies in order that the combined Kingdom could afford the necessary troops and baffler fortresses. The combination proved unworkable. The Dutch Calvinist administration in a R. Catholic area was intolerant, rapacious and oppressive. In 1830 a rebellion led to the creation of the separate KINGDOM OF THE BELGIANS and the barrier was supplemented by a treaty whereby the internationally guaranteed new kingdom was interposed between French and the Dutch, who obtained the territories on both sides of the Scheldt so as to be able to strangle Antwerp in favour of Amsterdam.

(13) As a small country with large colonies, the Netherlands entered an era of material but decadent prosperity and, unlike Belgium, escaped the ravages of World War I, while its territory became a channel of communication and espionage between the Allies and the Central Powers. The ancient habit of land reclamation re-emerged as construction of the Zuider Zee dam began

in 1923, and the great dam was ready just before the outbreak of World War II. In May 1940, the German outflanking swing through the Netherlands and Belgium was accompanied by an intimidating air offensive and the bombing of Rotterdam. Morale collapsed in four days and Q. Wilhelmina and the govt. fled to Britain whence they continued to administer the Indonesian empire. This in its turn was lost to the Japanese after a much stouter defence lasting three months in 1942. Only the oil- and sugar-rich Surinam was left.

(14) The empire having been effectively lost, Dutch attention after World War II was directed to the recovery of considerable territories in the Zuider Zee (now the fresh water Yssel Meer), the dyking and pumping of channels between the Zeeland islands and the development of European markets for the growing electrical and chemical industries and the banking houses. The first step was the formation of Benelux (q.v.), the second the formation of the European Community. *See also* BELGIUM; BURGUNDY; DUTCH WARS; FLANDERS; HOLLAND; INDONESIA; STATES GENERAL; SURINAM; ZEELAND.

NETLEY (Hants.) had a large Cistercian abbey founded in 1239. In 1863 the Royal Victoria Military Hospital was established there and became the training centre of the Royal Army Medical Corps.

NEUHOFF, Baron (?-1756). *See* CORSICA.

NEUILLY, T. of (signed Nov. 1919: in force Aug. 1920). *See* BULGARIA

NEUSTRIA. After 567 the western Frankish realm.

NEURATH, Baron Konstantin von (1873-1956) originally a diplomat, was German Ambassador to London from 1931-32 when he became Minister of Foreign Affairs. His responsibility for the German withdrawal from the League of Nations and for the reoccupation of the Rhineland was slight because Hitler meant to do these things anyway. On the other hand as German Protector of Bohemia and Moravia from 1939-41 he set up the oppressive state machinery which was later exploited by Reinhard Heydrich. Hitler dismissed him as too indulgent. *See* NUREMBERG TRIALS.

NEUTRAL ISLANDS (W. Indies 1732-63) Britain and France agreed to differ over the ownership of Dominica, Grenada, St. Lucia, St. Vincent and Tobago and evacuated their respective nationals, who promptly started to return. The running disputes were a factor in causing the Seven Years' War as a result of which the islands, save St. Lucia became British.

NEUTRALITY in a war was never a fixed and unalterable condition, for the acts of the neutral state would depend upon its own view of its interests and the belligerent's view of theirs and there was no means, save reprisals, to ensure impartiality. Nevertheless belligerents paid lip service and somctimes allegiance to ccrtain approximate norms viz: (a) a neutral ought not deliberately by its commercial or diplomatic policy, to support the war economy of one belligerent more than another, and if it does so the injured belligerent may take economic or diplomatic reprisals if it can. (b) Warlike intervention or collusion may result in the neutral being treated as a belligerent enemy. Hence belligerent troops and aircraft entering neutral territory must be disarmed and interned, and belligerent warships must not lie in a neutral port for more than 24 hours. Moreover, a neutral must not break a blockade which has been publicly proclaimed and actually enforced, but is not bound to respect a mere "paper blockade". Despite learned dispute and so-called international 'law', in this field the law is the law of the strongest or the most cunning, regulated by expediency e.g. in World War II Spain in breach of her neutrality entertained a German navigational radio beacon near Corunna, but the British took no diplomatic or other steps against it because they had learned how to 'bend' its emissions and use it for their own purposes.

NEUTRALITY PACT (1870). Austro-Hungary, Britain, Italy and Russia on British initiative agreed not to abandon neutrality in the Franco-German war without notice to the others.

NEUTRALITY PROCLAMATION (1793) by U.S. Pres. Washington, on the outbreak of War between Britain and France, declared that the U.S.A. would be "friendly and impartial towards belligerent powers" and warned U.S. citizens against involvement. It formed the precedent for U.S. attitudes to wars outside the Americas.

NEVILLE. Though claiming descent from one GILBERT, supposed commander of the Conqueror's fleet in 1066, the ascent of this formidable clan **(A)** began with Henry II's patronage of **(1) Alan (?-1176)** a Lincolnshire landowner, who became Chief Justice (C.J.) of the Forest in 1167. His son **(2) Geoffrey (?-1225)** was a royal Chamberlain from 1207-25, Sheriff of Wiltshire in 1207 and of Yorkshire in 1214 when he was sent to raise support for K. John among the barons of Poitou. In the winter of 1215-16 he held Scarborough castle against John's opponents. He was Seneschal of Poitou from 1215-19 and from 1223-25. This branch of the family died out in 1345.

(B) A more successful line was descended from one of Geoffrey's brothers **(3) Ralph (?-1222)** a companion of Richard I on crusade, C.J. of the Forest in 1198 and royal Treasurer in 1208. Both his sons **(4) Hugh (?-1234)** and grandson **(5) John (?-1246)** were C.J.s of the Forest, John being dismissed and fined for Forest infringements. These were the ancestors of the Lords NEVILLE of Essex of the 14th and 15th cents.

(C) The most important line stemmed from **(6) Gilbert (?- c. 1169)** a brother of Alan (1 above). His granddaughter and after the death of her brother **(7) Henry** in 1227, sole heiress married **(8) Robert fitz MALDRED Ld. of RABY (Co. Durham)** who was directly descended from Uchtred, son of E. Gospatrick (*see* NORTHUMBRIA, EARLDOM OF) and son-in-law of K. Ethelred the Unready, but his heirs took their mother's name. His grandson **(9) Robert (?1232-82)** was Warden of Bamburgh and Newcastle in 1258 and Governor of Norham and Wark castles. He became C.J. of the Forest beyond the Trent in 1261 and of all Forests in 1264. He was a guarantor of the Provisions of Oxford but supported Henry III in the Barons' War and commanded the royal troops north of the Trent. His brother **(10) Geoffrey (?-1285)** another royalist, became Constable of Dover (1265) and of Scarborough (1270). He also commanded in N. Wales in 1276-7 and in 1282. **(11) Ralph (?1291-1367) 4th Ld. NEVILLE of RABY (1331)** was Seneschal of Edward II's household and made a joint warden of the Scottish March with Henry Percy in 1334. In 1346 they won the spectacular victory at Neville's Cross in which they took the Scottish King. Of his sons **(12) John (?-1388)** the wealthy **5th Ld.,** commanded the fleet in 1370, signed the Breton alliance of 1372 and besieged Brest. He was one of the lords impeached in 1376 but the sentence was reversed in 1377 and he became a very successful military Lieutenant of Aquitaine. After 1381 he was constantly in demand on the Scottish border and he built the powerful fortifications of Raby Castle, besides adorning Durham Cathedral. His brother **(13) Sir William (?-?1389)** was a courtier, admiral in the North Sea and a Lollard, while another brother **(14) Alexander (?-1392)** became Abp. of York in 1373. He had a series of disputes with collegiate churches in the province, especially with Beverley. Richard II settled them in his favour in return for his political support; he witnessed the judges' formal opinions taken at Nottingham in Aug. 1387, and apparently favoured extreme courses, for he was one of the five appealed of treason by the Lords Appellant in Nov. He fled northwards and the Feb. 1388 Parliament (The Merciless) condemned him in absence. He reached

Flanders, and Urban VI was induced to translate him to St. Andrews.

John's son **(15) Ralph (1364-1425) 6th Ld. and 1st E. of WESTMORLAND (1397)** joint warden of the March from 1388 was also associated with the court party and assisted at the condemnation of Gloucester, Arundel and their associates in 1397. In 1399 however, his defection contributed strongly to Richards overthrow and he was prominent in the negotiations for his abdication. Henry IV made him marshal, gave him some of the Percy estates and added the Captaincy of Roxburgh to his wardenship in 1402. His strategic sense frustrated the rebellion of 1405, for he prevented the rebels uniting, dispersed those in Cleveland and took Scrope and Mowbray. Though much of his work as warden consisted in military and diplomatic dealings with the Scots, he was an executor of Henry VI's will and an assistant of the Regent Bedford. He raised the family to commanding national importance mainly through marriages. His daughters by his first wife married great northern barons, Mauley, Dacre of Gilsland, Umfraville of Kyme and Scrope of Bolton. His second wife (1396) was Joan Beaufort, half sister of Henry IV, who until his death regularly conferred lands, offices, wardships and pensions upon him or him and her jointly, including important royal rights in Yorkshire. This second marriage, however, led to a family feud. Ralph, by resettlements transferred many properties from his first wife's descendants (the E.s of Westmorland) to those of his Beaufort wife. Meanwhile her daughters married into Staffords, Despensers, Percys and Mowbrays and of the sons **(16) William (?-1463) Ld. FAUCONBERG (1424)** in right of his wife, **E. of KENT (1460)** was a mercenary commander mainly in Normandy; he held Calais for his nephew Warwick the Kingmaker in 1459 and fought at Towton. His brother **(17) Robert (1404-57)** was Bp. of Salisbury from 1427-38 and thereafter Bp. of Durham. His brother **(18) Edward (?-1476) 1st Ld. BERGAVENNY** (1450) obtained his large Welsh estates in 1436 through marriage with Elizabeth Beauchamp, but the lordship only in 1450. His brother **(19) Richard (1400-60) 1st E. of SALISBURY (1429)** in right of his wife Alice of Montacute, was warden of the West March from 1420, and of both Marches from 1434 and he inherited the properties resettled by his father. He was in conflict with his nephew **(20) Ralph (?-1484) 2nd E. of WESTMORLAND** who preferred violence to litigation and with whom he fought a series of minor wars in the Border country. Richard's enormous wealth and connections made him the natural support of the Yorkist connection (*see* HENRY VI; ROSES, WARS OF) but he tended later to follow in the wake of his famous *s.* **(21) Richard (1428-71) E. of WARWICK (1449) "the Kingmaker".** The father was murdered at Pontefract after the Lancastrian victory at Wakefield (1460). The son whose title and vast properties had come through his wife Anne Beauchamp, now added his father's even greater properties, and in 1470 betrothed his daughter **(22) Anne (1456-85)** to Edward P. of Wales (*see* below). The Kingmaker's brother **(23) John (?-1471) E. of NORTHUMBERLAND (1464)** was employed by Edward IV in the North, and after he defeated the Lancastrian-Percy forces at Hexham (1464) received the Percy estates and earldom. He changed sides with his brother, partly because he lost the estates, and both were killed at Barnet (1471). Another brother **(24) George (?1433-76)** became Bp. of Exeter in 1458. He did not openly support his family's policy in 1459 but benefited by becoming Chancellor in 1460, and Abp. of York in 1465. He was a dextrous diplomat who secured a Flemish commercial treaty (1463), French neutrality and a Scottish peace (1464). Like the Kingmaker, he drifted apart from the King as the Woodville's rose in influence. He was deprived of the Great Seal in 1467. In 1468 he was superficially reconciled to Edward IV, but took a prominent part in the conspiracies and risings of 1469-70 and became Chancellor during Henry VI's readeption. He surrendered Henry VI to Edward IV and was imprisoned at Hammes until 1475.

The death of the Kingmaker and John left Anne extremely rich. The death of P. Edward at Tewkesbury (1471) left her without a husband. In 1474 she married Richard D. of Gloucester and died during his reign as Richard III whereby her tremendous inheritance passed to the crown.

NEVIN. See CAERNARVONSHIRE.

NEVIS (W. Indies) was settled by the English in 1628 and occupied by the French from 1781-83. It was governed together with St. Kitts and Anguilla. Nelson was married there in 1787.

NEWALL, Cyril Norton (1886-1963) 1st Ld. (1940) as Chief of the Air Staff from 1937-40 was responsible for the rise of the R.A.F. before World War II. He was Gov. Gen. of New Zealand from 1941-46.

NEW AMSTERDAM. See NEW NETHERLAND; NEW YORK.

NEWARK (Notts.) at a crossing of the Trent and the intersection of the Fosse Way and the Great North Road, had a Roman, and on a different site, a Saxon fortification, replaced in 1125 by a powerful castle built by the Bps. of Lincoln and kept in regular repair because of its strategic importance. It withstood three sieges in the Civil War. K. John died there in 1216. Throughout the middle ages the town maintained a modest but steady prosperity as a local market and with industries, such as brewing, related to agriculture. After the coming of the railways engineering became important and also the quarrying and despatch of gypsum. After World War II the agricultural connection was further developed by the production of sugar beat, artificial manures, and agricultural machinery.

NEWARK, Ld. See LESLIE, DAVID.

NEW BRITAIN (Pac.) was discovered by Le Maire in 1616 and named by Carteret in 1767. German copra traders arrived in 1873 and had provoked native rebellion by 1878 when they were saved by a Wesleyan missionary. Annexed in 1884 by the Germans who established the capital at Rabaul, the island was seized by the Australians in 1914 and the German planters deported. It became an Australian mandate and was occupied by the Japanese from 1942-44. See NEW GUINEA.

NEW BRUNSWICK. See CANADA.

NEWBURY (Berks.) (i.e. the new settlement from the neighbouring village of Speen) was mostly part of the Domesday manor of Ulvriton owned by Ernulph of Hesdain, from whose family it passed to the Crown. There was a castle, and another castle at Donnington nearby, and the place was the centre of a wealthy area of farms and sheepruns supporting a cloth industry. The town owes much to the mediaeval cloth financier John of Winchcombe ("Jack of Newbury") who built the church, but there was already a hospital in the 13th cent. and K. John granted a fair in 1215 with whose profits he endowed almshouses. There was a prescriptive corporation which sent two M.P.s to Parliament from 1302 and a grammar school founded probably in 1466. Elizabeth I had the corporation's constitution reduced to writing in a charter of 1596 and in 1601 she chartered the Weaver's Co, which in due course, built itself a cloth hall. This turned out almost to mark the end of the cloth prosperity, for the industry moved to the natural sources of power, leaving Newbury as an agricultural market and flour milling centre. The race course too preserved some prosperity from the wreck of the surrounding horse breeders.

NEW CALEDONIA (S. Pac.) was discovered by Capt. Cook in 1774 but seized by the French in 1854. They used it as a penal colony until 1894. It is rich in precious metals, and in copper, lead, zinc, nickel, chrome, cobalt and manganese.

NEWCASTLE-under-LYME (Warw.) grew up as an agricultural market for the adjoining district, round a castle completed in 1146. It remained relatively unimportant until coal mining developed in the early 19th cent. when tile making (connected with the development of Birmingham) and a textile industry began. In the 20th cent. a complex of industries connected with electrical equipment caused the borough to expand and in 1932 to take in adjacent areas.

NEWCASTLE, D. of. See GEORGE I-7,10; PELHAM-5; WARS OF 1739-48.

NEWCASTLE COMMISSION (1858) reported on popular education. Children left school at eleven and about 95% of children under eleven were in the schools. The quality was low, state-aided and inspected schools being slightly better than the others. It recommended school boards for towns of over 40,000, examination in the Three Rs and payment by results. The govt. rejected the Boards but accepted the rest. See TAUNTON COMMISSION.

NEWCASTLE PROGRAMME (Oct. 1891) of the Liberal Party cobbled together Home Rule for Ireland, Church disestablishment for Wales and Scotland, abolition of the plural vote, triennial parliaments, payment of M.P.s, reform of leaseholds, the creation of district and parish councils, employer's accident liability, and shorter working hours. Designed to please the disparate elements within, its apparently incongruous components displeased powerful disparate elements outside the party. Its champions expounded it as the application of Liberal principles to different situations. See SALISBURY'S SECOND GOVT.-12.

NEWCASTLE-UPON-TYNE (Rom: *PONS AELII* = Aelian Bridge). As Aelius was the family name of the Emperor Hadrian, the town was doubtless founded in connection with the building of his wall (c. 118-26). Roman relics abound but little is known of Newcastle before the Norman Conquest. The New Castle was begun c. 1090 and a Norman church on the site of an earlier one in 1091. The Castle keep was not built until 1172-7. The church was burned down in 1216 but soon replaced.

(2) The Tyne is an excellent tidal haven. Wool exports became valuable in 13th cent and consequently the town was walled against the Scots probably in the 1280s. A shipbuilding industry grew up, particularly at Tynemouth, which in its turn created a traffic with the Baltic in spars, tar, copper and hemp, while the growing population, after the sudden migration of the herring from Scandia to the Dogger Bank, supported quickly prosperous fisheries.

(3) Coal was already being dug in the vicinity, and by 1380 was being exported to London where it was known as 'seacoal'. The wool exports fell off against competition from southern cloth but the coal trade flourished with improved mining and larger locally built colliers. By 1565 exports had risen to 35,000 tons. James I issued a proclamation against pollution by coal fires in London, and by Charles I's reign overseas as well as coastwise exports of coal had raised the trade to 400,000 tons.

(4) The advent of steam powered iron shipping and the ability of the new railways after 1838 to add unlimited iron to the local coal, revolutionised the local economy. The Tyne developed the engineering industries for building and repairing ships (including warships) and supplied coal to fuel them. These and ancillary industries soon diversified so that Newcastle was exporting (e.g.) metal goods, machinery, boilers and fire bricks, while the older sail-related industries went over to linen, cotton and coarse textiles. This headlong 19th cent. advance, however, proliferated slums and polluted the air and the river.

(5) Moreover it was checked by World War I which closed the Baltic and European (other than French) markets, while U-boats interrupted the already reduced shipping. Enlistment and then conscription masked

the underlying unemployment, but when the men returned from war there were not enough jobs (because the old markets did not reopen) nor good houses in which to live. A slow economic recovery was postponed by the 1929-31 slump, and its succeeding recovery by World War II, whose commercial and traffic effects were graver than those of World War I, and accompanied by destructive bombing. The wholesale sinkings did keep the shipyards busy on replacements, but British shipbuilding, as the war advanced, became supplementary to American mass-production and when the war and the sinkings ended, foreign-built ships were in possession, and the demand for Tyne-built ships fell rapidly. By 1980 the Tyne had almost ceased to build ships, while oil had superseded coal. The industries had had to be converted to lighter employments such as chemicals, plastics and electrical goods, bringing with them enormous retraining problems.

NEW CHURCHES, COMMISSION FOR (1711) was set up to erect 50 metropolitan churches but built only twelve. These however, included such interesting churches as Gibbs' St. Mary-le-Strand (1714-6) and St. Martins-in-the-Fields (1722-6), and Hawksmoor's Christ Church, Spitalfields (1714-29).

NEW COLLEGE, OXFORD. See WYKEHAM, WILLIAM OF.

NEWCOMEN, Thomas (1663-1729) designed, in about 1700, an atmospheric steam engine, which was used as the standard mine pumping engine until about 1775.

NEW COURTIERS. See COMMONWEALTH AND PROTECTORATE-17.

NEW DEAL was the name of economic and social programmes introduced by the U.S. Pres. Franklin Roosevelt to deal with the slump which had brought him to power in the 1932 elections. The First New Deal (1933-35) was opposed by conservatives and big business, and much of the legislation on which it was based was held to be unconstitutional by the Supreme Court. The Second New Deal (1935-8) was a deliberate bid for popular support on the basis of deficit financing and anti-trust measures. It introduced Americans to the idea of govt. intervention in moments of economic difficulty, and secured for Roosevelt his third term of office.

NEWDEGATE, Charles (1816-87) was Conservative M.P. for N. Warwickshire from 1843-85.

NEWDIGATE (1) Sir Richard (1602-78) Bt., was C.J. of the King's Bench from 1660. His great grandson **(2) Sir Roger (1719-1806) 5th Bt.** was M.P. for Middlesbrough from 1741-47 and for Oxford University from 1750-80. A traveller and collector of marbles, he was benefactor of University College Oxford and of the Radcliffe Library, and in 1805, endowed the Newdigate Prize for English verse.

NEW ECONOMIC POLICY (N.E.P.) (1921-27) was a tactical reversion to private enterprise devised by Lenin to head off the miseries inflicted by the Russian Revolution. Not in real terms very successful, it created an atmosphere of relative well-being after the previous horrors, and was cast aside, as Lenin intended, by his successors as soon as convenient. The term is used for any similar tactical reversion by a Marxist govt.

NEW ENGLAND (U.S.A.) now comprises Maine, New Hampshire, Vermont, Massachusetts, Rhode Island and Connecticut. **(1)** The Dutch explored the Connecticut River in 1614, and John Smith discovered the cod fisheries in 1616. A New England Company was chartered in 1620 (see CHARTERED COMPANIES). Settlements (partly under the auspices of the Council for New England) of English origin were made in all areas except Vermont between 1620 (The Pilgrims of Plymouth) and 1640. The Council faded out, weakened by royal interference and the English Civil War, which left the area unprotected against the Indians and the Dutch; Massachusetts, Connecticut, Plymouth and New Haven accordingly formed the virtually independent New England Confederation of 1643; this enabled them, under John

Endecott (Governor in 1644, 1649, 1651-3 and 1655-65) to hold their own, take the Dutch fort at Hartford (1654) and to weather Indian opposition.

(2) The Dutch New Netherland was conquered and English political suzerainty restored in 1664 but Indian hostility and power grew, culminating in the great Iroquois conflict known (after one of their chiefs) as King Philip's War (1673-6). The damage retarded the colonial advance by 50 years, but ended Iroquois aggressive capacity in the area. The Confederation was dissolved in 1684 when the Massachusetts charter was revoked. Soon the British Govt. perceived the dangers of French penetration by way of Canada and the Mississippi inspired by Louis XIV, and in 1686 attempted to form a more extensive co-ordinating body, called the Dominion of New England, under the presidency of Sir Edmund Andros. James II instructed Andros to rule without the local assemblies, but gave him insufficient money and troops to enforce his will; the scheme thus failed and Andros was deposed when his master abdicated.

(3) New England early developed a foreign trade and consequently benefited under the Navigation Acts of 1651 to 1696 and the later Trade Acts which supplemented them. The elimination of local French power in the Seven Years War removed the most compelling motive for loyalty, and the substitution of mild taxation for considerable subsidies inflamed local political sentiment. It was the New England states which led the rebellion.

(4) The area remained predominantly of British stock until after the American Civil War, when many French Canadians, Irish and Italians settled there.

NEW ENGLAND WAY. A puritan scheme (1640-60) whereby the franchise in the Massachusetts Bay Colony was limited to church members who chose their minister, who in turn chose the civil authorities.

NEW FOREST (Hants.). This substantial area was afforested under William I. Contemporary propaganda claimed that several villages were destroyed in the process, and William II's accidental death in it was, of course, divine retribution for this. Under Henry I it was farmed out to Waleran fitz William for the fairly high amount of £25 p.a. and in 1200 his son Walter was paying the same. The ancient Court of Verderers was reformed by Acts of 1677, 1879, 1964 and 1970. Though the forest law was abrogated within the boundary called The Perambulation of the Forest, save as to the appointment of verderers, in 1971, the wild character of the Forest and the limitations on private development continue.

NEWFOUNDLAND (1) The banks were fished by the Iberians and French from about 1496. European interest in the land began with the Cabot's visit in 1497 and Sir Humphrey Gilbert claimed it for England in 1583. Drake harried the Spanish and Portuguese fishermen, leaving the British and French as the main contenders for the fishery. There were unsuccessful British efforts, mostly through a Newfoundland Company chartered in 1611, to establish colonies in 1610-21. In 1713 (P. of Utrecht) the mainland was ceded to Britain by France, which however retained fishing rights, the Is. of St. Pierre and Miquelon and the right to land for the purpose of drying nets and curing fish. Spain abandoned her, by then minimal rights in 1763.

(2) Since the American colonists had fished there before the rebellion, they claimed to continue these rights after the British recognition of their independence.

(3) There was a non-resident British Governor from 1729, but the first resident Governor with a real administrative function was appointed only in 1824 when the I. began to develop from a fishery to a colony. By 1860 a local spirit of independence had developed. The Newfoundlanders held themselves aloof from Canadian federation at the Charlottetown Conference of 1864, and at subsequent negotiations in 1895. During all this time French and American claims in and connected with the fisheries were engendering increasing friction. The French problem was solved in 1904 when Britain bought out the landing rights. The alleged American rights were pronounced non-existent by the Hague International Court of 1910.

(4) Pronounced an independent dominion by the Statute of Westminster 1931, the world slump, acting on an overspecialised economy, bankrupted the govt. which turned to Britain for help. From 1934-49 accordingly Britain subsidised the island but ruled it through a commission of govt. During this time opinion slowly changed in favour of confederation with Canada, and after a vigorous political campaign waged in 1948 by Joseph Smallwood, a small majority voted for confederation. Newfoundland accordingly became a Canadian province in Mar. 1949.

NEW FRANCE. See CANADA.

NEWGATE PRISON (London) which already existed in 1190 was used for those charged with felonies and felons who had been reprieved from execution. It was overcrowded, short of water and pestilential. Dick Whittington left a fund to rebuild it and this was done in 1425. Thereafter debtors were often admitted. Though damaged in the Great Fire of 1667, this building was in use in 1767 when a further rebuilding was begun. The scaffold was moved from Tyburn to a place just outside it in 1773. The partially completed building was fired by the Gordon rioters in 1783, and most of the prisoners escaped. Debtors were sent elsewhere in 1815. Public executions ceased in 1868 and the place was used only for remands from the Central Criminal Court from 1881 until its demolition in 1902.

NEW GRANADA. See COLOMBIA.

NEW GUINEA (IRIAN) was discovered by the Portuguese in 1526. The Dutch occupied the western half in 1828. Queensland annexed the Eastern half in 1883 to anticipate the Germans, but abandoned the northern part to them in Nov. 1884 at the insistence of the Colonial Office. The North Eastern part with New Britain became German in 1884 under the name of Kaiser Wilhelms Land and the Bismarck Archipelago. The British part was renamed Papua in 1906. The German colonies were conquered by the Australians in Sept. 1914, became Australian Mandated Territories in 1921, Trust Territories in 1946 and were combined with Papua in 1946. They became independent in 1975. See INDONESIA.

NEW HAMPSHIRE (U.S.A.) publicised by John Smith in 1614, was part of the area granted in 1620 to the Council for New England which conferred rights upon John Mason (1586-1635), lately Governor of Newfoundland; he, in 1629 named the territory and began to settle it with English farmers and fishermen. Later colonists, who populated only the southern part, came from Massachusetts and Connecticut. From 1641-79 under Massachusetts it became a separate (if territorially ill-defined) province. It was soon involved in 150 years of boundary disputes. The first was compromised with Massachusetts in 1741. The second, with New York, began in 1749 over Governor Benning Wentworth's land grants in Vermont which was then called The New Hampshire Grants. In 1764 New York was awarded the disputed territory by a judgement which neither New Hampshire nor the grantees in possession would accept. Feeling ran high, and at the American revolt in 1776 New Hampshire was among the first to drive out the English govt. The Vermonters, however, declared their independence of all comers in 1777, and New Hampshire agreed a boundary with them in 1782. The boundary with Canada was defined only in the Ashburton T. of 1842. New Hampshire was one of the thirteen original members of the U.S.A. and supported the Union in the Civil War.

NEW HAVEN (Connecticut). This puritan theocratic colony was founded by John Davenport (1597-1670) and Theophilus Eaton (1590-1658) with other Massachusetts Co. colonists in 1638, without a charter. The smallest of the New England colonies, it joined the New England Confederation in 1643. In 1664 it was incorporated into Connecticut by charter, but resisted the change until the conquest of the New Netherland by the D. of York (later James II). Faced with the possibility of inclusion in New York, the colonists resigned themselves to Connecticut, and the colony, as a separate unit, faded out.

NEW HEBRIDES now VANUATU (Pac.) were discovered in 1606 and surveyed by Cook in 1774. European whalers made regular visits from 1800 and sandalwood traders from 1825. A British presbyterian mission was established in 1848 but French penetration also began and led in 1878 to an Anglo-French non-annexation agreement. In 1886, however, the New Caledonia Nickel Co. hoisted the French flag and the Australians induced the British in 1887 to join with the French in a Mixed Naval Commission which held the ring until it was converted into a condominium in 1907. The Americans used it as a base in World War II. Independence was achieved in 1981 against French opposition.

NEW HOLLAND. See AUSTRALIA.

NEW JERSEY (U.S.A.) was part of Dutch New Netherland until the D. of York's conquest of 1664. He granted it to Carteret (a Jerseyman) and Berkeley, who in 1676 divided it. South and West Jersey received mostly English Quakers; North and East mostly Scots and New England Calvinists under Carteret. In 1702 the parts were politically reunited, but the legislature met alternately in the two parts until 1790. Though a strong loyalist element later contributed substantial forces to the govt. a congress seized control in 1776 and declared independence. The strategic position of the colony attracted many misfortunes and much fighting. New Jersey was one of the original 13 states of the Union, which it supported in the Civil War.

NEW LABOUR. A Labour outlook, perhaps typified by that of Tony Blair, which is not committed to revolutionary or Fabian socialism, but is ostensibly concerned with adapting existing economic and political institutions so as to benefit a generally high proportion of the poor.

NEW LANARK. See OWEN, ROBERT.

NEW LEARNING. A term for the classically influenced, sharp sighted but primarily Christian Humanism of the Renaissance exemplified by Machiavelli, Polydore Vergil, Thomas More and Erasmus.

NEW or LITTLE CUSTOM. See CARTA MERCATORIA.

NEWMAN, Sir George (1870-1948) Medical Officer of Health (M.O.H.) for both Finsbury and Bedfordshire, became Chief M.O.H. to the Board of Education in 1907 and in addition to the Ministry of Health in 1919. Together with his writings on bacteriology (1904-8), infant mortality (1906), hygiene and public health (1917) and his *Outline and Practice of Preventive Medicine* (1919) he made himself the chief inspirer and architect of British public health administration and saved many thousands of lives.

NEWMAN, John Henry (1801-90) Card. (1879) vicar of Oxford University Church from 1828, became associated with the Anglo-Catholic Oxford Movement in 1833 and started contributing to *Tracts for the Times.* A strong and attractive character with a powerful and learned intellect, his activities were bound to attract controversy. In TRACT 90 (1841) he proposed an interpretation of the XXXIX Articles in congruity with the decrees of the Council of Trent. In the ensuing furore, he was forbidden to preach by the Bp. of Oxford and condemned by the University, from which he slowly withdrew. In Oct. 1845 he was received into the R. Catholic church, and ordained at Rome in 1846. He was rector of Dublin University from 1854-58 when he quarrelled with Cardinal Manning and was in disfavour for some years. In 1864 he published his *Apologia pro Vita Sua* as a result of a controversy with Charles Kingsley, who had said that he did not regard truth as a necessary Christian virtue. The *apologia* and his *Dream of Gerontius* (1865) won him considerable intellectual and popular sympathy, while his view that papal prerogative cannot affect the civil allegiance of R. Catholics finally allayed suspicions lingering from the 16th cent.

NEWMARKET. *See* HORSE RACING.

NEW MEXICO (U.S.A.) was from 1598 a Spanish Kingdom embracing the modern areas of California, Utah, Colorado, Arizona and parts of Texas and modern New Mexico. In 1771 it was attached to New Spain. It thus became part of the Republic of Mexico in 1821; most of the area passed to the U.S.A. (after the Mexican-American war) under the T. of Guadalupe Hidalgo in Feb. 1848; the rest under the Gadsden Purchase of 1853.

NEW MODEL ARMY *see* CIVIL WAR-19.

NEW NETHERLAND. This vaguely defined area between Albany (N.Y.) and Gloucester (New Jersey) was claimed by the Dutch upon the basis of Henry Hudson's explorations (1609) in the employ of the Dutch East India Co. A Dutch West India Co. was formed in 1621. Colonists began to arrive in 1624 and in 1626 Pieter Minuit the first Director-General bought Manhattan I. and founded New Amsterdam, later New York. The Co. was financed by selling large estates complete with control of public offices and private jurisdictions to rich men who were encouraged to settle. These, the *Patroons*, under the Directors-General, controlled the colony and established a form of feudalism. When New Netherland was conquered in 1664 by James, D. of York and Albany (after whom New York and Albany were named) the territory was divided into the colonies of New York and New Jersey. In the former the feudalism of the patroons remained undisturbed until 1775.

NEWNES, Sir George (1851-1910) launched *Tit-bits* at Manchester in 1881 and brought it to London in 1884. Its low-grade fragmented and gossip journalism combined with prize competitions and insurance policies appealed to an increasing literate but not educated public, and so impeded improvement in the standards of journalism generally. He became a liberal M.P. (Newmarket) in 1885. In 1891 he brought out the *Strand Magazine*. and in 1893 the *Westminster Gazette,* an organ of liberal opinion. He lost his seat in 1895 but sat for Cardiff from 1900-10.

NEW ORDER. Originally an expression naming the objectives of Japanese Eastern policy, its better known application related to the long-range policy of Nazi Germany, expressed in 1941 by Walther Funk, the Minister of Economics, that "the peacetime economy must guarantee to the Great German Reich a maximum of security and to the German people a maximum consumption ... to increase their welfare". The frontiers of the Greater Reich were to include not only Germany and Austria but the important contiguous industrial areas (with large non German populations) of Luxembourg, Alsace, Lorraine, Czechoslovakia, Teschen and Pless and parts of Poland including Lodz. The industries of Hungary, Roumania, Yugoslavia, Italy, France and the Low Countries were controlled or powerfully influenced by purchases of shareholdings, Jewish expropriations and diplomatic pressures. Elsewhere in German controlled territory only agriculture, mining and oil were to be encouraged: the general principle being that within a self supporting European unit the outer subject areas would feed and supply an industrialised Greater Reich. Naturally this predatory policy was locally resisted, especially as it was sharpened and distorted by wartime exigencies. These were held to justify requisitions enforced by the terrorist methods of the SS, which was not composed wholly of Germans. Thus the New Order envisaged the creation of a supranational Nazi organisation inconsistent with some of the proclaimed racialism of the original Nazi party.

NEW ORLEANS. *See* LOUISIANA.

NEW PARTY, was launched by Sir Oswald Mosley in Feb. 1931 to advocate his economic proposals which had attracted both Labour and Conservative support. Only four M.P.s joined him, including his wife, and the Party won no seats in the 1931 election.

NEW PROTECTION. *See* AUSTRALIA-15.

NEW RUSSIA. An 16th cent. name for the relatively empty areas adjacent to the Black Sea opened to colonisation from the north as a result of cession by Turkey. They rapidly attracted British maritime enterprise carrying W. European products in exchange for grain.

NEWS, THE. *See* L'ESTRANGE, SIR ROGER.

NEWS CHRONICLE (1930-60) was an amalgamation of the vaguely liberal *Daily Chronicle* and the *Daily News*. It tried to combine popular appeal with high journalistic standards and so fell victim to competition from less scrupulous rivals. It was absorbed by the *Daily Mail* in 1960.

NEWSHOLME, Sir Arthur (1857-1943) as medical officer of health (M.O.H.) at Brighton from 1888-1908 made a statistical study of diseases which, when M.O.H. to the Local Govt. Board (1908-1919) he used as the basis of the national health services related to maternity and child welfare, tuberculosis and venereal diseases.

NEW SHOREHAM ACT, 1771, for enlarging the parliamentary borough of Shoreham (Sussex) provided one of several conflicting precedents for reforming corruption in Parliamentary elections.

NEWSLETTERS were manuscript accounts of parliamentary and court events sent twice a week to subscribers by Henry Muddiman (fl. 1650-80) who, at Monck's request, was authorised by the Parliament as an official journalist. Their arrival was always a locally important event. He also started the *Parliamentary Intelligencer, Mercurius Politicus* and in 1665 under the direction of Sir Joseph Williamson (1633-1701) started the *Oxford Gazette*, the forerunner of the *London Gazette*.

NEWSOME REPORT (1965) by the Central Advisory Council on Education for England, of which Sir John Newsome (1910-71) was Chairman, recommended that the school leaving age be raised from 15 to 16 in 1965 and proposed widened curricula and more extra-curricular activities.

NEW SOUTH WALES. *See* AUSTRALIA.

NEW STATESMAN AND NATION now **NEW STATESMAN AND SOCIETY** and **SPEAKER.** The *Speaker* was founded in 1890 and supported the radical wing of the Liberal Party. In 1907 it was superseded by the *Nation* which followed the same line. The *New Statesman*, inspired by Sydney Webb and George Bernard Shaw, was launched in 1913 as a left wing political and literary review. In 1912 the *Nation* absorbed the *Athenaeum* and this combined weekly was in its turn swallowed by the *New Statesman* in 1931 which combined with *New Society* in 1988. The *New Statesman* has always retained a political stance well to the left of official Labour Party policy.

NEW STATUTES (*Nova Statuta*) are an edition, first printed by Pynson in 1497, of the statutes beginning in 1327.

NEW SWEDEN. *See* DELAWARE.

NEW TIPPERARY. A political migration in 1890, organised by William O'Brien, from Tipperary Town, owned by Smith Barry, a good landlord who supported another landlord in difficulties at Youghal. The new town, financed by world-wide subscription, failed and the inhabitants returned.

NEWTON, Sir Isaac (1642-1727) burst upon the intellectual world in 1666 after a retreat from Cambridge to escape the Great Plague of 1665. He worked out the binomial theorem, the integral and differential calculi and had postulated the notion of universal gravitation. In 1667 he began to study optics; by 1671 he had built two reflecting telescopes, and in 1672 he communicated his *New Theory about Light and Colours* to the Royal Society of which he had just become a Fellow. In the course of long and not always friendly correspondence with Robert Hooke he conceived the *Principia,* the most influential mathematical work until the 20th cent. This was, with Halley's help, published between 1686-87. By this time his abilities were much in demand, partly through the royal patronage accorded to the Royal Society. In particular he was employed to investigate the problems of coinage and currency, becoming an unusually active warden of the mint in 1695 and Master in 1699. By then personal problems had virtually ended his creative activities. From 1703 he was annually elected Pres. of the Royal Society until his death. In 1717 and 1718 he presented reports on the currency (*see* COINAGE). By now he was a legendary figure and when he died his body lay in state and was buried in Westminster Abbey. *See* RENAISSANCE-14.

NEW TOWNS. War destruction and a general feeling that big cities were getting too big prompted the govt. in 1945 to set up a committee to investigate the possibilities of planned decentralisation from congested areas, before attempts to rebuild bombed areas set the priorities irrevocably in a different direction. The Committee issued three reports as a result of which the New Towns Act, 1946, was passed. This created a Commission for the New Towns, set out the way in which New Town sites were to be determined, and required that each should be built and managed by a New Town Corporation financed by the Treasury. It was intended that once the work was substantially completed the New Town should be handed over to a local authority. Accordingly New Towns for populations of about 60,000 were commenced at between 20 and 30 miles from London. These were

Basildon	(Essex)	*Hatfield	(Herts)
Bracknell	(Berks)	*Hemel Hempstead	(Herts)
*Crawley	(Sussex)	Stevenage	(Herts)
Harlow	(Essex)	*Welwyn Garden City	(Herts)

Three were begun in Durham and Tyneside namely: Aycliffe, Peterlee and Washington.

Others of this type were:

Corby (Northants)	Telford (Salop)
Skelmersdale (Lancs)	Redditch (Worcs)
Runcorn (Ches)	Cwmbran (Gwent)

Meantime there were changes of policy. It was decided in 1959 that completed New Towns should pass not to a local authority but to the New Towns Commission and those which had so passed by 1976 when transfers ceased are marked *. The decentralisation policy was also to be carried on through either the construction of much bigger new towns or by extending existing towns. Of the new bigger type Milton Keynes (Bucks.) was expected to expand to 250,000 and the Central Lancashire New Town to 400,000. Of the new expanded towns, Warrington (Lancs.) Northampton and Peterborough would reach about 200,000. A small expanded town was also begun at Newtown (Powys). The six Scottish New Towns were all intended to relieve congestion in the Glasgow area. These and their designed populations were:

Cumbernauld	70,000	Irvine	120,000
East Kilbride	90,000	Livingstone	100,000
Glenrothes	70,000	Stonehouse	70,000

In addition, the Letchworth Garden City, begun in 1903, was reorganised on new town lines in 1967 and the Greater London Council began to develop Thamesmead for 48,000 people.

NEW YORK CITY. Verazzano saw Manhattan I. in 1524. In 1614 some Dutch merchants set up a fur trading post. In 1623 the Dutch W. India Co. adopted the I. as its trading centre and in 1626 Peter Munuit (1580-1638) a Director of the Co. bought the I. from the Indians for $24 worth of beads. As New Amsterdam it became the capital of the Dutch New Netherlands, but Minuit quarrelled with the Co. and in 1638 established, in Swedish service, a rival settlement at Wilmington on the Delaware. In 1647 Peter Stuyvesant (1610-1672) became Governor. He soon quarrelled with the prominent personalities (The Patroons) who complained of his violent temper and arbitrary rule. (He also had an ornamental silver leg.) By 1655 however, he had gained the Delaware forts and eliminated Swedish rivalry. Meanwhile the quarrels continued, and when a British expedition appeared in 1664, the population happily surrendered the town (Sept.) without a fight. It was renamed New York in honour of James D. of York (James II) then Lord High Admiral. He had received a Charter for the territory from Charles II and the city became the capital of the colony. It grew very slowly, being smaller than Boston until 1770 and Philadelphia until about 1810, but its splendid situation and harbour developed into a shipping and trading centre, so that the city achieved the basis of its modern form with its churches, schools, theatres and a population of 10,000 by 1750. Columbia University (then King's College) was founded in 1754. With its strong coastwise and trans-Atlantic shipping interests, the city became a nucleus of rebellious sentiment after the French defeat in the Seven Years' War had eliminated the need for British protection. The Governor (William Tryon 1725-88) was driven out with the aid of the terrorist Sons of Liberty in 1775, but the city was reoccupied in 1776 and remained in British hands until 1783. From 1789-90 the city was the American capital but in 1790 the govt. transferred to Philadelphia and in 1797 the state govt. to Albany. By 1810 the population was 96,000 and was soon expanding at a rate of 15,000 a year, especially after the opening of the Erie Canal (1825) and the creation of the railway networks (1840 onwards) which made the port the world distribution centre for the manufacture and agriculture of the north east. European immigrants poured in from 1850, negroes after the Civil War. By 1900 the population had swollen to 3.5M and the city had become the major financial centre of N. America.

NEW YORK COLONY (*See* NEW YORK CITY.) The British alliance with the Iroquois had theoretically opened the centre of the state to colonisation but real progress was slow because of tribal and military disturbances connected with the great wars between 1689-1783. Hence western New York remained a wilderness until the 1820s. Meanwhile though there was a Local Assembly, public opinion and provincial feeling, it remained muted, and in the American rebellion many New Yorkers at all levels remained loyal and ultimately migrated to Canada. Since the British retook the city in 1776, the colony, which had declared for independence, was governed from Kingston. The state abolished slavery in 1827 and joined the Union in the American Civil War.

NEW ZEALAND (N.Z.) (*see* COOK, JAMES) **(1)** Missionaries first met Maoris in 1814. An army officer, the Belgian Baron de Thieny, proposed a scheme of colonisation which the Colonial Office rejected in 1823 because N.Z. was not a British possession. Thierry then approached the Dutch and then the French. By now traders were exchanging whisky and firearms for the much prized preserved Maori heads. The result was disorder and missionary protests, mostly ignored until Gibbon Wakefield gave evidence to a parliamentary committee on the disposal of colonial lands. He remarked incidentally on the "slovenly and disgraceful" proceedings in N.Z. The banker, Francis Baring, and some associates took him up and founded a N.Z. Association in favour of systematic colonisation. The Pope too became interested and appointed a bishop. The Association ran into opposition despite missionary support, because of a sensational select committee report on the shameful treatment of aborigines in Australia. In 1837 Lord Glenelg (Colonial Sec.) concluded, however, that proper govt. was essential in the Maori interest; he was ready to use the Association if it became a chartered company and if the Crown could exclude undesirables and veto bad appointments. The Association's Parliamentary friends attacked Glenelg who found few defenders but stood firm. In Aug. 1838 members of the Association accordingly formed a joint stock co.

(2) Glenelg was succeeded by Lord Normanby (Feb. 1839) who agreed with him and refused to support the Co. The Co. then despatched a ship in spite of him. This excited the interest of the French govt. which remembered Thierry and the papal interest and had had complaints from its traders. The Paris press discussed intervention. The British govt. was alarmed and decided with extreme reluctance, to annex. The instructions to Capt. William Hobson (1795-1842) the local senior naval officer forcibly expressed this reluctance and were scooped by the *Globe*. The French govt. thereupon arranged to have settlers conveyed to N.Z. from Rochefort in Mar. 1840.

(3) Hobson, however, had made the Waitangi T. (6 Feb. 1840) with the Maori chiefs. He proclaimed British annexation before signature to forestall the company's settlers, and the French arrived too late. The under-capitalised Co. tried but failed to establish a separate German colony and to sell the Chatham Is. to Germans. Its colonists were poor or unscrupulous. There were misunderstandings and sharp practice about land sales. Disputes led to fighting (June 1843) in which settlers were killed. The govt. refused a punitive expedition because the settlers were in the wrong. The North I. Maoris, thinking this a sign of weakness, rebelled. They were suppressed and pardoned (1845).

(4) In 1846 the first Crown colony constitution, with the capital at Auckland, was established. This was superseded by a second in 1852 when the white population was rapidly increasing and the Maori falling. Though certain lands were reserved to the natives, Europeans were acquiring large tracts. The Maoris acquired some European material advantages but they had a poor opinion of Europeans and the chiefs feared the erosion of tribal custom and their own authority with it. In 1854 they launched a movement to unite the tribes under a paramount chief, to limit land sales and the liquor and arms traffic. Since the franchise was confined to those who could write English, the purely settler govt. was unhelpful. In 1856 the home govt. unwisely conceded ministerial responsibility and the Assembly tried to bring forward a bill which, by recognising private ownership of native land, broke the treaty. The two communities drifted towards violence, despite Maori restraint and the efforts of the churchmen.

(5) War broke out in 1860. The settlers already outnumbered the Maoris, but British regulars (without much local help) had to do the main fighting. The settlers govt's land grab made peace impossible until the home govt. which had paid for the war, pressurised it into modernisation. Hence in 1862 proof of land title before sale became necessary, and in 1865 (when the major war was over) a native land court was created. In 1867 the Maoris were given representation in the Lower House, and in the better atmosphere the war fizzled out in 1869. Sir Donald Maclean became Minister for Native Affairs, and achieved, before he retired in 1876 a great work of conciliation which included (1872) the nomination of two Maori chiefs to the Upper House.

(6) The two foundations of the N.Z. economy, sheep and gold, had already been well laid. The large land acquisitions were divided into pastoral crown leases and there were forest clearances and artificial grassing, especially in North Is. Gold was first discovered in 1852.

The big Tuapeka field in Otago was opened up in 1861, followed by exploitation in both Is. Many prospectors and their families settled, but found life hard during the 1867-71 slump. The country now established one of the earliest deliberate examples of successful deficit financing in a depression. Sir Julius Vogel (1835-99) the Treasurer in the Fox administration, persuaded the Assembly to borrow large sums to build roads, telegraph lines, railways and to import British immigrants. A rising wool market helped the scheme almost too well; the prosperity engendered not only much cereal planting by 1876 but speculation and bank failures when, in 1879, prices began to fall. All the same, the economy had been transformed in those eight years; the population had risen from 100,000 to half a million since 1861, and racial and constitutional disputes were giving way to political controversies of a different sort.

(7) In the first twelve years of the ensuing 16 year depression, the conservatives, led by Sir Harry Atkinson (1831-89) and mostly representing the landed interest, were in power. Sir George Grey (1812-98) a former Governor returned as a leader of a radical or liberal party, which he organised to such effect, that his successor, John Ballance (1829-93) led it to victory in 1890. Ballance was followed by 1893 by Richard Seddon (1845-1906). He had the fortune to enter a boom period. The Liberals under him and Sir Joseph Ward (1857-1930) held office until 1912, so that it was the conservative or Reform Party which had to take the country into World War I. In fact they formed a coalition, in which the Liberal William Massey (1856-1925) was Prime Minister with Ward as his finance minister. A very reliable volunteer force was raised and sent, as part of the A.N.Z.A.C. division, to the war, in which it caught public imagination in Gallipoli. The war debt (about 30% owed to Britain) was substantial, but in 1931 its British component was written off.

(8) The artificial wartime boom had speculative effects similar to those in the more natural conditions of 1871-89 and with similar results. The Liberals went into opposition in 1919. The Reformers had to face the price collapse of 1921 which brought farming and bank failures, exacerbated by the ex-soldiers' resettlement problems. The population had by now reached 1,250,000. Yet the Liberals were unable to gain a clear victory in the elections of 1922, mainly because of the Labour decision (dating from 1910) to be independent. Hence the Reformers, under Joseph Gordon Coates (1878-1943) a young farmer, won a landslide victory of 1925. His govt. inaugurated the famous policy of mass' farming exports. This period, too, saw major changes in the country's international status. It had taken the title of Dominion in 1907, by which time its local autonomy was complete. By the end of World War I its subjection to the imperial Govt. and Parliament was nominal. It signed the peace treaties, adhered to the League of Nations, the Kellogg Pact (1928) and the London Naval T. (1930). In 1931 the Statute of Westminster held out the prospect of formal independence whenever the Assembly should see fit to enact it. It did so in 1947.

(9) Sir Joseph Ward had succeeded Coates in 1928 and was followed by George William Forbes (1869-1947). The Coates Govt. had indirectly subsidised exports by devaluing the N.Z. pound, subsidising farm labour and placing farmers in a favourable credit and tax environment. This essentially protectionist policy now collided with the world-wide depression of 1929. In 1931 Forbes formed a coalition and at the Ottawa Conference (1932) agreed to enter the system of Commonwealth preference. As the slump deepened, wages and salaries (as in Britain) fell, and there was a net outward migration. This lasted until 1935, by which time the Labour Party, now led by Michael Joseph Savage (1872-1940) was able to organise an electoral triumph over the

coalition. The new Govt. was dedicated to a form of state socialism in which it controlled major finance through the nationalisation of the Reserve Bank (1936) and exports by becoming the sole purchaser of dairy products. The resulting effective guarantee of farm prices also held taxes steady, while the world climbed out of the slump. Hence Labour had another electoral victory in 1938.

(10) Savage was followed by Peter Fraser (1884-1950). The country was united in declaring war on Germany in 1939, and took great risks in coming to the aid of Britain during the Dunkirk period (1940) and of U.S.A. in the Pearl Harbor collapse (1942). Subsequently N.Z. became a major U.S. base. The essentially socialist character of any modern war effort had coincided with the state socialist spirit of the govt. Relief at victory, and accumulated shortages and difficulties caused impatience with the govt's methods. Sidney Holland's (1893-1961) National party ousted Labour at the polls in 1949. The result was new men rather than new methods. Atomic energy, the pulp industry, the laying of new grasslands were financed in a time of rising prices, from govt. sources. The result was a very large increase in export-based prosperity over the following 20 years. By 1961 the population was nearly 2,000,000.

(11) The British accession to the European Common Market brought with it, in N.Z. as elsewhere in the Commonwealth, a feeling of desertion exacerbated by an agricultural and economic decline caused by the imposition of European tariffs round N.Z.'s main market. Relations with Britain had to be conducted with an eye to the alternatives and there was a recovery while new markets were entered which enabled N.Z. to reestablish most of her position in Britain. It was symptomatic of the greater independence of outlook that in 1977 *God Defend New Zealand* took its place beside *God Save the Queen.*

NEY, Michel (1769-1815) D. of ELCHINGEN (1805) P. of the MOSCOWA (1812) Marshal of France. Only part of the career of this wildly brave headstrong cooper's son is germane to British history. He served in Spain in 1808-9, but quarrelled furiously with Masséna, his commander during the invasion of Portugal. His daring example saved the rearguard in the retreat from Moscow (1812) and he fought gallantly in Bonaparte's disastrous campaigns of 1813 and 1814. He then saw the futility of further suffering. He helped to impose Bonaparte's abdication of 1814 and took a respected place under the restored Bourbon monarchy. When Bonaparte returned from Elba he was sent with 4,000 troops to 'bring him back in a cage' but he and his men were bewitched by the usurper's magnetism and they all changed sides. He commanded and suffered from confused orders at the B. of Quatre Bras (16 June 1815). At Waterloo (18th) he directed the assault on Wellington's centre but failed to exploit the capture of La Haye Sainte so as to pierce it. After the rout, and fall of Paris, he was court-martialled and shot.

NGUNI. A collective name for Bantu-speaking tribes originating in Natal including the Zulu, Swazi, Pondo*, Xhosa* and Matabele+ who in the 1820s, apart from the Zulus, migrated outwards in the *Mfecane* and established themselves respectively in Swaziland, *The Cape and + Rhodesia.

NICENE CREED, whose wording constituted one of the most important of all spiritual, practical and political controversies was drawn up at the Council of Nicaea in 325 in the form (as set out in the Book of Common Prayer):

(1) "I believe in one God the Father Almighty, maker of Heaven and Earth And of all things visible and invisible; And in one Jesus Christ, the only begotten son of God, Begotten of His Father before all worlds, God of God, Light of Light, Very God of very God, Begotten not made, Being of one substance with the Father by whom all things were made; Who for us men and for our salvation came down from heaven and was incarnate by the Holy Ghost of the Virgin Mary; And was made Man; and was crucified also for us under Pontius Pilate. He suffered and was buried, And the third day he rose again according to the scriptures, And ascended into heaven, And sitteth on the right hand of the Father. And he shall come again with glory to judge both the quick and the dead; Whose kingdom shall have no end. And I believe in the Holy Ghost."

This was and is acceptable to all Christian churches and left the nature of the Holy Ghost undefined so that a worshipper was free to hold any reasonable opinion on it. At the Council of Constantinople in 381 the following was added to the end:

(2) "The lord and giver of life who proceedeth from the Father ... who with the Father and the Son together is worshipped and glorified, Who spake by the prophets."

(3) "And I believe one Catholick and Apostolick Church. I acknowledge one Baptism for the remission of sins. And I look for the Resurrection of the dead, And the life of the world to come."

This creed, relying on patristics and others to similar effect was developed to combat the powerful mostly Teutonic Arians whose primary tenet was that the Father created the Son, who with the Holy Ghost were subordinate to Him, and that Redemption could be attained through human free will.

The Roman church developed the opinion that, of the Constantinopolitan addition, para **(2)**, known as the Procession of the Holy Ghost, was inconsistent with the original because if the Father and the Son are of one substance as asserted at Nicaea, the Holy Ghost must proceed from both. As God (being of one substance with the Father) the Son might redeem the human race by his death on the Cross. Procession from the Father only might thus cast doubt on the Redemption. Accordingly the Roman Church, relying on biblical authority, added at the gap after 'Father' the words "and the Son". (Lat: *filioque*).

The controversy became important after Arianism had disappeared and other threats, notably Islam had developed in 7th cent. The Eastern churches held that the Constantinopolitan addition was a guideline which did not trench on the worshipper's free will, by means of which he could reach a proper opinion and through it make himself amenable to Redemption. This reduced the authoritarian aspect of the Church and implied the equality, within one universal (catholic) Church of its then five patriarchates (Alexandria, Antioch, Jerusalem, Constantinople and Rome) and the possibility that others might come into existence, while denying the supremacy, save of precedence, of one of them (Rome). By 1453 four of the five were in Islamic territory, but a sixth was created at Moscow under Ivan III (r. 1462-1505).

It will be seen that behind the words *filioque* lay major differences of outlook leading to a widening division between East and West Christendom, the mutual hostility of its parts and the decay of the unsupported Eastern Churches in the face of Islam.

NICHOLAS V, Pope. *See* RENAISSANCE-7.

NICHOLAS, Sir Edward (1593-1669) became sec. to the Lord Warden of the Cinque Ports in 1618 and was M.P. for Winchilsea from 1620-24. In 1625 he became Secretary to the Admiralty. He was M.P. for Dover in 1627. In 1635 he became clerk to the Council and in 1641 Sec. of State. He conducted the negotiations at Uxbridge in Feb. 1645 and for the surrender of Oxford in 1646 and then retired to Normandy, remaining in name Sec. of State, until the King's death in 1649. Q. Henrietta Maria disliked him and gave him an innocuous post with the D. of York in 1650. In 1654 Charles II formally appointed him Sec. of State, but pensioned him off after the Restoration.

NICHOLAS of FARNHAM (?-1257) A Professor of Medicine and physician to Henry III, was elected Bp. of Durham in 1241 and began the ambitious Chapel of the Nine Altars in the Cathedral. In 1248 he retired to the parish of Stockton.

NICHOLAS of HEREFORD (fl. 1380-1417), preacher and friend of John Wycliffe, and according to Lollard practice, a translator of the Old Testament, was excommunicated in 1382, appealed to the Pope and was imprisoned in Rome. He escaped in 1385 (after Wycliffe's death) was retaken in England and after further imprisonment led the Lollards until he recanted in 1391. He then held offices in Hereford Cathedral until 1417 and ended as a Carthusian.

NICHOLAS (KOLAS) of MEAUX (?-?1227), *de facto* abbot of Furness before 1207 was nominated Bp. of Sodor and Man by K. Olaf of the Isles, though the monks claimed the right of election. Consecrated by the Abp. of Trondheim in 1210, he remained a controversial figure and was driven into exile in 1217.

NIETZSCHE, Friedrich Wilhelm (1844-1900). German social theorist who suffered from nervous afflictions and went mad in 1889. He held that humanity was divisible into the weak, subservient mass and the strong, dominating minority; that there was a natural conflict between them in which each would seek to impose its ideals upon the other. The weak naturally extolled meekness, pity, poverty and renunciation; these Christian virtues were really symptoms of a slave morality which was undesirable and wrong. The future lay with a master race, whose strength would be justifiably used to dominate the rest and root out Christianity. The subject is expounded at inordinate length in his works, but also more lyrically and epigramatically in *Anti-Christ* and in *Thus Spake Zarathustra*. His views, widely known in Germany, created a favourable atmosphere for the Wilhelminian aggressiveness of pre-1914 Germany and, perhaps, for Nazism.

NIGEL or NEALE (?1100-68) Bp. of ELY (1133) nephew or son of Roger of Salisbury, was educated by Abbot Anselm of Laon before entering the service of Henry I. By 1130 he was the Royal Treasurer and had extensive land holdings. He was forced upon the reluctant monks of Ely but remained in London as Treasurer. He supported K. Stephen's accession (1135) and retained office until Roger of Salisbury fell in 1139. He then escaped to his castle at Devizes but had to surrender it. He supported the Empress Matilda at her arrival later in the same year and tried, but failed, to hold Ely for her. In 1142 he was formally reconciled with Stephen, but his loyalty was later doubted more than once. After Henry II's accession he apparently played a role in restoring the damaged apparatus of govt. and he bought the treasurership for his bastard Richard fitz Neale, served as a curial judge and was much involved in Exchequer business until he had a paralysing stroke in 1166. Unlike his uncle who kept a mistress, he was married.

NIGER. *See* AFRICA. WEST (EX-FRENCH).

NIGER, Ralph (fl. 1160-70) perhaps Archdeacon of Gloucester, left a derivative chronicle and a scandalous *Succinct Chronicle of the Vices of Emperors as well as the Kings of France and England* in which he carefully includes Henry II. He was a partisan of Becket.

NIGERIA. The Niger delta, mangrove swamps and coastal forests isolated the country from the sea, and early immigration, trade and Islam came via the Sahara caravan routes. In the 15th cent. Moslem Hausa states existed in the N.W., while an already old and prosperous Yoruba kingdom in the S. was visited but not exploited by the Portuguese in 1486 and the English in 1553. In the 17th cent. the country was destabilised by famines, political dissensions and by slave wars in which the tribes raided each other for slaves who were sold to European traders. In the confusion the interior was known only by repute to Europeans until Mungo Park reached the Niger in

1796. The suppression of the slave trade from 1807 had calming effects, encouraged innocent trade and brought explorers and missionaries to Calabar, Ibadan and even Abeokuta. Clapperton reached Sokoto in 1823 and the Lander brothers plotted the Niger in 1830. Unfortunately the Fulani from the Upper Nile invaded the Hausa areas and there was a reversion to confusion which continued until the British bought Lagos from a local chief in 1861. This was governed (if at all) from Sierra Leone, and then from the Gold Coast, but in 1886 it was declared a separate colony, just after a Berlin conference (1885) had recognised British claims further inland. The British proclaimed the **Oil Rivers Protectorate** which in due course became the **Niger Coast Protectorate** while the northern, mostly Hausa and Fulani areas were chartered to the United Africa Co. When the Co. was brought under govt. control in 1900, its northern areas became the **Northern Nigeria Protectorate** while the southern were united with the Niger Coast and added to Lagos in 1906. In 1914 the whole area became a united colony.

The adjacent German Cameroons fell rapidly to the Allies in 1914 and were mandated under the T. of Versailles (1920) mainly to France, but Britain added a 300 mile strip alongside the eastern frontier sometimes 80 miles wide from near Calabar, half way to L. Chad. In this form Nigeria developed into a country exporting enormous amounts of cocoa, with lesser amounts of ground nuts, timber, rubber and latterly cotton.

In World War II Lagos and Port Harcourt were aircraft staging points for the Middle East. As everywhere else, there were demands for local independence after it was over, but these were hard to satisfy because the political scene was divided between four major nations and cultures (Hausa, Fulani, Yoruba and Ibo) and a multiplicity of others, with several religions and English as the only common language. The result was a division followed by the creation of a federal state, which became independent in 1960. In 1961 the Southern Cameroons rejoined French Cameroun. In 1966 their Ibo neighbours tried to secede as the independent state of BIAFRA and in the ensuing civil war the Russians tried to stir the pot by helping the federal govt. with arms and advisers. Britain, fearing to be outbid, followed suit. Biafra was crushed by 1972.

NIGHTINGALE, Florence (1820-1910). *See* NURSING.

NILE, B. of the (28 July 1798) was fought in the Mediterranean Bay of Aboukir, 10 miles west of the Rosetta mouth of the Nile, where Admiral Brueys' 14 ships which had escorted Bonaparte's troops to Egypt, lay in anchored line of battle. Nelson's fleet of 14, which was expected but not on that day, rounded the point into the bay suddenly at dusk, divided and doubled Brueys' windward ships, which were crushed between two fires while the leeward ships were unable to come to their help. The French flagship, *L 'Orient* caught fire and blew up, taking the entire treasure of Malta with her. Only two escaped. The victory brought Turkey into the war, cut Bonaparte off from home and eventually frustrated his attempt to conquer Egypt (*see* MEDITERRANEAN WAR). The name of the battle, like that of Bonaparte's B. of the Pyramids (which were equally out of sight) is propagandist.

NILE (1) flows from L. Victoria and was navigable from the Sudan border to Khartoum (1100 miles) and from Assuan to the Delta, but between Khartoum and Assuan (c. 1400 miles) it was interrupted by six series of cataracts only navigable in flood time. The main river, called the WHITE NILE above Khartoum, flowed with a certain regularity because the floods from the south were restrained by a huge swampy district called the Suddh, but there are four major tributaries namely (from south to north) the BAHR AL GHAZAL, from the west, and the SOBAT, BLUE NILE and ATBARA from the east, and in Aug. these bring down huge quantities of rain water, and in the case of the last three meltwater from the Ethiopian highlands. This caused the annual floods in the narrow Egyptian Nile valley which benefited from the fertilising silt brought down with them.

(2) The annual flood cycle, whose true cause was long unknown, dominated Egyptian life and prosperity, and basin irrigation, nourishing one annual crop on flood borne silt, has been practised in Egypt since pharaonic times. Perennial irrigation permitting year round cultivation began in 1820 with Mehemet Ali's Delta canals, designed to extend the crop (especially cotton) areas. Water had to be raised mechanically from these canals which silted up quickly. In 1834 he decided to combat these problems with a barrage at the head of the Delta, but Egyptian efforts to build it failed until the British occupation of 1882. Their immense development programme, connected with the Lancashire cotton industry, was based on dam construction. The Delta barrage was completed in 1890. The Assuan Dam, completed in 1902, was raised in 1912 and again in 1934; the Jebel el Awliya (Sudan) Dam to impound part of the floods for later release, was finished in 1937. Meantime Indian competition was depressing the world market. The Russian financed Assuan High Dam, plans for which were politically entangled with the nationalisation of the Suez Canal, was completed in 1970. At that period about 750,000 acres were under basin irrigation and 5,000,000 under perennial to which the High Dam added a further 2,000,000. It also generated vast amounts of cheap electricity some of which is exported.

(3) Land under perennial irrigation does not receive the annual silt deposit and much artificial fertiliser has to be used. The cost and influence on quality and the spread of waterborne disease partly offset the advantages of year round cultivation, which has also changed the national way of life.

(4) The Aug. floodwaters are now allowed to flush the sluices in order to move the silt. The reservoirs are filled while the floods are subsiding in Nov. and Dec. and the stored water is released from Feb. to July. The disturbance of nature caused by the higher dams is leading to a gradual desiccation of the Delta, a lowering of the land levels, and consequent encroachment of the sea. The High Dam has altered the climate of Upper Egypt.

(5) As the silt annually accumulating in the 250-mile stretch (L. Nasser) above the High Dam may eventually cause the water level to overtop the Dam, plans are being canvassed for a 'parallel Nile' from near Abu Simbel to the Mediterranean near Alexandria. This might fertilise a huge hitherto desert area, and facilitate the exploitation of metallic resources under it.

NINE POWER TREATIES (1922) on China were signed by Britain, U.S.A., Japan, France, Italy, Belgium, the Netherlands, Portugal and China. Under one, the 8 powers undertook to respect Chinese sovereignty and territory, to aid her to develop, to give equal opportunities for other trading nations, and to refrain from taking advantage of the internal condition of China to secure special advantages for themselves. Under the other the question of control of the Chinese customs was referred to an international commission. The Japanese persistently violated them from 1931 and the other parties conferred ineffectually about the violations in 1937.

NINETEEN PROPOSITIONS (1 June 1642) were the unacceptable parliamentary ultimatum to Charles I. They demanded that parliamentary approval should be required for the appointment of privy councillors, great officers of state and Governors of fortresses and for the form of education and the marriage of the King's children; that the laws against papists should be strictly enforced; that the King should reform the church in accordance with parliamentary advice; that papists should be excluded from the Lords and that newly created peers should not take their seats without the consent of both houses; that 'delinquents' (i.e. the King's supporters) should not be shielded from attainder or impeachment by veto or pardon; and that by accepting the Militia Ordinance he should abandon control of the forces. There was no mention of taxation or extraordinary jurisdictions because legislation had already dealt with these matters.

The King's reply, that this amounted to a revolution and that the church, needing no reformation, would be defended against papists and sectaries alike, attracted much moderate support and became the foundation of later royalist doctrine.

NINETY-FIVE THESES (1517). See LUTHER, MARTIN- 2.

NINE WITCHES OF GLOUCESTER, in the Welsh legend of PEREDUR were apparently ladies who taught martial arts. See WARRIOR WOMEN (CELTIC).

NINIAN St. See MISSIONARIES IN BRITAIN AND IRELAND; CUMBERLAND-1.

NISI **(Lat: = unless).** Certain decrees of ecclesiastical courts were expressed to become final at a future date *unless* the successful party before then moved to rescind. The practice descended to the divorce jurisdiction of the High Court.

NISI PRIUS. See ASSIZES-2.

NITHING (A.S.: hateful). A person pronounced nithing was held to be socially and morally worthless; therefore he lost his Wergild and was no longer protected by the law or the church. Swein Godwinson was proclaimed nithing by Edward the Confessor in 1049 after he had murdered his cousin Beorn, and the threat of it was used by William II in 1088 to force people to assist him in the siege of Rochester.

NITHSDALE, William Maxwell, 5th E. of (1676-1744) and his wife **Winifred (?-1749).** He, a Scottish Jacobite, was captured at the B. of Preston (1715) and condemned to death. George I rejected her petition for his life so she engineered his escape from the Tower disguised as a woman, and they lived happily ever after in Rome.

NITRATES. Before 1911 the chief world source for artificial fertilisers and explosives was the disputed north Chilean provinces. In 1911 Fritz HABER (1868-1934) and Karl BOSCH (1874-1940), Berlin chemists, invented a process for the mass synthesisation of ammonia from hydrogen (in water) and nitrogen (in air). This made Germany independent of imported nitrates in both World Wars and ultimately ruined the British financed Chilean economy.

NITRATE WAR (Feb. 1879-Oct. 1883). See BOLIVIA.

NIZAM (al-MULK) (Arab = Governor of the Empire). The title of the rulers of Hyderabad (S. India) of the dynasty founded by Asaf Jab, Subadar of the Deccan from 1713-48.

NKRUMAH, Kwame. See GHANA-2,3.

NOBEL, Alfred Bernhard (1833-96) with his father studied explosives and invented nitroglycerine in 1861, dynamite in 1866 and gelignite in 1874. He left his immense fortune to provide the celebrated Nobel Prizes for physics, chemistry, medicine, literature and service to peace.

NOBILE OFFICIUM **(Lat: lofty obligation).** In Scots law the equivalent of English *Equity*.

NOBLE, GEORGE. See COINAGE-13; **ROSE.** See COINAGE-12; **SHIP.** See COINAGE-10.

NOBILITY in the sense of privilege heritable simply by virtue of blood relationship to a noble ancestor has never been part of English or Scots law; primo-geniture has always restricted titles to a very small circle.

NOLI ME TANGERE **(Lat = Do not touch me.)** The motto of the Scots Kings, associated with the thistle.

NOLLE PROSEQUI **(Lat = Do not prosecute)** is the formal refusal, made by the Attorney General on behalf of the Crown, to prosecute a person for crime. Unlike a free pardon it does not protect the person against the consequences, if he incriminates himself in evidence in another case.

NOLLEKENS, Joseph (1737-1823) sculptor, executed *inter alia* portraiture of most important English personalities of the 1770s.

NOLO EPISCOPARI **(Lat = I do not want to be bishoped).** The formal refusal of a bishopric. If repeated three times, it was believed, hence "What I say three times is true". (Lewis Carroll).

NOMINATED, LITTLE or BAREBONE'S (q.v.) PARLIA-MENT (4 July-12 Dec. 1653). (*See* COMMONWEALTH (1649-1653)-5,6.) The army invited congregations to name persons considered fit to be members and the council of the army then selected 129 of these for England, 6 for Ireland and S for Scotland. These 140 were then summoned. It was a totally inexperienced but godly body which thought that the law could be codified into a pocket book. It also wanted reforms which were too radical for Cromwell, the Army or the businessmen.

NONCONFORMITY. Originally the tenet of those who in the 17th cent. agreed with Anglican doctrine but would not conform with Anglican practice or discipline; the term came to embrace all protestant dissenters particularly English Presbyterians, Congregationalists and Methodists, Quakers and Baptists.

NON-CO-OPERATION MOVEMENT (India) was launched by Gandhi as a leader of the Indian National Congress in 1919, to bring pressure for Dominion Status. In theory a peaceful movement in which office holders resigned, courts refused to sit, pupils would not go to school, elections were ignored and so forth, it soon brought violence, as extremists tried to stop poor people from earning their living. There were consequently thousands of arrests. The movement continued until 1924, when the Muslims broke with Congress, whose members also quarrelled.

NON-IMPORTATION ACT (U.S.A.) (1806). *See* NON INTERCOURSE.

NON-IMPORTATION AGREEMENTS. *See* AMERICAN REBELLION-12.

NON INJURY, OATH OF. *See* FEUDALISM-16.

NON-INTERVENTION. *See* INTERVENTION; SPAIN.

NON INTERCOURSE ACTS (U.S.A.) were a series of Acts of Congress passed as a result of the effects of the Napoleonic wars on U.S. trade.

(**1**) The Non-importation Act (July 1806) in reply to the Orders in Council, forbade the importation of specified British goods and was designed to strengthen a mission to Britain about impressment and seizures. The mission failed, but in the meantime Bonaparte issued an interpretation of the Berlin decree requiring the arrest of neutral shipping carrying goods of British origin, even the property of a neutral. In reply (**2**) the Embargo Act (Dec. 1807) required all U.S. ships until Mar. 1809 to deposit a bond before sailing, that their cargoes would be landed only in another U.S. port. This caused far more damage to American commerce than to Britain or France; there was an outcry, and it was repealed by (**3**) the Non-Intercourse Act (Mar. 1809) which authorised (until May 1810) the seizure of British and French ships, and required U.S. ships to give bond that they would not enter British or French ports. The Act was in fact aimed at Britain, since few French ships were at large or French ports unblockaded. It failed to move either belligerent and was followed by (**4**) Macon's Bill No. 2 which offered exclusive U.S. trading rights to whichever should recognise U.S. trading claims first. This was also aimed at Britain (or naive) since Bonaparte's recognition could not affect the issue. Some shipping had all along evaded the acts, and a more open and profitable intercourse now sprang up with Britain, but when Bonaparte issued an ambiguously worded recognition, the Madison govt. accepted it and embargoed British trade. The British promptly reimposed the full rigour of the Orders in Council.

The primary effect of this harassment of British trade was to divert a substantial part of it to S. America before the two countries drifted into the war of 1812-15.

NON-JURORS. *See* CHARLES 11-9; DIVINE RIGHT OF KINGS.

NO MAN'S LAND (1) A narrow strip between Delaware and Pennsylvannia; (**2**) A name for Griqualand East (S. Africa); (**3**) A storage space in 18th cent. ships; (**4**) the land, mostly encumbered with barbed wire and shell craters, between opposing front lines of trenches in World War I; (**5**) a similar area to whose incumbrances mines had been added between front lines in World War II.

NON OBSTANTE **(Lat = notwithstanding).** *See* DISPENSATION.

NON POSSUMUS **(Lat = We cannot).** The papal way of saying 'No'.

NON-REGULATION PROVINCES (India). British Indian areas which, on annexation were not subjected to codes of English law.

NONSUCH (Cuddington, Surrey) was a top-heavy looking, as its name shows, extraordinary palace begun in 1538 and never quite completed, but a favourite abode of Elizabeth I who in 1585 confirmed the agreement there (*see* ELIZABETH 1-22) to assist the Dutch rebels. It was demolished under Charles II to provide materials for a canal.

NON SUIT. A court decision bringing civil proceedings to an end without determining the issue between the parties, thus enabling a plaintiff to start again. Not possible in the High Court since 1875.

NOOTKA SOUND and CONVENTION (Oct. 1790). This settlement on the W. Coast of Vancouver I. was founded by some British China merchants in the 1770s. In 1789 the Spaniards, to assert their claim to exclusive Pacific trading rights seized their ships. War was prevented by the revolutionary disorders in France, which was then Spain's ally. In the convention Spain abandoned her claims.

"NO PEACE WITHOUT SPAIN". *See* SPANISH SUCCESSION, WAR OF-17.

NORE. A sandbank outside the mouth of the Thames near which in the prevailing S.W. winds fleets were often stationed in days of sail; hence the C-in-C at the Nore was usually the flag officer responsible for the defence of the East Coast.

NORDBARUM. *See* STAPLE B-8.

NORD, CO. DU. French Co, chartered for whaling in 1644, secured govt. support, and so lucrative Danish concessions in Spitzbergen in 1663. Its activities added to the picturesque cosmopolitan violence which obtained in those waters throughout the 18th cent.

NORDEN, John (1546-1625), a surveyor, obtained royal support but no money for a projected set of county histories. His *Speculum Britanniae* (Lat: Mirror of Britain) reached only two published parts (Middlesex 1593 and Hertfordshire 1598) and five in manuscript (Essex, Surrey, Kent, Northampton and Cornwall) but he also engraved some good maps for the Middlesex volume which gives much interesting information on London and Westminster.

NORFOLK (AS. = Northern Folk, of the E. Angles). (1) A see for the North Folk was created at Elmham in 673 out of the original E. Anglian see at Dunwich. This probably represents a recognition of some pre-existing division between Norfolk and Suffolk whose origins, nature or purpose is not now known. The area was much fought over in the Danish wars and a Danish earldom of E. Anglia was formed in 1017. This was suppressed in 1076 after the rebellion of Ralph Gauder its last holder. Ralph's Norfolk lands went to the Bigod family who became until 1300 the dominating influence in the county. When their lands escheated, the Warennes succeeded to their influence but in 1310 the Bigod inheritance was granted to Thomas of Brotherton, Edward II's brother.

(**2**) Norfolk was perhaps more involved collectively

in the Peasants Revolt of 1381 than other counties. There were special local reasons for this, especially the grip which Flemings were supposed to have upon the Norwich cloth trade, and many Flemings were murdered. But many of the Norfolk gentry took park in the revolt, which isolated the area from the rest of the Kingdom for some weeks, and led to the wholesale destruction of monastic and aristocratic title deeds. The contrast between Norfolk stubbornness and the weakness of public authority thereafter long remained. In particular the violent assertion of claims, and the armed maintenance of litigants was a regular occurrence. Amongst others Pastons, Tudenhams, Fastolf and Pole fought each other for properties. In 1469 John Mowbray, D. of Norfolk for example, privately besieged Caistor Castle with 3000 men.

NORFOLK. *See* HOWARD; MOWBRAY.

NORFOLK BROADS are many shallow flint quarries worked from Neolithic times on a large scale along the rivers which concentrate fanwise from Geldeston, Brundal, Coltishall and Hickling upon Great Yarmouth. They were flooded perhaps by the great storms of the 1260s and became part of the navigable rivers. Quarrying virtually ceased, but they became a source of thatching reeds throughout E. Anglia, a huge breeding ground for birds, from which the unique practice of punt gunning developed, and from the 1870s, despite silting, a place for recreational boating which turned into a tourist industry by the 1970s.

NORFOLK REBELLION (1549). *See* KET'S REBELLION.

NORHAM CASTLE. Border fortress on the Tweed. *See* DURHAM-3.

NORHAM TREATIES 1209, 1212 and 1291. K. John was at the Border in 1209 with overwhelming force and William the Lion, rather than fight, wanted to secure the succession of his own family. He paid 15,000 marks, and handed over his daughters Isabel and Margaret to be married to John's sons Henry III and Richard. In 1212 William gave his earldom of Huntingdon to his son Alexander and sent him to England to be disposed in marriage. William and Alexander both did fealty to John, who sent a force to put down Cuthred MacWilliam's rebellion against them. The arrangements apparently led to a quiet succession between father and son in 1214. The exact terms of the agreement of 1212 are unknown but evidently provided for the subjection (of some kind) of the Scottish Kings to the English.

In about 1217 Alexander sent a copy to Pope Honorius asking that it be ratified or annulled and the Legate Pandulf came successfully to an agreement (1219) about this with Alexander, as a result of which he married John's daughter Joan in 1221. Honorius believed that the King of England had some kind of superiority over the King of the Scots and the treaty was still in force in 1237 and partly, perhaps, in 1279. In the treaty of 1291 the competitors for the Scottish crown, on submitting their claims to the arbitrament of Edward I were required by him and agreed to recognise his superior lordship. They surrendered the Kingdom to his keeping for restoration to the successful claimant, but he was to demand only homage from the claimants' successors. This conclusion was reached after a review of the records including, presumably, the treaty of 1212.

NORMANBY, M. of (first creation). *See* SHEFFIELD; **(second creation).** *See* PHILIPS.

NORMANDY (= Northmen's country) (*see* VIKINGS-15). **(1)** The R. Seine was the best access for 9th cent. Viking shipborne armies to Central Gaul, but in 88S-6 their advance was contained at Paris. Some, notably those clustered about ROLLO or ROLF (?-931) had been operating and sporadically settling in the area for years. Rollo's wife came from Bayeux. Prompted by the Duke of France at Paris, K. Charles the Simple changed from futile hostility to compromise. Rollo was to have the district about the Seine estuary as a fief. He would keep his followers in order and, in defending it, would automatically stop raiders penetrating to the Ile de France. Under the T. of St. Claire-sur-Epte (911) he was baptised and made Lord of the area as a tenant of the King. He and his successor WILLIAM LONGSWORD (r. 927-42) used various titles (count, marquis, prince) ending with duke from 940. The dukes owed bare homage to the French crown without defined services.

(2) Internal disorder was perennial, for the Duke's Norse (often pagan) subordinates had taken their lands by force, the rest resented mediatisation and immigration continued for another half century. The barons claimed an essentially unfeudal status, which even entitled them to levy private wars. To keep any sort of control the Dukes raised their prestige by good marriages (RICHARD the FEARLESS 942-96 married Hugh Capet's sister), they clung firmly to all rights of coinage, forfeiture and escheat and they diverted Norman superabundant energies to westward expansion. Rollo took in the Bessin (924) before abdicating in 927; Longsword, Avranches before he was assassinated; Richard the Fearless, the Contentin. Keeping order especially among pagans remained, however, the major problem. It generated a rudimentary central govt. and Exchequer, and though not always or wholly successful, the Dukes managed to erect feudally dependent counties (Arques, Eu, Evreux, Hiesmois, Mortain) in the hands of relatives.

These were embedded among about 20 bailiwicks each headed by a *vicomte,* who was a sort of sheriff employed by the Duke to manage his local estates, collect his rents and fines, maintain order and justice, and lead the local levies. The church's seven bishops and numerous conventual houses were mostly free of the count's and sometimes of the *vicomte's* jurisdiction but the Duke made every important church appointment himself regardless of the electing body, as often as possible in favour of a relative, and he habitually settled ecclesiastical disputes.

As power to control his wild men grew, those who disliked it began to seek fortunes elsewhere (e.g. Italy). The duchy was still ill defined and thinly populated. Border controls and coastguards did not exist.

(3) By the year 1020 the country was under a feudal order in which the baronies were held of the Duke mostly by knight service. The Norman aristocracy had abandoned the Scandinavian custom of fighting on foot, and came to war as quilted or partly armoured cavalry. The barons owed service for about 800 such knights but subenfeoffed for about double that number. Allowing 4 or 5 grooms, esquires and servants each, a Norman army might have amounted to 3,700 souls.

(4) There was cross-Channel trade and the duchy profited from the 10th cent. boom until the resumption of Viking activity at the end of it. Normans though increasingly Gallicised, sympathised with Scandinavians. Both Richard the Fearless in 968 and RICHARD (II) The GOOD (r. 996-1026) in 1017 took Danish second wives. Raiders by 989 were using Norman ports against English. An angry Anglo-Norman dispute (990) was composed by papal mediation. The T. of Rouen laid down that each would protect the traders and expel the enemies of each other. This worked well enough until a great Viking armament raided England in 1000; difficult to resist, it wintered (and doubtless recruited privately) in Normandy, and in 1001 returned to England. The coastal English retaliated by ravaging the Cotentin.

(5) Something more was needed than a police treaty such as the T. of Rouen. In 1001 Ethelred, K. of the English, married Emma the sister of the Norman Duke. Within a year, as it happened, the King and his family were fugitives. They claimed. D. Richard's hospitality. For 12 years the children, including the future Edward the Confessor, had besides a Norman mother, a Norman-

French education. One, Godgifu, married Drogo of the Vexin, a friend of the dukes' and in 1035 Eustace of Boulogne. When Canute took the English throne (1016) Edward returned to Normandy and stayed for 25 years, outlasting his host and Dukes RICHARD III (r. 1026-7) and ROBERT the MAGNIFICENT or the DEVIL (1027-35). When Edward succeeded in England (1042) he was as much the first Norman as almost the last English King. It was natural for him to appoint energetic Norman prelates such as Robert of Jumièges to English sees, and the occasional Norman noble to an English estate. He was used to them.

(6) Robert the Devil left the Duchy to his famous bastard WILLIAM (r. 103S-87) later the CONQUEROR who was eight years old (*see* WILLIAM I).

(7) After 1066 most Norman nobles acquired lands on both sides of the Channel, and a little later Norman religious houses followed suit or founded daughter establishments. When the kingdom and the duchy were in different hands (1087-96, 1101-6, 1144-54 and after the French Conquest in 1204) this posed difficult choices of loyalty and legal obligation. Norman families could and progressively did divide their inheritances. For religious orders the practical problems were greater because of the difficulties of alienation.

(8) The periods of war and confusion caused by the incompetence of Duke ROBERT II "COURTHOSE" (= short pants) during his two reigns (1087-96, 1101-B. of Tinchebray 1106), by sporadic border wars with the French King and by the Angevin occupation of 1144-54 retarded the growth of a modernised administration, until HENRY II (D. 1150-80) could build one under the protection of his vast European power. A Seneschal headed the financial and judicial system with its H.Q. at Caen. He, with justices, held all the *pleas of the sword*, relating to crime and the duke's rights, regardless of franchise. The local *vicomtes* had been grouped under the supervision of *baillis*, frequently local castellans, responsible to the treasury. Judging by contributions to Richard I's ransom, financially Normandy was worth about one eighth of England.

(9) For twenty years, while his son grew up, Normandy and the Channel trade were peaceful and prosperous. Even Breton piracy declined when Henry gained Brittany in 1158. The English and Norman govt's exchanged trained officials and could make safe financial transfers between Caen and Winchester. Norman abbeys established daughter houses in England and artists, craftsmen and architects worked in each other's countries.

(10) Apart from difficulties of communication, especially in the winter seas, the cohesion of Henry's estates depended too much upon a headstrong adventurous half savage military aristocracy, liable to be bored by a long peace. Eleanor, tempestuous and clever, was too like Henry. In their son, unsurprisingly, the faults and virtues of their king were exaggerated. When Henry and Eleanor finally quarrelled, there was no hope of controlling the son. Eleanor, adored by the Aquitainians, was an independent potentate upon whom her sons could rely. The French King had every reason to encourage their insubordination everywhere, but his principal target was Normandy. The pattern of subversion from without was resumed. The sons had been given nominal, but not real, authority over parts of Henry's dominions, HENRY the Young King (r. 1180-3) in Normandy, RICHARD in Aquitaine. They were encouraged to claim the substance. Their four rebellions (1173, 1181, 1184 and 1187-9) were really proxy attacks by the Capetian on the Plantagenet.

(11) With brief interludes these continued after K. Philip Augustus returned from the Crusade. The policy was now to incite John to rebel against K. Richard. The duchy had a sound administration which accustomed

Normans to orderly govt. While Richard reigned, its military protection and order were assured. When he died, John's unregulated habits and failure to pay or control his troops spread confusion and trouble. The defenders of Normandy were mostly not Normans, for the latter preferred the uninspired but more intelligent methods of K. Philip. He moved slowly, confirming privileges, replacing bad officials and untrustworthy military commanders. This erosive process culminated in the surrender of Rouen at midsummer 1204.

(12) English Kings continued to claim Normandy until the T. of Paris of 1259. *See also articles on the contemporary English and French Kings.*

NORMANDY CAMPAIGN (6th June-Aug. 1944) opened the long-awaited attack on Germany from the west under the overall command of the U.S. General Eisenhower with Field Marshal Montgomery commanding the land forces. It began with the bombing of the Seine bridges and airborne landings behind the German coastal defences, and then 2 British, 2 U.S. and a Canadian division came ashore between the R's Orne and Vire. These were soon reinforced (*see* MULBERRY HARBOURS) so that Montgomery's force totalled over 320,000 by 12 June. While British, Canadian and Polish troops attacked on the left of the Allied front and attracted most of the German resistance, the Americans, under Gen. Bradley on the right broke through the German defences to clear Brittany and advance towards Paris. Hitler's personal interference to forbid retreats presented Montgomery with a vulnerable enemy concentration which was shattered by bombing and nearly surrounded at Falaise. Badly mauled, the Germans' escape and northward flight ended the campaign.

NORMAN, Montagu Collett (1871-1950) D.S.O., 1st Ld. NORMAN of St. CLERE (1943) was Governor of the Bank of England from 1920-44. His main initial aim was to return to the monetary conditions of 1914, i.e. to enable industry to maintain its world position by processing cheap imported materials. This led to the overvaluation, with Churchill's support, of sterling by attachment in external dealings to the Gold Standard. This represented a misreading, in which he was not alone, of post-war international economics. In the overture to the 1929 slump, he worked hard, but ineffectually against economic movements which were too strong for him. His contribution to the collapse of 1931 was partly caused by an understandable obsession with the recent memory of the German wheelbarrow inflation from which, so he believed, attachment to a Gold Standard would have saved the Mark, and he proposed the printing of ration books by way of precaution. On the other hand his views were an important factor in the remarkable stability of the economy in World War II.

NORMAN RULERS 1087-1154. See APPENDIX GENEALOGY.

NORN (O.N. *Norroena mal* = northern speech) A Norwegian dialect influenced by Pictish, used in the Shetlands and Orkneys. It lost ground to Scots during the Reformation because it possessed neither Bible nor liturgy. By 1670 all the inhabitants spoke Scots, Norn being confined to four parishes, and by 1780 it was extinct, but many words are found in the local dialect. It survives in a more Norse form in the Faeroes.

NORREYS. See ELIZABETH I-24.

NORRIS or NORREYS. Three groups (of Fyfield, Rycote and Speke) of families sharing a common 14th cent. ancestor at Speke. See following entries.

NORRIS or NORREYS of RYCOTE (1) Sir Henry (?-1536) was a friend of Henry VIII and a supporter of Anne Boleyn against Wolsey. He was executed on trumped up charges of adultery with Anne, probably because he refused to implicate her in a false confession. His son **(2) Henry (?1525-1601) Ld. NORRIS of RYCOTE (1572)** shared with Sir Thomas Bedingfield the duty of guarding

P. Elizabeth during Mary's reign. He was kind to her, and she believed that his father had been unjustly executed. She restored all the family property at her accession and in 1570 used him as Ambassador to France in the Huguenot interest. His second *s.* **(3) Sir Edward (?-1603) a** quarrelsome soldier, became Sir Philip Sydney's deputy at Flushing in 158S and then Sir John Conway's at Ostend in 1587. Thenceforth as deputy or Governor he was almost continuously in charge of the defence of that important port until 1599. His brother **(4) Sir John (?1547-97)** a soldier, volunteered under the Huguenot Admiral Coligny in 1571, served with credit under Essex in Ireland and in 1573, and thence returned to the Low Countries in 1577, where his services in the field were in constant demand. He fought at Rymenant in 1578 and at Steenwyck in 1580. In 1584 he went to Ireland again where another brother **(5) Sir Thomas (1556-99)** had been campaigning since 1579, as acting Governor of Connaught (1580-1) and then Colonel of the Munster forces. Sir John now became Pres. of Munster but having appointed Sir Thomas as his deputy returned to the Low Countries to provide experience in Leicester's expedition which Leicester lacked. He won a victory at Grave in 1586, but Leicester was continually at loggerheads with his subordinates, particularly Sir John; the expedition came to a standstill, and the Queen recalled Sir John but with honour. Hence when Leicester came home, Sir John returned under Lord Willoughby in 1587, then was employed in setting up the defences against the Armada and became Ambassador to Holland in 1588. Meanwhile his brother was having trouble in Munster, where the plantations languished for lack of the resources employed in the Spanish war. In 1589 Sir John was joint (military) commander with Drake of the Spanish expedition, whose lack of success was attributed in part to their incompatibility. In 1591 and again in 1593 he commanded in Brittany (*see* ELIZABETH 1-26) but by 1595 it was time to return to his presidency of Munster, where Sir Thomas had had poor fortune but had amassed for the family behoof considerable lands. The brother managed to bring Tyrone's rebellion to a temporary end (1595-6) and having reached an accommodation with him at Dundalk, tried but failed to pacify Connaught. In fact neither side adhered to the truce. Worn out by a lifetime of exertion, Sir John returned to his estates at Mallow, where he died. Sir Thomas succeeded him in the warlike presidency, but died of wounds 18 months later. Their equally hot tempered nephew **(6) Francis (1579-1622) 2nd Ld. (1600) E. of BERKSHIRE (1621)** was a member of Nottingham's mission to Spain in 1605 and was primarily a Berkshire magnate. In 1621 he came to blows with Lord Scrope in the precincts of the House of Lords, who committed him to the Fleet prison. Mortified, it is said, by this, he killed himself with a crossbow.

NORRIS or NORREYS of SPEKE. Three brothers **(1) Thomas (1653-1700)** was M.P. for Liverpool from 1688-9S **(2) Sir William (1657-1702)** M.P. for Liverpool from 1698-1701 was sent to India to negotiate for (1698) trade on behalf of the English or London East India Co, with the Emperor Aurungzib. Opposed by the HEIC who offered to suppress piracy on the Aden and Basra routes, the mission failed. **(3) Sir John (?1660-1749),** sea officer trained by Sir Clowdisley Shovell, fought at Lagos (1693) and after a voyage to Hudson's Bay (1697) fought with distinction at Malaga (1704) and Barcelona (1705). He reached flag rank in 1707, and from 1708 he was continuously an M.P. He was in the Mediterranean in 1710-11 and in the Baltic from 1715-27. The latter was a difficult assignment for he had initially to support the Danes and then, after Charles XII's death to maintain the independence of Sweden. From 1718-30 he combined a lordship of the Admiralty with this and his Parliamentary work.

NORRIS, Admiral. *See* WARS OF. 1739-48-2.

NORTH, Frederick (1732-92) known by his courtesy title as **Ld. NORTH,** but only from 1790 **8th Ld. NORTH and 2nd E. of GUILDFORD,** became a Pelhamite M.P. in 1754 and a leading opponent of John Wilkes. He held the lucrative Paymastership of the Forces under the Elder Pitt and was Ch. of the Exch. in 1767. In 1770 he became prime minister. A respected House of Commons man and administrator, he was caught up in the unprecedented difficulties of the American Rebellion, in which, like George III he would have preferred to compromise. He was isolated between growing extremisms on both sides of the Atlantic and, though he several times offered to resign, the King kept him in office as the ablest man available. He resigned in 1782, returned with Fox under the D. of Portland in 1783, but was driven out on the issues raised by Fox's India Bill. Later he opposed the Younger Pitt and supported the Warren Hastings impeachment, but was forced into retirement by ill health and blindness.

NORTHAMPTON. *See* HOWARD.

NORTHAMPTON, ASSIZE of (1176) an expansion of the Assize of Clarendon of 1166, in the form of 13 instructions to six panels of justices who were to go on Eyre on newly delineated circuits. Penalties were increased in severity for those who failed to pass a trial by Ordeal, and some of the clauses related to the restoration of order in the counties in the aftermath of the rebellion of Henry the Young King (1172-73).

NORTHAMPTON-SHIRE. Local fertility has always supported a flourishing agriculture (especially animal husbandry) and associated industries such as leather-working and shoe making. There is continuous evidence of prosperity since the Early Iron Age. It was occupied by Mercians and then by the Danes but the town was not developed until the reconquest by Alfred's successors. This caused it to become the centre of the new, probably military shire. The Danes burned it in 1010 during Ethelred's wars, but it revived fairly rapidly. At the Conquest, Simon of Senlis (St. Liz) was made E. of Northampton and Huntingdon. He built the priory of St. Andrew at Northampton and also the castle whose convenience and strategically central position made it a regular resort for the Norman and Plantagenet Kings. This had disadvantages too, for the town and county were several times a focus of conflict in the mediaeval civil wars: for example the castle, held for John was besieged by the barons in 1215; it was stormed by the royalists in 1264 when held by the younger Simon de Montfort; and in 1460 Richard of York captured Henry VI there after a battle outside the town.

From the late 15th cent. the county was one of those most affected by inclosures, which bred much civil unrest; the displacement of population was, however, relatively small, because the rich corn trade with London made it possible to take in marginal lands. One result was the rise, in addition to Rockingham Castle and the royal manor of Fotheringhay, of substantial estates centred, eventually on great houses such as Althorpe, Burghley, Castle Ashby, Deene, Dingley Hall and Kirby Hall. The prosperity was further increased by the improvement of the main rivers, especially the Nene, Welland and Ouse and by the construction of the Grand Union Canal; this ushered in the industrial demand for Northamptonshire ironstone in Birmingham, and iron quarrying became an important activity around Kettering and Wellingborough and after 1933 spread to the neighbourhood of Corby. World War II increased the demand and urgency, with the result that foundries were established especially at Corby, which became an important industrial town.

The City of Northampton was a county borough from 1888-1974 when it, together with the Soke of Peterborough, were amalgamated into the new county of Northampton.

NORTHAMPTONSHIRE GELD ROLLS (written c. 1066-75) was a Danegeld survey by Hundreds and is the earliest surviving text of such a record. Of the 2663 Hides described, about one third were waste and only 631½ were assessed for payment.

NORTHAMPTON, STAT. OF (1328). See STAPLE B-2.

NORTH ATLANTIC TREATY ORGANISATION (N.A.T.O.) was set up under the Washington T. (Apr. 1949) between U.S.A., Britain, Canada, the W. European Allied Powers, Iceland, Italy and Portugal to resist Russian imperialism and subversion. The H.Q. was in Paris with Lord Ismay as its first Secretary General and a unified defence force was created. Greece and Turkey joined in 1952, W. Germany in 1954. France announced an intention to withdraw in 1969. Thereafter the main services components rested on German soil. The collapse of the Russian communist state in 1988 deprived it of some of its purposes but not, it seems, the will to live, despite the provisions of the T. of Maastricht which provided for the creation of a European army.

NORTH BRITAIN or NB = Scotland. An artificial usage virtually out of date.

NORTH BRITON. See WILKES, J and WILKES *v* WOOD.

NORTH CAROLINA. See CAROLINA.

NORTHCOTE. Devon family. **(1) Sir John (1599-1676) Bart. (1641)** rich Devon puritan M.P. 1641. He was excluded from the Commons because of his association with the presbyterians from 1648-54. He was M.P. for Barnstaple in the Cavalier Parliament from 1667-76. A descendent **(2) Sir Stafford Henry (1818-87) 8th Bart. (1851) 1st E. of IDDESLEIGH (1885)** was Gladstone's private secretary (1842) and helped him in his Oxford elections (1847, 1852 and 1853) but he became a Conservative M.P. in 1855. With Sir Charles Trevelyan he was responsible for the important Northcote-Trevelyan Report on the future civil service (1854). He was a confident Tory champion in opposition, and in 1866 became Disraeli's Pres. of the Board of Trade and in 1867 Sec. of State for India. As Chancellor of the Exchequer (1874-80) he accepted the permanence of Income Tax and so introduced exemptions and concessions for smaller incomes. He also set up and serviced a Sinking Fund. After 1876 he was also leader of the House. His arrogant abruptness probably increased the bitterness of Parliamentary obstruction at that time, and he failed to control the brilliant and derisive 'Fourth Party'. After a period in opposition, he became First Lord of the Treasury (i.e. joint Prime Minister) with Salisbury in the short govt. of 1885-6 and Foreign Secretary under Salisbury in 1886. As such he was weak, besides being intolerable in Cabinet, and at Goschen's insistence Salisbury required his resignation. He died in Salisbury's presence. His son **(3) Henry (1846-1911) 1st Ld. NORTHCOTE (1900)** was his father's secretary from 1877-80 and M.P. for Exeter from 1880-99, was from 1899-1903 a conscientious and sensible Governor of Bombay where he set up a standing famine and plague organisation and instituted land and local Govt. reforms. From 1903-7 he was Gov. Gen. of Australia.

NORTHCLIFFE. See HARMSWORTH.

NORTH, COUNCIL OF THE. Created by Richard III in the spring of 1484, initially as the Council of his heir Edward of Middleham who, however, died in Apr. Its presidency was entrusted to John de la Pole, E. of Lincoln, who became heir apparent on the death of the Prince. It included the E. of Northumberland (Percy), Lds. Greystoke, Scrope of Bolton and Scrope of Masham and Sir John Conyers. It was based at Sandal Castle near Wakefield, but the quarterly sessions were to be held in York. Although perhaps intended to emulate Edward IV's Council of Wales the extent of its authority in the Palatinates of Durham and Lancaster is unclear. It was empowered to keep the peace and punish lawbreaking. It could also take cognisance of land disputes if the parties agreed. It was discontinued by Henry VII in 1485 but in 1522 the northern English border counties were placed under a Lieutenant and Council. This was primarily a defence organisation with only incidental administrative and judicial functions. The Pilgrimage of Grace provoked an administrative and judicial reorganisation. The Council of the North was accordingly set up on the model of the Council for Wales and the Marches under the Presidency of Cuthbert Tunstall, Bp. of Durham in 1537, but its powers were not extensive. It never dealt with treasons. The territorial jurisdiction covered Yorkshire, Lancashire and the area northward (*see* DURHAM, PALATINATE OF) and it sat at York.

By 1600 it was attracting the professional animosity of the Common lawyers and like the Welsh Council its criminal and civil jurisdictions were attacked in 1604 and 1608, but except for Tunstall and Strafford who as Vist. Wentworth exercised the Presidency from 1626 until he went to Ireland in 1632, no major personality held office in it; hence its reputation and efficacy was always inferior to the Welsh Council. It was abolished in 1641.

NORTH EAST PASSAGE. In 1553 the Merchant Adventurers Co. of London sponsored a 3 ship expedition under Sir Hugh Willoughby to find a north about passage to China. He was wrecked on the Kola Peninsula but his second in command Richard Chancellor reached Archangel, and went overland to Moscow to meet the Czar. This contact bore fruit in the foundation of the Muscovy Co. in 1555. In 1594 a Dutch expedition under Willem Barents reached Novaya Zemlya and found the entrance to the Kara Sea. In 1596 Barents stumbled on Spitzbergen and in 1607 Henry Hudson, on behalf of the Muscovy Co attempted a passage by way of the North Pole. He found Jan Mayen I. on the way back, but more importantly he created an interest in the Spitzbergen whale fisheries which soon flourished. Between 1725-42 Russian govt. expeditions, mostly under the Danish seaman Vitus Behring, charted the N. Siberian coast, Kamchatka, Anadyr and reached America. The first through passage from the west was achieved by the Swedish Baron Nordensköld in 1878-9; the first from the east by the Russians in 1912-13.

The Russians developed the July-Oct. north Siberian shipping route between 1932-39.

NORTHERN CIRCARS. See CIRCAR.

NORTHERN REBELLION (Oct. 1569-Feb. 1570). (1) The countryside of this affair was the backward, poor and R. Catholic area of England north of the Trent. This was still feudally ruled by great nobles especially the Es. of Northumberland, Westmorland and Derby, and Lords Dacre, Lumley, Montague and Morley. These were all lords of wide lands and men but little money. The weak royal power was represented by the Council of the North under the E. of Sussex. There was discontent for a variety of reasons, unified by a desire to defend the old religion.

(2) The D. of Norfolk meant to exploit this for his own ends. Originally, with the Es. of Arundel and Leicester he proposed a *coup* against Cecil. This appealed to the northern magnates. The govt. was to be seized with Spanish help, to be procured by promises of a friendly settlement and a cessation of unofficial English succours to the Huguenots. The Spanish viceroy in the Netherlands, the D. of Alva, doubted if there was much substance in the plan, and advised Philip II against it. Leicester went over to Cecil. Norfolk abandoned the idea, but hatched a scheme to marry Mary Q. of Scots and secure the recognition of her right to the English succession and her liberation. Most of the council supported this, but Norfolk was also negotiating for French military help in Scotland and receiving French money.

(3) In Sept. 1569 Elizabeth I heard of the marriage plot and forbade the marriage. Norfolk left court in anger. Leicester was cowed by the Queen's personality, security measures were set on foot, French and Spanish diplomatic correspondence opened, and Arundel arrested. Thereupon Norfolk sued for pardon and tried to stop the avalanche. He was put into the Tower. On 10 Oct. Northumberland and Westmorland, who had heard of this, met and the latter persuaded all present to rise. Sussex, meanwhile started to mobilise but few answered his call. By 12 Nov. the northerners and borderers had assembled at Brancepeth; on 15 Nov. they took Durham, and issued a proclamation against the Queen's ill advisers. They were proclaimed rebels on 20 Nov. but were too strong for Sussex, who remained at York.

(4) The rebels now marched southwards to rescue Mary at Tutbury, while the govt. concentrated troops in Lincolnshire, Leicestershire and Warwickshire. On 24 Nov. they reached Selby: on 25 Nov. Mary was removed to Coventry. As a further southward movement would entrap them among several powerful royal armies, they retreated. They disbanded at Durham on 15 Dec. and the leaders made for Naworth and Dacre's country across the Pennines where they would be protected by the Scots border lords. Murray, the Anglophile Scots regent, captured Northumberland, but when Murray was assassinated on 23 Jan. 1570, Scots intervention became inevitable. On urgent orders from the Queen Lord Hunsdon, her cousin, marched from Berwick for Carlisle, passed Naworth in the dark, routed Dacre's larger force on the Gelt (20 Feb. 1570) and reached Carlisle just ahead of the Scots.

(5) Meanwhile the other southern armies overran and despoiled the country. About 500 minor rebels were hanged but there was wholesale looting of cattle and stores which the commanders were powerless to stop. Since, by Feb., stocks were low anyhow, the north starved.

(6) These events destroyed the political importance of the uncoordinate R. Catholic and feudal order in the north just before Pius V's bull *Regnans in Excelsis* deposing Elizabeth was published at Rome on 2S Feb. The main internal instrument for effecting the English counter-reformation was thus removed before it could be used. Norfolk was soon released. *See also* ELIZABETH I-11,12.

NORTHERN TERRITORY (Aust.) was part of N.S.W., then of Southern Australia and from 1911 administered from Darwin by the Commonwealth. Mostly desert with unascertained mineral resources, the population of this huge tract was only 129,000 in 1979.

NORTH GERMAN CONFEDERATION of 22 states north of the R. Main was formed in 1867 after the Prussian victory over Austria in 1866. It was wholly dominated by Prussia whose King was President and C-in-C. It was dissolved in 1871 to make way for the establishment of the German Empire.

NORTHMEN. *See* VIKINGS.

NORTH SEA OIL, discovered far offshore in 1969, was first pumped to land in 1975. It ended British dependence on overseas oil and transformed the balance of payments, and life on the Scots N.E. coast. Production reached a peak in the 1980s when Britain was an oil exporter, and then began a very slow decline.

NORTH SEA OUTRAGE or DOGGER BANK INCIDENT. In Oct. 1904 the Russian Second Pacific Squadron on the way from Reval to fight the Japanese, opened panic fire on some British trawlers and each other. This irrational incident helped to influence existing anti-Russian sentiment.

NORTHSTEAD. *See* CHILTERN HUNDREDS.

NORTHUMBERLAND (*see* DEIRA; NEWCASTLE UPON TYNE; NORTH, COUNCIL OF; NORTHUMBRIA; MARCHES, SCOTTISH) The area was always agriculturally poor, raising cattle and a few sheep, but coal was mined even in Roman times and the Tyne coal trade, mostly to London, developed prosperously in the 13th cent. There were also mediaeval lead and silver mines and iron was forged at Stretton in

14th cent. Salt was made in large amounts at Workworth and North and South Shields. All these developed towards the modern ironworks and furnaces, and chemical production. The area had a county council after 1888, but Newcastle and Tynemouth became independent county boroughs. In 1974 the southern part from Ponteland and Seton Delaval to the Tyne became part of the new county Tyne and Wear. The county disappeared as an administrative area as a result of the Tory determination to reduce the number of tiers of local government after 1993.

NORTHUMBERLAND, Ds. of. *See* DUDLEY; EDWARD VI; PERCY; SMITHSON.

NORTHUMBERLAND, Es. of. *See* PERCY.

NORTHUMBRIA, ANGLIAN KINGDOM. (1) Angles began to settle east Yorkshire in the late 5th cent. and reached York by about 500. They formed the Kingdom of **Deira** and their southward expansion was inhibited by the British Kingdom of Elmet. Further north other Angles later settled at Bamburgh and along the adjacent coast. These formed the Kingdom of **Bernicia.** The Kings of both tribes were descended from Woden through two brothers respectively Wegdaeg (Deira) and Baeldaeg (Bernicia). The Bernicians encountered grave difficulties until **Ida** the Flamebearer (r. 547-60) organised them and swept further north and west. Under his sons **Theodric** and **Hussa** the Bernicians were digesting an area which reached into the Lothians, while **Aelle** (r. 560-88) of Deira was penetrating Wharfedale.

(2) When Aelle died **Aethelric** of Bernicia (?-593) established himself as King of both countries. His energetic son **Aethelfrith** (594-616) carried the expansion further north and west. In 603 he overthrew an alliance of Strathclyde Britons, Scots and Dalriadans at **Degsastan** (location uncertain) and by 613 Anglian penetration across the Pennines brought on a war, and victory at Chester over Solomon ap Cynan, King of Powys. These events broke the territorial continuity of the Britons. They also perhaps, disturbed the southern English Kingdoms, for Raedwald of East Anglia, their paramount King had given asylum to **Edwin** (r. 616-32) son of Aelle. Asked to kill Edwin, he refused and was attacked but he defeated and killed Aethelfrith on the R. Idle (616).

(3) Aethelfrith's son **Oswald** fled to Dalriada, while the Deiran Edwin ruled. Oswald lived at Iona where he was educated as a Christian. In 625 Edwin married a Christian wife, Ethelburga, daughter of K. Ethelbert of Kent. He promised to respect her religion and she brought Paulinus, lately consecrated a bishop with her. He converted Edwin in 627 and he and his court set about the forcible conversion of the country. At the same time he founded Edinburgh and waged a series of wars against the Britons; he conquered Elmet, invaded North Wales, attacked the I. of Man, occupied Anglesey and drove Cadwallon, King of Gwynedd, into the I. of Priestholm. His activities provoked a reaction. Penda of Mercia intervened, and with Cadwallon killed Edwin at Heathfield or Hatfield Chase (632). For a year **Osric**, Edwin's cousin, maintained himself in Deira and **Eanfrith**, Aethelfrith's son, in Bernicia but Cadwallon killed them separately in 633; Penda killed Eadfrith one of Edwin's surviving sons and his other descendants died in Gaul, except Eanfled, queen to Oswiu (*see* 5 below.)

(4) Oswald (r. 633-41) now approached from Iona, gathering a force as he came. He met Cadwallon's army on the Rowley Burn near Hexham and there killed him. The men of both kingdoms accepted him at once; the Mercians fled; internal disputes interrupted the power of Gwynedd. This complex of events had however, dissolved the fragile Roman Christianity imposed by Edwin. In 634 Oswald imported a mission under the great St. Aidan from Iona, and established it at Lindisfarne. The conversion of Northumbria proceeded from the north, while Oswald's power overshadowed England. He married a daughter of the West Saxon K. Cynegils, who with other kings accepted him as overlord, but in 641 a quarrel with Penda of Mercia and perhaps with Welsh rulers provoked a war in which he was killed at Maserfield (Oswestry, Salop). Though a high handed ruler, his dismembered parts were quickly miraculous. His head, buried at Lindisfarne, ended up in St. Cuthbert's coffin. His body went to Bardney and in 909 to Gloucester. His many arms were kept at Bamburgh, Ely, St Paul's and Gloucester. Abp. Willibrord in the 8th cent and Judith of Northumbria took relics abroad. Cults grew up in N. Italy, Germany and Ireland. *Lives* were written, and he even figures in an Icelandic saga.

(5) Separatism reasserted itself. Oswald's brother **Oswy** or **Oswiu** (r. 641-70) took Bernicia but **Oswine** (r. 642-51) son of Osric (3 above) was acclaimed in Deira. The Mercians had penetrated the adjacent Elmet and when in 651, Oswiu murdered Oswine, the Deirans chose Oswald's son **Aethelwald** (r. 651-4) who preferred the protection of the heathen Penda to that of his Christian uncle. Hence Deira came under Mercian overlordship. Penda regarded Oswiu as a dangerous neighbour and sought to restrain him. One of Oswiu's sons was a hostage at Penda's court, another married Penda's daughter, while his daughter Alhflaeda married Penda's son Peada in 653. But the peace could not be kept. There had been at least two Mercian forays into Bernicia before Penda raised an army from all Mercia and summoned the E. Anglian King Aethelbere and some Welsh princes headed by Cadafael of Gwynedd. They staged a great invasion, guided by Aethelwald. The rival forces met at the Winwaedsfield near Leeds (654). Aethelwald stood by, while the Bernicians, against great odds defeated the allies. Penda and Aethelhere were killed, Cadafael escaped to Wales. For a short while, until the proclamation of Wulfhere in Mercia (651), Oswiu was overlord of all the English. Afterwards, as undisputed master of Northumbria he encroached incessantly upon the Picts, and at the Synod of Whitby (664) decided for Roman against Celtic church practices (*see* MISSIONARIES IN BRITAIN ETC 6-8).

(6) His son **Ecgfriths** (r. 670-85) reign began on a similar pattern. In 674 he beat off a Mercian invasion so decisively that he could annex Lindsey. In 678 he was himself defeated on the Trent, Lindsey reverted to Mercia, and he concentrated on the north, annexing much Pictish territory and pressing into Galloway. The east coast up to the Forth was ruled by one of his earldomen based in Dunbar. On the other hand in 672, as a result of matrilineal Pictish succession, Brude mac Beli, a son of the King of Strathclyde, became King of the Picts. Though Ecgfrith was the accepted overlord of the Strathclyde Britons, these soon seemed dangerous, especially combined with Dalriadan (Irish) unrest. In 684 he made a destructive foray into Ireland. In 685, against advice, he led another against the Picts. He perished at Nechtansmere near Forfar. Northumbrian overlordship in the north-west lapsed, the Picts regained much of their territory, and the northern frontier became a disputed land, which, however, **Aldfrith** (r. 685-704) a scholarly, Irish educated bastard of Oswiu, defended with ultimate success.

(7) In the long relative freedom of the Northumbrian heartland from warlike disturbances, Irish monasticism encouraged a notable flowering of learning, letters and design which Aldfrith himself helped to cultivate. Bede and Alcuin both acknowledged his influence. Unfortunately he died in 704 leaving his position to **Osred I** (r. 705-16) a child of eight, whose family had to put down an attempted usurpation. Another such attempt in 716 created a short interregnum before his brother **Osric** (r. 718-29) could take proper charge and at his death without heirs the throne was for a century the

object of competing ambition among representatives of collateral royal lines.

(8) After the death of **Ceolwulf** (r. 729-37) to whom Bede dedicated his *Ecclesiastical History* Northumbria was well ruled by **Eadberht** (r. 737-58) and his brother **Egbert,** Abp. of York from 732-66, cousins of Ceolwulf. The King campaigned in the north, unsuccessfully against the Picts, but successfully with them against the Strathclyde Britons, but he had to put down a rebellion on behalf of Offa, a son of Aldfrith. Meanwhile the Abp. founded and conducted a great school at York, where among others, he taught Alcuin. In 758 Eadberht retired to become a clerk in York Minster. In 759 **Oswulf** his son was murdered by his own followers, and **Aethelwald Moil** (r. 759-65), a provincial, ruled treacherously with the power of his local supporters. He was overthrown by **Alhred** (r. 765-74) and for the next forty years the feuding relatives of Aethelwald Moll and Eadberht disputed the leadership. Ahlred was deposed by household thanes of Aethelwald, for **Aethelred** (r. 774-9) who was himself expelled by **Aelfwald** (r. 779-88) Eadberht's grandson. This Aelfwald was the last Northumbrian King of good repute and was murdered. His successor **Osred II** (788-9) reigned only a year, for Aelthelred returned and drove him away. Aethelred was as murderous as his father, and unpopular. He married the daughter of Offa of Mercia possibly to acquire a powerful father-in-law. It was under him that the Vikings suddenly sacked Lindisfarne (793). His retainers murdered him, and after a period of confusion **Eardwulf** (r. 798-808) who had not taken part in the conspiracy, secured the kingship.

(9) Charlemagne, who treated Offa of Mercia with suspicion and as an equal, mistrusted Offa's matrimonial alliance; Eardwulf put himself under his protection, while the Mercians gave asylum to his enemies. In 801 Eardwulf was able to attack Cenwulf of Mercia with some hope of success, but the bishops and nobles patched up a peace; this lasted for about seven years when there was a revolt in which Charlemagne's representatives saved Eardwulf's life and brought him to the Frankish court, while one Aelfwald usurped the throne for about a year. The Franks, however, enabled Eardwulf to return (?-809) so that his son **Eanred** (r. 810-40) succeeded him quietly and ruled undisturbed by further conspiracies probably because the Mercians were too distracted by West Saxon movement to fish in Northumbrian troubled waters. It was Eanred who formally submitted to Egbert of Wessex at Dore in 829.

(10) Political confusion did not destroy the remarkable Northumbrian culture, but Viking piracy had become a condition of coastal life. By 835 the Vikings were more than pirates. In 844 K. **Raedwulf** was killed by a Viking army and under **Osberht** (r. 848-66) in 855 they had reached the Wrekin, presumably *via* the Humber. The Northumbrian crisis came in 866. Osberht had just been deposed in favour of one **Aelle.** The Viking Great Host, under Ivar the Boneless and Halfdan, taking advantage of the confusion, rode to York. Osberht and Aelle agreed upon a joint assault but were killed with eight of the earldormen in the attempt. Their armies were dispersed (Mar. 867) and the Vikings established an otherwise obscure puppet King called **Egbert.**

(11) The attempt to control Northumbria through a nominee was only temporarily successful. In 872 a revolt drove Egbert into Mercia, and the Northumbrians chose a certain **Ricsige** (r. 872-5) in his place. He was succeeded by **Egbert II** (r. ?-?) but in 876 Halfdan occupied most of the Deiran area around York and partitioned it among his followers. Egbert's territory and that of his successors and earldormen **Eadwulf** (r. ?-913) and **Ealdred** (fl. 927) who ruled from Bamburgh, were confined to the earlier Bernician area. By this time English Northumbria was a lordship of varying extent north of the Tees and cut off

from the south by the Danish and subsequently Ostman Kingdom of York.

NORTHUMBRIAN EARLDOMS (1) An isolated Anglian coastal lordship between the Tees and the Forth, based on Bamburgh, survived the Scandinavian Conquests (*see* YORK; SCANDINAVIAN KINGDOMS). Its rulers (e.g. Eadwulf ?-913, Ealdred fl. 927) were descended from the last Northumbrian Kings but they submitted to K. Athelstan and regarded themselves perforce as his representatives because they had to endure Scottish as well as Scandinavian aggression. His victory at Brunanburh (937) afforded some relief, but the Scottish seizure of Cumbria (945) increased their difficulties again. The dynamism of the descendents of Kenneth MacAlpin was a permanent problem.

(**2**) When the Danish Kingdom of York collapsed (9S4) K. Eadred naturally made **Oswulf**, Ealdred's son who had ruled at Bamburgh since 948, earl, but of the Danes as well as the English. His family, despite setbacks, maintained a hold on local loyalty for over a century. It made Danish marriages, for **Waltheof I** who again ruled from Bamburgh when the Ostmen were in York (c. 993) bore a Danish name. The Danish connection had a wider importance; **Aelfhelm** (?-1006) acquired lands in the midlands and his famous and notorious daughter **Aelfgifu** (fl. 1020-40), born at Northampton, reputedly the mistress of St. Olaf was the hand fasted wife of K. Canute.

(**3**) The year of Aelfhelm's death saw a determined Scottish invasion, which his brother or cousin **Uhtred** (r. 1006-16) defeated with slaughter at the siege and relief of Durham, but attrition and famine took their toll and when a Danish invasion occurred in 1013, Uhtred's resources no longer sufficed to hold Lothian. His murder in 1016 may have been connected with its abandonment at this time, for just after Canute's accession (1017) there was an effort to reconquer it, which came to grief at the B. of Carham (1018).

(**4**) Canute appointed the Norwegian **Eric** (r. 1018-20) and then **Hakon,** Eric's son (r. 1020-6) earls or perhaps military protectors. Northumbria, cut short at the Tweed was thus concurrently ruled by Uhtred's family and these nominees. In 1027 however, Malcolm II of Scots submission to Canute brought peace; the Scandinavian appointment was not refilled and **Eadwulf** (?-1041), a son or grandson of Uhtred, was the ruling earl. In the confusion which arose at Canute's death, however, Harold I (Herefoot) secured the regency and then the throne. As Aelfgifu's son he had local claims and he or Aelfgifu appointed the Danish **Siward** (v. 1035-55) as concurrent earl. Siward, who appears in Shakespeare's *Macbeth,* was a tremendous warrior, who held the Tweed, expanded the earldom westwards into modern Lancashire and expelled the Scottish authorities from Cumbria. He was also E. of Huntingdon and initiated the northern associations of that rich complex.

(**5**) Harold I's successor Harthacnut hated Aelfgifu, and though her relative Eadwulf was in his peace, he had him murdered. Siward was not impressed. He married, or had already married, into the family and named his son **Waltheof** (?-1076) after Uhtred's father. Fully identified with Northumbrian interests, he became a sort of adoptive representative of the dynasty, and protector of **Oswulf II** (?-1067) Eadwulf's son, but the earldom's preoccupations were with Scottish rather than internal English affairs, and in 1054 he intervened in the Scottish civil war and attacked Dunsinane.

(**6**) Siward's death in 1055 made Northumbria, despite Oswulfs office, a great prize in the political struggle between Godwin and his opponents. He secured it for his son **Tostig** (r. 1055-65) who enjoyed relative freedom from Scottish interference until after Malcolm of Scots had killed Macbeth (1057) and established himself (1058-61). Tostig ruled brutally and made himself unpopular,

probably among the Angles but he had to cope with a Scottish invasion in 1061 and they had no option but to support him until the danger was over. Opposition, however, accumulated around the family of Oswulf and its leader **Gospatrick** (?-1065) a son of Uhtred. Northumbrian politics developed into a faction feud. Tostig killed certain thanes, and his sister, Q. Edith, was suspected of murdering Gospatrick at court. A rebellion in Tostig's absence in 106S destroyed his following in York. The rebel thanes elected **Morcar** (v. 1065-67) a brother of Edwin, E. of Mercia and they, with Edwin's army, marched upon the court. From Northampton they forced the dying Edward the Confessor at Oxford to confirm the change. Tostig took refuge with his father-in-law the Count of Flanders. Oswulf was apparently recognised as earl under Morcar.

(**7**) The Northumbrians were thus hostile to Harold II (Tostig's brother) and after his accession he had to bring them round by a personal visit with Wulfstan, the saintly and forceful Bp. of Worcester. When Tostig and Harald Hardrada invaded the North, this work was undone, for at the B. of Fulford they destroyed Edwin and Morcar's military power to come to Harold II's assistance, though killed themselves a few days later. Hence Morcar (with Edwin) submitted to the Conqueror, and his place was given to **Copsige** (?-1067) a follower of Tostig. Copsige, however, on going north was killed by Oswulf, who a few months later was murdered by brigands. Oswulf's cousin Gospatrick's son Maldred (r. ?-1074) then purchased the earldom (*see* NEVILLE).

(**8**) The rebellions and devastations of 1068-69 effectively ended the old Northumbria. Edwin and Morcar left the court and they with Gospatrick supported the royal claims of Edgar the Atheling who was in Scotland. They destroyed an army under Robert of Comines at Durham (1068) but William I's counter measures brought the rebels to heel, and Gospatrick, having submitted, received back a divided territory in which Durham was to be ruled by its bishop with a largely depopulated area to the north and a devastated Yorkshire behind. He joined a further rebellion in 1072, fled to Scotland and ended as the Ld. of Dunbar. William then made Siward's son **Waltheof** E. of Northumberland but after he had been involved in a number of treasonable conspiracies, he was executed at Winchester.

NORTHUMBRIAN PRIEST'S LAW. A legal text of 67 clauses mainly concerned with the financial penalties (*Bot*) expressed in Scandinavian monetary terms, for offences committed by or against priests. It probably originated at York and dates from the beginning of 11th cent. but its current ascription to Abp. Wulfstan is tentative.

NORTH WEST COMPANY. *See* HUDSON BAY COMPANY.

NORTH WEST FRONTIER AND PROVINCE (India) The mountainous belt from the Pamirs to the Arabian Sea, is penetrated by five passes, viz. the Khyber, Kurram, Tochi, Gomal and Bolan, through which, especially the Khyber and Bolan, India has often been invaded since 600 B.C. When the British conquered Sind (1843) and the Punjab (1849) they acquired the territory of the tribal Pathans and Beluchis, became neighbours of Afghanistan and had to face the problem of Russian central Asian expansion. Masterly inactivity sufficed when the Russians were still far off, but Lord Lytton (Viceroy 1876-80) expected them soon to come uncomfortably close and advocated an advance to a more scientific frontier from Kabul, *via* Ghazni to Kandahar. This created trouble from the Afghans and ended with compromises and an Anglo-Russian agreement in 1907.

(**2**) The local or internal problems were less tractable. In the north, Afghan intrigues and pressure kept the Pathans in disorder, and a punitive, almost warlike policy had to be followed. In the south, Afghan influence (but not Arab gun-running) was negligible, but

Beluchis could be managed with allowances and a little backing from Quetta. In 1893 the Durand Agreement with Afghanistan drew a line across a northern No Man's Land, between the tribes for which the Amir of Afghanistan would be responsible and those under British supervision. The object was to apply the Beluchi method to the latter. In 1901 Lord Curzon created the Province under a Chief Commissioner at Peshawar. This included five settled districts of Bannu, Dera Ismail Khan, Hazara, Kohat and Peshawar and the tribal areas as far as the Durand line.

NORTH WEST PASSAGE. The analogy of a passage for shipping north of Asia led the Frobishers to try an approach N. of Canada. In 1576 they landed in Greenland and pressed into Frobisher Bay in the Baffin Is. bringing back iron pyriets (mistaken for gold) which led to mining attempts in 1577 and 1578. In 1583 John Davis systematically explored the Greenland coast, and in 1586-87 penetrated Baffin Bay. In 1611 Henry Hudson discovered Hudson's Bay where he was left to die, and in 1612 and 1615 Thomas Button explored the Bay as far as the Southampton Is. In 1616 William Baffin explored and named Baffin Bay and discovered the northward Jones, Lancaster and Smith Sounds. Further explorations of Hudson's Bay by Thomas James, Luke Foxe, and Jena Munk led in 1670 to the foundation of the Hudson's Bay Co, which opened up and explored the southerly adjacent lands. There was then a cessation of interest until Sir John Barrow, Secretary of the Admiralty, inspired further efforts; hence John Ross's voyage in 1818, William Parry's three attempts in 1819-20, 1821-23 and 1824-25 and Ross's private expedition of 1828-33 when his nephew James Clark Ross discovered the magnetic pole. John Franklin mapped parts of the N. Canadian coast in 1819-22 and 1825-27. His expedition of 1845 was trapped in ice and totally lost in 1847. In 1848 Sir James Clark Ross penetrated Lancaster Sound. The first passage, partly overland, was accomplished by McClure in 1853; the first wholly by ship by Amundsen in 1903-6.

NORTH WEST TERRITORIES (1) Canadian were the vast lands surrendered by the Hudson Bay Co. in June 1870 when the province of Manitoba was constituted from part of them. In 187S a Lieutenant Governor with appointed Council was established; by 1897 the Council had become elective and the govt. largely responsible. In 1905 the provinces of Saskatchewan and Alberta were constituted as far north as 60°N and in 1912 Quebec and Ontario were extended northwards to the sea and Manitoba to 60°N. Yellowstone became the administrative H.Q. in 1967. **(2) American** were the lands between Pennsylvannia and the Mississippi north of the Ohio.

NORTON, Caroline Elizabeth (1808-77) a granddaughter of Sheridan the playwright, was a poetess prompted by an unhappy marriage into an interest in improving the legal status and protection of women and children. Her poems on these subjects (*The Sorrows of Rosalie*, 1829; *The Undying One*, 1830; *A Voice from the Factories*, 1836 and *A Child of the Islands*, 1845) though hard to read now, caught the mood of her time and inspired much necessary legislation including the Custody of Infants Act 1839 and parts of the Matrimonial Causes Act 1857. Her novel *Lost and Sated* (1863) portrayed illicit feminine sexual passion, and created a Sensation.

NORWAY. *See* BALTIC; VIKINGS; HANSE.

NORWAY HOUSE (Ont.) This isolated trading settlement in the forests 1500 miles W. of Montreal was the central meeting place for the Hudson's Bay Co's local policymakers (The Governor in Chief, with the Chief Factors and Chief Traders) until 1880. It was the true capital of non-colonised Canada.

NORWICH (Norfolk) just above the confluence of the Wensum and the Yare, began with the three riverside fishing settlements of Conesford and Coslang (Anglian) and Westwick (Danish) which shared a market at Tombland. The Normans built the Castle and laid out the Mancroft market. In 1094 the see of Thetford was moved there and the cathedral was mostly built by 1101. The place developed an entrepot trade to Flanders and the Baltic mostly based on wool, and until 1299 there were important groups of Jewish financiers. Then from 1326 it acquired settlements of Flemish weavers who created a flourishing textile industry. The whole complex was enclosed between 1263-1342 in a four mile circuit of walls and its prosperity is attested by the splendour of even the parish churches.

(2) The internal history of the town was turbulent and sometimes destructive. From 1144 there were recurrent attacks on Jews, and there was running disputes culminating in arson between the citizens and the monks of the cathedral. In 1312 there had been systematic terrorism of foreign merchants. The difficulty was that Norwich had long been in competition with Flanders. The town had indeed been sacked by a Flemish expedition in 1174 and Flemings, even refugees, were not popular. Moreover Norwich as such was not popular with the surrounding countryside, and the sack of the city in the Peasants Revolt (1381) probably reflects the dislike of the producer for the middlemen.

(3) The city's prosperity however, continued well into the 18th cent. for though the cloth working trades had to give way to competition from Pennine water power, they were replaced by silk and tailoring, besides activities related to agriculture such as brewing. The coming of the railway had some important secondary effects. They superseded the coastal shipping links, especially to London, but helped to create a tourist industry based partly on the hitherto neglected Norfolk Broads.

NORWICH (1) Sir Walter of (?-1329) became a baron of the exchequer in 1311 and Chief Baron in 1312, but was treasurer from 1314-17 when he returned to the exchequer court. In 1321 he became keeper of the treasury but was reappointed Chief Baron in 1327. His son **(2) John (?-1362) Ld.** (1342) was admiral north of the Thames in 1336 and saw distinguished service in France between 1338-46.

NORWICH SCHOOL of painters, surrounding the Norwich Society of Artists, founded in 1803, was an influential body of landscape artists inspired by John Sell Cotman and John Crome.

NORWICH, William of, or William BATEMAN (?1298-1355) was auditor of the papal palace of Avignon under John XXII (r. 1316-34) and became Dean of Lincoln in 1340. Benedict XII (r. 1334-42) used him as a conciliator between Edward III and Philip VI of France and Edward III repeatedly employed his diplomatic talents. In 1350 he founded Trinity Hall, Cambridge to train the clergy in civil and canon law and in 1351 completed the establishment of Gonville College, left unfinished by Gonville's death.

NOSEY. Nickname of Oliver Cromwell, whose large nose was fleshy, and the first D. of Wellington, whose nose was thin but long.

NOTARY PUBLIC. An official originally appointed under papal authority and recognised in international commerce as a proper witness to formal transactions. Since the Reformation English notaries have been appointed by the Abp. of Canterbury; Scottish ones by the Court of Session. Their international function survives.

NOTITIA DIGNITATUM (Lat: Summary of Major Appointments) was an official Roman document drawn up after A.D. 395 listing the imperial military divisions and dispositions. The only preserved version is a Carolingian copy probably representing a western text partially revised c. 420-3. Thus its record of Roman units in Britain was anachronistic. *See* ROMAN BRITAIN.

NOTT, Sir William (1782-1845). *See* AFGHANISTAN- 6.

NOTTINGHAM, Es. of. *See* FINCH AND FINCH-HAFFON; GEORGE -3.

NOTTINGHAM-SHIRE (A.S. Snotingeham) (1) The area was penetrated *via* the R. Trent by successive movements of Angles and Danes with a few Norwegians but when ships grew larger, navigation ended at the city. This was originally a Saxon settlement on a bluff above the main river crossing but the Danes made it one of their five boroughs and dominated the whole area to an extent which resulted in privileged assessment for the Danegeld, and the division of most of it into 8 wapentakes, with 3 small Hundreds.

(2) The principal landowners in the 11th cent. after the King were the Abp. of York, Harold, E. of Wessex and one Stori. The royal lands passed to William the Conqueror, Harold's to the E. of Chester, Stori's to the ubiquitous Count of Mortain. The archbishop's lands, however, were mostly the liberty of the great collegiate church of Southwell, ascribed to the archbishop because of his close ecclesiastical association with that foundation. In addition, many manors were held by one Roger of Bush. These escheated in about 1098. Known as the honour of Tickhill, they became important in the hands of Robert of Bellême and of P. John for they supported Robert's important castle at Tickhill.

(3) The town and county suffered much damage in the risings under Stephen, Henry II, John and Henry III but the large quantity of undeveloped land made steady growth possible and incidentally gave rise to the legends of Robin Hood. Manorialisation began after the Conquest and was never complete. The county's central and strategic location made it inevitably an area of troop movement when there was trouble. One result was that it tended to have strong political views, favouring, for example Edward III against Mortimer, the Yorkists against the Lancastrians, and Charles I against the parliament. The town's attitudes, however, were not always in step with the county's: it was hostile to Charles I.

(4) As more land came into use, the town developed an export trade down the Trent, and industries, such as tanning, brewing, shoe and glove making related to agriculture. Wool was exported in large amounts and then, as everywhere else, a cloth working industry took over with associated dyers and bleachers. The area was however, unusual in having wealth in the ground. Coal was being mined and burned in sufficient amounts to pollute the town's atmosphere in 1257 and there was much quarrying and trade in building stone. It was natural for the various types of industry to diversify: the textile skills evolved in the 17th cent. to silk, flax and linen working and to hosiery, worsted and lace making: in the 18th cent. when coal began to provide power on a very large scale, came cotton. Mining led to the quarrying of gypsum and alabaster. The maladjustments caused by the coincidence of the Napoleonic Wars and the Industrial Revolution led to periodical riots between 1795 and 1816 and to Luddite outbreaks.

(5) These stresses were relieved by the coming of the railways in the 1830s. Canals had provided inland transport, but the growth of seagoing ships had partially isolated the area from the ports. After 1850 the products of Nottingham began to reach the sea and the world markets and some overseas producers found it convenient to process their products, such as tobacco there.

***NOVAE NARRATIONES* (Lat: New Readings)** an anonymous legal textbook, probably based on lectures (or 'readings') delivered at an Inn of Court, from the reign of Edward III, containing precedents of pleadings in actions commenced by the most commonly used writs. In the 15th cent. the equally anonymous *Articuli ad Novas Narrationes* (Lat: Notes on the New Readings) discussed the jurisdiction of the different courts and the forms of action employed in each.

NOVA SCOTIA. (Lat: New Scotland) (1) In 1621 Sir William Alexander obtained a Scottish charter to colonise the large country (to be called Nova Scotia) from the modern P. Edward I. and Nova Scotia to the St. Lawrence. The English New Plymouth Co. was coolly favourable because it might protect its lands from the French in Quebec without encroaching on its own territory. In 1624 James VI and I offered baronetcies to reputable investors. In 1629 Port Royal (later Annapolis) on the heavily tidal B. of Fundy was settled by Alexander, and C. Breton by Ld. Ochiltree. These colonies were very small because craftsmen and labourers were unwilling to go, and Lairds and their younger sons preferred mercenary opportunities in the Thirty Years' War. In the current French war they received naval protection but nevertheless ran downhill, and at the T. of St. Germain (1632) Charles I ceded them to improve his chances of getting payment of Q. Henrietta Maria's dowry. This seemed to Scots a betrayal (*cf* the later Darien Scheme) but was probably a sensible bargain.

NOVA STATUTA. See NEW STATUTES.

NOVAYA ZEMLYA. *See* ARCTIC EXPLORATION.

NOVEL in Roman law is new legislation supplementary to the main codex, especially by Justinian.

NOVEL DISSEISIN. *See* ASSIZES-1A.

NOVIBAZAR, Sanjak of. A small Turkish province adjacent to Bosnia, whose fate it tended to share in the Balkan politics of the 19th cent. It became important when the Serbs wanted to build a railway to the Adriatic across it. *See* AUSTRO-HUNGARY-13 *et seq.*

NOVIOMAGUS REGNENSIUM. *See* CHICHESTER.

***NOVODAMUS* (Sc. Lat = We regrant).** A fresh grant of lands or a peerage, either on surrender or failure of heirs defined in the original grant. It represented a means for altering the incidents of tenure or the line of inheritance, or for resolving doubts about the grant or its terms.

N-TOWN PLAYS are forty-two almost humourless religious plays performed in the 14th-15th cents. by travelling actors not on floats or wagons as in Mystery Plays (q.v.) but in open courts around which booths were set up for each of the plays. The place, called N Town in the text, was where the performances were taking place, the name being supplied by the actor (*cf* the Anglican catechism). A reference to Coventry in one of them has led to the series being called the COVENTRY CYCLE.

NUCLEAR FISSION, REACTOR, NUCLEUS. *See* ATOMIC THEORY AND ENERGY.

NUFFIELD. *See* MORRIS.

NUGENT. The ancestor, Sir Gilbert, came to Ireland with Hugh de Lacy and received the barony of Delvin. By reason of female successions the barony passed to the Fitzjohn's in 1180 and back in 1407 to **(1) Sir William NUGENT (?-c. 1415)** whose son **(2) Sir Richard (?-?1460) 10th Ld. DELVIN,** sheriff of Meath, long upheld English rule in wars with the native Irish and was Lord Deputy from 1444-52. His grandson **(3) Richard (?-?1538) 12th Ld. (1493)** a competent soldier but a weak Lord Deputy from 1527 was kidnapped by the O'Conor in 1528 and forced to pay him a pension. His greatgrandson. **(4) Sir Christopher (1544-1602) 14th Ld.,** a secondary Meath leader of moral courage, was imprisoned in 1576 in the Fleet for leading a deputation to protest against purveyance during a period of Irish inflation, but by 1579 he was commanding the forces of the Pale. He was a determined Romanist and was in custody in Ireland and England on unproved charges of treason from 1580-82. Thereafter he pursued his own affairs, and a feud with the Dillon family until the rebellion in 1600 of Tyrone, who harried his lands and forced him to submit, whereupon he was promptly arrested for treason and died awaiting trial. His son **(5) Sir Richard (1583-1642) 15th Ld.** was the **1st E. of WESTMEATH (1621).**

NUGENT, Robert (1702-88) 1st Vist. CLARE (1766) 1st E. NUGENT (1776) "a jovial and voluptuous Irishman who left Popery for the Protestant religion, money and

947

widows". He made a large fortune by marrying four in succession, was an M.P. (Bristol 1754-74, St. Mawes 1774-85) and acquired his Irish peerages because he could afford to lend money to George III as P. of Wales but George, as King could not afford to pay it back.

NULLIFY. *See* DIVORCE.

NULLUM TEMPUS. *See* LIMITATION OF LEGAL ACTIONS.

NUNCIO. A papal ambassador. *See* LEGATE.

NUREMBERG (locally NÜRNBERG) (Ger.) grew up round a fort at the junction of two major trade routes. It became an imperial city in 1219 and was soon immensely prosperous. The first German diet of each reign was held there but in 1525 it was one of the first German cities to adopt protestantism. Its prosperity was damaged in the Thirty Years' War and in 1806 it was annexed by Bavaria.

Its commanding position in German traditions made it a natural focus for Nazi propaganda and the Nazi Party Congresses were held there. It was at one of these that the notorious Nuremberg decrees were adopted in 1935. For similar reasons though it was severely damaged in World War II: the Allies used it for the venue for the War Crimes trials from Nov. 1945 to Oct. 1946.

NUREMBERG DECREES (15 Sept. 1935) passed by a Reichstag held during a Nazi Party Rally, deprived Jews of the rights of citizenship and all public employment and made sexual intercourse between Jews and non-Jews a criminal offence.

NUREMBERG TRIALS. *See* WAR CRIMES.

NURSERY RHYMES apart from those deliberately composed to amuse children, are sometimes survivals of May Day dances, or old aphorisms or preserve ancient or misunderstood memories, all reduced to childish form and handed down orally between children or through their uneducated nurses.

Ride a cock horse
To Banbury Cross
See a fine lady on a white horse
Rings on her fingers and bells on her toes
She shall have music wherever she goes

seems to record a child's memory of a Tudor royal progress. The bells would have been on the horse's reins. A cock horse is a child's hobby horse. The rhyme also preserves the older pronunciation of 'cross'.

NURSING was originally in the hands of monastic orders, and declined into disrepute after their dissolution. The renewed late 18th cent. interest in medicine and the casualties in Bonaparte's wars created an unorganised demand for nurses, especially in Germany, where eventually Pastor Fliedner founded the first modern nursing training school at Kaiserswerth in 1836. Societies for these purposes were soon being formed elsewhere; the London Society was founded in 1840 by Elizabeth Fry and sent its trainees to Guy's and St. Thomas's hospitals. Florence Nightingale (1820-1910) started visiting hospitals in London, Egypt and the Continent from 1844. In 1850 she visited Kaiserswerth and had herself trained as a sick nurse there until 1851. In 1853 she became superintendent of a Hospital for Gentlewomen and then in 1856 went to the Crimea. She was not alone (*see* SEACOAL) but her revelations, flare for publicity and practical steps to improve the military hospitals vastly improved public respect for nursing, and in 1860 the Nightingale Fund Training School was set up at St.

Thomas's, financed by public subscription. Thenceforth the movement was properly launched and began to develop defined professional standards. Nurses were appointed to military hospitals from 1866 and an army nursing service established with its H.Q. at Netley Hospital in 1881. District nursing began to develop, and a London Central Council for District Nursing was set up in 1914. World War I brought immense changes in scale, scope and techniques. One result was that the legal status of nursing as a profession was recognised by the Nurses Registration Act 1919 and a General Council of Nursing was set up. A Royal College of Nursing was founded in 1916 and amalgamated with the Council in 1963.

NYASALAND (1893-1907) or BRITISH CENTRAL AFRICA PROTECTORATE or (since 1964) MALAWI. Dr Livingstone provoked European Missionary interest when he reached the southern end of L. Nyasa in 1859 and in 1883 the African Lakes Corporation was founded to exploit the area. In 1884 the British S. African Co (B.S.A.) applied for a charter to trade there, but by now the neighbouring Portuguese were interested. Major Serpa Pinto was exploring the Upper Zambezi and Loangwa while Sir Hany Johnston was approaching the Arabs in the interior. Johnston was more active than Pinto. He progressively made treaties with the Makololo and Yaos, proclaimed a protectorate over the Shire in 1889 and then induced the rulers of Kota Kota, Mlosi and Wahenga to apply for protection. The Portuguese recognised a *fait accompli* by a Convention of 1891. The British protectorate was confined to Shire and Nyasa, the rest passed to B.S.A. In both parts the slave trade was quickly, and slavery more slowly, suppressed. The principal difficulty was the creation of an effective administration in a country with 1,000,000 Africans and only a few hundred Europeans. There was soon a large public debt which the home Govt. was anxious to dispose of. It proposed federation with the two Rhodesias. While they were not keen on shouldering the financial burdens, the local native population was opposed to federation with these powerful, European dominated entities. Hence the federation of 1953 (despite expropriation of B.S.A.) lasted only until 1964.

NYERERE, Julius. *See* TANZANIA.

NYMWEGEN, Ts. of, ended the Franco-Dutch war of 1672-78. **(1)** *Aug.-Sept. 1678* between France, the Netherlands and Spain. France returned her Dutch conquests and suppressed her anti-Dutch tariffs, but kept Franche Comté and 15 fortresses in Artois and Flanders.

(2) *Feb. 1679* between France and the Emperor settled the Rhine frontier. The treaties were conditional upon Denmark and Brandenburg restoring their Baltic conquests to Sweden. This was effected respectively by treaties signed at St. Germain and Fontainebleau.

NYON (Switz.) AGREEMENT (1937) Thinly disguised Italian assistance to the rebel General Franco in the Spanish civil war reached a point in the summer of 1937 where 'unknown' submarines were sinking non-Spanish ships bound for govt. ports. The British and French called a conference of Mediterranean powers and set up naval patrols. The sinkings ceased. In the 1930s this success represented the only occasion when the democracies seriously resisted Fascist, Nazi, Japanese or Communist aggression until World War II.

O

O' (prefix) **(Irish)** = grandson or descendant of.

OAK. The many species of this massive tree covered much of ancient Europe and Britain from Perthshire southwards. Its forests powerfully influenced primitive religion, e.g. Druidism, and legend. Its hard, durable timber was the essential material for the mediaeval system building which developed into the half-timbered house and of European shipbuilding, and so formed the basis of English political and commercial success between c. 1450 and 1830. In consequence widespread felling changed the landscape but because of the tree's slow growth replanting always lagged behind and virtually ceased in the 1850s when iron and steel ships were superseding wooden ones.

OAK APPLE DAY, 29 May is the anniversary of Charles II's restoration. Oak apples or leaves were worn in memory of his hiding in Boscobel oak on 6 Sept. 1651.

OAK BOYS (Ir.) were groups of peasant cattle slashers and farm burners in Ulster in 1764.

OAKELEY, Sir Charles (1751-1826) Bart. (1790) was Pres. of the Committee on the assigned revenue of the Nawab of Arcot from 1781 to 1784 and became gov. of Madras in 1790. As such he overhauled the administration and reformed the finances. He retired in 1795.

OAKELEY, Frederick (1802-80), cleric, translated the Latin hymn *Adeste fideles* as *O come all ye faithful* in 1841.

OAKHAM. See RUTLAND

OAKS, THE. See SUTTON (LONDON).

OAKUM was a fibre used in large amounts for caulking ships and made by picking old, especially tarred, rope. This work, which was tedious, was done by criminals and *picking oakum* became synonymous with prison.

OATES, Titus (1649-1705). See CHARLES II-21 *et seq*; 'POPISH PLOT'.

OASTLER, Richard (1789-1861), with Michael Sadler, John Fielden and the E. of Shaftesbury, waged a seventeen year campaign to reduce children's hours of work in woollen and worsted mills from thirteen or fifteen (or more) hours a day to ten, by the Ten Hours Act 1847. See FACTORY LEGISLATION.

OATHS, PERJURY, AFFIDAVITS, STATUTORY DECLARATIONS, etc. (1) In an oath the swearer undertook to risk divine vengeance if he lied or broke his sworn undertaking. There were four kinds, viz: **(a)** A statement made as evidence in a court of law. A lie in such circumstances was perjury and punishable as a felony. **(b)** A statement of belief in a defendant's plea in a trial by compurgation. Such a statement, if false, was theoretically punishable by amerciament but hardly ever punished. **(c)** The many promissory oaths were undertakings to perform the duties of an office and were the equivalent of contracts of employment. Until 1866 these were an important social factor especially in the 16th to 18th cents. The *Book of Oaths* of 1689 gives the text of 294; that of 1715, 349. They included oaths to be sworn by managers of a lottery and by a postman, and obsolete oaths such as those sworn by the Lieut. of Ruisbank and the Master Porter of Calais. Their real function in an illiterate age was to impress upon the deponent the nature of his duties. Some were framed, however, so that only an Anglican could conscientiously take them. Breach could lead, usually after long litigation, to forfeiture of the office. George III thought that R. Catholic relief would be a breach of his coronation oath. **(d)** An affidavit is a written statement under oath, under sanction of prosecution for perjury.

(2) Quakers were allowed as early as 1668 to affirm instead of swearing, but non-Christians and atheists were debarred from office and from giving evidence until 1838, when the methods of administering the oaths were altered to accommodate them. Meanwhile the consequences of perjury on affidavit were considered so excessive that in 1835 a form of statutory declaration not admissible in evidence was introduced.

(3) Most of the promissory oaths were abolished by statutes of 1866 to 1868. After 1888 anyone could demand, in the remaining cases, to affirm.

OATLANDS (Surrey) was acquired in 1538 by Henry VIII who built a brick palace for Anne of Cleves. It apparently resembled St. Johns Coll., Cambridge and covered nine acres. It was not used much until Elizabeth I who spent heavily on it; James I laid out gardens, vineyards and a silk farm and Charles I filled it with works of art. In 1649 Parliament sold it to Sir Richard Weston. He demolished it and used the materials for the Wey Navigation.

OBEAH or OBI. A remarkably successful form of W. African, and hence W. Indian, witchcraft for inducing sickness.

OBEDIENCE was a monastic office under the Superior; an OBEDIENTIARY one who exercised it.

OBLATE (1) A layman living according to the rules of a religious order **(2)** A child dedicated by his parents to become a Benedictine.

OBLIVION AND INDEMNITY, ACT OF (1660). *See* RESTORATION-6.

OBOTE, Milton. *See* UGANDA.

O'BRAEIN, Tighearnach (?-1088), abbot of Clonmacnoise and Roscommon, wrote an important Irish Latin Chronicle in which Irish events are synchronised with those of Europe.

O'BRIEN. The heads of this ancient sept were Kings of Munster until the end of the 12th cent; then successively Chiefs, Princes and from 1543 Es. or Ms. of Thomond down to 1855. A grandson of the 3rd E. became Vist. Clare in 1663. This branch became Jacobite. It raised the Clare Regiment for service with the French, and the 6th Vist. became a French marshal and died in 1761.

O'BRIEN (1) Murrough (?1614-74) 6th Ld. and 1st E. of INCHIQUIN (1654), a leading Munster protestant, was trained as a soldier in Spain and joined Strafford during the Irish massacre of 1641. In 1642, though without resources, he beat the Kilkenny Confederates by ingenuity at Lismore. His troops were disbanded at the truce of 1643 but he visited Charles I at Oxford in 1644 and then, on his return to Ireland he submitted to the parliament because it controlled the sea, and could alone bring help to the protestants against the Confederates. With arms brought him by Ld. Lisle he mastered Munster. In 1648 he declared for the King, made a truce with the Confederates and, with Ormonde, took Drogheda and Dundalk, but the Cromwellian sack of Drogheda destroyed his men's morale. Unable to stand, he made for France. He served under the French in Catalonia, was converted to R. Catholicism, captured and enslaved by Algerine pirates, but ransomed in 1660. He was High Steward to the dowager Q. Henrietta Maria until returning to Ireland in 1663. His son **(2) William (?1638-92),** also ransomed, was Gov. of Tangier from 1674 to 1678 and welcomed the Prince of Orange in 1688. Consequently he was attainted by the Irish (Patriot) parliament, but held out in Munster against the Jacobites. He was Gov. of Jamaica from 1690.

O'BRIEN, James Bronterre (1805-64), barrister and extremist writer in the *Poor Man's Guardian* and the *Northern Star*, advocated nationalisation of the land, if necessary by revolution. He took an important part in the Chartist movement and was imprisoned for sedition in 1840. By this time the movement was in decline; he quarrelled with its leaders, especially Feargus O'Connor, and retired into obscurity.

O'BRIEN, William (1852-1928) Irish Nationalist M.P. and anti-Parnellite, founded the United Irish League in 1898 and played a leading part in the reunification of the Irish party in 1900. After the Irish Land Act, 1903, he believed that Home Rule would come by agreement and left politics in 1918 when Sinn Fein ascendancy was plain.

O'BRIEN, William Smith (1803-64) as M.P. for Ennis in 1828 supported R. Catholic emancipation. He was M.P. for Limerick from 1835 to 1849. Disillusioned by the failures to relieve Irish poverty or improve education he joined 'Young Ireland' (q.v.). In 1846 he founded an Irish confederation dedicated to peaceful repeal of the union, but the growing misery and the belief that persuasion would never succeed led him to support the Young Ireland appeal to France (1848). Young Irelanders were prosecuted; he raised a wild peasant insurrection in Tipperary. Transported to Australia, he was pardoned in 1854 and settled in Brussels.

O'BROLCHAIN. Ulster family which, besides two poets, produced six learned churchmen between A.D. 1000 and c. 1240.

O'BRYAN, William (1778-1868), a strenuous preacher in Cornwall, was expelled from the Methodist church in 1810 and founded the Arminian Bible Christians in 1816. Most of them seceded to form the Bible Christians in 1829.

OBSCENITY was originally punished, if at all, by the Star Chamber, but the King's Bench hesitantly took over the jurisdiction after that court was abolished. In 1708 Holt C. J. thought that obscene words and libels were a purely ecclesiastical offence, but in 1727 the court held that an obscene book was punishable at Common Law. Obscene publications were forbidden but obscenity not defined in the Obscene Publications Act 1851 and the definition was hotly disputed in the 1950s. This led to the introduction of a literary defence of public good by the Act of 1959. *See* LADY CHATTERLEY'S LOVER.

OBSERVATOR, THE See L'ESTRANGE, SIR ROGER.

OBSERVATORY, ROYAL. *See* GREENWICH.

OBSERVER. Sunday newspaper founded in 1791 by W. S. and W. H. Bourne, had established a viable circulation by 1799 and in about 1814 was acquired by William Innell Clement (?-1852), a pioneer of pictorial journalism. His heir sold it in 1870 to Julius Beer and his son, who converted it into a quality newspaper. In 1905 Lord Northcliffe bought it and, having appointed James Louis Garvin (1868-1947) editor in 1908, sold it to Lord Astor in 1911. Garvin remained editor until 1942. The Astor family vested it in an independent trust in 1964, but sold it to the U.S. Atlantic Rackfield Corpn. in 1976. The trustees retained some shares and editorial independence.

OBSERVER CORPS, ROYAL. A uniformed, part-time 32,000 strong civilian body set up just before World War II to identify enemy aircraft and report their tracks to fighter command. It stood down in 1945 but was re-formed for the purpose of reporting nuclear explosions and radio-activity.

O'BYRNE, Fiagh MacHugh (?1544-97), the most colourful of the O'Byrnes of Wicklow, held the chieftaincy of that clan by a dubious claim. From 1571 he maintained by alternate violence and submission a bandit independence in the Wicklow mountains. He often raided the Pale and Wexford. In the end he was hunted down, but the O'Byrnes maintained their position in the mountains until the Commonwealth.

OCCASIONAL CONFORMITY ACTS (1) 1711. If an office holder attended a conventicle after admission, he was liable to pay £40 to a prosecutor, forfeit the office and be disqualified for it, but a year's conformity restored the qualification. The act came into force on 25 Mar. 1712. Its occasional conformity clauses were repealed in 1719. (*See* GEORGE -8.)

(2) 1713. This was aimed at teachers who took the sacraments to obtain a teacher's licence. They forfeited the licence and might be imprisoned for three months if they resorted to a conventicle. It was repealed in 1714.

OCHINO, Bernardino (1487-1564), Vicar-Gen. of the Capuchins, embraced Reformist doctrines, joined Calvin at Geneva, married and became a travelling preacher. Abp. Cranmer gave him a prebend at Canterbury, but his defence of polygamy and attack on trinitarianism destroyed his credit in England. He died in Moravia.

OCHTERLONY, Sir David (1758-1825) defended Delhi against Holkar in 1804, defeated the Nepalese in 1815 and commanded one of the columns in the Pindari War of 1817 to 1818.

OCKHAM or OCCAM, William of (?-?1349), English Franciscan nominalist philosopher, supported the Spirituals against Pope John XXII and in about 1330 wrote his *Opus Nonaginta Dierum* (The Ninety Day Tract), an extreme attack on John XXII. He had been summoned to Avignon, the Papal residence, and had fled to Munich in 1328 where he wrote the *Compendium errorum Papae Johannis XXII* (Collection of Pope John XXII's Errors) (about 1336), the *Dialogus super dignitate papali et regia* (Dialogue on Papal and Royal Pre-eminence) (1334-8) and the *Tractatus de imperatorum et pontificum potestate* (Treatise on Imperial and Papal Authority) (1338-42).

Holding that the existence and attributes of God could not be proved and that knowledge of them depended on faith, he also held that things were good because God willed them, not that God willed things because they were good. His theological and political views were not directly condemned by the Papacy though they were by the University of Paris. They formed much of the philosophical basis of the conciliar movement and foreshadowed the teachings of Martin Luther who was familiar with them.

O'CONNELL, Daniel. *See* PEEL'S SECOND GOVT.-4,5.

O'CONNELL (1) Count Daniel Charles (?1745-1833) entered the French army in 1760, joined the royalists in the revolution and suggested an Irish brigade to Pitt in 1796. His nephew **(2) Daniel (1775-1847)** famous as a barrister on the Munster circuit, entered politics in 1800 to protest against the govt's carefully planted rumour that the R. Catholics favoured Union. He was chairman of a sub-committee which examined the discriminatory laws in 1811; he opposed Grattan's emancipation bill in 1813 as being too restricted and ambiguous, while publicising the full case with great skill in defending Magee, the owner of the *Dublin Evening Post* on a charge of sedition. He continued to work for emancipation and in 1823 launched his most famous venture, the CATHOLIC ASSOCIATION, which from 1824 was allied to the 'Catholic Rent', a sum of 1s. a year which secured membership to any R. Catholic peasant who paid it. The Association dealt with practical problems as well as political grievances and soon attracted a vast following. In 1825 the Catholic Relief Bill was thrown out by the Lords and the Association suppressed by Act of Parliament, whereupon in 1826 he founded the Order of Liberators to prevent feuds and riots, discourage secret societies and make the franchise effective. This was really the Catholic Association in another form and in 1828 he was elected to Parliament. He refused to take the oath of supremacy, was excluded and returned again unopposed. He then formed a series of societies to repeal the Union, all of which were suppressed and in 1831 he was arrested, but personally prevented a riot in Dublin. The English reformers then got the prosecution withdrawn. He was returned for Dublin in 1832 and in 1834 moved for a committee to inquire into the state of the Union. He was defeated but with good will and this led in 1835 to the Lichfield House Compact and the appointment of Thos. Drummond to run Irish administration. The extremists promptly accused him of corruption because of his friendliness with govt. personalities and so in 1840 he founded the Repeal Association which was yet another copy of the Catholic Association. He was Lord Mayor of Dublin from 1841 to 1842 and afterwards resumed agitation supported by the new journal, *The Nation*. In 1843 he countermanded a great rally at Clontarf but was nevertheless arrested and convicted of sedition, but the conviction was reversed on appeal in 1844. In 1846 the potato rot overshadowed all other matters and in Feb. 1847 he made a last appeal in the Commons for the starving Irish. He was the creator of Irish national feeling and constitutionalism. A relative **(3) Sir Maurice Charles (?-1848)** was in French service until the Irish brigade was transferred to British service in 1794, and Lieut. Gov. of N.S.W. from 1809 to 1814 and thereafter GOC. the troops there. His son **(4) Sir Maurice Charles (1812-79)** became a commissioner of crown lands in N.S.W. in 1848 and was Pres. of the legislative council of Queensland from 1861-79. A son of **(2), (5) John (1810-58)** was an Irish M.P. from 1832 to 1851 and from 1853 to 1857. He helped his father in the repeal agitation and succeeded him as head of the Repeal Association which collapsed in 1848 through lack of funds. His brother **(6) Morgan (1804-55)** was M.P. for Meath from 1832 to 1840 and disagreed with his father on the repeal issue. He and a kinsman **(7) Baron Moritz (?1740-1830)** had both served in the Austrian army and Moritz was an Imperial chamberlain from 1781.

O'CONNOR. This Offaly clan, related to and allied with the Kildares, became prominent with the 15th cent. decline of English power in central Ireland. By 1500 the O'Connors had built up a power stretching from the Shannon to the Pale and even within the Pale where, by 1520, Meath and Kildare were paying the black rents. Their leader at this time was **Brian** or **Bernard (?1490-?1560)** who, with Kildare, was intermittently at war with the English. He was captured in 1548. In 1552 he escaped, was recaptured but released by Q. Mary I, only to be re-imprisoned in 1554. He died in Dublin Castle. Thereafter the clan declined.

O'CONNOR, Kings of CONNAUGHT. (1) Aedh (?-1167) took part in the defeat of Donnchad, K. of Munster, son of Brian Boroimh, but was himself killed by Art O'Rourke. His son **(2) Ruaidri (r. 1087-92)** established his rule over all Connaught only in 1087, but was blinded by his dynastic rivals, the O'Flaherty. Conflict between the Connaught dynasties and the O'Brien power in Munster kept the O'Connor weak until 1114 when **(3) Turlough (r. 1106-56)** emerged from O'Brien tutelage. He made Connaught dominant in Ireland and himself High King, but with opposition in Ulster, from 1120-1135 and from 1141-49. The conflicts of his son **(4) Ruaidri (?-1198)** with the King of Leinster led to the Anglo-Norman intervention and he did homage to Henry II in 1175. He was deposed in 1186 and proved to be the last High King. The clan continued powerful in Connaught and in frequent conflict with the incoming Normans. His bastard half-brother **(5) Cathal (r. 1201-24)** acknowledged K. John's supremacy in 1215, but fought the Lacys in 1220 and 1224.

OCTA. *See* KENT, KINGDOM-2.

OCTAVIANS (Sc.) were eight Exchequer Commissioners appointed in 1596 by James XI to revise the long obsolete tax assessments and economise expenditure. They were of course unpopular and the Edinburgh riots of Dec. 1596 were partly instigated by their opponents who spread rumours that they were Romanists. *See* LYON-3.

OCTENNIAL ACT 1767 (Ir.). An Irish parliament unless dissolved might last an entire reign, as that of George II had done. The members were secure so long as they did not vote the govt. down and openings to political ambition were restricted to bye-elections. The issue was raised in the new parliament of George III (1760), but it took seven years to get restrictive legislation passed. The

Act limited the life of a parliament to eight years from its first meeting day and the parliament which passed it was instantly dissolved. The Act began the political process which culminated in the constitution of 1782.

OCTOBER CLUB, a High Tory body, especially important after the 1710 election, determined with Henry St. John to force extreme policies upon the govt. and so oust the Whigs.

OCTOBER REVOLUTION (Nov. 1917). *See* RUSSIAN REVOLUTION.

OCTOROON. *See* MULATTO.

OCTROI (Fr.). A grant of authority (*auctoritas*) by a French govt. to a municipality to enforce an exclusive right or to levy a tax in the nature of customs at the municipal boundary.

OCZAKOV. *See* UKRAINE.

ODA (?-958), a Danish convert, was adopted by a thegn, Aethelhelm, who took him to Rome where he was ordained. K. Aethelstan made him Bp. of Ramsbury in 927 and he became Abp. of Canterbury in 942. His nephew St. Oswald, and St. Dunstan, owed their promotion to his discernment. He promoted church discipline and morals and held councils for the whole English church.

ODAL. *See* UDAL.

O'DALY. Irish family which, between 1200 and 1630, produced ten well known Gaelic poets.

ODDA, Earl (?-1056) a Mercian related to Edward the Confessor.

ODER, R. *See* BALTIC-1, and *passim*.

ODER-NEISSE LINE. The R. Oder and the Lusatian Neisse formed as a result of the Yalta agreement the controversial boundary between the new Poland and the German so-called Democratic Republic. This involved the partition of the Silesian industrial and mining zone. *See* POTSDAM AGREEMENT.

ODESSA, a Turkish fortress from 1764, was stormed by the Russians in 1789. It thus acquired a vast hinterland and as a free port from 1819 to 1879 rapidly became one of the greatest grain ports in the world and a principal destination of the British tramp steamer trade. It also harboured many Greek and Bulgarian political refugees and thus became a centre of Russian 19th cent. influence in the Balkans. In the 20th cent. its large Jewish population, which suffered intermittent violence, became a Zionist 'reservoir'.

ODIN, WODEN or WOTAN. The chief of the Teutonic gods, he was represented as wise, one-eyed and accompanied by two ravens. Wednesday and Wednesfield are named after him.

ODO of BAYEUX (?-1097) Bp. of BAYEUX (1049), E. of KENT (1066) was half-brother of William I. Pugnacious, able, unscrupulous but civilised, he fought at Hastings (with a club because *they that take the sword shall perish by the sword*) and then acted intermittently as William's vice-gerent in his frequent and sometimes prolonged absences. Between 1077 and 1080 he was issuing royal writs in his own name. In 1080 he commanded the army which devastated Durham. He also became very rich. In 1081 he was intriguing for the Papacy, proposing to go to Rome himself with a force of knights. This led to his arrest and trial in 1082. Deprived of his earldom, he was kept in custody at Rouen until William I died, when he returned to England to take part in the abortive opening rebellion of Rufus' reign. He was besieged at Tonbridge and then at Rochester. Driven to Normandy he held an influential position under D. Robert, with whom he thought it wise to go on crusade in 1096. He died at Palermo.

O'DONNELL, Chiefs of TYRCONNELL. (1) Ergh Dubh (fl. 1511) went on pilgrimage to Rome in 1511 leaving his son **(2) Manus (?-1564)** in charge. Manus established a personal ascendency and, with O'Neill's help, usurped his father, but when The O'Neill demanded submission in return he refused it, whereupon The O'Neill with other tribes and English help raided Tyrconnell, but father and son surprised them and drove them out. War continued intermittently until 1531 when Manus applied for English protection. In 1537, now entitled THE O'DONNELL, he married Lady Eleanor McCarthy who was seeking a protector for her nephew, the fugitive Gerald fitzGerald, E. of Kildare. As a result the O'Donnells, O'Neills and O'Briens of Thomond became allied against the English who defeated them in the B. of L. Bellahoc in Aug. 1539, so thereafter Manus concentrated on establishing a hegemony in Sligo but was deposed by his son **(3) Calvagh (?-1566)** with the aid of Scottish Macdonell kinsmen who surprised The O'Neill near Lough Swilly. In 1561, however, the O'Neill captured Calvagh and his wife (whom he raped) and kept them in prison until 1564 when he was released and appealed to the English govt. The Lord Deputy, Sir Henry Sydney, restored him to his rights in 1566. His half-brother **(4) Hugh (fl. 1557-92)** routed the O'Neills at Letterkenny and resigned in 1592 in favour of his son **(5) Hugh Roe (1572-1602) (Red Hugh)** who was imprisoned in Dublin Castle from 1588 to 1592 as an anti-Armada precaution. On release he expelled the English sheriff from Donegal and having cleared his rear by raiding the O'Neills, subdued most of Connaught between 1595 and 1597 but was then at war with the English whom he defeated in 1598 at the Yellow Ford and by whom he and The O'Neill were catastrophically defeated at Kinsale in Dec. 1601. He died in Spain. His cousin **(6) Sir Niall Garve (1569-1626)** disliked Hugh Roe's elevation to the chieftainship and in 1592 came to terms with the English, but in 1601 quarrelled with them because, though they were willing to support his claims in Tyrconnell, they would not do so in Inishowen. He went to London, was charged as a rebel and in 1608 put into the Tower, where he remained.

OEIL-DE-BOEUF (Fr. = bull's eye). A small oval window and so the antechamber to Louis XIV's bedroom lit by one; here courtiers waited for the king and meanwhile chatted and intrigued. Hence any similar group.

OFFA (5th cent.), K. of Angeln in Jutland, was the ancestor of the Mercian Kings. He is mentioned in *Widsith*.

OFFA (fl. 709) was a King of the E. Saxons who died in Rome.

OFFA (?-796). *See* MERCIA-6-8, KENT, KINGDOM-6.

OFFA'S DYKE runs from a point near Holywell on the Dee to the Severn near Chepstow with outliers near Prestatyn and round Montgomery. It was built by K. Offa of Mercia in about 785 as a defensible boundary against the Welsh and consists of a discontinuous ditch and earthwork (and sometimes more than one) covering the intervals between easily held natural features. It could not have been occupied continuously, nor held successfully, without standing patrols on the Welsh side. It has marked the approximate Border between English and Welsh ever since.

OFFALY or (1556-1921) KING'S COUNTY (Ir.) on the east bank of the Shannon was boggy with gravel lines or routes running east and west blocked by forts (or later Norman castles) between the two. With Leix (Queen's County), Kildare and part of Tipperary, it formed an ancient kingdom or country known in the later middle ages as GLENMALLERY. Poor and sparsely populated, it was a natural resort for monks and bandits. Sierkieran Abbey was founded in 5th cent. Clonmacnoise by St. Kieran, and Darrow by St. Columba in 6th cent. Originally ruled (if at all) by the O'Connors, the main local clan was the O'Carroll at Sierkieran. It was granted to the Mortimers in 12th cent. but not effectively ruled. It escheated in 13th cent. The country was shired into King's County (eastern) and Queen's County (western) in 1556 and many bogs were drained (save the Bog of

Allen) so that the area acquired good pasture besides crop rotation.

OFFENSIVE TRADES such as blood and soap boiling were first controlled under the Public Health Act 1875.

OFFICES, COMPULSORY. In the absence of a professional local administration, many necessary public functions were performed compulsorily and in rotation by unpaid amateurs. The offices concerned ranged from those of mayor, sheriff or alderman in a borough and such rural officers (petty in appearance but practically important) as the pinder and the hayward; high and petty constables (sometimes called headboroughs or tithingmen); church-wardens and guardians of the poor who existed both in town and country. The appointing authorities varied. High sheriffs were appointed by the crown; borough and parish officers were mostly elected respectively by the common council or the vestry, guardians by the county justices. To ensure that an officer could be brought to book for malfeasance, a property qualification was always required and he was liable to a fine if he refused office without a lawful excuse. To reduce the burden, tenure was limited to a year and mostly a man could, on laying down office, claim exemption until all others qualified had served, or been lawfully excused or fined. In some places the offices gave opportunities for just or unjust enrichment, so that exemptions were not always claimed. The system began to be dismantled after 1815, but a few such offices (e.g. those of High Sheriff and Lord Mayor of London) remain. *See* TYBURN TICKET.

OFFICES OF PROFIT. *See* PLACEMEN.

OFFICIAL SECRETS. A Foreign Office clerk copied an official document and gave the copy to a journalist. The clerk could not be charged with larceny because nothing had been physically removed. An Official Secrets Bill was introduced in Apr. 1889. The govt. tried to avoid explanations on the floor of the Commons and the committee proceedings were not properly recorded. M.P.s became suspicious and the bill was abandoned in July. A new version was introduced and pressed through at the end of the session. It created several offences, notably to enter govt. premises to copy anything, or to make copies in breach of an official trust, or to disclose matters capable of being so copied in circumstances which were not in the interests of the state. Acts of 1911, 1920 and 1939 reenacted it with extensions. An agitation to reform them resulted in an Act of 1989 which *inter alia* empowered a Sec. of State to notify somebody that he was dealing with matters which must not be disclosed.

OFFORD or UFFORD, John of (?-1349) was Dean of the Arches and by 1335 Archdeacon of Ely. In 1342 he was Keeper of the Privy Seal and from 1345 to 1349 Lord Chancellor. He was mostly employed as a diplomat. In 1348 he was nominated Abp. of Canterbury but died before he could be consecrated.

OGHAM ALPHABET was invented in Ireland in the 4th cent. for arcane purposes by persons familiar with a literate Latin Christian civilisation. The numerous inscriptions, which are all short and dull, are in Q-Celtic or Q-Celtic and Latin and commemorate persons. The highest density of Ogham inscriptions is in S. Ireland and Pembrokeshire, Brecon and Cornwall. It is commonly read from the bottom left corner upwards, as follows:-

A	·	B		H		M	
O	:	L		D		G	
U	⫶	V		T		NG	
E	⫶⫶	S		C		Z	
I	⫶⫶⫶	N		Q		R	

OGILVY. Banffshire family **(1) Alexander (?-1456) Ld. of INVERQUHARITY, a** sheriff of Kincardine, was a freebooting chief who sacked Bp. Kennedy's estates and came to a bad end in Finhaven Castle. **(2) Sir George of DUNLUGAS (?-1663) Ld. BANFF (1642)**, also violent, was a royalist who beat the Covenanters at Turriff in 1639. **(3) Sir Alexander (?-1727) Ld. FORGLEN (1706)** was M.P. for Banff burgh from 1702 and a commissioner for the union. He became a Lord of Session. *See next entry.*

OGILVY. Forfarshire family distantly related to the foregoing. **(1) Sir Walter (?-1440)** of Lintrathen was Treasurer of Scotland from 1425 to 1431 and Treasurer of the royal household thereafter. The family built Airlie Castle and **(2) James (?-1605) 5th or 6th Ld. OGILVY** was a consistent supporter of Mary Q. of Scots and secured lands by helping to overthrow Morton, the regent, in 1581. His grandson **(3) James (?1593-1666) 1st E. of AIRLIE (1639)** was a royalist supporter of Montrose together with his adventurous son **(4) James (?1615-1704) 2nd E.** who held Airlie against the Covenanters in 1640, took Montrose to Charles I in 1644, was released but recaptured in 1645 and condemned to death but escaped and was pardoned. He joined the Pluscarden insurrection in 1649, was captured again in 1651 and not released until 1657 when he retired to Forfar. He supported William at the Revolution of 1688.

(5) OGILVY, The Rt Hon. Sir Angus James Bruce (1928–) *s.* of the 12th E. of Airlie and Lady Alexandra Coke, *m.* P. Alexandra of Kent in 1963. A successful company director, he and the princess were concerned in the modest but active promotion of an important spectrum of charities.

OGLETHORPE, James Edward. *See* GEORGIA.

O'HANLON. Armagh clan which received grants in other parts of Ulster during the Plantations of James I but was ruined by the civil war and the subsequent Acts of Settlement and Explanation. Their last notable figure **Redmond (?-1681)** was a relatively romantic tory (i.e. bandit) who was treacherously killed.

O'HELY, James. *See* ELIZABETH -24.

O'HIGGINS (1) Don Ambrosio (1720-1801) Marquis de OSORNO (1792), of humble Irish family, served as a soldier in Chile where he built the road from Santiago to Valparaiso. He was Capt-Gen. of Chile from 1789 to 1796 and Viceroy of Peru from 1795 to 1801. For his son **(2) Bernardo** *see* CHILE-I 2.

OHIO (U.S.A.). La Salle explored the **River** in 1669-1670, but the country was mostly a Shawnee hunting ground until the 1740s. It was then disputed between the French, penetrating from the north and west and the Virginians, claiming English charter rights, from the east. In 1747 the latter formed the **Ohio Company** for purposes of land speculation and fur trading. In 1754 the French built Fort Duquesne (later Pittsburgh) in the north and rivalry between the two sides and their respective Indian allies grew into sporadic violence, amounting to open war in 1755 when Gen. Braddock was repulsed at Fort Duquesne. This was one of the causes of the Seven Years' War (1756-63). The British being victorious, the country was part of the territory ceded by France in the T. of Paris of 1763, but it was kept apart from the adjacent British colonies by proclamation and in 1774 incorporated into Quebec by the Quebec Act. The British policy represented by these measures, of limiting the westward movement of the eastern colonists, was a major cause of the dispute which ended in the American rebellion. It was ceded with the other French ceded territories to the U.S.A. at the T. of Paris of 1783. There being no continuing British occupation, U.S. exploitation began, led by the New England **Ohio Company of Associates** formed in 1786. The area was admitted to the Union as a state in 1803 and supported the Union in the Civil War. *See* GEORGE II.-15.

OHTHERE, (fl. 880) was a Norse explorer known to K. Alfred.

O'HURLEY, Dermot (?1519-84) originally a canon lawyer and philosopher at Rheims, went to Rome, became involved in Irish plots and in Sept. 1581 was ordained deacon, priest and Abp. of Cashel on the same day. He then went to Ireland but incriminating papers were taken by pirates and handed over to the govt. and he was himself eventually captured. He was tortured to reveal the extent of R. Catholic anti-govt. plans, but withstood all interrogation and was hanged under martial law.

OIL RIVERS PROTECTORATE. *See* NIGERIA.

OIL TANKERS. The first ship whose hull was itself an oil container was the *Glückauf* (2300 tons), launched on the Tyne in 1885. The first motor driven tanker was built in Holland in 1910. By 1990 some tankers of 200,000 tons were in use.

OIL WELLS were first drilled at Titusville (Penn.) in 1859.

OJIBWA or CHIPPEWA were farming Indians of Algonquian stock who drove the Sioux out of the area S. of L. Superior. They were allies of the French against the British and in 1812 of the British against the Americans.

OKEHAMPTON (Devon). Baldwin of Brionne founded the town in about 1085 as the head of his large Honour of the same name and also the castle. By marriage to Hawise, his heiress, it passed to Reginald of Courtenay and with Plympton became the main support of the influence of the Courtenay Es. of Devon. The town was incorporated in 1623 and represented in parliament from 1640 to 1832. It was the scene of a brilliant defeat of the Royalists under Hopton by a much smaller force under James Chudleigh in Mar. 1643.

O'KELLY or O'CEALLAIGH, Sean (1882-1966). A founder of Sinn Fein in 1905 and Gen. Sec. of the Gaelic League from 1915, he became an M.P. in 1918 (Dublin) and was elected the first Speaker of the Irish Dail. He opposed the 1921 treaty and helped to found the Fianna Fail party in 1926. He held various offices when the party came to power in 1932. He was Pres. of Ireland from 1945 to 1959.

OKEY, John (?-1662), independently minded regicide soldier, sat in parliament in 1654. He was cashiered for circulating a petition against the Protectorate. Suspected of Fifth Monarchist sympathies in 1656, in 1658 he was arrested for further opposition to Oliver, but restored to his command by Richard Cromwell's parliament, of which he was also a member. In 1659 he resisted Lambert who cashiered him, but he regained his regiment until yet again deprived in 1660 by Monck; he then joined Lambert, but fled, was arrested in Holland and eventually executed.

OLAF THE BLACK (?-1238). *See* MAN. I. OF-4.

OLAF GODFREY'S or GUTHFRITH'S SON (?-941) Ostman K. of DUBLIN (934), was involved in the defeat at Brunanburgh (937) but held parts of Deira until killed near Dunbar.

OLAF KUARAN (fl. 926-54) Ostman K. of YORK. *See* AETHILSTAN-L, AETHILSTAN'S SUCCESSORS-2.

OLAF, St. (?-1030) K. of NORWAY. *See* VIKINGS- 23.

OLAF THE RED (?-981) Ostman K. of DUBLIN. *See* AETHILSTAN'S SUCCESSORS-I.

OLAF THE WHITE (fl. 851-70) Norwegian Viking. *See* VIKINGS-9.

OLAF TRYGVASSON. *See* VIKINGS-19; ETHELRED 11-2- 5.

OLD AGE PENSIONS. *See* SOCIAL SECURITY.

OLD BAILEY (London) an originally fortified area and street at the western end of the City, overlooking the Fleet River and prison. The City Assizes were held there and it became the location of the Central Criminal Court.

OLDCASTLE. A Herefordshire knightly family much involved in Marcher administration. **Sir John (?-1417)**, captain of Builth and other castles was with P. Henry (later Henry V) at the siege of Aberystwyth (1406) and in 1409 he married Joan, Lady Cobham and was summoned to parliament as Lord Cobham, with large estates and Cooling Castle in Kent. He was a convinced Lollard and was accused of encouraging heresy in Herefordshire and on his Kentish estates. Having been condemned, he was handed over for execution (1413), but escaped and hid in London where he tried and failed to organise the seizure of the King and capital in Jan. 1414. Lollard troubles continued in London while he moved westwards. He was captured at Welshpool in 1417 and was hanged and his body burned.

OLD CONTEMPTIBLES were surviving members of the British Expeditionary Force of 1914. So called because a German politician had called it a 'contemptible little army'.

'OLD DOMINION'. Virginia.

OLDENBURG. *See* BALTIC *passim*; MOSCOW DISASTER 1812-1.

OLDHAM, Hugh (?-1519) founded Manchester Grammar School in 1503, was Bp. of Exeter from 1504 and was the main contributor to the foundation of Corpus Christi Coll., Oxford.

OLD IRISH. *See* CELTS.

OLD PRETENDER. *See* JACOBITES AND PRETENDERS-6 TO 22.

OLD Q. *See* DOUGLAS.

OLD ROWLEY, the name of a conspicuously masculine royal stallion, was a common contemporary nickname for Charles II.

OLD STATUTES (VETERA STATUTA) are an edition, first printed in 1588, of the statutes from the 1225 confirmation of Magna Carta to the accession of Edward III (1327). *See* STATUTES OF UNCERTAIN DATE and NEW STATUTES.

OLD STYLE. The method of dating before the Calendar Act 1752.

OLD VIC Theatre was opened as the *Royal Coburg* in the Waterloo Bridge Road, London in 1818 and renamed the *Victoria* in 1833. It declined into a music hall with a promenade for assignations, but restarted more respectably in 1880. Lilian Baylis became manager in 1912 and her Shakespearean productions were the foundation of a new classical London theatre movement.

OLÉRON I (Biscay) original seat of the Admiralty Court established in 1360. The maritime Laws of Oléron, derived from Amalfitan customs, formed the basis of English Admiralty law.

OLIGARCHY is a govt. by a small number exercising their power usually for selfish purposes. The **Iron Law of Oligarchy** is a sociological theory that all movements fall into the hands of a small group in the process of rationalisation and systemisation.

OLIPHANT, Francis Wilson (1818-59) and his wife and cousin **Margaret (1828-97).** He designed, with Pugin, the stained glass in the Houses of Parliament, Kings College Cambridge and Ely Cathedral. She wrote many quiet but much appreciated serial novels of professional and moneyed society, particularly *Chronicles of Carlingford* (1863-76); also a *Life of Edward Irving* (1862) and various works in literature and criticism.

OLIPHANT. Perthshire family. **(1) Sir Laurence (?-?1500) of Aberdalgie, 1st Ld. OLIPHANT (1467)** was a councillor and Lord of the Articles in 1488, supported the King in the 1489 rebellion and was ambassador to France and Castile in 1491. His great-grandson **(2) Laurence (1529-93) 4th Ld.** and a councillor from 1565, managed to be both a member of the assize for Bothwell's trial and a witness to his marriage agreement with Mary Q. of Scots, for whom he fought at Langside in 1569. He changed sides in 1572 and faded from prominence. A descendant **(3) Laurence (1691-1767)** Laird of Gask, a Jacobite who had fought at Sheriffmuir (1715) and became the Young Pretender's gov. of the north in 1745, and after fighting with his son at Falkirk and Culloden, escaped to Sweden. His forfeited lands at Gask were repurchased for his benefit in 1753 and he returned unmolested in 1763.

OLIPHANT, Laurence (1829-88), son of a Chief Justice of Ceylon, had a varied and eccentric career. He visited Nepal (1851) and the Black Sea (1853), was sec. to Lord Elgin in America and to Lord Stratford de Redcliffe in the Crimea. Then he returned to Elgin and was with him in China (1857- 9). After a period of plotting with Garibaldi at Genoa, he became sec. to the legation in Japan. In 1865 (when he was an M.P.) he wrote a satirical novel called *Piccadilly*. In 1867 he came under the influence of Thomas Lake Harris, an American prophet, to whom he gave much of his property. In 1870-1 he was *Times* correspondent in the Franco-Prussian War and was then commercially employed by Harris in America. Meanwhile he married (1872). He freed himself from Harris and recovered his property in 1881 and with his wife wrote (1883) a curious work, *Sympneumata*, which they believed to have been dictated by a spirit. They then went to Haifa and formed a Jewish proto-kibbutz.

OLIVE BRANCH PETITION (1775). John Dickinson, the author of the *Farmer's Letters* (1767-8), persuaded the Continental Congress to send this petition, setting out the American Colonists' grievances, to the British govt. who refused to accept it as coming from rebels.

OLIVER or OLIVIER (1) Isaac (?1556-1617) Huguenot pupil of Nicholas Hilliard, executed many portraits and miniatures of Tudor and Jacobean court personalities including Elizabeth I and James II. His son **(2) Peter (1594-1648)** was a highly successful miniaturist.

OLIVIER, LAURENCE (1907-89) Ld. OLIVER OF BRIGHTON (1970). Stage and screen actor. He directed and played in the powerful *Henry V* (1943) and was a founder-director of the N. Theatre Company.

OLLAMH **(Gael).** An Irishman of learning, usually attached to some important chief. *See* SENNACHIE.

OLYMPIA (London) was opened in 1886, originally for agricultural shows, but was soon used for other spectacles. It was enlarged in 1930.

OLYMPIAD. The four year period between OLYMPIC GAMES. **(1)** The first modern Games were held modestly at Athens in 1896. Those scheduled for 1916, 1940 and 1944 were cancelled because of world wars. The Games were held in London in 1908 and 1949, at Melbourne in 1956 and at Montreal in 1976. **(2)** The Nazi govt. made nationalist capital out of the Berlin Games of 1936, where carefully trained Germans won most of the events. By 1956, with incessant pressure to widen their scope, the Games had become vast business and quasi-political assemblies where many of the competitors (especially the Russians) were disguised professionals sponsored for reasons of national prestige and generating as much bad blood as the good-will for which their originator, Pierre de Coubertin, had hoped. At the Munich Games of 1972 several Israeli competitors were massacred. In 1992 there was a bribery scandal in connection with Salt Lake City.

O'MAHONY, John (1816-77), an active nationalist among Irish exiles after 1848, he founded the Fenian Brotherhood, later the Irish Republican Brotherhood, with James Stephens in 1858 and was its leader in the U.S.A.

O'MALLEY, Grace (?1530-1600). Irish lady pirate, married Richard Burke, Chief of Mayo in 1582. Captured but redeemed in 1586, she died in poverty.

OMAN. *See* ARABIA.

OMAR KHAYYAM (c. 1034-1130) a Persian, became famous in Britain because Edward Fitzgerald brilliantly translated his Quatrains (*Rubayyat*.) and set a lasting fashion for their blend of deterministic hedonism. Omar's Quatrains are much less respected in his own country, but his mathematical and astronomical gifts still are.

OMBUDSMAN (Sw: complaints man) was originally an official appointed (permanently after 1809) by the Swedish and Finnish Estates to collect grievances in the intervals between parliamentary sessions. He could investigate any administrative act and attend the deliberations of officials and judges; he reported to parliament and could initiate prosecutions. A military *ombudsman* was permanently instituted in 1915. The idea was adopted in Denmark in 1954, in the West German army in 1956 and in Norway and New Zealand in 1962. In Britain an Ombudsman under the title of **PARLIAMENTARY COMMISSIONER FOR ADMINISTRATION** was created in 1967, but his functions were more limited. He could act only on a complaint referred to him by an M.P. and only in relation to a limited group of central govt. departments. He could enforce his findings only by threatening to report a matter to parliament and he could not act if some other remedy was available. In 1974 **LOCAL COMMISSIONERS** for dealing with complaints against local authorities were created. Their powers and limitations within their field were analogous to those of the parliamentary commissioner but a complainant could approach them direct, if approach through a councillor failed.

OMDURMAN. *See* SUDAN.

OMNIBUS (Lat: for all). Geo. Shillibeer (1797-1866) built omnibuses in Paris (where they had been tried in the 1660s) in 1825 and introduced them in London in 1829. The pay-as-you-enter system was legalised by statute in 1832. The first double decker originated at the Great Exhibition (1851) and motor buses were tried from 1897, the first permanent route (Helston-Lizard) being established in 1903. Electric trolley buses were first operated in 1911. The advent of the private car challenged the bus between the World Wars and by 1970 buses were largely confined to towns but long distance coaches developed especially with the construction of motorways.

O'MORE. A turbulent clan of Leix, often allied to the Ormondes. Their most notable chiefs were **Rory Oge (?-1578)** and **Rory or Roger (?-1652).** The first was heavily engaged in fighting the Plantation of Queens County whereby most of his people lost their homes. After his death there were 19 successive outbreaks, in the later of which the second gradually emerged as a person of consequence. He was involved in the planning of the great Ulster rebellion of 1641 and the attempt to seize Dublin castle. Thereafter he was a Confederate leader and ultimately driven to Innishboffin, where he died.

ON DIT **(Fr. = It is said).** 18th and early 19th cent. term for a piece of scurrilous or salacious gossip, especially in London or Bath.

O'NEILL TRIBES. Niall of the Nine Hostages, High King of Ireland, who was killed on the coast of Gaul in 405, had 14 sons. Several tribes deduced their descent from them, in particular in Meath the O'Coindelbhain, O'Melaghiin, MacGeoghan, Malloy and O'Catharnaigh, and in the north the O'Cannanain, O'Donnel and the O'Neill who occupied the Tir Eoghan (the country of Niall's son Eoghan) or Tyrone (Ulster) and were also called the Cinel Eoghan. They had a pre-eminence over the others and their chief was called THE O'NEILL and was usually High King until the coming of the Normans. Hence these chiefs were regarded by the Irish as their national leader, and conversely they were treated alternately by the English with suspicion or enmity, or made the objects of attempts at Anglicisation. The use of the title was, indeed, made illegal. This curious relationship continued until the flight of Hugh O'Neill with the other earls in 1607.

O'NEILL, Shane The Proud (1530-67), 2nd E. of TYRONE, who was partly educated with the Sidneys at Penshurst, was the eldest son of **Con Bacach O'Neill (?1484-?1559)** who attempted to supersede him by his younger brother **Matthew.** He fought a civil war with and expelled them in 1556 and then had to face attack by the Irish and Scots Macdonald clans. He murdered Matthew in 1558, was recognised by the English govt., but remained at war with the Macdonalds who,

meanwhile, had secured English support. As a result his recognition was withdrawn. In 1562, however, he made a public submission but intrigued with Spain. His first object was to conquer an independent Ulster and by 1565 he had captured most of the chiefs of the Irish Macdonnells. His purposes could not be achieved without foreign help and he was soon intriguing with Mary Q. of Scots and the French. The result was war with the English. He unsuccessfully invaded the Pale, but burned Armagh. In 1567 the Macdonnells defeated him at Letterkenny and he was subsequently murdered. *See* ELIZABETH I-9.

O'NEILL, Shane. *See* ELIZABETH 1-17.

ONSLOW (1) Richard (1528-71) was Recorder of London in 1563, Solicitor-Gen. in 1566 and Speaker of the Commons from 1566 to 1571. His grandson **(2) Sir Richard (1601-1664)** was M.P. in the Short and Long parliaments, raised a regiment against the King in the Civil War, was purged in 1647, but sat in the Protectorate parliaments first in the Lower and then in the Upper House. He was also in the Convention parliaments of 1660. His grandson **(3) Richard (1654-1717) 1st Ld. ONSLOW (1716)** was almost continuously in the Commons from 1679. He was Speaker from 1708 to 1710 and Ch. of the Exchequer from 1714 to 1715. His nephew **(4) Arthur (1691-1768)** was Whig M.P. from 1720 and as Speaker from 1728 to 1761 established the main lines of modern parliamentary procedure. From 1734 to 1742 he was also Treasurer of the Navy. His nephew **(5) George (1731-92)** was an M.P. from 1760 to 1784, first as a supporter of Rockingham and later of North. Arthur's son **(6) George (1731-1814) 1st E. of ONSLOW (1801)** was an M.P. from 1754 and a Lord of the Treasury under Rockingham in 1765. In 1776 he inherited the Onslow peerage. From 1777 he worked mainly at court as Comptroller (1777), Treasurer (1779) and Lord of the Bedchamber from 1780. A great friend of the P. of Wales he was present at his marriage to Mrs Fitzherbert in 1785. His son **(7) Thomas (1755-1827) 2nd E.,** was an M.P. from 1775 to 1806.

ONTARIO. *See* CANADA.

OO. The prefix by which Marlborough identified his secret letters to the D. of Berwick.

OOTACAMUND (India). The summer station of the Madras govt. where snooker was invented.

OPEC = Organisation of Petroleum Exporting Countries.

OPEN DOOR. A type of agreement between western powers, relating usually to 19th cent. China, under which they agreed to compel the local gov. to admit the traders of the contracting powers upon equal terms.

OPEN FIELD CULTIVATION. A method, suitable in flat lands especially the Midlands, of combining some of the advantages of communal work with those of private ownership and used by the 10th cent. or even earlier.

A large unfenced field was divided into three and in each the manor tenants had individual holdings (*virgates*) consisting not of consolidated areas but of strips a furlong in length and a pole wide, scattered and intermingled with other such strips to make for equality of yield and fertility between virgate and virgate. One field was left fallow, the others sown with grain and beans, the use being rotated year by year. The whole labour force worked the entirety of each field, but owned cattle individually. The cattle were pastured on common lands outside the field and to some extent on the fallow. After the harvest the cattle were allowed to roam at will to fertilise the fields under crop. The bailiff was in charge of labour under the steward. Disputes were settled according to the custom of the manor in the customary court and between free tenants by the lord in the court baron.

These open fields were steadily, with a very few exceptions, swept away by approvements and enclosures.

OPEN UNIVERSITY was founded under the inspiration of Harold Wilson in 1971 with an H.Q. in Milton Keynes.

OPERA and ORATORIO have a common precursor in the medieval mystery, miracle and morality plays which normally included music and singing. Oratorio was foreshadowed in 15th cent. Florence and at Rome in 1556 by St. Philip Neri as a popular service for the young performed in an oratory. Opera came from a group of renaissance intellectuals who were trying at Florence to resurrect the original form of the classical Greek drama. The first deliberately composed example of each (Cavalieri's oratorio *Representation of Soul and Body* and Peri and Caccini's opera *Eurydice*) was performed in the same year in 1660. Opera reached England under the Commonwealth when spoken plays were prohibited; the first was *The Siege of Rhodes;* the music was by five different composers, the libretto by Sir Wm. Davenant, who had probably seen opera in Paris while attending Q. Henrietta Maria and who inspired the project. The Italian style of opera, with its disregard for anything but virtuoso singing, came to England with Handel in 1712, but in 1728 Gay's *Beggars Opera* represented a return to the synthesis of music and drama intended by the Florentines. Thereafter English Ballad Opera and Grand Opera remained in uneasy competition down to modern times.

Oratorio, however, only reached England in 1720 when the D. of Chandos commissioned Handel's *Haman and Mordecai* or *Esther. Israel in Egypt* appeared in 1738 and the *Messiah* in 1742. By 1795 'the rage for oratorio' had 'spread from the capital to every market town', aided by methodist and other revivalisms and in the 19th cent. many English oratorios were written. This movement has continued ever since.

Since 1930 opera has had to be subsidised by the govt.; oratorio, however, was still paying its way in 1993.

OPIUM was much cultivated in India and the Shan States of Burma. The Chinese were hostile to it on moral grounds and the **Opium Wars** (*see* CHINA-17) were fought largely to compel them to legalise it. They never did, but a huge illicit trade grew up with farming in Yunnan. In 1906 China made a Ten Years' Agreement with India by which cultivation would be stamped out in China in return for an ending over ten years of Indian exports. The agreement worked well until civil war broke out in China in 1917. Hague Conventions of 1912, with similar but wider objects, broke down at the outbreak of World War I. Large scale cultivation spread to Turkey and Colombia after World War II and had become a serious social problem and threat to international order by 1990.

OPORTO, ancient city which, as PORTUS CALE, gave its name to Portugal. There was a long standing trade in salt, olive oil and fruit, but the English trade in port began in 1703 during French wars, when Bordeaux was cut off from Bristol, and originated in the ingenuity of English shippers who established a Factory House, still extant in 1995. The trade was firmly grounded on the Methuen T. (1703), which gave a preference to Portuguese over French wines and later by the special relationship with Portugal which grew up in the Peninsular War. It led, too, to the improvement of the wines as beverage wines and eventually to an accumulation of capital and the establishment of textile, sugar, pottery and glass industries. *See* PENINSULAR WAR 1807-14, 4-5, 9.

OPPIDUM **(Lat. = town).** The word is often used of Celtic forts which were not always permanently occupied.

OPTIONAL CLAUSES (1) Until 1766 banknotes were payable on presentation or at the option of the directors six months later with interest. **(2)** Optional writs called upon a defendant to do something or show cause why he should not. **(3)** The requirement in educational legislation that a parent should send his child to school or otherwise provide for his education or **(4)** may choose not to allow the child to be given religious instruction.

ORANGE (-NASSAU) HOUSE OF. The family originated at Orange, a principality since 1163 near Avignon in S. France. By successive marriages it passed to the Chalon (Burgundian) family (1393) and to the Nassaus (1544). WILLIAM the SILENT (1544-84) was the first Nassau P. of Orange and from 1572 until his murder, Stadholder of Holland. The headship of the family and the title then passed to PHILIP WILLIAM (r. 1584-1618), then to his half-brother MAURICE (r. 1618-25) who succeeded William the Silent at Stadholder and was followed both in title and office by another half-brother FREDERICK HENRY (r. 1625-47). His son WILLIAM II (r. 1647-50) succeeded in both capacities and married MARY (1631-66) *d.* of K. Charles I. Their son WILLIAM III (1650-1702), Stadholder from 1672 and King of Great Britain from 1689, was thus half English. He married his cousin MARY II, *d.* of K. James II. In 1673, as a result of William's opposition to French policy, Louis XIV seized Orange and conferred it on the Longueville family, a junior branch of the Chalons. The direct Orange-Nassau line ended with William III, but the title passed to a distant cousin JOHN WILLEM FRISO (1687-1711), Stadholder of Frisia from 1696. The P. of Utrecht confirmed the separation of the title from the principality. Friso's son WILLIAM IV (1711-51) became hereditary Stadholder of all the Dutch Provinces in 1747. His son WILLIAM V (1746-1806), the last Stadholder, succeeded him but was in exile after 1795. His son was called to the throne of the Netherlands as King WILLIAM I (1815-40) and was the ancestor of the present royal house.

ORANGE FREE STATE (O.F.S.) (S. Africa). Europeans and semi-nomadic Dutch pastoralists were at large north of the Orange R. in the late 18th cent., but from 1836 the Great Trek brought in Boers in large numbers. The resulting confusion and native wars brought the British in and from 1848 to 1856 they kept order in an indeterminate area called the **Orange River Sovereignty.** They then withdrew and the Boers formed a sketchy O.F.S. which was harassed by Basuto to the east until the frontier was stabiised in the 1870s. The Free Staters joined the Transvaal Boers in the South African War and suffered annexation afterwards as the ORANGE RIVER COLONY. Self govt. was conferred in 1907 and the O.F.S. under its original name became a province of S. Africa in 1910.

ORANGEMEN. Politically organised protestants in Ireland since the time of William of Orange. Their ORANGE ORDER was formed on Masonic analogies in 1790 after the fight known as the Battle of the Diamond between the Protestant Peep o'Day Boys and the R. Catholic Defenders where some twenty of the latter were killed. Its purpose was to prevent R. Catholics from obtaining tenancies. It was directly influential with the Dublin govt. from the Union in 1800 until 1835 when Thomas Drummond put an end to its pretensions. It recovered some influence in Ulster when partition became an issue.

ORATORIO. *See* OPERA.

ORB. A golden ball surmounted by a cross signifying the sacredness of the power committed to Kings. In English practice it is held by the sovereign only very briefly at the Coronation.

ORDAINERS, LORDS were set up by Edward II on the demand of Thomas of Lancaster and four other earls in Mar. 1310. The bishops elected two earls, the earls two bishops. These four chose two barons and the six then co-opted fifteen others making twenty-one in all. They were the Abp. of Canterbury, the Bps. of London, Salisbury, Chichester, Norwich, St. Davids and Llandaff; the earls of Arundel, Gloucester, Hereford, Lancaster, Lincoln, Pembroke, Richmond and Warwick; Hugh de Vere, Robert Clifford, Hugh Courtenay, William Marshall and William Martin. The result was a fairly balanced body.

The forty-one **ordinances** which they drew up were

ratified in the parliament of Aug. 1311, They included **(1)** the banishment of Piers Gaveston, Henry de Beaumont, Lord of Man, his sister Isabella de Vesci Chatelaine of Bamborough and the financier Amerigo dei Frescbaldi; **(2)** Annulment and prohibition on alienations of crown land until the King's debts are paid; **(3)** All revenues to be paid into the Exchequer; **(4)** Prises abolished; **(5)** New customs and maltolts; and **(6)** Monetary changes to require the consent of Parliament; **(7)** The King not to quit the realm, appoint a keeper of the realm nor make war without the consent of Parliament; **(8)** No Chief Officers of State or Household to be appointed without the consent of Parliament and existing appointments to be reviewed; **(9)** Sheriffs to be appointed by the Chancellor, Treasurer and council or by the Treasurer, the barons of the Exchequer and the chief justices; **(10)** Only born Englishmen to be collectors of customs; **(11)** All officials to take an oath to uphold the ordinances; **(12)** Parliaments to be held annually or more often and to appoint a committee to hear complaints against ministers; **(13)** The use of the Privy Seal restricted; **(14)** Royal letters of protection to malefactors abolished and civil proceedings not to be delayed by royal letters; **(15)** Common law actions to be excluded from the Exchequer and the courts of the steward and marshal; **(16)** Bail to be more readily given; **(17)** Various detailed abuses in forest law remedied.

The whole was to be proclaimed in every shire and Cinque Port. *See* EDWARD 11-3.

ORDEAL, TRIAL BY. In Anglo-Saxon times if a person accused of crime could not find compurgators or if his oath burst, i.e. was imperfectly recited, he might insist on an ordeal supervised by the church. Freemen carried a hot iron three paces and were freed if there were no scars after three days under bandages. Bondmen were thrown bound into water and were freed if they sank. The clergy swallowed an accursed morsel (containing a feather) and were held guilty if they choked. The Normans permitted the alternative of trial by battle. In 1215 the Fourth Lateran Council forbade the clergy to assist at such ordeals and they rapidly ceased.

ORDENANZA. See PENINSULAR WAR 1807-14, 5-6.

ORDER in classical architecture is the unit of composition comprising entablature, column and base. The five orders, in ascending degrees of decorative complication, are known as Doric, Ionic and Corinthian which had Roman as well as Greek forms and Composite and Tuscan which were Roman. Attic orders are square columned versions of any of these. The Roman forms, much used in the Renaissance, are derived from descriptions by Vitruvius (c. 40 B.C.) and Palladios observations of Roman remains. The Greek orders reappeared in the Neo-classical revival.

ORDER BOOK of the House of Commons is the minute to minute register of matters which will be brought before the House and from which each day's **ORDER PAPER** (agenda) is prepared.

ORDERIC[US VITALIS] (1075-?1143), English born Norman monk at St. Ernoul, Normandy, wrote a Latin *Ecclesiastical History* from A.D. 1 to 1141, which is an important source. It contains a history of Normandy and of the reigns of the first three Norman kings together with sections on the wider history of Europe. He seems to have been influenced by the work of Bede.

ORDER IN COUNCIL is made by the Sovereign at a meeting of the Privy Council. Such orders are made either under the prerogative, e.g. to declare a wartime blockade, or as subordinate legislation authorised by an Act of Parliament, e.g. to close a churchyard. The minister concerned with the Order will generally be present together with the Lord Pres. and the Clerk.

ORDERS IN COUNCIL of 1793 to 1815 are the usual name for certain particular orders on the regulation of enemy trade. There were nine important ones viz: **(1)** *June 1793* ordered the arrest and compulsory purchase of all cargoes of flour and grain consigned to French ports. **(2)** *Nov. 1793* condemned all ships carrying cargoes from French colonies to France or provisions or supplies for the use of such colonies. **(3)** *Jan. 1794* limited (2) above to vessels bound from these colonies direct to Europe. **(4)** *Jan. 1798* limited (2) still further by excepting neutrals if the cargo had become neutral property destined for the neutral country or Britain. **(5)** *May 1806* proclaimed a blockade of the European coasts from Brest to the Elbe, exit and entry to ports between the Seine and Ostend being totally forbidden, but on either side neutrals being allowed free access if they had not loaded at, or were not destined for, another enemy port. **(6)** *Jan. 1807* forbade neutral sailings between enemy ports. **(7)** *Nov. 1807* declared a blockade of all ports from which British shipping was excluded but allowed neutrals **(i)** to trade with hostile colonies and **(ii)** between the latter and the free ports of British colonies and **(iii)** to sail from the U.K. direct to enemy ports and **(iv)** from an enemy port direct to the U.K. In other words all trade with enemy territory had to pass through Britain. **(8)** *Apr. 1809* restricted (7) to France, Holland and the ports of Italy under Bonaparte's control. **(9)** *June 1812* revoked (7) and (8) in so far as they affected the U.S.A. which had, however, already ceased to be neutral.

The system of 1807 was also modified in the interests of British trade by licences designed to protect against seizure neutral or fraudulently neutral ships with papers designed to deceive enemy customs authorities and which might therefore superficially seem to infringe the Orders. Many such licences were given 2,600 in 1807, 15,000 in 1809, 18,000 in 1810. Thereafter the numbers fell away because French methods of detection improved. *See also* ANGLO-AMERICAN WAR 1812-15; BLOCKADE (2 entries).

ORDINANCE. (1) An answer by the Crown to an inquiry from the Commons as to the law on a particular matter. **(2)** Some prerogative orders made before 1688. **(3)** Orders enforced as legislation, made by one branch of the legislature without the concurrence of the others, notably the ordinances of the House of Commons between 1642 and 1660. **(4)** The term is sometimes used of some early but regular enactments.

ORDINANCES (1311). *See* ORDAINERS, LORDS.

ORDINARY. The ecclesiastical official, usually the bishop, having primary judicial authority over a cause.

ORDINEM VESTRUM **(1245)** decretal of Innocent IV seizing Franciscan property.

ORDNANCE, BOARD OF. Armies were originally of feudal, i.e. semi-private, origin but gunpowder was intruded into the military scene from outside and kings kept a firm hand on the resulting artillery, which developed a separate organisation. Edward III's Crécy guns were kept by the Wardrobe. The first Master Gen. of the Ordnance was appointed by Henry V in 1414 and his dept. had close ties not only with the King, but with the guilds which provided the metal workers and fire masters. The effective organisation of the Board dated, however, from instructions drafted by James D. of York and issued by Charles II in July 1683. These were reissued at the start of each subsequent reign.

The Board was not subordinate to either armed service. It was headed by the Master Gen. and comprised a Lieut-Gen., Surveyor-Gen., Clerk of the Ordnance, Keeper of the Stores and Clerk of Deliveries, with about 160 senior officials and many Gentlemen of the Ordnance. None of these might buy or sell their commissions. Its primary function was to supply guns and other firearms to both services, but it also built and maintained fortresses and barracks, hired or supplied horses and wagons, trained and certified gunners and manufactured and tested weapons of all kinds. It owned a factory at Moorfields and later the Arsenal at Woolwich. An early combination of a ministry of supply and a nationalised industry, it presented a private financial estimate to the House of Commons; in emergencies the Master-Gen. (always a national figure) could authorise expenditure without the prior authority of a parliamentary vote.

The Board kept representatives, sometimes only a gunner and an armourer, sometimes a more substantial establishment in most fortresses throughout the U.K. and the colonies, but its strength and consequently its power to maintain standards and control abuses varied greatly as between wartime when money was forthcoming and peace when it was drastically cut. Peacetime retrenchment usually immobilised the artillery until the men could be recruited and the transport hired. This led in 1716 (when Marlborough was Master-Gen.) to the creation of a separate Royal Regiment of Artillery, because of the difficulties experienced in mobilising against the Jacobite rebellion.

The demands of naval and military commanders for equipment which would outclass that of an enemy forced the Board to maintain an interest in design, research and experiment. This ranged from new types of harness, split trails for light pieces and various types of bomb fuse, to the adoption in 1739 of a Swiss method of casting guns solid and boring them out. Later in the century greater ranges brought a need for ground survey, leading ultimately to the map making undertaking called the ORDNANCE SURVEY (see CARTOGRAPHY) established in 1791. The last Master-Gen. was Lord Raglan and on his appointment as C-in-C in the Crimea the Board was amalgamated with the War Office (1855) and the War Office and Admiralty thereafter pursued their own production policies, sometimes in competition.

ORDOVICES were a strong federation of pastoral clans in Snowdonia. They were finally conquered by the Romans in about A.D. 80. See BRITAIN, ROMAN-2.

OREGON was originally the name of a vaguely conceived but large area between (roughly) Russian America (Alaska) and Mexico (California) and stretching inland as far as the eastern foothills of the Rocky Mountains. It was first exploited at the end of the 18th cent. for furs and at Nootka Sound in 1789 the Spanish authorities attempted to assert a fur monopoly by arresting the English merchants there. Britain threatened reprisals and the ensuing Nootka Sound Convention (1790) opened the Pacific coast to British colonisation. It also awakened the U.S. State Dept., then under Thomas Jefferson, to the difficulties which might be created for the U.S.A by the New World colonial ambitions of Old World states. The Louisiana purchase, which Jefferson negotiated through Monroe in 1803 in pursuance of his solution to the problem, brought U.S. territory to the marches of the Oregon. The Russians meantime had been prospecting in Alaska, so that by 1815 there were four adjacent claimants, Spain, Britain, U.S.A. and Russia. In 1818 an Anglo-American boundary convention extended the Canadian boundary to the Rockies and provided for the joint occupation of the Oregon by the two powers. The Spanish (and so Mexican) claim north of Lat. 42° was abandoned to the U.S.A. by the Adams-Onis treaty of 1819. Russia gave up her claim south of Lat 54° 40° by separate treaties of 1824 with the U.S.A. and 1825 with Britain. Thus the serious claimants were reduced to two and the disputed area appreciably reduced. In 1827 Britain laid claim to the southern shores of the Vancouver Strait. Joint occupation continued until Americans began to move in from the East in substantial numbers along the Oregon Trail and made unsuccessful attempts to secure land titles. The biggest migrations occurred in 1843 to 1845 in circumstances of legendary hardship. Pres. Polk gave a year's notice to end the joint occupation in Apr. 1846. He was placed under strong popular pressure to go to war for the whole territory, but common sense prevailed and the Aberdeen govt's offer of a partition by extending the Canadian boundary directly to the Vancouver Sound was quickly accepted. The British claim of 1827 was settled by arbitration in favour of the U.S.A. in 1871. The Oregon Trail remained in use through the 1850s.

The American part of the territory now comprises the states of Oregon (admitted to the Union in 1859), Washington and part of Montana (both in 1889) and Idaho (1890). See BRITISH COLUMBIA.

ORFORD, E. of. See GEORGE 1-7; RUSSELL.

ORGAN. There was a 14th cent. organ (said to be deafening) at Winchester cathedral. Church organs were all destroyed during the Commonwealth and the first new one was built at the Temple Church (London) in 1661.

ORGANISATION OF AFRICAN UNITY (O.A.U.) was founded at Addis Ababa in 1963 against colonialism but was seldom very effective because of the Russian-induced instability of many of its member states which, even when proclaiming an anti-colonialist policy, were seldom able to do much about it. It mediated in the Algeria-Morocco dispute of 1964-5 and the border disputes between Somalia, Kenya and Ethiopia in 1965-7 but failed to settle the Nigerian (1968-70) and Chad (1982) civil wars. It proposed sanctions against S. Africa in 1982. Its main constructive concern in the 1980s has been the reform of African agriculture.

ORGANISATION OF AMERICAN STATES (O.A.S) originated at a Washington conference in 1890 to foster mutual co-operation and active support for the Monroe doctrine. It was not an effective body until a charter was adopted in 1948 and it began to be supported by large subventions from the U.S.A. These benefited the Latin countries. In 1961 an Alliance for Progress was formed to channel the funds and in 1962 Cuba, being by then Communist dominated, was expelled and the O.A.U. supported the stand against Russian missile bases in Cuba. In 1965 U.S. armed intervention in the right-wing Dominican Republic brought criticism from the members which replaced U.S. troops with their own. An Inter-American Court of Human Rights was set up in 1979.

ORGANISATION FOR EUROPEAN ECONOMIC CO-OPERATION (O.E.E.C.) was formed by 18 European states in response to the U.S. enactment of the Marshall Plan (Apr. 1948) in order to restore the war damaged economies by 1952 by solving the trade deficit with the U.S.A., developing mutual co-operation, establishing financial stability and maximum production. Western Germany joined in 1949, Spain in 1959. It encountered increasing difficulties in liberating inter-state trade and eventually divided into the group which eventually formed the E.E.C. and those, including Britain, which formed EFTA. In 1961 it was superseded by the **ORGANISATION FOR ECONOMIC CO-OPERATION AND DEVELOPMENT (O.E.C.D.).** This had the same members plus the U.S.A. and Canada. Its purpose was to raise the income of member states by 50% by 1970 and to collect and circulate economic information. The latter activity has become the most important activity since the T. of Maastricht came into force in 1993.

ORIANA. A poetic nickname for Elizabeth I.

ORIENT LINE. See PENINSULAR AND ORIENTAL, etc.

ORIFLAMME was an orange red banner presented by the Abbot of St. Denis to early French kings on setting out for war. One was captured at Crécy.

ORIGINAL SIN. A doctrine, in various forms common to nearly all Christian sects (save the Pelagians), that since the Fall of Adam sinfulness is inherent in the nature of humanity which needs redemption and can secure it only through the grace of Jesus Christ. Thus salvation is, at the most, only partly procurable by a person's own efforts or, according to extreme Calvinists, not so procurable at all.

ORINOCO R., whose delta represents the E. end of the Spanish Main, was a tempting avenue into northern S. America because, with a single break at the Atures cataracts, it is navigable for 1500 miles inland and was thought to approach the fabulous country of El Dorado. *See* RALEIGH.

ORISSA (India) was annexed to Bengal by the Moguls in 1572. In 1751 part of it was ceded to the Maratha Bhonsla and the rest came under British control with the cession of the *Diwani* in 1765. The two parts were reunited under British rule by the Anglo-Maratha T. of Deogaon (1803) and administered under Bengal until 1854. In 1912 it was united with Bihar but in 1935 it became a separate province on its own.

ORKNEY, Es. of. *See* HAMILTON; SINCLAIR; STEWART.

ORKNEY. *See* VILLIERS A.

ORKNEY Is. have many megalithic monuments testifying to a substantial pre-Christian population. In the 8th cent. A.D. the inhabitants were Pictish and Christian, but between 700 and 850 they were conquered by Norwegians in two waves, the first of landless people from Rogaland, the second a large expedition under Rognvald of Møre. This was probably an act of policy by K. Harald Finehair to use his surplus population to secure control of the Scandinavian-Irish traffic. Rognvald left his brother Sigurd the Mighty (?-?880) and the islands became, with the Shetlands, a powerful Norwegian sea earldom under his descendants, of whom Thorfinn the Mighty (?-1064) was the most notable. In 1231 this fell to John of Angus and thereafter was disputed between Norway and freebooting Scots whom the Scottish earls failed to drive out. Order was restored under the earls of the St. Clair (Sinclair) family, who ruled from 1379. By now Norwegian claims were almost valueless and in 1468 the Danish King of Norway, Christian I, pledged the islands to James III of Scots for the dowry of his daughter Margaret. The dowry was not paid in time, the Scots evaded later efforts to pay and in 1471 annexed the islands. The act of annexation forbade the King to give them away and consequently the crown leased them to a series of tenants who for the most part ruthlessly exploited the population into the 19th cent.

ORLEANISTS (Fr.) (1) *See* CHARLES XI AND XII OF FRANCE. **(2)** The adherents of the Duke of Orleans, younger brother of Louis XIV and his descendants, one of whom, Louis Philippe, was King of the French from 1830 to 1848.

ORLÉANS (France), apart from Paris the only substantial town of the French royal domain, was at a strategic point and also at an important crossing of the R. Loire. It was thus peculiarly important practically and psychologically to the French monarchy. Its Dukes were always princes; its relief by Joan of Arc in 1429 was the turning point in the Hundred Years War and it suffered severely in the Wars of Religion, the Franco-Prussian War and World War II, by which time it had become a focus of rail, road and water communications.

ORMULUM. Under this title, Orm, an early 13th cent. Augustinian, wrote some metrical homilies phonetically in the N.E Midlands dialect. The book is rare direct evidence of English pronunciation at the time.

ORMONDE, D. of. *See* GEORGE 1-2.

ORMONDE, E. of. *See* DOUGLAS ('RED')-12.

ORMUZ. *See* BANDAR ABBAS.

OROSIUS (fl. A.D. 500), Spanish disciple of SS Augustine and Jerome, author of *Historia adversus Paganos* (History in refutation of the Unbelievers), wrote a *Geography* which K. Alfred translated.

O'ROURKE. A large clan powerful in Leitrim and Cavan from the 12th cent. to the end of the 16th. Twenty chiefs or tanists were called **Tiernan.** The last chief of importance was **Sir BRIAN-NA-MURTHA** (?-1591) who secured substantial lands in Connaught but quarrelled with the govt., gave help to the survivors of the Armada and was taken and executed for treason at Tyburn.

ORRERY. *See* BOYLE-7 *et seq.*

ORSINI CONSPIRACY (1858). Count Felice Orsini (1819-58), an advanced Romagna liberal imprisoned for life in

1844, was amnestied by Pius IX in 1846 but became a member of the Roman Republican Govt. in 1849. He continued irreconcilable after its fall and in Jan. 1858 threw a bomb at Napoleon III in Paris, for which he was executed. This affair was a turning point in the reign of Napoleon III who, impressed by Orsini's patriotic determination, decided to espouse Italian liberation. *See* PALMERSTON'S FIRST GOVT.-9.

ORTHODOX CHURCHES. *See* EASTERN ORTHODOX CHURCH.

ORVILLIERS, Louis Comte d' (1708-92), French seaman, commanded the novel *escadre d'evolution* (Fr. = fleet training squadron) in 1774 and the Brest fleet when France entered the War of American Independence. Though inferior in numbers, he beat Keppel off Ushant (July 1778), causing the latter's disgrace. In June 1779 he commanded the ambitious operations to invade Britain with Spanish co-operation. These failed through head-winds and Spanish delays, the combined force being crippled by illness and shortages (June-Sept. 1779).

ORWELL, George or Eric BLAIR (1903-50) wrote, *inter alia, Down and Out in Paris and London* (1933), *Homage to Catalonia* (1938) after fighting in the Spanish Civil War where he was wounded. He then worked in the B.B.C. in World War II and published *Animal Farm* (1945), a satire on Marxist dictatorship, and *1984*, another on totalitarianism. Much discussed, liberal and Marxist-minded people have each sought to claim him for themselves.

OSBALDESTON (Squire) George (1787-1866), an irascible eccentric, was M.P. for Retford from 1812 to 1818 and a master of hounds, especially of the Quorn, from 1817 to 1828 and thereafter the Pytchley; he rode 200 miles in 10 hours and fought a duel with Lord George Bentinck in 1831.

OSBORNE HOUSE (I. of W.), a favourite summer residence of Q. Victoria, stimulated the prosperity of neighbouring Cowes. Edward VII gave it to the nation and it was used as a naval cadet school and hospital. The cadets were moved to Dartmouth in 1921.

OSBORNE'S CASE **[1910] AC 87.** The Amalgamated Society of Railway Servants made the furtherance of parliamentary representation one of their objects and made a compulsory annual levy on their members to maintain M.Ps. who should support the Labour Party. Osborne challenged this object and was upheld. Political objects were legalised by statute in 1913, but union members became entitled to contract out of any political levy.

OSBORNE (1) Sir Edward (?1530-91) married the daughter of Sir William Hewett, clothworker and Lord Mayor of London in 1559-60, succeeded to his fortune and vastly increased it through his trading operations in the Mediterranean (*see* LEVANT CO.). He was Lord Mayor in 1583 and M.P. for the City in 1586. For his great grandson **(2) Sir Thomas (1631-1712) 1st E. of DANBY (1674), M. of CARMARTHEN (1689) and D. of LEEDS (1694)** *See* CHARLES II-17 *to* 22.

OSBORNE, Ruth (1680-1751) was the last English victim of the belief in witchcraft. She died of a ducking at Longmarston, Bucks.

OSENEY PRIORY (1129) ABBEY (1154), Augustinian house at Oxford, was ultimately one of the richest and best managed English monasteries with properties in over 120 places and, in the 13th cent., a banking business. It was much used for councils and meetings. It fell into debt at the end of the 15th cent. but after the Dissolution its abbot became the first Bp. of Oxford.

O'SHEA. *See* PARNELL, CHARLES STEWART.

OSMANLI = the Ottoman Turks.

OSNABRÜCK (Ger.), in Eng. **OSNABURGH** (*see* THIRTY YEARS' WAR) at a centre of communications on a tributary of the R. Ems adjacent to Hanover was a prince-bishopric ruled after the P. of Westphalia (1648) alternately by protestant (often Guelph) and R. Catholic bishops. The town manufactured a coarse linen known as *Osnaburgh* which, throughout the 18th cent., competed in English and English colonial markets with the home produced equivalent, to the annoyance of British business. George I died on an urgent journey to secure it. It was annexed to Hanover in 1803. Hanoverian interest in it was a regular cause of friction between parliament and the Hanoverian kings.

OSMOND or OSMER St. (?-1099), *s.* of Henry of Seez and possibly a nephew of William I, became a royal chaplain and in 1072 Chancellor. In 1078 he became Bp. of Salisbury, a new see formed by the union of Sherborne and Ramsbury. He completed the cathedral at Old Sarum and established its chapter. He was unambitious but an excellent administrator and much involved in the preparation of the Domesday Book. He was also a copyist and bookbinder. At the Council of Rockingham (1095) he argued the King's case against Anselm, but without animosity. His canonisation, promoted in 1128 and completed in 1457, is reputed to have been the longest and most expensive cause of its kind.

OSSEWA-BRANDWAG (Afrik. = Oxwagon Sentinel). A quasi military organisation founded in S. Africa in 1938 to establish a nationalist republican state. Pro-Nazi and anti-semitic, its methods embarrassed the National Party with which, however, it merged in 1948.

OSSIAN = the Irish hero OISIN. *See* FORGERIES LITERARY.

OSSORY (Ir.), area centred on Kilkenny which long boasted the poorest Irish economy and bishopric.

OSTMARK. *See* AUSTRIA-ORIGINS, and -REPUBLICAN.

OSTMEN. Vikings, especially those settled in or operating from Ireland. The word is used exclusively in this narrower sense in this work.

OSTEND and OSTEND CO. This Flemish fishing village was first fortified in 1372. It suffered severely from inundations and also from military hostilities, particularly sieges by the Dutch in 1587, the Archduke Albert from 1601 to 1604 and the French in 1648. It was important after the separation of the Spanish from the United Netherlands because Belgian trade through it avoided the Dutch custom houses on the Scheldt. Hence, when Belgium passed to the Habsburgs under the P. of Utrecht, the Emperor Charles VI developed it and in 1722 chartered the Ostend Co. with a monopoly of trade with Africa and the East. Belgian enterprise had as early as 1718 established factory houses at Canton (China) and Cabelon (India). The Co. took these over and established others, e.g. at Bangibazar (India). It traded very successfully in Indian calicoes and silks and in tea, silk and porcelain from China, and Ostend became exceedingly prosperous. This attracted English, Dutch and French hostility and in 1727 the Emperor was forced to suspend the charter until 1734. In 1732, however, he withdrew it altogether as the price of the English and Dutch guarantee of the Pragmatic Sanction. There was another brief time of prosperity between 1781, when it became a Free Port, and the French occupation in 1795. It only revived permanently after Belgian independence in 1830. It was a German U-boat base in both World Wars, being connected with shelters at Bruges by canal. The British partly obstructed the canal by sinking an old cruiser in it during a raid in May 1918.

OSTORIUS SCAPULA, PUBLIUS. *See* BRITAIN, ROMAN-2.

OSTROGOTHS. *See* GOTHS.

OSWALD, K. of NORTHUMBRIA. *See* NORTHUMBRIA, ANGLIAN KINGDOM 3-4, and MISSIONARIES IN BRITAIN AND IRELAND-6.

OSWALD, St. (?-992), Benedictine of Danish parentage related to Abps. Oda of Canterbury and Osketil of York, was trained at Fleury and appointed Bp. of Worcester on Dunstan's recommendation in 961. In 962 he founded a monastery at Westbury-on-Trym. In 969 he reformed his chapter and in 971 he founded Ramsey Abbey outside his diocese with monks from Westbury. Ramsey established

the Severn Valley monasteries, especially Pershore and Evesham. By now he was a close political associate of K. Edgar. He managed most of the Border administration for the King and in 972 accepted the (then impoverished) archbishopric of York in plurality with Worcester in order to strengthen the King's northern influence. His monastic revivalism did not, however, extend so far. After Edgar's death (975) some of Oswald's monasteries were dispersed but Oswald continued, especially at Ramsey, to exercise his administrative talents on behalf of his two sons.

OSWIECIM. The Polish name of AUSCHWITZ. *See* CONCENTRATION CAMPS.

OSWIN of ESSEX. *See* KENT, KINGDOM-4.

OSWINE, King (?642-51). *See* NORTHUMBRIA-5.

OSWY or OSWIU K. of NORTHUMBRIA (r. 641-70). *See* NORTHUMBRIA 3 and 5; MISSIONARIES TO BRITAIN, etc. 6-8.

OSWULF I, Earl. *See* NORTHUMBRIAN EARLDOMS-2.

OSWULF I, Earl. *See* NORTHUMBRIAN EARLDOMS 5-7.

O'TOOLE, Laurence or Lorcan, St. (1123-80), one of the chieftainly O'Toole family and, as a boy, its hostage with Dermot MacMurrough, King of Leinster, was entrusted to the Bp. of Glendalough and in 1153 became Abbot of Glendalough, his family monastery and burial place. He enforced strict monastic rules. In 1162 he was elected Abp. of Dublin. He introduced the Rule of St. Augustine into Holy Trinity Cathedral which became the wealthiest monastery in Ireland. With the Abps. of Tuam and Cashel, he presided at the reforming Council of Cashel (1172) and in 1179 negotiated the T. of Windsor between Henry II and the High King RUAIDRI O'CONNOR. In 1179 he attended the Lateran Council, where he obtained privileges for his see and a legatine commission. He died at Eu in Normandy.

OTRANTO. *See* ADRIATIC; WORLD WAR I; OTTOMAN EMPIRE-3.

OTTAWA (Ont.). Originated in 1826 as a settlement round the H.Q. of Royal Engineers engaged in building the Rideau Canal. It was then called BYTOWN after Col. By, commanding at the time. The canal brought prosperity and the town was chartered as Ottawa in 1854. It became the capital of the Canadian province in 1858 and of the Dominion in 1867. It developed primarily as an administrative, parliamentary and educational centre but later acquired lumber, pulp, paper and cement industries.

OTTAWA AGREEMENTS. *See* RUNCIMAN-2.

OTTAWA CONFERENCE (July 1932). *See* COMMONWEALTH PREFERENCE.

OTTAWA INDIANS were an Algonquian tribe which the Iroquois had driven from their original Canadian area and were by 1755 mainly centred on Detroit. Under PONTIAC (?1720-69) they were allied to the French in the Seven Years' War. When the French surrendered after the B. of Quebec (1759) they decided to go it alone. Pontiac drew other clans into a confederacy and in the Spring of 1763 by co-ordinated attacks sacked the frontier settlements from Niagara to Virginia and destroyed every western fort except Pittsburgh and Detroit, which withstood a year's siege. The British counter-attack forced a peace in 1764. Pontiac was eventually murdered.

OTTERBURN or CHEVY CHASE, B. of (May 1388). The E. of Douglas disastrously defeated and captured Henry Percy the Younger at this battle, celebrated in song, south of Jedburgh.

OTTO, Card. See HENRY III-11.

OTTOMAN EMPIRE (1) named from the Amir OSMAN I (r. 1293-1324), had taken over the Byzantine territories in N.W. Asia Minor by 1346, when ORHAN (r. 1324-60) became the ally and supplier of mercenaries to the Emperor John VI. These troops originally crossed into Europe on imperial business. They looted Thrace and in 1354 converted Galipoli into a base which attracted recruits from all Islam. MURAD I (r. 1360-89) took Adrianople in 1361. He now controlled the food supply of Constantinople and the Mediterranean-Black Sea trade through it. The Emperor became a Turkish vassal.

(2) The neighbours of the Turks were obsessed with the effort and vigilance of resistance and sheer terror, but to the trading west the major feature of Turkish expansion was, on Murad I's model, the military control over trade routes and sources of supply. His Balkan offensive carried him to the Danube route. His successor the Sultan BAYAZID (r. 1389-1402) (*Balazeth* of Marlowe's *Tamburlaine the Great*) defeated a Hungarian-organised counter offensive at the B. of Nicopolis (1396) but himself perished fighting the Mongols at the B. of Ankara (1402). The Mongols did not stay but left the Turks in confusion. MEHMED or MOHAMMED I (r. 1413-20) had to reorganise. MURAD II (r. 1421-51) fought the first Turkish naval war against the Venetians (1423-30) and defeated the last formal crusade, at Varna (1444).

(3) MEHMED II (r. 1451-81) 'The Conqueror', using Murad's part slave army and powerful artillery, stormed Constantinople (1453) which, as Istanbul, became the capital. He restored and repeopled it and channelled trade to the vast new markets. He used Greek civil servants and organised the *Millets* and he systematised the celibate *Devshirmé*, the remarkable New Military (*Janissary*) and administrative system based on the conversion and training of Christian slave children. With this devoted and centralising machine he extended his frontiers from the Crimea to the edge of Syria. He fought another Venetian war (1463-79) and established full control of Balkan trade. In 1480, to papal consternation, his troops landed at Otranto. After him BAYAZID II (r. 1481-1512) occupied the mouths of the Danube and Dniester, took control of the riverborne trade to the Black Sea (1484) and with his Tartar vassals fought off a Polish counter attack (1483-9). He also took the last Venetian posts in Greece (1499-1503) but from 1504 the Safavid rise in Persia and its Anatolian religious and political effects led to a Persian war and related local insurrections. The Istanbul Janissaries had put him on the throne. They now deposed him in favour of SELIM I (r. 1512-20) 'The Grim'. These precedents were important. So was Selim's first act. To deprive the Janissaries of alternative candidates he murdered all the princes except Suleyman, the ablest of his own sons.

(4) At Chaldiran (1514) Selim's artillery discouraged Safavid ambitions for a generation. Between 1515 and 1520 he conquered Syria and Egypt. From the Ukraine to Suez the Ottoman realm could now take toll on every traditional route from Christendom to the East. SULEYMAN I (r. 1520-66) 'The Magnificent' or 'The Lawgiver' succeeded to a huge power and a fabulous revenue. He took the key fortress of Belgrade, conquered Hungary (1526) and besieged Vienna (1529). Against Habsburgs in Austria and the Mediterranean he naturally made alliances with the French. The capitulations of 1536 gave them a theoretical monopoly of European trade and attached their King, not always loosely, to Ottoman political policy. In the end it was to give them a sustained commercial advantage in the Levant, but meanwhile their production was inadequate for the immense Turkish market.

(5) Between 1522, when Suleyman drove the Hospitallers from Rhodes, and 1538, he beat a Habsburg-organised naval coalition at Preveza and his sea policy brought him Tunis, Algeria and the last Venetian islands in the Aegean. Thereafter Persian border wars distracted him into the conquest of Iraq and an interest in the Persian Gulf trade. From Basra and Egypt his fleets fought the Portuguese in the Indian Ocean.

(6) In 1560 the exhausted Suleyman was ready to delegate his work to his Grand Vizier. Till 1579 the executive was MEHMED SOKOLLÜ, while SELIM II (r. 1566-74) 'The Sot' enjoyed the flesh pots and MURAD III (r. 1574-95) the fleshly delights of the increasingly influential Harem. It was a watershed. The Spaniards and the Hospitallers had set a term to western aggression in 1565 by defending Malta with slaughter. A Christian coalition mauled the Turco-Barbary fleet at Lepanto in 1571. It nevertheless reappeared in 1572 in full strength and under the P. of Constantinople Venice confirmed the cession of Cyprus and paid tribute. The govt., however, was being infected by the irrelevant growth of the Sultan's huge household and the correlative parasitism of the *Devshirmé*, where marriage was now allowed and recruitment in decline. The Turkish reputation, meanwhile, held back the adjacent powers so that corruption spread, as in a hot house, unchecked for a while by external challenges.

(7) Meanwhile the lucrative oriental trade routes were being diverted or choked. Between 1600 and 1630 the spice routes via Egypt and Basra were superseded by the European big-ship route round the Cape. Then the Black Sea-Transasiatic route dried up because of disturbances in China and later in the 17th cent. the Russians interrupted it when it might have revived. Armed Protestant, especially English and Dutch, traders often in organised bodies such as the Turkey, Venice and Levant Cos., disputed the immense economic area with the Venetians and the French. In 1622 the Porte accepted the first English ambassador. The Venetians had lost most of their carrying trade by 1624 when the empire suffered, in Iraq, its first major loss, but the Turks recovered it in 1638 and between 1645 and 1669 conquered Venetian Crete. A family of Albanian Grand Viziers played an important role in these affairs, namely MEHMED KÖPRÖLÜ (1656-61), AHMED KÖPRÖLÜ (1661-76) and KARA MUSTAFA (1676-83), but the Cromwellian govt. smote the Barbary fleets (which did not attack the French) and the era of the Köprölü ended in defeat before Vienna (1683) and Kara Mustafa's execution.

(8) In astonished rejoicing, the Christians formed a counter-offensive Holy League. The Habsburgs recovered Hungary, the Venetians the Peloponnese (P. of Carlowitz 1699). The Russians appeared unsuccessfully if significantly and were repulsed in an attempt upon the Sultan's Tartar vassals in the Ukraine (P. of the Pruth 1711). The Janissaries, now a hereditary praetorian guard, accepted a compromise. Princes were no longer murdered at a Sultan's accession, but caged in gilded and untrained seclusion as an undesired reserve in case the Sultan might be murdered himself. A creeping central paralysis left imperial defence to independent or local commanders. The P. of PASSAROWITZ (1718) might have been worse, for the Turks had taken the Peloponnese from Venice, but had to cede to Austria, Belgrade, two provinces and commercial capitulations throughout the Empire. Revenge came in the war with Austria and Russia (1736-9). A series of victories recovered Belgrade and drove the Russians from all their gains save Azov (Ts. of BELGRADE Sept. 1739) and thereafter until 1768 these two enemies were preoccupied with the consequences of Prussian aggression. The Austrian capitulations remained to create, as against Russia, an Austrian interest in Turkish integrity.

(9) The self absorptions of Stambouli politics weakened authority over the provinces, beginning with the more distant. The offices of Dey of Algiers, Bey of Tunis, Pasha of Tripoli, of Egypt and of Syria passed into particular family groups, each new incumbent being he who was locally most acceptable, but willing to make the most suitable offerings to the Porte and its officials for his confirmatory *firman*. Within tolerances (such as war on Christians) understood by Moslems, these governors behaved as semi-autonomous rulers, though even at the last they were never free. In 1912 enormous sums were still being paid to Istanbul from provinces even under foreign protection. Central control was stronger in the European areas but, for that very reason, more abused.

Under the title of Interpreters (*Dragomen*) the Turks had always used Greeks in financial and diplomatic dealings. The Phanariot Greeks of Istanbul slowly acquired a monopoly of this work. If the Kapudan Pasha and the Reis Effendi, originally admirals, were in theory in charge of foreign policy, by 1730 their inferior, the Dragoman of the Porte, carried out their functions. Such Phanariots became very rich. The two Roumanian provinces were reserved for their sustenance; each governor (Hospodar) was really a tax farmer who became a millionaire in his three years.

(10) So many internal and foreign interests were concerned to preserve the Empire that it might have continued longer, but for Russian aggression. The Czarina Catharine the Great and Potemkin launched the Great War of 1768 to 1774 with the same objectives as Bayazid II (para. 3 above). The much discussed P. of KUCHUK KAINARDJI gave them the Crimea and a vaguely defined protectorship of the Millet-i-Rum. The Turks conceded the last because they calculated that it could never be enforced. The Peace also consolidated the Russians' southern acquisitions under the First Polish Partition (1772) and gave them access to the mouth of the Dnieper.

(11) The war had impoverished Turkey more than Russia and cut off long accustomed revenues. The political and economic factions at Istanbul fought each other for the balance without the slightest regard for imperial interests. Palace murder and street mutiny left provincial governors to fend, almost, for themselves while greedy foreign powers grew stronger. In 1787 Russia and Austria attacked and when in 1788 the Russians occupied Oczakov, there was anxious debate in the House of Commons. Ottoman power had been the long assumed guarantee of the Mediterranean as a commercial lake. It could be taken even less for granted when, in 1789, the Austrians took Belgrade. Similar doubts assailed responsible Turks. Another palace revolution installed, in SELIM III (r. 1789-1807), a reforming Sultan, one month before the Estates-General met at Versailles. The Ps. of Sistova (with Austria 1791) and Jassy (with Russia 1792) owed as much to French events as Turkish obstinacy, but the Ukrainian coast and Orsova with their recruiting grounds were lost.

(12) Bonaparte's Levantine adventure (1798) ultimately unhinged the African and Arabian dominion. Though half the Mediterranean coastline was nominally Turkish, others fought naval wars in it regardless of the Porte. The *sequelae* left Egypt virtually independent, and isolated the N. African provinces. The Wahabis of C. Arabia seized the Holy Cities (1804). Selim, wrestling with difficulties nearer home, had to leave such problems, which touched him both as Sultan and as Caliph, to other times or local men. In fact the last Janissary revolt destroyed him (1807) but unwittingly put a greater man, MAHMUD II (r. 1807-1839), in his place. By then the equally courageous Mehemet Ali had made himself Pasha in Egypt.

(13) Mahmud was losing an army to the Russians in 1811 when Mehemet Ali massacred his Mamelukes. The Empire, in Mahmud's view, had to be saved from itself and foreigners by a new military establishment. The European enemies were fighting each other or recovering from their wounds while this was patiently built up and financed. Mahmud, too, won over the *Ulema* who had too often co-operated with the Janissaries. In June 1826 the Janissaries were denounced, massacred by artillery in the streets and their barracks blown up. Their partisans in the palace were strangled, those in the provinces hunted down.

(14) This largest and swiftest political massacre of the 19th cent. (known as the *Auspicious Incident*) came too late. Europe had invented nationalism and the Greeks had discovered Themistocles. A Peloponnesian rebellion

of 1821 had embroiled the Orthodox Russians and the classically educated French and English. Mahmud invited Mehemet Ali to put it down. He had almost succeeded when classicism and orthodoxy combined in mutual suspicion to destroy his fleet at Navarino (Oct. 1827). Mahmud had to recognise Greek autonomy (1827) and then independence (1829). In 1830 he conceded Serbian autonomy too, but in 1831 he had to face a direct attack by Mehemet Ali. This was ultimately checked with Russian help (T. of Unkiar Skelessi July 1833) and western intervention. *See* EGYPT-4 *to* 7.

(15) The military reforms bred the *Tanzimat,* a programme of reorganisation undertaken, under ABD-EL-MEJID (r. 1839-61) and ABD-EL-AZIZ (r. 1861-76), to preserve the Empire by modernising law, education, the bureaucracy and technical training. The necessary money was, however, too often absorbed in fending off foreign aggression (e.g. in the Crimean War 1853-6, the Balkan Crisis and the Russo-Turkish War 1875-78). From 1854 it was necessary to borrow (*see* OTTOMAN PUBLIC DEBT), but meanwhile the Empire was penetrated by western ideas. Moreover western powers intermittently demanded concessions for minorities in which they were interested. The result was proclaimed reforms at moments of external crisis. It is no coincidence that the reforms called the Hatti Sherif of Gülhane (1839), the Hatt-i-Humayun (1856) and the Constitution of 1876 were each launched when the Sultan wanted western allies. None was wholly implemented but each weakened the prestige of autocracy, while educated western-influenced critics and watchful foreign businessmen multiplied.

(16) During the disturbed years 1875 to 1878 ABD-EL-HAMID II (r. 1876-1909) had established a precarious rule and elaborated a counter-policy based in part upon the notion of Pan-islamism latent in his office of Caliph. If the Czar had a protectorate over Orthodox Christians in his empire, it was reasonable that the Caliph should similarly protect Moslems outside it. This was a potent idea. Some Islamic leaders, notably Jamal-ed-Din Afghani (1839-97) even advocated an Islamic union of the Ottoman and Iranian empires and Afghanistan. The Hedjaz railway was built to bring to the Holy Cities shoals of pilgrims who might come from any point between Asiatic Russia and Zanzibar, or between Morocco and Malaysia. Fear of subversion might induce Islamic powers such as Britain and France to uphold Ottoman integrity. It might also rally more traditionalist Turkish opinion against the critics of the monarchy. Conversely the critics embraced nationalist doctrines involving the superiority of Turks within their own empire and the dissolution of the Millet system. Abd-el-Hamid's reign was a struggle between these ideas, in which his opponents slowly coalesced into a Committee of Union and Progress, known as the YOUNG TURKS. He drove most of them into exile, whence they bombarded the big cities with propaganda. They returned in 1908 when a Macedonian military mutiny of different origin overthrew him and took over most of the public offices.

(17) The Young Turk revolution was a disaster. Austro-Hungary annexed Bosnia and Herzogovina; Bulgaria shook off Turkish suzerainty (1908). The Italians seized Tripoli and the Dodecanese (1911-12). In the two Balkan Wars (1913-14) the European provinces, save Thrace, were lost. 'Turkification' provoked linguistic, racial and religious revolts and savage local repression. Diplomatic isolation led to increasing dependence upon Wilhelminian Germany, whose officers were retraining the army. The decision to enter World War I against the allies was a miscalculation compounded by a sense of recent humiliation.

OTTOMAN PUBLIC DEBT. Between 1854 and 1875 the Ottoman Empire had borrowed over £200M abroad, the service of which cost more than half the revenue. From 1873 (a year of world recession) it paid only half the interest. By 1880 it had defaulted altogether. By an agreement, called the DECREE OF MOHARREM (Dec. 1881) with the creditor govts. (mainly Britain and France), a European-managed Public Debt Administration was created and certain, notably customs, revenues assigned to it. This efficient body operated until World War I and though its activities were limited by tariff limitations under Capitulations, it could and did underwrite further borrowing on a large scale.

OUDH (India) an ancient holy land, was one of the 15 Mogul *Subas*. In 1724 its Subadar Saadat Khan (r. 1724-39) established himself as a virtually independent dynastic ruler or Nawab Wazir. He was followed by his son Safdar Khan (1739-54) and grandson Shuja-ud-Daulah (1754-75). As a result of confusion in Bengal (*see* MIR JAFAR) Shuja-ud-Daulah was involved in the military consequences and was beaten by the HEIC at the B. of Buxar. It was not, however, Warren Hastings's intention to weaken Oudh, for he wanted it as a buffer against the Marathas and Afghans. Hence in 1774 he encouraged the Nawab to conquer the Rohillas in the N.W. foothills of the Himalayas. Despite efforts by his enemies to reverse the policy (*see* FRANCIS, SIR PHILIP) this use of Oudh as a buffer state continued under the rule of Asaf-ud-Daulah (1775-97) and his brother Saadat Khan (1798-1814), who was placed on the throne by the British instead of an illegitimate usurper. Under Saadat British policy was effectively reversed: he paid an annual tribute to the HEIC, handed over the Allahabad fort and agreed to hold no communication with any foreign state. In return the HEIC undertook the defence of Oudh, but in 1801 Wellesley, in anticipation of a Maratha war but on the pretext of an Afghan invasion, demanded, for defence purposes, the cession of the Doab and Rohilkand and an increase in the British garrisons maintained at the Nawab's expense. This was logical, bearing in mind the reversal of policy, but Wellesley enforced it with a mixture of threats and insult which rankled.

The HEIC was now recruiting troops in Oudh. These men were privileged to have their grievances represented to the Nawab by the Company's residents, and their families benefited from the remittances. The administration, on the other hand, went from bad to worse and the country was overrun by speculators as well as gangsters. Sleeman, resident from 1848 to 1854 and Outram, his successor, sent sensational reports on local conditions. The Directors of the HEIC and Dalhousie, the Gov. Gen., concluded that drastic intervention was necessary, though both residents opposed annexation: but the Directors willed otherwise and Wazid Ali Shah, the last ruler, was deposed in Feb. 1856.

One result was that his disbanded troops were added to the gangs already at large. Another was that the many Oudh soldiers in the HEIC's armies suddenly lost their privileges, since there was no longer a resident to protect their families. *See* INDIAN MUTINY.

OUDH, BEGUMS OF were the rich mother and grandmother of Asaf-ud-Daulab, the Nawab of Oudh (r. 1775-97). By the T. of Faizabad (1775) he undertook to maintain the HEIC's army in Oudh. He got the initial sums from the Begums, but corruption and incompetence resulted in accumulating arrears. Warren Hastings, the Gov. Gen., pressed for funds required in the Maratha and Mysore wars, eventually demanded that the arrears should be cleared off. The Nawab professed poverty unless given possession of the Begum's fortune. They had been guaranteed (in 1775) by the Gov. Gen's. council which had over-ruled the Gov. Gen. In 1781 Warren Hastings put pressure upon the Begums, which was said to have included the imprisonment and starvation of their servants or ministers. In Dec. 1782 they gave way and handed over much, but not all, of their vast fortune. They remained on friendly terms with

Hastings throughout. Hastings was impeached but acquitted for this affair.

OUDH TENANCY ACT, 1868, inspired by Sir John Lawrence, reduced the exploitation of the peasant cultivators by their mostly Rajput landlords (Taluqdars). It provided for security of tenure and that rents could be raised only with the consent of the court, and then only with compensation for unexhausted improvements.

OUGHTRED, William (1575-1660), Cambridge mathematician published his *Clavis Mathematicae* (Lat = Mathematical Key) on arithmetic and geometry in 1631 and *Circles of Proportion* on trigonometry in 1632. In these he invented the multiplication, proportion and most of the trigonometrical signs and settled the basic principles of the three subjects. He was well known to other intellectuals of his time such as John Wallis.

OUNCE or INCH was one twelfth of a measure (pound or foot) and the ounce as the usual measure of silver was divided into 20 pennyweights. An OUNCELAND in the Scandinavian parts of Scotland was the amount of land which was expected to defray the cost of a ship. A PENNYLAND contributed one twentieth of such cost.

OUSELEY (1) Sir Gore (1770-1844) 1st Bart. (1808) was A.D.C. to the Vizier of Oudh and as British ambassador concluded the Anglo-Persian T. of 1812 and mediated between Russia and Persia in 1813. His brother **(2) Sir William** became a leading Persian scholar. Their cousin **(3) Sir Ralph (1772-1842)** entered the Portuguese army under Beresford in 1809 and took Pernambuco (Brazil) in 1817. Sir William's son **(4) Sir William Gore (1797-1860)** was *chargé d'affaires* in Brazil in 1838 and Minister to Argentina in 1844. In 1847 he mediated in the Argentine-Uruguay war and secured the evacuation of Uruguay.

OUSTER-LE-MAIN, at common law was a livery of land out of the hands of **(1)** a guardian on the wards' majority or **(2)** the King after a judgement founded upon a plea that he had no right to it.

OUTER SPACE. *See* SPACE LAW.

OUTLAWRY. (1) An outlaw was answerable to all, but none to him. He was civilly dead and could neither own property nor accept it. He had no defence to claims, and could bring none himself save as an executor or an administrator in right of someone else. Until about 1230 he could be killed with impunity. After that date only a sheriff with a warrant could do so. **(2)** A person could be outlawed if he failed to appear to a criminal indictment or to civil proceedings, or if he failed to satisfy a civil judgement. **(3)** The process for outlawry was long and complicated. Writs of *venire facias* (Lat: Make him come), *distringas* (Take his property), *capias* (seize him) having been successively issued without effect, a writ of *exigent* (they clamour) directed the sheriff to call upon the defendant five times in the (old) county court to appear upon pain of outlawry. If this failed a *writ of proclamation* was then issued and if this failed judgement of outlawry was pronounced by a coroner. A writ of *capias utlagatum* (seize the outlaw) might then be issued. By this time he would probably have gone overseas. **(4)** Long obsolete, it was abolished in civil proceedings in 1879 and in criminal proceedings virtually in 1870 but formally in 1938.

OUTRAM (pron. Ootrem) Sir James (1803-63), Indian soldier and legendary hunter, had captured Mategaon, subdued the Dhang country and put down a Bhil rising I before he was 20; after survey and political work he was employed in missions to Shah Shuja and then against Dost Mohammed (*see* AFGHANISTAN) and the Ghilzais and then in the S. of Kalat, all in 1839. After a hair-raising journey with despatches and disguised as an Afghan, to Bombay, he was Agent in Lower Sind until 1841 and then in Upper Sind whence he assisted the Afghan operations of Sir Chas. Napier and Gen. Nott. In 1843 he defended the Hyderabad (Sind) residency against many thousands of Sikhs. By now famous and well informed, he quarrelled with Napier over policy towards Sind, but this did not injure his standing and in 1844 he became chief of intelligence in the Maratha campaign and then Resident to the Gaekwad from 1847 to 1851. It was at this point that he suffered dismissal because of a report on perquisites which implicated a number of influential HEIC personalities, but three years later Dalhousie re-employed him in the key Residency to Oudh. It was his, subsequently controversial, recommendation which, against better opinion, led to the annexation of Oudh in 1855. After a successful foray into Persia in 1857 he found himself as Chief Commissioner in Sind, also commanding two divisions between Calcutta and Cawnpore. When the army mutinied he placed himself under Havelock for the first relief of Lucknow and then took command of the garrison there during its second and third sieges. By now he was a popular hero. He was military member of the Viceroy's council until 1860.

OUTREMER (Fr = beyond the sea) (1) was the mediaeval name for the Frankish Levant and its cosmopolitan states established by the First Crusade (1096-9).

(2) They began with a northern group comprising the Norman Principality of Antioch (1098), the County of Edessa (1098) inland of it, and that of Tripoli (1109) to the south. These were at first separated from the southern Kingdom of Jerusalem by coastal Moslem emirates. Jerusalem was stormed in July 1099, and Godfrey of Bouillon elected Defender of the Holy Sepulchre. He died in 1100. His successor, Baldwin I (r. 1100-18), Count of Edessa, took the title of King and was succeeded by Baldwin II (r. 1118-31). He was followed by Fulk of Anjou (r. 1131-43) (q.v.).

(3) The King had preeminence over the northern rulers and in a crisis took charge, but otherwise he and they lived of their own. By 1165 the intrusive emirates had been pinched out and the Kingdom proper stretched along the coast from the Tripolitan frontier just north of Beirut to Daron just south of Gaza. The landward frontiers ran thence to Aqaba, made a sweep 20 miles east of the Dead Sea back to the middle Jordan, up-river to its source and on again to the Tripolitan frontier.

(4) The King was not master of his country. The rich Church was independent of him. The four great feudatories, Jaffa, Galilee, Sidon and Oultrejourdain (Fr: beyond the Jordan) owed him service altogether of 360 knights (say 1800 men). At all times there was a shortage, even a dearth of Frankish manpower, only partly made up by visitors from the perenially interested west. Visitors together with the military orders of St. John, the Temple and the Teutonic Knights supplied the balance of troops from barracks and castles all over the Kingdom and in Europe. Of the 17 main towns of Outremer only Jerusalem, Nablus, Daron and Acre belonged to the King. The Venetians and the Genoese each had a street in Jerusalem. Genoa had autonomous trading quarters in 11 other towns, Venice in seven, Pisa in six, Marseilles in four, Amalfi in two and Barcelona in one. Only Nablus and Daron were wholly the King's. Acre, the chief southern port, was a patchwork of foreign jurisdictions. The foreign and entrepôt trade was in the hands of these socially unintegrated communities which spoke their own tongue and were backed by their quarrelling home states. If the trade brought considerable local benefits, Knights, visitors, traders and the Church all had outside allegiances and often incompatible objectives. Self interest in a military crisis would induce them to co-operate with the King, but as allies never wholly under command.

(5) These weak and chaotic states also made enemies of the Byzantines whom they should have cultivated. They at first survived because of moslem disunity, especially as between the rich but effete Fatimid Caliphate of Egypt and its fragmented rival at Baghdad, and between the various local Turkoman rulers in Anatolia, Iraq and at Hama, Homs and Damascus. The

Crusader intrusion brought these rivals slowly together save for Damascus which was allied to K. Fulk, but he was killed in an accident in 1143 and Baldwin III was a child under his mother's regency. There was a quarrel betwen Antioch and Edessa which Q. Melisende was too weak to compose. Imad-el-Din Zengi, the powerful *ata beg* of Mosul, pounced on Edessa.

(6) This provoked the Second Crusade (1144-9) which, as it attacked Damascus, the Christians' only ally, was worse than a fiasco. The decline of Outremer now began. Zengi was murdered and replaced by a greater man, Nur-ed-Din of Aleppo, who began to press Damascus. Meanwhile Baldwin III had taken over from his mother and demonstrated Fatimid decline by capturing their huge fortress at Ascalon. Within months Nur-ed-Din took Damascus. Constance, the Princess of Antioch, married the irresponsible but personable predator Reynald of Chatillon, who had come out with the Second Crusade. He made friends with the Templars, tortured the Patriarch to surrender his funds and used the funds to invade and pillage Byzantine Cyprus (1157). The Emperor Manuel came down to restore order and drive Nor-ed-Din back. The two potentates came to a sensible agreement, and then Nur-ed-Din captured Reynald, who was lifting cattle (1160). He did not emerge from prison until 1175.

(7) Baldwin III died unexpectedly in 1162 and was succeeded by his brother Amalric, Count of Jaffa. He and Nor-ed-Din had their eye on Egypt and Shawar its weak vizier, but after manoeouvres Amalric got in first and overthrew the Egyptians, whereupon Nor-ed-Din moved against Antioch and at the B. of Artah (1164) captured most of the northern Frankish princes. Amalric had to hasten to the rescue and with imperial help reestablished the position, but Nor-ed-Din's general Shirkub and his famous nephew entered Egypt. Shawar sent to AmaInc for help, and after battles and sieges it was agreed that Shirkoh and Amalric should both evacuate Egypt leaving a shaken Shawar in possession. Amalric accepted this because he needed to reorganise his northern defences against Nor-ed-Din but his barons, having seen the riches of Egypt, were dissatisfied. A strong Nivernais crusader company arrived. Amahic wanted to wait for imperial help. His vassals and the Nivernais would not wait and he gave way. The army reached Cairo but was manoeuvred out of Egypt by Shirkoh and Saladin. Shawar was seized and killed. Nor-ed-Din was now master of Egypt (1169) as well as inland Syria. A joint Byzantine and Frankish expedition against Damietta failed to dislodge him.

(8) In 1174 Amalric and Nor-ed-Din died within weeks of each other. Amalric's son Baldwin IV was a 13-year old leper. When Saladin marched swiftly north to secure his inheritance, the Kingdom was finding a regent. This was Raymond of Tripoli who, with the Hospitallers and the native nobility, wanted peace with the Moslems. They encountered a rising contradiction: westerners had come keen to fight the paynim, the aggressive Templars hated the Hospitallers and Reynald of Chatillon, released, neither better nor wiser, from captivity, supported his Templar friends. He married the heiress of Oultrejoordain, which became a nest of robbers.

(9) The faction-riven Kingdom was now deprived of its imperial ally. In Sept. 1187 the Emperor Manuel's great army was destroyed by the Turkish Sultan of Konya at the B. of Myriocephalum. The Byzantines were never again to help on land. Then Manuel died (1180) and there was intrigue and murder at Constantinople. The leper-King had taken over from his regent in 1177 but the factions survived. In 1180 he sensibly negotiated a two-year truce with Saladin because the whole of Syria was under drought and threatened by famine, and meantime his diplomats were seeking help from unheeding western rulers.

(10) Reynald of Chatillon now broke the truce by raiding an unarmed *haj*. Saladin complained, but Reynald's faction prevented Baldwin IV from enforcing retribution. Saladin seized a pilgrim caravan as hostages: Reynald was unmoved. Saladin mobilised and marched for N. Syria where he cleared his rear by reducing his Moslem rivals. Reynald promptly launched a pirate fleet which pillaged the Red Sea towns and destroyed pilgrim ships even in the ports of Mecca itself. Saladin's Egyptian forces hunted down the corsairs and he swore that the sacrilegious Reynald should never be forgiven. In Sept. 1183 he set out with a great army. His first operations were held up by Frankish fortresses and meanwhile the decaying King was gallantly arranging for his own succession. He died in Mar. 1185 during another famine. K. Baldwin V was a child and the new regency signed a four-year truce with Saladin, whose people were suffering too. In 1186 Baldwin V died and in a *coup d'état* Guy of Lusignan, husband of Amalric's daughter Sybilla, became a factional King with the support of Reynald. For the second time in mid-truce Reynald raided a peaceful caravan, a huge one from Cairo to Damascus. He would not restore the loot and K. Guy could not compel him. Saladin decided to make an end. On 4 July 1187 the Frankish army, incompetently commanded, was destroyed at the Horns of Hattin. The King and his knights were taken. Saladin himself struck off Reynald's head. On 2 Oct. Jerusalem surrendered. So did all the country save Tyre, safe on its peninsula and reinforced by Conrad of Monferrat. Saladin went into winter quarters.

(11) There now followed an extraordinary episode. The news had electrified the West and the western rulers were arming. Saladin released K. Guy, who arrived in Tyre and demanded admittance as King. Conrad refused him, so Guy recruited a force in order to lay siege. Suddenly he marched for Acre (Aug. 1189) and sat down to besiege it instead. Reinforcements began to arrive. Saladin attacked him and was beaten off. Each side was periodically reinforced and the siege within a siege snowballed. The city surrendered in July 1191. It became a nucleus of a different Outremer, delineated by a treaty between Saladin and Richard (Aug. 1192) and comprising only a 90-mile coastal strip from Tyre to Jaffa seldom even 10 miles wide, together with Antioch and its port at St. Symeon, the town of Tripoli, the Templar castle at Tortosa and the Hospitaller Krak des Chevaliers. Its mainstay was Cyprus seized by Richard I and ultimately passed to the ex-King Guy. With its food and resources the Kingdom survived, subject to attrition, for a century, helped between 1270 and 1272 by the future K. Edward I. The last of the Principality of Antioch fell in 1287; Tripoli in 1289. Acre fell after a desperate six-week defence in 1291 and Outremer was carefully devastated to make further invasion unattractive.

OVAL, KENNINGTON, previously a market garden, was laid out as a cricket ground in 1845 for the Montpelier Club which merged with the Surrey County Club.

OVERBURY, Sir Thomas (1581-1613) an Edinburgh friend of Robt. Carr since 1608, came to Court after the Union and was involved as go-between in Carr's (now Vist. Rochester's) affair with Frances, Countess of Essex; he opposed an intrigue to secure the Countess' divorce and remarriage to Rochester and perhaps threatened exposure. James I had a homosexual regard for Rochester. Overbury was imprisoned in the Tower and there poisoned by one of the Countess' agents. In 1615 four of her accomplices were hanged but she and Rochester were not charged. The scandal shook the prestige of the Court at a time of rising puritanism.

OVEREND AND GURNEY, bill brokers and discount house began as Richardson and Overend, the moving spirit being Thomas Richardson (1771-1853). Samuel Gurney (1786-1856) joined the partnership in 1807. Both quakers,

their families contributed much to the development of shorthand. Gurney was a brother of Elizabeth Fry and the firm supported criminal law reform and had philanthropic as well as financial motives in supporting the Niger expedition of 1841 and the foundation of Liberia. Gurney was Treas. of the British and Foreign School Society. The firm had a huge business: it was the most respected private institution in the financial world, sometimes called 'the bankers' banker'. After 1857 it became a Limited Co. and made a share issue. It was already in undisclosed difficulties, but, relying on its immense reputation, investors scrambled for the shares. The company failed in May 1866. This caused the collapse of many speculative ventures and a run on the banks. The Bank Charter Act was suspended, discount rates rose to 10% and foreign alarm resulted in an explanatory Foreign Office circular to British diplomatic missions.

OVERKIRK, Cornells Count of NASSAU (?-1708) rescued the British contingent abandoned by other Dutch generals at the B. of Steinkirk (Aug. 1692) and after William III's death became Dutch Veldt-Marschal. In the War of the Spanish Succession he was, after hesitations, Marlborough's ablest and most loyal Dutch military colleague beginning with actions at Tongres and Maastricht (Apr. 1703). He was prominent in Marlborough's complicated forcing of the Lines of Brabant (July 1705) and played vital roles in the victories of Ramillies (May 1706) and Oudenarde (July 1708).

OVERLANDER was one who in the 19th cent. journeyed from one Australian colony to another, usually driving cattle.

OVERLORD. *See* FEUDALISM-1.

OVERLORD. Code name for the Allied invasion of Normandy as carried out in June 1944. –

OVERSEERS. *See* LOCAL ADMINISTRATION – ENGLAND AND WALES.

OVERTON (1) Richard (?-1663) leveller pamphleteer against episcopacy in 1642 and 1643 and against the Westminster Assembly in 1646. He was imprisoned as a co-author with Lilborne of *England's New Chains Discovered* in 1649. In 1655 he fled abroad and was commissioned by Charles II but imprisoned again in 1659 and 1663. His kinsman **(2) Robert (?1609-68)** a Fifth-Monarchist friend of Milton and parliamentary commander, took Sandal in 1645, became Gov. of Hull in 1647, served at Dunbar and became Gov. of Edinburgh in 1650 and was military commander in W. Scotland from 1652 to 1653. He was imprisoned on charges of intended military opposition to the Protectorate and only released in 1659 when he was given a Yorkshire command by the Long Parliament. He refused to support Monck and ended his career in prison.

OVID (PUBLIUS OVIDIUS NASO) (43 B.C.-A.D. 18) Roman elegiac poet much read in the Middle Ages, especially the *Metamorphoses* and the *Amatory Art*.

OWAIN ap CADWGAN (?-1116), a Prince of Powys abducted the famous Nest in 1109 and murdered one of the leading Flemish colonists in Dyfed in 1110. After two politic visits to Ireland he succeeded his father Cadwgan ap Bleddyn in Powys in 1111, but in 1114 Henry I took him on a Norman expedition, the better to keep him under surveillance. On his return he was murdered by Flemings led by Nest's enraged husband.

OWAIN GLYNDWR. *See* GLENDOWER.

OWAIN ap GRUFFYDD (?-1236), whose mother was Matilda de Braose, was joint heir, with Rhys Ieuanc, of the Lord Rhys (Rhys ap Gruffydd) in Deheubarth and acquired much of Ceredigion in 1216 and 1222 by the good offices of Llywellyn ap Iorwerth of Gwynedd.

OWAIN GWYNEDD (?-1170) P. of GWYNEDD (1137). *See* GWYNEDD-24. The following uncertain account illustrates the confused violence of Welsh 12th cent. life, corresponding in part with the English confusion under Stephen. After Owain's victory over the Flemings at Cardigan, he made peace with the S. Welsh and married his daughter to his nephew Anarawd, son of Gruffydd ap Rhys of Deheubartli, but in 1143 Owain's brother and junior co-ruler Cadwaladr murdered Anarawd and abducted his wife. Owain expelled Cadwaladr, who, like his father, raised help from the Dublin Ostmen against Anglesey. The expedition was checked, so he tried to make peace with Owain, whereupon the Ostmen blinded him (probably partially) (1144). Cadwaladr then took refuge in England but soon returned to Anglesey. In 1149 Owain defeated Madog ap Maredudd, P. of Powys, and imprisoned his son Cynan. In 1151 he again expelled Cadwaladr, blinded his brother Cadwallon and blinded and castrated Cadwaladr's son, Cunedda. Naturally Madog and Cadwaladr joined Henry II's not very successful Basingwerk expedition of 1157. Owain, however, submitted, did homage and ceded certain lands. Thereafter he supported Anglo-Norman enterprises against S. Wales and in 1164 attended the Council of Woodstock, but in 1165 he allied with Rhys ap Gruffydd and Owain Cyfeiliog against an invasion by Henry which was abandoned because of bad weather. Henry consequently blinded two of Owain's sons whom he held as hostages. In 1166 when the King went to Normandy, Owain recovered most of the lands ceded in 1157 and in 1167 took Basingwerk and Rhuddlan. Just before his death he was negotiating with Louis VII of France against Henry.

OWAIN ap HYWEL DDA. *See* DEHEUBARTH-2.

OWAIN ap THOMAS ap RHODRI or OWAIN LAWGOCH (?-1378), descendant of Llywellyn ap Iorwerth and a great nephew of Llywellyn ap Gruffydd, was a successful mercenary in the service of Philip VI of France. He had an English estate of which he was deprived in 1369, but his hereditary claims on the principality of Wales became known at the French court. He was fitted out with a diversionary expedition which seems to have made clandestine contacts in Wales, though the force never got beyond Guernsey. He was assassinated at the siege of Mortagne.

OWEN family, originally of Bodowen (Anglesey), was influential in Anglesey until about 1720 and provided occasional sheriffs and M.Ps. Two brothers **(1) Hugh (?-?)** and **(2) Henry (?-?)** changed sides in the Civil War and then again during the Commonwealth and Restoration. Their grandfather **(3) Sir Hugh** had married a Pembrokeshire heiress in 1571 and as a result the family influence moved to that county and represented it in parliament 26 times after 1710, for the last time in the reform parliament of 1831.

OWEN, Aneurin (1792-1851) made the English translation of the Laws of Hywel Dda (1841) and edited the collections of Welsh legal material and part of the *Monumenta Historica Britannica* (1848) for the Record Office.

OWEN, Sir John (1600-66) was a Royalist commander mainly in Caernarvonshire and Merioneth. He raised royal troops for the second Civil War and was condemned to death, after a spirited defence, in Feb. 1649, but shortly reprieved by the intervention of many, including probably Cromwell and Ireton. He lived in seclusion but helped on the Restoration in 1659-60.

OWEN, Robert (1771-1858). Successful industrialist and philanthropist set up the industrial community at New Lanark in the 1790s.

OWENS' COLLEGE, MANCHESTER. John Owen (1790-1846), a radical nonconformist cotton merchant, was persuaded by his anglican tory partner George Faulkner (1790-1862) to leave his fortune for the foundation of a non-denominational college of higher education in Manchester. It was established in 1851 with Faulkner as its first chairman and ultimately inspired the foundation of Manchester University.

OXENSTIERNA, Axel (1583-1654). *See* THIRTY YEARS' WAR-13 *et seq.*

OXFAM, Short for Oxford Campaign for Famine Relief, was founded in 1942 with particular reference to the then starving Greeks. A huge world wide organisation mostly concerned with long term rather than emergency measures.

OXFORD, first occupied in Saxon times was a burgh and, in the 10th cent., a royal property. Robert d'Oilly, the first Norman lord, built the castle and the original bridges over the Thames and the Cherwell. The town was walled in the next 30 years. The university grew up within them and posed dangerous problems, leading to disorder and eventually to the great St. Scholastica's Day riot of 1355 when 61 members of the university were killed and the town govt. was made in many ways subordinate to the university by royal interposition. The town remained, however, an important market centre for S. Oxfordshire and N. Berks and its strategic position caused it to be the royal H.Q. in the Civil War until June 1646. In the 18th cent. the place became a regular meeting point of coach routes; and the Oxford canal, together with the other canals entering the Thames, gave it a central position in southern water traffic. It was thus natural to focus railways upon it in 1835, even though the university insisted on keeping the stations well away from the centre. These soon superseded the water traffic. Though the City subsisted mainly on the University before the 1850s, there had been a book and printing trade since the 16th cent. and the railway brought large supplies of fruit and oranges for the well known jam industry. The motor industry originated in a bicycle repair shop – the population being partial to bicycles. By the 1930s the factories at Cowley had attracted a labour force which far outnumbered the other population, and the motor industry continued to grow during World War II. With the Education Act 1944 the university expanded by a factor of five and a huge new polytechnic was created near Headington. By the 1970s this rivalled the university in size just as the motor industry began to decline. In 1993 this institution was renamed Brookes University.

OXFORD, E. of. *See* GEORGE 1-4; HARLEY and VERE.

OXFORD GROUP or MORAL REARMAMENT. Frank Buchman founded a movement of emotionally Christian affiliation in 1921, called it the Oxford Group in 1928 and Moral Rearmament in 1938.

OXFORD MOVEMENT. *See* ANGLICANISM-4C.

OXFORD PARLIAMENT 1681. *See* CHARLES 11-26.

OXFORD, PROVISIONS OF (Apr.-June 1258) (*see* HENRY III-19). The principal baronial leaders visited Henry III on 30 Apr. 1258 and offered to try and obtain a general *aide* on condition that the realm was reformed and foreign commitments reduced. By 8 May they had browbeaten the King into acceptance. Domestic reform was to be carried out by a council of 24, half appointed by Henry, half by the magnates; in foreign affairs Simon de Montfort, Peter of Savoy, Hugh Bigod with two of the Lusignans were to press the French peace negotiations, and proctors headed by Henry of Susa, Abp. of Embrun, were sent to the Curia. A treaty was initialled at Paris on 28 May.

A *parliamentum* was summoned to Oxford in June in an atmosphere of enthusiasm. The 24 could report a diplomatic success. Hugh Bigod was appointed Justiciar and immediately began to hold pleas. Four of the 24 chose a new council of 15 and castles were redistributed to castellans under its control. It was also to supervise the Chancellor and the Treasurer. There were to be three *parliamenta* a year on fixed dates, but the baronage was to elect 12 of their number to act with the council as or in a *parliamentum*. All important wardships and escheats were to be granted *in parliamento* only.

OXFORDSHIRE RISING (1596). Successive bad harvests combined with new inclosures, caused wide rural discontent, of which this rising was an extreme and sternly suppressed case.

OXFORD St., London, was called after Edward Harley, 2nd E. of Oxford, who obtained the Marylebone estate of the Newcastle family by marriage. It was the old Tyburn Rd. and followed the approximate line of Here St., the westward Roman road which crossed Watling St. at Marble Arch. This was the route by which condemned criminals were dragged on a hurdle from Newgate prison to be hanged or disembowelled at Tyburn.

OXFORD, UNIVERSITY OF (1) Contrary to a 17th cent. belief based on an interpolation in Asser, the Univ. was not founded by K. Alfred but originated in a scholarly migration from Paris (1167) and a royal decree depriving clerks of their benefices if they left the realm. By 1170 there was a *studium generale,* i.e. schools in more than one faculty recruiting from several regions. There was a trade in books by 1200. In 1209 town and gown riots (*see* OXFORD), led to a further scholarly migration to Cambridge. The loss of business led the Oxford townsmen to negotiate for a return and in 1214 the papal legate, Nicholas of Tusculum, arranged a compromise. The town was to make an annual payment for the murders and the Univ. was to return but its members, being all clerics, were to be subject to the discipline of a resident Chancellor, an ecclesiastical judge (under the diocesan, the Bp. of Lincoln), who was also to settle disputes between townsmen and scholars. Eventually the Univ. elected the Chancellor, especially when in Tudor times Oxford acquired its own bishopric.

(2) The Univ. was regarded as a corporation. The Masters developed a guild on Parisian lines with four faculties: Arts (*see* QUADRIVIUM), Divinity, Law both Civil and Canon, and Medicine. The *Previous Congregation* consisting only of Masters of Arts discussed all proposed university statutes and elected the two Proctors (first mentioned in 1248) who, as its executives, counted votes, announced decisions and enforced, by way of veto, the Arts Faculty's monopoly on the initiation of Univ. business. The *Second Congregation* consisted of the Regent Masters of the faculties meeting in the Univ. church to discuss studies and finance. The *Great Congregation,* consisting of all masters under the presidency of the Chancellor, voted on the drafts proposed by the Previous Congregation. The first statutes date from 1253.

Originally degrees depended on depositions by the Masters concerned, that the candidate had read the required works and made the stipulated public disputations. Undergraduates enrolled under a Master and paid him and he lectured them at least once a day. He had an interest, not always objective, in their success. The Univ. set up University College under four Masters to provide teaching and accommodation at about the same time as some other Masters set up halls of residence for their own students. This began the distinctive Oxford and Cambridge colleges which in due course required statutes of their own. The earliest such statutes belong to Merton College (q.v.). Other colleges were intended to support poor students. These included Balliol (q.v.), while some, e.g. Oriel (1324) and Queen's (1341), attracted initial royal patronage usually on a modest scale, the latter to attract scholars from the north. Simultaneously the Dominicans (1221), the Franciscans (1224) and the Carmelites (1255) all built houses as places of study for their own members. Robert Grosseteste, for example, was Lector to the Franciscans (1225-7) and soon the Univ. was numbering many distinguished students or masters including Roger Bacon, Edmund of Abingdon, John Pecham and John Wycliffe. This in its turn attracted more patronage. Bp. Cobham organised a library (1327) and some of the 14th and 15th cent. college foundations outstripped the earlier ones in wealth, notably William of Wykeham's New College (1379) and Abp. Chichele's All Souls (1438).

(4) Influential outside interest created the present Divinity School (1427-66) and between 1435 and 1444 the library was enlarged by a considerable gift of books by Humphrey D. of Gloucester. By 1488 this was housed in a new library abutting the Divinity School. Lay interest, however, laid the Univ. open to the winds of change. Renaissance humanists such as Grocyn, Linacre, More and Erasmus discredited the Schoolmen: the Reformation destroyed the monastic institutions and the town charities. After violent oscillations including the dispersal of the library and the burning of Latimer, Ridley and Cranmer, encouragement came from Elizabeth I who was learned and interested, and between 1598 and 1602 Sir Thomas Bodley restored the library, ever since called after him. Moreover, the wholesale destruction of the monasteries and chantries had left large gaps in the educational system. Hence six colleges (all save Christchurch very small) were Tudor foundations and two more followed under James I. One of these, Jesus, was designed for Welsh scholars.

(5) This little revival did not last. The Civil War created great difficulties, for Charles I used the town as his HQ; the colleges had to accommodate troops and melted down their plate, and many of their estates were occupied by parliamentarians. As a royalist centre the whole complex was out of favour with the Commonwealth and not much respected under the hedonistic Restoration. Learning languished while fellows struggled to recover endowments, and though one college was founded in 1714, indifference and mere wit displaced dedication until the end of the 18th cent.

(6) There followed the inevitable reaction, beginning with a statute of 1800 to establish Honours and Pass degree examinations, even if the opportunities were still limited to Divinity, Civil and Canon Law, Classics and Mathematics with Music as an afterthought. A new seriousness began to creep in with the emotional ferment of the Anglican Oxford Movement. A Royal Commission of 1850, though resisted and obstructed, proposed changes which began the process of turning the Univ. from a mere alliance of colleges into a more unitary institution. The universal movement away from religious exclusivity ended in the abolition of the religious qualifications (1871). This not only threw the Univ. open to men of all religions or none, but caused academics to think about teaching new subjects. This inevitably led to demands for more places. Women, on the periphery from 1879 onwards, were admitted to full membership in five colleges in 1920. Other colleges expanded. New colleges were founded. Still further subjects were added. The economic problems created by World War I resulted in 60% of the 2000 undergraduates of 1937 being supported from public funds. Those created by World War II, that all the 11,000 of 1990 were (meagerly) supported by the Dept. of Education. This placed the undergraduate at the mercy of the teacher. Consistently with this, a major constitutional change transferred ultimate authority from the Masters of Arts, i.e. those who had been educated at the Univ., to those who worked there in teaching and research, i.e. those who made a living by it.

OXFORD UNIVERSITY PRESS; CLARENDON PRESS. Independent printing began at Oxford in 1478. Printers to the Univ. were appointed from 1584 and legalised by Star Chamber Decree in 1586. A charter of 1632 permitted three presses and the right to print 'all manner of books', but Abp. Laud had to require the Univ. to set up a printing house in 1634. Nothing was done and the printing rights were let in 1672 to Dr. John Fell (1625-86), Dean of Christchurch, who enterprisingly obtained the best types and each year published a new classical author. He established international repute, despite being unaccountably unloved and left his equipment to the Univ., which in 1690 was thus able to carry out Laud's instruction. The Press became financially stable from the profits of Clarendon's *History* (1702), after which it developed steadily into the biggest publisher in the world. In 1829 it moved to a new building called the Clarendon Press, whose name was used as its imprint for its learned books until 1999. Printing had already ceased in 1995.

OXGANG, HORSEGANG (mostly Sc.). The nature of the soil determined the number of animals (up to 16 oxen or 8 horses) needed to draw a plough. In communal cultivation these terms connoted a tenant's obligation attached to his holding in proportion to its size, to contribute to the team (or ploughgang). The size of ploughgang influenced the number of joint tenants on such a farm and oxen were preferred. A *horse's foot* was a sixteenth of a four-horse ploughgang.

OXYGEN was first isolated by Priestley in England and Lavoisier in France in 1774.

OYER AND TERMINER, COMMISSIONS OF. *See* ASSIZES-2.

OYO, originally the capital of the N.W. Yoruba of Nigeria. Old Oyo, 35 miles SW. of Jebba, was superseded by the modern city 90 miles further south in 1837 and the word came to be used of all the culturally related inhabitants of SW. Nigeria. Old Oyo was a wealthy trade exchange for the W. Sudan, N. Africa, N. Nigeria and the European coastal settlements. The Oyo cavalry, using N. African horses, imposed a wide inland empire in the 17th and 18th cents; it began to break up in the early 19th cent. as the people migrated south. *See* YORUBA.

OZONE a sparse gas which intercepts the more damaging solar rays but is itself destroyed by C.F.C.s and halons; these have had to be reduced by international agreements in 1985.

P

PACE AND MILE. The Roman pace (Lat: *passus*) was measured from heel mark to heel mark of the same foot, i.e. about 5 ft. A mile was 1000 (Lat: *mille*) such paces. The English mile was 5280 ft.

PACIFIC or SOUTH SEA, was first sighted by a European (Vasco Nuñez de Balboa) from the Isthmus of Darien in Sept. 1513 and first crossed by the Portuguese Ferdinand Magellan from the Magellan Straits to Cebu (Philippines) between Nov. 1520 and Mar. 1521. The Spaniards claimed sovereignty over it and, owing to the dangers from other European powers besides Malay piracy, the trade and treasure route between the Philippines and Spain ran across it to Acapulco. The Spanish monopoly was sporadically challenged first by Sir Francis Drake, who raided the Spanish Pacific settlements in 1577-9. Others, mainly buccaneers, followed. The South Sea Co. was founded with such interventions in mind and Commodore Anson did immense damage in 1742 to 1743. In spite of this and the activities of Dutch prospectors such as Abel Tasman, who had made voyages to Australia in 1634, 1642 and 1644, the Spaniards maintained their predominant interest (insofar as the ocean was used at all) because they owned the American west coast ports and other nations were otherwise engaged. Systematic foreign interest began in the 18th cent. only with the explorations (1766-9) of the Frenchmen Louis Antoine de Bougainville (1729-1811) and Jean François de la Perouse and (1766-79) the Englishmen James Cook and (1767-8) Samuel Wallis (1728-95). It was the collapse of the Spanish Empire in the early 19th Cent. and the colonisation of Australasia which opened the area.

PACIFIC SCANDAL. British Columbia accepted union with Canada (1870) on condition that a railway from the east to the Pacific coast should be commenced in two years. The conservative Macdonald govt. of Canada negotiated the finance to win electors, who had been alienated by the boundary settlement with the U.S.A. (1871), for the 1872 general election. Despite charges of corruption in the method of raising the money, Macdonald won the election, but a R. Commission later investigated the charges and unearthed evidence that some members of the govt. had received campaign funds from the prospective railway concessionaires. The govt. resigned, though Macdonald's own reputation was unaffected.

PACIFICO, David ("Don") (1784-1854), a Portuguese Jew born at Gibraltar, traded in Athens where a mob burned his property in 1847. Palmerston, standing on Pacifico's British allegiance, demanded compensation from the Greek govt. which the latter delayed with French support. Palmerston indicated the possibility of naval intervention and forced the Greeks to give way. This was the occasion of his famous "Civis Romanus sum" speech in the Commons.

PACK TACTICS, U-BOAT. *See* COMMERCE PROTECTION, NAVAL c-3.

PADDINGTON, was a village of such unimportance N.W. of London that according to Canning: "Pitt is to Addington, As London is to Paddington." In 1801, however, it was connected with Uxbridge by canal and in 1805 *via* the Grand Junction Canal with the Thames. It burst into life when the Great Western Railway completed its terminus there in 1838 and, with the fashionable (or raffish) areas of Maida Vale and Bayswater, it had a population of 100,000 by 1900.

PADDLE STEAMERS. *See* SHIPS, POWER DRIVEN.

PADISHAH **(Pers = "imperial master").** A title applied to Ottoman Sultans, Persian rulers and the British sovereign as Emperor of India.

PAGANEL (L) or PAINEL. Of this family of Anglo-Norman landowners **(1) Ralph** was William II's sheriff in Yorkshire in 1088. His son **(2) William (?-c. 1140)** was involved in a battle at Moutiers with Geoffrey Plantaganet in 1136. His son **(3) Fulk (?-1182),** Ld. of Hambie in Normandy, was a regular attendant of Henry II when abroad. His son **(4) Fulk (?-?1210)** was accused of treachery to K. John in 1203. His son **(5) William (?-1216)** opposed K. John in 1216 and forfeited his lands. The Yorkshire line of this family died out in the 14th Cent. A Lincolnshire branch survived until the 16th cent.

PAGANISM (Lat: *paganus* **= peasant)** is not well recorded because most of the records were made by Christians. Its deities whether Celtic or Nordic were mostly related to the weather (e.g. Thunor the thunder god), or to fertility (e.g. the goddess Frigg), or to a human characteristic such as majesty (the god Odin), or cunning (Loki), or to the landscape, e.g. the sea (Aegir) or the forest (Tapio). It also tended to preserve memories of ancient migrations in which earlier races figure as giants or dwarves or wizards. The word itself commemorates the fact that its last practitioners were country people. Its decline may be inferred from the narrative in the entries on MISSIONARIES and MISSIONS but some pagan practices, often of forgotten provenance, were still used in the 19th cent.

PAGE, Walter Hines (1855-1918), a campaigner for American education and an early supporter of Pres. Wilson, he received the embassy to London as a political reward in 1913 and was an outspoken and popular advocate of the Allied cause there.

PAGET and BAILY. Two interlinked families originating with **(1) William (1505-63) 1st Ld. PAGET** (1549) one of Henry VIII's acquiescently rich new men. He was a skilled diplomat employed, *inter alia,* on the difficult charge (achieved satisfactorily) of explaining Q. Catherine Howard's execution to the French Court (1541). He became, on his return, a Sec. of State and Henry's chief foreign policy adviser and an adherent of the Seymours. He was Comptroller of the Household at Henry's death and proposed the Somerset Protectorate, by means of which Henry VIII's will was set aside and his own peerage secured. Naturally he fell foul of the Dudleys and was arrested (1551), fined and (on the pretext of insufficient birth) deprived of his Garter (1552) in the convulsions which set up Northumberland as Protector. At Edward XI's death he joined in proclaiming Lady Jane Grey Queen, doubtless under compulsion, for he signed Mary I's proclamation too (1553). He became Lord Privy Seal in 1556 but, suspected of R. Catholic leanings, was persuaded to retire when Elizabeth I came to the throne. He had acquired Beaudesert on the Cannock coalfield, the abbey of Burton with its widespread properties and estates at West Drayton and Uxbridge. Two of his sons were Romanists *viz* **(2) Thomas (?-1590) 3rd Ld.,** who fled abroad on the discovery of Throgmorton's plot in 1583, took service under Spain in Flanders and was attainted in 1587 and **(3) Charles (?-1612)** who became in 1572 sec. to and acted as a spy against James Beaton, Mary Q. of Scots ambassador in Paris. This was a cover for treasonable plots and he too was attainted in 1587. He also took service under Spain in Brussels but continued his double agency as a correspondent with Cecil, to whom he advocated James VI's English claims. In 1599 he abandoned Spanish service and in 1603 James VI and I had his and his brother's attainder reversed. Hence the barony revived. Thomas' grandson **(4) Sir William (1609-78) 5th Ld.** (1629) lost much of his patrimony as a royalist and his son **(5) William (1637-1713) 6th Ld.** was an ambassador first to Vienna (1689-93) and then to the Porte (1693-1702). He got on famously with the Sultan and rendered the important service of negotiating the Austro-Turkish P. of Carlovitz, which freed the Emperor for the War of the Spanish Succession. He undertook some other diplomatic missions and made money. His son **(6) Henry (?-1743) 1st Ld. BURTON (1711) and 1st E. of UXBRIDGE of the first creation (1714)**, a Tory Lord of the Treasury and privy councillor from 1711 to 1715, was a supporter of the P. of Utrecht. His grandson **(7) Henry (1719-69) 2nd E.** was notorious for money grubbing. The first earldom became extinct at his death. **(8) Sir Nicholas BAYLY (1707-82)** married **(9) Caroline PAGET (?-1766)**, a descendant of **(4)**, through whom the Paget lordship and properties descended to **(10) Henry BAILY (1744-1812) 9th Ld. and 1st E. of UXBRIDGE of the 2nd creation (1784)**. In 1780 he acquired large estates in Somerset and Dorset under the will of a Peter Walter, whose reasons for leaving them to him are unknown. In 1782 he inherited the Baily estates in Ireland and Anglesey. By this time, by reason of the Industrial Revolution, the Cannock coalfields were producing large royalties. He was one of the biggest and richest English landowners. He changed his name to Paget. Of his twelve children, one was the remarkable **(11) Henry William (1768-1854) 2nd E., 1st M. of ANGLESEY (1815)**, an M.P. from 1790 to 1810. He raised the 80th Foot from his father's Staffordshire tenants in 1793 and commanded them in the Dutch expedition of 1794. He married Lady Caroline Villiers in 1795 and commanded light dragoons in the D. of York's Dutch campaign of 1799. Thenceforth he was a recognised cavalry expert and was in charge of Moore's cavalry in the Peninsular (1808-9), winning brilliant actions at Sahagun and Benavente (Dec. 1808). In 1809 he caused one of the social scandals of the time by eloping with Lady Charlotte Wellesley, wife of the (later) D. of Wellington's brother; while the divorce bills were proceeding in parliament, he commanded the cavalry in the malaria-frustrated Walcheren expedition of 1809 and then married Charlotte in 1810. He had (under a clause) to devote five years to managing his father's disordered fortune and returned to the military life only in 1815 as Wellington's cavalry commander. He distinguished himself and lost a leg at Waterloo. He had long been a friend of the Prince Regent and supported him in the controversies with the Princess (later Queen) Caroline. In 1820, confronted by a pro-Caroline mob demanding that he should cheer for her replied, 'God save the Queen, and may all your wives be like her'. As a rich nobleman he took part in public functions but by 1826 he wanted more active work. He asked for the Mastership of the Ordnance and was appointed in 1827 with a seat in the Cabinet. His views, liberal for the period, were well known especially on the R. Catholic question and in 1828 he became a popular Lord Lieut. of Ireland. Wellington recalled him in 1829 but Grey reappointed him in 1830. In 1831 he set up a successful Irish National Education System but was constantly attacked by O'Connell (whom he put in custody). He was finally recalled in 1833. He was Master-Gen. of the Ordnance again under Ld. John Russell from 1846 to 1852. He had 14 legitimate children. His brother **(12) Sir Arthur (1771-1840)** was ambassador to Vienna from 1801 to 1806 and to the Porte from 1807 to 1809. His brother **(13) Sir Edward (1775-1849)** served as a general under Wellington in the Peninsular from 1809 to 1811 when he was captured. In 1824 he commanded in the invasion of Burma. A son of **(11) Ld. Clarence Edward (1811-95)**, M.P. from 1847 and Sec. to the Admiralty from 1859 to 1866 was C-in-C Mediterranean from 1866 to 1869.

PAGODA. A S. Indian coin worth 7s. current in 17th and early 18th cent.

PAGUS **(Lat = clan).** *See* BRITAIN, ROMAN-7.

PAHANG. *See* MALAYA.

PAIMPOL. *See* ELIZABETH 1-24.

PAINE, Thomas (1737-1809) went to America in 1774, edited the *Pennsylvania Magazine* until 1776 when he published his celebrated tract *Common Sense*, arguing for American independence and unification. From 1777 to 1779 he was sec. to the foreign affairs committee of the Continental Congress and then became Clerk of the Pennsylvania Assembly. In 1787 he returned to Britain and in 1792 published his *Rights of Man* in answer to Burke's *Reflections* This republican pamphlet was suppressed and Paine fled to France; he was elected to the Convention and convicted in *absentia* in England for treason. In 1796 he published his *Age of Reason* against biblical revelation. He retired to the U.S.A. in 1802.

PAINS AND PENALTIES. *See* ATTAINDER.

PAISLEY (Scot.) (Lat. VANDURA) was acquired by the Fitzalans in 12th cent. and Walter Fitzalan founded a Cluniac monastery which was destroyed in the English invasion of 1307, rebuilt and gradually destroyed again in the 16th cent. There is a good harbour on the White Cart R. and a fine weaving industry (silk, muslin and linen) grew up and made Paisley shawls famous until Indian competition drove them out in the 19th cent. Other industries related to textiles including linen thread, dyeing, bleaching and carpet-making survived, and there was always some shipbuilding and distilling, later diversified into engineering and chemicals.

PAISLEY, Ian (1926-), a charismatic personality, became the head of the Ulster Free Presbyterian Church in 1951 and leader of the loyalist Ulster Defence Committee in 1960. In 1970 he was elected M.P. for N. Antrim, founded the Democratic Unionist Party in 1971 and in 1974 organised the United Ulster Unionist Council with which he won 11 of the 12 parliamentary seats. He was long the main exponent of loyalism to the United Kingdom on national religious and economic grounds, particularly the fear that Union with Fire might make the N. Irish population into a small industrialised protestant minority, forced by its voting weakness to subsidise the R. Catholic agricultural south.

PAKENHAM. Originally a Norfolk family which moved to Berkshire and Hampshire. **(1) Sir William (?-1304)** was a judge. **(2) Hugh (?-c. 1478)** was a Lancastrian sheriff of Wiltshire and Constable of Odiham Castle. **(3) Sir Edmund (?-?)** was a gentleman usher to Q. Katherine of Aragon and his daughter married into the Pole family. **(4) Edmund (?1547-1605)** was long sec. until 1595 to his cousin Sir Henry Sidney, Ld. Deputy of Ireland. This began the family's deepening Irish connection. **(5) Sir Thomas (1649-1706)** was Prime Serjeant-at-Law in Ireland. His grandson was **(6) Thomas (1713-85) 1st Ld. LONGFORD (Ir. 1756)**. His third son **(7) Sir Thomas (1757-1836)** was a successful naval captain. His fifth son **(8) Sir Richard (1797-1868)** was a professional diplomat mainly in the Americas. He was minister in Mexico from 1835 to 1843 and then to Washington from 1843 to 1847. He thus had to deal with the highly irritating issues of the Oregon and Texas. He eventually went on leave and then retired rather than return, but from 1851 he was nevertheless Minister to Lisbon until 1855. His cousins **(9) Sir Edward (1778-1815)** and **(10) Sir Hercules (1781-1850)** were both good professional soldiers whose careers were advanced in part by the marriage of their sister **(11) Catherine (?-1831)** to the 1st D. of Wellington. Sir Edward was a divisional commander under the duke in the Peninsular from 1810 to 1813 and was then given command of the expedition against New Orleans where he fell. Sir Hercules was said to have been one of the best officers of rifles of his time.

PAKINGTON, John (seven knights and Bts.) (1) (?-1560) was a Welsh judge after 1553. His great-nephew **(2) (1549-1625)**, handsome, witty and athletic favourite of Q. Elizabeth lost and made a fortune at Court and was Sheriff of Worcs. His son **(3) (1600-24), Bart. 1620** was

M.P. for Aylesbury in 1623. His son **(4) (1620-80)** a royalist who fought at Kineton and in the Worcester Campaign of 1651, lost heavily through compounding but remade his fortune under the Restoration. He was M.P. for Worcs. from 1661 to 1679. His wife **(5) Dorothy (?-1679)** was (probably wrongly) reputed the author of the *Whole Duty of Man*. Their son **(6) (1649-88)** was a distinguished Anglo-Saxon scholar and M.P. for Worcs. from 1685 to 1687. His son **(7) (1671-1727),** a high Tory M.P. for Worcs. from 1690-1695 and from 1698, supported the Occasional Conformity Bill of 1703 and opposed the Union of 1707. He was falsely accused as a Jacobite in 1715. He is, without much evidence, supposed to have been the original of Addison's *Sir Roger de Coverley*. **(8) (1799-1880) 1st Ld. HAMPTON** (1874) was a maternal nephew of the 8th Bt. and took the name when he succeeded to the estates in 1831. He was a Conservative M.P. from 1837 to 1874, was Sec. of State for War and Colonies in 1852, 1st Ld. of the Admiralty in 1858 and 1866 and Sec. of State for War in 1867.

PAKISTAN (*see* MOSLEM LEAGUE) **(1)** The idea of achieving an independent Moslem state on Indian soil was latent in the existence of princely states of Mogul origin, but the Moslem League was concerned with the furtherance of Moslem interests in the two-thirds of India directly under the British. The Government of India Act 1935 reserved to Moslems there a proportion of the representation in most of the mixed but predominantly Hindu areas, i.e. in areas (other than E. Bengal) east of the Indus. The practical, if unintended effect was to make their minority status permanent and to give an increasingly strident political character to the long standing differences of tradition, education, religion and mode of life. The League's leaders foresaw that Moslems would have little future in a society dominated by large self-conscious Hindu majorities and their convictions were regularly strengthened by political rioting in the great cities which, though usually aimed by the Indian National Congress (INC.) at the British, were too often accompanied by sack, rape and arson aimed at Moslems.

(2) The League's leaders became obsessed with the need for a refuge for Indian Moslems under their own control and as early as 1938 circulated a proposal or aspiration for an independent Pakistan to consist roughly of the Moslem majority areas of the present republics of Pakistan and Bangladesh, plus the large S. Indian Hindu state of Hyderabad whose Nizam was a Moslem.

(3) At this period the balance between the rivals in most of British India was held by the British and as the Moslems were a large if proportionately small minority, the balance had to be held mostly by protecting them. In the much smaller Moslem majority areas the converse was the case, but the situation was complicated by a deep psychological factor. In religious riots here, Moslems often inflicted (tactfully named) forcible conversion (circumcision) on Hindus. This generated fears and hatreds far beyond the affected areas.

(4) Everything was changed by the I.N.C.'s. tactical decision to exploit the Japanese onrush in World War II by the *Quit India* agitation against the British. It was no longer certain that the latter would survive to protect the Moslems. When, as the Japanese tide receded, they indicated their willingness to consider Dominion status (i.e. to quit), the League naturally demanded a Moslem dominion as well. Pakistan was now firmly on the political agenda.

(5) The Labour govt. of Clement Attlee, ideologically anti-imperialist, came to power in July 1945. The Japanese surrendered in Aug. Indians could play politics and indulge their rancours free of outside interference and in particular the I.N.C. was suddenly pushing at an open door. The MOSLEM LEAGUE, on the other hand, faced a dire emergency. Legislative preparation was in

hand at Westminster. Britain might cease to rule the sub-continent in less than two parliamentary sessions. Dominion status for a singular India seemed to mean the servitude, if not the destruction, of 100M Moslems under Hindu triumphalism. The League, led by MOHAMMED ALI JINNAH and LIAQAT ALI KHAN, threatened to fight for partition. The principle was conceded by the British and the I.N.C. but not the details.

(6) The Indian revolution, complicated by the I.N.Cs. determination to obliterate the princely states (q.v.), was rushed through in a haste which caused a vast human disaster. The parties had agreed on such bureaucratic matters as the division of debts and balances, but boundary settlement was neglected and irrigation rights and military issues left vague (*see* AUCHINLECK). In heat and rain, minorities on both sides of imaginary frontiers trekked, thirsting and starving and often fighting in opposite directions towards supposed homelands. The police were inadequate; the army breaking up. The unknown number of deaths has been estimated between 10M and 20M. Hyderabad was lost and India seized Junagadh by force. Kashmir became, and in 1994 still was, a battle ground. The remaining frontiers were settled by local bargains.

(7) The Pakistan which came into being in Aug. 1947 comprised two parts separated by 1000 miles. The West (capital Karachi) consisted of Baluchistan, the N.W. Frontier, most of the Punjab and Sind with adjacent republicanised principalities; the East (capital Dacca) of parts of East Bengal and Assam. The arrangement was never satisfactory. Islam as a unifying factor was weaker than geography and the unifying personalities. Jinnah (died 1948) and Liaqat Ali Khan (assassinated 1951), were dead too soon. In 1954 the Moslem League was electorally overwhelmed in the East and coalitions of Islamic extremists, Marxists and republicans established an Islamic Republic in 1956.

(8) It could hardly be expected that the appalling circumstances of Pakistan's creation would lead to simple and speedy solutions to her difficulties. Her internal history from 1956 to the 1990s has only intermittently permitted this large nation to play an influential role in international affairs. In 1965 the smouldering hostilities in Kashmir broke out into local war and meanwhile East and West drifted steadily apart. In Mar. 1971 they came to blows. A Western effort to conquer the East with Western troops drove floods of refugees and many Eastern leaders into the surrounding Indian territory. In Dec. India intervened. The independent republic of BANGLADESH split off, leaving the West to bear the name of Pakistan.

(9) Internal politics in the new Islamic Pakistan now bore the marks of a guerrilla war between a military caste relying on arms and interested in administration, and politicians relying on votes and interested in popular parties. The popularist Zulfikar Bhutto succeeded the discredited military who had just lost Bangladesh, and ruled as Prime Minister until 1977, when his sweeping victory at the polls brought rioting and was denounced as a fraud. Thereupon Gen. Zia-ul-Huq, the Chief of Staff, put himself into office as martial law administrator (July 1977), arrested Bhutto (Sept.) on a charge of attempted murder and had him tried and hanged (Apr. 1979).

(10) At this point civil war provoked by a Russian supported *coup* broke out in Afghanistan. Between 1979 and the 1990s anti-communist Mujah-ed-Din refugees were received in huge numbers around Peshawar which became an anti-Russian crypto-base. The Mujah-ed-Din were powerfully supported on both sides of the frontier with U.S. arms and finance with the necessary Pakistani co-operation and an additional source of profit and finance grew up locally in the manufacture of heroin. Meanwhile the disturbed politics and unbalanced economy had brought about a large Pakistani emigration, notably to Britain. This helped to support the country with remittances. There was a period of artificially induced but real prosperity favourable to popular politics. The opportunity came in Aug. 1988 when Gen. Zia-ul-Huk with his leading generals and the U.S. ambassador were all killed in a contrived aeroplane crash. His associate, Ghulam Ishaq Khan, the Speaker of the Senate, proclaimed elections and Benazir Bhutto, Zulfikar's Oxford educated daughter, returned to lead her father's party. She won the most seats but not a majority and until Nov. 1990 was a Prime Minister with influence rather than authority.

PALACE COURT, created by James I, dealt with personal actions arising within the Verge. It was held, together with the Marshalsea Court, weekly. Abolished 1849.

PALATINATE. (1) The territory or office of a subordinate ruler with royal privileges, especially in England the Palatine Earldoms of Chester and Shropshire and the County of Durham. **(2)** The territory of the Count Palatine of the Rhine centred on Heidelberg. (*See* THIRTY YEARS' WAR.) In the frost and famine year 1709 some 12,000 refugees from religious persecution with memories of the role of Charles I's sister Mary, wife of the Palatine Elector during the Thirty Years' War, came to London where they were sparsely accomodated. Q. Anne sponsored an appeal, and most of them moved on to the colonies.

PALATINE PRINCES, sons of the Elector Frederick V and Elizabeth *d.* of James I (*see* THIRTY YEARS' WAR) **(1) Rupert (1619-82) D. of CUMBERLAND (1644),** served under William of Orange and, having been captured, came to England in 1642. He commanded the royalist cavalry brilliantly until 1644 when he became effective C-in-C (*see* CIVIL WAR). He left England in 1646, commanded English troops in French pay and went with Prince Charles to Holland in 1648. In 1649 he commanded the royalist naval expedition to Ireland; in 1650 Blake blockaded him in the Tagus, but he escaped to the Mediterranean where he indulged in piracy until 1652, ending at Barbados. He then went to France and Germany, returning to England in 1660 to become a Tangier commissioner and one of the founders of the Royal African Co. in 1663. He served as an admiral under the D. of York at Solebay (1665) and with Monck in 1666. In 1670 he became the gov. of the Hudson Bay Co. and was general-at-sea in the second Dutch war of 1672-3. He was First Ld. of the Admiralty from 1673 to 1679. His brother **(2) Maurice, Prince (1620-52)** was an unsuccessful royalist commander in the Civil War. Banished with his brother in 1646, he was drowned during his brother's piratical voyages.

PALAVICINO, Sir Horatio (?-1660), a Genoese, was appointed Collector of Papal Taxes by Q. Mary but when she died abjured R. Catholicism and appropriated the money, with which he laid the foundations of a European-wide business. From his huge fortune, he lent money to Protestant govts., including England, the Dutch and Navarre and supplied them with information through his contacts.

PALE, THE. (1) IRISH or DUBLIN, was the boundary of the defensible of Anglo-Norman citadel area centred on Dublin, and so the area itself. In the 14th cent. it comprised the six of the obedient shires (*see* KILKENNY, STATUTES OF) nearest to Dublin but by 1500 it had shrunk to roughly 50 miles north by 30 miles inland, with partly fortified zones. From Henry VIII's accession English administration began to be replanted outside the Pale in the Wild Irish areas and it ceased to have its defensive aspects and siege mentality, and became only a geographical and social expression (e.g. "beyond the Pale" = gone native). **(2) CALAIS.** (*See* CALAIS-3.)

PALESTINE (*see* CRUSADES, EGYPT) was ruled by Egyptian Mamelukes from 1260 until the Ottoman Sultan Selim I defeated them at Marj Dabiq in 1516. He converted most of Palestine into the Sanjak of Saida (Sidon) but the administrative centre was soon moved to Acre. The Turks

improved agriculture and the cultivation of cotton and silk and encouraged English and French merchants to supplant the Venetians and Genoese at Sidon. The French govt. encouraged R. Catholic missions and Turkish rule on the whole was favourable to the divided but substantial Christian minority. After about 1660, however, it degenerated at a time of agricultural recession. Disorder and Arab incursions broke up the trade routes and the European commercial colonies declined. Meanwhile, however, there had been a resurgence of a Mameluke type of govt. and between 1775 and 1804 this was firmly and ruthlessly led by the celebrated Ahmed el Djezzar Pasha who, with Sir Sydney Smith, held Acre against Bonaparte in 1799.

After Djezzar died, his puppet ruler in the Lebanon, Bashir II, began to encroach southwards and after 1810 the Wahhabis started to penetrate the country from the east. The Egyptian occupation of 1831 under Mehemet Ali's son Ibrahim was consequently welcome but the efficiency of his rule eventually was not. In any case the great powers were alarmed at Egyptian successes and in 1840 they forced Egypt to hand Palestine back to the Ottoman govt.

The succeeding 75 years were an era of confusion and decline. The Russians encouraged the Orthodox, and the French, especially of the Second Empire, the R. Catholics so that both minorities intrigued abroad for privileges at home and provoked Moslem hostility. European, especially British, goods poured in, to the detriment of the local, mainly Moslem craftsmen and the advantage of importers who were mostly Jews or Christians. In 1881 Palestine was incorporated in a new province of Beirut; but this increased the confusion, for the city was the epicentre of endemic civil war. The decline of the economy was driving people overseas especially to S. America; Russian anti-semitism and Zionism were bringing in Jewish immigrants on a sizeable scale while the Hedjaz railway (opened in 1908) to take pilgrims from Damascus to Mecca and Medina, was bringing Syrians into the Trans-Jordan. *See* ZIONISM; ISRAEL, STATE OF.

PALESTINE, CRUSADER, PILGRIMAGE CHURCHES. (1) Annunciation, Nazareth. There was a large church at the Grotto in 1106 whose rebuilding was begun after 1158, but not completed when the Saracens took Nazareth in 1187. There was also an Orthodox church at the Fountain. **(2) Holy Sepulchre, Jerusalem.** A Byzantine church completed in 634 was demolished by the Caliph al-Hakim in 1009 and partly rebuilt between 1048 and the earthquake of 1106. It was replaced by a new structure, finished in 1149. **(3) Nativity, Bethlehem.** The church was built under Justiian on foundations laid by Constantine and decorated with elaborate mosaics in 1169.

PALEY (1) William (1743-1805), Cumbrian parson, published *Principles of Morals and Political Philosophy* (1785) and the well known *Evidences of Christianity* (1794). The moral system was a Benthamite utilitarianism with religious sanctions, his *Evidences* a restatement and harmonisation of 18th Cent. anti-deistic writings. His grandson **(2) Frederick Abthorp (1815-88),** a Cambridge classical scholar, propounded the theory that the Homeric poems were put together from oral tradition in Periclean times.

PALGRAVE (1) Francis Turner (1824-97) was Asst. Sec. at the Education Dept. from 1855 to 1884. He published his celebrated *Golden Treasury* in 1864 and was Prof. of Poetry at Oxford from 1885 to 1895. **(2) William Gifford (1826-88)** became a Jesuit missionary in Arabia, but left the Jesuits in 1865 and embarked on an equally adventurous life as a British diplomatic agent. After two years in Ethiopia, he worked in Trebizond and other eastern areas of the Ottoman Empire from 1867 to 1872. His other assignments included the W. Indies (1873), the

Philippines (1876), Bulgaria (1878), Siam (1879) and Uruguay (1884). **(3) Sir Reginald Francis Douce (1829-1904)** was a clerk and procedural expert in the House of Commons.

PALIMPSEST. A manuscript in which a later writing has been written over, often across, an effaced earlier writing. Palimpsests were common in the Middle Ages. *See* PARCHMENT.

PALLADIANISM. *See* ARCHITECTURE-11.

PALLADIO, Andrea (1508-80), Italian architect, based his designs on classical models and detail; his work and his book 1 *quattro libri dell' architettura* (Ital: The Four Books of Architecture) (1570) influenced Inigo Jones; were made known to a wider public through the illustrations in Cohn Campbell's *Vitruvius Brittanicus* (1715-25) and strongly influenced the 3rd E. of Burlington and his friends. As a result many large houses were modelled on Palladios Venetian villas.

PALLES, Christopher (1831-1920), Irish Attorney-Gen. in 1872 and Chief Baron of the Exchequer from 1874 to 1916 was a leading educationalist and a fearless and impartial judge.

PALLISER, Sir Hugh (1723-96) fought with distinction under Anson at Ushant and then at Quebec (1759). In 1778 after the inconclusive engagement under Keppel again off Ushant, he preferred charges of neglect of duty against Keppel, who was honourably acquitted by a court martial. Palliser then applied for a court martial himself and was reprimanded. The incident illustrates the partisanship of naval affairs at the time.

PALLIUM. A narrow strip of white wool embroidered with crosses, lying over both shoulders with a short piece pendant front and back. It is the mark of metropolitical rank, conferred from 7th cent. exclusively by the Pope. Gregory I sent one to St. Augustine of Canterbury, but subsequently all metropolitans were required to go to the Pope and receive it in person. In cases of disputed archiepiscopal elections conferment of the *pallium* implied the Papal choice. In times of schism, an archbishop's visit implied the allegiance of his church to one Pope rather than another. Either event might have political implications.

PALL MALL (London) was developed from an alley in which the 17th cent. French game of *paillemaille* was played. A wooden ball (*palle*) was driven by means of a mallet (*maille*) through an iron ring set some height above the ground. Nell Gwyn and the painter Gainsborough both lived there.

PALL MALL GAZETTE. There were two inter-related publications of this name. **(1)** J. M. Thackeray's journal published by gentlemen for gentlemen and **(2)** a penny evening paper founded in 1865. It was owned by Thackeray's publisher and edited by Thackeray's assistant on the *Cornhill Magazine*. The *Evening Standard* took it over in 1923.

PALMER, John (1742-1818) established the mail coach service between 1784 and 1786. It cut postal delivery times between London and Bristol from 3 days to 12 hours and on other routes commensurably. Mail robberies ceased and costs were drastically reduced.

PALMER, Richard (?-1195) was Bp. of Syracuse from 1157, Abp. of Palermo from 1166, Chancellor of Sicily from 1166 to about 1170 and as Abp. of Messina from 1183 was present when Richard I seized the city in 1190.

PALMER. Of this Kentish family **(1) Sir John (?-?1545), Sheriff of Surrey (1533) and Sussex (1543)** habitually won money off Henry VIII and was hanged. His brother **(2) Sir Thomas (?-1553),** a court official of Henry VIII, held a number of military appointments at Calais from 1532. By 1547 he had gained a reputation for rash courage. In 1548 he served on the border without much success. In 1550 he betrayed Somerset to Northumberland and in 1553, being an adherent of Lady Jane Grey, was executed for treason. His brother **(3) Sir**

Henry **(?.1559)** held distinguished military commands at Calais from 1535 until the French captured it and him in 1558. His son **(4) Sir Thomas (1540-1626)** had three sons of whom **(5) Herbert (1601-47),** a Puritan divine, was a member of the Westminster Assembly of 1643 and drafted much of the Directory of Worship. From 1644 he was Master of Queen's Coll., Cambridge. His brother **(6) Sir James (?-1657),** a courtier of James I, became a personal friend of Charles I and advised him in forming the famous royal collection of pictures. His second wife was Catherine Herbert *d.* of Ld. Powis. Their son **(7) Roger (1632-1705) 1st E. of CASTLEMAINE (Ir.) (1661),** a R. Catholic, married Barbara Villiers, Charles II's mistress and gained his earldom on her account. They quarrelled over the religion of her eldest son and parted. He then served in the Venetian navy and under the D. of York in the Dutch War of 1665 to 1667. In 1668 he went on a diplomatic mission to the Sublime Porte and travelled the Levant and Holland until 1677 when he was denounced as a Jesuit by Titus Oates and further implicated by him in the 'Mealtub Plot'. At his trial in 1679 before a hostile court he discredited the prosecution and was acquitted. He nevertheless remained a close private adviser of James II as D. of York and King and was sent as his ambassador to the Holy See in 1686. The mission foundered on the Pope's intransigence and his own lack of tact and he was recalled. He witnessed the birth of the Prince of Wales in 1688 but, having been charged with treason in 1689 and 1695, retired from politics.

PALMER (1) Roundell (1812-95) 1st Ld. SELBOURNE (1872) 1st E. of (1882). Conservative M.P. and Anglican churchman in 1848 but moved steadily towards liberalism. He was Palmerston's Sol-Gen. in 1861 and Russell's Att.-Gen from 1863 to 1866. Disapproving of Irish church disendowment, he refused the Woolsack in 1868 but succeeded Ld. Hatherley on it from 1872 to 1874. A leading equity lawyer, his great achievement was the unification of the judicial system. He was Gladstone's Lord Chancellor from 1880 to 1885 but refused office in 1886 because he opposed Irish Home Rule. *See* JUDICATURE ACTS. His son **(2) William (1859-1942) 2nd E,** a Liberal and then a Liberal Unionist M.P. was Colonial Sec. from 1895 to 1900 and First Ld. of the Admiralty from 1900 to 1905. He backed Fisher at the Admiralty, particularly his policies of cadet training and the building of the *Dreadnought.* As High Commissioner in S. Africa from 1905 to 1910 he drafted and secured the Union.

PALMERSTON. *See* TEMPLE especially 10.

PALMERSTON'S FIRST GOVT. (Feb. 1855-Feb. 1858) (Fourteen in Cabinet under Vist. Palmerston with Gladstone Chancellor of the Exchequer; the E. of Clarendon Foreign Sec.; Ld. Panmure, Sec. for War; Sidney Herbert Sec. for the Colonies) *See* ABERDEEN'S GOVT.

(1) Aberdeen was the scapegoat for the Crimean disasters. The Queen asked Derby to form a govt. but he would not without Palmerston and Palmerston would not join him. She then tried Ld. John Russell, who could not drum up enough support. The country wanted Palmerston; the result seemed, with ten members of Aberdeen's govt. to be virtually a continuation of Aberdeen's coalition, but Palmerston was determined to have the popularly demanded inquiry into the conduct of the war and, within days, the Peelites Gladstone, Sydney Herbert and Sir James Graham (First Ld. of the Admiralty), the ministers most directly concerned, preferred to resign and were replaced by Sir George Cornewall Lewis, Ld. John Russell and Sir Charles Wood.

(2) Palmerston came to office as the expected saviour from a mood of public shame. He was at the summit of his popularity and the composition of Parliament seemed unlikely to make for stability. He demanded a dissolution and fought the election on personality alone. No issue of policy befogged the electors; he returned with an overall majority of 90, gained impartially at the expense of Conservatives and Peelites. His position was not, however, as strong as it seemed. Personal support for him did not, as events proved, mean commitment to any policies which he might adopt.

(3) In fact there was no coherent home policy, because public demand had not crystallised the need for one; important, in some cases, decisive reforms were made pragmatically without much panache or realisation of their long term consequences. The Merchant Shipping Act 1855 changed the status of seamen. The useful and overdue removal of testamentary and matrimonial affairs from the church courts (1857) incidentally breached the principle (which Parliament had annually acknowledged by a few private exceptions) of the indissolubility of marriage. On the other hand there was some pressure to extend the franchise but Palmerston, who sympathised with the principle, regarded the vote not as a right but as a trust and consequently opposed the ballot and could find no workable new qualifications for "trustees". Meanwhile he abolished the newspaper stamp tax.

(4) While the political public did not enjoy the hoped-for domestic inspiration, foreign and imperial affairs engrossed the govt's. attention. This was not surprising for the turn of these affairs had put Palmerston into power. In the first place, the Czar Nicholas I died in Mar. 1855 and Sevastopol fell in Sept. The fleet in the Baltic had stopped Russian trade and taken Bomarsund (Aland Is.). In Nov. 1855 the allies signed an alliance with Sweden. With civil disorder and sporadic Polish insurrections, the new Czar Alexander II had to face a radical change. There had been indirect contacts with the allies for some time.

(5) Secondly there was the nagging problem of colonial expansion, which seemed to continue by its own momentum despite doctrinal and practical objections. The colonists were a fact of life, but the colonies seemed too far off to control. The only alternative was, as before, to let them run their own affairs. In 1855 the Australian mainland colonies became virtually self-governing. In 1856 Tasmania joined them and a new colony was constituted in Natal.

(6) Thirdly, there was the immense complex of policies and problems arising from British interests in the Orient. The Russians took Kars, uncomfortably close to Persia, from the Turks in Nov. 1855, while Dalhousie was negotiating with the Afghans against Persia. In Feb. 1856, twelve days before the Paris peace conference, he annexed Oudh, yet for some time the Indian interests had been drifting towards a collision with China. The nature and extent of Ganges Valley discontents was at that time hardly suspected, but the Indian govt's. proceedings were open to criticism as ambitious and unjust. For these the govt. was really though not apparently responsible (*see* EAST INDIA COMPANY THE HONOURABLE OR HEIC).

(7) The Paris Peace Congress (Feb.-Mar. 1856) set the seal on negotiations which had been proceeding at Vienna since Aug. 1854. These, with Austrian diplomatic encouragement, had crystallised in the Vienna Points confirmed by treaty in Dec. when their principles had been accepted by Nicholas I. He had, however, refused to reduce his Black Sea fleet or evacuate Bessarabia. The war had continued but he had maintained the discussions in order to prevent the Austrians entering it, for freedom and the proper management of the Danubian navigation was an important interest of their own. The fall of Sevastopol changed the attitude of the powers. Napoleon III threatened to withdraw his army, which was four times the size of the British; an extension of the war (into the Ukraine?) was impracticable. He wanted to reduce the war to a blockade (mainly at British expense), or extend it by appealing to the sentiment of the Russian subject nationalities (which would have had repercussions in Austro-Hungary) or end it by Austrian mediation.

Palmerston had to accept this and the Austrians delivered an ultimatum to Russia in Jan. 1855. This forced the Czar to give way. The Peace Congress (apart from certain matters of maritime international law) was thus mainly a public ceremony.

(8) The Paris treaty came in for heavy criticism as a small result for a large effort. The trend of Indian affairs was equally heavily attacked and led to the supersession of Dalhousie by Vist. Canning. Since Canning was a cabinet minister and Ld. John Russell resigned from the Foreign Office at the same time, a govt. reconstruction followed. Canning, soon in the saddle in India, had to deal with the legacy of Dalhousie. In Oct. 1856 Britain and France became involved in the *Arrow* war with China; in Nov. there were hostilities with Persia and the British fleet bombarded Canton. The Persian war was liquidated in a treaty at Paris in Mar. 1857, just in time for the Indian Mutiny, which broke out three weeks later and which almost paralysed the operations against China.

(9) Uninterested in home affairs, Palmerston had chosen to stand on his external policies. He was forced to resign when the two became entangled as a result of Orsini's attempt, hatched in England, upon Napoleon III's life. French public opinion was enraged and Palmerston introduced legislation on conspiracies against foreign sovereigns. This was treated by the Commons as truckling to a Bonaparte and he was defeated (Feb. 1858).

PALMERSTON'S SECOND GOVT (June 1859-Oct. 1865) (Fifteen in Cabinet under Vist. Palmerston with Gladstone as Chancellor of the Exchequer; Ld. John Russell (from 1861 E. Russell) Foreign Sec; Sidney Herbert, from 1860 Sec. for War; D. of Newcastle Sec. for Colonies; Sir Chas. Wood Sec. for India; Edward Cardwell Chief Sec. for Ireland). (*See* DERBY'S SECOND GOVT.)

(1) This govt. operated against a background of worldwide confusion, war and doubt. It came to office between the French victories over the Austrians at Magenta and Solferino; and at a time when the French were beginning both to cut the Suez Canal and to build the first armoured battleship. It was, too, the year when Darwin published his *Origin of Species* and Tischendorf discovered the *Codex Sinaiticus* and when John Stuart Mill published *On Liberty*.

(2) British opinion, on the whole hostile to a Bonaparte adventurer, was nevertheless romantically favourable to the Italians, whose liberty Napoleon III's invasion of Lombardy was ensuring. It was doubtful if Britain, a sea power without an effective army, could do much to influence Lombard affairs. Instead Prussia, by mobilising (2 July), stopped the French in their tracks. The Preliminaries of Villafranca (11 July) gave only Lombardy and Parma to Sardinia-Piedmont. Cavour promptly resigned; for, as well he knew, Italian excitement and conspiracy were precipitating a landslide and he would have nothing less.

(3) In these circumstances there was a French scare in Britain. While the govt. and the royal family encouraged the Volunteers, the Cabinet argued about fortifications recommended by a royal commission on the south coast (*see* PALMERSTON'S FOLLIES). Gladstone doubted if the French danger was immediate. He thought that there was time to build armoured ships. He wanted to reduce or abolish the income tax and the paper duty, and encourage foreign trade by dismantling tariffs. Consistently with this, he thought that tension could be lowered by an Anglo-French commercial agreement and sent Cobden to negotiate it (Jan. 1860).

(4) Meanwhile with John Brown's Harper's Ferry raid (Oct. 1859) the U.S.A. was beginning to disintegrate, while Cavour's recall (Jan. 1860) portended further integration in Italy. In Mar. Tuscany, Parma, Modena and Romagna demanded union with Piedmont. In May Garibaldi and his Thousand sailed for Sicily. Napoleon III had destroyed his own Italian influence at Villafranca. The British, rightly or wrongly, reaped much credit for Garibaldi's safe landing; by June he was in Palermo. These were not the only Mediterranean disturbances. A Spanish-Moroccan war ended in the quasi-cession of the Riff to Spain (Apr. 1860); massacres of Christians in Syria brought, with pre-Crimean memories still fresh, hurried Anglo-French intervention (May-July). In Aug. a Montenegrin palace revolution seemed to threaten the entry to the Adriatic. Nor was this all. The Maori rising in New Zealand (Apr.) soon required the despatch of troops halfway round the world, yet at this time the British and French were conducting joint operations against China, beginning with the storming of the Taku forts (Aug.) and ending with the T. of Tientsin (Oct.). In fact Anglo-French commercial and armed co-operation and the supersession of the French by the British in Italian esteem was making Gladstone's task easier, especially as Piedmontese victory succeeded victory. By Oct. there was nothing left of the old Italian dispensation save the papal province of St. Peter's Patrimony which, to please the French clericals and still further upset the Italians, Napoleon III decided to guarantee. The year ended with Abraham Lincoln's election to the Presidency of the U.S.A. and the first secession (S. Carolina).

(5) In the absence of foreign threats Gladstone was free to carry on his financial policy. The free trade budget of 1860 which abolished customs duties on most articles, stimulated other sources of revenue. By meeting most of the cost of fortifications out of a loan, he met the new expenditure created by armed service demands and yet reduced taxation in six successive budgets.

(6) The govt. had inherited Irish religious feuds and rural distress but the Crimean War and the Indian Mutiny had distracted too much attention from them. Irish tenant right associations, founded in 1849, were demanding security and compensation for improvements, but the extremists were already taking the lead. The militant Fenian Brotherhood was founded in the U.S.A. In 1858. Cardwell introduced two ultimately ineffectual tenant right acts in 1860, by which time the internal troubles of the U.S.A. were distracting Irish Americans. The Fenians became dangerous only after the American Civil War.

(7) Palmerston was averse to legislation and virtually the govt's. only important measures designed, like its fiscal policies, to encourage commerce were the passage of the Companies Act 1861 and the foundation of the Post Office Savings Bank. The former greatly facilitated the employment of capital. The latter created a source of cheap govt. finance. Though the French scares had largely blown over, Palmerston's attention was still concentrated upon France which, by the T. of Saigon (Apr. 1862) had annexed Cochin China and acquired the protectorate of Annam. More apparently dangerous (in view of the French position at Suez) was her purchase of Obok as a coaling station opposite Aden. It was thus hardly surprising (especially since the death of the well-informed Prince Consort in Dec. 1861) that Bismarck's rise to power in Prussia (Sept. 1862) was insufficiently appreciated. Within a fortnight that statesman had secured a permanent military budget over the heads of the Prussian Lower House.

(8) In addition, there were difficulties arising from the American Civil War. British opinion favoured the anti-slavery north, for much the same romantic reasons as it cheered on the Italians, but the northern blockade of the Confederacy cut off cotton supplies to Lancashire, where there was widespread unemployment. It was natural for Palmerston to make an international gesture in such circumstances and so without recognising the Confederacy, the govt. nevertheless recognised Confederate belligerent rights. The blockade was too strong for this to help Lancashire much but it led to the unfortunate *Alabama* affair, which bedevilled Anglo-

American relations for some years. By July 1863 the Confederacy had reached its watershed at the key Bs. of Gettysburg and Vicksburg. Its defeat was suddenly certain.

(9) Bismarck joined with the Czar (who had emancipated his serfs in 1861) in suppressing the Polish rising of Jan. 1863. Palmerston openly sympathised with the Poles. Safe in the east, Bismarck could now concentrate upon the North Sea ports and the Isthmus of Jutland. His purpose, ultimately to supplant Austrian influence in Germany, was also to control the access of the European commercial river valleys to the open sea. He began with the complicated affair of Schleswig and Holstein, two duchies of which the Danish King was Duke (*see* BALTIC-56). The German Confederation (and therefore Austria) was stampeded into action against the Danes, who had been encouraged by the British govt. to resist. But Palmerston and Russell had assumed more French and Russian interest in the issues than they were prepared to show. The fleet could not fight the Prussian army or prevent it overrunning Jutland. The Prussians even seized the island of Alsen. The govt. withdrew, making sympathetic noises. It was heavily attacked in both Houses.

(10) These setbacks did not destroy the govt's. hold over the country. The minority electorate was only indirectly affected by mass unemployment, but directly affected by Gladstone's progressive tax reductions. The parliament was nearing the end of its seven year term. It was dissolved in July 1865 and the govt. won the General Election. In Oct., however, Palmerston died. *See* RUSSELL'S SECOND GOVT.

PALMERSTON'S FOLLIES. The chains of huge still surviving forts (facing inland) designed to defend Portsmouth and Plymouth against a French siege. They were built in 1859 when a French attack was feared. They were so-called because they added £11M to an average budget of £55M, when the Royal Navy, if properly financed, could ensure that the forts were never attacked.

PALSGRAVE a corruption of PFALZGRAF (Ger.) = Count Palatine of the Rhine.

PALSY. *See* POLIOMYELITIS.

PAMIRS COMMISSION (1895). Six years after the conclusion of the Penjdeh incident, the Russians in 1892 claimed the Pamirs on the unmarked frontier. Reminded of the Gladstone govt's. determination over Penjdeh they agreed to a demarcation commission which settled the rest of the Afghan northern frontier.

PANAMA CANAL and REPUBLIC. Of the many projects for a canal across the Isthmus of Panama, the first considered feasible was a sea-level scheme designed in 1879 by Ferdinand de Lesseps whose Suez Canal reputation ensured public interest. The Colombian govt. had made a concession to a Lieut. Wyse, who sold it to the French Panama Canal Co.; capital was raised and preliminary work begun. The work was to be completed at a cost of £M24 by 1888, but by 1889 £M74 had been spent and the Co. went bankrupt. It emerged (*The Panama Scandal*) in 1892 and 1893 that the causes were mismanagement and corruption in France and sickness at Panama. Lesseps was imprisoned. The Co's. concession was then offered to the U.S.A. and Colombia and bought for £M8 by the U.S.A. against Colombian opposition, under the Herran-Hay T. (1903). When the Colombians refused to ratify the Treaty, the Americans engineered a local insurrection, instantly recognised the new republic and signed the Panama Canal T. with it (18 Nov. 1903). This established the **CANAL ZONE** under U.S. police, judicial and sanitary control. Construction began in 1905 after the area had been rid of yellow fever and malarial mosquitoes and traffic began to pass the Canal in 1914. It was not fully open until 1920. The Canal's six flights of locks limit its capacity to 48 ships a day, the average passage being seven hours.

The U.S.A. fortified the Zone and controlled the sea approaches in both World Wars, but in 1964 anti-U.S. rioting led to the negotiation of a new treaty to establish Panamanian sovereignty and concede a share in the profits. A series of negotiations and treaties of the late 1970s abolished the Zone and established a commission to operate the Canal until 1999, when Panama would assume full ownership.

PAN AMERICAN UNION, founded in 1890 to publish commercial information about Latin American republics, developed into a commercial and diplomatic organisation for standardising such things as trade marks and private international law at the Buenos Aires Congress of 1911. The 9th (1948) Congress set up the ORGANISATION OF AMERICAN STATES with offices in Washington (q.v.).

PANCHAYATS were traditional village councils of five, mainly in S. India. Much of their work was settling disputes, but the establishment of courts with powers of enforcement led to their decline.

PANDECTS. The 6th cent. Compendium in which Tribonian assembled and systematised the most eminent Roman legal opinions and to which Justinian gave the force of law.

PAN-GERMANISM. A late 19th cent. movement seeking to unite countries in which Germanic languages were spoken, i.e. Germany, Holland, Flanders, Luxembourg, Switzerland and Austria.

PANDULF (?-1226), Subdeacon of the Roman Church, first came to England as a papal diplomat in 1211 to settle the incumbency of the See of Canterbury and excommunicated K. John for refusing to restore Langton. He left England but returned in 1213 when John made approaches for reconciliation; and he forbade K. Philip Augustus to attack England until the negotiations were completed. He was elected Bp. of Norwich in 1215 (but not consecrated until 1222). He was the most influential of the leaders who established Henry III (q.v.) on the throne and acted as effective Regent from William the Marshal's death in May 1219 until Langton and Hubert de Burgh made his position impossible. He resigned his legatine authority in 1221 but remained in the royal service till his death.

PANGKOR ENGAGEMENT (1874) was a British manoeuvre to detach the Malay tin mining state of Perak from Siamese allegiance. The British recognised as Sultan the candidate who would always take the advice of a British Resident on all matters other than Malay religion and custom. This imported an Indian precedent into Malaya. Pangkor is an island off the Perak coast.

PANISLAMISM. *See* OTTOMAN EMPIRE-16.

PANIZZI, Sir Antonio or Anthony (1797-1879), Italian liberal, fled from Parma in 1822 and became a librarian at the British Museum in 1831. As a result of a Commons select committee investigation he became Keeper of the Library in 1837. He retired in 1866, having established its fame and built the famous Reading Room.

PANKHURST (1) Emmeline (1859-1928) and her daughters **(2) Christabel Harriette (1880-1961); (3) Sylvia (1882-1960)** and **(4) Adela Mary (1885-1961).** In 1879 Emmeline married Richard Marsden Pankhurst, a radical Manchester barrister with left wing connections. They were not well off and after he died in 1898 Emmeline had to earn the family living. She also found time to work for the Independent Labour Party (I.L.P.) and for women's suffrage and she set Christabel to reading law at Manchester. Here she met Esther Roper and Eva Gore-Booth who had come north to organise the mill girls against the inferior position of women and their bad working conditions. While these three were penetrating the factories, Emmeline was trying to form a Women's Labour Representation Committee in London. On Christabel's suggestion the name was changed to the Women's Social and Political Union (W.S.P.U.) and launched in 1903. In the beginning the W.S.P.U.

concentrated on Lancashire (where they attracted Anne Kenney) but Sylvia was working in East London and Mary worked with her mother. These women were all strong-minded, attractive, witty and ingenious. They soon gathered a following by their sincerity, educated capacity for leadership and, as it proved, heroism.

By Oct. 1903 Christabel, by now the dominating personality, had concluded that the cause was developing too slowly. At a Liberal election meeting held for Winston Churchill by Sir Edward Grey, both of whom equally favoured women's suffrage, at the Free Trade Hall in Manchester, Anne Kenney demanded whether the Liberals, if successful, would bring it in. There was no reply and Christabel then unfurled a banner. Roughly expelled, Christabel tried to make a speech outside, was arrested and fined a few shillings which she refused to pay. She therefore stayed in prison, but was greeted on her release by an enormous demonstration at the Free Trade Hall, organised by the I.L.P. and Keir Hardie. She took the audience by storm with an accomplished and witty speech.

This was the beginning of her suffragette militancy and of her personal leadership, which she exercised while still reading for her degree. In 1906 she secured a first class in the Manchester LL.B. and in 1907 the H.Q. of the W.S.P.U. was established in London at Clements Inn with, after an internal revolution, herself as an authoritarian organising secretary. By June 1908 she was able to hold a huge rally in Hyde Park, where she made another famous speech. With this "physical" success behind her, she issued an appeal to the public to help her suffragettes rush the House of Commons. She and Emmeline were arrested, but when the case came up at Bow Street Police Court she caused another sensation. She had subpoenaed H. J. Gladstone, the Home Sec. and Lloyd George, the Chancellor of the Exchequer, and proceeded to cross-examine them at length. Of course she was convicted and sent to prison, but she had destroyed the myth of male superiority.

Militancy now gathered strength, progressing from suffragettes chaining themselves to railings, to fights with the police, arson, attacks on govt. property and picture slashing. In 1912 the govt. decided to arrest the entire leadership of the W.S.P.U. on charges of conspiracy, but Christabel escaped to Paris. At this point there was another controversy within the Union, the relatively moderate taking the journal *Votes for Women* with them; so Christabel founded *The Suffragette* in Paris and conducted it with single-minded, almost eccentric, fanaticism; but despite her apparently uncontrolled fury she had a cool vision and when World War I broke out (Aug. 1914) she came home, put her talents at the service of the country and became a powerful and effective recruiter of both sexes.

Sylvia, on the other hand, bitterly opposed the war and Emmeline publicly repudiated her. By 1918 it was clear that Emmeline and Christabel were right; the role which women had played in gaining the victory had gained them suffrage too. Accordingly they dissolved the W.S.P.U. and migrated to North America.

Sylvia and Mary, unable to live without a cause, pursued other forms of extremism. Sylvia first embraced communism and then the independence of African nations, particularly Ethiopia, where she died. Mary migrated to Australia in 1919 and organised first the Women's Party and then the Australian Socialist Party. She married Tom Walsh, the leader of the Australian Seaman's Union; the extremity of her political methods caused her to be interned in World War II.

PANNAGE. The right to pasture swine in woodland in return for a rent sometimes paid in kind in the form of an annual piglet. *See* LAND TENURE, ENGLAND-3.

PANSLAVISM was an unorganised movement for the unification of all orthodox Slavs under Russian protection.

It originated in 1867 and by 1869 Russian military writers were advocating attacks on the Ottoman and Habsburg empires. It had a strong anti-R. Catholic bias and was therefore unfriendly to the Poles. Its most influential advocate was Ignatiev, the Russian ambassador to the Porte, during the Eastern Crises of 1875 to 1885. Panslav feeling caused many Russian volunteers to join the Serbs in their war with Turkey in 1876 and this led to the Russo-Turkish War of 1877 and the abortive T. of San Stefano in 1878. The movement declined after 1885.

PAOLI, Pascal (1725-1807). *See* CORSICA.

"PAPAL AGGRESSION" (1850). The Pope decided that R. Catholic bishops in England should take territorial titles. There was an outcry, largely provoked by Card. Wiseman's orotund way of announcing it. Ld. Russell dubbed the decision "papal aggression" in a public letter and introduced the ineffectual Ecclesiastical Titles Act.

PAPAL or ROMAN CURIA is the papal govt. By the 11th cent. the authority of the ancient local synods had been transferred to the consistory of cardinals, but many administrative and secretarial offices and some judicial tribunals grew up with often overlapping functions. In 1588 Sixtus V instituted reforms which remain the basis of existing practice.

The administrative authorities are the CONGREGATIONS, each headed, save for three reserved to the Pope himself, by a Cardinal Prefect. The three are for *Doctrine*, the *Consistorial* for establishing dioceses and selecting bishops and for the *Oriental Church*. Of the eight others the most relevant to the matter of this work are those for *Propagation of the Faith* and for *Extraordinary Affairs* involving civil govts. The TRIBUNALS are *The Sacred Penitentiary* for matters of conscience, the *Rota* for appeals from diocesan and metropolitan courts and the *Signature* which is the highest court.

The OFFICES include the *Apostolic Chancery,* the *Camera* for temporal property and rights, the *Secretariat of State* whose head is a cardinal usually referred to as the Papal Prime Minister and which deals with much of the routine correspondence on behalf of the Congregations. In addition the Pope has at his personal disposal the *Secretariats* respectively for *Latin Letters* and *Briefs to Princes:* the former mainly drafts letters by the Pope to persons within the church; the latter drafts letters to the heads of govts. and other churches and drafts major documents such as encyclicals, allocutions and homilies. The Sec. for Briefs to Princes also usually preaches the sermon on the election of a Pope immediately before a conclave.

PAPAL CHANCERY. Most papal public documents are known by their opening words e.g. *Unam Sanctam.* The principal classes (which are not watertight) are **(1)** *Bulls,* so-called after the circular leaden seal (Bulla) affixed to them; these are the most solemn and formal documents and may e.g. define a doctrine, change a Vatican law, ratify a treaty or proclaim a jubilee. **(2)** *Apostolic constitutions* are solemn pronouncements or interpretations of existing doctrines. **(3)** *Encyclicals* are pastoral letters addressed to the church or a part of it. **(4)** *Briefs,* sealed under the Fishermans Ring (the Papal signet) are used to ratify administrative or constitutional arrangements such as the rules of an order. **(5)** A *Motu Proprio* is a document, informal in character, issued by a Pope to deal with a doctrinal or disciplinary issue. **(6)** A *decree* is an executive order issued by the Pope or a dept. of the Curia which binds those (who may be the whole church or two parties in a dispute) to whom it is addressed. **(7)** A *rescript* is a reply to a request or question. **(8)** A *chirograph* is a letter in the Pope's own hand, usually to a cardinal.

PAPAL ELECTIONS. Before the Third Lateran Council (1179) these were made by the dignitaries present in Rome or at the place of the late pope's death. Proceedings were sometimes tumultuary and not necessarily confined to churchmen. The Council decreed that only cardinals should be electors. There were very few and some, with the backing of great powers, carried more weight than others. An election was often in reality a diplomatic dispute and to hasten matters the cardinals were, for the first time, locked in a secret conclave in 1271. This became the invariable practice. *See* CARDINALS.

PAPAL STATES originated in a papal assumption of power in the Roman exarchate (province) of Ravenna, based upon an alleged grant by or arrangement with Pepin of Heristal to Stephen II in the 8th cent. They occupied central Italy between the Kingdom of Naples, Tuscany (on the N.W.) and Ravenna on the Adriatic, but Romagna and Emilia were not under proper control until after the 16th cent. northward extension to the R. Po. There were also two outliers at Benevento and Pontecorvo surrounded by Neapolitan territory. The malarial Tyrrhenian coastal province, including Rome, was called the Patrimony of St. Peter. The administration was seldom efficient or enlightened, but seems not to have provoked much internal opposition until French revolutionary times. Bonaparte incorporated the western parts into his Empire and the Adriatic parts into his Kingdom of Italy. Benevento and Pontecorvo became principalities of Talleyrand and Bernadotte respectively. In 1815 the Papacy re-established its sovereignty, but the seeds of Italian nationalism and French scepticism had been sown and the ecclesiastical governors could not have maintained their authority without Austrian support. The whole shaky structure collapsed during the 1848 revolutions and was re-established by French troops sent by Napoleon III in order to get the support of the French clericals. In 1860 there was popular demand for incorporation in the new Savoyard Kingdom of Italy, but Napoleon III saved the Patrimony for the Pope. In 1870 when he fell to the Germans, the Patrimony fell to Italy. *See* AVIGNON.

PAPER. Although named after the ancient Egyptian papyrus (made of a reed), true paper made from rag fibre was invented in China (c. 2nd cent. A.D.). In the 8th cent. the technique passed to the Arabs who brought it to Spain. It was also brought to Italy in the Crusades and spread to Germany where a paper mill had begun to operate by 1390. From Spain it spread to France and England where there was a mill at Hertford by 1490, but a German, Spielman, was licensed for 10 years to make paper at Dartford (Kent) where it has been made ever since. Continuous (as opposed to hand) paper making was begun in Hertfordshire in 1799. This brought on a demand for wood pulp and esparto, which had to be imported from Spain and America. *See* KOOPS.

PAPERBACK BOOKS, though normal elsewhere, were not much in use in Britain until Allen Lane launched his reissues of successful books at 6d (2½p) in 1935. He and his brother formed PENGUIN books (a £100 company) later in the year. The vast new, but not rich, reading public created by the educational system responded and by the Spring of 1937 he had issued 100 titles. Penguin Specials and Pelican books, new works on intellectual subjects, followed. When the company went public in 1962 the shares were 160 times oversubscribed.

PAPINEAU, Louis Joseph. *See* CANADA-13.

PAPUA. *See* NEW GUINEA.

PAPWORTH VILLAGE SETTLEMENT (Cambs) was founded by Sir Pendrill Varier-Jones in 1917. It was the pioneer attempt at social rehabilitation for those under a disability; it originally catered for the tuberculous but soon expanded to help others with persistent disabling conditions.

PARACELSUS (Theophrastus von HOHENHEIM) (1493-1541), city physician of Basel, was dismissed in 1528 as a quack because he preferred experiment to deduction from Avicenna and Galen, whose works he publicly burned. He was the initiator of modern chemistry.

PARACHUTE. The first human drop was from a hot-air balloon in Paris in 1787. There were showmen's acts in the 19th cent. In World War I they were used only to escape from observation balloons, until the Germans used them from aircraft in 1918. The first parachute troops were trained in Russia in 1936 and parachute formations took an important part in the German attacks on the Albert Canal (1940), Crete (1941) and in the British landings in N. Africa and Sicily (1942), Normandy (1943) and Arnhem (1944). Small-scale operations of great effect included the British raids on the Lofoten Is. and Bruneval (1941) and the rescue of Mussolini from the Gran Sasso by the Germans in 1943. The use of parachute troops led to the development of many kinds of specialised equipment including the recoilless gun and the folding motor-cycle.

PARAFFIN was used for household lighting from about 1847 and extensively after 1860 when American imports became cheap.

PARAGUAY (1) was first colonised by Spaniards under Juan de Salazar who founded Asuncion in 1537. Until 1776 it was organised in autonomous native communities called *reducciones* or *misiones* under Jesuit supervision. The dissolution of the Jesuits brought these under the distant Spanish viceroyalty of La Plata at Buenos Aires.

(2) When Buenos Aires declared its independence of Spain in 1810 it claimed jurisdiction within the old viceroyalty, but in May 1811 there was a revolution at Asuncion led by Pedro Caballero. After a period of instability the country was isolated from the rest of the world by a tranquil but absolute dictator, Jose Francia. until 1840. This paved the way for Carlos Antonia Lopez's declaration of independence in 1842. With Brazilian support this was finally accepted by Buenos Aires in 1852 and by the great powers shortly afterwards.

(3) Much European and N. American capital now entered the country whose boundaries were not, however, settled. There were perpetual warlike disputes which culminated, under Francisco Solano Lopez in a desperate war with Brazil and Argentina (1862-8) which devastated the country and wiped out most of the male Spanish speaking population. As a result Guarani became the majority language. The country's independence was saved because the victors quarrelled over the spoils and the U.S.A. imposed an award which favoured Paraguay (1877).

(4) Reconstruction was hampered by political instability and a further dispute over the Gran Chaco with Bolivia. This developed into the intermittent Chaco War (1924-1938). Further instability was due to the poverty engendered by this war. In 1954 a dictatorship under Gen. Alfred Stroessner established some kind of tranquillity, enabling development to continue, but the standard of living lagged and in the 1980s still lagged behind that of the rest of S. America.

PARAMOUNTCY was a doctrine elaborated but not invented as a principle of British rule in India under Ld. Dalhousie (Gov-Gen. 1848-56). The British, having taken responsibility for India by conquest, treaty or military protection, assured superiority in relation to the Indian princes. This took two forms. **(1)** In the case of *dependent princes*, i.e. those who owed their thrones to British action or to a grant (SUNNUD) from the Great Mogul (to whose position the British succeeded after 1858), there was a long-accepted right to settle disputed successions and this Dalhousie developed into a right to approve any succession. Where heirs failed, the state LAPSED to the Paramount power (*see* INDIAN MUTINY-5). Hindu families, in the absence of natural heirs, habitually adopted sons, amongst other things because only a son could perform the proper funeral rites. Dalhousie chose to ignore such adoptions, thereby offending religious as well as political susceptibilities. This doctrine of approval and lapse did not apply in those ancient, mostly Rajput,

states which antedated the British or even the Mogul appearance in India. **(2)** Where any state, dependent or not, had been long and persistently misgoverned the paramount power interfered. In the case of Oudh, Dalhousie annexed it in 1856 and precipitated the Indian Mutiny. After the Mutiny the Paramount power acted with greater tact. Successions were more tolerantly approved and interference for misgovernment, as in Alwar in 1936, was generally confined to occupation and reform. Moreover, the establishment of strong residencies to advise rulers usually anticipated any need for such interventions. *See* INDIAN PRINCELY STATES.

PARAVANES were successful devices resembling under-water kites developed in World War I to protect ships in movement against moored mines. They were towed in pairs and armed with cable cutters.

PARCHMENT was prepared by two long hand-processes involving both the skinner and the parchment maker, from the skins of sheep, goats or calves. The great expense led to expedients in writing, such as standard abbreviations, interlineation and reuse as palimpsests.

PARDO CONVENTION (1739) represented Walpole's attempt to avoid a Spanish war which the English public wanted. The Spaniards had long complained of English abuses of the Asiento and the South Sea Cos. ships, of English unlicensed traders in the Caribbean, salters at the Tortugas and logwood cutters in Honduras; their *guarda costas* (licensed revenue cruisers) harassed English shipping and often behaved like pirates. Between 1713 and 1731 18 English ships had been seized. The fundamental issue was that the Spaniards regarded the Caribbean as their closed preserve where no one else had rights without their licence. This was conceded by other govts. (especially in the T. of Utrecht) but never taken seriously by their public, whose more enterprising or piratical members could not be controlled from home. The convention did not deal with the fundamental issue: the mutual injuries were referred to commissioners who were to value them and strike a balance. Against £200,000 of English admitted claims was set-off £60,000 for the destruction of the Spanish fleet at C. Passaro and £45,000 for prompt cash, but the balance was conditional on the payment of £68,000 dues by the South Sea Co., leaving £27,000 for England. This paltry result inflamed English opinion still further.

PARDON (FREE) is a document issued by the Crown, now on the advice of the Home Sec., remitting every criminal consequence of a given act. It can be issued before, at or after trial or conviction and places a person, so far as criminal responsibility is concerned, in the same position as if the act had not happened. A pardon cannot be pleaded in bar of impeachment, but may be issued afterwards. The Crown cannot, however, by pardon absolve a person from the civil effects of the act in relation to third parties: e.g. it may pardon a theft, but cannot prevent the owner of the stolen property from recovering it.

PARDON AND OBLIVION, ORDINANCE OF, 1652, pardoned all offences against the state committed before the B. of Worcester (3 Sept. 1651) except high treason and rebellious acts since Charles I's death (30 Jan. 1649) and sums due to redeem sequestered lands.

PARDONERS. *See* INDULGENCES.

PARIS AIR CONVENTION, 1919. *See* AVIATION RULES-1.

PARIS CONFERENCE (1921). *See* REPARATIONS.

PARIS, CONGRESS OF (25 Feb.-16 Apr. 1856) was called at the end of the Crimean War. The peace treaty, based on the Vienna Points, was signed on 30 Mar.: it provided **(1)** that navigation of the Danube should be free; **(2)** that Russia drop her claim to protect the Millet-i-Rum; **(3)** that Turkey institute liberal reforms; **(4)** that neither Russia nor Turkey should maintain a fleet or naval bases in the Black Sea (the so-called BLACK SEA CLAUSES); **(5)** that the Aaland Is. should be demilitarised; **(6)** that Moldavia and Wallachia, under Turkish suzerainty, should enjoy an internal autonomy guaranteed by the Western powers. The treaty was signed by Britain, France, Austro-Hungary, Prussia, Turkey, Sardinia and Russia. Point (3) was a dead letter from the start. The Russians abrogated point (4) in 1871. The rest proved more durable and in particular point (6) led quickly to the formation of Roumania. **(7)** On 15 Apr. Britain, Austria and France concluded an alliance to guarantee the independence and integrity of Turkey, as defined by the peace treaty. **(8)** A declaration reaffirmed the abolition of privateering. It also declared illegal blockades unless effective, seizure of neutral goods other than contraband in enemy shipping and of enemy goods other than contraband in neutral shipping. **(9)** The Piedmontese made a statement on the Italian question and Clarendon, on behalf of the British, suggested compulsory mediation before the outbreak of war. This proposal to interfere in the internal affairs of Austro-Hungary incensed the Austrians.

PARIS, CONVENTION OF (1229). *See* AQUITAINE-6.

PARIS, DECLARATION OF (1856). *See* DECLARATIONS OF PARIS AND LONDON

PARIS GARDEN (Southwark). A noisy Tudor bull and bear-baiting resort owned by one Robert Paris.

PARIS, P. of (1259) between Henry III and Louis IX of France. Henry abandoned his claims to Normandy. Maine, Anjou and Poitou and did homage for Bordeaux, Bayonne, Gascony and for extensive lands to be determined in the dioceses of Limoges, Perigueux and Cahors. Saintonge was to return to him at the death of Louis' brother Alphonse of Poitou, the existing occupant, and Agenais on the death of Alphonse's wife Jeanne. In addition Quercy was to pass to him if it were proved that the title to it depended on a grant by Richard I. Alphonse and Jeanne died in 1271 and there was prolonged litigation eventually compromised in the *parlement* of Paris in 1286, whereby Saintonge and Agenais were joined to Gascony and the French crown paid an annuity in return for Quercy.

PARIS, P. of (10 Feb. 1763) between Britain, France. Spain and Portugal, with the P. of Hubertusburg ended the Seven Years' War by putting into formal shape the Preliminaries of Fontainebleau (Nov. 1762). **(1)** France (a) ceded Canada, C. Breton, Dominica, Grenada and the Grenadines, St. Vincent and Tobago, (b) ceded Minorca in exchange for Belle Isle, (c) was restricted to her Indian factories as at Jan. 1749 and undertook to keep no troops in India. **(2)** Britain restored to France (a) the Newfoundland fishing rights and drying grounds and Miguelon and St. Pierre, (b) Guadeloupe, Marie Galante, Martinique and St. Lucia, (c) Goree. These restorations were made without formal equivalent. Hence they weakened Prussia's diplomatic position and created a resentment in Frederick the Great's mind. This was handed down in German opinion as British treachery for over a century. **(3)** Spain (a) ceded Florida in exchange for Cuba, (b) and received back Manila without equivalent.

PARIS or VERSAILLES, Ts. of 1783. The collective names for several instruments signed at Paris and Versailles between Britain, the Americans, France and Spain. They established peace between the four countries. Florida but not Gibraltar was returned to Spain and Britain recognised the independence of the 13 colonies and in consequence settled the Canadian frontier and American fishing rights. It also provided that creditors might recover pre-war debts by court proceedings and that the Congress would earnestly recommend the states to return sequestrated loyalist property. The two latter provisions were almost a dead letter in the U.S.A. The British continued to occupy trading areas in Wisconsin until 1796.

PARIS, P. of (May 1814) between the Allies (Austria, Britain, Prussia, Russia, Sweden, Spain and Portugal) and

Restoration France. France publicly renounced all claims over Holland, Belgium, Germany, Switzerland, Italy and Malta; and ceded Tobago, Santa Lucia and Mauritius to Britain and San Domingo to Spain. She was reduced to her "ancient" frontiers with the addition of Chambery, Annecy, Avignon and Montbéliard. By secret articles, the German states were to be federated and the first four Allies named above alone were to regulate the future balance of Europe at the coming Congress, which it was agreed to convene at Vienna.

PARIS, P. of (Nov. 1815) (*see previous entry*) after the B. of Waterloo. This modified the Treaty of 1814. France lost Landau, Saarlouis, some minor territories on the Belgian and Genevan frontiers and most of Savoy. She had to pay an indemnity of 700M francs and was to support an allied army of occupation of 150,000 men for 5 years. This was reduced to 30,000 in 1817 and withdrawn altogether in 1818. A large number of looted works of art were retaken by their various owners.

PARIS PEACE CONFERENCE 1919-20. *See* VERSAILLES TREATIES.

PARIS, PRELIMINARIES OF (1727) negotiated between Walpole and Card. Fleury ended the minor hostilities of 1727. The Emperor agreed to suspend the Ostend Co.

PARIS, Matthew (?-1259) succeeded Roger of Wendover as chronicler of St. Alban's Abbey in 1235. In 1248 Innocent IV commissioned him to reform the Norwegian abbey of St. Benet Holm. He was a friend of Henry III and of the Norwegian royal house. His *Chronica Malora* (Lat: Greater Chronicles) ends in May 1259. He also wrote a summary of events from 1200 to 1250 called *Historia minor* or *Historia Anglorum* (Lat: Lesser History or History of the English) and compiled a *Vitae Abbatum S. Albani* (Lat: Lives of the Abbots of St. Albans). The *Vitae Duae Offarum* (Lat: Lives of the Two Offas) is also uncertainly attributed to him. *The Chronica Majora* was continued to 1272 by William Rishanger (?1250- ?1312) of the same abbey.

PARISH, PARISH COUNCILS, PARISH MEETINGS. (1) The word was originally synonymous with *diocese* but as the supply of clergy grew, it became possible to settle clergy locally and create sub-divisions mostly based upon the manors, whose lords provided the means to build the church and got the advowson in return. The parish from the early middle ages reflected the manorial organisation.

(2) While the manor declined, the parish with its weekly assembly of the faithful for divine service in the most important local building was relatively simple and durable. The inhabitants began to meet under the parson's direction for social and administrative purposes, often in the Vestry, after which the meetings came to be named. The old civil obligation of the Lord of the Manor to maintain his tenants was matched by the religious obligations of charity. The Church and especially the monasteries administered the only system of unemployment relief and it was the parson's duty to encourage almsgiving and the succour of the poor. Charity, however, remained a virtue and its organisation local. It was essential that the burden should be evenly spread and as early as the 14th cent. attempts were made to make vagrancy a crime.

(3) The dissolution of the monasteries and the improvement in communications made the voluntary system unworkable. Hence the legislators of 1601 conferred upon the vestries the power of levying a poor rate: in so doing they were strengthening machinery which existed already.

(4) But meetings of inhabitants in an expanding population became unwieldily large and so, especially but not exclusively in urban areas, authority tended to slip into the hands of so-called Select Vestries which claimed a separate existence by immemorial custom and which often were self-perpetuating. These could be more efficient than the open vestries and their number was increased by public and private legislation, but, in the absence of a proper auditing system, they became notoriously corrupt. By the Napoleonic Wars this had become important because the vestries were administering huge sums of money. By 1819 they were levying over £10M in rates: a reform was demanded: the Sturges Bourne Act enabled an open vestry, by adopting the Act, to create an annually elected committee (also called a Select Vestry) to administer poor relief.

(5) The vestry, in origin ecclesiastical, depended for its efficacy upon religious unity. The damage done to its reputation by its amateurishness and corruption was completed by the Methodist revival. In hundreds of parishes the parson had to preside over an assembly composed mostly of people hostile to his church. Over extensive areas the church rate (eventually abolished in 1868) ceased to be levied and parish administration was reduced to the barest legal minimum. The critics who prized efficiency above democracy found unexpected allies in the democratic assemblies themselves and the glaring injustices of the Poor Law cried out for reform. From the 1830s onwards public opinion turned, on the whole, against the parish. The Poor Law Act of 1834 withdrew much of the poor law administration from it (*see* UNIONS) and as new administrative services were created to meet the increasing elaboration of society, they were usually committed to specialised bodies. Local government, notorious in the 1820s for inefficiency and corruption, became notorious half a century later for inefficiency and complication. The confusion required twenty years of legislation and experiment to straighten out. The coping stone of the new edifice was the Local Government Act, 1894. This took a year to pass and the parish council clauses in it excited much controversy.

(6) It created institutions having a civil origin, status and affiliation – the *Parish Meeting* and the *Parish Council,* and it transferred the civil functions of the older parish authorities to the new institutions. As a result the church was excluded from formal participation in local government and the traditional functions of the parish, which had always had a "Christian" complexion, were to be administered by laymen. This caused perturbation and it was expected that the new parish councils would embark upon a stormy career. Events, however, belied expectations. They fell rapidly into obscurity.

(7) In 1894 the squire, the parson and sometimes the schoolmaster were the leaders of the village. Their influence depended upon their prestige, superior education, relative wealth and social standing. The vestries had followed their lead. The parish councils were regarded as an intrusion. Most of them began without the co-operation of the influential. Worse still, agriculture had entered upon the long decline which only ended with the Second World War. The revenues of parish councils came mainly from rates on agricultural land, which in 1895 was derated by fifty per cent. Nevertheless Parliament from time to time increased their functions and the tendency to give new functions to parish councils, whilst reducing their financial assets, was exaggerated during the period of the wars. Their spending powers, already attenuated by inflation, were again reduced by still further derating and by the new administrative methods introduced for collecting rates from nationalised industries. In the meantime their position in English social life had altered. Wars, taxation and educational reorganisation had destroyed the old leaders. On the other hand general standards of living and education rose and the commuter appeared. The old internal quarrels died and new problems had to be faced. *See* LOCAL ADMINISTRATION, ENGLAND.

PARK was an enclosed area held by prescription or royal grant for keeping game, but not subject to forest law. *See* CHASE.

PARK, Mungo (1771-1806) attracted interest in his botanical investigations on a voyage to Sumatra and in 1796 was employed by the African Assn. to penetrate the Niger, from which he returned in 1799. His published *Travels* caused a sensation and in 1805 he set out again for the Niger and was killed.

PARKE, Sir James. *See* WENSLEYDALE PEERAGE CASE.

PARKER, Hyde (1) (1714-82) 3rd Bt. (1782) entered the Royal Navy as a seaman in 1728 and was commissioned in 1745. He fought the Dutch at the Dogger Bank in 1781. His son **(2) (1739-1807)** served in N. America during the American rebellion and was C-in-C Jamaica from 1796 to 1800. He was then appointed to command the Baltic expedition. Nelson, his 2-in-C, turned a blind eye to his signals at Copenhagen. His subsequent timidity and procrastination caused his recall. His son **(3) (1784-1854)** was First Sea Ld. in 1853.

PARKER, Joseph (1830-1902) famously eloquent congregationalist preacher who built the City Temple.

PARKER, Matthew (1504-75) was from 1527 one of the "Cambridge Reformers" and a friend of Hugh Latimer but a learned and moderate one. He was licensed to preach in 1533 and became Anne Boleyn's chaplain in 1535, but spent much of his time at his living at Stoke by Clare until he became Master of Corpus Christi Coll., Cambridge in 1544. Here he was preoccupied until Henry VIII's death with royal efforts to despoil the colleges and thereafter he was in good odour with the new reforming govt. He became Dean of Lincoln in 1552. He supported Lady Jane Grey in 1553 and lived in hiding until Mary I died. Elizabeth I then made him Abp. of Canterbury (Dec. 1559) and he became the mentor of the middle road Anglicans. He revived convocation and published the XXXIX Articles through it and between 1563 and 1568 he published (himself substantially contributing) the Bishops' Bible. By 1565 he was at odds with the Puritan extremists, especially over church ceremonial as set forth in his *Book of Advertisements* (The Vestiarian Controversy) and thereafter used his powers of patronage to restrict Puritan influence in the church. Since this was contrary to the political purpose of Leicester, then influential at court, Parker went seldom to court himself after 1567. His interest in learning made him an important benefactor of Cambridge, where he laid out a new street, and he was responsible for the earliest printed editions of many chronicles including Gildas, Asser, Aelfric and Matthew Paris.

PARKER (1) Sir Thomas (?1666-1732) 1st Ld. MACCLESFIELD (1716) 1st E. of MACCLESFIELD (1721), brilliantly persuasive barrister, became Whig M.P. for Derby in 1705. As a result of his distinguished advocacy at Sacheverell's trial (1710) he became C.J. of the King's Bench and in 1711, being opposed to the peace, refused the Woolsack. Consequently he was in high favour with George I and became Ld. Chancellor in 1718. In 1724 an inquiry into suitors' funds in chancery threw suspicion not only on particular masters, but on him. He resigned (Jan. 1725) and on impeachment in May 1725 was fined £30,000. He took no further part in public life. His son **(2) George (1697-1764) 2nd E.,** an F.R.S. in 1722 and M.P. for Wallingford from 1722 to 1727 was a distinguished astronomer. He patronised Thomas Phelps and the Rev. James Bradley the Astronomer Royal and with the help of their calculations brought about the harmonisation of the English and Gregorian calendars by the Calendar Act, 1752.

PARKES, Sir Henry (1815-96) migrated to Australia and became notorious as a political agitator from about 1848. In 1850 he founded and until 1857 edited the liberal *Empire*. On the establishment of responsible govt. in 1858 he became N.S.W. M.P. for E. Sydney. He was Colonial Sec. from 1866 to 1868 and Prime Minister from 1872 to 1875, 1878 to 1882 and from 1887 to 1889. An advocate of federation, he presided over the Sydney convention which laid the foundation for it.

PARKINSON, Cyril Northcote (1909-93) brilliant conservative political economist whose perfectly serious books, notably *Parkinson's Law*, were too witty to be taken seriously by the British political public.

PARLEMENT or its equivalent a **CONSEIL SOUVERAIN** was in fact a high French law court under the old monarchy. Certain provinces preserved privileges or had local legal codes. These so-called *Pays d'état* had their own parlements, which sat at Arras (Artois), Valenciennes (Hainault), Metz (Verdun), Nancy (Lorraine), Colmar (Alsace), Besançon (Franche Comté), Dijon (Burgundy), Grenoble (Dauphine), Aix (Provence), Toulouse (Languedoc), Perpignan (Roussillon), Pau (Navarre) and Rennes (Brittany). The remaining two-thirds of the country was under a centralised control, there being, however, important *parlements* at Bordeaux and Rouen. Finally, the Parlement of Paris was in a different category from the others because it acted as a court of appeal in all judicial matters which might come before the King and its function of registering royal edicts gave it opportunities to protest against royal policy. If the parlement refused to register an edict it could be overridden by the King in person in a solemn session called a *Lit de Justice*.

PARLEMENTAIRE (Fr. = speaker). An envoy between opposing forces, to arrange some matter, e.g. a truce, exchange of prisoners or surrender.

PARLIAMENT (M.E. and O.F. = a conference, colloquy or discussion) (1) The medieval King carried on his routine business himself or with the aid of his familiars and council, but when a great matter such as peace or war, an alteration in the succession, the grant of a major or new fief or an important change in the law had to be decided, it was necessary to confer with the great lords, without whose support, consent or at least acquiescence the decision might be a dead letter or provoke civil war. In this practical sense there was little difference between the Witans and the early parliaments. Such conferences were inevitable rather than legal or institutional.

(2) At these meetings the King and his Council, i.e. those habitually at court, formed an obvious group distinct from the visitors. It was necessary to explain to the latter why they had been summoned and to propound the agenda. Conversely the visitors would have to seek information from the councillors and they would commonly express provincial points of view. This distinction between 'ins' and 'outs' is visible in the practice of petitioning the English King and Council in parliament, in James VI and I's account of Scottish parliamentary practice, in Richard Leatherhead's description of the Irish parliament of 1324, in the later organisation of many colonial legislatures into a Council and House of Assembly and in the nature of the Speech from the Throne; modern national organisations habitually hold periodical mass conferences in the presence of their managing executives.

(3) The magnates who were summoned to a parliament would naturally be those with great territorial possessions, private armies or powerful spiritual influence, or all three. The decisions might be regarded as bargains between them and the King with his council. They would harden into law when a later assembly investigated the way in which such bargains (e.g. Magna Carta and the Forest Charters) had been kept. This hardening process raised the issue of the formal qualifications of those entitled to take part. Hence the royal practice of summoning acceptable magnates developed, under pressure against 'packing', into rules governing the right to participate in making law. Their elaboration eventually constituted the English and Irish House of Lords and the Scottish Unicameral parliament (*see* PEERAGE).

(4) Much of the business of these original and feudal parliaments was judicial, because a magnate could seldom be brought to justice without the assent of his colleagues. He became entitled to be tried before them and eventually by them. This power of judicial decision influenced the way in which decisions were made generally, for some created precedents. A decision upon a petition might equally do so and either type of precedent might harden into law. The difference between such decisions and formal law making was not clear, save in the originally rare cases of the "statutory bargain" exemplified by Magna Carta.

(5) Financial necessity was the main reason for summoning the Commons but once present, they naturally submitted petitions which they had brought with them or which they drew up collectively. Parliament, before their coming, was the Crown-in-Council-in-Parliament. Apart from financial dealings with the Crown, it remained the deciding body and this explains why the English Commons were a separate house; they were a petitioning body. It was considered *necessary* to summon such a house after 1295 in England and 1370 in Ireland (where the Anglo-Normans self-consciously imported English customs), but this was a practical necessity because increasing sums were needed to finance policy. The principle that all legislation required the consent of Lords and Commons grew more slowly out of financial measures and – Scotland apart – from the assenting of petitions and finally from the procedure by bill, in which the propounder stated his exact requirement by offering a draft of the law which he believed would give effect to it. It was sometimes tactically convenient for the Crown to get the Commons to initiate legislation (e.g. the Irish Statute of Provisors 1454 or Edward IV's Act of Confirmation 1461), but the Lords might also prefer bills which they had passed to be agreed – or rejected – by the Commons. This became a legislative habit from about 1384, but it left the judicial functions of the Lords still imprecisely defined but almost unimpaired. The introduction of impeachment and bills of attainder represented a long lasting, but temporary, bi-cameral approach to high judicature.

(7) The balance between the English Houses continued to shift. The three readings of bill procedure was established by the 1430s. The Commons were already numerous and gaining experience as they returned year by year to meetings with a familiar routine. The Lords were few and suffered heavy casualties in the 15th cent. wars. The rule that only the Crown should originate a money bill was soon matched by the claim, conceded as early as 1407, that it must start in the Commons. This represented a special relationship tending to exclude the peers. By 1678 it was accepted that the Lords could reject but could not amend money bills.

(8) The Civil War, the Revolution and the Hanoverian succession established parliamentary superiority over the Crown and a preponderance of the Commons over the Lords, but these movements represented readjustments of balance rather than overthrows of principle. In 1707 the royal veto was used for the last time. This was the year when the Scottish parliament disappeared. In 1712 a ministry, with the support of the Crown and the Commons, defied the Lords by creating enough peers to approve the T. of Utrecht. Sir Robert Walpole's govt. of 1721 to 1742 was the first in which a recognisable prime minister maintained a govt. upon the financial support of the Commons, but he repudiated the title of prime minister (which, indeed, was not statutorily recognised until 1936) and relied for support upon noblemen and the King. The change in habit was caused by the growth, since the Restoration, of political parties operating within the constitution as a whole, rather than factions using one component of it against another. It was, for example, no longer necessary to withhold the Royal Assent, because ministers could use their influence to prevent bills ever reaching that stage.

(9) Political coherence was the fruit of private financial pressure. Nobles were still mostly very rich and the Crown extremely influential. The composition and votes of the Commons could be powerfully influenced because of open and openly bought voting by small, even minute electorates. Votes in both Houses were habitually influenced by jobbery, advancement or bribes. Such practices held govts. together for long periods in fair weather: they usually failed to do so at moments of crisis. The balance between the three components changed only slowly, if at all, under George I and II, because the functions of the Crown and the constitution of the Commons had become full of mutually supporting anomalies. It happened that the Crown's position was altered first. The Younger Pitt's dogged Benthamite economies from 1782 began very slowly to reduce the patronage in paid sinecures by which the Crown exerted its influence. The year 1782, though nobody realised it at the time, was also the decisive year when the Industrial Revolution took off. In the next 50 years the shift caused by that revolution in the springs of wealth and the location of settlement made Commons reform essential (see REFORM ACTS 1832). It had been the object of agitation since the late 1760s.

(10) Throughout the 18th and 19th cents. the Lords included only meagre legal talent and they had decided their Common Law appeals on the advice of the judges and in Equity on that of the Ld. Chancellor. The Reform legislation naturally cast doubt upon the hereditary principle and in 1856 Palmerston's govt. sought to kill two birds by using the prerogative. Sir James Parke, a distinguished judge, was made a life peer as Ld. Wensleydale and summoned to the Lords by writ. This thin end of a wedge was rejected by the Committee of Privileges: they held that a lord summoned by writ who actually took his seat became *ipso facto* a hereditary peer. Thus, the authority of the House of Commons increased steadily with the weight of successively enlarged electorates behind it, but that of the Lords remained nearly stationary and based upon a wealth which was changing in form from land to capitalism more slowly among its members than in society at large. From 1873 the problem of a judicial life peerage was solved by statute, leaving the principle of hereditary peerage untouched.

(11) The Whig secession from the Liberals after Gladstone's Home Rule Bill of 1886 reinforced the conservative majority in the House of Lords and accentuated its isolation. In 1892 Gladstone warned the Commons of the constitutional dangers of Lords' obstructionism and under the Liberal govt. of his successor Ld. Rosebery, the Upper House frequently threw out govt. bills and so continued from 1906 onwards. This drift led to the crisis of 1909-10 when, to meet the need to re-arm against Germany, new but provocatively framed taxes were required. Led by the M. of Lansdowne and encouraged by Balfour, the Lords proposed to revive their long dormant power to reject a finance bill. Lloyd George's demagoguery provoked a public clamour. Two successive electoral mandates and the common sense of Edward VII and George V prevented the use of this power by the threat to create additional Liberal peerages. The finance bill was forced through and also the Parliament Act of 1911 (q.v.).

PARLIAMENT ACTS 1911 and 1949. (*See* PARLIAMENT-11.) The Act of 1911 enabled a *public* bill to be presented for the Royal Assent without the Lords' agreement (a) if certified by the Speaker of the Commons as a money bill. within one month of passing the Commons and (b) in other cases if passed in two successive sessions by the Commons against the Lords and then a third time. It also reduced the legal life of a parliament from seven years to five. The Act did not apply to private or personal bills. It was seldom used in practice: the two major cases were

the Disestablishment of the Welsh Church (1914) and to force through the Parliament Act of 1949 which reduced the delaying power to one session and two passages by the Commons. The Speaker's power of certification is not always used, notably where the money clauses form a minor part of a larger bill needing detailed scrutiny or govt. amendment in the Second House. The Act of 1949 was used to override the Lords' objections to the 1991 War Crimes Bill which made offences committed fifty years ago outside the Kingdom triable in the Kingdom.

PARLIAMENT, IRELAND (to 1495) (1) was for most of its existence an institution of the Ascendancy in its successive forms, beginning as a meeting of the council with or in the presence of the magnates. By about 1300 about 80 of these, including 16 bishops and 14 abbots might be summoned but not all were; not all who were summoned attended and some attended only by proxy or proctor. Thus in addition to the 6 or 7 ministers (councillors) the average pre-tudor attendance of magnates was about 40, but the permanent need to summon them was not recognised before 1370.

(2) It is uncertain when Knights, burgesses and proctors for the lower clergy first attended. The earliest undoubted case was in 1275 but the permanent need to summon them was not established before 1370. The numbers summoned oscillated with the size of the area under Anglo-Norman control: between 1375 and 1394 writs were issued for the 14 counties of Carlow, Clare (once only), Cork, Dublin, Kerry, Kildare, Killarney, Limerick, Leath, Neath, Tipperary, Ulster, Waterford and Wexford and the 12 towns of Athenry, Cork, Drogheda, Dublin, Galway, Kilkenny, Kinsale (once only), Limerick, New Ross, Waterford, Wexford and Youghal making, at two representatives each, 52 members at most. In the 15th cent. only the four counties of the Pale and seven towns could be summoned. The number of members who actually obeyed was much smaller because of the expense, inconvenience or danger on the boggy bandit-infested tracks. In 1440 the Chancellor, Richard Wogan, inveighed against M.Ps. who represented more than one place. In 1463 it was noticed with interest that Knights came from Cork for the first time for many years.

(3) Meetings were held mostly at Dublin, Drogheda, Trim, occasionally at Castledermot until its destniction in 1440 and Kilkenny, and rarely at Kilmainham, Naas, Waterford and Kildare. Single meetings occurred in at least six other places. The meetings were short but frequent. Between 1264 and 1494 parliaments or great councils met over 250 times. In 1478 it was decided to meet only at Dublin or Drogheda (well within the Pale) because of the unsafety of the journeys.

(4) These parliaments were seldom concerned with legislation. They mainly discussed ways of upholding the common law, keeping the peace, fighting the 'wild Irish' and paying for such proceedings in a country where Celts and Anglo-Normans were at enmity and where Celtic tribes were constantly at feud with each other. They thus on the one side resembled police conferences rather than legislatures, while the declining jurisdiction of the courts brought much business before them which would now be called judicial.

PARLIAMENT, IRELAND (1495-1800)
(1) The membership of this body was as follows:-

	Bishops	Temporal Peers	Commons
1560	22	32	76
1585	22	32	126
1681	20	119	276
1790	20	178	276
1800	20	228	300

In 1793. 134 M.Ps. were nominated by peers and 94 by commoners who had the patronage of nomination boroughs. About 200 M.P.s were legally speaking elected by a total of about 100 electors. Only 72 represented anyone but their patrons.

(2) This state of affairs continued between 1782 and 1800 and made it relatively easy in 1800 to induce the parliament by corruption to abolish itself and vote the Union with Great Britain. (*See* POYNING'S LAW; GRATTAN'S PARLIAMENT; STEWART, ROBERT CASTLREAGH.)

(3) Membership, after 1560 in theory confined to Protestants, always included some R. Catholics and up to about 1670 as many as 50%.

PARLIAMENTARY PAPERS. Papers presented to Parliament began to be bound and indexed in 1801 (Commons) and 1804 (Lords).

PARLIAMENTARY PAPERS ACT, 1840. See STOCKDALE *v.* HANSARD.

PARLIAMENT ROLLS were records of parliamentary proceedings from 1278 to 1503, mainly in the form of petitions with the King's answers and decisions on difficult points of law. At the end of a parliament the judges drew them up into a statute which was entered on the statute rolls.

PARLIAMENT OF SCOTLAND (PRE-1707) was unicameral, originally consisting of prelates, nobles and tenants in chief to which in 1357 burgh representatives were admitted. Successive acts excused smaller tenants from personal attendance and by 1587 the tax paying burghs were appointing commissioners. From 1619 Edinburgh had two commissioners, other burghs one. Eight officers of state were members *ex officio*. The membership was always small. The rolls of 1567 show 83 of whom four were bishops, 30 were nobles and 14 were lay holders of monastic lands. In 1581 there were 55. In 1617, 152 of whom 12 were bishops and 44 nobles.

According to James VI a parliament would be proclaimed about 20 days in advance and a day fixed for bills to be deposited with the Clerk Register. He then laid them before the King or Regent who gaxe his fiat by giving them to the Ld. Chancellor "to be propounded to the Parliament and none others". Members could speak only to matters thus propounded and could be silenced if they raised any other issue. All business was subsequently referred to the Committee of the Articles. See ARTICLES, LORDS OF THE

PARLIAMENTARY BEHAVIOUR AND LANGUAGE. To preserve frankness of debate in the Commons, yet prevent passions from making debate impossible, members must not overstep a line on their side of the floor which is said to be two swords-lengths from the equivalent line opposite: they must address their speeches to the Speaker only, which forces them to refer to all other persons (including other M.P.s.) in the relatively cool third person: they must not mention another member by name, but only by description (e.g. "the Honourable Member for York" or "my Right Honourable friend"), nor do they mention the House of Lords or individual peers in it and they must not use certain words (called "unparliamentary expressions"), calculated to give offence or provoke disorder (e.g. "liar" is unparliamentary but "terminological inexactitude" is permissible). A member bows to the House on entering the Chamber; he must not remain standing if the Speaker is on his feet and must not interrupt or obstruct him.

The House listens in silence to a member's personal statement (i.e. one relating to his private conduct in a public matter) but his statement must be true. A maiden speech is similarly treated provided that it is uncontroversial. Speeches must not refer to private conversations between members outside the House. A member must declare an interest (if he has one) in a matter on which he wishes to speak.

The right to speak is determined by the Speaker, who gives priority to privy councillors. In practice he is informed about hopeful speakers and chooses them alternately from opposing sides.

The practices in the Lords are very similar, but in the more sedate atmosphere of that House are not reduced to so many rules and precedents.

PARLIAMENTARY TRAINS were trains which, by Gladstone's Railways Act 1844, had to run at least once a day on every line and provide accommodation at a charge not exceeding 1d. a mile. The rolling stock was apt to be uncomfortable, but some companies using better carriages and slightly higher charges attracted enormous numbers of potential travellers into 'Third Class' instead.

PARNELL, Charles Stewart (1846-91), (1) of an Irish political family was, with his sister **Fanny (1854-82),** brought up to Anglophobia in Co. Wicklow by his Irish-American mother. He was the first to perceive that the Ballot Act 1872, would emancipate the Irish voter from the English landlord; in 1874 he offered to help Isaac Butt's Home Rule party, formed in 1870. In 1875 he became M.P. for Meath in a by-election. His aristocratic *hauteur*, ruthless brilliance, good looks and Fenian connections soon made his name. As Butt's constitutionalism seemed to be ineffectual, he organised a militant group which in 1877 began to obstruct the business of the Commons, while achieving alliance at home with the R. Catholic hierarchy and the Irish Republican Brotherhood.

(2) In 1878 the group ousted Butt, with a programme of parliamentary obstruction, backed up in Ireland by various forms of civil disobedience and financed from the U.S.A. Parnell united all the hitherto warring anti-British factions and in Dec. 1878 went to America, where he agreed with the violent Clan-na-Gael (the extremist Fenians) on tactics designed to secure possession of the land by the Irish tenants. For this purpose the Irish National Land League was launched (Oct. 1879). Parnell was its first president. Fanny helped to organise it. Irresistible now among Irish nationalists, he became chairman of the parliamentary party (May 1880).

(3) (For the effect of Parnell's activities upon English politics see articles on the following govts.: DISRAELI'S SECOND; GLADSTONE'S SECOND; SALISBURY'S FIRST; GLADSTONE'S THIRD; SALISBURY'S SECOND.) Parnell's career was now and henceforth strongly influenced by a private factor. He and Katharine O'Shea fell in love at first sight. She was the sister of the (later) Field Marshal Sir Evelyn Wood V.C.; her cousin the first Ld. Justice Farwell and though she was married to the bankrupt and unpleasant Capt. O'Shea (by whom she had had three children), they had long lived apart. Katharine daily comforted an aged, wealthy, pious aunt, Mrs Benjamin Wood, who maintained her and the children; to estrange Mrs Wood would be disastrous for Katharine had no money. She and the Capt. agreed to keep up appearances and he visited her Eltham house weekly, in return for which she used her social position for his benefit. She became Parnell's mistress in 1880 and from 1881 they lived very privately as husband and wife, with O'Shea continuing his visits. She had three children by Parnell, and O'Shea in effect lived off Mrs Wood by blackmailing them). Mrs Wood, who was born in 1792, lived unexpectedly long and Parnell had to exclude his political colleagues entirely from his private life to keep the secret.

(4) The facts were, however, known or surmised by politicians as early as 1882 and in any case Katharine acted as a sort of political sec. for Parnell, on whose behalf she corresponded with Gladstone, especially on the Kilmainham Treaty. The extremist Irish resented Parnell's new willingness to compromise and attributed his "inaction" to her charms, whereas it was due to his poor health and sound policy. They, especially Biggar and Healy, were doubly furious when Parnell insisted on the Capt's. candidature at a Galway by-election in 1886, though they did not know that Gladstone had been

offered the Irish vote in four English constituencies in return.

(5) Mrs Wood died in 1889 and left Katharine her fortune. The Capt. was willing to be divorced for £20,000, but the Wood family disputed the will and Parnell could not raise the money. The Capt. then petitioned for a divorce on the ground of her adultery and it was impossible to stop him, for the suit was necessarily collusive. The public thus gathered from O'Shea that Parnell had been deceiving him for nine years. It was shocked.

(6) Parnell had for some time had difficulty in controlling his wild men. The divorce split the party by bringing the R. Catholic bishops out against him. This politically unnatural coincidence of the extremisLs and the hierarchy destroyed his power and his health was insufficient to support his desperate battles to retrieve the position. He married Katharine after the divorce was made absolute, but died shortly after.

(7) Since Parnell's children were born during the subsistence of the O'Shea marriage, they were technically O'Shea's and he had the custody of them. He used this after Parnell's death to extort more money and prevent the truth being published.

PARNELL COMMISSION (1888-9). *See* PIGOTT, RICHARD.

PARNELL, Thomas (1679-1718), Irish drunken but moral poet and friend of most of the Brothers' Club.

PAROCHIAL AGREEMENTS. *See* ADVOWSON AND TITHE-9.

PAROCHIAL CHURCH COUNCILS. *See* CHURCHWARDENS.

PAROLE (Fr. = word) (1) *adj.* Something spoken rather than written. **(2)** *sb.* A promise e.g. by a prisoner temporarily at liberty to return to captivity in a specified event. **(3)** A password.

PARR, Catherine (1512-48), respected daughter of Sir Thomas Parr of Kendal (Cumbria) was already the widow of **(1) Ld. Borough (d. 1529)** and **(2) Ld. Latimer (d. 1542).** He had brought her to court, where she fell in love after his death with Sir Thomas Seymour, brother of Q. Jane Seymour. Witty, well educated and kind, she was obliged to become the sixth Queen of Henry VIII in 1543. She acted as Regent for him in 1544 when he was on campaign, but was mostly concerned with bringing up and protecting the King's three children in the tidal intrigues of that steamy court. He died in Jan. 1547 and in July she secretly married Sir Thomas Seymour, now Ld. Seymour of Sudeley, who treated her and the Princess Elizabeth badly. She died in childbirth. Unappreciated by historians, she played an important role in maintaining the stable continuity of the dynasty.

PARR, Thomas (?1483-?1635) "OLD PARR" was said to have done penance for amorous exploits at the age of 105 and to have been sent from Shropshire to court by the E. of Arundel in 1635, where the mode of life killed him.

PARRY, Sir Hubert (1848-1918), composer, musical historian and, with Stanford and Sir Geo. Grove, one of the original professors at the R. College of Music founded in 1883. His social eminence and wide education enabled him to interest the hitherto uninterested influential in music.

PARSEES are the survivors in India of the ancient Persian Zoroastrian sect. They included some very rich families and were mostly centred in Bombay. *See* ALBIGENSIANS.

PARSONS or PERSONS, Robert (1546-1610), bursar and dean of Balliol Coll., Oxford in 1574, quarrelled with the fellows and left for Louvain, where he was received into the Roman Church and the Society of Jesus. In 1580 he returned with St. Edmund Campion to England, made converts and set up a clandestine printing press. He thought that the reconversion of the English would best be achieved by a Spanish conquest, and believed that many, perhaps most English R. Catholics, would welcome this. He was abroad from 1587 mostly in Spain promoting these ideas. The Castilian authorities were sceptical, but his many tactless publications helped to fuel the English govt's. suspicions of R. Catholics, already kindled by the papal bull *Regnans in Excelsis*. His ineffectual extremism ultimately brought about a change of papal policy from political action to missionary conversion, and in 1597 he was put out of harm's way as Rector of the English College in Rome.

PARSONS, Sir William (?1570-1650) succeeded his uncle Sir Geoffrey Fenton as Surveyor-Gen. of Ireland in 1602 and was thus a key figure in the plantations of Ulster, Wexford, Longford and Leitrim (1610-20), in the course of which he acquired wide estates. He was suspected of stimulating revolts to provide pretexts for new confiscations and was generally disliked in England as well as Ireland.

PARSONS, (1) William (1800-67) 3rd E. of ROSSE (1841), Irish M.P. from 1823 to 1834 but best known for his improvements in reflecting telescopes and his discovery, by means of his large telescope at Parsonstown (Offaly), of spiral nebulae. His son **(2) Sir Charles Algernon (1854-1913) F.R.S., O.M.,** invented the steam turbine in 1884. This revolutionised the propulsion of ships and facilitated the generation of electricity. He also invented an improved gramophone and a non-skid motor tyre.

PARTHENOPAEAN REPUBLIC (Jan.-June 1799). A revolutionary govt. in Naples encouraged and then abandoned by the French. *See* NAPLES, SICILY, TWO SICILIES.

PARTIAL TEST BAN TREATY (1963). *See* ATOMIC.

PARTISAN (1) properly anyone devoted to a cause or leader, the word has been virtually annexed by communist guerrillas in World War II, **(2)** A type of halberd.

PARTITION TREATIES. *See* SPANISH SUCCESSION.

PASCHAL CONTROVERSY. The dispute about the correct dating of Easter settled at the Synod of Whitby (664). The Irish use was not finally abandoned in the north of Ireland until well into the 8th cent.

PASHA, BASHAW or BASSO was a high ranking Ottoman, originally military, officer. There were three grades, distinguished respectively by one, two and three horsetails exhibited on their standards. A PASHALIK was a military district under a pasha, but civil and military functions tended to overlap. A pashalik of one horsetail might be the size of Yorkshire. At the end, the rank was as often honorific as functional. Mustafa Kemal (Atatürk) was made a Pasha for his military success at Galipoli.

PASQUINADE. Card. Carafa dug up a mutilated statue and set it up in 1501 near the Piazza Navona in Rome. It became known as Pasquino and it was customary to attach satirical anonymous verses often of a political flavour to it, called accordingly pasquinades.

PASSIVE RESISTANCE (1) Opposition to the Education Act 1902 by refusing to pay the new education rate. **(2)** The often explosively non-violent tactics of the Indian National Congress under Gandhi's leadership, against the British.

PASSCHENDAELE, B. of (Flanders) (July-Nov. 1917). *See* WORLD WAR I-8.

PASSIVE OBEDIENCE was a 17-18th cent. doctrine that subjects must not resist their lawful Prince, and that if he issued commands contrary to Divine Law they must accept punishment for refusing obedience, in the sure and certain hope of Divine reward. The difficulty was the lawful status of the Prince: in particular whether obedience was owed to James II or William and Mary. The Non-Jurors (mostly clergy) refused to swear allegiance to the latter because they held that they owed obedience to the former.

PASS LAWS (S. Africa) or VAGRANCY LAWS were originally imposed on Cape Hottentots in 1809 as part of a compromise related to the abolition of the slave trade. The British wanted to protect the Hottentots, the Dutch wanted an alternative labour supply. Hottentots were put under colonial law and courts entertained actions by them, but their migratory habits were to be restricted. They could not cross a district boundary without a pass from the Landdrost, or own land. These latter provisions were abolished by the 50th Ordinance of 1828, which proclaimed equality in connection with slave emancipation. In 1834 a draft Vagrancy Law was dissallowed by the Crown as inconsistent with the 50th Ordinance. Thenceforth a main difference between British colonies and Boer republics was that the latter had pass laws, the former did not. The Union of 1910 reopened the problem because it united the two types of area.

PASSPORT was originally a rare document which, as the wording made clear, gave privileged clearance to persons on international journeys and, outside Russia, were used only by diplomats. To 'send passports to an ambassador' was a polite term for expulsion. In 1914 ordinary passportless British subjects caught in Germany at the outbreak of World War I travelled home through neutral countries unhindered by the Germans. The perversion of the passport into a document of identity required of any foreigner entering a state territory was the effect of a French security panic in the war, combined with their already established requirement of identity papers for their own people. By 1920 the British govt. had so far acquiesced in this, that it began to issue passports to British subjects on demand.

PASS STAGE on a bill in either House of Parliament comes after Third Reading. The motion "that the bill do pass" is seldom debated. It is an instruction to the clerks to pass the master copy to the other House for consideration or, if already so considered, to the Crown for Assent.

PASTON, Norfolk businessmen and courtiers whose correspondence, amounting to about 1000 letters, is a major source for the lives of such people in the 15th cent. **(1) William** (1378-1444) of Paston became Steward of the Bp. of Norwich's courts in 1413, a serjeant-at-law in 1421 and a Justice of the Common Pleas in 1429. He had, for the period, an unusual reputation for integrity. He left six children and much property which he bought at Paston, elsewhere in Norfolk and in Suffolk and Hertfordshire. His daughter was the mother of Sir Edward Poynings. His son **(2) John (1421-66)** wrote many letters, married a Fastolf and was Sir John Fastolf's legal adviser. He was engaged much of his life in disputes, some violent, with neighbours and rivals, notably the Tuddenhams, the Moleyns and their patron the D. of Suffolk and the D. of Norfolk. Fastolf left him much of his property, but the will was disputed. The eldest of his seven children **(3) Sir John** (1442-79), also a letter writer, went to the court of Edward IV and knew everyone of importance there. The disputes were compromised through William of Waynflete in 1470. Sir John lived and amused himself in London, where a friend called him "the best Chooser of Gentlewomen he ever knew". He left a daughter but never married. The estates then passed to a brother, also called John, whose son **(4) Sir William (?1479-1554)** was a lawyer and courtier, besides sheriff in Norfolk and Suffolk.

***PASTOR AETERNUS* (1516)** bull of Leo X reaffirming *Unam Sanctam.*

PATEL. Two brothers **(1) Vithaldas Javeri (1873-1933),** Indian nationalist, was the first Indian pres. of the Legislative Assembly but resigned in 1930 in protest against the detention of the Congress leaders. He left a large sum to Netaji Subhas Bose, the nationalist extremist, but his brother **(2) Vallabhai Sardar (1875-1950)** had the bequest disallowed. He was pres. of the Indian National Congress in 1931 and was prominent in Gandhi's *Quit India* movement of 1942 to 1946.

PATENT ROLL. *See* LETTERS PATENT.

PATENTS. *See* ACONTIUS; MONOPOLIES.

PATENTS, DESIGNS AND TRADE MARKS ACT, 1883, repealed and codified previous statutes on these subjects,

created the Patent Office, transferred to it the business of granting patents from the Ld. Chancellor's Office and also the registration of designs and trade marks.

***PATER NOSTER* (Lat: Our Father)** The Lord's Prayer; hence any prayer and so a rosary. Paternoster Row near St. Paul's, London, was a resort for publishers until it was destroyed in World War II.

PATERSON, Emma (1848-86) inspired the pioneering Women's Protective and Provident (later) Women's Trade Union, League, and was the first woman delegate at the Trade Union Congress. She was interested in practical matters such as factory inspection. She taught herself printing and edited the *Woman's Union Journal.*

PATESHULL or PATT'ISHALL, Simon (?-1217) was C. J. in the *coram Rege* court under King John. **(2) Martin (?-1229)** was a justice at Westminster in 1217 and Dean of London in 1228. Simon's son **(3) Hugh (?-1241)** was the King's Treasurer in 1234 and became Bp. of Lichfield in 1239. **(4) Walter (?-1232)** was a justice in eyre for midland counties in 1218. Simon's grandson **(5) Sir Simon** (?-1274) was a justice in the Kings Bench in 1257 and a supporter of Montfort. **(6) Sir John (?1291-1349)** sat in Parliament in 1342.

PATHANS are mostly clans inhabiting the frontier areas between Pakistan and Afghanistan, the best known being the Afridis and the Waziris. They are also prominent as moneylenders in northern India.

PATIALA (India) was a Sikh state founded in 1763. It put itself under British protection in 1809 to avoid absorption by the main Sikh state under Ranjit Singh. The enlightened Maharaja Bhupindra Singh (r. 1891-1938) greatly developed the state, inspired the creation of the Indian Chamber of Princes and represented India at the League of Nations. He was popular and much respected in Britain.

PATNA (India), capital of Bihar, had an HEIC factory from 1760 which was responsible for exporting much rice abroad. The city became the capital of the joint province of Bihar and Orissa in 1912.

PATRIA. The Welsh lands of a lordship.

PATRIAL. A citizen of the U.K. and colonies who under the Immigration Act, 1971, had a right of abode in the U.K. *See* NATIONALITY-6.

PATRIARCH, originally a title of bishops generally, became restricted in the greatest denominations to bps. of the highest rank, namely those of Antioch, Alexandria, Rome, Constantinople and Jerusalem. The title always connoted a degree, claimed sometimes to be absolute, of autonomy. In the West the Roman patriarchate developed into the Papacy and three other patriarchates were eventually created at Venice, Lisbon and Lima. In the East, Constantinople achieved an honorific (but not jurisdictional) primacy through its association with the imperial and later with the Ottoman monarchy. A further orthodox patriarchate was set up in Moscow in the 16th cent. The chief bps. of certain other denominations, e.g. the Copts, are also known as Patriarchs but Armenian patriarchs are subordinate to the Catholicus. *See* NICENE CREED.

PATRICK, St. (?373-?464). *See* MISSIONARIES IN BRITAIN AND IRELAND.

PATRIOT PARLIAMENT. *See* JAMES II and VII-15.

PATRIOTS, THE. An opposition group headed by Sir William Wyndham and the Pulteneys. *See* GEORGE II 1-4.

PATTEN, the Rt Hon. Christopher Francis (1944-) PC 1989, was educated at Balliol Coll. Oxford and entered Tory politics *via* research in 1966. As MP for Bath (1972-92) he was in minor office between 1979 and 1985, when he became a Min. of State at the Dept of Education and Science and later at the Foreign and Commonwealth Office. In 1989-90 he was S. of State for the Environment and then held some Tory party positions. In 1992 he was made Gov. of Hong Kong in order to hand the Colony (which was untenable owing to water problems) over to the Chinese with as little damage as possible to western democratic and business interests. This was done with uncertain success in 1997. In 1998-9 he was employed by the Blair govt to investigate the Royal Ulster Constabulary and made recommendations broadly consistent with the cession of Ulster to Eire.

PAUL, Czar (r. 1796-1801) and Alexander I, Czar (r. 1801-25) (*see* RUSSIA, PETRINE) **(1)** By the accession of the Czar PAUL in a court which had been French educated by his mother, the French Revolution had already seven years' old. The attraction and repulsion of the new French ideas upon opinion was very great and, whether in hostility or friendship, enmeshed Russia in European affairs. Paul, like other monarchs, originally saw the Revolution as a threat to thrones, and by 1798 was ready to fight France (*see* SECOND COALITION, WAR). The Second Coalition, however, was defeated and French diplomacy convinced him that France's objectives were limited. To Russian ambitions against Turkey, Austria's defeat was welcome and the Anglo-Turkish victories in Egypt were not. Similarly if French continental objectives really were limited, Russia might have more to fear from Britain's control over seaborne commerce. Paul abandoned the Coalition and, by forming the Second Armed Neutrality (1800) on the model and with the objectives of the First (*see* RUSSIA, PETRINE-8), changed sides. An eccentric tyrant, he was not mad, but he alienated too many people who, threatened with commercial ruin, found it convenient to say that he was. He was deposed with his son's consent, but strangled.

(2) ALEXANDER I, never forgetting the murder and its commercial background, was disinclined to defy Britain. The Armed Neutrality was dissolved (1801) but Russia remained informally and then from Oct. 1803 formally at peace with France. The P. of Amiens had come (Mar. 1802) and gone (May 1803). Alexander, who believed in liberalisation from above and in the limited French objectives, was rudely jolted by the French annexation of Hanover (June 1803), the kidnapping and murder of the D. of Enghien (Mar. 1804) and Bonaparte's imperial coronation (Dec.). The liberal Czar would oppose the upstart tyrant. The Anglo-Russian T. of St. Petersburg (Apr. 1805) was joined by Austria (Aug.) (*see* THIRD COALITION, WAR OF), but in Dec. 1806 he was entangled in a Turkish war as well.

(3) The Ts. of Tilsit (July 1807) left Russia free to despoil the Swedes and fight the Turks at the expense of joining Bonaparte's Continental System. By Sept. 1809 Alexander had annexed Finland (P. of Frederikshamn) and was making for the Balkans, but the son of the strangled Paul dared not stop the wholesale smuggling of British goods or their re-export to French Europe. By Feb. 1811 the Russians had captured a Turkish army and Belgrade and were secretly negotiating with Britain. Bonaparte's invasion (May 1812) saved the Turks, who escaped with the cession of Bessarabia (T. of Bucharest, May 1812). Its disastrous conclusion and the subsequent campaigns ended in Bonaparte's overthrow, the occupation of France, the Congress of Vienna and the Holy Alliance.

(4) Finland kept its free constitution. Bonapartist Poland (i.e. the Grand Duchy of Warsaw) had been under the *Code Napoleon*. The Baltic provinces were Germanised. To the liberalising Czar these areas were obviously readier for reform than Russia proper. In theory correct, the position was unsustainable with the Finnish frontier a day's easy walk from the capital. and occupying soldiers learning about self-reliance in post-war France. The Polish Constitution (Nov. 1815) made things worse. The Czar of All the Russias seemed to favour non-Russians more than his own people. The result was military debate and conspiracy as the troops came home and this opened the Czar's mind to Metternich's views on conspiracy and liberalism in Germany. He lent his prestige to Metternich's Conference System, especially after the risings of 1820. The liberal *Decembrist* conspiracy, the last of the Palace revolts, was brewing when he died.

PAUL III (Pope 1534-49). *See* COUNTER-REFORMATION.

PAUL IV (Pope 1555-9). *See* COUNTER-REFORMATION.

PAUL V (Pope 1605-21) (Camillo Borghese) was involved in a dispute with Venice between 1604 and 1606 over a new Venetian law of mortmain: in this he was committed to a doctrine of temporal supremacy. He could not retreat from this when James I imposed an oath of allegiance and the result was a division of opinion within the R. Catholic church on papal claims, not only in England and Venice but in France, the Empire and Spain. His attempts to unite Europe against the Turks were pressed against a background of mounting political and intellectual confusion and he pursued a cautiously unpartisan policy towards the R. Catholic powers at the beginning of the Thirty Years' War.

PAULET, PAWLET or POULLET (1) Sir John (fl. 1497-1501) commanded at the B. of Blackheath in 1497.

A. (2) Sir Amyas (?-1538) also a soldier was attainted after Buckingham's rebellion in 1483, but restored in 1485 and served in France under Henry VIII. His son **(3) Sir Hugh** (?-1572) was Capt. of Jersey from 1550, Vice-Pres. of Wales from 1559 and in 1562 adviser to Warwick at the occupation of Le Havre. His puritan son **(4) Sir Amias (?1536-88)** was ambassador to Paris from 1576 to 1579 and from 1585 Mary Q. of Scots keeper at Tutbury, Chartley and Fotheringhay. She failed to suborn his loyalty and he assisted in the interception of her correspondence which led to her condemnation. He refused, however, to murder her. In 1587 he was ambassador to the Netherlands.

B. The eldest son of (1). **(5) Sir William (?1485-1572) 1st M. of WINCHESTER (1551), 1st E. of WILTSHIRE (1550) Ld. ST. JOHN (1539)** was successively Comptroller (1532), Treasurer (1537), Chamberlain (1543) and Great Master (1545) of the Household. In 1546 he became Ld. Pres. and was nominated one of the regents in Henry VIII's will. Under Somerset he became Ld. Keeper, but later supported his overthrow in favour of Northumberland and in 1550 became Ld. Treasurer. His sense of realism led him to proclaim Mary against Lady Jane Grey and he survived Mary's reign and retained his office under Elizabeth to whom he advised moderation. Consequently he opposed Cecil and in 1569 tried unsuccessfully to get rid of him. His descendant **(6) John (1598-1675) 5th M.** kept open house for Q. Henrietta Maria at Basing (q.v.) and after Cromwell stormed it in Oct. 1645 he was long imprisoned and lost much property. His son **(7) Charles (?1625-99) 6th M. and 1st D. of BOLTON (1689),** an intriguing politician, supported the Whigs on the Exclusion Bill, feigned insanity under James II, welcomed William III and in 1692 caused Marlborough's dismissal by relating to the K. a private conversation which he had had with Marlborough. His son **(8) Charles (1661-1722) 2nd D.,** was already with William III in Holland in 1688 and having held minor offices was Ld. Chamberlain in 1715 and Ld. Lieut. of Ireland from 1717 to 1722. His son **(9) Charles (1685-1754) Ld. BASING (1717) and 3rd D.,** held a variety of minor but lucrative jobs until 1733 when Walpole turned him out for persistent opposition. His nephew **(10) Harry (1719-94) 6th D. (1765)** became an Admiral.

PAULINUS. *See* KENT, KINGDOM-4, MISSIONARIES TO BRITAIN AND IRELAND-4-5.

PAUNCEFOTE, Julian (1828-1902) 1st Ld. PAUNCEFOTE (1899) had high legal experience at Hong Kong and the Leeward Is. before becoming legal U-Sec. at the Foreign Office in 1876. He became permanent U-Sec. of State in 1882, a commissioner at Paris on the free navigation of the Suez Canal in 1885 and minister (later ambassador) to

986

the U.S.A. in 1889. As such he dealt successfully with many American continental problems, especially the Canadian seal fisheries in the Bering Sea (1892), the Venezuela-British Guiana boundary dispute (1895-9), the Spanish American War (1899) and in the Hay-Pauncefote T. of 1901 the Panama Canal passage rights.

PAVISE (Med). A large oblong shield supported by a prop and used as cover by archers.

PAWNBROKERS. *See* USURY.

PAX or TREUGA DEI. *See* TRUCE OF GOD.

PAXTON, Sir Joseph (1801-1865), head gardener at Chatsworth from 1826, became a close friend of his employer the D. of Devonshire. He proposed him as the architect for the Great Exhibition of 1851, for which he designed the Crystal Palace.

PAY BEDS amounting to about 10% of the total were made available in state hospitals under the National Health Acts for patients who paid for their treatment. Being contrary to contemporaneous socialist doctrine, the Wilson govt. sought to abolish them in 1978. This pitted trade unions against doctors and encouraged a boom in the creation of all-private hospitals.

PAYMASTER-GENERAL. (1) Under Charles II four offices were established to deal with cash flows generated by services. These were the Army Pay Office under the Paymaster (General) of the Land Forces (P-M-G), the Paymaster and Accountant of Chelsea Hospital, the Treasurer of the Royal Navy (T.R.N.) and the Treasurer of the Ordnance. Besides their salary (the P-M-Gs: £4,000 a year), the annual sum which was to pass through their hands was paid over to them in a lump sum at the beginning of each year and openly invested for their private profit. In addition the P-M-G received over 4% on foreign military subsidies. Since especially in wartime the sums involved were enormous, the profits of office were huge and scandalous. The D. of Chandos (P-M-G 1707-1712) built Canons from his profits: Henry Fox (1757-65) created the Holland fortune from his and speculated in HEIC and other stock. It took 17 years to separate the public from his private accounts. Both the P-M-G and the T.R.N. were, not surprisingly, much coveted political appointments often conferred upon statesmen of high influence. The elder Pitt (P-M-G 1746-55) refused his profits by paying them into the Treasury account at the Bank of England and this arrangement was made statutory by Burke's Civil List Act, 1782. The arrangement was not water tight, for money could still be drawn from the Bank on imprests and in 1798 a T.R.Ns. official had used such an imprest for private purposes. The result was Melville's impeachment in 1805. After these events these offices ceased to have political importance. They were statutorily amalgamated into a single Pay Office in 1835. The functions of the Accountant Gen. in Chancery were also transferred to it in 1872.

PAYMENT BY RESULTS 1862-97. An elementary school might claim from the govt. 4s. a year for each pupil with a good attendance record plus 8s. for each one who had passed an examination in the Three Rs. Instituted when it was hard to get parents to send their children to school at all, the system also provided an automatic corrective to the size of staffs, but it orientated Inspectors of Schools towards attendance matters for many years after the system was abandoned, and tended to keep general standards low.

P-CELTIC. *See* CELTS.

PEABODY, George (1795-1869) made a fortune in groceries in Massachusetts, came to England in 1827, began a banking business in London and founded the Peabody Housing Trust in 1843.

PEACE AND WAR, ACT anent, 1703 (Scot) laid down that after Q. Anne's death the crown was not to declare war or make treaties on behalf of Scotland without the consent of the Scottish parliament.

PEACE BALLOT (1934-5) was a nationwide questionnaire issued by the League of Nations Union to restore the prestige of the League shaken by failures in Manchuria, the resignation of Germany and the collapse of the disarmament conference. About 11½M people answered the questions: most favoured the League and disarmament: about 90% favoured economic and 7000 military sanctions against aggressors. The organisers considered that the results showed support for collective security through the League and Baldwin made this part of his election platform in 1935. In fact newspaper controversy confused the public mind and the platitudinous nature of the questions created inevitable if spineless replies.

PEACE, Charles (1832-79), first convicted of robbery in 1851, confessed to many burglaries and the murder in 1876 of a constable, for which another man had been convicted. He was hanged for a different murder.

PEACE CONFERENCES. *See* HAGUE CONFERENCES.

PEACHAM'S CASE (1615). Edmond Peacham (?-1616) wrote but did not publish a sermon against James I's policy, foretelling rebellion and the King's sudden death. He was tortured and indicted on the unpublished manuscript. James I, through Bacon, in order to found proceedings for treason, ordered the judges to consult him individually on the case. Sir Edward Coke, C.J., rejected the order. James then threatened to stop the proceedings by a writ *de non procedendo rege inconsulto* (Lat: concerning a stay of process where the King has not been consulted). The judges stated that even where the royal interests were involved and even in the King's Bench (which theoretically sat in the King's presence) the King could not thus interfere. Before the council, the puisne judges gave way but Coke stood his ground and was dismissed.

PEADA (?-655). *See* MERCIA-4; MIDDLE ANGLES.

PEARCE, Patrick (1879-1916) a barrister, was leader of the Dublin Easter Rising of Apr. 1916 and President of the Provisional Govt. then proclaimed. Forced to surrender, he was executed in May.

PEARL COAST. A stretch of the Spanish Main between Trinidad and Cumaná, formerly studded with valuable pearl fisheries attractive to buccaneers.

PEARSON, Charles Henry (1830-94), Prof. of Mod. History at King's Coll., London, migrated to Australia in 1871 and, as Victorian Min. of Education from 1886 to 1890 reorganised the local educational system. In 1893 he published his powerful and original *National Life and Character* which expressed his fear of coloured, especially Mongolian, economic competition and proved the inspiration of the White Australia policy.

PEARSON, Sir Cyril Arthur (1866-1921), Winchester educated hack journalist, struck out on his own and founded a series of independent journals such as the *Ladies Magazine* and *Short Stories* and in 1900 launched the *Daily Express*. In 1905 he bought the *Standard* and a majority holding in the *St. James's Gazette*. His eyesight had long been troubling him and by 1911 he was blind. He now turned his talents to promoting the cause of the blind and in 1915 founded the St. Dunstan's Charity, originally for blinded servicemen, which later developed important work and experiment in opthalmology.

PEARSON, John (1613-86), post-Restoration Master of Jesus Coll., Cambridge and Bp. of Chester from 1673, wrote his *Exposition of the Creed* in 1659. This was long one of the best and most learned works on Anglican theology.

PEARSON, Lester. *See* CANADA-30.

PEARSON, Weetman Dickinson (1856-1927), Ld. COWDRAY OF MIDHURST (1910), Vist. (1916) was a contractor who made money in Mexican oil, became Liberal M.P. for Colchester (1895-1910) and was one of the businessmen brought by Lloyd George into his coalition govt. as Pres. of the Air Board for 11 months in 1917.

PEASANTS' REVOLT (1381) (*see* RICHARD II) **(1)** took place in an atmosphere of wartime failure, trade stoppages and suspicion of the govt. dating back to the Good Parliament (1376). Since 1377 the additional war funds had come from hitherto untried poll taxes: that of 1377 was for 4d. a bead, that of 1379 was graduated. The Northampton parliament imposed a shilling. A poll tax requires a census and investigations into personal and sometimes embarrassingly private circumstances. Officials were high handed. There was, too, biblical authority against a census. The very means used to raise the tax drew attention to the govt's. shortcomings. The tax was inequitable as between tax payers and it was widely believed that the proceeds were being wasted or embezzled by rapacious courtiers. The peasantry, whose relative power in society had been growing, were not so downtrodden as to be incapable of self-help. Some ancient pre-conquest affiliations and loyalties still trans-cended the manor horizons and agitation and organisation had been in progress since the first poll tax. Naturally other grievances became involved: villeinage was in retreat and villeins wished to follow those who had already escaped from it. Attempts at wage restraint, embodied in the Statute of Labourers, had their counterpart in demands for a fair rent at 4d. an acre. There was a substratum of egalitarianism in church teaching and the poorer but relatively articulate lower clergy envied the wealth and pride of the ecclesiastical princes.

(2) It had been intended to collect two-thirds of the tax by Jan. 1389 and the rest by June, but resistance and evasion reduced the inflow to a trickle while the govt's. indebtedness grew. In desperation collectors were appointed in Feb. to account for the full amount by Apr. and in Mar. commissions of inquiry followed them up. This engendered rumours that an additional unparliamentary tax was being exacted. In a country ripe for insurrection, the first risings (June) were in Essex, followed by Kent where the peasants assembled at Dartford. They marched *via* Rochester to Maidstone where they chose Wat Tyler as their leader. He then moved on Canterbury where they released the priest John Ball from the Abp's. prison and with Tyler as their leader and Ball as their prophet they turned back and marched to Blackheath (London) in two days. The Essex men reached Mile End next day (12 June). On hearing of their approach Richard II, now fourteen, moved from Windsor straight to the Tower where he was the only courtier not in a panic. Since the rebels proclaimed their intention of saving the King from evil councillors and had been killing such magnates as they could seize, the contrast was not surprising. Two attempts at parley failed and the rebels entered the City and started fires while the govt. looked on helplessly. Eventually Richard took charge. He would meet the rebels as they demanded at Mile End while his councillors escaped from the Tower in other directions. This he did, but the escape attempt failed; the Essex rebels entered the Tower unopposed and beheaded Abp. Sudbury, Sir Robert Hales the Treasurer and others. Some pages got the queen mother to Baynards Castle. At Mile End Richard had been faced in an atmosphere of adulation with demands that traitors be handed over, that villeinage be abolished, labour regulated by contract and that land should be let at 4d. per acre. He seems to have been carried away: he promised that all should be free and might seek out traitors and bring them to him. They believed him and he perhaps believed himself. After wandering unscathed all day in the riotous streets he joined his mother at Baynards Castle. The Essex men started to leave for their villages. Next day he met Wat Tyler and the Kentish men at Smithfield. Tyler's demands included those of the Essex men and also, at John Ball's inspiration, equality of all under the King, the distribution of church property

and the abolition of all but one bishopric. He behaved with gross insolence. Richard replied that all would be granted and told him to go home. Tyler was suspicious and the King's party were irritated beyond endurance. The mayor, William Walworth, pulled him off his horse and a squire killed him. The peasants prepared to shoot, but Richard simply rode to them, declared himself their captain and told them to follow him north, which they did. Walworth then hastened into the City, raised a force of volunteers and followed them up. Richard prevented all violence, declared that he forgave the peasants and advised them to disperse to their homes. This ended the London episode. He knighted Walworth and two aldermen on the way back.

(3) The revolt had, of course, spread, mainly in the Fenland and East Anglia, but there were murders in Sussex and a craftsmen's rising against the City authorities at Winchester. Many Middlesex villages were plundered or burned. There were movements at Dunstable and in Leicestershire and isolated outbreaks as far north as the Wirral, York and the East Riding. The rebels' hatred was directed primarily against those who seemed to obstruct the peasants' advance towards happiness as they saw it. These were some particularly oppressive magnates, the great churchmen, the larger monasteries with their crowds of lazy monks who ate up the people's substance and the lawyers who entrapped the simple into bonds which they understood only when it was too late. Everywhere rolls, charters and documents were burned. Among the victims were two judges and many lesser lawyers. St. Alban's Abbey was occupied; St. Edmund's sacked. The abbeys at Huntingdon and Ramsey repelled the men of Ely, but at Cambridge the townsmen gutted Corpus Christi Coll. and destroyed the university's records. The most important movement was in east Norfolk, where, under Geoffrey Lister, the rebels had Norwich under their control for a week and, using it as a base, captured Yarmouth and Lowestoft.

(4) Once London was cleared the counter attack could be organised. The King's euphoria did not last and his friends and councillors changed his attitude. When peasant delegations came to claim the protection of the charters promised at Mile End they were repudiated. The energetic Bp. of Norwich led a force across Norfolk and reoccupied his see. By the end of July the revolt was over. Commissions under Sir Robert Tressilian were trying prisoners. Save in Hertfordshire and Essex the number punished was surprisingly small. No wholesale reprisals or torture was allowed; the ringleaders, such as John Ball, Jack Straw and Roger Grindcob were executed but many were acquitted or lightly treated. All proceedings were stayed at the end of Aug.

PEASE, Edward Reynolds (1857-1955) with Frank Podmore founded the Fabian Society in Jan. 1884. George Bernard Shaw and the Webbs soon joined it. The earlier meetings were held in his rooms and he acted as sec., with intermissions in 1889 and 1913 to 1915, until 1918. The Liberal Newcastle Programme (1891) was a Fabian draft; he helped to form the Labour Representation Committee and later sat for 14 years on the Executive Committee of the Labour Party. Though retiring, he was possibly the most influential individual in developing the distinctive character of British socialism.

PECKHAM or PECHAM, John (?-1292), academic Franciscan, studied at Oxford and Paris, where he attracted the favour of the queen, returned to Oxford in 1270, was elected Franciscan Provincial in 1276 and in 1278 was called to Rome as theological Reader in the papal palace schools. Nicholas III nominated him to Canterbury in 1279 and he went reluctantly. Like other friars he was a papalist. He began with a council at Reading (1279) which legislated against pluralism and he set about enforcing this and other regulations by visitation. Since some of the new rules were inconsistent with the customs of England, a dispute with Edward I followed. He met his match and changed emphasis to other fields. He upheld friars wherever possible against monks and the Franciscans against the Dominicans, whose doctrine on the nature of the eucharist he condemned at Oxford (1284). All this time he was writing poetry and scientific and theological treatises. He was also trying with Edward's blessing to extend his jurisdiction to Wales, where the division of the dioceses between warring lordships and principalities made great difficulties for the bishops. He became sympathetic with the Welsh and tried to mediate in the last war which ended in the destruction of Gwynedd, but the fundamental cleavage between Welsh and English social law and the obduracy of both sides in upholding their own earned him abuse from both. Crown necessities, especially in the Welsh war and church wealth led to demands for money; the discussion and grant of ecclesiastical taxes in diocesan and provincial assemblies led Peckham to organise the latter into the convocations of later times.

PECOCK, Reginald (?-1461) became Bp. of St. Asaph in 1444 and of Chichester in 1450. He wrote several works against the Lollards, notably the *New English Creed* and *The Repressor of Overmuch Wilting (= criticism) of the Clergy*, but his anti-Yorkist bias brought charges of heresy in 1457, based upon his belief that the Scripture was supplementary to a natural law implanted in men by God. He was deprived and confined at Thorney Abbey, where he died.

PECSAETAN were a small Mercian folk settled about the Derbyshire Peak in the late 6th Cent.

PECULIAR INSTITUTION, THE. American euphemism for slavery.

PECULIAR PEOPLE. A small sect, rejecting medical aid, founded at Plumstead in 1838.

PECULIARS are ecclesiastical areas not subject to the jurisdiction of a bishop. The Court of Peculiars is the Abp. of Canterbury's court for cases which would otherwise come before a diocesan consistory. In the Middle Ages the abbeys of St. Albans, Beverley, Bridgnorth, Dorchester, Evesham, Glastonbury, Peterborough, Ripon, Southwell, Selby and Waltham were ecclesiastical peculiars; Westminster Abbey, Windsor Chapel, Bocking and Battle were royal. They are to be distinguished from **diocesan enclaves** under the jurisdiction of a bishop who was not the bishop of the surrounding diocese. There were many of which the most important were the following:-

NAME	DIOCESE	SURROUNDING DIOCESE
Ruthin	Bangor	St Asaph
Llandinam	Bangor	St Asaph
Sevenoaks	Canterbury	Rochester
Howden	Durham	York
Northallerton	Durham	York
Forde	Exeter	Bath & Wells
Huntingdon	London	Lincoln
Magdalen & New Colleges Oxford	Winchester	Lincoln
Hexham	York	Durham

In the Scottish coastal area between the Forth and Aberdeen the sees of Aberdeen, St. Andrews, Brechin, Dunkeld and Dunblane were partially intermingled.

PEEBLES, BURGH and COUNTY (Scot.). A hilly pastoral border area which became effectively Scottish in about 1018. The small burgh was chartered in 1367.

PEEL, John (1776-1854) eponymous hero of a famous song composed impromptu by a friend, maintained a pack of hounds at Caldbeck (Cumb.) from 1804.

PEEL'S FIRST GOVT. (Dec. 1834-Apr. 1835) (twelve in cabinet under Sir Robert Peel) included Wellington and Lyndhurst. The party confusion and the circumstances of Melbourne's resignation in Nov. decided Peel to ask for a general election, which was remarkable for the issue of the novel Tamworth Manifesto and for public lack of interest. He failed to secure a majority in the Commons and, after six defeats there, resigned.

PEEL'S SECOND GOVT. (Sept. 1841-July 1846) (fourteen in cabinet under Sir Robert Peel with Ld. Lyndhurst, Ld. Chancellor; the E. of Aberdeen, Foreign Sec; Vist. Stanley, Sec. for War and Colonies; the D. of Wellington, without portfolio) **(1)** held office after the collapse of the Melbourne Govt. during a period of recession and world-wide ferment. The First Afghan War was coming to its disastrous end. There was war with China. Carlyle had just published *Heroes and Hero Worship. Punch* had lately been established. There was trouble in Ireland and the Chartists were on the move again. Peel, with his business and industrial background, dominated a cabinet and party in which the old landed interest was powerful and with which he was out of sympathy. It was, too, a cabinet of strong men: five of his colleagues had been or were to be prime ministers, four were to be Govs.-Gen. of India. He himself was sensitive, bad at conciliating colleagues, enormously industrious and ready to be enlightened. Beneath the administrative and financial reforms and trade expansion which he fostered, opposition within his own party steadily grew, inspired by the Young England group and Benjamin Disraeli.

(2) The Second Chartist petition, with over three million signatures, was brought to the Commons and rejected in May 1842 and by Aug. there were riots in the industrial north. Peel's courageous and far-sighted measures to alleviate the widespread underlying poverty were not readily intelligible to the politically uneducated. His first great budget of 1842 reduced customs duties on three quarters of the 1046 dutiable goods and made up the difference by reimposing for three years the income tax repealed in 1815. The settlement of the Canadian frontier in the Ashburton Treaty (Aug.) created peaceful conditions for the growing Anglo-U.S. trade. The P. of Nanking opened China to British commercial penetration. Peel's support for Ashley's Mines Bill ended the labour of women and children underground. Only in India was it impossible to pacify troubles, for the internal prestige and stability of the *Raj* demanded revenge on the Afghans and, ultimately, the conquest of Sind (Feb-Mar. 1843) which in S. Africa was matched by the proclamation of Natal as a colony.

(3) Fiscal and financial reform was carried on through successive budgets in which the surpluses from direct and increasing buoyancy of indirect taxes were used to remit indirect taxes and reduce the national debt. The Bank Charter Act, 1844, stabilised the paper currency and rising confidence made it possible to bring down the interest on govt. stocks. These were great gains and were accompanied by the Factory Act, 1844, which, by limiting the working hours of women and children, indirectly limited those of all textile workers. Such matter of fact measures did not attract the support of Victorian romantics. Worse still, the most powerful interests in Peel's party were being made to pay for them. In 1844 Disraeli published *Coningsby*, in 1845 *Sybil*, both hostile to Peel's point of view. Internal opposition was growing: overseas affairs were not altogether smooth. In 1844 came the first of the Maori wars. Solicitude for the route to the east forced the govt. in 1845 to join the French in an expedition against Madagascar and the confusion of Sikh politics inaugurated a drift towards war, which broke out in Dec.

(4) But the overseas troubles in Ireland with its 100 members in the Commons had counterparts; its huge English-owned estates precariously tenanted by its teeming poor, its minority Protestant church and its weak executive. Under the Melbourne Govt. Daniel O'Connell had temporarily given up his demand for repeal of the Union in return for specific concessions. Under Peel he had no such expectations and reverted to full-blooded Repealism. The small body of Irish electors, however, had lost interest in repeal and returned mainly moderate M.Ps. O'Connell took to the fields and organised mob demonstrations. In two years he had recreated for himself and the govt. a familiar dilemma. To go forward meant civil war: to go back meant loss of face and position. His nearest associates and the Young Ireland Group disliked his rabble-rousing smugness, his carelessness of system and finance and besides, the giant had feet of clay. His son mismanaged business whenever he was away and he himself had fallen in love with a *Protestant* linen draper. Peel made it clear that he would not repeal the Union or disestablish the Protestant church and that rebellion would be put down. He sent troops to Ireland and prohibited a great mass meeting at Clontarf (Oct. 1843). O'Connell stepped back from the brink and told his people to go home. They went.

(5) Peel's Irish and English views ran parallel. The line must be held; the existing interests must be upheld, but abuses and anomalies must be eliminated and new, unprotected interests conciliated. O'Connell was prosecuted on charges of sedition, but the Devon Commission was set up to investigate Irish rural problems; a Charitable Bequests Act facilitated the endowment of the R. Catholic church and the Ld. Lieut. was told to exercise his patronage in favour of R. Catholics. In following the two latter policies he was heading for a collision with the inherited Anglicanism of the 1689 revolution in his own party. Discomfort grew with his educational policy. Parliament had continued a small grant, made originally by the old Irish parliament, to the R. Catholic seminary at Maynooth. In 1831 Stanley had set up a board of education composed of Protestants and R. Catholics to administer elementary schools at which priests of either church could teach. Peel now proposed to set up on similar religious lines three colleges to cater for those between the elementary and the university levels and since R. Catholics could enter Trinity Coll., Dublin, but not secular scholarships or prizes, he proposed to enlarge Maynooth, increase its annual grant from £9,000 to £26,000 a year and break down its exclusive concentration on priestly training. These sensible and moderate proposals were made when O'Connell, convicted at his trial, had successfully appealed. They were a spark in a powder magazine. The already irritable English Anglican Tories denounced them as trucking with the Devil, the Papacy pronounced the colleges dangerous to faith and morals. Then, on the Devon Commission's report, Peel proposed that tenants should be entitled to compensation (limited to £5 per acre) for fencing, draining and building. Parliamentary opposition to this was equally factious and heated. He had to withdraw the bill.

(6) The disarray of the govt. party was due both to Peel's abrasive personality and to his being ahead of his time. The landowners had for some time been harassed by the Anti-Corn Law League. In 1845 Peel persuaded the Commons to continue the income tax for a further three years; by 1846 he had abolished customs duties on 605 dutiable articles. Free trade was in the air when the potato rot appeared, in 1845 first in England and parts of Europe and then worst of all in Ireland. The repeal of the Corn Laws became entangled in an emergency which they could hardly affect. After five months' furious debate (Feb-June 1846) Peel's bill was carried. The same night a combination of Irish, Whigs, radicals and discontented Tories led by Disraeli and Ld. George Bentinck, destroyed one of the pillars of Peel's Irish policy by throwing out his temporary Irish Coercion Bill. Four days later he resigned.

PEELER. After Sir Robert Peel, a policeman. 'Bobby" had the same origin.

PEENEMÜNDE. *See* ROCKETS.

PEEP O'DAY BOYS were Ulster Protestants who from 1785 searched R. Catholic houses for arms and were resisted by Catholic Defenders. They mostly joined the new Orange Society in 1795.

PEERAGE (pre-reform) is a dignity whose holder had the right to a summons to sit and vote in Parliament. The five DEGREES are Dukes (first created 1337), Marquesses (1385), Earls (of Danish origin), Viscounts (1440). Barons (of Norman origin). The five CLASSES are Peers of England and Scotland (created before 1707), of Great Britain (1707-1800), of Ireland (*see below*), of the United Kingdom (since 1800). Lds. of Appeal in Ordinary (since 1876) and Life Peers (since 1958) are barons and peers of the United Kingdom. METHOD OF CREATION. A writ issued to an individual created a barony if he took his seat. The first creation by letters patent was in 1388. Some earldoms and above have been created by charter, the Dukedom of Cornwall and a few other peerages by Act of Parliament. A bishop ranked above a Baron and an Abp. above a Duke, but neither were peers, though the Abs. of Canterbury and York, the Bps. of London, Durham and Winchester and 21 other English bishops in order of consecration are summoned to Parliament.

DESCENT. Hereditary peerages descend to heirs general unless limited to a male line, under the terms of a patent or specially remaindered by statute (*see* ABEYANCE).

SCOTTISH PEERS were represented in the House between 1707 and 1958 by 16 of their number elected for the duration of a parliament by those not otherwise entitled to be summoned. Since 1958 all Scottish peers were summoned. No new Scottish peerages could be created. IRISH PEERS were represented by 28 of their number similarly elected but for life. After 1800 one Irish peerage could be created for every three which became extinct until the number fell to 100, when one for one creations became permissible. Irish peers not entitled to sit in the Lords might be elected to the Commons.

PEERAGE BILL of 1719 represented a Whig attempt permanently to dominate Parliament by ensuring that the wholesale peerage creations of 1712 could not be repeated. It was to provide that the Crown could create peerages (a) for princes, (b) to replace extinct peerages and (c) six new peerages of Great Britain only. In addition 25 Scottish peerages, as hereditary lordships of Parliament, were to replace the 16 Scottish representative peers, but could be replaced on extinction only from other Scots peerages. The House of Lords at the time had 178 lay peers and 26 bishops. The bill, moved by Stanhope and Sunderland, passed the Lords but was withdrawn in the face of public clamour. Reintroduced in the second session, it again passed the Lords, but Walpole persuaded the Commons to throw it out, mainly by appealing to those who might want to become peers themselves. The incident forced Stanhope to recognise the danger of keeping Walpole out of office.

PEERAGE, PRIVILEGE OF. Since Magna Carta laid down that a man must be tried by his equals, it followed that a peer had to be tried by other peers. This privilege of peerage was restricted to lay peers (and after 1442 to peeresses) and to cases of felony. The trial was held before the House of Lords when Parliament was sitting and before a Court of the Ld. High Steward appointed for the occasion with generally, 23 other peers. The last case occurred in 1933. The privilege was abolished in 1948. Life Peers are exempt from jury service and free from arrest on civil process, but they cannot vote in parliamentary elections or sit in the House of Commons.

PEERS, PETITION OF THE (published 28 Aug. 1640). After the dissolution of the Short Parliament, Charles I was against calling another, but his opponents. Bedford, Brooke, Essex, Saye and Sele and Warwick, with

Hampden and Pym, drafted this petition which classified the troubles of the kingdom under seven heads and asserted that a parliament could cure them. To evade the argument Charles summoned the last *Magnum Concilium*.

PEGU. *See* BURMA.

PEINE FORTE ET DURE (Fr: strong and hard pain). A felon might be appealed (i.e. challenged to mortal combat) by his victim or the victim's family but if, as often happened, no such challenge was made, he might submit the issue of his guilt to the verdict of a petty jury. The more dangerous or powerful criminals learned to obstruct justice by omitting to plead 'guilty' or 'not guilty', thereby depriving the jury of the very issue which it was supposed to try. This was done by standing mute when arraigned. Cap 12 of the Stat. of Westminster 1275 enacted that *notorious* (or in the French *proclaimed*) felons of openly evil name who thus stood mute of malice should be kept in *strong and hard prison* until they pleaded and this was interpreted as being tied down without clothes or heat and with daily increasing weights being piled on the chest. Some preferred to die under this treatment, for without a verdict of guilty there could be no forfeiture of land or goods and the family would not be left destitute. The practice was abolished in 1712 by entering a plea of 'not guilty' on behalf of one held mute of malice.

PEISHWA or PESHWA. *See* MARATHAS.

PEKIN, SUMMER PALACES. *See* CHINA-23.

PELAGIUS (fl. 410) PELAGIANISM. Pelagius was a Briton who settled in Rome, fled to Carthage in 410 and to Jerusalem in 415. He denied the existence of Original Sin and so held that sin and redemption were the product of free will, though redemption was much assisted by divine grace. His doctrines were condemned by the Papacy and the Imperial Govt. at the instance of St. Augustine of Hippo and the African church in 418.

PELE CASTLES were simple northern refuges against cross-border raids. They mostly comprised a small square keep with a walled enclosure and dated from the 14th and 15th cents. Many examples survive, notably at Chipchase, Corbridge and Sizergh.

PELHAM and PELHAM-HOLLES. Several members of this wealthy and distinguished Sussex family have made an impact on English history. **(1) John (?-1429),** a servant of John of Gaunt and Henry IV became Constable of Pevensey in 1393 and from there gradually extended his property and influence throughout the rapes of Pevensey and Hastings and the Sussex ports. He was Steward of the Duchy of Lancaster from 1405 and Treasurer of England from 1412 to 1415 and occasionally an M.P. His rents in 1403 were as much as £870. **(2) Sir William (?-1587),** a soldier and military engineer, served against the French and in 1578 was sent to Ireland to defend the Pale. The council made him Lord Justice *ad interim*. Fearing Spanish intervention in the Desmond revolt, he devastated Munster to frustrate their possible landings. He left Ireland in 1581 and served as marshal under Leicester in the Low Countries (1586-7). His brother **(3) Sir Edmund or Edward (?-1606)** was C.B. of the Irish Exchequer from 1602. **(4) Thomas (?1650-1712) 1st Ld. PELHAM of LAUGHTON (1706)** was a Sussex M.P. from 1678 to 1706. His second wife was Grace Holles, sister of the last Holles D. of Newcastle and they had two sons **(5) Thomas (1693-1768) 1st Vist. HAUGHTON and E. of CLARE (1714), D. of NEWCASTLE (1715)** and **(6) Henry (?1695-1754).** These two, known to political historians as "the Pelbams" went into politics together, Thomas having succeeded to his uncle's vast lands and rents in 1711. They were connected by marriage to the Godolphin, Churchill, Manners, Walpole and Townshend families and Thomas gave Henry part of his estates in 1726.

Their rise began with Thomas' support for the Hanoverian succession. In 1717 Henry became an M.P. in the Townshend interest, already favoured by Thomas in the other House. They both rose with Walpole. Thomas being Ld. Chamberlain from 1717 to 1724 and then Sec. of State: Henry a Ld. of the Treasury from 1721 to 1724 and then Sec. at War. In 1730 Henry became Paymaster of the Forces. He supported Walpole's excise scheme of 1733 and saved him from a mob in the lobby of the House at that time. He remained completely loyal to him throughout, whereas Thomas, as Walpole's interest declined, began to connive with the opposition. His best adviser was Philip Yorke but, like Walpole, he was no war minister and when the Bourbon Wars began to go badly Walpole, as Chief Minister, naturally attracted most of the criticism.

George III liked the Pelhams, partly for their conversation and good manners, and as a result of the political intrigues surrounding Walpole's resignation and Wilmington's death, Henry became First Ld. of the Treasury. Thomas remained a Sec. of State, with Carteret as the other. The result (July 1743) was a govt. with three heads or none, but in Nov. 1744 the Pelhams got enough parliamentary and cabinet support to force the King to dismiss Carteret (now Granville). Their joint rule lasted until Henry's death. Sometimes called the **Broad Bottom** administration, the govt. included Tories besides Whigs It had to deal with the Wars of 1739-46 and the Jacobite Rebellion of 1745 and it used the political methods inherited from Walpole, nowadays stigmatised as corrupt, i.e. the manipulation of Commons votes by the award or withdrawal of offices. In view of the distractions of the period, the Pelhams' achievement was considerable. Henry reduced the cost of the national debt and, incidentally, taught the Pitts much about debt management. Though there were hardly any other permanently influential general measures (save the Calendar Act, 1751), the accumulation of local legislation greatly improved the roads, rivers and harbours and effected enclosures and drainage. The movement towards the Industrial Revolution was beginning.

Thomas succeeded Henry at the Treasury but needed a spokesman in the Commons. He did not want Fox or Pitt and tried to use the unfortunate Robinson. As a result Fox and Pitt combined to make Robinson's life intolerable and Thomas had, in 1755, to accept Fox. By now the Seven Years' War required a govt. of a different sort and he resigned in 1756 and after further confusion resumed as First Ld. (June 1757) but under Pitt's leadership. This was a successful rearrangement, for Thomas managed the finances and the votes upon which Pitt's war leadership was founded (*see* PITT, WILLIAM THE ELDER). He stayed in office until May 1762 when Bute forced him out. He returned as Rockingham's Ld. Privy Seal and as such advocated the repeal of the American Stamp Act. The Pelhams' reputation has suffered from the hostility and half truths in Horace Walpole's *Memoirs*. **(7) Thomas (1756-1826) 2nd E. of CHICHESTER (1805)** was Home Sec. under Addington from 1801 to 1803. *See also* WAR OF 1739-48-5, GEORGE II.

PELLEW (1) Sir Edward (1757-1833) 1st Vist. EXMOUTH (1816) entered the Navy in 1770 and was repeatedly promoted for bravery. In 1797 he commanded two frigates in a famous success against the French 74, *Droits de l'Homme*. In 1799 he quelled a mutiny at Bantry with his bare hands. By 1804 he was C-in-C East Indies where in 1807 he destroyed the Dutch fleet. In 1811 he became C-in-C Mediterranean and in 1816 he bombarded Algiers and destroyed most of the Barbary fleet. His brother **(2) Sir Israel (1758-1832)** also a naval officer, captured the French flagship at Trafalgar in 1805. Sir Edward's son **(3) Sir Fleetwood Broughton Reynolds (1789-1861)** also entered the Navy and became C-in-C East Indies and China in 1852. His heedless severity provoked mutinies and in 1853 he was retired.

PELLS of issue and receipt were Exchequer journals of daily receipts and expenditure commenced in about 1272 and kept until the end of the 18th Cent. The **Clerks of the Pells** were paid fees calculated on the amounts of the entries, but had to provide the staff to do the work. As business expanded their offices became highly lucrative sinecures, until abolished by Pitt the Younger.

PEMBA. See ZANZIBAR.

PEMBERTON, Sir Francis (1625-97), an independent spirited lawyer, was arrested by the House of Commons in 1675 for appearing as counsel against an M.P. and, as C.J. of the Common Pleas, was dismissed for impartiality in the proceedings against Ld. Russell in 1683. He led the defence of the Seven Bishops in 1689. The Commons imprisoned him in 1689 for his views, expressed in 1682, on parliamentary privilege.

PEMBROKE, Earldom. (1) The important palatinate comprising Pembrokeshire was originally conferred with Pevensey upon Gilbert fitz Gilbert of CLARE (?-1148) in 1138. His son Richard (called Strongbow) lost the earldom but gained the Irish lordships of Leinster and Wexford, originally by conquest and then by surrender to Henry II and regrant in 1172. **(2)** At Richard's death in 1176 the inheritance on both sides of the Irish Sea passed by marriage to the MARSHAL family who also had Norman properties. William the Marshal increased the accumulation and after his death in 1219 it passed in succession to each of his five sons. One of these added the Breton lordship of Dinan, another the whole of Glamorgan and Carmarthen. At the death of Anselm, the youngest, in 1245 the huge accumulation was divided between his five sisters or their issue, but the earldom reverted to the Crown. **(3) Joan,** a daughter of the youngest sister, was married to **William of VALENCE (?-1296),** Henry III's half brother in 1247. He used the style "E. of Pembroke". His son **Aymer** was created Earl but of a diminished if still large inheritance (comprising Pembroke and Goodrich) at his mother's death in 1307. He died suddenly in 1324. **(4)** His sister **Isabel** married **Laurence HASTINGS (?-1348)** who in 1339 was created Earl Palatine. The earldom remained in this family until the death of John Hastings in 1389. **(5)** The earldom was next successively created (1414) for **Humphrey D. of GLOUCESTER (1390-1447),** (1447) for **William de la POLE, D. of SUFFOLK,** who were always known by the higher title, for (1452) **Jasper TUDOR** who was attainted in 1461. In 1468 it was created for **William HERBERT** the elder, but his son **William** resigned it in 1479 and it was created for **Edward P. of Wales** and merged in the Crown when he was briefly King as **EDWARD V.** It was recreated as a marquessate for **Anne BOLEYN** in Sept. 1532, but was forfeited at her condemnation in 1536. The palatinate was suppressed in the same year under the Act of Union. **(6) William HERBERT** the elder had a mistress Maude Graunt and the earldom was recreated for the tenth time in 1551 for their grandson **Richard** in whose descendants it remains. The Herbert property, however, was mainly in Wiltshire, with some later-acquired Irish estates.

PEMBROKE-SHIRE (1) There is a stone circle in the shire, in which the materials for Stonehenge were quarried. The local culture was little affected by Roman influences, but in the 3rd cent. A.D. there was an Irish (Deisi) settlement and the area was an important centre of Celtic Christianity and a staging point on the sea passage between the Irish sea "province", Cornwall and Brittany. Pilgrims habitually moved to and from St. David's.

(2) In the 9th cent. the area was nominally under the princes of Deheubarth after the death of Rhodri the Great (877), but they could not prevent some Scandinavian settlement along the S. coast and it was in this area that Arnulf of Montgomery began by building Pembroke Castle (c. 1096) to establish an Anglo-Norman colony. In about 1100 William fitz Martin built another castle at

Newport for his lordship of Cemaes (Kemes) and between 1106 and 1156 there were also at least four introductions of Flemish settlers for whose protection castles were built at Haverfordwest and Tenby. This colonisation of the southern part or Englishry continued. The Welsh, who fought hard against it, were mostly driven away. There was more castle building at Manorbier, Carew, Narberth, Picton, Benton, Upton and Cilgerran. This, together with the new monasteries at Pembroke, Tenby and especially at Haverfordwest (Austin) and St. Dogmael's (Benedictine), altered the landscape which became and largely remains typically English. The northern part, the *patria* or Welshry, remained however an area of scattered farms under Welsh law. Sporadic feuding and fighting continued in the shire, which was a palatinate from 1138 throughout the Middle Ages.

(3) The Marcher jurisdictions were all abolished in 1536, except Cemaes which still had a theoretical but honorary existence to it were accommodated at 1980. The area was entirely agricultural until 1814, when a naval dockyard was opened in Milford Haven. This developed into the Town of Pembroke Dock. The dockyard, closed in 1926, was reopened in 1931 and after 1945 became a development area for shipbuilding, textiles and light engineering. The splendid and placid fjord of Milford Haven also attracted attention as an anchorage for oil tankers and from 1966 it became an oil terminal.

PENANG. See MALAYA; THAILAND.

PENAL SERVITUDE, for periods of three years and upwards, was substituted for transportation in 1853. The prisoners sentenced to it were accommodated at Dartmoor, Parkhurst and Peterhead, with Aylesbury for women and Broadmoor for criminal lunatics. It consisted of three stages: separate confinement, associated labour itself in three gradually improving stages and release on licence (*ticket of leave*). Trades were taught. The system was ended in 1949.

PENANCE and PENITENTIALS. Penance was anciently a kind of second baptism. A sinner requested penance; he was enrolled in the order of Penitents and excluded from communion until he had undergone a course of almsgiving, fasting, prayer and possibly other inflictions. At the end of the course, whose duration and severity depended on the nature of his sin, he was readmitted to communion but could never thenceforth be a soldier or marry. In practice, therefore, this form of penance could be administered only once in a lifetime and was soon being postponed until shortly before death.

The inconvenience led to the development by the Celtic churches, perhaps originating with St. Patrick, of a new system laid down in the *Penitentials,* which were manuals of instructions and prayers for use by priests. They were disseminated by English missionaries and the best known is the Penitential of Theodore of Tarsus, Abp. of Canterbury (c. 670). Enrolment and perpetual continence were omitted from these and absolution was withheld until the public penance had been completed. The practice slowly changed to absolution on confession *followed* by private penance and this was finally approved by the Lateran Council of 1215. See INDULGENCES.

PENDA (?-655) K. of MERCIA according to the *Anglo-Saxon Chronicle* from 626; according to Bede from 633. See MERCIA, KINGDOM OF.

PENDEREL, Richard (?-1672) with his four brothers were the Staffordshire yeomen who hid Charles II in an oak tree at Boscobel and risked their lives to secure his escape after the B. of Worcester. They were rewarded after the Restoration. They were the heroes of Oak Apple Day (29 May) and given a coat of arms displaying an oak and three crowns, which their descendants still use.

PENENDEN HEATH near Maidstone (Kent) was the regular assembly place for the Kentish Men and the Kent Shire Court. It was the scene of one *cause célèbre*, when

Lanfranc, Abp. of Canterbury, recovered lands belonging to the see which had been lost in the interval between Stigand's deposition and his own election, mainly to Odo of Bayeux, and also other properties belonging to the See of Rochester.

PENICILLIN was first observed as an inhibitor of *staphylococci* by Sir Alex Fleming in 1928. It was later refined by Sir Howard Florey and Prof. E. Chain and produced in quantity in the U.S.A. for treatment of casualties in World War II. The penicillin resistant staphylococci were mostly overcome by a variant called celbenin in 1960.

PEN[N]INGTON (1) Isaac (?1587-1661), Puritan fishmonger, was Sheriff and Alderman of London in 1638, M.P. in the Short and Long Parliaments and Ld. Mayor in the crucial years 1642 and 1643 when his influence secured the City's allegiance to Parliament and finance for its armies. A member of the 'court' which tried Charles I, he refused to sign the death warrant. He became a member of Cromwell's Council of State in 1648. His kinsman **(2) Sir John (?1568-1646)** served under Raleigh to the Orinoco in 1617 and under Mansell at Algiers in 1621. In 1625 he commanded a squadron lent to the French and in 1639 he held the Downs command when the Dutch seized the Spanish treasure fleet there. He was superseded by Parliament in 1642. The son of **(1)**, **(3)** Isaac (1616-79) became a Quaker in 1657 to his father's disgust, was imprisoned for refusing the oath of allegiance and suffered other persecutions. His son **(4) Edward (1667-1711)** migrated to Pennsylvania where he was Surveyor-Gen.

PENINSULA, THE, is Spain and Portugal.

PENINSULAR AND ORIENTAL STEAM NAVIGATION CO. (P. and O.) opened regular services to Spain and Portugal in 1837 (whence its house flag combined the Spanish and then Portuguese colours). It soon extended its mail and passenger service to India *via* Egypt and added "Oriental" to its name. In the absence of a canal there was a transhipment organisation of river steamers, rest-houses and camels. The mail service was extended to Australia in 1852 and then to China and Japan. When the Suez Canal opened in 1869 the passages became much faster. The **ORIENT LINE** was set up in 1878 as a rival, superseding the sailing traffic to Australasia. In 1914 the "P. and O." took over the British India Steam Navigation Co., while the Orient Line successively acquired the New Zealand Shipping, the Union Steamship and the General Steam Navigation Cos. as well as the Hain and the Strick Lines. The P. and O. and the Orient Line began to operate their fleets jointly in 1960.

PENINSULAR WAR 1807-14 (1) arose out of French moves to exclude British trade from Portugal and Italy. Immediately after the T. of Tilsit (July 1807) Bonaparte demanded the closure of Portuguese ports and the seizure of British ships and goods by 1st Sept. The Portuguese resisted. He moved troops under Junot to Bayonne and agreed with Spain (T. of Fontainebleau, Oct.) on a partition with Spanish help of Portugal, which was to serve three purposes, bearing in mind that British goods were flooding in through Etruria and the Papal State. Part of Portugal was to go as a bribe to Godoy, the Spanish Prime Minister; part to the Spanish King of Etruria, who was to give up his state and its important port of Leghorn to the Bonaparte Kingdom of Italy and the rest was to remain in French occupation. Thus Spain was to be entangled in Bonapartist policies and the obstacles to British trade extended in two directions. Junot marched across Spain and reached Lisbon at the end of Nov. A British fleet overawed a hostile Russian squadron (Russia having declared war in Oct.) and had two days previously escorted the Portuguese Regent away.

(2) The British had already issued the last of the 1807 Orders in Council; in Dec. Bonaparte replied with the Milan Decree and in Jan. 1808 Etruria was duly annexed. Smuggling on a vast scale, however, continued on the Peninsular and Papal coasts. Bonaparte decided upon subjugation. French troops, on the pretext of communications duties towards Portugal, were introduced into Spain and managed to gain access to Basque and Catalan fortresses. Quarrels within the Spanish royal family were exploited and pretexts were sought for action against Etruria's papal neighbour. By Apr., when the Spanish Kings Charles IV (father) and Ferdinand VII (son) had been summoned to Bayonne for a so-called arbitration, Rome had been occupied and French troops under Bonaparte's brother-in-law Murat were in Madrid. Spanish opinion, however, was taking instinctive alarm as the signs of treachery multiplied. Moreover French activities offended conservative, religious, nationalist and liberal inclinations. French lack of a commissariat brought rural seizures and requisitions and their soldiers made themselves too free with Spanish wine and women. Thus while Bonaparte was summoning his brother Joseph from Naples to the Spanish throne and offering Murat Joseph's throne to secure better Italian military arrangements, an insurrection broke out in Madrid (2 May 1808). Four days later, however, he forced the two Spanish Kings to resign their crowns into his hands and in June Spain and Naples were duly allotted their Bonaparte monarchs (The Bayonne Decree). The circumstances could hardly have been worse for Joseph.

(3) The British, who had by now exchanged Portuguese Madeira for the Azores and Goa (Apr. 1808), were suffering from the commercial war and were looking for S. American markets by way of relief. They were, however, entertaining approaches from opposed interests. The Spanish-American Francisco Miranda had urged them to help to destroy Spanish authority in the Americas, i.e. to continue to treat Spain as an enemy. By June 1808 an expeditionary force under Maj. Gen. Sir Arthur Wellesley (later Wellington) was ready in Ireland for this purpose when a Spanish patriotic delegation appeared begging help against the French, i.e. to treat Spain as a friend. The Madrid insurrection had been suppressed but the countryside was in arms. The British Govt's. first move was to) extract some Spanish troops under the M. de la Romana from Denmark (where they had been moved by Bonaparte) and land them in Spain (July). Then a Portuguese home delegation arrived with similar requests and reports. There was insurrection, massacre and counter-massacre throughout the Peninsula. Romana's army quickly attracted support and in July won a great victory in Andalusia at Baylen. It was decided to reject Miranda's advice and switch Wellesley's Irish force to Portugal, reinforce it and replace him by two more senior officers.

(4) Wellesley landed at the R. Mondego (Aug.) and in quick succession beat Junot at Roliça and Vimiero, just as his seniors appeared. Faced with disaster, Junot applied for an armistice to which the seniors, Burrard and Dalrymple, readily agreed. By the Convention of Cintra the French were evacuated from Portugal in British ships, to Wellesley's annoyance and London's fury. There followed recriminations and official inquiries, which kept all three generals in England while the Portuguese borrowed Sir William Beresford to train their troops. The Portuguese disaster had, however, shaken Bonaparte. The lustre of his glorious Erfurt Congress (Oct. 1808), which was designed especially to cajole the Czar into further co-operation, was slightly but distinctly dimmed. The Emperor's personal attention would, of course, set all to rights. Large armies under his personal direction took Madrid and swept south and west (Nov.). The Spanish patriotic *fortes* took refuge in Cadiz. A small British expedition, under Sir John Moore, landed at Lisbon and, marching north and east, cut into Bonaparte's communications with France. The French turned upon him and pursued him to Corunna, where he was killed while embarking the troops (Jan. 1809). This event gained time. The Austrians were on the move and Bonaparte with considerable forces had to leave Spain to deal with them before Portugal could be fully reoccupied. In Feb. they (see FRANCO-ALLIANCE, WAR OF) declared war. Thus when the British had concentrated their available troops at Lisbon and put Wellesley in charge of them, the French under Soult were no nearer than Oporto (Apr.).

(5) Wellesley lost no time. In May (when Bonaparte was checked outside Vienna at Aspern-Essling), he drove Soult from Oporto with fearful losses into Spain. In July he balanced Napoleon's hard-won victory at Wagram by a triumph over K. Joseph and Victor at Talavera. Wagram, however, meant that an overwhelming counter-offensive was inevitable and Wellesley anticipated it by the nine-month construction across the Lisbon peninsula of the immense triple Lines of Torres Vedras and (inspired by Spanish *guerrillas*) the rehabilitation of the ancient Portuguese irregular militia called the *Ordenanza*.

(6) The French counter-attack soon developed. A month after the P. of Vienna (Oct. 1809) the Spanish armies were scattered at Ocaña and Tamames. The ensuing bill was occasioned by winter and diplomacy, but Spanish guerrilla activity gathered momentum. In Apr. 1810 Bonaparte married the Habsburg Archduchess Marie-Louise. In June Masséna, his ablest general, was C-in-C in Spain and began his powerful advance against N. Portugal with superior numbers and equipment. He took Ciudad Rodrigo in July and Almeida, whose magazine blew up, in Aug. A few days later Wellesley (now Wellington) halted his orderly retreat to inflict a sharp defensive reverse upon him at Busaco (Sept.). He then continued southwards, while the *Ordenanza* scorched the earth and closed in behind Masséna. By Oct. the British were safely in the Lines of Torres Vedras and Masséna was starving and isolated outside. He retired in Nov. to Santarem where, continually harassed, he remained until his ruinous retreat past Ciudad Rodrigo to Salamanca during Mar. 1811. He had lost half his army. For this, however, the treasonable Spanish surrender of Badajoz on the southern frontier to Soult was some compensation.

(7) Just before the betrayal of Badajoz, a detached Anglo-Spanish army under Sir Thomas Graham had won an opportune victory at Barrosa. Beresford had been sent south to succour, but now to besiege, Badajoz. Consequently Wellington had, with a part of his army, to stave off a newly reinforced onslaught from Salamanca at Fuentes de Oñoro and Beresford won another desperate battle at Albuera (May 1811), famous for the almost insane bravery of the combatants. Thereafter Badajoz, Almeida and Ciudad Rodrigo were blockaded. Soult retired to Andalusia and Marmont superseded Masséna. There were widespread epidemics in the armies and fights round Almeida and Ciudad Rodrigo (Sept.).

(8) Between Sept. and Jan. 1812 the armies recovered their health, the Czar opened his territories to British trade and Bonaparte gathered his immense forces to coerce him into closing them again. Wellington, meanwhile, prepared the two strokes essential to the conquest of Spain. In eleven January days he stormed Ciudad Rodrigo, in Apr. Badajoz. With Portugal now safe, he advanced upon Salamanca and after a month's manoeuvring won a great victory over Marmont (July). He entered Madrid (Aug.) just before Bonaparte reached Moscow. The advance was continued, but ultimately stopped through exhaustion, bad weather and the ingenious French defence of Burgos Castle. The campaign ended with a successful retreat past Salamanca, while Bonaparte made his disastrous one from Moscow.

(9) Wellington now organised his great strategic surprise. He planned to outflank all the French-held river lines to the Pyrenees by a rapid march well to the north of them. This required pontoons and a new administrative and material base. He arranged with the War Office and the Navy that as soon as his march began, the bases would be shifted from Lisbon and Oporto to Santander on the B. of Biscay. The pontoons came forward in total secrecy. At the end of May 1813 two forces set out. The lesser, a powerful feint accompanied by Wellington, moved through Salamanca where he left it quietly and rode 50 miles north over to the greater which, using its pontoons, crossed the otherwise impassable R. Esla. In June the two forces met at Toro and continued north-about. K. Joseph, now in command, abandoned first Valladolid and then Burgos as the flank of each was turned. In a fortnight he was in Vitoria. On 21 June combined frontal and northerly flanking attacks destroyed his army, his reputation and his Kingdom. Bonaparte, desperately fighting in Saxony, disgraced him and handed over his charge to Soult.

(10) Loot and exhaustion prevented the pursuit after Vitoria, and Soult managed to constitute an army of sorts on the Pyrenean frontier. He still held Pamplona and San Sebastian and counter-attacked, vigorously if ineffectually, at Sorauren (July) at the mouth of the Roncevalles and against the Spaniards at San Marcial (together called the B. of the Pyrenees), after which it was possible for Wellington to attack San Sebastian. The terrible storm and sack of this town culminated in a conflagration which destroyed it (Aug.). The troops crossed the R. Bidassoa into France (Oct.) while Bonaparte was experiencing his essential defeat at Leipzig.

(11) It was now becoming politically important to keep the goodwill of the French inhabitants. The advance was delayed while vengeful Spanish troops were sent back and Pamplona taken. Immediately Wellington advanced to and defeated Soult on the R. Nivelle (Nov.) and then on the R. Nive. In Feb. and Mar. he successively turned his positions on the Joyeuse, the Bidouse and the Gave d'Oloron. The last battle took place at Orthez, just before Paris fell and Wellington was in Toulouse when he heard of Bonaparte's abdication (11 Apr.).

(12) In the Peninsular War the French casualties exceeded their losses in the Moscow campaign, while the long struggle absorbed far greater French resources of other kinds. The seven most distinguished Napoleonic marshals were defeated and the D. of Wellington's, and with it Britain's, prestige reached commanding heights.

PENJDEH or PANJDEH INCIDENT (Mar. 1885) arose out of the Russian annexation of Merv (1884) and southward pressure towards the Pamirs. British protests made the Russians accept a delimitation commission but they delayed while their troops pressed on and drove the Afghans from Penjdeh. The Gladstone Govt. got the Commons to vote a war credit, which brought the Russians to their senses. In the end they kept Penjdeh: the Afghans kept the more important Zulficar pass just to the south and in 1886 the frontier from the Oxus to the Pass was formally marked. See PAMIRS COMMISSION.

PENN (1) Sir William (1621-70), parliamentary admiral, served under Blake at Portland (Feb. 1653) and in the victories of 2 June and 29-31 July 1653. After a short time as Navy and Admiralty Commissioner he became Joint Commander with Gen. Robert VENABLES (1612-87) of a W. Indies expedition against Hispaniola which took Jamaica instead (May 1654). In the summer he offered his services to Charles II who suggested that he wait. He and Venables were briefly imprisoned on their return. Penn retired to his Moinster estates, continued to correspond with the royalists and was knighted and made a Commissioner of the Navy at the Restoration. In 1665 he served under the D. of York at the B. of Lowestoft, was censored and not employed again afloat. His famous son

(2) William (1644-1718) joined the Quakers in 1667 and wrote his *No Cross No Crown* (on self sacrifice) in 1669 in prison, whence he was released by his father's influence through the D. of York. He suffered much for the benefit of persecuted minorities but, maintaining his links with the Court, became a friend of Charles II. From him he secured the Pennsylvania charter and was in Pennsylvania until 1684 when he returned to exploit the Duke's apparent views on toleration. He remained on such close terms with the Duke as King that he was variously courted as a favourite and reviled as a suspected Jesuit, whereas his main concern was to alleviate the condition of the oppressed, including the fellows of Magdalen (Oxford) and the Seven Bishops. Consequently he was under suspicion at the Revolution and it was not until 1693 that, through the influence of Ld. Sidney, William III formally assured him of his good will. Until 1699 he was an itinerant preacher, but was in Pennsylvania until 1701 when he returned to oppose a bill to convert it into a crown colony. His subsequent adventures included a period in prison for debt; his career ended with a stroke in 1712. His proprietary rights in Pennsylvania descended to his sons and then to his grandsons **(3) John (1729-95)** and **(4) Richard (1736-1811)**. John was Deputy Gov. from 1763 to 1771, Richard from 1771 to 1773 and John again until 1778 when the American rebellion ended the family's rights.

PENNSYLVANIA was founded by William Penn (1644-1718) under a charter from Charles II in 1681 as a proprietary colony and named after his father. It was intended for persecuted nonconformists and his propaganda secured 3000 settlers in the first year. Under the charter he was proprietor and governor invested with executive and legislative power, but he formed a 'Free Society of Traders of Pennsylvania' and with Algernon Sydney framed a constitution and laws under which all modes of worship compatible with monotheism and religious liberty were free. He was in Pennsylvania from 1682 to 1684 where he made a treaty with the local Indians and laid out Philadelphia, the capital, on the grid plan which Wren had abortively proposed for London. The colony was steadily enlarged by a stream of English and Welsh Quakers who settled the eastern areas and by Germans (the so-called Pennsylvania Dutch) from 1683 in Germantown and the south-east. After 1718 the colonists were joined by Scots and Irish Jacobites who pushed the frontier westwards and provoked the hostility of the hitherto friendly Indians. These sought protection from the Ohio French, with the result that the earliest battle of the colonial part of the Seven Years' War took place at Pittsburgh in 1754. Quaker pacifism and German indifference divided the colony in the rebellion which owed much, however, to distinguished Pennsylvanians such as Benjamin Franklin and to partisanship in Philadelphia. Nevertheless the state was the second to ratify the Union Constitution (Dec. 1787) and Philadelphia was the political and financial capital of the U.S.A. from 1790 to 1800. Pennsylvania supported the Union during the American Civil War.

PENNY. *See* COINAGE-4 *et seq.*

PENNY BANKS were set up under nonconformist inspiration in the 1850s to make possible saving by those who had little to save, such as children and the poor. There were 200 by 1860. By 1904 they (save the Yorkshire Penny Bank) were the object of benevolent legislation in the Savings Bank Act.

PENRUDDOCKS RISING (1655), part of a wide royalist conspiracy against the Commonwealth, was begun by John Penruddock (1619-55) in Wiltshire in Mar. 1655. The insurgents were never more than 400 strong and after marching through Dorset to Devon surrendered at Cullompton. It provided the pretext for govt. by major generals.

PENRY, John, Printer. *See* MARPRELATE.

PENSHURST PLACE, of 14th cent. origin, was granted in 1552 to Sir Henry Sydney in whose family it has ever since remained.

PENSIONARY was the chief magistrate of a Dutch city. He combined the functions of legal adviser and chairman or mayor. From 1619 to 1794 each province had a pensionary who was its chief political minister. In Holland and Zeeland he was called the Grand Pensionary and that of Holland, because of its wealth and power, was generally the leading civil minister of the United Provinces, especially in the conduct of foreign affairs.

PENSION PARLIAMENT. *See* RESTORATION-8.

PENTICE COURT (at Chester). *See* COURT OF RECORD, BOROUGH.

PENTLAND RISING 1666 of Covenanters was provoked by Lauderdale's repressive and episcopalian policies. About 1000 men marched on Edinburgh and were defeated at Rullion Green.

PENTONVILLE PRISON (London) was built in 1840-2 as part of the scheme for abolishing transportation.

PENZANCE (Cornwall) (Corn = Holy Head, from a seaman's chapel on a headland S. of the harbour). The place was a hamlet until the 14th cent. when it developed a fishing industry and Edward III conferred a market charter (1332). It farmed its own customs under a charter of 1512, was incorporated as a borough with its own quarter sessions in 1614 and was a tin staple from 1663 to 1838. It was always the port for the Scilly Is.

PEOPLE, The. Largely unpolitical Sunday newspaper founded in 1881.

PEPYS, Samuel (1633-1703), whose celebrated Diary has tended to obscure his remarkable public gifts, became clerk of the Acts to the Navy Board by the influence of Edward Montague, his father's cousin, in 1660. Despite a crippling shortage of funds, he managed to keep the fleet supplied mainly by rooting out corruption. After the Dutch raided the Medway, efforts were made to make him a scapegoat but he justified his conduct in a famous speech in the Commons. In 1673 he became Sec. to the Admiralty and after the Third Dutch War (1672-4) he developed a systematic programme for developing the Navy. As an M.P. he was the recognised service spokesman. Unfortunately his association with the D. of York as Ld. High Admiral made him one of the many victims of the Popish Plot and he was imprisoned in 1680. The charges were dropped, but he remained unemployed until 1685 when he became Sec. for Admiralty Affairs and so remained under James II. During this time he reorganised naval administration, which had fallen into confusion. Between 1685 and 1687 he was again an M.P. He lost his job at the Revolution and retired. His shorthand Diary was never meant for public scrutiny and remains a peculiarly authentic source on the life and manners of the time. His administration of the Navy is sometimes considered to have founded its later greatness. He was also an active member of the Royal Society and for a while its President.

PEQUOD, an Algonqouan tribe, dominated the area between Rhode Is. and the Connecticut in the early 17th cent. Maltreatment by frontiersmen caused them to plan a general insurrection in 1637. This was anticipated by a colonists' expedition, which massacred them near New Haven.

PERAK. *See* MALAYA.

PERAMBULATION. A settled boundary, especially of the New Forest.

PERCEVAL (1) Richard (1550-1620) was pensioned in 1586 for deciphering Spanish secret documents, published an Anglo-Spanish dictionary in 1591, invested in the Virginian Co. and was M.P. for Richmond in 1604. His son **(2) Sir Philip (1605-47)** had much property in Ireland but lost it through the rebellion of 1641, disliked Charles I's Irish policy and in 1644 went over to the Parliament and became, as M.P. for Newport (Cornwall), a political supporter of the moderate Presbyterians. The independents drove him into retirement just before he died. The family's Irish fortunes were re-established in the next generations and Sir Philip's great-grandson **(3) Sir John (1683-1748) 1st Ld. (Ir.) PERCEVAL (1715), 1st Vist. (Ir.) (1723), 1st E. of EGMONT (1733)** was Irish M.P. for Cork from 1704 to 1715 and English M.P. for Harwich from 1727 to 1734. He revived the family interest in America by assisting James Oglethorpe's philanthropic foundation of Georgia. His son **(4) Sir John (1711-70) 2nd E., 1st Ld. LOVEL (1763)** was an Irish M.P. from 1731 to 1748 and an English one from 1741. He was for a while in 1748-9 a noisy rather than prominent figure in the faction gathered round Frederick P. of Wales and First Ld. of the Admiralty during the years of demobilisation 1763-6. His second son **(5) Spencer (1762-1812)** first came to notice as junior prosecuting counsel in the trials of Thomas Paine (1792) and Home Tooke (1794). He became a Pittite M.P. in 1796, Addington's Sol-Gen. in 1801 and Att-Gen. in 1802. As such he was virtually the only effective champion of the Addington Govt. in the Commons against such talent as Fox, Pitt and Windham. He remained in office when Pitt resumed power, but resigned when he died in 1806. In 1807 he became Chancellor of the Exchequer in the Portland Govt. and won a considerable reputation for his handling of the national debt, now inflated by the French wars, by converting much of the stock into terminable annuities. He became Prime Minister (*see* PERCEVAL'S GOVT. 1809-12) in 1809 and, so far (1995) the only English prime minister to have been assassinated, died at the House of Commons by the hand of a demented bankrupt called John Bellingham.

PERCEVAL GOVT. Oct. 1809-May 1812. (12 in Cabinet, 13 from Apr. 1812. The main personalities under Spencer Perceval were Ld. Eldon, Ld. Chancellor; the M. Wellesley, Foreign See; the E. of Liverpool, War and Colonies; and E. Camden, Ld. Pres.) (*See* PORTLAND GOVT. 1807-9).

(1) The Portland Govt's. sudden collapse left the King without any outstanding leader. He commissioned Perceval, who tried to form a coalition. His efforts failed, for Castlereagh and Canning had just gone and the Whigs under Lds. Grey and Grenville, mindful of the King's treatment of All-the-Talents, reasonably doubted their future in a govt. where others had the royal ear. So Perceval had to make do with the remains of the previous administration. Its parliamentary prospects were regarded as poor. The international circumstances were daunting (*see* FRANCO RUSSIAN-ALLIANCE. WAR OF; FRENCH COASTAL ANNEXATIONS). The country was in the grip of a war-induced economic and social crisis and Opposition cat-calls have echoed down to modern times. Perceval's excessive modesty, in juxtaposition with the flamboyant public characters of the time, seemed to reduce the standing of the Prime Minister to nothing.

(2) In fact the govt. was remarkably successful. Liverpool at the War Office more than maintained the supplies and reinforcements upon which the brilliant Peninsular campaigns depended and, despite recruitment difficulties and timber shortages, the Navy could be expanded to keep pace with the growing demands of economic and colonial war. By Aug. 1811, at the depth of the war's second economic crisis, Britain was supreme in Indonesia, India and the settlements *en route* to them and also in the Caribbean; and the economic depression, to which the U.S. Non-Intercourse Act contributed and which was really the equivalent of casualties in a winning battle, was damaging Napoleon more than Britain.

(3) Early in 1811, however, the political outlook was grim. The French annexation of Oldenburg (Jan.) closed Emden and deprived the British Baltic trade of many neutral carriers. After Princess Amelia's death, George III finally went mad and, in view of the P. of Wales'

opinions, the institution of a regency seemed to threaten the govt. The Russians took Belgrade, captured a Turkish army and yet again seemed to threaten the route to India. The U.S. renewed the Non-Intercourse Act. The Austrian govt's finances collapsed (Feb.). The unemployment of the depression was now compounded, especially in the north, by Luddite machine smashing. But the storm abated. The Prince, as regent, was less adventurous than the prince as critic and his powers were limited for the first year. He did not post his friends into power after all. Then Wellington began a victorious advance in the Peninsula. By the end of the year (when news of the capture of Java reached London) British diplomacy was reaching an understanding with the Czar, who was ready to break out of the Continental System (*see* MOSCOW DISASTER). Trade began to flow again, especially after the secret Russo-Swedish T. of Abo (Apr. 1812). By now the Napoleonic armies stood ready for the great offensive against Russia. Ten days before it began, Perceval was assassinated.

PERCIVAL, John (1834-1918), a follower of Arnold, became first headmaster of Clifton in 1862 and raised it to a high status. From 1879 to 1886 he was Pres. of Trinity Coll., Oxford and then became headmaster of Rugby. He became Bp. of Hereford in 1895.

PERCY (1) William of PERCI (in the Cotentin) (?-1096) migrated to England in 1067. With many estates in Lincolnshire and Yorkshire the family became locally prominent, its first seven heads being reckoned barons by tenure. The fifth **(2) Richard (?1170-1244)** and his nephew the sixth **(3) William (?1183-1245)** were involved in litigation from 1212 to 1234 over the estates. Richard was an executor of Magna Carta and then reduced Yorkshire to order in the interests of Louis the Dauphin, until persuaded to change sides in 1217. William supported K. John in 1215 but retired to his estates in 1216. His son, the seventh baron, was **(4) Henry (?1228-72)** after whom all the heads of the family but one until 1632 were named. He supported the Crown against Simon de Montfort and brought up his children in the circle of the Ld. Edward who, as Edward I, employed his martial son **(5) Henry (?-1315) 1st Ld. PERCY of ALNWICK** by writ, in the Scottish wars. He began to fortify Alnwick, which became and in 1996 was still the family seat, and he acquired by local standards much wealth, extensive lands and a following. For this reason and the military prowess of himself and his son, he and his successors were often Wardens of the East March and Alnwick the military H.Q. down to 1537. He was present at Bannockburn, but his son **(6) Henry (?1299-1352) 2nd Ld.** was the principal victor and captor of the Scottish King at Neville's Cross (1346). Henceforth for centuries the family enjoyed a semi-royal prestige in Northumberland. His younger son **(7) Thomas (1333-69)** was Bp. of Worcester from 1356. With the advent of **(8) Henry (1342-1408) 4th Ld. and 1st E. of NORTHUMBERLAND (1377)** his brother **(9) Thomas (?1344-1403) E. of WORCESTER (1397)** and **(10) Sir Henry ("Hotspur") (1364-1403)** (q.v.) son of **(8)** the Percys became involved as principals in national as well as border politics. Henry supported John of Gaunt, D. of Lancaster, in the political crises of the Good Parliament; Richard II sought their support and conferred their earldoms; and having made matrimonial and political alliances with the Mortimers, they acquired lordships and prestige in the Welsh Marches. They had, however, an important quarrel with Lancaster over Scottish policy. Lancaster proposed to acquire the Lothians by taking the homage of local Scottish nobles, led by George, E. of Dunbar. This would have prevented Percy expansion (and freebooting) into the Scottish march. Meanwhile they became uneasy over Richard II's activities and when the Lancastrian rebellion overthrew him, they supported it. They soon regretted it for Henry IV's border policy continued that of John of Gaunt. As a result they were drawn into the civil wars at the beginning of his reign. Hotspur was killed at the B. of Shrewsbury, Worcester executed immediately afterwards (1403) and Northumberland after activity in Wales and intrigues in France and Scotland was killed at Brambam Moor (1408), all his vast estates having already been seized. Hotspur's son **(11) Henry (1394-1455) 2nd E.** was, however, restored in 1416 by Henry V and became a member of the subsequent regency. He and his son **(12) Henry (1421-61) 3rd E.** were important Lancastrian supporters and at feud with the Nevilles. The father fell fighting the Yorkists in the first B. of St Albans. The son defeated and killed York at Wakefield (1460), defeated Warwick at St. Albans (1461) but was himself killed at Towton. Consequently his son **(13) Henry (1446-89) 4th E.** was imprisoned by Edward IV but restored in 1469 and later accepted considerable emoluments from Richard III. Captured at Bosworth, he made his peace with Henry VII. He was killed in a riot at Thirsk. His son **(14) Henry (1478-1537) 5th E.** strongly supported the Tudor monarchy, helping to suppress the Cornish rebels in 1497 and serving in France in 1513.

The institution of the Council of the North marked a stage in the family's decline from virtual independence, even though the Earl was a member (1522) and his son **(15) Henry (?1502-37) 6th E.** Warden of both Marches (1527) and Pres. (1536). The 6th E. was a reliable Tudor officer who, unlike his relatives, refused to help the Pilgrimage of Grace. His nephews **(16) Thomas (1528-72) 7th E.** and **(17) Henry (?1532-85) 8th E.**, were both R. Catholic sons of a Percy attainted under Henry VIII and both were successively involved in R. Catholic politics. Q. Mary I lifted the attainder for Thomas, who rebelled on Mary Q. of Scots behalf in 1569, fled to Scotland but was extradited and put to death. His brother did not support him, but was later implicated in intrigues with Mary which led to his arrest (1571) and release (1573) and further arrest (1584). He was found shot in the Tower. **(18) Henry (1564-1632) 9th E.,** called "The Wizard" because of his chemical experiments, was a Protestant soldier who served in Walcheren (1585-6), against the Armada (1588) and at Ostend (1600). His distant kinsman **(19) Thomas (1560-1605)** was a R. Catholic who was disappointed at the outcome of certain assurances of toleration given by James VI and I in 1602. He took a leading part in the Gunpowder Plot and was killed resisting arrest at Holbeach. The 9th E. was (probably wrongly) charged in this connection with misprision and was imprisoned until 1621. His son **(20) Algernon (1602-68) 10th E.** had served in the parliament of 1624-6. He became Admiral in 1626 and commander of the forces S. of the Trent in the Bishops' Wars. Becoming increasingly suspicious of the King, he thought that the constitutional balance had to be redressed and that this required adequate parliamentary force. Thus he served on the Committee of Safety and on the Committee of Both Kingdoms, but tried to effect reconciliations with the King and opposed efforts to bring him to trial. During the interregnum he remained aloof from public affairs but became a P.C. in 1660.

The direct line of the family ended with his grand-daughter **(21) Elizabeth (1667-1722)** who married Henry Cavendish, E. of Ogle in 1679 and then allied both her fortunes to the wealthy Thomas Thynne of Longleat (1648-82), a strong supporter of Shaftesbury during the Popish Plot. Before this marriage was consummated, she ran away and Thynne was murdered by Count Königsmarck, a rival suitor. She instantly gave her hand to Charles Seymour, D. of Somerset (1662-1748).

PERCY, Sir Henry (called HOTSPUR) (1364-1403) (see PERCY-10) an outstanding figure of the 14th cent. was knighted by Edward III in 1377 and in 1384 became with his father joint Warden of all the Scottish Marches and in 1385 Gov. of Berwick. His ruthless speed in countering Scottish border forays earned him his nickname from the Scots and established relative quiet, so that he was despatched to Calais in 1386 and commanded a fleet in the Channel in 1387. He became a Knight of the Garter in 1388. Later that year during a major Scottish raid, having successfully held Newcastle, Hotspur surprised the retreating Scots, killed the E. of Douglas their commander but was himself captured. Ransomed in 1389, he was confined as Warden to the West March and then sent as Gov. to Bordeaux (1393-5). Back again in the East March in 1398, he supported Henry of Bolingbroke (see HENRY IV) in July 1399 in overthrowing Richard II. He was then appointed to the Chief Justiceships of N. Wales, Cheshire and Flint, the Constableships of Conwy and Caernarvon Castles and the Shrievalties of Northumberland and Flint besides his other offices, and obtained only a personal grant of Anglesey and Beaumaris. The latter were inadequate to support the weight of the responsibilities; he quarrelled with the King, resigned his Welsh responsibilities (Sept. 1401) and in 1402 was required to surrender Anglesey to the P. of Wales and Roxburgh Castle to the Nevilles. In Sept. 1402 he won a great victory over another major Scots raiding army at Homildon Hill. The King now demanded not only the prisoners, especially the E. of Douglas, but refused to ransom Hotspur's cousin, Edmund Mortimer, then a prisoner of the Welsh rebel, Owain Glyndwr. There was an altercation between Henry and Hotspur in Parliament (Oct. 1402). Hotspur, Glyndwr and Edmund Mortimer, with the knowledge of Hotspur's father and his uncle, Thomas Percy, E. of Westmorland, conspired to replace Henry IV with Edmund Mortimer, for it was known that Richard II was dead. In July 1403 Hotspur suddenly moved from the Border by forced marches towards Wales to unite his troops with Owain's, but Henry moved even more quickly and intercepted him at Shrewsbury where, in a hard fought battle, the Percys were defeated and Hotspur killed.

PERCY, previously SMITHSON (1) Hugh (1715-86) 1st D. of NORTHUMBERLAND (1766) in 1740 married Elizabeth Seymour, heiress of the ancient Percy properties as grand-daughter of Elizabeth Percy, Duchess of Somerset (see PERCY-21). He was a friend of the E. of Bute, became a P.C. in 1763 and Ld. Lieut. of Middlesex and as such fell foul of John Wilkes. From 1778 to 1780 he was Master of the Horse under North. His grandson **(2) Algernon (1792-1865) 1st Ld. PRUDHOE (1816) 4th D. (1847),** First Ld. of the Admiralty just before the Crimean War and an Admiral in 1862, was a distinguished traveller and philologist who financed Lane's immense *Arabic Lexicon* (1863). See also SMITHSON.

PERIGUEUX. See AQUITAINE-9,11.

PERIM. A hot barren waterless island in the Straits of Bab-el-Mandeb, occupied by the British in 1857 as a re-insurance against the French construction of the Suez Canal at the other end of the Red Sea. A military presence and some coaling facilities were maintained there from Aden until Aden became independent.

PERJURY. See OATHS.

PERKINS, William (1558-1602) widely read Cambridge Calvinist theologian.

PERLIS. See MALAYA.

PERNICIOUS ARTICLE. Victorian circumlocution for opium, lucratively exported from India to China.

PERPENDICULAR. A late phase of English Gothic. See ARCHITECTURE.

PERPETUAL CURATE. See ADVOWSON.

PERPETUITIES. See CHARITIES; LAND TENURE – ENGLAND.

PERRERS or of WINDSOR, Alice (?-1400), a maid of honour to Philippa of Hainault, became Edward III's mistress before 1369; influential and hated, she was believed to have influenced judges in deciding cases and was banished in 1376 by the Good Parliament; she returned after the Black Prince died in the same year, but was again banished in 1377 by Richard II's first parliament. This sentence was finally revoked by the parliament of 1379.

PERROT (1) Sir John (?1527-92) was knighted at the Coronation of Edward VI and became Pres. of Munster in 1570 (*see* ELIZABETH I-17). He returned to England without leave in 1573 and was briefly in partial disgrace. After several sea appointments, however, he returned to Ireland as Ld. Deputy in 1584 when he fought the Macdonnells of Antrim and prevented further settlements of mainly Hebridean Scots in Ulster. His experiences led him to the conclusion that Ireland might be better governed with moderation, but the wars in Munster and the north had depopulated vast areas which the English extremists wished to colonise. The result was a collision between Perrot and the extremists of the Irish Parliament of 1585-6 and a trial of strength between him and the Chancellor, Abp. Loftus, who accused him of partiality to R. Catholics. His great achievement, however, was the Composition of land titles in Connaught and Clare which was designed to substitute common law land holdings for the rights of clan chieftainship. This was itself suspect to English planters in Dublin. Moreover, he quarrelled incessantly with his council. The anti-Catholic excitement of the Armada year (1588) ensured his recall. He was eventually convicted of High Treason but died. His son **(2) Sir James (1571-1637)** was M.P. for Haverfordwest in 1597, 1604 and 1614, for Pembrokeshire in 1624 and again for Haverfordwest in 1628.

PER SALTUM (Lat = with a Limp). A promotion from one degree or rank to another, omitting intermediate stages, e.g. from archdeacon to Pope.

PERSHING, Gen. John Joseph (1860-1948) commanded the U.S. Expeditionary Force to Europe in World War I.

PERSIA or IRAN (1) has its modern form from the reconquest from the White Sheep Turkomans by Ismail, a Shiite from the Caucasus. He ruled from 1502 to 1524 and his SAFAVID dynasty benefited, in Shah Tahmasp (r. 1524-76) and Abbas the Great (1587-1629), from long reigns. The Safavid state exercised a strong indirect leverage on the Mediterranean through its military, religious and economic conflicts with the Turks. After the defeat at Chaldiran (1514) by Selim the Grim. who captured Tabriz, Ismail moved his capital to Kazvin and Selim turned his attention to Egypt. which he seized in 1519. Sporadic frontier fighting continued, but the main Turkish effort was directed westwards against Christendom for over forty years. while Tahmasp consolidated his rule and established his northern frontier against the Uzbegs. At the end of his reign the Turks changed to eastward aggression and this provoked a major change in Persia. Abbas moved the capital to Isfahan. This magnificent city had a more central location, better suited for the western and Indian trade which Abbas hoped to develop *via* the Persian Gulf. In 1622, with English help he took Ormuz from the Portuguese: and Englishmen, especially the brothers Robert and Anthony Sherley, cast his guns and reorganised his army. The Turks meanwhile were moving through Iraq to the head of the Gulf taking, incidentally, the Iraqi Shiite pilgrimage centres. Abbas anticipated this by developing the great centre at Meshed to reduce the export of gold to Turkey, for there was a longstanding war of specie between the Turkish silver based economy and the Persian, based on gold.

The Safavid decline after Abbas' death was delayed by the Turkish switch to western aggression which ultimately failed before Vienna in 1683. The collapse was due to internal causes, notably disorders in Khorassan and an Afghan revolt (1717) which ended in the death of Shah Hoseyn at Isfahan in 1722. The Turks promptly seized the opportunity. They occupied the Christian vassal state of Armenia and the war, complicated by civil disturbances, lasted for 13 years, during which the last Safavids were deposed by Nadir Shah Afshar (r. 1736-47). He established a military supremacy, invaded India and sacked Delhi (1738-9). In truth his regime was a predatory militarism and when he was murdered, the main corps of the army dispersed and seized such provinces as they could (*see* AFGANISTAN). The country was divided among contending princes and tribes until 1789 when Aga Mohammed Khan established a new govt. and his KAJAR dynasty (1779-1925).

(2) The Turks being now in decline, the Kajar state was mainly important because it was in the collision area of the British approaching from the south-east and the Russians from the north-west. The Persians were not far behind the Russians in military technology at the beginning: they overran Armenia (which had become a Russian protectorate) in 1795. When Bonaparte invaded Egypt there was Anglo-French competition for a Persian alliance. The British commercial treaty of 1800 for excluding French influence and forces was not ratified because of the French surrender in Egypt, so in 1807 the French renewed their approaches, offered (T. of Finkenstein) an alliance against Russia and sent a military mission. The British hoped, by supplanting the French, to anticipate the Russians, but in the short term to prevent Russia from being distracted from the European conflict by a Caucasian sideshow. By 1810 British officers were reorganising the army, but in 1812 the Russians resumed the war and forced the cession of Georgia and some Caucasian provinces (T. of Gulistan 1813). Hence Fath Ali Shah (r. 1797-1834) was glad to accept the British T. of Tehran (1814) neutralising Persia in return for British military or financial help in case of attack. He was, however, aggressive in his designs: a Turkish War (1822-3) achieved little (T. of Erzenim 1823) and an attack on Russia ended disastrously with the loss of Erivan and Nakhichevan (T. of Turkmanchai 1828) and the establishment of influential Russians at the Shah's court. They now sought to turn the tables on the British by encouraging eastward warlike adventures. Persian armies invaded Khorassan (1830) and Afghanistan (1834), but British threats forced them to raise the siege of Herat (1837).

(3) The successor to Mohammed Shah (r. 1834-48) was Nasir-ud-Din (r. 1848-96) who was faced with religious revolts at Meshed and among the Baha'i and then, at Russian instigation (related to the Crimean War), seized Herat. The British naval reaction and the fall of Sevastopol forced him to retreat (T. of Paris 1857). Persia was now falling behind the industrialised countries and Nasir-ud-Din, who visited Europe three times, sought like his Turkish and Egyptian colleagues, to modernise his country so as to provide a modern army for its defence. Autocracy combined with foreign loans, banking concessions and Russian tariff agreements and a Russian-trained Cossack force, repeated in the Russian interest the British pattern of penetration in Egypt and similarly a liberal western orientated opinion was forming underneath. In 1896 the old despot was murdered and his successor Muzaffar-ud-Din (r. 1896-1907) inherited a deepening financial crisis and a series of political agitations which became increasingly hard to control. In 1898 the British refused to lend any money. In 1900 the Russians did, but insisted on securing their loan on the customs. The British prospected for oil (1901), the Russians built roads towards Isfahan (1902) and secured new tariffs, which obstructed the Gulf trade (1903). Riots and unrest forced the Shah to concede a constitution (1906). His successor Mohammed Ali (1907-9) meant to overthrow the constitution with his Cossacks. The alarmed British now intervened with a Convention which created northern and southern spheres of explosive influence, leaving a central zone where Britain and Russia might compete. The arrangement failed to pacify the country or limit Russian ambitions, for the Russians assisted the anti-constitutionalists and, incidentally, bombarded the shrines at Meshed, while the constitutionalists were actuated by western nationalist theories and Russophobia and led by claimants to the throne. Mohammed Ali was deposed in favour of a regency in 1909, but made dangerous efforts to regain his position in 1911. At the outbreak of World War I the disordered, only partly governed country proclaimed a neutrality which she could not enforce.

(4) In 1925 the Cossack Reza Khan overthrew the last Kajar, took the throne and by proclaiming himself Reza Shah Pahlevi (the name of the ancient classical language) appealed to secular traditionalist sentiment while instituting a gradual westernisation (by authoritarian means), which in part competed with British and Russian penetration. Logically enough he made tentative approaches to their German opponent. In 1941 the British occupied the south and the Russians the north to create a safe supply route to Russia, now desperate under German invasion. They deposed Reza, who was succeeded by his son Mohammed Reza Pahlevi.

(5) This Shah, with U.S. encouragement sought to restore the old Iranian glories by becoming a regional power and developing the monuments of the ancient civilisation such as Persepolis. This in practice involved westernisation, especially in education. The regime ran into violent Shia opposition on all counts directed from Paris by the exiled Ayatollah Khomeini. Persistent rioting drove the Shah from the country in 1979 and religious leaders proclaimed an Islamic republic. *See next entry* ABADAN; AZERBAIJAN.

PERSIAN GULF. The riparian lands being mostly arid, the Gulf was until 1908 solely a shipping route (disturbed by piracy) between India and the Orient and the Iraqi port of Basra. The Royal Navy patrolled it and built special ships for the purpose. It produced only things associated with shipping. Oil was found in the Persian part of the N.W. in 1908 but not developed until after World War I (*see* ABADAN). The coalescence of orderly states on both sides of the Gulf made a British naval presence unnecessary after 1972, but British officers continued to train the forces of Oman and the United Arab Emirates. After the Iranian convulsions Iraq attacked Iran but failed to win the expected quick victory and the war dominated the life of the region in the 1980s. In 1990 Iraq attacked and overran the oil state of Kuwait but her troops were driven out by a United Nations (largely Anglo-American) force under American command. This was prevented for political reasons by the U.S. govt. from achieving the total victory which was in its grasp. *See also* HORMUZ; OTTOMAN EMPIRE.

PERSONA GRATA (Lat = a welcome character). A diplomat who is acceptable to a government to whom he is about to be accredited.

PERSONAL PROPERTY. *See* REALTY.

PERTH, -SHIRE (Scot.), a part highland part lowland county from early times much given over to forest, sheep and cattle, with consequent cottage industries in weaving and dying. There is a Roman site at Ardoch and Perth itself is said to have been founded by Agricola in about A.D. 70 and occupied by the Romans until about 340. The area was the most important centre of Pictish culture and power. Scone being the ancient coronation place at which, after the union of the Picts and Scots, the Scottish Kings were also crowned until 1437. Culdees penetrated the Tay Valley and established with royal support an important community at Dunkeld and also the Forth where they founded Dunblane. Both houses became cathedrals when the Scots church was reorganised on Romanist principles. There was an important royal residence at Dunsinane. The highland parts were colonised by restless Scottish clans, notably Menzies, Robertsons, Macnabs and Macgregors, together with

Campbells and Murrays, so that the King's govt. was only directly effective in the low country. This, however, was a major objective of English strategic policy during the attempted English conquest: the town was intermittently occupied by the English from about 1292 until 1340.

There were signs of Lollardy in 1407 and the importance of the area in Scottish opinion was emphasised when John Knox used Perth as the centre from which to propagate his reformist doctrines (1559). The lowlands soon joined the reformers, but of the six major clans, only the Campbells and the Murrays eventually did so. This sharpened the endemic feuds and in all the disturbances down to 1745 the county remained divided and, since these were frequent, poor. The "pacifications" made things worse, but the Napoleonic Wars raised agricultural prices and brought some prosperity back. As a result the town began to prosper and in addition to distilleries and glass manufactures developed iron foundries.

PERTH, FIVE ARTICLES OF (1618) imposed on the Scots church by James I, required kneeling at communion, observance of Easter and Christmas. confirmation, private communion for the dying and child baptism. They were enacted by the Scots parliament in 1621.

PERTH, PACIFICATION OF. *See* JAMES VI-3.

PERTH, T. of (1266). *See* ALEXANDER III OF SCOTS; MAN-4

PERU, REPUBLIC (*see* BOLIVAR). Peruvian independence after 1824 brought constant civil disturbance and political instability: the wars had damaged the economy and devastated some areas and the dominant Spanish found it increasingly difficuilt to maintain their position without Spanish inspiration. The resulting weakness showed up and was compounded in the great Nitrate War of 1879-83, when the Peruvians suffered resounding defeat at the hands of the fewer but better organised Chileans: they had to cede the valuable nitrate province of Tarapacá. and two others, Tacna and Arica, remained in dispute until 1929. One important consequence was that British investment flowed into Chile rather than Peru before 1914 and American investment mostly stopped short at Panama and Venezuela. *See* ALPACA.

PERU – SPANISH. The Inca culture extended to modern Bolivia (then Upper Peru) and Ecuador. Consequently the Spanish vice-royalty of Peru, established at Lima in 1732, covered these areas and eventually all Spanish America. Lima was the seat of the Patriarchate, the centre of much Jesuit missionising and from 1551 of the Univ. of San Marcus, the first in the Americas. The city was magnificent and the viceroy's reigned there, generally for two years at a time, in splendour. The vice-royalty enjoyed a politically uneventful and superficially prosperous history based on silver mining, the coastal production of cotton, rice, sugar and tobacco and the cattle, vicuña and later sheep of the mountains. No naval establishment burdened the economy. which very occasionally suffered lucrative English raids (e.g. by Drake and Anson) and the only armed land force sufficed to escort labourers to and silver from the mines. An annual silver tribute was sent *via* Panama to Spain, but enough remained locally to maintain, by a steady but gentle inflation, three centuries of Spanish euphoria. The two clouds over this idyllic picture were the use of compulsory, if technically free, labour in the mines and a number of appalling epidemics, mainly influenza and smallpox, imported from Europe. Despite the efforts of the distant crown and the present church the rounding up, movement and use of Indians for mining was conducted with a cruel ferocity which depopulated many upland areas. The epidemics are believed to have destroyed about 75% of the people.

PERUZZI, with the Bardi and Frescobaldi of Florence and the Riccardi of Lucca were banking syndicates which, formed or operative by 1275, reached a leading position in the English wool trade under Edward I. By 1336 the

Peruzzi had 15 branches in England. Edward III borrowed heavily from them to supplement the shaky finances of the opening of the Hundred Years' War. The change from commercial to war finance ruined the Peruzzi who went bankrupt in 1343.

PESCADORES Is. *See* CHINA-31.

PESHAWAR (Pak.) with its busy markets and flourishing orchards at the foot of the Khyber Pass was for centuries the main staging point for trade between India and C. Asia. The Sikhs took it from the Afghans in 1833, the British from the Sikhs in 1849. They built cantonments, made it the capital of their N.W. Frontier Province and the base for their military and diplomatic dealings with the frontier tribes.

PÉTAIN, Henri Philippe (1856–1951) Marshal of France, was of peasant stock but by 1914 a corps commander. In 1916 he commanded the heroic defence of Verdun and in 1917 became C-in-C in the justified expectation that his popularity would raise the morale of the mutinous French troops. In 1934 he was Minister of War. In 1939 he became ambassador to Spain but in June 1940 he was brought back because of his rank to become Prime Minister and entrusted with negotiating with the victorious Germans. A month later, as Prime Minister of the part of France based on Vichy, he instituted a regime under which he became Head of State and which, despite its subjection to the Germans, was devoted to combatting the moral decadence which had led to the defeat. In 1942 the Germans occupied Vichy and Pétain, aged 86, became a puppet. In 1945 he was sentenced to death for treason, commuted to life imprisonment. He was a sample of the many Frenchmen who believed that the Germans had become invincible and that some form of passivity was the only hope of saving something from the wreck. In his case, he lent his prestige to his country's enemies and especially caused the Navy and some of the colonies to declare against his country's friends. It is doubtful if he fully understood these issues.

PETER of BLOIS (fl. 1160-1204) was tutor to William II of Sicily from 1167 to 1170 and after holding ecclesiastical posts in Paris, became Abp's. Chancellor at Canterbury in 1173. In 1190 he became Q. Eleanor's sec. and in 1192 a Deacon of London. He wrote some historically important *Epistolae* (Letters). His complete works were edited in 1848.

PETERBOROUGH CHRONICLE. See ANGLO-SAXON CHRONICLE.

PETER of COURTENAY (?-1183). *See* CAPETIANS, EARLY-14.

"PETERLOO MASSACRE" (July 1819). A meeting of 50,000-60,000 was convened at St. Peter's Fields, Manchester, to draw up a petition for reform and the organisers drilled many men, according to them, to ensure an orderly march, to their opponents, as some kind of military preparation. Henry (Orator) Hunt was invited to address the meeting. The magistrates found an orderly meeting carrying revolutionary banners and lost their nerve. They ordered Hunt's arrest. The Yeomanry who tried to reach him were pressed by the mob and drew sabres. Hussars came to their rescue and there was a general panic in which eleven people were killed and about 400 injured. The affair caused widespread indignation on the one hand, while strengthening the govt's. case for disciplinary legislation on the other (*see* SIX ACTS). In the long term the event hastened parliamentary reform.

PETER the HERMIT or LITTLE PETER (fl. 1100) an eloquent Picard preacher, led a largely German expedition of poor people as part of the First Crusade to disaster in Asia Minor in 1096. He reached Jerusalem with the main body in 1099 and returned to Europe in 1101.

PETERLEE. *See* NEW TOWNS.

PETER MARTYR of ANGHIERA (fl. 1510) wrote *De Orbe Novo* (Lat = The New World), a history of Spanish explorations, translated by Richard Eden as *Decades of the Newe World or West India* (1555) and edited by

Hakluyt (1587). It stimulated English explorers and contributed to their knowledge of navigation.

PETER of SAVOY (1203-68) Count of ROMONT, E. of RICHMOND (1240-66), Count and Marquis of SAVOY (1263), uncle of Eleanor and Sanchia of Provence wives of Henry III and Richard D. of Cornwall, began as a cleric in the Rhone Valley but resigned his orders (1232), married (1234) and acquired estates in Bugey which he enlarged. Henry III invited him to England in 1240 and gave him the castles of Lewes, Dover and Rochester, with the Shrievalty of Kent and the Wardenship of the Cinque Ports. Effectively he was Henry's gov. of the S.E., but in 1241 he surrendered Dover, accompanied Henry to Aquitaine and after negotiating the marriage between Sanchia and Richard, went on to Savoy with some of Henry's money and men to repel (with advantage) a Genevan attack on his lands. He returned in 1247. In 1249 he acquired Hastings and Tickhill and in 1250 he went with Simon de Montfort to Paris to negotiate an extension of the subsisting truce. He then continued to Savoy where he settled further troubles in his own favour. At this period he was on good terms with both Montfort and the King and in 1252 he acted as one of the arbitrators on Montfort's Gascon expenses. In 1254 he was with Henry in Aquitaine and employed in French and Papal negotiations over Sicily. As before, he went on to Savoy, where his brother Andrew IV had died and there was a civil war. Hence he was not available for English business until 1257 when he, Montfort and John Mansel were sent to negotiate yet again over the Sicilian business with the Pope. He agreed (no doubt from experience) with Montfort and his party that the royal ambitions were overstretching the national resources and was prepared to support some measure of control over the royal policy; Montfort's determination to make that control permanent, however, trenched on the rights of many great feudatories and so when in 1259 Montfort quarrelled with Richard of Clare, Peter abandoned him and became Henry's ablest adviser. He reconciled the King and the Ld. Edward (later Edward I) in 1260 and guided Henry in the gradual erosion of the Oxford Provisions. During this time he negotiated a marriage between Henry's daughter, Beatrice, and John of Brittany who reasserted, as a condition, his ancient claim to Peter's earldom. The claim was sidetracked by means of a pension which Henry paid.

Despite growing English xenophobia, Peter remained in Henry's service until civil wars broke out simultaneously in England and Savoy. The latter claimed his attention, for the Count was dying and Peter was the next in succession. He quickly returned to the Channel coast and raised troops for the Queen, but took no part in the war. His English properties, seized by the barons, were returned in 1266 but his earldom was conferred on John of Brittany. His absences prevented Henry from benefiting properly from his intelligence and energy.

PETER DES ROCHES (?-1238) and his "nephew" **PETER DES RIVAUX (?-c. 1258)** were Poitevins of knightly family. The elder was clerk and chamberlain to Richard I and by 1198 Prior of Loches. He negotiated the truce with France in 1202 and was nominated by K. John to the Bishopric of Winchester; when the chapter objected he was confirmed and consecrated by Innocent III (1205). He stood by John throughout the struggle with the barons, even during the interdict, and in 1213 became Justiciar in succession to Geoffrey fitz Peter. He excommunicated Louis the Dauphin when he invaded England in May 1216, crowned the child Henry III in Oct. and led a force against the Dauphin with distinction at the B. of Lincoln in 1217. Until William the Marshal died in 1219 he acted mainly as Henry III's personal guardian and it was at this period that his young "nephew" got to know the King well. After the Marshal's death the uncle shared control of the govt. with Hubert de Burgh and the legate Pandulf, but quarrelled with Hubert, against whom he led a baronial faction. In 1221 he was elected Abp. of Damietta and set out for Egypt but returned on hearing that Damietta had fallen to the Mamelukes and continued in the quarrels. Dismissed in 1227, he joined the Emperor Frederick II's crusade of 1228 as a negotiator with the Papacy, but returned in 1231 and when Hubert de Burgh was extruded from the Justiciarship, he got some appointments for his countrymen from the half Poitevin king. In particular the "nephew" was given charge of the royal household in 1232 and in July of that year he became sheriff in 21 counties and was put in charge of such sources of royal revenue as the demesnes and the Jews. In Jan. 1233 he was also made Treasurer and began an appraisal of local accounts. It was clear that a reorganisation of the tax system was in hand, supported by closer Exchequer control of the profits of the shires. Naturally there was opposition which took the form of an outcry against Poitevin influence. Moreover the murder of Richard the Marshal in Ireland created a fearful scandal which forced the King to repudiate his ministers. The two Peters were required to account for their stewardship and took sanctuary at Winchester. By the intervention of Abp. Edmund of Canterbury they were pardoned. The elder went abroad in 1235 and commanded a Papal army which beat the Romans at Viterbo. He returned quietly to his see in 1236. The younger retained some influence on financial policy until about 1241.

PETER'S PENCE or ROM[E]SCOT started as a contribution levied on every hearth in Wessex, probably by Ine (r. 689-726), to sustain pilgrims to Rome, especially at the English pilgrims' hospice or *Schola Saxonum* (Ut = Guild of the Saxons). It spread to the rest of England with the widening power of the Wessex Kings, but by Ethelwulf's time (r. 832-58) it had ceased to be appropriated to the pilgrim traffic and was offered for Roman church expenses and general papal use. The English example was followed by Charlemagne. Canute (1014-33) introduced it into Denmark: the Normans into Sicily (1059). By 1144 it was widespread in mainland Europe. Card. Nicholas Breakspear (later Pope Hadrian IV) introduced it into Scandinavia. It had become, as a permanent papal tax, the most regular source of papal income. Henry VIII stopped payments from England to Rome in 1534. Mary I resumed them in 1556 but Elizabeth I finally stopped them in 1558. By 1680, owing to wars and the Reformation, Peter's Pence had ceased to be the mainstay of papal finances, which depended until about 1850 mainly on income from the Papal States. When these finally ceased to exist in 1870, Peter's Pence was reorganised as a system of world-wide voluntary collections made in churches generally on St. Peter's Day (29 June) or an adjacent Sunday. In this form it is again the largest single source of the papal income.

PETER PINDAR, pseudonym of John Wolcott (1733-1812) the poet, satirist and public goad.

PETERBOROUGH, Es. of. *See* MORDAUNT-3 *et seq.*

PETERBOROUGH (A.S. MEDESHAMSTEDE = Marsh town). In 655 Peada, K. of Mercia founded the Benedictine Abbey of St. Peter in the fens. Accessible to raiders from the Wash, it was burned by the Danes in 870 and then refounded by Bp. Aethelwold of Winchester in 966. Between 992 and 1000 Abbot Coenwulf fortified it and the enclosure became known as St. Peter's burh. Some time before the Conquest, the Abbots acquired the lordship (with outfangthief) of Nassaburh and this developed into the liberty or Soke of Peterborough. In 1116 the abbey was accidentally burned down; mostly rebuilt on a large scale by 1200, the great facade was added in the 13th cent. The monastery could afford this, for it was endowed with properties outside the Soke and the retreat of the sea was making the Soke itself more profitable. The town was growing and c. 1265 Abbot Robert of Sutton chartered it under a high bailiff

appointed by the abbot, with a court leet which elected the other officers. This, with the Reformation substitution of the Chapter for the Abbot, remained the town constitution until 1790.

At the Dissolution part of the assets were used to endow the Henry VIII school and the abbey was made the cathedral of a new diocese abstracted from that of Lincoln (1541). In 1576 the bishop sold the Soke to Q. Elizabeth I; she granted it to Ld. Burghley whose descendants retained a strong, especially political interest in the area and in the election of its M.Ps., first instituted in 1547. This Cecil interest is said to have accounted for the Soke's separate Quarter Sessions and for its erection into an administrative county in 1888. In the meantime the cathedral suffered severely from the Commonwealth's men who, *inter alia*, melted the lead roof for ammunition and destroyed the outbuildings. Subsequently, however, the town and Soke became very prosperous through land reclamation, the development of an immense brick industry on the Fletton clays and the establishment of the railway works and junction in the 19th cent. These in their turn encouraged engineering and such agriculturally based industries as food processing and beet sugar production. The Soke was amalgamated with Huntingdonshire in 1974.

PETERHEAD (Scot.) was developed as a harbour between 1886 and 1958. The fisheries and dependent industries developed after 1945.

PETHICK, Emmeline (1867-1954) and **LAWRENCE, Frederick (1871-1961)** married as **PETHICK-LAWRENCE (1901), Ld. (1945).** He edited the *Echo* (1902-5) and the *Labour Record and Review* (1905-7). In 1906 she joined and became very active in the Suffragette movement and he was prominently identified with them too and imprisoned in connection with his activities in 1912. They set up and edited *Votes for Women* in 1913 and in 1914 she went to the U.S.A. to set up a sister movement. In World War I the Suffragettes attained their substantial ends peacefully and the Pethick-Lawrences turned to a new cause, namely Indian self-rule. He took part in the Round Table Conference of 1931. Accordingly he became Attlee's Sec. of State for India in 1945 and under him prepared the necessary legislation and action for Indian partition and independence.

PETILLIUS CEREALIS, QUINTUS. *See* BRITAIN, ROMAN-9,11.

PETITION MOVEMENT (1779-80), influenced by the Rev. John Jebb (1736-86) and the Rev. Christopher Wyvill (1740-1822), began in Yorkshire by complaints against high taxation and then against excessive executive power secured through venal borough M.Ps. who outvoted the solid, independent county M.Ps. especially from Yorkshire. Wyvill organised a petition to the House of Commons demanding stringent economy, an additional 100 county M.Ps. and annual parliaments. Jebb organised county committees to recruit support, and there was a fluctuating national committee representing 12 counties and 4 cities at the highest. It decided to oppose all candidates who would not support the petition and soon attracted the support of opposition figures such as the younger Pitt, Shelburne (extremist), Charles James Fox and Rockingham (moderate). After the petition was presented (Jan. 1780) Burke introduced five economy bills (Feb.) and the House passed Dunning's famous resolution in Mar. He followed it in Apr. by an attempt to prevent a dissolution until the grievances were remedied. This failed. At the height of the excitement the Gordon Riots provoked a reaction and the movement fizzled out.

PETITION OF RIGHT. Since no ruler could be impleaded in his own court, a subject who had a claim which would be sustainable if made against another subject petitioned the Crown setting out his claim. If the Crown, through the Att.-Gen. endorsed it ('Let right be done'), it was tried like an ordinary case and the Crown, though not bound by the result, generally abided by it as a matter of policy.

The Crown Proceedings Act, 1947, made it possible to sue the Crown but not the Sovereign personally and made most such petitions unnecessary.

PETITION OF RIGHT (1628) The *Five Knights* case raised simultaneously the issue of forced loans and arbitrary punishment. Parliament was summoned by Charles I for 1628 to provide money needed as a result of the Protestant disasters in the Thirty Years' War. In fact it debated forced loans, arbitrary punishment and denial of *habeas corpus* and bail, on the basis of a declaratory and explanatory bill, but Charles would not place his prerogative at Parliament's disposal. Thereupon Sir Edward Coke suggested a petition of right in concert with the Lords. This begins with a preamble in nine clauses. **(1)** and **(2)** asserted by reference to *De Tallagio non concedendo*, to a statute of 25 Edward III against forced loans and to uncited enactments against benevolences, the right of a subject not to be taxed without parliamentary authority and set out recent breaches of these rights, particularly the levying of forced loans. **(3)** and **(4)** cite *Magna Carta* and 28 Edward III as establishing the right of trial and due process in matters of life, limb, liberty or property and **(5)** sets out recent breaches of these rights and particular evasions of *habeas corpus* by a return of *per specialem mandatum regis* (detention by special command of the King). **(6)** asserts that illegal quartering of troops is taking place and **(7)**, **(8)** and **(9)** cite *Magna Carta* and other statutes against a growing practice of issuing commissions of martial law to supersede ordinary processes, whereby persons are punished against the law, or rightly punished by the wrong law, or go unpunished for want of enforcement of the right laws. Clause **(10)** prays that these abuses cease and clause **(11)** that they be not drawn into precedent and that all officials shall act only according to the laws and statutes. The record ends with the enacting formula proper to a petition. The King could not dissolve Parliament because he needed money and his attempts at ambiguous or evasive answers were repelled until eventually he assented. It was held not to have made new, but only to have confirmed old law. Two remonstrances by the Commons alone on general grievances and against unparliamentary tonnage and poundage led to a prorogation. The immediate effect was thus small. *See* CHARLES -7.

PETRARCH (Francesco PETRARCA) (1304-74), Italian poet and humanist, travelled widely in France, Italy and central Europe, often at the instance of admiring princely patrons and he was also a friend of such figures as Boccaccio and Cola di Rienzo. His poems made him famous but he also wrote many letters and treatises and so began the revival of interest in classical literature and style. He is commonly regarded as the father of Italian humanism. *See* RENAISSANCE-2.

PETRE, Edward (1631-99), Jesuit from 1652, was sent on mission to England in 1671, committed to prison in 1679, freed at the instance of James D. of York and summoned to court in 1683 where he was well known as James' confessor then and throughout his short reign, when he was also a privy councillor. He fled with James. Much of James' catholicing policy has, perhaps too plausibly, been attributed to his influence.

PETROGRAD (Russia) = St. Petersburg during World War I.

PETROL[EUM] or GAS[OLINE]. The substance and some of its by-products such as bitumen were known in Biblical times and hand-dug wells are recorded in Burma in the 13th cent. The first modern oil well was drilled (with a percussion drill) by Edwin Drake in Pennsylvania in 1859. By 1938 the significant oil producing countries were the U.S.A. and Venezuela in the Americas, Russia and Roumania in Europe, Persia in Asia, and Indonesia. The shortage of oil in Europe forced the Germans to rely mainly on a horse-drawn army: the absence of it in Japan

tempted the Japanese into their attack on Indonesia. The war boosted demand among the Allies and with intensive exploration the existing producers vastly increased production by the 1960s, while Kuwait, Bahrain and Saudi Arabia added to the Asian sources, Canada to the American and new ones were developed, notably in N. Africa and in the North Sea. The huge supplies which became available in their turn permitted a vast and expanding supply of motor vehicles and aircraft, which in many areas superseded the railways and were by 1995 polluting the urban and rural environments so that serious consideration was being given internationally to other, less finite and cleaner power.

PETT (1) Peter (?-1589) was master shipwright at Deptford from about 1550. His son **(2) Phineas (1570-1647)** was master shipwright at Deptford (1605) and then at Woolwich from 1607 and was a distinguished naval architect much ahead of his time. He became a Navy Commissioner in 1630. His son **(3) Peter (1610-?70)**, as Navy Commissioner at Chatham from 1648, was largely responsible for the material efficiency of the Navy during the Dutch wars, but was made a scapegoat for the Chatham disaster of 1667 and dismissed.

PETTY or NEW CUSTOM (1303) was imposed by the *Carta Mercatoria* on foreign merchants in return for trading rights and protection in the courts. It was an additional imposition at half the rate of the Great Custom, plus 2s. a tun, in lieu of prise, on wine, similar amounts on cloth and wax and 3d. in the pound by value on all other imports and exports. It was suspended in 1309-10 and 1311-22. The wool levy died out with the Tudor prohibition on exports: the others in 1672 save the wine duty which lasted until 1809. Between 1303 and 1307 they yielded between £9,000 and £10,000 a year.

PETTY and PETTY-FITZMAURICE (1) Sir William (1623-87), a friend of Hobbes, carried out the Down Survey of Irish forfeited lands for the Commonwealth. This was the first scientifically conducted large scale survey since Roman times. He was a founder member of the Royal Society and wrote economic treatises including his *Political Arithmetic* (1690) in which, using statistical methods, he demonstrated the mercantilist fallacy of treating the availability of bullion as the criterion of prosperity and argued that wealth is based on land and labour. His descendant through a daughter **(2) Sir William (1737-1805) 2nd E. of SHELBURNE (1761), 1st M. of LANSDOWNE (1784)** served under Granby in the army, refused political office under Bute, but briefly, in 1763, held the B. of Trade under Grenville in 1763 and then became a Pittite. He sensibly refused to countenance the govt's. and Court's hysterical reaction to Wilkes. His remarkable unpopularity in political circles dates from this period. In many ways an impeccable Whig, even a radical, his personality seems to have alienated many of his contemporaries. As Sec. of State he had framed plans for America but opposed govt. policy on the American colonies, helped to repeal the Stamp Act in 1766 and then, as Pitt's Sec. of State for the southern dept., initiated a policy of conciliation which brought him public obloquy and royal obstruction. He resigned from frustration in 1768 and became a principal and courageous critic of govt. policy and, when Chatham died in 1778, the acknowledged leader of the Pittites. In 1782 he became Home Sec. under Rockingham and then Prime Minister at the latter's death. Though opposed to American independence, he saw that the trend of the war was irreversible and concluded the Ts. of 1783 with France, Spain and the U.S.A. which recognised it. Although enjoying the royal confidence, he was overthrown by the voting strength of the Fox-North coalition of 1783 and never held office again. He was very rich, a splendid patron of art and learning and a great Irish landowner. His son **(3) Sir Henry (1780-1863) 3rd M. (1809)** was an M.P. from 1802 and as

Grenville's Chancellor of the Exchequer from 1806 to 1807, raised the property tax to finance the war and reduce borrowing. In opposition from 1807 to 1827 he championed, from the standpoint of moderate Whiggery, such liberal causes as anti-slavery and parliamentary reform. In 1827 he joined the Whig-Canningite govt. which he had done much to organise, as a member of the Cabinet without office. He resigned in 1828 but became Ld. Pres. (1830) in Grey's reformist govt. and then held various offices until 1841. He was Ld. John Russell's Ld. Pres. from 1846 to 1852 and remained, again without office, in the Cabinet until he died. His son **(4) Sir Henry Thomas (1816-66) 4th M.** was an M.P. from 1847 and a govt. whip under Ld. John Russell from 1847 to 1849. He was Palmerston's U. Sec. of State for Foreign Affairs from 1856 to 1858. His son **(5) Sir Henry Charles Keith (1845-1927) 5th M.**, was Liberal U. Sec. for War from 1872 to 1874 and for India in 1880 but resigned over Gladstone's Irish land policy. From 1883 to 1888 he was Gov.-Gen. of Canada. During his eventful tenure the Canadian Pacific Railway was completed and the Newfoundland Fisheries dispute settled and in 1885 he also had to deal with Louis Riel's rebellion. His vice-royalty of India (1888-94) was, save for currency problems, relatively uneventful. From 1895 to 1900 he was Sec. of State for War and carried through many of the essential military reforms advocated by Wolseley, but was unreasonably attacked for the defeats at the start of the Boer War. He was transferred to the Foreign Office where he negotiated the Japanese understandings and Alliance of 1902, dealt with the belligerent Americans over Venezuela and Alaska in 1903 and made the French Alliance of 1904. Immensely respected, he was by now the leader of a prominent body of Tory peers who hardly appreciated his hereditary streak of liberalism. When the Liberals came to power in 1906, he favoured Lords' reform rather than constant collisions with the Commons and sought to introduce a bill to that effect in the constitutional crisis of 1911, but finding that the govt. was determined to reduce the Lords' powers, abstained on the Parliament Bill. In 1914 he brought the Tories into support for the govt. in prosecuting the war and became a member of the War Cabinet (1915). In 1916 his championship of a compromise peace led to the break-up of the govt., ostracism by his own party and retirement.

PETTY BAG OFFICE was the main office on the Common Law side of the Chancery. So called because in proceedings involving the Crown the record was not enrolled but kept in a little bag. Its main function was to issue the original writs commencing actions in the courts. It became part of the High Court in 1873 and ceased to exist at the death of its last Clerk in 1888.

PEUTINGER MAP is a 13th cent. copy (at Vienna) of a 4th cent. diagram of the Roman road system. The British part is incomplete.

PEVENSEY (Lat = ANDERIDA) (Sussex) had a Saxon Shore fort built c. 270 and garrisoned until c. 400. The South Saxons took it in the 6th cent. and it became a port for the Wealden iron industry. William the Conqueror found it a convenient landing place in 1066 and Robert of Mortain built the castle soon afterwards. This was extended in the 13th cent. and the ruins are still to be seen on the beach. The port was a limb of the Cinque Port of Hastings. With the decline of the iron industry it fell into disuse and the population dwindled away. The corporation was dissolved in 1866.

PEVEREL (Lat = PIPERELUS) of LONDON or HATFIELD. A large Honour of the Peverel family entitled to the service of 70 knights plus some parts of them. It comprised 25 manors in Nottinghamshire, 10 in Derbyshire and others in 4 other counties.

PHANARIOTS were Greeks of Constantinople near the Orthodox Patriarchate at the Phanar. They acquired high influence and important privileges as tax farmers and diplomats under the Ottoman Empire and the governorships of the Roumanian principalities were reserved to them. At the height of their prosperity in the 18th cent. many were very rich. Their influence was ended in Mahmoud II's revolution in 1821. Their complaints at the loss of their status contributed to the flood of anti-Turkish feeling in Western Europe at that time.

PHARMACEUTICAL SOCIETY was established in London in 1841.

PHILBY, HAROLD or KIM (1912-88) intellectually arrogant Cambridge Communist, was recruited as a Russian agent perhaps in Vienna in 1933, and built up a cover as *Times* correspondent in Francoist Spain during the Spanish Civil War. He joined MI6 in 1941, side-tracked outstation warnings of impending Russian aggression in the post-War years, and in 1949, as liaison officer with the CIA and FBI warned various other traitors, including Burgess and Maclean, of contemplated investigation. He was interrogated in 1963 but continued until 1975 as an ostensible Middle Eastern journalist to pass information and betray British agents to the Russians. Faced with discovery, he fled to Moscow, where he lived in comfort as a major-general in the KGB.

PHILIP (1921-), D. of EDINBURGH (1947), son of the Danish P. Andrew of Greece, served as a British Naval officer in World War II. In 1947 he was naturalised British, took the name of MOUNTBATTEN, renounced his rights of succession in Denmark and Greece and married the Princess Elizabeth, later Q. Elizabeth II.

PHILIP I of FRANCE. *See* CAPETIANS, EARLY-11.

PHILIP II of SPAIN. *See* ELIZABETH I-5 *et seq*, MARY I; SPAIN.

PHILIP (II) AUGUSTUS, King of FRANCE (r. 1180-1223) (*see* LOUIS VII) **(1)** continued his father's policy of subverting the great fiefs with single-minded ferocity. This ruthless, profligate, unsociable man succeeded at fifteen in a court which was torn between the Champagne faction of his mother Alice and the Flemish relatives of his queen, Isabel of Hainault, whose uncle was the powerful Count of Flanders. The T. of Gisors (June 1180) brought peace with England and represented an advantage for Flanders; Alice fled to the court of Eleanor of Aquitaine; but the King did not intend to be ruled by his wife's Flemish uncle, who formed a hostile coalition of northern and eastern vassals including both Flanders and Champagne. The skirmishes and intrigues ended advantageously for Philip at the T. of Boves (July 1185) in which he received small areas and other rights from all his neighbours, including the reversion of Artois. He now copied his father by fomenting rebellion among Henry II's sons, while threatening the Plantagenet frontiers. By 1189 he had shaken the structure of Plantagenet rule; he had acquired Norman frontier territories and Berry. At the T. of Azay, Henry II renounced the Auvergne; he then died. Richard Coeur de Lion succeeded him.

(2) *Local Effects of the Third Crusade (1189-93).* The fall of Jerusalem to Saladin (Oct. 1187) fell on Western Europe like a thunderclap. The Papacy seized the leadership of opinion. It was inconceivable that a Crusade should not set out. The next two years were a period of diplomatic deck clearing. Pope and Emperor made peace and the Emperor set out in May 1189. Richard and Philip, who knew each other only too well, agreed to go simultaneously in July 1190, by which time the Emperor Frederick Barbarossa had been drowned in Cilicia. The Crusader princes thus had no lay overlord on earth. Their Palestinian quarrels and the death of the Count of Flanders created the pretext for Philip (in June 1191) to secure Artois and to support the intrigues of Richard's notorious brother, John. A month later Richard stormed Acre and in Sept. 1192 made a truce with Saladin to free himself for his own return. In Dec., on the way home, he was imprisoned by Leopold of Austria.

(3) Philip's opportunism was restrained by a public opinion hostile to attacks on a crusading hero. An invasion of Normandy was beaten off. John, however, prepared rebellion and did homage to Philip for the fiefs and perhaps for England. A *coup d'état* was projected with Flemish mercenaries, a French squadron and the help of the K. of Denmark, whose sister Ingeborg Philip married. His plans miscarried. Q. Eleanor and the English justiciars organised an efficient defence and blockaded John's castles. Philip found Ingeborg repellent and repudiated her. His Danish alliance had angered the Germans; he now angered the Danes and embroiled himself with the Papacy. The Emperor disliked his ambitions and released Richard for a large ransom. John fled to Paris. Richard reached England in 1194. He defeated Philip at Frèteval in July and though by the T. of Louviers (1195) he lost the Norman Vexin, he built the castle of Chateau Gaillard at Les Andelys as a base for its reconquest. In 1198 Philip attacked again and took Aumale. The church patched up a further peace, during which Richard was killed in a private foray.

(4) Richard had designated John as his universal heir, but the Aquitainians did homage to Eleanor, while Anjou, Maine and Touraine, following local custom and the leadership of William des Roches their Seneschal, accepted the young Arthur of Brittany, for whom Constance, his mother, claimed all the Angevin lands. Philip promptly accepted his homage and garrisoned the places which recognised him. Outside pressures reduced the warlike ardour of the contestants. John's ally, the Count of Flanders, made peace with Philip at Péronne (Jan. 1200) and John was having trouble with Llywellyn the Great in Wales. William des Roches deserted Philip and, playing a lone hand, took Arthur with him; above all, the repudiation of Ingeborg of Denmark had brought an interdict on Philip's dominions. Even then, at the P. of le Goulet (May 1200) he managed to secure important advantages.

(5) *Fourth Crusade and Plantaganet Collapse.* John's quarrel with the Lusignans precipitated the triumph of Philip's reign. He had insulted that family by marrying Isabel of Angouleme, fiancé of its Head. In the ensuing disorders he had mishandled the Poitevin baronage, who appealed to Philip. The latter summoned him before his court and issued a sentence of deprivation when he did not appear (Apr. 1202). At this point Baldwin of Flanders, Thibaut of Champagne, Louis of Blois and other important feudatories left for the Fourth Crusade. The deprivation weakened John, the departures freed Philip. He attacked Normandy and Poitou and invested Arthur with John's possessions other than Normandy, which he intended to annex. John, however, captured Arthur at Mirebeau (Aug. 1202) but murdered him in Apr. 1203. Philip thus had no claimant ready to hand, but the vassals of the great fiefs were revolted by John's cruelties. Philip saw an opportunity to raise his sights. William des Roches brought over the feudatories of the Loire: Maine came over too. They thought that they preferred Philip's orderly despotism to the confused tyranny of John. Safe from interference near Paris, Philip's invasion of Normandy went forward. Chateau Gaillard fell in Mar. 1204. Rouen surrendered at midsummer.

Neither side considered these events decisive, but each had his distractions. John invaded Poitou in 1206 but had his quarrel with the Papacy over Stephen Langton's election. In 1208 England was under interdict. In 1209 he was excommunicated. In 1209 also the northern French baronage, led by Simon de Montfort the Elder, began their freebooting Albigensian Crusade. Philip, who could have stopped it, took no direct part. The territories of John's ally, Raymond VI of Toulouse, were overrun.

(6) The tide of southern events freed Philip for northern affairs. English trade, especially in wool, was vital to Flanders and the Rhineland. John was seeking to build an alliance with the Guelph Emperor Otto IV, his nephew, and with the Flemish princes. Philip and the Pope supported Otto's rivals, particularly Philip of Swabia and the Hohenstaufens. The Swabian was murdered in 1208 just when Otto's fortunes were at a low ebb, but the French threat to Flanders was evident and the Flemings were increasingly persuaded to throw in their lot with John, against whom Philip was preparing invasion. Through the interdict of Mar. 1208 and his excommunication in Nov. 1209, John lost his best administrators (who were churchmen) but he pillaged the church and spent the immense proceeds in successful campaigns in Scotland, Wales (1209) and Ireland (1210). With his back safe he was ready to face Philip, who had achieved a similar condition, for in Nov. 1210 Pope Innocent III excommunicated Otto IV, and Philip made an alliance with his rival Frederick of Hohenstaufen. This alliance was directed against Otto and John. Its force was increased by Philip's contacts with German princes and English barons. The war was delayed. John, through Raoul of Dammartin, Count of Boulogne, built up Flemish alliances. Philip prepared an invasion of England. Innocent in 1212 released the Welsh from John's allegiance. John promptly came to terms with Innocent by submitting the Kingdom to the Papacy as a fief. The Pope could not countenance a French attack on his new vassal. Philip's project lost its sacred character. The forces were turned against Flanders and advanced to the Zwyn, near Bruges. The Count of Flanders appealed to John, whose fleet entered the Zwyn and destroyed Philip's armada at Damme (June 1213).

(7) John intended to press the advantage by a joint operation. Otto and the Flemings would attack from the north; the English from Poitou. In July 1213 his force was assembled at Portsmouth but the barons, led by the northerners, twice refused to move. This was doubly advantageous for Philip, for Simon de Montfort overthrew the armies of Toulouse and Aragon, John's southern allies, at Muret (Sept. 1213); the delay also helped Philip to organise and deprived his opponents of strategic surprise. The result was the decisive BOUVINES campaign which ended the reign of Otto IV, destroyed John's hopes of recovering Normandy, established the French monarchy and put John at the mercy of his baronage.

(8) *Southern Orientations.* But southern affairs now required royal intervention. The Lateran Council of 1215 deposed Raymond VI of Toulouse and gave his estates to Simon de Montfort. The new Count, Raymond VII, put up a powerful resistance, supported by the population. Philip had to intervene to preserve his suzerainty against Papal encroachment and, when Simon was killed besieging Toulouse (1218), to prevent defeat. An official expedition reached Languedoc in 1219 under the future Louis VIII. He bought out Simon's son Amaury with money provided by the Papacy. *See* LOUIS VIII AND CRUSADES.

PHILIP III, King of FRANCE (r. 1270-85), son of Louis IX. His reign was dominated by the international activities of Charles of Anjou (*for whom see also* LOUIS IX) and coincided almost exactly with the rest of Charles' life.

The Tunis fever killed not only Louis IX but his brother Alphonse (whose vast possessions, including Poitou and Toulouse, were at once incorporated in the royal domain) and Thibaut V of Champagne and Navarre. This led, after a series of tragedies, to the T. of Orleans (1275) between Philip and Blanche, Dowager Queen of Navarre. Her infant daughter, Jeanne, was to many a French prince and until she came of age, Philip was to govern Navarre, and Blanche Champagne. Blanche married Edmund of Lancaster, who then administered this wealthy fief. Meanwhile the nominal union of the Eastern and Western churches was proclaimed at the Council of

Lyons (July 1274) and the Pope, Gregory X, accordingly forbade an expedition which Charles of Anjou intended against Constantinople. In Sept. Gregory recognised Rudolf of Habsburg as King of the Romans, thus ending the imperial interregnum, encouraging the Italian Ghibellines and destroying the legal basis of Charles' imperial vicariate in Tuscany. Though shaken, Charles proceeded with his ambitions. In 1277 he purchased the crown of Jerusalem (i.e. Acre). In 1281 the election of a French Pope (Martin IV) seemed to offer him his opportunity and he assembled an armada at Messina for his long planned attack on the Greeks. This was frustrated by the Sicilian Vespers (Mar. 1282). This successful Sicilian revolt arose from an international conspiracy financed from Constantinople and involving Peter III of Aragon, who seized the island. Martin proclaimed a crusade against Aragon, which brought Philip III into the war. Jeanne of Navarre's minority was terminated and in 1284 she married the future Philip the Fair, who took over Navarre and Champagne. Charles was defeated in Italy and then died. Philip III's crusade met disaster in Aragon and he died too.

PHILIP (IV) THE FAIR, King of FRANCE (r. 1285-1314) (see PHILLIP III) **(1)** had just acquired Navarre and Champagne by marrying Jeanne of Navarre and he added them to the possessions of the French crown at his accession. His father's crusading force against Aragon had just met with disaster and his uncle Charles of Anjou's son, Charles of Salerno, was a prisoner of the Aragonese. On the other hand Peter III of Aragon had just died too.

(2) The diplomacy of Philip's early years was thus directed towards settling the wars of the Sicilian Vespers which, since they raged about the frontiers of Aquitaine, were important too to Edward I of England. Edward did homage to Philip for his Gallic territories in 1286 and the two Kings were on excellent personal terms. The T. of OLORON (Béarn) (1287) between Edward and Alfonso of Aragon provided for Charles' release, but was repudiated in 1288 by the new Pope (Nicholas IV). A supplementary treaty of guarantee was signed between Edward, Alfonso and a number of their towns at CANFRAN in 1289. Charles of Salerno was at last released to his Neapolitan territories. Peace between the Papacy and Aragon was signed at TARASCON in 1291.

(3) Philip's disputed character combined an element of personal asceticism with willingness to listen to opportunist Angevin advice. His reign saw notable legal developments but he failed to control the profligacy of his court, which was shaken by sensational scandals. He engineered a series of large scale breaches of good faith.

(4) The limit which the Ts. of Oloron and Tarascon had set to Angevin ambitions diverted them into other channels. There were two permanent sources of friction in Anglo-French relations. The one was the tendency of the *parlement* of Paris to extend the scope of its jurisdiction (and the income of its members) over Aquitaine. The other was endemic piracy in the Narrow Seas and Biscay, amounting often to private wars. Sometime, probably in 1292, when Edward I was involved in the problems of the Scottish succession, Philip resolved to attack Aquitaine. Norman piracy had been particularly destructive and a combined fleet of the Cinque Ports and Bayonne concentrated to make reprisals. They defeated the Normans at Cap St. Mathieu in May 1293 and went on to sack La Rochelle. Philip demanded damages and the surrender of the responsible Bayonnais. This amounted to an extension of his *parlements* jurisdiction from appeals to matters of first instance. Edward, with the Gascons, proposed negotiations. In Oct. Philip issued a citation to Edward to appear before the *parlement* and discussions followed, ostensibly to effect a settlement out of court, but actually to enable Philip to mobilise. When he was ready the Duchy was declared forfeit and invaded (May 1294) and

in July 1295 Philip signed the treaty with the Bruce faction in Scotland, later known as the AULD ALLIANCE. Edward replied by organising a league of Flemish and Rhenish princes.

(5) But Philip was now in financial and ecclesiastical difficulties. He had already begun to debase the gold coinage and was seeking to tax the clergy. In Feb. 1296 Boniface VIII by the Bull CLERICIS LAICOS forbade the clergy to pay. By 1297 both Philip and Edward (entangled in Scots and Welsh warfare) wanted a rest. A truce, several times renewed, left most of Aquitaine in Philip's hands and brought a lull in Flanders.

(6) The quarrel with the Papacy gathered heat. Philip taxed such clergy as he could reach and in 1301 arrested the Bp. of Pamiers for treason. Boniface VIII demanded his release and issued the Bull *Ausculta Fili* (Lat = pay attention my son) against the King: Philip forbade clerics to go to Rome without a licence and in Apr. 1302 summoned an assembly, the first STATES GENERAL to approve his measures. At this point, however, his policy went awry. The Flemish urban oligarchies, upon which he relied to dominate Flanders, were overthrown in a series of popular uprisings and the Flemish artisans defeated his armies at Courtrai (July 1302).

(7) In Nov. Boniface VIII issued the Bull UNAM SANCTAM claiming temporal supremacy for the Papacy. In Dec. Philip's troops were expelled by popular risings from Aquitaine. He made a virtue of necessity and the T. of Paris (May 1302) returned Aquitaine to Edward I. In June the States General reaffirmed its support against the Pope and in Sept. Philip's adviser, Gillaume de Nogaret, and the mercenary, Sciarra Colonna, seized Boniface at Anagni. They made no impression on Boniface who was rescued, but he died a month later, leaving an alarmed sacred college. There was a partial reconciliation with the new Pope, Benedict XI, and at the same time Philip's forces inflicted a series of defeats on the Flemings. Benedict, however, died in 1304. After a six months conclave thick with French intrigue, Bertrand de Got, Abp. of Bordeaux, was elected as Clement V and crowned in Philip's presence at Lyons (June 1305). Almost simultaneously the Flemish war was ended by the T. of Athis in which Philip secured Lille and Douai.

(8) Clement was willing to comply with at least some of Philip's wishes. In Feb. 1306 the Bull *Meruit* made of France an exception to the principle of *Unam Sanctam*. *Clericis Laicos*, on the other hand, could not be so easily withdrawn since it would rupture the confidence of the clergy in the Papacy. It was resolved, as a compromise, to sacrifice the order of the Knights Templar. They were rounded up on charges of witchcraft, heresy and sodomy in Sept. 1307 and their vast wealth went to lighten the deficits of Philip's finances. Clement fixed the Papal residence at Avignon in 1309 and issued his final condemnation of the Templars in 1312. *See* CAPETIANS, LAST.

PHILIP V, King of FRANCE (r. 1316-22). *See* CAPETIANS, LAST.

PHILIP VI of FRANCE (r. 1328-50) (*see* VALOIS) took the throne by virtue of the newly discovered Salic Law, in preference to Edward III of England. Temporarily the English claim could not be pressed and the reign opened with a great victory over the Flemish burghers at Cassel (Aug. 1328) and disputes with Robert of Artois, a convicted forger suspected of murdering his aunt to secure the county. This interest in Flemish affairs was unwelcome in England, whither Robert fled. Meanwhile armaments were being assembled for a crusade which never materialised; in 1337 the ships were transferred to the Channel and as England was at war with the Scots, support was offered to them. The time was one of agricultural depression, aggravated by debasement of the coinage. The cost of warlike preparation had to be met from new taxes, especially the salt tax (*gabelle*) which was to weigh heavily on the poor for four centuries. In 1337 Philip declared Aquitaine forfeit. The ensuing collision was in every way disastrous. The English destroyed the French fleet at Sluys in 1340 and the feudal army at Crécy in 1346. Calais fell in 1347. The prestige of the Valois dynasty, with its doubtful claim and the unpopularity of the govt. were severely damaged. Thereafter, until 1351, the Black Death destroyed some 30% of the people. For this, the distant acquisitions of Montpellier from the K. of Majorca (1346) and of Dauphine (1347) were small recompense. There was a perceptible movement, prompted not wholly by self interest, of allegiance to the English claimant. The situation was not retrieved by the accession of John II (the Good).

PHILIP of POITOU (?-1208). See DURHAM-4.

PHILIPPA of ENGLAND (fl. 1409). See BALTIC-13.

PHILIPPA of HAINAULT (?1314-69) was married to Edward III in 1328 as part of a bargain with the Count of Hainault to supply Q. Isabel and Mortimer with troops against Edward II. This disreputable deal turned into an affectionate and useful partnership. She was charming and popular. As a Fleming she was a good intermediary with the Flemings who, in 1340, accepted her as a hostage for Edward's local debts. According to Froissart, her sec. from 1361, she harangued the troops before the victory at Neville's Cross (Oct. 1346). She joined the army before Calais by Christmas and made the famous intercession for its Burghers (who were Flemings too) in Aug. 1347. This was not the only occasion when she intervened on behalf of the weak. Though constantly in financial difficulties, she was as constantly praised as a "full noble and good woman" and she apparently turned a blind eye to Edward's infidelities. His character deteriorated after she died.

PHILIPPA of LANCASTER. See AVIS-1

PHILLIP, Arthur (1738-1814). See AUSTRALIA-3.

PHILIPPINE Is. Magellan's ship touched them in 1521 and the Spaniards took possession in 1571 but never established full control, save in Luzon and the coastal areas of the other Is. In 1896 the so-called Young Filipino Party staged a rebellion and in 1898 welcomed the Americans, who sank the local Spanish squadron at the B. of Manila. They instituted a local assembly in 1907 but American protection and economic penetration was strong, and, as a result of an Americanised educational system by 1929 more Filipinos spoke English than any other language. In 1933 the U.S. Congress fixed 1943 as the date for independence. The Filipinos rejected this but in 1934 accepted a ten-year Commonwealth with U.S.A. retaining control of defence and foreign affairs. As a result American as well as Filipino troops were involved in the Japanese invasion (Dec 1941). The defence was driven into Bataan and surrendered in Apr. 1942. The I. of Corregidor in Manila harbour surrendered a month later, but Filipino politicians collaborated with the Japanese, while communist inspired rural guerrillas sprang up. These had a greater influence in Filipino politics than they had on the Japanese. The Americans under Gen. MacArthur began their reconquest from the Leyte Gulf in Oct. 1944 but after the early surrender of the atom-bombed Japanese, events moved quickly and in July 1946 the country became theoretically independent. In practice war damage forced the Filipinos to ask for financial assistance which was accorded on condition of an eight-year free trade period and twenty further years of limited tariffs, a 99-year lease for certain sovereign forces' bases and American equality with Filipinos in the exploitation of their natural resources. U.S. sovereignty in the bases was ended in 1979 but meanwhile under U.S. economic domination there was a long struggle between the corrupt and authoritarian Pres. Marcos and the Aquinos, in which Benigno Aquino was murdered and his widow Corazon elected, and Marcus was driven into exile (1987).

PHILIPPS. Three brothers **(1) Sir John Wynford (Bt.) (1860-1938) 1st Ld. St. DAVIDS (1908), Vist. (1918)** was a Liberal M.P. (1888-1908) and financier who was Chairman of 12 trust cos. and many S. American railway cos. **(2) Sir Ivor (1861-1945)** served in the Indian Army (1883-1903) and was a Liberal M.P. (1906-22). He served in the 38th Division in France (1915-16) and was made an Hon. Maj.-Gen. in 1916. He subsequently became a Co. Director. **(3) Owen Cosby (1863-1937) 1st Ld. KYLSANT (1923)** was a Liberal M.P. (1906-10) and a Tory M.P. (1916-22). He was a shipping magnate. He founded the King Line (1888), became a Director and then Chairman of the R. Mail Steam Packet Co. (1902) and in 1912 amalgamated the Pacific Steam Navigation and the Union Castle Steamship Cos. In 1924 he acquired the Belfast shipbuilders Harland and Wolff and in 1927 the White Star Line. From this pinnacle he fell in 1928 when sent to prison for publishing a false prospectus.

PHILOSOPHES. A number of 18th cent., mostly French, writers who were sceptical of received opinion and materialist and hedonist in practical philosophy. They included Condorcet, D'Alembert, Diderot and Helvétius, influenced the Czarina Catherine II, Frederick the Great of Prussia and the Emperor Joseph II and were popularised by Voltaire. They laid the foundation of the *Encyclopedie* and inspired Bentham.

PHIPPS (1) Sir William (1651-95), ship's carpenter and American privateer, made a fortune by raising a Spanish wreck in the Bahamas and in 1687 was knighted and became Provost-Marshal of New England. In 1690 he captured Port Royal from the French and in 1691 became a supine gov. of Massachusetts. Summoned home to account for his neglect, he died while proceedings were pending. A cousin **(2) Sir Constantine (1656-1723)**, Jacobite barrister, defended Sacheverell in 1710, was knighted and appointed Ld. Chancellor of Ireland. This politically controversial appointment lapsed at Q. Anne's death. He defended Atterbury in 1723. A descendant **(3) Constantine John (1744-92) 2nd Ld. MULGRAVE (1775)**, commanded the *Racehorse* on the 1773 Polar expedition, with Nelson under him as midshipman, and was able to assist his rise when he became a Ld. of the Admiralty in 1777. His brother **(4) Sir Henry (1755-1831) 3rd Ld., 1st E. of MULGRAVE of the second creation (1812)**, was a soldier and politician. He became a Westminster M.P. in 1784 and was one of Pitt's ablest military advisers. In 1804 he became Chancellor of the Duchy of Lancaster, Foreign Sec. in 1805 but resigned at Pitt's death (1806). In 1807 he became 1st Ld. of the Admiralty and was thus directly responsible for the second attack on Copenhagen, the maritime conduct of the Waleheren expedition and Collingwood's Mediterranean operations. He was promoted to Gen. in 1809 and became Master of the Ordnance in 1810, retaining his seat in Cabinet. He passed the mastership to Wellington in 1818 and retired in 1820. Besides his successful wartime political career he was a minor artist and a distinguished patron of the arts and furthered the fortunes of painters such as Benjamin Haydon, Sir David Wilkie and John Jackson. His son **(5) Sir Constantine Henry (1797-1863) 2nd E., 1st M. of NORMANBY of the second creation (1838)** became a Whig M.P. in 1818, was Gov. of Jamaica from 1832 to 1834 and was Ld. Privy Seal in Melbourne's Cabinet of 1834. He was a successful, if bitterly traduced, liberal Ld. Lieut. of Ireland from 1835 to 1839, mainly because he understood O'Connell. In 1839 he became Sec. of State for War and Colonies and then Home Sec. until 1841. Thereafter he was not active in home politics, but from 1846 to 1852 he was Ambassador to Paris and from 1854 to 1856 Minister in Florence. Both posts were politically strenuous and exposed him to criticism. His son **(6) Sir George (1819-90) 2nd M.,** became a Liberal M.P. in 1847 and was a whip from 1853 to 1858. He was then successively Lieut.-

Gov. of Nova Scotia (1858-63), Guy, of Queensland (1871-74) and Gov. of New Zealand (1874-79), where he and Sir George Grey constantly quarrelled. He was Gov. of Victoria from 1879 to 1884.

PHOENIX PARK (Dublin) was also the exercise ground of the Dublin garrison. In 1882 Ld. Frederick Cavendish and T. H. Burke were murdered there. The murderers were brought to justice in 1883, largely on the evidence of one James Carey who was himself murdered at sea in the same year. *See* GLADSTONE'S SECOND GOVT.-6.

PHONEY WAR. American journalistic name for the quiescent phase of World War II from 1st Sept. 1939 to 9th Apr. 1940. *See* WORLD WAR II-3.

PHOSGENE. *See* CHEMICAL WARFARE.

PHOTOGRAPHY. Both the camera principle and the darkening of silver nitrate by light were known in the 16th cent., but the earliest photographic print was made by Niepce in 1822, the first Daguerrotypes in 1829 and the first Calotypes in 1839. The collodion silver bromide emulsion was developed from about 1850 by the London sculptor Frederick Archer. Enlargers were introduced in the 1860s as were gelatin dry plates. Lewis Carroll and Julia Margaret Cameron (1815-79) were important popularisers of the art. In the late 1870s their manufacture was monopolised by British firms, notably Wratten & Wainwright. The roll film arrived in 1884 and in 1888 the New Yorker George Eastman produced his *Kodak No. 1,* the first camera for popular use. Panchromatic emulsions appeared in 1904, colour emulsions soon after, notably by the Lumière establishment in Paris, but the first practical colour film was *Kodachrome,* which appeared in 1935.

PHTHISIS. *See* TUBERCULOSIS

PHYSICIANS, ROYAL COLLEGES. (1) ENGLAND founded 1518, **(2) EDINBURGH** founded 1681, **(3) DUBLIN** founded 1654.

PHYSIOCRATS. A group of French political economists founded by François Quenay (1694-1774). They held that society should be governed according to an inherent natural order to be secured by safe property rights and freedom of work and exchange, but financed in return solely by taxes on land which, properly regarded, was the only source of wealth. In other words, the church and the aristocracy should pay for their position. Their most important convert was Jacques Turgot (1727-81), Controller-Gen. of France, whose unsurprising dismissal in 1776 ended viable attempts at financial reform. The physiocratic doctrines strongly influenced Adam Smith.

PIACENZA, COUNCIL of (1095). *See* CRUSADES-2.

PIASTRE was **(1)** the Spanish piece of eight or its equivalent, **(2)** 1/100th of a Turkish pound.

PICARD SWEAT. *See* SWEATING SICKNESS.

PICKETING, i.e. the patrolling of workplaces by strikers to prevent people getting to work, was a criminal conspiracy at Common Law if force was used. Merely persuasive picketing became lawful in 1875, but the distinction between persuasion and forcible obstruction was blurred. Peaceful picketing became lawful in 1906 but peacefulness and obstruction were equally hard to distinguish. In 1927 picketing became unlawful if in support of a strike itself unlawful. In 1945 all picketing became lawful. Under the Thatcher Govt. it became lawful in the 1927 sense, but the requirement that a strike should be authorised by ballot made more strikes unlawful.

PICKLE the spy. Alastair Ruadh Macdonell (?1724-?61) of Glengarry, a secret messenger of the Highland Chiefs to the Young Pretender, was captured by the English, put in the Tower and from 1749 to 1754 acted as a double agent with the Pretender.

PICQUIGNY, T. of (1475) provided that all differences between the Kings of England and France were to be settled by four arbitrators, namely the Abps. of Canterbury and Lyon, the Count of Dunois and the D. of Clarence. There was to be a seven-year truce and in due course a permanent treaty of friendship. On payment of 75,000 gold crowns the English army was to leave and Louis XI was to pay Edward IV a joint life annuity of 25,000. Q. Margaret, widow of Henry VI, was ransomed for 50,000.

PICTON, Sir Thomas (1758-1815), having taken a leading part in the capture of St. Lucia in 1796, was appointed Mil.-Gov. of the newly captured island of Trinidad in 1797 and Civil Gov. as well in 1801. Having sanctioned an application of torture, permissible under the Spanish law of the island, he was strongly attacked and it was proposed to associate two others with him in a commission of govt. He promptly resigned, returned home and was prosecuted unsuccessfully in the Kings Bench. By 1808 he had risen to Maj.-Gen. and in 1809 he took part in the capture and became Mil.-Gov. of Flushing, from which he was invalided home.

In 1810 he was sent to the Peninsula and took command of the 3rd Division. He fought Masséna at the Pass of St. Antonio in Sept. and was prominent in the pursuit of him from the Lines of Torres Vedras. He then fought at Fuentes d'Oñoro (May 1811) and in Mar. 1812 conducted the siege of Badajoz; he led the storm in person and was badly wounded but soon returned to the army and distinguished himself at Vitoria (1813). In the Waterloo campaign he fought at Quatre Bras and was killed leading a charge at Waterloo itself. An eccentric and foul-mouthed man who went into battle in a top hat, he was always controversial and did not receive the recognition which his abilities deserved.

PICTS (poss: from Lat: *PICTI* **= painted, i.e. tattoed people).** A nation occupying the eastern half of Scotland from the Pentland (i.e. Pictland) Firth to the R. Forth and originating in two Iron Age migrations respectively N. and S. of the Moray Firth. Later the division between the two was the Mounth. The Romans called some of them Caledonians. They spoke a P-Celtic mixed with an indigenous Bronze age speech. Inscriptions but no literature have survived, and their internal history is almost unknown. Their kings had a matrilineal rule of succession which facilitated rule by strangers. In the 4th-5th cents, they replaced the Votadini in the Lothians but they were also pirates and some of their raids on the Romano-Britons were seaborne. Their 6th cent. K. Brude mac Maelchon ruled the Northern Picts from a stronghold near Inverness, where St Columba visited him and obtained the grant of Iona, and in 685 the Picts, perhaps unitedly, defeated and killed the Northumbrian K. Ecgfrith at Dunnichen Moss near Forfar. The southern Picts, however, dissolved into four states namely **(a) Atholl** or **Athfotla,** with a centre at Dunkeld and then at Scone. **(b) Circinn** (centre Forfar) in Angus, Kincardine and the Mearns. **(c) Fife** with most of Perthshire (Kilrymont, later called St Andrew's) and **(d) Fortrenn** (no fixed capital) on the upper Earn and Forth. There was territorial and matrimonial interpenetration between the Picts and the Scots from Ireland, but fusion was forced on both sides by the Viking invasions, the Picts having been much reduced by the plagues of 664-84. They became thin on the ground and by the political union under K. Kenneth mac Alpine of Scots (843), even their language was falling into disuse. *See* DALRIADA, SCOTS OR ALBAN KINGS.

PICTS' HOUSES. *See* WEEMS.

PIDGIN (Chinese corruption of English 'business'). PIDGIN ENGLISH was a jargon of mostly English words, corrupted in pronunciation and arranged according to Chinese syntax, used in dealings between Chinese and Westerners.

PIEDMONT. *See* SAVOY.

PIEPOWDER COURT was a summary court for dealing with disputes between itinerant ('dusty-footed' = *pieds poudreux*) merchants at markets and fairs.

PIERREPONT (1) Robert (1584-1643) Vist. NEWARK (1627), E. of KINGSTON-upon-HULL (1628), wealthy Yorkshire landowner, refused to lend money to Charles I and tried to remain neutral in the Civil War. He joined him eventually in 1643 but was accidentally killed. His son **(2) Henry (1606-80) 2nd E. and M. of DORCHESTER (1645)** was summoned to the Lords in 1641. He joined the Royalists, never fought and had to compound for his estates. His brother **(3) William (1607-78)** was M.P. for Much Wenlock and joined the Parliamentarians. He was an energetic member of the Committee of Both Kingdoms; a moderate independent who left politics after Pride's purge, he remained friendly with Cromwell. He sat for Notts. in the Convention Parliament and then retired. His grandson **(4) Evelyn (1665-1726) 1st D. of KINGSTON (1715)** was a Whig M.P. for Retford in the Convention Parliament of 1689 and again in 1690. A leader of fashion, he became prominent under George I and was Ld. Pres. in 1719 and 1720. His son **(5) Evelyn (1711-73) 2nd D.** is remembered chiefly for the affairs of his mistress, the bigamous Elizabeth Chudleigh. *See* KINGSTON'S CASES.

PIERS PLOWMAN. *See* LANGLAND.

PIETERMARITZBURG (S. Africa) was founded in 1839 by Voortrekers and named after two of them, Piet Retief and Gert Maritz. It became the capital of Natal when that colony was created in 1856.

PIGOT, George (1719-77) Ld. (Ir. 1766) was Gov. of Madras from 1755 to 1763 and from 1775. In the first period he quarrelled with Eyre Coote about the annexation of Pondichery. In the second he was involved in a furious faction dispute in his council between the supporters (or creditors) of the Nawab of Arcot and those of the Raja of Tanjore. Bitter and unseemly wrangles culminated in one of the factions seizing control of the presidency and placing him under arrest. He died before the home authorities could disentangle the *imbroglio*.

PIGOTT, Richard (?1828-89) and his **FORGERIES.** He was Manager, and from 1865 owner of the *Irishman;* he sold it to the Land League in 1879 and became a political blackmailer. In 1886 he started to sell information to *The Times,* connecting Irish Home Ruler politicians with terrorism. In Apr. 1887 *The Times* published in facsimile and in good faith a damaging letter, ascribed to Parnell, as part of its campaign against "Parnellism and Crime". In July 1888 an Irish ex-M.P. also mentioned by *The Times* sued it for libel and in defence *The Times* produced other letters ascribed to Parnell. Parnell got the govt. to set up a special commission of investigation which established that Pigot had forged all the letters. He absconded and committed suicide in Spain.

PIGS. Wild pigs survived in Britain until the 18th cent. These, crossed with Neapolitan and Chinese breeds, produced the modern British varieties. Systematic breeding apparently began with *Berkshires* in 1850 and the *Saddleback* breeds a little later. The National Pig Breeders' Assn. was formed in 1884.

PIG WAR 1859. A farcical Anglo-U.S. conflict, starting with the shooting of an American pig, on San Juan I. near Vancouver. It was settled by German arbitration in 1871.

PILE O'BONES. Now REGINA (Sask.).

PILGRIM. An original English settler in New Zealand, cf SHAGROON.

PILGRIMAGE (1) CHRISTIAN. The great mediaeval international centres were St. James of Compostela (Sp.), St. Michael at Monte Gargano (Italy), Rome and above all the Holy Places in Palestine and from about the 10th cent. onwards a pilgrimage to one of these places was considered a valuable penance. In England the main centres were Walsingham (Norfolk), where there was an 11th cent. replica of the Holy House of Nazareth, Glastonbury (Som.), which had legends and reputed relics of Joseph of Arimathaea, and especially Canterbury, after Becket's death and popular canonisation in 1170.

The English centres ended with the Dissolution of the Monasteries in 1539. (*See* PILGRIM'S WAY.) **(2) MOSLEM.** The great centres, generating vast traffic, were Mecca Medina, Jerusalem and Akrotiri (Cyprus).

PILGRIMAGE OF GRACE (Oct.-Dec. 1536). (1) The scandals surrounding Anne Boleyn's execution and Henry VIII's immediate marriage to Jane Seymour offended the old-fashioned north. The Welsh Act of Union (1536) and the coercion of Henry Percy, 6th E. of Northumberland, into barring his entails and surrendering his land in return for £1,000 a year was suspect in an area honeycombed with palatinates, baronies, honours and liberties overlaid, in the part near the Cheviots, with a highly self conscious tribalism. A Council of the North had existed since 1525, but its writ did not run outside Yorkshire or even in some parts within it. In these relatively primitive societies, as in Ireland, the monasteries still fulfilled a respected function as reclaimers of land, introducers of modern farming methods, dispensers of education, charity and hospitality. The North disliked Cromwell's policy against them. The West Riding clothiers were being harassed by a new Act for regulating weaving. There was a spate of inclosures, too, at a time when rents and premiums were rising.

(2) Northern discontents were provoked into fury by Cromwell's commissions, especially those for dissolving the smaller monasteries of which Lincolnshire and Yorkshire each had 40. A riot at Louth (Lincs.) was followed by mass risings in Yorkshire and elsewhere (Oct.). The demand was to leave the church alone, to levy no new taxes and to surrender Thomas Cromwell. Most of the gentry joined the Lincolnshire insurgents but persuaded them to wait at London until the King replied. Poor leadership, the King's stern terms and shortage of food caused them to disperse just as the Yorkshire rebels, supported by all the north, assembled in force under Robert Aske and took York. They too were joined by most of the gentry, some of the northern councillors and Abp. Lee. By Nov. they had taken Pontefract and Doncaster. Here the D. of Norfolk, whose force was minimal, suggested a conference. Their demands resembled the Lincolnshire demands, but they added the legitimation of the Princess Mary, the repeal of the Act of Succession and freedom of speech in the House of Commons and an end to royal interference in elections. At the conference (6 Dec.) Norfolk agreed to refer the demands to Parliament and produced a free pardon. Relying on his word, Aske got his host to disperse, but there were local riots in Jan. and Feb. 1537, some of which he and his friends suppressed. Thereupon Henry could now hold that the pardon had been rejected and some 200 people were executed by courts martial, including Aske (July 1537).

PILGRIM FATHERS were E. Anglian Puritans who in 1609 moved from Boston to Leyden in the Netherlands to avoid interference with their religion. In 1619 they obtained, through Sir Edwyn Sandys, a grant from the Virginia Co. and financed by a group of London merchants built the *Mayflower* at Plymouth, whence they sailed, in Sept. 1620, about 100 strong. They reached C. Cod on 9th Nov., signed the *Mayflower Compact,* elected John Carver (?1576-1621) as their gov. and after some prospecting abandoned their grant and settled at Plymouth on Massachusetts Bay. Despite a mild winter and friendly Indians, 47 died by the next spring, but the rest elected William Bradford (1590-1657) as gov. and held on. They were in contact with England, for the *Fortune* arrived in Nov. 1621 bringing reinforcements and a new charter, and this occasion was marked by the first American Thanksgiving. *See* MASSACHUSETTS.

PILGRIMS' WAY is a mediaeval term for the greater part of an Iron Age track from the Channel crossings such as Ebbsfleet and Stourport through Canterbury to Eastwell and then westwards *via* the ford at Snodland, the neighbourhood of Otford, Dorking and Guildford to

Farnham, where it bifurcates. The virtually obliterated route due west is called the HARROW WAY and continued to Old Sarum. The south-westerly track passes through Alton and close to Alresford and Itchen Abbas before curving south to end at Winchester.

The tracks mostly run along the south side of the Downs at a contour (roughly 400 feet) marking the line where the gentle gradient from the valley bottom suddenly steepens to reach the crest. The Pilgrims-Harrow route was a spinal trade route which fell into disuse as such when the Romans imposed a new road pattern. The much later Farnham-Winchester branch arose out of the growth of Winchester and of shipping at Southampton and there was pilgrim traffic to Winchester which had the relics of St. Swithun, a more popular saint than Sts. Augustine and Cuthbert at St. Augustine's, Canterbury. Luckily for the rival Christchurch Cathedral at Canterbury, Abp. Thomas Becket was murdered in it in 1170 and canonised in response to public demand in 1173. This reversed the traffic flow but unfortunately the Martyrdom and its anniversaries took place on 29 Dec., a bad travelling season. Accordingly in 1220 the monks of Christchurch translated the relics of St. Thomas to a splendid shrine in July and instituted the Festival of his Translation. Both festivals were celebrated, but the Translation became the occasion of high splendour and much roistering. Both put St. Augustine and St. Cuthbert in the shade, but many pilgrims, especially from the continent, visited St. Swithun on the way to or from St. Thomas. For three centuries the Pilgrims' Way but not the Harrow Way was beaten out by an extensive tourist traffic. This ceased with the Dissolution of the Monasteries in 1539. Chaucer's pilgrims from Southwark, if they ever reached Canterbury, would have gone through Rochester avoiding the Way altogether.

PILGRIM TRUST was founded in 1930 with £2M by the American railway magnate Edward Stephen Harkness. The money is to be spent for the benefit of Great Britain.

PILKINGTON'S CASE (c. 1447). The judges held that a subsidy enacted in the English parliament could not be levied in Ireland because the Irish were not summoned to it.

PILLNITZ, DECLARATION OF (Aug. 1791). The Emperor and the K. of Prussia, after consultation with French *emigrés*, found that the revolutionary situation of the French King was an object of common concern to all European rulers and invited them "to employ ... the most efficacious means, relative to their forces, to enable the King of France to consolidate in the most perfect liberty, the basis of a monarchical govt. equally suitable to the rights of sovereigns and the welfare of the French-nation".

PILLORY was a form of stocks into which the head or the head and hands of a culprit were thrust and in this state he was exposed to public ridicule or violence. Sometimes his ears were nailed to it. *See* JENKIN'S EAR.

PILOT-S-AGE. *See* TRINITY HOUSE.

PILTDOWN (Sussex). In 1912 certain alleged Pleistocene remains were found here. In 1953 these were proved to be forgeries.

PINDARIS, were originally Pathan mercenaries employed mostly by the Maratha rulers. As the authority of these rulers declined, the Pindaris developed into land pirates and roamed Rajputana and southern India in organised bodies, seizing and killing. Their bases were mainly on the Narbada R. Their worst period extended from the British defeat of the Scindia and Holkar in 1803 to 1817. In the Third Maratha or Pindari War (1817-19) the British, with Scindia, rounded them up. *See* MARATHAS C-8.

PINDER OF WAKEFIELD or GEORGE A' GREEN, probably a wood sprite like his neighbour Robin Hood whom with others he defeats at quarter staff. Like Robin he defied Prince John. A public house near Kings Cross, London, was named after him until 1985.

PINERO, Sir Arthur Wing (1855-1934) took to play-writing in 1881 with *The Money Spinner,* followed by three successful and well constructed farces. His established popularity then enabled him to break the hold of second-rate melodrama with the well known *Second Mrs Tanqueray* in 1893, after which he published many other plays. His work virtually revived English drama.

PINE-TREE SHILLINGS. In the 17th cent. it was illegal to export coin from Britain. Hence a currency famine in the American Colonies, which resorted to barter or used wampum, beaver skins, corn or QUIDS of tobacco as a substitute, or foreign dollars. From 1652 to 1668 the Massachusetts Mint illegally coined shillings marked with a pine tree, a practice with which Charles II, with his usual common sense, did not interfere.

PINK. *See* SHIPS. SAILING.

PIOZZI or THRALE, Mrs Hester (1741-1821) married Henry Thrale in 1763 and in 1764 began a partly intellectual friendship with Dr. Johnson. She used to whip him. Thrale died in 1781. In 1784 she married Gabriele Piozzi, an Italian R. Catholic musician. The marriage was not popular, Johnson sulked, and they went to Italy. In 1786 she wrote her best selling *Anecdotes of the late Samuel Johnson.* The Piozzis returned to England in 1787. She published her correspondence with Johnson in 1788. Piozzi died in 1806.

PIPELINES (GAS and OIL). The first successful crude oil pipeline was built in Pennsylvania in 1865. There were none of importance in Europe before 1939 (*see* PLUTO). The Iraqi and Saudi Arabian oil fields were connected to Mediterranean ports in the 1950s, but, being very vulnerable, were rendered virtually useless by local unrest and they were replaced by huge tankers.

PIPE ROLL was the Great Roll of the Exchequer upon which the sheriffs' and other similar accounts for a given year were entered. The relevant dept. was called the Pipe Office, its head, the Clerk of the Pipe. The earliest extant Pipe Roll is that for 1130; they are continuous from 1156 to 1834 when they ceased, with the abolition of the sheriff's account, to be made up.

PIRACY – BRITISH WATERS (*see* PIRACY-GENERAL; VIKINGS; HANSE; BARBARY) **(1)** The six conditions (*see* PIRACY-GENERAL) favourable to a pirate industry prevailed in the Channel and its Western and Northern Approaches from about 1200 until 1590. Before 1200 the rich and regular commerce was insufficiently available. Thereafter it was liable to professional attack by pirates from Castile (mainly Corunna), the Basque seaboard (Bilbao, Irun, San Sebastian, Fuentarrabia), Gascony (Bordeaux, Bayonne, La Rochelle), Brittany (St. Malo), Normandy (Caen, Le Havre), Flanders (Dunkirk, Ostend), Zeeland (Flushing), Frisia (The Jade). The English pirates operated from Cornwall (Fowey and later Helston), Devon (Plymouth), Dorset (Lyme, Weymouth, Portland, Melcombe, Poole), the Solent ports (Southampton, Hamble, Ryde and later Portsmouth), all the Cinque Ports, Essex (Harwich), Suffolk (Ipswich), Norfolk (Great Yarmouth, Little Yarmouth, Aldeborough, Gorleston, Lynn), Boston and the Humber. Of these the most active, with the best markets in their hinterlands, were those facing the Channel.

(2) These many groups not only preyed upon passing traders but attacked each other. Great Yarmouth, the Cinque Ports and the other Essex and E. Anglian ports were involved in three-sided wars which began in about 1219 and lasted well into the 14th cent., despite govt. interventions. The Dorset pirates were so active that Coast Keepers were appointed to keep order in 1224. In 1233 Royal writs were ordering Great Yarmouth not to molest Dunwich. Despite the appointment of Coast Keepers in Kent in 1234, the men of Winchelsea seized French ships under English govt. safe conduct in 1235. In this year a triangular war between the Cinque Ports, Bayonne and the Basques broke out and long continued, despite private treaties in 1277, 1341 and 1351. During the Barons' War, the Cinque Portsmen stopped most of the traffic in the Straits (1264).

(3) Apart from conventional sea robbery and reprisals, in some of these wars a policy objective, similar to a protection racket, may sometimes be discerned. Great Yarmouth, for example, was attempting to channel all East Coast trade, legitimate or otherwise, through herself, by raiding and blockading the other East Coast ports. The Biscay carriage of salt, wines and pilgrims engendered the bitter and prolonged conflict between the Basques and Bayonne. The northward issue of the same trade attracted efforts by the Cinque Ports to levy systematic tolls. The Portsmen were thus often in alliance with one side or the other (more often the Basques) and, of course, in conflict with others (e.g. the Cornishmen and Bretons) attempting to levy toll on the same trade.

(4) The private wars reached an astonishing climax in the period 1290-1340. In 1293 there was a pitched battle (apparently by arrangement) between the Portsmen with Irish, Dutch and Gascon allies and the Normans supported by Flemings and Genoese. This ended in the Cinque Ports being filled with prizes and plunder. In 1297 French corsairs burned Dover, while an English combined fleet at Sluys broke up in a furious combat between the Great Yarmouth and Cinque Ports contingents. From 1301 to 1303 ships of Great Yarmouth habitually blockaded and raided foreign vessels in Gorleston and Little Yarmouth. In 1309 Frisian and Dutch fishermen had to be protected against Harwich pirates. In 1315 the Portsmen were robbing Flemish ships in the Orwell. In 1316 the ships of Great Yarmouth virtually blockaded Kent. By 1320 the Cornishmen from Fowey, Polruan and Lostwithiel were entering the fray and were in another triangular war with Portsmouth and the Cinque Ports, which in 1327 added the Flemings to their enemies. An English squadron of Channel pirates occupied the Orwell in 1335 for three months and methodically pillaged all the shipping.

(5) Since the volume of seaborne trade at this time is uncertain, the burden of depredations is uncertain too. It was undoubtedly grave. In 1336 the govt. paid 8,000 marks (£5,300) compensation to Genoese shipowners; in 1340 £16,527 to Flemish. There was a battle with the Castilians off La Rochelle in 1372 and in 1375 they sacked Portsmouth and Rye and seized 39 merchantmen at Bourgneuf. Between 1377 and 1394 the French raided the Dorset coast so persistently that the ports there fell into decay. By 1403 Breton pirates had created such hazards that ships sailed only in convoy or with special armed guards. In 1410 Hamble was being used largely to lay up ships. In 1412 the ports from Southampton to Thanet made a private agreement with the French ports opposite, regulating the ransoming of ships taken by each other (cf Barbary). The cost of Mediterranean goods was raised enormously by the need to transport them in armed convoys, while prices oscillated from high scarcity levels between arrivals, to low glut levels just after the convoys made port. The practice of dividing cargoes between ships and of subdividing the ownership of ships became universal, as did the custom of maritime average. At a time when shipping movements could be predicted from the state of the wind, robbery (or worse) was as great a risk as shipwreck.

(6) There was a major shift in the early 15th cent. After a Commons' petition against sea-rovers in 1414. Conservators of Truces began to be appointed, beginning with Dorset. Their efficiency was variable, but Henry V's French wars put much of both Channel coasts for a while under the same crown and the rise in ship tonnages slowly sterilised the shallow Cinque Ports. The main infestations were now north of the Straits, where Essex

pirates caused Danish protests and were somewhat hopefully forbidden to go to the Iceland fisheries (1435): and in the Western Approaches where the Cornishmen. especially of Fowey, had taken the lead. From 1404 Fowey was at war with much of the western world. A combined Franco-Spanish fleet attacked it in 1405. In 1457 the Bretons made a planned attack. In 1470 its depredations on Spanish shipping created diplomatic difficulties and led to wholesale ship-arrests in the port. Though govts. were becoming uneasier about piracy and possessed greater resources with which to combat it, there was a long way to go. There were enough pickings for other Cornish ports to enter the business; and Harwich pirates were seizing slaves in the Orkneys.

(7) The advent of Henry VIII marked a further stage. The creation of a Royal Navy and the claim to sovereignty in the Four Seas was directed as much against his own seafarers as against foreign powers. An Anglo-French treaty against piracy (1525) was followed by the gradual creation of local Vice-Admiralty courts, who were now to try pirates by Common, not Civil Law; this improved the chances of conviction. Improvement was however impeded by the weakness and corruption of the govt's. chosen instruments. By 1560 the Helford R. was as important a base as Fowey. The wealth and beauty of St. Ives were due to its flourishing trade in stolen goods. In 1564, after angry directions from the council, many Dorset pirates and receivers were rounded up, but as the local authorities were hand in glove with them, none was executed. The prosperous Dorset trade attracted a French blockade in 1574. Meanwhile robberies in the Solent continued openly and the men of the East Coast could frustrate searches because some of the searchers were pirates themselves, e.g. at Aldeborough in 1597. In 1582 the lady pirate, Mary Killigrew, plundered a Spanish merchantman at Falmouth quay.

(8) Politics apart, the Elizabethan govt. had economic and police reasons for encouraging piratical expeditions against the Spanish Main. Large numbers of desperadoes vanished over the Atlantic horizon and left English waters relatively clear, or were absorbed into legitimate naval or commercial activities. Hence local English piracy languished at the end of the reign, but the resulting maritime prosperity attracted a new type of pirate. From the 1580s Flemings and Dutchmen (initially encouraged by Elizabeth against the Spaniards) based mainly on Dunkirk, made the Straits of Dover hazardous and inhibited growth in the port of London, while simultaneously Spanish preoccupations encouraged the Barbary (q.v.) corsairs, who took to slave raiding on the English Channel coast. Dunkirk, Algiers and Salee became international trouble spots. The Commonwealth solved the Dunkirk problem by occupying it. Charles II sold it and its fortifications remained a matter of diplomatic controversy until the P. of Utrecht (1713). By this time industrial, though not occasional piracy, had ceased in the Four Seas, replaced by the less risky if slightly less lucrative smuggling industry.

PIRACY – GENERAL (A) The *temptation* to piracy is always present in waters which are (1) unpatrolled and (2) used by a rich commerce. If these two conditions are alone present piracy will be sporadic and for personal consumption (like shop-lifting). The *opportunity for a pirate industry* to establish itself arises when, in addition, the adjacent ports (3) are inadequately policed and their populations can (4) build and (5) man suitable ships and (6) organise an efficient market for the plunder. A pirate industry is a form of organised crime, with its concomitant subornation and corruption of authorities and gang wars, resembling a *mafia,* but geographically widespread because of the mobility of ships. Consumer piracy is seldom, if ever, wholly suppressed (e.g. the piracy in the Gulf of Siam in 1980). Pirate industries have formed a major overhead of seaborne trade at certain historical epochs (*see* VIKINGS; BARBARY; PIRACY; BRITISH WATERS; MADAGASCAR; INDONESIA-5).

(B) Piracy has on the one hand at various periods been an aspect of lawful trade, in particular slave trading, and on the other of privateering in the nominal interest of a state at war. The intermittent legality of the activity has confused the terminology (and propaganda) and created lasting difficulties of analysis.

PIRACY – LEGAL Piracy *jure gentium* (Lat: by the law of nations) consists in sailing the seas for private ends without authorisation from any govt., with the object of committing depredations upon property or acts of violence against persons and it includes seizure of a ship by the passengers, crew or master and (since 1696) acts committed against British subjects by other British subjects acting under authority of a foreign state. Piracy was triable in Admiralty under Civil Law until 1536 when, because of the difficulty of securing convictions, the jurisdiction was transferred to the Common Law courts. *See* BUCCANEERS, PRIVATEERS, REPRISAL.

PIRATE COAST. *See* TRUCIAL OMAN.

PIROGUE or PIRAGUA. A seagoing canoe used in the G. of Mexico and on the American Pacific coast.

PISA (Italy) was a powerful maritime trading republic with settlements in Corsica, Sardinia and the Balearic Is. from the 11th cent. It maintained a great Levantine trade until its defeat by the Genoese off Meloria, near Leghorn, in 1284, after which it rapidly declined. Its political independence was ended by the Visconti in 1399. They sold it to Florence in 1405. There was a brief, French supported revolt ending in the permanent establishment of Florentine rule in 1409.

PISA, COUNCIL OF (1409). *See* SCHISMS 6-7.

PISCARY. A common right to fish in manorial waters. *See* LAND TENURE

PISTOLE or PISTOLET. *Pistolet* was the common name for certain foreign gold coins worth about 6s. in the 16th cent. *Pistole*, its abbreviation, was especially used of a Spanish gold coin worth about 17s. in the 17th cent.

PIT AND GALLOWS in Scotland was the highest kind of private criminal jurisdiction, i.e. to imprison or hang criminals. Abolished in 1746.

PITCAIRN I. and NORFOLK I. (Pac.). Pitcairn, uninhabited when it was discovered in 1767, was occupied in 1790 by the *Bounty* mutineers with some male and female Society Islanders under Fletcher Christian. In 1800 the survivors of quarrels and disease submitted to the leadership of John Adams (?-1829), the last mutineer. They then moved to Tahiti in 1831, but in 1832 they went to NORFOLK I. In 1863, 42 of them returned to Pitcairn, where their descendants remain. After 1952 it was administered under Fiji but after the independence of the latter it was transferred to the British High Commissioner to New Zealand. New Zealand currency was introduced in 1967. The land is still held by families on the lines laid down by Christian.

Norfolk I. passed to N.S.W. in 1900 and to the Australian Commonwealth in 1914. *See* BLIGH, V-ADM. WILLIAM.

PITMAN, Sir Isaac (1813-97) invented the phonographic system of shorthand and published it in 1837.

PITT, William the Elder (1708-78) 1st E. of CHATHAM (1766), grandson of Thomas Pitt (1653-1726) the successful E. India merchant who brought the Pitt Diamond to Europe, became M.P. for Old Sarum in 1735. He supported the "patriot", aggressive party against Walpole, and Frederick P. of Wales against George II. These were the standard nuisance tactics of contemporary office seekers, but Pitt was an epigrammatic and abusive orator with a magnetic personality and an instinct for the country's political advantage. He made political capital during the Wars of 1739-44 by attacking the system of foreign subsidies and supported the Broad Bottomed administration of 1744. In

1746 he achieved office as P.M.G; he could afford to take none of the customary profits and so gained credit. In 1747 he was returned for one of the D. of Newcastle's seats, but got no promotion and by 1755 had apparently returned to the nuisance tactics of 1739-42. Actually the colonial prologue to the Seven Years' War had already opened and in 1756 he was free to criticise its misconduct. His views got some support. In Dec. 1756 he became, as Sec. of State for the Southern Dept. and Leader of the Commons, the real premier under the D. of Devonshire. George II, whom he hectored and lectured, was still hostile and as the Commons only feebly acknowledged him, the King felt able to dismiss him in Apr. 1757. No one could be found to replace him and after nearly three months he returned, this time in powerful coalition with Newcastle. He was now in charge of the spectacularly victorious war until Oct. 1761 and made an overwhelming reputation which sustained the prosecution of the war after he resigned.

He had inherited gout of an increasingly excruciating kind so that when, in 1766, he was called to form a govt. to deal with the American crisis, he was physically and mentally partly disabled. He took a peerage to reduce the burden of parliamentary attendance and not only suffered in popularity thereby, but had trouble with his heterogeneous colleagues. His views on American affairs were in principle the same as his views on the Seven Years' War. He had no intention of losing a war, but since victory was possible in the latter but not against the Americans, he pursued a vigorous offensive in the latter but intended an equally vigorous policy of constructive concession to the Americans. In fact he went seldom to Parliament and from May 1767 to Oct. 1768 remained *incommunicado* in a darkened room. He then resigned.

In Jan. 1770 he was sufficiently recovered to attack in concert with the Rockingham Whigs the increasingly aimless govt. policy on America, but he was virtually disabled again until 1774, by which time the situation was already out of hand. He hotly opposed the coercive policy, though he believed that the colonies should not be independent. This view was most forcibly expressed on his motion in May 1777 to discontinue hostilities. The North govt. tried unsuccessfully to recruit him when war with France and Spain was imminent, but in Apr. 1779 he had a dramatic stroke while speaking in the Lords against a motion to withdraw troops from America. *See* GEORGE II; GEORGE III; AMERICAN REBELLION; SEVEN YEARS' WAR.

PITT, William the Younger (1759-1806), second *s.* of the above, became M.P. for Appleby in 1781. His abilities were already well known so that he could choose his time in accepting office. He supported the "Pittite" Shelburne and, at Rockingham's death, accepted the Chancellorship of the Exchequer, an office then less important than he made it. Shortly afterwards Fox and North contrived Shelburne's overthrow: the latter and George III pressed him to accept the Treasury, which he refused, but when the Fox-North coalition fell nine months later (Dec. 1783) he accepted it together with the Chancellorship of the Exchequer and became, to the amusement of the House of Commons, Prime Minister at the age of 24 (*for his public career see* PITT'S FIRST, SECOND GOVT; ADDINGTON'S GOVT; GEORGE III; FRENCH WARS (1793-1815).)

The Lords and the King supported him. As a result he could, despite defeats in the Commons, choose a favourable moment for a general election and was returned triumphantly in 1784. Though inexperienced, he inherited experienced men of business from North, such as John Robinson and Charles Jenkinson. Though as dramatic and gouty as his father, he was more mundane and had the advantage of over 20 years of office, interrupted, briefly, only once. This period, despite the wars, represents a watershed in the transition between the semi-mediaeval administrative system which he inherited and the modern one for which he cleared the way. This involved rationalising the financial system as well (see TREASURY). These improvements, in which he took a personal interest, laid the foundations for the victorious French war, the first half of which he directed. Many of the personalities who executed its naval and military actions received their promotion directly or indirectly through his encouragement. He died prematurely of gout, overwork, depression at Bonaparte's victory at Austerlitz, with his last breath demanding one of Bellamy's pork pies.

PITT GOVT – FIRST (Dec. 1783-July 1794) (Eight in Cabinet) (See GEORGE III-10 *et seq.*) **(1)** William Pitt the Younger was 24 when, after a factional period had almost halted govt. altogether, he was persuaded to undertake it as a non-party leader. He was also, until 1789, the only M.P. in his cabinet, but royal support helped to attract noble support provided that he shelved sweeping or theoretical reforms and balanced the budget.

(2) The first problem was India and the Commons threw out his first India Bill. Next he sought the support of Fox and North (or both) but they insisted on his resignation before a coalition was formed and on their motion the Commons bombarded the King with resolutions demanding the Minister's dismissal. They backed these up by postponing supply and the annual Mutiny Bill (Feb. 1784), i.e. by prolonging from opposition the confusion which they had brought about in office. Out of touch with opinion, they discredited themselves by their every move. Independents began to come over to Pitt. In March he got the Mutiny Bill passed. It was now safe to dissolve. With the backing of public opinion, the moneyed classes and the Crown, he overwhelmingly won the general election.

(3) Large majorities can afford to be independent. Parliament accepted Pitt's second India Bill because the difficulties had gone on too long. It then proceeded joyfully to clip the govt's. wings as in the good old days of conflict with the Crown. This began when Fox was admitted by a vote to his seat for Westminster. Then on a casting vote, it threw out proposals to fortify the dangerously unprotected Naval dockyards at a cost of £760,000 (Spring 1785). A powerful industrialists' agitation, led by Josiah Wedgwood, frustrated Pitt's plan to admit Ireland in return for an Irish contribution to the Navy, to the Anglo-imperial economy, by equalising the customs duties and in Apr. 1785 the Commons rejected his moderate parliamentary reform bill by 248 votes to 174. Yet they had no intention of forcing him out. They simply wished to limit the field of govt. and keep it cheap.

(4) Within this field there was much scope. Pitt's appetite for facts made him the best informed man in Parliament. He could thus be the most practical and calm, because he did not have to supplement ignorance with imagination. His logic and far-sightedness went together. £9M out of the £18M yield of taxes went in servicing the national debt, mostly incurred in the American War. Parliament expected the debt burden to be reduced. It could not be expected only to vote new taxes for the purpose. Pitt set about finding the money by quickly reducing overheads and waste. He avoided public gestures and the controversy which they would raise. Instead, as death vacated sinecures, he mostly left them unfilled; but where he had to act sooner, he compensated the holder. He instituted effective auditing and centralisation of services like printing and, when politically feasible, salaried rather than fee-paid posts. A system of inspection compelled officials to pay over taxes more quickly, a reorganisation enabled them to collect more cheaply. He ended the charging of loans on particular taxes and so reduced the necessary records by half. Commissioners were appointed to make the Crown lands pay; civil list appropriations were introduced; loan offers were to be made by sealed tender and a lottery

exploited the national passion for gambling in order to reduce the flow of Treasury bills. Many of these improvements could, however, affect the finances only slowly. Pitt's main hope was to stimulate trade and spread the tax burden, for example, by the Commutation Act of 1784.

(5) The total effect of these financial measures was to produce an annual surplus of about £1M. In 1786 independent Debt Commissioners were set up to redeem the National Debt and the Treasury required by statute to pay them £1M a year. This arrangement was, by 1792, a success. Thereafter war destroyed its foundations.

(6) Pitt's financial policy depended precariously upon peace, but he had inherited a dangerous diplomatic isolation. The Emperor Joseph II proposed in 1784 to exchange Belgium for Bavaria and when Frederick the Great of Prussia frustrated this plan he changed course and began in Belgium a policy of paternalistic capital investment which could succeed only by trenching on local privileges and the Dutch treaty right and British interest to keep the port of Antwerp closed. Pitt wanted to oppose the development both of Antwerp and Ostend and of Dutch trade; the Dutch appealed to France which was constructing the naval port at Cherbourg. In 1785 France and the United Provinces signed an alliance which appealed to and strengthened the aristocratic Dutch anti-Orange Party. In 1786 the States of Holland suspended the P. of Orange from his Stadholdership. In 1787 the Utrecht authorities publicly insulted his wife, the sister of Frederick William III of Prussia; thereupon the Prussian army moved in and the Franco-Dutch alliance was proved hollow, for the Dutch were unwilling to provide the battle ground and the French were bankrupt. The P. of Orange was restored.

(7) Pitt could now make a diplomatic re-entry into Europe. The French were glad to accept a trade treaty for the mutual reduction of customs. Since 1782 the English Industrial Revolution had "taken off". The treaty opened France to the new British mass production and Britain to French wines and spirits. A triple alliance (1788) with Orange and Prussia guaranteed Holland and the permanent closure of Antwerp. Belgium meanwhile was in confusion, for under Joseph II's modernistic paternalism, the local privileges remained in abeyance, but the compensating economic development had been frustrated. Insurrection followed, at a time when Britain was convulsed by the first Regency crisis and the beginning of Warren Hastings' impeachment.

(8) French weakness was not as self-evident as the Revolution was shortly to make it. The Russians, having reached the Black Sea at Kinburn in 1774, took Oczakov opposite in 1788. These distractions, besides being a scarcely apprehended Russian threat to the Mediterranean, seemed to isolate Britain in case of trouble with France. They threatened, too, the stability of the new Triple Alliance, since Prussia might indulge her Polish ambitions while Russia's and Austria's back was turned. For the time being these fears were allayed. The Swedes attacked Russia and were defeated. The Danes then attempted to recover their lost mainland provinces from Sweden. The members of the Triple Alliance had a common interest in the Baltic; imposed an armistice (1789), while the Russians took Bucharest and the Austrians Belgrade.

(9) These were resounding events, but the French Revolution deafened everybody and seemed to create a western power vacuum. In 1790 Spain, bereft of her French ally, had to give way to Britain over the Nootka Sound claims which ultimately dictated the shape of modern Canada. Then Joseph II died and his successor Leopold, to secure Prussian support in the imperial election, allowed the Triple Alliance to pour oil on Joseph's troubled waters, for he had on his hands not only a Turkish war and a Belgian revolt, but a Hungarian insurrection too. He joined the Triple Alliance in guaranteeing Belgian liberties and undertook (T. of Reichenbach, July 1790) to make peace with Turkey on the basis of a mutual restoration of conquests. Only towards Russia was there a diplomatic failure. To the D. of Leeds, the Foreign Sec., the Triple Alliance was vital and could be kept alive only by activity. At this stage this meant activity against Russia, whose threat to Ottoman stability was now evident. An ultimatum was delivered to the Czarina Catherine (Mar. 1791). She was to make peace on the same terms as Austria. She refused to relinquish Oczakov. An opposition resolution against the policy was defeated only because more than half the Commons abstained. There was in truth no way of attacking Russia and the Commons would not have voted the money if there had been. Pitt conceded Oczakov (Apr. 1791) and Leeds resigned. The Russo-Turkish P. of Jassy completed the transaction (Jan. 1792).

(10) Leeds was right about the means for keeping the Alliance together, but at the time it was uncertain whether it mattered. Its main object was to curb France, but France was in dissolution. It had pacified the Baltic and Belgium. To precipitate it into foreign adventures merely to keep it alive, might involve Britain in wars of no direct advantage to her and besides, they would upset Pitt's financial policy. The British taxpayer would not pay for war in the Black Sea or, as now seemed likely, in Poland whose remnant Russia and Prussia with Austria signing behind were preparing to destroy. Moreover the Germanic states were organising against France. At Pillnitz (q.v.) (Saxony) (Aug. 1791) the rulers of Saxony, Prussia and Austria produced their Declaration. In Dec. imperial troops marched slowly towards Trier (Trèves) in support. The French Assembly had repudiated foreign conquests: the Prussians would certainly co-operate with Britain if success against France gave Austria too much power in the Low Countries. Whoever else might be at war, there seemed solid reasons for thinking that Britain could look forward to a long tranquillity. In Feb. 1792 Pitt began to reduce taxation.

(11) There were other reasons for this too. The French Revolution had excited much sympathy. Anti-Jacobite and Orange societies applauded the new French liberalism. The old supporters of John Wilkes reappeared as sympathisers. The Society of Friends of the People was formed in Apr. 1792. Dissenters, excluded from public life, praised the concept of careers open to talent. Ideological as well as financial currents moved away from war, until French Revolutionary excesses justified the *Reflections* which Burke had published amid execration in Oct. 1790. English opinion now slowly began to grow wary of French ideologies just as the French Revolutionary wars broke out and threatened British strategic interests.

PITT GOVT. – SECOND (July 1794-Mar. 1801) (*see ditto,* FIRST) 13 in Cabinet. **(1)** Pitt, as a peacetime reformer, had gone into the French Revolutionary war (q.v.) reluctantly. The French seemed to be destroying themselves without any effort on Britain's part and neither he nor the opposition sympathised with the royalist programme of France's opponents. With most people, he thought that the British commitment should be limited to restoring Belgium to Austria and picking up French sugar colonies on the side. The forces were not, after ten years of economy, adequate for a major war. Pitt had just reduced them. Thus minded, Pitt made the mistake of not, initially prosecuting it with concentrated vigour or in a properly planned fashion. The dependence on militia, fencibles and Naval impressment starved the army (such as it was) of reliable material; and there was no single minister responsible for military business, let alone war policy. Since Dumouriez' defeat at Neerwinden (Mar. 1793), his desertion (Apr.) and the allied capture of Mainz and Valenciennes (July), it hardly seemed to matter.

(2) The result was a dispersal of effort. The Fleet entered the Mediterranean; there were attempts to bring over the French royalists in Haiti; Brittany was raided; a rebellion in the Loire Valley was aided; yet the Belgian campaign was to have priority at a time when the army amounted to 9000 men. Pitt assembled Hanoverians and hired Hessians; the G.O.C., the D. of York, made a junction with the Dutch to attack Dunkirk. He was beaten off at Hondschoote. A combined operation was needed but the ships were not available. In a civil war-torn France they, under Hood, had achieved a major success by occupying Toulon (Aug.), but the troops required to hold it had to be borrowed from Savoy and Naples. They were too few and too late. In Oct. the Austrians in Belgium were defeated at Wattignies and the D. of York had to retreat to Ostend. At the end of the year Hood evacuated Toulon.

(3) As Pichegru and Hoche pressed the Austrians and the Prussians towards the Rhine, the latter's political objectives began to change. Prussia, financially exhausted and in civil disorder, was using her resources and British subsidies to ensure her share of Poland. The Austrians, jealous of Prussia both on the Rhine and in Poland, were preparing to turn away from Belgium. Pitt decided to hire 60,000 Prussians, but before they could be ordered to Belgium, the Austrians were defeated at Tourcoing (May 1794). The battle involved the D. of York. In June they were overthrown at Fleurus and had to abandon Belgium precipitately. The Duke's army narrowly escaped.

(4) 1793 began a series of bad harvests which caused bread riots everywhere in Europe. If revolutionary excesses had shocked the public into supporting the patriotic line, French ideas inspired a new intellectual discontent among those in England who could afford bread. There were the Foxites adhering to a cool radicalism, professional opposition and the boudoirs of Bath. Fox, who thought that European hostility had provoked French violence, was thought a traitor by many. On the other hand there were the educated or self-educated upright men of skill – artisans, shopkeepers, dissenting ministers, schoolmasters, solicitors and other minor professional men, unprivileged but conscious of ability, to whom therefore *la carrière ouverte aux talens* appealed. Radical societies such as the Society for Constitutional Information disseminated radical literature. The Corresponding Society of London and its provincial affiliates bid for a mass membership in support of a programme of manhood suffrage, annual parliaments, simpler law and an end to unfair inclosures. In Scotland, panic stricken obscurantism resulted in one Thomas Muir of the Society of Friends of the People being transported for 14 years, but in London the trial of Horne Tooke and others for High Treason ended in an acquittal. Cooler heads entertained cooler ideas. Prosperity, perhaps derived from a successful war, might lower the temperature.

(5) Hence those who thought that the war had to be won either for external commercial or for internal social reasons had strong motives for uniting their efforts. Negotiations for bringing the Portland Whigs into the govt. took some time, but ended in a complete reconstruction in which, apart from Pitt, only Richmond and Hawkesbury survived.

(6) By this time Jervis had taken most of the French W. Indian islands and the French Brest fleet had been beaten on the Glorious 1 June (1794). The D. of York, vastly out-numbered, harassed by the Dutch population and hardly supported from home, then managed to evacuate his troops through Bremen (Mar. 1795). Prussia (Apr.) and Holland (May) made peace with France. In June a force of emigrés was landed at Quiberon to support the Vendean royalists, but was wiped out in July by Republican troops released from elsewhere. At the same time Spain made peace. Britain continued to mop up French and Dutch colonial establishments at the Cape, in India, Ceylon and Indonesia and to blockade the French coasts, but the French, free on the Rhine and the Pyrenees could concentrate on Italy. By July 1796 the Austrians had been driven to Venetia, the plundered Italian states had sued for peace or been destroyed. Military confrontation on land between Britain and France had ceased. It now seemed that the enemy could, after all, do serious damage at sea, for in Oct. 1796 Spain changed sides. Her materially important fleet and strategic position apparently made the W. Mediterranean untenable. Corsica and Elba were given up. The Fleet retreated to Gibraltar.

(7) The govt. had mistakenly charged the leaders of the Societies (Horne Tooke, Thelwall and others) with treason, of which they were acquitted (Dec. 1794). Jubilation and agitation went hand in hand. In reply the govt. secured the Seditious Meetings Act, 1795 almost unopposed. The agitation had width but no depth and the law was circumspectly treated alike by those who had to obey and to enforce it. The agitations died away. By 1797 the country, though depressed and often hungry, was quiescent (*see* SPEENHAMLAND). Charles Grey's and Fox's parliamentary reform proposals were thrown out on Pitt's argument that they were too hazardous in the circumstances. The argument was just. Only the weather had frustrated a winter invasion of Ireland (Dec. 1796) and though Jervis and Nelson had beaten and destroyed the reputation of the Spaniards at C. St. Vincent (Feb. 1797), in Apr. the Channel Fleet had mutinied (with great decorum). This was settled in a week, but in May the North Sea Fleet mutinied violently at the Nore, when Dutch preparations against Ireland were in hand. This outbreak was not suppressed until July. The Nore command in fact frustrated the Dutch in Oct. by the great victory at Camperdown (q.v.) but in such hazards, common-sense dictated that the govt. should not create yet more.

(8) Though Pitt and everyone else wanted peace, a very long war had to be assumed. This required a fiscal reorganisation to avoid excessive deficit financing. The proportion of indirect taxation was too high and the potential of the old direct taxes was, after trebling in 1793, exhausted. The taxable resources were increased by extending American imports of cotton and corn in exchange for manufactures, but it was imperative to raise revenue in new ways. In 1797 this was done by stabilising the Land Tax with redemption provisions which kept down the borrowing rate and by introducing an income tax. Other measures for more directly increasing the war potential were also pursued. The suspension of the Navigation Acts enabled the Navy to press more prime seamen to man the warships coming off the shipways. Bounties were used to attract militiamen into the regular army. Military and financial commitments were reduced in the W. Indies.

(9) In theory the govt. could now negotiate from strength. In fact, the Irish rebellion of 1798, by offering the French a prospect of victory, made peace impossible. The British plan to give Austria Lombardy in exchange for Belgium, to give Belgium to Holland, to give Russia a voice in reorganising Germany and protecting Malta, to enlarge Savoy-Sardinia, was not a basis for peace but a war aim which might be acceptable to a second coalition (q.v.). That coalition had yet to be formed and to win victories, but Bonaparte had seized Malta (June 1798) and had reached Egypt (July) (*see* MEDITERRANEAN WAR, OCT. 1797.-MAR. 1799). It was Nelson's victory of the Nile (Aug.) which inspired the coalition and the opening successes of the coalition induced Bonaparte (First Consul since Nov. 1799) to make overtures for peace. These were rejected because a permanent peace could be agreed only with a French govt. so secure that it would not need to indulge its public opinion with foreign adventures. Pitt did not

believe in Bonaparte's security or peaceful intentions. He also believed that the second coalition would win the war. The B. of Marengo (June 1800) undeceived him. Triumph in India was overbalanced by European disaster. The coalition broke up. Russia organised the Armed Neutrality which was dissolved by the Czar Paul's death and the B. of Copenhagen (Apr. 1801).

(10) The Irish rebellion (Feb-Aug. 1798) (*see* UNITED IRISHMEN) led indirectly to Pitt's fall. He thought that the cure for Irish troubles must arise from the true incorporation of the Irish into the English polity. This required two inseparable measures: a parliamentary union and the political emancipation of the R. Catholic majority, who would thus acquire a stake in the union. Bribes and patronage persuaded the Irish parliament to vote its own abolition (1800), but neither English political opinion nor the King would accept emancipation. War weariness also played its part. The King made contact with Addington, the Speaker, in Jan. 1801, to persuade Pitt, but Pitt's rationalism was out of step with the emotional protestantism of public opinion dating from the time of James II, while the King's interpretation of his oath to protect the Anglican church focused that opinion in high quarters. Pitt could not be persuaded. The King, in emotional terms asked Addington if he would form a govt. By Mar. Addington had found the necessary support, and in Mar. Pitt resigned. He believed that national safety was paramount and accordingly promised to support the new govt. and never to raise the issue again. "Nothing" the King said "could possibly be more honourable."

PITT-RIVERS, Gen. Augustus Henry (1827-1900) (b. LANE-FOX), after a conventional military career, succeeded to the Rivers' estate at Rushworth where, between 1880 and 1897, he originated the modern technique of archaeological excavation. He published the results in *Excavations at Cranborne Chase,* set up a museum at Farnham (Dorset) and left his immense collections to Oxford University.

PITTSBURGH (Penn.). George Washington built a stockade on the strategically important and tactically defensible site in 1753. The French destroyed it and built FORT DUQUESNE there in 1754. It was the objective of Braddock's disastrous expedition in July 1755, but was eventually taken and renamed Pittsburgh by Gen. Forbes and George Washington in Nov. 1758 and included in Pennsylvania.

PIUS II, Pope. *See* AENEAS SILVIUS.

PIUS V. *See* COUNTER REFORMATION.

PIZARRO, Francisco (1478-1541) with his three brothers conquered Peru for Spain between 1530 and 1535 with so small a force that they used the utmost brutality and treachery.

PLACAAT (Dutch = public notice). A law made by the Dutch local Council of Policy in the Cape and elsewhere.

PLACE, Francis (1771-1854) became sec. of several trade clubs after 1791 when his own trade as a leather breeches maker declined. In 1799 he became a tailor in London and a leading radical associate of Sir Francis Burdett. His long sustained campaign secured the repeal of the Combination Acts in 1824.

PLACEMEN, PLACE BILL. M.P.s, having accepted a paid employment held at the will of the Crown, might be influenced by it. The number of such "places" was so large under Charles II and James II that they were thought to endanger the independence of the Commons. Place Bills to reduce or abolish them) were introduced in 1675 and 1692, but the Act of Settlement 1700 enunciated the general rule that a person cannot be an M.P. and hold an office of profit under the Crown. The rigour of this was found to be highly inconvenient and therefore many, possibly too many, exceptions were made. Hence later Place Bills were designed to abolish the exceptions or to get rid of the parallel difficulty of places for M.Ps'.

friends and relatives. This could be done effectively only by abolishing the places themselves. Since most of them had become sinecures by the 1780s, the younger Pitt could get rid of them (usually with compensation) in the interests of efficiency and economy.

There has been a recrudescence of the problem in a different form in the multiplication of paid ministerial offices. In 1868 there were only 36. Under the second Wilson Govt. in 1966 there were 110: under the second Thatcher Govt. 99. i.e. at least a third of the majority party in the Commons was holding paid, sometimes very well paid, office in addition to their parliamentary salary. This has much simplified the task of the govt. whips whose numbers have nonetheless risen.

PLACE NAMES. Few subjects contain so many pitfalls and the following can be only a very rough indication of its main features.

A. Principal Influences (1) Personal Names: OE *Heregeard* (Harrietsham); Dan: *Tove* (Towton); Celtic *Ceadwalla* (Chardbury); post-Conquest: *Bagot* (Morton Bagot).

(2) Celtic Elements. *Stour* = powerful or rapid (R. Stour); *meneth* = mountain (Longmynde, Mendip, The Mounth), *Eve* or *Axe* = water or river.

(3) Romano-Celtic survivals. *Luguvalio* (Carlisle).

(4) English elements. These settled into four main dialects: Northumbrian, Mercian, West Saxon and Jutish and include 14 important types **(a)** Folk names: *Essex* = East Saxons; *Hwicce* (Wychwood), **(b)** Settlers' names: *Dorset* = The settlers at Dorn (Dorchester), **(c)** -ingas names *see* B below, **(d)** Survivals of Heathenism: *Hearg* = temple (Harrowden); *Wih* = idol (Weyhill); *Tiw* (Tysoe), *Thunor* (Thundersley) and *Woden* (*Wansdyke, Wednesbury*) all gods, **(e)** Introductions of Christianity *Minster* = monastery or Cathedral (Minster-in-Sheppey); *Church* or *Kirk* (Church Stretton; Kirkmichael); *Cristelmael* = cross (Christian Malford), **(f)** Habitation: *Tun* or *town* = farmstead (Ruyton of the Eleven Towns), **(g)** Secondary settlement: *Stoc* = outlying dairy farm (Stoke Charity, Chardstock), **(h)** Nature names: *Hoe* = hill or mound (Thingoe), **(i)** Types of Tenure: *Fifehead* = an estate of five hides, **(j)** Rank: *Ealdorman* (Aldermarston); *Cniht* = squire (Knighton), **(k)** Trades: *Smith* (Smethwick, Great Smeaton), **(l)** Farming and country pursuits: *Sheppey* = Sheep I., **(m)** Fishing: *Countess Weir*, **(n)** Law: *wearg* = felon *Wreighill*, **(o)** Sports: *Haffield Chase*.

(5) Scandinavian elements occur mainly in a Norse form in Man and the coastal counties from the Solway to the Dee and mainly in a Danish form north and east of Watling Street, but it is often impossible to attribute a given name to one or the other. Names ending in *by* (= village) are Norse; those in *thorpe* (= outlying settlement) Danish.

(6) French elements. These included not only words and names (*Beaulieu* = nice place; Stoke *Mandeville*) but affected the pronunciation of pre-existing names (Fr: *Diss* for OE Ditch).

B. Common Components

Beer, Bear, Beer (OE) = clearing (Bere Alston); *Borough, Brough, Burgh, Bury* (OE) = fortified place; *Borrow, Barrow* = hill; *Wick, Vick* = (i) creek or haven or (ii) settlement or dairy farm; *Breck* (OE) = periodically tilled waste; *Carl, Charl, Chorl* = serf (Chorley); *Chart* = thicket; *Chester* or *Caster* (Lat: Castra) = fortification; *Chet* (Celtic) = wood; *Chipping* or *Cheap* = market (Chipping Camden, Cheap St., Sherborne); *Den* or *Denn* (Jutish) = pasture or clearing, especially for swine (Tenterden); *Ham* (AS) = home or settlement; *Hope* (OE) = clearing in a fen (Alsop); *-ing* = followers of (Hastings i.e. Hasta's followers) or people (Avening, i.e. dwellers by the Avon); *Leigh* = clearing; *Llan* (Welsh) or *Lan* (Cornish) – holy place or church or place where a holy man preached (Llanilltyd i.e. St. Illtyd's place); *Moss* (Norw.) = marsh; *Sett* (Norw.) = summer pasture (Consett); *Vil* (AS) = field,

(Fr.) settlement; *Wal* = Welsh (Walton or Walbrook); *Wich* (Early Eng.) = saltings (Northwich).

PLACENTIA. See GREENWICH.

PLAGUE (BLACK DEATH or GOD'S TOKENS) is a disease of rodents, especially those like black rats and prairie dogs, which colonise equable habitats (such as human dwellings and underground warrens) or follow the transport of grain. The disease also attacks their fleas which thrive in the same middling temperatures and which communicate it from rodent to rodent. A major fatal rodent epidemic will deprive infected fleas of their usual hosts. They then migrate directly to and infect human beings or indirectly after emerging from cargoes of cloth or cotton.

The plague appears in a bubonic and a septicaemic or pneumonic form. The latter may possibly be communicated directly as well as through fleas. The disease is ancient; an outbreak is described in the Bible (I Samuel Ch. 5 and 6). Its ancient base was probably in Yunnan. There have been four pandemics in the Christian era. The ANTONINE PLAGUE (166-7) devastated the Roman Empire and ended the Antonine prosperity. The PLAGUE OF JUSTINIAN (542-600) was accompanied by smallpox. During its slow westward advance across the Roman Empire and western Europe it destroyed about half the populations. There was a terrible visitation to Britain in the years 664 to 684. Other epidemics, which were uncertainly plague, occurred in 829 and 897.

A long interval of perhaps relative quiescence was disturbed by the rise of the Mongols. They carried the fleas and perhaps some of the rats to the Middle East and the confines of Europe. This plague, called since 1823 the BLACK DEATH, was first reported in the west at Caffa (Crimea) in 1346. It was probably pneumonic and anthrax was also probably present. It travelled the trade routes to Asia Minor, the Levant and North Africa and by Genoese ships to Genoa; thence along the coasts to Marseilles and Barcelona and so inland across Italy, Spain and France. It entered England in Aug. 1348 by way of Dorset, was active in London by Nov., appeared at Norwich in Jan. 1349 and involved the whole country by Dec. when it died out. It then wheeled across the Low Countries, Northern Europe and eastwards across Russia and Asia. It struck China only in 1380.

In England this first epidemic killed mainly adults, including many prominent people. A second visitation, called the MORTALITÉ DES ENFANTS 1361-2, attacked the young and so did the third and fourth outbreaks in 1369 and, in the north, in 1379. By 1439 it had become an endemic urban disease.

This pandemic was the greatest human disaster in history. On the very moderate assumption that 20% of the people died in the first outbreak and smaller percentages in the three later ones (which affected fertility), the population of England must have fallen by 50% before 1400. Actually in the first visitation the mortality at Bristol was between 35% and 40% and about half of all the English clergy died.

Further epidemics occurred in 1479, 1486, 1499 (when 20,000 people died in London alone), 1509 (especially at Calais), 1530, 1535, 1563, 1593 (when a connection with cotton was noticed), 1603 (London mortality 33,000), 1625 (41,000); in 1665 the London GREAT PLAGUE carried off 68,000. Minor provincial outbreaks continued till 1679, but, despite an epidemic at Marseilles in 1720, it died down.

The reason for this interruption was the supersession in Europe of the housebound black rat by the outdoor brown rat in the years about 1727. The greater extremes of heat and cold to which this rat is accustomed shortens the life of the flea and so reduces the latter's ability to move from host to host. The disease retreated. Egyptian outbreaks, coinciding with the return of the Haj, drew further attention to the part of trade routes. It led to the creation of a quarantine board there in 1831 and to the widespread readoption of port health control.

Meanwhile it remained endemic in Yunnan, whence THE MODERN PANDEMIC emerged as a result of a civil war. It reached Canton and Hong Kong in 1894 and fanned out westwards to Bombay (1896) and Calcutta (1896), eastwards through Indonesia to Australia (1907) and California and northwards across China. Between 1898 and 1918 it killed, on average, 500,000 people a year. There was even a small but persistent outbreak in Suffolk (1910-18). It invaded Africa in 1926, but the average mortality declined to 170,000 a year in 1919-28, to 42,000 in 1929-38 and despite a noticeable return of the Black Rat in 1936, to 21,000 in 1939-48. *See* EPIDEMICS, HUMAN.

PLAID CYMRU (WELSH NATIONALIST PARTY) was founded in 1925 during the post-World War I recession. It first contested a parliamentary seat in 1929 and first gained one at a bye-election in 1966. Welsh Nationalism was primarily linguistic, designed to preserve the language and civilisation and by insisting upon Welsh as a qualification for official employment, to reserve Welsh official posts to Welshmen. On the other hand Welsh local govt. was consistently subsidised by the English taxpayer. Thus business opinion was mostly indifferent and when devolution proposals were put to the Welsh electorate in 1977 in a referendum, they failed to win approval because of the possible loss of subsidy implicit in autonomy. This was not a fatal blow to Plaid Cymru, which was still winning seats in local govt. elections in 1994.

PLAIN, THE. The more moderate members of the revolutionary French Convention, as opposed to the extremist "Mountain".

PLANNING AUTHORITIES. *See* TOWN AND COUNTRY PLANNING-4.

PLAN OF CAMPAIGN (1887-90) (*see* SALISBURY'S SECOND GOVT-2), was organised by William O'Brien and John Dillon, leaders of the Irish National League, against Parnell's wishes. It began in Nov. 1887. The tenants of each estate were to organise, make a united offer of rent to the landlord and if he refused it, pay the money to the League's campaign fund.

PLANTAGENETS. *See* ANGEVINS, ENGLISH (PLANTAGENETS).

PLANTATION (1) The division of forfeited Irish land and its allotment to and settlement by English or Scots; especially in the case of Ulster land forfeited by the Es. of Tyrconnell and Tyrone under James I.

(2) English settlements in N. America and the W. Indies. The term fell into disuse in the later part of the 18th cent. and was never used of other British possessions. *See* TRADE, BOARD OF.

PLANTATION, ARTICLES OF (1609). *See* JAMES I AND VI-7.

PLANTATION of ULSTER. *See* JAMES I AND VI-7.

PLANTATION DUTIES ACT, 1672, imposed a heavy tax on American exports unless landed in Britain, the exporters being required to give a bond before sailing.

PLANTATIONS, COUNCILS OF. In 1660 a council of unpaid commissioners was appointed to regulate colonial affairs ("Plantations"), but like the Council of Trade it languished after 1664 and was replaced from 1670 to 1672 by a new body partly of ministers *ex officio* and partly of paid commissioners, one of whom was designated President. *See* TRADE AND PLANTATIONS.

PLANT DISEASES. *Bunt* or *Smut* in wheat, and *Rust* in grains generally, were dangerous scourges of ancient origin. Matthieu du Tillet (1714-99) investigated Bunt in 1755, but Benedict Prevost (1755-1819) invented the copper sulphate treatment in 1807. Felice Fontana (1730-1805) observed the relationship of parasitic fungi to Rust in 1767 and Christiaan Persoon (1762-1837) systematised mycology as a science. These activities raised cereal productivity by very large though so far undetermined amounts.

A bacterial plant disease (*Twig Blight* in apples and pears) was first identified in 1878. The study of immunity and disease resistance, begun in about 1902, began to engender practical results in 1923. More recently chemical sprays against pathogens or virus vectors have been developed. Some of these, which are absorbed and transmitted within plants, are capable of being directly or indirectly harmful to animals or humans. On the other hand, while the breeding of immune or resistant strains is less likely to endanger vertebrates, pathogens often develop new varieties which can overcome such resistance. This has happened with rust-resistant British wheat.

PLASTICS. Natural plastics such as shellac and bitumen are of ancient use. Styrene was first prepared in 1831, acrylic acid in 1843, celluloid in 1865 and casein in 1904, but the plastics industry effectively began in 1916 with the manufacture of Bakelite. The development of the modern mass industry was strongly encouraged by World War II.

PLATONISTS, CAMBRIDGE. A group of Restoration theologians who reacted against Calvinism with an appeal to reason, science and the works of Plato and Platinus. They paved the way for Latitudinarianism.

PLATORIUS NEPOS, AULUS. *See* BRITAIN, ROMAN-14.

PLAUTIUS, AULUS. *See* BRITAIN. ROMAN-1.

PLAYFORD, John the Elder (1623-?86), the Younger (1656-86) and **Henry (1657-?1706)** operated the first English musical publishing business from about 1648. The shop was in the Temple. Under the Commonwealth the business had a virtual monopoly. Henry organised regular concerts from 1699 and weekly music clubs.

PLEA ROLLS were medieval court records, stitched together at the top, not in a continuous roll. The most important were **(1)** Curia Regis rolls from 1181. These were divided after 1233 into **(2)** Coram Rege (Kings Bench) and **(3)** De Banco (Common Pleas). **(4)** Exchequer rolls began in 1236. **(5)** Eyre and Assize rolls began in 1189. **(6)** Chancery non-judicial rolls in 1199. **(7)** Parliament rolls in 1290. These give, especially in the 12th-14th cents., first hand evidence of the workings of the bodies concerned, because they contain pleadings and decisions in actual cases.

PLEASANT SUNDAY AFTERNOON, a mainly secular type of meeting held in a nonconformist chapel with songs, music and a lecture by a journalist, traveller or politician. They were regular and widespread between 1895 and 1914 and contributed, especially among Congregationalists and Baptists, to the spread of socialist ideals.

PLEASAUNCE. A fine of £1000 or 1000 marks levied by Richard II on 17 counties in 1398 alleged to have supported the Appellants, as the price of recovering his favour.

PLEAS OF THE CROWN were cases in which the Crown might have a financial interest and as all crimes might involve a fine or forfeiture, the term came to include the criminal law. In practice such pleas were confined originally to acts considered to be against the Crown or the King's Peace, namely treason, counterfeiting the royal seals or coinage, breach of the peace, homicide, arson, robbery and rape. In 1066 there were lists of royal pleas which varied between counties, but these were standardised under the Normans; larceny, however, long remained a plea of the sheriff in some places. As these matters concerned the King, they became cognisable in the Kings Bench and so in the equivalent division of the High Court. The development of the doctrine and procedure was a strong element in the erosion of seigneurial jurisdictions. *See also* PRAECIPE.

PLEAS OF THE SWORD, though differing in detail, were the Norman equivalent of Pleas of the Crown.

PLEGMUND, St. (?-914), learned Mercian, helped K. Alfred with his version of St. Gregory's *Cura Pastoralis*. He became Abp. of Canterbury in 890 and went to Rome for his *pallium*. In 901 he crowned K. Edward the Elder. In 909 he went to Rome again and apparently brought back relics of St. Blaise. In the same year he reorganised the S. W. Wessex church from two dioceses (Winchester and Sherborne) into five (Winchester, Ramsbury, Sherborne, Wells and Crediton).

PLIMSOLL, Samuel (1824-98), a Sheffield clerk, became Hon. Sec. of the Great Exhibition of 1851 and set up as a London coal merchant in 1853. Passionately concerned with loss of life in unseaworthy ships, in 1868 he secured election as a Radical M.P. to campaign for improvements. This culminated in his Merchant Shipping Bill of 1875. When the shipping interests obstructed it, he created a violent scene, thought to have suggested later Irish obstruction and drove his bill through to become law in 1876. The Plimsoll or Load Line, his enduring monument, marked on the outside of a ship, indicates clearly whether she is overloaded. He resigned his seat in 1880 and devoted the rest of his life to the welfare of seamen, of whose union he was Pres. from 1890.

PLOESTI (Roumania). Its great oilfields, vital to the Germans in both World Wars, attracted their cupidity and aggression.

PLOMBIÈRES, PACT OF (July 1858) was an unsigned but effective secret agreement between Cavour and Napoleon III for the expulsion of Austrian influence from Italy.

PLOUGH. Traces of mould-board ploughs have been found in Romano-British sites. The *caruca* was the light medieval plough; the *aratrum* the more elaborate heavy plough which made the later tillage of heavy soils feasible. Both were drawn by oxen, usually eight.

PLOUGH ALMS (O.E. Sulli-aelmessan). An Anglo-Saxon ecclesiastical tax (found in the Laws of Edmund (c. 950) and the *Canons of Edgar*) of a penny a year for each plough or ploughland.

PLOUGHLAND (Lat: *Carrucata*). A N. and E. English unit of assessment based on the area capable of being tilled by an eight-ox plough team in a year. *See also* HIDE AND SULUNG.

PLOUGH MONDAY. On this, the first Monday after Twelfth Night, men with corn in their hats dragged a plough round the village and, accompanied by a man or boy swathed in straw (called the Straw Bear) or a man dressed as a woman called Bessy, they leaped as high as they could (to persuade the corn to grow high) in front of each house. Straw bears were seen at Whittlesea (Cambs.) as late as 1909, on the Tuesday.

PLOWDEN, Edmund (1518-85), jurist, became a member of the Council for Wales in 1553 and was an M.P. from 1553 to 1555 but, being a R. Catholic, retired from politics when Q. Mary I died and devoted himself to the law. His Commentaries (1571 and 1579) were famous for their lucidity and much quoted, especially by Coke.

PLUG PLOTS (1842) were strikes involving the unplugging of boilers among Staffordshire miners. With Chartist and Anti-Corn Law League help, they spread to mines and mills in Lancashire and S. Wales and there was some rioting which led to arrests of some Chartists. They and the League thenceforth avoided association with such movements.

PLUMPTON FAMILY, LETTERS and PAPERS. Of this West Riding family, dependants of the Percys **(1) Sir Robert (1383-1421)** married the heiress of the Foljambes. He was several times M.P. Their son **(2) Sir William (1404-80)** was twice a sheriff and was Constable of Knaresborough. 229 family letters between 1416 and 1552 survived into the 17th cent. when they were copied. The originals are lost. Most of them concern a family dispute over inheritances between 1483 and 1515. A few refer to national events such as Buckingham's revolt (1483) and the execution of Perkin Warbeck. There are also cowchers of charters, deeds and court rolls.

PLUNKET, John, alias ROGERS (1664-1734), a professional Jacobite agent between 1708 and 1723,

when he was unmasked through the penetration of another's plot.

PLUNKET, St. Oliver (1629-81), Prof. of Theology at the College for Propaganda of Rome, was appointed R. Catholic Abp. of Armagh in 1669. He was tolerated by the govt. until the Test Act was passed, when he tactfully disappeared, but re-emerged to resume work. Of a saintly disposition, he was one of the many innocent victims of the "Popish Plot"; arrested in 1678 he was executed for treason with the customary barbarities.

PLUNKET, Thomas (1716-79) Baron, Austrian general born in Ireland, shared the victory over Frederick the Great at Kollin in 1758 and was Gov. of Antwerp from 1770.

PLUNKET (1) William Conyngham (1764-1854) 1st Ld. PLUNKET (1827) became an Irish M.P. in 1798 and being only lukewarmly opposed to the Union of 1800, became Sol-Gen. in 1803 and Att.-Gen. in 1805. From 1807 to 1812 he conducted a rich practice at the bar, but became an M.P. in 1812 and, after Grattan, the foremost advocate of R. Catholic emancipation. In 1820 he succeeded to Grattan's position but in 1822 accepted the Irish Att.-Generalship from Ld. Liverpool. In 1827 he became C.J. of the Irish Common Pleas and in 1829 he was the principal advocate of the R. Catholic Emancipation Bill in the Lords. He was Irish Ld. Chancellor from 1830 to 1841. His grandson **(2) William Conyngham (1828-97) 4th Ld.** (1871) was Bp. of Meath from 1876 to 1884 and a leading exponent of Irish evangelical anti-disestablishmentarianism (a word sentence attributed to him). He was Abp. of Dublin from 1886.

PLURALISM. The holding of more than one church office by the same parson at one time.

PLURAL CANDIDATURE. It has always been lawful for a person to stand for election in more than one electoral area at the same time, but after a candidate has been elected in more than one area of the same authority or more than one parliamentary constituency, he must choose one and resign the others.

PLURAL VOTING, i.e. the giving by one elector of more than one vote for the same candidate in the same electoral area has never been lawful but subject to this **(1)** where there is more than one post to be filled (e.g. in a two member constituency) every elector has one vote in respect of each post, though he is not bound to give any or all of them and **(2)** a person who is qualified as an elector for more than one elected body (e.g. the councils of two different parishes or counties) may vote in all of them. **(3)** The possibility that a voter might be represented by more than one M.P. arose most often when the franchise depended upon the ownership of property, which might be situated in different constituencies. It also occurred because universities were separately represented in Parliament, originally by four, but eventually by 11 members elected by graduate postal ballot and proportional representation. This was abolished under the Attlee Govt. just after World War II.

PLUTO (= Pipe Line Under The Ocean) was a petrol pipeline from Liverpool across England and the Channel to Normandy after June 1944 to supply the Allied armies. It was one of the most important strategic surprises of the campaign and its identification in air photography over England was prevented by setting most of the army to dig and fill in random earthworks all over the country. The pipeline rapidly reached Antwerp once the Germans began to retreat.

PLYMOUTH (Devon). The minor Saxon settlements began to acquire importance as trade developed with Aquitaine, as a result of Henry II's marriage with Eleanor. The place had a market by 1253 but it belonged to the Priory of Plympton, which resisted its development until its men successfully petitioned for the first of all parliamentary charters in 1439. At this period it was still second to

Dartmouth as a western port, but African and transatlantic discoveries gave it a strong stimulus and it became the chief base in the wars against Spain (*see* ARMADAS). In 1690 Plymouth Dock (now Devonport) was founded as a naval base against France and extended into Stonehouse. These two soon outstripped Plymouth in population and Devonport was separately incorporated in 1837. The "Three Towns" were united in 1914.

PLYMOUTH BRETHREN, a Puritanical sect originally founded in 1827 in Ireland by an ex-Anglican priest, J. N. Darby (1800-82). They moved to Plymouth in 1830 and split in 1849 into 'Open Brethren' and 'Exclusive Brethren'.

PLYMOUTH COLONY (Mass.). Epidemics perhaps originating with European fishermen had carried off many of the Algonquian Indians so that the Pilgrim Fathers, on arriving at Plymouth in the *Mayflower* in 1620, started without human enemies. Other groups founded Salem in 1626. *See* MASSACHUSETTS.

PLYMOUTH CO. *See* VIRGINIA.

POCAHONTAS. *See* ROLFE. JOHN.

POCKET BOROUGHS. *See* REFORM BILLS (1831-1832)-2(C).

POCKET SHERIFF. A sheriff occasionally appointed by the Crown without previous nomination in the Exchequer.

POCOCKE, Edward (1604-91), Oxford orientalist, as chaplain to the Turkey merchants at Aleppo, collected many MSS. He was the first Laudian Prof. of Arabic (1636) and parliamentary Prof. of Hebrew from 1648. Widely admired for his learning, he published *inter alia* a text and Latin translation of Abu'l Faraj's *Dynastic History* and a polyglot dictionary.

POETS CORNER. The south end of the south transept of Westminster Abbey, originally so named in 1711 by Oliver Goldsmith because Chaucer is buried there. It has since become a literary necropolis.

POILU **(Fr: hairy man).** A French private soldier in World War I.

POITOU. See AQUITAINE-6 *et seq.*

POLACCA. See SHIPS, SAILING.

POLAND. See POLAND; POLISH PARTITIONS; PRUSSIA; SAXONY; VIENNA, CONGRESS OF.

POLARIS MISSILES were U.S. ballistic nuclear weapons fired from submarines. The 1959 type had a range of 1500 miles; the 1963 type 2500 miles. They were supplied to Britain in 1962 as a result of defects discovered in the U.S. *Skybolt* missiles in which the British govt. had invested when it cancelled the *Blue Streak* rocket project.

POLE ARCTIQUE, CO. DU. This French Co. was founded in 1609 to compete with the Muscovy Co. by fortifying posts along the North-East Passage. In fact it set up a whaling station at Spitzbergen from which the Muscovy Co. drove it in 1613. It returned in 1629 and held its own against the Dutch and the Muscovy Co., but was extruded by the Danes in 1636 and went into liquidation. *See* NORD, CO. DU.

POLE (1) Richard (?-1505) a Buckinghamshire landowner was married by Henry VII to Margaret *d.* of George, D. of Clarence in 1491 and niece of Henry IV and Richard III. Henry VIII made her Countess of Salisbury and governess to the Princess Mary. She refused to have anything to do with the Boleyns and was banished from the court until they fell in 1536. She and Richard had three children **(2) Henry (1492-1538) Ld. MONTAGUE, (3) Geoffrey (?1502-58)** and **(4) Reginald (1500-58) Card. (1536).** They were all opposed to Henry VIII's divorce and their royal descent exposed them to Henry VIII's suspicion. Geoffrey was implicated in the Northern rebellion of 1536 at a time when Reginald published his criticism of Henry VIII in his *Pro Ecclesia Unitatis Defensione* (Lat. = In Defence of Church Unity). This angered the King, shook the position of the mother and in 1538 led to Geoffrey's arrest. His confessions under threat of torture implicated his brother Henry, who was executed. The mother was attainted with Henry in 1539 and executed in 1541 as a

precaution during the Yorkshire rising of that year. Meanwhile Reginald, appointed Legate to England in 1536, had to turn back because Henry VIII tried to have him apprehended in France. He then engaged in forming an anti-English alliance. In 1540 he was one of the three Legates who opened the Council of Trent. His efforts to bring about an understanding with England failed under Edward VI, but he became Legate to Mary I. His fanaticism was distrusted by Charles V who hindered his arrival until after she had married Philip of Spain. He was much involved in the persecutions of the reign, but found that attempts to resettle the church encountered unexpectedly strong opposition on material, doctrinal and political grounds. Moreover Pope Paul IV, who disliked him, undermined his influence by cancelling his legation. He died the same day as the Queen.

POLE, DE LA or ATTE POOLE (1) Richard (?-1345) and his brother **(2) William (?-1366)** were merchant financiers of Hull who lent large sums to Q. Isabel and Mortimer and Edward III; they represented Hull in Parliament (1322, 1327, 1334, 1336 and 1338) and moved to London (c. 1333) where Richard was the King's Chief Butler (thereby entitled to the proceeds of butlerage, a customs duty on wine) while William became a baron of the Exchequer. His son **(3) Michael (?1330-89) 1st Ld. (1366) 1st E. of SUFFOLK (1385)** fought under the Black Prince in France, but emerged into politics as a supporter of John of Gaunt. When the latter left for Spain, Michael became an intimate of Richard II who made him Chancellor in 1383. His great wealth (often violently acquired) excited jealousy; the peace policy which he advocated, the opposition of the military aristocracy; and his humble origin the suspicion of the nobles. The opposition was led by Thomas of Gloucester and he was convicted and dismissed in the Wonderful Parliament (1386). Briefly reinstated, he fled to Paris before the parliament of 1387. His estates and dignities were forfeited. He died in Paris. His son **(4) Michael (?1361-1415) 2nd E. (1397)** was restored by Henry IV and died at the siege of Harfleur. His son **(5) Michael (1394-1415) 3rd E.** was killed at Agincourt. His brother **(6) William (1396-1450) 4th E., 1st M. (1444) and 1st D. (1448)** served in Henry V's French wars and as commander in Normandy after 1428 was captured at Jargeau (1429), but ransomed himself. He came home in 1431 and married Alice, grand-daughter of Geoffrey Chaucer, the poet, niece of Card. Beaufort and widow of the E. of Salisbury. In 1433 he became Steward of the Royal Household and custodian of the captured D. of Orleans. By 1437 he had become a leading and greedy politician and, generally favouring peace with France, in frequent dispute with Humphrey D. of Gloucester. His progress may be measured by his acquisitions beginning with Thames valley Crown lands and Welsh castles. By 1446 he had also become C. J. of Chester and N. Wales, Steward of the Royal Mines, of Wallingford and of the Chiltern Hundreds. To these offices were added in 1447 the Chamberlainship of England and the Wardenship of the New Forest. In 1447 he also acquired the Earldom of Pembroke and D. Humphrey's Welsh lands and in 1448 the lucrative captaincy of Calais. Despite his prominence in arranging the King's French marriage (1445-6) his peace policy failed and the English position in Aquitaine collapsed. He was impeached and forfeited but pardoned and sent into exile. His ship was intercepted by Kentish seamen who struck off his head. His son **(7) John (1442-91) 2nd D. (1455)** married Elizabeth, sister of Edward IV whom he supported throughout his life, but he transferred his allegiance to Richard III and then to Henry VII. Of his and Elizabeth's children **(8) John (?1464-87) E. of LINCOLN (1467)** also adhered to Richard III and became Pres. of the North in 1483 and Ld. Lieut. of Ireland in 1484. Richard recognised bin) as heir presumptive to the throne. Henry VII left him alone, but in 1487 he was involved in Simnel's rebellion and was killed at Stoke. His brother **(9) Edmund (1472-1513) E. of SUFFOLK (1493)** inherited his claims, fled in 1499 to Flanders, was pardoned by Henry VII, but went abroad in 1501 again to the Emperor's court and was outlawed. In 1504 the D. of Guelders arrested him and he was surrendered to Henry as part of a Spanish negotiation and kept in the Tower until Henry VIII executed him in 1513. His brother **(10) Richard (?-1525)** also went to the Imperial Court in 1501, but took service in the French army (until expelled after the peace of 1514) and was ultimately killed at the B. of Pavia.

POLES. See ANTARCTICA; ARCTIC.

POLESDEN LACEY. Regency villa in Surrey, bought and embellished by Richard Brinsley Sheridan in 1797.

POLICE (*see* BOW STREET). **(1)** Sir Robert Peel's Metropolitan Police Act, 1829, authorised a police force in London; the initial scheme was drawn up by his two Commissioners, Col. Charles Rowan and Richard Mayne and the force started work in Sept. The Act of 1839 extended its area to any parish within 15 miles of Charing Cross.

(2) The Metropolitan Police were used as a model for the voluntary creation, under the Municipal Corporations Act, 1835, of borough forces controlled by the borough watch committees and, under the County Police Act, 1839, of county forces controlled by the J.Ps. By 1856 most areas had a force of sorts; then the County and Borough Police Act, 1856 made total coverage compulsory and to raise efficiency introduced Inspectors of Constabulary on the basis of whose reports the Home Sec. could make an annual grant of 25% for pay and clothes. The Local Govt. Act, 1888, transferred control in the counties to Standing Joint Committees of magistrates and the new county councillors. In fact the standards were based upon the practices of the Metropolitan Police, whose celebrated branch at Scotland Yard provided, by way of loan, most of the best detective skill available. On the other hand pay and conditions of service were by no means uniform and this led in 1918 to a police strike.

(3) The resulting Report of the Desborough Committee was the foundation for the Police Act, 1919, which empowered the Home Sec. to standardise pay and conditions (including housing) and created the Police Federation. The arrangements were rounded off by a pensions system in 1921.

(4) Social unrest and increasing traffic soon required further reorganisation of a more technical kind. This was done in London by the successive commissioners, Lds. Byng and Trenchard between 1928 and 1933. The beat system was supplemented by wireless patrols and scientific equipment and Ld. Trenchard founded the, sometimes criticised, Police College at Hendon. As usual the metropolitan example spread to other forces which remodelled themselves with Home Office encouragement just in time for World War II.

(5) Hendon was closed in 1939 and in 1949 new colleges available to all forces were opened at Ryton near Coventry (transferred in 1961 to Hartley Wintney) and at Tulliallan near Kincardine. Hendon was reopened. Post-war recruiting problems were largely solved by raising salaries and in 1953 by setting up the **Police Council** to negotiate pay. From that time until 1979 the main limitation on the size of police forces was govt. willingness or lack of it to increase establishments, for which it provided 50% of the cost.

(6) The rising crime rate and the mobility of criminals produced much criticism and led to further improvements in centrally provided services (e.g. inspection and research) and some misconceived demands for a unified national force. The main result was the amalgamation of the small forces with their neighbours between 1948 and 1955 and the creation by further amalgamations of several regional forces after 1965. These measures (which did nothing to raise effective establishments) largely

failed to stem the tide of crime, so that by 1978 only 4% of known crimes in the Metropolis were being solved. Traffic problems, on the other hand, had been mostly solved. The truth was that the police were overburdened. This, and a lowering of entry standards caused by low pay seemed to cause departures from the previous high standards. The few, if disturbing cases of undue police violence, of fabricated evidence and in London of gainful collusion with criminals, received wide publicity which unduly blackened the reputation of the forces. Public confidence was further undermined by an unwise insistence on investigating such cases privately (and after 1976 by the Police Complaints Board), but in fact policemen were also charged before the courts. In the late 1970s the Police were also accused with increasing stridency of racial prejudice and Ld. Scarman's report (1982) after rioting in S. London, implied that such accusations were not without substance. In his 1999 report on a murder, Macpherson of Cluny made them directly if intemperately.

(7) Between 1900 and 1982 the police forces in England and Wales increased from 41,000 to only 109,900 (including some 11,000 women) and there were some 15,000 part-time Special Constables. In Scotland the figures were respectively 4900 and 12,500 (including 750 women). In N. Ireland the numbers increased between 1930 and 1977 from 2,800 to 5,700. *See* BURGHS-SCOTS-8

POLICE FEDERATION, representing constables below the rank of Superintendent, was created in 1919.

POLIOMYELITIS (INFANTILE PARALYSIS, PALSY) is an ancient disease originally of the very young; clubfootedness due to it seems to have been a feature of life. In 1773 it caused Sir Walter Scott's lifelong lameness, but it first attracted attention as an *epidemic* disease in 1789. There were important outbreaks in Nottinghamshire in 1835, in Scandinavia in 1890 to 1905, in New Zealand and the U.S.A in 1916 and during World War II it occasionally attacked troops, especially in the Middle East. It was sharply checked from 1955 by the Salk Vaccine. *See* EPIDEMICS, HUMAN.

POLISH PARTITIONS (*see* BALTIC; PRUSSIA) **(1)** The Seven Years' War and its aftermath were as decisive in the Baltic area as elsewhere. Augustus III of Saxony and Poland died in 1763 and the Czarina Catharine the Great, with Frederick of Prussia's connivance, bullied the Poles into electing her former lover, Stanislas Poniatowski (r. 1764-95). In so far as Poland had a govt., its head was now the Russian ambassador in Warsaw, but the war had warned Russian statesmen that further westward advances would require circumspection. With cosmopolitan Baltic Germans in powerful positions and a Czarina from Anhalt (next to Brandenburg), this was easy for them to understand, but the extent to which ability, ambition and lust influenced this extraordinary woman will never be known. Russian lovers (Orlov and Potemkin) coincided with a change from a western, freethinking European policy to a southern, orthodox Russian one.

(2) By 1768 Catharine's and Potemkin's great Turkish war had been launched; without renouncing northern ambitions she was committed to a northern peace, but meantime the powers observed her (British trained) Baltic fleet circumnavigate Europe and defeat the Turks in the Aegean (B. of Tschesmé, July 1770). Britain was distracted by Marathas and American unrest, France by the economic consequences of recent defeat. A suggestion by Frederick that Poland might be partitioned was a polite reminder that Russia could not, without western allies and against Austro-Prussian opposition, both fight the Turks and dominate all Poland. Moreover Sweden in 1771 acquired in Gustavus III (1771-92) an able monarch hostile to Russia. The Czarina adroitly offered an alliance and her Holstein claims (*see* BALTIC 42-3) to the Danes (who had seen the circumnavigation) in return for Oldenburg, but Prussia would not be frightened. The FIRST

PARTITION accordingly took place in Aug. 1772. The Empress Maria Theresa signed with reluctance, based on grounds of comity and ethics and unconvinced by her advisers and her son. Austria, in return for Galicia, gave up her free hand in the East. Russia got the lands east of the Dvina and Dnieper, but lost her threatening influence in the West. Prussia, by acquiring West Prussia and, with a stranglehold on Danzig, the control of the Vistula basin, was the real gainer.

(3) In fact exhaustion, plague and Pugachev's peasant revolts were ending the Turkish war. While the Swedes tried to protect themselves by a French alliance, in Feb. 1773, Oldenburg passed nominally to Russia in Oct. By July 1774 the Turkish war was over (P. of Kuchuk Kainardji), much to Catharine's relief, but she could not prevent Frederick of Prussia's advantageous commercial treaty with Poland in Mar. 1775. The special conditions of Swedish politics after 1782 created a permanent element of uncertainty. The Czarina relied, in Sweden as in Poland, on bribes and threats to nourish constitutional dissension which would keep both countries quiet, while she digested her southern gains. In both countries, therefore, the champions of strong govt. were both reformers and anti-Russian. Their hopes brightened when in a new war (1787-92) the Turks proved tougher than had been expected. Gustavus III attacked Russia in 1788: militarily a failure, this move prevented another Russian naval circumnavigation against the Turks and it enabled the King to establish an autocracy (Feb. 1789). The Poles tried to follow suit. A reforming Sejm was convened in Oct. 1788 and, encouraged by Prussia, debated a constitution with an hereditary monarchy and abolition of the *liberum veto*. But Austria and Russia renewed their alliance, defeated the Turks at Focsani and on the Rymnik and took Belgrade (July-Oct. 1789). Peace negotiations began and the Czarina was free to deal with the Poles. The Swedish peace was concluded at VERELA in Aug. 1790; the Austrian at SISTOVA in Aug. 1791; the Russian at JASSY in Jan. 1792.

(6) By this time the Poles had adopted their new constitution, but dissidents appealed to Catharine who invaded Poland in May, by which time Gustavus III had been assassinated. Left in the lurch by Prussia, the Poles capitulated. In Jan. 1793 Prussia and Russia agreed on the SECOND PARTITION. It gave Russia the lands east of the Dvina and Dnieper and Prussia Danzig, its hinterland and most of the territory west of the Vistula. The process was completed in Sept. and led to an explosion of Polish feeling led by Thaddaeus KOSCIUSZKO. He raised the flag of independence at Cracow in Mar. 1794 but his desperate and courageous supporters, after initial successes, were overwhelmed by Russian and Prussian armies by Nov. and in the THIRD PARTITION of Oct. 1795, Poland disappeared. Lithuania went to Russia, Cracow, Lublin and Sandomir to Austria and Warsaw to Prussia. These measures were completed in 1797.

(7) FOURTH PARTITION (1939). After Nazi-Germany had rearmed, she could close the western entrances to the Baltic and cut the "Versailles nationalities" off from western support against RUSSIA. They thus became totally dependent upon Hitler who could sell them to Russia when he liked. The Russians were ready to offer a price. By the Thieves Compact (The Ribbentrop-Molotov agreement of Aug. 1939), which precipitated World War II, the Russians promised material support for Hitler's adventures in return for the Baltic republics, Finland and a Polish partition. The latter was effected (not exactly as agreed) in Sept. 1939.

POLISH SUCCESSION, War of (1733-5). *See* BALTIC-44; LORRAINE; PARMA; SICILY; TUSCANY.

POLITICAL ARITHMETIC. The older term, originated by Sir William Petty in 1690, for statistics.

POLITICAL CORRECTNESS. Euphemism or ironical pejorative for a sacrifice of style by substituting words or manipulating grammar at the instance of a pressure group in the interests or supposed interest of a group which it is championing. The new expressions are commonly weaker and vaguer than the original and indifferent to moral absolutes e.g. *murder* becomes *unlawful killing;* adultery, *extramatrimonial intercourse.*

POLITICAL LEVY. The sum levied by a trade union from a member towards the cost of supporting a political party. The Trade Union Act, 1913, required trade unions to keep a separately accounted political fund and to identify separately the amount payable by a member as a subscription and as a political contribution and he could (by CONTRACTING OUT) refuse to pay the latter. *See* OSBORNE'S CASE.

POLITICAL UNIFORMS. *See* RIOT.

POLITIQUES were those who favoured practical compromise during the French Wars of Religion.

POLLEXFEN, Sir Henry (?1632-91). This professional lawyer prosecuted at the Bloody Assizes in 1685, defended the Seven Bishops in 1688, became Att.-Gen. in Feb. 1689 and C. J. of the Common Pleas in May.

POLLITT, Harry (1890-1960) opposed participation in World War I and organised strikes at Southampton in 1915 and in 1920 against intervention in Russia. He was a founder of the British Communist Party; in 1924 he was Sec. of the National Minority Movement, an organisation for penetrating the trade unions and in 1929 Sec. of the Communist Party. He did much to mobilise opinion in favour of the Spanish Republicans. As party leader he approved the declaration of war on Germany in 1939, only to be required within weeks as a result of the German Thieves Compact with Russia publicly to confess his error and declare his sympathy for Hitler. He was nevertheless demoted. When the thieves fell out and the Germans invaded Russia, he readopted his former opinion and became party Sec. again. From 1956 he was party Chairman.

POLL TAXES or POLL MONEY (1) 1377 This, like the Parish Tax of 1371 was an experiment due to the reduced yield and unfairness of the taxes on moveables. The Parliament of 1377 granted a poll tax of 4d. per head of the laity over 14 and the clergy offered 1s. for every beneficed clerk and 4d. a head for the rest. Uniformity irrespective of means created opposition. **(2) 1379** This poll tax was consequently graduated but proved less profitable. Hence **(3) 1380** Parliament returned to the ungraded tax and at 1s. a head. This higher rate and resentment at the collectors' inquiries led to evasion between 1377 and 1381 by as much as a third of the population and the demand for a return to the older system was prominent in the Peasants' Revolt. Poll taxes were not again imposed until **(4) 1640** This was an emergency tax to pay off the English and especially the Scottish armies. It was graduated according to social status, viz. peers £100-£40, down to freemen of any city company, 1s. **(5) 1666** For the Dutch War. It amounted to 1% of public pensions. Professional persons paid 15%, servants 10%. In addition, persons of higher social status paid £50 (for a duke) down to £5 for an esquire, **(6) 1678** This was raised for the French war and was similar to (5) above. **(7) 1688** For the reduction of Ireland. It amounted to over 2% of personal estate with additions similar to (5) above including gentlemen at £1. A later act added traders and artificers if they had not paid as gentlemen. **(8) 1689** This resembled (7). **(9) 1691** For the French War. This was payable in quarterly instalments at a rate of 4s. per head plus £4 for anyone between the degree of gentleman and peer with more than £300. Peers paid £40; it was expected to raise £1,342,000. **(10) 1694** For the French War. This resembled (9) save that those with £600 paid double. **(11) 1989** This was called the Community Charge and was payable to local authorities. It led to rioting and when it was abolished in 1993 over £1,000,000,000 remained uncollected.

POLO, Marco (?1254-1324), Venetian, set out with his father and uncle in 1271 *via* Persia, W. Asia and Tartary to the capital of the Mongol Khan, Kublai, which they reached in 1275. Marco stayed in Kublai's service and was employed in various missions in India and China. In 1292 the Polos went to Persia as ambassadors and reached home in 1295. His account is a very complete and accurate picture of his experiences and of the Asiatic world of the time.

POLLOCK (1) Sir David (1780-1847) was C. J. of Bombay from 1846 to 1847. His brother **(2) Sir Jonathan (1783-1870),** Tory M.P. for Huntingdon from 1831 to 1844, was Peel's Att.-Gen. from 1834 to 1835 and from 1841 to 1844 when he became C.B. of the Exchequer until 1866. His brother **(3) Sir George (1786-1872)** became a Maj.-Gen. in 1838 and having relieved Jelalabad (Afghanistan) in 1842, with Nott occupied Kabul (*see* AFGHANISTAN.) The son of (2), **(4) Sir Charles Edward (1823-97)** became in 1873 the last Baron of the Exchequer and wrote a number of legal works. His nephew **(5) Sir Frederick (1845-1937)** was Corpus Prof. of Jurisprudence at Oxford from 1883 to 1903 and wrote a number of legal works including the subsequently famous *Law of Torts* (1887) and with F. W. Maitland a *History of English Law*.

POLWARTH. *See* HUME.

POLYTECHNICS. *See* UNIVERSITIES.

POMPADOUR, Jeanne Antoinette Poisson, Marquise de (1721-64). *See* LOUIS XV.

POMPEY. Naval slang for Portsmouth.

PONDICHERRY (India) was the capital of the French East India Co's. possessions in India. It was occupied by the Dutch from 1693 to 1699; attacked by the British in 1748 and occupied by them from 1761 to 1765, 1778 to 1785 and 1793 to 1814. It was transferred to India in Nov. 1954.

PONSONBY. Two related families of Anglo-Irish landowners powerful in Fermanagh and Kilkenny.

A. (1) John (1713-87), M.P. in the Irish Parliament for Newtown from 1739, became Sec. of the Revenue Board in 1742 and first commissioner in 1744. By manipulating the Board's patronage he built himself the most influential and lucrative position in the Irish govt. and in 1736 had himself elected Speaker. His power, in collaboration with successive Lds. Lieut. and Deputies dominated Dublin until 1771, by which time he had quarrelled with the M. Townshend and was dismissed from the Board as part of the policy of broadening the base of the govt. beyond the narrow circle of "undertakers", by whose arts the system was managed. He resigned the Speakership later in the year and slowly faded out of politics. His son **(2) William Brabazon (1744-1806) 1st Ld. PONSONBY (1806),** a Foxite Whig, was an Irish M.P. from 1764 to 1800 and then M.P. for Kilkenny. His brother **(3) George (1755-1817)** was an Irish M.P. from 1776 to 1800. He was wholly opposed to the Anglo-Irish Union, but after it was accomplished he was M.P. for Wicklow in the U.K. Parliament from 1801 and for Co. Cork in 1806-7. As such he was Fox's Ld. Chancellor of Ireland in 1806. From 1808, as M.P. for Tavistock, he led the opposition until his death. A son of (2), **(4) Sir William (1772-1815),** a professional cavalry officer, commanded the Union Brigade at Waterloo, where he was killed in the course of a celebrated and disastrous charge.

B. A brother of (1), **(5) William (1704-93) 2nd E. of BESSBOROUGH (1758),** was Irish M.P. for Kilkenny from 1725 and British M.P. for Derby from 1742. Though an assiduous politician and holder of minor office, he is chiefly remarkable for making no recorded speech in any of the legislative houses of which he was a member. His grandson **(6) John William (1781-1847) 1st Ld. DUNCANNON (1834) 4th E. (1844)** usually known as Ld. Duncannon, was a British M.P. from 1805 and strong supporter of R. Catholic emancipation. He was first Commissioner of Woods and Forests under Grey (1831), Home Sec. under Melbourne in 1834 and First Commissioner and Privy Seal under Melbourne again from 1834 to 1839. As such he was responsible for rebuilding the Houses of Parliament. In 1846 he became a well liked Ld. Lieut. of Ireland, but died suddenly. His second son **(7) Frederick George Brabazon (1815-95) 6th E. (1880)** headed the Irish Royal Commission on Land appointed by Gladstone in 1880. The report, which recommended fixity of tenure, independently assessed rents and freedom of sale of long leases, was a landmark, first in Irish and later in English agricultural legislation.

PONTACK, ? (?1638-?1720), son of Arnaud de Pontac, Pres. of the *parlement* of Bordeaux, migrated to London and opened *The Pontack's Head,* a tavern in Abchurch Lane which was highly fashionable for its excellent food and the wit and learning of its host.

PONTEFRACT or POMFRET (W. Yorks.), a strategic point 5 miles from the junction of the Rs. Aire and Calder at Castleford and the Aire crossing at Ferrybridge, was the site of an important royal castle founded in 1069. Thomas of Lancaster (1322), Richard II (1400) and E. Rivers (1483) were put to death there. There was also a major abbey. After the monastic Dissolutions (1529) the place declined, but it revived with coal mining in the Industrial Revolution.

PONTHIEU, COUNTY OF (Fr.) with its port and capital of Abbeville passed in 1279, as a result of dynastic marriages, to Eleanor of Castile, Q. to Edward I, who organised its govt. and ruled it on her behalf. Philip of Valois seized it in 1336 and King John of France conferred it on James of Bourbon. In 1360 it was retroceded to England under the P. of Bretigny, but the French recovered it in 1369. From 1435 to 1463 and from 1465 to 1477 it was a Burgundian fief.

PONTIAC. *See* OTTAWA INDIANS.

POOLE (Dorset). The channels and anchorages in its apparently wide harbour are restricted and there is a shifting bar at the entrance. Hence Poole, though an important early port supplying shipping for royal use in 1224, tended to fall behind as ships grew in size. The flagging development of the place was stimulated in Tudor times by the Newfoundland fisheries. Piracy was endemic and practised until the 17th Cent. The town was a Puritan stronghold in the Civil War.

POONA (India), the Peishwa's capital from 1750, was occupied by Wellesley (later Wellington) in 1803 and ceded to the British in 1817. They built a large military cantonment and made it the summer capital of the govt. of Bombay. *See* MARATHAS.

POONA PACT (1932). *See* COMMUNAL AWARD.

POOR LAW ACT 1601 or "STATUTE OF ELIZABETH" followed exhortatory and ineffectual measures of 1563, 1572, 1576 and 1597 to deal with unemployment. It enjoined J.Ps. to nominate for each parish between two and four householders who, together with the churchwardens, were to be Overseers of the Poor. These, with the consent of two local J.Ps. were to arrange (a) to set to work children whose parents could not maintain them; (b) to set to work persons "having no means to maintain them and use no ordinary and daily trade of life to get their living by"; (c) to provide relief of "the lame, impotent, old, blind and such other ... being old and not able to work" and (d) "for the putting out of such children to be apprentices". The Overseers were to raise the necessary money "by taxation of every inhabitant, parson, vicar and other and of every occupier of lands, houses, tithes ... coalmines or saleable underwoods" to provide "a convenient stock flax, hemp, wool, thread, iron and other necessary ware and stuff". J.P.s. could subsidise a poor parish by rating other parishes in the same hundred and a poor hundred by rating other parishes elsewhere in the county. The Act was the effective foundation of the Poor Law until superseded by the new Poor Law of 1834 and of local govt. finance until superseded by the Community Charge in 1989. *See next entry and* SPEENHAMLAND; VAGRANCY.

POOR LAW INCORPORATIONS provided the precedent for the later Unions. Administration by urban parishes was muddled and wasteful, while rural parish resources could support a workhouse only seldom better than a ruinous cottage. The first incorporation, instigated by John Cary under a local Act of 1696, covered the 19 parishes of Bristol. Others followed haphazardly e.g. Sudhury (3 parishes) in 1702. Nine of the 10 (rural) hundreds of E. Suffolk were thus incorporated between 1756 and 1779, but this was peculiar to Suffolk. Each incorporation substituted a central House of Industry for the parish workhouses. In theory concentration would reduce overheads, provide better accommodation and make the system self supporting by improved production and the resulting sales. They provided a concentrated cottage industry such as wool spinning for local weavers, rug and coarse cloth and sack making and the winding of ropes, fishing nets and ploughlines. In practice their unskilled, aged, witless or feckless inmates were unable to compete with rising industrial production and after about 1782 (*see* GILBERT'S ACT) all the incorporations were running at substantial losses. Corruption, neglect and maladministration existed from the start and conditions were often scandalous: mortality rates varied from 7% to 26%. Some Houses were used by prostitutes as winter retreats and the authorities did their best to get rid of children by compulsory apprenticeship, often regardless of aptitudes. The Houses were exceedingly unpopular and their construction sometimes led to riots. The failure of the system was obvious by the 1830s when Acts of Disincorporation were being passed without opposition.

POOR LAW (SCOTS). An act of 1535 made every parish responsible for its own poor. Another of 1579 provided that sturdy beggars should be arrested and scourged and impotent poor placed in almshouses or given begging badges and that householders should be assessed to a rate for the relief of the poor. In 1597 poor relief was to be supervised by kirk sessions and from 1617 justices and constables were to punish vagrants and assess parishes. This fair seeming system was unworkable because householders would not pay. In 1625 the magistrates of E. Lothian refused to levy a rate. By 1700 only 2 or 3 parishes had adopted any assessment. The church was helpless in times of dearth and the landowners usually made provision themselves. The system remained thus backward in the Lowlands until the Industrial Revolution, and in the Highlands until the mid-19th cent.

POOR PERSONS LITIGATION. By an act of 1494 the Ld. Chancellor could issue writs for and assign counsel to poor persons *gratis* in civil suits. This remained the law until 1883. In criminal cases prisoners could obtain a defence at the public expense under an act of 1930. Down to 1951 barristers, however, commonly gave their services for one guinea in cases of obvious poverty.

POPE, Alexander (1688-1744), silver age poet of great wit, dexterity and Tory sympathies, published anonymously and under his own name a great variety of letters and works in verse, of which the earliest to be long remembered is the *Rape of the Lock* (1712). *Windsor Forest* (1713) *inter alia* praised the P. of Utrecht and led to a friendship with Swift, Gay, Atterbury and others of the same circle. In 1718 he completed a famous, partly paraphrased, translation of the *Iliad* and in 1717 he began his long affairs with Martha Blount and Lady Mary Wortley Montague, both South Sea speculators.

Of a waspish disposition, in 1723 he published a satire on Addison (dead since 1719) and in 1725 a critical edition of Shakespeare which was justly criticised by Lewis Theobald (1688-1744) in 1726. Pope promptly attacked Theobald in a satire of 1727 and then made him the preposterous hero of the *Dunciad* (1728), a sprightly and memorable epic on dullness. He continued to issue other, mainly moral or philosophical poems, but by 1733 he had quarrelled with Lady Mary and inserted a gratuitous attack on her in his *Satire I. His Epistle to Dr. Arbuthnot* contained invective against Addison, Hervey, Theobald and others. By 1737 he had plunged into pamphlet controversy with his *Grub Street Journal*. Meanwhile he had quarrelled with Colley Cibber and so in 1743 Theobald was degraded in favour of Cibber as the hero of the *Dunciad's* final version.

POPHAM (1) Sir John (?1531-1607) was an M.P. from 1571 to 1583, Speaker in 1580, Att.-Gen. in 1587 and C.J. of the Kings Bench from 1592. His son **(2) Sir Francis (1573-1644)** was an M.P. in every parliament except the Short Parliament from 1597 until his death and an active promoter of American colonisation. His son **(3) Edward (?1610-51),** M.P. and Parliamentary commander in the West Country, became a Commissioner of the Navy, commanded the fleet in the Downs in 1649 and helped to blockade the Palatine Princes in Lisbon in 1651.

"POPISH PLOT" (1678-81) was fictitious. Two clergymen, **Titus Oates (1649-1705)** who had been indicted for perjury in 1675 and **Israel Tonge (1621-80),** an anti-Papist pamphleteer, concocted allegations of a Jesuit plot to kill Charles II, to massacre Protestants and so to bring James II to the throne. Oates got his circumstantial detail while chaplain to the R. Catholic D. of Norfolk's protestant servants in 1676 and then through having, as a pretended convert, been in Jesuit establishments at Valladolid and St. Omer. Tonge worked it all up into a plausible narrative. Oates deposed to the well known protestant magistrate, Sir Edmund Berry Godfrey, on 6 Sept. 1678 and to the Privy Council some days later. Godfrey was found transfixed with his own sword on 22 Oct. In the intense and credulous public excitement, a Jesuit-educated adventurer, **William Bedloe (1650-80)** cashed in on the movement. He made similar allegations in which, so he said, Oates had anticipated him. The stories pointed to Edward Coleman, Mary of Modena's sec., who had been corresponding with French R. Catholics and had visited the nuncio in Brussels. He burned most of his papers, but those which were seized implicated yet others. The coincidence of perjury, murder, apparent corroboration and documentary evidence seemed conclusive. The E. of Shaftesbury now sensed an opportunity to use the 'plot' as a form of political terrorism. A R. Catholic goldsmith, Miles Prance, arrested on suspicion of murdering Godfrey, was bullied into a false confession. On 21 Nov. another, William Staley, was sentenced to death for treasonable words and then on Prance's and Bedloes' evidence, three others were convicted of the murder. Tonge, Bedloe and especially Oates were acclaimed as public heroes and lodged and paid at the public expense. The King disbelieved them entirely, but for nearly three years anyone else who expressed disbelief or favoured a policy which Shaftesbury disliked was likely to be hounded or put in danger of his life through false charges. Altogether some 35 people were put to death on perjured evidence. These included Oliver Plunket, Abp. of Armagh, and Vist. Stafford. The fury died down in 1681. *See* CHARLES II-24-26.

POPLAR, -ISM one of the earliest London borough councils to be controlled by Labour (under George Lansbury), in 1921 defied the govt. by refusing to pay its share of the London County Council's expenses, on the economically equitable ground that the rich boroughs should pay more. Moreover its totals of unemployment pay, made under the Poor Law to workers whose right to national benefits had run out, were higher than most, so that the council was particularly poor. The councillors were duly surcharged by the auditors. They refused to pay and were committed to prison for contempt. They went in gala procession with bands and banners.

POPULAR FRONT. Originally a construction of Spanish left-wing parties designed to entice the centre into collaboration with crypto-revolutionaries on the pretext of opposing a right-wing coalition in the elections of Feb. 1936; and generally any alliance designed to further left wing tactical interests.

POPULATION. Lack of statistical information makes exact assessments of medieval population impossible, but a 10th cent. copy of the *Senchus fer N-Alba* gives the 7th cent. military strength of Dalriada as over 1000 men. Allowing for women, children and old men this gives this Celtic Kingdom a population of no more than 5000. From Domesday Book (1086) a rough estimate of 1,250,000 has been made and the Poll Tax returns of 1377 suggest an increase to 2,500,000 by the late 14th cent., despite the Black Death. The population is surmised to have been still c. 2,500,000 in 1558, at between 4,000,000 and 4,500,000 in the reign of James I and at 5,600,000 in 1630. These figures may be inconsistent with each other. By 1750, for which more reliable evidence is available, the population including Scotland was probably a little over 7,000,000. The first census was made in 1801. The following are the decennial totals:-

Census	Eng. & W.		Scotland	
Year	Popu-lation	Females per 1000 males	Popu-lation	Females per 1000 males
1801	8.9	1057	1.6	1176
1811	10.2	1054	1.8	1185
1821	12.0	1036	2.1	1129
1831	13.9	1040	2.4	1122
1841	15.9	1046	2.6	1100
1851	17.9	1042	2.9	1100
1861	20.1	1053	3.1	1112
1871	22.7	1054	3.4	1096
1881	26.0	1055	3.7	1076
1891	29.0	1063	4.0	1072
1901	32.5	1068	4.5	1057
1911	36.0	1068	4.8	1062
1921	37.9	1096	4.9	1080
1931	40.0	1088	4.8	1083
1939	41.5	1081	5.0	1076
1951	43.8	1082	5.1	1094
1961	46.1	1067	5.2	1086
1971	48.6	1058	5.2	1078
1981	49.2	1051	5.1	1080
1991	49.9	1054	5.0	1088

POPULATION OF COLONIES. *See* EMIGRATION FROM U.K.

PORSON, Richard (1759-1808), son of a parish clerk, early attracted respect for his astonishing memory and was educated by private subscription and the help of friends. He took a fellowship of Trinity Coll., Cambridge in 1782, but forfeited it in 1792 for refusing to take orders, whereupon he was promptly elected Regius Professor of Greek. In fact he mostly engaged in private study at the Temple, London, where he was much sought out by authors. A somewhat Johnsonian figure, though occasionally drunk in later life, he greatly advanced the study of classical Greek.

PORT. *See* WINE TRADE.

PORT, PORTMAN, PORTMOTE, PORT REEVE. The word *port,* apart from its coastal meaning, was also the equivalent to borough or perhaps to walled or market town. A portman was thus a freeman, the portmote the burgess or freemen's assembly, a Capital or Head Portman an alderman and the Port Reeve the mayor. The Municipal Corporations Act 1835 left a few such corporations such as Ashburton in existence, not as local

authorities but as trusts for the benefit of their portmen. *See also* COURT OF RECORD, BOROUGH.

PORTAGE. A place, often strategically important, in America or Canada where a boat had to be carried or manhandled.

PORTAL, Charles Frederick (1893-1971) 1st Vist. PORTAL of HUNGERFORD (1946) was Chief of the Air Staff from 1940 to 1946 and as such exerted a prolonged and important influence on the highest direction of World War II. He was controller of Atomic Energy at the Ministry of Supply from 1946 to 1951 and Chairman of the British Aircraft Corporation from 1960 to 1968.

PORTCULLIS (1) A heavy wooden or metal grating the size of a gateway, which could be dropped rapidly down side grooves to block it, as one of the defences against surprise. It was introduced from the Levant in the Crusades. A generally successful device, it could be frustrated only in a peacetime surprise (as happened at Roxburgh Castle in 1307) by driving in and leaving a wagon under it. **(2)** For reasons unknown, a crowned portcullis is the symbol of Parliament.

PORTE. *See* SUBLIME PORT.

PORTEOUS, John (?-1736) and PORTEOUS RIOTS. As Capt. of the Edinburgh City Guard, he fired on the crowd during a disturbance at an execution and killed several. Tried and sentenced to death himself, he was reprieved whereupon the mob took him from prison and lynched him. The identity of his murderers was never discovered.

PORTER, Sir Charles (?-1696), a London apprentice who served as a Dutch private soldier and also kept a tavern, returned to England at the Restoration and was called to the bar. In 1675 he was put in custody with others in the *Dalmahoy Case* for contempt of the Commons but knighted. He habitually overspent and was liable to be pressurised by the ascendant political power. Thus, in 1686 he became James II's Irish Ld. Chancellor. He was dismissed at Tyrconnell's instance in 1687 but, increasingly a partisan of William III, returned to Ireland in 1690 and was the latter's Ld. Chancellor there until he died.

PORTER, Endymion (1587-1649) was brought up in Spain. He entered the service of the D. of Buckingham, became a Groom of the Bedchamber to P. Charles (Charles I) and conducted the Duke's Spanish correspondence. He was at Madrid in 1623 to prepare for Charles and the Duke's visit and again in 1628 with peace proposals. Temporarily rich, he was a friend and patron of poets and helped Charles I to form his picture collection. He was M.P. for Droitwich in the Long Parliament, opposed Strafford's attainder and joined the King when he left London. The Commons expelled him and he left England in 1645 in poverty.

PORTLAND, Es. of. *See* WESTON − ESSEX FAMILY.

PORTLAND, Earls and Dukes of. *See* BENTINCK.

PORTLAND GOVT. 1807-1809 (Eleven in Cabinet increased to 13 in 1809. The leading figures were Ld. Hawkesbury, Home Sec; George Canning, Foreign; Vist. Castlereagh, War and Colonies, under the Chairmanship of the ailing, slow witted but high ranking D. of Portland) (*See* ALL THE TALENTS.)

(1) It immediately increased its majority in a "No Popery" election, but had to face an attack on sinecures by way of a parliamentary select committee, followed by sensational attacks on all the royal family except the King and the D. of Cambridge. A privy council committee had to investigate whether the Princess of Wales had had an illegitimate child. Foreign events were depressing. There was news of Whitelocke's disaster at Buenos Aires and of Duckworth's failure at Constantinople. There were mutinies at Malta and Vellore (India). The victorious Maida force had been withdrawn, leaving the Calabrians to the mercy of the French. The Egyptian expedition had been a failure. On the Baltic the King's German Legion was isolated at Stralsund after Bonaparte's victory over the Russians at Friedland (June 1807). The T. of Tilsit (July) added Russia to the Continental System and secretly allotted Denmark to France and Finland to Russia.

(2) The secret clauses were, however, quickly known at Whitehall. The Legion was transported to Denmark to assist a combined operation, in which Copenhagen was taken and the Danish fleet seized (Aug-Oct. 1807). The govt. then sent an expeditionary force under Sir John Moore to assist Sweden (May 1808) but, frustrated by the oddities of the Swedish King. it returned. This was fortunate because the force became available for the Peninsula (*see* PENINSULAR WAR).

(3) In the meantime the economic clauses of the T. of Tilsit called for retaliation (*see* ORDERS IN COUNCIL) designed to channel all European trade through Britain. Napoleon replied by enacting the seizure of all goods touching at British ports. The U.S.A. tried to embargo trade with both sides. The resulting dislocations induced falls in exports and such reductions in imports (especially cotton) that there was serious unemployment and, with a poor harvest, a rapid rise in the price of bread. Moreover the standstill in the Baltic trade created a timber shortage and so a shortage of ships. The govt. accordingly sought to increase trade with areas free from hostile domination. Trade with S. America and the Levant increased by 50% annually using 1805 as the base.

(4) In Jan. 1809 G. L. Wardle, radical M.P. for Okehampton, revealed to the Commons the details of a traffic in military commissions by Mary Anne Clarke, the actress mistress of the C-in-C, the D. of York. The Duke was exonerated of personal knowledge or corruption by a vote in the Commons, but he had evidently told her too much and had to resign. The affair, pursued as a piece of sensational anti-royalism, occurred during Sir John Moore's tragic retreat to Corunna. It reflected on the conduct of the war and so upon the govt. rather than the Crown. Spencer Perceval, the Chancellor of the Exchequer, however, carried an act to penalise soliciting money for patronage, but the opposition in full cry unearthed an HEIC scandal involving Castlereagh and then another involving him and Perceval in allegations of corruption in the use of Treasury influence to affect Irish elections. The govt. defeated the resulting motions by whipped majorities, which still further damaged its reputation. It was forced to countenance Curwen's Bill against Treasury bargains for electoral support, thereby weakening its future hold upon the political system. For these political disasters, Wellesley's landing at Lisbon offered only speculative compensations and his brilliant defeat of Soult at Oporto was soon overshadowed by the Austrian defeat at Wagram (July 1809), the Russian annexation of Finland (P. of Frederickshamn, Sept.), the P. of Vienna and finally the British Walcheren disaster (July-Dec.)

(5) The govt. had hitherto survived because no one could find an alternative. It now came apart at the seams. Canning had attacked Castlereagh for inefficiency in a letter to Portland (Mar. 1809). Portland asked him to keep his views to himself until the end of the session. The Walcheren expedition was a great public disappointment reflecting on Castlereagh. In Sept. he discovered Canning's letter and challenged him to a duel. They both resigned and fought. Then Portland had a stroke.

PORT ROYAL now ANNAPOLIS ROYAL. *See* CANADA, A-2.

PORT ROYAL. *See* JAMAICA.

PORTSMOUTH, Es. of. *See* WALLOP

PORTSMOUTH, Duchess of. *See* KEROUALLE.

PORTUGAL AFTER 1640. (*See* AVIS *various* ANGLO-PORTUGUESE TS). (1) The popular *coup d'état* of Dec. 1640 ousted the Spaniards and brought the rich, semi- royal D. of Bragança to the throne as **João (John) IV (r. 1640-6).** French diplomacy had provided an impulse, but the Portuguese urgently needed allies. Britain was declining

into civil war. Of the other anti-Spanish powers, the Dutch held Brazil and other Portuguese colonies and the French did not want to offend the Dutch. Foreign armed help was ineffectual and only commercial agreements and truces could be settled. Luckily the Spaniards were preoccupied and the Portuguese maintained their defence in a war of small battles. In 1647 João confirmed the privileges granted to Englishmen at various times by his predecessors and these were formalised in a Treaty of 1654. This and the isolating effect of war with other powers gradually placed English traders in an enduring predominance in the economy.

(2) Portugal had been excluded from the P. of Westphalia (1648), which freed the weakened Spaniards and Dutch for war against her. In 1656 João IV died. His successor, **Afonso VI (1656-83)** was a dim-witted child. The Queen Regent **Luisa** continued the defence against mounting pressure. Negotiations for a French alliance failed, but Luisa gained the goodwill of Charles II who was about to be restored. Charles knew that English commercial interests could not be abandoned. Luisa was in military difficulties. The eventual result was the Marriage T. (June 1661) in which the Commonwealth T. of 1654 was partially revised. English forces occupied Tangier and campaigned with success on the Spanish frontier. Within a year, however, an aristocratic palace revolution overthrew Luisa. The Count of CASTELO MELHOR became the King's private sec. and effective dictator. In June 1663 an Anglo-Portuguese force drove back the Spaniards at Ameixial; in June 1665, Schomberg, a gen. in English service with a mixed army, decisively beat them in the Montes Claros and Spanish recognition became a matter of time. In fact Afonso was forcibly secluded in 1667. Castelo Melhor fell and the necessary treaty was signed in Feb. 1668 for the new Regent, who in 1683 ascended the throne as **Pedro II (1683-1706).**

(3) Meanwhile the Anglo-Dutch conflicts indirectly weakened Dutch hold on the colonies. Hence these were recovered too, but with a difference. In the face of French and English competition in India, Portugal switched her efforts to Brazil. The E. African staging points to India declined slowly; the W. African, especially Angola and Guinea, developed as sources of slave labour for Brazil. The seeds of the Brazilian boom were thus already sown when Portugal was attracted, through the medium of the Methuen T. (1703), into the War of the Spanish Succession. She emerged territorially intact at the Ts. of Utrecht.

(4) **João V (1706-50)** had a poor kingdom with a rich colony. Labour shortages hampered gold and sugar extraction until slave importation was fully developed in the 1720s. There was a gold rush to Minas Geraes and Cuiaba, followed by a diamond rush in 1728. By 1730 João was the richest King in Europe. He had no need to raise money by parliamentary means and was repaying the state loans. The Cortes fell into disuse. A new absolutism, floated on a flood of bullion, established academies, provided aqueducts and built huge monuments such as the monastery at Mafra. Much of the prosperity benefitted England, especially the cloth trade, and English imports ruined the budding textile industries in favour of the steadily spreading wines of Oporto. The economy was biased towards trade and luxury, while land went out of cultivation. When João was succeeded by **José I (r. 1750-77)** there were ominous signs of depression.

(5) José was not interested in govt. and his strong-minded minister, POMBAL, became the real ruler. Pombal had, as a diplomat, known England from 1740 to 1744 when he reported on the adverse balance of trade. He was a premature but not anti-British nationalist, yet determined to replace British economic domination by colonial mercantilism. He began by reforming the Brazilian mining system and establishing a diamond

market in Holland. Between 1752 and 1756 he reduced the English privileges under the treaty of 1654 and prohibited a long list of English imports. Then his purpose was deflected by the appalling Lisbon earthquake (Nov. 1755) which undermined contemporary religious beliefs and imposed a vast burden of rebuilding. Pombal accepted help from England, but refused it from France and Spain. The newly planned city is said to have been modelled on Covent Garden.

(6) The cloth trade fell by half in the next 10 years, but as agriculture had declined, English corn had to be imported for gold. Britain was preoccupied with the Seven Years' War; the increase in the volume of British trade left the Portuguese part of it proportionately smaller and in any case French wars always raised the profits of the Port wine trade. English capital cleared and planted the vine terraces of the Douro and focused the trade on the English Factory House at Oporto. Pombal's attempts to raise standards through a chartered wine monopoly led to a local revolt (Feb. 1757). He had other enemies. He had inherited a quarrel with the Jesuits over *reducciones* (settlements) which they governed in Paraguay and S. Brazil and he had alienated most of the nobles. In 1758 he used an attempt on King José's life to engineer the judicial murder of certain leading noblemen. In 1759 the same pretext was used to expel the Jesuits. Henceforth he ruled as a tyrant.

(7) In Aug. 1759 Rodney and Boscawen beat a French fleet at Lagos (Algarves). The French demanded that Portugal should defend her territorial waters (i.e. favour France in the war) and Pitt instantly offered amends. The quarrel continued into 1761 when the Franco-Spanish Family Compact created a potential overland threat. A demand that the ports be closed to English shipping was only to be expected. The army and navy being in decay, Pombal asked for British help, which was sent. The English-born Count William of Schaumburg-Lippe, with Gens. Loudoun and Burgoyne held off a Franco-Spanish invasion from Apr. 1762 until the truce of Nov. 1762 which heralded the end of the Seven Years' War.

(8) Pombal's increasingly brutal and unrealistic dictatorship lasted until Jose I died in 1777. **Maria I (1777-1816)** and her uncle and husband **Pedro III (1777-86)** immediately dismissed him, released or rehabilitated his victims and stopped his policies. Politically the atmosphere was much improved, economically the jolt of sudden retrenchment was too great. Moreover they had a colonial war with Spain on their hands and felt constrained to settle it by ceding Fernan do Po (P. of San Ildefonso, Oct. 1777). English commercial influence increased in the stagnant economy, which now also lacked vigorous govt.; Pedro was dying and Maria's eccentricities were turning to madness. In 1792 her son **João,** Prince of Brazil, was exercising a regency.

(9) The French Revolution was three years old and the govt. made a Spanish alliance which involved a Portuguese military expedition in Catalonia. The Spanish adventurer Manuel de Godoy, P. of the Peace, began to influence Portuguese fortunes. In July 1795 his secret peace agreement with France left the Portuguese troops stranded. In Jan. 1796 the French were demanding parts of Brazil and Amazonian trading rights. In Oct., while Franco-Portuguese negotiations were in progress in Paris, Spain declared war on England. The British victory at Cape St. Vincent (Feb. 1797) impressed the French with the importance of Portuguese ports to the British. They demanded closure. The Portuguese rearmed and English troops and ships arrived in Lisbon. Meanwhile Bonaparte's victories in Italy released troops: Godoy was offered 30,000 men to invade Portugal, but in July 1798 Portuguese ships helped the British to blockade Malta and Egypt. By Nov. 1800 the British had to withdraw

most of their forces, but a local treaty at Badajoz, followed by the T. of Amiens, brought a temporary peace.

(10) The situation was now complicated by the eccentricities of the Regent and Godoy's ambition to become a ruling prince. The end product was a nominally joint Franco-Spanish, but actually a French invasion. The royal family and treasure were rescued in the nick of time by the British fleet and conveyed to Brazil. The French military occupation was soon disturbed. In June 1808 a general revolt developed and its leaders appealed to Britain. Wellesley's expedition arrived on the Mondego in Aug. (*See* PENINSULAR WAR.)

(11) The British handled Portuguese interests in the T. of Paris (1814) but the Regent in Rio de Janeiro refused to ratify; the P. of Vienna left Portugal in much the same posture as before the war and a British T. of Jan. 1815 enabled her to continue the Africa-Brazil slave trade. In Dec., to anticipate local Spanish inspired secessionism, Brazil was proclaimed a Kingdom and in 1816 **João VI** succeeded to both thrones. He liked Brazil and was easily persuaded to stay there. Portuguese resentment at this was a factor in the liberal revolution at Lisbon in 1820. João was obliged to return to swear to the new constitution, whereupon a Brazilian constitutional movement proclaimed his son, **Pedro,** first as Defender and then as constitutional Emperor of Brazil (Oct. 1822).

(12) The metropolitan constitution was overthrown in May 1823 by conservatives led by P. Miguel, João's younger son. João died in 1826. The Emperor Pedro, now also King, executed in favour of his young daughter **Maria da Gloria,** an abdication on condition that a new constitution of his devising was accepted and that Miguel married her. The ensuing constitutional *imbroglios* first in Portugal and then in Brazil involved Spain (as neighbour), Austria (whose Emperor was Maria's grandfather) and of course Britain. A civil war broke out in 1828. In 1831 Pedro abdicated in Brazil and came with Maria to Europe to contest the throne. By May 1834 he had defeated Miguel, but he died in Sept. The 15-year-old **Maria II (1834-53)** thus succeeded neither by right of birth (being Brazilian), nor through her father's conditional abdication, but by his victory in a factional struggle. She married a Saxe-Coburg. Factionalism continued throughout her reign with *pronunciamentos* in 1836, 1837, 1840, a civil war in 1846-7 and another *pronunciamento* in 1851.

(13) Exhaustion, common sense and the end of a world recession combined to render her well-trained successor **Pedro V (r. 1853-61)** more fortunate and stability facilitated the modernisation of the country. This was the period of railway and telegraph building. Unfortunately he died of typhoid and under his successors **Luis (1861-89)** and **Carlos (1889-1908)** constitutionalism degenerated into a rotation of offices among entrenched parliamentary factions ("rotativism") decreasingly in touch with opinion.

(14) This might have been acceptable in a static world, but the Great Power scramble for Africa threatened the potentially large, old, but undefined colonies, which the Kingdom as a minor power could not defend on its own. It had to bargain continually for the retention of its own possessions and, in the stagnant political atmosphere of Lisbon, the traditional authorities progressively lost credit with the public. The first such event was the abortive treaty of 1884 about the mouth of the Congo. This was a British manoeuvre at once to check the Belgian Congo Association and the French. It also provoked protests from Bismarck who was seeking a quarrel in which he could side with the French. All the protests were based on a doctrine of effective occupation detrimental to Portuguese claims. Germans then "effectively occupied" Angra Pequeña by hoisting flags

and expanded their claim to all S.W. Africa. The Berlin Conference (Feb. 1885) accepted this, thus setting aside Portuguese claims based on prior discovery.

(15) The Portuguese felt betrayed by Britain and the Castro Govt. sought a new policy. There was to be a great East-West colony uniting Mozambique and Angola, guaranteed by France (May 1886) and, in return for Angolan concessions, Germany (Dec. 1886). The scheme, known as the *Pink Map*, was placed before the Cortes and provoked protests in 1887 and in 1888, based on effective occupation, from Britain which was expanding from the south to the north. Portuguese armed parties from both sides began to penetrate the disputed areas, but established no permanent presence. There were skirmishes in Mashonaland and Makalololand. In Jan. 1890 Britain threatened to break off diplomatic relations. This note, known in Portugal as *The Ultimatum,* provoked anti-British hysteria and was made a pretext for demonstrations against the govt. and Crown and, in Jan. 1891, a mutiny at Oporto.

(16) Rotativism was financially unsound, for nobody dared to pay the mounting debts by increasing taxation. The British hoped to win the Boer conflict without a war by controlling the Delagoa Bay-Pretoria Railway, now being built. The British proposed a loan to Portugal in return for such control. The Germans promptly objected and then sold their nuisance value for an agreement (Aug. 1898) to share any future loan with Britain on the security of a partition of the Portuguese Colonies. No such loan or partition occurred, because the British settled the control question direct with Lisbon by the T. of Windsor (Oct. 1899) but just after the Boers attacked. In 1903 and 1904 there were exchanges of state visits and an Arbitration Treaty.

(17) King Carlos and the able M. de Soveral, ambassador in London, had so far maintained the inheritance, but got no credit because the transactions were mostly secret. The overthrow of the Brazilian monarchy in 1891 naturally awakened Republicanism in Portugal, where the opposition could easily blame the Crown for the corruption of rotativism and the more obvious dangers of foreign policy. Their simplistic propaganda encountered a simplistic response. In 1906, when the Riberro Govt. collapsed, the monarchist João Franco attempted to govern by decree and the Cortes was dissolved in 1907. There were disorders and deportations, culminating in the assassination of the King and Crown Prince (Feb. 1908). Conspiracy and the subornation of the armed forces continued and in Oct. 1908 the monarchy was violently overthrown.

(18) The revolution made little difference to the attitude of foreign powers. In 1913 Britain revived the idea of colonial partition in the Anglo-German agreement of 1898, for the purpose of conciliation with Germany. This time the negotiations were frustrated by the French who, reasonably, feared that such conciliation might isolate them in the face of German aggression. Consequently when war broke out in 1914 Britain guaranteed Portugal against improbable German aggression and made such aggression even less probable by advising Portugal to stay out of the war. When the German colonies had been conquered by Britain, it was safe to enter it in 1916, thus enabling the Royal Navy to use Portuguese ports and the Azores in the anti-U-Boat war. Hence, Portugal emerged with her possessions intact, but peculiarly vulnerable to movements of international trade which was endangered by the Great Depression of 1928 onwards. In Mar. 1928 Gen. Carmona became a semi-dictatorial Pres. with Salazar as his Finance Minister. Salazar was financially exceptionally able and soon stabilised the economy. In 1932, when the world depression had deepened, he became Prime Minister with dictatorial powers and as such, during World War II, granted air and naval bases in the Azores

to the British between 1943 and 1946 under the treaty of 1373.

(19) After World War II the foundations of Portuguese policy crumbled under the impact of two major trends. The first was the Russian decision to destabilise Africa through the medium of Marxist inspired movements which, in the Portuguese cases, soon led to civil war and wholesale destruction in Angola by Cuban, but Russian financed forces. The second was the collapse of Britain as a world power upon which, therefore, Portugal could no longer rely for efficient support. Consequently it became necessary for Portugal to reduce her colonial commitments and transfer her confidence to N.A.T.O. and the U.N.O. British investment meanwhile remained at a high level, especially at Oporto.

PORTUGUESE INDIES (1) Vasco da Gama first reached Calicut (India) and encountered Arab inspired opposition in 1498. Pedro Cabral followed in Sept. 1500 but, driven away by the Zamorin (or local king), he entered into relations with the Zamorin's enemies, the Rajahs of Cochin and Cannanor. In 1501 João de Niva established a factory house at Cannanor and in 1502 Vasco da Gama signed treaties with the ruler of KILWA (E. Africa), reinforced Cochin and Cannanor and bombarded Calicut. When he left, the Zamorin drove the Portuguese and the Rajah out of Cochin, but in 1503 a fleet under Francisco de Albuquerque restored them and Cochin became a Portuguese client state. In 1505 the first Viceroy, Francisco de Almeida, was despatched with a substantial force. He built a fort at Kilwa, burnt Mombasa and defeated the Zamorin's fleet off Calicut. Hence Arab spice traders began to avoid the Indian coastal route from the east and sailed direct from Ceylon to the Red Sea and the Persian Gulf. In 1506 Afonso de Albuquerque set out with Trist o da Cunha to interfere with this new route. They seized Socotra and in 1507 stormed the great market city of Ormuz. Almeida, however, repudiated them: but meantime the Egyptians and Venetians became alarmed and an Egyptian armada was assembled. This, with the Zamorin's fleet, was defeated at the great B. of DIU (Feb. 1509) which established Portuguese naval predominance in the Indian Ocean for a century.

In Oct. 1509 Afonso de Albuquerque superseded Almeida and after an unsuccessful attempt on Calicut, took GOA in 1510 and there set up his capital. In May 1511 he took Malacca (Malaysia) and so forced terms upon the local Sumatran and Javanese rulers. In 1513 he revived his earlier projects, making an unsuccessful attack on Aden and in 1515 a successful one on Ormuz. His successors built a factory and fort at Colombo in 1518, took Basra (Iraq) in 1529, obtained Diu in return for military assistance to the Mogul in 1530, reached Suez in 1541, Liampo (China) in 1542 and built Macao in 1543. By 1545 they had settlements in Timor (Indonesia).

(2) The early profits were immense but there were three weaknesses. The Portuguese were too thin on the sea to control the spice trade completely, so that once they had got over their surprise the Arabs found means to continue the trade *via* Iraq, Egypt and Venice. Venetian competition thus brought the price of spices down just as costs were rising naturally through the appearance of pirates (especially French) in the Mozambique Channel. Lastly the territorial settlements entailed substantial (mostly warlike) expense at the end of communications many months and thousands of miles long.

(3) The Spanish rule in Portugal (1580-1640) created great difficulties because the enemies of Spain became automatically enemies of Portugal. The Dutch began to penetrate Java in 1595 (*see* INDONESIA) and the British followed. By 1650 most of the trade had been lost to other nations, Ceylon to the Dutch and the various staging posts had begun to decay. Bombay was ceded with Tangier to Britain as part of Charles II's Braganza marriage which was really a treaty to guarantee Portuguese independence.

(4) The Indian possessions remained Portuguese until 1962. The Timor until 1974.

PORT WINE. *See* OPORTO.

POSITIVISM, HISTORICAL and LOGICAL. Between 1830 and 1854 Auguste Comte proposed three stages in the evolution of human knowledge, namely the theological, the metaphysical and the Positive. The third involves the discovery without preconceptions of information; and as revealed religion is a preconception, it is abandoned. At this point logic must take over. All intellectual and moral development comes from logical conclusions drawn from facts. Human beings are the only vehicles for these processes, and their religion is replaced by a morality based on obligations between people. As a coherent philosophy, positivism made an impact in France, then in a period of emotional and social exhaustion. In Britain it bore a more practical and instinctive fruit in the form (e.g.) of the researches of Charles Darwin and other scientists, and the resulting debates.

POSSE COMITATUS **(Lat: 'power of the county')** was the body of men over 15 (other than peers, clergy and the infirm) who might be raised by the sheriff to defend the area or suppress disorder. Long since disused in England, they were still a feature of American practice in the 19th cent.

POSSESSORY ASSIZES. *See* ASSIZES-1.

POSTNATI (Latinism meaning *those born after* the accession of James VI of Scotland, in England as James I.) The two crowns were not united and so the subjects of each were thought to be foreigners in the country of the other. This carried economic disadvantages, especially inability to own land and prejudiced the Scots from the weaker country. James was anxious to bring about a proper union, but met with determined parliamentary opposition. In a collusive action, the *Case of the Postnati, Calvin's Case or Colville's Case* (1604), he secured a judgement that *postnati*, being born in allegiance to the same King, were in equal allegiance in both countries. Sir Edward Coke disagreed with the judgement and there was political opposition led by Sir Thomas Wentworth, but the decision gradually eliminated the problem.

POST OFFICE. Crown messengers carried mails between London and major towns such as York and Norwich from earliest times and a govt. monopoly was occasionally claimed and enacted under the Protectorate. This was replaced by an act of 1660 which enjoined the creation of a London letter office, empowered the King to appoint a Postmaster General (P.M.G.) and conferred a monopoly upon the latter in the movement of persons riding post and in the carriage of letters and parcels. The act also regulated the charges (payable on acceptance by the receiver). The basic inland letter rate was 2d. per sheet per 80 miles: foreign rates varied between 6d. and 1s. Charles II appointed his brother James D. of York.

This over-priced system was slow and inefficient. By the 1830s it was losing more money each year, despite the increase in population and industry. The cost of conveying a letter from London to Edinburgh was ½d. but the charge was 1s. 4½d. In 1837 Rowland Hill published his scheme based upon prepayment by adhesive stamps and a low uniform rate. It required a furious public agitation, the D. of Wellington's support and a chairman's casting vote to introduce it and three years' work to overcome internal opposition. In 1868 the P.M.G. was authorised to buy out private telegraph companies and in 1880 this was held to mean that telephone companies must obtain his licence to operate. By 1902 all the private cos. had been absorbed by the National Telephone Co. who sold their undertaking to him in 1905. Six boroughs still had licensed systems in 1912, but the only modern survivor is Hull. In 1923 the P.M.G. started licensing broadcasting. In 1969 the Post Office was converted into a corporation and the P.M.G. ceased to be a minister. In 1981 British Telecom took over its telephone and telegraph business and later closed down the latter. In the 1990s the govt. was preparing plans to sell off certain other parts of the business into the private sector.

POTATOES were introduced from Peru to Spain c. 1580 and by Sir Walter Raleigh into England c. 1585. They reached IRELAND c. 1610. *See* IRELAND, E.-5-6.

POTLATCH (Nootka *patshatl* = **give).** Pacific coast Red Indians, being prolific craftsmen in wood, stone, leather and textiles, tended to overstock their longhouses. This inspired their chiefs to give it all away to neighbouring chiefs at a great party, and the latter were morally obliged at some time to reply with equal or greater generosity. This reobliged the original host and so on. Potlatches, like fairs were socially or orgiastically significant. In 1921 a Kwakiutl potlatch lasted a week; gifts included 5 motor boats, 24 canoes, household goods, clothes, 400 blankets and 1000 sacks of flour. Paleface moralists got the Canadian government to prohibit this form of investment, but potlatches with cash gifts were still being held in the 1970s.

POTSDAM AGREEMENT (Aug. 1945) between Britain, U.S.A. and Russia, arising out of the German surrender, provided **(1)** that a committee of the foreign ministers of the three plus France and China should frame peace treaties with Germany's allies which should be submitted to the U.N.O.; **(2)** the respective C-in-C's should rule their occupied zones subject to directives from their govts. and, sitting together as a control council, should deal with affairs common to all Germany; **(3)** no German govt. was to be set up for the time being, while Nazism was extirpated, the German people made aware of their defeat and democratically re-educated and the country disarmed. Germany was nevertheless to be treated as a single economic unit; **(4)** war criminals were to be brought to trial; **(5)** Königsberg was to be annexed to Russia which was also to be entitled to material reparations (mostly already being looted) and the Oder-Neisse line was provisionally to be the Polish western frontier; **(6)** transfers of Germans from Poland, Hungary and Czechoslovakia should be humanely carried out. This was a dead letter.

POTTERIES. *See* STOKE ON TRENT.

POTWALLOPERS had the means (mostly a hearth) to boil a pot. This was a voting qualification in certain boroughs, notably Westminster and Preston which consequently had a very large electorates until the Reform Act 1832.

POUND, Alfred Dudley Pickman Rogers (1877-1943), Admiral of the Fleet and First Sea Ld. (1939-43) commanded the battleship *Colossus* at the B. of Jutland and had been C-in-C Mediterranean (1936-39). Steady and taciturn, he organised the Royal Navy and maintained its morale at the most critical periods of World War II and was the officer most concerned in fending off disaster in those dangerous times. He was naturally cautious, being conscious, as was Jellicoe, that the Navy could 'lose the war in an afternoon'. This probably influenced his much criticised order to disperse convoy PQ 17 which led to the worst convoy disaster of the war, for he believed (with some evidence) that the German battleship *Tirpitz* was approaching. He died of an unsuspected brain tumour.

POUND (OF ACCOUNT). *See* COINAGE-4.

POUNDAGE was an import and export tax levied on the value of goods, usually at a rate of 5% (but 10% on tin in the hands of strangers). It was invariably coupled with tonnage in parliamentary grants. First levied as a war tax in 1347, it was first granted for the king's life in 1472 and became perpetual in 1714. It was abolished in 1787. *See also* SUBSIDY.

POUNDMAKER (1826-86) Cree chief in the Canadian N.W. who led his people in the N.W. Rebellion of 1885.

POWDERHAM CASTLE (Devon) built about 1390 for the Courtenay family. It was damaged in the Civil War and restored in the 18th and 19th cents.

POWELL, Enoch (1912-98), Tory M.P. for Wolverhampton (1950-74) and for S. Down (Ulster) (1974-87) and Min. of Health in 1967-8. A man of strong character and intellect with rhetorical gifts and vast learning, he favoured the safe maintenance of the nation's special character, and so proposed the exclusion of most immigrants or their repatriation, independence from or separateness within the E.U., and continuing sovereignty over Ulster.

POWERSCOURT. *See* WINGFIELD-7.

POWNALL, Thomas (1722-1805) called GOV. POWNALL because he was successively Lieut.-Gov. of New Jersey (1757-9), of Massachusetts (1757-9) and S. Carolina (1759-60). In his *Administration of the Colonies* (1764) he foreshadowed the union of the American colonies and gave warning of their dislike of taxation by the British parliament. As an M.P. from 1767 to 1780 he was one of the few experts on America in the House. He supported the Whigs but when the American rebellion broke out, he supported vigorous military operations in order to obtain the best terms with the colonists, whose independence was, in his view, assured.

POWYS. The modern Welsh county was a combination of the Tudor border shires of Montgomery, Radnor with most of Brecknock. It came into existence in 1974 under the Local Govt. Act 1972. It was much larger than the ancient Powys.

POWYS (N. Central Wales) was a geographical rather than a political expression. Between c. 1050 and 1286 the principal Welsh rulers were the descendants of **Bleddyn ap Cynvyn**, probably of the royal house of Gwynedd, who carved out a shakily independent principality. He had three sons **Iorwerth (?-1112), Cadwgan (?-1112)** and **Maredudd (?-1132).** At this time Powys was being taken over piecemeal by Robert of Bellême, palatine E. of Shrewsbury, and Cadwgan obtained a grant from him but in 1102 joined in Robert's overthrow. Then Henry I suppressed the palatinate but other marcher lords continued the encroachment, aided after Cadwgan and Iorwerth were dead, by a major English invasion in 1121.

In 1152 **Madog (?-1160)** succeeded Maredudd and in his time the family possessions were divided with or were perhaps partly seized by a rival, **Owain Cyvelliog (?-1197).** The two parts continued under their respective descendants until the fall of Gwynedd, but their extent was always in doubt through marcher activity and internecine wars. From the beginning of the 14th cent. until Tudor times, Powys was ruled by Lds. Marcher who were mostly English in the east and mostly Welsh in the west. *See* WELSH LAW-2.

POX. *See* SYPHILIS.

POYNINGS ACTS 1465 (1) At the instance of Sir Edward Poynings, the Ld. Deputy, the Drogheda Parliament passed 49 Acts including the specifically known POYNINGS LAW, which had important effects in English occupied Ireland. Irish revenues were to be accounted for in the English Exchequer; Chief officers of the Irish Govt. were to be dismissable at pleasure; English statutes on Provisors and Livery were to apply in Ireland; the Statutes of Kilkenny (save those against riding bare-back or speaking Erse) were confirmed and English statutes were applied to Ireland and Irish Acts inconsistent with them were to be void. There were various Acts of Resumption, and documents issued by Lambert Simnel were declared void. **(2) POYNINGS LAW** was a constitutional enactment. It laid down that for a valid Irish parliament to be held, the Lieut. or Deputy had, under the Irish Great Seal, to apply to the King, giving reasons for calling it and listing the bills to be considered. Then the King, under the English Great Seal had to signify his consent. The bills as passed could receive the Royal Assent only after further submission to the Crown.

Exceptions were made in 1537 and 1569, but failure to carry out the proper procedure invalidated the legislation and oppositions sometimes manipulated the procedure to embarrass the govt. until the Law was mostly repealed in 1782.

PRAECIPE (Lat: 'notify'), WRIT OF. Was used originally to compel the lord of a seignorial court to hear and determine a suit concerning land. The sheriff was to notify the lord that a grievance existed and that if he did not do right, the King would. By allowing an impossibly short time for the lord's court to act, a case could be taken out of his hands altogether. This was one of the grievances cured by Clause 34 of Magna Carta. The inferiority of seignorial over royal justice was so obvious that by 1300 the clause came to be ignored by the expedient of issuing a writ of Right to the Lord followed by a Writ of Praecipe *Quia dominus remisit curiam* ("Because the Lord has remitted his court"), an allegation which the lord was seldom strong enough to contest.

PRAEMUNIENTES (Lat: "summoning") was an instruction first issued by Edward I in 1394 to bishops to summon to Parliament deans and archdeacons, one representative of each chapter and two representatives of the other clergy. The object was to oppose or circumvent the Papal prohibition on lay taxation of the clergy by creating a third House which could vote the taxes itself. The clergy refused to come or to vote taxes even in convocation, save by Papal mandate. By 1400 they voted taxes in convocation by the fiction that the money was a free gift.

PRAEMUNIRE (from Lat: *Praemunire facias* = forewarn him) is the offence of introducing a foreign power or jurisdiction into the country, paying obedience to alien processes, or directly or indirectly asserting Papal superiority over the Crown. It originated with the Statute of Provisors 1352 and was defined in the Statute of Praemunire 1392. The offence was punishable with forfeiture of land and goods and withdrawal of the Crown's protection (virtual outlawry). The Statute of 1392 was incorporated into many later acts; in particular it was *praemunire* for an archbishop to refuse to consecrate a duly elected bishop (1533), for anyone to assert that Parliament could legislate independently of the Crown (1661), or to send a prisoner beyond the seas (1679).

PRAESTITA ROLLS listed advances to royal officials by the Exchequer between 1199 and 1603.

PRAGMATIC SANCTION was a fundamental crown decree. **(1)** For that of Bourges (1438) *see* GALLICANISM. **(2)** For that of 1724 *see* AUSTRIA, POST-PRAGMATIC; GEORGE I-12; WARS OF 1739-48-3. **(3)** For that of 1830 *see* CARLISM.

PRAGUERIE (1440). French aristocratic revolt under Charles VII who bought it off by exempting the nobles from taxation.

PRATIQUE. The clearance given to an incoming ship which has either a clean bill of health or has performed its quarantine.

PRATT (1) Sir John (1657-1725) was M.P. for Midhurst from 1711 to 1715, Judge of the Kings Bench in 1714 and C.J. from 1718. His son **(2) Charles (1714-94) 1st Ld. CAMDEN (1765), 1st E. CAMDEN (1786)** was Pitt's Att.-Gen. and an M.P. from 1757. In 1761 he became C.J. of the Common Pleas. His ruling against general warrants in the *Wilkes* cases made him a popular hero (1763). In the Lords he opposed the taxation of the colonies and argued that the Stamp Tax was unconstitutional. In 1766 he became Ld. Chancellor under Pitt (Chatham) until dismissed in 1770. He then established a sort of comradeship of opposition with Chatham until the latter died (1778) when he withdrew slowly from politics. In 1782 however he returned as Rockingham's Ld. Pres.; he resigned in 1783 to assist the formation of the coalition and resumed in 1784 until he died. His son **(3) John (1759-1840) 2nd E. and 1st M. (1812)** was an M.P. from 1780 to 1794, a Ld. of the Admiralty in 1782 and 1783 and of the Treasury from 1789 to 1794 when he became Ld. Lieut. of Ireland. His reactionary attitude to Irish affairs made him unpopular and his advice to the Cabinet was an important cause of unrest, leading to martial law in Ulster in 1797 and the rebellion of 1798. At his own request he was replaced by a soldier (Cornwallis). He was Sec. at War from 1804 to 1805 and Ld. Pres. from 1805 to 1806 and from 1807 to 1812. He and his father made a fortune building Camden Town (London).

PRAYER BOOK. *See* COMMON PRAYER.

PREAMBLE in legislation is a statement of facts or aspirations at the beginning of a statute purporting to justify its substantive provisions. Where the wording of the latter is ambiguous the courts will have regard to the preamble to explain them. Since the mid-19th cent. preambles have been rare in public Acts. In private legislation, however, they are necessary and procedurally crucial, because if a promoter fails to prove his preamble, his bill will be rejected.

PREBEND, -ARY. A canon of a cathedral was a prebendary if a particular part or prebend of the cathedral endowment was appropriated to his support. Some prebends (e.g. at Durham) were more valuable than some bishoprics (e.g. in Wales). Though they have all been abolished the title is still used.

PRECEDENCE. In the House of Lords it is laid down by Act of Henry VIII. In most other cases it is established by the royal prerogative. Its symbolic importance is considerable in a hierarchical or deferential society, but it sometimes has other practical consequences. In law courts, precedence was regulated among barristers by date of call or order of appointment as King's or Queen's Counsel; seniority gave first choice of time for hearing and was pecuniarily valuable. In politics, privy councillors have precedence in speaking in the House of Commons where time is necessarily limited. Privy Councillors thus have more parliamentary opportunities than back benchers.

PRECEPT. An order or mandate, is especially used in local govt. finance where it is an order to an authority charged with levying a rate, community charge or council tax, requiring it to raise money from the persons liable to these imposts, for the purposes of the precepting authority. Precepting authorities included councils of counties and parishes, river boards and police authorities; the precepts were directed to district and municipal borough councils.

PREFAB[RICATED HOUSE]S were compact mass produced temporary bungalows with furniture, provided after World War II to replace buildings in badly damaged places so that the demobilised could be housed in their home town. Over 150,000 were erected and some are still in use.

PRELATE. An ecclesiastical dignatory with episcopal status, i.e. a mitred abbot, bishop or higher who, in England, might be summoned to the House of Lords.

PRELIMINARIES OF 1727. *See* GEORGE I-14.

PREMIUM BONDS. *See* NATIONAL SAVINGS MOVEMENT.

PRERAPHAELITE BROTHERHOOD, a small society led by William Holman Hunt, Dante Gabriel Rossetti and J. E. Millais, led a romantically inspired reaction against Victorian artistic canons in the late 19th cent. William Rossetti and F. G. Stephens argued its case persistently in the *Athenaeum* and *Spectator*. Their object was to return to the seriousness of the artists before Raphael's time and they attracted many followers. Their distinctive pictorial style and outlook remained dominant until World War I and influential for some years after.

PREROGATIVE (1) is the common law pre-eminence and power which the sovereign enjoys in right of the regal dignity. New prerogatives cannot be created and all are subject to such statutes as may be relevant to them. Hence a statutory power conferred on the Crown is not a prerogative and where the Crown has a statutory power to do something which it could do under the prerogative,

that statutory power prevails. A prerogative if surrendered to a legislature, cannot be recalled.

(2) (a) The sovereign is inviolable, incapable of wrong and never dies. **(b)** The sovereign is head of state and of the executive and directly or indirectly appoints public officers. **(c)** The sovereign summons, prorogues and dissolves Parliament and the royal assent is essential to all legislation. **(d)** The sovereign is the fountain of justice and of mercy. **(e)** The conduct of foreign policy is a royal prerogative and consequently the deployment and use of the armed forces. **(f)** All honours are conferred by the sovereign. **(g)** Other prerogatives include the right to create ports, harbours, markets and fairs, to control the coinage and to create corporations by charter.

(3) Statute, convention and the facts of politics make the foregoing statement a mere shell for underlying realities. The perfection of the sovereign means that a blameworthy act must be imputed to advisers. The prerogative includes no power of taxation and therefore, since the exercise of virtually all prerogatives involves expenditure, the Crown must in practice take the advice of the govt., which can through the House of Commons raise the money. In addition there are certain more direct, controls. The size of the armed forces is periodically enacted by statute. The prerogative of justice must be exercised in accordance with law and gives no right to deprive a person of life, liberty or property save by a lawful process.

PREROGATIVE WRITS were issued at the discretion of the Crown (exercised by the courts) upon extraordinary occasions and only for proper cause. There were six viz: **(1)** *certiorari* (Lat = To be made more sure), **(2)** *habeas corpus* (= Have the body), **(3)** *mandamus* (= We command), **(4)** *procedendo* (= to that which should be continued), **(5)** *prohibition,* **(6)** *Quo Warranto* (= by what warrant). In 1938 orders were substituted for writs in cases (1), (3) and (5). Since 1978 these, together with (2), injunctions, declaratory orders and damages, have been made the basis of the process called JUDICIAL REVIEW.

PRESBYTERIANISM is the govt. of the church through a hierarchy of meetings or committees. A congregation elects a minister *ad vitam aut culpam* (for life or until unworthy) and representative elders (presbyters). These together form the *consistory* or *kirk session*. The ministers and representative elders of several parishes form a body called the *colloquy, classis* or *presbytery,* several presbyteries similarly appoint a *synod* and the synods appoint a national *General Assembly* consisting of equal numbers of ministers and laymen. Most presbyterian churches, notably the Church of Scotland and the Welsh Methodists, are Calvinist in doctrine.

PRESCRIPTION. Use continued for a long time was held to confer a right in property. The time began at the coronation of Richard I (1189); but as this receded into the past the courts assumed that there had been a more recent grant which had been lost. This hardened into a presumption if 20 years' unexplained use could be proved. The defects in the doctrine were that the presumed grant had to be legally possible and not contrary to law or custom. These defects have been partially remedied by Prescription and Limitation Acts at various times since 1832.

PRESENTATION. *See* ADVOWSON.

PRESIDENCIES (Ir.). *See* ELIZABETH I-17.

PRESIDENCY. The heads of the HEIC trading establishments at Bombay, Madras and Calcutta (Bengal) were termed presidents and they exercised a certain control over other dependent factories. When the Co. became a territorial power, these commercial presidencies became the basis of three provinces; these had a precedence above the others of British India, signified by the higher rank and pay of their governors. The word remained in use until 1947.

PRESS ASSOCIATION. A London news agency founded in 1868 and jointly owned by the principal English and Irish newspapers.

PRESS GANG. *See* IMPRESSMENT.

PRESTON (Lancs) at the lowest crossing of the Ribble was a small possession of E. Tostig, which passed to Roger of Poictou and thence (1102) to the Crown. Though said to have had a charter of about 1100, the earliest demonstrable one dates from 1179; this set up the merchant guild. It became a significant market for the Fylde area after the 13th cent. pacification of Lancashire and was also a port with a growing woollen and linen weaving industry, besides glove making. By 1328 membership of the guild was valuable and it was decided to hold enrolments every 20 years. This is the origin of the 20-yearly processional festival called **Preston Guild,** which is still held. The stabilisation of the Scottish Border north of Carlisle and the peace which followed the accession of Henry VII greatly increased local prosperity: Elizabeth I extended the market rights in 1566, Charles II added a weekly market day in 1662 and a three day March fair in 1685.

The town's position on a river-crossing had meanwhile involved it in the later Civil Wars. It was the local centre of royalist feeling and consequently stormed by the Parliamentarians in Feb. 1643. In 1648 it was a Scottish objective and Cromwell defeated the Scots in a pitched battle in the town. In 1715 the Old Pretender's troops surrendered there after the inhabitants had intervened. This is the origin of the rhyme, quoted in *Alice Through the Looking Glass:*

"The Lion and the Unicorn were fighting for the Crown;
The Lion beat the Unicorn all round the Town;
Some gave them white bread and some gave them brown,
And some gave them plum cake and drummed them out of town."

The Young Pretender hoped to recruit there on his way south in 1745.

Preston sent two members to Parliament until 1331 and after 1529. These were elected on the potwalloper franchise; thus the Reform Act, 1832, disfranchised a large number of the electors. This, however, caused relatively little stir for the cotton boom had been in progress since the 1790s; by 1835 there were 40 mills and the port was growing. Other industries appeared, notably soap, chemicals, some shipbuilding and paper. Thus when Lancashire became an administrative county in 1889 it was preferred to Lancaster as the administrative centre even though it was, as a county borough, taken out of the county.

PRESTON'S INN. *See* KINGS INNS.

PRETENDERS, OLD and YOUNG. *See* JACOBITES.

PRETORIA. *See* SOUTH AFRICA, TRANSVAAL, *and next entry.*

PRETORLA CONVENTION (Aug. 1881) defined the present boundaries of the Transvaal and thereby excluded Swaziland. It conferred self-govt. on the Boers subject to British suzerainty, i.e. control of foreign affairs and a veto on native legislation; it also prohibited slavery and required equal rights for all. There was no provision on the franchise. There was to be a British Resident with a seat on a Native Locations Commission in which native land was to be vested. It was revived by the LONDON CONVENTION (Feb. 1884). Concluded after the defeat at Majuba Hill, the defeat made the Boers over-confident while the real effects of the convention made no impression on world opinion.

PRETORIUS (1) Andries Wilhehmus Jacobus (1799-1853), Trek leader, broke the Natal Zulus at the B. of the Blood R. (Dec. 1838), then set up the Natal Republic and became Pres. of its Volksraad. When the British annexed Natal, Pretorius led a further trek and set up the Orange and Vaal R. Republics. Resistance to further British annexation led to his defeat at Boomplaats (Aug. 1848) and he became a fugitive across the Vaal. His quarrel with Potgieter led to civil disorders in this trans-Vaal area and delayed its organisation as a republic, until after the British gave up the Orange area in 1852. His son **(2) Marthinus Wessels (1819-1901)** took over his position as Commandant-Gen., led successful expeditions against the Bantu and tried to conquer the O.F.S. He was Pres. of the S. African Republic three times (1857-69) and of the Transvaal from 1859 to 1863. His policy of uniting the Boers and extending their rule to Delagoa Bay and Bechuanaland was frustrated largely by Boer disunity. In 1877 he fought the British annexation of the Transvaal from which the British retreated in 1880. He founded Pretoria and named it after his father.

PREVENTION OF TERRORISM (TEMPORARY POWERS) ACT 1974 received the R. Assent on 29 Nov. 1974. **(1)** It made it an offence (a) to belong to, solicit for, organise or speak at a meeting of, the Irish Republican Army (I.R.A.) or any other organisation using terrorism for political purposes proscribed by the Home Sec., and it made the offender liable to a fine or five years imprisonment or both; (b) to wear or display anything likely to arouse reasonable apprehension of membership of or support for the I.R.A. (£200 or three months). It enabled **(2)** the Home Sec. to exclude any terrorist from Great Britain and **(3)** the police to detain a suspected terrorist for between 48 hours and a week. The act was to be in force only for six months i.e. until 28th May 1975 but could be prolonged by the Home Sec. for six months at a time. In 1996 it was still in force.

PREVENTIVE DETENTION (1) Detention of an accused to prevent his interfering with evidence before his trial. **(2)** Detention of an habitual criminal to prevent further depredations upon the public. This was first authorised by the Prevention of Crimes Act, 1908. The Criminal Justice Act, 1948, permitted the imposition of from 5 to 14 years' preventive detention in cases of a history of serious convictions. This was replaced in 1973 by a power to extend imprisonment for the protection of the public.

PRICES. Owing to early lack of statistics, variables in taste and weather and the appearance of new skills and inventions, the long term history of prices is controversial, uncertain and possibly unrewarding. The following is offered with hesitation as a summary of some of the results (all figures are very approximate).

(1) Prices of consumer goods reigning in 1260 still reigned in 1520, but there had been steady rises to 50% peaks in 1310 and 1420 with a relapse to normal in between. Thus the average price of wheat per quarter in 1260 was 5s. 9d. and only 6s. in 1520. On the other hand daily wages had risen from 3¼d. to 5⅞d. for skilled men and from 2½d. to 4d. for labourers.

(2) From 1520 to 1580 prices more than doubled. Wheat rose to 13s. 10d; but wages less than doubled to 10d. and 6½d.

(3) From 1580 to the Civil War (1642) prices of consumables nearly trebled. Wheat rose to 36s. 1d. On the other hand more durable things such as cloth and iron rose by much less, perhaps 40%. Wages rose by less still to 1s. ½d. and 9¾d.

(4) From 1642 to 1702 prices rose more slowly. Wheat to 41s. 11d. More durable things by 10%. Wages rose more buoyantly to 1s. 8¾d. and 1s. 0¾d.

(5) The London price of bread per 4 lb. varied between 4¼d. and 6¾d. between 1735 and 1755. It rose to 7d. in 1756, declined to 4d. in 1761 and reached 7½d. in 1767. It then fell slightly, touching 7d. occasionally until 1794. It rose steadily to peaks of 15½d. in 1801 and 17d. in 1812 and 15½d. in 1813. Between 1815 and 1832 it varied between 9½d.-10d. level until 1842, fell to 7½d.-8¼d. in 1854 to 1857 between 9d. and 10¾d. Except in 1861 (9d.), 1867 (10¼d.), 1868 (9¼d.) there was a gentle decline which reached 5d. in 1899 and then a slight increase which reached 6d. in 1910.

(6) Two differently constructed cost of living indices have shown (a) (using 1700-1 as 100) a decline from 137 in 1661 to 94 in 1703, variations up to 107 in 1771, a steady rise to 122 in 1792, a steep rise to 228 in 1801, a fall to 156 in 1803, a rapid rise to 243 in 1813 and then with variations to 128 in 1823 and (b) using 1767-77 as 100 a decline from 142 in 1818 to 100 in 1826. Thereafter, (save for 109-111 in 1872-3) it seldom reached 100 until 1913 and fell steadily from 102 in 1874 to 61 in 1896, after which it climbed slowly to 85 in 1912. *See* INFLATION AND DEFLATION; CORN LAWS.

PRICES AND INCOMES BOARD (Feb. 1965-Nov. 1970) was set up by George Brown. All price increases and wage claims were to be referred to it for advice to him. The sheer burden of the work led to a breakdown, and in 1966 a blanket moratorium was imposed for six months, and the Board faded out. The Heath govt. abolished it.

PRIDE'S PURGE. *See* CHARLES-29.

PRIESTLEY, John Boynton (1894-1984), essayist, playwright and novelist, known particularly for his novel *The Good Companions* (1929) had an affection for the Englishness of England, but noticed the emergence of a 'third nation' with new ideas from the old 'two nations' of rural and industrial England. During World War II his radio broadcasts raised morale without lapsing into propaganda or exhortation.

PRIESTLEY, Joseph (1733-1804), Yorkshireman, originally a Presbyterian minister and from 1772 to 1780 Shelburne's librarian, was already sufficiently known as a scientist to have been elected F.R.S. in 1766 and to the French scientific academy in 1772, through his work on *The History of Electricity* (1767) and studies of conduction. His studies of gas led to his isolation of oxygen (which he called dephlogisticated air). Meanwhile he had involved himself in a series of furious theological controversies and then in political arguments; he never made any secret of his extreme liberalism. His house at Birmingham was sacked in 1791 when he celebrated the fall of the Bastille. He migrated to the U.S.A. in 1794.

PRIMARY SCHOOLS. *See* ELEMENTARY SCHOOLS.

PRIMATE, is usually used of the Abp. of Canterbury as signifying his superiority over the other English Bishops. He bears the title 'Primate of All England', the Abp. of York that of 'Primate of England'; the similarity and difference recall an ancient dispute and its settlement.

PRIME MINISTER (1) The first recognisable prime minister was Sir Robert Walpole (1721), but the headship of the govt. was vested in the First Ld. of the Treasury and the title was officially unknown until Disraeli described himself as such in the T. of Berlin (1878). It was legally recognised in a Royal Warrant of 1905 conferring precedence below the Abp. of York. The Chequers Estate Act, 1917, gave him the use of a country house. Under the Ministers of the Crown Act, 1937, he was, for the first time, paid as such.

(2) The Sovereign chooses the Prime Minister, but in practice the choice is limited to the person who can rely upon the support of Parliament, or since 1922, of the House of Commons. The Sovereign requests the candidate to form a ministry and the latter retains office only so long as he can do so. The Sovereign is constitutionally bound by his advice, but it is seldom (if ever) tendered in choosing his successor. It is uncertain if the Sovereign is invariably bound by advice to hold a general election or to swamp the House of Lords with peerages. One effect of these conventions is that the Prime Minister controls the composition of the Cabinet and govt., all of whose members go out of office when he does.

PRIMER was originally a book of prayer or devotion for lay use. Mediaeval primers were copies or translations of parts of the Breviary; post-Reformation ones were based on the *Sarum Hours* or the B.C.P. and were issued from Henry VIII down to 1783. Johnson defined a primer as "a small prayer book in which children are taught to read".

PRIMER SEISIN was the King's right to take over the lands of a dead tenant in chief and keep them until the heir had paid a relief and done homage. It could be commuted for a year's profits. Abolished 1660.

PRIMOGENITURE is the English rule that landed property on intestacy before 1926 and hereditary titles passed to the eldest legitimate son at the death of the holder, to the exclusion of the younger sons and daughters. In the absence of sons the daughters took the property in equal shares. *See* ABEYANCE.

PRIMROSE (1) Sir Archibald (1616-79) Ld. CARRINGTON (1661) a Royalist and supporter of Montrose and of Charles II at the B. of Worcester. He became a Ld. of Session and drafted the Rescissory Act. His son **(2) Archibald (1661-1723) 1st Vist. (1700) and E. (1702) of ROSEBERY** was a Scottish commissioner for the Union and afterwards a Scottish representative peer in 1707-8 and 1713. A descendant **(3) Sir Archibald (1783- 1868) 4th E. (1814)** was a Whig M.P. from 1805 to 1807. He was given a U.K. peerage in 1828 and supported the Reform Bill of 1832. His grandson **(4) Archibald Philip (1847-1929) 5th E. (1868)** joined the Liberals in 1869 and in 1887 held the Scottish office brief in the Lords. In 1883 he propounded the idea of the British Commonwealth of Nations in speeches in Australia and New Zealand and in 1884 he was urging House of Lords reform. In 1885 he was in the Cabinet and Foreign Sec. in 1886. In 1889 he was the first chairman of the L.C.C. and in 1892 he became Foreign Sec. again. He was a handsome, eloquent, popular figure with three Derby winners to his credit. He was now asked by both sides to mediate in the great coal strike of 1893 and did so with great effect. Thus when Gladstone retired in 1894, Q. Victoria sensibly chose Rosebery to form a new govt. in preference to the overbearing Sir William Harcourt (*see* ROSEBERY'S GOVT., MAR. 1894-JUNE 1895). He resigned the leadership of the Liberal Party in Oct. 1896, mainly over Gladstone's attitude on the Armenian massacres. In the ensuing years he moved steadily in the direction of imperialism and in Feb. 1902 he helped to form and became Pres. of the Liberal League and so split the Liberals on the imperialist issue. In practice this meant opposition to Home Rule and in 1905 he left the Liberal Party altogether. He was thus caught in the dilemma of having to oppose Lloyd George's 1909 budget while proposing Lords reform, yet disliking the Parliament Bill which gave it effect.

PRIMROSE LEAGUE, a conservative fund-raising organisation founded in 1883 in memory of Disraeli, whose favourite flower the primrose was.

PRINCE, -ESS (1) *See* ROMAN EMPERORS. **(2)** In Britain this title is used only by children of a sovereign and the eldest son of such a son. **(3)** The word is also used, for lack of anything better, to translate certain non-royal foreign titles e.g. (Ger.) *Fürst* and (Rus.) *Kniaz.* **(4)** Between Machiavelli's time and the end of the 18th cent. *Prince* was often used in political philosophy or as a technical term to denote an effective ruler, e.g. *Restraints of Princes* is still the marine insurance term for govt. interference with shipping movements.

PRINCE EDWARD ISLAND. *See* CANADA-10.

PRINCES, CHAMBER OF (1921-47) was a consultative assembly of Indian princes consisting of 109 princes with salutes of 11 guns and over and 12 elected to represent 127 lesser rulers. The Viceroy presided, but the princes elected a Chancellor. Unfortunately some of the greatest rulers, notably the Nizam and the Maharajah of Mysore, refused to attend and this deprived it of prestige and initiative, but the successive chancellors were men of distinction. *See* INDIAN PRINCELY STATES.

PRINCES IN THE TOWER. *See* RICHARD III-4-6.

PRINCE'S TRUST was founded in 1976 with the small naval pension of Charles, P. of Wales to help people of real potential in difficulties. By 1999, when it was chartered, the annual turnover had grown to £55M and 140,000 people had been helped.

PRINCETOWN. *See* DARTMOOR.

PRINCIPALITY OF SCOTLAND. A number of estates in Ayr, Renfrew and Ross appropriated to the maintenance of the heir to the Scottish throne.

PRINGLE, Sir John (1707-82), Bart. (1766), F.R.S. (1745), Physician-Gen. to the British troops in Flanders, Germany and Scotland between 1742 and 1748, reorganised military hospitals, improved their sanitation and the care of the wounded and in his internationally reputed *Observations on the Diseases of the Army* (1752), set out highly modern views on these matters and described his experiments with toxic and antiseptic substances. He also persuaded Stair and Noailles, the opposing generals in the German war, to respect each other's military hospitals and so originated the principle of "Red Cross neutrality" enunciated in the Geneva Conventions over a century later.

PRINTING. *See* BOOKS, RENAISSANCE-8.

PRIODAWR PRIODOLDER, PRIODORION. See WELSH LAW-7.

PRIOR. *See* ABBOT.

PRIOR, Matthew (1664-1721), part educated at Westminster, had to be taken into his uncle's fashionable wine house in Cannon (then Channel) Row when his father died. The place was frequented by the E. of Dorset and his friends, who noticed the boy reading Horace and turning a pretty ode. Dorset paid for his return to school. Here he made the acquaintance of Charles and Jas. Montague.

His first (political) poem written at Cambridge appeared in 1686 and by 1690 he had sufficient interest to become sec. to Ld. Dursley (later the E. of Berkeley), ambassador at The Hague. This, in William III's reign, was the key diplomatic mission and Prior, while producing the clever silver age verse for which he is now remembered, was an active and successful diplomat and gained much favour with the King. In 1697 he was Sec. of the Ryswick negotiations and after a short time as Sec. of State in Ireland became Sec. to the embassy, successively under the Es. of Portland and Jersey in Paris, whither diplomatic interest had shifted. In 1699 he became U. Sec. of State and in 1700 M.P. in the parliament which impeached Halifax, Orford and Somers for their part in the Partition Treaty. Though Prior had been involved in the negotiations, he voted for the impeachment.

In 1702 he joined the Tories, thereby remaining out of office until 1711. He was then sent to Paris on the secret *pourparlers* which culminated in the betrayal of the allies and the P. of Utrecht. He was accidentally arrested on his return and the facts came out, but the French mission who came with him carried on the discussions at his house. He initialled the preliminaries (sometimes known as "Matt's Peace") and went to Paris to agree the military suspension. Not surprisingly, Walpole impeached him in 1715. Exempted from the Act of Grace in 1717, he was shortly released but was never publicly employed again. Nevertheless his personal popularity remained and his friends subscribed for a substantial volume of his poems and made other gifts.

PRISE was a tax on goods levied in kind or by means of a right to buy a certain quantity at a privileged price. The RECTA PRISA (Lat: proper or fair prise) was a royal right to a prise of two casks of wine per shipload. This was converted, as early as the 13th cent., into a small toll on every cask but the right to take this prise was maintained well into the 15th cent.

PRISON COMMISSION was set up in 1877 to superintend local prisons. It was an independent and, though responsible to the Home Sec., often outspoken body which did its best to keep prison conditions before the public and was abolished in 1963.

PRISONS were originally used for custody pending trial, though the courts at Westminster maintained their own prisons mainly for debtors. From 1552 workhouses or houses of correction were being set up to provide work for vagrants and paupers. These, often called Bridewells after Bridewell Palace (London) (converted into a house of correction in 1552) began to house petty criminals and this was statutorily recognised in 1720. Corruption and oppression in the Marshalsea and Fleet prisons was a scandal which reached the House of Commons in 1729. In 1773 John Howard (?1726-90), as sheriff of Bedfordshire, was so shocked by the condition of his county prison that he decided to make a general investigation. In 1774 he secured the suppression of a fundamental abuse, by procuring an act to forbid the remuneration of gaolers by prisoners' fees. He travelled the U.K. and in 1777 published *The State of the Prisons in England and Wales*. In 1788 after continental travels he published an appendix. The abuses and horrors which he exposed jolted the public conscience and inspired the later movements for prison and penal reform. The Gaols Act 1823 required visits by chaplains, gaolers paid from public funds, women staff for women prisoners and restricted the use of irons. These advances became fully effective only after the Prison Act 1853 created an inspectorate. In 1990 the Conservative govt. planned to transfer some prisons to private ownership and this was begun in 1992.

PRIVATE BILL (PARLIAMENTARY) is a bill introduced in one house or the other by means of a petition from someone who is not a member. Such bills deal with individual concerns (e.g. formerly, divorce or naturalisation, or land settlement outside the usual law of entails) or (since about 1700) local matters such as the creation of turnpikes, canals, railways or bridges, or the conferment upon a local authority or statutory undertakers of special powers. Private bills are treated in the same way as other bills except that in each house the committee stage is taken before a small select committee, which conducts a hearing similar to a trial, with witnesses and counsel for the promoters and opposers. *See* PETITIONS, PARLIAMENTARY, PREAMBLE.

PRIVATEERS were privately owned ships authorised by a belligerent to levy war upon the subjects of a hostile state and to seize and sell their property as prize. The document authorising their acts was called LETTERS OF MARQUE without which they might be treated as pirates. No letters of marque have been issued by a civilised country since 1815. *See* COMMERCE PROTECTION, NAVAL-A; PIRACY; REPRISAL.

PRIVATE EYE, a weekly journal founded in 1961, specialised in exposing in downright language matter which its victims preferred, sometimes reasonably, to keep private. It warned readers that "long boring letters will be cut".

PRIVATISATION (1) is a doctrinally based Tory counter attack on socialism involving the dissolution of public monopolies and the transfer of all manner of undertakings to private management. It is asserted that they will be more prosperous and innovative if conducted in competitive conditions by the enterprise of those with an interest in their success, rather than by indifferent publicly paid employees with no such interest. The prosperity thus generated will more than compensate for the low-level security of socialism, by a rising standard of living, while the govt. benefits from realisations on sale, rising tax yields, falling administrative payrolls and reduced inflation.

(2) A usual but not essential feature of the process is that ownership of an undertaking is transferred by sale.

Willing buyers with funds must be found and each undertaking must be brought to a point where it is commercially attractive to them at the moment of the intended sale. This may involve reorganisation into successful and saleable units, disposal of unprofitable departments and the writing off of debt. The public undertakings concerned were vast in scope and variety and owned huge properties (e.g. local authorities alone owned aggregate areas equivalent to six average counties). Hence sales had to be made slowly to avoid gluts and prevent privatisations in one sector absorbing free capital needed for another.

(3) The Thatcher govt. began the programme in 1978 and the first privatisations emerged in 1981. It required successive electoral victories because it could not be completed in one or even two parliaments and it needed a buoyant economy. The electorate was lukewarmly favourable, but the deep slump which began in 1989 created great difficulties, especially for mortgaged house-buyers and small businesses which often ended in the hands of building societies or banks.

(4) The following are examples of the various privatisation methods. (a) Broadcasting franchises were auctioned; (b) Water, Gas and Electricity were divided into territorial companies with millions of low denomination shares and floated on the stock market; (c) Some municipal undertakings were sold to their employees: housing estates to tenants; (d) The Post Office telegraph was closed; its telephone organisation sold to British Telecommunications which was required to share its lines with Mercury; (e) Direct labour organisations under public authorities were required to tender on level terms with private contractors; (f) Security firms took over the escort of prisoners and began to manage prisons.

(5) Foreign respect for Margaret Thatcher and the contrast between the early successes of privatisation and the inefficiency, corruption and oppression of Russo-socialism were major features in the European political overturns after 1988.

(6) In fact, inflation had to be controlled by other means; the administrative burden on the economy as a whole was not reduced; the era was notable for corruption scandals and huge frauds and for the highest unemployment in history. The relationship between these things and the effects of privatisation is uncertain.

(7) In the 1990s the advantages of competitiveness were partly eroded by inadequately policed takeovers.

PRIVILEGE. *See* GOODWIN *v* FORTESCUE; STOCKDALE *v* HANSARD.

PRIVY COUNCIL (1) was also called in mediaeval Latin or French the Secret, Large, Ordinary, Good, Wise, Full, Whole or Common Council, but all these were different ways of naming the King's Council which, especially under the Tudors, was often simply called The Council.

(2) No ruler can avoid asking his entourage for information or advice. The origin of the Council was thus natural rather than formal and its remit might relate to all the royal functions subsisting or in use at any given time. Its membership and work depended upon the ruler, who might be a strong King (William I, Edward I), a weak one (Stephen), a minor with a guardian or regent (Henry III with William Marshal and Guala) or a simpleton (Henry VI). Strong rulers consulted whom they pleased and settled agendas as they wished. In times of weakness, councillors from a previous dispensation might take over responsibility because someone had to do it. At such times certain magnates, perhaps previously out of favour, might assert a right to be of the Council and this focused attention upon its constitution. The need for an office (The Chancery) and an office routine tended also towards formalisation.

(3) Constitutional informality, however, remained because while Parliament had grown up by 1380 to take over supremacy in legislation and taxation, administrative business and interim legislation grew in quantity, novelty and complexity. The Council became like a govt., preparing business for Parliament, besides coping with daily minutiae. Conversely, when the country was under civil war, parliaments were packed, administration languished and the Council hardly functioned at all, particularly from 1460 to 1497, by which time Henry VII had revived it.

(4) The natural distinction between policy and detail was reflected in organisation. Judicial and local business tended to be hived off towards the Admiral and the Chancellor, the Star Chamber and Court of Requests and, latest of all, the Councils of the North and of Wales and the Marches. These had to have fixed seats while the rest of the council followed the King. By 1497 there was a Ld. Pres. who became a regular officer after 1529. Total membership was about 40, or whom 20 followed the King and of these 20, Henry VIII expected two or three to be in constant attendance. Between 1532 and 1540 the King's Principal Sec., Thomas Cromwell, did much to formalise an inner ring of some 20 policy-making councillors who dealt with all manner of business. Between 1558 and 1640 domestic business, for example, included disputes about hunting rights, regulation of the coal and wool trades, the granting of charters and the making of military assessments. External affairs included the silk trade, relations with France, Spain and Scotland, piracy and the Greenland fisheries. Since Poynings Law they had dealt with Irish legislation and a little later, with appeals from the Channel Is. They also dealt with ecclesiastical affairs after 1530. Finally the Council had a reserve power to maintain order, involving inquisitorial procedures, sometimes (not often) under torture.

(5) Under Edward VI the 40 included only 4 bishops, 10 peers and 4 great officers (who were peers). The rest were new men, which made the Council dependent on the monarch and set it apart. It had 5 committees viz: to hear suits and enforce forfeits and proclamations (Star Chamber), a committee on courts, another on defence and a committee for the State which was the equivalent of the councillors who followed the King. This committee practice has continued into modern times.

(6) Being a prerogative body, it continued after the Restoration to exercise those functions which had not been invaded by statute, but its political position was soon occupied by cabinets which could command parliamentary support. Hence it became in practice, though not in theory, a subordinate and experimental body overlapping with, but controlled by the govt. Its initial preoccupations were colonial policy and trade (*see* TRADE AND PLANTATIONS) based on the Irish precedents, and colonial appeals (*see* JUDICIAL COMMITTEE) based on Channel Is. precedents. In the Napoleonic Wars the vast policy operation concerned with economic warfare was carried through by prerogative orders in council. Subsequently the departments of education, health and local govt. originated as privy council committees.

PRIVY COUNCIL, JUDICIAL COMMITTEE (*see* CURIA REGIS; COUNCIL; previous entry and STAR CHAMBER). The Act 16 Car I cap. 10 (1641) of the Long Parliament abolished the Council's jurisdiction only over English Bills and Petitions, but the post-Commonwealth colonial expansion was extending its jurisdiction elsewhere. In 1667 the Council had a committee for trade, foreign plantations and for hearing appeals from Jersey and Guernsey assisted by the Att.-Gen. and the King's Advocate. The Committee heard appeals from other plantations, for in 1696 a committee was directed "as formerly" to hear them. It consisted usually of the chief legal authorities, a Sec. of State, the Bp. of London and interested privy councillors. Such committees were set up *ad hoc* but tended to have the same membership and in practice the council rubber-stamped their recommendations. These appeals were sometimes judicial, sometimes quasi-judicial or political.

As the empire expanded, business increased. Between 1720 and 1730 there was an appeal on average every six weeks; between 1760 and 1770 slightly over one a month. The creation of Indian and colonial supreme courts added to the number and generated rules of procedure, but the quasi-political function was still in evidence. In 1774 Benjamin Franklin, for example, argued a petition (contemptuously dismissed) for the removal of the Gov. and Lieut. Gov. of Massachusetts. The Council's proceedings were not always respected or popular and occasionally colonial authorities or courts disobeyed its orders, but in general the weight of opinion favoured it; the judges of colonial courts were sometimes too closely involved with local society, or insufficiently talented and there was a need for uniformity of rules throughout the Crown's dominions. By 1815 the judicial business had superseded the rest, which was being referred to the Board of Trade, or rather its Pres. The Committee was now in all essentials a court, sitting in public and after 1829 publishing its own reports. In 1832 the jurisdiction of the abolished High Court of Delegates was conferred upon it and in 1833 the Judicial Committee Act regularised its membership and functions and conferred Admiralty appellate jurisdiction as well. It was to consist of the Ld. Pres. and privy councillors who held or had held the highest English judicial offices and the quorum was 4, but the Crown could summon others. In 1871 the chief justices of Bengal, Bombay and Madras were added: in 1895 and 1913 their colleagues from Australia, Canada and S. Africa.

The Committee is not bound by all its own decisions and they do not bind courts in the U.K., though they are powerfully persuasive; many are made by judges sitting in U.K. courts in other capacities. In addition, since the Committee decisions are in theory advice to the Crown, minority opinion was never reported until 1960. The Committee's jurisdiction has been restricted or abolished by many of the independent members of the Commonwealth since the Statute of Westminster 1931. *See* DOMINION STATUS.

PRIVY PURSE is that part of the sovereign's funds which he may spend as he pleases. Now a very small proportion of the Civil List.

PRIVY SEAL, LORD. The Privy Seal was originally used to authenticate royal documents of lesser or private importance, or to authorise the use of the Great Seal. In the late 15th cent. it began to be used for criminal process issued by the conciliar courts, especially the Star Chamber, because its use was expeditious, informal and secret. Its Keeper, later Ld., was thus a leading member of the Star Chamber. After the Star Chamber's abolition the Seal continued to be used procedurally: the Lordship became and remains a ministry without portfolio. The Privy Seal itself was abolished by the Great Seal Act, 1884.

PRIZE is that part of maritime law which regulates the taking, condemnation and forfeiture of ships and goods in them on the way to a belligerent port. The proclamation of a blockade or of prize rules or regulations is a necessary precedent and seizures are brought before a prize court for investigation. This court was the Court of Admiralty or a local Court of Vice-Admiralty. Condemned prizes were sold and the proceeds paid originally to the commander and crew of the captor. In World Wars I and II they were paid into a prize fund and divided among the officers and men of the Royal Navy. This form of reward was prospectively abolished in 1949.

PROBATE. Originally only chattels could be left by will and the church tried to influence the dying to will these to pious or charitable purposes by denying final absolution. By the 13th cent. bequests were administered by the bishop and the authenticity of wills was settled by the ecclesiastical courts. Hence the law of probate was

developed in ecclesiastical courts until the creation of the Court of Probate in 1857. *See* DEATH DUTIES.

PROBATION. *See* FIRST OFFENDERS.

PROCEDENDO, **WRIT OF.** *See* PREROGATIVE WRITS.

PROCLAMATIONS "cannot make that an offence which was not an offence before", but disregard of a proclamation against an existing offence can attract heavier punishment. In 1539, however, Henry VIII was given a secondary power to create punishable offences by proclamation having statutory force, but not so as to prejudice a person's life, inheritance, offices, liberties, goods or chattels. The Act was repealed in 1547. James I wished to prohibit new buildings in London by proclamation but was advised by the Chief Justices and the Chief Baron (*The Case of Proclamations* 1611) as above.

PROCTOR, a representative in ecclesiastical matters and hence the equivalent, in an ecclesiastical court, of a solicitor or in the lower house of Convocation a deputy acting for a cathedral chapter. The Queen's or King's Proctor is an official entitled to intervene in divorce and nullity cases (which originated in canon law) if it appeared that the court might be deceived.

PROCTOR, Adelaide (1825-64), Q. Victoria's favourite poet and a philanthropist, was an influential supporter of the Soc. for the Employment of Women, and similar women's causes.

PROCURATOR AUGUSTI. See BRITAIN. ROMAN-5.

PRODUCTION, MINISTRY OF, was established for war purposes in 1942 and merged in the Board of Trade in 1945.

PROFUMO AFFAIR (1963). John Profumo, Sec. of State for War, was consorting with a Christine Keeler. Hints appeared in the press but as he threatened proceedings for libel, the matter was raised in the Commons. After discussion with ministers nominated by Harold Macmillan, the Prime Minister, he said in a personal statement to the Commons that his relationship with her had not been 'improper' (which was false) and had not compromised his ministerial duties (which was true). Journalists ferreted out evidence, including that of orgies at Cliveden (Berks), that in the first of these assertions he had been lying. The incidents gained piquancy, though not importance, when it emerged that Miss Keeler had had a sultry affair with the Russian Naval Attaché. The ill advised personal statement in response to press prurience brought this matter into the public domain, because it infringed the rule that personal statements in Parliament must be true. The need to make it had been forced upon him by wild allegations of breaches of security. He resigned and became for the next 30 years a well liked welfare worker in East London.

PROGRESSES, ROYAL. Any royal court comprises many hundreds of assorted people, horses (not to mention vehicles) which, before 1800 fouled the ground and exhausted local supplies. The means for keeping public order were minimal. A show of royal strength and splendour supported local peace, strengthened loyalties and checked abuses. Thus English and Scots monarchs had every ground of convenience and political expediency for going on progress, even if the arrangements were sometimes interrupted by wars. Until Tudor times they habitually (when not encamped) used large monasteries as hotels. Parliaments often met in them too. Hence mediaeval progresses commonly took in places (e.g. Worcester, Gloucester or Arbroath) where suitable monasteries were. After their Dissolution, other arrangements became necessary. Country palaces were built e.g. at Eltham, Nonsuch, Hampton Court, and Greenwich, and magnates now expected to be honoured with visits. A season's itinerary was planned and the public notifications ("Giests") of intended halts issued. Some greater magnates established permanent accommodation (or "prodigies") for them. The architect

Robert Smythson (1535-1614) specialised in these. They account for the great size of such country houses as Knowle, Longleat, Penshurst, Hatfield and Audley End. Prodigious building lasted as long as progresses continued to be expected; actually they faded out with the first two Georges (who preferred Germany), but travelling remains a feature of Royal practice.

PROHIBITION, in force in the U.S.A. from 1920 to 1933, created a general disrespect for law in that country and immense prosperity for certain Canadian border towns and the Bahamas.

PROHIBITION, WRIT OF. *See* PREROGATIVE WRITS.

PROHIBITIONS, CASE OF **(1607).** Abp. Bancroft complained to James I about interference in the proceedings of ecclesiastical courts by writs of prohibition issued by the Kings Bench. He argued that in determining the jurisdiction of ecclesiastical courts or in the exposition of certain statutes or in other cases where there is no express authority, the King may decide the matter personally and that as judges are only the King's delegates, he may take any case out of their hands and determine it himself. Sir Edward Coke, C.J., in the presence and with the consent of all the judges, replied that the King cannot do this because cases must be decided according to the law of England, which is that the court, even in the King's presence, gives the judgement. "The King said that he thought the law founded upon reason and that he and others had reason as well as the judges" to which Coke replied that "...causes... are not to be decided by natural reason, but by the artificial reason and judgement of law, which law is an art which requires long study and experience..." with which the King was greatly offended. The case is the foundation of the view that judicial functions should be separated from executive functions.

PROLETARIAT (Lat: proles = offspring). Those whose only economic asset is their offspring and so a communist propaganda term for any suitable object of communist benevolence.

PROMENADE CONCERTS were commenced by the London Philharmonic Society at Queens Hall (Upper Regent St., London) in 1894. The hall was destroyed in World War II and the concerts were revived at the R. Albert Hall after it.

PROMISSORY OATHS. *See* OATHS.

PROPAGANDA. The word is derived from a Papal congregation (ministry) *de Propaganda fide* (Lat: for the dissemination of the faith) set up in 1622 to deal with missions to the heathen and territories without a hierarchy. It was equipped with a missionary seminary, the Collegium Urbanum, in 1627. The word now represents the propagation, accurate or otherwise, of a particular point of view usually in support of a totalitarian purpose. Its negative counterpart is censorship. *See also* GOEBBELS, JOSEF.

PROPAGATION OF THE GOSPEL, SOCIETY FOR (S.P.G.) was chartered in 1701 to provide ministration for Anglicans abroad and to convert non-Christians.

PROPHESYINGS (*See* 1 COR. 14 vv3, 22, 29) (c. 1560-c. 1640) were puritan inspired conferences of clergy for purposes of biblical exposition, often along Zwinglian lines. They were commonly held in town churches and attracted much public interest, besides training for the often astonishingly ignorant clergy. Hence reforming Elizabethan bishops. sometimes encouraged them, provided that they only helped to wean the public away from the 'old religion'. Elizabeth I mistakenly thought them subversive and made Abp. Grindal suppress them in 1577. They were then revived under the less alarming name of **PREACHING EXERCISES.**

PROPRIETARY GOVERNMENTS were created under royal charters which conferred the ownership of a territory upon a person or persons, together with political and

sometimes virtually sovereign powers there. The most important British examples were: (in America) the Carolinas, the Hudson Bay Co's. Canadian territories, Maine, Maryland, New Jersey, New York and Pennsylvania; (in Africa) Rhodesia; (in Indonesia) British North Borneo. The Indian territories of the HEIC and the Irish lands of the Hon. Irish Society are not usually comprised in this class though they bore some of their characteristics.

PROROGATION is the termination of a parliamentary session without holding a general election. It is commonly effected by royal commission. It brings the existence of both Houses of Parliament to an end and therefore kills any business in progress in them. Hence a bill before either House has to be reintroduced from the start and go through both Houses again, after they are called into being by summons to the next session. Both Houses often save private bills (because of the expense to the promoters) in these circumstances, by taking the proceedings upon them formally up to the point which had been reached at prorogation. The period during which Parliament stands prorogued lengthens the time before which a statutory instrument subject to parliamentary procedure comes into force. *See* DISSOLUTION.

PROSTITUTION. *See* SEXUAL OFFENCES; BROTHELS.

PROTECTIONISM. A state policy of nurturing home industry by exclusion or taxation of foreign products. Since other states may retaliate, the long range effect is a constriction of international trade, excessive global investment and rising prices.

PROTECTIONS against impressment were issued by govt. departments (e.g. to officials in Crown service or the crews of Post Office packets) or by the consuls or diplomatic representatives of neutral states to their own subjects. During the longer wars between 1702 and 1815, there was a lucrative trade in protections obtained by personation, forgery or bribery.

PROTECTOR, LORD (A) A kind of surrogate kingship or guardianship conferred upon a close relative of the King during the King's incapacity, by infancy or infirmity, viz: **(1)** Humphrey, D. of Gloucester for Henry VI from 1422 to 1437; **(2)** Richard, D. of York also for Henry VI in 1454 and 1455; **(3)** Richard, D. of Gloucester (Richard III) for Edward V in 1483; **(4)** Edward, E. of Hertford and D. of Somerset for Edward VI from 1547 to 1549 and **(5)** John, E. of Warwick and D. of Northumberland from 1549 to 1553.

(B) The title of the head of the state under the Commonwealth held by **(1)** Oliver Cromwell from 1653 to 1658 and by **(2)** Richard Cromwell from Sept. 1658 to May 1659.

PROTECTORATE 1653-9. *See* COMMONWEALTH-9-18.

PROTECTORATE or PROTECTED STATE is a sovereign country which, by agreement, has secured the protection of a more powerful state and has in return surrendered, during the term of the agreement, certain rights of which the conduct of foreign policy is usual and the control of armed forces and frontier tariffs common. Often subjects of the protecting state have a privileged position there and its diplomatic representative may, as the only resident foreign envoy, be the local ruler's chief adviser or may, through the medium of strongly supported advice, be the real ruler himself.

PROTEST is the note of dissent which any peer may enter in the Journals of the House of Lords against one of its decisions.

PROTESTANT ASSN. *See* GORDON RIOTS.

PROTESTANT-ISM is the usual term for most forms of Christianity which grew up in the Reformation in opposition to the R. Catholic Church. The term originated in the PROTESTATIO of the reformers against the decisions of the R. Catholic majority at the diet of Speyer in 1529. *See* ANGLICANISM; CALVIN; LUTHER.

PROTESTANT SUCCESSION. The Act of Settlement 1701 requires that the Crown shall pass to the descendants, *being protestant*, of the Electress Sophia of Hanover.

PROTESTATION (18 Dec. 1621) of the Commons. James I needed funds for his Palatine and Spanish policy, but would not explain what that policy was. The Commons had already shaken his position by successfully impeaching Sir Francis Mitchell and Sir Giles Mompesson for abuse of monopolies and Bacon for peculation. The King told them to get on with voting supplies. They drew up a petition asserting that the proper foreign policy was to fight Spain and other R. Catholic powers and marry the P. of Wales to a Protestant. James, advised by Gondomar the Spanish ambassador, threatened to punish any who presumed to meddle with the govt. or matters of state or the Prince's marriage. The Commons admitted that war, peace and royal marriages were matters for the prerogative but said that they were only drawing attention to things which might have escaped the King's notice. He replied that they were really trying to usurp the prerogative by means of advice. In their Protestation in reply they asserted that matters concerning the King, the condition and defence of the realm and the Church were proper for parliamentary discussion and that their freedom from arrest protected them against interference with such discussion. In reply James adjourned and then dissolved Parliament and tore the Protestation from the Journals of the House.

PROTOCOL (1) A diplomatic document in draft, especially one whose wording is being negotiated between powers, **(2)** The code of international etiquette and ceremonial.

PROTONOTARY. A secretarial official. There were three in the Common Pleas and one in the Kings Bench. The office was abolished in 1837.

PROVIDENCE. *See* RHODE I.

PROVINCE. *See* CHURCH ORGANISATION.

PROVINCE WELLESLEY. *See* MALAYA; THAILAND.

PROVISIONAL ORDERS are local orders made by a govt. department at the request, usually, of a public body but which require confirmation by an act of Parliament. Public notice is given and a public inquiry is held beforehand and the order is then submitted to both Houses for confirmation by public bill; but if objected to, the bill is treated as a private bill at the committee stage. The object of the procedure was to reduce the number of private bills and to ensure that detailed information is obtained locally. It has been mostly superseded by Special Procedure Orders procedure, except for Scotland.

PROVISION, PROVISORS, STATS. OF. *See* ADVOWSON AND TITHE-.

PROVOST (1). *See* CATHEDRAL, **(2)** the head of certain Oxford and Cambridge colleges.

PRUDENTIAL INSURANCE CO. LTD began in 1848 as a mutual assurance and investment association. It added industrial insurance to its work in 1854 and developed phenomenally, absorbing other companies. It adopted the name in 1867 and broadened its business to general insurance in 1919.

PRUSSIA (*see* BRANDENBURG). **(1)** On Joachim von Blumenthal's advice the Great Elector Frederick William (r. 1640-88) reorganised his devastated territories by political bargains with the local nobilities. They ceded their right to vote taxes, their feudal obligations were transmuted into a monopoly of military commissions and in return their tenants became serfs. The local Estates henceforth seldom met and so made way for centralisation. The new dispensation was a success. A land reclamation boom contented the tenants and filled the treasury. The Elector could create a proper army. The electorate moved from unimportance to significance when he defeated the terrible Swedes at Fehrbellin (1675).

(2) Frederick III (r. 1688-1713, King in Prussia as Frederick I from 1701) continued the armed policy. His Gen., Leopold von Anhalt-Dessau, by introducing the military march and the iron ramrod, doubled manoeuvrabiity and the rate of fire. The somewhat vain Elector had civilised interests as well. He employed architects such as Andreas Schlüter and Fischer von Erlach, founded the Berlin Academies of Arts (1696) and Sciences (1700) and patronised Gottfried Leibnitz (1646-1716).

(3) Frederick stood between the Great Northern War (1700-21) and the southern War of the Spanish Succession (1701-13) and profited from both without being sucked into either. He traded troops to the Emperor for the southern conflict in return for royal status and thus confirmed his independence of Poland which was involved in the northern war (*see* BALTIC, 36-41). The burden upon his sparse resources of a wartime inflation and the expense of a crown and a corrupt court while trade languished, was too much. He left the inheritance virtually bankrupt.

(4) His son, Frederick William I (r. 1713-40), who had hated him, saw the defects of his policies. There was plenty of land but not enough people. Ruthless savings were made and intelligently invested. By total religious toleration, bounties and tax concessions, he attracted reliable and talented refugees. The wastes of E. Prussia were peopled from Salzburg (1730). Huguenots made Berlin half French. Such enlightenment and progress amassed a huge return. He built up a formidable army and a cash reserve. The reverse of the medal was tyrannical administration, personally animated by this restless, gout-tortured autocrat and barbarous economy at court.

(5) In 1715, with the southern war safely over and Sweden beaten by the Russians, he occupied Swedish Stettin and having obtained that port's definitive cession in 1720 set up the *Seehandelsgesellschaft* (Maritime Trading Co. – SHG – in 1722). Thereafter, since war cost money, his diplomacy was quiescent, influenced on the west by a personal dislike of George I and on the south by the Emperor Charles Xl's Pragmatic Sanction, designed to maintain, under Charles' daughter Maria Theresa, the unity of the Habsburg dominions. Like every other ruler, the King guaranteed the Pragmatic. Unlike them, he meant it. He died a few weeks before Charles' death put it to the test.

(6) Frederick II (The Great r. 1740-86) had hated his father too, so changes were to be expected; but Saxony and Bavaria, supported by France and also Spain, instantly made claims upon the Habsburg lands. Frederick, however, acted. He seized Silesia and Glatz, rich Protestant provinces economically related to Brandenburg and having held them through the two Wars of the Austrian Succession (1740-2, 1744-5), obtained them at the P. of Dresden (Dec. 1745).

(7) The Silesians generally welcomed the change and were soon incorporated into Frederick's system, which continued to develop (but more rapidly) along the lines laid down by his father. Particularly after the P. of Aix la Chapelle (1748) re-established European intercourse, land reclamation and settlement, especially along the Oder (1749-53), proceeded apace. New industries such as cotton spinning (1744) and silk weaving (1748) at Berlin profited from improved navigations: the Elbe-Havel canal (1742) had extended the Great Elector's Oder-Spree waterway through Berlin to the North Sea. Potatoes, soon to be the staple of Prussian diet, were now being grown in previously unusable soils and beet sugar was discovered, though not for a while exploited. The economic balance was provided from Silesian iron and foundries. The profits of the boom were accumulated through the S.H.G. (by now really a bank) or in such ventures as the Emden Trading Co. Between 1745 and 1747, too, Knobelsdorff built Frederick's remarkable palace of *Sans Souci* at Potsdam. Prussia was undergoing a managed economic revolution technically in some ways similar to, but preceding the British Industrial Revolution. The differences lay in scale, geography and armaments. Britain, an island, invested in a navy divorced from most of its internal social life; Prussia, on the mainland, in an army heavily involved in her's.

(8) This helps to explain the *Renversement des Alliances* and Anglo-Prussian co-operation in the Seven Years' War (1756-63). French protectionist imperialism threatened British commerce; an Austrian recovery of Silesia would dismantle the new Prussian economy and the threatened powers' striking forces were complementary as long as Britain, the richer partner, financed Prussia.

(9) Prussia emerged territorially unchanged (P. of Hubertusburg) from the Seven Years' War. Severely, but no more shaken than her neighbours, she had the advantage of Frederick's fiery energy. He meant to connect E. Prussia with the main bulk of his dominions and to control the Vistula Basin's exports. Both could be achieved by acquiring Polish W. Prussia, part of whose trade along the R. Netze he had already diverted. Augustus III of Poland and Saxony died in Oct. 1763. The Czarina Catharine the Great intended to prevent another Saxon election and to control all Poland through one of her lovers, Stanislas Poniatowski. Other courts were hostile. Frederick, who needed an ally, was prepared to help. Their agreement of Apr. 1764 gave Stanislas the throne in Sept.

(10) Poland was institutionally isolated, but Stanislas proved less amenable on a throne than in bed. Catharine's efforts to interfere in aid of Polish Orthodox minorities met R. Catholic resistance and nascent reformism. From 1768 her resources were increasingly diverted by a Turkish war. Frederick wanted W. Prussia and was prepared to trade other parts of Poland to rivals. To do this Catharine had to be convinced that her policy would fail; but Maria Theresa had to be overborne too, for she thought partition both immoral and unwise on grounds of international comity and internal balance. Her son, the Emperor Joseph II, now co-ruler with her of the Habsburg states, disagreed. To him and Frederick the Turkish war seemed to offer a fleeting opportunity and Frederick hoped that large Polish annexations would at last reconcile the House of Habsburg-Lorraine to the loss of Silesia – and Lorraine. The two monarchs met at Neisse (Silesia) in Aug. 1769 and Novy Mesto (Moravia) in Sept. 1770.

(11) By 1771 Russian victories forced a decision. The threat of Austrian alliance with the Turk convinced Catharine; the fear of Russian success, Maria Theresa's advisers. The compromise first Polish Partition (Aug. 1772) was distasteful to Maria Theresa, unsatisfactory to Catharine, but advantageous to Frederick, even if he did not get Danzig or Thorn (Torun). Characteristically he instantly commenced a canal from the Vistula to the Oder. A commercial treaty (Mar. 1775) with Poland, its natural consequence, was a further step in an ambitious eastern policy.

(12) Central Europe was convulsed in the early years of the American rebellion by Austrian claims to the Bavarian Succession (1777-9). Frederick took the lead in resisting these, for their admission would have given the Habsburgs permanent paramountcy in Germany. Brief hostilities (July 1778-May 1779) ended in a minor partition. Austria took the Innviertel, Frederick the reversion to Ansbach and Bayreuth (P. of Teschen). By now it was apparent that Britain might not, after all, put down the Americans, who secured French (1778) and then Spanish (1779) help. British interference with seaborne trade attracted Baltic retaliation. In May 1781 Prussia joined the Russian-inspired Armed Neutrality of 1780. In 1784 Joseph II again revived his Bavarian scheme by proposing to exchange it for the Austrian

Netherlands. Frederick organised a successful N. German league against this and also concluded an American commercial treaty (July and Sept. 1785). He died in Aug. 1786.

(13) His eastward policies with westward excursions continued as of their own momentum under his nephew Frederick William II (r. 1786-97). In the west he intervened between William V of Orange and the Dutch extremists (1787) and accepted the escheat of Ansbach and Bayreuth (1792). In the east, Polish affairs were the main reason why Prussia long remained sluggish towards French revolutionary events and joined so unenthusiastically in the Valmy Campaign (Sept. 1792) and the First Coalition (1793). Under the Second Polish Partition (May 1793) the Kingdom secured Danzig, Thorn, Poznania, Gniezno and Kalisz. The Polish rising of 1794 caused Prussia to withdraw from the coalition and the Third Partition (Oct. 1795) gave her further wide provinces including Warsaw. An E. European, Prusso-Polish state expressed in a political form the commercial developments and aristocratic intermarriages of the past 40 years. By comparison, the French treaty of Aug. 1796, whereby Prussia exchanged her possessions on the left bank of the Rhine for the lands of ecclesiastical states, was mere opportunism.

(14) This opportunism was a characteristic of Frederick William III (r. 1797-1840), with whose father the long succession of able Hohenzollerns had ended. He managed to stay out of the Second Coalition (Mar. 1799-Feb. 1801) and having occupied Hanover and Bremen in Apr. 1801, bought the ability to keep them from the victor of Austerlitz at the price of Cleves, Neuchatel and Ansbach (T. of Schönbrunn, Dec. 1805). There was, however, a deeper problem. The great Hohenzollerns down to 1786 had managed their country like a private estate, with a concentration of responsibility which was too much for their successors. Slack administration, ageing functionaries and generals now hid behind a facade of ossified military power. Prussia joined in alliance against Britain (T. of Paris, Feb. 1806) on the assumption that, Austria having been reduced to second class status, Prussia would have the primacy in Germany. The wholesale creation of Bonapartist states and the formation of the French protected Confederation of the Rhine forced the King to fight for it (Oct. 1806). Within a fortnight he and his Saxon ally were overwhelmed in the twin debacles of Jena and Auerstädt and in Feb. 1807 the remaining Prussians with the Russians were battered at Eylau. A Russian defeat at Friedland (June 1807) ended this war. To the new Bonapartist Kingdom of Westphalia, Prussia lost her lands west of the Elbe; to the new Saxo-Polish Grand Duchy of Warsaw, her gains from the Partitions of 1793 and 1795. She had to join the Continental System, limit her army to 42,000, pay a large indemnity and endure and pay for a French occupation by 160,000 troops (Ts. of Tilsit, July).

(15) French nationalism provoked a German patriotism, and defeat stimulated Prussian reforms designed to exploit that patriotism. The leading reformers were the products of Prussian cosmopolitanism: few were Prussians. The King commissioned Heinrich vom Stein, a Nassauer, to reorganise the civil institutions, Gerhard von Scharnhorst, a Hanoverian and Count Augustus Neithardt von Gneisenau, a Saxon who had fought in the British army, to rejuvenate the army. Between 1807 and 1813 they overhauled the administration, converted the SHG into a state bank, abolished serfdom, guilds and internal customs, created town councils, prepared a scheme of universal conscription using the 42,000 as a cadre and opened commissions to the educated bourgeoisie.

(16) The result was that when Bonaparte retreated from Moscow (Oct-Dec. 1812) Prussia was able to throw him over. Her adherence to the Allies had important effects. Large numbers of Prussians fought in the campaigns which twice defeated him; and resurgent military power enabled her to make great territorial claims. The future of Poland was the main issue at the Congress of Vienna. Austria had her territories from the partitions. Russia was in possession of most of the Duchy of Warsaw. Nobody was prepared to support Prussia in a war for its restitution. Posnania only was returned to her, but in pursuit of the political logic of the time she was compensated elsewhere: with half of Saxony, the non-Hanoverian parts of Bonaparte Westphalia and Berg (which included the Ruhr). The eastern policies of Frederick the Great and Frederick William II were thus abandoned.

(17) The Prussian method of advance to domination in Germany resembled the earlier method in Poland. It began with commercial measures originally technical in character (*see* ZOLLVEREIN) arising from the separation of her Rhenish and eastern areas by foreign territory, but now occurring in the context of an industrial revolution. One major object of Prussian policy was to bring together Silesian iron and Ruhr coal, which railway and canal building facilitated; others, after Bismarck became Minister-Pres. (1862) were to dominate the Elbe basin, the North Sea ports and, by extension, the Baltic entrances. None of these four objects could be fully achieved unless Hanover was subdued and, since the Elbe was a main trade route from Bohemia, Austria was bound to support Hanover. The expulsion of the Habsburg from Germany was a prerequisite of the advance to the ocean. The Danish war of 1864 put Prussian troops into the neck of Jutland; the Austro-Prussian war achieved the expulsion of Austria and by logical extension the annexation of Hanover. Prussia now occupied two thirds of a Germany in which Austria could no longer support the lesser states. Their future was bound up with Prussia's and they recognised it in 1870 by joining her in attacking France. The proclamation at Versailles (Jan. 1871) of a federative German Empire, with a crown vested in the Prussian King, formally expressed a pre-existing reality.

(18) The merger of Prussia with a greater Germany put the management of German international interests for a generation in the hands of a Berlin govt. and general staff. This gave great leverage to the mainly Rhineland industrial interests, which favoured the capture of overseas markets, the seizure of colonies and naval development, but it gave rise to the foreign belief that Prussian soldiers dominated policy. This belief persisted long after it ceased to be well founded; and because, in 1932, the Nazis captured the Prussian Republic's administrative machine and state police, the liquidation of Prussia as a component entity of Germany became an Allied, particularly Churchillian, war aim in World War II. This was carried into effect in Feb. 1946.

PRUSSIAN BLUE, a powerful deep blue pigment discovered in 1704 by Diesbach at Berlin and used for Prussian infantry uniforms and for marking Prussian territory on maps. Hence the ambiguous *Le bleu prussien mange tous les autres* (Fr. = Prussian blue absorbs all the others).

PRYNNE, William (1600-69), learned and furious extremist, was writing against Arminianism in 1627 and in 1632 published him immense *Histriomastix*, an attack on stage plays containing opprobrious innuendoes against Charles I and his Queen. The Star Chamber fined him £5000 and sentenced him to prison for life and to lose his ears in the pillory, probably also for his arrogance before the court. He continued to write in a similar vein in prison and in 1637 was fined a further £5000 and branded on the face. The Long Parliament released him as a convenient martyr and declared his excessive sentences illegal (which they were not). The Star Chamber proceedings represented, in part, a clash of wills between him and Abp. Laud and he now, understandably, took his revenge, pursuing the Abp.,

however, with indecent ferocity not only to his death but afterwards in *Canterbury's Doom* (1646), a gloating version of his trial.

He now provoked enemies on all hands, indifferently belabouring in speech and print Independents, Presbyterians, bishops and the army. Naturally Col. Pride took the opportunity to purge him along with others (1648). He then retreated into the country and published pamphlets arguing that taxes were not payable to the Commonwealth either in conscience, expediency or law. Since the argument was difficult to answer in the prevailing terms, the govt. took him into custody. When he was released (1653) he promptly compared Cromwell and Richard III, if anything to Cromwell's disadvantage. The political climate was, however, changing and his escapades were now regarded with more indulgence. In May 1658, when with some reason he forced his way into the House of Commons, that body got round the difficulty by adjourning. In 1660 he resumed with all the others living his lawful seat. His experienced intelligence had by now been converted to a balanced constitution which could be established, as he saw it, only under a restored monarchy. The flail of Charles I became the equally bold champion of Charles II. That comically minded monarch solemnly thanked him, while courtiers called him the Cato of the Age. As M.P. for Bath in the Convention Parliament of 1660, he tried without success to be more royalist than the King in restricting the ambit of the Act of Indemnity and in disbanding the army. These were symptoms of his natural extremism. He wanted to exclude the XXXIX Articles from the B.C.P. and was reprimanded by the Speaker for his behaviour on the Corporation Bill. By now Charles II had found a niche where such a learned man could be useful and harmless. From 1662 he became Keeper of the Records at the Tower and published works of uncontroversial scholarship.

PUBLIC ACCOUNTS are the accounts of all spending govt. departments. They were kept upon a receipts and payments basis for a year ending 31 Mar. and had to be submitted to the Comptroller and Auditor-Gen. by 30th Nov. He considered them and submitted them to the Committee of Public Accounts of the Commons in Jan. or Feb., with his comments. The Committee then considered them and reported their conclusions to the House, calling, if necessary, witnesses before it for the purpose. It has functioned since 1862 and in 1978 it began to hear evidence in public.

PUBLIC GENERAL STATUTES is an edition of statutes begun in 1831 and since published annually.

PUBLIC HEALTH. *See* CHOLERA; DISRAELI'S SECOND GOVT-2; EPIDEMICS; HOUSING; LOCAL ADMINISTRATION.

PUBLIC OPINION POLLS (GALLUP POLLS). George Gallup set up an Institute of Public Opinion in the U.S.A. in 1935 and in the U.K. in 1936. An impetus was given by the *Literary Digest Poll* of 1936 which was based upon 2.3M ballot papers, but failed to predict the result of the 1936 U.S. Presidential election. Scientific sampling now came to the fore. The public under consideration is called the UNIVERSE. Before 1952 most samples were constructed so as to reproduce in miniature the structure of their universe. This QUOTA SAMPLING was based upon the proportions of persons determined by age, sex, wealth, affiliation and so forth. Its advantage was that it could be applied in a fairly small area, its disadvantage that the interviewers would themselves have to find the right people in the sample. RANDOM SAMPLING in its simplest form involves only taking every nth person in a list and so eliminates the subjective judgements of the interviewers. A more sophisticated form of it is AREA SAMPLING, in which areas chosen at random are assigned each to an interviewer who then chooses every nth person. Area Sampling is much more expensive than Quota Sampling.

All such polls have been criticised. In some cases it was thought that premature publication of the results created the very effect that the results predicted. Moreover, polling techniques assumed that those interviewed are pleased to be interviewed and truthful. The failure of all the pollsters to predict the outcome of the British 1970 election suggests that this might not be so. When the unavoidable margin of error in a poll exceeds the margin between the opinions being measured, the result will be only accidentally significant.

PUBLIC ORDER ACT, 1936. *See* RIOT.

PUBLIC RECORD OFFICE (PRO) The master of the Rolls was, and to some extent is, in charge of public records, which were kept at the Rolls in Chancery Lane, London. In 1838 his functions were regularised and in 1851-90 the P.R.O. was built there with extensions at Kew in 1973-7. Scottish records are kept at the General Register Office in Edinburgh. The Dublin Record Office was destroyed in the Troubles of 1922.

PUBLIC RELATIONS (1) Philosophical and political systems, like technologies develop languages of their own. Technological vocabularies, if often barbarous, are mostly utilitarian and morally neutral, but elsewhere special ones are, as in theology or philosophy calculatedly distinctive or, as in advertising or public relations, persuasive or both. In all ages men have adapted or abused language to suit purposes, but the need to do so varies with the numbers who have to be persuaded. In ancient populist Athens, the ambitious studied rhetoric, but the narrow Spartan oligarchy was proverbially laconic. The Papacy, always on a world stage, accidentally invented the word *propaganda* and larded its pronouncements, like the bull against Luther beginning 'Let the Lord arise' with evocations. Its opponents replied with The Scarlet Woman and the Whore of Babylon. The Roundheads called Charles I 'the Man of Blood' and in World War I the Germans were accused of turning corpses into margarine.

(2) Since World War II the public relations industries have blossomed in the English speaking world with the dissemination of wealth and voting power. In 1996 over 670 firms of consultants in central London alone, specialised like the ancient rhetoricians, in adapting language and image to intention. Ministries had public relations men, and every business advertised. The burden on the economy and the effect on prices is unknown, and so on public standards is that of the traffic in half-truths. In authoritarian countries part of the cost finds its way into police budgets, and this provokes the thought that where societies are not governed by force, they are deceived. This may be justified as being less bruising than the truncheon.

(3) Among an infinity of examples, all of misuse, the following may help to elucidate the methods. (a) **Distinctive Uses:** *dialectic* = logic (Marxist); *sharing* = confession (Moral Rearment); **(b) Negatively persuasive forms:** *elitist* = having high minority standards (populist); *chauvinist* = hostile to women (feminist); (c) **Persuasive Uses:** 10% *extra free* = more for your money (commercial); *guaranteed* = probable (commercial); *democratic* = egalitarian (any speaker); *see also* EUROSPEAK; POLITICAL CORRECTNESS.

PUBLIC SAFETY, COMMITTEE OF (Fr.) (Apr. 1793-July 1794) was a ruthless collective dictatorship set up at Robespierre's instance by the French Convention after Dumouriez defected to the Austrians. It conducted the Reign of Terror, the destruction of the Girondists and of Hébert and Danton with their respective followings and the dissolution of the Church. Its power ended with Robespierre's overthrow on 28 July 1794.

PUBLIC SCHOOLS in Britain are endowed non-state secondary schools, originally available to pupils from the general public rather than from a particular area. The parents paid fees, but subsidised scholarships were made available by competitive examination. Some, such as St. Peter's, York (7th cent.) were very ancient. The first with the distinctive peculiarities of the public school system, i.e. a classical curriculum, boarding, playing fields and games and a recognised method of pupil administered discipline, was Winchester College (1382). Eton was founded on the Winchester model in 1440 and others followed. Except for Westminster, they all had a period of decadence and corruption between the Restoration and 1815 when they began to revive. Nine were investigated and reformed by the Clarendon Commission (1861-4), the rest by the Taunton Commission (1864-8). *See* HEADMASTERS CONEERENCE.

PUBLIC TRUSTEE, to act as ordinary or custodian trustee and also, by order, judicial trustee, was created by statute in 1906 and started operations in 1908.

PUBLIC UTILITIES. *See* GAS; ELECTRICITY; TRANSPORT; NATIONALISATION; PRIVATISATION.

PUBLIC WORKS LOANS BOARD. *See* LOCAL AND PUBLIC WORKS LOANS.

PUERTO RICO (Caribb.), Spanish settlement begun by Ponce de Leon in 1508, was a source of gold until about 1550 when sugar was introduced; but piracy and native rebellion inhibited its prosperity. By 1600 the city (known as St. Juan) was a strategic fortress rather than an investment, while the rural inhabitants throve on contraband with which the authorities never interfered.

Loyal, consequently, to Spain, the island resisted British, Dutch and French attacks; it became a haven for Spanish loyalists in the wars of South American independence and so acquired economic and political privileges. These in due course made it prosperous and created a demand for reforms, including representation in the Spanish Cortes. A commission recommended the abolition of slavery as a precondition of reform and the result was an abrupt change of local opinion in favour of autonomy. In 1868 there was a small insurrection; by 1874 slavery had been abolished and nothing except Spanish political incompetence stood in the way of integration. In 1887 some autonomists were brutally treated by the Spanish police and their movement gathered strength. By 1898 autonomy had been conceded, but the island was occupied by, and then ceded to the U.S.A. (P. of Paris).

The Americans permitted a very limited local autonomy in 1900, but the degree of control was progressively relaxed in 1909 and 1917. In 1949 Pres. Truman appointed the first native born Gov. and in 1952 the island acquired an independent constitution, but remained 'in association' with the U.S.A.

PUGIN (1) Augustus Charles (1762-1832), originally French, was employed by Nash to make drawings of Gothic buildings. He trained his son **(2) Augustus Welby Northmore (1812-52)** who became a famous expert on Gothic and acquired an immense ecclesiastical practice. Barry employed him on the detail of the Houses of Parliament. He was driven mad by overwork in 1851 and his son **(3) Edward Welby (1834-75)** took over his practice at the age of 17 and erected a very large number of, mostly R. Catholic, ecclesiastical buildings by 1865, when he retired.

PUISET or PUDSEY, Hugh de (?1125-9), a nephew of King Stephen and Henry of Blois became a youthful Treasurer of York in 1143 and Bp. of **Durham** in 1153. His election was disputed by the Abp. of York who had not consented (*see* MURDAC, HENRY). He played little part in Becket's conflicts with Henry II, but Pope Alexander III briefly suspended him for assisting at the coronation of Henry the Young King (*see* ROGER OF PONT L'EVEQUE). He was, perhaps unreasonably, suspected of complicity in the latter's revolt in 1173 and Henry seized his estates. In 1179 he attended the 2nd Lateran Council.

When Richard I was raising money for his crusade, Hugh bought the earldom and shrievalty of

Northumberland from him for £10,000. In Sept. 1189 he was appointed Justiciar jointly with William Mandeville and on the latter's death with William Longchamp. Disputes led Richard to divide the jurisdiction geographically, Hugh taking the area north of the Humber, but after Easter 1190, with Richard abroad, Longchamp arrested Hugh and deprived him of the Justiciarship and earldom. The King restored the estates and the earldom but not the Justiciarship. In 1191 Hugh refused to make a profession of obedience to Abp. Geoffrey of York because he had done so to his predecessor. Geoffrey disbelieved and excommunicated him, but a compromise was drafted by St. Hugh of Lincoln. On the revolt of John's partisans in 1193, Hugh forced the surrender of the rebel castle of Tickhill just before the King's return in 1194. Nevertheless he had to surrender his earldom for which he had not fully paid. Early in 1195 Richard reinstated him as Joint Justiciar, but he died at Howden on the way to resume office. *See* DURHAM, 3-4; RICHARD I.

PULPITS existed only in a minority of churches until the Reformation emphasised preaching. Parish churches were required to have one in 1603. They are placed in the nave for audibility.

PULTENEY (1) Daniel (?-1731) and his brother **(2) Sir William (1684-1764) 1st E. of BATH (1742)** (*see* GEORGE I-7). William, a wealthy Whig, became M.P. for Hedon in 1705 and soon made a reputation as a dangerous and influential orator. By 1714 he was Sec. at War and in 1717 resigned with Walpole. He drifted into opposition because of the latter's inability to tolerate able men. In 1721 when Daniel also became M.P. for Hedon, Walpole refused William office, but Daniel, who had married a sister-in-law of Sunderland's and disliked Walpole, secured a lordship of the Admiralty. By 1725 they had joined Bolingbroke's group at Uxbridge and added a witty and vituperative journalism to their parliamentary performances. William, in particular, wrote extensively for the *Craftsman*. They were also visitors to Leicester House, but George II disappointed them at his accession, for Q. Caroline supported Walpole. Hence in 1728 when Frederick, P. of Wales set up at Leicester House, the Pulteneys were to be seen there again and soon joined Sir William Wyndham in a faction, nicknamed The Patriots, dedicated (in a strictly tactical sense) to attacking the govt's. alleged Hanoverian bias. In 1731 Daniel died and William, struck off the Privy Council, seemed to be in eclipse, but he and his friends used Walpole's excise scheme as a heaven-sent means of inflicting a sharp reverse on him in 1733. It was an unscrupulous campaign: Walpole took his revenge in his electoral victory next year, but William nevertheless secured a seat for Middlesex. By now the association with Leicester House was becoming embarrassing because of the Prince's extravagant hatred of his father. Moreover Bolingbroke's camarilla had broken up. William thus became a leader rather than a follower and his participation in the bellicose agitation of 1739 brought on the war and contributed to Walpole's fall. In the consequent political negotiations of 1742 he was asked to form a govt., but declined on condition that he should have a cabinet post under Wilmington. He was accordingly raised to the peerage but edged out of influence when Wilmington died in 1746. George II tried to get him into a govt. to exclude Pitt but the effort failed and thereafter he concentrated on the development of Bath and the pleasures of grandeur and wealth.

PUNCH, a satirical weekly, was founded in 1841 during Peel's Second Govt. and survived until 1980.

PUNDIT (India). A Hindu law officer. *See* EAST INDIA CO. COURTS.

PUNIC (i.e. Carthaginian) FAITH, according to the Romans was faithlessness. Carthaginian views on Roman faith have not survived.

PUNISHMENT (*see* WERGILD-1) **(1)** MOST criminal acts were considered, before the 12th cent., to be personal wrongs. Prisons were regarded as places of custody pending trial and as the idea of punishment came in, the judges had a wide discretion strongly influenced by the church's dislike of capital punishments.

(2) Hence lesser MISDEMEANOURS came to be punished by comparatively light inflictions involving a degree of pain such as whipping, or ignominy such as the stocks or ducking stool. More serious cases might attract the pillory, where a man might be stoned to death by a hostile crowd or feted by a friendly one, or mutilation by cutting off the ears or hand. Originally a fine could not be imposed, but a criminal might be kept in prison and invited, by composing a fine with the Crown, to buy himself out. Later, imprisonment became a normal consequence of a misdemeanour.

(3) The judicial discretion in cases of FELONY, other than piracy, tended to be used on the side of leniency, but it was limited in the 13th cent. when all important crimes came to be regarded as felonies and the distinction between them and misdemeanours had hardened. In the late 15th cent. the increased population was not commensurable biddable and this led to greater reliance on capital punishment in public and sometimes with barbarous accompaniments as an alleged deterrent. The felon's punishment was death by slow hanging; a pirate's by slow drowning. In either case his land escheated to his lord and no heir could claim property through him. As these latter consequences might leave his family destitute, a defendant sometimes preferred *Peine Forte et Dure* (q.v.).

(4) Moreover since a felon had no property, he could not compose a fine. On the other hand he might, especially after the abolition of sanctuary, be pardoned on condition that he be sent to a colony. This is the origin of transportation. In the absence of a police force, 18th cent. parliaments steadily increased the number of felonious crimes, but enlightened opinion reacted against the regular public hangings at Tyburn and elsewhere. Benefit of clergy became an important branch of the criminal law; juries often deliberately undervalued a stolen object so as to make a theft a misdemeanour and the monarchs, particularly George II, exercised their prerogative of mercy with great attention. By 1790 there were 200 capital felonies, but death was inflicted in practice only in cases coming within 25 of them.

(5) In TREASON property was forfeited to the Crown and heirs could not claim through the traitor. In the case of more serious treasons the punishment was hanging, drawing and quartering for men and burning for women: for lesser ones, such as uxoricide and counterfeiting the coinage, it was drawing and hanging only.

(6) Through the ceaseless campaigning of Samuel Romilly and Jeremy Bentham, the number of capital offences was reduced to 15 between 1790 and 1834 and the cruel accompaniments had gone. The pillory disappeared in 1837. The institution of an efficient police soon demonstrated the purposelessness of most of the remaining 15 and by 1861 they had been reduced to 4, namely treason, piracy, arson in naval dockyards and murder. Public executions disappeared in 1868; forfeiture for treason and felony in 1870. The death penalty for murder was abolished in 1965; for arson in naval dockyards in 1968. These developments led to the substitution of sometimes capriciously calculated periods of imprisonment.

(7) After World War II, despite the vast rise in the crime rate, legislation tended to reduce the length of imprisonment. The maximum sentence (by 1978 seldom imposed) was under 7 years in 108 out of 192 indictable offences. On the other hand the abolition of felonies and misdemeanours as categorisations made feasible a wider alternative use of fines and the introduction of compulsory community service. These ameliorations were ineffectual perhaps because of the spread of drug related crime, and in 1995 legislation was passed against judicial opposition to increase periods of imprisonment.

PUNJAB (Pers. = Five rivers, i.e. the Jhelum, Chenab, Ravi, Beas and Sutlej, all affluents of the Indus) was ruled, with Lahore as its capital, by the Moguls from 1556 to 1707 when the Marathas overran it. They were subsequently turned out by a Moslem alliance, which in due course made way for the rule of the SIKHS. After the latter's overthrow in 1849, the British annexed it. It was ruled firmly by a Board of Three until 1853, then by a Chief Commissioner until 1859 and thereafter by a Lieut.-Gov. Henry Lawrence had been Resident at Lahore from 1847 to 1849. He and his brother John were members of the Board and John, as Chief Commissioner until 1857, held the loyalty of the area during the Indian Mutiny. Under their administration, backed by Dalhousie, a new network of military roads greatly raised the economic prosperity and the area was surveyed for irrigation so that the rivers could be made to replace the almost total lack of rain. The canal system was developed in the ensuing century and by 1946 had brought 15,000,000 acres under cultivation (about half cereals and the rest cotton, indigo, opium, rice, sugar and tobacco). The Punjab was divided between India and Pakistan in 1947 amid bloodshed.

PUNKS were 1960s youths who developed flamboyant dyed hairstyles and mostly wore black leather. They favoured loud syncopated music and seemed to be against everything.

PUPIL TEACHERS (*see* MONITORIAL SYSTEM) were recruited from pupils of at least 13, given a 5-year course and, after examination, sent to teacher training colleges. The system, inaugurated in 1846 by Sir John Kay-Shuttleworth, was a half-way house to higher education and the ancestor of the modern Teacher Training system.

PURBECK. *See* VILLIERS.

PURCELL, Henry (?1658-95), the ablest of a musical family, composed *Dido and Aeneas* in 1680, when he also became organist at Westminster Abbey. Most of his many compositions from then on were published after his death.

PURCHAS, Samuel (1577-1626?). *See* HAKLUYT.

PURCHASE TAX was introduced in 1940 as a revenue raiser levied mostly on wholesalers not dealing in exports, raw materials, food, drink, other things already heavily taxed or books. Originally proposed at a flat rate it was altered in 1940 so as to distinguish between luxuries, things whose replacement could be postponed and unnecessary things taxed at 33% and other things at 16⅔%. The tax yielded £99M in 1940-1 and £633M in 1964-5. It was abolished to make way for Value Added Tax.

PURGATORY, according to R. Catholic theology is a place where the souls of the departed remain if not already damned or admitted to the Beatific Vision. There they undergo a period of purgation for their sins, which can be shortened by Papal indulgence. The concept was one of the foundations of mediaeval Papal power.

PURITAN, -ISM, originally an Elizabethan derisive term, meant those who wished from within to purify the Anglican Church of popish survivals. Protestant extremists existed in England under Edward VI, but they and others fled abroad, particularly to Switzerland, under Mary I and then returned under Elizabeth I with systematic, often Calvinistic ideas on church reform. Despite Elizabeth's disapproval and the activities of Abp. Whitgift and the Court of High Commission (established in 1559), they gradually gained ground because ignorant, pluralist and simoniacal clergy were still common in the church which they attacked. A Puritan assembly published a statement of its views in 1582. The enforcement of stricter tests under Whitgift and Bancroft drove many Puritans out of the Church and into hostility to episcopacy and they also formed a strong parliamentary group under leaders such

as Peter Wentworth who were beginning to assert parliamentary pretensions.

Released from their awe of the great Queen at the accession of James I, the Puritans became more vigorous. In their Millenary Petition and at the Hampton Court conference they demanded and James rejected a Presbyterian form of church govt. The Puritans now became distinguishable between those (like Prynne and Pym) who were Anglican and meant to reform the church from within and those, already outside the church, who were either Presbyterians or Congregationalists. Both Calvinist in theology, the latter proposed a less strict form of church and state govt. than the Presbyterians and tended (influenced by Dutch models) to throw off sects which were not Calvinist at all, such as Baptists and Quakers. Laudian persecution, however, drove many moderates into the arms of the extremists.

Aided by Scottish military power, the Presbyterians (a minority) began to carry the day under Charles I. Bishops were excluded from Parliament in 1642 and abolished in 1645 when the Book of Common Prayer was rejected. A Presbyterian organisation in accordance with the Book of Discipline was attempted, but never fully established against army opposition and the growing weariness of intolerance, prudery and gloom. The political contradiction of the period that the Puritans and Parliament, in the name of liberty and freedom of conscience, were setting up an intolerant dictatorship, reflected upon the Puritans too and Presbyterian persecution now drove moderates into the arms of the Anglicans. Hence the ease with which the Church was re-established in a relatively tolerant form at the Restoration.

Nevertheless the Puritans left their mark. They were not destroyed and many of their attitudes became part of English life, notably a passion for integrity and material honesty, a belief that salvation might come through hard work and its consequent admiration for business success, the English Sunday, a certain insensitivity to artistic matters originating in the destruction of abbeys and the purification of churches, and sexual repressiveness.

PURLIEU. *See* FOREST-3.

PURPRESTURE was unlawful encroachment or enclosure upon royal, manorial, highway or common land, or forest.

PURSUIVANT. *See* HERALD.

PURVEYANCE was the prerogative of purchasing goods and hiring transport compulsorily at 'the King's price', a wholesale price below local market rates. There was a similar PRISAGE or purchase of wines at the ports for the King's use. It was much disliked and there was a common complaint that King's officers took too much and sold the balance for their own pockets. Under Magna Carta immediate payment was required and transport and timber were not to be taken. In 1258 there were complaints of underpayment and the Statute of Westminster I (1275) regulated prisages. The real problem was that administration and defence would be seriously hindered if it were abolished and so regulation and the punishment of dishonest purveyors became the object of kings and complainants alike. In 1376 the Commons demanded that J.Ps. should punish dishonest purveyors and this was enacted in 1441. By Tudor times the justices were bargaining with the Board of Green Cloth for prices and the difference between agreed and market prices was offset against the county assessments. All the same complaints were made in the Parliament of 1603. The system fell into disuse in the Civil War and was abolished in 1660. A relic of purveyance is the practice of granting Royal Warrants to traders who supply royal households. The warrants are a certificate of excellence and good for trade, but the holders generally sell to royal households at a discount.

PUSEY (1) Philip (1799-1855), M.P. from 1830 to 1852, started as a Tory protectionist but was converted to free trade and agricultural reform by 1847. He championed the agricultural tenant, especially in the matter of improvements and was a founder of the Royal Agricultural Society. His brother **(2) Edward Bouverie (1800-82),** a friend of Keble and Newman at Oriel College, Oxford, became Regius Prof. of Hebrew in 1828. Suspicious of Anglican rationalism, he collaborated with the Tractarians and supported Newman against the College Heads in the controversy over Tract XC (1841). He was suspended as university preacher on a charge of heresy in 1843, but continued to preach his views and in 1856 published his *Doctrine of the Real Presence* in support of High Anglicanism. He opposed university reform because it tended to intellectual rather than moral or religious development and in 1862 charged Jowett before the Vice-Chancellor's court with teaching heresy. Thereafter he was much concerned with unsuccessful attempts to unite the Anglican church with the Roman, Wesleyan and Oriental denominations. He held that Anglican doctrine is founded in patristic writings and is sometimes regarded as the founder of Anglo-Catholicism.

PUTNEY DEBATES were discussions held by the New Model Army in 1647-8, on the political future of the country. Though theoretically interesting, they came to very little.

PUTSCH **(Ger. = thrust).** An unexpected small revolt aimed at the overthrow of a govt.

PUTTA (?-688) was consecrated by Bp. Theodore of Rochester in 669 and went to Mercia, where Bp. Sexulf assigned him to the Hecanas of the later Herefordshire.

PUTTING OUT was a development of primitive capitalism. An entrepreneur bought a large stock of raw materials, put them out to and paid cottage workers to convert into finished goods, took the goods back and arranged for their transport and sale. It was common in the 14-15th cent. West Country woollen industry and in 17th cent. Yorkshire.

PYM, John (1584-1643), Somerset Puritan, from 1620 M.P. for Calne but with important City connections. He and other Puritans such as Lds. Brooke and Saye and Sele and the E. of Warwick, were associated in the Providence Co. for the colonisation of Caribbean islands with Puritans. This brought them into collision with the Spaniards and with any govt. policy friendly to Spain. Similarly the kind of business enterprise which Pym typified was bound to collide with a court which was seeking money and influence by granting monopolies. He thus represented the peculiar mixture of business and religion which characterised the growing opposition to the Crown. He attacked Buckingham and Arminian bps. with equal skill in the parliaments before Charles I's period of personal rule. In the Short Parliament (1640) he naturally took the lead as an old hand in a House of Commons, three quarters of whom had never sat before. His carefully moderate but comprehensive rehearsal of grievances met the royal demand for subsidies head on. The House followed him in discussing grievances before considering supply. In the crisis provoked by the Scottish war a dissolution was bound to be followed by a new general election in which public interest would run high. Pym

rode about the country electioneering. Many members of the Short Parliament were re-elected. Pym thus returned as the acknowledged leader against the court. He began with a similar moderately worded analysis of grievances and urged that those responsible should be found and punished. Since it was believed that Strafford was about to charge the leaders of the opposition with treasonable correspondence with the Scots, Articles of Impeachment were hurriedly voted against Strafford and sent to the Lords in the nick of time.

The impeachment itself, however, seemed likely to fail for lack of evidence and in Apr. 1641 extremists in the Commons, led by Sir Arthur Heselrige, went over Pym's head by passing a bill of attainder, subsequently forced upon the Lords and the King by political and mob pressure. This early division was postponed while Parliament dismantled the machinery of royal absolutism, but it became acute once such work had been done, and ecclesiastical policy was the main cause of division. Pym's concern was to maintain unity against Charles I, in whose good faith he did not believe. He was prepared to support a modified episcopacy in the interests of such unity, but the court thought him sufficiently a moderate to approach him with offers of office. They mistook their man. Hence when Irish outbreaks and their sequel revealed the fundamental hostility of the Court, he supported the Root and Branch Bill and took a leading part in refusing supply for the repression of the Irish. By now his political position was weak and he determined to promote, upon the precedent of remonstrances by his earlier parliaments, a GRAND REMONSTRANCE, which was to be an appeal to the public. The debates were excited, but significantly in the motion to print it the Commons nearly came to blows. The King soon reacted by trying to arrest the Five Members, of whom Pym was one. These events restored a relative unity under Pym's leadership (Jan. 1642). War being inevitable, it remained to create the means for waging it. In July the COMMITTEE OF SAFETY was created. In Mar. 1643 the Parliament assumed the power of taxation to support the armies which it meant to control. Worn out by exertion, Pym died. *See* CHARLES I; CIVIL WAR.

PYNCHON, William (1590-1662), Treasurer of the Massachusetts Bay Colony from 1632 to 1634 and from 1636 to 1652 the virtual controller of the economy and effective ruler. He returned to England as a result of religious quarrels.

PYNSON, Richard (?-1530), a Norman who learnt printing from an apprentice of Caxton, set up on his own c. 1490 printing mostly religious books, but after 1500 also law books. Altogether he printed some 300 works. He was King's printer from 1501.

PYX, TRIAL OF THE. The Royal Mint annually places random specimens of gold and silver coin in a locked box or pyx. These are assayed before a jury of the Goldsmiths' Co. in the presence of the Queen's Remembrancer. It was formerly held in Westminster Abbey, but was transferred to Goldsmiths' Hall in the 19th cent.

Q

QATAR (Persian Gulf) was under Persia until the early 19th cent. when it shook itself free and in 1868 its Sheikh accepted British protection. The agreement was renewed in 1916. Oil was discovered in 1939 and exploited from 1946; production reached a peak in 1961 and was thereafter kept steady only by the discovery of off-shore reserves.

QATTARA DEPRESSION (Egyptian W. Frontier). An area impassable to troops and surrounded by high cliffs. It was strategically vital in World War II.

Q-SHIPS. See CAMPBELL, GORDON (1886-1953).

QOSSEIR. See BERESFORD.-2.

QUADRA, Alvarez de, Bp. of AQUILA. See ELIZABETH I-7.

QUADRILATERAL. A fortified area based on four independent but mutually supporting fortresses. (1) The **Bulgarian** (Silistria, Plevna, Shumla and Varna) was an important factor in the maintenance of Turkish rule in the 19th cent. Balkans. (2) The **North Italian** or **Lombard** comprised Legnago, Verona, Peschiera and Mantua. Until 1797 Mantua was technically independent but in practice Austrian; the rest were Venetian. They all passed to Austria in 1797 and to the Bonaparte Kingdom of Italy in 1805. Returned to Austria in 1814, they were the vital base of Austrian power in Italy. In 1859 Mantua and Peschiera passed to Savoy after the Franco-Austrian War and so to the Kingdom of Italy, which acquired the others in 1866.

QUADRIPARTITUS (Lat: four-part) (c. 1113-8). An anonymous legal book. The first part contains Latin translations of Anglo-Saxon laws, especially those of K. Canute; the second, the Coronation Charter of Henry I and documents related to the Investiture controversy. The rest, on legal procedure and theft, is lost.

QUADRIVIUM, TRIVIUM (Lat: Quadruple, Triple Route). See LIBERAL ARTS.

QUADROON. See MULATTO.

QUADRUPLE ALLIANCES. (1) 1718 between Britain, France and the Emperor, so called because the Dutch were expected to join. The object was to frustrate Spanish operations in Sicily and Sardinia. The Emperor was to receive Sicily; Savoy to receive Sardinia, Monferrat and part of the Spanish Milanese and the Spanish Infante Don Carlos the succession in Parma and Tuscany. The Emperor and the King of Spain were to recognise each other's titles and the Utrecht guarantee of the succession to the English throne was reaffirmed. In pursuit of these objects a British fleet destroyed a Spanish force off C. Passaro in 1718.

(2) 1815 between Britain, Austria, Prussia and Russia. Signed simultaneously with the T. of PARIS, they undertook for 20 years to work together to maintain the Vienna and Paris settlements and to exclude the Bonapartes from France, *if* necessary by force (*see* VIENNA, CONGRESS-8). France acceded to the treaty in 1818, by which time the divergent outlooks and economic interests of Britain on the one hand and the continental monarchies on the other, had rendered it obsolete.

(3) 1834 between Britain, France, Spain and Portugal. In dynastic disputes in the Peninsula, Britain and France supported the constitutional candidates Isabella (Spain) and Maria (Portugal) against the conservative Carlos and Miguel. The object of the alliance was to end Anglo-French rivalry for the favour of the constitutionalists by establishing a peninsular peace in which there would be great advantages for both powers. The manoeuvre succeeded only partially, because the Carlist civil war continued in Spain.

QUAI D'ORSAY (Paris). The address of the French Foreign Office from the beginning of the 19th cent.

QUAKERS. See FRIENDS.

QUANGO (= Quasi Autonomous National Govt. Organisation) such as the National Coal Board and the Traffic Commissioners were said in 1979 to have proliferated to a number exceeding 400, with undesirable effects on patronage. Many, on scrutiny, turned out to be moribund and were abolished without visible consequences, but new ones came into being as the Tory govts. of 1978 onwards created supervisory bodies for privatised industries.

QUARE IMPEDIT. See ADVOWSON.

QUARNERO, ITALIAN REGENCY OF THE. See D'ANNUNZIO.

QUARTERLY REVIEW was founded in Feb. 1809 by John Murray (1778-1843), the publisher, as a Tory rival of the *Edinburgh Review*, with the encouragement of Sir Walter Scott. William Gifford (1756-1826), an ailing reactionary, was the first editor, but Scott and other enthusiasts kept him roughly to conciliatory and usually liberal courses, so that contributors could eventually include Canning, Southey, Salisbury and Gladstone. It gave Jane Austen her first favourable notice (by Scott on *Emma*). Croker's savage attack on Keats' *Endymion* is supposed to have hastened Keats' death. The next editor was John Gibson Lockhart (1794-1854), Scott's son-in-law, a furious critic of Keats and Shelley, but he admired Wordsworth and Coleridge, whose nephew J. T. Coleridge, the lawyer, was a contributor and editorial *locum tenens*.

QUARTER DAYS

England	Scotland
Lady Day 25 Mar.	Candlemas 2 Feb.
Midsummer 24 June	Whitsun 15 May
Michaelmas 29 Sept.	Lammas 1 August
Christmas 25 Dec.	Martinmas 11 Nov.

These days have always been used for many important purposes, especially the payment of rent and instalments of taxes. Before the Calendar Act 1752, the days, expressed in modern (New Style) terms, fell 12 days later and the year began on 25 Mar. The Act moved the beginning of the year to 1 Jan., but left the taxation year unaffected. Hence the taxation year now begins on 6 Apr.

QUARTER SESSIONS (1) i.e. the quarterly assembly of the county J.Ps., instituted very soon after the commissioning of J.Ps. themselves (1361). They took over much of the local business of the Eyre and its procedure for inquiring, by way of charge to a series of juries assembled by the sheriff to meet them.

(2) The articles of the charge required jurymen to present certain known cases. By 1617 the list of articles included 27 ecclesiastical offences (e.g. keeping a fair in a churchyard, maintaining a schoolmaster who refuses to go to church, aiding a Jesuit, perjury, or extolling the Bp. of Rome), 34 capital felonies (e.g. petty treason, buggery, purse cutting, rebellious assembly) and 165 lesser matters (e.g. extortion and taking payment instead of inflicting corporal punishment, abuse of Hue and Cry, forcible entries, taking of hawks' eggs, usury, evasion of navigation acts, eating flesh in Lent, butchers working as tanners, unrepaired bridges, failure to practise archery). As most articles contained more than one and sometimes many particulars and juries could seldom read, it is unlikely that they could always be sure of doing their whole duty.

(3) The administrative and judicial business had already grown under the Tudors by way, for example, of appeals against rates (from 1601) and there was work such as licensing. This was often done at times other than the quarterly sessions. Meantime the business of answering the articles was falling increasingly to the High Constables who gathered their information from the petty constables, thus relieving the inhabitants of a tiresome

duty. In the end the articles ceased to be read and constables made presentments when cases came to their notice.

(4) The parish was adopted as an administrative unit (e.g. for the Poor Law), but being weak it needed supervision, involving a large mass of detailed sessions' business. Until the Civil War this administrative business was itself supervised by the King's Council, but this could not be re-established at the Restoration. Statutes continued to impose new work on the sessions which required staff and the differentiation of administrative and judicial functions. The latter were performed openly with a jury: the former by the justices themselves in private, often in the local alehouse. Such habits persisted into the 1820s in remoter areas.

(5) The Local Govt. Acts of 1888 and 1894 transferred the administrative functions of Quarter Sessions to the new elected councils, except in matters of licensing (*see also* POLICE) and Corn Rents. The sessions became thus wholly judicial; the congestion of criminal business resulted in a progressive extension of their criminal powers and it became increasingly usual to appoint barristers or other professional lawyers as chairmen. When the Courts Act, 1971, created the Crown Courts and transferred Quarter Sessions' judicial functions to them, most of these chairmen re-emerged as Crown Court judges.

QUARTER-STAFF. An oaken staff, iron-shod at each end and from 6 to 9 feet long, used by English country folk, especially in Wiltshire and Berkshire, as a weapon until the early 19th Cent.

QUEBEC. *See* CANADA A, 2-3,9,11, *et seq.*

QUEBEC ACT 1774. *See* AMERICAN REBELLION-13.

QUEBEC CONFERENCE. *See* CANADA-17.

QUEEN (1) REGNANT has the same status as a King. **(2) CONSORT,** i.e. the King's wife, is a subject but it is treason to plot her death or have sexual connection with her (*see* MORGANATIC MARRIAGE). **(3) -MOTHER.** The title often given to a King's widow.

QUEEN ADELAIDE PROVINCE. *See* XHOSA.

QUEEN ANNE'S BOUNTY. *See* CHURCH COMMISSIONERS-1.

QUEEN ANNE'S FREE GIFT was an annual payment to naval surgeons to supplement a pay scale which was so low that no surgeon worth the name volunteered for the Navy. It represented an early reaction against the contempt in which surgeons were held.

QUEENBOROUGH. *See* SHEPPEY.

QUEEN MARY LAND, part of the Australian sector of Antarctica, was first explored by the Mawson Expedition in 1912-3.

QUEEN MAUD LAND (Antarctica) was claimed by Norway in 1939 and declared a Norwegian dependency in 1949.

QUEENSBERRY, Ms. and Ds. of. *See* DOUGLAS (QUEENSBERRY).

QUEEN'S BENCH. *See* KING'S BENCH.

QUEEN'S (or KING'S) CONSENT, which is different from the Royal Assent, must be signified by a privy councillor usually on Third Reading, to any bill affecting the Royal Prerogative, the personal property, interests or hereditary revenues of the Crown or the Duchy of Cornwall, otherwise the bill falls to the ground. If the sovereign's eldest son is of full age his consent is necessary in matters affecting the Duchy of Cornwall.

QUEEN'S COUNSEL. *See* KING'S COUNSEL.

QUEEN'S COUNTY. *See* LEIX.

QUEEN'S GOLD. When a tenant-in-chief paid a relief or other fine to the King, he had to pay 10% in addition to the Queen.

QUEEN'S (or KING'S) RECOMMENDATION is required before any bill imposing taxation or expenditure can proceed in the Commons. In practice this means that new taxes and expenditures can be moved only by the govt. though an M.P. can move to reduce them. *See* QUEEN'S (OR KING'S) CONSENT.

QUEENS MEN. *See* JAMES V1-2.

QUEENSBERRY RULES. *See* BOXING.

QUEENSLAND. *See* AUSTRALIA.

QUESTIONS IN PARLIAMENT began in the Commons in 1721, as a means of extracting information from ministers about the work of their departments. A refusal to answer or an unsatisfactory answer may attract political consequences, in particular the dissatisfied M.P. may raise the matter on the motion to adjourn the House. In the Lords "starred" questions are similar to those in the Commons; "unstarred" questions lead to a short debate. Questions may be answered in writing, but in the Commons the first hour of public business is devoted to oral answers, to which supplementary questions may be put.

QUETTA (Pakistan), was occupied by the British in 1877 as a result of the Sandeman T. with Kalat. The Indian Army Staff College was established in 1907. The place commands the route from the Indus to Kandahar and was a garrison town.

QUEUES. The queuing habit (previously almost unknown) started in England because of a wartime Order (1940) requiring more than five people at a bus stop to queue.

QUIA EMPTORES **(Lat: Because buyers).** *See* LAND TENURE, ENGLAND-2.

QUIBERON (Morbihan, Fr.) is a roadstead beyond gunshot of the mainland which, much to French annoyance, was habitually used when the wind was easterly by British blockading fleets during the 18th cent. French wars. It was the scene of Hawke's famous victory in 1759. *See also* SEVEN YEARS' WAR.

QUIBERON BAY EXPEDITION (1795), was a French royalist attempt to exploit the reaction in French politics after the fall of Robespierre and the extreme Jacobins in 1794. It failed through incompetent leadership and it, together with the insensitive manifesto issued by the Comte de Provence, the claimant to the throne, encouraged a republican revival.

QUIDAM VESTRUM **(1225),** Bull of Honorius III empowering the Scottish church to hold councils notwithstanding that it possessed no metropolitan and for a council to choose a *conservator* to preside and to enforce decrees until the next council.

QUIETUS **(Lat: quit).** An acquittance, particularly for a tenant-in-chief's scutage if he had attended the King in person and for a sheriff on settling his accounts at the Exchequer.

QUILLER-COUCH, Sir Arthur (1863-1944) became Prof. of English at Cambridge in 1912. He wrote extensively under the nom de plume 'Q' and made a far-reaching contribution to the study of English literature by publishing the anthological *Oxford Books,* viz: *of English Verse* (1900- and 1939), *of Ballads* (1910), *of Victorian Verse* (1912) and *of English Prose* (1925).

QUINCY (1) Josiah (1744-75), lawyer and pseudonymous writer in favour of American independence, defended with John Adams the British soldiers tried for the so-called Boston Massacre in Mar. 1770. In 1774 he was sent to England to negotiate on behalf of the colonies in an attempt to avoid violence. He achieved nothing and died on the way home. His son **(2) Josiah (1772-1864)** was Federalist leader in the U.S. House of Representatives from 1805 to 1813 when he resigned against the war with Britain. He subsequently had a distinguished career in Massachusetts state politics and as Pres. of Harvard University.

QUINCY, QUENCY DE (1) Saer (?-1219) E. of WINCHESTER (1207) succeeded through his wife to half the Beaumont inheritance. He joined the opposition to King John, was a party to the invitation to Louis the Dauphin and was captured at the B. of Lincoln (1217). He died on Crusade. His son **(2) Roger (?1195-1264) 2nd E.** obtained the honours on the death of his mother in 1235. He married Helen of Galloway and became

Constable of Scotland in right of her. He supported the baronial opposition to Henry III.

QUINN v *LEATHEM* (1901). An Irish trade union sought to enforce a closed shop by stopping the employer (a wholesale butcher) from trading with a particular customer whose men belonged to the union. This could be done only by their inducing the men or the customer or both to break contracts. The butcher sued the union leaders for conspiracy to injure him in his trade by inducing these breaches of contract. The jury found for the plaintiff. On appeal the Irish Court of Appeal and the House of Lords unanimously upheld the action and that the trade union could not claim the protection of the Trade Union Acts 1871 and 1876 or the Conspiracy Act, 1875.

QUINQUENNIAL ENACTMENT. *See* TRIENNIAL, ETC, ACTS.

QUINSEY. *See* SCARLET FEVER.

QUINT. A tax of one fifth.

QUINTAINE. *See* JOUSTING.

QUIRINAL. Papal summer palace at Rome until 1871 when it became the residence of the Italian Kings and subsequently of the Presidents. Hence a term for the Italian secular state, contrasted with the Papacy seated at the Vatican.

QUISLING, Vidkun (1887-1945), leader of the Norwegian Nazi Party, administered a pro-German govt. after the German conquest of Norway in 1940. It was not very effectual and the Norwegian Resistance contrived periodically to place thirty pieces of silver on his desk. He was executed.

QUI TAM (Lat: 'who as well') was an action brought by an informer upon a penal statute to recover a penalty 'as well for our sovereign Lord the King as for himself'.

QUITCLAIM is a release from an obligation.

QUITCLAIM OF CANTERBURY. *See* RICHARD I-3.

QUONIAM ATTACHIAMENTA, a manual of procedure in Scottish feudal courts by an unknown but practically experienced 14th cent. author. Often quoted in statutes and by legal expositors, it was first printed in 1609.

QUONIAM NULLA (1317), Bull of John XXII promulgating the canon law recension known as the Clementines.

QUORUM (Lat: 'of whom') (1) originally referred to certain individuals named in a commission of the peace, whose presence was necessary to constitute a court. (2) The quorum in the House of Commons is forty, but only if challenged; in the Lords it is three; in local authorities it is three or one third, whichever is the greater.

QUOTA. (1) The annual number of immigrants of any particular origin permitted into a country. Originally used in this sense in the U.S.A. (2) The quantity or proportion of goods from a particular country permitted into another country. Restrictions based on quotas are contrary to the T. of Rome. (3) The proportion of persons of any particular nation for whom employment must be made available on the staff of an international agency (e.g. the U.N.O.) of which the nation is a member.

QUOTA ACTS 1795 laid down the number of men which each county and borough was to provide to the Navy. Since enough volunteers could not be found, magistrates filled up with criminals, tramps, lunatics and layabouts who between them instigated the Naval mutinies of 1797. They were entitled to bounties (q.v.).

QUO WARRANTO (Lat: by what warrant). In 1274, in order to restore the powers of the Crown eroded in his absence on Crusade, Edward I issued commissions to inquire into private jurisdictions. The results were recorded in the Hundred Roll. Further commissions were then issued to ask by what warrant landowners were exercising the jurisdictions. If a charter could not be produced, the jurisdiction was forfeited and a fine might be levied. If a charter's wording did not cover the jurisdiction exercised, the rights were reduced to those covered by the words. *See also* CHARLES II-27; CHARTER.

R

RABAUL. See COMMERCE PROTECTION, NAVAL B-1; NEW GUINEA.

RABY CASTLE (Durham) fortified manor built by the Neville family in about 1380.

RACCONIGI AGREEMENT (1909). By a secret exchange of notes at this Italian country palace, Italy and Russia agreed to maintain the Balkan *status quo* and make no independent agreements with a third power. A week earlier, Italy had made a similar agreement with Russia's rival, Austria. This manoeuvre, prompted by the weakness of Italy during the Bosnian crisis of 1908, did nothing to strengthen her, but merely increased the general suspicion of Italian politicians.

RACHMANISM (1963). One Rachman (Arab = merciful), a slum landlord, was said to be using dogs and thugs to drive out tenants whom he replaced with others at high rents. The Labour Party said erroneously that this was a consequence of the Conservative Rent Act of 1957. Legislation made Rachmanism an offence.

RACISM or RACIALISM (1) is the pursuit or advocacy of a policy designed to give advantages to a particular (dominant) ethnic, linguistic or religious group over another (servient) group, or to create disadvantages for, or persecute or exterminate that servient group. The treatment of Jews in mediaeval and modern Europe and Russia is the most commonly cited case, but other examples may be found in the *Apartheid* policies of S. Africa, the Japanese treatment of the Ainu, American 19th cent. relations with Indian tribes, Congolese policies towards Europeans and Christians, and the Tutsi-Hutu civil wars in Rwanda and Burundi. The champions on both sides of the relevant controversies are generally more notable for their emotional fervour than for scientific or rational argument and the justifications advanced for the activities of dominant groups are usually baseless. Two practical considerations seem however, to be relevant: one, a common desire among govts. to distract their public from their own short-comings by offering them a scapegoat, the other a desire for quick or continuous profits at the expense of a servient group similar to the motives behind military imperialism. A third, possibly relevant consideration, is so far inadequately explored, namely, physical unease between human animals of different types.

(2) In 1965 the Wilson govt's. **RACE RELATIONS ACT** made discrimination on national or racial grounds in hotels and public places punishable and set up the Race Relations Board. The principles were extended to housing, employment, insurance and financial services in 1968 and 1976 when a permanent Race Relations Commission was created. The legislation was a response mainly to darker skinned extra-European immigration, and though some covert discrimination continued, it improved the circumstances of the immigrants, but the continuance of the Commission has tended to favour communal separatism as against immigrant integration. Further legislation was projected for 2000.

RACK. An instrument of torture used exceptionally only by authority of the Privy Council and the Council of the North. It was a horizontal frame with rollers or pulleys at each end; from these, ropes were attached to the victim's wrists and ankles and his body thus stretched, if necessary, to dislocation.

RACKHAM, John (?-1720). See READ, MARY.

RACK RENT. The full economic rent of a property.

RADAR. In 1887 Hertz proved that radio waves can be reflected and in 1924 Edward Appleton used this fact to investigate the upper atmosphere and discovered the "Appleton-Heaviside Layer". In 1935 Robert Watson Watt showed that radio waves could be used to detect aircraft and J. T. Randall and H. A. H. Boot had developed the cavity magnetron to generate high power micro-waves.

Research on similar lines was proceeding at a slower rate in the U.S.A., Russia and Germany, so that in 1940 Britain alone was equipped with a system of anti-aircraft radar (then called R.D.F.). It was also used to locate and target ships.

RADCLIFFE, John (1652-1714), renowned, wealthy, successful but tactless physician bequeathed funds by which St. Bartholomew's Hospital (London), the Radcliffe Infirmary and Observatory (Oxford) were built.

RADCLIFFE (1) John (1452-96) 1st Ld. FITZWALTER (1485) was attainted for participation in Perkin Warbeck's conspiracy in 1495 and executed. The attainder was reversed in favour of his son **(2) Robert (1483-1542) 2nd Ld. (1506) 1st Vist. (1525) 1st E. of SUSSEX (1529)** a courtier and friend of Henry VIII who made him Great Chamberlain in 1540. His son **(3) Sir Henry (?1506-57)** was Mary I's Capt.-Gen. His son **(4) Sir Thomas (?1526-83) 3rd E.**, also a soldier, helped to put down Wyatt's rebellion and from 1556 to 1564 was an unusually successful Lord Deputy of Ireland who overawed most of the Irish clans before 1559, reintroduced the Protestant ecclesiastical supremacy under Elizabeth I, but failed, after a long struggle (1560-3) to put down The O'Neill. After representing the Queen in the marriage negotiations with the Archduke Maximilian in 1567, he became in 1569 Ld. Pres. of the Council of the North and had to deal, at the outset with inadequate forces, with the Northern rebels whom in 1570 he chased across the Border. As a supporter of a French marriage for the Queen, he was seldom on good terms with her friend the E. of Leicester and has consequently received less acclaim than may have been his due. His brother **(5) Sir Henry (1530-93)** also served with him in Ireland from 1556 to 1565. His son **(6) Robert (?1569-1629) 5th E.** was one of the commission who tried Essex in 1601.

RADHAKRISHNAN, Sarvepalli (1888-1975) held many high academic appointments in India and England between 1918 and 1952. He led the Indian delegation to U.N.E.S.C.O. from 1946 to 1952 and was Indian ambassador at Moscow from 1949 to 1952. In 1952 he became Vice-Pres. of India and was Pres. from 1962 to 1967.

RADICAL JACK. The 1st E. of Durham (1792-1840).

RADICALISM (1) An element in the political thought of any progressive or left wing party, envisaging the wholesale or "root (*radix*) and branch" reform of some major aspect of public life. The term is commonly (if inaccurately) used to indicate those English reformers who lived in and after the period when their ideas might have been influenced by Rousseau, Voltaire and the French Revolutionaries. William Cobbett, Henry Hunt and their friends were apparently first termed "radical reformers" in their campaign to reform the constitution, and the first reformed House of Commons contained 55 M.Ps. professing to be radicals; but from this time forth their tendency to join with Liberals resulted in a mixing of their two outlooks like the water of different streams flowing in the same river bed. The Liberal Party still professed radicalism in the 1970s. **(2)** More rarely, the word is used for extreme right wing thought.

RADIO. See BROADCASTING.

RADIUM was discovered in 1898 by the Curies.

RADKNIGHTS held land under a form of serjeanty by which they had to ride with their lords, or on their lords' errands. They were fairly numerous in the 13th cent.

RADNOR-SHIRE was unorganised and disputed between the Welsh princes (mainly of Powys and Brychiniog) from about 400 to about 1000, by which time the eastern side had long been closed by Offa's Dyke. The Normans, led by the Mortimer and de Braose families, now entered, the first castle being built at New Radnor in about 1100. The Edwardian Conquest and shiring of N. Wales hardly touched Radnor, which remained Marcher territory until the Acts of Union of 1536 and 1542 joined the Warwick and Mortimer lordships to form the county. The area was royalist in the Civil War and the scene of Rebecca riots in the 1840s. It was amalgamated into the new county of Powys in 1974.

RADNOR. *See* PLEYDELL-BOUVERIE.

RAEBURN, Sir Henry (1756-1823) studied in Rome on the advice of Reynolds. When he returned to Edinburgh in 1787 he became the leading Scots portrait painter of his day and painted almost every contemporary of note.

RAFFLES, Sir (Thomas) Stamford (1781-1826) landed at Penang in 1805, reduced and became Lieut.-Gov. of Java in 1811 and persuaded the HEIC to buy Singapore in 1819. A vastly learned botanist and zoologist, his papers were lost in a ship's fire in 1824, but he founded and became the first Pres. of the Royal Zoological Society. *See* INDONESIA-4.

RAGEMAN, STAT. OF (1276) appointed justices to settle complaints (mostly of trespass) which had arisen since 1251. *See* TRAILBASTON.

RAGGED SCHOOLS were a secondary development from the Sunday Schools (*see* RAIKES). John Pounds started the first ragged school at Portsmouth in 1820, to provide free teaching and necessities for destitute children. Shaftesbury took a great interest and himself taught in them. In the 1850s Dr. Guthrie extended the idea to Scotland. The movement lost its force after the Education Act, 1870.

RAGHOBA. *See* MARATHAS-6.

RAGLAN. *See* SOMERSET.

RAGMAN(S) ROLL. The formal record of homage paid to Edward I by the King (John Balliol) and notables of Scotland in 1296.

RAGNAR LODBROK (Dan. = Hairy breeches), (fl. 9th cent.). Viking ruler or leader. He raided France in 845 and Northumbria in about 860. King Aelle captured and killed him, according to tradition, in a snakepit and his sons Halfdan, Ivar the Boneless and Ubbe invaded England in 865 ostensibly in revenge. The many mentions of him in Danish and Icelandic literature point to a remarkable if hardly likeable personality.

RAGUSA (now DUBROVNIK). 'Argosy' is a corruption of this name. *See* ADRIATIC.

RAHERE (?-1144). *See* ST. BARTHOLOMEW'S HOSPITAL.

RAIKES (1) Robert (1735-1811), a successful Gloucester printer developed and publicised the idea of cheap or free schools and himself opened in 1780 and taught in one of the earliest Sunday Schools. He was one of the most influential pioneers of mass education. His nephew **(2) Thomas (1777-1848),** the diarist, was a Gov. of the Bank of England and a well known clubland figure. His great-nephew **(3) Henry Cecil (1838-91)** became Tory M.P. for Chester in 1868, Chairman of Committees in 1874, sat for Preston in 1882 and therefore for Cambridge University and was Postmaster-Gen. from 1886-91.

RAILWAY AMALGAMATIONS (1923). State control of railways in World War I had seemed to improve services and encouraged the idea of permanent state control. Nationalisation was considered but other schemes were studied, involving grouping. The railways were handed back to the companies in 1921 and on 1 Jan. 1923 a Railways Act created four big companies out of the 14 large and a hundred-odd small ones.

The largest of the new companies was the London Midland and Scottish (L.M.S.) which incorporated the former London and N. Western, Midland, Lancashire and Yorkshire, Caledonian, and Highland Railways. The second was the London and N. Eastern Railway (L.N.E.R.), comprising the lines of the Great Northern, Great Eastern, Great Central, N. Eastern, N. British and Great N. of Scotland Railways. The Great Western

Railway (G.W.R.) comprised the old G.W.R. together with sundry smaller companies, mainly in Wales. The smallest was the mainly passenger-carrying Southern Railway (S.R.) comprising the old London and S. Western, S. Eastern and Chatham, and London Brighton and S. Coast Railways. Former jointly-owned lines became jointly owned by the new companies. Subject to very strict profit limitations during World War II, these arrangements lasted until nationalisation in 1948.

RAILWAY (1873) AND CANAL (1888) COMMISSION was a court established to enforce the obligations of the relevant companies to grant reasonable facilities to the public and to refrain from undue preferences. Abolished in 1949.

RAIL-WAYS, -ROAD. *See* TRANSPORT AND COMMUNICATIONS-7 onwards.

RAINSBOROUGH, or RAINBOROW [E] (1) William (?-1642) commanded a successful naval expedition against Salee (Morocco) in 1626 to secure the release of 340 English captives. His son **(2) Thomas (?-1648)** served in the *Swallow* of the Parliamentary fleet, but in 1646 received command of a land regiment, when he was M.P. for Droitwich. He sided with the army in the disbandment controversy of 1647 and with the Republicans in the Putney debates and he opposed further negotiations with Charles I. In 1648 he was sent to sea as Vice-Admiral but his political views caused a mutiny. On returning to the army he was killed at Pontefract. His social views have attracted more attention in the 20th cent. than in his own day.

RAISON D'ÉTAT **(Fr. = reason of state).** A continental doctrine that private interests can be justifiably overridden by state action, of whose propriety the state alone is the judge. Save in certain limited fields of foreign policy, there is no such rule in the English Common Law. *See* INDEMNITY, ACTS OF.

RAITH or IRISH RING FORTS were small, high banked and circular with a ditch, providing defences for a family settlement. They are mostly mediaeval.

RAJAGOPALACHARI, Chakravarti (1879-1972) was Gandhi's chief representative in Madras where he dominated the local Congress Party until 1939. He was also a member of the Congress Working Committee until 1942 when he resigned over the Pakistan issue. He returned in 1945, was a member of the Interim Govt. in 1947 and Gov. of W. Bengal from 1947 to 1948 and last Gov.-Gen. of India until 1950. He then became Home Minister until 1951 and thereafter Chief Minister of Madras until 1954.

RAJ, -AH. Raj means rule or sovereignty. A rajah meant an Indian King or ruling prince, but the title was sometimes conferred as an honorific upon Hindus and was also used by certain Malay and Indonesian rulers. A Maharajah was slightly grander. 'Raj' is cognate with the Lat: 'rex' and Erse: 'ri'.

RAJA RAM. *See* MARATHAS-3.

RAJPUTS, RAJPUTANA, RAJASTHAN (India). (1) The Rajputs (= sons of Kings) were some 11M landowners organised in patrilineal and patriarchal clans, mostly in central and northern India. They claimed (sometimes accurately) descent from the ancient ruling Kshatriya, but in the N.W. some were Moslem. They are famous for courage, ambition, pride of ancestry and a regard for honour, every rajput from a great ruler to a poor farmer being equally royal.

(2) At the beginning of the 16th cent. the Rana SANGA of MEWAR was the leading ruler of Rajputana until the Moghul Babur defeated him at Khanua in 1527. He abandoned further attempts at expansion and in the time of Akbar the area, apart from Mewar, came under Moghul rule. Jehangir subdued Mewar. The Moghul policy of conciliation was, however, interrupted by Aurungzeb who provoked a lengthy civil war in which Rajput disunion prevented liberation and in due course made them victims of first the Marathas, then of the Pindaris and finally the Pathan freebooter Amir Khan.

(3) The British struggle with the Marathas created opportunities for the Rajput states to assert themselves and from 1813 the Marquess Hastings (Gov-Gen. until 1823) cultivated them. By 1818 British protection extended to the 23 states, one chieftainship and one estate which composed the area. They rapidly increased in prosperity during the resulting peace, so that most of the rulers (if not always their troops) remained loyal during the Indian Mutiny.

(4) The principal Rajput states were, in the N.E., Alwar, Bharatpur, Dholpur and Karauli; in the SE. Bundi, Kotah, Tonk and Udaipur; and in the West Jaipur, Jodhpur, Bikaner and Jaisalmer. There was also a small British-administered enclave at Ajmer-Merwara. The British authority was represented by a diplomatic official called the Agent to the Gov-Gen., who was also Chief Commissioner in Ajmer.

(5) The rulers surrendered their powers to the Indian Govt. in 1948 and 1949 when the area became known as Rajasthan. *See also* JAIPUR; JODHPUR; MALWA; MARWAR; MEWAR.

RALE[I]GH, Sir Walter (pron: *Rawley*) **(?1552-1618) (1)** Devonian, was half-brother to Sir Humphrey and Adrian Gilbert, a cousin of Sir Richard Grenville and a kinsman of the Champernownes, with whom, after leaving Oxford, he campaigned for the Huguenots in France (1569-77). He returned to England an experienced soldier and reputed the finest swordsman in the country.

(2) Sir Humphrey Gilbert gave him a command in his abortive expedition of 1578 and in 1580 he commanded a company in Ireland. In the ruthless spirit of the French wars he was merciless to the Irish and to the Spanish invaders, whom he massacred at Smerwick, but he could attract the loyalty of his troops by his prowess and address. Early in 1581 he was chosen to take the victory despatches to London. This recognised honour made his fortune. He greatly impressed the Queen by his good looks and knightly gallantry, wit and capacity for exposition. The story that he laid down his new cloak in the mud for her is (true or false) characteristic. She employed him in confidential business, made him Warden of the Stannaries and Capt. of the Guard and put him in the way of many lucrative opportunities. He was a Devon M.P. in 1585 and 1586.

(3) In 1584, after Sir Humphrey Gilbert's death, he had received a charter to colonise America. Restrained from going in person, his two ships explored the fertile coast of Virginia. In 1585 a larger squadron under Sir Richard Grenville planted a settlement which was abandoned in 1586. Similar attempts in the area also failed because of inadequate preparation and the use of criminals and tramps as colonists. One by-product of these expeditions was the more extensive introduction of potatoes and tobacco (already known in the 1570s) and to their association with him. He had a capacity, noted at the time, for 'making things his own'. From 1586 he also exploited vast grants in Cork, Waterford and Tipperary and in the 1590s introduced the potato there as a garden plant.

(4) During the early Armada years he was at the Queen's side devising plans, but shortly afterwards she began to favour the dashing E. of Essex. Raleigh was not liked at Court: he was too ruthless, too well placed, too acquisitive of money and credit, too successful with women. In a quarrel with Essex he suddenly met danger, for Essex had the Queen's ear. In 1591 the affair which he had been carrying on with Elizabeth Throgmorton came to light because of her pregnancy. She was not only a Queen's lady-in-waiting, but by relationship with Queen Catherine Parr, a step- and foster-relative to the Queen herself. The Queen was outraged. She sent Raleigh to the Tower but called him in to restore order at Dartmouth during the looting of the great Carrack *Madre de Dios*. From this fabulous Spanish prize he saved some £75,000 for the Queen (1592). Thus released, he married the lady, but was still forbidden the Court, so he went to his estate at Sherborne but kept himself in the public eye by assiduous attendance at the House of Commons.

(5) In 1595 he set out on his Guiana expedition in search of El Dorado, seized Trinidad, but found the Orinoco currents a harder adversary than the Spaniard. He brought back some gold quartz which seems to have deceived everyone including himself. In 1596 he and Essex went together on the brilliant Cadiz expedition in which the *flota* was destroyed and the port burned. In 1597, frustrated in their attempt on the mainland, they set out against the Azores to try and intercept the new *flota*. A storm scattered the squadron and without waiting for orders, Raleigh carried Fayal himself to Essex's fury. Although the feud was suspended when Essex went to Ireland, the Earl's later disobediences and execution injured the Queen's Capt., for Essex had been in correspondence with James VI of Scots who now thought that Raleigh might oppose his succession. In this view Cecil encouraged James and as Raleigh was unpopular with the Spaniards (whom James wished to cultivate) he was sacrificed to the new policy in the new reign. Deprived of his offices and monopolies, he was put on trial for treasonable correspondence, through Ld. Cobham, with the Spanish Viceroy at Brussels, condemned to death but respited (Dec. 1603).

(6) He now lived in the Bloody Tower with his wife until 1616, writing poetry (mostly lost), political and other essays and a *History of the World*. In 1616 his friends persuaded James to let him go on a further gold prospecting expedition to the R. Orinoco but on the condition that he did nothing hostile to the Spaniards. The condition was impossible. In any case Raleigh was ill when they reached Guiana and could not control his subordinates, who sacked San Tomas. On his return *via* Newfoundland in 1618, Gondomar, the Spanish ambassador demanded his head and he was executed under his original conviction in 1603. On the scaffold someone said that the block should allow Raleigh to die facing east. He replied "What matter how the head lie, so the heart be right".

(7) Though an unscrupulous adventurer, Raleigh was also a good poet and a competent prose writer. With Selden and Cotton he was a member of the first Society of Antiquaries.

RALPH, Abbot of COGGESHALL (fl. 1210) chronicled English and crusading events between 1187 and 1224.

RALPH D'ESCURES or DE TURBINE (?-1122), driven from Normandy to England by Robert of Bellême in 1100, he became Bp. of Rochester in 1108, administrator of Canterbury on Anselm's death in 1109 and Abp. of Canterbury in 1114. He immediately plunged into controversy with Thurstan of York over the primacy of the two sees and for some years prevented Thurstan's consecration. He secured Henry I's support and though Pope Calixtus II consecrated Thurstan in 1119, the pre-eminence of Canterbury was generally recognised from his time onwards.

RALPH (?-1057) Earl (surnamed the Timid or the Shy) was a nephew of Edward the Confessor brought up in Normandy. He came to England in 1041, became E. of Worcester in 1042 and of Monmouth and Hereford in 1051 when Swein Godwin's son was extruded from it. Though his appointments were political, he was mostly concerned with the ordinary, if energetic affairs of the March. See EDWARD THE CONFESSOR, 10-11.

RALPH ROBINSON. *See* FARMER GEORGE.

RAMBOUILLET, Catherine de VIVONNE, Marquise de (1588-1665) held famous literary and social gatherings at her *Salon Bleu* from about 1617 to 1650 and then on a lesser scale until she died. Among those whom she thus brought together were the playwright Corneille, the later well known letter writer Mme de Sévigné and wits such as La Rochefoucauld, Mlle de Scudéry and Saint-Evremonde. She encouraged or imposed an element of good manners, intelligent intercourse and modesty of thought and expression which had been hitherto lacking in French social custom. These, despite aberrations such as those satirised by Molière in *Les Précieuses Ridicules* (Fr. = The Laughable Blue Stockings), became accepted conventions throughout educated Europe and survived as late as World War I.

RAMPUR. *See* ROHILLAS.

RAMSBURY (Wilts.). Anglo-Saxon bishopric created in 909 for Wiltshire and Berkshire. In 1075 the see was moved to Old Sarum and thence in 1220 to Salisbury.

RAMSAY of Dalhousie. Scottish military and border family, sometimes at feud with the Douglas. Three members called **Sir Alexander (1) ?-1342, (2) ?-1402** and **(3) ?-?1451** figure as commanders against the English. **(1)** took Roxburgh in 1342; **(2)** was killed at Homildon Hill; **(3)** won a minor victory at Piperden in 1435.

RAMSEY. The rich and important Benedictine abbey was founded by Aylwin, E. of the E. Angles and foster brother to K. Edgar, c. 969, with the help of **St. Oswald** who sent monks from Westbury. Until 1113, with two insignificant exceptions, the abbots were Saxon. The abbey lost some lands at the Conquest, but still owned 42 manors in 6 counties at Domesday, but it suffered under Stephen from occupation by Geoffrey de Mandeville, who turned it into a fortress. The effort of recovering losses and a natural litigiousness led to continual disputes with ecclesiastical neighbours, e.g. Thorney Abbey and the Bp. of Ely. Nevertheless in 1178, 50 churches were confirmed to it by Pope Alexander III in 8 counties.

RAND. *See* WITWATERSRAND.

RANDOLPH, family identified with Scottish patriotism. **(1) Sir Thomas (?-1332) 1st E. of MORAY,** friend of Robert the Bruce, joined his rebellion of 1306 after the murder of the Red Comyn. He was captured at the B. of Methven, affected to change sides and help to hunt Bruce in Carrick and suffered himself to be retaken by Sir James Douglas in 1308. Thereafter he was accepted as Robert's most steadfast and courageous supporter and a performer of heroic and ingenious feats of arms, including the escalade of Edinburgh Castle in 1314. He commanded a division at the B. of Bannockburn (1314) and in Edward Bruce's Irish invasion of 1315. In the succession settlement of 1315 he was nominated Guardian of Scotland in the event of a minority. In 1319 he and Sir James Douglas led a major raid into England. They helped to negotiate the French alliance (T. of Corbeil, Apr. 1326) and led another raid in 1327. He became Guardian when Bruce died (June 1329) and, faced with renewed Balliol claims, had David II crowned in Nov. 1331. He died at Musselburgh while preparing for an English invasion. His martial second son **(2) John (?-1346) 3rd E. (1332)** routed Edward Balliol at Annan in 1332, fought at Halidon Hill in 1333 and became joint regent in 1334. He, with Sir Archibald Douglas and Robert the Steward, held S.W. Scotland for David II until his capture (July 1335). Imprisoned in Winchester and London, he was exchanged for the Es. of Suffolk and Salisbury, both taken in France. He then regained Annandale, granted to his father in 1314, from the Bohuns and became Warden of the Scots West March. In the summer of 1346 he led a great raid into Cumbria but was killed during David II's invasion at the B. of Neville's Cross in Oct.

RANDOLPH, Edward (?1632-1703) was employed by the Privy Council to report on Massachusetts' conformity with the trade and navigation laws (1676). He correctly reported that they were ignored and was appointed Collector of Customs for New England (1678). As the local magistrates invariably acquitted illegal traders, he was both frustrated and unpopular. His views probably resulted in the annulment of the Massachusetts Charter in 1684. From 1686 to 1689 he served as Sec. under Gov. Andros for the Dominion of New England. In 1689 the rebels against Andros imprisoned him but in 1691 he returned as Surveyor Gen. of Customs for N. America. A strong champion of the exclusive British trading policy of the time, he lacked the resources to enforce it, merely increasing the colonial irritability and his own unpopularity.

RANDOLPH, Thomas (1523-90), had been Principal of Broadgates Hall, Oxford, from 1549 to 1553 but took refuge in France under Mary I. Elizabeth I employed him as a diplomat first in Germany, then in Scotland, until 1566. In 1568 he negotiated trading privileges in Russia. In 1573 and 1576 he was engaged on special missions to France, whence he returned too late (1580) to assist Morton in Scotland. He also negotiated the Scots treaty of 1586.

RANDOLPH, William (1650-1711), shipowner, emigrant to Virginia and planter since 1674, was one of the founders of William and Mary College at Williamsburg in 1693. He was mainly interested in civilising the Indians.

RAN[D]ULF of GERNONS (?-1153) E. of CHESTER (1130). His career illustrates the confusion and high level intrigues in King Stephen's reign. From his father Ranulf *le Meschin* he inherited, with Cheshire, wide lands in Lincolnshire and claims to Lincoln Castle and Carlisle. Carlisle was granted to Henry E. of Huntingdon instead (1135). In 1140 Ranulf tried unsuccessfully to ambush Henry *en route* to Scotland, but succeeded in taking Lincoln Castle by a ruse. There King Stephen besieged him. Ranulf appealed to his father-in-law Robert of Gloucester who was the principal supporter of the Empress Matilda. Robert's relief expedition led to the B. of Lincoln (Feb. 1141) and the capture of the King, but when the latter's fortunes improved, Ranulf went over to him and they were formally reconciled early in 1142, Ranulf being entrusted with the midland territory between Lincoln, Chester and Coventry. In 1146 he helped Stephen to take Bedford, but then Stephen had him arrested at Court and forced him to surrender his castles. Having failed in 1147 to retake Lincoln or Coventry, he joined Henry of Anjou on his arrival in 1149. As the latter was allied to Henry of Huntingdon, Ranulf gave up his claim to Carlisle in return for the promise of the Honour of Lancaster, but Stephen put in a counter-bid and returned Lincoln with Belvoir Castle and the lands between the Rs. Ribble and Mersey. In 1153 Henry of Anjou returned to England and repurchased Ranulf with Staffordshire to add to Cheshire and lands in Normandy. In Dec., however, William of Peveril, whose Staffordshire lands had just been granted to Ranulf, poisoned him. *See* CHESHIRE; STEPHEN.

RANELAGH (London) was a place of amusement by Chelsea Hospital called after the 1st E. of Ranelagh, who built the house and gardens. It had a Rotunda and flourished between 1742 and 1803. The RANELAGH CLUB was founded at Barn Elms in 1894.

RANGER. The keeper of a purlieu. *See* FOREST-3.

RANGOON (Burma) was first developed as a port by Alaungpra after 1755. It was taken by the British in 1824, restored in 1826 and finally annexed in 1852. It developed rapidly but by 1931 72% of the population was Indian. The Japanese invasion and Burmese independence reversed this trend and by 1958 75% were Burmese. *See* BURMA.

RANJIT SINGH. *See* SIKHS-3.

RANKEILLOUR. *See* HOPE.

RANULF DE BRIQUESSART (Le Mesquin – the nasty). *See* CHESHIRE; CUMBERLAND 6-7.

RANULF of BLUNDEVILLE. *See* CHESHIRE.

RAOUL of DAMMARTIN. *See* PHILIP (II) AUGUSTUS.

RAP. A debased halfpenny, particularly one of Wood's halfpence, worth half a farthing, circulating in Ireland from 1721.

RAPALLO, Ts. of (1) The T. of **Nov. 1920** represented an unsuccessful attempt to normalise Italo-Yugoslav relations. **(2)** That of **Apr. 1922** was a treaty of mutual diplomatic and economic co-operation between Germany and Russia (the two defeated powers) arising out of the P. of Versailles and the Russian defeat at the B. of Warsaw (1920). *See* GENOA CONFERENCE.

RAPE. One of 6 ancient Sussex districts, each comprising several hundreds. Five were centred on castles; the sixth on Chichester.

RAPE (1) both in the sense of abduction and of sexual penetration without consent was originally appealable by the woman and was a felony punishable with loss of limb, but the woman might compromise the appeal by marrying the ravisher. If she brought no appeal he might only be fined or imprisoned. The two concepts grew apart in the Middle Ages, through separate enumeration in statutes of 1275 and 1285. Rape by sexual penetration became a capital felony in 1828 and ceased to be capital in 1841. **(2)** In 1736 Hale CJ held that at marriage a wife consented irrevocably to intercourse with her husband. In 1888 with the progress in the status of wives, this was doubted by 4 out of 13 judges, and lay and legal opinion gathered momentum behind them. After World War II the courts admitted exceptions. In 1991 judges and the House of Lords held *Nem:Con* that the rule no longer applied.

RAPHAEL *See* RENAISSANCE-11.

RAPPAREES. The later name for the Irish guerrillas or bandits called Tories.

RAROTONGA. *See* COOK IS.

RASCAL. Originally an army camp follower and then the lean ill fed deer not worth chasing.

RASEE OR RAZEE (Fr. = cut down). A heavy frigate made by reducing a ship of the line by one deck.

RASTADT, P. of (Mar. 1714) (*see* UTRECHT, P. OF 1713) was negotiated between Marshal Villars for France and Bavaria, and P. Eugene for the Emperor as such and as head of the House of Habsburg. The French evacuated the right bank of the Rhine but kept Strasbourg and Landau. The Elector Max Emmanuel was restored to Bavaria. The Milanese, Naples and Sardinia went to the Habsburgs. The Treaty complemented that of Utrecht.

RASTELL (1) John (?-1536) published *Expositiones Terminorum Legum Anglorum* (Lat: Explanation of the Terms of English Laws) in 1527. His son **(2) William (?1508-65)** had translated it in 1563 into English. In 1620 this was published as a law dictionary in parallel Norman French and English called *Termes de la Ley* (= Legal Terms). This is an important source book.

RATAE CORITANORUM. *See* BRITAIN (ROMAN)-2; LEICESTER.

RATCLIFFE or RADCLIFFE, Sir Richard (?-1485), a Knight of Edward IV, became a close friend and adviser of Richard III, for whom he executed Rivers and others at Pontefract and from whom he received large estates and a Garter. (For a well known jingle *see* LOVE(L) 2.). He was killed at Bosworth.

RATES, a slightly less primitive form of income tax than the tithe, were first imposed by the Poor Law Statute of Elizabeth in 1600 to finance parish poor relief, because private charity and recusancy fines had failed to replace monastic charity and the number of unemployed had grown as the military scares decreased. They were assessed by the churchwardens under the supervision of Quarter Sessions and upon the value of occupied land and movable goods, but were soon confined to land. They were not leviable in any of the 800-odd places which were not parishes, and non-parochial status (e.g. of the Temples in London) was therefore prized. They provided almost the sole source of local govt. finance down to 1895 when the new local govt. system came into existence. By this time most non-parochial places had disappeared and assessment was made by assessment committees. In 1896 agricultural land was derated by 50% and shortly after the practice of paying Exchequer grants to local authorities began. Agricultural land was totally derated in 1929 with damaging results to rural administration; industry was derated at the same time. Grants had to be increased.

Valuations have always lagged far behind reality. The 1929 valuations remained the basis of rateability of older properties until well after World War II, during which Exchequer grants had risen rapidly to encourage local authorities to carry out their share of war policy. The grants became a system with a structure and by 1954 less than half the income of local authorities was derived from the rates. Industry again became rateable in 1958 and a far reaching revaluation came into effect in 1972. This was an important govt. motive for amalgamating rural and urban areas under the Local Govt. Act 1972, for the support which urban values might afford to the rural areas might be expected to compensate for reduced govt. grants. The expectation was disappointed.

Rates had never been popular and this unpopularity hardened into a Tory party doctrine that domestic rates should be abolished. Hence in 1989 they were replaced by a Community Charge or Poll Tax levied on individuals. This caused riots and in three years over £1,000,000,000 remained uncollected. Business rating, however, was pooled nationally and shared out among the councils. This made it look as if govt. grants had been preserved, whereas it deprived local authorities of a right to levy as they thought proper. In 1993 the Community Charge was replaced by the Council Tax which was a sort of head tax assessed upon banded valuations of the property in which people lived. The higher the band, the higher the proportion of it to be taken in tax. Not surprisingly there were a million appeals against valuations.

RATHBONE, Eleanor (1872-1946), campaigner for women's rights and for family allowances, was independent M.P. for the Combined Universities from 1929. The Family Allowances Act 1946 established them but its operation was restricted by the smallness of the sums paid.

RATIFICATION OF TREATIES (1) In older diplomatic practice a negotiator was given Full Powers by his Prince who was expected or obliged to ratify a treaty if its terms fell within the terms of his Full Power. Since different negotiators might have differing Full Powers, ratification by all parties could be expected only on those points in which their negotiator's Full Powers coincided; thus if

Prince A accorded full powers on points 1, (2, 3, 4)
Prince B accorded full powers on points (2, 3, 4,) 5

Prince A could refuse ratification if point 5 were included; Prince B if point 1 were. In practice Full Powers were hedged about with qualifications and exceptions and might involve problems of linguistic and semantic interpretation. Hence when envoys exchanged their Full Powers, consideration and discussion of them might occupy a large part of the conference and could, if there were insufficient coincidence, end in failure or in prolonged adjournments while a representative obtained new powers from his Prince. In times of slow and uncertain communication, negotiations might be prolonged for many months.

(2) Such practices were suitable as long as rulers were masters of their internal govts., but as and when Princes became subject to constitutional or other internal restraints, ratification on all points had, increasingly, to be reserved lest the negotiator committed his master to politically or constitutionally impossible obligations. In particular, though the conduct of foreign policy is an undoubted English royal prerogative, the Crown cannot, by a mere treaty, alter the internal law. Hence where a treaty may create such an alteration it must either in advance secure an Act of Parliament empowering it to ratify, or the ratification must be made by such an Act.

(3) The formal instrument of ratification is in either event issued by the Crown under the Great Seal. In the case of bilateral treaties the parties exchange instruments; a multilateral treaty formerly provided for the deposit of instruments with one of them or with some disinterested body or power. Since World War II this has been the U.N.O. A treaty comes into effect when all the parties have ratified it, unless it otherwise provides.

RATIONING was designed to save wartime shipping (*see for example* B. OF THE ATLANTIC) **(1)** In World War I it began with sugar in 1916 and embraced most major foodstuffs by 1918. **(2)** In World War II it began on a weekly basis with bacon, butter and sugar in Jan. 1940 and was extended to eggs, cheese, sweets, tea and later meat (but not offal or poultry). In June it was extended to clothing and shoes, based on an annual allotment of personal points. Restaurant meals were price-rationed at between 5s. and 7s 6d., pigeon casserole being often served near Trafalgar Square. Routine house repairs were restricted to £10 a year. Powdered eggs were often substituted for shell eggs, milk was restricted and cheese-making other than limited amounts of Cheddar was prohibited, and some cheese-making arts in consequence lost. The sea being a battlefield, fish was unobtainable. Petrol was closely rationed for essential journeys only, with the result that main line and commuter trains were packed out. The system was very successful. Its wartime necessity and fairness were generally acknowledged. **(3)** The Attlee govt's. attempt to continue it into peacetime created bitter discontent, and the system was dismantled between 1950 and 1953. Sweet rationing was the last go. **(4)** There was some brief petrol rationing during the Suez crisis of 1956.

RATIO STUDIORUM **(Lat: Purposive study).** *See* JESUITS.

RATISBON or REGENSBURG, Electoral Meeting (1630). *See* THIRTY YEARS' WAR-11.

RATTLESNAKE, **H.M.S.,** made an arduous and important survey in 1848-50 of the Torres Strait and the Louisiade Is., with T. H. Huxley aboard as surgeon and naturalist. These cruises introduced Huxley to scientific research, besides gathering biological material of great interest.

RATTRAY, Thomas (1684-1743) became non-juring Bp. of Brechin (Scot.) and helped to draft the Scots canons in 1727, but as the Old Pretender had not assented to his election he was not recognised by other non-juring bishops until 1731 when he became Bp. of Dunkeld. He became Primus in 1739.

RAVENSPUR was anciently a thriving Yorkshire port close to Spurn Head. The sea began to encroach after 1400 and by 1500 it had vanished.

RAWALPINDI (Pakistan) was settled by Sardar Milka Singh, a Sikh adventurer, in 1765. He invited traders from the Jhelum area there and it grew rapidly. It was for a time a centre from which Afghan malcontents such as Shah Suja agitated in their own country, but in 1849, when the Sikh army finally surrendered there after the B. of Gujarat, the British made it their own main cantonment in the N.W. and it so remained until independence.

RAWDON (1790) -HASTINGS, Francis (1754-1826), Ld. RAWDON (1783), 2nd E. of MOIRA (1783), M. of HASTINGS (1817), originally a soldier, fought in America and returned to England in 1782. He was an influential friend of the P. of Wales, whom he supported in the 1789 regency controversy. In 1793 he commanded the Brittany expedition, in 1794 the reinforcements for Flanders. After routine commands, he returned to politics and was Master-Gen. of the Ordnance in the All-the-Talents ministry in 1806 to 1807 and supported the P. of Wales again in the crisis of 1810. He tried, with Wellesley, to

form a ministry in 1812 and then accepted the Gov.-Generalship of India in 1813. It was a time of rapid territorial expansion, caused mainly by aggression and disorder among the native powers adjacent to the frontiers. He launched a successful campaign in Nepal from 1814 to 1815. In 1817 he pacified or destroyed the freebooting Pindaris of the Deccan and in 1818 went on to subjugate the adjacent Marathas who gave them sustenance. The pacification of S. India was thus virtually complete. He was also much concerned with the trade across the Bay of Bengal. He accepted the offer of Singapore in 1819 and had initiated trade with the royal Siamese trading monopoly in 1822. He then resigned because the Directors of the HEIC disallowed loans by Palmer's Bank to Hyderabad, which he had approved.

RAWSON, John (?-1547), Vist. CLONTARFF (1541), as Prior of Kilmainham from 1511 was head of the Irish Knights of St. John. He was active in the Irish Privy Council from 1527, supported the Crown in the Kildare rebellion (1534) and was considered by Thomas Cromwell as a possible Ld. Chancellor of Ireland in 1535. He received his peerage at the dissolution of the Knights and a pension of 500 marks.

RAY previously **WRAY, John (1627-1705), F.R.S. (1667),** the 'father of English natural history', made several botanical tours of the N. and W. of England and in 1662 agreed with Francis Willughby to undertake the description of plants for their projected joint description of the organic world. In 1670 he accordingly published his *Catalogus Plantorum Angliae.* Willughby died in 1672 leaving him £60 a year and he took on the latter's zoological work and studied both together, leaving at his death very complete classification of plants and insects.

RÉ, ILE DE. *See* ROCHELLE, LA.

REACH FAIR. *See* CAMBRIDGE.

READ, Mary (fl. 1710-20), enlisted as a private in the War of the Spanish Succession, but deserted for the excitements and prospects of piracy and joined Anne Bonny and her husband John Rackham or Calico Jack. They were all captured at Jamaica in 1720. He was hanged, the two lady pirates spared.

READEPTION. The restoration of Henry VI in 1470. *See* EDWARD IV.

READING (Berks.) first mentioned in the *Anglo-Saxon Chronicle* in 871, near the junction of the Thames and the R. Kennet, probably originated as a trading settlement on a royal demesne. The Danes sacked it in 1006. St. Martin's Abbey at Battle acquired part of it under William I. The great Abbey founded in 1121 acquired the whole, with Cholsey, and it was given a fair on St. Lawrence Day and presented with the hand of St. James. This attracted crowds of pilgrims. There had also been a castle from early times but it was destroyed in 1151. The place was governed by bailiffs appointed by the Abbot, who seems to have superseded such burghal institutions as existed, save for an ancient merchant guild which is first mentioned as a going concern in 1253. At this period there was already a thriving cloth trade and thriving jurisdictional disputes with the Abbot. He made good his claim, but the Crown compensated the guild in 1257 by making the members free of tolls throughout England. This caused disputes with Newbury in 1261 and periodically with London in the 14th cent. By now the head of the guild was called the mayor, the guildsmen (who never exceeded 50) were called burgesses and the Abbot was in debt and trying to tallage the town. By mid-century the local govt. was vested in their mayor and his bailiffs, but he chose the mayor from three candidates whom they presented. These arrangements, despite quarrels about minor offices, continued until the Reformation.

By 1529 trade had greatly increased, but the guild oligarchy had not and was in a position to prevent or regulate trade by others. In practice this meant that it levied an *octroi* and financed itself at "foreign" expense.

The cloth trade was the most important, but there was extensive business in shoes, provisions and harness. When the Abbey was dissolved in 1538 Reading reverted to the Crown and a royal steward stepped into the Abbot's shoes. In 1542 a new charter superseded the guild. Meanwhile the Crown neglected the administrative duties of the Abbey so that the many bridges fell down. Thus trade and pilgrimage fell away together. A charter of 1560, which remodelled the corporation, sought to subsidise it by the grant of various fees and properties, but meanwhile trade revived and there were now five flourishing livery companies, especially in clothing. William Laud's father was a Reading clothier and he obtained a new charter in 1638.

The town suffered disastrously in the Civil War and by about 1780 the cloth trade had vanished. On the other hand the improvement of the London-Bath road and the Kennet and Avon Canal, opened in 1810, placed it on a major trade route, strengthened when the railway came in the 1840s. The town began to expand as small manufacturing businesses accumulated there. By 1914 the population had reached 50,000 and it had become the effective capital of Berkshire, though as a county borough it was administratively independent of it. When its county borough status was abolished in 1974 its population had more than doubled. The area was extended in 1977.

READING, M. of. *See* ISAACS.

REALTY or REAL PROPERTY, at Common Law was freehold land, including easements such as rights of way but excluding leases, which were CHATTELS REAL. All the rest including copyholds were CHATTELS or PERSONAL PROPERTY. Realty was said to *lie in grant,* i.e. ownership depended upon a formal grant, whereas chattels were said to *lie in action,* i.e. ownership could ultimately be established only by success in litigation.

REALISM, CLASSICISM, ROMANTICISM. In art or literature *realism* connotes fidelity of representation, especially of disagreeable, sordid or indecent particulars and is sometimes equated with cynicism, in contrast with *idealism,* sometimes equated with an over-optimistic view of nature and life. *Classicism* involves a strong sense of self control and often the adoption of strict and intellectual forms or rules, by means of which the emotional force of a work of art is expected to be explicable to the spectator. In *romanticism* the matter which the artist displays is cast in a form which suits him and which often ignores the spectator. Classical modes tend to be authoritarian and social: romantic modes protestant and anarchic. Realism or idealism may be present in either.

In Britain the **Romantic Movement** arose in reaction to the classicism of the earlier 18th cent. and lasted until about the mid-19th cent.

REALPOLITIK (Ger. = practical policy). A political technique practised by Bismarck in which objectives were limited in order to achieve real, if unspectacular gains, not likely to arouse strong feelings. The term is often misused in English to mean cynically conducted power politics.

REARMAMENT. The belief that World War I might have ended war engendered the Ten Year Rule (q.v.) and throughout the 1920s limited warlike procurements. Reliance was directed to the League of Nations but the idea that member nations should support the League's purposes with arms was not taken seriously. In Britain the appalling memory of the war made the very idea of rearmament abhorrent to many, and Stanley Baldwin in particular, but not uniquely, exploited this sentiment, which was also financially convenient. The Ten Year Rule was dropped in 1932 during Hitler's advance to power in Germany, but with little effect on defence estimates. Some important technical work, however, was begun on radar and fighter design. Despite the Manchurian crisis' the

Italian attack on Abyssinia and the Spanish Civil War, politicians of all parties (and their constituents) only reluctantly accepted any need for rearmament. In the 1935 election campaign, Baldwin only hinted that it might be necessary, while his Labour opponents used his falsely alleged predilection for arms against him. A White Paper in Mar. 1935, however, acknowledged that the League of Nations might not be a reliable shield and in 1936 a Minister for the Co-ordination of Defence (Sir Thomas Inskip) was appointed mainly for propagandist reasons. Rearmament gradually acquired momentum and the R.A.F., especially, received important increments of funds. The traditionally pacifist Labour Party and the electorally timid Conservatives were slow to accept the situation. The trade union leadership, with Churchill, recognised the German dangers. In 1937 with the development of German military movements in Europe, the Chancellor of the Exchequer, Neville Chamberlain, accepted that defence might prevail over orthodoxly balanced budgets and the parliamentary Labour Party abstained, rather than vote against the defence estimates. In 1938 the Services were given the right to demand priority treatment by manufacturers. In 1939 conscription of a half-hearted kind was proposed by the govt., opposed by Labour and enacted.

REBECCA RIOTS (*see* Genesis 24 v. 60). The frequent and heavy tolls on S. Wales roads made it uneconomic to transport Pembrokeshire limestone to fertilise the inland farms and so created cumulative agricultural distress. In 1839, and between 1842 and 1844 bands of rioters led by a man or men called Rebecca and dressed in women's clothes destroyed toll gates and houses. The disturbances were eventually quelled, but the toll burdens in S. Wales were reduced by Ld. Cawdor's Act, 1844.

RÉCAMIER, Mme (1777-1849). reputedly witty and beautiful, but probably virginal, Parisian hostess of the Restoration and originator of a type of conversational *sofa*. Everybody who was anybody, including Chateaubriand, went to her salons. Her conversation is little recorded.

RECEIPT ROLLS (c. 1154-) contained accounts of money received; they were superseded by the Pells (-1834) after periods of much dislocation and omission in the reigns of Henry VI and Richard III.

RECEIVER-GENERAL was an official of the Inland Revenue. The money formerly paid to him could more conveniently be paid to the Bank of England and his office was abolished in 1891.

RECHABITES. A teetotal benefit society established in 1835. See Jeremiah 35.

RECIPROCITY, as under Huskisson's Reciprocity of Duties Act 1823, is the granting by treaty of mutual, usually economic concessions between states, to the disadvantage of other states. Such treaties are inconsistent with the General Agreement on Tariffs and Trade (G.A.T.T.).

RECOGNITION, DIPLOMATIC is a political act whereby a govt. publicly undertakes to treat a particular body of people as a govt. or international personality equal in status to itself. It has far reaching effects and confers great advantages; the recognised govt.'s. laws, passport, flag and currency must be taken into account in legal and administrative transactions and dealings with it must take place through representatives entitled to diplomatic immunity. Its subjects are entitled to the same treatment as other foreigners in the recognising state, which will not enforce against them any of the international rules against piracy or the like. Moreover the recognised govt. can no longer be impeached in the courts of the recognising power and its property and servants were until recently immune against private process. This was particularly important where the recognised state holds extreme socialist doctrines and claims to own all the national property and to employ all its subjects.

Recognition is of two kinds. **(1)** To recognise a

country's independence involves defining its area and to that extent repudiating previous obligations to another power claiming local sovereignty. A unilateral recognition of this kind is therefore an act of hostility towards the latter, which may take counter-measures. Recognition by one country commits no others and most states will hold back until there is little danger of retaliation, because either the new state becomes sufficiently strong to be able to protect its friends, or the previous sovereign recognises it and so abandons its right of retaliation, or the recognising state intends or is at war with the previous sovereign. Spanish recognition of the Dutch Republic implicit in the truce of 1609 brought recognition by most European powers; Spanish explicit recognition in 1648 brought full acceptance into the comity of nations. The U.S.A. was recognised by France, which was at war with Britain, in 1778. British recognition under the T. of Paris in 1782 was followed in 1783 by that of Prussia, Sweden and Spain.

(2) To recognise a new govt. established by revolutionary means in an existing state involves no territorial definition, but does involve other problems. It is said that the new govt. ought to control the whole or most of the national territory, but the facts may be in doubt if the revolution has been fomented by a foreign power and in cases of civil war expediency may require half measures. Hence there is an accepted distinction of practice between recognition *de facto* (in fact) and *de jure* (in law). In the former case there will be arrangements between the revolutionary regime and the recognising power protecting subjects and property and regulating trade. The wider the scope of such arrangements the more they are likely to be treated as hostile acts by the lawful govt.

Premature Recognition (3) In a case of rebellion early recognition is in fact, if not in form, an interference in the internal affairs of the country concerned; such 'premature recognitions' are designed to assist the rebels and represent, or may lead to, disturbance of international peace. Since World War I recognitions have often been made through international bodies such as the League of Nations or the U.N. The U.S.A. has, however, tended to be guided by puritanical considerations acceptable to American voters, such as that the new govt. should not have been established by immoral or revolutionary means and shall be ready to observe international law. Hence it did not recognise the Communist govt. of Russia until 1931 and in 1932, by the so-called STIMSON DOCTRINE, influenced the League of Nations to refuse recognition to new states and to territorial changes effected by illegal force. This was applied against Manchukuo (1933), the annexation of Ethiopia by Italy (1936) and of Austria by Germany (1938). These gestures probably caused hardship to the annexed peoples without harming the aggressors. Since World War II there have been many cases of collective recognition through the U.N., but the influence of American thought was still manifest in the acceptance between 1945 and 1971 of the govt. of Formosa as the govt. of a China actually ruled from Peking by Communists. In 1971 the Peking regime was admitted as possessing all the charter rights of China and the Formosa govt. was expelled by a resolution which declared that its positions in the U.N. had all along been held illegally. This seems to indicate that the Formosan regime, which certainly controlled Formosa, was not the govt. of that island at all.

RECONCILIATION PARLIAMENT (1554). The parliament called to effect the reunion with Rome under Mary I.

RECONSTRUCTION, MINISTRY OF, existed from Aug. 1917 to July 1919.

RECORDE, Robert (?1510-58), Fellow of All Souls, was the first writer in English on arithmetic, geometry and astronomy and apparently introduced algebra into England. Besides inventing the equality sign (=) and several ways of extracting square roots, he practised as a court physician under Edward VI and Mary I and was

General Surveyor of mines in 1551. He died in the Queen's Bench prison, probably as a debtor.

RECOVERY. *See* LAND TENURE (ENGLAND)-4.

RECTITUDINES SINGULARUM PERSONARUM (Lat: Rights of Particular Individuals), an early 11th cent. private compilation describing the various classes of persons to be found on an estate and some principles of estate management.

RECTOR. *See* ADVOWSON AND TITHE.

RECULVER (Lat: REGULBIUM) (Kent). Roman fortified station at the northern entrance to the Wantsum. It was a prosperous village in the early Middle Ages but declined as the Wantsum silted up.

RECUSANCY was refusal to attend religious service established by statute. The Act of Uniformity of 1552 enjoined Sunday church attendance subject to ecclesiastical censure and imposed heavy prison sentences for attending any service not contained in the B.C.P. Repealed by Mary in 1553, it was restored by Elizabeth's Act of Uniformity 1559, when recusancy became punishable in the alternative by forfeiture of one shilling to the churchwardens for the poor. As the rich could afford it and the poor were paying themselves, the enactment was, as Elizabeth intended, virtually a dead letter. In 1570, however, the Bull *Regnans in Excelsis* purported to release her subjects from her obedience and the seminarist and Jesuit missions encouraged their followers to demonstrate their faith. In 1581 the fine was increased to £20 a month and an offender had to find two sureties for £200 to be of good behaviour. Heavy fines and imprisonment were also imposed on those who heard mass willingly and in 1586 the Crown was empowered to seize and enjoy two thirds of a recusant's landed property. Popish recusancy was considered dangerous because it occurred especially in the north, which had been in rebellion some months before the issue of the Bull; but there were bodies of recusants also in Wales, the South Welsh border and in the Midland counties of Warwick, Stafford and Derby. The economic pressure of the fines was severe upon the gentry who might be expected to lead R. Catholic opinion and rebellion and this in its turn led exiles like Cardinal Allen to press urgently for naval action against England.

The number of recusants is believed to have been about 5% of the adult population and relaxations of the law at the end of the 17th cent. did not apparently increase it, probably because it had been inefficiently administered.

REDAN. *See* CRIMEAN WAR.

RED BOOK. *See* MABINOGION.

***RED BOOK OF THE EXCHEQUER* (c. 1230)** was compiled partly by Alexander of Swereford, a Baron of the Exchequer, as a record of royal tenants' liability to scutage, but it includes a register of surrenders to the Crown, the Black Book of the Exchequer, the *Dialogus de Scaccario*, the *Leges Henrici Primi* and some charters.

RED CROSS. The international society was founded under the inspiration of the Swiss HENRI DUNANT (1828-1910), who had witnessed the sufferings of the wounded in the Franco-Austrian war of 1859. His agitation resulted in the GENEVA CONVENTION of 1864, to which most states had adaered by 1907. It established the immunity of the Red Cross workers in war and laid down conditions for the treatment of prisoners. The BRITISH RED CROSS was founded in 1870. The convention was revised in 1906. The Japanese disregarded the Convention in World War II.

REDCLIFFE-MAUD, John Maud (1906-82), Ld. (1967) was permanent Sec. to the Ministry of Education from 1945 to 1952, Fuel and Power 1952 to 1959, Ambassador to S. Africa from 1961 to 1963, Chairman of the Local Govt. Management Committee from 1964 to 1967, of the Royal Commission on Local Govt. from 1966 to 1969 and of the Committee on Interests in Local Govt. from 1974 to 1974. *See* LOCAL ADMINISTRATION – ENGLAND AND WALES.

REDDITCH. *See* NEW TOWNS.

REDEMPTIONER. An immigrant who redeemed the cost of his passage by working in the ship, or from his earnings on arrival.

REDESDALE. *See* MITFORD.

"RED FRIDAY" (31 July 1925). In response to the threat by an alliance of the mining and transport unions to black coal shipments, the govt. agreed to set up the Samuel Commission to examine miners' conditions and to subsidise miners' wages. It was less of a union victory than was at first thought, for it strengthened the resolve of those govt. supporters who wanted a show-down with the unions and who had one in the General Strike of 1926.

REDISTRIBUTION OF SEATS ACT, 1885 (*see* REPRESENTATION OF THE PEOPLE ACT, 1885) was part of a sweeping package of legislation. It abolished the ancient method of parliamentary representation by communities and substituted representation by single-member constituencies (save in the City of London and the Universities). For this purpose 82 English, 2 Scottish groups and 24 Irish boroughs were thrown into their surrounding counties. 58 boroughs were to have a single member each. The larger boroughs were given more members (e.g. Birmingham 7, Liverpool 9, Dublin 4) but divided internally into single-member constituencies and the surrounding counties also acquired more members (e.g. Leicestershire 4, Lincoln 7) but were thus divided. Constituency boundaries did not cross county or the surviving parliamentary borough boundaries, which were to some extent an obstacle to equality of size.

REDMOND (1) John Eward (1856-1918), originally a clerk in the House of Commons, became an Irish M.P. (New Ross 1881, Waterford from 1891). Between 1882 and 1884 he raised large sums for the Irish Party in Canada and the U.S.A. After the O'Shea divorce he led the Parnellites, until the party reunited under his own leadership in 1900. He was primarily responsible on the Irish side for the success of the Land Conference which led to the Irish Land Act of 1903; and he eventually got the Liberals to introduce the Home Rule Bill of 1912. He was a strong constitutionalist, believing in advance through accepted forms and was taken by surprise by Carson's militant Ulster Unionism and by the reaction which led to the formation of the Irish National Volunteers. During World War I he encouraged Irishmen to join the forces of the Crown; consequently the 1916 rising was a bitter blow. Nevertheless he persevered, assembling a convention at Dublin to draft a constitution for Ireland within the Empire (July 1917-Mar. 1918), but he died suddenly. His brother **(2) William Hoey (1861-1917)** was also an Irish M.P. (N. Fermanagh 1885, E. Clare from 1891). He agreed with his brother, joined the British Army, made a celebrated appeal for Home Rule on behalf of "we who are about to die" (Mar. 1917) and was killed on the Western Front.

RED RIVER SETTLEMENT (Manitoba). After the British conquered Canada, Anglo-French Canadian rivalry continued through the operations of the English HUDSON BAY Co. operating from York Factory on Hudson Bay, southwards, and the N.W. Co. of Montreal operating westwards. Their routes intersected at the junction of the Red and Assiniboine Rivers, a place then called THE FORKS, later WINNIPEG: here the N.W. Co. built FORT GIBRALTAR in 1804. In 1811 Ld. Selkirk founded an agricultural settlement called ASSINIBOIA on the Red River. A violent struggle ensued. The Hudson Bay Co. destroyed Fort Gibraltar, the N.W. Co. the agricultural settlement, but independent colonists kept arriving and in 1821 the two companies amalgamated. By 1859 the Red River settlements were also receiving colonists by steam boat from the south and the American West. The Dominion acquired the area from the Hudson Bay Co. in 1869.

RED SEA. In this hot rainless channel about 1200 miles long, the prevailing winds are northerly in the north, southerly in the south and variable in the middle. It was thus a difficult trade route in the sailing era, though always significant until the 17th cent. Power driven ships conferred independence of the wind and made the building of the Suez Canal (1869) an economic proposition.

REDUNDANCY PAYMENTS ACTS, introduced by the Wilson govt. in 1965 created a right to a payment when a job ceased to exist. The amount depended on length of service beyond two years, and age. The employer was liable but could claim about 40% back from the govt. The object was to create flexibility of employment.

REDVERS (from Reviers in the Bessin). This family, descended from the Counts of Eu, received wide estates especially in Devon at the Conquest. **(1) Baldwin of Moeles (?-1100)** was Sheriff of Devon. For his brother **(2) Richard of Clare (?-1090)** *see* CLARE. Their cousin **(3) Baldwin of Clare (?-1145)** was captured with King Stephen at Lincoln in 1141, while the grandson of (1), **(4) Baldwin of Redvers (?-1155) E. of DEVON** raised Devon and the I. of Wight and held Corfe against Stephen in 1139. He also raised his Norman lands. The Redvers earldom became extinct in 1262 and the family in 1293.

REDWALD or RAEDWALD, King (r. 616-27). *See* EAST ANGLIA; KENT.

REEVE (A.S: overseer) (1) In a manor, the manager of the unfree labour. **(2)** In a Hundred (where he was sometimes called the HUNDRED MAN) he was responsible to the Sheriff for the farm of the Hundred. He originally held the Hundred Court monthly but from Henry II's time fortnightly. In addition he had to attend the County Court. **(3)** Sometimes the word meant a Sheriff's deputy. **(4)** In Canada he was the chairman of a village or town council.

RE-EXPORTS. *See* NAVIGATION ACTS; WALPOLE'S EXCISE and FINANCIAL REFORMS.

REFEREES, COURT OF. A body of 7 M.Ps. with the Speaker, his Counsel and the Deputy Speaker, which determines the right of a person to petition against a private bill, if his *locus standi* is challenged.

REFERENDUM. Provisions for referenda form part of the Australian constitution. In Britain 4 have been held, each under a special Act viz: **(1)** In N. Ireland in 1973. **(2)** For the U.K. generally on the Common Market as constituted in 1974. **(3 & 4)** In Wales and Scotland on Devolution in 1979. In addition referenda are held every 7 years in Welsh districts on the question of Sunday opening hours for public houses. In general electorates vote 'No' to any question put to them.

REFHAM, Richer (?-after 1321), Norfolk mercer, migrated to London and became an alderman in 1298. He made his fortune in the Flemish wool trade and invested it in city property, mostly bought from declining aldermanic families.

"REFORM ACT" 1867. *See* REPRESENTATION OF THE PEOPLE ACT, 1867.

REFORM ACT (IRELAND) 1832 (*see* REFORM HILLS, 1831-1832) increased Irish representation in the Commons from 100 to 105 by giving Belfast, Dublin University, Galway, Limerick and Waterford 2 members instead of one and it introduced a £10 householder franchise in the boroughs. Other changes were considered unnecessary because of the reforms made by the 1800 Act of Union.

REFORM BILLS (1831-32). There were in all 7 such bills. Three for England and subsequently one each for Scotland and Ireland settled the issues of principle, but the consequent English and Irish boundary changes required 2 more.

(1) R. Catholic emancipation had been forced on Wellington by 1829 by the prospect of Irish electoral revolt, if not actual rebellion. The Belgian revolution, the overthrow of Charles X of France and the death of

George IV (both reactionary Kings) followed close together in 1830. Reform had been canvassed intermittently for some time and agitated by the London Radical Reform Association and the Birmingham Political Union (Birmingham was unrepresented in the Commons); new change was generally in the air. Huskisson, for example, was killed by one of the new steam locomotives in Sept. 1830 and there were agricultural riots (for which 9 were hanged and 450 transported) in the autumn. The landed interest, it was argued, was anachronistically over-represented in the Constitution, even if the geography of representation had not been out of date. This had remained almost unchanged since the 1670s, i.e. over a century before the Industrial Revolution began to urbanise and redistribute the population northwards.

(2) The chief features of the pre-1832 system were:-

(a) England south of a line from the Wash to Tewkesbury was far over-represented, e.g. Cornwall, Devon and Dorset with their boroughs returned 90 members: the comparable 3 Ridings of Yorkshire 30.

(b) Many of the boroughs represented were tiny, sometimes non-existent, while important cities such as Birmingham, Bradford, Brighton, Leeds, Manchester, Sheffield and Wolverhampton, elected no-one. The London area was represented only by the 6 members for London, Westminster and Southwark.

(c) The few electors of the tiny so-called rotten or *pocket* boroughs could be bullied or bribed (they voted openly) and consequently some 276 seats could be (and were) bought and sold, often for cash, more often for political advancement and Crown jobs for relatives and friends. This was not wholly bad, because it enabled interests which might not otherwise gain a hearing (e.g. the HEIC and the Sugar Lobby) to buy their way in. In this odd fashion, for example, India was said to have been virtually represented by Old Sarum (a depopulated hilltop).

(d) The franchise varied from the excitable potwalloper democracy of Westminster and Preston, with some 50,000 electors each, to a substantial body of freemen (e.g. City of London, York), to narrow or self perpetuating oligarchies of aldermen or capital burgesses incorporated under a charter (*see* CORPORATIONS, MUNICIPAL PRE-1834, VARIETY), or finally to the burgage franchise confined to the owners of a few tenements, represented, in one case, by 7 stones in a wall. At Old Sarum the 7 burgess electors pitched a tent in which to elect their 2 M.Ps.

(e) Yorkshire had 4 M.P.s. after 1821; otherwise English and Irish county areas had two each, Scottish and Welsh one. The rural franchise was uniformly defined and vested in those owning freehold land worth the, by 1832, very low sum of 40s. a year. The county qualification was thus haphazard since it excluded copyholders (besides leaseholders and other tenants and inhabitants) whose property might be worth much more.

(f) About 4000 Scottish voters elected 45 M.P.s. Sutherland had only 128. In the burghs the franchise was mostly confined to members of the corporation, who normally appointed their successors. Edinburgh's sole M.P. was elected by 33 people. The other burghs were grouped for these elections and usually took it in turns to make the nomination. Three pairs of counties (Clackmannan and Kinross; Nairn and Cromarty; Bute and Caithness) also took turns. Of these Clackmannan is said to have had one voter who conscientiously voted for himself; Cromarty consisted of 12 rural enclaves scattered from end to end of Ross, while Caithness and Bute were 250 miles apart by the shortest route. The Scottish vote was virtually controlled by the Ld. Advocate.

(g) Welsh boroughs were grouped by counties.

(h) Of the 100 Irish M.P.s., 64 sat for counties, 2 each were elected by Dublin and Cork, one by Dublin University. Thirty-one mostly very small boroughs elected one each.

(3) The First bill (*see below*) was primarily drafted by Ld. John Russell and a Cabinet committee. Carefully designed to do some justice and to remedy scandals while maintaining the old balance of power, it was greeted when introduced by Grey (1st M.) as if it was much more revolutionary than it really was. The Tories were transported with fury. This produced a public ready to rise in indignation against obstructive Tories and only a few radical extremists thought that it did not go far enough. Irish members helped the bill through its second reading (23 Mar.) by a majority of one, but the govt. was defeated in committee and asked William IV for a dissolution. When he heard that the Lords were preparing to resolve against a dissolution he came down, despite obstruction ("Damme I'll go in a cab") and dissolved Parliament in person.

(4) The reformers secured a larger majority in the general election and the Second bill (*see below*) was brought in in June, passed the Commons with amendments in Sept. and was thrown out by the Lords on 8 Oct. Riots broke out at Derby and Nottingham at once; at Bristol three weeks later mobs sacked the major buildings. Huge demonstrations were planned for London and the govt., having announced its intention to persist, secured a prorogation. On reassembly they introduced the Third bill (Dec.).

(5) The govt's. difficulty was that an attempt to coerce the Lords might drive too many of the bill's supporters in the Commons to change sides. The bill therefore modified the proposals to win over some of the wavering peers. These were approached by the govt. while the King approached the bishops. He also agreed if necessary to create a dozen peers as a sign that more might follow. This persuaded the waverers and the bill passed its second reading in the Lords (Apr. 1832), but after Easter they decided to postpone the disfranchisement clauses until the rest of the bill had been considered. This procedural decision amounted to a claim to deal with the details as they pleased. Grey asked the King to create 50 peers: he refused to exceed 20. Grey resigned (9 May). The King sent for the Tory Ld. Lyndhurst. He advised that Wellington should be asked to form a govt. to introduce a more moderate bill. The Duke was willing but the country was not and Peel would not support him. In the prevailing disquiet the Tories agreed with Peel. Hence the King had to send for Grey again. He insisted that William IV should undertake to create enough peers to carry the bill and resumed office (16 May). The undertaking was made known to the peers and Wellington and Lyndhurst agreed not to vote. This ensured its passage (4 June). The Scottish, Irish and Boundary bills were then passed as a matter of routine.

REFORM BILLS – ENGLISH – SOME PARTICULARS (*see previous entry*). As will be seen from the table on the next page the differences between the first two and the final bill and Act were radical.

REFORM ACT (SCOTLAND) 1832 (*see* REFORM BILLS 1831-1832) raised Scottish M.P.s from 45 to 53 and gave the vote in the burghs to £10 householders.

(1) *Constituencies.* The paired counties of Elgin and Nairn, Ross and Cromarty, and Clackmannan and Kinross (with some adjacent Perthshire and Stirling areas) jointly elected one M.P. each. The other 27 counties elected one M.P. each; Edinburgh and Glasgow 2 each; Aberdeen, Dundee, Greenock, Paisley and Perth one each; and 69 small burghs and towns were arranged in 14 groups electing one each.

(2) *Franchise.* £10 householders were added to the burgh vote.

REFORMADO. An officer who, owing to the *reforming* or disbandment of his company, was left without a command, but was retained in his rank and pay; or a volunteer serving as an officer but without a commission.

A. FIRST ENGLISH BILL

1. Constituencies

Disfranchisements				*Enfranchisements*		
	Number	*seats*			*Number*	*New seats*
Boroughs wholly	60	119		Large towns and new	11	22
Reduced from two to one M.P.	47	47		London districts		
				Smaller towns	20	20
				Counties increased from 2 to 4	26	52
Borough reduced from 4 to two	1	2		Yorkshire increased from 4 to 6		2
Total seats abolished		168		I of Wight	1	1
				Total seats created		97
Net REDUCTION of English seats	71					

2. Electors' Qualifications

Boroughs	*Counties*
Occupation of buildings worth £10 a year.	40s free holders
	£10 copyholders
	£50 tenants for seven years or more.

B. SECOND ENGLISH BILL

Similar to the above but all £50 tenants including tenants-at-will added by amendment to the county franchise.

C. THIRD ENGLISH BILL AND ACT

1. Constituencies

	Seats abolished
(a) 56 two-member constituencies wholly disfranchised	112
(b) 30 two-member boroughs reduced to one member	30

	New seats
(c) 22 new boroughs given two members	44
(d) 20 new boroughs given one member	20
(e) 57 Welsh boroughs to share 13 seats	13
(f) 25 counties divided into two each with two members	25
(g) 7 counties divided into three returning one member each	14

but

(h) 13 cities and towns included electorally in their surrounding county.

Net INCREASE of English seats	4

2. Electors' Qualifications

Similar to the Second Bill

REFORMATION – GENERAL (*see* COUNTER-REFORMATION) **(1)** This complex change in European society and beliefs, particularly affecting relations between Church and State and between priesthood and laity, arose from a convergence of doubts and disputes over doctrines, ecclesiastical abuses and the political attitudes to the ambitions of new states. These were related to economic upheavals, the great Discoveries, especially in America and Turkish military expansion in Europe and Africa.

(2) There had already been important and sometimes armed heresies, such as the 13th cent. Albigensians in France, the 14th and 15th cent. Hussites in Bohemia and the English Lollards, but few doubted the Church's right to condemn them, or the duty of princes to enforce such condemnation. Most people, however, were aware of the Church's imperfections. A body concerned with moral and divine law contained far too many, often of the highest rank, who openly and scandalously flouted both. The Church manifestly failed to set the right example. In particular its wealth was an outrage in an organisation which preached the virtues of poverty, modesty and charity.

(3) The states rising upon the new technology and the ruins of feudalism needed funds for their expensive forces and administrations. There had always been a temptation to raid the ecclesiastical coffers (*see* K. JOHN;

WILLIAM II) by one means or another, but it had hitherto been accepted that this was, in principle, improper.

(4) The economic upheavals followed and had sometimes been accompanied by plagues of horrifying virulence. People who had not enough to eat might take what they could. Those living among the thousands painfully dying might doubt the goodness of the dispensation expounded by the Church. Moreover Asiatic and Levantine political disturbances were changing the pattern and subject matter of commerce.

(5) The Turks had overthrown the Christian empire of the East; they were in possession of the Holy Places and other Christian powers were falling before them. At the end of the 15th cent. they had raided northern Italy and briefly occupied Otranto. It seemed that secular power was more likely to defend Christendom than God.

(6) The geographical discoveries challenged the Church's claim as teacher by revealing vast and obvious facts which it had known nothing about. Scientific, particularly astronomical discoveries were soon to carry the process further and in many directions.

(7) Reform of the Church from within or in co-operation with the princes had long occupied the attention of the far-sighted or the well disposed. There had been many attempts, notably in connection with the Great Schism (1377-1417) but the downward slide continued. The widespread sale through bankers of indulgences, i.e. the sale of things eternal for things ephemeral (not a new practice) in the early 16th cent. to raise funds for a new St. Peter's church at Rome, involved a flagrant commercialism, by such papal salesmen as John Tetzel and Bernhardin Samson and the exploitation of the superstitious and the ignorant. To challenge the practice, Martin Luther, already a distinguished professor of theology, found it necessary to challenge the doctrinal foundations of papal authority and the church institutions based upon it. The publication at Wittenberg of his XCV Theses in 1517 created an intellectual and ideological basis for many different discontents and doubts. Within a year Huldreich Zwingli had adopted a similar position in Switzerland.

(8) The precedent for a divided Christendom had been set by the Hussites who had established a doctrinally and politically separate church in Bohemia in the 15th cent., but this had at least been contained. Luther's challenge succeeded initially because too many rulers supported it for it to be put down by force; but now the idea of a Christendom without a single doctrinal supremacy spread rapidly and it was open to anyone with coherent views and a talent for publicity to put forward doctrines and found sects. Attempts have been made to relate the effects to some kind of nationalism but there is little evidence for this hind-sighted view. It took some time for the concept of new sects to be accepted and when it was, their basis was neither country nor nation; but the rapid development of the new invention of printing accelerated the spread of such notions. The rulers, however, were as authoritarian as the Pope. They claimed to choose and chose their subjects' religion. This was the principle of the Religious Peace of Augsburg (1556) in Germany and of the fluctuations of religious legislation in England and Scotland.

(9) The theocratic republic established in 1541 by John Calvin at Geneva took a similar view, but with the gloss that it alone might make the choice. It set about subverting the authority of the rulers from below. Its printing presses flooded the west with propaganda. Its missionaries penetrated with decreasing secrecy to all levels. Between 1555 and 1560, through John Knox, it inspired the creation of a Calvinist political state in Scotland. The French Wars of Religion began in 1562. Calvinist organisation began to grip the Netherlands from 1563 and led, by way of Spanish over-reaction, to the outbreak of civil war in 1572. In 1564 the Puritans had begun to attack the Anglican settlement but their influence developed only slowly; they had to deal with an established Reformation Church; and with the Queen's personality and the national preoccupation with maritime prosperity and anti-Spanish feeling. Moreover it was unwise to undermine a principal ally, the insurgent Dutch.

(10) The 17th cent. English political controversies were in part a late secondary convulsion of the Reformation movements. Some Puritans were Calvinists, others held Low Church opinions, yet others (e.g. the Levellers) were social revolutionaries. They attacked the Anglican Church and the Crown, as it were, from the left. After a temporary supremacy the Calvinists were defeated but at the Restoration both they and their opponents were exhausted. In the generation which followed, these controversies took on a constitutional form involving a steady political resistance to a French and Catholic attack from the right. By the time of Q. Anne purely religious violence or oppression was (with interruptions) dying out. *See also* BIBLE; EXCLUSION BILL; LOLLARDY; LUTHERANISM; MONASTERIES – DISSOLUTION OF; NONCONFORMISTS; SIX ARTICLES; SUBMISSION OF THE CLERGY; SUPREMACY; SUPPLICATION AGAINST THE ORDINARIES; THIRTY-NINE ARTICLES; UNIFORMITY – ACTS OF; *and the articles on reigns from Henry VIII to James II.*

REFORM CLUB was founded in 1836 as a radical and Whig club in opposition to the Tory Carlton Club.

REFORM LEAGUE was a popular organisation of the 1860s dedicated to widening the franchise. It reached its summit in 1867 with a demonstration in Hyde Park 400,000 strong in favour of giving all ratepayers, compounders and non-compounders alike, the vote. The cautious but plausible Reform Acts of that year took the steam out of it.

REFORMATION PARLIAMENT (Scotland 1560). *See* MARY, Q. OF SCOTS-7.

REFORMATORY SCHOOLS for young offenders otherwise punishable with imprisonment, were set up by statute in 1854 on the lines of similar voluntary establishments functioning since 1818. They were thought to have greatly reduced juvenile and potential crime by segregating the inmates from the hardened prison population. *See* BORSTAL; APPROVED SCHOOLS.

REFRIGERATION, in so far as it was practised at all, depended before 1880 on the use of local natural ice in thatched ice pits. There was also a trade in ice in the Middle East from the Caucasus, in Europe from Scandinavia and in the U.S.A. from New England. In the 19th cent. this became highly developed. A mechanical ice maker was, however, first patented in Britain in 1834 and the first refrigerator ship came into use in 1879. This revolutionised the food, particularly meat, trades and resulted in the immense growth of cattle and sheep raising in the Argentine, Australia and New Zealand. *See* BACON, FRANCIS.

REFUGEES. Britain accepted religious refugees from 16th to 19th cents., particularly from the Low Countries and France. They brought important skills in textiles and jewellery and many settled in E. Anglia. In 20th cent. there were political and racial refugees from Nazi Germany, Basques, and Asians from Uganda. These brought business capacities and mostly settled in the big cities. In the 1990s, though the public remained tolerant, British immigration laws became less liberal and would-be refugees were sometimes maltreated while their background was investigated.

REGALIA **(Lat: Things appertaining to royalty). (1)** According to the civil lawyers, consisted of the powers of war and peace, life and death and judicature, the right to ownerless goods and minting of money and the power to make assessments; **(2)** MAJORA Regalia (Lat: The greater regalia) meant the sum of the royal rights, dignity and prerogative; **(3)** MINORA Regalia (Lat: The lesser regalia) meant the Revenue; **(4)** The word is now most commonly used for the Crown Jewels or other marks of royalty, especially those used at a coronation or opening of Parliament.

REGALITY was a territory within which the lord had the royal rights of justice. In England and Wales the regalities were all palatinates or lordships marcher and ceased to be important by Tudor times. In Scotland regalities covered much of the Highlands and Isles, besides the great Douglas holdings in the Lowlands. Though they were in decline from about 1500 they were not abolished until 1747.

REGARD. *See* FOREST-3.

REGENCY. *See* ARCHITECTURE, BRITISH; GEORGE IV.

REGENSBURG = RATISBON (q.v.).

REGENT and COUNCILLORS OF STATE (1) A regent performs the sovereign's functions during minority or other incapacity; councillors of state during absence. No advance statutory provision for such contingencies existed until 1937. Between 1689 and 1760 Kings appointed Lds. Justices to act for them during absences abroad and commonly bound them by detailed instructions. A similar practice obtained in Ireland during vacancies in the Lieutenancy or Deputyship. A regent is always the closest relative, councillors of state are also relatives, but Lds. Justices generally were not.

(2) George Augustus Frederick, P. of Wales (later George IV) became Prince-Regent for George III by an

Act of 1811 which conferred all the royal powers save those of creating peerages and granting reversions of offices before 1 Feb. 1812. If George III had been insane he could not have assented to the Act, which would therefore have been void. The Act recited that his indisposition had for the present so far interrupted the personal exercise of his authority that he required assistance and assent was given by a commission – to which his assent was also needed.

REGENT STREET and REGENT'S PARK (London) were laid out by John Nash as part of a scheme, begun in 1812, to connect Carlton House in the Mall with another royal residence to be built in a park, to consist of the old Marylebone gardens with some added land and surrounded by grand terraced residences such as Park Crescent and Cumberland Terrace. The second residence was never built. The park was opened in 1838.

REGIAM MAJESTATEM (Lat: the Royal Majesty) is an anonymous adaptation of the English lawbook *Glanvill* made in the 1330s to suit Scottish conditions. It was applied practically, if with occasional revisions, for the next 3 centuries.

REGICIDES. Of the 135 members of the 'court' set up to try Charles I, over one third did not act and sentence of death was agreed by 67 of them. Of these again only 59 could be induced to sign the execution warrant and these together with the executive officials are known as the *regicides*. At the Restoration 29 were brought to trial and sentenced to death, but only 10 were executed.

REGIMENT, in foreign armies, was usually a fighting unit roughly equivalent to a British brigade, but in the British army either (a) a fighting formation of cavalry tanks or artillery equivalent to an infantry battalion or (b) more importantly, a non-fighting organisation based on a barracks called a regimental depot and responsible for recruiting, training, records and background administration of a number of fighting units (infantry battalions, cavalry regiments, etc.). Under the Cardwell system, there were usually 2 fighting units in peacetime; one abroad, the other quartered at the depot which supplied trained recruits and officers. Each depot had a recruiting area usually in the county after which the regiment was named. Territorial (part-time) units also existed and were serviced by the regimental system.

REGINALD, E. of CORNWALL (?-1175), a bastard of Henry I, supported the Empress Matilda against Stephen from his important Cornish lands and she made him E. of Cornwall in 1141. He was no enthusiast for her, however, and loyally supported Henry II when Stephen died.

REGION is apparently any substantial area which does not coincide with other accepted jurisdictional or administrative areas. A **homogeneous** region (e.g. the S. Wales coalfields) is one in which, for the purposes for which the region is defined, the similarities from place to place are more significant than the differences. A **nodal** region (e.g. the Home Counties) is an area where effort, activities or elements concentrate upon a centre.

Eight regional COMMISSIONERS were appointed during World War II to carry on the functions of govt. in case of invasion or paralysis at the centre. The St. Lawrence Seaway involves a regional plan dealing with parts of 2 sovereign nations. Regional PLANNING BOARDS were set up in Britain in 1967 to attempt to co-ordinate planning and development by the exchange of information between county planning authorities and govt. departments. Nine **Scottish regions** replaced the counties in 1975.

REGIONALISM is local partisanship in politics or the presentation of local background as an important element in literary productions, e.g. in the works of D. H. Lawrence, Trollope or the Brontës.

REGISTER OF M.P.'s INTERESTS was set up in 1975. The 9 types of interest compulsorily registrable are employment, company directorships, clients for whom professional services are provided in relation to the House of Commons, financial sponsorship, overseas visits, benefits from foreign govts. or organisations, substantial land or property and companies in which the M.P. has a shareholding exceeding 1%. Even though an M.P. has registered an interest he must still declare it in debate.

REGISTRATION, POPULATION. Parish registers of *baptisms, marriages and burials* were required to be kept from 1538, though some earlier registers exist. Foolproof rules for preserving them have never been enacted, but a very large number survive in parish chests and churches, diocesan registries, county archives, etc. Family bibles were also recognised as evidence, as were registers kept by nonconformist chapels and denominations. In 1837 registers were put in the care of the General Register Office, which was also required to operate a centrally controlled system of registration of *births, marriages and deaths*. See SOMERSET HOUSE.

REGISTER OF SASINES (Scot.). All deeds dealing in Scottish land must be entered in this register established in 1617.

REGISTRATION, LAND. The Land Registry was set up in 1862 and reformed in 1875. In certain areas, especially London, registration at the first change of ownership was compulsory and voluntary registration was permissible everywhere at any time. After World War II it was decided to register all titles compulsorily in London, Surrey and certain other areas, but this entailed so much work that in 1967 voluntary registration elsewhere was suspended. It was in due course resumed in most counties by 1994.

REGIUM DONUM (Lat: royal gift) was a payment originally made by Charles II to English Presbyterian ministers after the Declaration of Indulgence of 1672. In Ireland it was regularly made from 1690. In England George I paid £500 to the Presbyterian historian Edmund Calamy III in 1723 and from 1727 the *Donum* was paid annually to the Presbyterian, Baptist and Congregationalist churches. It ceased in England in 1851 and in Ireland in 1869.

REGIUS PROFESSORSHIPS were first established at Cambridge by Henry VIII in 1540 and at Oxford in 1546, in Divinity, Law, Medicine, Hebrew and Greek. Others have since been added.

REGNANS IN EXCELSIS (1570) was the Bull issued by Pius V excommunicating Elizabeth I and purporting to absolve her subjects from their allegiance. See ELIZABETH I-11; RECUSANCY.

REGNENSES. See BRITAIN, ROMAN-7.

REGRATING was a monopolistic practice consisting in buying up all the goods of a given class destined for a particular market, withholding them to create a shortage and then selling slowly at a higher price. It was an offence until 1847, by which time railways had made it impracticable.

REGULAR CLERGY followed a rule, i.e. monks, friars and certain canons.

REGULARIS CONCORDIA (Lat: Rule Agreement) was a standardised monastic rule settled at the Council of Winchester under King Edgar and reflecting the views of Dunstan, Oswald and Aethelwold and precedents obtained from Fleury and Ghent. It is unlikely that it was ever uniformly imposed in practice. An epilogue by the King freed all monasteries from having to give *heriot* on the demise of their Abbot.

REGULATING or MASSACHUSETTS GOVT. ACT, 1774, revoked the Massachusetts Charter and abolished the colony's Town Meetings.

REGULATION OF RAILWAYS ACT 1889 arose from the great Armagh crash when carriages from a badly braked excursion train ran backwards down an incline into an unsignalled express train coming up. There were 330 casualties. The Act required continuous braking and block signalling systems.

REGULATORS were Carolina frontiersmen who in 1768 organised protests against their lack of representation in the local legislatures. They were crushed by force in 1771.

REGULATORS, BOARD OF (1687) was a committee under Sunderland, Jeffries and Sir Nicholas Butler appointed by James II to reorganise the political structure in the R. Catholic interest by remodelling the corporations (which elected most of the M.P.s) and membership of the Commissions of the Peace (responsible for local administration). It caused great alarm and was overtaken by the Revolution.

REICH. This curious German word, connected with "riches", means a sovereign state under a recognised individual ruler. Hence the *First Reich* was the Holy Roman Empire, the *Second Reich* the Hohenzollern empire from 1870 to 1918 and the *Third Reich* the rule of Adolf Hitler.

REICHENBACH AGREEMENTS. (1) July 1790, between Austria and Prussia at the prompting of Britain and Holland (allies of Prussia). Austria was to guarantee Belgian liberties and abandon her Turkish war and alliance with Russia. In return Prussia (and inferentially Hanover) would vote for Leopold of Austria at the imperial election and the allies would ensure that Austria would be free to put down the Belgian rebels.

(2) **June 1813.** Austria secretly agreed to join the allies against Bonaparte, if by 10 Aug. he had not accepted mediation upon the conditions which Austria had proposed to him, viz. the dissolution of the Grand Duchy of Warsaw, the reconstruction of Prussia, the restitution of the Illyrian provinces to Austria and the re-establishment of the Hanse ports. Britain agreed to pay Austria £500,000 when she entered the war.

REICHSRAT. The parliamentary assembly of the non-Hungarian part of the Habsburg Empire after 1867. The *Lands Represented in the Reichsrat* was a usual official designation of this part which included Austria proper and the Polish, Czech, Serbo-Croat and Italian areas.

REICHSTADT. D of. *See* BONAPARTE-14.

REICHSTADT MEETING (July 1876). Andrassy, the Austro-Hungarian Foreign Minister and Gorchakov, the Russian, met to co-ordinate policy as a result of the Serb and Montenegrin intervention in the Bosnian-Bulgarian revolts against the Turks. If the Turks defeated the invaders, they were not to be allowed to destroy them. If the Turks lost, Russia was to acquire S. Bessarabia as far as the Khilia (northern and main) channel of the Danube delta while Austro-Hungary was to occupy (but not annex) Bosnia, Herzegovina and Novibazar, thus keeping Serbia and Montenegro apart, maintaining the fictional unity of the Ottoman Empire and excluding the populations from Hungarian parliamentary rights. It sacrificed the interests of the non-Hungarian half of Austro-Hungary. *See* AUSTRO HUNGARY-7; BERLIN MEMORANDUM.

REICHSTAG. The Diet of the Holy Roman Empire; the Parliament of the Second German Empire and of the Republic.

REID, Robert Threshie (1846-1923) Ld. (1905) and E. (1911) LOREBURN, Liberal M.P. from 1880; Sol-Gen. and then Att.-Gen. in 1894. In 1899 he arbitrated in the Venezuela dispute and from 1899 to 1902 he was a persistent critic of the S. African War. In 1905 he became Ld. Chancellor. He established the Court of Criminal Appeal in 1907. He had to pilot the Parliament Bill through the Lords and preside over that body at the same time. He retired from politics in 1912.

REIGN OF TERROR (May 1792-July 1794). *See* FIRST COALITION, WAR OF (Feb. 1792-July 1795)-3.

REINSURANCE TREATY (1887). A secret agreement between Germany and Russia. Germany recognised that Bulgaria, Bessarabia and the Dobrudja fell within the Russian sphere of influence and consistently with this agreed to remain neutral if Austro-Hungary (Germany's

ally) attacked Russia. In return, Russia agreed to remain neutral if France attacked Germany. The treaty possibly avoided a war at the time. In the long run it sacrificed Austrian interests and encouraged Balkan nationalism.

REIS EFFENDI. The Ottoman Foreign Minister.

REITH, John Charles Walsham (1889-1971) 1st Ld. REITH OF STONEHAVEN (1940), originally a Scottish civil engineer, was wounded as a major in the Royal Engineers in World War I. In 1916-17 he was in the U.S.A. negotiating munitions contracts. He joined the British Broadcasting Corporation (B.B.C.) as Gen. Manager in 1922 and became Director-Gen. in 1927. Under his inspiration the B.B.C. did not take easy paths to popularity for he was determined that it should educate and inform as well as entertain. As a result it became the most highly respected media organisation of the world. In 1938 he became Chairman of Imperial Airways and supervised its absorption into the British Overseas Airways Corporation. In 1940 he became Minister of Information, then of Transport and then, until 1942, of Works. In 1943 to 1945 he directed the supply side of Combined Operations. His influence on the B.B.C's. integrity expired under rising attack only in the early 1990s.

REITZ, Deneys (1882-1944) was S. African Minister of Lands from 1920 to 1929. In 1929 he recounted his adventures in the Boer War in a celebrated book *Commando.* He held various ministries successively from 1933 to 1939 and was Deputy Prime Minister from 1939 to 1943 when he became High Commissioner in London.

RELAPSING FEVER (sometimes called Yellow Disease or misnamed Bilious Typhoid) seems to have had its base from ancient times in Ireland and the Scottish west coast. Epidemics coincided in both areas, but especially Dublin in 1739, 1741, 1745, 1748, 1764-5, 1799-80. 1817-19, 1826-7 and from 1842 to 1848. It spread to English cities with Irish minorities for the first time in 1847 and there was an outbreak which started among Irish immigrants in London, from 1868 to 1870. *See* EPIDEMICS, HUMAN.

RELATIVITY. *See* EINSTEIN.

RELIEF. *See* FEUDALISM-18.

RELIEF SYNOD. *See* SCOTLAND (PRESBYTERIAN) CHURCH.

RELIGIO MEDICI. *See* BROWNE, SIR THOMAS.

RELIGION, WARS OF. *See* HUGUENOTS.

RELIGIOUS ATTENDANCE, CENSUS OF. In Mar. 1851 it was found that 60% of the population, classified in 38 sects, went to church, less than half being Anglican.

RELIGIOUS TRACT SOCIETY was founded in 1799.

REMEMBRANCER. (1) In England the King's (or Queen's) Remembrancer and in Scotland the King's (or Queen's) and Ld. Treasurer's Remembrancer, were responsible for collecting Crown debts. Originally officials of the respective Exchequer Courts, they are now officers of the Supreme Court and Court of Session. (2) The City Remembrancer represents the Corporation of London in dealings with Parliament, the govt. and the Treasury.

REMITTANCE MAN. A colonial immigrant who, unable to come to terms with local life, depended on money from home.

REMONSTRANCE (Scot.) 1650, arose out of the widespread self questioning which followed the Covenanters' defeat at the B. of Dunbar. The extreme Presbyterians thought that the defeat was due to ungodliness in high places and presented a Remonstrance to the Estates demanding that Charles II (as yet uncrowned) should not be recognised as King until he had given proofs that his adherence to the Covenant was sincere. The estates condemned the document by resolution and the opposing parties became known as *Remonstrants* and *Resolutioners. See* CHARLES II-2.

REMONSTRANTS. *See* ARMINIANISM.

RENAISSANCE has provoked an infinity of books and disagreement. The following may perhaps be useful signposts.

(1) Mediaeval western man tended to assume that there was one united Christendom governed by the principles of one doctrine capable of embracing all things: religion, morals, politics, nature and aesthetics were all part of a single effort which, however imperfectly realised in practice, was aimed at the greater glory of God and guided by the Pope and the Emperor, His vice-gerents on earth. This concept underlay most thinking until well into the 13th cent., but it was shaken by certain premonitory events which created scepticism. The main events of this kind were: **(a)** the political war between the Popes and Emperors (who were supposed to guide the Christian world in co-ordinate amity) and its culmination in the judicial murder of Conradin (1268); **(b)** the abuse of the crusading principle by the Papacy in pursuit of worldly policies against Christian rulers, notably Aragon after 1282; **(c)** the introduction (c. 1280) of the mariners' compass which, by making winter navigation possible, doubled the volume of Mediterranean trade by 1300; **(d)** the degradation of the Avignon Papacy to the status of an arm of French ambition (1305-77), bringing with it the curtailment of Papal powers in England by the statutes of *Provisors* (1351) and *Praemunire* (1353); **(e)** the scandal of the Great Schism (1378-1417) which had to be healed by temporal pressure; **(f)** the lesser schisms which accompanied the Conciliar Movement (1417-60), and, finally and pervasively nearer home; **(g)** the spectacle of proud and unholy bishops, rich monasteries dedicated to poverty and illiterate and incompetent clergy teaching the people. If the well of truth was perceived to be muddied, inquirers might start looking for other wells, or might trace the contents of the existing well to an older and purer source.

(2) Unsurprisingly the Italians, who were physically closest to the centre of Christendom, led the search for new alternatives which began during the times mentioned above. DANTE Alighieri (1265-1321) argued the divine origin of the imperial office in his *De Monarchia* (1309-12) and finished the *Divina Commedia* just before he died. Giovanni BOCCACCIO (1313-75) expounded Dante and, among many works of learning also wrote fiction, a *genre* almost forgotten. He also propagated an interest in the classics which he acquired from his famous friend PETRARCH (1304-74). The philogical origins of the Renaissance lie in classical Latin, the speech of those ancients whose majestic ruins lay all about the 14th cent. Italians. It soon led to the study of classical Greek and the word 'Renaissance' sometimes refers to the rebirth of Greek linguistic and philosophical studies. Actually Greek philosophy, mainly Aristotle's, had long been part of the corpus of Christian doctrine, and classical and Byzantine science was at least rumoured in Europe through the Arabs, whose Spanish civilisation reached its apex in the last 60 years of the 14th cent. What seemed new was the rediscovery of Plato.

(3) Soon intellectual additions to the existing system were matched by challenges to some of its principles. John WYCLIF (1324-84) published his first polemic in 1366. His view of the divine origin of authority went much further than Dante's; he attacked transubstantiation and sought, by translating the Bible, to open a way of salvation where priestly guidance was unnecessary. He had high patronage. The Bohemian adherents of his doctrine under John HUS (?-1410) were, for a time, to become a political institution.

At the same time there was another challenge of a different sort. So long as war was ill disciplined and waged at handstrokes, the armoured knight and his retainers was bound to impose his will on the unarmoured peasant or townsman. But in 1346 (Crécy) and 1356 (Poictiers) disciplined professional English archers destroyed feudal armies; in 1386 (Sempach) and 1388 (Näfels) well drilled Swiss pikemen did the same; in 1415 (Agincourt) the English archers wiped out half the nobility of France. The prestige of an essentially military society was undermined.

(4) The ideas which focused towards personal effort rather than received authority, magnified the human being and made him the centre of interest. He, not God, became the measure of all things. They also drew attention away from the prevailing Gothic of ecclesiastical piety. A new realistic art observed nature rather than symbolised it. A new architecture arose, based on Roman and, incidentally, pagan models. The phenomenal rise of FLORENCE, the construction of its cathedral dome (1420-34) by BRUNELLESCHI (1377-1446) and of the bronze doors of its Baptistery (1403-34) by Lorenzo GHIBERTI (1378-1455) are commonly accepted seminal events of the aesthetic revolution, to which the MEDICI family, increasingly powerful from 1424, leant energetic and discriminating support.

(5) These trends received impetus from the Ottoman invasions which caused a migration of Byzantine scholars to the west through Venice and Genoa. Manuel Chrysoloras died at Constance in 1415. Moreover, Florence, by the conquest of Pisa in 1406, had acquired direct access to the sea; in 1434 it became a Papal residence and so in 1439, the scene of a church council attended by Byzantine statesmen and clerics. Greek scholarship and Romano-Byzantine architecture and engineering moved forward together.

(6) The interest in classical studies, the dissatisfaction with the existing social order, the perception of possible flaws in doctrine handed down by authority and the personal unworthiness of many of its representatives, together led men to seek truth at first, rather than second hand. Research began to replace deductive reasoning. One of the first casualties was the sacred mumbo jumbo of the church, which turned out to be bad Latin. In 1440 Lorenzo VALLA (?1406-57) proved that the Donation of Constantine was a forgery.

(7) When Martin V (r. 1417-31) returned to Rome in 1420, the spiritual capital of the world was ruinous and poor, but Florence, not far off, was in the spring tide of its wealth and inspiration. Its influence upon the Papacy would, in any case, have been profound, but in fact for 9 years (1434-43) the Papal Curia and 2 major church councils were located in Florence. The Papacy was strongly infected by the Renaissance spirit. The Popes, beginning with EUGENIUS IV (r. 1431-47) became for nearly 2 centuries patrons of art on a vast scale. NICHOLAS V (r. 1447-55) founded the Vatican library and favoured Lorenzo Valla, who was a heretic; from 1458 to 1464 the Tuscan AENEAS SYLVIUS Piccolomini (1405-64), the greatest humanist of his age, reigned as Pope under the name of Pius II; SIXTUS IV (r. 1471-84) built the Sistine Chapel and founded the Sistine Choir; from 1464 Rodrigo Borgia, a typical Renaissance politician of great acumen and personal immorality, dominated the Curia. Nephew of one Pope (Callixtus III v 1455-8) he secured the election at least of Sixtus IV and of himself as ALEXANDER VI (r. 1492-1503).

One paradoxical consequence followed. The Church, still the main European communications network, was itself a most important means for spreading Renaissance ideas. Alarming speculations were rife in the universities yet new universities were being regularly founded. The new styles were first apparent in religious art.

(8) The spread of the Renaissance had nevertheless proceeded slowly, but was now accelerated by two world shaking events. The first was the introduction of PRINTING, the second the discovery of AMERICA. Printing by movable type was probably invented for Europe in 1440. Gutenberg was printing at Mainz by 1453, Caxton at Westminster in 1476, Aldus Manutius at Venice in 1494. Hitherto, new aesthetic ideas had had the widest available audience in architecture, because anybody could see a new building. Now at last intellectual innovation had its popular medium. COLUMBUS returned from America in Mar. 1493. His printed 'Letter' describing his discovery caused European excitement. Accepted views of world geography were publicly discredited overnight, by a triumph on a vast scale of research over deduction and of the man of action over the armchair theorist.

(9) Movement, especially by ship, became easier and this improvement in communications was partly a cause and partly an effect of the growth of centralised states (which could police them) along the Baltic and Atlantic litorals. GUN POWDER had been used at Crécy (1346) but was hardly influential until Turkish artillery dominated the Bosphorus in the 1440s and French royal artillery appeared at the end of the Hundred Years' War. It was, however, so expensive that only Kings could afford it, while artillery-proof fortifications were beyond the pockets of even great noblemen – though not yet of second class powers. The upward leap of the Kings to power left all their subjects far below and gave them strength to levy new taxes. Roads, guns, trade and taxes were forming the physical structure within which the nation states developed their claim to supersede mediaeval cosmopolitanism.

(10) Renaissance classicism and aesthetics were beginning to reach N. and W. Europe by about 1500. Erasmus met the Blounts in Paris in 1496, but turned to Greek New Testament studies only after 1504. Torrigiani's tomb of Henry VII at Westminster Abbey (1512-8) is the earliest English surviving work of the Italian Renaissance. Erected at the instigation of that Renaissance man of action, Henry VIII, and completed the year after Luther touched off the Reformation, it is a fitting symbol of a moment of change in English history.

(11) St. Peter's, at Rome, is a symbol of another kind. The new styles were expensive and the money for them had to come from somewhere. Constantine's venerated basilica was demolished at the end of the 15th cent. The work of replacing it was first pursued in earnest by Julius II (1503-13), a warrior politician and patron of BRAMANTE (1444-1514), MICHELANGELO (1475-1564) and RAPHAEL (1483-1520). Erasmus attacked the Pope's warlike character in his In Praise of Folly (1509), but the indulgence pronounced in 1507 by whose sale the new cathedral was to be financed, was to come under more dangerous fire. Giovanni de'Medici, second son of Lorenzo the Magnificent, succeeded Julius as Leo X (r. 1513-21). Weak and sybaritic, this pontiff squandered money and offices, sold preferments, surrendered Papal rights to the French and, in return for a loan, gave the banking house of Fugger the concession for the sale of indulgences in Germany (1514). It was this financial manoeuvre which provoked the issue of Luther's LXXXIXV theses on 31 Oct. 1517 and rent the seamless robe of the Church. It seems likely that if the crisis had not come in this form, it would have come in some other. (See REFORMATION.)

(12) The rise of civil potentates and the seizure of ecclesiastical wealth, which took place all over Europe, was to force the intellectual and artistic practitioners to depend increasingly upon lay rather than ecclesiastical patronage. The break was not immediate, for the Church had long been as worldly as the politicians and these processes in any case extended over generations. All the same changes of emphasis were soon apparent. St. George's Chapel, Windsor, completed in 1537, was the last great church to be built in England until St. Paul's, London, over 150 years later. Secular building was soon the order of the day (see ARCHITECTURE, BRITISH). In literature the same trend became pronounced. There had, of course, always been some non-religious writing and since the 14th cent. at least some in the vernacular, but

the new literature was a secular literature appealing to a widening lay public. Macchiavelli published The Prince in 1513, Major his History of Scotland in 1521, Rabelais Pantagruel in 1532; Udall's Ralph Roister Doister, the first English comedy, was perhaps acted in 1541. Paré's surgical work and Aschams Toxophilus both appeared in 1545 and the Mirror for Magistrates in 1559.

(13) The change was founded upon the relative cheapness of printed books combined with an educational revolution. The schools and universities which had hitherto represented vestibules to a church career, now adopted classical curricula and catered for laymen. Literacy became common even if learning was a mark of professionalism. Parliamentary bills no longer had to be read, for members could read them. James Burbage (?-1597) built the first English theatre in 1576, for there were now people willing to pay to see plays, as well as people who could write them. Shakespeare's Henry VI appeared in 1590-1.

(14) The spread of education throughout secular society brought training to many different types of mind which previously would have been able to function, if at all, only within the strict physical discipline and mental compression of religion. It took generations for intellectual freedom to be achieved, nevertheless intellectual activity was nourished and could flourish with increasing vigour.

The speculative Montaigne died in 1592. GALILEO Galilei (1564-1642) was propounding his views on gravity in 1603 and Johan KEPLER (1571-1630) his theory of planetary movement in 1609. John NAPIER (1550-1617) in the last years of his life momentously adopted the decimal point, invented logarithms and experimented with the first calculating machine. In 1628 William HARVEY (1578-1657) published his discovery of blood circulation; in 1637 René DESCARTES (1596-1650) his celebrated Discours de la Méthode, and in 1651 Thomas HOBBES (1588-1679) his Leviathan. Thus the intellectual foundations of the later age of industrial materialism were consolidated in Sir Isaac NEWTON (1642-1727), their noblest exponent, who inter alia in 1666 set forth the differential and integral calculus and conceived the idea of universal gravitation. In 1672 he published his theory of light and colour and 1686-7 his Principia.

RENDEL (1) James Meadows (1799-1856), a pupil of Telford, was a famous engineer who built, inter alia, Portland Harbour and Birkenhead docks. Of his sons (2) Sir Alexander (1829-1918) succeeded in the practice and was consulting engineer to the Indian State Railways and (3) George Wightwick (1833-1902), a partner with Sir William Armstrong at Elswick, invented the hydraulic mountings for heavy naval guns and conceived the protected 'Elswick cruiser'. He was a professional civil Ld. of the Admiralty from 1882 to 1885 and then settled at Naples. He was a friend of the Empress Frederick.

RENFREW-SHIRE (Scot.). The area was inhabited by the Damnonii under the Romans, who built forts at Bishopton and Greenock to protect the flank of the Antonine wall. After the Roman evacuation (410) the area was incorporated into a British kingdom, eventually Strathclyde. The town grew up in the 11th cent., the whole coming under the Scottish Crown at the Union of 1124. Renfrew was Somerled's objective in the war of 1164 when he met his death nearby at the B. of Elderslie and by the 14th cent. the area was a Fitzalan barony. In 1314 Walter Fitzalan, High Steward of Scotland, married Marjorie Bruce. In 1396 their grandson, King Robert III conferred a charter on Renfrew and in 1404 combined the barony and the Stuart estates into a county, which with the barony of King's Kyle and the earldom of Carrick (both in Ayrshire) were to be held together by the heir to the throne. So far as the titles are concerned, this arrangement has subsisted ever since.

In the 18th cent. the county was rapidly

industrialised, the main industries being shipbuilding at Greenock, Port Glasgow and Paisley, machine tools at Johnstone and Greenock, weaving, thread, ropes and carpets.

RENGER. London city aldermanic family descended from BERENGAR, a servant of the first Norman Bp. of London. They were wine merchants, shipowners and royal dealers in foreign exchange who acquired many properties in Hertfordshire, Essex, Nottinghamshire and Suffolk. **Richard (?-1239)** was mayor from 1222 to 1227 and from 1238 and Master of the Exchange.

RENNELL. See RODD.

RENNIE (1) John (1761-1821) trained under James Watt, for whom he designed a steam engine in 1784, but practised on his own account as a civil engineer from 1791. He built or improved the London and Hull docks, the Sheerness and Chatham dockyards, the Plymouth Breakwater and Waterloo, London, Southwark and Kelso bridges. Of his sons **(2) Sir John (1794-1874)** carried on or completed many of the above; his brother and partner **(3) George (1791-1866)** managed the firm's mechanical business and became a well-known railway engineer. His son **(4) George (1802-60)** a sculptor and Liberal M.P. from 1846 to 1847, was Gov. of the Falkland Is. from 1847 to 1855 and greatly improved them.

RENT RESTRICTION. See HOUSING-6 et seq. **(1)** An Act of 1915 froze the rents of all privately owned unfurished houses with values or rents below the following figures:

Rateable Value or Recoverable Rent

In Greater London	£35
Scotland	£30
Elsewhere	£26

(2) The legislation did not apply to the Crown or local authorities (neither of whom were taxed) and in particular the district councils, as housing authorities, were soon after World War I in a better position to build, improve or repair than private landlords. There was an upswing of local authority housing when prosperity returned and people could afford better houses. This was consistent with Labour and socialist thought, but Conservative govts. wanted to avoid the artificial depression of private housing into slums. In this sensitive political and doctrinal area there was, thus, much legislative tinkering designed on the one hand to close the landlords' loopholes and on the other to improve their prospects. Such acts, under the title Increase of Rent and Mortgage Interest Restrictions Acts, were passed in 1920, 1923, 1924, 1925, 1933, 1935 and 1938. On the Labour side the most important (1924) prevented eviction without a County Court order, to be granted only in a limited number of cases and virtually converted tenancies into tenancies for the life of 2 members of a family; and in addition there were valuation limit increases to keep step with rating revaluations. On the other side there were enactments permitting rents to be raised for landlords' improvements and for enabling a new rent to be charged as from the commencement of a lease to a new tenant.

(3) In World War II legislation distinguished between Old Control, i.e. houses already controlled before 3 Sept. 1939 and New Control, which applied to other houses with rateable values of £100 in Greater London and £75 elsewhere. This extended the geography of the same problems as before. Amending acts or orders were passed in 1949, 1951, 1952, 1954, 1955 and 1957. The last of these started to decontrol houses in Greater London rated in 1957 at £40 and £30 elsewhere (i.e. most houses), whereupon standstill legislation was enacted in 1958, 1959, 1964 and 1965.

(4) By now the law was in confusion and most of it was repealed and codified in the Rent Act, 1968.

Naturally matters could not be allowed to rest there and the Act of 1968 was amended in 1969 (twice), 1971, 1972, 1973, 1974 (twice), 1975 and 1976. The Law Commission joined in and the Rent Act, 1977, consolidated the legislation since 1968 with changes which it suggested. This was not the end of the story. The Housing Act 1980 modified the Act of 1977 and there were later modifying Acts. It was left to the Thatcher govt. to let the system slowly expire by permitting market rents whenever there was a change of tenant.

RENUNCIATION, STAT. OF (1783). The British Parliament declared that only the Crown and the Irish Parliament could legislate for Ireland and that no appeals from Irish courts should be entertained in England.

RENVERSEMENT DES ALLIANCES (1756). See AUSTRIA, POST- PRAGMATIC-3 to 6; PRUSSIA.

RENVOI (Fr. = return, but the word is not used in French in the sense following). In a legal proceeding which involves foreign law, the latter may require that the *lex fori* should be applied and the court then returns to its own law.

REPEAL, STAT. OF (1782). This repealed the Sixth of George I. See IRELAND, ENGLISH LEGISLATION IN.

REPARATIONS and WAR or INTERALLIED DEBTS (WORLD WAR I). These financial relationships embittered world politics for 20 years. **(1)** During World War I Britain had lent large sums to her allies, especially Russia which declined into revolution from 1917. Britain was thus a major creditor with at least one major defaulter. **(2)** Mainly at French insistence, Germany was required under the T. of Versailles to pay reparations towards the Allies' war costs and damage. The greater part was assigned to France. The total was fixed without knowledge of the German economy which was in confusion, so France was a major creditor with an intermittently defaulting debtor. Moreover, other nations entitled to reparations were hoping to pay their debts to Britain from their share. **(3)** Britain had borrowed from the U.S.A. amounts equalling roughly half the sum owed her by her Allies; other countries had also borrowed. Britain was willing to repay to the extent that she was repaid herself. The Americans wanted repayment in full. **(4)** Britain sensibly proposed a general cancellation of War Debts which would have left only the reparations problem, but the Americans insisted on full and separate settlements and hinted at economic reprisals. The French were determined to enforce German reparations if necessary by military sanctions. Hence the American attitude to Britain resembled the French attitude to Germany and forced the British, much against their will, to support the French policy of pressure on debtors. **(5)** But the Germans could pay only if they redeveloped their industries, for which capital could be found only in the U.S.A. In the early period this part of the economic merry-go-round was slow in starting and the Germans only too gladly defaulted. The BRUSSELS CONFERENCE (Dec. 1920) had fixed their liability at £13,450M over 42 years. The PARIS CONFERENCE (Jan. 1921) reduced it to £11,300M. As nothing seemed to be forthcoming, the French occupied the Ruhr (Mar. 1921). The Allied Powers then delivered the LONDON ULTIMATUM demanding £6,600M (May 1921). The Germans agreed and the French withdrew (Sept. 1921) but again the Germans seemed unable to pay. Hence the CANNES CONFERENCE (Jan. 1922) postponed payment and the GENOA CONFERENCE (Apr-May 1922) ended inconclusively because the Germans had made the RAPALLO TREATY with Russia. The Reparations Commission having reported 2 deliberate defaults (Dec. 1922 and Jan. 1923), the French entered the Ruhr again (Feb. 1923) and other industrial areas such as Mannheim (Mar. 1923). **(6)** In these circumstances a commission of experts under the American Charles Dawes (1865-1951) proposed the DAWES PLAN. It proposed that an international gold loan should be made to a central bank partly under Allied control and that this bank should issue Rentenmarks to supersede the inflated marks hitherto in use. Reparations were now to be paid in instalments beginning with £40M and rising in 5 years to £100M, but these were to be paid in gold and partly raised from industrial and railway prior charges; no total was fixed. The plan was accepted in Aug. 1924 and the loan subscribed in Oct. In July 1925 the French evacuated the Ruhr and in Jan. 1926 Allied troops left part of the Rhineland which had been occupied since 1919. **(7)** Reparations continued to be paid until 1928 and British war debts payments to the U.S.A. continued, but U.S. investment in Germany began to slacken and in June 1928 Germany demanded a definitive settlement of her liabilities. This was a political agitation against the second class status imposed by the Versailles Treaty, of which the machinery of the Dawes Plan was a part. A commission under the American Owen D. Young (1874-1962) proposed the YOUNG PLAN; German liability was reduced to £1500M payable over 59 years by means of an annuity partly levied upon the railways; but the control of the central bank, the prior charges and the liability to pay in gold were to be abolished. This was adopted in Aug. 1929 and a second zone of the Rhineland was then evacuated. **(8)** In Oct. 1929 came the New York Stock Exchange crash and U.S. investment in Europe stopped. Since most of the machinery for enforcing reparations had been dismantled, Britain's debtors were soon dragging their feet and Britain did too. In June 1931 Pres. Hoover accepted a one-year moratorium on War Debts and reparations.

In 1932, with a rising Nazi party, reparations were dead and only Finland continued to service her (very small) war debt. **(9)** After World War II the Western Allies, mindful of these experiences, took no reparations from Germany or Japan. The Russians looted everything they could and used many Germans as slave labour.

REPINGTON, Charles À Court (1858-1925), able military staff officer until 1902, when he became an influential military journalist on the *Morning Post* and from 1904 to 1918 on *The Times*.

REPLEVIN. A Common Law process developed c. 1200 to obtain redelivery of a chattel distrained usually for rent, upon the owner giving security for the rent and undertaking to pursue an action to determine the distrainor's right to the distress. It was useful where the detention of the chattel (e.g. a cart) was holding up work. If the distrainor had made away with ('eloigned') the chattel, the tenant might by a Writ of Withernam take goods from the distrainor as a pledge for its return. Later the tools of a man's trade could not be distrained and in other cases an action for trespass to goods was usually more efficacious.

REPORT STAGE on a bill in either House of Parliament comes after the Committee stage. The bill is reported to the House in its new or unchanged form and the House as a whole then has an opportunity to amend it further. This is often the point when undertakings given in committee are honoured. The stage is sometimes nominal when the bill has been in committee of the whole House (which is generally the case in the Lords), but has become more important than formerly in the Commons since most bills have, since World War II, been reported from select committees of limited membership.

REPRESENTATION OF THE PEOPLE ACTS (1) 1867. This extended the borough franchise to rated occupiers and £10 lodgers and the borough franchise to £5 owners and to occupiers of land with a rateable value of £12. In addition it reduced the representation of 38 boroughs from 2 M.P.s to one, created 12 new boroughs and 35 new county areas to be represented by 2 M.P.s each. **(2) 1885.** This extended the urban lodger and household franchise created in 1867 to rural areas and assimilated the occupation qualification by conferring the franchise

on all occupiers of £10 (annual value) of property. Registration Acts of 1885 set up uniform systems of electoral registration in Britain and Ireland. These enactments were combined in a package with the Redistribution of Seats Act, 1885, and doubled the electorate. **(3) 1948.** This abolished university representation in the Commons and the business premises vote in parliamentary elections. **(4)** Many other Acts of this type have been passed, mainly on details, but European legislation requires all European citizens to be able to vote and stand as candidates in local elections for areas in which they reside.

REPRESENTATIVE PEERS, IRISH. Under the Act of Union, 1800, those Irish peers who were not entitled to sit in the English House of Lords by virtue of other peerages were represented in that House by 28 of their number whom they elected for life. The remainder might stand for the House of Commons and many did so. The Irish peerage was limited so that one new peerage might be created for every 3 which became extinct, until the number had fallen to 100, which number could then be maintained. No elections were held after 1919 and the Irish Crown and Hanaper Office, which conducted them, was abolished in 1922. The last representative peer died in 1961. A claim by 12 Irish peers to be represented was rejected by the House in 1966.

REPRESENTATIVE PEERS, SCOTTISH. Under the Act of Union, 1707, those Scottish peers who were not entitled to sit in the House of Lords as peers of England, Great Britain or the U.K. were represented in that House by 16 of their number, whom they elected for the duration of each parliament. The remainder were not entitled to stand for the House of Commons. New Scottish peerages could not be created. In the Peerage Bill of 1719 Stanhope proposed *inter alia* to make 25 Scots peers hereditary Lords of Parliament but the bill was frustrated by Walpole. Under the Peerage Act 1963 the few remaining Scottish peers became entitled to sit in the House of Lords and these elections were abolished.

REPRISAL. Where someone (usually a shipowner) was aggrieved by the action of a foreign state or its subjects and could not obtain redress, he might be granted Letters of Reprisal by his own govt., authorising him to exact forcible reparation. Such authority, in effect to wage a private war in peacetime, was needed to protect him from international hostility as a pirate.

REPTON (Derbys). Its 7th cent. double monastery dedicated to St. Wystan was a burial place of Mercian Kings. The Vikings sacked it.

REPTON, Humphry (1752-1818), landscape gardener much employed by estate owners. His ornamental style represented a reaction against that of Capability Brown and provided the atmosphere in which John Nash was trained.

REPUBLICAN PARTY (U.S.A.) was an amalgamation in 1854 of anti-slavery groups inspired by the memory of Jefferson's Democratic Republican Party. Abraham Lincoln was its first successful presidential candidate in 1860. Its leaders were in office from then until 1884, from 1885 to 1892, from 1896 to 1912, from 1920 to 1932, from 1952 to 1960, from 1972 to 1976 and then in 1980. It represents industrial expansion. sound money, protectionism, disengagement in foreign affairs and sometimes isolationism, besides administrative devolution.

REPUGNANCY. *See* COLONIAL LAWS, VALIDITY-8.

REQUESTS, COURT OF, was a court for poor litigants and royal servants, over which the Ld. Privy Seal presided. Set up, like the Star Chamber, as a branch of the Council in 1493, it was permanently settled by Cardinal Wolsey in the White Hall of Westminster Palace. Its legal assessors, the Masters of Requests, assumed entire control by 1547. Under Elizabeth I the ordinary masters accompanied her while the extraordinary sat permanently at Westminster and the court became wholly separate from the Council. It relieved the Chancery of a mass of minor equitable business. In 1590, however, the Common Pleas issued a writ of prohibition against it because its jurisdiction was founded neither in statute nor in prescription; in 1598 it was held to be illegal and in 1606 the King's Bench refused to punish perjury before it, on the ground that it was not a court. Nevertheless it throve because it was cheap and speedy. It was not specifically abolished with the conciliar courts in 1641 and continued until 1642, but at the Restoration it was not revived. *See also* CHANCERY-9 *et seq.*

REQUESTS, LOCAL COURTS OF, were unprofessional small debt courts for sums of less than 40s. There were petitions for them and 3 bills failed to pass the Lords between 1689 and 1692. In the 18th cent., however, many were set up under private Acts and by 1840 some 370 were functioning: the Birmingham Court was settling 130 cases a week. They were superseded by the new County Courts in 1846.

RESCISSORY ACTS 1661 (Scot.), annulled the proceedings of Scots parliaments from 1639 to 1648 and so restored the Scots episcopacy.

RESCRIPTS were originally replies by a Pope or Emperor to questions or difficulties propounded by their subordinates and then applied generally. *See* PAPAL CHANCERY.

RESERVATION. *See* COLONIAL LAWS, VALIDITY-7.

RESERVED SUBJECTS. *See* DYARCHY.

RESIDENT, RESIDENCY. In a country bound to another superior power entitled by treaty to intervene in its affairs, the diplomatic representative of the superior was usually called the Resident and his lodging and also the area of his charge the Residency. Residencies were established for all the Indian states and Gulf Sheikdoms under the British, some small states sharing one. In Indonesia most of the Dutch residents developed into provincial governors.

RESIGNATION of peerage. Before 1706 Scottish peers could resign their peerages and did so usually preparatory to a *Novodamus*. No other peerage could be resigned. *See, however,* DISCLAIMER.

RESISTANCE. Violent but covert opposition to a conqueror, notably to the Nazis in W. Europe.

RESOLUTIONERS. *See* REMONSTRANCE (SCOT.) 1650; CHARLES II-2.

RESPONSIBLE GOVERNMENT in English constitutional terminology is government in which the ministers are responsible to an elected legislature.

RESSALA, RISSALA. A squadron of Indian native cavalry. A risaldar was an Indian native cavalry captain.

RESTITUTION. *See* DIVORCE.

RESTITUTION, EDICT OF (1629). *See* THIRTY YEARS' WAR-10.

RESTORATION 1660. (*For events leading to the collapse of the Protectorate and Commonwealth see* COMMONWEALTH-14 *et seq.*) **(1)** The movement towards a Restoration started when the civilians responsible for the Humble Petition and Advice (Mar. 1657) urged Oliver Cromwell to take the Crown. The Puritan extremists and especially the all-important army were irreconcilable, but both had become intensely unpopular during the rule of the Major-Gens. At Oliver's death, the power of the Protectorate, the sense of directive statesmanship of the civilians and the unity of the army all fell to pieces at once, while the general public now longed for familiar ways and an end to experiments. If there was to be a head of state he might as well be a King as a Protector and if a King, then Charles II had a better claim than the agreeable but absurd Richard Cromwell, who very early left the scene.

(2) The task of Charles and his chancellor, Hyde, was to appeal in the right way to the ordinary English masses and to win over enough of the central machine's manpower to neutralise or destroy the rest. The amount of effort required for the second depended on the

success of the first: for if a strong governing element turned royalist with public opinion behind it, a peaceful change was possible, whereas a neutral or republican public might nerve the irreconcilables to fight. Royalists and moderates all played on public fear of further civil war.

(3) On his southward march Gen. Monck had been besieged with petitions for a free parliament. His experience at Westminster and the City convinced him that a restored monarchy was the only means of permanent stability, if not the only shield against chaos. The problem was that all office holders had sworn to a form of govt. without a King or a House of Lords and royalist ones were exposed to prosecution for treason if things went wrong and, as functionaries of a usurping govt., were equally exposed if the King returned. Charles and Hyde understood this too and were not surprised that Monck refused to receive their envoys until the Long Parliament was dissolved (16 Mar. 1660). Two days later, however, he accepted a letter from the King and replied with an oral message. He had always been loyal at heart but unable, hitherto, to serve the King. Charles should offer liberty of conscience (which would bring back the oppressed but numerous Anglicans without upsetting the largely military Independents), a free and general pardon (which would relieve all who had fought against the Crown and all who had held office in the Interregnum), the prompt settlement of the army's arrears of pay (without which the army would not disperse) and the confirmation of land sales made since the beginning of the civil war which would conciliate many newly vested interests. These principles were improved by Charles and Hyde. In the DECLARATION OF BREDA (4 Apr.) Charles shrewdly said that he would assent to anything which parliament proposed on these matters. In this way he proclaimed his support for parliamentary govt., gave no hostages to fortune and announced his trust in the electorate. With the country in the grip of a general election, the Royalists, taking their cue from him, preached conciliation and promised forgiveness for past sufferings. The electors responded with devotion; among an unusually large number of candidates, the Puritan influence was minimal and, the law against Royalist candidates widely flouted, the electors voted mostly for those who favoured a speedy return of the King.

(4) When the parliament met on 25 Apr. 1660, the preliminary issue was the composition of the two Houses. The Lords who had inherited their peerages since Jan. 1648 (*The Young Lords*) and those peers who had been expelled or created since 1641 (*The King's Lords*) were at first excluded; in the Commons, over 100 M.Ps. were open to challenge as Royalists or sons of Royalists. Thus it seemed that there might be an extremist Presbyterian majority in both Houses, pledged to a rigid insistence upon the Cromwellian status quo as a condition of Restoration. But Monck foresaw that this would destroy both religious toleration, which Charles supported, and Parliament's right to enact it. These Presbyterians were still claiming to be above the Constitution. Rightly concluding that the country had had enough of them he insisted that all peers must be admitted and no elections challenged. This was decisive. He then laid the Declaration of Breda and the King's letters before the Houses, who voted a return to the ancient constitution, proclaimed Charles King from the moment of his father's death, nominated commissioners to invite him home and sent him a large sum of money. The erstwhile so Republican fleet escorted him to Dover, where he came ashore on 25 May 1660 amid a haze of salutes. His progress to London was a triumphant political healing.

(5) The Restoration was based on a return to political institutions upon which Kings and Parliaments had agreed. The Commonwealth and Protectorate from the beginning of 1642 until Apr. 1660 were thus ignored: their functionaries accordingly had no function and their public debt was repudiated. But it was not feasible or desired to return entirely to the older dispensation: the realities and the theories had to be harmonised. Divine right had been proclaimed, but fortunately the King's father had assented in due form to the legislation of 1641, which abolished the machinery of royal absolutism. The paramountcy of the Common Law gave way to the supremacy of statute, without which reform and a settlement were unobtainable. Parliament now enacted the settlement.

(6) The first case was to dispose of the army; its arrears were paid at once and in full and with the exception of a few regiments it was disbanded. All sides agreed that a standing army was a public danger and must not be raised in peacetime without parliamentary consent. Consistently with this, the King was granted (against the surrender of the feudal incidents) a life income which would suffice for routine purposes, but not for extraordinary policies. Thus foreign adventure needing armed support would need parliamentary co-operation. Thirdly, the Act of Oblivion and Indemnity sweepingly quieteted private property titles and (with the exception of the Regicides) relieved all participants in the late disturbances from criminal liability. The Crown, the Church and those whose lands had been confiscated for the most part resumed their own. The soldiers, freed from fear of their neighbours, had no reason to stand together in arms and were absorbed into the general population. Those many people who had paid good money for Royalist estates sold to raise compositions kept them. The Cavaliers complained; but overborne in the general tumult of reconciliation these in the end had few real grievances, for Charles made shift to find them honours, pensions, sinecures, employments, or Irish and colonial grants. Nevertheless their influence was potent.

(7) The Parliaments of England and Scotland, composed as they were mostly of men who had fought the Crown, enthusiastically pursued scapegoats, contrary to the King's wishes. Two thirds of the English Regicides were dead or had fled abroad and Charles saved all but 9 of the rest. Lambert was condemned but reprieved on the D. of York's intervention; Sir Harry Vane, who purloined the Privy Council notes upon which Strafford's attainder was founded, on the other hand suffered the full extremity and so in Scotland did the great M. of Argyll.

By this time, however, the country gentry were becoming restive. It was clear that the Convention Parliament would never enact a religious settlement which satisfied them. If they could not get their old lands back, at least they would resume their advowsons. There was a defect in the constitutional status of the Parliament, for it had not been summoned by the Crown. Charles was ready to remedy this by retrospective sanction, but constitutional lawyers, interested Anglicans and smarting Royalists urged that this was not enough. Moreover, there were old scores to pay off: canting Presbyterian ministers held a fifth of all the livings and were an uncomfortable reminder of Puritan oppression. The beneficiaries of the Interregnum had had their advantages confirmed: the Royalists must now have their day.

(8) The Convention Parliament was dissolved on 29 Dec. 1660. In the ensuing general election the old Cavaliers or their representatives freed from the inhibitions of Republican law, came forward and were elected in droves. The CAVALIER or PENSION PARLIAMENT met on 8 May 1661. It began by confirming the enactments of the Convention and then turned to the agreeable task of rooting out the political opponents without whom the Restoration could not have happened. The Corporation Act, 1661, and the Act of Uniformity, 1662, were the first instalments of the later misnamed "Clarendon Code". The religious tests imposed by these enactments were intended to drive non- royalists and R. Catholics from political and ecclesiastical public life. In this they largely succeeded, but at the expense of creating an abiding division in State and Church. The Parliament lasted for 18 years.

RESTORATION COMEDY, in reaction against the high-minded or hyprocritical gloom of the Commonwealth, was witty, often bawdy and focused on sexual intrigue in fashionable society. The best known playwrights of the *genre* were Vanbrugh, Wycherley, Congreve and Farquhar. Some of the plays date from as late as the reigns of William and Mary, and Q. Anne.

RESTRAINING ORDERS (May 1712) were issued by St. John, the Tory Sec. of State to the D. of Ormonde, the C-in-C by whom Marlborough had been superseded, forbidding him to engage in any battle or siege pending secret negotiations with France to end the War of the Spanish Succession. They were communicated to Britain's enemies but kept secret from her allies. P. Eugene of Savoy soon guessed their nature.

RESTRAINT OF APPEALS, ACT IN (1533) declared that the English body politic was one and indivisible under a King who could yield justice without restraint by a foreign prince and that when a matter of divine law or spiritual learning came into question, it was to be decided by the spiritual part of the body politic, i.e. the English church. Thereupon Abp. Cranmer persuaded convocation to declare Henry VIII's marriage to Katharine of Aragon void and having assembled a court by royal licence to try the cause, pronounced for Henry and declared his marriage to Anne Boleyn valid (and her pregnancy legitimate). The philosophy of the Act was the foundation of the later Act of Supremacy (1534).

RESTRICTIVE PRACTICES COURT, set up in 1956, consists of judges and experienced laymen. It considers whether agreements registrable with the Registrar of Restrictive Trade Practices are contrary to the public interest.

RESUMPTION, ACTS OF, were Acts of Parliament resuming rights in lands, property, annuities, franchises, tax exemptions or other things granted away by the Crown, sometimes with but often without compensation. They usually attended efforts to force the Crown to 'live off its own' (i.e. not to demand taxes). In 1276 the Crown was authorised to resume usurpations during the life of the usurper; in 1335 to forfeit charters under which alien merchants were disturbed in trading; in 1397 annuities granted till further order were avoided if the grantee had accepted other favours. In 1413 all grants, especially of Richard II and Henry IV out of lands and revenues of Calais were resumed, save those to the D. of Clarence. In 1449 there was a general resumption of grants made since 1422, but this was made subject to exceptions in 1452. In 1489 grants of offices in the mint and all grants free of the tenth and fifteenth were resumed; in 1540 a variety of grants, licences, offices in reversion and life shrievalties; in 1693 pensions chargeable upon the surplus of certain loans. There were also a great many local or detailed resumptions or (cf Acts of Attainder) of the property of particular unpopular people, such as Empson and Dudley in 1509.

RESURRECTION MEN in the 18th cent. stole corpses and sold them to hospitals for dissection.

RÉUNION or BOURBON (Ind. Ocean), was settled by the French in 1642. Captured by the British in 1810, it was returned, with its mainly French population, in 1815. It became an overseas *département* of France in 1946.

REVALUATION. *See* DEVALUATION.

REVANCHISME (Fr.). A fanatical desire to avenge a lost war, notable in France after the Franco-Prussian War of 1870-1.

REVENGE, H.M.S. *See* GRENVILLE A-1.

REVESTMENT ACT (I. of Man) 1765. *See* MAN, I. OF-10.

REVETT, Nicholas (1720-84) and STUART, James (1713-88) made and published their drawings of the *Antiquities of Athens* which popularised a visual knowledge of classical architecture and ultimately strengthened public sympathy for the Greeks.

REVISING BARRISTERS (1843-1918) held annual courts in the autumn to revise the electoral rolls for parliamentary and local govt. elections. Their functions were transferred to town and county clerks.

REVOCATIONS BY THE CROWN (Scot.). Crown property was the obvious target for the ambitious or unscrupulous during the many Scottish civil wars and regencies. Since the govt. had, otherwise, to be financed by increased taxation, it was normal for grants of Crown property made during such periods to be revoked when a monarch assumed the govt. King David II set the precedent on his return from English captivity in 1357 and repeated it in 1367; of later revocations the most important were by James IV in 1489, James V in 1537 (ratified by Parliament in 1540), Mary in 1555, James VI in 1587 (ratified in 1592), Charles I in 1625 (ratified in 1633) and Charles II in 1660 (ratified in 1662). Some, e.g. those of 1587 and 1625, were in form far-reaching but in practice merely gave a discretion, not always exercised, to resume property if alienated contrary to law and by implication to confirm defective titles – at a price. In 1630 Parliament petitioned on the revocation of 1625, because it was feared that by charging exorbitant fees for confirmations the Crown was creating a new source of revenue. The Parliament of 1633 confirmed the revocation as part of a larger programme of religious, property and revenue legislation.

REVOLT OF THE FIELD (1874) a strike of some 6000 members of Joseph Arch's N. Agricultural Labourers Union provoked by a lock-out in Suffolk. Its failure led to the decline of the Union.

REWA (India), a small warlike Rajput state, entered into subsidiary treaty with Britain in 1812.

REYNOLDS, Walter (?-1327), originally a wardrobe clerk to Edward I, was friendly with Edward II, who made him Bp. of Worcester (1308), Treasurer (1307) and Ld. Chancellor (1310-14). In 1313 the Canterbury monks elected the learned diplomat Thomas of Cobham to the archbishopric, but Clement V quashed the election at Edward II's instance and presented Reynolds, the King's nominee. He supported the King against the Ordainers and several times attempted to compose the disputes. This drove him into association with Pembroke and others and ultimately into a reluctant role in deposing the King. In Feb. 1327 he crowned Edward III.

REYNOLDS, Sir Joshua (1723-95) was taken by Commodore Keppel to the Mediterranean in 1749 and studied in Italy. He returned to London in 1752 and from then until he went partly blind in 1790 he was the leading English portrait painter.

RHANDIR **(Welsh).** *See* CANTREF.

RHEGED. British post-Roman kingdom around the Solway Firth.

RHINE, CONFEDERATION OF THE (July 1806-Oct. 1813), raised on the ruins of the Holy Roman Empire consisted, with Bonaparte as Protector, originally of 16 states, viz: Baden, Bavaria, Berg, Hesse-Darmstadt, Regensburg and Wurttemberg together with 2 Nassau principalities, a prince primate who held the City of Frankfurt and some lesser states. The Code Napoléon was imposed and the Protector was entitled to call for 63,000 troops and to regulate trade and taxation in the interest of foreign policy. The rulers were induced to accept these arrangements by the cession (or so-called mediatisation) of the lands of former minor states, such as the Imperial Knights and the cities of Augsburg and Nuremberg. Saxony was joined to the Confederation in Dec. 1806 (P. of Posen); Westphalia, Oldenburg and Mecklenburg after the T. of Tilsit (July 1807). Bonaparte habitually levied

more troops than the 63,000: 147,000 went on the Moscow Campaign. The Confederation's dissolution was a war aim both of Prussia and Austria, achieved with Russian agreement after the B. of Leipzig (Oct. 1813).

RHINELAND. *See* HANSE-4; REPARATIONS-6 AND 7.

RHODE I. (AQUIDNECK) U.S.A. Roger Williams (?1603-83), a strongly individualist Puritan who believed in the separation of the powers of Church and State, quarrelled with the Massachusetts authorities at Salem and moved to PROVIDENCE where he bought land and founded a democratic nonconformist settlement in 1636. William Coddington (1601-78), also exiled from Massachusetts, founded settlements at PORTSMOUTH (1638) and NEWPORT (1640), and Samuel Gorton (?1572-1677) another at WARWICK (1643). These 4 communities jointly obtained a parliamentary charter in 1644 after they had previously been refused admittance to the more authoritarian New England Confederation of May 1643. Charles II guaranteed religious liberty in 1663 by the Charter of Rhode I. and Providence Plantations, the working constitution until 1842. The smallest American colony, economically dominated by Newport, its development was stunted by the British presence during the American rebellion. Separatist in outlook, it was the last to ratify the U.S. Constitution.

RHODES (Med.) and the **DODECANESE.** Rhodes was seized by the Knights of St. John in 1309. The Turks attacked it in 1480, and expelled the Knights after a long siege in 1522. They ceded the islands to Italy in 1912 and between 1922 and 1926 the Italians converted Leros into a fortress. This had some influence in keeping Turkey out of World War II. The islands passed to Greece in 1955.

RHODES, Cecil John (1853-1902), delicate but pertinacious, worked in the Kimberley diamond claims and at Oriel Coll., Oxford, from 1873 until he secured his degree in 1881. By then his holdings were considerable and he soon amalgamated them. He was already a Cape M.P. (1880) and wanted to unite or federate S. Africa under Britain with Dutch assent. He helped to secure Bechuanaland and in 1889 obtained a charter for his British S. Africa Co., which was to administer the territory north of the Transvaal and Bechuanaland. This area, **Rhodesia** (after himself), was much extended in a war against the Matabele in 1893-4. From 1890 Dr. L. S. Jameson had been his administrator in Rhodesia, while Rhodes was Prime Minister of the Cape. The Dutch of the two Boer republics understandably felt hemmed in, but equally the *Uitlanders* in the republics felt, even more understandably, oppressed by the Dutch. In 1895 Rhodes secretly encouraged the *Uitlanders* to stage a rebellion and after the disastrous Jameson Raid (1896) and revelations to the Cape and British parliaments, he was forced to resign. Henceforth he concentrated on developing Rhodesia and on Co. affairs. He was cut off and besieged in Kimberley during the S. African War. He died after a long heart illness. *See* ZAMBIA; ZIMBABWE.

RHODES SCHOLARSHIPS. By his will Cecil John Rhodes (*see above*) endowed 170 scholarships at Oxford for students from the Commonwealth, the U.S.A. and Germany.

RHODRI MOLWYNOG (?-754). *See* GWYNEDD-6.

RHODRI ab OWAIN (?-1195). *See* GWYNEDD B-25.

RHODRI H (the Great) (?-877). *See* GWYNEDD-12; DEHEUBARTH.

RHONDDA (Glam.) is an intensive mining valley, whose coal was peculiarly suitable for steamships. The population was minimal until the opening of the Treherbert Mine in 1855. In 1871 it was 24,000; in 1901 113,000 and in 1924 167,000. By this time oil fuel was being increasingly used and this and the slump of 1929 produced a crisis of unemployment and destitution. By 1951 the population was down to 111,000: but industrial diversification thereafter eased the situation. The oil crisis of 1972 also helped to bring prosperity.

RHONDDA, Viscountess Case (1922). *See* SEX DISQUALIFICATION REMOVAL ACT, 1919.

RHUDDLAN, STAT. OF (1284). *See* WALES, STAT. OF 1284.

RHUN ap MAELGWN GWYNEDD (fl. 550), a ruler of N. Wales of whom little is known.

RHYDDERCH HAEL or HEN (fl. 573), King of Alclyde, a friend of St. Columba and an enemy of Aldan, King of Scots.

RHYDDERCH ap IESTYN, usurper in Deheubarth from 999 to 1033.

RHYS ap GRUFFYDD (?-1356), landowner in S. Wales and Steward of Cardigan from 1309, supported the Despensers through whom he got Dinefwr, Dryslwyn, the Lordship of Narberth and the Shrievalty of Carmarthen. He married Joan of Somerville through whom he got many estates in England and Carmarthenshire and his wealth and Despenser connections involved him in the political troubles of Edward II, at whose abdication he fled to Scotland. Restored in 1329 he fled again because of involvement in the abortive *coup* of 1330. When Edward III established himself shortly after, he was recalled and became a leading military figure, raising and commanding Welsh bowmen in France. His great estates descended in his family until the end of the 15th cent.

RHYS ap GRUFFUDD ('The Lord RHYS') (1132-97). *See* DEHEUBARTH-16.

RHYS ap MAREDUDD (?-1291). *See* DEHEUHARTH-22.

RHYS ap TEWDWR (?-1093). *See* DEHEUBARTH-12.

RHYS ap THOMAS (1449-1525), a powerful landowner in Carmarthenshire, had been educated at the Burgundian Court. A supporter of Edward IV, he actively opposed Richard III and used his influence to smooth Henry VII's landing at Milford Haven in 1485. He commanded Welsh levies at Bosworth and was rewarded with the Stewardships of Builth and Brecknock, the Constableship of Brecknock and the chambers of Carmarthen and Cardigan. As the leading figure in S. Wales he commanded the horse at Simnel's defeat at Stoke (June 1487), took part in the Boulogne expedition of 1492, captured Ld. Audley at Blackheath and was present at Warbeck's surrender at Beaulca in 1497. In 1505 he was made a Knight of the Garter and held a famous tournament in celebration at Carew Castle. In 1513 he took part in the expedition against France.

RHYS GRYG ap RHYS (?-1234). *See* DEHEUBARTH-19.

RHYS MECHYLL ap RHYS GRYG (fl. 1260). *See* DEHEUBARTH-2 1.

RI (Celt. = King). An Irish tribal chief. The word 'chief is used in this work to signify these minor leaders.

RI RUIRECH. An Irish paramount chief, to whom a *ri* would give hostages.

RIALTO. A bridge at the centre of the Venetian business district: hence business districts generally.

RIBAULDEQUIN (Med.). Several small guns mounted on one platform.

RIBBONISM or RIBBON SOCIETIES (Ir.) were a R. Catholic rural terrorist movement, strongest in Ulster, which grew out of the Defenders and was probably provoked by aggressive Orange activities in the period 1811-1829.

RICARDO, David (1772-1823) inherited from his father, a Dutch Jew, a fortune which enabled him to devote much time to the scientific study of economics, in which by 1812 he was an acknowledged expert. He retired from business in 1814 and in 1817 he published his *Principles of Political Economy and Taxation* in which he formulated (*inter alia*) the well known theory of rent. He was an independent radical M.P. for Portarlington from 1819.

RICCIO or RIZZIO, David. *See* MARY Q. OF SCOTS-12.

RICH. Essex family with Mercer connections in the City. **(1) Richard (?1496-1567) 1st Ld. RICH (1548)** disreputable but clever lawyer, sought protection from Wolsey (whose Essex property he inventoried for Cromwell), became Att.-Gen for Wales in 1532 and Sol-Gen. in 1533. He was much engaged for Cromwell in prosecutions under the Acts of Succession and Supremacy and brought both Fisher and More to the block by personal breaches of faith or perjury. In 1536 he reaped his reward by becoming the first Chancellor of the new Court of Augmentations, by which he became wealthy. Hated in the country, he met, as a Groom of the Bedchamber, Anne of Cleves at Dover and then hurriedly abandoned Cromwell when the marriage seemed to be turning out ill. His new protector was Stephen Gardiner and he was now ready to help that prelate to persecute reformers. He and Wriothesley are said to have racked Anne Askew with their own hands.

Henry VIII appointed him one of his executors and in the new reign he managed to extrude Wriothesley from the Woolsack (Mar. 1547) by insinuations of popery. In Oct. he became Ld. Chancellor himself, holding the office until Dec. 1551. During this period he was heavily involved in politics; he secured Seymour's attainder and Protector Somerset's deprivation; forbade masses at P. Mary's house and instigated strong measures against R. Catholics. In Dec. 1551, however, he resigned for (genuine) reasons of health and was fortunately not prominent during the convulsions of Lady Jane Grey's attempt on the throne. During those days he contrived to sign Jane's proclamation but support Mary in Essex, and his wife accompanied Mary on her entry into London. He took little part in national affairs thereafter, but was apparently an embittered persecutor, to whose activities the high incidence of Protestant martyrs in Essex was ascribed. He had 14 legitimate and 4 illegitimate children. His grandson **(2) Robert (?-1619) 3rd Ld. and 1st E. of WARWICK (1618)** married **(3) Penelope DEVEREUX (?1562-1607)** who was Sir Philip Sydney's STELLA and sister to Robert, Q. Elizabeth's famous E. of Essex. Robert Rich seems to have made her unhappy but he evidently was entitled to complain, not only of Sydney but of Charles Blount, 8th Ld. Mountjoy who acknowledged the last 5 of her 12 children. Her younger contemporary **(4) Sir Nathaniel (?1585-1636)** was a son of the 1st Ld's. bastard Richard. He entertained a close relationship with other Richs including her son **(5) Robert (1587-1658) 2nd E.** Both were concerned in the Somers Is. Co., the colonisation of Bermuda and the New England Co. and Robert was closely involved in setting up Massachusetts and Connecticut. He also belonged to the Guinea Co. and went into privateering (or piracy) and this, with his colonial ventures, brought him Puritan connections. As a result of disputes about the Massachusetts and Connecticut patents, the New England Co. ceased to function and he turned his attention to the Providence Co. of which Pym was treasurer. Thus he moved into circles opposed to Charles I. He had personal reasons as well since, as a forest owner in Essex, the revival of the forest laws directly threatened his interests. He was also anti-Lutheran and patronised Puritan divines wherever he could. When the King left London, Warwick stayed as a champion protector of the Parliament and in Mar. 1642 the Commons resolved that Northumberland, the Ld. High Admiral, should appoint him to command the fleet. In June the King dismissed Northumberland. In July the House ordered Warwick to take command. This he did with enough determination to bring most of it over. It was due to him that Parliament (which starved him of money and ships) was always superior at sea, despite the mutiny of 1648. He could not, however, support the murder of Charles I or the abolition of the monarchy and though personally friendly with Cromwell, whom he admired, he took no further part in Commonwealth affairs. His brother **(6) Henry (1590-1649) 1st Ld. KENSINGTON (1623) 1st E. of HOLLAND (1624),** a courtier and reluctant object of James I's amorous advances, was a personal friend of Charles I. Originally employed in the French marriage negotiations of 1624, for which he was quite unsuited, he commanded Buckingham's belated naval and military reinforcements for the Isle de Ré. Like his brother he was involved in colonisation at Providence and Newfoundland but also made money by patents and monopolies. Since he accepted a justiceship in eyre too, he was adopting increasingly unpopular courses. Public outcry and his Puritan colonial acquaintances forced reconsideration and he found himself at odds with Strafford and Laud. By 1640 he was voting in the Privy Council against the dissolution of Parliament and when the King left London he stayed behind. He was, however, a leader of the peace party, but when no peace came in 1643 he went over to the King who treated him contemptuously, though he fought at the siege of Gloucester and the first B. of Newbury. In Jan. 1644 he returned to London where, not surprisingly, Parliament refused to vote him a pension. Consequently in Sept. 1645 he rejoined the King and in 1647 raised a standard for the second civil war and was taken by the Parliamentarians and executed.

RICHARD (?-1184), Abp., took part in a controverted election to the See of Canterbury, the monks having elected Odo their sub-prior while the Bps. elected Richard. Despite the objections of Henry the Young King, he received the pallium in 1174. He increased the wealth of the See, but was otherwise undistinguished.

RICHARD of BAYEUX (?-1133). *See* SAMSON-4.

RICHARD of CHESTER. *See* CHESHIRE.

RICHARD of CHICHESTER, St. (1197-1253) became Chancellor to his former tutor Edmund Rich when the latter became Abp. of Canterbury; the two held the same views of clerical reform and secular functions and he shared Edmund's exile. In 1243 Abp. Boniface of Savoy reappointed him Chancellor and in 1244 he was elected Bp. of Chichester by part of the chapter while the other elected Richard Passelew. The King rejected Richard, the Abp. Passelew. On appeal to Rome Innocent IV confirmed Richard, but he could obtain the temporalities, much wasted, only in 1247. He was enthusiastic for the Crusades and an efficient and accessible bishop.

RICHARD I (1157-99) (*COEUR DE LION* **Fr. = Lion Heart) D. of AQUITAINE (1169), King (1189).** *For previous history see* HENRY II (passim).

(1) The effect of Henry I's defeat and death was that Richard I succeeded to all his lands without opposition. He instantly released Q. Eleanor, long imprisoned by his father, and empowered her to act for him until he should come to England. Next he was installed as D. of Normandy and on 31 July 1189 he surrendered his claim to the Auvergne and part of Bern to K. Philip Augustus and agreed to go on crusade with him in the spring of 1190 (T. of Gisors). The crusade was his ruling passion, to which he now bent all his energies, with far reaching results. The greatest general of the age, he knew, as others might not have done, what an efficient hot weather expedition needed. The requirements could be satisfied only by immense purchases and the pay of many professional soldiers. No feudal levy could undertake a crusade. Thus money was the first priority and peace at home the second. Richard's activities in the ill-judged pursuit of these objectives shook the stability of the state.

(2) The T. of Gisors had set a pattern of appeasement. Richard's treatment of his political opponents followed suit, sometimes with success. His father's supporters such as William Marshal were rewarded for their loyalty. His bastard half brother, Geoffrey, became Abp. of York. Above all his brother John got an immense provision: the honours of Cornwall and Lancaster, marriage to Isabel of Gloucester, the county of Mortain, various scattered properties, the shires of Nottingham, Derby, Dorset, Somerset, Devon and Cornwall were absolutely in his hand, to rule as he pleased, making no returns (until 1194) to the Exchequer.

(3) To raise funds the King emptied the Exchequer where his father had left a substantial amount, took compounding fees from crusaders with second thoughts, released (*Quitclaimed*) William the Lion from the T. of Falaise for 10,000 marks at Canterbury and sold every asset which came to hand – powers, lordships, castles, property and offices. He achieved his purpose but left a substantial body of people with local vested interests and a govt. without adequate resources. Moreover the governmental arrangements for his absence were defective: there were two Justiciars whose spheres were divided by the Humber. The better man, Hugh de Puiset, Bp. of Durham, was in the weaker position with only the poverty stricken north to face the Scottish border. The other, William Longchamp, Bp. of Ely, was an unscrupulous upstart, faithful, however, to Richard and burdened with the intrusive power of John's immense estates. His prime object was supremacy and family aggrandisement. In Dec. 1189 Richard left England permanently and at Easter Longchamp met Puiset at Tickhill, seized him and forced him to surrender certain castles. On his way Puiset was again seized and held in custody. Richard in Aquitaine made the best of a bad job and got the Pope to send Longchamp a legatine commission in June 1190. In July his crusade set out (*see* CRUSADES 13-15).

(4) Longchamp was arrogant, oppressive and unpopular and opposition crystallised round the unworthy John. In the spring of 1191 there was a series of disputes about the control of castles, especially Lincoln where the sheriff flouted the Justiciar's authority. John himself seized Nottingham and Tickhill Castles, while his friend Mortimer expelled the Justiciar's representatives on the Welsh border. Longchamp promptly captured Mortimer's stronghold at Wigmore and in July besieged Lincoln. Meanwhile news of the confusion had reached the King at Messina, whence he despatched the distinguished Englishman Walter of Coutances, Abp. of Rouen, with commissions to act as Longchamp's colleague or supersede him, as the circumstances dictated. Walter arrived on 27 June. A cautious man, he found that one alleged issue between the factions was Arthur of Brittany, whom Richard had recognised as his presumptive heir and whose lawful claim Longchamp supported. The evil precedent set by Henry II in denying Richard's claims worked on through several channels. It implied that the ruler on the spot might determine future rights: in which case Henry II might have set John up against Richard and Longchamp might bargain away Arthur's rights. Walter of Coutances, anxious to establish his authority by agreement, let him keep his post by such a bargain. By this means Longchamp had made substantial progress. Longchamp now became involved, through his sister, in an imbroglio with Richard's bastard brother, Geoffrey, Abp. of York, who arrived at Dover on the way to his See and was seized and ill-treated at her orders. The memory of Becket was vivid: the outcry tremendous. John took advantage of it. A council at Reading urged Walter of Coutances to depose the Justicier who had fled to the Tower of London. In Oct. 1191 Walter replaced him and he left the kingdom.

(5) Walter's accession did not simplify the situation, for John was too well entrenched. Moreover early in 1192 Philip Augustus returned from Outremer and the two, for mutually incompatible reasons, were soon deep in conspiracies against Richard. At home John was trying to secure more castles and actually got his hands on Windsor and Wallingford. Abroad Philip offered to transfer the English continental dominions if John would marry his sister, Alice. Eleanor stopped the prince from taking this proposal seriously. When John accepted a bribe to help Longchamp to return, the partially effectual govt. could keep him out only by outbidding him. John's influence crept steadily across the land: but it was not a

popular influence, rather a power against which people could not set a principle nor, in the King's absence, look to a rallying point.

It was, however, early in 1193 that the news came that Richard, on his way home, had been captured by Leopold of Austria who in Feb. surrendered him to the Emperor Henry VI. The nation's attention was now focused on Richard and the wrangles of lesser men became, for that reason, less irksome. They were, however, dangerous enough. The Emperor's position was threatened by a combination. This consisted of the Guelfs whose head was Richard's brother-in-law; of Henry the Lion; of Rhenish rulers closely connected with England by trade and of Tancred of Sicily with whom Richard was in treaty relations. The Emperor's interest was to squeeze out of Richard diplomatic advantages which could not enure until he was free. An excessive ransom would thus hinder his diplomacy. Richard and the English govt. were anxious to get the King home. John and Philip and other disorderly persons wished to prevent or delay the return, but the Emperor had strong grounds for not aggrandising Philip at Richard's expense.

As soon as John heard the news he did homage to Philip and agreed to marry Alice. He then returned to organise rebellion, while Philip invaded Normandy. Neither got as far as he hoped. Eleanor and the Justiciars took strong precautions and prevented the landing of a Flemish force. Richard's French vassals would not rise against an absent crusader. Walter of Coutances besieged Windsor; Puiset, Tickhill; but at Easter 1193 Hubert Walter arrived direct from Richard to explain that he was still in custody and that a ransom must be raised. So that the necessary work could be done a truce was arranged in England and a peace with Philip for the cession of part of eastern Normandy (T. of Mantes, 9 July 1193). The ransom, 150,000 silver marks (£100,000), was large but not crippling and the continental possessions shared the burden. Normandy found £16,000. By the end of 1193 a large instalment had been delivered and John had abandoned further areas of Normandy and Touraine to Philip; when Richard was set free in Feb. 1194, John fled to Paris.

(6) The main term of the imperial treaty was that England was to be held as a fief of the Empire. This cut both ways, for if England was subject to the Emperor it was also entitled to his protection. Hence Philip Augustus' hostility to Richard necessarily involved imperial hostility to Philip. The Emperor's object was to subjugate the Kingdom of France: he therefore favoured the alliances which Richard made on his way home with the ecclesiastical and lay rulers of the Rhineland and the Low Countries, the Dukes of Austria and Swabia and the M. of Monferrat. These were temporarily inactive because England could not afford to finance them, but they mostly represented an economic reality and developed eventually into a genuine political movement.

(7) When Richard reached England (Mar. 1194) John's possessions had been overrun and most of his castles taken. A council at Nottingham disposed of his supporters, especially Bp. Hugh of Coventry. Longchamp, actively engaged in Richard's release, was reinstated as Chancellor. Walter of Coutances went back to Normandy. The very able Hubert Walter, Abp. of Canterbury since May 1193, was made Justiciar and in 1195 received a legatine commission. The King was recrowned in Apr. and left for France in May. Hubert Walter ruled England for him until the end of the reign. Eleanor effected a formal reconciliation between her sons at Lisieux, but John received back Mortain, Eye and Gloucester (without their castles) only in the summer of 1195.

(8) Richard had no illusions about Philip, whose royal aura was tarnished by breach of faith with crusaders. Philip meant to have the English continental possessions by diplomacy, subversion, fraud or force.

Richard's diplomacy and counter-subversion had been brilliantly successful. War was therefore certain and Richard was a master of war. Neither the militia which, under the Assize of Arms, superseded the *fyrd* nor the short service feudal host were suited to the long and wide ranging war which Richard expected. The experience of Outremer proposed a strong mobile professional force operating among modern safely fortified strong points. The expense of this type of war was tremendous; and though Richard was progressively successful, finance was a permanent clog on operations.

(9) Richard landed in Normandy in May 1194 and relieved Verneuil. By the capture of Loches he undid John's treachery in Touraine; at Fréteval (22 July) he routed the French King himself. There followed an ecclesiastically arranged truce at Tillières (23 July), while both sides girded themselves for further efforts. The Emperor urged Richard on and in June 1195 remitted the outstanding 17,000 marks of the ransom as a contribution to his war chest. Philip, alarmed at the possibility of German intervention, called off the truce. A war of mutual attrition ended in the P. of Louviers (Feb. 1196).

(10) To prepare for the next round Richard completed the safeguarding of the south; Sancho of Navarre, brother of his wife Berengaria, was already his ally. Now he married his widowed sister, Joanna, to Raymond VI of Toulouse.

In the Norman Vexin he began to construct for the safety of the Seine Valley, Château Gaillard, the fruit of his skill and experience and the most powerful small fortress in Europe. By a combination of economic pressure and concession, he half bullied, half induced the Counts of Flanders and Boulogne to abandon their treaties of 1196 with Philip and make alliances with him. Limburg joined in and so did Brabant, whose Duke was given the honour of Eye, taken from John. The Italian Boniface of Montferrat was subsidised from Normandy.

(11) Henry the Lion of Saxony had spent the years 1185 to 1189 at the English Court, where his sons were brought up. He died in 1195, by which time his son Henry had become Count Palatine. In 1196 Richard made the second son, Otto, Count of Poitou. The Emperor Henry VI attempted to make his throne hereditary in that year, but secured only the compromise election of his son Frederick II as King of Sicily (Christmas). He died, after putting down a Sicilian rebellion, in Sept. 1197, absolving Richard of his allegiance on his deathbed. In the following Jan. occurred an event of world importance, namely the election of Innocent III to the Papal throne. That wily saint, in which the ambitions of the Papacy received their supreme expression, was soon busy. In Mar. 1198 Henry VI's brother, Philip of Swabia, was elected King of the Romans. In May Innocent took Sicily and its young King under his protection. In between, the anti-Hohenstaufen princes with Innocent's encouragement, invited Richard to participate in a schismatic imperial election. In June Otto of Saxony and Poitou became a rival King of the Romans; a German civil war, fomented by the Vicar of Christ, broke out. Thereupon Philip and Richard went formally to war (Sept. 1198). Richard won at Vernon, captured Courcelles and on 13 Jan. 1199 arranged a truce on the basis of the *status quo*. In Apr. Richard was fatally wounded at Chaluz, attempting to enforce rights of treasure trove against one of his own vassals.

(12) This sudden decisive death removed from the English side the ablest general and one of the most experienced diplomats in Europe.

RICHARD II or of BORDEAUX (1367-1400), P. of WALES (1376) King (1377-99), younger son of the Black Prince (1) came to England in 1371 after his elder brother's death; brought up by his mother, the beautiful and peaceful Joan of Kent. The strongest influence in his early life was that of Robert de Vere, E. of Oxford and

Great Chamberlain who as a royal ward five years older than Richard was virtually an elder brother. He was a silly, vain, irresponsible man, but too strong for Richard during his impressionable years.

(2) The ablest and most influential statesman of the period was Richard's uncle, John of Gaunt, D. of Lancaster, who had been involved in the stormy disputes at the end of the previous reign. As the foremost Prince he was the natural head of the govt. during Richard's minority. The wars were going badly and the Duke, perhaps mindful of his father Edward III's example, seized the opportunity of a new reign to attempt a national reconciliation. It was centred this time on Richard's especially splendid coronation and associated with signal acts of clemency, such as the pardon of Peter de la Mare (see GOOD PARLIAMENT) and of generosity, including the creation of four earls. But the war would not wait. French and Castilian fleets raided the I. of Wight, attacked the Yarmouth herring fleets and burned Hastings and Rye. There was a French inspired insurrection in Wales and the Scots had invested Berwick. The first Parliament (Oct. 1377) made large war grants and Gaunt had managed to borrow £15,000 from four London financiers and the City itself; but ominously, two of the financiers (John Philipot and William Walworth) were made treasurers of the grants and some of the parliamentary petitions were couched in the language of the Ordinances of 1311.

(3) It was not easy to reverse the trend of the war. The Welsh revolt was, admittedly, put down, but Berwick surrendered and the Castilians raided Cornwall and burned Fowey. An English expedition indeed seized Cherbourg; John Philipot with a private fleet captured an important Scottish pirate, John Mercer, but then Gaunt himself was disastrously repulsed from St. Malo. At the same time a murder perpetrated by a King's knight at the altar of Westminster Abbey caused a public outcry and reopened the breaches between the magnates, the Church and the City. Under these sensational conditions the next parliament had to be summoned to the relative security of Gloucester (Oct. 1378) and the govt., with difficulty, extracted only a meagre grant.

(4) The election of Urban VI at Rome (Apr. 1378) and of a rival francophile Clement VII at Fondi (Sept.) not only divided Christians but exacerbated relations between states. Papal peace-making ceased and was replaced by the rivalry of ecclesiastical potentates recruiting military allies against each other. If France was Clementist, it was natural for Scotland to be so too and for England and other northern states to support Urban. The Great Schism was from the start entangled in the Hundred Years' War, which now took a turn for the better. In 1379 the Bretons rose against the French and Berwick was regained, but despite these events the govt. had, since the Gloucester Parliament, slipped deeper into debt. A parliament called for Jan. 1380 was strongly critical and administrative changes had to be made before it would grant supplies. In the summer a Franco-Castilian fleet was sharply defeated off Ireland, but this attracted less attention than an abortive and wasteful foray across France by Richard's youngest uncle, Thomas of Woodstock. The govt's. finances were now in chaos. Yet another parliament had to be held, in Nov. 1380, this time at Northampton. This parliament enacted the third and disastrous poll tax which provoked the Peasants' Revolt (q.v.) of June-July 1381.

(5) Richard's spectacular and decisive part in stopping the revolt, partly emancipated him from the magnate councillors whose skins he had saved and gave him a good conceit of himself. In practice this meant that his private friends had too much royal patronage and money. Anxiety about his surroundings, his extravagance and that of his household and his upbringing was voiced in the parliament of Nov. 1381 and Richard, E. of Arundel

(whom he could not abide) and the financier Sir Michael de la Pole, who turned out to be sympathetic, were appointed as his advisers and tutors. Pole won his friendship by arranging his marriage in Jan. 1382 with the docile Anne of Bohemia, who was plain, poor and initially unpopular, but whose virtues and charity gained her growing esteem. This marriage was part of an Urbanist combination. It also suited the Lancastrian policy of distracting attention from home by vigour abroad. Lancaster had negotiated a truce with the Scots and there was an English expedition under his son, Edmund, in Portugal (see AVIS). The object was to form an Anglo-Aragonese-Portuguese alliance against France's Clementist ally, Castile. This would promote the Urbanist cause, strengthen the English hold on Aquitaine and protect the English seaboard against Castilian raids. Parliament in Jan. of 1382 was unenthusiastic, partly because Crown resources, such as the March wardship, were still being dissipated and large sums consequently borrowed.

(6) By Oct., however, the Portuguese expedition had failed and Ferdinand of Portugal had come to terms with John of Castile. A French army was invading Flanders. Ypres fell. The Flemings were beaten, their leader, Philip van Artevelde killed at Roosebeke (Nov.) and by Dec. Charles VI and the D. of Burgundy had seized Bruges, confiscated all English goods, stopped the English trade and were threatening Calais and its staple. Until the staple could be transferred (to Middleburg) the wool trade, a main source of royal revenue, was at a halt. Military action was clearly necessary: and as France was Clementist, it could be called a crusade and financed by the Church and the alms of the people. Success would strengthen the Flemish connection and draw off French pressure upon Aquitaine. Henry Despenser, the Bp. of Norwich (see PEASANTS' REVOLT) had been advocating such a crusade for some months and had published the Urbanist Bulls on the subject. The Commons and the clergy, led by the primate's brothers Philip and Peter Courtenay induced the govt. to accept (Mar. 1383). The discreditable Norwich Crusade (May-Oct. 1383) was financed in part by a gross abuse of indulgences, the untrained troops preyed upon Urbanist Flemish populations and retreated before the rumour of a French army. It achieved no military or political purpose and injured the good name of the Church.

(7) The Lancastrians had had reservations about a Flemish expedition especially if led by a bishop and when Ferdinand of Portugal died in Oct. 1383, the ensuing change of dynasty broke his Castilian alliance and brought Portugal back to Urbanist allegiance. A return to an Iberian policy was obviously not immediately possible, but Lancaster began to clear the decks for one; he made a short expedition to Scotland and concluded the truce of Leulegheim with France (Jan. 1384). In the meantime, however, he had become involved in the City factional struggles between the capitalist victuallers represented by Walter Sibill and Nicholas Brembre, with whom he had long been at variance, and the smaller masters and journeymen behind John of Northampton, who was elected mayor after the Peasants' Revolt but replaced in 1383 by Brembre. He began to organise against Brembre; there were riots and in Jan. 1384 Brembre was bound over. These events all coincided with a growing estrangement between Lancaster and Richard, egged on by de Vere. They had a public quarrel at the Salisbury Parliament (Apr. 1384) arising out of the Latimer affair, when some of Lancaster's supporters threatened the King. In Aug. John of Northampton was tried before the Council and, protesting against judgement in the absence of his Lord, the D. of Lancaster, was sent to prison in Tintagel.

(8) These and similar events were symptoms of a *malaise*. Magnates, statesmen and politicians were conscious of the decline since Edward III's time. Civil

disorder and military humiliation could be ascribed to bad govt. It was politic to blame Richard's greedy and dissolute friends. Lancaster said what he thought to Richard and Richard hated him for it. The Court seemed to take too little notice of public feeling, especially that a King ought to be strong and capable of martial deeds. The autumn Parliament of 1384 granted funds for a French expedition, but the French got in first: they sent a force under Jean de Vienne to upset the Scottish truce; and so in 1385 a great army invaded Lothian and took Edinburgh, while Jean de Vienne crossed to the west and raided Carlisle. Richard, bored with the operations, went home, but while it was in progress Portuguese emissaries appeared to ask for help. A force of volunteers reached Lisbon in Apr. 1385 and in Aug. the Anglo-Portuguese defeated the Castilians at the B. of Aljubarota, the Portuguese Bannockburn. Lancaster could now, with some show of support, claim the Castilian crown. Richard, glad to see him go, recognised him as King of Castile in Mar. 1386. He sailed with a strong force from Plymouth in July.

(9) Lancaster's departure unleashed a crisis whose approach Richard had been too isolated to perceive. A Franco-Burgundian invasion armada was collecting in the Channel ports. The means to defeat it were either in Portugal or non-existent. A parliament (The Wonderful Parliament) had to be summoned to Westminster for Oct. There was great excitement, feelings against the favourites and a desire for scapegoats. The govt., headed by Michael de la Pole (now E. of Suffolk) had to ask for very large sums ($\frac{4}{15}$ths). Richard retired to Eltham and made de Vere D. of Ireland. The Parliament replied by demanding the dismissal of Suffolk (Chancellor) and John Fordham, Bp. of Durham (Treasurer). Richard truculently refused. They demanded that he should come to Westminster. Too late he consented to receive a deputation, which might perhaps be browbeaten. His youngest uncle, Thomas D. of Gloucester, saw to it that this could not happen. With Thomas Arundel, Bp. of Ely, he brought the parliamentary demands himself and with allusions to Edward II's deposition bullied Richard into concessions on condition that his personal friends should be saved harmless. He came to Westminster and appointed the Bps. of Ely and Hereford in place of Suffolk and Fordham and John Waltham to the Privy Seal in place of Walter Skirlaw. The Commons were now free to impeach Suffolk, who however, proved hard to attack for the case against him was weak and he was eventually fined and imprisoned – at the King's pleasure.

(10) In fact the battle had just begun. The Parliament sought to reform the state by establishing a standing council (on the analogy of the Roman *Decemviri*) for a year with comprehensive powers over the govt. and the household. Richard declared that nothing done in the Parliament could prejudice the Crown and made household appointments in defiance of the Council; then, however, the Council's credit was much improved when the Es. of Arundel and Nottingham won a great victory over a Franco-Castilian fleet off Margate, dismantled the war installations at Brest and brought home much captured wine. Since the Council controlled the centre Richard's friends persuaded him to seek support at the periphery. In Feb. 1387 he left for a tour (*The Gyration*) to recruit support based on de Vere's Irish palatinate, N. Wales and the Cheshire palatinate. In these regions he raised troops; the City protested loyalty, the Abp. of York supported him and several distinguished lawyers, including Sir Robert Tresilian (C.J. of the King's Bench) were with him. On their advice he arranged consultations at Shrewsbury and Nottingham in Aug. with the judges on the legality of certain recent events, notably the creation and powers of the Standing Council, the King's parliamentary powers and impeachments. Their answers were embodied in a secret document executed, amongst

others, by two Chief Justices and three Common Bench judges and witnessed by the two archbishops and three bishops. They were wholly, and as the law then stood correctly, favourable.

(11) Armed with his justification and his troops, Richard now returned to a triumphal reception in London (Nov. 1387). The Standing Council, whose year of office was nearly over, had not been popular and most of them wanted a settlement, but the secret had been betrayed to Gloucester, who with Arundel and Thomas Beauchamp, E. of Warwick, set up a camp at Harringay and issued a public manifesto. They had reason to believe that Richard was coming to terms with the French King, for Warwick's brother, Sir William, Captain of Calais, had disobeyed orders to surrender the port to him. Richard had, on a previous occasion, said that he might seek French help. Support for these magnates now poured in. Many of those ostensibly friendly to Richard, including the Londoners, were not prepared to fight for his favourites. Thus when the Lords formally appealed de Vere, Tresilian, Suffolk, Brembre and the Abp. of York a compromise had to be patched up with all civility at Westminster. The favourites were to be detained pending trial at a parliament to be summoned in Feb. 1388.

(12) Richard did not mean to keep his word; the prisoners all escaped except Brembre, and the sheriffs were instructed to return only M.P.s indifferent to recent dispute. When the Lords found that they had been tricked, some wanted to depose Richard, but Warwick advised that an army under Henry of Lancaster and Thomas Mowbray be sent against de Vere. These, with Gloucester, defeated de Vere at Radcot Bridge (Dec. 1387). He fled overseas and, after a stormy interview at the Tower, Richard withdrew the offending parliamentary writs, while the Standing Council purged his household and dismissed the five judges who had given their opinion at Nottingham (*see* 10 *above*). The Parliament (*The Merciless Parliament*) met in Feb. Brembre and Tresilian (who had been caught) were executed as traitors: the other three condemned in absence. Other officials and four chamber knights were impeached and executed despite the Queen's supplications, and the five judges were condemned but reprieved. These events created a dangerous precedent. There was a reconciliation founded on the fiction that now that good King Richard was freed from his evil councillors all would be well.

(13) It was assumed that the rule of the Appellants would not last indefinitely; they suffered a setback against the Scots at Otterburn (Aug. 1388) which led to a series of truces with the French and though they auctioned off the property of those recently condemned, Richard was able to declare his own emancipation in council in May 1389. Warwick went home; Henry of Lancaster and Gloucester planned to go crusading in Prussia, Arundel in the Levant. Some Appellant supporters were dismissed from the household and the King announced his action to a generally approving public. He set the seal on this reversion to an older situation by summoning Lancaster from Spain, whence he arrived amid scenes of enthusiasm in Nov. 1389. For the next nine years his prestige was Richard's best shield.

(14) Richard never deviated from his chosen line. He soon alarmed his advisers by considering pardons for de Vere. In 1390 he was trying to promote Edward II's canonisation. In Nov. 1392 he quarrelled with the City, put in Sir Edward Dallingridge as custodian and let them recover their liberties for a *pleasaunce* of £10,000. Gloucester had seen to it that it was so little: he was popular in the City. Then Gloucester's friend Arundel quarrelled furiously with Lancaster over sporadic northern revolts which Arundel had not tried to suppress, and Lancaster accused him at the Parliament of Hilary 1394 of aiding the rebels. Arundel retaliated (with some justification) on the Duke's mainly personal policy in

Spain and Aquitaine, but Richard forced him to a humiliating apology.

(15) The four year French truce (May 1394) created an opportunity to deal with Irish problems. Ineffectual lordship under ineffectual sovereignty was the obvious difficulty. Legislation against absenteeism was unenforceable and provoked Anglo-Norman demands for rulers of consequence or perhaps a visit by the King in person. The King took them at their word. He would bring a great army and put down the Irish rebels. Large funds were voted and the King, his army and all his greater magnates landed at Waterford in Oct. The E. of Ormonde was sent in pursuit of Art McMurrough and the Leinster rebels, while Richard marched via Kilkenny to Dublin. Here he and his advisers drew up a policy for Ireland. McMurrough was to be driven from Leinster and an English land or Pale created between the Irish Sea and a line from the Boyne to Waterford. There was to be a general pardon for those English who had risen with the Irish, and finally Irish chiefs were to be admitted to the status of tenants under the Crown, in return for oaths of allegiance to the King and to the Anglo-Norman lords. Richard's presence, charm and powerful army impressed the chiefs, the greatest of whom did homage early in 1395. This was the most general Irish recognition of English overlordship before 1541. Richard's reputation stood high when he returned to England in May 1395 in response to parliamentary demands: for his Irish excursion had been expensive and the Scots were threatening, but he had recruited a small household army; most of his relatives were now friendly, old or powerless though Gloucester and Arundel both hated Lancaster.

(16) The next step was to end the French war: a 28-year truce was made in Mar. 1396. Anne of Bohemia had died in 1394 and Richard now married the child Isabella of France (Oct.). The policy, sensible in itself, was vitiated by the past. Generations of soldiers and nobles were used to the spoils of France. Magnates had not forgotten the King's threat to secure French help against his subjects and were alarmed by a clause to that apparent effect in the first draft of the truce. There was a general fear that he might commit the country expensively to French policies, for he had sent a force to the Franco-Florentine war and had undertaken to support the Way of Cession to solve the Great Schism. Yet he was prepared to barter the French alliance for Roman Papal support in a bid for the imperial crown and was paying pensions to Imperial Electors. He was bored with English restraints and, intolerant of criticism, forced the Commons to apologise in the Hilary Parliament of 1397. He was successfully borrowing considerable sums.

(17) Confident and strong, he now engineered a treacherous coup d'état. He invited Warwick to a banquet and arrested him. He gave false assurances to Arundel and arrested him too and then seized Gloucester at Pleshey and had him conveyed to Calais. His other kinsmen, with Nottingham, Salisbury, Despenser and Sir William Scrope formally appealed them. The appeal was referred to a parliament called for Sept. 1397, which first repealed the pardons granted to the Lds. Appellant in 1388 and then condemned the three for notorious crimes. Gloucester had already been murdered at Calais. Arundel was executed, Warwick banished. Richard then created five dukedoms (Hereford for Henry of Lancaster; Norfolk for Thomas Mowbray; Exeter for his half-brother John Holland; Surrey for Thomas Holland and Aumale for Edward of Rutland), a Marquessate (Dorset for John Beaufort) and four earldoms. He also annexed the palatinate of Chester to the Crown and started giving away forfeited property. Parliament was adjourned to Shrewsbury (Jan. 1398); it reversed the proceedings of the Merciless Parliament, granted a subsidy and conferred the wool and leather customs for life.

(18) Richard's power was all on the surface. His extravagance and ostentation, his lack of realism and unreliability had always been known to a limited circle. He now stood revealed to a wide public as a rapacious and treacherous tyrant. Disaffection seethed below his horizon. He sensed it and frequently required influential people to take special oaths to uphold some act of his. Meanwhile he was levying *pleasaunces*, circumventing the Common Law by bringing cases against his critics in the Court of Chivalry and pursuing the imperial crown by concordats (Nov. 1398), which abandoned the legislation against Papal provisions and alienated the French. This was the first of a chain of events leading to his overthrow, for there had been a quarrel between Hereford and Norfolk which led to their banishment and Hereford was in Paris. Next Hereford's father, Lancaster, died (Feb. 1399), whereby the resources of the strongest supporter of the regime were transferred to a powerful and enterprising enemy. Immediately afterwards came the news that Art McMurrough had, on the death of the E. of March, risen again. Richard raised an army. As soon as it was known that he meant to go himself, Hereford began to plot his own return. Some Lancastrian castles were already held in his interest when Richard landed at Waterford on 1st June. At the end of June Hereford, having rejected French help (except for money), sailed from Boulogne, touched at Pevensey and went on to Ravenspur on the Humber. All the northerners flocked to him. The ineffectual Edmund of York, Keeper of the Realm, failed to call out the levies in time. By the end of July Hereford had captured Edmund, most of the Council and Bristol. On 9 Aug. he took Chester. On 11th Richard arrived at Conway from Pembroke to find that almost all his magnates (save Edward Beaufort) had betrayed him. He negotiated terms through the E. of Northumberland and Abp. Arundel but was seized and taken to Flint, then to meet Hereford at Chester and then to the Tower. Parliament met at the end of Sept. as an assembly of Estates and he was deposed (see ABDICATION – LEGAL; HENRY IV).

(19) His arbitrary and sly incompetence as a ruler has since been obscured by the reputation and monuments which he left as a patron. These were in a sense a byproduct of his passion for splendour; Westminster Hall and the Wilton Diptych are impressive examples both of his outlook and of its expense.

(20) He died or was murdered a few months after his deposition.

RICHARD III (1452-85, King 1483) D. of GLOUCESTER (1461), brother of Edward IV, (1) was brought up by Warwick at Middleham. He was given Richmond and Pembroke in 1462; in 1464 he became a Special Commissioner in the west and south-west against the Lancastrians and acquired the estates of the attainted Ld. Hungerford. Shortly after Edward's Woodville marriage (1464) he came to Court where he got on very well with the Queen and her ambitious relatives; yet he married Anne Neville, Warwick's daughter, but during Warwick's rebellion and the Readeption he sided with his brother and rode north to raise troops for his rescue. He commanded part of Edward's army at Barnet and at Tewkesbury.

(2) By now he was influential by rank and wealth. He had acquired much Warwick property, especially Middleham and Sheriff Hutton (Yorks.), but at this time he did much (no doubt at his wife's entreaty) to comfort the fallen Nevilles, championing the enlargement of Warwick's widow and in 1473 his brother Abp. George Neville, besides helping Warwick's Northumberland nephew and sister, the Countess of Oxford, whose husband he disliked. He also did his best for the ungrateful and silly Clarence whose execution he opposed. His strongest influence was in the City of York where he and Anne often resided and he was enrolled as a guildsman there.

(3) After Clarence's execution he was put in charge of the Scottish Border operations (1478) and given the West March (*see* EDWARD IV-17). His proceedings were both successful and sensible, culminating in the retrocession of Berwick.

(4) Edward IV died on 9 Apr. 1483 and his son Edward V at Ludlow was proclaimed on the 11th. The boy left for London on the 24th and Ld. Hastings, the Chamberlain, informed Richard at Middleham that the late King had appointed him Protector of the King and realm and urged him to take charge of the King's person quickly. He also reported that the magnates available at the deathbed had been divided between those who held that the Protector should govern, and those (including the Woodvilles) who preferred conciliar rule with the Protector only as chief councillor. They preferred to expedite the coronation and headed by E. Rivers marched speedily towards London with the King. Hastings warned Richard, who with the D. of Buckingham intercepted Rivers at Northampton, caught up with the King at Stony Stratford and dismissed his escort. The Queen Mother and other Woodvilles took sanctuary and on 4 May Richard and the King entered London where the council confirmed the Protectorship.

(5) The fleet was now won over from its admiral, Sir Edward Woodville, while Buckingham was put in charge of the west, Wales and the Marches. The King was lodged in the Tower, his brother went to the Queen. It soon seemed that Hastings was inclined to a reconciliation with the Woodvilles; he was communicating with the M. of Dorset, their main supporter, through Jane Shore who had been Edward IV's mistress, then Dorset's and now his own. On 13 June Richard arrested and executed Hastings. Meanwhile the Lords due in London for the coronation were told to bring small escorts and found themselves powerless when they reached it. Abp. Bourchier next persuaded the Queen to surrender the young D. of York from sanctuary and he was lodged with the King in the Tower. Richard had by now heard a story that the two boys were bastards by reason of an alleged precontract between their father and Lady Eleanor Butler daughter of the E. of Shrewsbury and widow of Sir Thomas Butler. Buckingham published this in a speech at Common Hall in the City and it was repeated with embroideries in sermons during June. On 25 June an assembly of lords and commons petitioned Richard to take the Crown and to this the same persons assembled as a Parliament assented. Next day Richard usurped the throne and was crowned in July. He then set out on a progress. By this time Edward V and his brother had ceased to be seen at the Tower.

(6) Everybody believed that he had murdered the boys and there was a national revulsion against him. Buckingham, without whom he would not have reached the throne, was himself of royal descent through Thomas of Woodstock and the Beauforts; moreover he was married to a Woodville. If Richard was prepared to slaughter two children lately declared illegitimate by Parliament, he might *a fortiori* try to strike Buckingham. The Duke decided to strike first. He had contacts with Henry Tudor, E. of Richmond, through the latter's mother, Margaret. Henry's claim was prior to Buckingham's and Buckingham thought that his own claim would be insufficiently supported. He would be a new King-maker instead. A great pro-Tudor operation was planned for mid-Oct. The mine was prematurely detonated by local popular uprisings in the south, which forced Richmond to sail from Brittany and Buckingham to mobilise in Wales, under storms which dispersed the fleet and flooded the western valleys. Richard had a powerful army centrally placed. The southern rebels were easily suppressed. Buckingham's unfed troops dispersed and he was caught and executed. Richmond returned to Brittany

where Richard nearly succeeded by bribery in having him apprehended.

(7) The parliamentary session of 1483, postponed by the insurrection, was opened and after dealing with the expected crop of attainders, passed acts against legal and administrative abuses such as clandestine feoffments to uses, the denial of bail, the qualifications of jurors and abuse of piepowder process. It also forbade benevolences and in the sphere of foreign trade it attempted to regulate the activities of Italian merchants. At the same time out of his northern experience, Richard set up the important Council of the North.

(8) In Apr. 1484 Richard's son died and he nominated John de la Pole, E. of Lincoln, as his heir. By this time Henry of Richmond had obtained French finance as well as a Breton base and encouragement and important personalities such as Bp. Morton were joining him. Richard expecting attack, organised defences based upon a central position at Nottingham with a radiating network of messengers and signals. He was at Nottingham until Nov. and then, unwilling to call a Parliament, had to finance his dispositions by borrowing. The desertions continued. Sir James Blount, Lieut. of Hammes, joined Richmond with his prisoner, the E. of Oxford.

(9) Richmond sailed from the Seine and landed at Milford Haven on 7 Aug. 1485. For K. Richard's defeat and death *see* BOSWORTH FIELD, B. OF.

RICHARD of CAMBRIDGE (?-1415) E. of CAMBRIDGE (1414), 2nd *s.* of Edmund D. of York, married Anne *d.* of Roger Mortimer and became involved in a plot to put her brother Edmund of March on the throne. Edmund, who was not a conspirator, told Henry V and Richard was attainted.

RICHARD, E. of CORNWALL (1209-72), King of the ROMANS (1257), 2nd *s.* of King John, was sent to Aquitaine in 1225 in nominal command of a successful expedition which ended in a truce in 1227. In 1231 he married Isabel *d.* of William the Marshal, but in the meantime he had several quarrels with his brother, Henry III, and efforts were made to entangle him in the political movement against Henry's foreign supporters. He took the cross in 1236, but his departure was delayed because of these troubles until 1239. In Palestine he took advantage of recent successes by Count Thibault of Champagne and in a treaty with the Egyptian Sultan, secured the return of E. Galilee and the coast about Jaffa and Ascalon. This and ransoming French knights gained him a reputation in Europe. On returning he took part in Henry III's unsuccessful expedition to Poitou in 1342, but a rift developed between them and Richard, on his way to England, was nearly wrecked. In fulfilment of a vow he founded Hailes Abbey, where he was later buried. Isabel died in 1240 and in 1243 he married the Queen's sister, Sanchia of Provence. Henry now entrusted him with important diplomatic missions, in 1244 to Scotland and in 1247 and 1250 to France. Being very rich, he lent large sums to Henry who in return gave him control over, and the profits of, the recoinage of 1247-8 and in 1255 the royal rights over the Jews. Being very rich also enabled him to adopt a quasi-independent attitude, especially in the disputes between native nobles and the King's Provencals, whom he probably understood better than most. Meanwhile Henry was seeking to raise his own prestige by furthering Richard's candidature in the Holy Roman Empire. At the end of a very expensive negotiation Richard was elected King of the Romans by four votes to three, but the minority refused to recognise him. Hence his efforts to establish his position (for which the English tax payer paid) embroiled England with Alfonso X of Castile, the other candidate, who was a neighbour of Aquitaine. The whole misconceived venture added to the grievances which the baronial opposition, now led by Simon de Montfort, had against the King. By 1259 his German supporters threatened to desert because he had run out of money. He returned to England to raise more, but returned in 1260 and was caught up in the furious disputes which led to the Barons' War. Irrevocably committed to his brother, he was captured at Lewes (1264) but freed after Simon de Montfort's death at Evesham (1265). In 1268 he presided at an Imperial Diet. Meanwhile he was suffering from a wasting disease whose effects were hastened by the murder of his son, Henry of Almaine, by the younger Simon de Montfort at Viterbo.

RICHARD of DEVIZES (late 12th cent.), a monk of St. Swithun's, Winchester, wrote a chronicle of English events from the coronation of Richard I (3 Sept. 1189) to his preparations to return to England from the Holy Land in Oct. 1192.

RICHARD of WALLINGFORD (1291-1336) leper and abbot of St. Albans (1326) was a mathematician and astronomer. He designed the St. Albans astronomical clock, the first clock known to have had an escapement.

RICHARDSON, Jonathan, father (1665-1745) and son (1694-1771), fashionable portrait painters who succeeded Kneller and Dahl. The father wrote a standard *Theory of Painting* in 1715. It is through them that the faces of many 18th cent. notabilities are (approximately) known.

RICHARDSON, Samuel (1689-1761), earnestly sentimental but realistic novelist, published *Pamela* in 1740-1, *Clarissa Harlowe* in 1747-8 and *Sir Charles Grandison* in 1753. These were promptly translated into Dutch and French and won him European fame. Their popularity helped to establish the recently conceived idea of circulating libraries.

RICHBOROUGH (Lat. RUTUPIAE). *See* BRITAIN, ROMAN-1. THANET.

RICHELIEU, Armand Du Plessis (1585-1642), Bp. of LUÇON (1607), Cardinal (1622), Duke (1631), (1) As almoner to Anne, Q. to Louis XIII, gained the favour of Marie de Medici, the powerful Queen Mother, and was Sec. of State from 1616 to 1617 just before the opening of the Thirty Years' War and was about the Court during the subsequent tumults and rebellions. In 1662 he helped to cut the ground from under the factions by reconciling the Q. Mother with the King. He was called to the council and by 1624 was in the saddle as Chief Minister.

(2) His purpose was the wholly secular one of elevating the French Crown above the world. For this he had to begin by ensuring its pre-eminence at home. He liquidated an English war by negotiating the marriage of the Princess Henrietta Maria to Charles I (1625). The borders being thus safe, he turned upon the two bodies of semi-independent power in France, namely the territorial nobles and the Huguenots. Each had influential ramifications among the highest in the land, each possessed fortified enclaves: the nobles their jurisdictions and castles, the Huguenots their chapel congregations and walled towns. To some extent they overlapped, for many nobles, especially in the south, were Huguenots. Noble intrigues, generally centring on the D. of Orléans, and Huguenot riots were parallel but complementary and so were the methods of dealing with them. Orléans, as a Prince of the Blood, could not be touched, but some very august non-royal noblemen such as Montmorency, were hanged. Castles and town walls were dismantled, if necessary by artillery. By Aug. 1627 the royal army was besieging the Huguenot 'capital' of La Rochelle.

(3) Nothing illustrates the secular nature of this internal war better than Richelieu's treatment of the virtually bankrupt, but Protestant Dutch. In return for French finance against Spanish aggression, he required them to co-operate against their co-religionists. English efforts to relieve La Rochelle met more than expected resistance, failed and ended with Buckingham's assassination (Aug. 1628). La Rochelle capitulated in Oct. 1628. The P. of Susa (Apr. 1629) ended this English

intervention. By the P. or Decree of Alais (June) the Huguenots' religious freedom was granted, but their political organisation liquidated.

(4) The Huguenot political collapse was complete, but the old nobility was less tractable and remained a problem even after its castles had gone. He encouraged absenteeism at Court and by service in the army and made their absence a pretext for raising up a local administration. He encouraged the pretensions of the rival nobility of lawyers (*Noblesse de la Robe*). In the meantime he felt strong enough to intervene in the Thirty Years' War (q.v.). The Cardinal understood diplomacy, but little of economics or war. The result was a struggle in which an impoverished France made the rest of Europe still poorer than herself. In this sense he achieved the pre-eminence of the French throne but left it perched upon an unsound internal structure.

(5) He had, however, time and despite constant ill health, the energy to leave enduring monuments. He rebuilt and re-endowed the Sorbonne, set up the Paris botanical gardens, founded the French Academy and established the important govt. printing industry.

RICHMOND, Ds. of. *See* FITZROY, HENRY.

RICHMOND (Yorks.) and the 200 manors associated with it, covered about one third of the North Riding and belonged to E. Edwin before William I gave it in 1071 to Alan of Penthièvre, who built the castle. The burgesses apparently had liberties before their first surviving charter of 1145. A fair was granted in 1278. The honour was owned by the rulers of Brittany for most of the 13th and 14th cents. but passed to the Crown in 1485. Though first summoned in 1328 it was not represented in the Commons until 1584, just after (1576) it had been incorporated. The mayoralty was established in 1668. It returned one M.P. from 1867 to 1885. *See* BRITTANY.

RICHMOND, Es. of. *See* PETER OF SAVOY; TUDOR.

RICHMOND ON THAMES (London). Sheen, a favourite manor of Henry VII (formerly E. of Richmond), was renamed by him and contains or contained many important royal properties, notably Richmond Palace, Hampton Court, Ham House and Kew.

RICHMOND COMMISSION (1879-82). In 1879 there was an apparently irremediable agricultural disaster due to the coincidence of a series of abnormally wet seasons, outbreaks of plant disease (mainly ergot and mould) and huge animal mortalities in a variety of epidemics. The Commission appointed in consequence reported that rising local taxation for sanitation and education combined with discriminatory railway charges imposed an insupportable burden upon an agriculture which could not recover in the face of rising costs and cheap, mostly N. American, imports. This unforeseen effect of repealing the Corn Laws was not, because of the pressure of urban electorates, remedied until strategic considerations forced a solution upon the govt. in World War II.

RICKETS, not to be confused with Rickettsia, is a deficiency affecting very young children in temperate climates. Probably ancient, it was first recognised in 1650 by Glisson who thought that it had first been seen in about 1630 in Dorset and Somerset. It was an important cause of many of the deformities pictured in 18th cent. prints. In the 1860s it accounted for about 30% of cases in children's departments of London and Manchester hospitals. The mainly nutritional treatment was known on the continent in the 18th cent. but not the reasons why it worked and it seems to have been forgotten until the 1920s, when detailed analysis proved the value of ultra-violet light and cod liver oil. *See* INFANTILE DIARRHOEA.

RICKMAN, JOHN (1771-1840), prepared the first census of 1800 and wrote the reports for the censuses of 1801, 1811, 1821 and 1831. He also compiled the annual Poor Law Abstracts from 1816 to 1836, was clerk assistant to the House of Commons and indexed its journals.

RICKMAN, Thomas (1776-1841), published in 1817 a scholarly and influential *Attempt to Discriminate the Styles of Architecture in England from the Conquest to the Reformation*. One of the intellectual foundations of the Gothic revival.

RIDLEY, Nicholas (?1500-55) became Master of Pembroke Hall, Cambs., and a King's Chaplain in 1540. He then observed the old rites but after he became Bp. of Rochester and a visitor to the University in 1547 he encouraged more reformist opinions and in 1550 replaced the repressive Bonner as Bp. of London. He worked on the first English Prayer Book and cherished the poor. When Edward VI died, he preached at St. Paul's Cross that the Princesses Mary and Elizabeth were illegitimate and Lady Jane Grey his proper heir. After the failure of the attempted *coup* in her name, he was imprisoned and deprived. In 1554, with Hugh Latimer and Thomas Cranmer, he was tried in the Divinity School at Oxford and pronounced heretic. With the passage of new capital laws against heresy in 1555, he was retried and burnt with Latimer opposite Balliol College.

RIDOLFI, Roberto (1531-1612), Florentine financier, was first involved in English politics in 1568 as an agent of the D. of Norfolk to the Spanish Ambassador, Don Guerau de Spes, in connection with a plot against Cecil (*see* NORTHERN REBELLION, OCT. 1569-FEB. 1570). The Papal Bull *Regnans in Excelsis* against Elizabeth I was published in 1570 and Ridolfi began to plan a *coup* against the Queen herself, known as his PLOT. He would recruit about 40 peers who would, with Spanish military help, make Mary Q. of Scots Queen of England after a marriage to the D. of Norfolk. In Feb. 1571 Mary assented and gave him letters to the Pope, the D. of Alva (Spanish Viceroy in the Netherlands) and K. Philip II. His chief assistant was to be the Bp. of Ross. In Mar. they won over Norfolk (already suspect for his part in the Northern Rebellion). Ridolfi went to Brussels in Apr., Rome in May and Madrid in June. Alva called him a big talker and tried to persuade Philip against the scheme. In fact the plot had already come to Cecil's knowledge when the Scots Regent, Lennox, took Dumbarton in Apr. and found evidence incriminating Mary. Other details came from the Grand Duke of Tuscany and the Calvinist Queen of Navarre who intercepted Spanish diplomatic mail. Hence it was possible to arrest couriers for the Bp. of Ross and Mary's Scottish supporters and in Sept. Norfolk himself was arrested. Threatened with torture, the Bp. implicated Norfolk who was condemned in Jan. 1572 and executed in June. The plot destroyed Mary's reputation, ensured that Elizabeth would not willingly set her at liberty and discredited the Howards. *See also* ELIZABETH I-11 to 13.

RIDOTTO, REDUIT, ROUT or REDOUBT was an entertainment or social gathering for music and dancing. It was introduced in 1722 at the Haymarket Opera House and became an outstanding feature of social life in the 18th cent. for which the Assembly Rooms in many towns were built.

RIEL, Louis. *See* CANADA-20 to 22.

RIEVAULX ABBEY (Yorks.), a powerful and progressive Cistercian house, was founded in 1131 and established influential daughter houses at Melrose (1136), Warden (1137), Dundrennan (1142), Revesby (1143) and Rufford (1148). The ruins are still impressive.

RIFLE. *See* FIREARMS.

RIG or RIDGE (mainly Scot.). A primitive method of land drainage under strip cultivation, whereby the land was ploughed from the outer edge lengthways and so the soil gradually pushed and heaped in the middle to form a ridge, usually shaped like a very flattened, which might be 200-300 yards long.

RIGDAMNA **(Celt: Suitability for royalty).** In Ireland, membership of any of the four generations sprung from a common great-grandfather. One who possessed *rigdamna* was entitled to a share of an inheritance and was liable to contribute to any fine. The word was peculiarly appropriate to kingship.

RIGHT. *See* LEFT.

RIGHTS BOYS. *See* WHITEBOYS.

RIGHTS OF MAN AND OF THE CITIZEN, DECLARATION OF, passed by the French Constituent Assembly in Aug. 1789, consisted of 17 articles. Descriptive of natural rights as then conceived and ignoring religion, tradition or the monarchy, they represented a change in the assumptions behind political institutions. As, however, they contained no sanctions for their enforcement, they were soon ignored in France and derided elsewhere as utopian or unnecessary.

RIGHT, WRIT OF was in form a royal order obtained by a plaintiff ("demandant") to a sheriff to put him in possession of land by virtue of his right. The defendant ("tenant") might refuse to give up the land on the ground that he had a better right. The question whether the writ should or should not be enforced would then be decided by the court.

RIJEKA. *See* D'ANNUNZIO; FIUME.

RINUCCINI, Giovanni Batista (1592-1653) Abp. of FERMO, was Papal Nuncio in Ireland from 1645 to 1649. *See* CIVIL WAR-23.

RIO DE ORO was annexed by Spain in 1860.

RIOT. An UNLAWFUL ASSEMBLY must consist of three or more persons for purposes forbidden by law or with intent to effect a common purpose, lawful or not, in such a way as to endanger the public peace or give firm and courageous persons nearby reasonable grounds for apprehending a breach of the peace; but the fact that an assembly may meet opposition of an unlawful kind will not make it unlawful even if a breach of the peace will probably result (*Beatty* v *Gillbanks* (1882) 9 Q.B.D. 308). RIOT is a tumultuous assembly of three or more persons intending to help each other to carry out a common private enterprise (lawful or not) against any opposition and who actually do so in a violent or turbulent manner. A ROUT appears to be an unlawful assembly in movement. AFFRAY is behaviour by more than one person (such as fighting or carrying unusual weapons) which puts bystanders in terror. At Common Law an unlawful assembly was a misdemeanour, but under the Riot Act, 1714, it could become a capital felony (*see* next entry). The Public Order Act, 1936 (provoked by Fascist demonstrations) forbade political uniforms, quasi military organisations and the carrying of offensive weapons at public meetings and processions and made it an offence to use threatening, abusive or insulting words or behaviour intended to provoke a breach of the peace. This superseded most of the previous law.

RIOT ACT (1715). Under this Act, 12 or more people assembled riotously together became felons if they failed to disperse within an hour after a J.P., having commanded silence, "openly and with loud voice" had made the following proclamation:

"Our sovereign Lord the King chargeth and commandeth all persons, being assembled, immediately to disperse themselves, and peaceably to depart to their habitations, or to their lawful business, upon the pains contained in the act made in the first year of King George, for preventing tumults and riotous assemblies. God Save the King."

The courts opposed this method of "creating felons" by "Reading the Riot Act" and insisted upon its exact execution, e.g. in *R* v *Child* (1830) the defendant was acquitted because the words "God Save the King" had not been read. It was repealed in 1973.

RIPON (Yorks.). A Celtic monastery was founded here from Melrose in about 655 and enlarged by St. Wilfrid (q.v.) its second Abbot in 661. This survived until the 9th cent. when the Danes destroyed it. A revived house was sacked by King Eadred of Wessex in 948. The church was re-established as a collegiate body and the (later)

Cathedral was built progressively between 1154 and 1500. It and the town's prosperity arose from the markets and fairs. These belonged to the Abps. of York, who owned properties in the town. The borough was incorporated in 1604, by which time a small paint and varnish industry had grown up. Ripon became a bishopric in 1838 and was made a City in a private gas Act.

RIPON. See ROBINSON.

RISORGIMENTO. The 19th cent. Italian nationalist movement which brought about the unification of Italy and the expulsion of foreign political powers. See CAVOUR.

RITCHIE. Two brothers **(1) John (1778-1870)** and **(2) William (1781-1831)**, journalists, joined with Charles Maclaren (1782-1866) in founding the *Scotsman* in 1817. William and Maclaren were joint editors until William died. John then became sole owner but Maclaren remained editor until 1845.

RITUALISM, ANGLICAN, a symptom of the Oxford Movement, was backed by most of the clergy against most of the laity at a time (1885) when Gladstone proposed one of their leaders, the able and saintly Dr. Edward King for the bishopric of Lincoln. In 1888 the Church Association, a low church body, moved against Dr. King for illegal practices. In the trial, before Abp. Benson and six exceptionally distinguished bps. (Feb. 1889), the court found for him on five of the seven charges and made both sides pay their own costs. This was effectively a victory for ritualism, which now tended to spread to country parishes. The affair discredited doctrinal prosecutions and tended to divide congregations.

RIVERS, Earls. See WOODVILLE or WYDEVILLE.

ROADS. See TRANSPORT AND COMMUNICATIONS.

ROANOKE I. See CAROLINA.

ROBERT OF BELLÊME. See BELLÊME.

ROBERT CURTHOSE, D. of NORMANDY (r. 1087-1106). See NORMANDY-8; WILLIAM II *passim*; HENRY I *passim; and* CRUSADES 1-4.

ROBERT the DEVIL, or the MAGNIFICENT, D. of NORMANDY (r. 1027-35). See NORMANDY-5.

ROBERT, E. of GLOUCESTER (?-1147), bastard of Henry I, was married to Mabel *d.* of Robert Fitzhamon and so acquired great estates in Normandy, England and Wales. He submitted to King Stephen at his accession, but quarrelled with him in 1137. Stephen forfeited his English and Welsh properties, so he went over to the Empress Matilda and became one of her ablest supporters. He captured Stephen at Lincoln in 1141, was then himself taken at Stockbridge and exchanged for the King, whom he again defeated at Wilton in 1143. Until his death he remained the principal military pillar of the Empress's declining party.

ROBERT of GLOUCESTER (fl. 1260-1300). The metrical Gloucester chronicle from early times to 1272 is by several monks, one of whom, Robert, has given his name to the whole. It is autobiographically illustrated and contains accounts of the St. Scholastica riot at Oxford and of Montfort's death at Evesham.

ROBERT of JUMIÈGES (?-after 1052), Abbot of Jumièges (Normandy) from 1037, accompanied Edward the Confessor to England in 1043 and became his Bp. of London in 1044. He was a leader of the centralising, reformist and partly Norman opposition to Godwin. In 1051 he became Abp. of Canterbury and an instigator of Godwin's exile. On Godwin's return in 1052 he fled to Normandy and was deposed in favour of Stigand. Even with Papal support he failed to recover the see.

ROBERT, Count of MORTAIN (?-1091), a half-brother of William I and easily the greatest private landowner in England. See WILLIAM I; WILLIAM II; HENRY I; STEPHEN.

ROBERT I of SCOTS (1274-1329) King (1306). *For the antecedents of this famous King see* BRUCE. His father, Robert (VII) had a claim to the throne. His mother, Margery, Countess of Carrick, came of turbulent Galwegian stock. As E. of Carrick (from 1292) and Ld. of Annandale (from 1304) his power base was in S.W. Scotland. In the 1290s he was primarily an English rebel who in 1296-7 refused Edward I's summons to military service, but the revolt gave him an opportunity to attack the followers of his enemy Baliol, Robert's potential rival for the Scottish Crown. In July 1297 Bruce and his party made their own terms with Edward and acknowledged their allegiance to him, while Sir William Wallace was still maintaining the rebellion which was to cost him his life. Within a few months Robert had gone to Wallace's support, whereupon Edward laid Annandale waste, but refrained from granting the Lordship to anyone else, perhaps because it was too severely damaged. Robert thereupon refrained from attacking the English. The result was a tacit truce between 1298 and 1304, which allowed Edward to overthrow Wallace at the B. of Falkirk (July 1298). Scottish resistance, however, continued in a guerrilla fashion and in practice, as the people of Annandale favoured Robert, most of the Lordship had fallen into his hands by the time that he could assert a title to it (1304). He entered into a secret compact with Wallace's friend Lamberton, Bp. of St. Andrews (June 1304) and in 1306 took an irretrievable step. He murdered the Red Comyn, the other great magnate of the south west, in Dumfries church. Then gathering his people he marched to Scone and was crowned (27 Mar. 1306), but unrecognised by the Papacy or the French he had to enforce his rights against rival Scots (some of whom had been eliminated by the English) and against the English. For this he had patience, cunning, tactical skill, courage and the necessary luck; in particular Edward I died on the way to Scotland against him and was succeeded by the weak Edward II (1307) just after the E. of Pembroke had defeated Robert at Methven near Perth (June 1306) and a Comyn had scattered his followers in a surprise in Aug. This was the winter when Robert wandered as a refugee in the western Highlands and escaped to the I. of Rathlin on the Antrim coast where, according to a perfectly credible story, he drew courage from the persistence of a spider in his cave. Many of his followers were rounded up at this period, including his wife and daughter, who were taken to England. A sister was caged at Roxburgh and three brothers were executed.

The tide, however, turned quickly. English weakening competence enabled him to assemble a force with which in May 1307 he beat Pembroke and when Edward II left for England, he and his brother Edward recovered Galloway and then in Dec. defeated another Comyn, the E. of Buchan, and started to reduce the eastern Highlands. By 1309 the English were offering a truce and this led naturally to the recognition of his kingship by the Scots clergy at Dundee in Feb. 1310. This immensely increased his moral authority. Doubters joined him and enabled him progressively to reduce the English-held castles so that by 1314 they held only Berwick and Stirling. It was the siege of the latter which provoked Edward II's attempt at relief and his resounding and decisive defeat within sight of the castle at Bannockburn (q.v.) on 24 June 1314. The battle not only ousted further English pretensions but secured Robert's throne against all Scottish rivals when his title was confirmed by the Scots Parliament (Apr. 1315).

The Bruce power base in Galloway and Annandale was much closer to Ireland than to most of Scotland and in 1317 Robert and Edward felt secure enough to make an attempt on Ireland, whose affairs were in confusion. It was an excessive ambition which failed, but in 1318 the Scots took Berwick. The result, after a truce in 1320-2 (*see* BOROUGHBRIDGE, B. of), was an English invasion. Robert could contain it only by guerrilla tactics which could not prevent it reaching Edinburgh. In the autumn of 1322, however, he was able to lead a devastating counter-raid into northern England, defeated Edward II at Byland Abbey and nearly captured him. This rout and the civil disturbances which had been endemic in the English northern shires since Bannockburn, apparently led many northerners to despair of protection from the English Crown and look to the King of Scots. This was probably the reason why the English effectively concluded the war with a 13 year truce (1323). Papal recognition put the seal on Robert's position a few months later.

In 1327, taking advantage of the confusion in England surrounding Edward II's abdication and murder, Robert invaded and occupied the northern counties from June to Aug. The new English rulers, Q. Isabel and Mortimer (qq:v) were preoccupied with English politics and Gascon affairs. Negotiations were accordingly set on foot which culminated in the T. of Northampton (May 1328), so-called because it was ratified by an English parliament which met there. This converted the truce into a peace, necessarily involving the recognition of Robert's right to the Scot's Crown and provided for the marriage of Edward III's infant sister, Joan of the Tower, to Robert's son and heir, David, who succeeded his father soon afterwards. The marriage took place after David II's accession.

With this diplomatic success the reign ended. Robert was buried at Dunfermline, but at his wish his friend "Good" Sir James Douglas took his heart with him on a crusade against the Spanish Moors. Douglas' descendants have borne a crowned heart on their arms ever since.

ROBERT II (1317-90) King of SCOTS (1371). See STEWART or STUART, ROYAL HOUSE OF (EARLY) 9-14.

ROBERT III (1337-1406) King of SCOTS (1390). See STEWART or STUART, ROYAL HOUSE OF (EARLY)-15 et seq and JAMES I, KING OF SCOTS-1.

ROBERTS, Bartholomew (1682-1722), teetotaller, sabbatarian and early riser, was the most successful recorded pirate. His hunting ground was the coast of Guinea and the W. Indies and he is said to have taken over 400 vessels. He was killed in action with Capt. Chaloner Ogle who had been sent to put down piracy on the Guinea coast.

ROBERTS, Frederick (1832-1914) E. ROBERTS of KANDAHAR, PRETORIA and WATERFORD. He was C-in-C in India from 1885 to 1893 (see AFGHANISTAN). He was sent to retrieve the position after the Black Week in the South African War, which he did. He was the last C-in-C (1900-4).

ROBERTS, Griffith (?-?1585) published the first Welsh printed grammar at Milan in 1567.

ROBERTS, Richard (1789-1864) converted the Horrocks metal powerloom into a factory machine in 1822 and invented a steam powered mule in 1825 able to spin 2000 threads at once. The result was that the cotton industry moved to the coal fields.

ROBERTS, Sir William (1605-62), Kt (1624), Bart (1661), a lawyer, supported the Parliament in the Civil War, became a member of the Council of State and a commissioner for forfeited estates in 1653 and was much concerned in the purchases of church lands in Middlesex, for which he became M.P. in 1656. He sat in the House of Peers in 1657. No regicide, he was easily reconciled to the restored monarchy.

ROBERTSON, Archibald (1765-1835) and his brother **Andrew (1777-1845)** were leading miniature painters, Archibald in Washington, Andrew in London.

ROBERTSON, James (1758-1820) entered the Scottish Benedictine monastery at Ratisbon in 1772 and eventually became a priest in Galloway, but Canning employed him on a secret mission to Denmark in 1808. He returned to Ratisbon in 1815 and devoted himself to teaching the deaf and dumb.

ROBERTSON, Sir William Robert (1860-1933), Field-Marshal (1920), privately educated, enlisted as a trooper in 1877 and was commissioned in 1888. By 1915 he was Chief of Staff of the British Army on the Western Front, but later that year he was appointed C.I.G.S. Not popular, and cunning rather than clever, he demanded professional rather than political control of strategy while Lloyd George believed in political control. In 1918 he got rid of Robertson by appointing Sir Henry Wilson British representative at Versailles contrary to Robertson's advice. He resigned in protest. His son **(2) Brian Hubert (1896-1974) Ld. ROBERTSON of OAKSBRIDGE (1961)** was on the staff of the 8th Army in World War II; C-in-C of the British Zone in Germany after the War and Chairman of the Transport Commission from 1961.

ROBERTSON, William (?-?1686). Hebrew lexicographer at Cambridge.

ROBETHON, Jean or John de (?-1722), a sagacious Huguenot, came to England in 1689 and became a private sec. and political factotum to William III. At his death he entered the service of George William, D. of Zelle, and in 1705 that of his son-in-law George Lewis, Elector of Hanover (later George I), under whom he was exceptionally well qualified to manage the correspondence with Marlborough and the Whigs. He bore important responsibilities in ensuring the smooth Hanoverian succession (see GEORGE 1-2) in 1714 and acted as the King's political adviser almost until the end of the reign. He also translated Pope's *Essay on Criticism* into French verse.

ROBIN HOOD was the outlawed hero (sometimes described as an Earl or the true E. of Huntingdon and thus of Saxon royal descent) of a mid-15th cent. group of ballads, some possibly based on real events in Barnsdale, Sherwood or Plumpton Park (Cambs.). Attempts have been made to identify the original Robin Hood but have failed on conclusive grounds, probably because he is more likely to represent a rationalised personification of, perhaps, a pagan wood sprite. The stories were known by 1296 and were doubtless spread by wandering minstrels. The elements of 'social protest', notably robbing the rich to give to the poor, are 16th cent. accretions but the stories probably developed not for political reasons but for fun.

ROBINSON, Geoffrey. See DAWSON.

ROBINSON, Henry Crabb (1775-1867), journalist, barrister and diarist was *Times* correspondent in the Peninsula in 1808 and 1809 and founded the Athenaeum and University Coll., London.

ROBINSON, Sir Hercules (1824-97) 1st Ld. ROSMEAD (1896) had a remarkable career after retiring from the army in 1846 as a Colonial Gov., beginning with Monserrat (1854) and then St. Kitts (1855), Hong Kong (1859-65), Ceylon (1865-72), N.S.W. (1872-9), New Zealand (1879-80) and finally Cape Colony (1880-7). See *passim.*

ROBINSON, John (1650-1723) was apprenticed to a trade but was found by his master to be so addicted to reading that he sent him to Oxford. He became Chaplain to the British Embassy at Stockholm and was occasional *chargé d'affaires* from 1680. He was with Charles XII at Narva and acted as Marlborough's Swedish interpreter in 1707. He became Dean of Windsor in 1709, Bp. of Bristol in 1710 and Ld. Privy Seal in 1711. He was a plenipotentiary at the P. of Utrecht (1712-3) and rewarded with the Bishopric of London in 1714.

ROBINSON, John (1727-1802), Sec. to the Treasury from 1770 to 1782, developed the art of electoral analysis for Ld. North, but helped to achieve the younger Pitt's victory of Mar. 1784.

ROBINSON née DARBY, Mary (1758-1800), called **PERDITA,** actress, was the mistress of the P. of Wales (later George IV) in 1778. There are many portraits of her.

ROBINSON, Richard (1709-94) 1st Ld. ROKEBY (1777), a chaplain to the D. of Dorset, Ld. Lieut. of Ireland, in 1751, became after various episcopal appointments,

Dean of Christchurch, Dublin, in 1761, Abp. of Armagh (which he improved) in 1765 and Ld. Justice of Ireland in 1787.

ROBINSON, (1) Thomas (1695-1770) 1st Ld. GRANTHAM (1761), Ambassador to Vienna from 1730 to 1748, represented Britain in the Austrian and Prussian disputes from 1740 to 1748 and was a plenipotentiary at the P. of Aix-la-Chappelle in 1748. He became an M.P. in 1748 and Sec. of State (South) and Newcastle's Leader of the Commons in 1754-5. As such he was not a success. His son **(2) Thomas (1738-86) 2nd Ld.** was 1st Ld. of Trade from 1780 to 1782 and Foreign Sec. from 1782 to 1783. His son **(3) Frederick John (1782-1859) Vist. GODERICH (1827) 1st E. of RIPON (1833)** was a Tory M.P. from 1806, after minor office became joint Paymaster-Gen. in 1815 and led on the Corn Bill of 1815. He was Chancellor of the Exchequer from 1823 to 1827, became Sec. at War and Leader of the Lords in 1827 and was briefly Prime Minister (1827-8) after Canning's death. In 1830 he became Colonial Sec. and in 1833 Ld. Privy Seal. In 1841 he was Pres. of the Board of Trade and from 1843 to 1846 Pres. of the Board of Control. His son **(4) George Frederick (1827-1909) 1st M. of RIPON (1871)**, Christian Socialist, was a Liberal M.P. from 1853. After minor offices he became Palmerston's Sec. for War in 1863 and Sec. for India in 1866 and then as Gladstone's Ld. Pres. from 1868 to 1873 he was Chairman of the Anglo-American Joint Commission (*see* ALABAMA). after a period in semi-retirement, he became Viceroy of India in 1880. He settled the current Afghan dispute, abolished most of the censorship and developed systems of tax settlements. He returned in 1884 and became Gladstone's 1st Ld. of the Admiralty in 1886. From 1882 to 1895 he was Colonial Sec. and from 1905 to 1908 he led the Liberal peers as Ld. Privy Seal.

ROBINSON CRUSOE. *See* DAMPIER.

ROBSART, Amy[e] (?1532-60). *See* DUDLEY; ELIZABETH I-7.

ROCHDALE. *See* MANCHESTER.

ROCHDALE PIONEERS. *See* CO-OPERATIVES.

ROCHE, Sir Boyle (1743-1807) Bt. (1782), Unionist opponent of R. Catholic emancipation but better known, perhaps apocryphally, as the originator of many "Irish Bulls" e.g. (on Unionism) "I would have the two sisters embrace like one brother"; "No man can be in two places at once, like a bird"; "Why should we do anything for posterity? What has posterity done for us?"

ROCHEFORT (Fr.), naval base established at the mouth of the Charente by Colbert, had to be continually blockaded by the British in the French wars after 1756. Bonaparte surrendered there to the *Bellerophon* in 1815.

ROCHELLE, LA (Fr.). *See* LA ROCHELLE.

ROCHES, Peter des. *See* PETER.

ROCHESTER (Kent) (Lat: DUROBRIVAE; A.S: HRO-FAECAESTRE; Norse: HROFI), at the crossing of the Canterbury-London Roman road over the Medway, had a fortified bridgehead. The substantial Roman bridge was apparently replaced twice before the bridge of 1392. The original cathedral was founded within the walls in 604 for the Bp. of the Kentish Men (q.v.) but was poor and stayed poor. After the Conquest Gundulf (r. 1077-1108), the second Norman Bp., began to rebuild the church and introduced Benedictine monks. He also began the castle in a riverside corner of the walls, but this was granted to Canterbury and Abp. William of Corbeil finished the great keep. The place was besieged and variously damaged and repaired under King John, Henry III and during the Peasants' Revolt. In 1227 a guild merchant was chartered and the city was incorporated with admiralty rights in 1446. It was not, however, a significant port until steam power made it easily accessible. Its rise as an industrial town dates from the coming of the railway in the 1850s.

ROCHESTER. *See* HYDE.

ROCHFORD. *See* ZUYLESTEIN.

ROCKERS. Leather clad motor cycle gangs of the 1960s who claimed devotion to rock music and hatred of Mods, whom they fought at seaside resorts.

ROCKETS, a 13th cent. Chinese invention, were much used as fireworks and, with more enthusiasm than success, as weapons; their large scale use in India at the end of the 17th cent. led Sir William Congreve to develop a form of highly unreliable rocket artillery; this operated in the Peninsula under Wellington, who thought little of it, but rockets had other practical uses, especially as emergency signals and for projecting lines in sea rescue. It was not until the 20th cent. realisation that rockets could move in a vacuum that further serious attention was paid to them. The liquid propelled funnel rocket was first developed in 1920 in the U.S.A. and in 1927 in Germany. In 1933 German development was taken over by the German army which established the great research station at PEENEMÜNDE. This was heavily bombed by the British in 1943, but production and research had advanced far enough to make it possible to bombard London and Antwerp with V2 ballistic rockets in 1944 and 1945. Many German experts later went to the U.S.A. and Russia which each developed Intercontinental Ballistic Missiles. These in their turn led to the launching of space rockets. The first satellites were launched by the Russians in Oct. 1957 and by the U.S.A. in Jan. 1958.

ROCKINGHAM, Charles Watson-Wentworth (1730-82), Vist. HIGHAM (1734), E. of MALTON (1746), 2nd M. of (1750), Ld. of the Bedchamber from 1751 to 1762 **(1)** slowly acquired the leadership of the Newcastle group in Parliament after it had passed into opposition. In July 1765 he was called, through the D. of Cumberland, to form an administration, with the ageing Newcastle as Privy Seal, the E. of Winchelsea as Ld. Pres. and the D. of Grafton and Gen. Conway as Secs. of State (*see* GEORGE 111-6).

(2) A good chairman and pacifier, he set about ending vendettas, calming the agitated Commons and making his colleagues work together. He refused to purge the many minor offices to reinstate Newcastle's extruded dependants; but he gratified M.Ps. through patronage, abolished Bute's irritating Cider excise and got a resolution against general warrants through the House, but refused to help Wilkes, exiled in Paris. He dealt with the King as a deferential adviser and pleased him by restoring his friend Ld. George Sackville, the scapegoat or offender of Minden. He helped the trading interest by opening free ports in the W. Indies, and the smaller householders by altering the incidence of the window tax. He was ready to accept recruits and kept negotiations with Pitt going.

(3) This tactful stability was upset by the Americans. Many retaliated for Grenville's Stamp Tax by non-importation agreements, which hit the British traders in the pocket. They supported Pitt's constitutional line against the tax. Rockingham and some colleagues favoured its repeal, but the powerful county M.P.s. (with whom some ministers agreed) were determined to maintain the imperial supremacy of Parliament and wanted America to pay for itself. A compromise was devised: a bill declaratory of Parliament's right to tax the colonies was to be passed, followed by another repealing the Stamp Tax itself. The compromise was unworkable. The ministry had no first rate speaker in the Commons, where Pitt thundered against the declaratory bill and frightened the gentry and then backed the repeal in a crowded House and so convinced the weaker ministers that no ministry could survive without him. Two (Grafton and Gen. Conway) resigned when Pitt was not called (Apr. 1766). Two months later the Ld. Chancellor (Northington) resigned. Rockingham proposed to replace him with the "anti-American" Charles Yorke. The King, alarmed by disunity in the ministry and disunion in the Empire, sent for Pitt instead.

(4) Rockingham and his group now spent most of the rest of his political life in opposition. In 1767 he received overtures when Pitt collapsed, but was unwilling to join the Cabinet without leading it. The period mostly covered by Ld. North's supremacy was one of high excitement, for it included the American rebellion, the demands for administrative and financial reform, Irish troubles, the Gordon Riots and the entry of France, Spain and Holland into the American war. Rockingham thus had radical objects of policy forced upon him by the circumstances, while his group was never big enough to form a govt. alone. North's fall in 1782 made it necessary, for the formation of a govt., to combine with Shelburne's group which had quite different ideas. Accordingly, Rockingham as Prime Minister formed a Cabinet from the two bodies, who agreed that the American war should be ended and the resources so released used to force a favourable peace on Europe. They also agreed upon internal autonomy for Ireland and a superficial reform of the Civil List. Unfortunately they disagreed about the manner of the peace: Shelburne was in charge of the American, Fox (of Rockingham's group) of the European negotiations, conducted by their separate representatives simultaneously in Paris. Fox accused Shelburne of undermining his side and demanded that both negotiations should be put in charge of his nominee. At this point Rockingham died, whereupon Fox resigned.

ROCKITES. Similar to WHITEFEET.

RODD, James Rennel (1858-1941) 1st Ld. RENNELL (1933), was Minister to Stockholm from 1904 to 1908 and as Ambassador to the Quirinal from 1908 to 1919 was a key figure in the Allied diplomacy, which detached Italy from her obligations to the central powers. He was British representative to the League of Nations in 1921 and 1923 and a Conservative M.P. from 1928 to 1932.

RODEN. See DOLLY'S BRAE.

RODNEY, George Brydges (1719-92) 1st Ld. RODNEY (1782), energetic but gouty and extravagant naval commander, bombarded Le Havre in 1759 and 1760 and then as C-in-C Leeward Is. took St. Lucia, Grenada, St. Vincent and Martinique in 1762. He was M.P. for Northampton in 1768 but lived in Paris from 1775 to 1778 where, until a French acquaintance paid, his debts hindered his return home until after the outbreak of war. He was then given command (1780) of a complex operation escorting convoys and squadrons, first to the relief of Gibraltar and then by dispersal to the E. and W. Indies. On the way he brilliantly took the greater part of two Spanish squadrons, relieved and supplied Gibraltar, despatched the E. India convoy and, having crossed the Atlantic and taken command of the Leeward Is., fought the French under de Guichen indecisively off Martinique. In 1781 he seized the Dutch I. of St. Eustatius, but had to go home for his health, leaving Sir Samuel Hood in command. In 1782 he returned and defeated the French under de Grasse (whom he captured) off Dominica. In this controversial battle he achieved his success by breaking the enemy line, but failed to pursue his victory properly. He was, however, hailed in the depressed state of the war as a national hero.

ROE, Sir Thomas (?1581-1644), Esquire to Elizabeth I (1602), explored the Amazon, Spanish Main and the W. Indies in 1609-11, became M.P. for Tamworth in 1614 and from 1615 to 1618 led an embassy to the Moghuls, securing a treaty with Jehangir which established the commercial foundations of the HEIC and its factory at Surat. He left for home *via* Persia. From 1621 to 1628 he was ambassador to the Sublime Porte where he obtained commercial privileges, improved relations with Algiers and liberated 600-700 English seamen in slavery there, and he temporarily persuaded Bethlen Gabor, P. of Transylvania, to intervene against the Habsburgs in the Thirty Years' War (1626). In 1630, having helped to free some Polish prisoners in Constantinople, he mediated

between Sweden and Poland. From 1638 he tried to negotiate a general European settlement. Finally he was Ambassador at Vienna in 1642-3. From 1630 on he tried to retire, mainly because the controversies of Charles I's reign deprived him of a just reward for all his work.

ROEBUCK (1) John (1718-94), invented the modern process for producing sulphuric acid in 1749, established the Carron gun factory in 1760 and patented a method of iron smelting, using coal, in 1762. His grandson **(2) John Arthur (1801-79)** was educated in Canada, became a successful barrister and was a flamboyantly independent M.P. for Bath (1832 to 1837 and 1841 to 1847) and for Sheffield (1849 to 1868 and 1874 to 1879). His motion for an inquiry into the conduct of the Crimean War in 1855 led to the fall of the Aberdeen Govt. and Palmerston then made him chairman of the Sebastopol Committee. The resulting exposures led directly to the military and administrative reforms of the late 19th cent. He supported Disraeli from 1877.

ROGER of HOWDEN. See HOVEDEN.

ROGER of MONTGOMERY (?-?1193) E. of CHICHESTER AND ARUNDEL (1067) and SHREWSBURY (1071), cousin of William the Conqueror and married to Mabel of Bellême (?-1182) was the most powerful of the Norman nobles. He was not at the B. of Hastings but remained in Normandy to assist Matilda's regency until William called him to England in Dec. 1067. From newly built castles, notably at Hen Domen near Montgomery, he began the Norman encroachments on Wales. At William's death he was, despite initial doubts, won over to William II. Later he led a Norman revolt to release his son Robert of Bellême (q.v.) which was very convenient to William II. He patronised the monasteries at Cluny and St. Evroul, restored the Abbey at Wenlock and founded that of Shrewsbury, where he took the tonsure just before he died.

ROGER of PONT L'EVEQUE (?-1181). Rising from a clerkship in Abp. Theobald's household to (1148) the Archdeaconry of Canterbury, he was King Stephen's envoy to Rome in 1152. In 1154 he was elected Abp. of York and became Thomas Becket's principal ecclesiastical opponent. His part in crowning Henry the Young King in 1170, perhaps emphasising the claims of York against Canterbury, led to his excommunication on Papal authority by Becket and so to the latter's murder. He took an oath of non-complicity in it and was absolved. His quarrels with Canterbury over primacy or autonomy continued with Becket's successor, Richard, and he also tried to claim primacy over the Scottish church.

ROGER (?-1139), Bp. of SALISBURY (1102), one of Henry I's chaplains, was Chancellor between Easter 1101 and his election to Salisbury. He was a Justiciar and in 1109 Chief Justiciar. Said to have been the second man in the Kingdom, he issued writs in his own name during Henry's absences. In 1135 he supported Stephen's accession, perhaps with misgivings, but he kept his offices with his nephews (or sons), Alexander Bp. of Lincoln; Nigel of Ely, the Tres; and Roger le Poer the Chancellor. In June 1139, however, after a perhaps staged quarrel with Alan of Brittany over the quartering of their followings, Stephen suddenly seized Roger and his relatives, made them surrender their castles at Sherborne, Devizes, Malmesbury and Newark and returned them to their Sees without secular authority. By this means Stephen got rid of his father's administration.

ROGERS, John alias Thomas MATTHEW (?1500-55), originally a R. Catholic priest, became a friend of William Tindal, whose Bible he helped to publish posthumously at Antwerp in 1537. He appears as Matthew on the title page. He became a prebendary of St. Paul's in 1551 and preached constantly against popery until arrested in 1554. By now an extreme Calvinist, he was the first to be burned (1555) as a heretic under Mary I.

ROGERS, William (1819-96) (known as 'Hang Theology Rogers'), parson from 1845 at St. Thomas', Charterhouse, London, founded many schools for "street arabs" and ragamuffins and progressed to several sorts of elementary schools. He became a Queen's chaplain in 1857, a member of the R. Commission on popular education in 1858 and from 1863 was a prebendary of St. Paul's and Rector of St. Botolph's, Bishopsgate. From these points of vantage he saw the need of more secondary schools, not necessarily for the poor, and proceeded to found them. In 1871 he became a first member of the London School Board and a gov. of the important Alleyn's Charity, which he reorganised to such purpose that its Dulwich Coll. turned into a great public school. Altogether he founded more private or charitable schools than any other person.

ROGERS, Woodes (?-1732), commanded the privateering squadron from Bristol which rescued Alexander Selkirk from Juan Fernandez in 1708 and until 1711 raided the Peruvian coast. He published a journal of his operations in 1712 and in 1717 rented the Bahamas from its Lds. Proprietors and became their first gov. With 300 men against 2000-odd pirates and 1500 disgruntled Spaniards, he resigned the governorship in 1721, having, however, hanged 10 pirates at once. He resumed office in 1729 and died at Nassau.

ROGNVALD or RONALD (?-1159) recovered the earldom of Orkney from his kinsman Paul and built Kirkwall Cathedral (1137).

ROHILLAS were Afghan settlers in ROHILKHAND who became virtually independent after 1707 and very rich. They staved off a Maratha attack in 1771 in concert with the Nawab Shuja-ud-Daulah of Oudh, but later failed to pay him the sums agreed for his help. He then got Warren Hastings to help to expel them. Though their leader, Hafiz Rahmat Khan, was killed in 1774, the joint campaign was only partly successful and his heir Faizullah Khan retained RAMPUR as a jagir. In 1801 Rohilkhand passed to the British; Rampur was recognised as a princely state and so remained until 1950.

ROI FAINÉANT **(Fr: "Do-nothing King")** originally referred to the last Merovingians.

ROI SOLEIL **(Fr: Sun King).** Louis XIV.

ROKEBY. Yorkshire family, mostly lawyers, with Irish connections. **(1) Sir Thomas (?-1356)** was Justiciar of Ireland from 1349. **(2) Thomas (?-1418)** defeated the E. of Northumberland at Bramham Moor (1408). **(3) William (?-1521)** was Abp. of Dublin and Irish Ld. Chancellor from 1512. **(4) John (?-1573),** a canonist, was counsel in Henry VIII's divorce proceedings. **(5) Ralph (?-1575)** became Sec. to the Council of the North. **(6) Ralph (?1527-96)** was a Master of Requests from 1576.

ROKEBY. *See* ROBINSON.

ROKESLE(Y), London City aldermanic family from Kent. **Gregory (?-1291)** migrated to London in about 1254. He was a goldsmith (i.e. a banker) but traded in wool, wine and other commodities for the Household. He also acted as a royal auditor and for the Crown in its Italian financial dealings, especially with the Riccardi.

ROLFE, John (1585-1622), arrived in Virginia in 1610 and married the well known **Pocahontas,** d. of Powhattan, a high Red Indian chief, in 1613. He brought her to England where she was a sensation in 1616. She died in 1617 and he returned to Virginia.

ROLFE, Robert Monsey (1790-1868) 1st Ld. CRANWORTH (1850), M.P. in 1832, became Sol-Gen. under Melbourne in 1834 and Vice-Chancellor in 1850. He was one of the first Lds. Justices in Chancery in 1851 and Ld. Chancellor from 1852 to 1858 and from 1865 to 1866. A lawyers' lawyer, he introduced Cranworth's Act, 1860, a technical and useful measure for shortening legal documents.

ROLLE, Richard (c. 1300-49), Oxford educated mystic of Thornton-le-Dale (Yorks.), fled his home to become a hermit and later became spiritual director of the Cistercian nuns of Hampole near Doncaster. He wrote scriptural commentaries and mystical treatises, of which the best known is the *Incendium Amoris* (Lat: Fire of Love) (1343). Some of his shorter works, including verses, were in English.

ROLLO or HROLF the GANGER (= strider), 1st D. of NORMANDY. *See* VIKINGS-15.

ROLLS, MASTER OF THE. (*For earlier history see* CHANCERY-8 *et seq.*) He is now head of the civil side of the Court of Appeal.

ROLLS SERIES. A collection in 99 parts of historical documents learnedly edited and reprinted between 1857 and 1898 for the Historical Manuscripts Commission, on the proposal of the Master of the Rolls.

ROMAN CATHOLIC RELIEF ACT, 1829. *See* TEST ACTS.

ROMAN-DUTCH LAW, a combination of Germanic custom and the Roman law of Justinian, was the law of the province of Holland as expounded by Hugo Grotius in 1620, Johannes Voet between 1698 and 1704, and Godefridus van der Keessel in 1800. It was followed, more or less, in the colonial territories, notably Ceylon (1656) and the Cape (1652) and so with a variety of barbarisms and some British Common Law improvements, became the foundation of the law of those countries. The major features which distinguish it from English law lie in the field of property, succession, persons (especially wives) and contract. It spread with English modifications and by statute to other S. African provinces and S. Rhodesia (Zimbabwe).

ROMAN EMPERORS. (1) *The Titles.* The political title 'Emperor' came from 'Imperator', meaning a Roman C-in-C who had been acclaimed by his troops after a victory. The German 'Kaiser' and the Russian 'Czar' came from 'Caesar'. This referred to Julius Caesar's family name. Octavian (Augustus), who claimed to be his heir, gave unofficial currency to the name as a title, but though considered to have been the first Roman Emperor, he used the title 'Princeps' (*see* PRINCE). The Senate conferred the appellation 'Augustus' upon Octavian and later rulers used this as the equivalent of 'Emperor'. Later still 'Caesar' became the title of a deputy emperor or imperial crown prince. In the later Eastern Empire the Greek equivalent of 'Augustus' was 'Autocrator' (used by the Russian Czars) or 'Basileus Autocrator' and of 'Caesar' usually 'Sebastocrator'. In the Holy Roman Empire the ruler's title was 'Imperator Romanorum Semper Augustus' (Emperor of the Romans Eternally August – I.R.S.A. on coins) and the designated successor, if any, bore the title 'King of the Romans'.

(2) *Jurisdiction.* Though the Empire was one, the imperial office was not always held by one person. Usurpers apart, there might be two or more Augusti and even several Caesars at once. Usually one of the Augusti was regarded as the senior. Sometimes they divided the work functionally, ruling from one centre; sometimes territorially, but in theory neither arrangement disturbed the essential unity of the state. Quarrels which sometimes developed into civil wars did, however, impair this unity.

(3) *Method of Appointment.* It was considered that a new Emperor had to be accepted by the Army (meaning the best placed force), the Senate (meaning the late ruler's most powerful advisers) and the People (the population of the capital). Succession was not hereditary, but an experienced and especially wealthy Caesar had a better chance than other claimants if he was on the spot to seize it. The arrangements made for tumult, which sometimes degenerated into riot or even civil war and some emperors tried to secure peaceful successions by nominating their successors or by creating a co-emperor during their lifetime. These expedients did not always work.

In the following list, the dynasties (where they existed) are shown but only the emperors directly related to the subject of this work, including the Crusades, are specified. Usurpers appear in *italics*.

CLAUDIO-JULIANS	27BC-AD68
Claudius	41-54
Civil War	68-69
FLAVIANS	69-96
Non-dynastic	96-138
Trajan	98-117
Hadrian	117-138
ANTONINES	138-192
Civil War	193
SEVIERI	193-217
Septimius Severus	193-198
Clodius Albinus in Britain	*196-197*
Septimius Severus and Caracalla	198-211
Caracalla and Geta	211-212
Caracalla	212-217
THE SYRIANS	218-235
Non Dynastic	235-268
Valerian and Gallienus	253-260
Postumus in Gaul and the West	*258-268*
Gallienus	260 268
Laelian and then Marius in Gaul and the West	*268*
THE ILLYRIANS	268-296
Diocletian	284-286
Diocletian and Maximian	286-305
Carausius in Britain	*286-293*
Allectus in Britain	*293-296*
CONSTANTINIANS	305-361
Constantius I and Galerius	305-306
Galerius and Severus	306
Constantine I	306-337
Maxentius, Severus,	306-312
Licinius	306-323
Maximin Daia	306 313

From 337 the Empire was ruled in two halves viz:

West

Constantius II Constantine II Constans	337-353
VALENTINIANS	364-425
Magnus Maximus in Britain, Gaul and Spain	*383-388*
Theodosius I	386-393
Honorius	395-423

East

Non-dynastic	450-518
JUSTINIANS	518-610
HERACLIANS	610-717
ISAURIANS	717-820
AMOMANS	820-867
MACEDONIANS	867-1034
Paphlagonian confusion	
DUCAS DYNASTY	1059-1081
Romanus Diogenes	1068-1071
COMNENIANS	1081-1185
Alexius I	1081-1152
John II	1092-1143
Manuel I	1143-1180
ANGELIDS	1185-1204

LATIN EMPERORS	
Baldwin I	*1204-1205*
Henry	*1206-1216*
Peter of Courtenay	*1216-1217*
Robert	*1221-1228*
Baldwin II and John of Brienne	*1228-1237*
Baldwin II alone	*1237-1261*
LASCARIDS at Nicaea	1204-1258
PALAEOLOGIANS	
At Nicaea	1258-1261
At Constantinople	1261-1453

ROMANESQUE. *See* ARCHITECTURE, BRITISH.

ROMANIA. The Eastern Roman Empire. In this work the modern country of that name is spelt ROUMANIA to avoid confusion.

ROMANO-BRITISH SUCCESSOR RULERS (*see* BRITAIN, ROMAN) **(1)** After the Roman evacuation (407-10), a central authority of some kind was maintained and passed into the charge of a Cornovian prince of unknown name, entitled the Vortigern or Sublime King. The main active enemies were the Picts. Their disruptive raids caused widespread devastation, the collapse of regular trade and exchange and the permanent abandonment of many cultivations. Save in a few localities, coinage went out of use. The Vortigern, unable to raise sufficient force against the Picts, had to moderate between rival opinions: to try to revert to Roman rule (showing signs of revival under Aetius), or to seek help from the growing numbers of Saxons who appeared on the coasts. The Pelagian controversy was raging and Pelagianism, by making headway in Britain, was isolating her from the Roman Church. The Vortigern preferred Saxon military settlements (c. 425). The bishops on the other hand sent calls for help against the Pelagians and the continental church responded by sending over (430) the remarkable St. Germanus of Auxerre, a strong minded ex-gen. He organised effective resistance not only to Pelagianism but to an Irish (Scots) invasion in N. Wales, for which he trained British levies (THE ALLELUTA VICTORY). If the Vortigern organised Cunedda's migration with the Votadini to Gwynedd at that time, it suggests some political co-operation between Germanus and himself, for the Votadini were settled there to protect the area against pirates.

(2) There was a plague in 433 which, though serious, did nothing to reduce the rate at which Saxon immigrants came into their settlements. These by now were to be found inland by rivers as well as on the coast. In 442 a Jutish revolt broke out in Kent and most other Teutonic settlements joined in. The speed of their success suggests an initial surprise. In 446 the Britons, or any rate those who favoured the Roman connection, petitioned Aetius for help. In this document, known as *The Groans of the Britons*, they say that they are being driven into the sea. St. Germanus made a second visit. If he rallied them, the success was relatively short-lived; by 460 Britons were migrating *en masse* from the west to Armorica, soon to be called Brittany.

(3) By 470 the Saxon offensive had blocked off the east from direct continental, other than Saxon, contacts so that communication with the Roman world ran from Spain and Southern Gaul *via* Brittany, across or round Cornwall and thence up the Irish Sea to Man, which became the centre of a Celtic sea province. The inhabitants on both shores had much in common and there was migration and countermigration. The Saxon advance had gone too far and the Britons, led by Ambrosius Aurelianus, probably a cavalry leader, began to resist more successfully. Under his successor Arthur they won a great victory at Mount Badon (near Swindon) in 490 and drove the Saxons back as far as London and the borders of Norfolk (*but see* ARTHUR). There followed a

60-year period of peaceful coexistence, interrupted by a serious epidemic in 530. In 550 the Saxon advance was resumed.

ROMAN REPUBLIC (1848-9). Pope Pius IX condemned the Italian nationalist and liberal movements in Apr. 1848. His Prime Minister, Count Rossi, was murdered and he himself driven to Gaeta in Nov. The Republican Giuseppe Mazzini (1805-72), who had been living mostly in London since 1837, now appeared from Florence. In Feb. 1849 he proclaimed the Republic with himself as a triumvir. Louis Napoleon Bonaparte, now French Pres. with clerical support, sent an expedition against it in Apr. In May Garibaldi with volunteers reached Rome and defended the City against the French until July, when they captured it and dissolved the Republic.

ROMANTIC MOVEMENT. *See* REALISM.

ROMILLY (1) Sir Samuel (1757-1818) ("MARTIN MADDEN") published the reformist *Thoughts on Executive Justice* in 1786. He became Sol-Gen. and an M.P. in 1806 and secured many reforms in criminal law, procedure and punishment. He also favoured R. Catholic emancipation and the abolition of slavery. His son **(2) John (1802-74) 1st Ld. ROMILLY (1865)** was Liberal M.P. from 1832 to 1835 and from 1846 to 1852. He was Sol-Gen. in 1848; Att.-Gen. in 1850 and Master of the Rolls from 1851 to 1873.

ROMNEY, George (1732-1802), fashionable portrait and story painter originally from Kendal and rival of Sir Joshua Reynolds; he was much patronised by Georgina, Duchess of Devonshire, and Emma, later Lady Hamilton.

ROMNEY MARSH (Kent, Sussex) is a remarkable 40 sq. mile area said to be the world's only breeding ground for eels. It was gradually reclaimed from the sea in the Middle Ages through the agency of the Corporation of the Lords of the Level, which embanked ('med') the recoveries, laid out the drainage and imposed upon each holding a proportion of the maintenance costs, calculated by reference to the footage of sea wall chargeable upon each. Since mining altered the length of maintainable wall from time to time, changes in footage could be made by an assembly of the tenants of the Manors involved. This elected Jurats to settle surveys and disputes. The Marsh is an exceedingly rich pasture, which has developed its own distinctive breed of long-wool sheep.

ROMNEY, NEW (Kent), in the Middle Ages protected by the Romney Marsh sea wall, was the leading Cinque Port, but in the 15th cent. its harbour began to silt up and trade had virtually ceased by the 18th.

ROM[E]SCOT. *See* PETER'S PENCE.

ROMSEY (Hants.) had a royal hunting lodge (for the New Forest) ascribed to King John and a rich 12th cent. Benedictine nunnery. It declined after the Reformation, until the foundation in the 1880s of the brewery.

ROOKE or ROOK, Sir George (1650-1709), fought in the confused battles of the Second Dutch War (1665-7) and commanded, in very dilatory fashion, the squadron which relieved Londonderry in 1689. He was a junior admiral at the Bs. of Beachy Head and Barfleur (1692), but after the latter, commanded the gallant boat attack in which many French ships of the line and transports were burned at La Hogue. In 1692, however, he lost most of the 400 ships of the Smyrna convoy to the French off Cape St. Vincent. In 1702, as C-in-C of the combined Anglo-Dutch fleet, he failed before Cadiz but destroyed, through a lucky fluke, the *Flota* at Vigo and in 1704 after another failure before Barcelona, took Gibraltar, and then beat the French off Malaga. Attempts to exploit this by his Tory political friends in order to upstage Marlborough's victory at Blenheim incurred Whig wrath. He was recalled and not re-employed. He was remarkable in his time for financial honesty.

ROOKERY, a slum and criminal resort at the present St. Giles' Circus in London. When demolished in 1852 its 47 houses were found to contain some 2200 people.

ROOSEVELT COROLLARY (1904-5) was an extension of the Monroe Doctrine expounded by Pres. Theodore Roosevelt in messages to Congress. Provoked by the chronic indebtedness of Santo Domingo, which might lead to foreign intervention, he argued that if a nation failed to maintain civilised standards, intervention by a civilised nation might in the last resort be justifiable, but that in the Americas the U.S.A. might have to be the intervening power to prevent action by extra-American states. In other words the U.S.A. might collect her debts anywhere, but Britain, France, Spain, Portugal and Holland might not collect theirs in the Americas.

ROOT AND BRANCH PETITION (11 Dec. 1640), from London to the Long Parliament, sought the abolition of episcopacy. It was supported and attacked in a debate in Feb. 1641 but nobody defended the existing bishops. A bill against clerical interference in secular matters was thrown out by the Lords in the Spring and a Commons bill to abolish bishops and chapters had to be dropped in the summer in the face of opposition and disagreement on what should take their place. Early in 1642, however, after the affair of the Five Members, there was enough popular pressure to secure an Act excluding bishops from the House of Lords. *See* BAWDY COURTS.

ROPE. This industry, vital to a maritime nation in days of sail, apparently originated in hemp growing around Bridport (Dorset) as early as the 12th cent. The hemp was sent to Plympton (Devon) to be made into yarn and then sent back to be twisted into ropes. Bridport rope makers were also sent elsewhere (e.g. Newcastle). In 1530 a statute gave Bridport market a monopoly of hemp sales within 5 miles, but meanwhile the weight of hawsers was inducing a demand for ropemakers near ports, e.g. on the Humber. The Statute of 1530 merely encouraged such movement. In 1610 a ropewalk was founded at Woolwich and shortly after, another at Portsmouth. Dorset could not supply enough hemp to meet the voracious demand and more and more was imported from Holland and Russia. The safety of the Baltic trade thus became essential to British shipping. In Tudor times the Newfoundland fisheries created an enormous demand for nets in which Bridport again had a near monopoly. This replaced the falling trade in hawsers (killed by the introduction of chain in 1811-1850) and rope proper (replaced by wire about 1900).

ROS, originally Norman family from Bonneville where **(1) Robert (?-1227)** was Castellan. He was involved in negotiations between King John and William the Lion, received Wark and other Northumbrian estates (1200) and settled permanently after the loss of Normandy. He married William the Lion's daughter Isabel. He was an opponent of John in the Magna Carta crisis and though excommunicated in 1216, was slow to submit. He witnessed the 1225 version of the Charter. His son **(2) Robert (?-1274)** was one of the guardians of Margaret daughter of Henry III and Alexander III's queen, but was deprived of lands on allegations that he had mistreated her. He was a supporter of the Barons in the Barons' War. His nephew **(3) William (1260-1307)** inherited Yorkshire properties and made a claim, later withdrawn, to the Scottish Crown in 1291. He served in Aquitaine in 1297 and against the Scots in 1307. His second son **(4) John (?-1338)** supported Isabella and Mortimer's *coup d'état*, but became Steward to Edward III and 1337 Admiral of the North Sea fleets. The family continued to live in affluence until the honours and estates passed by marriage to the Manners family in the 15th cent. The 13th Lord became 1st E. of Rutland in 1525.

ROSAMUND, FAHR. *See* CLIFFORD-2.

ROSCOMMON, town and county (Ireland). The area was partly Macdermott and partly O'Kelly country which retained its Irish speech and habits because, by the Composition of Connaught (1589), the local chiefs received tenure according to English law and were left undisturbed in the Cromwellian plantations. There was a well known monastery from the 7th cent. until the Reformation.

ROSE (1) George (1744-1818) was Sec. to the Treasury from 1782 to 1801 and a Pittite M.P. (Launceston 1784, Lymington 1788, Christchurch from 1790 to 1818). He held a number of minor offices and from 1807 the Treasurership of the Navy. He was mainly important as a financial "staff officer" to the younger Pitt. His son **(2) Sir George Henry (1771-1855)** was Minister at The Hague in 1792 and at Berlin in 1793 and 1794. He was an M.P. from 1794 to 1844, but also Minister in Munich in 1813 and at Berlin in 1815.

ROSE, Hugh Henry (1801-85) 1st Ld. STRATHNAIRNE (1866) went to Syria, served with the Ottoman Army and from 1841 to 1848 as British Consul-Gen. there, actively did justice and composed tribal feuds. In 1851 he became Sec. to the British Embassy to the Porte and in the Crimean War he was British liaison officer with the French H.Q. and became a Major-Gen. He then went to India and in the Mutiny took over the small Central India force which he commanded brilliantly. Between Jan. and Mar. 1858 he stormed the forts and forced the passes to Jhansi, which was defended by its celebrated Rani, Lakshmi Bhai. He defeated a relieving army under Tantia Topi and in Apr. stormed Jhansi itself. The Rani and Tantia Topi, driven from the state, then subverted Gwalior and seized the fortress, but Rose stormed it too. After the war he commanded the Poona Division and the Bombay Army and carried out the amalgamation of the Queen's and the Company's force in S. India.

ROSE, Sir John (1820-88), was Sol-Gen. for Lower Canada in 1857 and Minister of Public Works from 1858 to 1861. He represented the, mainly English, Protestants in the negotiations on federation and in 1868 became the first Dominion Finance Minister. He retired in 1868.

ROSEBERY. *See* PRIMROSE.

ROSEBERY'S GOVT. (Mar. 1894-June 1895). (Sixteen in Cabinet under the E. of Rosebery. The principal members were the same as in Gladstone's fourth govt., but the E. of Kimberley was Foreign Sec; H. H. Fowler Sec. for India; James Bryce Pres. of the Board of Trade and G. J. Shaw- Lefevre Pres. of the Local Govt. Board.)

(1) Queen Victoria invited Rosebery to form a govt. on Gladstone's resignation, because Harcourt, the apparently obvious choice, was personally intolerable to Cabinet colleagues. The fact was unknown to the public; the appointment damaged Rosebery's party authority. He was rich, handsome, winning and popular, but a Whig aristocrat who had never been an M.P. He upset the nonconformist Liberals by his addiction to aristocratic pleasures such as horse racing and, moreover, he was an imperialist.

(2) Believing, correctly, that public opinion was against a Liberal-Home Ruler govt. without Gladstone, the Lords set about making its position impossible by throwing out its bills. Hence finance was the only domestic area in which the govt. had any room to manoeuvre. Money had to be found for a naval building programme. 1d. on the income tax and 6d. on the excise were not enough. Harcourt, on Sir Alfred Milner's advice, established the death duties (1894). This important long-term innovation was introduced against a background of significant shifts in the balance of foreign affairs. A modest treaty (July 1894) with Japan provided for the ending of British consular jurisdiction by 1899.

(3) The Turks were massacring Armenians. The British public was horrified and Kimberley forced a commission of inquiry (Jan. 1895). The Russians would not countenance intervention, but were ready to join in a demand for reforms jointly with Britain and France. Thereupon the Germans decided to supplant British influence with the Porte and further their Baghdad railway schemes by supporting the Turks. The anti-

Russian policy of the Japanese treaty soon developed. After the Sino-Japanese War of 1894 Germany, Russia and France forced the Japanese to return their conquests, other than Formosa, ceded at the P. of Shimonoseki (Apr. 1895). From this Britain ostentatiously abstained. Thus the British acquired a friend in the Far East just as they lost one in the Levant.

(4) The govt. resigned after a snap defeat censuring Campbell-Bannerman for not procuring enough cordite for the army.

ROSE COFFEE HOUSE (1651-1766). A notorious tavern, the scene of many brawls, near Covent Garden (London), frequented by Pepys and Gibbon.

ROSES, WARS OF THE, so-called because most of them seemed to be struggles between the Houses of York, whose badge was a white rose, and Lancaster (red). **(1)** The factors in them included discontent and policy disagreements over the conduct of the Hundred Years' War, the growing involvement of court factions in local rivalries and a consequent escalation of local and national violence; also resorts to violence bred a violent habit of mind.

(2) In fact struggles between the factions surrounding descendants of the offspring of Edward III began with the rivalry between Richard D. of York and the Beauforts with Suffolk for the control of the intermittently insane Henry VI. This culminated in Suffolk's murder in 1450.

(3) The **first** war between York and the Beauforts supported by Queen Margaret occurred in 1455 (B. of St. Albans). The **second** in 1459. The **third** in 1460 ended with York's death at Wakefield. The **fourth** in 1461 culminated in Margaret's defeat at Towton and the supersession of Henry VI by York's son, Edward IV, with the help of Warwick (The Kingmaker), but Margaret kept the war going in the north from Scots territory until 1464. The **fifth** arose when Warwick quarrelled with Edward and, with French help, restored Henry VI and Margaret (1469-70). In the **sixth** (1471) Edward killed Warwick at Barnet, defeated Margaret at Tewkesbury and murdered Henry VI. In the **seventh** Henry VII killed Richard III at Bosworth Field (1485). In the **eighth** (The Lambert Simnel Rebellion) Henry VII killed Richard's heir, the E. of Lincoln, at Stoke (1487). *For the details and the politics, see entries for the personalities mentioned.*

ROSS (1) Alexander (1783-1856), fur trader and topographer with the Pacific Fur Co. in Oregon from 1810 to 1812, then with the N. W. Co. In 1821 he joined the Hudson Bay Co. and organised the Red River Settlement (Manitoba). His son **(2) James (1835-71),** who was also in the Red River Settlement, became C. J. of Manitoba in 1870.

ROSS. *See* CROMARTY.

ROSS, Euphemia (?-1387), second Queen of Robert III of Scots. *See* STEWART or STUART, ROYAL HOUSE, EARLY-12.

ROSS, Sir James Clark (1800-62), was a naval topographer who on Felix Booth's expedition (1829-33) discovered the magnetic pole (1829). In 1838 he made the British magnetic survey. From 1839 to 1843 he commanded the Antarctic expedition. The Ross Dependency is named after him.

ROSS, Sir John (1777-1856) surveyed the White Sea and in 1818 led an expedition to search for the N.W. Passage. On a further expedition in 1829-33, financed by the maker of Booth's Dry Gin, he found and named the Gulf of Boothia. He also surveyed the Boothia Peninsula and King William Land.

ROSS (OF BLADENSBURG) Robert (1766-1814), educated and enterprising soldier who was partly responsible for the victory at Maida (1807) and was with Moore in the N. Spanish campaign of 1809 and then in Walcheren. As A.D.C. to George III he was being groomed for high command and in 1814 he commanded the military part of Cochrane's expedition against Washington. He won the B. of Bladensburg (Aug. 1814) but died of a wound at Baltimore. His descendants were allowed to add "of Bladensburg" to their name.

ROSS, Sir Ronald. *See* MALARIA.

ROSSE, E. of. *See* PARSONS.

ROSSETTI. *See* PRE-RAPHAELITES.

ROSYTH (Fife). The naval base was founded in 1909 but full-size docks were available only from 1916. Closure was in progress in 1993.

ROSSLYN, Es. of. *See* ERSKINE; WEDDERBURN.

ROTATION OF CROPS. *See* CROP ROTATION.

ROTHAMSTED AGRICULTURAL EXPERIMENTAL STATION, originated in private experiments by Sir John Lawes (1814-1900) on his family estate at Rothamsted after he settled there in 1834. In 1843 he established it on a permanent basis, but maintained it at his own expense, having discovered and patented (1842) the superphosphate fertilisers whose manufacture he began simultaneously at Deptford. He published many reports on his experiments, which ultimately revolutionised agriculture.

ROTHERMERE. *See* HARMSWORTH.

ROTHES, Es. and D. of. *See* LESLIE (ROTHES).

ROTHESAY in the I. of Bute, was the centre of an area of islands, peninsulas and coast about the entrance to the Clyde supposed to have been settled by the Scots from Ireland. David the Steward, E. of CARRICK, son of Robert III was made D. of Rothesay in 1398. At his death in 1402 his dignities reverted to the Crown and were granted with the Barony of RENFREW to his brother, James, who succeeded as James I. Thereafter these dignities were always granted together to the heir to the Scottish throne and by virtue of an Act of 1469 they automatically belonged to him. Since the accession of James VI and I in England they have been held by the D. of Cornwall for the time being.

ROTHESAY, David D. of. *See* STEWART or STUART, ROYAL HOUSE, EARLY.-17.

ROTHSCHILD. This famous international banking family descends from **Mayer Anischel (1743-1812)** of Frankfurt. A son **Nathan (1777-1836)** settled in Manchester in 1800 and became an important British govt. financial agent and with his brother **James (1792-1868),** in Paris since 1812, helped to finance the British military effort, particularly in the Peninsular War. A third branch under **Karl (1788-1855)** was established at Naples in 1820 and a fourth under **Solomon** at Vienna in 1821. Their private communications and clearing house system put them far ahead of their rivals. Their backing was important to the French Restoration govt. and to the July monarchy and in due course their activities extended to the govt. finance of most of mainland Europe, and in the 1840s to 1860s the construction of many of its railways. James' son, **Alphonse (1827-1905)** negotiated a large reduction in the post-1871 French indemnity to Germany. He with his brothers **Gustave (1829-1911)** and **Edmund (1845-1934)** were notable Zionists. Alphonse and **Edouard (1868-1949)** were both governors of the Bank of France. The Frankfurt branch was wound up in 1901; the Viennese in 1931. Nathan's son **Lionel (1808-79)** was elected to the Commons but was not allowed to take his seat until 1858, but his son **Nathaniel Meyer (1840-1915)** was the **1st Ld. ROTHSCHILD (1885)** and another son **Alfred (1842-1918)** was a director of the Bank of England. **Lionel Walter (1868-1937) 2nd Ld.,** was an important figure in international Zionism and it was to him that A. J. Balfour addressed the letter known as the Balfour Declaration. The family endowed many public institutions such as hospitals and art galleries. Lionel Walter was a distinguished naturalist. **Henri (1872-1942)** was a doctor, patron and, under the name of *André Pascal,* a dramatist.

ROTTEN BOROUGHS. *See* REFORM BILLS (1831-1832)-2(C).

ROTTERDAM (S. Holland), though a municipality since the 14th cent., was not an important port until the transit trade *via* the Hook of Holland and the Rhine to central Germany and Switzerland began to develop in the mid-19th cent. By 1939, however, it had become the most important continental port but it suffered severely in World War II from German and Allied bombing and blockade stagnation. The end of the war, however, opened the floodgates of trade and by 1960 Rotterdam harbours had become one of the largest ship-handling complexes in the world. This process was much assisted by the freeing of the European hinterland through the establishment of the European Economic Community.

ROTURIER, in Quebec, was a landowner who paid a rent charge to a *seigneur.*

ROUBILIAC, Louis François (1695-1762), French sculptor, settled in London in about 1732 under the patronage of the younger Walpoles. He executed much work at Vauxhall for Jonathan Tyers, the owner of Vauxhall Pleasure Gardens, but after 1738 set up on his own and made memorials and busts of many well known people.

ROUBLE was the Russian equivalent of the English mark, i.e. 13s. 4d. Between 1897 and 1914 it was worth 2s. 1d.

ROUEN (Fr.) became the seat of the Ds. of Normandy in 912 and so remained under the English dukes until Philip Augustus captured it in 1204. It then prospered greatly, by reason of an agreement with the city of Paris for the maintenance of the Seine navigation. It resisted Henry V vigorously but was taken in 1419 and remained in English hands until 1449. It became a wealthy centre of arts and crafts, especially textiles, but suffered in the Wars of Religion, being sacked and then settled by Huguenots in 1562. The Revocation of the Edict of Nantes (1685) ruined the textile industry and drove away half the population, many to Britain. It did not recover until after 1750. As an outport of Paris it has always suffered in wars with Britain. *See also* ELIZABETH 1-24.

ROUEN, T. of (1517). *See* JAMES V OF SCOTS.

"ROUGH WOOING". *See* MARY QUEEN OF SCOTS-2.

ROUMANIA. (1) Moldavia and **Wallachia** were disputed between the Turks, the Austro-Hungarians and local princes who occasionally retreated into Transylvania when too hard pressed. By 1678 the Turks were appointing the princes from mainly Greek families and from 1714 to 1821 these rulers (hospodars) were Phanariot Greeks whose average tenure was three years and who were really tax farmers. The first Russian occupation began in 1769 and the T. of Kuchuk Kainardji (1774) converted the provinces into Russian semi-protectorates. From now on Russian penetration was continuous and the area was the scene of Russo-Turkish fighting whenever the two empires were at war. In 1802 the Turks agreed to extend the Hospodar's tenure to seven years and not to change him without Russian consent, but in the war of 1806 to 1812 the Russian occupation was so barbarous that it established a permanent dislike of Russians. Hence in 1821 the Turks allowed the people to elect their own Hospodars.

(2) Russian designs on the provinces were a factor in causing the Crimean War and in 1856 the T. of Paris enacted an unworkable compromise; they were to remain separate under Turkish suzerainty, with separate assemblies but a commission for common interests and justice sitting at Focsani. In 1858 the assemblies simply elected the same Prince (Alexander Cuza) but in 1866 he abdicated and Charles (Carol) of Hohenzollern-Sigmaringen was elected in his place.

(3) Constitutional and military reforms and economic development with Austrian capital, besides the growing Danube traffic to central Europe, placed the provinces at a collision point of Russian and Austrian interests fought at the expense of the Turks. In the Russo-Turkish War of

1877-8 the Roumanians were dragged in behind the Russians but ended by ceding Bessarabia to them and receiving the N. Dobrudja from Turkish Bulgaria as compensation (T. of Berlin 1878). This was liable to create friction with Austro-Hungary.

(4) In 1880 the powers recognised Roumania's unity and independence. It was proclaimed a Kingdom in 1881 with an autocephalous Orthodox Church in 1885. These events served to increase the sense of nationality based upon a Romance language and, despite or perhaps because of peasant uprisings in 1888 and 1907, Roumanian politicians began to preach an *irredentism* aimed at the great Hungarian province of Transylvania and the Bulgarian S. Dobrudja. She gained the latter by stabbing Bulgaria in the back during the Balkan War of 1912-3 and manoeuvred for Allied support against Austro-Hungary in World War I. She entered that war in 1916 and was overwhelmed (*see* WORLD WAR 1-9). The defeat of the Central Powers, however, gave her all the territory of her ambitions including the predominantly non-Roumanian Transylvania, which from 1920 formed about 35% of her territory and became highly contentious when the Hungarians were cajoled and bullied by Hitler into alliance with the Axis.

(5) The Szekler (Magyar) parts of Transylvania were returned to Hungary under an unmanageable boundary award which lasted until the collapse of the Axis in 1945. At the same time Bessarabia and N. Bukovina were taken (and ultimately kept) by Hitler's ally, Russia, and the S. Dobrudja by Bulgaria. King Carol abdicated in favour of his son Michael (whom he had supplanted in 1930) and an S.A. style Iron Guard govt. was formed under Gen. Antonescu (Sept. 1940). A German motorised division arrived and a large German mission armed the Iron Guard which murdered 64 gens. and politicians. Antonescu then persuaded Hitler to reverse his policy on the Iron Guard and in Jan. 1941 when huge German forces were on their way to the Russian frontier, the army was mobilised and a June 30th-like massacre of Iron Guards took place, on the pattern of Hitler's treatment of the S.A. Britain broke off diplomatic relations in Feb. In June the great German-Roumanian invasion of Russia began. Bessarabia was recovered and territory as far as Odessa annexed by Aug.

(6) When the war went badly, the parliamentary parties made contact with the Allies, and Antonescu, having no party of his own, was overthrown in a *coup* personally organised by King Michael (*cf* the action of the hereditary sovereigns in Italy and Japan) when the Russian counter attack neared the frontiers. In Mar. 1945 Andrei Vyshinski, the Russian public prosecutor turned Dep.-Foreign Minister, bullied the nation into accepting an unpopular communist minority under Petru Grosa and in Dec. 1947 their threats forced King Michael to abdicate. A creeping communist revolution was now imposed and led ultimately to the formation of the Ceausescus' corrupt and violent police state. This was overthrown, after an atrocity at Timisoara, in 1989 by liberal opinion, in itself instantly crushed by another communist govt. under Giorgiu Iliescu with the support of armed minors.

ROUNDHEAD. See ROYALISTS etc.

ROUND SHIPS. See SHIPS, SAILING.

ROUND TABLE, a mythical order of knights associated with King Arthur, perhaps a force of armoured cavalry. The table at Winchester was made under Edward III and painted for Henry VIII.

ROUND WOOLSTAPLE. The ancient market at Westminster. It occupied much of the present Parliament Square and was removed to make way for the northern end of Westminster Bridge in 1749.

ROUS, John (?1411-91), chaplain from 1445 of the Beauchamp chantry at Guy's Cliffe near Warwick, wrote a *History of the Earls of Warwick* (The Rous Roll) in two versions, that in English (1483-5) (H) being pro-Yorkist and complimentary to Richard III; that in Latin (c. 1485) (H) pro-Lancastrian to please Henry VII. He also wrote a Latin *History of the Kings of the English* for his friend John Seymour who wished to know of suitable historical figures to be commemorated in the statuary at St. George's Chapel, Windsor, and a *Life* of Richard Beauchamp, E. of Warwick, (H). The books marked (H) are notable for their heraldic illustrations.

ROUSILLON. See LOUIS XI; CHARLES VIII of France; SPAIN 1406-1516-2.

ROUSSEAU, Jean Jacques (1712-78), son of a Geneva watchmaker, lived fecklessly with a kitchen maid whose five bastards he abandoned to foundling hospitals. His polemics against the social order, in which he was a misfit, attracted attention early. He published: *Discourse on the Influence of Learning and Art* (1750), *Discourse on the Origin of Inequality* (1754). *La Nouvelle Heloïse* (1761) was a novel on the return to nature in relationships between the sexes. *Du Contrat Social* (1762) propounded the theory that society is founded upon contract or agreement and that govts. thus derive their authority from the people. *Emile* (1762) suggested that educational methods should appeal to a child's natural curiosity and stimulate his intelligence, not impose settled doctrine. This, of course, attracted the enmity of the French church and he was driven first to Geneva and then until 1767 to England where Hume befriended him. His *Confessions* appeared posthumously.

ROUT. See RIOT; RIDOTITO.

ROUTLEDGE, George (1812-88) began publishing in London in 1836 and in New York in 1854. His huge output of cheap editions contributed considerably to popular literacy.

ROWLANDS, Daniel. See METHODISM.

ROWLANDSON, Thomas (1756-1827) became celebrated as a caricaturist and cartoonist from about 1781.

ROWNTREE (1) Joseph (1801-59), a York grocer and Quaker philanthropist, made a fortune and declined the mayoralty in 1858. His son **(2) Joseph (1836-1925)** developed the famous cocoa business of H. I. Rowntree and Co. and devoted much of the profits to his employees' welfare and housing.

ROWNTREE, Benjamin Seebohm (1871-1954) made a study of scientific management and industrial welfare and tried out many of his innovations at his family chocolate business in York, including works councils and the 44-hour week (1919) and profit sharing (1923). His York business was a success primarily because it depended upon imports of subsidised sugar. His *Poverty: a Study of Town Life* (1901) and its follow-up volume *Poverty and Progress* (1941) were both based on York.

ROWTON HOUSES, poor man's hotels better than common lodging houses, were called after the 1st Ld. Rowton who opened the first at Vauxhall in 1892. It was a great success and others followed.

ROXBURGH, -SHIRE (Scot.) was a fertile unorganised border area dominated from the 12th cent. by the abbeys of Melrose, Jedburgh and Kelso, but much disturbed by the feuds of lowland clans based upon various castles. There was a flourishing agriculture and industries subsidiary to it, all encouraged by the monasteries. It was long doubtful if it belonged to England or Scotland.

The royal stronghold at Roxburgh slowly became the centre of administration. By the mid-12th cent. it was accepted as part of Scotland for it was occupied by the English as surety under the T. of Falaise from 1174 to 1189 and then released. The Burgh, perhaps of Anglian origin, was first chartered by David I (r. 1124-53) and soon had its own mint. By the mid-13th cent. it was one of six important burghs which in 1296 ratified the Franco-Scots treaty of alliance and by the mid-14th cent. it was one of the Four Burghs. Nevertheless it remained very small (perhaps 1000 inhabitants), its importance being largely strategic. In all the Anglo-Scots wars the castle was liable to be attacked; the English held it with relatively short intervals from 1296 until 1460 (when James II of Scots was killed there) and burned the burgh in 1541. The major change came in 1544 when the Reformation had destroyed inhibitions on direct attacks on churches. In the 'Rough Wooing' of that year the English burned Kelso and Melrose Abbeys, which never recovered and other monasteries. The lands began to pass into secular hands, especially the Ker family (from 1570 Earls and from 1707 Dukes of Roxburgh) who by the mid-18th cent. owned most of the county.

ROXBURGHE, Ds. of. *See* KER OF FERNIEHURST-7 and 8.

ROYAL ACADEMY OF ARTS (London) begun by Hogarth in about 1739 as the SOCIETY OF INCORPORATED ARTISTS, was refounded in 1768 with Sir Joshua Reynolds as Pres.

ROYAL AFRICAN CO. (1672-1750) included Charles II and James D. of York among its shareholders. It acquired the Co. of Royal Adventurers' W. African monopoly, forts and trading posts and its right to import slaves to the British W. Indies. Eventually it owned forts at Cape Coast Castle (its H.Q.), Cormantine, Winneba, Accra and Bence I; and, after 1713 when a Spanish concession (*Asiento*) was made, at Jamaica and Barbados. Apart from slaves, it traded in gold, ivory and tropical produce.

Despite its monopoly and powers of confiscation, interlopers abounded and besides, the W. Indians complained constantly of its inadequate deliveries and high prices. In 1698 the slave trade was thrown open to all on payment of 10% of the cargo values, for the maintenance of the forts, but between 1713 and 1721 the W. Indian Spaniards purchased their slaves exclusively from the Co. Bence I. was abandoned in 1728 but subsequently occupied by independent traders. The Charter, which was renewed in 1720, was abolished by statute and after 1750 the forts were maintained by the Crown. *See* CHARTERED COMPANIES.

ROYAL AIR FORCE. *See* AIR FORCES.

ROYAL ARMY MEDICAL CORPS (R.A.M.C.). Before 1854 field units recruited their own medical staff as best they could and in the H.Q. of the military C-in-C there was a Surgeon-Gen. who was mainly a medical staff officer. His authority depended wholly on the interest which his C-in-C took in the work, and his effectiveness on the provision made by the Medical Department of the War Office for hospitals and equipment. Since medicine was in its infancy, the needs were seldom foreseen or adequately anticipated. The Crimean War scandals resulted in the formation of a Medical Staff Corps. and in 1857 this became the all male Army Hospital Corps., soon officered from the War Office. After various changes of name the Corps. and the Medical Department were amalgamated to form the R.A.M.C. in 1898.

(ROYAL) ARMY SERVICE CORPS. (R.A.S.C.) (*See* WAGONERS.) The Land Transport Corps. was formed in the Crimean War, merged with the Military Train in 1856 and became the A.S.C. in 1870. In 1880 the ordnance stores branch was hived off and a new A.S.C. was formed in 1889. It has been responsible for getting supplies to the troops ever since.

ROYAL BURGHS (Scot.). *See* BURGHS-1.

ROYAL BURGHS, CONVENTION OF (Scot.). A voluntary association of royal burghs which grew up in the 16th cent. to consider parliamentary business. Other burghs were admitted in the 19th cent. It was replaced in 1975 (when burghs were abolished) by the Convention of Scottish Local Authorities. *See* BURGHS.

ROYAL COLLEGE OF MUSIC was founded in 1883. *See* PARRY; STANFORD.

ROYAL COMMISSION. The Crown (i.e. the govt. of the day) issues a warrant to a person or persons to do something on its behalf, e.g. to act as a military officer, a judge or governor of a part of the Commonwealth. Such warrants are also issued to a group of persons to investigate a matter of public concern and report with or without recommendations. They empower them to summon witnesses and call for papers. This practice was rare before 1830, the functions being performed, if at all, by parliamentary select committees. From 1830, however, it was common; commonly a commission (often after several years' labour) presented a report to the Crown which published it and laid it before the Houses. They, at their leisure, debated it. The govt. (which might have changed since the issue of the warrant) expressed its acceptance with or without reservations, or rejection, and if it accepted it and parliamentary time could be found, legislation, which might propose some or all the recommendations, would follow the usual course. The end result (if any) might differ considerably from the recommendations. The Poor Law Commission's Report (1832-4) was mostly enacted in 1834 and so were reports on judicial (1833) and municipal reforms (1835). The great Canal report of 1907 to 1911 was, on the other hand, wholly ignored: that on Commons (1958) only partly and mistakenly enacted. By 1914 the appointment of a Royal Commission was already suspect as a delaying manoeuvre.

ROYAL DECLARATION repudiating R. Catholicism is required of all sovereigns at their accession. It was first imposed upon William III and Mary II.

ROYAL EXCHANGE (London) was first built in imitation of the exchange at Amsterdam by Sir Thomas Gresham and opened in 1571. Destroyed in the Great Fire of 1666, it was reopened in 1669. This building was burned in 1838. The existing building was opened in 1842.

ROYAL FAMILY. Where there is a King the next person after him is the Queen (the exception was Mary I and Philip), who is either consort or dowager. The Sovereign's eldest son is D. of Cornwall by Act of Parliament and D. of Rothesay in Scotland. The life of the King and Duke and their consorts is protected by the Statute of Treasons 1352 and so is the chastity of the consorts, but not of dowagers. The Sovereign is guardian of all members of the Royal Family and he may confer the Principality of Wales and the Earldom of Chester upon the Duke whose other titles, however, are heritable. The sons of sovereigns are princes and so are their sons; the daughters are princesses, but their children do not have princely rank. *See* ROYAL MARRIAGES.

ROYAL FLYING CORPS. *See* AIR FORCES.

ROYAL GEORGE, ship of the line, foundered with most of her crew and Adm. Kempenfeldt, without warning while at anchor on a calm day in Spithead in 1782. This sensational and scandalous event drew attention to the contemporary corrupt mismanagement of naval material. Many public houses are still named after her.

ROYAL HIGHNESS. Style of princes by birth and their wives and of princesses, but not by the Duchess of Windsor (*see* EDWARD VIII) nor since 1996 by divorced wives or, necessarily by non-royal husbands of princesses.

ROYAL INSTITUTE OF BRITISH ARCHITECTS began as a dining club of London architects in 1791 and was chartered in 1837.

ROYALISTS, CAVALIERS, ROUNDHEADS were Civil War terms originating in 1641. The King's supporters called the parliament-men "Roundheads". This referred satirically to their presumably shaven pates at a time when hair was mostly worn long. The overtones included excessive piety and lice. "Cavalier", initially in the Spanish form *Caballero* was used of royalists by parliamentarians. The overtones were brainless violence and excessive interest in sex. The royalists adopted the term in the English form because of its suggestion of selfless courage.

ROYAL MARRIAGES. In 1717 the judges advised George I that royal grand-children committed an offence by marrying without the Sovereign's approval, but that the marriage itself was valid. In 1771 the D. of Cumberland married Mrs Horton and the D. of Gloucester published his previous secret marriage with the Dowager Countess Waldegrave. George III was in dispute with both and he, with Ld. North, forced through Parliament the Royal Marriages Act, 1772. This declared that no issue of George II, other than the issue of princesses married into foreign families, should be capable of marrying without the Sovereign's consent, save that if such a person was over 25 and gave a year's notice to the Privy Council, he or she might contract such a marriage, unless within the year both Houses of Parliament had disapproved it.

ROYAL MILITARY ACADEMY (WOOLWICH), R.M. COLLEGE (SANDHURST). The Woolwich (Kent) naval dockyard needed guns. By 1716 guns were being cast at Woolwich Warren when it naturally became the H.Q. of the Royal Artillery. In 1741, equally naturally the R.M.A. was founded as a gunnery school in Woolwich Arsenal, whence it was moved in 1806. In 1799 Col. J. G. le Marchant and the exiled French Gen. Francis Jarry organised an officers' training school at High Wycombe. This was converted into an official college for officers other than artillery (R.M.C.) at Great Marlow in 1802 and transferred to Sandhurst (Surrey) in 1812. It originally trained both cadets and staff officers, but the two functions were separated in 1858 and the separate Staff College was built in 1862. It was intended to amalgamate the R.M.A. with the R.M.C. in 1940 but World War II delayed this until 1947 when they were amalgamated simply as the ROYAL MILITARY ACADEMY.

ROYAL NAVAL AIR SERVICE. *See* AIR FORCES.

ROYAL NAVAL COLLEGE. *See* GREENWICH.

ROYAL OAK. *See* PENDEREL

ROYAL SOCIETY (London) originated in weekly meetings of scientists begun in 1645 in Oxford and London. It was more formally constituted in Nov. 1660 and received royal approval in Dec. It was incorporated in 1662 under the patronage of Charles II. Its earliest Fellows included John Wilkins, John Evelyn and Robert Boyle. Samuel Pepys became a Fellow in 1664, Isaac Newton in 1671. He was Pres. from 1703 to 1727. The Society was not an exclusively scientific body until 1848.

ROYAL SOCIETY OF ARTS, founded in 1754 as the Society for the Encouragement of Arts, Manufacture and Commerce, originally devoted much of its resources to fostering agriculture, forestry and mechanical invention, but also helped young artists. In 1759 the latter persuaded the Society to hold an art exhibition, which was visited by thousands and demonstrated the need for a permanent artists' forum. Disagreements resulted in the holding of two rival annual exhibitions until 1768, when the difficulties were resolved by the foundation of the Royal Academy. Meanwhile in 1761 it had held the first industrial exhibition and it tended after 1768 to concentrate on economic rather than purely aesthetic issues. It was largely responsible for the Great Exhibition of 1851 and has continually promoted industrial design.

ROYAL SUPREMACY. *See* SUPREMACY, ROYAL.

ROYAL WARRANTS. *See* PURVEYANCE.

ROYCE, Frederick Henry (1863-1933) (*see* ROLLS, CHARLES STEWART) began poor but, while working in an engineering firm, went to night school and then helped to found an engineering business himself. He built his first car because his own, French, car was beset with faults. Rolls, who had a London car sales firm, was enthusiastic about Royce's car and the Rolls Royce line of cars soon followed. From 1914 Royce designed and produced aero engines also and shortly before he died his products had been entered for the Schneider Trophy. He was not, apparently, very inventive but an improver of genius.

RUANDA or RWANDA (C. Africa) was part of German E.

Africa from 1884 and administered with Urundi by Belgium from 1919. It became an independent and disorderly republic separate from Urundi in 1962 and the scene of a terrible civil war in 1993-4.

RUBBER. The earliest rubber imports came from the Amazon area in 1836-7. This was wild rubber obtained from jungle trees. In 1876 Sir Henry Wickham obtained seeds from Brazil, bred them at Kew and replanted them in Ceylon. All the world's plantation rubber is descended from this event. Wild rubber continued to be the major source until about 1914, when plantation production overtook it. The latter was enormously stimulated, especially in Malaya, by World War I and was a major contributor to the prosperity of tropical countries until the rise of the plastics industry. Charles Goodyear (1800-60) had invented the vulcanisation process in 1839, but the commercial uses which this made possible developed in the 1890s only with the motor car. When the Japanese, by occupying Malaysia, cut off the main source of natural rubber, synthetic rubber began to replace it, especially in the U.S.A. By 1970 synthetic rubber filled about 85% of world requirements. *See* KEW GARDENS.

RUFFHEAD, Owen (1723-69) published a standard edition of *Statutes at Large* from 1215 to 1763, and 1762 to 1765.

RUGGLES-BRISE, Sir Evelyn (1857-1935) a reforming member (1892) and Chairman (1895-1921) of the Prison Commission. Through him, prison staffs were re-trained; prisoners were properly classified; and special treatment of mental defectives introduced. He also devised special treatment for young offenders, which coalesced with a reformed Borstal system and he improved the medical care of prisoners and the development of prisoners' aid societies. A man of "humanity and insight beyond the common".

RUHR (Ger.) river and its basin, the name denotes a larger, originally lignite mining area, partly in the disputed Duchies of Cleves, Mark, Berg and Guelders. These were acquired piecemeal by Prussia between 1614 and 1801. The T. of Vienna (1815) unified the area in Prussian hands. It comprised (with others) the towns of Duisburg, Essen, Gelsenkirchen, Bochum, Düsseldorf, Elberfeld and Krefeld. Industrialisation was made possible by the use of Silesian iron. The first Krupp steel works began operations at Essen in 1818. The *Zollverein* and the railways rapidly increased the ease and volume of production which was exported by rail, or along the Rhine, or later by canal. By 1914 Bochum, Dortmund and Essen were the main industrial cities of Germany and Krupps provided most of the German military supplies in World War I.

The P. of Versailles disarmed Germany, required the payment of reparations and empowered the Allies to distrain if they remained unpaid. The Ruhr industries had to be converted to non-military purposes, but in 1922 the Germans discontinued payments. The French and Belgians then occupied the Ruhr. The British disapproved but let them pass through their area of occupation. As the British govt. had forecast, the seizure weakened the local economy, strengthened German resentments and further reduced German payments. The French withdrew only on the eve of the Locarno treaty.

The area was enormously redeveloped mainly for armaments after Hitler's advent to power in 1933 and became the main industrial base of German aggression. Consequently it was savagely bombed in World War II. Individual targets were sometimes under ground as well as heavily defended by anti-aircraft artillery and fighter aircraft. In response the Allies resorted to carpet bombing which demolished whole urban areas. The area lay in the British zone at the end of the war and some drastic dismantling was also done.

RULE OF 1756. If seaborne trade between a state and its colonies is closed to third nations in peacetime, it is enemy trade in wartime even if carried in neutral bottoms.

RUM. *See* SUGAR.

RUMBOLD (1) Sir Thomas (1736-1801) 1st Bart. (1779) served under Lawrence and Clive in the HEIC and was a member of the Bengal Council from 1766 to 1769. In 1777 he was Gov. of Madras where he reorganised the finances, took Pondicherry and Mahé from the French, but in 1780 resigned for ill health just before Hyder Ali's invasion. Held responsible, he was dismissed, but exonerated by a parliamentary inquiry. He was an M.P. in 1781 and from 1784 to 1790. His son **(2) Sir George Berriman (1764-1807) 2nd Bart.** was Ambassador to the Hanse at Hamburg in 1803 and was arrested by the French. His grandson **(3) Sir Arthur Carlos (1820-69) 5th Bart.** was Administrator of St. Kitts in 1867. His cousin **(4) Sir Horace (1829-1913) 8th Bart.** was Ambassador at Vienna from 1896 to 1900. His son **(5) Sir Horace George Montague (1869-1941) 9th Bart.** was Minister at Berne from 1916 to 1919; at Warsaw from 1919 to 1920; at Constantinople from 1920 to 1924; he was also Ld. Curzon's deputy at the first Lausanne Conference in 1922 and 1923 and Chief Delegate at the second Conference in 1923 where he signed the treaty with Turkey. He was then Ambassador at Madrid from 1924 to 1928 and at Berlin from 1928 to 1933.

RUMELIA. The name of the 'Roman' i.e. European territories of the Ottoman Empire, particularly Thrace, as opposed to **ANATOLIA,** i.e. the Asiatic territories, particularly Asia Minor.

RUMP was the remnant of the Long Parliament from the time of Pride's Purge in Dec. 1648. Cromwell dissolved it in Apr. 1653. It was restored in May 1659 and finally dissolved by Monk in Feb. 1660.

RUMPSTEAK or LIBERTY CLUB was founded by Walpole's Whig opponents in Jan. 1734. Its leading members were the Ds. of Bedford, Bolton and Queensberry, the E. of Chesterfield and Vist. Carteret. It met weekly during parliamentary sessions to settle tactics.

RUMWOLD, St. (?-?650), a royal Northumbrian, honoured for reciting the creed immediately after his baptism in infancy.

RUNCIMAN (1) Walter (1847-1937) 1st Ld. (1933) ran away to sea in 1853 and stayed there until forced by health to go ashore in 1885. He then set up as a shipowner, buying second hand ships during the depression of the '80s. In 1889 he built his first ship and founded the Moor Line which owned 40 ships by 1914. It was liquidated in 1919 and a new similar co. started. Meanwhile he became Pres. of the U.K. Chamber of Shipping and the Shipping Federation, even though he sympathised with the objects of the Seamen's Union. He was also a strong Liberal and M.P. for Hartlepool from 1914 to 1918. His son **(2) Walter (1870-1949) 1st Vist. RUNCIMAN of DOXFORD (1937)** as a Liberal defeated Winston Churchill at Oldham in 1899, but lost it to him in 1900. After 1902 he was M.P. for Dewsbury. A forcible speaker on finance, he became Parliamentary Sec. to the Local Govt. Board in 1905, Financial Sec. to the Treasury in 1907 and in 1908 Asquith's govt. Pres. of the Board of Education. In 1910 he went to the Board of Agriculture and in 1914 to the vital wartime Board of Trade, where his grasp of economic warfare and understanding of shipping performed an essential service. He resigned with Asquith in 1916, lost his seat in 1918, returning only in 1924. As a Liberal National, like his father no longer wedded to free trade, he returned to the Board of Trade and helped to negotiate the Ottawa Agreements. In 1938 Halifax asked him to go to Prague as an independent mediator in the Sudeten Crisis. His experience of German aggression and bad faith left him in permanent depression. He was Ld. Pres. until the declaration of war.

RUNCORN. *See* NEW TOWNS.

RUNES were letters of a Teutonic alphabet; the earliest dated from the 2nd or 3rd cent. and were Roman or Greek characters adapted for carving or scratching on wood or stone. They were used most extensively by the Scandinavians and Anglo-Saxons and the letters were sometimes thought to be magical.

RUNNYMEDE on the south bank of the Thames near Egham where King John was forced to confirm *Magna Carta.*

RUOTSI. *See* VIKINGS.

RUPEE. An Indian silver coin first minted in 1542 and used also in Afghanistan, Mauritius and British E. Africa. Under the British *raj* the rate of exchange was 15 to the £1 sterling.

> 1 Rupee equalled 16 Annas
> 1 Anna equalled 4 Pice
> 1 Pice equalled 5 Gundas
> 1 Gunda equalled 4 cowrie shells. *See* LAKH; CRORE.

RUPERT, Prince. *See* PALATINE PRINCES.

"RUPERT OF DEBATE", a nickname of Edward Stanley (1799-1869) 14th E. of Derby from 1851, attributed to Disraeli who said "in his charge he is resistless, but when he returns from the pursuit he always finds his camp in the possession of the enemy".

RUPERTS LAND, a vast tract of N. Canada stretching from Newfoundland to the Saskatchewan, was granted to the Hudson Bay Co. in 1670 and sold to Canada in 1869 for £300,000 and 5% of the arable land.

RURAL DISTRICT COUNCILS. *See* LOCAL ADMINISTRATION – ENGLAND AND WALES.

RURAL RIDES. *See* COBBETT.

RUS. *See* VIKINGS-1.

RUSH-BAGOT TREATY (1817) between Britain and the U.S.A. very strictly limited the number and size of warships permitted on Lakes Champlain, Ontario and the Upper Lakes. Ratified in 1818, it has ever since remained in force.

RUSHEN. *See* MAN, I. OF-6.

RUSKIN, John (1819-1900), wine merchant, won the Newdigate Prize at Oxford in 1839, got to know J. M. W. Turner in 1840 and published, anonymously, the first vol. of *Modern Painters* in 1843 partly in his defence. In 1849 he published the *Seven Lamps of Architecture,* in 1851 he made the acquaintance of (Sir) John Everett MILLAIS (1829-96) and other pre-Raphaelites whom he defended in pamphlets and letters to *The Times.* His *Stones of Venice* appeared between 1851 and 1853, when he lectured on Architecture and Painting at Edinburgh. He began to interest himself in the connection of other activities with the arts, lecturing at Manchester in 1857 on the Political Economy of Art and in 1859, in *Two Paths,* on the relevance of organic nature. Between 1860 and 1863 he contributed articles on pure economics to the *Cornhill* and *Frazers* and on social questions. He attacked the indifference of the state to such issues, favoured state education and trade unionism and denounced the pursuit of wealth as an end in itself. He inherited his father's large fortune in 1864 and had provoked strong opposition to his political views, which however he continued to propagate in *Sesame and Lilies* (1865) and *The Crown of Wild Olive* (1866). In 1871 he settled at Coniston where, in *Fors Clavigera* he addressed monthly letters to "the workmen and labourers of Great Britain" and founded the Guild of St. George to glorify labour and honesty. Its members were supposed to contribute a tenth of their income to philanthropy and Ruskin himself contributed generously and also engaged in industrial experiments, such as the revival of hand-made linen in Langdale. His unfinished auto-biographical *Praeterita* appeared between 1885 and 1889.

RUSSELL, Edward (1653-1727) E. of ORFORD (1687), one of the first gentleman officers bred to the sea, was a disloyal subordinate and perhaps a traitor both to James II and William III whom he joined in 1683. He came to

England with him and in 1689 became an M.P. and Treasurer of the Navy. He served under, intrigued against and then succeeded Torrington and in 1692 joined with the Dutch in the victory at Barfleur; but was dismissed in 1693 for not pressing the destruction of the French fleet. He was soon reinstated. He was 1st Ld. of the Admiralty from 1694 to 1699, an English Commissioner for the Union in 1706, 1st Ld. again from 1709 to 1710 and from 1714 to 1717. He also served as one of the Lords Justices during royal absences in 1697, 1698 and 1714.

RUSSELL, John (?-1494), diplomat and Ambassador to Burgundy in 1470, was Privy Seal from 1474 to 1483 and Bp. of Rochester from 1476 to 1480; he negotiated the Scots marriage treaty of 1474. From 1480 he was Bp. of Lincoln and in 1483 Ld. Chancellor. Trusted professionally both by Richard III and by Henry VII, he managed the negotiations with the Scots in 1484 and the Breton and Scots negotiations of 1486. From 1483 he was Chancellor of Oxford University.

RUSSELL'S FIRST GOVT. (July 1846-Feb. 1852) (Sixteen in Cabinet under Ld. John Russell, with Vist. Palmerston as Foreign Sec., the E. of Clarendon Pres. of the Board of Trade, Henry Labouchere Chief Sec. for Ireland and T. B. Macaulay P-M-G.)

(1) This govt. succeeded that of Peel, which broke up at the repeal of the Corn Laws, on an Irish Coercion Bill. It inherited Irish disorder and famine, but a successful war with the Sikhs in India. It then quarrelled with King Louis Philippe of France over the Spanish marriages and so destroyed the understanding necessary for the survival of his monarchy. Depending for its tenure upon the irreconcilable antagonism between protectionist and Peelite Tories, the govt's. position was not improved by the general election of 1847. In the meantime, if labour agitation was partly assuaged by the passage of the Ten Hours Bill, it soon revived when this legislation began to be circumvented by a system of relay working.

(2) The Irish disaster was the most important feature of the political landscape. It obsessed the hundred noisy Irish M.P.s; relief, public works and food distribution were costing many millions, which the English had to find because Ireland could not; thousands of deaths from disease and starvation-induced disease were horrifying the evangelical conscience; transatlantic emigration was taking on the aspect of a wholesale flight and re-awakening the latent anti-British spirit of the U.S.A. The underlying problem was said to be one of land tenure, to which the govt. directed its attention. In the meantime it sent the very able E. of Dalhousie to govern India; and the quarrel with France caused Palmerston to send a special mission under the E. of Minto to encourage the Italian liberals. The govt. was entangled in contradictions. It was liberal in outlook, yet imperially responsible; it had quarrelled with the nearest constitutional power and was now undermining Italian autocratic regimes, which leaned upon that power. Neither it, nor the Crown, was fully in control of its own Foreign Sec., nor was it in control of the House of Commons.

(3) The Sicilians, encouraged by Palmerston, now revolted against the tyranny of Louis Philippe's Bourbon relatives (Jan. 1848); and Europe, in which the revolutionary temperature had been rising for some years, boiled over. By the end of the year France was a republic; new ministers and a new Emperor ruled in Austria, which was involved in civil war with Hungary. Revolt and repression in the Slav areas was matched by a similar sequence in Italy. Germany too was convulsed. In these circumstances it would not be easy to solve Irish problems in which a war between landlord and tenant had been in progress for half a century. If the Irish had been less debilitated and oppressed they might have staged a revolt. In fact their leaders sent delegations to France and were transported for their pains (*see* YOUNG IRELAND). By this time the Govt's. Irish Tenant Right Bill

had been thrown out and Russell had to rely upon the pacifying effect of a successful royal state visit to Dublin, while he tried again.

(4) In 1848 Dalhousie had annexed Satara under the doctrine of lapse. The event, emotionally significant to the Marathas, was followed by the last of the Sikh wars (1849) and the annexation of the Punjab. Such events were much closer to home than they had been. Since 1840 the P. and O. Co. had been running a steamship service to India (overland at Suez), which had cut the voyage time by 70%. Irish events were closer too. Steam had reduced the time between London and Dublin from two and a half days to 15 hours. The Govt. got an Irish Encumbered Estates Act through Parliament to attract new capital, which it failed to do. It also tried to wind up the Dublin Castle administration, but encountered emotional appeals to memories of past independence and abandoned the idea. There were other troubles. Trade unions were becoming more effective and were pressing to close the loopholes in the Ten Hours Act. The "Papal Aggression" exacerbated the Irish problem because the Ecclesiastical Titles Bill alienated R. Catholic M.P.s. Then the *Gorham* judgement seemed to incite an Anglican secession to Rome. In 1850 the Govt. passed the important Factory Act.

(5) The Reform Acts of 1832 were too arbitrary in their franchise provisions ever to be acceptably final. Here again the internal contradictions in the Govt. placed a strain upon Russell. Liberal principles supported a similar electorate in town and country, but most of the Liberals were Whig landowners who wanted things as they were. The issue had been intermittently canvassed for some years. In 1851 a motion in favour of similar electorates was carried in the Commons against Russell's advice. He resigned. The old Tories could not form a govt. without the Peelites (whom they hated), and the Peelites knew that they could not get a majority. Peel had died in 1850. Thus, *faute de mieux,* Russell was back in a fortnight.

(6) Much maligned, imperial expansion continued. Sambalpur had lapsed in 1849. Disputes with Burma brought further war and annexations in 1852. Foreign policy and its constitutional aspect destroyed the Govt. at home. British opinion had been incensed by Austrian and Russian methods of suppressing the Hungarian revolt; Palmerston had supported the Turks in giving asylum to the Hungarian leaders. When the Austrian Gen. Haynau was mobbed on a visit to England, Palmerston replied in insulting terms to Austrian protests. Apart from angering the court, his demagoguery amounted to a claim to run the Foreign Office independently of the Cabinet. It was French politics which caused the final rupture and breakdown of the Govt. On 2 Dec. 1851 Louis Napoleon Bonaparte overthrew the French Republic. Next day Palmerston, without consulting anyone, expressed his personal approval. The court and Russell demanded his resignation. The Cabinet did not support him. He resigned. The matter did not end there. A potentially hostile Bonaparte in command of France required a more extensive defence establishment than a friendly one. The Govt. decided to introduce a National Militia Bill. Palmerston, logically enough, saw to its defeat. On this the Govt. resigned.

RUSSELL'S SECOND GOVT. (Oct. 1865-June 1866) (*see* PALMERSTON'S SECOND GOVT) (Fifteen in Cabinet under Earl Russell, with the E. of Clarendon as Foreign Sec; after Sir Charles Wood resigned in Feb. 1866, Earl de Grey became Sec. for India. Otherwise this Govt's. composition resembled the previous one). This Govt. came into office on Palmerston's death, with the support of a majority created by the 1865 general election. The German Crisis was getting under way with Bismarck's Biarritz meeting with Napoleon III (Oct. 1865) and the Govt. subsisted until the Prussians were well on their way to their victory over the Austrians at Koniggratz (3 July 1866). It and Parliament were preoccupied with Fenianism and the domestic issue of electoral reform, for only about 19% of adult males had the franchise and there was gross maldistribution of parliamentary seats. The Govt. decided on separate bills and was defeated on an amendment to its Franchise Bill. Since so early a general election would be unpopular and would deepen the divisions within the Govt's. supporters, Russell resigned.

RUSSIA CO. was chartered in 1555 as a joint stock venture with exclusive trading rights between England and Russia. In the north it exported cloth in return for furs and ships' stores, especially hemp, and had to contend with the rivalry of the Dutch until their defeat in the Dutch Wars. It then became a regulated trading assn. and as such dominated the Russian northern trade in the mid-18th cent. It also made much profit *via* a southern route through Persia (circumventing the Ottoman Empire) but in practice competed with the Levant Co. which had a similar but less well organised monopoly towards these areas before S. Russian territory could be reached. The profits of the route declined with the decline of Persian royal power and order and the Russian advance to the Black Sea. *See* CHARTERED COMPANIES.

RUSSIA, KIEVAN or VARANGIAN (*see* VIKINGS). **(1)** The preindustrial history of European Russia was dominated by two geographical peculiarities, viz: the division between deep forest to the north and open steppe of the Ukraine eastwards and two major river systems. The *Water Road* from the Gulf of Finland to Kiev and thence *via* the Dnieper to the Black Sea was the trade route from the North Sea and the Baltic to Constantinople. (*For the other, see paragraph* **(4)** *below.*) The Varangian princes traded in furs, wax, honey and slaves. They established major posts at Novgorod, Smolensk, Chernigov and Kiev. From Kiev, escorted convoys fought their way once or twice a year past the 60-mile rapids and the savage Petchenegs who infested them, to the mouth of the Dnieper and so to the Constantinople markets in exchange for textiles, armaments and bullion, which often found its way to England.

(2) This route functioned from about 865 and it was in the interest of the princes, who were numerous and related, to maintain its unity. The capital was Kiev from about 882 and the history of Kievan Russia is mainly that of this Road. The princes of Kiev became rich. Vladimir was converted to Orthodoxy in 989; Yaroslav married three daughters in the West, including Elizabeth to Harald Hardrada.

(3) In the mid-11th cent. the Polovtsian or Cuman Turks appeared in the southern Steppes and began a crescendo of annual raids. Crusades of 1101, 1108 and 1111 failed to suppress them and princely disunity compounded the difficulty of defending the Road. The rural population began to disperse northwards into the forests. The Water Road, and with it the southern towns, declined. Novgorod, beyond Polovtsian reach, survived. By the early 12th cent. it had made itself rich by substituting an East-West trade for the North-South Trade of the Water Road and had acquired a monopoly of vaguely-defined tracts of cold trappers' forest stretching, over 100 miles wide, almost to the Urals.

(4) It was in the forest river system to the south of this tract that the southern refugees settled, especially at Moscow, already stockaded in 1155. It had long distance water communication northward, south-west, south-east and eastward and it was close to the Steppe, but far enough inside the forest for protection against Polovtsian cavalry.

(5) This process of resettlement was already advanced when the Mongols rolled out of Asia between 1228 and 1241 and overwhelmed the Varangians and the Polovtsy together. They turned back from the Novgorod marches, but elsewhere imposed a tribute which for 150 years reduced the people to a bare subsistence and made the princes into tax collectors' agents. Kiev was ruined and in 1299 the Church moved its metropolitical See to Moscow, whose princes under the Mongol shadow expanded their territories among their down-trodden kinsmen by marriage, purchase or violence. The fact that they had a metropolitan in their pocket made them conscious of a unifying mission and they could lighten the burden of tribute by interfering in the affairs of Novgorod. They found this all the easier when Poland-Lithuania finally blocked the Water Road in 1370 (*see* MUSCOVY). N. European and English interest in the Mediterranean consequently expanded at this period. *See also* BALTIC-13 *et seq.*

RUSSIAN REVOLUTIONS (1) The huge casualties in World War I and the general incompetence of Nicholas II's govt. created a disillusioned weariness and indiscipline visible to foreign observers. On 4 Mar. 1917 the British Ambassador warned the Czar, who saw no need for apprehension. On 8th-14th (OS. 23 Feb-1 Mar) rioting and military desertions brought the govt. and economy to a halt and Nicholas II abdicated. As a result of this **FEBRUARY REVOLUTION,** Pr. Lvov formed a govt. with Miliukov and Kerensky and organised a general election for a Duma which met in St. Petersburg. On 22 Aug. Kerensky became Prime Minister and on 13 Sept. he proclaimed a republic. The Allies supported him in the hope of keeping Russia in the war, and a final offensive under Gen. Brusilov made some progress at great loss.

(2) The Germans, in reply, sent Vladymir Ilyitch Ulianov (alias LENIN) to Russia *via* Finland. He arrived in St. Petersburg and immediately organised a plot against the popular, budding but inexperienced democracy. This matured into the bloody **OCTOBER REVOLUTION** (7 Nov. 1917-05. 26 Oct.) in which the Bolsheviks obtained adequate local acquiescence by promising peace. Three weeks later an armistice was offered to the Central Powers and a peace conference began at Brest Litovsk (22 Dec.) while the forces dissolved, the Baltic states and the Ukraine seceded and White armies began to form in non-acquiescent areas. The area immediately dangerous to Lenin was Finland and his first military success was to occupy Helsinki (Jan. 1918). Emboldened by German troop transfers to the Western Front, the Brest Litovsk negotiators hardened, whereupon the Germans resumed their offensives. Russian troops surrendered in droves. The T. of Brest Litovsk was hurriedly signed (Mar.) but the Germans continued to Helsinki (Apr.), Sevastopol and Rostov (May). By now the German western offensives were consuming their resources, while British troops landed at Murmansk to protect the depots first against the Germans and then against the Bolsheviks, who had in Allied eyes become German allies. Moreover in Mar. 1919 they established the Third International.

(3) Acquiescence was so incomplete that a number of White armies, uncoordinated and with different objectives, assembled. Lenin and Lev Bronstein (alias TROTSKY), his military adviser, had to fight on several fronts, notably about St. Petersburg; in Siberia, where the Japanese intervened; in the Ukraine; in the Caucasus (*see* DUNSTERVILLE) and towards Poland. Between Oct. 1919 and Apr. 1920 these wars, save in Poland and the Ukraine, had been liquidated and the British had left Murmansk and Baku. Typhus broke out in central Russia and was conveniently exported to the Ukraine by trainloads of infected refugees. A vast epidemic destroyed unnumbered Ukrainians and their White organisation; and the Baltic states being left to their independence, Lenin was free to concentrate against the Poles, who had been trying to push their frontier eastwards in the confusion.

(4) Germany was in near dissolution. Trotsky, who favoured revolution by conquest, launched a great offensive into Poland (July 1920) under Tukhachevsky. This was proclaimed as a counter-offensive, but was aimed at Germany. Marshal Pilsudski resoundingly defeated it south of Warsaw by ignoring the advice of the French Gen. Weygand. The defeat was used by partisans of the Third International (which favoured revolution by subversion) to discredit Trotsky's political doctrines. Nevertheless such military resources as remained were used successfully to end the war in the south (Nov. 1920). *See* U.S.S.R.

RUSSIA, PETRINE or ST. PETERSBURG. (*See* MUSCOVY.) **(1)** The Czar **ALEXIS (r. 1645-76)** left children by two wives, Maria Miloslavskaya and Natalia Naryshkina. This stunted Russian development; in 11 reigns or regencies up to the 19th cent., periods of Crown strength alternated with times when factions used imperial puppets to pursue sectional interests and dilute reforms. In strong periods Russia usually preyed on her neighbours; during weak ones factions preyed on the rural populations. The cost of aggression and misgovernment absorbed resources and obstructed the way out of barbarism. The period is one of military, courtly and social violence.

(2) Maria's son **FEDOR II (r. 1676-82)** began the reforms by abolishing the right of a noble to enter upon his public career in the highest administrative rank enjoyed by any of his ancestors. The joint reign of the dim-witted Miloslavski Ivan V (r. 1682-96) and the Naryshkin 10-year-old **PETER I (The Great) (r. 1682-1725)** began, after a palace revolution, with the regency of Ivan's able sister **SOPHIA (r. 1682-9).** She and her minister P. Basil Galitsyn pursued limited foreign objectives. A Polish alliance legalised the illegal annexation of Kiev and stabilised the Tartar-Turkish frontier. The T. of Nerchinsk settled the Siberian frontier with China (1689).

(3) Germans were influential at the court of Moscow where they had a populous quarter near the Kremlin. Peter I educated himself through them and built up a new model bodyguard. Helped by foreign officers, notably the Scot Patrick Gordon, in 1689 he overthrew Sophia, installed his mother **NATALIA (r. 1689-94)** in the regency, but continued his self-education. His direct rule began when she died. He was a huge, abnormally strong, violent genius. His first important step was to create a Black Sea flotilla, so as to cut off and storm the Turkish fortress of Azov (1696). His second (1696-8) was a famous, thinly incognito journey to the west. He made friends with the Electors of Brandenburg and Hanover, hired over 1000 experts and craftsmen in Holland, worked as a shipwright at Zaandam and Deptford (where he wrecked John Evelyn's house) and came home *via* Vienna. A conspiracy gave him a pretext for eliminating the conservative opposition; reform and re-education began with the massacre of the ancient privileged bodyguard (*Streltzy* = Archers).

(4) From 1700 until 1721 he conducted a broadening aggression initially designed to secure free access to the ocean *via* the Baltic. This involved war with Sweden (*see* BALTIC-36 *et seq*). The main landmarks were the defeat at Narva (1700); the foundation in 1703 on Swedish territory of St. Petersburg; the decisive victory over Charles XII at Poltava in 1709; and the establishment of an English-trained Baltic fleet in 1713. Estonia, Livonia and S. Finland fell to him directly. Poland by interference and Courland by marriage became client states. In 1716 a political marriage treaty gave him, in Mecklenburg, a potential military base near the Sound. In comparison with this, the loss of Azov in 1711 seemed petty.

(5) The true political heir of Ivan the Dread (*see* MUSCOVY-3), Peter brought in western technology, but his furious revolutionary spirit could touch only the top level of society, a level which he tried to deepen by compulsory state service with promotion for ability. Prince Menshikov, his last minister, had been a pieman;

his second Empress, the Estonian Catharine, a housemaid. He put his only son to death, proclaimed the right of Czars to choose their successors and died without choosing one. His widespread but skin deep reforms were instantly jeopardised in a period of faction ridden weakness. The puppets (*see paragraph* (1) *above*) had mostly married into German princely families. They sustained the German influence and his educational programmes, but their manipulators emptied out the content of his social reforms. His service gentry made themselves into an upstart oligarchy, while tempests, famine and epidemics (1733-4), the War of the Polish Succession (1733-5) and a Turkish war in alliance with Austria and Persia (1735-9) consumed the economy.

(6) With the advent of Peter's daughter **ELIZABETH (r. 1741-62)** Russia acquired a no less predatory, but a stronger govt. The familiar pattern – foreign aggression creating internal tyranny – continued, but the Czarina, less intelligent and lazier than her father, was cajoled or driven still further from his social policies, tolerated enormous financial maladministration and strayed so far from his foreign aims as to become involved, with much blood or honour, in the Seven Years' War (*see also* BALTIC-42 *et seq*, PRUSSIA; AUSTRIA). The dangerous precedent was remembered by western statesmen and her own successors.

(7) Elizabeth's sudden death ended the war against Prussia but put the Crown on the head of a German princess with no lawful claims, who murdered her husband Peter III for it. **CATHERINE II (The Great) (r. 1762-96)** of Anhalt-Zerbst had first been advanced by the British Ambassador Sir Charles Hanbury Williams as a possible Czarina-Consort in 1756. Inheretrix of disaster, she astonished and shocked even that sophisticated and profligate age. Her legendary sexual appetite was matched by gifts of intellect, courage, application and a power to inspire or terrify. She had read Blackstone and Buffon; she was an engraver, painter, sculptor and writer. She corresponded with all the ablest minds and contributed to the *Encyclopedie*. Her court was a school of French culture. Nevertheless she was a professional ruler, specialising in foreign affairs. This was unfortunate, for her barbarous and violent peoples needed civilisation and repose. Allowing for overlapping, in the first part of her reign the main activity was westward aggression (*see* AUSTRIA-4 *et seq*; BALTIC-49 *et seq*; POLISH PARTITIONS; PRUSSIA-9 *et seq*), in the second Turkish wars (*see* OTTOMAN EMPIRE), all against a background of palace and city conspiracies, impersonated pretenders and rural revolts. Pugachev's great rising (1773-5) nearly destroyed her.

(8) Despite the brilliance and disorder, Russian seaborne trade, mostly carried under British and Danish and in wartimes, convenient flags, blossomed. All western seaboard countries wanted Russian furs, or hides and leather, wax, timber and hemp which nourished their naval and military power. During the American rebellion the British intercepted such cargoes in neutral bottoms and so interrupted Russian trade with France and Spain. British war and merchant ships depended on Baltic supplies to keep afloat. Catharine organised the First Armed Neutrality (1780) to exploit the dependence. This was not wholly successful; it created a recession at St. Petersburg and added the dislike of the trading communities to the existing unpopularity of the govt. The dependence of the Russian import and export trades upon the goodwill of Britain, now reaching a critical phase in the Industrial Revolution, was to have profound effects during the next 35 years, because Catharine was developing internal communications along which British manufactures penetrated, through St. Petersburg middlemen, into the hinterland and created influential vested interests.

(9) During the Wars of 1768-74 and 1788-92 the

subversion and overthrow of the Cossacks and the Krim Tartars, the annexation of the Crimea, the seizure of the Black Sea ports and victories over the Turks coincided with a period of Turkish decadence. The Ps. of Kutchuk Kainardji (July 1714), Sistova (Aug. 1791) and Jassy (Jan. 1792) mapped the future of the Straits or Eastern question. Turkish strength was taken for granted by English politicians before 1768, when the Russian frontier was a long way from Sebastopol. By 1794 Catherine's Black Sea Navy was two days away from the ill defended Bosphorus and she had, in three mouthfuls, swallowed the largest share of Poland. Her reign filled out the foreign policies of Peter the Great and provoked both the alarmed European preoccupation with Poland and the British concern over Levantine stability.

RUSSIA 1825-1918 (*see* PAUL, CZAR (r. 1796-1801) *and* ALEXANDER I, CZAR (r. 1801-25).) **(1)** A comic opera interlude, when the Grand Dukes Constantine and Nicholas proclaimed each other Czar, preceded Nicholas I's accession and the *Decembrist* outbreak of liberal guards officers. This confirmed Nicholas' conservatism and Orthodoxy. A strong govt. with a strong bureaucracy and police was to take charge while a strong army drove away the infidel. The programme began awkwardly and too early, for the Greeks were in revolt and Orthodox (in this case nationalist) opinion would not allow them to be suppressed. A Russian squadron had to take part in the B. of Navarino (Oct. 1827). The Turkish war had to be launched in 1828. It led to the autonomy of the Roumanian provinces (P. of Adrianople, Sept. 1829), the penetration of the Caucasus and the closure of the Straits to all but Russian warships. It also opened a phase in the Balkan rivalry with Austria.

(2) The revolutionary year 1830 brought insurrections in Poland where Nicholas solved Alexander I's problem by suppressing the constitution. He also entertained wider ambitions towards the world of Islam. The P. of Turkmanchai (Feb. 1828), after a three-year war with Persia, had given him Persian Armenia. The Ottoman Empire might be absorbed whole rather than partitioned. The Prussian, Russian and Austrian autocrats negotiated the Convention of Münchengraetz (Sept. 1833) but Nicholas had undertaken to protect the Grand Turk against his dangerous Egyptian vassal (T. Unkiar Skelessi July 1833). The Convention expired in 1841 and was replaced by the international Straits Convention (a success for Turkish diplomacy), but meanwhile migrants were penetrating Turkestan. When Nicholas was helping to destroy the Hungarian revolutionaries in 1848, his people were founding new towns by the gigantic Sea of Aral. Far to the east, in 1853, he annexed the northern half of the Japanese island of Sakhalin (Karafuto).

(3) It was not safe for statesmen to credit Russia with a desire only to be left in peace, like a boa constrictor digesting another goat. The Crimean War (1854-6) reflected this suspicion; fought for a variety of reasons by an alliance of French, Savoyards, Turks and British in a Ukrainian peninsula, it ended with Nicholas' death, the accession of the reforming **ALEXANDER II (1855-81)**, and the P. of Paris (1856) which demilitarised the Black Sea. The war destroyed the reputation of the conservative autocracy and almost ruined the state finances, but it made little impression on the massive economy. The controversies on U.S. slavery and Russian serfdom were reaching their climax together. Alexander had time to annex the Amur (1858) and Pacific Maritime (1860) provinces and subjugate the Caucasian princes (1859) before launching his great state-financed manumission programme (1861-94), which was also a land revolution. The Polish insurrection of 1863-4 did not impede its progress nor the advance into Turkestan. Tashkent fell in 1864, Samarkand and Bokhara in 1868, Khiva in 1873. He annexed Ferghana in 1876. This release of energy was accompanied after 1862 by a railway boom, but between 1870 and 1873 by local famines, which the railways would end.

(4) The Franco-Prussian war of 1870-1 and the Paris Commune had important consequences. After the first, Russia had a unitary Germany along her western frontier. The second reinforced the extremism absorbed from France and spawned an enlarged generation of terrorists. These fed on prosperity and feared the stability which the Throne and the rising businessmen and smallholders together might achieve. The war had also enabled Alexander to denounce the Black Sea Clauses and build up a naval potential against Turkey. With the annexation of Ferghana (1876) Russia had, at the Afghan frontier, reached a line about which the British in India were sensitive. They were equally sensitive when he attacked Turkey in 1877. His victorious P. of San Stefano (1877) delighted Orthodox and Slavophil opinion in Russia. Its Greater Bulgaria with an Aegean port represented a working compromise between the "absorbers" and the "partitioners" of Turkey and besides, Old Bulgar was the language of the Russian Orthodox scriptures. Hence the Berlin Congress of 1878, which tore up the P. of San Stefano, was a political debacle for the Throne. Nor was the shaky protectorate over Afghanistan, established under the T. of Kabul in the same year, any compensation: it is a long way from Kabul to Czarigrad (Constantinople) and the treaty kept British hostility alive. Alexander and his minister Loris-Melikov saw that liberal goodwill was now essential for orderly progress and took effective steps to secure it. The terrorists were well aware of this too and killed him (1881).

(5) The addition of a reforming liberal to the list of murdered Czars upset accepted beliefs. **ALEXANDER III (r. 1881-94)** was minded to continue his internal policies, but in the field of ideas and education was sharply checked by strongly held court opinion, led by his old tutor Pobedonstsev. The inefficient use of force to repress ideas, employed by this incorruptible but stupid man, soon drained the autocracy of its moral authority, even though its other policies were a distinct and often (e.g. the factory laws) liberal success. In Europe Bismarck's *Dreikaiserbund* gave support to Alexander's shaken nerve. In nearer Asia he continued Nicholas' Transcaspian advance: he cleared the Persian military feudatories from Goek Tepe and occupied Merv in 1884. The Penjdeh affair, when he tried to bully the Afghans, occurred in 1885. In the Balkans, Alexander tried to dominate Bulgaria by a naked violence, which even descended, in 1886, to kidnapping the Prince.

(6) 1886 represented a watershed. The continuing railway boom had brought in foreign, mainly French, capital. Prospectors had uncovered the iron and coal of the Donetz, where production now increased spectacularly. The American Civil War cotton famine created an indigenous textile industry, especially in the Moscow area. After 1887 this began to draw upon the new cotton fields of Turkestan: after 1891, the Donetz supplied the huge quantities of steel needed for the new Trans Siberian railway. The upswing in Russian internal and external trade made the Turkish Straits a principal highway of S. Russia. Much of all this was nourished on French capital, while French shipbuilders built prototypes for Russian ships. These activities began to restrict the rate of English commercial expansion. More importantly, they had created a practice of Franco-Russian business co-operation which suggested an alliance, in the new era of aggressive Wilhelminian Germany. Military conversations began in 1893, while Sergius Witte, the new finance minister, negotiated on tariffs with Germany. The apparent contradiction hastened the secret Franco-Russian alliance of 1894.

(7) NICHOLAS II (r. 1894-1917) succeeded during the Sino-Japanese War in an atmosphere of ill omen, terrorist explosions and confused policy. His father's strong will could co-ordinate the inconsistencies of departmental action. Nicholas had no will and no willingness to delegate. State action slipped into a morass of personal and often corrupt intrigue. Under the Japanese-dictated First T. of Shimonoseki (Apr. 1895) China ceded Formosa and the Liaotung Peninsula. A concert of France, Germany and the Russian military and railway interests forced the Japanese to give up Liaotung (Second T., May). In the ensuing scramble for China, the Russians seized Liaotung to provide a warmer water port for Siberia than Vladivostok. It was to be connected with the Tran-Siberian by a short cut across Manchuria, the home of the Chinese imperial dynasty. This opened up unlimited vistas of interference in China and Korea and the certainty of war with Japan. A fortified naval base was lethargically built at Port Arthur and a vulnerable commercial port at Dalny 20 miles away. The Japanese naturally strengthened their army, came to an understanding with Britain, the only uncommitted great power, and got her to build their warships. The Russians saw no reason to improve their military efficiency and expected a short victorious war, which would settle opinion at home.

(8) In the upshot the Japanese launched a surprise attack (Feb. 1904). Dalny proved very useful to them; they destroyed the Russian's Pacific fleet in Port Arthur, beat their armies in Manchuria by Mar. 1905, sank their Baltic fleet at Tsushima (May 1905) and made peace by U.S. mediation (T. of Portsmouth, Sept. 1905). Competence and a patriotic upsurge might have given Russia the victory, but few could be enthusiastic for the unintelligent, virtually autonomous, police regime. General strikes and demonstrations, some provoked by police agents, turned into bloody street battles. The Black Sea fleet mutinied. The possible dissolution of Russian society became a factor in the calculations of European chancelleries.

(9) Like Alexander II, but without conviction, the court now sought the co-operation of the less extreme, and conceded, in three successive *Dumas* (Parliaments), popular representation in govt. Abroad, after an aberration at Bjorkö, the analogy of the *Entente* was followed. Izvolsky, the Foreign Minister, reached settlements with Britain and her Japanese ally: the integrity of Persia, Afghanistan and Tibet were to be respected by Britain and Russia, but Afghanistan was to be wholly within the British sphere of influence, Tibet wholly outside that of either power, while each was to have a sphere of its own in Persia (Sept. 1907). This was followed by settlements of outstanding issues with Japan.

(10) Liberal opinion strongly favoured a British alliance for which, as France and Russia were already allied, the way was now clear. The Bosnian Crisis of 1908 hastened the movement (*see* AUSTRO-HUNGARY), for Russian statesmen were determined not to lose the patronage of Balkan slavism and thought a war with the Central Powers inevitable. The Kiev military district was put permanently on 48 hours alert and in 1910, when Sazonov became Foreign Minister, Izvolsky became Ambassador in Paris. Meanwhile conservative opposition to the extensive, parliamentary inspired reforms, was growing. If terrorists financed themselves by bank robberies ("Expropriations"), reactionaries now murdered Stolypin, the Prime Minister and principal architect of orderly advance (Sept. 1911). The govt. was in disarray when the Balkan Wars (1912-3) ushered in the final tragedy. *See* WORLD WAR I; RUSSIAN REVOLUTIONS.

RUSSIAN SECRET SERVICES were not always wholly obedient servants of the state. This and their huge financial, material and manpower resources gave them a special position (for which allowance had to be made) in international, as well as home affairs. Their names were portmanteaux of long Russian titles. **(1)** The Czarist service was called the OKHRANA. **(2)** Lenin created the

CHEKA under the Pole Felix Dzherzhinski in Dec. 1917, within six weeks of the Revolution, to put down political dissidence. This pervasive terrorist body, successively renamed NKVD, MVD and KGB operated from the LUBIANKA building and prison in central Moscow. It exerted great and sometimes decisive leverage as the cutting edge and disciplinary organism of, amongst others, the also successively named, Comintern, Cominform and International Dept of the Soviet Communist Central Committee. It had troops of its own and applied without moral scruple every type of cruelty, violence, blackmail, corruption, espionage or organised lies deemed technically appropriate to any given objective. It trained the members of similar services in subordinate states. Its and their victims ran into millions. At the fall of the U.S.S.R. much of its wider organisation was apparently dispersed, but the Russian State Police took over the Lubianka and promptly acquired a large building next door. **(3)** Like every major force, the Red Army had a military intelligence dept (the GRU) but because of the Red Army's constitution with political commissars down to battalion level, it was not always certain whether the GRU and the others were really separate.

RUSTENBURG GRONDWET (Dutch = Fundamental Law of Rustenburg). The Transvaal constitution adopted in Dec. 1856 under the inspiration of Marthinus Pretorius and the young Paul Kruger.

RUTHERFURD, Andrew (1791-1854) Ld. RUTHERFURD (1851) was Sol-Gen. for Scotland in 1837. He became a Tory M.P. in 1839 and also Lord Advocate until 1841, and from 1846. As such he carried through a reform of the Scots Law of Tailzie. He became a Lord of Session in 1851.

RUTHERFORD, Daniel (1749-1819), chemist, physician and botanist, adumbrated the discovery of nitrogen in 1772.

RUTHERFORD, Ernest (1871-1937) 1st Ld. RUTHERFORD, Nobel Prizeman (1908). He was a New Zealander and director of the Cavendish Laboratory (q.v.) from 1919 to 1937. *See* ATOMIC.

RUTHVEN (pron: Riven), Perthshire family. **(1) William (?-1552) 2nd Ld.,** was a Scots privy councillor in 1543 and a guardian of the infant Mary Q. of Scots in 1543. His son **(2) Patrick (?1522-66) 3rd Ld.,** was a soldier until he succeeded to the peerage and was then annually elected Provost of Perth. He supported the Scots reformation, the overthrow of Mary of Guise's regency in 1559 and helped to negotiate the T. of Berwick with England in 1560. In 1563, though a Protestant he was a councillor to Mary Q. of Scots, advised the Darnley marriage and supported her in Moray's insurrection (1565). In 1566 he was art and part of the murder of Rizzio and fled to England. His *Relation* is a description of the murder, intended to excuse it to Q. Elizabeth I. His son **(3) William (?1541-84) 4th Ld. and 1st E. of GOWRIE (1581)** was in the Rizzio conspiracy, fled with his father and later, with Ld. Lindsay, had custody of Mary at Lochieven and helped to bully her into abdication (1567). In 1582 he was involved in the strange affair known as the Ruthven Raid or Gowrie Conspiracy, but pardoned. In 1584, disillusioned with Arran's influence over the King, he joined the Stirling conspiracy with Angus, Mar and others and was convicted and executed for treason. His sons **(4) Alexander (?1580-1600)** and **(5) John (?1578-1600)** were involved (according to James VI) in a plot to kidnap James VI at Gowrie and were killed. A relative **(6) Patrick (?1573-1651) Ld. RUTHVEN of ETTRICK (1639), E. of FORTH (1642)** was a professional soldier trained in the Swedish army. He was Charles I's Muster-Master-Gen. in Scotland in 1638; was forced to surrender Berwick to the Covenanters in 1640; fought at Edgehill and became royalist C-in-C but was wounded at Reading in 1643. He won the victory at Lostwithiel in 1644 but, being wounded again at the second B. of Newbury, Prince Rupert superseded him. In 1646 he became chamberlain to Prince Charles whom he accompanied to Jersey and France and for whom he sought help from Q. Christina of Sweden.

RUTHWELL CROSS (Northumberland). This remarkable sculpture (c. 680-720) has four carved sides. Two are decorated with inhabited vine scroll; the others with panels and inscriptions. The subjects depicted are, sometimes allegorical, monastic themes. One, a runic inscription, contains an early short version of the *Dream of the Rood*. The Mediterranean style of the carving shows no sign of Celtic influence. The present transom is a 19th cent. reconstruction.

RUTLAND with its county town of Oakham developed into a separate shire from the late Anglo-Saxon practice of allotting the northern part as an honour for the sustenance of the queen. The previous Northamptonshire hundred or wapentake of Witchley was added in the 13th cent. The area included Lyfield Forest and Beaumont Chase but was otherwise highly productive cattle and sheep country and good arable. Limestone is the local building material. There was a castle at Oakham, whose Norman hall is still used for law courts, where every visiting peer is expected to give a horse shoe. The county became a district of Leicestershire in 1974.

RUTLAND, Es. and Ds. of. *See* MANNERS.

RUTUPIAE. A Roman signal station at Richborough (Kent) built as a navigational aid and as part of the Saxon shore defences. *See* BRITAIN ROMAN-1.

RUVIGNY. *See* GALWAY.

RYAL. *See* COINAGE-12.

RYDER (1) Sir Dudley (1691-1756), an M.P. in 1733 and 1734 was Sol-Gen. from 1733 to 1737 when he became Att.-Gen. and, as such, prosecuted the rebels of the '45. In 1754 he became C.J. of the King's Bench. A patent for his peerage was drawn but he died before the formalities were completed. His son **(2) Nathaniel (1735-1803) 1st Ld. HARROWBY (1776)** was an M.P. (Tiverton) from 1756. His son **(3) Dudley (1762-1847) 2nd Ld. and 1st E. of HARROWBY (1809)** was M.P. for Tiverton from 1778; he was Foreign U/Sec. in 1789, Paymaster of the Forces and Vice-Pres. of the Board of Trade in 1791 and Treasurer of the Navy from 1800 to 1801. In 1804 he was Foreign Sec. under Pitt and in 1805 Chancellor of the Duchy of Lancaster, but in the Cabinet. As such he visited Berlin, Vienna and St. Petersburg on a peace mission. In 1809 he was Pres. of the Board of Control and from 1812 to 1827 Ld. Pres., retiring at Canning's death. His brother **(4) Richard (1766-1832),** M.P. for Tiverton from 1795 to 1830, was a whip and Judge Advocate Gen. in 1807 and Home Sec. from 1809 to 1812. His nephew **(5) Dudley (1798-1882)** M.P. for Tiverton in 1819, 1820, 1826 and 1830 was a Ld. of the Admiralty from 1827 to 1828 and Sec. of the India Board from 1830 to 1831 when he became M.P. for Liverpool. Like his father, he favoured parliamentary reform and supported the Reform Bill of 1832. He also supported Peel's attitude to the Corn Laws and instigated the creation of the first Cabinet standing committee. He was Ld. Privy Seal from 1855 to 1857. In 1869 he moved the rejection of Gladstone's Irish Church Bill. He was also a member of the Oxford University Commission. His son **(6) Dudley Francis Stuart (1831-1900), 3rd E.,** was a Palmerstonian M.P. from 1856 to 1859 and from 1868 to 1882. In 1874 he was V-P. of the

Committee on Education; and was mainly responsible for the Education Act of 1876; from 1878 to 1880 he was Pres. of the Board of Trade and from 1885 to 1886 Ld. Privy Seal.

RYE (Sussex), a mediaeval fortified port chartered in 1289, joined the Cinque Ports confederation in 1350. It was long the main exporting centre for Wealden iron and timber and maintained a cross channel trade and a continental mail service until the Civil War. Its cave cellars were used for smuggling brandy, on which its many customs men turned, for a consideration, a blind eye. This formed the background of the leading case of *Coggs* v. *Bernard* (1703), where Coggs established that his temporary transfer (bailment) of a barrel of brandy to Bernard to escape a raid was not contractual and that therefore its illegal purpose was no defence for Bernard, who had smashed the barrel and was sued for its value.

RYE HOUSE PLOT 1683. The D. of Monmouth had Whig political associates with whom he schemed to seize the Crown by insurrection, and friends in a seedy underworld of criminals, disreputable lawyers and old Cromwellian soldiers who plotted the King's murder. One of the latter, Richard Rumbold, an extreme Republican, owned the Rye House (Hoddesdon) at a cutting on the Newmarket Road. He planned to overpower Charles II and James D. of York in the cutting on their return from Newmarket races in Apr. 1683, but a fire at Newmarket burned half the town and the King returned before the conspirators were ready. In June the plot was betrayed and the confessions and revelations implicated many Whig grandees. Monmouth went into hiding; Ld. Grey of Warke fled to Holland; Ld. Howard of Escrick turned King's Evidence as a result of which the E. of Essex committed suicide and William, Ld. Russell, and Algernon Sydney were executed (*see* CHARLES II-27). Rumbold escaped to Holland but was captured in 1685 fighting for Argyll in Scotland and executed.

RYOTWARI **(India)** was a system whereby in return for 30 years' assessment and security, the cultivator (Ryot or Rayat) paid a fixed annual tax to a govt. collector. *See* ZAMINDAR.

RYSBRACK, John Michael (?1693-1770), Flemish sculptor, settled in England in 1720 and executed many monuments in Westminster Abbey and elsewhere.

RYSWICK, P. of (May-Oct. 1697) between France, Spain, Britain, the Netherlands and the Emperor, under Swedish mediation, ended the War of the League of Augsburg (1688-97). Louis XIV recognised the Protestant succession in Britain, undertook to evacuate Catalonia and Luxemburg, relaxed his tariffs against the Dutch and handed over the Belgian (Spanish) Barrier fortresses to Dutch garrisons. These concessions were acceptable to Britain, Holland and Spain, leaving the Emperor to negotiate virtually alone. His hand had, however, been strengthened by victories over the Turks. Thus a compromise was reached on the Rhine. The right bank fortresses were restored to the Empire, and Lorraine, except Saarlouis, to D. Charles' son Leopold Joseph. In return France was confirmed in her sovereignty of Alsace and Strasbourg. The treaty cleared the way for Louis XIV's attempt on the Spanish Empire. *See also* BALTIC-36.

RYU-KYU or RIU-KIU (Chin: LU-CHU) Is. were seized by Japan in 1879. One of the Is., Okinawa, was desperately defended by them against the Americans in World War II and later became a U.S. base under Japanese sovereignty.

S

S.A. (Ger: *Sturmabteilung* = storm detachment). The brown shirted members of the German Nazi Party. They represented the militant wing of the Party until June 1934 when their leader Ernst Röhm was murdered by Hitler's orders. Thereafter they became a kind of pre-training organisation.

SAAR (Ger.). Under the T. of Versailles (1919) parts of Rhenish Prussia and the Bavarian Palatinate were combined as the Saar Territory and placed under League of Nations' trusteeship to enable the French to exploit the coal mines. It was included in the French customs area in 1925 and the mines were cheaply over-exploited regardless of surface subsidence. The relatively poor-quality coal was artificially so much cheaper than the good S. Welsh coal hitherto imported, that coal traffic from Cardiff ceased and there was serious unemployment in the Welsh Valleys. After an overwhelmingly pro-German plebiscite in 1935, the area was retroceded and the German govt. bought the mines back. In 1945 the area, slightly enlarged, was occupied by the French who proposed economic incorporation in France subject to local autonomy. The mines were leased for 50 years to France and anti-French parties and agitation suppressed. By now, the S. Wales mines had so far declined that this made little difference. In 1954 a Franco-German joint regime was rejected in a referendum and in 1959 the area was reincorporated as a *Land* in Germany.

SABBATH was originally (*see* Gen. c.2. v.2. *and* Fourth Commandment) the seventh day of the week and the day of religion i.e. Saturday but Protestants often applied the term to the Lord's Day, obviously the first day. A *Sabbath day's journey,* the maximum rabbinically permitted Sabbath journey, was 1125 yards, but in Presbyterian Scotland a mile.

SABBATH BREAKING (Scot.). (*See* also SUNDAY OBSERVANCE; DISCIPLINE, BOOK OF.) A Scots Act of 1579 forbade labour, physical recreation and drinking on Sundays and the General Assembly condemned dancing and travel. These prohibitions were often evaded by particular classes, e.g. by harvesters and fishermen, or in particular places, e.g. the Highlands. Charles I's bishops relaxed the rules considerably but the Covenanter Revolution of 1638 brought renewed impositions. An Act of 1656 forbade all worldly business, attendance at taverns, dancing, listening to profane music, household chores such as baking and laundering, travel and walking, save to kirk. Such provisions, of course, encouraged wholesale delation. They were re-enacted in 1661, but the abolition of civil and penal consequences of excommunication in 1690 and 1712 left enforcement to public opinion, which only slowly became more tolerant.

SACHEVERELL, Henry (?1674-1724), had a gift for invective which he used, as a preacher, in favour of Toryism and non-resistance and against Whigs, Dissenters and broad and low churchmen. He became increasingly notorious or in demand and in 1709 preached a violent sermon against the Whig govt. before the London Court of Aldermen. The govt. made itself ridiculous by impeaching him. Amid great excitement and rioting the Lords found him guilty by 69 to 52 and forbade him to preach for three years. The derisory penalty prepared the way for the collapse of a declining govt.

SACK (apparently Fr: 'sec') was the usual 16th cent. term for the white wine of Spain and the Canaries. It was not always dry. *See* WINE TRADE-3.

SACKVILLE-WEST, originally WEST. This family is descended from **George John West,** a younger son of the **5th E. de la WARR,** and **Elizabeth SACKVILLE, Lady BUCKHURST,** sister and co-heiress of the **4th and last D. of DORSET** Their son **(1) Mortimer (1820-88) 1st Ld. SACKVILLE of KNOLE (1876),** guards officer

and courtier, inherited all the Sackville estates in Gloucestershire, Kent, Sussex and Warwickshire (especially the vast house at Knole). His brother **(2) Lionel (1827-1908) 2nd Ld.,** a diplomat, was Minister plenipotentiary in Paris in 1869, 1871 and 1872; Minister to the Argentine from 1872 to 1878; to Spain 1878 to 1881 and then to Washington from 1881 to 1888. Here he was popular and successful, but fell victim of a dishonest Republican political trick in the course of a presidential election and was sent his passports. The British govt. raised him a degree in the knighthood as a mark of confidence. His Spanish illegitimate daughter Victoria Josefa married his cousin **(3) Lionel Edward (?-1928) 3rd Ld.** and their daughter **(4) Victoria (1892-1962)** was the celebrated writer.

SACRED COLLEGE. *See* CARDINALS.

SACROSANCTA (1415). A decree of the Council of Constance asserting the supremacy of general councils of the Church in matters of faith and morals (cf DICTATUS PAPAE). The complementary decree *FREQUENS* (1417) enjoined at least decennial councils. It never took effect, but *Sacrosancta,* though formally ignored, had some practical results, for many later Papal pronouncements were made in or in consultation with general councils or the episcopate.

SADAR DEWANI and NIZAMAT ADALAT. *See* EAST INDIA CO. COURTS.

SADLER (1) Michael Thomas (1780-1835), Tory reformer with Irish interests, opposed R. Catholic emancipation in 1813, but favoured an Irish poor law and improvements in English rural welfare. Radical working people trusted him and in 1831 he introduced legislation against the exploitation of young people in factories. His grandson **(2) Sir Michael Ernest (1861-1943)** was a member of the R. Commission on Education (1894-5) and then Director of Special Inquiries and Reports (i.e. research) at the Department of Education from 1895 to 1903. He virtually invented modern educational research. When govts. ceased to consult him, he resigned and became Prof. of Education at Birmingham. As Pres. of the Calcutta University Commission from 1917 to 1919 his reports governed the form which Indian university and secondary education was to take until Independence. He was Master of University Coll., Oxford from 1923 to 1934.

SADLERS WELLS (London). A Mr. Sadler opened a hydro at these wells in 1683 and entertainments were soon added. In 1765 a theatre was opened, at which Joseph Grimaldi the pantomimist performed for many years. Mesdames Warner and Phelps managed it and gave their famous Shakespeare productions from 1844 to 1859. It later fell on evil days, but was rebuilt largely at the expense of the Carnegie Trust and since 1931 has shown good plays at popular prices. By 1939 it had become the home of the Vic-Wells Ballet which changed its name to the Sadlers' Wells Ballet. A second Sadlers' Wells Ballet took its place when it became the Royal Ballet.

SAD PALM SUNDAY (29 Mar. 1461) when the bloody B. of Towton was fought.

SAFETY FIRST. An influential road safety slogan of the late 1920s, appropriated by the Conservative Party in the 1929 general election. With its undertone of over-caution it probably lost them votes in the long run.

SAGA (Norw.) or SAGE (Ger.) ('recital') is an account of historical or presumed historical events in the primitive and mediaeval Germanic and Scandinavian world. Originally composed by a court bard or historian to be spoken among the descendants and followers of those whom a saga concerns, it usually centres events around particular rulers, kings, heroes or other personalities and their aspirations, failings and feuds. Many are in verse, some in prose and some (*see* SNORRI STURLUSON) are the product of research. Their interpretation has yielded much historical information.

SAHARA. The gradually desiccating interior was known only by rumour to Europeans until the 19th cent., despite the regular, though declining caravan routes radiating from Timbuktu to Morocco, Algeria, Tunisia and Nigeria and those from Tripoli to Kano, L. Chad and Zinder. Alexander Gordon LANG (1793-1826), originally a Gold Coast military administrator, tried to ascertain the route from Tripoli to the Niger in 1826 but was murdered at Timbuktu. John DAVIDSON (1797-1836) travelled Morocco as a doctor in 1835 and was murdered on the way to Timbuktu in 1836. James RICHARDSON (1806-51) travelled for the Anti-Slavery Society from Algiers and Tripoli and in 1845 reached Ghadames and Ghat. He died of fever on the way to L. Chad. The French occupation of Algeria rapidly increased European knowledge and French opportunities after 1855.

SAHIB (Urdu). An Indian title of respect: 'Lord', 'Sir'.

SAILOR WILLIAM or BILL = William IV.

SAINTS (and Judas), SYMBOLS OF. The following are frequently found in religious art. Those marked ‡ relate to the manner of martyrdom.

Andrew	An X-shaped cross‡
Bartholomew	A knife‡
Catherine	A chaff cutters wheel‡
James the Great	A scallop shell, pilgrim's staff or water gourd
James the Less	A fullers' pole‡
John the Apostle	A cup with a winged serpent flying from it
John the Evangelist	An eagle
Judas Ischariot	A money bag
Jude	A club‡
Laurence	A grill‡, or two flowering trees
Luke	A man
Matthew	An ox
Mark	A winged lion
Matthias	A battleaxe‡
Paul	A sword‡
Peter	Keys, or a cock or a reversed cross‡
Philip	A long staff surmounted by a cross‡
Simon	A saw‡
Thomas	A lance‡

ST. ALBANS (*see* VERULAMIUM) **(Herts.)** is very ancient and was probably partly occupied throughout the Dark Ages. There was a church at the traditional site of St. Alban's martyrdom (c. 200), before 670, and in 794 Offa of Mercia founded the great monastery in expiation of the recent murder of St. Ethelbert, King of the E. Angles. The town grew up around it and in about 950 Abbot Wulsin built three parish churches and the Abbey school. Abbot Paul of Caen began to rebuild the Abbey in 1077 and Adrian IV (perhaps educated there) gave it immunity from episcopal jurisdiction and made it the premier English abbey. Its wealth continued to grow and so did the buildings which could adequately house church councils and parliaments. The nave was one of the longest in Europe. In the 13th cent. it was a centre of historical writing (*see* MATTHEW PARIS; WENDOVER; RISHANGER). Humphrey D. of Gloucester was arrested at a parliament there. The dissolution destroyed the school, which was refounded in 1545, but the town's prosperity as a market and entrepôt for Hertfordshire continued into modern times and its closeness to London has now made it virtually an out-suburb of the Metropolis.

ST. ALBAN'S COUNCIL OF (July-Aug. 1213) held after King John's absolution. Abp. Langton had made him renew his coronation oath and promise to maintain the ancient laws. To leave nothing to chance, the barons with the Abp. in council at St. Albans ordered in his name that the laws of Henry I should be observed, and adjourned

to St. Paul's, London, where Henry I's charter was read aloud.

ST. ALBANS, Dukes of. *See* BEAUCLERK; MELLON.

ST. ALBANS, Earls of. *See* JERMYN.

ST. ALBANS TAVERN (Pall Mall, London) was the meeting place of a number of loosely associated non-party M.P.s between 1778 and 1800. They helped to vote down Ld. North in 1782.

ST. ALDWYN. *See* HICKS and HICKS-BEACH.

ST. ANDREWS (Fife) was originally a 6th cent. Culdee settlement. In the 8th cent. Angus MacFergus, King of the Picts built a church to St. Andrew. In 908 the bishops of the Scots moved there from Dunkeld. Some of them professed obedience to York. Augustinians established a church (1160-1318). In addition the bishops built a strong castle (c. 1200) nearby and they chartered and laid out the burgh (1140-80) which also received royal privileges. After the pre-eminence of York had been ended (*see* YORK, ARCHBISHOPRIC), the bishopric was regarded as the chief Scottish See and became an archbishopric in 1472. By now St. Andrews was the largest town in Scotland, with a UNIVERSITY founded in 1410.

Its decline began with the Reformation (1560), when the cathedral and priory were abandoned, and continued with the Union which shifted trade southwards away from the port. It began to revive in the middle 19th cent. as a centre of learning and local govt. and as a seaside resort inspired by the Royal and Ancient Golf Club, founded in 1754.

ST. ASAPH (Clwyd) was founded as a Welsh bishopric in about 560 but after the Reformation the poverty of its endowments led the bishops to seek livings in plurality elsewhere (e.g. canonries at Durham) and they were often absentees.

ST. BARTHOLOMEW'S DAY. *See* HUGUENOTS-9 to 11.

ST. BRICE'S DAY MASSACRE (Nov. 1002). The details of this sensational event are unknown. King Swein Forkbeard of Denmark had designs upon England and it seems that he bid for the support of the many Danes already settled there. The govt. of King Ethelred the Unready may have thought that there was a plot among the English Danes against the King's life and organised a counter plot. Many English Danes were attacked throughout England, Swein's sister, apparently, among them. Swein himself landed with a small force in Hampshire very soon afterwards and sacked Wilton unopposed. The local alderman, Aelfric, possibly conspired with him.

ST. CLAIR-SUR-EPTE, T. of. *See* VIKINGS-15.

ST. CYR (France). In 1686 Louis XIV, prompted by Mme. de Maintenon, established a girls' college which survived until the Revolution. In 1802 Bonaparte established an officers' training school there, which continues. Col. Martinet, one of its commandants, has given his name to a type of disciplinarianism and to a soft multitailed whip which he invented.

ST. DAVIDS, MENEVIA or MYNWY (Pembs.), the headland to which St. David moved from Caerleon in the 6th cent., became a Welsh bishopric and pilgrimage centre associated with the tribal kingdom in S.W. Wales. When the Welsh Church was integrated into the Anglo-Norman Church at the turn of the 11th and 12th cents., the diocese was reorganised into a territorially based administration, a process begun by Bp. Bernard who exercised his authority under Canterbury. Efforts notably by its Dean, Gerald of Wales, the historian, to emancipate it from Canterbury as a metropolitical See failed. The See of Swansea and Brecon was carved out of it in 1923 and it is now conterminous with the old shires of Cardigan, Carmarthen and Pembroke.

ST. DAVIDS, Vist. *See* PHILIPPS.

ST. DUNSTAN'S (1) Institution for the Blind was founded by Sir Arthur Pearson in 1915 as a result of eye casualties in World War I. **(2)** St. Dunstan's-in-the-West in the

Strand, London, with its statue of Q. Elizabeth I was long the starting point of riotous anti-papist demonstrations. **(3)** *For the eponymous saint see* DUNSTAN.

ST. ETHELREDA'S or AUDREY'S monastery at Ely, apart from lands in the I. of Ely, acquired from King Edgar (959-75) the Liberty of the five and a half Hundreds of E. Suffolk, centred on Woodbridge. It and the Liberty passed at the Dissolution to the Dean and Chapter of Ely and the Liberty became the area of the Woodbridge Quarter Sessions which lasted until 1970.

ST. GALLEN (Switzerland). The monastery, reputedly founded by a 7th cent. Irish missionary later known as St. Gall, contains in its thousand year old library, many manuscripts important to the study of Celtic language and history.

ST. GERMAIN, T. of. *See* AUSTRIA (REPUBLICAN).

ST. HELENA I. Discovered by the Portuguese in 1502, it was seized by the Dutch in 1600 and later acquired by the HEIC. Bonaparte was exiled there in 1815 (*see* LOWE, SIR HUDSON). It became a Crown Colony in 1834.

ST. IVES or ST. UBES. Setubal (Portugal).

ST. JAMES' PALACE (London) was originally built by Henry VIII between 1530 and 1536 on the site of the leper hospital of St. James the Less. His gateway survives. Charles I was kept there on the night before his death. The grounds, now St. James' Park, were enlarged by Charles II and when Whitehall Palace was burned down in 1698, the court moved there and many alterations were made to accommodate it. Queen Victoria moved to Buckingham Palace in 1837, but the Court officials with their offices mostly remained and the palace was thenceforth used for formal functions and royal administration.

ST. JEAN DE MAURIENNE, SECRET T. of (1917) between Britain, France, Russia and Italy, allocated to Italy the Smyrna area of Asia Minor to balance allocations of other parts of the Ottoman Empire to France and Russia. The collapse of Czarist Russia invalidated the treaty and Lloyd George's predilection for the Greeks, who wanted Smyrna and had a large minority there, prevented any similar replacement agreement.

ST. JOHN (Pron: Sinjun). Several related families. **(1) Sir Oliver (1559-1630) 1st Vist. GRANDISON (Ir. 1621) Ld. TREGOZ (Eng. 1626)** killed the navigator George Best in a duel and fled abroad (1584), became a soldier and commanded Essex's horse at the S. of Rouen (1591). He became an M.P. (1593), fought at the B. of Nieuport (1600) and then went with Mountjoy to Ireland where he was knighted. He was an M.P. again (1604-7); became Irish Master of the Ordnance and an Irish Privy Councillor in 1605 and a Commissioner of Plantations for Ulster in 1608. An Irish M.P. in 1613, he was Lord Deputy from 1616 to 1622. **(2) Oliver (1580-1646) 4th Ld. ST. JOHN OF BLETSHO (1618) 1st E. of BOLINGBROKE (1624)** went over to the Parliamentarians and was a lay member of the Westminster Assembly. He was also a Commissioner for the Parliamentary Great Seal. **(3) Oliver (1598-1673),** related to Cromwell by marriage and an exceptionally able barrister, was connected with the Providence Co. He defended Hampden in *The Case of Shipmoney* (1637), propounded the fundamental constitutional doctrine, then rejected but accepted after the Restoration, of the irretractibility of prerogative grants. He was M.P. for Totnes in the Short and Long Parliaments where he led the attack on Shipmoney in 1640 and was not silenced by being appointed Sol-Gen. in 1641. He promoted Strafford's attainder when the impeachment faltered. In 1644 the Commons made him Att.-Gen. by ordinance. He took the Solemn League and Covenant and was a peace negotiator at Uxbridge in 1645. He took the side of the army in 1647, became C.J. of the Common Pleas in 1648 but refused a seat on the court which 'tried' the King. He and Walter Strickland acted in the failed Dutch negotiations of 1651 and in 1654 he was a

Commissioner of the Treasury. Thereafter he acted exclusively as a judge. He was permanently disqualified for office at the Restoration and left England in 1662. A parliamentarian son of **(2)**, **(4) Oliver (1603-42)** died at the head of his regiment at the B. of Edgehill. **(5) Henry (1678-1751) Vist. BOLINGBROKE and Ld. ST. JOHN of LYDIARD TREGOZE (1712-14)** sometimes called "Bolingbroke" in the books, was the son of Sir Henry St. John and Penelope Rich, daughter of the E. of Warwick. Brilliant, unscrupulous and profligate, he had money, married more and needed it all. He became an M.P. in 1701, supported Harley and the Tories and brought in the bill to secure the Protestant succession and the successive and divisive Occasional Conformity Bills. In 1704 when Harley succeeded Nottingham as Sec. of State, St. John became Sec. at War. He and Harley left office together in Feb. 1708 and St. John was out of Parliament in 1709 but they corresponded, so that when the Whigs were overthrown in 1710, Harley became Chancellor of the Exchequer and St. John (Foreign) Sec. of State. In Mar. Harley became E. of Oxford and Lord Treasurer, leaving St. John with the entire management of the Commons.

This govt. now diverted troops to Canada and opened secret negotiations for peace with France. They promised to desert their allies and dismissed Marlborough from the Command-in-Chief. These proceedings were driven through the Lords by the creation of 12 peers (Dec. 1711). St. John next issued the restraining orders (q.v.) to the new C-in-C, the D. of Ormonde. St. John had been promised a peerage in Dec. 1711 and hoped for the Bolingbroke earldom which had become extinct in his family in Oct. 1711. He received it as a Viscountcy and thus, in July 1712, quitted the House of Commons for a more exalted sphere "with the chagrin and latent malice of one who instead of 30 pieces of silver, had received only 25" (Churchill: *Life of Marlborough*). The P. of Utrecht was signed in Mar. 1713. Naturally this infuriated George of Hanover, the heir presumptive, so Bolingbroke now tried to negotiate a Stuart succession on the basis of the Pretender giving up his religion. Honesty was unfamiliar to St. John. Queen Anne died in Aug. 1714 and Bolingbroke, attainted, fled to St. Germains and became the Pretender's Sec. of State (July 1715). Suspecting that he had betrayed the 1715 rebellion, the Pretender dismissed him in 1716. He contrived to get himself partially pardoned in 1723 and settled, a semi-political semi-literary figure at Uxbridge. He retired to France in 1733.

ST. KITTS or CHRISTOPHER. *See* WEST INDIAN ISLAND COLONIES.

ST. LAURENT, Louis Stephen. *See* CANADA.

St LAWRENCE SEAWAY (Can.-U.S.A.). The treaty to establish it was signed in 1932 but opposition by U.S. railroads and the port of New York obstructed work which was not commenced until 1954. It was opened in 1959 and conferred hydro-electric benefits on both countries, but the channel was too small for the largest types of ocean going ships and it remains underused.

ST. LEGER (Pron: Selinjer) **(1) Sir Anthony (?1496-1559)** served on a commission to investigate Irish affairs and rose by the favour of Thomas Cromwell to be a gentleman of the King's Privy Chamber in 1538. In 1539 he escorted Anne of Cleves to England and in 1540 became Lord Deputy of Ireland. He overcame most of the Irish chiefs by force or fraud and in 1541 made the Irish Parliament acknowledge Henry VIII as King of Ireland. Confirmed as Lord Deputy at Edward VI's accession, he was recalled in 1548, but was again appointed in 1550. In 1551 he was accused of papistry, but acquitted and reappointed in 1553. In 1556 he was again recalled on a charge of malversation. His son **(2) Sir Warham (?1525-97)** became an Irish Privy Councillor, but when appointed Pres. of Munster, Queen Elizabeth refused to confirm. His son **(3) Sir William (?-1642)** was Pres. of

Munster from 1627 to 1642. He campaigned ceaselessly against Irish rebels and also helped Wentworth to raise his main army in 1640-1.

ST. LEGER STAKES, horse race at Doncaster (Yorks.) was founded in 1776.

ST. LEONARDS, Ld. *See* SUGDEN.

ST. LUCIA. *See* PARIS, P. OF (10 FEB. 1763); SEVEN YEARS' WAR, 10-13; WEST INDIAN ISLAND COLONIES.

ST. LUSSON, Simon d'Aumont, Sieur de. *See* CANADA.

ST. MARTIN (?315-97), as an officer at Amiens, experienced a sudden conversion (337) always pictured as sharing his cloak with a naked beggar in whom he saw Christ. He obtained his military discharge and lived as a hermit in Italy and Dalmatia but in 360 joined the clergy at Poitiers and founded the first (semi-eremitical) Gallic convent at Ligugé nearby. In 370 or 371 he became Bp. of Tours and established the convent at Marmoutier, encouraged many others and broke out of his eremitical habits to become an outspoken, spiritually overwhelming and sometimes violent missionary who penetrated to the most isolated places. His courage was famous. He was the true establisher of the Gallic Church and the father of French monasticism. His influence and popularity, attested by many church dedications (e.g. St. Martin's in the Fields, London and St. Martin's, Canterbury) spread from Ireland to Syria. The great monastery at Tours dedicated to him was long the richest in Europe and minted the French *livre tournois*.

ST. MARYLEBONE (London) consisted of the two Domesday manors of Lilestone or Lisson and Tyburn, named after the Tyburn stream. The village of Tyburn and its notorious gibbet were at the modern Marble Arch. The name St. Marylebone refers to the church of St. Mary-le-bourne (i.e. the Tyburn). There were pleasure gardens from 1650 to 1778 when Beaumont Street and Devonshire Place were built over them. Cavendish Square, the first fashionable area, was built in 1717; the Harley-Oxford estate was built up by 1780, the Portman estate between 1760 and 1810, Nash's Regents Park (Crown) estate between 1815 and 1830 and the Eyre estate at St. John's Wood, the first garden suburb, between 1830 and 1850. The affluence of the inhabitants attracted well known institutions including the M.C.C. at Lords, the Zoo, Madame Tussauds and the shopping area of Oxford Street.

ST. OLAF. *See* VIKINGS-23 *et seq.*

ST. OMER. *See* STAPLE B-2.

SAINTONGE. *See* AQUITAINE; JAMES I OF SCOTS.

ST. PAUL'S CATHEDRAL (London). King Ethelbert of Kent built a church for Mellitus, the first bishop, in about 607. It was destroyed in 675 and St. Erconwald replaced it in stone by 685. His shrine became a pilgrimage centre. The church was again destroyed in the Viking sack of London in 962 and again rebuilt. This building was much used for synods. It was destroyed in a great London fire of 1087. A fourth, mainly Norman cathedral, was instantly begun but, delayed by another fire, was completed only in 1332. It covered 3½ acres and with a 500 ft. spire and a nave 596 ft. long, was the biggest church in the world. The bishop's palace extended the complex from the N.W. end and St. Paul's Cross was to the N.E. Its vast nave, known as Paul's Walk, was put partly to secular uses. Lawyers, clothiers, writers and prostitutes had their accepted positions, wits and businessmen met there and the Smithfield porters had a right of way across it even during services. The spire, several times struck by lightning, fell down in the 16th cent. and by the 17th the church was badly decayed. Abp. Laud employed Inigo Jones to propose improvements (which were to include a Baroque facade); the Commonwealth's men converted the Lady Chapel into a preaching house and the nave into stables. The whole ruinous range was fortunately burned in the Great Fire of 1666.

Sir Christopher Wren's impressive building was begun in 1675 and finished in 1711, with carved woodwork by Griming Gibbons and ironwork by Jean Tijou. It first became a focus of national religious sentiment under the Regency, mainly because of the burial of Nelson there. Later Wellington was buried there and it became the church where monarchs customanly celebrate their jubilees. The building (by now nearly black) was declared unsafe in 1937, bombed in the Blitz, but well reconstructed and cleaned between 1965 and 1980.

ST. PAUL'S, COVENT GARDEN, built by Inigo Jones in 1635 and rebuilt according to his design after a fire in 1795, sometimes called the Actors' Church, contains the graves of many literary figures.

ST. PAUL'S CROSS (London) in the N.E. part of St. Paul's Close was originally the site for a folk moot and from the mid-13th cent. until 1633 its three tiered pulpit was the most important centre for public sermons, disputations and religious and political pronouncements; crowds often gathered in thousands and words spoken there had an effect similar to broadcasting in modern times. Charles I stopped its use for these purposes and the cross was pulled down in 1643.

ST. PAUL'S SCHOOL was founded adjacent to St. Paul's Cathedral by its Dean, John Colet, in 1509 and financed by the Mercers Co. who took an equal interest in founding the girls' school in 1904.

ST. PETERSBURG, founded 1703. Russian capital 1731-1918. *See* BALTIC-38; RUSSIA, PETRINE.

ST. PETERSBURG, T. of (Dec. 1800). Russia, Sweden, Prussia and Denmark undertook to uphold by force the rules that neutrals could carry on the coastal and colonial trade of belligerents; that enemy goods under a neutral flag should not be seized and that in any case naval stores were not contraband. The treaty, which invaded a major British war interest, was the immediate occasion of the B. of Copenhagen (Apr. 1801).

ST. PETER'S PATRIMONY. *See* PAPAL STATES.

ST. PIERRE and MIQUELON (Newfoundland) with their important cod fisheries have been French since 1635. *See* P. OF PARIS (1763); SEVEN YEARS' WAR-13.

ST. SARDOS WAR (1324). *See* AQUITAINE-11; CHARLES IV OF FRANCE.

ST. THOMAS. *See* MALABAR CHRISTIANS.

ST. THOMAS' HOSPITAL (London) was founded in about 1200 for the sick and poor originally within the monastery of St. Mary Overy, from which it was removed after a fire in 1215 to buildings provided by Peter des Roches, who also increased the endowment. It was largely self-governing under a master and brethren. The Augustinian rule was imposed in 1323. In the later Middle Ages it resembled other religious houses in its preoccupation with corporate self-interest. In 1535 the annual income was about £309 of which only £42 was spent on the sick and poor. Its revival as a hospital began only after the Reformation.

ST. VINCENT. *See* JERVIS.

ST. VINCENT. *See* WEST INDIAN ISLAND COLONIES.

SAC AND SOC, or SAKE AND SOKE (A.S. sacu = cause socn = suit) in 10th cent. land grants, conferred on the grantee private jurisdiction mostly concerned with theft, petty crime, property disputes and miscellaneous pleas by freemen. They applied both territorially (e.g. over an estate) and personally e.g., under Ethelred the Unready sac and soc over royal thegns was a royal prerogative. *See* IN-AND OUT-FANGTHEOF.

SAIVITISM. *See* HINDUISM.

SAKHALIN (U.S.S.R.) or KARAFUTO, was unclaimed until 1855 when Japan and Russia both had settlements there. In 1875 the Russians annexed it. In 1905 Japan took the southern half, which was retroceded to Russia in 1945.

SALADIN. *See* CRUSADES-9-14.

SALADIN TITHE. *See* CRUSADES-31.

SALAR JUNG, Sir, or MIR TURAB ALI (1829-83), became Dewan of Hyderabad in 1853 and regent in 1869. He believed in the possibilities of Indian state's govt., but maintained the British alliance during the Mutiny. He subsequently developed the state's economy with roads and railways; improved agriculture and water supplies and made a beginning with public education. In 1876 (when he visited London) he tried, but failed, to obtain the cancellation of the Berar lease, but maintained the Hyderabad claims, which survived until the overthrow of the principalities at Indian Independence.

SALBAI, T. of (1782). See MARATHAS-7.

SALEM (Mass.), previously NAUMKEAG, founded in 1626, was the head settlement of the Massachusetts Bay Colony and had the first Puritan church (1629). Its status was superseded by Boston in 1630. It was a prosperous trading port, but the scene of the notorious witchcraft hysteria of 1692, during which 150 were arrested and 19 executed by a special court. The bereaved families were later indemnified. The port's prosperity continued until about 1850.

SALE OF FOOD AND DRUGS ACT, 1875 provided for the appointment of public analysts.

SALFORD. See MANCHESTER.

SALIC LAW is a special rule, erroneously attributed to the Salian Franks, that a throne could not be inherited by or through a woman. It forms no part of feudal custom and applied only in certain continental monarchies, the most important being France. Here direct male succession from father to son was unbroken from the election of Hugh Capet in 987 until the death of Louis X in 1316. He left a daughter Jeanne and a pregnant queen who gave birth to a posthumous son. Both these children were set aside in favour of the late King's brother Philip V. He died in 1322 leaving only daughters, who again were set aside in favour of another brother, Charles IV. He died childless in 1328 and the choice now lay between his sister, Isabel, Queen to Edward II of England and mother of Edward III, or Philip of Valois, her uncle, and his descendants. The problem was basically political. The union of the Crowns of England and France would end the Aquitainian troubles of the English Kings, but involved asserting not merely that Philip V and Charles IV were usurpers, but finding means to sidetrack the claims of Jeanne which would have priority over Isabel's. Moreover Isabel was disreputable not only as the cause of her husband's murder. She had brought herself closer to the succession by denouncing the *amours* at the Tour de Nesle of the daughters of Philip III, yet endangered the legitimacy of any offspring of her own by her open liaison with Mortimer. The union would also threaten the influence of Angevins and legists now so important at the French Court. Their case accordingly was that the Salic Law was ancient, but that the issue had never arisen until modern times when the acceptance of Philip V and Charles IV illustrated its operation and constituted modern precedents. Their weakness was that the rule of the Salian Franks to which they pointed was concerned with the devolution of certain lands and not with the Crown at all. The validity of the Salic Law was settled by the arbitrament of war.

SALISBURY or NEW SARUM (Wilts.). Richard le Poer, 7th Bp. of Old Sarum, laid out Salisbury on a gridiron plan in 1218 and transferred the population and the See of Old Sarum (two miles to the N.) to the new site. The new Cathedral was begun in 1220 and completed in 1258, using material where possible from Old Sarum. The famous spire was added between 1330 and 1360. The new city was a great success and quickly developed into an important trading centre with guilds, some of whose halls survive. The base of its prosperity was wool and cattle and the related tanning and leather working industries, but the making and export of broadcloth became increasingly important in the 14th cent. As communications improved, its importance as a diverse agricultural market has continued to grow into modern

times and other associated industries, such as brewing, have appeared. It is said to be the model for Trollope's Barchester.

SALISBURY Es. and Ms. of. See CECIL-4 *et seq and* GASCOIGNE-CECIL.

SALISBURY AGREEMENT (Nov. 1289). See BRIGHAM *and* SALISBURY TREATIES.

SALISBURY (A) (1) Patrick of (?-1168) called **E. of SALISBURY (c. 1140)** was a partisan of the Empress Matilda (*see* STEPHEN). In 1196 his grand-daughter **(2) Isabella (?-1261)** married **William LONGSWORD (?-1226),** a bastard of Henry II who took the title. Their son **(3) William (?-1250)** twice a Crusader (1240-2 and 1249-50) was killed at the B. of Mansourah. Isabella's rights passed to her great-grand-daughter **(4) Margaret (?-1306-10)** and her daughter **(5) Alice de LACY (?-1348)** the wife of Thomas of Lancaster (q.v.), but in 1337 Edward III took the earldom for his friend **(6) William MONTAGUE (?-1344).** With an interlude from 1400 to 1409, when out of favour with Henry IV, the Montagues held the title until **(7) Thomas (?-1428)** the leading English commander in France, was killed at Orleans. The title then passed to his son-in-law **(8) Richard NEVILLE (?-1460)** and then to his son **(9) WARWICK the Kingmaker.** **(10)** George of CLARENCE **(?-1478)** was made E. of Salisbury in 1472, and a son of Richard III from 1472 to 1484. In 1513 the title was revived for Clarence's daughter **(11) Margaret (?-1541)** who was beheaded for her royal blood.

(B) Es. and Ms. of. *See* CECIL.

SALISBURY (Rhod.). See RHODESIA.

SALISBURY. MEETINGS AND COUNCILS. Royal meetings in this area mostly took place at the large nearby royal country residence at Clarendon, but if this was unusable or the meeting too large, the town was used. In particular Wilham I's Great Assembly of 1086 at which the *Oath of Salisbury* was administered consisted of most substantial landowners. Parliaments were held there in the 14th cent. if the King was residing at Clarendon, especially that of 1328 when Mortimer was made E. of March.

SALISBURY or SALESBURY. N. Welsh family of Tudor R. Catholics besides poets and grammarians **(1) William (?1520-?1600)** published, in the *Proverbs of Gruffydd Hiraethog,* the first Welsh printed book (1546) and he translated the Bible and the Prayer Book into Welsh. **(2) Thomas (?1555-86)** was implicated in Babington's conspiracy and executed. **(3) John (1575-1625)** was a Jesuit who also made translations into Welsh. **(4) Thomas (?1567-?1620)** printed the Psalms in Welsh meter.

SALISBURY, OATH OF. See WILLIAM I-9.

SALISBURY'S FIRST GOVT. (June 1885-Feb. 1886) (under the M. of Salisbury who was also Foreign Sec; with Sir Stafford Northcote, E. of Iddesleigh, 1st Ld. of the Treasury; Ld. Halsbury, Ld. Chancellor; Sir Michael Hicks Beach, Chancellor of the Exchequer; Sir R. A. Cross Home Sec; Sir F. A. Stanley, Colonial Sec; Ld. Randolph Churchill, Sec. for India; E. of Carnarvon, Ld. Lieut. of Ireland; W. H. Smith, Sec. for War.) (*See* GLADSTONE'S SECOND GOVT.)

(1) Salisbury took office because the Tory leadership was disputed between Ld. Randolph Churchill, a democrat entrenched in the National Union of Conservative Associations and Northcote who then accepted an earldom. Churchill was denied the leadership of the Commons which went to Hicks Beach. Salisbury's elevation, in a sense accidental, gave him the Conservative leadership for the ensuing 17 years.

(2) To redeem promises to Parnell and the Irish, Gladstone's "firm govt." or coercion was abandoned and Ld. Ashbourne's Act (Aug. 1885) set up a state-assisted scheme of Irish land purchase. To allay a certain restiveness in Scotland, caused by the public preoccupation with Ireland, a Secretaryship of State for Scotland was created with the D. of Richmond as its first holder (also Aug.), but meanwhile, secretly, Carnarvon on Salisbury's behalf was discussing with Parnell and Justin McCarthy the possibility of a local Irish legislature. In his public utterances Parnell was, however, demanding independence and he was also negotiating with Gladstone.

(3) Gladstone's anti-imperialism and the Irish troubles had enabled other powers to prosecute their colonial ambitions, Russia in Central Asia, France and Germany in Africa, the Far East and the Pacific. The intrigues of the Annamese French with the Burmese court at Mandalay persuaded King Theebaw to hand over British assets to the French, who, however, changed their minds. He, unaware of this, refused arbitration and a British expedition (Oct-Dec. 1884) deposed him and annexed his kingdom (Jan. 1885).

(4) Gladstone had been secretly converted to Irish Home Rule, but believed that a Conservative govt. should carry it out, if necessary with liberal support against the diehards. This was not a view which could be published and in any case he was unwilling to bid for Irish support. Hence Parnell, who could get no sense out of him, made a deal with Salisbury. Parliament was dissolved and Parnell told his followers in England to vote Conservative. This tipped the balance in the towns, but the new rural electorate voted for those who had enfranchised it and was stirred, too, by Chamberlain's social oratory. Thus the Liberals had 86 more seats than the Conservatives, but the Irish had 86 too.

(5) Parnell could now keep both the other parties out of effective power or put the Liberals in. In Dec. Gladstone's conversion became publicly known through an indiscretion of his son, Herbert. The Tory-Irish alliance was broken and Salisbury resigned.

SALISBURY'S SECOND GOVT. (Aug. 1886-Aug. 1892) (14

in Cabinet under the M. of Salisbury. Ld. Halsbury, Ld. Chancellor; Ld. Randolph Churchill, Chancellor of the Exchequer; Henry Matthews, Home Sec; W. H. Smith, Sec. for War; Sir Michael Hicks Beach, Ch. Sec. for Ireland; the E. of Iddesleigh, Foreign Sec; Ld. Ashbourne, Ld. Chancellor of Ireland) (*see* GLADSTONE'S THIRD GOVT.)
(1) was formed after a general election with the support of 316 Conservatives and 78 unionist Liberals against 191 Liberals and Parnell's 85 Irish nationalists. Hartington, the Liberal unionist leader refused office. Churchill was leader of the Commons.

(2) Parnell's Irish Tenants' Relief Bill was defeated while sensational events occurred in the Balkans. In 1885 the two parts of Bulgaria had united under Prince Alexander and defeated a Serb invasion. In Aug. 1886 the Russians kidnapped Alexander and European war threatened. Churchill disagreed with Iddesleigh's handling of this affair and in Oct. at Dartford, outlined a policy of support for Germany and Austria in the interests of the Balkan nations, combined with a programme of reformist legislation at home. There was Conservative criticism, but he carried the party conference at the end of the month.

(3) Meanwhile there had been a Cabinet controversy about the forthcoming and radical budget. On a total of £94.5M Churchill proposed to raise £4.5M by increased taxes, mostly death and house duties, save £8.4M by raiding the sinking fund, stopping existing local govt. grants and by direct economies. From this surplus he would reduce income tax, tea and tobacco duties and provide double the previous amounts for local govt. by a new grant system. He hoped to secure the direct economies (£1.3M) from the Admiralty and the War Office. The War Office objected because of the European crisis. In Dec. he wrote that he must resign unless they were overruled. Salisbury replied that they would not be overruled. Churchill affected to consider this an acceptance of his resignation. He published a provocative

rejoinder in *The Times*. Since the Cabinet discussions were confidential, nobody understood what had happened and he found himself without support.

(4) Salisbury now offered the leadership of the Commons to Hartington, who again refused; he then appointed the Liberal Unionist Goschen, a financier with wide European contacts in Churchill's place. Goschen, like Churchill, objected to Iddesleigh at the Foreign Office. Salisbury took over from Iddesleigh who died of a heart attack in Salisbury's presence. Then Goschen lost the bye-election necessitated by his appointment (Jan. 1887) and had to be put into a safe Conservative seat. In Mar. Hicks Beach went blind and resigned.

(5) The govt's. disarray was re-ordered by W. H. Smith, who took the leadership of the Commons, and Salisbury's nephew A. J. Balfour, who took over from Hicks Beach (Mar. 1887). Their abilities dashed Churchill's hopes of a return. They had to exercise them in the context of the Irish extremists' 'Plan of Campaign' against the landlords; there was a spate of evictions, and public order was disrupted by murder and arson. Balfour resorted to a new Crimes Bill, with a Tenants' Relief Bill of his own in tandem. These had to be helped through by closure and Kangaroo resolutions, but in an atmosphere of growing govt. popularity. The nation rejoiced in the Queen's Golden Jubilee, which also brought all the colonial statesmen together in the first and successful Colonial Conference (Apr.). Zululand was annexed (June). Bismarck and Salisbury co-operated to reduce the Bulgarian tensions, which ended in the accession of Ferdinand of Coburg. There was an Anglo-Russian compromise on Afghanistan (July). Moreover in May *The Times,* having innocently published the Pigott forgeries, profoundly influenced opinion in a series of articles on "Parnellism and Crime". Parnell denounced the forgeries, but was not believed. By Aug. the bills were passed.

(6) There followed a long period of Irish civil violence. Balfour determinedly enforced the law but could not wholly restrain evicting landlords; the Irish extremists, led by O'Brien and Dillon against Parnell's judgement, defied it. This period began with the notorious Mitchelstown affray (Sept. 1887) and Bloody Sunday (13 November 1887), in Trafalgar Square. Matthews, the Home Sec., incurred much odium for the latter, but there was no sequel, for Parnell had at last understood the need for English popular goodwill, which murder and cattle maiming were unlikely to secure and there was a sudden trade improvement, connected with the Rand gold rush; between May and Dec. 1887 the Rand multiplied its production tenfold. Finally (Dec. 1887) the Eastern Mediterranean problems were calmed by a secret triple treaty (Britain, Italy, Austria) to maintain the *status quo,* Italy agreeing to support British Egyptian interests, Britain agreeing to protect Italy against the French fleet. On the Indian western frontier the British influence in Afghanistan and Persia was strengthened by the acquisition of Baluchistan.

(7) The Balkan diplomatic defeat of Russia put her into the arms of an Anglophobe France and the first fruit of this new *entente* was the French Trans-Siberian Railway loan (1888). The French, for their part, resented discouragement of their expansion into S. E. Asia by the British, who had already annexed Burma and now (May 1888) established protectorates in northern Borneo. The scramble (the British East African Co. was chartered) for the world's emptier territories was in full swing, but the powers had not yet collided in them and within the naval shield the govt. could improve local administration, education and finance. It created (1888) county councils to take over the administrative work of the J.Ps; and the Technical Instruction Act, 1889, set the precedent for conferring educational powers upon them. Meanwhile Goschen converted and consolidated £558M national debt from 3% to 2¾% (2½% after 15 years) and followed

the principles of Churchill's budgetary proposals without forcing economies on his colleagues; his cautious approach was successful. By 1889 he was financing increased naval, military and local govt. expenditure upon lowered taxation rates established in 1887 and 1888. In 1891, when the govt. abolished elementary school fees, he found the additional money from the same buoyant source.

(8) The background prosperity highlighted the contrasts between the wealthy and the very poor. There had lately been strikes to secure some of the benefits of the prosperity. Ben Tillett's London Dock Strike (Aug-Sept. 1889) was of a new kind, for he and the Amalgamated Society of Engineers, a skilled workers' union, recruited unskilled labourers and by their victory with the aid of public opinion, shifted trade unionism from organisation by crafts to organisation by industries and added political action to its techniques.

(9) The deaths in 1888 of the German Emperors, William I (Mar.) and Frederick III (June) inaugurated a change in the international climate, for their successor William II represented a younger, less inhibited, more adventurous and inevitably anti-British generation. In Nov. 1887 Bismarck had written to Salisbury that Germany, along with Britain and Austro-Hungary, was a "satisfied power". By July 1888 this was no longer true. William II and his banking and industrialist friends were irritated by Arab risings in German E. Africa and jealous of foreign colonial successes. The autumn of 1888 had seen Cecil Rhodes' amalgamation of the Kimberley diamond companies and the Rudd Concession in Matabeleland. In Feb. 1889 four new states were added to the U.S.A. In May came the Italo-Ethiopian T. of Ucciali. While German financiers planned railway concessions in Turkey, pressure increased on Bismarck. The Samoa condominium agreement with Britain and the U.S.A. (June 1889) by no means satisfied the prestige-hungry court of Potsdam and Bismarck's proposals for an Anglo-German alliance broke down because Britain wanted to direct it against Russia, but Germany against France. The African advance continued with the chartering of the British S. Africa Co. Anglo-German arguments over Africa were now inevitable.

(10) The French had reached the Congo by lapping around Nigeria and the German Cameroons. By 1890 the Germans were advancing eastwards from S. W. Africa and towards the Upper Nile from Tanganyika. In the middle of the demarcation negotiations William II replaced Bismarck (Mar. 1890) with Caprivi. This instituted a sinister trend, for the new Germans were prepared to forego large African ambitions for the tiny islet of Heligoland (opposite Hamburg), British since 1807. The results were formalised in conventions with Germany (July 1890) and France and Portugal (Aug.). The vaguely ambitious but ancient Portuguese claims were given a more limited but more practical definition. The French secured the largest territorial share. The British got Mashonaland and Nyasaland from Portugal, Zanzibar from Germany and Kenya and Uganda. The British and German public both thought that it had received a poor bargain, but the German govt. set about. fortifying Heligoland on a vast scale, while the British occupied their new areas and extended the Charter of the British S. Africa Co. northwards (1891).

(11) The Anglo-German *rapprochement,* though unreal, provoked a Franco-Russian demonstration. The Trans-Siberian Railway was commenced (May 1891). Then a French fleet visited Kronstadt and an agreement was signed at St. Petersburg (July-Aug. 1891). In Britain, however, these events were overshadowed by the recovery and sudden fall of Parnell. The nonconformist Liberals would not associate with the Irish nationalists so long as the adulterous Parnell led them. Gladstone intimated privately that unless they changed their leader,

he would cease to lead the Liberals. His letter arrived too late. They had re-elected him and it was published. Parnell refused to back down and issued a manifesto charging Gladstone with betraying Home Rule. This decisive document convinced many of his followers that he was no longer a responsible leader. The Irish bishops intervened against him. His party split, 26 remaining with him, 44 seceding. Immediately he lost a bye-election at Kilkenny (Dec. 1890) and then two more (North Sligo, Apr. 1891; Carlow, July). His struggles undermined his health and in Oct. he died, his cause in ruins. W. H. Smith died the same day.

(12) Balfour succeeded Smith as leader of the House and in Dec. Hartington succeeded to his father's dukedom. This had the effect of consolidating the Conservatives, who, however, had been losing bye-elections. The Liberals too had been consolidating. In Oct. 1891 their Newcastle conference adopted a long-term Programme which was to have damaging later results, for most of the Old Whigs and the wealthier supporters had left the party over Home Rule and so had the Chamberlain radicals. The extreme radicals went over to socialism; the others were mostly Welsh or Scots. The Newcastle Programme alienated many who might have broadened the party's over-narrow base. In the circumstances Salisbury decided to try his luck. Parliament was dissolved in the summer of 1892 and he lost. In Aug. he resigned after a defeat in the new Commons.

SALISBURY'S THIRD GOVT. (June 1895-Oct. 1900) (Nineteen in Cabinet under the M. of Salisbury who also took the Foreign Office; A. J. Balfour led the Commons as 1st Ld. of the Treasury; E. of Halsbury, Ld. Chancellor; D. of Devonshire, Ld. Pres; Sir Michael Hicks Beach, Chancellor of the Exchequer; Sir Matthew Ridley, Home Sec; Joseph Chamberlain, Colonial Sec; M. of Lansdowne, Sec. for War; E. Cadogan, Irish Ld. Lieut; G. J. Goseher, 1st Ld. of the Admiralty; C. T. Ritchie, Pres. Board of Trade; H. Chaplin, Pres. Local Govt. Board; Walter Long, Pres. Board of Agriculture). **(1)** came into office on Rosebery's resignation, dissolved and obtained a majority of 340 Conservatives and 71 Liberal unionists against 177 Liberals and 82 Irish nationalists. In practice Chamberlain had a virtual equality of leadership with Salisbury and Balfour.

(2) Inspired by Chamberlain, the govt. intended social reform and colonial development. While it was drafting its Workmen's Compensation Bill and with the German Emperor William II in England on a state visit, Chamberlain announced (Aug. 1895) an abrupt change in colonial policy. Instead of *laissez-faire* there was to be "judicious investment of British (i.e. public) money" for the development of the colonies "for the benefit of their population and ... of the greater population which is outside". As Rosebery had transferred British E. Africa to the Foreign Office (Jan. 1895), the African investment in practice went mostly to Nigeria, the Gold Coast and Sierra Leone for ports, railways, roads and schools of tropical agriculture and medicine, but Chamberlain also subsidised new steamship services to the W. Indies. In the Gold Coast a preliminary clearance of the slave raiding and human sacrificing Ashanti had to be made and a (mostly Hausa) force under Sir Evelyn Wood was soon on its way.

(3) A S. African storm was approaching. It centred on the Boer Republics and Cecil Rhodes. Rhodes was the managing director of the British S. Africa Co., Premier, with the support of the Cape Dutch, of the Cape, and the owner of large interests in the Republics. He was negotiating for Bechuanaland, so that his company might build a railway outside the Republics to Rhodesia. It had been promised to the Cape but, save for the railway strip, withheld on the petition of the natives. The Boers, hemmed in from north, west and south were seeking outlets eastwards. The Swaziland Convention (Dec. 1894) had denied them the Tongaland coast, so when the Pretoria-Portuguese East Railway was opened (July 1895) Paul Kruger, their Pres., stopped traffic across the Vaal to the Cape to encourage its use. This infringed the 1884 London Convention. He gave way angrily before Chamberlain's ultimatum (Nov. 1895). The extraordinary interlinked episodes of the U.S. Pres. Cleveland's Message, the Jameson "Raid" and the German Kaiser's Kruger telegram (Dec. 1895-Jan. 1896) ensued.

(4) Sir Evelyn Wood was marching on Kumasi, the Ashanti capital, at this very time. The Kruger telegram suddenly disillusioned the British with the Germany of Queen Victoria's grandson. The govt. sent a powerful squadron to sea. Then as Kumasi fell, there was an outburst of angry patriotic pride. Chamberlain, whose wife was American, was dealing with the American crisis behind the scenes and the govt. was properly putting Jameson and his officers on trial, but the London public made heroes of them and confirmed foreign, especially Boer, suspicions that Britain had instigated Jameson's venture. Progressive and reactionary Boers united. Marthinus Steyn, a Krugerite, was elected Pres. of the Orange Free State (Mar. 1896). Rhodes lost the confidence of the Cape Dutch.

(5) The govt. meantime pressed ahead with the first instalment of its social programme, the Workmen's Compensation Bill, but foreign affairs maintained a high temperature. The Turks continued to slaughter Armenians and with Britain internationally hated and the Germans friendly, felt able to do so with impunity. The first stretch of their Anatolian Railway (Bosphorus-Konia) opened in July 1896. In Aug. a three-day massacre in Constantinople recalled Gladstone to the hustings to demand unilateral British action. Many Liberals agreed. Rosebery promptly resigned the Liberal leadership to Harcourt. Tactically the govt. was strengthened by this split in the opposition. It carried the bill (Aug. 1897) but the rest of its social programme was hamstrung by the cost of foreign policy.

(6) The expansion of British trade was, in the face of protectionist competition, slowing down and changing its composition. Textile exports were declining slightly, while coal and capital goods, such as machinery and ships (which helped to equip rivals), were increasing. Britain no longer outdistanced the world commercially and her 1891 population, though about equal to the French (38M) or the American (62M) or the German (49M). These relative weaknesses were partly concealed by the prestige of her industrial past and the wide extent of her Empire, but the latter feature was unhelpful without a powerful (but expensive) fleet which, itself, was essential during a period of diplomatic isolation (see ROSEBERY'S GOVT.). Queen Victoria's Diamond Jubilee (June 1897) was thus celebrated with subconsciously shaken confidence, as the publication of Kipling's *Recessional* showed; its splendour, which impressed all witnesses, had something of the nature of a defiance and the Third Colonial Conference (June-July) which it occasioned emphasised rather than solved the imperial problems.

(7) The balance of rival imperialisms was changing too. The Mekong Agreement (Jan. 1896) had contained the French in S.E. Asia, but their aggressive, govt.-organised expansion continued elsewhere. The Italians, beaten by the Ethiopians at Adowa (Mar. 1896) had had to concede the protector's claims in Tunisia to the French (Sept.) while the latter annexed Madagascar (Aug.), which had been developed by the British. They were also encroaching upon the economic hinterlands of the British W. African colonies, which they had undertaken to respect. On the Gambia this encroachment became permanent; in Sierra Leone it was slightly less damaging. The Jubilee Exhibition of military and naval power strengthened British diplomacy a little and other powers

were chary of provoking the British in the Mediterranean, yet the disadvantages of isolation were apparent there too. The British were expected to take the lead over the Cretan crisis (Mar-Dec. 1897) but the related Turkish-Greek land war had to be liquidated by the pressure of the land powers, Austria and Russia.

(8) The rise of Admiral von Tirpitz was now moving German policy into collision courses with other powers. He became ministerial head of the German Navy in June 1897. On his advice (for he had been there) the Germans occupied Kiao-Chau in Nov. This reopened the scramble for China. The Russians promptly seized Port Arthur and Dalny (Dec.), the British Wei-Hai-Wei, the French Kwang-chow-wan. Such commitments demanded an ocean-going navy. Tirpitz and his Kaiser's plans were already laid. In Mar. 1898 the first German Navy Law authorised the trebling of their fleet. In Apr. Tirpitz founded the aggressive German Navy League. Under such conditions Chamberlain's suggestion (Feb. 1895) of an Anglo-German alliance were foredoomed. On the other hand both the fact and the boorish manners of German ambitions were dispelling the anti-British climate, for Britain was not the only target and, as it happened, because of traditional British anti-Spanish feeling, Britain alone sympathised with the U.S.A. in the Spanish American War (Aug-Dec. 1898). American hostility suddenly evaporated as a result of the Manila incident.

(9) Chamberlain had organised the W. African Frontier Force under Lugard to counter-penetrate the French-threatened Nigerian interior. This stiffening of British and German aggressiveness made the French pause. In the autumn of 1897 an Anglo-French conference about the Niger Basin was convened in Paris, while rival detachments continued, without mutual hostility, to earmark areas in the disputed territories. Meanwhile Kitchener, the Egyptian Sirdar, had in 1896 undertaken to relieve the Italians who, after their defeat at Adowa, were besieged in Kassala by Sudanese dervishes. He had long planned the reconquest of the Sudan, but since France and Russia vetoed Egyptian expenditure on the project, the British govt. had, reluctantly, to advance the money. By Apr. 1898 he had beaten the dervishes at the Atbara. France and Britain signed the Paris Agreement on Nigeria and the Gold Coast in June. In July, however, a French military mission had occupied Fashoda on the White Nile, far to the south of Khartoum. In Sept. Kitchener destroyed the dervish army at Omdurman and took Khartoum. Three days later he heard of the French at Fashoda and went there in person. He courteously handed them a protest and left an Egyptian garrison.

(10) Metropolitan feelings ran high, but when the French got no German or Russian support, it became possible to delimit the respective interests along a line representing the Congo-Nile watershed (Mar. 1899). Thenceforth Anglo-French competition became less bitter. This was fortunate because trouble was brewing in S. Africa again. The more the *Uitlanders* developed the mining potential of the Transvaal, the less the Boers liked them and attempted to oppress them by alien and pass laws, discriminatory taxation and police brutality. In Mar. 1897 Sir Hercules Robinson had given way to Sir Alfred Milner as High Commissioner. Milner had every gift except patience and he arrived just as Chamberlain had forced Kruger to repeal some especially obnoxious alien laws. It is likely that war would have ensued whatever Milner's temperament, for Kruger began importing armaments on a very large scale at this time. In Feb. 1898 Kruger, having been overwhelmingly re-elected Pres. in the Transvaal, dismissed the Chief Justice and made himself effective dictator. Milner was alarmed and in Mar. warned the Cape Dutch that Krugerism was the cause of strife and that if they wanted peace they must exert their

influence against it. Their response was muted by the re-emergence as leader of the English settlers of Cecil Rhodes, who recovered his directorship of the British S. Africa Co. in Apr. Hence the Sprigg ministry lost the Cape autumn elections and was succeeded by that of W. P. Schreiner, a Dutch moderate, dependent upon the extremist wing of the Dutch *Bond*. The situation had become politically favourable for Boer aggression.

(11) During Milner's absence on leave (Nov.), the Edgar affair focused Uitlander working men's indignation against the Boers, and the resulting *Uitlander Petition* signed by 21,684 of them and delivered to the Queen in Mar. 1899, decisively changed the balance of political opinion in Britain and the Empire. In response to inquiries, Milner forcibly stated the issue in the well-known "helot's despatch" (May 1899). The govt. took up the petition. Chamberlain, the Cabinet and Milner hoped for success by negotiation. Milner did not expect it. After five days of the devious Kruger at Bloemfontein (May-June) he broke off discussions. Encouragement from Chamberlain arrived too late. There followed a six weeks' wrangle about franchise bills pending in the Transvaal legislature, ending in a proposal, welcomed by the Cape Dutch but rejected by Kruger, for a joint inquiry (Aug.).

(12) The favourable season for Boer mounted armies (late Sept., when the rains had renewed the Veldt grass) was approaching. To gain the necessary weeks, the Boers suddenly made liberal and satisfactory offers through J. C. Smuts, the Transvaal State Attorney (mid-Aug.), but Kruger later added unacceptable conditions and withdrew in Sept. Thereafter he rejected all proposals, including some approved by the Cape Dutch and both sides prepared, he for war, Britain for the worst. His ultimatum, demanding in truculent language, that the British should withdraw their troops, followed in Oct. (*See* S. AFRICAN WAR.)

(13) If Britain was isolated, other powers were in diplomatic confusion. The public of most of them loudly favoured pro-Boer intervention and the Russians suggested it several times, but French govts. were politically too busy with the clerical (Dreyfus) controversy and with the digestion of their vast new possessions, and the German navy was still on the stocks. The Russians' attitude was consistent (in their own eyes at least) with their peace policy, which had brought about the first Hague Conference (May-July 1899). The Germans were pursuing other ambitions temporarily inconsistent with a world conflict. They bought various Spanish Pacific Is. (Feb. 1899). They got the British to hand over their rights in Samoa (Nov.) and they acquired the Konia-Baghdad railway concession (Dec.). In June 1900 the Boxers murdered their ambassador to Peking and they found that they had to depend on the Royal Navy and British coaling stations to get their expeditionary force there. They talked alliances with Britain (Nov. 1899 and autumn 1900) and made an agreement to keep other powers out of the Yangtze Basin while the Russians occupied Manchuria. Hence no interventionist combination disturbed the course of the war.

(14) The colonies conceived the war issue as whether the Empire should stand up for its people. By engaging the Boers the U.K. rescured their respect, especially as the Cape Dutch govt. gave no help. Canada (after initial French Canadian doubts) sent 8400 men, the Australians 16,400, New Zealand 6000. There were 30,000 S. African volunteers. This increased the self consciousness of these countries as well as their military effectiveness. In the case of the six Australian colonies it materially assisted federation, enacted in July 1900 as a result of a constitutional convention in 1897 and 1898.

(15) The war concealed one of the periodical European depressions, which made trade unionism more attractive and the govt. decreasingly popular. Since Gladstone's retirement and death (May 1898) the

association of Labour politics with the Liberals had weakened and in Feb. 1900 socialist societies and major trade unions formed the Labour Representation Committee (q.v.). The new body, the origin of the Labour Party, had no time to do much before Salisbury (prompted by Chamberlain), hoping to profit from the victories in S. Africa, annexed the Transvaal (Sept.) and called a general election (Oct.). This so-called Khaki election signally failed of its purpose. *See next entry*-1.

SALISBURY'S FOURTH GOVT. (Oct. 1900-July 1902) (20 in Cabinet under the M. of Salisbury. This was a reconstruction of his third govt. in which the M. of Lansdowne took over the Foreign Office, C. T. Ritchie the Home Office, the Hon. St. Juhn Brodrick the War Office, the second E. of Shelborne the Admiralty, G. W. Balfour the Bd. of Trade and Walter Long the Local Govt. Board. The M. of Londonderry was brought in as P.M.G. Ridley, Goschen and Chaplin retired.) (1) It took office after the Khaki election with, therefore, a past but no defined mandate for the future. Its position was not enviable. It had gained only 3 seats in the election. The S. African war, believed to have been won, took on a new and awkward guerrilla life. Salisbury himself was ageing and losing his grip. The depression was creating urban unrest. The Queen, too, was suddenly failing. She had visited Ireland in Apr. 1900 and was still reviewing colonial troops in Nov. Few remembered a time without her. In Jan. 1901 she died. The sense of change and slackening confidence was powerful and dangerous, reinforced by the social criticism of G. B. Shaw's plays. Kipling's brilliant *Kim*, published at this time, was already out of date.

(2) Much of the cost of the war and of increased regular naval expenditure had been born in Hicks Beach budgets by raising taxes; but by adding £135M to the national debt he had burdened future taxpayers. The budget of 1901 was the first which allowed for more direct than indirect taxation. Foreign tariffs were restricting the markets for British consumer goods in Europe and America. The taxable resources were still apparently expanding, but that part of the expansion not attributable to inflation depended increasingly upon the oriental, especially the China, trade. There was growing official disquiet at the drain of armaments upon the national resources. A. J. Balfour, in particular, thought that security and prosperity required an end to isolation. German behaviour over the Yang-tze Agreement (*see previous* entry-13) and the doubling of the German naval programme had ended any serious belief in a German alliance. The Russian advance into Manchuria threatened the British China trade and also Korea, whose autonomy was vital to Japan. The Japanese approached the govt. for an alliance, while despatching the Marquess Ito to St. Petersburg for direct negotiations. Lansdowne refused to continue the discussions unless the Ito mission was withdrawn. Ito, who had had no success in St. Petersburg, therefore came to England and signed the alliance (T. of London, Jan. 1902).

(3) Edward VII, a charming tactful extrovert, had caught public imagination by his splendour. His coronation was to be a tremendous public event and the occasion of another (the fourth) colonial conference, which was to emphasise the re-established stability hoped from the end of the S. African War (P. of Vereeniging, May 1901). The King, however, fell ill with appendicitis and the celebrations were postponed. The conference from the start exhibited parochial attitudes. Salisbury's health was declining fast and as soon as the King's recovery was assured he resigned in favour of A. J. Balfour. The change came in the middle of the conference.

SALLEE. See BARBARY.

SALMASIUS or SAUMAISE, Claude de (1588-1653), French scholar and Prof. at Leyden, was commissioned in 1649 by Charles II to write a defence of his father and an attack on the regicide govt. His Latin *Defensio Regia* (= Royal Case) soon reached England and the Council commissioned Milton to reply. His *Pro Populo Anglicano Defensio* (Lat = Case on behalf of the English People), which appeared in 1651, was little more than a scurrilous personal attack on Salmasius who, in his *Responsio* (= reply) answered in kind.

SALO, REPUBLIC OF. The Italian Fascist regime from Sept. 1943 to Apr. 1945. Its H.Q. was in this small N. Italian lake resort.

SALONIKA (Gr.) FRONT (World War I). An Austro-German offensive across the Danube against Serbia early in Oct. 1915 came after the conclusion of a German-Bulgar military convention. An Anglo-French force under Gen. Sarrail was hurriedly sent from Galipoli to seize the neutral (Greek) port of Salonika to serve as a base of assistance. The Bulgars struck westwards across S. Serbia and the communications of the northward facing Serb armies, and forced Sarrail to retreat. The line was held with British, French, Italian and Russian reinforcements but the Serb army had to be evacuated through Albania. It was reformed at Corfu and ferried round to join the Salonika force. Sarrail made two half-hearted offensives (Nov. 1916 and Apr. 1917) but otherwise about 500,000 allied troops remained immobile. Sarrail even failed to interfere with the German-Bulgar offensive against Bucharest, which destroyed Roumania (Aug.-Dec. 1917). He was relieved by Guillaumat in Dec. 1917 who prepared an offensive plan. Recalled to be gov. of Paris in June 1918, he persuaded the allies to allow his successor, Franchet d'Esperey, to try. The attack, launched on 15 Sept. 1918, forced the Bulgars to an armistice by 29 Sept. This broke up the Balkan position of the central powers, and opened Austro-Hungary to penetration from the south. *See* WORLD WAR 1-15.

SALSETTE (India), now part of Bombay, was a Maratha city taken by the Portuguese in 1739, then by the HEIC from 1774. An ancient Buddhist centre.

SALT. This essential was produced in Britain by evaporation from salt springs or from brine pumping at Northwich, Middlewich and Nantwich in Cheshire, Droitwich (Worcs.) and Barton (Lincs.) and also, since the 17th cent., to a limited extent by quarrying. As no settlement could do without it, it (with iron) permanently supported a widespread pack trade throughout the Middle Ages and originated a considerable traffic on Watling St. (to London) and to Ireland *via* Chester and Liverpool. In India it was a govt. monopoly and its price a universal tax. Australia is an important salt exporter and a large salt lake in Cyprus has been exploited since, at least, the beginning of the Christian era. *See* BROUAGE.

S.A.L.T. *See* NORTH ATLANTIC TREATY ORGANISATION.

SALTASH (Cornwall) belonged to the Valletort family in 11th cent., from whom it passed to the Duchy of Cornwall. It was represented in parliament from 1548 until 1832. *See* BRUNEL.

SALTER, Sir Arthur Clavell (1859-1928) K.C. 1904 was conservative M.P. for Basingstoke from 1906 to 1917, when he became a King's Bench judge and chairman of the Railway and Canal Commission.

SALVADOR (C. America) declared its independence of Spain in Sept. 1821 but from 1823 until 1839 formed part of the Central American Federation. Independent from 1840 again it was in turmoil until 1863. By 1870 coffee was being produced in large quantities. An attempt to resurrect the federation was frustrated in 1885 and thenceforth until 1931 coffee represented the principal, almost only, asset. From 1931 to 1944 there was a brutal military dictatorship under Gen. MARTINEZ and after a period of confusion a further series of military or authoritarian govts. was installed in 1950. By this time cotton was also being grown but the country was in a state of fluctuating rebellion intensified after 1979 by a peasant guerrilla movement.

SALVAGE is an ancient rule of international maritime law, that a person who saves another's life or property from destruction at sea is entitled to payment for his efforts when the person is no longer in charge. The rule is one of public policy to prevent waste and piracy. The law was well developed by the English Admiralty Court because of the enormous British seaborne trade, but since most maritime insurance was effected through Lloyds of London and salvage disputes usually involved insurance policy holders, Lloyds developed an internationally recognised arbitration procedure called "No Cure – No Pay", under which almost all salvage cases are settled. A professional salvor is entitled to a proportionately higher award than a casual salvor, as an inducement to maintain his equipment in readiness. Awards amount to between 4% and 12% for casual and 8% and 16% for professional salvors.

SALVATION ARMY. *See* BOOTH, "GENERAL" WILLIAM.

SALVIDGE, Sir Archibald Tutton James (1863-1928), brewer and leading organiser of Conservatism in Lancs., he was Chairman of the N. Union of Conservative, etc., Associations in 1913. A powerful backroom figure. *See* CHURCHILL, WINSTON. S.

SAMBUJI. *See* MARATHAS-2.

SAMHAIN. The Irish Halloween. All fires were extinguished and first relit at Tlachtga, a rath on a hill near Athboy (Meath), which is said to have been a druidical centre.

SAMOA (Pac.). American traders appeared in 1830, Germans in 1850 and the British soon after. All these traders made so-called treaties with the natives and the resulting conflicts had to be resolved by a conference in 1889. In Dec. 1889 a three-power treaty divided the islands between Germany and the U.S.A. The German (Western) parts, occupied by New Zealand in Aug. 1914, were mandated to her in 1920 and committed to her in Trust in 1945. It became autonomous in 1962. *See* SALISBURY'S THIRD GOVT-13.

SAMOS (Med.). Turkish after 1475, became tributary to Turkey under a Greek gov. in 1832 and was united with Greece in 1912.

SAMSON, St. (?-565), important Welsh itinerant missionary, offered to St. Illtyd at Llantwit as a child, retired to Caldey where he became Abbot. After reforming an Irish house and becoming Abbot of a monastery on the Severn, he moved to Cornwall where he travelled and preached as far as the Scilly Is. After a time he went to Brittany where he founded a monastery and became Bp. at Dol. He also visited Normandy and Guernsey and was present at the Council of Paris in 557. *See* MISSIONARIES IN BRITAIN AND IRELAND-5.

SAMSON (?-1112) (1) a Norman of noble origin, was educated by Odo of Bayeux and became a personal friend of William I who offered him the See of Le Mans, which he refused, in 1073. He probably organised the final compilation of Domesday Book at Winchester. He accepted the See of Worcester in 1096. His brother **(2) Thomas of Bayeux (?-1100)** was similarly educated and having travelled widely in W. Europe became a well known scholar. He also became one of William's chaplains. In 1170 he was made Abp. of York, but Abp. Lanfranc would not consecrate him without a profession of obedience to Canterbury, which he refused. After negotiations at Court and in Rome the issue was settled in favour of Canterbury by a church council at Windsor in 1072. Of Samson's sons **(3) Thomas of York (?-1114)** was educated by his uncle Thomas at York and in 1108 became Abp. He and Anselm quarrelled over the respective jurisdictions of Canterbury and York and Thomas was eventually compelled by the King to submit. In his time the influence of York extended into Scotland where the Bps. of Glasgow, Man and Orkney made him professions of obedience. His brother **(4) Richard (?-1133)** was Bp. of Bayeux from 1108.

SAMSON OF BURY ST. EDMUNDS (1135-1211) Abbot (1182) was educated at Paris and was spokesman for the monks of Bury in an appeal to Rome against their Abbot (1160). He was tonsured at Bury only in 1166 and proved an able monastic administrator. As Abbot he reformed the abbey's estates, restored the finances, rebuilt extensively, encouraged the liberties of the townspeople of Bury and was a strong defender of the abbey's ecclesiastical privileges. He was also much involved in national politics, notably in the 1190s when he defended the administration left in England by Richard I. His relations with King John were, naturally, turbulent. He was no saint but a useful and efficient administrator.

SAMUEL, Herbert Lewis (1870-1963) 1st Vist. SAMUEL of MT. CARMEL and TOXTETH (1937), a Jew who learned Hebrew but renounced Jewish orthodoxy, entered politics with a legacy from his father and in 1902 took advantage of the Chinese Labour controversy to become Liberal M.P. for Cleveland. As U/Sec. at the Home Office in the Asquith Govt. he was much involved in the Children Act, 1908, the Eight Hour Act and the establishment of industrial injury compensation. In 1910 he was Postmaster-Gen. but his name was unfairly involved in the Marconi scandal, and though he got damages for libel against a hostile French newspaper, some of the mud stuck. Defeated in the 1918 election, he was appointed High Commissioner in the newly mandated Palestine (*for the Samuel Commission on the coal industry in the mid-1920s see* GENERAL STRIKE 1926). In the crisis of 1931, Lloyd George being ill, Samuel was temporary leader of the Liberals and recommended a National Govt., but he led his wing of his party in attacking the govt's. hesitation in pursuing disarmament and in 1935 was defeated at Darwen. In 1938 he refused office under Chamberlain and thereafter remained a respected but not a powerful figure.

SAMUEL, Sir Marcus (1853-1927) 1st Vist. BEARSTEAD (1921) formed the Shell Transport and Trading Co. in 1897 naming it after his father's shell shop. He was Lord Mayor of London in 1902-3, when he was concerned mainly with shipping oil between Russia and the Far East. His discovery of a means of cleaning oil-ships so that they could carry other cargo on return voyages, made the Co's. fortune. In 1907 he negotiated the amalgamation of the Dutch and British oil interests in Borneo and during World War I managed the business so that despite Dutch neutrality most of the oil came into British not enemy hands.

SANAD. *See* SUNNUD.

SANCROFT, Abp. William (1617-93), a Laudian opponent of Calvinism, studied at Padua during the Commonwealth and returned at the Restoration to become Bp. Cosins' sec. in the Savoy Conference and in 1661 Charles II's chaplain. He was Master of Emmanuel Coll., Cambridge, from 1662 to 1664 and then Dean of St. Paul's until 1666. He was responsible for employing Wren to rebuild it and took a life-long interest in the works. From 1668 to 1670 he was Archdeacon of Canterbury and from 1678 Abp. Willing to crown James II in 1685, he refused to sit on his Court of High Commission or to publish his Declaration of Indulgence, and as one of the Seven Bishops, was tried and acquitted in 1688. He signed the declaration requesting William of Orange to assist in procuring a free parliament, but favoured his appointment as Guardian of the Realm not his elevation as King. These legitimist views caused him to be suspended in 1689 and deprived in 1690.

SANCTIONS was the technical term used for the means by which the Covenant of the League of Nations was to be enforced against a power who went to war in breach of it. It was thought that an economic embargo especially on oil would stop a war, or destroy an aggressor's war potential. Such sanctions were imposed in July 1936 against Italy after it attacked Ethiopia. They could not be

properly enforced without a naval blockade to exclude oil from the U.S.A. which was not a member of the League. For fear of offending the U.S.A. no such blockade was set up; the Italians conquered and annexed Ethiopia and world-wide faith in international peace-keeping was destroyed.

SANCTUARY. *See* BENEFIT OF CLERGY.

SAND RIVER CONVENTION (Jan. 1852) between the Transvaalers and Sir Harry Smith for the British govt., left the Transvaalers to manage their own affairs. It fixed the R. Vaal as the frontier, but both parties undertook to allow movement across the river, to facilitate trade and extradite criminals. The Transvaalers renounced slavery; the British any alliances with native nations north of the river.

SANDYS (Pron: sands), Duncan (1908-87) Ld. DUNCAN-SANDYS (1974) became a son-in-law of Winston S. Churchill and an M.P. in 1935, having been a diplomat. He was a successful soldier but disabled on active service in 1941, and became Financial Sec. to the War Office until 1943. After various middle rank ministerial posts he was Min. of Housing and Local Govt. from 1954 to 1957 and for Aviation from 1959 to 1960. He then became Sec. of State for Commonwealth Relations until 1964. He had always been interested in heritage problems and he founded the Civic Trust.

SAN FIORENZO or ST. FLORENT (Corsica). *See* FIRST COALITION, WAR OF (FEB. 1792-JULY 1795)-5.

SAN FRANCISCO CONFERENCE (Apr.-June 1945) was called by the victorious United Nations in conformity with their declaration of 12 June, to act together for peaceful purposes after the War. Fifty nations were represented. They drew up the United Nations Charter and the new Statute of the International Court of Justice and created the preparatory commission to set up the U.N. Organisation.

SANDGROPERS. *See* T'OTHERSIDERS.

SANDHURST. *See* ROYAL MILITARY ACADEMY, *etc.*

SANDRINGHAM (Norfolk). A royal country estate acquired by Edward VII as P. of Wales who built the main house there.

SANDWICH, Es. of. *See* MONTAGUE *or* MOUNTAGU (SANDWICH) *et seq.*

SANDWICH Is. *See* HAWAII.

SANGER'S CIRCUS. A spectacular feature of Victorian entertainment from 1871 at Astley's.

SANITARY AUTHORITIES. *See* HEALTH. PUBLIC-2; LOCAL ADMINISTRATION-A3.

SANKEY, John (1866-1948), 1st Ld. SANKEY (1929), Vist. (1932) and SANKEY COMMISSION. He was a King's Bench judge from 1914 to 1928. In 1919 coalminers threatened direct action to obtain higher wages and nationalisation of the mines. The govt. appointed a R. Commission under Sankey to examine the miners' case. As the members disagreed Sankey imposed his own view that the mines should be nationalised. By that time the govt. had recovered from its fears and rejected the recommendation. This was accepted by the miners, perhaps because a 7-hour day had been conceded too. In 1928 he became a Lord Justice of Appeal and in 1929 (-35) Lord Chancellor. He was Chairman of the Inter-Imperial Relations Committee of the Imperial Conference and of the Federal Structure Committee of the Indian Round Table Conference. Always constructively at the boundary between law and politics and intellectually respected on both sides of it, he was not much liked.

SANQUHAR DECLARATIONS (1) (June 1680), affixed to the Market Cross at Sanquhar (Dumfries) by some Cameronians, disowned Charles II as King. **(2) (Nov. 1684)** (*The Apologetical Declaration*) was also affixed by them on several market crosses in the neighbourhood. It stated that every servant of the govt. who sought the lives of Cameronians, did so at the risk of his own. Suspects would then be asked by govt. officers to abjure the declaration. Anyone who refused was instantly shot.

SANS CULOTTES (Fr: breechless). See BREECHES.

SAN STEFANO, T. of (1878). See BULGARIA; BERLIN CONGRESS.

SANTANDER. See PENINSULAR WAR 1807-14, 9.

SANTIAGO (ST. JAMES) of COMPOSTELA (N. W. Spain) was one of the most important places of pilgrimage in the Middle Ages, providing much custom for shipping. Pilgrims (palmers) picked up scallop shells on the beaches at nearby ports and used them as badges; hence the frequency of scallops in heraldry. See also HANSE.

SANTO or SAN DOMINGO. See HISPANIOLA.

SARIHAD. A Welshman's honour price. See WELSH LAW-7.

SARACEN: SARSEN. A Byzantine word for the nomads of the Syro-Arabian deserts and hence an Arab or, to the Crusaders, a Moslem. 'Sarsen' stones are the large monoliths mostly in Wiltshire ascribed in the Middle Ages to the Saracens.

SARAGOSSA or ZARAGOZA, prosperous capital of Aragon from 1118 to 1468, sustained a famous French siege in 1808-9 celebrated in Byron's *Childe Harold*.

SARAGOSSA, T. of (1529) defined the Spanish-Portuguese frontier in the east, leaving the Spice Is. to Portugal.

SARAJEVO (Yugoslavia), capital of Bosnia since the Ottoman Conquest in the 16th cent., was the place where Gavrilo Princip assassinated the Archduke Franz Ferdinand and his wife in June 1914 and so precipitated World War I. It became the centre of a sanguinary civil war between the Serbs and the Muslims after the break-up of Yugoslavia in 1990.

SARAWAK became a separate state when the Muda Hassim, Regent of Brunei, conferred it upon Sir James BROOKE (1803-68) as Rajah (1842). Sir James, who had been an HEIC servant, had visited the area privately in 1838 and helped to put down a revolt in 1841. He substituted a simple tax for the existing system of forced labour and trade and put down piracy in the adjacent waters with a high hand. Complaints of cruelty and illegality were made, but a British Commission at Singapore could not establish them, neither could it have proceeded if it had. He went home in 1863 leaving his nephew Sir Charles Anthony JOHNSON (1829-1917) as Rajah Muda. He succeeded as Rajah in 1868 and assumed the surname of Brooke. Under him various accessions were made and in 1888 a treaty formally converted Sarawak into a British protectorate. He made much progress in developing the state which by his death was exporting coffee, pepper, rubber, sago and timber. In 1941 it was occupied by the Japanese and soon after their departure the Rajah made a doubtfully legal cession of the state to the British Crown (1946). It became a constituent part of the newly-created Malaysia in 1946.

SARDINIA (loc: SARDEGNA) (Med.). This large island's cereals, cheeses, wood and fisheries were an important prize much disputed over the centuries between firstly, Pisa and Genoa and then between Genoa and Aragon. Aragonese supremacy was eventually established in 1478 but the island's prosperity and importance declined until the rise of strategic interest once the European wars spread to the Mediterranean; hence an unsuccessful French attack in 1637 and the English occupation of 1708. By the T. of Rastatt the I. was transferred to Austria; in 1717 the Spaniards reoccupied it but, as a result of their defeat by the British at C. Passaro, it was ceded under the T. of London (1718) to Savoy which gave Sicily to the Habsburg King of Naples in exchange. Thenceforth the Savoyard rulers were called Kings of Sardinia. They went there only during the French occupation of Savoy between 1799 and 1814. Sardinia became part of Italy in 1861.

SARGENT, John Singer (1856-1925) achieved notoriety at the Paris Salon in 1884, settled in London in 1885 and until 1914 was the most fashionable portrait painter of his time.

SARK. See CHANNEL IS.

SARMATIA was the ancient term for the steppes from the Vistula eastwards to the Volga. It was sometimes used as a name for Poland, especially at its widest extent.

SARMIENTO DE ACUÑA. See GONDOMAR.

SARSFIELD, Patrick (?-1693), French educated Commander of James II's Irish troops in England, went with him *via* France to Ireland, where he secured the west for him and was his Gov. of Galway and Connaught. He was made titular **E. of LUCAN** in 1691. He commanded the Jacobite reserve at Aughrim and afterwards joined the French service with many of his men. He commanded the Irish in the projected expedition against England in 1692 (see JACOBITES-5), fought at Steenkirk in the same year and was mortally wounded at Landen.

SARUM was the ecclesiastical name for Salisbury, **OLD SARUM** being the abandoned hill-top city outside the present town, which sprang up round the new cathedral begun in 1220. The SARUM USE was an order of Divine service used at Salisbury from the 13th cent. to the Reformation. It spread to other parts of England and was the basis of the first Book of Common Prayer.

SASKATCHEWAN. See CANADA-22.

SASSENACH (= Saxon) was the Gaelic name for Englishmen.

SASSOON (1) David (1792-1864), merchant of Baghdad, moved first to Bushire and then to Bombay where he founded Sassoon and Co., of which his son **(2) Sir Albert (1818-96) Bt. (1890)** became Chairman. The firm largely built the Bombay docks and developed the Indian cotton industry and Sir Albert was a member of the Bombay Legislative Council. He eventually settled in England and spent much of his huge fortune on philanthropy. His son **(3) Sir Jacob Elias (1844-1916)** was, in addition to being associated in his ventures, a distinguished and successful banker. His son **(4) Sir Philip Albert (1888-1938)** was a Conservative M.P. from 1912 and Haig's private sec. during World War I. He was also U/Sec. of State for Air from 1924 to 1929 and from 1931 to 1937. He was an advocate of the development of civil aviation and a patron of arts. His brother **(5) Siegfried Lorraine (1886-1967)** was the leading (and pacifist) poet of World War I and novelist.

SATARA. See MARATHAS-A.

SATIS COGNITUM (1896), encyclical by Leo XIII, expresses a desire for Christian unity, but only on the basis that the Pope is the sole source of jurisdiction and so the necessary centre of unity.

SATRAP. An ancient Persian imperial delegate or governor and hence an abusive term for any governor.

SATURDAY REVIEW, a weekly journal of intellectual political opinion founded in 1855. Its contributors included Max Beerbohm, E. G. Freeman, J. R. Green, Sir H. Maine, G. B. Shaw, Sir J. F. Stephen and Lord Salisbury.

SAUDI ARABIA. See ARABIA-2 et seq.

SAUMAREZ. Guernsey family. **Sir James (1757-1836) Ld. DE SAUMAREZ (1831)** after very active service in the blockade of Brest (1795-6), the Bs. of St. Vincent (1797) and the Nile (1798), fought the French and Spanish twice in a week off the Spanish coast and, after routine commands, commanded the Baltic Fleet from 1808-1813 with great tact and discretion in pursuing the object of protecting Sweden against Bonaparte, whether that country was friendly or hostile to Britain. See BALTIC EXPEDITIONS, BRITISH.

SAUNDERS, Sir Charles (?1713-75) was with Anson on his famous circumnavigation from 1740 to 1744 and commanded H.M.S. *Yarmouth* with great gallantry at the B. of C. Finisterre in 1747. He was an M.P. in 1750 and Commodore on the Newfoundland station in 1752. M.P. again from 1754 and Comptroller of the Navy in 1755. At the opening of the Seven Years' War he was specially promoted Rear-Admiral and sent under Hawke to the Mediterranean. When Hawke went home he remained as C-in-C. Anson was by now 1st Lord of the Admiralty and Saunders was the obvious choice to be Wolfe's colleague in the attack on Quebec. This partnership of two brilliant friends ensured the ensuing victory. From 1760 until the end of the war, he was C-in-C Mediterranean again.

SAUNDERS, William (1823-95) founded the *Western Morning News* in 1860, the *Eastern Morning News* in 1864 and the Central News Agency in 1863. He was a Liberal M.P. from 1885.

SAURASHTRA. See KATHIAWAR.

SAVAGE CLUB, founded in 1857 for well-travelled men of artistic, literary or scientific bent.

SAVAGE, Richard (?-1743) claimed improbably to be a bastard of the 4th E. Rivers and Anne, wife of the 2nd E. of Macclesfield. They took it ill; he took to writing, including some unpleasant accounts in prose (*The Plain Dealer,* 1724) and in verse (*The Bastard,* 1728) of his own supposed origin, and allowed himself to be bought off with a pension from the E. of Tyrconnel. His plays appeared in London and his undoubted talent brought him to Queen Caroline's notice. He had applied for the Laureateship, which had been given to Cibber (1730), so she pensioned him on condition that he celebrated her birthdays with an ode.

SAVAGE, Thomas (?-1507), lawyer and chaplain to Henry VII, negotiated the T. of Medina del Campo in 1488 and represented the King at the Boulogne negotiations in 1490. He was Bp. of Rochester from 1492 to 1496, of London from 1496 to 1501 and Abp. of York from 1501.

SAVANNAH. See GEORGIA.

SAVARY DE MAULÉON (?-1236), Poitevin minor noble and soldier of fortune, led the Poitevins in their efforts to play off the Kings of England and France against each other in 1206 and 1212, when he betrayed King John, for whom he was providing troops. In 1216 on the pretence of John's service, his troops looted many English midland villages. The regency got rid of him to S. France, where his bandit mercenaries remained a nuisance until his death.

SAVERNAKE FOREST (Wilts.). The hereditary wardenship was granted to the Esturmy family in 1083, but the forest remained royal until 1550, when the descendants of that family acquired it. They leased the woodland to the Forestry Commission in 1939.

SAVILE CLUB, originally the NEW CLUB, founded for conversational purposes in 1868.

SAVILE, Sir George (1633-95) 1st Vist. HALIFAX (1668), E. (1679), M. (1682), *s.* of a Yorkshire royalist, was M.P. for Pontefract in 1660 and a Privy Councillor in 1672 when he went on a mission to Louis XIV. He became famous as the one major statesman who was willing to risk accusations of time serving or treachery in order to maintain political stability during the long period of high excitement after 1672. He opposed the Test Acts and the Exclusion Bill yet voted against Stafford's execution in 1679. By 1682 he was in communication with William of Orange. At this period he was Lord Privy Seal and trying to rid the King of the D. of York's influence. He was Lord President when the Duke became King and, at considerable risk, opposed the repeal of the Tests. He was dismissed but at the crisis of James II's reign led an influential demand for a new parliament. James II now commissioned him, with Nottingham and Godolphin, to argue a compromise with William of Orange, a hopeless commission which he loyally tried to carry out. Meanwhile James' govt. had collapsed and Halifax summoned some 20 available peers to form a committee to maintain order in London. These with others under his chairmanship asked William to establish a provisional framework of order while a Convention was summoned. The peers of the Convention elected him to the key post of permanent Speaker (1689) and he

managed the procedure for offering the Crown to the P. and Princess of Orange and for legalising the result as far as possible. He was Lord Privy Seal until 1690 and was struck off the council in 1692. He is sometimes called The Great Trimmer and justified his tactics in a well-known pamphlet (1688) *The Character of a Trimmer...*

Jotham of piercing wit and pregnant thought
Endued by nature and by learning taught
To move assemblies, who but only tried
The worse a while, then chose the better side;
Nor chose alone, but turned the balance too,
So much the weight of one brave man can do.
Dryden *Absalom and Achitophel*

SAVILE, Sir Henry (1549-1622) taught Queen Elizabeth I Greek, was Warden of Merton Coll., Oxford, from 1585, the Queen's Latin sec. from 1595 and Provost of Eton from 1596. He was one of those commissioned to make the Authorised Version and in addition helped Bodley to found his library and endowed the Savilian professorships of Geometry and Astronomy at Oxford.

SAVILE, Thomas (?1590-?1658) Vist. (Ir.) SAVILE OF CASTLEBAR (1628), 2nd Ld. SAVILE of PONTEFRACT (1630), 1st E. of SUSSEX (1644), influential Yorkshire royalist, organised the Yorkshire gentry for the King and tried to prevent the spread of Fairfax influence for Parliament. He was suspected of treachery by Newcastle who arrested him in 1643, but the King pardoned him. In 1645 he was again accused and this time changed sides, took the Covenant (1646) and retired. Clarendon called him a highly undependable character.

SAVINGS BANKS originated at Vienna under the inspiration of the Emperor Joseph II (r. 1765-90). The idea spread over Germany, reaching Hamburg in 1778. The first in Britain was opened at Ruthwell (Dumfries) in 1810. The Post Office Savings Bank was instituted by Gladstone in 1861. It became a separate body (the National Savings Bank) operating through the Post Office in 1969.

SAVINGS CERTIFICATES, NATIONAL. See NATIONAL SAVINGS MOVEMENT.

SAVOY, PIEDMONT, SARDINIA. The mountain county of Savoy owed its importance to the ingenuity of its rulers in balancing between French and Italian powers in the use of the W. Alpine passes. Piedmont belonged to a branch of the family from the mid-13th cent (see HENRY III-10 *et seq*). By 1440 when Amadeus VIII died, Savoy and Piedmont were united in a duchy with a port at Nice. The remarkable D. Emmanuel Philibert transferred the capital and the Holy Shroud from Chambery to Turin in 1563, after the P. of Cateau Cambresis (1559) had ended a long French occupation. His successors, by slowly increasing the Italian territory, turned the state into an Italian principality with a French appendix. Victor Amadeus II (r. 1675-1730) was an important, indeed key figure in certain phases of the War of the Spanish Succession and ended by becoming King of Sicily. In 1720 he exchanged this crown for that of Sardinia and he and Charles Emmanuel III (r. 1730-73) continued eastward acquisitions and reached the R. Ticino by 1748. The possession of Sardinia saved the House when the French occupied the rest from 1792 to 1815, and its harbours, notably Maddalena and Palmas, were valuable to the British fleet in those wars. Victor Emmanuel I (r. 1802-21) and by the T. of Vienna (1815) added Genoa and Liguria. He was forced by liberals to abdicate in 1821 but from the accession of Charles Albert, P. of Carignano (r. 1831-49), the family's acquisitive talent was manifested in the modernisation of the state and army, combined with espousal of Italian nationalism. This enabled him to postpone the issue of liberalism, to unite opinion against the Austrians. He was defeated by them and abdicated in the revolutionary period 1848-9, but his successor Victor Emmanual II (r.

1849-61: King of Italy 1861-78) and Cavour achieved the unification of Italy in 1859-61 into which Piedmont and Sardinia were merged. Savoy and Nice, however, were ceded to France in payment for the alliance of 1859 which brought it about.

SAVOY (London). In 1246 Henry III gave this precinct and liberty between the Strand and the Thames to his wife's uncle, Peter of Savoy. He built a palace in which King John of France was lodged during his captivity in 1357, but which was burned down in Wat Tyler's insurrection. Under Henry IV the buildings were restored as a hospital of St. John the Baptist, but after passing through various hands the hospital reverted to the Crown, was dissolved in 1702 and became a military prison. The buildings other than the chapel were demolished in the early 19th cent.

SAVOYARDS. Count Thomas I of Savoy had eight adventurous sons, who were uncles of Eleanor of Provence, Queen to Henry III. Of these Peter became E. of Richmond, Boniface became Abp. of Canterbury, William (of Valence) was a close personal friend of the King's and Amadeus IV as count did homage in 1246 for fiefs at both ends of the Great St. Bernard. Other Savoyards came with them or secured offices through them, including Peter of Aigueblanche, who became Bp. of Hereford in 1260. They tended to be confused in the public mind with Eleanor's unpopular Poitevin relatives and adherents. *See* SAVOY (LONDON).

SAVOY CONFERENCE 1661. *See* CHARLES 11-6.

SAVOY DECLARATION (1658). *See* CONGREGATIONALISM.

SAWTREY, William (?-1401). *See* LOLLARDY-4.

SAXE-COBURG-GOTHA (Ger.). Two scattered interdependent Ernestine Saxon Duchies, from whose ruling family sprang the Belgian royal house and the Prince Consort. When his elder brother, D. Ernest II died in 1893, the Duchy passed to Alfred, D. of Edinburgh, the Prince Consort's and Queen Victoria's second son, and at his death in 1900, to his nephew, Leopold, D. of Albany. *See* WETTIN.

SAXE-WEIMAR-EISENACH (Ger.). Two interdependent Ernestine Saxon Duchies, which included the University at Jena and the brilliant intellectual 18th-19th cent. courts of D. Carl-August, where Goethe was Prime Minister at Weimar and Schiller a respected member. This small, highly fragmented state with a total area no bigger than Cambridgeshire, had a remarkable European influence through the abilities and style of its people.

SAXO (GRAMMATICUS) (fl. 1200) wrote the *Gesta Danorum* (History of the Danes), in 15 vols., stretching from mythical times to 1222.

SAXON AND SALIAN EMPERORS (911-1126) (*see* HOLY ROMAN EMPIRE). **(1)** From 840 to about 940 Western Europe was being damagingly raided from north (The Vikings), south (The Saracens) and east (The Magyars). The Partition of Mersen (870) had defined the long lasting western frontier of Germany (which included Italy) but the Eastern Marches remained fluid. Weak Frankish kings reigned until 911.

(2) In these desperate circumstances the Germans elected to their throne **Conrad I (r. 911-18) D. of Franconia,** and then **Henry I THE FOWLER (918-36) D. of the Saxons.** Henry had, however, to overawe the other four military commands or Duchies. He succeeded in three; in Bavaria he failed, but Magyar raids in 924 ended the struggle. He built up Saxony and counterattacked from it in 933. The Magyars were beaten on the Unstrutt; the Danes chased back to the Eider.

(3) Under his son **Otto (I) THE GREAT (r. 936-73)** authority depended on an equilibrium between the Dukes, but a Lombard female succession tempted the Bavarian Duke to extend his power into Italy by marriage. To prevent this, Otto invaded Lombardy and married the lady, Adelaide, himself (951). The affair angered other disappointed contestants including Berengar of Ivrea, the elected King of Italy, and Liudolf,

D. of Suabia, Otto's son. His Italian absence gave the disaffected, including the Abp. of Mainz, their opportunity. Germany was in turmoil until foreign raids brought everyone to their senses. United behind their King, they crushed the Magyars on the Lechfeld and the Slavs in Mecklenburg (955).

(4) Taking advantage of the glory, Otto instituted durable reforms. Since 840 royal powers had been widely usurped by the Dukes or their subordinates. Where these could not be directly resumed, Otto conferred territorial immunities from royal (i.e. ducal) jurisdiction upon great ecclesiastics who, in a religious age, could keep lay trespassers out. These priestly princes were royal nominees and could not found dynasties; but they were irremovable and the episcopal ones, especially The Primate, the Abp. of the expanding province of Mainz, might overbalance the lay authorities. Otto planned an internal balance among the churchmen. A new missionary archbishopric at Magdeburg was to reduce and stabilise Mainz and the greater abbeys were to be immune from episcopal jurisdiction. Only the Pope could do these things. Again German organisation became entangled with Italian politics. Pope John XII, young head of a noble faction, was precariously at war with Berengar of Ivrea. Otto rescued him (961) and John crowned Otto Emperor, authorised the new archbishopric and embarked upon the immunities. In return Otto, by the *Privilegium Ottonianum* confirmed the Donations of Constantine and Pepin, defined the Papal territory and readopted the imperial protectorate of Christendom.

(5) They soon quarrelled over the inconsistencies in the *Ottonianum*. To Otto, the Holy See was the grandest of the imperial bishoprics. To John XII it was undoubtedly independent. He changed sides in the war with Berengar and called in the heathen Magyars. Otto thought this treason to the King of Kings besides himself. He occupied Rome. John fled and a synod under Otto deposed him and elected Leo VIII (Dec. 963). The *coup* was only a partial success. In a counter-synod John annulled the acts of Otto's synod. The Romans, maltreated by the German troops, rose in his support. Unexpectedly, John died. They defiantly elected the learned and saintly Benedict V. Otto reoccupied the City and reinstalled Leo (964). In the next years he campaigned in Italy and, by threatening the Italian Byzantine provinces, forced the other Emperor to recognise his imperial status. His son, Otto, married Theophano, a Byzantine princess (972). His secular prestige was enormous, but many thought it wrong for an Emperor to hold the Pope in thrall.

(6) As a Christian warrior **Otto II (r. 973-83)** was less successful. In attempting to turn the Byzantines out of Italy he collided with the Sicilian Moslems, who defeated him (982). When the news reached Germany, Slav revolts and invasions destroyed Christianity and German colonisation from the Oder to the Elbe (983). Yet it was safe to elect **Otto III (983-1002),** a child of three, with an unprecedented but successful joint regency under the Empresses Adelaide and Theophano. The half Byzantine young Emperor was instructed by the learned Gerbert of Aurillac, whom as Silvester II (r. 999-1003) he made Pope, but he died early. **Henry II (r. 1002-24) Emperor (1014),** and **Conrad II (r. 1024-39, Emperor 1027)** had problems on two military fronts similar to Otto II's, but with complications. The Normans appeared in Apulia in 1016 and the Papacy had become a prize of scandalous Roman family competition, at the very period of St. Odilo's long rule (994-1048) at Cluny. Reform was bound to come from Cluniac spiritual regeneration. Some of the discredit for the state of the Papacy stuck to its imperial protectors.

(7) The Cluniac inspired attack on universal simony, of which the Continental Investiture Dispute was a phase, began after **Henry III (r. 1039-56, Emperor 1046)** had deposed two out of three rival Popes and regularised elections (Synod of Sutri, 1046). The Synod of Rome (1047) denounced simony. **Leo IX (r. 1048-54),** a Lorrainer, went on to a spectacular progress in the Rhineland and France to enforce it. Such a campaign was bound to upset the German political balance, for if the church princes ceased to be rulers, the lay princes would overpower the King, but if they remained lay rulers, the abolition of lay investiture would transfer their appointment from the King to the Pope. Hence the Kings had to resist a reforming Papacy and its powerful Cluniac public relations organisation.

(8) The struggle began after Henry III died. Another child **(Henry IV, r. 1056-1105, Emperor 1084)** was elected under the weak regency (until 1062) of the Empress Agnes. The Romans acclaimed a reforming Pope (Stephen IX, r. 1057-8) without consulting her. His brother, by a marriage, ruled Tuscany and could protect Rome from the north. The Empress bowed to the *fait accompli*. The precedent prevented her from resisting the election of Nicholas II (r. 1058-61) and in 1059 he issued the Election Decree, transferring the right to elect his successors to the seven cardinal bps. The Empress summoned a synod to annul it. Nicholas sought protection where he could. In addition to his predecessor's Tuscan ally, he established an *entente* with the French King (Philip I) and, in 1059, at Melfi accepted the Norman Robert Guiscard (?-1085) as his vassal and D. of Apulia and Calabria; in return Guiscard swore to uphold the Election Decree. This adoption of a secular as well as imperial prerogative was a turning point. War, though long in coming, was certain. The hitherto intermittent Franco-Papal co-operation became a standing feature of mediaeval politics; the Normans were launched upon their southern campaigns which, in a generation, extruded the Byzantines, subdued the Sicilian Moslems and transferred half of Italy from Imperial to Papal suzerainty.

(9) The extremist Archdeacon Hildebrand, popularly acclaimed, not under the Decree, as Gregory VII (r. 1073-85) precipitated the major war. In 1075 he forbade lay investiture, but went further. He instructed the Germans to disobey bishops who did not forbid clerical celibacy and the Dukes to prevent simoniacal or married priests from officiating. Such an incitement to attack ecclesiastical rulers had to be resisted. After a civic revolution in the strategic and commercial centre of Milan, a Papalist archbishop had (like Gregory) been acclaimed contrary, in this case, to the imperial prerogative. Henry IV replaced him. Gregory threatened excommunication. The German bishops summoned by Henry to Worms (Jan. 1076) denounced Gregory as a usurper and disturber of the peace. Gregory, as the guardian of morality, issued the anathema against Henry and released his subjects from his obedience.

(10) The Pope had already set the Germans at each other's throats; now he touched a sensitive spot of Henry's. For two generations the Saxon dynasty had been building up an economic base by depressing the status of the free, colonising Saxon peasants. Rudolf of Swabia, Otto of Nordheim and other magnates had been meditating revolt; for this the anathema was the perfect excuse and it also enabled them to tamper with the Saxon peasantry. By Oct. 1076 a double revolt had Henry in its power. The magnates required him to appear in Feb. 1077 at Augsburg, before the Pope and a Diet and, on pain of deposition, to be reconciled with the Holy See within a fortnight thereafter. They did their best to hinder a reconciliation by blocking the passes, but Henry escaped and found the Pope, delayed by lack of an escort, at Canossa in the Apennines. Here Gregory the priest overcame Gregory the politician. Henry, after three barefoot days in the snow, was forgiven, but in terms so ambiguous that the Pope's abandoned allies elected

Rudolf of Swabia as anti-King. A further civil war ensued. In the winter of 1079 Gregory tried to mediate, but when Henry obstructed the necessary conference, Gregory anathematised and deposed him again and recognised his rival (Mar. 1080).

(11) With the quarrel now irreconcilable, Henry summoned a synod to Bressanone (Brixen) to depose Gregory again. The Lombard bishops came in force, the German attendance was thin, but the necessary decree was passed and an anti-Pope, Clement III (r. 1080-1100) elected. Henry now had greater worldly success. His German rivals were killed or died; in June 1083 he captured Rome; in Mar. 1084 Clement III crowned him Emperor while Gregory held out in the Castello St. Angelo nearby. Six weeks later, however, the Normans relieved the Castello, but sacked and fired the City. They escorted Gregory to Salerno, where in 1085 he died.

(12) Despite Henry's respectable following of cardinals, the reformers would have nothing to do with Clement III. They elected first Victor III (r. 1086-7) Abbot of Cassino, and then the religious and astute Frenchman Urban II (r. 1088-99) who had been a legate in Germany. In the meanwhile Henry pacified Saxony and in 1087, as a step in securing the German throne to his family, had his son Conrad crowned. In 1088 Hermann of Salm, the anti-King who had succeeded Rudolf of Swabia, died. Hence from 1090 to 1097 Henry could again campaign in Italy. He was not entirely successful. Urban was securing the sympathy of the wealthy Aragonese and Catalans; in 1093 he detached Conrad from his father and recovered Rome. He was now preparing the greatest diplomatic stroke of the Middle Ages. In 1095, at Clermont safely in France, he proclaimed the First Crusade. The Crusade was largely a French affair. Apart from its other repercussions the Pope wrested the military leadership of all Christians from the Emperor.

(13) After Henry IV's return to Germany in 1097, local affairs went badly. In 1099 he had his second son **Henry V (r. 1105-25, Emperor 1117)** elected King, but in 1104 Henry V headed a great rebellion and forced his father to abdicate (1105). Willy nilly he inherited his policies, for investiture was still in issue and the Papacy, leaning on French support, was still encouraging trouble especially in Saxony, where Lothair of Supplinburg (grandson of Otto of Nordheim) was Duke. Accordingly in 1110 Henry seized Pope Paschal II, forced him to concede all the rights of investiture and to crown him Emperor (1111). He also acquired, by way of reinsurance, the reversion of nearby Tuscany. French support for the Papacy now became important. In 1112, at Papal instigation, a synod at Vienne excommunicated him. In reply (Jan. 1114) he married Matilda, daughter of Henry I of England, the French King's dangerous enemy, but a Saxon rebellion supervened behind him. By 1115 Saxony was virtually independent. Nevertheless he went to Italy because the Tuscan inheritance had fallen in. Paschal II, however, felt himself strong enough to denounce the forced agreement of 1111 and in 1118 Pope Gelasius II (r. 1118-9) excommunicated him. Henry set up another anti-Pope, Gregory VIII (11 18-21).

(14) Three years later the German confusion had become intolerable and the Princes at Wurzburg (1121) imposed a settlement. The anti-Pope was deposed and the Concordat of Worms (1122) established a compromise. Ratified at the First Lateran Council in 1123, it resembled the English Compromise of 1172.

(15) The Concordat did not bring peace. Henry V, in alliance with Henry I of England, was involved in a humiliating military check and then died childless. *See* HOHENSTAUFEN; HENRY I; STEPHEN.

SAXONS, SAXONY. (1) The Germanic tribe named (perhaps by their enemies) after their *saex* or short sword, were in the 4th cent. in occupation of N.W. Germany, whence the Anglo-Saxons migrated to Britain, while the Old Saxons remained. Thus the early mediaeval Duchy of Saxony embraced an area between the Ems and the Elbe. (*For the Anglo-Saxon tribes, see* EAST, MIDDLE, SOUTH, WEST SAXONS, etc.) **(2)** It was divided between the **Ernestine** and **Albertine** branches of the House of **WETTIN** in 1485. The electoral bonnet passed from the Ernestines to the Albertines in 1547. The area became Lutheran and, until the Thirty Years' War, prosperous, but its northward expansion was inhibited after 1680 when Prussia acquired Magdeburg. Post-war revival, especially through the Leipzig fairs, financed by the silver mines, made electoral Saxony into a European economic, especially exchange, centre and Dresden, the capital, one of the richest and most civilised cities. The electorate was at the cross-roads of the Bohemian-Baltic and the Rheinland-Polish trades. It was logical for AUGUSTUS (tactfully called THE STRONG) (r. 1694-1735) to bid for, and secure the elective Crown of Poland (1697), but he had to profess Romanism for the purpose. This upset some Saxons: it also brought Saxony into conflicts with other powers (greedy for Polish corn) and devastation and humiliation at Swedish hands, but the Polish connection remained sufficiently attractive for his successor AUGUSTUS II (r. 1733-63) to secure election in 1733. Frederick of Prussia, however, by seizing Silesia in 1740 interrupted the Polish route. Saxony was sucked into the ensuing wars (1740-5, 1756-63) and occupied for long years by the Prussians, while Russian armies made free of Poland and Russian influence became predominant there.

(3) All the same the century saw the development of the Dresden art collections, the great Saxon musical and architectural flowering, the Meissen potteries. The trade and finances of Leipzig formed a noticeable element of London commercial dealings. After the French conquest of Germany in 1806, Saxony became a Kingdom dependent on France and after the formation of the Bonaparte Grand Duchy of Warsaw, AUGUSTUS III became its largely titular Grand Duke. Poles and Saxons, thus reintroduced, naturally sided with France and were involved in Bonaparte's downfall. The very existence of Saxony was in issue at the Congress of Vienna (1814–5) and eventually Prussia took half. This was resented and Saxon policy was thereafter guided by the anti-Prussian Baron von Beust. Saxony supported Austria in the disastrous War of 1866; Beust was forced to move to Austria and she was forced to join the Prussian-dominated N. German Confederation and in 1871 the German Empire. British connections, however, remained active; e.g. the Dresden tramways were British operated until 1914. The Saxon cultural reputation, enhanced by the architectural beauties of Leipzig and Dresden remained high and formed the basis of the controversy provoked by the destruction of Dresden by western air forces on Russian insistence at the end of World War II. The Communist govt. made no effort to repair the cultural damage. *See also* BALTIC-38 *and thereafter passim.*

SAXON SHORE (Lat: Litus Saxonicum). The *Classis Britannica* (Lat: British fleet) was originally based at Boulogne but acquired an additional base at Dover in the 2nd cent. When Saxon sea raiding became dangerous in the 3rd cent., a unified system of garrisoned bases was created for its use. These were (Channel) at Portchester (Portus Magnus), Pevensey (Anderida), Lympne (Portus Lemanis), Dover (Dubrae), Richborough (Rutupiae); (Thames Estuary) Reculver (Regulbium), Bradwell (Othona); (East Coast) Walton Castle and near Lowestoft and at Brancaster (Branodunum). They were administered by a Count, who in the 4th cent. became responsible for coastal signal stations as far as Wallsend on the Tyne. *See* BRITAIN, ROMAN-21.

SAXTON, Christopher (?1509-96) published his county by county atlas of England and Wales in 1579. This was the first complete work of its kind.

SAYE AND SELE. *See* FIENNES.

SCALA-CHRONICA, a history by Sir Thomas Gray (?-?1369) who was a high English border official, is an important source on Anglo-Scots wars.

SCALLOP SHELLS. *See* SANTIAGO (ST. JAMES) OF COMPOSTELA.

SCAPA FLOW (Orkneys). This anchorage was the principal base of the Home Fleet in World Wars I and II. It was not ready for this function at the beginning of either war and had to be hurriedly fortified. The German High Seas Fleet was interned (1918) and sank itself there (1919). A German U-Boat sank the battleship *Royal Oak* there in 1939.

SCARBOROUGH (Yorks.) is said to be named after a Viking Scarthi who set up a fort in about 965. Harald Hardrada raided it in 1066 and Stephen built the castle in about 1136. It was first chartered in 1181. Gaveston was seized there in 1312. It was held for the King in the Civil War and taken by Parliamentary troops in 1645 and 1648. From 1660 it began to be used as a health resort and from 1908 as a conference town. German battle cruisers bombarded it in 1915.

SCARLET FEVER ("ANGINA" or QUINSEY) was anciently confused with Diphtheria and in the 17th and 18th cents. with measles. It was described in the Middle Ages and was already endemic in a mild form in England in 1661. Sometime before 1727 a malignant strain developed and there were important lethal epidemics in England in 1727, Scotland in 1732, N. America in 1735, England again in 1739 and in the Low Countries in 1742. After an interval there were further outbreaks in London in 1770 and 1777, in Ireland in 18014 and in 1831-4. The first all-England epidemic occurred in 1839-40. Thereafter there were similar outbreaks in 1844, 1848, 1858-9, 1863-4 (mortality 61,000), 1868-70 (82,000) and 1874 (25,000). No year and no area was completely free, but the worst affected parts were the industrial and mining towns. On average six times as many victims were between the ages of 1 and 5 as all the rest put together. Though the disease continued to take its toll, later epidemics were noticeably less dangerous. *See* EPIDEMICS, HUMAN.

SCARLETT (1) James (1769-1844) 1st Ld. ABINGER (1835) was a Whig M.P. from 1819, Att.-Gen. under Canning from 1827 to 1829 and under Wellington from 1829 to 1830. He successfully brought in a law reform bill in 1830, but opposed Parliamentary reform. He became C. B. of the Exchequer in 1834. His myopic son **(2) Sir James Yorke (1799-1871)** led the Heavy Brigade at Balaclava in Oct. 1854.

SCEAT. *See* COINAGE-3.

SCHARNHORST (Battlecruiser). *See* COMMERCE PROTECTION NAVAL, C-6.

SCHEDULED TERRITORIES. *See* STERLING AREA.

SCHEEMACKERS, Sculptors, **(1) Peter (1691-1770),** originally from Antwerp, settled in London in 1735 and executed many monuments especially in Westminster Abbey. His son **(2) Thomas (1740-1808)** was active between 1765 and 1804.

SCHELDT R. (1) is the most southerly natural haven and entry to Europe from the North Sea. Flushing on the I. of Walcheren at its mouth was favourably placed for inward traffic before the prevailing wind and for tacking outwards. Breskens, opposite, was long the entry *via* Sluys (The Sluice) to Bruges. The wide estuary (Wester Schelde) continues 40 miles inland to Lillo and Antwerp. The river with its navigable tributaries, the Senne and the Dyle, then joins Antwerp with the Flemish towns (Dendermonde, Ghent, Oudenarde and Tournai) and those of Brabant (Malines, Louvain and Brussels).

(2) Improvement in mediaeval navigation elevated the sea entry of this inland arterial system to European status, converted its basin into the first western industrial area and Antwerp, in Tudor times, into the major financial centre of the continent. Its affairs were of primary interest to the Hanse, the Holy Roman Empire,

France, Spain and Britain. From earliest times both Flushing and Breskens belonged to Zeeland which, if adequately armed or supported, could thus levy tolls on all the seaborne commerce of the two provinces. England made several attempts to secure direct control (e.g. 1337, B. of Cadsand; 1340, B. of Sluys; the Waicheren expeditions of 1585 and 1809), but these proving too expensive, the usual policy was to ensure that control was divided. In this the adhesion of Zeeland to the United Provinces, when the inland territories were or might be in other hands, was vital. *See* ELIZABETH I-18.

SCHILTRON. *See* HEDGEHOG.

SCHISM ACTS (1) 1713 required prospective teachers (other than teachers of the three Rs) to be licensed by the bishop and forbade the bishops to grant such licences unless the applicant had signed a declaration of conformity with the Anglican liturgy and had taken the Anglican sacrament. It also disqualified licensed teachers found in conventicles.

(2) **1714,** an extreme Tory measure, required declarations of conformity and non-resistance under pain of imprisonment and added oaths of allegiance, abjuration and supremacy as preconditions of a licence. It came into force the day Queen Anne died. George I sensibly took no steps to enforce it and it was repealed in 1719.

SCHISMS (1) The principal schisms have been the following. Dates of double elections are printed **bold.**

Popes		Anti-Popes	
Leo VIII	963-5	964	Benedict V
Gregory V	996-9	997-8	John XVI
*Benedict IX	1032-45		
Gregory VI	**1045**-46	**1045**	Sylvester III
Clement II	1046-47		
Damasus II	**1047**-48	**1047**-48	*Benedict IX returned
Alexander II	**1061**-73	**1061**-64	Honorius II
Gregory VII	1073-85	1080-1100	Clement III
Victor III	1086-87		
Urban II	1088-99		
Paschal II	1099-1118		
Gelasius II	**1118**-19	1118-21	Gregory VIII
Calixtus II	1119-24		
Innocent II	**1130**-43	**1130**-38	Anacletus II
Alexander III	**1159**-81	**1159**-64	Victor IV
		1164-68	Paschal III
		1168-78	Calixtus III
John XXII	1316-34	1328-30	Nicholas V

(2) The reasons for the schisms were primarily political, those between 1061 and 1178 arising out of disputes between the Papacy and the Emperor.

(3) The Great Schism followed the sojourn of the Popes at Avignon from 1309 to 1377. Avignon had been convenient. An efficient, impressive and mainly French ecclesiastical administration had grown up there. Its staff

and cardinals did not want to move. When Gregory XI went to Rome in 1377 it was not possible to transfer them all at once. Gregory died in 1378. The new Pope, Urban VI, was an Italian outsider and, as it emerged, an unintelligent and provocative Puritan. The cardinals assembled at Anagni, denounced his election and elected Clement VII (Sept. 1378). He and his cardinals returned to the still existing Avignon establishment in 1379, while Urban VI made do with those brought by Gregory XI to Rome and created cardinals and an Italian administration of his own. The two Papacies bid for European support. Of the Italian powers Naples originally supported Avignon, Milan, Rome. Elsewhere France, whose intrigues had started the trouble, and the Scots favoured Avignon, while the Emperor and England, being anti-French, supported Rome. In addition, in 1381, Avignon secured the obedience of Castle, whose King was threatened by the claims of John of Gaunt and then of Aragon (1389) and Navarre (1390), while Rome was relatively successful in the Low Countries.

(4) The differences between the Great and previous Schisms were that Europe was for the first time split between two churches each with well developed institutions, adminstrations and settled capitals, but embracing rival alliances of political powers whom each Papal court incited against the other. The Papal peace-making function virtually disappeared from the diplomatic scene. Secondly, the split in the administrations at local level dislocated the financial machinery at a time when local clergy were finding it increasingly hard to raise funds for their Papal dues. Thirdly many, and as time went on, more people found the spectacle of rival Vicars of Christ assailing each other with propaganda, anathema and arms, degrading and scandalous. The Schism weakened the institutional, financial and especially the moral standing of Popes.

(5) Superficially Avignon, with its powerful compact obedience was stronger than Rome, but the University of Paris focused the moral disquiet of Christians and propagated the idea, called the *Way of Cession,* that both Popes should resign and that the dispute should be settled by a general council. This found favour at the French Court in 1394 also for political reasons. Charles VI, weak but devout, was dominated by uncles, of whom Philip of Burgundy ruled powerful states divided in their obedience; the *Way of Cession* would strengthen the bonds of the scattered Burgundian inheritance. Hence Benedict XIII, the new Avignon Pope, was progressively deprived of his main French support. In 1398 the French clergy proposed to repudiate him and shortly afterwards French troops blockaded Avignon. The Burgundian influence then waned and Benedict's fortunes improved. In 1405 he moved to Genoa.

(6) Meanwhile the Roman Papacy was not only unable to control the confused and fragmented Papal states, but was dominated and bullied by the Neapolitan King, Ladislas. In their sense of local helplessness the cardinals undertook, before the election of Gregory XII,

GREAT SCHISM

Rome		Avignon		Pisa	
Urban VI	**1378**-89	**1378**-94	Clement VII (Pisa)		
Boniface IX	1389-1404	1394-1417	Benedict XIII		
Innocent VII	1404-06				
Gregory XII	1406-15			1409-10	Alexander X
				1410-15	John XXIII
Martin V	1417-31			*Basel*	
Eugenius IV	1431-47			1439-49	Felix V
Nicholas V	1447-55				

not to enlarge their College if elected and to work for a double abdication. In 1407 a Neapolitan raid drove Gregory to Siena, not far distant from Genoa. Thus both Popes, deprived of their abode, were visibly the sport of uncontrolled lay powers. Negotiations between them began, but when Gregory broke his pre-election undertaking, nine of his cardinals and six from Avignon met and summoned a general council.

(7) The Council of Pisa (Mar.-Aug. 1409), an international assembly, included several hundred bishops and proctors and some representatives of secular powers, but Benedict XIII had taken refuge in Aragon, while Gregory XII could depend on Ladislas and Sigismund of Hungary, his relative by marriage, besides Rupert, the Palatine anti-King in Germany. When the Council deposed both Popes and the combined Colleges elected another, they both defied the sentence. There were now three.

(8) Benedict and Gregory had mainly nuisance value. John XXIII, the second Pisan Pope, was at the centre of affairs and tried to turn Ladislas out of the Papal states. In 1413 the Neapolitans sacked Rome and John, fleeing north, sought the help of Sigismund, who was now bidding for the German and Bohemian Crowns against his brother Wenceslas. Sigismund needed a compliant Pope to validate his claims and a means of pacifying the religious disorders surrounding the Bohemian and Moravian Hussites. In 1413 he persuaded John to accept his conciiar policy. In 1414 Ladislas suddenly died. John, with misgivings, came to the Council.

(9) The shifting membership of the Council of Constance (1414-18) ran into thousands and included most of the important western clergy and many princes or their proxies, including Sigismund himself. It reflected three main strands of European opinion: a real desire to cleanse the church, local hostility to Papal exactions and middle of the road opposition to (expensive) Papal ambitions on the one hand and to (destructive) heretical extremism on the other. It began with a confrontation between the numerous Italian clergy and the rest. After Sigismund arrived (Dec. 1414) it decided to vote by nations (English, French, Germans, Italians) and so deprived John of his majority. It reopened the *Way of Cession* and pressed John to abdicate. He did so on condition that the others (who were absent) did so. Pressed to make it unconditional, he fled to Austria. He was brought back and deposed (May 1415). A month later Gregory XII abdicated. Benedict remained obdurate.

(10) The English Parliament, which had passed the Statute *de Haeretico Comburendo* in 1401, had in May 1414 passed some more legislation against Lollardy, from which the Hussites derived some of their inspiration. The Council had invited John Hus and he agreed when provided with a safe conduct guaranteed by Sigismund. But the Council reflected the savage temper of the English authorities. It and Sigismund broke their word and burnt him (July 1415) and his friend, Jerome of Prague (May 1416). This destroyed all hope of a Bohemian religious peace; but meanwhile the political background was changing. Sigismund travelled south to persuade the Spanish powers to abandon Benedict XIII and the English struck the French down at Agincourt (Oct. 1415). The Spaniards eventually agreed and appeared at Constance as a fifth nation in a faction-ridden assembly. French and English clerics fought each other; English and Germans struggled with cardinals to reduce Papal powers. Lay diplomacy, in the absence of an effective French govt., was bound to prevail. Anglo-German-Burgundian treaties achieved some effects. The Council deposed Benedict. It agreed a method of electing his successor by a two-thirds majority and elected Martin V, an aristocratic Roman cardinal. *See* SACROSANCTA.

SCHLEGEL, August Wilhelm von (1767-1845) published, with **Johann Ludwig TIECK (1773-1853)** a famous translation of Shakespeare's plays (1798-1810) which was itself a classic of the German language and made them widely known to German speakers. His less well known Spanish translations are almost as good. He was also a lover of Madame de Stael from 1804, except when he was sec. to Bernadotte as Crown Prince of Sweden in 1813 and 1814. He and his equally distinguished brother **Karl Wilhelm (1772-1829),** the founder of Indo-European philology and a court sec. at Vienna, were the acknowledged leaders of German romanticism, which profoundly influenced English intellectual attitudes in the mid-19th cent.

SCHLESWIG or SLESVIG. *See* BALTIC *passim.*

SCHLIEFFEN, Count Alfred von (1833-1913) and his PLAN (*see* CANNAE). As Chief of the German General Staff, he worked out a plan to defeat a Franco-Russian alliance. His design was to exploit the distances and slow mobilisation of the enemy on the Russian front so as to concentrate upon and destroy the French army by a turning march through Belgium and Holland in overwhelming strength. This force having won its French Cannae would then be transferred by rail to the East. It was uncertain whether this plan of Schlieffen, an intellectual soldier who had never held a major command in war, would succeed, but his successor, the younger Moltke, increased the uncertainties by shortening the outer flank of the western swing to avoid involving Holland and by strengthening the eastern front. In fact the Russians came into action sooner and the Anglo-French resistance was stronger and more supple than expected and the western swing was partly mishandled by the local commanders. Thus the Plan was not attempted and Moltke's plan, despite notable victories, had more success in the east than the west.

SCHNEIDER TROPHY instituted in 1913 for seaplanes of all nations. The winners were:

		mph			*mph*
1913	France	45	1923	USA	177
1914	Britain	86	1925	USA	232
	– – –		1926	Italy	246
1920	Italy	107	1927	Britain	281
1921	Italy	111	1929	Britain	328
1922	Britain	145	1931	Britain	340

This third win gave the Trophy permanently to Britain. The relevant aircraft was the ancestor of the Supermarine Spitfire which decisively influenced the B. of Britain in 1940.

SCHNITZER. *See* EMIN PASHA.

SCHOLASTICISM was a mediaeval body of philosophical theology in which a variety of different and not always compatible attempts were made to reconcile reason, especially as expounded by Aristotle (originally known through Arabic versions), with faith and revelation as known through scripture, the fathers and the tradition of the church. The starting point was the controversy between Abelard (1079-1142) and St. Bernard, but the outlook took its name from the Schoolmen or products of the (primarily) Italian schools or universities. Of the more important, the Italian Peter Lombard (?1100-1160) published his *Sententiae* (opinions), a collection of annotated opinions of the Fathers in about 1150. Albert the Great (1193-1280), a Swabian Dominican expounded Aristotle at Cologne and Paris. His famous pupil, the Italian St. Thomas Aquinas (?1225-74) never completed his immense *Summa Totius Theologiae* (Effect of All Theology). Duns (?1265-1308), a Scottish Franciscan, lectured at Oxford (1300-4), Paris (1304-7) and died at Cologne. He upheld a theory of universal matter, yet attacked the validity of natural theology, thereby unwittingly opening the way for the separation between science and religion. William Ockham or Occam (?-1349), English Franciscan, first at Paris and then at Munich, was a strong critic of Duns and argued that likenesses were to be deduced from observation of nature. After his time scholasticism developed mainly into arid intellectual pursuit of logic, regardless of sense, while more practical people moved slowly towards the scientific method.

SCHOMBERG or SCHÖNBERG, Friedrich Hermann (1615-90), D. of (1689). His father was Court Marshal to James I's son-in-law the Elector Palatine Frederick V and his mother Anne, daughter of the 5th Ld. Dudley. As a mercenary he served Bernard of Saxe-Weimar from 1634-7, Holland (1639-42), France (1650-60) and Portugal (1660-8). He was naturalised French in 1668. In 1673 he took command of the French in Catalonia and was made a Marshal of France in 1675. In 1676 he commanded in the Low Countries. The Revocation of the Edict of Nantes (1685) drove him to take service under the Great Elector of Prussia and he came to England with Prussian troops with William of Orange in 1688. He was naturalised British and took a small defensive command in Ulster. He was killed at the B. of the Boyne.

SCHOOLING, COMPULSORY AGE. In 1880 attendance was made compulsory from five to 10; in 1893 to 11; in 1899 to 12; in 1920 to 14; in 1944 to 15; in 1973 to 16.

SCHREINER, William Philip (1857-1919) was Prime Minister of the Cape from 1898 to 1900 and S. African High Commissioner in London from 1914 to 1919.

SCHRIFT **(Ger: writing).** The remarkably illegible system of handwriting practised by all Germans until 1900. A serious obstacle to communication, it was slowly and with setbacks between 1914 and 1920 and 1936 to 1942 superseded by a Latin script, but was still occasionally found in the 1980s. It is not a written version of the German Gothic printed alphabet.

SCHULENBURG, Countess Ehrengard (1667-1743), Duchess of MUNSTER (1716) and of KENDAL (1719), a large mistress of George, later George I, from 1692 until his death. Said to have been rapacious and believed, without much reason, to have been politically influential.

SCHULENBURG-OEYNHAUSEN, Matthias von der (1661-1747), Count (1715), (the letter 'Y' is not pronounced) Hanoverian professional soldier and political ally of Marlborough and P. Eugene, under both of whom he served. After George I's accession in Britain he went to Venice, whose forces he commanded against the Turks until 1718. He then retired in Venice and built up a great picture collection, much of it acquired from the executors of the last Gonzaga D. of Mantua. This was auctioned at Christie's (London) in 1775, when many pieces passed to British royal and private collections.

SCHUSTER. Germans naturalised in 1875. **(1) Sir Arthur (1851-1934),** Prof. of Applied Mathematics and expert in spectroscopy, electricity and magnetism was Sec. of the Royal Society from 1912 to 1919. His brother **(2) Sir Felix Otto (1854-1936),** Gov. of the Union Bank of London from 1895 to 1918 and finance member of the Council of India from 1906 to 1916, carried through the multiple bank amalgamations which created the post-World War I National Provincial Bank. A cousin **(3) Claud (1869-1956) Ld. SCHUSTER (1944)** was educated at Winchester and became Sec. of the London Govt. Commission from 1899 to 1902. He impressed the formidable Sir Robt. Morant and worked under him at the Bd. of Education until 1911 when Morant took Schuster with him to administer the new N. Insurance. In 1915 Schuster moved over and became Clerk of the Crown in Chancery under Haldane, and then under the E. of Birkenhead and then under eight successive Lords Chancellor. The work included the property law reforms of 1922-5, Law Revision and in 1944 the creation of the legal aid system. From 1944 he was head of the legal branch of the British Zone Control Commission in Austria. He died at an old school dinner, leaving his huge library to the N. Library of Canada.

SCHWEITZER, Albert (1875-1965), O.M (1955). Alsatian musician, religious philosopher and physician set up a tropical hospital (financed from his own resources) in French Equatorial Africa in 1913 to combat leprosy and sleeping sickness. He published many works on such diverse subjects as Johan Sebastian Bach, Jesus Christ, Civilisation and African tribal custom.

SCILLY ISLES. About 40 islands and 100 islets 25 miles S.W. of Lands End. Submerged field walls in some of the shallows give some colour to the legend connecting them with the drowned land of Lyonesse. They were certainly occupied in the 10th cent., for King Olaf Tryggvasson was converted to Christianity by a local hermit. Henry I gave the Is. to Tavistock Abbey but under Edward I the monks began to share the lordship with the Blanchminster family. The latter excluded the Corish coroner and were granted one of their own in 1319. By 1345 the joint lordship was held by the earldom of Cornwall. By the dissolution of the monasteries, half the lordship fell to the Crown. In 1547 Silvester Danvers, the heir of the Blanchminsters sold their interest to the Admiral Sir Thomas Seymour by whose attainder it too fell to the Crown in 1549. In 1591 Elizabeth I leased the Is. to Francis Godolphin who fortified High Town in 1593. The Godolphins remained tenants until 1834, but meanwhile the Is. were strongly royalist in the Civil War and made their living at other times by piracy and smuggling. In 1834 Augustus Smith took over the tenancy and introduced compulsory education. The lease remained in his family until 1933 but the Is. were subject to a very sketchy mostly judicial control by Cornwall Quarter Sessions. Hence the creation of Cornwall County Council had only a very limited effect. A council of the Is. was set up in 1933 when the lease of the four major Is. was surrendered.

SCIMUS, FILII **(1299) (Lat: We know, my sons).** Bull of Boniface VIII asserting Papal overlordship over Scotland.

SCIRE FACIAS **(Lat: make known)** was a writ issued from the Petty Bag Office upon the Att.-Gen's. *fiat* at the request of an aggrieved subject. It directed the sheriff to make known to the holder of a charter or letters patent that he must show cause why they should not be cancelled.

S[C]IROCCO. Mediterranean south wind, often dust laden and liable to endure for long periods in summer.

SCOBELL, Henry (?-1660) was clerk of the Parliaments from Jan. 1648 until its dissolution by Cromwell in Apr. 1653. He was Asst.-Sec. to the Council of State from Dec. 1653 and clerk of Cromwell's first Parliament from Sept. 1654. The restored Rump tried to dismiss him. He published collections of Acts and Ordinances from 3 Nov. 1640 to 17 Sept. 1756, besides some constitutional tracts.

SCONCE (1) A fort or earthwork usually to defend a narrow place or harbour entrance. **(2)** At Oxford University a penalty involving drinking $2\frac{1}{4}$ pints of beer for an offence against table etiquette.

SCONE (pron: Skoon) (Perthshire) was a place of Pictish religious importance by the 8th cent. Pictish and Scots Kings were enthroned by the Seven Earls with pre-Christian ritual (e.g. bathing in blood) on the Moot Hill, probably a barrow. David I objected to some of the rites, but enthronements on the Stone of Scone and acclamations by the people continued until 1295 when Edward I deposed John Balliol and removed the Stone to Westminster Abbey. Nevertheless in 1306, Robert the Bruce had himself crowned here and coronations with acclamations were continued for his successors. Eighty pipers played at the last occasion (Charles II) in 1651.

SCORESBY (1) William (1760-1829) was an Arctic navigator from 1785 to 1823. His son **(2) William (1789-1857)** studied at Edinburgh, was also an Arctic navigator and scientist, but after studying at Cambridge in 1823 was ordained and was vicar of Bradford from 1839 to 1847. In 1856 he went to Australia to pursue magnetic investigations.

SCOT (AND LOT). *Scot* **(1)** was a local tax payable for the use of a sheriff or bailiff; **(2)** a special drainage tax levied to maintain Romney Marsh. *Scot and Lot* was a charge levied by a municipal corporation proportionately upon its members. Liability and discharge of Scot and Lot was in some boroughs, the qualification for a parliamentary vote.

SCOTALE was a mediaeval village jollification usually at festivals of pagan origin such as May Day, Twelfth Night or Midsummer. The hero of the hour was the man who drank the most and made his friends drunk too.

SCOT, Reginald or Reynald (?1538-99), published the first systematic treatise on Hop cultivation in 1574 and in 1584 his *Discoverie of Witchcraft* attempted to discredit the behef in witchcraft and the methods whereby people were induced to confess it. His wholly convincing arguments fell on ears so deaf that Shakespeare used his book for the witches scene in *Macbeth*. James VI of Scots tried to refute them in his *Demonologie* (1597) but had all accessible copies burnt. He was an M.P. in 1588.

SCOTLAND, 1603-25 (1) James VI and I began the habitual absenteeism seldom broken, of the monarchs. During long previous absences and minorities the Estates had appointed or recognised regents who, while acting in most ways as monarchs, were trustees of the Royal State. James VI set a new course when, in appointing the D. of Lennox, he appointed a Royal Commissioner who was his agent. Lennox, with Thomas Hamilton (later Ld. Haddington and E. of Melrose) as Ld. President, the E. of Dunbar until 1616 and then the E. of Mar as Treasurers with Gideon Murray as Treasurer-Depute, carried on the civil govt. while John Spottiswood, Abp. of Glasgow, managed the Kirk. They used the Es. of Argyll and Caithness as enforcing officers respectively in the west and north. It was an efficient reflection of policies increasingly originated in London.

(2) In the west, the Macgregors having in 1603 raided the Lennoxes in Glen Fruin, Argyll caught their chief under safe conduct and had him hanged. He then moved against the Macdonalds of Isla but had to be reinforced by Ld. Ochiltree with the blessing of Andrew Knox, Bp. of the Isles. The chiefs were kidnapped at a parley and in 1609 constrained to accept the Statutes of Icolmkill from Knox. Contemporary plantations of Ulster were interfering with Macdonald power and they continued restive. The Macgregors, now landless, meanwhile moved south and were raiding the Borders. Under Letters of Fire and Sword (1610) they and other bandits were rounded up and deported to the Cautionary Towns, and mostly became mercenaries. The Scottish ex-Marches could now be policed with only a small force under Sir William Cranston. There was however renewed trouble in 1614 with Angus Og Macdonald who kidnapped Bishop Knox to hold him hostage for a cession of Crown Lands. Argyll took him by a trick and hanged him too. Argyll's operations incidentally served the interests of his Campbell clansmen: his methods laid foundations of dangerous tribal mistrust, but he pacified his circumscription.

(3) In the outer Islands attempts to plant Lewis failed against Macleod opposition, and the investors ("Adventurers") sold their rights to the Mackenzies of Kintail. They were resisted for nearly a century. The Minch isolated these conflicts from the mainland, as the Pentland Firth did those in the Orkneys (q.v.).

(4) Thus by 1616 Scotland had civil peace for the first tIme.

SCOTLAND 1625-60. *See* CHARLES I; CIVIL WAR; COMMON-WEALTH; NATIONAL COVENANT RESTORATION 1660.

SCOTLAND 1660-89 (1) On 19 June the fountains at the Edinburgh Cross ran claret and at the Castle a firework tableau portrayed Cromwell being pursued by the Devil into one vast explosion, but the restored Charles II had probably had enough of the Scots in the negotiations,

humiliations and defeats of 1650-1. He never visited their country again and having formally asserted that he would preserve and protect the Kirk "as is settled by law without violation", he appointed Glencairn Chancellor and Rothes Lord President, together with Privy Councillors, some of whom were called to London. Lauderdale obtained the secretaryship of this London Council which acted alongside and sometimes with the English Council. The Edinburgh executive was headed by a series of Royal Commissioners, each reflecting the contemporary temper of London politics, the King's purpose being to keep Scotland in quiet conformity with England while he coped with successive English crises.

(2) The first Commissioner, the E. of Middleton, met the Estates in Jan. 1661. Two of the four victims selected for vengeance, Argyll and James Guthrie, were the leading covenanters of their time. In London the acts of the Interregnum were simply and logically treated as void; in Edinburgh there had to be legislation to effect a similar result. Of the 393 Acts passed in the next six months, the earliest re-established the Lords of the Articles, and the important Act Rescissory repealed all legislation passed since 1633. Another Act, however, preserved the kirk sessions, presbyteries and synods. The "law" by which the Kirk had been "settled" was altered by the Act Rescissory: an episcopacy could replace the Assembly and, as before through the bishops, the composition of the Articles could be controlled. Charles II was driven to the same mistake as his father. The Scottish bishops were to be more political than spiritual leaders. In 1662 their old powers were restored, but by then the honeymoon was over. An Act to expel from livings all ministers who had not been episcopally collated was flatly disobeyed by 270 of them. Charles II was sensitive to straws in the wind and when a further Act required office holders to declare the Covenant seditious, he foresaw inexpedient trouble within the govt. machine and replaced Middleton with Rothes.

(3) Rothes got provision for a small army, and for fining non-attenders at Kirk, and then dissolved the parliament. The legal instruments for the royal policy being now available, the Council tried to use them. They broke in its hand. Govt. appointed curates were put into the manses of expelled ministers. The congregations sought out the old ministers. The ministers were ordered into banishment. The congregations hid them. The curates tried to collect fines and suffered bloody noses. In truth the Edinburgh govt. was out of step with the people. In Nov. 1666 the small Pentland Rising which originated in Galloway, was an explosive symptom. It was defeated at Rullion Green. The govt. went back on a promise of quarter, and though the King urged leniency there were hangings and deportations. Rothes was replaced by Lauderdale in 1667.

(4) In England popular opinion was represented by and through political institutions: in Scotland by and through the Kirk. The King meant to control both or reduce their power, but the object of doing so was less certain. A realist with no intention of going on his travels again, he knew that whatever his convictions, the universal imposition of Romanism was impossible and so not to be attempted. On the other hand the quasi-Anglican episcopalianisation of a popularly managed Kirk, if difficult, seemed feasible. Lauderdale, well informed confidant of the King's though he had been, was greedy and coarse. He bored the King in later life and perhaps Charles was already glad to see him off to Edinburgh. His methods were a mixture of limited toleration and violence. Letters of Indulgence were issued in 1669 and 1672. Expelled ministers might be readmitted if peaceable. No liturgy was made compulsory. The Five Articles of Perth were not enforced. Yet over 150 ministers refused the indulgences, and if some bishops, such as Leighton, tried to co-operate with presbyteries, they met invincible indifference. The obstinacy was confined to the south and Fife, but these were the decisive areas.

(5) As efforts at compromise failed, violence replaced them. Field preaching became capital. In 1674 landowners and employers were made responsible for their tenants and employees. Fines bankrupted some nonconformist gentry. There were Letters of Intercommuning. In 1677 landowners were required to give bonds for everyone residing on their lands. Many refused the impossible burden. In 1678 came the affair of the Highland Host (q.v.), a forerunner of Louis XIV's dragonnades: 6000 Highlanders and 3000 Lowland militia were quartered on South-western households to exact fines and bonds and search for arms.

(6) In May 1679 Abp. Sharp was murdered outside St. Andrews. The perpetrators were on their way to murder someone else when they met his coach. They spread the good news. Dumfries rose. At Drumclog an armed conventicle repulsed Graham of Claverhouse with loss. The insurgents, 5000 strong, were driven back from Glasgow. Monmouth, sent up urgently, routed them at Bothwell Brig. Some were hanged: 250 deported to Barbados. Vicious though he was, Monmouth favoured clemency and obtained an Act of Indemnity and another Letter of Indulgence. Lauderdale was sent on holiday.

(7) Charles II, in the thick of the Exclusion crisis found it wise to send his brother James, D. of York, out of London. He joined the Scots Privy Council in Dec. 1679, made two reconnaissances to Scotland and finally appeared as Royal Commissioner in July 1681. He held a parliament which began by enacting that no difference of religion could alter the succession and that every office holder should take a highly confused test oath, apparently in favour of non-resistance. Argyll agreed to take it insofar as it was consistent with itself. He escaped from prison disguised as his daughter-in-law's train bearer. James had inherited general unrest and the specific problem of Cameronian unrest. His strong fanatical Romanist hand made things worse even if many Highlanders were Romanist, and when Charles II died (Feb. 1685) he omitted to take the oath to defend the Protestant religion. The parliament of Apr. 1685 declared taking the covenant treasonable and made mere attendance at a conventicle capital. It granted a perpetual excise and promised an army. When Argyll tried to raise his country in support of Monmouth, he was easily defeated in June 1685.

(8) The strength of James' regimes was superficial and it collapsed when the P. of Orange landed at Torbay. The divided Privy Council was powerless because the regular troops had gone south and the levies refused to act. The Lord Chancellor, the E. of Perth, was chased out of Edinburgh; the curates out of the manses, before James fled, Episcopalian clergy immediately after. When the news broke, a large all-party delegation rode to London. William undertook the govt. *pro tem*: and summoned the Estates for Mar. 1689. There being no King there could be no Commissioner, so the Estates elected the Williamite D. of Hamilton as President while the Jacobite D. of Gordon held the Castle. Claverhouse (now Dundee) tried to hold a rival Convention at Stirling but failed and went into the Highlands.

(9) Left alone, the Estates issued a Declaration containing a Claim of Right (q.v.) and offering the crown to William and Mary. Two days later they issued Articles of Grievances against the machinery of the previous regime. Both documents followed the English pattern and neither mentioned the Covenant. William accepted the offer at Whitehall.

SCOTLAND ACT 1998 (*see* DEVOLUTION-2) created a Scots parliament composed of normally elected members for each U.K. parliamentary constituency plus regional members elected from registered party lists by single transferable vote. It was to be elected quadrennially but might be dissolved sooner if it so resolved or if there was a failure to appoint a First Minister. There was provision for separating Scots finances and borrowing arrangements from those of the U.K., with a power to vary the basic rate of income tax within Scotland by not more than 3%, and it was empowered to pass Acts (requiring the Royal Assent) which would not be law insofar as they would affect law outside Scotland or touch Reserved Matters. These, with some detailed exceptions, included the Crown, the Union of Scotland with England, the U.K. Parliament, the continued existence of the Courts of Session and Justiciary, the registration of political parties, Foreign Affairs, defence and treason, and the public service. In addition there were 67 detailed reservations whose main purpose was to prevent or discourage encroachments on services established upon a uniform U.K. basis. Disputes concerning such so-called Devolution Issues could be raised in the English and N. Ireland courts by the Att-Gen and defended by the Lord Advocate, the final appeal being to the Judicial Committee of the Privy Council.

SCOTLAND, KIRK or CHURCH OF, REFORMED (1) In Apr. 1547, after the siege of St. Andrews, the Protestant leaders there urged John Knox to accept the office of preacher and he accepted a call from the congregation and preached a furiously anti-Papal sermon. His and Balnave's treatise on predestination was composed in France and sent to St. Andrews in 1548. The Kirk sprang from these seminal events. The influence of his preaching and study spread in Switzerland, France and Scotland. In 1560 he and others were commissioned by the Scots Parliament to summarise the reformed doctrine. It was adopted on 17 Aug. and three Acts were passed on 24th to abolish Papal authority and the mass, and consequentially to repeal, as idolatrous, much previous legislation. Parliament then rose and Knox was commissioned to write the (First) *Book of Discipline* which sets out in essence and principle the organisation of the Kirk into Kirk Sessions, Synods and the General Assembly. It also regulated worship, ecclesiastical penal law and Kirk property. In 1561 this was supplemented by rules for electing superintendents, elders and deacons. His *Book of Common Order* or liturgy with metrical psalms and Calvin's Catechism was published in 1564.

(2) Andrew Melville succeeded Knox in the leadership in 1572 and presbyteries began to be systematically erected only in 1580, but there was constant dispute about the authority of the Kirk (claiming Divine sanction as expounded by Knox) and that of the episcopal Church (claiming Divine origin from the Apostles). *See* JAMES VI AND I; CHARLES I; CHARLES II; CIVIL WAR; WILLIAM III; ARTICLES, LORDS OF THE *and* WESTMINSTER CONFESSION.

(3) Episcopacy was reimposed by Act in 1584, abolished again in 1592. As part of an integrated policy, James VI and I re-established episcopacy in stages between 1606 and 1610 and by the FIVE ARTICLES OF PERTH (1618) approximated some usages to those of the Church of England. Laud imposed the Book of Common Prayer in 1637. This last led to strong reaction viz: the NATIONAL COVENANT, subscribed at the Edinburgh General Assembly in 1638, the Assembly's abolition of episcopacy and the Bishops' Wars. In 1643 the Covenanters and the English Long Parliament made the SOLEMN LEAGUE AND COVENANT and convened the WESTMINSTER ASSEMBLY at which a general scheme of church govt. and practices was agreed for both Kingdoms. This was embodied in the DIRECTORIES OF CHURCH GOVERNMENT and of PUBLIC WORSHIP and the WESTMINSTER CONFESSION and CATECHISMS. In England these norms were not long acceptable, but they have remained the standards of Scottish churches ever since.

(4) Episcopacy was reintroduced in 1660 and there followed a sanguinary conflict ending with the abolition of patronage in 1689 and the lasting abolition of episcopacy in 1690. The General Assembly's BARRIER ACT (1697) impeded speedy future alterations in Church law by requiring approval from the presbyteries as well as the Assembly.

(5) Infringement of popular rights by the Patronage Act, 1712, led to the establishment in 1733 of the SECESSION CHURCH, which in 1747 split into the BURGHER and ANTI-BURGHER factions on the question of taking the new Burgess oath imposed after the 1745 rebellion. In 1761 a further secession from the main church led to the establishment of the RELIEF SYNOD. At this period the Burghers divided into the AULD and NEW LICHTS (= lights), but reunited in 1820 into the UNITED SECESSION CHURCH. In 1834 the so-called Veto Act was passed by the General Assembly of the main church to amend the Patronage Act, 1712, by giving presbyteries a right to object to presentations on reasonable grounds. This led to the DISRUPTION of 1843 when a third of the ministers led by Thomas Chalmers seceded and formed the FREE CHURCH OF SCOTLAND. In 1847 the United Secession Church joined with the Relief Synod to form the UNITED PRESBYTERIAN CHURCH, which in 1900 joined with the Free Church to form the UNITED FREE CHURCH OF SCOTLAND. This, in its turn, ended the Scottish schism in 1929 by uniting with the Church of Scotland. The General Assembly must still meet in the presence of a royally appointed Lord High Commissioner.

SCOTLAND YARD (London), off Whitehall near Charing Cross, was a palace used by Kings and great men of Scotland in the Middle Ages and in particular by Henry VII's sister, Margaret of Scotland, before her marriage to the E. of Angus. From 1842 to 1890 it was the H.Q. of the Metropolitan Police and the term came to mean the Criminal Investigation Department of that body, often called in by other police forces. The H.Q. was moved to a building between Cannon Row and Westminster Bridge in 1890 and called New Scotland Yard; under that name the H.Q. was moved again to St. James' Park Station in 1967.

SCOTS or ALBAN KINGS, EARLY. The royal succession in the house of Alpin apparently passed at first from the King to his eldest male relative. Thus **(1) Kenneth MacALPIN (r. 843-58)** first King of both the Scots and the Picts, was followed by his brother **(2) Donald I (r. 858-62).** Kenneth's son **(3) Constantine I (r. 862-71)** was followed by his brother **(4) Aed (r. 877-8).** Aed's nephew **(5) Eochaid (r. 878-89)** was probably a minor and the real ruler was GIRIC, his foster father. It was during this time that Norse raids and colonisation cut off Irish Dalriada where the Alban Kings ceased to rule. After Eochaid's death, the throne descended to Constantine I's son* **(6) Donald II (r. 889-900)** and then to Aed's son **(7) Constantine II (r. 903-43)**, defeated at Brunanburgh by Aethelstan in 937. It then alternated between the families of these two until 1005, each King being killed by or on behalf of his successor, whether ritually or in feud being unknown. **+(8) Malcolm I (r. 943-54)** partitioned Cumbria with Edmund of England in 945. He was followed by *(9) Indulf (r. 954-62)**, **+(10) Dub (r. 962-6).** *(11) Culen (r. 966-71).** **+(12) Kenneth II (r. 971-95)**, who acquired Lothian from Edgar of England. *(13) Constantine III (r. 995-7).** **+(14) Kenneth III (r. 997-1005).** There being no further descendants of *Constantine II, Kenneth III was killed by Kenneth II's son **++(15) Malcolm II (r. 1005-34)** who died in his bed, having killed a grandson of +Kenneth III. In 1018 he defeated the Northumbrians at Carham. In his reign the House of the virtually independent Mormaers (q.v.) of Moray rose to national importance by the marriage of FINDLAECH OF MORAY to one of his sisters, while his cousin Gillacomgain of Moray married GRUOCH, a

grand-daughter of +Kenneth III by whom he had a son, Lulach. Findlaech also had a son, the legendary Macbeth whom Gruoch took as a second husband. These two were thus cousins on both sides and likely to found a combined monarchy of Moray and Alban, strong enough to deny the succession to the descendants of ++Malcolm II. Malcolm's daughter, Bethoc, had married Crinan, Abbot of Dunkeld. Their son, for whom Malcolm III secured the throne, had since 1018 been King of Strathclyde by a dynastic arrangement. He was **++(16) Duncan I (r. 1034-40)**, the first King of all Scotland, who was killed by **(17) Macbeth (r. 1040-57).** Malcolm II's policy, which tended towards primogeniture and a single royal line, was pressed by Duncan's elder son. He killed firstly Macbeth who was succeeded by **(18) Lulach (r. 1057-8)** and then, having killed Lulach, he succeeded as **++(19) Malcolm III (1058-93).** In the course of a comparatively long life he married firstly INGEBJORG OF ORKNEY, a grand-daughter of Bethoc's sister who had married an E. of Orkney; and secondly in 1069 the West Saxon princess MARGARET who had fled to Scotland after the Norman Conquest. At his death his brother **++(20) Donald Bane (r. 1093-4, 1094-7)** seized or was placed on the throne. He had to defend it against Ingebjorg's son **++(21) Duncan II (r. 1094)** who ruled briefly with Norman help from England, but was killed by Donald Bane. The latter was overthrown and blinded by **(22) Edgar (r. 1097-1107)** who also had Anglo-Norman help. Henceforth the claims of Ingebjorg's descendants were ignored at Court and Edgar's brothers **(23) Alexander I (r. 1107-24)** and **(24) David I (r. 1124-53)** succeeded him. David's son, Henry, was designated successor, but in 1152 predeceased his father who immediately designated Henry's young son. This boy **(25) Malcolm IV (r. 1153-65)** was eleven at his accession and died childless. The establishment of primogeniture against the older Celtic rule of descent was not achieved without opposition, based partly on the claims of Ingebjorg's family and partly on hostility to Anglo-Norman customs and policies introduced by Malcolm III, Margaret and their children. There were five rebellions against David I and two under Malcolm IV, whose brother **(26) William the Lion (r. 1165-1214)** had to endure sporadic insurrection led by Ingebjorg's great grandson Donald MacWilliam (killed in 1187) and later by Guthred Donald's son (killed in 1212). The last challenge of this kind ended with Donald Bane, the brother of Guthred, who was killed in 1214 immediately after the accession of William the Lion's son **(27) Alexander II (r. 1214-49).**

SCOTS LAW is, apart from statute, a combination of elements from feudal law imported by Anglo-Norman colonists and Roman and Canon law derived from the practice, which began in the 15th cent. and ended in the 18th, of sending Scots lawyers to French and Dutch universities. Hence Scots lawyers depend less on precedent than English and more on deductions from principles. This difference has been preserved by the maintenance of the indigenous system of courts (*see* SESSION, JUSTICIARY) which pay attention not only to statute and decisions on appeal, but to Institutional Writings (q.v.) where the principles are expounded. The system has suffered since 1707 from decisions by a House of Lords devoid, until 1866, of any Scottish lawyers and by legislation largely based upon English assumptions not always applicable or apt for the Scots situation. Since World War I, however, the intellectual eminence of Scots lawyers in the Lords has tended to reverse the flow.

SCOTSMAN. *See* RITCHIE.

SCOT[T], Cuthbert (?-1564), Master of Christ's Coll., Cambridge from 1553 to 1556, was one of the disputants at Oxford with Cranmer, Ridley and Latimer in 1554 who brought them to the stake. He became Bp. of Chester in 1556. He publicly opposed Queen Elizabeth's ecclesiastical policy and was fined, and imprisoned for non-payment from 1559 to 1563. He died at Louvain.

SCOTT. This name often indicates the Scottish ancestry of a migrant elsewhere and is common in Co. Durham.

SCOTT AND ANOTHER v *SCOTT* **(1913).** The House of Lords redeclared the rule that with three narrow exceptions a court cannot be held in secret.

SCOTT family settled in Kent since the 14th cent. when **(1) Sir William (?-1350),** Judge of the Common Pleas since 1337, built Scot's Hall at Orlestone. **(2) Sir John (?-1485)** was Comptroller to Edward IV from 1461, M.P. for Kent in 1467 and simultaneously Lieut. of Dover Castle, Warden of the Cinque Ports and Marshal of Calais. He was employed on occasional diplomacy. **(3) Sir William (1459-1524),** a Privy Councillor and Comptroller from 1489 held the same group of Channel coast offices from 1491. He was three times Sheriff of Kent. **(4) Sir Thomas (1535-94),** Sheriff in 1576 and M.P. in 1571 and 1586 commanded the shire levy during the Armada crisis. **(6) Sir John (1570-1616)** fought in the Low Countries and became M.P. from 1604 to 1611. In 1607 he became a member of the Council of Virginia and in 1609 of the Virginia Co. in London. He was M.P. for Maidstone in 1614.

SCOTT, FITZROY or CROFTS, James (1649-85), D. of MONMOUTH and BUCCLEUCH. *See* MONMOUTH AND BUCCLEUCH.

SCOTT, GILBERT. Of this architectural family **(1) Sir George (1811-78),** a pupil of Sir Robert Smirke, won an open competition for St. Nicholas Church at Hamburg in 1844 and was then commissioned to restore cathedrals at Ely (1847), Hereford, Lichfield, Ripon, Salisbury and elsewhere, as well as Westminster Abbey. Forced to abandon his Gothic design for the Foreign Office (1858-1862), he used much of it for St. Pancras Station. He also designed the daring Albert Memorial. His activities as a restorer provoked the establishment in 1877 of the Society for the Preservation of Ancient Buildings. His grandson **(2) Sir Giles (1880-1960)** won the competition for the immense Anglican cathedral at Liverpool at the age of 22, built a variety of neo-Gothic churches, the neo Jacobean Bodleian extension at Oxford, the splendid new Waterloo Bridge (completed in 1945) and between 1948 and 1950 rebuilt the House of Commons.

SCOTT, Henry Darracott (1822-83), an officer of Royal Engineers, was sec. to the Commissioners for the Great Exhibition and in 1866 built the Albert Hall, London.

SCOTT or SCOT, Michael (?1175-1236), scholar and scientist educated at Oxford, Paris, Bologna, Palermo and Toledo, wrote an Abbreviation of Avicenna at Toledo and was called to the Court of the Emperor Frederick II, at whose request he wrote *Liber Physiognomiae* (Book of Physiognomy), a translation of Aristotle's *Animals,* and several works on alchemy and astronomy. The Emperor sent him to a number of universities on mission to communicate new translations of Aristotle. He was regarded with some alarm in his time and suspected as a wizard.

SCOTT (1) Robert Falcon (1868-1912) led two Antarctic expeditions (1901-4 and 1910-12). The latter ended in his death and that of his companions. As a result of the recovery of his diary and the account by a survivor, E.R.G. Evans ("of the Broke") (later Ld. Mountevans), Scott became a national hero. After World War II attempts were made to denigrate him as a bungler. His son **(2) Sir Peter (1909-89),** painter and ornithologist, founded the Severn Wildfowl Trust.

SCOTT, Thomas (?-1660), regicide and parliamentary opponent of Oliver Cromwell who excluded him from his first and second Parliaments, but became a Sec. of State under Richard. He was executed.

SCOTT, Sir Walter (1771-1832) ("Malachi Malagrowther"), poet, novelist, literary critic and also a publisher, was a successful Edinburgh advocate. He married in 1797, became Sheriff-depute of Selkirk in 1799 and was for some years sec. of the R. Commission on Scots law. His first literary venture was a translation of German ballads, and he became interested in such narrative poetry and published three volumes of *Border Ballads* (1802-3), and then *Marmion* (1808) and *The Lady of the Lake* (1810). His first (anonymous) novel was *Waverley* (1814) and in the next 18 years he wrote 32 more, plus much literary criticism, a life of *Napoleon* and pseudonymous banking polemics. He exactly caught the romantic mood of the time, and emerged from anonymity in 1819. His novels, particularly, became the rage. Now famous, he would have been rich had he not been burdened with huge publishing debts, not all his own. His house at Abbotsford became a rural salon, and his Edinburgh memorial (1841) was more conspicuous, if less sumptuous, than the later Albert Memorial in London.

SCOTTISH GRAND COMMITTEE of the House of Commons consists of all Scottish M.P.s., plus enough others to ensure that it reflects the balance of parties in the House. It considers the Scottish estimates for not more than six days in a session. In addition, unless there is objection it considers the principles of purely Scottish bills as if on second reading and any other purely Scottish matters referred to it.

SCOTTISH LAND COURT, set up in 1911, consists of a lawyer chairman and four members familiar with agriculture. It deals with landholding issues arising under the crofters' and landholders' legislation and the Agricultural Holdings and Agriculture Acts, originally only in the crofting areas but since World War II, in all Scotland. Appeals lie to the Court of Session.

SCOTTISH NATIONAL PARTIES. The Irish nationalist agitation inspired the Liberals to create a Scottish Home Rule Association in 1886, and in 1894, during the passage of the Local Govt. Bill, the Commons passed a resolution in favour of a Scots legislature. With the Liberal decline this came to nothing. In 1910 20 M.P.s. formed a Scottish National Committee, which in 1912 persuaded the Commons to accept the principle that Irish Home Rule should be matched by Scottish Home Rule. World War I then supervened and the issue was put into cold storage. In 1924 the Scottish Liberal Federation demanded a local parliament but, provoked by the recession, from 1927 a Scots National League demanded a total separation. In 1928 the Scottish National Party came into existence and gradually absorbed the others. It agitated, even in World War II, and in 1947 a movement for a Scottish Convention received wide support. In 1950 a govt. committee investigated the financial problems which might arise if there were a separate Scots legislature and found that the two economies were so entangled that no separation was practicable. Meanwhile off-shore oil brought advantages which muted further demands.

SCOTTISH STANDING COMMITTEE of the House of Commons consists of 30 Scottish members plus up to 20 others. It considers purely Scottish bills at the committee stage. The Committee of Selection changes its membership for each bill.

SCOURERS (17th and 18th cent.) were gangs of riotous drunks.

SCRIBLERUS CLUB. A club dedicated to the satirical publication of the memoirs of the fictitious Martinus Scriblerus, German antiquary, a man of capacity enough, who had dipped into every art and science but injudiciously in each. Arbuthnot, Atterbury, Congreve, Gay, Pope and Swift all belonged. Arbuthnot did most of the work.

SCRIPTORES HISTORIAE ANGLICANAE (Lat: authors of English history) *DECEM* (= Ten). A compilation of ten English historical chronicles edited by Sir Roger Twysden (1597-1672). *QUINQUE* (= Five). A similar compilation by Thomas Gale (?1635-1702) in 1687. *QUINDECIM* (= fifteen). A further compilation by him in 1691.

SCRIVENERS were lay public writers in the days before printing, and being mostly used in formal dealings, amassed routine legal knowledge. Their customers came to rely on it and used them as agents in the transactions as well as writing them out, including taking deposit of money or goods involved. They could not, however, act in court proceedings and when business became contentious they had to hand it over to professional attorneys or solicitors who employed writers of their own, and to whom clients found it increasingly convenient to confide their negotiations. Moreover, printing took over the standard forms which had been their staple. Since the mid 17th cent. they have been little used, but their 14th cent. livery co. still exists.

SCROFULA or KINGS EVIL. The English monarchs were supposed to be able to cure scrofula by touch and habitually touched sufferers for the purpose. The practice ended with the death of Queen Anne. *See* TUBERCULOSIS.

SCROGGS, William (?1623-83), son of a rich butcher, as C.J. of the King's Bench from 1678 to 1681, was notorious for his brutal partiality in the 'Popish Plot' trials, but in Nov. 1680 the Commons impeached him on counts which might be read as attempted impartiality in Sir George Wakeham's acquittal. In Apr. 1681 he was dismissed.

SCROPE (pron: Scroop) Richard (?1350-1405) was Bp. of Coventry in 1386 and Abp. of York from 1398. He regarded Henry IV's clerical taxation as sacrilegious and raised troops in support of the Percy rebellion, but disbanded them (1403). Two years later he with Thomas Mowbray and others raised another rebellion. His troops faced the royal forces for three days, when their commander got possession of Mowbray and Scrope by pretending a parley. They were tried at Bishopthorpe. The King ordered Gascoigne C.J., to pass sentence of death. Gascoigne resigned from the court which passed sentence without him, and Scrope was beheaded. His tomb in York Minster attracted a cult and many ascribed Henry IV's later illnesses to God's vengeance.

SCRYMGEOUR, Sir James (?1550-1612) was a favourite of James VI save between 1582 and 1586 when he was entangled with the Gowrie party. His descendants were the **Vists. DUDHOPE** (from 1641) and **Es. of DUNDEE** (from 1660). They hold the hereditary office of standard bearer.

SCRYMGEOUR or (as pronounced) SCRYMGER, Henry (1506-72) was Prof. of Civil Law at Geneva and coadjutor of Calvin, George Buchanan and Theodore Beza.

SCURVY, a dangerous condition caused by long absence of Vitamin C in the diet. It appeared during the Second and later Crusades and often during bad winters in N. Europe and Scotland. It became a major problem with the institution of long voyages in the late 15th cent. Vasco da Gama lost 100 out of 160 men by it in 1498 while rounding Africa. The Dutch used oranges as a preventive in 1564 and habitually carried sauerkraut in their ships from 1593; they also cultivated vegetables in their ships and settled bases along the Eastern trade route such as Cape Town, Mauritius and St. Helena, where fresh vegetables could be obtained. As a result their ships were relatively free of it. The HEIC followed their example with much success from 1600. Woodall, one of the Co's., surgeons reported on this in 1617, but the English and French Admiralties took no notice and continued to lose seamen by thousands. Anson lost 80% of his men during his circumnavigation of 1740-44. In 1747 James Lind again proved the value of citrus fruits and published his conclusions, but it was not until 1772 that James Cook, using all the recommended preventives, returned from his longest voyage having lost only one man. Despite the acclamations, it took until 1794 for the naval surgeons Gilbert Blane and Thomas Trotter to persuade the Admiralty to introduce citrus fruit juice into the naval rations. Scurvy then quickly vanished and its disappearance was a factor in the naval successes of the French Wars. The condition is also apt to occur during wars and sieges, e.g. at Quebec (1759), in the Crimea (1856) and at Kut-el-Amara (1916).

SCUTAGE. *See* FEUDALISM; LAND TENURES.

SEA BEGGARS or *GUEUX DE MER.* See ELIZABETH 1-14; HUGUENOTS-6.

SEACOLE, Mary (1805-81), born a Jamaican slave, came to Britain in 1854 and went on, against official obstruction and private prejudice to the Crimean War in which, as an unsponsored volunteer, she tended the sick and wounded and risked her life rescuing wounded soldiers. She returned to England and gained the respect and liking of Queen Victoria. She published a widely read autobiography in 1857.

SEA FENCIBLES were a maritime militia raised for limited service and fixed duration between 1798 and 1801 and from 1803 to 1815. Mostly fishermen and coastal residents, they were protected from impressment. At their peak in 1810 they numbered 23,000.

SEAFORTH. *See* MACKENZIE.

SEALED KNOT. A not very effective royalist secret organisation under the Commonwealth.

SEAL OF CAUSE (Scot.). A charter granted by a royal burgh generally to a society or association of craftsmen.

SEAL (Lat: *BULLA***).** The first surviving sealed writ dates from Edward the Confessor. Seals were used to authenticate documents because few people had a distinctive signature. Early seals commonly have a pictorial or armorial device and the sealer's name. The usual materials were wax or lead, melted and poured into a matrix containing the design or stamped with the design (as with a signet ring) and then attached by a ribbon to the document or placed on it. Sealing began as a Royal and Papal usage (hence 'Papal Bull') in the late 12th and early 13th cents. and spread down through society even to serfs. The main seals of govt. were the Great Seal, held by the Chancery from the time of William I, the Privy Seal introduced by King John probably to authorise uses of the Great Seal from a distance and abolished in 1882 (*see* REQUESTS, COURT OF) and the Signet, an innovation of Richard II, ultimately kept by the Sec. of State (now the Home Sec.).

S.E.A.T.O. (SOUTH-EAST ASIA TREATY ORGANISATION) was a U.S.-inspired anti-communist pact, based on the N.A.T.O. example, to which Britain subscribed in 1954.

SEATON DELAVAL (N'land), an immense Baroque mansion erected by Vanbrugh between 1718 and 1728 for Admiral Delaval.

SEBERT (?-616) King. *See* EAST ANGLIA.

SECESSION CHURCH. *See* SCOTLAND, KIRK OR CHURCH OF-5.

SECKER, Thomas (1693-1768) studied for the dissenting ministry and became a doctor of medicine at Leyden (1721) but then a D.D. at Oxford and in 1727 became a prebendary of Durham. In 1732 his excellent reputation brought him to the notice of Queen Caroline. He became a D.C.L. in 1733 and through her influence Bp. of Bristol in 1734; he was translated to Oxford in 1737 and Dean of St. Paul's in 1750. In 1758 he became Abp. of Canterbury and had to face growing outbursts of Methodism, whose adherents his breadth of vision taught him to treat with tolerance and humour even though he disapproved of them.

SECONDARY EDUCATION was the term applied by the Education Act, 1902, to the stage after elementary education; the dividing line being at about eleven years of age.

SECOND BUREAU. The intelligence branch of any French military staff.

SECOND COALITION, WAR OF (Mar. 1799-Feb. 1801). (*See* MEDITERRANEAN WAR 1797-99.) **(1)** Encouraged by internal French disorders, by the British return to the Mediterranean and by the isolation of a French army in the Levant, the Austrians followed (but with better luck) the Neapolitans into the war, defeating the French at Stockach (Mar. 1799) and Magnano (Apr.). Bonaparte got his army back from Acre to Egypt by May (when the British defeated and killed Tippoo Sahib in India) and in June the belligerents were joined by Russia, Turkey and Portugal in a formal alliance. The French, who had overrun most of the Neapolitan mainland, had hurriedly to withdraw. The Austrians defeated them in the north again at Novi (Aug.) and by Oct. the French had been hustled out of Italy.

(2) Two series of events now transformed the situation. Bonaparte abandoned his Egyptian army, evaded the British cruisers and reached France (Aug-Oct. 1799). During the same period the mutually jealous Russians and Austrians suffered reverses in Switzerland at Zürich and the British and the Russians were defeated in Holland at Bergen (Sept.). These were major French successes, for the Russians, in dudgeon, deserted the coalition in Oct. The success was all the more necessary because the French Directory was discredited, at loggerheads with the legislature, unable to meet the expenses of administration or war and unable to keep order or put down rebellion. Bonaparte now cut the Gordian knot by seizing power with the title of First Consul in the revolution of Brumaire 18 (9 Nov. 1799).

(3) There was now a strong hand on the reins. Inducements and force put down the provincial rebellions. The ragged armies were paid, equipped and put under Moreau and Masséna, the ablest commanders. The administration was centralised (Feb.). On the allied side only the British prospered. The Union of Britain and Ireland was nearing consummation: the blockade of French-occupied Malta was soon to force a surrender. By June, however, the First Consul was in Italy. While Moreau conquered S. Germany, he resoundingly defeated the Austrians at Marengo (June 1800) and established the puppet Cisalpine Republic. The Austrians obtained an armistice. For this the Anglo-Irish Union (July), the murder of Kléber in Egypt (June) and the fall of Malta (Sept.) seemed small compensation. Moreover, as peace discussions with Austria proceeded, Bonaparte was seeking other ways of imposing upon Britain. To secure a foothold in Brazil, he offered Tuscany to a Spanish infante in return for a Spanish attack on Portugal and by the same agreement he bought Louisiana from Spain. These northerly and southerly threats to the British West Indies might in theory be traded for Egypt, Malta and Minorca. In fact British command of the sea had just been emphasised by Saumarez' victory at Algeçiras and landings in Egypt (*see* ABERCROMBY).

(4) The British blockade bore heavily upon neutrals, especially in the Baltic. The unbalanced Czar Paul had moved from alliance, through discontented neutrality, to sullen dislike of British policy. French shipping being driven from the seas, neutrals carried French trade. The British therefore searched neutrals, which threatened to deprive the latter (both carriers and producers) of their huge war profits. Bonaparte judiciously flattered Paul: he proposed that he should become protector of the Knights of Malta. He released Danish shipping seized by the Directory. The Danes started to convoy their merchantmen. There was a small fight with the Royal Navy and a British battle squadron arrived at Copenhagen to support the representations of the British Minister there (Aug. 1800). In Sept. 1800 Malta surrendered and Paul, finding that he could not have it, embargoed British shipping. This induced Prussia to move against the British by occupying the Hamburg outport of Cuxhaven, to which prizes were sometimes taken. The Prussian threat, of course, involved Hanover which was virtually indefensible. Paul now took the lead in reviving the Armed Neutrality of 1780, by the Russo-Swedish T. of St. Petersburg (Dec. 1800) to which Denmark and Prussia instantly adhered.

(5) Franco-Austrian peace negotiations at Lunéville had been suspended in Nov. On 3 Dec. 1801 Moreau won his great victory at Hohenlinden and advanced on Vienna. An armistice was signed at Christmas and peace at Lunéville in Feb. 1801. Britain was now alone. A counter-attack was determined. A fleet under Sir Hyde Parker and Nelson sailed for the Baltic. While on its way, the Czar Paul was murdered, a fact unknown when Nelson reached Copenhagen. A furious battle ended in a Danish capitulation (Apr. 1801). The new Czar Alexander I hastened to make a complete change of policy. The Armed Neutrality was dissolved by compromise treaties of June and Oct. 1801 and Mar. 1802. The Danish fleet, too, had been denied to Bonaparte. On the other hand Prussia occupied Hanover (Apr. 1801), while in Italy the French exacted the closure of Neapolitan and Sicilian ports to British ships as the price of peace with Naples. With the British now in Egypt, Bonaparte was anxious to conclude a peace before the outcome of their operations was known. Discussions had begun in Mar. 1801 when the Addington ministry replaced Pitt's. The preliminaries were signed in London on 1 Oct., but provided that hostilities should cease upon their ratification. They were therefore regarded as the definitive treaty. The French surrender in Egypt was known only next day. The final treaty was signed at Amiens in Mar. 1802.

SECOND EMPIRE. The Bonaparte Empire of 1851 to 1870.

SECOND FRONT. The Russian propagandist name for the support which they were demanding against Hitler through a Western invasion of Atlantic Europe. The name was deliberately misleading since a second front already existed in the Mediterranean, together with a third in Burma and a fourth in the Pacific against Japan, with whom Russia was at peace.

SECOND READING in either House of Parliament is the debate in which the general aspects of a bill are discussed. A member who wishes to act in the committee stage of the bill is customarily expected (especially in the Lords) to say something in the second reading debate. The motion before the House is "that the bill be read a second time". If defeated, the bill is killed and cannot be reintroduced in the same session. A politer way of throwing it out is a motion to postpone second reading for six months. This has the same practical effect because there will not be enough time before prorogation to pass all the stages.

SECOND REPUBLIC – FRANCE 1848-52. King Louis Philippe was driven out in Feb. 1848 and replaced by a self-appointed govt. of idealists. These brought in universal suffrage, press freedom, *habeas corpus,* security of employment, the right of combination, a limited working day and national workshops for the many unemployed. This programme was unreal. The countryside and many cities were in insurrection. The administrative apparatus did not exist and as the taxable resources dwindled, the new policy had to be financed by much higher and wider taxation, borrowing and inflation. Bankruptcies put half the urban voters on the street. By June money had run out and the workshops were being closed. Revolutionary barricades rose in Paris. The Constituent Assembly commissioned Gen. Cavaignac to restore its authority. He did so in a three day storm of Paris with thousands of casualties, which disillusioned the moderate voters. Appointed Prime Minister, he proclaimed a new constitution and held the first office in Dec. 1848. *For subsequent events see* BONAPARTE (CHARLES) LOUIS NAPOLEON.

SECOND SIGHT. A form of premonition long and widely credited among the Highland Scots. It is said to be a gift and neither acquired nor inherited. It takes forms ranging from the well known sensation of unease to a clear perception of sight or sound and the events foretold range from the trivial to the historically decisive. Most well known Scottish heroes were believed to have it;

seventh sons of seventh sons were supposed to be prone to it and there were a number of Highland prophets who were reputed almost as oracles. A form, perhaps, of Napoleon Bonaparte's "general's luck"?

SECRETARY-AT-WAR, i.e. the Secretary at and in charge of the War Office, was originally appointed under Charles I as the C-in-C's secretary. From 1704 he was always a minister of the second rank, in charge primarily of such military administration as was not performed by the Board of Ordnance, or interrupted by royal or political intrigue or the demands or vagaries of the commanders in the field or the C-in-C. The office was merged in that of the Secretary of State for War in 1855 and abolished in 1863.

SECRETARY OF STATE. The King had a secretary from the time of Henry III, but the King's Secretary became a high public officer only under Henry VIII and the office became effectively supreme under Elizabeth I who appointed, in the two Cecils and Walsingham, men of outstanding ability and prestige. The office declined with the decline of the monarch under the first two Stuarts, but rose again with the increase in public and parliamentary business under Charles II. From 1689 there were two, one for the Northern Department (N. European powers) and one for the Southern, which included Home, Irish, Colonial and Southern European affairs. From 1709 to 1746 there was a third for Scotland and from 1768 to 1782 a third for the colonies. In 1782 the Northern Department was converted into the Foreign Office, the Southern into the Home Office. In 1794 a third, for War, was established and in 1801 he took over colonial affairs, but in 1854 a separate Secretary of State for the Colonies was appointed and in 1858 another for India.

In 1917 a Secretary of State for Air was added; from 1925 there were occasional appointments for the Dominions and since 1926 there has been one for Scotland. A new Secretary of State for Defence superseded those for War and Air and took over the Admiralty in 1964 and another for Wales was created. The Colonial and Dominion Offices were merged under a Secretary of State for Commonwealth Relations in 1966, whose functions were combined with the Foreign Office in 1968. Further appointments were made for Employment and for Social Services in 1968, for the Environment in 1970, for Energy and for Industry in 1974 and also to replace the old Board of Trade. Prices and Consumer Protection followed in 1974, Northern Ireland in 1975, Transport in 1980.

By now the title simply connotes a minister of higher dignity or political importance with a seat in the Cabinet.

Constitutionally the Secretaries of State are holders of a single joint office and, save where a (rare) statute otherwise provides, any one can act for any other. The Home Secretary, as holder of the Royal Signet, is the first in precedence and the person through whom subjects may approach the Sovereign.

SECRETARY OF STATE (Papal). The Pope's Prime Minister. Some Popes, notably Pius XII, did without one.

SECRETARY OF STATE (U.S.A.) has, since 1849, been the Foreign Minister of the Union.

SECULAR CLERGY lived in the world, i.e. bishops and parish clergy.

SECURITY (1) is restriction (raising important issues) of civil liberty in the alleged interest of public safety. Since the 1970s it has been increasingly invoked as a result of (a) the highjacking of aircraft (beginning in America) and at least two passenger ships, by armed or bluffing criminals, refugees or political hostage takers; (b) political murders (e.g. of Earl Mountbatten in 1979) often by radio controlled bombs, or attempts such as the farcical bombardment of 10 Downing St; (c) Bank robberies, sometimes politically related; (d) public terrorism like the Canary Wharfe explosion in Feb. 1996.

(2) The casualties, if sometimes serious, have been minute in numbers, but the popular reaction has generated a security industry comprising bafflers in streets, public buildings and airports, electronic, photographic and X-ray search and surveillance devices, all sorts of passes and identification procedures, a proliferations of locks and grills, and staffs of uniformed pseudo-officials from security firms interested in increasing public fears. 138 firms were listed in central London alone in 1996. This unconstructive deployment of resources is matched by a waste of ordinary people's time, mostly in queues.

(3) Some firms have private armies which govt. depts. or their own contractors have so far used to move prisoners and evict motorway protestors.

(4) The non-essential cost to the economy has not so far been computed.

SECURITY, ACT OF, 1704 (Scot.). The bill was intended to bring pressure on England by laying down that on Queen Anne's death the Scottish Crown should pass to such Protestant member of the Scots royal line as might be chosen by the Scottish Estates but that he must not be the King (or Queen) of England unless "there be such conditions of government enacted as may secure" Scottish sovereignty the "freedom, frequency and power of parliaments" and Scottish religion, trade and freedom. Anne refused her assent in 1703 but the Scots Parliament forced it through in 1704 by refusing supply. The English Parliament replied with the Aliens Act.

SECURITY COUNCIL (U.N.O.) consists of five permanent members (China, France, the U.S.S.R. until Dec. 1991, then Russia, Britain and the U.S.A.) and ten others elected for two years each by a two thirds majority of the General Assembly. Retiring members are not eligible for immediate re-election. The affirmative vote of nine members is necessary to decide a procedural question; other decisions may be vetoed by a single permanent member. The Chair is held for one month in rotation. The Council functions continuously. It bears the primary responsibility for maintaining peace and also for those trust territories considered to be strategic areas, and it can call on member states for forces.

Habitual Russian vetoes between 1945 and 1950 brought the Council to a virtual standstill and in 1950 the General Assembly decided that if through lack of unanimity of the permanent members the Council fails to exercise its primary responsibility where there appears to be a threat to peace or an act of aggression, the Assembly may recommend members to take appropriate (including armed) measures.

SECURITY SERVICE. See MI.

SEDBERGH. See DURHAM-4.

SEDDON, Richard John (1845-1906) went from England to Australia in 1863 and then to New Zealand as a gold prospector in 1866. He acquired notoriety as a miners' advocate and became a Liberal Member of Parliament in 1879. He was Minister of Mines in the Ballance govt. (1891-3) and Prime Minister from 1893. Under him women were enfranchised (1893), industrial arbitration and small holdings (1894) and old age pensions (1898) were introduced. The land policy required wholesale purchases from the Maoris and attempts also to annex Pacific Islands. He was determinedly pro-British, an advocate of Empire preference and a military supporter of the British in the S. African War.

SEDERUNT (Lat: The [Following] sat) (1) The beginning of a Scottish minute stating who was present. **(2)** Thence the minutes themselves. **(3)** Hence BOOKS OF SEDERUNT were the official records of Scottish governmental bodies, especially the Court of Session and **(4)** ACTS OF SEDERUNT are orders, such as rules of procedure, made by the Court in the exercise of delegated powers of legislation.

SEDITIOUS MEETINGS ACT, 1795, was in force until the ending of the parliamentary session after 18 Dec. 1798. It required that a public unofficial meeting of more than 50 to consider a petition to the Crown or Parliament should be advertised in a newspaper by seven householders and if such a meeting discussed a proposal to alter anything in church or state by means other than statute, it could be ordered to disperse and those who failed to leave could be arrested and condemned to death. It was hardly ever applied.

SEELÖWE (Ger = sealion). The code name for the World War II German invasion of Britain which never happened.

SEELY, John Edward Bernard (1868-1947), 1st Ld. MOTTISTONE (1933), Conservative M.P. for the I. of Wight 1900, crossed the floor to the Liberals in 1904 and from 1906 represented Liverpool (until 1910), Ilkeston until 1922 and the I. of Wight until 1924. He was Sec. of State for War in 1912 to 1914 and ordered Irish troop movements which appeared to threaten action against the Ulster loyalists and led to the "Curragh Mutiny". He added a sentence to the Cabinet's statement that troops would not be used to enforce home rule and was compelled to resign as having bargained with mutinous officers. He commanded a Canadian cavalry brigade from 1914 to 1918 and was chairman of the important National Savings Committee from 1926 to 1943.

SEGRAVE (1) Stephen (?-1241) was a justice in eyre from 1217, one of the Justiciars in 1230 and Chief Justiciar in 1232. Dismissed in 1234 but restored in 1236, he was relegated to Chester and then retired into a monastery. His son **(2) Gilbert (?-1254)** was Justice of the Forest from 1242 but died as a prisoner of war in Gascony. His son **(3) Nicholas (?1238-95) 1st Ld.** consistently supported Simon de Montfort from 1258 and, in particular, seized and held Northampton against the King in 1263. He was at Lewes and Evesham and suffered both forfeiture and excommunication. He was reconciled with the Lord Edward on the surrender of Ely and restored to most of his lands. Later he served against the Welsh (1277 and 1282) and was nominated one of the judges in the Scottish succession dispute. Of his sons **(4) Gilbert (?-1316)** was Bp. of London from 1313 and **(5) Nicholas (?-1322) Ld. of STOWE,** took part in all Edward I's Scottish campaigns from 1298 and then supported Edward II and Gaveston. He was briefly marshal in 1309, but in 1310 he returned to the Scottish wars, where after 1316 his local experience was valuable in the operations of Thomas of Lancaster. A kinsman **(6) Stephen (?-1333),** Rector of Stowe from 1300 to 1318, was Chancellor of Cambridge University from 1306 to 1307, Dean of Glasgow about 1309 and was Abp. of Armagh from 1323. Another relative **(7) Sir Hugh (?-?1385),** a Gloucestershire landowner, was a member of Richard II's council from 1377, Steward of his Household from 1380 and, after briefly acting as Keeper of the Great Seal during the Peasants' Revolt, was Lord Treasurer from 1381.

SEIGNEUR (1) The ruler of Sark. **(2)** A direct grantee by the French Crown of land in Quebec.

SEIGNORAGE. The percentage claimed by the Crown on bullion brought into the Mint for exchange or coining.

SEISIN or (Sc.) SASINE (Fr: *saisir* = take) meant the right to possession of land. It provided the basis of land law and came to be applied to the best right to possession of a free tenement. Villeins could not claim seisin because their land was unfree. By the 13th cent. it had come to mean the ultimate title, not necessarily the possession or enjoyment. Thus a lord retained seisin of his tenant's land and the seisin of an infant in wardship was not transferable to the guardian. An owner's seisin might be enforced by a real action. *See* ASSIZE.

SEISYLL ap CLYDOG (fl. 730) a descendant of Ceredig ap Cunedda was ruler of Ceredigion (Cardigan) to which he added the three Cantrefs of Ystrad Tywi, to make the area known later as Deheubarth.

SELANGOR. *See* MALAYA.

SELDEN, John (158?-1654), learned and humorous lawyer and parliamentarian, published his *Titles of Honour* in 1614 and became well known as an orientalist by his *De Diis Syris* (Lat: Syrian Gods) (1617) as well as by later studies in rabbinical law. In 1617 his *History of Tythes* offended many clergymen and it was suppressed. In 1621 he helped very actively to prepare the Protestation of the Commons and was briefly in custody, but in 1623 he became an M.P. and in 1626 took a prominent part in Buckingham's impeachment. By now he was much respected as a professional but liberal lawyer and was briefed for Hampden in the *Case of Shipmoney* (1626) and against *General Warrants* (1627). His opposition to imprisonment without cause shown censorship of books and unparliamentary tonnage and poundage were all based upon his studies of the Common Law. His book *Mare Clausum* (The Closed Seas) (1635) against Grotius *Mare Liberum* (Freedom of the Seas) proceeded by similar methods in a wider field with less happy results. Imprisoned from 1629 to 1631, he became M.P. for Oxford University in the Long Parliament and drafted Laud's Articles of Impeachment, but his loyalty was to the law. In 1640 he published *De Jure Naturali* (Natural Law) and *Judicature in Parliament;* at the outbreak of the Civil War he pointed out that the King's Commissions of Array and the parliamentary militia were alike illegal and in 1643 at the Westminster Assembly he told the Scots and their Puritan friends that certain English church practices were part of the law "which we have sworn to uphold". Later when the Presbyterians claimed immunity from reform by the civil power because of their authority from Jesus Christ, he blandly asked them to identify the scriptural passages in which that authority was conferred. Consistently with such an attitude he took no part in public life after the obviously illegal proceedings against Charles I in 1649. His great reputation rests upon his intellectual reasonableness and personal charm.

SELDEN SOCIETY was founded by F. W. Maitland in 1887 for the publication of old legal records.

SELECT COMMITTEES are appointed by each House of Parliament. It defines their terms of reference and they investigate and make reports and recommendations to their House. They are set up by resolution, generally moved by a govt. whip and their membership reflects the party balance in the House. They have power to summon witnesses and call for papers, but not to act.

There are three types of such committees. **(1)** The Sessional Committees are appointed mainly under standing orders. In the *Commons* these include the Committees on Public Petitions, Nationalised Industries, Public Accounts, Public Expenditure (formerly Estimates) and Business. In the *Lords* these include Committees on Special Orders, Personal Bills, Procedure, Offices and Journals. *Each House* also has a Committee of Selection which chooses the members of the other Committees, a Committee on Standing Orders and a Committee of Privileges whose function is quasi-judicial and deals with issues relating to the privileges of the House. The *Houses Jointly* appoint a committee on Statutory Instruments. **(2)** Occasionally a Select Committee is appointed to examine a bill before it is considered in Committee of the whole House. **(3)** Select Committees are also appointed for particular inquiries. Since 1966 such bodies have been appointed to consider policy in special areas of govt: since 1978 to keep a watch on individual govt. departments.

The Chairman of each Committee is theoretically appointed by the Speaker from a panel of Chairmen maintained for the purpose, but in the case of departmental committees tenure is said to be limited to two sessions.

SELECTIVE EMPLOYMENT TAX (1966-73) was levied on employers in respect of each employee, but refunded in supposedly productive industries or in certain less prosperous districts. Local authorities were treated as productive. The tax, championed by the economist N. Kaldor, was imposed so that, incidentally, it amounted to a large forced loan from the ratepayers and it was immensely complicated to administer.

SELF-DENYING ORDINANCE (3 Apr. 1645) provided that no member of the Lords or Commons should hold any military or naval command awarded since 20 Nov. 1640. Probably devised by Harry Vane and moved by Zouche, Tate and Oliver Cromwell, it would ostensibly purge the army of politics; but actually it gave commoners a choice denied to peers, who could not resign their seats. It therefore worked against Cromwell's opponents Essex and Manchester. It was introduced in the Commons on 9 Dec. 1644 and rejected by the Lords on 13 Jan. 1645. Reintroduced in the Commons in a slightly amended form, it was pressed home and eventually passed. Cromwell was excepted. The name was coined at the time. *See* CIVIL WAR-16.

SELF DETERMINATION, part of the American doctrine for settling the issues raised by World War I, required that aspiring nationalities should be able to determine whether they should be sovereign and the form of their own govt. Calculated as a political weapon against the Habsburg monarchy, which it helped to dissolve, it was applied with caution outside Europe. *See* MANDATE.

SELF HELP **(1859)** by Samuel Smiles (1812-1904) was a best seller translated into many languages. It advocated hard work, thrift and self improvement as individually the way to success and collectively to social prosperity. In part, it confirmed the American work ethic. In Britain it was tactically derided by socialists who fastened on the author's unfortunate name.

SELFRIDGE, Harry Gordon (1858-1947) American businessman, retired to London in 1906 and saw an opportunity for a large department store, which he opened in Oxford St. in 1909.

SELGOVAE. *See* BRITAIN, ROMAN-12.

SELKIRK. Small town and county which formed a part of Ettrick Forest and was in the Scots Middle March. It had castles at Buccleuch, Dryhope, Newark, Oakwood and Tushielaw and the main occupations of the people were always cattle raising (and lifting), tanning and sheep and the making of tweeds. Even in 1961 the town population was only 6700 and the county's 22,800. They had to share an M.P. with Roxburgh and Peebles.

SELKIRK, Alexander (1676-1721). *See* DAMPIER.

"SELSDON MAN" was briefly journalistic jargon for a right-wing Tory because just before the 1970 general election. Tory leaders held a policy meeting at the Selsdon Park Hotel, Croydon, at which, according to Labour sources, there was to be a rightward swing to market forces, stronger police powers and less govt. intervention. This foreshadowed parts of the Tory programme of later years. *See* PRIVATISATION; THATCHER, MARGARET.

SELSEY (Sussex) was the See of the Bp. of the South Saxons from the 7th cent. until 1075 when encroaching sea forced removal to Chichester.

SELVACH (?-729), Dalriadan King from c. 695, defeated the Britons of Strathclyde in 717 but was himself driven to take the tonsure in 719.

SELWYN (1) George Augustus (1719-91), M.P. through family connections from 1747 to 1780, accumulated sinecures and a comfortable living, but was renowned for his wit and urbanity which secured him election to Whites and the Jockey Club, in whose ostensible purposes he was not specially interested. His kinsman **(2) William (1775-1855)** was a well known barrister and legal writer whose son **(3) Sir Charles Jasper (1813-69)** was M.P. for Cambridge University from 1859-68, Sol-Gen. in 1867 and a Ld. Justice of Appeal from 1868. His brother **(4) George Augustus (1809-78)** as Bp. of New Zealand from 1841 to 1868 strongly influenced colonial

Anglicanism and was Bp. of Lichfield from 1868. He published many religious works and Selwyn Coll., Cambridge, was erected in his memory.

SEMAPHORE. *See* SIGNALLING.

SEMIRAMIS, mythical Assyrian queen distinguished alike for her abilities and profligacy. The term "Semiramis of the North" refers, on the basis of the first characteristic, to Queen Margaret (1353-1412), ruler of Norway, Sweden and Denmark and on the basis of both to the Czarina Catharine 11(1729-96).

SEMPILL or SEMPLE (1) Robert (?-1572) 3rd Ld. SEMPILL (1548), Gov. of Castle Douglas, initially a supporter of Mary of Guise and then of Mary Queen of Scots and Darnley, went over to the Congregation when Darnley was murdered and fought Mary at Carberry Hill. He was joint-Lieut. in the west from 1568 until seized by the Hamiltons in 1570. A kinsman **(2) Sir James (1566-1625)** was educated with James VI who employed him as his agent in London in 1599 and as ambassador in Paris in 1601.

SEMPRINGHAM, St. Gilbert of (1083-1189) founded the Gilbertine Order at Sempringham (Lincs.) in 1139 with the support of St. Bernard and St. Malachy. Greatly respected by Henry II, he nevertheless supported Abp. Becket in his controversies. The Order, originally of nuns, became a double Order with canons regular in 1148. At his death there were nine double houses and four for canons only. At the Dissolution there were 25.

SENANAYAKE. *See* CEYLON-9 & 10.

SENATE. A common term for the upper house of a modern bicameral legislature set up under a written constitution and differently constituted from the lower, popularly elected house. Most senates have lesser powers than lower houses, but the U.S. Senate, the earliest of them, is particularly powerful because of its control of the President's treaty-making powers.

SENEGAL. *See* AFRICA, WEST (EX-FRENCH).

SENEGAMBIA (W. Africa), a French possession, was taken by the British in the Seven Years' War and returned under the P. of Paris in 1783.

SENESCHAL (O. Teut. = senior servant), at the court of a King or magnate was a high officer in charge of justice and palace management. Sometimes, however, he was a provincial viceroy or, as in Aquitaine and Sark, the chief civil and financial officer. *See also* STEWARD.

SENIOR, Nassau William (1790-1864), a brilliant scholar and lawyer, had a talent for gaining the respect and friendship of the distinguished. Son of a clergyman, he had been impressed by the dangers of indiscriminate outdoor relief and in 1815 resolved to 'reform the English Poor Law'. He was interested in and well informed on economics and in 1825 became the first Prof. of Political Economy at Oxford. He also wrote extensively for the *Quarterly Review,* the *Edinburgh Review* and other political and literary journals. In 1839 he wrote a report for Ld. Melbourne on *Trade Combinations,* and in 1833 he became a member of the Poor Law Commission whose report he drafted. This became the foundation of the Poor Law Act of 1834. He refused many honours and died a master in Chancery.

SENLIS or ST. LIZ. (1) Simon (I) (?-1109) a Norman magnate came to England c. 1085. The Conqueror offered him Judith, widow of the Saxon E. Waltheof of Huntingdon but she would not have him, it is said because he was lame. The King then conferred the Earldoms of Huntingdon and Northampton upon him and he married Maud, daughter of Waltheof and Judith (about 1089). In 1098 he fought for William Rufus in Normandy and was captured by the French, but he was present at Henry I's Coronation (1100). He subsequently went crusading but died in Touraine. His son **(2) Simon (H) (?-1153)** had to compete with King David of Scotland, who married his mother and took Northampton; and in about 1136 King Stephen granted Huntingdon to Simon's half brother Henry of Scotland. When, however, the latter deserted the King for the Empress Maud, Stephen transferred Northampton to Simon, who became one of his most important supporters, and in 1152 Huntingdon as well. By Isabel de Beaumont, daughter of the E. of Leicester, he had a son **(3) Simon (III) (1138-84)** who was recognised as E. of Northampton in 1159 and secured Huntingdon after the forfeiture of the Earldom from William the Lion in 1174. He died childless.

SENUSSI. *See* LIBYA.

SEPARATION. *See* DIVORCE.

SEPARATION OF POWERS. A doctrine, or constitutional arrangement, whereby the legislative, executive and judicial functions in a state should be in different hands. The idea is an old one. It was adumbrated by Locke but received its most powerful exposition in Montesquieu's *Esprit des Lois* (1748). He contended that such a separation was the best safeguard of liberty and attempted to prove it by grossly inaccurate observations of the contemporary British constitution. Since more foreigners read him than observed the British political system, the book was immensely if spuriously influential. In particular the constitution of the U.S.A. was a republicanised version of what its draftsman thought the British Constitution was, after they had read about it through Montesquieu. *See* PROHIBITIONS, CASE OF

SEPHARDIM. *See* JEWS.

SEPOY. An Indian foot soldier.

SEPPINGS, Sir Robert (1767-1840), working shipwright, became master shipwright at Chatham in 1804 and was Surveyor of the Navy from 1813 to 1832. He invented Seppings blocks for suspending ships in dock, the diagonal system for bracing frame timbers and other improvements generally adopted. He was virtually the last designer of big sailing warships.

SEPTEMBER MASSACRES (1792). The wholesale murder of political prisoners in France. *See* FRENCH REVOLUTIONARY WAR (APR. 1792-FEB. 1793)-1

SEPTENNIAL ACT, 1716 extended the legal life of a Parliament from three years (since 1694) to seven. A Whig tactical and administrative measure designed to avoid a general election in the aftermath of the Jacobite rising of 1715, it survived until 1911. *See* TRIENNIAL ACTS.

SEPTIMIUS SEVERUS. *See* BRITAIN, ROMAN-16-17; YORK-1.

SEQUESTRATION is the taking control of assets belonging to an office or person in order to preserve them in the interest of someone who may have rights in them, e.g. on the vacancy of a benefice, the bishop sequestrates the temporalities so that they can be given to the next incumbent.

SERAGLIO (Ital: harem). The common western term for the palace of the Turkish Sultan.

SERASKIER. The Ottoman Minister of War.

SERBIA or SERVIA. The Serbs, an orthodox Cyrillic writing race of slav peasants around and S. of Belgrade, were under the Turks from 1389 (B. of Kossovo Polye) until one Black George (Karageorge) set up a petty state in about 1804. The Russo-Turkish T. of Bucharest (1812) recognised the existence of this by recognising Turkish Suzerainty and Russian religious (i.e. political protection. In ensuing sanguinary feuds, complicated by pro- and anti-Russian sentiment, the Turkish Sultan favoured Karageorge's opponent, Milos Obrenovic, and in 1830 conferred upon him the office of Prince. This offended the Russians, who in 1839 forced a legislature of his enemies upon him. He abdicated and in 1842 it elected Alexander Karageorgevic. The Crimean War temporarily ended Russian meddling and the P. of Paris, by recognising Turkish garrison rights and forbidding intervention without the consent of the contracting powers, substituted an international guarantee for Russian protection. This was ended by the action of the Serbs themselves in taking part with Russia in the attack on Turkey in 1877. By the abortive P. of San Stefano the Russians favoured Bulgaria and denied Serbian ambitions. International intervention destroyed the San Stefano settlement and the T. of Berlin (1878) recognised Serbia's independence but allowed Austro-Hungary to outflank her in Bosnia and Herzogovina. Milan Obrenovic was first King of the independent state. He abdicated in 1889. His son and successor, Alexander, with Draga, his unpopular Queen, were murdered in 1903 and Peter Karageorgevic was proclaimed King. The dynastic alternations represented not so much a family feud as a symbol of factional confusion, in which aggressive nationalists now had the upper hand. Their object was to unite all the Balkan slavs under Belgrade. As Turkish power declined they thus fell foul of Turkey's successors, the Bulgars and the Austro-Hungarians. In alliance with the former, the Turks were driven from most of the Balkans in 1912 but the allies fought over the spoils in 1913 (*see* BALKAN WARS) and Serbia gained Kossovo and much of Macedonia. Matters were in this posture when World War I broke out (1914) as a direct result of Serbian subversion in Austro-Hungarian Bosnia. Serbia was overthrown by combined Austro-German offensives and only restored by allied action. The Austro-Hungarian, Turkish and Bulgarian collapse and disintegration in 1918 left large slav areas with no effective authority. These gravitated, not always happily towards the Serbs and this coalescence resulted in the conversion of the area into a federative Yugoslavia (Dec. 1918). When Communism collapsed in the late 1980s, Yugoslavia dissolved and Serbia then tried to take the Serb-inhabited areas of Bosnia and as much else as she could get. The resulting military conflict was not resolved in 1998. *See* KOSSOVO.

SERENDIB. Ceylon.

SERFDOM or VILLEINAGE, (1) was a personally unfree status superior to slavery. In its extreme form the serf was attached to the land of an estate or manor; he was said to be *adscriptus glebae* (Lat: registered with the field) and his lord was the person who happened to own the land. He owed menial service to the lord personally, usually in the form of labour on the demesne and he had to pay certain dues, particularly *heriot* and *merchet*. The payment of merchet and the performance of service undefined in amount or kind were regarded as conclusive evidence of status as a serf. The rights and duties of serfs amongst themselves were regulated in the customary court which they had to attend and over which the steward of the manor presided. Their land was held of the manor by its customs, and title to it was conferred by admission in the court itself. These admissions took the form of a small ceremony (occasionally involving a minor humiliation) and the fact of an admission was recorded in the court rolls. From the later Middle Ages a copy of the relevant entry in the rolls was given to the tenant and was used as his title deed – hence COPYHOLD.

(2) A serf could not implead his lord in his own court, neither, initially would the King's Courts protect him directly against the lord. He was not, however, wholly without rights, for the Church might intervene on his behalf; escape was not too difficult and a year and a day within a borough conferred freedom; and the royal authority might be invoked by third parties in the event of a breach of the peace, however technical.

(3) The watershed in the history of villeinage was the Black Death (1346 *et seq*) which reduced the population and put labour at a premium. The personal serfdom disappeared with varying speed in different parts of the country, depending largely on the power of the lord i.e. sooner from the estates of small and even large lay lords and later from lands belonging to the Church and the Crown. The dissolution of the monasteries indirectly hastened its demise, but crown serfs and serfs on large northern estates still existed at the end of the century; the personal status was finally ended in the upheavals of the Civil War.

(4) On the other hand there was no bar to copyhold land being owned by a free man; it was often convenient to do so in order to round off a farm holding, especially in enclosed land. Moreover the lord had rights in connection with copyhold, especially the minerals which, from his point of view made the status worth preserving. Hence copyhold land survived as a tenure, though lords sometimes enfranchised it for ready money. All copyholds were enfranchised compulsorily in 1926 (Law of Property Act, 1925) but with reservation of mineral rights to the previous owners.

SERGEANT (Med.). A man-at-arms below the rank of Knight.

SERGEANT-AT-ARMS (Med.). A member of a royal bodyguard.

SERJEANTS-AT-LAW. Every year the judges collectively nominated the seven or eight best barristers with at least 16 years' experience to the Lord Chancellor, who then called upon them by writ to take the degree of serjeant (otherwise called the Order-of-the-Coif). This was equal in status to a knighthood and involved resignation from one's Inn of Court and joining Serjeants Inn. It was a great public occasion. The serjeants had a monopoly of the Courts of Common Pleas and the Marshalsea; they acted as itinerant justices and they were commonly consulted by Parliament. The more distinguished were appointed King's Serjeants and were always summoned especially to Parliament.

From the mid-14th cent. only serjeants were made Judges and this soon hardened into a rule. By the 16th cent., however, the Coif became mainly a condition precedent to the Bench, Lyster C.B. in 1545 being made a serjeant and then C.J. of the King's Bench successively on the same day. Such arrangements became necessary when it was recognised that the Att.-Gen. and Sol-Gen. (neither of whom could be serjeants) had a claim to a judgeship. These arrangements persisted until 1873.

SERJEANTY. *See* FEUDALISM; LAND TENURE.

SERVICE, DOMESTIC. Household servants were normal and sometimes numerous in richer households before World War I. They often remained all their lives in the same family, of which they became a respected part. Their decline began in World War I when younger men went or were called into the forces, high death duties destroyed households especially if deaths occurred in quick succession, and high income taxes reduced funds available for wages. Moreover industrial employments held out prospects of freer lives. In 1939 there were still 1.2M, mainly older women, but World War II more than halved the total which continued to decline, as other employments paid better than households. The spread of labour-saving machines reduced the employer's need, while some forms of domestic help, once provided by specialised servants, were provided by the welfare state. The changes put an end to the mythical helpless wife.

SERVICE INDENTURES were contracts between the Crown and magnates or between magnates and lesser men for specified services. They are occasionally found in the early 12th cent., but began to supplant serjeanties and knight service early in the 13th because professionalism was more efficient than the amateur resources of feudalism made obsolete by inflation. Edward I's wars were fought largely with indentured troops hired from barons, who equally hired retainers. This set the pattern for later armies. By the 14th cent. military indentures, comparable with Italian *condotti* (*see* HAWKWOOD, SIR JOHN) regulated the size and composition of the force, the time, duration and place of service, distribution of booty, pay, bonuses, compensation for loss and arrangements for transport.

Beginning under Edward II, lords sometimes engaged men under written indenture to wear their livery and perform services in return for an annual wage. The service might be rendered in council or as accountants or clerks and even in the courts or parliament as well as in war, but the element of dependence being primarily consensual, a man might be indentured to more than one lord at once. Such arrangements gave a lord a visible following without taking labour away from his land and it gave landless men security. The lord's public importance thus might depend upon the number of his indentured and therefore liveried retainers. Disputes were increasingly fought out in court, where the lord might support his man's cause by maintenance, champerty or liveried intimidation. Complaints against such perversions of justice were frequent in the 14th and 15th cents. They gave rise to legislation and were resisted only sporadically until Tudor times by exceptionally strong-minded judges with armed escorts. This gangsterism has been mistakenly called *Bastard Feudalism*.

SERVITIUM DEBITUM. *See* FEUDALISM-12.

SERVITIUM FORINSECUM. *See* DURHAM-5.

SERVITUDE IN MINES AND SALTPANS (Scot.). By ancient custom workers in coal and lead mines and in saltpans could be bound to their employers as quasi-serfs. Under an Act of 1606 they might be forcibly returned within a year and a day to their employer if found elsewhere without a certificate from him. The rule applied to a man's family as well as himself and in 1672 masters were empowered to seize vagabonds and families and set them to work. The men hewed, the women carried. They formed part of the inventory and were sold or leased with the undertaking (but not separately). They were regarded as pariahs and were often refused burial in the cemetery. The Scottish Habeas Corpus Act, 1701, did not apply to them. Children were bound on the receipt at christening of an employer's gift or ARLES. By the mid-18th cent. the supply of workers in this developing, if high wage industry, had understandably fallen off. People avoided Fife and E. Lothian where it mostly obtained. In 1774 an Emancipation Act promoted by mineowners forbade new servitudes and empowered Sheriff Courts to decree emancipation of an existing worker under 21 who had served for seven years; between 21 and 35, ten years; between 35 and 45, seven years; or over 45, three years. He might have to serve an extra three years if he failed to teach an apprentice, or two if he joined an unlawful combination. Emancipation of a man automatically freed his family. The first decree was made in 1778, but progress was slow apparently because wage levels made workers slow to apply for decrees. An Act of 1799 freed all miners, but there was a shortage of workers in these industries until the influx during the recession after the Napoleonic Wars. *See* ARLES.

SESSION, COURT OF (Scot.). Committees of the Scots Parliament in its judicial aspect were first set up in 1370. That for Causes and Complaints became a court for original business which sat irregularly between parliaments. The Committee for Dooms heard appeals only while the parliament was sitting. Under an Act of 1426 the Chancellor with others chosen by the King from the three Estates was to hold originating sessions thrice yearly, but as the others could be paid only from the irregular profits of justice it was difficult to hold the sessions regularly. In 1478 Councillors (who were more often available) began to hold them and to deal with the extensive business of *spuilzie* (dispossession from land), and this brought in more money. By 1511 the court, by then called the Lords of Council and Session, was sitting regularly and in Edinburgh. In 1532 the Chancellor, Gavin Dunbar, Abp. of Glasgow (1525-47), proposed a College of Justice (q.v.) comprising amongst others, seven clerical and seven lay judges with a President. Papal authority was procured for the clerical salaries to be paid by a levy on the church. Parliament found the rest in 1541 and the judges were long immune from municipal taxation. The shortage of educated manpower caused the College to be somewhat inbred and occasionally partial to relatives. The situation was not improved when the Scots Parliament disappeared in 1707 and the local means of appeal disappeared; but in 1710 the House of Lords in London assumed the appeal jurisdiction though devoid of Scots lawyers. The Court of Session remained in this unsatisfactory state until Acts of 1808, 1815 and 1824 established two divisions and made appeals from the Lords Ordinary sitting alone to the Inner House possible.

The Lords of Council and Session are also judges of the High Court of Justiciary (q.v.).

SÉT. Ancient Irish unit of exchange worth half a cow.

SETH. *See* JAGAT SETH.

SETTLED LAND ACT, 1882, enabled entailed land to be sold, by the device of transferring the entail to the purchase price.

SETTLEMENT. The Poor Law Acts (1660 onwards) required that a pauper should be maintained by his parish, i.e. the ratepayers of the parish in which he had his settlement. An elaborate jurisprudence developed around this concept. Chargeable ratepayers did not wish to maintain more paupers than they could help. The mass migration of paupers towards the towns arising from the inclosures and the Industrial Revolution created a novel social and local financial problem. The solution tried after 1661 was to deport them to their original settlement, where the workhouse was little better than a prison. This aggravated the difficulties still further, for those seeking jobs naturally found arguments in support of new settlements. A person's settlement was initially the parish where his parents had a settlement, or if illegitimate where his mother was settled, or if a foundling, where he was found. Provided that he showed an unequivocal determination to abandon his settlement, he might establish a new one, for example, by serving an apprenticeship elsewhere; hence apprentices had to be bound before the local magistrates who, amongst other things, administered the Poor Law. A married woman's settlement was that of her husband. Settlements could also be acquired by becoming a ratepayer, or by being employed in the new parish for a year. There was a perpetual conflict between those seeking to make good and those who feared unemployment and deportation, as well as those who wished to avoid further impositions on the rates.

SETTLEMENT, IRELAND 1653-8 (A) (1) The (Commonwealth) Settlement Act 1653 reserved to the govt. all the church property and the counties of Carlow, Dublin, Kildare and Cork. From the lands and tithes it was proposed to satisfy public debts, reward the most active English anti-royalists and maintain godly ministers. **(2)** It allotted ten counties (Waterford, Limerick and Tipperary in Munster; Meath, Westmeath, King's and Queen's in Leinster; Antrim, Down and Armagh in Ulster) divided by baronies into two roughly equal lots, one for Adventurers to whom the govt. owed £360,000, the other for soldiers who might help to protect the Adventurers. **(3)** The rest, other than Connaught, was divided among soldiers in satisfaction of £1,550,000 arrears of pay and of contractors for £1,750,000 of debts. **(4)** It required all Irish to move to Connaught, less a four mile coastal belt, by 1 May 1654 (*see* TRANSPLANTATION).

(B) (5) The transplantation of the Irish being well on its way, it remained for the govt. progressively to settle the evacuated lands. The unpaid troops and contractors had been given debentures which would now be redeemed in Irish land. Many needed cash for current spending and had sold their debentures, usually to officers through regular debenture agents. This traffic was illegal but unavoidable and recognised by the govt. In addition many soldiers did not want the land and sold their debentures to get rid of their rights. A third class was prepared to settle the land only if there remained enough Irish to work it, but (depending on circumstances) many or most Irish had been transplanted

or had taken to the woods as tories (bandits). Worse still, soldiers were severely punished for taking Irish women to bed or marrying them. The scheme for redeeming pay debentures with Irish land was largely promoted by the officers, and the soldiers as willing sellers found ready buyers at knock down prices, e.g. 36 men of Steephen's company in Axtell's regiment sold their holdings to their ensign for a total of £136 and a troop in the Lord Deputy's regiment sold their's to a Capt. Bassett for a barrel of beer.

(6) The mechanism for settling the diminished remainder was as follows: the lands were first surveyed and then measured. They were then revalued so as to produce some equality of value rather than size. Next they were arranged in sequences called files or strings of contiguity and lots were drawn regiment by regiment, each one taking possession from the lands of the area where the previous lot had fallen. A similar process was followed at sub regimental level and so on until the individual soldier had his plot. **(7)** In the case of the contractors and Adventurers, the method, though similar in principle was managed from Grocer's Hall, London. There were many conflicting or awkward allotments and long delays in settling them; and the officer settlers disliked them and often refused to help them to clear the Irish out.

(8) The inconvenience of an empty country was such that English settlers habitually allowed previous owners to remain as open or secret tenants. *See also* TORIES (IRELAND).

SETTLEMENT, ACTS OF 1662 and 1665 (Ir.) The 108 page Act of 1662 vested the lands of all rebels since 23 Oct. 1641 in the Crown and then enacted their disposition in accordance with the King's Declaration of 30 Nov. 1660 and Instructions to Commissioners for putting it into effect. The two latter documents are set out in detail and were drawn up after inquiry. Many loyal previous Protestant owners were put back in possession and those turned out for them compensated with lands elsewhere, at the expense of Papists. Where the previous owner had been disloyal or a Papist, those in possession (often Cromwellian veterans) were left in possession. In general transactions such as the payment of rent between 1641 and 1660 were left undisturbed. Most of the lands belonging to Oliver Cromwell and other regicides were conferred on the D. of York. Detailed amendments in 135 pages were made in the **ACT OF EXPLANATION 1665**, together with an interpretation by the Ld. Lieut. and Council. The act of 1665 also empowered the Lord Lieut. to make within seven years rules for the election and conduct of town corporations. This power was exercised in 1672 for Dublin, Drogheda, Limerick, Galway and 17 other towns. All the rules required stranger merchants to be treated as freemen and those for the four larger towns forbade the town assembly to debate anything unless it had passed the common council. *See* TRANSPLANTATION.

SETTLEMENT, ACT OF (1700) recited that the Act of 1689 had settled the Crown upon William III and Mary II and in default of heirs upon the P. Anne whose only surviving son had just died, and that it was necessary to make further provision for the Protestant succession. It then settled the Crown after her upon the Electress Sophia of Hanover (a grand-daughter of James I) and her heirs being Protestants and if married, married to Protestants. Certain other provisions, as a result of early repeals never came into force. These were that after the death of Anne the nation should not be obliged to go to war without parliamentary consent; that the sovereign should not leave the Kingdom without parliamentary consent; that all privy council acts should be signed by those responsible for them; that no one born out of the Kingdom should hold public office or be a member of either House of Parliament; that all office holders were to be disqualified from being M.P.s.

Provisions that judges should hold their commissions during good behaviour and receive a salary instead of fees and that pardons could not be pleaded in bar of impeachment ultimately became law by other enactments.

SETTLEMENT, ACT OF (1704) (Manx). Originally Manx landholders were yearly tenants only, but the leases slowly became automatically renewable at the same rent (the Lords Rent) and saleable: the seller gave the purchaser a straw in the presence of the Lord's steward and paid an alienation fine to the lord. This custom was confirmed by King James I of England in 1607. The Great Stanley, however, introduced leases for 21 years or three lives, which ended family security and made it possible to raise rents. This led to half a century of dispute, composed by the Act of Tynwald of 1704, which with some modernisations restored the custom. After 1913 the Lords Rent could be bought out.

SETTLEMENT ESTATE DUTY. See DEATH DUTIES.

SETON, Sir Alexander (?-1470) was the first holder of the later Gordon earldom of Huntly. See GORDON.

SETON, Lds. SETON, Lowland Scots first ennobled in 1448 **(1) George (?1530-85) 5th Ld.,** Lord Provost of Edinburgh in 1557 and 1559, became Mary Queen of Scots' Master of the Household in 1561, remained her devoted supporter, helped her to escape from Loch Leven in 1568 and was taken at Langside. Subsequently an opponent of the regent Morton who had deprived his son Alexander of the Priory of Pluscarden, he helped James VI to assert his authority and was a member of the court which tried Morton in 1581. His son **(2) Sir John (?-1594) Ld. BARNS,** Master of the Stable to James VI, became a Lord of Session in 1588. His brother, the Jesuit educated **(3) Alexander (?-1555-1622) 1st E. of DUNFERMLINE (1606)** was Pres. of the Court of Session from 1593. In 1604 he became V-Chancellor of Scotland and a commissioner for the abortive union negotiations with England. He was Chancellor from 1604 to 1608 and James I's Commissioner to the Scots Parliament in 1612. His son **(4) Charles (?-1673) 2nd E.,** who had known Charles I as a young man, was a leading Covenanter in 1639 and regularly negotiated with the King at that period. His ambiguous attitude resulted in his being Commissioner to the General Assembly of the Kirk in 1642 yet being appointed to treat with the King after the latter had surrendered at Newcastle in 1646. In 1648 he left for France and next appeared with Charles II in Scotland in 1651. He supported the Restoration and having served as a Lord of the Articles in 1667, became Lord Privy Seal in 1671.

SEVASTOPOL. See CRIMEAN WAR.

SEVEN BISHOPS, TRIAL OF. (See JAMES II AND VII-11.) They were Abp. Sancroft and Bps. Ken (Bath and Wells), Lake (Chichester), Lloyd (St. Asaph), Trelawney (Bristol), Turner (Ely) and White (Peterborough), all acquitted. *For Trelawney in this context q.v.*

SEVEN SEAS were the Arctic, North and South Atlantic, Indian, North and South Pacific and Antarctic Oceans.

SEVEN WEEKS' WAR. The Austro-Prussian War of 1866.

SEVEN YEARS' WAR (1756-63), so-called after its European duration, began in N. America in 1753, continued with defeats there and was heralded by the *Renversement des Alliances* (*Jan. and May* 1756) (*see* BALTIC 47-9; GEORGE II, 16-20).

(1) The Cabinet knew in Feb. 1756 of French aggressive plans, so that Admiral Byng and La Galissonière both sailed for Minorca in Apr. La Galissonière fended Byng off in May. In June the French in India under Bussy took the British factories in the Four Northern Circars, while their ally, Suraj-ud-Dowla, the new *subadar* of Bengal captured first Kasimbazar and then Calcutta. His prisoners perished in the guardhouse (*Black Hole*). Minorca surrendered at the end of the month. Montcalm, the French Gov-Gen. of Canada, took

Oswego in Aug. When the embroidered news of Minorca reached the angry London public it caused the supersession of the D. of Newcastle's govt. by that of Devonshire and Pitt.

(2) The new administration had to ride out the storm and try to lay the foundations of future action. Fortunately Frederick the Great of Prussia had entered the war. He occupied Saxony as a stepping stone to Bohemia (Aug.-Oct.) and the ensuing Austrian diplomatic activity induced a diversion of French resources. In the interval Pitt got Parliament to vote 55,000 seamen and a Militia Act. The Hanoverian and Hessian troops brought in by Newcastle could then be sent back to Hanover to guard Frederick's exposed flank. He was put under the ban of the Empire (Jan. 1757) which meant in practice, that if the French entered Germany in strength the south German states would reinforce them. Sweden declared against Prussia, thereby threatening Stettin, and so did Russia and (for the purposes of Russian troop movements) Poland.

(3) At this point Britain had a spasm of inbred insular politics. The D. of Cumberland, designated C-in-C in Hanover, refused to serve under Pitt. George II dismissed Pitt. The Hanoverian force was for some weeks without a commander and the country, until the end of June, without a govt. while hostile action gathered momentum. France and Austria agreed on a partition of Prussia (T. of Versailles) and Frederick sought to anticipate his enemies. He took Prague (May 1757), while the French moved on Hanover, the Austrians assembled for a direct counter attack and a Russian army lumbered towards Königsberg. On June 18th the Austrians shattered Frederick's army at Kolin. The news of this and of the Black Hole of Calcutta reached London on the day (29 June) when the new Pitt-Newcastle govt. took office. For a while the tide of defeat continued to flow. In July the French under Richelieu beat Cumberland at Hastenbeck. In Aug. the Russians beat the Prussians at Gross Jägersdorf and occupied E. Prussia, while a British expedition under Loudoun and Holborne failed before Louisbourg. In Sept. Cumberland, driven into a trap, neutralised the Electorate by the Convention of Kloster Zeven, whereupon the Swedes invaded Prussian Pomerania; and finally came news that Montcalm, aided by local British incompetence, had taken Fort William Henry above the Hudson Valley.

(4) The atmosphere of drama was heightened by Pitt's histrionic character and appeals to public patriotism. In fact the tide was turning through action taken independently of the home govt. In the previous autumn the Madras Council had risked sending all its European troops under Clive to Bengal. In Jan. 1757 he retook Calcutta. A week after Frederick's disaster at Kolin, he destroyed Suraj-ud-Dowla's great army at Plassey (June). French influence in N. India collapsed. The news reached England just after Frederick had won the first of his two most spectacular triumphs: the superior French and Imperial army under Soubise was destroyed at Rossbach (Nov.), the Austrian under P. Charles of Lorraine at Leuthen (Dec.).

(5) Pitt's comprehensive plans now began to take effect. It was safe to go to war again in Hanover. Emden was seized and, to command the strengthened Hanoverian forces, Pitt borrowed the able P. Ferdinand of Brunswick from Frederick. He was soon hustling Richelieu across the Weser. Amherst and Wolfe had replaced Loudoun before Louisbourg and to cut off French succours, a squadron under Osborn and Saunders drove the Toulon fleet into (neutral) Cartagena and Hawke the French Atlantic fleet into Rochefort. By the time Pitt had signed a new subsidy convention at London with Frederick (Apr. 1758), Richelieu had retreated to the Rhine. When, with reinforcements, he started back, P. Ferdinand roundly beat him at Rheinberg and Crefeld. A month later Louisbourg fell to Amherst, but though Abercrombie failed incompetently before Ticonderoga to press the advantage, Bradstreet reached and reduced Forts Oswego and Frontenac on Lake Ontario and John Forbes hacked his way towards Fort Duquesne.

(6) The vein of success continued to run overseas but dried up in Europe. In Aug. 1758 Frederick drove back but did not defeat Fermor's Russian army at the expensive B. of Zorndorf. In Oct. the Austrian Daun surprised him in a night attack at Hochkirch. He was in no position to achieve much recovery during the ensuing winter, whereas his enemies were. On the other hand the dying Forbes captured Fort Duquesne (renaming it Pittsburg); Howe raided St. Malo twice and Cherbourg, doing serious damage; and two forces under Captain Marsh and Commodore Keppel took Goree, Senegal and all the other French establishments on the W. African coast, incidentally disorganising French communication with S. India, where the final struggle was about to open. These French defeats led to the appointment of Choiseul as the Chief French Minister.

(7) The *Annus Mirabilis* of 1759 was somewhat less marvellous than tradition remembers. In India Eyre Coote captured Masulipatam, but long before this could be known, the French had won a battle at Bergen near Frankfurt (on Main) and the Russians under Soltykoff started to advance towards Berlin (Apr.) The London public was distracted from the slow strangulation of their only ally, by the capture of Guadeloupe (May) and Marie Galante (June). These rich sugar islands were dangerous privateer bases. More important, they constituted a pledge for the return of Minorca. Then the French, under Contades, pushed P. Ferdinand across Hesse while Soltykoff beat a Prussian army at Kay (July). In Aug., however, P. Ferdinand ended French designs on Germany by his brilliant victory at Minden, but Frederick, now too weak to keep the Austrians and Russians apart, was overwhelmed by Soltykoff and Laudon at Künersdorf. Had they followed up their victory Prussia must have been extinguished, but the Russians were obstructive and demanding allies. By the time they were willing to move, Frederick had raised enough troops eventually to manoeuvre Soltykoff out of Silesia.

(8) Choiseul had assembled many troops and invasion barges along the Channel coast. There was no hope of secrecy. In July the Navy blockaded Dunkirk and Rodney bombarded the barges in Le Havre. The whole French battle fleet was to be used. De La Clue emerged from Toulon and passed the Straits. Boscawen chased and drove him onto a lee shore at Lagos, where most of his ships were lost or taken (Aug.). A month later Wolfe and Saunders, at Quebec since July, found the weak spot and captured the city, both Wolfe and Montcalm dying in the battle. The event, which conquered Canada, might have been undone by Choiseul's projected invasion and in Nov., despite Lagos, de Conflans sailed from Brest to cover it. Intercepted by Sir Edward Hawke during a violent gale, he was driven pell mell into Quiberon Bay, where two thirds of his fleet were wrecked, burned or taken. This ended the threat to Britain and America, but Prussia was still in trouble. The day after Quiberon, Daun captured a Prussian army at Maxen in Saxony. Only winter saved Frederick.

(9) The following years echoed the pattern of 1759. After adventurous operations, Eyre Coote overthrew the French in S. India at Wandewash (Jan.). In June, however, the Prussians lost the B. of Landshut to the Austrians and the Silesian plain with it. Frederick was desperate, for the Russians were coming on and there yet remained four months of campaigning weather. But they came slowly and he managed to pull off a spectacular night victory over Daun at Liegnitz (Aug.). Then the British mopped up in Canada and India. They took Montreal and in Bengal got their nominee, Mir Kasim

made Nawab (Sept.). The Prussian ended his season by beating the Austrians at Torgau (Nov.), the British theirs by capturing Pondichery in Jan. 1761.

(10) Overseas glory was all very well, but its practical advantages would become apparent, if at all, much later. The present reality was high taxation, a growing national debt, dislocated trade and ever more active press gangs. George II had grown used to Pitt, who was fighting so successfully for Hanover. He died in Oct. 1760. The young George III 'gloried in the name of Britain'. He was, with his entourage, sensitive to the cost of the war and morally out of phase with Newcastle's older, rather corrupt, political generation. He was naturally ready to see the war won and Pitt's financial morals were above suspicion. It was assumed that George would make ministerial changes, but any changes which he was likely to make were certain to disturb the direction of the war. In Mar. 1761 he made his mentor, the pacific E. of Bute, Sec. of State in place of Holderness. Shortly afterwards P. Galitzin, the Russian ambassador, proposed peace negotiations on behalf of France and her allies and Pitt agreed to treat while pressing ahead with the war, for he meant to have bargaining assets in hand for the benefit of Prussia. Thus in June Dominica in the Caribbean and Belle Isle off the French coast were taken and plans were laid against Grenada, Martinique and Santa Lucia. The Russians and the Austrians also continued with their war for the converse reason: by Oct. the latter had taken Schweidnitz, the principal and only remaining fortress in Silesia, and had Frederick's army blockaded. The Russians, marching along the Baltic coast, had taken Kolberg by Christmas.

(11) Choiseul offered Minorca in return for Guadeloupe, Marie Galante and Goree, the restoration of all French conquests at the expense of Hanover and Prussia and the cession of Canada north and west of Niagara, except C. Breton I. and the Newfoundland fisheries. Pitt opposed any French foothold anywhere in Canada or the fisheries and there was controversy about Guadeloupe. An important dynastic death had, however, occurred in 1759 which now affected the situation. The Anglophil Ferdinand VI had been succeeded on the Spanish throne by his half brother Charles III of Naples. The latter inherited the Farnese policy (*see* GEORGE II, 5-8; WARS OF 1739-48, 3-8) and was ready for French offers. Secret negotiations for a Third Family Compact were soon on foot, but their details were known to Pitt through examination of the Spanish diplomatic bag. Choiseul had to demonstrate his sincerity to the Spaniards by making difficulties in London. In July 1761 he withdrew all his offers and demanded satisfaction for certain Spanish grievances. Pitt rejected these in terms designed to cover his source of information. The Compact was signed in Aug. Convinced that Spain would go to war as soon as her treasure fleet arrived, Pitt proposed an immediate attack on her (Sept.). The Cabinet rejected the proposal and reconsidered and rejected it twice more on reference from the King. In Oct. Pitt resigned, accepted a pension and a peerage for his wife.

(12) Pitt was right. The treasure reached Spain in Dec. and the Spaniards immediately rejected British protests against unfriendly action. Bute declared war (4 Jan. 1762). The next day the Czarina Elizabeth, Frederick's most implacable enemy, was succeeded by Peter III, his most fanatical admirer. The Russians began to evacuate Prussian territory. The expeditions planned by Pitt against the French Antilles were launched and soon conquered Cuba as well; and another force captured Manila but, in the belief that the Spaniards were threatening Portugal, Bute switched the Prussian subsidy to her and reduced the army in Germany. The Prussian alliance was not renewed, but in May Prussia signed a favourable peace with Russia and Sweden.

(13) The change in strategic emphasis was not enough to provoke disaster in Europe; indeed Frederick beat the Austrians at Bürkersdorf in July (just as Catharine the Great had Peter III murdered) and P. Ferdinand forced a French army to capitulate at Cassel (Nov.), but it had an effect in N. America. Pitt's advice to reinforce Canada was neglected and the French seized St. John's, Newfoundland. The war by now was petering out. Bute had made peace approaches through Sardinian diplomats before he had superseded Newcastle at the Treasury in May; the D. of Bedford went to Paris in Sept. The Preliminaries of Fontainebleau and a truce between Prussia, Saxony and Austria were signed in Nov., the peace Ts. of Paris and Hubertusburg in Feb. 1763.

SEVERN R., BRIDGE, TUNNEL Shifting sands and difficult tides made a sea approach hazardous and the lowest bridge was at Gloucester. From Gloucester to Worcester the river was navigable by large barges and by smaller ones from Worcester to Stourport. Towing up river was done by contractors whose charges depended upon the expected strength of the current. Such towage bargains were sealed by drinking a mug of ale, hence the phrase "Had for a mug" if the strength unexpectedly changed. Nevertheless the peculiar conditions long made the Severn an obstacle to intercourse below Gloucester.

In the late 18th cent. it was connected at Stourport with the Trent and Mersey *via* the Staffordshire and Worcester Canal and with the Birmingham Navigations *via* the Worcester and Birmingham Canal, but these lateral communications could not be properly exploited until the Gloucester-Sharpness Canal had been built in 1827 to circumvent the estuarial hazards. Apart from inefficient ferries the first crossing below Gloucester was the railway bridge (1879) followed by the railway tunnel opened in 1886; the third was the remarkable mile long suspension toll bridge for the M4 at Beachley close to Bristol, opened in 1966. A levy, still collected in 1956 was imposed on coal passing the tunnel in order to prevent the ruin of the seaborne colliers between Cardiff and Cornwall. In 1995 a second bridge was being built.

SÈVRES, T. of (1920). See CHANAK.

SEWERS in older technical parlance meant arrangements for managing harbours and protecting and recovering land from water. The elaborate law and local customs on the subject dealt with land drainage, coast protection and river embankments more than with sanitation. Various local arrangements (such as the Lords of the Level of Romney Marsh) had existed in the Middle Ages and occasionally prerogative commissions of sewers had been issued. The former broke down because of the inflexibility of their financial arrangements: the latter because they lacked them altogether. The same applied to statutory commissions under an Act of 1428. The Statute of Sewers, 1531, however, empowered the Crown to appoint commissions for five years at a time with power to assess and collect charges based upon the value of local properties. Originally enacted only for 20 years it was made perpetual in 1551 and the duration of commissions extended to ten years in 1571. The whole subject was minutely described in 1622 at Grays Inn by Serjeant Callis in the most learned law reading ever delivered. Republished in 1824 it remained the basic statement of the law and system until the Land Drainage Act, 1930 replaced Commissions of Sewers by Drainage Authorities. The process of replacement was not uniform and some Commissions still existed in 1965.

SEXBURGA, St. (?-699), sister of St. Ethelreda or Audrey was the Queen of Erconbert of Kent. She founded and became Abbess of Minster in Sheppey after he died and when Ethelreda died in 679 she succeeded her as Abbess of Ely.

SEX DISCRIMINATION. See FEMINISM.

SEX DISQUALIFICATION (REMOVAL) ACT, 1919, provided that with certain minor exceptions "a person shall not be disqualified by sex or marriage from the exercise of any public function or from being appointed to or holding any civil or judicial office or post, or from entering or assuming or carrying on any civil profession or vocation or for admission to any incorporated society..."

In 1922 Viscountess Rhondda claimed, as a peeress in her own right, to be summoned to the House of Lords. The Committee for Privileges of the House of Lords on the motion of Ld. Birkenhead rejected the claim by 22 votes to 4 because the right to sit in the Lords was not incidental to a peerage and therefore it was not Lady Rhondda's sex which disqualified her.

SEXTANT. See NAVIGATION.

SEYCHELLES Is., though apparently discovered by the Portuguese in 1505, were first explored by pirates about 1700 and then in 1742 by the French, who took possession in 1756 and started to colonise from Mauritius. The result was a French speaking population of pirate and European Mauritian ancestry together with African negro slaves. The British took over in 1794, the last French Gov. acting as the first British one. When the British took Mauritius in 1810, the Seychelles became a dependency of that colony and were much used as a refuge for slaves freed by the Royal Navy. Their descendants became a majority of the population. The European and Indian demand for spices such as cinnamon and vanilla, fertilisers such as guano and ornamental tortoiseshell gave the islands an export trade and by 1897 they were effectively separated from Mauritius. Their formal constitution as a colony followed in 1903. They were used by the British as a place for distinguished exiles including King Prempeh of Ashanti (1897), the Palestine Arab leaders (1937) and Abp. Makarios (1956). They became independent within the Commonwealth in 1975.

SEYMOUR. The fortunes of this distinguished family were grounded by **(1) Jane (?150?-37),** daughter of a Sir John Seymour of Savernake. She was a lady in waiting to Katharine of Aragon and Anne Boleyn. Put forward by Thomas Cromwell in an intrigue against Anne, she resisted Henry VIII's advances until after she married him in May 1536. She reconciled the P. Mary with her father, but died giving birth to the future Edward VI. Thus her brother **(2) Edward (?1506-52)** became D. of Somerset and Ld. Protector (*see* SEYMOUR, EDWARD, ?1506-52) and another brother **(3) Thomas (?1508-49), Ld. SEYMOUR of SUDELEY (1547)** became Lord Admiral. He tried to seduce the P. Elizabeth and then married the Dowager Queen Catherine Parr. He was executed for attempting to usurp his brother's Protectorship. The son of (2), **(4) Edward (?1539-1621), E. of HERTFORD** secretly married **(5) Catherine (?1538-68)** sister of Lady Jane Grey in 1560. Both were imprisoned by Elizabeth I, who already had had reason to fear Seymour ambition for marrying without royal consent and the marriage was dissolved (1562). She died in custody. He was released in 1571 but lived a quiet life until James I made him Ambassador to Brussels in 1605 and Queen Anne of Denmark's steward in 1612. His illegitimate son **(6) Edward (1561-1612) Ld. BEAUCHAMP** made many attempts to establish his descent from Catherine and would have inherited the throne if he had succeeded. His son **(7) Frands (?1590-1664) 1st Ld. SEYMOUR of TROWBRIDGE (1641)** was M.P. for Wiltshire in the parliaments of 1628 and 1640. A Royalist, he was Chancellor of the Duchy of Lancaster in 1645 and 1660. The son of (5), **(8) William (1588-1660) 2nd E. and 1st M. of HERTFORD (1640), D. of SOMERSET (1660),** married Arabella Stuart in 1610 and was put into the Tower whence he escaped and in 1615 went to France. His wife died and he returned to favour in 1616. He was Gov. to the future Charles II in 1641 and then became a successful Royalist commander, capturing Hereford

(1642), Cirencester (Feb. 1643), defeating Waller at Lansdowne and taking Bristol (July). He attended Charles I during his imprisonment and was restored to his estates in 1660. The grandson of (7), **(9) Charles (1662-1748) 6th D. (1678)** married Elizabeth, Countess Ogle, heiress of the last Percy E. of Northumberland. Indolent but rich, influential and courageous, he was dismissed from his offices in 1687 for refusing to introduce a Papal nuncio to court. His support was decisive for the revolution of 1688. In 1690 he was Speaker of the Lords and in 1706 a commissioner for union with Scotland. A supporter of Marlborough's, he was driven from office in 1711 but briefly reinstated in 1714, retiring in 1716. His son **(10) Algernon (1684-1750) 7th D.** was Gov. of Minorca from 1737 to 1742 and died without an heir.

SEYMOUR, Edward (?1506-52) Vist. BEAUCHAMP (1536) 1st E. of HERTFORD (1537) D. of SOMERSET (1547) (*see previous entry*-2). **(1)** After a variety of minor posts at Court or with Cardinal Wolsey, was elevated to the peerage and became Gov. of Jersey at his sister Jane's marriage to Henry VIII. Thereafter he was employed mainly on military tasks, organising the defences of the Calais Pale in 1539, acting as Warden of the Scottish Marches and Ld. Admiral in 1543. In 1544 he commanded against the Scots and took Edinburgh and was then with Henry VIII at the capture of Boulogne, which he defended against French counter attacks in 1545 and 1546.

(2) At Edward VI's accession, as the King's uncle, he took steps to secure the Protectorship (Mar. 1547) and before Henry VIII's death was made public, rode to Hertford to secure Edward VI's person. He faced governmental problems which had been kept in suspense alone by Henry VIII's iron will. Doctrinally he favoured Cranmer's moderate reformism but admitted many continental reformers to England, who were often more extremist than Cranmer; and the interest of his political association in reform was the acquisition of more church property. There was, from the first, a tendency for things to get out of hand and this was compounded by an apparent economic crisis, or revolution brought on or accelerated by Henry VIII's debasement of the coinage, the shift from subsistence to market agriculture and cloth trading, the concomitant inclosures and the rise of a primitive capitalism. While titled politicians feathered their nests, articulate and sometimes highly placed idealists such as Latimer championed the poor, whose public welfare apparatus had been destroyed by the dissolution of the monasteries. The 1547 Parliament opened the floodgates by abolishing the legislation against heresy, destroying the chantries and substituting appointment by letters patent for election to bishoprics. On the other hand, bills which Somerset favoured against inclosures, against the eviction of lease, and copyholders and for apprenticing poor men's sons, failed to pass and the provision of revenue was inadequate.

(3) The Protector was distracted from applying his energy to the solution of these difficulties by the threatening international situation. Henry VIII's forcible acquisition of Boulogne was enshrined only until 1554 in a treaty from which he had excluded the Scots. The French would obviously move against Boulogne and Calais when they could. But Somerset still had a French-aided Scottish war on his hands and the pro-English party in Scotland had, since the surrender of St. Andrews to the French (July 1547), been virtually destroyed by Henry's ineptitude. Something had to be done quickly before Scotland fell wholly under French domination. So Somerset offered to negotiate an early return of Boulogne to keep the French quiet and then attacked Scotland (Sept. 1547) with a large army and fleet. He won a great victory at Pinkie (10 Sept. 1547) and then retired, leaving garrisons on Inchholm and at Broughty, Home, Roxburgh and Haddington. The invasion united the Scots against

the English. They welcomed more French troops (May 1548) and sent their child Queen (Mary) to France (July). The French, meanwhile, were threatening war in the Boulonnais.

(4) Somerset's Scottish retreat was due to political and economic deterioration in England. His brother, Thomas, the Lord Admiral, had married the Dowager Queen Katharine Parr who was guardian of the P. Elizabeth. Katharine died in Sept. 1548. The Admiral had made advances to Elizabeth and, to win over Dorset, proposed that Lady Jane Grey should marry the King. He had also been taking a share in the profits of piracy: and had forced Sir William Sharington to share certain clandestine profits of the Bristol mint. Sharington denounced him (Jan. 1549) and the council, with the King's leave but without asking the Protector, had him attainted in Parliament and beheaded without a hearing (Mar.). The Protector's standing at the centre was severely damaged. Next he incurred the positive hostility of the political camarilla by instituting, contrary to the Parliamentary decision, commissions to inquire into inclosures. These excited popular agitation and his personal following among the poor without strengthening his position.

(5) The same Parliament (Nov. 1548-Mar. 1549) passed the momentous Act of Uniformity which established a book of Common Prayer for general use and the right of marriage to the clergy and communion in both kinds to the laity. The book was susceptible of different interpretations, and the compromise which it was meant to effect was rudely shaken by an influx of foreign reformers on the one hand, and on the other by separate risings against the supersession of the old familiar mass in the West (1549) and in the Thames Valley (May-Aug.), where Grey hanged priests from church steeples, and then by a third, mainly of agrarian origin, in East Anglia (July 1549) led by Robert Kett. It was an orderly affair, the rebels (who proclaimed their loyalty to Somerset) being concerned mostly with reversing inclosures, and there was no looting or disorder. The ambitious E. of Warwick with a force of German mercenaries put it down and hanged Kett. One result of these conflicts between rapacious armed politicians and the poor or old fashioned was that the French attacked Boulogne (Aug.) and the govt. could send no reinforcements. The troops in Scotland had to be withdrawn (Sept.). The other result was that the politicians, who had long ceased to trust Somerset, were now able to discredit and supersede him (Oct. 1549). Warwick committed him to the Tower. The rot, however, accelerated. Boulogne fell (Jan. 1550).

(6) Warwick' now proposed a seeming alliance. He released Somerset (Feb. 1550): made peace with the French (Mar.) and married his son, John Dudley, to Somerset's daughter Anne (June). In fact he was building a party of dictatorship, religious extremism and a French connection against Somerset's policy of secular and ecclesiastical moderation, an imperialist-Burgundian alliance and some accommodation for P. Mary. Warwick encouraged private armies, flattered the King and, by prolonging the commissions of lieutenancy, superseded the military authority of the sheriffs. By Oct. 1551 he was ready. Somerset was again arrested and while Warwick was created D. of Northumberland and his other supporters given offices and titles, Somerset was condemned for felony (Dec.) and executed (Jan. 1551).

SHAA or SHAW, Sir Edmund (?-1488), financier, Master of the Goldsmiths Co. and Sheriff of London in 1474, was an important friend and supporter of Edward IV, Mayor of London in 1482 and an adviser to Richard III.

SHACKLETON, Sir Ernest Henry (1874-1922), Lieut. in the Antarctic Expedition of 1901, commanded that of 1908-9 with H.M.S. *Nimrod* and attained a point 97 miles from the S. Pole. In 1914-6 while trying to cross from

Coats Land to McMurdo Sound his ship *Endurance* was crushed in the ice and he with five others reached S. Georgia by boat. He died on a further voyage in the *Quest*.

SHADOW CABINET. Phrase first used c. 1907 but ex-ministers in the main opposition party met to decide on policy and share out tasks from the 1930s. The Conservative Shadow Cabinet acquired a regular status and secretariat in 1924; the Labour Party established one in 1945. A member who deals in opposition with the affairs of a particular govt. department has no customary claim to that department when his party comes into power.

SHAFTESBURY (Dorset) SHASTON, SCEPTESBURIE or ST. EDWARDESTOWE, ancient hilltop town, was fortified by Alfred c. 880, who founded a Benedictine nunnery under his *d*. Ethelgiva. The remains of King Edward the Martyr were buried there in 981 and it became a pilgrimage shrine, as well as a trading centre. Under the Normans it was the most important place west of Salisbury and it was chartered in 1252. Thereafter it ceased to develop in comparison with the coastal towns, to which improved shipping and safer trade routes diverted an increasing share of traffic. There were supplementary charters in 1604 and 1644 and it had two M.Ps. until 1832.

SHAFTESBURY, Es. of. *See* COOPER.

SHAGROON. An original, but not English settler in New Zealand. *cf* PILGRIM.

SHAH ALAM. *See* MOGULS.

SHAH JEHAN. *See* MOGULS; BENGAL.

SHAHU. *See* MARATHAS-5.

SHAKA or CHAKA. *See* ZULUS-1.

SHAKESPEARE, William (1564-1616) was educated at Stratford-on-Avon Free Grammar School, married Anne Hathaway in 1582, was probably a schoolmaster in a neighbouring village in 1585 and came to London in 1586. He apparently got a job in either the *Globe* or the *Curtain* Theatre, made the acquaintance of the E. of Southampton and later became an acting member of the Lord Chamberlain's Men, a company of players renamed the King's Men at the accession of James I. His earliest play is *Henry VI* (1591) followed by *Richard III* (1592). These may, with their propagandist flavour, have earned him favour at Court. His other works included the *Taming of the Shrew* (1593), *Venus and Adonis* (1593) and *Lucrece* (1594); the two latter were dedicated to Southampton. Most of the *Sonnets* appeared between 1593 and 1596 and are, by some, connected with that nobleman but others hold that the dark lady of them was Luce or Lucy Morgan or Negro (fl. 1593) a handsome African black who kept a brothel in Clerkenwell. There followed *Two Gentlemen of Verona, Love's Labours Lost* and *Romeo and Juliet* (1594-5), *Richard II* and *Midsummer Night's Dream* (1595-6). By this time he was no longer poor and bought a large town house at Stratford in 1597. *King John* and *The Merchant of Venice* also appeared at about this time and *Henry IV* a year later. Then followed *Much Ado About Nothing, As You Like It, Twelfth Night, Henry V* and *Julius Caesar* (1598-1600). *Hamlet* dates from 1600 or 1601 and so does *The Merry Wives of Windsor* which was traditionally written at the Queen's command. His Jacobean plays were *Measure for Measure* and *Othello* (160?-5), *King Lear* and *Macbeth* (1605-6), *Anthony and Cleopatra* (1606-7), *Coriolanus* and *Timon of Athens* (1607-8), *Pericles, Cymbeline* and *The Winter's Tale* (1608-11) and *The Tempest* (1612). He then retired, bought a house at Blackfriars and spent the rest of his life between Stratford and London.

SHANGHAI. *See* CHINA-22 *et seq*; CHINESE TREATY PORTS.

SHANS. *See* BURMA.

SHARIA or SHERIA is the sacred law of Islam based upon the *Koran*, the *Sunna* or practice of Mohammed, and the *Hadith* or traditions.

SHARP[E], Bartholomew (?1650-82) led the 1679 buccaneer attack on Santa Maria, Panama, crossed the Isthmus and seized a Spanish ship with which he cruised the American Pacific coast. In 1680 he found an atlas of the South Seas in a Spanish prize and used it to reach the W. Indies round the Horn. The translation which he presented to the King was the first source of information on the South Seas available in England. Appointed, by way of reward, to the command of a sloop, he deserted and died a buccaneer at Anguilla.

SHARP, Cecil James (1859-1924) began research into traditional English music in 1903, published his *Folk Songs of Somerset* in 1904 and founded the English Folk Dance Society in 1911.

SHARP, James (1613-79), Royalist Scottish divine, relative of the E. of Rothes, leader of the Resolutioners, was put in the Tower for a year by Cromwell in 1651. He lay low until Richard Cromwell's resignation and then made contact with Gen. Monck, on whose behalf and that of moderate Scottish church opinion he visited Charles II at Breda in 1660. One of his purposes, as Charles knew, was to re-establish episcopacy in Scotland and he became one of the King's chaplains (a necessary preliminary), ecclesiastical adviser to John Maitland (later D. of Lauderdale) and on his return to Scotland a Prof. of Divinity at St. Andrews. He was then immediately consecrated Abp. of St. Andrews and he, with Maitland and Rothes, became joint Vice-regents of Scotland. The Commonwealth period had polarised Scottish church opinion: the smug democracy of the Presbyterians and Kirk Sessions had alienated magnates and gentry and the latter's defection tended to create fanaticism among certain of the Covenanters, depressed by the worsening economics after the Restoration re-separation of the Kingdoms. Sharp now required ministers to seek their authority from bishops or patrons. About a third (mostly in the South-West) refused and were ejected. The four South-West counties became seriously disaffected (*see* PENTLAND REBELLION). The 1669 Letter of Indugence and Act of Supremacy followed by various methods of enforcement drove the opposition into further resistance (*see* INTERCOMMUNING; HIGHLAND HOST). He had already been shot at in 1668. Some Fifeshire Covenanters, on their way to murder the Sheriff-substitute of Fife, fortuitously met him and killed him instead.

SHARPE, Granville (1734-1813), born of an ecclesiastical family, was a confused libertarian. Originally concerned over the maltreatment of Jonathan Strong, a slave, he published a philippic against slavery in 1769, yet supported the American rebels, most of whose leaders owned slaves. In 1787 he became Pres. of the Anti-Slavery Society and helped to found Freetown. He also wanted to convert the Jews, and though he favoured Irish parliamentary autonomy and British parliamentary reform, he became chairman of the Protestant Union against R. Catholic emancipation.

SHAUGHNESSY, Thomas George (1853-1923) 1st Ld. SHAUGHNESSY (1916) worked in N. American railways all his life and as Vice-Pres. (1891-99) and Pres. (1899-1918) of the Canadian Pacific Railway, was mainly responsible for the development of its network and fleet.

SHAW, George Bernard (1856-1950), born in Dublin, came to London in 1876 and joined the Fabian Society for which he wrote tracts. In 1885 he took to journalism, beginning with brilliant musical criticism. His first play to be performed was *Widowers' Houses* (1892). He also took up dramatic criticism in 1895. His many plays, mostly political or social in content included *Mrs Warren's Profession* (1898), *John Bull's Other Island* (1907), *Pygmalion* (1912) and *St. Joan* (1924). He expounded his doctrines in *Prefaces* to his plays and in *The Intelligent Woman's Guide to Socialism and Capitalism.* His powerful intellect combined with a sardonic humour and a capacity for contriving paradoxical situations made him the most dangerous opponent of Edwardian complacency. He died a rich man, leaving part of his fortune for research into the possibilities of a phonetic alphabet and another large part to the British Museum, which also profited enormously from *My Fair Lady,* the musical version of *Pygmalion.*

SHAWE, John (1608-72), a Puritan, was chaplain to the Herbert family until 1641, then to Henry Rich, E. of Holland and then to the Parliamentary Commissioners to the King at Newcastle in 1646. His work thereafter centred upon Hull and Rotherham. Charles II made him a royal chaplain in 1660, but learning that he was a Puritan clerical politician in the north, had him prohibited from preaching in Hull after 1662. Thereafter he ministered only in private.

SHAW, (Richard) Norman (1831-1912), leading late Victorian architect, built many studios and country houses and New Scotland Yard on the Victoria Embankment (London).

SHAW, William (1749-1831) published his Gaelic Dictionary in 1780.

SHAW-LEFEVRE, Charles (1794-1888) 1st Vist. EVERSLEY (1857), M.P. from 1830 to 1857 was Chairman of the Commons Select Committee on Procedure in 1838 and as a result, became Speaker in 1839. He carried through many detailed and technical changes which made it easier for the Commons to deal with their growing volume of business, but which have been largely unacknowledged because of other noisier political events in the House over which he presided.

SHAWNEES, an 18th cent. Algonquian nomadic tribe on the R. Ohio, constituted a barrier against American penetration of the North West ceded to them under the T. of Paris (1783), but still occupied long after by the British. Their famous leaders **Tecumseh (1768-1813)** and his twin **Tenskwatawa (1768-1837)** (called the Prophet), organised a league on the principle that American soil was the common property of all the tribes, no one of which could alienate any part of it. They favoured peaceful settlement of disputes with the whites and banned the lucrative and corrupting trade in spirits. The immediate and long range possibilities of their policy alarmed the Indianans, whose Gov. William Henry Harrison attacked them in 1811 and defeated them at Tippecanoe. This calculated aggression won the next presidential election for Harrison and drove the Shawnees into alliance with the British in 1812 when Tecumseh, as a British Brig-Gen., was killed. The league broke up after further defeats in 1813 and with it the influence of his tribe.

SHEADING. One of the six divisions of the I. of Man, possibly created each to equip a warship. Later the landowners of each appointed four of the Keys. *See* DUNCE; SHIPSOKE TYNWALD.

SHEBEEN. An unlicensed Irish drinking house.

SHEEP. It seems that BRITAIN has always in historical times produced more sheep absolutely and relatively to the size of the country than any other European country. These, until modern times, consisted of the Scottish blackfaced varieties for coarse carpet wool; the long wool breeds (e.g. the Leicesters, Lincoln, Romney Marsh) most of which originated in Britain, for cloth and meat; the medium or short wool breeds (e.g. the Cheviots, Southdowns, the Dorsets and Clun Forest) many of which also originated in Britain, for meat. Various efforts were made as early as the Middle Ages to introduce the fine-wool *merino* from Spain, but apparently without success until late in the 18th cent (*see* SOMERVILLE).

AUSTRALIAN sheep raising began with the purchase by the First Fleet of some Cape Sheep at the Cape in 1788. Some Silesian merinos were brought in in 1797 and in 1802 Gov. Kent of N.S.W. sent a selection of fleeces to England with John Macarthur. British woollen manu-facturers were impressed and a Board of Trade inquiry reported favourably. As a result Macarthur and a partner were given 7000 acres in N.S.W. and some stud animals from the King's Merino stud at Kew. By 1813 there were 65,000 sheep in N.S.W. and 19,000 in Tasmania. By 1840 Tasmanian sheep alone numbered 1 million. There was then a setback due to droughts, overstocking and low world prices, but the 1850s gold rush brought a revival. In 1860 Australia had about 20M sheep: by 1890 there were nearly 110M. There followed a slump which by 1902 had brought numbers down to 53M. By 1910 they had risen to nearly 100M and thereafter, with oscillations, there has been an upward trend.

SHEERNESS. *See* SHEPPEY.

SHEFFIELD grew up around the 12th cent. church and castle in a part of the large manor of Hallam. Thomas of Furnival, the Lord of Hallam, granted a charter to the free tenants. They acquired other property which they lost under the Chantries Act of 1547. Mary I restored it but chartered a body of 12 capital burgesses to rule the town. Meanwhile the coincidence of iron, water power, plenty of fuel and millstone grit had already engendered a Hallam cutlery industry, most of whose products were sold at Sheffield. There was an informal Hallamshire Cutlers Co. or Guild by 1554, when it was marking goods, and this was incorporated in 1624 with juris-diction for six miles round Hallamshire. In 1740 Benjamin Huntsman moved to Handsworth in the manor and developed his crucible steel, while Thomas Bolsover developed silver plating. This resulted in Sheffield becoming the centre for finished high-grade steel and plated ware. The Co. gave up its regulating functions in 1812, but in 1856 Henry Bessemer set up his steel works at Sheffield and the production of cheap steel by his method made Sheffield a world centre. Electroplating came in in 1850 and caused a parallel development in plated goods. The town became a borough in 1843 and a county borough in 1893. The close relationship between the industries and their isolation in an enclosed valley made the craftsmen an inward looking and strongly unionised body and the use of capital-intensive plant after 1856 created strains in relations between craftsmen and capitalists later in the century.

SHEFFIELD (1) Sir Robert (?-1518), knighted after the B. of Stoke (1487) was Speaker in 1512. His grandson **(2) Edmund** (152?-49) **1st Ld. SHEFFIELD (1547)** was killed in Kett's rebellion. His grandson **(3) Sir Edmund (?1564-1646) 3rd Ld. (1568) 1st E. of MULGRAVE (1626)** was given Mulgrave for services against the second Armada (1591), became Gov. of Brill in 1599 and was Pres. of the Council of the North from 1603 to 1619. As a major investor in the Virginia and New England Cos. he naturally drifted into opposition to Charles I. His grandson **(4) Edmund (?1611-58) 2nd E.** was a member of Cromwell's Council of State. His son **(5) John (1648-1721) 3rd E., M. of NORMANBY (1694), D. of BUCKINGHAM and NORMANBY (1703),** a dashing individual, commanded the Tangier expedition of 1680, paid exaggerated court to the P. Anne in 1682 and was banished, but was recalled and made Lord Chamberlain by James II in 1685 and a member of the High Commission in 1686. William III, nevertheless, received him into favour until 1696 when he was dismissed in connection with the Fenwick affair. Anne at her accession made him Lord Privy Seal (which he resigned in 1705) and he was an English commissioner for the Union in 1706. He was extremely rich, privately influential but intermittently retiring and more interested in literary pursuits and the country life. Nevertheless he was a known supporter of the Hanoverian Succession, and Queen Anne's trust in him probably decided that George I should succeed. He was a patron of Dryden and Pope and left a number of literary works.

SHEIKH (1) The chief of an Arab tribe or clan. **(2)** Hence the ruler of certain Arab states. **(3)** The chief Moslem religious functionary in a non-tribal area or state, especially the *Sheikh-ul-Islam* who was the professional head in the Ottoman Empire. (4) A Moslem landowner in parts of N.W. India and Kashmir whose title was deduced from an original conquest.

SHELBURNE. See PETTY; PETTY-FITZMAURICE.

SHELBURNE GOVT. (July 1782-Apr. 1783). Eleven in Cabinet including the Younger Pitt (*see* GEORGE III-9). It could muster the reliable support of 140 M.P.s. (against Fox's 90 and North's 120) and attracted reformers, though Shelburne hoped to employ the prerogative for reform. His first innovation was to announce a programme. This consisted in an increase in county M.P.s., debt amortizations, a wider spread of taxation, lower customs and peace with America based upon economic co-operation and wide cessions on the Ohio. The French wanted the U.S.A. as a client unlikely to penetrate their Mississippi interests. The Americans abandoned them for Shelburne's territorial offer and this, with Rodney's victory off the Saints, left the French in a weak position (*see* P. OF PARIS 1783). The peace therefore represented a diplomatic success, but the Ohio cessions displeased patriotic feeling, while the economic complement to them (which required legislation) representing the abandonment of the long cherished mercantiism was ahead of its time. Worse still Shelburne would not explain the unity of his concept in public because he feared the votes of nationalists (North) and reforming businessmen (Fox). He could survive if supported by either. In fact they united to overthrow him. *See* PETTY, SIR WILLIAM.

SHELDON, Gilbert (1598-1677) became Warden of All Souls', Oxford in 1626, was ejected by the parliament-men in 1648, reinstated in 1659 and became Bp. of London in 1660. He presided ably over the Savoy Conference and in 1663 became Abp. of Canterbury. With his practical sense, he abandoned the clerical claim not to be taxed by parliament in 1664, carried through the difficult administrative task of re-establishing the Anglican Church and financed the Sheldonian Theatre, the beautiful meeting hall of Oxford University.

SHELL TRANSPORT & TRADING CO. See SAMUEL, SIR MARCUS.

SHELLEY, Percy Bysshe (1792-1822), poet and *enfant terrible,* was sent down from Oxford in 1811 for publishing *The Necessity of Atheism* and knew most of the contemporary literary figures. His *The Cenci* appeared in 1819, *Prometheus Unbound* in 1820 and *Adonais* in 1821. He was drowned at sea.

SHENANDOAH INCIDENTS. The Shenandoah, a Confederate warship, was repaired and allowed to recruit seamen by Sir Charles Darling, Gov. of Victoria, at Port Phillip (Australia), against U.S. protests. The British govt. had to pay compensation as a result of subsequent arbitrations. *See* ALABAMA.

SHEPHERD, George Robert (1881-1954) 1st Ld. SHEPHERD (1946) was national agent of the Labour Party from 1929 until 1945. His organising and managerial ability ensured that his party was ready for its tremendous victory in 1945.

SHEPPEY (Kent) on the Thames estuary, lies E. of the Medway and is separated from the mainland by the narrow but navigable Swale. In early times Elmley and Harty Isles, now part of it, were cut off at high tides. The whole was not thickly populated in Roman or Anglo-Saxon times. Sexburga, wife of Erconbert, King of Kent, founded a nunnery at Minster in 670, but the island was a favourite Viking landing place. The nunnery was several times sacked. It nevertheless maintained a tenuous but quarrelsome existence until the Dissolution. The two small manors belonged in 1084 to Odo of Bayeux and the Abp. of Canterbury. QUEENBOROUGH was founded on marshes drained in 1339. William of Wykeham built a castle nearby on the Swale in 1361 and in 1366 Edward III chartered Queenborough and named it in honour of

his Queen. It was a Tudor wool staple after the loss of Calais and in 1579 a chemical industry was begun. In 1582 the castle became the H.Q. of the Ld. Warden of the Cinque Ports, but it was demolished in the Civil War. Meanwhile the growing size of ships and the silting of the Medway led the Admiralty to transfer the Chatham Docks to SHEERNESS with the result that the Dutch attacked the island in 1667. This dock soon attracted the population away from Queenborough which began to decline. It was amalgamated with other Sheppey local govt. areas to form the borough of QUEENBOROUGH-IN-SHEPPEY in 1966. The naval dockyard remained in use until the forces reductions began in the 1980s.

SHEPWAY, COURT OF. A court under the Lord Warden, which entertained appeals from the Mayor and Jurats of the seven Cinque Port towns. Abolished after long inactivity in 1835.

SHERATON, Thomas (1751-1806), celebrated maker and designer of furniture, published his *Cabinet Makers' and Upholsterers' Drawing Book in* 1791 and his *Cabinet Dictionary* in 1803. He advocated a simple classical style from which he departed only at the end of his life. Many works attributed to him are copied from his books.

SHERBORNE (Dorset) founded by St. Aldhelm, was the bishopric of the W. Saxons west of Selwood from 705 to 1075. The abbey and school came into existence in 705, the Benedictine rule being introduced in 978. The abbey was rebuilt twice, the final 15th cent. structure having an irregular fan vault. The school suffered in the dissolution but was refounded in 1550. The castle, an Elizabethan mansion of 1594 near the site of a Norman castle, was built by Sir Walter Raleigh but became the seat of the Digby family which it remains.

SHERBROOKE, Vist. See LOWE, ROBERT.

SHERIDAN, Richard Brinsley (1751-1816) wrote a succession of famous comedies between 1775 and 1780 including *The Rivals* and *The Duenna* (both 1775), *School for Scandal* (1777) and *The Critic* (1779). He had, meanwhile, acquired Garrick's share in the Drury Lane Theatre in 1776. In 1780 he entered Parliament as a Foxite Whig and thereafter concentrated on politics. In 1787 and 1788 he managed the impeachment of Warren Hastings, making (*inter alia*) two still celebrated philipics against that statesman. In 1794 he opened his new theatre and from 1806 to 1807 he was Treasurer of the Navy in the Ministry of All the Talents. When his theatre caught fire in 1809 the Commons adjourned. In 1813 he was arrested for debt and ended his days suffering hallucinations.

SHERIFF (A.S. SCIREGEREFA = shire reeve). (1) A royal estate had to have a reeve or manager and it was convenient that debts and services due to the King from neighbouring landowners be paid to this reeve. He would naturally be a person of social standing able to face any debtor and once the practice of giving him extra-territorial functions was established, more duties might be added, including collection and consequently adjudication and then enforcement, whence it is a short step to a duty of keeping order. Originally there might be several in a shire, but the tendency was for one to overshadow the others and to act with the earl or alderman and the bishop, if any, in the shire moot. Such a reeve, holding a shire moot, first appears between 964 and 988. The policy behind this was the need to have a local officer of standing who could supervise the hundreds and provide the aldermen, who began to rule more than one shire, with a deputy in each. The sheriff's judicial powers began as those of the alderman. His military function as leader of the shire levy were the King's. Godric, Sheriff of Berkshire, was killed at Hastings.

(2) Some English sheriffs, e.g. Tofig in Somerset, retained office after the Conquest, but by 1071 nearly all were Norman barons (familiar with the Norman *vicomte*) and these were considered the head of their shire and mostly had large grants of land. Some shrievalties became hereditary, e.g. that of Worcestershire in the family of Urse d'Abetot, others ran in a family in practice, but the danger of such hereditary offices was recognised early and new ones were not created. The Norman sheriff was the King's executive as well as the chief judicial officer and consequently the recipient of writs. He was also, by now, the chief tax collector and accounted for the county *ferme*, eventually at the Exchequer. This was an extortionate process and by the 12th cent. outcry against shrieval malpractice was general. The compilers of Domesday had sworn the sheriffs as well as the local witnesses. This inquisition was not repeated, but Henry I began to employ new and less exalted men e.g. Osbert the Priest in Lincolnshire dependent upon himself. In some cases the office continued in a family and the new men were permitted to buy their rights by a *gersoma* or *fine pro comitatu habendo* (Lat: for having the county). This increased the Crown revenue, but did little for the oppressed until the appearance of itinerant justices, but meanwhile court administrators began to take the shrievalty of several counties and operate through under-sheriffs who could be dismissed easily. In 1129 Aubrey de Vere and Richard Basset jointly held eleven. Not surprisingly boroughs and others with ready cash would offer money for the privilege of paying their taxes direct.

(3) As the Exchequer became more efficient and knowledgeable it took advantage of the sheriffs' position, holding, for example, a sheriff accountable for his predecessor's arrears or fining him heavily for an escaped prisoner. In 1130 the four sheriffs of London paid 100 marks to quit office. The greatest change came at this period, however, for another reason. Until then many or most of the King's pleas had been held before the sheriff; they now began to be heard before itinerant justices (*see* EYRE) who could inquire into their doings or listen to local complainants against them. This would have reduced their prestige quickly if the civil wars of King Stephen had not interrupted ordinary life. Many sheriffs were still accounting for their *ferme*. Neither Stephen nor Matilda could supervise them properly. For example between 1140 and 1142 Geoffrey de Mandeville had the shrievalties of Essex, London, Middlesex and Hertfordshire combined with the justiciarship of those counties and the custody of the Tower of London. He was uncontrollable and his cruelties were legendary. Some sheriffs, e.g. those in Glamorgan and the Warenne sheriff in the Rape of Lewes even became baronial not royal officers.

(4) Henry II reasserted royal control and by 1170 sheriffs were his personal executives who had, besides their previous functions, become responsible for the feudal levy, or the correlative collection of scutage, the maintenance of castles and the execution of judgements. Richard I's financial demands accelerated these developments, but the shrievalty remained lucrative under him and his successor, John.

(5) During the confusions and difficulties of John's reign and the minority of Henry III, the sheriffs became increasingly institutionalised, serving govt. as such, rather than the particular monarch and becoming practically responsible to a govt. institution, the Exchequer. By Edward I's time the burden of work upon them and Exchequer pressure was imposing a work force. They had permanent offices as well as messengers. They were, if anything, even less popular than before. In 1300 (*Articuli Super Cartas c.* 8) Edward I enacted piously that they should be persons who will not make charges or sell offices or lodge too often in one place or with poor persons or monasteries. This enactment failed. The local populations did not want to appoint these despots themselves, they wanted no despots. They therefore welcomed arrangements which reduced their power. This

had been begun by itinerant justices. It was continued by custodians and justices of the peace who were taking over the control of public order, but a fruitful line of attack was to reduce their period of office. In 1334 it was enacted that they should not hold office for two consecutive years. This was confirmed in 1368 but was ineffectual for lack of sanctions. Consequently in 1444 it was enacted that a sheriff holding office contrary to law should forfeit £200 a year, half to the Crown, half to any private prosecutor, of whom there was no shortage. Such an annual officer could not be head of the police system or effective commander of the county force. Thenceforth he became a ceremonial officer with only routine duties mostly performed by someone else.

SHERIFFS, INQUEST OF (1170) was an inquiry into the conduct of local officials (not only sheriffs or royal appointees). Large misapplied funds were recovered and many of the lords holding shrievalties were replaced by trained Exchequer officials.

SHERIFS are descendants of Mohammed. The word was also used as a title of certain Moslem rulers, notably the Sultan of Morocco and the Gov. of Mecca.

SHERRY. *See* WINE TRADE-3.

SHETLAND Is. were settled from Norway, of which they became a dependency in 875. They were ceded to Scotland in 1469. *See* JAMES III OF SCOTS ORKNEYS.

SHIITES. *See* CALIPHATE.

SHILLELAGH (Wicklow, Ire.). The wood nearby gave its name to the well known knobbly Irish club.

SHILLIBEER, George. *See* OMNIBUS.

SHILLING (OF ACCOUNT). *See* COINAGE-4.

SHILLING (COIN). *See* COINAGE-14.

SHINTO. A Japanese religious system in which all things have their eternal divinity. There is hence no important difference between life and death and also a natural polytheism and an ability to incorporate concepts from other religious philosophies (e.g. Buddhism) or polytheistic systems (e.g. Hinduism). One branch of these doctrines led to the deification of the Emperor (*Tenno,* or in European usage *Mikado*) who, besides, traces his descent from the Sun Goddess Amaterasu; another was the basis of the selfless bravery of the Japanese soldier; a third, the custom now in decline, of committing suicide (*Sepuku* or in European usage *Harakiri*) in order to make a point or obtain release from a hereditary obligation; a fourth, a remarkably delicate aestheticism in art, food and manners. Shinto was naturally inconsistent with monotheistic religions such as Christianity which was, after a short period of tolerant misunderstanding, persecuted from the early 18th cent. until the Meiji restoration. *See* BUSHIDO.

SHIP MONEY, CASE OF or R. v HAMPDEN (1637-8). *See* CHARLES I-9-11.

SHIP MONEY FLEETS were sent out annually between 1635 and 1641 to clear the Narrow Seas of pirates and the Dutch fishing boats from the English east coast fishing grounds. They were successful, but grew increasingly expensive until the levy of shipmoney on inland communities provoked the ship money crisis.

SHIPPING, MINISTRIES OF (1) 1916-19; (2) 1939-46 were both concerned with the direction of shipping and related resources in wartime.

SHIP SOKE. An Anglo-Saxon coastal district assessed to support one warship (cf SHEADING).

SHIPS, POWER DRIVEN. The first steam boats were J. C. Perier's on the R. Seine in 1775 and Patrick Miller's, a twin hulled centre paddle boat on the Clyde in 1788. The first practical steamboat was Hart's and Symington's stern-wheeler *Charlotte Dundas,* which pulled two 70 ton barges some 19 miles on the Forth and Clyde Canal in 1802, but was not put into service. In 1807 Robert Fulton started a regular service between Albany and New York with the paddle steamer *Clermont.* This is generally regarded as opening the new era. Henry Bell's (1767-

1830) *Comet* introduced the first European commercial service on the Clyde in 1811. The first iron steamship was the *Aaron Manby* built in 1821. The first naval steamer was the paddleship H.M.S. *Lightning* (1823). Ericsson's experiment with screws (1837) was adopted by Brunel in 1840 and the Royal Navy built its first screw vessel in 1843, but the screw superseded paddles in commercial practice only in the '60s. The delay arose from the revolutionary effect on ship construction and design, for the slow acting transverse high level paddle system necessarily required a different sort of ship from the fast rotating longitudinal screw, low down in the hull.

Until 1837, when the paddle ship *Sirius* crossed the Atlantic under continuous steam, seagoing steamships were, in fact, sailing ships with auxiliary means of rounding navigational hazards in difficult winds. The need to de-salt boilers used much coal and made engine operation intermittent; moreover coaling stations were rare. It was the invention of a practical condenser which made the *Sirius* voyage possible. In 1838 the paddleship *Great Western* (1778 tons), the first ship designed for the Atlantic run, crossed in 15 days, 5 hours. The same owners commissioned I. K. Brunel's beautiful *Great Britain* (3448 tons): the first transatlantic screw steamer, she crossed in 14 days 21 hours in 1845. From 1847 the British Admiralty was extending screw propulsion to existing ships of the line. The first specially designed screw propelled battleship was the *Agamemnon*, launched in 1852. The last important oceanic paddle-steamer was the *Scotia* which crossed the Atlantic in 8 days in 1862, her record being matched by the screw *City of Paris* in 1867. In the 1880s some govts. began to subsidise larger liners for use as auxiliary cruisers in wartime. Ships became larger and faster and with more than one screw. The *Lucania* (12,950 tons) could do 22 knots.

(2) The decisive change from sail and wood to steam and metal occurred between 1870 (when British registered tonnage was: sail 4.5M, steam 0.9M) and 1885 (sail 3.4M, steam 4.00 M). Ships of all kinds were built of wood, or wood on iron frames ("composite") or of iron, but steel was superseding iron. The changes were related to considerations of fire safety and vibration, but the use of steel was due to cheapening of steel production by the Bessemer and Siemens-Martin processes after 1879.

(3) The fastest sailing ships, the clippers (e.g. the *Cutty Sark,* 1869), lost their most profitable runs when the Suez Canal was opened in 1869, but the introduction, between 1863 and 1872 of successively improved compound engines, was already cutting their rivals' fuel consumption by half and increasing speed and reliability. The new steamers cost less to propel and space saved from coal bunkers could be used for cargo. Steamships now began to carry bulk, such as grain, instead of being confined to passengers and light valuable goods. In 1881 triple expansion engines suddenly increased speeds. In 1884 the Cunarder *Umbria* made the crossing in under six days. The expansion of steam shipping denoted a much larger expansion of seaborne trade, for steamers were not only faster than sailing ships, but less influenced by adverse weather.

(4) In 1872 the Navy introduced vertical reciprocating engines behind armour and varieties of these with improved boilers and condensers came into use. Propellers of better shape, sometimes in sets, were developed, but it was found that above 2000 r.p.m. they needed large increases in power to achieve small gains in speed. Parsons elaborated a new principle in the steam turbine; this was relatively light and (unlike reciprocating engines) could be accommodated on a single deck. He demonstrated his *Turbinia* to the Admiralty in 1897. The first turbine-driven warship (H.M.S. *Viper*) followed in 1900, the first battleship (H.M.S. *Dreadnought*) in 1906. The turbine propelled Cunarder *Carmania* plied the

Atlantic in the same year, followed by the 27-knot *Mauretania* in 1907.

(5) British world power had to be supported on many well placed coaling stations (e.g. Gibraltar, Cape Town, Aden, Colombo) and a big fleet of commercial colliers to supply them with 'Best Welsh' (S. Wales anthracite) which the Admiralty preferred. The coal carrying trade was a prominent feature of British shipping until the 1920s. Meanwhile Fisher at the Admiralty had gone over to oil firing with the *Dreadnought* for technical reasons; hence British interest in the Persian Gulf and the development of the oil-tanker. The diesel engine had been invented in 1897 but it had to await large oil supplies to develop, and remained a source of low rather than high power until World War II. Ships continued to grow in size but not significantly in speed: the liner *Queen Elizabeth* (1940) was over 83,000 tons, but could make only 27½ knots. The typical large or fast ship between the wars was oil fired and turbine powered, sometimes, as in U.S. warships, through electric motors, while low powered or small ships used reciprocating or diesel engines.

(6) In World War II the performance of diesels was notably improved and after it aircraft began to take over the carriage of passengers and light valuables. The smaller ocean-going ships were driven out of business and superseded by immense carriers for oil, ores and other bulk. The colliers virtually disappeared, but smaller efficient diesel driven ships appeared in large numbers to serve specialised purposes, such as the Dutch-English vegetable trade to Boston, or harbours such as Marseilles inaccessible to very large ships.

SHIPS, SAILING. (1) Mediterranean *carvel* building dates from earliest times. The planks were laid edge to edge onto prealigned ribs. In the early Middle Ages such ships mostly had lateen sails. N. European ship building developed independently and dates from the 6th cent. The ships were *clinker* built; the planks overlapped, the ribs were inserted afterwards and the sails were always square.

Early Nordic. The boats used for the Anglo-Saxon invasion must have been small and therefore numerous. The reliable evidence dates from later periods when nordic ships were already larger. The *Oseberg ship* (9th cent.) is about 69 ft. long, the *Gokstad ship* (10th cent.) 76 ft. and Olav Trygvasson's exceptional *Long Serpent* (*Ormen Lange*) (11th cent.) about 150 ft. These are all Scandinavian and were basically warships. They were known as *Drakkar, Skeid* or **Longships.** By the 10th cent. they were classified: the smallest warship was "20-roomed", i.e. it had 20 oars a side and 40 rowers. The *Long Serpent* was 34-roomed. There were external steering paddles. Fighting was hand to hand.

(2) Merchantmen called *Knorr,* or later **Cogs,** were wider and shorter than warships and relied on sail. The rudder was introduced in the 12th cent. The 13th cent. *Kalmar boat* is about 36 ft. long; the *Bremen cog* 77 ft. long, could load about 130 tons.

(3) *Early Mediterranean.* In the comparatively windless Mediterranean the early mediaeval warship was the **galley** and its relatives. It had a ram and was distinguished by the large number of its rowers and so could keep going for some while in a calm. The rowing speed was not great: in calm weather a galley could make about five miles headway in the first hour, falling to about one mile in the third and later hours.

The merchant ship was the so-called **Roundship** which unlike the cog had a rounded bow, two or sometimes three masts and a bowsprit. Most Western Mediterranean roundships came from five ports, namely Venice, Pisa and Genoa, Marseilles and Barcelona.

(4) *Interpenetration of types.* Piracy was a normal part or hazard of trade. The Venetians habitually used warships to carry cargoes of low bulk and high value.

Conversely merchantmen developed warlike arrangements, of which the fore-and-stern-castles were the most obvious. Moreover the tempestuous ocean challenged the northern and Atlantic shipbuilder to continual development. The cog with its rudder and square sail reached Marseilles in 1304, where it was promptly copied. The lateen rigged *mizzen* mast, to facilitate the steering of square rigged ships, appeared in the 1360s. The Portuguese had three-masted cogs with lateen mizzens in the early 15th cent. By 1470 **Carracks** or Kraeks of this type were also being built in the Low Countries. They had guns and were the ancestors of the later sailing warships. Fairly soon the handling difficulties created by the high castles resulted in big ships having four masts, the fourth or *bonaventure* being lateen rigged like the mizzen. The English *Henri Grace a Dieu* or *Great Harry*, built in 1514, was of this type. She was rebuilt between 1536 and 1539 with lower castles and armed with heavy guns between decks.

(5) Meantime Venetian experiments with oar-driven sailing ships called **galleasses** produced a slimmer hull and shifted the forecastle within the bows. The **Galleon** was an ocean going oarless combination of the major features of the galleasse and of the new type of carrack. Galleasses distinguished themselves at Lepanto (1572) and though four of them played a sensational but not very effective role with the Armada, the principal ships on both sides were galleons.

(6) Almost all later sailing warships developed from galleons. Phineas Pett's *Prince Royal* (1610) had 56 guns on three decks. By 1626 the lowering of the castles had made a reversion to three masts possible. The great *Sovereign of the Seas* (later *Royal Sovereign*) launched in 1637 was a three-masted 100 gunner. She was a century ahead of her time and her expense had a connection with the shipmoney crisis. In 1653 the Admiralty directed that ships should fight in line ahead. This presupposed a certain uniformity of armament and speed and it became necessary to classify ships according to their ability to take their place in a given **Line of Battle**, as well as for other purposes such as supply and officers' promotion. The result was the following system of rating:

Ships of the Line

First Rates	90 guns and over
Second Rates	80-88
Third Rates	50-78

Ships not of the Line

Fourth Rates	38-48
Fifth Rates	20-36
Sixth Rates	8-18

(7) A **Frigate**, originally any small warship, came to be a full rigged ship with one complete gun-deck and no more. A **Pinnace** then became a miniature full rigged ship, but was also used for trade. Its commonest mercantile rival was the **Flute** or **Fluyt**, a small Dutch full rigged vessel with a rounded stern. At this time there were over 10,000 Dutch merchantmen and they engrossed more than half the Baltic trade. The method of tonnage measurement employed by the Danish customs on the Sound distorted the hull design of the flute until the method was altered in 1669. It eventually developed into the very common **Pink.** Throughout the sailing era merchant ships were much smaller, on average, than warships. The largest merchant ships were employed on the East India route, where the very largest Dutchmen ran to 54 guns and the largest British were frigates somewhat smaller.

(8) *18th Century*. In France Colbert engaged the best naval architects of the time, while in England the Admiralty hamstrung its own by conservative regulations. The result was that from 1670 for 150 years French warships were mostly better than English. In particular

they were slightly wider and the extra buoyancy raised the lower deck gun-ports (where the heaviest guns were) higher above water. Hence in anything above a very moderate breeze a French two-decker could fire as much metal as an English three-decker. The French then concentrated on two-deckers of 76 and 80 guns which outclassed and could outsail the standard English two-decker, the 74, and which could hold their own against much bigger ships. The French naval failures against Britain were due to a misconceived naval policy, poor leadership and bad training, not to poor design or equipment. French ships were designed partly for service against the agile Barbary and Dalmatian pirates, who used small fast **Xebecs** or chebecks and **Polaccas**. Both developed from the galley, the Xebec being lateen rigged, the polacca having a square rigged main mast. They operated in hundreds mainly from N. African strongholds. To counter them, the **Sloop** was a frigate-rigged ship of about 18 guns which could be rowed, while the **Bomb Ketch,** a broad ship with the foremast removed, mounted heavy mortars in its place on reinforced beams. The French first used such ketches to bombard Algiers in 1682 and European bombardments of pirate nests were a feature of naval warfare until the powers occupied N. Africa in the mid-19th cent.

(9) By the end of the Seven Years' War (1756-63) most British Line of Battle ships were 74s, with a few larger three-deckers like the *Victory* being built between 1759 and 1765. The 64 was still reckoned as fit for the Line, but the 50 gunship was not. All ships had strong sides, but weak ends with only a bulkhead behind the beak and windows in the stern galleries. A single well-aimed raking broadside could put a ship out of action. This was the principle behind the manoeuvre of breaking the enemies' lines practised by British admirals in the later 18th cent. At Trafalgar the leading British ships suffered severely before they could break through and get under their enemies' sterns. Hence the last sailing fleet action, at Navarino in 1827, was fought by ships whose ends had been enclosed.

(10) The advent of steam ended the sailing warship era in about 1861 (*see* IRONCLADS), but sailing merchant ships continued for some time, getting larger and larger and equipped with devices for saving manpower. The first **Clipper** in modern parlance was the *Rainbow*, launched at New York in 1845. The tea clippers raced from the East each year from this time and rigs were simplified, steel masts and ropes came in and steam winches were used to operate the sails. All the same the main sail era ended, save for training and sport in about 1900, though the five-masted *Preussen* was launched in 1902 and the three-masted barque *Pommern* in 1903. Coastal traffic continued regularly until 1914 and irregularly until 1939.

SHIRE (A.S. *Scire* **= care or official charge)** could originally mean an office and so the area (e.g. province, bishopric, region) over which it was exercised and thence a union of hundreds, wapentakes or wards for purposes of justice, taxation or military administration. *See* COUNTY.

SHIRE MOOT. *See* COUNTY COURT.

SHIRLEY or SHERLEY (1) Sir Anthony (1565-?1635) and **(2) Sir Robert (?1581-1628)** sons of Sir Thomas (of *Shirley's Case*) were adventurers. Anthony, initially a fellow of All Souls' College, Oxford, turned to military adventure and, after a piratical interlude with Essex against the Portuguese (1506-7), went to Persia as a supposed diplomatic agent and was returned as a Persian ambassador-at-large to European powers (1607-14). The reason for these singular and ineffectual arrangements was that Persia wanted allies against Turkey but did not understand European conditions, whereas Essex wished to attract Persian interest in a European attack on Turkey, leading to the acquisition of English trading advantages in the Mediterranean. When Essex fell, Anthony was forbidden the realm. He died at the Spanish Court in poverty.

SHIRLEY'S CASE (1604). Sir Thomas Shirley, an M.P., was held in the Fleet prison for debt. The Commons imprisoned the Warden of the Fleet and passed a declaratory bill asserting their privilege from arrest save for treason, felony and breach of the peace. The bill was passed by the Lords and received the Royal Assent, Shirley being released. The principle was occasionally transgressed in Stuart times and also deeply eroded by the regular creation of new statutory felonies.

SHIRLEY v FAGG 6 St. Tr 1122. This case established the House of Lords' jurisdiction to hear appeals from the Court of Chancery.

SHOGUNS. See JAPAN.

SHOPS HOURS. An Act of 1892 protected *young persons* from working in a shop for more than 74 hours a week and obliged county and borough councils to enforce it by inspection. An Act of 1911 required meal intervals and one half-holiday a week for *all* shop assistants. From 1928 closure at 9 p.m. was permitted on one day a week, 8 p.m. on the other days. In 1934 young persons were restricted to 48 hours a week and the legislation included provisions on heat, light and ventilation. In 1938 persons under 16 were restricted to 44 hours and during World War II all shops had to close at 6 p.m. This was made permanent in 1950 with a one-day exception until 7.30 p.m. After 1960 there was a tendency to relax these limitations, often extra-legally. An Act of 1995 legalised the *fait accompli*, save in relation to Sunday sales of alcohol. *See* SUNDAY OBSERVANCE.

SHOP STEWARDS MOVEMENT. *See* TRADE UNIONS-5.

SHORE, Jane (?-1527), beautiful and witty daughter of a London mercer and wife of a goldsmith, was Edward IV's mistress from about 1470 until his death. She was also mistress of Thomas Grey, 1st M. of Dorset, elder son of Elizabeth Woodvile and then of William, Lord Hastings, Chamberlain to Edward V. She was thus involved in the politics leading to Richard III's *coup d'état*. After Hastings' execution (1483) Richard accused her of sorcery and forced her to do a public penance. She died in obscurity.

SHORE, John (1751-1834) 1st Ld. TEIGNMOUTH (Ir.) (1798), Asst. to the Revenue at Murshidabad in 1770, he found himself at 19 in charge of a large district. Promoted in 1772, he was also Persian interpreter to the Murshidabad Revenue in 1773. From June 1775 a member of the Bengal Revenue Council until its dissolution in 1780, he was appointed to its successor the Bengal Revenue Committee, by Warren Hastings, to whom he had previously been opposed. This was due to his hardworking selflessness and phenomenal knowledge. In 1784, as a result of a breach of confidence by John Macpherson, Shore resigned and returned home with Hastings.

The directors now appointed him to a seat on the supreme council and in 1789 he made the decennial but in the event permanent Land Revenue Settlement of Bengal, Bihar and Orissa. Its permanence was due to his misunderstood decision to treat Zamindars as landowners. He then returned to England to give evidence for Hastings at his impeachment.

In 1793, despite Burke's protests, he returned to Bengal to succeed Cornwallis as Gov.-Gen. The period was one of great difficulty. He was temperamentally more interested in trade and economics than in politics and this chimed in with the views of the HEIC, which instructed him to maintain a strictly pacific policy. On the other hand Indian powers with French advisers, and British political figures were adopting more aggressive attitudes. Thus British territorial prosperity grew at a time when the dangers outside were growing too. In particular Maratha and Sikh influence was expanding at the expense of Britain's allies and so were the resources and intrigues of Tippoo Sahib. He resigned in 1798, before these

movements had reached a flash point and devoted the residue of his life to learned and charitable pursuits.

SHOREDITCH (London) an always poor square mile immediately to the north of the City, had the first English theatres (*The Theatre* 1576, *The Curtain* c. 1577). These were soon moved to Southwark. By 1740 when the mediaeval church was rebuilt, the area had an important timber trade which naturally led to furniture making, and the population was about 10,000. 19th cent. industrialisation created overcrowding and some of the worst slums in Britain. By 1939 the population was 40,000. The health and slum problems were solved by German bombing in World War II and the need to rebuild.

SHORT PARLIAMENT (13 Apr.-5 May 1640) was summoned by Charles I to raise money for the second Bishops' War. The Lord Keeper, Finch, invited members to grant the money before debating other matters. Pym in a studiedly moderate speech enumerated all the grievances raised under the previous 11 years of unparliamentary govt. and they insisted on discussing other matters first. A debate on the Scots was scheduled for 7 May. Charles learned that it might produce a petition against the war. There being no hope of obtaining the 12 subsidies requested in return for the abandonment of ship money, he hurriedly dissolved this parliament.

SHOVELL, Sir Cloudesley or Clowdisley (1650-1707), seaman, cut out the corsairs at Tripoli (1676) and cruised against the Barbary pirates until 1686. He was Rear Admiral in the Irish Sea in 1690 and 2-in-C at Barfleur (1692), where he broke the French line. He was C-in-C in the Channel in 1686-7, became M.P. for Rochester from 1698 and was Comptroller of Victualling as well as C-in-C in the Channel from 1699 to 1704 when, with Rooke, he captured Gibraltar and fought the B. of Malaga. Next he co-operated with Peterborough at Barcelona (1705) and with the Austrians and Savoyards before Toulon (1707), where he destroyed the French Mediterranean Fleet. His brilliant career ended abruptly in a shipwreck on the Scillies when he reached the beach exhausted and a woman murdered him for his ring.

SHRAPNEL, Henry (1761-1842) invented the explosive shell loaded with bullets named after him, with an extra L, and secured its adoption by the British army in 1803.

SHREWSBURY (A.S. SCROBBESBYRIG, Welsh AMWYTHIG). (1) In the 5th to the 6th cents. was the seat of the Princes of Powys until the Mercians took it (c. 778). It was fortified at an early date and under Edward the Elder had a mint. Roger of Montgomery made it the H.Q. of his Shropshire palatinate in 1071; he improved and extended the castle and founded the abbey. The city's position in a loop of the Severn gave it great strength so that it functioned for two centuries as a border fortress until the conquest of Gwynedd (1282-4). All the same Edward I rebuilt the castle at this time and it remained a royal fortress until 1690 when the Crown sold it.

(2) The pacification of Wales brought great prosperity especially from the wool and cattle trade, evidenced in the town's many fine mediaeval buildings. The public school was founded in 1552 from the assets of other dissolved schools, chantries and the abbey. The town was Royalist in the Civil War.

(3) The Industrial Revolution extended the scope of the already well developed markets and brought locomotive and then general engineering industries.

SHREWSBURY, B. of (21 July 1403) between rebels led by Sir Henry Percy ('Hotspur'), his uncle the E. of Worcester and the E. of Douglas, and the Royal forces led by Henry IV, the Prince of Wales, and the E. of Stafford. By a forced march to Shrewsbury, the King arrived before Hotspur's father, the E. of Northumberland, and Glendower, the Welsh prince, could reinforce the rebels. The King offered to treat but was refused and after a long and bloody battle in which both sides suffered 4500 casualties, the King at nightfall held the field, though isolated skirmishing continued. Hotspur was killed, Worcester (later executed) and Douglas captured. The battle ended the Percy-Glendower rebellion.

SHREWSBURY, D. of. *See* GEORGE I-3.

SHREWSBURY, Es. of. *See* TALBOT.

SHRIEVALTY. The office of sheriff.

SHROPSHIRE or SALOP (1) was thinly populated in pre-Roman and Roman times by the Cornovii; the Roman and indeed the only urban centre was Viroconium (Wroxeter) on the Severn, some 7 miles S.W. of modern Shrewsbury. It was stormed and left deserted at the turn of the 4th-5th cents., presumably by Anglo-Saxons.

(2) In due course the area became part of Mercia with a fluctuating frontier towards Wales and special arrangements, including a privileged sheriff, for keeping order. After the Conquest, Saxon resistance was overcome by 1070 and in 1074 William I erected the shire into a palatinate for **Roger of Montgomery (?-1094)** who had interests elsewhere. His sheriff, Warin the Bald (?-?1085) had a large block of manors along the N.W. border and he and his stepson Hugh were the effective defenders of the frontier. The palatinate passed from Roger to his sons **Hugh (?-1098)** and **Robert of Bellême (r. 1098-1102),** but William Rufus suppressed it in 1102 and placed it under local justiciars. These held it until 1126 when it was granted to Queen Adela. As a result Shropshire had no Earl and the important local official continued to be the sheriff, whose office became hereditary in the FitzAlan family and then continued with the Le Strange.

(3) It was impossible to pursue criminals across the border or into the neighbouring palatinates and liberties. Hence Shropshire successfully claimed exemption from frank pledge and its associated *murdrum* and presentment of Englishry. On the other hand there was a special duty (Stretward A.S. = highway watch) between Michaelmas and Martinmas designed to catch stolen cattle. This had been commuted for money by 1255, probably because the marcher lordships erected by then formed an effective block.

(4) Of the 15 Domesday hundreds, the whole, or the greater part of the five border hundreds had been converted into marcher lordships and withdrawn from the county by about 1200. Three families were involved: of these the FitzAlans (Oswestry) and the Mortimers (Wigmore) had interests elsewhere and in national politics. The Corbets (Caus) were exclusively a marcher family. Within the county there were a number of private and ecclesiastical franchises free of their hundreds and the three substantial borough franchises of Bridgnorth, Much Wenlock and Shrewsbury. The conquest of Gwynedd destroyed the purpose of marcher lordships and other special frontier arrangements, with the result that from about 1327 the Crown took stronger hold of the administration and occasionally challenged the franchises. *See* MARCHER LORDSHIPS: WALES AND THE MARCHES, COUNCIL OF; UNION, ACTS OF.

SHROVE TIDE, before the Reformation corresponded with Carnival or *Fasching* on the Continent, when people had a final fling before Lent. The extremely violent shrovetide football survived into the 1950s in some midland villages.

SHUTE. *See* BARRINGTON.

SIBBALD, Sir Robert (1641-1722), educated at Edinburgh, Leyden and Angers, founded the Edinburgh Royal Coll, of Physicians in 1681 and the Scottish Botanical Gardens there in 1667. In 1682 Charles II appointed him one of his physicians and also Geographer of Scotland and in 1685 Prof. of Medicine at Edinburgh. The mob hounded him out of Edinburgh in 1686 for his temporary and politic conversion to R. Catholicism and he moved permanently to London.

SIBBENS. *See* SYPHILIS.

SIBERIA. Russian penetration across the Urals began in 1581, mostly by independent parties of huntsmen and trappers engaged in the lucrative fur trade. They followed a narrow eastward line of development, founding Tomsk on the Ob in 1604, Yakutsk on the middle Lena in 1632 and reaching the Sea of Okhotsk in 1639. The L. Baikal area had to be subdued (1641-52), but the Chinese forced the Russians to relinquish the Amur valley (T. of Nerchinsk 1689). Iron and non-ferrous mining began in the 18th cent., gold in the 19th, but the area was inhabited (as opposed to settled) only by nomads whom the Russians treated as subjects in an imperial province. The Amur became the Russo-Chinese frontier in 1858 (T. of Aigun) and Vladivostok was founded in 1860. The first Tran-Siberian railway was completed between 1891 and, save at L. Baikal, 1894. This was decisive for the sub-continent's development, whose population in 1897, at 7.75M, was still only 2 per sq. mile. The fertile soil supported a prosperous agriculture which was soon exporting dairy products westwards, even to Britain. Industrialisation began during World War I. The local prosperity and foreign connections were destroyed in the Revolution and by agricultural collectivisation, and industrial development was pursued regardless of the environment after 1950. By 1990 the Sea of Aral had shrunk to a mere lake and L. Baikal was suffering from grave pollution.

Siberia was a place of banishment of a relatively free type under the Empire, but afterwards it contained the slave or 'corrective' labour camps described by Solzhenitzyn.

SICCA (RUPEE) originally a newly coined rupee of full weight, but between 1793 and 1836 the Bengal govt. coined so-called sicca rupees which were of greater weight than HEIC rupees.

SICILY (1) with its Arab and Greek population, was conquered under Papal auspices by the Norman **Robert Guiscard (r. 1059-85)** and his brother **Count Roger I (r. 1085-1101)** between 1060 and 1091. Roger established a tolerant govt. in which Greeks, Arabs and other Normans, including Anglo-Normans, were employed. His successors conquered Apulia and Calabria (1127-39), obtained a royal title (1130 and 1138) and between 1146 and 1160 even occupied a large part of the N. African coast. These conquests were due to the large Sicilian navy; Sicilian Mediterranean ambitions brought the Kingdom into conflict with the Byzantines which lasted intermittently until 1185.

(2) The Kingdom (by now very rich) became entangled in the conflict between the Papacy and the Hohenstaufen. There had always been a fairly active connection between English and Sicilian Normans, so that when the Papacy, as suzerain, sought rival candidates for the Sicilian throne, acceptance by Henry III on behalf of his son Edmund (1252) was not strange; but English political opinion would not support the expense of the necessary war and in 1265 the Kingdom was allotted to Charles of Anjou, who was evicted from the island in the Sicilian Vespers (1282) (*see* LOUIS IX; PHILIP III OF FRANCE) in favour of Peter III of Aragon. Hence until 1442 the island had Aragonese rulers, while the mainland (called the Kingdom of Naples) had Angevin. In that year Alphonso V of Aragon expelled René of Anjou and the two parts were reunited, but from 1458 to 1500 and from 1500 to 1503 Naples was held by an illegitimate son of Alphonso's. Thereafter the two parts were united until 1707.

(3) The island passed to Savoy in 1713, to Spain in 1718 and to Austria in 1720. In 1733 under the T. of Escorial between France, Savoy and Spain, both parts were conquered by Don Carlos of Spain, who in 1738 took the title of the King of the Two Sicilies. His son Ferdinand married the strong minded Archduchess Maria Carolina in 1767 and she, with the English general Acton,

was the effective but not sole ruler in a govt. which was becoming effete. The Kingdom was by now becoming important to the British strategically and because English traders were investing in Sicily. In the Napoleonic Wars Sicily formed an important British protective position against Bonapartist oriental ambitions, and though Joachim Murat established himself as King in Naples, he was never able to cross the straits of Messina, and the increasingly oppressive Bourbon regime was re-established after the Congress of Vienna. It was the corruption, incompetence and cruelty of this regime which inspired Italian liberals to treat Italian unification as an essential part of their liberalism. With some minor English voluntary aid, the whole establishment collapsed like a house of cards when Garibaldi and his Thousand attacked it in 1860. *See* MARSALA RICHARD I; WORLD WAR II-13.

SICKERT, Walter (1860-1942) assistant to Whistler and a friend of Degas was an English impressionist painter contemporary with the French impressionists (*but see* TURNER, J.M.W.).

"SICK MAN OF EUROPE", the Czar Nicholas I's description of Turkey in a conversation with the British Ambassador in 1853.

SIDDONS and KEMBLE. The most notable members of this acting dynasty were **(1) Roger KEMBLE (1721-1802)** travelling actor-manager from 1753. Of his children **(a) John Philip (1757-1823)** was the chief founder of the declamatory style and flourished at Drury Lane from 1783 to 1802, his wife **(b) Priscilla (1756-1845)** acting with him. **(c) Stephen (1758-1822)** and his wife **Elizabeth (1763-1841)** were actor-managers and launched John Kemble and Mrs Siddons at Edinburgh. **(d) Charles (1775-1854)** was actor-manager at Covent Garden from 1822 to 1832; his wife **Marie Therese (de CAMP) (1774-1838)** acted with him. He was primarily a comedian. His daughter **(e) Fanny (Frances) (1809-93)** frequently appeared with him, but spent much of her life in America. Roger's daughter **(2) Sarah or Mrs SIDDONS (1755-1831)** was engaged by Garrick in 1775, reached celebrity in 1783 and acted permanently at Covent Garden from 1806 to 1812 when she retired. Her son **(a) Henry (1774-1815)** was manager at Edinburgh where he was much helped by Sir Walter Scott. His wife **(b) Harriet (1783-1844)** played Shakespearian leads at Covent Garden and Drury Lane from 1798 to 1809.

SIDGWICK, Henry (1838-1900). Cambridge philosopher, resigned the lectureship in moral philosophy at Trinity to which he had just been appointed because he favoured the abolition of religious tests for office (1869). He returned in 1875 and campaigned vigorously for women's higher education. This led to the foundation of Newnham Hall (later Coll.) in 1876 when he married Eleanor Balfour (sister of A. J.) who became Pres. of Newnham in 1892. In 1881 he secured the admission of women to the University. A disciple of John Stuart Mill, he wrote extensively on ethics and politics.

SIDMOUTH, Viscount. *See* ADDINGTON.

SIDNEY (1) Sir William (?1482-1554), soldier, sailor and courtier, descended from an Angevin chamberlain to Henry II, commanded the *Great Bark* at Brest (1513) and the English right wing at Flodden (1513). He went to France on a diplomatic mission in 1515 and attended Henry VIII at the Field of the Cloth of Gold in 1520. In 1523 he was with Suffolk's French expedition. In 1538 he became Steward and tutor to P. Edward and in 1552 acquired through Court favour the manor of Penshurst, which still remains in the family. He was by now a great landowner in Kent and Sussex. His distinguished son **(2) Sir Henry (1529-1838)** grew up at the Court of Edward VI, to whom he was a friend. Fearing his influence, the Protector Northumberland had him married to his *d.* Mary, but this did not prevent him from deserting Northumberland to support the accession of Mary I. He was rewarded with the Irish Vice-Treasurership in 1556.

By 1558 he was one of Sussex's Lords Justices in his absence and from 1559 he was Pres. of the Council of Wales. As a result of a quarrel with Cecil, he supported the idea of a marriage between the Queen and Leicester. In 1562 he went on diplomatic missions to Scotland and France.

In 1565 he began his first term as Lord Deputy of Ireland. He faced confusion caused mainly by his old friend Shane O'Neill, Captain of Tyrone, who had been brought up at Penshurst. Shane was supreme in Ulster but his ambitions reached further. In 1566 he was appealing to Charles IX of France, the Guises and the Pope; his tribesmen were raiding Meath, while he burned Armagh and its cathedral. Sidney obtained supplies, garrisoned Deny, rallied the Ulster tribes and destroyed Shane's fortress at Benburb. Meanwhile, in an inter-tribal conflict, Calvagh O'Donnell beat Shane at the B. of Lough Swily, and the Scots of Clandeboy murdering him in a drunken brawl (June 1567). Luckily for Sidney the E. of Desmond, with whom Shane had been in contact, had not co-ordinated his movements with him and in a rapid campaign in the autumn he seized the Earl and imprisoned him at Dublin. He reported that the disorders had wasted Munster. Meanwhile Meath and the Pale had to be re-secured, so he refortified Dublin Castle.

Sidney began his second period as Lord Deputy in 1568. He recommended English presidencies in Munster and Connaught to replace the Anglo-Irish palatinates; the abolition of coign and livery to reduce the armed followings of the chiefs; the resumption of the policy of surrender of lands and feudal regrant; the construction of roads and bridges in Ulster combined with strategic English colonies and castles and the provision of English teachers in schools. Sir Edward Fitton was made Pres. of Connaught, Sir John Perrot of Munster. Longford was shired and Flemish settlers brought in. Unfortunately Sir Peter Carew's brutal efforts to bring in English colonists provoked united opposition from Irish and Anglo-Irish and civil war. As the English govt. could neither stop the colonisation nor provide Sidney with money and troops, he resigned in 1571 and spent the next years in Wales and at Court. During his absence further colonisations in Ulster provoked the same violence as those in Munster. In 1575 he was therefore sent back as Lord Deputy for a third term, this time undertaking, in return for a guarantee of £20,000 a year, to make no demands on the English Exchequer. He pacified Ulster, shired Connaught and Clare, crushed the Clanricards, forced the gentry of the Pale to pay taxes and pacified Munster. His recall (1578) was nevertheless probably due to the unavoidable cost of his activities; but his name was canvassed in 1582 for a fourth term. Meanwhile he was busy in Wales and died at Ludlow (*see also* ELIZABETH I-9,17). His famous and accomplished son **(3) Sir Philip (1554-86)** was widely admired for his gallantry and youthful good looks. He was favoured by Cecil and became a friend of Essex. In 1577, on diplomatic missions to the Emperor and the German Protestants, he impressed William the Silent. He was his father's best advocate at Court and the associate and patron of most of the best known poets. At Court during 1578-80, he resisted the E. of Oxford's pretensions and challenged him to a duel, and sent the Queen a memorandum against her proposed marriage to the D. of Anjou. She was furious and he retired to the country and wrote *Arcadia* for his sister. By 1581, when he was M.P. for Kent, he had adopted an anti-Spanish point of view. In 1583 he became Master of the Horse and in 1585, though attached to 'Stella' (Penelope Devereux) married Walsingham's daughter. By now he was advocating open war. He joined Drake's fleet but was recalled to join Leicester's expedition to the Low Countries where, as Gov. of Flushing, he was mortally wounded at Zutphen. A considerable and much appreciated poet, he was one of the brilliant stars of the time. His brother **(4) Robert**

(1563-1626) Ld. SIDNEY (1603), Vist. LISLE (1605), 1st E. of LEICESTER (1618), originally a soldier, campaigned mainly in Flanders; but because of the family friendship with Essex, he acted as Essex's advocate at Court during his insurrection. This did him no harm then or later. He invested heavily and successfully in the HEIC and the Virginia Co. As Gov. of Flushing from 1603 he arranged its retrocession in 1616 and in 1621 he was appointed to the Council of War which considered the feasibility of intervention in favour of Frederick V the Elector Palatine (*see* THIRTY YEARS' WAR). His son **(5) Robert (1595-1677) 2nd E.** was an undistinguished character but a splendid figure. His son **(6) Algernon (1622-83)** joined the Parliamentary side in the Civil War and was wounded at Marston Moor (1644). He became M.P. for Cardiff in 1646, Lieut.-Gen. of Horse in Ireland in 1647 and Gov. of Dover from 1648 to 1650. Though nominated, he refused to serve on the court for Charles I's trial but joined the Council of State in 1653, mainly acting in the Foreign Affairs Committee. After the dissolution of the Rump he withdrew from politics. He rejoined the Council of State and was a mediator between Denmark and Sweden in 1659. As a republican, he refused allegiance and went to Italy and in 1666, believing that he might be assassinated, he had discussions with the French govt. about raising a revolt in England. In 1677 he returned to London and was personally reconciled with Charles II, but remained intimate with republicans and for a while with Shaftesbury. In 1683, indirectly implicated in the Rye House Plot, he was convicted of treason on the basis of his unpublished *Discourses concerning Governement,* an intended refutation of Filmer's *Patriarcha,* found in his desk. At his execution he told the sheriffs that he was pleased to die for the 'good old cause' of republicanism. His brother **(7) Henry (1641-1704) Vist. SIDNEY (1689), E. of ROMNEY (1694),** an exceptionally handsome court official, had been Master of the Horse to the Duchess of York and knew her and the Duke (later James II) very well. As Ambassador to The Hague from 1679 to 1681 he also gained the regard of William of Orange. From 1681 to 1685 he was Gen. of the British troops in Dutch service and became one of the channels between the Whigs and William. He was their messenger for the invitation to come to England. Not surprisingly, he became one of William's few English private advisers. From 1690 to 1691 he was Sec. of State; in 1692 Lord Lieut. of Ireland and in 1693 Master-Gen. of the Ordnance. He was William's Groom of the Stole from 1700 to 1702.

SIEGE WARFARE. *See* MILITARY ARCHITECTURE, MEDIAEVAL-3.

SIEGFRIED LINE (1) In World War I a reserve part of the German Hindenburg Line in 1917. **(2)** A German fortified line built in 1937 from Basel to Cleves.

SIERRA LEONE, discovered by Pedro de Cintra in 1462, was a hunting ground for slaves until the British Anti-Slavery Society bought coastal lands there in 1787. The venture failed but the survivors obtained a charter for the Sierra Leone Co. in 1791 and this founded Free Town in 1792. In 1807 it became a Crown colony, whose influence slowly expanded inland between the frontiers of Liberia and French Guinea. In 1896 Britain proclaimed a protectorate over the interior, thereby fixing the boundary of the coastal area. The produce was agricultural until 1930 when chrome, diamonds, platinum and lignite began to be extracted. The colony became an independent member of the Commonwealth in 1961.

SIFTON, Sir Clifford (1861-1929), Att.-Gen. and Minister of Education in Manitoba 1891, became Minister of the Interior in 1896. He was one of the most powerful and energetic leaders of the movement for opening up the Canadian west, but resigned in 1905 against Sir Wilfrid Laurier's more conservative (i.e. eastern) policies. He

developed the commission for the conservation of resources in 1909 and led the movement which defeated the liberals in the general election of 1911.

SIGEBERT, King (?631-7). *See* EAST ANGLIA.

SIGERIC (?-994) was Abbot of St. Augustine's, Canterbury, from 980, Bp. of Ramsbury from 985 and Abp. of Canterbury from 990.

SIGFRID, St. *See* MISSIONS TO EUROPE-5.

SIGN MANUAL. The Royal signature, normally written at the top of a document.

SIGNALLING, VISUAL In 1795 the Admiralty accepted a shutter system invented by Ld. George Murray. A chain of 15 stations between the Admiralty and Deal, with a branch to Sheerness and a similar chain of 10 stations to Portsmouth began operating successfully in 1796. In 1806 22 further stations extended the system to Plymouth. A message could be transmitted to Deal and acknowledged back to London in two minutes, to Plymouth and back in three. In 1823-5 this system was superseded by Sir Home Popham's semaphore, using different lines of stations, which, however, never reached Plymouth. The systems operated only in daylight. They were superseded by electric telegraph in 1849.

Popham's signals remain in use for short distance naval communication.

SIGNALS (ROYAL) CORPS OF, formed in 1920, took over the military signals service from the Royal Engineers and in 1927 absorbed the Indian Signal Corps.

SIGNET (Eng.) is a Royal seal used by a Sec. of State on the Sovereign's behalf. The smallest signet is called the Cachet. Delivery of this to a person constitutes him Sec. of State. Redelivery is the means of resignation.

SIGNIFICAVIT (Lat: He has stated). A stage, represented by a bishop's certificate, or one of two Chancery writs, in proceedings either to commit an excommunicate to prison, or to stop a suit in which one is involved as plaintiff.

SIGNOR. Variations of this Italian term of respect ('Lord', 'Sir') had specialised applications. The GRAND SIGNOR was the Sultan of Turkey: a SIGNORY was the govt. of certain Italian states, notably Venice, or sometimes a fief.

SIGTRYGGR or SIHTRIC (?-927) brought a combined Danish and Norwegian fleet to Dublin in 888 and then operated in the Irish and adjacent seas for many years. In 916 he won a victory at Wexford and plundered Leinster. In 919 he killed King Niall of Ailech, the High King, at Kilmashoge and from 925 he was King of York. He apparently married Athelstan's sister. *See* YORK, SCANDINAVIAN KINGDOMS OF-B.

SIGTRYGGR or SIHTRIC, the name of two Danish earls killed at Ashdown (871).

SIGTRYGGR or SIHTRIC (?-1042) SILK-BEARD, son of Olaf Sitricson, was King of Dublin by 1000 when King Brian defeated him at Glenmama and he married Brian's daughter. The Dublin Ostmen were too few at this time to effect any conquests and though Sigtryggr plundered Kells in 1019, he was defeated on land in Leinster (1020) and at sea by Niall of Ulidia (1022). After a pilgrimage to Rome (1028) he returned to sea roving.

SIGTRYGG GALE O'IVAR (fl. 923). Ostman King of York. *See* EDWARD THE ELDER; VIKINGS-16,17.

SIGURD THE STOUT (?-1014). Orcadian Viking.

SIKHS, KHALSA (1) The mystical Hindu Vaishnava Bhakhtis and the Persian Moslem Sufis both doubted the exclusiveness of religion and the Bhakhtis did not accept the Brahmin dominated Hindu caste organisation. Both kinds of devotees tended to seek each other's company and worship. This was institutionalised by the revelation of **Nanak (1469-1539),** the first of the Sikh TEN GURUS (teachers). He travelled, according to tradition, as far as Assam, Mecca, Ceylon and Tibet, but worked mostly, and died, at Kartarpur in the Punjab. He nominated a disciple as Guru and thereafter each Guru nominated his successor. The office remained in the family of the fourth *guru* **Ram Das Sodhi (r. 1574-81)** until **Gobind Rai (Tenth and Last 1675-1708).**

(2) The 17th cent. had been stormy: the fifth and ninth *gurus* had perished in Mogul persecutions. This primarily pacifist sect had to take up arms or go under. In Apr. 1699 Gobind established the *Khalsa* (= pure) and named all male Sikhs Singh and female Sikhs Kaur (= Lion and Lioness). This was a military sect and Gobind consequently terminated the succession of the *gurus*. Neither he nor his military successor were particularly successful in the field and in 1716 the Khalsa had to take refuge in the hills. It emerged during the Persian invasions of 1738, invasions by the Afghans from 1747 onwards and the latters' defeat of the Marathas at Panipat in 1761. The Khalsa stepped into the resulting political vacuum.

(3) Khalsa units called *misls* had been extracting *Chauth* from Punjab villages since 1739. By 1761, when they took Lahore, the *misls* were established in two main groups divided by the Sutlej. In 1799 **Ranjit Singh's (1780-1839)** *misl* from Gujranwala, N. of Lahore, seized the city and in 1801 he declared himself Maharajah of the Punjab. The British, however, took the states E. of the Sutlej under their protection and forced him (T. of Amritsar 1809) to accept the river as his S.E. frontier. With a European trained Khalsa he moved in the opposite direction, taking Multan in 1818 and Kashmir in 1819. By his death he had extended his power to the Khyber Pass.

(4) Dynastic confusion now reigned at Lahore. The British were preoccupied with the First Afghan War and its disastrous end, while five rulers (one a woman) were murdered in turn. Power fell into the hands of the Panchayat (Council) of the Khalsa, which murdered Hira Singh Dogra the chief minister, leaving a boy Maharajah, Duleep Singh, under a puppet Regent, Jindan Kaur. The defeat of the British in Afghanistan had injured their prestige. The Khalsa thought that the moment had come to cross the Sutlej and unite all the Sikhs under their banner.

(5) The FIRST SIKH WAR arose when the British anticipated the Sikhs by bringing up troops to the Sutlej. The Khalsa attacked at Moodkee and was attacked at Ferozeshah (Dec. 1845), Aliwal (Jan. 1846) and Sobraon (Feb. 1846). It was honourably defeated in these desperately contested battles. By the T. of Lahore the British annexed the Jullundur Doab (between the Sutlej and the Beas) of which John Lawrence became Administrator; they forced the Sikhs to reduce their army to 20,000 infantry and 12,000 cavalry and imposed an indemnity of Rs. 1½ crores. Since the money could not be found, they accepted ½ crore and Jammu and Kashmir instead and then sold them for 1 crore to a Punjab Hindu noble (T. of Amritsar 1846). A British resident, Henry Lawrence, brother of John, was also to be established at Lahore during Duleep Singh's minority. In fact the Khalsa had not admitted defeat and Jindan Kaur refused to accept her practical supersession by a foreign Resident. The British soon had wind of intrigues and caused her to be banished from the court. An uprising (The SECOND SIKH WAR) at Multan spread everywhere and the local absence of British troops enabled the Khalsa to organise. It was, however, totally defeated in the two great Bs. of Chilianwallah (Jan. 1849) and Gujrat (Feb. 1849) and surrendered. The Punjab was annexed.

(6) Henry Lawrence, who had always opposed annexation, was put in charge as Pres. of the Board of Administration, with John in charge of finance. The brothers after a while disagreed over the role of Taluqdars or Sirdars. These hereditary tax officials represented the older Sikh leadership. Henry thought it wise to conciliate them; John believed that reconstruction could be advanced by a moderate tax system from which they were eliminated. As a result Henry was transferred to the Residency of Rajputana, while John revolutionised

the Punjab. He created 32 territorial divisions and settled the condition of 36 tributary states. He established a police, enforced justice and order and built roads, barrages and canals. By the Indian Mutiny (1857) the Sikhs were so completely loyal that they disarmed mutineers and he could raise an army for the siege of Delhi.

(7) One consequence of John Lawrence's policy was that Sikhs were recruited in numbers into the army, another that in the irrigation and reclamation schemes they became the favoured settler aristocrats of the Punjab. By 1900, though representing only 12% of the Punjab population, they paid 40% of its taxes.

In World War I they provided 20% of the Indian Army. It was only after 1919, when depression and pressure on the land began to impoverish them, that their loyalty to the British began to cool; this process was accelerated by such incidents as the Amritsar shootings and the encouragement of democratic institutions which trenched upon their privileged status. As the local Moslem population became more fanatical and insecure, there were religious disputes too over Sikh holy places. In these circumstances the partition of 1947 left half the Sikhs unprotected at the mercy of the Moslem majority. Savage rioting ended in a wholesale migration to India.

SIKKIM, a small Himalayan state, was founded in 1641 as a Tibetan dependency. British treaty relationships commenced in 1817; the British purchased Darjeeling in 1839 and annexed the southern area in 1849. British protection became more active between 1861 and 1888 and was recognised by China in 1890. The Maharajah was taken into custody and so remained until his death in 1914. His successor was reinstated in 1918. India succeeded to the protectorate in 1947.

SILCHESTER (Lat: CALLEVA ATREBATIUM). *See* ATREBATES.

SILESIA (locally SCHLESIEN) (*see also* BOHEMIA), fertile basin of the Upper Oder with important coal and iron mines, was a Habsburg province until seized by Frederick the Great of Prussia in 1740 to increase Prussian resources and interrupt communications between Saxony and Poland. Fought over in 1742 and again from 1756 to 1763, it, other than Opava, was finally ceded to Prussia at the P. of Hubertusburg. In 1921 the Pless coalfields were ceded to Poland. Under the Potsdam Agreement (1945) the whole, other than a small part west of the Neisse, followed and the German population was driven out. *See also* WARS OF 1739-48.

SILK, a minor English industry, developed suddenly and quickly when 30,000 Huguenot silk weavers migrated to England between 1690 and 1700. During the French wars of William III and Anne, French silk imports were strictly prohibited and this prohibition continued into peacetime. Bounties were also paid to exporters. In 1716 John Lombe (1693-1722) smuggled in the design of an Italian silk throwing machine; in 1718 his half-brother Thomas (1685-1739) established such machines on the Derwent and by 1733 he had made a fortune. In 1732 Parliament voted him £14,000 for his patent and the industry spread to Macclesfield, Spitalfield (London) and to a lesser degree to Coventry, Derby and Stockport. By 1760 development, restricted only by the supply of raw silk, had spread to Dorset, Cheshire and Glos.

SILK. *See* COIF.

SILURES. A British tribe centred on the Glamorgan coastal strip and the valleys of the Wye and Usk, which fiercely resisted the Romans. From A.D. 46 when Caractacus led them, they were remarkably successful, even raiding into territory already occupied by the Romans to the east of the Wye. By A.D. 60, however, they had been broken by the governors Didius and Veranius, but their final overthrow was achieved only by Frontinus in the mid-70s.

SILVER (*see* COINAGE) was mined in Alsace and the Black Forest in the Early Middle Ages and in Saxony from the

10th cent. From the 11th cent. Bohemia and the Erz became important centres of supply (*see* DOLLAR) and from the 13th cent., Sweden. Veins were also found in other Habsburg states and in Norway. There were a few small workings in Wales and Cornwall but English supplies came mainly as profits from the wool trade. The enormous deposits in Peru and Mexico were worked with decreasing profit by the Spaniards until the mercury process was discovered in the 18th cent. These mines were the main world source until the discovery of the Comstock lode (USA) in 1889.

SILVERMAN, Sydney (1895-1968), lawyer and politician, was imprisoned as a conscientious objector in World War I and emerged as a penal reformer. Unable to get a teaching post in Britain, he taught for some years at Helsinki University and then practised as a poor man's solicitor. As a Labour M.P. he was a fearless critic of all govts. and so never gained office. In 1956 his Bill to abolish capital punishment for murder passed the Commons but was rejected by the Lords, but the Eden govt. restarted the progress towards abolition with the Homicide Act, which restricted capital punishment to a few situations. In 1965 the suspension of capital punishment effectively ended it.

SIMEON of DURHAM was Precentor of Durham Cathedral in the early 12th cent. His *Historia Regum* (Lat: History of the Kings) is a compilation from other historians from the 7th cent. to 1129, but the material after 1119 is apparently original. It may contain matter collected in the 10th cent. and thus be a good source for Anglo-Saxon, especially Northumbrian, history. It contains a long justification of the claims of the Abps. of York. The *Historia Dunel-mensis Ecclesiae,* a history of the See of Durham to 1096 and some smaller works, are also attributed to him.

SIMLA (India). The summer location of the govt. of India.

SIMLA DEPUTATION (Oct. 1906), an Indian Muslim deputation led by the Aga Khan presented to the Viceroy, Lord Minto, a summary of their political demands viz: that Muslims should be separately represented by elected not nominated representatives, that their representation should be proportionately greater than that of the Hindu community and that they should have an equivalent quota of administrative and judicial appointments. *See* MORLEY-MINTO REFORMS.

SIMNEL, Lambert (c. 1477-after 1534), son of an Oxford joiner, was coached for an imposture as the E. of Warwick (Clarence's son) by the priest Richard Simonds, as part of a conspiracy fomented by John de la Pole, E. of Lincoln, and involving the Queen Dowager, Elizabeth Woodville. The object was a Yorkist restoration. When Henry VII produced the real E. from the Tower, Lincoln fled to Flanders and then to Ireland. In May 1487 Lincoln and Irish Yorkists led by the Es. of Desmond and Kildare recognised Simnel and crowned him King as Edward VI. With German troops provided by Edward VI's sister, Margaret of Burgundy, Lincoln landed in Lancashire, supported by the Irish lords and Richard III's favourite, Ld. Lovell. They were defeated at Stoke-on-Trent (16 June 1487), Lincoln, Lovell and Kildare's brother Thomas being killed. Simonds and Simnel were captured. Simonds was imprisoned for life, but Simnel, who had been no more than a child dupe, was put to work in the Royal household. He rose to be the King's falconer.

SIMON, Sir John (1816-1904) was the first London Medical Officer of Health (M.O.H.) appointed in 1848 and then as chief M.O.H. to the Privy Council was the first professional adviser on public health to the govt. He was indirectly one of the most influential men of his time.

SIMON, John Allsebrook (1873-1954) 1st Vist. (1940), a revenue practitioner at the bar, became Liberal M.P. for Walthamstow in 1906, Q.C. in 1908, Sol-Gen. in 1910 and Att.-Gen. (in the Cabinet) in 1913. Though favouring neutrality in 1914, he refrained from resigning on the declaration of war. In 1915 he refused the Woolsack and

became Home Sec., but resigned in Jan. 1916 against conscription. He then pursued his lucrative legal practice as a backbench M.P. until 1926 when he scored an unusual parliamentary success, by a speech on the illegality of the General Strike which helped to end it. In 1927 he became Chairman of the statutory commission on the progress of the Montague-Chelmsford reforms in India and the possibilities of further constitutional progress. The work was stillborn because the Labour govt. announced its adherence to the principle of Indian Dominion Status (Oct. 1929) before the commission could report. Nevertheless it reported in 1930 with the general assent of Indian politicians and then Simon returned to the bar. In 1931 he led an anti-socialist secession from the Liberal Party in support of Ramsay MacDonald's National Govt. and became Foreign Sec. As such he bore much responsibility for the fatuity of British policy, firstly in not supporting the League of Nations against Japanese aggression in Manchuria and Jehol, and then in steadfastly refusing to be embroiled, in the era of Hitler, in central Europe. Baldwin transferred him to the Home Office in 1935; in 1936 he was prominent in the affairs which led up to Edward VIII's abdication and in 1937 he became Chancellor of the Exchequer in Neville Chamberlain's first govt. Uninspiring, apparently arrogant and believed to be devious, his deepening personal unpopularity contributed to growing public distrust of the Chamberlain govt. and helped to break it in May 1940. He had, however, been on good terms with Churchill since they were colleagues under Asquith and he now accepted the Woolsack, but with no part in the direction of the war.

He was thus able to concentrate, apart from his functions as govt. spokesman, on the primarily legal functions of the Lords and presided with distinction until 1945 over an exceptionally strong House, both in its appellate capacity and as a legislative chamber in "lawyers' legislation".

SIMON STOCK (d. 1265) was probably the English hermit who lived in a tree-trunk (stock). In the early 13th cent. he went to Palestine and joined the hermits on Mount Carmel, who were later organised as the Order of Our Lady of Mount Carmel. In 1237 he was prior of the order in Palestine. He returned to Europe and in 1247 was elected Prior-Gen. at a chapter held at Aylesford. In 1248 he secured approval for the order from Innocent IV and in about 1250 it received its rule and began to attend the schools at Oxford, Cambridge, Paris and Bologna. This distressed the older, eremitic members but Simon's generalship established the Carmelites as a significant mendicant order in W. Europe.

SIMONSTOWN (S. Africa), AGREEMENTS 1922 and 1955. The British naval base was established in 1814 and became the most important in the area. Under the 1922 agreement the Union govt. became responsible for manning the fortifications. Under the 1955 agreement the base was transferred to the Union, but in return for a regular supply of certain armaments by Britain the British were to have full naval use in peace and war. The supplementary base at Mombasa in Kenya was never completed and with the loss of bases in Aden, Ceylon, Malaysia and Singapore, Simonstown became increasingly important to British interests. In 1975, however, the Labour govt., unwilling to continue the agreed arms supply, abandoned the base.

SIMONY is the purchase of sacraments or ecclesiastical positions. It has always been illegal, but at times widely practised. *See* ACTS, 5 VV 18-19.

SIMOON. A long-enduring hot southerly wind in the Red Sea which delayed southward traffic.

SIMPSON, Sir George (1792-1860) as Administrator of the Hudson's Bay Co's. territory (most of Canada W. of Ontario) from 1826 to 1841 revealed much of its, hitherto sketchily known, geography and resources.

SINAI, the scene of the Biblical enactment of the Ten Commandments, has been exploited by Egyptian miners since prehistoric times. The area contains copper, iron and lead. Petrol, first found in 1910, began to be developed in 1935; deep drilling began in 1944 and by 1965 production was 3,000,000 tons. In addition it is between the Suez Canal and the ports of Aqaba and Eilat. Not surprisingly it became an object of Israeli-Egyptian dispute after the establishment of Israel, being occupied by Israel after the 1967 war, until retroceded by agreement in 1982.

SINCLAIR, Sir Archibald Henry Macdonald (1890-1970) 1st Vist. THURSO (1952), Liberal leader and M.P. (1922-45) was for a time Churchill's regimental 2-in-C on the Western Front in World War I, and in World War II, as the leading Liberal, became Sec. of State for Air in the Wartime Coalition. He advocated strategic bombing, but his role was administrative rather than policy making.

SINCLAIR (or ST. CLAIR). Lowland Scots family of Norman origin. Its fortunes were founded by **(1) Sir William (fl. 1266-1303)** of Roslin, a court personality who was a guardian or tutor to Alexander, P. of Scotland (later Alexander III) and became Steward of Dumfries and justiciar in Galloway. When Alexander died he supported the candidature of his neighbour Baliol, but not to the point of arms; he was captured fighting the English at Dunbar in 1294 and imprisoned at Gloucester whence he escaped in 1303. His son **(2) Sir Henry (?-?1330)** was captured at Dunbar in 1296, exchanged in 1299, became Sheriff of Lanark and fought for Robert the Bruce at Bannockburn and elsewhere. His brother **(3) William (?-1337)** became Bp. of Dunkeld in 1312, commanded the force which repulsed the English at Donibristle in 1317 but crowned Edward Baliol in 1332. The son of (2), **(4) Sir William (?-1330)** went with Good Sir James Douglas to take Robert the Bruce's heart to the Holy Land, but was killed by the Moors in Spain. His son (2), **(5) Sir Henry (?-1404) E. of ORKNEY (1379),** a seafarer or pirate, acquired Orkney (then Norwegian) and was recognised as Jan by King Haakon VI. He then went on to conquer the rest of the sea earldom, reaching the Faroes in 1391, and investigated, with the Venetian navigator Antonio Zen, the east coast of Greenland. His son **(6) Henry (?-1418) 2nd E.** became Admiral of Scotland but was captured in a more military capacity at Homildon Hill in 1402. Soon ransomed, he accompanied James I on his unlucky voyage to France in 1406, was captured with him and died in England. His son **(7) Sir William (?1404-80) 3rd E. (until 1479), 1st Ld. SINCLAIR (1449), 1st E. of CAITHNESS (1455)** stood hostage for James I on his release in 1421. He acknowledged the Norwegian rights when he took over the sea earldom in 1434, but remained Admiral of Scotland and as such escorted the P. Margaret to France in 1436. In 1446, with a view to asserting Norwegian rights, he was summoned to Norway but, like his father, his interests went further south. He rebuilt Roslin in 1446 and fought the English on the Border in 1448. He was Lord Chancellor from 1454 to 1456 and an opponent of the Douglases. In 1461 he was one of the Regents and, with his English experience, a negotiator with England. In 1471 he exchanged Orkney, which had become a bone of contention, for estates in Fife. He was again negotiating in England in 1472 and 1473. Of his descendants **(8) George (?-1582) 4th E.** was a R. Catholic who opposed the Confession of Faith of 1560 and joined in the invitation to Mary Queen of Scots. He was made hereditary justiciar of Caithness in 1566, an office which the family retained until 1746. He was said to have been implicated in Darnley's murder but contrived to preside over Bothwell's trial for it. His grandson **(9) George (?1566-1643) 5th E.,** really a brigand, fought or pillaged all his neighbours, especially Sutherland, Orkney and Forbes and was driven out under Letters of Fire and Sword in 1623.

SINCLAIR, Sir John (1754-1835), an M.P. from 1780 to 1811, was a scientific agriculturalist and statistician particularly interested in northern agriculture. With Arthur Young he secured the creation in 1793 of the Board of Agriculture and was its President until 1798. By collecting and publishing information, the Board did much to encourage the best farming practices and techniques.

SIND (Pak.) was a Mogul province until 1700 when the local Kalhora dynasties ruled increasingly loosely until 1782; then a Beluchi Taipur dynasty maintained itself amid chaos until 1843. Apart from the principality of Khairpur the British annexed it after a furious battle at Meeanee in 1843 to the Bombay Presidency, from which it was separated only in 1937. Sind and Khairpur became part of Pakistan in 1947.

SINDHIA (GWALIOR). See MARATHAS-C.

SIN EATING. A quasi-magical rite practised until the 20th cent. in Wales and the Welsh border. Men took food and drink, commonly bread and ale, in the presence of a corpse to lighten its soul's burden of sin and facilitate its passage to heaven.

SINECURES. Offices without duties became common in the 17th and 18th cents. because, though their remuneration (usually by fees) remained, social and administrative movements had rendered their functions obsolete or so simple that the work could be done by an underpaid deputy. These posts were habitually conferred as political *douceurs* and exercised an important function for that reason. They varied in importance from the minor but local to the national and financially fabulous. Pitt the Younger greatly reduced them, mainly by not filling them as they fell vacant (1784-1806). *For examples see* PAYMASTER-GEN.

SINGAPORE (*see* MALAYSIA, MALAYA) is one of the largest ports in the world because of its position on the routes from India, southern Africa and Europe to the Far East and Australasia. The 1980 population of about 2.4M was three quarters Chinese. It joined Malaysia in 1963 and left by agreement in 1965 and became an independent republic within the British Commonwealth. *See also* WORLD WAR II-9 & 10.

SINHA, Satyendra Prasanna (1863-1930) 1st Ld. SINHA of RAIPUR (1919) successful Indian lawyer, entered politics as a moderate. He became a member of the Viceroy's Council in 1909, presided over the Indian National Congress in 1915 and was Gov. of Bihar and Orissa from 1920 to 1924.

SINHALESE. See CEYLON.

SINKIANG or CHINESE TURKESTAN (Cap. Urumchi). Of this mixed racial area, the largest and usually ruling group has been the Moslem Uighurs, an agricultural and pastoral people. It was a remote, largely autonomous dominion of China under the Manchus who, however, permitted the Kalmucks to rule it in the 18th cent. It became a proper Chinese province in 1884 and fell to the Chinese Communists in 1949.

SINKING FUNDS. (1) The principle was incorporated in legislation (1717) on particular loans such as the Bank of England, South Sea Annuities, Lottery Annuities and the Exchequer Bills. An Act of 1718 consolidated the funds for these and other debts. Govts. were tempted from time to time to raid the fund and the revenues, whose surplus was appropriated to it, were inadequate for the debts (especially war debts) accumulated in the 18th cent. *See* GEORGE I-11.

(2) In 1786 Pitt's Act altered the administrative principles. It created an independent body of National Debt Commissioners, vested the sinking fund in them and legally obliged the Exchequer to pay them £250,000 a quarter. At that time particular revenues ceased to be appropriated for debt redemption. This made the fund difficult to raid and would have greatly reduced the debt under a prolonged peace. The practice enjoined by the Act had, however, to be carried on during the French Wars which ended in 1815, so in 1816 the Commissioners' authority was extended to Irish Debts and surpluses. It was soon apparent that the provision was inadequate and in 1819 the Commons resolved that general revenue should exceed govt. expenditure by £5M. Accordingly in 1823 the old payments to the Commissioners were repealed, the stock owned by and annuities charged to them were cancelled and they were to receive £1.25M a quarter with a limited power to cancel stock and annuities acquired.

(3) In 1875 these strong arrangements were superseded by the weaker provision of the Sinking Fund Act, that the Treasury should pay over to the Commissioners any surplus of income over expenditure for the preceding financial year.

(4) In 1928 the Sinking Fund was divided into two: the Old, to which the arrangements of 1875 applied and the New, which consisted of the surplus of an annual payment to the Commissioners of £355M for National Debt management. From 1954 payments applicable to the Old Sinking Fund were used to reduce national indebtedness in the year in which it arises and the Fund thus ceased to operate as a fund; the New Fund was abolished.

(5) Meanwhile a number of loans and obligations had been raised with specific sinking funds of their own. These were War Loan and Victory Bonds (1919), the 4% Funding Loan (1928), Govt. and Savings Banks Annuities (1929), 3½% Conversion Loan (1934). These continued to be managed by the Commissioners.

(6) The Commissioners are the Speaker, the Chancellor of the Exchequer, the Lord Chief Justice (replacing the Chief Baron of the Exchequer), the Master of the Rolls, the Accountant-Gen. of the Supreme Court (replacing the Accountant-Gen. in Chancery) and the Gov. and Deputy-Gov. of the Bank of England. In practice the functions are exercised by the Comptroller of the National Debt Office.

SINN FEIN (Pron: Shin fane, Ir. = Ourselves alone or Self reliance) (1) An organisation founded by Arthur Griffith, editor of the *United Irishman*. The name was suggested by an anonymous nun. It first came to notice when it won two seats at the Dublin municipal elections of 1902. He formed a national council in 1905 and launched his programme at the Dublin Rotunda in Nov. 1905. The policy was abstention by Irish M.P.s. in the work of Parliament, but as Irish M.P.s. had gained great successes, the idea was not popular. Though by 1908, they had 16 Dublin councillors, they were defeated in parliamentary bye-elections (*see* IRISH VOLUNTEERS).

(2) At the 1916 Easter Rising, Sinn Fein bid for support with an extreme appeal for a united Irish republic. At the General Election of 1918 it won 73 out of 108 Irish seats and in Jan. 1919 these 73 proclaimed themselves the govt. of Ireland. Sinn Fein refused to accept the partition of 1921 or the authority of the *Dail Eireann*. In 1926 its leader Eamonn De Valera seceded with most of the membership which he formed into the Fianna Fail. Thereafter in parliamentary elections it never gained more than 3% of the vote.

(3) Its relationship with the Irish Republican Army (I.R.A.), a terrorist organisation, is uncertain but membership has overlapped heavily; hence Sinn Fein cannot escape much of the responsibility for the campaign of murder and extortion waged by the I.R.A. with Libyan and American money and Czech explosives and weapons in Ulster and sometimes in mainland Britain. This cost over 3,000 lives between 1969 and 1994 when it was brought to a halt by Anglo-Irish diplomatic (and other) action.

SINO-JAPANESE WAR 1894-5. *See* CHINA-31; JAPAN-3 & 4.

SION COLLEGE (London) was established in 1623 near London Wall as a college, guild and almshouse for the City of London parochial clergy and accumulated a valuable library. The almshouse was abolished in 1884 and the college moved to the Embankment in 1886.

SIOUX. An unorganised group of tribes found on the upper Great Lakes of N. America in the 17th cent. Their most important branches were the Dakotas (whose dress and profile were the model for the popular western image of the Indian) and Assiniboin to the north and the Crows to the south. They spread gradually southwards along the west bank of the Mississippi as far as Louisiana and also into the plains. They were constantly at war not only with the Europeans and the Iroquois and Algonquin, but with each other.

SIR GAWAIN AND THE GREEN KNIGHT is a narrative verse romance of some 2500 lines written in N.W. Midland dialect between 1360 and 1400. It survives as one of four related poems in a single MS. and exhibits the same courtly and chivalric ideals as the 12th cent. Chrestien de Troyes, but with a close alliterative structure. It is uncertain whether the four poems were exceptional or representative of a larger vernacular literature.

SIVAJI I. *See* MARATHAS.

SIWARD (?-1048), Abp. of Canterbury. *See* EDWARD THE CONFESSOR-3.

SIWARD (?-1055) the Strong, a follower of Canute, became E. of Deira and after Canute's death, Earl of all Northumbria after killing the incumbent E. of Bernicia, his wife's uncle. He also acquired the lands of Huntingdon and became a semi-autonomous ruler, interfering successfully in the Scottish civil war by establishing Malcolm III in Cumbria. *See* EDWARD THE CONFESSOR-11.

SIX ACTS (1819) or GAGGING ACTS. 60 George III and I George IV caps. 1, 2, 4, 6, 8 and 9. **(1)** Prohibited assemblies for unauthorised military exercises; **(2)** authorised magistrates until 25 Mar. 1822 to search for and seize weapons and to impose bail upon suspected persons carrying arms; **(4)** accelerated the trial of misdemeanours by forcing defendants to plead within four days (or such longer time as the court allowed) or have judgement given against them; **(6)** *inter alia* forbade, until 24 Dec. 1824, meetings of more than 50 people outside a parish, strengthened the Riot Act and made those who refused to disperse when so ordered liable to seven years' transportation; **(8)** empowered courts upon conviction to order the seizure of any blasphemous or seditious libel against the Crown, Constitution, either House of Parliament, or tending to incite to attempted alteration "of any matter in Church or State as by law established otherwise than by lawful means" and to imprison or banish those convicted a second time; **(9)** imposed the existing newspaper stamp duty upon periodical news, pamphlets and news sheets of less than two sheets or costing less than sixpence. (8) and (9) were both repealable in the session in which they were passed, but parts of (1) and (8) were unrepealed in the mid-1980s. These acts have had a bad press.

SIX ARTICLES (1539), properly the *Act for Abolishing Diversity of Opinions. See* TEN ARTICLES.

SIX CLERKS, SIXTY CLERKS. *See* CHANCERY-8 *et seq.*

SKEFFINGTON and CLOTWORTHY (1) Sir John CLOTWORTHY (?-1665) 1st Ld. LOUGHNEAGH and Vist. MASSEREENE (1661) was a Parliamentary commander in N. Ireland and acquired most of the enormous forfeited estates of the Es. of Antrim. He changed sides at the right moment and for his useful activity in furthering the Restoration he was ennobled without having to give up the estates. By an exceptional special remainder the honours passed to his son-in-law **(2) Sir John SKEFFINGTON (?-1695),** a zealous Protestant. The titles and estates passed through his descendants (between 1756 and 1816 Es. of Massereene) to **(3) Harriet (?-1831)** who married Thomas Foster. He changed his name to Skeffington and in 1828 inherited the U.K. peerage of **ORIEL OF FERRARD.** By virtue of this peerage the family entered Westminster politics.

SKELMERSDALE. *See* NEW TOWNS.

SKIMMINGTON, RIDING. A scornful rustic punishment for scolds and adulterers. An absurd procession with cacophonous music paraded through the village. It included a man riding with his face to his horse's tail; he was belaboured by a woman with a skimming ladle. The procession swept the doorstep of any suspect's house. When a man ill-treated his wife, he might be borne astride a pole in a similar procession. This was called riding the STANG (cf Ger. *Stange* = pole).

SKINHEADS were young close-shaven headed youths in black leather jackets who began to appear in the 1970s. They had a loud-mouthed quasi-fascist aura (but without the leadership), and were associated, often by others, with attacks on Asians.

***SKINNER v EAST INDIA CO.* (1666-9).** Skinner, an interloping trader, petitioned against the Co. for damages incurred at Surat in 1659 and the case was referred to the House of Lords. They awarded him £5000 damages. The Co. complained to the Commons and a prolonged quarrel between the Houses ensued. Eventually Charles II suggested that all the proceedings be erased from the journals of both Houses and the Lords tacitly abandoned their claim to try civil cases at first instance.

SKINNER (1) Hercules (?-1803) married a Rajput girl and had substantial Indian lands. Of their children **(2) James (1778-1841)** ran away from school and was commissioned by de Boigne, Scindia's French military adviser, in the Maratha army. As a Maratha he took part in the capture of Delhi in 1798 and of Jhansi in 1799. In 1803 he was dismissed when the British attacked Aligarh and having joined them, took command of some cavalry which had also left Maratha service. This was the origin of the famous unit called Skinner's Horse with which he distinguished himself in the campaign against Holkar in 1825. The British govt. rewarded him with estates upon which he spent large sums and where he lived royally and had at least 14 wives.

SKIPPON, Philip (?-1660), a professional and religious soldier was twice wounded in the Netherlands and the Palatinate. He returned to England in 1639, joined the Hon. Artillery Co. and was soon recognised as an inspiring leader of troops. In Jan. 1642 (just after Charles I tried to seize the Five Members), the Common Council made him free of the City and then Parliament over the head of the Royalist Ld. Mayor, put him in command of the City train bands. He was appointed Serjeant-Major-Gen. and as such became a key figure in the rebellion, for he trained the apprentices and journeymen composing the Parliamentary infantry against powerful Royalist obstruction in the City. By 1643 his men could undertake more distant assignments and he accompanied Essex at the S. of Reading (Apr.), the relief of Gloucester and in the Cornish battles (Aug-Sept.). He also fought at both Bs. of Newbury, commanded the left-centre and was wounded at Naseby (May 1645) and retired ill, but recovered to be made Gov. of Bristol on its capture. He rejoined Fairfax for the capture of Oxford (May 1646). After taking over the custody of the King from the Scots, he was appointed to organise a proposed expedition against Ireland, but meanwhile was involved as a mediator in the controversies between godly but sometimes levelling officers and the politicians, for he was now M.P. for Barnstaple. His attitude remained professional: discipline must be maintained but the soldiers' legitimate grievances redressed.

Skippon was a member of all the Councils of State except the fourth and as Commander of the London Militia seems to have been the only officer to have retained much public respect. He was granted substantial lands in 1651 and called to Cromwell's Upper House in 1657. The restored Parliament reappointed him to the London command just before his death.

SKIRLAW, Walter (?-1406) was employed as a diplomat in Italy from 1381 to 1383 until he became Keeper of the Privy Seal. Provided to the See of Lichfield in 1385 he was translated to Bath and Wells and to Durham in 1388. In Co. Durham he built important works of engineering, particularly bridges, but he continued his diplomatic activity, with Scotland, France and Flanders under Richard III and as chief negotiator in France for Henry IV.

SKUPSHTINA. A Serb, Montenegrin or Yugoslav parliament.

SKYBOLT. *See* POLARIS.

SKYE. This large island was devastated (794) and then colonised (875) by Norsemen, who ruled it until the B. of Largs (1263) when it passed to the Lords of the Isles. They regranted it to the representative of the Norwegian house, Leod. The Clan Macleod was in two parts: of Lewis and Harris. Both held land in Skye, but Macleod of Harris held the greater part from Dunvegan. In the 14th cent. the Macdonalds crossed from the mainland and established themselves in Sleat. The forfeiture of the Lordship of the Isles (1493) and the weakness of the Scottish Crown after Flodden left the Isles without a govt. There was war between the clans; the Macdonalds, with mainland reinforcements, seized Trotternish in 1539 and the feud was not pacified until James VI and I intervened, after a major battle in the Cuillins, in 1601. The Macdonalds retained Trotternish until 1715 when it was forfeited for participation in the Jacobite rising. Nevertheless Macdonalds continued, for Lady Margaret Macdonald organised Bonnie Prince Charlie's escape from Trotternish after Culloden. The island's prosperity increased, as a result of peace, sound farming and the fisheries, but in 1830 the herring inexplicably ceased to come and in the 1840s the potato crops persistently failed. To stave off ruin the landowners introduced sheep farming (now, with tourism, the main activity) and the population fell from 23,000 (1841) to 7500 in a century.

SLANDER. *See* LIBEL.

SLANE HILL (Co. Meath, Ir.). Traditionally the place where, in 433, St. Patrick lit the Paschal beacon and proclaimed Christianity.

SLAVE REGISTRATION. To prevent secret slave trading William Wilberforce introduced a bill in 1815 requiring all slave owners to register their slaves. The W. India lobby resisted the proposal strongly on, *inter alia,* constitutional grounds, but undertook if the bill were dropped to get the W. Indian legislatures to introduce their own. Hence from 1817 to 1832 a system of triennial returns prevailed in the W. Indies.

SLAVERY is a form of property. **(1)** The master or *dominus* has much the same rights in the slave as he has in his cattle. Roman law developed a jurisprudence on the subject and its spirit (if not the details) was generally followed in slave-holding western colonies. The rights of a *dominus* over his property (*dominium*) were initially defined as the right to use, abuse or destroy. Nothing in law restrained his dealings with his property save self-interest. Moreover since property (e.g. a table) cannot have rights, a slave had no rights even against or in favour of another slave. A slave could not own anything, or make a bargain, or marry. Legally a slave had no father and the child of a slave mother was a slave and owned by the mother's owner.

(2) *Use.* The strong and the stupid were put to laborious or unpleasant tasks and served the purpose of, as yet uninvented, machinery. The vast majority were used for plantation labour, but a minority was needed for more skilled purposes such as carting, or for more polite ones such as household service.

(3) *Abuse.* As slave labourers obtained no benefit from their work, they could not be expected to do any unless driven. Slaves who were recalcitrant or lazy (or lethargic from hookworm) were thrashed or tortured by professional overseers. This did not happen much to the more skilled or household slaves; for them the main sanction was the threat of being returned to the fields. The masters and their families seldom inflicted punishment themselves. There was commonly a house of correction, sometimes shared with several plantations, where a slave would be sent to be beaten for his or her owner's account. Women slaves, especially if attractive, were liable to sexual abuse: in particular there were masters who made fortunes in slave brothels and the large number of half castes is evidence of less regular abuse. In law a slave woman could not be raped, since she committed an offence if she resisted a free man.

(4) *Destruction.* Self interest generally prevented the killing of slaves, but overwork and lack of medical care shortened life. Hookworm and lack of shoes was the misery of the tropical slave's life. If slaves were cheap, some masters calculated the advantages of working them to death and in times of famine, the slaves died first. Conversely, if they were dear there might be an incentive to make a quick profit by selling a slave elsewhere.

(5) *Sale.* Slave markets existed in ports and major towns and were mostly operated by commission agents. The merchandise had to be kept under lock and key, but the agents had an interest in its apparent physical condition, which affected the price.

(6) *Natural modifications.* Though the extreme principles might be invoked at any moment, practical improvements appealed to the masters' self interest and became customary. Christianity undoubtedly helped. Moreover the inability of a slave to own anything or make a contract (save for the master) was often highly inconvenient. An intelligent trading slave might make more for the master if able to keep some of the profits. Thus a sort of quasi-property arose, set aside for the benefit of the slave and respected by the master. A slave might accumulate enough to be able to purchase freedom, if the master were willing to sell. Generally speaking, but for reasons not wholly clear, the more temperate the climate, the better the condition of the slaves. The threat, in a more northern slave state of the U.S.A. to "sell you down the river", i.e. in Louisiana, was serious. Conditions were still worse in the sugar colonies (especially the Dutch ones) and Mexico.

(7) *Geography.* Slavery existed in all Spanish, Portuguese and Dutch possessions and in British colonies in the New World from New York southwards (except Pennsylvania) to Guiana.

(8) *Later History.* Home govts. tended to try and improve the lot of slaves against local colonial opposition. Hence the condition of British American slaves remained stationary after Independence, while legislation, e.g. forbidding the whipping of females and for investigating complaints, combined with the high price of sugar to ameliorate conditions in the British colonial Is. In the Latin American colonies the position was much worse. Attempts by the home govt. to raise standards were a cause of colonial revolt.

(9) Slavery was always wasteful and inefficient. The suppression of the legal and the harrying of the illegal slave trade from 1807 inflated the cost of slave labour at the very time when the Industrial Revolution was, by other means, bringing down the cost of production. The British were able to emancipate all their colonial slaves in 1834 with compensation to their owners, but in American states north of Pennsylvania slaves died out because it was too expensive to own one. Significantly, in the American Civil War four slave states sided with the Union. *See* BLACK CODES; SLAVE TRADE.

SLAVERY IN BRITAIN was a feature of Anglo-Saxon rural society. Servility could derive from birth, capture in war, punishment for crime, sale by a parent or self-sale because of poverty. The slave (A.S: *Theow;* Dan: *Thraell*)

was legally his master's chattel and by Domesday Book, was normally part of a lord's demesnal equipment. Many worked as domestic servants, labourers, herdsmen, bee-keepers and corn-grinders. Though slavery was in decline, Domesday Book records 9% of those counted as slaves, the highest incidence (20%) being in the West. From the 6th to the 11th cents. a slave trade within England and for export throve, possibly constituting the major export after wool.

Freedom could be obtained by manumission by the master, often granted in his will. The Church opposed slavery and in the 11th and 12th cents. it died out as much for economic as for social reasons. Also, according to the *Rectitudines singularum personarum,* a master had to provide his slave with the necessities for survival, which could drain his resources. So slaves were increasingly given their own holdings (*servi casati*), thus ceasing to be chattels without possessions or rights, whilst remaining servile. From slaves, these became serfs.

After its mediaeval disappearance, slavery in England reappeared only with the discovery of the New World, the opening of the African coasts and the 17th cent. overseas colonisations. In *Butts* v *Penny* (1677) it is reported that "negroes being usually bought and sold among merchants as merchandise and also being infidels, there might be a property in them ..." and this was followed in *Gully* v *Cleeve* (1694). In *Smith* v *Gould* (1707), however, Holt C.J. held that a negro taken by the defendant from the plaintiff could not be a chattel but at most a villein. In *Sommersetts Case* (1771), counsel for the negro said that *Butts* v *Penny* concerned negroes in India and that *Gully* v *Cleeve* had not been argued. Lord Mansfield held that once a slave set foot in England he was free and in *Knight* v *Wedderburn* (1778) the Scottish courts agreed, if in more prosaic terms, but Mary Prince (1788-after 1831) a slave born in Bermuda was brought to England in 1828 and had to escape. In 1831, with the aid of the Anti-Slavery Soc. she published, in a *History* of herself, an influential account of the barbarities which she had suffered.

SLAVE TRADE (1) Owing to the long periods of gestation, immaturity and old age of the human species, breeding cannot economically supply the demands of a slave economy; it needs human beings enslaved as adults by process of law, capture in war or kidnapping and any slave trade will deal mainly in stolen human goods. It therefore depends on war and disorder and breeds it.

(2) The western slave traffic became a major international trade after the great Spanish American epidemics of 1546-7 and 1576-9, which destroyed vast numbers of indigenous labourers. Spanish govts. tried to maintain the Castilian monopoly (*see* ASIENTO) in this, as in other colonial commerce, but the colossal profits attracted foreign interlopers and meanwhile the traffic spread to Portuguese America, the Caribbean Is. and the warmer British American colonies. The first interlopers were French and Dutch, quickly followed by the English, mainly from Bristol and other West Country ports. British maritime superiority put much of the trade into British hands by the mid-18th cent.

(3) The triangular pattern of the traffic, licit or illicit, was to ship knickknacks such as beads, mirrors, small knives and gaudy headgear to the West African (Gold and Slave) Coasts. Here coastal chiefs, who had seized the bodies from the interior tribes, kept them in stockades and traded them for these goods to the ship-masters through local agents. The slaves were packed recumbent, three or four tiers to a deck, and chained head to the centre line. The average slaver, of about 400 tons, might carry as many as 600. They could not leave their tiers, save in very small parties for rare and short periods of exercise, weather permitting. A slaver to windward could be smelt a mile away. The Middle Passage, from Africa to the Caribbean or Spanish Main, took between three and six weeks. The number of deaths depended upon the skill of the slave captains. The slaves, being as yet unbroken, were sold as raw material yet at profitable prices, and the money immediately reinvested in rum, indigo, cotton, tobacco and other colonial products. These were brought back to Britain (or elsewhere). A shipowner might expect a profit of 2000% on a round trip.

(4) The rise of evangelicalism and Quaker influence changed the climate of opinion after 1760 and in 1782 the first Abolition Bill was moved, unsuccessfully, in the Commons. Thereafter bills were moved annually, while the agitation gathered momentum. The Slave Trade Abolition Act, 1806, came into effect in 1807. It prohibited the trade and every transaction remotely connected with it, to British subjects and ships. This increased the profits of successful racketeers and, after 1814, drove the trade into continental hands. British naval supremacy was now used to suppress it and to support efforts to get other countries to do so. France agreed to phase it out by 1819, Spain (in return for £400,000) by 1820, Portugal (£300,000) by 1830. In fact slave smuggling continued on a large scale and with even more cruelty, as smugglers sought to compensate for the risks (they were hanged) by crowding their ships. Large numbers were brought into Brazil and, mainly by Americans, into Cuba. Britain alone made serious efforts to suppress it and the Royal Navy maintained regular W. African anti-slavery patrols.

(5) The E. African slave trade, mainly through Zanzibar to the Arab world, was less known to Europeans who were little involved in it. All the same the British govt. induced the Sultan of Zanzibar to restrict it in 1822. The havoc caused by this trade only became public through Livingstone's journeys (1852-6, 1858-64) and demonstrated yet again Samuel Wilberforce's and Thomas Buxton's thesis, urged a generation earlier, that a slave trade always grows up if there is a slave economy to use its goods. The first British measures against colonial slavery (the prohibition of slavery in Albany, S. Africa, in 1820) arose out of the difficulties inherent in intercepting slavers on the high seas. The British naval patrols were maintained until 1861, when the U.S. Civil War destroyed the principal surviving western market other than Brazil, but other measures included the removal of the British Gold Coast settlements from private to govt. control in 1843 and purchase of the Danish (1850) and Dutch (1871) settlements there and the settlement of Lagos (1861). The large Zanzibar slave market was closed in 1873, but the traffic continued across central Africa to the Red Sea for a century longer and probably still exists. *See* SLAVERY.

SLEEMAN, Sir William Henry (1788-1856) in addition to suppressing thugee, was a very successful resident at Gwalior from 1843 to 1849.

SLEEPING SICKNESS. *See* TRYPANOSOMIASIS.

SLIDE RULE. A circular version was described by Richard Delamain the Elder (fl. 1630-1), Charles I's mathematical tutor, in his *Grammelogia or the Mathematicall Ring* in 1631.

SLIGO (Ir.) PORT and COUNTY on the Irish W. Coast. Anciently MacDermott country, the de Burghs conquered it in the 12th cent., but by 1333 the O'Donnells had taken over effective lordship with O'Connor Sligo in the Port and the O'Dowds in the west. In 1567 by surrender and regrant the O'Connors received the whole area, which was shired in 1579. The borough was chartered in 1613. As it was in W. Connaught the shire was not touched by the Cromwellian plantations and remained typically old Irish until well into the 19th cent.

SLIM, William Joseph (1891-1970) Vist. SLIM of YARRALUMBA (1960), much loved soldier, joined the army in 1914, was commissioned and fought at Gallipoli and in Mesopotamia and then joined the Indian army.

When the Japanese invaded Burma in 1942, he commanded the 1st Burma Corps in a hair-raising fighting retreat from Rangoon to the Indian frontier. Both rugged and clever, he developed the tactics of deep penetration fed by airborne drops and commanded the 15th Indian Corps' Arakan operations (Oct. 1943). His ability to administer and lead large formations and to inspire troops was appreciated and he was given command of the 14th Army with which, under Mountbatten, he reconquered Burma between Mar. 1944 and May 1945. In Sept. 1945 he became C-in-C Allied Land Forces, S.E. Asia. After the war he was successively Commandant of the Imperial Defence Coll., Chairman of the Railway Executive and C.I.G.S. and from 1953 to 1960 Gov.-Gen. of Australia. *See* WORLD WAR II-10 & 16.

SLOANE, Sir Hans (1660-1753) was Sec. of the Royal Society from 1693 to 1712 and revived the *Transactions*. In 1712 he bought the manor of Chelsea and in 1725 he founded the Botanical Gardens there. He was Pres. of the Royal Coll, of Physicians from 1719 to 1735 and of the Royal Society from 1727 to 1741.

SLOGAN. Originally a Scottish clan war cry.

SLOOP. *See* SHIPS, SAILING.

SLOUGH (Bucks.) had a wartime mechanical transport depot in World War I and this was converted into an industrial estate afterwards. It and the town expanded rapidly and many Welshmen migrated there from the S. Wales depression of the '30s. In 1938 it was chartered.

SLUMS. To accommodate the townward migrations of an industrial revolution, cheaply built mass produced houses were rapidly erected. These when new were probably better than the hovels and cottages which these countrymen had left but, through their porous bricks, poor timber, plaster and plumbing and inefficient water-proofing, they succumbed in fifty years to pollution, damp and mistreatment and suffered infestations from dry rot to cockroaches, mice and rats. They were creating concern by the 1880s and various philanthropical bodies entered the housing market such as the Peabody Trust and self-help organisations like the R. Catholic inspired Somers Town Housing Assn. The size of the problem was uncomfortably understood, but World War I provoked radical solutions. Enormous casualties and repeated death duties deprived many landlords of resources, and the prospect of demobilisation brought a demand for 'homes fit for heroes'. To replace the worn out stock, legislation empowered local councils to make wholesale compulsory purchases and slum clearances, aided by govt. subsidies. By World War II some 2M people had been rehoused. The process was then accelerated by enemy bombing which affected over 3M buildings. *See* HOUSING.

SMALL HOLDINGS. The rural slump after 1865 still left many people who preferred the country but could get no or no adequate employment in it. The long established village allotments helped to supplement inadequate wages but did not much help the totally unemployed. In 1892 and 1907 the allotments legislation was codified and, to provide work for existing skilled agricultural labour, County Councils were empowered compulsorily to acquire land for letting in 5-acre holdings. By 1914 some 14,000 had been let. The system continued until well after World War II.

SMALLPOX, of uncertain origin or antiquity and often confused with measles and syphilis, reached Europe *via* Spain and Constantinople as a result of the Mohammedan invasions. It was relatively benign until the 14th cent. when virulent outbreaks began, especially in Ireland (1327), London (1366-7) and on the Scottish Border (1474). It was widespread in Europe by 1513; Europeans brought it to Hispaniola in 1517 and to the American mainland in 1520. It facilitated the Spanish mainland conquests, for it wiped out entire tribes and depopulated towns. On the other hand it greatly reduced the value of the conquests, for the casualties ran into millions.

In Europe malignancy became dangerously widespread in about 1590. A continental epidemic of 1614 reached England in 1616. Orlando Gibbons died of smallpox in 1625 and from 1629 the London Bills of Mortality itemised it. These show peaks (over 1000) in 1634, 1649, 1652, 1655, 1659, 1661 and 1664. It now caused serious concern especially as it was no respecter of rank: two of Charles II's brothers died of it in 1661, William II of Orange in 1680 and Queen Mary II in 1694. By 1700 it had replaced plague as the killer epidemic. Counter-measures excited great interest.

INOCULATION had been practised, unnoticed, in S. Wales at least as early as 1650. It was also in use in Turkey and Africa and was reported from China to the Royal Society in 1700. Cotton Mather of Boston learned of a method from an African slave in 1716 and tried it. Lady MARY WORTLEY MONTAGU interested George I in the Turkish method in 1719. Experiments on prisoners (who were pardoned) in Newgate were successful in 1721. Inoculation became compulsory at the Foundling Hospital in 1743. Meanwhile the disease had temporarily retreated, but after a serious epidemic in 1746 the Middlesex Small Pox Hospital was founded by Isaac Maddox, Bp. of Worcester, and an outbreak of 1752 gave him an opportunity to spread the practice. Nevertheless development could not keep up with population. In the 18th cent. the disease caused over 5% of all deaths in 87 years, the highest (18.4%) being in 1798. It was in 1796 that Edward Jenner made his first successful VACCINATION. After 1801 the practice spread very rapidly. The average deaths fell in 1811-20 to 4.2%, in 1821-30 to 3.3%. In the rest of the 19th cent. apart from the pandemics in 1838 and 1871 the decline was steady. Vaccination, free in every parochial union from 1840, was made compulsory in infancy in 1853, enforced by penalties in 1867 and by inspection in 1871. In 1900 the total of deaths in all England was 84. By 1948 the disease was believed extinct. *See* EPIDEMICS, HUMAN.

SMART, Christopher (1722-70), poet and acquaintance of Dr. Burney and Dr. Johnson was, though occasionally demented, one of the earliest to break with the classical style imposed by Dryden and Pope. His main achievements were *Spring* and the *Song to David*.

SMEATON, John (1724-92), engineer and astronomer, was elected F.R.S. for his work on the mariner's compass; he did much research on wind and water mills, studied the Dutch canals and harbours and made great improvements in the design and manufacture of pulleys and blocks, all-important in sailing ships. Between 1756 and 1759 he built the third Eddystone lighthouse which survived for 120 years; he also built bridges at Perth, Banff and Coldstream and designed and built the Forth and Clyde Canal.

SMERWICK (1580). *See* ELIZABETH I-20; RALEIGH.

SMILES, Samuel. *See* SELF HELP.

SMIRKE (1) Sir Robert (1781-1867), architect, built the British Museum, the G.P.O., Covent Garden Market, the Inner Temple Hall and restored York Minster. His brother **(2) Sydney (1798-1877)** restored the Temple Church (1841), built the Reading Room of the British Museum (1854 to 1857) and completed the Burlington House Galleries in 1870.

SMITH, Adam (1723-90) became Prof. of Logic at Glasgow in 1751 and of moral philosophy in 1752. He lectured *inter alia* on jurisprudence and politics, became a friend of Hume and foreign tutor to the D. of Buccleuch, whereby he got to know Turgot, Voltaire and the physiocrats. In 1767 he settled at Kirkcaldy on a pension from the Duke and in 1776 published his classic *Wealth of Nations,* an economic treatise of world wide influence. With the physiocrats he rejected mercantilism, but thought that their view of land as the source of all wealth was evidently too narrow. He considered that its principal source was labour, which was the original determinant of price, until civilisation advanced and brought in capital, profit and rent. The book contains the first scientific discussion of these three and in particular of capital, its accumulation and use and its function in increasing the productivity of labour and its tendency to claim lower rates of interest as economic efficiency rises. He regarded division of labour and the free movement of capital as vital to a healthy economy and therefore advocated free trade and uncontrolled industry and entry to the labour market. The pursuit of self interest contributed, in his view, to the public interest. This economic individualism was probably based upon the unspoken assumption that natural resources and living space were unlimited.

SMITH, Donald Alexander (1820-1914) 1st Ld. STRATHCONA and MOUNTROYAL (1897) was a Manitoba M.P. and the Hudson Bay Co's. Chief Commissioner in Canada from 1870 to 1874. He was a Canadian M.P. from 1871 and helped to overthrow the Macdonald govt. in 1873 over the Pacific scandal. Macdonald kept him out of the syndicate which built the Canadian Pacific Railway, to which, however, his background financial support proved essential. By 1889 he was the largest shareholder in the Hudson Bay Co. and Gov. from then on. He retired from Canadian politics in 1896 and became High Commissioner in London. He raised and equipped a cavalry regiment for the Boer War.

SMITH, Frederick Edwin ("FE") (1872-1930) 1st Ld. BIRKENHEAD (1919), Vist. (1921), E. of (1922) was a rumbustuous barrister and became Unionist M.P. for Walton (1906-19). Well aware of his own exceptional intellect, his mastery of epigram and invective amused the bystanders without endearing him to his equals, even though his maiden speech in the Commons was a much needed triumph for his lately defeated Party. He became Sol-Gen. in 1915. As Att.-Gen. (1915-9) he prosecuted Sir Roger Casement. As Ld. Chancellor (1919-22) he performed an enduring social and public service by reforming and codifying the law of landed property (*see* SCHUSTER-3). As a conservative coalitionist he rejected the decision of the Carlton Club Meeting and refused office under Bonar Law. He also made a stand on behalf of Ulster at this time but rejoined the Conservatives in 1924. He was Sec. of State for India during the transfer of the capital from Calcutta to New Delhi. During his final years he drank heavily. He wrote many books, some of which influenced public opinion.

SMITH, George (1831-95), brickmaker of gypsy origin, discovered a clay at Coalville (Staffs.) and developed a large brickmaking firm. In 1871 he published a book against the employment of children in the brickfields which led to legislation. He later worked to improve the condition of gypsy children and canal boat families.

SMITH, Sir Harry George Wakelyn (1787-1860), Bt. (1846), as a subaltern at the sack of Badajoz protected and married a fiery Spanish girl. He fought through the Peninsular War, then in America and at Waterloo, served in S. Africa in 1836 and went to India as Gough's Adjutant-Gen. In 1846 he led the charge which won the B. of Aliwal (Jan. 1846) and commanded a division at Sobraon. In 1847 he became Gov. of the Cape and in 1848 defeated Pretorius at Boomplatz and drove his men over the Vaal. In 1850 he put down a Kaffir rebellion. He retired in 1852, but Harrysmith and Aliwal North commemorate him, and Ladysmith his wife.

SMITH, Ian (1919-), Rhodesian who served in the R.A.F. (1941-6), became a United Federal Party M.P. (1953-61) in the Southern Rhodesian Parliament and in 1961 founded the Rhodesian Front against premature majority rule. He won power in 1962 and became Prime Minister in 1964. Unable to reach agreement with London on the future of the country, he promulgated a Rhodesian Declaration of Independence (modelled on the American). The new regime weathered international sanctions and diplomatic isolation, but rising guerrilla activity wore it down until finally Britain imposed majority rule and Southern Rhodesia became independent as Zimbabwe. Smith remained an M.P. in the new legislature.

SMITH, John (1580-1631). After military adventures in France, Italy, Hungary and Turkey, where he escaped from slavery, he returned to England *via* Morocco and in 1605 joined the original 106 Virginia settlers, mostly neer-do-wells who would have been lost but for his ingenuity and leadership in dealing with the Red Indians, by whom he was captured (Dec. 1607). By his own account they spared him from burning by the intercession of the Princess Pocahontas, whom he married. John Rolfe (q.v.) had a different story. From Sept. 1608 he was Gov. of Virginia and as such saved the colony by imposing order on the settlement (later called Jamestown) and by securing peaceful trading relationships with the Indians. He also explored much of the northern end of the American Atlantic coast, naming the part south of the Hudson 'New England'. Deposed from the governorship in 1609, he later returned to England.

SMITH, Joseph (1682-1770), was British Consul in Venice from 1710 to 1760 where he made a large collection of books and art treasures. Sold to George III in 1765, they became an important part of the British Museum.

SMITH, Sydney (1771-1845), parson and friend of Jeffrey and Brougham at Edinburgh, started the *Edinburgh Review* in 1802. He lectured on moral philosophy in London from 1804 to 1806 and was one of the Holland House Whigs. In 1807 he published the *Plymley Letters* in favour of R. Catholic emancipation. He settled in a country living in 1808 and only reappeared in London in 1831 when he became a canon of St. Paul's. Amusing and popular, he once described Heaven as "eating paté de foie gras to the sound of trumpets".

SMITH, Sir Sydney. *See* MEDITERRANEAN WAR-3.

SMITH, Sir Thomas (?1558-1625) of the Haberdashers' and Skinners' Cos., was the first Gov. of the HEIC (from 1600 to 1621 with a break in the Tower, 1601-3). He was also interested with one of its founders, his grandfather Andrew Judd, in the Muscovy Co. and in 1609 obtained a charter for the Virginia Co., whose treasurer he was until 1620. A very wealthy businessman, he was persistently accused of malversation but the accusations were pronounced false and James I trusted him until his death and employed him, also, as Receiver of the Duchy of Cornwall throughout his reign. Much of his large fortune benefited the Skinners' charities and Tonbridge School.

SMITH or SMYTHE, Sir Thomas (1513-77), polymath of Queen's Coll., Cambridge, attempted to restore the pronunciation of ancient Greek and became Prof. of Civil Law in 1544. He had been a protégé of Thomas Cromwell and, as a Protestant, he protected the reformers at Cambridge. At Edward VI's accession he became an adviser to Somerset, who made him Clerk of the Privy Council and Master of Requests. In 1548 he became Provost of Eton, Dean of Carlisle and joint Sec. of State with Sir William Petre. His work included diplomacy, visiting universities, reforming canon law, investigating the currency debasement and formulating English claims to suzerainty over Scotland. He fell with Somerset. In 1550 he was summoned as a witness against Bp. Gardiner, but used his influence in his favour. In return, Gardiner kept Smith out of harm's way during Mary I's reign.

Under Elizabeth he was back in favour. He helped to revise the Prayer Book, was employed in Swedish affairs and then, jointly with Sir Nicholas Throgmorton, as Ambassador in Paris (1563-6). After three years of retirement he became a P.C. in 1571 and was on the commission which inquired into Norfolk's conspiracy. In 1572 he was again in France to negotiate the Alençon marriage and then again became Sec. of State and persuaded Elizabeth to help the Scottish Protestants.

He wrote a famous account, *De Republica Anglorum* or *the Maner of Government or Policie of the Realm of England* (published in 1583). He also wrote on the wages of the Roman infantry and the coinage. He knew most of the scholars of his time and was said to have been an accomplished 'physician, mathematician, astronomer, architect, historian and orator'. He was also, typically of his time, interested in astrology and the transmutation of metals.

SMITH, Thomas Southwood (1788-1861), physician, investigated epidemics, especially typhus and his advice to the Poor Law Commission (and others) persuaded the authorities and the world at large to take public health and especially drains seriously. Much of the sanitary improvement in towns everywhere in the 19th cent. is founded upon his work.

SMITH, Vivian Hugh (1867-1956) 1st Ld. BICESTER (1938), banker, became a member of Morgan Grenfell & Co., who in association with J. P. Morgan & Co. of New York, acted as bankers and buyers for the British and French govts. before the U.S.A. entered World War I. He also built up the Royal Exchange Assurance Co. during a period of 60 years as director and governor.

SMITH, William (1769-1839). *See* GEOLOGY.

SMITH, W. H & Son Ltd. founded in 1792 by **Henry and Anna Smith,** was developed as a wholesale newspaper business by their son, **William Henry,** who despatched newspapers by morning instead of evening coach and then by rail as the railways developed. The second **William Henry (1825-91),** against his father's opposition, made the fortune of the business by obtaining bookstall concessions on stations, beginning in 1851 with a monopoly of the London & North Western Railway. Other, but not all, companies followed suit. He also profited from leasing the walls of railway stations for poster advertising. He refused to handle 'harmful' publications and was irreverently known as the North-Western Missionary. Such censorship long remained a feature of the business, which benefited from increased literacy arising out of the educational expansion at the turn of the century. Originally a Liberal, he left that party after being black-balled for the Reform Club, but devoted much wealth in Westminster to his election as a Liberal-Conservative M.P. His interest in social questions, his competence and determination soon earned him office. He became Disraeli's Sec. of the Treasury in 1874. In 1877 he became First Lord of the Admiralty and was mockingly commemorated by Gilbert and Sullivan in *HMS Pinafore.* In 1885 he was Sec. of State for War and in 1886, Leader of the Commons.

SMITH-DORRIEN, Sir Horace Lockwood (1858-1930), controversial soldier who became a major-gen. in the Boer War, commanded II Corps at Mons and on his own responsibility stood at Le Câteau (Aug. 1914). He disagreed with G.H.Q. on the desirability of immediate offensives before Kitchener's armies were ready; in Apr. 1915 his Second Army had to withstand the first German gas attack without anti-gas equipment and he urged a minor withdrawal before Ypres. This was not approved and he resigned in May; thereafter he occupied routine posts.

SMITHFIELD (originally SMOOTHE FIELD) (London) was used as a training and jousting ground in the Middle Ages and for the ancient Bartholomew Fair, where *inter ala* live cattle were sold from all over the kingdom. The cattle trade was moved to the Caledonian Market in Islington in 1855 and from 1860 onwards markets for meat, poultry, provisions, fruit and fish were successively established at Smithfield.

SMITHSON or MACIE, James Lewis (1765-1829), illegitimate son of the 1st D. of Northumberland (*see* PERCY previously SMITHSON) became a distinguished mineralogist and chemist and left his fortune to found the Smithsonian Institution at Washington.

SMOLLETT (1) Sir James (1648-1731), an active Scots supporter of William III, was one of the commissioners of the Union in 1707 and thereafter M.P. for Dumbarton. His grandson (2) Tobias George (1721-71) settled as a surgeon in Downing St. in 1741, published *Roderick Random* in 1748, founded the *Critical Review* in 1756 and published a *History of England* in 1757. From 1763 he was mostly abroad. He published *Humphrey Clinker* in 1771.

SMUGGLING is the human reaction to prohibitions or high taxes on cross-frontier movement of profitably saleable goods. From about 1700 American tobacco and rum, and French brandy were the commonest such goods, and later in the century, tea. In Britain customs men were so badly paid that they mostly collaborated (for a consideration) with the smugglers. In the American colonies, but for the Boston Tea Party, direct importation of cheaper tea by the HEIC would have destroyed the smugglers' market. Free trade and a properly organised and paid customs service reduced British smuggling to small amounts after 1840 until the rise of the dangerous and lucrative drug traffic at ferry- and air-ports in the 1980s.

SMUTS, Jan Christiaan (1870-1950) was State Attorney of the Transvaal in 1898 and an important Boer general in the S. African War of 1899 to 1902, who led raids deep into the Cape Colony to try to raise the Boers resident in it. He helped to draft the P. of Vereeniging and persuaded his people to accept it on the basis that Africans in the two former republics would not be given the franchise. In 1906 he was sent to England to negotiate for responsible govt. and, as Louis Botha's deputy, organised the triumph of HET VOLK (Dutch = The People), the nationalist party in the Transvaal elections of 1907, and he was Botha's Minister of Education. He and Botha next negotiated the Union of 1910 and he and Churchill became life-long friends. He became the Union's first Minister of Defence. As such he organised the force which crushed the Rand strike and also the rebellion of 1914. He was a respected, if occasional member of the War Cabinets in both World Wars. From 1919 to 1924 he was Prime Minister of the Union and Minister of Native Affairs. He was Justice Minister from 1933 to 1939. His United Party was split on the question of joining the war against Germany, but he became Prime Minister and Minister for External Affairs in 1939 after gaining a small majority in his party in favour of entry. He lost office on the electoral victory of the Nationalists in 1948.

SMYRNA (Turk: IZMIR) (Turkey) after vicissitudes finally became an Ottoman Turkish port in 1425. A large Christian population remained and the rich hinterland attracted western trade, notably later, in tobacco, cotton, carpets and silk. It became an important port with many seamen and Smyrna convoys were a feature of Dutch trade (*see* DUTCH WARS). It suffered from pirates, who also recruited there, and also from earthquakes which flattened it, in 1688 and 1778. The Greek army, with British encouragement, occupied it in 1919 but was driven out with the entire Greek population amid massacre in 1922.

SMYTH, Dame Ethel (1858-1944), courageous large scale composer, in her day suspect because her highly original style deviated widely from the commonly observed line of musical advance, and because she was a woman. Not surprisingly she became a stone-throwing suffragette. Her music was acclaimed in Leipzig, where she was trained, and in Prague, but despite the Albert Hall success of her *Mass in D* (1893) and Sir Thomas Beecham's efforts in 1916, she has not so far commanded much British interest.

SMYTH, Patrick James (1826-85), Irish Nationalist, joined the Repeal Association in 1844 and also Young Ireland. Implicated in the 1848 rebellion, he escaped to the U.S.A.

where he wrote for Irish journals. In 1856 he returned and briefly owned *The Irishman*. He was M.P. for Westmeath from 1871 to 1880 and for Tipperary until 1882, but as he opposed Parnell and the Land League, he destroyed his own popularity.

SMYTH (1) Percy Clinton Sydney (1780-1855) 6th Vist. STRANGFORD, diplomat and friend of Thomas Moore and Croker. As *chargé d'affaires* at Lisbon in 1807 he persuaded the Portuguese regent to go to Brazil and was Ambassador successfully at Stockholm (1817), Constantinople (1820) and St. Petersburg in 1824. His son (2) George Augustus (1818-57) 7th Vist., M.P. from 1840, was a supporter of Disraeli's Young England and is the model for Disraeli's *Coningsby*. He was Peel's Foreign U/Sec. and broke with Disraeli in 1846. Thereafter he was a successful political journalist. In 1852 he fought the last duel in England. His brother (3) Percy (1826-69) 8th Vist., was a brilliant oriental linguist who also wrote, mainly for the *Pall Mall Gazette*, on oriental subjects. His wife (4) Emily Anne (?-1887) *née* BEAUFORT, archaeologist and welfare worker, raised funds for Bulgarian relief in 1876 and organised a Turkish hospital in 1877.

SNELL, Hannah (1723-92), supposedly a martial and naval lady, said to have enlisted in 1745 and been pensioned for wounds received at Pondicherry. She later appeared on the stage, published some memoirs and kept a pub at Wapping called *The Female Soldier*. Thrice married, she died in Bedlam.

SNORRI STURLASON (1179-1241), statesman, historian and poet, was Law Speaker of the Icelandic Althing (Parliament) from 1215 to 1218 and again from 1222 to 1231. He also spent much time in Norway and Sweden, where he was an honoured guest of Kings and probably visited many ancient burial sites. His writings are the principal source for early Scandinavian history and civilisation. They include (1) the PROSE EDDA, a text book on versification and poetic diction, to which is appended (2) the HATTATAL, a summary of the Scandinavian metres written in the metres themselves; (3) HELMSKRINGLA. Parts I and III of this great work constitute a Scandinavian, primarily Norwegian, history from the most ancient times to 1177, cast in the form of a series of royal biographies. Part II is a full length biography of St. Olaf. In the preface and elsewhere Snorri discussed the reliability of his many sources, generally preferring contemporaneous accounts and poems published in the presence of those whom they concern; (4) he also probably wrote EGIL'S SAGA about his ancestor, the pirate poet, Egil Skalla Grimsson. Like so many Scandinavian politicians, Snorri was murdered.

SNOWDEN, Philip (1864-1937) Vist. SNOWDEN (1931), son of a weaver and permanently crippled by a spinal inflammation in 1891, became an active member of the Independent Labour Party in 1895, Chairman in 1903-6 and M.P. for Blackburn (1906-18) and for Colne Valley (1922-31). He was a pacifist and champion of conscientious objectors. He had mastered many aspects of national finance when he became Chancellor of the Exchequer in the brief Labour govt. of 1924. He held the same office in the Labour govt. of 1929 (*see* MACDONALD'S SECOND GOVT.) and, having brought off a successful deal in the Young Plan (1929), was faced with the Great Slump. He did not like, or perhaps did not understand, deficit financing and determinedly balanced the budget by raising taxes and cutting expenditure and suspending the Gold Standard. This, though few realised it, probably made things worse. Having thus become a fiscal conservative, he logically, if with distaste, remained with the National Govt. as Lord Privy Seal, but resigned on the tariff issue (1932).

SOANE (orig. SWAN), Sir John (1753-1837), son of a bricklayer, was sent to the Royal Academy by his father and distinguished himself as a pupil of George Dance.

After travels in Italy he set up as a private architect and in 1788 became architect to the Bank of England, which he rebuilt. This gave him wide connections and a vast practice. He was Prof. of Architecture at the Royal Academy from 1806. In 1835 he gave his curious house in Lincoln's Inn Fields (London) with its collections to the public.

SOAPY SAM = Samuel Wilberforce. *See* WILBERFORCE-2.

SOBRANIE. A Bulgarian parliament.

SOCAGE. *See* LAND TENURE (ENGLAND)-1.

SOCIAL CONTRACT. This phrase, purloined from Rousseau (q.v.) by the Wilson govt. of 1974, meant an arrangement whereby existing restrictions on trade unions were repealed but the unions were to moderate their demands as if restrictions still existed. There being nothing to stop them breaking their word and the govt. being not averse to maintaining employment by soaking the rich, the govt's good faith began to be doubted. Inflationary claims in fact grew until the collapse of the Callaghan govt. in 1978.

SOCIAL CREDIT, was based on an economic doctrine of the 1930s that the cost of production was not balanced by an equivalent purchasing power among potential users. The imbalance should be cured by monetary gifts by the state to individuals in the form of rapidly declining notes, which the receiver would wish to spend quickly. This attempt to remedy the 1930s depression by artificial stimulation of the currency had a serious political appeal only in Canada, where Social Credit govts. were set up in Alberta and British Columbia but could not carry out their programme because of the constitutional reservation of currency matters to the Dominion govt. In 1948 the Alberta party repudiated the doctrine.

SOCIALISM (1) in the sense of the vesting or appropriation of resources in a community for Common social purposes and the consequent exclusion or limitation of private ownership, is very ancient and natural, especially under tribal conditions (*see* WELSH LAW). Common lands and Charity (in the legal sense) are manifestations of the same idea and so, in a narrow form is monasticism. Well disciplined armies are large socialistic organisations.

(2) Theoretical socialism may (perhaps) have begun with theorists whose work could be widely circulated. St. Thomas More published *Utopia* in 1516. Thomas Muntzer (?-1525) led a revolutionary peasant army in Germany, the Anabaptists, who had everything in common including sexual relations, and terrorised Monster (1534-5). Gerrard Winstanley's (1649) God moved him and his followers to seize lands and cultivate them in common. All these denounced private property as an historic evil and (except More) claimed a God-conferred moral superiority which entitled them to enforce their ideas. These theological socialisms held the field as long as religion was not itself rejected. Ludwig Feuerbach thought, however (1841), that religion was simply the product of the human mind and Karl Marx paid much attention to Feuerbach.

(3) Marx substituted inevitability for God, but thought that revolutionary activity was necessary to overthrow the capitalist society. Since the propertyless masses (or proletariat) were excluded from the benefits of society, they would have a direct interest in such overthrow and should be trained to effect it. His analysis was propagandist and self-contradictory, but seductive. The poor were to inherit the earth not by work, but by violence.

(4) Since labour was his criterion of value and capitalism was bound to collapse under the weight of its own success, it followed that violent revolution might, probably would not achieve its real purpose, but would consume more than a justifiable proportion of the resources released from the clutches of capitalism. This suspicion led to the contentions of the English Fabians and, later, was apparently confirmed by the results of the

Russian Revolution in Russia and elsewhere. It appeared also that revolutionary socialism in due course created a new class of ruling party bureaucrats who, in the analysis of Milovan Djilas, had become the true proprietors of the sources of wealth.

SOCIAL DEMOCRATIC AND LABOUR PARTY (S.D.L.P.). a non-violent, mainly R. Catholic party in Ulster formed by Gerry Fitt M.P. in 1970 and led after 1983 by John Hume.

SOCIALIST LEAGUE, a small extremist group which, led by William Morris, broke away from the Social Democratic Federation in 1884. Increasingly infiltrated by anarchists, it soon broke up. Morris resigned in 1890.

SOCIALIST PARTIES (1) France. By 1900 there were five rival parties which attempted some co-ordination in 1901. The two principal ones united in 1905 under Jean Jaurès. **(2) Germany.** A Social Democrat was elected to the German Diet in 1864. The combined socialists held 110 seats out of 397 by 1912. **(3) Italy.** The main socialist party was formed in 1892. There were 40 socialist deputies by 1909. *See* LABOUR PARTY.

SOCIAL SECURITY (*for definition see* BEVERIDGE REPORT). In 1908 the Asquith govt. created pensions as of right for the over-70s. These were small but enough to keep the aged poor out of the workhouse. In 1911 Winston Churchill and Lloyd George created a separate contributory health insurance scheme involving friendly societies, trade unions and insurance cos., under which capitation payments were made to doctors listed in panels; they also instituted a contributory unemployment scheme combined with labour exchanges (now called Job Centres) for certain, mainly building and engineering workers. As a result of inflation and rising life expectations these schemes could be supported only by additional finance, which was obtained by making new retirement pensions contributory (1925) and by progressively increasing the classes required to join (and contribute to) schemes. None of them dealt adequately with the long term unemployed who, until 1929, were supported on locally financed Poor Law and after 1929 by public assistance committees to which the Exchequer contributed.

By World War II all the available classes of possible contributories had been brought in, but it was clear that the systems needed to be rationalised. Sir William Beveridge's Report, produced at the instance of the wartime govt. of Sir Winston Churchill, who had known him since 1911, proposed a unified social security scheme with unified contributions. This was enacted under the Attlee govt. in 1946 and it also created the National Health Service (N.H.S.) designed to underpin the system with free medical, dental and eye services for all. The N.H.S. was financed mainly and soon wholly from taxation.

Difficulties soon appeared. N.H.S. patients multiplied unexpectedly and the N.H.S. developed increasingly expensive techniques. In part the cost could be met and economies made by prescription charges, which despite political excitement were tolerated as long as they stayed low. In fact they rose. Hence after 1992 the Major govt. began to reduce services by, for example, closing relatively unnoticeable cottage hospitals and, by rationing funds. Later, however, it started to close such teaching hospitals as St. Bartholomew's in London.

Then, during periods of high unemployment, the unemployment and pensions insurance aspects were not self-financing without raising contributions, which developed into a burdensome poll tax upon employers and employed. On the pretext of European anti-sex discrimination legislation, it was decided gradually to equalise the retiring ages of men (65) and women (60) at 65.

SOCIETY FOR CONSTITUTIONAL INFORMATION (1770) led by John Horne (Tooke) split off from the Society for the Defence of the Bill of Rights after a quarrel between Home and John Wilkes. It attracted the wealthier and more intellectual radicals. Suspended in 1784, it revived in 1791 and began sponsoring radical pamphlets. It declined after 1796.

SOCIETY FOR THE DEFENCE OF THE BILL OF RIGHTS. See WILKES-2.

SOCIETY OF DILETTANTI began in 1754 as a dining club for those who had been to Italy on a Grand Tour (q.v.). Members had to pay 4% of the first year's increase of income from a legacy, marriage or preferment. The Society became rich. It supported Italian opera in 1750, planned a R. Academy, financed scholarships to Italy and Greece, and Chandler, Pars and Revett's expedition to Asia Minor in 1764 and the consequent publication (1769-97) of their *Ionian Antiquities*. The Society's funds and the social distinction of its members gave it exceptional influence on aesthetic style.

SOCIETY Is. See TAHITI.

SOCIETY PEOPLE (Sc.) = Cameronians (q.v.).

SOCMAN or SOKEMAN. A tenant in socage. See LAND TENURE (ENGLAND)-1.

SOCOTRA (Indian Ocean) was connected with the Yemeni MAHRI, whose Sultan exercised the functions mainly of an intertribal arbitrator on the mainland, but ruled absolutely in Socotra where he preferred to live. In 1834 the British made a coaling agreement with him and tried, but failed, to buy the island. In 1838 he proposed a lease but by this time the British were more interested in Aden. In 1876 he agreed not to sell Socotra to any other power and by Treaties of 1886 and 1888 accepted British protection until 1954, when the protectorate was replaced by an advisory relationship. In 1967 the Sultanate was abolished and the island became part of the People's Republic of S. Yemen.

SODOMY. See BUGGERY.

SODOR AND MAN, a diocese which includes the I. of Man and the Sudreys or Hebrides. The earliest episcopal evidence dates from the 9th cent. Ecclesiastical jurisdiction over the See was contested in the 12th and 13th cents. between the Abps. of Trondheim and York, the local chapter, clergy and people and latterly after Norway ceded overlordship to Scotland (1266) by the Kings of Scots. Such international pressure confused the episcopal succession and at times allowed the local clergy a certain freedom. During the Great Schism, the Sudreys adhered to Avignon, whereas Man, under English influence, followed the Roman Pope. The division of the Sudreys from Man continued until 1542 when the whole diocese was included in the See of York, but a separate bishop for the Isles existed until 1702.

SOHO (London). The name is said to be derived from a hunting cry used in the open fields of which it consisted until 1643, when the Parliamentarians built a fort where Oxford St. and Wardour St. now join. The area was laid out in building plots and King's Square (now Soho Square) built in 1681. After the Revocation of the Edict of Nantes (1685) Huguenot refugees made it a French quarter with a, still surviving, French Protestant church. Italians replaced them at the end of the 19th cent. There was also a Portuguese embassy. Soho was a haunt of prostitutes until the mid-1980s.

SOKEN or SOKE. A customary lordship (peculiar to the Danelaw) over men, perhaps originally settlers from a particular Danish band, who might be scattered over an area. It sometimes developed into a territorial jurisdiction. See PETERBOROUGH.

SOKOTO. See HAUSA.

SOLANDER, Daniel (1733-82), pupil of Linnaeus, sailed with Joseph Banks as a scientist in Cook's *Endeavour* expedition and became his sec. and librarian.

SOLAR ENERGY. In 1747 Buffon tested the possibility that Archimedes had burned Roman ships in 214 B.C. by means of mirrors and himself fired wood at 75 yards. At 20 feet he melted silver. In 1755 Hoesen constructed a 5 foot parabolic mirror with which he quickly melted coins. In 1834-8 Sir John Herschel made a workable solar oven at the Cape. Water was pumped in Algeria by solar engines in the 1870s. A boiler was heated to high pressure in California in 1902. By 1950 solar heating was commonplace in Cyprus and Israel and other Levantine countries.

SOLDAN. See SULTAN.

SOLICITOR-GENERAL. See ATTORNEY-GENERAL.

SOLDIERS', SAILORS' AND AIRMEN'S FAMILIES' ASSOCIATION (S.S.A.F.A.), a voluntary welfare organisation, was founded in 1885 to deal with the many difficulties arising from the prolonged absences of service men from their homes. It was an important element in service morale during World War II.

SOLEMN ENGAGEMENT (June 1647) was a mutual undertaking by all the New Model Army at Newmarket, that they would not disband until they received such treatment from Parliament as might be approved by a council consisting of the generals and two officers and two private men from each regiment.

SOLEMN LEAGUE AND COVENANT. See SCOTLAND, (PRESBYTERIAN) CHURCH.

SOLOMON Is. (Pac.). The Spaniards attempted colonisation in 1595, but the islands were properly surveyed by British and French explorers only between 1766 and 1792. The Germans claimed a protectorate in the north in 1885; the British in the south in 1893, but in 1895 the German islands except Buka and Bougainville were transferred to Britain in return for a German free hand in W. Samoa. Buka and Bougainvile were seized by Australia in 1914 and they, with the northern islands, were mandated to Australia in 1920. The islands, especially Guadalcanal, were the scene of furious fighting in World War II and in 1978 they became independent within the Commonwealth.

SOMALI-A,-LAND (1) The history after 1542 relates mainly to the drive of Somali Mohammedan tribes from the coast of the G. of Aden and the Red Sea towards the Arab coastal trading settlements. By 1800 these were mostly Somali dominated.

(2) When the British established their coaling station at Aden in 1839, they became interested in the Somali coast, especially Berbera opposite, because it supplied Aden with meat. The French made their coaling station at Obok I. in 1862 and then developed the Somali port of Djibouti. Further north the Italians occupied Assab in 1869 and began to develop and settle Eritrea and the trade along the south coast. In 1870 the Egyptians revived a Turkish claim to the suzerainty over Berbera dating from 1542 and raised their flag there to the initial annoyance of the British; but by 1877 the latter were favouring Egyptian pretensions as a way of creating difficulties for other European claimants. The Mahdist revolt in the Sudan caused Egypt to abandon Harar and other Somali possessions in 1885 and the British, solely to keep others out, established a special hybrid regime over BRITISH SOMALILAND; it became *vis-à-vis* other powers a British protectorate, but the independence of the inland tribes was guaranteed and the ports were controlled only through consuls. A conflict over the expanding French colony of Djibouti was averted by a boundary convention in 1888.

(3) In 1889 the Ethiopians seized Harar and concluded the T. of Ucciali with Italy; at the same time the British E. Africa Co., which had obtained a lease of the southern coast, made a sublease to an Italian Co. From 1892. This was held directly of the Sultan.

(4) The Ethiopian victory over Italy in 1896 radically changed the situation and the three European powers agreed with Ethiopia to curtail their interests. Ethiopia acquired the Somali Ogaden and the British abandoned their protection of the Haud tribes without ceding them.

In 1899, however, the British faced a religious revolt led by Mohammed bin Abdullah Hassan (The "Mad Mullah"). By 1904 the interior was under his control. In 1905 the Italian cos. in the south went bankrupt and their rights were taken over by their govt. and in 1910 the British cut their losses and abandoned their jurisdiction in their interior. At this period then the Somali areas from Assab to Harar were firmly under Italian, French and Ethiopian control, while the rest consisted of British northern coastal and Italian southern coastal strips, with a vast uncontrolled and undemarcated hinterland partly claimed by Italy and Ethiopia.

(5) After World War I the attitude of the adjacent powers hardened. The British put down the Mad Mullah in 1920; from 1923 Fascist Italy conquered the southern interior to which, by treaty with Britain, the port of Kismayu was added in 1925. Italian Somalia was pacified by 1926 and northward pressure towards the southward moving Ethiopians began. The result was a collision in 1934 at WALWAL which brought on the Italo-Ethiopian war.

(6) In 1940 the British evacuated their protectorate in the face of Italian invasion, but when the British conquered the Italian E. African Empire in 1941, the whole of Somalia except Djibouti came under their military administration. British Somaliland reverted to colonial office control in 1948; the Ogaden and the Haud were ceded to Ethiopia by 1950; the Italians were allowed to return to their parts in 1950 and, under U.N. trusteeship, to prepare the country for independence. In June 1960 the British protectorate became independent and in July it united with the Italian area to become the SOMALI REPUBLIC. In 1969 the parliamentary govt. was overthrown by a military one, which changed the name to 'Somali Democratic Republic'. This slowly broke up into a series of bandit armies.

SOMERLED. *See* ISLES, LORDSHIP OF THE; MAN.

SOMERSET (An elliptical form of Sumortunsaetan A.S. = the men of the area dependent on Somerton.) **(1)** Has many pre-Roman remains, particularly tracks, tumuli and fortified places on or along the crests of the Mendips, Poldens, Exmoor Forest and other eminences and at Bath, Bristol, Glastonbury and Taunton. The Roman pattern was different. They built towns at Avonmouth, Bath, Somerton and llchester and connected them by road, the last three being on the Fosseway from Cirencester to Exeter. There were many Roman villas round Somerton and in the north. They used slave labour in the Mendip lead mines. The area was Romano-British until the 7th cent.

(2) The B. of Deorham (577) heralded the Saxon Conquest of the Bristol Avon valley and after a victory at Bradford-on-Avon (652) King Cenwalh advanced inland to the R. Parret and his successors reached its mouth by 682. The West Saxon King Ine took over the eastern part. He drove the British King Geraint into the Exmoor hills in about 710 and founded Taunton. Athelney, near the confluence of the Parret and the Tone was a Royal border stronghold, later used as a refuge by King Alfred from dangers from the opposite direction. Saxon authority in the west had not long been established at that time and differences of outlook, custom and physique between the areas east and west of the Parret survived into modern times.

(3) Aldhelm (?-709), a relative of Ine, settled as a missionary at Malmesbury in about 675 and in 704 Ine made him Bp. of Sherborne. He built churches at Frome and Bruton, while other churches were built at Bath and Taunton. The Saxon area rose in population and ecclesiastical establishments, but by 909 the bishopric of Sherborne was obviously too large and a specifically Somerset diocese was established at Wells.

(4) By the Conquest Somerset was divided into 36 hundreds based on Royal estates and an honour belonging to Wells. They varied greatly in size and resources: the Honour, and Frome and Bruton being assessed at near or over £200 for geld, but Bedminster about £6 and Brompton Ralph at £5. The Count of Mortain was the largest landowner with a great concentration of manors covering a 10 mile wide strip along the Dorset and Devon boundaries as far as the Tone. The Royal holdings were much smaller and scattered. The ecclesiastical holdings too were scattered and divided between six bishops (including those of Bayeux and Coutances) and eight churches (including St. Peter's at Rome). All these between them accounted for less than 25% of the land.

(5) The bishopric was transferred from Wells to Bath between 1090 and 1111 and the bishop then became *ex officio* Abbot of Bath. Ecclesiastical holdings multiplied during the Middle Ages; by the Dissolution the Benedictines and the Austin Canons had seven houses each, the military orders and the Friars three each. There were 13 hospitals and seven other establishments.

(6) The shire was remarkably untroubled in the Middle Ages save for a local civil war around Taunton between the Yorkist E. of Devon and the Lancastrian Ld. Bonville of Chewton in 1451 and the levying of heavy fines after Perkin Warbeck's revolt of 1497. Similarly, though there were casualties in the Black Death (1346-7) recovery was extremely rapid. Apart from a fertile agriculture, which in the western part yielded easily to inclosure, and much forestry, there were important industries including the winning of clay, fullers earth and limestone, the great Mendip lead, zinc and coal mines and iron workings. There was always much wool and by 1336 (when there was a Flemish colonisation at Taunton) cloth making was far advanced. This industry was prosperous until the mid-17th cent. Otherwise it has remained a farming area for stock and dairy products such as the well known Cheddar Cheese. In 1965 a nuclear power station was opened at Hinckley Point.

SOMERSET HOUSE. The Protector Somerset had a palace on the Strand (London). This was superseded in 1776-86 by a govt. building which housed the Inland Revenue Valuation Office, the Probate Registry and especially the General Register Office, with which the name became identified. This office was moved to Aldwych in the 1980s. The East Wing has always been occupied by Kings College. The West Wing now houses the Courtauld Institute.

SOMERSETT'S CASE (1772). *See* SLAVERY IN BRITAIN.

SOMERVELL, Donald Bradley (1889-1960) Ld. SOMERVELL of HARROW (1954) took a degree in chemistry and in 1916 was called to the bar. He became a pupil of the Socialist W. A. Jowitt and a friend of the Liberal Cyril Asquith, but after becoming a K.C. in 1929 he entered politics as a Conservative and in 1931 became M.P. for Crewe. In 1933 he was Sol-Gen. under Inskip and in 1936 Att.-Gen. with Jowitt and then with Maxwell Fife under him. He held this office until 1945 and so had to cope with all the legal problems arising from the abdication and World War II. In 1945 he was Home Sec. in the caretaker govt; and thereafter became a Lord Justice of Appeal and in 1954 a Law Lord.

SOMERVILLE. Ancient Scots Lowland family and **Lords SOMERVILLE. (1)** Hugh (?1483-1549) **5th Ld.** captured at Solway Moss in 1542 took an English pension and became one of the "English Lords". A descendant **(2) John Southey (1765-1819) 15th Ld. (1796)** helped George III to reintroduce the Merino sheep.

SOMERVILLE, Sir James Fownes (1882-1949) had a distinguished naval career in World War I, was invalided out for tuberculosis in 1938, but from 1939 busied himself with naval technical problems especially radar. During the Dunkirk evacuation, still in retirement, he took charge at Dover where the Admiral in command was intermittently indisposed. In June 1940 he was returned to active service as Commander of Force H at Gibraltar running convoys through the Mediterranean and participating in the *Bismarck* episode. From 1942 to 1944 he was C-in-C of the weak Eastern Fleet, which he saved from disaster, and at the end of the war conducted an offensive against the Japanese in Java and Sumatra.

SOM[M]ERS, John (1651-1716) Ld. (1697) originally made his public reputation as junior counsel for the Seven Bishops in June 1688. He was M.P. for Worcester (his home county) from 1689 to 1697 and the principal Commons draughtsman of the Declaration of Rights. Consequently he became Sol-Gen. after William III and Mary II had accepted the throne and in 1693 Lord Keeper. Much liked for his apparent youthfulness, his literary and scientific interests, he belonged to the Kit Cat Club and was a patron of Addison, Congreve, Steele and Vertue. With Montagu, Locke and Newton he planned a currency reform in 1695 and so influenced Newton's management of the Mint and his later reports on the coinage. Respected for his legal abilities, he became Lord Chancellor in 1697 and supported Rymer and his successor Madox. He favoured William III's anti-French policies despite their expense and was one of the few Englishmen whom William trusted. Consequently he was driven from office in 1700 and unsuccessfully impeached for his part in the Partition Treaties of 1698-9. He was Pres. of the Royal Society from 1699 to 1704. When William died he joined the Whigs and effected an important service during the wars by drafting an acceptable Act of Union with Scotland in 1707. He was Lord President in 1708 and, as one of the Junto, advised his colleagues not to impeach Sacheverell, but fell with them in 1710.

SOMME, B. of the (June-Nov. 1916). For this battle, in which Anglo-French casualties amounted to some 600,000 for a gain of 125 square miles against German losses of 300,000 *see* WORLD WAR I-8.

SONS OF LIBERTY were an American terrorist society, founded in about 1765, whose main activity was to interfere with trade and taxation. They forced the resignation of all the agents for the stamp tax, organised boycotts of British goods and harried officials. Their symbol was the liberty tree or pine to which officials were sometimes brought and interrogated.

SOPHY, THE. The Shah of Persia, especially between 1500 and 1736.

SOPWITH, Sir Thomas Octave Murdoch (1888-1989) founded his aviation co. in 1912 and designed and built many British military aircraft in World War I. His firm was amalgamated with the Hawker-Siddeley Group of which he became chairman in 1935. The group produced the *Hurricane* fighter, the *Lancaster* bomber and the first jet aircraft.

SORBONNE. In about 1257 Robert de Sorbon founded a theological college at Paris and the name came to mean the important and influential theological faculty of the old Paris university.

SOTHEBY'S. These celebrated auctioneers were founded by Samuel Baker in 1744. The King St. book auctions began in 1754.

SOUDAN. *See* AFRICA, WEST (EX-FRENCH).

SOULBURY. *See* CEYLON.

SOUME (Sc.) was the number (generally fixed by custom) of animals which a tenant might pasture on the local common. In Inverness-shire $1\frac{1}{2}$ cows = 8 sheep = 40 goats. In Perthshire $1\frac{1}{2}$ cows = 8 sheep or 8 goats.

SOUND TOLLS. *See* BALTIC-7 to 8, 24, 50-56; SHIPS, SAILING.

SOUS-ALLIÉS (Fr. = subsidiary allies). Early 19th cent. diplomatic term for the allies against Bonaparte other than Austria, Britain, Prussia and Russia.

SOUTH AFRICAN REPUBLIC (1) The occasionally defined S.W. part of the Transvaal which accepted the Rustenburg Grondwet under Marthinus Pretorius in 1856. It extended its area into most of the Transvaal by 1864 and was annexed by the British in 1877. **(2)** The name of the Transvaal from 1884 to 1900.

SOUTH AFRICA, UNION later REPUBLIC (*see* SOUTH AFRICAN WAR) **(1)** The P. of Vereeniging (31 May 1902) brought the two Boer ex-republics (now the Transvaal and the Orange River Colony) and the two British colonies (Natal and Cape Province) separately under the same imperial sovereignty. Mindful of their investments and respecting the Boers, the victors in the persons of Chamberlain (Colonial Sec.) and Milner (High Commissioner) preached reconciliation and practical reconstruction. Milner got 450,000 people home and his ploughing teams had turned the soil for them by Jan. 1903. Large rebuilding grants and cheap loans were provided, but it was evident that properly geared progress required self-administration and Milner was soon setting up municipalities and nominated legislative councils in the ex-republics. It also required the removal of artificial bafflers. His Bloemfontein Customs Conference (1903) cleared away mutual tariffs. This was the decisive step towards union. The Conference also observed that mining labour shortages were hindering reconstruction and recommended recruitment of indentured labour in Asia. This engendered the 'Chinese Slavery' controversy which convulsed the British general election of 1905.

(2) A commission had reviewed court-martial sentences. Martial law was soon lifted and the army mostly withdrawn. A Boer revival began with linguistic and educational agitations. Politics soon followed. Jan Hofmeyr renamed the Afrikaner Bond the S. African Party to attract British votes (1904). Louis Botha launched *Het Volk* at Pretoria (1905). The Rand Uitlanders (mostly British) began to organise. All these thought in terms of S. Africa as a whole. They met a ready response at Westminster and from the new High Commissioner, Ld. Selborne, but the four colonies had differing motives. A Zulu insurrection had warned Natal that its native problems might not be soluble without help. The Cape wanted the rich mining Transvaal to support its tax burden. Some Boers of the ex-republics hoped to achieve peacefully the victory which had eluded them in war, and the essential railways, planned for an historical fragmentation, needed rationalisation. This need directed discussions towards political combination. Unlike the Boers, the British govt. could put closer union on the agenda. The Selborne Memorandum (July 1907) on railway problems, blessed by British and Boer leaders, implied closer union.

(3) Under the treaty, constitutional arrangements were to precede native enfranchisement and the ex-republics soon had legislatures. There was a need for haste when a railway and customs conference met in July 1908, because the Westminster Liberals were in decline. The four legislatures appointed politically representative delegations to a constitutional convention which sat from Oct. 1908 to May 1909 successively at Durban, Cape Town and Bloemfontein.

(4) They agreed (a) a unionist not a federalist constitution composed, under the Crown, of a 10-year Senate of eight indirectly elected for each province plus eight Gov-Gen's. nominees, and an Assembly of 121, in which the Cape was much underweighted with 51 seats, while the Transvaal received 36 and the others 17 each. Automatic upward or downward redistribution was to be based on quinquennial census quotas consisting of the 1904 European male adult population divided by 121. This also worked against the Cape which in 1904 had been crowded with white refugees and migrants heading for the Transvaal. (b) Disagreements between the Houses might be settled in joint session. (c) The provincial courts became divisions of a unified Supreme Court, administering mostly Roman Dutch law, from which appeals to the Privy Council might be made only with the special leave of the King in Council. (d) In response to British pressure the protectorate regimes and tribal lands in Basutoland, Swaziland and Bechuanaland were specially protected. (e) The railways were to be separately budgeted on business principles, 30% of the traffic passing through Natal.

(5) The necessary bill was passed uncontroversially at Westminster in Sept. 1909. Ld. Gladstone, the first Gov-Gen., summoned Louis Botha to form an interim govt. pending elections. His combined Nationalists and *Het Volk* had been renamed the S. African National Party. Independents campaigned in Natal. Elsewhere a Unionist or moderate party emerged. The Nationals won 66 seats, the Unionists 39, the Independents 12 and Labour 4. In fact Botha shared out cabinet offices on a provincial rather than a party basis, while the Unionist opposition were concerned to save him from his own extremists.

(6) In the next four years these inexperienced parliamentarians had to learn the novel task of guiding S. Africa as a whole, while coping with linguistic and educational controversies and a rising cost of living. Of the two languages, English was English but it was doubtful whether the other was Netherlands Dutch or a simplified version of it, or the Afrikaan's vernacular being systematised by Steyn's Suid-Afrikaanse Akademie. Language was related to politics: English-speakers often favoured the Anglo-Imperial settlement: the non-English were equally often unreconciled republicans. The teaching language, especially of the very young, was near to every mother's heart. Who should pay for which sort of school, to every father's. Thus, animosities put to sleep by the Treaty woke up with the Union.

(7) After the London Imperial Conference of 1911, a small army was created, supplemented by compulsory service in defence regiments and membership of rifle clubs. This reanimated the Boer tradition of the Armed Nation and created Boer confidence against the black millions, but meanwhile Jan Hertzog was becoming suspicious of Louis Botha's immigration and imperial co-operation policies as likely to destroy the old Boer way of life. This old way had been in decline for a generation, but the myth provided emotional appeal. In 1912 they quarrelled and in Dec. Botha reconstituted his cabinet without Hertzog who made inflammatory speeches. Thus when World War I broke out and the govt. took over defence from the British, there was opposition to anything save passive defence. A plan to attack two German radio stations in S.W. Africa and perhaps German E. Africa provoked a rebellion which, after scattered fights, was ended by Dec. 1914 (*see* BOTHA, LOUIS). S.W. Africa was then conquered by July 1915, but in E. Africa Gen. Smuts failed to defeat von Lettow-Vorbeck, who maintained his resistance until Dec. 1918.

(8) Rebellion advertised nationalism: the sinking of the *Lusitania* strengthened the Unionists. At the polls the polarisation wiped out Labour, and Botha's S. Africa Party lost heavily. He had to depend on Unionist support, while Nationalists talked republicanism and trumped up anti-British accusations over wool. In 1916 farmers the world over had made fortunes clothing the vast allied armies. The 1917 U-boat campaign constricted the S. African exports. The British govt. offered to buy the whole clip, whether shipped or not, at 55% above pre-war prices. This was less than the current price for those amounts of it which might safely be shipped. This was represented as oppressive and many farmers refused the offer and never sold their clips at all. The war seemed to be going badly and, with native strikes, Botha was barely able to keep order. When the war ended, a Nationalist delegation to the Peace Conference demanded independence or independence for the ex-republics or at least for the Orange Free State. Nobody outside S. Africa took this propagandist demonstration seriously, for the country already had the substance of independence and signed the Peace treaty in its own right. In 1919 Botha died and was succeeded by Jan Christiaan Smuts.

(9) The Boers' dilemma was that European immigration, if unrestricted, would overwhelm themselves but if stopped would result in whites being overwhelmed by blacks. The 1921 census showed: Europeans 1.5M; Coloured 0.5M; Asiatics 0.16M; 'Bantu' 4.7M. Save among the Zulus, detribalisation was far advanced. Blacks lived (i) in poverty on reservations whence many had to go out to work to sustain life; (ii) as squatters or labour tenants on European farms; (iii) as short term migrants from Mozambique and the protectorates in compounds and townships for mineworkers. There was also (iv) a slowly growing number who were educated. Labour felt threatened by the first three groups; Nationalists by all. There was a common drift towards a police state where Europeans would be kept out and blacks kept down — and out of the trade unions. In the sanguinary strikes of 1922 Rand Communist-directed gangs attacked native compounds; the trade unions struck for higher employment ratios of well paid whites to low paid blacks, and armed white bands terrorised moderates.

(10) Smuts personally restored order. Neither Nationalists nor Labour thanked him. His essential liberalism was at variance with their combination of re-emergent racialism and, during a post-war slump, labour poverty. He sought to annex S. Rhodesia but met furious opposition, for Rhodesian whites were British not Boer and the million blacks would raise the black population by 19%. Moreover his party had been in power too long. In the 1924 elections Nationalists and Labour in an alliance called The Pact had a majority of 27. Smuts gave way to Hertzog.

(11) In the world recovery of 1924 to 1930, many countries with S. Africa returned to the Gold Standard and vastly raised the profits of gold mining, while the principle of international collective security seemed to make it safe to move away from imperially guaranteed security towards both internal and external sovereign self-reliance. The Nationalists protected primary producers, subsidised fruit exports, joined diamond cartels and restricted British preferences. This economic nationalism went hand in hand with racialist legislation. The Senate threw out the Colour Bar Bill in 1925 but in 1926 it was overridden at a joint sitting where, to prepare for the future, the Nationalists forced through constitutional amendments so that the Gov.-Gen's. senatorial nominees had to vacate their seats on a dissolution or a change of prime minister. Further signs of the times included the recognition of Afrikaans as an official language and the partial concession in 1928 of most favoured nation treatment to Germany.

(12) There was also a furious and ramifying controversy about symbolism. The Nationalists wanted more than the substance of independence. They wanted parliamentary omnicompetence proclaimed from the house tops. Nationality legislation was uncontroversial, for Union citizens would have to be British subjects, but a proposed new flag brought uproar which ended only in 1928 with an agreement to fly alongside the Union Jack an amended Dutch flag. As usual internals and externals were interlinked. By 1929 the govt. had its majority in the Senate. British S. Africans began to feel a drift towards alienation and the new flag symbolised racialism but, with the Balfour Declaration and the raised diplomatic status of Canada, the whole white population wished S. Africa to stand on her own feet. A Minister of External Affairs was created (1927) and the govt. urged Westminster to turn the Balfour Declaration into law.

(13) It took until 1931 to pass the Statute of Westminster, by which time a new world slump had darkened the scene. Gold exports protected the Union from an immediate crash, but the economy could in the long term support excessively high pay for whites only by depressing the pay of blacks, who were soon to be ill-protected under the law. Nationalists were determined to maintain the white standard of living. As the blacks were multiplying, their standard was bound to decline. Nationalists beheld this prospect without qualms or fear of the consequences.

(14) In 1933 Hertzog and Smuts formed a coalition which swept the polls and in 1934 they fused their parties into an United Party, from which D.F. Malan's Purified Nationalists and C.F. Stallard's Anglophile Dominion Party were excluded. The Status and Seals Acts having complemented the Statute of Westminster, the Hertzog-Smuts govt. started to carry out Hertzog's policy of segregation. Cape Coloureds were allowed to vote only for white candidates and Africans might elect four white members of the powerless Senate. Next in 1936 the native reserves were enlarged so that native movement to the towns could be prevented and native urban residential areas separated from white. Non-whites became restive at this creeping social reorganisation which depressed their standard of living and shut them, by law, out of places where they could get the best work. Prosecutions were running at 500,000 a year, but the unrest gave the Nationalists a pretext for urging that white society could not be safe without still wider and deeper segregation. The resolution of this issue (which was to reappear as *apartheid*) was postponed by World War II.

(15) In answer to Hertzog's Assembly motion (4 Sept. 1939) to stay neutral, Smuts, understanding the implications of Nazism, carried the House on the basis of S. Africa's interests and next day formed, with most of the United Party and the Labour and Dominion Parties, a govt. which declared war. Some 325,000 S. African troops eventually fought in Ethiopia, the Mediterranean and Madagascar. In the 1943 elections, however, his majority was reduced while Malan's Nationalists won all the 43 opposition seats (out of 153). An industrial revolution in progress since 1938 and a wartime boom were raising the prosperity and confidence of skilled (white) workers and (white) capitalists who between them composed the effective electorate. The non-whites, though economically backward, despite police action by now outnumbered the whites in the towns. In the 1948 election the African National Congress (A.N.C.) demanded an end to discrimination, in conformity with the U.N. Charter. The Indians attacked S. Africa in the U.N. General Assembly. In an electoral appeal to a white electorate the Nationalists neatly combined fear of blacks, dissociation from Britain and the U.N. and repeal of wartime controls. In 1948 they obtained a majority of 5, in 1953 of 54, in 1958 of 72 and in 1961 of 76.

(16) Nakedly racialist policies followed. Constitutional provisions were manipulated to maintain Nationalist majorities. Thirty-three native political organisations were proscribed and their leaders fled the country. The population was classified by race. Mixed marriages became illegal, mixed sexual intercourse criminal. Single race ('Group') areas were laid out and natives deported to them. Mission schools were closed: blacks excluded from universities and given inferior colleges. Particular kinds of work were reserved to whites. Apartheid was enforced on transport, in cinemas and theatres, post offices and libraries.

(17) In 1971 the country was prospectively converted into a republic and at the Commonwealth Conference the govt. requested continued membership of the Commonwealth. Others present inveighed against racialism and the request was withdrawn. S. Africa accordingly became a republic and left the Commonwealth on 31 May 1961.

(18) International reaction had been gathering for some time. The Russian policy of destabilising Africa fitted well with the nationalisms of the new African states.

Communist and Black African countries got the U.N. Assembly to call for economic sanctions in 1962, for a diplomatic boycott in 1964. It revoked the S.W. Africa Trusteeship in 1966 and in 1968 renamed it Namibia and demanded the withdrawal of the S. African administration. The largely political campaign against racism' served many Russian purposes not only in Africa. In the meantime the Nationalists lived in a world of their own, enforcing and widening racialist laws; setting up an army and a militarised police which perceptibly moved towards becoming a state within the state. The only S. African policy which received any (mostly tacit) support was the intervention in favour of the Angolan govt. against Russo-Cuban invasion.

(19) In 1976 the watershed was reached with three weeks of bloody riots at Soweto, the great native slum township near Johannesburg, and a Russian-fomented rising in Namibia. The Nationalist reply was distinguished for its irrelevance. In 1984 they tried to bring the coloureds and Indians into the same camp as the whites against the unrepresented blacks by substituting for the bicameral parliament a tricameral one in which whites, coloureds and Indians should each elect a House. This, of course, failed. Violence became endemic. With a short interval, the country was under a state of emergency from 1985 to 1990.

(20) In 1989 Frederik W. de Klerk succeeded P.W. Botha as Prime Minister and with a new realism and discretion converted the National Party to constitutional negotiations with all groups, including the Africans. Many whites, tired of insecurity and having their attention drawn to the writing on the wall, actually read it. Hence, though the National Party maintained its majority, it shed its extremists in favour of conservatives and liberal democrats. It became feasible to lift restrictions on native political organisations and attract their leaders back from the countries to which they had fled. This essential preliminary to negotiation was given substance when Nelson Mandela, the A.N.C. leader imprisoned in 1962, was released in 1990. Racial classification and geographical separation were abolished; 17 police generals dismissed. The Communist collapse in Russia and the end of Russian-funded subversion in Africa generally made it easier to cajole the white electorate into common sense. In Mar. 1992 an interim multi-racial cabinet was formed and a white-only referendum favoured reforms based on universal equality before the law. A new multi-racial parliament was elected in Apr. 1994. Mandela and de Klerk became Pres. and Vice-Pres. respectively and were awarded a joint Nobel Peace Prize. The country was readmitted to the Commonwealth later in the year.

SOUTH AFRICAN WAR (12 Oct. 1899-31 May 1902) (1)

The British had foreseen the war; they had only 50,000 troops on the spot (against about 87,000 Boers) but reinforcements were coming. The Boers had the advantage of mobility, accurate rifle shooting and familiarity with the ground; but the disadvantage in regular warfare of an incompetent high command under Joubert, who was too old, and Cronje who was not clever.

(2) The war passed through two phases. The first comprised the regular fighting and ended with the defeat of the Boer formations and the annexation of the Transvaal in Sept. 1900. The second, the guerrilla period, ended in May 1902.

The regular war (3) Basutoland being treated as neutral, there were (from the British point of view) three fronts. The right, east of Basutoland, was in Natal and faced north. The centre, west of Basutoland, was about Stormberg and Colesberg and also faced north. The left from De Aar *via* Kimberley to Mafeking faced east. The Boers, that is, commandos from the Orange Free State and the S. African Republic, attacked on all three. The first British reinforcements were already landing, so that the only hope for the Boers was a speedy and ruthless advance, but after stubbornly contested victories at Talana Hill and Elandslaagte, the invaders of Natal settled down to besiege Ladysmith. The advance in the centre halted near Stormberg. On the left the campaign degenerated into investments of Kimberley and Mafeking.

(4) In Dec. the British launched a counter-attack simultaneously on all three fronts; it failed. During the 'Black Week' (9-15 Dec.) Methuen on the left was defeated at Magersfontein, Gatacre in the centre at Stormberg and Buller on the right at Colenso. Boer risings in the Cape Colony followed and all the territory north of the Orange was annexed to the Free State. In Feb. 1900 a further effort by Buller in Natal brought defeats at Spion Kop and Vaal Krantz.

(5) The British govt. had learned its lesson. Roberts and Kitchener were despatched with large reinforcements. While Buller was holding the Boers at Vaal Krantz on the right, Roberts with 30,000 men began a wide turning movement on the left. Political interference forced him to relieve Kimberley but Cronje, who was besieging it, was encumbered by wagons and was caught and surrounded at Paardeberg on 27 Feb. This damaged the morale of the Free Staters who abandoned the Colony and deserted their allies before Ladysmith. Buller was now able to force the Tugela and relieve the town, while Roberts broke the Free State army at Poplar Grove and Abraham's Kraal and occupied Bloemfontein. The remaining Free State commandos dispersed; and Roberts offered to release his many prisoners (other than the leaders) on parole.

(6) There was now a delay. Roberts' force was immobilized by enteric at Bloemfontein, and Joubert, who died, was succeeded by Botha. Christian de Wet revived Boer morale by successful raids at Sannah's Post and Reddersburg. By the time Roberts was ready to march, the Boers were in the field again. Roberts' advance began in May 1900: Mafeking was relieved; by 5 June Johannesburg and Pretoria had been taken and shortly afterwards Buller came north from Natal and joined hands with him. Much of de Wet's force was cut off against the north side of Basutoland and captured; in Aug. Pres. Kruger sailed for Europe in a Dutch warship from Lourenço Marques and in Sept. Roberts annexed the Transvaal.

Reconstruction and Guerrilla (7) In the Cape Colony there were many Boers and sympathisers and the Cape govt. was disposed to leniency. In Britain the conduct of the war was acutely controversial and produced a parliamentary election. The issue was the manner in which the ex-republics should be managed after the war; and the troops were going home. But the war went on. The Boers hid their weapons in times of danger and raided by night or at a distance. With sympathisers everywhere in the ex-republics and in many places in the Colony, their commandos ranged far: Hertzog even came within 50 miles of Cape Town. In reply Kitchener erected wire fences and blockhouses along the railways and burned every farm from which shots were fired or near which a blockhouse had been attacked.

(8) This sort of warfare bore hardly on the non-combatants for whom the British set up the so-called concentration camps. These were hurriedly formed and, at the beginning, badly administered: the death rate among inmates and camp staff was alike high until public indignation in England compelled improvements. Farm burning and the camps which resulted left a mark, and yet the camps prolonged the war by relieving the Boers of the need to look after their families. Nevertheless the commandos were slowly worn down and captured in detail. Kruger's attempts to rouse a friendly Europe against the hated British broke down in the face of the immense power of the Royal Navy. Negotiations had

gone on sporadically since the fall of Bloemfontein. A last effort to raise a rebellion in the Colony failed in May 1902. On 31st of that month representatives of the two republics signed the "Peace of Vereeniging" at Pretoria.

SOUTHAMPTON (A.S: HAMTUN) (Hants.). There was a Roman port (Clausentum) at Bitterne on the east bank of the Itchen, through which metals and other goods were exported from the Itchen valley and Wiltshire areas. The Jutes who settled in S. Hampshire built a village opposite and this was in due course superseded by a town on the promontory half a mile further south. By 709 the town was part of Wessex and by 755 it had given its name to Hampshire. The trading connection with Wiltshire subsisted into modern times.

Southampton Water was an excellent haven: ships were seldom wind-bound owing to the double entrance, and the double tides were increasingly important as ships grew bigger.

The Danes plundered it in 837 to 842 and again in 860. Athelstan established a mint when the town had already been fortified. There were more Danish raids in 980 and 994 and Southampton was, briefly, a Danish base. In 1016 the English swore allegiance to King Canute there.

The Norman Conquest stimulated pre-existing cross-Channel trade and in the late 12th cent. the Royal galley, the *Esnecca* (Snake), was stationed there. The Guild Merchant received a Charter of Liberties from Henry I and this was confirmed and extended by most later kings into the 15th cent. From the 12th cent. the trade passing through the port was dominated by the import of Biscay wines in exchange for Wiltshire wool. By the early 13th cent. it was third by value after London and Boston. It remained a significant port for the rest of the Middle Ages, maintaining close links with Aquitaine, Spain and the Mediterranean. The French raided it in 1338. In 1415 it was the scene of the conspiracy between the E. of Cambridge, Ld. Scrope, and Sir Thomas Grey immediately before Henry V embarked for the Agincourt campaign. Henry's French ambitions gave a special stimulus to shipbuilding, which in turn created a demand for crews. The port began to acquire a population of indigenous seamen as well as builders. Meanwhile the metal trade expanded. On the other hand cloth had almost superseded wool and the end of the 15th cent. saw a trade recession which the establishment of a metals' Staple (1492) did little to combat.

Meanwhile the town had been constituted a county of itself (1447), mainly to facilitate the collection of dues, which were controlled by Cardinal Beaufort as a means of repaying his large loans to the Crown. The customs and farm were thus for a considerable period under Beaufort receivership.

The end of the Middle Ages saw the Mediterranean trade fall off. The last Venetian ship called in 1569, by which time the Iberian and Dutch shipping had mostly disappeared too. The port stagnated until power driven large transatlantic ships began to take advantage of the double tides in the early 20th cent.

SOUTHAMPTON, E. of. *See* FITZWILLIAM, WILLIAM; WRIOTHESLEY.

SOUTH AUSTRALIA. *See* AUSTRALIA.

SOUTH BANK or BANKSIDE. *See* SOUTHWARK.

SOUTH CAROLINA. *See* CAROLINA.

SOUTHERN WHALE FISHERY. *See* WHALING.

SOUTH POLE. *See* ANTARCTICA.

SOUTH SAXONS. *See* SUSSEX.

SOUTH SEA CO., founded by Robert Harley under an Act of 1710, was a public speculation on the outcome of the War of the Spanish Succession. Govt. stock and outstanding interest of £8,971,000 was converted into South Sea Stock at 6% tax free and the Treasury was to pay the Co. £568,279 a year until Christmas 1713, plus £8,000 until redemption. In return the Co. was entitled to a monopoly of trade with Spanish American possessions from the R. Orinoco south-about Tierra del Fuego and so to the northernmost point of the Pacific coast, but within 300 leagues. It could also trade in unwrought iron with Spain. The assumption was that a lucrative slave trading concession (*Asiento*) would be secured from Spain in the peace treaty. In fact the Asiento was restricted to a single ship confined to the Atlantic. Though various dishonest expedients were used to increase the value of this, the first voyage in 1717 was only moderately profitable. Accordingly the Act was amended to enable the King to become Gov. which he did in 1718. This boosted an existing speculation wave in which many projectors and swindlers unloaded bogus stock, mostly on unsuspecting investors unable to secure real South Sea Stock. In the meantime the Co. proposed to take over 60% of the outstanding national debt, £7M, accepting 5% from the govt. until 1727 and 4% thereafter. These attractive terms caused a stampede. In 1720 the stock rose from 128 in Jan. to 1000 in Aug. This was the notorious BUBBLE.

It burst, and by Dec. the stock had fallen to 124, leaving some fabulous fortunes and a trail of smaller ruined investors. Three ministers (John Aislabie, Sunderland and Charles Stanhope) and both King's mistresses were implicated in bribery and corrupt speculation. Walpole restored confidence by a scheme, never in fact put into effect, for transferring £9Ms worth of South Sea Stock each to the HEIC and the Bank (*see* GEORGE I-9).

The Co. remained profitable until 1732; sold most of its rights to Spain in 1750, operated in the Greenland fishery until about 1807 and was wound up in 1853.

SOUTH SHIELDS. *See* DURHAM-13.

SOUTHWARK (London) or THE BOROUGH was a disorganised suburb which grew up around the convergence of the southerly roads upon London Bridge and its fortification. It included fairs, brothels, many inns (including Chaucer's *Tabard*), markets and prisons such as the Clink, the Marshalsea and the King's Bench, besides the Priory of St. Mary Overie in about 1106, burned in 1212 and rebuilt in about 1300. It contained also a palace of the bps. of Winchester. It was granted by charter to the City Corporation in 1327 so that it could regulate the markets and, as Bridge Without, became in part a ward of the City in 1550. By this time the Priory had been dissolved and renamed St. Saviours and the area was acquiring theatres such as Shakespeare's *Globe*, bearpits and other popular amusements. Its history as a sort of dumping ground for doubtful activities continued with the foundation of Guy's Hospital in 1722 and the transfer of the Bedlam in 1815. The City Corporation took little interest in it until it built Southwark Bridge (1815-19). It was transferred from the diocese of Winchester to that of Rochester in 1877. In 1888 it became a borough in the County of London and its connections with the City became mainly ceremonial. It was erected into a diocese in 1905 with St. Saviours as its cathedral. In 1965 it was (under the same name) amalgamated with Bermondsey and Camberwell as a London Borough.

SOUTH WEST AFRICA (NAMIBIA). In this poor tribal area the British seized Walvis Bay, the only harbour, in 1878 and the Germans proclaimed annexation between Angola and the Orange River in 1884. Their police and settlers worked their way inland until the territory, including the Caprivi Strip, was defined by a convention with Britain in 1891. Disputes over the very sparse water soon led to a rebellion of the Herreros, whom the Germans massacred. The country was still in some disorder when occupied by a British and S. African force in 1915. It, with Walvis Bay, became S. African mandated territory in 1920 and a U.N. Trust territory in consequence. In 1949 S. Africa in effect annexed it, by permitting it to be represented in its parliament. In 1966 the S. African security and apartheid

laws were extended to it retrospectively to 1950. In 1971 the International Court of Justice held that the S. African presence was illegal and in Dec. 1973 the U.N. appointed a Commissioner. This did not deter the S. Africans who had already set up legislative councils for the Ovambos and the Kavangos, and they repeatedly postponed promised general elections because they feared a victory by the South West African People's Organisation (S.W.A.P.O.) which would have taken the uranium mines out of S. African hands. The retreat of the Cubans and the Communists in neighbouring Angola (both of whom had infiltrated S.W.A.P.O.) reduced the risk, and in due course the U.N. supervised elections which led to Namibian independence in 1990.

SOVEREIGN. *See* COINAGE-13.

SOVIET **(Russ.).** A council, especially in former times a council of four village elders. Since the Russian Revolution the word was used to suggest that the Russian dominated areas had popularly supported regimes.

SOYER, Alexis Benoit (1809-58), French chef to the D. of Cambridge from 1830 to 1837 and then at the influential liberal Reform Club. There was strong criticism of the Crimean army's feeding arrangements and with official permission he visited the Crimea and Florence Nightingale's hospital at Scutari. He invented a mobile kitchen and the "Soyer stove". His recommendations and his books designed to help the poor in matters of diet and cooking created a permanent improvement in the military commissariats and in eating habits.

S.P.A.B. (Society for the Protection of Ancient Buildings). *See* MORRIS, WILLIAM.

SPACE LAW. As a result of the first space flights in 1957 the U.N. established a committee on space law in 1958. This became the Permanent Committee on the Peaceful Uses of Outer Space in 1959 and in 1963 its Declaration of Legal Principles was adopted by the General Assembly. Most states signed an Outer Space Treaty in 1966. The general principles are that space and celestial bodies are free for exploration but not subject to appropriation, that no military installations are to be established in space or on the bodies and that states are answerable for the activities of their subjects. It is doubtful, especially in the case of satellites, if these rules are being fully heeded.

SPA FIELDS RIOTS (1818). A public meeting called by revolutionaries resolved to stage a revolution. A few shops were sacked, but otherwise nothing happened. The govt., whose spies had given early warning, suspended *habeas corpus* and arrested only one of the main organisers, Arthur Thistlewood. The Att.-Gen. called no evidence at his trial and he was acquitted.

SPAs (from Spa, the Belgian watering place). Medicinal or at least healthy water was sought because most water was polluted and people drank and knew that they drank too much beer, wine or spirits instead. As spas were uncommon many people concentrated upon them with their families (if they could afford it) so that 'taking the waters' was socially agreeable, often amorous as well as healthy. At Bath, the oldest, the season was specially marked because London Society went there when parliament rose, and macadamisation had made the Bath Road easy. Cheltenham, nearby was another favourite. In the north there were Scarborough and, despite the sulphurous taste, Harrogate for local people; in the midlands Leamington. In Kent people went to Tunbridge Wells if they had political reasons for avoiding Bath. The spas began to be superseded as drinking water came in pipes from the 1860s, and people could risk drinking it.

There was also a cosmopolitan spa habit and people went, besides Spa, to Vichy, Biarritz, Plombières, Carlsbad, Marienbad, Baden Baden, Gastein or Rapallo. The spa era ran from about 1720, was encouraged by railways after 1860, and continued to 1914. One reason why it persisted after the advent of good water was that it gave statesmen, politicians, businessmen and their entourages, and people seeking them, opportunities to meet in buildings adapted to gatherings without the commitments engendered by formalities and publicity. It has left its general architectural mark, and such institutions as Pump and Assembly rooms and *Kurhäuser*.

SPAIN 1406-1516 (1) John II succeeded in Castile in 1406. The native dynasty in the three states (Aragon, Valencia and Catalonia) of the Crown of Aragon ended with the death of King Martin (1410). By the Compromise of Caspe, 1412, they accepted Ferdinand I of Antequera, a cousin of John II, and he was followed by Alfonso the Magnanimous in 1416. Despite its Mediterranean and Italian possessions, the Crown of Aragon was in decline through piracy, constitutional disorder and, after 1416, recurrent plagues. Meanwhile Castile was making headway against the Moors and Portugal was commencing her adventurous colonialism (*see* AVIS) by taking Ceuta (1415), the Canaries (1425) and the Azores (1445). When Henry IV succeeded John II in Castile (1454), the English had just been driven from Bordeaux, but the Valois were still settling specifically French problems. Castile was free to concentrate upon the surviving Moorish Kingdom of Granada and to seek dynastic union with Portugal.

(2) In 1458 another John II succeeded in Aragon. His attempts to rationalise the govt. and its finances provoked a Catalan revolt (1462), which in its turn attracted French intervention. Louis XI seized (1463) the counties of Rosselo (Roussillon) and Cerdanya (Cerdagne), the cradles of the Catalan nation, but John had to concentrate his energies on liquidating the rebellion. In the circumstances he needed an alliance, preferably a marriage alliance, with his Castilian relatives.

(3) In Castile, however, Henry IV's queen had a daughter Juana (*la Beltraneja*) who was widely believed not to have been his. If she were legitimate, a marriage with King Afonso V might eventually unite Portugal and Castile; if illegitimate, Henry's sister Isabella would inherit and a marriage with King Ferdinand of Sicily (John II's heir) might bring about a union with Aragon. Powerful factions, supported by Portuguese, French and Aragonese agents and money gathered round these two women. In 1468 Henry was bullied into recognising Isabella as his heir. In Oct. 1469 Isabella (18) and Ferdinand (17) made a runaway marriage supported by the Abp. of Toledo, who, with John II and Ferdinand, forged the necessary Papal dispensation. Henry IV, the French and the Portuguese party were furious, but the deed was done and nothing in Castile could be changed while Henry lived. This gave John of Aragon enough years to master his rebels. They were pacified by 1472. Henry IV died in 1474. Isabella proclaimed herself queen. Some French supported Castilian and Andalusian nobles proclaimed Juana. The French soon faded out, to be replaced by the Portuguese. Isabella, however, could rely upon other areas, upon the towns whose commerce and industry were injured by aristocratic disorder, upon the wily sagacity of John II and Ferdinand and most of all upon her own intrepidity In 1476 she beat the Portuguese at Toro and by 1479, when Ferdinand succeeded to the Crown of Aragon, Castile had been reduced to order, Juana was in a convent and the Crown was taking control over the vast lands of the military orders and resuming usurped estates.

(4) Ferdinand and Isabella's marriage, an outstanding personal and public success, created a central nucleus of statesmanship and strength, but their union did not unite their countries. The Castilian monarchy, in essence authoritarian, crusading and military, ruled a large area which was densely populated and dynamic. The Aragonese Kings, by contrast, reigned gingerly over three small, differently organised but fiercely constitutional trading states, whose population and commerce were in decline. Ferdinand's first act was to guarantee the Catalan constitutional liberties (1480). The Castilians, in furtherance of their Portuguese war, built an Atlantic squadron at Seville and seized the Canaries (1482). With sea power, Castilian anarchical energy was diverted to the destruction of Moorish Granada (1482-92). Ferdinand's diplomatic genius ensured that the casualties were not too high, but in Aragon he was distracted by rural social problems. The Crown of Aragon thus contributed little to the enterprise and the Castilians reaped the dividends. This, until the Bourbon succession in 1700, was (with some deviations) to set the pattern. Castilians provided the resources for and monopolised (by law) the advantages of colonial extension, and since this left the weaker partners undisturbed in the pursuit of their Mediterranean interests, they cheerfully acquiesced in it. On the other hand when, later, international politics placed an excessive burden upon Castile, their parliaments (Cortes) refused, as far as they could, to assist and imperial collapse was accompanied by internal disruption. There was no such country as "Spain" until after the P. of Utrecht (1713).

(5) But in the morning of inspiration almost anything was possible. Within seven months of the Moorish surrender (Jan. 1492), the Genoese Columbus had signed his contract with Isabella and Ferdinand and disappeared over the Atlantic horizon. At home the struggle against the infidel was metamorphosed into an expulsion of unconverted Jews. Castilian resources, used against the French, achieved (T. of Barcelona, 1493) the recovery of Roussillon and Cerdagne for Catalonia. This, after all, had been Ferdinand's original motive in marrying Isabella. Then came Columbus' sensational news which overshadowed, yet interacted with, continuing European events. As a result of the French incursion into Italy (*see* CHARLES VIII OF FRANCE) the Pope and the Spanish sovereigns needed each other. The T. of Tordesillas and a Papal Bull divided the undiscovered world between Castile and Portugal. The Pope conceded a third of the Castilian tithes to the treasury and while the sovereigns reorganised their wool trade with Flanders, reformed their coinage and created a new, soon to be famous army, a Holy League (1495) sealed by Habsburg marriages, chased the French out of Italy. By 1498 Melilla on the Moroccan coast had been taken, the three military orders and their huge resources were under Crown control and the possibilities of America were being actively explored. This process was hardly interrupted by the first Moorish rising in the Alpujarras of Granada and the consequent expulsion of the unconverted Moors (1499-1502), for in 1503 the sovereigns established the *Casa de la Contratacion* (House of Trade) at Seville to control the Castilian commercial monopoly in the Caribbean.

(6) This heroic period, which was to continue awhile, had however its darker side. The Habsburg marriages, followed by a series of unforeseeable deaths, had passed the succession to another Juana, the sovereign's mentally unstable daughter and her husband, the Archduke Philip (*see* HENRY VII-17-20), through whom the crowns would presumably pass to the Habsburgs. To these potential uncertainties the sovereigns created, unperceived at the time, a dangerous certainty by fixing (1502), for the benefit of the towns and the detriment of the great nobles, the price of corn at a low level. The *Tasa del trigo* ultimately ruined Castilian cereal agriculture. At the same time the expulsions, which were not the last, deprived the urban economies of an irreplaceable element of ingenuity and diligence. Meanwhile, however, affairs prospered. The French were defeated at Cerignola (1503). The Neapolitan Kings were driven away and their territory annexed (1504). Good administration had raised the Castilian revenue 30-fold since Isabella's accession, but in 1504 she died.

(7) Under his marriage contract Ferdinand ceased to

be King in Castile and, while the crown passed to Juana, under Isabella's will the regency passed to a council. The Archduke Philip reached Spain in 1505 to claim the regency but died in 1506. Juana then went irremediably mad and the right of succession passed to their Dutch educated infant son, Charles of Ghent. The regency was capably discharged by Cardinal Ximenez de Cisneros, but disputed by Ferdinand who eventually took it over in 1510. In his hands the European prosperity of the Spanish crowns reached a new level with the annexation by Aragon of southern Navarre in 1512 and its transfer to Castile in 1515. In America Balboa had crossed the Isthmus of Darien in 1513. Ferdinand died in 1516. Charles of Ghent was of age to take over his inheritance. See CHARLES V 1500-1559.

SPAIN (HABSBURG) 1556-1700. (See SPAIN 1406-1516; CHARLES V 1500-1559.) **(1) Don Philip (1527-98, King as Philip II, 1556)** was the son of Charles V and Isabel of Portugal. In 1543, when his father left for Flanders and Germany, he became titular Spanish regent, assisted by Charles' trusted Sec. of State, Francisco de los Cobos, who later found him Gonzalo Perez as his sec., in 1566. Amidst depression and inflation the govt. had to extract money from Castile and America to finance Charles' policies elsewhere. Philip idolised his absent father, but protested constantly at policies which seemed to be creating misery in Spain. His first wife, Maria of Portugal, died in 1545 giving birth to Don Carlos. In 1548 Philip was summoned to Flanders and from there, in 1554, he married Mary I of England in an effort to strengthen the Spanish hold on the increasingly restless and heretical Netherlands. His father handed them over with his Spanish crowns and their dependencies in 1556 and Philip's first act was to default on the Castilian debts (1557) of about 20M ducats.

(2) Philip was not a strong character and though subscribing to the mediaeval moralities in matters of justice and religion, was financially unscrupulous and politically timid. He inherited great difficulties (including a French war) of which heresy seemed to him to be the worst. This and bankruptcy made peace essential. Moreover in 1558 Mary I died and the new English ruler, Elizabeth, though politically uncommitted, was doctrinally suspect. To prevent the spread of heretical infection from Flanders to Spain he issued a decree against importing books. The panic atmosphere was heightened in 1559 (when the P. of Cateau Cambresis was signed) when the Inquisition arrested the Abp. of Toledo on suspicion of heresy. After Philip returned to Spain he placed the Netherlands under the governorship of Margaret of Parma with a council whose most prominent figure was the Burgundian Antoine Perrenot, Bp. of Arras, from 1561 Cardinal Granvelle.

(3) The Turks and their Barbary protégés threatened Christendom too, from Leghorn to the Channel. The transatlantic trade was protected by regular convoy from 1560, when a great and disastrous attack was launched against Djerba (Nr. Tunis). The financial consequences of naval and African war as well as growing turbulence in the Netherlands might have been damaging sooner than they were, but for an expansion after 1565 in American silver extraction using mercury, of which the Almaden workings in Spain were the only European source. In 1564 Dutch nobles and court intriguers forced or cajoled Philip into sacrificing Granvelle and in 1565 the greatest Moslem fleet ever seen appeared in the Sicilian narrows and attacked Malta. After an epic defence the island was relieved from Sicily, but dangerous Turkish armaments continued to threaten, especially the Venetian islands from Cyprus westwards. Hence peace in the north was increasingly important. This involved a contradiction, for the govt. of Queen Elizabeth had to be preserved from the Franco-Scottish menace, but Elizabeth survived by supporting Scottish heretics. In 1566 peace became

impossible for, emboldened by Granvelle's removal, the Dutch Calvinists rose.

(4) In 1566, too, Gonzalo Perez was succeeded in office by his corrupt illegitimate son, Antonio. Govts. now seemed to lose partial control of their people. The trouble in Flanders was spreading. In 1568 Hawkins made his first freebooting expedition to the W. Indies: there was a major Morisco (Moorish convert) rebellion on the Granada coast and the Bretons seized all the King's shipping on the Flanders route. Then Elizabeth of Valois, the best loved of Philip's wives, died and he also found it necessary to imprison his incurably wayward and vicious son, Don Carlos, who shortly died leaving improbable rumours of murder. Fortunately the Turks did not exploit the Morisco rising; it was put down and the Moriscos dispersed throughout Spain in 1570. The Turks attacked Venetian Cyprus; after excessively prolonged negotiations a combined Veneto-Papal-Spanish fleet under Philip's half-brother, Don John of Austria, spectacularly defeated the Turks at Lepanto in the mouth of the G. of Corinth. Cyprus, however, had already fallen; it was too late in the season to follow up the victory and in 1572 the Turks were again at sea in full strength. In fact the Mediterranean war declined into a perennial summer skirmish of pirates (see BARBARY; MALTA GC) because the Sultan and the King were dragged apart, the one by Persian War, the other by Dutch revolution. The Dutch Sea Beggars had seized Brill. See ELIZABETH I-14.

(5) Since 1568 Philip had found it hard to pay his troops in the Netherlands. In 1574 they mutinied. In 1575 Philip for the second time defaulted on the Castilian debts and in 1576 the unpaid troops sacked Antwerp (The Spanish Fury). These events destroyed all hope either of conquering the Dutch or of reconciling them. There was, too, a redoubled outbreak of American plague (see CHARLES V. 1500-1559-5). The court, settled since 1561 in Madrid, was faction ridden. Perez favoured compromise solutions analogous to the multiplicity of Iberian Kingdoms. Don John of Austria, now Gov. of the Netherlands (who mistrusted Perez) and the Castilians, against whom the balance of imperial advantage was now turning, wanted a free hand towards the Dutch and the states of the Crown of Aragon (see SPAIN 1406-1516, 1 & 4). Philip seems to have feared that Don John was planning to invade England after first overthrowing himself, and Perez tricked the King into complicity in the murder (1578) of Don John's Sec., Escobedo. Philip later discovered that Perez was selling state secrets. At this point King Sebastian of Portugal and most of his nobles perished at the B. of Alcaza-kebir in Morocco. His successor was an aged and invalid Cardinal and thereafter the Portuguese Crown would fall to one of three claimants. Action was urgent, for with rebellion in Flanders and treachery at Madrid, Philip might well fear the difficulties of enforcing his legally pre-eminent claim against Portuguese popular hostility, especially as Perez had formed a liaison with the Princess of Eboli who had her own plans for the Portuguese Crown. In 1579 he sent for the long retired Cardinal Granvelle and then imprisoned Perez and the Princess.

(6) Hard upon these sensational events came the death (1580) of the Cardinal-King. Philip and Granvelle were prepared with bribes and troops; he swore to respect Portuguese privileges. Save in the Azores, the take-over was almost bloodless and in the Azores a French fleet of intervention was destroyed (July 1582) at Terceira. Thus another addition was made to the constitutional multiplicity of the Crown, but with a vast necklace of materially weak but commercially wealthy oriental trading stations. There were advantages for Philip: he had raised his prestige at French expense and had acquired a new coastline, a new navy and trading benefits. The benefits were less obvious to the Portuguese who were now involved in Castilian policies.

Despite the civil war, trade between Flanders and the Iberian ports had continued and had even been protected by Spanish convoy. In 1585 Philip embargoed Dutch shipping. Apart from causing a commercial crisis in Castile and Portugal, this led the Dutch to emulate the English defiance of the monopoly to America and to raid the Portuguese trade routes. The struggle against Dutch rebellion and English intervention could not now be won unless the Channel was cleared. The strategically inevitable war with England was, with the decline of France into civil war, politically feasible, and besides, the captive Mary Queen of Scots' intrigues failed. The preparation of the Enterprise of England provoked Drake's attack on Cadiz and a summer long interruption of the coastal trade (1587), but the first Armada (q.v.) whose most important fighting component was Portuguese, was launched nevertheless. Its defeat (1588) ensured the ultimate independence of Holland.

(7) The years 1588 to 1608 marked the summit of the Sevillan trading splendour and the downturn of the N. Castilian wool trade. New taxes were raised for the war (1590) and the Castilians demanded contributions from the states of the Aragonese Crown. The result was an Aragonese rebellion (1591-2) in which the French intervened. Moreover Antonio Perez escaped from prison and joined the rebels. Their fiscal advantages had to be confirmed. A last effort against the Dutch by means of another embargo again damaged the trade of Seville and four bad harvests (1595-8) in a country which had imported grain since 1570 brought famine. In 1596 Philip, by handing over the Netherlands to the Archduke Albert in life sovereignty, began the Spanish withdrawal. For the third time he defaulted on the Castilian debts, but he prosecuted the English war with a second and a third Armada (1596 and 1597), both scattered by storms. Plague now trod on the heels of famine. He liquidated another commitment by concluding the P. of Vervins (1598) with France and then, worn out, he died.

(8) During the last three Habsburg reigns (Philip III 1598-1621, Philip IV 1621-65, and Charles II 1621-1700) the active ruler was a royal nominee or minister known as the *Privado* or *Valido*, or abroad as the *favourite*. The first (1598-1618) was the D. of Lerma who promoted his relatives, while the Dutch seized Caribbean saltings and the plague raged. Nevertheless a fourth Armada was despatched and came to grief in 1602. Fortunately the accession in England of a King of Scots who was not at war with Spain facilitated a settlement. Peace with England (The T. of London) was signed in 1604 and was followed by a fourth default in 1607. It was now born in upon Lerma that there was no hope of beating the Dutch. The 12-year truce of 1608 was a face-saving device. To distract from its announcement in Spain, the Moriscos were expelled at the same time. This reduced tensions between landowners who employed them and those who did not, but it ruined the economy of Valencia, where most of them were and so accelerated the piecemeal decline.

(9) The Mediterranean trade languished and banditry grew unchecked in the depressed states of the Crown of Aragon. Castile staggered on, supporting an extravagant court and an incompetent govt. on debased currency, mortgaged revenues and commandeered American private silver. Despite the truce the Dutch persistently attacked the Portuguese Indies and the Portuguese consoled themselves with a Brazilian sugar and slave trade. In 1618 Lerma's son overthrew him and in 1621 when the Dutch truce ended, it was not renewed (*see* THIRTY YEARS' WAR). All parties agreed that open war everywhere was better than covert war in Indonesia alone.

(10) Philip IV (1621-65) succeeded his colourless father and brought in a new favourite, the remarkable and controversial Count of Olivares, from 1625 D. of

San Lucar la mayor (hence often known as the Count-Duke). He had vision, energy and a policy. Unfortunately the war, which he inherited, absorbed the resources which might have made the policy work. A curtailment of extra-Castilian privilege could not be achieved all at once without force, but the process might begin with a limited sharing of military burdens. The Catalans resisted even this (1624). In 1625 an English attack on Cadiz was easily beaten off and in 1626 Olivares halted the Castilian inflation by suspending the debased coinage. Since the means of current payment were now too short, the Crown suspended service of the Castilian debts (1627). These foundations for a financial reconstruction had been laid in relatively favourable circumstances, for Richelieu was preoccupied with a civil war and Spain's Austrian allies were victorious in Germany. Unfortunately Spain became involved in an unsuccessful Mantuan War (1628-31) and in Aug. 1628 the Dutch captured the year's silver fleet. Olivares sought for yet other new sources of revenue and began to reconstruct the cumbersome administration. The latter provoked enmities among the vested office holders. A salt tax injured the Biscay cod trade and provoked a Basque rebellion (1631).

(11) Depression too reigned in Portugal, whose Brazilian interests had been taken by the Dutch. Two Portuguese-commanded naval expeditions to Brazil failed (1634 and 1635) and in 1635 war broke out once more with France. In 1637 the Dutch took Breda and there were Portuguese riots; in 1638 the French interrupted the essential land route to Belgium by taking Breisach and then invaded Catalonia. Attempts to mobilise Catalan resistance resulted in civil war. There were even Castilian desertions. The Dutch destroyed Oquendo's fleet in the Downs and with naval action in progress off Pernambuco, the silver fleet never sailed. Olivares decided to mobilise all the remaining military resources to clear Catalonia of rebels and the French. A well laid Portuguese conspiracy while the country was denuded of troops overthrew the govt. and proclaimed the D. of Braganza King as Joao IV (1640). The operations in Catalonia failed at Montjuich (1641). The famous Spanish infantry went down in disaster at Rocroi in 1643 (*see* THIRTY YEARS' WAR-16).

(12) Olivares fell in 1643, but Richelieu and Louis XIII both died and leisurely peace negotiations were begun in Westphalia. The new favourite (1643-61), Don Luis de Haro, a latter day Lerma in a hurricane, could at first do nothing. For the sixth time the Crown defaulted; Catalonia was effectively a French protected state and there were insurrections in Spanish Naples and Sicily (1647). The monarchy avoided dissolution mainly because the P. of Westphalia (1648) and the weakness of the French regency during the Fronde (1648-53) reduced foreign commitments and the Crown was ready to respect local sentiment. By 1653, at the cost of another default, Barcelona had been retaken and Catalonia was quiet. Only Portugal, saved by the reconquest of Brazil (1654) and a native dynasty, remained unconquered.

(13) The thinly spread authority remained weak. The France of Louis XIV soon showed its aggressive intentions and Cromwell's Britain joined in. There were more defeats. In 1657 Blake destroyed the silver fleet. By the P. of the Pyrenees Rousillon, Cerdagne and Artois passed to France (*see also* SPANISH SUCCESSION). Then faction struggles at court disorganised the direction of the war in Portugal. With two resounding defeats (Ameixial, 1663 and Villaviciosa, 1665) the reign closed. The Queen Regent in the name of the diseased and eccentric Charles II was dominated by Fr. Nithard, her confessor, who became the favourite (1665-9) in practice. After elaborate hesitations the govt. recognised Portuguese independence (T. of Lisbon 1668).

(14) During the ineffectual apathy of Charles II's reign the political existence of Spain depended upon the

restraint which predatory foreign powers could impose upon each other. The French occupied Franche Comté in 1673; there was a Sicilian revolt in 1674 and Franche Comté was definitively ceded in 1678 (P. of Nimwegen). Foreign interest centred increasingly upon the problems of succession to the impotent King. Louis XIV had followed a policy of piecemeal annexation. In the 1690s the possibility of total absorption became a reality. His European opponents thereupon favoured partition, but here Castilian opinion became important. However abhorrent foreign domination might be, partition of the still astounding empire seemed worse: and in any case Spain had Hispanicised the present dynasty. Why not the next? Thus the end of the drama was played out in Madrid among factions and ambassadors trying to persuade Charles II to make his will. In 1700 he opted for the Bourbon succession and died. Louis XIV accepted on behalf of his grandson, who succeeded as Philip V on condition that the Crowns of France and Spain should never be united. Louis' subsequent disingenuous behaviour made it clear that the condition would be nominal only. This provoked the great War of the Spanish Succession.

(15) From the Spanish point of view the war was opened in the Spanish Netherlands and involved between 1705 and 1714 an attempt, largely British in conception, to use the liberties of the Crown of Aragon in support of an Austrian Habsburg claim. In this Peninsular War Philip V thus fought for the integrity of his dominions against allied efforts to disrupt it. By the P. of Utrecht (1713) he lost European outliers, but since the British Tories abandoned the Austrian claimant and his Catalan supporters, Philip could concentrate against them. After a desperate defence, Barcelona fell in 1714 and the Aragonese privileges were abolished. Spain had become one country. *See* CARLISM; USSR (7-8).

SPANISH BLANKS. *See* JAMES VI-12.

SPANISH INFLUENZA. *See* INFLUENZA.

SPANISH MAIN was the coastal territory of S. America along the Caribbean especially between Panama and the Orinoco. The term was later applied to the adjacent seas and later still to the routes permitted to ships entitled to trade with the Spanish possessions ("ships on the Spanish register").

SPANISH MARRIAGES (1840-6). The Carlist defeat left the Spanish throne occupied by Queen Isabella (b. 1830) whose marriage would be internationally important. In discussions between Aberdeen (Foreign Sec.) and Guizot, the British objected to any son of King Louis Philippe; the French to any Coburg relative of the P. Consort. By way of compromise it was proposed that Isabella should marry her cousin, Don Francisco, and that after they had had children, her sister should marry a son of Louis Philippe. Don Francisco, however, was thought to be impotent, which would prevent the second marriage. Simultaneous weddings were proposed, but Louis Philippe thought them dishonourable. In June 1846 Peel resigned and Palmerston succeeded Aberdeen at the Foreign Office. In a rudely direct despatch, he assumed that the French prince was excluded and recommended Don Francisco's liberal and ne'er do well brother, Henriques. This caused offence in Madrid and Paris and both govts. promptly announced the arrangements rejected by Louis Philippe. The resulting rift between Britain and France, both constitutional states, enabled the Russians with their autocratic Prussian and Austrian allies' connivance to destroy the Polish republic of Cracow, guaranteed under the T. of Vienna (1815).

SPANISH MATCH. *See* JAMES I-17-18.

SPANISH SICKNESS. *See* SYPHILIS.

SPANISH SUCCESSION (*see* SPAIN, HABSBURG. 14-15). when it became clear in the 1690s that the Habsburg Charles II of Spain would die childless, there were three possible claimants, all descended from daughters of his father Philip IV. **(a)** The child prince, Joseph Ferdinand of Bavaria; **(b)** the Habsburg Archduke Charles of Austria, brother of the Emperor Joseph. These two were both descended by different marriages from the Emperor Leopold; **(c)** Philip of Anjou, grandson of Louis XIV of France. England and Holland preferred the Bavarian, as least likely to upset the balance of power. In the First (Secret) Partition Treaty (1698) Louis and William III agreed to recognise him as Charles II's heir; the Dauphin, Philip of Anjou's father, was to have Naples and Sicily and the Archduke Charles, Milan. When this agreement became public, the Emperor rejected it since Naples and Sicily would eventually pass to the French Crown. There was uproar in Spain, whose political classes refused to tolerate any partition. Hence Charles by will conferred the entire dominions on the Bavarian (Nov. 1698) but in Feb. 1699 the child died.

In Europe the situation of the individual powers had also changed. The Emperor, no longer at war with Turkey (P. of Carlovitz, 1699) was in a stronger position. William III was weaker because Parliament had disbanded the army. By the Second Partition Treaty (June 1699) the Archduke Charles was to be the main heir, provided that the Spanish territories should never be united with the Empire, while the Dauphin was to keep Naples and Sicily, receive Milan but exchange the latter for Lorraine. The Emperor sensibly rejected this, which would have denied lands for ever to Austria but given others eventually to France.

Throughout 1699 Louis was organising a party at Madrid in favour of Anjou. Since the Emperor would not accept this partition, the Spaniards felt free to reject it. In Oct. 1700 the dying Charles II was persuaded to make over his *entire* dominions to Anjou. On 1 Nov. he died. On 16th Louis publicly accepted them on his behalf. Anjou now became Philip V of Spain, but in Feb. 1701 Louis reserved his rights in the French succession and, under colour of Spanish authorisation, occupied the Belgian Barrier Fortresses. While the European powers might have been willing to accept Anjou's accession, they now realised that Louis had never intended to abide by the separation of the French and Spanish dominions and that the international balance could be maintained only by war. *See* SPANISH SUCCESSION, WAR OF (1702-13).

SPANISH SUCCESSION, WAR OF (1701-14) (*See previous entry,* ANNE; WILLIAM III.)

French Aggressions **(1)** Philip V (formerly D. of Anjou) entered Madrid in state in Apr. 1701, French troops, ostensibly on his authority, having already occupied the Spanish Netherlands and Barrier Fortresses and also positions in Venetian territory covering Spanish Milan and Mantua. In a whirlwind campaign the Austrians, under P. Eugene of Savoy, drove the French back halfway across Lombardy (Apr.-Sept. 1701). This heartened the British and Dutch and accelerated their negotiations for a triple alliance with Austria. Signed on 7 Sept. this did not commit Britain to immediate war, but on the 16th when James II died at St. Germain, Louis XIV, against all advice and in breach of the P. of Ryswick, recognised the Old Pretender as King of England. This united British opinion. In Mar. 1702 William III died and in May the three powers declared war.

(2) In July 1702 Marlborough, already Ambassador to the States-General, became English C-in-C and Dutch Deputy Captain-Gen. He, with the Dutch Grand Pensionary, Antonie Heinsius, and the Austrian, Count Wratislaw, acted (so far as distance and their govts. permitted) as co-ordinators of war policy, but Marlborough's authority was restricted by the presence of Dutch civilian Field-Deputies, without whose consent he could not fight a battle. In Sept. the Imperial Diet declared war on France and the Margrave of Baden took command of their motley forces on the Rhine, but troubles in Hungary and the Turkish Marches prevented the Emperor from reinforcing the Margrave or P. Eugene. Hence the French, under Villars and Vendôme, were now much stronger than Eugene, while the best French army under Boufflers, based on the Belgian fortresses other than Maestricht, threatened Holland and Germany from Xanten near Cleves. On the other hand the English Admiralty was planning a combined attack on Cadiz preliminary to a naval invasion of the Mediterranean.

(3) In the latter half of 1702 the French gained a predominance in northern Italy. Marlborough, hampered by the Field-Deputies, nevertheless manoeuvred Boufflers out of the Meuse fortresses as far west as Liège and cleared the Rhine to Bonn; Admiral Rooke and the D. of Ormonde, however, failed ignominiously at Cadiz, but redeemed their reputation if not the strategic balance, by sinking the *Flota* at Vigo and bringing home £1,000,000 of bullion. Political developments overshadowed these events. The Hungarians broke into revolt and P. Eugene was withdrawn to deal with them, but on the other side, so did the Protestant Camisards in the Cevennes. Bavaria and Savoy had each been plotting treachery, the Bavarian Elector Max Emmanuel against the Emperor, D. Victor Amadeus of Savoy against his sons-in-law of France and Spain. Both plots partly miscarried. The Bavarian seized Ulm, but an imperial diplomat intercepted his correspondence so that the French failed to co-ordinate with him. Meantime, the French got to know of the Savoyards' intentions through the incompetence of two British diplomats, and three French armies planned to move on Turin in the Spring of 1703. Thus each side had a rebellious ulcer and an enemy enclave within its sphere.

(4) More important was the Portuguese conversion, upon terms, from a silent alliance with France to an open alliance against her. The Portuguese throne was unstable amid court tumults, noble and official corruption and the savage Lisbon mob. An Anglo-Dutch blockade might cause revolution. Conversely the allies wanted a base against the French King of Spain in Spain. A bargain (*see* METHUEN T. MAY 1703) was ultimately to transform the war. An Anglo-Dutch-Portuguese force of 30,000 (28,000 of them Portuguese), mostly at British expense, was to invade Spain with the Archduke Charles, the Habsburg claimant, in its midst. Portugal was to receive two Castilian provinces, Badajoz and preferential trade terms as a reward. The Dutch were doubtful, the Austrians unenthusiastic, but English money and warships had their way. The Alliance was thus committed to imposing its own King on a hostile nation and to a partition not merely of the Castilian empire but Castile itself. Since Castilians despised the Portuguese, their French King suddenly became a symbol of national self-respect, while English ministers found that they had miscalculated Portuguese effectiveness.

(5) The French now put their Belgian armies on the defensive and concentrated on Austria. Vendôme had reached L. Garda, while Marshal Villars had advanced from the Rhine and joined the Bavarians. Menaced from east, west and south, Austria was desperate. Villars proposed a march on Vienna, but the Elector wished first to gain the Tyrol. Villars should hold off the Margrave to his northwest, while the Elector and Vendôme pinched the Tyrol out from north and south. They miscalculated. The Tyrolese stopped Vendôme near Trent and turned the Elector out of Innsbruck.

(6) Having wasted the 1703 season, the French had to commit larger resources to re-attempt Villars' purpose in 1704. Villars, by now reduced to bad terms with the Elector, was relieved by de Marsin who, with the Elector and Marshal Tallard, was overthrown at Blenheim (Aug. 1704 q.v.).

Allied Offensives and French Counter-measures (7) As sanguine in Spain as their enemies had been in the Tyrol, allied attempts to cross into Portugal had similar local results but, like the Cadiz expedition, collected unintended benefits. Nine days before Blenheim, Rooke took Gibraltar against minor resistance; a fortnight after Blenheim he crippled the Franco-Spanish fleet in a furious battle off Malaga. Hence the enemy had to attempt recovery of the Rock by land. They moved slowly and Rooke reinforced the garrison. The ensuing three-year siege diverted Franco-Spanish resources with important effects.

(8) The Castilians had not eliminated Aragonese separatism. Thus, to follow up the successes of 1704, the allies planned to invade France *via* the Moselle and switch naval efforts to the Mediterranean. The Moselle plan failed because the Margrave would not co-operate and Marlborough therefore returned to the Meuse, bloodlessly demolished the French fortified Lines of Brabant and beat a part of the enemy in a brilliant action at Elixem (July 1705). Meanwhile in Apr. a combined force under Sir Cloudesley Shovell and the vainglorious and aggressive E. of Peterborough had taken Barcelona (Apr.-May 1705). By the autumn the *Cortes* of Aragon, Catalonia and Valencia had saluted the Archduke as King, but operations were paralysed by Peterborough's quarrels with him and his advisers. Such frictions made opportunities for the French. By taking Nice (Jan. 1706) they cut off Savoy from naval help. Marshal Tessé, advancing from Madrid, met the French fleet before Barcelona (Apr. 1706). Peterborough was in Valencia, his troops scattered among the three states. The 21-year old Archduke Charles made a desperate defence of Barcelona and was relieved by Admiral Leake (May). Grave dangers now threatened in Italy. After a victory at Calcinato (Mar.) Vendôme had driven the Austrians back to the Trentino. P. Eugene arrived in the nick of time.

(9) The Dutch now agreed to reinforce Eugene and to give Marlborough a free hand in the Low Countries, where Louis XIV planned an offensive. Marshal Villeroy, believing that he had a superiority, provoked a battle at Ramillies (May 1706) just after Leake relieved Barcelona; this savage contest included the greatest cavalry battle in history, but Marlborough dispersed or captured Villeroy's troops and in a week conquered Flanders. To rebuild his northern defences, Louis diverted resources from all fronts and recalled Vendôme from Italy.

(10) The E. of Galway with an Anglo-Portuguese force, had already entered Spain in Apr. He, the Archduke from Barcelona and Peterborough from Valencia converged on Madrid, which Philip V and the Jacobite D. of Berwick abandoned. The three forces, much wasted, met at Guadalajara (Aug.) while Berwick was joined by the entire Castilian nobility at Burgos. A popular Castilian uprising destroyed Galway's communications. The combined armies retreated perforce to Valencia (Sept.). This was the watershed of the Spanish war. For this, however, P. Eugene made a spectacular compensation. In a second brilliant Lombard campaign, he joined Victor Amadeus and drove the French who were besieging Turin into France (Sept. 1706).

(11) These events shook the cohesion of the alliance. The Whigs forced Sunderland into a Secretaryship of State. The Habsburgs wished to profit from the Turin success by seizing Naples. A Franco-Austrian convention at Milan (Mar. 1707) established a local peace and allowed the remaining French garrisons to go elsewhere. With reinforcements released from Lombardy, Berwick beat Galway at Almanza (Apr. 1707) and in May Villars surprised the Lines of Stollhofen from Strasbourg, broke into Germany and pillaged the south German states.

(12) In reply Marlborough proposed an assault from north and south. In the north he could depend on Belgian bases, but in the south Toulon had to be seized and made into a depot for an advance up the Rhone. There were delays before the Emperor could be coerced into any operation. Eugene advanced along the Provençal coast aided by Shovell's fleet. The land operations against

Toulon failed (July-Aug. 1707) but Shovell destroyed the naval base with the French fleet in it. The threat was enough to bring the French back from Germany and Spain, but the failure was an expensive strategic defeat.

(13) Early in 1708 both sides planned offensives in Flanders. Eugene was to command an army on the Moselle, a third army was to be formed on the Rhine under the Elector of Hanover and Eugene was to join Marlborough suddenly and fall upon Vendôme in Flanders before he could be reinforced. Meanwhile the French had fomented conspiracies in the Flemish fortress cities and meant their field army to cover a series of popular seizures. The roots of discontent lay in the rapacity of Dutch taxation. The opposed policies collided head on. The French indeed surprised Ghent and Bruges, the keys to the waterways, but Eugene also joined Marlborough and together they destroyed half of Vendôme's army in a pell-mell battle at Oudenarde (July 1708).

(14) Vendôme retired north to Ghent so as to deny the waterways for the movement of siege artillery, because the allies would obviously attack the French frontier zone where Berwick led a strong army. Marlborough and Eugene ("The Princes") made do without waterborne carriage. Convoys, which included 16,000 horses, brought the siege trains from Brussels to Menin. All the allied troops covered them. Louis XIV forbade Berwick to intervene and Vendôme's army was too shaken to do so.

(15) The Princes immediately invested Lille, the earliest prize of Louis XIV's aggressions and the second city of France, now commanded by Marshal Boufflers. Frustrated in an attempt to relieve it, Vendôme and Berwick cut the allied land communications through Brussels to Holland. The Princes shifted their supply line to the 50-mile route, partly through inundations, from Ostend. At Wynendael Gen. Webb bloodily repulsed an attempt to cut it. In subsequent amphibious fighting, war stores continued to come through to sustain the bombardment. Boufflers retired to his citadel in Oct. The Ostend line was then cut, but the Princes reopened the line through Brussels. In Dec. Boufflers surrendered. Ghent was also retaken.

(16) Lille distracted European attention from the by-products of Toulon. With French sea power in eclipse, the English made important gains. In Aug. 1708 Admiral Leake took over Sardinia. In Sept. he and Stanhope took Minorca, which was to remain a British base for some 48 years. All these events, however, were soon over-shadowed by a natural disaster. The Great Frost of 1709 was followed, especially in France, by famines, disease and riots. Louis XIV resolved to come to terms.

Allied Disunity **(17)** The ensuing negotiations broke down on the obduracy of the British. As the only principal ally involved in the Peninsula, all English parties agreed that there must be "No Peace without Spain". But Philip V had been accepted by the Castilians and a war of conquest would be needed to impose the Archduke Charles. The Dutch and the Germans were not interested in a war in Spain; the Emperor had not the resources. The British therefore demanded a guarantee from Louis XIV that his grandson would leave Spain. Louis naturally refused and represented the case as a demand that he should make war on his own family. The French rallied to him and the war was resumed.

(18) Allied victories continued. Tournai fell (July 1709). The Princes won a pyrrhic victory at Malplaquet (Sept.). Mons fell (Oct.), but the year 1710 saw dangerous changes and apparent stagnation. After an apparently fortunate entry by the Archduke Charles into Madrid (Sept.), Queen Anne had dismissed the Whigs from office. The election of a Tory parliament (Nov.) just preceded decisive Franco-Spanish victories at Brihuega and Villa Viciosa (Dec.). To set against these, not only

fortresses continued to fall in Flanders, but the allies continued to gnaw their way through the French defensive area. In July 1711 Marlborough forced the *Ne Plus Ultra* Lines (Lat: No further) and took Bouchain in Sept. With his dismissal in Dec. the war petered out because the Tory govt. was determined to negotiate a separate peace. *See* UTRECHT, P. OF.

SPARHAFOC, Abbot (fl. 1050). *See* EDWARD THE CONFESSOR-6.

SPEAKER (occasionally PARLOUR, PROLOCUTOR) is the presiding officer of a House of Parliament or Convocation. In the Lords the office is combined with that of Lord Chancellor. The term derives from his duty to *speak* to the Crown on behalf of his House. *See next entries.*

SPEAKERSHIP OF THE HOUSE OF COMMONS. A (1) The Speaker is elected before the Speech from the Throne at the opening of a new parliament, on the proposal of a back bencher, and confirmed in the Lords by Commissioners representing the Crown, to whom he makes a formal claim to the ancient rights and privileges of the House of Commons. These are instantly confirmed. He then returns to the Commons' Chamber and is the first to take the oath of allegiance.

(2) Though he must be re-elected for each parliament, it is customary, regardless of the political complexion of the House, to treat his office as continuous, so long as he is willing to stand. This habit follows from his duty of impartiality.

(3) His principal duties are to preserve the privileges of the House and of its individual members. Of these, the most important are freedom of speech and the rights of minorities: he must ensure that a member, once called to speak, is given a hearing. He has a necessary discretion (in a House of some 600) to call whom he pleases and generally calls members from opposite sides of the House alternately, giving preference as a rule to maiden speeches and privy councillors and having regard to whether a member has already spoken on the same subject at another stage in the proceedings.

(4) He also has the duty of selecting amendments to bills after they have passed their committee stage.

(5) In addition he must ensure that the procedure of the House, embodied in elaborate standing orders, is adhered to.

(6) To carry out his duties he is entitled to require respect for the chair and obedience to his rulings, enforceable if necessary by expulsion. He must therefore act fairly and in fact acts judicially, basing his decisions on existing rules and on precedents. He must also, under the Parliament Acts, certify whether a bill is a money bill and this is done judicially too.

(7) He has a casting but no deliberative vote. By custom he casts his vote, if possible so as to ensure that the question can be reopened. He does not preside over a Committee of the whole House.

(8) He presides over a Speaker's Conference customarily called whenever legislation on electoral reforms or redistribution of seats is contemplated.

B. (9) The earlier presiding officers were appointed or irresistibly recommended by the Crown and invariably, until 1533, sat for a county. The earliest known is Peter de Montfort in the Oxford or Mad Parliament (1258). Some, e.g. Sir Geoffrey le Scrope (1332), William of Thorpe (1348), William of Shareshull (1351 and 1352) were Chief Justices. The first undoubtedly chosen by the House itself was Sir Peter de la Mare (1376). Sir Thomas Hungerford (1377) was first to be styled Speaker. Sir John Cheyne (1399, a dangerous year) resigned after two days and was followed by John Dorewood, the first lawyer. Thomas Chaucer (1407, 1410 and 1421) was the son of the poet Geoffrey Chaucer. Speakers occasionally continued to hold other offices. Roger Hunt (1420) was a Baron of the Exchequer, Sir Thomas Lovell (1485) was

Chancellor of the Exchequer, Sir Thomas Audley (1529-33) Chancellor the Duchy of Lancaster.

(10) Sir Humphrey Wingfield (1533-6), M.P. for Great Yarmouth, was the first Speaker from a borough and Sir Robert Brooke (1554) the first from the City of London.

(11) A majority between the Reformation and the Revolution were lawyers, many of whom later held high judicial office. These included Sir Edward Coke (1593), Sir Christopher Yelverton (1597-8), Sir John Finch (1629), Sir Harbottle Grimston (1660) and, the last, Sir John Trevor (1687 and 1695) who was Master of the Rolls but contrived to be expelled from the House for taking a bribe.

(12) Thereafter Speakers for a while aspired to, and often achieved, high political office after their tenure, for example, Robert Harley (1701, 1702 to 1705) and Sir Spencer Compton (1715-22 and 1722-7). The long and single-minded speakership of the able Arthur Onslow (1734-61) helped to raise the prestige of the office, though William Grenville (1789) and Henry Addington (1790 to 1801) both became Prime Minister.

(13) With Charles Abbot (1802-17), the first to receive a peerage for his pains, the era of professional Speakers began and average tenure lengthened. This was fortunate, for the business of the House was becoming more complex and the character of its membership radically changed by successive reforms. Charles Manners-Sutton held office from 1817 to 1834. Charles Shaw-Lefevre (1839-57) was an expert on procedural reform. John Denison (1859-72) presided over the second Reform Bill. Henry Brand (1872-84) by a largely forgotten exercise of personal authority, ended many days of Irish obstruction (Jan. 1881) by putting the question after an all night debate, on condition that the House reconsidered its procedure (*see* CLOSURE). Arthur Peel (1885-95), a powerful personality, dominated the House in a period of peculiar stress and raised the prestige of his office to a level which survived the relative weakness of William Gully (1895-1905). The urbane and witty James Lowther (1905-21) held the office throughout the constitutional and ecclesiastical controversies before World War I, during the war and also the depressed period afterwards.

(14) Of the Speakers since 1921, Edward Fitzroy (1928-43) was respected for his tact and commanding presence and he, with Clifton Brown (1943-51), shared the years of World War II. From 1959 Speakers have come, apparently fortuitously, from the Conservative and Labour benches alternately, regardless of the complexion of the govt. In 1992 Betty Boothroyd was the first woman elected to the office.

SPECIAL AREAS were named in an Act of 1934. They were the same as the later Development Areas (q.v.). The Act created commissioners to make suggestions for their improvement and assist job creation. It was continued in force until 1939 by Acts of 1937.

SPECIAL ORDERS is the House of Lords' term for a statutory instrument requiring confirmation by affirmative resolution of both Houses. Such an order must be referred to the House's Special Orders Committee and the confirmatory resolution cannot be moved until it has reported.

SPECIAL ROADS ACT 1949. *See* HIGHWAY.

S.P.C.K. (SOCIETY FOR PROMOTING CHRISTIAN KNOWLEDGE) was founded by Thomas Bray in 1698 to encourage the formation of Anglican schools and the dissemination of Christian literature.

SPECTATOR was founded in 1828 and owned and edited by Stephen Rintoul; he took the title and the idea of a non-party family weekly from the Addison and Steele *Spectator* which had ended in 1712. It was generally to the left of centre, coming out strongly for the Reform Bill (1832), Gibbon Wakefield's colonialism (182946) and for trade unionism, but its highly informed and critical articles appealed to a limited readership of decreasing

political importance. In the 20th cent. it was of an independent conservative persuasion.

SPEENHAMLAND "ACT". In 1795 (a bad year) the J.P.s of Speenhamland, a parish adjacent to Newbury (Berks.) decided, in the interests of humanity and public order, to supplement wages from the poor rate by calculating a family survival level and making up the difference between wages and that level. They reckoned that when the quartern (81b 1 loz) loaf cost 1s., a wage earner needed 3s. a week plus 1s. 6d. for each dependant, and that a rise of 1d. in the cost would need to be met by an extra 3d. plus 1d. per dependant. They gave outdoor relief on this basis and their example was quickly followed in Berkshire and soon spread; by 1815 it was normal in the south other than Kent; the west, other than Cornwall; the Midlands, E. Anglia and the Fens, and in the E. and N. of Yorkshire. In 1801 the average rural labourer's weekly income was 9s. wages plus 6s. poor relief.

The system tended to keep wages low and impede labour movement, but contemporary opinion held that it had prevented a catastrophe during the Napoleonic Wars.

SPECIAL OPERATIONS EXECUTIVE (S.O.E.) was founded in July 1940 to organise sabotage and subversion and create resistance movements in enemy controlled and occasionally neutral countries. Its greatest practical successes in Europe were in Poland and Norway and in Asia, in Burma and Malaya. Save that it forced the enemy to divert considerable resources to police work and brought hope to oppressed populations, its operational achievements were, in a warlike sense, trivial even when, as often happened, it enjoyed wide local support. Its operations and those of M.I.6 were kept distinct to prevent mutual compromise.

"SPECIAL RELATIONSHIP" (ANGLO-U.S.). Post World War II. Conscious that Britain's warlike strength had been eroded by two World Wars and especially by the abandonment of Indian manpower, yet still having vast interests to defend somehow, alliances had become, in the absence of dominating power, the only available means to do so. The bedrock of this policy was that however much British and U.S. interests were likely to clash, the two countries would never go to war with each other and that therefore no ally of the one need fear war with the other. It was presented to the British public as an underlying convergence of interests, culture and good natured personal relationships between kinsfolk, even though the U.S.A. was born in rebellion and American tradition and educational atmosphere was hostile to Britain. The concept was fostered by British govts. to disguise the increasing subordination of London to Washington, particularly after the Suez Crisis. American policy makers hardly acknowledged the special relationship save where no important American objectives were involved.

SPEED, John (c. 1552-1629) published between 1607 and 1611 a series of good county maps giving an excellent vision of the England of his time. He also wrote a history.

SPEKE, John Hanning (1827-64), Indian army officer, discovered L. Victoria during his expedition with Richard Burton in search of the sources of the Nile in 1857.

SPELMAN, Sir Henry (?1564-1641) wrote a *Glossary* of obsolete English and Latin words (1626) and works on *The Councils of the Church* (1639) and *Tenures by Knight Service* (1641). *An earlier History of Sacrilege* and a *Treatise of Tithes* found after his death were intended to refute Selden's view that the Church and its rights were only legitimised by the state. He was an original member of the Society of Antiquaries, an M.P. for Castle Rising in 1597 and a Commissioner for unsettled Irish tithes in 1617.

SPENCER (1) Henry (1620-43) 1st E. of SUNDERLAND (1643), royalist killed at the first B. of Newbury, had married (1639) **(2) Dorothy SIDNEY of Permshurst**

(1617-84), the SACHARISSA of Edmund Waller's poetic courtship. She succoured distressed clergy and Royalists from her house at Althorp and was a friend of Halifax. Their son **(3) Robert (1640-1702) 2nd E.** married the rich Anne Digby in 1665. Educated abroad, he got diplomatic employments in Madrid and Paris through the King's mistresses (1671-1673). In 1679 he became Sec. of State (north) but intrigued with Shaftesbury and the exclusionists and was dismissed in Feb. 1681 at the fall of that statesman. He then contrived to make his peace with James, D. of York, and returned to favour in 1683, mainly to supersede the influence of Halifax and the Hydes. He thus became James' main adviser at his succession. He favoured extension of the prerogative mainly for patronage, and the repeal of the Test Acts. He advocated severe measures against Monmouth's rebels (1685) but his sense of the possible told him that James II was going too fast and might go too far. Accordingly he maintained a correspondence with William of Orange, but under-estimated that Prince's support in the country or his ability to invade. Hence he was taken by surprise, but thought that he could mediate. The hurried reversal of James' policies had no effect and he, like his master, fled. At Rotterdam he soon reverted to his Protestant upbringing. He partially justified himself by negotiating the purely Whig ministry, instead of the coalition which William had favoured. He thus held office until 1697 and remained:-

A Proteus, ever acting in disguise;
A finished statesman, intricately wise;
A second Machiavel who soared above
The little tyes of gratitude and love.

His son **(4) Charles (1674-1722) 3rd E.**, a Whig M.P. in 1695, married Anne, daughter of the 1st D. of Marlborough in 1700 and was Ambassador to Vienna in 1705. He was Sec. of State (south) from 1706 to 1710 when his dismissal became a strategic political objective of Harley and the Tories in their campaign against Marlborough. In opposition he was discovered in contact with Hanover, which prejudiced the Queen still further against the pro-Hanoverian Whigs. Consequently George I and Robethon doubted his political value and sent him to Ireland as Lord Lieut., but then (1715) made him Lord Privy Seal. He still had some political nuisance value; by 1717 he had ousted Townshend and Walpole and became Sec. of State (north); in 1718 he became 1st Lord of the Treasury and proposed to pay off the National Debt by selling stock in the South Sea Co. He resigned in 1721. A bibliophile, he founded the library at Althorp. In his third son **(5) Charles (1706-58) 5th E. (1729) and 3rd D. of MARLBOROUGH** the Spencer and Churchill interests and titles were united. Otherwise unremarkable, he commanded the abortive expedition against St. Malo in 1758.

SPENCER, Herbert (1820-1903), either "the most immeasurable ass in Christendom" (Carlyle) or the prophet of a scientific philosophy and ethics, had a contempt for classical studies. Trained as an engineer, he issued his *Principles of Psychology* in 1855, *First Principles* in 1862, *Principles of Biology* between 1864 and 1867, *Principles of Sociology* in 1876 to 1896 and *Principles of Ethics* between 1879 and 1896. There were also works on *Education* (1861), *Classification of the Sciences* (1864), *The Study of Sociology* (1873) and *Factors of Organic Evolution* (1887). This enormous, if opaque, corpus was widely read among the international disciples of the Germanic philosophical masters, who probably understood his definition of the Laws of Evolution as "an integration of matter and concomitant dissipation of emotion during which matter passes from an indefinite incoherent homogeneity to a definite coherent heterogeneity, and during which the retained motion undergoes a parallel transformation". He had difficulty in applying this universal principle to ethics. His *The Man versus the State* (1884) is sometimes read.

SPENS, Sir John (?1520-73) simultaneously a Scots judge of session and Queen's Advocate from 1560, supported Queen Mary and prosecuted the murderers of Riccio and Darnley. He seems, however, to have had some traffic or sympathy with Knox and the Reformers and kept his offices until his death. In 1566 he was appointed to a commission to revise Scots law.

SPENS, Thomas (?1415-80) became Bp. of Aberdeen in 1449 and Keeper of the Scots Privy Seal in 1458. He was much employed as a diplomat, especially to Edward IV (with whom he was *persona grata*) and the Court of Burgundy. In 1471 he negotiated the T. of Alnwick, signed in 1473, and in 1474 the betrothal of P. James (later James IV) to Edward IV's daughter Cecilia. He also helped to endow Aberdeen Cathedral and rebuilt the palace there.

SPENSER, Edmund (?1552-99) obtained a place in the E. of Leicester's household in 1578 and associated with Sir Philip Sidney and Dyer in a literary group called The Areopagus. His *Shepeard's Calendar* appeared in 1579. In 1580 he went to Ireland as Sec. to the Lord Deputy, Ld. Grey of Wilton, and spent nearly the rest of his life there. He wrote the first part of the *Faerie Queen* between 1579 and 1589, the *Epithalamium* in 1595; the rest of the *Faerie Queen* appeared in 1596 and his *View of the State of Ireland* in 1597.

SPERRY, Elmer Ambrose (1860-1930) was a U.S. scientific technician who invented many things, but especially the gyroscopic compass, thus making navigation independent of magnetic variation, and gyroscopic stabilisers for ships and aircraft.

SPES, Don Guerau de. *See* ELIZABETH I-11.

SPICE Is. *See* INDONESIA.

SPICE TRADE, ORIENTAL. In the Middle Ages meat and fish were extremely short out of season and were (more or less) preserved by salting, smoking or drying. The idea of making them palatable with spices, which sometimes seemed to assist preservation, was perhaps learned by westerners during the Crusades. Pepper, ginger, cloves, turmeric, cinnamon, certain kinds of capsicum and caraway were brought to the Levant from southern India, Ceylon and Indonesia (especially the Moluccas) by Arab traders through Basra and Egypt. Since a small amount went a very long way and the demand was great, spice cargoes and even small (horseborne) consignments were extremely valuable (cf. the modern drug trade). The Venetians early specialised in this trade; they found it worth while to ship the goods in armed galleys and despatched them over the Alps to German marts such as Augsburg, whence they were further dispersed. The present city of Venice represents the enormous profits.

The crusading impulse apart, these profits were an important motive in the Portuguese efforts to find a way east round Africa. The Portuguese irruption into the E. Indies brought huge wealth to Lisbon at the beginning of the 16th cent., but the European demand was so large that the Venetian trade, after a short set-back, continued to increase until about 1595. Their system was destroyed by a decline in shipping resources, piracy and Ottoman obstruction. Meanwhile the Dutch intervened in the Portuguese East, after which they competed on decreasingly favourable terms with the French and the English.

From about 1700 W. Indian spices, besides sugar, began to reach the markets and the 18th cent. triumph of the British over the French in India and the W. Indies resulted in a *modus vivendi* with the Dutch. This was sealed in the end by improved cattle breeding and greater opportunities to eat fresh meat.

SPIN DOCTOR. A public relations adviser, especially one skilled in presenting his employer's intentions to the public as more favourable than they really are, or even in concealing their reality altogether. *See* GOEBBELS.

SPINNING. See WEAVING AND SPINNING.

SPIRITUALITIES. See INVESTITURE.

SPITALFIELDS in Stepney, London, became the centre of an important Huguenot silk weaving industry from 1685, surrounding a vegetable market. The industry survived until 1900. Clothing and provisions were still made and sold in 1990.

SPITHEAD MUTINY. See MUTINIES, NAVAL 1797.

SPITZBERGEN. See JAMES I AND VI-10.

SPIVS were mostly young black-marketeers and dealers in scarce goods who in the later 1940s made no real contribution to society and dressed flashily to advertise success or availability for deals.

SPLENDID ISOLATION, a phrase of the Canadian G. E. Forster and popularised by Vist. Goschen in 1896 to signify a free hand in foreign policy and, in face of the rise of German power and the scramble for Africa and China, the avoidance of international commitments. The policy depended upon overwhelming naval superiority, which became too expensive when Germany started to build a fleet in earnest.

SPORTS, BOOK OF (1618). Puritan magistrates in Somerset and Lancashire had tried to suppress Sunday games and Morris Dances in 1616 and 1617. Protests and confusion led James I and VI to define and permit certain sports after Sunday church in the *Book,* which angered narrower Puritans, but was reissued in 1663.

SPRAGGE, Sir Edward (?1629-73) served under P. Rupert in the Four Days' Battle (June 1666) and was in command at Sheerness when the Dutch forced the Medway (June 1667). In 1671 he destroyed the Algerine fleet at Bougie and in 1673 he fought brilliantly against the Dutch at Solebay, as Admiral of the Blue. Probably to avenge the Medway disaster, which had affected him personally, he grappled with the powerful Dutch flagship and went down with his own.

SPRING-RICE (1) Thomas (1790-1866) 1st Ld. (Ir.) MONTEAGLE (1839), Whig M.P. for Limerick, supported Irish reforms under Canning. He was Sec. to the Treasury under Grey from 1830 to 1834 and Chancellor of the Exchequer from 1835 to 1839 under Melbourne. He introduced Rowland Hill's penny postage scheme but sought the Speakership which, owing to radical opposition, he failed to get. He then retired. His grandson **(2) Sir Cecil (1859-1918)** was British Commissioner to the Egyptian *Caisse de la Dette* from 1901 to 1903, Minister to Persia from 1906 to 1908 and to Sweden from 1908 to 1913, when he became a very successful Ambassador to Washington until the end of World War I.

SPURGEON, Charles Haddon (1834-92) became Baptist Pastor at Waterbeach in 1852, came to London in 1854 and ministered at the Metropolitan Tabernacle from 1861. His sermons, which combined fervour, demagoguery and humour attracted thousands and were a major weekly public spectacle. He left the Baptist Union in 1887.

SPY. See WARD, SIR LESLIE.

SQUADRONE VOLANTE (Fr: flying picket) or NEW PARTY (Sc.) comprised rural Presbyterian politicians led by the M. of Tweeddale in the Scots parliament during the early years of the War of the Spanish Succession. They were concerned to preserve the existing Scots Presbyterian society against English and Anglican encroachments, but thought that defeat by the Caesaro-Papalist Louis XIV might be much worse. Hence they mistrusted the tactics of the extremists, who, in the parliament of 1703, had refused war funds and tried to force a Bill of Security, separating the Crowns of the two Kingdoms upon the govt. (which had refused Assent), because such disunity might let in the French. In the next parliament, Tweeddale was Royal Commissioner. Godolphin in London offered Assent in return for war funds and Tweeddale, holding the balance with the Squadrone, accepted the bargain. The funds were conceded and the Squadrone committed to the Bill of Security, which was duly assented. Thereupon the English parliament threatened to treat Scots as aliens and cut off trade unless they accepted the Hanoverian succession by Christmas 1705. The Squadrone now had to execute a somersault by voting to repeal the Act of Security and its credit as a party was destroyed. Nevertheless their watchfulness persisted in a party sometimes called the PATRIOTS led by the D. of Roxburgh, Sec. of State under George I until ousted by Walpole in 1725 in favour of Argyll.

SRI LANKA. Ceylon.

STADHOLDER (Dutch: STADHOUDER) originally one to whom is delegated the 'state' of a prince and thus a viceroy, but in the Dutch provinces he was also the chief magistrate. The office in five of the provinces, especially Holland, became hereditary in the Orange-Nassau family and formed the basis of their rise to power.

STAFF COLLEGE. See ROYAL MILITARY ACADEMY etc.

STAFFORD. See HOWARD.

STAFFORD, Ds. of BUCKINGHAM (1) Humphrey (?-1460) Ld. STAFFORD, a grandson of Thomas of Woodstock, became 1st Duke in 1444. His grandson **(2) Henry (?-1483) 2nd D. (1460)** was a supporter of Richard III but rebelled and was attainted and executed. The dukedom was restored to his son **(3) Henry (?-1521) 3rd D.** (1485). He too was executed, on trumped up charges, but really because he was related to the throne.

STAFFORD, Ms. of. See LEVESON-GOWER.

STAFFORD -SHIRE (1) The area was sparsely populated under the Romans and because of its position at the heart of Mercia, its history is subsumed in that of the Mercian bishopric at Lichfield and of the Mercian Kingdom, until its collapse in the 9th cent. As an entity it came into existence in 913, when Ethelfleda, Lady of the Mercians, founded *burhs* at Tamworth and Stafford as part of her programme of reconquest. The shire remained poor and for that reason relatively undisturbed in the political upheavals until after the Conquest, when it was devastated as part of William I's reprisals against the rebels of 1069. William built the castle at Stafford in 1070.

(2) Roger of Toeni or of STAFFORD became the Castellan and at Domesday was the largest landowner. The Montgomeries and the Ferrers also had lands, besides the bishops and the Abbot of Westminster. The shire's poverty was such that the sheriffs *ferme* was less than half the average. This state of affairs continued and until about 1750 the county was a backwater.

(3) It was the Industrial Revolution with its enormous demand for coal and iron which activated the county and its hitherto largely unexploited mines and led to the creation of the canal network, beginning in 1777, and the improvement of the roads. The 19th cent. population rose fivefold and unimportant villages such as Wolverhampton and Wednesbury grew into substantial cities. Conditions in the south Staffordshire collieries were exceptionally good, but that of children in the associated industries notably bad. Public health was so poorly managed that cholera killed hundreds in 1832 and 1849. In the Potteries on the other hand conditions were generally better despite industrial diseases, but employment was much influenced by successive inventions. Thus diversification such as the harness and saddlery trade, the making of tinned and japanned ware and the manufacture of bicycles and motor cars helped to keep employment stable.

STAGE CARRIAGES were first licensed, along with post horses, in 1779 in order to raise revenue, since the carriageable roads were either turnpikes or maintained by the parishes. Later acts made amendments, restricted the numbers carried and laid down rules about plating and numbering. Much of the Consolidating Act of 1832 became the model for later vehicle taxation and licensing.

STAIR. *See* DALRYMPLE.

STALIN, Josif Vissarionovich (orig: DJUGASHVILI), a Georgian who intrigued his way upward during Lenin's physical decline and in 1922 became Communist Party Sec. As brutal and unscrupulous as his master, he climbed to a dominant position in Soviet Russia. He continued Lenin's industrialisation, a murderous and inefficient rural collectivisation and the purge technique for the mass elimination of potential or imagined opposition. His misjudgement in allying himself with Hitler nearly led to disaster when Hitler turned on him. He then directed the defence against invasion and at conferences with the western leaders at Teheran, Yalta and Potsdam his attitude was wholly predatory. After his death, the Communist regime became somewhat less cruel and a process of de-Stalinisation was set in motion by Khrushchev, but his legacy of slave labour and environmental pollution continued until the overthrow of the Russian Communists in the 1980s.

STALLER. A Court officer under Edward the Confessor, perhaps a translation of the ducal constable in Normandy, where Edward had spent many years.

STAMFORD, STATUTE OF (1309). *See* EDWARD II-2.

STAMP ACT 1764. *See* AMERICAN REBELLION-9.

STAMP DUTY was first imposed (on legal proceedings) in 1670. It was extended for four years to most official documents, conveyances, etc. in 1694 and increased in scope and amount and made permanent by a series of Acts beginning in 1697. It was, in effect, a sporadic flat rate capital tax. Its imposition on the American colonies was an occasion of their rebellion. After 1894 the duty was related to the value of certain, particularly land, transactions. Modern estate and capital gains duties have eliminated the need for it, but it still (1996) survives as a cumbrous nuisance.

STANDARD, B. of the (Aug. 1138) on Cowton Moor, north of Northallerton (Yorks.). Abp. Thurstan of York and some northern barons led by Walter Espec of Helmsley organised local resistance to a particularly savage incursion by the Scots under King David I. The English were apparently filled with religious fervour and the battle was fought round a ship's mast placed on a cart to which were fixed a pyx and the banners of St. John of Beverley, St. Peter of York and St. Wilfrid of Ripon. The Scots and Picts were routed in three hours.

STANDING ARMY in peacetime. Control was a major issue between the executive and Parliament, culminating under the Commonwealth and Protectorate in military rule of an oppressive, godly but licentious kind. At the Restoration this army was paid off and replaced by an innocuous militia under local control. The fears generated by the experiences under the interregnum raised opposition to James II when it became obvious that he meant to form a standing force officered by R. Catholics. This was not illegal at the time, but it was declared illegal to maintain a standing army in time of peace without parliamentary consent in the Declaration and Bill of Rights 1689, and thenceforth practical control was maintained by limiting the validity of the Mutiny Act (upon which discipline depended) to a year at a time. The period was extended to five years after World War II. *See also* CHARLES I.

STANDING COMMITTEES (HOUSE OF COMMONS) are composed of 20 to 50 M.Ps. (usually about 45) appointed by the Committee of Selection in proportion to the party strengths in the House. The chairman is appointed by the Speaker from a panel of committee chairmen. They take the Committee Stage of public bills other than finance bills and the rare bills of major constitutional importance, and their procedure is the same as that of the House. The membership is changed for each bill. As many as nine such committees may be sitting simultaneously. They meet in the mornings whereas the full House meets in the afternoon. Their systematic creation by the Attlee govt. after World War II amounted to a major constitutional amendment and converted an M.P.'s position into a full time occupation.

STANDING JOINT COMMITTEES. *See* POLICE.

STANDING ORDERS, in Parliament. Both Houses have separate codes for private and public business, based upon custom or upon recommendations of select committees, and both have Standing Orders Committees to consider whether orders may be dispensed with in particular cases. Those on private business are nearly identical in both Houses. On public business the Commons orders are much more elaborate than the Lords.

STANFORD, Sir Charles (1852-1924), composer, especially of church music, conductor and with Parry and Sir Geoffrey Grove, Prof. at the Royal College of Music from its inception (1883) until his death.

STANG, RIDING THE. *See* SKIMMINGTON.

STANHOPE. The next three articles deal with three Nottingham and Derbyshire families, which received three earldoms and were founded by two half-brothers perhaps **Philip (1584-1656), 1st E. of CHESTERFIELD,** and **Sir John (?-1638)** the ancestor of the **Es. of HARRINGTON.** The Es. STANHOPE were descended from the Es. of Chesterfield.

STANHOPE (CHESTERFIELD) (1) Philip (1584-1656) 1st Ld. STANHOPE (1616), 1st E. of CHESTERFIELD (1628) was heavily fined by the parliament as a strong Royalist. Two of his Royalist sons perished in the Civil War. His grandson **(2) Philip (1633-1713) 2nd E.** was a perplexed constitutional moderate who opposed James II's policies, helped to guard the Princess Anne at the Revolution and welcomed William III, but refused either to take the oath to William or to fight James. He was a patron of the poet Dryden. His son Alexander was the ancestor of the Es. Stanhope (*see below*). Of his grandchildren **(3) William (1702-72)** and **(4) John (1705-48)** were both M.P.s from 1727. Their elder brother **(5) Philip Dormer (1694-1773),** the celebrated **4th E. (1726)** was elected to the House of Commons in 1715 before coming of age, with the political support of his kinsman, Gen. (later 1st E.) Stanhope. His urbanity and tact became legendary: he even maintained good relations simultaneously with George I and the P. of Wales and after the latter's accession he was sent to The Hague, despite Walpole's dislike, as Ambassador (1728) and there conducted negotiations for an Anglo-Dutch royal marriage and the (1731) adherence to the second T. of Vienna. He also acquired a mistress, a Mlle du Bouchet, whose son, Philip Stanhope, was the addressee of his father's famous letters.

In 1732 he returned to London politics, having been Ld. Steward since 1730. He soon clashed with Walpole. The two men were profoundly divided by temperament and style as well as political principle. His was a strong influence in frustrating Walpole's excise scheme in 1733 and the Minister with Queen Caroline in retaliation engineered his dismissal from the Stewardship. There was a spectacular public quarrel. Philip refused to attend the Court of St. James and became a leading figure at the Prince of Wales' court at Leicester House. As if this were not enough, he infuriated the King by marrying the King's bastard half-sister, Melusine von der Schulenburg. The marriage was solely a political and financial arrangement: they lived apart and Philip took a new mistress. He continued to quarrel financially with the King and politically with the govt. After 1737, when Queen Caroline died, his ability to embarrass Walpole grew. He had a strong following in the Commons and a famous wit and he patronised Pope and the other Leicester House literary men, besides being on excellent terms with Voltaire.

In 1742, in alliance with Pulteney and Carteret, he contrived Walpole's overthrow, but being out of sympathy and contemptuous of the cypher Spencer

Compton, E. of Wilmington, he stayed in opposition alongside the rising Pitt. This earned them each commendation and, ultimately, a legacy from the still formidable Duchess of Marlborough.

The issue upon which Philip based his opposition was the indirect subsidisation of Hanover mainly by paying the Hanoverian army. The policy was in fact justifiable in British interests, because the electorate's rivers were important avenues for British trade into middle Europe, but disregarding this consideration, he waged throughout 1743 and 1744 a relentless campaign in the press (thinly disguised as "Broad Bottom") and in the Lords. In July 1743 Wilmington's death brought the Pelhams into greater power and by Nov. 1744 they, with Philip, drove Carteret from office. Popular opinion recognised his role. The new govt. was known as the Broad Bottom Administration. Philip became Lord Lieut. of Ireland, but preceded his assumption of office by negotiating an Anglo-Dutch intervention in the War of the Austrian Succession (Jan. 1745). He was in Ireland, however, at the decisive period of the 1745 Jacobite rebellion. He believed that poverty, not Popery, was Ireland's bane and that Irish landlordism was the curse of the rural areas. He instituted public works (including the planting of Phoenix Park in Dublin) and flatly refused to apply repression when the Jacobites rose. Through this sense and sympathy the rebellion never affected Ireland at all, but his health broke down and he was laid up in England until Oct. 1746.

The Pelhams now found that they needed him and George II was becoming reconciled to the witty friend of his youth. Philip was persuaded to exchange Ireland for the northern Secretaryship of State with his relative, the E. of Harrington (Oct. 1746). The arrangement failed. The Pelhams were prepared to countenance brilliance in Dublin, but not nearer home, and he now wanted peace while they wanted the advantage of his influence yet a continuance of the war. In Feb. 1748 he resigned, much to the regret of the King who offered him a dukedom; and the usual furious press controversy followed. He never took office again, but remained a feared elder statesman, capable, despite advancing deafness, of two further feats of statesmanship. He brought in the Calendar Act of 1751 in a speech whose astronomy (he cheerfully admitted) he did not understand, and in 1757 he reconciled Newcastle and Pitt so as to make the formation of their famous administration feasible.

Philip built Chesterfield House in London, assembled two remarkable picture collections and helped many in the literary world, including booksellers and publishers as well as writers. Though one of the greatest Englishmen of his age, his reputation has suffered for he shunned office and because of Dr. Johnson's dislike, the malice of Walpole and Hervey and Victorian moral criticism of his letters. At his death the earldom and fortune passed to collaterals.

STANHOPE (HARRINGTON) (1) William (?1690-1756) 1st E. of HARRINGTON (1742), M.P. in 1715, was a special envoy to Madrid in 1717-8 and at Turin in 1718. After a short service in the French army, he was Ambassador to Madrid from 1719 to 1726. As such, much of his energy was engaged in dealing with Spanish demands for Gibraltar. In 1726 he obtained particulars of the secret T. of Vienna and from 1728 to 1730 he was plenipotentiary to the Congresses of Aix-la-Chapelle and Soissons. In 1729 he negotiated the triple T. of Seville with France and Spain.

In 1730 he became Northern Sec. of State to advance Walpole's peaceful trading and pro-Hanoverian policy, which provoked Chesterfield's opposition. By 1740 the policy was breaking down, especially when Prussia attacked Austria, and Hamington, with the King, negotiated Hanoverian neutrality independently of Walpole who was being forced into a war which he

disliked. There was, in fact, no alternative, but his action kept him in office after Walpole's fall and in due course the Pelhams put him into Carteret's Secretaryship of State (Nov. 1744). He was dependent on the Pelhams because, unlike other Stanhopes, he had little private means. All the same, when he resigned and returned with them in Feb. 1746, he was so offensive to the King that he increased his dependence and it was only through their pressure that he was allowed to retain office (safely away from London) by exchanging his seals for Ireland with his relative, Chesterfield. During his four years at Dublin he had the misfortune to encounter the first organised Irish parliamentary opposition and his invincible laziness did not improve matters. He retired in 1751 in a haze of insults and burning effigies. His grandson **(2) Charles (1753-1829) 3rd E. (1779)** was C-in-C in Ireland from 1805 to 1812 but also acted as a special military envoy in Berlin in 1805 and to Vienna in 1806. **(3) Charles (1780-1851) 4th E.,** usually called by the family courtesy title **Ld. PETERSHAM,** a popular eccentric, invented an overcoat, a snuff mixture and his own blacking and was an expert on tea. He patronised the stage and married the actress Maria Foote. His brother **(4) Leicester (1784-1862) 5th E.,** soldier of liberal opinions, was agent of the British Committee for the Liberation of Greece in 1823-4. He encountered great difficulties because of Greek corruption and factionalism and he and Byron disliked each other. It was impracticable to be neutral and he was driven to a preference for the Western faction, led by one Odysseus, as against the Aegeans preferred by Byron and his friend, Mavrogordato. He tried to reconcile the two sides, but Byron was dying and when the Ottoman govt. complained, he was, as an army officer, ordered home. He had, however, managed to organise a Greek newspaper, an artillery regiment and a postal service to London before he left. These were probably of more practical use than Byron's posturings.

STANHOPE (STANHOPE) (*see* STANHOPE-CHESTERFIELD) **(1) James (1673-1721) 1st Vist. STANHOPE (1717) 1st E. STANHOPE (1718)** was born in Paris and spent the years 1690-1 in Madrid with his father. He became a professional soldier and was naturalised by Act in 1696. He became a Whig M.P. in 1701, served against Cadiz in 1702, under Marlborough in 1703 and in Portugal in 1704. He was made a Brig.-Gen. and went to Spain with Peterborough. He earned widespread acclaim and in 1706 replaced Sir Paul Methuen as Minister to Charles VI, while retaining his subordinate military position. Hence, against his advice, he was involved in the Spanish defeats of 1707, but he earned Marlborough's respect and in 1708 became C-in-C of the weakened British army in Spain. He made the important capture of Minorca (Sept. 1708) and in 1710 led the offensive *via* victories at Almenara (July) and Saragossa (Aug.) which culminated in the short occupation of Madrid. He was captured at Brihuega (Mar. 1711) in Vendôme's counter-offensive.

On his return (Aug. 1712) to a Tory-governed England, he became a champion of Whig Hanoverianism and even arranged with Marlborough and Cadogan (as it turned out, superfluously) to bring over Hanoverian troops to secure the Protestant succession. Hence, under the new dynasty he became, with Vist. Townshend, a Sec. of State and leader of the Commons. He was thus the main civil authority when he was commissioned with the military task of putting down the Jacobite rebellion of 1715 (*see* GEORGE I-3).

With the crisis past, he turned to diplomacy for which his family urbanity, cosmopolitanism and the King's favour suited him; but political and bureaucratic delays hindered the signature of the Baffler Treaty and the French Treaty of Guarantee and led to the reconstruction of the govt. with himself as 1st Lord of the Treasury. In 1718 he exchanged this post for the Southern Secretaryship of State. Either way he was the most powerful of the ministers and so chiefly responsible for the defeat of Cardinal Alberoni's Sicilian adventure at the peaceable naval victory off C. Passaro (Aug. 1718), and for the repulse of a Russian attempt on Sweden in 1719. He died of a stroke during the South Sea Bubble crisis.

His grandson **(2) Charles (1753-1816) 3rd E. (1786)**, Dutch and Swiss educated mathematician and friend of the younger Pitt, became a Whig M.P. in 1780, refused office under Pitt in 1783 and quarrelled with him over financial policy (beginning with a tax on bricks) in 1784. By 1789 he was favouring the French Revolution and supporting Fox and in 1794 he moved to recognise the French Republic. He was so unpopular that he withdrew from the House of Lords until 1800, by which time liberal opinions were more fashionable and he could pursue causes of his own such as the abolition of slavery and the defence of the currency.

During all these years he had exercised his remarkable scientific and mechanical talents on, amongst others, marine steam propulsion, printing, instrument tuning, calculating machines and canal engineering. His sister **(3) Hester (1776-1839)**, eccentric Society wit, beauty and friend of the younger Pitt, went to the Levant in 1810. In 1814 she settled among the Lebanon Druses and became a local potentate who protected Christians and lectured her many visitors at exhausting length. The son of (2), **(4) Philip Henry (1805-75) 5th E.**, a Conservative M.P. in 1830 and Peel's U/Sec. of State (1834-5), was mainly distinguished for his work on copyright legislation, passed in 1843. In 1844 he became Peel's Sec. to the Board of Control (India) and resigned with him after the repeal of the Corn Laws. His later life was devoted to promoting learning and the arts. He wrote many long historical works and inspired the establishment of the National Portrait Gallery. His son **(5) Edward (1840-93)**, Tory M.P. from 1874, became U/Sec. for India in 1878. From 1880 he was a leading opponent of Gladstone and in 1885 he was effectively Salisbury's Minister of Education. In 1886 he became Sec. of State for the Colonies, but went to the War Office and between 1887 and 1892 began the modernisation of the army.

STANLEY. The fortunes of this family were founded upon the career of **(1) Sir John (1350-1414)** who acquired Knowsley and Latham by marriage in 1385 and governed Ireland as de Vere's deputy and then as Lieut. from 1386 to 1391, again from 1399 to 1401 and from 1413. He also held military appointments on the Welsh and Scottish borders and in 1405 was granted the I. of Man. His son **(2) Thomas (1406-59) 1st Ld. STANLEY** (1456) maintained the Irish service as Deputy from 1431 to 1437. He was a powerful Lancashire figure, representing it in Parliament from 1446 to 1455 and he was also a household official and, from 1455, Lord Chamberlain. His son **(3) Thomas (1435-1504) 2nd Ld., 1st E. of DERBY (1485)** married Eleanor Neville and became Edward IV's C.J. of Chester in 1461, but dexterously survived Henry VI's readeption and Edward IV's recovery and became Ld. Steward after Warwick's defeat. After military commands in France in 1475 and against Scotland in 1482 he married Margaret Beaufort, Countess of Richmond, thus becoming stepfather to the future Henry VII, then a fugitive. Richard III put him briefly in custody at the beginning of his reign because of his legitimism, and though he was made Constable, he rightly did not trust him. When Henry VII invaded Wales in 1485, Richard, by taking Thomas' son, Ld. Strange, as a hostage, thought that he could rely upon him, but he was unaware of the depth of his commitment to Henry (*see* BOSWORTH FIELD). Thomas crowned Henry after his victory and Henry made him E. of Derby. His brother **(4) Sir William (?-1495)** had a parallel career and became Henry's chamberlain after Bosworth. Thomas' son **(5) James (1465-1515)** became Bp. of Ely by provision in 1506. Protestants denounced his lechery, but he has a claim to fame as his

stepmother's (Lady Margaret's) adviser and executant in her important Cambridge foundations. *See also* MAN, I. OF-6 -10; DERBY GOVTS; EPSOM.

STANLEY, Arthur Penrhyn (1815-81) DEAN STANLEY, Prof. of Ecclesiastical History and Dean of Westminster, was the leading Broad Churchman of his day and an early champion of Anglican ecumenism.

STANLEY, Henry Morton. *See* LIVINGSTON, DR DAVID.

STANNARIES (1) were the tin mines and later certain courts in Devon and Cornwall which, perhaps as early as King Athelstan, had jurisdiction over the tinners. Because of their economic muscle, they came to be exempt from all other jurisdictions save in cases of life, limb and land. These privileges were confirmed by a Royal Charter of 1305. From the 14th cent. the Cornish Stannary Parliament was held at Truro, the Devonian at Crockern Tor (Dartmoor). They were controlled by an official of the Duchy of Cornwall.

(2) The tinners might mark out areas which they intended to mine, by digging a line of turves along its boundary. This was called *tin-bounding* and could be done anywhere, but if the land were cultivated they had to give notice to the court. They could dig as long as they rendered *toll tin*, namely one fifteenth of their production to the Duchy of Cornwall. The tin was smelted into blocks: Devon tin being taken for certification (*coinage*) to Ashburton, Chagford or Tavistock; Cornish to Bodmin, Helston, Liskeard, Lostwithiel or Truro. It was done by cutting off a corner and stamping it.

(3) The last Cornish Stannary Parliament was held in 1752. The whole complex of customs and courts was abolished in 1896.

STANSFIELD, Sir James (1820-98), was Pres. of the Local Govt. Board and in the Cabinet from 1871 to 1874, but gave up his prospects to promote Josephine Butler's campaigns on prostitution and against the related Contagious Diseases Acts. Though pressed to take office he refused until these Acts had been repealed in 1886. "A front rank statesman who threw up" his ambitions for a thankless crusade of mercy in "a rewardless and repellent field".

STAPLE. A. A place where all goods of a certain type, destination or origin are required to be sold.

B. (1) To finance his war in 1294 Edward I, advised by the merchant Laurence of Ludlow, channelled wool and hides to a limited number of ports where merchants were elected and assigned to buy them; some were requisitioned for the King against compensation. A heavy ("New") custom or maletolt (5 marks per last of leather, 3 marks per sack of wool or 300 wool fells) was levied and the goods were then consigned to a staple at Dordrecht. The King's goods, being untaxed, were used either as gifts for, or the increased profits on sale applied to, the Count of Holland and the D. of Brabant. In 1295 this staple was moved to the Duke's town of Malines (because of the Dutch defection) and in 1296 to Antwerp. This system and its maletolt constituted a major factor in the political crisis of 1297 when the maletolt was abolished. Since simplicity of tax collection was a prime object of the scheme, Royal pressure to maintain the Antwerp monopoly was much reduced and it became effectively a preferential staple for the southerly goods.

(2) In May 1313 for the preferential staple at Antwerp an ordinance substituted a compulsory staple as from 1314 at St. Omer for wool destined for Flanders, Brabant and Artois. Edward II's adviser was another Shropshire wool merchant, Richard Stury; the King had just been deprived of the services of Italian bankers and was searching for new sources of credit. The merchants paid heavily for the arrangement and the King could expect fines from disobedient exporters and payments for exemptions. In 1319 a merchant assembly unsuccessfully demanded the substitution of two English staples but in

1323 the St. Omer staple had hurriedly to be moved to Bruges because of the war of St. Sardos. Meanwhile opposition to Royal policy blew hot and cold; in 1321 Thomas of Lancaster had championed the foreign merchants who were the main victims of St. Omer. In May 1326 the Despensers' ordinance of Kenilworth substituted home staples for Bruges. These were at York, Newcastle, Lincoln, Norwich, London, Winchester, Exeter, Bristol and Shrewsbury; Carmarthen and Cardiff; Dublin, Drogheda and Cork. The arrangement, pleasing to merchants in these towns, was unpopular with most others and growers, so Isabella and Mortimer suspended and then abolished them (Statute of Northampton, 1328), whereupon wool exports rose. This was beneficial to the economy but detrimental to the interests of the larger merchants and the conflicting interest of the Crown. By 1332 a 'voluntary' staple or black market had been organised at Bruges, whereupon the home staples were reintroduced and as promptly abolished by the York Parliament (Feb. 1334).

(3) Edward III's wars soon stilled these controversies. In 1337 he established a compulsory staple at Antwerp which in 1340 he moved to Bruges, the location of the Hanseatic Kontor, and started using the monopoly as security for Lombard and English loans. Unfortunately the Flemings prevented native and foreign access to the Staple, which lowered wool prices and in 1348 Edward moved it to Middleburg (Zeeland) while establishing a staple for cloth, lead and tin at newly-captured Calais. Piracy and the Black Death dislocated this system and ruined several English finance houses. After the agitation against monopolists, a compromise was reached in the great Ordinance (1353) and Statute (1354) of the Staple in return for a three year wool subsidy.

Staple Organisation (4) The statute confirmed the authority of a Mayor of the Staple who with two Constables and in the presence of two alien merchants was to administer the law merchant within any staple town. In pleas of land the common law was to be applied, but the mayor and constables were to be the justices for enforcing it. The mayor must have knowledge of the law; the first mayor and constables were to be appointed by the Crown, but thereafter by local election of the merchants. Local Royal justices and officials were excluded, but appeals lay to the King's Council. The Mayor and Constables could also control rents so as to make sojourn attractive to merchants and there were special arrangements for handling debts. Alien merchants alone were allowed to export the goods but had to surrender their foreign bullion to the local mint and receive an equal amount in new coin; they were forbidden to export their old coin.

(5) The Statute applied to wool, wool fells, leather and lead and forbade exports of the first three to Scotland. It returned the Staple to home and named the same places as in the Ordinance of Kenilworth except London, Shrewsbury and Cardiff, but it added Canterbury, Chichester, Westminster and Waterford and required goods from York to be shipped through Hull, from Lincoln through Boston, from Norwich through Yarmouth, from Westminster through London, for Canterbury through Sandwich and from Winchester through Southampton.

(6) The alien export monopolists were unpopular when prices were high and ceased to come when they fell towards the conclusion of peace in 1360. The Commons wanted to abolish the system, the Crown to retain a lucrative source of revenue and profit. Hence a further compromise in 1363. The Home Staple was transferred to Calais, now English but adjacent to Flanders and France; it was to be under the control of 26 important merchants incorporated as the Merchants of the Staple, but the home staples and their ports became sub-staples for Calais in wool.

(7) Until the loss of Calais in 1558 the Staple remained there in principle, but its actual operation and location were affected by evasion, Royal licensing, internal dissension and the vicissitudes of war. War compelled a temporary suspension in 1369-70 and evasions, whether illegal or by licence, led to complaints in the Good Parliament of 1376 which reconfirmed the Calais staples. In 1378 a statutory blanket licence had to be given to all goods passing the "Straits of Marrock" (Gibraltar). In 1382 the Flemings stipulated for a removal to Bruges as a condition of a projected alliance, but the French captured Bruges so that in 1384 the Staple had to go to Middleburg. Parliament required its removal home in 1385 but nothing was done and in 1388 it came back to Calais. In 1390, in the hope of popular support, Richard II moved it to the home towns in return for a three year wool subsidy, but by now he was negotiating for a French peace and in order to be able to finance the defences he returned it to Calais in 1392. These politically motivated interferences apparently had adverse effects, uncertain in scope, on the wool trade which boomed during periods of home staple and fell away under foreign, but like the Mediterranean trade, evasions from the north to Germany had to be licensed too and the English cloth trade was developing so that wool was beginning to be exported by Merchant Adventurers in manufactured form, leaving only the metals and hides unaffected.

(8) Henry V's belligerent plans led to a recurrence of the older pattern. The Calais staple was enforced and licences revoked in 1414; a mint was established there in 1421, but, with the slackening of the war effort, evasions brought new enforcement and revocations of licences in 1424, 1430 and 1432. In 1433 sales were required to be made in cash, but the northern leakages continued and in 1440, when the Danes set up a staple at Nordbarum, the Danish (i.e. northern) wool trade was made to use it. This arrangement continued until 1509. Henceforth the Staple served mainly to finance the Calais garrisons and fortifications (*see also* CALMS).

C. There was a Scottish staple for the Low Countries at Veere on the I. of Walcheren in the 16th and 17th cents. It was supervised by the Convention of Royal Burghs. The Scots exported mostly raw materials including grain, skins, hides, lead, iron ore, coal and, considering the location, a surprising amount of fish and salt, besides some textiles and leather. They imported timber, bar and wrought metals, weapons and luxuries. The merchants could lend large sums to the Crown.

D. Britain was the staple for a large variety of traffic with the colonies between 1660 and 1782. *See* AMERICAN REBELLION; NAVIGATION ACTS.

STAPLEDON, Walter (c. 1260-1326) Bp. of EXETER (1308), West countryman educated at Oxford, began in diocesan administration at Exeter and rose to be Canon, Precentor (1305) and finally Bishop. He was employed as a diplomat but became prominent only when he was made Edward II's Treasurer in Feb. 1320 and as such, one of the chief ministers. He overhauled the operations of the Royal finances, defined the functions of the departments and his reorganisation of the Exchequer made it the centre of financial administration. The reforms were prompted by the King's need for money at a time when lay and clerical assemblies were disinclined to grant taxes. His exploitation, through the new machinery of Royal rights and his stringent recovery of Crown debts were unpopular, but a central factor in Edward II's political supremacy between 1322 and 1326. Unavoidably he became identified with the govt's. rapacity and unsurprisingly after Isabella's invasion of 1326, he was hacked to death by a London mob, the first English bishop to be murdered since Becket. Isabella and Mortimer abandoned his potentially far-reaching reforms. His most lasting legacy was Stapledon Hall, Oxford, which he founded in 1314 and which was later called Exeter College.

STAPLETON or STAPILTON, Sir Philip (1603-47), Presbyterian soldier, was M.P. for Boroughbridge in the Long Parliament and an associate of Hampden, with whom he attended the King to Scotland in 1641. In 1642, as Parliamentary commissioner, he helped to prevent the wholesale recruitment of Yorkshire for the King. He then became a colonel and commander of Essex's bodyguard and fought at Edgehill (1642), Chalgrove Field (1643), where Hampden was killed, and at the first B. of Newbury (1643). He had been a member of the Committee of Safety from 1642 and became increasingly involved in politics, which he found distastefully extreme, especially when sent by Essex to give an account of the western armies in 1643. In 1644 he became a member of the Committee of Both Kingdoms. He was by now an increasingly isolated moderate, opposed to the Self Denying ordinance and Cromwell's rising power. Impeached, with other Presbyterian leaders, by the army he fled to Calais where he died on arrival.

STAPLETON or STAPYLTON, Sir Robert (?-1669), a Yorkshireman and a Douai Benedictine converted to Anglicanism, joined the Royalists after the B. of Edgehill and was at Charles I's court at Oxford. At the Restoration he became a gentleman usher to Charles II and wrote many plays and translations including *The History of the Low Countrey Warres* (1650 and 1667).

STARRA or STARRS (Sing: STARRUM: Heb: *Shetar***).** Before their expulsion in 1290, English Jews, on repayment of a loan, made out a quittance written in Hebrew and Latin, Latin only or French. The Jewish creditor signed it in Hebrew and sealed it. From the mid-13th cent. such starra had to be enrolled in the Exchequer of the Jews, whose influence enforced them.

STAR (or STARRED) CHAMBER (1), a room in Westminster Palace with, since at least 1348, a star spangled ceiling. The decor may have been suggested by the name of the Jewish *Starra* stored in parts of the palace.

(2) The King's Council met there and when it began to divide into the Council with the King and the Council at Westminster, the latter used it (c. 1380). The two bodies, though identifiable, remained different parts of the same organism, the Council with the King being political, the Council at Westminster concerned with routine matters. It was the nature of the age that much of this routine was judicial or quasi-judicial.

(3) The Council included the most powerful statesmen of the day and the monarch might be present. It exercised the extraordinary prerogative of the Crown in matters pertaining to the safety and peace of the realm. The nature and limits of this were not then known, but public disorder and foreign wars pointed to a need for something more expeditious in particular instances than Parliament, and more effective than the courts. Thus the *Lords of the Council Sitting in the Star Chamber* began to develop a method and to use the whole resources of the Council to back it. Since the extraordinary prerogative were their foundation and many, such as bishops, were canon lawyers, the members did not feel bound by Common Law procedure and developed one nearer to the inquisitorial systems of the continent with their use of torture. They were a feature of metropolitical life by Lancastrian times, sitting regularly in term time under the name of the Court of Star Chamber. Its usual members were regarded as *ordinary* rather than *full* members of the Council. Their *Book* begins to run continuously from 1421, but the breakdown of govt. after 1435 interrupted the work, which revived only under Edward IV and Richard III.

(4) Parliaments had been suspicious of the Council from early times. There were petitions to exclude cases of life, limb or free tenement in 1351 and these were partially confirmed by Acts of 1354 and 1368. By 1378 the point on free tenements had been conceded but the Crown reserved and continued to reserve its position on the rest. In practice, however, judgements of life and limb were left to Parliament or the courts. By 1420 parliamentary petitions were being treated as if the Council were a parliamentary committee. The later 15th cent. disorders changed all this. People now wanted a strong and speedy central body and the Council dealt unchallenged with foreigners and their trade, admiralty and prize and matters related to the stability of the state, from great conspiracy to petty libel. Henry VII found it necessary to rationalise the means for dealing with the flood of work. The Statute *pro Camera Stellata* (Lat: on the Starred Chamber) 1487 allowed much of the Council's jurisdiction to a specially powerful group viz: the Lord Chancellor, Treasurer and Privy Seal calling to them a bishop and a temporal lord of the Council and two chief justices. The Ld. Pres. was added in 1530. The Statute raised the courts' prestige by substituting full for ordinary councillors. It took nothing from the Council itself, but it inferentially confirmed the Council's inquisitorial powers, especially in matters of livery, maintenance, subornation of jurors, sheriffs' false returns, riots and unlawful assemblies. In Ordinances of 1526, however, the old distinction between the political and the routine bodies had reappeared and soon there was a tendency to man the court again with ordinary councillors.

(5) In 1553 the mass of private business in the Council was already excessive because of its cheapness, expedition and relative purity. In 1582 the Council decided that no private business capable of decision in another court should come before the Council unless it raised an issue of public order or govt., but by 1589 suitors were still pressing at the doors and the order had to be repeated. There was, in effect, a working balance between the court, the legislature and the common law.

(6) The watershed of the court's high reputation was the accession of a Scottish King, with an inclination to disregard the law or bend it to his own purposes, a penchant for foreign favourites and a conceited capacity for irritating councillors abler than himself. The court's right to imprison had already been challenged in 1591 by the judges. There was now a tendency to blur the distinction between the two sides of the Council. Parliament, the common lawyers, the low churchmen and the Puritans were arrayed against Crown, prerogative and the high churchmen. The Star Chamber could be represented as a political court endowed with odious powers to interrogate parties and to force men to incriminate themselves, if necessary by torture. Efficient in ordinary cases (by far the greatest part of its daily work) the political cases attracted the obloquy in the morning of the era of printing. Its savage proceedings against such men as Prynne, Burton and Bastwick, though not out of line with the savagery of the times, excited a newly widespread indignation. As the most powerful instrument of prerogative govt. it became the target of the parliamentary leaders and they secured its abolition and the Council's jurisdiction in England and Wales in 1641.

(7) This was the end of the court, but not of the principle. Commonwealth Ordinances of 1650, 1653 and 1654 created a similar court with much greater powers. The real end came when these lapsed at the Restoration. *See* PRIVY COUNCIL; PRIVY SEAL; COUNCIL OF WALES AND THE MARCHES; COUNCIL OF THE NORTH REQUESTS, COURT OF.

STARS AND STRIPES. The flag of the U.S.A. was introduced in 1777. Based upon the arms of the Washington family, it had 13 stars and stripes for the original 13 states, but the number of stars was increased for each state which joined the Union.

[E]STATES-GENERAL. French legislative assembly of uncertain powers occasionally convoked by the Crown. That of 1789 transmuted itself into the National Assembly.

STATES-GENERAL. Each province of the Low Countries had a legislative court called the States. A meeting of representatives of all the states was called a States-General. It had no legislative sovereignty, but resembled a diplomatic congress or a negotiating committee. When the northern provinces (Holland, Zeeland, Utrecht, Gelderland, Overyssel, Drenthe, Gröningen and Friesland) rejected Spanish sovereignty, they kept a States-General in regular session and the word became synonymous with the Netherlands. It was dominated by the representatives of Holland, much the richest, most populous and best placed of the provinces and the detailed conduct of foreign policy was generally left to the Grand Pensionary of that province. In war or crisis the provinces (or most of them) achieved a certain functional unity by electing the same person to important local state offices, e.g. the Princes of Orange were usually stadholders in five. The whole cumbersome arrangement disappeared in 1795. The term is now used for the Dutch Parliament.

STATE TRIALS. 1st Ed. apparently by Thomas Salmon was published in 4 vols. in 1719. The 2nd and 3rd (6 vols.) by Sollom Emlyn in 1730 and 1742, contain a survey of the contemporary state of English law. The 7th and 8th volume had appeared in 1735, the 9th and 10th in 1766. Hargrave's 4th Ed. of 1781 had his additional (11th) vol. Thomas Bayley Howell produced 21 vols. of the 5th Ed. by 1815 and his son, Thomas Jones Howell, 12 more by 1820. This final Ed. also contained proceedings notable for their curiosity or for those involved and represents a quarry of material on contemporary speech and habits as well as law. A NEW SERIES was begun in 1885 as from 1858.

STATIONERS HALL (London). Stationers Co. of London was incorporated in 1557. All printers had to serve an apprenticeship through it and all printed works had to be registered (*entered*) at the hall until the Copyright Act, 1911. Originally intended to assist the licensing, i.e. censorship of books, compulsory entry became the standard method of proving copyright and remained in Canada as late as 1956.

STATIONERY OFFICE, H.M. was set up in a building opposite Westminster Abbey in 1786 as one of Pitt's economies to centralise govt. printing and stationery supplies. Since 1888 the Controller has been the Queen's Printer of Acts of Parliament and responsible for dealings in Crown copyrights. Since the strengthening of Crown copyright and the creation of a parliamentary copyright in 1988 it has become a lucrative monopoly of statutory knowledge.

STATISTICAL ACCOUNT (1791-8) and NEW STATISTICAL ACCOUNT (1834-45) were valuable Scottish parish surveys promoted by the Kirk and carried out through the ministers. They embraced population and migration, economics and communications and education, manners, dress and morality. The results were published in many volumes.

STATUTE (1) All the decisions of a given parliament were engrossed on a roll which represented the record of a single 'policy' and was divided into chapters. The unity of this concept made it impossible without special mention for one chapter to amend or repeal another chapter in the same roll.

(2) Subsequently chapters came to be called 'Acts' and then, more loosely still, 'statutes'. This did not affect the technical unity of the roll until the Interpretation Act 1978 abolished it.

(3) Scottish rolls were named after the Calendar years: English and United Kingdom rolls after the regnal year until 1963 when the Calendar year was adopted. If two parliaments are held in the same year, the later roll is called the Second Statute. *See* Appendix A.

STATUTE LAW COMMISSIONS (1) 1833-45. This Royal Commission was to digest into two bills respectively the criminal statutes and the common law on crime, to consider whether the two could be combined and what other branches of the law might be profitably consolidated. It made a general report in 1835 and seven reports on the criminal law. (2) **1845-9.** This commission completed its predecessor's eighth report, made five more of its own, and published a draft bill which consolidated all the law on crimes and punishment. No progress was made and this led to much public criticism. (3) **1853-4** a temporary Statute Law Board made three reports and was superseded by another commission. (4) **1854-59** which made four more reports. It included many distinguished judges and as a result a Register of Public General Acts 1800-58 was drawn up, the first major Statute Law Revision Act (1861) and seven criminal law consolidation Acts (based upon the reports since 1833) were passed. Statute Law Revision Acts have continued to be passed intermittently ever since.

STATUTE MERCHANT (1285) and STATUTE STAPLE (1354) (*for the former see* ACTON BURNELL). The latter extended the Acton Burnell principle to stapler courts. Long obsolete, the Acts were repealed in 1863.

STATUTES AT LARGE is the title of several printed collections of Acts of Parliament all beginning at 1215. *Keble's* runs to 1667, later continued to 1733; *Hawkins* to 1734 continued to 1757; *Cays* to 1757 continued to 1773; *Ruffhead's* to 1764 continued to 1800; *Tomlin's and Raithby* to 1800 continued to 1869 and *Pickering's* 1215 to 1761 continued to 1806 and then to 1869. None are complete, but the best is probably *Ruffhead* which contains summaries where Acts are not printed. *See* STATUTES OF THE REALM.

STATUTES IN FORCE, begun in 1972, is a growing loose-leaf edition of the unrepealed statutes, printed as amended and periodically replaced when further amended. The up-dating process generally lags far behind the convenience of users.

STATUTES OF THE REALM **(1215-1713)** published by the Record Commissioners is the most accurate and the fullest edition of the statutes between those dates. *See* STATUTES AT LARGE.

STATUTES REVISED, by the Statute Law Committee consists only of public Acts; it omits repealed matter and the text is printed, if necessary, as amended. There are three editions **(1) 1236-1878; (2) 1236-1886** continued to **1920** and **(3) 1236-1948.**

STATUTE ROLLS. *See* PARLIAMENT ROLLS.

STATUTES OF UNCERTAIN DATE represent a collection of 44 documents included at the end of the *Vetera Statuta* (Old Statutes). Only three, the Statute of the Exchequer (probably 1275), of the Jewry (probably 1275) and of Exeter (1292) were true statutes. Two are extracts from treaties and eight are useful summaries of particular legal topics. The rest are notes on administrative or court procedure.

STATUTORY INDIAN CIVIL SERVICE (1879-85) represented an unsuccessful attempt to bring Indians of good family into administration. They showed little disposition to apply for posts because the pay was inferior to that of the Covenanted service and because the scheme was unpopular with the much larger body of educated Indians.

STEAD, William Thomas (1849-1912), editor of the *Northern Echo* from 1871 to 1880 and asst. editor of the *Pall Mall Gazette* from 1880 to 1883 and its editor until 1890 was the earliest of the new mass agitational journalists. He bore much responsibility for the despatch of Gen. Gordon to Khartoum and, by purchasing child prostitutes and publishing the fact, helped Josephine Butler in securing the prohibition of brothels.

STEAM. *See principally* INDUSTRIAL REVOLUTION; NEWCOMEN; PARSONS; SHIPS, POWER DRIVEN; STEPHENSON; TREVITHICK; WAFT.

STEEL, Sir David (1938-) M.P. from 1963. As leader of the Liberals kept the Labour minority govt. in power (1977-

8); went into alliance with the Social Democrats in 1981 and in 1988 merged the two parties as the Liberal Democrats.

STEELBOW. A form of Scottish tenancy in which the landlord provided stock and seed and was paid by a share of the crop.

STEELBOYS. Irish rural terrorists in 1771.

STEELE, Sir Richard (1672-1729) began in the Horse Guards in 1694 and was sec. to Ld. Cutts from 1696 to 1697. He published *The Christian Hero* in 1701 and his *Lying Lover* was performed at Drury Lane in 1701. In 1706 he became a member of P. George of Denmark's household. Under the name of **Isaac Bickerstaffe** he and Addison wrote most of the *Tatler* between 1709 and 1711, the *Spectator* from 1711 to 1712 and the *Guardian* until 1713, when he became Whig M.P. for Stockbridge. They produced the Whig paper *The Englishman* from Oct. 1713 to Feb. 1714 when he also issued *The Crisis* on his own. This was a telling pamphlet in favour of the Hanoverian succession. Expelled from the Commons for sedition, he naturally came back into favour at the accession of George I and in 1716 became a commissioner for forfeited Scottish estates. In 1718 he denounced Sunderland's Peerage Bill and finally quarrelled with Addison. His later activities were mostly literary, his last play being produced in 1722.

STEELYARD (Ger: *Stalhof* = pattern or sample yard). *See* HANSE-1,2,3,8.

STEGAN or STIGAND, Abp. *See* EDWARD THE CONFESSOR.

STELLA was the nickname of two celebrated ladies **(1) Penelope Devereux**, daughter of the first E. of Essex, originally affianced to Sir Philip Sydney, who dedicated his sonnets to her. Then married to and divorced by Robert, Ld. Rich, she finally married Charles Blount, Ld. Mountjoy, later E. of Devonshire. **(2) Esther Johnson**, to whom Jonathan Swift addressed his *Journal to Stella*.

STELLALAND and GOSHEN were two small republics set up by Boers from the Transvaal in Bechuana territory in 1882. Cecil Rhodes believed that with the Transvaal they blocked communications between the Cape and the area later called Rhodesia which he wished to exploit. He persuaded the Cape govt. to have them dissolved and this was effected by establishing a protectorate over Bechuanaland with troops under Sir Charles Warren in 1885.

STEPHEN (c. 1096-1154) King (1135) (*see genealogy. For the arrival of Henry I's daughter, the Empress MATILDA, at court see* HENRY I-12). **(1)** At Henry's death on campaign in Normandy the long-standing Norman-Angevin feud influenced events. The Norman baronage assembled at Neubourg to elect Theobald of Blois, but his younger brother, Stephen, had the advantage of an English upbringing, the English honours of Lancaster and Eye and the possession of his wife's fief of Boulogne. He slipped across the Channel, had himself elected at London, moved to Winchester, of which his brother HENRY of BLOIS was bishop, and seized the Treasury. The brother got him the support of the church, in the person of Abp. William, and of the administration controlled by Roger, Bp. of Salisbury (?-1139) and his nephews Nigel (?-1169) Bp. of Ely and Alexander (?-1148) Bp. of Lincoln. By Christmas he was crowned in London. Theobald withdrew from the Norman election. Early in 1136 the Pope (Innocent II) confirmed Stephen's position and impliedly absolved the barons from their oath to Matilda.

(2) Stephen had won his Crown by quick action and by over hasty concessions. He gave undertakings to the Church, and Scottish threats were rewarded with most of Cumbria. He pacified Matilda's most powerful champion and half-brother, Robert E. of Gloucester, and other magnates with large grants of land. This policy was recognised as weakness.

(3) Many Normans had acknowledged Stephen,

though important fortresses had been handed over to Matilda at Henry's death. Geoffrey of Anjou's troops plundered the Duchy and increased the Norman hatred of the Angevins. In 1137 Stephen went to Normandy with Flemish mercenaries, who behaved as badly as the Angevins. The Normans refused to co-operate; their goodwill was lost and, after Theobald had arranged a truce, Stephen in Dec. left the Duchy to its own devices. After the truce expired it fell increasingly under Angevin domination.

(4) *The First Civil War 1138-41* Matilda had probably been organising a conspiracy for some time. There had been Scots raids, Welsh rebellions and sporadic English disturbances all the early part of 1138. In the summer she appealed to the Pope, while her half-brother, Gloucester, renounced his allegiance. He got much armed support in the south and west, but in the opening campaign Stephen took Shrewsbury and Hereford together with Dover and Wareham. He thought, rightly or wrongly, that the powerful Roger of Salisbury, with his son, Roger le Poer the chancellor and his nephews of Ely and Lincoln intended to desert him. At midsummer 1139 he had them arrested and seized their vast wealth and castles. The Church and even his brother Henry, now Papal Legate, was bitterly offended and the govt. which the arrested prelates had managed was temporarily disorganised. In Aug. a church council at Winchester considered reprisals but adjourned. A month later Matilda arrived at her stepmother's castle of Arundel, while Gloucester went to Bristol. The King marched about the south west making ineffectual assaults on castles. When he caught up with Matilda he let her go – to Bristol.

(5) At Bristol the Empress and Gloucester were gathering support. This included the Constable Miles of Gloucester (?-1143) and Brian Fitz Count (fl. 1130-50), son of the Count of Brittany, who occupied Wallingford. Moreover, Stephen's alienation of Cumbria had offended Rannulf E. Palatine of Chester, who had hereditary claims on Carlisle and was married to Gloucester's daughter. Rannulf and his brother William of Roumare had immense Lincolnshire estates. At the end of 1140 they seized Lincoln itself. Stephen arrived, confirmed the seizure and then changed his mind. Gloucester arrived with reinforcements for Rannulf and in Feb. 1141, after a pitched battle, Stephen was taken. He was hustled off in chains to Bristol.

(6) *The Second Civil War 1141* Matilda went to Winchester and after agreeing to leave church affairs to the Legate, was elected Lady of the English in April, preparatory to coronation. The Londoners would not vote for her. When she reached London in June her financial demands and arrogance infuriated the unfriendly citizens. Moreover Stephen's Queen, **Matilda of BOULOGNE (?1103-52)** had reached Southwark with an army. The citizens rose and expelled the Empress who fled towards Oxford. The Queen raised loans to subvert the Empress' supporters and at Guildford won over the Legate. The Empress and Gloucester counter-attacked by moving on his town of Winchester. She besieged the Legate in Wolvesey Palace and the town was burned. Then the Queen arrived and established a counter-siege. Menaced in Sept. by starvation, the Empress broke out. The retreat developed into a rout in which Gloucester was captured at Stockbridge. He was exchanged for the King in Nov. Stephen's restoration was recognised by a church council in Dec.

(7) *The Third Civil War 1142-45.* A serious illness prevented Stephen from moving until June 1142. Gloucester went to Normandy to ask Geoffrey of Anjou for reinforcements and Geoffrey constrained him to help with his conquest of the Duchy. Meantime Stephen took Wareham, occupied the river crossings west of Oxford and besieged the deserted Empress in Oxford Castle. She escaped by night over the ice to Wallingford in Dec.

before Gloucester could rescue her. He then established himself in the four western counties as an independent potentate and repulsed all attacks. In 1143, however, Henry of Blois' legatine commission expired by the death of Innocent II and thereafter the Papacy became pro-Angevin; when Geoffrey conquered Normandy this helped him in 1144 to obtain recognition as Duke.

(8) *Anarchy.* During the nine years of civil war, govt. broke down in many areas. Local lords or robber chiefs, changing allegiance as often as they pleased, used their nominal participation as a pretext to tyrannise and plunder, while rival towns such as Gloucester and Worcester, or the Cinque Ports and Yarmouth, fought private wars. The horrible outrages perpetrated by Geoffrey de Mandeville (?-1144) in E. Anglia and Essex between 1140 and 1144 have often been quoted from the Peterborough Chronicle and these were repeated in the north Midlands by Rannulf of Chester in 1146. There was widespread damage, especially in the west, but attempts to deduce its extent and incidence from the Danegeld returns of 1156 (i.e. eight years after the end) are probably unreliable. There was a spectacular increase in monastic, particularly Cistercian and Premonstratensian foundations, in the setting up of hospitals and alms-houses, in the spread of the Templars and Hospitallers and in secular church endowments.

(9) *The End of the Wars 1145-8.* In 1145 Stephen's important victory at Faringdon cut off the Angevin supporters on the Thames from Bristol. Their defence now became largely passive, while Geoffrey of Anjou and his son, Henry Plantagenet, consolidated their hold on Normandy. When Henry came to England early in 1147, the Empress' party was disintegrating. A new crusade was being preached by St. Bernard and some, including Philip (?-?), Gloucester's nasty son, decided to join it. Gloucester died in Oct. Henry was defeated in skirmishes and shipped back to Normandy at Stephen's expense. In Feb. 1148 the Empress followed him.

(10) *The End of the Reign 1148-54.* Though without a rival, there were many areas and some departments of life in which the King could not enforce his will. There was sporadic fighting. The greatest earls, such as Chester and Leicester, ruled their territories, usurped Royal revenues and made treaties with each other. The Church's increasing wealth made it more and more dangerous and Stephen was engaged in a dispute about the succession to the See of York, in which his nephew and nominee William fitz Herbert was kept out until the death of his opponents in 1153.

Developments abroad were more important. Geoffrey of Anjou, taking account of local prejudices, wisely ruled Normandy as Regent for Henry Plantagenet who had a title to it through his mother. Henry was fighting in England in 1149, but returned to Normandy in 1150 and was given the Duchy outright. He was then attacked by the King of France who was endeavouring to enforce the cession of Gisors, promised by Geoffrey in 1144 as the price of recognition as Duke. In 1151 Henry bought peace by ceding it and the Norman Vexin, but in Sept. his father died and he became Count of Anjou and Tours.

(11) There followed the greatest dynastic revolution of the Middle Ages. Louis VII and the high spirited Eleanor of Aquitaine had long been uncomfortable bedfellows. In Mar. 1152 their marriage was annulled for consanguinity. In May she married Henry; with the joint possessions stretching from Spain to the Channel Henry was a great potentate. Early in 1153 he invaded England and after overrunning half the country, confronted Stephen at Wallingford. Mediators prevented a battle, but in Aug. Stephen's eldest son **Eustace (?-1153)** died. The Church then intervened to negotiate a settlement. By the miscalled T. of Wallingford (negotiated at Winchester and ratified at Westminster) in Nov. 1153 Stephen's second son, **William (?-?)** was secured in Stephen's private

English and Norman estates, Henry was recognised as heir to the Kingdom and unlicensed castles were to be destroyed. Eleven months later Stephen died.

STEPHEN (1) James (1758-1832) a prize lawyer from St. Kitts and William Wilberforce's brother-in-law, supplied the latter with expert information on the slave trade and as an M.P. from 1808 to 1815 supported abolition of slavery, resigning his seat when the govt. refused to enact registration of slaves. His *Slavery in the British West India Colonies Delineated* appeared in 1824 and 1830. Of his sons **(2) Sir James (1789-1859)** was a powerful U. Sec. of State for colonies. He prepared the bill which abolished colonial slavery in 1833 and was also a leading figure in the introduction of responsible govt. in Canada. He was Prof. of Modern History at Cambridge from 1849 and at the East India College between 1855 and 1857. **(3) Sir George (1794-1879)** was also in the anti-slavery movement, but emigrated to Australia in 1855. A nephew of (1), **(4) Sir Alfred (1802-94)** set up the legal system of Tasmania between 1825 and 1837, was C.J. of N.S.W. from 1844 to 1873 and Lieut.-Gov. from 1875 to 1891. A son of (2), **(5) Sir James FITZJAMES (1829-94) Bt. (1891)**, a far-sighted reformer and writer in intellectual periodicals, was Sec. of the Education Commission from 1858 to 1861. He was legal member of the Council of India from 1869 to 1872 and responsible for the Indian Evidence Act, 1872, a member of several legal commissions between 1876 and 1878 and a judge from 1879 to 1891. Amongst other works he published a *History of the Criminal Law* in 1883.

STEPHENS, James (1825-1901), chief founder of the Fenians in 1856, raised much money for them in 1863. He promised his American friends that he would lead a rising in 1865, but had to postpone it because their dissensions delayed the arms. He was arrested and escaped, but the U.S. Fenians denounced him as a traitor and he went to ground.

STEPHENS, Joseph Rayner (1805-79), Methodist minister from 1829 but suspended in 1834 for advocating disestablishment, was inspired by moral indignation at the new Poor Law to champion the Chartists whose political objectives he disliked. His fiery speeches landed him in prison from 1839 to 1840 and subsequently he took up the cause of the miners' trades unionism in Lancashire where he knew everyone, spoke the dialect and had a deep understanding of the local customs. He was the most effective of the northern Tory or practical radicals.

STEPHEN HARDING, St. (?-1134) was born at Sherborne (Dorset) and travelled widely as a young man in Europe. Returning from a pilgrimage to Rome, he entered the Abbey of Molesme where he rose to be sub-prior. In 1098 he was one of the monks who left Molesme to found Citeaux for a more ascetic life based on the pure Rule of St. Benedict. When Alberic became Abbot of Citeaux in 1099, Harding became Prior and, on Alberic's death (1109), Abbot. Although Cistercian popularity was secured by St. Bernard who had entered Citeaux only in 1112, Harding established the early ideals and rules of the Order in his *Exordium Cisterciensis Coenobii* (Lat: Description of the Cistercian Community, c. 1115) and the *Carta Caritatis* (Charter of Love) of 1119. With the *Consuetudines* (Customs) of Abbot Alberic, these documents prescribed the pattern of life which made the Cistercians popular and successful in 12th cent. Europe.

STEPHENSON (1) George (1781-1848), as a Northumbrian colliery engineer invented a miner's safety lamp superior to that of Humphrey Davy, but received no credit for it. Having built a steam locomotive for his colliery, he was chosen as the Superintendent Engineer of the Stockton & Darlington (S.&D.) Railway. As a railway surveyor he was less of a success and he did not always behave scrupulously towards other railway engineers, whom he regarded as commercial rivals. He advocated a standard gauge for all railways but, unlike Brunel, opted for the 4ft 8½in gauge. He was almost illiterate but he ensured that his son **(2) Robert (1803-59)** had a full education and father and son together designed early locomotives. Their *Locomotion* (1825) performed well on the S.&D. Railway, while their *Rocket* (1829) won the Rainhill Locomotive Competition sponsored by the Liverpool & Manchester Railway. Robert was an excellent civil engineer, surveying many main lines, including the pioneer London & Birmingham Railway and constructing bridges, tunnels and viaducts, of which many are still in use. From 1847 he was Conservative M.P. for Whitby.

STERLING. *See* COINAGE.

STERLING AREA or BLOC (1) emerged as a named but informal entity in 1931 after the collapse of the gold standard. It comprised the Commonwealth other than Canada, Portugal with its large empire, to which were added the Scandinavian countries in 1933 and Persia and Latvia in 1936. Japan and Argentina, though not in the area, conformed to its practices which were (a) to maintain their currencies in a fixed ratio with Sterling; (b) to keep their exchange reserves mostly in Sterling and in London. In fact most countries previously on the gold standard had long maintained stable sterling ratios.

(2) At the outbreak of World War II, most non-British members left, and the rest pooled their dollars in London and drew only essential amounts from the pool. Some countries (both member and non-member) especially India increased their Sterling balances during the war and these were frozen and annual releases were rationed by agreement.

(3) The area continued after the war under the name of Scheduled Territories with formal rather than informal controls imposed in the interests of Labour Party policy, but some, mainly gold producing, countries ceased to pay their dollars to the pool. The system effectively included Austria.

(4) It was dismantled after Britain, having joined the E.E.C., had to go over to floating rates. In 1996 it comprised only the U.K., the Channel Is., Gibraltar and the I. of Man.

STERNE (1) Richard (?1596-1683), Master of Jesus Coll., Cambridge (1634-44) until ejected in the Civil War, was Abp. Laud's faithful and learned chaplain and then taught at school, but became Bp. of Carlisle at the Restoration and Abp. of York from 1664. A reviser of the Prayer Book of 1662, he made endowments at Cambridge and was wrongly credited with Richard Allestree's *Whole Duty of Man*. His great-grandson **(2) The Rev. Laurence (1712-68),** profligate and humorist, owed his early advancement to relatives whom he alienated by an affair with a maid in 1758. Between 1759 and 1767 he published his celebrated satirical novel *Tristram Shandy* in parts. His *Sentimental Journey* appeared in 1768. Denounced by Dr. Johnson, Horace Walpole, Smollett and others for indecency and facility, he achieved a *succès de scandal* in Britain and in France and was defended by Bp. Warburton, Garrick and Rockingham. Voltaire even subscribed to his *Sermons*.

STETTIN or SZECZIN (Poland), a Hanseatic city at the mouth of the R. Oder, commanded the Silesian grain and coal traffic and was the capital of Pomerania until it passed to Brandenburg in 1637. Seized by Sweden in 1648, it remained Swedish until 1720 when it was returned to Brandenburg Prussia. It was taken by Poland at the end of World War II.

STEVENAGE. *See* NEW TOWNS.

STEVENSON, Robert (1772-1850) designed some 20 lighthouses (including the Bell Rock 1812) and invented much of their modern equipment.

STEWARD (O.E. perhaps = Housekeeper) DAPIFER (Lat = Cupbearer) SENESCHAL (O. Teut = Old Servant) DISH THANE. (1) Every large household needs a caterer.

In Royal establishments this person was respected but not a state officer. He ordinarily waited on the King at table and might be in his confidence. Kings often had several. The above titles were used interchangeably but their connotations varied with time and place.

(2) On state occasions such as a coronation, Kings, to lend dignity to themselves, had the table service performed by noblemen who took the title *pro tem*. Moreover from 1047 to 1191 the French royal *dapifer* was a powerful noble and recognised as the chief royal officer. This inspired the Ds. of Normandy (soon Kings of England) some of whose Norman *dapiferi* (e.g. Osbern son of Herfast) rose to eminence. The working stewards continued as before: the noble stewardship, valued for its prestige, meanwhile became hereditary in the Beaumont family and so descended to the Montfort Es. of Leicester but was merged in the Crown at the death of E. Simon at the B. of Evesham (1265). The office was then occasionally granted for life, the last such holder being Thomas of Clarence who was killed at the B. of Baugé (1421). Thereafter it was conferred only to perform certain coronation ceremonies and to preside at trials of peers.

(3) Peers were supposed to be tried for felony or treason by their peers, i.e. the House of Lords, but if (but only if) Parliament was not sitting, some 19 to 23 peers were summoned to constitute a special court over which, by special appointment, the Steward (by now dignified as Lord High Steward) in either case presided. The special court became known as his court. The precedent for it, allegedly a trial of the E. of Huntingdon in 1400, is a forgery probably dating from c. 1499 but a similar court tried the E. of Cambridge and Ld. Scrope in 1415. The court was easy to pack and the rule that 12 must be agreed was squared with a rule of majority verdicts by summoning 23 members. Henry VII did this for the trial of the E. of Warwick in 1499 but as he pleaded guilty there was no need for a verdict. In 1521 Buckingham pleaded not guilty and was found guilty. Actually the court almost always found for the Crown. On the other hand as parliamentary sessions lengthened, the opportunities for summoning it diminished and Parliament became progressively less frightened of the Crown. In 1690 the House of Lords questioned the legality of these trials and in 1695 an Act prevented further packing by requiring all peers to be summoned.

(4) Meanwhile the palace developed a Lord Steward who was a peer appointed during pleasure. This officer still exists. His functions have always been ceremonial save that he presided over the Board of Green Cloth, a kind of managerial committee dealing with non-routine matters such as (in 1937) the issue of permissions to view the Coronation procession from inside the forecourt of Buckingham Palace.

STEWART, Alexander (c. 1454-85) D. of ALBANY, second *s.* of James II of Scots. *See* JAMES III OF SCOTS.

STEWART, Dugald (1753-1828), learned philosopher and political economist at Edinburgh University with a continental training, he became famous during the Napoleonic Wars for his expository gifts. Called "the educator of a generation", he attracted large audiences and his histrionic hold on them was said to exceed that of Mrs Siddons (qv). His many influential pupils included Henry Brougham, Lord Cochrane, Henry Erskine, Francis Horner, Lord Palmerston, Lord John Russell and Sir Walter Scott.

STEWART, Francis E. of BOTHWELL. *See* JAMES VI OF SCOTS.

STEWART, James (?1499-1544) E. of MORAY (1501), bastard of James IV, a R. Catholic and anti-English partisan, first emerged into public affairs through a quarrel with the Homes whom he suspected of connivance with the English. By 1523 he was a guardian of James V and nominal commander of the French troops. In 1531 he was employed in putting down a revolt in the Isles and Ross and from 1532 to 1536 he superseded the Homes as Warden of the E. and Middle Marches. He was a late champion of the French connection, supporting Cardinal Beaton's internal policies and helping to negotiate James V's marriage (1538) with Mary of Guise who brought a large sum as a dowry. After James' death he stood by Beaton and fought Hertford's invasion (1544), but died suddenly.

STEWART, (1) James (?1531-70) E. of MAR and MORAY (1562) usually known as **THE LORD JAMES**, a bastard of James V and half-brother of Mary Queen of Scots, was legitimated in 1551 and therefore came into the Scottish line of succession. He had originally favoured the French connection and Cardinal Beaton's policy, but had acquired large monastic properties and in 1555 was apparently converted to Calvinism by John Knox. In 1557 as a Prince he witnessed his half-sister's French marriage in Paris, but, as a Protestant he signed the invitation to John Knox to return to Scotland. This document, the founding manifesto of the Lords of the Congregation, placed him in a special position. He might at any time become a Protestant candidate for the Crown. Hence he opposed Mary's supporters Darnley and Rizzio and the French alliance, and maintained a friendly relationship with the English govt., but was not prepared to destroy the position of a Crown which he might inherit.

At Mary's abdication he became Regent for James VI with Elizabeth I's support and helped her to round up the English northern rebels (1569). The weakness in his position was that he was a party leader in a peculiarly bitter period of party and religious controversy, besides acting head of the Kingdom. A leading figure in the opposing party, James Hamilton of Bothwellhaugh, assassinated him (*see* MARY QUEEN OF SCOTS, JAMES VI).

A kinsman **(2) James (?-1592) 2nd E. (1580)** by the marriage with his daughter, followed the English and Protestant policy and fell equally a victim to party fury. By 1590 James VI was in a position to take action against the Presbyterian domination over the Crown and Moray was killed by the R. Catholic E. of Huntly. A descendant **(3) Alexander (?-1700) 5th E.**, was Lord Justice General in 1674. As Sec. of State from 1680 to 1688 and Commissioner to the Scottish Parliament in 1686 he was virtually Viceroy of Scotland and concerned primarily to maintain the Royal authority. Since Presbyterianism had become temporarily identified with local separatism, he was entangled for political reasons in religious controversies and is remembered as a persecutor of Covenanters. He was deprived of office at the Revolution of 1688.

STEWART, Sir John (?-1659) 1st Ld. STEWART (1628), 1st E. of TRAQUAIR (1633), a descendant of the Black Knight of Lorne, sat for Tweeddale in the Scots Parliament of 1621 and was sworn of the Scots P.C. In 1630 he became Treasurer-Depute and in 1636 Lord Treasurer. As a politician he attempted compromise between an increasingly obstinate King and increasingly obdurate Covenanters. He helped to introduce the Laudian liturgy, but after the riot in St. Giles advised Charles that it could not be imposed. Ordered, nevertheless, to enforce it, he was met with widespread opposition and so set about arming Edinburgh Castle (Mar. 1639) but the Covenanters took the Castle, seizing him and the arms at Dalkeith. He then joined Charles at York, but was at first kept in custody. In Aug. 1639, however, he was appointed Commissioner to the Scots Assembly. An Act abolishing episcopacy was introduced and forced him to undertake to have the Act confirmed by Parliament. When Parliament met (Nov.) he had to adjourn it to July 1640. Neither Covenanters nor King now trusted him. The Scots Parliament passed an act against him in 1641, tried him in his absence and sentenced him to death. The King compromised by issuing a pardon but depriving him of office. In 1644 the Scots seized his property but he bought it back for 40,000 merks. In 1645 his son, Ld. Linton, joined Montrose's rising and Traquair undertook to supply Montrose with information about Gen. Leslie's movements. As Linton and his force deserted, it seems possible that Traquair was acting as a double agent. Whatever the truth, Traquair came back into favour, for in 1648 Charles II had him readmitted to the Scots Parliament; he raised cavalry for the Royalists, was taken prisoner at Preston (1648), freed by Cromwell in 1654 and returned to Scotland.

STEWART or STUART, ROYAL HOUSE (EARLY), originally a Breton family, held office as Butlers (*dapifer*) of Dol and one member **(1) Flaald (fl. 1100)** settled in Monmouthshire in about 1101. One of his sons **(2) Alan (?-?)** was the ancestor of the **FITZALANS**, later Es. of Arundel. Another son **(3) Walter (?-1177)** was given lands in Shropshire by Henry I and got to know K. David I of Scots who was in England during King Stephen's reign, for David and the Shropshire feudality sided with the Empress Maud in the civil wars. David introduced feudal offices into Scotland and between 1134 and 1140 made Walter his High Steward; he also gave him for life the Barony of Renfrew. Walter imported Cluniac monks from Wenlock to Paisley where he founded an important abbey. He was succeeded in the Stewartry and at Renfrew (both of which had been made hereditary between 1153 and 1164) by his son **(4) Alan (?-1204)** who was followed by his son **(5) Walter (?-1246)**. His son **(6) Alexander (?-1283)** was an active soldier and commanded in the great victory over the Norsemen at Largs in 1263. His successor in office was his son **(7) James (?-1309)**. A guardian of Scotland in 1286 and a partisan of Scots independence, he was leader of the council which effected the *coup* of 1295 and negotiated the French alliance in defiance of John Balliol and Edward I. He escaped the disaster at Dunbar (Apr. 1296) and with Bruce and Sir James Douglas remained in arms in the west until the truce at Irvine (July 1297). By this time William Wallace's movement was in full swing. Wallace rose in Balliol's name to free his King from English constraints. James the Steward, though ready to take advantage of Wallace's popularity, favoured Bruce's claim especially as the experiment of ruling in Balliol's name but against English policy had already proved unworkable. Wallace's victory at Stirling Bridge (Sept. 1297) put the govt. into Wallace's hands, but all knew that without national unity independence would not survive the English counter-attack once Edward had freed himself from his French and internal embarrassments. There were unsuccessful negotiations, in which James was prominent and then in July 1298 Wallace was disastrously beaten at Falkirk. The result was a compromise joint regency vested in Bruce and the Red Comyn, who was a nephew of John Balliol. The arrangement could not last, Bruce resigning in 1300. In 1302 James was in France but shortly, like Bruce, made his peace with Edward. English control hardly extended beyond the Lowlands and when Bruce murdered the Red Comyn (Feb. 1306), raised a Lowland revolt and was crowned at Scone (Mar.), James promptly recognised him and remained his faithful supporter.

This had the important result that his son **(8) Walter (1293-1326)** married Bruce's daughter **(9) Margery (?-1315)**. By Acts of 1315, 1318 and 1324 the Scots Parliament settled the Crown upon Robert the Bruce and in default of sons, upon his brother Edward (who died in 1318) and failing male heirs of either, upon the heirs of Margery and Walter. He had jointly commanded a wing at Bannockburn (1314) and from 1316 acted as Robert's lieutenant and manager of the Lowland defences during Royal absences. Robert died in 1329 but his son David II's accession inaugurated a recurrent feature of Scots history, namely, makeshift govt. caused by the minority, absence, captivity or incapacity of the monarchs. The lawful regents were dead by 1332; the appointed Regent, Mar, was killed at Dupplin fighting Edward Balliol; his successor Douglas at Halidon Hill (July 1333); hence the anti-English party sent David II to France for safety in May 1334. At this time Walter's son **(10) Robert II (1316-90) King (1371)** was associated with Sir Andrew Moray in a fugitive regency. This began to make headway in 1335 when Moray, Dunbar and Douglas beat Balliol's supporter Atholl in the Forest of Culblean. By 1338 England was again at war with France and the tide had turned. Most of the English castles had fallen by 1341 when Edinburgh was retaken and David returned and took over the govt. In 1346, however, he was captured at NEVILLE'S CROSS and Robert became Regent alone.

There was hatred between David and Robert and partisanship among their supporters. Robert was accused of deserting the King at Neville's Cross and dragging out the negotiations for his release; this was to take place in 1354 under the T. of Newcastle, in return for a ransom of 90,000 merks (£60,000 Scots) payable over nine years. Thereupon the French intervened with bribes and a small force. The Scots seized Berwick. In 1356 the English burned the country from Roxburgh to Edinburgh (*The Burnt Candlemas*) and in 1357 the T. of Berwick restored the Truce of Newcastle with an extra 10,000 merks and 20 hostages. Since current revenue roughly balanced expenditure the instalments had to be raised by an unprecedented annual tax which made the King unpopular. In 1363 he offered the succession (legally Robert's) to Edward III in return for a remission. Robert and his sons raised an insurrection and were put in custody. The proposed bargain was laid before the Estates who would have none of it; the tax had been raised but the ransom delayed, leaving balances in the King's hands and anyhow they were not dissatisfied with Robert. He, however, remained in custody. In 1369, however, England, again at war with France, agreed to spread the outstanding 56,000 merks over 14 years and Robert's detention by an old and childless King became pointless. Released in 1370, he succeeded quickly in the next year.

By his kinswoman **(11) Elizabeth MURE (?-?)** Robert had since 1337 had four children. In 1347, just after the commencement of his sole regency, he had obtained a Papal dispensation and married her. After she died he married **(12) Euphemia ROSS (?-?)** by whom he had two sons born in wedlock **(13) David (?-1389) E. of STRATHEARN** and **(14) Walter (?-1437) E. of ATHOLL**. The Scone Parliament of 1371 assured the Crown, despite doubtful legitimacy to Elizabeth's son **(15) John (?1337-1406) E. of CARRICK (1368)** who became King as **Robert III (1390)**, and his other full brothers and their respective heirs, as against the undoubtedly legitimate descendants of Euphemia. This started a dangerous Royal feud. It also imported the doctrine of legitimation by subsequent marriage into Scots law.

When Edward III died in 1377 the unstable truce and the annual payments ended and the Scots seized Berwick (1378). John of Gaunt drove them out and renewed the truce, but in 1384 Carrick took over the govt. on the ground of his father's incapacity and attacked. John of Gaunt now penetrated to Edinburgh, but retired when French reinforcements and subsidies reached Carrick. In 1388 Douglas defeated the Percies in an unusually important private war at the poetically celebrated B. of Otterburn or Chevy Chase. In the same year, 1388, Carrick was permanently injured by a kicking horse and in 1389 the second son of (11), **(16) Robert (?1341-1420) Ld. of MENTEITH (1361) E. of FIFE (1371) D. of ALBANY (1389)** superseded him in the govt. A hostage in 1360, he had become Castellan of Stirling in 1373, Chamberlain in 1382 and Commander on the border in

1385. Carrick succeeded as King (Robert III) in 1390 but Albany relinquished his power only in 1393. English wars and court politics had by now so distracted the central personalities that many tribal and territorial magnates had established a virtual autonomy which Robert III could not break. By 1399 his bodily infirmities, too, were so serious that his son **(17) David (?1378-1402) D. of ROTHESAY (1389)** was appointed Lieut. and started putting down rebellious highlanders, among whom the worst was his brother, **(18) Alexander (?-1406) the 'WOLF of BADENOCH'.** The northern operations were only partially successful and meanwhile Rothesay repudiated his wife Elizabeth of March, antagonising her powerful relatives, and took Marjory of Douglas (whom he mistreated) and whose relatives were defeated at Homildon Hill in 1402. In his isolation a *coup d'état* by Albany was easy. Rothesay, imprisoned at Falkland, is said to have starved to death. Albany now began his long regency. *See* JAMES I OF SCOTS, 1394-1437, and others; DARNLEY.

STEWART, Robert (?-1592) 1st E. of ORKNEY (of 1st Scottish creation 1581), a bastard of James V, was made Abbot of Holyrood as a baby (1539). He supported the Lords of the Congregation politically and in fighting the French in 1559. He is said to have warned Darnley of Bothwell's plot. In 1569 he exchanged the Holyrood properties for those of the See of Orkney; accused of offering the Isles to the King of Denmark, he was imprisoned by the Regent Morton and was one of those who profited from Morton's overthrow in 1580. His second son **(2) Patrick (?-1614),** the ill-tutored **2nd E.,** acquired a charter for Orkney and Zetland in 1600, but his misrule ended with his forfeiture and eventual execution.

STEWART, Robert (1769-1822) known as **Vist. CASTLEREAGH (Ir.) from 1796, 2nd M. of LONDONDERRY (1821).** Irish M.P. in 1790. English M.P. from 1794, he favoured, like his patron Pitt, a combination of Union with Ireland and R. Catholic enfranchisement. He became Irish Privy Seal in 1797 and so, in practice, the Lord-Lieut's. chief executive, for which his knowledge of the country and his father's interest suited him. He anticipated the Irish rebellion by seizing most of the leaders and by replacing the Irish militia with English regulars. The event convinced him of the urgent military need for Union and Pitt promoted him to Chief Sec. for Ireland to carry it through. He did it by promising honours, sinecures, jobs or pensions to everyone who might make difficulties and when the govt. hesitated to honour his promises, he threatened a scandalous resignation. On the Union of the Parliaments he became M.P. for his old Irish constituency in the U.K. Parliament and having pressed for the R. Catholic Emancipation Bill which represented the other part of the policy, resigned in Mar. 1801 with Pitt and, like him, gave unofficial support to Addington in war policy and Irish legislation: in particular he proposed to pay R. Catholic priests and phase out the tithe system.

In 1802 he became Pres. of the Board of Control and as such supported the warlike but inevitable policies of the M. Wellesley (Gov.-Gen.) against his war-weary colleagues and the Directors of the HEIC. He also opened negotiations with Persia. Of handsome aspect and with a high reputation, in 1805 he added the Secretaryship for War and Colonies to the Board of Control. He was thus responsible for the Elbe raid of 1805 and for the other military undertakings until 1809. *See* THIRD COALITION; PENINSULAR WAR; FRANCO-RUSSIAN ALLIANCE; FRENCH COASTAL ANNEXATIONS.

He and George Canning disagreed and disliked each other. In 1809, as a result of Canning's intrigues, he resigned and wounded him in a duel, but he continued to support the war policy and in 1812 returned as Foreign Sec. and also, after Spencer Perceval's murder, as Leader of the House of Commons.

His first measure was by reinforcing the highly successful Spanish war, to distract the enemy and increase the authority of Britain among her friends or allies. His second was to pacify the Baltic and the Black Sea, so as to focus the efforts of Russia and Sweden on the defeat of Bonaparte. He concluded alliances with them, increased the war subsidies and encouraged Austria and Prussia. It was largely by his determination, as expressed in the T. of Chaumont (Mar. 1814) and preliminaries of Dijon, that the alliance was maintained until Bonaparte's abdication in 1814.

Castlereagh thought that Britain's interests were bound up with commerce, production, markets, colonies and sea power, to which a durable European peace was essential. Durability was more important than particular ambitions or acquisitions and he was ready not only to force sacrifices upon other states but to make them himself. The result was the longest settlement of modern times (*see* VIENNA, CONGRESS OF), and he was universally admired on the continent for his statesmanship.

At home, once the post-war slump had set in, he was less popular. Forceful and elegant on paper and across the negotiating table, he was a poor, sometimes boring speaker. As leader of the House he had to bring in or defend internal legislation for which Sidmouth's govt. was collectively responsible, which he helped to moderate, but for which he was personally blamed. This included the suspension of *Habeas Corpus* (Feb. 1817), the return to the gold standard in 1819, and the Six Acts (1819-20). His work as a peacemaker (which continued) was hidden from later opinion by Shelley's ill-informed squib:

I met Murder on the way
It had a face like Castlereagh.

In fact he was negotiating to *abolish* the Spanish and Dutch slave trade, arranging a Hispano-Portuguese arbitration, getting allied troops out of France (1819), preserving constitutionalism in the Peninsula (*see* CARLISTS), dissociating Britain from the repressive policies of the Holy Alliance. Overwork, gout and unscrupulous personal abuse slowly wore him down. He committed suicide. His half-brother **(2) Charles (1778-1854) Ld. STEWART (1814), E. VANE (1823) 3rd M.,** was briefly his U/Sec. for War in 1807; he was a successful but deaf and shortsighted cavalry officer in the Peninsula until 1812 and in 1813, when his brother returned to office, he became a kind of military ambassador to Prussia and Sweden and commanded Blucher's reserve cavalry at the B. of Dresden. He also kept the Swedes in the war, in particular preventing a Franco-Swedish convention which would have released the French garrison at Hamburg. In 1814 he became Ambassador to Vienna and to the Congresses of Troppau (1820), Laibach (1821) and Verona (1822). He had acquired very large estates in Ireland and Durham in 1819 through his second wife Frances Vane-Tempest and he spent the next 13 years developing the collieries and harbour at Seaham and building the Durham railway.

STEWART (LENNOX), especially MATTHEW. *See* JAMES IV, V AND VI OF SCOTS.

STEWS were originally mediaeval Turkish baths (in which both sexes *stewed* together). They became houses of assignation or brothels or both. *See* FLEET (LONDON).

STIGAND or STEGAN (?-1072), Bp. of ELMHAM (1043-52), Bp. of WORCESTER (1043-70) and Abp. of CANTERBURY (1052-70) was a Royal priest under Canute and rose through the hierarchy by his involvement in govt. from his earliest known benefice at Ashingdon. As a pluralist controlling many monasteries and the two richest Sees, he has been represented as epitomising the faults of the later Anglo-Saxon church, but he was a competent administrator and a patron of the arts. In the 1050s he was increasingly identified with E.

Godwin and his family, to whom he probably owed his elevation to Canterbury in place of Robert of Jumèges and he received his pallium from the anti-Pope Benedict IIX in 1058. Though supporting Harold's assumption of the throne in 1066, he managed to stay in office until deposed in 1070 as a preliminary to the Conqueror's intended church reforms. Pluralism, briefly interrupted, remained a problem for centuries.

STIGMATA (Gr: brands). Bodily marks corresponding to those received by Jesus in the course of His Passion. Many people are known to have developed them. The only modern English case is that of Mary Anne Girling (1827-86) who founded a chiliastic sect at Battersea (London).

STILLINGFLEET (1) Robert (?-1491) Bp. of Bath and Wells from 1466, was Yorkist Keeper of the Privy Seal in 1460 and Lord Chancellor for most of 1467-75. An opponent of the Woodvilles and a supporter of Richard III, he was pardoned by Henry VII but imprisoned in connection with the Simnel rising. A kinsman **(2) Edward (1635-99)** was a popular preacher and friend of Charles II from 1667. He became Dean of St. Paul's in 1678 and Bp. of Worcester from 1689. A frequent speaker in the Lords, he also reformed consistorial procedure.

STIPENDIARY. *See* MAGISTRATE.

STIRLING, E. of. *See* ALEXANDER.

STIRLING, James (1692-1770) *THE VENETIAN,* a mathematician, studied in Venice from 1715 to 1725, where he learned the secret of Murano glass making and of the control of silt in navigable channels, besides corresponding with Newton, Euler and Bernoulli. He returned to England and in 1726 became F.R.S. Apart from developing the Newtonian Calculus, he successfully managed the Leadhills mines and surveyed and developed the Port of Glasgow.

STIVER. A Dutch coin worth a penny.

STOCKDALE v HANSARD (1839) 9 Ad. & El. **(1)** Stockdale published a medical book. A copy found in a prison was described by two inspectors of prisons as "disgusting and obscene". Hansard published this report by order of the House of Commons. Stockdale sued Hansard for libel. Hansard pleaded parliamentary privilege. Stockdale contended that in asserting parliamentary privilege the court was being asked to recognise a change in the law made not by Statute but by a simple resolution of one House. The court gave judgement for Stockdale.

(2) The principle of the case stands, though the law specifically on the publication of parliamentary proceedings was altered so as to conform with Hansard's contention by the Parliamentary Papers Act, 1840.

STOCK EXCHANGE (London). Before 1773 brokers and jobbers did business informally at various coffee houses and in the Old Royal Exchange. In that year those who habitually met at Jonathan's Coffee House in Change Alley moved to a specially hired room in Sweeting's Alley. This was called the Stock Exchange and the building containing it, the Stock Exchange Tavern. In 1801 some members raised capital and built a new building in Capel Court which was opened in 1802. It had about 500 members and, like a club, admitted new members by ballot. It was progressively extended in the 19th cent. and developed an increasingly refined organisation. The property was vested in trustees and managers, but dealings and members were regulated by a separate committee which developed a practice and professional custom and ethics of great importance in the business world, particularly the segregation of brokers from jobbers or dealers and the rules against dealing and broking on own account. These rules and customs were backed by the threat of expulsion which became increasingly effective as the Stock Exchange began to engross most of the stock market.

The development after 1970 of world-wide electronic communications made it possible to trace anywhere and deal in saleable stock almost instantaneously. A single world stock market was developing to which the major local markets (e.g. at New York or Tokyo) were really points of access. A jobber-orientated exchange could not operate quickly enough in this environment. In 1986 the London Stock Exchange was revolutionised in the so-called **Big Bang** by the abolition of the segregation, the reorganisation of the firms into broker-dealers and market makers, and the introduction of Stock Exchange Automated Quotations (S.E.A.Q.).

STOCKHOLM, Ts. (1719). Britain undertook to protect Sweden with her fleet against Russia, to help her to recover Russian occupied territories and to pay her a subsidy. In return Sweden promised freedom of British trade in the Baltic and ceded Pomerania and Stettin to Prussia, Bremen and Verden to Hanover. *See* HANOVER-8.

STOCKMAR, Christian Friedrich, Baron von (1787-1863) became physician to Prince Leopold of Saxe-Coburg in 1816 and 1817 his secretary. Actively engaged in promoting the Prince's interests, he led the negotiations which brought the Prince to the Belgian throne in 1831. Until 1837 he acted mainly as the Belgian King's agent in Britain and when Victoria, Leopold's niece, came to the throne he acted as her unofficial adviser and negotiated the match with the Prince Consort in 1840. Until 1857, when he retired, he was Victoria and Albert's adviser and contributed greatly to their strictly constitutional approach to their duties.

STOCKPORT (Ches.) had a castle which was held against Henry II by his son, Geoffrey, in 1172. It was chartered in 1220 and had a market in 1260. After the coming of the cotton industry in the 18th cent. there were persistent industrial disturbances. In 1800 the weavers demanded statutory wage regulation; in 1808 a fixed price for their goods. Local bankruptcies and unemployment caused riots in 1812. Demonstrators in 1846 seized the work-house. Excessive reliance on cotton continued to create problems until the diversifications of the post World War II period. *See also* MANCHESTER.

STOCKTON. *See* MACMILLAN.

STOCKTON AND DARLINGTON RAILWAY. *See* TRANSPORT AND COMMUNICATIONS; STEPHENSON.

STOCKTON ON TEES. *See* MIDDLESBROUGH.

STOKE-ON-TRENT (Staffs.) was a small Potteries town until 1910, when it was amalgamated with TUNSTALL, BURSLEM, HANLEY and FENTON, as a county borough of the same name. It was extended in 1922, 1925 and 1929. The University of Keele was opened in 1949. The British Ceramic Research Laboratories in 1951. The whole has been given over to the manufacture of ceramics since about 1730.

STOKESAY CASTLE (Salop), fortified manor begun in 1291 but converted to a still occupied house in Tudor times.

STOKES INCIDENT (1911). The Persian govt. proposed to put a British Capt. Stokes in charge of their financial gendarmerie. The Russians, projecting onto the British their own Byzantine outlook, objected. The British govt. vetoed the appointment in order to keep Russian goodwill in the Agadir crisis.

STONE, George (?1708-64) rose through the Irish church to become Abp. of Armagh, a Lord Justice and an Irish P.C. in 1747. He ousted Henry Boyle from power by supporting the Crown's claim in 1751 to the Irish revenue surplus and in 1753 used the Crown patronage to drive a confirmatory bill through the Irish Parliament. Thereafter until his death he was the effective ruler of Ireland, together, after 1758, with Boyle (now E. of Shannon) and Ponsonby.

STONE or CALCULUS. A disease mainly of males, affecting most often the young and poor, but also the rich and elderly who, being literate, made more of it than seems

to have been statistically justified. Samuel Pepys had it. In the 1860s the English mortality varied between one in 63,000 and in 210,000 of the population. It was somewhat higher in Scotland but apparently unknown or unnoticed in Ireland.

STONEHENGE (Wilts.) was probably built in four main phases. A circular bank and ditch with a 35 ton "heel stone" in 19th cent. B.C; a two mile avenue of banks and ditches with two concentric circles of standing stones (brought from Pembrokeshire) in the 17th cent. B.C; and a circle of standing stones with lintels around five large trilithons arranged in a horseshoe in 16th cent. B.C. In about 1400 B.C. there was much dismantling and rearrangement, some of which caused the present rather confused appearance. It is assumed, from the solar alignments of some of the stones, that the building was a sun temple, but the nature of the cults practised there is unknown. It has been the subject of much fanciful speculation.

STONEHOUSE. *See* NEW TOWNS.

STONOR FAMILY AND PAPERS. This family already lived near Henley-on-Thames by 1300 but its fortunes were established by **Sir John (c. 1285-1354)** who was C.J. of the Common Pleas (1320-54). Over 350 family papers dating between 1290 and 1483 survive including private letters and estate records, but the major interest dates from the time of **Thomas (?-1431).** The papers ended up in the Royal archives after a law suit over the inheritance of **William (?-1494).** They provide details of the lives of substantial gentry uninvolved in national affairs.

STOPES, Marie Charlotte Carmichael (1880-1958) originally made her name in classifying ancient plants and the composition of coal on which she was a world expert, but the failure of her first marriage led her to publish *Married Love* (1918), a sensational success, followed immediately by *Wise Parenthood,* an even greater one. They brought birth control for the first time into frank public discussion. In 1921 she and her second husband, Humphrey Verdon-Roe, opened the Mothers' Clinic for Birth Control in London and she continued to publish influential books on sexual behaviour and ethics, primarily to make the life of women happier than it was. Arrogant, vain and prickly, she yet remained an idealist and to the end of her life a campaigner who, with Freud, perhaps influenced moral attitudes more than anyone in the 20th cent.

STOPFORD, Sir Robert (1768-1847) after a busy but conventional naval career became Commander of the Rochefort blockade in 1808; C-in-C at the Cape in 1810 and of the Java Expedition in 1811. As C-in-C Mediterranean from 1837 to 1841 he commanded the operations against Mehemet Ali in 1840.

STOP OF THE EXCHEQUER. *See* CHARLES II-14.

STORMONT, (N.I) the meeting place of the N. Irish Parliament until 1971, hence the regime under which N. Ireland was governed.

STOUR. *See* TRANSPORT AND COMMUNICATIONS.

STOURBRIDGE FAIR (Cambs.). Important horse fair until the 18th cent. *See* CAMBRIDGE.

STOW, John (?1525-1605), tradesman and Merchant Taylor, retired c. 1560 to devote himself to learning. A hard working chronicler and antiquary, he wrote an original *Summarie of Englyshe Chronicles* (1565), published editions of *Chronicles* by Matthew Paris (1571), Thomas Walsingham (1574) and Holinshed (1585-7) and wrote the well-known *Survey of London* (1598 and 1603). In the end his great expenditure on books left him destitute, supported only by alms and a small Merchant Taylors' pension.

STRACHAN, Sir Richard John (1760-1828) Naval Commander, took four French ships of the line which had escaped from the B. of Trafalgar. In 1809 he was, with the E. of Chatham, Joint Commander of the fever ridden Walcheren expedition.

The Earl of Chatham with his sword drawn
Stood waiting for Sir Richard Strachan.
Sir Richard, longing to get at 'em,
Stood waiting for the Earl of Chatham.

STRACHEY, (Evelyn) John (St. Loe), Etonian left wing ideologue was the son of an editor of the *Spectator*. In the 1920s he collaborated with another energetic socialist, Sir Oswald Mosley, and also edited the *Socialist Review*. When Mosley left the Labour Party, Strachey followed him into his New Party, but left it because of Mosley's hostility to Communist Russia. He began to write for Communist publications and his *Theory and Practice of Socialism* (1936) inspired the Labour left wing. The Nazi-Soviet alliance, however, shook his faith and he joined the R.A.F. where he became Air Ministry radio spokesman and well-known to the public. This helped his election as an M.P. in 1945. As Attlee's Minister of Food (1946-50) he instituted one of the govt's. large scale enterprises in planned development, namely the E. African groundnuts (or monkey nuts) scheme. This incompetently handled venture showed that his ideology was no substitute for administrative competence.

STRACHEY (1) Sir Henry Bt. (1736-1810) Sec. to Ld. Clive in India in 1764 was intermittently an M.P. and became Master of the Household in 1794. Of his descendants **(2) Sir Edward (1812-1901) Bt. (1858)** was an oriental philologist. His brother **(3) Sir Richard (1817-1908),** originally a soldier, was Sec. to the Central Provs. in 1856 and became a versatile civil engineer. He was a member of the Council for India in 1875 and Chairman from 1889 to 1906. He organised the purchase of the E. India Railway in 1877 and initiated the scientific study of oriental meteorology, for which he invented several instruments. His brother **(4) Sir John (1823-1907)** a distinguished Indian civil servant, was Lieut.-Gov. of the N.W. Frontier Prov.; created the Indian agricultural department and was finance member of the Gov.-Gen's. council. He was retired in 1880 for under-estimating the cost of the Afghan War. The son of (3), **(5) Lytton (1880-1932)** was the brilliant and ironical writer and member of the Bloomsbury Group. He published *Eminent Victorians* (1918), *Queen Victoria* (1921) and *Elizabeth and Essex* (1928).

STRAFFORD. *See* BYNG; WENTWORTH.

STRAITS QUESTION. The phrase refers to the Bosphorus and the Dardanelles and the control of naval and commercial traffic through them. The question is very ancient: some hold that the Trojan War arose out of it. In more modern times, imperial powers (Byzantium, Ottoman Turkey) in possession have taxed commercial traffic and stopped warships, but as their power weakened they tended to make concessions or grant free passage to particular and then to all maritime commercial shipping and to allow warships to pass after notice and in limited numbers in peacetime. The STRAITS CONVENTION (July 1841) between Britain, France, Russia, Austria, Prussia, Naples, Sardinia-Savoy and Turkey guaranteed Turkish independence and the ancient rule that the Turks should permit free passage of the Bosphorus and Dardanelles to merchant shipping only in peacetime, but might close them to any flag they chose in time of war. Since 1878 the Straits have (harbour dues apart) been a free international highway for commercial shipping. Since World War II only one warship has been allowed in the Straits at a time.

STRAITS SETTLEMENTS. The collective name for the Crown Colony composed of Malacca, Penang and Singapore (Malaya), Labuan (Borneo) and the Indian Ocean Cocos Is. and Christmas I. Dissolved in 1946 when Singapore became a separate colony. Penang and Malacca passed to Malaya, Labuan to Sabah and the islands first to Singapore and then, in 1955 and 1958 respectively, to Australia.

STRAND (London), ancient road from Temple Bar to Charing Cross, along the top of the north bank (strand) of the Thames. It was continuously built up by the end of the 13th cent. and paved in the 14th. In Tudor and Stuart times it was lined with important mansions such as Somerset House. *See* SAVOY.

STRANGE, Ld. *See* RICHARD III-9.

STRANGE, Sir Robert (1721-92), engraver, achieved distinction under Le Bas at Paris whither he had, as a Jacobite, fled. He returned to England in 1750, but had difficulties because of his Jacobitism until 1784 when Benjamin West introduced him to the King. By this time he had become the leading European line engraver of his time.

STRANGFORD. *See* SMYTHE.

STRATA FLORIDA or YSTRADFLUR (Cardigan) had the largest Welsh Cistercian Abbey, founded in 1164 but badly damaged in 1294.

STRATFORD-ON-AVON (Warwicks.), at a river crossing, was an ancient borough of no particular note until Shakespeare was born there in 1564. Since the tourist industry arose in the mid 20th cent. it has flourished mainly on American pilgrimages to the shrine of the Bard.

STRATHCLYDE. Kingdom in S.W. Scotland, perhaps a British survival from the Roman evacuation. It disputed territory with the Picts and the Scots to the N.E. and N.W., but they combined under the House of Alpin and this led by unknown means to a kind of throne-sharing between the descendents of Constantine I (r. 862-71) and his brother Aed (r. 877-8) (*for the descent see* SCOTS AND ALBAN KINGS, EARLY). Strathclyde British aggression was now diverted southwards into Cumbria where Athelstan decisively checked it at the B. of Brunanburgh in 937. Thereafter they remained weak but distinct until absorbed into the Scots monarchy in 1034 under Duncan I, who had ruled in Strathclyde from 1018.

STRATHCONA AND MOUNTROYAL. *See* SMITH, DONALD ALEXANDER.

STRATHEARN, David E. of (?-1389). *See* STEWART OR STUART, ROYAL-13.

STRATHMORE. *See* BOWES-LYON; LYON.

STRATHNAIRNE. *See* ROSE, HUGH HENRY.

STRAW, JACK or RACK (?-1381) a possibly pseudonymous leader of the Peasants' Revolt and the only one mentioned by Chaucer. He figured in the London violence in June 1381 and was summarily executed.

STRAWBERRY HILL (Twickenham) was a romantic stuccoed Gothic house built by Horace Walpole between 1747 and 1755. It gave its name to a Gothic revival style of the period. *See* WALDEGRAVE.

STREET, George Edmund (1824-81), neo-Gothic architect and influential pupil of Sir Geoffrey Gilbert Scott, trained, *inter alios* Norman Shaw and Philip Webb.

STREET OFFENCES ACT 1959. *See* PROSTITUTION.

STRESA CONFERENCE (Apr. 1935) on an island in L. Maggiore, was held to consider the effect of Hitler's rearmament. The participants were Ramsay MacDonald and Sir J. Simon for Britain, Flandin and Laval for France and Benito Mussolini for Italy. It reaffirmed the independence of Austria but said nothing about Mussolini's current pressure on Ethiopia.

STRETFORD. *See* MANCHESTER.

STRICKLAND. Related northern families. **(1) William (?-1419)** was provided to the bishopric of Carlisle in 1400 but Henry IV insisted on capitular election and confirmation by himself. Having thus asserted a principle, he employed William to negotiate a peace with the Scots in 1401. Of the Protestant Stricklands **(2) Sir William (1598-1673) 1st Bt. (1641)** was a Yorkshire M.P. and supporter of the Long Parliament. His brother **(3) Walter (?-1670),** also a Yorkshire M.P., was Parliamentary agent to Holland from 1642 to 1650. He was Oliver St. John's adviser in the abortive Dutch negotiations of 1651 and a member of Cromwell's Upper House in 1657. Of the R. Catholic Stricklands **(4) Sir Roger (1640-1717),** a seaman, fought successfully as a Captain in the Four Days (June 1666) and at Solebay (1672); was knighted in 1673 and as Admiral of the Blue in command of the fleet in the Narrow Seas in 1687 provoked a mutiny by having mass celebrated on board. He had to be superseded (1688). He died at St. Germain. A relative **(5) Thomas John** known as the **Abbe Strickland (1679-1740),** educated at Douai, tried unsuccessfully to reconcile English R. Catholics with the govt. He became Bp. of Namur in 1727 yet lived mostly at Rome as agent of the British govt. to the Curia and was once employed as a diplomatic agent in London by the Emperor Charles VI.

STRICT SETTLEMENTS. *See* ENTAILS.

STRIKES. The word originated in seamen and dock-workers preventing ships from going to sea by *striking* (= lowering) their topmasts and yards. The major 19th cent. strike years were 1834 (the year of the Tolpuddle Martyrs), 1842 and 1889 (London Docks). In the 20th cent. the major strike years were 1906 (Miners), 1911 (Transport and seamen), 1912 (Miners), 1920 (Miners), 1921 (Miners), 1922 (Engineering workers), 1926 (Miners and General), 1972 (Miners). Some are known to have lost more than 10 million working days. The General Strike of 1926 lost 160M. Working days lost diminished in World War I, increased seriously in 1919-23, but did not in World War II repeat the reduction of World War I.

The many trivial strikes and near-strikes seem to have made the British strike record bulk larger in the public mind than the figures of days lost seem to justify. Particularly, the overfrequent disputes of 1978-9 antagonised the long suffering public and probably contributed to the Tory victory in 1979 and the reforms of trade union legislation.

The euphemism 'INDUSTRIAL ACTION' first appeared in the 1970s. *See also* GENERAL STRIKE, 1926; POLITICAL CORRECTNESS.

STRODE'S CASE **(1629) and William STRODE (1599-1645),** M.P. for Beeralston, stopped the Speaker from adjourning the House to prevent Eliot's manifesto being read. Summoned before the Council, he refused to attend, was arrested and when charged in the Star Chamber repudiated its jurisdiction, refusing to answer outside Parliament for words spoken in Parliament. Refusing also to be bound over, he was imprisoned until 1640, when the Long Parliament voted the proceedings a breach of privilege and gave him compensation. Embittered by his experiences he was the most vengeful of Strafford's, Finch's and Laud's accusers (1644). He was generally recognised in his own time as one of the most violent ("bloody") of the Parliamentarians. *See* FIVE MEMBERS.

STRONGBOW. *See* CLARE.

STROUDWATER CANAL. *See* TRANSPORT AND COMMUNICATIONS.

STRUTT (1) Jedediah (1726-97), cotton spinner and inventor, made a fortune in partnership with Sir Richard Arkwright. His son **(2) William (1756-1830) 1st Ld BELPER (1856),** a radical and friend of Bentham, Macaulay and J. S. Mill, was M.P. for Derby from 1830 to 1847, for Arundel from 1851 to 1852 and for Nottingham until 1856. He held office as Chancellor of the Duchy of Lancaster in the Aberdeen govt. of 1852 to 1854.

STUART, Esmé, D. of LENNOX. *See* JAMES VI-7 *et seq.*

STUART, Matthew (1516-71) 4th E. of LENNOX. *See* JAMES VI-3.

STUART, James (1713-88). *See* REVETT, NICHOLAS.

STUART of DARNLEY (1) Sir John (?1365-1429) 1st Seigneur d'AUBIGNY (1422), commander of a Scots contingent, helped the French to defeat the English at Beaugé in 1421. His grandson **(2) Bernard (?1447-1508) 3rd Seigneur,** commanded a French contingent which helped Henry VII to defeat Richard III at Bosworth in 1485. He also fought in the Italian wars between 1494 and 1503 and was then employed on French diplomatic missions in Scotland where he died. The Seigneurie devolved through his brother or half brother. *See* STEWART OR STUART (LENNOX).

STUART-WORTLEY (-MACKENZIE), James Archibald (1776-1845) 1st Ld. WHARNCLIFFE (1826), was the grandson of the 3rd E. of Bute and nephew of the 1st M. of Bute. He inherited the Wortley properties in Cornwall and Yorkshire and the Scottish estates of the Mackenzies of Rosehaugh. He was a Tory M.P. from 1797. In 1812 he moved the resolution calling for an efficient administration and brought about the resignation of ministers after Percival's assassination. In 1820 he seconded the motion for a reconciliation between George IV and his queen: in 1818 he proposed a property tax to relieve the poor; in 1820 he declared against agricultural protection and in 1823 he supported R. Catholic emancipation. As a result he lost his seat in 1826 but was made a peer. In the Lords he was the most skilful opponent of the Reform Bill, to which he objected not on principle but on method. Hence when it became clear that further opposition might lead to revolution he and his friends helped to carry the bill to avoid a wholesale creation of peers. In the new parliament he became Peel's Privy Seal (1834) but went into opposition in Apr. 1835. He was Peel's Lord President from 1841 but in Cabinet discussion opposed the repeal of the Corn Laws.

STUBBS, George (1724-1806), painter with an equine bias, of aristocratic and popular rural life.

STUBB[E]S, Philip (fl. 1583-91), a Puritan who, in a pamphlet called *The Anatomie of Abuses,* described and denounced those evil customs of his time which he thought should be abolished. The descriptions are a valuable source of social and economic information.

STUPOR MUNDI **(Lat. = The Astonisher of the World).** The Emperor Frederick II (?-1250).

STURDEE, Sir Frederick Charles (1859-1925), Admiral of the Fleet (1921), was Chief of the Naval War Staff in 1914 and then commanded the force which sank Admiral Count Spee's squadron at the Falkland Is. in Dec. 1914. He commanded a battleship squadron at the B. of Jutland (1916).

STURM UND DRANG (Ger: Assault and Charge, or Storm and Stress), the name of a late 18th cent. German literary ferment inspired by American Independence and by Rousseau's reaction against convention and his call to nature. Schiller, Goethe and Herder were strongly influenced by and helped to shape it.

STUYVESANT, Peter (1592-1672). *See* NEW YORK CITY.

SUBA[H]DAR. A *subah* was a Moghul province and a subahdar its governor. Subsequently a subahdar was the chief native officer of a sepoy company.

SUBLIME PORTE (Istanbul). The Ottoman Turkish Foreign Office or sometimes (more loosely) govt.

SUBMARINES, SUBMERSIBLES, U-BOATS. (1) Many attempts to build such ships were made before Robert Fulton's first success in the Seine and off Brest in 1780. Two awash boats were tried in the American Civil War. Garrett and Nordenfelt sold one to the Russians and another to the Turks in 1877, but the forerunner of the modern submarine was the French *Gustave Zédé* built in 1898 with electric motors. The British acquired American Holland boats in 1899, but most submarines of all nationalities were ultimately derived from French and Italian designs of 1911. These were all based upon oil or petrol driven surface motors which also recharged the batteries for electric drive underwater.

(2) In World War I the Germans built 343 using them mainly for commerce destroying. They lost 178 and their maximum operational strength was 45 in 1915, 97 in 1916, 140 in 1917 and 132 in 1918. These used torpedoes for underwater attack but some were minelayers. Nearly all had a gun which, used on the surface, was the preferred method (because cheapest) of destroying merchantmen. Their surface tonnage varied from 127 to 1930.

(3) The Germans were forbidden submarines between the wars and development elsewhere was sluggish. After rearmament began they built large numbers. During World War II underwater charging with the use of the *schnorkel* was developed and also a high powered underwater peroxide driven motor, but these were perfected too late to affect the course of the war. About 1150 U-boats were built, of which 781 were destroyed. Surface tonnage varied from 600 to 2,500.

(4) In the 1950s the Americans and their allies and subsequently the Russians developed nuclear powered boats which required only a single type of engine and did not need to re-charge on the surface. These could stay underwater indefinitely. Large submarines capable of launching long range guided missiles from underwater were introduced first by the Americans and then by Russia, Britain and France. Long range target-seeking torpedoes were developed against naval targets. The Argentine cruiser *General Belgrano* was sunk by a Royal Navy nuclear driven submarine with one of these during the Falklands War. See COMMERCE PROTECTION, NAVAL B (2-4), C.

SUBMISSION OF THE CLERGY (1532). Following upon the Supplication against the Ordinaries, Convocation undertook that it would make no new canons, constitutions or ordinances without Royal licence; that existing canon law should be reviewed by a committee of 32 nominated by the King and that canons so approved should come into force only with the King's consent.

SUB POENA (Lat: **'under penalty').** A Chancery writ requiring a person to attend any court as a witness or the Chancery court as defendant in a suit.

SUBSIDY meant originally any parliamentary grant to assist or *subsidise* the Crown in performing its functions; then more specifically, indirect taxes in the form of tonnage and poundage levied for that purpose. Meanwhile the mediaeval direct tax of the Tenth and Fifteenth (2s. in the pound on land, 1s. 6d. on movables) had with the obsolescence of assessment become uneconomic. It became usual to double it under Edward VI and this doubled amount became known as "one" or "one entire" subsidy. More than one might be voted. The last such subsidy was granted in 1663.

SUCCESSION (1) Under the early Anglo-Saxons succession passed within the kin-group; there were few patterns or rules of inheritance. The strongest generally got the biggest share. Hence estates were likely to pass from brother to brother rather than from father to son, but the kin often intervened in favour of a woman. By the 11th cent. there was a theoretical acceptance of the rights of children but not of primogeniture. The greater Norman magnates seem to have thought that land inherited by a father should go to the eldest son, but land acquired in his lifetime might pass to a younger. The rights of women to independent inheritance were eroded, but where daughters only survived, the estates were divided between them. The desire, however, for integrity of estates and security of inheritance in a time of increasing Royal interference and shortage of male heirs led to a gradual acceptance (save in Kent and certain boroughs) by the mid 13th cent. of primogeniture for all parts of the inheritance. This presumption permeated society from King to serf. In the 14th cent. even greater security of succession was sometimes achieved through an increase in Royal licences to entail estates (*see* GAVEL-KIND, BOROUGH ENGLISH).

(2) Succession to the Crown developed on similar lines. Brother to brother succession was common in 9th and 10th cent. Wessex and no eldest surviving son succeeded his father to an English throne from 1040 to 1189 and in 1199 it was not clear whether Richard I's brother, John, or his nephew, Arthur of Brittany, had the better claim. Although primogeniture was the established presumption by the end of the 13th cent., some doubts were raised about the succession of a grandson in 1377. From 1399 to 1485 succession to the throne depended as often as not upon political muscle, on which to a degree it always had, and on which it continued to depend until the Act of Succession of 1701. See however, SUCCESSION, ACTS OF (HENRY VIII).

SUCCESSION, ACTS OF (Henry VIII). This singular series of Acts arose out of the matrimonial vagaries of Henry VIII and some of his wives. **1534** Two Acts declared his marriage to Katharine of Aragon void, by reason of her previous marriage with Arthur P. of Wales, and his marriage to Anne Boleyn valid and entailed the Crown upon her issue including the Princess Elizabeth. They made it treasonable to impugn the latter marriage and required anyone to swear allegiance to this settlement on demand. **1536** This Act irrationally declared that Henry's marriage to Anne Boleyn had never been lawful and anyhow that she, inflamed by carnal desires, had perpetrated abominable treasons already found to be adulterous. It declared that both the Princesses Mary and Elizabeth were now illegitimate and that Henry's marriage to Jane Seymour was valid; it entailed the Crown upon her issue but empowered Henry by letters patent or will to identify, in the absence of such issue, the person to whom the Crown should come. It was declared treasonable to believe that either of the two previous marriages were valid or that either of the Princesses were legitimate and required all subjects to swear to the new dispensation. **1544** This Act entirely ignored the statutory illegitimacy of the Princesses and settled the Crown, in default of further issue of Henry or P. Edward, son of Jane Seymour, firstly upon the Princess Mary and her issue, then upon Princess Elizabeth and hers and then upon such person as Henry should name by letters patent or will. It also enacted that those who had sworn to the Act of 1536 should be deemed to have sworn to the Act of 1544.

SUCCESSION DUTY. *See* DEATH DUTIES.

SUCCESSION, PICTISH RULE, still in force in the 8th cent. The choice of a successor to the throne lay between men whose mothers were daughters or grand-daughters of a King.

SUCCESSION STATES were the states created after World War I from the territories of Austro-Hungary, Germany and Russia, namely Poland (later shifted westwards); Austria, Lithuania, Latvia and Esthonia (which existed interruptedly); Finland (which lost territory to Russia); Hungary and Roumania (whose frontiers fluctuated wildly); and Czechoslovakia and Yugoslavia (which broke up).

SUDAN or SOUDAN. This name has been used in two senses. **(1)** A huge vaguely defined tract between the latitude of Khartoum and Uganda, stretching from Abyssinia westwards as far as L. Chad, or even further.

(2) That part of the above, south of Khartoum which, combined with the provinces northward as far as the Egyptian frontier and the Red Sea coast centring on Port Sudan and Suakin, now constitute the Sudanese Republic. The term MILITARY SUDAN occasionally appeared to describe these northerly areas.

(3) Much of the Sudan (in either sense) is desert with a few, often seasonal, springs, but going southwards the land changes first to scrub and thorn thicket and then to equatorial jungle. The southerly equatorial area is separated from the rest by the spongy virtually impassable waterlogged SUDDH, which by storing some of the flow of the Nile, acts as a flood regulator.

(4) The original population was black, upon which tribal Arabs were superimposed as conquerors. These imported from all directions or took locally large

numbers of slaves whose descendants form a distinctive element in the population. *See next two entries.*

SUDAN AGREEMENT (19 Jan. 1899) between Britain and Egypt vested the Sudanese military and civil command in a single Gov-Gen. who was to be jointly appointed and removed. He alone was to legislate (by proclamation); Egyptian law was to apply only if applied by proclamation, but this comprehensive power was limited in four ways. *European* rights were regulated by a mostfavoured nation clause; the Egyptian Mixed Tribunals were never to have jurisdiction in the Sudan; for purposes of tariffs, Egypt and the Sudan were to be one economic area; the slave trade was to be declared illegal. The British flag was always to be flown beside the Egyptian save at Suakin, but no foreign consular officers were to be allowed without British consent. The two govts. also undertook to co-operate in enforcing the Brussels Act of July 1890 against trafficking in arms and liquor.

SUDAN (1) In 1819 Ibrahim, *s.* of Mehemet Ali, Pasha of Egypt, garrisoned Suakin and eight major and many minor points along the Nile, including Khartoum and Calso. This virtually unresisted conquest secured control of the rich slave trade, which funnelled into the great Arabian slave market at Jiddah, besides the trade in Equatorian Ivory, ostrich feathers from Kordofan, guns from Darfur and grain from Dongola and Sennar. The poverty-stricken population had to support a luxurious viceregal court at Khartoum, a rapacious bureaucracy, a large undisciplined and disintegrating army and heavy tributes for the Egyptian treasury. These expenses, assessed upon the Sheikhs, could not be met without redoubling their efforts as slave hunters and traders. Disorder was endemic (*see* SLAVE TRADE) and the govt's. weakness was compounded by the existence of a govt. irregular force as well armed as the army (*The Bazingers*), and of armed desert Arab and jungle negroid tribes. Bazingers and tribes alike hated the Egyptians, but ignorance and lack of a unifying spirit long prevented them from combining to destroy their infamous system.

(2) Two prophets now successively arose. Conditions were unknown in the West in 1869 when the horrors of the slave trade were reaching a climax through the operations of Zubehr Rahamna, the biggest slave trader in modern history, and a confederacy of slave merchants. By 1869 Zubehr with his private army ruled the Bahr-el-Ghazal. He refused to pay the tribute and routed an Egyptian force. He and the Khedive made a face saving peace and jointly attacked Darfur. Its ruler was killed and the inhabitants enslaved. Zubehr became a Pasha. But the affair was on so large a scale that rumours reached the great powers. In reply to increasingly suspicious inquiries the Khedive in 1874 appointed the already famous CHARLES ("Chinese") GORDON Gov. of the equatorial province in succession to Sir Samuel Baker. His province was one of the victim areas. His appointment may originally have been a pretence, but the Khedive was soon surprised. Gordon scattered justice and liberty regally and energetically, protecting the weak, feeding the sick, rescuing the kidnapped and executing the wicked. He acquired slaves, trained them as soldiers and with them raided the slave caravans. The unenthusiastic Egyptian govt. was however stimulated to support him because the Bahr-el-Gazal slavers still omitted to pay their tribute. In 1877 he went home, while the Khedive's ministers enticed Zubehr to Cairo. When Gordon returned as Gov-Gen. the Pasha was in comfortable but effective custody. His son, Suleiman, raised a revolt which the Gov-Gen., riding into his camp alone in full uniform, quelled single-handed. In 1878 Suleiman revolted again. Defeated by an Egyptian force he surrendered on terms but was shot with ten associates by Gessi Pasha in breach of them. Meanwhile Gordon rode thousands of miles on his camel with a charmed, or

rather a respected life, going where armed forces dared not go, righting wrongs and, since slavery was the greatest of Sudanese institutions, undermining the whole social and economic system. He taught the tribes, both Arab and black, that they had rights and they noticed that only the Egyptians stood in the way of them. He left in 1879.

(3) The second unifying prophet appeared: Mohammed Ahmad, a saintly recluse of Abba I (south of Khartoum) quarrelled with his spiritual director and acquired in Abdullah a very able disciple. The two became the centre of an anti-Egyptian and religious conspiracy. Mohammed Ahmad was to be the MAHDI. He received assurances from tribes in his native Kordofan. When Raouf Pasha, the new Gov-Gen., heard of it he sent a force to Abba. The Mahdi's small following destroyed it (Aug. 1881). Revolt was now opened. The Mahdi retired to Kordofan, triumphantly gathering adherents. In Dec. 1881 they ambushed the Bey of Fashoda. In June 1882 they wiped out an Egyptian force of 4000 and captured stores and weapons. A mass revolt began just as the British were bombarding Alexandria and scattering the Egyptian home army. This was decisive if coincidental. The British restored order in Egypt while the Mahdi's Dervishes massacred the small Sudan garrisons and blockaded the rest. The British rounded up 8000 Egyptian troops, placed them under Gen. Hicks and sent them to rescue the Austrian Slatin Bey, who was still holding out in Darfur. The Mahdi destroyed this force with little loss at El Obeid (Nov. 1883).

(4) The British had been in Egypt only 13 months at the B. of El Obeid: they had gone there only to enforce certain international debts; they did not mean to stay, even in Egypt, and their purpose towards the Sudan was to liquidate a ruinous entanglement which might prevent Egypt paying her debts altogether. Therefore they advised the unwilling Khedive to evacuate the surviving garrisons and offered the miracle working Gordon to do it. Gordon arrived without resources. He soon discovered that Zubehr Pasha, still in custody, was (though he detested him) the only one with the ability and power to help. The Gladstone govt. was horrified and vetoed the proposal. It also vetoed the use of British troops and meanwhile the Mahdi's forces closed in on Khartoum. The British public was disturbed at the plight of its abandoned hero. A furious agitation compelled the govt. to act. A relief column was organised and set out. The Dervishes stormed Khartoum after a ten months' siege and sacked it. Gordon was killed (Jan. 1885) two days before the column arrived. It struggled back and the other garrisons were massacred. Only Suakin remained.

(5) The Mahdi died of typhus five months later and Abdulla succeeded him as KHALIFA. He spent his first year putting down rivals, in process of which he established a military monarchy based upon his own tribe, the Baggara Arab. He abandoned the ruins of Khartoum and settled the population and the Baggara in the adjacent new-built city of Omdurman. He converted the black *Bazingers* into the *Jehadia* (the makers of holy war). Together the Baggara and the Jehadia, armed with modern rifles and even artillery, dominated the rest of a huge, partially disaffected army. Such a mixture was too explosive. War was necessary to survival. A *Jehad* was launched against Christian Abyssinia. Intermittent but heavy fighting around Gallabat lasted for three years and culminated in slaughter and in the death of the Emperor John at a tremendous battle (Mar. 1889) involving 200,000 men. In this pyrrhic victory, Abdulla lost most of his faithful troops. It was politically necessary to engage less faithful ones. Capitalising on the victory, Arabs from Omdurman were sent to their destruction against Egypt (B. of Toski).

(6) Besides Egyptian imperialism it was realised by most authorities that the internal state of the Dervish empire would make peace in the long run impossible. The British-Egyptian command was well informed of conditions and intrigues at Omdurman, for there were many willing to act as spies. A catastrophic famine felt also in Egypt devastated the Sudan in 1890 and was followed by locusts and swarms of mice. The population died in tens of thousands. The best and presumably best fed fighting force lost 80% of its strength. There thus was a period of quiescence while the British developed Egypt and its army. In Mar. 1895 Slatin, who had accepted Islam and had become a confident of the Khalifa, escaped to Egypt bringing all his wealth of experience and detailed knowledge. He also published a book, *Fire and Sword in the Sudan* which awakened the British public to the cruelties of Sudanese internal politics and to the decline of the Khalifa's power. British opinion was ready to support the new conservative govt. in a more forward policy which was desirable for other reasons (*see* EGYPT-14). It was resolved to occupy Dongola, the most fertile and the nearest province of the Dervish Empire. In Mar. 1896 the Sirdar (Sir Herbert Kitchener) was instructed to do so.

(7) In practice the war could not be thus limited. It lasted until Dec. 1899 and was distinguished, as far as the fall of Omdurman (Sept. 1898) by two features. The first was Kitchener's determination to ensure continuous supplies from a base 1000 miles to the north for his large force in this barren country. It was an engineer's war. The troops built a railway as they advanced and armed steamers were brought up, sometimes in parts and built. The railway was needed for the periods when the Nile (qv) was low and to circumvent the many cataracts. The second feature was the strategic incompetence of the Dervish military command. They never tried to interrupt Kitchener's lengthening communications but awaited defeat at fixed points. The first such was at Firket (June 1896). Some of the *Jehadia* fraternised with the British Sudanese and were recruited into their army. There was now a pause, for the force had outrun its communications.

(8) The fall of Dongola caused many Arabs to flee from Omdurman; but galvanised the Khalifa, who ordered up troops from all parts. He mistrusted the Jaalin and Barabara tribes around Metemma and decided to occupy it with a large but loyal and savage force from Kordofan. Foreseeing sack and rape, the Jaalin protested. He overruled them. They bid him defiance, but before the British could reach them, they were massacred (May-June 1897). With the railway further advanced and the high Nile of July, Abu Hamed and then Berber, 100 miles further on, were seized by flying columns. Berber is the closest Nile town to British-held Suakin. The tribes between immediately submitted and a new supply route was opened *via* the Red Sea. The Dervish Empire was falling apart.

(9) Expecting a direct attack on his capital and fearing further defection, the Khalifa again left the British in peace to perfect their next moves; but when he realised that they would wait until the high Nile of 1898 he changed his mind and moved forward to attack. But the subordinate rival commanders, to whom troops had personal allegiances, quarrelled. The large expectant army returned disconsolate, leaving a part of it to try its hand. This detachment, 20,000 strong, was destroyed at the B. of the Atbara (Apr. 1898). The decisive concentration and advance could now begin. It ended with the overthrow of the main Dervish army (about 60,000) at Omdurman (Sept. 1898).

(10) The Khalifa escaped to Kordofan. Kitchener was distracted by the Fashoda incident. Pursuits and surrenders proceeded all over the south-east, but the Khalifa still had a faithful following, protected by 120 miles of scrub and desert. Attempts in Jan. and Oct. 1899 against him failed for lack of water, while he organised and plundered. There was unrest and rumoured conspiracy at Omdurman. Then suddenly in Nov. he started to march for its recapture. He

was brought to battle near Abba and fell with his leading emirs (Dec. 1899).

(11) The B. of Omdurman raised the problem of the future status of the Sudans (*see previous entry*). The lost provinces had been reconquered in the name of the Khedive by a force only 30% of which was British, though in practice the British paid. World, let alone British, opinion would never tolerate the reimposition of a govt. of the previous Egyptian character. At the same time the Fashoda incident showed that if the British washed their hands of the reconquered provinces, the Egyptians would lose them. It precipitated therefore the Anglo-Egyptian Sudan Agreement (19 Jan. 1899), which settled their status, while other influences compelled the Salisbury-Cambon Declaration of London (21 Mar. 1899) which, though Egypt was not a party, settled the western boundary.

(12) Evidently the role of the slave trade in the economy had to be replaced with something else and this was rapidly supplied by cotton, for which there was an expanding world market. The British disarmed and settled the population and the need of a guaranteed grain supply was met by great irrigation schemes based upon Sennar. Half starved disorder gave way rapidly to a relative prosperity, which the population had never known before. But the British never corrected an imbalance which resulted from the Dervish, Kordofani-led defeat. The Christian and pagan south was the source of most of the wealth, but the Mohammedan Arabs of Khartoum and the barren north were the more politically sophisticated. As long as the British remained, the balance stayed approximately level, but when Independence came in 1956 there seemed to be in new terms a repetition of the older pre-Dervish pattern, with the real wealth being exploited for the benefit of a ruling Arab minority.

SUDBURY, Simon (?-1381) Bp. of LONDON (1362-75), Abp. of CANTERBURY from 1372, had been a Papal auditor. In 1376, after pressure from the Good Parliament, he became a councillor but was already faced with a break-down of discipline among the lower clergy and the rise of dissent and Lollardy. In 1378 he attempted to try Wycliffe at Lambert. The attempt made him unpopular, the failure destroyed his public prestige. Nevertheless in 1380 he was made Chancellor as a result of court manoeuvres. In 1381 the Kentish rebels concentrated their hatred upon him as symbolising the evils of govt. and the Church and, during their occupation of London, they dragged him from the chapel in the Tower and hacked off his head. A conscientious diocesan, he initiated a fund to rebuild the nave of Canterbury Cathedral.

SUDELEY (Glos.) originally 12th cent. mansion much enlarged in the 16th when Queen Catherine Parr lived there, and damaged in the Civil War (1643).

SUDETENLAND was that part of Bohemia inhabited by a majority of German speaking people. Hitler made this the pretext for his territorial demands, which really had a military purpose, upon Czechoslovakia in 1938. *See* WORLD WAR II.

SUDRA. *See* CASTE.

SUETONIUS PAULLINUS, GAIUS. *See* BRITAIN. ROMAN-4.

SUEZ AFFAIR. *See* EDEN GOVIT; EGYPT-24.

SUEZ CANAL. The Egyptian concession was granted to Ferdinand de Lesseps (1805-94) in 1854 and revised in Jan. 1856. He formed the Suez Canal Co. in 1858; this was a French concern with a substantial Egyptian govt. minority interest. After much British obstruction the Canal was opened in 1869. In 1875 Disraeli bought the Egyptian shareholding and in 1882 intervened in Egypt. France, still feeling the effects of her 1870 disaster, could not prevent this, but by 1888 European opinion had been aroused to the danger of British predominance in a route carrying 7% of world trade and the SUEZ CANAL or CONSTANTINOPLE CONVENTION 1888 between Britain,

France, Germany, Austro-Hungary, Italy, Russia, Spain, Turkey and the Netherlands vested the Canal in a company with 32 directors appointed proportionately by the powers and declared that the Canal should be "free and open in time of war without distinction". This rule was applied until 1914. There was always more northward than southward traffic. In fact two thirds of the tonnage using the Canal was British and it soon became a vital imperial interest to safeguard it, for it immensely cheapened the terms of trade between Britain, India, China, the Far East and Australasia and brought prosperity to the Punjab and Malaysia. Hence heavy British naval investment at Gibraltar and Malta and the permanent establishment of a large up-to-date Mediterranean fleet.

Turkish entry against the Allies in World War I ended the nominal Turkish suzerainty of Egypt and the Canal, defended by British troops, was open only to friendly and neutral traffic. After 1919 the proportion of world trade using the Canal rose steadily, but the diplomatic imbroglio of 1935-6 enabled the Italians to take advantage of the Constantinople Convention to further their aggressive designs on Ethiopia. Between the appearance of German troops in N. Africa (Jan. 1941) and their defeat in 1943, the Canal was virtually unusable by large ships through parachute mining. Thereafter the proportion of world trade rose steadily with the new oil shipments and by 1953 had reached 15%. In 1953 the British evacuated the area, following the Egyptian revolution. In 1956 the Egyptians seized the assets and the Canal was again closed. It was closed after the Israeli War of 1967 until 1975. This long closure speeded the development of the long-distance super tanker. *See* EGYPT-24; WAGHORN.

SUFFOLK (The South Folk of the Angles) (1) The area had a considerable Romano-British agricultural population, but the only significant port was Dunwich (possibly called Sitomagus) which is now under the sea. When the E. Angles had settled the district, Dunwich became their bishopric. The E. Angles were, temperamentally or otherwise, isolated from the E. Saxons to their south and, if they built the Devil's Dyke, from inland tribes as well. It is uncertain when the North and South Folks were separated: Domesday deals with Norfolk and Suffolk separately, but for most fiscal purposes the two shires were administered together until Tudor times. The Danes dominated Suffolk in the late 9th and early 10th cents., but did not strongly colonise it. It was, however, the most densely populated shire except Middlesex.

(2) The shire was, by Domesday, divided into 24 hundreds. The seven western ones belonged to the Abbot of St. Edmundsbury from the 7th cent. and six others belonged to St. Etheldreda of Ely. These two liberties paid half the geld while the eleven geldable hundreds were proportionately assessed to the other half. The two Abbots were much the largest landowners, the next being the Crown and Robert Malet, but the Bigod family, beside holdings of its own, had the custody of some forfeited Crown land. In fact, the typical Suffolk land holder was a freeman of small estate. Suffolk contained 7460 of the 12,423 freemen mentioned in the whole of Domesday, besides 1060 socmen, and the proportion of cottars and villeins was less than half that normal elsewhere. The mere serfs were on the decline. Though many people's status was reduced by the Conquest, Suffolk remained an area with many relatively independent people, who needed an unusually large number of markets. There were seven (Beccles, Caramhall, Clare, Eye, Haverhill, Hoxne and Sudbury) and a fair at Aspall. The annual cloth fair at Bury St. Edmunds was of European dimensions and as Dunwich, mainly a fishing port, was destroyed by the sea, Ipswich, which had suffered severely during the Conquest, replaced it. By the 14th cent. Dunwich was virtually abandoned.

(3) The trade through Ipswich was carried mostly by Flemings and Dutchmen. It was initially confined to comestibles and wool in exchange for wine, groceries, tallow, pitch, salt, leather and iron, but cloth from Coggeshall, Colchester, Maldon and Sudbury became an increasingly valuable part, in exchange for Italian and Flemish fabrics and French and German cutlery.

(4) The weak governmental fabric left much to violence. Gorleston was regularly at war with Yarmouth. In 1335 a fleet of Harwich privateers blockaded Ipswich. The Abbot of Bury was often prevented from collecting his rents. The many Suffolk freemen with bargaining power after the Black Death (1346-7) were inevitably prominent in the Peasants' Revolt of 1381.

(5) The prosperity of the cloth industry expanded the towns, which needed food. The redistribution of land after the Dissolution of the Monasteries and the Elizabethan inclosures revolutionised Suffolk agriculture. Rents rose under the early Stuarts, but farming profits kept well ahead of them. All sections of the population benefited. The villages and private houses were rebuilt so that the county became famous for its domestic architecture.

(6) The importation of cheap oriental textiles and the industrial movement towards Pennine water power ended this prosperity soon after the Restoration. By the Napoleonic Wars depression was deep and the workhouses full, but the wars induced a prolonged, if artificial boom so that the largest population increase recorded in the 19th cent. took place between 1811 and 1821, whereas the arrival of cheap N. American grain led to the only recorded fall between 1851 and 1861. This rural depression continued, if interrupted by the two World Wars, into the 1950s when local industries began to develop.

SUFFOLK, Ds. of. *See* BRANDON; POLE.

SUFFOLK RESOLVES. *See* AMERICAN REBELLION-14.

SUFFRAGAN. A bishop in his capacity as the subordinate of another bishop or archbishop.

SUFFRAGETTES. *See* PANKHURST.

SUFFRAGISTS, RADICAL. *Ex post facto* term for Lancashire and Yorkshire women who disliked suffragette violence and favoured a trade union approach to womens' claims rather than through the N. Union of Women's Suffrage Societies.

SUGAR. The cane, an Asiatic plant from Bengal, was brought to Syria in Roman times and was much appreciated by the Crusaders who took it to Cyprus. It thrives in hot damp climates and was introduced by the Spaniards into the obviously suitable W. Indies and Guianas in the 16th cent., by the Portuguese into Brazil and by the English at Barbados in the 17th. Apart from crushing, which was done by windmills, production, especially harvesting, was labour intensive but the relevant climates were unsuitable for European drudges. On the other hand, the European markets for sugar and its derivatives, rum and molasses, were insatiable and the prospective profits, even after cooperage, an Atlantic crossing and the middlemen, were gigantic. It paid to cultivate on the widest scale and to incur risks and high expense to import black slaves, more inured to the climate, from Africa to America. There was a scramble in which Spaniards, English, French, Dutch and some others took part. The sugar islands frequently changed hands (*see* WEST INDIES) and were the objects of war and anxious diplomacy. Glasgow, Liverpool and Bristol owe their 18th cent. development to the profits of a transatlantic trade in which, with tobacco and slaves, sugar was a major component. By 1800 Britain consumed 15 times as much sugar as she had in 1700. Many great houses were built on the sugar trade, as were the fortunes of great (slightly later) Quaker confectionery businesses such as Fry's, Cadbury's and Rowntree. Everything was done to encourage the trade by discriminatory sugar duties and direct and indirect subsidies. The govt. supplied rum free to the lower decks of the Royal Navy (a huge organisation during most of that warlike century) and private shipowners found it necessary to do the same. Processed sugar was also an important re-export to continental, especially Baltic, areas engendering competition, especially with the French and Dutch, in which the windward position of the British Is. was an important factor.

The French wars from 1793 onwards made a radical change. Sugar beet was long known in W. Europe, but the extraction of solid sugar from it had only just been discovered. The British blockade raised cane sugar to famine prices on the continent. Beet sugar became profitable and acquired established markets which W. Indian sugar could not regain after 1815. Moreover the slave trade was being put down and slavery was to be abolished in the British W. Indies within a generation. The cane sugar industry experienced a set-back whose effects were diminished by the rapid 19th cent. rise of the British population. Marginal plantations had to diversify, for example, into bananas and coconuts, but despite fluctuations, W. Indian sugar maintained a hold on the British market until World War I. After 1920 there was a steady decline.

SUGAR ACT, 1764. *See* AMERICAN REBELLION-9.
SUGDEN, Edward Burtenshaw (1781-1875) 1st Ld. ST. LEONARDS (1852), a very learned lawyer, originally made his name by publishing legal treatises. In 1828 he became a Tory M.P. and in 1829 Sol-Gen. Professionally opposed to Brougham, whose manners and jobbing habits he disliked, he nevertheless recognised his legal abilities and they eventually became friends. From 1834 to 1855 and from 1841 to 1846 he was Ld. Chancellor of Ireland and in 1852 briefly of Great Britain. He continued thereafter very active in the judicial business of the Lords, whose legal standing and prestige he enhanced.
SUGER (?1081-1151), Abbot of St. Denis from 1122, friend and adviser of Louis VI and Louis VII of France. A diminutive fireball, he was an ecclesiastical and political reformer and popularised (if he did not invent) Gothic architecture. *See* CAPETIANS, EARLY; LOUIS VII.
SUICIDE or *FELO DE SE* (self felony) could not (obviously) be absolved and brought eternal damnation. Being a felony all property was forfeited, and nothing was payable under policies of life or endowment insurance. These effects could not be avoided by the previous creation of a trust, for a trust in contemplation of crime is void. Hence the family would inevitably be ruined. Murder, however, must be deliberate and so a verdict of death while the self-inflicter's mind was disturbed was not a verdict of *felo-de-se*. Verdicts thus depended on the jury's sympathy for the family. A suicide could not be buried in consecrated ground, but was often buried at a cross-road. A failed attempt, like any other attempted felony, was only a misdemeanour having no property effects. Efforts to decriminalise suicide were successfully resisted by insurance interests until after World War II.
SULLIVAN, Sir A. *See* GILBERT.
SULPHURIC ACID. The demand was first precipitated by the invention of Glaubers Salts, but production was complicated and expensive. In 1736 the quack Joshua Ward set up a factory at Twickenham and brought the price down by 95%. This stimulated demand and the invention of new substances and processes requiring it. In 1736 John Roebuck established an even more efficient factory at Birmingham and in 1739 at Prestonpans, which undercut Ward's price by 75% and by 1820 there were 23 factories in production and yet greater demand.
SULU. This Philippine sultanate was first attacked by the Spaniards in 1578 but continued to expand southwards and achieved a suzerainty over N. Borneo in the 17th cent. Spanish authority was established only in 1878,

when the Sultan granted Sabah to the British N. Borneo Co. Whether the grant was absolute or by way of lease has been in controversy ever since.
SULUNG, SULING or SOLIN (related to O.E. *SULH* = plough) was a Kentish unit of as much land as could be cultivated with a single plough team of 8 oxen (about 160 to 200 acres). It had defined boundaries and was usually continuous. It was about twice as large as a Mercian hide and being self-contained, usually had a name. A quarter-sulung was called a YOKE.
SULTAN or SOLDAN. Sultan was the title of a secular or military, usually Moslem, ruler especially of Turkey, Johore and Zanzibar. *Soldan,* the mediaeval form of the word, was used primarily of the ruler of Egypt.
SUMATRA. *See* INDONESIA.
SUMMER TIME (*see* WILLIAM WILLET) or **DAYLIGHT SAVING** was introduced in Britain in 1916 and became permanent from spring to autumn. In 1941 it applied all the year round, with double time in the summer. This continued until 1944 when the winter advance was abandoned. Double time continued in the summer until 1947. The Summer Time Act fixed a single hour from mid-Mar. to late Oct.
***SUMMIS DESIDERANTIBUS* (1484) (Lat = Amongst the most important factors)** Bull of Innocent VIII against witchcraft.
SUMNER. Two dissimilar brothers who were liberal prelates **(1) John Bird (1780-1862),** evangelical theologian, became Bp. of Chester in 1828, voted for R. Catholic relief in 1829 and for the Reform Bill in 1832. He was Abp. of Canterbury from 1848. **(2) Charles Richard (1790-1874)** had been tutor to the sons of the notorious Conynghams, who introduced him to George IV in 1820. He received a variety of court preferments, much to Ld. Liverpool's annoyance, but in 1826 became Bp. of Llandaff and Dean of St. Paul's and in 1827 Bp. of Winchester. He too voted for R. Catholic relief in 1829 which upset George IV. He was an excellent diocesan who built schools and churches. He also edited and translated Milton's *De Doctrina Christiana.*
SUN newspaper. *See* DAILY HERALD.
SUNDAY OBSERVANCE. The first English statute (1625) recites that "the true service of God ... in very many places hath been and now is profaned ... by a disorderly sort of people in exercising and frequenting bear baiting, bull baiting, interludes, common plays and other unlawful exercises and pastimes upon the Lord's Day and that many quarrels, bloodshed and other great inconveniences have grown by the resort and concourse of people going out of their own parishes to such disordered and unlawful exercises and pastimes ..." It forbade Sunday assemblies outside the parish for sports or pastimes and bear and bull baiting, interludes, common plays altogether. An Act of 1627 forbade carriers and drovers travelling and butchers slaughtering or selling on Sundays and awarded a third of the fine to the informer. Since cheerfulness kept creeping in, statutory prohibitions of this type together with awards to informers were extended by a number of later acts, e.g. in 1668, 1775, 1780; the Lord's Day Observance Society derived a substantial income from prosecutions until the Common Informers Act, 1951 abolished the informer's right to a share of the fine. *See* SABBATH BREAKING (SC.).
SUNDAY SCHOOLS, probably first opened by Methodists at High Wycombe in about 1770, soon spread through the advocacy of Robert Raikes and the *Gentleman's Magazine.* The idea attracted sensible or idealistic people everywhere and particularly employers, because children could acquire the rudiments of literacy yet work six days a week; Christians, because the Scriptures would be the vehicle of literacy; and parents, because they would have the children taken off their hands for part of their only day off. The SUNDAY SCHOOL SOCIETY, established in 1785, in 1803 developed into the SUNDAY SCHOOL

UNION. It ran schools through county committees composed equally of Anglicans and Nonconformists. By 1787 there were 250,000 pupils and the number volunteering to teach was so large that paid teachers became unnecessary. Immense sums were raised by voluntary contribution. Unfortunately the association of nonconformity with radicalism and the rise of the High Church Oxford Movement led to gradual Anglican withdrawal from the Society's committees. In 1843 the Anglican SUNDAY SCHOOL INSTITUTE was consequently founded. Sunday schools, however, continued to flourish and at pupil level were never entirely denominational. The movement was still active in 1914, but declined between the World Wars.

SUNDERLAND (*see* DURHAM-13) was part of the lands of a monastery founded by Benedict Biscop in 674 and known as MONKWEARMOUTH. Sunderland (i.e. the separate land) was on the other side of the R. Wear and was long identified with BISHOPSWEARMOUTH, the property since 930 of the Bishops of Durham. It acquired an episcopal charter in about 1190. The area was agricultural, but shipbuilding was practised and coal exported by the 14th cent. The charter privileges were increased by Bp. Thomas Morton in 1634. As Newcastle was Royalist and Sunderland Parliamentarian in the Civil War, the blockade diverted much of the trade to Sunderland, where it remained in conjunction with the coal trade. Consequently a body of harbour commissioners was set up in 1717 to improve the port. Modern shipyards were established in 1775 and developed rapidly in 1795. In 1796 the, for the period, enormous iron bridge was opened. Shipbuilding and coal remained the backbone of local life until the decline of both from the 1930s. Diversification into other industries only began in earnest in the 1960s.

SUNDERLAND. *See* GEORGE I-3; SPENCER.

SUNNA. *See* ISLAM.

SUNNINGDALE AGREEMENT (1973). An Anglo-Irish accord to create a power-sharing executive for Ulster and a Council of Ireland, but to maintain Ulster in the U.K. as long as a majority of its people so wished. The Executive was formed in Jan. 1974. As the protestants would always be in a minority on the Council, and within Ulster have to share official power with terrorists, they organised a strike which destroyed the arrangement by June. *See* PAISLEY, IAN.

SUNNIS. *See* CALIPHATE.

SUNNUD or SANAD was a formal grant or charter by an Indian ruler. It was often engraved on a silver or golden plate and was mostly concerned with the terms upon which the recipient should hold a country, or local fief. Most of the greater princes had Moghul *sunnuds. See* PARAMOUNTCY.

SUPERSEDEAS (**Lat: That you stay**). A writ staying the exercise of a jurisdiction or withdrawing a charter.

SUPERTAX, SURTAX. Supertax was first imposed in 1910 at a rate of 6d. in the pound on the top slice of incomes above £3000 provided that the taxpayer's total income exceeded £5000. It was raised in amount and lowered in threshold during and after World War I and in 1927 it was replaced by surtax. This was a graduated additional income tax upon income tax payers whose total income in any year exceeded a stated sum (in 1929 £2000). The combined effect of income and surtax was to tax high incomes at very high rates amounting, for example, throughout World War II to a tax of 97½% on layers of income above £20,000. Surtax and income tax were replaced in 1973 by a single graduated unified income tax though the graduations varied from budget to budget.

SUPPLICATION AGAINST THE ORDINARIES (1530) was a virulently-worded petition by the Commons against the abuses and partiality of the ecclesiastical courts and against legislation by convocation without Royal or parliamentary consent. There are several drafts by Thomas Cromwell. *See* SUBMISSION OF THE CLERGY.

SUPPLY, COMMISSIONERS OF (Scot.) were originally set up in each county by statute to collect the Land Tax. They included the sheriff, his substitute, the parliamentary representatives of the burghs and some landowners. Various administrative duties, e.g. the preparation of rolls of valuations and electors, the provision of court houses and prisons and the management of the police were imposed upon them. They were superseded by county councils in 1889.

SUPPLY, COMMITTEE OF. A committee of the whole House of Commons which before 1966 dealt with estimates. A similar committee dealt with Financial or Money Resolutions, without which any bill involving expenditure could not proceed beyond second reading.

SUPPLY, MINISTRY OF was set up in 1937 to ensure a proper flow of warlike supplies other than aircraft. It acquired the functions of the Ministry of Aircraft Production in 1946. It built up an immense fund of experience in industrial planning and control during World War II and its personnel therefore played a key role in the implementation of the Labour govt's. nationalisation programme after the war. Thereafter its functions were progressively dispersed among other departments, particularly the Board of Trade and the Ministry of Defence. In 1959 the title was changed to Ministry of Aviation, whose functions were transferred to the Ministry of Technology in 1967.

SUPREMACY, ACTS OF (1534) recited that the King ought to be supreme head of the English Church, that he had been so recognised by convocation and that "for corroboration and confirmation thereof" Parliament declared that he and his successors should be the only supreme head and, in effect (though not in form) the Crown should, in the govt. of the Church, step into the shoes of the Papacy. Henry VIII formally took the title of Supreme Head of the English Church in Jan. 1535. The Act was repealed under Mary in 1553.

(**1558**) repealed the repeal of 1553 but approached the position under the Act of 1534 only indirectly, by conferring all powers of ecclesiastical correction upon the Crown and requiring all holders of public and ecclesiastical offices to recognise the Queen as supreme Governor (not Head) by oath under penalty of loss of office. *See* ELIZABETH I; HENRY VIII.

SUPREME COURT OF JUDICATURE (ENGLAND). (**1**) The Judicature Act, 1873, was intended to consolidate eight separate courts into a single Supreme Court (in a number of divisions) with a Court of Appeal and to abolish the appellate jurisdiction of the House of Lords. It was amended to preserve the latter because otherwise there would have been no co-ordinating court of appeal for both English and Scots law.

(**2**) The new arrangements and amalgamations came into force as follows:

Old Court	New Division
Chancery	Chancery 1875
Queen's Bench	
Common Pleas	Queen's Bench 1880
Exchequer	
Admiralty	
Probate	Probate Divorce &
Divorce and	Admiralty (PDA) 1875
Matrimonial Causes	
London Court	
of Bankruptcy	Chancery 1883

(**3**) In 1971 the P.D.A. Division was dissolved, a new Family Division was created and business was reorganised as follows:

Matrimonial and domestic business from P.D.A. and Chancery to Family Division, Admiralty and Commercial to Queen's Bench, Contentious Probate to Chancery.

SURAJ-UD-DAULA (MIRZA MOHAMMAD). *See* BENGAL AND PLASSEY, B. OF.

SURAT (Gujarat, India), a substantial port when the Portuguese burned it in 1512 and 1530, was refortified by the local ruler in 1546 but stormed in 1573 by Mogul troops. Thereafter it became a great emporium, producing textiles and building ships and enjoying a rich seaborne trade in silks and gold with the Yemen (Mocha), Basra and Sumatra (Achin.). The Portuguese tried to control this trade from stations such as Goa or Hormuz along the main routes. The first English factory house in India was set up there in 1608. Surat declined after serious disturbances occurred in its hinterland, notably Maratha raids between 1664 and 1684, and the collapse of Mogul authority after 1707. Business began to move to Bombay, British since 1660, and the Turks closed the Basra trade in 1776. It passed to Britain in 1800, by which time it had ceased to be important. *See* EAST INDIA CO.-1,4.

SURBITON. *See* KINGSTON UPON THAMES.

SURCOUF, Robert (1773-1827), French slave trader, took to privateering in 1796 and until 1800 did much damage in the Bay of Bengal, where he took, among others, two of the largest East Indiamen, despite opposition from the French govt. of Ile de France. He came home and when the war was resumed in 1803 he fitted out privateers from St. Malo until 1807, when he went to the Indian Ocean again in his own ship. He returned in 1810 and continued his activities at St. Malo until the war ended. A romantic, almost heroic figure, his material influence on the naval war was slight.

SÛRETÉ. The French Criminal Investigation Department.

SURFEIT. *See* DYSENTERY.

SURGERY. (1) Primarily for amputations, was part of Roman military practice and used in Roman 3rd cent. hospitals. The latter, with Greek manuals, survived in the Eastern Empire and were organised by the invading Arabs. They and Greek speaking 11th cent. Sicilians accumulated some knowledge at Palermo, whence Constantine the African (?1010-87) brought his skill and clumsily translated Arabic texts to Salerno. Salerno was the foremost medical school in Europe until the end of the 13th cent. By this time the surgical and anatomical school at Bologna had been in existence for nearly a century; the Norman Henri de Mondeville (?1260-?1335) was trained there and in 1301 joined the school at Montpellier. The detailed observation of anatomy was strongly encouraged by the Renaissance artists, especially Dürer, Leonardo da Vinci, Michelangelo and Raphael. This led ultimately to the migration of Vesalius of Brussels (1514-64) to PADUA and the publication in 1543 of his revolutionary illustrated *De humani corporis fabrica* (Lat: Workings of the Human Body) and this, in its turn, influenced the French military surgeon Ambroise Paré (1510-90) and challenged the deductions hitherto blindly made from inaccurate observations of ancient authorities such as Galen.

(2) Though instruments of increasing elegance continued to be developed, surgery remained barbarous for the next 250 years, because without reliable anaesthetics, a patient could not be kept still and might succumb to shock, and without an understanding of sepsis he all too often died of unanticipated poisonous effects. Opium, mandrake, Indian hemp and hyoscamus were sometimes used as early as the 9th cent., as soporifics or sedatives, and alcohol was used with the advent of rum. James Esdaile (1808-59) often used hypnotism successfully on Indians, but could not make it work on Scots. The first operations under general anaesthetic (using ether) were performed by William Morton (1819-68) in the U.S.A. in Sept. 1846 and Robert

Liston (1794-1847) in London in Dec. Joseph (later Ld.) Lister (1827-1912) initiated his antiseptic technique in 1867 and instantly reduced his percentage of fatal amputations from 46% to 15%. Sir William Macewen (1848-1924) established the standard aseptic routine at Glasgow in 1879.

SURINAM. *See* GUIANA; GUYANA.

SURRENDER AND REGRANT, an important technical feature of English policy in Ireland (and also, earlier, in Wales) in late mediaeval and Tudor times. Under Celtic laws and custom, land was held for or by the clan, and the chiefs had rights only over their people and produce. Accordingly the feudal incidents did not apply and there was a strong clan interest in maintaining the clan's 'country'. If, however, the clan and its chief could be persuaded or bullied into surrendering the lands, these were then regranted to the chief (who usually became an earl or lord), who in turn subinfeudated to his clan sub-chiefs. This let in the feudal incidents and obligations, substituted individual for collective rights and so tended to break up the clan. The question whether a sufficient surrender had been made was often hotly disputed and many regranted territories were in practice re-occupied by partisans of the older custom. *See* FEUDALISM.

SURREY, Es. of. From 1088 to 1347 the title was held by the Warenne family, whence it descended to the FitzAlans from 1361 and thence to the Howard Ds. of Norfolk after 1483. Other Earls of Surrey were John Mowbray (1451-76) and Edward IV's second son, Richard (1477-?83). Richard II created his nephew Thomas de Holland D. of Surrey (1397-99).

SURREY (A.S. = southern district) was mostly wild in Roman and early Saxon times, so that the main settlements and most of the place names are Saxon. The word suggests that colonisation came from the north, i.e. Middlesex and the Thames Valley; the greatest ecclesiastical foundations, Chertsey Abbey (660, later Benedictine), Bermondsey (1082, Cluniac), Merton (1117, Augustinian) and Reigate (1220, Augustinian) were on or near the Thames, the Royal town of Kingston, where Wessex Kings were crowned, and the Royal manor of Sheen (later Richmond), were too. The rural area to the south was partly heath, later celebrated for bandits, or sheep runs in the area of Farnham, Godalming and Guildford which, in conjunction with the Nutfield fuller's earth developed a cloth trade. In the Weald there was smelting by charcoal made from the trees and since this was connected with gun founding, powder mills were established in the 16th cent. at such places as Albury, Chilworth and Godstone. There was also an ancient glass-making industry at Chiddingfold, which flourished down to 1914. The Wey was canalised in 1653 from Guildford to the Thames (*see* OATLANDS) and greatly simplified transport to London and this, together with 18th cent. inclosures, led to the development of a lucrative farming interest. Farnham was said to have been the biggest market in England outside London.

Canal extensions up to 1816 and the opening of railways after 1837 led to intense building at places such as Woking, Wimbledon and Caterham in the next 20 years.

Wandsworth, Brixton, Lambeth, Camberwell and Southwark became part of the County of London in 1889. The crescent of territory from Purley to Kingston became part of Greater London in 1965.

SURROGATE. A deputy appointed by an ecclesiastical (or sometimes other) authority to administer justice or legal procedure.

SURTEES, Robert Smith (1805-64), comic novelist, published the sketches of Mr. Jorrocks, the hunting grocer, from 1831 onwards. *Handley Cross* came out in 1843, *Ask Mamma* in 1858 and *Mr Facey Romford's*

Hounds in 1865. They enjoyed a huge Victorian and small enduring public.

SUSPENDING POWER. *See* BILL OF RIGHTS 1688; DISPENSATION.

SUSSEX (A.S. = South Saxons) was raided by AELLE and his sons in 477 and again in 485. He and CISSA stormed Anderida (Pevensey) in 491. The Kingdom, which they set up, was a string of coastal settlements from which pioneers slowly hacked their way northwards into the Weald. There was a war with Wessex in 607. When WILFRID (q.v.) arrived on a mission in 681 he found that the King, AETHELWALH, had been baptised and had acquired the I. of Wight and the Meon Valley through the influence of King Wulfhere of Mercia, but that the rest of the people were heathen. He based himself on Selsey, where he built and obtained endowments for a monastery. In 684 a South Saxon army was involved in a dynastic war in Kent and, probably as a result, Ceadwalla of Wessex invaded and subjugated Sussex in 685. Thereafter it was divided among a number of petty Kings, some of whom had ruled in the area about Hastings for a long time. The only unifying factor was the Church which established a bishopric at Selsey in 709, when King NUNNA or NOTHELM was described as a relative of King Ine of Wessex. Ine attacked in 722 and again in 725. By the time of the Mercian Offa, the Kings were in decline and the last seems to have been ALDWULF, who towards the end of Offa's reign called himself only an earl. The South Saxons finally submitted to Egbert of Wessex in 825 and thereafter were ruled through Royal nominees. The area was divided into five RAPES running from the coast to the northern edge and each included a port and a river. After the Norman Conquest these were allotted to trusted barons who built castles at Hastings, Pevensey, Lewes, Bramber and Arundel. A special liberty was also created for Battle Abbey; the bishopric was moved to Chichester and in about 1250 a sixth rape for Chichester was carved out of Arundel. The inland areas were hardly settled and the northern boundary was still indeterminate until the mid-13th cent.

The area mostly supported the Peasants' Revolt and also Jack Cade. Protestantism caught on in the Reformation and Puritanism later. It was Parliamentarian in the Civil War. It was divided into two administrative counties in 1888 and this arrangement, with some boundary revisions, was still extant in 1994.

Sussex has always maintained an obstinate identity symbolised by the pig symbol and the motto 'won't be druv'. *See* WEALD.

SUSSEX, D. of. *See* AUGUSTUS FREDERICK.

SUSSEX, ES. of. *See* RADCLIFFE.

SUTHERLAND (Norse = South land, i.e. south of Orkney), was with Caithness dominated in the early 11th cent. by the Es. of Orkney, one of whom, Thorfinn, was the grandson through his mother, of King Malcolm II. Orcadian rule lasted until the line of **William the Lion (r. 1165-1214).** He conquered the area and placed it under one **Hugh FRESKIN (?1214-22)** whose son **William,** became first E. in 1235. The family ruled in semi-independence until **William (?-?1370), 5th E.,** married Margaret, daughter of Robert the Bruce. After King David II died, the Es. resumed their autonomy until John, 9th E., died childless in 1514. His sister **Elizabeth (?-1535)** married **Adam GORDON** in 1515 and the title passed to her Gordon descendents. Adam was the second son of the E. of Huntly and the family's history was thereafter much entangled with that of the Gordons until **John (1609-79) 14th E.,** a Covenanter who fought Montrose at Auldearn in 1645. His grandson **John (1661-1733) 16th E.** supported the revolution of 1688 and the union of 1707 and as the King's Lieut. in the six northern counties vigorously put down the Jacobites in 1715. His grandson **William (1708-50) 17th E.** did likewise in 1745. When **William (1735-66) 18th E.** died, the

earldom passed to his daughter **Elizabeth (1765-1839).** In 1785 she married **George Granville LEVESON-GOWER (1758-1833)** who became the 2nd M. of Stafford in 1803 as well as **19th E.** in right of his wife. He evicted many thousands of tenants from the interior so as to convert it into sheep runs and settled them in new coastal villages where they were to live on fishing and kelp burning. These *Sutherland Clearances* provoked bitterness and criticism at the time; the new alkali industry superseded kelp and the potato famine of 1846 completed the ruin of these people. George meantime had inherited the D. of Bridgwater's fortune and spent much money on improving the roads and attempting to prevent emigration. He became **1st D. of Sutherland** in 1833.

The county has always been backward, only about 2% of the land being arable, so that there was some economic justification for the clearances. In the 20th cent. forestry has helped to diversify the means of livelihood. *See* LEVESON-GOWER.

SUTTEE (Hindi = good wife) was an Indian widow who was burned alive with her dead husband or in expectation of his death in battle. It was an ancient practice in high caste Hindu families, particularly the Rajputs and Bengali Brahmins. It was supposed to be voluntary, but in places such as Bengal where widows inherited the property, heavy family pressure was often exerted and very slight gestures interpreted as acquiescence. Escapes and rescues were not uncommon. The Moguls tried to suppress it and so, from 1829, did the British, neither with complete success.

SUTTON (London). The Oaks, an estate belonging to the Es. of Derby, gave its name to the race of that title first held at Epsom nearby in 1779. The Derby was first run in 1780. The place was a borough from 1934 until it was amalgamated with Cheam, Beddington, Wallington and Carshalton to form the London Borough of Sutton in 1964.

SUTTON, Sir Richard (?-1524) made an early fortune in the law, together with William Smith, Bp. of Lincoln, endowed Brasenose College, Oxford (1508-23) and probably contributed to Corpus Christi College, Oxford, in 1516.

SUTTON, Sir Richard (1798-1855) 2nd Bt., one of the fabulously rich Suttons, devoted himself to fox hunting as Master of the Burton from 1822 and of the Quorn (whose expenses he bore) from 1848.

SUTTON, Thomas (1532-1611), educated at Lincoln's Inn, used his opportunities as Surveyor of Ordnance in the North (1574-93) to obtain coal leases in Durham. From these mines he made a fortune shipping coal to London and this fortune he increased by marrying Elizabeth, the wealthy widow of his kinsman, John Dudley. He was reckoned the richest commoner in England and gave liberally to London charities. Just before his death he bought the old Charterhouse and endowed it as the famous Hospital and School.

SUTTON HOO (Suffolk). In 1939 an Anglo-Saxon Royal ship burial was uncovered here. The King's body was not found, but the grave is attributed through Merovingian coins to the period 650 to 670 and was probably erected for Aethelhere who was killed, very likely by drowning, at the B. of Winwaedsfield nearby in 654. The grave goods are of unexampled splendour and include many gold cloisonnee ornaments and fittings, an immense Byzantine silver tray and other silver objects, some of Levantine make.

SUZERAINTY is a type of overlordship in which the inferior lord usually owes a duty of assistance or non-injury and of deference and sometimes pays tribute to the superior, but the latter has no right to interfere habitually in the internal govt. of the inferior's territory, or to entertain appeals from his subjects. It is essentially a relationship between powerful states. The determination of Edward I to convert his suzerainty over Scotland into something more active provoked the Scottish War of Independence.

Turkish suzerainty over the Barbary States (other than Morocco) complicated Mediterranean politics from about 1600 to 1914. British PARAMOUNTCY over the Indian princely states (q.v.) amounted, even in the case of the largest, to more than mere suzerainty, because a British resident or agent at the court of the local ruler could tender advice in the interest of the British govt. and he, if not always legally obliged, usually had to comply with it in general terms. Paramountcy was based upon the theory that a ruler's powers could be forfeited for misgovernment. Suzerainty was not so based and, significantly, only suzerainty was claimed over border states like Bhutan.

SWABIAN LEAGUES. The first Towns League lasted from 1331 to 1372; the Knights or Schiegler League from 1366 to 1395; the second Towns League from 1376 to 1388. The great Swabian League of 1488 was a power of European importance organised by the Emperor Frederick III and included 22 cities, the Knights and local prelates, the Electors of the Palatinate, Mainz and Trier and later Baden, Hesse, Bavaria, Ansbach and Bayreuth. It controlled the Rhine trade, had a constitution and a standing army and was the foundation of Habsburg power in S. Germany. It suppressed the Rhenish knights in 1523 and the Peasants' Revolt of 1524. It split on religious lines in 1534 and broke up.

SWADESHI **(Bengali = patriotic)** was a Hindu political movement provoked by the partition, in 1905, of Bengal. It spread to other provinces and adopted, as a primary tactic, the encouragement of Indian-made goods, especially cloth. Since these were more expensive than those imported, it took to picketing shops, boycotting dealers, burning foreign goods and other violence. The movement undoubtedly stimulated Indian industry, especially the Tata metals complex, but it split the Indian National Congress at Surat in 1907 because the moderates distinguished between the promotion of the Indian economy and the use of boycotts and other methods to redress Bengali grievances, while the extremists favoured the use of both tactics to further the cause of Indian self govt. *See* YUGANTAR.

SWAFFHEARD of ESSEX. *See* KENT, KINGDGM-4.

SWAN, Sir Joseph Wilson (1828-1914), one of the most important inventors of modern times. In photography he developed the collodion process, invented autotype and the modern bromides. He invented also the original electric light bulb and the appropriate method of making filaments by extrusion and so originated the processes for making artificial silk, nylon, etc.

SWANIMOTE. *See* FOREST-3.

SWANSEA (A.S. SWEYNSEY = Sweyns I.; Welsh = ABERTAWE). The English name is thought to refer to King Sweyn Forkbeard. Henry of Beaumont or Newburgh built a castle in the 11th cent. and the town grew up around it. There was a market charter c. 1180 and an incorporation by King John in 1215. The Welsh name is first recorded at about this time. A charter of 1306 granted lumber rights for shipbuilding. There was already some surface coal working.

The shipbuilding industry and the port grew in importance, but slowly, until the opening of the Llansamlet coalmines in the 18th cent. stimulated an older copper smelting industry. The coal supply was much improved by a canal, which in its turn resulted in large scale harbour improvements (1789-91). The canal by 1798 served the whole coal valley and the city grew steadily, especially after the establishment of the enormous maritime demand for anthracite, of which Swansea had a virtual monopoly. Copper, steel and tinplate industries followed in their wake at the end of the 19th cent. and to some extent offset the fall in demand for coal, which resulted from the naval changeover to oil.

SWAZI-LAND (Africa). This tribe settled between the Pongola and the Great Usutu rivers in the 16th cent., but in the time of **King Sobhuza I (r?-1836)** the Zulus drove them north to the Little Usutu and his successor **Mswazi II,** was driven still further north. In 1846 he ceded land north of the Crocodile R. to the Lydenburg Republic and also sought British aid against the Zulus. The Boers got further concessions in 1855 and 1875, but were then halted by the annexation of the Transvaaal (1877) and the Pretoria and London Conventions (1881 and 1884), which affirmed Swazi independence. When gold was found on the Rand, Kruger planned a direct outlet to the sea. Swaziland was the only area south of Portuguese Mozambique not in British hands and Boer farmers and prospectors overran the country. The British in 1888 set up a protectorate to prevent further breaches of the Conventions and in 1890 established Anglo-Boer joint administration. This lapsed with the Boer War and from 1903 the country was under the Transvaal govt., but with British protected status. In 1968 it became an independent member of the British Commonwealth.

SWEATED LABOUR is apt to occur where the state ignores the condition of a mass of unskilled, uneducated and unorganised labour subject to management heedless of humanity. The first British inquiry by a select committee of the House of Lords, reported in 1890 on conditions among bootmakers, certain types of garment makers and leather workers, dock labour, chain makers, cutlers and hardware workers. It found that work was monotonous, excessive and grossly underpaid and that working and related living conditions were insanitary or otherwise injurious. The report eventually bore fruit in the Trade Boards Act, 1909, which created wage fixing boards for certain specified industries namely wholesale tailoring, boxing, lacing, and chain making. The scope of the Act was extended in 1918 to any trade where the Ministry of Labour thought that machinery for wage regulation was ineffective, and in 1922 there were 44 British and 19 Irish Boards. Supervening depressions and World War II prevented further extensions and in 1945 their functions were transferred to Wages Councils.

SWEATING SICKNESS (ENGLISH). There were violent epidemics in England and Scotland attacking mainly men in their prime, but never children or old people. Ireland was not affected and Europe only once. There were five visitations each lasting about four months and associated with heavy rains. The first was in 1486; the next three in 1507, 1518 and 1529 all began in London, that of 1529 spreading to northern Europe. The last began at Shrewsbury in 1551. A noticeable proportion of those who died were persons of consequence. An 18th-19th cent. variety known as the PICARD SWEAT was rife in France and Italy, but apparently never reached England. *See* EPIDEMICS, HUMAN.

SWEDEN. *See passim* BALTIC; HANSE; VIKINGS.

SWEIN (?-1052) E., son of Godwin. *See* EDWARD THE CONFESSOR-6.

SWEIN FORKBEARD, King of the DANES (r. 986-1014). *See* ETHELRED THE UNREADY; VIKINGS-19-25.

SWETTENHAM, Sir Frank (1851-1946), pioneered British influence in Perak and Selangor (Malaya) (*see* PANGKOR ENGAGEMENT) from 1874 to 1896, became Resident-Gen. at Kuala Lumpur in 1896 and established the Federated Malay States; he was Gov. of the Straits Settlements and High Commissioner to the Malay States from 1901 to 1904 and as such secured the abrogation of Siamese suzerainty over Kedali, Kelantan, Patani and Trengganu in 1902.

SWIFT, Jonathan (1667-1745), Irish and educated in Ireland, came to England in 1689 and became sec. to Sir William Temple (c. 1692) and through him met most influential people from William III downwards. His outspokenness probably hindered the promotion which his abilities would have justified and in 1694 he was ordained and given a minor Irish prebend. From 1696 to

1699 he was again in Temple's service and met 'Stella' (Esther Johnson). In 1699 he became a prebendary of St. Patrick's, Dublin, and in 1701 published his first (pro-Whig) political pamphlet. He visited London in 1705 and 1707 when he became acquainted with the Kitcat Club. He also negotiated for some of Queen Anne's Bounty for the Irish Church; but in 1708 he published an attack on the Irish Presbyterians and by 1710 he could stand the Whig-Dissenter alliance no longer and joined the Tories. He published attacks on the govt. in the Tory *Examiner* in 1710 and 1711 when he also wrote the *Conduct of the Allies*. Intimate with Tory ministers, in 1713 he became Dean of St. Patrick's and one of their ablest propagandists. In 1715, after they had fallen, he retired to Ireland and devoted himself largely to the welfare of the Dublin poor. He published *Draper's Letters* (an attack on Wood's halfpence) in 1724 and *Gulliver's Travels* in 1726. He remained for the rest of his life in regular correspondence with ministers and never failed to urge the case for fair treatment for Ireland. He spent a third of his income to relieve distress and saved another third to endow St. Patrick's Hospital. The Irish adored him.

SWINBURNE, Algernon Charles (1837-1909) learned and poetic champion of political individualism, suffered from epilepsy after 1862 and lived in seclusion with Theodore Watts-Dunton after 1879.

SWINDON (Wilts.) grew up round the Great Western Railway workshops built in 1841 at the junction of the S. Wales and W. of England lines. The post-World War II shrinkage of the railways led to the decline of the workshops and to industrial diversification after 1952.

SWING RIOTERS (1830) were agricultural Luddites reacting to economic change, unemployment and the bad harvest of 1829. Preceded by warning letters signed 'Captain Swing' they smashed machines and burned barns and ricks, beginning in Kent and spreading as far as Dorset and Wiltshire and into the midlands and E. Anglia between June and Nov. They were not wholly spontaneous but were not directed. 19 poor people were hanged and 1149 transported or imprisoned. *See* THRESHING MACHINES.

SWITHIN or SWITHUN, St. (?-862), a counsellor of Egbert and Ethelwulf of Wessex, he became Bp. of Winchester in 852. It is said that the weather on his feast day (15 July) will hold for the next 40 days. Hence he is sometimes considered to be the patron saint of the English climate. The great Cathedral at Winchester is dedicated to him. *See* PILGRIM'S WAY.

SWITZERLAND (locally SCHWEIZ, SUISSE or SVIZZERA) has long exerted great influence through its strategic and tactical advantages, financial acumen concentration on limited objectives, and willingness to shelter powerful ideas.

(1) *Formation of the Nucleus*. This stagnant area of peasants and shepherds was first dragged into European politics by German ambitions in Italy and the opening of the St. Gotthard. In the incessant bargaining of imperial politics, bailiwicks were often sold to feudatories and the peasants then had no local official protector against oppressive lords. Peasant guilds conspired in self-defence. Their ability to close the pass embarrassed imperial policies. By this means URI, in 1231, and SCHWYZ and UNTERWALDEN in 1240 obtained charters of self-govt. These constituted the THREE FOREST STATES, whose existence portended social revolution as well as independence.

(2) In 1291 the northern Swiss towns, aided by Uri and Schwyz, staged a successful revolt against the Habsburgs. Anticipating retaliation, the Three signed an EVERLASTING LEAGUE for military support and mutual arbitration. In Nov. 1315 they routed the first major Habsburg attack in the Pass of Morgarten.

(3) *City Participation*. This brought revolution in Lucerne which adhered to the League, henceforth called

the FOUR FOREST STATES. Meanwhile in BERNE and ZÜRICH, patrician families with artisan support had established new institutions and were fighting the Austrian supported feudatories. The latter were overthrown in 1339 at Laupen by a force from Berne and the Four States.

(4) In 1351 Zürich made an alliance with the Four States, who guaranteed her internal constitution. This treaty defined the five parties' spheres of influence as extending well beyond their own confines and was taken as a *casus belli* by the Habsburgs. In the ensuing war the latter were expelled from GLARUS, which in 1352 entered an Everlasting League with Zürich and the Three Forest States. ZUG also signed a League with Zürich and the Four.

(5) Bernese social policy differed from that of the others; the patrician govt. sought to establish an internal oligarchy, which the men of Unterwalden tried to subvert. But both sides feared the Habsburgs more than each other. The League of 1353 between Berne and the Three Forest States was essentially a treaty of territorial guarantee. This completed the LEAGUE OF EIGHT PLACES. Established only by partial treaties, it had no common fund, constitution, legislature, army or capital and the cities reserved the right to enter foreign alliances. It was, however, kept together by outside pressure and a habit of arbitration and regular conference. The members called themselves EIDGENOSSEN (= Sworn Friends, hence *Huguenots*), but externally, because of the military prowess of the men of Schwyz, they became known as SWISS.

(6) *Outward Extension*. In 1370 the states agreed to exclude the jurisdiction of foreign (i.e. Austrian influenced) ecclesiastical courts (*cf Praemunire*) and to outlaw unauthorised mercenary expeditions. The age of the Swiss mercenary was about to begin. Foreign policy, however, tended to be conducted by the Cities. The Swabian Towns and their surrounding nobility were in conflict.

(7) Between 1370 and 1500 the League gradually expanded by accretions, accessions and aggression to the areas now forming it and in 1500 Austria abdicated any claims which she had and with the promotion of Appenzell to full membership in 1513, the "old confederation" was complete. Officially called the THIRTEEN RULING PLACES, it comprised, with them, five distinct classes of territory. There were subject lands and the *common sovereignties*. Neuchatel, the Abbey and City of St. Gallen, Valais and, later, the Bp. of Basel and the City of Geneva became Dependent Places, internally autonomous but under various forms of protection; The Grisons, known as a Dependency, occasionally acted independently. The stability of the confederation depended upon the observance of the STANS ENGAGEMENT to uphold each other's constitutions, and a French alliance. The Reformation shook both.

(8) *The Reformation*. Anti-clericalism began early in Switzerland; several bishops had been driven out before Luther published his theses in 1519. Basel had become an European centre of humanism under Erasmus, Reuchlin and Zwingli. Ulrich Zwingli (1484-1531), as field chaplain in Italy had been horrified by the fundamental baseness of Swiss activities. He entered public life as a politician in Zürich and campaigned successfully against the French alliance. Converted by Luther's manifesto, by 1523 he had established Protestantism in Zürich. Meanwhile the printing presses at Basel were flooding Middle Europe with Lutheran tracts. By 1529 Berne, Basel, Zürich, Schaffhausen and some other small places had become Protestant by political resolution. The Forest States, however, held to the Old Religion, but, since religion was still regarded as a matter for authority, the religious future of the Common Sovereignties was bitterly disputed. The Confederacy was divided into Protestant and R. Catholic unions which fought each other and hired mercenaries to rival European powers. City Protestantism was connected with bourgeois liberties against the episcopal jurisdictions to which the townsmen laid claim. One such quarrel had world-wide consequences. Geneva rose against its Savoyard bps. The Bernese intervened. By 1536 they had established the Reformation in Geneva. The way was open for the rise of Calvin.

(9) Throughout the 16th cent. Switzerland was a political vacuum in which the Catholic states counterbalanced the Protestant majority by Habsburg alliances, and French protection was rendered nugatory by the Wars of Religion. Only the preoccupations of powerful neighbours prevented foreign invasion. This could not last.

(10) *The Thirty Years' War and Neutrality.* In the Thirty Years' War the R. Catholic states gave passage to Spanish troops, but the re-establishment of French Crown authority made France dangerous again. The French gained rights of passage through the Protestant states. The imminent disruption of the League was too serious a matter and in 1647 the first federal military arrangements (THE DEFENSIONALE OF WILS) were set up to defend it against all comers. Switzerland, if not the Grisons, had escaped a war which devastated much of central Europe.

(11) Swiss independence received formal recognition in the P. of Westphalia (1648), but the reality depended on European exhaustion and the Swiss military reputation. France was soon exerting, under Louis XIV, great influence. French money and pensions and commercial privileges at Lyons dragged the Confederacy into the French political and economic orbit. In 1663 all the states signed a treaty at Paris. This nullified the alliance of the older states with the Habsburgs and prevented their intervention when France seized the Franche Comté in 1674 and Strassburg in 1681.

(12) France now marched with Switzerland from Basel to Geneva and French power extended to Milan. Only in 1707 was further encroachment prevented: Berne defended NEUCHATEL, whose dynasty had died out, and persuaded the local assembly to elect the King of Prussia as its prince instead. The French, now involved in the War of the Spanish Succession, avoided a conflict. Swiss disunion, however, prevented other effective action and actually broke out in a minor civil war. Independence was saved by the P. of Utrecht (1713) which transferred Milan from French to Austrian rule. The weak and divided Confederacy maintained its autonomy by the tolerance of its neighbours.

(13) *Collapse.* The French Revolution brought division. In 1792 the Swiss Guard was massacred, all Swiss troops were sent home without their pay and Swiss commercial privileges were abolished. A war party at Berne favoured the defence of treaty rights. Its influence was nullified by neutralists at Basel and Zürich, but meantime a third or revolutionary party was growing up in the subject territories, especially in Vaud, and at Basel too. The French exploited this. In 1797 they seized the Valtelline from the Grisons and annexed it to their Cisalpine Republic and in the same year the well-known Vaudois exile Frederic La Harpe (1754-1838) submitted a petition to Paris from Vaudois malcontents. Bonaparte was rapturously welcomed on a journey through Switzerland and the Basel revolutionary Peter Ochs (1752-1821) was invited to Paris and persuaded to draft a Swiss unitary constitution. He fell into the trap. In Jan. 1798 French troops crossed the Jura to 'liberate' the Vaudois. The strategic defiles once in their hands, the conquest commenced in earnest. By Mar. it was complete. Switzerland became the HELVETIC REPUBLIC, looted of its assets and bound hand and foot to the French state, whose main purpose was to control the two great military routes by way of L. Constance to S. Germany and to avoid the British fleet by way of the Valais towards Lombardy and the Adriatic.

(14) The country now became a scene of European conflict, for France's opponents sought to block these routes, vital to France since Britain dominated the Mediterranean after the B. of the Nile. In 1799 Austrian and Russian armies fought the French at Zürich and were driven out. Until the fall of Bonaparte in 1814 the Helvetic Republic was a French client state. Its future was thus at the disposal of the victors.

(15) *The Modern Federation.* It was mainly the Czar Alexander who secured Swiss independence and neutrality, probably because La Harpe had once been a tutor at the Czarist Court. The powers refused to countenance the reduction of the subject territories to their previous inferiority; they, together with the old ruling places, numbered 22 and all were equally represented at the LONG SESSION which eventually concluded the FEDERAL PACT of 7 Aug. 1815. The 22 states took the French title of CANTONS and were recognised as sovereign, but they signed a single document establishing a federal administration and army. The modern constitution developed by fits and starts from this treaty, the most important stage being the adoption of the formal federal constitution of 1848. This recognised 25 states, of which six were and are half-Cantons. A 26th was created in the Jura after World War II.

(16) *International Influence and Status.* The Swiss understood that their neutrality could survive only if infringement was more inconvenient than respect. They established a powerful citizen conscript army to defend their formidable mountains, while creating international vested interests in local peace. BANKING with political objects had begun at Zürich as early as 1772, when the Bank Leu was set up to influence foreign govts., and in the 19th cent. Zürich was a ready refuge for foreign capital. In 1863 Henri Dunant, who had witnessed the carnage at Solferino in 1859, established the INTERNATIONAL RED CROSS at Geneva with the aid of the Swiss army. Between 1872 and 1906 the great (and easily closed) trunk railways over St. Gotthard and the Simplon and towards the Arlberg were completed. These routes were better and cheaper than the French and Austrian routes to the east and west. They practically guaranteed Swiss neutrality in the World Wars, particularly the second.

(17) In pursuit of similar objects the LEAGUE OF NATIONS, created by the T. of Versailles (1919) was established in 1920 with its headquarters at Geneva along with the INTERNATIONAL LABOUR OFFICE, and Swiss diplomacy championed the admission of the defeated powers to the League.

A further vital step in the policy of neutrality for a country devoid of minerals was the development of hydro-electricity. This was completed by 1935.

SWORD, KNIGHTS OF THE. *See* BALTIC-10-17.

SWYNFORD, Katherine. *See* BEAUFORT.

SYDNEY (Aust.) (previously PORT JACKSON) was founded by Gov. Phillip in 1788 and until 1833 the small population consisted mostly of serving and released convicts. By 1842 a sufficient free commercial life had developed for a council to be created and the Australian gold rush led to an enormous expansion. The population rose 10-fold by 1861 to 95,000, to 380,000 by 1891 and to over 4m by 1931. Capital of N.S.W., it was also the capital of Australia until 1927. The famous bridge was opened in 1932 and the remarkable Opera House in 1973.

SYDNEY, alternative spelling for SIDNEY.

SYDNEY. *See* TOWNSHEND-10.

SYKES. Of this varied family (1) **Sir Mark, 3rd Bt. (1771-1823)** was a famous book collector. His brother (2) **Sir Tatton, (4th Bt. 1772-1873)** was a boxer, breeder of sheep, racehorse owner and for 40 years, M.F.H. (3) **Sir Mark, (6th Bt. 1879-1919)** travelled the Levant, was a Tory M.P. and signed the **Sykes-Picot Agreement** (*see*

SYRIA-3). From 1916 he was Chief Near Eastern Adviser to the Foreign Office. He contrived to favour both Arab Independence and Zionism.

SYKES, Sir Frederick Hugh (1877-1954) commanded the military wing of the Royal Flying Corps (R.F.C.) in 1912 and in 1914 was succeeded by Trenchard. They disliked each other. Sykes became C-of-Staff to the R.F.C. in France but after various intrigues was sent to command the Royal Naval Air Service in the E. Mediterranean, which included Gallipoli. Highly successful, he returned to England and was employed in a series of military staff appointments. When Trenchard quarrelled with Rothermere and resigned (Apr. 1918) Sykes succeeded him as Chief of the Air Staff. Like Trenchard he believed in an independent air force, but Churchill, who became Sec. of State in Jan. 1919, thought his plans too expensive, consulted Trenchard behind his back and eventually superseded him with Trenchard. He then became Controller of Civil Aviation, which involved resigning from the R.A.F. but, dissatisfied with aviation policy, resigned in 1922 and also refused the Governorship of S. Australia. From 1922 to 1928 he was a Conservative M.P. and from 1923 to 1927 Chairman of the Broadcasting Board. He then accepted the Governorship of Bombay, in circumstances of civil disobedience, industrial unrest and financial difficulty He was an effective conciliator, though he preferred stronger methods which were not authorised until 1932. By this time the civil disobedience campaign was losing its momentum. Sykes believed that these troubles originated in social deprivation and economic depression to which he now gave vigorous and effective attention. He was, however, replaced in 1933 and from 1934 to 1946 he was Chairman of the Miners' Welfare Commission. From 1940 to 1945 he was an M.P. again.

SYKES-PICOT AGREEMENT. See SYRIA-3.

SYLLABUS, PAPAL. Two lists, published respectively in 1864 by Pius IX and in 1907 by Pius X, of heresies and errors condemned by the Papacy.

SYLVESTER II (?-1003) Pope (999), originally Gerbert of Aurillac, confessor to the Emperor Otto III and an experimental scientist. See CAPETIANS or ROBERTINES, EARLY 6-7; CLOCKS.

SYNDICALISM is a programme for replacing capitalism by autonomous working groups in control of production units such as factories and farms. This was to be achieved through direct industrial action. It was closer to anarchism than to socialism, inasmuch as it was not intended to seize control of the state and impose the programme through a dictatorship. The movement flourished in France and other Latin countries between 1900 and 1914 and again in France in the 1970s. Though it hardly influenced British socialists and trade unionists, there were signs in the 1970s that it was favoured by some Liberals. In the course of the Tory privatisations of the 1990s workers' and management buy-outs amounted to a form of syndicalism.

SYNOD (1) A CHURCH COUNCIL is an assembly of the highest clergy of an entire church or several. A synod is an assembly of the clergy of part of one. In modern R. Catholic practice such assemblies must be summoned by the chief bishop concerned and its acts must be confirmed by him. This was not always so. Many of the earlier ones were summoned by the chief lay ruler; and laymen often played leading and sometimes dominant roles, e.g. the First Council of Constantinople (381) was convoked by the Emperor Theodosius; King Oswy not only convened the Synod of Whitby (664), but made the major decisions. **(2)** In the Presbyterian churches a synod is the authority above the presbyteries and consists of ministers and elders representing them. **(3)** The GENERAL SYNOD OF THE CHURCH OF ENGLAND is the legislative body of the church which replaced the Church Assembly. Its proceedings are parliamentary in form.

SYNODUS. See WITAN.

SYON HOUSE. A 15th cent. nunnery converted by the Protector Somerset into a mansion between 1548 and 1551. Robert Adam began rebuilding it in 1762 for Hugh Smithson, D. of Northumberland. The grounds are by Capability Brown.

SYPHILIS or SIBBENS (otherwise called (Sc.) GRANDGORE, POX, SPANISH SICKNESS, SICKNESS OF NAPLES, FRENCH DISEASE) and YAWS. Syphilis and Yaws are caused by the same spirochete, Yaws being communicated through the skin by contact with a sufferer, Syphilis through the genitals. Both have been widely and anciently endemic. It seems that Yaws, often mistaken for leprosy, was common in Europe before the mid-14th cent., possibly because of nocturnal huddling for winter warmth, but that the onset of a cold period led to people wearing more clothes, with better heating and less habitual naked contact. Hence Yaws virtually died out, but the spirochete reappeared as syphilis in an outbreak which began in France in 1488, passed to Spain in 1493 and to Italy *via* Naples in 1494. It reached England in 1496 and Scotland in 1497. It remained an alarming European epidemic until about 1520 and was soon imported into America. Thereafter the incidence fell for a century, but there were renewed epidemics in the second half of the 17th cent., Scotland, in particular, being reinfected by Cromwellian troops. It remained endemic from about 1720, but was definitively distinguished from gonorrhoea in 1905. Salvarsan, the most effective cure, was invented in 1909. *See* EPIDEMICS, HUMAN; VENEREAL DISEASES.

SYRIA. *See* CRUSADE; OUTREMER; PALESTINE; JORDAN. **(1)** After the collapse of Outremer in 1291, Syria formed part of the Mameluke state of Egypt and enjoyed prosperity and the benefits of Venetian trade until 1401 when the Mongols under Tamerlane devastated it. Mameluke rule continued until the Ottoman conquest in 1516 when it was separated from Egypt and organised into the four provinces of Damascus, Aleppo, Tripoli and Saida. The local semi-independent religious minorities were simply watched and not molested unless they failed to pay their taxes. The Turks encouraged agriculture and the manufactories and marts at Aleppo and Tripoli had trading connections with Europe mostly through Venice. This prosperous condition declined after 1690, when the system of govt. broke down and lawless troops and uncontrolled Bedouin levied exactions on all productive activity, which declined. European trade disappeared. By about 1720, however, order, if not prosperity, was restored through the rise of a number of local hereditary rulers, notably the Azm family at Damascus, who behaved independently but were loyal to the Ottoman govt. It was one of these, Ahmed-al-Jezzar (1775-1804), Bosnian Pasha of Saida, who with British help held Acre against Bonaparte in 1799. This state of semi-feudal administrative fragmentation continued until 1831, when Mehemet Ali, Pasha of Egypt, sent his son Ibrahim to conquer the country. European disquiet over the growth of Egyptian power at Turkish expense brought Franco-Anglo-Austrian intervention in 1840; and Egypt was compelled to return Syria to Ottoman rule.

(2) The new Ottoman system of taxation and military conscription conflicted with older ideas; there was a power struggle between Druzes and Maronites in Mount Lebanon; European manufactured goods put local craftsmen out of work and raised the status of the merchants and bankers; and R. Catholic and orthodox minorities began to look respectively to France and Russia for protection. In 1860 violent disorder led to massacres of Christians which the Ottoman govt. suppressed. The French sent troops and a western commission persuaded the govt. to convert Mount Lebanon into a separate administration. Thereafter there was a steadily rising prosperity encouraged by railway building, but the population outpaced resources and emigration began.

(3) The Young Turk revolution of 1908 brought a fundamental change from an Islamic state to a Turkish nationalistic one. The result was Arab counter-nationalism and Christian localism, as well as Jewish aspirations in Palestine. These disruptive tendencies were naturally encouraged by the Allies in World War I and the Sykes-Picot Agreement (1916) divided Syria between British and French spheres. This resulted, against Arab wishes, in territorial division between French Syria, which was divided into four states under French mandate and the British mandates of PALESTINE and TRANSJORDAN (q.v.).

(4) In French Syria there was a Druze revolt from 1923 to 1927 and a Lebanese Republic was set up in 1926. There was local agreement in 1932 to set up a Syrian state as a republic incorporating the other three states, but France did not ratify it and when World War II broke out, the French took steps to ensure their own supremacy in the whole area. Hence when France surrendered in 1940, French Syria became an appendage of the Vichy govt. and a threat to the British position in the Middle East. British and Free French forces occupied it in 1941 and in Feb. 1942 the British recognised at least the potential independence of Syria and Lebanon. The Free French, however, did not, and combined Arab-British pressure was needed before they did so in Mar. 1943. Even then the French would not transfer their powers and it took a Lebanese general strike in 1943 to make them see reason. In 1945 there were clashes, a bombardment of Damascus and British intervention, leading to complete independence of both countries.

(5) Political confusion led to a series of military dictatorships from 1949 until 1958, when until 1961 there was an ineffectual union with Egypt. In Lebanon a single govt. under Bishara al Khoury, based on Maronite and Sunni co-operation, ruled from 1943 to 1952 when a general strike forced its resignation in favour of Camille Chamoun. The 1958 crisis, however, did not lead to union with Egypt but, with U.S. intervention, in the creation, after local fighting, of a compromise regime under Gen. Shehab. This lasted until 1964, since when the Lebanon has been in confusion caused by Israeli and Syrian intrigues.

T

TAAFFE. This Irish-Austrian family, descended from a Welsh follower of Strongbow, settled in Co. Louth. **(1) Sir William (?-1627)** was protestant sheriff of Sligo. An active commander against Irish rebels and the Spaniards (at Kinsale in 1601) he was well rewarded with confiscated estates. His grandson **(2) Theobald (?-1677) 2nd Vist. and 1st E. of CARLINGFORD (1661)** was a prominent R. Catholic politician and in 1651 and 1652 was involved in Ormonde's abortive effort to hire troops from the D. of Lorraine. He was excluded from the parliamentary amnesty and restored to his lands and honours in 1661. In 1665 he was Charles II's envoy to the Emperor. His son **(3) Francis (1639-1704) 4th Vist. and 3rd E.** became an Austrian field marshal. **(4) Nicholas (1677-1769) Count (1729)** became an Austrian general and introduced the potato into central Europe by planting his Silesian estates. In 1766 he published a moderate scheme for toleration for Irish R. Catholics. Another descendent **(5) Count Charles Rudolf (1823-73) 10th Vist.** successfully claimed the peerage in 1860. **(6) Count Eduard (1833-95) 11th Vist.** was Austrian Prime Minister from 1868-70 and from 1879-93 and had to grapple with many of the racial and linguistic problems of the Habsburg Empire. The peerage was extinguished by Order in Council in 1919. *See* AUSTRO-HUNGARY-9 to 12.

TABARD was a short usually sleeveless surcoat worn over armour, or by a herald. It was embellished with the arms of the wearer, or in the case of a herald with those of his employer.

TABARD INN (Southwark) was the point where Chaucer's Canterbury Pilgrims assembled. It survived until 1875.

TABBY (from *Attabiy,* a quarter of Baghdad) was a kind of striped or shot silk.

TABLET, THE. R. Catholic intellectual weekly founded in 1840 acquired by Herbert Vaughan, the future Cardinal in 1868. It had a semi-official status until 1936 when Cardinal Hinsley sold it.

TABOO or TAPU. A Polynesian concept, meaning 'supernaturally set apart' and hence 'sacred', 'untouchable', or 'forbidden', applicable to people, actions, places, occasions or totems.

TACITUS, PUBLIUS CORNELIUS (A.D. c. 5?-c. 120) historian, was Agricola's son-in-law and a friend of Pliny. He was Praetor in 88, consul in 97-8 and Pro-Consul of Asia in 112-3. Thus well informed, he wrote many works of which his valuable *Agricola* and *Germania* (a description) survive complete. His other historical books survive only in part.

TACK, TACKSMAN (Scots Law). A lease, especially in the Highlands a headlease taken by the tacksman for subletting.

TACKING is the parliamentary device of inserting a proposal into a bill, usually a finance bill, about something quite different, either to over-ride the Lords *via* their constitutional weakness in money matters, or to force it through under threat of other serious disadvantages. It has been disapproved in controversial matters since 1704, when the High Tories tried to tack measures against occasional conformity to a bill to finance the War of the Spanish Succession. In minor matters it will probably never die out: Ripon was made a City in a Gas Act.

TAEL (Malay) the Chinese silver ounce used in Malaya and the East as a money of account, whose value fluctuated with the silver supply.

TAEOG. See WELSH LAW-1,9.

TAFFETA (the word is Persian). A particularly smooth woven silk introduced into England in 14th cent.

TAFF VALE CASE **[1901] AC 426.** Two trade union officials organised a strike on the plaintiff company's railway and induced strike breakers, in breach of their contracts, not to replace workers on strike. The company sued the union as such. It was held that the two officials were acting in the course of their employment by the union which was, therefore, liable for their unlawful acts. *See* TRADE DISPUTES.

TAFT (1) William Howard (1857-1930) Theodore Roosevelt's Sec. for War from 1904-8 and Republican Pres. of the U.S. from 1909-13. His support of protectionism alienated the progressive Republicans; his party lost ground in the 1910 elections; he quarrelled publicly with Roosevelt and in the resulting split the Democrat Woodrow Wilson was elected in 1913. He was C.J. of the U.S. from 1921-30. His son **(2) Robert Alonzo (1889-1953)** led the conservative Republican opposition in Congress from 1938 when he became a Senator.

TAGORE, Sir Rabindranath (1861-1941) Indian lyrical poet and philosopher, led the Bengali literary revival while seeking to synthesise Indian and Western thought and to promote world unity. He won a Nobel Prize in 1913. His talents and fame greatly contributed to the growth of Indian self-confidence under the British although he did not support his friend Gandhi's political nationalism.

TAHITI (Pacific) was discovered by Samuel Willis in 1767. The London Missionary Society established a mission at Matavai in 1797 and became friendly with the TU or POMARE clan, which secured firearms and in 1812 embraced Christianity. In 1815 the clan conquered the islands and set up a missionary kingdom with a scriptural law code. European traders, disease, alcohol and cheerful sexual customs undermined the missionary influence. In 1836 two French R. Catholic priests arrived, but were promptly deported by Q. Pomare IV. In 1842 a French frigate arrived with a demand for reparations, and established a protectorate in which the English mission was replaced by French naval officers. Govt. weakness and financial difficulties led eventually to the abdication of the last Pomare ruler in 1880 and French annexation. The islands adhered to the Gaulists in World War II and in 1958 became part of an Overseas Territory of the French community.

TAHSILDAR (Urdu) was the chief revenue collector of a Moghul and British subdivision of a district.

TAIL (Eng.) TAILZIE (Scots.). *See* LAND TENURE – ENGLAND-4.

TAILORS OF TOOLEY St Three, probably apocryphal, tailors who began a petition to the House of Commons with the words, "We, the people of England..."

TAILLEFER. William the Conqueror's minstrel who, according to mostly later accounts, led the Normans into battle at Hastings singing and juggling with his sword.

TAIPING 'REBELLION' (1850-64). *See* CHINA-18 TO 25; GORDON, CHARLES.

TAIT, Archibald Campbell (1811-82) Bp. of LONDON (1856-69) Abp. of CANTERBURY (from 1869) succeeded Arnold as headmaster of Rugby. Throughout his career he was a vigorous disciplinarian and evangelist, and noted for his charitable works, preaching in the open air and working among the sick. He eventually supported the Irish Church Bill as Abp. on grounds of common sense.

TAIWAN. *See* FORMOSA.

TAJ MAHAL. *See* AGRA.

TAKORADI (Ghana) was opened as a port in 1928. The only fully effective big ship port in the area, it rapidly developed the local economy and was an important staging point for unloaded aircraft in World War II. *See* GHANA-1.

TAKU FORTS at the mouth of the Pei-Ho channel to Tientsin and Peking (Beijing) were attacked by the Anglo-French force in 1860 and occupied until 1865; and again taken in 1900 by the international force on its way to relieve the Peking legations during the Boxer War. They were demolished in 1901.

TALAINGS. *See* BURMA.

TALBOT. A breed of hunting or tracking hound of obscure origin and now believed to be extinct. It was associated from the 15th cent. with the Talbot family whose heraldic device it was. A dog called Talbot is mentioned in Chaucer's *Nun's Priest's Tale.*

TALBOT. (1) Gilbert (1276-1345) 1st Ld., a landowner in Wales and Gloucestershire, campaigned with Edward I in Scotland and opposed the Despensers under Edward II. He and his son **(2) Richard (c. 1305-56)** were both captured at Boroughbridge in 1322. In 1326 he joined Mortimer and Isabella in their coup against Edward II. In the 1330s Richard campaigned for the Balliols in Scotland, claiming Scottish estates in his wife's right. Later he served in France and fought at Crécy. His great-grandson **(3) John (?1384-1453) E. of SHREWSBURY (1442),** despite early suspicions of Lollardy, played a major part in the Lancastrian wars in Wales, Ireland and especially France. He was Lieutenant of Ireland from 1414-16, 1414-19 and from 1445-48 but he won his reputation as the feared and respected *Roi Talbot* in the French wars from 1420. He fought at Verneuil (1424), Orleans (1428-29) and was captured at Patay (1429). On his release he defended English Normandy and Maine successfully in the 1430s and 1440s. The leading English field commander after the deaths of Salisbury (1428) and Bedford (1435) his efforts encouraged English optimism, but he could not overcome govt. political incompetence and diplomatic folly which was at the root of French success. He stood hostage for the surrender of Harfleur in 1450. In 1453 he led a small force to attempt the recovery of Gascony, lost in 1451, but was killed at the B. of Castillon, which ended English rule.

TALBOT, Mary Ann (1778-1808) the 'British Amazon' served as a drummer in Flanders in 1792 and then as a cabin boy was wounded aboard the *Brunswick* on the Glorious First of June 1794. After further adventures she entered service and was pensioned.

TALBOT, Richard (1630-91) E. of TYRCONNEL (2nd creation 1685) titular **D. (1689)** and Irish landowner, fought the parliamentmen in Ireland, escaped abroad and returned to England. Arrested there, he eventually reached Holland where Clarendon affected to believe that he was a double agent. He became a gentleman of the D. of York's bedchamber at the Restoration and fought under him at the B. of Sole Bay (1665). He and the D. of Ormonde disliked each other and he had been imprisoned for challenging Ormonde in 1661. In 1670 he was again imprisoned for heatedly championing the Irish R. Catholics against him. In 1678 he was a target of the 'Popish Plot'. In 1685 he superseded Ormonde in command of the Irish army and started to discharge protestant soldiers. In 1687 he became Ld. Lieut., dispensed with oaths of Supremacy and sent some Irish troops to England. This helped to precipitate James II's deposition and flight to France, and his voyage to Kinsale where Tyrconnel met him. James could not and Tyrconnel did not restrain the unwisely divisive proceedings of the Patriot Parliament, partly because he was organising the defences. He was routed at the B. of the Boyne and advised James to depart for France. After raising the siege of Limerick he followed, secured funds and arms from Louis XIV and returned. A month after Sarsfield's disaster at Aughrim, he died of a stroke.

TALFOURD, Sir Thomas Noon (179?-1854) M.P. for Reading (1833-44) introduced the important Copyright Bill of 1857, wrote many plays, was Charles Lamb's literary executor and became a judge.

TALIESIN a British poet who lived in Strathclyde in about 550. He is mentioned in Nennius's *Historia Britonum.* Regarded as the founding literary figure of the Welsh, but the 14th cent. Book of *Taliesin* consists of poems of differing date and authorship.

TALLAGE was a capricious levy which a feudal superior might impose upon his tenants of mean or unfree birth or the crown upon its own manors and towns. Very unpopular and often resisted, lords had ceased to attempt tallages by 1250. The crown's claim was abandoned in 1340.

TALLARD. *See* BLENHEIM.

TALLEYRAND-PERIGORD, Charles Maurice, Comte de (1754-1838) (Bonapartist) Pr. of BENEVENTO (1806) **(1)** This famous statesman, being club-footed and ugly, was destined for the Church and was sent to the seminary of St. Sulpice in 1770 whence, having acquired his first mistress, he was expelled in 1775. He was distinguished in that sophisticated society for his wit, urbanity and charm. He also showed signs of a supple yet profound intellect which was the foundation of his skill as a negotiator. Having, despite the expulsion, gone on to the Sorbonne and been ordained (1779) he was appointed Vicar-General to his uncle, the Abp. of Rheims and in 1780 he became Agent of the Clergy. This officer represented to the state authorities the vast and varied interests of the French Church during the five year intervals between meetings of its Assembly and Talleyrand became a determined and skilful defender of even the least excusable ones. In 1788, he became Bp. of Autun and as such Speaker of the Estates of Burgundy, a semi-autonomous local Parliament.

(2) Thus when he went to Paris to the Estates General in 1789, he was thirty-five and better versed in public affairs and debate than most. He also brought with him a *cahier* (catalogue) of grievances which largely corresponded with other *cahiers* and of whose urgency he was well-informed. These included universal fiscal equality and therefore the end of church privileges.

(3) He became prominent at once. The Estates had been called to deal with govt. bankruptcy. The only fund from which the debts could be paid consisted of the huge possessions of the Church. The only hope of future solvency lay in the taxability of the nobles as well as the Commons. With characteristic attention to essentials, he persuaded the Estates to sit as a single body, where the Third Estate (Commons) could outvote the others, rather than in three Houses where nobles and clergy would outweigh the Third Estate, and he proposed the abolition of tithes and the surrender of all church property to the Crown. This was voted in Nov. 1789, and within days also the Civil Constitution of the Clergy, to which Talleyrand swore and under which he consecrated the first bishops. The Pope promptly excommunicated him and he became a layman (1790).

(4) His subtlety had become widely known. In Jan. 1792 he was sent to London to persuade the British govt. to stay neutral in the impending conflict between an Austrian-led coalition and France. He proposed mutual territorial guarantees to Pitt, but an answer was delayed and in Mar. he returned without one. He persuaded the govt. to appoint the personable Marquis de Chauvelin Ambassador and went with him as Councillor. They arrived in May when war had already broken out and on the 25th secured a British declaration of neutrality, but on 20 June the Paris mob stormed the Tuileries. There was a revulsion of British feeling and Talleyrand left for Paris in July. The monarchy was overthrown in Aug. and many nobles were massacred in the prisons in Sept. As a high aristocrat himself, it became essential to leave Paris. After drafting a circular to European capitals blaming the King for his own overthrow, he obtained a passport for England as a private traveller, but again tried to keep Pitt neutral. The French invasion of Belgium and the guillotining of Louis XVI (Jan. 1793) made war inevitable. He became *persona non grata* in Britain and was also denounced in the French Convention. In Jan. 1794 he left for the U.S.A. where, until Sept. 1796, he repaired his finances by successful speculation.

(5) Having left France on a lawful passport, he obtained leave to return, reached Paris (now the seat of the Directorate) and in July 1797 read an able paper before the *Institut National* contending that France could not recover her American colonies and should therefore seek to colonise Africa. The well-timed thesis was acclaimed: he was on friendly terms with the Director Siéyès who nominated him Foreign Minister and was a friend of Napoleon Bonaparte. Accordingly Talleyrand ratified Bonaparte's T. of Camp Formio and consistently with his paper to the *Institut*, joined him in persuading the Directors to authorise his Egyptian expedition. Early in 1799 he resigned to manage his large fortune, partly derived in that openly corrupt dispensation, from bribes. He resumed office in Nov. after Bonaparte's return from Egypt and *coup d'état* of Brumaire.

(6) From now on Talleyrand and Bonaparte slowly diverged. Talleyrand believed in peace. He negotiated the Ts. of Luneville and Amiens and the Papal Concordat of 1801 to pacify Europe but he was forced to concur in policies in Italy, Germany and Switzerland which must necessarily lead to war and if he supported the Life Consulate and Bonaparte's imperial dignity and was perhaps privy to the murder of the D. d'Enghien, his service was received without pleasure, for Bonaparte's ambition envisaged war as the only solution to international problems. Accordingly he resigned in Aug. 1807.

(7) The Emperor, however, consulted him and took him to the Erfurt Congress (Sept. 1808) where he opened secret private relations with the Czar and the Austrian Emperor. Fouché, the Police Minister, and Talleyrand had both lost faith in Bonaparte's statesmanship, in which they saw only catastrophe. They were right and when in 1814 the Allies took Paris, Talleyrand persuaded the Czar, who was staying with him, that a Bourbon restoration was essential to the public peace. At his insistence the Senate deposed Bonaparte and appointed himself and four others as the provisional Govt. This body recalled Louis XVIII, who appointed him Foreign Minister for the third time.

(8) His first task was to attend the Congress of Vienna and rescue something from the misfortunes of his defeated country. He raised France from submission to membership of the concert of great powers by calling in aid the British concern for the balance of power. He supported Britain and Austria to prevent Russia and Prussia becoming too strong in Saxo-Poland, in return for support against a dangerous weakening of France by excessive annexations and reparations. He remained in Vienna during the Waterloo campaign, returned to Paris but not withstanding his remarkable recent services, was forced to resign by the extreme royalists. He retired until 1829.

(9) In 1830, clear-sighted as ever, he assisted the liberals to set up the Orléanist July Monarchy in preference to the deeply reactionary Govt. of Charles X, and became Ambassador in London. As such he negotiated the Belgian independence treaty and the alliance with Britain, Spain and Portugal, both important to European stability.

(10) Wily yet principled and civilised, deeply read and uniquely experienced, Talleyrand served France and peace rather than successive French rulers. He believed in calm, comfort and good cooks for objective diplomacy and in 1816 boasted that he had, he hoped, purged the staff of his Foreign Office of the least trace of enthusiasm.

TALLINN or REVAL (Estonia) important grain and timber port in the Middles Ages (*see* BALTIC *passim*) passed in 1710 to Russia. It was the main Russian naval base until 1918 and from 1946.

TALLIS, Thomas (c. 150?-85) organist, teacher of William Byrd and a prolific and original composer of church music inspired by the demand for it created by the second Prayer Book of Edward VI (1552).

TALLOW, rendered from beef or mutton fat, was used for various purposes such as calking and lubrication and especially for candles. These were smelly and smokey and darkened walls and ceilings; hence the gloomy backgrounds of many 18th cent. indoor prints. Tallow candles were superseded by the more expensive but cleaner wax candles over a long period ending c. 1900 when electric light began to supersede both.

TALLY, EXCHEQUER. *See* EXCHEQUER TALLIES.

TALMAN, William (fl. 1670-1700), architect and enemy of Wren, built Chatsworth and made many alterations at Hampton Court.

TALMUD (Heb: study) consists of the *Torah* or Pentateuch of Moses, explained after the Jewish dispersion (A.D. 70) in a great corpus of teaching and rabbinical tradition called the *Mishna* (= learning by heart) compiled in Palestine and Babylonia to preserve the culture and identity of the Jews and itself the subject of criticism, study and explanation incorporated in divergent *Gemara* (= Completions) made respectively at Tiberias (Palestine) in the 3rd cent. and in Babylonia in the 5th. The JERUSALEM and the BABYLONIAN TALMUDS thus have the Torah and Mishna in common but differ in their Gemara. The Babylonian was first published in Europe at Venice in 1520-23, the Jerusalem in 1524. The latter was much used in E. Europe. The first authoritative English versions were published in 1949.

TALUQ,-DAR (Urdu = estate owner). Under the Moguls N. Indian villages were grouped to form divisions of a district for purposes of tax collection. These taluqs tended to descend in the family of the collector, who originally received a commission, but whose position increasingly resembled that of an owner or feudal lord, until the British mistakenly recognised it as such.

TAMAR, R. is described by Cornishmen as the boundary between Cornwall and England.

TAMILS are a Dravidian race inhabiting southern India and part of Ceylon. *See* CEYLON.

TAMMANY ('affable') was a Delaware chief from whom William Penn obtained land. In 1789 a New York benevolent society adopted his name. It soon became politically involved, and built Tammany Hall, long the H.Q. of a Democratic organisation which corruptly dominated the city's politics.

TAMWORTH MANIFESTO (1834) in form addressed by the Tory leader Sir Robert Peel to the 586 electors of his constituency for the general election, was discussed in cabinet before issue and gathered, as intended, a wider readership partly because such a manifesto issued by a prime minister in office was a novelty. The election, however, attracted little interest and though the Tories gained 94 seats, they failed of a majority and Peel had to resign after six defeats in the Commons. The document committed the Tories to the irrevocability of the Reform Acts and, while not abjuring conservative principles, declared their readiness to combine "the firm maintenance of established rights, the correction of proved abuses and the redress of real grievances". Reaction was thus repudiated.

TANDY, James Napper (1740-1803) helped Wolfe Tone and Thomas Russell to found the Dublin United Irishmen in 1791. In 1793, charged with taking an illegal oath, he fled. In 1795 he reached U.S.A. and in 1798 France. He was sent as a French general to raise a revolt in Ireland in Sept. 1798, but was ashore for only one day. In Nov. he reached Hamburg, whence he was extradited to Ireland and sentenced to death, but released. He died in France.

TANGANYIKA. *See* TANZANIA.

TANGIER. *See* MOROCCO; CATHERINE OF BRAGANZA; CHARLES II.

TANISTRY. *See* DERBFINE.

TANKERVILLE, E. of. *See* GREY OR GRAY-2 AND GREY.

TANJORE (Madras, India) a prosperous Brahmin religious, political and literary centre.

TANKS. These armoured vehicles were developed from caterpillar tractors by a largely naval committee inspired by Winston Churchill. The first tanks came into action on the Somme in Sept. 1916, but they were first used *en masse* at Cambrai in Nov. 1917. *See* TENNYSON D'EYNCOURT; WORLD WAR I-4,14.

TANTALLON CASTLE (Berwicks, Scot.) Douglas fortress destroyed by Cromwell in 1651.

TANTIA TOPEE. *See* INDIAN MUTINY-9.

TANTIVY, TO RIDE was to ride breakneck. The word 'Tantivy' was applied in 1687 to high churchmen and Tories, as a result of a cartoon representing them mounted upon the Church of England, riding tantivy behind the D. of York to Rome.

TANTRISM. *See* BUDDHISM; HINDUISM.

TANZANIA – TANGANYIKA AND ZANZIBAR – GERMAN EAST AFRICA. The Portuguese maintained a certain shadowy influence at Zanzibar from 1503 to 1698 when Arabs of Oman took Mombasa and established Zanzibar as a tributary province. The first Omani Sultan settled there in 1830 but in 1856 his African dominions passed to one son while Muscat and Oman went to another. In 1860 as a result of an arbitration by Ld. Canning, Viceroy of India, Zanzibar became independent of Oman, but the connection remained close. By 1866 it was under strong British influence through Sir John Kirk, British Consul General until 1888. He persuaded the Sultan to abolish the slave trade in 1873.

(2) Meantime European exploration was proceeding in the mainland territories over which Zanzibar claimed ineffectual suzerainty. Burton and Speke reached L. Tanganyika in 1857, Speke went to L. Victoria in 1860 and Livingstone reached L. Nyassa in 1866. The Germans also became interested and in 1884 Karl Peters, supported by Bismarck obtained land grants near the coastal areas claimed by Zanzibar.

(3) By an Anglo-German agreement of 1886, the Sultan's claims were limited to a ten-mile coastal strip under British influence while the German East Africa Co. was allowed to exploit Tanganyika. By 1891 its activities had caused a rebellion and the German govt. took over the territory as German East Africa. They built a railway from Dar-es-Salaam to L. Tanganyika and introduced Florida sisal and coffee.

(4) The territory was invaded in 1914 by British and S. African troops and brilliantly defended by General von Lettow-Vorbeck, who, though outnumbered by 30 to 1, did not surrender until a fortnight after the armistice in Nov. 1918.

(5) In 1920 Tanganyika became a British mandated territory and in 1947 a U.N. Trust territory with Britain as trustee. By 1960 there was a legislature with an elected majority under the leadership of Julius Nyerere; in 1961 Tanganyika became an independent member of the Commonwealth and in 1962 a republic. In Dec. 1963 Zanzibar similarly became independent, but in Jan. 1964 the Sultan was violently overthrown by a communist trained cadre under John Okello. This led in Apr. 1964 to the signature of an Act of Union between the two countries which became known in Oct. as the United Republic of Tanzania. The govt. of Zanzibar appeared, however, to remain internally autonomous.

TAPESTRY was imported into England in quantities from Flanders especially Arras, the earliest English tapestry weaving shops were those of William Sheldon (?-1570). There was a distinguished factory at Mortlake from 1619-1703, which flourished before the civil war and made cloths to designs by Vandyck. These weavers were mostly Flemings. In 1703 the rest of the Mortlake crafts-men moved to Soho under the brothers *Poyntz*. By 1750 English commercial tapestry was extinct.

TAPROBANE. Usually Ceylon, sometimes Sumatra.

TARA (Ireland). Religious and ceremonial seat of Meath and of the Irish High King. *See* ARD-RI.

TARA BAI. *See* MARATHAS-9.

TARDIEU, André (1876-1945) had an influential part in drafting the T. of Versailles and was a disciple of Clemenceau, under whom he served briefly as a Minister. He was strongly against any revision of the treaty but after 1926 served under Poincaré. He was Prime Minister from Nov. 1929 to Feb. 1930 and from Mar. to Dec. 1930. He then served under Laval in 1931 and 1930 and was again premier from Feb. to Mar. 1932 when he retired in disgust.

TARIFA (Sp.) Through this small port Ballesteros' anti-French guerrillas in the Sierra Ronda drew their supplies from the British. A small Anglo-Spanish garrison with-stood a violent siege from Oct. 1811 to Jan. 1812.

TARGE[T], originally a small often round shield which, suitably painted, could be used as a practice aiming-mark.

TARIFF (Arab: notification) and **BOUNTY.** In politics, 'tariff came to mean a list of import or export duties (or both), originally called a Book of Rates in English 16th-18th cent. fiscal practice. A *tariff-wall* was an import duty designed to exclude goods rather than raise revenue. Such walls often provoked foreign counter-tariffs which had then to be overleaped by export subsidies or bounties, i.e. by a govt. paying to an exporter a sum which would enable him to lower his price by the amount of the foreign duty.

TARIFF REFORM LEAGUE was founded by Joseph Chamberlain in 1903 to modify free trade in favour of imperial preference and solidarity.

TARLETON, Sir Banastre (1754-1833) Bart. (1815) one of the ablest of the English generals in the War of American Independence, served under Clinton from 1778-80. In 1781 he defeated Lafayette at Jamestown, but had to capitulate with Cornwallis at Yorktown. He was M.P. for Liverpool from 1790-1812.

TARLTON, Richard (?-1588) celebrated clown, humorist and dancer, said to have inspired some of Shakespeare's comics such as Bottom and Dogberry.

TARPAULIN was used, *inter alia,* to cover seamen's hats. Hence the word came to mean a seaman ("Jack Tar") or a sea officer as contrasted with a military officer appointed to command a ship.

TARTAN. *See* CLANS.

TARTARS was the name originally applied indiscriminately to the races which made up Genghis Khan's forces in the 13th cent. and then equally vaguely to their actual or supposed descendants. More strictly, the Tartars were the Turkic branch of the Turanian family, their principal representatives being the Kirghiz Tartars and the Turks.

TASCIOVANUS. *See* CATUVELLAUNI.

TASHKENT (C. Asia) was seized by the Russians in 1867.

TASMAN, Abel Janszoon (?1603-?59) sent by the Dutch East India Co. to explore Australian waters, made two famous voyages. **(1)** 1642-3. He sailed from Batavia anti-clockwise, discovered Tasmania, New Zealand, Tonga and Fiji and so proved that Australia (which he never sighted) was separated from any hypothetical southern continent of which he thought that New Zealand might be a part. **(2)** 1644. He sailed clockwise along the Australian coast to Lat. 22° and back.

TASMANIA. *See* AUSTRALIA.

TASS. Russian propaganda and news agency established as part of the propaganda department in 1925.

TATA (1) Jamsetji Nasarwanji (1839-1904) visited Lancashire in 1872 and opened the Nagpur cotton mills in 1878. He acclimatised Egyptian cotton in India and from 1901 developed the Bombay industries using the monsoon rainfall in the Western Ghats as a source of electricity. His son **(2) Sir Dorabji Jamsetji (1859-1932)** established the great steelworks of Jamshedpur in 1911.

TATE, Sir Henry (1819-99) and TATE GALLERY. Sir Henry Tate, a sugar merchant who invented a sugar cubing machine, founded the firm of Tate and Lyle. Several modern picture collections had been given to the nation but were unsatisfactorily housed. These included the Vernon Collection (1847), the Turner Bequest (1856), the Chantrey Bequest (1841) and the Watts Gift. Sir Henry Tate financed a gallery for them and himself gave pictures to it. It was opened in 1897 and extended by Sir Joseph Duveen in 1910. The Lane Bequest (1915) was the foundation of the foreign modern art collection, which was endowed by Samuel Courtauld in 1923. The building was extended in 1927 and 1977. *See* BANKSIDE.

TATE, Nahum (1652-1715) Irishman settled in London from 1672. He wrote a second part of Dryden's *Absalom and Achitophel* (1682) and with Nicholas Brady published (1696) metrical psalms, some of which remain in use. He was also Historiographer Royal and, as Poet Laureate, ridiculed by Pope.

TATTERSALL, Richard (1724-95), stud groom to the D. of Kingston, set up as a horse auctioneer at Knightsbridge Green in 1766. His honesty and businesslike methods, in a trade where neither was common, soon brought *Tattersalls,* nationwide and eventually world-wide patronage. The business moved in 1961.

TATTOOING. (1) Until 1876 soldiers were tattooed (if appropriate) with 'D' = deserter or 'BC' = bad conduct. A form of registration. **(2)** The Polynesians and Maoris used patterns some of which were hereditary.

TATWIN or TADWIN (?-734) of Bredon became Abp. of Canterbury in 731.

TAUNTON (Som.) founded c. 710 by Ine, it had a market by the 9th cent. It belonged in 11th cent. to the Bps. of Winchester who built the castle and priory. It became very prosperous during the 14th cent. wool boom. Bp. Fox founded the grammar school in 1522. Perkin Warbeck's insurrection collapsed there in 1499. It sustained, under the command of Robert Blake, three sieges in the Civil War. Monmouth's rebellion and Jeffrey's Bloody Assize focused on it. Apart from the agricultural products and industries such as spinning, weaving and tanning associated with them, the town has long had specialist trades such as glove making.

TAUNTON COMMISSION (1864) found that secondary schools were lacking in over 100 towns with less than 5000 people and that many existing schools had failed to up-date their curricula. They proposed that there should be rate-aided secondary schools partly controlled by school boards. The proposal was not accepted. *See* NEWCASTLE COMMISSION.

TAUROGGEN CONVENTION (30 Dec. 1812) between the Russian General Diebitsch and the Prussian General Yorck von Wartenburg, whereby Yorck's troops ceased, despite the alliance of their King with Bonaparte, to fight the allies. This mutinous act was wildly popular in Prussia and began the crystallisation of German opinion against Bonaparte.

TAVERNER, Richard (?1505-75) originally a protégé of Wolsey, he wrote protestant tracts for Thomas Cromwell. He was clerk to the Privy Seal from 1536-64, during which period he wrote a revised edition of "Matthew's" bible. In 1545 he was M.P. for Liverpool and under Elizabeth sheriff of Oxfordshire.

TAVISTOCK (Devon). Its important Benedictine Abbey was founded in 961. Henry I gave the Scilly Is. to it and chartered a Goose Fair (1105) where maids were also hired. The place was a mediaeval stannary and centre for tin and copper mining and it became rich enough for much fine building. Sir Francis Drake was born there. The Russell family acquired the Abbey at its dissolution and mostly demolished it.

TAWNEY, Richard Henry (1880-1962) amongst other works wrote the powerful *Religion and the Rise of Capitalism* (1926), an analysis of the religiously based work ethic and its social effects in an industrial society.

TAXATIO PAPAE NICHOLAI (Lat: Valuation of Pope Nicholas). Nicholas IV's valuation (1291) of ecclesiastical property to replace that of 1254. It contains the fullest mediaeval survey of English church property and was the basis for later clerical grants of taxation.

TAY, R. is navigable to Perth. The first railway bridge was blown down (with a train on it) in 1879 and replaced in 1887. The Newport-Dundee road bridge was opened in 1966.

TAYLOR, Jeremy (1613-67) born, educated and ordained at Cambridge, attracted Abp. Laud's attention and became a Chaplain to Charles I in 1636 and in 1642 a chaplain in the royal army. He was briefly imprisoned after its defeat and then went to Wales as chaplain at Lord Carbery's house, Golden Grove. Here he wrote five works celebrated for their persuasive skill: *Liberty of Prophesying* (1646) an argument for toleration; *Holy Living* (1650), *Holy Dying* (1651), *The Golden Grove* and *Unum Necessarium* (1655) on repentance. In 1658 he went to Lisburn in N. Ireland as a lecturer and in 1660 became Bp. of Down and Vice-Chancellor of Dublin University where he firmly enforced discipline. He also became Bp. of Dromore in 1661. He was involved in bitter conflicts with R. Catholics on the one hand and the nonconformists whom he treated harshly. One result was the publication of his invective *Dissuasive from Popery* (1664).

TAYLOR. (1) Sir Robert (1714-88) the architect of Stone Buildings at Lincoln's Inn and the Bank of England, left most of his fortune to found the Taylorian or modern language institute at Oxford University. His son **(2) Michael Angelo (1757-1834)** entered the Commons as a Tory in 1784, but voted with the Whigs in 1797 and was one of the managers of the Warren Hastings impeachment. He was responsible for the passing of the Metropolitan Paving Act, 1817.

TEA, CHA or BOHEA. ("Tea" is from the Amoy dialect used by China merchants; 'Cha' from northern or mandarin and adopted by soldiers of the Indian army. Both originally meant green tea, as opposed to bohea which was black.) The Dutch started to carry tea from China to Bantam and thence to Holland in about 1610. The HEIC started re-exporting from Hirado (Japan) in 1615. Europeans began adding milk in about 1655 but tea became fashionable only with the advent of Catharine of Braganza in 1662. By 1760 London had many teahouses. In 1823 a Major Robert Bruce discovered accidentally that the plant was indigenous to the Assam forests and with the help of the Indian govt. the great Indian teagardens were founded in the following years. It was not realised in Europe that black is the fermented leaf of the green variety until Robert Fortune established the fact in 1843. Black tea had virtually superseded green in Europe by 1900. *See* CEYLON.

TEACH, Edward (?-1718) "Blackbeard", a reputedly sadistic pirate in 1716, operated in the Caribbean and on the coasts of Virginia and Carolina where in 1718 he set up a base and shared his profits with Charles Eden, the Governor. The local planters appealed to Virginia and in Nov. 1718 he was killed in a fight with two Virginian sloops.

TEAGUE. A 17th cent. pejorative for an Irishman.

TECHNICAL EDUCATION AGE 1889. *See* WHISKEY MONEY.

TECUMSEH. *See* SHAWNEES.

TEDDER, Sir Arthur William (1890-1967) 1st Ld. (1946) became C-in-C, R.A.F. Middle East in 1941. He developed the essential techniques of army-air-force tactical co-operation and in 1942 established a close liaison with the Americans to which his calm temperament was well suited. From 1944-45 he was Eisenhower's Deputy and Commander of Air Operations in the invasion of Europe and from 1946-55 Chief of the Air Staff.

TE DEUM. A Latin hymn ascribed to St. Ambrose and St. Augustine at the baptism of the latter but probably composed by Nicetas in the 5th cent. As the centre piece of a thanksgiving service, it has often been set to music e.g. by Handel to celebrate the Peace of Utrecht, or the victory at Dettingen.

TEES and TEESSIDE. The river was never navigable above Stockton and it was accessible from the sea only with difficulty until the channel was straightened in the early 19th cent. The Stockton & Darlington Rly opened in 1823 and as the first railway operated with steam locomotives, originated the local industrial development which caused Teesside to become a separate county in 1974.

TEHERAN CONFERENCE (Nov.-Dec. 1943) was a meeting of Winston Churchill, Pres. Roosevelt and Stalin on war policy. Churchill wanted full scale western allied invasions of Europe based on the Mediterranean and carried out through Italy and the Balkans. This was unacceptable to Stalin because it might finish the war too soon and place large parts of Europe in western, not Russian, hands. The Americans also objected because it was contrary to their industrialised conception of warfare. It was eventually agreed that there should be an invasion of Normandy followed by a further invasion up the Rhone Valley. As a logical consequence the W. frontier of a restored Poland should be along the Oder and Neisse, thus giving the Russians a pretext for taking over the East Polish territories. Germany should be dismembered but the exact method was not agreed. There were preliminary discussions about the creation of a permanent U.N.O. The conference also guaranteed Persian integrity and independence.

TEIND (Scots Law) a Scottish tithe or that part of property liable to be assessed for tithe.

TEL AVIV. See ISRAEL.

TELECOMMUNICATIONS, ELECTRIC (see SIGNALLING, VISUAL). **(1)** The first experimental instruments were made by Francis Ronalds (1788-1873) in 1816. The first **telegraph** line was probably the Russian govt. line from St. Petersburg to the naval base at Kronstadt laid in 1835. W. F. Cooke (1806-79) and C. Wheatstone (1802-75) developed a better system in 1837 and the Morse Code was applied to it in the same year. Outside Russia, the first line was laid along the Gt. Western Rly from Paddington to Slough in 1844 and knowledge was widely diffused by the Great Exhibition of 1852. An unsuccessful Transatlantic cable was laid in 1858, a successful one in 1866. Punched tape, developed by Wheatstone, came into use in 1867. The French were experimenting with **teleprinting** in 1874 but it was established in general use only in 1900. **(2)** The **telephone** was patented in 1876. The first English exchange was opened in London in 1879 and the courts held telephonic communication to be a form of telegraph and so a post-office monopoly in 1880. Several systems were licensed and in 1891 a cable was laid to France. The Post Office acquired the trunk lines in 1896, began to establish exchanges in 1902 and acquired all telephone systems except that in Hull in 1912. Radio telephony between Britain and U.S.A. commenced in 1927. There were 3000 telephones in use in 1900, 122,000 in 1910 and about 23,000,000 in 1959. The telecommunications branch of the Post Office had in effect become a separate business at the end of World War II. Amplified by satellite in 1957 it was transferred to British Telecom in 1981. The Hull system was and remains independent. **(3) Facsimile** was introduced after World War II but became widespread only in 1987.

TELESCOPE. See GALILEO.

TELEVISION. See BROADCASTING.

TELFORD (Salop) named after the Scottish engineer. See NEW TOWNS.

TELFORD, Thomas (1757-1834) became a surveyor of works in Shropshire in 1783; he built the Ellesmere Canal with its spectacular aqueducts between 1793-1805, and between 1805-10 cut the Caledonian Canal, built 920 miles of roads in the Highlands and deepened and improved six northern Scottish ports. He began the Menai Suspension Bridge in 1819 and completed plans for improving Dover harbour just before his death.

TELUGU. The most widespread Dravidian language, spoken from Madras to Orissa.

TEMPEST, Dame Marie alias Mary Etherington (1864-1942) Belgian educated English actress, drew large audiences for light opera between 1895-1900 and then took equally successfully to comedy until 1939.

TEMPLAR, KNIGHTS originated in Outremer in about 1118 as a small body of poor celibate soldiers subject to the Patriarch of Jerusalem and employed to escort pilgrims. K. Baldwin II (1118-31) gave them quarters in the area of the Temple in Jerusalem. The order was approved at the Council of Troyes (1128). Bernard of Clairvaux redrafted their Rule and wrote *De Laude Novae Militiae* (Lat: In Praise of the New Chivalry) in their honour. In 1139 they were exempted from tithes and episcopal jurisdiction. Their first leader, Hugh of Payens, visited England after the Council of Troyes, and after Q. Matilda (Stephen's wife) had given the Order land at Cressing (Essex) in 1137, it received large estates throughout England. Each Templar establishment (Commandery) was ruled by a Commander who was subject to the Preceptor or Visitor of his country; he in turn was subordinate to the Grand Master elected by a special committee of the Chapter of the Order. The Grand Master was the military commander to whom the Knights swore absolute obedience but he had to consult the Chapter on major policy or constitutional matters. By mid-12th cent. the Templars were crucial to the defence of Outremer, holding many castles, and providing a professional fighting force. With its international holdings and membership, the Order soon operated a banking system notably in France, because it could safeguard and circulate large sums. The Knights played an important part in collecting the Saladin Tithe, and were often used by Henry III as financial agents. Such a role, their notorious arrogance and their wealth exposed them to slander and unpopularity, especially after the fall of Acre (1291), when their H.Q. moved to Cyprus. In 1307 the French Templars were arrested, accused by K. Philip IV of lurid, trumped-up charges ranging from heresy and embezzlement to sorcery and sodomy. Harried by torture, false-witness and harsh imprisonment most French and Cypriot Knights confessed and many were executed. Jacques de Molai, the last Grand Master, was burned alive, calling down the wrath of God upon the King. In England, though Edward II reluctantly agreed to the arrests, there was no systematic torture or effective inquisition and few Knights confessed or were convicted. In 1312 the Order was suppressed by the Pope at the Council of Vienne. Templar lands passed mostly to the Order of St John (The Hospitallers) or the Crowns of the various countries.

TEMPLE survives as the name of sites (e.g. in London, Bristol, Cambridge and Paris) formerly occupied by the Knights Templar. In London they originally had a site in Holborn (The Old Temple) but in the 1160s they moved to the New Temple between Fleet St. and the Thames. In 1312 the land was granted to the Hospitallers. From 1346 lawyers began to take leases there and developed two building syndicates called, respectively, the Societies of the Inner and Middle Temple. These became separated in 1609 but their buildings in the Temple still interpenetrate. Templar churches are distinguished by a circular part which served as the meeting place of the Knights. The London Temple was not rateable. Most families called Temple are descended from foundlings left there and brought up at the private expense of the two Societies. Foundlings were normally maintained at the expense of the ratepayers but this private arrangement avoided admitting that there were any ratepayers in the Temple.

Since 1924 the London Temple Church has been the focus of a notable revival, under Dr Geo. Thalben Ball and Stephen Layton of choral music.

TEMPLE. Buckinghamshire family originating at Stowe, where the senior branch remained, while the junior went to Ireland. **A.** Of the Stowe Branch **(1) Sir Peter (1592-1653)** was a parliamentarian M.P. so was his son **(2) Sir Richard (1634-97)** but he was converted to the Restoration and as an M.P. continuously from 1660, he was a supporter of Shaftesbury in the "Popish Plot", an exclusionist and a supporter of William III. His son **(3) Sir Richard (1669-1749) 1st Ld. COBHAM (1714) Vist. (1718)** became an M.P. in 1697 but already a soldier in 1689, served under Marlborough, distinguishing himself at the siege of Lille (1708). As a Whig he was out of favour during the D. of Ormonde's restrained command (1710-13) but George I sent him to Vienna to announce his accession and in 1719 he commanded the expedition against Corunna which sacked Vigo. As a peer he supported Walpole until 1733 but opposed his excise scheme and the govt's later handling of the South Sea Co. He was sensationally dismissed from his regiments, but politically supported in both Houses, gaining both public esteem and the favour of the P. of Wales. He also formed the Whig association known as the Boy Patriots. After Walpole's resignation, he briefly joined Wilmington's coalition (Mar. 1742) but resigned against military involvement in Hanoverian interests (Dec.). His considerable fame, however, rests upon, in his own eyes, secondary activities. He was a literary patron, especially of Congreve and Pope, and a member of the Kit-Kat Club and he built the great house and laid out the gardens at Stowe in their modern form.

B. Of the Irish Branch **(4) Sir William (1555-1627)** was secretary to Sir Philip Sydney in 1585-86 and then to Essex and in 1597 M.P. for Tamworth. His fortunes collapsed with those of Essex but he had previously had a small academic reputation and in 1609 James I made him provost of Trinity College, Dublin. His son **(5) Sir John (1600-77)** was Irish Master of the Rolls from 1640-43 and from 1655 but sided with the Parliament in the interval. His book on the Irish Rebellion (1646) inflamed anti-Irish opinion and contributed to knowledge of R. Catholic barbarity in 1641. Having voted as an Irish M.P. for a compromise with Charles I in 1647, he was sufficiently trusted at the Restoration to be confirmed in office and given extensive lands. His son **(6) Sir John (1632-1704)** was Speaker of the Irish Commons in 1661 and Irish Attorney General in 1690. The son of (5), **(7) Sir William (1628-99)** moved to Sheen (Middlesex) in 1663 and was employed as a diplomat at Monster (1665) and at Brussels (1666) whence by assiduous visits to The Hague he made friends with John de Witt and other Dutch republican notables. He negotiated the Triple Alliance in 1668 and was appointed Ambassador to The Hague. This assignment was difficult, for he differed from Charles II on policy but the King had his own reasons for not advertising the difference. Hence in 1670 Charles dismissed him but told him to go privately. He retired to Sheen and wrote, until he was re-employed on more congenial diplomacy in 1674 again at The Hague, arranging for the marriage (which took place in 1677) of the P. Mary with William of Orange. In 1677 he refused a secretaryship of state, probably to avoid being entangled in a foreign policy conducted mainly by the King. This was fortunate, for the "Popish Plot" agitation broke out in 1678 and threatened many lives. He thus had even stronger reasons for refusing office in 1679. Nevertheless Charles consulted him for some while as a privy councillor until 1681 when they disagreed and he again retreated to Sheen. He was not involved in the Revolution and consequently William III refused him office when he asked for it. He left a number of literary works, especially *Memoirs* which Swift helped him to write. His brother **(8) Henry (?1673-1757) 1st Vist. (Ir.) PALMERSTON (1723)** was an English M.P. from 1727-47 and a consistent Walpoleite. He improved the houses at Sheen and Broadlands. His grandson **(9) Henry (1739-1802) 2nd Vist.** was an M.P. from 1762, a lord of the Admiralty from 1766 and a Lord of the Treasury in 1777. His house in Hanover Square, was a famous social and artistic centre, where such figures as Gibbon and Reynolds habitually appeared. He was also an enthusiastic traveller. His son, the famous **(10) Henry John (1784-1865) 3rd Vist.** was an M.P. from 1807. His abilities were already known and he at once became a Lord of the Admiralty. In 1809 he became Secretary at War and so remained until 1828. He was thus executively responsible for the military climax of the French wars and their aftermath. He was attracted to the foreign policy views of George Canning, who wanted to offer him the Exchequer in 1827 but was over-ridden by the King. He resigned with the other Canningites in 1828 and then emerged into popular view with attacks on govt. foreign policy. In 1830 he became Grey's Foreign Sec. and held this office, save for four months in 1835, until 1841. He was a truculent, moralising and demagogic foreign secretary, combining hostility to the European autocracies, with imperial and commercial opportunism from the Mediterranean to the Far East. (*See* GREY'S AND MELBOURNE'S FIRST AND SECOND GOVTS. *besides* BELGIUM; CARLISTS; CHINA; GREECE; EGYPT; OTTOMAN EMPIRE; RUSSIA, ETC.) In opposition from 1841-46, he resumed the Foreign Office under Ld. John Russell from 1846-51 and followed the same aggressive popular style, to the growing concern of informed opinion, the cabinet and the Queen. He upset his predecessor Aberdeen's rapport with the French July monarchy and quarrelled with it over the Spanish marriages (1846-47). He encouraged liberal movements in Spain, Portugal and Italy, yet bullied Greece in the Don Pacifico Affair. He upset the Austrians by gleefully supporting the London draymen who horsewhipped their General Haynau, and by welcoming Lajos Kossuth, the Hungarian nationalist to England. When he recognised the French Second Empire without consulting the Queen Russell dismissed him. He promptly engineered the overthrow of Russell's Govt. and after a short intermission, reappeared as Home Sec. (1853-5) under Aberdeen. Despite his call for firm preventive action, the govt. drifted slowly into war in the Crimea and broke up over its conduct. He was accordingly called upon to form a new one, as much by popular demand as by Q. Victoria. The fall of Sevastopol and the P. of Paris (1856) gave him much prestige, which enabled him to deal sensibly with the Indian Mutiny (1857) but meanwhile he entertained an old fashioned opposition to France, whereas opinion was veering towards a greater degree of European co-operation. As a result he was defeated over the (*Arrow*) China War in 1858. He won the general election, was defeated on a Conspiracy Bill, resigned and then returned (1859).

His principal achievement was to obstruct French efforts to stop Garibaldi's conquest of S. Italy and to maintain neutrality in the U.S. Civil War. He tried but failed for lack of an army, to save the Poles from Russia (1863) and the Danes from Prussia (1864).

TEMPLE (1) Frederick (1821-1902) born in the Ionian Is. and a friend of Matthew Arnold and of A. H. Clough, was employed under the Education Dept, and was then headmaster of Rugby from 1857-69. He was also involved in ecclesiastical controversies and his contribution to *Essays and Reviews* (1860) created opposition to his preferment to the see of Exeter where he was consecrated in 1869. He was a reformer in social and educational fields: at Rugby he had widened the curriculum and enlarged the school; at Exeter he founded secondary schools and helped to create the new diocese of Truro; in the Lords he favoured abolishing the university tests. As Bp. of London (1885-96) he was a member of the Royal Commission on Education (1888) and was mainly responsible for building Church House. He also acted as a conciliator in the London Strike of 1889. As Abp. of Canterbury from 1896, he made two metropolitical visitations mainly to dissuade incumbents from using high ceremonial. He supported the Education Bill of 1902. He was as clever, rugged and honest as his son **(2) William (1881-1944)** who was Headmaster of Repton from 1910-14; and Pres. of the Workers Educational Association from 1908-24. As Bp. of Manchester from 1921-29 he tried to mediate in the General Strike (1926). He was Abp. of York from 1929-42 and Abp. of Canterbury from 1942. His determination helped to frame the Education Act of 1944. He was an early exponent of Oecumenism.

TEMPLE BAR, the City gate in the Strand, London, was removed to Theobalds Park in 1878.

TEMPLE NEWSAM (Yorks), a Templar property acquired by the d'Arcy family on the dissolution of the Order, passed to the Crown and then to the Ingram and Irwin families. Its size made it a resort of northern politicians and the present Jacobean and Georgian house is immense.

TEMPORALITIES. The income and estates, especially those owing feudal military obligations, which form part of the possessions of an ecclesiastical office and for which a holder does homage. See INVESTITURE.

TEMPORARY ESTATE DUTY. See DEATH DUTIES.

TENANT RIGHT PARTY (Ir.) arose briefly out of the collapse of the Repeal (1847) and Young Ireland (1848) movements. *The Nation* had been ventilating the Irish land question since 1842 but Gavan Duffy and other Young Irelanders who had escaped the disasters now tried to base a nationwide land movement on the *Three Fs*, viz. fixity of tenure, fair rent and free sale. It gained the support of all denominations and nominated parliamentary candidates, but it failed to gain popular support and collapsed in 1852.

TENANTS-IN-CHIEF were tenants holding land directly of the King and owing direct service (whether military or other) to him. Domesday Book (1086) records of some 180 of them but in respect of many different holdings. See FEUDALISM-6 *et seq.*

TEN ARTICLES (1536) were issued by Convocation at the request of Henry VIII and enforced by Cromwell's injunctions. The first English reformation articles of faith, they upheld Baptism, Penance and the Eucharist, which was defined on a basis of consubstantiation. Justification was considered attainable by contrition, faith and charity. Images could be displayed but not worshipped. Prayers and masses for the dead were enjoined and the intercession of saints permitted. These articles were followed by the more Romanist **Bishops' Book** (1537) or *Institution of a Christen Man* which was an exposition of the Creed, the Seven Sacraments, the Ten Commandments, the Lords Prayer and the Ave Maria, with consequential teachings on justification, purgatory and relations with the Papacy. Drawn up by a committee of bishops and divines it never received royal authority, but superseded the Ten Articles in practice. It was followed by the **Six Articles** (1539) a purely Romanist act of parliament enforcing transubstantiation, communion in one kind, clerical celibacy, monastic vows, private masses and the confessional. The laymen voted for it; some of the bishops against; Latimer resigned his see and Cranmer sent away his wife. It was almost a dead letter. The **Kings Book** (1543) or *Necessary Doctrine and Erudition for any Christian Man* was equally Romanist. It defined transubstantiation, free will and good words; Henry VIII wrote the preface and presented it to Convocation.

TENASSERIM. See BURMA.

TENBY (Pembs.) originally a Welsh settlement but fortified as a Flemish colony planted by Henry V and chartered in 1402.

TEN GURUS. See SIKHS-1.

TEN HOURS MOVEMENT to reduce working hours, was initiated by Chartists and other Radicals, and supported by enlightened industrialists e.g. Richard Oastler and John Fielden. It gained parliamentary clout from the championship of the respected 3rd E. of Shaftesbury and with evidence supplied from Lancashire and Yorkshire mills. The first bill of 1832, introduced during the Reform Bill excitement, was intended to apply to both women and children, the sponsors calculating that cutting off both sources of cheap labour would force employers to reduce the hours for their consequently enlarged and more expensive male work-force. The greedier industrialists saw this too, and the Act of 1833 was confined to children. The principle (if with many exceptions) of the bill of 1832 was conceded in 1847. See FACTORY LEGISLATION.

TENISON (1) Abp. Thomas (1636-1715) first gained public respect through his services at Cambridge during the plague in 1667. He published several polemical works against Hobbes and the Jesuits. In 1685 he ministered to Monmouth at his execution; in 1688 he associated himself with the Seven Bishops and later supported William III. He became Bp. of Lincoln in 1691 and Abp. of Canterbury in 1694. Among his many philanthropic works were the foundation of the Society for the Propagation of the Gospel, a school at St. Martins in the Fields, and in 1695 the first public library. He also preached at Nell Gwynn's funeral and strongly favoured moderation towards dissenters. In 1696 he voted for the Fenwick attainder. Though largely outside politics under Q. Anne, he took part in ensuring George I's peaceful accession. A relative **(2) Richard (?1640-1705)** was Essex's chaplain in Ireland and then Bp. successively of Killala (1682), Clogher (1691) and Meath (1697). A cousin **(3) Edward (1673-1735)** was Bp. of Ossory from 1731-35.

TEN MINUTE RULE. A method of having a quick debate on a specific subject involving legislation in the House of Commons. A motion for leave to bring in a bill is proposed at the beginning of public business after question time. The proposer and opposer may speak for ten minutes each, the question is put and if carried the proposer will then bring in his bill for First Reading. Not more than one such motion is proposed in a day.

TENNANT (1) Charles (1768-1838) chemist, established the great chemical (especially sulphuric acid) works at St. Rollox near Glasgow in 1800. His grandson **(2) Sir Charles (1823-1906)** became chairman of the United Alkali Co. which took over the St. Rollox business. He was a liberal M.P. from 1879-86 and a collector of English pictures.

TENNESSEE was part of Charles II's Carolina, but permanent settlement (from Virginia and the Carolinas) began only in 1770. It was ceded by N. Carolina to the U.S.A. in 1784 and was part of the U.S. South West Territory until it entered the Union as a state in 1796. It supported the Confederacy in the Civil War.

TENNIS (1) ROYAL, REAL or COURT was played in 11th cent. It probably originated in a convent yard or cloister. The Hampton Court Tennis Court was built in 1529 and was the model for all later courts. **(2) LAWN** was originated under the name *Sphairistike* by a Major Walter Wingfield in 1874. The All England Croquet Club at Wimbledon added 'Lawn Tennis' to its title, and tennis courts to its facilities in 1877, when the first tournament took place. The Lawn Tennis (L.T.) Association was founded in 1886, the International Lawn Tennis Federation in 1912.

TENNIS COURT OATH (20 June 1789). The deputies of the Third Estate of the French Estates General demanded a constitution. Excluded from their usual chamber, they took over a nearby (Royal) tennis court and swore not to separate until France had a constitution. This defiance of the autocracy was the seminal event of the Revolution, preceding the storming of the Bastille (14 July).

TENNYSON-D'EYNCOURT, Sir Eustace Henry William, Bt. (1868-1951) trained as a naval architect at Armstrong's Elswick shipyard in its heyday and was the firm's chief designer from 1902-12 when Winston Churchill appointed him Director of Naval Construction. As such, he designed and constructed 21 capital ships beginning with the *Royal Sovereign*, including the battle cruiser *Hood* and ending with the Washington Treaty Battleships *Nelson* and *Rodney*. He also designed 53 cruisers and eleven types of submarine. He invented the successful bulge form of protection against underwater explosion and originated the design of all aircraft carriers. His extraordinary talent extended, however, in 1915 to naval airships, and in 1916 to the first tanks. He left the Admiralty in 1924 to design merchant ships for Armstrong.

TENNYSON, Alfred (1809-1892) 1st Ld. TENNYSON (1884) became acquainted with Arthur Hallam at Cambridge on whose death in 1833 he wrote the earlier parts of *In Memoriam*. He met Gladstone in 1837, and his Poems published in 1847, were attacked by Lord Lytton. Peel pensioned him shortly after and *In Memoriam* (more popular with the public than the critics) was published in 1850 when he succeeded Wordsworth as Poet Laureate. *Maud* was coldly received in 1855 but his treatment of Arthurian romance in *Idylls of the King* ensured his popularity from 1859 onwards. He published work regularly until his death, *Crossing the Bar* coming out in 1889 and *Robin Hood* in 1891.

TENTERDEN (Kent) (A.S: the swine pasture of the men of Thanet) was combined with Rye in 1449 and then separated from it in 1600 as a distinct corporation. This led to its becoming a borough under the Municipal Corporations Act, 1834. There is a legend that funds for the sea defences of Goodwin's I were diverted to repair the steeple and that the consequent inundations in 1099 converted the island into the Goodwin Sands.

TENTERDEN (1) Charles Abbot (1762-1832) 1st Ld. (1827) became a judge of the Common Pleas in 1816 without having taken silk, and was quickly moved to the King's Bench. In Sept. 1819 the chief justiceship fell vacant and no better candidate being in sight, Abbott was appointed. Neither intellectual as a lawyer nor distinguished as a speaker he nevertheless raised the reputation of the court by common-sense, despatch and attention to detail. As a peer he introduced a number of useful practical improvements. **(2) Charles Stuart (1834-82) 3rd Ld.** was permanent U/Sec. of State for Foreign Affairs from 1873.

TENTH AND FIFTEENTH was a tax on lay rents and movables. Originally levied at varying but flat rates with towns and royal demesnes being tallaged in addition, the amounts and incidence created endless disputes especially in the early 14th cent. Accordingly when the tallage was abandoned, it was fixed at 10th for the towns and royal demesnes and a 15th for the rest. The global amount of a single 10th and 15th was settled as at 1334, and this figure was divided up *pro rata* between the counties. The actual amount paid by individuals was originally settled by a sort of county conference but liability thereafter clung to the same properties regardless of their condition. Changes of ownership and land use caused the yield to decline while inflation destroyed much of its value:

1225	$\frac{1}{15}$th only	£58,000
1229	$\frac{1}{15}$th only	£117,000
1334	$\frac{1}{10}$th & $\frac{1}{15}$th	£38,170
1436	" "	£34,170
1486	" "	£30,000
1540	" "	£29,000

It ceased to be levied at the outbreak of the civil war, and technically was superseded by the Land Tax in 1688. *See* SUBSIDY.

TEN YEAR RULE. In 1919 Lloyd George, in response to inquiries, told the Chiefs of Staff that they might plan on the assumption that no major war would happen within ten years. In 1925 they inquired again and received the same answer from Baldwin. This was repeated in 1926 and 1927. In 1928, on Churchill's proposal, they were told that the period was daily renewable. In Mar. 1932 the rule was formally abandoned and the Chiefs of Staff were told to make recommendations for remedying deficiencies. This took two years but the Cabinet meanwhile pinned its faith to collective security and the League of Nations and had accepted Neville Chamberlain's Budget estimates for the lowest arms expenditure since 1918. There was thus no means with which to carry out the recommendations.

TEPEE. The Sioux or Dakota word for wigwam.

TE RANGITAKE or WIREMU KINGI (?1795-1882) Maori High Chief who stopped the sale of the Waitara (N.Z.) tribal lands in 1859 and so precipitated the Taranaki War.

TEREDO or SHIP WORM. A warm water mollusc very destructive of wooden ships whose cost was much increased by the need for copper underwater sheathing against it.

TERMES DE LA LEY. See RASTELL.

TERRIER was a register of land showing vassals, tenants, the particulars of their holdings, and the services or rents due. Such inventories were kept for private as well as official purposes.

TERRITORIAL ARMY. Cardwell's reforms in 1881 territorialised the British infantry and linked each local volunteer rifle corps to a local regular regiment. These corps became known as territorial units and with some famous exceptions, took the name of their parent regiment. This relationship was formalised under Haldane's Territorial and Reserve Forces Act, 1907. Though intended for home service, territorials could volunteer to go overseas, and in 1914 nearly all the 12,000 officers and 300,000 other ranks did; consequently they went to war as complete units: the World War I territorial infantry divisions were numbered 42-56. The cavalry units were distributed or formed into the 74th division. In 1939 the Territorial Army was about 405,000 strong and overseas service was obligatory. The system was re-established in 1947.

TERRITORIAL WATERS. Anciently the sea within lines drawn from headland to headland and known as the Queen's Chambers was considered under English rule but not part of the realm, but the Scots claimed, at any rate for fishing, the sea from which any part of their coast was visible from the masthead. This was later defined as 14 miles. Other states, notably Denmark and Spain adopted a similar opinion. In days of sail such an area could not be efficiently controlled and in 1609 Grotius proposed the more practical criterion of control which could be maintained without leaving land, in other words gun range. This was optimistically estimated at 6 miles and by 1789 (still optimistically) at 3. Between 1798-1828 Lord Stowell, as Judge of the Admiralty, consistently applied the Three Mile Rule which was thus received into English Law and statutorily recognised in 1878. By this time it had become ballistically realistic. A state is considered to have sovereign rights in the sea bed, the water and in the air over territorial waters, but it may also have special rights in so-called Contiguous Zones if specifically claimed. This is the basis of the, often much wider fishery zones, the Continental Shelf legislation and the North Sea and other off-shore oil and gas exploitations. In legal proceedings a Sec. of State's certificate is conclusive as to the extent of territorial waters. From the 1950s coastal states began to claim 12-mile territorial and 200 mile economic zones. Fishing states such as Iceland and Peru led the way. Iceland's Cod Wars with Britain in 1972-73 and 1975-76 were one consequence. Conferences at Geneva in 1958, 1960 and 1975 failed to secure international agreement on new limits.

TERRITORY (1) The soil of the country. **(2)** A part of a state where conditions do not permit the usual organs of govt. to function adequately and where, in consequence, public authority is usually vested in persons or bodies responsible to a national authority, not to the local population e.g. the Northern Territories of Australia, the North Western Territories of Canada.

TERRY ALTS. A ribbon society similar to Whitefeet. They infested Co. Clare.

TESCHEN (Poland, Czechoslovakia) is rich in coal and was heavily industrialised by World War I. The population was roughly half Polish and a quarter Czech. At the collapse of the Habsburg Empire in 1918, the local Polish and Czech politicians fixed an ethnic frontier, but the Czech govt. at Prague claimed the whole and occupied it. The Allied Supreme Council proposed a plebiscite, which the Czechs prevented. In 1920 the Poles, in danger from Russia, were forced to let the Czechs take all the industrial zone and 140,000 Poles. In 1938 at the time of Munich, the Poles secured a rectification along the ethnic line of 1918. In 1945 the Russians re-established the line of 1920. *See* SILESIA.

TEST ACTS (ENGLISH) were based partly on a Commonwealth Act of 1657 against Popish recusants. **(1) The Act of 1672** (*see* CHARLES II-16) required all persons holding any office under, or any fee, salary or wages from, the crown, and anyone employed by the D. of York and resident within 30 miles of London, to take the oaths of supremacy and allegiance, publicly, in the courts of Chancery or King's Bench and at the same time to sign a declaration that they believe "that there is not any transubstantiation in the sacrament of the Lords Supper, or in the elements of bread and wine, at or after the consecration thereof by any person whatsoever". The declaration took this form because, being against a R. Catholic article of faith, the Pope could not grant a dispensation for making it. The Act also disqualified all persons who allowed their children to be brought up as Papists from public office and in order to exclude certain non-conformist Protestants, required the taking of the Holy Communion in the Anglican manner. **(2) The Act of 1677** imposed similar requirements upon peers and M.P.'s with some additional wording against invocation of saints and papal dispensations. **(3)** These acts became the centre of the controversy about the royal dispensing power under James II. (*See also* GODDEN *v* HALES.) **(4) The Act of 1702** imposed the requirement upon all persons at the age of 18 if they expected to inherit land, and disqualified them from so doing if they refused. This soon became a dead letter. **(5)** In so far as the Acts discriminated against Protestants it became usual from 1727 onwards to pass an act annually to indemnify them against the consequences of failure to take the sacrament. This part of the Acts was permanently repealed in 1828; the rest in 1829 by the R. Catholic Relief Act. **(6)** The Acts operated in Ireland to keep R. Catholics out of office and to some extent, property, much longer than in Britain.

TEST ACT (SCOTS) 1681 required office holders to swear to the Confession of 1560 and the Royal Supremacy.

TESTA DE NEVILL or ***LIBER FEODORUM* (Lat: Book of Fees) (c. 1220)** named either from Jollan de Nevill (?-1246) a Justice in Eyre, or Ralph de Nevill, a contemporary Accountant of the Exchequer. It contained a list of fees held in chief by knight service, serjeanty, or frankalmoign and whether, if alienated or escheated, to whom granted (if anyone) together with a note of wards and widows and the amounts payable by each tenant for aids and scutage. It was derived from inquisitions. Only a copy of part of it now exists.

TEST BAN TREATY (1963). The U.S.A., Britain and the U.S.S.R. agreed to cease testing atom bombs above ground because of their world-wide environmental effects. France and China, which were still developing their own bombs, refused to sign.

TEST MATCHES. *See* CRICKET.

TESTOON. *See* COINAGE-13.

TEULU. *See* WELSH LAW-4.

TEUTONIC KNIGHTS. This order, founded at Acre in 1190, was regularised by Innocent III in 1198. Mainly German, from 1211-1215 it campaigned in Hungary. Having secured an invitation to Prussia from the D. of Poland, it acquired Kulm (1226) and from the Emperor Frederick II, sovereignty over future conquests. It was never exclusively aristocratic, and recruits were secured from all over, but mostly from northern Europe and England. Paganism was exterminated and towns were settled with German colonists so that they had a firm grip on East Prussia by 1237 when they absorbed the KNIGHTS of the SWORD with their lands in Livonia and Courland. The Prussian territories were ruled by the *Deutschmeister* (German Master) of the order; the Livonian by the *Landmeister* (Land Master). The High Master remained at Acre until its fall, when he moved to Venice. In 1255 the Knights founded Königsberg and in 1308 took Danzig. The High Master moved to Marienburg in 1309. They carried on a vigorous policy of state trading in consort with the Hanse and of land settlement and founded some 90 towns. (*See* BALTIC.-9-28; BRANDENBURG; HANSE.) They formed a secure and reliable partner for English trade in the late middle ages.

TEW, GREAT (Oxon). This beautiful village represents one of the earliest cases of planning, the stone houses being all possibly executed by John Loudon.

TEWKESBURY (Glos.) B. of (4 May 1471) Edward VI, fresh from his victory over the E. of Warwick at Barnet (14 Apr.), completed the destruction of the Lancastrians by routing the forces of Q. Margaret and Edmund D. of Somerset. Edward, P. of Wales, son and heir of Henry VI, was killed in the fighting (not as Shakespeare has it in *Henry VI Pt III*), and Somerset and other leading Lancastrians were executed on 6 May. A few days later the captive K. Henry VI was murdered in the Tower.

TEXAS (U.S.A.) Spanish settled occupation was slight, but when the territory passed to an independent Mexico in 1821 Americans began to colonise it, and by 1835 the 30,000 Americans outnumbered the Mexicans by four to one. The Mexican govt., suspecting conspiracy, tried to disarm the Americans; they resisted and formed a provisional govt. The war lasted six months, including the siege of the Alamo, the massacre of the Texans at Goliad and the B. of San Jacinto, when the Mexicans were surprised during the siesta. From 1836-46 accordingly Texas was independent, but in 1846 it was annexed to the U.S.A. at the end of the American-Mexican War. It supported the Confederacy in the Civil War.

TEXTILES-BRITAIN (1) Basketry and then fish netting anciently inspired weaving, which in its turn created a quantity need for thread, produced eventually by distaff spinning. These crafts, using wool and linen together with dying, were established in Mediterranean countries and W. Europe by 200 B.C. Silk at this time was confined to China, cotton to India.

(2) Coarse woollens were being made for local or household use in Roman Britain and it is unlikely that this craft ever died out. There were sheep in abundance, especially in the West Country, E. Anglia, Wessex, Kent, Warwickshire and Gloucestershire but the skilled use of wool was retarded by the disturbances of the Anglo-Saxon and Scandinavian invasions. Hence 11th and 12th cent. England exported raw wool and fells to Flanders and N. France where more skilled techniques had become available, and received fine dyed cloth and good leather back. (*See* STAPLE.)

(3) By the 6th cent. silk had reached the Byzantine empire, whose craftsmen had also learned Persian tapestry making. The Seljuk invaders of Asia Minor were skilled makers of carpets, felt and towelling. The Arabs quickly disseminated these methods and their conquest of Sicily (A.D. 827) is a major landmark. Palermo became a centre of high quality production which the Norman rulers and the Emperor Frederick II developed with Greek and Turkish craftsmen. Travellers and crusaders brought samples and the Indian spinning wheel to the west; ideas migrated, particularly when French 13th cent. aggression drove Sicilian weavers up Italy and so *via* Lucca and Florence (where nearly 50,000 were employed), their techniques reached Cologne, Artois and Flanders. The name of Arras became synonymous with tapestry (made also at Brussels); Arras also produced silks and velvets. Linen damasks were developed at Courtrai, Ghent, Ypres and Cambrai ("Cambric").

(4) Flemish woollen weavers had long been in England. In 13th cent. the main English sheep breeding areas (*see* (2) above) were beginning to produce a surplus of good cloth, which was sold as far away as the Mediterranean, but this export trade collapsed in the face of continental competition and in the early 14th cent. foreign merchants were importing 12,000 cloths annually. These imports in their turn fell away in the 1330s and ceased in the 1340s through warlike disruption.

(5) Fulling was first done by covering the material with fuller's earth and trampling it underfoot, but from the early 13th cent. water-powered fulling mills came into use. They stimulated the revival of the industry and attracted it to locations near the swift-flowing upper reaches of rivers in the wool producing countrysides. **Spinning** also and **weaving** mostly had been feminine occupations which could be carried on nearby, but the finishing stages from **dyeing** onwards tended to be carried on in the towns. In the 14th cent. the biggest and finest production was in Somerset and Wiltshire but cloth-making increasingly took place in E. Anglia and the West Riding of Yorkshire. The relatively cheap kerseys, worsteds, mendips and aylshams from these areas virtually equalled, by mid cent. the amount of imported cloths and were supplemented in the later 14th cent. by broadcloths. Between 1300 and 1380 cloth imports almost halved the export of raw wool and English cloths began to oust Flemish in the French and Italian markets (*see* MERCHANT VENTURERS). The Cotswolds, which specialised in fine broadcloths, prospered notably as the fine village churches and houses of Gloucestershire and Somerset testify, and the industry continued to move into the countryside in the 15th and 16th cents.

(6) Wealth and improved skills also created a demand for home grown **flax**, cultivated in Gloucestershire for fine linens. The rising seaborne commerce stimulated the cultivation (in Dorset) of **hemp** for ropes and nets.

(7) Flemish immigration continued. Flemings were weaving silk at Norwich in 1455, some 25 years before the industry was fully established at Lyons. England was taking its share of European development, reinaugurated by the foot-powered Saxony spinning wheel, in the later 15th cent. A guild of Norwich silk weavers was set up in 1564. English and French producers were for a while in competition and Flemings were migrating to France, especially to the new crown carpet and tapestry works at Savonnières founded in 1589, the year when the English invented the **frame knitting** machine. The long warlike devastations in France and Germany, however, disturbed industry, but England, even in the Civil War, remained relatively quiet while a rapid rise in production and quality was financed through the inflow of piratical and more legitimate capital from Africa and the Spanish Main. By 1626 English cloth was a major import into the Ottoman Empire, and through Venice and Leghorn into N. Italy.

(8) Until 1685 French textiles, especially the fancy varieties, combined with tariffs and bounties to engross the French domestic and adjacent markets. The Revocation of the Edict of Nantes initiated a decline which subsequent wars completed. Shoals of Huguenot textile workers deserted France for her rivals, notably England, where in Norwich, Braintree (Essex) and Spitalfields (London) they formed busy colonies. British maritime supremacy carried the products to a widening circle of lucrative and hitherto unexploited markets. The immense unit profits encouraged ingenuity, and social experiment. The concentration of cottage workers under one roof began at Derby in 1717. The **flying shuttle** was invented in 1733. (*See* INDUSTRIAL REVOLUTION.)

(9) Though cotton had been known in Europe for centuries, Anglo-French enterprise and conflict in India were responsible for its introduction in the 18th cent. as a crop in the American colonies and as an industrial material in Europe. The French defeat in the Seven Years' War (1756-63) diverted it increasingly to Britain which, through the industrial revolution was equipping herself to use it. By 1800 British textile production in which cotton predominated, came from a steampowered, coal-fired industry. The latter had abandoned its ancient seats and had migrated to the neighbourhood of the mines in Yorkshire, Lanark and Lancashire where also the damp climate was especially suitable for cotton spinning. "Cotton" indeed "was King". The English textile industry was the biggest production complex the world had ever seen. Despite the post-war recession of 1815-50 it continued to expand, but it then faced stagnation through technological backwardness in the making of apparel (*see* CLOTHING). The solution of these problems in Britain and U.S.A. in the second half of the 19th cent. lent a new impetus to a world leadership which lasted until after World War II, and the industrial development of artificial fibres.

TEXTILES-IRELAND. The plantations of Ireland had led to the rise of important Protestant controlled cloth industries in Ulster and elsewhere; William III brought in Huguenot weavers and spinners, especially the brothers Crommelin (q.v.) and Dutch flax growers to encourage the small existing linen industry around Lisburn, and with promises to encourage linen, induced the Irish parliament to impose from 1799 an additional export duty of 20% on broad-cloth and 10% on other woollens except frize. In 1799 an English statute prohibited the export of Irish woollens from any Irish port save Dublin, Waterford, Youghal, Kinsale, Cork and Drogheda to any place in the world save the English ports of Bideford, Barnstaple, Minehead, Bridgwater, Bristol, Milford Haven, Chester and Liverpool. As there was no useful home market and English woollens could easily undersell Irish in England, the Irish woollens manufactories were ruined. This has been a smouldering historical grievance ever since but the chief sufferers were the Protestant colonists, and the chief gainers the Irish tenantry whose land was not converted into sheepwalks. The promise to encourage linen was kept. The industry at Lisburn was rapidly expanded and new ones at Kilkenny, and in Cos. Cork, Waterford and Dublin, besides sail cloth manufactories at Cork, Waterford and Rathbride were established.

THACKERAY, William Makepeace (1811-63) After unsuccessful ventures, began to write for *The Times* in 1837. His celebrity began with his *Snob Papers* contributed to *Punch* from 1842. *Vanity Fair* came out in 1847, *Pendennis* between 1848-50 and *Esmond* in 1852. He lectured in America and the Continent from 1852-54, published *The Virginians* from 1857-59 and edited the *Cornhill* from 1960-62.

THAILAND (locally MUANG-THAI = Land of the Free) or SIAM (a European corruption of SHAN). **(1)** contains a majority of the Thai peoples which also include the Shans, Karens and Laos. The Siamese language is related to ancient Chinese, but with Indian, Javanese and Khmer accretions. The alphabet is derived from Sanskrit. The people are 95% Hinayana Buddhist with some Moslems. The alluvial flood basin of the Chao Phya or Menam R. is fertile, producing a surplus of rice, fruit and vegetables. Communication here was, until modern times by boat, most of the people living either in boats or in stilted houses along the winding river banks. The up-country teak forests are worked by elephants, the logs being floated down the rivers.

(2) When the Portuguese, the first Europeans to arrive, took Malacca in 1511, there was a declining northern Kingdom centred on Chiengmai, and an immensely rich Menam-based Kingdom of Ayuthaya (its capital). This included Malaya, Tavoy and Tenasserim on the B. of Bengal, and suzerainty in Cambodia. It was the meeting point of the vast China and Japan trade with the trade of India and Persia. The wind conditions and piracy in Malaysian waters strengthened the mercantile tendency to establish exchanges further north. The western trade used Mergui, a ten-day journey from Ayuthaya, or else Junk Ceylon (now Pukhet) and thence across the Isthmus of Kra to Sonkhla (Singora). Most eastern ships came up to Ayuthaya on the S.W. Monsoon (May-Sept.), stayed six months and sailed in the winter.

(3) External history in the 16th to 19th cents. was dominated by three factors. On *land,* recurrent Burmese aggression from the west and Cambodian sedition or rebellion on the east. On *the sea,* successive western powers tried to divert the trade through Indonesian waters where they could control it. *Internally* foreign adventurers and rival religious missions sought, often with foreign help, to cut out careers or dominate opinion. The common factor was the royal monopoly of foreign trade, which was exercised through a system of pre-emptive prises on all goods landed. Foreign traders were compelled to use the King as their broker. The enormous profits, so long as they were maintained, rendered the govt. virtually independent of taxation. Conversely inroads upon them from whatever direction might lead to social upheaval. At the same time the monarchs early recognised western technological superiority; they became adept at balancing the various external threats against each other and tried to acquire, from a safe variety of sources, the more useful western skills.

(4) The Portuguese helped the Burmese with artillery and gunners. In a series of wars, the Burmese took Chiengmai, penetrated Laos and in 1569 sacked Ayuthaya. A P. Naresuan, who had escaped, became King (r. 1569-1604) and waged a long war of liberation. In 1580 the Spaniards annexed Portugal, and the Portuguese possessions became victims of English and Dutch aggression. By 1599 Naresuan had pressed on to victory despite Cambodian efforts to get Spanish help from Manila. The lesson was not lost. Naresuan's successor (Ekatotsarot r. 1604-10) made contact with anti-Spanish powers and signed a commercial treaty with the Dutch at The Hague (1608). Dutch traders soon appeared (1610) followed by English (1612).

(5) The English (i.e. the HEIC) concentrated on India and closed their factory at Ayuthaya in 1622. The Dutch forged ahead and by 1660 their predominance was giving concern. Moreover, there was a Moslem problem. Moslems dominated the shipping at Mergui and held important govt. posts. Moslem powers such as Achin, Golconda and Persia were sending religious missions to the court. K. Narai (r. 1656-88) reacted by countenancing French missionaries and English commercial interlopers. The Dutch now felt strong enough to use force. In 1664 they blockaded the Menam and compelled the King to surrender the export trade in hides and to place the China and Japan carrying trade in their hands.

(6) French missionaries and engineers suggested a French alliance; the interloper Constantine Gerakis

(otherwise Falcon or Phaulcon) a Venetian Greek brought up in England, had become the King's favourite and controller of foreign trade. He was hostile to the HEIC. Diplomatic exchanges resulted in 1686 in the appearance of small French garrisons at Bangkok and Mergui; but this combined with suspicions of the missionaries and official jealousy of Phaulcon, led to a palace revolution, Phaulcon's death and the expulsion of the French (1688).

(7) The revolution inaugurated an era of disputed successions and governmental weakness. There was a successful Cambodian revolt (1709-17) and while the European powers fought each other elsewhere, a Burmese revival brought renewed wars and the final sack of the capital (1767). This time no prince escaped, but the Chinese drove the Burmese out, and a surviving General, Taksin, made his H.Q. at Dhonburi opposite Bangkok and was proclaimed King (1768).

(8) The disaster left Mergui in Burmese (and so ultimately in British) hands, and encouraged the diversion of trade round Malaya. Taksin reasserted Thai authority over the Malay sultanates, but a further Burmese war distracted him when Kedah ceded Penang to the British (1771). The latter, victorious in the Seven Years' War, with their large armed East Indiamen and huge navy were a greater threat than their predecessors, for they could police the Indonesian seas and make them commercially attractive. Meanwhile, Taksin recovered Chiengmai (1773), Laos (1778) and Cambodia (1779).

(9) Taksin was murdered in 1782 and replaced by the Chao Phaya Chakri who, as conqueror of Laos had brought back the long lost Emerald Buddha. As Yodfah Chulaloke or Rama I (r. 1782-1809) he transferred the capital across the Menam to Bangkok for greater safety in the Burmese war. At its climax in 1785-86, he ended the Penang Is. dispute by recognising the British occupation. In 1791 the British demanded a mainland area opposite (later called Province Wellesley) so that Penang could be fed without piratical disturbance. In view of events in Vietnam he made the cession in 1800.

(10) Ambitious Vietnamese, helped by French adventurers using the rumour of French support, had forced Cambodia to pay tribute (1807). The Burmese were threatening, and then launched a war. K. Lert Lah (Rama II r. 1809-24) approached the Chinese Court, repelled the Burmese and drove the Cambodian King into exile in Saigon (1810). This was the last Burmese invasion, for Burmese royal authority was crumbling; moreover as a result of the Vienna settlement western trade revived. In 1822 Sir John Crawford came to discuss Kedah and left with a commercial agreement. In 1826 K. Nang Klao (r 1824-51) agreed with John Burney, during a Vietnamese fomented revolt in Laos, not to obstruct trade in Kelantan or Trengganu, that is, not to enforce the royal monopoly there. In 1833 the U.S. obtained a treaty similar to Crawford's treaty. A long Cambodian war (settled in 1847) created the usual further opportunities for pressure. The western powers were demanding extra-territorial privileges for their subjects. Nang Klao refused them (1850).

(11) The next King was the remarkable K. Mongkut (Rama IV 1851-68) made famous yet misrepresented in a western book and musical. He had been a monk for 27 years; he was learned in sciences, and western languages and was, because of the Buddhist monastic custom of daily begging, very familiar with his subjects. Unself-consciously enlightened, he saw at once that without modernisation Thailand could neither resist the west nor justify rejection of western privileges. For example, the legal system still depended upon trial by ordeal. There was no properly minted currency. The thread-bare royal trading monopoly no longer supported the state expenditure, and the taxes were in the hands of Chinese tax farmers. Slavery was still common. Mongkut and his

even abler son Chulalongkorn (Rama V 1868-1910) proceeded, in the face of international difficulties, to consolidate a national consciousness and to hurry the country out of mediaevalism.

(12) In 1855 to their surprised pleasure Mongkut agreed on extra-territoriality with Sir John Bowing and the American Townshend Harris. A Thai embassy visited London and Paris in 1857. In 1859, however, the French seized Saigon and egged on by the new colonials at Singapore, the British interpreted Burney's treaty (1826) as recognising the independence of Kelantan and Trengganu. By 1862 they were bombarding Trengganu, while in 1863 the French proclaimed (despite the presence of a Thai resident) a protectorate over Cambodia. By an abuse of their customs agreement, they had acquired a predominance in the spirit trade with grave moral as well as financial consequences. In the end (1867) Mongkut recognised the French protectorate (save over Angkor) in return for the right to tax French spirits.

(13) Sir Harry Orde, the sensible governor of Singapore, saw in this an opportunity to win Thai good will, and forcibly advised his govt. just after Chulalongkorn's accession, that the Malay sultanates were under Thai suzerainty. In 1873, when Chulalongkorn came of age, the tempo of modernisation was accelerated, but ten years later French imperialism made itself felt in Vietnam. The British, who had held Lower Burma since 1827, reacted by annexing Upper Burma in 1885. Meanwhile, events in the Nomansland of the Vietnam-Laos-Chinese border gave the French a pretext for further encroachments. The Hos, survivors of the Chinese Taiping rebels, created disorders which the Thais put down (1886) but the French demanded Laos on grounds of public peace and because Laos had once paid tribute to Vietnam. Their gunboats penetrated to Bangkok, and they blockaded the G. of Siam. The dispute dragged on until 1893 when Chulalongkorn at length ceded Laos, but he got the British to mark out the Burmese frontier (1894) and to recognise the advantage of Thailand as a buffer state. They were already moving towards the idea of the *Entente Cordialé*, in 1896 they secured a joint Anglo-French declaration on the integrity of the Menam basin. This did not cover Thailand as a whole. Hence when Chulalongkorn had reformed the law and wanted to get rid of extra-territoriality, he had to buy it with territorial cessions: in 1907 with Angkor to the French, in 1909 with the four Malay Sultanates to the British.

(14) K. Vajiravudha (Rama VI r. 1910-25) was educated in England. Like Yodfah and Mongkut, of a strongly literary cast of mind, he translated Shakespeare. He also founded a modernised state trading and banking system. In 1917 he joined the Allies in World War I and at Versailles took advantage of the Fourteen Points to get U.S. support for the ending of the remaining unequal treaties. He had founded a University in 1916 and put the existing plans for universal education into effect in 1921. Unfortunately his expanding expenditure coincided with a world-wide depression. The Treasury was empty when Prajadhipok (Rama VII 1925-34) succeeded him. The new King's economies put many of the rising European educated state employees out of work. They had new western ideas and had witnessed the European revolutions. In 1932, led by Pridi Panomyong, they staged a *coup d'état* which ended the autocracy. In 1934 the King abdicated in favour of his eldest child Ananta Mahidol (Rama VIII 1934-46) who was at school in Switzerland. The Regency and the new politicians were able to carry on unobstructed by the monarch, whose office still had great popular appeal.

(15) When World War II broke out the British and French sought to neutralise Thailand by non-aggression pacts. The Thais wanted the retrocession of the Angkor area. A French ultimatum erupted into a pointless war

during which the French surprised and wiped out the Thai navy (1940). Hence when the Japanese demanded their right of way to Malaya in Dec. 1941 the Thais, though unwilling, were already psychologically prepared by allied mistakes. The allied bombing of Bangkok (Jan. 1942) created a pretext for declaring war on Britain and U.S.A. The Songgram Govt., negotiated the return of parts of Cambodia, the four Malay Sultanates and even the Shan states with the Japanese, while Seni Pramoj organised in Britain and U.S.A. a Free Thai movement which, through Prince Svasti, had direct contact with the Govt. Hence at the Japanese surrender Seni Pramoj slipped quietly into office.

(16) The French required the return of their former territories, the British 1.5M tons of rice for their starving colonies as a condition of peace. The U.S.A., which had lost nothing, demonstratively demanded nothing and stole a diplomatic march upon them. Meanwhile K. Ananta had returned from Switzerland. He was found shot in bed and a public revulsion against left-wing politics ensued (1946). This almost coincided with the creation of the South East Asia Treaty Organisation (S.E.A.T.O.) with its H.Q. in Bangkok. Almost immediately Thailand was indirectly involved in the Vietnamese and Cambodian Civil Wars. Successive govts. supplied necessaries to the royalists and the anti-communists, and the U.S. established bases on Thai soil. The communists reacted (1956) by attempting to penetrate the north-east and by subverting the growing student movements. These secured the evacuation of U.S. troops in 1973, but the govt. did not allow itself to be reorientated politically but encouraged western investment. This resulted in a modern economic, mainly industrialised, revolution with the townward migrations characteristic of such changes and Bangkok, in particular, grew to an enormous area.

THALER. *See* DOLLAR.

THAMES. The conservancy belonged, but was scarcely exercised by the Crown until 1389 when it was conferred below Staines upon the Mayor or Warden (as the case might be) of London. In 1751 it was conferred above Staines on Navigation Commissioners consisting of the riparian borough magistrates and landowners assessed to land tax at £100 a year. The functions of the two bodies were radically different, since the conservancy existed mainly to protect fisheries, the Commissioners to improve navigation. Since, however, improved navigation involved raising water levels, and risking floods on riparian owners lands, progress by this unwieldy body was slow. The river was notoriously mismanaged and stank until a new more expert Conservancy of 31 members was created in 1857 above Teddington. The Lord Mayor's rights passed in 1908 to the Port of London Authority whose duty was to improve navigation and manage the vast docks which had grown up from Tower Bridge onwards. Changes in the nature of maritime traffic and the rise of aviation diverted the trade into other channels and the docks were progressively converted to other uses after 1960.

THAMES AND SEVERN CANAL. *See* TRANSPORT AND COMMUNICATIONS.

THANET (Kent). Originally an island in the delta of the Kentish Stour, cut off from the mainland by a navigable channel (The Wantsum) from Richborough (Lat: Rutupiae) on the Straits of Dover to Reculver (Lat: Regulbium) on the Thames estuary. The Wantsum was a navigational short cut, and the Romans had garrisons and signal stations at each end. The Stour progressively silted it up, so that after the 5th cent. Jutish landings (which traditionally took place first in Thanet) Richborough and Reculver ceased to serve their purpose and Sandwich developed near Richborough as the outport of Canterbury. The area was agriculturally well developed and its inhabitants had swine pastures (*a denn*) on the

Sussex border at Tenterden. There was a monastery at Ebbsfleet. The trade routes bypassed it increasingly so that by 16th cent. it was, save for smuggling at Ramsgate, purely agricultural. Ramsgate began to develop in the 18th cent. in connection with the peacetime cross Channel tourist trade, and the wartime shipping concentrations in Pegwell Bay and the Downs. Margate and Broadstairs began to develop as Londoners' seaside resorts after the coming of the South Eastern and Chatham Railway in the 1850s. Manston Airfield was the most advanced fighter base in World War II and many of the inhabitants were evacuated from the coastal towns, which did not recover their previous holiday prosperity.

THANET, Es. of. *See* TUFTON.

THATCHED HOUSE [CLUB] originally a tavern at the foot of St. James's London, was a resort of politicians and men of fashion. It was pulled down in 1814.

THATCHERISM; THATCHER, Margaret Hilda (née ROBERTS) (1925-) Lady THATCHER of KESTEVEN (1992) (1) Daughter of a Grantham shopkeeper, qualified as an Oxford Chemist. She married a wealthy industrialist and was called to the Bar, but was always primarily interested in politics. In 1959 she became Conservative M.P. for Finchley and held minor office from 1961-64. In the Heath govt. of 1970-74 she was a successful Sec. of State for Education and Science. She was elected Leader of her party against Edward Heath in 1975 and in 1979 led it, assisted by the Labour Govt.'s inept handling of industrial relations, to the first of her electoral victories.

(2) She and a small group of colleagues, including the E. of Gowrie, formulated a theoretically coherent plan to drive back the frontiers of state activity, initially by returning public property to private hands, and then replacing the officially guided, relatively safe society which had grown up since 1939 by a competitively orientated one in which social safety could be achieved by working success and private savings. The energies released by these liberations would generate higher prosperity than had so far been experienced and this, and the expected withering away of bureaucracies would justify reductions in the absolute and relative amounts taken by the state in taxes. It was a necessary feature of the policy that there should be no economic distortions or obstructions in the way of competition, therefore Trade Union power and immunities, official subsidies and grants and selective taxes were equally objectionable and should be abolished. It was consistent with this view that tariffs and export bounties should at least be confined to non-European countries, but this, of course, was injurious to the Commonwealth.

(3) Competition was to be the motor of economic efficiency in the private sector and by keeping prices down, would control inflation. In the public services a new concept of **accountability** was to govern administration by limiting each activity by the funds available, it being understood that profits were desirable and the use of public funds limited. The state was to do things by contract rather than direct labour and it was not to be a provider of capital. The public debt was to be paid off as opportunity offered. In consequence capital operations were to be left to the banks and other financial institutions centred on the City of London.

(4) The combined objectives during Margaret Thatcher's 12 year prime ministership were only partially achieved and then only at the expense of great hardship. There was a fundamental contradiction, compounded by many factors including her autocratic habits and the obstinacy of the civil service, in trying to impose freedom from above. Moreover the policy, launched on the assumption that the world economy would either expand or remain stable, ran into the worst slump of the century, so that resources which might have contributed to prosperity were eroded in business failures and mortgage

foreclosures; unemployment rose, at 3M, to unprecedented heights; the cost of the dole and the contraction of the tax-paying public prevented taxation from falling and as buyers for public property proved harder to find than expected, privatisations had to be spaced out at wider intervals than originally intended; they were not complete in 1995. They did not reduce bureaucracy as such, merely transferring most of the bureaucrats to other paymasters, and the doctrine of accountability in practice meant responsibility to accountants who multiplied in thousands. Inflation too, was a serious mystery which despite many theories, nobody understood. People looked to the govt. to control it, that is, they demanded the central action which the govt. was trying to avoid, and as it had abandoned direct intervention, it had to resort to indirect, namely the manipulation of interest rates (which made life more expensive) or the raising of taxes (which made people poorer).

(5) In these circumstances the Falklands War (1982) and other external excitements particularly on the Continent, came as a godsend. A form of Bonapartism was forced upon Margaret Thatcher by Argentinian aggression and European greed. She stood forth (very properly) as the defender of a small British country at the other end of the world, and the resounding victory enhanced her prestige in coping with Brussels, the communist powers and the U.S.A. With this, her robust clarity and oratorical gifts engendered internal and international respect unequalled since Churchill. The oppressed and maladministered populations of Russia and its satellites understood that the precedent for a retreat from socialist corruption had been set in Britain and might be repeated. The relatively tranquil Thatcherite Revolution was thus as influential as the Russian and French Revolutions of 1917 and 1789. It led, with other factors, notably religion, to the overthrow of the governing communist parties everywhere save in China, the disruption of the U.S.S.R. and the ending of Russian promoted destabilisation in Africa.

(6) Her time of office also had other seamier sides. Crime reached new heights and the prisons consequently were overflowing, and financial corruption reached astonishing levels with such affairs as the Bank of Commerce and Credit International and the Maxwell frauds and the writing off by the clearing banks of vast sums incautiously lent to banana republics. None of such events can be directly ascribed to her, but they seem to have been the product of the type of materialistic society which Thatcherite policies encouraged.

(7) Meanwhile her popular image as an Iron Lady evoked decreasingly favourable responses among her colleagues in the cabinet which she hectored and domineered. She had a ruthlessness and a disregard for common misfortune which did not come well from a rich man's wife living at free quarters in two official residences (though she never accepted an increase of salary), and she derisively stigmatised more sympathetic colleagues as 'wet'. She had made powerful enemies in and outside the cabinet. By 1990 it contained no members serving with her in 1979. Her abrasive manner, combined with disagreements within her party over European integration, led to a party conspiracy which forced her to resign (1991). She signalised the event with one of the most brilliant Commons speeches of modern times. She was succeeded by John Major.

THATCHER, FIRST GOVT. (May 1979-83) (1) 22 in cabinet. Sir Geoffrey Howe, Chancellor of the Exchequer; Secs. of State: William Whitelaw (Home), Ld. Carrington (Foreign), Francis Pym (Defence), James Prior (Employment), Sir Keith Joseph (Industry) and John Nott (Trade). In 1982 Pym replaced Carrington after the Falklands War. Pym had already been replaced by Nott who was himself replaced by Howe after the 1983 election. Prior took the N. Ireland office in 1981 and was replaced at Employment by Norman Tebbitt. A feature of this govt. was the domineering character of the Prime Minister who progressively replaced ministers who disagreed with her. Hence conservative parliamentarians with minds of their own accumulated with Sir Edward Heath outside the govt. including Francis Pym and her former Lord Privy Seal, Sir Ian Gilmour.

(2) She entered office with clear assumptions. Govt. was costing and doing too much, and govt. spending should be limited; and market forces should shape the economy and society (see THATCHERISM), while market orientated indirect taxation should replace direct. Some of this was inherited from the mostly discarded doctrines of the Heath Govt. but Margaret Thatcher had unusual determination and the public was ready for strong leadership and was ready to accept some sacrifices in tackling the difficulties.

(3) Doctrinally it was necessary to influence the economy indirectly through manipulation of the money supply, exchange rates and rates of interest, but the public did not expect the resulting drop in living standards, increased unemployment, bankruptcies or foreclosures of mortgages taken out for the benefit of a property-owning democracy. Fortunately off-shore oil and gas were expected to and did cushion some of the effects and tended oft most balance of payments problems, but the govt. accepted rising unemployment as the price of draconian measures against inflation and rising labour productivity. In 1979 the minimum lending rate stood as high as 17% which bankrupted many not necessarily inefficient businesses and put hundreds of thousands of not necessarily lazy or incompetent workers out of work. By 1983 unemployment, at 3.5M exceeded the scale of the 1929 slump, but because of stronger welfare services (whose soaring costs prevented tax reductions) the social effects seemed less degrading; but the demoralisation of younger people without apparent hope of work, was an important factor in the inner city riots of 1981.

(4) With a partial abandonment of non-intervention the govt. set up the Youth Opportunities Programme, which, though a palliative, did not quite live up to its name, and to attract work into neglected urban centres, a scheme of temporary Enterprise Zones (q.v.) was established. In 1980 business failures approached 7000 and the govt. sought means to help small firms while, logically, opposing large pay increases in the large industries. A long steelworkers' strike in 1980 hurt the steelworkers more than the govt., for the industry cut its labour force and created distress in some steel towns. Subsidies, however, continued for among others, the motor, railway and steel industries but selectively and on condition of higher productivity, in practice involving work-force reductions. In 1981 the civil service also (without much public sympathy) had to submit to an efficiency drive and in 1982 a similar drive brought out the engine drivers. Meanwhile nationalised industries, beginning with electricity and gas were made to raise their prices so as to be able to borrow internally. After threats from the National Union of Mineworkers, however, the govt. made a tactical change of course when it temporarily reversed a decision to close some uneconomic coal mines. There were further moves to increase control of local govt. This became inevitable when it was decided to impose reductions in spending on local authorities. Central grants to those which exceeded certain expenditure norms were withheld.

(5) Privatisation of state-owned industries reduced govt. expenditure primarily by paying off, as opportunity offered, the long term debt. State shareholdings in British Petroleum, British Aerospace, Cable and Wireless and Britoil were wholly or partly sold, yet social services were poorly financed and efforts made, sometimes with tragic

incidents, to restrict the open-ended expense of the National Health Service. The Post Office, long divided into postal and telecommunications depts, was formally divided into different entities and legislation prepared to sell the Telecommunications enterprise. Coach services were progressively deregulated, bringing substantial, if not always sustained fare reductions.

(6) In its efforts to curb trade union power, the govt. had the advantage that over the previous 20 years, union leaderships had made themselves unpopular with the population at large and even with their own members. James Prior's Employment Act had restricted the more extreme forms of picketing and given rights to individual workers against closed shops, by making them illegal unless supported by an 85% majority in a secret ballot. When he was replaced at the Dept. of Employment by Norman Tebbitt, further legislation removed the immunities enjoyed by trade unions; in particular employers hurt by secondary strikes, i.e. strikes in disputes to which they were not a party acquired a limited right to sue the unions responsible.

(7) The pay of servicemen and police rose markedly, but the Brixton riots of 1981 brought to light (in an investigation by Mr Justice Scarman) evidence of police misbehaviour. In Ulster, republican and loyalist terrorism continued without prospect of an early end. A withdrawal of Britain was unacceptable to govt., public and Ulster protestants alike. Southern Irish in Britain, though foreigners continued to enjoy full rights including the local govt. franchise, but the British Nationality Act denied a right of abode to two of the three categories of British citizens which it created. This complex change was ill received by domestic liberal or Commonwealth opinion or by established immigrant minorities.

(8) Overseas the govt. unexpectedly accepted an independent Rhodesia (Zimbabwe) under the Marxist Robert Mugabe, but the keystone of policy remained the alliance with the U.S.A., and in disputes with the U.S.S.R. Margaret Thatcher sometimes led rather than followed the U.S. Govt. and sometimes voiced her irritation with ill-considered U.S. actions. In the Bonapartist Argentinian invasion of the Falklands Is. (1982) she achieved public and international respect, despite strident minority criticism, by her defence of British sovereignty, and though her reported operational interferences were probably unfortunate, the victory (achieved mostly by the Admiralty) contributed to the success of her demand that the unfair financial obligations placed on Britain by the E.E.C. be rectified by repayments. This paid for 75% of the cost of the Falklands War. By this time she had acquired the journalistic sobriquet of 'iron lady'. This enhanced her appeal in the 1983 general election which the conservatives won.

THATCHER, LATER GOVTS. (June 1983-7; 1987-Nov. 1990) (1) 21 in cabinet. Ld Pres: Vist. Whitelaw; Chancellor of the Exchequer; Nigel Lawson; Secs. of State: Home, Leon Brittan; Foreign, Sir Geoffrey Howe; Education, Sir Keith Joseph; Defence, Michael Heseltine; Environment, Patrick Jenkin; Employment, Norman Tebbitt; Trade, Cecil Parkinson; Transport, Tom King; Leader of the Commons, John Biffen.

(2) The Falklands victory, skilfully attributed to Margaret Thatcher, created a national self-respect unknown since 1946 and the grateful electors gave her and her party a large majority in 1983. Despite the enormous continued unemployment, bankruptcies and repossessions the policy of Thatcherism (q.v.) was pressed, and spread into every corner of life, especially housing and health. The govt., agreeably to the public mood, maintained its own nuclear deterrent and support for N.A.T.O. and its essentially doctrinaire domestic policies were mostly hidden from a public distracted by a further instalment of defensive Bonapartism in numerous Ulster murders (given much space in the media) and the

Brighton Bomb explosion (1984) which failed to kill her but gravely injured Mrs Tebbitt. This caused Norman Tebbitt to leave politics. Margaret Thatcher thus progressed from near-heroine to near-martyr.

(3) Negotiations centring on European integration remained largely unnoticed but were crystallised into the irreversible Single European Act signed at Luxembourg in 1986, which transformed the E.E.C. into a European Union, and in which the 12 signatory states undertook to make 'concrete progress towards European unity' by, amongst other things, co-operation on foreign policy, twice yearly meetings of heads of govt. and quarterly meetings of foreign ministers.

(4) The details were largely hidden from the public so that this cession of national sovereignty remained unappreciated for some time, mainly because it was not much understood by the media; but public disquiet began to filter through. The opposition parties welcomed the Single European Act: the Tories, being the responsible group in power, began to entertain doubts. There was a latent split between those who held that the direct ability to influence Europe from within for Britain's benefit was of paramount importance, while a strong minority believed that Europe was hoping to be carried by Britain and anyhow the strong patriotic streak in the electorate would turn votes against them. Two further considerations supervened. The fall of the Berlin Wall and the union of the Germanys, admirable though they were, induced the *Bundesbank* (German Federal Bank) as the strongest bank in Europe to keep its interest rates high, thereby drawing in large foreign funds for the revival of the ruined E. German economy. The Bank of England could thus not lower its own rates to the accepted desirable level. Hence the British, and to a less extent non-British economies were financing German reunification. Secondly, the slump having hit Britain first, was engulfing European countries where conditions were soon even worse than in Britain. It began to be doubted if there was much advantage in pressing to unify such a run-down organisation. Hence Margaret Thatcher began to retreat from the 'concrete progress towards European unity' to which the country (by the signature of Linda Chalker, a junior minister) was pledged.

(5) The govt. won the 1987 elections with a reduced parliamentary majority and a minority vote (40%) while critics of Europeanism became more articulate. To abandon integration, however, meant retreat from treaty obligations with the support only of a minority of M.P.s and a minority of a minority of voters. It seems likely that Margaret Thatcher understood the issues better than anyone else, but it was clear that if she were right and pursued her view openly, the Tory Party would burst into fragments. Unfortunately, she had made many enemies. She could neither compromise nor overbear her opponents. She resigned after a Tory Party internal leadership election had given her, in John Major, a person whom she could recommend to the Queen as her successor. John Major therefore became head of the govt. not with parliamentary or popular participation but by a Tory Party intrigue.

THAXTED (Essex) important mediaeval cutlery centre, is now simply a large village. Its old prosperity is attested by its great perpendicular church and three-storied timbered guildhall.

THEATRE (1) In 11th-13th cents. there were many troubadours, *jongleurs* and wandering unfrocked priests and scholars moving between great continental mansions and fairs as acrobats, ballad singers and minstrels, puppeteers and esters. These disreputable folk nevertheless partly inspired the development of the biblical stories into the church play cycles, lives of saints and Morality plays. The church plays, originally in Latin, thus became secularised through presentation at markets and fairs and by the influence of comic interludes.

(2) The presentation of religious plays, to prevent total degradation or excessive church influence, became an important duty of the guilds, who acted them on travelling floats, often as part of a function such as the London Lord Mayor's Show; but meanwhile companies of players proper were acting short comic and moral plays in noble mansions. One of these, led by James Burbage (?-1597) built *The Theatre* (the first) (1576) and the *Curtain* (c. 1580) in Shoreditch. Philip Henslowe (?-1616) built the *Rose* on Bankside (1592). By this time theatre was popular. Amongst others, Burbage built another in the ruins of the *Blackfriars* (1596). In 1599 his son Richard (?1567-1619) moved the *Globe* to Bankside. In 1613 Henslowe built the *Hope,* part bear-pit part theatre, also on Bankside. These men were the earliest English impresarios outside the court, and besides acting themselves, employed almost all the contemporary actors whose names have survived.

(3) The mobile Guild plays had as their setting simultaneous representations of all the places needed in a play. This was not possible in a theatre where the pieces became more concentrated and less narrative in character. These playhouses were open to the sky with an apron stage projecting into a pit (standing room only) surrounded with tiers of galleries. The entry price was ld to the pit, with additional fees for going upstairs. The audiences habitually ate and drank. In addition, there were small private and court theatres which developed, in continental practice, into the familiar roofed type of theatre with proscenium arch, horse-shoe auditorium, boxes and stalls.

(4) Shakespeare (sometimes) apart, Tudor and early Stuart tended to the bloodily horrific and anyhow from about 1615 the theatres were under increasing pressure from puritan critics. In 1642 the Parliament suppressed them, probably because they were mostly royalist. The open playhouses fell into ruin, and at the Restoration the returned cavaliers, who were used to continental theatres, did not revive them. Thomas Killigrew received a patent for *Drury Lane* and Sir William Davenant another for *Covent Garden* in 1663; these enjoyed almost a monopoly until it became an actual monopoly under Walpole's Licensing Act, 1737. The standard of the plays until the appearance of Goldsmith's *She Stoops to Conquer* (1773) was poor, yet the standard of acting by such practitioners as Garrick, Macklin, Macready, the Kembles, Mrs. Siddons and Kean was extremely high. The monopoly led to successive reconstructions and enlargements. To fill these huge buildings spectacular production, loud voices and declamatory characterisation were needed, and became a feature of theatrical presentation until the Licensing Act, 1843, virtually ended the monopoly and made smaller theatres and a more natural style possible. The older habit, however, lasted as late as the Irving and Ellen Terry productions at the *Lyceum* (1878-1902).

(5) The modern 'Theatre of Ideas' was meanwhile being developed, originally abroad, by such playwrights as Ibsen, Strindberg and Chekhov, and then by G. B. Shaw. It required a new type of actor with a new training and possibly a new theatre. A new fashion of theatre design started to alter the 25-odd London theatres. Apron stages reappeared; theatre-in-the-round was tried in the early 1950s. Scenery was often abandoned in pursuit of theories which sometimes concealed shortage of cash; apart from spectaculars, many plays were experimental or intentionally banal in setting or dialogue. Such plays could not survive long without subsidies and these came from the govt. through the Arts Council (founded in 1940). Rising costs soon created great difficulties. To make a theatre pay required either a subsidy or an indefinitely long run of a popular kind. Since only a few theatres could be subsidised, such long runs, in the 1960s and 1970s were monopolising theatres and withdrawing

them from the field in which original talent could practice. Hence the state became a necessary patron.

THELLUSSON (Pron: 'Telissen') **Peter (1737-97)** left his £500,000 fortune to be accumulated at compound interest during the lives of his descendants living at his death. It would probably have reached £140M before distribution, which, at the money values of the time, was considered a potential danger, and the Accumulations (or *Thelluson*) Act, 1800 limited such accumulations to 21 years.

***THEGN* or THANE (A.S: boy or young man)** in the Anglo-Saxon world was a, usually well born, helper to someone greater than himself (cf. the modern personal assistant). His public standing depended mainly on his master's importance (e.g. a King's stood higher than an earl's, abbot's or bishop's and they higher than a thegn of another thegn) but additionally on the length of his service, his achievements, wealth, personal character and age. Thegns were necessarily young only in the mythical past. Thanehood carried a wergild of 1200 shillings, and in the Danelaw sometimes even higher. It was not hereditary but it was natural for a master to take on the son of a trusted thegn. Most were rewarded with land, usually *bocland,* which tended to pass in the same family. By the 10th cent. the word had replaced GESITH to describe a local landed noble, but some, apart from their rank, were indistinguishable from small free farmers. They never formed a caste; a ceorl or merchant might become a thegn if taken on as such by a master, especially in a military service where casualties accelerated promotion. A ship's captain became a thegn after three successful overseas voyages. They were never numerous, and when Canute was recruiting *huscarles* of thegnly standing, their military function was in decline. Many were killed in the three battles of 1066, and the rest were mostly superseded or destroyed in the reprisals and forfeitures after the rebellions of 1067-71. Some became outlaws (e.g. Hereward), some migrated to Lothian or overseas (e.g. to Constantinople as members of the Varangian Guard). The lesser ones remaining were depressed into the status of manorial tenants. Domesday Book (1086) records only two holding large estates directly of the King.

***THE NATION* (Ir.)** *See* YOUNG IRELAND.

THEOBALD (TEDBALDUS) of BEC (?-1161) became Abbot of Bec in 1137, and in 1138 was elected Abp. of Canterbury at K. Stephen's instance in preference to Henry of Blois, Bp. of Winchester, Stephen's brother. In the ensuing civil wars he avoided supporting Matilda as far as he could, even when, after the B. of Lincoln her claims were recognised (Apr. 1141) by Henry, acting as papal legate. Nevertheless, he was with her at Winchester (Sept.) and was roughly handled when her party broke out of the siege. In Dec. the legate changed sides, and Theobald recrowned Stephen and his Queen at Canterbury. The division and vacillation in the English Church continued until Henry's legatine commission lapsed at the death of Innocent II in 1143. In the meantime, Theobald had begun recruiting into his household talented and later famous men, eventually, Roger of Pont l'Eveque (Abp. of York from 1154), Thomas à Becket, John Belmeis (Abp. of Lyons from 1182), John of Salisbury the humanist (Bp. of Chartres from 1176) and the Mantuan canonist Vacarius, who went to York with Roger of Pont l'Eveque. After 1143 the papacy increasingly favoured an Angevin succession, and this naturally affected the English Abp. who went to Rome for a while, originally to obtain a settlement of one of the many disputes with St. Augustine's Canterbury. In 1148, mainly by Henry's influence, Stephen forbade Theobald to attend a papal council at Rheims, but Theobald defied him. On his return Stephen seized his temporalities and forced him to go back. In 1150, however, Theobald had a legatine commission of his own and he and Stephen found it politic to be

reconciled. On the other hand in 1152, on papal orders, he refused to crown Stephen's son Eustace of Boulogne. He was arrested but escaped to Flanders and was recalled only when the Pope threatened an interdict. This course of policy enabled Theobald to mediate in 1153 between Stephen and Henry of Anjou, who in 1154 took the throne without incident as Henry II. He and Theobald co-operated amicably over political and church affairs and Theobald suggested his secretary Thomas à Becket for the Chancellorship. The civil wars had created much corruption and bad discipline among the clergy. The encouragement (not unique to England) of the canonists led to more appeals to Rome, but Henry and Theobald thought that civil and ecclesiastical jurisdiction should complement not encroach upon each other, and maintained mutual respect by give and take. They had progressively improved the state of the English church when Theobald died.

THEOBALD of BLOIS, elder brother of K. Stephen. *See* GENEALOGY; HENRY I-10; STEPHEN-I 3.

THEODORE of TARSUS (c. 602-90). Pope Vitalian appointed him Abp. of Canterbury in 668 on the advice of Hadrian, later Abbot of St. Augustine's Canterbury. A Greek, he was also educated in Latin. When he reached Kent in 669, the church was in confusion with most sees vacant or disputed. He set the common-sense tone of his rule after appointing Chad to Mercia. Chad objected to riding as a luxury so he bodily lifted him onto a horse. By the Synod of Hertford (672) Theodore had six suffragans and tried to raise the number by dividing the traditional tribal sees, but was resisted possibly, by Bp. Wilfrid of York. Theodore, however, seized opportunities such as a vacancy in E. Anglia (673) and the expulsion of Wilfrid from Northumbria (678) to divide E. Anglia into two (Dunwich and Elmham), Mercia into three (Lichfield, Worcester and Hereford) and Northumbria first into three (York, Lindisfarne with Hexham and Lindsey) and later five (York, Hexham, Lindisfarne, Ripon and Abercorn). He stressed episcopal dignity as well as setting bishops to work in tribally homogeneous dioceses. Drawing on his Asiatic experience these were to be based on towns. His other preoccupation was learning. He and Abbot Hadrian made Canterbury a major centre for Roman Law and the classics, and a channel for communicating Mediterranean influences. His scholarship too, informed his **Penitentials,** a collection of canons and rules of life compiled from his records after his death.

THEODORE, Etienne (Baron NEUHOFF) (?-1756). *See* CORSICA.

THEODOSIUS the ELDER, Count. *See* BRITAIN, ROMAN-24.

***THERMIDOR* (COUP D'ÉTAT OF) (27 July 1794).** The fall of Robespierre.

THERMOMETERS. Fahrenheit of Danzig invented his scale and thermometer in 1714. Réaumur the 80 scale in 1730; Celsius the centigrade scale in 1742.

THESIGER (1) Sir Frederick (?-1805) an expert on the Baltic, having served in the Russian navy, was Nelson's adviser at Copenhagen. His nephew **(2) Frederick (1794-1878) 1st Ld. CHELMSFORD (1858)** became conservative M.P. in 1840, Sol-Gen. in 1844, Att-Gen. 1845-46, and 1852-58 when he became Lord Chancellor until 1859 and again from 1866-68. Of his sons **(3) Frederick Augustus (1827-1905) 2nd Ld.** commanded the troops in the Zulu Wars (1879) and **(4) Alfred Henry (1838-80)** was a Lord Justice of Appeal from 1877. The son of (3), **(5) Frederick John Napier (1868-1933) 3rd Ld. and 1st Vist. (1921)** was Governor of Queensland from 1905-9, of N.S.W. from 1909-13 and Viceroy of India from 1916-21. The Montagu-Chelmsford Report of 1918 opened the way to Indian self govt. He was First Lord of the Admiralty in 1924, and Warden of All Souls from 1932.

THETFORD (Norfolk) was a Saxon town of some importance with a mint and some industry. It was also the seat of the East Anglian diocese from 1072-95. There was a Norman palace and castle and a grammar school. The town had municipal charters before 1272 and by the 14th cent. there were 8 monastic houses and 20 churches. It then began to decline, the process being hastened by the dissolution of the monasteries, but a new charter was granted in 1573, and its quiet existence was scarcely disturbed when it became a borough under the Municipal Corporations Act 1834.

THING (A.S.). A judicial or deliberative assembly or a matter or issue brought before such as assembly.

THIRD COALITION, WAR OF, PRELIMINARIES (Mar. 1801-May 1803). (*See* SECOND COALITION, WAR OF, 1799–1801.) **(1)** The Franco-Austrian P. of Lunéville (Feb. 1801) left Bonaparte with only one antagonist, Britain, and no means of attacking her save by economic warfare which could be carried on only through diplomacy. The Armed Neutrality was destroyed by Czar Paul's death and the B. of Copenhagen, but French secret diplomacy was exceedingly active.

(2) In Mar. 1801 France secured Louisiana from Spain and by agreements with Naples and Tuscany obtained the strategically important I. of Elba.

(3) In Sept. 1801 by a Franco-Portuguese T. of Madrid, the boundaries of French Guiana were extended to the mouth of the Amazon and by a Franco-Turkish P. in Oct. the French agreed to hand back Egypt (which unknown to the Turks had already been surrendered to the British) in return for commercial privileges.

(4) The French surrender in Egypt was not known in England and the above treaties were not disclosed in the negotiations leading to the Anglo-French Preliminaries signed in Oct. as a Peace Treaty in London (*see* AMIENS. P. OF). The latter included the British retrocession of Guiana and large additions to the Cisalpine Republic. In Dec. a powerful French battlefleet and military expedition sailed for the Caribbean, in order to reduce Haiti, while a Cisalpine constitutional convention was assembled by Bonaparte at Lyon. In Jan 1802 this body made him Pres. of the Cisalpine Republic, whose name was changed to the more aggressive title of the Italian Republic. Thus when the definitive T. of Amiens was signed in Mar. the British ministers who knew of the Louisiana agreement but not the rest, realised that they had been tricked but were constrained by pacific English opinion.

(5) Bonaparte now invited the new Czar Alexander to participate in the reorganisation of Germany, arising out of the P. of Lunéville. The two held Austria powerless, while dispossessed rulers were compensated and Prussia enlarged at the expense of Austria's friends. By Aug. Bonaparte was ready for the next step in his domestic career. He was proclaimed First Consul (and incidentally Pres. of Italy) for life.

(6) British opinion was at last alarmed. Contrary to the treaties, French troops still, despite protests, occupied Holland. Bonaparte now celebrated his new status by large Italian annexations. In Aug. and Sept. Elba, Piedmont, Parma and Piacenza were seized. Then French troops entered Switzerland. It was now clear that France intended to dominate Italy by way of routes which could not be interrupted by naval action.

(7) The Addington govt. retaliated (Oct.) by stopping colonial restitutions prescribed by the P. of Amiens. Such orders would take many weeks to reach their destinations. Then it changed its mind (Nov.) but the effect of this was subject to the same delays. Meanwhile, Bonaparte's public pronouncements were becoming increasingly belligerent and in Jan. 1803, a Col. Sebastiani, who had been on a fact-finding mission in the Levant, reported that the area was ready and willing to be taken over by France. Bonaparte published the report in the official *Moniteur*. It being now obvious that he intended war at his convenience, the govt. called out the militia, mobilised the fleet (Feb.) and on hearing reports of his preparations, declared war. (Mar.).

THIRD COALITION, WAR OF, FIRST PHASE (May 1803-Aug. 1806). (1) Bonaparte had intended war in 1804, but the British observed his preparations on the Channel coast and mobilised the fleet in Mar. 1803. The French expedition to Haiti was a failure from which Bonaparte wished to be free: he ended his commitment there, and in Apr. sold Louisiana, the main source of supplies to Haiti, to the U.S.A. He also erected coastal batteries along the Channel, the Riviera and on Elba to protect the water movements of his troops. The British accordingly anticipated his convenience by declaring war in May on France and her Dutch satellite. Ld. Keith blockaded Holland from the Nore; Ld. Cornwallis Brest from Torbay and Ld. Nelson Toulon from Maddalena (Sardinia). These naval undertakings were difficult because St. Vincent at the Admiralty had during the short peace, unduly reduced the fleet. The British had also to contend with a dangerous Indian war with the Maratha Scindiah, which broke out in May.

(2) Within a month French troops occupied Hanover (which offended Prussia) and S. Italy; large forces also moved to the Channel ports of Boulogne, Wimereux and Ambleteuse where (and elsewhere) huge fleets of ill-designed invasion boats were being constructed. The invasion preparations diverted resources from the French navy, but on the other hand the Toulon fleet represented a threat to Egypt and distant support for the Marathas, for Bonaparte believed that India was Britain's primary resource. In July Robert Emmet's Irish rebellion complicated the British situation and led to great efforts to increase the fleet. By Sept. however, Emmet had been captured and Wellesley (later Wellington) had won his great victory over Scindiah at Assaye.

(3) A head-on collision now seemed inevitable, but until the invasion project had either succeeded or failed, the contestants had no direct means of attacking each other. Spain was bound by treaty to aid France, but Bonaparte accepted a large subsidy and the use of Spanish ports instead (Oct.) Meanwhile he dealt with a royalist plot (Feb.) and arrested the two important Generals Moreau and Pichegru, who were involved and then kidnapped the Bourbon D. d'Enghien and had him shot. The duke had been living privately in Baden and this ruthless disregard of German frontiers offended not only Prussia, but the Czar, who had been a party to the reorganisation of Germany. The First Consul's attention was, however, fixed on France where he played on national feeling to have himself declared Emperor (May 1804).

(4) British diplomacy was much concerned to stop the Spanish subsidies (mainly of S. American bullion) and the arming of French ships in Spanish ports, but the Duke's murder and Bonaparte's imperial elevation braced British opinion for a decisive war, for which the Addington govt. was unsuitable. William Pitt accordingly returned to power in the same month as the imperial proclamation, with his friend Ld. Melville (Dundas) as First Lord of the Admiralty. The navy was vigorously enlarged in the ensuing months and in July an ultimatum was presented to Spain. Spanish negotiations nevertheless proceeded for Madrid was scarcely its own master and it and Pitt hoped for an accommodation.

(5) The German reorganisation had made the imperial constitution formally unworkable and the Emperor, in anticipation of the Holy Roman Empire's demise, took the title of Emperor for his hereditary lands (Aug. 1804). This amounted to the political abandonment of S. Germany under existing conditions for Austria was not ready for another war. Two other events of future significance then occurred. Bonaparte's ablest Admiral, Latouche-Tréville died and in Oct. the British seized the Spanish treasure ships. The negotiations at Madrid broke down, though the British and Spanish diplomats had no knowledge of the seizure. In Dec. Spain declared war and in Jan. concluded a further war alliance with France.

(6) The murder of the D. d'Enghien had ruptured Franco-Prussian diplomatic relations and a special Russian embassy arrived in London in Jan. 1805. Its original, unsuccessful purpose was to discuss European reorganisation in the event of peace, but the negotiations ended in a treaty signed at St. Petersburg (Apr. 1805) to promote a league against further French encroachments. In blithe disregard of the signs, Bonaparte crowned himself King of Italy in May and in June carried out the annexation of Genoa which he had contemplated since 1799. This latter event persuaded Austria to join Britain and Russia. Sweden joined too (Aug.)

(7) Bonaparte's intention was to attack England but if his naval combination failed, to turn upon Austria. In the event (see TRAFALGAR, CAMPAIGN AND B. OF) it failed and his Channel army marched east in Sept. The decisive naval battle off C. Trafalgar was fought two days after the Austrian advanced force was rounded up at Ulm. Russian succours arrived too late for the opening, and precipitated the Austrians into their common disaster at Austerlitz (Dec. 1805). The Turks promptly began to arm against Russia.

(8) Bonaparte's reorganisation of Europe commenced without delay. Thirteen days after Austerlitz the Franco-Prussian T. of Schönbrunn gave Hanover to Prussia in exchange for Prussia's detached western territories. On Boxing Day, by the P. of Pressburg, Bavaria and Württemberg became Kingdoms and Baden a Grand Duchy, while Austria ceded the Tyrol to Bavaria and Venice to Italy. Pitt prophetically told his secretary to roll up the map of Europe, for the process had just begun. Worn out with exertion and disappointment, he died (Jan. 1806). Three weeks later at the T. of Paris Prussia agreed to exclude British trade. In Mar. began the creation of the new Bonapartist states. Of Napoleon's brothers, Joseph became King of Naples and Louis King of Holland. Two of his sisters became rulers of Italian duchies. His marshals Murat and Berthier secured Berg and Neuchâtel. In July the S. German states were formed into the French protected confederation of the Rhine, from which Austria and Prussia were excluded. In Aug. the last Holy Roman Emperor abdicated.

THIRD COALITION, WAR OF, SECOND PHASE (Oct. 1806-July 1807). (See PREVIOUS ARTICLE.) **(1)** The new British ministry (see ALL THE TALENTS) had begun by negotiating with Bonaparte who, having just given Hanover to Prussia, offered to give it back to George III. In his negotiations with the Czar, the Emperor agreed to resist Prussian claims on Swedish Pomerania. By such means, Prussia was bullied into the anti-British Franco-Prussian T. of Paris (Feb. 1806), which deprived her people of the huge profits of the distorted wartime overseas trade, diverted from French ports by the British. As the effects began covertly to be evaded, Bonaparte's brother-in-law, Murat was invested with Cleves and Berg, former Prussian territories on the Hanoverian frontier (Mar. 1806). The British Order in Council of May 1806 (see ORDERS IN COUNCIL) was the counterblast to the T. of February. In reply, under the protection of French troops, the S. German Confederation of the Rhine was formed, and its component states taken out of Prussian influence (July). Next Bonaparte indicated that Prussia should cease to bring pressure upon the N. German, especially coastal states, across which the overseas trade was reaching her and in particular, that the Hanseatic port republics of Hamburg, Bremen and Lübeck were now under his protection. The Prussians, who had never meant to honour the T. of Feb. now found that Bonaparte meant to compel them to do so.

(2) It was obvious that the troops moving in honour of the Rhenish confederation were equally a threat. Bonaparte needed an abject or conquered Prussia before the Czar could rearm and recruit. He had every reason, besides his economic war with Britain, to precipitate a

Prussian conflict, for he still had to beat the Czar. The Prussians faced a dilemma, to lose all peacefully by waiting for Russia, or to fight alone. In Oct. they chose the latter course; with the Saxons they were overwhelmed at Jena and Auerstadt in a fortnight and Berlin fell 12 days later. That economic warfare against Britain was uppermost in Bonapartist policy is shown by the sequel. In Nov. Bonaparte issued the Berlin Decree (see CONTINENTAL SYSTEM).

(3) The French now moved east. At Posen in Prussian Poland (Dec. 1806) Bonaparte reached a settlement with Saxony, which incorporated that country, as a Kingdom, into the Rhenish Confederation. The Turks, egged on by French diplomacy, invaded Russia and delayed still further the Russian approach. The first (drawn) engagement was at Eylau on the E. Prussian frontier (Feb. 1807).

(4) The May 1806 Order in Council was a warlike measure, but the Govt. was also trying to compensate for trading losses by development elsewhere. After Sir Home Popham had taken the Cape (Jan. 1806) he crossed the Atlantic and attacked the R. Plate. Montevideo and Buenos Aires (see ARGENTINA; URUGUAY) both fell (June) and Spanish S. America seemed open to exploitation, but the inhabitants of Buenos Aires joined with French-led Spanish troops to expel Popham's small force, and new and more powerful armaments were sent out under Gen. Whitelocke. These came to grief (June-July) at the same time as the Russian disaster at Friedland (June) and the two Ts. of Tilsit (July) (q.v.). Of equal importance to their territorial clauses were the Russian (and the formal Prussian) adherence to the Berlin Decree, a Russo-Turkish armistice aided by the accession of a new Sultan (Mahmoud II) and agreements to secure the closure of the Baltic and the Ottoman Empire to British trade.

(5) France and Russia now made war upon Sweden: the Russians invading Finland (Aug.) the French, Pomerania (Sept.) with its important port at Stralsund. The British could not interfere in these operations but could, at least, keep the Danish fleet out of French hands. Once again a British force, under Admiral Gambier, appeared and this time invested and bombarded Copenhagen (Sept.). The Danish fleet was carried off and Denmark, with signs of spontaneity, joined Bonaparte's system into which she would, in any case, have been coerced.

THIRD ESTATE (*TIERS ÉTAT*). A French term meaning those who were not nobles or clergy.

THIRD INTERNATIONAL. See COMINTERN.

THIRD READING of a bill in either House of Parliament comes after the Report Stage. It is a general debate on a bill in the form settled as a result of amendment (if any) in committee or on report. Such a debate will generally be short if the bill was not amended (since everything will already have been said on Second Reading) unless an opposition wants to make political capital. Only drafting amendments are allowed. If the motion for a third reading is carried, a motion to pass the bill (i.e. to some other branch of the legislature) is generally put at once.

THIRD REICH. See REICH.

THIRLAGE (Scots Law) was a requirement that tenants or inhabitants of certain places should restrict their custom to a particular forge, bakery or, especially in later times, grind their corn at a particular mill, for which a customary payment called MULTURE was due.

THIRLBY, Thomas (?1506-70) through Cranmer's interest became Archdeacon of Ely and a member of the Convocation of 1534 which recognised Henry VIII's supremacy. As prolocutor he signed the Cleves annulment in 1540 and then became the only Bp. of Westminster. He was an ambassador to Spain in 1542 and 1545 and voted against the Act of Uniformity in 1549 becoming nevertheless Bp. of Norwich in 1550.

Translated by Mary I to Ely in 1554 he presided over the trial of Bp. Hooper in 1555. In 1558 he refused to take the oath of Supremacy to Q. Elizabeth and was deposed.

THIRTY-NINE ARTICLES were founded on the FORTY-TWO ARTICLES drawn up by Cranmer in 1552, promulgated by Royal Mandate in June 1553 but never enforced because of the R. Catholic reaction under Mary I. At Elizabeth's instance, Art. 29 against 'The Wicked which eat not the body of Christ' was originally omitted to avoid offence to R. Catholics and Art. 20 includes an assertion of the church's right to prescribe ceremonies. They were issued in 1563 and Art. 29 was restored in 1571 after the Bull *Regnans in Excelsis* (Feb. 1570) had purported to depose the Queen. From then on they had to be signed by all clergy and members of the two universities until 1865 when the university rule was abolished and a slightly less stringent requirement was imposed on the clergy. The articles are short summaries of dogmatic issues not narrow definitions and, doubtless intentionally, allow for the variety of interpretation. For example, Art. 6 states that "Holy Scripture containeth all things necessary to salvation". They nevertheless set forth the Anglican relationship to R. Catholics, Calvinists, Anabaptists and the State; rejecting transubstantiation and works of supererogation. *See also* ELIZABETH I-6.

THIRTY-THREE ARTICLES. A primitive constitution adopted by Voortrekkers who moved from Natal across the Vaal in 1844.

THIRTY YEARS' WAR (1618-48) (1) The Hispano-Dutch truce of 1609 was due to expire in 1621 when the Spaniards (as everyone knew) meant to attack. The Spanish Habsburgs presided over a patchwork of R Catholic powers which included their own world empire with Belgium and Milan and the European states of their much less affluent Austrian cousins. But they had a problem of communications. Their Netherlands army under Spinola needed money and supplies; these could not come across France, nor by sea against the Dutch and probably the English. Therefore they would have to come by northern Italy, through the **Valtelline** and down the Rhine. This route might be closed by the Savoyards, the Swiss, the Venetians and others and it was interrupted for 50 miles on the Rhine by the **Palatinate** under its young Calvinist Elector Frederick V. His minister, Christian of Anhalt, hoped through him and a so-called Protestant Union of German Calvinist states, to become the leader of protestant Germany. Venice supported the Union, the Dutch gave money and Britain was apparently committed, for James I had married his daughter **Elizabeth** ("The Winter Queen") to Frederick V. The war may, with all caution, be considered in eight phases.

Phase I. The Palatinate and Bohemia.

(2) The Habsburg Emperor Matthias was dying. Of the seven Electors three were R. Catholic prelates, three (Saxony, Brandenburg and Palatinate) were protestant princes and the seventh, the King of Bohemia, was Matthias himself. The Bohemian crown was elective and most of the Bohemian voting nobility was protestant. Their religion was protected by the *Letter of Majesty,* and a charter granted by Matthias. Their choice would fall upon a candidate ready to uphold it. The Habsburg candidate was the fanatical Archduke Ferdinand of Styria. Always short of money, he agreed to make way for Spanish troops across Germany in return for Spanish support and finance in the elections. In June 1617 he was pre-elected King and confirmed the Letter of Majesty, but in the autumn it was infringed by a protestant assembly which pushed his regents out of a window of the Hradcin (*The Defenestration of Prague*). These protestants sought help from the Protestant Union, and Anhalt got the Duke of Savoy to hire out his mercenary army (under **Mansfeld).** His and Austrian movements began the war in Aug. In Mar. 1619 Matthias died. Other provinces sprang into revolt and Ferdinand was besieged in Vienna.

In June, however, he was relieved, and Mansfeld was checked at Sablat. The estates of Lusatia, Silesia, Moravia and Bohemia signed a compact, and when Bethlen Gabor, the Calvinist Prince of Transylvannia invaded Hungary as their ally in Aug., they declared Ferdinand deposed and offered their Crown to Frederick of the Palatinate. Ferdinand however, was at Frankfort where he was unanimously elected Emperor. The news of his deposition arrived minutes after he had been sworn. In Sept. Frederick accepted the Bohemian crown.

(3) Maximilian, the R. Catholic D. of Bavaria, ruled a strong military state. He opposed both the extension of protestant power to Bohemia, and the probable increase in Habsburg power by Spanish troops. He therefore offered to overthrow Mansfeld and the Bohemians himself in return, *inter alia,* for his expenses and Frederick's electorate. Bohemia, hitherto considered outside the Empire, was pronounced within it by a meeting of rulers at Mulhouse in Mar. 1620. This converted Frederick legally into a rebel. The meeting included Lutherans, and was a diplomatic triumph for Ferdinand, who guaranteed the Upper Saxon religious liberties to gain it. In June, therefore, the Palatinate was sequestrated. Simultaneously John George, the Lutheran Elector of Saxony, from motives similar to Maximilian's offered to attack Frederick in return for Lusatia and Lutheran religious freedom in Bohemia. In Aug. 1620 Spinola's Spaniards overran the Palatinate except for English garrisons at Mannheim and Frankenthal. The Bohemians succumbed to simultaneous invasions from north and south, and the Bavarian General **Tilly** routed them at the White Hill (8 Nov. 1620). So ended Bohemian independence.

(4) Frederick and Elizabeth fled to Holland but would not yield, so the Spaniards remained in the Palatinate. Peace now hinged on the fate of Mansfeld's undamaged mercenary army, and Ferdinand's huge obligations to Bavaria. The Dutch, whose truce was running out, financed Frederick to rehire Mansfeld for the reconquest of the Palatinate. Ferdinand pawned Upper Austria to Bavaria, but Maximilian insisted on his Electorate. To satisfy him, Ferdinand in Jan. 1621, unconstitutionally pronounced the imperial ban against Frederick without the consent of the Diet. Protests ensued from the Protestant Union, Britain, Holland and now Denmark whose King, as Duke of Holstein, feared growing Habsburg power in the trans-German trade routes. The Union collapsed under threats from Spinola.

Phase II. The Dutch War and Imperial Reorganisation.

(5) On 9 Apr. 1621 the Hispano-Dutch truce expired. There were now two wars and a conflict between Austrian and Spanish policy. Spain wished to impose a local peace by restoring Frederick and Elizabeth in the Palatinate under Spanish protection. This would clear their Rhine route, please James I and promote their Dutch war. Ferdinand, however, wanted to pay Maximilian out of Palatine lands. The Spanish scheme foundered. Mansfeld, driven by famine joined the English at Frankenthal. He was hotly pursued by Tilly and his Bavarians and crossed into Alsace seeking food and bringing plague. Meantime, Frederick had obtained new allies in Christian of Brunswick, Administrator of **Halberstadt** in the north and George Frederick of Baden-Dürlach in the south. Tilly defeated the latter at Wimpfen and Christian at Hoechst (May-June 1622). After plundering Alsace they resigned their Palatine commissions and then unexpectedly marched against Spinola, who was besieging the key Dutch fortress of Bergen-op-Zoom. Tilly was clearing the Palatinate, and in Sept. he took Heidelberg, the capital. In Oct. Mansfeld relieved Bergen. The Dutch were saved at the expense of Frederick and Elizabeth, now bereft of army, money and lands. In Feb. 1623 at an electoral meeting at Ratisbon, Ferdinand secured their deposition and transferred the electorate to Maximilian for life.

(6) Albrecht v. Waldstein or **Wallenstein,** military Governor of Prague, had speculated in the confiscated lands of the Bohemian protestants, and by 1623 he had organised a compact industrial state round Gitschin, had married Isabella v. Harrach, was lending large sums to Ferdinand and had been made Count of Friedland. His rise was a product, in part, of a Habsburg policy of governmental reorganisation, intended to revive the Holy, and especially R. Catholic, Empire. The Habsburg lands, other than Tyrol, were henceforth to descend as a unity in Ferdinand's family and other territorial rearrangements were contemplated which must violate the imperial constitution. These had already begun with the cession of Lusatia and the transfer of an electorate to Bavaria. They were continued with the dispossession of the Margrave of Baden-Dürlach and the return of certain Rhenish lands to ecclesiastical princes. Resistance was bound to grow, as indeed it did when Ferdinand proposed to appoint his son Leopold as administrator of two wealthy Lower Saxon secularised bishoprics, namely **Osnabrück** and Christian of Brunswick's Halberstadt. Tilly, however, defeated Christian at Stadtlohn (6 Aug. 1623) and as a result Frederick V at last was persuaded (by James I) to sign a truce with Ferdinand. This could not last, for Mansfeld, looking for a paymaster, arrived in London. James I had linked the Spanish scheme for restoring Frederick on the Rhine with a proposed Spanish marriage, but the Londoners received Mansfeld rapturously as the defender of their princess and the negotiations collapsed.

Phase III. French Diplomacy and the Baltic.
(7) For the first time France, with Cardinal **Richelieu** newly in charge, entered the arena. He offered Henrietta Maria as a bride for the Prince of Wales and she was accepted. The King of Denmark accepted French subsidies, claimed Osnabrück for his son and offered protection to the Lower Saxon Estates. In June 1624 a Franco-Dutch treaty was signed at **Compiègne** to which James I acceded. In July Venice and Savoy agreed to block the Valtelline. Ferdinand and Maximilian turned to Wallenstein who had offered to raise an army; in Apr. 1625 Habsburg diplomacy was seeking naval facilities against Denmark and possibly Sweden in the Baltic ports of the Hanse. Wallenstein's commission was enlarged to the Baltic coast to overcome their hesitations. Meantime the Spaniards had taken Breda; there was a Huguenot revolt in France and the French occupation of the Valtelline quickly broke down. By 1626 Mansfeld and the Danes were the only effective protestant forces in the field, but in Apr. Wallenstein defeated Mansfeld at Dessau, and in Aug. Tilly beat the Danes at Lutter.

Phase IV. The Rise of Wallenstein.
(8) These victories made Ferdinand more aggressive, yet delivered him from Bavaria into the hands of Wallenstein. The latter now occupied neutral Brandenburg, overran Mecklenburg, an ally of Denmark, and wintered in Jutland. In Apr. 1628 Ferdinand transferred the Duchy of Mecklenburg to him. This elevation of an imperial creature to princely status staggered public opinion. Ferdinand's autocratic ambitions stood nakedly revealed. The greater princes changed sides. Prompted by Bavaria, the Electors refused the Kingship of the Romans to his son. Ferdinand now saw that he could obtain their support only by abandoning Wallenstein. They, unable to coerce the Emperor, looked for allies elsewhere: two might be available – France and Sweden but Sweden was at war with Poland.

(9) In 1628 Wallenstein, too strong to be directly attacked, planned a further northward expansion. Meanwhile France and Spain were drifting into an Italian war over the succession to Mantua. In July Wallenstein appeared before the Hanseatic city of **Stralsund,** but three days earlier the city had signed a Swedish alliance. French diplomacy had secured a truce between Sweden

and Poland. Sweden, with France behind her, was now in the war. Moreover Stralsund held out and for this a victory over the Danes at Wolgast (28 Sept. 1628) was only partial compensation. The Swedes dominated the Baltic. Through Stralsund they could enter Germany; Wallenstein could not reach Sweden.

(10) Wallenstein had made Ferdinand supreme within Germany, but had passed his peak. In Mar. 1629 the policy of re-organisation was pressed a stage further. By the **Edict of Restitution,** R. Catholic lands alienated to protestants since 1555 were to be restored. Wallenstein's troops were used to enforce it. Bavaria, aspiring to Catholic leadership could hardly object, but in the ensuing upheavals (affecting all north and central Germany) much of the unpopularity clung to Wallenstein. It was becoming safer for the Emperor to sacrifice his general. Meanwhile, Wallenstein himself, preoccupied with the Spanish threat, prompted the T. of Lübeck (May 1629) which effectively removed Denmark from the war.

Phase V. Spanish Insistence and Swedish Intervention.
(11) The Spaniards were in trouble. Dutch fleets intercepted their bullion and their unpaid and ill supplied troops were mutinous. Philip IV and his minister Olivarez called on Ferdinand to intervene in Holland and Italy. Policy and family loyalty inclined him to do so. Constitutionally the Electors had to consent to war with the Dutch. Wallenstein's dismissal might persuade them. Some of his troops were sent to Italy and during the **Ratisbon** electoral meeting of 1630 he was persuaded to resign. The Electors, however, would not declare war on the Dutch. Bavarian power over Ferdinand was greatly increased and the interference with the north German military arrangements opened the road to the Swedes. On 4 July 1630 King **Gustavus Adolfus** landed in Pomerania. The Ratisbon meeting marked the transformation of the war into a European conflict between the Habsburgs on the one side and Sweden and Holland backed by France on the other. It also indicates the moment when for a while British and European History practically parted company. Distracted respectively by constitutional and warlike preoccupations, neither Britain nor the continental powers could intervene effectively in each others' affairs.

(12) In Aug. 1630 Charles William, the deposed protestant administrator of **Magdeburg,** re-entered his wealthy and strategic city with Swedish troops and in Jan. 1631 in the **T. of Bärwalde,** France undertook to subsidise Gustavus Adolfus. Meantime, the protestant German states, alarmed at the Swedish invasion, called upon the Emperor to withdraw the Edict of Restitution and restore the constitution (the Leipzig Manifesto). They began to arm under one of Wallenstein's former generals, Hans Georg v. Arnim, and their purpose was to unite Germany against the foreigner. But the Emperor would not listen. Faced with the prospect of becoming a battleground between Catholic and Swede, they could only join the Swede. This isolated Tilly the Bavarian now in charge of Wallenstein's army, for Wallenstein would not supply troops no longer his and no one else could. Tilly therefore made for Magdeburg and stormed it in May 1631. Massacre, rape and looting culminated in the destruction of the city by fire, together with all its stores. Tilly was no better off materially and the sack horrified Europe and steeled resistance to the Habsburgs. The Dutch immediately acceded to the T. of Bärwalde. In desperation Tilly invaded Saxony, where in 18 Sept. 1631 his army was destroyed by a Swedish-Saxon force at the first B. of the Breitenfeld. By Nov. the Saxons were in Prague, the Swedes at Frankfort, the Spanish communications on the Rhine were disrupted, and Gustavus was proposing to reorganise the Empire under Swedish protection.

(13) Ferdinand, to the horror of Maximilian, had to recall Wallenstein. Gustavus beat Maximilian and Tilly on the Lech (14 Apr. 1632) but this marked the limit of his fortune. His German dependants were suspicious and Arnim, probably suborned by Wallenstein, retreated from Prague to Silesia. When Wallenstein invaded Saxony, its Elector called on Gustavus. On 16 Nov. 1632 in an indecisive battle at Lützen near Leipzig, Gustavus was killed. The management of Swedish policy now fell to his formidable and unruffled Chancellor **Oxenstierna** as Regent for the child Q. Christina. Despite Saxon desertion, he managed to establish the protestant **League of Heilbronn** in Apr. 1633 under his direction. This deprived Saxony of the protestant leadership, and prevented any return to the Leipzig manifesto but he had to accept France as a co-equal protector of the League, and henceforth the Bärwalde subsidies were to be paid to Sweden for the League's behoof.

Phase VI. Habsburg Revival and Wallenstein's Death.

(14) Two younger Habsburg leaders now came forward. These were Ferdinand, K. of Hungary and Bohemia, the Emperor's son and the warlike Cardinal-Infant Ferdinand, brother of Philip IV, appointed Governor of the Spanish Netherlands in Nov. 1632. It was planned that the Cardinal-Infant should reach his province from Italy with an army which should clear the Rhine on the way, while the King of Hungary should raise another to co-operate with him. This would free Austria of the power alike of Bavaria and of Wallenstein as well as striking at the protestants. The only available force was Wallenstein's; therefore, it was necessary to get rid of him without disrupting his army. In this the Ferdinands were justified, for he was not only refusing to fight the Swedes; he was plotting to seize Bohemia. His ambitious arrogance and brutality alienated even his brutal troops; an irrational streak destroyed the respect of his officers. He was dismissed. In Feb. 1634 English, Scots and Irish officers murdered him at Eger and his army passed to Gallas, serving the K. of Hungary. On 6 Sept. 1634 the two Ferdinands overthrew the Swedes and their allies at **Nördlingen.** The remnants of the League of Heilbronn turned to France for protection and in Nov., the Cardinal Infant reached Brussels.

(14) The King of Hungary now tried to end the war by adopting the policy of the Leipzig manifesto. A truce with Saxony accompanied negotiations, involving the withdrawal of the Edict of Restitution, in Prague. But Oxenstierna had to achieve some compensation for all the Swedish losses, and Richelieu belatedly appreciated the dangers of Swedish defeat and Habsburg triumph on the Rhine. They resolved at the **T. of Compiègne** (30 Apr. 1635) to continue the war; but, in return for the left bank of the Rhine, France was openly to declare war on Spain. This was done in May. The so-called **P. of Prague,** signed nearly simultaneously, therefore became an alliance for further war, in which Catholic Habsburgs and protestant Germans were allied against Catholic France and Protestant Holland and Sweden. Politics had superseded religion.

Phase VII. The Spanish Collapse.

(15) The Habsburgs entered the new phase with the advantage of recent victory and almost united support. In Feb. 1637 the King of Hungary succeeded his father as Emperor, but the situation changed quickly. The Swedes had defeated the Saxons at Wittstock in Oct. 1636. In Oct. 1637 the Dutch captured Breda, and during 1638 French mercenaries defeated the Imperialists at Rheinfelden, cleared Alsace and took the key fortress of Breisach. In Oct. 1639 the Dutch Admiral Tromp destroyed the main Spanish fleet in the Downs. In 1640 Portugal reasserted her independence of Spain, helped by French support, Dutch neutrality and English and Swedish commercial agreements. Revolution broke out in Catalonia, and Spanish subsidies to Austria began to dry up. An imperial diet called to Ratisbon in Sept. 1640 almost achieved German unity, but suddenly the front was broken:

Frederick William, known later as the **Great Elector,** succeeded in Brandenburg-Prussia, suspended hostilities with Sweden and publicly accused the Emperor of furthering his German ambitions under cover of a foreign war. The lesser protestant princes followed suit. The diet after resolving on further negotiations was dissolved in Nov. 1641 by which time the Catalans had elected Louis XIII as their Duke. Spain, while insisting on control of local policy, could give the Cardinal Infant no help. Overburdened with work, uncertainty and a war on two fronts he died in Nov. 1641.

(16) Negotiations began at Hamburg, but French and Habsburgs each played for time, to the disadvantage of the latter. A Swedish campaign in central Germany ended in a great victory at the Second B. of the Breitenfeld (2 Nov. 1642). Within a month, Richelieu was dead but the Spaniards contrived to alienate the Austrians and their Flemish subjects by a series of inept appointments. Cardinal Mazarin, who immediately succeeded Richelieu, continued his policy, but on 15 May 1643, Louis XIII also died, leaving a regency for Louis XIV who was only five. On 19th the Duc d'Enghien, a young commander appointed by Richelieu, destroyed the flower of the Spanish army at Rocroi. There was now no doubt that the Habsburgs would have to accept a compromise.

Phase VIII. The Slow Approach to Peace.

(17) After an interlude when Turenne and Enghien defeated the Bavarians at Freiburg (July 1644) and the Swedes had a brief war with the Danes, the **peace congress of Westphalia** opened at Münster and Osnabrück in Dec. 1644. The diplomats were in no haste, and as hostilities continued, negotiations were constantly swayed by the fortunes of war. The 135 delegates sat under two 'mediators' or chairmen, Chigi the Papal Nuncio (the future Pope Alexander VII) and Contarini the Venetian.

(18) Congress had to deal with three main groups of issues: (a) *The complaints of the imperial estates.* The principal problem was the distribution of land between R. Catholic and Protestant rulers in Germany. This was settled at the *status quo* of 1624 and the Edict of Restitution became a dead letter; (b) *Conditions of Amnesty towards rebels.* The main issue was the restitution of the Palatinate. The son of Frederick V received part of his lands, for which a new Electorate was created; (c) *Satisfaction for the allies and compensation for the dispossessed.* This, the major international problem, had to be solved to secure peace at all. France, by receiving Alsace and Breisach obtained her power to control the Rhine. Sweden took part of Pomerania with Stettin from Brandenburg, which acquired the bishoprics of Halberstadt, Minden and Magdeburg instead. The independence of the Swiss and the United Provinces was recognised and the Austrians paid off the Swedish army. The Scheldt was closed and Antwerp ruined.

(19) The P. of Münster between Spain and the United Provinces was signed on 30 June 1648. The P. of Westphalia was signed at Osnabrück on 24 Oct. The troops were not finally rounded up and demobilised and the final garrisons withdrawn until May 1654.

THISTLEWOOD, Arthur (1770-1820) a revolutionary said to have been unsettled by incautious reading of Tom Paine, organised the Spa Fields Riot of 1816, was imprisoned and then acquitted. In 1818 he was im-prisoned for challenging Ld. Sidmouth and in 1820 he planned the Cato St. conspiracy and was executed for High Treason.

THOMAS of BAYEUX (?-1100). *See* SAMSON (?-1112)-2.

THOMAS or St. THOMAS. *See* BECKET.

THOMAS of BROTHERTON (1300-38) E. of NORFOLK (1312) Marshal (1316) son of Edward I and Margaret of France, was warden of England during Edward II's

Scottish absence in 1319 and though he was an opponent of Thomas of Lancaster in 1321, and profited by grants from the Despensers, he quickly joined Mortimer and Isabella in 1326 and married his son to Mortimer's daughter By 1329 however, he had watched the wind change again and was one of the London Conference which welcomed Mortimer's overthrow. Naturally Edward III did not trust him and he retired.

THOMAS (?1388-1421) D. of CLARENCE (1412) second son of Henry VI and Mary of Bohun, became titular Lieutenant of Ireland in 1401 and Captain of Guines in 1407. In 1408 he visited Ireland to put down one of the Kildare rebellions and to try to re-establish the English in the former obedient shires. He was not successful. By now he was regarded simply as a soldier, and differences on military policy between Henry IV and his heir resulted in 1412 in Thomas becoming Pres. of the Council. In the same year he led an army to the assistance of the Orleanist party in the French Civil War. In 1415 he was one of Henry V's commanders at Harfleur, but returned to England with the wounded before the B. of Agincourt. He played a leading role in the conquest of Normandy (1417-19) and on Henry's return to England, he became the King's Lieutenant in France. In Mar 1421 he imprudently engaged a French force at Baugé and was killed.

THOMAS, David Alfred (1856-1918) 1st Ld. (1916) and 1st Vist. RHONDDA (1918) liberal M.P. for Merthyr Tydfil from 1888-1910 and Rhondda colliery owner, was Pres. of the Local Govt. Board in 1916 and Minister of Food from 1917.

THOMAS, George (?1756-1802) deserted from the navy and became army commander first for the Begum of Sirdhana (1787) and then for Appa Rao. By 1792 he was Gov. of Meerut and invading the Punjab, whence the Sikhs drove him with French help. A brilliant and impetuous tactician.

THOMAS, James Henry (1874-1949) Pres. of the Amalgamated Society of Railway Servants from 1905-6 and then organising and assistant secretary, led the national railway strike of 1911. He had become Labour M.P. for Derby in 1910 and organised the N. Union of Railwaymen from 1913. He was Pres. of the T.U.C. in 1920 but refused to support the extremist miners in 1921. He was Colonial Sec. in 1924. In 1926 he tried but failed to prevent the general strike, and then joined the National Govt. in which he was Lord Privy Seal from 1929-30 and Dominions Sec. from 1930-35. This was resented by his old associates, who expelled him from his union and the Labour Party. In 1935, he again became Colonial Sec., but in 1936 his career ended suddenly when it appeared that he had privately disclosed budget proposals.

THOMAS of LANCASTER. *See* LANCASTER − FIRST FAMILY-2; EDWARD II-6.

THOMAS, Sidney Gilchrist (1850-85), self taught metallurgist, made a fortune by inventing the method for eliminating phosphorus from pig-iron in the Bessemer process.

THOMAS v SORRELL **(1674).** In this case, it was held that the King could dispense with an individual breach of a penal statute by which no one was injured, or with a continuing breach of a penal statute enacted for the King's benefit. Though a clause in the Bill of Rights 1689 condemned as illegal only recent uses of the power, the clause has been considered to abolish the power altogether.

THOMAS, Thomas (1553-88) first printer to Cambridge University from 1582.

THOMAS, William (?-1554) published the first English-Italian grammar in 1550 when he was made Clerk of the Privy Council. He was ambassador to France in 1551 and political instructor to Edward VI until the latter's death. He then lost his preferments. As an active member of Wyatt's conspiracy in 1553, he was executed.

THOMAS, William Luson (1830-1900) originally an engraver, founded the *Graphic* weekly in 1869 and the *Daily Graphic,* the first daily illustrated paper in 1890.

THOMAS of WOODSTOCK (1355-97) E. of BUCKINGHAM (1377) D. of GLOUCESTER (1385) youngest son of Edward III and Philippa of Hainault, married Eleanor Bohun and in her right became **E. of ESSEX.** In 1376 he became Constable of England. A leading opponent of Richard II and a prominent Lord Appellant in 1388, he favoured greater baronial control of royal policy and Govt. and despite a poor showing on campaign, a vigorous prosecution of the French war. An aggressive and vindictive politician, especially when his elder brother John of Gaunt was away, his influence steadily declined in the early 1390s. In 1397 he was arrested for alleged treason and imprisoned at Calais, where he died, probably murdered.

THOMAS of YORK (?-1114). *See* SAMSON (?-1112)-3.

THOMOND. *See* O'BRIEN.

THOMPSON, William Frank (1919-44) Wykehamist poet and communist, was parachuted from Britain to the Bulgarian resistance in World War II and betrayed. At his trial he made a rousing speech before being shot.

THOMSON (1) James (1800-83) architect, designed, amongst other things, Cumberland Terrace and Cumberland Place in Regent's Park and planned the Notting Hill estates in London. His son **(2) James (1822-92)** engineer and expert on fluids, invented a variety of water turbine and air fans and pioneered the study of the relationship of heat and pressure on liquefaction.

THOMSON, James Bruce (1810-73) resident surgeon at Perth Prison from 1858, pioneered the scientific investigation of crime as a symptom of disease and heredity.

THOMSON, James (1700-48) poet of Scottish origin acquainted with most of the members of the Brothers' Club but remembered not as a politician, but as the first user of natural diction in 18th cent. poetical style. He was much admired for it on the continent. He did, however, perpetrate the line "Oh Sophonisba, Sophonisba Oh!"

THOMSON, Joseph (1858-94) African explorer, discovered L. Leopold in 1880, explored the environs of L. Victoria in 1882, made treaties with rulers from Nigeria to the Nile in 1884, explored the Atlas Mountains in 1888 and Nyassaland in 1890.

THOMSON, William (1819-90) provost of Queen's College, Oxford from 1855, became Bp. of Gloucester in 1861 and Abp. of York from 1861. He was a compelling preacher and a very active administrator who, though a strong disciplinarian, preferred reasonable courses in legislation. He considered Bp. Colenso's deposition illegal.

THORFINN THE MIGHTY, E. of the ORKNEYS (?-1064). *See* ORKNEY IS.

THORKEL. *See* ETHELRED II.

THORLAC, St. *See* MISSIONS TO EUROPE-5.

THORNE, William (fl. 1397) a monk of St. Augustine's, Canterbury, wrote its history and also an account of the papal court which he visited in 1387.

THORNEYCROFT (Edward George) Peter (1909-94) Ld. THORNEYCROFT of DUNSTON (1967), educated at Eton and the Bar, became Conservative M.P. for Stafford (1938-45) and then for Monmouth (1945-66). He was Pres. of the Board of Trade (1951-57) and Chancellor of the Exchequer (1957-58) in the Macmillan Govt. As such, he faced rapid growth leading to price rises. As an early adherent of the view that if the volume of money in circulation is limited, wages generally speaking will not rise save when justified by production increases, he disagreed with Macmillan who hated the hardships of unemployment and thought that expansion was necessary to deal with it. Accordingly Thorneycroft was dismissed in 1958. In the early 1960s he was Min. of

Aviation, then (1962-64), Sec. of State for Defence. In 1975 he became Chairman of the Conservative Party organisation.

THORNEYCROFT, Sir John Isaac (1843-1928) pioneer of naval architecture, designed many high speed warships, especially torpedo boats and destroyers from 1871 and introduced general improvements in ship and propeller design and in boilers and propulsion.

THORNHILL, Sir James (1675-1734) portrait painter and decorator *inter alia* of St. Paul's Cathedral, Greenwich Palace and Blenheim, was also Hogarth's father-in-law.

THOROUGH was Strafford's motto. He meant a total devotion to King and state regardless of private interests. It seems to have been suggested by his friend Laud.

THORPE, the Rt. Hon. Jeremy (1929-) M.P. for N. Devon from 1959 to 1979 succeeded Joe Grimond as Leader of the Liberal Party in 1967 but was driven from that position in 1976.

THORPE'S CASE (1454). The Lords imprisoned Thorpe, who was at once Speaker of the Commons and a Baron of the Exchequer, for not paying a fine for trespass in seizing the D. of York's goods. The Commons demanded his release. The Lords consulted the judges who thought that he should be released but declined to declare the privilege of parliament. The Lords refused to release him and the King ordered the Commons to elect a new Speaker. The case illustrates the low status of the Commons at this period.

THRALE. See PIOZZI.

THRASHERS or THRESHERS (Ir.) were gangs of Connaught rural terrorists who, armed with flails, attacked any Orangeman or tenant who paid more in rent, rates or cess than amounts fixed by themselves. They virtually controlled the province in 1806 and had to be put down by troops.

THREADNEEDLE ST. (London) was called Three Needle St. in Tudor Times. The presence of Merchant Taylors in the lane seems to have brought about a possibly jocular change in the name. The Old Lady of Threadneedle St. is the Bank of England.

THREAPLAND. Land asserted not to be part of the Debateable Land. See CUMBERLAND-10 *et seq.*

THREE CHOIRS FESTIVAL has been held annually in rotation in the Cathedrals of Gloucester, Hereford and Worcester since 1724.

"THREE Fs". See GLADSTONE'S SECOND GOVT.-4.

THREE RESOLUTIONS (1629). In the second session of the 1628 Parliament the Commons began to discuss Arminianism and Episcopal govt. Charles I ordered the Speaker to adjourn. He was held down in his chair until the House resolved that anyone was a capital enemy of the King and Kingdom who **(1)** introduced Popery or Arminianism; **(2)** advised levying; or **(3)** who paid, tonnage and poundage without Parliamentary sanction. This mixture of religion and fiscal law arose because Charles had asked the clergy to preach in favour of the forced loan of 1627 and the Arminian clergy had responded with a will.

THREE TEINDS (1531-53). See JAMES V OF SCOTS-5.

THREE WEEKS [or WEEKEN] COURT (at Yeovil). See COURT OF RECORD, BOROUGH.

THRESHING MACHINES. The hand flail began to be superseded in about 1786 by a hand worked and then a steam worked machine and then by locomotive machines. The development caused rural unemployment long before the agricultural slump of the 1860s, and combined with a harvest failure in 1829 provoked the Swing riots of 1830.

THRING, Edward (1821-87) headmaster of Uppingham and inspirer of the Headmasters' Conference, was an influential educator who believed in small (up to 400) boarding schools with varied curricula and small classes. His *Theory and Practice of Teaching* was long a standard professional textbook.

THROCKMORTON or THROGMORTON (1) Thomas (fl. 14th cent.) was a Worcestershire retainer of Thomas, Beauchamp **D.** of Warwick. His son **(2) Sir John (?-1445)** by the Beauchamp interest became a clerk in the Treasury, and M.P. for Warwickshire; in 1431 he became a member of the Earl's Council and in 1432 he was M.P. again. When the earl died in 1439, he became a custodian of his lands and by 1440 he was under-Treasurer of England. His grandson **(3) Sir Robert (?-1519)** was privy councillor to Henry VII. His son **(4) Sir George (?-1553)** married a connection of Q. Katharine Parr, by whom he was supported in a (nearly fatal) quarrel with Thomas Cromwell. His brother **(5) Michael (?-1558)** became in 1537 Secretary to Cardinal Pole in Rome as a spy of Cromwell, but turned R. Catholic. A son of (4), **(6) Sir Robert (?-1570)** was also a R. Catholic and suffered much from the recusancy laws under Elizabeth. His brother **(7) Sir Nicholas (1515-71)** a protestant, was brought up in the household of Q. Katherine Parr and was an M.P. for various places from 1545-67. He was a personal friend of Edward VI who gave him estates and annuities. He signed the letters patent for the succession of Lady Jane Grey, but warned Mary of Edward's death. In 1554 he was tried and acquitted, despite strong evidence, for complicity in Wyatt's rebellion, but imprisoned for some time. He then became a frequenter of Elizabeth's court and so at her accession he was made Chief Butler and Chamberlain of the Exchequer. In Jan. 1560 he went to Paris as Ambassador, to induce Mary Q. of Scots not to claim the English throne nor, when her husband died, to go immediately to Scotland. He and Mary became personal friends despite their religious and political differences but this did not prevent Throckmorton advising Elizabeth of the danger represented by the Guises, and the need to support the Huguenots. In 1562 he was with an Anglo-Huguenot force and was captured at Dreux in Dec. In 1564 he helped to negotiate the P. of Troyes and in 1565 he went to Scotland to try, unsuccessfully, to prevent Mary's marriage to Darnley. Darnley's murder, Mary's marriage to Bothwell and the consequent rebellion caused Throckmorton again to be sent to Scotland. Though given contradictory instructions, he tried to induce Mary to throw Bothwell over. She refused and when taxed by Elizabeth for failing to secure her release, he tried to get a compromise by disclosing all his instructions to the Scots lords. This did not please Elizabeth either. He retired in 1568 through ill health, but was briefly imprisoned in Sept. 1569, because of his sympathy with Mary, during the rebellion of the northern R. Catholics. His brother **(8) Sir John (?-1580)** was an M.P. from 1553, C.J. of Chester and a member of the council for Wales until 1576. He was an ardent R. Catholic. He was convicted in the Star Chamber of partiality in the administration of justice and dismissed in 1576. His son **(9) Francis (1554-84)** acted in 1583 as the link between Mary Q. of Scots, the Spanish ambassador in London and the R. Catholic malcontents in Paris. He was arrested and executed for treason. See ELIZABETH -20.

THRYMSA. See COINAGE-2.

THUGGEE was a religious murder in honour of the Indian goddess Kali performed by secret roving bands of stranglers not entirely for profit. Lord William Bentinck (Gov. Gen. from 1827-35) employed William Sleeman to suppress them and between 1831-37, over 3000 Thugs were caught. The fraternity or caste was inactive by 1852 and extinct by 1890. The **THUGEE DAFTAR** (= Thug Office) was the Intelligence Bureau at Simla, originally established in this connection. The name survived into World War II.

THULE. A Greek and Roman name for a territory north of Britain; conjectured to have been the Orkneys, Shetlands, Iceland or possibly W. Norway, but the Greek navigator Pytheas (4th cent. B.C.) reported that the seas were too thick for rowing and that days and nights were six months long.

THURKILL, THORKILL or TURGESIUS (?-845) took Dublin with the Danish fleet in 832, became ruler of the Ostmen, took over the see and abbey of Armagh and thence invaded Meath and Connaught. He is said to have installed his wife as a kind of sybil on the high altar at Clonmacnoise. By 845 he had garrisons at Limerick, Dundalk, Dublin and on the Ree, Neagh and Carlingford Loughs. Ruthless and energetic, he seemed ready for a great future when he was taken by Maelsachlann, K. of Meath, who had him drowned. Some authorities have identified him with Ragnar Lothbrok.

THURKILL or THORKILL, E. (before 990-after 1024) arrived with a Danish fleet in 1009 and he with the fleets of Eglaf and Heming carried out most of the campaigns in S. and E. England up to 1012, when he was present at the murder of St. Alphege whom he tried to save. Apparently converted, he then entered the service of K. Ethelred and was one of the most effective commanders against K. Sweyn of Denmark. In 1015, however, he and Edric Streona went over to Canute. He was evidently a man of major importance for Canute trusted him and he acted as one of the King's independent lieutenants. In 1017 he was given the earldom of E. Anglia (the nearest to Denmark) and at some time unknown he made a royal marriage to Edith, daughter of K. Ethelred and widow of Edric Streona. This marriage may have caused difficulties, for he and Edith were banished for a while in 1021. In 1023, however, he became Canute's lieutenant in Denmark. His later career is unknown.

THURLOW, Edward (1731-1806) 1st Ld. (1778) became a K.C. in 1762 and Tory M.P. for Tamworth in 1765. His brilliant oratorical powers were used against Wilkes and in the *Junius* Affair. In 1770 he became Sol-Gen. In 1771 he was Att. Gen. and became the chief party spokesman against Clive, the American colonists and in favour of the slave trade. He became Lord Chancellor in 1778 and with a few months gap in 1783, held that office under North, Rockingham, Shelburne and Pitt until 1792. He was a friend of Crabbe and Samuel Johnson and he recognised the abilities of and sponsored the later Lord Eldon, but was detested by almost every politician of importance.

THURSO (Caithness) was the Norwegians' mainland centre in Scotland from the 11th cent. until their defeat at the B. of Largs in 1263. It had a bishopric and remained of sufficient commercial importance for its system of weights and measures to be adopted for the whole of Scotland in 1330. In 1633 it became a burgh of Barony. In common with the rest of the far north, it suffered a decline after the Highland depopulations of 1745 and this was arrested only in 1954 by the construction of the Dounreay atomic power station.

THURSTAN or THURSTIN (?-1140) Abp. of YORK (1114) was educated at Bayeux and rose through the royal chapel, becoming a clerk to William II, then Henry I's almoner and a canon of St. Paul's and eventually Abp. of York. His early years were spent in controversy with Canterbury, to whose primacy he refused to submit. Some Popes supported him, but only in 1119 was he consecrated by Calixtus II and he was enthroned at York only in 1121. A temporary compromise with Canterbury was reached in 1125 when the southern metropolitan was given a legatine commission over the English church, but York as such was not required to submit to Canterbury as such. Pious and capable, his later patronage of the Augustinian canons led to the creation of the diocese of Carlisle, and he encouraged the early Yorkshire Cistercians at Fountains Abbey from 1133. Almost his last act (1138) was to organise the victorious force against the barbaric Scottish and Galwegian invasion at the B. of the Standard.

THYNNE (1) Sir John (?-1580) became steward to Edward Seymour, later D. of Somerset, and in 1541 acquired Longleat. During Mary's reign he was comptroller to Elizabeth. Between 1567-69 he built the great mansion at Longleat. **(2) Sir Thomas (1640-1714) 1st Vist. WEYMOUTH (1682)** was Minister to Sweden in 1666, and an M.P. from 1674-82. He was opposed to the policy of James II, and in 1688 was one of four who conveyed the invitation to William III to take over the govt. He also, as a high Tory, opposed William's policies and so received office only at Anne's accession. **(3) Thomas (1734-96) 3rd Vist. (1751) and 1st M. of BATH (1789)** was briefly a non-resident Lord Lieut. of Ireland in 1765 and in 1768 by the interest of the Bedfords, he became Sec. of State (Northern Dept) with Shelburne. When Shelburne resigned in the same year he transferred to the Southern Dept. and in 1769 tried to establish govt. control over the HEIC. He resigned during the Falklands Is. dispute of 1770. After a period of spasmodic opposition, he was reappointed in 1775 and acted as govt. manager in the Lords throughout the American rebellion. When it threatened the stability of the govt. after Chatham's dying attack in April 1778, he was the King's principal negotiator for a coalition, but the negotiation failed, and as Weymouth disliked the continuance of the War, he resigned in Nov. 1779. His great-grandson **(4) John Alexander (1831-96) 4th M.** was ambassador at Lisbon in 1858 and at Vienna in 1867. He became an expert in Balkan affairs (on which he wrote) and was opposed to Disraeli's eastern policy.

TIBET. A dual theocracy under the Dalai Lama and the Panchen Lama, the two rulers succeeding by reincarnation and discovery, was under a Chinese suzerainty of varying effectiveness when the first British diplomatic approach was made in 1772. The Chinese excluded all foreigners in 1792, and the first British mission thereafter, under Colonel Francis Younghusband, fought its way to Lhasa in 1903-4. The country declared its independence in 1911 after the Manchus were overthrown in China, and this remained their *de facto* condition, recognised by the British but not by the Chinese, until the latter overran Tibet in 1951 and the Dalai Lama fled and eventually established himself in Wales.

TICHBORNE CASES (1871-73). Arthur Orton (1834-98) claimed to be the long lost Roger Charles Tichborne, heir to the baronetcy and fortune of Sir Roger Tichborne who died 1862. Orton was heavily in debt. The trial of his claim lasted 102 days and he was revealed as an impostor. He was then tried for perjury. This trial lasted 188 days. He was found guilty and sentenced to 14 years penal servitude. The affair created tremendous excitement and a sort of class partisanship. Orton's leading and very learned counsel Dr. Edward Kenealy Q.C. (1819-80) conducted his cases rudely and aggressively and afterwards published pamphlets in which he attacked the integrity of Cockburn C.J. and counsel on the other side. For this he was disbarred in 1874. He then became an M.P. but was widely shunned.

TICKHILL. Honour entitled to the service of 70½ knights in 1208-13.

TICONDEROGA (N.Y.) a strategic fort in colonial times, was held by the French until 1759, by the British until 1775 when Ethan Allen took it and Burgoyne retook it. After Burgoyne's surrender it was abandoned but reoccupied by the British in 1780 until 1785.

TIDES. The relationship of tidal movements to the sun and moon has so long been evident that predictions based on experience have been regularly made for particular localities, such as Liverpool, from early times. Systematic theory began only with Sir Isaac Newton, but the first generalised work relating to world tides was by Pierre Laplace in 1773. Kelvin's tidal predictor was invented in 1872.

Using the tidal periodicity at Dover, which has long been known, the tides at any other place in the world can be predicted from the tidal time difference, or **tidal**

constant, between Dover and that place. The discovery and publication of these constants was a feature of 19th cent. hydrography.

TIERNEY George (1761-1830) of a wealthy Mediterranean merchant and banking family, entered politics in a radical interest by contesting the corrupt borough of Colchester in 1788. He was an M.P. from 1789-90 and from 1797, much of the intervening time being spent in electoral disputes. He then joined Fox's opposition as M.P. for Southwark, but when the Foxites seceded from the Commons in 1798 he insisted on staying and so achieved the notoriety of being Pitt's only opponent. This annoyed both sides, but a parliamentary quarrel with Pitt led to a duel at Putney where both contestants missed twice. An able besides pugnacious critic of Pitt described by Wilberforce as "truly Jacobiical" he concentrated on financial policy. Pitt recommended Addington to secure his support, which he did, and Tierney held the lucrative treasureship of the navy under Addingtron. In Aug. 1804 Pitt offered him the Chief Secretaryship for Ireland, which he would have accepted without a seat in the Commons because he did not want to be committed to supporting Pitt. In Sept. 1806, however, he took the Board of Control, but lost his seat and had to buy one in Ireland. He sat for Irish boroughs until 1812, then for English ones again. After 1810 he was, by virtue of his abilities, the leading member but not the acknowledged leader of the Opposition, for which his personality disqualified him.

TIERRA del FUEGO. Magellan named it in 1520. C. Horn was first rounded by Drake in 1578, but not so named until 1616. The area was first surveyed by King and Fitzroy from 1826-36. European colonisation began in 1880.

THAK, Bal Gangadhar (1857-1920) learned Indian journalist and nationalist politician, organised in the Congress meeting of 1907 extremists who favoured total independence by revolutionary means. In 1916 he founded the Home Rule League. Implacably hostile to the British govt. and inclined to calumniate it, he spent a considerable time in prison.

TILBURY and THURROCK (Essex). Henry VIII built Tilbury Fort and Docks to create a protective base for London, and the London defence forces were assembled there in the Armada crisis. Charles II enlarged the installations, but they were later superseded for naval purposes by Chatham and Sheerness. In the 19th cent. seaborne traffic to London grew in tonnage and quantity, and the London and India Dock Co. built commercial docks, which were opened in 1886. The Port of London Authority extended them between 1917-29 to compete for oceanic traffic. Other industries such as soap, oil refining, cement and margarine grew up in the neighbouring areas of Grays, Thurrock and Purfleet, and Tilbury with Orsett was amalgamated with these into Thurrock Urban District in 1936.

TILLETT, Ben[jamin] (1860-1943) formed the Dockers Union in 1887, led the London dock strike of 1889 and formed the National Transport Workers Federation in 1910. When the two unions were united as the Transport and General Workers Union in 1922 he became Secretary for its political and international affairs. He was M.P. for N. Salford from 1917-24 and from 1929-31.

TILLEY, Vesta, alias Alice POWLES (1864-1952) was a celebrated music hall star between 1873-1920. Her songs included *Burlington Bertie* and *The Girl who loved a Soldier*. She was a male impersonator.

TUSIT, Ts. of (*see* BALTIC; THIRD COALITION. WAR OF, SECOND PHASE-4). After the B. of Friedland (June 1807) the Czar Alexander I feared a Polish insurrection while Bonaparte wanted a Russian alliance against Britain. They opened their discussions by a private meeting on a raft in the R. Niemen and two treaties resulted. **(1) 7 July 1807.** The Czar secretly agreed to declare war on Britain should she refuse his mediation, and meantime to join Bonaparte's continental system, to give up his claims to the Ionian Is. and to recognise the Confederation of the Rhine. He also agreed to evacuate the Danubian principalities (which were under Turkey). Bonaparte for his part offered largely illusory assistance in a Russian war with Turkey. **(2) 9 July 1807.** Prussia surrendered her Polish territories for conversion into the new Grand Duchy of Warsaw, her territories W. of the Elbe for annexation by the new Bonapartist Kingdom of Westphalia and had to pay an indemnity or submit to military occupation until payment. The secret terms were known to the British govt. very soon after signature.

TIMBER PREFERENCE. In 18th cent., European, mostly Baltic timber was taxed, but Canadian timber received a bounty. The effect at home was small as long as home produced timber supplied most of the demand, but the French Wars from 1793 consumed most of the U.K. tlmber reserves, and to minimise the strategic danger of relying upon the Baltic, the duty was doubled to encourage Canadian supplies, which in fact it did; but Baltic timber continued to be imported in quantity because of the huge post-war demand. The result was that English timber prices were fixed by Canadian supplies and the duty was an important source of revenue in the nature of an indirect tax on investment. The duty was halved in 1851 and abolished in 1866.

TIMBUKTU (Mali) was the southern junction of the trans-Saharan caravan routes to the Niger and the W. Sudan. It became a trading centre in 12th cent. and by 1500 had risen to great splendour with a university and, it is said, 1,000,000 inhabitants. The trade was mainly in gold, slaves and salt. In 1591 it was captured by the Moroccans, whose weak authority failed to establish a settled govt. Climatic and political changes also contributed to its decline, and after 1800 it was largely ruinous and tributary to surrounding Tuareg clans. The French took it in 1893.

TIME OF TROUBLES (Russia) (1584-1625 and later) (*see* MUSCOVY). Ivan the Dread's death in 1584 precipitated civil wars between rival Shuisky and Romanov, Orthodox branches of his house and the partly Tartar Boris Godunov. These were complicated by Swedish (Protestant), Polish (R. Catholic) interventions and incessant raids by Moslem Crimean Tartars. The material organisation of society and commerce fell apart, and so continued after Michael Romanoff (r. 1613-45) was elected to the vacant throne. He presided over bloody conflicts between rural populations on the move and those seeking to pin them to fixed habitations. Under Czar Alexis (r. 1645-76) there were widespread tax riots (1648) and wars with the Poles and the Cossacks (1656-67). In 1662 the coinage debasement wrecked the reviving urban trading economies; and from 1667-71 the Volga catchment was ruled by the Cossack pirate Stenka Razin, and reconquered only at a cost of 100,000 deaths. The period stunted Russian development, for order and foreign defence required burdensome centralisation which was biased towards the military life, beginning with foreign weapons, officers (e.g. a Colonel Leslie) and training manuals. But the degradation was not total or continuous. In 1632 a Dutch Co. helped to found a state ordnance factory; in 1634 Saxon experts investigated the copper deposits; and after 1670 as a result of Baltic frustrations, Archangel developed rapidly as a port. *See* RUSSIA PETRINE.

TIMES, THE. Newspaper. *See* WALTER DELANE.

TIMES EDUCATIONAl SUPPLEMENT was begun as a monthly inset in *The Times* in 1910 and became a separate weekly in 1916.

TIMES LITERARY SUPPLEMENT, weekly review founded in 1902.

TIMETABLE MOTION. See CLOSURE.

TIMOR (Indonesia). The Portuguese arrived in 1520, the Dutch in 1613, and the curious political geography of the island dates from this time. The British occupied it from 1812-15.

TIN with COPPER is an essential constituent of **BRONZE** which came into increasingly common use in the 3rd millennium B.C. The only large European tin deposits were in Cornwall, where the mines, worked probably from 2000 B.C., were the basis of a growing trade, itself fundamental to Bronze Age civilisation. Tinned vessels were known to the Romans. Tinned iron and steel sheeting first appeared in 15th cent. Bohemia, and the modern tinning industry commenced in the 1870s. *See* BRITAIN BEFORE THE ROMAN CONQUEST-1 3; STANNARIES.

TINCHEBRAY, B. of (28 Sept. 1106) was fought between Henry I and his elder brother Robert Curthose when the latter tried to relieve the siege of Tinchebray which is 35 miles E. of Avranches. The battle, mostly between dismounted knights and infantry, was short and Robert was captured. He spent the rest of his life in prison while Henry took over his duchy.

TINCOMMIUS. *See* BRITAIN BEFORE THE ROMAN CONQUEST- 3 *et seq.*

TINTAGEL (or BOSSINEY, which was part of it) was represented in Parliament by two M.P.s under a charter of 1685. The voting qualifications were so restricted that in 1784 the vicar of Tintagel as mayor of Bossiney was the only elector. The castle is connected, somewhat obscurely, with Arthurian legend.

TIPPERARY, County and Town (Ireland) was organised by John (later King) who came in 1185; he built the castle forming the nucleus of the town, and gave lands in the south to Philip of Worcester and in the north to Theobald Walter, Butler of Ireland. This originated the division into north and south ridings which still persists. It also founded the fortunes of the Butler family, who also acquired the Worcester lands and Kilkenny. In 1328 the whole became a Butler (Ormonde) palatinate, but in 1339 the O'Briens burned the town. The Butlers remained pillars of the English supremacy down to the civil war when they supported the King. They later supported the Stuarts, and after the second D. of Ormonde was impeached in 1715, the palatinate, the last in Ireland, was abolished though the family was later restored to its estates.

TIPPETT, Sir Michael (1905-98), highly original and widely influenced English composer, sprang to notice with his *Concerto for Double String Orchestra* (1938-9). His many works included *King Priam* (1962) and *The New Year* (1989).

TIPPOO SULTAN (?-1799) *See* MYSORE.

TIPTOFT or TIBETOT (1) Robert (?-1298) inherited his estates in 1250 and was from youth a friend of the Lord Edward (later Edward I) whom he tried to rescue from captivity in Wallingford Castle in 1264. Closely involved in all Edward's policies, he went on crusade with him, was an executor of his will and played a prominent part in his wars in Gascony, Scotland, and especially Wales, where he negotiated the T. of Rhuddlan (1277), suppressed the rising of Rhys ap Maredudd (1288) and served as justiciar for S. Wales (1281-98). His 15th cent. descendants were prominent Lancastrians especially **(2) John (c. 1375-1443)** Speaker of the Commons (1406), the first lay Treasurer of the Household (1428-32) and his son **(3) John (1427-70) E. of WORCESTER (1449)** Lord Deputy of Ireland and Constable, a humanist patron and scholar, whose pleasure in impaling criminals and enemies earned him notoriety and retribution.

TIRAH EXPEDITION (1897). *See* KHYBER PASS.

TIR CYFRIF. *See* WELSH LAW-9.

TIREL, Walter (fl. 1100) Ld. of POIX, received English estates from William the Conqueror and was an associate of William Rufus. He was supposed to have shot and killed Rufus accidentally at a deer hunt in the New Forest (2 Aug. 1100). His hasty flight from the scene suggested guilt to many contemporaries, but he always denied any connection with the arrow which killed the King and he may have understandably mistrusted contemporary legal processes, or it may have been encouraged by Henry I and Gilbert of Clare to distract attention while they seized the Winchester treasury. *See* TYRRELL, SIR JAMES.

TIR EOGHAN. *See* TYRONE.

TIROL. *See* TYROL.

TIRONENSIAN MONKS (Scotland). David I (r. 1124-53) founded an abbey at Selkirk, which moved to Kelso in 1128. Under Malcolm V (r. 1153-65) and William (r. 1165-1214) further foundations included the abbeys at Arbroath, Lindores and Kilwinning. The abbot of Arbroath was always a significant figure in church and secular politics and the abbey often housed parliaments and other similar meetings and provided the necessary secretarial facilities. *For later development cf* CISTERCIANS (SCOTLAND).

TIRPITZ, Alfred Peter Friedrich von (1849-1930) German naval officer, took Tsingtao in 1896; became Sec. of State for the navy in 1897, and with his bill of 1898 began the expansion of the German navy. His bill of 1900 started the naval armament race with Britain. He resigned in 1916.

TIRPITZ **(Battleship).** *See* COMMERCE PROTECTION, NAVAL-6-9.

TITANIC **DISASTER.** This immense liner, believed unsinkable, hit an iceberg on her maiden voyage in Apr. 1912 and sank with nearly 1600 people.

TIT-BITS. *See* NEWNES, GEORGE.

TITHE, TITHE AWARDS. *See* ADVOWSON AND TITHE-5-9.

TITHE PROCTORS were church officials common in Ireland, who collected (violently if necessary) tithes and were paid a commission. Their functions were transferred to the govt. in 1832.

TITHING. In the system of frankpledge, groups of people who were decreed to be mutually responsible for each other's good behaviour (usually ten to twelve men) were called tithings and were directed by a tithingman. Numbers were not standardised so that a tithing might encompass a whole village.

TITYRE-TU or TITTYRY. A well-to-do London 17th cent. rough.

TIVERTON (Devon) was given to the Redvers family in about 1105 when they built the castle. William de Vernon, E. of Devon granted a charter in about 1200. Peter Blundell founded the school named after him in 1604. The town was incorporated and represented in Parliament under a charter of 1615 and almost depopulated by an epidemic in 1644.

TIZARD, Sir Henry Thomas (1885-1959) aeronautical scientist, was largely responsible for the exploitation of radar, as a result of his committee, formed in 1935, on radiolocation. As chairman of the Aeronautical Research Committee he encouraged Whittle's jet engine but resigned from his responsibilities in 1940 as a result of policy differences with Professor Lindemann (Lord Cherwell) the Prime Minister's wartime scientific adviser. Nevertheless, he opposed the bombing of urban populations in 1942. He was thereafter until 1952 Chairman of the Advisory Council on Scientific Policy and then became Pres. of Magdalen College, Oxford.

TOBACCO, observed in the Antilles on Columbus' second expedition in 1497, was introduced to Spain in 1559 and to France in 1560 by way of Portugal, through the French ambassador Jean Nicot, after whom nicotine is named. It reached England in 1565 and became the foundation of the economy of Virginia which it reached in 1612. Heavy import duties led to cultivation in England, especially about Cheltenham, but this was forcibly suppressed under Cromwell and Charles II. Cigarette smoking was introduced into England in about 1857 by soldiers returning through Turkey from the Crimea. By 1914 cigarette and pipe tobacco were smoked in equal quantities. The revenue from tobacco duty expanded from about £11M in 1900 to £602M in 1949 and to

£3500M in 1982-3. A propaganda campaign in which the tobacco companies were forced to take part, against the health risks of cigarette smoking, began in the 1970s and by the 1990s adults were smoking much less than in the 1960s.

TOBAGO (W. Indies), discovered by Columbus in 1498 and visited by Leicester in 1580, the first settlement was attempted in 1615 by Englishmen, but the first to succeed was Dutch in 1632. The island was disputed between Dutch, Courlanders, French and British until 1672. It was then a sort of no-man's land spasmodically occupied by British and French forces until 1814 when it was ceded to Britain. *See* TRINIDAD.

TOBRUK (Cyrenaica) The British took this Italian colonial port in Jan. 1941 but in the spring it was isolated by the Italo-German counter attack under Rommel. It was relieved in Auchinleck's offensive in early 1942, but was not well organised and in another offensive Rommel unexpectedly stormed it (June 1942). This injury to British prestige was made good by the end of the year by Rommel's defeat at Alamein and final retreat.

TOC H (= signallers jargon for the initials T.H.) In 1915 the Rev. P.B. ('Tubby') Clayton, M.C. an army chaplain, founded **T**albot **H**ouse, as a soldier's club at Poperinghe (Belgium). Refounded in London in 1920 as a Christian fellowship, it spread throughout the English speaking world.

TOCQUEVILLE, Alexis de (1805-59) French historical philosopher was a deputy from 1839-51 and served briefly as Foreign Minister in 1849. His *De La Démocratie en Amerique* (Democracy in America) appeared in 1835 and 1840; *L'Ancien Régime et la Revolution* in 1856.

TOEPLITZ, T. of (Sept. 1813). Austria, Prussia and Russia agreed to settle the Polish question amicably between themselves. This was not consistent with the Kalisch Convention or the Second T. of Reichenbach.

TOGODUMNUS. *See* BRITAIN BEFORE THE ROMAN CONQUEST-5,6; BRITAIN, ROMAN-2,3; CATUVELLAUNI.

TOGOLAND was partly occupied by the Danes in 18th cent. German missionaries and traders came in 1847 and a German protectorate was imposed in 1885. The boundaries were settled by treaties with France (1897) and Britain (1899). It was occupied by Anglo-French forces in 1914, partitioned and mandated to the two countries in 1922. The British territory was part of the Gold Coast in 1956 and so part of Ghana. The French part became independent in 1960.

TOKYO TRIALS. *See* WAR CRIMES.

TOLBOOTH (Sc.). A building at which fair or market tolls were collected and in which market offenders were detained. The close connection of Scots burgh corporations with trading often caused the Tolbooth to be the principal municipal building and in Edinburgh an important govt. building too, used for meetings of councils and assemblies, and law courts as well as a prison. It was called the Heart of Midlothian by Scot. It stood near St. Giles cathedral until 1817 when it was demolished.

TOLEDO was the principal Arab city of Spain from 712 to 1085 and thereafter the capital of Castile. It declined after Madrid became the capital in 1560. It was a famous mediaeval centre of learning, civilisation, steel and silk.

TOLER, John (1745-1831) 1st Ld. (1800) 1st E. of NORBURY (1821) entered the Irish parliament in 1776 and was one of the most ruthless upholders of the unreformed Ascendancy. He was Irish Sol-Gen. in 1789, Att-Gen. in 1798 and C.J. of the Irish Common Pleas from 1800. A famous wit, and as a judge still an influential politician, he was notorious for impropriety, particularly on the bench, and for ignorance of the law.

TOLERATION ACTS (Eng.) (*see* TEST ACTS) relieved English non-conformists from the Acts of Supremacy and Uniformity of 1559 and acts against non attendance at church (1583), other similar enactments of 1593 and 1606,

the Act of Uniformity 1662, the Corporation Act, 1661, the Conventicle Acts of 1664 and 1671, the Five Mile Act, 1665 and the Test Acts. The Toleration Act, 1688, relieved from penal consequences, those who took the oaths of allegiance and supremacy and made the declaration against popery, and it required dissenting chapels to be registered. The Dissenting Ministers Act, 1779, exempted nonconformists from the bans on teaching. Other major issues were settled by the repeal of the Test Acts and by a number of minor acts.

TOLERATION ACT 1712 (Scots) forbade Scottish magistrates to enforce kirk censures or summonses. This ended state enforcement of kirk rule, and effectively, the quasi-legislative powers of the General Assembly of the Church of Scotland. *See* BOOK OF DISCIPLINE.

TOLL and TEAM were late A.S. associated legal terms. Toll was a landowner's right to levy a payment on the sale of goods or cattle, or on the passage of cattle across his land. Team was the right to hold a court to determine their ownership and therefore the identity of the person liable to the toll. The rights were conferred by royal grant, and usually formed a fascicule of jurisdictional grants along with Sake and Soke, and Infangthief and Outfangthief.

TOLLS (*see* TOLL AND TEAM; TURNPIKE). **(1)** i.e. charges only marginally related to the giving of a service were a very common source of local and private income until the late 19th cent. They burdened the economy and delayed movement. In 1498 Coventry complained of tolls at Bristol, Gloucester and Worcester. The main types, paid in money were *passage, traverse* or *thorough tolls* to cross land, especially a borough, or to cross a bridge; *mooring* tolls against ships and on landing or shipping cargo; *market* tolls on removing goods sold in a market and *canal tolls* for the passage of privately owned barges. The D. of Nassau was still levying tolls on the Rhine in 1838. A toll was levied at the Severn Tunnel to prevent the railway co. from undercutting colliers between S. Wales and Devon and Cornwall. Some municipalities depended for much of their finance on tolls, and the City of London accumulated a large still existing capital fund from a toll on Newcastle coal. **(2)** Charges for a monopoly service (e.g. to have corn ground or bread baked by the manor miller or baker) were often rendered in kind as a customary proportion of the material treated. *See* BALTIC-7 to 9; SHIPS. SAILING.

TOLPUDDLE MARTYRS. Seven methodists led by George and James Loveless formed a trade union called the Friendly Society of Agricultural Labourers at Tolpuddle in Dorset in Oct. 1833 and began to agitate for a strike against the low wages then prevailing. Arrested for administering illegal oaths, they were sentenced in Mar. 1834 to seven years' transportation. Public demonstrations in favour of clemency resulted in Melbourne securing a remission of their sentences in Mar. 1836.

TOMAN (Tartar = 10,000). A Persian gold coin originally worth 10,000 dinars, also used in India.

TOMATOES were brought to Europe from Peru, being first grown for food in Italy in about 1550, and in England in about 1690 where they were called **Love Apples.** They were not extensively cultivated in Britain until about 1870.

TOM O'BEDLAM, a wandering beggar affecting madness, common after the dissolution of the monasteries had thrown many simpletons onto the streets.

TOMMY ATKINS. Familiar name for a British private soldier, especially in World War I, arising out of the use of the name after 1815 in specimen army forms to show how they should be completed. The term was seldom used in World War II.

TOMSAETAN were a Mercian folk who settled the area about Tamworth in the late 6th cent.

TON. *See* WEIGHTS AND MEASURES.

TONBRIDGE (Kent) grew up round a Norman Castle built

at the end of the Medway navigation. Of some mediaeval importance, a school was founded there in 1553 by Sir Andrew Judd, who placed it in the care of the London Skinner Co. The principal industries were tanning, bricks and sawmilling.

TONE, R. *See* TRANSPORT AND COMMUNICATIONS.

TONE, Theobald Wolfe (1763-98) Irish barrister, helped to found the United Irishmen in 1791. He became Sec. of the Catholic Committee in 1792, and organised the Catholic Convention which met in Dublin in Dec., and forced the govt. to pass the Catholic Relief Act, 1793. He was in fact anti-clerical; the steam went out of the Catholic Convention in 1794 and in Apr. he gave William Jackson, an English emissary of the French Govt. to the United Irishmen, a memorandum arguing that Ireland was ready for revolt. Jackson was arrested, the document was found and Tone was also arrested, but confessed and was released. In June 1795 he left, and reached Paris *via* U.S.A. in Feb. 1796. He persuaded Carnot and Delacroix to send a force to Ireland and sailed with it under the command of General Hoche in Dec. The expedition was frustrated by the Royal Navy and bad weather and he returned in Jan. 1797. A similar expedition from Holland was abandoned in Sept. but when the Irish revolt broke out in May 1798 he accompanied a small expedition under Commodore Bompart which was captured in Lough Swilly. He made a defiant speech at his trial and committed suicide.

TONGA (Pacific) though visited by Lemaire in 1616 and by Tasman in 1643, enjoyed no effective European contacts until James Cook's visits in 1773 and 1777. From 1799 and 1852 the islands were in a state of dynastic civil war which was ended by **(1) Taufa'ahau (r. 1852-93)** the representative of the third or Tu'i Kanokupolu dynasty. He adopted methodism and the title of King George Tupou I in 1845 and had subdued the islands by 1852. He established a legal, administrative and constitutional structure. He was succeeded by his grandson **(2) George II (r. 1893-1918)** who placed Tonga under British protection. His impressive daughter **(3) Salote (r. 1918-65)** signed a revised treaty in 1958 which left the Kingdom internally autonomous. Her son **(4) Taufa'ahau Tupou IV (r. 1965-)** negotiated the end of British protection in 1970 when Tonga became an independent member of the Commonwealth.

TONGKING. *See* INDOCHINA.

TONK. *See* RAJPUTS.

TONNAGE, or more correctly Tunnage, was an import tax of 3s per tun of wine or 6s per tun of sweet wine. Invariably associated with Poundage it had the same history. *See* SUBSIDY.

TONSON (1) Jacob (?1656-1736) was the publisher of Dryden, Addison, Pope and Steele. He was also secretary of the Kit Cat Club and made a fortune from South Sea and Mississippi stock. His great-nephew **(2) Jacob (?-1767)**, also a publisher, was a friend of Dr. Johnson. His brother **(3) Richard (?-1772)** was M.P. for Wallingford from 1747 and for Windsor from 1768.

TONSURE proclaimed dedication to monastic life. In the Roman tonsure the head is shaved, leaving a fringe all round; in the Celtic only in front of a line from ear to ear. The difference was a mark of doctrinal allegiance and even of offence in the controversies before the Synod of Whitby (664).

TONTINE. A loan in which a fixed sum is divided by way of annuity between such subscribers as are living at any given time, so that each survivor's sum increases with the death of the others. Believed to encourage murder, the last British govt. tontine was raised in 1789.

TOOKE, (John) Horne, The Rev. (1736-1812) called Home until 1782, brilliant and pugnacious son of a well-to-do poulterer, was ordained but soon found radical politics more interesting. He travelled abroad besides as a tutor and by 1767 knew Voltaire, Sterne, and especially John Wilkes whose Middlesex Election campaign of 1768 he organised. George Onslow moved the annulment of Wilkes' election: Tooke accused Onslow of selling offices and was fined £400 but got the judgement set aside on technical grounds. He then helped to found the Society for the Bill of Rights but quarrelled with Wilkes and formed a rival Constitutional Society. In 1774 he was summoned before the Commons for libelling the Speaker, but no action was taken. In 1778 he was imprisoned for trying to raise a subscription for American colonists. By now he had inherited his father's money and was able to entertain. His political suppers included many radicals such as Bentham, Paine, Coleridge, Godwin but also Thurlow and Erskine. He had belonged to the Society for Constitutional Information since 1780. In 1788 he supported Pitt against Fox and stood against Fox at Westminster in 1790. His feud with the Whigs got him into further trouble in 1794 when he was charged and acquitted of High Treason. In 1796 he again failed at Westminster, but in 1801 was returned for Old Sarum but disqualified as a clergyman by a supervening act. Though famous as an adventurous old fashioned radical, he was also interested in Anglo-Saxon philology the study of which he did much to advance.

TOOM TABARD (Scots. = empty jacket). A derisive nickname for K. John Balliol.

TORCH. Code name for the Anglo-American invasion of Algeria. *See* WORLD WAR II-13.

TORCY, Jean-Baptiste Colbert, M. de (1665-1745) son of Charles Colbert de Croissy, Louis XIV's Foreign Minister, who trained him. For his diplomatic skill he succeeded his father in 1696 and held the post until Louis XIV died (1715). He negotiated all the major diplomatic events from the succession to the Spanish throne to the Ts. of Utrecht and Rastadt. At Louis' death, the Regent dismissed him.

TORDESILLAS, T. of (1494). In May 1493 to settle conflicts arising from Spanish and Portuguese exploration, Pope Alexander VI, by the bull *Inter Caetera* (Lat: Amongst other matters) fixed a line from Pole to Pole 100 leagues west of the C. Verde Is. In return for converting the heathen, Spain was to have exclusive rights to the west of the line, and expeditions by the Portuguese were to keep to the east, but their rights were not specifically affirmed. This, and the fact that the line did not allow enough sea room for African voyages, caused dissatisfaction in Portugal, and the two govts. negotiated a treaty direct at Tordesillas which affirmed Portuguese rights and moved the line 270 leagues westward. This was confirmed by the Papacy in 1506. As the new line intersected the South American coast at the longitude of Santos, Portugal was able, in right of Cabral's discoveries in 1500, to claim Brazil. *See* SPAIN (1406-1516)-5.

TORIES (Ir.) (1653 onwards) (*see separately* TORY AND WHIG). Tories were Irish who refused to be transplanted or who, after transplantation, returned from Connaught and, led by nobles and gentry, waged a guerrilla against the new settlers in the empty, partly devastated country with its woods, bogs and thickets. Their main objectives were cattle and horses for sustenance. Their kindred, or if not identified, the people of the barony were supposed to make satisfaction, but it was more effective to pay head-money or to foment feuds between Tories. The endemic war continued after the Restoration and the Revolution of 1689 because the dispossessed did not receive their property back on either occasion. Most of the leaders as they died off, were not replaced. The remainder became known under the Hanoverians as RAPPAREES.

TORONTO (Ft. ROUILLÉ, YORK) (Ont.) There was a French trading post from 1750 to 1759 but the British purchased the site from the Missisanga Indians in 1787 and settlement began in 1793, when it was made the capital of Upper Canada, and called York. The Americans burnt it in 1813. It remained a small village until 1825, but by 1834 when it was incorporated as Toronto, it had 9000 people. It grew rapidly after 1850, numbering 120,000 by 1885 and exceeding 2M in the 1970s.

TORPEDOES were invented by Robert Whitehead, an English engineer, at Fiume in 1866. Gyroscopic control was introduced in 1895. First effectively used by the Japanese against the Chinese in 1894 and against the Russians in 1904-5, they revolutionised naval warfare by providing a true long range underwater weapon which could be used by surface and submarine ships, aircraft and as at Oslo in World War II, shore forts. Homing torpedoes came into use after World War II.

TORRENS (1) Sir Henry (1779-1828) had a busy military career beginning under Abercrombie in the W. Indies (1796) and then in Portugal (1798), Holland (1799), Nova Scotia (1800-1), against the Marathas, and then at Buenos Aires (1807). In Holland and India he knew Sir Arthur Wellesley (later Wellington) who took him to Portugal as his mil. sec. in 1808. After the brilliant opening at Roliça and Vimeiro Wellesley was superseded by incompetents, and Torrens in 1809 went home and became mil. sec. to the royal C-in-C. In practice this meant that Torrens did the C-in-C's routine work. As he knew Wellesley's mind he ensured that his army got (most) of what it needed during his later campaigns. He was an important cog in the machine which defeated Bonaparte. His admiration for Wellesley may be gauged from the names of his second son **(2) Sir Arthur Wellesley (1809-55)** who commanded an infantry brigade in the Crimea, fought at the Alma and Balaclava and was badly wounded at Inkerman. A cousin of (1), **(3) Robert (1780-1864)** economist, wrote an *Essay on the External Corn Trade* (1815) and an *Essay on the Production of Wealth* (1821). The first influenced Peel, the second anticipated J. S. Mill and Ricardo. In 1835 he was made Chairman of the South Australia Commission and delineated its territorial layout. He was also editor of the *Globe*. His son **(4) Sir Robert Acland (1814-84)** was an official nominee on the South Australian Legislative Council in 1851 and became a member for Adelaide in 1858. He introduced conveyancing by registration in 1858 for the first time anywhere in the British Empire. He was M.P. for Cambridge from 1868-74.

TORRES VEDRAS. *See* PENINSULAR WAR (1807-14)-5,6.

TORRINGTON, E. of. *See* BYNG.

TORRINGTON, Vist. *See* HERBERT.

TORT (Fr = Wrong) is a civil wrong for which the injured party now claimant may obtain unliquidated damages (i.e. the monetary award separate from itemised expenses) from the person (defendant) who inflicted the wrong. Many torts are also crimes but not all crimes are torts. In 1990 there were 33 known types of tort and 4 more which seemed to be emerging. The law of tort is a law of conflict, and as the human condition becomes more complicated, opportunities for conflict arise which nobody foresaw. Hence though a tort is defined by the Common Law, it cannot necessarily be defined in advance, and new torts come into existence when a court has an opportunity to consider a new situation e.g. Malicious Prosecution in 1698, Inducing a Wife to Leave Her Husband in 1745, Deceit in 1789, Inciting a Breach of Contract in 1853, Negligence in 1932, Conspiracy in 1941 and Intimidation in 1964. Torts are classifiable into (a) those which are actionable *per se* (by themselves) simply because a right has been infringed or into those (b) actionable *per quod* (by reason of which) on proof that the act has caused identifiable damage. (a) includes trespass to land, person or goods, conversion (i.e. appropriation of property), escapes of dangerous things, libel and certain grave slanders. (b) includes negligence, nuisance, conspiracy, intimidation, slander and certain injurious lies.

TORTUGA. *See* BUCCANEERS; HISPANIOLA.

TORTURE. Apart from *peine forte et dure* (q.v.) the Common Law has never countenanced torture and has refused to listen to evidence procured under it or even procured by threats or duress. Church authorities investigating heresy were entitled to use torture under canon law, but there was little heresy in England before the Lollards, and the Inquisition was admitted only for a short period under Edward II to investigate the Templars. Unofficially, however, and especially in troubled times, torture cannot have been uncommon because scanty policing and private cruelty created the right conditions for it. Outside the more lurid propaganda, there is evidence (e.g. Pipe Roll 34 Henry II) that Angevin govts. resorted to it, but as an 'engine of state' it became fashionable only in the 16th cent. and then only under the strict control of the Privy Council.

TORY (Irish, *toiridbe*) WHIG (Scots., *whiggamore*) (1) These rival party denominations both meant thief, rustler or plunderer. They were given to each by their opponents in 17th cent.

(2) The Tories (many of them country gentry) originally favoured Charles II and legitimism in the controversies surrounding the Exclusion Bills, but as supporters of the C. of E. were equally opposed to R. Catholics and non-conformists. The Whigs (many of them great nobles) favoured exclusion, the Hanoverian succession, toleration for nonconformists and parliamentary hegemony. The Tories had some Irish R. Catholic support, the Whigs some Scottish Presbyterian.

(3) The Whigs engineered the Glorious Revolution. Some of the extreme Tories became Jacobites and save between 1712-14 the Whigs were continuously in power from 1689 to 1783. The Tories were thereafter in power until 1830 and from 1834.

(4) The parties named were not monolithic organisations. The epithets connoted outlooks rather than allegiances, and it did not follow that because a govt. was of a particular persuasion all those of the same persuasion supported it. The Tories were transmuted by 1850 into the Conservatives, the Whigs into the Liberals. The Conservatives revived the use of the word Tory after World War II. *See* TORIES (IR.) 1653 ONWARDS.

TORY DEMOCRACY is a phrase used in at least four senses. **(1)** retrospectively and least convincingly of Disraeli's extension of the franchise in the Reform Act, 1867; **(2)** more democratic control over the party machine, notably in the 1870's by the urban householders and villa Tories; **(3)** Conservative party policies intended to appeal to workers, especially in the towns, such as the Public Health Legislation of 1875; **(4)** wider opportunities for property ownership as opposed to post World War II socialism. *See* CHURCHILL, LORD RANDOLPH.

TOSTI[G] (?-1066) E. (1055) brother of K. Harold II. With his father E. Godwin he fled in 1051 to Flanders, where he married Judith, daughter of Baldwin IV of Flanders. In 1052 he returned and in 1055 when Siward of Northumbria died without heirs, Harold secured the earldom and the lands of Huntingdon for him. He was now a despotic semi-autonomous potentate, intervening successfully in the Scottish Civil War in which Malcolm III overthrew Macbeth. After a visit to Rome (1061) he joined with Harold in an invasion of Wales, but his Northumbrian rule created increasing unrest. In 1064 he treacherously murdered two Northumbrian thegns and was deposed by his own witan. On Harold's advice Edward the Confessor confirmed their action and Tostig retired to Flanders where he gathered a following. In 1066 he unsuccessfully raided the south and east coasts, was driven to Scotland and then joined Harold Hardrada's invasion and was killed at Stamford Bridge.

TOTAL ABSTINENCE MOVEMENT (Ir.). The Quakers founded the first society at Preston (Lancs) in 1832 and some of them suggested the idea to Theobald Mathew (1790-1856) a Capuchin at Cork. He launched the movement in Apr. 1838 and by 1844 serious crime was reduced by a third, and the production of taxed Irish whiskey by 55%. The movement declined after he had a stroke in 1847.

TOTALISATORS were invented in France in 1872, introduced to New Zealand horse racing in 1880 and to British in 1929.

T'OTHERSIDERS, a Western Australian name for migrants from the east during the 1890's gold rush. The T'othersiders retaliated by calling the Western Australians **Sandgropers.** T'othersider influence probably decided W. Australia to join the Commonwealth.

TOTHILL FIELDS was the 19th cent. Westminster Bridewell, a stern but not inhumane institution.

TOTNES (Devon) had a Saxon mint and a royal portreeve. In Domesday it appears as a mesne borough under a Breton Knight called Juhel, who built a castle. It was also a port, and was later fortified. The earliest charter dates from 1205. The fortifications were dismantled by Henry VII. The town became a borough under the Municipal Corporations Act, 1835.

TOUCHET, Lds. AUDLEY (or ALDITHLEY) of HELEIGH (or HELY) descended from **(1) Adam (temp. Henry I)** 1st of nine lords by tenure. **(2) Nicholas (?-1317)** was the first lord by writ. **(3) John (?-1408) 4th Ld.** served against Owain Glyndwr. His son **(4) James (?-1458) 5th Ld.** was killed by Yorkists at Blore Heath. His son **(5) John (?-1491) 6th Ld.** was summoned to all Edward IV's parliaments, became a P.C. in 1471 and Richard II's Lord Treasurer in 1484. His son **(6) James (1465-97)** came out in support of the Cornish (Flammock's) rebellion, which he joined at Black Heath. Defeated by Oxford and Daubeny he was executed but the family was restored in blood in 1512. His grandson **(7) George (?1550-1617) 1st E. (Ir.) of CASTLEHAVEN,** had been Gov. of Utrecht and one of the planters of Ulster. His son **(8) Mervyn (?1592-1631) 2nd E.** contracted parts of two fortunes by marrying Ann Brydges, daughter of the E. of Derby and widow of Lord Chandos, but was executed for buggery in 1631. His son by his first wife was **(9) James (?1617-84) 3rd E.** He was married off at 13 to his stepsister, Elizabeth Brydges, who had been raped, at his father's instance, by his mother's lover. Neglected and horrified, he was a principal in the prosecution of his father. The English barony was restored to him in 1633 as a mark of royal approval, confirmed by Statute in 1678 but most of the English (but not the Irish) properties had fallen into other hands and he became a soldier. He happened to be in Ireland in 1641 when the Civil War broke out in earnest, but being a R. Catholic he was suspect to the Lords Justices and eventually imprisoned. In Sept. 1642 he escaped, apparently meaning to get to England, but finding the R. Catholic confederate H.Q. at Kilkenny, he accepted their generalship of the horse under Sir Thomas Preston. He was very successful, but sensibly desired to come to terms with the royalists proper, so that the northern Irish suspected that his escape had been contrived by Ormonde (a relative) to gain a foot in the R. Catholic side. In any case after the Cessation (Sept. 1643) he organised the shipment of Irish royal troops to England, took command of the reinforcements against Gen. Monro's Scots in Ulster, and subsequently campaigned with great effect in the south. When eventually faced with the choice between allegiance to the extreme confederates with Rinuccini the nuncio, or with the peace party courted by Ormonde, he chose the latter, and, consistently, he favoured coming to terms with Parliament, rather than lose Ireland to the English connection altogether. Nevertheless, he left Ireland before the Parliamentary commissioners arrived. In Sept. 1648 he returned with Ormonde and maintained a dangerous but dwindling resistance to the Parliamentarians until Oct. 1651 when he went to

France. Here he commanded one of Conde's cavalry regiments in the Spanish service. He was very active in the Flanders wars until the P. of the Pyrenees, returned to England at the Restoration, and then fought intermittently in Flanders until 1678.

TOULON passed to France in 1481; the naval arsenal was founded by Henri IV in 1600 and enlarged by Richelieu, Colbert and Vauban. It has always been the chief French base in the Mediterranean. It successfully resisted an Anglo-Austrian attack in 1707; there was an indecisive naval battle between the French and the Anglo-Spanish fleet in 1744; in July 1793 royalists handed the place over to the British (*see* FIRST COALITION, WAR OF 1792-2 *et seq*). In Nov. 1942 the French fleet was scuttled there to prevent German seizure.

TOULOUSE. See ALBIGENSIANS; AQUITAINE; LOUIS VII; PHILIP (II) AUGUSTUS; LOUIS XIII.

TOULOUSE, Louis Alexandre de BOURBON, Comte de (1678-1737), bastard of Louis XIV and Mme. de Montespan, Admiral of France from the age of five, commanded the French fleet with success from 1702-13 and had the better of Sir George Rooke at the bitterly fought B. of Velez Malaga (Aug. 1704) but his decision to take his damaged fleet back to base helped to consolidate the British hold on Gibraltar.

TOURAINE. See AQUITAINE.

TOURISM (*see* GRAND TOUR) as an industry began in 1841 with Thomas Cook's organisation of railway excursions from Leicester in the interests of temperance. He published the periodical *Excursionist* and tourist handbooks from 1846. He moved to London in 1864, by which time he had interested Swiss bankers and hoteliers and was running package tours there. As railways spread across Europe and America, the idea was taken up by increasing numbers, encouraged by the travels of crowned heads and other prominent or notorious persons. By 1914 many places, mostly in Europe, had hotels which catered entirely for a tourist, mostly summer season. Winter sports were established after 1918. London had many hotels from the mid-19th cent. but a fully grown trade for tourists developed with aviation only after World War II.

TOURN, SHERIFF'S. A special twice-yearly session of the Hundred Court at which the sheriff presided to take the view of Frankpledge and bring the tithings up to strength. The 1217 re-issue of Magna Carta reduced the compulsory attendance of suitors at the Hundred Court to two occasions a year, and thereafter business at the other sessions declined, while the rise of effective J.P's rendered Frankpledge and tithings slowly obsolete.

TOURNAI (Belgium) was annexed by France in 1187 and acquired important privileges which led it to resist an Anglo-Flemish siege in 1340. It remained determinedly Francophile after the T. of Troyes (1420). It was briefly in English hands in 1473 and ceded to Spanish Flanders by the T. of Madrid (1526). Louis XIV's troops took it in 1667, but it was retaken in 1709 and incorporated in the Austrian Netherlands and so eventually into Belgium.

TOURNAMENTS or TOURNEYS. See JOUSTING.

TOURNOIS, POUND or LIVRE, minted at St. Martin de Tours Abbey consisted of 20 silver *sous* which each consisted of 12 *deniers*. It was widely used in the west in the middle ages and tended to be at a premium over other French currencies.

TOURVILLE, Anne-Hilarion de COTENTIN, Comte de (1642-1701) trained with the Knights of Malta and served in the Third Dutch War under Duquesne. He was C-in-C against England in the War of the League of Augsburg. Tactically over-cautious, he failed to make the victory at Beachy Head (1690) decisive, by declining a general chase. In 1692 he was committed in the Channel by Louis XIV against heavy odds and suffered the twin disasters of Harfleur and La Hogue. In 1693 he tricked the escort and intercepted the 400 ships of the Smyrna convoy off C. St.

Vincent, but though he did £6M worth of damage, his caution allowed some of it to escape. He was not employed at sea again.

TOVEY, John (1895-1971) Ld. TOVEY of LANGTON MATRAVERS (1945), a distinguished destroyer commander, particularly at the B. of Jutland (1916), commanded the Home Fleet at a critical stage of World War II (1940-43), especially in the destruction of the *Bismarck* (1941) and he supervised and protected the many convoys between Britain and Murmansk.

TOWER BRIDGE (London) was built between 1886 and 1894.

TOWER CRANES, by their ability to move great weights within building sites, markedly accelerated, after 1958, construction and environmental change.

TOWER HILL, an open slope by the Tower of London convenient for executions before a large public; most of the victims were condemned traitors. For smaller audiences Tower Green, within the castle was considered more suitable.

TOWER OF LONDON. William I began fortifying the site just outside the S.E. corner of the City in 1066. New, stronger fortifications dominated by the stone keep, the White Tower, were begun under the direction of Bp. Gundulf of Rochester, sometime after 1077 and completed in 1090s. More buildings were added in 12th cent. especially by William Longchamp in the 1190s. Henry III and Edward I converted the Tower into a large concentric fortress and royal palace with a moat and watergate. The 14th cent. curtain wall had six bastions facing the Thames. It contained the notorious royal prison and from the 14th cent. the Privy Wardrobe which housed the royal armoury. Under Henry VIII the bastions were redesigned for artillery, and a wall was built beyond the moat, which until 1843 was fed by the Thames. Access until then was through the water or Traitor's Gate and a land gate at the S.W. corner. The Tower was a royal residence until the time of James I (*see* WARDROBE) and the Crown jewels together with the royal boatmen who kept them, and the Gentlemen Pensioners (or Yeomen of the Guard) are established there. The principal Mint was there until 1811; the menagerie until 1834; the public records until 1860. The moat, a long stinking nuisance, was drained in 1843 by the D. of Wellington as Constable. The use of the Tower as a state prison has given it a rather sinister reputation, but it virtually ceased to be used as such at about the same time as the last execution took place on Tower Green in 1747, save that the supposed Rudolf Hess was kept there briefly in 1941.

TOWN. (1) In earlier usage, a farm, as in Ruyton-of-the-Eleven-Towns (Salop). **(2)** In common midlands usage till the 19th cent., any village. **(3)** A place whose parish council has declared it to be a town since 1974.

TOWN AND COUNTRY PLANNING (T&CP) (1) From 1909 urban authorities could make planning schemes for land under development. In 1919 they could be compelled to make them, and were given interim control of development pending approval of the scheme. In 1932 this was extended to rural areas. The Ribbon Development Act was passed in 1935. In 1943 all land was made subject to interim development control, and in 1944 planning authorities received powers of acquisition and redevelopment because of World War II damage.

(2) During World War II Mr Justice Uthwatt was commissioned to enquire into compensation and betterment, and his report became the basis of later planning legislation. The T&CP Act, 1947, nationalised all development rights, compensating owners with £300M, and it followed that owners could no longer develop their property without permission. Such a permission, when obtained, would increase the value of the private property, therefore a development charge was imposed, payable before the work was done, and representing the amount by which property would appreciate. These logical but unpopular financial provisions had to be repealed in 1954, when the development charge was abolished, and compensation became payable only as and when development permission was refused.

(3) The method of control was to require that, subject to exceptions, every change of use of land or buildings should require permission from the planning authority. The exceptions were minor alterations to buildings, roadworks, and agriculture; but ministers were empowered to create new (and eventually numerous) exceptions by General Development Orders, and by Use Classes Orders which group certain uses together and gave an owner in a group deemed permission to change to another use in the same group. An applicant who had been refused a planning permission could appeal to the Sec. of State; by 1968 appeals were running at over 500,000 a year. A person who developed without permission could be compelled to return the property to its previous condition. On the whole this was laxly enforced.

(4) The planning authorities under the 1947 Act were county councils and they had to make a county development plan and get it approved by the govt. These plans amounted to public notice of the sort of planning permissions which might be obtained in particular places. The procedure for making and revising them was complicated and bedevilled by shortages of staff. Some took 12 years to make.

(5) The procedure for dealing with applications was supposed to take two months, but invariably took over five. Since the numbers increased with rising economic activity, the system appeared to be a clog on enterprise. The Local Govt. Act, 1972, transferred the control (but not the planning) function from county to the more numerous district councils, with only moderate success. *See* NEW TOWNS; NATIONAL PARKS.

TOWN AND GOWN. Phrase representing the sometimes hostile contrast between the inhabitants and the academics of university towns, especially at Oxford where there were several dangerous riots.

TOWNSEND, John (1757-1826), an independent minister in Bermondsey and Kingston, founded the Deaf and Dumb Asylum at Bermondsey in 1792 and helped to establish the London Missionary Soc. in 1794.

TOWN[E]SEND, Richard (?1618-92), helped, in the parliamentary interest, to defend Lyme Regis in 1644 and Pendennis in 1646. He was sent to Ireland in 1647 where he served under, and changed sides with, Inchiquin but returned and in 1649 tried to obtain the surrender of Youghal. He sat in the Irish parliament after the Restoration and was an important English figure in S. Ireland, where he organised protestant defences in 1685 and was forced to surrender to the Jacobites in 1690.

TOWNSHEND. The fortunes of this rich and influential family were established by **(1) Sir Roger (?-1493)** a respected Lincoln's Inn Lawyer and advisor of the Pastons, who became Kings Serjeant in 1483 and a Judge of the Common Pleas shortly afterwards, and by **(2) Sir Roger (?1543-90)** an Elizabethan courtier who was knighted during the Armada campaign. **(3) Sir Roger (1588-1637)** could afford a baronetcy. His son **(4) Sir Horatio (?1630-87) 1st Ld. TOWNSHEND (1661) Vist. (1682)** was a Norfolk M.P. in 1659 and a member of the Protector's Council of State, but actively promoted the Restoration and was a member of the deputation to The Hague which invited the King to return. His able son **(5) Charles (1674-1738) 2nd Vist.** became a whig party politician and, having opposed the Occasional Conformity Bill, was a commissioner in 1706 for the union with Scotland. In 1709 he became British representative at The Hague and was entangled in the peace negotiations aborted by the excessive demands of the allies. In 1711 he was recalled on the change of govt. and publicly disgraced, even though the new govt. was negotiating with the French behind its allies' back. In the circumstances he spared no effort to embarrass the govt., even to the extent of raising the repeal of the Union. The tactical nature of his manoeuvres became plain as the queen's health declined, and his allegiance to the Hanoverian succession was well understood at the Hanoverian court. He became Sec. of State (Northern) in the new reign. He had married Walpole's sister in 1713 and furthered Walpole's career by procuring the lucrative Paymastership for him. Meanwhile, as virtual head of the govt. he was faced with several interlocking problems. The opponents of the new dynasty had to be neutralised, the Jacobite threat defeated, and English continental security established. The first was achieved by proceedings against the negotiators of the P. of Utrecht, which drove their leaders overseas. Prompt, initially draconian, measures and Dutch help defeated the Jacobite rebellion of 1715, while the Septennial Act postponed potentially threatening elections. A proper Barrier Treaty (1715) and an Imperial Alliance completed the strongly Marlburian pattern. This also posed a problem for George I, who disliked English Constitutional restraints and regarded with suspicion any individual who might become a minister independent of royal backing. The King was thus ready to listen to insinuations, particularly that Townshend was intriguing with the P. of Wales in the habitual Guelf father and son quarrels. He was shifted to the Lieutenancy of Ireland in 1717 and then dismissed. In 1720 he became Lord Pres. under Stanhope and returned to the northern secretaryship when Stanhope died in 1721. He was promptly faced with another Jacobite crisis (Atterbury's Plot) complicated by the South Sea Bubble, and its aftermath. He came through the financial scandal unscathed, but the credit for dealing with it belonged to Walpole, who thereafter slowly superseded him in the leadership. Thus Townshend became the effective Foreign Sec., while his brother-in-law managed home affairs with the Commons. The partnership remained stable until after George II's accession (1727) when he disagreed with Walpole, and Q. Caroline on the Franco-Spanish alliance (T. of Seville) of 1729 and resigned in 1730. He spent the rest of his life improving his wide estates in Essex notably by the use of turnips, by reason of which he became known as Turnip Townshend. Of his children **(6) George (1715-69)** a seaman, incompetently commanded a squadron supporting the Corsican revolt of 1747; **(7) Thomas (1701-80)** was an M.P. from 1722-74 and lived comfortably as a sinecurist from 1727 and **(8) Roger (1708-60)** a soldier, was an M.P. from 1737-48 and George II's A.D.C. at the B. of Dettingen (1743). The grandson of (5), **(9) George (1724-1807) 4th Vist (1764) and 1st M. (1786)** another soldier, became a royal A.D.C. in 1748 but lost the appointment in 1750 owing to disagreements with Cumberland, whose capacity he doubted. When Cumberland was forced to retire after the Convention of Klosterzeven (1757), Townshend returned as A.D.C. and so became a Brigadier-General under Wolfe in the Quebec expedition (1759) and took command after Wolfe's death. Despite criticism, he took some of the credit for the conquest of Canada. He became a P.C. in the new reign (1761) Lieutenant of the Ordnance in 1763 and Lord Lieut. of Ireland in 1767. Here he encountered all the frustrations of Irish govt. His efforts to improve public services failed for lack of money, his efforts to economise on places and pensions and to liberalise the system brought parliamentary obstruction. To secure the necessary parliamentary powers he had to create new peerages and grant more pensions and sinecures, which attracted strong criticism in England. Not surprisingly he took to drink. Recalled in 1772 he was out of office until 1786 when he became Master-General of the Ordnance. His brother **(10) Charles (1725-67),** M.P. from 1747 and the finest speaker of his time, was educated with John Wilkes

in Leyden. He became a Lord of the Admiralty in 1754 but resigned in 1755 to be free to attack the war policy of the Newcastle Govt. in 1755. He became Secretary at War in 1761, resigned in 1762, became Pres. of the Board of Trade in 1763 but refusing office under Grenville, made, on behalf of his friend Wilkes, a famous attack on general warrants in 1764. He succeeded Fox as Paymaster-General in 1765 and became Chatham's Chancellor of the Exchequer in 1766. (*See* AMERICAN REBELLION; GEORGE III; PITT.) His cousin, the son of (7), **(11) Thomas (1733-1800) 1st Ld. SYDNEY (1783) 1st Vist. SYDNEY (1789)** was an M.P. from 1754. An opponent of North, he was Sec. at War under Rockingham in 1782 and then from 1783 Home Sec. successively under Shelbourne and Pitt; he eventually resigned in 1789 mainly against Pitt's Indian and slavery policy. Sydney (Australia) is named after him. The son of (9), **(12) George (1755-1811) E. of LEICESTER (1784), 2nd M.** held sinecure and court office but is chiefly remembered as a Pres. of Society of Antiquaries and a Trustee of the British Museum. He quarrelled irreconcilably with his son **(13) George (1778-1855) 3rd M.** As a result the properties were diverted away from the family honours.

TOWNSHEND ACTS or DUTIES 1767. *See* AMERICAN REBELLION-11.

TOWNSHIP was, technically, a part of a manor for which a separate constable or headborough was appointed.

TOWN TENANTS ACT 1906 (Ir.) passed as a result of the M. of Clanricarde evicting a shopkeeper for his political opinions, gave business and residential tenants a right to compensation for improvements and for eviction without good and sufficient cause. At first sight a reasonable measure, it deterred the investment of money in urban building.

TOYNBEE, Arnold Joseph (1889-1975) historical theorist was a member of the British delegation to the Peace Conferences of 1919 and 1945. His 10 volume *Study of History* appeared between 1934 and 1954. His theory is that the intelligible unit of history is a civilisation, of which he distinguishes 21. All these came to fruition through successful responses by creative minorities to the challenge of a time of troubles. The responses lead in practice to the creation of a universal "church"; this in its turn gives birth to the high period of a civilisation whose decline is ushered in by the rise of a universal state. This, in its turn, may collapse into a time of troubles from which a new creative minority arises. Toynbee's theory is accordingly a moral not an economic science.

TOYNBEE HALL (Whitechapel, London) was founded in 1884 by Canon Barnett, Vicar of St. Jude's Whitechapel to enable graduates to work among the East End poor. Others included Hubert Llewellyn Smith, Sir Cyril Jackson, Clement Attlee, William Beveridge and Alfred Milner. Their experience brought to light the crying need for affordable legal advice and housing and how to provide them, and the demand for educational and artistic opportunities above the simpler levels. A modest but influential institution.

TRACTARIANISM. *See* ANGLICANISM.

TRADE ACTS. *See* NAVIGATION ACTS.

TRADE BOARDS. *See* SWEATED LABOUR.

TRADE AND PLANTATIONS, COUNCIL and COMMITTEE or LORDS OF. Using the model of the last Council of Plantations, the functions of that body and of the Council of Trade were transferred from 1672-74 to a unified council. In 1675 this was superseded by a Committee of nine of the Privy Council but any other councillor could attend; many habitually did. This arrangement lasted until 1695, save in 1688 when the business was done by a committee of the whole council. In 1696 William III reverted to the earlier conciliar pattern, but with some unpaid, as well as paid and ex officio members. The President was known as the First Ld, but between 1768-1779 the Sec. of State for the Colonies presided. This body was abolished in 1782 and replaced in 1784 by the Board of Trade which was a committee of 19 unpaid privy councillors. In 1786 this was in its turn reconstituted with a President and Committee of the Council. The Board, as such, never met and the Pres. was really a minister, whose functions were confined increasingly to commercial administration of very diverse kinds. These included Corn Returns (1826), Statistics (1832), Railways (1840-46), Merchant Shipping (1850), Meteorology (1854-65), Weights and Measures (1865), Schools of Industrial Design and Practical Art (1837-57), Registration of Seamen (1835), Designs (1839) and Companies (1844).

TRADE, COUNCILS OF. In 1660 a council of 62 unpaid members was appointed to regulate trade; by 1664 it was virtually moribund and from 1668-72 was replaced by a new body of 42 commissioners. *See* TRADE AND PLANTATIONS.

TRADE or BUSINESS CYCLES recur in industrial economies. Rising production and employment engender rising prices, and then a consequent slackening of demand and business decisions to restrict output. Unemployment then grows and its relief throws a rising burden on the surviving taxed earners. The cost of labour now falls and production then rises into a new cycle. Between 1815 and 1939 (war years apart) the cycles lasted between 7 and 10 years; since 1948 between 5 and 8. The effects invade morality, for high levels of unemployment create boredom and crime, while in politics the discontented generally vote against the govt.

TRADE ROUTES. *See* MAPS.

TRADEMARKS were first protected by injunction in 1838 (*Millington v Fox*). The Merchandise Marks Act, 1862, made fraudulent use of trademarks an offence. Registration was introduced by the Trade Marks Registration Act, 1875. Both Acts were amended at intervals, the criminal side of the law being in the Merchandise Marks Act, 1862 to 1953, the registration provisions in the Trade Marks Act, 1938. *See* PATENTS; COPYRIGHT ETC.

TRADESCANT, John (?-?1637) and his son **John (1608-62).** The father, gardener successively to Salisbury, Wotton and the D. of Buckingham, visited Archangel (Russia) in 1618 and brought back the larch and other trees, and enlisted against the Algerines to secure the Algiers apricot. He became Charles I's gardener and with his son helped to finance a Virginia expedition, from which the son returned with the Michaelmas daisy, phlox, and the Virginia creeper. The son succeeded the father, who meanwhile had established the first English botanic garden near Lambeth. He introduced the acacia lilac and the London plane. The garden and associated collections were the first English public museum and became famous. By less than scrupulous means, Elias Ashmole secured possession of them in 1657 and gave them to Oxford University in 1683.

TRADE DISPUTES ACT 1906. *See* TRADE UNIONS-3.

TRADE UNIONS (1) Combinations to protect jobs, pay or profits are natural. In 1664 London brewers were convicted of conspiring to defraud the Revenue by brewing only small (untaxed) beer which as individuals they were entitled to do. In 1721 the journeymen tailors of Cambridge collectively struck for higher pay and were convicted of conspiracy though again, as individuals they were entitled to refuse to work. By now Britain was the first country moving towards industrialisation, and the consequent trade unions were designed to face a novel situation. These began as artisans' local mutual benefit clubs which soon discussed and then began to act in defence of jobs threatened by the new steam-powered mass production.

(2) There being no police, the authorities were always sensitive to any type of combination to achieve an advantage by pressure. It was conceived as an interference with the contractual freedom to hire and be hired upon negotiated terms, just as perpetual entails interfered with the free market in land. Trade Unions might have grown peacefully if the French Revolutionary wars had not injected an element of panic into the atmosphere. By 1799 labour was restive; the law of conspiracy by itself was considered inadequate and the so-called Combination Act 1799, replaced by another in 1800, rendered agreements by employees to obtain better wages or restrict hours of work void, and rendered parties to them liable to imprisonment, while membership of combinations, attendance at meetings and subscriptions to support strikers could be punished by fines. Prosecutions had to be started within three months, but all cases could be tried by two J.P.s who, though they could not be employers of defendants, would mostly be employers. There were also provisions to settle disputes by arbitration. The Act was repealed in 1824 (after the wars and the post-war slump were over) and a trade union movement became possible. There were strikes, lock-outs and violence. In 1830 an agrarian revolt in S. and S.E. England was suppressed with 9 hangings, 400 imprisonments and 457 transportations. Four years later came the affair of the Tolpuddle Martyrs (q.v.). In the same year Robert Owen tried to launch a Grand National Consolidated Trades Union, which failed for lack of interest.

(3) In 1851 the Amalgamated Society of Engineers was launched as the first national union for skilled workers recruited through apprenticeship. Such craft unions provided sickness benefits and support for emigration, but maintained the prosperity of their members by closed shops and restricting the numbers of apprentices. Mass, unskilled unionism had to await the Trade Union Act 1871 which declared that Unions should be neither criminally nor civilly liable merely because their purposes were in restraint of trade and it set up a register of them. This led to recruitments amounting to 2M and wage bargaining based on threatened or actual strikes, including the successful docks strikes of 1889. Employers sought legal protection, and in the *Taff Vale Case* (1901) the courts held that a trade union could be liable for damage done to an employer by its actions. This struck from their hands the very weapon which they had been formed to use. Disorderly agitation and the advent of a Liberal govt. led to an extreme oscillation in the opposite direction. The Trades Disputes Act 1906 forbade a court to entertain any action against a trade union for any act done in contemplation of a trade dispute. This placed unions above the law. Not surprisingly between 1910-20 membership quadrupled and union leaders were suspected of preparing to dominate the state.

(4) The post-World War I slump tempted this great army of unskilled workers to rely upon their unions to maintain their standard of living, but the leaders had only the economically damaging strike weapon with which to effect that purpose. In 1926 they proclaimed the General Strike (q.v.) It collapsed against determined opposition. The Trades Disputes Act of 1927 made secondary strikes, lock-outs and strikes to coerce the govt. illegal besides various forms of intimidation and the levying of subscriptions for political purposes unless a member applied to pay ('Contracting in') (*see* TRADE UNION ACT 1913). This struck at the Labour Party's finances. More importantly, the failure of the strike led to 4M desertions by 1933. A genuine recovery had to await the end of World War II.

(5) After the War an element of disorder crept into industrial relations through the rise of a movement for local shop stewards, many being influenced by Marxism. While unions and employers' organisations fixed national wage agreements, shop-stewards and local managers settled local rates at higher levels than the agreements. This was calculated to disrupt the national bodies on both sides or drag them by the tail into industrial action. Moreover the Attlee Govt. had repealed the Act of 1927 and returned to legal immunity and contracting out. The result was sporadic if persistent industrial warfare which assisted inflation, damaged the balance of payments and infuriated the consumers. It contributed importantly to the Tory victory of 1979 and the Thatcher Govt's legislation which returned to contracting in, permitted civil actions against trade unions for secondary strikes and required closed shops to be supported by 85% of those voting in a secret ballot. *See* THATCHERISM.

TRADE UNION ACT, 1913 legalised the use of trade union funds for political purposes provided that the majority of members consented but required that there should be a political fund to which dissenting members need not contribute. *See* TRADE UNIONS-4.

TRADE UNION CONGRESS (T.U.C.) (*see previous entries and* GENERAL STRIKE 1926) was founded at Manchester in 1868 by craft unions and set up a parliamentary committee in 1871. By 1900 its affiliated unions comprised about 1M mostly unskilled workers who outnumbered the craftsmen. By 1914 the membership was 2.5M and it was effectively financing the Labour Party. In the 1920s continental events created a belief that the T.U.C. could rely on strikes to exert political power, but the quick defeat of the General Strike of 1926 disabused the leadership of this, and they began to exert indirect influence by way of the Labour Party through a N. Joint Council in which both sides were equally represented but the T.U.C. members represented most of the money. It opposed communism and, in due course, Nazism, and from 1936 supported rearmament which, incidentally, created employment.

World War II gave the T.U.C. direct influence in govt. and the conduct of the war, particularly through Ernest Bevin of the Transport & General Workers' Union as Min. of Labour and N. Service. The first post-war Labour electoral victory put it into a dominating position while the wholesale nationalisations were carried out. This put trade union leaders into responsible positions for which, mostly, they were unfitted by habit and temperament. Stoppages bedevilled the economy and disenchanted the consumer-voters, so that the 1979 electoral defeat of Labour represented a vote against the T.U.C. The Tory govts. of 1979-96 shouldered the T.U.C. aside.

TRADE WINDS especially those of the Atlantic and Indian Oceans formed the chief motive power of inter-continental trade from 1500 until the steamship era and strongly affected its pattern. They blow steadily at about 10-15 knots, diagonally from N.E. to S.W. north of the Equator and from S.E. to N.W. south of it but with a greater tendency to blow westwards in the Summer and equatorwards in the Winter. Hence the summer was relatively favourable for voyages starting from Europe to the Caribbean (returning north-about using the Westerlies) and the late winter for voyages towards the far east, so as to catch the early summer trades and S.W. Monsoon (a reverse trade) in the Indian Ocean. Westward voyages from China usually commenced in the winter so as to catch the N.E. monsoon (a true trade). The Atlantic wind pattern made it easier and so cheaper to ply between Europe and the Caribbean than N. America. *See* DIAGRAM.

TRAFALGAR, CAMPAIGN and B. (21 Oct. 1805) (1) To win the war after the short-lived P. of Amiens, Bonaparte could only invade England. An army and hundreds of badly built landing barges began to concentrate in 1803 at Boulogne and the lesser ports of Étaples, Wimereux and Ambleteuse. The shoals enabled barges to move coastwise, and combined with batteries, prevented British warships from destroying the concentrations; these had to be attacked, if at all, by boats and drifting mines ('torpedoes'). These attacks, gallantly pressed, were not effectual.

(2) On the other hand the Royal Navy dominated the open water of the Straits which the barges would have to cross, but a fortunate combination of wind, tide and fleet movements might interrupt the British domination for the 30 hours which might make the crossing feasible. Hence the British set up additional lines of defence such as harbour fortifications and Martello towers and they trained and embodied a large and expensive militia. Bonaparte had no doubt that he could defeat these amateurs. The principal defence, however, was the BLOCKADE (*see* BLOCKADE; SAILING).

(3) In Mar. 1805 Admiral Ganteaume with 21 ships of the line and 6 frigates was being blockaded in Brest (Atlantic) by Cornwallis. Admiral Villeneuve with 11 and 6 was blockaded in Toulon (Mediterranean) by Nelson and in between were French and Spanish squadrons blockaded in Ferrol and Cadiz (Atlantic) and Cartagena (Mediterranean). A small force was in the Atlantic under Admiral Missiessy. On 2 Mar. Bonaparte ordered Villeneuve to sail; he was to go west; liberating ships at Cartagena and perhaps Cadiz, and then make for Martinique (W. Indies) where Missiessy was to join him. Ganteaume was also ordered to Martinique, and Villeneuve was to wait 40 days there for him. The great combined armada was then to return, sweep the Royal Navy out of the Channel and convoy the army of invasion. (*See* TRADE WINDS.)

(4) Villeneuve sailed on 30 Mar. and evaded Nelson. Ganteaume tried, but failing to evade Cornwallis, stayed in port. It was not until 10 May that Nelson was certain which way Villeneuve had gone. Meanwhile Bonaparte thought that Nelson was looking for Villeneuve off Egypt and made his second plan. Villeneuve was now to spend 30 days capturing British Caribbean Is.; he was then to recross the Atlantic, pick up 15 Spanish ships of the line at Ferrol and liberate Ganteaume. The Channel was then to be swept as before. This order was impracticable, because Villeneuve would have had to fight Cornwallis before he could unite with Ganteaume.

(5) But things never even reached that point. No sooner had operations against the British W. Indies begun than Villeneuve learned that Nelson was hot behind him. He promptly sailed for Europe, and was brought to battle off the Biscay by Sir Robert Calder, who took two of his ships on 22 July. He ended up in Vigo, whence he made his way to Ferrol and picked up his allies. They all put to sea, but contrary winds and a mistaken belief that he had sighted a northward bound British fleet in the night, decided him not to risk his ill found combined fleet in the Channel. He turned south, and on 22 Aug. reached Cadiz, where Admiral Collingwood, eventually with 27 of the line, blockaded him. He reported his position to Bonaparte.

(6) The second plan had thus failed but Bonaparte had decided on another war, and on 27 Aug. before he knew that Villeneuve was not at sea, he ordered the army of invasion to march for S. Germany, on the campaign which ended at Ulm and Austerlitz.

(7) Nelson, back from the W. Indies, had gone home, but on 28 Sept. he took command of the fleet off Cadiz. On the same day, Bonaparte issued a third and final directive connected with his new war. The combined fleet was to sail for the Mediterranean, land 4000 troops in Italy and retire to Toulon. Secret orders enjoined Villeneuve to treat Austrian and Russian shipping as hostile. Since Villeneuve had been at Cadiz, personal letters from General Lauriston, commanding the French troops in the fleet, were going to Bonaparte, for Lauriston was one of his A.D.C.s. He falsely accused Villeneuve of cowardice and disobedience. On 8 Oct. Villeneuve held a council of war to consider the new orders. It was a stormy meeting; he and the French accused the Spaniards of cowardice and the Spaniards made accusations of incompetence and bad faith, but all agreed that the fleet should not sail until Nelson was blown off station or something happened to divide his fleet. At about the same time Bonaparte reacted to Lauriston's letters by ordering Admiral Rosily to supersede Villeneuve and send him to Paris. Rosily set out but Villeneuve was not told. Rosily was delayed at Madrid, but Villeneuve perhaps instinctively realising that false but unanswerable charges were pending, took the plunge, when the wind turned fair.

(8) Owing to the very light airs it took Villeneuve's 33 sail of the line all 19 and 20 Oct. to get out of Cadiz and sail for the Straits. The movement was reported to Nelson who first made for the Straits; he then assembled 27 of the line and turned towards Cadiz, keeping well out to sea. Until the evening of 20 Oct. the fleets were moving slowly on opposite courses about 10 miles apart. During the night Nelson could only calculate where the enemy were. He turned south. At 6.30 am on 21st the fleets were in sight. Nelson turned to attack and Villeneuve reversed his course towards Cadiz. The speed of the fleets was between ½ and 3 knots only. There was a heavy swell from the west which tended to make the British ships pitch and the enemy role. This adversely affected enemy gunnery. The French opened fire at 11.50. Collingwood's *Royal Sovereign* at noon. (*See Chart of the Straits of Gibraltar.*)

(9) The *Royal Sovereign* cut the enemy line at 12.30; Nelson's *Victory* at 12.45. Collingwood's column fanned out slightly to the south engaging any ships they met in the smoke. Nelson's column forced their way into the enemy line rather closer to their flagship. The last British did not reach the engagement until nearly 3 hours after the first. Meantime the leading 10 ships of the enemy under Admiral Dumanoir, with no one to fight, sailed slowly north. Villeneuve recalled them but was not obeyed until 2.15 and in the very light airs they never came into action. Hence the rear two-thirds of the enemy fleet were overpowered by the full force of the British. Nelson fell at 1.00 p.m. and by 3.30 p.m. the battle was over. Sixteen enemy ships were taken and one blew up. In the appalling four day hurricane after the battle most of the prizes were lost and only 4 were brought into port.

(10) The battle did not frustrate Bonaparte's invasion plan, which had already been abandoned; it made it impossible for him ever to contemplate another and so forced him to attempt the defeat of the British by means of the CONTINENTAL SYSTEM whose enforcement ultimately brought his downfall.

TRAFALGAR SQUARE (London) designed by Sir Charles Barry, was laid out on a smaller space, an old royal mews and miscellaneous shops and slums. Work began in 1829; William Railton's Nelson's Column with its 9-foot statue was erected in 1842, and Sir William Landseer's lions were added in 1867. During most of this period the site, together with various other neighbouring constructions and reconstructions such as the Admiralty, Charing Cross and Whitehall, was a scandalous eyesore and hindrance to traffic. *See* WESTMINSTER

TRAHEARN ab Caradog. *See* GWYNEDD-22.

TRAILBASTON **(One who carries a cudgel) COMMISSION OF,** dates from 1305. It authorised itinerant justices to put down bands of bullies (*trailbastons*) who extorted gifts, women and concessions and suborned juries. With the institution of Commissions of the Peace in 1361 the need for such commissions faded out.

TRAINED BANDS were the best of the Tudor General Levy, the London Band being trained by the Hon. Artillery Co; provincial bands were modelled on the London ones, but there being no guild to stiffen them, they declined. By 1585 the London Bands included 4000 musketeers and pikemen. In 1614 they were organised into 4 regiments under the Lord Mayor and in 1643, in the Civil War, they rose to 9 regiments of 1270 men and 5 regiments of auxiliaries of 1000. These were the London

parliamentary garrison which also relieved Gloucester and won the Bs. of Newbury and Worcester. Charles II abolished all remaining provincial bands; William III required all officers of the London Band to be members of the Hon. Artillery Co. This continued until 1779. In 1794 the four regiments were amalgamated into two militia regiments.

TRAMWAYS, perhaps OUTRAMWAYS named after Benjamin Outram (1764-1805) adviser to the D. of Norfolk. He laid L-section rails across sleepers at the Duke's Sheffield colliery in 1776.

TRANSFERRED SUBJECTS. *See* DYARCHY.

TRANSJORDAN. *See* JORDAN.

TRANSPLANTATION (Ir.) (1653-58) (*See* SETTLEMENT ACT OF 1653 (Ir.).) **(1)** The Act required all Irish to move to Connaught by 1 May 1654 save children under puberty and it was proposed to fortify the crossings of the Shannon to wall them in. The timing of the move prevented crops being sown either in the evacuated lands or in Connaught, which was wasted. Incoming colonists and outgoing Irish found it impossible to carry out the operations: many colonists were not used to farming and wanted to keep tenants to work the land; thus in practice proprietors and their closer adherents were deported first, and the army complained of the dangers of leaving the rest. In theory anyone who refused to transplant could be hanged by court martial and some were but mostly the condemned were sent to Barbados or other American colonies instead.

(2) For Connaught there were two commissions (i) the **Athlone Commission** valued the claims of incoming Irish as measured by the property they had left behind and then discriminated their guilt according as (a) they had been nobles or gentry who had borne arms for the King, (b) persons ("Swordsmen") under that rank who had done so, (c) R. Catholics who had taken no part on either side in the war, (d) protestants similarly placed, (e) those who by outward acts had manifested a constant loyalty to the parliament. (a) got nothing, (b) forfeited two thirds, (c) forfeited one third, (d) forfeited one fifth but might compound and avoid transplantation, (e) might obtain a Decree of Constant Good Affection and be entitled to be restored to their estates. (ii) The **Loughrea Commission** then allotted properties in Connaught in accordance with the entitlements of those liable to transplantation. These were called final settlements as distinguished from those which transplantees received on first arrival for temporary shelter and sustenance of the stock.

(3) In fact not all the area west of the Shannon was given to the Irish. Leitrim, Sligo, part of Mayo and the Barony of Clare, plus the coastal belt, and the islands received military settlers or were reserved for the govt. The rest was divided into seven not wholly continuous blocks of baronies, each block being settled from particular exporting areas. Of these Ulstermen got most of the north and west, Leinstermen the south and Roscommon, and Munstermen the area from Galway Bay to Athlone.

TRANSPORT AND COMMUNICATIONS (BRITAIN) (1) Until Tudor times bulk transport was economic only by coastal shipping and along parts of eight major waterways, viz: the **Clyde,** the **Fen Rivers,** the **Fossdyke** and the **Severn, Tees, Thames, Trent** and **Tyne.** The roads were so bad that the expense of conveying goods, which had to be done by packhorses, was prohibitive beyond a day's journey (about 15 miles) from the point of landing. Trade and industry kept to sea and river ports and more than half the country (especially the hill areas) was backward and out of reach. Moreover, waterways enjoyed uses, especially land drainage, fishery and corn milling which conflicted with transport. The two latter had an interest in preventing water from being lost above their weirs to allow boats to pass; the riparian landowners in preventing water levels rising high enough to make navigation easy.

(2) The Tudors tried not very successfully to improve the roads by making the parishes collectively responsible; Leonardo da Vinci's invention of the water-saving pound lock was introduced into England in Elizabeth I's time, which also saw the construction (1563-66) of the **Exeter Canal** to evade the local weirs. In 1630 a general agreement called the **Lynn Law** led to great improvements in the Fens. By the Civil War there were about 680 miles of navigable waterway.

(3) Continental, particularly Dutch practice had awakened exiled Cavaliers to the advantages of river transport and there followed three periods of vigorous river improvement, viz: 1662-66 **(Itchen, Medway, Stour, Wiltshire Avon, Wye)**, 1697-1701 **(Aire, Calder, Bristol Avon, Tone, Trent)**, and 1719-24 **(Derbyshire Derwent, Douglas, Idle, Kennet, Mersey, Weaver)**. By 1724 the navigable mileage had risen by nearly 500 miles and the isolated areas had greatly shrunk.

(4) This in its turn facilitated the establishment of the new textile industries. The spinning and weaving inventions, in the absence of steam, needed water power more of which was now within a day's reach of a landing point. The growth of the metal industries also stimulated the demand for coal; in 1737 the **1st D. of Bridgwater** projected a canal from his mines at Worsley to Manchester but dropped the idea, at a time when Newcastle coal was cheaper in Leeds than coal from mines 20 miles off. There was also a movement to improve and harden road surfaces through the agency of **Turnpike Trusts,** and wheeled transport was beginning to replace the packhorse on some major highways. The roads, though generally bad, were already regarded as the best in Europe. *See* CARRIAGES.

(5) In 1759 the **3rd D. of Bridgwater** with **James Brindley,** his engineer, revived his father's scheme. The Bridgwater Canal, with its spectacular aqueduct over the Irwell, ushered in the **Canal Era** which lasted until 1840. This may be conveniently divided into four periods. From 1759-1774 the inspiration flowed outwards from S. Lancashire where the Mersey Navigations were connected southwards with the Severn and Eastwards with the Trent, Aire and Calder. In 1774-1789 interest became more diffused and resulted in the Basingstoke, Birmingham Navigations, the Stroudwater and Thames and Severn Canals in England and after much argument, the Forth and Clyde in Scotland.

(6) The period from 1789-1815 saw complications. Previous successes in seller's markets led to the **Canal mania** of 1789-1797 and the building of the Dearne and Dove, the Warwick Canals and Grand Junction and the Kennet and Avon, all of which though costing much more than their estimates, were financially viable. There were also speculative ventures especially in coal mining areas. These were kept in business by the industrial change from water to steampower, which altered the location of industry by increasing industrial output, but especially by the hothouse conditions created by the Napoleonic Wars. Prices rose. Troops as well as goods could be moved by waterway at twice the accepted speed. Moreover a single barge-horse could pull over 50 times the weight which it could pull on even a good road. The Turnpike Trusts, which by 1815 were maintaining 20,000 out of 120,000 miles of road, had already surfaced many by the methods perfected by John Loudon **McAdam** (1756-1836) and Telford between 1798-1815, but the reputation of the canals as bulk carriers overcame all competition save in passenger and mail traffic. Turnpike dividends declined after 1797 and did not recover until 1830.

(7) There were two other factors. French privateering created a demand for inland routes and stimulated the building of the Caledonian and the Crinan canals, and

canal companies associated with mining began to build horse powered **railways** as feeders from 1797 onwards because they were cheaper to build than branch canals. By 1816 there was a railtrack from Gloucester to Cheltenham, another from Merthyr to Cardiff and over 200 miles of them on the Tyneside.

(8) The canal decline began when the Napoleonic stimulus was removed; 1815-30 was the golden age of the **stagecoach,** made possible by McAdam's hard roads; the opening of the **Stockton and Darlington Railway** in 1825 showed that steam locomotion was suitable for railways, in which there was already a generation of experience. The canal companies spent money on improvements and cut prices to maintain their traffic but profits disappeared. Moreover railways had special advantages. Unaffected by weather they were fast and self advertising, and their managements were confident and modern. The canals were parochial and never co-operated sensibly; they even failed to make clearing arrangements for through fares.

(9) Meanwhile by 1840 railways were already operating from London to Bristol, Southampton, Portsmouth, Brighton, Dover, Colchester, Cambridge, Lincoln, York, Birmingham and Lancashire. The **Railway Mania** (1840-47) increased their mileage to 5000. By 1868 nearly all the network (except the Great Central's access to London) had been built. Railways took away the traffic from highways and canals alike, made inroads into horsebreeding and livery and steadily altered the uses and population of the extensive mews, and the layouts of new urban building. The railways created new suburbs like St. Pancras (London) and new railway towns like Crewe, Swindon, Ashford (Kent), Grantham and Doncaster.

(10) The railway promoters could not close the public roads, but they could and did attack the canals. By 1870 they had bought and sabotaged enough to create fears of monopoly. The consequent Railway and Canal Regulation Act 1873 obliged navigations to be kept open and tolls to be classified and published. An influential conference in 1885 concluded that there was a future for canals in certain areas. Between 1887 and 1894 Manchester was converted into the country's fourth largest port by the completion of its **Ship Canal**. The Aire and Calder navigation was improved and the Grand Junction Canal was completed. These successful under-takings did not reverse the trend. The railways continued their advance by successive amalgamations such as the **North Eastern** (1854) and the **Great Eastern** (1862). They absorbed increases in traffic created by rising production and population, and continued to divert canal customers. This process, despite a Royal Commission on Canals (1906-9) continued until 1914. Moreover local public transport in the form of horse 'buses (which began to operate in 1820) had been mostly superseded in towns first by steam and then by electric trains.

(11) The **motor car** (first introduced by Benz at Paris in 1887) became a feature of life only in 1894 but being still hand made, offered no competition to rail-tracked transport until after 1919. The latter kept ahead through a great **amalgamation** into four groups (Southern, Great Western, London Midland and Scottish, and London and North Eastern) in 1922 when, though there were already 200,000 registered private cars there were still 96 different manufacturers. In 1922, however, the Austin Seven appeared and the mass produced car, despite an absurd taxation system and hampering, but largely ignored, speed limits, began to forge ahead. The rail tracked undertakings had to maintain their ways out of their own funds, whereas the cost of road maintenance fell on the rate and tax payer who was thus subsidising the car. Nevertheless, tracked mileage increased slightly and reached its peak both for rail and tramways in 1928-29, just before the great slump. By that time, however, there were nearly 1,000,000 cars. In 1930 all speed restrictions were abolished (save in Oxford). In 1934 driving tests were imposed on newcomers and a speed limit was reimposed in built-up areas, defined as places with street lamps less than 200 yards apart. Improvement in the internal combustion engine also brought back the 'bus whose flexibility and tax subsidisation created a rapid urban revolution. By 1932 buses were carrying more people than trains.

(12) After the depression lifted in 1933, the effects of the new mobility and freedom became manifest in ribbon development, the movement of industries out of the older cities and the depopulation of town centres in favour of suburbs. It also created the opportunities for a mass holiday industry.

(13) World War II with its petrol rationing and diversion of industry to warlike production thrust the burden of movement back onto the still very comprehensive railway system, which until 1945 functioned fully for the last time. Peace brought a Labour Govt. with ideas on transport co-ordination and in 1947 railways, canals, and most large 'bus undertakings were nationalised under a single **TRANSPORT COMMISSION.** The result was a gigantic failure. The disparate attitudes and rival staffs of the commission's mutually incompatible acquisitions failed to produce modernisation or even co-ordination while the advance of the motor vehicle on the publicly maintained road and after 1961 on the **motorway** was redoubled, and drained away the commission's customers. A statutory reorganisation in 1953 made little difference; statutory permission in 1957 to work on unbalanced budgets made little difference; neither did successive extensions of borrowing powers. By 1961 the Beeching Commission found, not without contradiction, that the virtual bankruptcy of the system required radical surgery. The Transport Act of 1962 dissolved the Commission, replaced it by four **Boards** (Railways, London, Docks and Waterways) and a Transport Holding Co, and released these bodies from certain previous obligations of carriage and maintenance. This enabled the railway and waterways boards to set about the liquidation of their undertakings with a will. By 1971 most of the branch railways and most of the canal system had been closed or was in disuse, while motor-ways all but connected Glasgow, Birmingham, Cardiff and Newcastle with each other and with London. This led to a great increase in the numbers and size of commercial vehicles which in their turn were beginning to elbow the vastly more numerous smaller vehicles off the main roads across country. The result was a rising repairs bill for the local highway authorities. The social, administrative and demographic consequences of the motor vehicle were beginning to create alarm. They were in fact one of the arguments for reorganising Local Government put forward by the Redcliffe Maud Commission in 1969 and they have been the subject of controversy ever since. *See* TRANSPORT ACTS.

TRANSPORT ACTS (1) That of **1946** nationalised all forms of inland transport for profit except short distance road transport, road vehicles belonging to non-transport undertakings and restricted to company use, and municipal bus services. Boards were established for each form of transport, with the British Transport Commission supervising them. **(2)** The **1953** Act denationalised road transport, but some could not be sold and were (1956) subordinated to the British Road Services. **(3)** The Act of **1962,** eliminated the British Transport Commission. **(4)** The **1968** Act moved back towards centralisation with the National Bus Company running the state-owned road passenger services. The National Freight Corporation was set up to coordinate rail and road freight services, while the way was opened for public transport authorities to provide local co-ordinated rail and road passenger services. Post-1979 legislation was mostly concerned with progressive denationalisation and privatisation.

TRANSPORTATION for crime began under Charles II who granted pardons to persons sentenced to death, conditionally upon their being transported to a colony for a fixed period (usually 7 years) for penal labour or as indentured servants. As a separate punishment it was first enacted in 1717. Convicts were sent to Australia from 1784-1840 and to Tasmania up to 1853. It was phased out after 1853 because the colonies objected to it, and penal servitude or imprisonment were substituted. The system could not, however, end entirely until 1867 when enough prisons had been built in Britain.

TRANSUBSTANTIATION is the R. Catholic doctrine that the bread and wine are at the Eucharist turned into the body and blood of Christ, only their appearances remaining. This doctrine, which places the priest in a pre-eminent position as the exclusive channel of a miraculous power, has always been the chief point at which R. Catholic and Protestant doctrines diverge.

TRANSVAAL (S. Africa) (1) Originally the undefined area N. of the R. Vaal colonised by irreconcilables of the Great Trek (1835-45) who had pressed beyond Natal and the Orange River Sovereignty, together with military deserters, adventurers, hopeful slavers and others. Mutual forbearance as between the Transvaalers and the British, and the setting of the Vaal as the frontier were agreed in the Sand River Convention (Jan. 1852). In Feb. 1854 the British abandoned the O.R. Sovereignty, and the Vaal became the frontier between two Boer Republics.

(2) The widely scattered farms were roughly divided into two groups; in the S.W. under Andries Pretorius based on Potchefstroom and Rustenburg, and in the E. under Hendrik Potgieter based on Lydenburg. There were personal feuds, especially between Pretorius and Potgieter, political differences between Pretorius who wanted a unified republic and the others given to anarchism and the XXXIII articles, and ecclesiastical controversies besides. These were all continued by Marthinus Pretorius and Piet Potgieter after their fathers died in 1853.

(3) Externally Pretorius' objects were to expand northwards and westwards and to obtain access to the sea, through (modern) Natal or the Portuguese port of Inhambane. Potgieter was interested in northward expansion only, but wanted his seaward access through Swaziland. Tsetse fly defeated the Inhambane project. The others meant clashes with powerful tribes backed or protected by the British.

(4) Meanwhile the country was without a govt., so Pretorius persuaded the Volksraad to adopt a constitution (*The Rustenburg Grondwet* Dec. 1856). Lydenburg rejected it and declared its independence. So did the Commandant-General-Elect who lived in the Zoutpansberg. Hence the constitutional govt. operated (under the title of the South African Republic) only in the S.W. The different parts pursued their own policies, fought their own native wars and in 1864 their own civil war which ended with Pretorius as President and Kruger as Commandant-General in a vast area thinly peopled by Dutch, among a huge mobile, often hostile, population of tribes.

(5) In fact the north had to be abandoned, but in 1868 gold and diamonds were found in unclaimed territory to the west and along the Vaal, besides the discoveries at Tati (*see* MATABELE). The result was a many sided dispute over Griqualand West, in which the British, the Griqua tribes, the Orange Free State (O.F.S.), Pretorius, the Transvaalers, not to mention sundry prospectors were involved. Pretorius annexed as much as he could and pushed a diamond monopoly through his legislature for his friends. The diggers promptly proclaimed a Diamond Field Republic (1870). While the British policed and eventually annexed most of its area, there was a gold rush to Lydenburg (1872). Thus the European population was suddenly expanded by non-

Boers (*uitlanders*) mostly English and Australians who were soon in a majority over the Boers.

(6) T. F. Burgers became President in July 1872 and revived the efforts to secure access to the Portuguese port on Delagoa Bay. Diamonds and gold were, however, encouraging British railway building from the Cape and Port Elizabeth towards Griqualand West. Natal began to build a railway northwards (1873-74). The Transvaal risked becoming dependent on these, before it could open a route eastwards, and at a time when the tribes were crowding in, and fighting in the north and northeast was endemic.

(7) The railways awakened a strong movement for South African confederation. The old Transvaalers were, by the facts of their origin, opposed to this: others were not, but the obstacle was native policy, since the British accepted and the Dutch rejected any present or future equality among the races. Transvaal policy seemed to cause disorders which might break out into a major native war and engulf the British as well as the Dutch. Accordingly in 1877 the British annexed the Transvaal.

(8) This move failed. The Transvaalers were uncooperative and in 1880 rioted over a tax dispute. The riot developed into a rebellion. The old Volksraad reproclaimed the Republic and appointed a triumvirate of Kruger, Pretorius and Joubert. The small British garrisons were besieged in Pretoria and Potchefstroom. The Boer riflemen beat off Sir George Colley's troops at Laing's Nek (Jan. 1881) and routed them at Majuba (Feb.), while responsible people on both sides were trying to negotiate. Their efforts bore fruit in the Pretoria Convention (July-Oct. 1881) modified by the London Convention (Feb. 1884).

(9) Paul Kruger, elected President in 1883, inherited the Pretorian policy with the differences since Burger's election that the British railways had reached Aliwal North, Kimberley and Richmond, that the Transvaal's finances were in better shape and that gold quartz at Lydenburg demanded heavy machinery. A cheap and tse-tse proof connection with Delagoa Bay had become urgent. He gave a concession to the Netherlands' Railway Co, stopped the Kimberley line at his frontier and tried to persuade the O.F.S. to delay the Port Elizabeth line for 10 years. Cecil Rhodes, Alfred Beit and their new British South African Co, wanted to take the Kimberley line north to the Tati ("Rhodesia") gold fields, across the Transvaal but as Kruger would not have it, they built it just inside the Bechuanaland frontier, where it attracted W. Transvaal traffic without profit to the Republic.

(10) *Uitlanders* continued to pour in, encouraged by the opening of the deep levels under the Rand (1894) and were now demanding franchise rights since they paid most of the taxes. To the Dutch the fear of Rhodes was becoming obsessive. He was supreme in the Cape to the south and in "Rhodesia" to the north of them; the two areas were connected by his railway; the concessions to *Uitlanders* meant surrender of the cherished hope of Dutch autonomy. The Jameson Raid (Dec. 1895-Jan. 1896) confirmed Dutch belief in Rhodes' evil ambitions. War, which had always been in Kruger's mind, now seemed the only alternative and he began to arm. (*See* SOUTH AFRICAN WAR.)

(11) The P. of Vereeniging (1902) incorporated the Transvaal into the British dominions, and it received a constitution. The first elections were held in 1906 and the nationalist Afrikanders secured a majority.

TRAQUAIR. *See* STEWART, SIR JOHN (?-1659).

TREASON (cf Fr: trahison = betrayal) is essentially betrayal of good faith or fealty which is owed to one's lord or protector. Alfred and Ethelred II prescribed death for plotting against the King's life and the *Leges Henrici Primi* extended treason to slaying royal emissaries. Glanvill described treason as encompassing the King's death or betraying the realm or the army. As lands of traitors were forfeit to the Crown, there was a royal temptation to extend the concept which was expanded in 13th cent. under the ostensible influence of Roman Law. Under Edward I armed resistance to the King was treated as treason and it was as traitors rather than enemies that David of Wales (1283) and William Wallace (1305) were executed. Under Edward II, Thomas of Lancaster was executed for raising his banner against the King (1322); Piers Gaveston (1308) and the Despensers (1326) on the pretext of accroaching the prerogative. Thus the law of treason was used for political assassination. As a result of pressure from the Commons the 1352 Statute of Treasons defined treason restrictively to plotting the King's death, killing the King or Queen, raping the Queen or the King's eldest daughter, killing judges or the Chancellor in the performance of their duties, and importing forged coins. Most felonies were expressly excluded so that felons' lands could be forfeited to their lord rather than the Crown. Nevertheless each political crisis (e.g. 1386-88) and (1397-99) brought its manipulations. Moreover throughout the 14th and 15th cents. treason in war could be deemed to fall under the laws of war administered summarily in the Constable's court; the excesses of 1308-30 and in the 1460s were validated in this way outside the Common Law. Treason by words was added in 1534. In 1688 attempting to prevent a lawful succession was added and maintaining the right of any person to the throne other than those mentioned in the Bill of Rights, and the Act of Settlement 1700. Sovereigns regnant lawfully or unlawfully for the time being, are protected, rightful sovereigns out of possession are not. Two witnesses are required. Until 1814 the punishment was hanging, drawing and quartering for men and burning for women. Since then it has been hanging only, but a man may still be beheaded.

TREACHERY was a capital offence between 23 May 1940, and 24 Feb. 1946. It consisted in doing, attempting or conspiring to do anything likely to assist enemy operations, to impede the forces of the crown, or to endanger life. See JOYCE, WILLIAM.

TREASONABLE PRACTICES ACT 1793 forbade trading relations with France on pain of death.

TREASON ACT, 1794 empowered the authorities to hold until 1 Feb. 1795, without trial, anyone accused of treason. Extended in 1795 to 1 July.

TREASURER OF THE NAVY. *See* PAYMASTER-GENERAL.

TREASURE TROVE. If gold or silver has been hidden in the ground and its owner cannot be discovered, it passed, after inquest and verdict, to the Crown. The rule does not apply to things which have been abandoned or lost. These belong to the finder unless found upon a municipal rubbish dump, in which case they belong to the local authority. Changes in the law were being canvassed in 1996.

TREASUR-Y, -ER (1) Kings had places where they kept their money, but 11th cent. Kings were constantly on the move. Once the business of collection, accountancy and expenditure had reached a critical volume, a permanent seat had to be found. The royal treasury was separated from the travelling household financial depts and settled, near the end of the 12th cent. at Winchester which was not too far from London but accessible, then by sea, from Normandy. It then developed a staff and a procedure with comparative ease, and somebody soon called the Treasurer had to be in local charge.

(2) The Treasurer naturally knew more about the national finances than anyone else and habitually sat with the Justiciar and the Chancellor when decisions had to be taken. The demise of the Justiciarship was followed by the diversion of the Chancellor's energies elsewhere. The Treasurer then became a powerful minister standing alone, while the over-the-counter business was managed increasingly by the Chancellor's representative, later known as the Chancellor of the Exchequer.

(3) Meanwhile Westminster was gradually becoming the permanent seat of the govt. the Exchequer and certain courts. When Normandy was lost (1207) the surviving reason for maintaining the Treasury at Winchester disappeared and it was moved to London where it maintained a separate existence under two subordinate officials called, reminiscently of the primitive household arrangements, Chamberlains. It also became a repository for public documents, court rolls and other records such as Feet of Fines.

(4) By mid-13th cent. the Treasurer was the head of a relatively complex organisation mostly but not wholly concerned with the collection, care and disbursement of the royal funds, but he and it had rivals because those with policy notions differing from the King's tended to try and enforce control of the Crown through the Treasury system while Kings tried to evade such controls by passing large sums through household departments, notably the Chamber, the Wardrobe, the Duchy of Lancaster and later the Privy Purse. A technical justification for this was that the Exchequer procedure was becoming elaborate and slow.

(5) The political disturbances during the cent. after 1386 shook the stability of the Crown and consequently the ill-defined influence of the Crown's household depts., while the quasi-independent Treasury organisation plodded on and by staying power acquired increasing prestige. The Treasurer became the Lord High Treasurer of England and a Great Officer of State. The power of the office was consolidated by Ld. Burghley, the mainstay of Elizabeth I's Govt. and Lord Treasurer from 1572 until his death in 1598.

(6) Burghley appointed a Secretary, Sir Henry Maynard, who was an M.P. in the Parliaments of 1586-1601. Maynard not only gave instructions on Burghley's behalf to the Exchequer but also dealt continuously with those responsible for expenditure on the Navy, the land forces and the Royal Household.

(7) In 1612, 1614 and 1618 James I put the Treasure-ship into commission and entrusted the duties to a Board of five or six. Abp. Laud was Chairman of such a commission appointed in 1635 by Charles I. The motive seems to have been hesitation about appointing any particular individual, but it had important results. A regular procedure and an effective secretary with a department were even more needed by a Board of six than by a single Ld Treasurer. By 1714 the Treasurership had become obsolete. The last holder, the E. of Shrewsbury, resigned and the office has been in commission ever since.

(8) The Commissions of James I and Charles I, and the Restoration Commission of 1660, were Committees of the Privy Council, including usually the Lord Chancellor, the Secretaries of State, the Chancellor of the Exchequer and the Abp. of Canterbury. The Secretary of these Commissions was a Privy Council clerk.

(9) In 1667, however, Charles II made a clean break by appointing a new type of commission, which did not include any of the principal Privy Councillors, except the Chancellor of the Exchequer, with Sir George Downing (of Downing Street) as its Secretary. Charles II was influenced by his French and Dutch experience and by Commonwealth constitutional practice. He wanted such persons, whether Privy Counsellors or not, who might have nothing else to do, and 'were rough and ill-natured men, not to be moved with civilities or importunities in the payment of money'. Downing's appointment was of a piece with this. He was nasty but efficient and stingy. He had amassed a fortune which eventually financed Downing College, Cambridge, and was an effective House of Commons man.

(10) The events of 1667 were important. Though Downing did not long continue as Secretary he had organised the first real system of Treasury records and the administration which went with them. The Treasury Minute Books begin with him and he departmentalised the records with separate books of warrants drawn on the separate branches of the revenue, an order book of directions by the Treasury Lords, and letter books classified according to topic. These reflected the work of a regular staff. Downing and the members of the 1667 Commission made great efforts from their seats in the Commons to explain the needs of the Crown to Parliament and obtain support, and they habitually concerted their interventions in the Commons on financial issues.

(11) The practice of putting the Treasury into commission, and of making that commission independent of the Privy Council had other consequences. The First Lord of the Treasury Commission, soon became the leading minister, and secondly, it started the rise of the Chancellor of the Exchequer to the position of Minister of Finance. As the value of the royal permanent revenues declined and parliamentary grants were enacted for shorter and shorter periods, the Treasury became increasingly concerned with **Ways and Means** of financing govt. policies. Many of these were devised by William Lowndes, Secretary from 1695-1724. The period saw the beginning of a long term, or national, debt and of short term indebtedness through the discounting of bills. Lowndes was a major influence in the rise of the Bank of England and of the money market.

(12) Treasury control of public servants scarcely existed before 1780 because their emoluments were separately charged upon the revenues (e.g. from fees) of their offices. It was Edmund Burke's polemics on the waste and corruption shown up by the American debacle which set reform in motion. It began with the abolition of sinecures, and then it became necessary to consider how essential work could best be done. Parliamentary committees looked to the Treasury for evidence and suggestions and anyhow the Treasury controlled, through the Customs and Excise, the tax gatherers who formed the largest single group of public servants. The first important measure, designed at once to get rid of the sale of offices and of 'passengers' was a custom's pensions scheme of 1803, widened to the whole service in 1810. In 1816 Civil List pensions were transferred. This, of course, exerted some pressure upon salaries, which could be rationalised after the institution in 1870 of a competitively recruited Civil Service (q.v.) also in effect, under Treasury control.

TREASURY BILLS are a means by which the govt., through the Bank of England, raises money for short periods seldom exceeding three months. These consist of written undertakings to pay a sum of money (calculated in multiples of £5000) on a certain day, and are offered for sale each Friday. When tenders have been received the Bank allots bills which will raise the amount needed for the week, at the best (i.e. the highest) price. In the 1960s and 1970s bills worth between £250M and £300M were allotted weekly. *See* WALPOLE'S FINANCIAL REFORMS.

TREASURY NOTES ("GREENBACKS") with a picture of the Houses of Parliament on the back were issued by the Treasury without limit during World War I, backed by a Currency Redemption Account. The issue was limited in 1920 and transferred with the Account other than govt. stocks, to the Bank of England in 1928.

TREASURY SOLICITOR, originally a Cromwellian official, became in time responsible for preparing state trials and generally for the legal business of most govt. departments. In 1883 he became effectively the Director of Public Prosecutions, but the latter's function was separated from his in 1908.

TREATY PORTS. See CHINESE TREATY PORTS.

TREBUCHET. The largest mediaeval siege engine. Its arm was operated by a counterweight, and it threw large objects such as boulders (or a dead donkey) up to half a mile.

TREF (Welsh). *See* CANTREF.

TRELAWNEY (1) Sir Jonathan (3rd Bt) (1650-1721) one of the builders of Tom Tower at Christchurch, Oxford, became Bp. of Bristol in 1685, refused to declare in favour of James II's Declaration of Indulgence, presented the Bishop's Petition against it for which he and six others were tried. He was the subject of the song:

"And shall Trelawney die?
There's twenty thousand Cornishmen
Will know the reason why."

Actually the offence (seditious libel) of which they were acquitted, was not capital. He supported William III, became Bp. of Exeter in 1689, supported Anne and the Churchills in 1691 and was Bp. of Winchester from 1707. His brother **(2) Charles (1654-1731)** served William III in Ireland as an army officer and Gov. of Dublin from 1688-92. The son of (1), **(3) Edward (1699-1754)** was a very efficient Gov. of Jamaica from 1738-52 and settled the maroon problem.

TRENCHARD, Hugh Montague (1873-1956) Vist. TRENCHARD (1936) a soldier, learned, on a friend's recommendation, to fly in July 1912 and was promptly transferred to the new Royal Flying Corps (R.F.C.). He played a leading part in developing instructional techniques and standards for flying and then in 1914 as commandant of the military wing at Farnborough, he laid the foundations of the flying force. By Aug. 1915 he was in command of the R.F.C. in France and by 1917 he had installed the aggressive spirit which later made the R.A.F. famous. Meanwhile, the Smuts Committee had persuaded the Govt. to convert the R.F.C. into an independent third service with Ld. Rothermere as Secretary of State, and Trenchard as C. of Staff (Jan. 1918), but they disagreed so acutely that Trenchard resigned (Apr.) and returned to France as Commander of the Inter-Allied Independent Air Force designed to carry the war into Germany. It never operated as intended and Trenchard doubted its efficacy, but immediately after the war Churchill, as Sec. of State, asked him to return as C. of Staff (Feb. 1919). He had simultaneously to create (doing nearly everything himself) an Air Force out of the ruins of precipitate disarmament, and to defend it against reabsorption by the other services. In both tasks he was greatly helped by his successful scheme for air control of Iraq (1922-25) whereby, with airfields, and a few aircraft and armoured cars he kept the peace as efficiently as three times the number of troops. The Royal Navy, however, acquired an airforce (R.N.A.S.) of its own. Meanwhile he developed the R.A.F. mainly by insistence on quality, spending much money on an Apprentice School and Cadet and Staff Colleges. This policy, criticised at the time, paid handsomely when pre-war and then wartime expansion began. The R.A.F. which fought World War II was his creation. He retired in 1929 and was asked in Nov. 1931 to take charge of the Metropolitan Police which was in difficulties. He instituted important reforms aimed at raising quality: these included the Hendon Police College and Forensic Laboratory, and a scheme of 10 year service for senior officers. He retired a second time in 1935 to become Chairman of the United Africa Co. (until 1953) but in 1939 he returned to the R.A.F. as a travelling representative of the Air Council and general adviser.

TRENGGANU. *See* MALAYA.

TRENT, COUNCIL OF, was summoned in 1542 at the wish of the Emperor Charles V, to try to heal the divisions of Christendom caused by the Reformation. It met in Dec. 1545, and adjourned to Bologna from Feb. 1547 to May 1548. There was a second series of sessions at Trent from May 1551 to April 1552, and a third from Jan. 1562 to Dec. 1563. Its decrees were confirmed by bull in 1564. The original object of reconciliation was driven into the background early in the first series and wholly abandoned in the second, when the council's doctrinal conclusions made reconciliation with the protestants impossible. In the third series, a jurisdictional rift which might have threatened the supremacy of the Holy See was averted in favour of decrees on useful subjects such as the establishment of seminaries. *See* COUNTER-REFORMATION; ELIZABETH I-6.

TRENT, Ld. *See* BOOT.

TRENT, R. *See* TRANSPORT AND COMMUNICATIONS.

TRESPASS is a civil wrong (tort) involving originally the use of force. Its best known form, trespass to land, is the foundation of the law of property since the right to bring an action against a trespasser and his defence could be made to settle an issue of ownership. Trespasses to the person are *assault* (a threat of violence), *battery* (actual violence), and *false imprisonment*. In addition there is trespass to goods by damage or destruction or by *conversion* which is the civil aspect of theft.

TREVELYAN (1) Sir George Otto (1838-1928) 2nd Bt, O.M. (1911) a nephew of Lord Macaulay, became financial member of the Governor General of India's Council in 1863. He was an enthusiastic liberal and supporter of the Italian Risorgimento. M.P. in 1865, he was civil Lord at the Admiralty from 1868-70. In opposition he advocated the equalisation of the rural with the urban franchise, but found time to write large scale historical works. In 1887 he returned to the Admiralty as Parly Sec; from 1882-84 he was Chief Sec. for Ireland and in 1884 he joined the Cabinet as Chancellor of the Duchy of Lancaster. In 1886 he was briefly Sec. of State for Scotland, but resigned against Irish Home Rule. He was soon converted. From 1887 he was M.P. for Glasgow and was again at the Scottish Office from 1887-95. He retired from politics in 1897. Of his sons **(2) Sir Charles Philips (1870-1958)** became secretary to the Lord Lieut. of Ireland in 1892, stood unsuccessfully for Parliament in 1895 and joined the London School Board in 1896. In 1899 he became Liberal M.P. for Elland (Yorks) and a leader of the movement to open commons for public use. From 1906-08 he was Parliamentary Charity Commissioner and from 1908 Parliamentary Sec. to the Board of Education, for which his London experience was useful. He advocated purely secular teaching, but his strong liberalism also inclined him to the Russia Committee (for exposing Czarist maltreatment of the 1905 revolutionaries) and against Russian aggression in Persia. In 1913 as a result of the Anglo-French naval undertakings, he joined a movement against secret treaties, partly because of the Franco-Russian alliance, to which Britain was now morally committed. He disapproved of Grey's balancing policies and resigned at the outbreak of World War I. He then, with Arthur Ponsonby and Ramsay Macdonald helped to create the Union of Democratic Control, and he continued to advocate peace by negotiation and inveigh against secret treaties. As a result he lost his seat in 1918 and then joined the Labour Party. In 1922 he became Labour M.P. for Central Newcastle, and was Pres. of the Board of Education in the first Labour Govt. (1924) and then educational spokesman of the opposition. He also became a somewhat uncritical champion of Soviet Russia. In the 1929 Labour Govt. he returned to the Board of Education and tried to raise the school leaving age to 15 and provide grants for poorer parents and for school development. He opposed such grants for denominational schools but had to accept them on an amendment from his own party; in Feb. 1931, however, the Lords threw out the bill on the grounds of expense in the slump; in Mar. he resigned, suspecting that his colleagues meant to reduce expenditure on other doctrinally important projects. He lost his seat in the following general election and left national politics. As Lord Lieut. of Northumberland from 1930 he set an important precedent by recruiting magistrates from all sections of local society.

TREVELYAN-NORTHCOTE REPORT (1853). *See* CIVIL SERVICE.

TREVITHICK, Richard (1771-1833) introduced the double acting vacuum water pressure engine into Cornish mines in 1800. He built the first passenger carrying steam-engine in 1801, and the first railway locomotive in 1804. In 1812 he erected the first 'Cornish' engine, and sent some to the Peruvian mines in 1814. He then went to central America, made and lost a fortune and returned penniless in 1827.

TREVOR, Sir John (1637). *See* SPEAKERSHIP-(11).

TREVOR and HAMPDEN-TREVOR. Denbighshire family **(1) Sir John (?-1673)** M.P. in the Parliaments from 1620 until the dissolution of the Rump, was a member of Cromwell's Council of State in 1651. He managed to be agreeable and make profits, and favoured the Restoration. His son **(2) Sir John (1626-72)** was an M.P. in 1646, 1654 and in the Convention and Cavalier Parliaments. He was negotiator at Paris with France, Holland and Spain and was a Sec. of State from 1668. His son **(3) Thomas (1658-1730) 1st Ld. TREVOR (1712)** Sol-Gen. in 1692, M.P. from 1692 and Attorney General in 1695, opposed the Fenwick attainder in 1696, became C.J. of the Common Pleas in 1701, was a commissioner for union in 1706-7 (mainly as a legal adviser) and was created a peer to force through the T. of Utrecht. George I naturally disfavoured him and he did not return to office until he became Lord Privy Seal from 1726. He was briefly Lord Pres. in 1730.

TRIAL by (1) BATTLE *see* APPEAL OF FELONY; **(2) JURY** *see* JURY; **(3) ORDEAL** *see* ORDEAL; **(4)** *see also* COMPURGATION.

TRIANGULAR TRADE. *See* SLAVE TRADE.

TRIANON, T. of (June 1920) confined modern Hungary to the area solidly settled by 7M Magyars, leaving some 3M as minorities in neighbouring states.

TRIBAL HIDAGE is a late 10th cent. Mercian list of Anglo-Saxon tribes as settled S. of the Humber before the Viking wars, with the number of hides then belonging to each. The text is corrupt and the figures probably conjectural though they are some evidence of the *relative* importance of the units listed. The principal figures are Mercians, and E. Anglians, 30,000 each; E. Saxons 15,000; S. Saxons 7000; W. Saxons 100,000; the Hwicce, the Wreocensaetan and the men of Lindsey 7000 each; the Fenmen 1200; and the Cilternsaetan 4000. Other minor tribes appear with hidages as low as 300.

TRIBUNAL is a person or body which adjudicates on a special type of issue by procedures which are less formal than those of a law court. Tribunals mostly have a legally qualified chairman and lay members who have some personal knowledge or experience of the tribunal's remit. They are supposed to operate locally, cheaply, and quickly though they do not always do so. Rights of appeal, if any, are usually confined to points of law, and the High Court or Court of Session restricts its supervision to ensuring that a tribunal observes the Rules of Natural Justice, does not overstep its jurisdiction and does not act illegally or in an illegal manner. In 1981 it was said that there were over 2000 tribunals, most of which have grown up since 1918. Important examples of these bodies are Traffic Commissioners, Social Security, Industrial and Pensions Appeals Tribunals. *See next entries.*

TRIBUNAL OF INQUIRY, can be set up under an Act of 1921 by the govt. to inquire into some matter of public concern. The chairman or only member is often a judge, the Attorney-General calls the evidence, and persons who may be directly affected may be represented by counsel. The Tribunal has no power save to compel witnesses, require the production of documents and make a Report. This is generally published and since these tribunals are rare and the events which call them forth usually sensational, creates great interest. Among the best known instances were the Tribunal of 1936 on budget leakages,

the Lynskey Tribunal of 1948 on allegations of political corruption and the so-called Vassall Tribunal of 1963 on betrayal of state secrets.

TRIBUNALS, COUNCIL ON (1958) is not a tribunal of appeal, but a body which reviews the constitution and working of most of the 2000+ tribunals (but not the Courts) and of inquiries held by inspectors on behalf of ministers. It must be consulted before any procedural rules are made. It makes an annual report and also special reports on such matters as are referred to it.

TRIBUNE and its **GROUP.** A practical and intellectual weekly founded in 1937 which after World War II focused the views of Aneurin Bevan and his wife Jenny Lee, Harold Wilson, Michael Foot, Richard Crossman and others. They favoured socialisation towards a classless society. This would involve reliance on Communist Russian friendship, making nuclear armaments and membership of the E.E.C. alike unnecessary, so that resources could be freed for further nationalisations, social engineering through a reformed education, and a high level of social and health security. The group's cohesion did not survive the responsibilities of office. Mr and Mrs Bevan resigned against health charges: the others discovered the dangers of Russian policy. The ideas, however, remain potent.

TRIBUTUM. *See* BRITAIN, ROMAN-6.

TRICHINOPOLY (locally TIRUCHIRAPALLI) (India). S. Mysore fortress city disputed (*see* GEORGE II-15) between England and France and their respective supporters. The French were defeated there in 1753 and the place was incorporated into British India after the defeat of Tippoo Sultan in 1799.

TRIENNIAL, SEPTENNIAL AND QUINQUENNIAL ACTS. (1) 1641. This provided that if in every third year parliament had not been summoned by 3 Sept. it was to meet without summons on the second Monday in Nov. It was repealed by the Act of **(2) 1664** which laid down that Parliaments should "not be intermitted or discontinued above three years" but left it to the crown to carry it out. The substance of this was re-enacted in the Act of **(3) 1694** which, however, added that no parliament could continue for more than three years from its first meeting. The (Septennial) Act of **(4) 1715** extended this period to seven years. **(5)** The Parliament Act 1911 reduced this to five.

TRIERS AND EJECTORS were protestant non-Anglican part-lay bodies created under the Commonwealth to purge the Anglican Church of its Anglicanism. From Mar. 1654 the Triers sat in London to test candidates for parochial and teaching duties. From Aug. county committees ejected unsuitable incumbents and teachers to make room for the new men. This slow and unpopular process ended at the Restoration.

TRIESTE (Adriatic) Venetian from 1302-79 and Habsburg from 1382 became prosperous as the transit port between Venice and the Habsburg Empire and declined as Venice declined and also as the Dutch and Baltic trade increased. In 1719 it became a free port and the H.Q. of the Austrian Levant and East India Cos; its prosperity began to increase slowly, and after the opening of the Suez Canal in 1869, rapidly. When the Italians seized it in 1918 and deprived of its hinterland, it declined. It was taken by the Yugoslavs in 1945, and after much local controversy the city passed to Italy as a free port in 1954 while the surrounding countryside (Istria) passed to Yugoslavia.

TRIMMER. One who trims between opposing political parties. *See* SAVILE, SIR GEORGE (1633-95).

TRINCOMALEE (Ceylon) was the principal British Naval base in the Indian Ocean from 1795 to 1956.

TRINIDAD, though seen by Columbus in 1498, was left to the internecine warfare of Caribs and Arawaks with occasional visits by European ships seeking asphalt for calking at the La Brea pitch lake on the W. Coast. There were small Spanish settlements after 1530 but the island was largely wild until about 1690 when the Spaniards introduced cocoa. This was destroyed by blight in 1725 and there was no progress until 1783 when the govt. offered advantages to foreign R. Catholic immigrants. This brought Europeans and Creoles especially from France and the French Antilles after the French Revolution. In Feb. 1797 the island was seized by Britain and ceded at the T. of Amiens in 1802. The British developed cocoa and sugar in the 19th cent. and oil from 1910. In 1941 they leased an area to U.S.A. for 99 years for a base. Trinidad, with Tobago, were given limited local autonomy in 1956, joined the West Indies Federation in 1958, achieved full internal self govt. in 1961 and independence within the Commonwealth on the dissolution of the Federation in May 1962.

TRINITARIANS or RED FRIARS were an order of Canons Regular founded in 1198 to raise means for redeeming captives from the Saracens and Moors. Their houses were mostly in ports.

TRINITY COLLEGES (1) Cambridge. This was set up by the fusion in 1546 of Michaelhouse (1324) and Kings Hall (1337). (2) Dublin. Adam Loftus, Abp. of Dublin persuaded the corporation of Dublin to give the old Augustinian buildings for the purpose, and the College was incorporated in Mar. 1592 with Lord Burghley as Chancellor. It was intended as the beginning of a university, but as no other colleges were founded, it and the University were identical. (3) Oxford. This was founded in 1555 in the Durham College of the dissolved Benedictine Priory at Durham. It was Jacobite in sentiment.

TRINITY HOUSES were maritime corporations at Dundee, Hull, Leith, Newcastle upon Tyne and London (strictly Deptford Strond). Of these the first four soon became merely mariners' charities. The London house, however, was chartered in 1514 to maintain lights and seamarks, to train and govern pilots and to regulate pilotage, and its later parliamentary powers made it the principal authority on the English coasts for these matters. It is governed by a Master, Deputy Master and Elder Brethren, who habitually sit as assessors in shipping cases. (See LIGHTHOUSES.) Since 1894 lighthouse maintenance has been systematised in England under Trinity House; in Scotland under the Commissioners for Northern Lights and in Ireland under Commissioners for Irish Lights.

TRINODA (really TRIMODA) NECESSITAS (Lat: three forms of essential duty) were obligations which from at least the 8th cent. nobody could avoid, namely service in the fyrd, the maintenance of the local fort or burh (see BURGHAL HIDAGE) and the repair of bridges.

TRINOVANTES. This British tribe occupied modern Essex, with their capital at Camulodunun (Colchester). They submitted to Julius Caesar (54 B.C.) thereby forcing the main British leader Cassivelaunus, to come to terms. Between A.D. 5-10 they fell under the control of the Catuvellauni to the west. In A.D. 43 new Roman invaders soon captured Camulodunum, and the lands of the Trinovantes were among the earliest to be colonised by the Romans, whose harsh behaviour provoked the tribe into joining Boadicea's rising in A.D. 60

TRIPARTITE PACT (Sept. 1940) after the fall of France, between Germany, Italy and Japan was directed against the possibility of U.S.A. entering the war. Within a few weeks Hungary, Roumania, Slovakia, Bulgaria and Serbia joined it. When the Japanese attacked Pearl Harbor (Dec. 1941) Hitler declared war on U.S.A. gratuitously and dragged the other signatories in.

TRIPLE ALLIANCE (1668) negotiated by Arlington with Holland and Sweden to force peace upon Louis XIV and Spain, by laying down a Flemish frontier already agreed between Holland and France and requiring the French evacuation of Franche Comté The French gains, primarily Lille, facilitated further aggressions later on.

TRIPLE ALLIANCE (1716-17) between Britain, France, with Holland acceding, provided that the succession to the English and French thrones should be mutually guaranteed; that the Jacobite pretender be forced to leave Avignon and settle in Italy, and that the fortifications and sluices at Dunkirk and Mardyk should be destroyed.

TRIPLE ALLIANCE (1788). See PITT'S GOVT-FIRST-7.

TRIPLE ALLIANCE. See GEORGE II-17.

TRIPLE ALLIANCE (1854) of Austria, Britain and France was intended to force Russia to make peace at the end of the Crimean War. The negotiations for it probably produced that effect, but it was signed after Russia had given in. The French tried to revive it in 1863 to protect the rebellious Poles.

TRIPLE ALLIANCE (1869) of France, Italy and Austro-Hungary was intended to protect France against Prussia, and Austro-Hungary against Russia, with the Italians receiving the Trentino for joining the guarantees; but the negotiations broke down because France and Austro-Hungary did not want to be committed to wars and the Italians wanted the French to evacuate Rome.

TRIPLE ALLIANCE (May 1882). Austro-Hungary, Germany and Italy agreed to assist any one of them if attacked by two great powers and to remain neutral if attacked by one, but Germany and Austro-Hungary would assist Italy if attacked by France and Italy would assist Germany if similarly attacked. The alliances were expressed not to be against Britain. It therefore envisaged unlikely dangers from France and Russia. Its main effect was to raise Italian prestige. It was renewed in Feb. 1887 but supplemented by separate treaties between Italy and the other two. The Austro-Hungarian treaty provided for reciprocal compensations if the Balkan *status quo* were disturbed but defined nothing; and as Italy wanted the Trentino but Austro-Hungary meant to offer rights in Albania, the parties were at cross-purposes. Under the Italo-German treaty, Germany was to assist Italy if France tried to extend her occupation, protectorate or sovereignty in Tripoli or Morocco. The main treaty was renewed in May 1891, because Italy hoped, but failed to secure British support for her Tripolitan ambitions. In Mar. 1899 an Anglo-French agreement made the Italians fear that they would not secure Tripoli after all but in Dec. 1900 the French offered to support their seizure of Tripoli, provided that they let France take Morocco first, and changed the terms of the Triple Alliance in senses favourable to France. In June 1902 the treaty was renewed unaltered but the Italians assured the French that they were in no way committed ever to fight the French. It was renewed again in 1907 and 1913 without the exception on Britain. In World War I Italy repudiated it on the ostensible ground that is applied only in a defensive war, but really because Austro-Hungary had offered no compensations.

"TRIPLE ALLIANCE" was a name for the informal alliance of the miners', railwaymen' and Transport and General Workers' Unions which developed in World War I. It declined in 1920.

TRIPLE ENTENTE. See ENTENTE.

TRIPOLI. See LIBYA.

TRISTAN or TRISTRAM was a hero of the Brythonic Celts of Scotland, who later became known in Wales. The scene of Tristram's intrigue with Iseult, wife of his uncle, K. Mark, is laid mainly in Cornwall, in the modern version of the story, which owes its form to a French 12th cent. poet.

TRISTAN DA CUNHA Is. was named for its Portuguese discoverer in 1506. The Dutch tried to settle it in 1656, and the HEIC in 1686. It had a British garrison in 1816-17 and on its withdrawal the Glass family remained. They were joined by occasional shipwrecked people. Occupation was interrupted for two years by a volcanic eruption in 1961.

TRIVET or TREVET, Nicholas (1258-c. 1334) son of Thomas Trivet, one of Henry III's justices in eyre. He became an Oxford Dominican and taught there and at Paris. He got an international reputation by his commentaries on scripture and on patristic and classical works. In later life at the London Dominican friary, he began to write history. His two *Histories* are derivative but his patriotic *Annales Sex Regum Angliae* (i.e. K. Stephen to K. Edward I) (c. 1320) contains original material, uses official documents such as Boniface VIII's Scottish letters and includes anecdotes and eye witness accounts of Henry III and Edward I.

TRIVIUM (Lat: Triple Way). *See* LIBERAL ARTS.

TROLLOPE, Anthony (1815-82). Post Office official from 1834; in Ireland from 1841 to 1859, in England (with missions to Egypt and most of the major British speaking colonies) until 1866. He originated the pillar box. He also found time for a very large literary output. His Irish novels are forgotten. The eight *Barsetshire* novels, based on contemporary life in Salisbury, appeared between 1855-67 and were and are immensely successful. Of the five political novels (1867-75) the best known are *Phineas Finn* and *The Way We Live Now*. There was also an *Autobiography* (1876) and accounts of places he had visited. His practice was to write 250 words every 15 minutes by the clock.

TROMP. Dutch naval family of which **(1) Maarten Harpertszoon (1598-1653)** defeated the Spaniards in 1639 off Dunkirk and in the Downs and helped the French to take Dunkirk in 1646. In May 1652 he was battered by Blake and relieved of command. Restored in Dec. he defeated the English off Dover, and signified a boast that he had swept the seas by hoisting a broom at the masthead. In Feb. 1653 however, Blake defeated him in the Three Days Battle off Portland. In June he fought an indecisive action with Monk and Deane (who fell) off the Flemish coast. On 8 Aug. there was an indecisive action off Terheijde; reinforced by De Witt, he resumed action next day and was killed in the ensuing defeat. He is said to have originated the close-hauled line ahead formation for battleships. His son **(2) Cornelius (1629-91)** commanded against the Algerian corsairs and then in the Baltic in 1656 against the Swedes. In 1662 and 1663 he convoyed Dutch trading fleets to the Mediterranean. In the Second Dutch War he commanded a squadron at the B. of Lowestoft where his manoeuvres were not supported by some of his captains. He then became C-in-C, but was soon superseded by De Ruyter with whom he quarrelled. De Ruyter accused him of failing to support him. William of Orange reconciled them after the B. of Solebay (June 1672) and in June 1673 they won a joint victory over an Anglo-French fleet. In 1674-75 he commanded operations against the French coast. In 1676 he commanded in the Baltic in support of the Danes against the Swedes whom he defeated at Christianstad. He spent the rest of his campaigning life in the Baltic.

TROOPING SEASON. Late February to the end of April, when the annual reliefs of troops in India used to be made.

TROPPAU, CONGRESS OF. *See* HOLY ALLIANCE.

TROT OF TURRIFF (May 1639). The first skirmish, outside Perth, in the Bishops' Wars.

TROTSKY (originally BRONSTEIN) **Lev Davidovitch (1879-1940); TROTSKYISM; TROTSKYITES.** Trotsky was initially a Menshevik but had a genius for organising violence and conducted the seizure of power at St. Petersburg in 1917. He became Lenin's Foreign commissar, but refused to agree the T. of Brest-Litovsk, resigned and became War Commissar. As such he organised the Red Armies in the victorious civil war and in the defeated invasion of Poland. He held the doctrine (Trotskyism) that socialist countries should be ready to spread world revolution by conquest rather than revolution, but hated Lenin's autocratic tendencies and he

was still more objectionable to Stalin who, after Lenin's death, had him expelled from the Communist Party (1927), from the U.S.S.R. (1929) and murdered in Mexico. The term Trotskyite became a Stalinist derogatory and later a fatal smear epithet. Later still in the west it was used by socialist dissidents and their opponents to describe with equal inaccuracy, those whose socialism was a form of violent subversion.

TROUBADOURS or TROUVÈRES. *See* LANGUE D-OIL-OC.

TROUBLES (1) Irish. The name given to two periods (a) the first (Jan. 1919 to July 1921) when the Irish Republican Army (I.R.A.) fought a guerrilla war in the name of an Irish Republic without the authority of the Dail, against the British who sought to maintain order in the name of the sovereignty which had disappeared, and used in the later stages a form of counter-terrorism. It ended with the Irish response to George V's plea for civil peace at the opening of the Ulster Parliament in June 1921 and the Irish Treaty of Dec. 1921. (b) In the second period (June 1922 to Apr. 1923) the I.R.A., disliking the treaty, attacked the Irish govt. and was eventually worn down. In these two periods some 2000 Irishmen and 1000 British troops and police were killed and most of the country mansions burned down.

(2) Russian. *See* TIME OF TROUBLES (RUSSIA).

TROUBRIDGE, Sir Thomas (1758-1807) joined the navy as a seaman in 1773 and was commissioned by Sir Edward Hughes in 1781 and by 1785 had become his flag captain. In 1790 as a frigate captain he was captured and then recaptured on the Glorious First of June. In 1797 he commanded the *Culloden* at St. Vincent, and then under Nelson at Santa Cruz and the Nile. From 1801-4 he was a Lord of the Admiralty. He went down in a hurricane off Java.

TROY WEIGHT. *See* WEIGHTS AND MEASURES.

TROYES T. of (1420) This momentous treaty, after repeating the provisions of the convention of Arras, provided that Henry V with the advice of the nobles and wise men (i.e. the Burgundians) of France, was to be regent of France during the life of Charles VI, who with his Q. Isabel was to be maintained in proper estate and that at Charles VI's death, Henry or his heir was to inherit the French crown. The crowns of England and France were always to descend to the same person, but the two Kingdoms were to remain distinct and the King in governing France should have only French advisers. For his part he undertook to conquer Dauphinist France: all conquests outside Normandy were to be made for the profit of the French crown, and at the death of Charles VI Normandy was to revert to France. Dispossessed supporters of Charles VI or of Burgundy in conquered lands and Normandy were to be restored to their property or benefices. *See also* CHARLES VII OF FRANCE; JOAN OF ARC.

TROYES, T. of (Apr. 1564) (*see* HUGUENOTS). In Oct. 1562 the English under the E. of Warwick occupied Le Havre with the aid of the Huguenot P. of Condé both to help the Huguenots and as a pledge for the return of Calais. In Mar. 1563 Huguenots and Catholics signed the P. of Amboise and united against the English. 20,000 French troops attacked Warwick's 5000, who held out heroically until June when a sudden plague started to kill 200 a week. By 28th Warwick had to capitulate. By the treaty the French paid 120,000 Crowns to redeem their hostages but were relieved of their nominal obligations under the T. of Câteau Cambrésis, especially in relation to Calais.

TRUCE. *See* ARMISTICE.

TRUCE CONSERVATORS. *See* MARCHES, ANGLO-SCOTS-4.

TRUCE OF GOD. An attempt by the church to limit endemic warfare by forbidding it on certain occasions. The Council of Elne (1027) denounced fighting between Saturday night and Monday morning. Lent, Advent and Whitsun were added hopefully later.

TRUCIAL OMAN or PIRATE COAST (Persian Gulf). The Kawasim were sea traders until about 1805 when, under Wahabi influence, they took to piracy. In 1820 they plundered two British vessels; this brought reprisals and the sheikhs signed a general peace treaty. At this period there were 5 states **(1) Abu Dhabi: (2) Sharja; (3) Ajman; (4) Umm al Qaiwain; (5) Fujaira.** In 1853 they all signed, under British compulsion, a General Maritime Truce (hence *trucial*). In 1866 Sharja was split into four states, one retaining the name, the other being **(6) Ras al Khaima (7) Dubai and (8) Kalma.** In 1892 the states agreed to restrict their foreign relations to Britain. Kalma was reabsorbed into Sharja in 1952. In 1962 oil was found in Abu Dhabi and it and the deep water port of Dubai began to develop. These two states rapidly became wealthy, and in 1971 British troops and protection were withdrawn.

TRUCK was payment of wages in kind or most often by tokens exchangeable for goods only at Truck or Tommy shops, usually owned by the employer, who might overcharge or sell poor quality goods. Sometimes arising from a shortage of coin (*see* COINAGE), truck when personal mobility was difficult could be a gross abuse. The Truck Act 1831, required certain workers to be paid wholly in coin, and this was extended in 1887 to all manual workers but with special arrangements for farm workers. An early consequence was that perquisites (e.g. the miners' free coal, the dustman's pickings or the gardener's potatoes) could not legally be regarded as remuneration and when wages rose in the 20th cent. could not be taxed. A later consequence, remedied in 1960, was that workers could not be paid by cheque.

TRUDEAU, Pierre Elliott. *See* CANADA-30 *et seq.*

TRUE LAW OF FREE MONARCHIES (1603). A treatise expounding the divine right of Kings written against George Buchanan's *De jure regni* (Lat: The Law of the Kingdom – 1579). It was attributed to James I, his pupil, who detested him.

TRUMAN DOCTRINE (1947). When Greece and Turkey were menaced by communist subversion. Pres. Truman of the U.S.A. declared that it was U.S. policy 'to support free peoples who are resisting attempted subjugation by armed minorities or by outside pressures'. The practical consequence was that the American public accepted the need for a large warlike establishment to provide the means of enforcement.

TRURO (Cornwall) has been discontinuously represented in Parliament since 1295. It was an important Stannaries (q.v.) centre. Its 12th cent. charter was replaced in 1589 and the new charter remained the governing document until the Municipal Corporations Act 1834. It became the cathedral city for Cornwall in 1876 and the huge cathedral was built between 1880 and 1910.

TRUSTS. *See* USES AND TRUSTS.

TRUSTEESHIP, U.N. *See* MANDATE, INTERNATIONAL.

TRYON, Sir George (1832-93) a naval officer had a number of successful experimental commands, including the *Warrior* (1861-64) and the *Raleigh* (1874-7); and he revised the signal book. Unfortunately he is remembered for the collision which, as C-in-C Mediterranean, cost him his life and for which, before his flagship went down, he blamed himself.

TRYON, William (1725-88). *See* NEW YORK.

TRYPANOSOMIASIS (or SLEEPING SICKNESS in humans and NAGANA in cattle) exists in two varieties, the Gambian and the less widespread Rhodesian. It is a chronic and often lethal infection peculiar for humans to tropical Africa, though the animal form is found in S. and C. America. Several sub-species of the **Tsetse fly** (*Glossina*) attack quadrupeds and humans in swarms and carry it from one to the other. It was known in Mali in the 14th cent. and a Portuguese expedition was driven back on the Zambezi by the death of its horses in 1569. An English surgeon described it in 1734 and another in

Sierra Leone in 1792-96. At that time the main areas of *Gambiense* were on the Upper Niger and Benue, whence it spread to L. Chad in 1859, to the Volta in 1880 and to Nigeria in 1890. It also followed the track of Stanley's 1887 expedition and from 1896-1906 a fearful epidemic raged on the Congo. This spread in 1898-1908 to Uganda and in 1900-11 to Kenya with enormous adult mortalities. L. Victoria virtually ceased to be a highway. Meanwhile *Rhodesiense* in the period 1837-51 held up the Boer Voortrekkers, especially in Bechuanaland and Rhodesia. Trypanosomiasis in cattle was first identified in 1894, but the slow progress against the disease has so far depended upon laborious and seldom wholly effectual campaigns against the fly. *See* EPIDEMICS, ANIMAL, HUMAN.

TRYSTING PLACES. *See* MARCHES, ANGLO-SCOTS-3,5,6.

TSINGTAO. *See* CHINESE TREATY PORTS; COMMERCE PROTECTION, NAVAL B-1.

TSR-2 was a swing wing fighter and attack aircraft. Its development was stopped by the Labour Govt. in 1964 for reasons of economy and U.S. aircraft bought instead.

TSUNG-LI YAMEN **(1861-1901)** a sort of staffed permanent conference of Chinese ministers which considered "Western" problems such as internal modernisation and relations with great powers. It had influence because many of its members belonged to the imperial council but no decision-making power of its own. Also its functions were circumscribed because provincial governors had dealings with foreign powers. Western govts. erroneously thought of it as a foreign office.

TUAM (Galway, Ir.) The archbishopric of Connaught dating from the Synod of Kells (1152).

TUATH **(Ir. = people)** A tribe or its territory.

TUBERCULOSIS, otherwise CONSUMPTION, PHTHISIS, SCROFULA or KING'S EVIL, *LUMOR ALBUS,* is ancient and was reckoned by the 16th cent. to be a major agent of mortality. It has claimed amongst its many others Calvin, Richelieu, Spinoza, Keats, R. L. Stevenson and Cecil Rhodes. In 1665 the London mortality was approximately 20% of all deaths, in 1715 13% and in 1780 when industrialism was advancing but its disadvantages were not being tackled, 35%. It fell to 30% in 1801. It rose everywhere in war years. Recorded deaths in England were 57,000 between 1840 and 1847. Robert Koch, who isolated the tubercle bacillus in 1882, reckoned that the disease in his time accounted for 14-15% of *all* deaths. Its communication from cows to humans *via* milk was discovered soon afterwards and in 1917 wholesale pasteurisation of milk began to interrupt this avenue. The spread of tuberculosis was thus hindered and the incidence of new infections rapidly reduced. Streptomycin, invented in 1943, came into general use in 1947 for the cure of sufferers. The primary effect was in a few years to increase the expectation of life and therefore a revolutionary change in the balance of age groups. *See* EPIDEMICS, HUMAN.

TUCKER, Josiah (1722-99). Domestic chaplain to Bp. Butler and Dean of Gloucester from 1758, anticipated Adam Smith in his opposition to monopolies and state interference in economic processes but derived his views from the conduct of foreign policy. Turgot, with whom he corresponded, translated his work *Going to War for the Sake of Trade* (1763). He attacked the war with the American colonies and in 1781 addressed *Cui Bono?* (Lat: = who benefits?) to Necker, arguing that the American war was a mistake for all concerned including the French and Spaniards. His many political, economic and religious writings also include a defence of clerical subscription.

TUDOR. English royal dynasty (1485-1603) descended from the N. Welsh **(1) Ednyfed Fychan (?-1246)** adviser to Llewellyn the Great. His son **(2) Twdwr ap Ednyfed (?-?)** helped to negotiate the T. of Conway (1277) between Llewellyn II ap Gryffyd and Edward I. Two of Twdwr's great-great nephews **(3) Gwilym** and **(4) Rhys** son of Twdwr ap Goronwy were associated with Richard II and joined the revolts of their first cousin Owain Glendower against Henry IV. Under Henry V, the son of their youngest brother **(5) Meredith (6) Owen (?-1461)** was employed about the royal household, and in 1420 was in Sir Walter Hungerford's retinue in France. In this way he met Henry V's young widow **(7) Catherine of Valois** and at an unknown date, perhaps 1429 or 1432, secretly married her. The *mésalliance* is said to have become known only shortly before her death in 1437, but as they had two sons it can only have been the identity of the husband which was uncertain. These two sons were **(8) Edmund (?-1456)** and **(9) Jasper (?-1495)** and in 1449 they were knighted by their half-brother Henry VI and in 1455 created respectively **Es. of Richmond and Pembroke.** After a chequered career their father was captured at the B. of Mortimer's Cross (1461) and beheaded at Hereford. In 1455 Edmund had married his 12 year old ward the fabulously wealthy Margaret Beaufort (*see* BEAUFORT). He died in 1456; his son **(10) Henry (1457-1509) 2nd E.** (later Henry VII) was born post-humously. Henry's royalty was thus derived from his Valois grandmother and Beaufort mother whose rights to the succession were, however, statutorily barred. As only one of his grandparents was Welsh, his self-proclaimed Welshness was probably derived from his seven year sojourn as a boy at Harlech under the protection of his uncle Jasper, an active Lancastrian who helped him to escape to France in 1471 and supported him in the unsuccessful revolt against Richard III in 1483 and in the victorious Bosworth campaign of 1485. Jasper who had no heir, was created **D. of BEDFORD** in 1485 and was Lord Deputy of Ireland from 1486-94.

TUDOR ARCHITECTURE. *See* ARCHITECTURE, BRITISH.

TUFTON. There were eleven Tufton **Earls of THANET** between Nicholas of Hothfield (Kent), created first earl in 1628 and Henry the last earl who died in 1849. None was of any particular distinction. The family still owned Hothfield in 1973.

TULL, Jethro (1674-1741) a barrister, invented the seed drill at Wallingford in about 1705 and on his travels in Europe was so impressed with the virtues of vine cultivation that he invented a horse hoe. His ideas on plant nutrition were the foundation of most modern husbandry.

TUMULTS and PETITIONS. To prevent people being bullied into signing petitions to the Crown or Parliament, an Act of 1661 forbade them to be signed by more than 20 unless agreed by the Common Council of London or a Grand Jury. To reduce pressure on the addressee no petition was to be presented by more than ten. The Seditious Meetings Act 1817 forbade assemblies within a mile of Westminster Hall when Parliament was sitting. As the Chartist agitation shows, these enactments were evaded or laxly enforced. They were repealed as recently as 1986.

TUNBRIDGE WELLS (ROYAL) (Kent). The springs were discovered in 1606 and became popular in 1690. The Pantiles were paved in 1700. The place remained a fashionable resort of London society until the rise of Brighton at the end of the century. *See* SPAS.

TUNIS-IA was seized by the Turks in 1574 but in 1590 the local Janissaries took over effective govt. ("Regency") under a **Dey** whose Second in Command was the **Bey**. Both these offices became hereditary, the Dey being the nominal, the Bey the actual ruler, but both maintaining deference to the Sultan of Turkey. The Dey was imprisoned in 1671 by the last Bey of the first dynasty; the first Bey of the second dynasty abolished the office in 1705. In fact the govt.'s authority was confined to the larger cities, the countryside being in the hands of tribes supported by the neighbouring regency of Algiers. Since they held the towns to ransom by cutting off food supplies, the towns took to piracy to raise the cash necessary to feed themselves. The English sent punitive

expeditions at intervals; the French obtained trading concessions. French interest grew especially after the annexation of Algeria (1850); the regency had become financially embarrassed by the suppression of the local slave trade in 1819 and of piracy in 1824. The Beys called in foreign (mainly French and English) advisers, who reorganised the army in 1837. Railways and telegraphs were in operation by 1857 and an ineffective constitution was issued in 1861. Italian immigration began in 1868. Financial incompetence brought excessive borrowing needing new taxes, which brought revolt and bankruptcy. In 1869 an Anglo-French-Italian debt commission was imposed by international action. In 1878, as part of the Berlin settlement, Britain took Cyprus and renounced her Tunisian interests. This left France and Italy facing each other. In 1881 France decided to forestall the Italians by sending an expedition; this imposed a protectorate (T. of **Bardo** May 1881) which placed Tunisian military and foreign affairs under a French resident. This continued until 1939 by which time French economic penetration had created a nationalist middle class. While Tunisia was occupied by the Germans this was ineffective, but after World War II ended the Tunisians, led by Hassan **Bourguiba,** compelled France to abolish the protectorate in 1956 and he abolished the Beylik in 1957.

TUNNAGE and POUNDAGE. See TONNAGE.

TUNNELS. The first English tunnels were built: for a canal by Brindley in 1761; for a railway by Kilsby and Robert Stephenson in 1838 and for pedestrians, under the Thames by Marc Brunel in 1843. This last was the first to be shield-driven. The Severn Tunnel, at 4 miles 628 yards, is the longest in Britain. The Channel Tunnel, first proposed in 1882, was finished in 1994.

TUNSTALL. *See* STOKE-ON-TRENT.

TUNSTALL, Cuthbert (1474-1559) became Bp. of London in 1522 but in 1530 was translated to Durham. A prominent King's man and friend of Erasmus, he became the leading figure in the Council of the North, formed in 1531 to keep order among the traditionalist northern population. He would not, however, support the doctrinal protestantism of Edward VI's reign and was deprived. Mary restored him, but he refused to take the oath of supremacy to Elizabeth and was again deprived.

TURBARY. See LAND TENURE, ENGLAND-3.

TURBERVILLE, George (c. 1540-1610) Wykehamist and sec. to Thomas Randolph on the embassy to Russia in 1540. He wrote books on Falconry and Hunting and also much pioneering blank verse.

TURBERVILLE or TRUBLEVILLE, Henry of (?-1239) of a Norman family settled in Dorset, was Seneschal of Gascony from Oct. 1226 until 1231. He had succeeded Richard of Cornwall, whose inefficiency he did something to remedy. He then went to Wales, where in 1233 he put down local disorders and in 1234 returned to Gascony and, having campaigned in Brittany took, in 1238 an army to Lombardy to repress rebels against the rule of the Queen's Savoyard relatives.

TURBINES. (1) Steam (*see* PARSONS, SIR CHARLES). **(2) Gas** (*see* WHITTLE, SIR FRANK).

TURENNE, Henri de la Tour d'Auvergne, Vist. de (1611-75) nephew of Maurice of Nassau, took service under France in 1630, triumphantly commanded French armies from 1640 in Italy, Spain and Germany and conquered much of Belgium. In 1658 he commanded at the B. of the Dunes and in 1672 against the Dutch. He laid waste the Palatinate and Alsace and was killed on the Sassbach.

TURGESIUS. *See* THURKILL; VIKINGS-7.

TURKANA. See KENYA.

TURKESTAN was subjected by the Russians in 1885.

TURKEY (*see* OTTOMAN EMPIRE) rose through a nationalist revolt against the treaty imposed upon the Sultan's govt. after World War I. It was led by Mustafa Kemal (Ataturk), particularly against the Greek cessions in Thrace and Asia

Minor. The capital was moved away from Allied naval guns on the Straits and Stambouli corruption, to Ankara. A strong patriotic army swept the Greeks, amid massacres, out of Thrace and Asia Minor (*see* CHANAK INCIDENT). The cosmopolitan Sultanate and Caliphate (q.v.) were abolished. The Ataturk became the first Pres. of a secular and specifically Turkish republic. Education was his first priority and having substituted a western alphabet phonetically adapted to Turkish for the incompatible Arabic script hitherto in use, the literacy rate was raised from 10% to 70% by 1990. The country was engaged in internal modernisation and investment to the virtual exclusion of other pre-occupations and so stayed out of World War II, but afterwards experienced a series of constitutional and politico-military upheavals, mainly affecting the still narrow ruling groups. Disputes, however, with Greece over Cyprus (q.v.) led in 1963 nearly, and in 1974 actually to war in Cyprus, and the creation of a Turkish Cypriot state recognised only by Turkey. Subsequently two new bridges were built over the Bosphorus in the 1980s which for the first time directly connected Asia Minor with Europe and increased the chances of Turkish admission to the European Union.

TURKEY COMPANY. *See* LEVANT CO.

TURKS AND CAICOS Is. were uninhabited until 1678 when Bermudans established saltpans. In 1799 they were annexed to the Bahamas. In 1848 they received a separate charter and from 1874 they were dependent on Jamaica. In 1962 they became a crown colony again but as Jamaica had become independent, they were re-attached to the Bahamas and then, when the latter became independent, they became a separate colony altogether.

TURNBULL, William (?-1454) Bp. of Glasgow from 1447, founded the University there in 1451.

TURNER, Francis (?1658-1700) became Bp. of Rochester in 1683 and was translated to Ely in 1684. A legitimist, he was nevertheless one of the Seven Bishops; he refused allegiance to William III and in 1690 was deprived. He remained an active but harmless Jacobite until his death.

TURNER, Joseph Mallord William (1775-1851) first exhibited at the Royal Academy in 1798. His first or imitative style lasted from 1800-20. In 1832 he visited Italy, particularly Venice and with the completion in 1839 of the *Fighting Téméraire* he reached his final, impressionist, development for which he was much ridiculed but trenchantly defended by Ruskin. The *Snowstorm* was painted in 1842 and *Rain, Steam and Speed* in 1844.

TURNHAM, De. Two brothers **(1) Robert (?-1211)** and **(2) Stephen (?1215)** accompanied Richard I on crusade. Robert became justiciar of Cyprus after its conquest in 1191; Stephen escorted Richard's queen, Berengaria, to Rome after their wedding in Cyprus. Stephen was a justice in Eyre in England while Robert, after commanding Richard's forces in Anjou in 1197, was John's seneschal of Poitou and Gascony from 1201-5.

TURNIPS as a fallow field crop, were in use in England by 1650 but were popularised as part of a four year rotation by Vist. Townshend ("Turnip Townshend") in the 1730s. They help to improve soil fertility and by providing winter cattle feed, trebled the cattle.

TURNPIKE ROADS AND TRUSTS. A turnpike was a tollgate (usually with a keeper's cottage) on a road maintainable by users' tolls. These originated in the early 18th cent. They were mostly by-roads, regulated by a temporary local act, which however, was almost automatically renewed. Their unpopularity led as early as 1728 to penal legislation against breaking turnpikes down. The growing number of private acts followed a pattern of vesting each road in trustees, commonly self perpetuating £100 freeholders with fairly stereotyped powers. Hence public general acts could be passed applying to all of them. These provided for weigh-

bridges, differentiated between charges for vehicles according to the width of their wheels, weight and number of horses, and regulated the raising of capital, besides closing penal loopholes. They were frequently evaded and so amended or consolidated. By the last major general Turnpike Act in 1822, there were many thousands of turnpike roads. There was a rapid decline with the coming of steam railways: renewals ceased to be automatic: but in 1864 there were still over 1000; by 1879 there were only 200 and by 1890 they were extinct. *See* TRANSPORT AND COMMUNICATIONS.

TURPIN, Dick (Richard) (alias PALMER) (1706-39) an Essex gangster and cattle rustler reached his peak (or bottom) in partnership with one King after 1735. After he accidentally killed King he went to Yorkshire and was there caught and hanged.

TUSCANY. Alexander dei Medici became D. of Florence in 1532. His son Cosmo I annexed Siena in 1555 and was created Grand D. of Tuscany by Pius V in 1569(-74). He and Ferdinand I (r. 1587-1609) neglected Florence, but developed Leghorn (*see* DUDLEY), reclaimed the marshes, and played (like the earlier Medici) important roles as international financiers. From 1609 until 1723, however, the Grand Dukes left the administration in financially incompetent ecclesiastical hands and between 1723-37 Tuscany was overrun by successive invasions arising from a disputed succession. Eventually at the death of the last Medici ruler (1737) it passed to Francis of Lorraine, husband of the Empress Maria Theresa and so to the house of Austria. Francis and his son Leopold (r. 1765-90) established a successful enlightened despotism. Leopold, on becoming Emperor, left Tuscany to his son. Ferdinand who, having allowed the British to use Leghorn, was expelled by the French in 1800. It was then erected into the Kingdom of Etruria for Louis, D. of Parma and in 1807 became a grand duchy again for Napoleon's sister Elisa. Ferdinand returned in 1814 and Lucca was added in 1847. In 1848 Leopold II (r. 1824-59) granted a constitution, fled in 1849, returned with an Austrian army and abolished the constitution in 1852. His attempt to stay neutral in the Franco-Austrian war of 1859 cost him his throne. In 1860 Tuscany was united to Italy.

TUSSAUD, Mme Marie (1760-1850) helped her uncle at his wax works at the Palais Royal in Paris and there modelled heads of victims of the revolutionary Terror. She migrated to London in 1800.

TUTCHIN, John (?1661-1707). A Whig pamphleteer, attacked William III in *The Foreigners* in 1700. This provoked Defoe's *True-Born Englishman*. In 1702 he established the *Observator* and made friends with Defoe. In 1704 he attacked the naval administration (now under Q. Anne's consort, Prince George of Denmark) and was unsuccessfully prosecuted. His "deadly malice and admirable prose" continuing to be published, he was flogged. He died in the Queens Bench Prison.

TUTICORIN (S. India) from 1549 a Portuguese trading station, was taken in 1658 by the Dutch who used it (despite its open roadstead) as a port for their Ceylon trade. They ceded it to Britain in 1825.

TWEED or TWEEL. A woollen cloth originally made in Scotland and the Tweed Valley is a variety of twill and is said to derive its name from a London clerk in 1826 who wrote 'tweed' instead of 'tweel'.

TWEEDDALE. *See* HAY (TWEEDDALE).

TWEEDSMUIR, Ld. *See* BUCHAN.

TWM SHON CATTI (1530-1609) Cardiganshire landowner, antiquary and apocryphal Welsh Robin Hood.

TWNS. *See* GWESTFA.

TWO POWER NAVAL STANDARD was an alleged principle that the Royal Navy must be at least equal to the next two strongest navies together. Until 1904-5 it was theoretical, for the only major foreign navies belonged to France, Russia, Japan and the U.S.A. In 1904-5 Japan and Russia were fighting each other, and U.S.A.

and France had no reason to combine against Britain. By 1902 Germany was beginning her threatening naval expansion in earnest, and it was her navy alone which needed to be outgunned, while the others would combine with Britain under the *entente*.

TWO SICILIES. The official name of the Bourbon Kingdom of Naples and Sicily.

TWYSDEN or TWISDEN. Two brothers **(1) Sir Roger (1597-1679)** refused to pay ship-money and was a member of the Short Parliament, but subsequently opposed the proceedings of the Long Parliament and was summoned, imprisoned and sequestrated as a delinquent (1642-43). Released in 1650 he occupied himself in pioneering studies of mediaeval and church history (*see* SCRIPTURES). **(2) Sir Thomas (1602-83)** lawyer and M.P. in 1647 and 1660 though a royalist, became a Commonwealth serjeant-at-law, but was imprisoned for his outspoken defences in the courts. He was made a King's Bench judge at the Restoration.

TYBURN was one of two manors of St Marylebone, N.W. of the City of London, called after the Tybourne, a tributary of the Thames to the W. of Bond St. From the 12th cent. the Middlesex gallows stood near the stream but in the 16th cent. it was moved and replaced by a triangle supported on three legs at a place near the modern Marble Arch. Three felons could thus be hanged at once. Public executions on the eight annual hanging days were a tremendous popular spectacle for which spectators stands were erected and apprentices given a day off. They continued here until 1783.

TYBURN TICKET. Under an act of 1699, to discourage the then prevalent crimes of burglary, horse stealing, and shop lifting a man who successfully prosecuted for one of them, was entitled to life exemption from compulsory offices in the parish where it had been committed. These being time-consuming and unpaid, the exemption was valuable especially to small tradesmen. A ticket might be sold once and could fetch as much as £280 in 1818, when saving existing tickets, the act was repealed. *See* OFFICES, COMPULSORY.

TYLER, TEGHELER, TYGHLER or HELIER, Wat (?-1381) of unknown origin, led the Kentish rebels in the Peasants' Revolt of 1381. He emerged as their head probably at Maidstone on 7 June 1381 and organised widespread violence, the entry into Canterbury, the burning of the sheriff's records and the rebel march to Blackheath. He evidently possessed prestige and powers of leadership during this 70 mile march. On 12 June he tried unsuccessfully to open talks with Richard II. On 13th the Thanet rebels issued a proclamation in his name. On 14th he led the combined rebels of Kent and Essex in their demands for an end to serfdom and under his command the Tower was stormed and Sudbury and Hales murdered. At Smithfield on 15 June he presented extreme demands including the end of outlawry and of all lordship save the monarchy, and the disendowment of the Church. He became abusive, seemed to want to touch the King (perhaps he was drunk) and was cut down by William Walworth, the Mayor of London. Walworth had consistently urged strong action but the stroke seemed to have been opportunistic. With Tyler dead, the rebels broke up. He seems to have been a typical mob leader thrown into prominence by heated events rather than a champion of liberty, even of socialism, and little is known of him.

TYLOR, Sir Edward Burnett (1832-1917) published his seminal anthropological work *Primitive Culture* in 1871 and was the first Oxford Professor of Anthropology from 1896-1909.

TYNDALE or TINDAL, William (?1494-1536) (*see* BIBLE) being out of sympathy with the contemporary English church and suspected of heresy, left England in 1522 and matriculated at Wittenberg in 1524. Here he got to know Luther. He translated the N.T. in 1525, the Pentateuch by

1531 and had reached the book of Jonah when he was burned for heresy at Vilvorde near Brussels.

TYNE R. The lowest bridging point was 8 miles from the sea, and the river was navigable for a further 25 miles inland until the introduction of larger steam powered ships, which mostly could go no higher than Newcastle. The river flows above a coalfield whose outcrop workings were therefore easy to load into boats. Hence a primitive mining industry existed in the early middle ages and was exporting coal ('seacoal') to London from 13th cent.

TYNEDALE. *See* MARCHES, ANGLO-SCOTS-1-2.

TYNWALD COURT (related to *Thingvollr*, O.N. = Assembly Field) is the Manx midsummer assembly held publicly on a mound near St John's church, now on 5 July. Its purpose was to proclaim the laws (and sometimes to make them) and to settle taxes and disputes. It consisted of the King or Lord, now usually represented by the Lieutenant Governor, the Chief Priest, now the Bishop, the two Deemsters who were expected to know the laws by heart and the Keys, now corresponding to the House of Commons, of whom there were originally 16 representing Man, and 16 the Inner and Outer Hebrides. These were reduced to 24 when the Mull and Islay groups were lost, but remained at 24 after the loss of the other islands. Four are now elected by each sheading. In addition, the vicars and the captains of the parishes are present within the fence, and the rest of the freemen (i.e. the Manx nation) outside. Formerly an ancient midsummer fair was held there at the same time. Until 1690 Manx laws were not written down and until 1914 new laws did not come into force until read in English and Manx at Tynwald.

TYPEWRITER. One Henry Mill patented a writing machine, of which nothing is known in 1714. Early 19th cent. designers were concerned mainly to help the blind, the most successful being the **braille** system still in use. The Americans, Carlos GLIDDEN (1834-77) and Christopher Latham SHOLES (1819-90) were the first to develop a practical machine, which they licensed REMINGTON & SONS to manufacture in 1873. This had only capitals but the introduction of the **shift key** in 1880 made a compact double alphabetical machine feasible. Portables were on sale by 1893 and the first electric machines were in use in 1935. **Word Processors** came into the market in 1978.

TYPHOID. A sometimes fatal disease caused by a Salmonella bacillus most often spread by faecally contaminated water. It was not distinguished from typhus until after 1830. There was a serious epidemic among royal troops at Oxford in 1643 and a widespread one in 1690. The bacillus was identified in 1829 but the vector was not. The latter's nature was inferred negatively from the virtual disappearance of the disease between 1854-72 from Millbank prison whose water supply was artesian, and positively by matching the location of victims with particular water supplies and then identifying the manner of pollution, as in the twin outbreaks at Caterham and Redhill (Surrey) in 1879. Work of this type had already been done in Germany in 1872. All the same, English outbreaks killed 74,000 people between 1869-1877, after which the great improvements in town water supplies steadily reduced mortality to minor proportions. A vaccine was discovered in 1896 but the disease can easily be reintroduced by carriers. *See* EPIDEMICS, HUMAN; SPAS.

TYPHUS (HEAD PAINS) and TRENCH FEVER. (1) Typhus is a cold weather disease, dangerous when a population's resistance is weakened by famines or other calamities. Being louse borne, it breeds in squalor and dirt and propagates rapidly under overcrowding in, for example, slums, ships and military formations. It is apt to accompany the appearance of vermin or locusts. It was described at Salerno in 1083 and was endemic in Ireland from ancient times. As it can kill an *apparently* healthy adult in 12 hours, it is a creator of panic.

(2) English epidemics occurred in the period 1480-1504 if not before. There were continental outbreaks associated with famines especially in 1505-12 in Italy, Germany and Scandinavia and in association with wars in 1572-74 in much of western Europe. In the Thirty Years' War (1618-48) it killed tens of thousands. It spread to Britain during the Civil War (1640-49) and killed far more than the war itself. (*See* TIVERTON.)

(3) The disease returned to England in 1688 and thereafter (if not before) there was a distinct relationship between Irish conditions and prevalence in Britain. Irish epidemics spread to Britain in 1708-10, 1718-21, 1728-31. An Irish famine in 1741 was followed by a typhus disaster in both countries. On the other hand in the Seven Years' War (1756-63) the British Is. suffered little but Germany severely. The next important Irish-British epidemic was in 1770-72.

(4) The Irish famine and disorders of 1797 ushered in a long and disastrous era. The disease invaded England and Scotland and also exacerbated the Continental effects of the French wars. More especially, a Polish and Russian outbreak killed large numbers in the French invasion of 1812, and the survivors spread the disease all over Europe, where there were virulent epidemics in 1815. There were further Irish-British outbreaks in 1816-19, 1821-22, 1826-28 (mainly in Scotland) and 1836-42 when the English mortality alone was 92,000. The greatest disaster, however, came with the Irish **Potato Famine** of 1846, in the course of which about one million Irish were ill and the disease killed hundreds of thousands in Ireland and Britain. It strengthened the panic resolve of the Irish flight to America, killed many at sea in the process and caused serious outbreaks in the eastern seaboard of the U.S.A.

(5) Typhus was rife on both sides in the Crimean War, but the last major Irish epidemic was delayed until 1862-64.

(6) In World War I it virtually incapacitated the Serbian Army in 1914, and attacked with rising virulence, the increasingly lousy Western Front trench armies which also suffered from the very similar, and also louse-born **Trench Fever**. There were too, serious outbreaks on the Russian fronts which, in due course, developed into urban and village epidemics during the revolutionary civil wars. These repeated themselves on the Russian fronts in World War II but the allied invasion of Western Europe was free of the disease, because of the wholesale issue of D.D.T. impregnated clothes to the allied troops. *See* GAOL FEVER; EPIDEMICS, HUMAN.

TYRES, RUBBER. Pneumatic tyres were first patented in England in 1845 and revived by John Dunlop in 1888 for bicycles, which then ceased to be bone-shaking rarities. By 1896 they were becoming common on all types of vehicles and facilitated high speeds. *See* WESTWOOD.

TYRANNY is rule by a ruler in his own interest against the consent of his subjects.

TYRCONNEL, Richard, E. of (1630-91). *See* TALBOT.

TYRCONNEL or TIRCONAILL (Irish = Connel's Land) now Donegal. Anciently a central part of the kingdom of Ailech, it was divided early from TIREOGHAINT (TYRONE) and was ruled by the O'DONNELLS. The town of Donegal ('the Foreigners' Fort') was probably of Norse origin, but by 11th cent. it was in the hands of the O'Donnells. Owing to its remoteness Tyrconnell escaped Norman subjugation and in 14th cent. the O'Donnells had extended their power to most of Fermanagh and Sligo. They supported Hugh O'Neill under Elizabeth I; but the area was shired in 1585 and Rory O'Neill was created 1st E. of Tyrconnell in 1604. After the Flight of the Earls in 1607, the county was included in the Plantation of Ulster.

TYROL, TIROL (Austria). Its intensely stubborn people resisted Franco-Bavarian rule from 1805-10 when their hero Andreas **Hofer** was shot at Mantua. Tyrol was returned to Austria in 1815. In 1914 Italy claimed the southern part of the Brenner as her price for supporting the central powers, but Austria offered only the Italian speaking Trentino. By the secret T. of London (1915) the allies accepted her extreme demands and these were granted by the T. of St. Germain (1919). The annexation was resented by Austrians and Germans as well as Tyrolese especially when the Italians began to suppress local customs and the German language. Hatred of Italian rule was a cause of difficulty between Germany and Italy after 1937 and by a T. of 1939 the Tyrolese were given the chance to migrate to Germany, which about 25% did. Italy was permitted to keep the area after World War II, but in 1947 a special regime was set up for the German speaking areas, and many migrants returned.

TYRONE, Co. (Ulster) (*Tir Eoghan* = poss. Euan's land). A county of fertile river valleys and barren heaths originally ruled by the O'Neills from Tullahogue near Dungannon. Eoghan, traditionally was a son of the eponymous Niall of the Nine Hostages. O'Neill power remained in possession until the Flight of the Earls (1607) when the area was incorporated in the Plantations of Ulster and was heavily colonised by Scots.

TYRONE, O'Neill, E. of. *See* ELIZABETH 1-26,28 *et seq;* O'NEILL.

TYRRELL, Sir James (?-1502) said to be descended from Walter Tirel, William II's possible assassin, was an active Yorkist. He was knighted after the B. of Tewkesbury and fought for Edward IV against the Scots. It is possible that he murdered the Princes in the Tower on Richard III's instructions in 1483 but in 1486 he received two pardons from Henry VII (who benefited from the two murders) and he remained in court favour until 1494. Some later Yorkist activities led in 1502 to his execution at which he is said to have confessed to the murders.

TYRWHITT, Sir Reginald Yorke Bt. (1870-1951) began as a commander of torpedo craft in 1896 and by 1914 was Commodore of all Destroyer flotillas and commanded the light Harwich force throughout World War I. He planned, with Keyes, the successful Heligoland Bight action (28 Aug. 1914) and covered the Cuxhaven air raid on 25 Dec. He also played an important part in the B. of the Dogger Bank (Jan. 1915). He was an influential supporter of naval aviation.

U

UBANGI-SHARI. *See* EQUATORIAL (EX-FRENCH) AFRICA.

UBI PERICULUM MAIUS (Lat = The situation of the main danger) (1274), decree of the Second Council of Lyons regulating Papal elections.

U-BOAT (Ger. *Unterseeboot* = submarine). *See* COMMERCE PROTECTION; NAVAL B-2-4, C; SUBMARINES.

UCHELWYR. See WELSH LAW-1.

UDAIPUR. *See* MEWAR.

UDAL or ODAL. A quasi-allodial land tenure brought to the Orkney and Shetland Is. by 9th cent. Vikings. An odal comprises a farmstead and common rights and may be let. It is perpetual and, being absolute is subject to no homage or service save for *skat* (a fixed payment) and an obligation to attend the *Thing* and the Host, neither of which now exist. Not surprisingly, Kings, the Earls and the Bishops disfavoured it and from the 15th cent. took available opportunities to feudalise odals by charter. Hence feudal and odal properties co-exist in the islands.

UDALL or UVEDALE (1) John (?1560-92), a puritan and contributor to the Marprelate tracts, was in 1590 convicted of seditious libel in connection with puritan propaganda whose authorship he refused to deny. Sentence was not carried out and he was released in 1592. His son (2) Ephraim (?-1647) was a royalist divine much persecuted by London puritans.

UDALL or UVEDALE, Nicholas (1505-56). *See* UVEDALE.

UFFINGTON. *See* HILL FIGURES.

UFFORD. *See* OFFORD.

UFFORD (1) Robert (?-1298), was with Edward I on crusade and between 1276 and 1281 was Justice in Ireland and built Roscommon Castle. Of his grandsons (2) Robert (1298-1369), 1st Ld. UFFORD (1322) and 1st E. of SUFFOLK (1337), was employed by Mortimer and Q. Isabel on a variety of local business giving him much land and the control of castles and garrisons in E. Anglia. He was thus a powerful ally of Salisbury when the latter seized Mortimer at Nottingham in 1331. There after he was one of Edward III's most trusted officers. He took a leading part in the invasion of Brittany in 1342 and fought at Crécy (1346). He was also admiral in the Channel and defeated the Spaniards off Winchilsea in 1350. In 1355 he went with the Black Prince to Aquitaine and bore the brunt of the fighting at the B. of Poitiers (1356). In 1359 he was in Champagne. Thereafter he slowly retired. His brother (3) Sir Ralph (?-1346), had married the daughter of Henry of Lancaster and was a vigorous lord justice in Ireland from 1344. (4) William (?1339-82), also 1st Ld. UFFORD (1364), and 2nd E. served in France from 1370 to 1375 under Warwick, Edward III and John of Gaunt. In 1376, however, he opposed Gaunt in the Good Parliament and so acquired unwanted popularity, for at the Peasants' rising in 1381 they attempted to kidnap him and make him their leader. He escaped and took part in their suppression. In the quarrel between Gaunt and Northumberland in 1382 he acted as surety for the latter and in the subsequent Parliament acted as spokesman in the Lords for the Commons.

UGANDA (1) had by the 16th cent., three main kingdoms viz: BUNYORO the most powerful, BUGANDA and ANKOLE. When Arab slavers arrived in 1844, Bunyoro was in decline and in 1862 the explorers Speke and Grant found that Mutesa I (r. 1856-84) Kabaka of Buganda was the greatest local ruler. In 1869 the throne of Bunyoro fell vacant and most of it was conquered by the Kabarega, who were warlike immigrants, assisted by the Sudanese slavers. In the 1870s the area was a target for Egyptian ambitions, but fortunately the principal Egyptian officer was Charles Gordon and Mutesa persuaded him to retire. Christian missionaries appeared in 1875. Mutesa was soon hostile both to them and to the Moslem *Ulema,* because they seemed to detract from loyalty to him. His weaker successor, Mwanga thought the same. Mwanga, moreover, was homosexually profligate, and there was a conflict in 1885-7 when he beheaded or burned 24 pages and officials who had refused him favours. This outrage to the missionary ethic permanently damaged his reputation. In the next 16 years Mwanga and his brothers Kiwewa and Kalema fought civil wars in which religious allegiances were directly or indirectly involved.

(2) The Imperial British East Africa Co., was chartered in 1890, and Capt. Lugard appeared in Dec. on its behalf and induced Mwanga to allow the Co. to keep order. In fact he did not have the resources, and a further civil war between so-called Anglicans and R. Catholics ended in 1892 in a shaky partition between them. Thereupon the Rosebery Govt. sent Sir Gerald Portal to investigate. He proclaimed a provisional protectorate in Mar. 1893 and this was converted into a formal protectorate over Buganda in June 1894. This ended the Co's rights, but Moslem discontent resulted in a war with and proclamation of a protectorate over Bunyoro in June 1896. In 1897 Mwanga tried to repudiate Portal's treaty and after defeat in battle, fled to German E. Africa and was replaced by his infant son Daudi Chwa under a regency. He returned during a Sudanese mutiny, and in 1899 was taken and deported to the Seychelles Is.

(3) By now a chasm in Ugandan history was opening. Between 1898 and 1908 a fearful visitation of Trypanosomiasis (q.v.) carried off 60% of the people and virtually closed L. Victoria to navigation. When Sir Harry Johnstone was sent to establish a govt. he was dealing with enfeebled and still declining nations. In Mar. 1900 he concluded an agreement with the regency and the chiefs, and later with the chiefs of Toro and Ankole, to set up a British administration which could make laws other than on subjects specified in the agreement; that the Kabaka and other Kings would rule their people under the agreement, and that the sub-chiefs would become owners of about half the land instead of being tenants of their Kings. A railway had rapidly to be built from the coast. It reached L. Victoria by 1902, and by 1914 cotton was being exported. Recovery, confused by two World Wars, was slow. The effect of the British geographical approach was that much of it was concentrated in the south, populated by Bantu-speaking Ganda, the largest national group. On the other hand the armed services, who had to be paid, were mostly recruited in the Niotic speaking, sometimes Moslem north. This had serious effects in the 1960s.

(4) In 1961 Uganda became a federation with internal self-govt. Full independence followed in 1962 and in 1967 it became, as a result of a quasi-coup, a presidential republic in the British Commonwealth, under Milton Obote who was a northerner. He was overthrown by an army coup in 1971 and there ensued chaotic and bloody years under Idi Amin. In 1979 exiles with Tanzanian troops overthrew him and thereafter the country was under Tanzanian occupation while puppet presidents came and went. In 1980, however, general elections were held and Milton Obote was restored. *See* AMIN, IDI; GLADSTONE'S FOURTH GOVT.

UGANDA or KENYA RAILWAY, from the seaport of Mombasa *via* Nairobi and Nakuru to the lakeport of Kismayu, was built between 1896 and 1903. It opened the Kenyan Rift Valley to development and, with lake shipping to Entebbe (Port Alice) and Kampala, gave Uganda access to the ocean. *See* TRYPANOSOMIASIS.

UHLAN (Pol.). A Polish and, until 1918, a Prussian lancer.

UHTRED or UCHTRED. *s.* of WALTHEOF. *See* DURHAM-1; NORTHUMBRIA, EARLDOM OF.

UI equivalent of O' in old Irish names.

UIST, NORTH AND SOUTH. *See* HEBRIDES.

***UITLANDERS* (S.A. Dutch = foreigners).** The non-Boer, mainly British, residents in the Boer republics of the Orange Free State and the Transvaal (*see* JAMESON RAID). Their **Petition** (Jan-Mar. 1899) by some 21,000 Uitlanders in the Transvaal to Q. Victoria, requested British intervention to cure the injustices inflicted by Paul Kruger's Govt. *See* SALISBURY'S THIRD GOVT-11.

UJIJI. *See* TANGANYIKA.

UKRAINE (Russ: March), or **LITTLE RUSSIA,** until 1640 was a thinly settled steppe between Muscovy, Poland and Crimean Tartary, divided by the R. Dnieper into Right Bank (Polish, with Polish landowners) and Left Bank (more Russian) ungoverned areas containing auto-nomous Cossack communities which attracted runaway serfs. A Right Bank rebellion against the Poles soon involved Russia, and the whole area became a theatre of intermittent war, between the Poles, the Russians and the Tartars. Catherine the Great took Oczakov in 1788 and ousted Tartar and Turkish rights in the T. of JASSY (1792). She ousted Polish rights in the Second Polish Partition (1793).

The Ukraine was now free to develop its rich soil for agriculture and its immense untapped mineral resources in peace. In the 19th cent., it became the main supplier of cereals, coal and iron to the Russian Empire (and later the U.S.S.R.) and a considerable exporter of them. The population multiplied, cities grew and the Black Sea ports developed and were much frequented by British tramp shipping. This emphasised the mutual importance of the Straits to the British and Ukrainian economies. It also gave rise to separatist movements because the Russian (and also the USSR) govts., manipulated tariffs and communications to exploit Ukrainian resources. Separatist agitations were violently suppressed in 1905; by artificially induced famine in 1929-30 and again violently in 1946. The devastation caused by the Chernobyl nuclear explosion (Apr. 1986) gave a further fillip to separatism since the installations were U.S.S.R. managed. The break-up of the U.S.S.R. after June 1990 led to a lengthy dispute with the Russian Federated Republic over the control of the naval ports and the ownership of the Black Sea fleet.

ULCERA SYRIACA. *See* DIPHTHERIA.

ULEMA or ULAMA. Islam having no priesthood, Moslem lawyers (MUFTI) and theologians (in Iran AYATOLLAHS) are collectively known as Ulema, and often exert great power. In the Ottoman Empire the Ulema was headed by the Sheikh-ul-Islam, a mufti, whose *fetva* (formal opinion) carried great weight. He could, e.g. pronounce whether a particular ruler might lawfully be deposed. In Iran the same authority to issue *fetvas* was used to condemn the monarchy and to encourage the murder of the British author Salman Rushdie. A *fetva,* being a formal and considered statement of religious truth, cannot be changed or recalled.

ULFKELL (ULFKETEL or ULFCYTEL) SNILLING (?-1016), E. of the E. Angles paid a composition to K. Sweyn in 1004, but fought the Danes determinedly at Thetford in 1010, and fell fighting for Edmund Ironside at Assendun.

ULIDIA. *See* ULSTER.

ULLSWATER, Vist. *See* LOWTHER.

ULNAGE, AULNAGE, was inspection of cloth for quality and measure and levy of a tax on it.

ULSTER, ULADH or ULIDIA, kingdom or province comprising anciently Ireland N. of a line along the Boyne to the mouth of the Erne. Uladh was the part east of Lough Neagh. It had its own dynasty until the mid-13th cent. The metropolitical see was at Armagh. The principal clans were the O'Connell, the immigrant McDonnell (*see* DALRIADA) and the O'Neill, reckoned the chief in precedence of all Ireland. Dalriada was long separate from the rest and when Meath disappeared, the areas of

Monaghan and Cavan were added. These two and Donegal were detached when the rest became Northern Ireland.

ULSTER COVENANT. Properly **SOLEMN LEAGUE AND COVENANT (Sept. 1912),** drawn up by Carson, was signed by 200,000 protestant Ulstermen, and a similar covenant of association was signed by 200,000 women. The main document was signed with theatrical publicity in Belfast Cathedral, the first four signatories being Carson himself, the M. of Londonderry, the Anglican Bp. of Down and Connor, and the Moderator of the Presbyterian Assembly. It pledged the signatories "to stand by one another in using all means which may be found necessary to defeat the present conspiracy to set up a Home Rule Parliament, and in event of such a Parliament being forced upon us we further solemnly pledge ourselves to refuse to recognise its authority".

ULSTER CUSTOM of land holding represented a survival from the conditions imposed by James I in the Planta-tion of Ulster. These were that the Undertakers were forbidden to let lands at uncertain rents or for less than 21 years or three lives, and the Crown reserved a right of resumption if the conditions were broken. The conditions were broken and the Crown was generally unable to enforce its rights, but because of the Scottish Presbyterian background and the mutual feeling which this created, understandings grew up between landlords and tenants, which varied as between estates, but had five leading features: **(1)** Yearly tenants remained undisturbed so long as they paid their rent and behaved; **(2)** The landlord, correctively, might periodically raise the rent to give him a fair participation in the increased value of the land, but not by so much as to take the tenants share of it; **(3)** Yearly tenants might sell their interest but **(4)** the landlord had to be consulted about the identity of the purchaser and **(5)** if the landlord took the land for himself he paid fair compensation for the tenant right.

The custom was a model for the early Irish land agitations, and bills to enforce point **(5)** were introduced, mostly by Irish landlords, and thrown out of parliament in 1853, 1854, 1855, 1856 and 1858. The Irish Landlord and Tenant Act, 1860, applied only to future improve-ments. The Act of 1870 enforced the custom in Ulster and any like custom elsewhere in Ireland. It also entitled a tenant to damages for eviction and provided state loans (repayable by 35 year annuity) to tenants who wanted to buy their holdings.

ULSTER CYCLE. A group of mostly sanguinary oral traditions, recorded between 8th and 11th cents., of court and warrior life in Ulster and Connaught in pre-Christian times. It centres on the lives of K. Conor or Conchobar in Ulster, his nephew the hero Cuchulainn, and of Q. Maeve of the rival court of Connaught.

ULSTER DEFENCE ASSN. The re-emergence of Irish Republican Army terrorism and the rise of the Civil Rights Association in the 1960s provoked the formation of local protestant Defence Assns. and then of the Ulster Defence Assn. which co-ordinated them. They were paramilitary.

ULSTER, EARLDOM, centred on Downpatrick, was roughly conterminous with the modern counties of Antrim, Down, and Louth. The area was originally subdued by John de Courci between 1177 and 1180, but he was ejected by K. John, who gave it to HUGH DE LACY (?-?1242) and erected it into the earldom. It escheated at Hugh's death, and was regranted in 1263 to WALTER DE BURGH, and remained in his family until the death in 1333 of his grandson WILLIAM. William's daughter ELIZABETH (1332-63) had married Edward III's son LIONEL of CLARENCE who took the earldom in right of his wife. Through them it descended to Edward D. of York, and merged with the crown on his accession as Edward IV in 1461. The title (but not the lands) has since been occasionally borne by princes.

ULSTER UNIONIST PARTY was descended from Carson's signatories of the Ulster Covenant and his Ulster Volunteers. It dominated the Ulster Parliament and local authorities from 1921 to 1970 and supported the Tories at Westminster. Irish Republican Army terrorism restarted in the mid-1950s and the leader of the Ulster Unionists (Terence O'Neill) sought accommodation with the Ulster R. Catholics. This provoked the formation of Ian Paisley's Democratic Unionists, who doubted R. Catholic good faith and thought that no relationship should be entertained with them as long as they connived at terrorism. The two parties have tended to drift together since 1985.

ULSTER VOLUNTEERS or ULSTER VOLUNTEER FORCE (U.V.F.) was raised and armed by Sir Edw. Carson in 1912 to back the Ulster Covenant (q.v.). The name was appropriated in 1966 by a protestant terrorist group opposed to the I.R.A. and nearly as murderous. It was instantly proscribed under the Prevention of Terrorism Act and was still proscribed in 1996.

ULSTER WORKERS COUNCIL was an organisation of protestant trade unionists which, particularly in 1974, organised strikes against efforts to reduce tension in Ulster by Anglo-Irish governmental co-operation.

ULTAN, St. *See* MISSIONS TO EUROPE.

ULTRA. English code word for ENIGMA (q.v.).

ULTRA-MONTANISTS (Lat. = beyond the Alps). (1). The continental politicians who supported the temporal claims of the Papacy. Hence any French right wing extremist. **(2)**. More generally, those who accept the doctrine that Papal supremacy in religious matters supersedes the rights of the state. A 19th cent. word conveying a very old idea. *See* UNAM SANCTAM.

ULTRAS. The extreme right wing Tories in 1820 to 1850.

ULTRA VIRES (Lat = beyond the powers). This important sub-constitutional doctrine lays down that where a person (or corporate body) has powers conferred by statute, its functions are confined to those powers. Even a properly conferred power, if exercised for a purpose not contemplated by the statute is unlawful. Action by way of injunction or other process may be taken by an aggrieved person to prevent or reverse an *ultra vires* act, and those who authorise it can be made to repay any money spent in carrying it through and an *ultra vires* order or bylaw can be disobeyed.

In theory the rule applies to all statutory bodies including limited companies, local authorities, and even Mins. In practice large loopholes have been created in recent times. Judicial interpretation since 1922 has widened the scope of company directors' powers. Since 1972 local authorities have been empowered to spend a limited amount on things which would otherwise be *ultra vires,* and a person who deliberately breaks a bylaw or statutory instrument which he believes to be *ultra vires,* has to set up his case as a defence to a prosecution. *See also* CHARTER.

UMAIYIDS. *See* CALIPHATE.

UMBRELLAS (1) are an ancient emblem of the very highest rank. At the coronation of Elizabeth II, the Queen of Tonga would not, despite the rain, put hers up in the vicinity of the Queen of Great Britain. **(2)** As a protection against English rain, it is mentioned in 1620. The steel-ribbed, easily raised umbrella appeared in 1840 and, when tightly rolled, soon became a symbol of English-ness second only to the bowler hat.

UMFREVILLE FAMILY, of Norman origin, was established in Redesdale (Northumberland) by the mid 13th cent. **(1) Gilbert (fl. 1227-45)** married the heiress of the E. of Angus and his son **(2) Gilbert (c. 1244-1307)**, an erstwhile supporter of Simon de Montfort, was recognised as E. of Angus in 1267. He was Gov. of Dundee, Forfar and Angus in 1291, but the Scottish lands were lost after the B. of Bannockbum (1314). **(3) Gilbert (1310-81)** tried to recover them by force when he joined Edward Balliol's 'Disinherited' in 1332, but Umfreville

power remained based in N. England. Another **(4) Gilbert (1390-1421)** was an important commander of Lancastrian armies in 1415 and 1417. He helped to negotiate the T. of Troyes and was made a Marshal of France (1421), but was killed with Thomas of Clarence at the B. of Baugé in the same year. Sometimes called the E. of KYME from one of his Lincolnshire estates. The family became extinct in 1436.

UNAM SANCTAM (Lat = one Holy) (1302). This bull by Boniface VIII proclaimed that there was One church, outside which there was neither salvation nor remission of sins, that the Pope was its head and that to reject his authority was to cease to be a member of the church. The spiritual and temporal swords were alike in the hands of the church, but the temporal sword was delegated to the civil powers solely to be wielded under ecclesiastical direction, for which the church was responsible to God alone. It ended with the statement that it was necessary to salvation for every human creature to be subject to the Supreme Pontiff. The bull, though provoked by a quarrel with Philip IV of France, represented the extreme statement of papal claims.

UNCONSTITUTIONAL means in U.S. law any action or law which infringes the terms of the written constitution (possessed by every state of the union as well as the Union itself), and is therefore void. The Supreme Court has the power to pass judgment in such cases, and can, within the wording of the constitution, set aside the intentions of the legislature or the acts of the Executive. No such legal doctrine has ever existed in Britain (*see, however,* COKE) where the term applies to activities deemed in a **political** sense to be contrary to the spirit of the constitution as interpreted at any given moment, and for which the remedy is political not judicial e.g. the threat by the House of Lords to interfere with the budget in 1909 resulted in general elections leading to the reduction of its powers by the Parliament Act. If the elections had brought in the opposition, the Act would not have been passed. Conversely the rule that public expenditure can be authorised only by a provision introduced in the Commons is sometimes so inconvenient that the Commons' privilege is waived or deliberately circumvented with Commons' agreement.

UNDERGROUND (Amer: Subway). The first underground railways in the world were the London lines from Paddington to Farringdon, opened in 1863, and from Gloucester Road to Westminster in 1868. These and their extensions were in covered cuttings. The first tube or tunnel line in London (1890) ran from the City to Stockwell and was the first to be electrified, but steam traction using special smoke-consuming engines continued on some lines till 1929. In 1900 the Central line was opened. These were all operated by different companies, some of which were amalgamated into the Underground Electric Co., which opened the Baker Street to Waterloo (Bakerloo), the Northern, the Piccadilly and Brompton lines in 1906, and the Charing Cross to Hampstead in 1907. In 1910 these were united into the London Electric Co., which methodically acquired the others and the 'bus cos. The lines converted a hitherto minor commuter habit into vast daily tidal movements which, in their turn, led to further outward extensions. The haphazard layout set the residential and working pattern of London until World War II. The first new underground, the Victoria Line, was begun across central London in 1962, and was operating ten years later.

UNDERTAKER. (1) Statutory is a person, or more usually a company, who *undertakes* for profit to provide a public service (e.g. water) under the authority of an Act of Parliament. This confers privileges and usually imposes duties and often dividend limitation. When the field of public provision was invaded by the nationalisations after World War II, the number of statutory undertakers declined. The privatisations of the Thatcher govts. (1978 onwards) increased them but without obligations to limit dividends.

(2) In **Ireland** the term was used of those (e.g. John Ponsonby 1713-87) who occupied locally influential positions and could be relied upon to get the British govt's. policies carried through in the administration or as the case might require, in the Irish parliament, usually by jobbery.

UNEMPLOYMENT (*see also* POOR LAW), in an industrial society is a condition in which people are willing to work but cannot find jobs. The figures became certainly known (rather than guessed) only with the appearance of centralised systems of relief or insurance. It seems that between 1870 and 1914 the average British percentage was 21%; in 1921, 13%; in 1931, 21%; in 1932, with 2,947,000 unemployed it reached 22%. In 1941 (wartime) it had fallen to 6½% and from 1946 to 1964 the average was below 2%. It then rose irregularly but persistently with the introduction of electronics, computerisation, and interest manipulation to a number approximating to that of 1932. The figures are hard to calculate because of problems of definition arising from a shift towards part-time employment, and the exclusion from the unemployment figures of certain retrainees. Statisticians of equal respectability have arrived at totals for 1990 between 250,000 above and below 3M.

UNEMPLOYMENT INSURANCE was first established compulsorily by the National Insurance Act, 1911, in conjunction with a system of labour exchanges. It applied only in certain employments and covered about 4M people. Administration, originally by the Board of Trade, was transferred to the Min. of Labour in 1917. The Unemployment Insurance Act, 1920, was, with some exceptions, of general application and increased the numbers insured to 12M. Unemployment brought legislation for uncovenanted benefit, but by 1927 the fund was heavily in debt. The Blainsborough Committee recommended adding persons between 18 and 21 and abolishing uncovenanted benefit. This was done by the Act of 1927. Meantime mass unemployment continued to deplete the fund; by 1931 payments out were four times payments in: the administration was made more stringent whereupon applications for outdoor relief under the Poor Law rapidly increased. The Guardians were then employed to make transitional payments charged to the Exchequer and subject to a means test. As a result of a political outcry the Unemployment Assistance Act, 1934, set up a national Board to administer supplementary benefits. The post World War II Beveridge report was enacted as the National Insurance Act, 1946. It covered all persons between 16 and 65 employed under a contract. The National Assistance Act, 1948, extended the Act of 1934.

UNGAVA. *See* LABRADOR.

UNICORN. (1) A mythical animal; two support the Scots royal arms, and one those of the U.K. **(2)** A Scots gold coin worth 18s. Scots, current in the 15th and 16th cents.

UNIFORMITY, ACTS OF. 1549, 1552, 1558, and 1662. Each of these prescribed a slightly differing book of Common Prayer, and enjoined parsons, under penalty, to use it and to perform certain duties regularly. The present Book is a schedule to the Act of 1662. An Act of 1872 permitted other services subject to conditions and with the sanction of the bishop. *See* ANGLICANISM-5; ELIZABETH-4; CHARLES II-8 TO 9; CLARENDON "CODE" 1661-5.

UNIGENITUS. There were two papal documents of this name. **(1)** Clement VI's bull of 1343 approved the scholastic doctrine that indulgences depended upon the Pope's dispensation of the accumulated merits of the church. **(2)** Clement IX's constitution of 1713 condemned 101 Jansenist propositions, some already condemned in previous pronouncements.

UNION, ACT OF (Ireland) 1800, recited eight Articles viz: **I.** Great Britain to be united into a single Kingdom on 1st

Jan. 1801. **II.** The Succession to the crown to remain unaltered. **III.** The United Kingdom to be represented in one parliament. **IV.** Ireland to be represented in parliament by four bishops by rotation of sessions, 28 peers elected for life by the Irish peers, and 100 M.P.s. The method of returning these representatives to be settled by an Act of the Irish Parliament to be passed before the union. The Crown to have power to create only one Irish peerage for every three peerages extinguished until the number is reduced to 100 when one peerage may be created for every one extinguished. **V.** The Churches of England and Ireland to be united. **VI.** Subject to a schedule of countervailing duties and drawbacks, trade between the two countries to be free without prohibitions or bounties. **VII.** The existing public debts of the two kingdoms to be managed separately, but new debt to be managed as a single fund. **VIII.** Existing law to remain, until altered by act of the united parliament.

The Act then recites the Irish Act mentioned in Article III and proceeds to enact it and the articles in England.

UNION, ACTS OF (Wales) 1536 and 1543. Mainly, the 1536 Act suppressed the local marcher jurisdictions. Except for Cemaes (or Kemes), they were annexed either to their surrounding, newly created, Welsh counties (Monmouth, Brecon, Radnor, Montgomery, Denbigh, Glamorgan, Carmarthen, Pembroke and Merioneth) or to the English counties of Shropshire, Hereford and Gloucester. Monmouthshire was transferred to England. The normal organisations for English shires were set up, together with a special court of Great Sessions which acted as assizes twice a year in each county. There was provision for representation in Parliament. The county towns were named, but division into hundreds was left to a future royal commission. The Lords Marcher were not deprived of their property nor of their manorial or customary rights.

The Act of 1543 confirmed the hundredal division, and the authority of the Council of Wales and the Marches, but recited that many of the lordships had since 1536 fallen to the Crown by suppression of monasteries, purchase or attainder. It otherwise completed the scheme of English institutions partially created in 1536. Cemaes continued in nominal existence into modern times.

UNION, ANGLO-SCOTTISH – SCOTTISH ATTITUDES. (1) The mere personal union of the Crowns was workable only if the Crown pursued a co-ordinated policy for both countries. Once it had to focus the views of two unpredictable parliaments the choice lay between parliamentary union and national separation. William III needed English support for the Dutch. He was mainly interested in Scotland to prevent the Jacobites from distracting the English.

(2) The Revolution Settlements had opponents. William, used to the authoritarianism of war, himself ignored parts of the Scottish Claim of Right. He recalled the Convention of Estates as a parliament nine times. He imposed a new Oath of Allegiance and dissolved the General Assembly without fixing a date for the reassembly. He may have been necessary, but he was disliked. The Episcopalians resented the re-establishment of Presbyterianism; the Cameronians the failure to re-enact the Covenant, and there were disappointed politicians who talked patriotism. The strength of Jacobitism was shown when Dundee gathered the R. Catholic clans and routed the Williamites at Killiecrankie. Luckily for William he was killed. These groups had different objectives and tended to cancel each other out, but other events began to unite Scottish discontents. In 1692 the Glencoe affair enraged many who otherwise favoured the govt. The French war was contrary to Scots tradition, and the high Scots casualties, especially at the B. of Steenkerk, were offensive to that tradition. There was the terrible failure of the Darien Scheme, which was

blamed with at least partial justification on the English; and, finally, the English settled the Crown on the Hanoverians without any reference to the Scots at all.

(3) The War of the Spanish Succession brought these strands together. Louis XIV's recognition of the Old Pretender as James III and VIII infuriated the English but it appealed to the Scots. Scotland as a separate state might become a danger to the English war effort even if the predominant Presbyterians mistrusted French Caesaro-Papalism.

UNION-CASTLE LINE. The Union (shipping) Line was founded in 1853 and operated progressively extended mail services to S. Africa from 1857. The Castle Line, founded in 1862, began to compete for the same business in 1872 and shared the mail contract from 1876. They amalgamated in 1900. In 1956 the Clan Line came in and the group was acquired by the British and Commonwealth Shipping Co.

UNIONIST. (1) In Britain, those who advocated the continuance of the parliamentary union of Britain and Ireland. They were formed from a coalition of Tories and Liberal Unionists in 1886, and the Tory Party later called itself both conservative and unionist, because some conservative politicians felt that they continued to belong to a liberal if unionist tradition. After the creation of Eire, unionism remained significant in relation to the six counties of Ulster. When the Irish Republican Army (I.R.A.) launched terrorism on a large scale in the 1960s, the term, in association with 'conservative' indicated a commitment not to give way to republican pretensions. **(2)** In the U.S.A., the opponents of Secession, especially before the civil war of 1861-5.

UNION JACK. *See* FLAGS, NATIONAL.

UNION OF THE CROWNS (1603) – IMMEDIATE EFFECTS. These were not unimportant. **(1)** The Border laws and march organisations disappeared (*see* MARCHES, SCOTTISH) with large savings in costs and facilitation of local traffic and trade. **(2)** A single allegiance for those born after the Union as a result of *Calvin's Case* 1607 (*The Case of the Postnati*). This eventually enabled all English and Scots to own property in each other's country. **(3)** The two countries shared a common foreign policy. As Scotland was at peace with Spain but England at war, an Anglo-Spanish peace quickly followed. **(4)** Commissioners to negotiate a full union were appointed by both sides but the negotiations broke down on the obdurate Caledonophobia of the English Commons. **(5)** James VI and I was at first well received in England but his accent and conceit grated, and the many Scots who followed him were not liked. *See* SCOTLAND, POST 1603 entries and UNION, ANGLO-SCOTTISH-SCOTTISH ATTITUDES and UNION TREATY AND ACTS OF (SCOTLAND) 1707.

UNIONS of parishes for Poor Law purposes were effected under an Act of 1834. Each parish continued to defray the cost of its own poor but they jointly elected a Board of Guardians which then provided a workhouse at their joint expense. The poor with rare exceptions had to go into the workhouse for relief, and workhouse conditions were spartan and sometimes cruel to deter persons from becoming a charge on the rates. The word 'Union' came to mean 'workhouse' and originated the 'Union Streets' in many towns.

UNION, TREATY AND ACTS OF (SCOTLAND) 1707 provided as follows: **(1)** Scotland and England were to be united as Great Britain with a common monarchy, flag, coinage and Great Seal. The two parliaments ceased to exist and were replaced by a new Parliament of Great Britain.

(2) The new parliament was composed of the existing 190 English peers and 513 M.P.s plus 16 Scots peers representing the 154-strong Scots peerage and 45 Scots M.P.s. These proportions were based both on population (about 5:1) and taxable capacity (about 36:1). New Scots peerages were not to be created but before the Union came into force the manner of election was to be settled by a Scottish Act forming part of the Treaty. By this the 16 peers should for each parliament be openly elected from and by the Scots peers but the arrangements for the M.P.s were less straightforward. 30 were allotted to the shires and 15 to the royal burghs. Six smaller shires were paired to send one member alternately. Edinburgh elected one, the other 65 royal burghs were formed into 9 groups of five and 5 groups of four sending one each. The burghs each elected a single delegate to vote on its behalf. Non-royal burghs were not represented, though some (e.g. Paisley) were larger than some royal burghs, and the equal representative vote put large royal burghs (e.g. Glasgow) on a level with small ones. By 1800 the population of Glasgow was 70 times that of Dumbarton.

(3) The two parliaments were to pass Acts for securing the respective churches of the two countries and these were to form part of the Treaty.

(4) The Scots Privy Council and Court of Exchequer were to remain until the new Parliament should otherwise decide. The Privy Council was in fact abolished in 1708.

(5) Scotland was to retain the noble heritable jurisdictions and burgh privileges, and her own law and judicature free of any appeal to any court sitting in Westminster Hall. In 1710, in *Greenshield's Case* it was held that this did not prevent appeals to the House of Lords which, of course, never sits in Westminster Hall and which, until nearly two centuries later, contained no Scots lawyers.

(6) For financial arrangements *see* EQUIVALENT.

UNITARIANS reject the doctrines of the divinity of Chnst and of the Trinity, and (like Mohammedans) favour a single divine personality. This post-Reformation continental sect established its first English conventicle under John Biddle (1615-66) only in 1652, and until 1773 there was still only one. In the 18th cent. those of Unitarian views were widely accepted in other dissenting, particularly Presbyterian, congregations. In 1773 Theophilus Lindsey (1723-1808) seceded from the Church of England, founded the Unitarian denomination as such, and in 1774 opened the Essex chapel in London. The Penal Acts applied to Unitarians until 1813. There were prolonged disputes about chapel endowments. These were settled in the Non-conformist Chapels Act, 1844, which permitted Unitarians to keep chapels founded under open trusts, if they could prove 25 years usage according to their beliefs.

UNIT, in military parlance, is a force capable of carrying out its specialist function by itself: in the Infantry this is a battalion, in cavalry, artillery or tanks a regiment, but some specialised units are much smaller.

UNITE. *See* COINAGE-15.

UNITED AFRICAN CO. *See* ROYAL NIGER CO.

UNITED ARAB REPUBLIC (U.A.R.). The short lived nominal union between Egypt and Syria.

UNITED BRITONS, ENGLISHMEN, SCOTSMEN were respectively small organisations which tried to model themselves upon the United Irishmen and exploit the opportunities of the French Revolutionary Wars for radical objectives. Having no true nationalist base they attracted little support, though they alarmed the govt. enough to include them in the statutory suppression of the United Irishmen and the Corresponding Societies in July 1799.

UNITED EMPIRE LOYALISTS were Americans who preferred British allegiance to citizenship of the U.S.A. when that country's independence had been recognised by the T. of Paris (1783). There had been a steady migration to Canada and the Bahamas ever since the Declaration of Independence (1776). After the treaty 40,000 souls moved. About 10,000 settled in Quebec. The settlement in Nova Scotia led to the erection of part of that colony into the colony of New Brunswick (1784); that into the territories west of Quebec into the creation of the colony of Upper Canada (later Ontario), in 1791. *See* CANADA-11 *et seq.*

UNITED FREE CHURCH OF SCOTLAND. *See* SCOTLAND, (PRESBYTERIAN) CHURCH.

UNITED IRISHMEN, properly **UNITED IRISH SOCIETY** was founded in Belfast and Dublin in 1791. The leading personalities were Lord Edw. Fitzgerald, Arthur O'Connor, Wm. McNevins, Oliver Bond, Robt. Emmet, The Rev. James O'Coigley, Cornelius Grogan, Bagenal Harvey, Henry and John Sheares and, above all, Wolfe Tone, who drafted the manifesto. This stated, *inter alia* "We have no national government. We are ruled by Englishmen and the servants of Englishmen..." and it called for "equal representation of all people in Parliament". It functioned openly until 1794, by which time the extremists were taking control and issuing seditious newspapers and pamphlets, importing arms and drilling by night. It was then proclaimed unlawful and went underground as a network of county and district organisations under a Dublin Committee. In 1795 Edward John Lewis was sent as its permanent envoy to the French govt., and in the summer of 1796 Fitzgerald and O'Connor planned arrangements with Gen. Hoche for a French invasion. A detailed military organisation was set up but not in time for Hoche's large expedition to Bantry Bay which was dispersed by fog, battered by gales and driven home without being sighted by the British fleet. A general revolt was now planned for Mar. 1798, and in Apr. 1797 the French were asked for another expedition. This was assembled at the Texel, but intercepted (*see* CAMPERDOWN, B. OF) in Oct. 1797, but preparations went ahead. The Society's enrolled membership in Ulster alone was nearly 100,000. The total armed membership was nearly 280,000, but the character of the movement, originally bipartisan, was changing because of protestant aggression, the formation of the Orange Society in Ulster, and the mendacious propaganda of the extremists against it. The govt. was already aware of nocturnal assemblies, drills, and stores of arms, and Gen. Lake was sent to Ulster to disarm the people. A merciless search in Mar. 1797 involving house burning and the lash, revealed 70,000 pikes, 50,000 muskets and 22 guns. The most dangerous part of the Society was thus disarmed, but Leinster rose in late May 1798. The Irish military and Yeomanry (mostly R. Catholic) remained loyal, but by June, Wexford was in rebel hands. This was the high point. In mid June, 4000 were defeated at Ballynahinch; a week later some 20,000, short of ammunition, were beaten at Vinegar Hill, and a week later still some 15,000 at Kilcomny. The rebellion was over by July. Though many were killed and there were atrocities on both sides, there were only 21 executions afterwards.

In Aug. a small French force landed at Killala and was soon rounded up. In early Oct. a French squadron with some 4000 troops aboard was destroyed at Lough Swilly and Wolfe Tone captured. In late Oct. another appeared at Killala but made off.

UNITED IRISH LEAGUE was founded by William O'Brien in 1897 to force larger landowners and grazing farmers to give up part of their land for tilled smallholdings. It began in Connaught where graziers were common. Its methods of persuasion were boycott, cattle houghing and other forms of terrorism. By 1900 it had spread to the East, and by 1902 it had over 1200 branches, and was headed by John Redmond. The owners retaliated by bringing actions for conspiracy or taking county court proceedings in circumstances where no jury could be claimed. This restrained the League and heartened moderates. A western landowner, suggested a conference of landowners and League representatives which unanimously agreed upon a state aided system of tenants' voluntary land purchase. *See* IRISH LAND ACT, 1903.

UNITED KINGDOM (U.K.). (*see* GREAT BRITAIN). Great Britain and Ireland became a U.K. under the Anglo-Irish Act of Union 1800. After the Irish treaty of 1921 it became the U.K. of Great Britain and Northern Ireland.

UNITED NATIONS EDUCATIONAL SCIENTIFIC AND CULTURAL ORGANISATION (U.N.E.S.C.O.), came into existence (on Anglo-French initiative at London in 1945) in Nov. 1946 and was established at Paris, but its General Assembly meets in a different capital each year. It is a specialised agency of U.N.O. and apart from certain grandiose projects (e.g. a *Scientific and Cultural History of Mankind*) it is supposed to support educational projects in under-developed countries. Increasingly criticised in the 1970s for grandiloquence, left wing propaganda and waste, its affairs reached a point of crisis when the U.S.A. and Britain refused to finance it any further in the 1980s.

UNITED NATIONS RELIEF AND REHABILITATION ADMIN. (U.N.R.R.A.), was founded at Atlantic City in 1943 to assist war devastated countries with emergency action. It was dissolved in 1947, unfinished policies being passed to the International Refugee Org., the U.N. Children's Fund, and the World Health Org.

UNITED NATIONS ORGANISATION (U.N.O.). (1) Proposals were adumbrated at the Dumbarton Oaks diplomatic conference in 1944, modified at Yalta by Churchill, Roosevelt and Stalin and eventually turned into the Charter of the U.N. at the San Francisco Conference (Apr-Oct. 1945). The H.Q. was fixed at New York to maintain American interest. The original members were the 46 countries which had declared war on Germany before Mar. 1945, plus the Ukraine, Belorussia, Argentina, Denmark and Poland. In 1971 the membership rights of Nationalist China (i.e. Formosa) were transferred to Communist China. Between 1945 and 1991 120 other states joined, of which 37 were ex-British, 18 ex-French and 8 Portugal and ex-Portuguese.

(2) (a) Every member country is represented in the **Gen. Assembly,** which decides important issues by a two-thirds majority and others by a majority. Its main functions were to receive reports, and to elect the non-permanent members of the Security Council and all the members of the Economic and Social and the Trusteeship Councils. Its functions have widened by reaction to conduct in the (b) **Security Council,** composed of five permanent members (Britain, China, France, U.S.A. and the U.S.S.R.) together with, between 1945 and 1965, six and since 1965 ten non-permanent members chosen as to 5 from Africa and Asia, one from E. Europe, 2 from Latin America and 2 from W. Europe. The Council was intended to control the maintenance of peace by investigating disputes and if necessary imposing sanctions. It acted by seven affirmative votes before 1965 and has acted by nine since, but any permanent member has a veto. Russia habitually paralysed the council by veto, but in Nov. 1950 the Assembly provided that if the Security Council, because of disunity among its permanent members, had failed to exercise its primary responsibility, the Assembly should immediately consider a threat to or breach of the peace with a view to recommending measures, including force; and strengthened this by creating a **Peace Observation Commission** and a **Collective Measures Committee.** (c) The **Trusteeship Council** took over the League of Nations functions in former Mandated territories. The successive independence of most of these has drastically attenuated its importance.

(d) The **Economic and Social Council** has with varying success organised or encouraged post-war economic reconstruction, a voluntarily finance programme of technical assistance (1949), various financial organs including the International Finance Corporation (1956) the supplementation of the Gen. Agreement on Trade and Tariffs (G.A.T.T.) by the U.N.

Conference on Trade and Development (1964), the succour of refugees through a commissioner for refugees, and has somewhat sketchily supported commissions on Human Rights (1976) and Narcotics. This Council also acts as protector of the International Labour Organisation (1919), the World Bank (1945), the International Monetary Fund (1946), the Food and Agriculture Organisation (F.A.O.), U.N.E.S.C.O., the U.N. Children's Fund (1946) and the World Health Organisation (W.H.O.) (1948).

(3) An important political feature of the Organisation is the Secretary General who may bring to the attention of any of its organs any event which he believes that it should consider.

(4). Originally conceived to prevent or arrest wars between states, it has been increasingly faced with costly and distressing disturbances within them. These have dragged in neighbours through secessions (e.g. Bangladesh), frontier violations (Indo-China), mass refugee flights (e.g. from Afghanistan to Pakistan or Burundi to Zaire), or insidiously through the drug traffic (from Medellin in Colombia or the Burmese Golden Triangle), or by outside but indirect or covert interventions (see DESTABILISATION). Such breakdowns have been as inter-nationally injurious as wars, without being wars in the originally accepted sense. To deal with them the U.N.O. has had tentatively, even experimentally, to evolve methods different from those needed to stop wars. This has strained its institutions, in particular because the member countries who are bound to finance the U.N.O. for the purposes of its charter (though some have long defaulted) are not obliged to do so for purposes not contemplated in it. Moreover, they have been attended by varying success. U.N. peace keeping forces kept Cyprus calm for several years before the Turkish invasion but failed in Somalia. One feature of the U.N. operations is that considerable peace keeping forces have been supplied by lesser powers such as Finland and Italy which would otherwise play no very significant role on the world stage.

(5) In addition the U.N.O. seems naturally to have become a forum for concepts which transcend nation states, including the movements towards equal status and opportunities, particularly as between the sexes.

UNITED PRESBYTERIAN CHURCH. See SCOTLAND (PRESBYTERIAN) CHURCH.

UNITED PROVINCES (now UTTAR PRADESH) were formed in 1856 by the union of the Presidency of Agra (formed in 1833) with Oudh (annexed in 1856) under the name, until 1902, of the North-Western Province. Its language, Hindustani, developed round the Mogul court in an Arabicised version (Urdu) and a Devanagari version (Hindi) which are the Indian *linguae francae*. The area is thickly populated and fertile. Cawnpore (Kanpur) is the biggest city, Lucknow the capital.

UNITED SECESSION CHURCH. See SCOTLAND (PRESBYTERIAN) CHURCH.

UNITED STATES OF AMERICA. (1) The peace treaties of Paris (Sept. 1783) between Britain, the Americans, France and Spain divided N. America between them. Britain kept Canada, though the boundary was not clearly settled. The Americans now had their independence, but their country was in confusion. Eventually a convention was held at Philadelphia (1787) to draft a constitution and form the permanent govt. The constitution emerged as a series of compromises, and there were vigorous contests before the states ratified it, the last being Rhode Island in 1790. The voting for the first president (George Washington) and vice-president (John Adams) took place in Jan. 1789. New York became the temporary capital and Congress passed various laws necessary for the establishment of central organs of govt., including a Tariff Act, a National Debt and the national capital at Washington D.C. The first real test of the new govt's. power came in 1794. Farmers

in Pennsylvania resisted the whisky tax. George Washington sent to Pennsylvania, and three other states for troops and the rebellion collapsed.

(2) The eight years of his presidency saw the rise of political parties. Alexander Hamilton founded the Federalists, Thomas Jefferson, the Democratic Republicans (later known as Democrats). When Washington retired the first real campaign for the presidency began. John Adams, the Federalist was chosen with Jefferson as his vice-president. At the election of 1800 Jefferson became president.

(3) Jefferson presided over a rapidly growing country. The 1790 census showed 3,900,000 of whom nearly 700,000 were slaves, and over 500,000 had settled in the Mississippi Valley by 1800. The greatest of his achievements was the Louisiana Purchase from France (Apr. 1803), which added a greater domain than the 13 original states combined. When Jefferson was triumphantly re-elected in 1804, France and Britain were once more at war. Bonaparte's Berlin Decrees and the British Orders in Council were paralysing U.S. seaborne commerce. In Dec. 1807 he initiated successive enactments designed to force the British to abandon the Orders, because he thought that they needed U.S. commerce. He was mistaken; farm products accumulated in warehouses, and ships lay rotting in harbours.

(4) In 1808 his Sec. of State, James Madison, was elected fourth president. There were fights with the Shawnee Indians under Tecumseh and then the Anglo-American War of 1812-15 supervened (q.v.). The peace treaty (Dec. 1814) merely ended hostilities; disputes about boundaries, fisheries and Mississippi navigation were left open for later settlement.

(5) James Monroe (1758-1831) (Pres. 1816-1824), began with a war with the Seminole Indians on the Florida frontier. Though speedily ended by Andrew Jackson, it brought the U.S.A. into a conflict with Spain, which in 1819 was compromised. The U.S.A. gave up its spurious claim to Texas and bought Florida for $15M. The West was also being settled. New states had been admitted to the Union, including Louisiana, an organised part of the much larger area subject to Jefferson's Purchase, and Indiana. Now came the question of admitting Missouri, and with it the slavery issue. The North wanted to stop the admission of states in which slavery was allowed; the South wanted the opposite. Under **The Missouri Compromise** Missouri was admitted in 1820 on condition that slavery should be prohibited in the Louisiana territory north of the Mason-Dixon Line (36°-30N).

(6) In Dec. 1823 Monroe signed the message to Congress enunciating the Monroe Doctrine (q.v.).

(7) The 1824 election ended in John Quincy Adams (1767-1848) son of the second Pres. being elected against Andrew Jackson, but unable to establish a policy against a deadlocked Congress. Consequently Andrew Jackson (1767-1845) defeated him in 1828.

(8) Jackson and his successor Martin Van Buren (1782-1862) (Pres. 1836-40) gave U.S. politics a specially inward looking flavour which lasted until at least 1916. The nation was too busy colonising the West to think of much else, but shortly after Van Buren's induction came the financial panic of 1837, for which his Democratic party was blamed. His reply, which passed Congress in 1840 was to replace the U.S. Bank with an independent Treasury. In 1840 the Whigs nominated Wm. Henry Harrison (1773-1841) with John Tyler for V-Pres. These were elected, but Harrison died within a month and Tyler (1790-1862) took over. One feature of his administration was the Anglo-U.S. Webster-Ashburton Treaty which settled the boundaries between Maine and New Brunswick.

(9) Meanwhile in 1827 Mexico had freed her slaves, but her province of Texas, suborned by U.S. immigrants,

refused to do so, and in 1836 declared independence. This was recognised by the U.S.A. and some European powers; and having defeated the Mexicans in the B. of San Jacinto, Texas applied for admission to the U.S.A. In 1844 the Senate rejected Tyler's annexation treaty as a breach of the Missouri Compromise. The question thus became a main issue in the 1844 presidential campaign. The Democrats favoured annexation and their candidate James K. Polk (1795-1849) was chosen. Congress admitted Texas to the Union by a joint resolution before he took office. In 1846 he signed a Tariff Bill which lowered many of the duties. He now turned his attention to the west. Firstly to the great **Oregon** area occupied jointly by Britain and the U.S.A. After acrimonious exchanges and popular threats of war, a compromise was reached. Instead of the extreme American demand (54°-40N) the mainland frontier was fixed at 49°N, the U.S.A. thus securing 300,000 sq. m. of territory and Britain a sea coast on the Pacific and the whole of Vancouver I. Secondly he conquered California and the wide lands north of the Rio Grande from Mexico. A pretext for war was found and a series of battles resulted in total Mexican defeat and the cessions under the T. of Guadaloupe-Hidalgo (Feb. 1848).

(10) Nine days before the treaty, gold was found in California, and the famous GOLD RUSH began. The Whigs, Zachary Taylor (1784-1850) and Millard Filmore (1800-74) were elected Pres. and Vice-Pres. The slavery question at once became prominent. California was claiming entrance into the Union as a free state. Taylor was a southerner and slave owner, but recommended admission. Clay brought into the Senate a compromise package including Californian admission, prohibition of slavery in Washington D.C. and a new fugitive slave law. While the debate was pending, Pres. Taylor died and Filmore succeeded him. Most of Clay's package was enacted.

(11) In the election of 1852, the Democrat Franklin Pierce (1804-69) won a sweeping victory and Stephen A. Douglas attacked the Missouri Compromise. He introduced a Bill to admit Kansas and Nebraska without first determining whether they should be slave or free. This threatened the Compromise which had almost acquired the status of a treaty, for the two areas were north of the Mason-Dixon Line. It alienated the free-soil states which had hitherto been Democrat, brought the Illinois Republican Abraham Lincoln to the fore, and so paved the way for the new Republican party.

(12) In the election of 1856 the Democrats nominated James Buchanan (1791-1868) and endorsed the Kansas-Nebraska Bill, He was elected. After the Bill was passed, people from Missouri poured into Kansas for the purpose of making it a slave state, and the North sent bodies of immigrants determined on free soil. In the ensuing virtual civil war, John Brown the abolitionist led a night raid on Pottawatomie and killed some adherents of slavery. Rival armed bands roamed the state. A pro-slavery convention adopted a constitution which would have made Kansas a slave state. Buchanan recommended it to Congress. At this juncture Douglas, who now saw that the Kansas-Nebraska Bill had been a mistake, defied his party and denounced the Kansas constitution which made him once more the favourite of the northern Democrats and defeated the bill, not in the Senate, where he spoke, but in the House.

In Oct. 1859, John Brown and a crowd of abolitionists and Negroes seized the U.S. arsenal at Harper's Ferry (Virginia). Federal troops under Cols. Robert E. Lee and J. E. B. Stewart (later distinguished Confederate generals) arrested Brown for treason and murder. He was tried and hanged and became a martyr-hero of the northern Republicans.

(13) Next came the election of 1860. The Democrats were divided. The Republican anti-slavers nominated

Abraham Lincoln who obtained 180 votes in the electoral college, while needing only 152. The threats of secession made by southern orators for 40 years now became real. Some months before Lincoln's inauguration, the S. Carolinans held a convention and in Dec. 1860 passed secessionist resolutions. Alabama, Florida, Georgia, Louisiana, Mississippi and Texas soon followed. The seven states, in a joint convention at Montgomery, Alabama in Feb. 1861, formed a **CONFEDERACY** with a temporary constitution and appointed Jefferson Davis and A.H. Stevens of Georgia Pres. and Vice-Pres. They took over national forts, arsenals and munitions everywhere with a few exceptions, the chief being the harbour forts at Charleston (S. Carolina). Robert Alderson occupied one of these, Fort Sumter, which he prepared to hold with regular troops. Pres. Buchanan, in his last days of office, sent *The Star of the West* with ammunition, but the ship was fired upon by the Confederate shore batteries. These were the first shots in the Civil War.

(14) The North ultimately had decisive advantages. It had four times as many white people as the South. Its industry was immeasurably more advanced and could meet its own civilian and military needs. It could, by command of the sea, deny supplies to the South. If there were to be a long war, numbers and industrial power would win. The South had to rely on sporadic purchases or a quick victory, and the Union forces were routed at the first clash at Bull Run (July 1861). Relations with Britain now assumed great importance. The British proclamation of neutrality (May) had already accorded belligerent rights to the Confederacy. Other European nations now followed suit (*see* TRENT AFFAIR), but the North was beginning to gather strength, and the South could import materials only by smuggling cotton through the Federal blockade. A huge clandestine trade brought a febrile prosperity to the British Bahamas. World cotton prices rose and alternative supplies from Egypt and Russia came onto the market. Despite occasional unemployment in Lancashire, British opinion backed the North.

By Aug. 1862, though the Confederates had won brilliant victories, the Federals had overrun Arkansas and Tennessee, had taken New Orleans and had fought their enemy to a standstill at Antietam (Sept.). Lincoln now took a decisive step. Hitherto he had merely struggled to preserve the Union. Now he issued his famous proclamation of emancipation (Sept. 1862). Its effect was confined to confederate territories but European reaction was immediate, for most nations opposed slavery. There was now no chance that a foreign power would intervene to break the blockade. Sooner or later the Confederates were bound to succumb. It took over two further years before the Union armies entered the Confederates' capital at Richmond (Apr. 1865) and their Gen. Lee, surrounded at Appomatox Court House, surrendered. By the end of May the war was over but Pres. Lincoln had been murdered.

(15) Half a million lives had been lost and tens of thousands went home with broken health. The public debt of the Union had risen to nearly $3 billion. The Confederate debt had been repudiated. While the North was stronger than ever, the South was ruined. Because of the northern vindictiveness and rapacity (which Lincoln would have restrained) in the post-war years, real union was not attained, and many of the racial and social problems of the 20th cent. U.S.A. stem from this so-called Carpet-bagger era, which engendered the defensive white counter-terrorism exemplified by the Ku-Klux-Klan. Moreover in 1868 the Republican war victor, Gen. Grant became Pres; his eight years were marked by administrative corruption which was a political reflection of the licence which carpet-baggers and industrialists allowed themselves. The period of "reconstruction" was the beginning of Big Business and produced J. D.

Rockefeller, Andrew Carnegie, J. Pierpont Morgan and other controllers of vast enterprises. Rapidly built new railways such as the Union Pacific (completed in 1869) accelerated industrialisation. The West was opened up, and farmers followed the pioneers. The 'Wild West' disappeared and huge acreages of soft wheat supplied not only the spectacularly growing towns, but the industrial workers of urban England. The Repeal of the British corn laws was now consummated, bringing slow ruin to the English countryside. Labour movements, the control of investment and the economics of agriculture formed the three major problems confronting successive presidents. Presidential elections turned principally upon tariffs, pensions and the Silver Standard, but, save for Grover Cleveland's two periods of office (1884-8 and 1892-6) Republicans occupied the White House until 1912. During this long period, the west was colonised and organised into states, and people began to look abroad for further fields of enterprise. The U.S.A. built a powerful navy which was used in 1898, on the pretext of aid and comfort to the oppressed, to seize Cuba (made nominally independent) and the Philippines from Spain. Then came the Panama affair which put the Central American republics under American investors, notably the United Fruit Co., and doubled the effectiveness of the U.S. fleet. Not surprisingly Pres. Taft (r. 1908-12) (1857-1930) signed a high tariff bill to protect the profits.

(16) In 1912 the Republicans were split between a Taft faction and Theodore Roosevelt's Bull Moose party. This split was to be important later, but meanwhile it let in the Democrat Woodrow Wilson, with a large majority. His prejudices and weaknesses were to be of world importance. He began with an ideological intervention in Mexico. The murderous Gen. Victorino Huerta had killed Pres. Francisco Madero, whose liberal revolution Wilson admired. Wilson aided Madero's follower Venustiano Carranza by occupying (Apr. 1914) Vera Cruz and cutting off Huerta's supplies. Carranza took the capital, but his faction split and there was a long civil war between him and his well-known Gen. Pancho Villa. This might have disillusioned Wilson. It did not.

(17) World War I (q.v. especially 7 onwards) broke out in Aug. 1914. The first U.S. concern was a neutrality in which Americans could make profits from both sides. The Royal Navy, however, stopped U.S-German trade, but this created little heat because the British bought the seized property. In fact they soon became the main market for U.S. arms, raw materials and food, and they borrowed large sums to finance this trade. In Feb. 1915 the Germans replied with an entirely new type of submarine-enforced blockade, and in May they did themselves much damage by sinking the liner *Lusitania* and drowning 128 Americans. American opinion now began to move over to the Allied side, but Wilson's moral ambitions encountered difficulties with the Allies because to him both sides were fighting to dominate the World. In Dec. 1916 he asked both sides to state their peace terms and secretly proposed a peace conference. On 9 Jan 1917 the Germans replied with unrestricted U-boat warfare. On 22nd he addressed the Senate on "peace without victory" and a League of Nations. Diplomatic relations with Germany were broken off (Feb.) and war declared (Apr.), and in Jan. 1918 he set forth his views on a future world order in his well-known or notorious FOURTEEN POINTS (q.v.). The result was that after the German defeat, the Pres. of the U.S.A., supposedly the most powerful man in the world, had already influenced the post-war settlements in particular directions, but his country was now divided behind him and he could not secure the two-thirds Senatorial majority required to ratify the Covenant of the League of Nations. Thus the treaties embodied the worst features of the 14 Points and the U.S.A. did not support the best.

(18) This understandable isolationism arose partly out of relief at the ending of the war and partly out of a desire to return to the pre-war economic liberty called 'normalcy' by Pres. Warren Harding (r. 1920-3). Govt. activity was to be reduced, business encouraged, and the 1921 Washington Disarmament Conference was to be a kind of substitute for failure to support the League. As it weakened the British who supported the League, and strengthened the Japanese, it was mainly of economic significance to Americans.

(19) In 1919 Prohibition had been enacted in the 18th Amendment, and it developed during the presidency of the much loved and genial Harding. It became the incubator of organised crime, as the nation enthusiastically drank hooch made locally or smuggled from Canada and the Bahamas, which experienced another boom. Then Harding died and his govt. was found to have been deeply corrupt. There was a reaction towards the austerity of his Vice-Pres. Calvin Coolidge, who won the 1924 election, and an even further reaction when the Republican Herbert Hoover won the election of 1928 with the support of the rural prohibitionist vote.

(20) Hoover was inaugurated in Mar. 1929. In Oct. came the WALL STREET CRASH which started the great Slump. Americans ceased to invest in Europe and foreigners were prevented from earning dollars by the 50% tariff increase of the Smoot-Hawley Act. World trade contracted. In the panic election of 1930 the President's enemies carried both Houses and left him without real power. In 1931, the Germans defaulted on their reparations and pushed the house of cards of international credit over. European govts. devalued and withdrew gold from the U.S. banks, which in turn called in business loans. This caused business bankruptcies which then set off bank failures. By Dec. 1932, 25% of the workforce was out of work. Hoover refused direct relief, spoke platitudes and drove unemployed veterans from Washington with the bayonet. A Democrat victory at the 1932 elections was certain.

(21) The victor was Franklin Delano Roosevelt (r. 1932-45), crippled Gov. of New York, who came with a detailed programme, the NEW DEAL, beginning on 9 Mar. 1933 with an Emergency Banking Bill, which passed both Houses in eight hours, and continuing until 16 June. The width of the programme equalled the energy which Roosevelt instilled into the administrators. Despite often powerful opposition and constitutional setbacks in the courts, by 1940 the New Deal had established, what had hitherto been lacking, federal responsibility for welfare and for the economy even where it had failed fully to revive it. In addition it placed the U.S.A. on a strong industrial platform which was soon to be of great importance in international affairs.

(22) In these years, however, isolationism reached malign levels. The Italian attack on Ethiopia provoked the 1935 Neutrality Act which forbade arms exports to both sides i.e. to Italy which had an arms industry and to Ethiopia, which had not. In the Spanish civil war the same rule favoured the rebels armed by Italy and Germany. An attempt to impede Japanese aggression in China broke down on isolationist opinion even when the Japanese sank an American gunboat, but when World War II broke out, the so-called Cash and Carry Act permitted arms to be sold (at a large profit) to the Allies, who could collect them but not to the Germans, who could not, and it made Americans begin to see that the U.S.A. was part of a warring world. It was the fall of U.S.A's oldest friend, France, which broke down the opposition, and the Japanese raid on Pearl Harbor which precipitated the U.S.A. into War (see WORLD WAR II-7 et seq).

(23) Four times elected, Roosevelt died in Apr. 1945, and his V-Pres. Harry S. Truman succeeded him. The Germans surrendered in May. The Cold War with U.S.S.R. began almost at once. In 1947, owing to Russian pressure

in Greece and Turkey, Truman came forward as the protector of free nations, and in the particular case with $400M in cash (*see* TRUMAN DOCTRINE). Shortly afterwards in the same spirit, his Sec. of State, Gen. George Marshall, proposed the European Recovery Programme or MARSHALL PLAN, whose principle was extended to underdeveloped countries in 1949. By 1953, Congress had voted $13,000M towards it. By reducing the influence of local communist parties, it was a form of containment of Russian aggression, as exemplified in the Berlin Blockade (1948-9), and it culminated in the creation of N.A.T.O.

(24) It was harder to contain the Chinese communists, for there were no free nations to support, only an inefficient nationalist faction which fled to Formosa (Taiwan) in 1949. For the time being, U.S. aid was focused on Japan, but in June 1950 the Russian-supported N. Korean communists invaded S. Korea, and Truman, backed by a U.N. Security Council resolution passed when Russia was not present to veto it, cobbled together an Anglo-U.S. force under Gen. MacArthur. Driven to the sea, it counter-attacked and forced the N. Koreans back to the Chinese frontier. The Chinese now intervened and drove MacArthur south to the 38th parallel, where an armistice was called (July 1951). This was converted into permanent form by the Eisenhower administration in 1953. Pres. Dwight D. Eisenhower (r. 1956-60), the former Allied Supreme Commander in Europe also had to deal with the Suez crisis, the Hungarian uprising of 1956, and in 1958 conflicts in the Lebanon, the off-shore Chinese islands and Berlin.

(25) The 1960 elections were distinguished by the comparative youth of the Democrat John F. Kennedy (43) who defeated the Republican Richard Nixon (47). Within a year, Kennedy was involved in the Cuban imbroglio. An American force made a bungled landing (planned under Pres. Eisenhower) which was captured at the Bay of Pigs (Apr. 1961), and in Oct. 1962 the Russians were found to be setting up nuclear rocket bases in Cuba. Kennedy compelled them to withdraw by a show of force so powerful that the Khrushchev govt. abruptly changed direction (*see* U.S.S.R-15).

(26) With the international scene now relatively quiescent and the U.S. economy buoyant, it seemed that the administration had a fair future. So it had, but not as expected. In Nov. 1963, Kennedy was assassinated in a carefully laid street ambush at Dallas. He was succeeded by his V-Pres. Lyndon B. Johnson (r. 1963-8), a middle-aged highly skilled politician whose Great Society programme extended Kennedy's New Frontier with civil rights, race relations, educational and regional development legislation. Meanwhile U.S. involvement in Indo-China suddenly developed into war. The French had left in 1954 leaving a not wholly uncorrupt anti-Communist govt. in S. Vietnam existing mainly on American support. By 1964 the insurgent Vietcong, supplied by the govt. of N. Vietnam, was defeating the American financed South. The only alternatives were withdrawal or full blooded participation. The opportunity came with an attack on some U.S. warships in the G. of Tongking. With almost unanimous congressional support for all necessary warlike action, Johnson commenced operations against Vietnam and Vietcong. They moved their southward communications into the nominally neutral territory of Cambodia. By 1967, 500,000 U.S. troops were on the ground with enormous air and naval forces, but they could not overcome an agile and well-organised guerrilla, which in the so-called Tet Offensive (Jan. 1968) simultaneously attacked every major town in S. Vietnam. The attacks were beaten back, but strongly influenced U.S. opinion to despair of victory and stop the war. With elections approaching, Pres. Johnson suspended bombing and opened negotiations.

(27) The war was the main issue in the 1968 elections, which Richard Nixon, a former Republican V-Pres. won. It was not feasible instantly to abandon the war, but Nixon and Henry Kissinger, his Sec. of State, pressed a tripartitie policy. They called upon their allies to take greater responsibility for their own defence (i.e. replace U.S. troops). They made tentative approaches to the U.S.S.R. and they widened the geography of the war by seeking to block the Vietcong's communications in Cambodia. The latter backfired. In May 1970 there were furious student demonstrations, upon which the Ohio National Guard fired. There was a revulsion against the war policy, strengthened in 1971 by reports of misbehaviour by American troops and of some of the war-methods being used. The Vietcong were winning the war on the campuses of the Middle West.

(28) On the other hand relations with the U.S.S.R. now bore the important Strategic Arms Limitation Talks, which reduced arms expenditure, and in July 1971 Kissinger went secretly to Peking and, while negotiating an interim agreement with the U.S.S.R. against the deployment of offensive missiles, prepared a visit to Peking by Nixon himself. Natural anxieties in Moscow made him a welcome guest there too. In Oct. 1973, however, the Yom Kippur (Arab-Israeli) war interrupted the smooth course of diplomacy, for the U.S.A. supported the Jews and the U.S.S.R. the Arabs. Common moderation, however, prevailed and Nixon answered the Russian bid for Arab allegiance by negotiating a truce.

(29) Nixon and Kissinger had by now changed the technique of U.S. foreign policy to a reliance on the Sino-Russian balance of power rather the more confrontational alliances. Meanwhile negotiations with Hanoi had been in progress, hastened by an unpopular resumption of bombing in 1972. In Jan. 1973 an armistice provided for an exchange of prisoners and the withdrawal of U.S. troops. Relief at the war's end distracted attention from this admission of defeat, and wholesale massacres of well affected Vietnamese followed.

(30) In June 1972, burglars were arrested in the Democratic Party H.Q. in the Watergate Building in Washington. They had been set on by a Republican Committee for Nixon's re-election, and this, with accusations of tax frauds led eventually to a threatened impeachment. Nixon resigned (9 Aug. 1974) and was succeeded by his congressionally appointed V-Pres. Gerald Ford with a promise of unconditional pardon. Ford lacked electoral backing and had an inflation to face. Hence in 1976 he lost the elections to the little known, by his own account inexperienced Southern Democrat Jimmy Carter, in a multi- candidate election.

(31) Pres. Carter (r. 1976-80) and his appeal to electoral naïveté were less naïve than they seemed. He had little understanding of or perhaps interest in economics, but an idealistic concern (reminiscent of Woodrow Wilson) for human rights in other countries, such as S. Korea, Argentina, S. Africa and Zimbabwe. This was a useful moral base for dealing with the U.S.S.R. which had switched its aggressions by mounting medium range missiles in Europe, invading Afghanistan and organising subversion in Africa. He pressed on doggedly with this theme while the world economy declined. In 1977 he agreed to hand over the Great Canal to Panama in the year 2000 and between Sept. 1977 and Mar. 1978 he promoted the Israeli-Egyptian Peace Treaty. This was probably his most important achievement, yet matched by even further improved relations with China established in 1979; but unfortunately he received a slap in the face from the Iranians, whose religious extremists had overthrown their monarchy and had gone on to permit a mob (Nov. 1979) to seize the U.S. embassy in Teheran. Its staff was held in a sort of popular custody, and an attempt at a military rescue failed through incompetence. The odium clung unjustly to Carter in the approach to the 1980 election, which was also influenced

by high interest rates and unemployment. The Republican Ronald Reagan, a film actor and successful Gov. of California, defeated him resoundingly.

(32) The Teheran diplomats were released at Ronald Reagan's accession (r. 1980-8) and the economy, whose poor showing had carried him to office, began to mend without much intervention. His difficulties arose through a combination of left-wing or Russian-inspired rebellions in Central America especially Nicaragua, a strong current of populist opinion inherited from the Vietnam years and inept or immoral handling of Latin American affairs by U.S. agencies, over which he seemed to exert inadequate supervision. That the Russians and their Cuban subsidiary were making trouble for the U.S.A. is shown by the Grenada affair. On this island, a member of the British Commonwealth, a huge airfield was being constructed for a purpose which can only have been military. It was deemed a threat to the U.S.A. and seized without any notification to the Queen or the Foreign Office. Curiously enough this expedition excited less criticism in Britain than in most other countries where the Communist propaganda machine whipped up much indignation.

(33) Reagan's international unpopularity abated with the conclusion (1987) of a sensible treaty against inter-mediate range nuclear missiles which the U.S.A. and the U.S.S.R. had mounted against each other in Europe. This began the rapid improvement in East-West relations begun by the Gorbachov govt. in 1988, when Reagan was succeeded by his V-Pres. George Bush (r. 1988-92).

UNITED STATES PARTIES. American presidents are often described by their party affiliation. The parties started to form during George Washington's Presidency and the following is a brief account of them.

The Federalist party favoured a strong federal union and were opposed by the Democratic Republicans. The Federalists became increasingly reactionary; they ceased in 1800 to be a major party and vanished in 1825. The Democratic-Republicans came to power in 1800; a coalition of southern planters and northern farmers supported by merchants, frontiersmen and artisans, they were often colloquially called 'Republicans'. This party gradually split into two wings: the more conservative planters and merchants against the more radical frontiers-men and artisans. In 1828 the latter, led by Andrew Jackson, won, and the party was thereafter called the DEMOCRATIC PARTY. The conservatives were then sometimes known as the National Republicans and from 1834 as Whigs; they lasted as a national party until 1852. The REPUBLICAN PARTY arose from a coalition of anti-slavery whigs and Independent Democrats. The party was founded in 1854, the name being a reference to the alleged principles of the original Democratic Republican Party.

Republicans having won the civil war and imposed the oppressive original settlements upon the defeated southern states, the people of the latter embraced a Democratic platform peculiar to themselves, which was in fact as conservative as the Republicans elsewhere.

UNIVERSITIES, BRITISH, GENERAL. The oldest English Univs. are Oxford, traceable to a 12th cent. *studium,* and Cambridge, established early in 13th cent., by a migration from Oxford. Both developed on Parisian lines, being ruled by the *Universitas Magistrorum* (Lat: teachers' collective). From 13th cent., both developed colleges which began to dominate intellectual life and from the 14th cent. controlled the entry of junior members. In Scotland the three Univs. of St. Andrew's (1410), Glasgow (1451) and Aberdeen (1495) adopted the model of Bologna where authority devolved upon the *Universitas Scholarium* (Lat: Gen. Body of Learners). After the 13th cent., arrival of the friars, Oxford was a major inter-national centre of learning. In the 14th cent. King's Hall, Cambridge, started teaching undergraduates in college. This was later expanded and popularised by Wm. of

Wykeham who instituted linkage with a feeder school. The 15th cent. curriculum was based on the *trivium* and *quadrivium* with higher studies in theology and later canon law. Despite secular links the mediaeval univs. remained essentially ecclesiastical and the change to the New Learning was made with difficulty and controversy, so that a gentleman who sought a secular education preferred the Inns of Court near the centres of power and commerce. Despite Sir Thos. Gresham's encouragement this did not lead, as it nearly did, to the foundation of a Univ. of London until the 19th cent. *See next three entries.*

UNIVERSITIES, ENGLAND (Letters denote initial asso-ciation.) Movements to found universities fall into seven distinct periods: **(1)** Oxford and Cambridge (q.v.) are mediaeval in origin but acquired additions in all the periods.

(2) 1832–52
a   Durham 1832
     London 1836
b   Victoria Manchester 1851
a   Newcastle 1952

(3) 1893-1909
     Wales (with colleges at Bangor, Cardiff
     and Swansea) 1893
     Birmingham 1900
b   Liverpool 1903
b   Leeds 1904
     Sheffield 1905
     Bristol 1909

(4) 1926
     Reading

(5) 1948-1969
     Twenty Universities were founded mostly in county towns, together with two technological Institutes and the Open University.

(6) 1967
     University Coll: Buckingham

(7) 1992-1993
     Thirty-two Polytechnics were elevated to university status.

UNIVERSITIES, IRELAND. The following are the dates of foundation:-

(1)   Trinity Coll: Dublin 1592
       National University 1908

       Queen's University Belfast 1908
       New University of Ulster, Coleraine 1965

UNIVERSITIES, SCOTLAND. The following are the dates of foundation:-

(2)   St. Andrews 1411
       Glasgow 1451
       Aberdeen 1495
       Edinburgh 1583

       Strathclyde 1964
       Heriot-Watt 1966
       Dundee 1967
       Stirling 1967

In 1992-3 four Polytechnics were elevated to Univ. status, making 12 in all.

UNIVERSITY GRANTS COMMITTEE for canalising govt. funds towards university education, was set up in 1911 and amplified and reorganised in 1920. By 1975 it was dealing with some 75% of university income.

UNIVERSITY TESTS ACT 1871, abolished liability, at Oxford, Cambridge and Durham, to subscribe the XXXIX

Articles and to compulsory attendance at Divine Service. Thereupon some colleges, instead of recording those who failed to attend service, recorded those who attended, and this continued sporadically with decreasing disciplinary effect until World War II.

UNIVERSITY WITS were Elizabethan novelists and pamphleteers, of whom the principal were Thomas Nashe (1567-1601) educated at St. John's Coll. Cambridge, his friend Robert Greene (?1560-92) at Clare Hall, Gabriel Harvey (?1545-1630), at Christ's Coll. and Christopher Marlowe (1564-93) Corpus Christi Coll.; the Oxford Wits were John Lyly (1554-1606) at Magdalen, and Thomas Lodge (?1558-1625) at Trinity. They occasionally shared a fantastic allusive style: Lyly wrote *Euphues,* and others imitated it from time to time. They all took sides against the Marprelate authors (1588-9), but they sometimes attacked each other, or the govt., or contemporary social abuses.

UNKNOWN WARRIOR. An unidentified soldier buried in Westminster Abbey on 11 November 1920, to honour all the war dead.

UNLAWFUL ASSEMBLY. *See* RIOT.

UNLAWFUL OATHS. It was an offence to administer, assist in, or consent to the administration of an oath to engage in a mutinous or seditious purpose, to disturb the peace, to be of an association formed for such a purpose or to obey anybody not lawfully constituted, and not to reveal the existence of any such body or illegal act. Early trade unions often administered such oaths, and as their activities were tortious and so unlawful, their members were frequently prosecuted under these rules in the early 19th cent. *See* TOLPUDDLE MARTYRS; OATHS.

***UNTER DEN LINDEN* (= Under the Limes),** is an avenue in Berlin. The name was sometimes used to connote the Prussian ruling caste.

UNTOUCHABLES. *See* CASTE.

UPPER CANADA (ONTARIO). *See* CANADA.

URANIA COTTAGE (Shepherds Bush, London) was a house for reforming prostitutes established in 1846 and associated with Charles Dickens and Baroness Burdett-Coutts.

URANIUM was recognised as an element in 1789 and as a metal in 1841. The main western producers in 1970 were U.S.A. (50%), Canada and S. Africa (15% each), France (6%) with significant quantities from the Gabon, Australia, Portugal, Sweden and Argentina.

URBAN. Of the Popes of this name **(1) II (r. 1088-99)** a French pupil of St. Bruno was Gregory VII's legate in France and Germany after 1078. As the imperial antipope Clement III was in possession of Rome, much of his reign was spent elsewhere (*see* CRUSADES-2,3). **(2) V (r. 1362-70)** *see* AVIGNON POPES. **(3) VI (r. 1378-89)** an Italian, was elected to end the Avignon period, but within months the cardinals declared the election void and at Anagni elected the French Clement VII, thus inaugurating the Great Schism. **(4) VIII (r. 1623-44)** greatly strengthened the material and military power of the Papal states and, as a politician, feared Austrian domination in Italy to the extent of supporting Richelieu (and so his Lutheran allies) in the Thirty Years' War. This deprived that war of its ideological character.

URBAN DISTRICT COUNCILS. See LOCAL ADMINISTRATION – ENGLAND AND WALES.

URDU (Pers. = camp) or HINDUSTANI is an Indian *Lingua Franca* originally of the Moslem conquerors of India. It consists of Hindi with much Arabic, Persian and Turkish.

URICONIUM or VIROCONIUM (WROXETER, Salop), was a Roman town stormed and burned by the Mercians at about the turn of the 5th-6th cent. *See* BRITAIN, ROMAN-3.

URIEL (Lat: corruption of OIRGHIALLA). The southern part of ancient Ulster represented by the modern Counties of Louth, Armagh and Monaghan.

URQUHART. Small clan of the Great Glen. **(1) Sir Thomas (1611-60),** a learned and eccentric royalist, published works on trigonometry, a universal language, an invective against Presbyterianism and translated most of Rabelais. **(2) Sir Brian (1918-)** joined the staff of the United Nations Organisation at its foundation and retired as its Dep-Sec-Gen. in 1985.

URRAGHT. An Anglo-Irish term for an important vassal of a great lord or Prince, or sometimes for an assembly of such vassals.

URSULA, St. (?238 or 283 or 451), was a daughter of a British prince, who, with 11,000 other virgins, went to Rome and was slaughtered by the Hungarians at Cologne. The meaning of this tradition is unclear.

URUGUAY or BANDA ORIENTAL (= East Bank). The area was cut off from the Spanish Argentine by the Paraná and the Plate with their swamps, so that the wandering cattlemen (*gauchos*) who occupied the east bank were not under effective Spanish control. Hence the Portuguese were able to penetrate from the north, and by 1680 had built a fort at Colonia opposite Buenos Aires. More permanent settlers spread slowly north, establishing ranches and displacing the *gauchos*. In 1726 the Spaniards of Buenos Aires founded Montevideo and the Banda Oriental's govt., was languidly disputed between Spain and Portugal until the independence movements of the early 19th cent. In 1822 Brazil declared its independence and proclaimed the Banda Oriental part of its territory. In 1825 the Argentinians drove the Brazilians out, but by now British trade was so strongly established that the British intervened to prevent the Argentine from controlling both sides of the Plate estuary. By British armed mediation, Argentina and Brazil were induced to recognise Uruguayan independence in 1828. It became highly prosperous as a sort of British economic appanage assisted by the navigability of the Uruguay River, mainly in cattle, hides and agricultural produce and it was politically stable until the 1960s, when a conflict broke out between the militarised govt. and the so-called Tupamoros, which cost many lives. Their military triumph in 1973 ended in a somewhat dictatorial stability.

USE CLASSES ORDERS. See TOWN AND COUNTRY PLANNING-3.

USES AND TRUSTS, were and are ways in which the Common Law ownership of property could be vested in one person for the benefit of others (of whom he might be one), or for some specific purpose. Uses might circumvent the common law rules against devises of land and mortmain, avoid liability for feudal burdens and forfeiture for treason, and defraud creditors. They became common in mid-15th cent., to avoid losses in the Wars of the Roses, when, it was said, that most land was held in use. The reason was that the Common Law took no notice of a Use, which was enforceable only in Chancery, but the Use itself emptied the Common Law ownership of its valuable content. Among the many effects was a large loss to the Exchequer, which Henry VIII was determined to stop in view of the wholesale distribution of monastic lands. The STATUTE OF USES (1535) accordingly enacted that a person who has a Use shall be deemed to have a common law estate of the same extent, by operation of the Statute. For technical reasons it increased the flexibility of land law, but after the abolition of feudal incidents in 1661 the objections to Uses evaporated and the Chancery began to enforce them again under the name of trusts. The jurisprudence was systematised mainly under Lord Eldon (q.v.). In the 20th cent. there has been a vast growth in the number and scope of trusts (both private and charitable), and it is said that every third person is a trustee.

USHANT or OUESSANT (Brittany). This important navigational landmark and, for sailing ships, hazard is near Brest and forms the most westerly extremity of France. In Anglo-French wars British blockading fleets naturally cruised near it. Many prizes were caught and three major battles (Quiberon Bay 1759, Ushant 1778 and the Glorious First of June 1794) were fought nearby.

USK (Lat: BURRIUM, Welsh CAER WYSG), was a Roman settlement probably destroyed in 5th cent. A Norman Castle was built in 11th cent. and the town was chartered in 1324. Owain Glyndwr stormed it in 1402.

USK, Thomas (?-1388), was a royal supporter in the struggle between Richard II and the barons in the 1380s. In 1384 his evidence convicted his former employer, John of Northampton, Mayor of London and so secured his own freedom, but in 1387, as Under-Sheriff of Middlesex, he fell with his patron, Nicholas Brembre also Mayor of London. In prison, he wrote the *Testament of Love,* a self-justificatory allegory. He seems to have been a man of some stature, for the Merciless Parliament found him worth impeaching and he was executed.

USSHER, James (1581-1656), drafted the Irish Convocation Articles of 1615, became V-Chancellor of Trinity College, Dublin in 1617 and Bp. of Meath in 1621. He lived in England until just after he became Abp of Armagh in 1625, and in 1634 accepted the XXXIX Articles, but not the English canons, for the Irish church. He besought Charles I not to sacrifice Strafford. His biblical chronology was used in England until the 20th cent. It fixed the year of the creation at 4004 B.C.

U.S.S.R. (UNION OF SOVIET SOCIALIST REPUBLICS)
(1) was, from 1922, the name of the Russian empire under Communist Party rule, after the ruinous civil war of 1918 to 1921. The Communists had won through a combination of crude promises, ruthless violence, the disunity of their enemies and typhus epidemics. Over 20M lives were lost. Disunity and discontent appeared among their supporters because the collectivist policies failed and the promises were not met. Vladimir Ilyitch Ulyanov (alias LENIN) instituted a tactical shift into capitalism, which for propaganda reasons was called the New Economic Policy (N.E.P.). This lasted until 1927, but he died in 1924 and was succeeded as Sec. of the Party by the Georgian Josip Vissarionovitch Djugashvili (alias STALIN).

(2) It was a Marxist tenet that class interests transcended nationality. The urge to bring revolution to the oppressed workers of the world had been checked by the Poles at the B. of Warsaw in 1920. There was a sometimes murderous dispute between the champions of world revolution by military means, defeated at Warsaw, or by subversion alone, which the COMINTERN had been founded to promote, or of socialism in one country, apparently eclipsed by N.E.P. Subversion and socialism in one country were not, practically, incompatible, but both would break down if N.E.P. continued for long.

(3) Lenin meant to abandon N.E.P. From 1928 Stalin did so, with a violence and cruelty which foreshadowed later events, in favour of rapid heavy industrialisation through a Five Year Plan. Lenin had set up a State Planning Commission (GOSPLAN) in 1921 to formulate it. The rural populations had to be driven into the towns to provide the labour, and agriculture had to provide the cheap food to make overcrowded town life tolerable. The collectivisation and mechanisation of farming would serve both purposes. The third, intellectual sector of society had to be revolutionised too. Technical and managerial training would replace education. Art and literature would subserve policy with propaganda. Firing squads took care of most of the older *intelligentsia.*

(4) The Stalin govt. doubted if the Plan (1927-32) would attain its objects, and Gosplan was told to prepare a second (1933-8), which came into force without an interval save for the dislocation caused by drought and famine in 1932-3. It was followed by a Third Plan, which was distorted by rearmament and war. The Plans threw up administrative and enforcement problems. Collectivi-sation, fiercely resisted, provoked another bloody, if scattered civil war, and urban hunger. Factory building

fell behind. Accommodation for the new urban immigrants was inadequate and badly built. The Marxist principle "from each according to his labour, to each according to his need" meant in practice that each economic unit and worker had to produce a set amount in a set time (the NORM), and be rewarded by an allotment of consumables unrelated to the norm. In a professedly materialistic state, material prosperity was too obviously lacking, and, there being thus no material incentives, the workers had to be indoctrinated or bullied by a coercive apparatus. As, however, the members of the apparatus **(Apparatchiks)** would be disinclined to press policies as bleak in their effects upon themselves as on everyone else, they were exempted from its effects by special passes, shops and other concessions. It comprised two interlocking bodies, the Communist Party of the Soviet Union [Bolshevik] (CPSU[B]) and the State Police, variously named the OGPU, GPU, NKVD, or MVD, and candidates for either elite were specially trained, often from an early age. They resembled the Church and *Oprishchina* of Ivan the Dread. The CPSU manipulated ideas; police action was more practical. In a society directed towards classlessness, they, jointly, were a new class.

(5) Despite the perfection of Marxist intentions and the excellence of its planning principles, the policies based on them did not seem to work. Neither ideology nor policemen could make the crops grow. Private cottage plots were more productive than the collective lands, and factory output was measured not in units but by tonnage. Sabotage was presumed. The Dictatorship of the Proletariat could not have eliminated as much of bourgeois culture, including various nationalisms, as had been supposed. Stricter action to root out Enemies of the People filled the death pits and corrective labour camps. Action brigades seized crops and provoked a Ukrainian famine. Inconvenient minorities were deported to hitherto unexploited lands. The economic miracle did not, however, occur, and also there was criticism from within the apparatus which might be evidence of treason, deviation or slackness. The apparatus was necessary to the system and had to be protected as an institution, but it could be refined. The only likely threat to it was the Red Army, which was purged of most of its best generals. Refinement now came to the Party which, in 1929, 1933 and 1935-6 suffered expulsions, arrests, show trials and executions. These sensational events were meant to impress, and the outside world often took the trumped up and preposterous charges seriously. Many victims, for reasons unlikely to be known, openly admitted them. Between 1937 and 1938 there were further purges of the party hierarchy below the Politburo.

(6) Conscientious Marxist hostility to capitalism imposed revolutionary foreign policies. The destabilisation of Europe was an obvious objective once the first post-World War I revolutionary tide had ebbed. An early experiment was the secret convention with the German crypto-Gen. Staff, which, to evade the service clauses of the T. of Versailles, permitted German officers and N.C.O.s to be trained with the Red Army.

(7) The Spanish civil war (1936-9) was a watershed. It was begun by a military mutiny against a govt. strongly influenced by left wing and communist parties, which the Stalin govt. could hardly refuse to support. The Germans and Italians, to embarrass the French, supported Gen. Franco. Suddenly all the Communist world adopted a new, strident policy against Fascism which, in Italy, had been in uncriticised existence for 14 years. This was a major tactical shift. The international proletariat was to hate an undefined 'fascism' rather than love socialism, and even to equate hatred of one with love of the other. Ultimately 'fascist' became an umbrella term for any group which disagreed with the prevailing mood in the Comintern.

(8) In the short term, the change was remarkably successful: it is easier to hate an object than love an abstraction. In the West there was a burgeoning of young enthusiasm symbolised by the volunteer International Brigades which fought and died for the Spanish govt. while the govt. parties quarrelled and murdered each other, but it soon had damaging effects. The most promising contradiction in western capitalism was the rising Nazi govt. of Germany which had seized Austria. Stalin's govt. allowed it to seize Czechoslovakia and encouraged it with the Ribbentrop-Molotov Pact (for the general course of WORLD WAR II q.v.). In return for a free hand and Russian supplies against the West, Poland was to be partitioned for a fourth time, and the U.S.S.R. was also to take the Baltic states and Finland. Doctrinally, this might be represented as a return to Trotskyism (q.v.) whose great originator the govt. had exiled and was about to murder. Actually it was nakedly opportunistic. As an alliance with the most obvious 'fascists', it destroyed the repute of the foreign communist parties and the moral idealism of the Russians; and the details exposed defects in the system. The vast Russian power deployed to conquer unresisting victims could not, initially, overcome the tiny army of the resisting Finns.

(9) Stalin had had a monastic education and had never been outside Russia. The condition of foreign countries was not understood in the jargon- and doctrine-ridden parochialism of the Kremlin. A huge German military deployment against Russia took months. It was inherently difficult to conceal and the British warned the govt. of an impending invasion. Nevertheless the Russians were surprised and the attack nearly succeeded. The country was saved because it began too late in the year.

(10) In this ferocious death grapple, the morally poverty-stricken regime resorted to a kind of moral N.E.P. It preached patriotism, which the interests of the international working class were supposed to transcend, and it even cultivated the long persecuted Orthodox Church. In W. Russia and the Ukraine many collectivised rural workers welcomed the invaders in the hope of retrieving their lands. When the Germans failed to fall in with them, these people "preferred their own bastard to a foreign bastard" and reverted to nationalism. Meanwhile the regime's essential hostility to capitalism was maintained. British sacrifices and material aid were meticulously concealed from the Russian population, and there were increasingly strident demands for a premature SECOND FRONT designed at least to belittle the existing fronts in Africa and the Atlantic, and at best to involve the Allied enemy and the Germany enemy in a common catastrophe.

(11) The German defeat was thus only a partial success. The Allies were not destroyed, while at home the supremacy of the morally bankrupt CPSU could be maintained only by police terrorism and a disregard for anything but the main chance. This was the era of the forced labour camps in the Siberian Tundra, and environmental degradation such as the incipient desiccation of the Sea of Aral. Its counterpart was the so-called COLD WAR which included such episodes as the Berlin blockade (1948-9), designed to incorporate West Berlin in E. Germany, and the Allied airlift (*see* BERLIN). It failed directly to overcome the Western powers but provided a shield behind which the regime fastened its friends upon six European states and Cuba, and nurtured "Anti-Fascist People's Fronts" wherever it could.

(12) Stalin's death (1953) was followed by convulsions. His designated successor, the *apparatchik* Malenkov was soon packed off, and was followed by Nikolai Sergeyevich KHRUSHCHEV (r. 1953-64) who had been political commissar at the defence of Stalingrad, and later had Ukrainian experience of the miseries of Stalin's farming policies. He had Lavrenti Beria, Stalin's head of

the MVD, who had once been refused *agrément* by Britain, arrested at an armed meeting of the Politburo (Dec. 1953) and this importantly symbolic event was followed by major changes of posture. In May 1955 he simultaneously made overtures to Yugoslavia (with which Stalin had quarrelled) and signed the Austrian State Treaty. This had important indirect political effects, for the withdrawal of Russian troops from Vienna thinned out the lines of communication across the satellite states. In July, Khrushchev met the U.S. Pres. Eisenhower at Geneva. There was a switch from European aggression to pressure elsewhere. Khrushchev was in India at the end of 1955 and had by then intervened in Middle Eastern politics by agreeing to supply arms to Egypt (q.v. and *see* EDEN GOVT.).

(13) The new direction was signalised by a remarkable leaked speech to a private session of the 20th Party Congress, in which Stalin's methods and crimes were exposed in some detail. A world sensation, it released a ferment among intelligentsia and youth in Russia and E. Europe. A Hungarian revulsion, fed on traditions of the Capitulation of Vilagos (1849), against all things Russian, was bloodily suppressed by Red troops. This damaged the precarious understanding with Yugoslavia as well as Khrushchev's general credit. In May 1957 the Presidium by 7 votes to 4 demanded his resignation. He appealed to the large Central Committee and got Molotov, Malenkov and Kaganovitch, distinguished Stalinists, expelled. This was an important event in the progress against the past.

(14) In Oct. 1957 the U.S.S.R., having launched its first Intercontinental Ballistic Missile (ICBM), also launched its first astronautical satellite. Khrushchev claimed that this altered the balance of power and demanded that western troops be withdrawn from Berlin. He had other reasons for doing so. The best minds and labour in E. Europe were fleeing to the West. The Berlin Wall and its Iron Curtain extensions, with their mines and machine-guns were rapidly built from the Baltic to Yugoslavia, to keep them in. Fairly effective in Germany, they were habitually flouted in Hungary, so that fugitives still got away by a roundabout route. Nevertheless it advertised the heartlessness of Russian society, whose aggressiveness was emphasised in 1962 by an attempt, frustrated by Pres. Kennedy, to establish rocket bases in Cuba.

(15) The Cuban retreat was caused by the warlike superiority of the U.S.A. The Chinese wanted Russian help in spheres (Japan, Korea, Formosa and Indo-China) which encroached on U.S. interests. They talked uncomprehendingly of American paper tigers, and Khrushchev feared they might drag him into an American war. He withdrew specialists, restricted trade, refused nuclear weapons and demanded that they cease their attacks on the govt. of the U.S.S.R. They retaliated by seeking support within international communism. He promptly signed a Test Ban Treaty (1963) (q.v.), established a hotline to Washington, restrained the Cubans, and set about tranquillising relations with W. Germany.

(16) His main purposes were to redirect most resources away from war or subversion into raising the Russian living standards. Unfortunately farming under-investment, unremedied since Stalin, coincided with bad weather, a drought in 1963 and a grain shortfall of 12M tons. A decision to raise the fertilizer output came too late. A reorganisation of the CPSU into urban and rural sectors upset local leaders and was otherwise irrelevant. He was overthrown in favour of a 'collective' leadership led by Leonid Ilyitch BREZHNEV and Alexei Kosygin. Their rehabilitation of Stalin was a short step to elevating Brezhnev (r. 1964-82), who soon eclipsed the others, but, as the Party's moral authority had gone with Stalin, Brezhnev, save in physique a much weaker man was unlikely to revive it. Khrushchev's administration having been dismantled, agriculture was sensibly offered real incentives which, by reason of alternating bad (1967 and 1969) and good (1968 and 1970) harvests were difficult to enjoy. In industry a correlative concession of greater managerial freedom broke down on the ingrained bureaucratic habits of the Party which had become corrupt and exploitative. Not surprisingly it feared and oppressed free thought as likely to lead openly to the criticism muttered beneath; despite labour camp sentences on distinguished writers, many gallant intellectuals stood up for their colleagues. The CPSU was increasingly perceived as an obstacle to prosperity.

(17) The foreign problems deviated from those previously experienced. Brezhnev inherited the Chinese quarrel. In 1969 fighting broke out on the R. Ussuri and the Sinkiang frontier. A truce for negotiations did not stop him from giving military aid to India, Pakistan and Vietnam against Chinese penetration. Knowing that another great Communist power might be interested, the E. European satellites had caught the de-Stalinist infection. Roumania had persisted since 1964 in an autarky inconsistent with Russian planned specialisations in E. Europe. In 1969 came the PRAGUE SPRING. The populace overthrew the Party leader Antonin Novotny in favour of the more liberal Alexander Dubcek. Fearing the effect on other E. European regimes, Brezhnev announced (in the later-named Brezhnev Doctrine) that the U.S.S.R. was entitled to intervene militarily in any E. European state whenever its interests or those of its allies were threatened; he then put the Red Army in. These troops, believing that they had been sent on a rescue mission, were surprised at the execration in which they were held. E. Europe could no longer be held by conviction, only by force, and the force was beginning to doubt its own convictions.

(18) It was now thought wise to reduce direct friction with the West. The self-contradictory "fight for peace" was switched in 1969 towards DETENTE, that is, away from direct confrontation. In 1970 the German Govt. was induced to recognise existing frontiers and therefore the territory of E. Germany. In May 1972 there were Strategic Arms Limitation Talks (S.A.L.T.) with U.S.A. In Aug. 1975 all the signatory states to the Helsinki Accords recognised the existing European frontiers and also international concern with human rights within them. Nobody believed that the Brezhnev govt. would respect these rights (and it did not) but the Accords created a juridical status for critics of Russian oppression. Meanwhile foreign trade agreements improved the internal economy.

(19) Brezhnev's illness (1979) and death (1982) were followed by two other sick rulers. Y.A. Andropov (r. 1982-4) and K.U. Chernenko (1984-5). Thus for six years weak govts. did little to restrain the growing corruption, absenteeism, and drunkenness, or mend the shrinking economy. They got themselves, however, embroiled in the proverbially lethal uproar of Afghan affairs, and concealed their failures from their own people with lies. They also expended large resources in destabilising Africa, notably in civil wars in Ethiopia and Mozambique and in instigating and financing Cuban intervention in Angola.

(20) This was the situation faced by Mikhail Sergeyevitch GORBACHOV on his election. He neutralised the remaining Stalinists, and after a deep survey of Russia's ills, concluded that the Party and Police having worse then failed, radical reconstruction (*Perestroika*) and openness (*Glasnost*), namely public rather than secret scrutiny, alone could save the situation. In this he was paradoxically fortunate. The appalling Chernobyl nuclear explosion (Apr. 1986) demonstrated the disastrous inefficiencies which secretiveness might harbour. In May his announcement of the extent of the disaster was coupled, *a fortiori,* with promises of glasnost

on lesser matters such as crime, drugs and corruption. Suddenly a new freedom began to erode the Party's infallibility, while *Perestroika* envisaged un-Marxist economic practices and semi-private enterprises such as no Dictatorship of the Proletariat would tolerate. Russians were, however, inexperienced in market economics. Well-intentioned reforms were ill co-ordinated. There followed an old-fashioned slump.

(21) Gorbachov's govt. had from the start been convinced of the need for genuinely rather than spuriously peaceful policies. The consumption of resources in fomenting world revolution, which also obstructed trade and destroyed markets, had now to end, in order to keep the Russian economy afloat. The troops were withdrawn from Afghanistan. African destabilisation was dropped. The Brezhnev Doctrine was repudiated. Troops were withdrawn from Europe. In Mar. 1991 the Warsaw Pact Alliance (the Communist counterpart of N.A.T.O.), and in June the organisation for economic aid in E. Europe (COMECOM) were dismantled. All this made Gorbachov wildly popular in the West. Margaret Thatcher promoted his reputation. E. European satellite countries, notably Poland, Czechoslovakia and Hungary, began to shake off their shackles and the two Germanys were rapturously reunited; but the deepening economic home crisis, with which the govt. was not yet equipped to deal, made him equally unpopular at home.

(22) Gorbachov's solution was to widen the public right and duty to solve the difficulties by a political *perestroika* which was itself related to *glasnost.* A new constitution brought the first free elections since 1917 (Mar. 1989). Early in 1990 the C.P.S.U. formally abdicated its eroded supremacy and open multiparty politics became possible. The new Congress of Peoples' Deputies elected Gorbachov to a presidency theoretically comparable with that of the U.S.A. There was, however one grave imbalance. Hitherto the U.S.S.R. had in fact been a Great Russian empire. With the collapse of All-Union authority there was disorder and war in the non-Russian peripheral areas such as Central Asia and the Caucasus, followed by secessionist movements in the three Baltic states. The latter refused to send deputies to the Congress. The people of Vilna and Riga fought the Red Army. Then the whole structure was blown apart in June 1990 when the Russian Soviet Federative Socialist Republic (R.S.F.S.R.) declared the superiority of its own laws over those of the U.S.S.R. and adopted the pre-Revolutionary flag. By Dec. the other 15 republics had done the same. Leningrad became St. Petersburg again.

(23) Gorbachov now began to lose support at both ends of the political spectrum. With the Union in dissolution, he sought to negotiate a new, freely signed multinational treaty. This angered the surviving, still influential authoritarian Communists. At the same time he would not repudiate his Marxism, and by continuing Communists in high office, alienated the reformers. In Aug. 1991 he was on holiday in the Crimea when a Communist group staged a *coup* in Moscow timed for the day before the signature of the Treaty. They had him detained and ordered troops and tanks into the City. It was at this point that Boris YELTSIN, already well-known in Russia and slightly in the West, leapt into world prominence. He had left the C.P.S.U. in July 1990 and had won the R.S.F.S.R.'s presidential election in June. He called out the citizenry, who erected barricades. He jumped from tank to tank shouting, in an evocation of the *Battleship Potemkin,* "don't shoot!". They did not shoot. The *coup* collapsed. Gorbachov was now free to return to Moscow but found Yeltsin effectively in charge. The other republics were liquidating their Communist parties. Gorbachov resigned his party posts (24 Aug. 1991), and got the deputies to take over the assets of the Party.

(24) Amid these events the three Baltic states declared their independence, which was recognised by many Western states, if not in Moscow. On 5 Sept. 1991, however, the Congress, on Gorbachov's recommendation transferred governmental authority to an interim govt., and on 6th this recognised their independence.

USURY was canonically forbidden and practised legally only by Jews. After their expulsion (about 1290) business men had difficulty in raising capital without paying for it and it became customary to avoid the usury laws by buying bills at a discount repayable at a future date. This distinction without a difference was inconvenient especially in times of money shortage, and the usury laws were habitually ignored. A considerable brokerage grew up, and when rates were high attracted popular indignation and hostile legislation. Brokers were liable to the pillory under an Act of 1486. In 1494 this was repealed but the lender was liable to forfeit half the capital. Meanwhile the law was circumvented by fictitious bargains: a borrower sold goods to the lender and later bought them back at a higher price, or the lender gave him money in exchange for a bond to pay back more at a later date. In 1545 the first type of transaction was made illegal and in the second the difference (now called **Interest)** was limited to 10%, and this limit was also applied to mortgages. Offenders were liable to a triple forfeiture and imprisonment, half the money passing to anyone suing for it. In 1552 this was repealed, and usury was again totally forbidden on pain of forfeiture, fine and imprisonment. In 1570 parliament returned to the Act of 1545. In 1623 the legal rate of interest was reduced to 8%, and in 1660 to 6%. By 1713 even this was embarrassing the Govt., which was trying to borrow large sums at 5%. Accordingly this was made the legal rate. The legislation continued to impede Govt. borrowing at intervals and there was special legislation on govt. annuities in 1813, 1823 and 1827. The law continued to be flouted, increasingly as the industrial revolution brought an insatiable demand for capital; in 1835 usurious bargains ceased to be void, but became only legally unenforceable, and in 1837 bills of exchange and promissory notes were exempted even from this.

The way was now open for the whole absurd system to be swept away, which was done in 1854, except in the case of moneylenders' and pawnbrokers' transactions, which could be reopened if the conditions were harsh and unconscionable or if the interest exceeded 48%. Pawnbrokers' activities were regulated by an Act of 1872. Literacy, higher wages and the practice of hire-purchase had driven most of them out of business by 1950, but a small revival was visible in the hard 1990s.

UTHER PENDRAGON. See ARTHUR, KING.

UTHWATT. See TOWN AND COUNTRY PLANNING.

UTILITARIANISM. The view largely developed and popularised by Jeremy Bentham and J.S Mill, that all public conduct and public institutions are to be appraised by the consideration whether they conduce to the greatest happiness of the greatest number. Bentham thought that all happiness was somehow measurable; Mill recognised forms of happiness which were not. The doctrine, being easy to grasp in an elementary form, created much popular support for the 19th cent. administrative and constitutional reforms.

"UTILITY". Official epithet for manufactures devoid of ornament made to govt. specification and sold at controlled prices during World War II.

UTI POSSIDETIS (Lat = as you possess). The basic legal principle that in the absence of a reason to the contrary, he who has a property should keep it; in international practice, a peace or truce based on the territories currently occupied by the contending powers.

UTOPIA (= Nowhere), by Sir Thos. More was a Latin political essay published at Louvain in 1516 with Erasmus' help. A traveller describes a land where communism, universal education and total religious toleration are practised. A best seller, it was translated into French in 1530 and into English and most other European languages by 1551.

UTRAQUISM (Lat = Uterque = both). The Bohemian doctrine that the laity should take communion in both kinds. It was strongly held by the Hussites, who influenced the English Lollards and at a greater remove, the protestant sects.

UTRECHT (CITY AND PROVINCE), was an ecclesiastical state until 1527, when the bishop ceded the temporal rights to Charles V. Spanish rule prevailed until 1577 when the population demolished the fortress. Thereafter it supported the House of Orange. The UNION OF UTRECHT (1579) was a treaty by the seven Dutch provinces to drive out the Spaniards from the Netherlands.

UTRECHT, P. of (Mar. 1713) (see SPANISH SUCCESSION, WAR) was a series of separate agreements between France, Spain and Britain, Holland, Prussia, Portugal and Savoy, engineered between the Tory govt. of Bolingbroke and the French. Their collective effect was **(1)** Philip V (previously the Bourbon D. of Anjou) remained K. of Spain and kept Spanish America, but covenanted to cede no territory to France. **(2)** The French and Spanish crowns were never to be united. **(3)** The French recognised the British Protestant Succession and expelled the Pretender. **(4)** Britain acquired, from France, Hudson's Bay, Newfoundland, Nova Scotia and St. Kitts, and from Spain, Minorca and Gibraltar. Consistent with this **(5)** Spain conceded trading privileges and a 30 year Asiento to Britain. **(6)** Madame des Ursins, the effective ruler of Spain, received the duchy of Limburg. **(7)** The Catalans were abandoned to Castilian vengeance. In southern Europe **(8)** Savoy received fortresses against France, and the Kingdom of Sicily. On the west **(9)** the French were to demolish Dunkirk and the Dutch to receive a new Barrier of nine fortresses from Furnes to Namur, plus Ghent and the estuarial forts of the R. Scheldt. Other Low Country fortresses including the Lille were handed back to France. **(10)** Britain and Holland were to share the Belgian trade; **(11)** Prussia secured Gelderland. **(12)** Portuguese Amazonion claims were recognised. Since the policy of these treaties involved leaving the Emperor to fight France alone, they could not and did not deal with the Rhine Frontiers or the future of Milan and Bavaria, all of which were still in issue between France and Austria. See RASTADT, P. OF 1714.

UTRECHT, T. of (1474) (see HANSE). The Hansards gave up their steelyard at Boston and undertook to support Edward IV. In return they paid a third of the cloth export duty paid by aliens and were exempted from poundage.

UTRUM. See ASSIZES-1C.

UTTAR PRADESH (India). See NORTH WEST PROVINCES AND UNITED PROVINCES.

UTWARE (A.S.; cf 'outward'). A free cultivator owed services to his Lord and might owe others to some higher person, mostly the King but sometimes a Palatine or Marcher Lord. From the immediate Lord's point of view, these other services were *utware*. They were slowly reduced to purely military ones. See DURHAM-5.

UVEDALE or UDALL, Nicholas (1505-56), a flogging headmaster of Eton from 1534, wrote *Ralph Roister Doister* the first English comedy before 1541, when he was dismissed for unnatural vice. He helped to translate Erasmus' *Paraphrase of the New Testament* in 1548, yet managed to retain Q. Mary's favour, and in 1554 became Headmaster of Westminster.

UVEDALE or WOODHALL, John (?-1549), a speculator in mining leases, was Sec. to Henry D. of Richmond from 1525 to 1528, to Anne Boleyn from 1533 to 1535 and to the Council of the North from 1536 to 1539.

UXBRIDGE (London), formerly in Middlesex had a market charter as early as 1170 and developed into a significant agricultural market with mills and breweries, a well endowed ecclesiastical living, and successful market gardening. Swakeleys is a substantial mansion built between 1629 and 1638. Prosperity was only briefly interrupted during the Civil War by broken communications towards the midlands, and later expansion created a brickmaking industry of more than local importance. Some iron founding started in the 19th cent. The place was chartered in 1955 (when the population exceeded 60,000) but taken into the London borough of Hillingdon in 1963.

UXBRIDGE. *See* PAGET AND BAILEY-6 *et seq.*

V

V.1 and V.2 (V = Victory), were long distance weapons used by the Germans from June 1944. They were developed at Peenemünde on the Baltic coast but the British heavily bombed it and set back production by over six months. Hence they were too late and too few. The **V.1** was a small pilotless jet-propelled explosive aircraft whose noisy and predictable course from a pre-constructed launching ramp made it easy to shoot down. Of 8000 launched at London and 2000 at Antwerp only 2000 and 350 respectively reached their target area. The **V.2** was a peroxide propelled 10 ton ballistic rocket which could be fired from any hard surface such as a road and descended almost vertically from the stratosphere ahead of its own sound. Only about 2000 were ever fired. The V.1's sensitive fuses made it explode above ground causing widespread hardship through rendering houses no longer weather-proof. V.2s mostly buried themselves deep before exploding and sometimes damaged substructure installations like water and gas mains but caused few casualties save for 400 killed by a direct hit on an Antwerp cinema. Aerial action and capture of launching sites eliminated V.1s. The Germans ran out of V.2s.

VACARIUS (?1115-1200), Lombard civilian attracted to England from Bologna by Abp. Theobald in 1143. He lectured on Justinian at Oxford, and made a nine book abridgement of his Digest and Code known as the *Summa Pauperum de Legibus* (Lat: The Poor Men's Legal Primer) which was widely known. K. Stephen suppressed the study of Italian law in about 1152 and Vacarius went to York as an ecclesiastical judge.

VACCINATION. *See* JENNER; SMALLPOX.

VAGRANCY (1) From the Black Death (1346) onwards masterless men and their families travelled the roads because they had lost their home or job. The causes in their respective periods were the collapse of feudalism, the urge to escape villeinage, the failure of official wage fixing, the disappearance, after the Dissolution of the monasteries, of monastic charity, the Inclosures, the effects of the industrial revolution, and the failure to provide for discharged soldiers and sailors at the ends of wars. The first effort to deal with the problem arose in the Stat. of Labourers (1394) but by the end of the Wars of the Roses these people were a recognised and dangerous element in society. An Act of 1494 directed that vagabonds and idle and suspected persons should be put in the stocks for three days and then turned out of the town and that beggars unable to work must remain in the Hundred of their birth or where they last lived or were well known.

In 1530 an act distinguished between the aged, the poor and the impotent on the one hand and punished vagabonds and beggars on the other. The Act of 1535 threatened sturdy (i.e. persistent) vagabonds with whipping, mutilation and, at the third offence, with death, while in 1547 it was enacted that idle vagabonds should be enslaved.

(2) This was repealed in 1549, and in 1553 a committee of 24 London citizens investigated the whole question and settled the principles upon which the policy of much later legislation was based. It held that these people were either poor by impotency or casualty or thriftless. The latter class comprised "the rioter that consumeth all", "the vagabond that will abide in no place", "the idle person, as the strumpet, and others". The tendency was to help the poor by impotency or casualty, and to punish the thriftless, and further acts to effect the latter purpose were passed in 1572, and 1597. They provided too for houses of correction where the thriftless might be compelled to work, but this last was ineffectual through lack of funds, and the Act of 1600 accordingly

instituted the rating system. In 1609 a further act threatened further retribution, but by the Restoration the burden of dealing with unemployed vagrants was falling too heavily on certain places, such as Westminster, where they congregated, and the Act of 1661 required that they should be returned to their last place of settlement. The law on vagrancy was codified in 1739, and further amended in 1744, 1792. The Act of 1824 contains most of the remaining penal provisions including the definitions of idle and disorderly persons, rogues and vagabonds, and incorrigible rogues. The Poor Law legislation after 1834 dealt with the welfare aspects of the problem.

VAISHNAVITISM. *See* HINDUISM.

VAISYA. *See* CASTE.

VAKIL, VAKEEL (Urdu). An Indian agent or representative, hence an ambassador or a court attorney.

VALENCE. (*See* MARSHAL; PEMBROKE.) Isabel of Angoulême, widow of K. John, married Hugh X of Lusignan, Count of La Marche. The two Valence children of this marriage owed their prominence to the fact that they were half brothers of Henry III. They came to the English court in 1247. **(1) William (?1226-96),** was married to Joan, grand-daughter and coheiress of William, E. of Pembroke. Though he never was, he was sometimes known as E. of Pembroke. A consistent supporter of his half-brother, he acted as envoy to France in 1249; and as his nominee under the Provisions of Oxford (1258), upon the committee then set up. He opposed Montfort as much from temperament as from policy, and was with Henry at the siege of Northampton (1263) and the B. of Lewes (1264), whence he escaped to France, returning to assist in the overthrow of Montfort in 1265. In 1250 he had taken the cross, and when the Lord Edward resolved to do so, he could hardly evade the obligation. They were away for three years, and when they returned, Edward, now King, made him a member of his council and gave him a variety of appointments. He acted for the King in Picardy under the T. of Amiens in 1279, commanded in West Wales in 1282-3 and was one of the negotiators in the Scottish treaty of Salisbury (1289). His younger brother **(2) Aymer or Athelmar (?-1260),** a frivolous cleric, was, at Henry III's instance elected Bp. of Winchester in 1250 and confirmed by Innocent IV in 1251. His life style was that of a prodigal secular but foreign noble, and he was mainly concerned to preserve the episcopal revenues which supported it. He managed to make himself and, by association, his brother un-popular with everyone, Englishmen, serious churchmen, his own tenants whom he oppressed, and the crown to whom he avoided payment. William's son **(3) Aymer (?1324),** succeeded to his English lands in 1307. He was, throughout his career closely involved with France by blood, marriage and property. He served Edward I as a diplomat and soldier in Flanders (1297) and Scotland, fighting at Falkirk (1298) and being appointed Lieut. and Capt. of the North (1306-7). He then continued in the service of Edward II, being especially useful in diplomacy with France. He also fought at Bannockburn (1314). He opposed Lancaster's extremism, but disliked Piers Gaveston whose sharp tongue nicknamed him Joseph the Jew. Between 1310 and 1312 he became a prominent Ordainer, but after the E. of Warwick hanged Gaveston in breach of Aymer's safe conduct, Aymer returned to the King's service (1312). His diplomatic talents played a part in the reconciliations of the King with Lancaster in 1313 and especially in the T. of Leake in 1318. He was probably not the leader of a moderate 'middle party', but rather a respected upholder of orderly society, necessarily allied with Edward II who as King was its head. After 1318 the distrust of the Despensers reduced his influence, but he supported

Edward against Lancaster and the rebels, and assisted at Lancaster's condemnation to death. Thereafter he played only a minor role in English politics until his childless death. *See* LUSIGNAN.

VALENTIA. *See* ANNESLEY.

VALERA, Eamon De (1882-1975), born in New York, was brought up in Ireland from 1885 and early became a nationalist. Captured and sentenced to death during the Easter Rising (1916) he was spared as a foreigner. In 1918 he was imprisoned in England, but escaped to U.S.A. In 1919 he was elected President of the Dail, and in 1921 returned to Ireland to lead the negotiations for the Anglo-Irish T. These, however, were relegated to representatives whom he later tried to repudiate. When the Dail, against his opposition, approved the treaty in Jan. 1922, he led a republican insurrection; this petered out in 1923 and kept the republicans out of legitimate politics until 1927. In that year he re-emerged at the head of the republican Fianna Fail, whose fanatical unity of purpose carried the elections of 1932 against Cosgrave's confused coalition, and thereafter he dominated Irish politics for a generation.

He began by repudiating the Irish Land Annuities, a popular measure during the current economic depression; then he overhauled the constitution upon a republican basis, and in 1937 proclaimed the, implicitly all-Irish, R. Catholic state of Eire. Since the Irish economy had always been primitive, British economic counter-measures made little difference, and by 1938 the German danger drove the British to an accommodation in which, expecting Irish support in a German war, they unwisely gave up the Irish naval bases. True to form, de Valera declared Irish neutrality in World War II and so denied the bases to Britain. This type of nationalism did not prevent many Irishmen from joining the British forces, and these were neither discouraged nor publicised, but it helped to distract attention from the worsening economy which was driving increasing numbers to work abroad, particularly in Britain.

His long period of continuous office ended with defeat in 1948, after which he was in office alternately with J.A. Costello's coalition from 1951 to 1954, and from 1957 to 1959. From 1959 he was President.

VALETTA. *See* MALTA G.C.

VALLA, Lorenzo (?1406-57), as Prof. of Eloquence at Pavia, wrote a defence of sensory pleasure (*de Voluptate*) in 1431. Driven from Pavia, he settled at Naples in 1436 as a protégé of K. Alfonso I. In 1440 he proved the spuriousness of the *Donation of Constantine*; in 1442 he published his *De elegantiis Linguae Latinae*, long the standard work on Latin style, and in 1444 a critical comparison between the Vulgate and the Greek New Testament. A trenchant and effective opponent of scholasticism and monasticism, he denied the possibility of harmonising divine omnipotence with human free will. Though suspected of heresy he secured, in 1447, a post at the papal court of Nicolas V as scriptor, then as Apostolic Secretary and finally as Prof. of Eloquence. He deeply influenced renaissance and all later scholarship and created much of the intellectual groundwork of Luther's thinking. *See* RENAISSANCE-6,7.

VALLUM (Lat. = wall or earthwork). The entrenchment sometimes found some distance to the rear of Roman frontier fortifications, especially Hadrian's Wall.

VALOGNES, Philip of (?-1215). Anglo-Norman noble, had migrated to Scotland by 1165 and was a friend of William the Lion, for whom he stood hostage in 1174. He was William's High Chamberlain from 1180 and hostage again in 1209.

VALOIS, FRENCH ROYAL HOUSE (1328-1589). (1) Descended from Charles of Valois, next brother to the Capetian K. Philip IV (r. 1285-1314). He and Philip IV's last male descendent, Charles IV, both died in 1328.

(2) The dynasty had a stormy history. The claim of Philip VI (r. 1328-50), Charles of Valois' son, and his descendants was legally doubtful, depending upon a Salic Law in favour of males set up to justify the desire of the French court and its dependent baronage for a French succession. A closer line of inheritance through females would have given the throne to Edward III of England, and his claims were supported by other baronages.

(3) Opinion was at the outset divided throughout a France, whose contemporary eastern frontier was still 100 miles from the Rhine, and of which the Paris Govt controlled only about 60%. The rest was in the hands of feudal dynasts, whose allegiance was in practice nominal or worse. Apart from lesser fiefs such as the N.E. frontier constellation about Rethel, and the more important Pyrenean states of Béarn, Armagnac, and Foix, there were *in the north* Flanders, *in the east* Burgundy, Nivernais and Bourbon, *near Orléans,* Blois, *in the west* Brittany and *in the south,* the largest, Aquitaine. The most dangerous was Aquitaine, because its Duke was the King of England, who besides a strong legal claim to the French crown, possessed, separately, in Ponthieu, the mouth of the Somme, only 80 miles to the north of Paris.

(4) The human quality of these thirteen Kings oscillated from the flawed genius of Francis I (r. 1515-47) and the ruthless practical sense of Charles V (r. 1364-80), Charles VII (r. 1422-61) and Louis XI (r. 1461-83) to the fatuity of John II (r. 1350-64), Charles IX (r. 1560-74) and Henry III (r. 1574-89), and the hopeless madness of Charles VI's (r. 1380-1422) latter years. Regencies accounted for 63 years between 1328 and 1589.

(5) Agricultural depression, the Black Death and disastrous defeats by the English, loosened the bonds of society and the authority of the rulers during the first thirty years. Royal France was twice partitioned: firstly John II created appanages for his younger sons in the shape of Berry (escheated 1415), Anjou (escheated 1480) and a new Burgundy (escheated 1477), which nearly became an independent Rhenanian state. Secondly Henry V's operations and the T. of Troyes (1420) for a while put Paris and the north, as well as Aquitaine, into English hands. The dynasty at this period was saved by Joan of Arc and English internal troubles.

(6) The expulsion of the English, together with escheats and suitable marriages had unified the territories of the ancient Kingdom by 1491, but this unity was fragile and soon overstrained, economically by Charles VIII's and Francis I's Italian adventures, and then politically by the Reformation, the spread of the Huguenots and the savage civil wars of Religion. During the last three reigns France was not a European power. *See* articles on those mentioned above and on CHARLES VIII; LOUIS XI; HUGUENOTS; JAMES IV AND V OF SCOS; HUNDRED YEARS' WAR and on the contemporary English sovereigns.

VALOR BENEFICIORUM **(Lat. = Valuation of Benefices),** or **KINGS BOOKS.** An assessment made originally under Elizabeth I, of ecclesiastical livings, to regulate the amount of First Fruits.

VALOR ECCLESIASTICUS **(1535)** (Lat: Ecclesiastical Resources). Was an inventory of church property made under Thos. Cromwell, ostensibly for tax purposes but actually as a preliminary to the Dissolution of the Monasteries.

VALUE ADDED TAX (V.A.T.), was introduced in Europe as a base upon which the E.E.C. could be financed, and into Britain in 1972 to conform with Europe. It is a sales tax on the supply of all goods and services except those which are exempt. Every sale is taxed, but any purchaser in business save the ultimate consumer can reclaim the tax which he has paid (the input tax) by deducting it from the tax (output tax) which he has received from the next purchaser. In this way the true incidence of the tax ultimately rests upon the consumer, and the businesses through which the goods and services reach him are mere collectors on behalf of the Board of Customs and Excise. In the case of an exempt supply the supplier will have paid input tax but cannot reclaim it because there is no output tax from which it can be deducted. In the case of a zero rated supply (e.g. food or books) the position is reversed: output tax is recovered though no input tax has been paid.

One practical effect is to place the administrative burden of a vast tax system upon industry and commerce.

VANBRUGH, Sir John (1664-1726), playwright, architect, wit and herald brought out *The Relapse* in 1696 and the *Provok'd Wife* in 1697. In 1702 he became controller of the Board of Works and in 1705 manager of the Haymarket Theatre. While continuing to write plays he practised as an architect (*see* BAROQUE). His works included Castle Howard, the Haymarket Theatre and Blenheim Palace. From 1704 to 1726 he was also Clarenceux King of Arms.

VANCOUVER, VANCOUVER ISLAND. *See* BRITISH COLUMBIA.

VANCOUVER, George (1758-98), sailed twice (1772 and 1780) under James Cook. Commissioned in 1781 he had a conventional naval career until 1791 when he sailed on a voyage of discovery via the C. of Good Hope, surveyed the S.W. coast of Australia and New Zealand, and between 1792 and 1794 the Pacific Coast of N. America and Vancouver I. He returned via C. Horn in 1795. His *Voyage* was published in 1798.

VANDALS. This Germanic tribe entered Gaul in 406, and Spain in 409 where they adopted Arian Christianity. In 429 they crossed to Africa and by 439 had conquered the province. They interrupted communications between Rome and the West, persecuted Catholic and Orthodox Christians and disrupted West Mediterranean trade, until they were overthrown by Justinian in 534.

VAN DE VELDE, Willem. (1) The Elder (1610-93) originally a Dutch sailor and his son **(2) The Younger (1633-1707)** came to England c. 1675 and worked as marine painters for Charles II and James II. Their pictures give a faithful account of marine activity and warfare, some being eye-witness pictures in which the artist figures unconcernedly with his easel in a boat amidst the uproar.

VAN DIEMEN'S LAND later **TASMANIA.** *See* AUSTRALIA.

VAN DYCK, Sir Anthony (1599-1641), a friend of Rubens, first visited England in 1620, and after travelling in Italy was brought to England in 1626 by Charles I, who knighted him in 1632. He visited Antwerp in 1634 and 1635 and then worked as a painter almost entirely in England.

VANE, Anne (1705-36), was the mistress to Frederick P. of Wales. He, Lord Harvey and Lord Hamington all claimed to be the father of her child born in 1732.

VANE, Frances Anne (1713-88), wife of the 2nd Vist. Vane, known as Lady Fanny, and notorious for her seductive beauty, extravagance and promiscuity, was the subject of ribald gossip from 1735 until 1768 when struck down by illness. She was the author of *Memoirs of a Lady of Quality* inserted by Smollett into *Peregrine Pickle.*

VANE, Sir Henry the Elder (1589-1655), and his son Sir **Henry the Younger (1613-62). (1)** The Elder, an undistinguished M.P., reached prominence and wealth through a succession of household offices. He was employed unsuccessfully to negotiate a Dutch-Spanish peace (1629) and with Sweden (1631), in order to secure the return of the Palatinate to the King's brother-in-law the Elector Frederick. In 1630 he became a councillor and was employed until 1640 on various commissions including the Admiralty and the Plantations. When the Scottish troubles began, he was one of the eight councillors appointed to deal with them, and favoured peaceful solutions which commended him to the Scots, especially Hamilton. Strafford therefore resented his appointment as Sec. of State in Feb. 1640, and they

became increasingly estranged. At a council meeting in May 1640 on the Scottish crisis Strafford advised the King to employ the Irish army "to reduce this Kingdom".

(2) Meanwhile the Younger, converted to Puritanism in 1628, had pursued an independent career, and in Mar. 1637 became gov. of Massachusetts. His tenure, involving Indian wars and religious disputes, was stormy, and he left for England in Aug. 1637. In 1639 the Elder got him the lucrative joint Treasurership of the Navy, and, on his marriage, settled upon him large estates including Raby. While searching for documents connected with this settlement, he accidentally came across the Elder's record of the Council Meeting of May 1640. He transcribed it, and allowed Pym to copy his transcription. Pym's copy was used as evidence in Strafford's attainder that Strafford intended to use the Irish army against England. The Elder Vane, who knew what had happened, refused to offer any other interpretation (Apr. 1641). He seems to have thought that Strafford's attainder would bring peace. Not surprisingly the King got rid of him at the first convenient time (Nov. 1641), whereupon he joined his son *in the opposition.*

(3) The Younger had become an extremist member of the Committee on church affairs in Feb. 1641. The Elder now joined the Irish Committee and in Feb. 1642 became parliamentary Lord Lieut. of Durham. As the country drifted towards civil war, the Younger took the lead, especially when the flight of the Five Members temporarily deprived the opposition of its main figures. He was the principal inspirer of the war party and succeeded to Pym's authority when the latter died. It was he who inserted the important amendment in the Solemn League and Covenant which protected the Independents, and he and St. John carried the establishment and were the main personalities of the Committee of Both Kingdom (Feb. 1644). As the breach between parliament and the Scots widened, Vane took up military reform to balance the power of the Scots army. He seconded the Self Denying Ordinance (Dec. 1644) and with Cromwell was a teller for Fairfax's appointment as Lord General.

(4) By this time the Elder Vane was in semi-retirement, while the Younger's experiences had altered his convictions. He was willing to treat with the King and to reach religious compromises because factional bitterness was tearing society apart. Hence he took no part in the final breach with the King or in his trial and execution. On the other hand he was elected to the Council of State (Feb. 1649) of which he was an energetic and resourceful member until the Restoration. He was also a close friend to Cromwell. He was versatile. He took a leading part in colonial affairs and foreign diplomacy, and favoured religious toleration and a limited reform of parliament. These latter views estranged him from Cromwell and after the expulsion of the House of Commons (1653) he retired for a while to Raby. He was even imprisoned from Sept. to Dec. 1656.

(5) The final acts of the Younger Vane's career began with his election for Whitchurch (Hants) to Richard Cromwell's parliament in 1659. His wide experience and talents were at the service of republicans who opposed efforts to strengthen the new Protector or to concede any legislative veto to an upper house. His efforts were thus directed to reconciling those politicians and soldiers who might be trusted to keep the monarchy out. Monck's march from the north and the revolt of the Navy destroyed his position. At the Restoration he was seized, as too dangerous to be allowed to escape, and after hesitations was tried and executed.

VANE. *See* STEWART.

VANE-TEMPEST-STEWART (*see* STEWART). **(1) Charles (1852-1915) 6th M. of LONDONDERRY (1884)** was conservative M.P. for Co. Down, Ld. Lieut. of Ireland from 1886 to 1889 and first pres. of the Board of Education from 1902 to 1905. He signed the Ulster

Covenant in 1912. His son **(2) Charles Stewart (1878-1949) 7th M.** was conservative M.P. for Maidstone from 1906 to 1915.

VANITY FAIR, the famous novel of Regency manners, by W.M. Thackeray was published serially in 1847 and 1848.

VAN LEUWENHOEK, Anthony (1632-1723), originally a draper of Delft was a pioneer of microscopy and biology He accurately described the capillaries (1668) and the red blood corpuscles (1674), investigated the structure of teeth and muscle and did much research into animal, plant and insect life. He corresponded with the Paris Academy of Sciences and wrote over 100 papers for the Royal Society, of which he became a fellow in 1680.

VAN MILDERT, William (1765-1836). *See* DURHAM-12.

VANSITTART family of Dutch origin. **(1) Henry (1732-70),** a profligate official in the HEIC, made friends with Clive at Fort St. Davids between 1746 and 1751 when he returned to Leadenhall St. In 1754 he was sent to negotiate with the French HEIC and this opened the way to membership of the Madras Council in 1757. He took part in the defence of Madras in 1759 and became its temporary gov. in 1760. From then until 1764 he was gov. of Bengal, but his dealings with the subadar and dewani at Murshidabad (*see* MIR JAFAR) were much disliked by Clive and the Directors, so that after he returned he published his *Narrative* (1766), a justification of his conduct. He became an M.P. in 1768 and a Director of the HEIC in 1769. He vanished at sea on the way to India. His son **(2) Nicholas (1766-1851) Ld. BEXLEY (1823),** a Pittite Tory M.P. from 1796, supported the Addington Govt. and was the very astute Min. to Copenhagen at the time of the battle in 1801. He immediately became Sec. to the Treasury (until 1804), then Chief Sec. for Ireland in 1805, reverted to the Treasury from 1806 to 1807 and then went into opposition, until he became Liverpool's Ch. of the Exchequer in 1812. He was Castlereagh's ablest critic in the cabinet, and also prepared the way for the union of the British and Irish treasuries. His long tenure was a significant step in the rise of his office, which from 1823 to 1828 he exchanged for the Duchy of Lancaster. He retired in 1828. A descendent **(3) Robert Gilbert (1881-1957) Ld. VANSITTART (1941)** Etonian and brilliant linguist (unsuspected under a pseudonym, he was a successful French playwright and poet) entered diplomacy in 1903 and the Foreign Office in 1911. In World War I he was joint head of the Contraband Dept and then of the Prisoners of War Dept. He attended the Paris Peace Conference (1920) and was private sec. to the Sec. of State Lintil 1924, and private Sec. to the Prime Min. from 1928 to 1930 when he became head of the Foreign Office. Until 1938 he never ceased to warn govts. of the aggressive dangers of Italian and German policy, so that in 1938 he was removed to the largely honorific specially created post of Chief Diplomatic Adviser, while the Chamberlain Govt. pursued appeasement against his advice. He retired in 1941.

VAN SOMER, Paul (1576-1621), Flemish portraitist, came to England in about 1606 and became the most fashionable painter at the Jacobean court.

VANUATU. *See* NEW HEBRIDES.

VARANGIANS. *See* RUSSIA, KIEVAN.

VARENNES, FLIGHT TO. Louis XVI fled towards the frontier in June 1791 and was arrested at Varennes in the Argonne.

VATICAN (Rome), became an occasional Papal residence after 1376, but the permanent one only in 1870. The territory of the Vatican City became a sovereign papal enclave in Rome in 1929.

VATICAN COUNCILS and DECREES (1) 1869-70 under Pius IX. It issued two major DECREES viz: *Dei Filius* against the effects of rationalism and *Pastor Aeternus* enunciating the doctrine of papal infallibility and so subordinating general councils to the Pope. **(2) 1962-65.**

This was summoned by John XXIII and its second, third and fourth sessions continued by Paul VI. Amongst a large number of decrees *Lumen Gentium* (Lat: The Light of the Nations) propounded a theory of church organisation based on the collegiality of the bishops under the Pope and *Sacrosanctum Concilium* encouraged the translation of the liturgy into vernacular languages.

VAUBAN, Sebastian le PRÊTRE, Sieur de (1633-1707) when young was Turenne's chief engineer. In 1678 he became French Commissioner for fortifications. On the basis of the most thorough study of them ever made, he built or improved over 150 fortresses and himself conducted some 40 sieges. Until the introduction of rifled explosive shells, fortifications everywhere were built on his principles and they in turn dominated the layout of many towns even after the fortifications had been demolished.

VAUGHAN. Carmarthenshire family. **(1) John (?1572-1634), 1st Ld. (1621) and 1st E. of CARBERRY (1629)** served in Ireland in 1599 and was M.P. for Carmarthenshire (Carms) in 1601 and 1620 to 1622, when he became comptroller to P. Charles with whom he went to Madrid in 1623. His son **(2) Richard (?1600-86), 2nd E.** was M.P. for Carms. from 1624 to 1629 and royalist commander in S. Wales. Defeated by Rowland Laugharne in 1644, he had to compound heavily as a delinquent in 1644, and again in 1645. He nevertheless sheltered Jeremy Taylor. From the Restoration until 1672 he was Pres. of the Marches. His second son **(3) John (1640-1713),** was M.P. for Carmarthen from 1661 to 1679, Gov. of Jamaica from 1674 to 1678, and M.P. for Carms. from 1679 to 1681 and from 1685 to 1687.

VAUGHAN, Sir John (1603-74), lawyer, Welsh landowner and politician, was distinguished under Charles I and the Protectorate for his unwillingness to commit himself to any side. After the Restoration he became a leader of the country party in the Commons and in 1667 promoted Clarendon's impeachment. In 1668 he became C.J. of the Common Pleas, but his main work was the summary adjudication of the many disputes arising out of the Fire of London.

VAUGHAN or VYCHAN (i.e. the Younger), Sir Griffith (?-1447), Welsh soldier, made banneret at Agincourt, in 1417 captured the Lollard rebel Sir John Oldcastle. He was a wealthy landowner, and at feud with the Greys of Powys, one of whom murdered him.

VAUGHAN (1) Benjamin (1751-1835) was a friend of Shelburne's and of Benjamin Franklin. He favoured the colonists in the American revolution and Shelburne used him as an intermediary in the peace negotiations with them. In 1790 he was in contact with the French revolutionaries. In 1792 he became M.P. for Calne, but his career came to an abrupt end with the discovery of some documents apparently implicating him in anti-govt. conspiracies. He went to America in 1798. His brother **(2) William (1752-1850),** a London businessman, was mainly responsible for the development of docks, on which he was an expert, and particularly of the London Docks.

VAUGHAN, Charles John (1816-97) as headmaster from 1844 to 1859, reformed Harrow School.

VAUGHAN, Herbert (1832-1903) R. Catholic Abp. of Westminster (1892), Card. (1893), owned *The Tablet* and the *Dublin Review* and commissioned the building of Westminster Cathedral (1895) with the instruction that it was to be "nothing like Westminster Abbey".

VAUGHAN (1) Sir John (1769-1839) a barrister who prosecuted Burdett (1820) and the Birmingham rioters (1821), became a Baron of the Exchequer in 1827 and a Judge of the Common Pleas from 1834. He was much respected as a constitutional authority. His brother **(2) Sir Charles (1774-1849)** started as an explorer in the Levant and S. Russia, then, after adventures in Spain, became private Sec. to the Foreign Sec. (1809), and was subsequently employed in diplomacy in Spain. From 1825 to 1835 he was a very successful Minister to the U.S.A.

VAUGHAN WILLIAMS, Ralph (1872-1958), O.M. (1935), studied under Parry, Stanford and later with Max Bruch and Ravel, but became a composer against family opposition. His English nationalist musical interest was fed by folksong, his editorship of the *English Hymnal* and some work for the Purcell Society. In 1910 his choral *Sea Symphony* brought him into prominence, and there after he developed his considerable output along lines which, whether or not characteristically English, were emancipated from continental models, and influenced the work of later English composers. It can be argued that he founded rather than typified an orchestral and choral style.

VAUX (1) Sir William (?-1471) of Harrowden, Northants, was a Lancastrian attainted by Edward IV's parliament in 1461 and killed at the B. of Tewkesbury. His son **(2) Sir Nicholas (?-1523), 1st Ld. VAUX of HARROWDEN (1523),** a page to Margaret, Countess of Richmond, had the attainder reversed in 1485 and between 1490 and 1509 inclosed great tracts in Bucks. and Northants. From 1502 to 1523 he was also Gov. of Guines and in 1507 he married Anne Green who had immense estates. In 1511 they entertained Henry VIII at Harrowden. He served in France in 1513, was a member of the diplomatic mission to Paris in 1518, and attended the King in France in 1520. His son **(3) Thomas, 2nd Ld. (1510-56),** was a poet and courtier. His son **(4) William, 3rd Ld. (?1542-95),** was imprisoned in 1581 for harbouring Edmund Campion.

VAUXHALL (London). The (New) Spring Gardens, or Vauxhall Gardens were laid out in 1661 and became a favourite resort. They were improved in 1728; the Prince Regent frequented them; they declined after 1840 and were closed and built over in 1859.

VAVASSOUR. An inferior baron, or more often, a vassal of a baron.

V-BOMBERS, viz VALIANT, VICTOR and VULCAN, were types of 1950s long distance R.A.F. bombers able to deliver atom bombs. Vulcans were still in use in the Falklands War of 1982.

VEDANTA and VEDAS. See HINDUISM.

VEGETARIANISM. A Vegetarian Society was founded in London in 1847.

VELD or VELDT (Dutch). Unenclosed or pasture land in S. Africa.

VELLORE MUTINY (July 1806). The widows, sons and retainers of Tippoo, the Sultan of Mysore, killed at Seringapatam in 1799, had lived ever since as pensioners of the HEIC in a palace at Vellore (Madras). Wellesley's defeat of the Marathas in 1803 was followed by a reduction in the local British forces and Tippoo's sons thought that they might regain his throne by subverting the rest. Sir John Craddock, C-in-C Madras, issued a series of religiously offensive orders to the troops in Nov. 1805 substituting hats for turbans, introducing leather stocks and requiring the removal of face marks and earrings. The palace faction used religious fears to attempt a *coup d'état*. The initial stroke was well organised and successful, but no plans had been made to follow it up, and the mutineers took to looting. The British counter-stroke, organised within hours, caught them disunited and ended the affair. The obnoxious orders were cancelled, but three regiments were disbanded. *See* INDIAN MUTINY.

VENDÉE, LA (Fr.). The royalist revolt of the Chouans in Brittany in 1792, spread to La Vendée and adjacent areas in Mar. 1793. The peasant leader Cathelineau took Saumur and in June Angers. A full scale civil war led to a pitched battle, where the Chouans were defeated, at Cholet (Oct.). Guerrilla war and widespread devastation continued until 1795. There were brief risings also in 1796, 1799, 1815 and 1832. *See* FIRST COALITION, WAR OF (1792-5).

VENDÔME, Louis Joseph D. of (1654-1712), a French professional soldier, took Barcelona in 1697, commanded with some success against the Austrians in Italy from 1702, was defeated by Marlborough at Oudenarde in 1708, but in 1710 commanded in Spain, where he forced Stanhope to surrender at Brihuega and decisively beat the Austrians at Villavicosa next day (9-10 Dec.), thereby establishing the Bourbon Spanish dynasty.

VENDÔME, TREATIES OF (1227). *See* AQUITAINE- 6.

VENEREAL DISEASES. Gonorrhoea is very ancient and widespread. It is possible that some mediaeval so-called leprosy was syphilis, since it was occasionally said to be highly contagious, sexually communicable, heritable and yielding to mercury. There was an acute European outbreak of syphilis just after Columbus returned from America and this, with evidence from skeletons of pre-Columbian Indians, has led to suggestions that the disease was imported from the New World. Syphilis was not considered distinct from gonorrhoea until 1790 nor from Chancroid until 1850. For syphilis, mercury was the accepted medium of treatment until 1909 when Salvarsan 606 was introduced; this was superseded in 1943 by penicillin, which was also found to be very effective against gonorrhoea.

VENETI. See BRITAIN BEFORE THE ROMAN CONQUEST-1.

VENEZUELA (*see* BOLIVAR). **(1)** became independent of Greater Colombia in 1830 under Gen. Paez, but civil war was endemic until 1864. The federal organisation then adopted survived only until the dictatorship (1870 to 1887) of Gen. Guzman Blancos.

(2) Meanwhile the discovery of oil, and chronic unwillingness to pay debts, led to growing friction with foreign powers. In 1895 there was a boundary dispute with Britain over Guiana which led to intervention by the U.S. Govt. of Pres. Grover Cleveland under an extension of the Monroe doctrine, and an arbitration. This affair gave the U.S.A. a brief access of prestige in S. American eyes, but did nothing to save the civil administration, which had replaced that of Blancos, from being over-thrown in 1899 by Gen. Cipriano Castro. His high handed treatment of mainly European interests led to a joint Anglo-German-Italian blockade in 1902. His govt. was succeeded by another more intelligent dictatorship under Gen. Juan Vicente Gomez (r. 1908-35), which established order and respected investors' rights. The result was an enormous and continuing development of the oil industry, which brought an industrial revolution and great prosperity, and permitted the liquidation of state indebtedness.

(3) After Gomez' death, Lopez Contreras enacted a new constitution under which the extreme left was soon in power (1937). This was superseded (1945) by a more right-wing govt. under Roberto Betancourt and Ramon Gallegos, which was overthrown in a military *coup* in Nov. 1948. The dictatorship of Gen. Jimenez lasted until it was overthrown by Adm. Larrazabal in 1957. The country was by now in disorder, fomented by professional guerrillas of Fidelist persuasion but Betancourt persuaded most of the moderate parties to co-operate in a new constitution which, in 1963, resulted in the first constitutional presidential succession in Venezuela's history.

(4) Despite the political instability of the past the industrial upswing continued and broadened. By 1970 Venezuela had not only a huge oil and gas industry but was producing significant amounts of salt, steel and sugar.

VENICE was a business which happened to be a state. Its importance lay in its mediaeval supremacy in finance and exchange, as a carrier, as a channel for Greek and oriental thought, and as a focus of arts and applied sciences such as surgery, law and accountancy. It had the first state industries and funded national debt and a much admired stable constitution.

(1) With commercial privileges (in return for help against the Saracens) throughout the Eastern Empire, and trading posts at the foot of the Alps, the Venetians, after 996 were the biggest intermediaries in international trade. They were already large scale ship builders, underpinned by the conquest of Istria and Dalmatia (other than Ragusa) for anti-piracy, timber, and later, building stone. By 1070 there were agents in most Levantine ports, and the overland commerce extended across the Alps to Ulm, whence secondary traders dispersed the goods towards the Champagne fairs and further west. The expense of overland movement restricted this trade mostly to goods, such as spices, of small bulk and high value, sold for specie.

(2) A western seaborne traffic to the Languedoc isthmus was potentially important to England and promised greater symmetry. Besides spices, bulkier cargoes such as silk, alum and cotton might be exchanged for clothes from Flanders, coming *via* Bordeaux and resold in the East. The profit margins were enormous, but so were the risks of navigation, disease, piracy and predatory rulers, besides trade rivals, especially the so-called Apulians led by Amalfi, and, between 1070 and 1095 the Normans, who threatened to control the Straits of Otranto.

(3) To maintain her momentum Venice developed an efficient diplomatic and consular system backed by a powerful navy. In 1104 the Arsenal was established to build the ships and manufacture their equipment. Initially suspicious of the crusades, Venice exploited them to get extra-territorial quarters at Constantinople and the ports of the Frankish states, while extending her voyages to the Crimea and maintaining strained but profitable relations with Egypt. The object was to ensure access to, or a monopoly of, the three major channels (S. Russia, Iraq, Red Sea) between which oriental trade fluctuated as a result of events far to the east. The western trade continued to expand as Amalfitan and then Pisan competition declined, and in 1204 Venice secured from the Latin dismemberment (which she instigated) of the Byzantine Empire, Peloponnesian fortresses, Aegean islands including Euboea and Crete, a large quarter in Constantinople and Gallipoli.

(4) The international boom offered opportunities to others, especially Genoa, with which there were recurrent disputes; the Genoese now courted the renascent Byzantines; both cities expanded and fought, but Venetian strength was able to absorb the effects of the Latin overthrow in 1261.

(5) By 1270 Venetians were penetrating the Atlantic, and the advent of the mariners' compass (c. 1290) made winter navigation possible. This doubled the opportunities, and represented "a great leap forward", at a time when the Languedoc route was politically disturbed. From 1319 a regular convoy, the FLANDERS GALLEYS left Venice in March with spices (particularly pepper), silk, sweet Greek wine (*Malvoisie*) and Cypriot and Syrian sugar. The ships called at Southampton, Margate and Boston, exchanging the cargo for wool. This was taken to Bruges or Antwerp and re-exchanged for finished cloth, with which the fleet returned, dropping off pilgrims for Compostella on the way, to Venice at Christmas. If not sold in Italy, the cloth, with armaments and glass, might be shipped in Apr. to the Crimea or with armaments, timber and slaves to Egypt, and exchanged for silk and spices which returned to Venice in the autumn. These convoys were not necessarily large, but a ship's round trip might be worth a fortune. It was during this boom that the wealthier families turned themselves into a hereditary nobility (1297-1317).

(6) From 1330 the oriental trade began to change. In 1354 the Ottoman Turks seized Gallipoli and began to interfere in the passage of the Dardanelles. After 1364 the Mongols began to disrupt the Asiatic land routes. In the west the prosperity of Lyons increased the importance of Genoa, which now competed for products brought *via* the Indian Ocean. The Venetians had immense Cypriot investments in sugar, cotton, corn and salt, and their trade now passed mainly through Egypt. The Genoese trade came *via* Iraq to Lesser Armenia, whence their Cyprus based shipping collected it. A brawl at the coronation of Peter II of Cyprus in 1372 developed into a series of wars involving the Eastern Empire, Hungary, Austria and Naples on the side of Genoa, Milan on the side of Venice. In 1379 the Genoese attempted to penetrate the Venetian lagoon, but after a long struggle at CHIOGGIA (from which the war is named) were destroyed. Venice now had no western rival in the Eastern Mediterranean.

(7) At the summit of her fortunes, Venice now exploited the petty Italian wars to build up a mainland territory (The *Terraferma*) to control at once the East Alpine passes and her own food supply. Profits were now increasingly invested in building and land. In a properly aristocratic fashion, the nobility spent their money on a magnificence which survives in the glories of Venetian Gothic.

(8) There was, however, a change of spirit. In the East the republic's trade was becoming dependent upon potentially hostile Moslem powers: in the West the Hundred Years' War, the Spanish Reconquest and the Wars of the Roses disorganised some markets, while Aragonese and Hanseatic competition cut profit margins in others. The difficulties were partly masked by the supersession of the labour intensive galley by the bulk-carrying cog or roundship; nevertheless the western seaborne trade in Venetian hands slowly retreated. Profits now came through the control of the overland routes: the city's riches were being maintained less on its contributions to the volume of world trade, and more on the sums which it extracted from it. This began to provoke retaliation. From 1411 Venice had to pay an annual tribute to the Turks. After 1415 German emperors tried periodically to block the Transalpine routes or close the market at Ulm. The republic, nonetheless, continued to expand its *terraferma*, and many nobles to buy estates instead of investing in commerce.

(9) When Constantinople fell in 1453, Venice, as the principal survivor of the Byzantine world, became an object of Turkish acquisitiveness. The Turks mounted their first planned offensive in 1470 and by 1479 they had taken Euboea (Negropont) and most Peloponnesian fortresses, and had inflicted financial penalties; but there was a partial compensation. By a curious piece of legalism, Venice acquired control of Cyprus in 1474, and annexed it in 1489.

(10) All the same the strain had told, and bank failures preceded another wasteful, indecisive, Turkish war (1499-1502) in the middle of which Pedro Cabral's arrival at Lisbon with spices direct from Calicut (June 1501) caused a panic. If Venice and Egypt had been each others' customers before, they became allies now. German and French spice purchases at Lisbon finally took the heart out of the languishing western convoys, and the Flanders Galleys declined after 1515. Venetian-supported Egyptian intrigues at Calicut brought on an Indian War, in which, at the B. of Diu (1509) the Portuguese were victorious. In this year there was another disaster nearer home. The Venetians lost the B. of Agnadello and temporarily the *Terraferma* in the War of the League of Cambrai. (*See* LOUIS XII.)

(11) The position was, however, retrieved by diplomacy, patience, diversification and the Venetian business sense. The Venetian commercial privileges were renewed in 1513. The French wars and the decline of the Flanders galleys deprived Italy of Flemish and English

textiles. From 1516 a Venetian textile industry began a lucrative expansion, 200-fold by 1569. A famous printing industry and glass works arose. Cyprus and Crete were vigorously exploited, and it soon appeared that Portugal could not, after all, control the spice trade; it began to revive through Syria and Egypt, which the Turks conquered in 1517. In 1522 they had also driven the Knights of St. John from Rhodes: the elimination of these holy pirates, who intercepted non-Christian cargoes on Christian ships, benefited Venice commercially, but uncovered Cyprus and Crete militarily. More than ever Venice was dependent upon the good graces of the Porte, and after a Third and creditable War (1537-50) had to cede minor Aegean islands and the last footholds in the Peloponnese. The wartime economy had, however, to be maintained because further wars seemed inevitable; by 1560 the Alexandria spice trade had returned to the volume of 1490, but an immense programme of fortification was started in the colonies in 1564.

(12) The epidemics and recessions of the 1560s culminated in a great famine in 1569. The Turks, who had been preoccupied with Malta, now demanded Cyprus. A combined Venetian, Genoese and Papal fleet failed to reach Cyprus before the Turks landed. The last garrison capitulated at Famagusta in Sept. 1571: the allied fleet, however, won an immense but strictly tactical victory at Lepanto in Oct. It did not recover Cyprus.

(13) While Venice had put her resources into Levantine defence, her strength was being sapped in other and ultimately decisive ways. Inflation caused by American gold reduced the purchasing power of her famous currency (ducats). English and Dutch galleons began to compete in the carrying trade. The Barbary corsairs, the Knights of Malta and of St. Stephen, the English and Dutch carriers themselves, the Spanish Neapolitans and the Dalmatians preyed on the shipping. As if this were not enough, local ship timber gave out; more and more Venetian ships had to be built abroad. Moreover the Dutch had taken over the Portuguese spice trade and more efficiently than they. Venice's share began its definitive decline in 1595. By 1610 Venetian commerce had shrunk to the radius of Crete and in 1630 a plague destroyed a sixth of the population.

(14) One reason for the collapse of the Levantine trade had been political upheavals in the Turkish empire. These ended in a species of 'Bonapartism'. In 1635 the Turks went to war. Both contestants were weaker than before but still matched. The long War of Candia lasted until the surrender of that Cretan fortress in 1669. It should have exhausted the republic. In fact a renewed Turkish offensive in 1684 culminated in the victorious P. of Carlowitz (1699) when the Peloponnese, Sta Maura, Zante and Aegina fell to Venice. Most of these were lost in another war from 1714 to 1718.

(15) Thereafter Venice subsisted on its prestige, in the architectural form which has survived to this day, as a financial centre, manufacturing luxury goods, visited by increasing numbers of wealthy tourists. The republic was destroyed by Bonaparte in 1797, and the city and province thenceforth became an international bone of contention. *See also* ADRIATIC.

VENICE COMPANY. *See* LEVANT CO.

VENN, John (1586-1650), a wealthy wool-merchant in business in the West and in Ireland was a member, from 1629 to 1640 of the Massachusetts Co. In 1640 he was Warden of the Merchant Taylors Co. and M.P. for London. He served as a parliamentary colonel and was Gov. of Windsor from 1642 to 1645. After commanding at Northampton in 1646 he attended Parliament assiduously as a supporter of Cromwell and signed Charles I's death warrant.

VENTA BELGARUM. *See* WINCHESTER.

VENTA SILURUM (CAERWENT), was built by the Romans in A.D. 75 to 100 to replace local native strongholds.

VENUTIUS. *See* BRITAIN, ROMAN-4.

VENVHLE. *See* DARTMOOR

VERANIUS, QUINTUS. *See* BRITAIN, ROMAN-4.

VERCELLI BOOK is a codex of O.E. MSS owned by the Chapter of Vercelli (Italy). It is not known how they came by it. It contains sermons and religious poetry, notably the *Dream of the Rood.*

VERDERERS were judicial officials of royal forests, who acted as keepers of the rolls and held courts to deal with civil infringements of forest law. Courts of Verderers still (1973) sit for the New Forest and the Forest of Dean. *See* FOREST-2.

VERE, DE. Norman family from Bayeux settled by the Conqueror in Essex where Castle Hedingham was their stronghold, with wide estates previously owned by the Saxon thegn Wulfwine. **(1) Aubrey (?-1141),** was joint sheriff of eleven midland counties from 1130 and Great Chamberlain from 1133. This office became hereditary. He was an adherent of K. Stephen and was killed in London. His son **(2) Aubrey (?-1194), 1st E. of OXFORD** and **Count of GUINES** in right of his wife, adhered to the Empress Matilda who gave him the earldom in 1142. Henry II confirmed it in 1156. His younger son **(3) Robert (?1170-1221), 3rd E. (1214)** acquired large Buckinghamshire estates by marriage in 1208. A powerful nobleman, he was one of the executors of Magna Carta. The family, though continuing rich, remained uninteresting until **(4) Robert (1362-92) 9th E. (1371)** who married the semi- royal Philippa de Couci in 1378. He was a domineering but frivolous friend to the young Richard II from 1381 and the latter rewarded him with lands and grants beyond his reasonable desserts. This and his growing political influence, provoked angry opposition, but he and Richard set about creating a western based power against the midland based magnates. In 1385 he became M. of Dublin and in 1386 D. of Ireland with viceregal powers which he exercised through a Lord Deputy, Sir John Stanley, while Richard strengthened his hold on Cheshire. Appealed of treason in 1387, he raised men in Cheshire, but they deserted on the march to London, and he was defeated by the Es. of Derby (the future Henry IV) and Gloucester at Radcot Bridge (1388); he fled to the Low Countries, and was attainted. His uncle **(5) Aubrey (?1340-1400), 1st (1393) and 10th E.** (1397), squire to the Black Prince in Aquitaine and from 1375 Steward of Wallingford, was ambassador to France in 1376, became a household chamberlain in 1381, went to France again in 1383 and fought in Scotland in 1385. The Merciless Parliament treated him with hostility on account of his nephew and drove him from court. Richard II recreated the earldom for him; he took his nephew's earldom by succession when the attainder was reversed, but forfeited it by another attainder of 1399. **(6) John (1433-1513), 13th E. (1464)** by reversal of the previous attainders (*see* 4 and 5 above), was imprisoned as a suspected Lancastrian in 1468, helped to restore Henry VI in 1470, escaped to France from the B. of Barnet (1471), made an unsuccessful attempt on Cornwall in 1475 but escaped in 1484 to the E. of Richmond's party in Paris and then helped to establish him as Henry VII. His attainders were once again reversed in 1485. He was an active military supporter of Henry VII throughout his life. The earldom and office of Great Chamberlain continued until the death of the 20th earl in 1703.

VEREENIGING, P. of. *See* S. AFRICA; SOUTH AFRICAN WAR-8.

VERELST. Family of flower painters originally Dutch. These included **Harmen (?1643-1700),** his younger brother the fashionable and insufferable **Simon (1644-1721),** his son **Cornelius (1667-1734),** his son **Willem (fl. 1640-56).** The grandson of the last, **Harry (?-1785),** was a competent Gov. of Bengal in succession to Clive from 1766 to 1769. He returned with a fair fortune but was sued and driven abroad by those, especially one Willem

Bolts, whose corruption and incompetence he had tried to limit. He was opposed to the political expansion of the HEIC.

VERGE (1) Anciently the area within twelve miles from the King's court (wherever it was) which was under the jurisdiction of the Lord High Steward and the Coroner of the Household. **(2)** The precincts of the palaces of Whitehall and the Savoy considered as sanctuaries. **(3)** Land adjacent to a road which though unmetalled is legally part of the public highway.

VERICA. *See* BRITAIN, ROMAN-2,7; REGNUM.

***VERITATIS SPLENDOR* (Lat = The splendour of truth) (1993)** is a closely argued 176 page (in the English version) encyclical of Pope John Paul II on his Church's moral teaching. It begins with an analysis of Jesus' conversation with the rich young men who asked "what good must I do to have eternal life?" It then sets out the principles for discerning what is contrary to sound doctrine. The following summary by a respectful Anglican must be read with caution. Freedom is not itself a source of values and conscience recognises but does not create the criteria of morality. Conversely the behavioural sciences, if they deny freedom, deny morality for morality is inseparable from choice. Morality, however, is a given or revealed universal law and its immutability is not to be denied. In particular "there is a grave danger in an alliance between democracy and ethical relativism which would remove any sure moral reference point from political and social life and on a deeper level make the acknowledgement of truth impossible ... A democracy without values easily turns into open or thinly disguised totalitarianism". The path to the moral act is through rational choice of the act and some acts are intrinsically evil, for example reducing persons by violence to a source of profit or forcing up prices by trading on ignorance or hardship. The fundamental moral option is inseparable from this choice, hence a good intention is not by itself enough and an evil act performed that good may come, such as rendering the conjugal act deliberately infertile, is against the moral order. But obedience to the moral order is elevating not degrading. "A man's history of sin begins when he no longer acknowledges the Lord as his creator and himself wishes to be the one who determines ... what is good and what is evil." The Church's defence of morality is the defence of freedom and it is the duty of pastors to teach right, and shield people from false doctrine, however seemingly hopeful. In this the theologians have an important function as the scientific component of the church's conscience. The writer then outlines a programme of new evangelism, and ends with a prayer to Mary the Mother of Mercy.

VERMONT (U.S.A.) was reached by Champlain from Canada in 1609. The first English settlement was built in 1690. In 1749 the area was claimed both by New Hampshire and New York, and Govs. Wentworth and Bennington of New Hampshire issued charters to many places in the territory. These became known as the **New Hampshire Grants** and were challenged by New York, which obtained judgement in 1764. Purchasers with New Hampshire titles refused to give up their land, and, led by ETHAN ALLEN, revolted against New York in 1771. They continued till the uprising against Britain. Allen's followers joined the rebels, and with Connecticut's help took Ticonderoga in 1775 and joined the attack on Canada. In 1777 a convention of the towns issued a Declaration of Independence and later adopted a constitution. These documents were presented to the Continental Congress. Neither New York nor New Hampshire had, however relinquished their claims, and they now agreed secretly to partition Vermont between themselves. This agreement was frustrated by the obstinacy of the Vermonters, whose territory was for some years a sovereign but unrecognised state. In 1782

New Hampshire accepted the Connecticut River as their frontier, and the New York claims were abandoned in 1790. There being now no further obstacle to recognition, Vermont was the first state, after the original 13, to be admitted to the Union (1791). This created precedents for similar operations in the subsequent expansion of the U.S.A. Vermont supported the Union in the Civil War.

VERMUYDEN, Sir Cornelius (?1595-1683), a Dutch engineer was employed to embank the Thames in 1621, to drain the Axholme marshes in 1626, and the Bedford Levels of the Fens from 1629 to 1637 and 1649 to 1656.

VERNEY (1) Sir Edmund (1590-1642), servant and friend of Charles I as prince and King, was with him in Madrid. He was M.P. for Buckingham in 1624, for Aylesbury in 1628 and for High Wycombe in the Short and Long Parliament. He was loyal to Charles, lent him money and was frank about the dangers of his policies. He was with Charles in most of his movements and was killed at Edgehill as his standard bearer. His eldest son **(2) Sir Ralph (1613-96), Bart (1661)** was M.P. for Aylesbury in the Short and Long Parliaments and took important notes of the proceedings in the latter. He opposed Laud's ecclesiastical policy as impracticable and unwise, but refused the Covenant and went into exile in 1643. His estates were seized in 1646, but he reacquired them through agents in 1650 and came home in 1653. He was still at variance with current political opinion and was imprisoned in 1656. He was M.P. for Buckingham in 1680, 1685 and 1689.

VERNON, a Norman family **(1)** acquired Haddon Hall in 13th cent. It remained with the senior line until **Dorothy (?-1584),** daughter of the last of the line eloped with Sir John Manners. He and she were the ancestors of the Ds. of Rutland whose residence it thus became. Of their kinsfolk **(2) James (1646-1727)** was a diplomat and from 1674 to 1678 sec. to Monmouth. In 1678 he was M.P. for Cambridge Univ., and from 1693 to 1705 a commissioner of prizes. From 1695 to 1798 and from 1705 to 1710 he was M.P. for Penrhyn; in between for Westminster. In 1696 he worked out the details of the Fenwick plot. He was a Sec. of State from 1698 to 1702. His son **(3) Edward (1684-1759)** ("OLD GROG") also M.P. for Penrhyn from 1722 and a conventional naval officer, advocated offensive action against the Spanish Main in 1739 and, taken at his word, was sent there. He seized Porto Bello, but disagreements with Wentworth, the military commander caused failure before Cartagena, Santiago and Panama. His nickname came from a very durable but distinctive cloth called *grogram* of which he had his clothes made, and passed into the language for his issues of rum and water. In 1745 he became M.P. for Ipswich and C-in-C at the Nore. He wrote anonymous pamphlets against Admiralty inefficiency at this time and was cashiered in 1746. *See* WARS OF 1739-48-2,4.

VERONA, CONGRESS OF (1822). *See* CANNING.

VERRIO, Antonio (?1639-1707), south Italian history painter, was brought over to England from France by Charles II and employed by successive monarchs to decorate walls and ceilings at Windsor, Hampton Court, besides large private houses. The paintings are often enormous.

VERSAILLES, T. of (1) (May 1756) (*see* RENVERSEMENT DES ALLIANCES), between France and Austria consisted of three documents, viz: a treaty of mutual non-aggression; a treaty of mutual guarantee except in relation to the Anglo-French war then in progress; and a secret treaty of mutual aid if either party were attacked by an ally of Britain (i.e. Prussia). **(2) (1757 and 1759).** The first was a military convention amplifying the treaty of 1756; the second prolonged the first.

VERSAILLES, P. of (1919-20) (1) The term is sometimes loosely used for the post-World War I settlement embodied in the major T. of Versailles between the Allies and Germany and three lesser treaties with Austria (St.

Germain Sept. 1919), Bulgaria (Neuilly Nov. 1919) and Hungary (Trianon June 1920).

(2) The Versailles Treaty (known in Germany as the *Versailles Diktat*) was a hybrid document in 440 clauses, beginning with a fascicule setting out the Covenant of the League of Nations. This was in reality a separate treaty between the Allies only, concerning an organisation which Germany was not invited to join. The rest was also settled between the Allies without the Germans. The whole was presented to them on 7 May 1919. The German parliament of 375 agreed with 138 dissentients, to accept it and on 28 June the German delegates signed. In view of its contents they were in great distress.

(3) The following German territories were ceded: (a) Alsace-Lorraine to France; (b) most of W. Prussia, Posen and E. Silesia and part of E. Prussia to Poland; thereby creating the Polish Corridor; (c) Part of Upper Silesia to Czechoslovakia; (d) Memel to Lithuania; (e) part of Schleswig to Denmark; (f) Eupen and Malmedy to Belgium. The countries marked had taken no part in the war, and of these Denmark alone existed during it. In addition Danzig became a Free State under League of Nations protection, and the German colonies, subject to League mandates, were shared out between (in Africa) Britain, France, Belgium and S. Africa; (in the Pacific) Australia and Japan. These last provisions explain why Germany was made to accept the League clauses.

(4) The German army was limited to 100,000 men and the Rhineland was to be demilitarised. The navy was limited to 8 old battleships and 8 cruisers with a limit of 10,000 tons on new ships. Gen. Staff, submarines, an airforce and (somewhat whimsically) a secret service were forbidden. The Heligoland fortresses were blown up.

(5) The German Govt. was to admit guilt for the war and liability for damage to France and Belgium. This was to be made good by reparations in cash or kind. The Brussels Conference of Dec. 1920 fixed their value at the then vast amount of £13,450M, and France was to occupy the Saar and exploit the coal mines until 1935. There was a provision, which no one took seriously, to try the ex-Kaiser Wilhelm II, then living in Holland.

(6) China refused to sign. Ratifications followed in Jan. 1920. The U.S.A. did not ratify, but signed separate treaties later.

(7) All Germans as individuals regarded it as a moral duty, by any means fair or foul to evade or frustrate these provisions, which collectively were one major cause of the rise of Hitler.

VERULAM. *See* BACON-2.

VERULAMIUM, capital of the Catuvellauni, was a Belgic settlement, with fields and dwellings scattered inside extensive embankments S.W. of modern St. Albans (Herts), and possibly the site of Cassivelaunus' stronghold in 54 B.C. The Romans (c. A.D. 47-52) made it the cross-road of Watling St. and the road from Colchester to Alchester and Cirencester. At the time of Boadicea's revolt (A.D. 60), when it was burned, the population was about 15,000. It was reconstructed in A.D. 75 and became a *municipium,* probably of Latin status. A disastrous fire (A.D. 155) led to further reconstruction. St. Alban was martyred there (c. 208-9). Though it suffered from the widespread troubles of urban decline, it was still important as an urban and religious centre when St. Germanus of Auxerre visited it in 429 for his victorious disputation with the Pelagians, which took place in the presence of a great assembly. *See* ST. ALBANS.

VESCI or VESCY of Alnwick and later Kildare. Influential 13th cent. nobles whose large properties, being close to or in hostile areas, made them less powerful than they seemed. **(1) Eustace (?1170-1216),** while a fugitive from K. John, married a bastard of William the Lion, K. of Scots. He returned to England, joined the opposition to K. John and became an executor of Magna Carta. He was

killed, excommunicate, at Barnard Castle, in the upheavals after John's death. His grandsons **(2) John (?-1289)** and **(3) William (?1249-97),** supported Simon de Montfort in the Barons' Wars, but John, wounded at the B. of Evesham, made his peace with the Lord Edward and crusaded with him. The brothers served in both Edward's Welsh campaigns 1277 and 1282, when John was an envoy to Aragon and in 1285 to Holland. William, having succeeded to Alnwick at John's death, inherited Kildare in 1290 at the death of his mother Agnes Marshall and was an Irish Lord Justice until 1294 when Edward sent him to Aquitaine. He had a bastard **(4) William the Younger (?-1314),** born at Kildare to whom just before his death he gave his N. English estates but had to surrender Kildare to the Crown in return for the licence to do so. William the Younger served against the Scots in 1300, sold Alnwick to the Percies in 1309 and was killed at Bannockburn.

VESPASIAN. *See* BRITAIN, ROMAN-2.

VESPUCCI, Amerigo (1451-1512), a Florentine who sailed in westward expeditions in 1499 and 1501, claimed in a book published in 1507 to have discovered a terra firma in 1497 which he named America after himself. There is no corroboration for this claim, but the German geographer Waldseemüller popularised the linguistic usage.

VESTIARIAN CONTROVERSY. A dispute about clerical vestments began under Edward VI. One party thought the issue unimportant and therefore suitable for legislation: the other that vestments smacked of Popery. In 1566 Abp. Parker imposed the use of some very moderate vestments in his *Book of Advertisements* but 37 London clergy refused to conform and there were riots. The matter was taken up by puritans as a means of objecting to episcopal authority and the controversy slowly merged into that greater issue.

VESTRIS, Lucia Elizabeth or Lucy Eliza (1797-1856), singer in light opera in London and Paris, became theatre manageress at the Olympic Theatre where she staged spectacular burlesques on the Parisian model, with many innovations in dress and scenery which have survived.

VESTRY was a meeting of the parish ratepayers under the chairmanship of the incumbent, held in the vestry or parish church to elect churchwardens and after 1600 to nominate guardians of the poor and raise a sufficient rate to maintain the poor (in or out of the workhouse), the roads, the church and churchyard and such things as cattle pounds, pumps, stocks and that part of the land drainage carried by the public sewers. Its activities were supervised if not directed by the local J.P.s. Where landowners had large estates a vestry might comprise only half a dozen people. There were about 9000 vestries but the system was not uniform. Over 700 places were not parishes. In many places there were oligarchic select vestries which had grown up and usurped the functions of the popular ones, or which had been created under local Acts of Parliament; and in some towns the chartered corporation effectively superseded them. A vast number of local enactments created local variations in their powers, so that some, especially in London, were lighting and paving streets. Between them they were levying £10m in rates by 1815. They were notoriously corrupt because there was no effective audit system. For poor-law purposes many areas were amalgamated into Unions in 1834. Their secular functions were transferred to parish and district councils in 1894. *See* LOCAL ADMINISTRATION – ENGLAND AND WALES.

VETERA STATUTA. See OLD STATUTES.

VETERINARY SCIENCE, depended much on traditional and empirical lore and the writings of the Roman Vegetius until the opening of the French veterinary colleges at Lyons (1762) and Alfort (1766) whence the Frenchman St. Bel founded the R. Veterinary College in London in 1790.

VEXIN, FRENCH (Cap: Pontoise) and NORMAN (Cap: Gisors), were separated in 911. The latter as the strategic key to Rouen was much fought over between English and French Kings, until 1195 when it was ceded to France. Richard I built Chateau Gaillard at Les Andelys to replace it.

VÉZELAY (Fr), had a great Cluniac abbey from 9th cent., and became an important pilgrimage centre in 11th. After a fire the church was rebuilt with strange magnificence, and structurally on the model of St Mark's in Venice, in 1120; St. Bernard preached the Second Crusade there in 1146.

VIAN, Sir Philip (1894-1968), commanded H.M.S. *Cossack* which rescued 299 seamen from the German *Altmark* in Norwegian waters in Feb. 1940. In May 1941 he commanded the destroyers in the destruction of the *Bismarck*, in Mar. 1942 the light forces in the B. of Sirte (Med), and in 1944 the British force covering the Normandy landings.

VICAR. *See* ADVOWSON AND TITHE-7.

VICAR APOSTOLIC. A R. Catholic bishop in a country where there is no normal hierarchy or where episcopal functions are impeded, e.g. in Britain until 1850.

VICAR-GENERAL. A bishop's deputy. In the Anglican church usually the Diocesan Chancellor.

VICAR OF CHRIST. The Pope.

VICE CHANCELLOR. (1) The Lord Chancellor's deputy to whom much of his litigious business was delegated before 1876. The office was recreated to provide a regular head of the Chancery Division of the High Court. **(2)** The judge of the Chancery Court of Lancashire before 1970. **(3)** The active, as opposed to the honorific, head of an English university.

VICEROY. This title, more convenient in common speech than 'governor-general' or 'crown representative' or 'Lord Lieutenant' was customarily used of the gov-gen. of India after 1857, and sometimes of the Ld. Lieut. of Ireland, especially in the Indian case because after 1857 he officially represented the Crown and not the HEIC. In fact the title was never official and even the Government of India Act 1935 calls him the Governor General in relation to British India and the Crown Representative in relation to the Princes.

VICE SOCIETY (1802), whimsically named Anglican body which encouraged prosecutions for sexual and similar offences, blasphemous offences and illegal lotteries. It prosecuted Carlyle for blasphemy. In 1886 it merged with the N. Vigilance Assn.

VICHY, a French watering place favoured by Napoleon III, was the seat of the French Govt. under Marshal Pétain from 1940 to 1944.

VICINAGE. *See* COMMONS.

VICKERS, Alfred (1) father (1786-1868), (2) son (1810-37), landscape and marine painters.

VICTOR, Prince of HOHENLOHE-LANGENBURG (1833-91), usually called **Count GLEICHEN,** a half nephew of Q. Victoria, was an admiral and a successful sculptor.

VICTORIA (1819-1901) (Queen 1837, Empress of India 1877), daughter of Edward Augustus D. of Kent, 4th son of George III and Mary Louisa Victoria of Saxe-Coburg and widow of Ernest Charles of Leiningen. Her early education was committed to Louise (later baroness) Lehzen, and from 1827 to the Rev. Geo. Days and a bevy of tutors and teachers. The personal union with Hanover was dissolved at her accession, and she firmly extruded her mother from her own quarters. Lehzen continued in a private secretarial capacity, and Ld. Melbourne acted as mentor as well as Prime Min. K. Leopold of the Belgians also recommended the able Baron Stockmar to her. She opened parliament herself in Nov. 1837.

(2) In 1839 Melbourne resigned and Sir Robt. Peel, being commissioned to form a govt., wanted to replace some of the Queen's Ladies of the Bedchamber. She rejected, on personal grounds, his constitutional view, which was somewhat old fashioned; he refused to proceed and the whigs returned to office.

(3) In 1840 she married her cousin, P. Albert of Saxe-Coburg (The Prince Consort), K. Leopold having brought them together, and he became, in effect, her confidant and secretary, to the eventual exclusion of Lehzen and Stockmar. In the next two years their first two children were born, and three attempts were made on her life. In 1841 she also came into conflict with Palmerston, whose policy seemed likely to alienate France. The new Peel govt. of 1841 agreed with her and Albert on this issue: in 1843 she visited K. Louis Philippe of the French, and he returned the visit in 1844.

(4) She was, by the standards of the day, a modern woman and set other precedents. Since 1848 she had become a railway traveller, and in 1844 acquired Osborne (I. of W.), and in 1848 Balmoral (Scotland). She had visited Germany in 1845, she went to Ireland in 1849. She also upset conservative churchmen by giving birth to her later children under anaesthesia. In 1850 to 1851 she was energetically encouraging the revolutionary Great Exhibition. If her influence on matters of feminine fashion and household taste was prodigious, her views on morality showed more common-sense than the Victorianism invented for her contemporaries: her embarrassing questions are said to have prevented lesbian acts being made an offence.

(5) In politics her work was influenced by a strong sense of the dignity of the throne, and by such factors as the personal charm (or otherwise) of a minister. She could respond to the raffish urbanity of the Whig Ld. Melbourne and the unreliable courtliness of the conservative Disraeli, but she disliked the moral hectoring of the Tory Peel and the Liberal Gladstone's olympian evangelicalism. In internal secular affairs she was a constitutional sovereign, but she held strongly by her prerogatives in overseas affairs, considering that she was entitled to be consulted on every policy step and that there should be no departure from a policy, once settled, without further consultation. This brought her and Palmerston into conflicts, for he was apt to manage foreign policy as if it were his private concern. In such matters other ministers sympathised with her, for they wanted to know what was happening as much as she. Disputes of this sort occurred in 1850 and 1851.

(6) Her sense of dignity and of the sole right of the crown to represent the country in foreign affairs, indirectly influenced imperial affairs too. To add to the empire was (despite liberal misgivings) to add jewels to her crown; imperial, especially Indian, affairs always claimed her attention. This, in its turn, created an interest in the naval and military instruments of policy, both in their human aspect and for their splendour. She initiated the first Crimean schemes of military welfare and helped to create the atmosphere which made Florence Nightingale's nursing revolution possible. She instituted the Victoria Cross (June 1856), and inaugurated the National Rifle Assoc. and the Queen's Prize. In matters of this sort she differed from many of her wiser statesmen, but instinctively reflected public opinion.

(7) The effects but not the intentions of her imperialism were aggressive, but she understood very well that the pursuit of empire needed peace with other great powers. The personal consideration, that she was related to many continental rulers gave her natural private contacts not so easily available to others, but her desire for European peace went beyond this. She feared, reasonably, the upheavals attending Italian and German unification and distrusted bellicose Foreign Secretaries.

(8) In 1861 both her mother and her adored (if somewhat priggish) husband died. She withdrew into mourning and social self isolation. This had significant effects. She continued to carry on her constitutional business and made her late husband's sec., the Hon.

Charles Grey, her private sec., and so almost accidentally created an important constitutional office. Her with-drawal left a gap in Society which had to be filled, especially after his marriage in 1863, by the P. of Wales. After several years, her seclusion excited widespread criticism which continued intermittently until her death, but she began slowly to emerge in 1866, when she opened parliament in person, and in 1867 when she founded the Royal Albert Hall and received the Khedive of Egypt and the Sultan of Turkey. In 1869, through Abp. Tait, she influenced the Lords (despite her own disapproval) in favour of Gladstone's Irish Disestablishment Bill. She did not come out of her desolate isolation until 1879 when she made her first journey to Italy, by which time imperial expansion engrossed much public attention. In 1885-6 she encouraged the Imperial and Colonial Exhibition, which was to leave as its legacy the great complex of institutes and museums in South Kensington, set up to com-memorate her Golden Jubilee in 1887.

(9) By this time people were showing a greater toleration of her peculiarities and her long experience was valued by her ministers. She developed imper-ceptibly into a national representative, perhaps mother-figure, which was suddenly demonstrated by an almost hysterical outburst of public adulation at her Diamond Jubilee in 1897. She died before the close of the Boer War.

(10) She was a short figure, inclined in later life to stoutness. She was not clever but she became well informed. Her political judgement, if not always right, was usually sensible. She was masterful and inconsiderate with her entourage, but utterly conscientious in her endless work, from which she never desisted until the few days of her last illness.

VICTORIA. *See* AUSTRALIA.

VICTORIA AND ALBERT MUSEUM, was founded in 1835 as the SOUTH KENSINGTON MUSEUM, and renamed in 1899.

VICTORIA ADELAIDE Princess ("Empress Frederick") (1840-1901), daughter of Q. Victoria, married Crown Prince Frederick of Prussia in 1858. Her liberal influence over him made her unpopular and after Frederick's short reign in 1888 their son, the Emperor Wilhelm II, encouraged the Prussianism which she found most distasteful, rifled her correspondence and drove her into retirement.

VICTORIA CROSS (V.C.) for conspicuous gallantry in battle, was founded in 1856. It carries a small pension.

VICTORIA FALLS (Africa) were discovered by Livingstone in 1855. The road and rail bridge was completed in 1906.

VICTORIA FALLS CONFERENCE (1963), agreed the dissolution of the Federation of Rhodesia and Nyasaland.

VICTORIA, L. (Africa) was discovered by Speke in 1858. Stanley explored it in 1875 and it was thoroughly surveyed in 1901 by Sir Wm. Garston. The great Owen Falls Dam was built to raise its level in 1954. *See* TRYPANOSOMIASIS; UGANDA.

VICTORIAN ARCHITECTURE. *See* ARCHITECTURE, BRITISH.

VICTORIA UNIVERSITY, a combination of colleges at Manchester, Leeds and Liverpool, became a degree-giving institution in 1884. Women participated equally with men. Manchester and Liverpool were chartered as separate universities in 1903, Leeds in 1904.

VICTORY, H.M.S. 100-gun ship launched at Chatham in 1765 and commissioned in 1778. She was Nelson's flagship from 1803 until his death at Trafalgar in 1805. Paid off in 1812, she remained afloat at Portsmouth until 1928, when she was permanently docked and restored to her Trafalgar appearance.

VICTUALLING BOARD, NAVY, a subsidiary of the Navy Board, bought and supplied food and clothing to the fleet and appointed ship's pursers. In its earlier years high level peculation on contracts made many illicit fortunes, and pursers became richer than most ships officers by

reckoning 14oz to the pound. Sailors' food and clothing varied from the bad to the abominable, and were a matter of endless official complaint and a major cause of desertion. Most of the worst abuses had, however, been removed in time for the Seven Years' War. It was dissolved in 1832.

VICUS. *See* BRITAIN, ROMAN-7.

VIENNA AWARD (Aug. 1940). An arbitration by Hitler between Hungary and Roumania on their running dispute over Transylvania. Most of the Szekler (Magyar speaking) areas were returned to Hungary in such a way as to make Hungary little stronger but Roumania distinctly weaker.

VIENNA, CONGRESS OF (Sept. 1814-Sept. 1815) (*see* LANGRES PROTOCOL; PARIS, T. OF MAY 1814) **(1)** All the European states accepted the Austrian invitation to this Congress (which was to open on 1 Oct. 1814), but none of the minor powers was told of the secret articles of the Paris T. The four major and numerous other powers were thus at cross purposes, since the former were bound to each other to settle everything themselves, while the latter thought that they would have a voice. The Congress and its entertainments overcrowded Vienna, and cost the Austrian treasury some 30M florins. Apart from reigning houses, over 200 royal and princely families with their ministers, mistresses, staffs and retinues appeared. The Hofburg had to accommodate 1400 horses and the stone deaf Beethoven conducted his 7th Symphony.

(2) The main public personalities were:-

Austria	**Metternich**
Britain	**Castlereagh** later **Wellington**
France	**Talleyrand**
Prussia	**Hardenberg** K. Frederick William III Humboldt
Russia	Nesselrode **Czar Alexander III** Razumovski

The Congress secretary was the Austrian FRIEDRICH VON GENTZ. There were also some personalities of a distinct but secondary importance viz:-

Hanover	Count Münster
The Pope	Card. Consalvi
The Sultan	Mavrojeni Pasha

Saxony, which had not been invited, was unofficially represented by Friedrich von der Schulenburg. *Naples* had rival Bourbon and Muratist delegations. The *Spanish* representative, Don Pedro Gomez Labrador, was an insufferable nuisance. The exhausting festivities were supplemented by weekly salons of well known Viennese hostesses (e.g. the Princesses Metternich, Trautmannsdorf, Fürstenberg and Esterhazy) and by bedroom intrigues and rivalries, at least one of which envenomed relations between Metternich and the Czar.

(3) The four allied ministers began their procedural discussions only a fortnight before the official opening date. Then Talleyrand arrived and unanswerably pointed out that the directing body could only be the eight signatories of the P. of Paris, and that they must get their authority from the whole congress. He secured the enthusiastic support of the minor powers; the convening powers hurriedly postponed the formal opening indefinitely, and by so doing admitted France to the inner discussions. The Congress then proceeded *de facto* or informally. It appointed ten committees viz:-

(i)   Germany
(ii)   The Slave trade
(iii)   Switzerland
(iv)   Tuscany (see 5 below)
(v)   Sardinia and Genoa (see 5 below)
(vi)   Duchy of Bouillon
(vii)   International rivers
(viii)   Diplomatic precedence
(ix)   Statistics
(x)   Drafting

The major issues were, from Jan. 1815 onwards, kept in the hands of the Council of Five (the four major allies and France). These were Poland with Saxony, Germany and Italy.

(4) With romantic schizophrenia, the Czar proposed that Austria and Prussia should surrender their Polish provinces, which should be added to Russian-occupied Poland and together constitute a Polish state under his tutelage. In return for this Prussia would demand all Saxony and considerable Rhineland territories with the fortress of Mainz, and Austria would be expected to seek compensations in Italy and Illyria. Prussia was willing to co-operate in principle (see KALISCH CONVENTION) since German acquisitions might be more digestible, and were certainly richer than Poland. Austria was not, because her so-called compensations would amount merely to recovery of previous assets, to which she considered herself entitled anyway. Moreover she, France and Britain feared that the proposal would in reality bring Russian power within striking distance of W. Europe and Vienna. There were barbarous Russian troops in France at this time. Moreover Talleyrand opposed the extinction of Saxony, as infringing the principle of legitimacy, upon which his own Bourbon and every other govt. depended and because Prussia, over-mighty in Germany, could be a menace to France and to Austria. By Dec. 1814 feelings were running high when Prince Repnin, the Russian commander in occupied Saxony, handed over the civil administration to the Prussians and the Russian Grand Duke Constantine issued a proclamation calling on the Poles to unite and fight for their fatherland. It was now suspected that Castlereagh's strong stance was stronger than his govt. was apparently prepared to support. The cabinet had instructed him not to go to war "for any objects which have been hitherto under discussion at Vienna". Talleyrand, however, denounced the extinction of Saxony and got all the minor German states to support him. There was much sympathy for the old Saxon King too in Britain. Hence when the Prussians lost their temper and threatened war if their demands for all Saxony were not met, Talleyrand proposed a secret military alliance to Metterich and Castlereagh. This was signed in Jan. 1815 despite Castlereagh's instructions, and Hanover, Sardinia, Bavaria and Hesse were invited to accede. Its existence was, of course, leaked. The Czar, with disaffected troops and homesick generals, gave way. So did the Prussians. The result was a compromise (Feb. 1815). (See PRUSSIA.)

(5) The cabinet wanted Castlereagh home to explain his policies in a captious but ill-informed House of Commons. Accordingly Wellington replaced him at Vienna (Feb. 1815), but meanwhile Metternich had secretly agreed with Louis XVIII behind Talleyrand's back to expel Murat from Naples in favour of a Bourbon, but in exchange for some adjustments in N. Italy. Castlereagh confirmed this on Metternich's behalf at Paris on his way to London. The general Italian settlement gave the Papacy its old states plus the Three Legations; Genoa went to Savoy – Sardinia; Austria took Lombardy and Venetia, while Austrian princes or clients obtained the smaller duchies. The result was Austrian supremacy throughout Italy.

(6) Since Oct. 1814 the German Committee had wrestled with many sensible and preposterous proposals.

It suffered from its composition, which was restricted to Austria, Bavaria, Hanover, Prussia and Würtemberg. In Feb. 1815 a detailed Prussian scheme of Feb. 1805 was being hotly disputed but on 7 Mar. the news came that Bonaparte had escaped from Elba. The German committee was hurriedly enlarged by Saxony, Hesse, the Netherlands for Luxembourg, Denmark for Holstein, various minor princes, and the Free Cities. This body agreed that a German Diet of all 38 German states, under Austrian presidency, should meet at Frankfort and draft a federal constitution.

(7) Since the decisions of principle had been taken, Bonaparte's Hundred Days and the hasty departure of the leading personalities hardly affected the work, and Gentz had the text of the Final Act in 121 articles ready a fortnight before the B. of Waterloo. It was signed on behalf of Austria, Britain, France, Portugal, Prussia, Russia and Sweden on 9 June, 1815. Spain was left out. Most of the others, save Turkey and the Pope, acceded later.

(8) Castlereagh wanted to support it with a separate Five Power T. of Guarantee but Metterich, apprehensive of Russia, sought instead to renew the secret alliance of Jan. 1815 (see para (5) above). Castlereagh did not wish to divide Europe permanently in this way and in Sept. Austria, Prussia and Russia signed the Holy Alliance. Accordingly Castlereagh adopted the limited objective of a Quadruple Alliance to guarantee the new P. of Paris, with a provision that the signatories would confer at fixed periods to discuss measures "most salutary for the repose and prosperity of nations" (Nov. 1815). See CONFERENCE SYSTEM.

VIENNA, P. of (1809), between France and Austria, transferred W. Galicia to the new Grand Duchy of Warsaw, made some German frontier adjustments, imposed a large war indemnity on Austria and limited her army to 150,000.

VIENNA POINTS 1854-6, represented the war aims (strongly influenced by Austria) of the allies in the Crimean War, viz: **(1)** a European guarantee instead of a Russian protectorate for the two Danubian Principalities; **(2)** Improvement of the Danube Navigation; **(3)** Revision of the Straits Convention of 1841 in western interests, with a limitation on the Russian Black Sea Fleet; **(4)** abandonment of the Russian claim to protect the *millet-i-Rum*. With a Russian abandonment of the Danube delta, and the neutralisation of the Black Sea, these became the basis of the P. of Paris 1856 and made Austria the main practical beneficiary of the Russian defeat.

VIENNA, PRELIMINARIES and T. (Aug. and Oct. 1864) ended the Austro-Prussian war with Denmark, which ceded Schleswig, Holstein and Lauenburg to them jointly. See GASTEIN CONVENTION.

VIENNA, SIEGES of 1529 and 1683. The period between these Ottoman failures represents the European high tide of Turkish power.

VIENNA, T. (1738), settled the War of the Polish Succession. France secured the reversion of Lorraine, the Spanish Bourbons received Naples in appanage in exchange for Parma and Tuscany, which passed to the future Empress Maria Theresa's husband. It isolated Britain diplomatically and altered the maritime balance in the Mediterranean.

VIENNA, T. of (1689). See GRAND ALLIANCE.

VIENNA, Ts. of (Apr. and Nov. 1725). Spain guaranteed the Pragmatic Sanction; the emperor promised his good offices in recovering Minorca and Gibraltar for Spain; Spain was to give trading facilities to the Austrian Ostend Co. The Nov. treaty strengthened these provisions. Bavaria and the ecclesiastical electorates joined the treaty which was supported by Russia and joined later by Prussia. See HANOVER, T. OF (1725).

VIENNE, Jean de (1341-96), Admiral of France from 1373, created the fleet of galleys which, in 1377 with a Castilian force, raided the south coast ports from Folkestone to Plymouth. In June 1378 he beat off English attempted reprisals at Harfleur and Cherbourg. In 1380 he put the I. of Wight and the Channel Is. to ransom sailed up the Thames and burned Gravesend. In 1383 he defeated an English squadron at Gravelines and sacked the commercial base at Sluys. In 1384 he took an amphibious expedition to Scotland. This was inadequate for its purpose and, after ravaging the north of England, he had to retreat past Carlisle. Meanwhile the Ghent citizen militia surprised his reinforcements in the Zwijn (B. of Damme July 1385), and he had to re-embark at Perth for lack of supplies. During the truce after 1389 he was employed against Tunis (1390-1). He was killed on crusade at Nicopolis.

VIET NAM. *See* INDOCHINA; U.S.A.-25 *et seq.*

VIEUXPONT, Robert of (?-1228), partisan and adviser of K. John. Custodian of Arthur of Brittany at Rouen in 1203 and then Lord of Appleby and other northern and Norman fiefs. He also acted as one of John's sheriffs in the north, but went with him to Ireland in 1210 and consequently campaigned in Wales in 1212. In 1216 he was John's joint warden of the Yorkshire Castles.

VIGO. *See* ELIZABETH I-24; SPANISH SUCCESSION, WAR OF-3.

VIKINGS (c. 720-1100) (1) The meaning of the word is contested. Frankish Latin chroniclers called them NORMANNI = Northmen; the English, DANI = Danes (then interchangeable terms); the German, ASCOMANNI; the Irish GALL = stranger namely WHITE for Norwegians or BLACK for Danes, or LOCHLANNACH = northerners. Finns called them RUOTSI 'rowers' whence the Slavonic RUS, the origin of RUSSIA. The Byzantine emperors had VARANGIAN (VAERINGJAR) guards, an old Norse word which appears in WIERINGERMEER, now a drained part of the Zuider Zee. OSTMEN were Vikings who had settled in Ireland.

(2) They began as ship-borne Scandinavian traders in mostly female, slaves which were valuable but obtainable only by violence, and re-exported them for exchange at sources of furs, textiles, bullion and metals. They got ship timber and built excellent ships in Sweden, Denmark and Norway. The Swedish Vikings operated S.E.-wards from the early 8th cent. *via* Estonia, the G. of Finland and the Russian river systems, across the Black Sea to Byzantium and Iraq. Vast amounts of Roman and Arabic, besides English Danegeld coinage have been found at their home settlements. They shared the Baltic as a thoroughfare with the Danes who, however, faced S.W. and in mid-8th cent. began exploiting the ill-defended prosperity of the inheritors of the W. Roman Empire in the Low Countries and the British east coast. The Norwegians at this time were learning blue-water seamanship and moving step by step via the Faeroe Is., the Shetlands and the Orkneys north about Scotland to the Western Is., Man and Ireland, and thence penetrating S. Scotland and N. England from the west. Thus Danish based place names are common in eastern Britain: Norwegian in the N.W. The Norwegians also accidentally found and began to colonise Iceland, then Greenland and finally Canada. There were also powerful Norwegian-led thrusts down beyond the Channel.

(3) During their **piratical stage** small private expeditions temporarily occupied safe places (e.g. off-shore islands or river confluences) not too far from their intended prey and then surprised them, slaughtered the men, looted the valuables and saleable women and made off to their base. When it was full of merchandise, they evacuated it and disposed of the goods elsewhere.

(4) The Norwegians had bases in Caithness and probably the Western Is. when they opened the British Viking era by the sensational sack of Holy I. in 793. From 794 to 806 they raided down both coasts: Jarrow in 794, Iona and N. Wales in 795, Kintyre and Man in 797; Iona again in 802 and 806. Enterprises of this sort continued throughout the era but against mounting precaution and resistance.

(5) The earliest **state organised** forays started from Denmark. Its position across the Baltic-North Sea trade route and the virtually sea-level continuity of Jutland with N. Germany exposed it to attacks which had to be met by a war organisation. The Danish world then included the Kattegat coasts and the Oslofjord. To protect their rear during westward anti-Carolingian expeditions the Kings first attacked the Slavonic Wends and Obotrites to the E. of the neck of Jutland, while building a 10-mile wall (The Danevirke) across it to safeguard their base and the easy route across the isthmus. These precautions taken, K. Guthfrith (or Godfred) the Proud made a massed raid on Frisia and the Carolingian Low Countries in 803 and began to prepare a greater expedition.

(6) He had, however, succeeded to the position of Sigurd Hring, a Norwegian who had become King by a victory at Bravik in about 777. Sigurd had married Alfhild by whom he had a famous son, Ragnar Lodbrok (hairy breeches) (?-862-6). Sigurd died after a battle in 797 and Guthfrith then married Alfhild and they had children. She died a few years later, Guthfrith now demanded the hand of Ase, daughter of Harald, the Chief of Agder on the Skagerrack in the Norwegian south. It was refused and he killed Harald and took her by force. She waited until the resulting son, Halfdan the Black, was born and then had Guthfrith murdered. The second attack was thus never launched and the ensuing sanguinary Dano-Norwegian internal politics led eventually to the rise of a recognisable Norway through Halfdan the Black. The process interrupted major westward sea-faring aggression for a generation.

(7) Halfdan's elder kinsman Ragnar Lodbrok may best be described as a sea-king who, though still in part a pirate, initiated Viking **colonisations.** In 831 he was in Ireland, then a gold-producing area. Wicklow (835) and Dublin (836) were founded and in 838 Cornwall raided. In 839 a fleet under one Thurkill built a base at Lough Rea and seized Armagh and Clonmacnoise. Ragnar's much larger fleet tested England from Lindsey to Portland, crossed to the Seine, sacked Rouen and in 845 reached Paris which bought him off for 7000 lb of silver. His crews, however, were depleted during their withdrawal by dysentery; storms overtook the under-manned ships; the withdrawal became a, perhaps superstitious, flight. Thurkill had, meanwhile been taken in 843 and drowned by the Irish High King Maelseachlann, but Ragnar's sons explored the route from Ireland to Spain and made two-way contact with the Spanish Moors.

(8) During Ragnar's 19-year absence, Danish leaders had become inconveniently independent, so in 850 he returned to re-assert himself. In 851, having sent a reconnaissance to Thanet which K. Aethilwulf's son Aethilstan expelled at the cost of his life, his main force of 350 ships stormed Canterbury and Rochester, beat K. Beortwulf of Mercia at London, and then marched, probably through topographical ignorance, south along Stane Street towards Chichester. K. Aethilwulf with the Wessex troops met it at Ockley near Dorking and virtually destroyed it (852).

(9) The disaster diverted Ragnar to softer targets. In the track of his sons, he entered the Mediterranean and raided the mouths of the Rhone and Tuscany. Behind him Norwegian colonists were filling the Irish ports. In 852 some of them attempted Shropshire through Wales. Thereupon K. Aethilwulf and K. Buhred of Mercia forced the Prince, Rhodri ap Merfyn, to set up efficient defences. Thus, in 855 Rhodri defeated a further incursion and slew its leader. Thenceforth Vikings avoided Wales, which thus shielded central England from the west.

(10) The piratical habit of raiding from a local base was now imported into grand strategy. Frankish wealth made the Seine attractive. Reconnaissance parties under Ragnar's son Hingwar entered Sheppey and Thanet. Ragnar died between 862 and 864. In 865 an advance force wintered in Thanet and levied supplies. In 866 Hingwar arrived with a large fleet. The B. of Ockley had shown that conquest by full scale operations could alone make Wessex into a base against N. France. Hingwar's approach was indirect. He crossed to E. Anglia, stayed a year collecting information and horses; rode into Northumbria, then in political confusion (Autumn 867) and seized York. The Northumbrians composed their differences and unitedly attacked him. They were lured into the City and ambushed (B. of York Gate, Mar. 868). Hingwar set up a collaborative King. It was at last clear that he intended conquest not plunder. He and his brother Hubba came south, were bought off at Nottingham by K. Buhred and moved to E. Anglia. The E. Anglian K. Edmund made a disastrous assault on their entrenchments at Thetford, was captured and, tied to a cross, was used as an archery target (Nov. 870). Leaving their brother Halfdan in charge, they went north, met Olaf the White of Dublin and with him subdued Strathclyde and went on to Dublin in 871. The main army now rode from Thetford to the conquest of Wessex, but was slaughtered by Alfred (not yet King) at the B. of Ashdown (q.v. Jan. 871).

(11) The remnants retreated upon reinforcements which brought them forward again. In a long series of engagements, during which K. Aethilwulf died of wounds, the W. Saxons, now under the great K. Alfred, retreated steadily leaving an empty land. The Vikings took Winchester and reached Wilton just beyond Salisbury but it availed them nothing. By the autumn they had arranged an armistice and retired to London. From 872 to 874 they left Wessex alone. Hingwar died in Dublin.

(12) As before, they switched to a softer target. They forced Buhred to supply them by threatening devastation and then, when fully recruited, attacked him. The Mercian collapse was sudden and complete. Buhred retired to Rome, while they set up a collaborator and reorganised. Halfdan, like Hingwar and Hubba, went north to continue the operations in Strathclyde; another brother Guthrum (Guthorm) seized Wareham, where Alfred besieged the crews. They swore to leave, but in the Spring of 877 rode for Exeter. He came upon their heels and his fleet blockaded the Exe. The Viking fleet left Poole to relieve the siege but its 120 ships were wrecked off Swanage. The Exeter Vikings gave hostages and oaths, and left Wessex overland for Gloucester.

(13) Alfred had to disband for the harvest, while Guthrum, not involved in agriculture, could assemble a new army. He rode into Wessex at the New Year 878 and simultaneously K. Hubba appeared in the Severn with Ragnar's raven standard, the *Land Ravager*. Caught off balance, Alfred retired to the Somerset marsh island of Athelney, which he fortified, within sight of the coast. As K. Hubba landed, Eorlderman Odda surprised and killed him and took the Land Ravager. Guthrum's detachments were already concentrating on Athelney. Odda's importantly symbolic victory depressed them and heartened the West Saxons. Alfred, outside Athelney, drew together a large army. He smote Guthrum at Ethandun (Edington), drove him to Chippenham and invested him.

(14) Alfred's Christianity, skill, courage and luck had impressed Guthrum. He now applied for baptism, and at Wedmore Alfred stood godfather to him and thirty of his chiefs. They agreed to leave Wessex, and either set up as provincial men of consequence in E. Anglia or left for the Low Countries where the main Danish host under Sigfrith Snake-Eye, Ragnar's successor in Denmark landed in 880. In eleven years the area was devastated, but in 891 the Germans stormed Sigfrith's camp at Louvain. He perished. The survivors were brought to Sussex by K. Bjorn Ironside and Hastein. The latter's men, driven hither and thither by Alfred, ended in London whence some left or took service under the French King.

(15) By 899, when Alfred died, the Danish Vikings had lost heavily, and Britain and the Low Countries had become risky for their enterprises. K. Edward the Elder and his sister Aethelfleda could reconquer the Scandinavian areas of England for they were not reinforced because the remaining Viking resources were deployed by Hrolf or Rollo the Ganger (Strider) *via* the Seine against another soft target, the realm of K. Charles the Simple. The Northmen liked the Seine area and in 911 by the T. of St. Claire-sur-Epte Charles gave it to them as the Duchy of Normandy with Rollo as the first Duke, thereby setting up a Scandinavian vested interest against further Viking raids. This brought comparative peace in the Channel while Anglo-Saxon campaigns against midland Vikings proceeded. The latter were thin on the ground and mainly concentrated in towns. By 922 when Edward built a fort at Manchester, all the towns south of the Humber had submitted.

(16) Norwegian settlements in Cumbria and on the Solway, linked Dublin with the Viking kingdom of York. Edward was closing all the other links and threatening both Cumbria and York. In 918 Ragnvald Olvar, K. of Dublin, landed in Cumbria, fought a battle on the Stainmoor with Constantine, K. of Scots and the Bernician Angles, and next year took York. In 921 he died. One of his brothers, Guthfrith, drove another brother, Sigtrygg Gale, from Dublin and the latter succeeded to the weak inheritance. Hence, when Edward built a bridge at Nottingham and a fort at Bakewell, Sigtrygg, Constantine, the Anglian eorldermen Edred and Uhtred and the Northumbrians submitted to him at Bakewell (923).

(17) K. Aethilstan (r. 925-39) having had Siggtrygg baptised and married to his sister, took over Northumbria when he died a year later, and drove his sons Guthfrith and Olaf Kuaran, who tried to interfere into Scotland. The T. of Emmett (or Eamont) (926) which included the Welsh, ratified the surrender of Bakewell, and Eorlderman Edred became Aethilstan's gov. of Northumbria.

(18) The Dublin Ostmen did not intend to relinquish Northumbria. In nine ensuing years of military preparation and diplomacy, they secured allies within Britain, and Aethilstan isolated them from their continental friends. In 937 the allied Ostmen, Scots and Picts confronted the English at Brunanburh (probably in Cumbria) but the latter won a tremendous victory, celebrated in song, which marked a distinct stage in Anglo-Viking relations. For forty-three years, no Scandinavian power supported attacks on England (*see* AETHILSTAN'S SUCCESSORS).

(19) In 978 the ten-year old Ethelred the Unready came unluckily to the throne in discreditable circumstances and England became a soft target. Vikings attacked Chester, Southampton and Thanet in 980; in 981-2, Devon and S. Wales. A violent, piratical and heathen reaction took place in Scandinavia with the rise of K. Swein Forkbeard (r. 955-1014) in Denmark and Earl Hakon of Ladi in Norway. Swein, like Guthfrith the Proud, covered his back by paying off the Wends and settling disputes with the Jomsborgers, a kind of praetorian garrison at the mouth of the Oder. He then prepared an invasion of England. In 991 a reconnaissance in force under Olaf Trygyasson coasted *via* the mouths of the Scheldt to Sandwich, sacked Ipswich and passed north-about to the Ostmen strongholds of the Irish Sea, having, as urged by the churchmen, been paid 10,000 lb of silver to go away. This *gafol*, raised by the first Danegeld, represented a misreading of Viking intentions. They could not be bought off because they intended conquest. On the other hand the churchmen doubted the competence and even the loyalty of the court eorldermen and saw silver as a substitute for ineffectual deaths. In 992 eorlderman Alfric lost the fleet. In 993 two Viking fleets appeared. One ravaged Lincolnshire and Northumbria: the other was frustrated by Essex troops

under eorlderman Brihtnoth at Maldon where he lost his life, but became the hero of an epic poem. In 994 K. Swein came himself with Olaf and the main force. Their attack on London was beaten off but, without interference from the eorldermen, they devastated the home counties. The govt. now made peace feelers in pursuance of a new diplomatic policy. The spokesmen were Bp. Alphege (Alfheah) of Winchester and the royal Eorlderman and chronicler Aethilweard.

(20) They offered 16,000 lb of silver. They also approached Olaf Trygvasson separately. His father had been a Norwegian under-king of K. Hakon the Good and, being descended from K. Harald Fairhair was entitled to the Norwegian throne. He had supporters at home. The English diplomats persuaded him to break with Swein and, with English finance, to recover Norway for himself. He gave hostages and was baptised at Aethilred's court at Southampton where he received rich gifts and undertook never to attack England again. How he deceived Swein is unknown, but having taken his fleet to Ireland and paid it off, he went to Norway, easily overthrew Hakon of Ladi and took the throne.

(21) This English diplomatic success prevented an immediate debacle but Swein changed from a strategy of occupation to one of attrition for which Vikings were peculiarly well qualified. Ship-borne and mounted raids from ports on both sides of the Irish Sea were widespread and worryingly devastating. The govt. made a combined attack on Cumbria, but the enemy coasted round to Normandy, refitted, and then, having devastated Hampshire and S. Devon, occupied the I. of Wight. They were given 24,000 lb while Aethilred approached the Normans and fatefully married Emma, sister of D. Richard.

(22) The problem was that the Kingdom's warlike resources did not include an adequate fleet, while repeated Danegelds exacerbated without stopping the devastation. Men were beginning to despair and some English-born Danes supported Swein anyway. In 1002 the govt. uncovered a plot against the King's life. Swein appeared off the I. of Wight. The govt. organised a counter-conspiracy and on St. Brice's Day (12 Nov.) Danes (mostly English subjects) including Swein's sister Gunnhild, were simultaneously killed. The massacres were a European sensation. Swein landed and sacked Wilton and Sarum, Eorlderman Aelfric declining to stop him. By 1005 his devastations were causing a famine. The Govt. negotiated a truce for 30,000 lb and set about reorganisation. Alphege, now Abp. of Canterbury, went to Rome for his *pallium*. One Edric Streona became Eorlderman of the Mercians. A fleet was built. New systems of mobilisation were established. Danish designs were never in doubt. A fleet under Thorkel, Earl of the Jomsborgers, was refitting on the Scheldt. In the spring of 1008 the English fleet and King concentrated at Sandwich for a major test. They broke up amid denunciations of treachery. In particular eorlderman Brihtric, brother of Edric Streona denounced Wulfnoth, a squadron commander who promptly deserted with his ships. Brihtric went in pursuit and lost his own ships in a storm. The King retired with the outnumbered remnant to London, whereupon Thorkel seized Sandwich.

(23) Besides Thorkel, the fleet had two other leaders, his brother Hemming in charge of the Danes and Olaf Harald's son (later known as St. Olaf), who had Norwegian claims similar to those of the late Olaf Trygvasson. Olaf unsuccessfully attacked London. Thorkel fortified Greenwich and the whole force abandoned the siege of the City and devastated the Home Counties again. In 1010, having beaten Ulfketel Snilling and the E. Anglians at Rondham Heath, it devastated E. Anglia. Chaos ensued. The govt. negotiated on the basis of a further *gafol*, but meantime Olaf stormed Canterbury (1011) and captured Abp. Alphege.

He, refusing to ransom himself, was taken to Greenwich. He was steadfast, and for almost a year followed the same diplomatic policy towards Olaf Harald's son as he had with Olaf Trygvasson, with similar results. He converted Olaf and some of his men. The Greenwich Vikings expected a large ransom for an Abp; just before Easter 1012 the King paid no less than 48,000 lb. The Danes, in particular, got very drunk on it and battered Alphege to death. Olaf quarrelled with Thorkel and his men fought a battle with the Jomsborgers, after which he left England with his share of the *gafol* and went south, while Thorkel and the Jomsborgers took service under K. Aetlidred in London. This has never been explained for they were in the sworn service of K. Swein who was known to be coming. Conceivably part of the exceptionally large *gafol* was paid for their temporary adhesion, perhaps as a kind of police. The unwisdom of the transaction is plain.

(24) In 1013 Sweyn arrived *via* Sandwich and the Humber, and set up his H.Q. at Gainsborough, where he took hostages from Lindsey, Northumbria and the Danish Five Boroughs. Leaving his young son Canute in charge of the fleet, he rode *via* Oxford to Winchester, moved upon London, which resisted him, and doubled back to Bath where he took hostages from Wessex. In the face of this London gave up the struggle. Aethilred, unsupported by his Jomsborger bodyguard, fled with his family to the court of D. Richard, his Norman brother-in-law.

(25) There was now another reversal of fortune. Olaf, Harald's son, was in Normandy: his councillor Rani in England watching events. On 2 Feb. 1014 K. Swein died of a stroke or was slain in a dream by K. Edward the Martyr. Oaths sworn to him lapsed, and the English magnates, free to invite Aethilred back, did so, while at Gainsborough there was a delay for the fleet to accept Canute. Olaf exploited it. Landing at the Lyme Bay end of the Fosse Way he rode ahead of rumour to Gainsborough at the other end. Canute just avoided disaster by taking to his ships, and having collected such men as he could, sailed for the Scheldt where Thorkel, bringing 21,000 lb of silver, joined him from Greenwich. Aethilred celebrated a prematurely joyful restoration.

(26) In his physical decline and with the precedent of St. Brice's Day (*see* 22 above), he accepted unwisely unscrupulous advice to depose Sigfrith and Morcar, the Lawmen of the Five Danish Boroughs which had submitted to Swein in 1013. Edric Streona undertook the task by inviting them to dinner, murdering them, putting Sigfrith's widow Aldgytha into Malmesbury Abbey and seizing their great estates. Nothing more provocative was conceivable. The strong minded Aetheling Edmund (later King) perceived this and in his first public act defied his father and Edric. He rode to Malmesbury, married Aldgytha, rode to the Five Boroughs and took over the properties. The pleasure in the Boroughs healed the rift, but created another in the English leadership. Canute returned to Lyme Bay. Aethilred broke down. Edric raised the men of Wessex; Edmund brought an army from the midlands. They opposed Canute not in unison but in rivalry. Edric seems to have wanted to be the real ruler under a nominal King such as Aethilred had become or as the young Canute might be. Faced with a determined heir apparent, he deserted to Canute with his men, to ensure Canute's victory and his own importance.

(27) Edmund would not give up. While Edric was trying to bring over Edmund's Wessex to the enemy, he with E. Ughtred of Northumbria started to recruit in Edric's Mercia. Canute rode to York, thus turning Edmund's position. Ughtred deserted to Canute who slew him and put Eirik Hakon's son in his place. He then returned to the fleet, coasted round to London to find that Aethilred was dead and Edmund Ironside King. He laid siege to the City. Edmund recovered Wessex loyalty and marched to the rescue. Edric met him at Aylesford

and there was some kind of reconciliation. After long convoluted marches, the semi-amateur English and the professional Danish armies met at Assendun (Assington) N.W. of Colchester, and "there King Canute had the victory, though all England fought against him" – save Edric who fled with his Mercians. By the T. of Olney Edmund gave a *gafol* of 72,000 lb, divided the Kingdom with Canute along Watling Street subject to a pact of mutual succession. London paid 10500 lb. Within six months Edmund was dead. Canute took the whole. Thorkel became E. of E. Anglia. Canute sensibly slew Edric Streona.

(28) For later Viking history *see entries on* CANUTE AND HIS SONS; EDWARD THE CONFESSOR; HAROLD II; HASTINGS, CAMPAIGN AND B.

(29) Viking history, as opposed to the history of states peopled by them, effectively ended as regards England with the B. of Hastings. In Scotland it lasted a little longer with K. Magnus Barefoot's seizure of the Western Isles between 1098 and 1104.

VILAYET. A large Ottoman province ruled by a VALI.

VILL was technically a collection of houses which has or had an active church, and a name by reputation, usually a village or township and its vicinity.

VILLAFRANCA, CONVENTION or TRUCE (11 Aug. 1859) brought the fighting in the Franco-Austrian war to an end.

VILLAGES. There are no rules for establishing the location or foundation date of any of the 9000 villages in England and Wales, but certain classifications are possible. **(1)** Nucleated residential association near a resource such as, most often, an open field but also a fishery, or mine. **(2)** Roadside or seaside linear building. **(3)** Congregation at a cross-road or **(4)** in disturbed areas, a castle. **(5)** Resort to isolated hard sites in otherwise soft ground. **(6)** Later planned building. The presence or absence of water was often decisive. About 1000 Domesday villages disappeared during the Black Death.

VILLARET (DE) JOYEUSE, Louis Thomas (1750-1812), French admiral trained under Suffren, reorganised the navy, and commanded the fleet on the Glorious First of June (1794, Fr. = Combat of Prairial Year II.). He later fell under political suspicion and hid at Oleron until the establishment of the Consulate, when he was sent with a fleet and army to San Domingo and then become Capt. Gen. of Martinique, which he defended heroically until forced to surrender in 1809. He ended as gov. of Venice.

VILLARS, Claude Louis Hector, Duc de (1658-1734), distinguished French Marshal, defeated the Margrave of Baden at Friedlingen in 1702 but was defeated and badly wounded by Marlborough and P. Eugene at Malplaquet in 1709. In 1712, however, he recovered and drove P. Eugene back to Brussels and settled the P. of Rastadt.

VILLAS, ROMAN, were unitary establishments and centres of, mostly lowland estates, usually but not always based on agriculture. They varied from modest farmsteads to a luxury complex such as that at Fishbourne (Sussex) and presumably represented the reinvestment of profits. It has been suggested that in some areas later parishes followed villa estate boundaries and that the many Coldharbours marked on ordnance maps often recall their roofless ruins used as cattle pounds.

VILLEINAGE. *See* FEUDALISM.

VILLEHARDOUIN, Geoffroi de (?1152-?1212), marshal of Champagne and Romania wrote, as an eyewitness, the *Conquête de Constantinople,* an account of the Fourth Crusade, the election of Baldwin of Flanders as Latin Emperor and the subsequent partitions. He knew all the leading figures concerned.

VILLENEUVE, Pierre Charles, Comte de (1763-1806), French Admiral escaped from Brueys' disaster at the B. of the Nile (Aug. 1796) and was given command of the Toulon squadron in Nov. 1804, 50 as to play the main role in Bonaparte's elaborate plan to invade Britain (*see*

TRAFALGAR, CAMPAIGN AND B.). He was taken prisoner at Trafalgar, released on parole and stabbed at Rennes.

VILLEROI, Francois de Neuville, Duc de (1644-1730), French Marshal and childhood friend of Louis XIV, was defeated and captured by P. Eugene in Italy in 1701 and defeated by Marlborough at Ramillies in 1706.

VILLIERS (pron: Villers), old Leicestershire family, whose fame or notoriety began with **Sir George (?-1606),** and his two wives. **A. Audrey (?-1587),** the first, bore him, *inter alios,* **Sir Edward (?1585-1626),** master of the mint and comptroller of the court of wards (lucrative offices). He married Barbara St. John, and by a special remainder, their eldest son William (?-1643), became the **2nd Vist. GRANDISON.** He was the father of **Barbara (1641-1709), D. of CLEVELAND,** mistress of many men, especially Charles II and John Churchill, later D. of Marlborough. William's brother, another **Sir Edward (1620-89),** married Frances Howard, whose father was the second E. of Suffolk. Strong royalists, they were rewarded with the royal manor at Richmond, while Frances was governess to the princesses (later Queens) Mary and Anne. Of their children **Edward (1656-1711),** a dull man, was the **1st E. of JERSEY** while **Elizabeth (?1607-1733),** an accomplished and vivacious woman, who squinted like a dragon, was mistress of William III. He gave her most of James II's Irish property, and after they parted in 1695, he arranged for her to marry Ld. George Hamilton, and created him **E. of ORKNEY.** She is said to have entertained a dangerous hatred for John Churchill. Her brother's eldest grandson was the ancestor of the other Es. of Jersey, while the younger, **Thomas (1709-86),** a diplomat, became **1st E. of CLARENDON** of the second creation, and founded a family of diplomats and politicians.

B. Sir George's (*see* above) second wife **Mary (?-1632), Countess of BUCKINGHAM for life (1618)** bore him **John (?1591-1657), Vist. PURBECK (1619)** who married a daughter of Sir Edw. Coke and went mad; **George (1592-1628), 1st D. of BUCKINGHAM,** whom James I and Charles I made rich and notorious; **Christopher (1593-1630),** monopolist and **1st E. of ANGLESEY (1623);** and **Susan (?-after 1651)** who married William Feilding **1st E. of DENBIGH** and secured rich and highborn marriages for all her children. The Stuart courts were thus pervaded by the determination, beauty and occasional brilliance of this formidable family See succeeding entries.

VILLIERS (BUCKINGHAM). (1) George (1592-1628), Vist. VILLIERS (1616) E. (1617) and 1st D. of BUCKINGHAM (1623) owed his first fortune to his good temper and beauty, and to a political intrigue designed to oust James I's reigning favourite, the D. of Somerset. In Apr. 1615, against Somerset's hostility, he became a gentleman of the bedchamber with £1000 a year, and (Somerset having fallen) Master of the Horse in Jan. 1616. He was more interested in influence for its own sake than in policy and used it to benefit his relatives and friends, but without risk. Thus he repudiated his brothers Christopher and Edward in the monopolies which he had obtained for them, and manoeuvred himself into a neutral position over the peculations of his friend Bacon. He favoured the P. of Wales' Spanish marriage as a way of helping James to secure a R. Catholic evacuation of the Palatinate (*see* THIRTY YEARS' WAR). In 1623 he went with the Prince on the abortive journey to Spain and when they returned he tried to whip up anti-Spanish war fever, combined with a French marriage and alliance. Richelieu frustrated him, and he then resolved to catch Protestant fervour by naval help for Richelieu's rebels, the Huguenots of La Rochelle. His expensive lack of principle in an age of principles, his extraordinary failure to understand the effects of his actions, and his unrealistic and sanguine temperament combined to infuriate all responsible public men. He was assassinated before setting out on his second expedition to La Rochelle. His son **(2) George (1628-87), 2nd D.** was brought up by Charles I, took an impetuous part in the later Civil Wars, and so lost his vast estates. He became one of Charles II privy councillors in 1650 and had the good sense to try and reconcile the King with the Scottish Presbyterians. He escaped to Holland after the B. of Worcester (1651), where he alarmed Nicholas and Hyde by intrigues for a restoration with the help of the Levellers. Eventually in 1657 he went to England, swept Fairfax's daughter Mary off her feet and married her. The object was to get his estates back by the Fairfax influence, but the Protector thought that it was a presbyterian plot and, after a long search, arrested him (Apr. 1658). He was bound over in Feb. 1659 and was thus at liberty and claiming credit, at the Restoration. His estates were restored and he was suddenly very rich, but distrusted by Clarendon, whom he cordially disliked. He took a leading part in bringing about Clarendon's fall and thereafter, though he held nothing more than the Mastership of the Horse, was so widely regarded as the King's first minister, that Charles had to deny it. It was largely due to his ideas of toleration that Charles published his Declaration of Indulgence; he tried to get rid of Romanist influence at court, and was involved in a long feud with the D. of York. Not surprisingly he was one of the Cabal who was not let into the secret of the T. of Dover (1670), so that when it began to leak out and he was attacked by the Commons in Parliament, his revelations were too few for them, but too many for Charles. He was dismissed. For some years he was now engaged in promoting toleration and opposing the doctrines of non-resistance then much canvassed. Consequently he found himself in some initial sympathy with Shaftesbury, but by 1680 he had seen the dangers of the "Popish Plot" agitation and absented himself from the debates on the Exclusion Bill. Thereafter he retired. He was one of the handsomest and wittiest men of his generation.

VILLIERS (CLARENDON) (*see* VILLIERS). **(1) Thomas (1709-86), 1st E. of CLARENDON (second creation) (1782)** was ambassador to Warsaw in 1737 and also to Dresden in 1740. In 1743, being well informed on Austro-Prussian affairs, he was sent to Vienna and then in 1744 back to Poland, where the Saxon elector-King was. Frederick the Great used him as a peace negotiator with Saxony, to such purpose that it was found convenient to appoint him British Ambassador to Berlin (1745). He was an M.P. from 1747, left diplomacy in 1748 but held offices under Ld. North. His wife was a daughter of the last Hyde E. of Clarendon. His grandson **(2) George William (1800-70), 4th E. (1838)** began as a diplomat, then worked in the Irish customs and in 1831 negotiated a commercial treaty with France. His reward was the important legation at Madrid (1833) where he negotiated the Quadruple Alliance (Britain, France, Portugal, Spain) for preventing interventions in the Spanish and Portuguese Civil Wars. This won him much regard at home and abroad; in 1839 he was offered and refused the Governor-Generalship of Canada and then entered the cabinet as Lord Privy Seal, and promptly found himself at variance with Palmerston over Levantine policy. He resigned with the govt. in 1841 and became known as a free trader, who favoured a Liberal treatment of Ireland (on which he was well informed). In 1846 he became the Whig Pres. of the Board of Trade, but in 1847 accepted the Irish Lord Lieutenancy. This was a popular appointment, but he was soon in conflict with all parties, because he had to deal firmly with both Romanist and Orange disturbances, and import cheap food to relieve starvation, yet maintain the solvency of Anglo-Irish landlords. His life, of course, was in constant danger, while Westminster politicians attacked him for doing too little or too much. All the same he had retained public

respect when he left Ireland in 1852, and was canvassed for, but rejected, the prime ministership. In Feb. 1853 he succeeded Ld. John Russell at the Foreign Office, and was there throughout the Crimean War and the peace negotiations. His diplomatic experience was very valuable, particularly in his handling of Napoleon III, and much of the P. of Paris was his work, but politicians at home also relied upon him to solve the dangerous crisis which replaced Aberdeen by Palmerston. He remained Foreign Sec. until 1858, and returned to the post in 1865-6. He became Liberal Foreign Sec. in 1868 and negotiated the *Alabama* settlement with the U.S.A. in 1869. He died in office.

VILLIERS (then PALMER), Barbara (1641-1709), Countess of CASTLEMAINE (1660), D. of CLEVELAND (1669) (*see* VILLIERS A) married Roger Palmer, soon made E. of Castlemaine, in 1659 and became Charles II's mistress in May 1660. Though she undoubtedly had side affairs with Charles Berkeley, James Hamilton, John Churchill and probably with the E. of Chesterfield, she remained the *maitresse en titre* until 1671, when she was slowly superseded by Louise de Keroualle. Her political influence, based mainly on personal considerations, is uncertain but she had a part in the dismissal of Clarendon's friend Sir Edw. Nicholas, in the promotion of Sir Henry Bennet (later Arlington), in Churchill's earlier advancement and in the fall of Clarendon himself. Accustomed in bed to communication and appraisal of character, her influence on policy was not necessarily malign, despite her extravagance and rapacity. Charles II was, on matters of calculated policy, hard to move. Besides the five already mentioned, the names of seven other lovers are known, and she had at least seven children, none apparently by her husband. In 1705 she married a Denbigh relative (*see* above) Robert Feilding but the marriage was void because he was already married. For her royal bastards *see* FITZROY.

VILLIERS, Christopher (?159?-1630), 1st E. of ANGLESEY (1623), was a friend of James I, who gave him a number of reversions and an income through monopolies of gold and silver wire and ale houses. Considered a worthless person, he was one of the targets of the complaints by the Commons about monopolies.

VINCENT, Henry (1813-78), chartist champion, was convicted of sedition at Newport (Mon.) in Nov. 1839. This caused a sanguinary miners' riot, which proved the summit of his career. He was imprisoned again in 1840 but thereafter, though a very effective publicist on social questions, he held public interest decreasingly.

VINCENT (1) Sir Howard (1849-1908) was first director of the C.I.D. at Scotland Yard and from 1885 to 1908 Conservative M.P. for Sheffield. He secured the reform of the law on alien immigration and the creation of the Public Trustee. His brother **(2) Sir Edgar (1857-1941), Ld. (1914) and 1st Vist. D'ABERNON (1926)** was financial adviser to the Egyptian govt. from 1883 to 1889, Gov. of the Ottoman Bank from 1889 to 1897 and M.P. for Exeter from 1899 to 1906. He was in Poland during the Russian invasion of 1920 and Ambassador to Berlin from 1920 to 1926. Through his friendship with Stresemann, he negotiated the Anglo-German commercial agreement of 1924 and the Locarno agreement of 1926. He also headed an economic mission in S. America and did much work for art galleries and museums.

VINCENT, William (1739-1815) was associated with the Westminster Abbey foundation almost all his life, beginning as a pupil at the school in 1747 and ending as Dean from 1802. He superintended the restoration of the Abbey and laid out Vincent Square.

VINDICATION. A procedure in legal systems based upon Roman law whereby one who claimed the ownership of land, cattle and certain other things could, if he adduced sufficient evidence, obtain a judgement which was conclusive against all comers. No such procedure exists in common law jurisdictions, the nearest equivalents being (private) Acts of Parliament and, formerly, Recoveries.

VINER, Charles (1678-1756), published a celebrated *Abridgment of Law and Equity* between 1742 and 1753 and founded the Vinerian Professorship of Law at Oxford.

VINEYARDS. *See* KNATCHBULL-HUGESSEN; WINE TRADE.

VINLAND. *See* CANADA-1.

VINTRY. A Thames-side ward of the City of London, mostly occupied in the middle ages by Bordeaux wine merchants and their cellars. Vintners Hall is still there.

VIOLIN FAMILY OF INSTRUMENTS. These enormously influential melodic stringed instruments were first made in a recognisable modern form near L. Garda in N. Italy in the 1560s, first at Salo, then at Brescia and Cremona where the Amatis, notably Nicolo (1596-1684) taught the later famous Antonio Stradivari (1644-1737). Tirolese makers, notably Lukas Stainer, preferred the pre-Stradivarius Amati type and these are still made at Mittenwald. These instruments reached England in mid-17th cent.

VIRGINIA and WEST VIRGINIA. (1) Virginia, a vague coastal territory named after Elizabeth I (The Virgin Queen) by Sir Walter Raleigh in 1584, originally included all English N. American possessions. In 1606 two interlinked Virginia Cos were formed. The LONDON (or South Virginia) COMPANY with planting rights from modern S. Carolina to New York; the PLYMOUTH (or N. Virginia) COMPANY with similar rights from Virginia to Maine, but the respective Co. plantations were to be at least a 100 miles apart. *See* CHARTERED COMPANIES.

(2) In 1607, the London Co. founded Jamestown. The Plymouth Co's interests were mostly in Maine and in fisheries further north, and being rechartered by the Council for New England in 1620, brought out the so-called Pilgrims to Cape Cod. Jurisdiction was divided in the other part of Virginia between the London Co. which imported goods and settlers and had the right to plant, and a local gov. in the settlement. There were inevitable clashes and the London Co. languished while Ld. de la Warr, Sir Thos. Gates and George Percy successively led the settlement to greater prosperity.

(3) The more liberal charter of 1612 trenched on the Co's passenger monopoly and brought colonists to the Tidewater. Meanwhile Sir Thos. Smith, the Co's Treasurer (1609-19), the foremost financier of the time, failed to improve the Co's position. In 1619, when Sir Francis Yeardley became Gov., Smith was superseded by Sir Edwin Sandys (until 1621) and then by Sir Francis Wyatt. Yeardley and his allies strengthened the settlement. In 1619 he called the first local assembly. In 1620 they brought in a shipment of girls. The colony throve, but in 1624 the Co. went bankrupt and Virginia was constituted a chartered colony with Wyatt as Gov. He was succeeded until 1627 by Yeardley.

(4) By 1640 there were 7000 settlers plus indentured negro labourers, growing tobacco for export and maize for subsistence, and there was a developing fur trade. In 1642 Sir Wm. Berkeley became Gov. The Colony, ignored in the Civil War at home, became a virtually independent trading state, so that when a Cromwellian expedition forced Berkeley to retire in 1652, it was thought sensible to leave things otherwise as they were. At the Restoration, however, Berkeley was reinstated, and set about enforcing the originally Cromwellian policy of the Trade and Navigation Acts. This made immense profits for the Tidewater tobacco planters, but created difficulties for the frontier farmers, who, in addition, suffered from Indian raids. The Tidewater politicians refused to protect them, and the result in 1676 was Bacon's rebellion, which began as a self help movement against the Indians, but soon developed into a civil war. The savagery of Berkeley's repression led Charles II to dismiss him, but

for the next century political control remained in the hands of the Tidewater politicians and planters. Negro slavery now increased rapidly and some families established huge *latifundia,* or made fortunes in land speculation.

(5) Emigrants driven away by these operations as well as newcomers, soon struck inland and the Shenandoah began to be settled in 1730s. The planters then formed the OHIO CO. (1747) to deal in land and furs further west. This Co.'s activities led to clashes with the Mississippi French and was one cause of the Seven Years' War of 1756 to 1763 which here broke out a year earlier. The British victory brought great advantages because all the inland areas as far as the Mississippi were now under British control and open to Virginian exploitation and land speculation. The Virginians were glad of the profits but objected to taxation designed to help pay to protect them against a French and Indian resurgence. Virginia and Massachusetts led the opposition to British colonial policies, and in 1773 the Virginian House of Burgesses organised one of the important Committees of Correspondence, which rallied many colonists to the rebellion. Virginia also proposed the creation of an inter colonial assembly, and the Virginian, Peyton RANDOLPH (1721-75) was the first Pres. of the Continental Congress of 1774. In 1775 the colony drove out its last British gov. (The E. of Dunsmore) and declared its independence in 1776. Many leaders of the rebellion were Virginians including seven of the first twelve pres. of the U.S.A. and its third C.J.

(6) In 1784 Virginia ceded its western lands north of the Ohio to the U.S.A., and these became the NORTHWEST TERRITORY. In 1789 it ceded part of its Potomac lands to help form Washington D.C. In 1792 the Virginia County of KENTUCKY was admitted to the Union as a state. Virginia and Kentucky joined the Confederates in the Civil War, but the up-country farmers rebelled against the planters across the mountains. They seceded in 1863, and were admitted to the (Federal) Union as the state of **WEST VIRGINIA.**

VIRGIN Is. were reached by Columbus in 1493. The Dutch settled Tortola in 1648, but in 1666 the British took it and kept it. The Danes settled St. Thomas, St. John and St. Croix in 1754, and these islands were occupied by the British in 1801, and from 1807 to 1815, but returned. They were sold to the U.S.A. in 1917.

VIROCONIUM. *See* URICONIUM.

VIRTUOSI OF ST. LUKE was a club founded by Van Dyck after 1620, as a forum for artists, who dined periodically in a tavern and raffled for pictures. It petered out in 1744.

VIRUSES, being mostly too small to be seen under the optical microscope, were not recognised until 1892, before which it was not feasible to make progress in combating animal distempers, foot-and-mouth, or rabies, or influenza, measles, poliomyelitis or yellow fever.

VISIT AND SEARCH. *See* BLOCKADE.

VIS or LISSA (Adriatic) I., was seized by the French when they dissolved the Venetian Republic in 1797. As a result of Sir William Hoste's naval victory (Mar. 1811) it fell to the British. They held it until 1815 when it passed to Austria. In 1866 it was the scene of an Austrian naval victory over the Italians, in which the Austrians used the bows of their ships as rams. This influenced naval design for a generation. In 1918 it passed to Yugoslavia and was occupied in 1940 by the Italians. In 1943 the allies expelled them and it then became the H.Q. of the Yugoslav partisan supreme command.

VISBY (Sweden), capital of Gotland, as the centre of Baltic and Russian trade, was one of Europe's richest cities in 10th and 11th cents. and in the 14th it was the leading factory and member of the Hanseatic League. In 1361, however, it was stormed and sacked by K. Valdemar Atterdag of Denmark and later a series of epidemics prevented its recovery.

VISCOUNT, *VICOMTE, VICECOMES*. The *vicomte* was an official in the Duchy of Normandy resembling the English sheriff. Hence after the conquest, in official English documents in Latin *vicecomes* meant sheriff. *Viscount,* as a title of nobility higher than baron but lower than earl (Lat: *comes),* was first conferred on John, Lord Beaumont, in 1440. *See also* FEUDALISM.

VISIGOTHS. *See* GOTHS.

VISITATION (1) In canon law "to visit is ... to inquire into excesses and mistakes, to denounce ... and mend them by suitable remedies, to ensure the observance of obligations ... and the preservation or restoration of property to whomever it may belong". "The right and power of visitation belongs to all prelates with ordinary jurisdiction", and firstly to the Pope, to legates *a latere,* to *legati nati* but only to other legates and nuncii if specially commissioned. Metropolitans and bishops have the right in their own areas, but monasteries often hotly resisted this, and from the 12th cent. some monastic orders followed Cistercian example in visiting their own houses.

(2) The reformation statutes transferred the papal visitatorial powers to the crown. By a pre-1634 agreement the Abp. of Canterbury does not visit the diocese of London. Episcopal regular visitations must be carried out annually on the bishop's behalf by his archdeacon, unless inhibited by the Bp. or Abp. Royal peculiars are visited only by the crown. Disciplinary measures can be taken only by the proper legal procedures.

(3) The right of visitation of universities, colleges and similar charities arose from their connection with the church, but usually arises from the charter or trust deed governing their constitution.

VITA **(Lat = life).** Lives of saints, originally inspired by St. Athanasius' *Life of St. Anthony,* were a feature of Celtic church literature from the early 7th cent. onwards, especially in Ireland. The fashion spread, via St. Illtyd's monastery in S. Wales, to Brittany.

VITA EDWARDI REGIS **(Lat = Life of K. Edward)** by an anonymous Flemish monk, was written in two parts. The first (1065-6) recounts the King's reign and the deeds of Earls Godwin, Harold and Tostig, the second (after 1066) deals with his religious life.

VITERBO (Italy), was given to the Papacy in 11th cent. and was the main papal residence from 1257 until 1309.

VITTORIOSA. *See* MALTA G.C.

VITRIFIED FORTS, are early Iron Age hill forts in Scotland. The walls comprised a front and back of roughly squared stones tied together with closely spaced timber baulks and filled in with rubble. Some were burned in war and the combustion of the baulks vitrified the rubble.

VITRUVIUS (1st cent. B.C.). a Roman military engineer, wrote *De Architectura* which, apart from direct observation, is the main surviving source on classical building.

VIVES, Johannes Ludovicus (1492-1540), voluminous writer on theology, philology, philosophy, law and history, was born in Spain. He met Henry VIII in 1521. Wolsey settled him at Oxford but he occasionally went to Flanders. He was entangled in Henry VIII's matrimonial controversy and imprisoned for advocating Katharine of Aragon's case. He was also the P. Mary's tutor. The liberal ideas in his *De Ratione Studii Puerilis* (Lat = Sensible Education for Boys) had wide currency and probably influenced Ascham and Colet.

VIVIAN (1) Sir Richard Hussey (1775-1842), 1st Ld. (1841) soldier and M.P. from 1820 to 1831 and 1837 to 1841 was C-in-C in Ireland in 1831. His bastard **(2) Sir Robert John Hussey (1802-87),** Indian soldier, commanded the Turkish contingent in the Crimea in 1855 and 1856. The grandson of (1), **(3) Sir Hussey Crespigny (1834-93), 3rd Ld. (1886),** a diplomat in the Levant and the Balkans, was British plenipotentiary to the Brussels slave trade conference on 1889.

VIZIER (Turk = minister). The Turkish title of the chief known in the West as the Grand Vizier was SADR AZAM (= First Breast i.e. leader of the army).

VLADIVOSTOK, founded in 1860, became the main Russian Pacific naval base in 1872, was linked *via* the Chinese Eastern Rly. to the Tran-Siberian Rly. in 1897, and was reconnected to it *via* the Amur Valley in 1908.

VOGUE. The British version of this influential American fashion magazine was launched in 1916.

VOLKSDEUTSCH **(Ger. = German by race).** This emotive word, much used by the Nazis, refers to those German speaking communities living outside the boundaries, at any given moment, of the German Reich especially to the Sudeten Germans of Bohemia, the Roumanian Saxons, the inhabitants of Danzig and Memel, the since-destroyed German Volga Commune and the many pockets of the diaspora in the former Baltic provinces, Russia and the Ukraine.

VOLKSRAAD **(Dutch = Council of the People).** A legislature, often sketchily constituted, of a South African Boer republic.

VOLTAIRE, François-Marie Arouet (1694-1778), was already well known in Paris *salons* when his jibes at the govt. earned him a year in the Bastille in 1717. In 1726 he was thrashed by the servants of the Chevalier de Rohan and sent to Calais. He went on to England, learned English and a superficial understanding of English politics and political philosophy. He returned in 1729 and thenceforth based his criticism of French institutions on English models. He published his *Lettres Philosophiques* in 1734. Compelled by the outcry to leave Paris, he took refuge at Cirey with Madame du Châtelet, with whom he maintained a friendship until she died in 1749. She had reopened the court for him but his indiscretions had again shut him out. In 1750 he went to the Berlin Court of his correspondent Frederick the Great. In 1751 he published *Le Siècle de Louis XIV* (The Century of Louis XIV). He and Frederick began as friends but Voltaire applied his talent for infuriating people to the King and in 1753 he left, eventually taking refuge in 1755 at Geneva and Lausanne. In 1757 further indiscretions forced him to settle at Ferney on the border. Here he wrote *Candide* (1758), *Histoire de la Russie sous Pierre le Grand* (1759-63) and the *Philosophie de l'Histoire* (1765) and many other works including numerous attacks on the church. An unrivalled propagandist, he probably did more to shake common acceptance of existing institutions than anyone before the American revolution.

VOLUNTEER MOVEMENT (*see* MILITIA), was part of the public reaction to the French scare of 1859. Many thousands became Sunday soldiers and were reviewed by Q. Victoria on Bagshot Heath.

von in German surnames indicates nobility. Noble families by prescription abbreviate it 'v' e.g. the v. Blumenthals are an ancient noble family unrelated to the von Blumenthals ennobled in the 19th cent.

VOORTREKERS (S.A. Dutch = pioneers). *See* GREAT TREK.

VORTIGERN or GWTHEYRN (= ? Sublime Ruler) was used by Bede and Nennius as the name rather than the title of a British ruler who, in the mid-5th cent, invited Saxon mercenaries to Thanet, thereby initiating the Anglo-Saxon settlements in England. This probably preserves an authentic tradition, perhaps through Gildas, who mentions a 'proud tyrant', but this ruler's name and career are unknown. *See* BRITAIN, ROMANO-BRITISH.

VOTADINI. *See* BRITAIN, ROMAN-12 *et seq*; GWYNEDD.

"VOTE, THE". The collective name of the papers issued daily to an M.P. when the House is sitting.

"VOTES AND PROCEEDINGS". The daily minutes of the House of Commons.

VOYAGEURS were canoeists employed by the Hudson Bay and N.W. Cos. to keep their outposts supplied. They were Indians, half breeds or French.

VRYHEID (Natal) was founded as an independent Voortrecker republic by Lucas Meyer in 1884 but absorbed into the S. African Republic in 1887. The surrounding area is rich agriculturally and in coal.

VULGATE. *See* BIBLE.

VURICH, CLAN. *See* CLANS, SCOTTISH.

VYNE, THE (Hants). Tudor mansion built for the Sandys family about 1530. Altered in 1654 by John Webb and sold to the Chute family in 1659.

VYRNWY, L. (C. Wales), a 5 mile long reservoir built between 1890 and 1905 to supply Liverpool.

W

WAAD or WADE (1) Armagil (?-1568) sailed to Newfoundland in 1536, became Clerk to the council in Calais in 1540, M.P. in 1547 and chief clerk of the Privy Council in 1552-3. He was employed on a diplomatic mission to Holstein in 1559. His son **(2) Sir William (1546-1623)** was one of Burghley's continental agents from 1576 to 1581. In 1583 he went on an abortive diplomatic mission to Spain. From 1583 to 1613 he was a clerk of the Privy Council and employed, largely as a detective, examining Mary Q. of Scots papers in 1586 and of other R. Catholic conspirators including the Gun Powder Plotters of 1605 and Raleigh. In his later years he was a subscriber to the Virginia Co. and by 1613 fell foul of Robert Carr and the Countess of Essex.

WACE (fl. 1170) wrote French narrative poems and began, at Henry II's request, the *Roman de Rou* (Norman Fr. = Story of Rollo), a history of the House of Normandy to 1107.

WACHT AM RHEIN, DIE (Ger. = Watch on the Rhine). A German patriotic song whose words, composed by Schneckenburger in 1840, recalled French aggressiveness.

WADAT (C. Africa) a Sultanate near L. Chad, conquered Baghirmi in about 1815 and established a direct route via Kufra to Tripoli and Egypt. On good terms with Mehemet Ali and the Senussi, the sultans carried on a thriving slave trade. In the 1880s their power was shaken by the Mahdists of the Sudan and the area was conquered by the French in 1906.

WADE, George (1673-1748) a soldier, was stationed at Bath in 1715 to overawe the western Jacobites and served in the Vigo expedition of 1719. He was M.P. for Bath from 1722. He began a military survey of the Highlands in 1724 and built the military roads there from 1726 to 1733. In 1743 he became a field-marshal and commanded in Flanders in the next year. His failure to stop the Young Pretender in 1745 led to his supersession as C-in-C. He demolished 20 miles of Hadrian's Wall for roadstone.

WADHAM COLLEGE (Oxford) founded in 1612 was the first venue of the Royal Society (1652-9). In the 1860s it defeated Cambridge Univ. in a race and its boat club has used the Cambridge Univ. colours ever since.

WADSETTER was a creditor of a Scottish landowner. He occupied and worked on the land free until the debt was paid off. He was often a neighbour.

WAFER, Lionel (?1660-1705) a surgeon with Bartholomew Sharp's Panama expedition in 1680, after piratical adventures on both sides of the Isthmus, returned to England in 1690 and published a *Description of the Isthmus of America* (1699) and was appointed an adviser to the disastrous Darien Scheme, though it is not clear how much his advice was heeded.

WAGER OF LAW. *See* COMPURGATION.

WAGES COUNCILS. *See* SWEATED LABOUR.

WAGHORN, Thomas (1800-50), naval officer and then a Hooghli pilot, became familiar with the state of British goods and travellers between England and India *via* the Cape. In 1825 he left India without resources save a singleminded determination to establish a route *via* Suez. By 1841 he had set up a part river, part overland service for passengers, coal and later mails between Alexandria, Cairo (where Shepherd's Hotel was built for the purpose) and Suez and had inspired the Anglo-Indian scheduled steamer services which lasted until 1970. His overland route passed to the P. & O. in 1847.

WAGNER, Richard (1813-83) brilliant, if greedy and treacherous, mainly operatic composer whose work influenced German, and eventually all musicology, and the literary atmosphere from about 1860 to 1914. *Lohengrin* was his first work to be performed in Britain (1875) but Hans Richter fully introduced his music at a Wagner festival at the Albert Hall in 1877, just after the *Ring* cycle had been performed in Bayreuth. The political teachings in the latter were lost in the music.

WAGONERS, CORPS OF and ROYAL WAGON TRAIN (R.W.T.). The corps was formed in 1794 to supply the deficiencies in the army's transport, shortly disbanded and then resuscitated as the R.W.T. in 1799. Its main fields of operation were the Peninsular and the Waterloo campaigns. It was disbanded in 1833, leaving the army without a regular transport organisation for 20 years. *See* (ROYAL) ARMY SERVICE CORPS.

WAHHABIS. *See* ARABIA; EGYPT.

WAILING or WESTERN WALL (Jerusalem). The only surviving part of the Herodian Temple, sacred both to Jews and Moslems and claimed by both.

WAITANGI TREATY (Feb. 1840). (1) between Capt. William Hobson on behalf of the Crown and 46 Maori chiefs advised by missionaries. Copies were then carried through New Zealand and over 500 other chiefs signed, each receiving a blanket and some tobacco. It is uncertain how well they understood the document.

(2) By the treaty the Maoris ceded sovereignty over New Zealand to the Crown. The Crown in return gave them the full status of British subjects, guaranteed to them the full and exclusive possession of their lands but reserved to the Crown the exclusive right to purchase them.

WAITERS, TIDE- and COASTING. These were customs officers who boarded ships respectively in and out of port to collect dues and search out contraband.

WAITS were originally night watchmen at big houses or in wealthy districts who called or piped the time during their rounds. From this, more or less musical, custom the word was applied to carol singers making their Christmas rounds.

WAKE, Thomas (1297-1349) Ld., a Lincolnshire magnate, was married to Blanche, daughter of Henry of Lancaster, in 1317. He joined the rising against the Despensers in 1326 and became Constable of the Tower. In 1328 he rose against Isabella and Mortimer and was deprived. Restored in 1331 he became gov. of the Channel Is. but was imprisoned in 1340.

WAKE, William (1657-1737) became Bp. of Lincoln in 1705 and Abp. of Canterbury in 1716. From 1717 to 1720 he tried to negotiate for the entry of the French Jansenists into the Anglican Church.

WAKEFIELD (A.S. = WACAFELD) (Yorks) was a royal manor until about 1088 when it was granted away as the head of a liberty extending westwards into Lancs and Cheshire. A fair was established in 1204, when a merchant or guild organisation apparently began. It had a wool market at least by 1308 and a bridge toll in 1342. Flemish weavers settled there in about 1470. It was captured by Fairfax in 1643 but Sandal Castle nearby held out until 1644. Despite its trading and industrial importance it remained a township under a manorial constable until it was first enfranchised in 1832. It was chartered in 1848 and was a county borough from 1888 to 1974.

WAKEFIELD, Charles Cheers (1859-1941) 1st Ld. (1930) 1st Vist. (1934). Made a fortune through C.C. Wakefield and Co. (Castrol) lubricating oils. A great public benefactor, he financed the flights by Sir Alan Cobham and Amy Johnson and Sir Henry Segrave's motor speed trials.

WAKEFIELD (1) Mrs Priscilla (1751-1832) a Quaker philanthropist, instituted a lying-in charity and a savings bank at Tottenham. Her grandson **(2) Edward Gibbon (1796- 1862)** worked in the legation at Turin from 1816 to 1819 when he eloped with a ward of court. From 1820 he was at the embassy in Paris until 1826 when he abducted an heiress and was in prison until 1829, the marriage meanwhile being dissolved by private Act of Parliament. He then began to take an interest in colonial and land reform on which he published pamphlets. His arguments brought a discontinuance of free land grants in N.S.W. in 1831; in 1834 he inspired the founding of the S. Australian Assoc. which planted its first colony in 1836. From 1839 to 1846 he was London agent of the New Zealand Land Co. and in 1853 he migrated to New Zealand whither his brothers had already gone in 1840 and 1851.

WAKE-WALKER, Adm. Sir William Frederick (1888-1945) was director of torpedoes and mining at the Admiralty from 1935 to 1938 and co-ordinated measures against the German magnetic mines. In May and June 1940 he commanded the naval side of the Dunkirk operations. In May 1941 he took part in the destruction of the *Bismarck* and, as Third Sea Lord from 1942 to 1945, was responsible for landing craft development.

WALBROOK (London) (A.S. = the stream of the Britons), rose beyond Moorgate, passed through the city wall and entered the Thames at Dowgate.

WALBURGA. *See* MISSIONS TO EUROPE-3.

WALCHER. *See* DURHAM-2.

WALCHEREN (Netherlands). Strategically important but formerly malarial island at the mouth of the E. and W. Scheldt. It contained the town of Middleburgh, to which the mediaeval English Staple was occasionally moved, its port of Flushing (Vlissingen), the fort of Ramekens and the Scottish Staple at Veere. The approach to Antwerp could be controlled from it and for this reason English expeditions occupied it in 1585 and 1809 and the Germans made special efforts to hold it until Nov. 1944. *See* ELIZABETH-14; FRANCO-RUSSIAN ALLIANCE, WAR OF-3; PORTLAND GOVT. 1809-12-4 and 5.

WALDECK, George Frederick, Prince of (1620-92), a soldier and diplomat, had a distinguished military career under Austria and then entered the service of the P. of Orange. He used him to organise German resistance to Louis XIV and then left him as military deputy when he came to England to assume the throne in 1689. In that year Waldeck beat the French at Walcourt but was himself later defeated at Fleurus (1690) and Steenkirk (1692).

WALDEGRAVE (HARCOURT or FORTESCUE), Frances, Elizabeth Anne (1821-79) always known as the **COUNTESS WALDEGRAVE** from the 2nd of her four marriages (1840-6) to the 7th E. WALDEGRAVE, who died in 1846. She was the vivacious political daughter of John BRAHAM (1774-1856) in his day a famous operatic tenor who in 1835 built and lost money on the St. James's Theatre. She inherited the Earl's fortune and with her third marriage to George HARCOURT of Nuneham became a leading Society hostess. Her salon was the meeting place of all the major liberals of the period. She also restored Horace Walpole's house at Strawberry Hill. Harcourt died in 1861 and in 1863 she married Chichester PARKINSON FORTHSCUE (1823-98) Ld. CARLINGFORD (1874) who, as Gladstone's Chief Sec. for Ireland, carried through Irish Church Disestablishment, and two Irish Land Acts.

WALDEGRAVE, Sir Richard (?-1402) was M.P. for Suffolk in most of the parliaments from 1376 to 1390 and Speaker in 1381-2.

WALDEN. *See* HAY. (TWEEDDALE)-7.

WALER. A powerful horse bred in New South *Wales* for the Indian army.

WALES *see under* surnames of Welsh people and ABERGAVENNY, ABERFAN, *ANNALES CAMBRIAE*, ANTHRACITE, BARDS, BORDER, BRECON, BRITAIN, BRUT, entries beginning CAER-, CAMBRIA, CANTREF, CARDIFF, CARDIGAN, CARMARTHEN, CELTS, CELTIC, entries beginning CY-, DEHEUBARTH, DEVOLUTION, DRUIDS, EDWARDIAN CASTLES, FLINT, GLAMORGAN, GODODDIN, entries beginning GW-, LL, MABINOGION, MARCHER LORDSHIPS (WALES), MERIONETH, MERTHYR, METHODISM, MISSIONARIES IN BRITAIN, MONMOUTH, MONTGOMERY, MORGANNYG, OGHAMS, PEMBROKE, RADNOR, RHONDDA, ROMANO-BRITISH, SURRENDER AND REGRANT, SWANSEA, UNION ACTS OF (WALES), VOTADINI, WELSH LAW. *See also* UNION ACTS OF 1536, 1543.

WALES, PRINCE OF. In the mid-13th cent. the advance of the rulers of Gwynedd was reflected in their titles. In 1230 Llywelyn ap Iorwerth (?-1240) called himself 'Prince of Aberffraw and Lord of Snowdon'. His son David ap Llywelyn (?-1246) assumed the title of Prince of Wales. His nephew Llywelyn ap Gruffudd (?-1282) called himself Prince of Wales from 1258 and was recognised as such by Henry III in 1267. Edward I's conquest ended his power and on his death his brother David (1282) assumed the now empty title. The story that Edward I presented his baby son Edward of Caernarvon to the Welsh as their Prince is a myth. He was created first English Prince of Wales in 1301. The title was always associated with the eldest son of a monarch but required a new creation on each occasion. The 1376 parliament had to petition for the creation of Richard of Bordeaux as Prince of Wales. The sons of Edward III, Henry IV, Richard III and Arthur, son of Henry VII, were all princes of Wales who never succeeded to the throne and Edward III, Henry IV, Edward IV, Richard III, Henry VII and George VI were all kings who had not been Princes of Wales. The English princes seldom had much influence as such on the principality (*see* WALES AND THE MARCHES, COUNCIL OF). Other princes were as follows. Those who became Kings are marked (K).

Edward	1454-71	George (K)	1751-60
Henry Frederick	1610-12	George (K)	1783-1820
Charles (K)	1616-25	Edward (K)	1841-1901
Charles (K)	1638-49	George (K)	1901-10
George (K)	1714-27	Edward (K)	1910-36
Frederick	1729-51	Charles	1956-

WALES AND THE MARCHES, COUNCIL OF (1) was originally set up by Edward I to assist his son Edward in his new principality. From the first it tried to interfere as much as possible in the Welsh Marcher Lordships. Under Edward IV its powers began to be extended beyond the administration of the Prince's possessions to embrace the functions of a court. In 1476 it took power to appoint commissioners of oyer and terminer and its jurisdiction was extended to the English counties of Cheshire, Shropshire, Hereford and Gloucester. It lapsed c. 1483 but was revived for Prince Arthur, who had received wide estates and jurisdictions in Wales in 1493, and continued after his death (1501). By then it was functioning as an outpost or agent of the King's Council and the Star Chamber and it also dealt with some ecclesiastical matters such as legacies and sexual offences. From 1501 it sat permanently at Ludlow. As a result of the (Welsh) Acts of Union it was reconstituted in the 1530s and 1540s.

(2) Most of the early presidents were bishops and after the establishment of the Welsh Courts of the Great Sessions (1536) the Justices of Chester and of N. Wales were, *inter alia,* members. The President was Lord Lieut. of all Welsh counties. Since its jurisdiction was concurrent with that of Great Sessions whose decisions it occasionally reviewed, friction, sometimes personal, naturally occurred within the Council.

(3) The existence and function of the Council were confirmed by Act of 1543 but in 1604 (*Fairley's Case*) the judges held that its criminal jurisdiction did not extend to the four English counties. In 1608 its civil jurisdiction in these counties was similarly impugned but James I suppressed the judges' conclusions. The agitation continued but in 1617 its instructions conferred most of the full powers. In 1629 Charles I ordered it to ignore writs of prohibition as long as it kept within its jurisdiction but writs continued to be ineffectually issued throughout his eleven years of personal rule.

(4) The Council's Star Chamber powers were abolished along with the Star Chamber in 1641 but it continued to carry out administrative functions and exercise civil and equitable jurisdiction against mounting resistance until the Civil War when it fell into abeyance. At the Restoration there was a demand for a strengthened provincial govt. and the Council was revived upon the post-1641 basis. It was not popular, partly because of anti-Star Chamber prejudice and partly because it was ill accommodated and had become expensive. A bill to abolish it passed the Commons in 1680 but was dropped. It was abolished in 1689.

WALES, Charles Philip Arthur George (1948–) D. of CORNWALL, P. of (1968) and **Lady Diana Frances née Spencer (1961-97). (1)** He was educated at Gordonstoun, Geelong (Australia), Cambridge and Aberystwyth, and had the unpaid services' appointments usual for an heir to the Throne. He was interested in the arts and welfare: he supported the Welsh Nat. Opera, created his own Inst. of Architecture; set up his Committee for Wales (1971) and The Prince's Trust (1975), and continually improved the Duchy of Cornwall Estates. **(2)** In 1981 he married Diana, a temperamental, ambitious, beautiful but not intellectual kindergarten teacher, d. of the 8th E. Spencer and Frances, his first (divorced) Countess. The Prince had another affectionate commitment (to a married woman), and was warned against the marriage. He tried to make it a love match. After the birth of their sons in 1982 and 1984, they were slowly estranged through differing temperaments, interests and intellectual levels. Divorced in 1996, his adultery figured as an element in their irreconcilability; she settled for £17M and life residence in Kensington Palace. **(3)** Her motherly love, courage, star quality and ruthless self-publicity now expanded into the championship of spectacular causes such as Children with AIDS or mutilated by Cambodian land mines. She also cultivated or was pursued by the very rich. All this attracted intrusive journalists whom she disliked but needed. Attempting to escape at 120mph from reporters, she was killed with a wealthy friend in a motor smash in Paris. **(4)** This provoked an outburst of public grief (evidenced by the deposit everywhere of millions of flowers), and a revulsion against the recent commercially inspired media denigration of royalty. Her brother, the 9th E's frank televised valediction contained criticisms of both the Royal Family and the sneering press. Her memory became for a while a minor industry. The Prince continued to pursue his concerns with his usual modesty.

WALES, CHURCH IN. Before 1920 the dioceses of Wales (St. Asaph, Bangor, St. David's Llandaff and Swansea) were in the province of Canterbury. They were poor and often held by absentees in plurality with rich prebends, especially at Durham. Methodism and a demand for disestablishment gained ground quickly in the 19th cent. A Royal Commission in 1906 found that less than 25% of the people professed to belong to it. In 1914 a disestablishment bill received the Royal Assent under the Parliament Act but was promptly suspended at the outbreak of World War I. It came into force on 31 Mar. 1920 when a sixth diocese (Brecon) was created and an archbishopric to which one of the bishops is elected. Much of the property was vested in Welsh Church Committees mostly appointed by local authorities and was applied to non-religious purposes.

WALES, GOVT OF, ACT 1998 (*see* DEVOLUTION-2) created a quadrennially elected Welsh Assembly composed of a member, elected normally, for each parliamentary constituency plus members for each E.U. constituency, to be elected from registered part lists. The Assembly's function was to undertake Welsh administrative reforms. A minister with Welsh functions might transfer them to the Assembly or in future execute them concurrently with

it or without its concurrence. The S. of State was to provide the finance and should participate in its deliberations but not vote. There was to be an executive committee composed of officials, and also subject committees. The Assembly was empowered to reform the Health Authorities and 22 other miscellaneous (mostly minor) bodies.

WALES, STATUTE OF, or OF RHUDDLAN (Mar. 1284) was issued at the end of Welsh resistance to Edward I after the death of Llywelyn II ap Gruffydd (1282) and the execution of his brother David (1283). It organised the administration of N. and Central Wales on English lines. It set up a new county of Flint under the control of the Justiciar of Chester and divided Snowdonia into the counties of Anglesey, Caernarvon and Merioneth. They, with the older counties of Carmarthen and Cardigan, received laws, sheriffs and coroners. The new counties and their hundreds were based on existing commotes and cantrefs. The statute directly or implicitly introduced many Common Law procedures.

WALEWSKI. *See* BONAPARTE-16.

WALKER. The name (Flemish 'weaver' or 'warp maker') commemorates migrations of weavers mainly to E. Anglia in the later middle ages. Of the many of this name the following are probably *not* related. **(1) Sir Alexander 1st Bt. (1764-1831)** was political agent in Baroda from 1800 to 1808 and left a collection of oriental manuscripts to the Bodleian. **(2) Sir Baldwin (1802-76) or YAVIR PASHA** served in the Turkish navy from 1838 to 1845 and was surveyor of the Navy from 1848 to 1860. **(3) George (1618-90)** raised a regiment for William III and was gov. of Derry during the siege from Apr. to July 1689 and then organised the financial relief in London which caused Derry to change its name. He became Bp. designate but was killed at the Boyne. **(4) George (?-1777)** commanded a privateer from 1739 to 1744 and a privateer squadron from 1744 to 1748, mostly in American and French waters. **(5) Sir George Townshend (1764-1842)** was C-in-C at Madras from 1826 to 1831. **(6) James Thomas (1826-96)** Indian soldier, was engaged in the Indian survey from 1849 until 1883, from 1871 as superintendent and from 1875 as surveyor-gen. **(7) Obadiah (1616-99)** was Romanist Master of University College, Oxford and propagandist for James II. **(8) Sir Samuel (1932-1911) Bart. (1906)** a barrister, defended Parnell in 1881 and was Irish sol-gen. in 1883 and an Irish Liberal M.P. from 1884. He was Irish att-gen. in 1885 and again in 1886 and Lord Chancellor of Ireland from 1892 to 1895.

WALKER, Sir Emery (1951-33), process engraver and, with William Morris, was the refounder of English fine printing and book production.

WALKER, Robert (?-?1658) puritan artist, painted portraits of parliamentarian notables including Oliver Cromwell and John Hampden.

WALLACE COLLECTION (London) was commenced by Richard, 4th M. of Hertford (1800-70), who collected French 18th cent. art. His son, Sir Richard Wallace (1818-90) added mediaeval and renaissance work and armour, plate and other objects. His widow left it to the nation in 1897.

WALLACE, Alfred (1823-1913). *See* DARWIN-2.

WALLACE, Edgar (1875-1932), destitute orphan saved by a fish porter, after various adventures fought as a private in the Boer War and then decided to become a journalist and returned to S. Africa on behalf of Reuter's Agency. He published his first novel, *The Four Just Men,* himself in 1905 and then wrote or dictated over 150 others in 20 years. He effectively created the popular taste for thrillers, which he called 'pirate stories in modern dress'.

WALLACE LINE. The frontier between the distinctive fauna and flora of the Australian region (which stretches as far as Lombok and Gilolo) and that of the Indo-Malaysian region to the west.

WALLACE, Sir William (?-1305), second son of Sir Malcolm Wallace of Elderslie, swore fealty to John Balliol and refused it to Edward I after Balliol was captured in 1296. Following an affray at Lanark, he murdered the English sheriff, Sir William Hazelrigg, and was outlawed. In 1297 Wallace, with Sir William Douglas, attacked the English Justiciar at Scone. Soon he was in alliance with other, more influential, resistance leaders viz. Robert Bruce, James the Steward and Bp. Robert Wishart of Glasgow, but he neither shared their interests nor sympathised with Bruce's ambition, for he still felt bound by his allegiance to Balliol. When the rebel magnates came to terms at Irvine with Edward I (June 1297) Wallace maintained a separate popular struggle. In two months he and Andrew Moray were besieging Dundee. In Sept. 1297 they defeated the English at Stirling Bridge but Moray was mortally wounded, leaving Wallace in sole command. He styled himself 'Guardian of Scotland for John Balliol', led a raid into England and dispensed ecclesiastical patronage but his power depended upon success and loot to attract popular interest. At the B. of Falkirk (22 July 1298) he had to rely heavily on the schiltron formation because he was short of cavalry and was routed; whereupon magnates such as Bruce and Comyn stepped in. He remained active, maintained a guerrilla resistance for a year and then went overseas to get aid from France, Norway and the Pope. By 1302 his diplomacy had failed and he returned to guerrilla in Scotland. Betrayed near Glasgow he was tried at Westminster. He is said to have been the first to have been hanged, drawn and quartered.

WALLASEY (Cheshire) was a well-to-do Merseyside residential settlement which grew with the prosperity of Liverpool opposite and slowly linked up with similar villages at Egremont, Liscard and Pulton-cum-Seacombe and with the more popular resort at New Brighton. These were combined as the borough of Wallasey in 1910 and made a county borough in 1913.

WALLER family originally of Groombridge (Kent). **(1) Richard (?1395-1462)** soldier, captured the D. of Orleans at Agincourt (1415) thus founding the family's fortunes. From 1439 he was Card. Beaufort's master of the household but secured preferment under Henry IV. Of his descendants **(2) Sir William (?1597-1668)**, an able but unlucky parliamentary general and unpopular presbyterian politician in the Civil War, ultimately helped to promote the Restoration. His son **(3) Sir William (?-1699)**, M.P. for Westminster in 1679 and 1680, was a manufacturer of evidence in the Popish and Mealtub plots and much mistrusted by Charles II. He was in exile from 1681 until the accession of William III, who refused to employ him. A cousin **(4) Sir Hardress (?1604-?66)**, a military supporter of Cromwell and a regicide, was mainly employed in the military subjugation of Ireland. An opponent of the Restoration, he surrendered, was condemned for treason but reprieved and died in prison. Another kinsman **(5) Edmund (1606-87)** the poet, was related to John Hampden and became an M.P. at the age of sixteen and, though opposed to the royal abuses, remained attached to the monarchical principle even while continuing in the Commons during the Civil War. In 1643 he was involved in the plot named after him to subvert the City, arrested, imprisoned and in 1644 was banished. He returned with Charles II, was elected M.P. for Hastings and so remained until his death.

WALLINGFORD (Berks). Town and Honour. **(1)** The town, at an important Thames ford, was a fortified Roman settlement and was later disputed between Mercia and Wessex. Offa of Mercia annexed it after the B. of Benson in 779. The fortifications were maintained, for Athelstan (924-40) allowed a mint there and the Danes had to storm the town in 1006. A royal borough and possibly residence under Edward the Confessor, it was then and for three centuries the largest town in Berkshire. The mint survived to the 13th cent.

(2) Wigod, K. Edward's cupbearer, owned it at the Conquest. He supported the Conqueror and helped to build the castle. His grand-daughter married Robert Doyli, to whom his many estates passed in about 1087. The Honour passed to Brian fitz Count who was three times besieged in the castle by K. Stephen and eventually entered a monastery leaving no heir. Henry II took it over and granted a borough charter (1156) recognising a gild merchant. In 1189 Richard I granted the Honour to P. John so that it reverted to the Crown when the latter became King. From about 1220 until 1307 it was part of the lands of the E. of Cornwall. It was then given to Piers Gaveston (1307-12), to Q. Isabel (1317-76) and to John, E. of Cornwall (1330-4). In 1335 it was included in the lands of the Duchy of Cornwall until 1385. By this time the town had declined and the value of the estates was much diminished. The castle and Honour continued in royal hands and intermittently in royal use until 1490. From then until 1540 it was again part of the Duchy of Cornwall.

WALLINGFORD, Vist. See KNOLLYS-5.

WALLINGFORD HOUSE PARTY. See COMMONWEALTH-16.

WALLIS, Barnes Neville (1887-1974) versatile aviation inventor, helped to design the airship R100, evolved the geodetic airframe and the swing wing and designed the huge bombs used, by ricochet off reservoir surfaces, to destroy German dams in World War II.

WALLIS, John (1616-1703), mathematician, was domestic chaplain to Lady Vere in London and occasionally employed between 1642 and 1645 by the parliamentary govt. to decipher captured despatches. He was also sec. of the Westminster Assembly in 1644 and intruded into a fellowship at Queens College, Cambridge, but settled in London where he habitually met the ablest scientists and mathematicians. From 1649 he was Savilian Prof. of Geometry at Oxford and in 1655 he published his *Arithmetica Infinitorum* (Lat = Arithmetic of Infinities) in which he invented the mathematical sign for infinity. He inspired Newton's differential calculus. He was confirmed in his places at the Restoration and in 1690 William III again made use of his cryptographic ability. His introduction of analogy and continuity into mathematical analysis marked a distinguished stage in scientific study.

WALLMODEN née von WENDT, Amalie Sophia Marianne (1704-65) Countess of YARMOUTH (1740) became George II's mistress at Hanover in 1735 and was installed at St. James' in 1738. She was divorced in 1739. She went home to Hanover when the King died.

WALLOP. Hampshire family **(1) Sir John (?-1551)** served on land and sea between 1511 and 1523 against the French and the Moors and in Ireland. In 1524 he became marshal of Calais and a diplomat, serving in Holland, Germany, Poland and Austria in 1526-7 and at Paris in 1528 and in 1540, when he was recalled on suspicion of treason. He cleared himself; was Capt. of Guisnes from 1541 and commanded troops in France in 1543. He received large grants of church lands. His son **(2) Sir Henry (?1540-99)** was an active planter in Munster from 1580 but quarrelled with the Lord Deputy (Sir John Perrot) and lived at Farleigh Wallop from 1589 to 1595, discharging his Irish offices by deputy. He returned to Ireland to treat (unsuccessfully) with the 2nd E. of Tyrone in 1596 and died in Dublin. A kinsman **(3) Robert (1601-67)** was an active puritan M.P. in the Long Parliament and sat as a judge in Charles I's trial. He was a member of the Commonwealth and Protectorate councils of state and was imprisoned at the Restoration but not released. **(4) John (1690-1762) 1st E. of PORTSMOUTH** (1743) was a minor whig politician.

WALLSEND. See TYNE.

WALMER (Kent). The artillery castle was built by Henry VIII in 1539 and it became the H.Q. for the Kent coastal defences and so the official residence of the Lord Warden of the Cinque Ports which in 1995 it still was.

WALPOLE (1) Sir Robert (1676-1745) 1st E. of ORFORD (1742) whose father had been Whig M.P. for Castle Rising, was supported by Sarah, Duchess of Marlborough, in entering parliament for it in 1701. He was M.P. for King's Lynn in 1702-12 and 1713-42 and soon made his mark as a Whig favouring religious toleration. He was one of the Lord High Admiral's council in 1705, Sec. at War from 1708 to 1710 and Treas. of the Navy from 1710 to 1711. By this time his financial skill had won wide recognition but he fell with Marlborough in 1711 and in 1712 was expelled from the Commons and imprisoned on a charge of peculation. Though he favoured the Hanoverian succession, George I originally disliked him but he showed his mettle in the impeachment of the Tory leaders in 1715 and as leading minister in dealing with the Jacobite rebellion (for *his political career see* GEORGE I-3 *et seq*; GEORGE II WARS OF 1739-48-1) and also the next two entries). He rebuilt his great house at Houghton between 1722 and 1738 and filled it with an imposing if not necessarily good collection of pictures and statuary (later sold to Catherine the Great of Russia) and he took great interest throughout his long and busy political life in the management of his estates, especially in the four-course rotation of crops which had been practised in Norfolk since 1670. He was gross in his conversation and his political methods were, by modern standards if not those of his day, corrupt, yet he died poorer than when he entered politics. His brother **(2) Horace (1678-1757) 1st Ld. WALPOLE of WOLTERTON (1756),** notorious for his coarse speech, was intermittently an M.P. and held a number of minor govt. posts, but was primarily a diplomat, being ambassador to The Hague in 1722 and in Paris from 1723 to 1730 where he and Card. Fleury got on well together. He returned to The Hague for seven years in 1733 and was always in favour, in the Hanoverian interest, of a Prussian alliance. The accepted fourth son of (1), **(3) Horatio or Horace (1717-97) 4th E. (1791)** lived comfortably on some lucrative sinecures procured for him by his father and was an M.P. from 1741 to 1767. Strongly whig, sometimes republican, he was notable as a literary *dilettante* and patron, particularly of Thomas Gray. He built Strawberry Hill and amassed pictures for it, together with minor statuary and *virtu*. His enormous collection of letters are an entertaining and deep quarry of political, social and literary material drawn from his wide and well-informed acquaintanceship. A grandson of (2), **(4) George (1758-1835),** a soldier, put down the Jamaica rebellion of 17?-6. He was a Foxite M.P. from 1797 to 1820 and Foreign U/Sec. of State from 1806 to 1807.

WALPOLE'S EXCISE SCHEME (1732-3). Walpole proposed to extend the bonded warehouse system to wine and tobacco; an excise, payable only as and when goods were released from bond, would replace the lump sums hitherto payable as customs by the importers; the vast smuggling industry would thus be put out of business and the profits could be used to abolish the land tax. Pitt and his cronies, in pursuit of office, defeated the bill which, however, remained the model for later reforms.

WALPOLE'S FINANCIAL REFORMS (1723-41) (*see* GEORGE I). Walpole initiated his financial reforms with short term, instead of yearly, Treasury Bills. His Sinking Fund had already been set up in 1717; now it became the backbone of investors' confidence. It permitted him to standardise the interest on the national debt at 4% instead of rates varying up to 9%, to reduce the capital from £54M to £47½M and the cost of servicing by 1739 from £3.35M to £2M. While making such economies, he developed and rationalised the revenue. The customs Book of Rates, not revised since 1660, was brought up to date and the various duties on the same item were consolidated into a single levy which was often much less than the previous total. He also developed and systematised the bonded warehouses and abolished or greatly reduced duties on imported raw materials. The combined result was that lower duties produced higher revenue, leading to cuts in the land tax in 1723 from 3s. to 2s. and to 1s. in 1732 and 1733. In the war years 1727, 1740 and 1741 he had to raise it to 4s. Consistently with the favourable treatment of imported raw materials he made a virtual clean sweep of export duties and even gave export bounties on grain, refined sugar and spirits and on silk and sail cloth. England was being groomed for the invasion of foreign markets.

WALSALL (Staffs.). An ancient ironworking centre, belonged to the church at Wolverhampton in 996 and was a royal manor under Edward the Confessor. There was a charter of 1159 but it passed to the Beauchamps in the 14th cent. though it had a mayoralty from 1377 and a merchant guild from 1390. Another charter was granted in 1399. In 1538 Henry VIII granted Walsall to the Northumberlands but a further charter was granted in 1627: this was superseded by yet another of 1674 which remained in effect until 1835. The town was first represented in Parliament in 1832.

WALSINGHAM (Norfolk) became a European pilgrimage centre through the foundation of a shrine in honour of the Annunciation in 1061 by Richeldis, a local noble-woman, on the instructions of the Virgin Mary. It was dismantled during the dissolution of the monasteries in 1538-40.

WALSINGHAM, Sir Francis. *See* ELIZABETH I-23.

WALSINGHAM, Thomas (?-?1422) precentor of St. Albans, compiled the lost *Chronica Majora* (Principal Histories) and the *Chronicon Angliae* (History of England) for the years 1328 to 1388. From 1394 to 1409 he was prior of Wymondham. Between 1409 and 1419 he compiled at St. Albans the *Ypodigma Neustriae* (Notes on Neustria), a Norman chronicle, and the *Historia Anglicana* (English History). These are all important sources for the period 1377 to 1421.

WALSINGHAM, Petronilla Melusina v. der Schulenburg, Countess of (1693-1778), bastard of George I and the Duchess of Kendal; her marriage with the 4th E. of Chesterfield in 1733 estranged him from George II.

WALTER. Three High Stewards of Scotland. *See* STEWART OR STUART, ROYAL HOUSE, EARLY-3,5,8.

WALTER, Hubert. *See* HUBERT WALTER.

WALTER or BARLOW, Lucy (1630-58) seductive and energetic daughter of William Walter of Haverfordwest, became the mistress of Col. Robt. Sidney at The Hague in 1644 and then of Charles II from 1648 to 1650 when Henry Bennet (later E. of Arlington) shared her with others. She represented a personal bond between Charles and Bennet. The King was the father of her son James, D. of Monmouth (b. 1649) and, less likely, of her daughter Mary (b. 1651). In 1656 she returned to England from Cologne and was promptly deported as a spy. She died in Paris. It was strenuously asserted between 1673 and 1680, and three times publicly denied by Charles II, that he had married her.

WALTER (1) John (1739-1812), originally a prosperous London coal merchant, inspired the foundation of the Coal Exchange, became a Lloyd's underwriter and in 1782 failed. He then acquired Henry Johnson's logotypes, improved them, bought an old printer's at Blackfriars and in Jan. 1785 started the *Daily Universal Register* which he renamed *The Times* in Jan. 1788. He was twice convicted of criminal libel and in 1785 handed over the business to his son William who in 1803 transferred it to his brother **(2) John (1776-1847).** In 1810 he made *The Times* into a famous and feared journal mainly by delegating editorial supervision to a succession of able journalists: Sir John Stodart, then to Thomas Barnes and finally in 1841 to J.T.

Delane. He maintained an all-over direction of policy and protected his staff against indignant officials and angry politicians. He became an M.P. himself in 1832. He also made great technical improvements in the printing processes which his son **(3) John (1818-94)** followed up. Save between 1865 and 1868 he was a Liberal M.P. from 1847 to 1885 but meanwhile he had developed the Walter press, the prototype of all modern newspaper presses. For this reason *The Times* was for a long while ahead of other papers anywhere in Europe. He retired in 1885 and his son **(4) Arthur Fraser (1846-1910)** remained Chief Proprietor until 1908 when he converted the business into a limited Co. with himself as Chairman. The chairmanship was held by his son **(5) John (1873-1968)** from 1910 to 1923.

WALTHAM, ABBEY, FOREST, HOLY CROSS, -STOW (Essex). The abbey was founded by a miraculous cross found at Montacute (Som.) in the 9th cent. King Harold, Godwin's son, refounded and endowed it in 1060 and was buried there. Henry II increased the endowments. Waltham Holy Cross and Walthamstow became thriving centres, partly because of the fertility of the soil and so remained, despite the dissolution of the abbey. The forest was a favoured Tudor chase. Walthamstow in due course became a borough, Waltham Holy Cross an Urban District. The former was merged in the Outer London Borough of Waltham Forest in 1963. The latter became a parish in 1974.

WALTHEOF (?-1076) E. of HUNTINGDON (c. 1065), younger son of Earl Siward of Northumbria (?-1055) was initially quiescent under William I but in 1069 joined the Danes in their invasion of Yorkshire and helped them to take York. The movement was defeated in William's winter campaign of 1069-70 and in 1070 Waltheof submitted and was restored to favour. In 1072 he added Northumbria to his other earldom. In 1075 he was implicated in the revolt of Ralph, E. of Norfolk, and Roger, E. of Hereford and, despite apparent contrition and Lanfranc's advocacy, was executed. His death marked the effective end of Norman co-operation with Anglo-Saxon magnates. He was buried at Crowland where his tomb became a place of pilgrimage. His daughter Matilda later married K. David I of Scots and through this marriage there was an association between the earldom of Huntingdon and the Scots crown and also a confused popular idea that the E. of Huntingdon (if not Robin Hood) was the rightful *English* King.

WALTON, Izaak (1593-1683) wrote lives of *Sir Henry Wotton* (1651), *Richard Hooker* (1665) and *George Herbert* (1670). The first edition of the celebrated *Compleat Angler* appeared in 1653, the fifth or *Universal Angler* in 1676.

WALTON (on the Naze) ORDINANCES (1338) were issued by Edward III when embarking for the French War. **(1)** They cancelled existing exemptions from taxation and respites of debts due to the crown and postponed crown debts incurred by Edward's predecessors to those incurred by himself. **(2)** They then altered the position of the Exchequer and the Chancery by requiring payments and applications of the Great Seal to be authorised by warrants or writs of Privy Seal (which the King kept with him) and by imposing upon the Chamberlains of the Exchequer an annual audit under a royal nominee. **(3)** They also provided that sheriffs should be elected in their bailiwicks, not nominated in the Exchequer. This reduction of the home offices to mainly ministerial functions was probably intended to simplify the conduct of the war but the fiscal measures (*see* (1) *above*) provoked protests in the parliaments of 1339 and 1340 and these widened out and led to the repeal of the rule on sheriffs (*see* (3) *above*) as well. The permanent effect was to raise the status of the Privy Seal, put the Great Seal in the custody of the Keeper during royal absences and convert the Keeper into a sort of Sec. of

State. In the longer run it complicated the procedure and expense of using the Great Seal.

WALTON, Sir William (1902-83) individualistic but influential English composer, particularly of *Façade*, a curious recitation of Edith Sitwell's verse to a chamber orchestra, and the dramatic oratorio-cantata *Belshazzar's Feast.*

WALVIS or WALFISCH BAY (S.W. Africa) was first settled by Europeans in 1844. Annexed to Cape Colony in 1878, it remained an enclave in German S.W. Africa until the latter was mandated to the Union in 1922.

WALWAL (1935). *See* ABYSSINIA-6; SOMALIA-5.

WALWORTH, Sir William (?-1385) came from Durham to London, was apprenticed to John Lovekyn and joined the Fishmongers Co. He was alderman of Bridge in 1368, sheriff in 1370 and mayor in 1374. He had made a fortune in victualling and made loans to the crown. By 1377 he was treasurer of the parliamentary subsidy and in 1380 he was a member of the parliamentary committee on the govt's finances. In 1381 he supported the King against the rebels, himself striking down Wat Tyler at Smithfield in June. Part of his fortune was invested in the Southwark brothels.

WAMPANOAG were the first Indian tribe encountered by the Pilgrim Fathers, with whose chief, MASSASOIT, they made friends. His son METACOMET or KING PHILIP (?1640-76) became hostile and he, with his Iroquois allies, precipitated the Indian war in which he was killed, many settlements destroyed and the tribe itself exterminated. *See* NEW ENGLAND.

WAMPUM was strings of black or white shell beads used by red Indians as ornaments and ceremonial gifts and in early days as a sort of currency between them and Europeans on the Atlantic and Pacific coasts.

WANDERER, THE This anonymous poem in the Exeter Book describes the thoughts and adventures of a well born seeker after a noble war band. The nostalgic poet transplants a society long before his own time into his contemporary circumstances.

WANSDYKE, a probably Romano-British, set of northward facing earthworks covering the 60 miles from Inkpen (Berks.) to Maesburgh (Somerset).

WANTAGE (Berks). Small country town, was the birthplace of K. Alfred.

WAPENSHAW (Sc.). In the middle ages, the production of arms for inspection.

WAPENTAKE (Dan: vapnatak = clash of weapons). The Danelaw administrative division equivalent to the Hundred elsewhere. Those attending the meetings had to bring their weapons for inspection and expressed their vote by brandishing them.

WAQF or VAKUF. (Arab = pious foundation) is an Islamic endowment similar in character to an English charity. It comes into force as soon as its founder has set aside the fund and declared the objects and it is perpetual and irrevocable. It is administered by a **Nazir** who may be the founder himself and his descendants. A *waqf* must be pleasing to God, i.e. it must serve the religious, moral or social ends of Islam, for example the establishment of mosques or schools, the support of the poor or the provision of public works. Very widespread in Mohammedan countries, *waqf* forms the economic foundation of the power of the Ulema and its control or seizure (cf. the dissolution of the monasteries) one of the objects of reforming oriental parties.

WARBECK, Perkin (1474-99) son of John Osbeck or Werbeck of Tournai, travelled as a page to a Yorkist lady in Portugal and then in 1491 with a Breton merchant to Cork (Ireland) where some bystanders thought that he was a Yorkist prince. The Es. of Desmond and Kildare were prepared to take him at this valuation and he gave out that he was Richard, D. of York, son of Edward IV. In 1492 he wrote to James IV of Scots. In Oct. he went by invitation to the French Court and in Nov. was recognised by Margaret of Burgundy as her nephew. Henry VII brought pressure for his banishment and in Nov. 1493 he reached Vienna where Maximilian I recognised him as Richard IV and financed his claim. *For later history see* HENRY VII; JAMES IV OF SCOTS.

WAR CABINET. *See* CABINET.

WAR CRIMES (1) are acts which go beyond those necessary for the prosecution of a war. The concept is old, dating from at least the 15th cent., but varying from age to age with changes in the manner and equipment of war. A surrendered armed enemy is not entitled to his life but if the victor expressly or inferentially grants it to him the grant is irrevocable and subsequent massacre is, for example, a war crime. Injury or death of non-combatants incidental to the course of operations is legitimate; their death as part of them is probably not and massacre or sack after operations have ceased or passed by is certainly not. The victor's right to punish war crimes is founded upon his right to grant life. The grant in such a case is conditional upon the prisoner facing his trial and proving his innocence. This is a concession or grace, considerably more respectable than the outright and large scale (if technically legitimate) massacres perpetrated by the Germans, the Japanese and the Russians in World War II.

(2) The victor's own war crimes, if any, are usually forgotten. This has tended, intellectually, to discredit the concept but, practically, the possibility of losing a war and submitting to enemy justice has probably mitigated excesses and so reduced innocent suffering. The biggest judicial operations on war crimes arose out of World War II. The allied powers set up a War Crimes Commission in 1943 to digest the jurisprudence and sift the evidence. The London Agreement of Aug. 1945 created an international tribunal of one judge each from Britain, France, Russia and the U.S.A. under the presidency of Lord Justice Lawrence from Britain. The tribunal was to follow English procedure and to try certain Germans and German organisations for (1) conspiracy; (2) crimes against peace; (3) war crimes and (4) crimes against humanity, of the persons concerned (death = *). Göring*, Ribbentrop*, v. Neurath (15 years), Keitel*, Jodl* and Rosenberg* were charged under all four counts; Hess (life) was charged under counts (1) and (2); Raeder (life), Frick*, Seyss-Inquart* and Funk (life) under counts (2) to (4); Dönitz (ten years) under counts (2) and (3); v. Schirach (20 years) and Streicher* under count (4); Kaltenbrunner*, Frank* and Sauckel* under counts (3) and (4); Speer (20 years) under counts (2) and (4); v. Papen and Schacht were acquitted. In addition Bormann* was tried *in absentia;* Ley committed suicide before trial and Krupp was found unfit to plead. Of the organisations concerned, the Nazi Party leadership, the Gestapo, the S.S. and the S.D. (Security Service) were found to be criminal organisations, membership of which was an offence in itself.

(3) The Tribunal of Four sat at Nuremberg in 1945-6 for a year's careful proceedings. Its judgements are the foundation of an important corpus of international law. Subsequently military courts guided by these judgements were set up by at least the three western occupying powers in Germany to deal with other similar offenders in their respective zones.

(4) After the Japanese surrender a U.S. C-in- C set up a Military Tribunal at Tokyo which tried the leading Japanese statesmen and soldiers. The Tokyo proceedings seem, in certain cases, notably that of Gen. Homma, to have been less objective than those at Nuremberg.

WARD (1) The area for which a councillor or common councilman is elected. Wards were originally community or traditional areas. Legislation, from the Municipal Corporations Act, 1834, related them to units of local govt. but attempted increasingly to secure equality of electorates, not necessarily with success. The Local Govt.

Act, 1972, instituted a wholesale review based primarily on mathematical criteria.

(2) The equivalent, in Northumberland, Durham and Cumberland, of a Hundred or Wapentake.

WARD, Joshua (1685-1761). *See* SULPHURIC ACID.

WARD, Sir Leslie (1851-1922) under the pseudonym 'SPY' contributed a famous series of weekly portraits to *Vanity Fair* from 1873 to 1909.

WARD, Mrs Humphrey (Mary Augusta) (1857-1920), novelist, philanthropist and opponent of women's suffrage, wrote with almost clinical accuracy on the lives of the ruling English. Of her novels *Robert Elsmere* (1888), *Marcella* (1894) and *The Case of Richard Meynell* (1911) are the best remembered.

WAR DEBTS. *See* REPARATIONS.

WARDEN. *See* FOREST-2; MARCHES-3 *et seq.*

WARDHA (C. India). The site of Gandhis *ashram.*

WARDHOLDING was the Scottish equivalent of tenure by knight service unmodified by a statute equivalent to *Quia Emptores*. By 1690 it had almost died out in the lowlands but it remained characteristic of the highlands until abolished in 1746. *See* FEUFERME.

WARDMOTE. An assembly of the electors of a ward in certain cities, notably the City of London, where they meet annually on 21 Dec. under the chairmanship of the Alderman.

WARDOUR CASTLE (Wilts), Palladian mansion built by James Paine in 1768 for the 8th Ld. Arundell of Wardour, whose family had been in possession of the manor since the 16th cent.

WARDROBE, ROYAL, where the King's clothes, jewels, bed-linen and documents were held, was distinct from the royal store houses and the two arms stores called the Great Wardrobe (at Baynard Castle) and the Privy Wardrobe (at the Tower). It became an important financial dept. of the Household, and by 1224 it had developed its own accounts with the Exchequer and was headed by a Keeper. Under Henry III its influence increased in two ways. Peter des Rivaux, in his period of power (1232-34) made it the administrative and financial centre of his household reforms and it became central in funding foreign wars because it was conveniently accessible, the depository of the Privy Seal and account-able to but not hindered by the Exchequer. Hence it attracted criticism from opponents of Henry III. By the 1290s its staff acted as paymasters and victuallers for Edward I's forces and received funds from the Exchequer and taxes directly from the sheriffs while its Keeper, John Droxford, raised loans and issued bills cashable at the Exchequer. Secret and diplomatic correspondence was also enrolled separately at the Wardrobe and diplomats were briefed and de-briefed there. These activities continued for the next half century but the 14th cent. saw an erosion of its authority. In 1311 the Ordainers wanted the Keeper to be confirmed by parliament. Between 1318 and 1324 receivers of stores, the Butler, the Great Wardrobe, the Keeper of the King's Horses and royal messengers were all made to render their accounts to the Exchequer and the keeperships of the Privy Seal and the Wardrobe were separated. Its domestic operations continued and in early campaigns of the Hundred Years' War, its military role was maintained. After 1359-60 Kings ceased to campaign in person and an indenture system established the magnates and military commanders as army paymasters under the Exchequer, whence they got their funds. By the end of the 14th cent. the Wardrobe had almost reverted to its original functions and in the 13th and 14th cents. its financial business was taken over almost entirely by the Chamber.

WARDSHIP was the duty of a lord to protect a vassal during minority and, in return, to enjoy the profits of the vassal's estates but, in theory, without waste or diminishing their value. In practice the minor was often shamelessly exploited for the Lord's profit and a wardship was often a valuable saleable asset. The abuses and corruption surrounding, in particular, royal wardships, were a standing grievance throughout the 12th cent. and featured in Magna Carta (1215) but the profits accruing to the Crown ensured its survival and led to the creation of a Court of Wards highly profitable to its Masters and staff. The system came to an end in the civil war.

WARELWAST, William of (?-1137), a Norman royal secretary and ecclesiastical diplomat, negotiated with the Papacy in 1095 on behalf of William Rufus, who employed him to search Anselm's baggage in 1097. He went on further missions to the Pope in 1098, 1103, 1105, mostly connected with Anselm's affairs. In 1107 he became Bp. of Exeter and attended the Council of Troyes. He began to rebuild Exeter Cathedral and founded or refounded priories at Plympton, Launceston and Bodmin. In 1119 he again visited the Curia and also the Council of Rheims, returning to the Curia in 1120. He later became blind but nevertheless was at the Council of Northampton in 1131.

WARENNE or WARREN. Norman family which, by the operation of wardship and marriage, became semi-royal. **(1) William of (?-1088) 1st E. of SURREY (c. 1088)** fought for William the Conqueror at Mortemer (1054) and, having married the wealthy Gundrada of Flanders, was given Mortemer Castle. He fought at Hastings and was richly rewarded. He built castles at Lewes (Sussex), Reigate (Surrey), Castle Acre (Norfolk) and in 1069 Conisborough (Yorks). In 1071 he ended the Saxon resistance in the Fens and in 1075, as joint justiciar, suppressed the conspiracy of the Es. of Norfolk and Hereford. He and Gundrada founded important Cluniac monasteries at Lewes and Castle Acre in about 1077. He was one of William Rufus' supporters at his accession but was killed besieging Pevensey. His enormous estates passed to his son **(2) William (?-1138) 2nd E.,** known as **Earl WARENNE,** who held Coucy against Robert of Normandy in 1091 but, having been worsted in his suit for Matilda of Scotland by the future Henry I in 1094, became entangled in Robert's politics and helped him to invade England in 1101. He was reconciled with Henry in 1103 but lived mainly in Normandy. He supported Stephen's accession. His son **(3) William (?-1148) 3rd E.,** too supported Stephen and was involved in the B. of Lincoln (1141). In 1147 he took the Cross and was killed at Laodicaea. The inheritance now passed to his daughter **(4) Isabel (?-1199)** whom K. Stephen married to his second son William (c. 1152). He died without issue in 1159 and Henry II married her to his half-brother **(5) Hamelin (?-1202) 4th E. (c. 1163).** He took her name and titles and was one of the most splendid noblemen of the time. He was a good supporter of royal govt., hostile to Becket in 1164 and to the rebel sons of Henry II in 1174 and 1189, yet present at Richard I's coronation in 1189. In 1191 he opposed John but supported his coronation in 1199. He built the curious great keep at Conisborough. His son **(6) William (?-1240) 5th E.,** on losing his Norman estates at the French conquest, was given Grantham and Stamford (1206). He stood surety for John at Magna Carta in 1215 and at his submission to the Papacy. He seems to have acquiesced in P. Louis' French invasion but by Apr. 1217 he had rejoined his allegiance. In 1225 he married Matilda, co-heiress of William Marshall, the great first E. of Pembroke, and by 1230 he was one of the most important Lords of the Realm and a co-regent. In 1232 he stood surety for Hubert de Burgh at his dismissal on the intrigues of Peter des Roches. His son **(7) John (?1231-1304) 6th E. and E. of SUSSEX (1282),** long a royal ward under the guardianship of Peter of Savoy, had inherited the earldom of Sussex in 1243 but did not use the title until his sister Isabel died in 1282; he was married to Henry III's half-sister Alice of Lusignan in 1247. Brought up in the royal family, he was

with the Lord Edward in Aquitaine and Spain (1254) and opposed to the barons who imposed the Provisions of Oxford upon the King. From 1260, however, he supported Simon de Montfort in his less extreme courses but rejoined the King after the Mise of Amiens (1263). He held Rochester against de Montfort in 1264 and, involved in the defeat at Lewes, fled to France while his opponents seized his lands. He made his way to Edward at Ludlow, was with him at Evesham and went on to reduce Kent. He spent the next few years recovering his estates, not always peacefully. He took the cross in 1268 and did not go. He was fined in 1270 but gladly swore allegiance to his friend Edward I at his accession (1272). For the next 13 years he was mostly in Wales, acquiring the Honour of Bromfield and Yale in 1282, and building castles on the Dee. In 1279 in reply to writs of *Quo warranto* inquiring *by what warrant* he did certain things, he cheerfully returned the writs marked "by the sword". In 1285 Edward began to employ him in the north, at first on a diplomatic mission to Edinburgh. After a further Welsh campaign (1287) he took part in the Salisbury and Brigham treaties (1289 and 1290). In 1294, however, he was back in Wales whence in 1296 he emerged with troops to support Edward in Scotland and took Dunbar. By Aug. he was Custodian of Scotland. In 1297 he was replaced, but instantly reappointed to deal with Wallace's revolt. His defeat at Stirling Bridge (Sept. 1297) did not reduce Edward's confidence in him. He had to take command of the Dec. counter attack, raised the siege of Roxburgh (Jan.), played an important role in the victory at Falkirk (July 1298) and ended his life clearing the Lowlands. His grandson **(8) John (1286-1347) 7th E.,** succeeded him and married Joan of Bar in 1306. He quarrelled with Piers Gaveston at Edward II's accession (1307) but made it up two years later. He was with Edward in Scotland in 1310 and 1311, by which time he had decided to join in Gaveston's overthrow. Gaveston surrendered to him at Scarbrough on promise of safe conduct and when his allies murdered Gaveston later he honourably repudiated them. This probably saved Edward, but he was no uncritical royal supporter, and declined to take part in the Bannockburn campaign. He was, however, embroiled in a quarrel with his wife and in another with Thomas of Lancaster, whose wife he encouraged to elope, and suffered severe losses of lands in a private war with him from 1317 to 1319. Hence he supported Edward and the Despensers in the Boroughbridge campaign. He recovered his Welsh lands after Lancaster's execution and the rest after an Aquitainian campaign in 1326. His support for Edward II in Mortimer and Isabella's revolt, however, came too late and after he had been reconciled to them he advised Edward to abdicate, attended Edward III's coronation and then negotiated a Scottish peace (1327-8). In the next five years he acquired many more estates but in 1333 he struck out with Edward Balliol who, as King of Scotland, made him E. of Strathearn. Until the end of 1335 he was in the Scottish wars after which he retired to his English properties. The family became extinct at his death. The huge estates escheated but the titles passed to the Fitzalans.

WAR GRAVES, IMPERIAL, later COMMONWEALTH, COMMISSION established in 1917 was, by 1972, maintaining over 1M graves in over 23,600 cemeteries in 150 countries.

WARHAM, William (c. 1456-1532) Oxford lawyer and leading advocate in the Court of Arches, went to Rome and Antwerp on legal business and then in 1493 to Brussels as a diplomat. In 1494 he became Master of the Rolls, but in 1497 reverted to diplomacy as joint ambassador to Edinburgh and then as ambassador to Burgundy and in 1499 and again in 1501-2 to the Emperor. He became Bp. of London and Keeper of the Great Seal in 1502 and Abp. of Canterbury and Lord

Chancellor in 1504. His brilliant rise was due to the conditions prevailing under Henry VII. He was a friend of humanists such as Erasmus and Grocyn, learned rather than strong and half convinced of the inadequacies of the church well before Luther's XCV theses crystallised opinion against its moral standing. Consequently he was easily bullied and in the new circumstances after 1509 had the misfortune to encounter an autocrat in Thomas Wolsey and a popular tyrant in Henry VIII. He crowned Henry and Katharine of Aragon. In 1512 he weakened his position by a worldly quarrel with his bishops over the lucrative probate jurisdictions and in 1515 Wolsey superseded him as Chancellor. Warham soon found Wolsey (who, as a Cardinal, outranked him) interfering in English church affairs proper to himself and, from 1523, when the Cardinal received his legatine commission, he ruled the English church over Warham's head. It was he who proposed that the annulment of Henry's marriage with Katharine of Aragon be pronounced by an English archiepiscopal court. On the Cardinal's fall Warham resumed the headship of a church now under attack as an institution and was soon humiliated first by being forced himself schismatically to pronounce the annulment under an Act of Parliament and then, in 1531, to preside at the Convocation which made the Submission of the Clergy. Just before he died he published a protest against the last three years political and legislative anticlericalism. He left his large library to Winchester and New Colleges where he had been educated.

WAR LOAN. About £2000M worth of 3% and 5% stock with, like Consols, no specific redemption date was issued to help finance World War I. In the 1931 slump the interest was reduced to 2½% and 4%. Its price is often regarded as the indicator of the state of the gilt-edged market.

WARMING PAN. A long handled brass pan filled with hot ashes used formerly for warming beds and, in a particular case, alleged to have been used to introduce a suppositious child, later the Old Pretender, into Mary of Modena's bed. A convenient protestant myth, long exploded.

WAR OFFICE. George Monck, D. of Albemarle, as Lord General used The Cockpit in Whitehall as his official H.Q. This was moved to the Horse Guards in 1684 and the terms 'Horse Guards' and 'War Office' became virtually interchangeable (see SECRETARY AT WAR). In 1794 a Sec. of State for War was created and in 1801, because armies were so often employed in the colonies, they were transferred to his responsibility. The Adjutant-Gen. (in charge of personnel) was originally a Cromwellian officer, the first royal one being appointed in 1685. The first Quartermaster-Gen. (in charge of material) was appointed a year later. A Commissary-Gen. of musters existed from 1661 to 1818. In 1855 the Sec. of State ceased to be responsible for colonies and the War Office absorbed the old commissariat, medical dept and Board of Ordnance. Control was divided between the C-in-C and the Sec. of State, who was responsible to parliament. This dual arrangement subsisted because the C-in-C, the D. of Cambridge, was a prince. He obstructed military improvements and though in 1870 the Sec. of State became fully responsible, military efficiency lagged behind that of continental armies. The test came in the Boer War which led, in 1904, to the abolition of the C-in-C's office and the creation of an Army Council on the analogy of the Board of Admiralty, and an Imperial General Staff. The president of the Council was the Sec. of State; the Chief of the Imperial General Staff corresponded to the First Sea Lord. The War Office became a dept. of the unified Ministry of Defence in 1964.

WARRANT (The word is connected with *guarantee*.) A constitutional document issued by a person having authority in the matter, authorising another to do something and exonerating him from the consequences, unless he knew or should have known that it was unlawful, unlawfully issued or issued by a person without authority: for example a hangman can plead his warrant signed by the sovereign in bar of a charge of murder; a bailiff his warrant for the distress of goods in bar of proceedings for trespass or robbery. Similarly the application of the Great Seal or other state seals to public documents such as treaties and royal commissions was authorised by warrant as a safeguard against forgery and irresponsibility.

WARREN, Sir (Thomas) Herbert (1853-1930) Fellow (1877) and from 1885 to 1925 a celebrated President of Magdalen College, Oxford and Vice-Chancellor from 1906 to 1910.

WARREN, Samuel (1) (1781-1862) Lancashire Methodist preacher, was expelled for faction in 1835 and with his followers joined other methodist seceders to form the United Methodist Free Churches, but promptly took Anglican orders and was rector of Ancoats from 1840. His son **(2)** (1807-77), successful barrister, writer of law books, F.R.S. (1835), M.P. (1856-9) and master in Lunacy from 1859, published three widely read novels, *Passages from the Diary of a Late Physician* (1830), *Ten Thousand a Year* (1839) and *Now and Then* (1847) which influenced Dickens.

WARRINGTON (Lancs) (Lat: VERATINUM; A.S: WALINTUNE) at the lowest and so strategic ford on the Mersey and the main connection between Cheshire and the area northward towards the Border, developed a mediaeval flax and linen industry besides armoury and tools. By the 18th cent. there was shipbuilding and instrument making which developed into metal-related industries such as engineering and also chemicals, all of which profited from the vicinity of the coalfields. It was a prominent centre of nonconformism and its circulating library, founded in 1760, was the model for the municipal library, the first of its kind.

WARRIOR WOMEN (CELTIC) e.g. Boadicea, Cartimandua and Maeve, were taken for granted and classical writers mention Gallic women in battle. Men often learned martial skills from women or at training schools run by them. The Irish hero CuChulainn is said to have been trained in two such schools. Arthur fought a desperate battle with such a woman. *See also* NINE WITCHES OF GLOUCESTER.

WARS OF 1739-48 viz: OF JENKIN'S EAR, and OF THE AUSTRIAN SUCCESSION or FIRST AND SECOND SILESIAN WARS. *See* BALTIC; GEORGE II-9-11; JACOBITES-16-21. **(1)** This first of the world wars had four phases namely the opening Anglo-Spanish war (Oct. 1739-Dec. 1740); secondly the Prussian seizure of Silesia (Dec. 1740-July 1742) and the attempt by France, Spain, Prussia and Bavaria to partition the Habsburg inheritance. In these two France was, as against Britain, a neutral auxiliary of Spain but in the second she was a principal against Austria while Britain, as against France, was only an Austrian auxiliary and Hanover was neutral. After, thirdly, a bellicose interlude (July 1742-Mar. 1744) France and Britain entered the fourth phase (Mar. 1744-Apr. 1748) as principals on opposite sides and fought indecisively until the P. of Aix-la-Chapelle. In the first three phases Walpole and Card. Fleury, the French minister, hoped to avoid direct conflict, Walpole by keeping to maritime aggression, Fleury to continental. The fact that Spain, a maritime power with continental ambitions, was the enemy of Britain and the ally of France ultimately brought about the collision in the fourth phase.

(2) Walpole was driven without preparation, enthusiasm or allies into a war for which he had no gifts. Offensive action had been decided in June 1739 but no plans or recruiting had been initiated until Jan. 1740. The small fleet was undermanned, badly equipped and late. Adm. Haddock, at Minorca, had 10 ships-of-the-line to watch the Mediterranean and Atlantic coasts of Spain. Commodore Brown had 8 between Trinidad and Labrador, Adm. Norris a fluctuating but ill-found squadron in the Channel to reinforce them and watch the theoretically neutral French. There was nothing for Indian waters. The fleet naturally failed to intercept the *Flota* and could not stop Spanish reinforcements for the W. Indies because the French convoyed them. Adm. Vernon's victorious stroke against Porto Bello had to be made with six ships. Anson's celebrated small expedition for the Spanish Pacific had to wait until Nov. 1740.

(3) The super-imposition of the continental war arose from two royal accessions. In May 1740 the brilliant and unscrupulous Frederick the Great of Prussia came to his father's well armed throne; in Oct. the Archduchess Maria-Theresia succeeded the Emperor Charles VI in his hereditary lands under the universally guaranteed Pragmatic Sanction. With the maritime powers distracted and the Austrians lately humiliated in a Turkish war, Frederick calculated on an easy stroke. In Dec. he invaded Silesia, one of the guaranteed lands and, having narrowly beaten the Austrians at Mollwitz (Apr. 1741) overran it. Others awoke to the pickings. Spain, with an eye to Italy, and Bavaria, ambitious for territory and the vacant imperial throne, signed an alliance in May; France and Prussia in June. Adm. Haddock could not stop a French escorted Spanish expeditionary force to Italy. By Aug. French troops were in S. Germany. George II hurriedly neutralised Hanover. By Nov. the French with their Saxon and Bavarian allies were in Prague. The Bohemian estates recognised the Bavarian Elector Charles Albert as King.

(4) English mercantile losses in a war launched to expand the mercantile sphere were not popular. There was public shame at the incompetent war direction, for after Vernon's victory at Porto Bello had come disaster at Cartagena (1741). There was romantic sympathy for the young Archduchess-Queen, radiantly courageous amid overwhelming enemies. The country was determined to have a change. Walpole had moved a niggardly subsidy (£300,000) for Austria. In the winter general election of 1741 he lost control of parliament and considered resignation. The election of the Bavarian, for whom George II cast his electoral vote, as Emperor (24 Jan. 1742) was the decisive event: defeat on a constituency election petition the pretext. He went to the Lords as E. of Orford.

(5) The new govt., nominally headed by George II's crony Sir Spencer Compton, now E. of Wilmington, was a coalition of disparate family groups in which Henry Pelham and his brother, the D. of Newcastle (long a Sec. of State under Walpole) were the leading domestic figures. But energetic foreign policy and war leadership were the needs of the moment and for this they, as political pupils of Walpole, were unsuited. In his well informed Anglo-Hanoverian perplexities the King turned to their rival, Lord Carteret, who for the second time played a decisive international role. Carteret spoke most European languages, including German with his master. He was energetic, confident, almost brilliant. He was also an aristocratic individualist and careless of popular politics.

(6) For the moment, as Sec. of State, this did not matter. What did matter was that Britain's isolation must be ended. Somehow the Archduchess must be saved and to this end Carteret concentrated Britain's resources. The subsidy was raised to £500,000. The King was persuaded to abandon Hanoverian neutrality; Hessians and Hanoverians were taken into British pay and a composite Pragmatic Army was sent to the Austrian Netherlands. A strengthened Mediterranean fleet chased Spanish galleys into French ports. Commodore Martin, watch in hand*,

gave the Neapolitans an hour to withdraw from the war or be bombarded. At Genoa a similar threat by Adm. Mathews, who doubled the Chief Command in the Mediterranean with the legation at Turin, persuaded the Savoyard ruler into amenability. The Spaniards could now reinforce N. Italy only minimally and their military operations ground to a snail's pace. Meanwhile Carteret had perceived that a powerful French presence in Germany and Bohemia would not please Frederick and with military arguments, persuaded Maria Theresia to accept a Prussian peace by ceding Silesia and Glatz (P. of Berlin, July 1742). British-Prussian negotiations now threatened the isolated Franco-Bavarian armies in Bohemia. The Anglo-Prussian T. of Westminster (Nov.) sent them into hurried retirement (Dec.) and might protect Hanover. It also enabled the Austrians to overrun Bavaria. At this point (Jan. 1743) Card. Fleury died.

(7) For want of Dutch support the Pragmatic Army had been idle throughout 1742 but early in 1743 Carteret at length secured Dutch and also Austrian reinforcements. The whole under the personal command of George II lay at Aschaffenburg on the north side of the Main, facing a much larger Franco-Bavarian force opposite. After parallel westward marches, part of the neutral French crossed the river and were defeated at Dettingen (June 1743) by the neutral British. The victorious King failed to develop his local strategic advantages but the wider consequences were substantial, especially for the Austrians who were given time to recruit and train new troops.

(8) The next task was to end the Bourbon menace in Italy by transforming the Sardinian (Savoyard) neutrality convention into an alliance. The French offered the Savoyard the prospective sovereignty of Milan. Carteret persuaded the Austrians to offer the actual cession of something less and the Savoyard to accept it (T. of Worms, Sept. 1743). By now the Bourbon powers beheld the prospect of defeat unless they undertook a more energetic policy. The second Family Compact of Fontainebleau (Oct 1743) supplemented a secret naval agreement made by Fleury early in 1742; the French were to choose their moment. In the meantime the cabinet repudiated subsidies promised until the end of the war to Maria Theresia, while Frederick the Great disapproved of the territorial compensation for Silesia also promised her at Worms. Thus the British political position in Europe was weakening while the French secretly prepared their Jacobite stroke and sheltered another Spanish convoy in Toulon. The latter emerged but Mathews failed, owing to the misbehaviour of his subordinates, to destroy it (B. of Hyères or Toulon, Feb. 1744). A fortnight later the Jacobite operation dispersed in a Channel storm and in Mar. the pretences were dropped and the major powers declared war.

(9) Freed from inhibitions, the belligerents and the ambitious soon altered the scope of operations. An accident of succession in E. Frisia brought Prussia a window on the North Sea in May and in June Frederick signed an alliance with the French; their ablest commander, Prince Maurice of Saxony (the Maréchal de Saxe), baulked of his English invasion, had turned his forces upon the Austrian Netherlands. In Aug. Frederick's powerful armies marched suddenly upon Prague across neutral Saxony. The overstretched Austrians had to leave the defence of their Netherlands to the British, Dutch and Hanoverians under the D. of Cumberland. In Britain these set-backs brought about the fall of Carteret (who on his mother's death had become E. Granville) but the Pelhams, who had intrigued him out of office, had to continue his work. They signed a Quadruple Alliance (Britain, Holland, Austria and Saxony) in Jan. 1745.

(10) A fortnight later the fugitive Bavarian Emperor Charles VII died. The new electoral govt., under the pressure of Austrian occupation, abandoned his disastrous claims and the war at the P. of Füssen

---

*If this famous anecdote is not true it ought to be.

(Apr. 1745). This enormous gain was hardly offset by two defeats. In May Cumberland was beaten, but with honour, at Fontenoy: in June Frederick proudly defeated the Austrians at Hohenfriedberg. Both battles have left their mark in military tradition; they did not put an end to allied confidence. When the electoral representatives assembled at Frankfurt it was clear that Maria Theresia's husband, Francis of Lorraine, would succeed to the Imperial throne.

(11) The declarations of war in Mar. 1744 had extended hostilities to N. America and potentially to India, where the rival E. India Cos. managed policy as well as commerce. Like Fleury and Walpole four years earlier, the two Cos. hoped to maintain a specialised mutual neutrality and so agreed. Dupleix, the French gov., meant meanwhile to build up a powerful connection with the south Indian princes with whom to expel the British in a land-based movement. In the absence of the Royal Navy, La Bourdonnais, the naval commander and gov. of Mauritius, cherished the more dangerous hope of destroying British Indian influence by maritime pressure. Thus when the English Co. agreed, without binding the English govt., to local neutrality it was acting on balance to its own advantage. Meanwhile no similar considerations obtained in N. America. William Shirley, gov. of Massachusetts, with the aid of Commodore Warren, prepared an expedition from colonial resources against the fortress of Louisbourg at the mouth of the St. Lawrence. Louisbourg and C. Breton I. thus fell into British hands simultaneously (May-June 1745) with the defeats of Fontenoy and Hohenfriedberg. Nor was this all. The Admiralty had despatched a force under Commodore Peyton to the Far East which began by interrupting the French trade between India and China and then appeared off Pondicherry, the French Indian capital, in July.

(12) The Imperial election of Francis of Lorraine was tarnished by the remarkable enterprise of Bonnie Prince Charlie, whose landing in Scotland (Aug.) and success among the Highland clans constituted the major strategic surprise (to his friends as much as his enemies) of the war. British and Dutch troops were hurried north and Maurice de Saxe's conquest of the Austrian Netherlands could now proceed. On the other hand Frederick was sensitive to the European balance, now tipping too far towards the Bourbons, and after another victory at Kesselsdorf just after the Young Pretender reached Derby (Dec. 1745) he signed the P. of Dresden (Christmas). This represented a retreat from his enlarged aims. Saxony was restored; he kept Silesia and Glatz but (for what it was worth) reguaranteed the Pragmatic Sanction.

(13) Peyton's preparations against Pondicherry were averted by Dupleix's political skill; his ally the Nawab of the Carnatic threatened to attack Madras and drew Peyton off. In 1746, however, La Bourdonnais appeared and attacked him. The battle was drawn but Peyton, short of timber and spars, retired to Ceylon. La Bourdonnais and Dupleix now quarrelled at Pondicherry from temperament and strategic outlook, as well as conflicts in their instructions. Eventually La Bourdonnais sailed for Madras which he carried by assault (Sept. 1746) but agreed to retrocede it for a large ransom. Dupleix claimed the right to repudiate this stipulation and during the ferocious quarrel which delayed further operations a cyclone wrecked part of the fleet. La Bourdonnais then went home, Dupleix broke the capitulation, drove out the British settlers and went on to attack Fort St. David.

(14) The Jacobite crisis enabled the Pelhams to force Wm. Pitt upon the King in Feb. 1746. The small British army was fully engaged in dealing with the Jacobites, and the navy in intercepting Bourbon succours for them. The French continued their penetration of Belgium, which culminated after their victory over the Austrians at Rocoux (Oct.) in a wholesale occupation. Baulked of the direct route to Holland by the fortress of Bergen-op-Zoom and Anglo-Dutch fleets, Saxe threatened the Dutch inland by laying siege to Maestricht. After Culloden (Apr.), however, the navy could engage in a more offensive role. Reinforcements went to the Mediterranean and the Far East. Squadrons were formed for the Atlantic. There were, besides, two other important events. In June an Austro-Russian treaty ensured that Frederick would not re-enter the war; at the end of the year a change in Spanish politics by the accession of Ferdinand VI made Spain more inclined to leave it. In these circumstances the reorientation of British naval strategy had its effect. A squadron forced Dupleix to raise the siege of Fort St. David. Two Atlantic engagements destroyed France's battle strength and put her commerce and colonies at Britain's mercy. On the other hand the French advance into the Netherlands continued. Cumberland, with his retransferred army, was beaten at Lauffeld (July 1747) and so the maritime powers sought the use of Russian troops (T. of St. Petersburg, Dec. 1747).

(15) Each belligerent now had decisive reasons for terminating the struggle. The financially exhausted French faced the loss of Canada, their Newfoundland fisheries, their E. Indian investments and, above all, their W. Indian sugar colonies, for Haitian production alone exceeded that of the entire British W. Indies and formed an important component in the French European balance of payments. The British feared the domination of the Low Countries by France, the military and political dangers which that implied and their unpredictable commercial consequences. War weariness too after eight years played its part. Negotiations were set on foot in the winter, which developed into the Preliminaries (Apr.) and then the P. of Aix-la-Chapelle.

WARSAW AIR CONVENTION (1929). *See* AVIATION RULES-1.

WARSAW, GRAND DUCHY. This Napoleonic state was carved mainly out of Prussian Poland under the T. of Tilsit (1807). The arrangement whereby the King of Saxony was its Grand Duke revived the Polish-Saxon nexus of the previous century and was a factor in maintaining Saxon support for Bonaparte later in the wars. The Grand Duchy provided him with cavalry and loyally conformed to his political and economic policies. It was suppressed after the Moscow disaster (1812) and most of it passed to Russia in 1815.

WARTON (1) Thomas (?1688-1745) Jacobite and Prof. of Poetry at Oxford 1718-28. His elder son **(2) Joseph (1722-1800),** literary critic and editor, was a friend of Dr. Johnson and a disastrous headmaster of Winchester (where he caused a rebellion) from 1766 to 1793. His brother **(3) Thomas (1728-90),** also a friend of Dr. Johnson, was Prof. of Poetry at Oxford from 1756 to 1766 and published a *History of English Poetry* (1774-81). From 1785 to 1790 he was both Camden Prof. of Ancient History at Oxford and Poet Laureate. He was a serious critic and satirist but his official odes attracted humorous comment which unfairly blighted his reputation.

WARWICK-SHIRE (1) The town, on a crossing of the Avon, was fortified by Aethilflaed in 914 and the shire was the military district dependent upon it. It was divided physically into the open or Feldon and the forest or Arden. The Feldon was fertile and the Arden, as it was progressively felled, was found to be as well.

(2) The royal holdings were not large. The Conqueror took over but regranted many of those to Earl Edwin. There survived also, Turchil, one of the few remaining large landowners of Edward the Confessor's time; his descendants, under the name of Arden, continued there for several centuries. Much the largest landowners, however, were the Beaumont brothers Robert, Count of Meulan and Henry, E. of Warwick, who ultimately acquired Robert's holding and Warwick Castle. This great honour dominated Warwickshire until Tudor times. It passed to the Beauchamps and then, by the marriage of Anne Beauchamp to Warwick the Kingmaker.

(3) Until the 17th cent. the main places were Warwick and Kenilworth, both with immense castles, and Coventry with its cathedral. Warwick had a grammar school dating at least to Henry I. The splendid St. Mary's church contains the famous Beauchamp (chantry) Chapel, and Robert Dudley, E. of Leicester, endowed Lord Leicester's Hospital in 1571. Such signs of prosperity were due to fertility, ironstone and limestone and in due course the opening up of immense underlying coal deposits, but the communications were poor, until the canal era and the inventions of Macadam. Nevertheless, the metal working industries of Birmingham, Coventry and Rugby early created a demand for fuel which led to progressive clearance and rising agricultural production in Arden. Hence the county developed as a cereal and fruit producing region. In the meantime coal began to be exploited and this in its turn stimulated the towns into modern industrialisation.

(4) Stratford-on-Avon, though Shakespeare's birth-place, contributed little to the county until railways and roads and the Shakespeare Memorial Trust created a mid-20th cent. tourist traffic.

(5) In addition to the county, Warwick and Coventry were represented in parliament from 1295 and Tamworth from 1584.

WARWICK, Es. and D. of. See BEAUCHAMP; DUDLEY, RICH-5.

WASH. See PENS.

WASHINGTON (Durham). This village was the probable origin of the Washington family. See NEW TOWNS.

WASHINGTON (1) Augustine (?-1743) was a planter in Westmoreland, Virginia. By his first wife, one son **(2) Lawrence (?-1752)** was educated in England from which he returned in 1738. He acted as father of both families after Augustine's death and married a Fairfax. Augustine's second wife's son **(3) George (1732-99)** was thus introduced to the 6th Lord Fairfax, who owned vast estates W. of the Blue Ridge and employed him to survey them. This powerful patronage brought him a majority and an assignment to warn off French encroachments on the Ohio (1753) and, as a lieut-col., to protect the building of Fort Duquesne which, however, was taken (1754) before he could arrive. He built Fort Necessity nearby but the French captured it too (1755). After participating in Braddock's disaster against Fort Duquesne in 1755, he was given command of the Virginia militia on the W. frontier and helped to capture Fort Duquesne in 1758. He then settled down as a tobacco planter at Mt. Vernon and served in the Virginian House of Burgesses from 1759 to 1774. His personal vitality and intelligence were kept well in the public eye. He blamed the British for the terms of trade which reduced the profits on his tobacco, but probably his main quarrel with the home govt. was related to the policy of restricting migration beyond the Appalachians. This was an area which he knew well, where he had large investments and where many Virginians under his wartime command had settled on his advice. He had the regimental officer's conscience about his men. He early concluded that the issues could be settled only by violence. He was one of the first to boycott British taxed goods and led the Virginian delegation to the Continental Congress (1774-5) (see AMERICAN REBELLION). When fighting started at Lexington (Apr. 1775) he appeared at the sessions in uniform and was nominated as rebel C-in-C in July. He and his opponents muddled along until French local naval intervention enabled him to starve Burgoyne into surrender at Yorktown (1781). He retired, a sort of secular saint, from the army in 1783 and Mt. Vernon became a kind of American Delphic oracle. In 1787 he presided at the Constitutional convention which, much by his influence, adopted the constitution of the U.S.A. and in 1789 he became first President. He believed that the President should be above party and, in the manner of the later Stuarts and early Hanoverians, appointed men of opposed political outlooks to his cabinet. In 1797 he refused a third term as Pres, a precedent which was followed until F.D.R. Roosevelt. He then retired. See UNITED STATES OF AMERICA-1-3.

WASHINGTON CONFERENCE (1921-2) was called to reduce tension in the Far East and to limit naval armaments; to induce Japan to co-operate, Britain and the U.S.A. fatefully agreed not to strengthen fortifications between Singapore and Hawaii. See WASHINGTON TREATIES.

WASHINGTON D. C. was established on land ceded by Virginia and Maryland. The White House was commenced in 1792 and the Capitol in 1793. It became the seat of govt. of the U.S.A. in 1800 but was burned by the British in 1814. It remained a somewhat muddy village until about 1870. In 1900 its authority began to lay it out in accordance with the original plans drawn up by Pierre l'Enfant in 1791.

WASHINGTON STATE (U.S.A.). See OREGON.

WASHINGTON TREATIES (1) 1871 was the outcome of Anglo-U.S. negotiations on the U.S. *Alabama* claims against Britain, the Pacific coast fisheries disputes, U.S. Canadian commercial reciprocity (which had lapsed in 1866) and Canadian claims for damage by Fenian incursions from U.S. territory. Only the first two were settled by the treaty which, however, helped to stabilise Anglo-American relations for a generation. **(2) Dec. 1921 (THE FOUR POWER PACT)** with a supplementary declaration and a supplementary agreement of 6 Feb. 1922, was a treaty for consultation on Pacific questions between Britain, U.S.A., Japan and France. It formally ended the Anglo-Japanese alliance of 1902. **(3)** See NAVAL LIMITATION. **(4)** See NINE POWER TREATIES (1922).

WASON v WALTER (1868) LR 4QB 73. In this case it was held that a fair and accurate newspaper report of a parliamentary debate was privileged in an action for libel and that comment upon it, being a matter of public concern, was privileged in the absence of malice.

WATCH AND WARD was **(1)** a petty serjeanty, performed by providing a sentinel or watchman for specific periods in border or coastal castles; **(2)** a burgess obligation to form part of a town peace patrol.

WATER COLOURS. This pictorial art in which the English excelled originated in Germany in the 15th cent. The main landmarks in England were William Taverner (1703-72), Paul Sandby (1725-1809), Thomas Rowlandson (1757-1827), David Cox (1783-1859), John Sell Cotman (1782-1842), Peter de Wint (1784-1849), Joseph Mallord William Turner (1775-1851) and Samuel Palmer (1805-81).

WATERFORD, TOWN AND COUNTY. Ostmen fortified the town in the 10th cent. and held it until Raymond le Gros, one of Strongbow's commanders, took it in 1170. It was chartered in 1205 and long remained the second English town in Ireland. It supported the Tudor govt. down to 1603, by which time the fall of the Fitzgeralds had ended feudal rule in the surrounding areas. The town now became the centre of the county and the local outlook changed. It opposed the Stuart (protestant) succession, resisted Cromwell and supported James II against William III. Thereafter it was generally peaceful. The glass industry flourished from 1783 to 1851 and was revived after World War II. Brewing and bacon curing were established in 1820.

WATER FRAME. See ARKWRIGHT; INDUSTRIAL REVOLUTION.

WATERLOO (Fr: MONT ST. JEAN; Ger: BELLE ALLIANCE) B. of (18 June 1815) and CAMPAIGN (4 Apr.-19 June 1815) (1) For this famous event Bonaparte mobilised a northern army during May 1815 and assumed personal command at Beaumont near the frontier on 14 June. The D. of Wellington had already reached Brussels on 4 Apr and disposed his polyglot force of about 50,000 infantry, 13,000 cavalry and 156 guns on a wide front south of the city ready to

WATLING STREET

concentrate when the route of Bonaparte's approach was known. The British communications ran westwards to the Channel. The powerful Prussian army under Blücher was camped around Namur with its communications stretching eastwards through Liège to Germany.

(2) Bonaparte, operating behind a dense security screen, intended to hold Wellington stationary by a bluffed threat to his westward communications while attacking Blücher in force. Success here might drive Blücher eastwards away from Wellington, and Bonaparte would then be free to concentrate against the latter and, having defeated him, to occupy Brussels. This strategic plan failed through miscalculations and blunders. Wellington received confirmation of Bonaparte's true movements in time to draw in most of his westward troops. The Prussians, when attacked, withdrew to Ligny and, despite many unnecessary casualties in the ensuing battle, proved tougher than expected and, by retreating further, remained in distant contact with Wellington. On the same day (16 June) Bonaparte's direct advance on Wellington developed into an indecisive encounter battle at Quatre Bras in which Marshal Ney was denied adequate reinforcements because confused orders and bad staff work caused Drouet d'Erlon's large corps to march back and forth between the two battles without taking part in either.

(3) Wellington concentrated most of his troops on the Mont St. Jean position 12 miles in front of Brussels but Bonaparte reduced his own available force by detaching Grouchy's corps to shepherd the retreating Blücher eastwards. Through confused orders Grouchy imitated Drouet d'Erlon's movements on the east, thus missing both Blücher and the main battle.

(4) The allied army (only 24,000 of which was British) lay in a typically Wellingtonian position mostly on the reverse slope of a ridge where it could not be directly bombarded; it had two outlying posts: the more advanced in front of the right (westward) wing in a farm and orchard called Hougoumont: the nearer in front of the centre in a farm and gravel-pit called La Haye Sainte. Bonaparte, with 49,000 infantry, nearly 16,000 cavalry and 246 guns, planned a powerful feint against Hougoumont followed, when Wellington's centre had been denuded to reinforce Hougoumont, by a massed assault prepared by his artillery and designed to smash in Wellington's centre. This tactical plan also failed through miscalculations and blunders. It had rained all night and the ground was so sodden that operations had to wait until 11.30 a.m. for it to dry out. Then the Hougoumont feint under Pr. Jerome Bonaparte was allowed to develop into a furious sub-battle where the obsessed Prince drew in two additional divisions destined for other purposes, and it lasted longer than originally intended. Consequently the extreme Prussian advance guard was already descried from Bonaparte's H.Q., La Belle Alliance (opposite La Haye Sainte) at 1.30 p.m., before the central attack had begun. Moreover Bonaparte (an artilleryman) had not appreciated the subtlety of the Wellingtonian position which his massed guns had mostly failed to hit, and when his infantry assault was launched it was less powerful than planned while Wellington, who had not denuded his centre, was stronger there than expected. This first assault was dispersed by the British cavalry, which was itself scattered by a French counter-charge. A second assault failed and Ney now launched a series of massed cavalry charges unsupported by guns. These encountered the British infantry drawn up in squares just behind the crest of the ridge and fell victim to their steady platoon firing. One square repelled 23 attacks. Ney had four horses shot under him.

(5) By now the Prussians were approaching a point dangerously close to and rather behind Bonaparte's right wing. The Imperial Guard and the VIth Corps under Gen. Lobau were massed as a reserve behind La Belle Alliance.

At about 4.30 p.m. Lobau was ordered away to move behind the French right wing, meet Blücher's Prussians and contain them. Extremely heavy fighting developed here while the need for a French success in the centre had become urgent. At about 6.00 p.m. Drouet d'Erlon at last took La Haye Sainte and began to bring up guns to support a general breakthrough. Wellington reorganised his centre. Lobau had to be reinforced with the Young Guard but Bonaparte ordered a general assault which was to include the hitherto invincible Middle Guard. It encountered the British infantry which rose suddenly in line from concealment in the corn and treated it to its routine platoon firing with Col. Colbourne with the 52nd outflanked it and poured volleys into its left. The Guard fled and this brought about within minutes a widespread collapse of French morale. Sensing this Wellington launched a general advance and Bonaparte's army disintegrated. The comparatively fresh Prussians relieved Wellington's exhausted troops in an all-night pursuit. The Old Guard refused to surrender and enabled Bonaparte to escape.

WATERLOO BRIDGE and STATION (London). Sir John Rennie's Bridge was begun in 1811, named after the battle in 1815 and opened in 1817. The railway station was named after it. The bridge began to subside in 1924 and was replaced between 1925 and 1945. This operation was politically controversial for reasons which have long been obscure.

WATERLOW, Sir Sydney Hedley (1822-1906) was apprenticed to his uncle Thos. Harrison, the govt. printer, in 1836 and in 1844 added printing to the family stationery business which, as Waterlow and Co., became a limited Co. in 1876 with him as managing director until 1895. He was Lord Mayor in 1872 and a liberal M.P. from 1868 to 1869 and from 1874 to 1885. The firm has done much govt. printing ever since.

WATER POWER. An English water mill is mentioned in the 8th cent. and many appear in Domesday, at first to grind corn and much later to provide power for early factories, still, in Yorkshire called mills. The result was an industrial migration to foothills, especially the Pennines. Steam superseded water power after about 1840 but water power on an infinitely grander scale returned for hydro-electricity, at first in Switzerland and then in Scotland in the 1930s.

WATERWAYS, INTERNATIONAL (1) The Rhine was opened to free navigation by the T. of Mainz (1831) but non-discriminatory navigation was not established until the Act of Mannheim (1868). **(2)** The Danube was opened by the T. of Paris 1856. **(3)** The Elbe, Vltava, Oder, Niemen and Danube were declared international by the P. of Versailles but those parts of these rivers dominated by Russia and her satellites ceased to be so between 1945 and 1989. **(4)** The Congo and Niger were internationalised by the T. of Berlin 1885. **(5)** Other waterways important to international commerce have also been internationalised, notably the R. Scheldt and the Panama and Suez canals.

WATIER'S. A dining club in Piccadilly founded at the Prince Regent's suggestion by Watier, his chef, and noted for its elaborate cuisine. Everybody who was anybody went there and it became a gambling centre. It was closed in 1819.

WATLING STREET (O.E. WAECLINGA STREET) was called after an English clan whose name also appears in Waeclingaceaster (= St. Albans). It was a Roman road running from Dover *via* Canterbury to the ford at Westminster, thence along the modern Edgware Road, through St. Albans and *via* Lichfield and Shrewsbury to Chester. It was one of the four great roads subject to the King's Peace. Watling St. London was probably a diversion. A number of stages dedicated to St. Laurence (represented standing between blossoming trees) were places where companies of merchants foregathered for the journey: Blossoms Inn, London and the Blossoms Hotel, Chester recall these. The saint was painted out at the Reformation. *See* BRITAIN, ROMAN-2,3.

WAT'S DYKE was a line of tactical earthworks from the R. Dee to Morda Brook near Oswestry (Salop) built under K. Aethelbald of Mercia in c. 716-20 to block raids from Gwynedd which had been particularly frequent and damaging between 705 and 709.

WATSON-WATT, Sir Robert Alexander (1892-1973), after working at the Meterological Office and the Dept. of Scientific and Industrial Research became, in 1933, superintendent of the radio dept. of the N. Physical Laboratory, where he developed the military uses of radar (then called radio-location). From 1938 to 1940 his inventiveness was transferred as director of communications and then as scientific adviser to the Air Ministry and in 1942 as Vice-Controller to the Min. of Aircraft Production.

WATT, James (1736-1819) A remarkably integrated inventor, was first employed in Scotland for canals and improving harbours. This led him naturally to the power employed in using them and so, to substituting steam (already used in mine pumping) for wind propulsion and animal towage. While repairing a Newcomen pumping engine in 1764 he concluded that its efficiency would be much improved if the steam were condensed separately rather than in a cylinder. He obtained the necessary data on steam properties and specific heat by experiments which he designed himself and built the first separately condensed engine in 1765. He now set up a firm with Matthew Boulton of Birmingham and they made reciprocating engines to his 1765 design but quickly saw that the primitive state of these machines gave wide scope for improvement. Watt accordingly designed a crank to deliver power by rotating shaft but one Pickard, one of his employees, had done so too and had patented it. Watt, therefore, designed the alternative sun-and-planet gear and went on to double-acting engines, the engine indicator, the centrifugal governor and his straight-line Watt mechanism. As a by-product of his drawing office he invented a copying ink.

WATTS, Isaac (1674-1748), nonconformist schoolmaster and minister (from 1702) in London, composed over 600 hymns including *Oh God, Our help in ages past* and *Jesus shall reign.* He also wrote educational manuals on such subjects as logic and biblical history.

WAUGH (1) Alexander (Alec) (1898-1981) a prolific novelist who first scandalised the educated public in 1917 with the *Loom of Youth,* a realistic novel about public school life. His equally prolific brother **(2) Evelyn Arthur (1903-66)** wrote most amusing satirical novels of inter-war life and some others of wartime and post-war life which were famous in their time.

WAVELL, Archibald Percival (1883-1950) (1) 1st Vist. (1943) 1st E. (1947) WAVELL of CYRENAICA and WINCHESTER considered, with reason, the most brilliant military commander of the century, was attaché with the Russian army of the Caucasus in 1916 and was then posted to Allenby's H.Q. in the Middle East. From 1935-7 he held the Aldershot divisional command, which became legendary for the ingenuity of its training programme and then, after a period as G.O.C. Palestine, he took over Southern Command in 1938 and in June 1939 became C-in-C Middle East.

(2) With the French collapse and the loss of most of the British Army's equipment in Norway and Dunkirk, he was expected to defend the Middle East on two fronts (W. and S.) against 20 to 1 odds on the ground and 100 to 1 in the air. He therefore surprised and destroyed the large Italian army at Sidi Barrani in Dec. 1940 and then, leaving a small force to conquer Cyrenaica, switched his main body against Abyssinia. He had, however, already been compelled by the Cabinet to detach troops to Greece (Oct.). The southern operations

proceeded to a rapid triumph, Italian Ethiopia and Somalia being overrun by May 1941 but meanwhile enemy counter measures developed and he was, despite the R. Navy's remarkable successes at Taranto (Nov. 1940) and C. Matapan (Mar. 1941) too weak to anticipate them. Rommel with his Afrika Korps, attacked from Libya (Mar. 1941). In Apr. the Germans invaded Yugoslavia and Greece and there was a pro-Axis coup in his rear at Baghdad. The war took on the aspect of a desperate rearguard action yet Wavell managed to keep up some offensive spirit. The Vichy French were threatening from Syria. In conjunction with the Free French he expelled them (June). An Anglo-Russian occupation of Persia followed (Aug.). Greece and Crete had been lost by June but Rommel was stopped at the frontier and a counter attack drove him back to Libya (Nov.-Dec.).

(3) Wavell and Churchill irritated each other but Churchill implicitly acknowledged his greatness by transferring him to the even weaker Allied Supreme Command against the Japanese, who had occupied Siam and crippled or sunk the U.S. and British eastern fleets. The Japanese momentum was overwhelming in Indonesia and S.E. Asia and by Apr. 1942 they were overrunning Burma and raiding Ceylon. The Allied Supreme Command was dissolved and Wavell moved to India to organise defence against the inevitable thrust from Burma. In Jan. 1943 he was promoted F-M and appointed Viceroy.

(4) He now had the responsibilities of a statesman rather than those of a military commander. His six year viceroyalty was devoted to keeping India (much disturbed politically) calm, raising production and recruiting and dealing with dangerous and inopportune famines, especially in Bengal, just behind the front. The organisation of India was the foundation upon which others were able to win their later victories. On the other hand wartime paternalism was deemed the wrong approach to the post-war political problems which the new Labour govt. was determined to solve by grants of independence to a united or divided sub-continent. Wavell was unwilling to risk the probable casualties. The govt. thought that the risk had to be taken and superseded him.

(5) Besides his public career, Wavell was a poet, a linguist and, as an author, found time to publish two studies of Allenby (1940 and 1943), books on *Generalship* (published in several languages), a poetical anthology (1944) and *The Good Soldier* (1948).

WAYLAND or WELAND the Smith. A hero, who in Swedish mythology worked as a smith after his Valkyrie wife left him. He was mutilated and enslaved by a Swedish King whose children he contrived to murder. As WIELAND in German mythology he was a great swordsmith. In England his forge was at a dolmen near the Wantage White Horse.

WAYNFLETE, William of (?1395-1486) became a master at Winchester College in 1429 and, traditionally, brought half the scholars of that place with him to found Eton in 1442. In 1443 he became Provost of Eton and in 1447 Bp. of Winchester. He founded Magdalen College, Oxford, in 1448. He was Lord Chancellor from 1457 to 1460.

WAYS AND MEANS, COMMITTEE OF. A committee of the whole House of Commons which until 1966 considered resolutions for raising new taxes, continuing an expiring tax or increasing or extending the scope of an existing tax and matters ancillary thereto. The budget was always moved in this committee. The effect of the resolutions would subsequently be embodied in Finance Bills.

WAZIRISTAN (Pakistan). Inhabited by two Pathan tribal groups, the Darwesh Khel or **Waziris** (north) and the **Mahsuds** (south) this area lay on the Indo-Afghan frontier between the Khyber and Bolan passes and, being off the main routes, was not administered by the British Indian govt. Hence tribal raiding provoked only minor punitive expeditions between 1860 and 1914. The Mahsuds, however, supported the Afghans in the Third Afghan War (1919) and were not suppressed until 1923. There was further fighting in 1936-7 following the activities of the Fakir of Ipi and again during World War II.

WEALD (A.S. = forest) or ANDRAEDSWEALD (= Forest of Anderida or Pevensey) extending from Hampshire through Sussex and Kent nearly to Canterbury and from the North Downs in Surrey almost to the coast, was important for its deposits of iron, which its timber was used to smelt. The iron was exported in Romano-British times through the fortified port of Pevensey which consequently attracted Saxon interest and was stormed by Aelle and Cissa in about 477. The forest also constituted a barrier against settlement which, in Sussex, was felled only slowly from the coast northwards and in Kent by means of sporadic clearances. Iron working continued on a substantial scale into Tudor times; it was largely responsible for the destruction of the trees but it declined thereafter as the deposits were worked out.

WEALTH OF NATIONS. *See* SMITH, ADAM.

WEAVER, R. *See* TRANSPORT AND COMMUNICATIONS.

WEAVING AND SPINNING. John Kay of Bury invented the flying shuttle in 1733. By enabling a single person to work a wide loom it increased the demand for yarn and led to the inventions connected with machine spinning. Paul and Wyatt tried roller spinning unsuccessfully as early as 1738. In 1760 Robt. Kay invented the drop box loom using more than one shuttle and in 1764 James Hargreaves his spinning jenny, which was an instant success; Richard Arkwright introduced his water frame in 1769 and in 1779 Samuel Crompton combined Hargreaves' and Arkwright's principles in the so-called mule. This opened the way for Cartwright's power loom introduced in 1785 and in 1808 Joseph Jacquard of Lyons invented his handloom for weaving elaborate designs. Power looms became common only after 1815 but by 1850 they had wholly superseded handlooms. Automatic looms came into use after 1900.

WEBB, Sir Aston (1849-1930), architect, mainly remembered for his Victoria and Albert Museum and Royal College of Science in Kensington.

WEBB, John Richmond (1667-1724) vain, brave and picturesque soldier and Tory M.P. (1690-1710, 1715, 1722) fought with distinction as brig-gen. and maj-gen. at Blenheim, Ramillies and Oudenarde. During the siege of Lille in 1708 he won a brilliant victory at Wynendael with 8000 men against 22,000 French which, by preserving a main supply convoy, decided the siege. The first *London Gazette* report by the Prince of Hesse-Cassel accidentally described the victory to Cadogan and started a furious attack by Tories, other than Webb, on Marlborough's supposed political bias. Marlborough was, in fact, trying to have him promoted for the victory. He was badly wounded at Malplaquet and in 1712 became the Tory C-in-C of the home army. He was abruptly dismissed from his post when George I arrived from Hanover.

WEBB, Matthew (1848-83) merchant seaman, was the first to swim the Channel (Dover-Calais in 22 hours, Aug. 1875). He was drowned trying to swim below the Niagara Falls.

WEBB, Philip (1831-1915), architect trained by George Edmund Street (1824-81), the exponent of neo-Gothic who built the London Law Courts, was one of Wm. Morris original partners in the design firm of Morris, Marshall and Faulkner, founded in 1864. He was a house builder but the firm designed mainly for churches at that time, save for wall papers. *See also* PRE-RAPHAELITES.

WEBB, Sidney James (1859-1947) Ld. PASSFIELD (1929) and **Beatrice neé POTTER (1858-1943),** his wife from 1892. **(1)** He was educated as a lawyer and was one of the earliest (1885) members of the Fabian Society which his sense and erudition, as well as G. B. Shaw's

brilliance, did much to form. He became a Progressive Councillor for Deptford on the L.C.C. in 1892. She was the daughter of a rich industrialist but with ideas of her own and they met in connection with her co-operative studies. Since they shared similar collectivist ideas and a passion for information the first public fruit of the (childless) marriage was their *History of Trade Unionism* (1894). Meanwhile, with R. B. Haldane and others, they had agitated for and now secured the foundation of the London School of Economics (1895). In 1897 they published *Industrial Democracy*.

(2) From 1905 until 1909 Beatrice served on the R. Commission on the Poor Law and this helped with and also helped to inspire their *History of English Local Government,* whose nine volumes emerged at intervals until 1929. Beatrice also drafted the R. Commission's minority report and they waged a nationwide but unsuccessful campaign for its adoption. In 1913 they helped to found the *New Statesman.* By now the Labour Party had substantially adopted the minority report as part of its social policy and in 1918 Sydney, who had become a member of its executive in 1915, drafted the party policy statement, *Labour and the New Social Order.* Public discontent with the Liberals and distrust of Lloyd George now gave Labour its opening. Sydney's successful election campaign at Seaham (Durham) in 1922 contributed powerfully to electoral successes and he became Pres. of the Bd. of Trade in the first short Labour Govt. He continued to hold Seaham until 1929 when he took a peerage and was successively Sec. of State for the Dominions and Colonies (1929-30) and then for the Colonies alone (1930-1). He never held office again and the couple reacted against the formation of the National Coalition Govt. by visiting Russia in 1932. This resulted in their naïve *Soviet Communism: a New Civilisation* (1935).

(3) The Webbs were enormously respected for their integrity, learning and total commitment to English or Fabian socialism. They were also personally liked by most people with whom they ever had to deal.

WEBBE, Edward (fl. 1566-90) a gunner and servant of Anthony Jenkinson at Moscow, was enslaved by the Krim Tartars when they sacked the city in 1571 and was consequently a Turkish master-gunner at Tunis at its capture by Don John of Austria in 1572. He remained a Turkish slave until ransomed in 1588. He then took service under Henry IV of France and fought at his victory at Ivry in 1590.

WEBB[E], John (1611-72) pupil of Inigo Jones, supervised the building of Greenwich Palace (1661-6), Burlington House, London (1664-8) and country houses.

WEBB[E], Samuel (1740-1816) and his son **(2) Samuel (1770-1843),** organists at the Spanish embassy in London, composed many glees, madrigals, motets and much church music. The younger was considered the finest organist of his time.

WEBSTER, John (c. 1560-c. 1625) playwright, collaborated between 1602 and 1607 with Dekker, Middleton and Rowley in roistering comedies but on his own wrote macabre and violent tragedies, of which *The White Devil* (1612) and *The Duchess of Malfi* (1616) are still played.

WEDDERBURN. Dundee family. Its best known members were **(1) James (?1495-1553)** the godly vernacular poet. **(2) James (1585-1639)** Laudian Bp. of Dunblane from 1636 until deposed by the Glasgow assembly. **(3) Sir Peter (?1616-79) Ld. GOSFORD (1668),** royalist advocate, became clerk to the Scottish Privy Council in 1661 and a distinguished Lord of Session from 1668. **(4) Sir John (1704-46),** Jacobite, was taken at Culloden and executed. **(5) Alexander (1733-1805) 1st Ld. LOUGHBOROUGH (1780), 1st E. of ROSSLYN (1801),** left the Scottish bar after publicly insulting the Lord Pres. of the Court of Session and was called to the English bar (1757). He attracted Bute's favour and was an M.P. from

1761 to 1778; originally a Tory, he spoke for John Wilkes in 1769 and attacked Lord North in 1770. These nuisance tactics gained promotion. He returned to the Tories as Sol-Gen. in 1771, became Att-Gen. in 1778 and accepted the customary offer to be C.J. of the Common Pleas in 1780. His distinguished tenure of this office did not prevent political promotion and from 1793 to 1801 he was Lord Chancellor. *See* ERSKINE.

WEDGWOOD. (1) Sir Josiah (1730-95), educated, partly crippled potter, established his first independent business at Burslem in 1759. His efficiency, understanding of material and design, inventiveness and ability to handle people brought quick success and by 1762 he was the Queen's potter. He opened the famous Etruria factory and settlement in 1769 and promoted road and canal building in the area. This compounded the prosperity of all the local potters while his inventions revolutionised their work. His epitaph correctly states that he "converted a rude and inconsiderable manufactory into an elegant art and an important part of national commerce". A son **(2) Thomas (1771-1805)** propounded the earliest method of photography in 1802.

WEDMORE, T of. *See* ALFRED.

WEE FREES (1) The minority of the Free Church of Scotland which remained separate after it merged with the United Presbyterian Church in 1900. **(2)** By analogy, the Asquith Liberals who disastrously opposed Lloyd George's coalition Liberals in the Coupon Election of 1918.

WEEMS or PICTS HOUSES are subterranean chambers of unknown date found mostly in the Pictish territory of Scotland. *See* BROCHS.

WEIGHTS AND MEASURES (*see also* COINAGE; DECIMALISATION). In this entry the reader is assumed to know the metric system. Though criminalised in 1995, the following, mostly of ancient origin, are used. Those in *italics* were or are of specialised rather than common application.

(1) Length on land

1 inch (25.4cm)	× 12	= 1 foot
1 foot	× 3	= 1 yard
1 yard	×5½	= 1 rod, pole or perch
1 rod, pole or perch	× 4	= 1 *chain*
1 *chain*	× 10	= 1 *furlong*
1 furlong	× 8	= 1 mile (1760 yards or 5280 feet)
1 mile	× 3	= 1 league
	BUT	
1 sea mile		= 6080 feet
1 knot		= 1 sea mile per hour

(2) Area

1 square yard	×30¼	= 1 pole
1 pole	× 4	= 1 *rood*
1 *rood*	× 4	= 1 acre

(3) Liquid capacity

1 gill	× 2	= 1 pint
1 pint	× 2	= 1 quart
1 quart	× 4	= 1 gallon (= 4.546 dm³)

(4) Dry capacity

1 pint	× 2	= 1 quart
1 quart	× 8	= 1 *peck*
1 *peck*	× 4	= 1 bushel (= 35.24 dm³)
	Apothecaries only	
1 minim	× 60	= 1 drachm (= 35.24 cm³)

(5) Weights

Avoirdupois (the usual commercial system)

1 ounce (oz)	× 16	= 1 pound (lb)
1 lb	× 14	= 1 stone (st)
1 st	× 2	= 1 *quarter (qr)*
1 *qr*	× 4	= 1 hundredweight (cwt)

1 cwt	× 20	= 1 ton or long ton as opposed to the US short ton of 2000 lb.

Troy (used by apothecaries only and jewellers)

1 grain	× 20	= 1 scruple
1 scruple	× 3	= 1 ounce (31.1 grams)

There were at various times four accepted weights whose proportions to each other are as set out below

Tower Pound	540	Mercantile Pound	720
Troy Pound	575	Avoirdupois Pound	700

The first two were related to the original currency (*see* COINAGE). The Tower mint changed from Tower to Troy in 1529 as a barely concealed inflation excused as conformity with mainly French uses. The mark was ⅔rds of a Tower Pound. The Mercantile Pound = 2 Marks.

(6) Other Special units. (Mostly used by port or customs authorities)

1 Fotmal (72 lb)	× 15	= 1 hogshead	Wine not otherwise specified
1 hogshead	× 4	= 1 puncheon	
1 puncheon	× 2	= 1 pipe	
1 pipe	× 2	= 1 tun	

This tun was related to the ton through ships in the Bristol wine trade being rated by the number of tuns which they could carry.

	BUT	
1 gallon	× 30	= 1 Aum (Hock)
	× 36	= 1 Barrel (beer)
	×106	= 1 Butt (Sherry; Whisky)
	× 48	= 1 Hogshead (Burgundy; Claret)
	× 92	= 1 Pipe (Madeira)
	×115	= 1 Pipe (Port)
	×120	= 1 Puncheon (Brandy)
1 inch	× 45	= 1 ell (cloth)

(7) Paper quantities

1 sheet	× 24	= 1 quire
1 quire	× 20	= 1 ream

(8) Coal

1 cwt	×28½	= 1 chaldron (London)
	× 53	= 1 chaldron (Newcastle)

WEI-HAI-WEI (China) naval base on the south side of the G. of Pechihli, was taken by the Japanese in 1895. They were forced to relinquish it by the western powers and in 1898 Britain took a 25 year lease. Owing to the disturbed state of China in the 1920s the place was not returned until 1930. *See* CHINA-29,31-2.

WEIMAR (Ger.) before 1919 capital of the Duchy of Saxe-Weimar-Eisenach, was famous through its association with Cranach, with Goethe, Schiller, Herder and other German thinkers and so with the German publishing trade of which it was the centre. In 1919 the post-imperial republican constitution was signed there.

WEIZMAN, Chaim (1874-1952). *See* ZIONISM.

WELBECK ABBEY (Notts.) the immense seat of the Dukes of Portland, was built mainly in the late 17th cent; the underground rooms date from 1734 onwards.

WELENSKY, Roy. *See* CENTRAL AFRICAN FEDERATION.

WELFARE STATE, namely a state which makes provision for all against the uncertainties of human weakness, particularly in health, housing, unemployment and old age, was effectively established to cope with the personal emergencies of World War II, accepted by all parties as a peacetime principle by 1945 and established and extended legislatively as well as organisationally in the years thereafter. By the 1980s its bureaucracies and expense were under fire from the Conservatives who sought, after the advent of the Thatcher govt., to maintain the benefits by contractual rather than administrative means. Their erosion of the structure had by the 1990s made popularly disliked changes which, especially in the field of health, seemed to recreate the uncertainties which the Welfare State was supposed to prevent.

WELFENFONDS. The enormous family trust of the Hanoverian ruling family, seized by Bismarck and used to induce K. Ludwig of Bavaria to propose the elevation of the King of Prussia into German Emperor.

WELLESLEY and WELLESLEY-POLE (*see* COLLEY OR COWLEY); **(1) William (1763-1845) 1st Ld. MARYBOROUGH (1821), 3rd E. of MORNINGTON** acquired the Pole estates and took their name. He was an Irish M.P. from 1783 to 1790, an English M.P. from 1790 to 1794 and an Irish M.P. in the U.K. parliament from 1801 to 1821. He was a vigorous parliamentary defender of his more famous brothers (*see* WELLESLEY. M. and WELLINGTON, D. OF) and contributed to Wellington's success. He was Chief Sec. for Ireland from 1809 to 1812 and, being against R. Catholic relief, clashed with his brother, the M. Wellesley. In 1814 he became a member of the Cabinet as Master of the Mint where he was chiefly distinguished by a common sense dislike of repression. He was driven from office in 1823 by the intrigue which put Huskisson in. His brother **(2) Henry (1773-1847) 1st Ld. COWLEY (1828)** went to India in 1797 as private Sec. to the M. Wellesley, Gov-Gen. (his brother) and they, with Sir Arthur Wellesley (later Wellington, another brother) settled the Mysore problem. Henry was then sent home to explain matters but returned (1799-1801) and negotiated the Oudh cessions, of which until Mar. 1802 he was Lieut-Gov. In 1807 he became an M.P.; in 1809 he went to Spain as the M. Wellesley's embassy sec. and became *chargé d'affaires* after Wellesley's return to England and ambassador in Oct. 1811. His services with the difficult Spaniards in the Peninsular War were important to Wellington, who was heavily burdened with military, supply and financial matters. He persuaded the Spanish King to renounce future family compacts in 1814, negotiated the commercial treaty of 1815 and the treaty for the abolition of the slave trade in 1817. From 1823 to 1831 he was ambassador to Vienna. In 1835 Peel nominated him for the embassy at Paris but the govt. changed and he did not go. He was reappointed in 1841 and resigned in 1846. His son **(3) Henry Richard Charles (1804-84) 2nd Ld. and 1st E.** (1857), also a diplomat, was minister to the German Confederation in 1851 when he was appointed ambassador to Paris unexpectedly and arrived two months after Napoleon III's *coup d'etat*. He was thus the key figure in British diplomacy on the Crimean War, the Congress of Paris, the Persian T. of Paris (1956), the consequent detailed issues in the Balkans and on the Danube and the Paris Declaration on maritime warfare. He also had to calm the ruffled Anglo-French susceptibilities over the Orsini affair. In Feb. 1859 he was despatched on a special mission to Vienna to try to prevent the Franco-Austrian war which, through no fault of his, broke out shortly afterwards. On his return to Paris he had to deal with the problems arising out of it, notably popular British suspicions of Napoleon III's intentions on the Channel as well as in Italy, and he helped Cobden to negotiate the valuable commercial agreement of 1860. His familiarity with French political conditions and his personal acquaintance with all the leading French personalities made him by now almost a leading French statesman but able from his point of vantage to speak his mind to the emperor. He retired in 1867.

WELLESLEY (*see* COLLEY OR COWLEY and previous entry). **Richard COLLEY (1760-1842) 2nd E. of MORNINGTON (1781) 1st M. WELLESLEY (1799)** became in 1784 an M.P. of a reforming conservative type and in 1793

member of the Board of Control. He became gov-gen. of India in 1797 and arrived there in May 1798 to be faced with the Mysore crisis. He doubted the possibility of maintaining a peaceful balance in the South, with the French fomenting trouble, or in the North where the Marathas might, and the Afghans and Sikhs certainly would do so. A forward or aggressive (and expensive) policy seemed necessary but was disliked or misunderstood at home. His southern solution was the system of subsidiary treaties, the first with Hyderabad, the military overthrow of Mysore, further subsidiary treaties with Tanjore and Surat and the effective annexation of the Carnatic. In the north he reversed the previous policy in Oudh and incited the Persians to attack Afghanistan. At this point the P. of Amiens (1802) required him to hand back the captured French possessions. Believing that peace would be short he delayed the transfer on various pretexts until war broke out again and relieved him of the responsibility. This incident typified an independent and autocratic attitude which from time to time brought him into collision with the directors of the HEIC. He offered his resignation in 1802 and again in 1803. The HEIC could not dispense with him and, because of the developing Maratha crisis, it could not control him. In Dec. 1802 he had forced another subsidiary treaty (T. of Bassein) upon the Peishwa, which strained the loyalty of his nominal vassals. In the ensuing second Maratha War (1802-4) his brother Arthur (later Wellington) overthrew Scindia and Bhonsla at the Bs. of Laswari, Assaye and Argaum (1803) but Col. Monson under Gen. Lake suffered a defeat at the hands of Holkar and this was made the excuse for superseding the Gov-Gen. He reached England in 1806 and was hotly attacked in parliament but a motion for an impeachment was thrown out.

In 1809 he was briefly ambassador in Spain but was recalled to become Foreign Sec. under Perceval. He was not popular in the cabinet, which he seldom attended, for he was moodily arrogant and also led a scandalous sexual life, but he resolutely supported his brother's campaigns in Spain from his office. When Perceval was murdered, the Prince Regent commissioned him to discover who would form a govt. and then secondly to form one. He failed in both assignments and remained out of office until 1821.

In that year he became Lord Lieut. of Ireland, then in disorder. He had much multi-partisan good will but much bigotry to contend with. He suppressed the Whiteboys, reorganised the police (such as it was), purged the bench of its more grossly prejudiced members, raised nearly £1M for famine relief in 1822 and secured the passage of a Tithe Composition Act, but when his brother (Wellington) became Prime Minister in 1828 they disagreed on R. Catholic relief and he resigned. He retired from public life in 1835. An orotund English stylist and a libertine, he had a considerable sense of humour.

WELLINGTON (N.Z.) (Port Nicholson 1826-40) was first surveyed in 1826. The New Zealand Co. founded the first settlement in 1840. The seat of govt. was transferred there from Auckland in 1865.

WELLINGTON (*see* COLLEY OR COWLEY LATER WESLEY). **Arthur WELLESLEY (1762-1852) Vist. DOURO (1809), E. (1812), Duque da VICTORIA (Port. 1812), D. (1814),** also a Dutch Prince and Spanish grandee, was an Irish M.P. from 1790 to 1795 and commanded the 33rd Foot in the 1794 Flanders expedition, where he was one of two officers to acquit himself well. He extracted his troops *via* the mouth of the R. Weser.

(2) In Apr. 1796 he was sent to India, which he reached in Feb. 1797. In May his brother Mornington arrived as Gov-Gen. and put him in charge at Vellore. In 1799 he commanded a division against Mysore and, after its conquest, was gov. until 1802. During this time he put down bandits (Pindaris) and reduced the country to order. In 1803 he commanded a division to Poona to reinstate the Peishwa and then beat Holkar and Scindia at the great Bs. of Assaye (Sept.) and Argaum (Nov.) and forced peace on the Rajah of Berar. After pursuing further bandits he came home in 1805. He was an English M.P. from 1806 and chief sec. for Ireland from 1807 to 1809 but commanded the troops in the successful Danish expedition of 1807.

(3) His celebrated Peninsular War (q.v.) career (1808 to Apr. 1814) made him the most respected figure in Europe. This was due not only to his military genius but to his special ability to discern the purpose of an action and his willingness, regardless of self interest, to do what was necessary to achieve it. The splendour of his talents contrasted strongly with his personal modesty and kindness and his manners were, in that ceremonious age, faultless. Though his marriage was not a success, his eye for pretty women was discerning and popular. He was much sought in the salons of Paris, which he reached soon after Bonaparte's abdication.

(4) After a flying return to Spain where he failed to reconcile the reactionary Ferdinand VII with the liberals, he was appointed ambassador to Paris (Aug. 1814) and then plenipotentiary with Castlereagh at the Vienna Congress. It was here that he heard of Bonaparte's escape from Elba and was entrusted with the operations which culminated in the B. of Waterloo. He dissuaded the Prussians from sacking French towns or other reprisals as likely to jeopardise peace and the stability of the restored Bourbons; for similar reasons he resisted major cessions of French territory, kept the army of occupation, of which he was C- in-C, as inconspicuous as possible with its H.Q. at Cambrai instead of Paris and, since violent incidents exacerbated feeling, recommended its withdrawal at the Aix-la-Chapelle congress of 1818. Such military statesmanship contributed powerfully to the willingness of the liberal maritime countries jointly to resist the claims of the more authoritarian monarchies.

(5) Meanwhile he had been voted a lump sum and the house at Strathfieldsaye (Hants) and had acquired Apsley House at Hyde Park Corner. With various Treasury annuities and the lucrative Mastership of the Ordnance, which he held from 1818 to 1827, he was rich as well as famous.

(6) The basis of his political view was that a society had to be stable. He recognised, as any observant man, that the contemporary industrial and technological leap forward would bring vast human changes, but he had spent half a life time fighting the French social disturbers and knew too much about death and destruction to risk civil disturbance at home. Though ready to put down riots, he disliked force. He thought that a strong landed, especially rural, interest was the foundation of stability and was ready to defend apparent abuses if they strengthened that foundation. Hence he defended the landowner-dominated constitution of the unreformed House of Commons, the Corn Laws and the purchase of military commissions and, as an Anglo-Irishman, he knew what effect R. Catholic emancipation would have on the position of Irish landowners. He therefore had to bear some blame for the earlier post-war repressions. That he was no reactionary can be demonstrated from his record in foreign policy and his readiness to sacrifice long cherished institutions when their continuance provoked real dangers to stability.

(7) At the Verona Congress (1822) he tried, but failed, to prevent armed intervention in favour of Spanish reaction but in 1824, despite his dislike of that reaction, he disliked recognising the independence of the Spanish S. American colonies because he rightly doubted their stability (see BOLIVAR). Similarly in 1826 he opposed intervention by Russia or any other power in favour of the Greek rebels, not only because intervention might serve Russian interests, but because it might open up

limitless confusion in the huge Ottoman dominions. His attitude to Portuguese and Spanish (see CARLISTS) affairs was similarly consistent: he obstructed volunteers in support of so-called liberal pretenders, but when the Portuguese "liberal" Don Pedro gained the throne he would not countenance attempts to turn him out (1826). Hence also he refused office under the adventurous Canning in 1827 and during his reluctant premiership of 1828-30 carried R. Catholic emancipation against the Crown, the royal brothers and his own religious convictions because the disorders were undermining the stability of Ireland. During the Grey govt. he opposed the Reform Bill, but when a similar situation arose in England he helped the govt. to get it passed. Neither in his opposition nor in his change of mind did he pay the least attention to the personal obloquy (crowds broke his windows) and his long term repute did not suffer. In 1834 he briefly carried on almost the whole of the govt. himself because the confusion of politics created a governmental hiatus, and he served under Peel in two administrations and helped him to repeal the Corn Laws, again for reasons of stability, in 1846.

(8) Many offices of honour, usually regarded as ceremonial, naturally came his way but he took them seriously and, whether it was the Lieutenancy of Hampshire (1820-52), the Constableship of the Tower (1826-52), the Wardenship of the Cinque Ports (1829-52) or the Chancellorship of Oxford Univ. (1834-52) or anything else he used his position to confer practical benefits upon those within range of the office concerned. His practical bent never left him. He designed the Wellington boot, proposed sparrowhawks when all else failed to extrude a plague of sparrows from Crystal Palace and became a frequent, almost habitual, visitor to the Great Exhibition in 1851. For many years after he died people in perplexity would ask "What would the Duke have done?" *See succeeding entries.*

WELLINGTON COLLEGE (Berks.) was opened in 1853 as a school for the sons of officers in memory of the 1st D. of Wellington.

WELLINGTON GOVT. (Jan. 1828-Nov. 1830) (13 in Cabinet under the D. of Wellington) was formed on the ignominious demise of the Goderich govt. It included Peel (Home Sec.), Huskisson (War), some Canningites and also some extreme Tories. Its members quarrelled incessantly. It inherited the Greek War of Independence but believed that Turkey should be supported against Russia. Huskisson resigned (May 1828) over a dispute about the transfer of four parliamentary seats; in the reshuffle Vesey Fitzgerald, appointed to the Bd. of Trade, was defeated by O'Connell in the Clare bye-election, which made an Irish electoral revolt a certainty; therefore the govt. had to accept R. Catholic emancipation, in which it did not believe either. Unable to secure any western support the Turks signed away the mouths of the Danube and the Circassian fortresses at the P. of Adrianople (Sept. 1829) and the powers, assuming that an independent Greece would be dominated by Russia ensured (London Protocols Feb. 1830) that it should be as small as possible. By this time parliamentary reform had become the major political topic. The Duke refused to countenance it and the govt. broke up. *See* REFORM BILLS 1831-2; TEST ACTS.

WELLINGTON'S STOP-GAP ADMINISTRATION (Nov.-Dec. 1834). When Melbourne resigned (Nov. 1834) Peel, his only possible successor, was in Rome. The D. of Wellington, therefore, agreed to carry on the routine affairs until Peel could return. Ld. Lyndhurst was Lord Chancellor, Ld. Denman Chancellor of the Exchequer. The Duke took over all the other major posts and drove from office to office dealing with their business.

WELLS, Herbert George (1866-1946), born poor, studied under T. H. Huxley and began writing imaginative novels in 1895 when the *Time Machine* appeared. Increasingly socialist in his idealism, he published more realistic works beginning with *Kipps* in 1905. Free love attracted his attention in 1909 (*Ann Veronica*); World union in 1914 (*The War That Will End War*). In 1920 he began publishing didactic works (*Outline of History*) but never lost his imaginative ability, issuing *The Shape of Things To Come* as late as 1933. His pervasive influence was due as much to his ability to summarise and compress as to his extraordinary prophetic sense.

WELLS (Som.) existed before the time of Ine (688-726) who built a church there. It became a see in 909 when the diocese of Sherborne was divided. The see was moved to Bath in 1088 but in 1192 Bp. Jocelin, a native of Wells, returned there. He chartered the town in 1201. The famous Cathedral was mostly built by Reginald Fitzjocelin at the turn of the 12th cent.

WELLS, SACRED were fairly common, mostly pre-Christian, objects of cult worship or magic. The mediaeval church often converted the local god into a saint or substituted a saint for him (or her). The best known cases are at Tissington (Derbys), St. Chad's at Lichfield, St. Anthony's at Maybole, St. Keyne (Cornwall) and St. Elian (Denbigh). The Celtic goddess Sul of the hot spring at Bath was never so converted nor the Roman Conventina at Carrawburgh on Hadrian's Wall.

WELSER FAMILY, bankers of Augsburg and Antwerp, dealers in metals and cloth, by 1519 were lending to Charles V for his wars and the imperial election. In 1528 they acquired the right to colonise the Spanish Main; they traded with other colonies through an agency at Santo Domingo; and they owned silver mines in Mexico. Their colonising patent was, however, revoked in 1546 and the Spanish American colonies were closed to non-Castilians in 1560. They continued to deal extensively in the exchange markets but unsound investment, the decline of the German towns, the prosperous and aggressive enterprise of the Dutch during the 12 Years Truce (1609-21) and the little understood phenomenon of inflation brought a spectacular bankruptcy in 1614.

WELSH CHURCH ACT (1914). *See* WALES, CHURCH IN.

WELSH GRAND COMMITTEE consists of all Welsh M.P.s plus enough others to reflect the political composition of the House. It deals with purely Welsh questions.

WELSH LANGUAGE. *See* CELTIC.

WELSH LAW, SOCIAL (*see* HYWEL DDA, LAWS OF) **(1)** recognised five main classes of persons. (a) The King (*Brenin*) or Kings, or territorial Lord (*Arglwydd*) and their following; (b) The Free (*Boneddig*) of which gentlefolk (*Uchelwyr*) were respected but had no special rights; (c) The Unfree (*Aillt, Taeog*) (cf Cornish *tyack* = farmer), or *bilein* (from *villein*); (d) Resident Foreigners (*Alltud*); (e) Bondsmen or slaves (*Caeth*).

(2) The Isle of Britain was considered a unity. Its head was the King of London, to whom the King (Prince) of Wales was subordinate, but Wales was not subordinate to England. Wales was considered a unity too, but it had three (sometimes four) parts: Gwynedd (capital Aberffraw), Powys (Mathrafal), Deheubarth (Dinefwr) and sometimes Gwent (Caerleon). The King at Aberffraw, of the long surviving House of Cunedda took precedence. Succession was hereditary, passing in the male line to the ablest, who was called the Edling (cf A.S. *atheling*).

(3) Subject to defined rules the King could claim allegiance, obedience, a temporal supremacy over the church and military service. He was the source of land rights and coinage. For his support he had a demesne (*maerdref*) and the disposal of all wild forest and he was entitled to certain land levies (*see* DAWN BWYD, GWESTEA, TWNC) succession payments (*see* EBEDIW, CYNHASEDD) and miscellaneous fees such as *amobr*. In addition he could take flotsam, waste and unowned property, property abandoned by wandering strangers, fines, particularly for theft, estates of childless intestates save bishops and judges and the whole estate of the Court Usher. The

Queen was entitled to a third of the income from the *maerdref*. The *Edling* lived entirely at the King's bounty and might lose his position if he struck out and acquired land on his own.

(4) The laws lay down the duties, payment and precedence of 24 royal officers. Of these the most important were the *Penteulu*, invariably a near relative, who as captain of the Household presided in the King's absence and commanded his military following (*teulu*); the priest, who also acted as the King's secretary, the steward and the Court judge. The rules and privileges of the court were in force not only where the King was present but where the priest, the steward and the judge happened to be together.

(5) The *arglwyddi* might possess superiority or jurisdiction in a commote (*cymwd*) or *cantref* or several and the laws related to them were much the same as those on Kings (whose local power they often exercised) but as subjects they had no power over the church, no right of coinage or legislation and no power to punish crimes committed on the highway.

(6) The Free (*Boneddig*) according to the Venedotian Code "is one who shall be of entire Welsh origin, both by the father and the mother" and the other codes add "without bond, without foreign, without mean descent". They comprised more than half the 11th cent. population and belonged to often shadowy tribes (*cenedl*). These were divided into, more practically important, clans (*cenhedloedd*) which might, but did not necessarily, have a chief (*pencenedl*). Membership was by male descent. The really important body was the extended family (*gwely*) which might embrace a whole clan or merely form part of one and was liable to split up from human or economic causes. The freedom of the members consisted in a right to move anywhere in Wales. Such movements tended to be clan or *gwely* migrations, or transhumance.

(7) Land (*but see below*) was, in principle, a fact of nature incapable of full ownership even by the King, and any free Welshman might get his living at large from it as he wanted. But in practice people wanted to have a base holding (*gafael*) or home. Thus rules about rights of exclusive occupation, their acquisition, transmission and loss grew up. (*See* 9 (a).)

(8) Everything, including a person's life and honour had a value, the honour price (*sarhad*) and the blood fine (*galanas*) varying with his social rank. *Sarhad* and *galanas* were expressed mainly in cattle (later usually recalculated at 60 silver pence a head) plus some additional silver, the *galanas* being roughly 12 times the *sarhad*. A King's *sarhad* and *galanas* were enormous and probably fanciful, the highest being the King at Aberffraw. The *Edling's* was two thirds of the cattle component of a King's; the Queen's and Penteulu's one third. Since affronts to or the murder of such people usually brought war these amounts were academic. Other *sarhads* varied from between 27 cows and 540 pence for a serious insult to a *Pencenedl* through eleven gradations of status multiplied by three of gravity to 12 pence (payable to the master) for a trivial affront to a slave. A woman's *sarhad* was half her brother's or one third of her husband's.

(9) Emphasising the nomadic origins and corporate responsibility of the free there was a system of computable relationships *via* a common ancestor in (i) nine degrees, usually through males (sometimes confusingly called a man's *cenedl*); (ii) seven degrees through males and females and (iii) four degrees through males only (approximating with the clan or *gwely*). In particular cases a person was entitled to support from, or owed duties towards, the others within the appropriate degrees, viz. (a) a *gwely* held a *gafael* in common and undivided. If it came peacefully and continued there to the fourth generation it was termed *priodawr* and the *gafael* was earmarked for its exclusive possession (*priodolder*). If it abandoned the land sooner the process had to begin again; if later it was entitled to put in a claim for it until the extinction of the ninth degree. There might thus be two rival *gwelys* entitled to exclude or drive out a *non priodor* but in the case of an unsettled dispute between them the *gafael* would be partitioned in proportion to the number of generations each had been *priodorion*. (b) In cases of crime and tort, and especially *sarhad* and *galanas*, a man was entitled to contribution from and had to share with his kin to the seventh degree (known as *galanas* kin). In very gross cases he might also appeal to the eighth and ninth for a penny, the spear penny each. A *galanas,* if underpaid by a farthing, was not only ineffectual to prevent blood feud, but lost. *Sarhad* was important in relation to foreigners (*see* 11 below).

(10) The Unfree (*Aillt* or *Taeog*) were probably descended from aboriginals conquered by the Free. They could not move from their land. This scattered unfree land thus had to be distinguished by boundaries, like a modern native reservation. Most unfree lands were agricultural and called *gwelyau*. They were held by unfree *gwelys* which, since they could not migrate, remained small (18 men is the largest known) and there was a tendency for them to break down into individual *priodolder* holdings. A minority of unfree lands were *tir cyfrif* however; they could never be so appropriated, but were subject to the management of a royal officer called the *maer*. The tenants were really serfs but, as between sons, they had an equal undivided share, save the youngest who remained with the father but stepped into the father's share and homestead. When a tenant died his property otherwise went back into the common stock. Unfree *gwelys* never held land in more than one vill. The unfree were liable to build and maintain royal buildings and, under the Normans, to porterage. *See also* CYLCH.

(11) A foreigner, whether merely passing through, or engaged on some more than passing purpose, or resident (*alltud*) had to place himself under the commendation of a lord or a free man or unfree man, who had to feed and protect him and was responsible for his behaviour. Injury to the foreigner was an affront to the protector who was also entitled to his *galanas*. Conversely the protector had to pay his fines. The foreigner could leave the protector only by leaving Wales.

(12) Slaves (*caeth*) were acquired through capture or purchase at the Viking slave markets in Ireland, Bristol and Chester or through surrender for debt, or apparently as a punishment for certain crimes. They had no rights.

(13) Promotion of status was possible in five cases. An unfree man could become free if the King conferred one of the court offices upon him and all unfree men in an unfree *tref* became free if, with the King's permission, a church was built in the *tref*. In both cases their descendants were free. In addition a man would be free for his lifetime only if, with his lord's consent, he became a proficient (i.e. tonsured) scholar or a bard or a smith, since these professions were divorced from the land.

(14) The erosion of Welsh law began with the creation of marcher lordships and continued with the Stat. of Rhuddlan which shired half of Wales. Subsequent surrenders of land and regrants altered many tenures from Welsh to English and there were detailed amendments by statute in 1360. Much of Welsh law, however, was in force until the Acts of Union and traces of it remained in practical effect as custom (mostly related to commons) even into the 20th cent.

WELSH METHODISM. *See* METHODISM.

WELWYN. *See* GARDEN CITIES; NEW TOWNS.

WEMBLEY (London). The Association Football final has been played there since 1923. The British Empire Exhibition was held there in 1924 and 1925.

WEMYSS (pron. Weems) **(1) David (1610-79) Ld. ELCHO and 2nd E. of WEMYSS (Sc.) (1649)** was defeated by Montrose at Tippermuir in 1644 and Kilsyth in 1645. **(2) David (1678-1720) 3rd E. (1705)** was a commissioner for the Union with England. His grandson **(3) David (1721-87)** visited Britain in 1744 as a Jacobite agent, commanded the Young Pretender's guards in 1745 and 1746 and was attainted.

WENDOVER, Roger of (?-1236) monk of St. Albans and prior of Belvoir compiled *Flores Historiarum* (= Flowers of the Histories) covering the period from the creation to 1234. The part from 1202 is a major source and was used extensively by his fellow St. Albans monk Matthew Paris.

WENLOCK (Salop) had a 7th cent. monastery which was superseded in 1017 by the great Cluniac Priory of St. Milburga. The monks developed agriculture, quarrying and a market. These remained important after the dissolution. *See* IRONBRIDGE.

WENSLEYDALE (N. Yorks), the catchment of the R. Ure, contained powerful castles at Middleham and Bolton and originated a long-wooled sheep and a well-known cheese.

WENSLEYDALE PEERAGE CASE **(1856)** represented the defeat of an attempt to reform the House of Lords by the use of prerogative. Sir James Parke (1782-1868), a distinguished judge, was granted a life peerage as Ld. Wensleydale and called to the Lords by writ to strengthen it in its judicial functions. The Lords Committee of Privileges decided that the issue of a writ to sit in the Lords automatically created a hereditary barony, provided that the original recipient had actually taken his seat.

WENTWORTH. Yorkshire family whose most famous or notorious member was **Sir Thomas (1593-1640) Vist. WENTWORTH (1628), Ld. RABY and E. of STRAFFORD (1640).** Able, determined, irascible and lacking charm, he became a Yorkshire M.P. in 1614 and provoked a feud with the Saviles in 1617. He disliked puritanism, but opposed the inept and corrupt administration of the D. of Buckingham at the end of James I's reign. He was a parliamentary opposition leader in 1621 and attacked the Spanish war in 1624. In 1625 Sir John Savile unseated him on petition but he was re-elected. He still opposed the war and hotly objected to the dissolution of the parliament. He was appointed sheriff to disqualify him in the next election but continued to inveigh against the crown's financial demands. Not surprisingly he was dismissed from the Commission of the Peace (he had been Custos Rotulorum since 1615) and replaced by Savile. He next refused to contribute to the forced loan of 1627 and was briefly imprisoned. In the 1628 parliament he tried, with some skill, to induce the King to accept the modified propositions which were later set out in a strong form in June, in the Petition of Right. He probably increased Charles' obduracy, also, by proposing a form of appropriation of subsidies, but by now he had become disenchanted with opposition. Buckingham's assassination removed a cause of the govt's incompetence and extravagance, and the extremism of the new leaders such as Sir John Eliot and Digges did much to bring moderates over to the King. Wentworth's role in the passage of the Petition of Right was passive. Abp. Laud, realising that Wentworth's motive was neither contumacy nor self interest but a passion for good administration, persuaded the King to take him into the govt. He was made Pres. of the Council of the North in 1628 and a privy councillor in 1629. In the north he was a just, if forbidding, protector of the poor and landless, earning thereby some merited general popularity but the hatred of the large landowners and gentry fanned, of course, by the Saviles.

By 1632 the King was becoming short of funds through mismanagement at the Treasury and corruption at court. Wentworth hoped for the Treasurership and Laud tried to get it for him. He and Laud were by now personal friends and much the ablest and most honest members of Charles' entourage. Court intrigue, however, frustrated them. Wentworth was appointed Lord Deputy of Ireland and in 1633 went to Dublin without relinquishing his Northern post. He decided to make Ireland a profitable instead of expensive possession. He began by disciplining the riotous armed forces and easing Anglo-Irish trade by suppressing piracy. He encouraged industry, especially linen weaving. He began to resume illegally acquired church property and attacked govt. corruption. The Court of Castle Chamber became popular by its justice and expedition, especially when the weak were opposed to the great. He bought out the tax farmers and farmed the taxes himself. The result resembled his continuing northern administration, popularity with the public, hostility of the well to do. He was also disliked by many courtiers because he refused Irish pensions to the Queen's nominees. In 1635 on his instigation the Star Chamber forfeited the Londonderry Plantation (granted to the City of London) on valid grounds of neglect, but against his advice Charles began to alienate the vast lands and fisheries so acquired. This had been inconsistent with Wentworth's agreed, and so far successful, policy of colonising Ireland, for it involved pursuing the controversial Connaught plantations in fact if not in theory and this alienated the native Irish. The Irish revenue, however, continued to rise and in 1637 Wentworth laid plans for developing, and made a triumphal progress, in Munster.

Individual enmities mounted. In 1635 he moved against the Irish vice-treasurer, Ld. Mountnorris, whom he disgraced and in 1638 he had the corrupt Lord Chancellor, Loftus, tried in the Castle Chamber. These actions were reversed in the Long Parliament. Meanwhile the Scottish crisis was impinging on his northern circumscription. He favoured suppressing the Scots opposition to the prayer book for he agreed with Laud. But he saw that the northern troops were valueless. Either they had to be trained or his own Irish army had to do the job. By Sept. 1639 he was the King's chief adviser. He offered a personal loan and promised subsidies from the Irish parliament but Charles would not take his considered advice nor fully adopt some other policy. Thus Wentworth (by now Strafford) felt bound to agree to the dissolution of the Short Parliament (May 1640). *For his fall, impeachment and attainder see* CHARLES I; VANE.

WENTWORTH. Radical Oxfordshire family. **(1) Peter (?1530-96)**, M.P. in 1571-2, 1576-83 and 1586-7 was an early puritan critic of the court. He asserted the right of the House of Commons to discuss ecclesiastical policy and faith in 1571 and was persistently critical of the XXXIX Articles. He made a sensational attack on crown influence in the Commons in 1576. The speech was interrupted and he was sent to the Tower. In 1587 he again attacked royal absolutism in church affairs and was again imprisoned. From 1593 he changed his tactics, argued for the Queen to name her successor and championed the rights of Lord Edward Seymour. This made him no more popular at court and he was again in the Tower, possibly until his death. During this final imprisonment he wrote *A Pithy Exhortation to Her Majesty* on the succession. His brother **(2) Paul (1533-93)**, M.P. 1563-7 and 1572-83 also promoted a petition for the naming of a successor and wanted the Commons to hear a sermon before each meeting. A son of Peter **(3) Thomas (?1568-1628)**, Recorder (1607-23) and M.P. (1604-28) for Oxford was an equally rumbustuous critic of the court; he was imprisoned in 1614 for attacking unparliamentary levies and advocated war with Spain in 1624. His nephew **(4) Sir Peter (1592-1675)** M.P. for Tamworth in 1641, was a parliament man but refused to sit as a judge at Charles I's trial. He was a member of Cromwell's council of state.

WENTWORTH. Suffolk political family. **(1) Thomas (1505-51) 1st Ld. (1529)** soldier, was converted to protestantism and became an advocate of Katharine of Aragon's divorce in 1530. He was much at court and in 1549 helped to put down the Norfolk disturbances and to overthrow the Protector Somerset. Thereafter he was a prominent member of the govt. and Lord Chamberlain from 1550, enriching himself in the process. His son **(2) Thomas (1525-84) 2nd Ld.** was M.P. for Suffolk from 1547 to 1551 and helped his father by voting for Somerset's attainder. He became a member of Mary I's council and assisted at the trial of Northumberland. From 1553 he was deputy and last resident gov. of Calais. Having failed to anticipate the attack by which it fell he was tried, but acquitted, of treason in 1559. Thereafter of little credit, he was employed only in 1572 on the Commission which tried Norfolk. His grandson **(3) Thomas (1591-1667) 4th Ld. (1593), 1st E. of CLEVELAND (1626)** was a friend of the D. of Buckingham and was with him at La Rochelle (1627) and at his assassination (1628). A staunch if extravagant loyalist, he had lost his entire fortune by the outbreak of the Civil War. He served against the Scots; attended Strafford at his execution; commanded royalist cavalry in the Civil War and, having joined Charles II, was with him in France and Scotland and covered his flight from the B. of Worcester (1651). His son **(4) Thomas (1613-65) 5th Ld. (called up 1640)** was M.P. for Bedfordshire in the Short and Long Parliaments and as determined a royalist as his father. He served in Wilmot's and Goring's cavalry in 1644 to 1645 and was then put in command (when it was too late) in the west. Defeated at Torrington he followed Charles II in his journeys and became col. of the Guards from 1656. His only child **(5) Henrietta (1657-86) Lady (1667)** was the D. of Monmouth's mistress.

WENTWORTH, Sir John (1737-1820) loyalist gov. of New Hampshire from 1766 to 1776, was extruded by the rebels, lived in London from 1778 to 1783, became surveyor of the royal forests in Nova Scotia from 1783 to 1792 and gov. from 1792-1808.

WENTWORTH, William Charles (1793-1872) explored across the Blue Mountains (Australia) in 1813, went to Cambridge Univ. where as an undergraduate he published a *Statistical Account of the British Settlements in Australasia* (1819) and, after being called to the English bar, became joint proprietor of the nationalistic *Australian*. He advocated the franchise for emancipists and the discouragement of interlopers. In 1831 he raised a popular agitation against the gov., Sir Ralph Darling, for alleged favouritism in the distribution of land and secured his recall. The new gov., Sir Richard Bourke, was careful to take his advice, especially on the immigration scheme which he devised. Meanwhile he was speculating covertly in New Zealand land; this came to light under the next gov., Sir George Gipps, and Wentworth was temporarily excluded from influence. He forced his way back by getting himself elected in 1843 to the new N.S.W. legislature and becoming the leader of the pastoralists or squatters. Regarding those already in possession as a sort of colonial aristocracy, he advocated the continuance of transported labour which could be assigned to private persons as virtual slaves. Consistently with this he opposed the reduction of franchise qualifications and even argued for an Australian peerage. In the meantime he had founded Sydney Univ. (1852) and in 1857 suggested a federal constitution. He retired to England in 1862.

WENTWORTH WOODHOUSE (Yorks.), a property of the E. of Strafford, passed to the Rockingham family. The first marquess employed Flitcroft to build the immense mansion there, completed in about 1740.

WERBURGA or WERBURGH, St. (?-?700), *d.* of K. Wulfhere of Mercia, was abbess of Sheppey, Ely and some Mercian convents. Her remains were moved to Chester in about 875 and Chester Cathedral is the church of her shrine.

WERGILD (A.S. = man money). An early way of preventing the disorders of retaliation and feud. If a person injured or killed another he might pay him (or if a serf, his master) or as the case might be, his relatives or master, a sum which was originally negotiable but became fixed by law according to the rank of the victim. If the money was accepted, retaliation or feud was outlawed. A 7th cent. free man's (*ceorl*'s) wergild was generally 200 shillings (= 1000 silver pence); an earl's or bishop's 1200 (= 6000) but in Kent the value of the ceorl's at 20 gold shillings (= 2000) was higher but the earl's was the same as elsewhere. In 10th cent. Northumbria the ceorl's wergild was 266 thrymsas (= 798 pence), a thegn's 2000 thrymsas, an earl's or bishop's 8000. After a time the correct wergild, if offered, had to be accepted. Later part became payable to the King and eventually the system gave way to royally enforced criminal law.

WESLEY (1) John, (2) Charles. *See* METHODISM.

WESLEY (1) Samuel (1766-1837) and his son **(2) Samuel Sebastian (1810-76)**, famous cathedral organists. The father wrote an oratorio at the age of eight and popularised the music of J. S. Bach; the son wrote much church music of considerable splendour.

WESLEYAN METHODIST ASSOCIATION. *See* METHODISM.

WESSEX. *See* WEST SAXONS; ENGLISH MONARCHY, EARLY.

WESSEX, P. Edward Anthony Richard Louis (1960-) E of (June 1999) Documentary film producer. The earldom was conferred on his marriage to Sophie Rhys-Jones and was the first such earldom created since K. Harold II's accession by coronation on 7 Jan. 1066.

WEST, THE or THE WESTERN WORLD. This vague but sometimes useful expression signifies the group of nations or states whose culture is derived from European civilisation as distinct from **(1)** oriental nations, especially the Chinese; **(2)** African non-Islamic nation states; **(3)** Communist states generally. Thus New Zealand though far to the east of most oriental and all African states, belongs to the "West" but communist Cuba, though west of most of the "West" does not. Users of the expression often seem to be uncertain whether it includes the Iberian speaking countries or excludes the Islamic. Not to be confused with the (WILD) WEST, to which young men are bidden to go.

WEST, Benjamin (1738-1820), Pennsylvanian painter who exhibited in London from 1764, settled there, was much employed by George III and was a founder member of the Royal Academy and Pres. in 1792. Many of his pictures, which were mostly historical, were engraved. *See* WOOLLETT.

WEST. Hampshire family. **(1) Thomas (1577-1618) 3rd or 12th Ld. DE LA WARR (1602),** first gov. of Virginia in 1610-11 rescued the despairing colonists and later advised the govt. on colonial policy. He died on a second voyage to Virginia. His descendant **(2) John (1693-1766) 7th or 16th Ld. (1723), 1st E. (1761),** absentee gov. of New York and New Jersey from 1737, was also a gov. of the Turkey Co. and twice Speaker of the Lords, where he was a weighty authority on financial and commercial issues. He also pursued a successful military career, commanding a brigade at Dettingen and ending as a General of Horse.

WEST, COUNCIL OF THE, was set up in 1540 on the principle of the Council for Wales and the Marches but was shortly abolished because of local opposition.

WEST AFRICA. (1) The 15th cent. Portuguese navigators hoped to reach India and also divert the Trans-Saharan gold route from Barbary direct to Christendom. From 1458 their Cape Verde Is. colony provided a trading base with Mali and in 1471 they reached Ghana (El Mina or the Gold Coast) where the Akan tribes were ready to trade gold for iron, copper and cloth. This was not an end in itself. The policy was to realise profits which would make the discovery of the Indian route self-financing but as Portugal produced neither metals nor cloth in exportable quantities they had to be bought. Hence the Portuguese became traders between the Akans, Benin and the Niger delta but kept their material commitments to the minimum necessary to exclude or intimidate European rivals. They built a system of forts beginning at São Jorge de Mina (1482) and advancing step by step to Aiyim, Shama, Accra and the I. of São Tomé. Their often brutal attempts to control the trade of the native states were not always successful. They could not muster enough troops in that appalling climate and had to rely on allies. Benin expelled them in 1520 and destroyed their fort at Accra in 1570. Meanwhile a form of basic Portuguese became the language of W. African commerce.

(2) After Portugal became a Spanish possession (1580) the insurgent Dutch felt free to attack her interests. The first Dutch trading posts appeared and were locally welcomed in 1598, but their disruption of the Portuguese monopoly was a by-product of the Dutch West India Co's assault on Brazil and the Caribbean, after its formation in 1621. The Portuguese had always traded, to a small but growing extent, in slaves for Madeira, for the Cape Verdes and their off-shore bases and, since 1520, towards the W. Indies and, since 1570, to Brazil. The Dutch co. now determined to monopolise this trade. By 1642 it had taken all the forts but by 1660 the Portuguese had recovered São Tomé and had expelled the Dutch from Brazil. The two countries shared a slave trade which was exporting about 15,000 souls a year to the Americas.

(3) The colossal profits attracted the attention of all Europe, but more especially that of France and Britain who both had W. Indian colonies. The great prize of the 17th cent. Dutch wars was the W. African trade. By 1677 the French controlled it north of the Gambia from their new bases at Goree (near the Cape Verdes) and St. Louis at the mouth of the Senegal R. Slaves being scarce in this area, the French dealt mainly in guns, hides and alluvial gold but subject, in the face of British sea supremacy, to British toleration. The British seized the French bases in every Anglo-French war and attempted between 1758 and 1779 to establish a Senegambia colony. This failed because the British came, like the Portuguese, to prefer minimal territorial commitments and the Royal African Co. like them, built forts. By 1790, though the Dutch still had more forts (especially on the Gold Coast) than anyone else, almost every Dutch fort (e.g. El Mina) had a British double (e.g. Cape Coast Castle) nearby and there were, besides the French, the one time Swedish, Prussian and Danish establishments. A ship sailing that 300 mile stretch of coast was never out of sight of a European post.

(4) In fact the great monopoly companies with their high military and administrative overheads were being superseded by large numbers of private interlopers without these expenses. Their commercial zone was initially to the east of the Gold Coast where Co. control was weak or non-existent and they could outbid and undersell their clumsy rivals. Since Britain had displaced Holland as the principal naval and carrying trader, this trade passed by this means steadily into British and Anglo-American hands. Its volume was very large. About 50,000 slaves a year were being exported at the peak of 1780-90, in return, besides the traditional goods, for luxuries and, especially, firearms, and the resultant inflow of wealth had created powerful native states, especially Dahomey, Ashanti and the Nigerian Hausa.

(5) Inland an important series of Moslem revolutions had been taking place through the agency of the pastoral, often nomadic, Fulani. These, by a series of *Jehads* between 1750 and 1860, created a belt of Moslem states from the Cameroons to Upper Senegal at a time when progressive suppression of the slave trade (1803-65) and of slavery was affecting the coastal economies. The large British anti-slave trade establishment required naval bases, jurisdictions for dealing with captured slavers and lands and welfare organisers for the benefit of rescued slaves. The British bases became the most noticeable and powerful political as well as economic influence on the coast. The main H.Q. was in Sierra Leone and especially Freetown (i.e. the Town of Freed Slaves). By 1811 it had a, mainly emancipated, population of over 2000 growing at 1000 a year. Between 1814 and 1824 when Sir Charles M'Carthy was gov. the British policy was to occupy the worst outlets for the slave trade, for British naval activities only touched about 10%. In 1821 the Gambia and Gold Coast forts were transferred to the jurisdiction of Freetown but the policy was proving expensive and producing no commensurate increase in trade. When M'Carthy was killed in 1824 in a war with the Ashanti, the policy was confined to Sierra Leone. Meanwhile, however, a prosperous trade mostly in palm oil (for British soap) was growing up especially with the Niger delta and the Niger itself was being explored; and as the population of Sierra Leone could not achieve local riches there was a re-migration of liberated slaves from Sierra Leone to the prosperous entrepôts of the Nigerian and Ghanaian coasts. The British, who had abandoned the Gold Coast forts in 1828 and reoccupied them in 1843, bought out the Danish forts in 1850. They also annexed Lagos in 1861, got the Dutch to leave the Gold Coast in 1872 and, having defeated the Ashanti, declared the Gold Coast a Colony. This represented the first major European annexation.

(6) The so-called Scramble for Africa took a generation. For descriptive purposes the British, German and Portuguese colonies may be regarded as enclaves in a much larger, but not necessarily richer, French area. The frontiers of the Gambia (Br.) were settled in 1889, of Portuguese Guinea between 1884 and 1897, of Sierra Leone (Br.) between 1889 and 1895, of Liberia 1885 to 1907, of the Gold Coast (Br.) and Togoland (Ger.) between 1893 and 1898, of Nigeria (Br.) between 1893 and 1906 and of the Cameroons (Ger.) between 1884 and 1894.

(7) The settlement of frontiers did not complete but often rather began the operations of colonisation. Wars within almost all the areas continued up to and sometimes after 1914.

(8) After World War II the British West African colonies gained their independence and eventually became republics within the British Commonwealth, the Gold Coast (Ghana) in 1957; Nigeria in 1960; Sierra Leone in 1961 and Gambia in 1965.

WEST AFRICAN TROOPS AND FRONTIER FORCE. Trading companies raised guards for their fortified coastal factories in the 18th cent. In 1822 Sir Chas. M'Carthy formed the African Colonial Light Infantry, the Cape Coast Militia and the Cape Coast Volunteers, all for the Gold Coast area. In 1862 troops were raised from the Nigerian Hausas: these were known successively as Glover's Hausas, the Hausa Militia and the Lagos Constabulary. The last fought in the Ashanti War of 1873 and part of it became the nucleus of the Gold Coast Regt. The Royal Niger Constabulary which was both Hausa and Yoruba also fought in the Ashanti Wars. These various units were grouped in 1901 by Lugard into the W. African Frontier force, which by 1914 was composed of Gold Coast and Nigerian Regiments and Gambia and Sierra Leone Battalions.

WESTBURY, Ld. *See* BETHELL.

WESTERN DESERT, i.e. the eastern end of the Great Libyan Desert, is the western desert of Egypt as opposed to its Eastern or Sinai Desert.

WESTERNE were a Mercian folk who settled the Cheshire plains in the 7th cent.

WESTERN MAIL. Conservative newspaper founded at Cardiff in 1869.

WESTERN PROVINCES (India). The name given to a combination of Ceded and Conquered Provinces, situated to the *west* of Bengal, after their administrative and judicial separation from Bengal in 1833.

WESTERN UNION. A defence organisation based on the five Brussels treaty powers and then extended into the North Atlantic. In Mar. 1954 W. Germany and Italy were invited to join and in May 1955 a formal organisation based on N.A.T.O. was created.

WEST FLORIDA. *See* MISSISSIPPI.

WEST INDIA COMPANIES (1) DUTCH. Founded in 1621 with a monopoly of the Dutch W. African and American trade, it had practically sovereign rights in the Dutch American colonies and, until the English interfered, it dominated the slave trade. Well established in the Caribbean and the Guianas between 1634 and 1648, it held Pernambuco and other Brazilian settlements between 1630 and 1654. It lost its American colonies in 1664 and English competition undermined the slave trade. A financial reconstruction took place in 1675 and thereafter the Co. enjoyed a steady, if unspectacular, prosperity until 1791 when the colonies were vested in the state. The Co. was dissolved in 1794. **(2) FRENCH.** Founded by Colbert in 1664 in imitation of the Dutch Co., with similar rights in the equivalent French possessions and a 40 year trading monopoly save in Newfoundland fish, it failed, against British and Dutch competition, to supply enough slaves to the French American colonies and its monopoly was revoked in 1674. It was amalgamated with the French East India Co. in 1719.

WEST INDIAN INCUMBERED ESTATES ACT (1854). Through competition from beet sugar, a world recession and the disturbances after the liberation of the slaves, many W. Indian planters were in debt and their properties so mortgaged that they were difficult to realise. This was an obstacle to land reforms needed to provide landless ex-slaves and their families with holdings. The Act set up commissioners to sell land on which mortgage interest exceeded half the annual value, clear off the existing mortgages, pay the purchase money into a special account and then pay off the mortgages and share out the residue among previous owners. The act was locally adoptive.

WEST INDIES – GENERAL. The first Spanish settlement was Isabela (1493) in Hispaniola, but until 1530 the islands were used mainly as bases for mainland expeditions and revictualling, exporting also small amounts of hides, sugar and tallow to Europe. As the Mexican silver shipments increased many islands became pirate lairs. The Spaniards in reply built fortresses at Cartagena, San Juan and Havana and organised convoys (*see* FLOTA; GALEONES). The overworked local natives died out and slave importation (legal and illegal) from Africa became profitable. English and Dutch piracy, though often individually profitable, achieved little until as late as 1620. In 1621, however, the Dutch W. India Co. was incorporated specifically for conquest and plunder as well as trade and under cover of its activities (which were also directed at Brazil) foreigners began to settle vacant islands. The first actually Spanish island to be seized was Jamaica (by the British) in 1656 (*see also* BUCCANEERS; HISPANIOLA). The early settlers grew tobacco, using European convict or indentured labour, but by 1660 they had turned to cane sugar, using slaves imported by the Dutch, who in interfering in Brazil had taken over the Portuguese slave depots in W. Africa. The sugar islands were fabulously prosperous and the object of much jealousy and ambition until the 19th cent; there was heavy fighting in the W. Indies in all the wars and sugar islands figured largely in the peace treaties (*see next entry*). The populations, apart from minute numbers of planters and overseers, were soon composed of uprooted

Africans and their descendants. The French wars of 1793 to 1815 inhibited the sugar trade to Europe, established the production of beet sugar and reduced prices. The slave trade was suppressed between 1807 and 1861. British slaves were freed between 1833 and 1838; French in 1848 and British sugar preferences disappeared in 1846. The prosperity ended save in Trinidad and British Guiana, where Indian indentured labour was in use and in Cuba, where slavery survived until 1886. Elsewhere neglect and stagnation prevailed until oil and asphalt began to be exploited at Trinidad and Curaçao and the invention of refrigerator ships enabled Jamaica to export bananas.

WEST INDIES – ISLAND COLONIES. The most important islands were settled, or permanently ceded, as follows. Most of them also changed hands (with damage) for short periods during wars (*see passim*).

B = British; F = French; D = Dutch; S = Spaniards

Island	Settled by & year	Ceded to & year
Antigua	B 1632	
Barbados	B 1624	
Cuba	S 1511	Independent 1898
Curacao	D 1630	
Dominica	F 1750	B 1763
Grenada	F 1650	B 1763
Guadaloupe	F 1635	
Hispaniola	S 1493	San Domingo to F
Jamaica	S 1509	B 1670
Martinique	F 1635	
Monserrat	B 1632	
Nevis	B 1628	
Puerto Rico	S 1508	
St Croix	B 1625	
St Kitts	B 1623	
St Lucia	Disputed between B and F 1605–1803	B 1815
St Vincent	Disputed between B, F and D 1627–1762	B 1763
Tobago	D 1632	B 1763 F 1783 B 1815
Tortola	D 1648	B 1666
Trinidad	S 1498-1530	B 1802

WEST INDIAN MERCHANTS, SOCIETY OF, was a pressure group. In 1783 it combined with the Society of West Indian Planters and Merchants. This W. India Lobby's main objective was to defend the profitability of the sugar trade and was opposed to Abolitionism and sugar extraction from beet.

WESTMACOTT, Sir Richard (1775-1856) sculptor, pupil of Canova, left many statues at St. Paul's and Westminster Abbey and the Duke of York's column (London).

WEST MARCH (ENGLISH). See CUMBERLAND-10 *et seq.*

WESTMEATH. See NUGENT.

WESTMINSTER (London) already had a monastery in the 9th cent. and a royal palace by 1015. The monastery or ABBEY, refounded by Edward the Confessor, became the coronation place of English kings. ST. MARGARET'S CHURCH was founded c. 1100. Henry III, who was especially devoted to the shrine of Edward the Confessor, began a major rebuilding of the Abbey and it remained under almost continuous reconstruction until c. 1740. The MANOR was governed by the Abbot until the Dissolution. The mediaeval PALACE was composed of a large rectangular moated fortification with towers (one of which, the JEWEL TOWER, survives) with the Hall and various buildings, chapels and later inns and coffee houses irregularly scattered about the interior.

WESTMINSTER HALL was originally built in 1097 but the present dimensions and hammer-beam roof date from 1394 to 1399. In the 12th cent. the Exchequer and later the Common Law Courts were sited at Westminster which, when the royal treasury moved there from Winchester in the late 12th cent., became the administrative capital. From the 13th cent. the Kings Bench and Common Pleas sat in, or in rooms off, the Hall until 1882 but the Palace gradually ceased to be used as a palace from the 15th cent., when the House of Lords and various state departments settled there. Until the 16th cent. it was not the exclusive venue for parliaments. Henry VIII built WHITEHALL PALACE, probably using materials from Westminster Palace, which he finally abandoned. Hence the House of Commons, which had hitherto sat in the Abbey CHAPTER HOUSE, moved to ST. STEPHENS CHAPEL in 1547 when also the manor was constituted a parliamentary borough. James I wished to rebuild Whitehall but only completed, in 1622, the BANQUETING HOUSE. The rest of Whitehall Palace was burned down in 1698 and thereafter monarchs divided their time mainly between Windsor, Hampton Court and St. James'. The first bridge was finished in 1750. The much altered old Palace of Westminster was also burnt down in 1834 (*see* EXCHEQUER TALLIES) and the new HOUSES OF PARLIAMENT which replaced it were completed in 1857, while new PUBLIC OFFICES were constructed along Whitehall in the following 20 years. TRAFALGAR SQUARE was built between 1829 and 1867. Westminster Hall was damaged by a terrorist bomb in 1974. The Westminster parliamentary constituency had, down to the 19th cent. reforms, the largest and widest electorate in the country, the electors being 'pot-wallopers'. Westminster elections were often wild events and used by opponents of the govt. to test the govt's popularity.

"WESTMINSTER-ARDTORNISH", T. of. See JAMES III OF SCOTS-1.

WESTMINSTER ASSEMBLY. See SCOTLAND, (PRESBYTERIAN) CHURCH.

WESTMINSTER CONFESSION. See SCOTLAND, (PRESBYTERIAN) CHURCH.

WESTMINSTER GAZETTE. See NEWNES.

WESTMINSTER, PROVISIONS OF (1259) were settled by the Council created under the Provisions of Oxford and notified to Parliament in Oct. They were to standardise the laws administered by the local seignorial courts, primarily suit of court, exemptions from royal justice and the access by sub-tenants to royal justice. They were not automatically enforced until substantially enacted in the Stat. of Marlborough (1267).

WESTMINSTER I, STATUTE OF (1275) dealt (besides miscellaneous matters) with a variety of abuses and types of violence which had grown up during the Barons' wars, notably quartering on religious houses, the treatment of criminous clerks, excessive purveyance, the pursuit of felons, abuse of bail, mainprise and distress, extortion by officials, maintenance, champerty and the circulation of scandalous news.

WESTMINSTER II, STATUTE OF (1285) contained the regulating provision (*De Donis Condicionalibus* – Lat = Conditional Grants) on entails, for which it is best known, and also other provisions on property, judicial procedure (*see* ASSIZE) and fees.

WESTMINSTER III, STATUTE OF or *QUIA EMPTORES* (1290) was issued by Edward I at the request mainly of tenants in chief, to give practical protection for their economic rights from subinfeudation by their tenants. By such subinfeudations, a tenant might divest himself of possession of the tenement and therefore be unable to discharge his obligations to the Tenant in Chief, while benefiting from the services of his own sub-tenants, with whom the Tenant in Chief had no legal nexus and against whom he therefore had no right of action. The statute enacted that any new tenant should hold of and render services to the Lord of the tenant from whom he had acquired the land. This prevented any *new* subinfeudations and gradually extinguished mesne tenures. *See* LAND TENURE, ENGLAND-2.

WESTMINSTER, STATUTE OF (1931) recited, as a result of the Imperial Conferences of 1926 and 1930, that the crown is the symbol of the free association of members of the British Commonwealth; that it is in accordance with the established constitutional position that changes in the law of Succession and the Royal Style and Titles require the assent of Dominion parliaments; and that United Kingdom statutes should apply in Dominions only with the consent and the request of their govts. It then proceeds to turn these principles into law. A (s.1) "Dominion" is defined as Canada, Australia, New Zealand, S. Africa, the Irish Free State and New-foundland, (ss.2-3, 5 and 6) within a Dominion the Colonial Laws Validity Act, 1865, is not to apply nor is any dominion law present or future to be void because repugnant to English law. (s.4) No British Act is to apply in a Dominion unless it is expressly declared therein that the Dominion has requested and consented to it. There follow a certain number of exceptions viz: (s.7). The Statute did not enable the Canadian constitution (contained in the British North America Acts) to be altered by Canadian legislation, nor (ss.8-9) the Australian and New Zealand Constitutions save in accordance with their local constitutional law and (s. 10) ss. 2-6 of the Statute did not apply in Australia, New Zealand or Newfoundland until adopted by their own parliaments.

WESTMINSTER, Ts. (24 Jan. 1502) between Henry VII and James IV of Scotland, provided for peace and alliance and the repudiation of the Auld Alliance; for the marriage of James IV and Henry's daughter Margaret; and for regulating the Borders.

WESTMINSTER, T. of (Jan. 1554) for the marriage of Mary I and Philip of Spain. He was to have the title of King and might "assist" in the govt. but Mary alone was to confer secular and church offices which might be held only by Englishmen. English laws and customs were to remain. Mary was to receive a jointure of £60,000 a year and might not leave England without her own consent. If she died childless Philip's interest in England lapsed. If there were children they would inherit Burgundy and the Low Countries besides England. If Philip's elder brother Don Carlos died childless they were to inherit Spain and its possessions too.

WESTMINSTER, T. of (May 1716). The Emperor guaranteed the Hanoverian succession. Britain in return guaranteed his gains under the Ps. of Utrecht and Baden.

WESTMORLAND was crossed by a Roman road connecting forts at Stainmore, Brough (Verterae), Crackenthorpe, Kirkby Thore (Braboniacum) and Brougham (Brocavium) and by another connecting Brougham with the forts at Low Borrow, Kendal (Alone) and Ambleside (Galava). Angles and Danes made slight penetrations from Yorkshire and Ostmen rather more. By the end of the 10th cent. the name *Westmorland* applied to the area of the later barony of Appleby, as far as the Cumberland boundary at Eamont. This until 1092 was part of the honour of Carlisle and was sometimes claimed by the Scots. In 1131 the baronies of Appleby and Kendal were combined administratively to form the county with the chief centre at Appleby. In 1133 the Appleby area was included in the new diocese of Carlisle but Kendal remained in the diocese of York. After the Scottish sack of Appleby in 1388 the town was not rebuilt and the administration was moved to Kendal. The county was Lancastrian in the Wars of the Roses. Kendal was transferred to the new diocese of Chester in 1543. The county was amalgamated into Cumbria in 1974.

WESTMORLAND, Earls of. *See* PANE; NEVILLE-9.

WESTON. Essex family **(1) Richard (1577-1635) Ld. WESTON (1628) 1st E. of PORTLAND (1633)** courtier and minor office holder until 1620 when he was sent as envoy, with Sir Edw. Conway, to Brussels and then through the Empire to try to settle the Palatine problems at the opening of the Thirty Years' War. He arrived in Prague in time to witness the B. of the White Mountain and was then recalled. He became Chancellor of the Exchequer in Jan. 1621 and M.P. for Arundel. He was in Brussels on further unsuccessful Palatine business in that year and in 1623 found himself in opposition to Buckingham's War, yet bound as Chancellor of the Exchequer to try to find funds to support it. He also had to try to defend the Crown in Eliot's case. All the same he managed to pay the fleet. After he went to the Lords he persuaded them to moderate their support for the Petition of Right and in July 1628 he became Lord Treasurer. Entirely in favour of peace and release from foreign entanglements and willing to resist the pecuniary demands of the queen's establishment, he succeeded in balancing the royal books during the first five years of Charles I's personal rule. His son **(2) Sir Jerome (1605-63) 2nd E.,** M.P. in the parliament of 1627 defended his father in the Commons and in 1629 was sent as ambassador to Paris and in 1632 to Paris and Turin. After his father died his mediocre talents received little employment.

WESTON. Lincolnshire family connected in the 15th cent. with the Knights of St. John, for whom two brothers had served as Turcopoliers, another had fought in the defence of Rhodes (1480) and a fourth was Lord Prior of England from 1476 to 1489. **(1) Sir William (?-1540)** was one of the few English survivors of the fall of Rhodes (1522) and having commanded the *Great Carrack,* was appointed Lord Prior by papal bull in 1527. He died the day that the English order was dissolved. His brother **(2) Sir Richard (?1466-1542)** also a soldier, served in Spain in 1511 and was a personal Knight to Henry VIII from 1516 to 1520 when he served on the jury at Buckingham's trial and was given the latter's manor of Sutton (Surrey) in 1521. In 1525 he became treasurer of Calais and from 1528 he was U/Treasurer of England. He died rich. His son **(3) Sir Francis (?1511-36),** a courtier, was implicated by some of Q. Anne Boleyn's confessions and executed. His son **(4) Henry (1535-92)** was restored in blood and estates. His grandson **(5) Sir Richard (1591-1652),** agriculturalist and engineer, introduced the canal lock from Holland into England on the Wey navigation. His properties were seized by the parliamentarians during the Civil War but by 1651 he had compounded and obtained an act for his Wey scheme with a grant of materials from the royal estates. Oatlands was demolished as a result. He also introduced the raising of crops of Nonesuch hay on irrigated meadows and a crop rotation of clover, flax and turnips.

WESTPHALIA (Ger) was a Kingdom under Jerome Bonaparte from 1807 to 1813. For the P. of Westphalia *see* THIRTY YEARS' WAR-17.

WEST SAXONS, EARLY or *GEWISSAE* (= probably, Confederates). (1) The later W. Saxon Kings traced their ancestry through Baeldaeg to the God Woden, the ancestors, borrowed or actual, of the Kings of Bernicia, but early W. Saxon history may concern two power centres or clans, one on the Upper Thames, the other in Wiltshire and Hampshire.

A. The first of the "C" kings was the fourth in descent from Baeldaeg, a leader with a British name **(1) Cerdic (519-34)** who began his career or landed near Southampton in 495, defeated the Britons in 508, acquired more men or organised a group of clans in 514, defeated the Britons again at Charford (Hants) in 519 and took the title of King in 520 but was defeated at Badbury (Dorset) and in 530, by recoil, took the I. of Wight from the Jutes. Nothing is known of his son **(2) Creoda (?-?)**

but Creoda's alleged son (3) **Cynric (534-60)** advanced westwards and took Sarum in 552. In 556 the great (4) **Ceawlin (r. 560-93),** reputedly Cerdic's great grandson, beat the British at Banbury. He succeeded to Cynric's position. Later he took Silchester and after a great victory at Deorham (577) the Gewissae expanded into the West Midlands. In principle after him the succession moved from the King to the next eldest or perhaps most competent relative, an arrangement reflecting the needs of a nomadic or mobile society. Thus Ceawlin was succeeded by his nephew (5) **Ceol (r. 591-7)** who was followed by his brother (6) **Ceolwulf (r. 597-611)** and then only by Ceol's son (7) **Cynegils (r. 611-43)** who won a victory at Beandun (616). Next came (8) **Cenwalh (r. 643-74)** a Christian convert who took a great interest in the see of Winchester and then briefly a descendant of Ceolwulf (9) **Aescwine (r. 674-6)** followed by Cenwalh's brother (10) **Centwine (r. 676-85).** During the period of this group of kings the Gewissae came under pressure from the aggressive Mercian power of Ks. Penda, Wulfhere and Ethelred and were driven south and west from the upper Thames into Somerset and later Dorset and Devon, conquering the local Britons as they moved. Then an adventurer, the British named (11) **Caedwalla (r. 685-8)** having failed to carve out a separate state in Sussex, fought his way to the throne and, after a violent reign, abandoned it and died, baptised at Rome (Apr. 689). He had claimed descent from Ceawlin.

B. There was now an interval beginning with the Christian (12) **Ine (r. 688-726)** of the fifth generation from Ceawlin. He reigned in the lifetime of his father Cenred, who advised him and he established a power nucleus comprising Hampshire, Dorset and Wiltshire which was the core of the later WESSEX; in particular he founded the see of Sherborne with St. Aldhelm as the first bishop, enlarged the endowments of Glastonbury Abbey and published for his people the important code called the LAWS OF INE. He abdicated and was followed by his brother (13) **Ingild (?-?)** of whom nothing is known.

C. The "E" Kings began with apparent descendants of Ingild named (14) **Eoppa (?-?),** (15) **Eaffa (?-?)** and (16) **Ealhmund (?-?)** an under-king in Kent. His son (17) **Egbert (r. 802-39)** is the ancestor of all later English monarchs. *See* ENGLISH MONARCHY, EARLY.

WEST WALL. The German Atlantic coastal fortifications in World War II.

WESTWOOD, Frederick (1858-1935), a pioneer of the safety bicycle and the motor car, invented the Westwood Rim to hold pneumatic tyres secure under their own pressure and so made inflatable tyres practicable. When car head lamps became sufficiently powerful he started to fit red rear reflectors to bicycles. He also collaborated with Louis Bledot in bringing in early motor cars during the 'red flag' era.

WEST WYCOMBE (Bucks.). Palladian and oriental mansion built by Sir Francis Dashwood between 1745 and 1771. *See* HELLFIRE CLUB.

WETTIN. This family became Margraves of Meissen in the 10th cent., added Lusatia in the 12th, Thuringia in the 13th and the electoral Duchy of Saxe-Wittenberg in 1423. In 1485 the family divided into ERNESTINES and ALBERTINES, the electorate passing from the Ernestines to the Albertines in 1547. The Albertines remained rulers of Saxony until 1918. The Ernestines ruled a collection of constantly redivided central German duchies and would have sunk into insignificance but for a series of successful dynastic operations, viz: (1) Leopold of Saxe-Coburg became King of the Belgians in 1831 and his descendants have held that throne ever since. His brother (2) Albert married Queen Victoria. Another brother (3) Ferdinand married Q. Maria II of Portugal and his descendants reigned in Portugal until 1910 and another (4) also Ferdinand became ruler of Bulgaria in 1887, his descendants reigning there until 1946.

W.E.U. *See* BRUSSELS TREATY 1948.

WEXFORD, TOWN and COUNTY (Ireland). The 10th cent. Ostman settlement was seized by Robert FitzStephen in 1169. The surrounding countryside was disputed between the Irish and the Normans so that the town lived a separate existence until the destruction of feudalism in the 17th cent. Cromwell's storm of Wexford was an atrocity long remembered by the Irish. *See also* FITZGERALDS; LEINSTER.

WEYMOUTH (Dorset). The ancient, probably pre-Roman, settlement was first mentioned in a charter of Athelstan in 938. It developed a port (*see* DORSET) after the Norman Conquest and had an extensive trade with the Biscay. In the 16th cent. it developed links with America and in 1616 it was chartered. It declined in the Civil War and by 1750 it was only a fishing village. It was revived by George III who first went there for his health in 1789 and bathed to the sound of a brass band. In the 19th cent. naval establishments and the naval harbour were built, and in 1944 it was the chief base for the Normandy invasion.

WHALING. Though trapping or luring of smaller cetaceans is ancient, whale hunting (mostly of the **Right Whale**) by harpoon was originated by the Basques in the 10th cent. Due to overfishing their offshore fisheries were very lucrative in the 12th and 13th cents. and then declined. By the 16th cent. they were seeking more distant hunting grounds, reaching Newfoundland by the 1570s. From 1610, as a result of Willem Barents' (?1550-97) discovery of **Spitzbergen,** then called **Greenland,** the Muscovy Co. fitted out expeditions, hired Basque experts and tried to establish a monopoly. This was challenged by Danes, other English, especially from Hull, the Dutch and other Basques. The parliamentary attack on monopolies from about 1620 followed by the upheavals under Charles I brought about a decline first in the Muscovy Co's activities and then by the English generally. By 1630 the Dutch predominated, though each nation had its own harbour which functioned as a modern factory ship. Smeerenburg, the Dutch base, was visited by over 1000 whalers a year and had shops and a church.

Overfishing again caused a decline and in the 18th cent. the Germans and Dutch moved to the Davis Straits; here their predominance, affected by the general Dutch recession, was again challenged by the British who operated under a system of govt. bounties, primarily from Hull, London and Whitby. Meanwhile from about 1712 American colonists, mainly of Nantucket, New Bedford and Newfoundland, began to hunt the Cachalot or **Sperm Whale** along the Atlantic coast. This **Southern Whale Fishery** as usual overfished, was extended steadily southwards as far as Brazil until the American rebellion called a halt and, under the bounty system, English whalers overreached them. By 1787 they had rounded the Horn but the Americans soon caught up and reached Japan in 1821 and Zanzibar in 1828. Right Whales were being caught in the N. Pacific and the Arctic in 1840s. By this time, however, both Atlantic and Pacific fisheries were being set back by the substitution of coal gas for whale oil for lighting and then by the American civil war (1861-5) and, in 1871, by the loss of most American North Pacific whalers in the pack-ice. The Atlantic Right Whale, moreover, was dying out.

Rationalisation was necessary to save the industry if not the whale. The harpoon gun was introduced in 1864 and steampowered whale catchers in the 1890s. Hunting moved to the Antarctic, where the Norwegians, acting under British licence, had from 1904 a base at South Georgia. The **Whale Factory ship,** which came into use in 1927, gave independence of shore bases. By 1937 overfishing was leading to international concern and there were agreements, not always honoured, limiting the seasons and settling minimum sizes. An International Whaling Commission was created in 1946 with expert and advisory powers and there were attempts to negotiate *moratoria* (which failed) and quotas, which the now dominant Russians and Japanese habitually evaded. Certain species were threatened with extinction. Conventions drawn up at Washington on endangered species generally (1973), at Bonn on migratory species (1979) and on Antarctic living resources (1980) failed to create an effective system of limitation on whaling in the 1980s.

WHARNCLIFFE. *See* STUART-WORTHLEY-MACKENZIE.

WHARTON. (1) Thomas (?1495-1568) 1st Ld. WHARTON (1544), three times sheriff of Cumberland, was a trusted expert on Border affairs, holding various commands all his life after 1531. He defeated James V at Solway Moss and five years later created much indignation by hanging the Scottish Maxwell hostages. His great-grandson **(2) Philip (1615-96) 4th Ld. (1625)** organised Yorkshire opposition to Charles I, but having been parliamentary Lord Lieut. in Lancashire and Buckinghamshire abandoned the military life when his regiment was routed at the B. of Edgehill (1642). As an Independent he voted for the Self-Denying Ordinance but refused to take part in public affairs during the Interregnum. His puritan son **(3) Thomas (1648-1715) 1st M. *of* WHARTON (1715)** published *Lillibulero* (q.v.) in 1687. He joined William of Orange at Exeter in 1688 and was his Comptroller of the Household until 1702 when Q. Anne dismissed him. He was Ld. Lieut. of Ireland in 1708-10. In 1714 he was one of the Lords who came unbidden to the crucial Privy Council meeting just before Q. Anne's death. His son **(4) Philip (1698-1731) D. of WHARTON (1718)** became a Jacobite and died penniless in Spain.

WHATELEY, Abp. Richard (1787-1863) eccentric and outspoken divine, was prof. of political economy at Oxford from 1829 and Abp. of Dublin from 1831. Though a convinced Anglican, he supported Irish church reform, the endowment of the Irish R. Catholic clergy and a national non-sectarian system of education.

WHEATLEY, John (1869-1930), a miner who became Labour (I.L.P.) M.P. for Shettleston in 1922.

WHEATSTONE, Sir Charles (1802-75) (*see* TELEGRAPH, ELECTRIC) was a distinguished electro-physicist, but originally a musical instrument maker and then an investigator into the properties of sound and light. He proposed the stereoscope and spectrum analysis before improving dynamos and making electric recorders.

WHEEL, BREAKING ON THE. A mostly continental capital punishment. The condemned was tied saltire-wise across a horizontal cartwheel and slowly rotated, while the executioner progressively broke his bones with an iron bar. It was sometimes mitigated by an early fatal blow called the *coup de grâce*. It was occasionally used in Scotland until the 17th cent.

WHEELS (1) for carts were a Bronze Age invention; **(2)** for pottery making, were brought to Britain by Belgic tribes c. 75 B.C.

WHETHAMSTEDE or BOSTOCK, John (c. 1393-1465) monk of St. Albans, had a meteoric career at Oxford and returned to St. Albans in 1417 as prior. He was first elected Abbot in 1420. In 1421 he was at the Chapter of Black Monks and, having attended the Council of Pavia as its representative in 1423, was its president from 1426 to 1432. As a result of his absences, literary, intellectual and other preoccupations, conventual discipline was neglected and in 1440 he resigned or was deposed having, however, repaired the buildings but involved the Abbey in many lawsuits. In 1451, however, the monks re-elected him. In these difficult years the Abbey was involved, geographically and as a great landowner in the Wars of the Roses, a series of emergencies with which he was not well fitted to cope.

WHIG. *See* TORY.

WHIMSICAL An early 18th cent. pejorative for someone who deviated from his party norm or regular opinion,

e.g. by voting with the party to which he is usually opposed.

WHIP (1) A disciplinary officer of a political party especially in Parliament. The govt. Whips are always Lords of the Treasury and officers of the Household. The Chief Whip manages the party funds.

(2) A document issued by a party whip to members of his party indicating the times at which they are expected to be present and the way they should vote. The importance attached to an occasion by the party leadership is indicated by the number of times that a given request is underlined. A *single line whip* means that if the member is there he should vote as indicated; a *two line whip* that he must be present until 10 p.m. at least; a *three line whip* that he must be present at all costs.

WHIPPING, a common law public punishment for misdemeanour was abolished for women in 1820. Its use became decreasingly common thereafter and it was abolished in 1948.

WHIPPING BOY. A boy kept to be whipped when a prince or other young nobleman deserved punishment. They often exerted strong, not invariably moral, pressure on their principals. The practice died out at the end of the 17th cent.

WHIPSNADE (Herts.) was laid out as an open air zoo in 1927 and opened in 1930.

WHISKY MONEY. In 1890 6d per gallon was levied on spirits to form a compensation fund to licensees of redundant public houses. So few publicans surrendered their licences that the money was diverted, under the Technical Instruction Act 1889, to county and county borough councils for education.

WHIST originated in England in the 16th cent. and became immensely popular after the publication of Edmund Hoyles book on it in 1742.

WHITAKER, Sir Frederick (1812-91) went to New Zealand in 1840, became a member of the first General Assembly in 1853 and was prime minister in 1863-4 and 1882-3.

WHITAKER, Joseph (1820-95) edited the *Gentleman's Magazine* from 1856 to 1859, founded the *Bookseller* in 1858 and started the annual WHITAKERS ALMANAC in 1868.

WHITBREAD. Bedfordshire non-conformist family. **(1) Samuel (?-1796)** entered a London brewery as a clerk and eventually became its owner. He gave his son **(2) Samuel (1758-1815)** a stern and religious education and the latter married Elizabeth, a sister of the Whig second Earl Grey. He was elected as a Whig for Bedfordshire in 1790. In a year he made himself one of the leading and best informed members of Fox's opposition. He was by contemporary standards an extreme radical, advocating liberation of slaves, religious toleration, free education and, as early as 1793, constitutional reform. He attacked the war administration on the principle that the war was both wrong and incompetently waged. He welcomed the P. of Amiens and seems to have been over-persuaded by Bonapartist diplomacy. When the war was resumed he led the attack on and impeachment of Pitt's friend Melville and later bid successfully for popularity by exposing the D. of York. By 1807 he was advocating poor law reform but his insistence on peace at any price was alienating Grey's whigs. He now insisted on championing the Prince Regent's hoydenish wife to a point where some of his allegations were evidently nonsense. He was also becoming voluble, vulgar and vain. His ill-judged activity was counter-productive. He thought (not without reason) that his public life was ending and committed suicide.

WHITBY, ABBEY and SYNOD. (A.S. STREANAESHEALH. Whitby = Dan. White Town). The double monastery for men and women was founded by St. Hilda c. 650 on a northern French model. It was ruled by an aristocratic, usually Northumbrian, Abbess. K. Oswy's queen Eanfled lived there for some years and his daughter Aeffled was a nun and Abbess there. It supplied bishops and became the royal mausoleum. Its powerful and ultramontane influence on the local church was demonstrated at the famous Synod of 664 when Oswy accepted the arguments of St. Wilfred and embraced the Roman rules rather than the Irish traditions and customs, primarily on the inconvenient differences caused by rival methods of calculating the date of Easter. The Synod ended the already declining Irish and Ionan predominance in the Northumbrian church and was an important stage in the attraction of the north English churches into the fold of western Christendom.

WHITE BOOK or *LIBER ALBUS*, a collection of City of London records compiled by John Carpenter, Town Clerk from 1417 to 1438.

WHITEBOYS were secret Irish rural terrorists during the agricultural depressions, particularly in Tipperary and Limerick in 1765, in Munster in 1785 and again in 1821-3. They were also widespread in 1860 and 1885. They were poor and, though condemned by the R. Catholic clergy, they attacked those whom they considered oppressors. These, depending on the area, were landlords, Protestant clergy, tax-, tithe- and rent-collectors and other unpopular persons. The Whiteboys' method was to assemble by night in white shirts (cf Ku Klux Klan) and burn their enemies' property, sometimes with them in it.

WHITECHAPEL (Stepney, London) named after a white chapel to St. Mary, had a clothing industry which in the 19th cent. employed much sweated labour in slums. Its people became the objects of Victorian solicitude taking the form, amongst other things, of the establishment of the London Hospital and Toynbee Hall. Clement Attlee was at one time Sec. of the latter. The area proved a fertile recruiting ground of Labour supporters throughout the 20th cent. Despite local govt. changes and heavy bombing in World War II it has maintained a distinct identity.

WHITEFEET. Early 19th cent. Irish local agrarian terrorist organisations, designed to combat evictions, often by murdering anyone who took a tenancy of a holding from which someone had been evicted. *See* RIBBONISM.

WHITEFIELD, George. *See* METHODISM.

WHITEFRIARS (London) was a former sanctuary between the Temple and Blackfriars.

WHITE GALL or GAEL Irish name for Norwegians.

WHITEHALL (Westminster). Hubert de Burgh built a residence with a white hall in the early 13th cent. He left it to the Dominicans who sold it in about 1250 to Walter Gray, Abp. of York. Hence it became the London residence of the Abp. of York down to Card. Wolsey's time. Wolsey extended it and made it the seat of the Court of Requests but, with all his other property, it fell into Henry VIII's hands in 1529. He and later monarchs extended it in a rough and ready fashion and it became the principal royal palace or rather a sprawling official village with ministerial offices jumbled among royal apartments. It occupied an irregular area between the Thames, the modern limits of St. James' Park and Trafalgar Square with a main gate near the present site of the Cenotaph. Thus the King with his large entourage of relatives, courtiers, guards, servants, officials and hangers-on lived cheek by jowl with parliament a few hundred yards to the west. This helps to explain some of the Tudor and Stuart political events, especially the royal raid on the Commons which led to the flight of the Five Members. James I built the surviving Banqueting Hall from which Charles I stepped to his execution. This faced onto a very large yard which accommodated an enormous crowd.

Apart from the Banqueting Hall this palace was mostly destroyed in a widespread fire in 1697. William III had always disliked it and the damage gave him a heaven sent excuse to live elsewhere. So did Q. Anne. The area

was not rebuilt as a palace but a wide street of the same name was driven through the site and slowly lined with an irregular collection of govt. offices.

WHITEHAVEN (Cumbs.). The Lowther family developed the collieries and built the pier between 1634 and 1670. It also became a tobacco port for Maryland and Virginia (*see* JONES, PAUL). It had shipbuilding and pottery industries throughout the 19th cent.

WHITE HORSE CELLAR at the corner of Piccadilly and Dover St., London, was a starting place for stage coaches, especially to Edinburgh.

WHITE HORSES. *See* HILL FIGURES.

WHITE HOUSE (1) The place in central Wales where, traditionally, the Laws of Hywel Dda were compiled. **(2)** The Executive Mansion of the Pres. of the U.S.A., so-called because it was painted white to hide the fire marks when the British burned it in 1812.

WHITELOCKE (1) Edmund (1565-1608), a soldier who fought in the French Wars of Religion, was implicated in Essex's rebellion of 1601 but released and suspected of complicity in the Gunpowder Plot but again released. His brother **(2) Sir James (1570-1632)** was M.P. for Woodstock in 1610, 1614 and 1622 and in 1624 became a judge of the King's Bench but refused to certify the legality of forced loans (1626). His son **(3) Bulstrode (1605-75)** was M.P. for Stafford in 1626 and for Marlow throughout the Long Parliament. He chaired the managers of Strafford's impeachment but afterwards was much concerned in attempts at pacification. In 1648 he became a commissioner of the Great Seal. He was a member of the committee which drew up charges against Charles I, but refused to take part in the 'trial'. He was then a member of the Council of State and in 1653 Ambassador to Sweden. In 1655 he was dismissed from the Great Seal because he opposed Chancery reforms but became a member of the Committee for Trade and Navigation. He was also chairman of the committee which offered the Crown to Cromwell in 1659. He was briefly Pres. of the Council of State after the fall of Richard Cromwell and then retired unmolested. He left several historical memoirs.

WHITGIFT, Abp. John (?1530-1604) became prominent at Cambridge after the death of Mary I, becoming in 1657 Regius Prof. of Divinity, Master of Trinity and Chaplain to Q. Elizabeth. He vigorously opposed the presbyterians and from 1572 to 1576, as prolocutor of the Lower House of Canterbury convocation helped to draw up the canons of 1576; he also wrote the official answer to the presbyterian *Admonition to the Parliament*. From 1577 he was a vigorous and efficient Bp. of Worcester and also (until 1580) Vice-pres. of the Council for the Marches and Wales. He became Abp. of Canterbury in 1583.

As Abp. he refused to co-operate with the presbyterians, rejected interference by the privy council and, by a system of clerical subscription of three articles (on Supremacy, Book of Common Prayer and the XXXIX Articles), secured a fair uniformity among his clergy. Though he used ecclesiastical jurisdiction to expose secret puritanism and puritan propaganda (such as the Marprelate Tracts) he was not a persecutor. Q. Elizabeth appointed him to the Privy Council and liked and trusted him. He was a key figure in the peaceful succession of James I, whom he crowned, and his protégé and ally Bancroft became the buttress of the Jacobean Anglican church.

WHITHORN or CANDIDA CASA (Galloway) (Eng. and Lat. = White House). St. Ninian built a stone church in the 5th cent. dedicated to St. Martin of Tours and it became the centre of a British diocese from which he converted the southern Picts and Britons. As a result of late 7th cent. Anglo-Saxon expansion it became a Northumbrian see in 731. In the 11th cent. it became the Scottish diocese of Galloway.

WHITLEY COUNCILS. *See* INDUSTRIAL COUNCILS AND COURT.

WHITE SHIP DISASTER. On 25 Nov. 1120 the *White Ship*, with important court personalities, many of them drunk, and William Audelin, only legitimate son of Henry I, on board left Barfleur for England and shortly struck a rock. She quickly sank and the life boat carrying William, which had returned for his half-sister, was swamped by people trying to climb in and sank too. There was only one survivor. The prince's death left Henry with no direct male heir and led to his attempts to secure the succession of his daughter Matilda and the civil wars under Stephen. There is a poem by D. G. Rossetti.

WHITE SLAVING became an offence in 1885 as a result of the efforts of W. T. Stead, Josephine Butler and, especially, Sir James Stansfeld.

WHITTINGTON, Richard (Dick) (?-1423) born at Pauntley, Glos., youngest son of Sir William Whittington, a landowner, had become a London mercer by 1379, trading with the court during the 1380s and 90s and becoming heavily involved in court finance. A common councilman in 1384, he became an Alderman in 1393 and sheriff in 1394. In 1397 Richard II, then engaged in trying to raise money from the City, appointed him mayor and he loyally tried to secure the City's support for the King's attack on the former Appellants. The royal financier gradually superseded the trader and between 1388 and 1422 he lent the crown over £33,000. This gave him influence and authority. After Richard's fall in 1399 Henry IV made him a royal councillor and he was mayor again in 1406-7 and 1419-20. He was a City M.P. in 1416. He was also a commissioner of Oyer and Terminer fifteen times and a special commissioner against the Lollards after the 1414 rising; and from 1413 to 1421 he was joint supervisor and accountant of the rebuilding of Westminster Abbey. As a major crown creditor he was drawn into the wool export trade because his loans were often secured on the wool custom and subsidy. He collected these in the City in 1401-3 and 1407-10 and was mayor of the Calais Staple in 1406-7, 1409 and 1413. He was also master of the Mercers' Company three times. Married to Alice FitzWaryn, he had no children and left his huge fortune for endowments and benefactions in the City such as almshouses and priests' colleges and the rebuilding of Newgate gaol. Contemporaries saw his career as a spectacular success story, which it was, and his memory attracted a rags-to-riches legend in the 16th cent. The story of the cat is now sometimes prosaically explained by his interests in Newcastle coal, brought to London by coasters called catts.

WHITTLE, Sir Frank (1907-96) became interested in jet propulsion (q.v.) as an R.A.F. cadet, but was first encouraged in 1936 when he was permanently assigned to experimental work. His first engine ran in 1937.

W[H]ITTLESEY, William (d. 1374), Abp. of Canterbury (1368-74), a nephew of Abp. Simon Islip whose vicar-gen. he became. Warden of Peterhouse, Cambridge (1349-51), Bp. of Rochester (1360-64) and Worcester (1364-8), he achieved little at Canterbury except the hostility of the monks over his support for secular priests at Canterbury College, Oxford, and he managed to persuade the clergy to satisfy royal demands for subsidies.

WHO'S WHO. An annual biographical dictionary of contemporary people first issued in 1849 and, since 1901, incorporating *Men and Women of the Time*.

WHO? WHO? MINISTRY was the Derby Administration of Feb. 1852. It contained many inexperienced figures. When Derby tried in the House of Lords to tell the (now somewhat deaf) Duke of Wellington their names the duke constantly and loudly said "Who? Who?".

WIDDRINGTON (1) Sir Thomas (?-1664) barrister and M.P. for Berwick in 1640, was a commissioner for the great seal in 1648-9, a member of the council of state in 1651, commissioner again from 1654 to 1655 and then a Treasury Commissioner from 1654 to 1659. He was also

Speaker of the House in 1656 and C.B. of the Exchequer in 1660 but lost his offices at the Restoration. He became M.P. for Berwick again in 1661. His brother **(2) Ralph (?-1688)** was Regius Prof. of Greek at Cambridge from 1654 and Lady Margaret Prof. of Divinity from 1673.

WIDDRINGTON (1) William (1610-81) 1st Ld. (1643), a soldier, fought for the King in the north of England. He went to Hamburg with Newcastle and later joined Charles II in his 1650-1 campaign and died of wounds at Wigan. **(2) William (1678-1743) 4th Ld. (1695)** joined the Jacobite Rebellion of 1715 and was attainted but not executed.

WIDOW OF WINDSOR. A slight pejorative for Q. Victoria after her widowhood had lasted some time. The phrase is attributed to Kipling.

WIDSITH, an O.E. poem probably of the 7th cent. describes the European wanderings of a court minstrel.

WIGAN (Lancs) (probably Roman COCCIUM) was taken into the barony of Newton after the Conquest but is said to have become a borough in 1100. The manor became attached to the parish and in about 1246 the rector obtained a charter constituting Wigan a free borough with a guild merchant A weekly market and a half yearly fair were added in 1258. The town had two M.P.s in 1295 and 1307, when the right went into abeyance but in 1314 the town received a new charter. Shortly afterwards outcrop mining for cannel coal began and industries requiring heat such as pewter, pottery and bell founding were started. By 1547 the place was important enough to be represented again in Parliament. Modern coal mining began in the 17th cent. and led to the development of iron works.

WIGHT, I. of (Lat: VECTIS), an early Roman conquest after A.D. 43, has many Roman remains. It was settled by Jutes in the 6th cent. but in the 7th cent. it passed under Sussex, Wessex and briefly Mercia until finally becoming part of Wessex. It was occasionally raided by the Danes, who occupied it in 998. William I granted the island to one of his close advisors, William fitz Osbern (?-1071) and in c. 1110 Henry I granted it to Richard de Redvers, in whose family it remained until Isabella de Forz sold it to Edward I in 1293. The island produced and produces salt and good building stone. Its peaceful life was interrupted when the French sacked Yarmouth and Newport in 1377. In 1404 and 1419 they attacked again and in 1545 a French fleet did great damage around Brading. As a result artillery castles were built at Cowes, Sandown, Freshwater and Yarmouth and a governor was installed at Carisbrooke Castle. These local defences ceased to matter to the island once Portsmouth became a major naval base in the 17th cent. but coastal batteries for the defence of the base were built at the beginning of the 20th cent. on the Solent coast. The island has always had a ship-building industry, besides being the centre for an important yachting activity.

WIGMORE. See MORTIMER.

WIGRAM, Clive (1873-1960) 1st Ld. (1935), became A.D.C. to the Viceroy (Lord Elgin) in 1895 and with Curzon until 1904, though seeing some active service on the N.W. frontier and S. Africa. He was included in the P. of Wales' staff on the latter's first visit to India in 1905, became his equerry in 1906, mil-sec. to the C-in-C at Aldershot in 1908 and then asst. private sec. to George V on his accession. He held this post under Lord Stamfordham until 1931 and took over the secretaryship when he died. He and the King had always been great friends and he communicated to George V much of his own interest in sport and young people's welfare. He also had to advise in the difficult questions arising out of the economic crisis and the formation of the "National" govt., the consequences to the crown of the Statute of Westminster, 1931, and the Indian problems leading up to the Govt. of India Act, 1935. He was not in sympathy with Edward, P. of Wales, and retired in favour of

Alexander Hardinge six months after his accession as Edward VIII.

WIGTOWN (Scot.) was ruled from Cruggleton by a Scots-Norse line of Kings, of whom FERGUS (?-?) re-constituted the bishopric of Whithorn in 1120 and married a daughter of Henry I. His son UCHTRED, like his father, settled Anglo-Normans on the land but lost his life in a revolt led by his brother GILBERT in about 1170. Uchtred's son ROLAND, however, continued the policy of his father. By a succession of marriages the land passed to the Balliols and when they were discredited by their support of the English, to the Douglases who bought the earldom in 1372. In 1426 they superseded the old Galwegian laws by the general law of Scotland. The Kennedys succeeded to the influence of the Douglases when the latter fell in 1455.

WIHTRAED, LAWS OF (c. 695). A Kentish code of money penalties giving a special position to the clergy and incorporating some procedural rules, especially on oaths. *See* ETHELBERT, LAWS OF; KENT, KINGDOM OF-4.

WILBERFORCE (1) William (1759-1833) became M.P. for Hull and a close friend of William Pitt in 1780. In 1784 he experienced a moral conversion and thereafter sought worthy causes to support. He began with the Proclamation Society which prosecuted blasphemy and indecency. In 1785 Thomas Clarkson interested him in the slavery question and in 1787 a largely Quaker committee was formed. Pitt advised parliamentary action and Wilberforce began by trying to secure some anti-slave clauses in the Anglo-French P. treaty. Thenceforth he and his friends kept the slave trade and slavery before one House of Parliament or the other by bills or resolutions continually for many years. His moral earnestness was beginning to be respected when he published *Practical Christianity* in 1797 and he was the most prominent member of the Clapham Sect. Once, in 1802, his zeal outran his judgement: his *Society for the Suppression of Vice* incurred legitimate ridicule. Meanwhile the anti-slavery campaign gathered strength much aided after 1800 by the 100 new Irish M.P.s. In Mar. 1807 the great Slave Trade Act abolished it and rendered void or criminal every collateral transaction. Wilberforce was now a sort of moral mascot widely cherished (he was never in good health) and respected by the highest and the lowest. Slavery (rather than the trade) continued to occupy him but his authority was powerfully exercised in moderating public indignation over the D. of Cambridge's scandal (1809), in the introduction of Christian teaching in India and in supporting the Corn Law of 1815. He also supported the suspension of Habeas Corpus in 1817 (when he fell foul of Burdett) and tried to arrange a compromise in the affairs of Q. Caroline. In 1823 his public appeal led to the formation of the Anti-Slavery Society. Ill health, which had forced him to exchange Hull for the quiet pocket borough of Bramber in 1812, forced him to retire in 1825. Personally one of the most charming public characters, he was distinguished for his versatility and sociable gaiety. Of his sons the best known was **(2) Samuel (1805-73)** a celebrated preacher and divine who became Bp. of Oxford in 1845. Here he had to cope with Pusey, Newman, the Tractarians and with a disorganised and badly funded diocese. He disciplined his clergy, established Church Building Societies, founded Cuddesdon College for theological students and Culham for school masters, collected for missionary bodies, raised funds and aided the education of the poor. He was also an active member of the Lords and successfully promoted, from 1852 to 1865, the revival of Convocation. In 1869 he became Bp. of Winchester and continued, with the same extraordinary energy, his works, to which was added the revision of the New Testament. The most considerable and best known of Anglican prelates of his time, his career ended abruptly when his horse threw and killed him.

WILD, Jonathan (?1682-1725), head of a London criminal network, ran a public office for the return of property stolen by his associates and became a famous delator of thieves not in his ring. He was eventually hanged for receiving.

WILDE, Oscar Fingall O'Flaherty Wills (1854-1900) was already famous as an Oxford undergraduate, being satirised by Gilbert and Sullivan in *Patience* in 1881. He published the *Picture of Dorian Gray* in 1891, *Salome* (in French) in 1893 and *The Importance of Being Earnest* in 1895 when he was involved in a series of spectacular trials culminating in his imprisonment for buggery. In 1898 he published the *Ballad of Reading Gaol* and *De Profundis* was published posthumously in 1905. His vicissitudes and likeable character sparked off a controversy about sexual law reform which continued for more than 60 years.

WILDMAN, Sir John (?1621-93) highly individualistic politician, served under Fairfax in 1646 and 1647 but was imprisoned with John Lilburne for supporting the dissentient regiments against Cromwell in 1648. Major in Reynolds regiment in Ireland in 1649, he speculated in forfeited lands there. In 1655 he was imprisoned for plotting against Cromwell and from 1661 to 1667 for plotting against Charles II. He was also involved with Algernon Sydney and others in 1681 and was again imprisoned in 1683 in connection with the Rye House Plot. In 1685 he became Monmouth's agent in England but refused to join him and joined William of Orange instead. He was M.P. in the Convention Parliament and Postmaster-Gen. from 1689 to 1691 when he was dismissed on suspicion of intriguing with the Jacobites.

WILFRID, St. (c. 633-709), a Northumbrian, was in teenage at Lindisfarne under St. Aldan and was then educated at Rome and Lyons. K. Alchfrith of Deira, son of K. Oswiu, made him Abbot of Ripon (c. 663). An energetic and awkward person of strong convictions, he led the successful Romanist attack on Irish practices at the Synod of Whitby (664) and Alchfrith then made him Bp. of York where he developed a high view of episcopal status and independence and, though ascetic, favoured episcopal splendour and ceremony. Consistently with this he disliked outer interference. Consequently when Oswiu had Chad consecrated to the see of the Northumbrians, Abp. Theodore in 669 had tactfully to discover a defect in Chad's consecration. In 678, because of a quarrel with K. Ecgfrith and Theodore's wish to divide the Northumbrian diocese, Wilfrid appealed ineffectually to Rome, returned, was imprisoned at Dunbar (680-1) and went into exile. He occupied his time converting the South Saxons and establishing a monastery at Selsey and is said to have taught them how to fish. Restoration to York provoked further disputes and exile, this time to Mercia where he acted as bishop (at Leicester from 962). In 702 he appealed to Rome again, was reconciled with the Northumbrians and was Bp. of Hexham (out of harms way) until he died. He built or rebuilt many churches, especially at York, Hexham and Ripon, and presided over a large monastic organisation.

WILHELMSHAVEN (Ger.) was built on land bought by Prussia from Oldenburg in 1853. The name dates from 1869 when it began to be developed as a naval base. The base was demolished in 1945 but by 1960 there was an oil harbour with a pipeline to Cologne.

***WILHELMSTRASSE* (Berlin).** The address of the German Foreign Office between 1870 and 1939.

WILKES, John (1727-97). (1) Son of a distiller and educated at Leyden, he was a member of the Hellfire Club and became M.P. for Aylesbury in 1757. His vicious life brought him into debt, his character to extremist courses encouraged by Pitt and Temple against the Bute govt. In 1762 he founded the *North Briton* with Charles Churchill to lampoon and slander ministers. In No. 45 he called the speech from the Throne a lie. The govt's reaction led to a series of court cases (*see WILKES v WOOD*). Failing a printer to continue his operations he set up a press himself and issued, not only the *North Briton* but an obscene *Essay on Women* by Thos. Potter. The Commons voted that these were not protected by members' privilege (Nov. 1763). Faced with prosecution he fled to France, was expelled from the Commons (Jan. 1764) and outlawed (Oct.). He remained in France until 1768 using up his money.

(2) He reappeared, still an outlaw and desperate, to stand in the general election of 1768 first in the City, where he failed, and then in the tumultuous constituency of Middlesex. Home Tooke and Serjeant Glynn organised his campaign. Temple gave him qualifying land. He came first in the poll and then insisted on being arrested so as to become a popular martyr. The Lord Chief Justice, Lord Mansfield, cancelled the outlawry on a technicality (Apr. 1768) but he was heavily fined on the charges which he had evaded and sent to prison. From prison he triumphantly continued to direct his supporters. In Feb. 1769 he was, on govt. initiative but with wide backing, expelled from the Commons again. He and Horne Tooke then organised a *Society for the Defence of the Bill of Rights*. He was elected an alderman of the City and in Middlesex he was re-elected M.P. without opposition. Expelled again, he was re-elected again and for a third time expelled. At the next round rival candidates were found but he led the poll. He was expelled yet again but this time the House declared Col. Luttrell, his leading opponent, elected instead.

(3) This associated Wilkes with a major constitutional issue between those who held, with Chas. James Fox and Grafton, that the Commons should be independent of both crown and popular pressure, and those who held with Chatham that the Commons were already unduly influenced by the crown and should seek popular support. A Wilkes' Society campaigned in the country and organised petitions for the dissolution of the corrupted parliament. Varyingly offensive in their wording, these poured into the palace throughout 1770. Meanwhile the Society split between Wilkes' excessively personal adherents and those such as Horne Tooke, who foresaw the growth of a permanent popular movement. The latter seceded. Wilkes abandoned part of his radicalism and appealed to mob passions. At the shrieval elections of 1771 he successfully fought the Tories, Horne Tooke and his progressives and the parliamentary opposition, advocating abolition of impressment and control of bread prices.

(4) The technical secrecy of parliamentary debates had long been ignored. It was now resolved to protect the House of Commons from agitations based on proceedings in it by denying knowledge of them to the public. Three journalists were summoned for breach of privilege. Prompted by Tooke one (Miller) took refuge in the City, whose authorities arrested the messenger sent to fetch him. Brought before Wilkes as alderman and ex-officio magistrate, the deputy serjeant of the Commons was forced to bail him. The Commons summoned the Lord Mayor, Alderman Oliver M.P., and Alderman Wilkes for contempt. Wilkes refused to accept a summons unless made out to him as M.P. for Middlesex. The Lord Mayor and Oliver were committed to the Tower: but Lord North's govt. refused to be drawn. Wilkes' summons was dated for a day when the House was in recess. Thereafter the House ceased to proceed against those who resisted it and reporters were excluded with decreasing frequency. The battle between Wilkes and parliament subsided.

(5) Wilkes now combined London with national politics and in 1774, after two failures, became Lord Mayor and also, with eleven supporters, was elected to parliament in the general election. He took his seat without disturbance. The Wilkesite M.P.s had a serious

programme: shorter parliaments, bills against placemen and crown contractors and the redress of grievances at home, in Ireland and in the colonies, but Wilkes was less serious than they; they could not make an impression without his irrepressibility; but he was bored and inert. The reforming initiative passed to others, notably Chatham and Shelburne. His parliamentary performances became undistinguished.

(6) Affairs remained in this posture until 1779 when the American disaster awoke public indignation against Lord North. At a Middlesex bye-election a moderate Mr Tufnell took the Chiltern Hundreds in order to stand. The Wilkesite George Bynd also applied for the Chiltern Hundreds in order to stand and was denied them. This revived memories of Luttrell's "co-option" to the Commons in 1769. While Wilkesism thus revived in the south a Petition Movement (q.v.) started independently further north on the pattern of the Wilkesite petitions of 1770. The storm centre was Yorkshire. It set up local committees and in 1780 a national assembly. Opposition politicians hurried up in support, the younger Pitt, Chas. James Fox and, of course, Wilkes, among them. The result was Dunning's celebrated motion in the Commons (Apr. 1780) against the Crown. The House was prepared to accept it but threw out the bill which might have implemented it because members wanted peace at home and abroad and, moreover, they were frightened by the ferocious Gordon riots. So was Wilkes. He became a supporter of established order, perhaps because in 1779 he had been elected to the lucrative financial office of City Chamberlain, and the destructive rioting affected the City's rateability and his pocket. The rest of his public life was, accordingly, respectable.

WILKES v WOOD (1763) or the **CASE OF GENERAL WARRANTS**. The Sec. of State issued a general warrant to "search for the authors printers and publishers of a seditious and treasonable paper entitled the *North Briton No. 45* and these ... to apprehend and seize together with their papers". Wood, acting under the warrant, broke into John Wilkes' house and seized his papers. Wilkes sued for trespass. The Court of Common Pleas held that the power claimed in the warrant where no offenders names are specified and no inventory given "may affect the persons and property of every man in the Kingdom and is totally subversive of the liberty of the subject" and urged the jury to award exemplary damages, which it did.

WILKINSON, Ellen Cicely (1891-1947), trade unionist and suffragette, was an early (1912) member of the Independent Labour Party, of the Communist Party (1920-4) and then became a Labour M.P. for Jarrow. She led the celebrated hunger march on London in 1936. In 1938 she carried a private members' bill against the abuse of hire purchase schemes. As Min. of Education (1945-7) she was responsible for ensuring that the Tory 1944 Education Act came into force.

WILKINSON, John (1728-1808) set up a blast furnace at Bilston (Staffs) in about 1748 but perfected his cylinder boring and finishing processes in 1756. His immediate profits arose from armaments contracts but his work was essential to the steam and internal combustion engine, besides spreading the use of iron piping. He was buried in an iron coffin.

WILLEHAD (?-789). *See* MISSIONS TO EUROPE.

WILLETT, William (1856-1915), the advocate of Summer Time, after many attempts succeeded posthumously in getting the first daylight saving Act passed in 1916. *See* SUMMER TIME.

WILLIAM I (1027-87) D. of NORMANDY (1035) King of ENGLAND (1066), the CONQUEROR or the BASTARD (1) was the son of D. Robert (the Devil) and Herleva, daughter of William the Tanner, later Robert's Chamberlain. She (c. 1028) married Herluin de Conteville by whom she had ROBERT, Count of Mortain, and ODO,

Bp. of Bayeux. William's great-aunt Emma had been Ethelred the Unready's Queen, and Ethelred and his son, Edward the Confessor, William's cousin, had spent many years as exiles until 1042 at the Norman court.

(2) Robert the Devil left on pilgrimage in 1035 and died at Nicaea leaving the Duchy to William, who was put under the protection of Alan, Count of Brittany and Gilbert of Brionne with, more immediately, Osbern the Seneschal. This regency was murderously assaulted by the great freebooting house of Bellême. William of Bellême missed William but killed Osbern, to be himself killed by one of Osbern's servants. After an interval certain leading, especially W. Norman, nobles brought forward the claims of Guy of Burgundy, a legitimate descendant in the female line of earlier dukes. Aided by K. Henry I of France, William defeated these rebels at the cavalry battle of Val-és-Dunes (1047).

(3) The vigorous and resourceful young duke now needed a politically suitable wife, who was found in the person of MATILDA or MAHAUT (?-1083) of the adjacent county of Flanders and a descendant of K. Alfred. There was, however, a so far unidentified, canonical impediment and the Papacy forbade the marriage. Flanders was the scene of some of the political intrigues of the House of Godwin. William, however, was determined. Though he favoured the new reformism of Pope Leo IX (r. 1048-54) he strengthened his own popular power by appointing warrior bishops (Geoffrey and his half-brother Odo) to Coutances and Bayeux. Geoffrey was penanced at Leo IX's council of Rheims but William sacrificed his disreputable uncle Malger, who had to give up the archbishopric of Rouen to one Maurilius of Leo's choosing. A decisive event was the election of the strong minded Italian scholar, Lanfranc, to the priory at Bec. He and William contracted a lifelong, if stormy, friendship. In 1053 when William married Matilda, Lanfranc denounced the union but on his way out they met by chance. They were reconciled and Lanfranc even agreed to plead William's cause with the Pope.

(4) This and the Flemish alliance were as well, for K. Henry with the Counts of Anjou and Champagne, were hoping to partition Normandy or at least clear the Seine Valley to its mouth. Half their divided force was surprised at Mortemer (1054); the other half retired. The war had a bearing on the English succession. In 1051 Edward the Confessor designated William as his heir. He had appointed the Norman Robert of Jumièges to the see of Canterbury and William had paid him a state visit. Then came the reassertion of the power of the House of Godwin; Robert of Jumièges was deposed and Stigand put in his place. They would undoubtedly fight for the English crown. Defeat, or even war, in Normandy at the critical time would destroy William's chances. To what extent his policies took this into account is unknown, but he (and no doubt Matilda) never lost sight of the possibilities. In 1057 he defeated the last French invasion (B. of Varaville) and went over to the offensive. In 1060 two events powerfully assisted him. Henry I of France died and the regency passed to William's father-in-law; more locally, the Count of Anjou died. By 1063 William had conquered the Angevin territory of Maine. The Duchy frontiers were safe. Widely respected, he could recruit for his English venture from all the Channel states.

(5) In 1064 Harold Godwin's son fell into William's hands by shipwreck and was made to swear an oath to William upon the relics of Bayeux Cathedral. The circumstances and the nature of the oath are conjectural. There was an element of duress, if not trickery. Nevertheless when Harold accepted the English crown in Jan. 1066 he could be represented as perjured and, because perjured, as a schismatic since William had, through Lanfranc, the support of the reforming papacy. He also had extraordinary luck.

(6) William defeated and killed Harold and two of his brothers at Hastings on 18 Oct. 1066 and after devastating the home counties was crowned at Westminster on Christmas Day. He was not, however, in full control. His followers had to be rewarded and this he began from the lands of the House of Godwin and thanes killed at Hastings. One result was that the new owners received scattered estates, not consolidated fiefs, but the process naturally provoked resistance from followers and families of former owners. There was much minor campaigning in Wessex and Mercia in 1067-8 and castle building. The new dispensation was in some ways revolutionary. William was not merely stepping into the Kingship in Anglo-Saxon society; he was bringing in a French-speaking warrior and clerical following which, not too gently, shouldered aside the older families. The castles demonstrated the determination of the new armed minority to hold its takings. The reservation of game in the forests was enormously resented, especially by the poor. The New Forest was a name of reproach.

(7) After the initial shock and subjugations of 1066-8 resistance began to solidify and organise. The years 1069-72 were a period of civil war with interventions. In 1069 a Danish fleet supported the northern rising which Earls Waltheof, Edwin and Morcar joined. William's answer was a devastation so frightful that much of the north became almost worthless and had to be recolonised in the 12th cent. Waltheof submitted, Edwin was killed by his own men, Morcar went into hiding. Then the army crossed to Chester. The Welsh fled and the city hurriedly surrendered. The damage done in these operations virtually restricted the English Kingdom to an area west of Wales and south of Yorkshire. In 1070 E. Anglian insurgents were driven into the Fens, among whose reeds and islets they maintained themselves under Hereward the Wake until 1072. In many cases William could forfeit rebel lands and give them to Normans so that the alien aristocratic diaspora spread even more widely.

(8) Holding down the English nation by means of a tiny body of armed foreigners could succeed in the long run only if the govt. was efficient and just enough to attract native allegiance. The problems were compounded by wars and rebellions in Normandy which threatened the home properties of the new aristocracy. The French King Philip I encouraged, at Le Mans, a commune whose example was soon followed (1072). This threatened the feudal organisation as well as William's authority. At the time when, with Lanfranc since 1070 at Canterbury, he might reorganise the English church, he had to cross the Channel to suppress these embryonic municipalities. In 1074 there was a Norman baronial rebellion; during his absence Ralph Guader, E. of Norfolk, conspired with Roger, E. of Hereford, his brother-in-law and E. Waltheof. They expected Danish help but the rebellion failed before it could arrive. Ralph escaped to Brittany. Roger was deprived and imprisoned. Waltheof was executed (1075). Significantly, it was the English who came out in support of the King, whom they began to recognise as their defence against anarchy. In 1076 there was a dangerous border war with Philip who in 1077 helped William's eldest son Robert to head another Norman rebellion. Such distractions and rumours of them provoked trouble on other parts of the periphery. Welsh chieftains and the Scottish K. Malcolm began to encroach. In 1079 when William defeated Robert at Gerberoi Malcolm was in Northumberland. The quarrel with Robert was patched up and he was sent out of harm's way on a northern expedition; he invaded Scotland and founded Newcastle-upon-Tyne. In 1081 William himself commanded an expedition against Wales while Robert went home and made more trouble. So did Odo, now fabulously rich and E. of Kent. William imprisoned him at Rouen for the rest of his reign.

(9) Though Norman troubles pursued William to the end, Odo's adventure marked their conclusion in

England, where relative tranquillity and orderly administration were bringing a change of atmosphere. William's magnificence, enormous bulk and terrifying personality all contributed to an established prestige derived mainly from an understanding that order and justice (however rough) went hand in hand. At the Gloucester Court of 1085 he ordered the compilation of Domesday Book. In 1086, when a Flemish and Viking invasion threatened, he could summon a great assembly of his tenants to Salisbury and take an oath from each. At the end of the year he left to fight K. Philip for the French Vexin and met his death in Sept. 1087 in a riding accident during the sack of Nantes.

WILLIAM II RUFUS (Lat = red faced) (?1056-1100) King (1087) *see* genealogy. **(1)** William the Conqueror left Normandy to the agreeable but incompetent Robert and England to the vicious and violent Rufus. Adela had married Stephen of Meaux (later Count of Blois) in 1080. Henry got £5000 of silver. Robert succeeded in Normandy (where primogeniture obtained) without incident. William succeeded in England (where an election was possible) through Abp. Lanfranc's influence and then had to face a rebellion nominally in favour of Robert, led by his uncles Odo of Bayeux and Robert of Mortain. Outbreaks in E. Anglia, Leicestershire and the Welsh border were easily suppressed but a campaign was needed in the principal disturbed areas, namely Kent centring on Rochester, and Sussex centring on Pevensey, where in each case the rebels could get help from Normandy. Odo and Robert were banished to Normandy after Rochester fell (*see* NITHING) and never returned. William triumphed because the English and the church supported him against the barons.

(2) Robert being short of cash sold the Cotentin and Avranches to Henry for £3000 in 1088. Most Norman lords had lands in Normandy as well as England. Therefore the rulers of the two countries could stir up trouble for each other. Rufus resolved to have Normandy. His method was pressure and bribery for which large sums were needed. Lanfranc died in 1089 and the revenues of Canterbury were in the King's hands. The owners of important ports and castles were subverted. By the T. of Rouen (1091) he compelled Duke Robert to concede Eu, Aumale, Gournai, Fécamp and Conches together with parts of the Cotentin already sold to Henry. Rufus and Robert now combined to drive Henry out, but Henry, invited by the inhabitants to take over the fortress of Domfront, used it as a base to re-establish himself. By 1095 he ruled the Cotentin again and Rufus put him in charge of his Norman affairs while he himself faced another baronial revolt. This was led by Robert de Mowbray, ostensibly in the interests of Rufus' cousin, Stephen of Aumâle. The scene of operations was Northumberland; they took several months.

(3) Rufus' financial adviser and chaplain Rannulf FLAMBARD (?1064-1128) encouraged his tallages and other exactions, especially the milking of the church by keeping benefices vacant. Canterbury was vacant until the King's illness in 1093 when, believing himself about to die, he at last appointed Anselm. There followed the long quarrel with Anselm in which finance was, from the King's side, an element. In 1096 the money was particularly needed when Duke Robert, to go on crusade, pawned Normandy to Rufus for 10,000 marks. He went east with Odo, who died in Sicily in 1097.

(4) Rufus, who did not intend to let the pledge be redeemed, set about enlarging the Duchy. Anselm went to Rome without his permission in 1097 and the Canterbury revenues were again available to the King. He fought the French unsuccessfully in the Vexin and while his agents in Rome strove to keep Anselm there he made temporarily successful wars in Maine. He and Robert of Bellême also built the fortress of Gisors. Duke Robert then started home and in 1099 married a rich heiress on

the way. He could now redeem the Duchy. Flambard at this time was made Bp. of Durham.

(5) A clash between Duke Robert and Rufus was prevented by Rufus' accidental or engineered death in the New Forest in Aug. 1100. Murder or not, Henry seized the throne just before the Duke reached Normandy in Sept. Other beneficiaries from the death were Henry's friends the Clares, who had been present.

WILLIAM III (1650-1702) P. of ORANGE, King (1689) posthumous son of William II of Orange and Charles II's sister Mary, **(1)** was coldly brought up by his strong minded grandmother, Amalia of Solms, and educated at Leyden under the supervision of a series of committees often nominated by the de Witts, political opponents of his family. This loveless consumptive and partly crippled orphan had, however, a strong intellect, high courage and political shrewdness. Moreover, the French threat echoed the Spanish threat from which his ancestor William the Silent had saved the Dutch some 80 years before. William had not only estates and followers but a name to conjure with. Hence it was impossible to exclude him from the Dutch Council of State when he reached seventeen at the height of the Second War with England.

(2) In 1670 he visited England to test and, perhaps, exploit, the controversies surrounding Charles II's desire for independence from parliament and his brother James' Catholicism. He was received with respect and, sometimes, enthusiasm and thereafter his English claims were never forgotten. In the meantime Charles had to pay the price of Louis XIV's support by joining his attack on Holland. The Dutch republican policy of trade and appeasement collapsed. The nation turned again to a Prince of Orange in a revolution which restored the Captaincy and Admiralty-General and the Stadholdership to him (July 1672) and brought about the murder of the de Witts (Aug.). Now identified as the European champion against French tyranny, he was seen by many as a leader against French supported tyranny in England. His assumption of power was moreover marked by an inspiring act of Dutch self-sacrifice: they let in the sea and so stopped the French advance.

(3) Dutch determination was a rock on which William could build a system of alliances and compensations. An indifferent soldier but a brilliant and well informed diplomat, his combinations retrieved his lack of military success while his victorious enemy always failed to secure a military decision. In the bloody victory at Seneffe (Aug. 1674) the French had to defeat Spaniards who had just entered the war; England had just left it and (Dec.) the Swedes attacked France's Prussian ally. There followed a stroke of luck. Turenne, victorious in Alsace, met his death on the Sassbach (July 1675). The inspiration went out of the French leadership. 1676 was, nevertheless, a disaster. There was the secret agreement between Louis and Charles II (Feb.) and then the defeat and death of Adm. de Ruyter at Messina (Apr.). William's attempt a year later to re-establish the position failed (Apr.) before Cassel, yet this was the time when he achieved, with the aid of a popular agitation, his fateful marriage (Nov.) with James' daughter Mary.

(4) By 1678 the belligerents had had enough and Louis offered trade concessions and the *status quo ante* with Holland, whose republicans were thus induced to abandon William's allies (P. of Nymegen-1 Aug.). The deserted Spaniards made the best of things and ceded Franche Comté (11 Sept.) while Louis held onto Flemish fortresses which he had promised to give up; somewhat later the Empire ceded Freiburg and Breisach (Feb. 1679). While England was put out of action, first by the fall of Danby engineered by Louis and then by the 'Popish Plot', the novel *Chambers of Reunion* at Metz, Breisach, Besançon and Tournai began to assimilate the new provinces to the French monarchy. The temporary quality of the Ts. of Nymegen was soon demonstrated by Louis' peace time seizure of Strasbourg and Casale (Sept. 1681) (thus threatening central Germany, Savoy, Spanish Milan and Genoa) and the investment of Luxemburg. A Dutch-Swedish treaty founded a new anti-French coalition, whereupon Louis raised the siege and offered to submit his Spanish quarrel to Charles II's arbitration.

(5) Western dissensions encouraged the Turks and their last attempt at Vienna (July-Sept. 1683) encouraged Louis. While the Emperor struggled to relieve the starving city Louis invaded Spanish Flanders. Spain declared war but England would not move and without her William could not persuade the Dutch to do so. French forces again appeared before Luxemburg and others bombarded Genoa into submission, thereby isolating Milan from Spain. By the summer of 1684, however, the Turks were being driven down the Danube and the victorious Habsburg preferred a standstill in the west. Hence the twenty-year Truce of Ratisbon (Aug.) left Strasbourg and Luxemburg under French occupation but reserved imperial claims. English prevarication convinced the Dutch that the overthrow of Charles' apparently Francophil govt. was a matter of vital concern to them.

(6) James II's accession seemed to strengthen the pro-French govt, supported as he was by a friendly, even co-operative, parliament; and when the D. of Monmouth, expelled from the Spanish Netherlands, arrived in Amsterdam William advised him to take service against the Turks. The collapse of Monmouth and Argyll's venture seemed to demonstrate that James' throne was unshakeable. Yet Louis XIV's German encroachments were developing into a threat to the Dutch; when the Elector Palatine Charles died childless in 1685 Louis occupied Zweibrücken on behalf of Louis' sister-in-law, to whom it had passed. He was meddling with the affairs of Cologne, whose Elector-Abp. also held Münster and Liège. Such moves seemed to foreshadow interference in the next imperial election and a northward extension of the French military presence from Strasbourg. There was alarm in Germany. The Great Elector of Brandenburg lent his troops to the Emperor and became an imperial pensioner; the Emperor, with Spain, Bavaria, Sweden and some minor German states, negotiated at Augsburg for the defence of S. Germany. The so-called League of Augsburg (July 1686) was ineffectual, for Spain was weak and Austria and Bavaria still distracted by the Turkish war. Louis so far disregarded it as to build forts on German soil and secure the election of a pro-French coadjutor bishop at Cologne. The Dutch saw themselves beleaguered without a useful friend and this feeling was reinforced by Louis' persecuting catholicism. The Edict of Nantes had been revoked in 1685; despite Papal doubts French instigated persecutions were beginning in Savoy and the Palatinate.

(7) Dykveld, a high ranking ambassador from the States-General, came to England (Feb-May 1687), ostensibly to seek assurance from James II about the purpose of his armaments. He also exploited the growing sympathy between those endangered by Louis' or James' political policy and those threatened in conscience by them. James' political opponents, thereafter, remained in communication with William. The change in the climate of English opinion after the Bloody Assize lent reality to such communications but William refused to repeat Monmouth's mistake and intervene in England without assurances of support. It was not only the risk of failure which deterred him. Failure would jeopardise his brave, obstinate, Dutch to whose safety he had devoted his life. It was as the leader of Dutch foreign policy that he accepted the invitation (July 1688) from the English lords to turn his father-in-law out. The venture succeeded (Nov-Dec.) mainly because Louis' fleet was laid up and his army since Sept. engaged near Switzerland. Louis' declaration of war on the Dutch (Nov. 1688) could not

affect this outcome (see LEAGUE OF AUGSBURG, WAR OF 1688-97).

(8) The English thus had to accept involvement with Dutch foreign policy as the price of their Glorious Revolution. The settlement (see BILL OF RIGHTS) once attained, the war shelved the political issues between James and his erstwhile people. There could, for example, be no controversy about a standing army in peacetime for the country was at war. Parliament consolidated its own importance but the need for strong wartime direction prevented it from extending its power. Dutch William distrusted the English and maintained some 5000 Dutch guards in London; he admitted none to his personal life or confidence and openly exhibited his poor opinion. They, conversely, disliked him and the uninhibited court ladies regarded their misogynist master as a boor. William and the English were no more than necessary to each other but the needs of war required a strong executive and a tranquil society. William exercised all the royal power and reserved the conduct of foreign and military affairs to himself. During the joint reign with Mary (until 1694) he was the real King, though he delegated functions to her during his frequent absences and she virtually controlled the church appointments. They effected a practical religious toleration; R. Catholics and Nonconformists were legally excluded from public affairs but Catholics were seldom persecuted and their general condition of life improved, while a Toleration Act legalised, under certain conditions, non-conformist chapels, preachers and schools. The secession of the Nonjurors enabled Mary to make ecclesiastical appointments favourable to the regime and her choices were sound and, in Tillotson the Abp. of Canterbury, distinguished.

(9) The years 1696-1700 exhibited major changes in the conditions of world politics. The down-turn of Turkish aggressive power became definitive with the Russian capture of Azov (July 1696), P. Eugene's great victory at Zenta (Sept. 1697) and wholesale Turkish cessions under the P. of Carlowitz, and their ability to divert Habsburg attention from the west was much reduced and no longer forced Austria and Bavaria to cling together. Secondly, the election of Augustus the Strong of Saxony to the Polish throne (June 1697) and the simultaneous rise of Peter the Great in Russia and Charles XII of Sweden created an independent storm centre in the north-east. Thirdly, and to some extent consequently, Louis' W. European ambitions had to be sustained or contained by the fate of the Spanish empire, now in the hands of the dying and childless Habsburg K. Charles II. The problem of the Spanish Succession touched the interests of every western power. Harmless under weak govt., in strong hands Spanish Flanders would endanger Britain and Holland; the American and other overseas territories, the growing English trade; Milan and Naples, the security of Austria, Venice, Genoa and Savoy; the Iberian Peninsula with its harbours, the eastern Atlantic and the western Mediterranean. The bullion of Mexico and Potosí might similarly reinforce the strength of the overmighty. With all these territories in French hands all other states, their backs to the wall, would have to fight. The diplomacy of the three years was concerned to prevent this by neatly balanced partitions of the great inheritance. Two Partition Treaties (Oct. 1698 and Mar. 1700) failed in the face of Spanish determination to preserve their empire intact and of Louis' opportunism in exploiting that determination. In Oct. 1700 the Spanish King was induced to devise his entire possessions to Louis' grandson, Philip of Anjou, and in Nov., just after the Second Northern War broke out, he died.

(10) The Emperor regarded his family claim as paramount and hastened to improve his position by a stroke which had immense long term effects. The Prussian Crown Treaty (Nov. 1700), in return for military

friendliness, recognised the Elector of Brandenburg as King in Prussia and therefore no longer a feudatory of Poland under its Saxon King. Other countries, while appreciating the dangers, were less anxious to try conclusions with France and by the time Philip reached Madrid (Feb. 1701) most western nations had recognised his accession. Louis had, after all, accepted the permanent separation of the French and Spanish monarchies, but he never thought that war could be avoided and decided to get in first. Acting under the legal cover of the new Spanish King's authority, French troops immediately replaced the Dutch in the Belgian barrier fortresses. The Abp. Elector of Cologne, who held the Prince-bishopric of Liège, instantly declared for Louis and, as war broke out with Austria, Bavaria did so too (Mar. 1701). The Dutch and English, however, still held back. Louis' triumph, however, was short. In Italy P. Eugene brilliantly drove the French headlong westwards (Apt-Sept.). At St. Germain James II died (Sept.) and, in a moment of arrogance and contrary to the T. of Ryswick, Louis recognised his son James Edward as King of England. This produced an explosion of English feeling. The childless William's health had deteriorated and it had just been necessary by the Act of Settlement (June 1701) to entail the crown to Anne and, after her, to the House of Hanover. The stadholder-King had now no difficulty in uniting Britain with Holland behind the Habsburg and the Anglican settlement (Sept.). Six months later he was dead.

WILLIAM IV (1765-1837) D. of CLARENCE (1789) King (1830) son of George III. He served in the navy in 1780 as an able seaman and, after commissioning, had an active naval career occasionally interrupted between 1791 and 1811 by dalliance at Bushey Park with Mrs Jordan, by whom he had nine children (the FitzClarences). In 1818, however, he married Adelaide of Saxe-Meiningen. From 1827 until his accession he was the last Lord High Admiral. Known as 'Silly Billy' because of his amiable but rambling chatter, he was enormously popular and no fool. He never wholly lost the common touch. Consequently he played a sensible moderating role in the great Reform Bill crises of 1831-2, on the one hand refusing to overpower the Lords by a mass creation of peers and, on the other, using his influence to stop them throwing the bill out. *See* REFORM BILLS (1831-2)-3 *et seq*.

WILLIAM, son of King Stephen (q.v.).

WILLIAM of Sta. BARBARA. *See* DURHAM-3.

WILLIAM, Prince (1103-20). *See* HENRY I-11; WHITE SHIP DISASTER.

WILLIAM the CLITO (= prince or atheling) (c. 1100-28) son of Robert Curthose, D. of Normandy, was present as a child when Henry I defeated his father at Tinchebrai (1106). Henry released him and he was used, through the hope of recovering Normandy, by Louis VI of France and Fulk of Anjou to stir up trouble for Henry, especially after the latter had lost his male heir in the *White Ship* disaster (1120). In 1127 Louis made him Count of Flanders, to which he had a claim through his grandmother Matilda, the Conqueror's wife, but as Thierry of Alsace was in possession he had to fight for the honour and in 1128, while besieging Alost, was mortally wounded.

WILLIAM the LION (1143-1214) King of Scots (1165). *See* SCOTS AND ALBAN KINGS, EARLY; HENRY II; RICHARD I; JOHN; DURHAM. His purpose was to enlarge the authority and territory of the Scottish monarchy in all directions from its centre on the Forth. For this reason he intervened in the rebellions of Henry II's sons in order to acquire the four English northern counties, but this plan came eventually to grief when he was captured near Alnwiek (1173) and was forced by the T. of Falaise (1174) to acknowledge English suzerainty. Baulked in this field, he devoted his considerable energies to securing the independence of the Scottish church from the archbishopric of York, in subduing rebels in the Moray Highlands and in asserting

Scottish sovereignty in the Norwegian areas of Sutherland and Caithness. His efforts to control the Church, especially the elections to the see of St. Andrews were resisted by the Papacy, and Scotland was briefly put under interdict. In 1189 Richard I quit claimed to him the English rights under the T. of Falaise for 10,000 merks. At K. John's accession in 1199 he perceived an English opportunity similar to that which had obtained at the end of Henry II's reign and demanded the four northern counties but he could not raise the force to make his claim good and in 1212 was overawed militarily into making peace.

WILLIAM (fl. 1051) Bp. of LONDON. *See* EDWARD THE CONFESSOR-7.

WILLIAM of MALMESBURY (c. 1095-?1143), of Anglo-Norman parentage and librarian at Malmesbury Abbey, wrote *Gesta Regum Anglorum* (Lat = History of the Kings of the English) from the arrival of the Saxons to 1120 and its sequel, the *Historia Novella* (Lat = Later History) from 1128 to 1142, the *Gesta Pontificum Anglorum* (Lat = History of the Church Rulers of the English) to 1125, the *De Antiquitate Glastoniensis Ecclesiae* (Lat = The Ancient Origins of Glastonbury Abbey) and parts of a hagiographical *Life* of St. Dunstan. He was critical of his sources and a selective user of topography and architecture as evidence and he treated the history of pre- and post-Conquest England as one sequence. This made him not only influential but popular.

WILLIAM of NEWBURGH (1136-?98) a Yorkshire Augustinian, finished his *Historia Rerum Anglicanum* (History of English Events) in 1198. It covers the period from 1066 to 1198.

WILLIAM of NORWICH (?1095-1174) prior and then, from 1146, Bp. of Norwich, was a partisan of Becket and a disseminator of the legend of Little St. William.

WILLIAM of NORWICH, Little St. (1132-44), said to have been ritually murdered by Jews, his tomb at Norwich was long a disreputable pilgrim centre.

WILLIAM of St. CARILEF or St. CALAIS (?-1096) was trained at Bayeux and rose through his diplomatic and administrative abilities. In 1080 William the Conqueror appointed him to the border state and see of Durham after the murder of Bp. Walcher. He was a conscientious and efficient ruler and bishop, who introduced monks to his cathedral, but the ambivalence of the position was illustrated by his well-known trial. In the revolt of 1088 he refused to fight the rebels under Robert Courthose. In the consequent trial at Salisbury K. William Rufus, with the support of Abp. Lanfranc, charged him as a secular baron (which he was). The bishop demanded to be tried as a bishop (which he also was). He appealed to Rome. His temporalities were forfeited but he was allowed to go into exile. He did not, perhaps wisely, go to Rome. He and Rufus were reconciled in 1091 and he was restored to his temporalities. *See also* DURMAM-2.

WILLIAM of TYRE (?1130-?86), a Frankish diplomat of Outremer, became Abp. of Tyre in 1175. Much involved in high level Levantine politics, he wrote a well informed *Historia rerum in partibus transmarinis gestarum* (Lat = History of Outremer) most of which survives and other works which survive only in quotation. His works are important for the study of the mediaeval outlook as well as for the study of Crusader politics.

WILLIAM of VALENCE. *See* HENRY III-10 *et seq*.

WILLIAM of YPRES (?-?1166), bastard of Philip of Loo and grandson of Count Robert of Flanders, was a competitor for the County of Flanders in 1127-8 against William the Clito. Expelled in 1133 he came to England and from 1135 to about 1145 was Capt. of K. Stephen's Flemish mercenaries and a loyal and effective, if ruthless and violent, commander. It was by his tactical skill that Robert of Gloucester was taken at the Rout of Winchester in 1141. In the mid 1140s, however, he became blind and turned his energies to church patronage and polities.

He mediated between Stephen and Abp. Theobald, both of whom he knew well. In 1148 Stephen had given him large estates and revenues in Kent which Henry II allowed him to keep only until 1156-7. He spent his last years in the Flemish monastery at Loo. His military career exemplifies the growing 12th cent. importance of paid troops.

WILLIAMS, Charles (1838-1904) celebrated reporter of Franco-Prussian War 1870, the Armenian affairs of 1877, the Berlin Congress 1878 and Afghanistan 1879-80. He became editor of the *Evening News* in 1881 but reported the Nile Expedition of 1884. In 1885 and in 1897 he reported for the *Daily Chronicle* in Eastern Europe. He founded the Press Club in 1896.

WILLIAMS, David (1738-1816) founded in 1788 the Literary Fund which became the Royal Literary Fund in 1842.

WILLIAMS, Sir Edward Leader (1828-1910) engineer of the Admiralty pier at Dover (1852-5) built the Manchester Ship Canal between 1882 and 1894.

WILLIAMS, Sir George (1821-1915) founded the Y.M.C.A. in 1844.

WILLIAMS. (1) Henry (1792-1829) was a missionary at Waiapu in New Zealand from 1822. Much trusted by the Maoris, he induced many of their chiefs to sign the Waitangi T. (184) and was much blamed (probably wrongly) for the hopes which led to the Maori War. His brother **(2) William (1800-79)** became 1st Bp. of Waiapu in 1859.

WILLIAMS, John (?1500-59) 1st Ld. (1554), a relative and protégé of Thos. Cromwell, was sheriff of Oxon in 1538 and from 1544 to 1553 Treas. of the Court of Augmentations. He was also M.P. for Oxon in 1542 and from 1547 to 1552. He and Wingfield arrested Somerset in 1549. He supported Q. Mary's claim in 1553 and was Chamberlain to Philip II. He also had respectful custody of the P. Elizabeth who, as Queen, made him Lord Pres. of Wales.

WILLIAMS, John (1582-1650) Bp. of LINCOLN (1621) Abp. of YORK (1641) came to notice as dean of Salisbury in 1619 and then of Westminster in 1620. In 1621 he became Lord Keeper and was a close associate of Buckingham, but lost the Keepership when opposing the Spanish War. He tried to reconcile the factions over the Petition of Right and to oppose Laud's Arminianism. He was then charged in the Star Chamber for betraying royal confidences, fined and later imprisoned until 1640 for subornation of penury. On the outbreak of the Civil War he retired to N. Wales but, as principal dignatory there, made terms with the parliamentarians at the general royalist collapse after Naseby.

WILLIAMS (1) John (1757-1810) sergeant at law, brought out the 10th (1787) and 11th (1791) editions of Blackstone's Commentaries. His son **(2) Sir Edward (1797-1879)** was a Judge of the Common Pleas from 1846 and P.C. from 1865.

WILLIAMS, John (1796-1839), missionary mostly in the Society Is., built his own ship and made many voyages in the Pacific. In 1834 his visit to England inspired great interest in missionary activity. He was eaten at Erromanga.

WILLIAMS, Robert (1810-81). Celtic, especially Cornish, scholar.

WILLIAMS, Sir Roger (?1540-95) Lieut. to Sir John Norris in the Low Countries from 1577 to 1584, served under Leicester in 1585, fought at Zutphen in 1586, unsuccessfully defended Sluys against Parma in 1587 and commanded the horse at Tilbury in the Armada year. He was with Willoughby at Dieppe in 1589 and was then allowed to go on campaign with Henry of Navarre. In 1592 he succeeded Essex in command before Rouen.

WILLIAMS, Roger (?1604-83) often persecuted pioneer of religious liberty. *See* RHODE I.

WILLIAMS, Thomas (?1513-66) M.P. for Bodmin in 1555,

Saltash in 1558 and Exeter in 1563, was elected Speaker in 1563.

WILLIAMS, Sir William (1634-1700) M.P. for Chester, was Speaker in 1680 and 1681. He was a notable champion of Commons independence but though fined in 1686 at Jeffrey's instance for licensing Dangerfield's *Narrative,* was sol-gen. from 1687 to 1689 and appeared against the Seven Bishops. He sat in the Convention and later Parliaments and was Queen's Sol-Gen. in 1692.

WILLIAMS, Sir William Fenwick Bt. of KARS (1800-83) artillery general and British commissioner for the Turko-Persian frontier in 1848, was commissioner to the Turkish army in the Crimean War and held Kars with great credit against the Russians until he ran out of supplies. He was M.P. for Calne from 1856 to 1859 and thereafter held colonial governorships

WILLIAMSON, Sir Joseph (1633-1701) M.P. for Thetford in 1669, became Clerk of the Council in 1672, joint plenipotentiary at the Congress of Cologne in 1673 and Sec. of State in 1674. Accused in the Popish Plot in 1678, he was nevertheless Pres. of the Royal Society until 1680. In 1696 he was one of the negotiators of the P. of Nimwegen and in 1698 a signatory of the First Partition Treaty.

WILLIBALD, St. *See* MISSIONS TO EUROPE-3.

WILLIBRORD, St. (c. 657-739). *See* MISSIONS TO EUROPE-2.

WILLIKEN of the WEALD. *See* HENRY III-2.

WILLOUGHBY (1) Francis (1613-66) 5th Ld. WILLOUGHBY of PARHAM, a parliamentary commander in Lincolnshire and presbyterian leader, was impeached by the Independents in 1647, imprisoned and in 1648 sought revenge with the royalists in Holland but then became briefly Vice-Adm. of the mutinous parliamentary fleet in the Downs (1648). In 1650 he became gov. of Barbados, where he rejected parliamentary jurisdiction on the ground of non-representation, but had to give way when parliamentary forces landed. Naturally he was imprisoned. After the Restoration he was made gov. (1663) of not only Barbados but St. Kitts, Montserrat and Antigua. He was drowned on the way to recover St. Kitts from the French. He was succeeded in the governorships by his brother **(2) William (?-1673) 6th Ld.,** who recovered Antigua and Montserrat from the French and seized Cayenne from them and Surinam from the Dutch.

WILLOUGHBY of ERESBY. *See* BERTIE.

WILL'S COFFEE HOUSE (Bow St., Covent Garden, London), literary and gambling rendezvous in the 17th and 18th cents. Addison, Congreve, Pope, Prior, Steele and Wycherley habitually went there and Dryden dominated it until 1700. The *Tatler* was planned there. The owner was called William Unwin. *See* BUTTON'S COFFEE HOUSE.

WILLS AND LETTERS OF ADMINISTRATION. (1) As few were literate, early wills are rare but some survive from Anglo-Saxon times onward. Only a minority make wills now. **(2)** The inheritance of *real* property was governed by strict rules applying to the property as such. It could not be left by a will, which could only pass *personal* (i.e. mostly movable) property. Practical exceptions to this inconvenience began to develop. Leases were deemed personal, and when Uses (q.v.) were invented they could be devised because they were not real. The Statute of Uses 1535 was meant to abolish them, but this theoretically revived the inconveniences, and the Statute of Wills 1540 made some not very useful and complicated exceptions. In the 17th cent. the courts found ways round the Statute of 1535 which made that of 1540 unnecessary, and later legislation removed the technical obstacles. **(3)** The Church often had rights on death and so in the 13th cent. it took over testamentary administration. It developed a commonsense practice for establishing the genuineness of a will and the identity of the executor, and for preserving it in a diocesan register (*see* PROBATE). **(4)** In 1857 a Court of Probate was created.

This took over all English testamentary business from the church courts including their law.

(5) An English will must be in writing signed by the testator and by two witnesses, but soldiers, sailors and airmen on service may make informal, even spoken, wills. In Scotland, in addition, a will is valid without witnesses if it is wholly in the testator's handwriting and signed by him, and small legacies can be left by nuncupative (i.e. spoken) wills. Wills are revoked by other wills or destruction, and in England by marriage.

(6) Letters of Administration authorise someone to deal with a deceased's property where there is no will or named executor.

WILLS (1) William Henry (1830-1911) 1st Ld. WINTERSTOKE (1906) and his cousin **(2) Sir George Alfred (1854-1928) Bt. (1923)** were directors of the W. D. & H. O. Wills, tobacco merchants, and in 1901 negotiated the formation of the Imperial Tobacco Co, of which Sir George was chairman until 1911. They both made immense benefactions to Bristol and its university.

WILLUGHBY, Francis (1635-72). *See* RAY, JOHN.

WILMINGTON, LONG MAN OF. *See* HILL FIGURES.

WILMOT (1) Charles (?1570-?1644) 1st Vist. WILMOT of ATHLONE (1621) served in the Irish wars under Sir Thos. Norris. In 1600 he was sworn of the Munster Council. By 1602 he was gov. of Kerry. In 1607 he became a member of the Irish Council and in 1616 Pres. of Connaught. His reconstruction of Athlone led to accusations of embezzlement, but in 1625 he was pardoned. In 1629 he became C-in-C of the Irish forces. He hoped for the Lord Deputyship but was angered by Wentworth's (Strafford's) appointment in 1631, especially when Wentworth revived the accusations concerning Athlone. He was forced to restore considerable tracts of land to the Crown and in retaliation assisted petitions against Wentworth who, however, in 1636 compelled him to submit. He was now elderly by the standards of the time and, though he retained his office in Connaught, he took part only in civil administration until he died. His able son **(2) Henry (?1612-58) 1st Ld. WILMOT (1643) 1st E. of ROCHESTER (1652)** began as a soldier in the royal army against the Scots and was M.P. for Tamworth but was expelled from the Commons in 1641 as a result of the so-called Army Plot. He reformed the royal army as commissary-gen., commanded the left wing at Edgehill and in July 1643 inflicted the damaging defeat on Waller at Roundway Down. Neither the King nor P. Rupert liked him and he feuded with Digby. Temporarily in command in 1644 he beat Waller at Cropredy Bridge (June). He thought, however, that the war might be ended only by Charles I's abdication and was arrested in Aug. as a result of private communications between him and Essex, the parliamentary commander. The officers, however, intervened and he was allowed to retire to France where, in 1647, he fought a duel with Digby. He became Charles II's principal confidant after Charles I's death and accompanied him to Scotland (1650) and was with him at the B. of Worcester and in his subsequent adventures. He thus became Charles' most important adviser, negotiating on his behalf with the D. of Lorraine (1652), the Imperial Diet (1652-3) and the Elector of Brandenburg (1654). In 1655 he was in England co-ordinating the attempted rising of that year. His son **(3) John (1647-80) 2nd E.,** was the wit, poet and libertine who amused Charles II, bedded many women and wrote some of the least decent verse of that frank era. He was also a useful patron of minor poets and actors (and actresses).

WILSON, Sir Henry Hughes (1864-1922) Anglo-Irish Gen. and intriguer, was Dir. of Mil. Operations at the War Office (1910-14) and conducted much of the joint planning with the French before the outbreak of World War I. In 1914 he tacitly encouraged officers at the Curragh in the line of conduct which led to the 'Curragh Mutiny' and he advised Carson on the formation of the Ulster Volunteers. He had ingratiated himself with Lloyd George and consequently supplanted Robertson as C.I.G.S. in 1918. Parliament voted him a substantial gratuity in 1919 and in 1922 he became a Conservative M.P. but soon after the I.R.A. shot him on his doorstep at Michael Collins' orders. The reason and timing for this remains unclear.

WILSON, Sir Horace John (1882-1972) joined the Civil Service from the London School of Economies specialising in industrial and financial matters. He had been seconded to the Treasury in 1935 and his advice was trusted by Neville Chamberlain, even outside matters in which Wilson had expertise and experience such as foreign affairs, where his advice was taken as a substitute for, rather than a complement to, advice from professionals. He was head of the Civil Service from 1939 to 1942.

WILSON, [James] Harold (1916-95) Ld. WILSON of RIEVAULX (1983) became a lecturer at Oxford and in World War II worked as a planner in the Min. of Fuel. He became Labour M.P. for Ormskirk in 1945 and for Huyton from 1950. After junior office under Attlee, he became Pres. of the Board of Trade in 1947 but resigned in 1951 with Aneurin Bevan on the ground that the new rearmament programme was more than the economy could sustain. After Hugh Gaitskell's death he became leader of the Labour Party and then prime minister in 1964-70 and 1974-6. He was said to be devious but compassionate and had a respectful devotion to the Queen. His resignation in 1976 and the honours list which accompanied it aroused suspicions which were never substantiated or even defined. *See* next entries.

WILSON'S FIRST GOVT. (Oct. 1964-June 1970) (1) As Labour had been out of office for 13 years most of Attlee's ministers had retired and this govt. was composed largely of new men. Only Dennis Healey (Defence) and Ross (Scottish Office) retained their offices throughout. George Brown began as First Sec. of State and Min. of Economic Affairs but in 1966 moved to the Foreign Office following, first, Patrick Gordon Walker and then Michael Stewart, who succeeded George Brown at Economic Affairs until 1967 when Peter Shore took over. James Callaghan was Ch. of the Exch. until 1967 when Roy Jenkins succeeded him. Sir Frank Soskice, a survivor from the Attlee era, was Home Sec. until late in 1965 when he was followed by Roy Jenkins and then (1967) by James Callaghan. The Board of Trade went first to Douglas Jay and then (1967) to Anthony Crosland and (1969) to Roy Mason. The Dept. of Education and Science had four transient ministers but Wilson established a new Dept. of Technology, headed first by the trade unionist Frank Cousins and then, from 1966, by the radical Anthony Wedgwood Benn. The Min. of Labour was transformed into a Min. of Employment and Productivity under Barbara Castle. Richard Crossman held the Dept. of Housing and Local Govt. until 1968 and then went to the Dept. of Health. In 1969 a new Dept. of Local Govt. and Planning was created under Anthony Crosland and a Min. of Overseas Development replaced the defunct Colonial Office and was held successively by Barbara Castle, Anthony Greenwood, Arthur Bottomley and (out of the Cabinet) by Reginald Prentice.

(2) The govt. faced economic problems while its small majority made radical measures difficult. In one early bye-election the Foreign Sec. Patrick Gordon Walker even failed to win a seat. It relied on economic improvement to raise its standing for another general election when the opportunity arose. Callaghan opposed another devaluation of sterling and so an import surcharge was levied instead and a Prices and Incomes Board set up. Income tax was raised but the poorer obtained a pensions increase, and health service prescription charges, then ideologically suspect to socialists, were abolished. The trade unions were flattered by, *inter alia,* a Trades Disputes Act (1965) which gave trade unions even more protection from the law in closed shop cases. A more popular measure was the Redundancy Payments Act 1965 which required employees dismissed for reasons other than misbehaviour to be compensated jointly by the employer and the state.

(3) Meanwhile George Brown had committed a large staff to drawing up a national plan of long term development and at the same time the balance of payments eased. Accordingly Wilson called an election for 1966 and won 363 seats against the conservatives 253 and the Liberals 12, but these results and the Seamen's strike of May-July did not create confidence among international bankers, and the govt. had to return to deflation and temporary wage and price fixing. This was unacceptable to George Brown who changed places with Michael Stewart, the Foreign Sec.

(4) With the improved balance of payments the import surcharges were withdrawn at the end of 1966 but there was another cyclic crisis compounded by a Dock strike in the autumn of 1967 and in Oct. Sterling was devalued, Harold Wilson transparently assuring the public that this would make no 'difference to the pound in your pocket'. Consequently James Callaghan changed places with Roy Jenkins who insisted on reducing expenditure and raising taxes and prescription charges. The National Plan was now dead and George Brown resigned from the govt. in 1968. With the approach of the 1970 election the economy was improving but the public was irritated by persistent strikes arising out of obsolete trade union organisation and provocation by left wing shop stewards' movements. The unnecessary strikes impeded the govt's policy of wage control by voluntary agreement. Moreover, Barbara Castle's proposals, *In Place of Strife,* split the cabinet and could not be transformed into legislation.

(5) The govt. accordingly switched to another approach to economic problems, namely industrial modernisation through an Industrial Re-organisation Corporation to encourage company amalgamations and modern technology. British Leyland was the prominent, but ultimately least successful, result. Consistently with this, nationalisation was not pursued save in the ease of iron and steel which was formed into a British Steel Corporation. This part of the programme was facilitated by a considerable reduction in defence deployment. Spending was reduced by cancelling the excellent, but expensive, TSR-2 aircraft and on military prototypes, and defence industries were forced to convert to other production or seek overseas markets. The changes were made possible by withdrawing from military commitments east of Suez except in the Persian Gulf (which came later) and Hong Kong and by a very tepid support for U.S. policy in Vietnam. At the same time *détente* with the U.S.S.R. simplified the military situation and while credits for British imports were readily granted to Moscow, Britain signed two nuclear weapons control treaties.

(6) There was, meantime, a subtle change of emphasis and attitude. Decolonisation in one form was interrupted by the Declaration of Independence by the Smith govt. in Rhodesia in another. After abortive negotiations Britain instigated international sanctions. There had been in 1967 an unsuccessful attempt to join the European Common Market and immediately Gen. de Gaulle died (1969) a fresh application was made. Thus the process of abdication from overseas responsibilities was intensified by internationalist merger policies in embryo. As it happened the I.R.A. launched its policy of terrorism in Ulster and troops released from elsewhere had to be sent there.

(7) All the same social expenditure policies were pursued against a background of heavy spending on existing such policies. An ideologically based Rent Act of

1967 repealed the Conservatives' Act of 1965 but probably made the housing situation worse, while increased urban renewals allocations did not make up the difference. On the other hand driver breathalisation, not popular at the time, was soon accommodated by public opinion; the creation of the Swedish-inspired Ombudsmen (significantly called the Parliamentary Commissioner) made less of an impact because he was made inaccessible save through an M.P. Other miscellaneous social changes included the suspension of the death penalty, an investigation of the Civil Service by the Fulton Commission, two Race Relations Acts, moves towards comprehensive, and expanded Higher, Education and most importantly, the reduction of the age of majority from 21 to 18.

(8) Labour lost the 1970 election mainly through failure to deal with the trade union problem and immigration.

WILSON'S SECOND GOVT. (Mar. 1974-Apr. 1976). (1) The Feb. general election was held amid conflict between the Heath govt. and the miners. Labour won 301 seats, the Conservatives 297 and the Liberals 14 with others (notably Scots and Welsh nationalists) winning 23. A Liberal-Tory coalition being soon clearly impossible, Edward Heath resigned and Harold Wilson formed a Labour govt. with Dennis Healey as Ch. of the Exch., James Callaghan Foreign Sec. and Roy Jenkins Home Sec. Roy Mason at Defence, Reginald Prentice and then Ted Mulley at Education and Science. Anthony Wedgwood Benn at Industry and Varley at Energy changed places in 1975. Michael Foot was at Employment and Anthony Crosland at Environment. The arduous Northern Ireland Office was taken with considerable success by Merlyn Rees. Peter Shore took on Trade and Industry, Barbara Castle, Health and Social Security. In addition a Price and Consumer Protection department was created and put under Shirley Williams.

(2) The first move was to end the coal dispute by paying the miners more. The previous govt's Industrial Relations Act was repealed and its Pay Board abolished. The govt. intended to rely on a voluntary so-called Social Contract to control prices and wages. This began well but as the strong and greedy might disagree with it, its long term prospects were poor. In the election called for Oct. 1977, however, Labour increased its seats to 319 at the expense of the other parties, save the Welsh and Scots nationalists.

(3) In the remainder of its term the govt. hardly solved the economic problems, though movement from expedient to expedient helped to identify the issues. Voluntary restraint was a partial failure and there was an increasing component of compulsion, first applied *via* rent standstills and a Price Code, to prices. Faster growth might have solved the inflation difficulties but could not be obtained. If the British National Oil Corporation and the new oil taxation were signs of a better future, industrial modernisation *via* a new National Enterprise Board seemed like creeping nationalisation when the Board started making advances to ailing industries. The main issues being apparently insoluble, employment palliatives were deployed, notably the Health and Safety at Work Act, 1974, which imposed a drain on the short available private capital and the Employment Protection Act, 1975, which, by making it harder to change staff, hindered industrial change. The Sex Discrimination Act had a similar effect despite its evident justice. On the other hand the creation of A.C.A.S. (q.v.) to help settle industrial disputes added a permanently useful feature to the economy.

(4) Having got some concessions from the European trading partners and perhaps to obtain them, the govt. held a referendum to decide if Britain should continue in the Common Market. The bemused public response was affirmative. Elsewhere the abandonment of the colonial

empire proceeded but the Rhodesian problem remained unresolved because the international economic sanctions were easily evaded by all concerned.

(5) In the spring of 1976 Harold Wilson suddenly retired in favour of James Callaghan.

WILSON, (1) James Maurice (1836-1931), one of the earliest school science teachers (at Rugby from 1859 to 1879) and as headmaster of Clifton (1879-90), the first to introduce summer camps for poor children. His son **(2) Talbot (1884-1940)** was acting civil commissioner in the Persian Gulf from 1918 to 1920 and then with Anglo-Persian Oil until 1932. From 1933 he was conservative M.P. for Hitchin and a champion of rearmament against Germany and of industrial insurance and workmen's compensation. He was killed as an air gunner in the B. of Britain.

WILSON, John (1785-1854) was prof. of moral philosophy at Edinburgh from 1820 to 1851 and as *Christopher North* edited the Tory *Blackwood's Magazine* with Lockhart from 1817.

WILTON (Wilts). Small town, ancient royal manor with a favourite and rich royal nunnery founded in about 870 and, until 1075, a bishopric, was granted to the Es. of Pembroke who built Wilton House. The carpet industry dates from Elizabeth I. *See also* CARPETS; WILTSHIRE.

WILTON DIPTYCH, a sumptuous picture in the Franco-Flemish style dating probably from 1395, was commissioned by Richard II. It depicts him being presented by St. Edmund the Martyr, Edward the Confessor and John the Baptist to the Virgin and Child, who are surrounded by angels, one of whom holds a banner. The three saints resemble respectively Edward II, Edward III and the Black Prince. Richard II's White Hart motif appears on most of the clothes, and the angels and the King wear collars of broom pods, perhaps a reference to a revival of the name Plantagenet. The Diptych is the most striking of all later mediaeval English paintings.

WILTON, Joseph (1722-1803). Sculptor and pupil of Delvaux, settled in London in 1755, was a founder member of the Royal Academy and was responsible for much of the decorative sculpture in the works (such as Somerset House) of Sir Wm. Chambers.

WILTSHIRE (A.S. WILTLUNSCIRE = the district about Wilton.) (1) is so thickly studded with monuments, archaeological sites (including the complexes at Stonehenge and the much larger Avebury) and hilltop entrenchments, that large populations and a well developed agriculture from about 2000 B.C. must be deduced. The people were apparently hostile to the Romans, who established a town at Old Sarum, the meeting point of several roads and built the Fosse Way. The Romanised inhabitants repulsed the Saxons until about A.D. 540 but were subdued by 600. The leading elements were either killed or fled westwards, leaving behind a depressed labouring population. There is some place-name evidence of temporary bilingualism, but the Celtic speech was entirely superseded by the 9th cent.

(2) The shire was W. Saxon in the 8th cent. and it was the scene of much fighting then and in the Danish wars. The damage was less serious than might have been expected. The bishopric, moved from Wilton to Old Sarum in 1078, could afford a large Norman hilltop cathedral and Domesday and the *Inquisitio Geldae* give a prosperous impression.

(3) The shire had been divided by the conquest into 39 hundreds and at the time of Domesday there were, with the crown, 60 important landowners, of whom 5 were episcopal (including the Norman bishoprics of Bayeux, Coutances and Lisieux) and 12 monastic (including Bec and Lisieux). The ecclesiastical establishments increased in number and, like the abbeys at Malmesbury and Lacock, in size throughout the middle ages and the bishopric became exceedingly rich. It was able not only to support another move, to Salisbury and

the construction (1220-66) of its splendid cathedral, but was habitually used by the Crown as a reward for its more important servants. Between the Conquest and the Reformation the see seldom had a resident bishop. At the same time the lay tenants found it worthwhile to engross the local jurisdictions. There were so many franchises that by 1280 only 11½ hundreds were in crown hands. Mediaeval Wiltshire "lived of its own".

(4) The mixed farming which was practised once the valleys had been drained was supplemented by very extensive cattle and sheep raising on the downland. Much wool was produced and exported *via* Southampton but from the 14th cent. a broadcloth industry grew up at Bradford on Avon, Trowbridge and Wilton which, later still, made and makes carpets. There is also much good building stone.

(5) The county apparently recovered quickly from the Black Death (1346-8) and until the 18th cent. was one of the most thickly populated areas in Britain. Other areas overtook it, and its prosperity in the industrial and agricultural revolution which, however, did not depress it. Improved agriculture brought dairy farming and a cheese industry. The railways created Swindon with its locomotive and carriage works and brought engineering to Chippenham. Oceanic shipping indirectly created a tobacco industry at Devizes and rubber at Bradford on Avon and Melksham. The modern setback in Wiltshire history, however, arose from the agricultural depression which began after 1870 and lasted until after World War II. This brought about a net decline in the rural population.

WILTSHIRE, Es. of. *See* BOLEYN.

WIMBLEDON, originally a Surrey manor and then a fashionable London suburb. *See* TENNIS-2.

WIMBLEDON, Ld. *See* CECIL-6.

WIMBORNE MINSTER (Dorset). Cuthburgha and Cwenburh, sisters of K. Ine, founded a famous nunnery in 718 and in 871 K. Ethelred I was buried there. In about 1010 the whole place was destroyed by the Danes and Edward the Confessor replaced the nunnery by a college of secular canons; this became a royal free chapel to which, in 1496, Lady Margaret Beaufort added a chantry and seminary. This establishment was dissolved in 1547 but refounded as a grammar school in 1560. It remained a royal peculiar until 1846.

WINCHELSEA (Sussex), an important Cinque Port, was overwhelmed by the sea in 1297. Edward I built a new town on a spur 3 miles to the north by a large inlet which by 1500 had silted up. The population soon drifted away. The vaults for the Gascony wine trade were thereafter used extensively for smuggling (its only remaining industry) but it was represented in Parliament from 1386 to 1832.

WINCHESTER or WINTON (Lat: VENTA BELGARUM, Welsh: CAER GWENT). (1) Urban settlement in the city or just outside it on St. Catherine's Hill and other downs, dates from c. 1000 B.C., the Itchen valley being fertile and well watered. The place became the chief town of the Belgae and of their Romano-British canton and had a clothworking industry. There is a mythical link with K. Arthur.

(2) When the Gewissae (W. Saxons) conquered Hampshire (5th-6th cent.) it naturally became their chief seat and in the late 7th cent. the see of their bishop. Its royal and episcopal importance grew with that of the W. Saxon kings. K. Alfred founded Hyde Abbey (The Minster) where he was buried; his court and church were important centres of learning; and from his time, if not earlier, the royal treasure was kept there. The Saxon cathedral was built and enlarged by such famous men as Sts. Swithun (Bp. 852-62), Ethelwold (Bp. 963-84) and Alphege (Bp. 984-1005). Insofar as England had a capital, Winchester occupied the position; and this continued in the prosperity after the Conquest. There was easy communication down the Itchen via Southampton to Normandy and to the I. of Wight for building stone; there was a royal palace; the Kings' hunting grounds in the New Forest were not far off and one of the three yearly ceremonial courts was held at Winchester. The town's special position is suggested by its omission (with London) from Domesday.

(3) The prosperity was based upon the woollen and related trades and is evidenced by the extensive buildings of the time. In addition to a palace the Kings built a castle at the top of the town, which they refortified, while rather later the bishops built another, much larger, castle-palace (Wolvesey) at the bottom and they, especially Walkelin (Bp. 1070-98), rebuilt the cathedral on a large scale.

(4) The govt. of the city was shared between the bishop, who had a privileged enclave around the cathedral and was its titular abbot, and the Guild Merchant, which probably replaced a Saxon *cnihts* (Knights) guild, and which performed the function of a city corporation down to 1834. The right to keep order was thus vested in the main trading body, with the exception of the three weeks period of the St. Giles Fair, when under a charter of William Rufus the entire management, policing and justice of the town were handed over to the bishop. The St. Giles Fair was an international event and this privilege was lucrative. The presence of the royal treasury was important in the local exchange operations, especially at the fair, and it attracted a large well known and respected colony of Jews.

(5) The prosperity continued to increase throughout the 12th, 13th and 14th cents. though the rate of increase was checked by the damage done in the civil wars under K. Stephen and by the loss of Normandy under John. All the same Henry of Blois (Bp. 1129-71) completed Wolvesey and began the remarkable hospital of St. Cross; William of Edington (Bp. 1346-66) and William of Wykeham (Bp. 1367-1404) rebuilt the cathedral again and made it one of the most splendid and the longest in Christendom; Wykeham also built the College and Card. Beaufort (Bp. 1405-47) enlarged and embellished St. Cross and other buildings. In fact the bishopric at this period was a statesman's rich reward or the foundation of his power.

(6) The town's decline was connected with the rise of London, which resulted in the transfer of govt. institutions there and by shifts in the trade pattern which interrupted the prosperity of Tudor Southampton. Mary I and Philip of Spain were married in the Cathedral because it was convenient for Philip's arrival at that port. It was already only a rural centre when Cromwell besieged and bombarded it in the civil war.

(7) Attempts after the Restoration to make good the economic difficulties and, incidentally, the damage by canalising the Itchen and building a royal residence failed mainly because Southampton would not revive. Stagnation continued until after World War II when an extensive tourist industry began to develop.

WINCHESTER COLLEGE founded in 1382 by William of Wykeham, was opened together with NEW COLLEGE, Oxford, in 1394 to which it was designed to supply undergraduates. The curriculum, method of promotion, system of discipline through prefects, encouragement of outdoor exercise and attachment of outsiders or commoners for education alongside the scholars, formed the basis from which later public schools were developed. Moreover entry was not confined to local families. The College still had a considerable reputation in Elizabethan times but, like many other such institutions, fell on evil days especially towards the end of the 18th cent. when there were several rebellions (*see* WARTON). It was reorganised in 1868-9 and intelligent stewardship soon made the scholarships so valuable that intense competition gave it a supreme reputation among public schools for learning. The connection with New College was broken in the 1980s.

WINCHESTER, Marquesses of. *See* PAULET; BASING HOUSE.

WINCHESTER, ORDINANCE OF (Sept. 1265) (*see* BARONS' WAR) was made the day after peace was declared. The property of every accomplice of the late E. Simon de Montfort was to be taken into the King's hands and any already seized by others was to be surrendered to the King. Knights were appointed in each shire to make extents of these lands. Since Henry III had made some prospective grants and now precipitately made new ones to his followers, the Ordinance operated, not as an administrative standstill, but as a transfer of loot from one party to another. It was locally resisted; it confused the settlement of legitimate wartime transactions and the trial of post-war cases of robbery and other violence, it caused the organised bodies of rebels to withhold their surrender and prolong the war by over a year. *See* KENILWORTH, DICTUM OF.

WINCHESTER, STATUTE OF (1285) imposed collective fines upon counties and hundreds which did not produce a felon within 40 days of the felony, imposed curfews from 9 p.m. until sunrise and enjoined the clearance of cover within 200 feet of major highways. An inquiry into its administration was ordered in 1306.

WINCHILSEA, Earls of. *See* FINCH and FINCH-HATTON; QUINCY.

WINCHILSEY, Robert of (?-1313) was Chancellor of Oxford University in 1288, elected Abp. of Canterbury in 1293 and received his pallium at Rome in 1294. The delay was due to papal interregna and he reached England in Jan. 1295. His predecessor, Pecham, had helped Edward I in the creation of constitutional machinery for raising taxes and Edward's needs due to Welsh and Aquitanian wars and a threat of French invasion, in Winchilsey's absence, were pressing. He had summoned the clergy himself and had bullied them into granting a subsidy. Winchilsey was anxious to be helpful. His time abroad had opened his eyes to Edward's difficulties. The King needed still more money and proposed to summon the clergy to a full parliament at Bury St. Edmunds for Nov. 1296. Unfortunately Boniface VIII issued the bull *Clericis Laicos* in Feb. and Winchilsey was bound to resist the financial demands. Edward understood his dilemma and a year was allowed for debate. Convocation (Jan. 1297) could find no way out and decided to resist taxation. Edward levied it nonetheless. Winchilsey excom-municated those who touched church property but was assisted by the publication of the bull *Etsi de Statu*. The issue now became entangled with the *Confirmatio Cartarum* crisis, in which Winchilsey and the magnates acted together, and they continued to press the King for the next three years. Edward was by now an elderly, embittered and thwarted widower who felt that Winchilsey was the prime cause of his difficulties. Bishops in royal service (e.g. Winchester) were encouraged to obtain papal immunity from his jurisdiction. In 1305 the Aquitainian Bertrand Got was elected Pope as Clement V and Edward sent Walter Langton, Bp. of Coventry, his principal minister to Clement, to demand Winchilsey's removal. The archbishop was suspended, left England and returned only at the request of Edward II in 1308. As a churchman and an associate of elder statesmen he found Piers Gaveston's affair with Edward intolerable, supported the opposition and was one of the Ordainers in 1310. Consequently he excom-municated Gaveston when he returned in 1312. Winchilsey's death greatly strengthened Edward. His manner being brusque and sometimes ill-tempered and his attitude being determined and principled, he was not popular.

WINDEYER. (1) Charles (1780-1855) was the first recognised parliamentary correspondent. He migrated to

Australia and his son **(2) Richard** (1806-47) became a member of the N.S.W. legislature in 1843 and advocated popular as well as bureaucratic govt. His son **(3) Sir William Charles (1834-97)** became a N.S.W. Liberal M.P. in 1859, sol-gen. in 1870 and att-gen. from 1877 to 1879 when he became a judge.

WINDHAM, William (1750-1810) a friend of Burke and Dr. Johnson, was sec. to the Lord Lieut. of Ireland in 1783 and M.P. for Norwich from 1784 to 1802. He was one of the managers of Warren Hastings' impeachment but in 1794 became Sec. at War in Pitt's Cabinet. He was opposed to the P. of Amiens and he and Wm. Cobbett founded the *Political Register*. From 1802 to 1806 he was M.P. for St. Mawes, in 1806 for New Romney when he became Sec. of State for War and Colonies until 1807. He improved the principles of the military administration but, being himself not a good administrator, his reforms had little effect. From 1807 he was M.P. for Higham Ferrers.

WINDMILLS. The earliest, dating from the late 12th cent., were post mills whose sails and machinery were mounted on a housing or body pivoting as a whole on a central post and turned to face the wind by hand. Such mills could be used only for grinding corn. The tower mill, invented in Holland, came into use in England in the mid 14th cent. Tower mill machinery is housed in a stationary tower, surmounted by a cap which supports the sails and which alone is turned. Such mills are easier to handle and more versatile; they made large scale fen pumping feasible. All windmills needed constant supervision to keep them facing the wind: Edmund Lee, however, invented the tail fan in 1745. This turned the cap by a ratchet mechanism whenever the wind caught it. The sails remained of canvas drawn by hand across a wooden framework and were dangerous and difficult to handle in a high wind, but in 1772 Andrew Meikle invented the spring sail, a sort of venetian blind closed by springs of adjustable tension which would automatically spill the wind if it became too strong. A better version using weights and levers was introduced by Sir William Cubitt in 1807. At this period there were some 10,000 windmills in use but better designed drainage and steam power was beginning to make inroads, as well as the huge international flour milling businesses at Budapest which had taken over the markets by 1900.

"WIND OF CHANGE". Harold Macmillan's striking phrase about resurgent indigenous consciousness in a speech to the S. African Parliament in Feb. 1960. It was a warning that S. Africa could not survive indefinitely as a stubbornly racialist state.

WINDOW TAX was first imposed in 1796 upon houses with more than nine windows, the rate as well as the amount rising with the number of windows. It was obvious to assess, required no entry by officials into private houses and was easy to collect. The poor were seldom liable at all. It varied from time to time and had a noticeable effect on architecture. It was repealed in 1851. *See* MONTAGU-HALIFAX.

WINDSCALE or SELLAFIELD (Cumbria). In Oct. 1957 a fire at the plutonium plant here spread radiation over adjacent areas, and some deaths were attributed to long term exposure to it.

WINDSOR. Old Windsor was a Saxon royal manor and hunting lodge which Edward the Confessor gave to Westminster Abbey. King Harold built a fort on the bluff at Clewer and William I a castle which he called New Windsor. The town grew up around this castle, which sustained its only siege in 1216, and was progressively extended as a fortress-palace by Henry II, Henry III and Edward III. The town was first chartered in 1277 but there had already been a market there for some time. The castle, owing to its great strength, had virtually no military history but Edward III held a celebrated tournament there in 1344 and established the Order of

the Garter there four years later. The splendid St. George's Chapel was built for it by Edward IV in about 1475 and then given its collegiate constitution. Charles II partly remodelled the royal apartments but it was George IV who made a true palace out of it. There was a serious fire in the 1980s.

WINDSOR. Surname of the Royal Family since 1917.

WINDSOR, Ts. (1506) were signed between Henry VII and Philip of Burgundy who, on his way to Spain, had been driven into Melcombe Regis by a storm. **(1) Feb.** Each party agreed to maintain the other in his actual and rightful dominions, to arrest and, on demand, hand over the other's rebels and not to make peace separately in any joint war. This closed the Low Countries to the Yorkists without imposing any important obligation on Henry. **(2) Mar.** Philip was to support a marriage between Henry and Philip's niece, Margaret of Savoy. This treaty was ineffectual because Margaret refused to marry Henry. *See also* MALUS INTERCURSUS; SPAIN; HABSBURG.

WINDSOR, T. of (Oct. 1899) was a secret Anglo-Portuguese declaration reviving the ancient alliances and therefore imposing upon Portugal an obligation to close the Delagoa Bay-Pretoria railway to arms traffic for the Boers, who had just attacked the British colonies.

WINDWARD Is., BRITISH, though separate colonies, shared the same governor. From 1833 St. Lucia, St. Vincent, Grenada and Tobago were under the gov. of Barbados. In 1875 an attempt was made to federate the isles with Barbados but the Barbadians frustrated this. From 1885 the governorship was separated from Barbados. In 1889 Tobago was transferred to Trinidad and in 1940 Dominica from the Leeward Is. to the Windwards. They entered the W. Indies Federation separately in 1958 and became associated states with Britain in 1970. In 1979 St. Lucia became the first to gain its independence.

WINEBALD, St. *See* MISSIONS TO EUROPE-3.

WINEFRID or GWENFREWI, St. (7th cent.), an apparently unimportant Welsh virgin and niece of St. Beuno, became the object of a widespread mediaeval cult and of pilgrimages to Shrewsbury and her miraculous spring at Holywell (Flint). These were encouraged by Roger Walden and Henry Chichele, Abps. of Canterbury, and performed among others by Henry V and Edward IV. Lady Margaret Beaufort built a chapel at Holywell after the B. of Bosworth in 1485. There were special arrangements for pilgrims and a guesthouse at Ludlow. The cures and pilgrimages continued on a large scale after the Reformation and were witnessed by Dr. Johnson in 1774. They brought much prosperity to the area which was an important centre of recusancy.

WINE TRADE (1) Importation became a major English business and developed an Anglicised nomenclature. It was probably established at least from the 11th cent. and in the middle ages wine was popular and comparatively cheap (as late as 1610 six carpenters refused to pay 7d for a quart of claret at the Queen's Head, Cripplegate) but had to be drunk quickly so that mediaeval claret was unmatured. It probably lasted longer than Ale (*see* ALE AND BEER and also paras 5 and 6 below).

(2) The trade in French wines was established before Henry II's marriage (1152) to Eleanor of Aquitaine brought these vineyards under English political influence. It began mostly with Poitevin wines through La Rochelle until 1224 when the French annexed the port but thereafter Bordeaux wines predominated. This *Claret* (Fr: *Clairette*) trade had, by the 14th cent., reached 90,000 tuns and even in 1415 it still amounted to 38,000 tuns despite the wars. It was virtually monopolised by English merchants who shipped mainly to Bristol, but most ports as far north as Hull handled it, especially Southampton and London. The loss of Bordeaux (1451-3) halted the traffic, which was resumed on a reduced scale from the 1480s. French shippers then handled much of it, English monopolists having suffered in the Wars of the Roses. Thereafter it was seriously interrupted only in the 18th cent. and Napoleonic wars and in World War II.

(3) The trade in sweet wines was originally incidental to seaborne trade in other goods. *Malmsey* or Malvoisie (from Monemvasia, a Peloponnesian port) and *Sherry* (from Xeres near Cadiz) or Sack came in the 15th cent. with Venetian and Genoese ships to Southampton; Portuguese wines to Dover and London perhaps a little earlier by Hanseatic shipping. Canary and Madeira wines were stowed in 16th and 17th cents. as additional cargo on returning Indiamen. The development of the British and Dutch E. India trade and the collapse of the Hanse (15th cent) and Venice (16th cent.) extended these practices to Sherry and especially to the *Port* (from Oporto) trade, soon favoured by the Methuen treaty and substantially in English hands.

(4) Rhenish and Moselle wines (later known from *Hochheim* as *Hock*) were brought down river from the 15th cent. by the Hanse and the Dutch direct to London. This trade was much interrupted by wars involving the Low Countries and the Rhineland. In any event the climate made wine production on the Rhine and its tributaries more expensive and intermittent than elsewhere.

(5) Primitive vinification and poor barrels caused much wine to spoil and, in the absence of glass bottles, once started, it had to be drunk quickly. Hence the many recipes for the use of spoilt wine and the tremendous drinking bouts of the 16-18th cents. The production of cheap glass bottles and the cultivation of cork oaks at vineyards in the late 18th cent. facilitated, for the first time, the laying down of wine, the establishment of vintages and the drinking by the individual of more quality and less quantity and resulted in 18th and 19th cent. gentlemen's houses being built with wine cellars.

(6) Many of the technical improvements applied as much to beer as to wine but beer, being brewed in Britain, was relatively cheap and the supply not interrupted by wars. As the population rose, the proportion of beer drinkers rose too (leaving the wine trade stationary) and this was assisted by the heavy taxation stringencies from the turn of the 20th cent. and by shipping stringencies in the World Wars. After 1960, however, the habit of package holidays in Europe began to spread the taste for wine again, wine bars and wine imports rapidly increased and were still increasing in 1990. *See* KNATCHBULL-HUGESSON.

WINGATE, Orde Charles (1903-44) in the late 1930s created Jewish *night squads* to protect Palestinian pipelines against sabotage. *See* CHINDITS. In 1940 he organised Abyssinian resistance on Italy entering World War II and accompanied the Emperor Haile Selassie on his return to Addis Ababa (Jan-May 1941). He then proposed the formation of Long Range Penetration Groups to operate behind the Japanese in Burma and commanded one such in Feb.-Mar. 1943. In Mar. 1944 he was killed while leading a similar but much larger operation. *See* CHINDITS.

WINGFIELD. Three brothers **(1) Sir Richard (?1469-1525)** was with Sir Edward Poynings in the negotiations on the Holy League of 1512 and also held a succession of offices at Calais until 1519 during which time he was employed in diplomacy at Brussels and Antwerp (1513) and in connection with royal marriage negotiations (1514-5), to Paris (1515) and again to Brussels (1516). As English Ambassador in Paris he acted as mediator in the Franco-Habsburg disputes of 1521-3. **(2) Sir Robert (?146?-1539)**, also a diplomat and Calais official, was sent on missions to the Emperor and the papacy and also to Brussels from 1522 to 1526. **(3) Sir Humphrey (d. 1545)**, barrister, was sheriff of Norfolk and Suffolk in 1520, a member of the Council from 1526, M.P. for Great Yarmouth from 1529 and Speaker from 1533 to 1536. His nephew **(4) Sir Anthony (?1485-1552)** was a Suffolk

M.P. (1529-35 and 1547-52). He was Vice-Chamberlain and Capt. of the Guard; as such he arrested Somerset in 1549. He was comptroller of the Household from 1550. His grandson **(5) Sir John (?-1596)** was a Capt. of Foot in Leicester's Walcheren Expedition (1585), master of ordnance in Brittany (1591) and was killed as Essex's campmaster at Cadiz. His brother **(6) Anthony (?1550-1615)** was Greek reader to Elizabeth I and was with Lord Willoughby's Danish Embassy in 1582. **(7) Sir Richard (?-1634) 1st Vist. (Ir.) POWERSCOURT (1619)** served in the Netherlands, Breton and Cadiz expeditions but from 1600 his work lay wholly in Ireland, where he settled.

WINNIPEG. *See* CANADA, D.

WINSTANLEY, Gerrard (?-1652) a prolific leveller pamphleteer, led a party to cultivate the waste at St. George's Hill, Walton-on-Thames, asserting that this was the people's right.

WINTER OF DISCONTENT (1978-9). Phrase borrowed by the Tories from the first line of Shakespeare's *Richard III* to characterise the coincidence of extreme cold and a succession of strikes against the Callaghan govt's. 5% pay-rise limit. It decisively influenced the election of 1979 in favour of the Tories.

WINTER or WYNTER. (1) Sir William (?-1589) Surveyor of the Navy from 1549 and master of naval ordnance from 1557, bore much credit for the nature of the new English fleet. He commanded the Forth blockade in 1559, the attack on Le Havre in 1563 and the Dover squadron in the Armada campaign. He was on bad terms with the Hawkinses. His son married a daughter of the E. of Worcester, by whom he had **(2) Sir John (?1600-?73)**. He gave large sums to Charles I who sold him the mining rights in the Forest of Dean. He fought as a royalist in the Civil War and during his parliamentary imprisonment from 1650 to 1653 conducted experiments in the production of coke; for this he got a monopoly at the Restoration and so became a successful mineowner in the Forest of Dean until his death.

WINTER or WINTOUR, Robert (?-1606) and **Thomas (1572-1606)** were active members of the Guy Fawkes conspiracy and both executed.

WINTHROP (1) John (1588-1649), an attorney, went to Massachusetts in 1630, being given acting gubernatorial powers by Gov. Endecott and founded Boston. He was elected gov. in 1631 and 1632, life councillor in 1636 and gov. again in 1637, 1642 and 1646. His *Journal* (1630-49) was published in 1825. His son **(2) John (1606-76)** joined his father in 1631 and became gov. of the New River Settlement in 1632. This was absorbed into Connecticut, of which he became a magistrate in 1651. In 1659 he was deputy gov. of Connecticut and from 1660 to 1667 gov.

WINTON, an alternative name for Winchester still to be seen on old milestones.

WIRELESS. *See* BROADCASTING.

WISCONSIN (U.S.A.), visited by French explorers in 1634, was settled in the 1660s. By 1690 it was dotted with their fortified and trading posts. Prosperity was checked by Indian wars from 1712 to 1740 and by the Seven Years' War, in which the Indians supported the British. It was ceded to Britain in 1763 and the population was loyalist during the American rebellion. It passed to the U.S.A. in 1783 but British military posts were not evacuated until 1796 and the British continued to exploit the fur trade until 1816. Admitted to the Union as a state in 1848, it supported the Federals in the Civil War.

WISEMAN, Nicholas Patrick Stephen (1802-65) Card. (1850). Born in Spain, this learned priest was engaged in orientalist studies in Rome until 1828, when he became Rector of the English College. In 1835 he came to the U.K., founded the *Dublin Review* in 1836 and in 1839 became Bp-coadjutor of the English Central district. In 1848 he undertook a papal diplomatic approach to

Palmerston; in 1849 he was vicar-apostolic; and from 1850 Abp. of Westminster. He left a great body of literary work and criticism and was the principal refounder of the R. Catholic organisation in England.

WISHART, George (?1513-46), a Montrose schoolmaster, fled from Scotland as a heretic but returned and preached vigorously all over the Lowlands from 1543. He taught and befriended John Knox in 1544. In 1546 he was arrested by Bothwell and burned.

WITAN-AGEMOT (A.S. Witan = wise man, Gemot = assembly) (1) Receiving the advice of leading figures is a natural feature of all rule. Anglo-Saxon Kings might summon the *witan* to debate important issues of state or major local disputes or for a festivity. There was no right to or regularity of summons, the *gemot* being essentially *ad hoc* and a practical supplement to the business of daily administration in the royal household. As an assembly of powerful lay and church leaders it could, on occasions such as a disputed succession or under a weak or unpopular king, wield great influence but this was personal to the members present as magnates and was not institutional. The *witangemot* of the late Anglo-Saxons is recognisable in the *curia regis* of the Normans in its informal as well as occasionally ceremonial role. Counsel was central to good kingship: Etheldred II was called *unraed,* without counsel. Harald Hardraada was hard to advise.

(2) The Kings of Essex, Kent, Mercia, Northumbria, Sussex and Wessex and the under-Kings of the Hwiccas certainly had witans, to whose *gemots* they summoned their more important people and over which they presided. They were important: for example they might mark a chronological era, but not large. An 11th cent. witan even for all England seldom reached a membership of 100. Before the Danish wars it might happen that several witans met together, e.g. that of Wessex and Essex in 680, Mercia, Kent and Wessex in 705 and Mercia and Kent in 756. When Wessex became supreme its Kings assembled *witans* from all areas but the older surviving submonarchies still had their own, e.g. Kentish *gemots* were held in 809 and 842, Mercian *gemots* by royal licence in 809, 842, 896 and 950. In 1004 an E. Anglian witan agreed separately to pay tribute to the Danes; in 1065 a Northumbrian witan deposed its earl.

(3) High rank or important office were indispensable for summons and these were held for life and conferred by the King; but it did not follow that everyone who had been summoned had a right to be summoned again. Some such as the greater earldormen, the bishops, the court chaplain, high court officers were inevitably summoned; others might be called only a few times or even once; including a representative of the town of meeting. Royal ladies were sometimes included.

(4) Witans met at least once a year between 920 and 1066 and commonly more often. The most usual date was Easter, followed by Christmas and then Whitsun but there were many single occasions on other dates. Of the 116 named meeting places 20 have not been identified and 76 occur only once. Such places would in any case be well known, often perhaps ancient pagan, sites. They included rocks, hills, meadows and famous trees, for some meetings were held in the open. Some 50 were at royal estates or residences or at royal foundations. Between 811 and 1044, 13 were in London, between 1044 and 1066, nine. There were 10 at Winchester and three at Gloucester between 811 and 1066. Meetings lasted several days and though the records were usually drawn up by clerics in Latin, English was spoken. Voting, when it took place, did not necessarily result in a majority decision by heads; power counted. There was invariably a banquet. The members were specially protected during *gemots* by a doubling of their *wergild.*

(5) The main types of ordinary business transacted at a *gemot* were the settlement of judicial disputes between magnates, the passing of legislation, the granting of charters, lands and approval of taxation on the King's motion and political discussions, often related to these matters. In addition there were other less usual but momentous types of business. When a King died the witan elected his successor from among his relatives, unless he had already caused them to do so in his lifetime. Several kings (e.g. Sigeberht of Wessex in 755, Ethelwald of Northumbria in 765) were deposed by their witans. The witan sometimes agreed foreign treaties (e.g. the peace with Normandy in 990) and dealings with the church and papacy including the nomination or confirmation of prelates. In later times appointments to ealdermanries were made in it.

(6) Ecclesiastical transactions by an ecclesiastical synod were sometimes confirmed by a witan perhaps sitting at the same place and period, for membership of the two bodies was partly interchangeable.

(7) The word *witan* continued to be used well into the 12th cent. for the King's *curia* and continuity was assumed, but its character changed in the face of feudalism and the despotic nature of the Norman royal incursion into Anglo-Saxon society.

WITCHCRAFT, insofar as definable, is the practice of contracting or compelling occult forces to act upon a person other than a witch. The forces might, for example, be old pre-Christian gods (equating the practice with heathenism) and belief in the practice doubtless arose to explain, in the existing state of knowledge, otherwise inexplicable events. The Fathers of the Church were sceptical and canon law moderate on the subject but in 1486 the German Dominicans Kraemer and Sprenger published *Malleus Maleficarum* (Lat: The Hammer of Evil Women) in which they elaborated a theory that witches' powers arose from links or compacts with the Devil. Persecutions, official and related to heresy and popular and prurient, soon began. Witches were also suspected of mundane activities such as abortion. Between 1542 and 1547 it was a felony and English and Scottish Acts of 1563 made it capital. James VI and I believed in and wrote against witches. English popular fury occurred mainly in 1603-18 and 1642-9 when there were many hangings (*see* HOPKINS, MATTHEW). At Salem (Mass.) there was an outburst in 1692. Burning ended in 1712 in England and in 1722 in Scotland. Prosecutions were prohibited in 1736. *See* MAGIC.

WITE (A.S.) A penalty payable to the King.

WITNEY (Oxon) drew wool from the neighbouring Cotswold sheep runs for its ancient woollen, particularly blanket making, industry which was already in existence in the 10th cent. The manor was an important property of the see of Winchester until leased to the Ds. of Marlborough in the 18th cent.

WITTELSBACH. *See* BAVARIA AND PALATINATE.

WITTENBERG. *See* LUTHER.

WITWATERSRAND or simply THE RAND (S. Transvaal) (which includes JOHANNESBURG) is a gold-bearing 1000 ft. ridge about 130 miles long, which has been worked since 1885 and had produced annually about a third of the world's gold. The local prosperity attracted many other industries and the area was by 1970 almost continuously built-up.

WOAD. A blue dye made from the fermented leaves of *Isatis Tinctoria* much cultivated, particularly near Toulouse, until superseded by indigo. The Celts used it for personal decoration.

WOBURN ABBEY (Beds.) the seat of the Ds. of Bedford, was built largely by Henry Flitcroft (1697-1769) out of the remains of a former Cistercian Abbey.

WODEHOUSE, John (1826-1902) 3rd Ld. WODEHOUSE (1846) 1st E. of KIMBERLEY (1866) was Foreign U/Sec. of State from 1852 to 1856, ambassador at St. Petersburg until 1858 and then Foreign U/Sec. again until 1861. In 1863 he was in Sehleswig Holstein and from 1864 to

1866, as Lord Lieut. of Ireland, he had to deal with the Fenians. He was in the Gladstone Cabinet as Lord Privy Seal from 1868 to 1870 and then Colonial Sec. until 1874. Hence the name of Kimberley (S. Africa) which was annexed with Griqualand West in 1871. Cape Colony secured responsible govt. in 1872. He despatched the Ashanti expedition of 1873; converted Rupert's Land into Manitoba and brought British Columbia under Canada. He held the same office from 1880 to 1885 and in 1886 but he had to manage some of the Home Office business in the Lords, especially the franchise and redistribution legislation. He became Liberal leader in the Lords in 1891, held the Presidency of the Council and the India Office from 1892 to 1894 and then became Lord Rosebery's Foreign Sec. As such he signed the Congo Treaty of 1894.

WOFFINGTON, Peg (?1714-60) came to Covent Garden as an actress in 1740 from Dublin and remained in the public eye until 1751. She had many lovers including Garrick and ended with a quarrel (on stage) with the playwright Mrs Bellamy, whom she stabbed (off stage).

WOGAN, A Brecon family which moved to Pembroke after marriage with the heiress of Wizo, a Fleming. **(1) Sir John (?- 1321)** was introduced by William of Valence, E. of Pembroke, to Edward I who, in 1285, encouraged him to go to Ireland. By 1295, as C.J. and gov. of Ireland, he enforced a truce between the Burkes and the Geraldines and made the Kilkenny parliament pass enactments against the use of Irish names by English settlers. He was a strong and effective ruler until 1312 during which time the country was peaceful enough for him to be able to lead expeditions to Scotland in 1296 and 1300. **(2) Thomas (?-after 1666),** one of the regicides, was excepted from execution at the Restoration, escaped to Holland and disappeared.

WOKINGHAM (Berks.) originally OAKINGHAM or OCKINGHAM, was the head town and market of Windsor Forest from the Conquest until the late 18th cent. Bull baiting survived there until 1821.

WOLCOT, John (1738-1819) physician and, from 1778, satirist under the name of *Peter Pinclar* attacked, *inter alios,* George III and the court.

WOLFE, James (1727-59) was Mordaunt's brigade major in the Netherlands in 1747 and took command of the 20th Foot in 1750. He studied in Paris in 1753 and then introduced a new drill and manoeuvre system, which was widely copied and long practised. In 1757 he was Q.M.G. in Ireland. In 1758 he was Mordaunt's Q.M.G. in the attack on Rochefort and then brig-gen. in the expedition against Louisbourg. In 1759 he was appointed to command the St. Lawrence expedition and was killed in Sept. at the moment of victory at Quebec. *See* CANADA-9; SEVEN YEARS' WAR-8.

WOLFENDEN, Sir John Frederick (1906-85) Ld. WOLFENDEN (1974). Witty headmaster of Uppingham (1934) and of Shrewsbury (1944), V-Chanc. of Reading Univ. (1950-63) presided over the sensational Home Office Committee on homosexuality and prostitution. Its report was published in 1957 Legislation on the first confused the law; on the second, degraded the practitioners.

WOLSELEY. (1) Sir Charles (?1630-1714) M.P. in 1653, was a member of both Councils of State and in 1657 of Cromwell's House of Lords. In 1660 he was a member of the Convention Parliament and pardoned at the Restoration. His brother **(2) William (?1640-97),** a soldier, took a leading part in the Irish campaign of 1689 to 1691 and ended as a Lord Justice in Ireland in 1696.

WOLSELEY, Sir Garnet Joseph (1833-1913) 1st Ld. (1882) and Vist. (1885) WOLSELEY commanded the Red R. expedition against Louis Riel in 1870 and the victorious Ashanti expedition of 1873-4. He was the first administrator of Cyprus in 1878. In 1879 he was sent to retrieve the situation in the Zulu war and captured Cetewayo. He then established the Zululand and Transvaal colonial administrations. In 1880 he became Q.M.G. and in 1882 Adj-Gen. His policy of preparation for war was carried through against opposition from the C-in-C, the D. of Cambridge. In 1882 he crushed Arabi Pasha's revolt in Egypt and in 1884-5 led a campaign to relieve Gordon. He was C-in-C in Ireland from 1890 to 1895 and C-in-C from 1895 to 1899. A perfectionist with an eye for the important, he was the modern recreator of the British Army. "All Sir Garnet" was a military equivalent of "Shipshape and Bristol fashion".

WOLSEY, Thomas (1472 or 3-1530) Abp. of YORK (1514) Card. (1515) Legate (1518) (1) Son of an aggressive Ipswich butcher began brilliantly at Magdalen College, Oxford, where he took his B.A. in 1487. He was ordained on becoming a fellow in 1497. Through the influence of the sons, at Magdalen College School, of the M. of Dorset he secured the latter's patronage. After Dorset died (1501) he became Chaplain to Henry Deane, Abp. of Canterbury, and at Deane's death (1503) to Sir Richard Nanfan, Deputy Lieut. of Calais. Nanfan was old and ill and Wolsey did his work; Calais was his early school in politics and administration. Nanfan commended him to Henry VII whose chaplain he became in 1507. He became Dean of Lincoln in 1509. Henry's death in that year and the unpopularity of his protégés failed to restrain Wolsey's skilled careerism. He already knew the new King and on Richard Fox's nomination he immediately became Royal Almoner, a member of the Council and in 1513 Dean of Hereford. During the Scottish war of 1512-4 (B. of Flodden 1513) he contrived to become Dean of York while managing the administration of the war. His success was rewarded with the bishopries of Lincoln and Tournai and when Card. Bainbridge, Abp. of York, was poisoned in Rome he exchanged Lincoln for his archbishopric and helped himself to Bainbridge's estate to pay the dues (1514). Despite the Lateran Council's prohibition of *commendams* he retained Tournai until 1518 and held Bath and Wells (1518) and then, by exchange, the successively richer sees of Durham (1524) and Winchester (1529). He also obtained the wealthy abbacy of St. Albans and had the profits of Salisbury, Worcester and Llandaff, paying their Italian bishops fixed allowances. In 1515, by constant interference in the King's name, he supplanted Abp. Warham as Lord Chancellor and added the fees of that lucrative office to his riches. Besides York House (Whitehall), his London residence, he had Moor Park and Cawood and between 1514 and 1520 he built Hampton Court where he could entertain 300 guests. He encouraged ecclesiastical splendour but lived as a renaissance magnate, preferring riding clothes to vestments and the body of his mistress to that of Christ.

(2) As Warham was unlikely to die, Wolsey meant to override him. As a cardinal he would outrank him. As Legate *a latere* he might rule the English church. The Cardinal's hat arrived in 1515. The legation was another matter. Meanwhile as Chancellor he activated the Star Chamber and Court of Requests (then popular) while as cardinal he began to interfere with diocesan patronage. Govt. was moving towards a centralised, if surrogate, autocracy.

(3) Wolsey knew how to make Henry think as he did himself, so long as others were kept away from the royal ear. They were alike in their colourful ruthlessness and ambition. As a King, Henry was an international figure by birth; Wolsey was one by virtue of his rank. As Henry's chief minister he conducted foreign policy. He hoped to make his master the greatest of Kings, perhaps Emperor, but he shaped his diplomacy to serve his own ambitions, first to secure the legation for life and then to become Pope. The Anglo-French peace and marriage treaty of Aug. 1514 was his first major achievement. It did not last, for Louis XII died in Dec. and Francis I, having suborned Scotland and allied himself with Burgundy to keep England busy, invaded Italy. Wolsey hired expensive mercenaries for Francis' opponent, the Emperor, who left them in the lurch and came to terms (T. of Noyon 1516) and in Mar. 1517 agreed with France and Spain on a partition of Italy. Wolsey's efforts to ingratiate himself with the Papacy seemed to have failed. In fact the new combination broke up and by 1518 he was being courted by all parties. Card. Campeggio arrived outside Calais to negotiate on the Pope's behalf for a European peace and alliance against the increasingly threatening Turks. Wolsey, by keeping him waiting beyond the Pale for months, forced the Pope to associate him with Campeggio as legate. Thereafter successive extensions of his commission achieved his first objective. The treaty, signed at London, gave him European prestige.

(4) Political conditions were changing beyond conventional experience. Luther's XCV Theses (1517) coincided with a time of economic recession and inflation, while the Turks hammered on the land and sea frontiers of a disunited Christendom. The Emperor Maximilian died in 1519 and Charles V succeeded to a vast inheritance and, after a sharp diplomatic struggle with Francis I, was elected Emperor. In these convulsions the T. of London evaporated. The Habsburg and the Valois again courted England. 520 marked the watershed of Wolsey's fortunes. The Pope conferred on his master the resounding title of Defender of the Faith. Francis and Henry met at the Field of the Cloth of Gold, which Wolsey magnificently staged, and then the Emperor visited England.

(5) Charles V's visit forced Wolsey off the fence – aided by an imperial pension. English opinion was Francophobe and Wolsey committed England to an attack on France (1522-3) which was expensive and ineffectual; Charles had held out hopes of imperial support for Wolsey at the next papal election. In 1523 his candidature was canvassed. He received only seven votes. Meanwhile the Cardinal was alienating many sections of the public. He bullied the nobles in the Star Chamber; extracted forced loans from the mercantile community; attempted in person to browbeat the House of Commons; used his legatine powers to override episcopal patronage and monastic elections and publicly insulted Abp. Warham by sending for convocation (over which Warham presided) to attend him. His power now depended solely on the King, whom he was beginning to deceive. His expedients were not only failing to provide Henry with the sinews of magnificence but his so-called Amicable Grant of 1525 (a demand for one sixth of lay and one third of ecclesiastical movables) provoked a nationwide demonstration, similar to a general strike, which ended when, for the first time, the King publicly repudiated his minister's policy.

(6) Since 1524 Henry had worried about the succession, for Q. Catherine's only live child was Mary. The only English female succession, that of the Empress Matilda, was not an encouraging precedent and the collateral relatives had all died or been destroyed. Annulment and remarriage was the only solution but the necessary negotiations with the Papacy were now in the hands of a minister with a shaken reputation and, besides, they involved a diplomatic anomaly. The Queen was the Emperor's aunt. Legalism apart, the Papacy would never grant the necessary bulls if dominated by the Emperor. The annulment must therefore depend on the ability of England's enemy, France, to protect the Pope. It might, too, enmesh England in unpopular Italian wars. To bring *The King's Great Matter* to a fortunate outcome was virtually impossible even before Charles V captured Francis I at the B. of Pavia (1525) yet Wolsey had to persist because *The Great Matter* represented his surviving hold on power. In May 1527 he opened

collusive proceedings by summoning Henry before his legatine court to answer questions on the lawfulness of his marriage. This could be only a preliminary hearing because the matrimonial status of princes was always reserved to the Holy See. But Henry had fallen in love with Anne Boleyn (who hated Wolsey) and allowed himself to be convinced by academic canonists. In June he separated from the Queen on the pretext of mortal sin. It was at this point that the news of Charles V's occupation of Rome (and its mutinous sack by his unpaid troops) reached England. The Pope would never be free to proceed against the Emperor's aunt.

(7) The Cardinal now pursued desperate courses. On the ground that the Pope was sacrilegiously imprisoned, he would summon the cardinals to France and have the papal powers transferred to himself as Vicar-General. He would also stir the French to fresh efforts and offered to join them in the war. They had some initial success. Without telling Henry he sent a formal defiance to Charles V's court at Madrid. These moves failed. Only four cardinals joined him at Compiègne; the English would not fight and the French were routed at Landriano. Unknown to Wolsey the contestants were negotiating. Charles had deliberately allowed the Pope to escape (Dec. 1528) and came to terms with him (T. of Barcelona June 1529). The Ladies' Peace of Cambrai (June 1529) temporarily ended the Habsburg-Valois conflict. The Cardinal was outwitted.

(8) The legatine proceedings in England reflected his decline. While the French were having some success, the Pope had issued a decretal commission to Wolsey and Campeggio to hear the case and pronounce sentence. Campeggio had been long in coming and the court opened only in May 1529. Wolsey tried to expedite the matter but the continental events (para 7) had overtaken him. Campeggio adjourned until Oct. (on valid procedural grounds). Everyone knew that this was the end.

(9) The King had decided with Anne Boleyn's help. The hated Cardinal was too rich, too arrogant and too powerful. Henry wanted his power and needed his wealth, which equalled a third of the ordinary revenues of the Crown. In Oct. 1529 he was indicted for using his legatine powers contrary to the statutes of *Praemunire* and Provisors and offered the choice of answering in Parliament or in the King's Bench. Fearing a possible attainder in Parliament, he pleaded guilty in the King's Bench which could not sentence him to death. He received a pardon in Feb. 1530 and the return of some of his property and he was allowed to keep his archbishopric.

(10) He remained ambitious. He went north and planned a magnificent enthronement at York for Nov. He sought the aid of the French and Imperial courts and asked the Pope to prevent Henry from consorting with Anne Boleyn. The Pope merely forbade Henry to remarry while the annulment proceedings were pending. When the news reached England Henry knew or suspected Wolsey's part in it. He had him arrested but the Cardinal died at Leicester on the way to the Tower.

WOLSTENHOLME, Sir John (1562-1639), an incorporator of the HEIC in 1600, was a member of the Council of the Virginia Co. in 1609 and helped to finance the N.W. Passage exploration. In 1619 he was a navy commissioner, in 1624 a member of the Council for Virginia and in 1631 a commissioner for the plantation of Virginia. An associate of the 3rd E. of Southampton.

WOLVERHAMPTON (Staffs) grew up round a collegiate church founded by Wulfruna in 996. The church was well endowed and from 1204 until the Dissolution, the manor was held by its dean. From 1258 there was a weekly market and an annual fair and from 1510 a grammar school. The manor was given to the D. of Northumberland in 1553 but Mary I restored it to the college. Coal mining began in the 18th cent. and the place rapidly developed into an industrial town. In 1848 it was incorporated and in 1888 it became a county borough which was extended in 1927, 1933 and 1966.

WOLVERTON. See GLYN.

WOLVES, common in Anglo-Saxon times, were largely brought under control in the 10th cent. but persisted in small numbers in England until about 1580, in Scotland until 1743 and in Ireland until 1770.

WOMEN, EDUCATION OF. The 140 mediaeval English nunneries provided some education not exclusively for religious; renaissance courts and court personages educated their women, such as Lady Jane Grey and Q. Elizabeth I (who once blasted a Polish ambassador with unrehearsed invective in Latin) but in the 17th cent. there seems to have been a decline, if the propagandist works of Makins, Mary Astell and Daniel Defoe are any guide. A century later Mary Wollstonecraft (1759-97) and Erasmus Darwin were still complaining and John Stuart Mill published his *On the Subjection of Women* as late as 1869. All the same there were boarding schools for young ladies, sometimes of a showy superficiality, in 18th cent. towns, and influential people were interesting themselves in the matter. Amelia Murray and friends at King's College, London, opened Queen's College in 1848. Bedford College opened in 1849, Girton (near Hitchin) in 1869. Lady Stanley of Alderley, Emily Shirrett and Mary Gurney founded the National Union for the Education of Women in 1871 and the Girls Public Day School Co. (later Trust) opened its first school in 1873 and had 33 functioning in 1900. By 1914 Oxford had five colleges and Cambridge two.

WOMEN'S FRANCHISE (1) Women received the vote in local govt. elections in 1894 on the same terms as men. In 1918 the male franchise was extended and simplified and women received the local govt. franchise upon those same terms, but the parliamentary franchise only if they were over thirty. In 1928 both franchises were unified with the same age qualification as from May 1929.

(2) Women could be elected to parish and district councils from 1894, to borough and county councils from 1907 and to parliament from 1919. *See* FEMINISM.

WOMEN'S INSTITUTES originated in Canada in 1897; the first in Britain was founded in 1915 and the National Federation and movement inspired by Lady Denman were launched in 1916 as a successful means of self-help and self-education for women in villages.

WOMEN'S LABOUR REPRESENTATION COMMITTEE. *See* PANKHURST.

WOMEN'S LAND ARMY originally enrolled 18,000 women to work on the land in 1917. Disbanded at the end of World War I, it was quickly set up at the beginning of World War II and recruited and trained women in large numbers, the peak strength (Aug. 1943) being 80,000. It was disbanded in Nov. 1950.

WOMEN'S PROPERTY. Originally only single women of full age could own property. The N.T. derived doctrine (Matthew chap.19 v.5) that husband and wife were one, vested everything a woman possessed in her husband, including even her clothes and earnings after marriage. In real life subjection was often less and sometimes much less than this, since some men are more tolerant and some women less weak than others and in any ease a woman could always pledge her husband's credit for necessaries (unless she had committed adultery) for otherwise she could not manage the family household, and he had to pay any damages for which she was liable. Moreover, to prevent destitution a widow was entitled to dower amounting, as a rule to a third of her husband's property, during her life. The invention of the equitable use, a primitive form of trust, in the 14th cent. made it feasible to set aside property for a wife so that her husband had no power over it, by vesting the bare ownership in a trustee for her benefit, but this was rare

even among propertied people until Tudor times. It became, however, a feature of marriage agreements and family settlements after the Restoration.

With the institution of divorce in 1857 divorced and separated women became entitled to be treated as single in property matters, or their husband, if the guilty party, could be made to pay maintenance. In 1870 women became entitled to keep property owned before marriage and earnings after it. In 1882 they became entitled to acquire property during marriage and in 1893 to make contracts binding their separate property. In 1926 all women became entitled to deal with property on the same terms as men and in 1935 a married woman was enabled to deal with her property by will in the same way as a single woman. From 1970 on divorce the spouses had to share property acquired during marriage fairly. *See* FEMINISM.

WOMEN'S SOCIAL AND POLITICAL UNION. *See* PANKHURST.

WOMEN'S WAR SERVICES (1) AIR. A Women's Royal Air Force (W.R.A.F.) of World War I was reformed as the Women's Auxiliary Air Force (W.A.A.F.) in June 1939 and expanded into a very large body carrying on, *inter alia,* highly skilled operational ground activities in communications and plotting essential to defensive and offensive operations in all theatres. It was renamed W.R.A.F. in 1946. **(2) ARMY.** The Army Territorial Service (A.T.S.) was formed in 1938 and by the middle of World War II exceeded 100,000 serving in many operational capacities other than the actual handling of personal weapons in battle in every theatre save the Far East. **(3)** **CIVIL DEFENCE.** The Women's Royal Voluntary Service for Civil Defence (W.R.V.S.) was formed in June 1938 at Home Office instigation, initially in connection with air-raid precautions; but it soon expanded its scope to the manifold personal and welfare problems arising out of the pressure of war and the effects of bombing. **(4)** **NAVAL.** The Women's Royal Naval Service (W.R.N.S.) was a World War I organisation which was revived in 1939. A much smaller body than the others, its work included administration, cypher, meteorology, radio plotting and photographic interpretation.

WONDERFUL or MERCILESS PARLIAMENT. The parliament of Feb.-June 1388 in which the Lords Appellant prosecuted the supporters of Richard II.

WOOD. Yorkshire family **(1) Sir Charles (1800-85) 1st Vist. HALIFAX (1866)** as liberal M.P. from 1826 to 1866 mostly for Halifax, held minor office from 1832 to 1839 and was Lord John Russell's Ch. of the Exch. from 1846 to 1852. He hated new expenditure and new taxes so that, though a late convert to repealing the Corn Laws, he did nothing else to alleviate Irish distress. He did, however, approve the important Canadian railway loan and, more doubtfully, repealed the window tax in 1851. He was exceptionally well informed on India and as Aberdeen's Pres. of the Board of Control from Dec. 1852 was responsible for the India Act, 1853. In 1855 he became Palmerston's First Lord of the Admiralty and prevented naval reductions after the end of the Crimean War. In June 1859 he returned to the India Office, this time in the new post of Sec. of State, with the difficult task of adapting the Indian administration to the new conditions created by the Indian Mutiny and the abolition of the HEIC. He settled the number of European troops to be stationed there (1859), reorganised the Indian Army (1860), reconstituted the legislative council, regulated the High Court (1861) and improved the Indian Civil Service. He believed in railways and allowed heavy and, as it proved, controversial borrowing to finance them and this led to the public resignation of Stephen Laing, the Indian Finance Member. In fact Wood was right: revenue buoyancy in 1863-5 enabled him to cut expenditure and pay off debt. He resigned in 1866 after losing his seat and a hunting accident, went to the Lords and was Lord Privy

Seal from 1870 to 1874. He was an excellent, knowledge-able and industrious administrator, but a boring and ineffective speaker. His son **(2) Sir Charles Lindley (1839-1934) 2nd Vist.,** social worker and tractarian ecclesiastical politician, spent a lifetime promoting ecumenism. His son **(3) Edward Frederick (1881-1959) Ld. IRWIN (1925), 3rd Vist. and 1st E. (1944)** was Conservative M.P. for Ripon (1910-25), Pres. of the Board of Education (1922-4), Min. of Agriculture (1924-5) and one of the influential Conservatives opposed to a prompt reconciliation with Germany. As Ld. Irwin he became **Viceroy of India.** He sympathised with Indian nationalism, but tried to divert it into evolutionary courses. His term coincided with the reappearance of Gandhi, whose civil disobedience tactics soon em-barrassed the govt. After a visit to London Irwin returned and announced that Dominion Status was envisaged for India. Owing to dissensions within the Indian Congress, rivalries between Moslems and Hindus led finally to the acceptance by Congress of Gandhi's demand for full independence. Agitation was conducted on a large scale and included the demonstration known as the Salt March and in 1930 there was widespread civil disobedience and some violence. Irwin, who displayed great patience, finally had Gandhi and some of his supporters interned but towards the end of his viceroyalty freed the political prisoners and concluded what was known as the Delhi Pact with Gandhi. For his moderation he was hotly criticised by right-wing Conservatives; the *Daily Mail* said he was weak, yet it is hard to see what else could have been done in the very difficult circumstances in which he yet contrived to gain the affection of the Indians with whom he dealt. After this he held a number of ministerial posts (Education, War, Privy Seal, Lord Pres.) and was Foreign Sec. (1938-40) in succession to the resigned Eden. He was therefore closely associated with Chamberlain's dealings with the dictators. When Chamberlain decided to resign Halifax was thought to be a possible successor but was not thought strong enough and Churchill was chosen instead. Halifax was in Churchill's War Cabinet but was soon sent to Washington to conduct as Ambassador a permanent War Cabinet outstation (1941-6).

WOOD (1) Sir Andrew (?-1515), a popular sea captain, rescued James III from the rebels of 1488 and built Dunbar Castle. His son **(2) John (?-1570)** was sec. to Ld. James Stewart (later E. of Moray) on a mission to Mary Q. of Scots in 1561; became a Lord of Session in 1562; and was Moray's confidential sec. as regent. Made Bp. of Moray in 1569 he was shortly murdered.

WOOD, Sir Henry (1869-1944), originally an organist, conducted the Carl Rosa opera company from 1889 and in 1895 was engaged by Robert Newman to conduct the promenade concerts at Queen's Hall, London. These, in which he pioneered much new or little known music, became famous. When the hall was destroyed by bombing in World War II the Promenade Concerts were moved to the Royal Albert Hall.

WOOD, Howard Kingsley (1881-1943), was Conservative M.P. for W. Woolwich (1918-43) and, as Postmaster General, gained a seat in the Cabinet in 1933. He was Min. of Health (1935-8), Sec. for Air (1938-40), Lord Privy Seal 1940 and Ch. of the Exch. (1940-3) in Churchill's Coalition administration and in the War Cabinet (1940-2). As Sec. for Air he presided over the decisive pre-war preparations of the R.A.F. In May 1940, though a Chamberlain protégé, he urged Chamberlain to resign. He was a most successful Ch. of the Exch., achieving the unique feat of financing the war without much recourse to inflation. This was done by a balance of high taxes on luxuries and on excess profits and higher incomes, together with post-war credits, judicious borrowing and the institution of the relatively fair method of levying income tax by 'Pay-as-you-Earn'. An essential yet modest

figure in the conduct of the war, his remarkable career has so far remained unappreciated.

WOOD, John, father (?1705-54) and son (?-1782) were between them responsible for designing and laying out, from 1727 onwards, in the Palladian style the greater part of Bath.

WOOD'S HALFPENCE. The Duchess of Kendal, George I's mistress, obtained patents to supply Ireland and the American colonies each with £100,800 of halfpence and farthings. In 1722 she sold them to Wm. Wood (1671-1730), an ironmaster, for £10,000. He expected a profit of £36,000 but the deal leaked out. Swift attacked it in *Drapier's Letters* in 1724 and though Sir Isaac Newton certified the standard of the coins the Irish parliament forced the govt. to cancel the patents. The uproar partly reflected popular dislike of George I and Irish dissatisfaction with England.

WOODSTOCK (Oxon). This Saxon royal manor, well watered from the R. Glyne, was a frequent court resort. Henry I built a new house and enclosed a large deer park. Henry II's mistress, Fair Rosamund Clifford, died (if she was not murdered) there. Edward III's sons Edward the Black Prince (1330) and Thomas D. of Gloucester (1355) were born there. The place housed a royal zoo and nourished court crafts such as glove making and book binding. The little town received a charter under Henry VI and always elected two M.Ps. Elizabeth I as princess was kept there in semi-custody from 1555 to 1556. Thereafter the manor was less used because the growing importance of London kept monarchs in the Home Counties. It does not seem to have suffered much in the Civil War and formed part of a munificent gift to the 1st D. of Marlborough who, with his formidable duchess, employed Vanbrugh to build Blenheim Palace, the seat of the Dukes ever since, and laid out the great park. In 1832 the borough representation was reduced to one and in 1885 it was thrown into the Banbury constituency. Sir Winston Churchill was partly brought up at Blenheim, which happens to be in the parish of Bladon, and he was buried in Bladon churchyard.

WOODVILLE or WYDEVILLE. High Northamptonshire gentry. **(1) Richard (?-1441)** became Seneschal of Normandy (1421), Lieut. of Calais (1435) and chamberlain to John, the royal D. of Bedford. His son **(2) Richard (?-1469) 1st Ld. SCALES (1448), 1st E. RIVERS (1466)** married Bedford's widow, Jacquetta of Luxemburg and St. Pol, in 1437 and rose steadily, being Seneschal of Aquitaine in 1450 and Lieut. of Calais in 1451. He fought for Henry VI at Towton (1461) and was taken into favour by the victor, Edward VI, who three years later secretly married one of his 12 children **(3) Elizabeth (?-1492),** widow of Lord Ferrets of Groby. Once the marriage became public the family's rise to prominence and power was rapid but resented, especially by the E. of Warwick whose political schemes the marriage frustrated. Rivers became Treasurer (1466) and Constable (1467) but was beheaded with his brother Sir John during Warwick's rebellion. Elizabeth's sisters made spectacular marriages particularly to the heirs of the Es. of Arundel, Buckingham, Essex, Kent and Pembroke. Her eldest brother **(4) Anthony (?-1483) 2nd E. RIVERS,** was Lieut. of Calais, fought for Edward IV in 1470-1, became Chief Butler of England (1473) entitling him to a lucrative prise of wines and Protector of the P. of Wales (1473). The family fell suddenly for on Edward IV's death Richard of Gloucester, having secured the person of Edward V, Elizabeth's son, hurried her brother Anthony to execution at Pontefract; his assumption of the Crown as Richard III and the disappearance of Edward V and his brother Richard (The Princes in the Tower) finished the immediate business. Another brother **(5) Lionel (?1446-84),** Dean of EXETER in 1478 and Chanc. of Oxford Univ. in 1479, became Bp. of Salisbury in 1482. He helped to organise Buckingham's abortive revolt (*see*

RICHARD III) and fled to Henry of Richmond (the future Henry VII) in Brittany where he died. Henry VII's marriage to Edward V's sister **(6) Elizabeth (1465-1503)**, designed to symbolise the reconciliation of York and Lancaster, had the incidental effect of restoring the remaining Woodvilles to a moderate standing which included the marriage of **(7) Catherine (?-?)** to the King's uncle, Jasper D. of Bedford.

WOODWARD. *See* FOREST.

WOOL. *See* CLOTHING; INCLOSURES; INDUSTRIAL REVOLUTION-4,5; MERCHANT VENTURERS; SHEEP; STAPLE; TEXTILES.

WOOLF, Harry Kenneth (1933-) Lord WOOLF OF BARNES (1992) became a QBD judge in 1979, a Lord Justice of Appeal in 1986, and a Lord of Appeal in Ordinary in 1992. In 1996 he was appointed Master of the Rolls. During these times he held in addition many public and voluntary positions and from 1997 he was caught up in the movement for legal reforms generated by the upsurge in litigation and its cost. In particular he formulated the new civil procedures (known as the **WOOLF REFORMS**) intended to make civil law cheaper, speedier and more intelligible. These came into full use in 2000. It seems possible that the good will behind these reforms may be in part side tracked by the Treasury's determination to make the legal system a source of revenue.

WOOLFSON, Sir Isaac (1897-1991) Bt. amassed a huge fortune, gave liberally to British and Israeli charities, established the Woolfson Foundation for education, health and youth and endowed Woolfson College, Oxford.

WOOLLETT, William (1735-85) originally a landscape engraver, achieved in addition a European reputation as an historical line engraver, e.g. of Benjamin West's *Death of General Wolfe*.

WOOLSACK, a large couch stuffed with wool which from early times has been the official seat of the Lord Chancellor when presiding over the House of Lords. It is technically outside the House and so can be occupied (as sometimes happens) by somebody who is not a peer. It is uncomfortable and now contains microphones to improve acoustics.

WOOLTON, Frederick James Marquis (1883-1964) 1st Ld. (1939) 1st E. (1956). After taking a science degree at Manchester University he became warden of a dockers' club. In World War I he was a War Office economist and this gave him his opportunity for, through his contacts, he was asked to join John Lewis, of which, by 1938, he had become chairman. Neville Chamberlain appointed him Min. of Food in 1940. Charged with the potentially unpopular task of imposing rationing, he achieved widespread respect for the efficiency and equity with which it was handled and the smoothness with which the slow transition from unavoidable excess to near starvation was managed. He moved to the new Min. of Reconstruction in 1943 to plan the post-war future. In 1951 he was Lord Pres. but much of his post-war work was concerned with organisation of the Tory party.

WOOLWICH (Kent), a fishing village near the royal palace at Eltham, achieved importance when a royal dockyard and Powder House were established there in the 15th cent. A carriage dept. was soon added and after a time a royal laboratory. The whole was combined into the Royal Arsenal, to which the govt. foundry was moved in 1717 from Moorfields. The Royal Military Academy (R.M.A.) was founded in the Arsenal in 1741. The dockyard was closed in 1869 but the Crimean and First World Wars brought much industrialisation and population. The R.M.A. was combined with Sandhurst in 1946.

WOOMERA (C. Australia) (= spear thrower). The name given to an Anglo-Australian rocket testing centre and range 2700 miles long established in 1946.

WORCESTER,-SHIRE (A.S. WIGRANCEASTRE). The town was strategically important at a ford over the Severn and it became the seat of a bishopric c. 680. The surrounding area was rich, especially for cattle, sheep, cereals and orchards, all of which were steadily developed as clearances proceeded by intelligent monastic farmers, their tenants and serfs. The see stretched from Dudley to Bristol and the bishops were powerful figures, expected to rally the countryside against the Welsh when the border defences collapsed.

St. Oswald founded the Benedictine Abbey Cathedral in 964 and 13 monastic houses held most of the spreading workable land. Apart from the Cathedral (which owned the franchise in the scattered hundred of Oswaldslow) and Westminster Abbey, which shared in Pershore Abbey the Hundred of Pershore, the most important were Evesham (whose abbot held Blackenhurst both as hundred or and as a peculiar), Great Malvern, Bordesley and Halesowen. The town was burned by Harvhacnut in 1041 for refusing to pay its taxes. The fearless Saxon post-conquest bishop, St. Wulfstan, added greatly to the prestige of the see, whose wealth was increased by the salt of Droitwich and later by the Bristol wine trade. The Crown, however, had large forests in Wyre and Malvern Chase besides the Hundred of Doddingtree and half that of Hlafshire. Certain families, e.g. the Beauchamps and Lyttletons, held numerous manors as Crown or monastic sub-tenants or in unity of management.

The agriculture naturally created dependent industries such as cider-making and cloth and leather working – the latter developing at the town in the later middle ages into a fine leather industry producing mostly gloves. Political and military disturbances and border incursions did not interrupt progress. The town, for example, was sacked by Derby in 1263 and there was endemic banditry in the 14th and 15th cents, but there are impressive, mainly ecclesiastical, survivals of mediaeval prosperity and also of royal interest. King John was buried in the Cathedral and Henry VII built a chantry and screen in memory of his son Arthur.

The Tudor revolution had profound effects. By the dissolution of the monasteries much land changed hands and many tenants now held direct of the Crown. The Pershore endowments passed to Westminster Abbey, Evesham to the Hoby family, Dudley to the Dudleys, Halesowen to the Lyttletons and Bordesley to the Windsors. The cathedral and episcopal endowments were much diminished and the bishop's authority too was destroyed. His leadership was no longer desired against the Welsh and the shire was put under the Council for the Marches. Henry VIII divided the see establishing bishoprics at Gloucester and Bristol in 1541. The pacified border enabled the enriched landowners to live in style. These royal partisans (who took no part in the rebellion of 1536) built country houses as centres for newly inclosed estates. Tudor, Jacobean and classical country houses abound: the materials were usually quarried from the ruined monasteries. In the city, which continued to grow, the 13th cent. school, previously supported by the Trinity Merchants Guild, was endowed with monastic property and called the Royal Grammar School (1561). The Cathedral School was similarly treated and chartered as the King's School in 1541. Q. Elizabeth I received an enraptured welcome there in 1574 and the whole area, unlike Gloucester, was strongly, if not quite single-mindedly, royalist during the Civil War.

Limestone quarrying had long been carried on. In the early 18th cent. ironstone became viable through the supply of suitable fuel in the form of coal from newly opened mines. Thus an iron industry with offshoots grew up in the city and at Dudley and Netherton, which slowly merged into the 'Black Country' as the century proceeded. The coal also made possible the rise of the Royal Worcester porcelain industry (started by John Wall and Wm. Davis in 1751) and the manufacture of glass at

Stourbridge. All these activities received powerful stimuli when the canals (q.v.) connected the Severn with the midlands at the end of the 18th cent., bringing cheap coal in one direction and moving the fragile goods safely – in contrast with the still appalling roads – in the other. Road improvements and, later, the coming of the railways naturally affected the prosperity of the canals but simply quickened that of the locally well balanced economy, where the industries had been well established for a long time. Further diversification followed: carpets at Kidderminster, small hard steels at Redditch, printing, shoes and agricultural machinery at Worcester – not to mention Worcester sauce – and when electricity came in the 20th cent. electrical engineering naturally followed. Worcester and Dudley became county boroughs in 1888 but Worcester, its shire and Herefordshire were amalgamated, to the indignation of all three, in 1974.

WORCESTER RIOT (Edinburgh, 1705). The crew of an English ship, the *Worcester,* was wrongly convicted of piracy against a ship belonging to the Company of Scotland. A well organised mob prevented their release and hanged them.

WORCESTER, William (1415-82), from 1438 to 1459 sec. to Sir John Fastolf, was mainly a manager of Sir John's and his own affairs but wrote the *Boke of Noblesse* (begun 1451) to urge the govt. to greater belligerency in France and the *Deeds of Sir John Fastolf* (begun 1459). He presented a copy of the *Boke* to Edward IV on the eve of his 1475 French expedition. His *Itinerary,* a commonplace book on his English journeys between 1477 and 1482, illumines the life of his time with its anecdotes, observations on architecture, topography, geography and nature and his assorted thoughts.

WORCESTER, Es. of. Waleran of Meulan may have been Earl briefly under K. Stephen. Others included Thomas Percy (cr. 1397-d. 1403), Richard Beauchamp, Lord Abergavenny (cr. 1421-d. 1422), John Tiptoft (cr. 1449) and his son Edward (d. 1485). The earldom was revived in 1514 for Charles Somerset, a bastard of Henry Beaufort, 3rd D. of Somerset, and descended in his family until raised to a marquessate during the Civil War.

WORDE, Wynkyn de (fl. 1477-1535), an Alsatian printer, came to London in 1477 and inherited Caxton's business in 1491. He printed some 800 books.

WORDSWORTH, William (1770-1850), became interested in revolutionary doctrines in 1792 and settled at Grasmere in 1799; by 1812 his revolutionary fervour had ebbed; he accepted a sinecure and took to simple things. In 1842 he accepted a civil list pension. Critical and uncritical reactions to his poetry have varied from romantic devotion to hilarity.

WORKHOUSES, PARISH (*see* FIRMIN, THOMAS; HOUSE OF CORRECTION; POOR LAW ACT; POOR LAW INCORPORATIONS; CORPORATIONS OF THE POOR). If the unemployed were set to work at home they were hard to supervise, and if a parish workhouse were provided the overheads absorbed the profits, the building became ruinous and the unemployed could not work there.

WORKMEN'S COMPENSATION, INDUSTRIAL ACCIDENTS AND INJURIES. (1) Under ordinary principles of contract law a person who accepted an employment accepted the risks arising out of, or in the course of it. The risks had been much diminished by the Factory Acts but the rule became increasingly inconvenient with the advance of industrialisation and trade unionism; it might bear heavily upon an employee in the case of an unknown or disputed risk, for the employer was generally in a stronger position in a lawsuit. Moreover feelings were apt to run high in such disputes and occasioned frequent strikes.

(2) The Workmen's Compensation Act, 1897, conferred upon employees an alternative resort to their rights at common law, viz: the option in certain cases of choosing to 'refer a serious accident to arbitration and

subsequent compensation by an employer in accordance with a statutory scale; but an employer could contract out if he satisfied the Registrar of Friendly Societies that he had a compensation scheme at least as favourable to employees as the Act (*see* SALISBURY'S THIRD ADMINISTRATION-2,5). These principles, which originally applied only to railways, factories, mines and quarries, engineering and major construction work and to power driven machinery, were extended by Acts of 1900 and 1906 to merchant shipping and six specified diseases. There was then much statutory tinkering and the whole subject was consolidated into one Act in 1925 which also made it possible to extend the principles to aircraft and to conventions with foreign states. Later acts made detailed improvements and added such diseases as Byssinosis (1940) and Pneumoconiosis (1945).

(3) There had always been the possibility that an employer could not pay and World War II created many such cases. The National Insurance Act, 1946, which came into effect in July 1948, substituted a state Industrial Injuries Scheme whereby compensation is paid from an insurance fund to which employers, employees and the exchequer must all contribute. The act received much detailed amendment and the law was again consolidated in 1965 and 1975 incorporated in the Social Security Act.

WORKERS EDUCATIONAL ASSOCIATION (W.E.A.) founded by Albert Mansbridge (1876-1952) in 1904, began with university standard courses at Derby. In 1907 co-operation with university teachers began, with the help of Prof. R. H. Tawney. In 1919 the Min. of Reconstruction proposed grants for courses below university standard and the number of students grew. A joint agreement was made with the Trade Union Congress in 1920. Always sporadic in its influence, the W.E.A. declined as the educational system, especially the Further Education Colleges, developed. It was still functioning in certain areas in the 1970s.

WORKS, MINISTRY etc. In 1814 the control of public buildings and works was given to a Surveyor of Works and in 1832 transferred to the Commissioners for Woods, Forests and Land Revenues. This made it too easy to spend crown revenues on works without parliamentary control and in 1851 a Board of Works under a political First Commissioner (sometimes in the Cabinet) was set up. This body also managed the Royal Parks. As a board it was a fiction: all the functions were exercised by the First Commissioner and in 1945 it became an ordinary Ministry, but with certain powers of control over the building industry conferred by the Labour govt. In 1970 it was absorbed into the Dept. of the Environment.

WORLD COUNCIL OF CHURCHES was established in 1948. In the 1980s it still did not include the R. Catholics or certain evangelical bodies and was being criticised by the Orthodox churches.

WORLD HEALTH ORGANISATION (W.H.O.), based on a treaty of 1946, came into existence in 1948 and became an agency of U.N.O. in 1950. It is mainly an advisory body, seeking to establish (e.g.) common international standards for drugs, vaccines and sera and medical terminology but it also encourages national health organisations by negotiating exchanges of practitioners and it occasionally administers international quarantine measures.

WORLD WAR I (July 1914-Nov. 1918) (1) This immense conflict was fought upon (a) a Western Front in France and Belgium; (b) an Eastern Front mostly in Poland and Galicia (Aug. 1914-Nov. 1917); (c) Southern Fronts in the Balkans (Aug. 1914-Sept. 1918), Roumania (Dec. 1916-Jan. 1917) and Italy (May 1915-Nov. 1918); (d) Turkish Fronts in the Caucasus (Dec. 1914-Sept. 1918), Mesopotamia (Nov. 1914-Sept. 1917), the Hejaz and Syria (Feb. 1915-Oct. 1918) and the Dardanelles (Mar. 1915-Jan. 1916); and (e) at sea, involving battles, commerce destruction and the incidental liquidation of the German colonies.

(2) Apart from the Serbs all the participants bungled their opening moves. The Austro-Hungarians began (12 Aug.) with an unsuccessful southward attack on Serbia. Soon afterwards the Russians, earlier than their enemies expected, advanced westwards against the Central Powers, who had made no arrangements for co-operation. The Russians suffered a disaster at German hands in the B. of "Tannenberg" (26-31 Aug.). In the meantime 80% of the German strength was executing an anti-clockwise attack, through Belgium, on the French and British (Bs. of Mons and le Câteau) while a considerable French force was attacking the Germans near the Swiss frontier. The French and the Austrians discontinued their offensives to deal with the strategic surprise sprung on them by their respective German and Russian opponent. The German swing was stopped at the B. of the Marne (6-9 Sept.) and the contestants subsequent efforts to outflank each other north-westwards extended their lines to the sea near Ostend. The Austro-Hungarians and the Russians collided in Galicia and, after confused fighting on a huge scale, the latter, reinforced too late from the southern front, suffered a shattering defeat and, save for the fortresses of Przymsl and Lemberg, abandoned Galicia. This was the only major overthrow in 1914.

(3) The three fronts now became static: the east and the south through local exhaustion, the west bogged down among trenches, mud and barbed-wire entanglements made impassable by machine guns firing from ground level. Neither side appreciated the defensive strength of this combination and each thought that the decisive theatre was in the west. The result was a succession of western battles (e.g. at Ypres) of an industrial character which uselessly drew in most of the output of the expanding war factories, while sacrificing casualties in hundreds of thousands for gains of a few hundred yards.

(4) On 29 Oct. 1914 the Turks had entered or were bounced into the war. This cut off Allied supplies to Russia and threatened her in the Caucasus. By Dec. the bloody western deadlock was causing heart searchings. Both sides thought along two lines: the tactical (to punch a way through the embattled western front) and the strategic (to go round it). British tactical thought revolved controversially round the tank, first mooted in Oct. 1914. The Germans experimented with gas. The tank, however, had a prolonged argumentative gestation and meanwhile the Russians appealed for help in the Caucasus. Accordingly the British, with some French help, began on a strategic alternative, namely a campaign to force the Dardanelles (Mar. 1915) while the Germans launched chlorine gas near Ypres (22 Apr.). Both efforts failed through mismanagement: each side lacked faith in its chosen actions, confused its objectives and so failed to press its initial success.

(5) With the Dardanelles deadlocked the Allies reverted to the Western front offensives which proved as bloodily disastrous as before and only convinced the Germans that the front could be held with ease. They had planned the reverse of 1914, for which the gas attack had been a feint. 80% of the armies would go east, destroy the Russians and then return for a final decision in France. Nine days after the Ypres gas attack and after a concealed approach, they sprang a brilliant surprise at Tarnow in W. Galicia by storming the Russian entrenchments after a short, but extremely violent, bombardment. The Russians panicked and the Germanic armies, to their surprise, advanced, taking prisoners all the way to Lemberg (mid June). Here, however, their supplies lagged behind and once again the influence of a southern front was felt. The Allies had lengthened the southern front by persuading Italy to join them (24 May 1915). Though the Italian mobilisation was slow and their strategic position difficult, this extension absorbed some

Austrian resources but, as on the western front, was soon bogged down.

(6) The offensive against Russia got a second wind which almost achieved a decision but the Russians, at a cost of 750,000 casualties, eluded annihilation by retreating as far as a line from the Gulf of Riga to Austrian Bukovina (Sept. 1915). The German attack was now called off in favour of a stroke against Serbia, which had thus far stood her ground behind the gigantic Danube. The new feature was that the Bulgars had been bribed to join in with the promise of Macedonia. The Austro-Germans attacked from the north and west. The Anglo-French sent a rescue force under Gen. Sarrail from Gallipoli. The Bulgars entered S. Serbia between the northward facing Serbian main armies and Sarrail, whom they drove into Salonika. The desperate Serbs fought their way to the Adriatic. The Allies evacuated them to Corfu, revived and rearmed them and shipped them round to Salonika. Thus by Jan. 1916 (when Gallipoli was evacuated) Russia was half crippled, the southern front pushed back almost to the Mediterranean, the Central Powers had a continuous communications zone from Hamburg to Baghdad and, by way of a bonus, a British expedition sent to protect the Gulf oilfields had ventured too far and was trapped at Kut-el-Amara in central Iraq.

(7) The industrial character of the western battles was a grave strain on the rival economies, especially on the well organised but blockaded Central Powers. The Royal Navy dominated the surface of the seas. It raided the Heligoland Bight in the first days of the war. After a defeat in the minor B. of Coronel (Nov. 1914) it destroyed Count Spee's armoured cruisers at the Falkland Is. (Dec.) and hunted down his commerce raiders. The German colonies, isolated by the blockade, were seized or neutralised. In Jan. 1915 the German armoured cruiser *Blücher* was sunk in a pursuit engagement off the Dogger Bank. The British Grand Fleet was the first in the world: the German High Seas Fleet only the second. Its command, encouraged when a single submarine (U-boat) sank three British cruisers (Sept. 1914) turned to submarine operations of a novel kind. If the British could stop the Reich's commerce by surface measures, the Reich should retaliate under water. In Feb. 1915 U-boats began to attack merchant shipping. These blockades and counter-blockades did little immediate damage to the war potentials: the govts. diverted the effects to the civilians. A harvest failure in 1915, however, precipitated the long-term damage to the Central Powers which was ultimately decisive. Diplomatically the U-boat war also did them serious harm. The British, naturally unpopular in the U.S.A., became even more so when their surface blockade interfered with American profits. The German attack on freighters had no equivalent effect, for the American goods were sunk after they had been paid for but in May 1915 a U-boat torpedoed a passenger liner, the *Lusitania,* on the way to New York and drowned 1100 civilians, including 128 Americans. This began the reluctant conversion of American opinion.

(8) By 1916 the war industries were geared up to immense outputs. The war directions of both sides had learned nothing from their own best or the enemy's worst performances and could think only of throwing huge volumes of explosives at their opponents and thousands of helpless men against their machine guns. The Anglo-French planned an offensive on the Somme for June. The Germans anticipated it with an attack on the French in Feb. at Verdun. This battle lasted nine months and sucked in the French troops earmarked for the Somme. The British began the Somme offensive virtually alone in July. This battle, known collectively as Passchendaele, lasted over four months. These muddy holocausts, which cost the attackers (the Germans at Verdun, the British on the Somme) twice as many casualties as the defenders, were accompanied at intervals by six week long conflicts

in Italy. It was only on the Eastern and Turkish fronts that sense prevailed. The Russians, to help the Western Allies, started two offensives: one in Feb. in the Caucasus supported by an attack across Persia in Mar. The other was in Poland towards Austro-Hungary. The Persian advance reached Ispahan but failed to save Kut-el-Amara where the British surrendered in Apr. The Caucasian advance reached Trebizond before the Turkish counter-attack developed. Meanwhile the greatest leverage was being exerted by the smallest force of all. A group of Arabists, among whom T.E. Lawrence made himself famous, had been fomenting an Arab revolt in the Hejaz. In June British diplomacy, dynamite and the Grand Sherif forced a Turkish retreat from Mecca up the Hejaz railway amid clouds of belligerent tribes. The Turks, however, concentrated on the threat nearer home. By the end of the year they had driven the Russians back in Persia and the Caucasus.

(9) The Russian offensive towards Austro-Hungary brought in its trail a forseeable catastrophe. Using the Hungarian province of Transylvania as a bribe, the Allies persuaded Roumania to enter the war. Strategically the country was in an impossible position with the summits of the frontier passes down into the Roumanian plains in the hands of the Hungarians, and the Bulgars on the Danube 30 miles from Bucharest. Her only hope lay in a quick Russian victory before she entered the fray but the Russians wanted her help in winning it. She took a chance and on 28 Aug. her army, delayed only by demolitions, invaded Transylvania but its sluggish movements enabled the Austro-Germans to throw active forces together and drive it down the passes while outflanking it from Bulgaria. Bucharest fell on 6 Dec. By Jan. 1917 most of Roumania, with her corn and oil, was in German hands.

(10) In the context of the tremendous and sanguinary events of 1916 the sea B. of Jutland (31 May-1 June 1916) in which 258 ships took part, seems like an uncomfortable appendix. The two fleets met cautiously in semi-fog and inflicted damage which the British could but the Germans could not afford. The German naval effort was now diverted to the mounting commerce destruction by U-boats. The High Seas Fleet, with reduced U-boat operational support and the Grand Fleet under assumed U-boat threat, kept away as entities from mutual contact but raided each others areas. In practice the large German units stayed in port where their morale slowly deteriorated.

(11) By the end of Jan. 1917 the U-boat campaign had forced Britain to introduce rationing. It, and industrial sabotage, had also angered the U.S.A. Realising that sooner or later the U.S.A. would enter the war, the Germans had rationalised their war machine. On 1 Feb. they proclaimed unrestricted U-boat warfare and began to sink neutral (mostly American) ships. On 3 Feb. the U.S.A. broke off diplomatic relations. On 4 Feb. the Germans withdrew some 20 miles to the heavily fortified Siegfried (or Hindenburg) Line to accumulate reserves. The stage was now set for major military decisions but political events supervened. On 8 Mar. the February (Old Style) Revolution began in Russia. On 11 Mar. the British took the symbolic city of Baghdad. On 16 Mar. the Czar abdicated. On 31 Mar. the new Austrian Emperor Charles made a peace offer. This general softening of fibre was followed by a hardening. On 6 Apr. the U.S.A. declared war. The disastrous Allied western offensives began again and continued until the French army mutinied in June but the Germans were then occupied by further British operations (3rd B. of Ypres) and by the last Russian offensive (delivered by the new republicans) against Austro-Hungary. At this moment there was an ominous naval mutiny at Kiel and the *Reichstag* demanded peace. With social revolution in the air and the first U.S. troops arriving, time was running against the German rulers.

Their first reaction was a blow against Italy. This had been foreseen and the French Gen. Foch had made contingency plans. The Austro-German attack on Caporetto, based on the Tarnow principle (see para 5) began exhilaratingly. The Italians dissolved. The headlong advance crossed the Tagliamento but was halted decisively on the Piave (10 Nov.) by British troops despatched in accordance with Foch's plan.

(12) The disappointment caused by this unexpected check was acute but short. The liquidation of the Russians was in the forefront of German war policy. The Russians now did it for them. The (Bolshevik) October (O.S.) Revolution took place in Petrograd on 7 Nov. and the new rulers sued for an armistice. Against this, however, the British and their Arab friends had penetrated the Turkish Palestinian front and on 9 Dec. triumphantly entered Jerusalem. Bad harvests and shortages of farm labour had brought Austro-Hungary to the verge of famine: the German cities were little better. Turkey was suddenly tottering and soon the Americans would be fit to fight.

(13) The Allies had not grasped the full truth about their enemies. Themselves depressed by the Russian collapse they planned with weary determination for war in 1919. The Germans, by contrast, wanted immediate peace or immediate victory. The publication of Pres. Wilson's Fourteen Points in Jan. 1918 shut out peace. While negotiations with the Bolsheviks proceeded at Brest-Litovsk, most of the German eastern armies entrained for the west. This emboldened the Bolsheviks. The negotiations were deadlocked. With reduced forces the Germans resumed hostilities. Revolution had turned the Russian troops into undisciplined mobs. By early Mar. Reval and Kiev had fallen. On 3 Mar. the Bolsheviks hurriedly accepted terms but the Germans pressed on.

(14) The Germans planned four huge, violent, western onslaughts on the Tarnow principle, firstly opposite Amiens, secondly on the Lys in Flanders, thirdly across the Chemin des Dames to the Maine. These having confused and disrupted the Allies, the final blow was to crush the British against the Flemish coast. The preparations for the first could not be concealed but the Allies failed to interpret the signs. Aided by a providential fog the German storm burst on 21 Mar. at the point of junction of the surprised Anglo-French. The Germans lurched through the gap, advanced 40 miles in a week and then stopped because of the contrast between the smiling prosperity of the Allied back areas and their own years of deprivation. Discipline broke down in an orgy of food, drink and loot. Allied reinforcements closed the gap during the delay. The initial excessive successes had sucked in more German troops than the economy of the plans allowed and had disorganised the arrangements for transferring troops to the second (Lys) assault. Here the untried Portuguese, who happened to be in line, ran away (9 Apr.) and again the Germans lurched through but this time, to avoid excessive involvement, their command fed the reinforcements in too slowly. This attack could thus be contained and was abandoned on 29 Apr. The third diversionary assault was delivered on 27 May and had reached the Maine on the fourth day. Its unexpected success, as at Amiens, sucked in reinforcements intended for elsewhere and it similarly collapsed in drunkenness and indiscipline, but it tempted the Germans into a further effort on the Maine (15-17 July) which the Allies frustrated. The aggregate results were that the Germans had temporarily used up the resources needed for their fourth and final assault on the British but before they could regroup for it the British sprang a devastating surprise with massed tanks near Amiens on 8 Aug. From this shattering event the German will to victory never recovered. The fourth assault was never made. The Allies went over to the offensive.

(15) Actual defeat came, however, from other

quarters and in the third week of Sept. On 15 Sept. the Allies attacked the Bulgars in Macedonia. Between 19 and 22 Sept. Gen. Allenby brilliantly wiped out the Turkish armies in the B. of Megiddo. The Bulgars sued for an armistice on 25 Sept. Allenby entered Damascus on 1 Oct. The Bulgarian surrender simultaneously, if in opposite directions, exposed the Turkish and the Austro-Hungarian rear. The convergence of defeats on all fronts penetrated German opinion. The Allies attacked in Italy on 26 Oct. On 28 Oct. a mutiny began in a German battleship. The Turks surrendered on 30 Oct. There was revolution in Vienna the next day and the Austro-Hungarians obtained an armistice on 3 Nov. The same day the whole High Seas Fleet mutinied. On 7 Nov. the Germans requested an armistice. There was revolution in Munich on 8 Nov; in Berlin on 9 Nov. William II and the other German monarchs abdicated on 10 Nov. The German Armistice was signed in a railway carriage at Compiègne for 11 Nov. 1918.

WORLD WAR II (a) 11 Mar. 1938-30 Aug. 1939; (b) 1 Sept. 1939-23 Sept. 1945. (1) German aggressions were planned firstly to secure unresisted advantages; secondly if resistance were generated, to avoid wars on two fronts; the third stage was to secure favourable conditions for an attack on Britain or British complaisance and fourthly to establish a new order in Europe as a springboard for the conquest of Russia. This orderly development was confused and eventually frustrated by unexpected British determination; by the poor war performance of Germany's ally Italy; the unco-ordinated Japanese intervention which provoked the U.S.A. and miscalculations in German high policy.

(2) Period (a) above began with the unresisted seizure of Austria, which outflanked the defences of Czechoslovakia. Within a fortnight the Sudeten Germans who lived in the areas of those defences demanded autonomy and, Czechoslovakia having been betrayed by the British and French, German troops entered the Sudeten areas also unresisted in Sept. With Czechoslovakia at their mercy the Germans partitioned her and started to digest Bohemia and Moravia. They were declared a protectorate on 16 Mar. 1939. This outflanked S. Poland. On 22 Mar. the Germans, also unresisted, seized the Lithuanian port of Klaipeda (Memel). As Nazis had controlled Danzig since 1933 Poland's only outlet to the Baltic was now the exposed port of Gdynia (Gdingen). In Aug. 1939 the Ribbentrop-Molotov (or Thieves') Compact freed Germany for an attack on Poland by leaving the Baltic republics to the mercy of the Russians, who duly occupied them.

(3) Period (b) above, the conventional period of the war, began with the German attack on Poland on 1 Sept. and the British and French declarations of war on 3 Sept. The Russians invaded, not wholly to the Germans liking, on 17 Sept. and the country was partitioned between them on 28 Sept. There followed six months of apparent repose while the western allies wondered what to do about the W. German fortified zone called the Siegfried Line. The Germans matured their arrangements for their third stage; the Russians made, in a disastrous side-show, an attack on Finland and a weak British cruiser squadron brilliantly defeated the German pocket battleship *Graf Spee* in the R. Plate (Dec.).

(4) On 9 Apr. 1940 bodies of German troops concealed in cargo ships or escorted by their navy surprised Norway at many points while others overran Denmark. On 10 May they opened a western offensive of great violence by invading the Low Countries. The results were not as the belligerents expected. The Anglo-Norwegian defence was prolonged until 10 June, by which time the greater part of the German surface fleet had been sunk, while the other western countries, save Britain, capitulated (Holland 15 May; Belgium 28 May; France 22 June). Most of the British and about an equal

number of French troops had been evacuated amid fire and smoke from Dunkirk (30 May-3 June). Then the British, suspecting that the French had really changed sides, interned or, at Mers-el-Kebir (Oran), sank important units of the French fleet. In Sept. they unsuccessfully attacked Dakar.

(5) While the Germans now faced Britain from the North Cape to the Pyrenees and prepared the aerial onslaught which was to precede the storm of the British Is., the Italians had extended the conflict first to Africa where their army advanced cautiously to Sidi Barrani (Egypt) and then to the Balkans where they attacked Greece (28 Oct.). On 8 Aug. the Germans had begun the aerial bombardment of Britain (*see* BRITAIN, B. OF). Italian operations did not prosper. The Greeks drove them back into Albania. The British sank some of their battleships by aerial torpedo in Taranto harbour (11 Nov.) and on 8 Dec. Gen. Wavell opened his astounding double offensive which, against odds of five to one, virtually eliminated their Libyan armies by Feb. 1941 and conquered their Ethiopian empire by Apr.

(6) The air offensive against Britain was manifestly failing. The Germans had indeed been conducting U-boat warfare since Sept. 1939 but now found that they had to change over from a mainly military to a naval policy (requiring industrial and manpower redeployments) against the British Is. and at the same time rescue their ally. They had occupied Roumania (Oct. 1940) before the Italians attacked Greece. In 1941 they occupied Bulgaria and began to ferry troops to Africa. Two other developments were also changing the trend of the war. The British won a diplomatic triumph by persuading the U.S.A. to pass the Lend-Lease Act, through which they could gain access to American armaments production without actually having to buy the products. At the same time the Germans had decided to launch their long intended attack on their Russian ally. Immense troop and material movements had to begin and their battered airforce had to be redirected. The ineffectiveness of the gallant but ill-equipped Italian fleet for squadron warfare was at this time demonstrated at the B. of C. Matapan (28 Mar. 1941).

(7) The Germans now made decisive miscalculations. They needed a long summer for total victory in Russia but, observing the poor Russian performance against Finland (Nov. 1939-Mar. 1940) under-estimated Russian military capacity. They decided to risk an attack later in the summer, using the interval to liquidate the Mediterranean war. Accordingly in Mar. their Gen. Rommel initiated the German-Italian counter-attack on the thinly spread British in Libya and in Apr. they engineered a pro-Axis *coup* in Iraq (3 Apr.), overran Yugoslavia in a week and drove the British from mainland Greece in a fortnight. By May Rommel was well into Egypt, though at the end of a long supply line harassed by the Royal Navy from Malta; and Wavell, also threatened by pro-German changes in French Syria, was having to sustain four fronts with a German attack on Crete impending. He managed to hold Rommel; using small forces he regained Iraq and Syria with their essential oil supplies and finished off the Ethiopian conquests. Meanwhile the German attack on Crete (19 May-1 June), though victorious, was qualitatively a disaster. The whole of their limited force of highly trained airborne troops was committed and mostly lost. The Cretan defeat was also psychologically balanced for the British by the destruction of the huge German battleship *Bismarck* in the Atlantic (28 May).

(8) Thus at the moment when German war policy towards Russia was reaching a point of no return the Mediterranean war had not been liquidated and the airborne component was not available when the attack on Russia was due. It was, at all hazards, launched on 22 June and, aided by the incompetence of the Russian high command, made alarming strides only alleviated by an Anglo-Russian operation to secure Persia. On 4 Sept. the Germans reached the suburbs of Leningrad (St. Petersburg); on 17 Sept. they took Kiev. The Russians, however, had learned quickly. In the battle for Moscow they fought their enemy to a standstill. In the middle of it they began a counter-offensive in the Ukraine (Nov.) Then came, for the Germans, a fatal winter.

(9) At this period there were three major theatres, all affected by air power, in which the combatants were locked in bloody, fluctuating fortunes, namely Russia, a land conflict, the Atlantic, a sea conflict and Africa, which was both. The Atlantic balance had been much improved in July 1941 when the Americans occupied Iceland. In Sept. their naval patrols had been ordered to shoot U-boats at sight. They were now precipitated out of neutral participation into active war by the Japanese who suddenly attacked Western and American positions in Dec. The surprise raid on Pearl Harbor (7 Dec.) was more an American humiliation than a material disaster. The invasion of Siam and Malaya next day was more serious for it threatened the rear of the improvidently designed naval base at Singapore at a time when the British had no effective air force locally available. Adm. Phillips, without air cover, made a brave but foredoomed sortie with two battle cruisers to try and inflict damage on the invaders before being sunk himself but was sunk too soon (10 Dec.).

(10) The seemingly irresistible Japanese onrush garnered the Philippines (Jan. 1942) and Singapore (Feb.). They invaded Burma and Java. A scratch Anglo-Dutch force was mostly destroyed. Rangoon and Batavia surrendered (Mar.). In Apr. there were air raids on Ceylon, New Guinea and the Australian W. Coast. In fact the Japanese were becoming involved in a war on four fronts. They had long been entangled in their Chinese war; on the Western or Indo-Chinese and the Australian fronts they were overstretched; on the east or Pacific the inadequacy of their Pearl Harbor operation had exposed them to transoceanic counter attack. In the west, Anglo-Indian retirement upon the Indian industrial base simplified logistics and hardened resistance, but Japanese logistic problems multiplied and their offensive capacity softened. By mid 1942 the Burmese front was more or less stationary along the line of the Indian frontier and if the Japanese navally based expansion helped to isolate China, the U.S. Pacific counter-attack was developing. Tokyo had been raided in Apr. During the summer there were tremendous aircraft carrier battles in the Coral Sea (May) and off Midway I. (June) in which the two sides never saw each other but which eroded the irreplaceable Japanese carrier force.

(11) The war in Russia was meanwhile causing fearful damage. The Russians, mindful of their Marxist analyses, were hoping for some relief while yet entrapping their Allied enemy into a common disaster with their German enemy. There were strident appeals through diplomatic and all propaganda channels for a 'Second Front Now', intended to belittle the existing second front in Africa and the three in the Far East. The western allies, though anxious to help, were determined not to compromise the major offensives which they were planning by premature exposure. They sought to influence immediate events by other means, primarily the bombing of Germany. A thousand bombers attacked Cologne in May. In addition in Aug. the British and Canadians made a controversial raid on Dieppe to test their amphibious techniques and deceive the Germans into keeping more troops in the west than they really needed.

(12) The period Aug. 1942 to Feb. 1943 decided the war, though the major events were so far apart that they occurred without co-ordination. The American landing on Guadalcanal I. and the British defeat of the Axis navies in the Mediterranean began it. In Sept. the long Stalingrad battle began. In Oct-Nov. came Gen. Montgomery's expensive but important victory over the supply-starved Axis armies at El Alamein. A week later the Anglo-Americans landed in Algeria. At the end of the year the B. of Kotelnikovo cut off the Germans in Stalingrad. Then the allies began full scale daylight as well as night raids on Germany. In Feb. 1943 the Germans at Stalingrad surrendered. This began the long campaign which, despite embittered fighting, was to carry the Russian armies into central Germany.

(13) The Anglo-American invasion of French N. Africa was followed by a major German policy mistake. Instead of cutting their losses they reinforced their N. African forces. The 300,000 troops and airmen which might have nourished the Eastern Front were thus lost, together with most of the Italian fleet. Their African surrender took place in May. They had not enough with which to hold Sicily, which fell in a month (July-Aug.) or to defend S. Italy where landings began in Sept (B. of Salerno); nevertheless, they committed large additional forces to the defence of a line just north of Naples (B. of Cassino).

(14) These forces were now entangled in much worsening politics and communications. The Italians have always hated the Germans. The landings on the Italian mainland precipitated the collapse of the govt. which had forced them into alliance with Germany. K. Victor Emmanuel III, with Marshal Badoglio, Count Grandi and the D. of Acquarone, arrested the dictator Mussolini and abolished Fascism overnight. The rest of the fleet came over to the Allies. Prisoners were released in hundreds. Civil populations seized arms from paralysed authorities and began sporadic guerrilla against the Germans. The latter had to intensify the policing or occupation of their back areas. They managed one spectacular, if trivial, *coup* in rescuing Mussolini and setting him up in Salo on L. Garda in a gimcrack govt. which nobody heeded. From Jan. to June 1944 the Germans were engaged in a costly war in Italy while the Russians hammered in the east. Thus by the time Rome fell (4 June) their forces had been mostly driven from Russian national territory, yet there was no weakening of the pressure on either of the two fronts. On 6 June an immense Allied armada covered by overwhelming air support crossed the Channel and began to land the armies which constituted the Fifth Front. Much of this had been made possible by the successes in the Far East, whereby undue diversions of resources from the western fronts had been avoided.

(15) By Aug., when the Allies entered Florence, the main German forces in the west had been compelled, after enormous losses on both sides, to retreat northwards, hastened by Allied landings on the Riviera and advances up the Rhone. Paris was abandoned on 25 Aug: Brussels on 3 Sept. The Germans now hoped, by denying the use of the Belgian and Dutch ports to the Allies, to be able to hold the West easily while they stabilised the Russian front: the Allies, by using airborne troops, to pierce the front and make the storm of the ports unnecessary. Neither side calculated accurately. The Allied airborne offensive at Arnhem failed at the end of Sept. The German port garrisons had surrendered by Nov and the British, after clearing the Scheldt and Walcheren, opened Antwerp in Nov. German defeat in the west (and so in the east) was now certain unless somehow the ports could be closed again. Antwerp was more heavily bombed with V1s and V2s than London and, this proving useless, a last German western offensive took place in the Ardennes (Bastogne) at the turn of the years 1944-5. It was quickly defeated, mainly by a new technical invention, the radar operated air-burst shell-fuse.

(16) The Germans now had little fighting capacity left. Pressed on all sides they surrendered in Italy on 29

Apr; in Berlin (with Hitler's suicide) and N. Germany between 30 Apr. and 7 May; in Norway on 8 May.

(17) The Americans had begun the reconquest of the Philippines during the Oct. when the Germans were surrendering Belgian ports. The Japanese battlefleet was decisively beaten in the Philippine Sea at the end of the month. Japanese and German defeat thus became inevitable at the same time. There were, however, two differences. The distances in the Far East were many times greater and, save in Burma, across water, and the Japanese moral background based on Shinto (q.v.) created an unequalled warlike desperation. Japanese island garrisons could not be forced to surrender: they had to be wiped out, and their dive-bombers, loaded with explosives, were suicidally crashed onto Allied ships. Progress was therefore slow.

(18) Lord Mountbatten, Allied C-in-C in S. E. Asia since Aug. 1943, had been preparing a great Burmese offensive. In Mar. 1944 this began in Manipur. The Americans landed near Manila in Jan. 1945. It took them until Mar. to take Manila itself. In Apr. the Russians denounced their non-aggression pact with Japan by which, at no cost, they restrained the Japanese from transferring forces from Manchuria to the active fronts. In May Mountbatten took Rangoon.

(19) It had become clear that, helpless though the Japanese had now become, they could not be subdued by conventional means without an invasion of the Japanese archipelago involving terrible carnage on both sides, even though the Allied air forces were already ranging over it without opposition. Atomic research had been pursued by the Anglo-Americans since 1939. It had now developed two bombs. It was resolved to use them in the hope of persuading the Japanese to give up a defence which, however heroic, would be futile. Accordingly a bomb was dropped on Hiroshima on 6 Aug; the Russians declared war on 8 Aug. On 9 Aug. a second bomb hit Nagasaki. As with the Italians, the Japanese nation was saved by the realism of its hereditary sovereign who obtained the emotional acquiescence of the politicians and soldiers and broadcast defeat and surrender to his people a week later. The local military capitulation was formally signed on 2 Sept., whereupon the Russians invaded Manchuria. Surrenders in China and S.E. Asia were completed by 12 Sept. The Russians completed their operations on 23 Sept.

WORMS, CONCORDAT OF (1122). See INVESTITURE.

WORMS, DIET OF (1521). See LUTHER, MARTIN-3.

WOTTON (1) Sir Edward (1489-1551) sheriff of Kent in 1529, went with Henry VIII in 1532 to Calais of which, from 1540, he was treasurer. His brother **(2) Nicholas (?1497-1567),** a diplomat, was Cranmer's commissary in 1538 and negotiated the Cleves marriage in 1539. In 1540 he became a Sec. of State and was employed on missions to the Regent of the Netherlands in 1543 and then to Charles V and, in 1546, to arrange peace with France, where he was resident ambassador until 1549. A further mission to Charles V followed in 1551 and a further residence in France from 1553 to 1557. In 1558 he negotiated the P. of Cateau Cambrésis with France and a peace in 1560 with Scotland. He ended his busy diplomatic life in 1565 in the Netherlands arranging the terms of trade. Of his great-nephews **(3) Edward (1548-1626) 1st Ld. WOTTON (1603)** was one of Walsingham's diplomats, being employed in Vienna in 1574-5, in Scotland in 1585 and in France in 1586. He was a privy councillor and Comptroller of the Household in 1602. He was ambassador to France in 1610. His brother **(4) Sir Henry (1568-1639)** became Essex's Sec. and editor of foreign intelligence in 1595. He settled in Venice where he was ambassador from 1604 to 1612, 1616 to 1619 and from 1621 to 1624, after which he became Provost of Eton. He was also a delicate and well known poet. He defined an ambassador as *peregre missus*

ad mentiendum reipublicae causa: one sent abroad to lie for his country's good.

WRECK. See DROITS OF ADMIRALTY.

WREN (1) Sir Christopher (1591-1658) was Dean of Windsor from 1635 to 1658. His famous son **(2) Sir Christopher (1632-1723)** was Prof. of Astronomy at Gresham's College from 1657 to 1661 and at Oxford from 1661 to 1673. His interest in architecture began early for he was the King's Surveyor-Gen. of Works in 1661. He began the Sheldonian Theatre (Oxford) in 1664 was engaged in replanning London after the Fire in 1666 and completed his design for St. Paul's in 1673. He also built 52 city churches, the Monument, Chelsea Hospital (1682) and supervised repairs to Westminster Abbey. He started an ambitious rebuilding of Hampton Court Palace which had proceeded half way when he was dismissed in 1718. He also did much medical and anatomical work, initiated barometrical researches and was a founder of the Royal Society.

WREOCENSAETAN were a large Mercian folk who settled westwards of the Wrekin in the late 6th cent.

WRIGHT, Edward (1558-1615), Cambridge mathematician interested in navigation. He went to sea and, having experienced the amateurishness of navigation still in vogue, published *Certaine Errors in Navigation Detected and Corrected* (1599). This included a Mercator's chart of the North Atlantic and a clear exposition of the advantages of Mercator's projection.

WRIGHT, John Michael (?1625-1700) London portrait painter and rival of Lely.

WRIGHT, Joseph (1734-97) "of DERBY", painter mainly of candle and fire-lit subjects and conflagrations, achieved a great reputation in London from 1781.

WRIOTHESLEY originally WRITH or WRITHE. Of this distinguished courtier family **(1) Sir John Writh (?-1504),** herald to Henry VI and Edward IV, Garter King of Arms, was the first head of the College of Arms in 1483. His son **(2) Sir Thomas (?-1534)** succeeded him as Garter and organised the Tournai jousts of 1513. He changed the family name and was knighted by Ferdinand of Austria. His nephew **(3) Sir Thomas (1505-50) 1st Ld. WRIOTHESLEY (1544) 1st E. of SOUTHAMPTON** (1547) was ambassador to the Netherlands regency in 1538 to negotiate the abortive marriage proposal with the Duchess of Milan. M.P. for Hants in 1539, he became a joint Sec. of State in 1540. He advised the alliance with Charles V in 1543, which led to the invasion of France in 1544. He then became Lord Chancellor and was appointed one of Henry VIII's executors and a counsellor to Edward VI in 1547. He was immediately attacked and dismissed but readmitted to the Council in 1548. He joined the opposition to the Seymours but was sacrificed at the reconciliation of 1550 and dismissed just before his death. His son **(4) Henry (1545-81) 2nd E.,** was involved in a scheme to marry Mary Q. of Scots to Norfolk and spent the years 1569 to 1573 in prison. His son **(5) Henry (1573-1624) 3rd E.,** was the patron of Shakespeare who dedicated *Venus and Adonis* to him in 1593; they were on such close terms that he has been considered to be the friend of the *Sonnets*. He withdrew from Court in 1595 because of an affair with Elizabeth Vernon, whom he secretly married in 1599 to the Queen's displeasure. Accordingly he went with Essex to Ireland and so got involved in Essex's conspiracy, for which he was condemned to death; but the sentence was commuted and in 1603 James I released him and restored his honours. He financed Weymouth's Virginia expedition in 1605 and became increasingly interested in colonial development. In 1609 he became a member of the Virginia Co's Council and of that of the HEIC. He was an incorporator of the N.W. Passage Co. in 1612. of the Somers I. Co. in 1615 and from 1620 to 1624 treasurer of the Virginia Co. He had become a privy councillor in 1619 and was an opponent of Buckingham whose growing influence made it wise to go abroad. He died in command of a troop of volunteers at Bergen op Zoom. His son **(6) Thomas (1607-67) 4th E.**, supported the parliamentary doctrine that redress of grievances should precede supply but refused to countenance rebellion and became a close friend of the King, for whom he tried persistently to negotiate compromises. He retired after the King's murder but was Charles II's Lord Treasurer from 1660 to 1667. Honest and disinterested, he had great difficulty in managing the Govt's financial business efficiently because of the bad system which he inherited, the lack of statistics and the trade recession.

WRITERS TO THE SIGNET were clerks who drafted documents for the Scottish Kings' Secretary of State. When the Court of Session was created in 1532 they were recognised as part of it and, as writs under the signet then superseded brieves of chancery, their sphere of activity was much enlarged and they began to be sought as advisers and solicitors. This was, however, prohibited in 1594 and subsequently but the prohibitions fell into disuse and they were permitted to practice in the court of session along with solicitors and advocates' first clerks in 1754. The latter were amalgamated with the solicitors in 1850.

WRITS, ORIGINAL were issued by the Chancery upon the petition of a litigant to *originate* a legal proceeding. **(1)** The writ set out in standardised language the plaintiff's grievance and ordered the sheriff or appropriate officer to remedy it. The defendant could then resist the writ by requiring a court to pronounce whether or not the sheriff must obey it. The defendant might do this on the ground (i) that the grievance was not proved; (ii) that the sheriff was required to apply the wrong remedy; (iii) that the defendant was the wrong defendant; (iv) that the writ was addressed to the wrong officer; (v) that it was too late; (vi) on various technical grounds; (vii) that the writ disclosed a grievance unknown to the law or (viiii) which ought not to be remedied because he was entitled to do what was alleged. If the sheriff enforced an illegal writ he might himself be sued for damages for trespass or as the case might be, false imprisonment.

(2) The issue of an unprecedented writ thus amounted to the first step in making new law and if a court pronounced in favour of it, the new law was in effect "made" by the chancery and judges together. The barons regarded this with suspicion, for the number of standard original writs ("writs of course") increased rapidly with changes in society particularly in the 13th cent. The Provisions of Oxford (1258) required that the Chancellor "should seal no writ save writs of course without the command of the King and his council being present". The Statute of Westminster II (1285) permitted the Chancery to issue new writs *in consimili casu cadente sub eodem jure* (in a similar case falling under the same right) but required important or difficult cases to be referred in writing to the next parliament. By the mid-14th cent. parliament was recognised as the legislature and new writs ceased to be issued save *in consimili casu* or by authority of new legislation. *See* WRITS, REGISTER OF ORIGINAL.

WRITS, REGISTER OF ORIGINAL was a collection of original writs in use at a given time. It was kept by the Chancery but courts, sheriffs, bishops and even large landowners had copies, for in early times it was the only law book. Glanville's register (1187) contained 39 writs; the Cambridge Register Ti.vi 13 (c. 1230) 58; the Cambridge Register KK v 33 c. 1255 contains 121 writs but many are not original. The St. John's College Register (c. 1430) 215 plus many supplementary ("judicial") writs.

WROXETER. *See* URICONIUM.

WULFRED (?-832) became Abp. of Canterbury in 805. Wealthy, pluralist and influential, he fell foul of K. Cenwulf of Mercia, who deprived him of the monasteries at Reculver and Minster and laid charges against him at Rome. He was, however, on good terms with Cenwulfs successors and with Egbert.

WULFHERE, K. of the MERCIANS (r. c. 659-74). *See* MERCIA-4.

WULFSTAN (?-1023), Bp. of LONDON (996), Abp. of YORK and Bp. of WORCESTER in plurality (1002-16) York alone (1016-23), wrote homilies, many in Anglo-Saxon under the punning pseudonym *Lupus* (Lat = Wolf). In his *Sermo Lupi ad Anglos* (Lat = Wolf's Sermon to the English) (1014) he attributed the Danish invasions to the sins of the English. In a more practical vein he composed tracts on law, administration and society such as the *Institutes of Polity* (q.v.). His most important work was the drafting of the law codes of Ethelred II and Canute between 1008 and 1023.

WULFSTAN, St. (c. 1012-95) (Canonised 1203), son of a servant of the Bp. of Worcester, was educated at Evesham and Peterborough Abbeys and then returned to Worcester, firstly to Bp. Brihtheah's household where he was ordained. He soon became a monk at Worcester and later Prior. In 1062 he became bishop of this border diocese where the duties were both military and diocesan. He was fearless and known for his common sense as well as piety, simplicity of life and energy in perambulating the diocese. He accepted the changes wrought under the Conquest. Hence he survived the purges of 1070-2 and was a trusted associate of Abp. Lanfranc. In 1075 he helped to put down the revolt of the Es. of Norfolk and Hereford and he made a point of protecting and accommodating the many orphans of the disturbances. He died the last Anglo-Saxon bishop and a local cult sprang up for him which led to his canonisation. In 1216 K. John chose to be buried at his shrine in Worcester Cathedral.

WYANDOTS. *See* HURONS.

WYATT and WYATTVILLE. Influential practical artists, the best known being **(1) James (1746-1813)** who studied architecture in Rome and Venice. His first, and widely known commission, was to adapt the Oxford Street Pantheon (London) for stage performances (1770-2). He became Surveyor of Westminster Abbey in 1776 and this seminal event brought commissions to restore the cathedrals at Salisbury, Lincoln, Hereford and Lichfield. In the process he studied and helped to revive interest in Gothic (already inspired by Horace Walpole's Strawberry Hill). In 1796 he built the Royal Military Academy at Woolwich and became Surveyor-Gen. to the Board of Works. In 1796, also, the millionaire Wm. Beckford commissioned him to build the vast and improbable neo-Gothic mansion at Fonthill. His son **(2) Matthew Cotes (1777-1862)**, sculptor, executed equestrian statues, notably of George III, in Pall Mall East and of Wellington at Aldershot. A nephew of (1), **(3) Sir Jeffrey (1766-1840) later WYATTVILLE**, designed neo-Gothic additions to Sydney Sussex Coll., Cambridge and was then employed by George IV on the huge task of rebuilding Windsor Castle into its modern form (1824-8).

WYATT. Practical artists, possibly related to the above (1) Thomas Henry (1807-80), architect, built the Byzantine church at Wilton, Knightsbridge barracks and the Adelphi Theatre, Charing Cross. His brother **(2) Sir Matthew Digby (1820-77)**, expositor, published works on mediaeval mosaics, was Sec. to the committee of the Great Exhibition of 1851 and designed courts at the Crystal Palace, Sydenham, to exhibit the features of various architectural periods. He became the first Slade Prof. of Fine Arts at Cambridge in 1870.

WYATT (1) Sir Henry (?-1537) a Tudor politician, was imprisoned by Richard III but rescued by Henry VII. He was a supporter of the Boleyns and from 1524 to 1528 Treasurer of the King's Chamber. His son **(2) Sir Thomas (?1503-42)** one of Henry VIII's esquires, was a member of Russell's mission to the Curia in 1527, became Marshal of Calais in 1529 and a Privy Councillor in 1533.

Said to have been a lover of Anne Boleyn before her marriage, he was imprisoned on suspicion in 1536 but fought against the Pilgrimage of Grace, was knighted in 1537 and was ambassador to Charles V until 1539. In 1541 he again fell under suspicion as a supporter of Cromwell but was elected M.P. for Kent just before he died. His son **(3) Sir Thomas the younger (?1521-54)**, a friend of the Howards, was a member of the council at Boulogne in 1545. He supported the E. of Devon's attempts to prevent Q. Mary's marriage to Philip of Spain and, having raised Kent, was deserted at Southwark and executed. *See also* ELIZABETH I-2.

WYCLIF[FE], John (?1329-84). *See* LOLLARDY.

WYDEVILLE. *See* WOODVILLE.

WYKEHAM, William of (1324-1404), a protégé of Bp. Edington of Winchester, began his association with the King's Works (and enjoyed at least 14 prebends) as Surveyor of royal castles, especially Windsor (1359-63) where he administered much of Edward III's rebuilding. A talented and energetic organiser, he gained the King's confidence, becoming receiver of the Chamber (1361) and King's Sec. (1361-3). He was ordained in 1362 and became archdeacon of Lincoln in 1363 as well as Keeper of the Privy Seal (until 1367) while rebuilding at Wells Cathedral. He became Chancellor in 1367 just as Edward III secured (by way of reward) papal approval for his election as Bp. of Winchester. He could hold himself apart from contemporary factions because his see was rich and little affected by Lollardy or peasant discontents. Initially on good terms with John of Gaunt, the latter ousted him from the Chancery in 1371, but he seems to have been regarded as a man of independence and objectivity. The Good Parliament (1376) consequently appointed him as one of the councillors to control the King but this exposed him to John of Gaunt's full hostility. Accused of corruption and mismanagement as Chancellor, he was driven from court and deprived for a while of his temporalities. He was restored to favour and reconciled with John of Gaunt only after Edward III's death. He belonged, but only nominally, to the regency commission of 1386, but, retaining Richard II's trust, was Chancellor again from 1389 to 1391. These political difficulties, however, disturbed neither his activity as a builder nor in education. As Surveyor of Castles he made the acquaintance of leading master-masons (effectively architects) such as Hugh Herland, William Wynford and the great Henry Yevele. In 1378 he became Clerk of the King's Works as well as a splendid rebuilder of Winchester cathedral and also he designed and built his linked educational foundations of Winchester College (1378) and New College, Oxford (1379). This educational model, financed largely from his temporalities, eventually revolutionised university foundations and in the 15th cent. inspired, for example, Henry VI at Eton and King's College Cambridge while its physical aspects powerfully influenced Gothic design.

WYKES, Thomas (122-?93), priest and landowner, became an Augustinian canon at Osney Abbey, Oxford in 1282. Here he wrote a chronicle for 1066 to 1289 and probably continued the Osney Abbey chronicle to 1290 or 1293. He was interested in secular affairs such as government, finance and trade and, unusually, favoured Henry III against the barons.

WYLD (1) James (1790-1836), Geographer Royal, introduced lithography into Britain in the form of plans illustrating Peninsular War battles. His son **(2) James (1812-87)** continued the father's interest and also, as M.P. for Bodmin (1847-52, 1857-68), did much to advance technical education.

WYLIE, Alexander (1815-87) superintendent of the London Missionary Society's printworks at Shanghai from 1847, was the Society's agent with Lord Elgin's Yangtse expedition in 1858 and its permanent agent in China from 1863 to 1877. He was a notable Chinese scholar who

translated many works both ways and he proved that 14th cent. Chinese mathematicians had anticipated William Homer's (1786-1837) method of solving numerical equations by continuous approximation.

WYLIE, Sir James (1768-1854) became a Russian army doctor in 1790 and doctor to the Czar and the Grand Duke Alexander (later Alexander I) in 1799. He founded and was president (1804-34) of the Russian medical academy and effective director of military health. He came with Alexander I to England in 1814 when the Prince Regent knighted him.

WYNDHAM'S ACT (Ir.). *See* LAND PURCHASE ACT, 1903.

WYNDHAM. (1) Sir Hugh (?1603-84) serjeant and circuit judge under the Commonwealth, was deprived and then restored at the Restoration. His brother **(2) Sir Wadham (1610-68)** having, as serjeant, prosecuted the regicides, became a Justice of the King's Bench in 1660. His grandson **(3) Thomas (1681-1745) Ld. WYNDHAM of FINGLASS (1731)** became C.J. of the Irish Common Pleas in 1724 and was Lord Chancellor of Ireland from 1726 to 1739.

WYNDHAM (1) Sir William (1687-1740) 3rd Bart. Jacobite Tory M.P. for Somerset from 1710, was Sec. at War in 1712 and had some personal responsibility for the restraining orders which compromised the war of the Spanish Succession. George I regarded him as a dangerous enemy. He was Ch. of the Exch. in 1713-4. Arrested by way of precaution at the outbreak of the Jacobite rebellion in 1715, he was never brought to trial but remained an honest Tory though converted by Bolingbroke to the Hanoverian monarchy in 1723. He originally inspired and, with the Pulteneys and Bolingbroke, formed the important Patriot faction against excessive Hanoverianism in policy. In this he was almost certainly sincere. His second son **(2) Sir Charles (1710-63) 2nd E. of EGREMONT (1750)** started as Tory M.P. for Bridgwater in 1735 but went over to the Whigs and, after inheriting the earldom from an uncle, was much concerned with the local affairs of Cumberland. He also became a close friend of George III. As Sec. of State from 1761 he was concerned in the peace negotiations of 1762 and in the prosecutions of John Wilkes. His son **(3) Sir George (1751-1837) 3rd E.,** a minor politician and from 1819 Lord Lieut. of Sussex, settled at Petworth and became a munificent and advanced patron of the arts. He gave J. W. M. Turner a studio there and supported or helped many others including Constable, Flaxman, Robt. Haydon and Nollekens.

WYNDHAM-QUIN, Sir Edwin Richard Windham (1812-71) 3rd (Ir.) E. of DUNRAVEN (1850), 1st Ld. KENRY (U.K.) (1866) was Tory M.P. for Glamorgan from 1837 to 1851. A well known archaeologist and writer on architectural history.

WYNFORD, William (?-1403) architect (Master Mason) was Mason at Windsor when William of Wykeham was surveyor there in 1360. When Wykeham moved to Wells (1363) Wynford, though remaining in charge at Windsor, designed the Vicars' Close at Wells. As Bp. of Winchester from 1366 Wykeham regularly consulted him. In 1377 he finished at Windsor and in 1378 was put in charge of the defences of Southampton (in Wykeham's diocese). Subsequently he worked almost exclusively for his patron and was responsible for the radical designs of Winchester College and New College, Oxford, and the astounding nave and chancel of Winchester cathedral. *See* HULLE.

WYNN and WILLIAMS. (1) Sir William WILLIAMS (1634-1700), recorder of Chester from 1667 to 1684, became M.P. for Chester in 1675. An outspoken champion of parliamentary privilege against the crown he was Speaker in 1680 and 1681 and licensed Dangerfield's *Narrative*. In 1686 he was Algernon Sydney's counsel and Jeffreys had him fined for the licence of 1680. In 1687, however, he became sol-gen. and prosecuted the Seven Bishops in 1688. M.P. for Beaumaris in the Convention

Parliament he was a draftsman of the Bill of Rights (1689). His grandson **(2) Sir Watkin Williams (1692-1749) WYNN (from 1719)** was M.P. for Denbighshire from 1716 to 1749. He was suspected of Jacobitism. His descendants included **(3) Sir Henry Watkin Williams (1783-1856)** minister at Dresden (1803-7) and at Copenhagen (1824-53). His brother **(4) Charles Watkin Williams (1775-1850)**, a friend of Southey, was M.P. in 1797 and again from 1799 to 1850. He was in the Cabinet as Pres. of the Bd. of Control from 1822 to 1828.

WYNTOUN, Andrew of (c. 1350-1420) (Sc.) Prior of St. Serf on Lochleven, wrote a metrical *Orygynal Cronykil of Scotland* recording Scots history from the Creation to 1406.

WYON, George (?-1796) was a Sheffield engraver. His sons and their sons (seven in all) between 1787 and 1891 were leading engravers, especially of seals, at the Royal Mint. Their styles dominated official medal and coinage design until about 1960.

WYSE, Sir Thomas (1791-1862) married Laetitia, daughter of Lucien Bonaparte in 1821 but they separated in 1828. In 1830 he became M.P. for Tipperary and from 1835 to 1847 for Waterford. A strong Catholic emancipationist, he was also a leading educational reformer. From 1846 to 1849 he was Sec. of the Bd. of Control and from 1849 until 1859 Minister in Athens, where his mission was a complete success, being mainly concerned with Greek financial affairs.

X

XANTEN, T. of (1614). *See* JÜLICH.

XEBEC. *See* SHIPS, SAILING.

XENOPHON (?430-after 362 B.C.) Greek general successively in Athenian, Persian and Spartan service and historian. His many stylistically lucid works, especially the *Anabasis* (Gr = March North), formed the foundation of the classically based higher instruction which from 1700 to 1914 gave most educated Englishmen a common background, as well as a knowledge of 4th cent. B.C. Greek and Persian politics.

XERES or JEREZ de la FRONTERA (SHERRY) (Sp.). *See* WINE TRADE.

XHOSA, XOSA or KAFFIRS (Arab = Unbelievers) were a group of E. Natal cattle-raising tribes organised in patrilineal clans. When the Dutch settlers moved east from the Cape in the 1770s they collided near the Great Fish River with the Xhosa who, under pressure from other tribes, were moving west. The Gov. van Plettenberg fixed the frontier at the river in 1778 and in 1779 expelled the Xhosa and provoked the *First* of the **KAFFIR WARS**. They did not give up and he fought a *Second* War in 1789. The British continued the Dutch policy and fought the *Third* (1799). Xhosa persistence, however, gave rise to Sir John Craddock's punitive expedition (The *Fourth* War) of 1812 and a *Fifth* war in 1819, after which the river was guarded by a chain of expensive and ineffectual military posts and a neutral zone to the Keiskama. The pressure, however, continued and a drought brought a mass migration, repulsed in the *Sixth* War (1834-5) by Sir Benjamin d'Urban: he now advanced the frontier to the Great Kei and expelled the Xhosa within it. The annexed territory was briefly known as **QUEEN ADELAIDE PROVINCE.** This arrangement was worse than before, for the Xhosa continued to multiply in a more constricted area and the province was soon abandoned. The result was the *Seventh* War (1846) and the province was reannexed as **BRITISH KAFFRARIA** in 1847. Attempts to interfere with the chiefs' prerogatives here provoked the long *Eighth* War (1850-3) after which British Kaffraria became a Crown Colony. The despair thus engendered brought messianic visions, culminating in the great slaughter of 1857, when the Xhosa killed their cattle, destroyed their crops and died in thousands. Hence the frontiers between the two Kaffrarias remained quiescent and British Kaffraria was taken into Cape Colony in 1865. Meanwhile the Xhosa began to multiply again and to acquire firearms. The frontier became unsettled; the *Ninth* and last war broke out in 1877 and lasted until 1879. The tribes were disarmed and native Kaffraria was progressively annexed between 1879 and 1894. The appellation *Kaffir* was probably applied because of the British difficulty in pronouncing the click represented by the letter X.

XIMENES DE CISNEROS, Francisco (1436-1517) Card. (1507) became confessor to Q. Isabella the Catholic in 1494 and Spanish Franciscan Provincial. In 1495 he accepted the Archbishopric of Toledo at express papal command and thenceforth was the most powerful man in Spain. He instigated the expulsion of the Moors in 1497; he organised and financed the capture of Mers-el-Kebir in 1505 and Oran in 1509, and instituted important military and financial reforms.

X-RAYS were discovered by Röntgen in 1895.

XYZ COMPANY was the common name for the Canadian New N.W. Co. founded in 1798 and absorbed into the North West Co. in 1804.

Y

YACHTING. The Dutch gave Charles II two lee-board yachts at the Restoration but English builders promptly designed proper keeled yachts, in two of which Charles and his brother James raced between Greenwich and Gravesend for £100 in 1661. This was the first such race recorded in English waters. The first club was founded at Cork in 1720; the Cumberland Fleet or Sailing Society, later the Royal Thames Yacht Club, in 1775; the Yacht Racing Assoc. in 1875. Many different types of yacht were designed and discarded up to 1939 but after World War II designs suitable for mass production came onto the market and small boat racing became a growth industry not only in salt waters but in reservoirs, rivers and flooded gravel pits.

YALE. Elihu Yale (1649-1721), born at Boston (Mass.) entered the HEIC and from 1687 to 1692 was gov. of Fort St. George (Madras). In 1699 he became a gov. of the Co. In 1701 a group of Congregationalist ministers founded – with benefactions from him – a **college** under a colonial charter at Saybrook (Conn.) whence it moved eventually, in 1716, to New Haven (Conn.). It was given a royal charter in 1745 and, by the rebellion, had established faculties of divinity, mathematics, astronomy and physics. One of the most advanced liberal universities of its time, it developed very rapidly after independence.

YALTA CONFERENCE (Feb. 1945) between Pres. Roosevelt, Winston Churchill and Joseph Stalin, reaffirmed the decision to accept only unconditional surrender from Germany and agreed separate four-power occupations of Germany, Berlin, Austria and Vienna. Russia was to attack Japan after the German surrender and they agreed on a meeting at San Francisco to set up the U.N.O. A great diplomatic success for the Russians, it ensured the domination of Eastern Europe by their army and police until the upheavals of 1989-90.

YANDABO, T. of (Feb. 1826). *See* BURMA-8.

YANKEE possibly derived from the Dutch *Janke* (= Jack) was used by New Englanders derisorily; then of North Americans by the English in the 18th cent; and finally by southerners of New Englanders or Unionists as an insult.

YARDLAND. (1) ¼ share. **(2)** An area, varying in extent according to the district, but most commonly of 30 acres and considered to be a quarter of a hide.

YARM. *See* MIDDLESBROUGH.

YARMOUTH (I. of W.) was chartered in 1334 and returned two M.Ps. until 1832. It was the ferry terminal between the I. of Wight and Hampshire and a Tudor artillery fort corresponding with the Calshot battery on the mainland was built there to protect the western approach to Southampton Water.

YARMOUTH, GREAT (Norfolk) was founded in the 11th cent. at the common mouth of the Norfolk Broads rivers, and K. John chartered it. The Fair attracted much business away from the Cinque Ports, whose ships often attacked and sometimes blockaded it. This intermittent private war continued into Tudor times when Henry VIII's fleet combined with shifts in trade routes and patterns ended it and the town declined into a fishing port. It returned two M.Ps. from 1295 to 1867 and one until 1948. It became a county borough in 1888.

YARROW, Sir Alfred Fernandez (1842-1932) Bart (1916) began building torpedo boats in 1876. He invented the high-pressure water tube boiler and made a world-wide reputation as a builder of fast warships. In 1907 his shipyard was moved from the Thames to the Clyde.

YAWS. *See* SYPHILIS.

YEAR BOOKS are a collection of reports of legal cases, extending from 1292 to 1534, written mostly in law French. Abridgments were made by Sir Anthony Fitzherbert in 1516 and by Sir Richard Brooke in 1568.

YEAR, DAY AND WASTE. A royal right to enjoy a felon's property, as indicated by the name, before returning it to the lord of the fee to whom it was forfeited.

YEATS, William Butler (1860-1939), of a protestant artistic family, trained as a painter but realised his poetic genius in English to reflect the mystic and religious atmosphere of the Co. Sligo of his formative years. His first major work was *The Wanderings of Oisin* (1889), his last, other than the posthumous *Last Poems and Plays* (1940) was *The Winding Star* (1929). He also encouraged and wrote for the Abbey Theatre in Dublin. A poet of international stature and timelessness, his portrayal of atmosphere was unique in modern times.

YEAVERING (N'land) had a palace of K. Edwin of Northumbria (r. 617-33) which was the scene of preaching and mass baptism by Paulinus in 627. Excavations have shown, among other buildings, four wooden halls each nearly 100 feet long.

YELLOW BACKS, so called from their binding, were the cheap 'railway novels' of the '80s and '90s of the 19th cent.

YELLOW DISEASE. *See* RELAPSING FEVER.

YELLOW FEVER. An acute disease of hot climates carried by mosquitoes, mainly *Aedes Aegypti,* originally confused with Dengue and associated with the slave trade. It appears that negroes carry but resist it, for Yellow Fever epidemics occurred among Europeans after dysentery among blacks at Guadeloupe in 1635, Barbados and St. Kitts in 1647 and at Jamaica in 1655. Thereafter it became endemic in the Caribbean, the Spanish Main and, in the 18th cent., in adjacent parts of N. America and was carried back to Spain (1730), W. Africa (1778) and Morocco (1793). European garrisons and fleets in the American area always suffered heavily, sometimes to the point of total ineffectiveness. A British expedition to the Spanish Main in 1741 lost about 8500 out of 12,000. The French lost 30,000 troops in the Caribbean islands between 1795 and 1798. In the Antilles outbreak of 1837 40 losses in the British garrisons varied between 15% and 69%. There were serious outbreaks in the Antilles which began in 1852, spread to the U.S.A. and even reached Swansea in 1865. Others occurred in 1866-9, 1875-8 and 1905. *See* EPIDEMICS, HUMAN.

YELLOW JOURNALISM or YELLOW PRESS. This term for sensational journalism originated in 1895 with an experimental coloured issue of the *New York World.*

YELLOW PERIL. The danger, much discussed in the 19th cent., of an Asiatic invasion of Europe. The idea was publicised in Oswald Spengler's *Decline of the West* and by a speech of Kaiser William II at Bremerhafen in 1900. The phrase returned to use in Australia during World War II.

YELVERTON. (1) Sir William (c. 1400-c. 1472) became Recorder of Norwich in 1433, M.P. for Great Yarmouth in 1435 and 1436 and a King's Bench judge in 1443. In 1450 he conducted an unsuccessful judicial tour of E. Anglia in pursuit of the Tuddenham-Haydon gang. As one of Sir John Fastolf's executors he was in conflict with the Pastons. He had been opposed to Edward IV, but after a reconciliation, nevertheless supported Henry VI's readeption (1470-1) and was demoted to the court of Common Pleas. His descendent **(2) Sir Christopher (?1535-1612)** was M.P. for Brackley in 1562 and for Northampton in 1572 when he made a strong defence of Commons' privilege. He became a serjeant-at-law in 1589. He was M.P. for Northamptonshire in 1592 and again in 1597 when he was elected Speaker. In 1598 he became Queen's Serjeant and was prominent in the prosecution of Essex for treason in 1600. He became a Queen's Bench judge in 1602. His son **(3) Sir Henry (1566-1629)** was M.P. for Northampton for the first time in 1603 and had an erratic career. He opposed the royal view in *Goodwin's Case* (1604) and attacked Dunbar, and the bills for uniting the Kingdoms in 1606 and 1607 but he refused to speak against the royal case on the *Post Nati* and in 1610 defended the prerogative to impose duties on imports on the extreme ground that as the Common Law extended only to low water mark the King could deny goods before they reached it. In 1613 he succeeded Bacon as Sol-Gen. but refrained from speaking on impositions in the Addled Parliament (1614). When Bacon became Lord Keeper, Yelverton became Att-Gen. (1617) after a wrangle with Buckingham which ended with the latter recommending him to James. Almost immediately he was, at Buckingham's instance, prosecuting infringements of monopolies in the Star Chamber. In 1619, however, as a Star Chamber commissioner himself, he refused to continue the imprisonment of some silkmen for such infringements unless Bacon supported him. Bacon thereupon had him prosecuted in the Star Chamber for irregularities in the issue of a charter to the City of London; in 1621 he was relieved of the Attorneyship and prosecuted in the Lords in connection with the monopolies. Condemned and fined, he was released into retirement. In May 1625, however, Charles I made him a judge of the Common Pleas. He compiled an important set of King's Bench Reports.

YELVERTON CASES. Maria (Theresa) LONGWORTH (?1832-81), the author, married William Charles YELVERTON (1824-83) 4th Vist. AVONMORE, in 1857 by a R. Catholic priest at his chapel in Ireland. He repudiated the marriage and remarried in Scotland in 1858. The first marriage was upheld by the Irish courts in 1861; the second by the Scottish courts in 1862. The Scottish court was upheld by the House of Lords in 1864. She published several novels and the *Yelverton Correspondence* between 1861 and 1875.

YEMEN (*see* ARABIA). After the Ottoman Empire broke up in 1918 the Zaydi Imam Yahya ibn Mohammed (?-1948) established a primitive autocracy. He was succeeded by his son Ahmad (r. 1948-62). There had been family conspiracies or tribal revolts in 1948, 1955, 1960 and 1961. In 1962 an Egyptian inspired cabal of army officers led by Abdulla al Sallal, with townsmen and southern sheikhs, overthrew Ahmad's successor, Mohammad al Badr who, however, escaped northwards. There followed a civil war between the royalists supported by Saudi Arabia, and Sallal with the republicans supported by Egypt. Saudi and Egyptian forces were eventually withdrawn in the face of the Israeli threat in 1968. Sallal was deposed in 1968 after the republican victory. *See* ADEN AND YEMEN.

YEOMAN originally meant a free man above the status of a villein but less than a gentleman or one who, being above a villein, had prospects, or was an important servant of an important person. By the early 16th cent. the word was acquiring the technical meaning of one who owned freehold land worth 40s. a year or more and who, therefore, had, outside a borough, a parliamentary vote.

YEOMEN OF THE GUARD ('BEEFEATERS') were first raised in 1485.

YEOMANRY were mounted auxiliary troops first raised for home defence in 1761 and organised in county regiments in 1794. IMPERIAL YEOMANRY for overseas service were raised for the Boer War (1900-1902).

YESILKÖY, otherwise SAN STEFANO. *See* BULGARIA.

YEVELE, Henry (?-1400) Master Mason (architect) of parts of Windsor Castle under William of Wykeham and later architect of Westminster Hall, the naves of Westminster Abbey and Canterbury Cathedral and other places. Because of the association with Wykeham, it is not certain how much of his work was really by Wykeham's masters Hugh Herland or William Wynford or vice-versa.

Y.M.C.A., Y.W.C.A. (YOUNG MEN'S, or WOMEN'S, CHRISTIAN ASSOC.). The Y.M.C.A. was founded by Sir George Williams (1821-1905) in 1844. It spread to the U.S.A. in 1851. The Y.W.C.A. was founded in 1857 and spread to the U.S.A. in 1858. Both bodies became famous for soldiers' welfare in both World Wars.

YOGA. *See* HINDUISM.

YONGE, Charlotte Mary (1823-1901), a disciple of her neighbour John Keble, expounded his religious views in many works of fiction, notably *The Heir of Redcliffe* (1853), *Heartsease* (1854), *The Daisy Chain* and *The Trial* (1856). She also wrote historical romances and histories, 160 works in all.

YORK (Lat: EBORACUM; Dan: JORVIK) was founded in about A.D. 72 for the IXth Legion as a fortress and *Colonia*, the IXth being replaced by the VIth in the 2nd cent. The fortress, on the left bank of the Ouse, was on the site of the present Minster: the *colonia* was on the right bank. They were the military and administrative focus of N. Britain. Of the Emperors, Hadrian and Constantius improved the walls, Septimius Severus (211) and Constantius died there and Constantine was proclaimed there in 306. The Roman occupation lasted until about A.D. 400 and though little is known about York in the next two centuries it remained a place of some prestige. For the Roman missionary church it was the obvious place for a provincial see (625) and K. Edwin of Northumbria was baptised there and made it his capital (627) (*see* NORTHUMBRIA; YORK, ARCHBISHOPRIC; YORK, SCANDINAVIAN KINGDOMS OF).

(2) The city's position, in a fertile hinterland, is at the head of the Humber on the junction of the Foss and the Ouse and at the crossing of the northern highway over the latter. It had a large trade based (as is shown by the recent Coppergate excavations) on wool towards the Low Countries, Frisia and the Baltic so that the damage which it suffered in William the Conqueror's northern devastation was more easily made up than elsewhere in the area (*see* STAPLE). In fact it was a magnet for the north with its huge, if slowly built, Minster and dozens of churches and monastic institutions. Eleven parliaments met there between 1298 and 1335 and the Common Law Courts and Exchequer were several times established there, notably in 1298-1304 and 1333-8. The prosperity, however, began to fall away as ships grew bigger and found it harder to reach the quays and by Tudor times the trade pattern had changed from export of wool to making and exporting the more labour intensive cloth. The dissolution of the monasteries also had a marked effect, for much monastic property was concentrated within the walls. Nevertheless its prestige remained high not only as an economic centre. Later, as the seat of the Council of the North (q.v.) it retained the functions of a real northern capital until the union of the crowns in 1603 which abolished an external challenge and the need for a response to it.

(3) The Civil War, in which royalist York was elaborately besieged, hastened a stagnation which had already begun; the wholesale movement of the cloth industry to the Pennine foothills depriving the city of most of its economic foundation. Nevertheless its position on the Great North Road still gave it importance as a communications centre and this in turn brought the railway, the 19th cent. establishment of locomotive and coach works and, in due course, an extensive revival based upon engineering. The population grew from 16,000 in 1801 to 78,000 in 1901 and to 105,000 in 1951.

YORK, ARCHBISHOPRIC. (1) A Celtic bishop went from York to the Council of Arles in 314 but the more recent see began with Paulinus' consecration in 625 and his baptism of K. Edwin in 627. The pre-reformation see is intimately connected with northern secular as well as ecclesiastical politics. In particular its function was long disputed with (a) the Irish monks, originally from Iona, who had bishops at Lindisfarne and Hexham; then (b) with the Scots over jurisdiction; (c) with Canterbury over primacy; and (d) with the bishops of Durham over their immunities. In the background and foreground was the endless poverty, disorder, depopulation and sometimes devastation of the province caused by Scandinavian, Scottish and civil wars, the feuds of magnates such as the Percys with the Nevilles or of clans such as the Reeds with the Halls and the habitual banditry of the marches. The see, though high in rank and claims, was so poor that Saxon and early Norman archbishops often held it in plurality especially (for uncertain, perhaps family, reasons) with Worcester. *See* SAMSON.

(2) The noticeable differentiation of the North from the adjacent Scots and southern English areas sometimes caused the Archbishops to champion the North because they were its greatest figures. In the 10th cent. they supported Scandinavian rather than West Saxon Kings, and Abp. Scrope was involved in rebellions against Henry IV. They also had defence business. The turbulent Border included the Franchise of Hexham which belonged to the see; and Abps. Thurstan in 1138 and Bowet in 1417 mobilised and commanded armies.

(3) After the Synod of Whitby (664) the retreat of Celtic Christianity was only a matter of time and the bishop's jurisdiction was felt in such areas as were under the Northumbrian Kingdom. York first became the effective centre under Abp. Egbert (r. 732-66), who founded the famous school, but as a result of political boundary fluctuations, especially during the Scandinavian invasions, the ecclesiastical and civil areas ceased to coincide. After he received the *pallium* (735) he had consecrated a bishop for the Galwegian see of Whithorn which remained dependent upon York for centuries and this led to further consecrations of, and occasional professions of obedience by, other Scottish bishops. The metropolitan claims in Scotland could be supported by early papal pronouncements, which had envisaged the division of Britain into two co-equal provinces, each with twelve bishops. In practice the influence of York became shadowy once the Scottish church ceased to be merely missionary and the Scottish monarchy had become an effective institution, frequently hostile to England. Moreover, poverty inhibited energetic action at a distance. When in 1188 Clement III agreed at the request of William the Lion to make the Scottish church directly dependent upon the Holy See, he was only giving formal expression to practicalities.

(4) The same papal pronouncements supported the independence of York from Canterbury or even primacy. The controversy began after the Conquest between Abp. Thomas of Bayeux and Lanfranc. The papacy supported Lanfranc (1071) but Calixtus III released Thurstan from obedience in 1118. Canterbury, however, was rich, better located and had a recognised position as the King's first adviser and the only prelate entitled to crown him. Moreover he had twelve English and, after 1187, four Welsh suffragans while York had only the often hostile bishop of Durham and the remote and sometimes Scottish occupied suffragan sees at Carlisle and at Whithorn. Thus the real, if not the formal, primacy slowly passed to Canterbury despite protests, occasional quarrels and brawls. Innocent VI finally approved a compromise giving each the precedence over the whole country but excluding the interference of each in the Province of the other.

(5) The difficulties with Durham arose partly as an inheritance from Lindisfarne (which Durham succeeded), partly from the secular functions of the bishop as a palatine and military ruler and partly because many mediaeval bishops of Durham were court politicians who, while neglecting their spiritual duties, could make trouble with the King. Hence the archiepiscopal authority

was only gradually asserted as the secular usefulness of the bishopric declined in the 15th cent.

(6) The primitive conditions and, perhaps, the Celtic monastic tradition gave the York Province a different religious character from that of Canterbury. Monasticism was exceedingly strong and relatively uncorrupt down to Tudor times. Yorkshire then alone had 21 friaries, the Benedictines and Cistercians had 20 houses each (*see* YORKSHIRE-2), the Augustinians had 13 and there were 16 collegiate churches and 91 hospitals. Elsewhere the monastic density was comparable with the populations. The heads of these houses did the work of bishops and the monks exerted a powerful economic and technological, as well as religious, influence. Their existence probably inhibited the creation of suffragan sees. Their dissolution (1536-8) had a revolutionary effect not felt elsewhere and provoked the peculiarly provincial rebellion of the Pilgrimage of Grace. It also resulted (1541) in the endowment of the new see of Chester involving the transfer of part of Lichfield to York, but its general effect was to weaken the influence of the church without strengthening the metropolitan power.

(7) The long range consequence of this was that when industrialisation started to raise the population of the northern church, which had in any case harboured puritans as well as adherents of the old religion, was unable to keep up with the rising fervour of 18th cent. non-conformity. York itself became a citadel of Methodism.

YORK, Card. of. *See* JACOBITES.

YORK, DUKE OF. Apart from the mediaeval House of this royal title, it was also borne by Henry Tudor (Henry VII) from 1494; by James II before his accession; and by George V and George VI before theirs'. The princes Ernest Augustus (1674-1728) and Frederick Augustus were Ds. of York and Albany. It was revived for Elizabeth II's son Andrew.

YORK, HOUSE OF. The strength of this branch of the royal family in the Wars of the Roses lay in the midlands and the south, not in Yorkshire. It originated with **(1) Edmund of Langley (1341-1402) E. of CAMBRIDGE (1362) 1st D. of YORK (1385)**, 5th son of K. Edward III He served under his father in France in 1359 and under his brother, the Black Prince, in Spain in 1367 and at the sack of Limoges in 1370. He married Isabella, daughter of Pedro the Cruel of Castile, in 1372. In 1374 he became Lieut. in Brittany, Constable of Dover in 1376 and one of the council of regency for Richard II in 1377. In 1385, when he went with the King on the Scottish expedition, Richard made him D. of York to counter-balance the great influence of York's brother, John of Gaunt, D. of Lancaster and he occasionally acted as the King's Lieut. during his absence but he would not be drawn into quarrels with his brother and gave his allegiance to Lancaster's son Henry IV willingly. He retired after Henry's coronation. His son **(2) Edward of Norwich (?1373-1415) E. of RUTLAND (1390), of CORK (1396) 2nd D.** was Admiral of England from 1392 to 1398 and Constable of the Tower from Jan. 1392. He accompanied Richard II to Ireland in 1394. In 1396 he became Warden of the Cinque Ports and in 1397 Warden and Justice of the Forests S. of the Trent and Lord of the I. of Wight. As a royal partisan he led the arrest of the D. of Gloucester and the Es. of Warwick and Arundel in June 1397. He received Gloucester's Constableship of England and his former Dukedom of Albemarle. These and all royal grants to him since June 1397 were revoked by Henry IV immediately after his usurpation and he received 20 challenges to combat as the supposed murderer of Gloucester. By Dec. 1399, however, he was restored to the Council and in 1401 he became Lieut. of Aquitaine. In 1403 he became Lieut. in S. Wales. For his part in the plot to abduct the Mortimers, whose royal claims equalled those of Henry IV, he was cosmetically arrested in 1405 and in 1406 reappointed Constable of the Tower. In 1412 he went to France under the D. of Clarence and while there made a claim to the throne of Aragon in right of his mother. Under Henry V he returned to S. Wales and in 1414 became Warden of the East March as well. In due course he joined the King on his expedition to France, commanded the right wing at the B. of Agincourt and was killed. His brother **(3) Richard (?-1415), E. of CAMBRIDGE (1414)** married Anne Mortimer and was executed for his part in the plot of 1415 against Henry V. His son **(4) Richard (1411-60) 3rd D. (1415)** inherited the Mortimer possessions in 1425 and married Cicely Neville in 1438. In 1440 he became Lieut. in France and on his return in 1445 became the head of the anti-Neville and Somerset faction (*see* HENRY VI; ROSES, WARS OF). He was killed at the B. of Wakefield. His eldest child was **(5) Edward IV (1461-83)** whose children were **(6) Edward V (1483)** and **Richard, D. of York,** the princes in the Tower. The eleventh child of (4), **(8)** was **Richard III (1452-85), King (1483).**

YORK (Ont.). *See* TORONTO.

YORK (Pennsylvania). In June 1777, when the British advanced on Philadelphia, the Continental Congress moved to York which became the rebel capital until Sept. 1778.

YORK, SCANDINAVIAN KINGDOMS OF. A. DANISH. (1) When in 875 the English K. Ricsige died HALFDAN, a son of Ragnar Lothbrok, had settled a large part of the Danish Great Host in the Vale of York. Its members formed a military aristocracy superimposed upon the depressed and sometimes enslaved population. Halfdan himself left in 877 for Ireland where he was killed. The identity of his immediate successors is uncertain but K. GUTHFRITH (?-895), a Christian, was probably responsible for assisting the Danish invasion led by Haeste in 892.

(2) The county of Yorkshire roughly represented this Kingdom's extent. It was powerful at sea and had close connections with northern France. The otherwise unknown Kings CNUT and SEIFRED, who followed Guthfrith, minted coins both at York and at Quentovic on the French R. Canche. York Danish support saved other Danish invaders from disaster and their seaborne raids prompted Alfred to create his own navy. Under K. Edward the Elder they sheltered his rebel cousin Aethilwold (c. 900) who fell in an E. Anglian battle in 902. After seven years of peace war broke out again and ended in the destruction of the York-Danish army at the B. of Wednesfield (Staffs) in 910.

B. OSTMEN. (3) After Wednesfield the West Saxons subdued the midland Danes but the battle left the Kingdom of York open to aggression by the Ostmen who were settling the Wirral and pillaging the area between the Mersey and the Ribble. Piracy and banditry turned into colonisation, while further north the Strathclyde Britons took over Cumbria from the English of Bamburgh. These English, the Britons and the Scots soon had a joint enemy in the Ostman RAENGVALD, who defeated the Scots and English at Corbridge in 915 and then in 918. After wintering in Northumbria he stormed York and became its King (919). A year later his cousin Sygtryg of Dublin invaded Cheshire but achieved little against Edward the Elder's defence works: and later in that year Raegnvald, Ealdred of Bamburgh and the King of Scots acknowledged Edward's overlordship at Bakewell. Raegnvald I died in 921 and SYGTRYG (?-927) succeeded him at York. The compact of Bakewell held until he died.

(4) OLAF, his son, succeeded him. His kinsman Guthfrith, K. of Dublin, came in support but Athelstan drove them both out. At an assembly at Eamont the Scots, the Strathclyde Britons and the English of Bamburgh submitted to him and undertook to suppress heathenism; Guthfrith, however, made an unsuccessful attempt on York and then fled to Ireland. Athelstan seized York for himself.

(5) The ensuing peace was precarious and trouble led Athelstan in 931 to mount a combined operation which reached Kincardine by land and Caithness (a Viking staging area) by sea. Then OLAF GUTHFRITHSON succeeded in Dublin and in reply formed a grand alliance with the Scots and Britons of Strathclyde. This materialised in a major invasion, stopped with heavy fighting at Brunanburgh (937). Athelstan died in 939, whereupon Olaf seized York and during a combined invasion and southern Danish revolt in 940, the magnates made K. Edmund cede the Mercian territory north of Watling St. Olaf died and in 941 OLAF SYGTRIG'S SON started to clear the isolated Anglian earldom centred on Bamburgh. His resources were inadequate: Edmund attacked him from the south and forced him to abandon his new Mercian area. Some of his people deposed him for RAGNVAELD II, a brother of Olaf Guthfrithson, and each intrigued with Edmund, who was only too happy to have both of them baptised. In 944 Ragnvaeld raised an insurrection whereupon Edmund drove them both away, retook York and attacked Strathclyde (945).

(6) After Edmund's assassination (945) the York Norse and Ostmen accepted Eadred for want of a better and in 947 swore oaths to him at Tanshelf. Within months the better appeared in the person of K. ERIC BLOODAXE, who had been driven from Norway after a short, bloody reign and they changed their mind. Eadred promptly marched north, burned Ripon Minster and, after a setback at Castleford in Airedale, forced them to change their mind again. A few months later, when he had gone south, Olaf Sigtryg's son reappeared from Dublin and was accepted as King. Eric Bloodaxe, however, ended his second reign (949-52) by chasing him out. Relying on a local Norse minority he maintained a saga heroes' warrior court at York but in 954 the Northumbrian English and Ostmen revolted and he was slain on Stainmore, at the head of Edendale. This enabled Edred to return; he conferred the Scandinavian area upon Oswulf, the Earl at Bamburgh of the English Northumbrians.

YORKE. (1) Philip (1690-1764) 1st Ld. (1733) and 1st. E. of HARDWICKE (1754) became M.P. for Lewes in 1719, sol-gen. in 1720 and att-gen. in 1724. In 1733 he became C.J. of the King's Bench and in 1737 Lord Chancellor. He was one of George II's regents in 1740 and a determined Hanoverian during the 45. He presided as Lord High Steward at the trial of the rebel lords and was mainly responsible for the abolition of Scots heritable jurisdictions and the proscription of the tartan. He resigned in 1756 as a result of the Minorca crisis. His main professional achievement was the conversion of Equity from a collection of precedents into a system. His younger son **(2) Charles (1722-70)** was M.P. for Reigate from 1747, counsel for the HEIC in 1751, sol-gen. from 1756 to 1761 and att-gen. in 1762 when he had to deal with Wilkes *North Briton No. 45*. In 1765 he resigned, became a Rockingham Whig and was again att-gen. from 1765 to 1767. He drafted the Quebec Act and was Lord Chancellor for a few days before he died suddenly. His brother **(3) Joseph (1724-92) 1st Ld. DOVER** (1788), a soldier and diplomat, was not only an M.P. from 1751 to 1780 but also minister or ambassador at The Hague, as well as rising steadily through the army, in which by 1777 he was a gen. Of the sons of (2), **(4) Charles Philip (1764-1834)** was Sec. at War from 1801 to 1803, Home Sec. from 1803 to 1804 and 1st Lord of the Admiralty from 1810 to 1811. His brother **(5) Sir Joseph Sydner (1768-1831)** was M.P. almost continuously from 1790 to 1831; a professional seaman, he was a Lord of the Admiralty from 1810 to 1818. His son **(6) Charles Philip (1799-1873) 4th E. of HARDWICKE (1834),** also a sailor, was M.P. from 1831 to 1834, P.M.G. (in the Cabinet) in 1852 and became a Rear Admiral in 1854.

YORKSHIRE (1) The area of the old shire, its division into Ridings (Dan: *thrydings* = thirds) and subdivision into wapentakes were the legacy of the Scandinavian kingdoms of York (q.v.). It was devastated in 1069 by William the Conqueror and, apart from York itself took some years to recover but great honours were created at Richmond (for Alan Rufus), Pontefract (for Ilbert de Lacy), Sherburn-in-Elmet (for the Abp. of York) and Howden for the Bps. of Durham who already had Crayke and received Northallerton from William II. Richmond long belonged to the rulers of Brittany: the great castles at Conisbrough and Sandal to the Warennes.

(2) Cereal cultivation and cattle and sheep-raising created a theoretically balanced economy with a rising surplus of wool and leather exported through the port of York. The wildernesses were cleared or reclaimed and turned into rich farms and ranches by the many regular and secular bodies, notably the monasteries at Fountains, Rievaulx, Jervaulx, Byland, Whitby, Selby, Easby, Roche, Kirkstall, Bridlington, Bolton and Beverley. The resulting supply of cheap food as well as the exportables created the prosperity of York whose population rose as clothmaking and cloth exporting replaced the export of raw wool. The interlock between agriculture and religion and between religious bodies and welfare remained close well into the 16th cent. so that the Dissolution of the Monasteries provoked, in the Pilgrimage of Grace (1536-7) a social revolt against a social, as well as a religious, revolution and its suppression did not prevent another more religious revolt in the Northern Rebellion of 1569.

(3) The appearance of water-driven machines such as the 13th cent. fulling mill in the serial processes of clothmaking so much reduced costs that the textile industry could afford the extra distance from the port of York and go up to the Dales to obtain good heads of water. Hence the foundation of Bradford, Huddersfield and Halifax.

(4) Coal was mined in the 13th cent. and facilitated iron working, particularly cutlery, at Sheffield and the surrounding Hallamshire. 18th cent. coal mining and its derivative, steam power, brought the textile industry back eastwards towards Leeds and the pitheads (though factories continued to be called mills) and with the increase of ship tonnages, the port facilities of Edward I's outport at Hull mostly superseded those at York. The combination of metal working and steam soon inspired engineering industries. The first locomotive powered railway ran between Stockton and Darlington on Teesside. Locomotive and carriage works sprang up at the railway junction at Doncaster and reanimated York.

(5) The three ridings shared a single sheriff but were otherwise treated as shires for administrative and judicial purposes. Consequently they had separate county councils from 1888 to 1974 when other local govt. counties superseded them. Some of these disappeared in 1995.

(6) Yorkshiremen have long been marked off by a hard-headed yet generous common sense and a downright pithy dialect (*Y'can't 'ave owt for nowt*) containing Scandinavian and Celtic elements and so hard for others to understand as to make them seem a different nation in alliance with rather than part of their neighbours to the north and south of them. If something is not done in Yorkshire it is probably not worth doing. Such stubbornness is unlikely to give way to mere administrative rearrangements. *See* entries on other aspects and the places mentioned.

YORKSHIRE POST originally *THE LEEDS INTELLIGENCER* was a weekly started in 1754. In 1866, as *The Yorkshire Post and Leeds Intelligencer*, it became a conservative daily. It was the first English newspaper to report on Edward VIII's affair with Mrs Simpson and opposed appeasement of Hitler.

YORUBA. People speaking this and the related AJA languages are found from Lagos (Nigeria) to N. Togo and traces of Yoruba custom and culture are, due to the slave trade, discernible in the Gambia, Cuba and N.E. Brazil. The 13 major groups of Yoruba in Nigeria included forest and coastal dwellers and, inland, horsemasters, and the dynastic traditions of all their states agree in a common origin at Ile-Ife in the period A.D. 900-1200. They all had a well developed urban life and a distinctive art. Islam, introduced in the 17th cent., made little headway against a divine pantheon ruled by a sky god. Though not politically united, the common ancestry of the royal houses and the predominance of one of them, the OYO, seems to have kept the peace until the early 19th cent. when the Oyo moved south and caused a series of wars in their passage to the coast. At this period Islam began to spread in competition with Christianity. It was the confusion caused by the decline of Oyo hegemony which created the opportunity for European intervention.

YOUGHAL (Co. Cork) and its harbour owed its rise to the Benedictine and Dominican abbeys which developed and exported cattle and grain along the Blackwater.

YOUNG, Arthur (1741-1820) published his excitable *Farmers Letters* in 1767; his various agricultural *Tours of England* in 1768-71; his *Tour in Ireland* in 1780. In 1784 he began publishing the monthly magazine *Annals of Agriculture* and in 1792 his *Travels in France*. In 1793 he became Sec. of the new Board of Agriculture and compiled a series of very comprehensive agricultural reports county by county. His writings are the principal source of agricultural information for the period.

YOUNG ENGLAND was a romantic conservative group led by Geo. Smythe (1818-57), later 7th Vist. Strangford, Lord John Manners and Disraeli. It favoured a paternal aristocracy as agents of social justice, as against the blind economic forces represented by the industrialists. Disraeli shook Sir Robt. Peel's Tory leadership through it between 1842 and 1846 when the group dissolved in disagreement over the Maynooth grant and the Corn Laws.

YOUNGHUSBAND, Sir Francis Edward (1863-1942) explored the Karakoram and Pamirs and travelled from Peking to Rawalpindi *via* Chinese Turkestan in 1887 and up to Kashgar and back in 1890-2. He was political officer at Hunza in 1892, Chitral in 1893-4, Tonk in 1898-1902 and Resident at Indore in 1902-3. He then headed the armed mission to Tibet and negotiated the Tibetan treaty and ended as Resident in Kashmir from 1906 to 1909. He also inspired the Everest expeditions.

YOUNG IRELAND was originally a group of young patriot intellectuals formed in 1841 as a departure from O'Connell's demagoguery and inspired by Mazzini's Young Italy. Its leaders were Thomas Davis (1814-45), John Blake Dillon (1816-66), Charles Gavan Duffy (1816-1903), Fintan Lalor (1807-49), John Martin (1812-75), Thomas Meagher (1823-67) and John Mitchel (1815-75). It favoured a programme of national regeneration including the revival of Erse and launched *The Nation* in Oct. 1842 with Duffy as editor, assisted by Davis and Dillon. The general atmosphere was romantic, courageous and disorganised but as O'Connell became less extreme, they became more so. They distrusted R. Catholic church support for O'Connell but his prosecution for sedition in Jan. 1844 greatly raised the circulation of *The Nation,* which helped to discredit him. After the collapse of the repealers in 1845 Young Ireland began to foment rebellion, *The Nation* publishing articles on such topics as railway wrecking. Repealers and priests opposed this and a furious quarrel occurred in 1846 which went largely unnoticed because of the famine. In Jan. 1847 the Young Irelanders founded the IRISH CONFEDERATION which was intended to be a sort of Liberation Army and saw in the continental revolutionary movements of 1848 an opportunity for an Irish rising. The govt. became aware of preparations and seized John Mitchel and others. The Confederates launched an appeal for a National Guard (to be paid in land) and for a Council of Three Hundred to function as a shadow parliament. Confederate clubs were formed in most towns and large meetings assembled but there were no arms and no staff work. The rebellion, in Aug. 1848, was heroic and farcical and collapsed after a fight with 40 policemen known as the B. of Widow McCormack's Cabbage Patch.

YOUNG LORDS. *See* RESTORATION-4.

YOUNG PLAN (1930). *See* REPARATIONS.

YOUNG PRETENDER. *See* JACOBITES AND PRETENDERS.

YOUNG, Thomas (1773-1829), polymath, had a vast knowledge of ancient and modern languages but became known in 1793 by a brilliant paper before the Royal Society on the muscular structure of the eye. He propounded the basic theory of colour and interference of light in 1801 and of the nature of capillary action in 1804. He was physician to St. George's Hospital from 1811 to 1829, superintendent of the *Nautical Almanac* and Sec. of the Board of Longitude from 1818. He also wrote on ancient Egyptian grammar, the Egyptian articles in the *Encyclopaedia Britannica* and translated the demotic part of the Rosetta Stone.

YOUNG TURKS. Brutally nationalistic Turkish politicians who wished to convert the Ottoman Empire into a unified and standardised Turkish state. In so doing they came into collision with, and in 1907 deposed, the Sultan Abdul Hamid II and also with the numerous subject nationalities which during World War I were the more easily subverted by the Allies. *See* OTTOMAN EMPIRE-16.

YOUTH HOSTELS arose out of the traditional wandering habits of German apprentices and journeymen and the collapse of the German guilds which had catered for them. The first hostel was opened there in 1910. The first in Britain in 1920. The English Youth Hostels Association was founded in 1930, the Scottish in 1931. By 1965 there were nearly 400 hostels in the U.K.

YPRES (*see* FLANDERS-2). In the first battle (Oct-Nov. 1914) the professional British Expeditionary Force was destroyed. *For the second battle see* WORLD WAR 1-4.

YUGANTAR (Bengali = New Era). A numerous body of minor Bengali professionals and smallholders known as **Badralok** was committed to English education and established many Anglo-Bengali schools. In 1902 the brothers Arabindo Ghosh and Barindra Kumar tried to interest them in revolutionary ideas and naturally failed but disillusionment set in when Curzon's Universities Bill of 1904 seemed to limit the numbers of Indians to be educated in English and, additionally, in 1905 Bengal was partitioned. Ghosh and Kumar now formed **Anusilan Samiti**, a revolutionary society, and published *Yugantar*. They attracted a small hyperactive Badralok support which carried on robbery and terrorism. *Yugantar* was suppressed in 1907 but urban terrorism called after it continued until 1916.

YUGOSLAVIA (Serb-Cr: South Slavia) (1) While the orthodox (Cyrillic writing) Serbs and Montenegrins had their own independent kingdoms in 1914, the largely R. Catholic (Latin writing) Croats and Slovenes and the Moslem Bosnians and Illyrians formed part of the Habsburg empire, to which most of them were loyal. The union of Southern Slays was a primarily Serb ambition. In 1915, after the Austro-German conquest of Serbia, however, the Croat A. Trumbic formed a Yugoslavia Committtee in London and this issued at Corfu a joint declaration with the exiled Pasic govt. of Serbia demanding a united Yugoslavia. The Slovene deputies in the Austrian *Reichsrat*, by way of counterblast, demanded a Slovene kingdom under the Habsburg crown. When it became clear that Austro-Hungary would be defeated in World War I these deputies joined the PanSerb movement and in Nov. 1918 pronounced for union with Serbia and Montenegro. In Dec. the Serbian regent Alexander proclaimed the Serb-Croat-Slovene Kingdom, otherwise Yugoslavia, under the Serb Karageorgevich dynasty. The boundaries were ultimately fixed by the Ts. of St. Germain, Neuilly and Trianon. These left 500,000

Slovenes under Italy (*see* QUARNERO) which also acquired the port of Zara as an enclave. In Nov. 1919 d'Annnunzio seized Fiume (Rijeka) for Italy (*see* QUARNERO) and this was recognised by Yugoslavia in 1924.

(2) The centralised constitution proved unworkable because the Yugoslavia committee's non-Serb members did not represent any worthwhile body of opinion. Until 1924 the Croats refused to co-operate. Their leaders, the brothers Radic, were then reconciled with the Pasic govt. but in June 1928 they were shot in parliament by a Montenegrin deputy and the opposition seceded to Zagreb. The Serbs and Montenegrins wanted a unitary state: the ex-Habsburg subjects a federation and as neither side would make any concessions Alexander, now King, suppressed the constitution and ruled as a autocrat (Jan. 1929). He was assassinated in 1934 and a regency for the new King Peter under Pr. Paul took over his powers.

(3) The inveterate enmity between Yugoslavia and Italy was exacerbated after 1922 by Italian fascism and diplomacy. Yugoslavia could do nothing to prevent the establishment of the virtual Italian protectorate over Albania in 1926 or the alliance with Bulgaria (1927) and Greece (1928). If, from 1927, Yugoslavia had to rely upon a French alliance, the rise of Hitler's Germany and its economic penetration of the Balkans brought Yugoslavia, Bulgaria and Italy for a while together (1937) but the German victories in 1940 destroyed France and the Italian will to resist Germany. Hence the Stoyadinovitch govt., so far neutral in the war, decided to abandon previous diplomatic commitments. In Apr. 1941 Gen Simovitch seized power from Stoyadinovitch whereupon the Germans, poised for the attack upon Greece, took the route through Yugoslavia, compelled the army to capitulate in a fortnight and set up a so-called Independent Croat State.

(4) In W. Serbia the royalist Chetnik militia under Gen. Mihailovitch rose in May 1941 and in July there was a Montenegrin rising which the Germans suppressed in Oct. As long as Germany and Russia were allies there was no other opposition but the German attack upon Russia in June 1941 caused the illegal communists to emerge suddenly and bid for a national leadership under the Montenegrin Josip Broz, known as TITO. Their earliest care was to elbow out or destroy the Chetniks after which, with British arms and liaison officers, they fought the Germans and Italians with some effect. The civil and guerrilla war of 1941 to 1944 inflicted fearful losses through starvation, disease as well as military action. Over 10% of the population perished.

(5) In Nov. 1942 Tito formed the Anti-fascist People's Liberation Council (AFPLC) at a meeting at Bihac and this was converted into a provisional govt. at the Jajce conference (Nov. 1943). Meanwhile Britain tried to mediate a reconciliation with the govt. in exile in London (Nov. 1944) and the resulting fusion of the AFPLC and the pre-war politicians became a provisional parliament (Aug. 1945) in which the communist-dominated People's Front won an 88% majority in the Nov. elections. As it had been carrying through a classical Marxist revolution involving the murder of political opponents and the seizure of property, this was a foregone conclusion. On the other hand its prestige and strength enabled Tito to take an independent line towards the Russians who had done nothing for it. He refused to accept Russian dictatorship on internal matters and broke with Moscow in 1948.

(6) The frontiers had been re-established as before, save on the Italian side. Zara (Zadar) and Fiume (Rijeka) had been recovered but Istria remained in dispute until the diplomatic isolation of Yugoslavia brought a compromise. In 1954 therefore Italy retained Trieste at the end of a militarily vulnerable corridor and Yugoslavia took the rest. By this time, too, she had been forced to establish close trading relations with the west in order to maintain herself against the Russians, and she made agreements with Greece and Turkey (Aug. 1954). A short reconciliation with Khrushchev's Russia was abruptly ended with the Russian invasion of Hungary in Oct. 1956 and thereafter Tito sought to identify with the "uncommitted" states while establishing a friendly partnership with the E. Germans. In 1962 he visited Moscow and persuaded the Russians to accept the possibility of separate routes to socialism, and in the ensuing Russo-Chinese controversies he backed the Russians, partly because the Chinese backed Albania. In practice the new friendship was again interrupted by the Russian attack on Czechoslovakia in 1968.

(7) A new constitution in 1974 purported to confirm the rights of the constituent republics and autonomous provinces. The centrifugal tendencies of the component peoples differed as between the North and West and the South-East. In the former the Croats and Slovenes as ever, wished to be rid of a party bureaucracy which was Serb dominated and were slowly realising their own power to do it. In the S.E. the Albanians and Macedonians were minorities within Serbia itself and might prefer to secede to neighbouring countries. There was a risk of foreign intervention. In the case of the Albanians this touched a sensitive nerve for an Albanian secession would entail the loss of the Kossovo Polye, an area sacred in the annals of Serb nationhood. In Greece, meanwhile, there was a growing tendency, despite the Philippics of the classical orator Demosthenes, to represent Macedonia as really Hellenic. By 1993 this had become a Greek irredentist movement.

(8) The obvious contrast between Marxist doctrinaire inefficiency and western prosperity (Yugoslavia not being isolated by an Iron Curtain) was creating stresses, notably student riots in Belgrade, and renewed Croat mass-movements for local autonomy alongside Albanian nationalist riots. Tito's Montenegrin origin and strength of personality and apparent (if cosmetically induced) bodily vigour were some guarantee of impartiality and constructive action but in May 1980 he died.

(9) Latent fissures now became patent, beginning with disputes over the structure of Serbia where Albanians and Macedonians rioted. Unrest spread to the Vovyodina, Montenegro, Croatia and Slovenia. In Bosnia and Herzegovina the situation was complicated by religious geography. There were large intermingled tracts populated respectively by Serbs and Moslems but over the area as a whole there was a Moslem majority. For a while there were at least seven parties, namely the six states and the army, but by June 1990 the last was suffering from desertions of non-Serbs. Croatia and Slovenia proclaimed plebiscite-based independence. The army was chased out of Slovenia and Germany recognised both states. The Russian- or Ukrainian-supplied forces became an instrument designed to prevent the break-up or partition of Serbia and to recover what else was recoverable elsewhere. In practice this meant the consolidation of Bosnian Serb areas by the "ethnic cleansing" (by massacre or expulsion) of Moslem areas. Naturally the Moslem govt. of Bosnia-Herzegovina resisted and Bosnia declined into a savage race war in which no attempted U.N., E.U. or Anglo-U.S. mediation (led by Lord Owen) could effect anything against persistent, often daily, breaches of faith, and large, mostly British and French peace-keeping forces, mostly under British command, were not allowed to shoot. By 1995 they had probably saved thousands of lives but could not do more.

YUKON (Canada) was explored between 1840 and 1850 by Robt. Campbell who established Hudson Bay Co. posts at Frances Lake and Pelly Banks. It passed to Canada and became part of the N.W. Territories in 1870 but the **Klondike** gold rush of 1898 suddenly raised the population and created social problems. It was then made a separate territory with an appointed council sitting at Dawson. From 1905 it was represented in the Dominion House of Commons. It stagnated until the strategic American Alaska Highway brought new employment and easier outside contact in 1942. In 1944 the Canol pipeline brought crude oil for refining to White Horse which became the capital and the population rose steadily through oil prospecting, the N.A.T.O. defensive installations and minor tourism.

YULE (Norw: *Jul.*). A, usually, 12-day Scandinavian fertility festival involving also the banishment of mischief, commonly by fire. Transferred to Britain, it became confused with Christmas and the Plough Monday fertility rites. The **Yule Log** (sometimes **Block** or **Candle**) was widely burned on Christmas Eve well into the 19th cent. A part was saved to kindle the next year's log and meanwhile was considered a talisman *against* fire.

ZAHAROFF, Sir Basil (alias Prince GORTZAKOFF, alias Z. WILLIAMSON) (?-1936) a Greek born in Turkey, after unfortunate business ventures in England became Balkan agent for Nordenfeldt machine-guns in 1875. When Maxim joined Nordenfeldt in 1888 he became agent also for central Europe and Russia and when their business was acquired by Vickers in 1895 his agency included all sides of the Vickers business. A millionaire, he was the probable origin of the idea or myth of the sinister war-fomenting international arms dealer. In World War I he probably acted as a high level allied intelligence agent and he was credited with promoting the Greco-Turkish war of 1920-1. Such an improbability was doubtless the consequence of his shady reputation.

ZAIRE previously **BELGIAN CONGO. (1)** The basin of the Congo R. was virtually unknown until Stanley, bringing the Tse-tse fly, reached the Portuguese settlements at its mouth from the interior in 1877. The Belgian K. Leopold II instantly took the lead in exploring and exploiting the territory which was allotted to him as sovereign of the Congo Free State by the Berlin Conference of 1885.

(2) Financial scandals and human outrages in the rubber plantations caused stimulated anger in Belgium; by a treaty between the King as sovereign and Belgium the latter annexed the Congo and enacted a constitutional charter which, with amendments, remained sketchily in force until June 1960. In the interval the country was exploited, primarily for its minerals and timber, by the use of cheap labour financed through the Brussels banks. Very little was done to educate the people or to create professions save by charitable and missionary bodies. The administration was carried on by Belgians.

(3) After World War II agitation for independence developed in such strength that maintenance of the colonial status seemed likely to be uneconomic. Accordingly independence was granted as from June 1960 and most of the Belgians left. A governmental breakdown instantly followed. The party leaders, including the Moscow trained Patrice Lumumba, were really tribal leaders superimposing rival doctrines upon old feuds. Neither he, as prime minister, nor Joseph Kasavubu, the Head of State, could impose order and meanwhile Moise Tschombe was setting up an independent state in Katanga where most of the mines were. Then the army mutinied and drove out the last Belgians. Lumumba appealed to the U.S.S.R., Kasavubu to the United Nations and an Asian and African U.N. force arrived but not in time to prevent Katanga tribesmen eating Lumumba (Feb. 1961).

(4) Lumumba's lieutenant Antoine Gizenga now set up a factional govt. in the capital but the U.N.O. recognised Kasavubus successor Joseph Adoula, whose forces compelled Gizenga to surrender (Aug. 1961-Jan. 1962). U.N. forces, meanwhile, invaded Katanga and compelled it to reunite with Zaire (Dec. 1962-Jan. 1964). Then Gizenga raised a further rebellion involving widespread massacres of foreigners (Sept. 1964). This was put down only in Apr. 1965.

(5) Almost immediately Gen. Mobutu overthrew Pres. Kasavubu, established an approximate order, quelled the Katangan country rebellion and in 1977 repelled an invasion of Katanganese emigrés from Angola. His rule was not otherwise a success and by 1991 corruption and mismanagement had reduced the people to a poverty as abject as those of Haiti.

ZAMBIA (formerly NORTHERN RHODESIA). (1) The N.W. was settled by Ngoni refugees from Zululand c. 1835; Barotseland by the Kololo a little later. Livingstone reached it in 1855 when Arab slavers were beginning to penetrate from the north. By the 1880s slave raiding was creating a demand for British protection and in 1890 Cecil Rhodes and the British United Co. began to make treaties with the chiefs. It took several years to drive out the Arabs and subdue their ally, the Bembas. Under Orders in Council of 1899 and 1900 the Co. administered the area as two separate protectorates (N.W. and N.E. Rhodesia). Large deposits of lead, zinc, silver and vanadium were found at Broken Hill in 1902 and copper at Bwana Mkubwa in 1910, just after the railway from Bulawayo was completed. The two protectorates were amalgamated in 1911 but developed slowly. The European population was only 4000 in 1924 when the Co. ceased to administer the area. It retained its mining rights. **(2)** Development of the copper belt now began in earnest, huge profits were reaped, stimulated by wars and electricity industries and by 1945 the European population exceeded 50,000. The African population, meantime, was growing spectacularly and had reached 2,500,000. **(3)** There was now a divergence of political outlook between settlers and Africans. The settlers, who had had a monopoly of political power, feared to be swamped by the African majority and favoured association with Southern Rhodesia (later Zimbabwe) where Europeans were established in large numbers. The Africans, for converse reasons, were opposed to such association. In 1953 accession to the Federation of Rhodesia and Nyasaland represented a victory for the Europeans, but political advance among the Africans, led by Kenneth KAUNDA eventually gave them a majority in the legislature in 1962. **(4)** The federation was dissolved, Northern Rhodesia became internally autonomous in Jan. 1964 and, as Zambia, an independent republic in Oct. The declaration of independence of (Southern) Rhodesia by the Ian Smith govt. in 1965 and the subsequent sanctions created great difficulties because all Zambia's seaward communications ran through Rhodesia, with whom most of her trade was carried on. Hence the blockade hurt Zambia more than Rhodesia and it became necessary for friendly countries to give economic aid and to interrupt ordinary development to realign the communications in a northerly direction. The new railway was completed in 1973. Kenneth Kaunda soon transformed the country into a one party state with a programme of wholesale expropriations. As the best farmers left for S. Africa Zambia became increasingly dependent on copper exports in a falling world market. Moreover it became a refuge or base for guerrilla fighters conducting civil wars in neighbouring countries and a focus for the Russian policy of African destabilisation. This aspect of the situation became less important with the collapse of Russian communism which drove Kaunda to anticipate trouble, in 1990, by legalising opposition.

ZAMBO or SAMBO. A person of part negro, part local (non-European) descent.

ZAMINDAR (= land holder). In the Moghul parts of India an official of Persian origin who collected the land revenue. The office tended to become hereditary and acquired differing characteristics in different areas. Because liability to land tax connoted a title to the land itself the Zamindars began to be regarded as superior landowners. In Bengal and Bihar they collected the revenue keeping 10% commission and were eventually converted by the British into landowners. In other parts they became owners of the soil by a sort of prescription. In the Maratha (i.e. non-Moghul) areas, on the other hand, the word meant simply a revenue official.

ZAMINDAR'S COURT. See EAST INDIA CO. COURTS.

***THE ZAMORA* [1916] 2 AC 77.** A British cruiser seized a neutral ship laden with contraband copper but bound for Stockholm. The War Office requisitioned the copper, now in the custody of the Prize Court, under one of the Prize Court Rules. It was held that Prize Law was international and that the Crown could relinquish its rights under it but could not alter it to other's detriment. The requisition was, therefore, illegal.

ZAMORIN. The title of the ruler of Calicut when the first Europeans reached India.

ZANGWILL, Israel (1864-1926) Jewish writer whose powerful works on ghetto life might have made more impact in Britain if the Nazi type of racialism had arisen in his day.

ZANTE or ZAKYNTHOS. *See* IONIAN IS.

ZANZIBAR. *See* TANZANIA.

ZEALOTS. In 17th cent. parlance, puritan militants.

ZEEBRUGGE and OSTEND RAIDS (Apr. 1918). This combined operation commanded by Sir Roger Keyes was intended to block the entrances to the canals at Ostend and Zeebrugge (Bel.) which were sea outlets from the German bomb-proofed U-boat bases at Bruges. At Zeebrugge an old converted cruiser, H.M.S. *Vindictive* was to land infantry on the Mole to destroy the harbour batteries while an old submarine packed with explosives, cut it off from the town by blowing up the bridge at the landward end. Three blockships were then to be sunk in the mouth of the canal. The plan was carried out against furious resistance in smoke and uproar but the blockships were imperfectly placed and only hindered rather than stopped passage by the U-boats. At Ostend navigational difficulties caused total failure. The affair, novel in conception and pressed with enormous courage even though it failed, fired public imagination in the dark days of the great German spring offensives (*see* WORLD WAR I-14). It also provided a precedent for such ingenious raids, often inspired by Keyes himself, in World War II.

ZEELAND. (1) A Dutch province, of seven marshy main islands and three navigable channels, constituted the central part of the Scheldt and Rhine joint delta. Some of these islands have been joined or enlarged. The channels are a mass of navigational hazards, the marshes malarial. No vessel can approach Antwerp or Bergen-op-Zoom without co-operation from Zeeland or enter the Rhine against joint opposition of Zeeland and Holland. The principal towns are Middleburg and Flushing (locally Vlissingen) on Walcheren which, with Schouwen, faces the North Sea. The small population of seafarers could provide a navy exceptionally large for its resources. It had its own Admiralty from early times but no other effective govt.

(2) Zeeland was naturally disputed between the rulers of Holland, who wanted to divert the commerce to the Rhine, and those of Flanders who favoured the Scheldt. By the 13th cent. the struggle had developed into a customs war in which the revenues were more important than the exiguous islands. By 1323 the Counts of Holland emerged victorious and became Counts of Zeeland, which retained its own identity. Politically its history was now tied to that of the other Dutch provinces but its position exposed it to much English aggression and the local politics of the Staple (occasionally moved to Middleburg) and the Hanse. Moreover Middleburg branches of the Dutch East and West India Cos. were exceptionally active and successful and brought much prosperity until the Anglo-Dutch Wars and the War of the Spanish Succession ruined them. By 1809 Walcheren was the passive victim of a British attack on Antwerp which was defeated by the mosquitoes. *See* JACQUELINE OF HAINAULT; HUMPHREY, D. OF GLOUCESTER.

ZEITGEIST (Ger = spirit of the period), the spirit or subconscious consensus which lends identity to a period.

ZELO DOMUS DEI (Lat = By the zeal of the House of God) (1648, published 1651) bull of Innocent X repudiating the P. of Westphalia.

ZEN (from Sansk: Dyana = meditation, through Chin: Chan). A type of Japanese meditational Buddhism which has attracted western youth since World War II. It assumes that enlightenment (Jap = *Satori*) can be reached in this life and differs from other forms of Buddhism less in doctrine than by an apparent irrationality of method exemplified in the occasion when the Buddha, instead of preaching a sermon silently held up a flower.

ZEPPELIN, Ferdinand Count (1838-1917) flew his first airship at Friedrichshafen on L. Constance in 1900 and his name became synonymous with German dirigibles which formed a spectacular but ineffective part of the German airforce in World War I. Commercial Zeppelins flew until 1937.

ZETLAND. *See* SHETLAND IS.

ZETLAND, M. *See* DUNDAS.

ZIMBABWE (1923-63 SOUTHERN RHODESIA; 1963-80 RHODESIA) (1) as S. Rhodesia refused, by a majority of its 14,500 voters, to join S. Africa and in 1923 became, though a Crown Colony, a quasi-Dominion with a parliamentary constitution in which only colonists had votes. In general they held a benevolently paternalistic view of the Mashonas and Matabele among whom they lived and disliked the increasingly oppressive S. African policies later encapsulated in *Apartheid*. Though the local law was Roman-Dutch, the country drifted away from S. African attitudes mainly because the colonists were almost uniformly of British stock.

(2) Under the intelligent leadership of Sir Godfrey Huggins, the premier, S. Rhodesia flourished mightily, mostly on tobacco which, as an export overtopped everything else (save gold) put together, but there was actual and potential diversification into citrus fruits and maize on the one hand and into coal and base metal mining as well as high grade asbestos. The climate is benign and the country beautiful. It became the target for mass immigration of Africans from N. Rhodesia and Nyasaland seeking better paid work than they could get at home; of whites from S. Africa and Britain seeking to invest and to enjoy the happy liberty of the wide open spaces. British immigration swelled after World War II. By 1964 the white population had increased 15-fold: the much larger African population had trebled.

(3) Benevolent paternalism was by then obsolescent through education and the circulation of attractively packaged radical and left-wing ideas among the Africans. They were no longer content to accept what they were given when it might be within their power to take much more. Relations on the whole remained friendly but the colonists were determined to maintain their supremacy with the reasonable ground that it was their capital and enterprise which had created the prosperity.

(4) The Labour govt. in Britain meant to liquidate the Empire and had indeed ended the *Raj* in India amid carnage. In 1953 the colonists of the two Rhodesias and Nyasaland, seeing the writing on the wall, sought to strengthen their position by entering into a Central African Federation in which their aggregate numbers and economic power could most effectively dominate the total. For the opposite reasons the Africans opposed federation and sought its dissolution. In S. Rhodesia their National Democratic Party split along unavowed tribal lines into the Zimbabwe Peoples' Union (Z.A.P.U. – Matabele) led by Joshua Nkomo and the Zimbabwe African National Union (Z.A.N.U. – Mashona) led by Ndabaningi Sithole and then by Robert Mugabe. Z.A.N.U. was the more extreme or better armed of the two. By 1963 they, with the help of Malawi and the blessing of the Wilson govt. had forced the dissolution of the Federation.

(5) The dangers of haste (not only in India) had become clear. Rapid Africanisations in neighbouring ex-colonies such as Zaire, Mozambique, Angola and Zanzibar were interpreted in opposed directions by Africans and colonists. To Africans they were encouraging; to colonists the massacres and seizures a terrifying disaster. The case for delay seemed overwhelming. The country having again become a

Crown Colony in 1963, the Wilson govt. sought to force majority (i.e. African) rule upon it. The Rhodesian Front govt. of Winston Field tried to negotiate for gradual change. This was thought too weak by his backers and he was superseded by Ian Smith who, finding no sympathy in Britain, proclaimed the country's independence (1965). In reply the British imposed economic sanctions and got the U.N. to follow suit while Mozambique and Zambia gave facilities for Russian supplied Z.A.P.U. and Z.A.N.U. guerrilla organisations which could thus attack Rhodesia with fair impunity. Economically, with S. African help, the sanctions were not very successful and did at least as much damage to Zambia as to S. Rhodesia, but militantly the S. African connection was less effective. Thousands perished in the civil war, for which Britain must accept some responsibility, and nearly a million were driven from their homes. The Smith regime could not hold out and in 1980 agreed with Robert Mugabe on nationwide elections under British supervision. Z.A.N.U. and Mugabe, backed by sporadic popular terrorism, won 80% of the seats and formed a nominal coalition which was soon converted into a Marxist one-party state. In 1990, however, the collapse of the Russian communists led to liberalisation.

ZIMBABWE, GREAT (Zim.), a huge stone structure one of many scattered in the area of Mashonaland. Their origin and purpose is disputed but carbon tests of certain wooden parts indicate a date around 1820. This does not exclude other dates for stone parts. As they seem stylistically and engineering-wise unrelated to other architecture, they are more likely to have been built by indigenous people than by gold-prospecting Arabs or Indians or Ethiopians or others speculatively proposed by archaeologists, but there seems to be no interpretable local tradition about them. The masonry holds itself together without cement or filler. The name was adopted as the African official name for Southern Rhodesia as a proud symbol of past achievement.

ZIMMERMANN TELEGRAM (Jan. 1917). Arthur Zimmermann became German Foreign Minister from Nov. 1916 in succession to Gotlieb von Jagow who had resigned against the policy of unrestricted U-boat warfare on the ground that it would provoke the U.S.A. into the war. Zimmermann proposed to divert American power by making trouble in Mexico. He proposed an alliance with Mexico and Japan for an attack on the U.S.A., the Mexicans to annex the areas lost to the U.S.A. in the 19th cent. The enciphered telegram conveying this to Pres. Carranza was decoded by British Admiralty Intelligence and given to Pres. Wilson who used it to convince the American public of the need to enter the war.

ZINC (or SPELTER) was used in Roman times as a component of brass. It was first produced in a pure form in commercial quantities only in the 16th cent. in India and in Britain in 1738.

ZINOVIEV LETTER (1924) was written on behalf of the Comintern by Grigory Yevseyevich Zinoviev, the chairman of its central committee, urging subversion of the British armed forces. Published by the London press, its terms contributed to the Labour Party's electoral defeat. Long denied by left-wing publicists, its authenticity was established in 1977.

ZIONISM began among persecuted Russian Jews in the 1880s. Many migrated to the west but a few set up small farming communities with the help of Edmond de Rothschild in Palestine. The Russian Jews developed a new Hebrew literature and also elevated Yiddish, an eastern derivative of mediaeval German, into a literary medium. Political Zionism began as a reaction to anti-Semitic outbursts in the west. The basic text was *The Jewish State* a pamphlet published in 1896 by Theodore HERZL (1860-1904), an Austrian journalist who thought that assimilation was desirable but impracticable and that, therefore, the only available solution was a return to

Jerusalem. In 1897 he convened the first or BASEL CONGRESS which resolved that "Zionism strives to create for the Jewish people a home in Palestine secured by public law" and established an H.Q. at Vienna. As a consequence of a British offer of territory in Uganda (1903), the majority of the SEVENTH CONGRESS (1905) rejected colonisation outside Palestine and its neighbourhood and so laid the foundations of later conflicts with the Arabs. By 1914 there were 90,000 Jews in Palestine (then Turkish) of whom 13,000 were in 43 *kibbutzim* (agricultural colonies).

World War I and its political upheavals in the Levant made radical changes. The leadership passed to Russian Jews living in London, notably Chaim WEIZMANN (1874-1952) and Nahum SOKOLOW (1861-1936) because Austria, Germany and Turkey were allies. The manpower came increasingly from Poland but the finance from the Jewish Community in the U.S.A. Moreover the British govt., the only one really sympathetic to Zionism, was considering annexing Palestine to protect the Suez Canal. Hence the issue of the Balfour Declaration (q.v.) in Nov. 1917 to rally Jewish world opinion. In July 1922 the British position was consolidated by a League of Nations' mandate which made special provision for Jewish immigration. This alarmed Arab opinion and the British then stated that they "did not contemplate the disappearance or subordination of the Arab population". Since this was precisely what the Zionist extremists did contemplate, British policy was attacked by powerful American interests whenever it seemed pro-Arab and by local and other Arabs whenever the immigration rate rose. The advance of Nazism brought a persistent rise in that rate. There were Arab insurrections in 1936 to 1939. World War II brought a temporary cessation of disorder but as soon as the U.S.A. entered it Zionist organisations (especially the NEW YORK CONGRESS of 1942) began to demand the creation of a Jewish state. When the German danger had been fought off, the British and Arabs became the target of, largely American financed, Zionist violence. The British proposed first Anglo-U.S. discussions and then submission to the United Nations which in Nov. 1947 resolved in favour of partition. Civil war broke out; the state of Israel was proclaimed in May 1948 and promptly recognised by the U.S.A. *See* ISRAEL.

ZOFFAN-Y (or -II) Johann or John (1733-1810) attracted notice as a portraitist in 1760 and until 1772 painted many English (mostly stage) portraits. He was in Italy from 1772 to 1779 and in India from 1783 to 1790.

ZOLLVEREIN (Ger = customs union) began in 1819 as a Prussian administrative simplification. Instead of levying excises and imposing tolls, customs were levied at external frontiers and the proceeds shared with the non-Prussian enclaves on a population basis. The savings and convenience in a territorially confused Germany were soon apparent. Hessen-Darmstadt joined the Rhineland part of the Prussian system in 1828; Bavaria, Baden and Württemberg set up their own, thereby linking the economies of the divided Bavarian territories, and Saxony, Hanover, the Thuringian states and Hesse-Cassel a third. In 1829 the three groups agreed on a North-South road building programme and in 1831 the vital state of Hesse-Cassel, which divided the Prussian Rhineland from the rest, went over to the Prussian system thus dividing the Saxon. The Prussian economists rightly believed that the middle and long term benefits of economic union would be so great that it would pay to obtain accessions by giving favourable terms. In this way the southern and Saxon unions were induced to join the Prussian system in 1833. This left Hanover and the north-western states, particularly Oldenburg and the Hanseatic ports, outside. The Prussian Union was managed by a representative conference. As this had to be unanimous changes were seldom made except when the treaties were due for renewal. On these occasions Prussia ensured renewal by assuring to the other states higher *per capita* payments than she took herself. This made their govts. beholden to her and helped to delay the growth of inconvenient parliamentary liberalism in territories which she did not directly rule. Moreover the size of the union favoured not only road but, from 1840, rail and canal development which opened up new markets and resources such as the Pless coalfields. Initially administrative, then economic, the Prussian policy was not originally anti-Austrian but as growing Prussian influence challenged Austria's position in the German Confederation and as the Austrians reacted, the *Zollverein* was increasingly an instrument of Prussian ambition. Before 1850 Austria, which had not attained internal freedom of trade, could not have joined anyhow; after that date Austrian attempts to do so were prevented by Prussia, which by 1854 had brought in Hanover and Oldenburg. Austrian efforts to detach the S. German states were also foiled and a further consequence of the Austro-Prussian war of 1866 was the creation of a reformed *Zollverein* which extended additionally to the four Baltic duchies. The half century of administrative experience and commercial and travelling habits engendered by the Union were prime factors in achieving the united Germany which superseded it in 1871.

ZOO. There was a royal menagerie at Woodstock (Oxon) under Henry I, later transferred to the Tower of London and maintained there until taken over by the Royal Zoological Society of London in 1829 and transferred to Regent's Park.

ZOROASTRIANISM. The prophet Zoroaster or ZARA-THUSTRA lived c. 628-551 B.C. He preached a cosmology and doctrine now mostly contained in scriptural texts called AVESTA or ZEND-AVESTA. At one period this developed a strong dualistic tendency which influenced the rise of Bogomilism and Albigensianism. The doctrines are now professed only by the Parsees.

ZOUCHE, DE LA (1) Alan (?-1270), Ld., served with Henry III in Aquitaine in 1242, was made Justice of Chester and the Four Cantreds in 1250 and in 1255-8 he was Justice of Ireland. He was loyal to Henry in the Barons' War, acted as Justice of the Forests S. of the Trent from 1261 and Sheriff of Northamptonshire in 1261-4. He also became King's Seneschal in 1263. Trusted both by the King and the Lord Edward, he was one of the arbitrators at the surrender of Kenilworth (1266) and Warden of London and Constable of the Tower in 1267-8. **(2)** The life of **William (?-1352),** chaplain to Edward III, illustrates the widely travelled and confusedly semi-secular life of an educated mediaeval churchman. He was purveyor and then Keeper of the Great Wardrobe; Keeper of the Privy Seal and Treasurer of the Exchequer and then of England (1330-40). Meanwhile he had steadily risen in the Church, beginning with a canonry at Exeter in 1328 and the Archidiaconate in 1330. In 1335 he accepted a prebend and in 1336 the Deanery at York besides stalls at Ripon and Lincoln. In 1340 he was though Edward favoured William of Kildesley, elected Abp. of York and hastened to Avignon for his pallium but was waylaid by brigands and arrived in 1341 to find Kildesley already there. Benedict XII kept them both waiting but when he died Clement VI favoured Zouche and confirmed the election. He returned to York, was soon embroiled in the running archiepiscopal dispute with the chapter about the Deanery. In 1346 he became a Warden of the March just in time to take part in the victory at Neville's Cross. In 1349 he questioned a papal award in the dispute over the Deanery and died excommunicate. **(3) Edward (1556-1625) 11th Ld.** was a trier of Mary Q. of Scots in 1586, went abroad until 1593 and held various diplomatic, financial and administrative posts. In 1609 he became a member of the Council of Virginia, in 1620 of New England and he was Lord Warden of the Cinque Ports from 1615. Always well

off, he patronised poets and Ben Jonson. **(4) Richard (1590-1661)** Regius Prof. of Civil Law at Oxford and Admiralty Judge, published *Jus Feciale* (Lat = Internationally Ratified Law) (1650), the first English scientific exposition of the Law of Nations.

ZUCCARELLI, Francesco (1704-88), Venetian-trained landscape and pastoral painter, worked in England in 1751-62; was a founder member of the Royal Academy in 1768 and worked on in England until 1772.

ZUIDER ZEE (now YSSELMEER) was formed in the 13th cent. when the North Sea broke through the coastal dunes now represented by the islands from the Texel to the Ems, flooded the adjacent plain and connected up with an existing lake. The same storms did great damage to the English east coast and overwhelmed Winchelsea. The event caused migrations mainly towards the east but some towards E. Anglia. In 1918 reclamation of the Zee was begun. The enclosing dam was completed in 1932 and the land progressively exposed by pumping.

ZULUS. The Mtetwa, a Nguni Bantu clan of Natal, built up a subject confederacy under the statesman chief **Dingiswayo (r. 1810-18)** of local clans including the Zulus who were settled in the Umfolozi country. **(1) Shaka or Chaka (?1787-1828)** was the irregular offspring of a Zulu chief and a beautiful royal virago of a neighbouring clan; he was a huge man noted for his hunting prowess. The Bantu clans were organised in iNtangas (age groups) and when Shaka's iNtanga was called up into the Mtetwa army (c. 1810) he soon became a regimental commander. He devised new tactics, drills and weapons, superseding the throwing *assegai* by the stabbing spear (iKlwa), introducing the left handed shield-sweep and the pincer movement and he created a separate commissariat to increase mobility. His victories attracted Dingiswayo's attention: he helped him to take the leadership of the Zulu clan in 1816. Shaka promptly organised the Zulus on his new model and started to attack neighbouring tribes not under Mtetwa paramountcy. Unlike Dingiswayo, who preferred the submission of a clan as such, he would smash it, kill the leaders and incorporate the rest into the Zulus. Thus the Zulu clan grew. Dingiswayo was killed in a war with the powerful **Ndwandwe** and had weak successors. By 1821 Shaka had shattered the Ndwandwe and took over the Mtetwa paramountcy. His rule was a reign of terror.

(2) The Ndwandwe wars and Zulu pressure set off a chain reaction across the Drakensberg Mts. which brought widespread massacre and famine to the area of the modern Orange Free State. For this the Zulus were not directly responsible but one of Shaka's commanders, Mzilikazi, defected northwards and ultimately founded the **Matabele.** Shaka's operations were directed into S.W. Natal. Much of the population fled towards Xhosa territory on the British Cape Colony frontier. In 1828, when Shaka was assassinated, Zulu territory covered the area between the Pongola and the Tugela Rivers. His assassin and successor was his half-brother **(3) Dingane (?1798-1840)** a self indulgent and treacherous ruler unfitted to deal with aggressive and well armed Boers who, from 1835, were engaged in the Great Trek. These had migrated from Cape Colony N.E. into the modern Orange Free State and some were now descending (after victories over the Matabele) easterly into Natal over the Drakensberg Mts. to make contact with the tiny European trading settlement of PORT NATAL (Durban). Their main leader was Piet RETIEF who arrived there in Oct. 1837 and made an agreement to cooperate with settlers. He then negotiated, as he thought, the cession of most of Central Natal by Dingane and the Boer wagons started to pour in. On 4 Feb. 1838 Dingane invited them to a feast and massacred them including Retief ("DINGAANS DAY"). Many Boer leaguers elsewhere were wiped out. Boer reinforcements, however, arrived over the passes and a counter-attack saved Durban. These events forced the British to occupy Durban in Dec. 1838 but the Boers refused to be controlled and under Andries PRETORIUS they waged an independent war, defeated the Zulus at the Blood River, sacked the royal Kraal at emGungundhlovu and set up an independent republic with its centre at Pietermaritzburg. A peace was patched up. Dingane now mobilised his army to attack the Swazis. His half brother **(4) Mpande (?-1872),** suspecting treachery, fled to Boer territory with 17,000 followers and was recognised by them as Prince of the Emigrant Zulus. In Dec. 1839 the British left and the Boers, now unrestrained, provoked a war with Dingane, in the course of which he was killed by his own people and they recognised Mpande as King of all the Zulus (1840). Mpande was weak, the Boers were rapacious and uncontrolled and the area in confusion. In 1842 the British reoccupied Durban and held it against Boer resistance. In May 1843 Natal became a Crown Colony and the Boer republic was dissolved. In 1845 it was annexed to the Cape and an agreement made the Tugela the boundary with the Zulus. Mpande retained his rights over Zulus living south of it.

British migration in Natal started on a substantial scale but Mpande's weakness, and confusion and population pressure in Zululand brought Zulu southward migration at a far greater rate. By 1849 5000 Europeans were settled among 150,000 Zulus. Under the influence of Theophilus SHEPSTONE, it was decided to move them to reserves where they were to live under native law with the Lieut. Gov. as supreme chief *vice* the Zulu King. This social concept created a permanent barrier between native and European and also infringed Mpande's rights. But Mpande's laziness caused power to slip into the hands of outlying chiefs. Moreover, he had neglected to marry a Chief Wife so that his two eldest sons by commoners had equal claims to the succession. The favourite was MBULAZI, the other was **(5) Cetshwayo (1827-84)** and factions grew up around them. In Dec. 1856 Mbulazi and his faction were wiped out in a great battle near the Tugela and Cetshwayo became the effective ruler of Zululand. More intelligent and energetic than his father, he realised that the only hope for his Kingdom lay in playing off the British in Natal against the Transvaal Boers. In Mar. 1861, in return for the surrender of a rebel chief, he ceded some land to the Transvaal (T. of WAAIHOEK). In July Shepstone, to win his friendship, proclaimed him heir to the Zulu throne; the move was not popular for it involved resurrecting the suzerainty which the Natal Boers had once claimed over Mpande. When Mpande died in 1872 Cetshwayo's position was still weak. Shepstone came to Zululand to crown him and so drove the Zulus into unanimous recognition of his title before he arrived. His attempt to impose Natal native law on Zululand merely created hostility.

The discovery of diamonds in the Boer territories brought a rush of, mostly British, miners into these ill-organised republics. By 1877 their institutions were collapsing and, though the miners were doing well, the republics were bankrupt. In Apr. Shepstone proclaimed their annexation, thus encircling Zululand. It was generally agreed in British politics that some kind of S. African confederation would follow and that Zululand would have to be part of it. As a barbarous native state this was inconceivable. Moreover, Natal was open to invasion by the large Zulu army. It was, therefore, resolved to fight the Zulus on their own ground. Troops were brought in under Gen. Thesiger (Lord Chelmsford) and a war which the Zulus did not want was provoked on flimsy pretexts. There was a gallant defence of Rorke's Drift but the first invasion (Jan. 1879) was beaten back and met disaster at Isandlhwana. The second destroyed the Zulu army and burned the royal Kraal at Ulundi in July. Cetshwayo was deported and Zululand was divided between 13 rival chiefs. There was a revulsion of opinion in England where it was soon realised that the attack on Zululand had been unprovoked. Cetshwayo persuaded the govt. to let him go to England where he arrived in July 1882 and received a popular welcome. He was given a large part of his Kingdom back but died of wounds in a civil war. He was succeeded by **(6) Dinizulu (1868-1913).** Zululand became a British protectorate in 1887 and Dinizulu was deported in 1889. In 1897, when Dinizulu returned, Zululand was annexed to Natal and in 1902 opened to European settlement. In 1906 the last Zulu rising was easily suppressed and Dinizulu imprisoned until 1910. His son **(6) Solomon (?-1933)** was recognised as paramount chief in 1916 and his son **(7) Bhekezulu** in 1945.

ZUYLESTEIN or ZULESTEIN, NASSAU DE (1) Frederick (1608-72) bastard of, P. Henry Frederick of Orange, was tutor to William III whom he accompanied to England in 1670. His son **(2) William Henry (1645-1709) 1st E. of ROCHFORD (1695)** came to England in 1688 as William III's negotiator with the protestant party, was naturalised and was William III's Master of the Robes from 1689 to 1695. His son **(3) William (1681-1710) 2nd E.,** was A.D.C. to Marlborough, became an Irish M.P. in 1705 and English M.P. in 1708. He was killed as a Brig-Gen. in Spain. His nephew **(4) William Henry (1717-81) 4th E.,** was min. to Sardinia from 1749 to 1755 and ambassador to Spain from 1763 to 1766. In 1768 he was Sec. of State for the Northern Dept. and in 1769 opposed the repeal of the American taxes. In 1770 he was moved to the Southern Dept. He resigned in 1775 as a result of the American crisis.

ZWINGLI, Ulrich. *See* SWITZERLAND.

Appendix A

English Regnal Years

Regnal years were used for dating documents and also parliamentary sessions until 1963 when A.D. dating came into use for statutes. The table shows the number, beginning and end of the first year of a reign, from which, save as shown, the other years including the penultimate can be deduced. It also shows the number and dates of the last year, which ends, unless otherwise shown with the death of the sovereign.

Before Edward II, regnal years began on the coronation day. Then save as noted, on the day after the predecessor's death. The following notes to the table deal with the irregularities.

(1) Date of coronation. (2) K. John was crowned on Ascension Day and his regnal years ran from one Ascension to the next. (3) Date of Proclamation. Edward I was on Crusade. (4) Between 25 Jan. 1327 and 28 Nov. 1330 the rulers were Edward II's Queen Isabel and Mortimer, her lover. They had Edward II murdered on or about 21 September 1327. Documents dated with the name of a K. Edward, do not always distinguish between the first three. (5) Date of Deposition. (6) In 1340 Edward III claimed the French crown and added French regnal years to his English ones. In 1360 he renounced the claim. In 1369 he resumed it and counted his subsequent regnal years as if it had not been renounced. After him English and French regnal years were the same until the French title was renounced in 1806. (7) Edward IV was recognised as King on the day when Henry VI was deposed. (8) Henry VI's short restored reign was reckoned both from his original accession in 1422 and from his readeption in 1470, but Edward IV reckoned his regnal years as if the readeption had not occurred. (9) Murdered in the Tower. (10) Mary I reckoned her *second* and later years as if Jane had never been Queen. (11) Mary I married Philip, K. of Naples and Jerusalem and from 16 Jan. 1556, of the Spanish kingdoms, on this day. His English titles lapsed at her death. (12) Jac = Jacobus. James VI began his Scots reign on this day. Both Scots and English regnal years commonly appear in documents after 24 March 1603. (13) Under the Commonwealth and Protectorate, documents were dated A.D. (14) Charles II dated his reign from the day of his father's death on the scaffold, but seldom used regnal years in dating during his exile i.e. before 29 May 1660, when he was restored. (15) Fled. (16) Mary II died in the night of 27-8 December 1694. (17) The Calendar Act omitted eleven days in September 1752, so eleven days were added to the end of the regnal year. (18) Date of abdication.

No.	Sovereign	Begin	End	No.	Sovereign	Begin	End
1	Will. I	25 Dec. 1066(1)	24 Dec. 1067	1	Edw. I	20 Nov. 1272(3)	19 Nov. 1273
21	Will. I	25 Dec. 1086	9 Sept. 1087	35	Edw. I	20 Nov. 1306	7 Jul. 1307
1	Will. II	26 Sept. 1087(1)	25 Sept. 1088	1	Edw. II	8 Jul. 1307	7 Jul. 1308
13	Will. II	26 Sept. 1099	2 Aug. 1100	20	Edw. II	8 Jul. 1326	20 Jan. 1327(5)
1	Hen. I	5 Aug. 1100(1)	4 Aug. 1101	1	Edw. III(4)	25 Jan. 1327	24 Jan. 1328
36	Hen. I	5 Aug. 1100	1 Dec. 1135	13	Edw. III	25 Jan. 1339	24 Jan. 1340
1	Steph.	22 Dec. 1135(1)	21 Dec. 1136	14 & 1	Edw. III(6)	25 Jan. 1340	24 Jan. 1341
19	Steph.	22 Dec. 1153	25 Oct. 1154	34 & 21	Edw. III	25 Jan. 1360	8 May 1360(6)
1	Hen. II	19 Dec. 115(1)	18 Dec. 1155	34	Edw. III(6)	9 May 1360	24 Jan. 1361
35	Hen. II	19 Dec. 1188	6 Jul. 1189	43	Edw. III	25 Jan. 1369	10 Jun. 1369
1	Ric. I	3 Sept. 1189(1)	2 Sept. 1190	43 & 30	Edw. III(6)	11 Jun. 1369	24 Jan. 1370
10	Ric. I	3 Sept. 1198	6 Apr. 1199	51 & 38	Edw. III(6)	25 Jan. 1377	21 Jun. 1377
1	John	27 May 1199(2)	17 May 1200	1	Ric. II	22 Jun. 1377	21 Jun. 1378(6)
2	John	18 May 1200	2 May 1201	23	Ric. II	22 Jun. 1399	29 Sept. 1399(5)
3	John	3 May 1201	22 May 1202	1	Hen. IV	30 Sept. 1399	29 Sept. 1400
4	John	23 May 1202	14 May 1203	14	Hen. IV	30 Sept. 1412	20 Mar. 1413
5	John	15 May 1203	2 May 1204	1	Hen. V	21 Mar. 1413	20 Mar. 1414
6	John	3 Jun. 1204	18 May 1205	10	Hen. V	21 Mar. 1422	31 Aug. 1422
7	John	19 May 1205	10 May 1206	1	Hen. VI	1 Sept. 1422	31 Aug. 1423
8	John	11 May 1206	30 May 1207	39	Hen. VI	1 Sept. 1460	4 Mar. 1461(5)
9	John	31 May 1207	14 May 1208	1	Edw. IV	4 Mar. 1461(7)	3 Mar. 1462
10	John	15 May 1208	6 May 1209	10	Edw. IV	4 Mar. 1470	3 Mar. 1471
11	John	7 May 1209	26 May 1210	49 & 1	Hen. VI(8)	9 Oct. 1470	14 Apr. 1471
12	John	27 May 1210	11 May 1211	11	Edw. IV	4 Mar. 1471	3 Mar. 1472(8)
13	John	12 May 1211	2 May 1212	23	Edw. IV	4 Mar. 1483	9 Apr. 1483
14	John	3 May 1212	22 May 1213	1	Edw. V	9 Apr. 1483	25 Jun. 1483(9)
15	John	23 May 1213	7 May 1214	1	Ric. III	26 Jun. 1483	25 Jun. 1484
16	John	8 May 1214	27 May 1215	3	Ric. III	26 Jun. 1485	22 Aug. 1485
17	John	28 May 1215	18 May 1216	1	Hen. VII	22 Aug. 1485	21 Aug. 1486
18	John	19 May 1216	19 Oct. 1216	24	Hen. VII	22 Aug. 1508	21 Apr. 1509
1	Hen. III	28 Oct. 1216(1)	27 Oct. 1217	1	Hen. VIII	22 Apr. 1509	21 Apr. 1510
57	Hen. III	28 Oct. 1272	16 Nov. 1272	38	Hen. VIII	22 Apr. 1546	28 Jan. 1547

1	Edw. VI	28 Jan. 1547	27 Jan. 1548
7	Edw. VI	28 Jan. 1553	6 Jul. 1553
1	Jane	6 Jul. 1553	19 Jul. 1553
1	Mary I	19 Jul. 1553 (10)	5 Jul. 1554
2	Mary I	6 Jul. 1554 (10)	24 Jul. 1554
1 & 2	P. & M.	25 Jul. 1554 (11)	5 Jul. 1555
1 & 3	P. & M.	6 Jul. 1555	24 Jul. 1555
2 & 3	P. & M.	25 Jul. 1555	5 Jul. 1556
2 & 4	P. & M.	6 Jul. 1556	24 Jul. 1556
3 & 4	P. & M.	25 Jul. 1556	5 Jul. 1557
3 & 5	P. & M.	6 Jul. 1557	24 Jul. 1557
4 & 5	P. & M.	25 Jul. 1557	5 Jul. 1558
4 & 6	P. & M.	6 Jul. 1558	24 Jul. 1558
5 & 6	P. & M.	25 Jul. 1558	17Nov.1558
1	Eliz. I	17 Nov. 1558	16 Nov. 1559
45	Eliz. I	17 Nov. 1602	23 Mar. 1603
1	*Jac. VI(Scots)*	*24 Jul. 1567*	*23 Jul. 1568(12)*
1 & 36	Jac. I	24 Mar. 1603	23 Jul. 1603
1 & 37	Jac. I	24 Jul. 1603	23 Mar. 1604
2 & 37	Jac. I	24 Mar. 1604	23 Jul. 1604
2 & 38	Jac. I	24 Jul. 1604	23 Mar. 1605
3 & 38	Jac. I	24 Mar. 1605	23 Jul. 1605
3 & 39	Jac. I	24 Jul. 1605	23 Mar. 1606
4 & 39	Jac. I	24 Mar. 1606	23 Jul. 1606
4 & 40	Jac. I	24 Jul. 1606	23 Mar. 1607
5 & 40	Jac. I	24 Mar. 1607	23 Jul. 1607
5 & 41	Jac. I	24 Jul. 1607	23 Mar. 1608
6 & 41	Jac. I	24 Mar. 1608	23 Jul. 1608
6 & 42	Jac. I	24 Jul. 1608	23 Mar. 1609
7 & 42	Jac. I	24 Mar. 1609	23 Jul. 1609
7 & 43	Jac. I	24 Jul. 1609	23 Mar. 1610
8 & 43	Jac. I	24 Mar. 1610	23 Jul. 1610
8 & 44	Jac. I	24 Jul. 1610	23 Mar. 1611
9 & 44	Jac. I	24 Mar. 1611	23 Jul. 1611
9 & 45	Jac. I	24 Jul. 1611	23 Mar. 1612
10 & 45	Jac. I	24 Mar. 1612	23 Jul. 1612
10 & 46	Jac. I	24 Jul. 1612	23 Mar. 1613
11 & 46	Jac. I	24 Mar. 1613	23 Jul. 1613
11 & 47	Jac. I	24 Jul. 1613	23 Mar. 1614
12 & 47	Jac. I	24 Mar. 1614	23 Jul. 1614
12 & 48	Jac. I	24 Jul. 1614	23 Mar. 1615
13 & 48	Jac. I	24 Mar. 1615	23 Jul. 1615
13 & 49	Jac. I	24 Jul. 1615	23 Mar. 1616
14 & 49	Jac. I	24 Mar. 1616	23 Jul. 1616
14 & 50	Jac. I	24 Jul. 1616	23 Mar. 1617
15 & 50	Jac. I	24 Mar. 1617	23 Jul. 1617
15 & 51	Jac. I	24 Jul. 1617	23 Mar. 1618
16 & 51	Jac. I	24 Mar. 1618	23 Jul. 1618
16 & 52	Jac. I	24 Jul. 1618	23 Mar. 1619
17 & 52	Jac. I	24 Mar. 1619	23 Jul. 1619
17 & 53	Jac. I	24 Jul. 1619	23 Mar. 1620
18 & 53	Jac. I	24 Mar. 1620	23 Jul. 1620
18 & 54	Jac. I	24 Jul. 1620	23 Mar. 1621
19 & 54	Jac. I	24 Mar. 1621	23 Jul. 1621

19 & 55	Jac. I	24 Jul. 1621	23 Mar. 1622
20 & 55	Jac. I	24 Mar. 1622	23 Jul. 1622
20 & 56	Jac. I	24 Jul. 1622	23 Mar. 1623
22 & 56	Jac. I	24 Mar. 1623	23 Jul. 1623
22 & 57	Jac. I	24 Jul. 1623	23 Mar. 1624
22 & 57	Jac. I	24 Mar. 1624	23 Jul. 1624
22 & 58	Jac. I	24 Jul. 1624	23 Mar. 1625
23 & 58	Jac. I	24 Mar. 1625	27 Mar. 1625
1	Car. I	27 Mar. 1625	26 Mar. 1626
24	Car. I	27 Mar 1648	30 Jan. 1649

Commonwealth and Protectorate (13)

1	Car. II	30 Jan. 1649	29 Jan. 1650
11	Car. II	30 Jan. 1659	29 Jan. 1660
12	Car. II	30 Jan. 1660	29 Jan. 1661
37	Car. II	30 Jan. 1685	6 Feb. 1685
1	Jac. II	6 Feb. 1685	5 Feb. 1686
4	Jac. II	6 Feb. 1688	11 Dec. 1688(15)

Interregnum		12 Dec. 1688	12 Feb. 1689
1	Wm. & Mar.	13 Feb. 1689	12 Feb. 1690
6	Wm. & Mar.	13 Feb. 1694	27 Dec. 1694(16)
6	Wm. III	28 Dec. 1694	12 Feb. 1695
14	Wm. III	13 Feb. 1702	8 Mar 1702
1	Anne	8 Mar. 1702	7 Mar. 1703
13	Anne	8 Mar. 1714	1 Aug. 1714
1	Geo. I	1 Aug. 1714	31 Jul. 1715
13	Geo. I	1 Aug. 1726	11 Jun. 1727
1	Geo. II	11 Jun. 1727	10 Jun. 1728
2S	Geo. II	11 Jun. 1751	10 Jun. 1752
26	Geo. II	11 Jun. 1752	21 Jun. 1753(17)
27	Geo. II	22 Jun. 1753	21 Jun. 1754
34	Geo. II	22 Jun. 1760	25 Oct. 1760
1	Geo. III	25 Oct. 1760	24 Oct. 1761
60	Geo. III	25 Oct. 1819	29 Jan. 1820
1	Geo. IV	29 Jan. 1820	28 Jan. 1821
11	Geo. IV	29 Jan. 1830	26 Jun. 1830
1	Wm. IV	26 Jun. 1830	25 Jun. 1831
7	Win. IV	26 Jun. 1836	20 Jun. 1837
1	Vic.	20 Jun. 1837	19 Jun. 1838
64	Vic.	20 Jun. 1900	22 Jan. 1901
1	Edw. VII	22 Jan. 1901	21 Jan. 1902
10	Edw. VII	22 Jan. 1910	6 May 1910
1	Geo. V	6 May 1910	5 May 1911
26	Geo. V	6 May 1935	20 Jan. 1936
1	Edw. VIII	20 Jan. 1936	11 Dec. 1936(18)
1	Geo. VI	11 Dec. 1936	10 Dec. 1937
16	Geo. VI	11 Dec. 1951	6 Feb. 1952
1	Eliz. II	6 Feb. 1952	5 Feb. 1953
49	Eliz. II	6 Feb. 2000	Q.D.S.

APPENDIX B – SELECTED WARLIKE EVENTS

Events are land battles unless marked A (= Air), N (= Naval), B (= Bombardment)

NAME	COUNTY, COUNTRY, OR U.S. STATE	DATE	CONTESTANTS (Victor marked *)	REFERENCES (NMN = Related to reference but not mentioned by name)
A				
Aberdeen	Aberdeen	13 Sept 1644	Royalists* : Covenantors	CIVIL WAR (14)
Aboukir	Egypt	(1) 25 July 1799	French* : Turks	
		(2) 21 March 1801		ABERCROMBY (1)
		(3) See **Nile**		
Acre	Palestine	(1) July 1191	Crusaders* : Egyptians	ACRE; CRUSADES (13)
		(2) March-May 1799	British & Turks* : French	ACRE
		(3) 3 Nov 1840	Egyptians : Turks	EGYPT (7-NMN)
Adrianople	Thrace	(1) 20 Jan 1878	Russians* : Turks	
		(2) Jan-March 1913	Bulgars* : Turks	BALKAN WARS (2)
Adwalton Moor	Lancashire	30 June 1643	Royalists* : Parliamentarians	CIVIL WAR (6); FAIRFAX (4), (6)
Agincourt	France	25 Oct 1415	English* : French	AGINCOURT; HENRY V (2)
Aix or Basque Roads	N. France	11-12 Apr 1809	British* : French	COCHRANE (5); GAMBIER (2)
Alamein	Egypt	23 Oct-3 Nov 1942	British* : Germans and Italians	WORLD WAR II (12)
Albuera	Spain	16 May 1811	British* : French	COLE, SIR LOWRY; BERESFORD (2); PENINSULAR WAR (7)
Alcazar Kebir	Morocco	1578	Moroccans* : Portuguese	AVIZ (8-9)
Aliwal	Punjab	January 1846	British* : Sikhs	SIKHS (5)
Alexandria (B)	Egypt	(1) 21 March 1801	British* : French	ABERCROMBY
		(2) 11-13 July 1882	British : Egyptians	GLADSTONE'S SECOND GOVT. (7)
Algeciras (N)	Spain	5 July 1801	British : French 1799-1801	2ND COALITION, WAR OF
Algiers (N)	N. Africa	1816	British* : Barbaresques	PELLEW (1)
Aljubarrota	Portugal	14 August 1385	Portuguese : Castilians	AVIS (1); RICHARD II (8); CASTILE
"Alleluja"	Britain	429 or 430	British* : Picts & Scots	MISSIONARIES IN BRITAIN ETC. (1); BRITAIN, ROMANO-BRITISH (2)
Alma, R	Crimea	20 Sept 1854	British & French : Russians	CRIMEAN WAR (7)
Almanza	Spain	25 April 1707	French* : British	GALWAY; BERWICK
Alnwick	Northumberland	13 July 1174	English* : Scots	GLANVILLE, RANULF; DURHAM (4)
Alresford	Hampshire	29 March 1644	Roundheads* : Cavaliers	CIVIL WAR (11); HOPTON (2)
Altimarlich	Caithness	1680	Campbells* : Sinclairs	CAITHNESS
Ambur	India	August 1749	British : Indo-French	ARCOT
Ameixial	Portugal	8 June 1663	Anglo-Portuguese* : Spaniards	CHARLES II(9)
Ancrum	Scotland	27 Feb 1545	Scots* : English	HENRY VIII (19)
Anderida (Pevensey)	Sussex	491	S.Saxons* : Britons	AELLE
Anjou - see Baugé				
Anzio	Italy	Jan-Feb 1944	Anglo-Americans* : Germans	WORLD WAR II (4 NMN)
Ardennes, The	Belgium	16-22 Dec 1944	Anglo-Americans* : Germans	WORLD WAR II (15)
Argaum	India	29 Nov 1803	British : Marathas	MARATHAS; WELLINGTON (2)
Arkinholme	Scotland	1455	Scots King : Douglases	JAMES II OF SCOTS (6)
Armada, The (N)	Four Seas	May-Sept 1588	English* : Spaniards	ARMADAS (1); ELIZABETH I (22)
Arnhem	Netherlands	17-26 Sept 1944	British* : Germans	WORLD WAR II (15)
Arsuf	Palestine	7 Sept 1191	Franks : Egyptians	CRUSADES (14)
Ashdown	Wiltshire	8 Jan 871	W. Saxons* : Danes	ALFRED THE GREAT; ASHDOWN; VIKINGS (10)
Assaye	India	25 Sept 1803	British* : Marathas	MARATHAS (8); 3RD COALITION WAR, FIRST PHASE (2); WELLINGTON (2)
Assendum or Assingdon	Essex	June 1016	Danes* : English	EDMUND IRONSIDE; EAST ANGLIA (18); ULFKELL
Atbara, The	Sudan	8 April 1898	British* : Dervishes	SALISBURY'S 3RD GOVT.
Athenry	Ireland	August 1316	English* : Connaughtmen	BURGH, DE

NAME	COUNTY, COUNTRY, OR U.S. STATE	DATE	CONTESTANTS (Victor marked *)	REFERENCES (NMN = Related to reference but not mentioned by name)
Atlantic, The: see separate entry				
Auberoche	France	Oct 1345	English* : French	EDWARD III
Aughrim	Galway	12 July 1691	William III : Jacobites	AUGHRIM, GINKEL
Auldearn	Scotland	9 May 1645	Royalists* : Parliamentarians	CIVIL WAR (21)
Auray	Britanny	September 1364	English* : French	BRITTANY, CHANDOS, EDWARD III (14)
Austerlitz	Moravia	2 Dec 1805	French* : Austrians and Russians	ALEXANDER I, 3RD COALITION, FIRST PHASE
Aylesford	Kent	455	Jutes* : Britons	KENT (1)
Azov (S)	Ukraine	March-Sept 1796	Russians* : Turks	AUGSBURG, WAR OF LEAGUE OF; AZOV
B				
Badajoz (S)	Spain	(1) 1705	British* : French	GALWAY
		(2) April 1812	British* : French	BADAJOZ; PICTON; PENINSULAR WAR 1807-14 (8)
Badbury	Dorset	520	W. Saxons* : Britons	WEST SAXONS, EARLY (1)
Badon, Mt.	? Wilts	Between 490 and 517	Britons* : Angles	BADON MT.; DEVIL'S DYKE (3), ICKNIELD WAY
Baggot Rath	Ireland	13 August 1649	Parliamentarians* : Irish Royalists	COMMONWEALTH (2); JONES (2)
Balaclava	Crimea	25 Oct 1854	Anglo-French : Russians	BALACLAVA; BINGHAM (5); CRIMEAN WAR (8)
Ballynahinch	Ireland	June 1798	British* : Irish Rebels	UNITED IRISHMEN
Banbury	Oxfordshire	556	Gewissae* : Britons	WEST SAXONS, EARLY (4)
Bannockburn	Stirling	24 June 1314	Scots* : English	BANNOCKBURN; EDWARD II;
Bantry Bay (N)	Ireland	(1) 11 May 1689	English : French	AUGSBURG, WAR OF THE LEAGUE OF
		(2) Dec 1796	French : English	2ND COALITION, WAR OF
Barfleur - see La Hogue				
Barnet	Hertfordshire	14 April 1471	York* : Lancaster	BARNET; EDWARD IV (14)
Barrosa	Spain	5 March 1811	British* : French	PENINSULAR WAR 1807-14 (7); GRAHAM (2); THOMAS (7)
Basing House (S)	Hampshire	1644	Royalists : Parliamentarians	BASING "HOUSE"
Basque Roads - see Aix Roads				
Bastogne	Belgium	December 1944	Anglo-Americans : Germans	WORLD WAR II (15)
Batalha- see Aljubarrota				
Baugé	France	22 March 1421	Angevins* : English	CHARLES VI OF FRANCE (15)
Baylen	Spain	20 July 1808	Spanish* : French	PENINSULAR WAR 1807-14 (3)
Beachy Head (N)	Channel	10 July 1690	Anglo-Dutch : French	AUGSBURG WAR OF LEAGUE (2); EVERTSEN (4)
Beandun	S. England	616	W. Saxons* : Britons	WEST SAXONS, EARLY (7)
Beersheba	Palestine	31 Oct 1917	British* : Turks	ALLENBY
Belle Isle (N)	France	June 1761	British* : French	SEVEN YEARS' WAR (10)
Benburb	Ireland	5 June 1646	Irish Confederates* : Scots	CIVIL WAR (25)
Bergen	Germany	(1) 13 April 1759	French* : Anglo-Hanoverian	SEVEN YEARS' WAR (7)
	Holland	(2) 19 Sept 1799	French* : Anglo-Russians	2ND COALITION WAR 1795-1801
	Holland	(3) 2 Oct 1799	French* : Anglo-Russians	2ND COALITION WAR 1795-1801
Berwick	Northumberland	30 March 1296	English* : Scots	BALIOL
Blackheath	Kent	17 June 1497	Henry VII* : Cornish Rebels	HENRY VII (14); PAULET (1)
Blenheim	Bavaria	13 August 1704	Anglo-Austrians* : Franco Bavarians	BAVARIA (2); BLENHEIM
Blood R	Natal	December 1838	Boers* : Zulus	ZULUS (2)
Bloody Marsh	Georgia	1742	English* : Spaniards	GEORGIA, (USA)
Blore Heath	Salop	23 Sept 1459	Lancastrians* : Yorkists	HENRY VI (14)

NAME	COUNTY, COUNTRY, OR U.S. STATE	DATE	CONTESTANTS (Victor marked *)	REFERENCES (NMN = Related to reference but not mentioned by name)
Boomplatz	South Africa	29 August 1848	British* : Boers	GREAT TREK (NMN)
Boroughbridge	England	16 March 1322	Edward II* : Lancaster	ADAM OF ORLTON; BOHUN (8); EDWARD II (8)
Bosworth Field	England	22 August 1485	Henry VII* : Richard III	HENRY VII (2); BOSWORTH FIELD; RICHARD III (9)
Bothwell Brig	Scotland	22 June 1679	English* : Covenanters	
Bourgneuf (N)	Biscay	1371	English* : Flemings	EDWARD III (15)
Bouvines	France	27 July 1214	French : Germans and Flemings	BOUVINES; FLANDERS (9); JOHN
Boyne, The	Ireland	11 July 1690	William III* : James II	SCHOMBERG; BOYNE; BUTLER (19); JAMES II and VII (15)
Brandywine	Pennsylvania	11 Sept 1777	British* : Rebels	HOWE (4)
Brechin	Scotland	1452	Gordons: Crawford	JAMES II OF SCOTS (5)
Brémule	France	20 August 1119	English* : French	ANDELYS; HENRY I (10); LOUIS VI
Brest - see Camaret Bay				
Brihuega	Spain	9 Dec 1710	French* : British	VENDÔME
Britain (A)	Britain	10 July-15 Sept 1940	British* : Germans	BRITAIN, B OF; MACHINE GUNS
Bristol (S)	Britain	(1) 26 June 1643	Royalists* : Parliamentarians	CIVIL WAR (6)
		(2) 21 Aug-10 Sept 1645	Royalists* : Parliamentarians	CIVIL WAR (21)
Brunanburh	England	937	English* : Celts, Scots and Vikings	SCOTS AND ALBAN KINGS, EARLY (6); VIKINGS (18); CUMBERLAND (3); YORK, SCANDINAVIAN KINGDOMS. B (5)
Bunker Hill	Massachusetts	17 June 1775	British* : Americans	HOWE (4); AMERICAN REBELLION (5)
Burnt Candlemas	S. Scotland	February 1356	English : Scots	EDWARD III (12)
Busaco	Portugal	27 Sept 1810	British* : French	PENINSULAR WAR 1807-14 (6)
Buxar	India	23 Oct 1764	British : Oudh & Moguls	BENARES; MOGULS (10); BUXAR
C				
Cadiz (N)	Spain	(1) 19 April 1587	English* : Spaniards	ARMADAS (1)
	Spain	(2) 30 June 1596	English* : Spaniards	ARMADAS (2)
	Spain	(2) 1702		
Cadzand (N)	Belgium	Nov 1337	English* : Flemish	PHILIP VI; JOHN II OF FRANCE; EDWARD III
Calais (S)	France	1346	English* : French	CALAIS; EDWARD III
Camaret Bay (N)	France	June 1694	French* : English	AUGSBURG, WAR OF LEAGUE (4); BERKELEY (7)
Cambrai	France	20-30 Nov 1917	British : Germans	WORLD WAR I (11 NMN)
Camden	South	(1) 10 Sept 1780	British* : Americans	AMERICAN REBELLION (20)
	Carolina	(2) 25 April 1791	British : Americans	AMERICAN REBELLION (20)
Camelford	Cornwall	825	W. Saxons* : Cornish	ENGLISH MONARCHY, EARLY (1)
Camlan		537	Saxons* : Britons	ARTHUR, KING; FAMINE
Camperdown (N)	Dutch Coast	(1) 21 August 1673	British : Dutch	DUTCH WARS, 3RD (4)
	Dutch Coast	(2) 11 Oct 1797	British* : Dutch	
Canterbury	(S) Kent	1011	Danes* : English	ALPHEGE
Cantysgol	Northumberland	December 633	Northumbrians* : Welsh	GWYNEDD
Caporetto	Italy	23 Oct-10 Nov 1917	Austro-Germans : Italians	WORLD WAR I
Carberry Hill	Scotland	15 June 1567	Scots Protestants: Roman Catholics	MARY Q. OF SCOTS (14)
Carham	Northumberland	1018	Scots* : Northumbrians	DURHAM (2)
Carrick on Suir	Ireland	1462	Desmond* : Butler	BUTLER (12)
Cartagena	Spanish Main	1741	Spaniards* : British	WARS OF 1739-48 (4)
Cassel	France	23 August 1328	French* : Flemings	FLANDERS (10); PHILIP VI
Cassel	Germany	1 Nov 1762	Anglo-Hanoverians* : French	SEVEN YEARS' WAR (13)

NAME	COUNTY, COUNTRY, OR U.S. STATE	DATE	CONTESTANTS (Victor marked *)	REFERENCES (NMN = Related to reference but not mentioned by name)
Cassino	Italy	11-21 May 1944	Allies : Germans	WORLD WAR II(13)
Castillon	France	17 July 1453	French* : English	AQUITAINE (16); BUREAU; HENRY VI
Castlebar	Ireland	7 August 1798	British* : Irish	IRELAND D (5 NMN); TONE (NMN)
Cateau Le	France	25-6 August 1914	British : Germans	WORLD WAR I (2)
Cawnpore (S)	India	July - Dec 1857	Indian Mutineers* : British	HAVELOCK (2)
Caya R	Portugal	1709	Portuguese* : Spaniards	GALWAY
Chalgrove Field	Oxfordshire	18 June 1643	Royalists* : Parliamentarians	HAMPDEN (1)
Charford	Hampshire	519	West Saxons* : Britons	WEST SAXONS, EARLY (1)
Charmouth	Dorset	835	Vikings* : West Saxons	ENGLISH MONARCHY, EARLY (1)
Chase About Raid	Scotland	August 1565	Mary of Scots* : Dissidents	MARY Q. OF SCOTS (11)
Cherbourg (N)	France	1758	British : French	HOWE (3)
Cheriton - see Alresford				
Chernaya R	Crimea	16 August 1855	French : Russians	CRIMEAN WAR (8)
Chevy Chase or Otterburn	Northumberland	19 August 1388	Scots* : English	STEWART (15); CHARLES VI (2)
Chilianwallah	India	13 Jan 1849	British : Sikhs	SIKHS (5)
Cholet	France	16 Oct 1793	Republicans* : Royalists	1ST COALITION WAR OF (3); VENDÉE
Ciudad Rodrigo (S)	Spain	19 Jan 1812	British* : French	PENINSULAR WAR 1807-14 (8)
Cleanse the Causeway	Edinburgh	1520	Angus* : Arran	JAMES V OF SCOTS (1)
Clontarf	Ireland	23 April 1014	Irish* : Ostman	DUBLIN; BRIAN BORU
Colenso	South Africa	15 Dec 1899	Boers* : British	BOTHA; BULLER
Colonsay	Hebrides	1156	Somerled* : Manx	MAN, ISLE OF (3)
Connor	Ireland	September 1315	Scots* : de Burgh	BURGH, DE (6)
Conway, R	Wales	(1) 881	N. Welsh* : Mercians	GWYNEDD (13)
		(2) Jan 1295	English* : Welsh	EDWARD I (15)
Copenhagen (B)	Denmark	(1) 21 May 1801	British* : Danes	2ND COALITION WAR 1799-1801 (5); JERVIS (1).
(S)		(2) 25 Sept 1807	British* : Danes	FRANCO-RUSSIAN ALLIANCE, WAR OF (1); PORTLAND GOVT. (2)
Coral Sea (N)	Pacific	26 May-1 June 1942	US* : Japanese	WORLD WAR II (10)
Coronel (N)	N. Pacific	1 Nov 1914	Germans* : British	WORLD WAR I (7)
Corunna	Spain	16 Jan 1809	British : French	PENINSULAR WAR 1807-14 (4)
Corrichie	Scotland	1562	Moray* : Gordons	GORDON (HUNTLEY) (2)
Courtrai	Belgium	11 July 1302	Flemings* : French	FLANDERS (9); EDWARD I(21)
Coutras	France	20 Oct 1587	Huguenots* : Catholics	HUGUENOTS (13)
Coventry	Warwickshire	AD 61	Romans* : Iceni	ICENI
Craon	France	May 1592	French* : English	ELIZABETH I(26)
Crayford	Kent	456	Jutes* : Britons	KENT, KINGDOM (1)
Cravant	France	July 1424	English* : French	CHARLES VII OF FRANCE (1)
Crécy	France	26 August 1346	English* : French	ICH DIEN; BLACK PRINCE; EDWARD III (9)
Crefeld	Germany	23 June 1758	French : Anglo-Hanoverians	SEVEN YEARS' WAR (5)
Crete	Mediterranean	20-30 May 1941	Germans* : British	WORLD WAR II (7)
Cropredy Br.	Oxfordshire	20 Jan 1644	Royalists: Parliamentarians	CIVIL WAR (13)
Crossford - see Rhyd-y-groes				
Ctesiphon	Iraq	22-24 Nov 1915	Turks* : British	WORLD WAR I (6 NMN)
Culblean	Scotland	1335	Scots: Balliol's Men	BAL[L]IOL, EDWARD
Culloden	Scotland	16 April 1746	English* : Jacobites	JACOBITES (20); WARS OF 1739-48 (14)
D				
Dakar	W. Africa	23-25 Sept 1940	French* : British	WORLD WAR II (4)

NAME	COUNTY, COUNTRY, OR U.S. STATE	DATE	CONTESTANTS (Victor marked *)	REFERENCES (NMN = Related to reference but not mentioned by name)
Dalry	Scotland	July 1306	Anglo-Scots* : Bruce	EDWARD I (22)
Damme (N)	Belgium	28 May 1213	English* : French	FLANDERS (9)
Dangan	Ireland	August 1647	Parliamentarians* : Irish	JONES (2)
Deeg	India	November 1804	British* : Holkar	MARATHAS (8)
Degsastan	Northumberland	603	Northumbrians* : Scots	DALRIADA (3)
Deorham	Avon	577	English* : Britons	WEST SAXONS, EARLY (4)
Dettingen	Germany	27 June 1743	British* : French	DALRYMPLE (6); HANOVER (1); GEORGE II; WARS OF 1739-48 (7)
Devizes	Wiltshire	13 July 1643	Royalists* : Parliamentarians	HOPTON (2); CIVIL WAR (6)
Diamond Hill	Orange Free State	June 1900	British : Boers	BOTHA (1)
Dieppe	France	14 August 1942	British and Canadians : Germans	DIEPPE (2); WORLD WAR II (11)
Diu (N)	India	February 1509	Portuguese* : Egyptians and Indians	PORTUGUESE INDIES (1)
Dixmude	Flanders	13 June 1489	English* : French	HENRY VII (6)
Dogger Bank (N)	North Sea	24 March 1917	British : Germans	BEATTY; WORLD WAR I (7)
Dominica (N)	Caribbean	(1) June 1761	British* : French	SEVEN YEARS' WAR (10)
Doornkop	South Africa	May 1900	Boers : British	BOTHA (1)
Douro, R	Portugal	12 May 1809	Anglo-Portuguese* : French	PENINSULAR WAR (5 NMN)
Dover (N)	Channel	(1) 19 May 1652	Dutch : English	DUTCH WAR, 1ST (1)
		(2) 2-3 June 1653	Dutch : English	DUTCH WAR, 1ST
Downs, The (N)	Channel	(1) Oct 1639	Dutch* : Spanish	THIRTY YEARS' WAR (15);
		(2) 3 June 1666	Dutch : English	TROMP (2)
Drogheda (S)	Ireland	11 Sept 1649	Parliamentarians* : Irish	COMMONWEALTH (2)
Dunbar	Scotland	(1) 27 April 1296	English* : Scots	EDWARD I(17)
		(2) 3 Sept 1650	English* : Scots	FLEETWOOD (2); COMMONWEALTH (4)
Dunes, The	France	13 June 1658	Anglo-French* : Spaniards	JOHN OF AUSTRIA 1629-79; COMMONWEALTH (16)
Dungeness (N)	Channel	30 Nov-10 Dec 1652	English : Dutch	BLAKE (2); DUTCH WARS, FIRST (15); EVERTSEN (1)
Dunkirk (N)	Channel	(1) see Four Days (N)		WORLD WAR II (4)
		(2) 30 May-3 June 1940	Germans* : British and French	
Dunnichen	Forfar	685	Picts* : Angles	DALRIADA (3)
Dunsinane	Scotland	27 July 1054	Northumbrians* : Macbeth	
Dupplin Moor	Scotland	12 August 1332	Anglo-Scots* : Scots	BALIOL (5); EDWARD III (2); DAVID II); DISINHERITED (SCOTLAND)

E

NAME	COUNTY, COUNTRY, OR U.S. STATE	DATE	CONTESTANTS (Victor marked *)	REFERENCES
Edgehill	Warwickshire	23 Oct 1642	Royalists : Parliamentarians	CIVIL WAR (5); MELDRUM
Edington	Wiltshire	878	W. Saxons* : Danes	ALFRED THE GREAT; VIKINGS (13)
Elandslaagte	South Africa	November 1899	Boers* : British	SOUTH AFRICAN WAR (3)
Elderslie	Renfrew	1164	Scots* : Islanders	RENFREW
Ellandun	Wiltshire	825	W. Saxons* : Mercians	ENGLISH MONARCHY, EARLY (1)
"Espagnols-sur-mer" - see Winchelsea				
Ethandun - see Edington				
Evesham	Worcester	4 August 1265	Royalists* : Barons	BARONS' WAR (4); GIFFARD (1); KENILWORTH
Eylau	Prussia	7-9 Feb 1807	French* : Russians and Prussians	3RD COALITION, FIRST PHASE (3)

F

NAME	COUNTY, COUNTRY, OR U.S. STATE	DATE	CONTESTANTS (Victor marked *)	REFERENCES
Falkirk	Scotland	22 July 1298	English* : Scots	EDWARD I (19)
		17 Jan 1746	English* : Scots	JACOBITES (20)

NAME	COUNTY, COUNTRY, OR U.S. STATE	DATE	CONTESTANTS (Victor marked *)	REFERENCES (NMN = Related to reference but not mentioned by name)
Falkland Islands (N)	S. Atlantic	(1) 8 Dec 1914	British* : Germans	STURDEE (7); WORLD WAR I
		(2) 1982	British* : Argentinians	ARGENTINA 10-12; FALKLANDS IS.
Faughart	Ireland	1318	Irish* : Scots	ISLES, LORDSHIP OF (9); BURGH, DE (6); EDWARD II (6)
Ferozeshah	India	21-22 Dec 1845	British : Sikhs	SIKHS (5)
Finisterre (N)	N. Atlantic	(1) 3 May 1747		
		(2) 14 Oct 1747	British* : French	BOSCAWEN
Flodden	Northumberland	9 Sept 1513	English* : Scots	JAMES IV (6); HENRY VIII (7)
Flores (N)	Azores	1591	Spaniards* : English	ELIZABETH I (24)
Fontenoy	France	25 June 841		
		11 May 1745	Germans* : Lorrainers	
			French* : British	WARS OF 1739-48 (10); JACOBITES (18)
Formigny	France	15 April 1450	French* : English	BUREAU; HENRY VI (7)
Fort Duquesne (S)	USA	November 1759	British* : French	AMHERST (1); JOHNSON, SIR WILLIAM; SEVEN YEARS' WAR (6)
Foul Raid	Northumherland	1417	English* : Scots	JAMES I OF SCOTS (2)
Four Days (N)	North Sea	11-14 June 1666	English : Dutch	DUTCH WARS (SECOND) (5); EVERTSEN (2)
Fréteval	France	July 1194	English* : French	PHILIP II AUGUSTUS
Friedland	East Prussia	14 June 1807	French* : Russians	3RD COALITION, SECOND STAGE (4)
Frontenac, Fort	Quebec	August 1758	British* : French	SEVEN YEARS' WAR (5)
Fuentes d'Oñoro	Spain	3-5 May 1811	British* : French	PICTON; PENINSULAR WAR 1807-14 (7)
Fulford	Yorkshire	20 Sept 1066	Hardrada* : Tostig : Morcar	HAROLD II (2)
G				
Gabbard, The (N)	Thames	12-13 June 1653	British : Dutch	BLAKE (3); DUTCH WARS, FIRST (4)
Gaza	Palestine	(1) 26-28 March - 18-19 April 1917	Turks : British	MURRAY ALLENBY; WORLD WAR I (12 NMN)
		(2) Oct 1917	British* : Turks	
Gelt, R	Cumberland	20 Feb. 1570	Royal Troops* : Rebels	NORTHERN REBELLION (4)
Gembloux	Belgium	June 1578	Spaniards* : Dutch	BELGIUM (1) HUGUENOTS (12); GHENT, PACIFICATION OF; ELIZABETH I (19)
Gerberoi	Normandy	1079	William I : Baronage	WILLIAM I (8)
Ghazni (S)	Afghanistan	July 1839	British* : Afghans	AFGHANISTAN (16)
Gibraltar (S)	Straits	1779-83	British* : Spaniards	HOWE (30), ELIOTT GEORGE; GIBRALTAR
Gisors	France	1198	English* : French	WILLIAM II(4)
Glenlivet	Scotland	October 1594	Huntly* : Argyll	CAMPBELL OF LOCHOW, B (7)
Glenmama	Ireland	1000	Irish* : Ostmen	BRIAN BORU
Glenshiel	Scotland	10 June 1719	Jacobites : British*	JACOBITES (14)
Glorious 1st June (N)	Atlantic	1 June 1794	British* : French	GAMBIER (1); HOWE (3); USHANT
Gloucester (S)	England	August-Sept 1643	Parliamentarians* : Royalists	CIVIL WAR (8)
Graupius, Mona	Scotland	AD 84	Romans : Caledonians	BRITAIN, ROMAN (15-17)
Gravelines (N)	North Sea	7-8 August 1588	English* : Spaniards	ARMADAS (1)
Grenada (N)	Caribbean	1779	British* : French	BARRINGTON (4)
Gretna	Scotland	1448	Scots* : English	JAMES II OF SCOTS (3)
Guadalcanal	Pacific	August 1942	US* : Japanese	WORLD WAR II (12)
Guadaloupe (N)		(1) May 1759		
		(2) See Saints (N)	British* : French	SEVEN YEARS' WAR (7)
Guinegatte	France	16 August 1513	Anglo-Hapsburgs : French	HENRY VIII (7)
Gujerat or Gujrat	India	21 Feb 1849	British* : Sikhs	RAWALPINDI; SIKHS (5)

NAME	COUNTY, COUNTRY, OR U.S. STATE	DATE	CONTESTANTS (Victor marked *)	REFERENCES (NMN = Related to reference but not mentioned by name)
H				
Halidon Hill	Berwick	19 July 1333	English* : Scots	EDWARD III (2); STEWARTS (9); BALIOL, EDWARD
'Hallelujah' Victory	Britain	429 or 430	British* : Picts and Saxons	BRITAIN, ROMANO-BRITISH (2); MISSIONARIES IN BRITAIN & IRELAND (1)
Harfleur (S)	Normandy	August-Sept 1415	English* : French	HENRY V (2)
Harlaw	Aberdeen	24 July 1411	Lord of the Isles : Scots Royal Forces	ABERDEENSHIRE
Hastenbeck	Hanover	26 July 1757	French* : British	CUMBERLAND, DUKES OF (3); HASTENBECK, HANOVER (11) SEVEN YEARS' WAR (3)
Hastings	Sussex	14 Oct 1066	Normans* : English	HAROLD II; WILLIAM I
Hattin, Horns of	Palestine	4 July 1197	Egyptians* : Franks	CRUSADES (9)
Heathfield	Yorkshire	October 632	Welsh, Mercians* : Northumbrians	GWYNEDD (4); NORTHUMBRIA (3)
Hedgeley Moor	Durham	March 1464	Yorkists* : Lancastrians	EDWARD IV (4)
Heligoland (N)	North Sea	28 August 1914	British : Germans	BEATTY; WORLD WAR I (7)
Hexham	Northumberland	8 May 1464	English* : Scots	EDWARD IV (4)
Hingston Down	Devon	823	English* : Cornish, Vikings	CORNWALL
Homildon Hill	Northumberland	14 Sept 1402	English* : Scots	HENRY IV (4)
Hyères (N)	Mediterranean	February 1744	British : Franco-Spanish	WARS OF 1739-48 (8)
I				
Idle, R	Lincolnshire	617	Deirans* : Bernicions	EAST ANGLIA (3)
Imphal	Manipur	May 1944	British : Japanese	WORLD WAR II (18 NMN)
Inkerman	Crimea	5 Nov 1854	British : Russians	CRIMEAN WAR (18)
Inverlochy	Scotland	2 Feb 1645	Royalists* : Covenanters	CIVIL WAR (18)
Isandhlwana	South Africa	22 Jan 1879	Zulus* : British	ZULUS (4)
J				
Jargeau	France	12 June 1429	French* : English	JOAN OF ARC (2)
Jena	Germany	14 Oct 1806	French* : Prussians	3RD COALITION WAR, SECOND PHASE (2)
Jutland (N)	North Sea	31 May-1 June 1916	British : Germans	BEATTY; WORLD WAR I (10)
K				
Kandahar	Afghanistan	1 Sept 1880	British* : Afghans	AFGHANISTAN (9)
Kashgil	Sudan	1883	Mahdists* : British	KORDOFAN
Kells	Ireland	November 1315	Scots : Irish	BURGH, DE (6)
Kentish Knock (N)	Thames	28-29 Sept 1652	English : Dutch	BLAKE, ROBERT (3); EVERTSEN (1)
Keren	Eritrea	Feb-April 1941	British : Italians	WORLD WAR II (5 NMN)
Khanua	India	16 March 1527	Moguls* : Rajputs	RAJPUTS (2);
Kharda	India	1795	Marathas* : Nizam	MARATHAS (7); HYDERABAD
Kilcomny	Ireland	June 1798	British* : Irish Rebels	UNITED IRISHMEN
Killiecrankie	Scotland	27 July 1689	Jacobites : English	AUGSBURG, WAR OF LEAGUE (1)
Kilsyth	Scotland	16 August 1645	Royalists* : Covenanters	CIVIL WAR (21)
Kimberley (S)	South Africa	Oct 1899-Feb 1900	British : Boers	S. AFRICAN WAR (3), (5)
Kinsale (S)	Ireland	Sept 1601-Jan 1602	English* : Spaniards	ELIZABETH I (35)
Kohima	Manipur	May 1944	British : Japanese	WORLD WAR II (18)
Kotah	India	17 June 1858	British* : Kotians	JHANSI
Kut el Amara (S)	Iraq	(1) April 1916	Turks* : British	WORLD WAR I (6 and 8)
		(2) 24 Feb 1917	British* : Turks	WORLD WAR I (10 NMN)

NAME	COUNTY, COUNTRY, OR U.S. STATE	DATE	CONTESTANTS (Victor marked *)	REFERENCES (NMN = Related to reference but not mentioned by name)
L				
Ladysmith (S)	South Africa	Nov 1809-Mar 1900	British* : Boers	S. AFRICAN WAR (3), (5)
Lagos (N)	Portugal	18 Aug 1759	British* : French	SEVEN YEARS' WAR (8)
La Hogue (N)	Channel	19 May 1692	English* : French	AUGSBURG, WAR OF LEAGUE (3); JAMES II & VII (16); BARFLEUR
Laings Nek	South Africa	28 Jan 1881	Boers* : British	GLADSTONE'S SECOND GOVT (3)
Landen	Belgium	29 July 1693	French* : Dutch/Allies	BERWICK, JAMES (1)
Lansdown	Somerset	5 July 1643	Royalists* : Parliamentarians	HOPTON (2)
Langport	Somerset	10 July 1645	Parliamentarians* : Royalists	GORING (2); CIVIL WAR (21)
Langside	Glasgow	13 May 1568	Scots Protestants : Catholics	MARY Q. OF SCOTS (15)
Largs (N)	Scotland	2 Oct 1263	Scots* : Norwegians	ISLE OF MAN (4); ALEXANDER III OF SCOTS
Laroche	Brittany	June 1347	English* : French	EDWARD III (9)
Laswari	India	1 Nov 1803	British* : Marathas	MARATHAS (8)
Lauffeld	Germany	July 1747	French* : British	CUMBERLAND, D OF (3); WARS OF 1736-48 (14);
Leipzig	Saxony	16-18 Oct 1813	Austrians, Russians, etc* : French	4TH COALITION, WAR OF (4)
Leominster	Salop	1052	Welsh* : Saxons	GWYNEDD (20)
Leuthen	Silesia	5 Dec 1757	Prussians* : Austrians	GEORGE II (21); SEVEN YEARS' WAR (4)
Lewes	Sussex	14 May 1264	Barons* : Royalists	BALIOL; BARONS' WAR (3) BOHUN, JOHN (? 1269)
Lexington	Massachusetts	19 April 1775	Rebels* : British	AMERICAN REBELLION (15)
Ligny	Belgium	16 June 1815	French* : Prussians	WATERLOO
Limerick (S)	Ireland	27 Oct 1651	Parliamentarians* : Irish	COMMONWEALTH (5)
Lincoln	England	(1) 2 Feb 1141	Matilda : Stephen	STEPHEN (5)
		(2) 20 May 1217	English* : French	HENRY III (12)
Linlithgow	Scotland	1526	Angus* : Lennox	JAMES V OF SCOTS (3)
Lisbon (S)	Portugal	October 1147	Anglo-Portuguese* : Moors	CRUSADES (8)
Liscarrol	Ireland	3 Sept 1642	English* : Irish	BOYLE (2)
Lissa (N)	Adriatic	(1) 1811	British* : French	HOSTE
		(2) 1866	Austrians* : Italians	ADRIATIC (6); IRONCLAD (4)
Lizard, The (N)	Channel	August 1652	Dutch* : British	DUTCH WARS, FIRST (1)
Lofoten Is. (N)	Norway	(1) 6 March 1941	British* : Germans	LOFOTEN IS.
		(2) 29 Dec 1941		LOFOTEN IS.
Loos	France	Sept-Oct 1915	Germans : British	LAMBART (4); LOOS
Louisbourg (S)	Nova Scotia	July 1758	British* : French	AMHERST (1); COLVILLE (5); SEVEN YEARS' WAR (4)
Lostwithiel	Cornwall	1 Sept 1644	Royalists* : Parliamentarians	CIVIL WAR (14)
Louvain	Belgium	Sept 891	Germans : Danes	VIKINGS (14)
Lowestoft (N)	N. Sea	13 June 1665	British* : Dutch	DUTCH WARS, SECOND (4)
Lucknow (S)	India	1857	British* : Indians	HAVELOCK; INDIAN MUTINY (8), (9)
Ludford Bridge	Salop	12 Oct 1459	Lancastrians* : Yorkists	HENRY VI (14)
Lundy's Lane	Ontario, Canada	25 July 1814	British : USA	ANGLO-AMERICAN WAR (5a, NMN)
M				
Madras (S)	India	September 1746	French* : English	WARS OF 1739-48 (13)
Mafeking (S)	South Africa	Oct 1899-May 1900	British : Boers	MAFEKING, S. AFRICAN WAR (6)
Magdala	Ethiopia	1868	British* : Ethiopians	ABYSSINIA (1)
Magersfontein	South Africa	11 Dec 1899	Boers* : British	S. AFRICAN WAR (4)
Maharajpur	Gwalior, India	29 Dec 1843	British : Marathas	NMN
Maida	Italy	4 July 1806	British* : French	COLE, SIR GALBRAITH
Maiwand	Afghanistan	July 1880	Afghans* : British	AFGHANISTAN (9)

NAME	COUNTY, COUNTRY, OR U.S. STATE	DATE	CONTESTANTS (Victor marked *)	REFERENCES (NMN = Related to reference but not mentioned by name)
Majuba Hill	South Africa	27 Feb 1881	Boers* : British	GLADSTONE'S SECOND GOVT (3)
Malaga (N)	Spain	13 August 1704	British* : Spaniards	SPANISH SUCCESSION, WAR OF (7)
Maldon	Essex	993	Vikings* : English	VIKINGS (19)
Malplaquet	Belgium	11 Sept 1709	British/Allies* : French	DALRYMPLE (6); SPANISH SUCCESSION, WAR OF (18)
Manila (N)	Philippines	February 1762	British* : French	SEVEN YEARS' WAR (12)
Marie Galante (N)	Caribbean	June 1759	British* : French	SEVEN YEARS' WAR (7)
Marne, R	France	4-9 Sept 1914	Allies* : Germans	WORLD WAR I (2)
Marston Moor	Yorkshire	2 July 1644	Parliamentarians* : Royalists	CIVIL WAR (13); FAIRFAX (4), (6); GORING (2);
Masulipatam	S. India	7 April 1759	British* : French	SEVEN YEARS' WAR (7)
Matapan, C (N)	Mediterranean	28 March 1941	British* : Italians	AIRCRAFT CARRIER; ITALY, KINGDOM-13; WORLD WAR II (6)
Medway, R (N)	Kent	11 June 1667	Dutch* : British	DUTCH WARS, SECOND (7)
Meeanee	India	17 Feb 1843	British* : Sind Amirs	SIND
Mcgiddo	Palestine	September 1918	British* : Turks	ALLENBY
Meigen - see Heathfield				
Merchain	Wales	1070	Welsh : Welsh	BLEDDYN AF CYNFYN
Mers-el-Kebir - see Oran				
Messines	France	June 1917	British : Germans	WORLD WAR I (11 NMN)
Metemma	Ethiopia	March 1889	Mahdists* : Abyssinians	ABYSSINIA (2)
Methven	Scotland	June 1306	Anglo-Scots* : Bruce	EDWARD I (22)
Miani - see Meeanee				
Midway (N)	Pacific	3-6 June 1942	US* : Japanese	AIRCRAFT CARRIER; WORLD WAR II (10)
Minden	Germany	1 August 1759	British* : French	HANOVER (11); SEVEN YEARS' WAR (7)
Minorca (N)	Mediterranean	28 June 1756	French* : English	MINORCA; SEVEN YEARS' WAR (1)
Mons	Belgium	23 August 1914	British : Germans	WORLD WAR I (2)
Montargis	France	1427	French* : English	DUNOIS
Montes Claros	Portugal	17 June 1665	Anglo-Portuguese* : Spaniards	PORTUGAL AFTER 1640 (2)
Moodkee	India	18 Dec 1845	British : Sikhs	SIKHS (5)
Mortemer	Normandy	1054	Normans* : French	CAPETIANS (9); WILLIAM I (4)
Mortimer's Cross	Yorkshire	2 Feb 1461	Yorkists* : Lancastrians	HENRY VI (17)
Multan	India	7 Nov 1848	British* : Sikhs	SIKHS (5)
Musselburgh	Scotland	10 Sept 1547	English* : Scots	SEYMOUR, EDWARD (3) NMN
Mynydd Carn	Wales	1081	Welsh : Welsh	DEHEUBARTH (11); GWYNEDD (22)
N				
Najera	Spain	3 April 1367	English : Henry of Trastamara	BLACK PRINCE; AQUITAINE (14); EDWARD III (14)
Namur (S)	Belgium	September 1695	English* : French	AUGSBURG, WAR OF LEAGUE (4); CUTTS
Nancy	France	5 Jan 1477	Swiss* : Burgundians	BURGUNDY (7); LOUIS XI
Nantwich	Cheshire	25-8 January 1644	Parliamentarians* : Royalists	BUTLER (18)
Narvik (N)	Norway	(1) 10 April 1940	British* : Germans	WORLD WAR II
		(2) 13 April 1940	British* : Germans	
Naseby	Northants	14 June 1645	Parliamentarians* : Royalists	DEANE, RICHARD; CIVIL WAR (21)
Navarino (N)	Greece	20 Oct. 1827	British, French, Russians* : Turks	GREECE (4)
Nechtansmere - see Dunichen				
Nesbit	Northumberland	August 1355	Scots* : English	EDWARD III (12)
Nesbit Moor	Northumberland	22 June 1402	English* : Scots	HENRY IV (4)

NAME	COUNTY, COUNTRY, OR U.S. STATE	DATE	CONTESTANTS (Victor marked *)	REFERENCES (NMN = Related to reference but not mentioned by name)
Neville's Cross	Yorkshire	17 Oct 1346	English* : Scots	BALIOL, EDWARD; DURHAM (9); EDWARD III (9); STEWART or STUART (EARLY) (10)
Newburn	Northumberland	28 August 1640	Scots* : English	CHARLES I (12 NMN)
Newbury	Berkshire (1)	10 Sept 1643	Parliamentarians* : Royalists	CIVIL WAR (8)
	(2)	27 Oct 1644	Royalists : Parliamentarians	CIVIL WAR (15)
New Orleans	Louisiana	8 Jan 1815	Americans* : British	ANGLO-AMERICAN WAR 1812-15
Newark	England	24 March 1644	Royalists* : Parliamentarians	CIVIL WAR (11); MELDRUM
"Nile, The" (N)	Egypt	1 August 1798	British* : French	FOLEY (4); JERVIS (1); MALTA (3) MEDITERRANEAN WAR 1797-99 (2)
Nive	France	9-13 Dec 1813	British* : French	PENINSULAR WAR 1807-14 (11)
Nivelle	France	10 Nov 1813	British* : French	PENINSULAR WAR 1807-14 (11)
Nombre de Dios (N)	Spanish Main	1567	Spaniards* : English	DRAKE
Northampton	England	10 July 1460	Yorkists* : Lancastrians	HENRY VI (15)
North Cape (N)	North Atlantic	26 Dec 1943	British* : Germans	ATLANTIC, B OF (3);
North Foreland Channel (N)		4 August 1666	English* : Dutch	DUTCH WAR, SECOND (6) NMN

O

Ocaña	Spain	November 1809	French* : Spaniards	PENINSULAR WAR 1807-14 (6)
Ockley	Surrey	852	English* : Danes	ENGLISH MONARCHY EARLY (2); VIKINGS (10)
Omdurman	Sudan	2 Sept 1898	British* : Sudanese	DAFEUR; KORDOFAN; SALISBURY'S THIRD GOVT (9)
Oporto	Portugal	12 May 1809	British* : French	PENINSULAR WAR 1807-14 (5); PORTLAND GOVT. (4)
Oran (N)	Algeria	3 July 1940	British* : French	MERS-EL-KEBIR; WORLD WAR II (4)
Orfordness (N)		25 July 1666	British* : Dutch	DUTCH WARS, SECOND (6)
Orléans (S)	France	Oct 1428-May 1429	French* : English	JOAN OF ARC (2)
Orthez	France	27 Feb 1814	British* : French	PENINSULAR WAR 1807-14 (11)
Oswego	New York (1)	August 1756	French* : British	SEVEN YEARS' WAR (1)
	(2)	August 1758	British* : French	SEVEN YEARS' WAR (5)
Otterburn - see Chevy Chase				
Otford	Kent	774	Mercians* : Kentishmen	KENT, KINGDOM (5)
Oudenarde	Belgium	11 July 1708	British, Allies* : French	DALRYMPLE (6); VENDÔME; SPANISH SUCCESSION, WAR OF (13)

P

Paardeberg	South Africa	27 Feb 1900	British* : Boers	SOUTH AFRICAN WAR (5)
Panipat	India	14 Jan 1761	Afghans* : Marathas	AFGHANISTAN (2); MARATHAS (3)
Passaro, Cape (N)	Mediterranean	11 August 1718	British : Spaniards	HADDOCK (2); QUADRUPLE ALLIANCE (1); BYNG (1); JACOBITES (14); GEORGE I (8)
Passchendael	France	July-Nov 1916	Allies : Germans	WORLD WAR I (8)
Patay	France	18 June 1429	French* : English	JOAN OF ARC (2)
Patna	India	15 Jan 1761	British : Moguls	MOGULS (10)
Pearl Harbour (N)	Hawaii, USA	7 Dec 1941	Japanese* : Americans	WORLD WAR II (9)
Philiphaugh	Scotland	15 Sept 1645	Covenanters* : Royalists	CIVIL WAR (22)
Pinkie	Scotland	September 1547	English* : Scots	DURIE; SEYMOUR, EDW. (3)
Plassce	Bengal, India	23 June 1757	British* : Bengalis	BENGAL; CALCUTTA; CLIVE (1); COOTE (2); SEVEN YEARS' WAR (4)
Plate, River (N)	South Atlantic	14 Dec 1939	British* : Germans	WORLD WAR II (3)
Poitiers	France	19 Sept 1356	English* : French	EDWARD III (12)
Pondichery	S. India	Jan 1761	British* : French	SEVEN YEARS' WAR (9)
Poona	India	23 Oct 1801	Holkar* : Peishwa, Scindia	MARATHAS (8)

NAME	COUNTY, COUNTRY, OR U.S. STATE		DATE	CONTESTANTS (Victor marked *)	REFERENCES (NMN = Related to reference but not mentioned by name)
Portland (N)	Channel		28 Feb-2 Mar 1653	English : Dutch	DUTCH WARS, FIRST (4); BLAKE; TROMP (1); PENN, DEAN RICHARD; EVERTSEN (2)
Porto Bello (N)	Panama		November 1739	British* : Spaniards	WARS OF 1739-48 (2);
Porto Novo	India		1 July 1781	British : Hyder Ali	COOTE (2)
Prairiai - see Glorious 1st June					
Preston	Lancashire	(1)	17 August 1648	Parliamentarians* : Scots	CHARLES I (26)
		(2)	12 Nov 1715	Government* : Jacobites	GEORGE II; JACOBITES (12)
Prestonpans	Scotland		21 Sept 1745	Jacobites* : English	JACOBITES (19)
Pyrenees	Spain		25 July-2 August 1813	British* : French	PENINSULAR WAR (10)
Q					
Quatre Bras	Belgium		16 June 1815	British, Allies : French	WATERLOO
Quebec	Canada		18 Sept 1759	British* : French	SEVEN YEARS' WAR (8); CANADA (9); OTTAWA INDIANS
Quiberon Bay (N)	France		20 Nov 1759	British* : French	HARDY (3); HAWKE; SEVEN YEARS' WAR (8); USHANT
R					
Radcot Br.	Oxfordshire		December 1387	Appellants : de Vere	APPELLANT, LORDS; RICHARD II (6)
Ramillies	Belgium		23 May 1706	British, Allies* : French	SPANISH SUCCESSION, WAR OF (9)
Rathamines - see Baggot Rath					
Renfrew	Scotland		1164	Scots* : Islanders	ISLES, LORDSHIP OF (2)
Rheinberg	Germany		June 1758	British and Hanoverians* : French	SEVEN YEARS' WAR (5)
Rhyd-y-groes (Crossford)	Wales		1039	Welsh* : Mercians	GWYNEDD (20)
Roche, La	Brittany		June 1347	English* : French	EDWARD III (9)
Roche aux Moines, La	France		July 1214	French* : English	JOHN (14 NMN)
Rochelle La (N)	France		June 1372	French : Castilians	CHARLES V OF FRANCE
Roliça	Portugal		17 August 1808	British* : French	PENINSULAR WAR 1807-14 (4)
Ronaldsway	Isle of Man		1275	Scots : Manx	MAN, ISLE OF (5)
Rorke's Drift	South Africa		22 Jan 1879	Zulus : British	ZULUS (4)
Ross	Ireland		March 1643	Royalists* : Parliamentarians	BUTLER (18)
Rossbach	Saxony		5 Nov 1757	Prussians* : French, Imperialists	GEORGE II (21); SEVEN YEARS' WAR (4)
"Rough Wooing"	Scotland		May-June 1545	English: Scots	MELROSE (2); HENRY VIII (20)
Roundway Down - see Devizes					
Rowton Heath	Chester		24 Sepl 1645	Parliamentarians* : Royalists	GERARD (3); CIVIL WAR (22)
S					
St. Albans	Hertfordshire		22 May 1455	Yorkists : Lancastrians	ROSES, WARS OF (3)
St. Aubin du Cormier	France		28 July 1488	French* : Bretons	HENRY VII (5)
St. Augustine	Florida		1740	Spaniards* : British	GEORGIA
St. Fagans	Glamorgan		1648	Parliamentarians* : Royalists	JONES, PHILIP (NMN)
St. George's Bay	Belize		10 Sept 1798	British* : Spaniards	BELIZE
St. Malo (N)	France	(1)	1693	English : French	
		(2)	1758	British : French	AUGSBURG, WAR OF LEAGUE OF HOWE (3)
St. Mahé (N)	Biscay		May 1293	English : Bretons	EDWARD I (15); AQUITAINE (10)
St. Nazaire (N)	France		27 March 1942	British* : Germans	COMBINED OPERATIONS (3)
St. Vincent, Cape (N)	Atlantic		14 Feb 1797	British* : Spaniards	JERVIS (1); FRANCO-AUSTRIAN WAR (5)
Saintes	France		22 July 1242	French* : English	AQUITAINE (7)
Saints, The (N)	Caribbean		12 April 1782	British* : French	JAMAICA (3); AMERICAN REBELLION (22)

NAME	COUNTY, COUNTRY, OR U.S. STATE	DATE	CONTESTANTS (Victor marked *)	REFERENCES (NMN = Related to reference but not mentioned by name)
Sakaria, R	Anatolia	23 Aug-13 Sept 1921	Turks* : Greeks	CHANAK; GREECE (7)
Salamanca	Spain	22 July 1812	British* : French	PENINSULAR WAR 1807-14 (8)
Saldanha Bay	S.W. Africa	1796	British* : Dutch	ELPHINSTONE (1)
Salerno	Italy	10 Sept-10 Oct 1943	Allies : Germans	WORLD WAR II (13)
San Domingo (N)	Caribbean	1806	British : French	DUCKWORTH
Sandwich (N)	Channel	24 August 1217	English* : French	HENRY III (2)
San Sebastian (S)	Spain	July-August 1813	British* : French	PENINSULAR WAR 1807-14 (10)
Santa Cruz (N)	Tenerife	20 April 1657	British* : Spaniards	BLAKE (6); COMMONWEALTH (14)
Saragossa	Spain	20 August 1710	British* : French	SPANISH SUCCESSION, WAR (18) NMN
Saratoga	New York	17 Oct 1777	Americans* : British	GATES; BURGOYNE
Schellenberg, The	Bavaria	2 July 1704	British* : Franco-Bavarians	BLENHEIM
Scheveningen (N) - see Texel				
Schoneveldt (N)	Channel	7 and 14 June 1673	Dutch : British	DUTCH WARS, THIRD (4)
Sedgemoor	Somerset	6 July 1685	James II* : Monmouth	MONMOUTH; JAMES II & VII (5)
Seine, R (N)	France	15 August 1416	English* : Genoese	HENRY V (3);
Selby	Yorkshire	11 April 1644	Parliamentarians* : Royalists	CIVIL WAR (12)
Seringapatam (S)	Mysore, India	(1) 15 May 1791	British : Indians	MYSORE
		(2) 6 Feb 1792	British* : Indians	MYSORE
Sheriff Muir	Perthshire	13 Nov 1715	Jacobites: English	JACOBITES (12)
Shrewsbury	Salop	21 July 1403	Henry IV* : Percies	HENRY IV (7)
Sinope (N)	Black Sea	30 Nov 1853	Russians* : Turks	CRIMEAN WAR (2); IRONCLAD (1)
Sirte (N)	Mediterranean	March 1942	British* : Italians	VIAN
Sluys (N)	Belgium	(1) 24 June 1340	English* : French	BOHUN (11); FLANDERS (11); EDWARD III (5);
Sluys	Belgium	1604	English* : Spaniards	FAIRFAX (2)
Sobraon	India	10 Feb 1846	British* : Sikhs	ABBOT (2); SIKHS (5)
Sole Bay (N)	North Sea	7 June 1672	Dutch : Anglo-French	DEANE; HADDOCK (1); TROMP (2); DUTCH WARS, THIRD (3); JAMES II & VII (2); EVERTSEN (3)
Solway Moss	Cumberland	25 Nov 1542	English* : Scots	JAMES V OF SCOTS (7)
Somme	France	July-Nov 1916	British : Germans	WORLD WAR I (8)
Sorauren	Spain	28-30 July 1813	British* : French	PENINSULAR WAR (10)
Southwold - see Sole Bay				
Spion Kop	South Africa	February 1900	Boers* : British	BOTHA (1); S AFRICAN WAR (4)
Spurs, The - see Courtrai, Gurinegatte				
Stainmoor	Yorkshire	954	Norse : Ostmen	YORK B. (6)
Stamford Bridge	Yorkshire	25 Sept 1066	English* : Norsemen	HAROLD II (3)
Standard, The	Yorkshire	22 August 1138	English* : Scots	BRUCE (2); DURHAM (3); THORSTAN ABP.
Steenkerk	Belgium	3 August 1692	French* : Dutch	BERWICK, JAMES (1); AUGSBURG, WAR OF LEAGUE (3)
Sticklestead	Norway	31 August 1030	Canute* : Olaf Haraldsson	CANUTE AND HIS SONS (1)
Stirling Bridge	Scotland	September 1297	Wallace* : English	EDWARD I (18); WALLACE, SIR WM.
Stoke	Staffordshire	16 June 1487	Henry VII* : Lambert Simnel	RHYS AP THOMAS; HENRY VII (3)
Stormberg	Natal, S Africa	10 Dec 1899	Boers* : British	SOUTH AFRICAN WAR (4)
Stow on the Wold	Gloucestershire	21 March 1646	Parliamentarians* : Royalists	CIVIL WAR (24)
Stratton	Somerset	16 March 1643	Royalists* : Parliamentarians	CIVIL WAR (6)
Swanage	Dorset	877	English : Danes	VIKINGS (12)
Swilly, L	Ireland	1567	O'Donnells* : O'Neills	ELIZABETH I (10)
T				
Tachov	Bohemia	11 July 1427	Hussites* : English	BOHEMIA

NAME	COUNTY, COUNTRY, OR U.S. STATE	DATE	CONTESTANTS (Victor marked *)	REFERENCES (NMN = Related to reference but not mentioned by name)
Taku Forts	China	(1) May 1858	Anglo-French* : Chinese	CHINA (21)
		(2) June 1859	Anglo-French : Chinese*	CHINA (22)
		(3) Aug 1860	Anglo-French* : Chinese	CHINA (22)
		(4) July 1900	International Force : Chinese	CHINA (33 NMN)
Talana Hill	South Afnca	October 1899	Boers* : British	SOUTH AFRICAN WAR (3)
Talavera	Spain	27-8 July 1809	British* : French	PENINSULAR WAR 1807-14 (5)
Tamames	Spain	Nov 1809	French* : Spaniards	PENINSULAR WAR 1807-14 (6)
Tannenberg	E. Prussia	15 July 1410	Poles* : Teutonic Knights	HANSE (5)
"Tannenberg"	E. Prussia	25-31 August 1914	Germans* : Russians	HINDENBURG; WORLD WAR I (2)
Taranto (N)	Italy	11 Nov 1940	British* : Italians	AIRCRAFT CARRIER; WORLD WAR I (5)
Tarbes	France	20 Mar 1814	British* : French	PENINSULAR WAR (11 NMN)
Tel el Kebir	Egypt	13 Sept 1882	British* : Egyptians	GLADSTONE'S SECOND GOVT. (7)
Ter Heijde (N) - see Texel				
Tewkesbury	Gloucestershire	4 May 1471	Edward IV : Queen Margaret	DYMOKE (2); EDWARD IV (13)
Texel, The (N)	North Sea	10 August 1653	English* : Dutch	COMMONWEALTH (9); DUTCH WARS, FIRST (4); EVERTSEN (3)
Thames, R	USA	Oct 1813	US* : British and Shawnees	ANGLO-AMERICAN WAR 1812-15 HARRISON (1)
Three Days (N) - see Portland				
Tibbermore	Perth	September 1644	Royalist : Covenanters	CIVIL WAR (14)
Ticonderoga (S)	USA	(1) July 1758	French* : British	SEVEN YEARS' WAR (5)
		(2) July 1759	British* : French	AMHERST (1); GAGE (7)
Tinchebrai	Normandy	28 Sept 1106	Henry I* : Robert of Normandy	NORMANDY (7); HENRY I
Torrington	Devon	16 Feb 1646	Parliamentarians* : Royalists	HOPTON (2)
Toulon - see Hyères				
Toulouse	France	10 April 1814	British* : French	BERESFORD (2)
Towton	Yorkshire	29 March 1561	Yorkists* : Lancastrians	BUTLER (11); HENRY VI (18)
Towy, R	Wales	1044	N. Welsh* : Danes, S. Welsh	GWYNEDD (19)
Trafalgar (N)	N. Atlantic	21 Oct 1805	British : Franco-Spanish	BARHAM; TRAFALGAR
Tugela R.	South Africa	December 1856	Cetewayo* : Mbulazi	ZULUS (4)
Tynwald Hill	Isle of Man	1210	Olaf* : Reginald	MAN, ISLE OF (14)
U				
Ulundi	South Africa	3 Jan 1879	British* : Zulus	ZULUS (4)
Urchingfield	Hereford	917	English* : Brittany Danes	
Ushant (N)		(1) July 1778	British* : French	ORVILLIERS
		(2) 1781	British* : French	KEMPENFELT
		(3) see Glorious 1st June		
V				
Vaalkrantz	Natal	December 1899	Boers* : British	BOTHA 10
Val ès Dunes	Normandy	1047	D. William* : Norman Rebels	WILLIAM I (2)
Valmy	France	20 Sept 1792	French* : Austro-Prussians	FRENCH REVOLUTIONARY WAR (2)
Varaville	France	August 1058	Normans* : Angevins	WILLIAM I (4)
Verneuil	France	1 August 1424	English* : French	CHARLES VII OF FRANCE
Vimeiro	Portugal	21 August 1808	British* : French	PENINSULAR WAR 1807-14 (4)
Vimy Ridge	France	9 Apr-5 Aug 1917	British : Germans	BYNG (4)
Vinegar Hill	Ireland	June 1798	British* : Irish Rebels	UNITED IRISHMEN
Vitoria	Spain	21 June 1813	British* : French	PICTON; PENINSULAR WAR 1807-14 (9)

NAME	COUNTY, COUNTRY, OR U.S. STATE	DATE	CONTESTANTS (Victor marked *)	REFERENCES (NMN = Related to reference but not mentioned by name)
W				
Wagram	Austria	6 July 1809	French* : Austrians	FRANCO-RUSSIAN ALLIANCE, WAR 1807-14 (3); PORTLAND GOVT. (4)
Wakefield	Yorkshire	30 Dec 1460	Lancastrians* : Yorkists	HENRY VI (16)
Wandewash	S. India	22 June 1766	British* : French	LALLY; COOTE (2); SEVEN YEARS' WAR (9)
Wargaon	India	1779	Marathas* : British	BOMBAY (2); MARATHAS (7)
Waterloo	Belgium	18 June 1815	British, Prussians* : French	WATERLOO
Wednesfield	Warwickshire	910	English* : Danes	YORK, SCANDINAVIAN KINGDOMS. A (2)
Wexford (S)	Ireland	11 Oct 1649	Parliamentarians* : Irish	COMMONWEALTH (2)
White Mountain	Bohemia	8 Nov 1620	Austrians* : Bohemians	THIRTY YEARS' WAR (3);
White Plains	New York	28 Oct 1776	British : Americans	HOWE (4)
Wijk-aan-Zee (N)	North Sea	13 June 1653	British* : Dutch	DUTCH WARS, FIRST (4)
Winceby	Lincolnshire	October 1643	Parliamentarians* : Royalists	CIVIL WAR (9)
Winchelsea (N)	Channel	1350	English* : Spaniards	EDWARD III (10)
Winwaedsfield	Yorkshire	654	Northumbrians* : Mercians, Welsh	EAST ANGLIA (8); GWYNEDD (5); MERCIA-3
Worcester		3 Sept 1651	Parliamentarians* : Royalists	COMMONWEALTH (4); FLEETWOOD (2); LANE
Wimbledon	Surrey	568	Jutes* : W. Saxons	KENT KINGDOM (2)
Wippedesfleot	Kent	465	Jutes* : Britons	KENT KINGDOM (1)
Y				
Yellow Ford	Ulster	1598	Irish* : English	ELIZABETH I (31); O'DONNELL-5
York Gate	Yorkshire	1 March 868	Danes* : Northumbrians	VIKINGS (9)
Yorktown	Virginia	19 Oct 1781	Americans* : British	AMERICAN REBELLION (21)
Ypres	Belgium	(1) Oct-Nov 1914	British : Germans	WORLD WAR I (3)
		(2) Apr-May 1915	British : Germans	WORLD WAR I (4)
		(3) July-Nov 1917	British : Germans	WORLD WAR I (11)
Z				
Zeebrugge (N)	Belgium	23 April 1918	British : Germans	DOVER PATROL; ZEEBRUGGE RAID
Zutphen	Netherlands	1586	English : Spaniards	ELIZABETH I (22); SIDNEY (3)

APPENDIX C
GENEALOGIES AND DIAGRAMS
Interest in the English Crown 1035-66
(Kings of the English in CAPITALS)

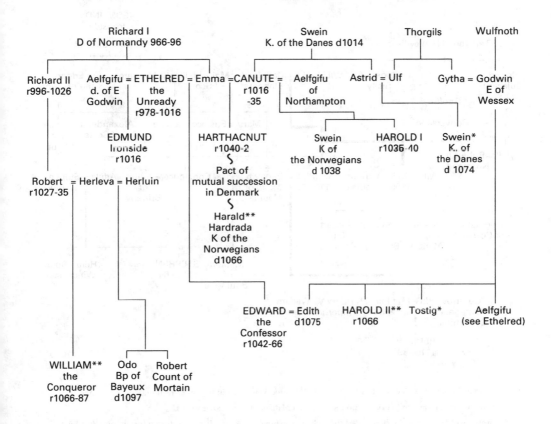

*Possible, **actual competitors at the death of Edward the Confessor. William the Conqueror had a distant blood relationship to him which is not shown. Godwin's sons were Edward's brothers-in-law. Swein of Denmark was Canute's nephew and stepson. Harald Hardrada claimed that his mutual succession pact applied to England.

The Norman-Angevin Transition

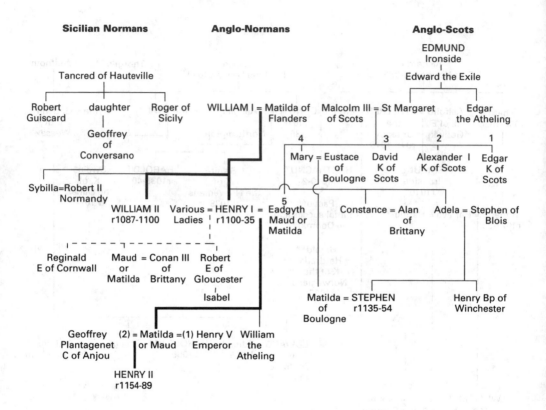

Notes. The five children of Malcolm III of Scots and St Margaret were born in the order of numbers above their names.

Matilda is the Church Latin version of the northern French Mahaut, Anglicised as Maud.

The Empress Matilda was royally descended through both parents: Stephen, her rival, through only one, but his wife was royally descended.

Isabel, daughter of the Empress' half-brother and partisan, Robert of Gloucester, eventually married K. John (see table 3)

The children and grandchildren, surviving infancy, of Henry II and Eleanor of Aquitaine

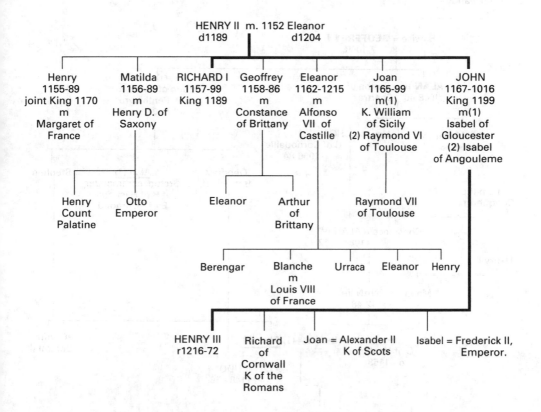

HENRY II m. 1152 Eleanor
d1189 d1204

Henry
1155-89
joint King 1170
m
Margaret of
France

Matilda
1156-89
m
Henry D. of
Saxony

RICHARD I
1157-99
King 1189

Geoffrey
1158-86
m
Constance
of Brittany

Eleanor
1162-1215
m
Alfonso
VII of
Castille

Joan
1165-99
m(1)
K. William
of Sicily
(2) Raymond VI
of Toulouse

JOHN
1167-1016
King 1199
m(1)
Isabel of
Gloucester
(2) Isabel
of Angouleme

Henry
Count
Palatine

Otto
Emperor

Eleanor

Arthur
of
Brittany

Raymond VII
of Toulouse

Berengar

Blanche
m
Louis VIII
of France

Urraca

Eleanor

Henry

HENRY III
r1216-72

Richard
of
Cornwall
K of the
Romans

Joan = Alexander II
K of Scots

Isabel = Frederick II,
Emperor.

Henry II had bastards by various ladies. The most distinguished were Geoffrey, Abp. of York, and William, E. of Salisbury.

K. John also had many ladies. His most distinguished bastard was Johanna, who married Llywellyn ap Iowerth of Gwynedd.

Brittany, Richmond and Anglo-Norman Ambitions

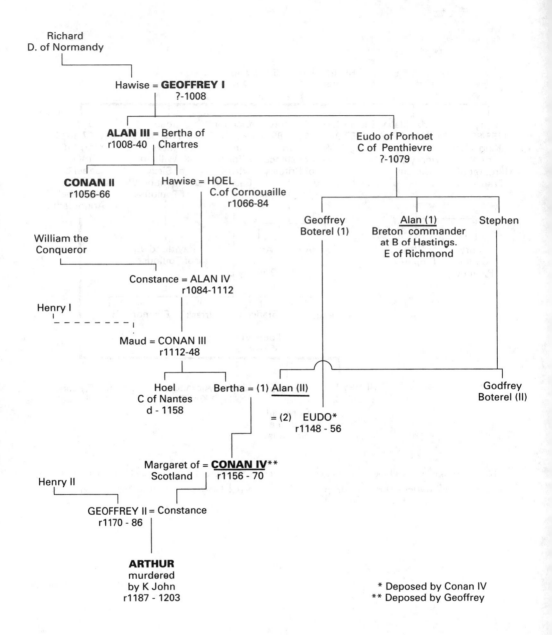

Richard
D. of Normandy

Hawise = **GEOFFREY I**
?-1008

ALAN III = Bertha of
r1008-40 | Chartres

Eudo of Porhoet
C of Penthievre
?-1079

CONAN II
r1056-66

Hawise = HOEL
C.of Cornouaille
r1066-84

Geoffrey
Boterel (1)

Alan (1)
Breton commander
at B of Hastings.
E of Richmond

Stephen

William the
Conqueror

Constance = ALAN IV
r1084-1112

Henry I

Maud = CONAN III
r1112-48

Hoel
C of Nantes
d - 1158

Bertha = (1) Alan (II)

Godfrey
Boterel (II)

= (2) EUDO*
r1148 - 56

Margaret of = **CONAN IV****
Scotland | r1156 - 70

Henry II

GEOFFREY II = Constance
r1170 - 86

ARTHUR
murdered
by K John
r1187 - 1203

* Deposed by Conan IV
** Deposed by Geoffrey

Rulers (usually Dukes) of Brittany in CAPITALS: those by succession **Bold:** those by marriage Roman: Earls of Richmond underlined

The Plantagenets, The Three Families of John of Gaunt and the Transition to Lancaster

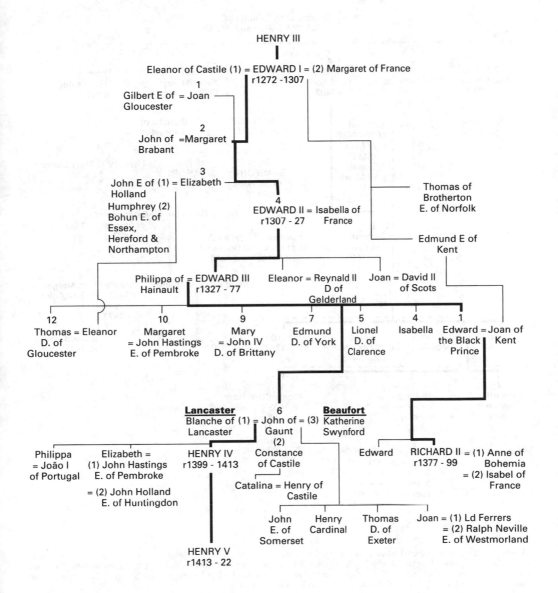

HENRY III

Eleanor of Castile (1) = EDWARD I = (2) Margaret of France
r1272 -1307

1
Gilbert E of = Joan
Gloucester

2
John of =Margaret
Brabant

3
John E of (1) = Elizabeth
Holland
Humphrey (2)
Bohun E. of
Essex,
Hereford &
Northampton

4
EDWARD II = Isabella of
r1307 - 27   France

Thomas of
Brotherton
E. of Norfolk

Edmund E of
Kent

Philippa of = EDWARD III   Eleanor = Reynald II   Joan = David II
Hainault   r1327 - 77   D of   of Scots
                                  Gelderland

12
Thomas = Eleanor
D. of
Gloucester

10
Margaret
= John Hastings
E. of Pembroke

9
Mary
= John IV
D. of Brittany

7
Edmund
D. of York

5
Lionel
D. of
Clarence

4
Isabella

1
Edward = Joan of
the Black   Kent
Prince

Lancaster
Blanche of (1) = John of = (3) Katherine
Lancaster   Gaunt   Swynford   **Beaufort**
                  (2)

6

Philippa
= João I
of Portugal

Elizabeth =
(1) John Hastings
E. of Pembroke

= (2) John Holland
E. of Huntingdon

HENRY IV
r1399 - 1413

Constance
of Castile

Catalina = Henry of
Castile

Edward

RICHARD II = (1) Anne of
r1377 - 99   Bohemia
         = (2) Isabel of
              France

John
E. of
Somerset

Henry
Cardinal

Thomas
D. of
Exeter

Joan = (1) Ld Ferrers
     = (2) Ralph Neville
     E. of Westmorland

HENRY V
r1413 - 22

Note Edward II had three powerfully married elder sisters besides a wife (Shakespeare's "She-Wolf of France") who took Roger of Mortimer as a lover and had Edward done to death.

The Factions in the Lineage of King Henry VIII

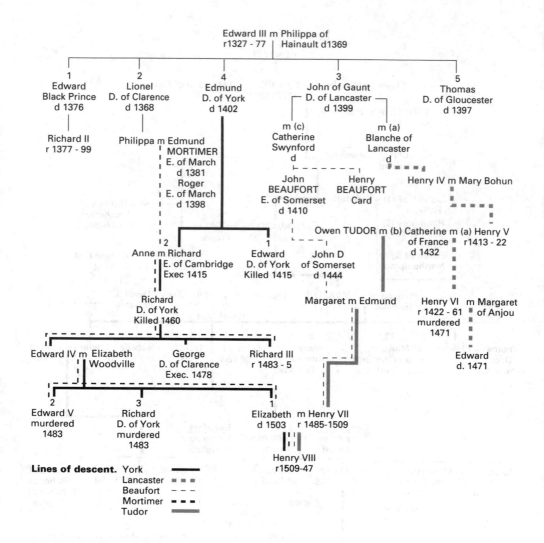

Notes (1) Catherine Swynford had at least three other children not shown. (2) John D. of Somerset's brother Edmund succeeded to the dukedom and died in 1455. (3) As will be seen, Henry VII, though claiming to represent both York and Lancaster (a claim symbolised by the combined and white Tudor rose) had in fact no Lancastrian rights save through the Clarence and York lines by default of heirs to the Lancaster family in 1471.

Transitions from Tudor to Stuart and then to Hanover

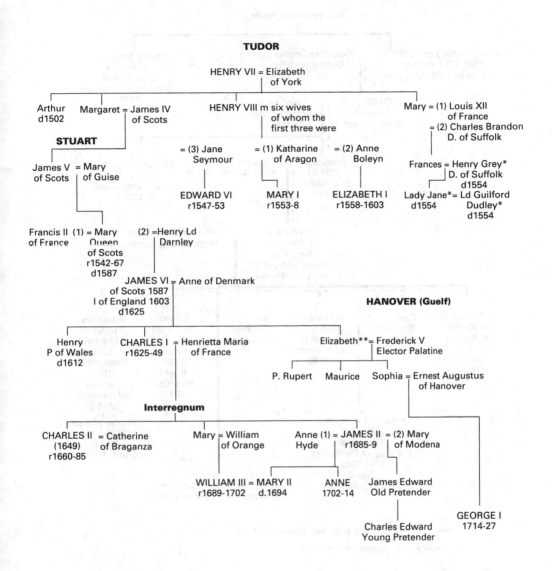

TUDOR

HENRY VII = Elizabeth of York

Arthur d1502   Margaret = James IV of Scots   HENRY VIII m six wives of whom the first three were   Mary = (1) Louis XII of France
= (2) Charles Brandon D. of Suffolk

STUART

James V = Mary of Scots | of Guise   = (3) Jane Seymour   = (1) Katharine of Aragon   = (2) Anne Boleyn   Frances = Henry Grey* D. of Suffolk d1554

EDWARD VI r1547-53   MARY I r1553-8   ELIZABETH I r1558-1603   Lady Jane* = Ld Guilford d1554   Dudley* d1554

Francis II (1) = Mary of France   Queen of Scots r1542-67 d1587   (2) = Henry Ld Darnley

JAMES VI = Anne of Denmark of Scots 1587 I of England 1603 d1625

HANOVER (Guelf)

Henry P of Wales d1612   CHARLES I = Henrietta Maria r1625-49   of France   Elizabeth** = Frederick V Elector Palatine

P. Rupert   Maurice   Sophia = Ernest Augustus of Hanover

Interregnum

CHARLES II (1649) r1660-85   = Catherine of Braganza   Mary = William of Orange   Anne (1) = JAMES II = (2) Mary Hyde | r1685-9 | of Modena

WILLIAM III = MARY II r1689-1702   d.1694   ANNE 1702-14   James Edward Old Pretender   GEORGE I 1714-27

Charles Edward Young Pretender

Notes. *These were executed after Northumberland's attempt to put Lady Jane Grey on the throne. ** The "Winter Queen"

Britain, Hanover and Osnabrück

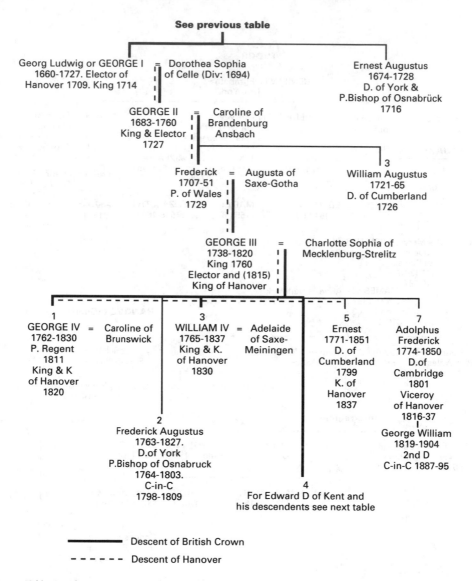

See previous table

Georg Ludwig or GEORGE I 1660-1727. Elector of Hanover 1709. King 1714 = **Dorothea Sophia** of Celle (Div: 1694)

Ernest Augustus 1674-1728 D. of York & P.Bishop of Osnabrück 1716

GEORGE II 1683-1760 King & Elector 1727 = **Caroline of Brandenburg Ansbach**

Frederick 1707-51 P. of Wales 1729 = **Augusta of Saxe-Gotha**

3 **William Augustus** 1721-65 D. of Cumberland 1726

GEORGE III 1738-1820 King 1760 Elector and (1815) King of Hanover = **Charlotte Sophia of Mecklenburg-Strelitz**

1 **GEORGE IV** 1762-1830 P. Regent 1811 King & K of Hanover 1820 = **Caroline of Brunswick**

2 **Frederick Augustus** 1763-1827. D.of York P.Bishop of Osnabruck 1764-1803. C-in-C 1798-1809

3 **WILLIAM IV** 1765-1837 King & K. of Hanover 1830 = **Adelaide of Saxe-Meiningen**

4 For Edward D of Kent and his descendents see next table

5 **Ernest** 1771-1851 D. of Cumberland 1799 K. of Hanover 1837

7 **Adolphus Frederick** 1774-1850 D.of Cambridge 1801 Viceroy of Hanover 1816-37

George William 1819-1904 2nd D C-in-C 1887-95

———— Descent of British Crown

- - - - - Descent of Hanover

Note on Tables 8 and 9

(1) The *Act of Settlement* required (and still requires) sovereigns and their consorts to be protestant, and custom that a royal spouse should come from a sovereign house of traditional ancestry. Hence British royalties mostly made arranged marriages into north German, particularly Saxon, states until George V. Edward VII instituted a Danish connection. The Swedish Bernadottes, being descended from a revolutionary Bordelais pork butcher, were not considered suitable. The German revolution of 1918 destroyed the reservoir of German marriageable royalties, and though efforts to maintain a habit of royal marriages were made, the custom under George V was abandoned, and British royalties married subjects, except for Elizabeth II.

(2) Save for George III, V and VI most men of this family had, often respected, mistresses. George I arrived with two. Before Q. Victoria's reign there were many royal bastards. See FITZROY and FITZCLARENCE.

(3) After 1760 no British King visited Hanover, and they delegated their functions to royal viceroys, save during the Bonapartist occupation. In 1837 Hanover passed under Salic Law to Ernest D. of Cumberland instead to Q. Victoria, but the connection remained commercially and socially strong until 1866, and social relations with north Germany remained active until 1914.

(4) Until 1803 Hanoverian rulers appointed alternate prince-bishops of Osnabrück.

Hanover (from 1837 to 1901), Saxe-Coburg-Gotha (to 1917) and Windsor (1917 onwards)

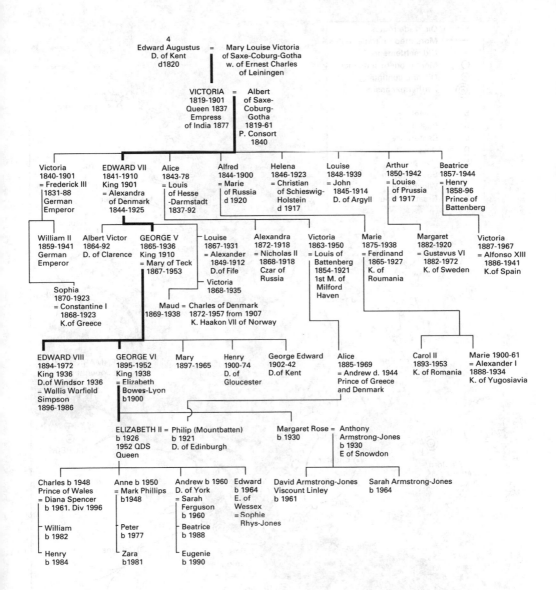

4
Edward Augustus = Mary Louise Victoria
D. of Kent   of Saxe-Coburg-Gotha
d1820   w. of Ernest Charles
                  of Leiningen

VICTORIA = Albert
1819-1901   of Saxe-
Queen 1837 Coburg-
Empress   Gotha
of India 1877 1819-61
            P. Consort
            1840

Victoria   EDWARD VII   Alice   Alfred   Helena   Louise   Arthur   Beatrice
1840-1901   1841-1910   1843-78   1844-1900   1846-1923   1848-1939   1850-1942   1857-1944
= Frederick III   King 1901   = Louis   = Marie   = Christian   = John   = Louise   = Henry
1831-88   = Alexandra   of Hesse   of Russia   of Schieswig-   1845-1914   of Prussia   1858-96
German   of Denmark   -Darmstadt   d 1920   Holstein   D. of Argyll   d 1917   Prince of
Emperor   1844-1925   1837-92   d 1917   Battenberg

William II   Albert Victor   GEORGE V   Louise   Alexandra   Victoria   Marie   Margaret   Victoria
1859-1941   1864-92   1865-1936   1867-1931   1872-1918   1863-1950   1875-1938   1882-1920   1887-1967
German   D. of Clarence King 1910   = Alexander   = Nicholas II   = Louis of   = Ferdinand   = Gustavus VI   = Alfonso XIII
Emperor   = Mary of Teck 1849-1912   1868-1918   Battenberg   1865-1927   1882-1972   1886-1941
                                  1867-1953   D.of Fife   Czar of   1854-1921   K. of   K. of Sweden   K.of Spain
                                                                  Russia   1st M. of   Roumania
Sophia   Victoria   Milford
1870-1923   1868-1935   Haven
= Constantine I   Maud = Charles of Denmark
1868-1923   1869-1938 1872-1957 from 1907
K.of Greece   K. Haakon VII of Norway

EDWARD VIII   GEORGE VI   Mary   Henry   George Edward   Alice   Carol II   Marie 1900-61
1894-1972   1895-1952   1897-1965   1900-74   1902-42   1885-1969   1893-1953   = Alexander I
King 1936   King 1938   D. of   D.of Kent   D.of Kent   = Andrew d. 1944   K. of Romania   1888-1934
D.of Windsor 1936 = Elizabeth   Gloucester   Prince of Greece   K. of Yugosiavia
– Wallis Warfield Bowes-Lyon   and Denmark
Simpson   b1900
1896-1986

ELIZABETH II = Philip (Mountbatten)   Margaret Rose = Anthony
b 1926   b 1921   b 1930   Armstrong-Jones
1952 QDS   D. of Edinburgh   b 1930
Queen   E of Snowdon

Charles b 1948   Anne b 1950   Andrew b 1960   Edward   David Armstrong-Jones   Sarah Armstrong-Jones
Prince of Wales   = Mark Phillips D. of York   b 1964   Viscount Linley   b 1964
= Diana Spencer   b1948   = Sarah   E. of   b 1961
b 1961. Div 1996   Ferguson   Wessex
                                  b 1960   = Sophie
                                                  Rhys-Jones
William   Peter   Beatrice
b 1982   b 1977   b 1988

Henry   Zara   Eugenie
b 1984   b1981   b 1990

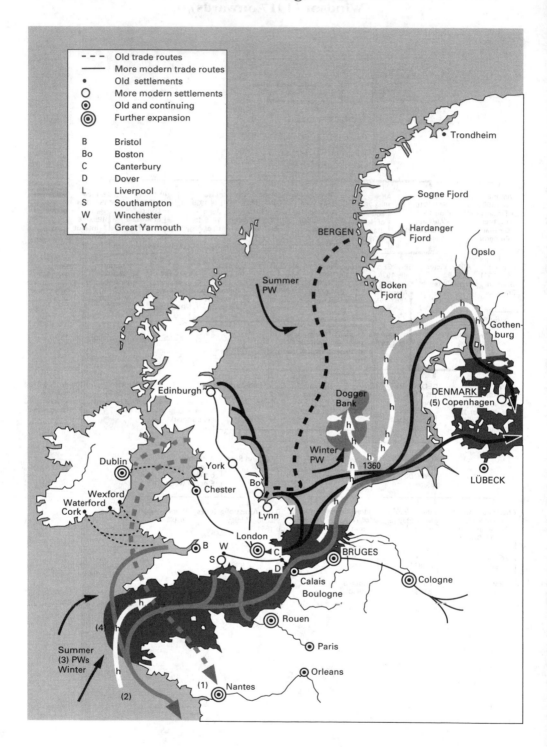

Trade in the Age of Sail

Legend:

- – – – Old trade routes
- ——— More modern trade routes
- • Old settlements
- ○ More modern settlements
- ◉ Old and continuing
- ◎ Further expansion

B	Bristol
Bo	Boston
C	Canterbury
D	Dover
L	Liverpool
S	Southampton
W	Winchester
Y	Great Yarmouth

Trondheim

Sogne Fjord

BERGEN

Hardanger Fjord

Opslo

Summer PW

Boken Fjord

Gothenburg

Edinburgh

Dogger Bank

DENMARK
(5) Copenhagen

Winter PW

LÜBECK

Dublin

York

L

Chester

Bo

h 1360

Wexford
Waterford
Cork

Lynn

Y

London

BRUGES

B W

C

Cologne

S

D

Calais
Boulogne

Summer
(3) PWs
Winter

(4)

Rouen

Paris

(2)

(1) Nantes

Orleans

Trade in the Age of Sail
Notes

(1) • • = Ancient and Iron Age trade route from Biscay and perhaps the Mediterranean to the Irish Sea. It avoided Atlantic storms by crossing Brittany and Cornwall where the traders bought tin.

(2) h h = Herring movements. Till about 1360 herring shoals swarmed off Scania. Thereafter they stopped short at the Dogger Bank and commercial fishing moved from Danzig to Holland and then to English east coast ports with important social and exchange effects.

(3) PW = Prevailing Winds. They were in the western quadrant and so cargoes could be expected to move more quickly east than west e.g. Lynn to Copenhagen 6½-7 days but 7½-9 days back. The Mediterranean was reckoned at six weeks from the Straits to Alexandria but exceptionally fair or foul winds might upset calculations by as much as a fortnight each way.

(4) ⎱ Darkened ⎰ = Channel pirate zone (Normans, Bretons, Portsmen, Devonians and Cornish). This lasted till about 1520,
    Sea   Sea being intermittently policed, if at all, from Calais.
(5) ⎰ Areas ⎱ = Danish pirate zone suppressed by the Danish Kings who ruled both sides of the Sound till 1658 and from the 12th cent. substituted a toll which lasted till 1857. This was based on ship measurements and permanently influenced merchant ship design.

(6) CAPITAL names denote the major finance and exchange centres. The Lynn Hanse depended on Bergen.

(7) In summer overland journeys on not impossible roads might average 20 miles a day but the Pilgrims Way between Winchester and Canterbury was probably a strollers' route. Rivers, where navigable, might permit downstream speeds of 40-50 miles a day and upstream of 7-10 miles.

Principal Routes and Goods
Southwards

From England				To England
Wool and Textiles	Pilgrims	Bourgneuf	Pilgrims	Salt
Bullion		Bordeaux		Wine
Tin		Vigo and		
		Santiago		
		Mediterranean		Art works, Silks, luxuries, oriental goods

Eastwards

From England			To England
Wool and Textiles		Baltic Ports	Hemp, Timber, Furs
Salt		Novgorod	Bow staves.
Tin		Russia	Later, base metals
(Slaves picked up en route)			

Colonisations 5-10th cent.

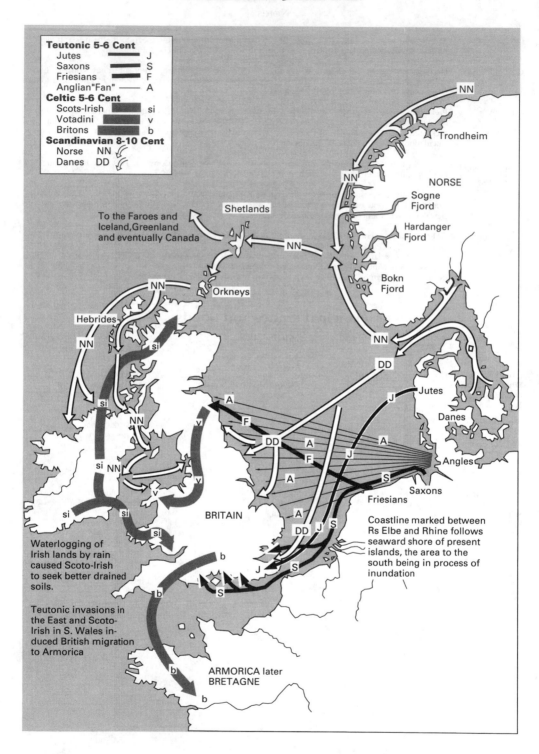

Teutonic 5-6 Cent
- Jutes ▬▬▬ J
- Saxons ▬▬▬ S
- Friesians ▬▬▬ F
- Anglian"Fan" ——— A

Celtic 5-6 Cent
- Scots-Irish ▬▬▬ si
- Votadini ▬▬▬ v
- Britons ▬▬▬ b

Scandinavian 8-10 Cent
- Norse NN
- Danes DD

To the Faroes and Iceland, Greenland and eventually Canada

Shetlands

NORSE
Sogne Fjord
Hardanger Fjord
Bokn Fjord
Trondheim

Orkneys

Hebrides

Jutes
Danes
Angles
Saxons
Friesians

BRITAIN

Waterlogging of Irish lands by rain caused Scoto-Irish to seek better drained soils.

Teutonic invasions in the East and Scoto-Irish in S. Wales induced British migration to Armorica

Coastline marked between Rs Elbe and Rhine follows seaward shore of present islands, the area to the south being in process of inundation

ARMORICA later BRETAGNE

Motte and bailey castles heavily adapted

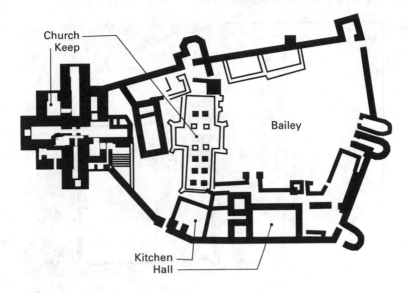

Warkworth for use as a residence

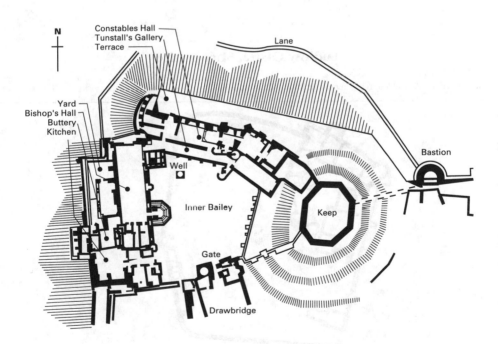

Durham for use as a palace

Portchester near Portsmouth, Hampshire

Norman castle with a tall corner-keep in a Roman legionary depot seven hundred years older.

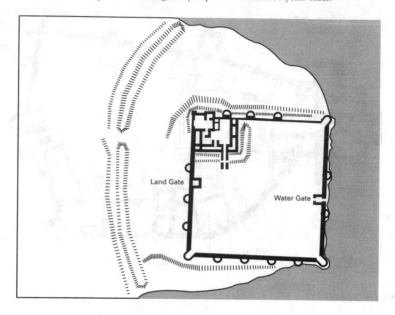

Land Gate

Water Gate

Ludlow Castle, Shropshire

Castle with later bailey added to accommodate Welsh administration.

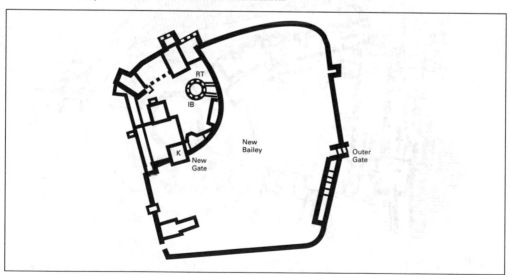

RT

IB

New
Bailey

K

New
Gate

Outer
Gate

IB = Inner, originally the only, bailey
RT = later round tower
K = Gatehouse converted into a keep

Battle of Hastings 1066 about 9am to noon

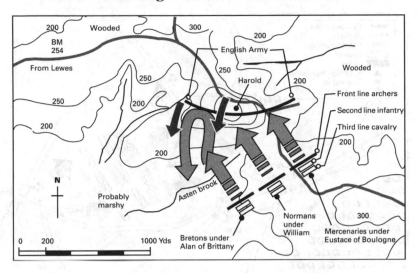

ARTILLERY FORTIFICATIONS

Some of the HOSPITALLER Fortifications at Malta GC indicating the components of artillery fortifications and also why various powers coveted the islands.

FLORIANA

Two middle bastions (B) connected by a curtain (C) and with outer demibastions (D) by gated N and S curtains. Middle curtain covered by a lower outer bastion (OB). The very wide ditch contains two ravelins (R) (or demi-lunes) to cover the two gates, and on the glacis beyond the ditch, lunettes (L) cover the re-entrant angles.

VALETTA

Two middle bastions (B) surmounted by cavaliers (Cav) (to gain height against the Floriana plateau) protect the only gate and are connected outwards to demibastions (D). Immediately outside, the Great Ditch is 150 feet deep. The gate is covered by a Lunette (L), the bastions and demibastions by counterguards (G) (probably manned by forlorn hopes) with wide ditches outside.

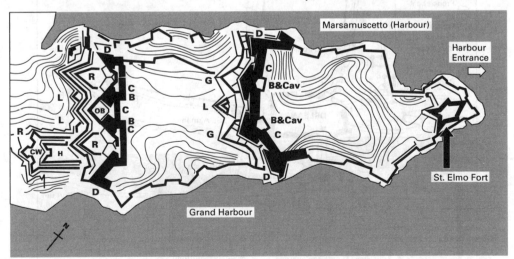

A hornwork (H) with ditches within a crownwork (CW) with ditches and a ravelin (R), placed on the highest ground prevents a landing near the capital line from the south and any approach to it from the north until it has itself been taken.

Guns in St. Elmo cover harbour entrance and any approach to the south side of the Harbour.

Battle of Crécy 1346 about 6pm

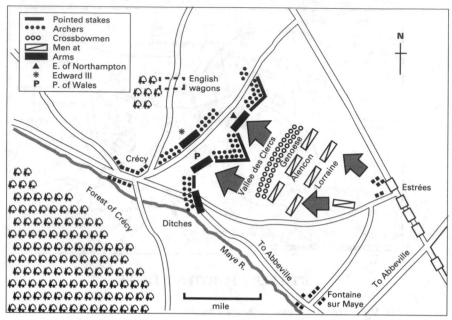

Note. The ill-disciplined French knights were probably disposed less tidily than the plan suggests. They charged prematurely and without warning through the Genoese who (confusion apart) could not shoot without hitting their own side once the knights were through. The latter then had to labour up hill from the Vallée des Clercs against archery cross fire.

Relief of Orléans 1429

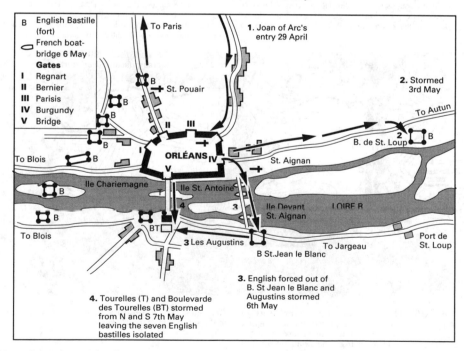

Arabic numbers indicate order of events.

The Mediaeval Anglo-Scottish Marches as a diplomatic Quasi-Condominium

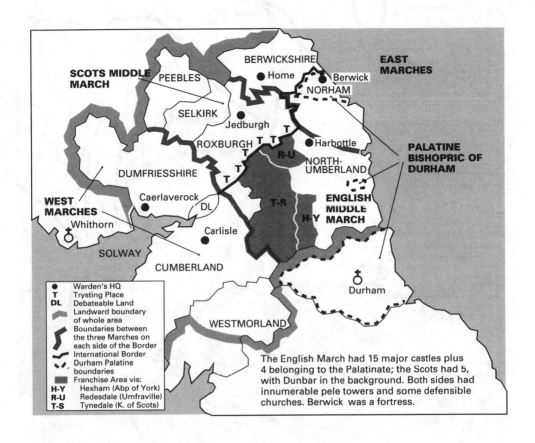

SCOTS MIDDLE MARCH
PEEBLES
BERWICKSHIRE
EAST MARCHES
Home
Berwick
NORHAM
SELKIRK
Jedburgh
ROXBURGH
Harbottle
T
T
T
T
R-U
NORTH-UMBERLAND
PALATINE BISHOPRIC OF DURHAM
DUMFRIESSHIRE
T
T
Caerlaverock
DL
T-S
ENGLISH MIDDLE MARCH
H-Y
WEST MARCHES
Whithorn
Carlisle
SOLWAY
CUMBERLAND
Durham
WESTMORLAND

Legend:

- ● Warden's HQ
- T Trysting Place
- DL Debateable Land
- Landward boundary of whole area
- Boundaries between the three Marches on each side of the Border
- International Border
- Durham Palatine boundaries
- Franchise Area vis:
- H-Y Hexham (Abp of York)
- R-U Redesdale (Umfraville)
- T-S Tynedale (K. of Scots)

The English March had 15 major castles plus 4 belonging to the Palatinate; the Scots had 5, with Dunbar in the background. Both sides had innumerable pele towers and some defensible churches. Berwick was a fortress.

The Gibraltar Area and the Battle of Trafalgar 21 October 1805

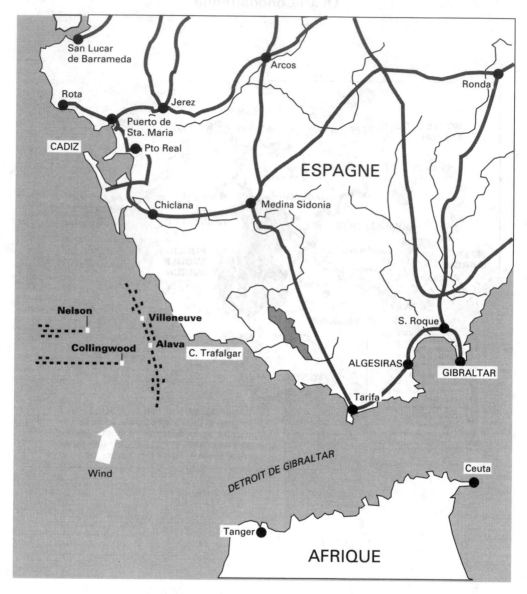

This French chart shows an area of widespread historical importance in peace and war. Columbus sailed from Palos, fifty miles west of San Lucar de Barrameda, the outport of Seville. Cadiz, almost impregnable on its spit, protects the splendid anchorage and main Spanish naval base, raided by Drake in 1587, through which Sherry (named after Jerez) is exported. The commander of the first Armada lived at Medina Sidonia. The current, representing less evaporation, the output of the Mediterranean and Black Sea rivers, flows strongly westward through the Straits. The *Levanter*, a warm damp wind also blows westwards often for days and the two stopped square-rigged shipping from the Atlantic and forced it to anchor off Tarifa or Tangier. Hence their importance. Tangier, a Portuguese anti-piracy base, was British from 1661 to 1684 when it became untenable against the Moors. Ceuta, on its peninsula, was Portuguese but has been Spanish since 1580. Ronda was a centre of brigandage and revolt between 1550 and 1850. Most of the citrus fruits used as anti-scorbutics by the Royal Navy came from Tangier (tangerines) or from the area between Medina Sidonia and Algeçiras where, in 1801 the Royal Navy incurred a rare defeat. The Royal Calpe hunted foxes around San Roque until 1939. In World War II Gibraltar was the essential staging point for British convoys to Malta GC, Egypt and round Africa.

At Trafalgar most British ships save flagships (100 guns) were 74s. Most French were 80s including their flagship. The Spanish *Santissima Trinidad* (136) immediately ahead of Villeneuve was the biggest ship afloat and the other Spaniards were 76s with two 112s. The battle was fought in a calm, the ships being unable to make more than two knots.

The Thirteen Colonies and Subsequent U.S. Continental Expansion

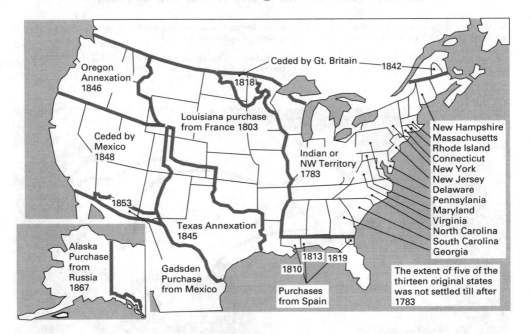

Oregon Annexation 1846

Ceded by Gt. Britain — 1842

1818

Louisiana purchase from France 1803

Ceded by Mexico 1848

Indian or NW Territory 1783

1853

Texas Annexation 1845

Alaska Purchase from Russia 1867

Gadsden Purchase from Mexico

1813 1819

1810

Purchases from Spain

New Hampshire
Massachusetts
Rhode Island
Connecticut
New York
New Jersey
Delaware
Pennsylania
Maryland
Virginia
North Carolina
South Carolina
Georgia

The extent of five of the thirteen original states was not settled till after 1783

Difficulties of Long Distance Navigation under Sail

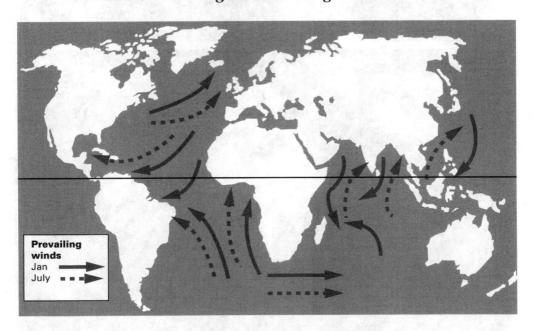

Prevailing winds
Jan ▬▬▶
July ▬ ▬ ▬▶

(1) In the North Atlantic conditions remained basically the same all the year round. Hence it was normal to go well south before turning west for the West Indies, while the return journey to Europe was made further to the north.

(2) On the eastern voyages a long run had to be made, often as far as Brazil before tacking towards the Cape of Good Hope. Once round it, the probability of a speedy voyage depended on the time of year. Outward bound ships tried to round the Cape in the Spring or early summer (European reckoning). Homeward bound ships preferred to start in the Autumn. Ships tended, therefore, to sail in convoy.

Britain's relationship to the World and to Trade

Tucked away at the end of the known world, Britain gets the leavings of the world's goods. These are expensive because they need much overland transport and pass through the hands of many middlemen.

With the discovery of new continents and new sea routes (which are cheap), the old land routes begin to dry up just as Britain becomes a sea power. Thus everything at once conspires to put Britain at the CENTRE of the world.

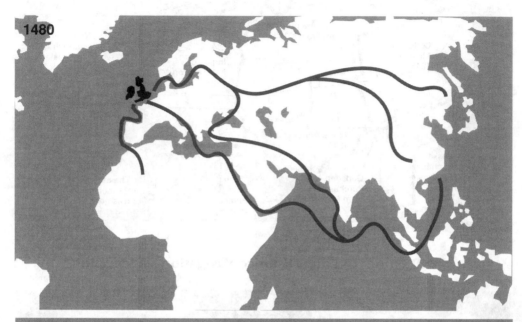

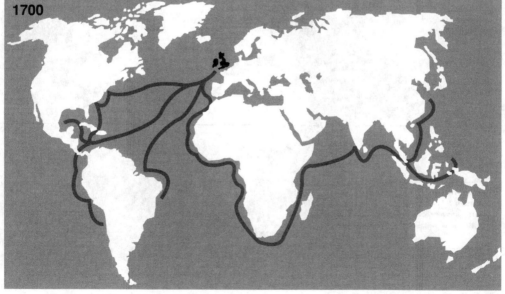

BEFORE 1272

LOTHIAN

SCOTLAND

Note: Scots ruled the
Lothians by 1150

Durham

The North

●YORK

Chester

Shropshire

WALES

ENGLAND

Wales and
the Marches

1272-1642

SCOTLAND

NORTHUMBERLAND

CUMBERLAND   COUNTY
DURHAM

YORKSHIRE

YORK ●

Lancaster

ANGLESEY

DENBIGH

CAERNARVON

MERIONETH

●LUDLOW

Rutland

CARDIGAN

WALES   ENGLAND

CARMARTHEN

Cornwall

'English' frontier in Anglo-Saxon times

Counties originating as Kingdoms

Counties originating as West Saxon military Districts

Counties originating as Norman military Palatinates

Counties originating as special jurisdictions
connected with the Royal House

Counties imposed by conquest under Edward I

Counties created by the Tudors

Areas of the council for Wales and the Marches
(Ludlow) and the council of the North (York) until 1642

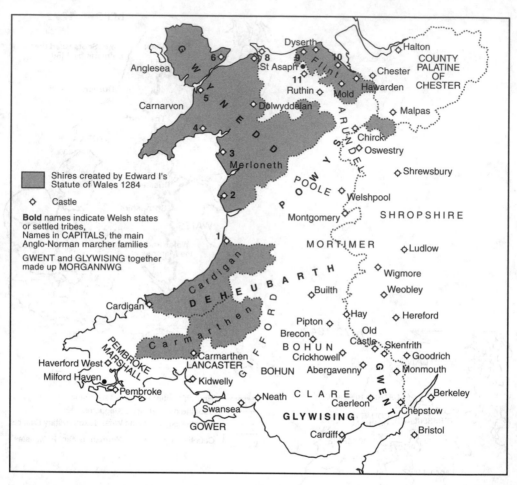

The core principality of
GWYNEDD covered the
three shires of Anglesea,
Caernarvon and Merioneth
but sometimes extended
east to Ruthin and south
as far as Brecon. Edward I's
castles to control it after the
conquest were:

1. Aberystwyth
2. Bere
3. Harlech
4. Criccieth
5. Caernarfon
6. Beaumaris
7. Conway
8. Deganwy
9. Rhuddlan
10. Flint
11. Denbigh

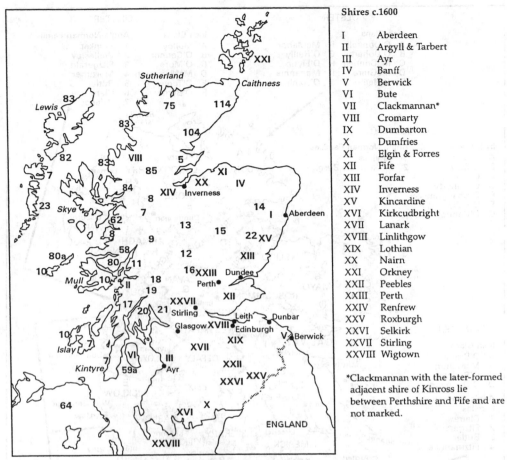

*Clackmannan with the later-formed adjacent shire of Kinross lie between Perthshire and Fife and are not marked.

Most of the shires south and east of Inverness were formed by the 14th century but James VI & I (1567–1625) constituted the separate shires of Inverness, Caithness, Sutherland and the intermixed areas of Ross & Cromarty with Lewis.

Highland clans as at 1745 are represented by arabic numbers which will be found in the entry CLANS, SCOTS. Only the most powerful or best placed are shown.

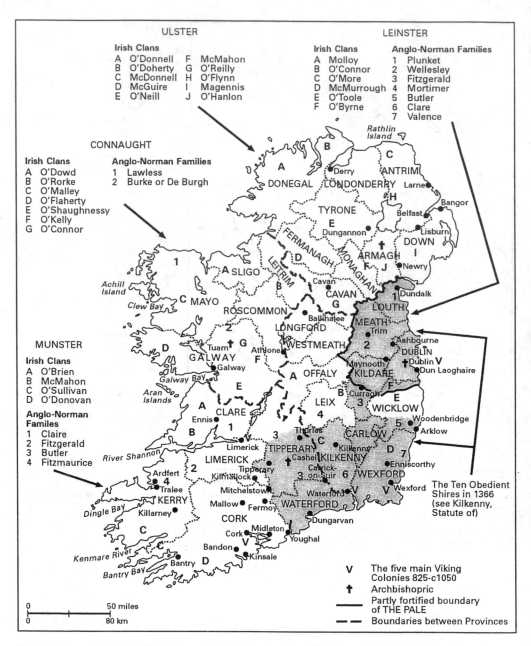

ULSTER

Irish Clans
A O'Donnell   F McMahon
B O'Doherty   G O'Reilly
C McDonnell   H O'Flynn
D McGuire   I Magennis
E O'Neill   J O'Hanlon

LEINSTER

Irish Clans
A Molloy
B O'Connor
C O'More
D McMurrough
E O'Toole
F O'Byrne

Anglo-Norman Families
1 Plunket
2 Wellesley
3 Fitzgerald
4 Mortimer
5 Butler
6 Clare
7 Valence

CONNAUGHT

Irish Clans
A O'Dowd
B O'Rorke
C O'Malley
D O'Flaherty
E O'Shaughnessy
F O'Kelly
G O'Connor

Anglo-Norman Families
1 Lawless
2 Burke or De Burgh

MUNSTER

Irish Clans
A O'Brien
B McMahon
C O'Sullivan
D O'Donovan

Anglo-Norman
Familes
1 Claire
2 Fitzgerald
3 Butler
4 Fitzmaurice

The Ten Obedient
Shires in 1366
(see Kilkenny,
Statute of)

V   The five main Viking
     Colonies 825-c1050
†   Archbishopric
──   Partly fortified boundary
     of THE PALE
·─·─ Boundaries between Provinces

There is an uncertain relationship between the Scots Macdonalds and Macdonnells, and the Macdonnells and O'Donnells of Ulster. There was mediaeval inter-migration between Ulster and the Isles, and in the 16th and 17th centuries of Protestant Scots to Down, Antrim and Londonderry, and more thinly in Armagh. These plantations alone succeeded.

Continental Countries of Immediate Concern

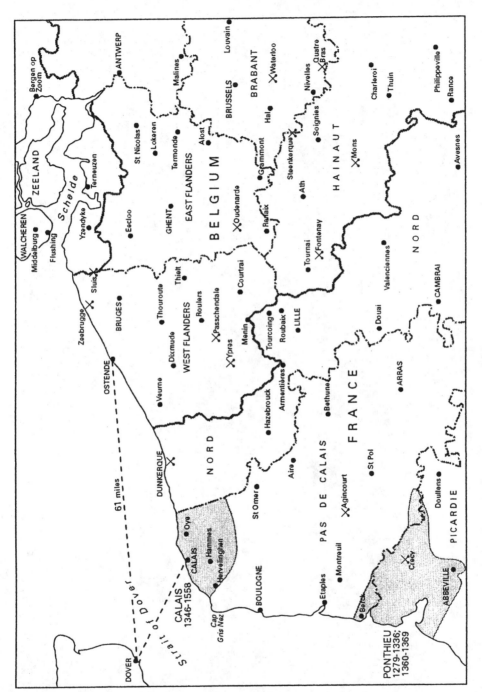

Many places have separate entries in the text but for ABBEVILLE *see* PONTHIEU and for BRUGES *see* FLANDERS, HANSE *and* STAPLE-B. X represents a battle.